The International WHO'S WHO

2015

The International WHO'S WHO

78th Edition

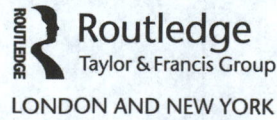

Routledge
Taylor & Francis Group

LONDON AND NEW YORK

Seventy-eighth edition published 2014
by Routledge
2 Park Square, Milton Park, Abingdon, Oxon., OX14 4RN, United Kingdom

and by Routledge
711 Third Avenue, New York, NY 10017, USA

www.routledge.com

Routledge is an imprint of the Taylor & Francis Group, an informa business

First published 1935

ISBN: 978-1-85743-713-3
ISSN: 0074-9613

Typeset in Frome by Data Standards Limited

Senior Editor: Robert J. Elster
Editorial Researchers: Ankita Baruah (Team Leader), Tanmoyee Rajkhowa (Editorial Researcher), Arsheen Kaur (Editorial Researcher), Herina Gangmei (Editorial Researcher)
Consulting Editors: Gerard Delaney, Annabella Gabb, Sue Leckey, Justin Lewis
Editorial Assistant: Lydia de Cruz
Editorial Director: Paul Kelly

PUBLISHER'S NOTE

The *International Who's Who* has been published annually since 1935 and provides biographical information on the most famous and talented men and women in the world today. We select the entries entirely on merit and our book is recognised by librarians in every country as a standard reference source in its field. We wish to make it clear that the Europa Biographical Reference Series has no connection with any other business purporting to produce a publication with the same title or a similar title to ours.

FOREWORD TO THE 78th EDITION

This is the 78th edition of THE INTERNATIONAL WHO'S WHO, which since its first publication in 1935 has become the standard reference work on the world's most famous and influential men and women. The current edition contains more than 25,000 entries, of which more than 1,000 appear here for the first time.

In compiling THE INTERNATIONAL WHO'S WHO, our aim is to create a reference book that answers the needs of readers seeking information on the lives of our most gifted contemporaries. We choose the entries entirely on merit and for their continuing interest and importance. Some are household names in every continent. Others are noted for their contributions in specialized fields or for their role in the political, economic, social or cultural life of their particular countries. The scope and diversity of the book is reflected in the range of activities represented, which includes architecture, art, business, cinema, diplomacy, engineering, fashion, journalism, law, literature, medicine, music, photography, politics, science, sport, technology and theatre.

Each year new entrants are sent questionnaires with a request to supply biographical details. All existing entrants are also contacted, so that they may have an opportunity to make necessary additions and amendments. Supplementary research is done by the Editor and the Europa editorial department to ensure that the book is as up-to-date as possible upon publication. Valuable assistance is also provided by consultants and experts in particular fields or with specialized knowledge of certain countries.

The introduction contains a list of abbreviations and international telephone codes. The names of entrants whose death has been reported over the past year are included in the Obituary. There is also a section on Reigning Royal Families.

The biographical information contained in this 78th edition, as well as information on past entrants, deceased entrants and entrants from the wide range of other Europa biographical sources, is provided online in WORLD WHO'S WHO. Using the product's sophisticated search functions, researchers can easily and quickly access the rich biographical data in the comprehensive Europa biographical database. As well, online users can take advantage of the quarterly updating cycle that ensures the data is as current as possible. Details of this resource are available at www.worldwhoswho.com

Not many countries have their own who's who, and not all national who's whos are published annually. THE INTERNATIONAL WHO'S WHO 2015 represents in one volume a library of information from all countries that is not found elsewhere and is unrivalled in its balance and coverage.

May 2014

ALPHABETIZATION KEY

The list of names is alphabetical, with the entrants listed under surnames. If part of an entrant's first given name is in parentheses, this will not affect his or her alphabetical listing.

All names beginning Mc and Mac are treated as though they began Mac, e.g. McDowell before MacEachen, MacFarlane after McFadyen, Macharski before McHenry.

Names with Arabic prefixes are normally listed after the prefix except when requested by the entrant. In the case of surnames beginning De, Des, Du, van or von the entries are normally found under the prefix. Names beginning St are listed as if they began Saint, e.g. St Aubin de Teran after Sainsbury. As a general rule Chinese names are alphabetized under the last name.

In the case of an entrant whose name is spelt in a variety of ways, who is known by a pseudonym or best known by another name, a cross reference is provided, e.g.:

Kadhafi, Col Mu'ammar Muhammed al- (see Gaddafi, Col Mu'ammar Muhammed al-).

Le Carré, John (see Cornwell, David John Moore).

Lloyd, Chris(tine) Marie Evert (see Evert, Chris(tine) Marie).

ABBREVIATIONS

AAA	Agricultural Adjustment Administration	ASSR	Autonomous Soviet Socialist Republic
AAAS	American Association for the Advancement of Science	Asst	Assistant
AAF	Army Air Force	ATV	Associated Television
AASA	Associate of the Australian Society of Accountants	Aug.	August
AB	Bachelor of Arts; Aktiebolag; Alberta	autobiog.	autobiography
ABA	American Bar Association	AZ	Arizona
AC	Companion of the Order of Australia		
ACA	Associate of the Institute of Chartered Accountants	b.	born
ACCA	Associate of the Association of Certified Accountants	BA	Bachelor of Arts; British Airways
Acad.	Academy; Académie	BAAS	British Association for the Advancement of Science
Accad.	Accademia	BAFTA	British Academy of Film and Television Arts
accred	accredited	BAgr	Bachelor of Agriculture
ACIS	Associate of the Chartered Institute of Secretaries	BAgrSc	Bachelor of Agricultural Science
ACP	American College of Physicians	BAO	Bachelor of Obstetrics
ACS	American Chemical Society	BAOR	British Army of the Rhine
ACT	Australian Capital Territory	BArch	Bachelor of Architecture
ADC	Aide-de-camp	Bart	Baronet
Adm.	Admiral	BAS	Bachelor in Agricultural Science
Admin(.)	Administrative; Administration; Administrator	BASc	Bachelor of Applied Science
AE	Air Efficiency Award	BBA	Bachelor of Business Administration
AERE	Atomic Energy Research Establishment	BBC	British Broadcasting Corporation
AF	Air Force	BC	British Columbia
AFC	Air Force Cross	BCC	British Council of Churches
ADB	African Development Bank	BCE	Bachelor of Civil Engineering
affil.	affiliated	BChir	Bachelor of Surgery
AFL	American Federation of Labor	BCL	Bachelor of Civil Law; Bachelor of Canon Law
AFM	Air Force Medal	BCom(m)	Bachelor of Commerce
AG	Aktiengesellschaft (Joint Stock Company)	BCS	Bachelor of Commercial Sciences
Agric.	Agriculture	BD	Bachelor of Divinity
a.i.	ad interim	Bd	Board
AIA	Associate of the Institute of Actuaries; American Institute of Architects	BDS	Bachelor of Dental Surgery
AIAA	American Institute of Aeronautics and Astronautics	BE	Bachelor of Education; Bachelor of Engineering
AIB	Associate of the Institute of Bankers	BEA	British European Airways
AICC	All-India Congress Committee	BEcons	Bachelor of Economics
AICE	Associate of the Institute of Civil Engineers	BEd	Bachelor of Education
AIChE	American Institute of Chemical Engineers	Beds.	Bedfordshire
AIDS	Acquired Immune Deficiency Syndrome	BEE	Bachelor of Electrical Engineering
AIEE	American Institute of Electrical Engineers	BEM	British Empire Medal
AIME	American Institute of Mining Engineers; Associate of the Institution of Mining Engineers	BEng	Bachelor of Engineering
		Berks.	Berkshire
AIMechE	Associate of the Institution of Mechanical Engineers	BFA	Bachelor of Fine Arts
AIR	All-India Radio	BFI	British Film Institute
AK	Alaska; Knight of the Order of Australia	BIM	British Institute of Management
Akad.	Akademie	biog.	biography
AL	Alabama	BIS	Bank for International Settlements
Ala	Alabama	BL	Bachelor of Laws
ALS	Associate of the Linnaean Society	BLA	Bachelor of Landscape Architecture
Alt.	Alternate	Bldg	Building
AM	Alpes Maritimes; Albert Medal; Master of Arts; Member of the Order of Australia	BLit(t)	Bachelor of Letters; Bachelor of Literature
		BLL	Bachelor of Laws
Amb.	Ambassador	BLS	Bachelor in Library Science
AMICE	Associate Member of the Institution of Civil Engineers	blvd	boulevard
AMIEE	Associate Member of the Institution of Electrical Engineers	BM	Bachelor of Medicine
AMIMechE	Associate Member of the Institution of Mechanical Engineers	BMA	British Medical Association
		BMus	Bachelor of Music
ANC	African National Congress	Bn	Battalion
ANU	Australian National University	BNOC	British National Oil Corporation
AO	Officer of the Order of Australia	BOAC	British Overseas Airways Corporation
AP	Andhra Pradesh	BP	Boîte Postale
Apdo	Apartado	BPA	Bachelor of Public Administration
APEC	Asia and Pacific Economic Co-operation	BPharm	Batchelor of Pharmacy
approx.	approximately	BPhil	Bachelor of Philosophy
appt	appointment	Br.	Branch
apptd	appointed	Brig.	Brigadier
apt	apartment	BS	Bachelor of Science; Bachelor of Surgery
AR	Arkansas	BSA	Bachelor of Scientific Agriculture
ARA	Associate of the Royal Academy	BSc	Bachelor of Science
ARAM	Associate of the Royal Academy of Music	Bt	Baronet
ARAS	Associate of the Royal Astronomical Society	Bucks.	Buckinghamshire
ARC	Agriculture Research Council		
ARCA	Associate of the Royal College of Art	c.	child; children; circa
ARCM	Associate of the Royal College of Music	CA	California; Chartered Accountant
ARCO	Associate of the Royal College of Organists	Calif.	California
ARCS	Associate of the Royal College of Science	Cambs.	Cambridgeshire
ARIBA	Associate of the Royal Institute of British Architects	Cand.	Candidate; Candidature
Ariz.	Arizona	Cantab.	of Cambridge University
Ark.	Arkansas	Capt.	Captain
ARSA	Associate of the Royal Scottish Academy; Associate of the Royal Society of Arts	Cards.	Cardiganshire
		CB	Companion of the (Order of the) Bath
ASEAN	Association of South-East Asian Nations	CBC	Canadian Broadcasting Corporation
ASLIB	Association of Special Libraries and Information Bureaux	CBE	Commander of the (Order of the) British Empire
ASME	American Society of Mechanical Engineers	CBI	Confederation of British Industry
Asoc.	Asociación	CBiol	Chartered Biologist
Ass.	Assembly	CBIM	Companion of the British Institute of Management
Asscn	Association	CBS	Columbia Broadcasting System
Assoc.	Associate	CC	Companion of the Order of Canada

CChem	Chartered Chemist
CCMI	Companion of the Chartered Management Institute (formerly CIMgt)
CCP	Chinese Communist Party
CD	Canadian Forces Decoration; Commander Order of Distinction
Cdre	Commodore
CDU	Christlich-Demokratische Union
CE	Civil Engineer; Chartered Engineer
CEAO	Communauté Economique de l'Afrique de l'Ouest
Cen.	Central
CEng	Chartered Engineer
CENTO	Central Treaty Organization
CEO	Chief Executive Officer
CERN	Conseil (now Organisation) Européen(ne) pour la Recherche Nucléaire
CFR	Commander of the Federal Republic of Nigeria
CGM	Conspicuous Gallantry Medal
CGT	Confédération Général du Travail
CH	Companion of Honour
Chair.	Chairman; Chairwoman; Chairperson
CHB	Companion of Honour of Barbados
ChB	Bachelor of Surgery
Chem.	Chemistry
ChM	Master of Surgery
CI	Channel Islands
CIA	Central Intelligence Agency
Cia	Compagnia (Company)
Cía	Compañía (Company)
CID	Criminal Investigation Department
CIE	Companion of the (Order of the) Indian Empire
Cie	Compagnie (Company)
CIEE	Companion of the Institution of Electrical Engineers
CIMgt	Companion of the Institute of Management (now CCMI)
C-in-C	Commander-in-Chief
CIO	Congress of Industrial Organizations
CIOMS	Council of International Organizations of Medical Science
CIS	Commonwealth of Independent States
CLD	Doctor of Civil Law (USA)
CLit	Companion of Literature
CM	Canada Medal; Master in Surgery
CMEA	Council for Mutual Economic Assistance
CMG	Companion of (the Order of) St Michael and St George
CNAA	Council for National Academic Awards
CNRS	Centre National de la Recherche Scientifique
CO	Colorado; Commanding Officer
Co.	Company; County
COI	Central Office of Information
Col	Colonel
Coll.	College
Colo	Colorado
COMECON	Council for Mutual Economic Assistance
COMESA	Common Market for Eastern and Southern Asia
Comm.	Commission
Commdg	Commanding
Commdr	Commander; Commandeur
Commdt	Commandant
Commr	Commissioner
CON	Commander of Order of Nigeria
Conf.	Conference
Confed.	Confederation
Conn.	Connecticut
Contrib.	Contributor; contribution
COO	Chief Operating Officer
Corp.	Corporate
Corpn	Corporation
Corresp.	Correspondent; Corresponding
CP	Communist Party; Caixa Postal (Post Office Box)
CPA	Certified Public Accountant; Commonwealth Parliamentary Association
CPhys	Chartered Physicist
CPP	Convention People's Party (Ghana)
CPPCC	Chinese People's Political Consultative Conference
CPSU	Communist Party of the Soviet Union
cr.	created
CSc	Candidate of Sciences
CSCE	Conference on Security and Co-operation in Europe
CSI	Companion of the (Order of the) Star of India
CSIRO	Commonwealth Scientific and Industrial Research Organization
CSSR	Czechoslovak Socialist Republic
CStJ	Commander of (the Order of) St John of Jerusalem
CT	Connecticut
Cttee	Committee
CUNY	City University of New York
CV	Commanditaire Vennootschap
CVO	Commander of the Royal Victorian Order
d.	daughter(s)
DArch	Doctor of Architecture
DB	Bachelor of Divinity
DBA	Doctor of Business Administration
DBE	Dame Commander of (the Order of) the British Empire
DC	District of Columbia
DCE	Doctor of Civil Engineering
DCL	Doctor of Civil Law; Doctor of Canon Law
DCM	Distinguished Conduct Medal
DCMG	Dame Commander of (the Order of) St Michael and St George
DCnL	Doctor of Canon Law
DComm	Doctor of Commerce
DCS	Doctor of Commercial Sciences
DCT	Doctor of Christian Theology
DCVO	Dame Commander of the Royal Victorian Order
DD	Doctor of Divinity
DDR	Deutsche Demokratische Republik (German Democratic Republic)
DDS	Doctor of Dental Surgery
DE	Delaware
Dec.	December
DEcon	Doctor of Economics
DEd	Doctor of Education
DEFRA	Department for Environment, Food and Rural Affairs
Del.	Delegate; Delegation; Delaware
Denbighs.	Denbighshire
DenD	Docteur en Droit
DenM	Docteur en Medicine
DEng	Doctor of Engineering
Dep.	Deputy
Dept	Department
DES	Department of Education and Science
Desig.	Designate
DèsL	Docteur ès Lettres
DèsSc	Docteur ès Sciences
Devt	Development
DF	Distrito Federal
DFA	Doctor of Fine Arts; Diploma of Fine Arts
DFC	Distinguished Flying Cross
DFM	Distinguished Flying Medal
DH	Doctor of Humanities
DHist	Doctor of History
DHL	Doctor of Hebrew Literature
DHSS	Department of Health and Social Security
DHumLitt	Doctor of Humane Letters
DIC	Diploma of Imperial College
DipAD	Diploma in Art and Design
DipAgr	Diploma in Agriculture
DipArch	Diploma in Architecture
DipEd	Diploma in Education
DipEng	Diploma in Engineering
DipMus	Diploma in Music
DipScEconSc	Diploma of Social and Economic Science
DipTh	Doctor of Theology
Dir	Director
Dist	District
DIur	Doctor of Law
DIurUtr	Doctor of both Civil and Canon Law
Div.	Division; divisional
DJur	Doctor of Law
DK	Most Esteemed Family (Malaysia)
DL	Deputy Lieutenant
DLit(t)	Doctor of Letters; Doctor of Literature
DLS	Doctor of Library Science
DM	Doctor of Medicine (Oxford)
DMD	Doctor of Dental Medicine
DMedSc	Doctor of Medical Science
DMilSc	Doctor of Military Science
DMunSci	Doctor of Municipal Science
DMS	Director of Medical Services
DMus	Doctor of Music
DMV	Doctor of Veterinary Medicine
DO	Doctor of Ophthalmology
DPH	Diploma in Public Health
DPhil	Doctor of Philosophy
DPM	Diploma in Psychological Medicine
DPS	Doctor of Public Service
Dr	Doctor
DrAgr	Doctor of Agriculture
DrIng	Doctor of Engineering
DrIur	Doctor of Laws
DrMed	Doctor of Medicine
DrOecPol	Doctor of Political Economy
DrOecPubl	Doctor of (Public) Economy
DrPhilNat	Doctor of Natural Philosophy
Dr rer. nat	Doctor of Natural Sciences
Dr rer. pol	Doctor of Political Science
DrSc(i)	Doctor of Sciences
DrScNat	Doctor of Natural Sciences
DS	Doctor of Science
DSC	Distinguished Service Cross
DSc(i)	Doctor of Sciences
DScS	Doctor of Social Science
DSM	Distinguished Service Medal
DSO	Companion of the Distinguished Service Order
DSocSc	Doctor of Social Science
DST	Doctor of Sacred Theology
DTech	Doctor of Technology
DTechSc(i)	Doctor of Technical Sciences
DTheol	Doctor of Theology
DTM	Diploma in Tropical Medicine
DTM&H	Diploma in Tropical Medicine and Hygiene
DUP	Diploma of the University of Paris
DUniv	Doctor of the University

E	East; Eastern
EBRD	European Bank for Reconstruction and Development
EC	European Commission; European Community
ECA	Economic Co-operation Administration; Economic Commission for Africa
ECAFE	Economic Commission for Asia and the Far East
ECE	Economic Commission for Europe
ECLA	Economic Commission for Latin America
ECLAC	Economic Commission for Latin America and the Caribbean
ECO	Economic Co-operation Organization
Econ.	Economic
Econs	Economics
ECOSOC	Economic and Social Council
ECSC	European Coal and Steel Community
ECWA	Economic Commission for Western Asia
ed	educated; edited
Ed.	Editor
ED	Efficiency Decoration; Doctor of Engineering (USA)
EdD	Doctor of Education
Edin.	Edinburgh
EdM	Master of Education
Edn	Edition
Educ.	Education
EEC	European Economic Community
EFTA	European Free Trade Association
eh	Ehrenhalben (Honorary)
EIB	European Investment Bank
EM	Edward Medal; Master of Engineering (USA)
Emer.	Emerita; Emeritus
Eng	Engineering
EngD	Doctor of Engineering
ENO	English National Opera
EPLF	Eritrean People's Liberation Front
ESA	European Space Agency
ESCAP	Economic and Social Commission for Asia and the Pacific
ESCWA	Economic and Social Commission for Western Asia
est.	established
ETH	Eidgenössische Technische Hochschule (Swiss Federal Institute of Technology)
Ets	Etablissements
EU	European Union
EURATOM	European Atomic Energy Community
Exec.	Executive
Exhbn	Exhibition
Ext.	Extension
f.	founded
FAA	Fellow of Australian Academy of Science
FAAS	Fellow of the American Association for the Advancement of Science
FAATS	Fellow of the Australian Academy of Technological Sciences
FACC	Fellow of the American College of Cardiology
FACCA	Fellow of the Association of Certified and Corporate Accountants
FACE	Fellow of the Australian College of Education
FACP	Fellow of American College of Physicians
FACS	Fellow of the American College of Surgeons
FAHA	Fellow Australian Academy of the Humanities
FAIA	Fellow of the American Institute of Architects
FAIAS	Fellow of the Australian Institute of Agricultural Science
FAIM	Fellow of the Australian Institute of Management
FAO	Food and Agriculture Organization
FAS	Fellow of the Antiquarian Society
FASE	Fellow of Antiquarian Society, Edinburgh
FASSA	Fellow Academy of Social Sciences of Australia
FBA	Fellow of the British Academy
FBI	Federal Bureau of Investigation
FBIM	Fellow of the British Institute of Management
FBIP	Fellow of the British Institute of Physics
FCA	Fellow of the Institute of Chartered Accountants
FCAE	Fellow Canadian Academy of Engineering
FCGI	Fellow of the City and Guilds of London Institute
FCIA	Fellow of the Chartered Institute of Arbitrators
FCIB	Fellow of the Chartered Institute of Bankers
FCIC	Fellow of the Chemical Institute of Canada
FCIM	Fellow of the Chartered Institute of Management
FCIS	Fellow of the Chartered Institute of Secretaries
FCMA	Fellow of the Chartered Institute of Management Accountants
FCO	Foreign and Commonwealth Office
FCSD	Fellow of the Chartered Society of Designers
FCT	Federal Capital Territory
FCWA	Fellow of the Institute of Cost and Works Accountants (now FCMA)
FDGB	Freier Deutscher Gewerkschaftsbund
FDP	Freier Demokratische Partei
Feb.	February
Fed.	Federation; Federal
FEng	Fellow(ship) of Engineering
FFCM	Fellow of the Faculty of Community Medicine
FFPHM	Fellow of the Faculty of Public Health Medicine
FGS	Fellow of the Geological Society
FGSM	Fellow of the Guildhall School of Music
FIA	Fellow of the Institute of Actuaries
FIAL	Fellow of the International Institute of Arts and Letters

FIAM	Fellow of the International Academy of Management
FIAMS	Fellow of the Indian Academy of Medical Sciences
FIAP	Fellow of the Institution of Analysts and Programmers
FIArb	Fellow of the Institute of Arbitrators
FIB	Fellow of the Institute of Bankers
FIBA	Fellow of the Institute of Banking Associations
FIBiol	Fellow of the Institute of Biologists
FICE	Fellow of the Institution of Civil Engineers
FIChemE	Fellow of the Institute of Chemical Engineers
FID	Fellow of the Institute of Directors
FIE	Fellow of the Institute of Engineers
FIEE	Fellow of the Institution of Electrical Engineers
FIEEE	Fellow of the Institute of Electrical and Electronics Engineers
FIFA	Fédération Internationale de Football Association
FIJ	Fellow of the Institute of Journalists
FilLic	Licentiate in Philosophy
FIM	Fellow of the Institute of Metallurgists
FIME	Fellow of the Institute of Mining Engineers
FIMechE	Fellow of the Institute of Mechanical Engineers
FIMI	Fellow of the Institute of the Motor Industry
FInstF	Fellow of the Institute of Fuel
FInstM	Fellow of the Institute of Marketing
FInstP	Fellow of the Institute of Physics
FInstPet	Fellow of the Institute of Petroleum
FIPM	Fellow of the Institute of Personnel Management
FIRE	Fellow of the Institution of Radio Engineers
FITD	Fellow of the Institute of Training and Development
FL	Florida
Fla	Florida
FLA	Fellow of the Library Association
FLN	Front de Libération Nationale
FLS	Fellow of the Linnaean Society
FMedSci	Fellow of the Academy of Medical Sciences
fmr(ly)	former(ly)
FNI	Fellow of the National Institute of Sciences of India
FNZIA	Fellow of the New Zealand Institute of Architects
FRACP	Fellow of the Royal Australasian College of Physicians
FRACS	Fellow of the Royal Australasian College of Surgeons
FRAeS	Fellow of the Royal Aeronautical Society
FRAI	Fellow of the Royal Anthropological Institute
FRAIA	Fellow of the Royal Australian Institute of Architects
FRAIC	Fellow of the Royal Architectural Institute of Canada
FRAM	Fellow of the Royal Academy of Music
FRAS	Fellow of the Royal Astronomical Society; Fellow of the Royal Asiatic Society
FRBS	Fellow of the Royal Society of British Sculptors
FRCA	Fellow of the Royal College of Anaesthetists
FRCM	Fellow of the Royal College of Music
FRCO	Fellow of the Royal College of Organists
FRCOG	Fellow of the Royal College of Obstetricians and Gynaecologists
FRCP	Fellow of the Royal College of Physicians
FRCPE	Fellow of the Royal College of Physicians, Edinburgh
FRCPGlas	Fellow of the Royal College of Physicians (Glasgow)
FRCPI	Fellow of the Royal College of Physicians of Ireland
FRCPath	Fellow Royal College of Pathologists
FRCR	Fellow Royal College of Radiology
FRCS	Fellow of the Royal College of Surgeons
FRCSE	Fellow of the Royal College of Surgeons, Edinburgh
FRCVS	Fellow of the Royal College of Veterinary Surgeons
FREconS	Fellow of the Royal Economic Society
FREng	Fellow of the Royal Academy of Engineering
FRES	Fellow of the Royal Entomological Society
FRFPS	Fellow of the Royal Faculty of Physicians and Surgeons
FRG	Federal Republic of Germany
FRGS	Fellow of the Royal Geographical Society
FRHistS	Fellow of the Royal Historical Society
FRHortS	Fellow of the Royal Horticultural Society
FRIBA	Fellow of the Royal Institute of British Architects
FRIC	Fellow of the Royal Institute of Chemists
FRICS	Fellow of the Royal Institute of Chartered Surveyors
FRMetS	Fellow of the Royal Meteorological Society
FRNCM	Fellow of the Royal Northern College of Music
FRPS	Fellow of the Royal Photographic Society
FRS	Fellow of the Royal Society
FRSA	Fellow of the Royal Society of Arts
FRSAMD	Fellow of the Royal Scottish Academy of Music and Drama
FRSC	Fellow of the Royal Society of Canada; Fellow of the Royal Society of Chemistry
FRSE	Fellow of the Royal Society of Edinburgh
FRSL	Fellow of the Royal Society of Literature
FRSM	Fellow of the Royal Society of Medicine
FRSNZ	Fellow of the Royal Society of New Zealand
FRSS	Fellow of the Royal Statistical Society
FRSSA	Fellow of the Royal Society of South Africa
FRTS	Fellow of the Royal Television Society
FSA	Fellow of the Society of Antiquaries
FSIAD	Fellow of the Society of Industrial Artists and Designers
FTI	Fellow of the Textile Institute
FTS	Fellow of Technological Sciences
FWAAS	Fellow of the World Academy of Arts and Sciences
FZS	Fellow of the Zoological Society
GA	Georgia
Ga	Georgia
GATT	General Agreement on Tariffs and Trade

GB	Great Britain
GBE	Knight (or Dame) Grand Cross of (the Order of) the British Empire
GC	George Cross
GCB	Knight Grand Cross of (the Order of) the Bath
GCIE	Knight Grand Commander of (the Order of) the Indian Empire
GCMG	Knight (or Dame) Grand Cross of (the Order of) St Michael and St George
GCSI	Knight Grand Commander of (the Order of) the Star of India
GCVO	Knight (or Dame) Grand Cross of the Royal Victorian Order
GDR	German Democratic Republic
Gen.	General
GHQ	General Headquarters
GLA	Greater London Authority
Glam.	Glamorganshire
GLC	Greater London Council
Glos.	Gloucestershire
GM	George Medal
GmbH	Gesellschaft mit beschränkter Haftung (Limited Liability Company)
GOC	General Officer Commanding
GOC-in-C	General Officer Commanding-in-Chief
Gov.	Governor
Govt	Government
GPO	General Post Office
Grad.	Graduate
GRSM	Graduate of the Royal School of Music
GSO	General Staff Officer
Hants.	Hampshire
hc	honoris causa
HE	His Eminence; His (or Her) Excellency
Herefords.	Herefordshire
Herts.	Hertfordshire
HH	His (or Her) Highness
HI	Hawaii
HIV	human immunodeficiency virus
HLD	Doctor of Humane Letters
HM	His (or Her) Majesty
HMS	His (or Her) Majesty's Ship
Hon.	Honorary; Honourable
Hons	Honours
Hosp.	Hospital
HQ	Headquarters
HRH	His (or Her) Royal Highness
HSH	His (or Her) Serene Highness
HSP	Hungarian Socialist Party
HSWP	Hungarian Socialist Workers' Party
Hunts.	Huntingdonshire
IA	Iowa
Ia	Iowa
IAAF	International Association of Athletics Federations
IAEA	International Atomic Energy Agency
IATA	International Air Transport Association
IBA	Independent Broadcasting Authority
IBRD	International Bank for Reconstruction and Development (World Bank)
ICAO	International Civil Aviation Organization
ICC	International Chamber of Commerce
ICE	Institution of Civil Engineers
ICEM	Intergovernmental Committee for European Migration
ICFTU	International Confederation of Free Trade Unions
ICI	Imperial Chemical Industries
ICOM	International Council of Museums
ICRC	International Committee for the Red Cross
ICS	Indian Civil Service
ICSID	International Centre for Settlement of Investment Disputes
ICSU	International Council of Scientific Unions
ID	Idaho
Ida	Idaho
IDA	International Development Association
IDB	Inter-American Development Bank
IEA	International Energy Agency
IEE	Institution of Electrical Engineers
IEEE	Institution of Electrical and Electronic Engineers
IFAD	International Fund for Agricultural Development
IFC	International Finance Corporation
IGAD	Intergovernmental Authority on Development
IISS	International Institute for Strategic Studies
IL	Illinois
Ill.	Illinois
ILO	International Labour Organization
IMCO	Inter-Governmental Maritime Consultative Organization
IMechE	Institution of Mechanical Engineers
IMF	International Monetary Fund
IMO	International Maritime Organization
IN	Indiana
Inc.	Incorporated
Ind.	Indiana; Independent
Insp.	Inspector
Inst.	Institute; Institution
Int.	International
INTERPOL	International Criminal Police Organization
INTUC	Indian National Trades Union Congress
IOC	International Olympic Committee
IPU	Inter-Parliamentary Union
ISO	Companion of the Imperial Service Order
ITA	Independent Television Authority
ITU	International Telecommunications Union
ITV	Independent Television
IUPAC	International Union of Pure and Applied Chemistry
IUPAP	International Union of Pure and Applied Physics
Jan.	January
JCB	Bachelor of Canon Law
JCD	Doctor of Canon Law
JD	Doctor of Jurisprudence
JMK	Johan Mangku Negara (Malaysia)
JP	Justice of the Peace
Jr	Junior
JSD	Doctor of Juristic Science
Jt(ly)	Joint(ly)
JUD	Juris utriusque Doctor (Doctor of both Civil and Canon Law)
JuD	Doctor of Law
JUDr	Juris utriusque Doctor (Doctor of both Civil and Canon Law); Doctor of Law
Kan.	Kansas
KBE	Knight Commander of (the Order of) the British Empire
KC	King's Counsel
KCB	Knight Commander of (the Order of) the Bath
KCIE	Knight Commander of (the Order of) the Indian Empire
KCMG	Knight Commander of (the Order of) St Michael and St George
KCSI	Knight Commander of (the Order of) the Star of India
KCVO	Knight Commander of the Royal Victorian Order
KG	Royal Knight of the Most Noble Order of the Garter
KGB	Committee of State Security (USSR)
KK	Kaien Kaisha
KLM	Koninklijke Luchtvaart Maatschappij (Royal Dutch Airlines)
KNZM	Knight of the New Zealand Order of Merit
KP	Knight of (the Order of) St Patrick
KS	Kansas
KStJ	Knight of (the Order of) St John of Jerusalem
KT	Knight of (the Order of) the Thistle
Kt	Knight
KY	Kentucky
Ky	Kentucky
LA	Louisiana; Los Angeles
La	Louisiana
Lab.	Laboratory
Lancs.	Lancashire
LDP	Liberal Democratic Party
LDS	Licentiate in Dental Surgery
Legis.	Legislative
Leics.	Leicestershire
LenD	Licencié en Droit
LèsL	Licencié ès Lettres
LèsSc	Licencié ès Sciences
LG	Lady of (the Order of) the Garter
LHD	Doctor of Humane Letters
LI	Long Island
LicenDer	Licenciado en Derecho
LicenFil	Licenciado en Filosofia
LicMed	Licentiate in Medicine
Lincs.	Lincolnshire
LittD	Doctor of Letters
LLB	Bachelor of Laws
LLC	Limited Liability Company
LLD	Doctor of Laws
LLL	Licentiate of Laws
LLM	Master of Laws
LLP	Limited Liability Partnership
LM	Licentiate of Medicine; Licentiate Midwifery
LN	League of Nations
LPh	Licentiate of Philosophy
LRAM	Licentiate of the Royal Academy of Music
LRCP	Licentiate of the Royal College of Physicians
LSE	London School of Economics and Political Science
Lt	Lieutenant
Ltd	Limited
Ltda	Limitada
LTh	Licentiate in Theology
LVO	Lieutenant, Royal Victorian Order
m.	married; marriage; metre(s)
MA	Massachusetts; Master of Arts
MAgr	Master of Agriculture (USA)
Maj.	Major
MALD	Master of Arts in Law and Diplomacy
Man.	Management; Manager; Managing; Manitoba
MArch	Master of Architecture
Mass	Massachusetts
Math.	Mathematics; Mathematical
MB	Bachelor of Medicine; Manitoba
MBA	Master of Business Administration
MBE	Member of (the Order of) the British Empire
MBS	Master of Business Studies
MC	Military Cross
MCC	Marylebone Cricket Club

MCE	Master of Civil Engineering	Neb.	Nebraska
MCh	Master of Surgery	NEDC	National Economic Development Council
MChD	Master of Dental Surgery	NERC	Natural Environment Research Council
MCL	Master of Civil Law	Nev.	Nevada
MCom(m)	Master of Commerce	NF	Newfoundland
MCP	Master of City Planning	NGO	Non-Governmental Organization
MD	Maryland; Doctor of Medicine	NH	New Hampshire
Md	Maryland	NHS	National Health Service
MDiv	Master of Divinity	NI	Northern Ireland
MDS	Master of Dental Surgery	NIH	National Institutes of Health
ME	Maine; Myalgic Encephalomyelitis	NJ	New Jersey
Me	Maine	NL	Newfoundland and Labrador
MEconSc	Master of Economic Sciences	NM	New Mexico
MEd	Master in Education	Northants.	Northamptonshire
mem.	member	Notts.	Nottinghamshire
MEng	Master of Engineering (Dublin)	Nov.	November
MEP	Member of European Parliament	NPC	National People's Congress
MFA	Master of Fine Arts	nr	near
Mfg	Manufacturing	NRC	Nuclear Research Council
Mfrs	Manufacturers	NS	Nova Scotia
Mgr	Monseigneur; Monsignor	NSF	National Science Foundation
MI	Michigan; Marshall Islands	NSW	New South Wales
MIA	Master of International Affairs	NT	Northern Territory
MICE	Member of the Institution of Civil Engineers	NU	Nunavut Territory
MIChemE	Member of the Institution of Chemical Engineers	NV	Naamloze Vennootschap; Nevada
Mich.	Michigan	NW	North West
Middx	Middlesex	NWT	North West Territories
MIEE	Member of the Institution of Electrical Engineers	NY	New York (State)
Mil.	Military	NZ	New Zealand
MIMarE	Member of the Institute of Marine Engineers	NZIC	New Zealand Institute of Chemistry
MIMechE	Member of the Institution of Mechanical Engineers		
MIMinE	Member of the Institution of Mining Engineers	O	Ohio
Minn.	Minnesota	OAPEC	Organization of Arab Petroleum Exporting Countries
MInstT	Member of the Institute of Transport	OAS	Organization of American States
Miss.	Mississippi	OAU	Organization of African Unity
MIStructE	Member of the Institution of Structural Engineers	OBE	Officer of (the Order of) the British Empire
MIT	Massachusetts Institute of Technology	OC	Officer of the Order of Canada
MJ	Master of Jurisprudence	Oct.	October
MLA	Member of the Legislative Assembly; Master of Landscape Architecture	OE	Order of Excellence (Guyana)
		OECD	Organisation for Economic Co-operation and Development
MLC	Member of the Legislative Council	OEEC	Organization for European Economic Co-operation
MM	Military Medal	OFS	Orange Free State
MLitt	Master in Letters	OH	Ohio
MM	Military Medal	OHCHR	Office of the United Nations High Commissioner for Human Rights
MMus	Master of Music		
MN	Minnesota	OIC	Organization of the Islamic Conference
MNOC	Movement of Non-Aligned Countries	OJ	Order of Jamaica
MO	Missouri	OK	Oklahoma
Mo.	Missouri	Okla	Oklahoma
MOH	Medical Officer of Health	OM	Member of the Order of Merit
Mon.	Monmouthshire	ON	Ontario; Order of Nigeria
Mont.	Montana	Ont.	Ontario
Movt	Movement	ONZ	Order of New Zealand
MP	Member of Parliament; Madhya Pradesh	OP	Ordo Praedicatorum (Dominicans)
MPA	Master of Public Administration (Harvard)	OPCW	Organization for the Prohibition of Chemical Weapons
MPh	Master of Philosophy (USA)	OPEC	Organization of the Petroleum Exporting Countries
MPhil	Master of Philosophy	OPM	Office of Production Management
MPolSci	Master of Political Science	OQ	Officer National Order of Québec
MPP	Member of Provincial Parliament (Canada)	OR	Oregon
MRAS	Member of the Royal Asiatic Society	Ore.	Oregon
MRC	Medical Research Council	Org.	Organization
MRCP	Member of the Royal College of Physicians	OSB	Order of St Benedict
MRCPE	Member of the Royal College of Physicians, Edinburgh	OSCE	Organization for Security and Co-operation in Europe
MRCS	Member of the Royal College of Surgeons	Oxon.	of Oxford University; Oxfordshire
MRCSE	Member of the Royal College of Surgeons, Edinburgh		
MRCVS	Member of the Royal College of Veterinary Surgeons	PA	Pennsylvania
MRI	Member of the Royal Institution	Pa	Pennsylvania
MRIA	Member of the Royal Irish Academy	Parl.	Parliament; Parliamentary
MRIC	Member of the Royal Institute of Chemistry	PC	Privy Councillor
MRP	Mouvement Républicain Populaire	PCC	Provincial Congress Committee
MS	Mississippi; Master of Science; Master of Surgery	PdB	Bachelor of Pedagogy
MSc	Master of Science	PdD	Doctor of Pedagogy
MScS	Master of Social Science	PdM	Master of Pedagogy
MSP	Member Scottish Parliament	PDS	Partei des Demokratischen Sozialismus
MT	Montana	PE	Prince Edward Island
MTS	Master of Theological Studies	PEI	Prince Edward Island
MUDr	Doctor of Medicine	Pembs.	Pembrokeshire
MusB(ac)	Bachelor of Music	PEN	Poets, Playwrights, Essayists and Novelists (Club)
MusD(oc)	Doctor of Music	Perm.	Permanent
MusM	Master of Music (Cambridge)	PGCE	Postgraduate Certificate in Education
MVD	Master of Veterinary Medicine	PhB	Bachelor of Philosophy
MVO	Member of the Royal Victorian Order	PhD(r)	Doctor of Philosophy
MW	Master of Wine	PharmD	Docteur en Pharmacie
		Phila	Philadelphia
N	North; Northern	PhL	Licentiate of Philosophy
NAS	National Academy of Sciences (USA)	PLA	People's Liberation Army; Port of London Authority
NASA	National Aeronautics and Space Administration	PLC	Public Limited Company
Nat.	National	PLO	Palestine Liberation Organization
NATO	North Atlantic Treaty Organization	PMB	Private Mail Bag
Naz.	Nazionale	pnr	partner
NB	New Brunswick	PO(B)	Post Office (Box)
NBC	National Broadcasting Corporation	POW	Prisoner of War
NC	North Carolina	PPR	Polish Workers' Party
ND	North Dakota	PPRA	Past President of the Royal Academy
NE	Nebraska; North East	PQ	Province of Québec
NEA	National Endowment for the Arts	PR	Puerto Rico

PRA	President of the Royal Academy
Pref.	Prefecture
Prep.	Preparatory
Pres.	President
PRI	President of the Royal Institute (of Painters in Water Colours)
PRIBA	President of the Royal Institute of British Architects
Prin.	Principal
Priv Doz	Privat Dozent (recognized teacher not on the regular staff)
PRO	Public Relations Officer
Proc.	Proceedings
prod.	producer
Prof.	Professor
Propr	Proprietor
Prov.	Province; Provincial
PRS	President of the Royal Society
PRSA	President of the Royal Scottish Academy
PSM	Panglima Setia Mahota
Pty	Proprietary
Publ.(s)	Publication(s)
Publr	Publisher
Pvt.	Private
PZPR	Polish United Workers' Party
QC	Québec; Queen's Counsel
QGM	Queen's Gallantry Medal
Qld	Queensland
QPM	Queen's Police Medal
QSO	Queen's Service Order
q.v.	quod vide (to which refer)
RA	Royal Academy; Royal Academician; Royal Artillery
RAAF	Royal Australian Air Force
RAC	Royal Armoured Corps
RACP	Royal Australasian College of Physicians
RADA	Royal Academy of Dramatic Art
RAF	Royal Air Force
RAFVR	Royal Air Force Volunteer Reserve
RAM	Royal Academy of Music
RAMC	Royal Army Medical Corps
RAOC	Royal Army Ordnance Corps
RC	Roman Catholic
RCA	Radio Corporation of America; Royal Canadian Academy; Royal College of Art
RCAF	Royal Canadian Air Force
RCM	Royal College of Music
RCP	Romanian Communist Party
RCP	Royal College of Physicians
RCPI	Royal College of Physicians of Ireland
Regt	Regiment
REME	Royal Electric and Mechanical Engineers
Rep.	Representative; represented
Repub.	Republic
resgnd	resigned
retd	retired
Rev.	Reverend
RI	Rhode Island
RIBA	Royal Institute of British Architects
RMA	Royal Military Academy
RN	Royal Navy
RNR	Royal Naval Reserve
RNVR	Royal Naval Volunteer Reserve
RNZAF	Royal New Zealand Air Force
RP	Member Royal Society of Portrait Painters
RPR	Rassemblement pour la République
RSA	Royal Scottish Academy; Royal Society of Arts
RSC	Royal Shakespeare Company; Royal Society of Canada
RSDr	Doctor of Social Sciences
RSFSR	Russian Soviet Federative Socialist Republic
RSL	Royal Society of Literature
Rt Hon.	Right Honourable
Rt Rev.	Right Reverend
RVO	Royal Victorian Order
RWS	Royal Society of Painters in Water Colours
s.	son(s)
S	South; Southern
SA	Sociedad Anónima; Société Anonyme; South Africa; South Australia
SAARC	South Asian Association for Regional Co-operation
SADC	South African Development Community
SAE	Society of Aeronautical Engineers
Salop.	Shropshire
SALT	Strategic Arms Limitation Treaty
Sask.	Saskatchewan
SB	Bachelor of Science (USA)
SC	Senior Counsel; South Carolina
SCAP	Supreme Command Allied Powers
ScB	Bachelor of Science
ScD	Doctor of Science
SD	South Dakota
SDak	South Dakota
SDLP	Social and Democratic Liberal Party
SDP	Social Democratic Party
SE	South East
SEATO	South East Asia Treaty Organization

Sec.	Secretary
SEC	Securities and Exchange Commission
Secr.	Secretariat
SED	Sozialistische Einheitspartei Deutschlands (Socialist Unity Party of the German Democratic Republic)
Sept.	September
S-et-O	Seine-et-Oise
SHAEF	Supreme Headquarters Allied Expeditionary Force
SHAPE	Supreme Headquarters Allied Powers in Europe
SJ	Society of Jesus (Jesuits)
SJD	Doctor of Juristic Science
SK	Saskatchewan
SLD	Social and Liberal Democrats
SM	Master of Science
SOAS	School of Oriental and African Studies
Soc.	Society; Société
SpA	Societá per Azioni
SPD	Sozialdemokratische Partei Deutschlands
Sr	Senior
SRC	Science Research Council
SRL	Societé a responsabilité
SSM	Seria Seta Mahkota (Malaysia)
SSR	Soviet Socialist Republic
St	Saint
Staffs.	Staffordshire
STB	Bachelor of Sacred Theology
STD	Doctor of Sacred Theology
STL	Licentiate of Sacred Theology
STM	Master of Sacred Theology
str.	strasse
Supt	Superintendent
SW	South West
SWAPO	South West Africa People's Organization
TA	Territorial Army
TD	Teachta Dála (member of the Dáil); Territorial Decoration
Tech.	Technical; Technology
Temp.	Temporary
Tenn.	Tennessee
Tex.	Texas
ThB	Bachelor of Theology
ThD	Doctor of Theology
THDr	Doctor of Theology
ThM	Master of Theology
TN	Tennessee
Trans.	Translation; Translator
Treas.	Treasurer
TU(C)	Trades Union (Congress)
TV	television
TX	Texas
UAE	United Arab Emirates
UAR	United Arab Republic
UCLA	University of California at Los Angeles
UDEAC	L'Union Douanière et Economique de l'Afrique Centrale
UDR	Union des Démocrates pour la République
UED	University Education Diploma
UK	United Kingdom (of Great Britain and Northern Ireland)
UKAEA	United Kingdom Atomic Energy Authority
UMIST	University of Manchester Institute of Science and Technology
UMNO	United Malays National Organization
UN(O)	United Nations (Organization)
UNA	United Nations Association
UNCED	United Nations Council for Education and Development
UNCHS	United Nations Centre for Human Settlements (Habitat)
UNCTAD	United Nations Conference on Trade and Development
UNDCP	United Nations International Drug Control Programme
UNDP	United Nations Development Programme
UNDRO	United Nations Disaster Relief Office
UNEF	United Nations Emergency Force
UNEP	United Nations Environment Programme
UNESCO	United Nations Educational, Scientific and Cultural Organisation
UNFPA	United Nations Population Fund
UNHCR	United Nations High Commissioner for Refugees
UNICEF	United Nations International Children's Emergency Fund
UNIDO	United Nations Industrial Development Organization
UNIFEM	United Nations Development Fund for Women
UNITAR	United Nations Institute for Training and Research
Univ.	University
UNKRA	United Nations Korean Relief Administration
UNRRA	United Nations Relief and Rehabilitation Administration
UNRWA	United Nations Relief and Works Agency
UNU	United Nations University
UP	United Provinces; Uttar Pradesh
UPU	Universal Postal Union
Urb.	Urbanizacion
US	United States
USA	United States of America
USAAF	United States Army Air Force
USAF	United States Air Force
USAID	United States Agency for International Development
USN	United States Navy
USNR	United States Navy Reserve
USPHS	United States Public Health Service
USS	United States Ship

ABBREVIATIONS

USSR	Union of Soviet Socialist Republics	WFTU	World Federation of Trade Unions
UT	Utah	WHO	World Health Organization
UWI	University of the West Indies	WI	Wisconsin
		Wilts.	Wiltshire
VA	Virginia	WIPO	World Intellectual Property Organization
Va	Virginia	Wis.	Wisconsin
VC	Victoria Cross	WMO	World Meteorological Organization
VI	(US) Virgin Islands	WNO	Welsh National Opera
Vic.	Victoria	Worcs.	Worcestershire
Vol.(s)	Volume(s)	WRAC	Women's Royal Army Corps
VSO	Voluntary Services Overseas	WRNS	Women's Royal Naval Service
VT	Vermont	WTO	World Trade Organization
Vt	Vermont	WV	West Virginia
		WVa	West Virginia
W	West; Western	WWF	World Wildlife Fund
WA	Washington (State); Western Australia	WY	Wyoming
Warwicks.	Warwickshire	Wyo.	Wyoming
Wash.	Washington (State)		
WCC	World Council of Churches	YMCA	Young Men's Christian Association
WCT	World Championship Tennis	Yorks.	Yorkshire
WEU	Western European Union	YT	Yukon Territory
WFP	World Food Programme	YWCA	Young Women's Christian Association

INTERNATIONAL TELEPHONE CODES

To make international calls to telephone and fax numbers listed in the book, dial the international code of the country from which you are calling, followed by the appropriate code for the country you wish to call (listed below), followed by the area code (if applicable) and telephone or fax number listed in the entry.

	Country code	+ or – GMT*		Country code	+ or – GMT*
Abkhazia	7	+4	Egypt	20	+2
Afghanistan	93	+4½	El Salvador	503	–6
Åland Islands	358	+2	Equatorial Guinea	240	+1
Albania	355	+1	Eritrea	291	+3
Algeria	213	+1	Estonia	372	+2
American Samoa	1 684	–11	Ethiopia	251	+3
Andorra	376	+1	Falkland Islands	500	–4
Angola	244	+1	Faroe Islands	298	0
Anguilla	1 264	–4	Fiji	679	+12
Antigua and Barbuda	1 268	–4	Finland	358	+2
Argentina	54	–3	France	33	+1
Armenia	374	+4	French Guiana	594	–3
Aruba	297	–4	French Polynesia	689	–9 to –10
Ascension Island	247	0	Gabon	241	+1
Australia	61	+8 to +10	Gambia	220	0
Austria	43	+1	Georgia	995	+4
Azerbaijan	994	+5	Germany	49	+1
Bahamas	1 242	–5	Ghana	233	0
Bahrain	973	+3	Gibraltar	350	+1
Bangladesh	880	+6	Greece	30	+2
Barbados	1 246	–4	Greenland	299	–1 to –4
Belarus	375	+2	Grenada	1 473	–4
Belgium	32	+1	Guadeloupe	590	–4
Belize	501	–6	Guam	1 671	+10
Benin	229	+1	Guatemala	502	–6
Bermuda	1 441	–4	Guernsey	44	0
Bhutan	975	+6	Guinea	224	0
Bolivia	591	–4	Guinea-Bissau	245	0
Bonaire	599	–4	Guyana	592	–4
Bosnia and Herzegovina	387	+1	Haiti	509	–5
Botswana	267	+2	Honduras	504	–6
Brazil	55	–3 to –4	Hong Kong	852	+8
British Indian Ocean Territory			Hungary	36	+1
(Diego Garcia)	246	+5	Iceland	354	0
British Virgin Islands	1 284	–4	India	91	+5½
Brunei	673	+8	Indonesia	62	+7 to +9
Bulgaria	359	+2	Iran	98	+3½
Burkina Faso	226	0	Iraq	964	+3
Burundi	257	+2	Ireland	353	0
Cambodia	855	+7	Isle of Man	44	0
Cameroon	237	+1	Israel	972	+2
Canada	1	–3 to –8	Italy	39	+1
Cape Verde	238	–1	Jamaica	1 876	–5
Cayman Islands	1 345	–5	Japan	81	+9
Central African Republic	236	+1	Jersey	44	0
Ceuta	34	+1	Jordan	962	+2
Chad	235	+1	Kazakhstan	7	+6
Chile	56	–4	Kenya	254	+3
China, People's Republic	86	+8	Kiribati	686	+12 to +13
Christmas Island	61	+7	Korea, Democratic People's Republic		
Cocos (Keeling) Islands	61	+6½	(North Korea)	850	+9
Colombia	57	–5	Korea, Republic (South Korea)	82	+9
Comoros	269	+3	Kosovo	381†	+3
Congo, Democratic Republic	243	+1	Kuwait	965	+3
Congo, Republic	242	+1	Kyrgyzstan	996	+5
Cook Islands	682	–10	Laos	856	+7
Costa Rica	506	–6	Latvia	371	+2
Côte d'Ivoire	225	0	Lebanon	961	+2
Croatia	385	+1	Lesotho	266	+2
Cuba	53	–5	Liberia	231	0
Curaçao	599	–4	Libya	218	+1
Cyprus	357	+2	Liechtenstein	423	+1
Czech Republic	420	+1	Lithuania	370	+2
Denmark	45	+1	Luxembourg	352	+1
Djibouti	253	+3	Macao	853	+8
Dominica	1 767	–4	Macedonia, former Yugoslav republic	389	+1
Dominican Republic	1 809	–4	Madagascar	261	+3
Ecuador	593	–5	Malawi	265	+2

	Country code	+ or – GMT*		Country code	+ or – GMT*
Malaysia	60	+8	Singapore	65	+8
Maldives	960	+5	Sint Eustatius	1721	–4
Mali	223	0	Sint Maarten	1721	–4
Malta	356	+1	Slovakia	421	+1
Marshall Islands	692	+12	Slovenia	386	+1
Martinique	596	–4	Solomon Islands	677	+11
Mauritania	222	0	Somalia	252	+3
Mauritius	230	+4	South Africa	27	+2
Mayotte	262	+3	South Ossetia	7	+4
Melilla	34	+1	South Sudan	211	+2
Mexico	52	–6 to –7	Spain	34	+1
Micronesia, Federated States	691	+10 to +11	Sri Lanka	94	+5½
Moldova	373	+2	Sudan	249	+2
Monaco	377	+1	Suriname	597	–3
Mongolia	976	+7 to +9	Svalbard	47	+1
Montenegro	382	+1	Swaziland	268	+2
Montserrat	1 664	–4	Sweden	46	+1
Morocco	212	0	Switzerland	41	+1
Mozambique	258	+2	Syria	963	+2
Myanmar	95	+6½	Taiwan	886	+8
Nagornyi Karabakh	374	+4	Tajikistan	992	+5
Namibia	264	+2	Tanzania	255	+3
Nauru	674	+12	Thailand	66	+7
Nepal	977	+5¾	Timor-Leste	670	+9
Netherlands	31	+1	Togo	228	0
New Caledonia	687	+11	Tokelau	690	+15
New Zealand	64	+12	Tonga	676	+13
Nicaragua	505	–6	Transnistria	373	+2
Niger	227	+1	Trinidad and Tobago	1 868	–4
Nigeria	234	+1	Tristan da Cunha	290	0
Niue	683	–11	Tunisia	216	+1
Norfolk Island	672	+11½	Turkey	90	+2
Northern Mariana Islands	1 670	+10	'Turkish Republic of Northern Cyprus'	90 392	+2
Norway	47	+1	Turkmenistan	993	+5
Oman	968	+4	Turks and Caicos Islands	1 649	–5
Pakistan	92	+5	Tuvalu	688	+12
Palau	680	+9	Uganda	256	+3
Palestinian Territories	970 or 972	+2	Ukraine‡	380	+2
Panama	507	–5	United Arab Emirates	971	+4
Papua New Guinea	675	+10	United Kingdom	44	0
Paraguay	595	–4	United States of America	1	–5 to –10
Peru	51	–5	United States Virgin Islands	1 340	–4
Philippines	63	+8	Uruguay	598	–3
Pitcairn Islands	872	–8	Uzbekistan	998	+5
Poland	48	+1	Vanuatu	678	+11
Portugal	351	0	Vatican City	39	+1
Puerto Rico	1 787	–4	Venezuela	58	–4½
Qatar	974	+3	Viet Nam	84	+7
Réunion	262	+4	Wallis and Futuna Islands	681	+12
Romania	40	+2	Yemen	967	+3
Russian Federation	7	+3 to +12	Zambia	260	+2
Rwanda	250	+2	Zimbabwe	263	+2
Saba	599	–4			
Saint-Barthélemy	590	–4			
Saint Christopher and Nevis	1 869	–4			
Saint Helena	290	0			
Saint Lucia	1 758	–4			
Saint-Martin	590	–4			
Saint Pierre and Miquelon	508	–3			
Saint Vincent and the Grenadines	1 784	–4			
Samoa	685	+13			
San Marino	378	+1			
São Tomé and Príncipe	239	0			
Saudi Arabia	966	+3			
Senegal	221	0			
Serbia	381	+1			
Seychelles	248	+4			
Sierra Leone	232	0			

* The times listed compare the standard (winter) times in the various countries. Some countries adopt Summer (Daylight Saving) Time—i.e. +1 hour—for part of the year.

† Mobile telephone numbers for Kosovo use either the country code for Monaco (377) or the country code for Slovenia (386).

‡ The Republic of Crimea and the City of Sevastopol were placed in the time zone GMT+4 following their annexation by Russia in 2014.

Note: Telephone and fax numbers using the Inmarsat ocean region code 870 are listed in full. No country or area code is required, but it is necessary to precede the number with the international access code of the country from which the call is made.

REIGNING ROYAL FAMILIES OF THE WORLD

Biographical entries of most of the reigning monarchs and of certain other members of the reigning royal families will be found in their appropriate alphabetical order in the biographical section of this book. The name under which they can be found in the text of the book will be listed in this section in bold type.

BAHRAIN

Reigning King

HM SHEIKH HAMAD BIN ISA AL-**KHALIFA**; b. 28 January 1950; succeeded 6 March 1999 as Ruler of Bahrain on the death of his father, Sheikh Isa bin Sulman al-Khalifa; acceded as Amir 6 March 1999; proclaimed King 14 February 2002; married 9 October 1968, Shaikha Sabeeka bint Ibrahim al-Khalifa; three sons, one daughter; four sons, four daughters with his three other wives.

Crown Prince

HRH Sheikh Salman bin Hamad bin Isa al-**Khalifa**, b. 21 October 1969 ; married Hala bint D'aij al-Khalifa; two sons, two daughters.

BELGIUM

Reigning King

HM KING **PHILIPPE** I; b. 15 April 1960; succeeded to the throne 21 July 2013, on the abdication of his father, King Albert II; married 4 December 1999, Mathilde Marie Christiane Ghislaine d'Udekem d'Acoz (Queen Mathilde) (b. 20 January 1973).

Children of the King

HRH Princess Elisabeth, Duchess of Brabant, b. 25 October 2001

HRH Prince Gabriel, b. 20 August 2003

HRH Prince Emmanuel, b. 4 October 2005

HRH Princess Eléonore, b. 16 April 2008

Parents of the King

King Albert II, b. 6 June 1934; succeeded to the throne 9 August 1993, on the death of his brother, King Baudouin I; married 2 July 1959, Donna Paola Ruffo di Calabria (Queen Paola) (b. 11 September 1937); abdicated 21 July 2013 in favour of his son, Crown Prince Philippe; three children.

Brother and Sister of the King

Princess Astrid, b. 5 June 1962; married 22 September 1984, Archduke Lorenz; son, Prince Amedeo, b. February 1986; daughter, Princess Maria Laura, b. August 1988; son, Prince Joachim, b. December 1991; daughter, Princess Louisa-Maria, b. October 1995; daughter, Princess Laetitia Maria, b. 23 April 2003.

Prince Laurent, b. 19 October 1963; married 12 April 2003, Claire Coombs; daughter, Princess Louise, b. February 2004; son, Prince Aymeric, b. December 2005; son, Prince Nicolas, b. December 2005.

BHUTAN

The Druk Gyalpo (Dragon King)

HM DASHO JIGME KHESAR NAMGYAL **WANGCHUCK**; b. 21 February 1980; succeeded to the throne 14 December 2006, on the abdication of his father, the Druk Gyalpo Jigme Singye Wangchuk.

Parents of the King

King Jigme Singye **Wangchuck**, b. 11 November 1955; succeeded to the throne 24 July 1972; crowned 2 June 1974; abdicated 14 December 2006; married Queen Ashi Tshering Yandon Wangchuck (b. 21 June 1959); two sons, one daughter; three sons, four daughters with his three other wives.

Brothers and Sisters of the King

HRH Princess Chimi Yangzom Wangchuck, b. 10 January 1980.

HRH Princess Sonam Dechen Wangchuck, b. 5 August 1981.

HRH Princess Dechen Yangzom Wangchuck, b. 2 December 1981.

HRH Princess Kesang Choden Wangchuck, b. 23 January 1982.

HRH Prince Jigyel Ugyen Wangchuck, b. 16 July 1984.

HRH Prince Khamsum Singye Wangchuck, b. 6 October 1985.

HRH Prince Jigme Dorji Wangchuck, b. 14 April 1986.

HRH Princess Euphelma Choden Wangchuck, b. 6 June 1993.

HRH Prince Ugyen Jigme Wangchuck, b. 11 November 1994.

BRUNEI

Reigning Sultan and Yang di-Pertuan

HM Sultan Haji HASSANAL **BOLKIAH MU'IZUDDIN WADDAULAH**; b. 15 July 1946; succeeded as 29th Sultan 5 October 1967, on the abdication of his father, Sultan Haji Omar Ali Saifuddien II; crowned 1 August 1968; married 29 July 1965, HM Raja Isteri Pengiran Anak Hajjah Saleha; two sons, four daughters; also married 28 October 1981, Mariam Abd Aziz (divorced 2003); two sons, two daughters; also married 19 August 2005, HRH Pengiran Isteri Azrinaz Mazhar Hakim (divorced 2010); one son, one daughter.

Crown Prince

HRH Prince Haji al-**Muhtadee Billah**, b. 17 February 1974; proclaimed Crown Prince 10 August 1998; married 9 September 2004, HRH Pengiran Anak Isteri Pengiran Anak Sarah binti Pengiran Salleh Ab Rahaman; one son, one daughter.

Brothers of the Sultan

HRH Prince Mohamed **Bolkiah**, b. 27 August 1947.

HRH Prince Haji Sufri Bolkiah, b. 31 July 1951.

HRH Prince Haji Jefri **Bolkiah**, b. 6 November 1954.

CAMBODIA

Reigning King

KING **NORODOM SIHAMONI**; b. 14 May 1953; appointed King by the Royal Council of the Throne October 2004, following the abdication of his father, the late King Norodom Sihanouk.

Parents of the King

King Norodom Sihanouk, b. 31 October 1922, died 15 October 2012; elected King 1941; abdicated 1955; took oath of fidelity to vacant throne 1960; elected Head of State 1960, on the death of his father; deposed 1970; elected as King 24 September 1993; abdicated October 2004; married Queen Norodom Monineath Sihanouk.

Brothers and Sisters of the King

Princess Buppha Devi, b. 8 January 1943.

Prince Yuvaneath, b. 17 October 1943.

Prince **Norodom Ranariddh**, b. 2 January 1944.

Prince Ravivong, b. 1944, died 1973.

Prince Chakrapong, b. 21 October 1945.

Prince Naradipo, b. 10 February 1946, died 1976.

Princess Soriya Roeungsey, b. 1947, died 1976.

Princess Kantha Bopha, b. 1948, died 14 December 1952.

Prince Khemanourak, b. 1949, died 1975.

Princess Botum Bopha, b. 1951, died 1976.

Princess Socheata, b. 1953, died 1975.

Prince Narindrapong, b. 18 September 1954, died 8 October 2003.

Princess Arunrasmy, b. 2 October 1955.

DENMARK

Reigning Queen

HM QUEEN **MARGRETHE II**; b. 16 April 1940; succeeded to the throne 14 January 1972, on the death of her father, King Frederik IX; married 10 June 1967, Count Henri Marie Jean André de Laborde de Monpezat (HRH Prince Consort Henrik) (b. 11 June 1934).

Children of the Queen

HRH Crown Prince **Frederik André Henrik Christian**, b. 26 May 1968; married 14 May 2004, Mary Elizabeth Donaldson (HRH Crown Princess Mary Elizabeth) (b. 5 February 1972); son, HRH Prince Christian Valdemar Henri John, b. 15 October 2005; daughter, HRH Princess Isabella Henrietta Ingrid Margrethe, b. 21 April 2007; son, HRH Prince Vincent Frederik Minik Alexander, b. 8 January 2011; daughter, HRH Princess Josephine Sophia Ivalo Mathilda, b. 8 January 2011.

HRH Prince Joachim Holger Waldemar Christian, b. 7 June 1969; married 1st 18 November 1995, Alexandra Christina Manley (Alexandra Christina, Countess of Frederiksborg) (b. 30 June 1964) (divorced 2005); son, HH Prince Nikolai William Alexander Frederik, b. 28 August 1999; son, HH Prince Felix Henrik Valdemar Christian, b. 22 July 2002; married 2nd 24 May 2008, Marie Cavallier (Princess Marie of Denmark); son, HH Prince Henrik Carl Joachim Alain, b. 4 May 2009; daughter, HH Princess Athena Marguerite Françoise Marie, b. 24 January 2012.

Parents of the Queen

King Frederik IX, b. 11 March 1899 (son of King Christian X and Queen Alexandrine), died 14 January 1972; married 24 May 1935, Princess Ingrid of Sweden (b. 28 March 1910, died 7 November 2000).

Sisters of the Queen

HRH Princess Benedikte Astrid Ingeborg Ingrid, b. 29 April 1944; married 3 February 1968, Prince Richard zu Sayn-Wittgenstein-Berleburg (b. 29 October 1934); son, Prince Gustav, b. 12 January 1969; daughter, Countess von Pfeil und Klein-Ellguth (formerly Princess Alexandra), b. 20 November 1970, (married, two children); daughter, Princess Nathalie, b. 2 May 1975, (married, one son).

HM Queen Anne-Marie Dagmar Ingrid of the Hellenes, b. 30 August 1946; married 18 September 1964, HM King **Constantine II** of the Hellenes (b. 2 June 1940); daughter, Princess Alexia, b. 10 July 1965, (married, four children); son, Prince Pavlos, b. 20 May 1967, (married, five children); son, Prince Nikolaos, b. 1 October 1969, (married); daughter, Princess Theodora, b. 9 June 1983; son, Prince Philippos, b. 26 April 1986.

JAPAN

Reigning Emperor

His Imperial Majesty EMPEROR **AKIHITO**; b. 23 December 1933; succeeded to the throne 7 January 1989, on the death of his father, Emperor Hirohito; enthroned 12 November 1990; married 10 April 1959, Shoda Michiko (Empress Michiko) (b. 20 October 1934).

Children of the Emperor

The Crown Prince **Naruhito** (fmrly Hiro no Miya), b. 23 February 1960; married 9 June 1993, Owada Masako (The Crown Princess Masako) (b. 9 December 1963); daughter, Princess Aiko (Toshi no Miya), b. 1 December 2001.

Prince Akishino (Fumihito, fmrly Aya no Miya), b. 30 November 1965; married 29 June 1990, Kawashima Kiko (Princess Kiko) (b. 11 September 1966); daughter, Princess Mako, b. 23 October 1991; daughter, Princess Kako, b. 29 December 1994; son, Prince Hisahito, b. 6 September 2006.

Sayako Kuroda (fmrly Nori no Miya, then Princess Sayako), b. 18 April 1969; married 15 November 2005 (relinquished Imperial claim), Yoshiki Kuroda (b. 17April 1965).

Parents of the Emperor

Emperor Hirohito, b. 29 April 1901, died 7 January 1989 (known as Emperor Showa); married 26 January 1924, Princess Kuni Nagako (b. 6 March 1903, died 16 June 2000); seven children.

JORDAN

Reigning King

KING **ABDULLAH II IBN AL-HUSSEIN**; b. 30 January 1962; succeeded to the throne 7 February 1999, on the death of his father, King Hussein Ibn Talal; married 10 June 1993, Rania al-Yassin (Queen **Rania al-Abdullah**) (b. 31 August 1970).

Children of the King

HRH Crown Prince Hussein, b. 28 June 1994.

HRH Princess Iman, b. 27 September 1996.

HRH Princess Salma, b. 26 September 2000.

HRH Prince Hashem, b. 30 January 2005.

Parents of the King

King Hussein ibn Talal, b. 14 November 1935, died 7 February 1999; married 1st Dina bint Abdelhamid (Queen Dina) (divorced), one child; married 2nd Antoinette Gardner (Princess Muna) (divorced 1972), four children; married 3rd Alia Toukan (Queen Alia) (deceased), two children; married 4th Lisa Najeeb Halaby (**Queen Noor**) (b. 23 August 1951), four children.

Brothers and Sisters of the King

Princess Alia, b. 13 February 1956; married 1st 11 July 1977, Nasser Wasfi Mirza (divorced 1983); son, Prince Hussein Mirza, b. 12 February 1981; married 2nd 30 July 1988, Mohammad Farid as-Saleh; son, Talal as-Saleh, b. 12 September 1989; son, Abdel Hamid as-Saleh, b. 15 November 1991.

Prince Feisal, b. 11 October 1963; married 1st 10 August 1987, Alia at-Tabaa (Princess Alia) (divorced April 2008); daughter, Princess Ayah, b. 11 February 1990; son, Prince Omar, b. 22 October 1993; daughter, Princess Aisha, b. 27 March 1996; daughter, Princess Sarah, b. 27 March 1996; married 2nd 24 May 2010, Sara Qabbani (Princess Sara) (divorced 14 September 2013).

Princess Zein, b. 23 April 1968; married 3 August 1989, Majdi Farid as-Saleh; son, Jaafar as-Saleh, b. 9 November 1990; daughter, Jumana as-Saleh.

Princess Aisha, b. 23 April 1968; married 26 July 1990, Zeid Juma'a (divorced); son, Aoun Juma'a, b. 27 May 1992; daughter, Muna Juma'a, b. 18 July 1996 .

Princess Haya bint al-Hussein, b. 3 May 1974; married 10 April 2004, Sheikh Muhammad bin Rashid al-Maktoum (Ruler of Dubai); daughter, Sheikha Al Jalila, b. 2 December 2007; son, Sheikh Zayed, b. 7 January 2012.

Prince Ali, b. 23 December 1975; married 23 April 2004, Rym Brahimi; daughter, Princess Jalilah, b. 16 September 2005; son, Prince Abdullah, b. 19 March 2007.

Prince Hamzah, b. 29 March 1980; named Crown Prince of Jordan 1999 (title rescinded by King Abdullah 2004); married 1st 29 August 2003 (official wedding 27 May 2004), Princess Noor bint Asem Ben Nayef (divorced 9 September 2009); daughter, Princess Haya, b. 18 April 2007; married 2nd 12 January 2012, Princess Basmah Bani Ahmad; daughter, Princess Zein, b. 3 November 2012.

Prince Hashim, b. 10 June 1981; married 15 April 2006, Fahdah Mohammed Abu Neyan; daughter, Princess Haalah, b. 6 April 2007; daughter, Princess Rayet, b. 4 July 2008; daughter, Princess Fatima al-Alia, b. 5 November 2011.

Princess Iman, b. 24 April 1983; married 22 March 2013, Zaid Azmi Mirza.

Princess Raiyah, b. 9 February 1986.

KUWAIT

Reigning Amir

SHEIKH SABAH AL-AHMAD AL-JABER AS-**SABAH**; b. 16 June 1929; married Fatuwah bint Salman (died 1990); four children (two deceased); succeeded as Amir 29 January 2006, following the abdication of Sheikh Saad al-Abdullah as-Salim as-**Sabah**.

Crown Prince

HH Sheikh Nawaf al-Ahmad al-Jaber as-**Sabah**; b. 25 June 1937; four sons, one daughter; proclaimed Crown Prince 20 February 2006.

LESOTHO

Reigning King

KING **LETSIE III**; b. 17 July 1963; installed as King 12 November 1990, abdicated 25 January 1995, reinstalled 7 February 1996, following the death of his father, King Moshoeshoe II on 15 January, crowned 31 October 1997; married 18 February 2000, Karabo Anna Mots'oeneng (Queen 'Masenate Mohato Bereng Seeiso).

Children of the King

Princess Senate Mary Mohato Seeiso, b. 7 October 2001.

Princess 'MaSeeiso Mohato Seeiso, b. 20 November 2004.

Crown Prince Lerotholi Mohato Seeiso, b. 18 April 2007.

LIECHTENSTEIN

Reigning Prince

HSH PRINCE **HANS-ADAM II**, Duke of Troppau and Jägerndorf, Count of Rietberg; b. 14 February 1945; succeeded 13 November 1989, on the death of his father, Prince Franz Josef II; married 30 July 1967, Countess Marie Aglaë Kinsky von Wchinitz und Tettau (Princess Marie) (b. 1940).

Children of the Prince

Hereditary Prince **Alois Philipp Maria**, b. 11 June 1968; appointed permanent representative 15 August 2004, performing the duties of Head of State from that time; married 3 July 1993, Duchess Sophie of Bavaria (b. 28 October 1967); son, Prince Joseph Wenzel, b. 24 May 1995; daughter, Princess Marie Caroline, b. 17 October 1996; son, Prince Georg, b. 20 April 1999; son, Prince Nikolaus, b. 6 December 2000.

Prince Maximilian, b. 16 May 1969; married 29 January 2000, Angela Gisela Brown; son, Prince Alfons, b. 18 May 2001.

Prince Constantin, b. 15 March 1972; married 18 July 1999, Countess Marie Kalnoky; son, Prince Moritz, b. 27 May 2003; daughter, Princess Georgina, b. 23 July 2005; son Prince Benedikt, b. 18 May 2008.

Princess Tatjana, b. 10 April 1973; married 5 June 1999, Philipp von Lattorff; son, Lukas, b. 13 May 2000; daughter, Elisabeth, b. 25 January 2002; daughter, Marie Teresa, b. 18 January 2004; daughter, Camilla, b.

14 November 2005; daughter, Anna, b. 3 August 2007; daughter, Sophia, b. 30 October 2009; son, Maximilian, b. 17 December 2011.

Brothers and Sisters of the Prince

Prince Philipp, b. 19 August 1946; married 11 September 1971, Isabelle de l'Arbre de Malander; son, Prince Alexander, b. 19 May 1972; son, Prince Wenzeslaus, b. 12 May 1974; son, Prince Rudolf, b. 7 September 1975.

Prince Nikolaus, b. 24 October 1947; married 20 March 1982, Princess Margaretha of Luxembourg (b. 15 May 1957); son, Prince Leopold Emmanuel, b. 20 May 1984 (deceased); daughter, Princess Maria-Annunciata, b. 12 May 1985; daughter, Princess Marie-Astrid, b. 26 June 1987; son, Prince Joseph-Emmanuel, b. 7 May 1989.

Princess Nora, b. 31 October 1950; married 11 June 1988, Vicente Marques de Mariño (died 22 July 2002); daughter, María Teresa, b. 21 November 1992.

Prince Wenzel, b. 19 November 1962, died 28 February 1991.

LUXEMBOURG

Reigning Monarch

HRH GRAND DUKE **HENRI ALBERT FÉLIX MARIE GUILLAUME**; b. 16 April 1955; succeeded 7 October 2000, on the abdication of his father, Grand Duke Jean; married 14 February 1981, Maria Teresa Mestre y Batista-Falla, b. 22 March 1956.

Children of the Grand Duke

HRH Prince **Guillaume Jean Joseph Marie**, b. 11 November 1981; proclaimed Hereditary Grand Duke of Luxembourg 18 December 2000; married 20 October 2012, Countess Stéphanie de Lannoy, 18 February 1984.

Prince Félix Léopold Marie Guillaume, b. 3 June 1984; married 21 September 2013, Claire Margareta Lademacher (Princess Claire), b. 21 March 1985.

Prince Louis Xavier Marie Guillaume, b. 3 August 1986; married 29 September 2006, Tessy Antony, b. 28 October 1985; son, Prince Gabriel, b. 12 March 2006; son, Prince Noah, b. 21 September 2007.

Princess Alexandra Joséphine Teresa Charlotte Marie Wilhelmine, b. 16 February 1991.

Prince Sébastien Henri Marie Guillaume, b. 16 April 1992.

Parents of the Grand Duke

Former Grand Duke **Jean Benoit Guillaume Marie Robert Louis Antoine Adolphe Marc d'Aviano**, b. 5 January 1921; married 9 April 1953, Joséphine Charlotte, Princess of Belgium (b. 11 October 1927, died 10 January 2005).

Brothers and Sisters of the Grand Duke

Archduchess Marie-Astrid of Austria, b. 17 February 1954; married 6 February 1982, Carl Christian of Habsburg Lorraine, Archduke of Austria; daughter, Archduchess Marie-Christine Anne Astrid Zita Charlotte of Austria, b. 31 July 1983; son, Archduke Imre, b. 8 December 1985; son, Archduke Christophe, b. 2 February 1988; son, Archduke Alexander, b. 26 September 1990; daughter, Archduchess Gabriella, b. 26 March 1994.

Prince Jean, b. 15 May 1957; married 1st 27 May 1987, Hélène Suzanne Vestur (divorced 2004); daughter, Marie-Gabrielle, b. 8 December 1986; son, Constantin Jean Philippe, b. 22 July 1988; son, Wenceslas, b. 17 November 1990; son, Carl-Johann, b. 15 August 1992; married 2nd 18 March 2009, Diane de Guerre.

Princess Margaretha, b. 15 May 1957; married 20 March 1982, Prince Nikolaus of Liechtenstein (b. 24 October 1947); son, Prince Leopold Emmanuel, b. 20 May 1984 (deceased); daughter, Princess Maria-Annunciata, b. 12 May 1985; daughter, Princess Marie-Astrid, b. 26 June 1987; son, Prince Joseph-Emmanuel, b. 7 May 1989.

Prince Guillaume, b. 1 May 1963; married 24 September 1994, Sibilla Sandra Weiller (y Torlonia) (b. 12 June 1968); son, Prince Paul-Louis, b. 4 March 1998; son, Prince Léopold, b. 2 May 2000; daughter, Princess Charlotte, b. 2 May 2000; son, Prince Jean, b. 13 July 2004.

MALAYSIA

Yang di-Pertuan Agong (Supreme Head of State)

HM The Sultan of **Kedah**, Tuanku Haji Abdul Halim Mu'adzam Shah ibni al-Marhum Sultan Badlishah ; b. 28 November 1927; elected as 14th Yang di-Pertuan Agong 13 December 2011, crowned 11 April 2012.

Timbalan Yang di-Pertuan Agong (Deputy Supreme Head of State)

HRH The Sultan of **Kelantan**, Tengku Muhammad Faris Petra ibni Sultan Ismail Petra.

The Hereditary Rulers

There are nine hereditary rulers who qualify for and elect the positions of Yang di-Pertuan Agong and Timbalan Yang di-Pertuan Agong.

The Yang di-Pertuan Besar of **Negeri Sembilan**, Tuanku Muhriz ibni al-Marhum Tunku Munawir.

HRH The Sultan of **Selangor**, Tuanku Sharafuddin Idris Shah Salahuddin Abdul Aziz Shah.

HRH Tuanku Syed Sirajuddin al-Marhum Syed Putra Jamalullail, The Raja of **Perlis**.

HRH The Sultan of **Terengganu**, Tuanku Mizan Zainal Abidin.

HRH The Sultan of **Pahang**, Haji Ahmad Shah al-Musta'in Billah ibni al-Marhum Sultan Abu Bakar Ri'ayatuddin al-Mu'adzam Shah.

HRH The Sultan of **Johor**, Sultan Ibrahim Ismail ibni al-Marhum Sultan Mahmud Iskandar.

HRH The Sultan of **Perak**, Tuanku Azlan Muhibuddin Shah ibni al-Marhum Sultan Yusuf Izuddin Ghafarullah Shah.

MONACO

Reigning Monarch

HSH PRINCE **ALBERT II**, Albert Alexandre Louis Pierre Grimaldi; b. 14 March 1958; succeeded 6 April 2005, on the death of his father, Prince Rainier III ; married 2 July 2011, Charlene Lynette Wittstock (Charlene, Princess of Monaco), b. 25 January 1978.

Parents of the Prince

HSH Prince Rainier III, Rainier Louis Henri Maxence Bertrand Grimaldi, b. 31 May 1923, died 6 April 2005; married 18 April 1956, Grace Patricia Kelly (b. 12 November 1929, died 14 September 1982).

Sisters of the Prince

Princess Caroline Louise Marguerite, b. 23 January 1957; married 1st 28 June 1978, Philippe Junot (divorced 1980, marriage annulled 1992); married 2nd 29 December 1983, Stefano Casiraghi (died 3 October 1990); son, Andrea Albert Pierre, b. 8 June 1984; daughter, Charlotte Marie Pomeline, b. 3 August 1986; son, Pierre Rainier Stefano, b. 5 September 1987; married 3rd 23 January 1999, Prince Ernst August of Hanover; stepson, Prince Ernst August of Hanover, b. 19 July 1983, stepson, Prince Christian of Hanover, b. 1 June 1985; daughter, Princess Alexandra of Hanover, b. 20 July 1999.

Princess Stéphanie Marie Elisabeth, b. 1 February 1965; married 1st 1 July 1995, Daniel Ducruet (divorced 1996); son, Louis Robert Paul, b. 26 November 1992; daughter, Pauline Grace Maguy, b. 4 May 1994; daughter, Camille Marie Kelly Gottlieb, b. 15 July 1998; married 2nd 10 September 2003, Adans Lopez Peres (divorced 2004).

MOROCCO

Reigning King

HM KING **MOHAMMED VI**; b. 21 August 1963; succeeded to the throne 23 July 1999, on the death of his father, King Hassan II; married 21 March 2002, HRH Princess Lalla Salma Bennani.

Children of the King

HRH Crown Prince Moulay Hassan, b. 8 May 2003.

HRH Princess Lalla Khadija, b. 28 February 2007.

Parents of the King

HM King Hassan II, b. 9 July 1929, died 23 July 1999; married 1st 1961, Lalla Latifa Hammou (five children); married 2nd 1961, Lalla Fatima bint Qaid Amhourok.

Brothers and Sisters of the King

HRH Princess Lalla Meryem, b. 26 August 1962; married September 1984, Fouad Filali (divorced 1999); daughter, Lalla Soukaïna, b. 1986; son, Moulay Idriss, b. 1988.

HRH Princess Lalla Asma, b. 29 September 1965; married 7 June 1987, Khalid Bouchentouf; son, Moulay Yazid, b. 1988; daughter, Lalla Nuhail, b. 1992.

HRH Princess Lalla Hasna, b. 19 November 1967; married 13 December 1991, Khalid Benharbit; daughter, Lalla Oumaïma, b. 15 December 1995; daughter, Lalla Oulaya, b. 20 October 1997.

HRH Prince Moulay Rachid, b. 20 June 1970.

THE NETHERLANDS

Reigning King

HM KING **WILLEM-ALEXANDER** CLAUS GEORGE FERDINAND; b. 27 April 1967; succeeded to the throne 30 April 2013, on the abdication of his mother, Queen Beatrix (now HRH Princess **Beatrix**); married 2 February 2002, Máxima Zorreguieta (b. 17 May 1971); daughter, HRH

Princess Catharina-Amalia Beatrix Carmen Victoria, b. 7 December 2003; daughter, HRH Princess Alexia Juliana Marcella Laurentien, b. 26 June 2005; daughter, HRH Ariane Wilhelmina Máxima Inés, b. 10 April 2007.

Brothers of the King

HRH Prince (Johan) Friso Bernhard Christiaan David, b. 25 September 1968, died 12 August 2013; married 24 April 2004 (relinquished right to the throne and membership of the Royal House), Mabel Wisse Smit; daughter, Countess Luana, b. 26 March 2005; daughter, Countess Zaria, b. 18 June 2006.

HRH Prince Constantijn Christof Frederik Aschwin, b. 11 October 1969; married 17 May 2001, Laurentien Brinkhorst (b. 25 May 1966); daughter, Countess Eloise, b. 8 June 2002; son, Count Claus-Casimir, b. 21 March 2004; daughter, Countess Leonore, b. 3 June 2006.

Parents of the King

HRH Princess **Beatrix** of The Netherlands, b. 31 January 1938; married 10 March 1966, Prince Claus George Willem Otto Frederik Geert Jonkheer van Amsberg (b. 6 September 1926, died 6 October 2002).

NORWAY

Reigning King

HM KING **HARALD V**; b. 21 February 1937; succeeded to the throne 17 January 1991, on the death of his father, King Olav V; sworn in 21 January 1991; married 29 August 1968, Sonja Haraldsen (HM Queen Sonja) (b. 4 July 1937).

Children of the King

Princess Märtha Louise, b. 22 September 1971; married 24 May 2002, Ari Mikael Behn (formerly Ari Mikael Bjørshol, b. 30 September 1972); daughter, Maud Angelica Behn, b. 29 April 2003; daughter, Leah Isadora Behn, b. 8 April 2005; daughter, Emma Tallulah Behn, b. 29 September 2008.

HRH Crown Prince **Haakon**, b. 20 July 1973; married 25 August 2001, Mette-Marit Tjessem Høiby (HRH Crown Princess Mette-Marit) (b. 19 August 1973); stepson, Marius Borg Høiby, b. 13 January 1997; daughter, HRH Princess Ingrid Alexandra, b. 21 January 2004; son, HH Prince Sverre Magnus, b. 3 December 2005.

Sisters of the King

Princess Ragnhild, b. 9 June 1930, died 16 September 2012; married 15 May 1953, Erling Lorentzen; three children.

Princess Astrid, b. 12 February 1932; married 12 January 1961, Johan Martin Ferner; five children.

OMAN

Reigning Sultan

SULTAN **QABOOS BIN SAID AS-SAID**; b. 18 November 1940; assumed power 23 July 1970, after deposing his father, Sultan Said bin Taimur (b. 13 August 1910, died 19 October 1972); married 1976, Sayyidah Nawwal bint Tariq (divorced 1977).

QATAR

Reigning Amir

HH SHEIKH TAMIM BIN HAMAD BIN KHALIFA ATH-**THANI**; b. 3 June 1980; proclaimed heir apparent 8 August 2003, succeeded to the throne 25 June 2013 on the abdication of his father; married 1st 8 January 2005, Sheikha Jawahar bint Hamad bin Sohaim ath-Thani; married 2nd 3 March 2009, Sheikha Anoud bint Mana Al-Hajri.

Children of the Amir by His First Wife

HE Sheikha Almayassa bint Tamim ath-Thani, b. 2006

HE Sheikh Hamad bin Tamim ath-Thani, b. 2008

HE Sheikha Aisha bint Tamim ath-Thani, b. 2010

HE Sheikh Jassim bin Tamim ath-Thani, b. 2012

Children of the Amir by His Second Wife

HE Sheikha Nayla bint Tamim ath-Thani, b. 2010

HE Sheikh Abdullah bin Tamim ath-Thani, b. 29 September 2012

Parents of the Amir

HH Sheikh Hamad bin Khalifa ath-**Thani**, b. 1 January 1952; assumed power 27 June 1995, after deposing his father, Sheikh Khalifa bin Hamad ath-**Thani** (b. 17 September 1932), abdicated 25 June 2013 in favour of his son, HH Sheikh Tamim bin Hamad bin Khalifa ath-Thani; married 1st Sheikha Mariam bint Muhammad ath-Thani (two sons, six daughters); married 2nd Sheikha Mozah bint Nasser al-**Missned** (five sons, two daughters); married 3rd Sheikha Noora bint Khalid ath-Thani (four sons, five daughters).

SAMOA

O le Ao o le Malo (Head of State)

HH Tuiatua Tupua Tamasese **EFI**; b. 1 March 1938; elected Head of State 15 June 2007; married HH Masiofo Filifilia Imo.

SAUDI ARABIA

Reigning King

HM KING ABDULLAH IBN ABD AL-AZIZ AS-**SA'UD**; b. 1 August 1924; succeeded to the throne, 1 August 2005, on the death of his brother, King Fahd.

Brothers of the King include

King Saud ibn Abd al-Aziz as-Sa'ud, b. 15 January 1902, acceded 9 November 1953 (following the death of his father, King Abd al-Aziz as-Sa'ud), relinquished the throne 2 November 1964, died 24 January 1969.

King Faisal ibn Abd al-Aziz as-Sa'ud, b. April 1906, acceded 2 November 1964, died 25 March 1975; children include son, Prince Sa'ud al-Faisal as-**Sa'ud**, b. 1941; son, Prince Turki al-Faisal ibn Abd al-Aziz as-**Sa'ud**, b. 15 February 1945.

HRH Prince Mohammed ibn Abd al-Aziz as-Sa'ud, b. 4 March 1910, died 25 November 1988.

King Khalid ibn Abd al-Aziz as-Sa'ud, b. 13 February 1913, acceded 25 March 1975, died 13 June 1982.

King Fahd ibn Abd al-Aziz as-**Sa'ud**, b. 16 March 1921, acceded 13 June 1982, died 1 August 2005.

HRH Crown Prince Sultan ibn Abd al-Aziz as-**Sa'ud**, b. 5 January 1928, died 22 October 2011; children include son, HRH Prince Bandar ibn Sultan ibn Abd al-Aziz as-**Sa'ud**, b. 2 March 1949.

HRH Prince Talal ibn Abd al-Aziz as-**Sa'ud**, b. 15 August 1931; children include son, Prince Walid ibn **Talal**.

HRH Prince Nayef ibn Abd al-Aziz as-**Sa'ud**, b. 1934, died 16 June 2012.

HRH Crown Prince Salman ibn Abd al-Aziz as-**Sa'ud**, b. 13 December 1935.

SPAIN

Reigning King

HM KING **JUAN CARLOS I**; b. 5 January 1938; succeeded to the throne 22 November 1975; married 14 May 1962, Princess Sofia of Greece (HM Queen Sofia) (b. 2 November 1938, daughter of the late King Paul of the Hellenes and Queen Frederica).

Children of the King

HRH Princess (Infanta) Elena, b. 20 December 1963; married 18 March 1995, Don Jaime de Marichalar y Sáenz de Tejada (divorced 21 January 2010); son, Felipe Juan Froilán de Todos los Santos, b. 17 July 1998; daughter, Victoria Federica, b. 9 September 2000.

HRH Princess (Infanta) Cristina, b. 13 June 1965; married 4 October 1997, Iñaki Urdangarin (b. 15 January 1968); son, Juan Valentín, b. 29 September 1999; son, Pablo Nicolás Sebastián, b. 6 December 2000; son, Miguel, b. 30 April 2002; daughter, Irene, b. 5 June 2005.

HRH Prince Felipe de Borbón, The Prince of **Asturias**, Prince of Girona, Prince of Viana, Duke of Montblanc, Count of Cervera, Lord of Balaguer, b. 30 January 1968; married 22 May 2004, HRH Princess Letizia Ortiz Rocasolano (Princess of Asturias) (b. 15 September 1972); daughter, Princess (Infanta) Leonor, b. 31 October 2005; daughter, Princess (Infanta) Sofía, b. 29 April 2007.

Parents of the King

Don Juan de Borbón y Battenberg, Count of Barcelona, b. 20 June 1913, died 1 April 1993; married 12 October 1935, Doña María de las Mercedes de Borbón-Dos Sicilias y Orléans, b. 23 December 1910, died 2 January 2000.

SWAZILAND

Reigning Monarch

KING **MSWATI III**; b. 19 April 1968; proclaimed Crown Prince September 1983, following the death of his father the previous year; installed as head of state 25 April 1986.

Father of the King

King Sobhuza II, b. 22 July 1899, died 21 August 1982.

SWEDEN

Reigning King

HM KING **CARL XVI GUSTAF**; b. 30 April 1946; succeeded to the throne 15 September 1973, on the death of his grandfather, King Gustaf VI Adolf; married 19 June 1976, Silvia Renate Sommerlath (HM Queen **Silvia**) (b. 23 December 1943).

Children of the King

HRH Crown Princess **Victoria Ingrid Alice Désirée**, Duchess of Västergötland, b. 14 July 1977; married 19 June 2010, Olof Daniel Westling Bernadotte (Prince Daniel, Duke of Västergötland), b. 15 September 1973; daughter, Princess Estelle, Duchess of Östergötland, b. 23 February 2012.

HRH Prince Carl Philip Edmund Bertil, Duke of Varmland, b. 13 May 1979.

HRH Princess Madeleine Thérèse Amelie Josephine, Duchess of Hälsingland and Gästrikland, b. 10 June 1982; married 8 June 2013, Christopher O'Neill, b. 27 June 1974.

Parents of the King

Prince Gustaf Adolf, Duke of Västerbotten, b. 22 April 1906, died 26 January 1947; married 20 October 1932, Sibylla, Princess of Saxe-Coburg and Gotha (b. 18 January 1908, died 28 November 1972).

Sisters of the King

Princess Margaretha, b. 31 October 1934; married 30 June 1964, John Ambler (b. 6 June 1924, died 31 May 2008); daughter, Sibylla Louise, b. 14 April 1965; son, Charles Edward, b. 14 July 1966; son, James Patrick, b. 10 June 1969.

Princess Birgitta, b. 19 January 1937; married 25 May 1961, Prince Johann Georg of Hohenzollern (b. 31 July 1932); son, Carl Christian, b. 5 April 1962; daughter, Desirée, b. 27 November 1963; son, Hubertus, b. 10 June 1966.

Princess Désirée, b. 2 June 1938; married 5 June 1964, Baron Nils-August Otto Carl Niclas Silfverschiöld (b. 31 May 1934); son, Carl Otto Edmund, b. 22 March 1965; daughter, Kristina Louise Ewa Madeleine, b. 29 September 1966; daughter, Hélène Ingeborg Sibylla, b. 20 September 1968.

Princess Christina, b. 3 August 1943; married 15 June 1974, Tord Magnuson (b. 7 April 1941); son, Carl Gustaf Victor, b. 8 August 1975; son, Tord Oscar Fredrik, b. 20 June 1977; son, Victor Edmund Lennart, b. 10 September 1980.

THAILAND

Reigning King

HM KING **BHUMIBOL ADULYADEJ**, (King Rama IX); b. 5 December 1927; succeeded to the throne 9 June 1946, on the death of his brother, King Ananda Mahidol; crowned 5 May 1950; married 28 April 1950, Mom Rajawongse Sirikit Kitiyakara (Queen Sirikit) (b. 12 August 1932).

Children of the King

Princess Ubol Ratana, b. 5 April 1951; married August 1972, Peter Ladd Jensen (relinquished royal claim) (divorced 1998); daughter, Khun Ploypailin, b. 12 February 1981; son, Khun Poomi, b. 16 August 1983, died 26 December 2004; daughter, Khun Sirikittiya, b. 18 March 1985.

HRH Crown Prince **Maha Vajiralongkorn**, b. 28 July 1952; proclaimed Crown Prince 28 December 1972; married 1st 3 January 1977, Mom Luang Soamsawali Kitiyakara (b. 13 July 1957) (divorced 1991); daughter, Princess Bajrakitiyabha, b. 7 December 1978; partner, Yuvadhida Polpraserth; four sons (no royal claim); daughter, HRH Princess Siriwanwari Nariratana, b. 8 January 1987 (elevated status by royal command 15 June 2005); married 2nd 10 February 2001, Mom Srirasmi Mahidol na Ayudhya (HRH Princess Srirasmi, The Royal Consort) (b. 9 December 1971); son, HRH Prince Teepangkorn Rasmichoti, b. 29 April 2005.

HRH Princess Maha Chakri Sirindhorn, b. 2 April 1955.

HRH Princess **Chulabhorn**, b. 4 July 1957; married 7 January 1982, Flight Lieutenant Virayuth Didyasarin (divorced 1984); daughter, Princess Siribhachudabhorn, b. 8 October 1982; daughter, Princess Aditayadornkitikhun, b. 5 May 1984.

Parents of the King

Prince Mahidol Adulyadej of Songkla, b. 1 January 1892, died 24 September 1929; married 1920, Sangwal Talabhat (Princess Mahidol of Songkla) (b. 21 October 1900, died 18 July 1995).

Brother and Sister of the King

Princess Galyani Vadhana Krom Luang Naradhiwas Rajanagarindra, b. 6 May 1923, died 2 January 2008.

King Ananda Mahidol, b. 20 September 1925, died 9 June 1946; elected to succeed to the throne 2 March 1935.

TONGA

Reigning King

HM KING **Tupou VI**; b. 12 July 1959; proclaimed Crown Prince 11 September 2006; succeeded to the throne 18 March 2012, on the death of his elder brother, King George Tupou V; married 11 December 1982, Nanasipau'u Vaea (Princess Nanasipau'u).

Children of the King

Princess Latufuipeka Tuku'aho, b. 17 November 1983.

Crown Prince Tupouto'a 'Ulukalala, b. 17 September 1985, married 12 July 2012, Sinaitakala Fakafanua (b. 1987); son, Prince Taufa'ahau Manumataongo, b. 10 May 2013.

Prince Viliami Tuku'aho, The Prince Ata, b. 1988.

Parents of the King

King **Taufa'ahau Tupou IV**, b. 4 July 1918, died 10 September 2006; succeeded to the throne 15 December 1965; married 1947, Princess Halaevalu Mata'aho 'Ahome'e (Queen Halaevalu Mata'aho) (b. 29 May 1926).

Brothers and Sisters of the King

HRH Princess Salote Mafile'o Pilolevu Tuku'aho Tuita, Princess Regent, b. 17 November 1951; married 21 July 1976, Captain Ma'ulupekotofa Tuita (known as Honourable Tuita) (four daughters, one adopted son).

HRH Prince Fatafehi Alaivahamama'o Tuku'aho (known as Honourable Matu), b. 17 December 1954, died 17 February 2004; married (relinquished royal claim).

UNITED ARAB EMIRATES

Reigning Rulers

Ruler of Abu Dhabi: HH Sheikh KHALIFA BIN ZAYED AN-**NAHYAN**; b. 25 January 1948; succeeded to the throne 2 November 2004.

Ruler of Dubai: HH Sheikh MUHAMMAD BIN RASHID AL-**MAKTOUM**; b. 15 July 1949; succeeded to the throne 4 January 2006; married 2nd 10 April 2004, HRH Princess Haya bint al-Hussein of Jordan.

Ruler of Sharjah: HH Sheikh SULTAN BIN MUHAMMAD AL-**QASIMI**; b. 6 July 1939; succeeded to the throne 25 January 1972.

Ruler of Ras al-Khaimah: HH Sheikh SAUD IBN SAQR AL-**QASIMI**; b. 10 February 1956; succeeded to the throne 27 October 2010.

Ruler of Umm al-Qaiwain: HH Sheikh SAUD BIN RASHID AL-**MU'ALLA**; b. 1 October 1952; succeeded to the throne 2 January 2009.

Ruler of Ajman: HH Sheikh HUMAID BIN RASHID AN-**NUAIMI**; b. 1931; succeeded to the throne 6 September 1981.

Ruler of Fujairah: HH Sheikh HAMAD BIN MUHAMMAD ASH-**SHARQI**; b. 25 May 1948; succeeded to the throne 18 September 1974.

UNITED KINGDOM

Reigning Queen

HM QUEEN **ELIZABETH II**; b. 21 April 1926; succeeded to the throne 6 February 1952, on the death of her father, King George VI; crowned 2 June 1953; married 20 November 1947, HRH Prince Philip, Duke of **Edinburgh**, Earl of Merioneth, Baron Greenwich, KG, KT, OM, GBE, AC, QSO (b. 10 June 1921), son of Prince Andrew of Greece and Princess Alice of Battenberg (Mountbatten).

Children of the Queen

HRH Prince Charles Philip Arthur George, The Prince of **Wales**, Duke of Cornwall, Duke of Rothesay, Earl of Chester, Earl of Carrick, Baron Renfrew, Lord of the Isles and Great Steward of Scotland, KG, KT, GCB, OM, AK, QSO, ADC (heir-apparent), b. 14 November 1948; married 1st 29 July 1981, Lady Diana Frances Spencer (The Princess of Wales) (divorced 1996, died 31 August 1997); son, HRH Prince **William** Arthur Philip Louis of Wales (HRH The Duke of **Cambridge**), b. 21 June 1982; married 29 April 2011, Catherine Elizabeth Middleton (HRH The Duchess of Cambridge) (son, Prince George Alexander Louis of Cambridge, b. 22 July 2013); son, HRH Prince Henry Charles Albert David of Wales, b. 15 September 1984; married 2nd 9 April 2005, Camilla Parker Bowles (HRH The Duchess of **Cornwall**) (b. 17 July 1947).

HRH Princess Anne Elizabeth Alice Louise, The Princess **Royal**, KG, KT, GCVO, QSO, b. 15 August 1950; married 1st 14 November 1973, Captain Mark Phillips (divorced 1992); son, Peter Mark Andrew Phillips, b. 15 November 1977; daughter, Zara Anne Elizabeth Phillips, b. 15 May 1981; married 2nd 12 December 1992, Vice-Admiral Timothy Laurence, CB, MVO, ADC.

HRH Prince Andrew Albert Christian Edward, The Duke of **York**, Earl of Inverness, Baron Killyleagh, KS, KCVO, ADC, b. 19 February 1960; married 23 July 1986, Sarah Ferguson (The Duchess of York) (b. 15 October 1959) (divorced 1996); daughter, Princess Beatrice Elizabeth Mary of York, b. 8 August 1988; daughter, Princess Eugenie Victoria Helena of York, b. 23 March 1990.

HRH Prince Edward Antony Richard Louis, The Earl of **Wessex**, KS, KCVO, ADC, b. 10 March 1964; married 19 June 1999, Sophie Rhys-Jones (HRH The Countess of Wessex) (b. 20 January 1965); daughter, Lady

Louise Alice Elizabeth Mary Windsor, b. 8 November 2003; son, James Alexander Philip Theo, Viscount Severn, b. 17 December 2007.

Parents of the Queen

King George VI, b. 14 December 1895 (son of King George V and Queen Mary), died 6 February 1952; married 26 April 1923, Lady Elizabeth Angela Marguerite Bowes-Lyon (Queen Elizabeth The Queen Mother) (b. 4 August 1900, died 30 March 2002).

Sister of the Queen

Princess Margaret Rose, Countess of Snowdon, CI, GCVO, b. 21 August 1930, died 9 February 2002; married 6 May 1960, Antony Armstrong-Jones (Earl of Snowdon, GCVO) (divorced 1978); son, David Albert Charles, Viscount Linley, b. 3 November 1961, (married, two children); daughter, Lady Sarah Frances Elizabeth Chatto (née Armstrong-Jones), b. 1 May 1964, (married, two children).

The full titles of Queen Elizabeth II are as follows:

United Kingdom
"Elizabeth the Second, by the Grace of God, of the United Kingdom of Great Britain and Northern Ireland and of Her other Realms and Territories Queen, Head of the Commonwealth, Defender of the Faith."

Canada
"Elizabeth the Second, by the Grace of God, of the United Kingdom, Canada and Her other Realms and Territories Queen, Head of the Commonwealth, Defender of the Faith."

Australia
"Elizabeth the Second, by the Grace of God, Queen of Australia and Her other Realms and Territories, Head of the Commonwealth."

New Zealand
"Elizabeth the Second, by the Grace of God, Queen of New Zealand and Her other Realms and Territories, Head of the Commonwealth, Defender of the Faith."

Jamaica
"Elizabeth the Second, by the Grace of God, Queen of Jamaica and of Her other Realms and Territories Queen, Head of the Commonwealth."

Barbados
"Elizabeth the Second, by the Grace of God, Queen of Barbados and of Her other Realms and Territories, Head of the Commonwealth."

The Bahamas
"Elizabeth the Second, by the Grace of God, Queen of the Commonwealth of The Bahamas and of Her other Realms and Territories, Head of the Commonwealth."

Grenada
"Elizabeth the Second, by the Grace of God, Queen of the United Kingdom of Great Britain and Northern Ireland and of Grenada and Her other Realms and Territories, Head of the Commonwealth."

Papua New Guinea
"Elizabeth the Second, Queen of Papua New Guinea and of Her other Realms and Territories, Head of the Commonwealth."

Solomon Islands
"Elizabeth the Second, by the Grace of God, Queen of the Solomon Islands and of Her other Realms and Territories, Head of the Commonwealth."

Tuvalu
"Elizabeth the Second, by the Grace of God, Queen of Tuvalu and of Her other Realms and Territories, Head of the Commonwealth."

Saint Lucia
"Elizabeth the Second, by the Grace of God, Queen of Saint Lucia and of Her other Realms and Territories, Head of the Commonwealth."

Saint Vincent and the Grenadines
"Elizabeth the Second, by the Grace of God, Queen of Saint Vincent and the Grenadines and of Her other Realms and Territories, Head of the Commonwealth."

Belize
"Elizabeth the Second, by the Grace of God, Queen of Belize and of Her other Realms and Territories, Head of the Commonwealth."

Antigua and Barbuda
"Elizabeth the Second, by the Grace of God, Queen of Antigua and Barbuda and of Her other Realms and Territories, Head of the Commonwealth."

Saint Christopher and Nevis
"Elizabeth the Second, by the Grace of God, Queen of Saint Christopher and Nevis and of Her other Realms and Territories, Head of the Commonwealth."

The Republics of India, Ghana, Cyprus, Tanzania, Uganda, Kenya, Zambia, Malawi, Singapore, Botswana, Guyana, Nauru, The Gambia, Sierra Leone, Bangladesh, Sri Lanka, Malta, Trinidad and Tobago, Seychelles, Dominica, Kiribati, Vanuatu, Maldives, Namibia, Mauritius, South Africa, Fiji, Pakistan, Cameroon and Mozambique, together with the Federation of Malaysia, the Kingdom of Lesotho, the Kingdom of Swaziland, the Kingdom of Tonga, the Independent State of Samoa and the Sultanate of Brunei, recognize the Queen as "Head of the Commonwealth".

OBITUARY

Abbado, Claudio	20 January 2014
Abdel Meguid, Ahmed Esmat	21 December 2013
Agakhanov, Khalnazar Amannazarovich	29 June 2013
Agnew, Harold Melvin	29 September 2013
Albery, Wyndham John	3 December 2013
Alfaro, Andreu	13 December 2012
Allison, Herbert M.	14 July 2013
Aloni, Shulamit	24 January 2014
Anthony, Polly	29 September 2013
Askew, Reubin O'Donovan	13 March 2014
Auletta, Mino	5 October 2012
Azim, Syed Aftab	25 March 2013
Azuela, Arturo	7 June 2012
Bai, Zhongren	4 January 2014
Balabanov, Alexei O.	18 May 2013
Banks, Iain Menzies	9 June 2013
Barbour, Ian Graeme	24 December 2013
Barker, David James Purslove	27 August 2013
Bartolucci, Domenico	11 November 2013
Barton, Anne	11 November 2013
Baruch, Jordan J	26 October 2011
Batten, John Charles	7 October 2013
Baudis, Dominique	10 April 2014
Becker, Gary Stanley	3 May 2014
Beckett, Terence	2 May 2013
Beitz, Berthold	30 July 2013
Bellany, John	28 August 2013
Belyakov, Rostislav Apollosovich	28 February 2014
Benerito, Ruth	5 October 2013
Benn, Anthony (Tony) Neil Wedgwood	14 March 2014
Bernard, Robert	19 September 2013
Bertuccelli, Jean-Louis Augusto	6 March 2014
Betts, Donald Drysdale	23 October 2012
Bilby, Bruce Alexander	20 November 2013
Bishop, Bernardine	4 July 2013
Biteo Borico, Miguel Abia	6 December 2012
Black, Shirley Temple	10 February 2014
Blandy, John Peter	23 July 2011
Bonello Dupuis, George	19 February 2010
Bord, Andre	13 May 2013
Boularès, Mohamed Habib	18 April 2014
Brewer, Richard George	22 July 2012
Bridges, Alan	7 December 2013
Bronfman, Edgar, Sr	21 December 2013
Brout, Robert H.	3 May 2011
Bryant, Gyude	16 August 2014
Bryant, Thomas Edward	9 December 2011
Burgh, John Charles	12 April 2013
Butler, Marilyn Speers	11 March 2014
Butler, Michael Dacres	24 December 2013
Butterworth, Ian	29 November 2013
Byrd, Harry Flood, Jr	30 July 2013
Caldwell, Philip	10 July 2013
Callaway, Howard Hollis (Bo)	15 March 2014
Camara, Assan Musa	15 September 2013
Campbell, Iain Donald	5 March 2014
Caro, Anthony	24 October 2013
Carrington, Alan	30 September 2013
Casselton, Lorna Ann	13 February 2014
Castellet, Josep María	9 January 2014
Cecil, Henry Richard	11 June 2013
Cellucci, (Argeo) Paul	8 June 2013
Chatah, Mohamad	27 December 2013
Chen, Muhua	13 August 2012
Chéreau, Patrice	7 October 2013
Chikvaidze, Alexander Davidovich	4 May 2012
Chryssa	23 December 2013
Civita, Roberto	26 May 2013
Clarke, Bryan Campbell	27 February 2014
Clerides, Glafcos	15 November 2013
Cloudsley Thompson, John-Leonard	4 October 2013
Clyne, Michael George	29 January 2010
Coase, Ronald Harry	2 September 2013
Coleman, Douglas L.	16 April 2014
Colombo, Emilio	24 June 2013
Conte, Arthur	26 December 2013
Coveney, James	12 July 2013
Crichton- Brown, Robert	11 July 2013
Dahl, Robert Alan	5 February 2014
Davenport, (Arthur) Nigel	25 October 2013
Davie, Alan	5 April 2014
de Duve, Christian	4 May 2013
de Tricornot de Rose, François	23 March 2014
Delly, Emmanuel-Karim	8 April 2014
Deryabin, Yuri Stepanovich	1 August 2013
Desmarias, Paul	8 October 2013
Dretske, Frederick Irwin	24 July 2013
Dubinin, Yuri	20 December 2013
Dutilleux, Henri	22 May 2013
Ebert, Peter	31 December 2012
Eglin, Colin	30 November 2013
Eisenhower, John	21 December 2013
Emanuel, James Andrew	28 September 2013
Etrog, Sorel	26 February 2014
Fahim Khan, Mohammad Qassim	9 March 2014
Falise, Michel	December 2012
Faure, Maurice Henri	6 March 2014
Finney, Thomas (Tom)	14 February 2014
Fischer, Paul Henning	26 September 2013
Flaherty, James (Jim) Michael	10 April 2014
Fogel, Robert William	11 June 2013
Foley, Thomas Stephen	18 October 2013
Forbes, Bryan	8 May 2013
Ford, William Clay	9 March 2014
Fox, Frederick Donald	11 December 2013
Fraser of Carmyllie, Peter Lovat Fraser	23 June 2013
Fromstein, Mitchell S.	7 November 2013
Frost, David Paradine	31 August 2013
Frye, Richard Nelson	27 March 2014
Funcke, Liselotte	1 August 2012
Gandolfini, James Joseph, Jr	19 June 2013
Ganev, Stoyan	2 July 2013
García Márquez, Gabriel José	17 April 2014
Geach, Peter	21 December 2013
Gibb, Frank (Francis Ross)	4 June 2013
Gibbons, David	30 March 2014
Gitari, David-Mukuba	30 September 2013
Goldman, John Michael	24 December 2013
Grams, Rodney (Rod) Dwight	8 October 2013
Gray, Herb E	21 April 2014
Gray, Robert Keith	18 April 2014
Greenland, Dennis James	23 December 2012
Greenwood, Duncan Joseph	13 February 2010
Greet, Kenneth Gerald	11 February 2014
Hackney, (Francis) Sheldon	12 September 2013
Haekkerup, Hans	22 December 2013
Haid, Djama Mahamoud	11 January 2013
Handy, Nicholas C.	2 October 2012
Harris, Julie	24 August 2013
Harryhausen, Ray	7 May 2013
Hayami, Yujiro	24 December 2012
Heaney, Seamus	30 August 2013
Heilmeier, George Harry	21 April 2014
Hennessy, John Basil	27 October 2013
Herbig, George Howard	12 October 2013
Herzenberg, Leonard (Len) Arthur	27 October 2013
Hightower, John B.	6 July 2013
Hijuelos, Oscar	12 October 2013
Hill, Robert Lee	29 November 2012
Hiquily, Philippe	27 March 2013
Hoffman, Philip	2 February 2014
Hoggart, Richard	10 April 2014
Hollander, John	17 August 2013
Hollein, Hans	24 April 2014
Holliday, Robin	9 April 2014
Hopkins, Antony	6 May 2014
Horn, Gyula	19 June 2013
Horn, Gabriel	2 August 2012
Hoskins, Robert (Bob) William, Jr	29 April 2014
Howard, Elizabeth Jane	2 January 2014
Huang, Weilu	23 November 2013
Hudson-Phillips, Karl Terrence	16 January 2014
Huizenga, John R.	25 January 2014
Hurnik, Ilja	7 September 2013
Hussein, Abdirizak Haji	31 January 2014
Huxley, Hugh Esmor	25 July 2013
Igarashi, Kozo	7 May 2013
Ignatius Zakka I Iwas	21 March 2014
Izrael, Yury Antonievich	23 January 2014
Jack, Kenneth Henderson	28 January 2013
Jancso, Mikles	31 January 2014
Jens, Walter	9 June 2013

OBITUARY

Jin Luxian, Aloysius	27 April 2013	Noma, Sawako	31 March 2011
Jolowicz, John Anthony	17 January 2012	Noonan, Michael	17 September 2013
Jones, David Charles	10 August 2013	Nugis, Ülo	18 November 2013
Jones, Douglas Samuel	27 November 2013	Nungesser, Roland	30 March 2011
Kabbah, Ahmad Tejan	13 March 2014	O'Reilly, Frances Joseph	11 August 2013
Kalashnikov, Mikhail	23 December 2013	Ogata, Shijuro	14 April 2014
Karle, Jerome	6 June 2013	Olins, Wallace	14 April 2014
Katritzky, Alan Roy	10 February 2014	Oliva, L. Jay	17 April 2014
Keilis-Borok, Vladimir Isaakovich	19 October 2013	Olive, David Ian	7 November 2012
Kernan, Roderick Patrick	10 January 2014	Oliver, Roland Anthony	9 February 2014
Khan, Khurshed Alam	20 July 2013	Orbelian, Konstantin Agaparonovich	24 April 2014
Kikutake, Kiyonori	26 December 2011	O'Toole, Peter	14 December 2013
Kilar, Wojciech	29 December 2013	Overhauser, Albert Warner	10 December 2011
Kingsdown, Robert Leigh-Pemberton	24 November 2013	Pacheco, José Emilio	26 January 2014
Klein, Lawrence Robert	20 October 2013	Paffrath, Hans-Georg	18 September 2013
Knackstedt, Gunter Wilhelm Karl	27 May 2012	Pashin, Valentin Mikhailovich	15 December 2013
Kojima, Kiyoshi	7 January 2010	Pawson, Anthony James	7 August 2013
Kolodkin, Anatoliy Lazarevich	24 February 2011	Pellegrino, Edmund	13 June 2013
Krkobabic, Jovan	22 April 2014	Perin, François	26 September 2013
Kulikov, Viktor Georgiyevich	28 May 2013	Perry, Robert Palese	15 July 2013
Kumin, Maxine Winokur	6 February 2014	Phelan, John Joseph, Jr	4 August 2012
Kuznetsov, Anatoly Borisovich	7 March 2014	Philipson, Lennart Carl	26 June 2011
Kuznetsov, Fedor Andreyevich	4 February 2014	Phillips, Owen Martin	13 October 2010
Lafont, Bernadette Paule Anne	25 July 2013	Pimenta, Simon Ignatius	19 July 2013
Lal, Devendra	1 December 2012	Policarpo, José da Cruz	12 March 2014
Lalive d'Epinay, Pierre	8 March 2014	Ranis, Gustav	15 October 2013
Lalla Aicha, Princess	4 September 2011	Ray, Ajit Nath	25 December 2010
Landes, David S	17 August 2013	Reed, Lou	27 October 2013
Lappert, Michael F	28 March 2014	Reichmann, Paul	25 October 2013
Larsen, Kai	23 August 2012	Reich-Ranicki, Marcel	18 September 2013
Lautenberg, Frank R.	3 June 2013	Resnais, Alain	1 March 2014
Lautner, George Charles	22 November 2013	Resnik, Regina	8 August 2013
Lazorthes, Guy Aman Felix	26 March 2014	Reynolds, Anna	24 February 2014
Le Goff, Jacques	1 April 2014	Roberts, Bernard	3 November 2013
Le Goy, Raymond Edgar Michel	30 September 2011	Roberts, Denys Tudor Emil	19 May 2013
Le Portz, Yves	8 December 2013	Robinson, (Arthur Napoleon) Raymond	9 April 2014
Lecat, Jean-Philippe	26 March 2011	Rogers, Paul	8 October 2013
Leclerc, Edouard	17 September 2012	Rohrer, Hans Heinrich	16 May 2013
Leman, Alexander B.	28 April 2010	Romaszewski, Zbigniew	13 February 2014
Leonard, Elmore	20 August 2013	Rooney, Mickey	6 April 2014
Lessing, Doris May	17 November 2013	Rosenthal, Thomas Gabriel	3 January 2014
Lewandowski, Janusz	13 August 2013	Roux, Jean-Louis	28 November 2013
Lewis, Peter B	23 November 2013	Rowley, Janet Davison	17 December 2013
Lewis, Samuel Winfield	10 March 2014	Rozewicz, Tadeusz	24 April 2014
Li, Moran	8 November 2012	Rubin, Louis Decimus, Jr.	16 November 2013
Liem Sioe Liong	10 June 2012	Ruggiero, Renato	4 August 2013
Lilov, Alexander Vassilev	20 July 2013	Rustin, Jean	24 December 2013
Lin, Ruo	7 October 2012	Ryrie, William Sinclair	6 July 2012
Liu, Danzhai	3 March 2011	Samoilova, Tatyana Yevgeniyevna	4 May 2014
Liu, Zhengwei	9 August 2012	Sanger, Frederick	19 November 2013
Llewellyn, John	2 July 2013	Sargsyan, Sos Artashesovich	26 September 2013
Lopes, António Simões	18 December 2012	Sarkisyan, Fadey Tachatovich	10 January 2010
Louët, Philippe Marie Alexandre Gabriel	4 November 2010	Sarraj, Eyad Rajab el	17 December 2013
Lu, Xueyi	13 May 2013	Schell, Jonathan	25 March 2014
Luce, Robert Duncan	11 August 2012	Schell, Maximilian	1 February 2014
Mackay, Graham	18 December 2013	Scheman, L. Ronald	1 April 2013
McKennon, Keith Robert	14 September 2013	Schiffrin, Andre	1 December 2013
McPherson, Harry Cummings, Jr	16 February 2012	Schloter, Carsten	23 July 2013
Maiorescu, Mircea	19 May 2010	Schulz, Peter	17 May 2013
Malone, Thomas Francis	6 July 2013	Scoon, Paul	2 September 2013
Mandela, Nelson Rolihlahla	5 December 2013	Scotchmer, Suzanne	30 January 2014
Marques de La Plata Irarrazaval, Alfonso	22 April 2014	Scranton, William Warren	28 July 2013
Marshall of Knightsbridge, Colin (Marsh) Marshall	5 July 2012	Seaman, Keith Douglas	30 June 2013
Matthiessen, Peter	5 April 2014	Serrin, James B	23 August 2012
Mauroy, Pierre	7 June 2013	Sharon, Ariel	11 January 2014
Maxwell, Hamish	19 April 2014	Sharpe, Thomas (Tom) Ridley	6 June 2013
Mazowiecki, Tadeusz	28 October 2013	Shatkin, Aaron Jeffrey	4 June 2012
Mera Goyenechea, Rosalia	15 August 2013	Shaw, Run Run	7 January 2014
Messer, Thomas Maria	15 May 2013	Shirley-Quirk, John	7 April 2014
Middlemas, Robert Keith	25 August 2013	Shukla, Vidya Charan	11 June 2013
Middleton, Peter	15 March 2014	Siddiqui, Kazi Abu Zafar Mohammad	15 October 2012
Mifflin, Fred J.	5 October 2013	Singh, Khushwant	20 March 2014
Mlynarik, Ján	26 March 2012	Slym, Karl	25 January 2014
Morales, Armando	16 November 2011	Speakes, Larry	10 January 2014
Moran, John McMoran Wilson	14 February 2014	Stafford, Godfrey-Harry	16 September 2013
Mortier, Gerard	9 March 2014	Stansfield- Smith, Colin	19 June 2013
Mossbauer, Rudolf L.	14 September 2011	Still, Ray	12 March 2014
Mowat, Farley	6 May 2014	Stoker, Michael George Parke	13 August 2013
Mrozek, Slawomir	15 August 2013	Stone, Francis Gordon Albert	6 April 2011
Mu, Guoguang	12 April 2012	Strauss, Robert Schwarz	19 March 2014
Murray, Noreen Elizabeth	12 May 2011	Suckling, Charles W.	31 October 2013
Nairne, Patrick Dalmahoy	4 June 2013	Świerzy, Waldemar	27 November 2013
Nam, Duck-woo	18 May 2013	Tait, James Francis	2 February 2014
Nashashibi, Nassiriddin	17 May 2013	Tavener, John	12 November 2013
Neuberger, Michael S	26 October 2013	Thirsk, (Irene) Joan	3 October 2013
Newton, (Charles) Wilfrid	28 November 2012	Thomson, Thomas James	20 July 2013
Ney, Edward Noonan	8 January 2014	Todorovsky, Piotr Yefimovich	24 May 2013
Nguyen, Khanh	11 January 2013	Townsend, Susan (Sue) Lilian	10 April 2014
Ni, Zhifu	24 April 2013	Turro, Nicholas John	24 November 2012
Nicholson, Ernest Wilson	22 December 2013	Umarov, Doku (Dokka) Khamatovich	18 March 2014

OBITUARY

Vago, Constant	6 February 2012	Wiin-Nielsen, Aksel Christopher	26 April 2010
Vasile, Radu	3 July 2013	Wilkes, Michael (John)	27 October 2013
Velasquez-Gáztelu Ruiz, Cándido	8 November 2012	Wilson, Colin Henry	5 December 2013
Verges, Jacques	15 August 2013	Wilson, Kenneth G.	15 June 2013
Vest, Charles Marstiller	12 December 2013	Woodhouse, Owen	15 April 2014
Videla, Jorge Rafael	17 May 2013	Wran, Neville Kenneth	20 April 2014
Vo, Nguyen-Giap	4 September 2013	Wu, Renbao	18 March 2013
Wade, Kenneth	16 March 2014	Wu, Tianming	4 March 2014
Walker, David Alan	12 February 2012	Wunderlich, Paul	6 June 2010
Walker, David Maxwell	5 January 2014	Yakovlev, Yuri	30 November 2013
Wallot, Jean-Pierre	30 August 2010	Yalá, Kumba	4 April 2014
Walsh, Lawrence Edward	19 March 2014	Yamauchi, Hiroshi	19 September 2013
Wang, Zhongcheng	30 September 2012	Yang, Huaiqing	12 December 2012
Warnke, Jürgen Walter Franz Karl	27 April 2013	Yap, Emilio	7 April 2014
Weidenbaum, Murray Lew	20 March 2014	Zaentz, Saul	3 January 2014
Weinberg, Felix Jiri	6 December 2012	Zaffaroni, Alejandro	1 March 2014
Werder, Felix	3 May 2012	Zaslavskaya, Tatiana Ivanovna	24 August 2013
Whicker, Alan Donald	12 July 2013	Zen, E-An	29 March 2014
Whitehead, John Stainton	8 November 2013	Zimmerman, Howard Elliot	12 February 2012
Whitham, Gerald Beresford	26 January 2014		

THE INTERNATIONAL WHO'S WHO

2015

A

AARON, David L., MA; American diplomatist; *Senior International Adviser, Dorsey & Whitney LLP;* b. 21 Aug. 1938, Chicago; m. Chloe W. Aaron; one c.; ed Occidental Coll. Calif. and Princeton Univ.; entered Foreign Service 1962; Political and Econ. Officer, Guayaquil, Ecuador; Int. Relations Officer, Dept of State 1964–66; Political Officer, NATO, Paris 1966; Arms Control and Disarmament Agency; Sr Staff mem. Nat. Security Council 1972–74; Legis. Asst to Senator Walter Mondale 1974–75; Task Force Leader, Senate Select Cttee on Intelligence 1975–76; mem. staff, Carter-Mondale presidential campaign; Transition Dir with Nat. Security Council and CIA 1976–77; Deputy Asst to Pres. for Nat. Security Affairs 1977–81; Vice-Pres. Oppenheimer & Co. Inc. 1981–85, Dir Oppenheimer Int. 1984; Sr Adviser, Mondale presidential campaign; writer and lecturer, Lantz-Harris Agency 1985–93; consultant, 20th Century Fund 1990–92, Sr Fellow 1992–93; US Rep. to OECD 1993; US Special Envoy for Cryptography 1996; Under-Sec. of Commerce for Int. Trade 1997–2001; Sr Int. Adviser, Int. Trade Practice Group, Dorsey & Whitney LLP 2000–; Dr hc (Occidental Coll.); Nat. Defense Medal. *Television:* The Gulf War (script), Miracle on 44th Street: The Action Studio (script). *Publications:* State Scarlet 1987, Agent of Influence 1989, Crossing by Night 1993; articles in newspapers and journals. *Address:* Dorsey & Whitney LLP, 1001 Pennsylvania Avenue, NW, Suite 300, Washington, DC 20004, USA (office). *Telephone:* (202) 442-3000 (office); (202) 442-3645. *Fax:* (202) 442-3199 (office). *E-mail:* aaron.david@dorseylaw.com (office). *Website:* www.dorseylaw.com (office).

ABAGA NCHAMA, Lucas, DEA; Equatorial Guinean economist and central banker; *Governor, Banque des Etats de l'Afrique Centrale;* b. 4 March 1961, Ebebiyín, Río Muni; m.; three c.; ed Univ. Jean Monnet, St Etienne, France, Univ. Lyon II; joined Banque des Etats de l'Afrique Centrale (BEAC) 1998, with Bata br. 1999–2003, Pres., BEAC Audit Cttee 2007–08, Dir-Gen. of Operations 2008, Gov. BEAC 2010–; Dir-Gen. of Economy, Ministry of Economy and Trade 2003–06; Sec.-Gen., Ministry of Finance and Budget 2006–08. *Address:* Office of the Governor, Banque des Etats de l'Afrique Centrale, BP 112, Libreville, Gabon (office). *Telephone:* 01-76-13-52 (office). *Fax:* 01-74-45-63 (office). *E-mail:* beaclbv@beac.int (office). *Website:* www.beac.int (office).

ABAKANOWICZ, Magdalena; Polish artist, weaver and sculptor; b. 20 June 1930, Falenty, nr Warsaw; d. of Konstanty Abakanowicz and Helena Abakanowicz; m. Jan Kosmowski 1956; ed Acad. of Fine Arts, Warsaw; mem. Soc. of Authors ZAIKS; work includes monumental space forms of woven fibres, cycles of figurative sculptures of burlap, wood and clay, cast metal, stone, drawings, paintings with collage and gouache; Prof., Acad. of Fine Arts, Poznań 1979–90; mem. Presidential Council for Culture 1992; Hon. mem. American Acad. of Arts and Letters 1996; Commdr's Cross with Star, Order of Polonia Restituta 1998, Officier des Arts et Lettres, Paris 1999, Cavaliere nell Ordine Al Merito della Repubblica Italiana 2000; Dr hc (RCA, London) 1974, (Rhode Island School of Design, Providence) 1992, (Acad. of Fine Arts, Łódź) 1997, (Pratt Inst., New York) 2000, (Massachusetts Coll. of Art, Boston) 2001, (School of the Art Inst. of Chicago) 2002, (Acad. of Fine Arts, Poznań) 2002; Minister of Culture and Art Prize (1st Class) 1965, Gold Medal VIIIth Int. Biennale of Arts, São Paulo 1965, Gottfried von Herder Prize 1979, Alfred Jurzykowski Foundation Award 1982, New York Sculpture Center Award 1993, Leonardo da Vinci World Award of Arts 1997, Visionaries! Award, American Craft Museum 2000, Lifetime Achievement Award, International Sculpture Center, New York 2005. *Works include:* Sculpture for Elbląg, relief woven composition for North Brabant Prov. Bldg, Netherlands; three-dimensional woven forms: Abakans Figurative sculptures, seated figures, Backs, Incarnations, War Games, Crowds, Hands-like Trees, Mutants, Birds; large outdoor installations: Katarsis, Italy, Negev, Israel, Space of Dragon, S Korea, Space of Nine Figures, Germany, Becalmed Beings, Hiroshima, Japan and others. *Leisure interests:* swimming, walking in the countryside and forests. *Address:* ul. Bzowa 1, 02-708 Warsaw, Poland. *Telephone:* (22) 8486379 (home). *Fax:* (22) 8486379 (home). *E-mail:* magdalena@abakanowicz.art.pl. *Website:* www.abakanowicz.art.pl.

A-BAKI, Ivonne, BA, BArch, MPA; Ecuadorean diplomatist and artist; *Goodwill Ambassador, UNESCO;* b. Guayaquil; m. Sammi A-Baki; two s. one d.; ed Sorbonne Univ., Paris, France and Harvard Univ., USA; fmr Dir Conflict Man. Group, Harvard Univ., del. to confs in Geneva 1984, Lausanne 1985; Adviser to Pres. on Ecuador–Peru peace negotiations –1998; Consul-Gen., then Hon. Consul in Lebanon; Consul-Gen. in Boston, Mass; apptd Amb. to USA 1999; unsuccessful cand. for Pres. of Ecuador 2002; Minister of Foreign Trade, Industrialization, Fishing and Competition 2003–05; Pres. Andean Parl., Bogotá, Colombia 2007–09; UNESCO Goodwill Amb. 2010–; Ecuadorean negotiator for Yasuní-ITT Initiative and Pres.'s special envoy in charge of preserving the Yasuni National Park and Head, YNP Foundation; painter, numerous exhbns in museums, galleries and pvt. collections in Europe, N and S America and Middle East; f. Harvard Foundation for the Arts; Artist-in-Residence, Harvard Univ. 1991–98; Pres. Arts and Community Renewal Coalition, Boston, Beyond Boundaries Foundation; Order of Merit, Honorato Vasquez Order; numerous other awards. *Address:* Yasuní-ITT Initiative, Av 6 de Diciembre, N33-42 and Ignacio Bossano Edif Titanium Piso 7, Quito, Ecuador (office). *E-mail:* yasuni.itt@presidencia.gob.ec (office). *Website:* yasuni-itt.gob.ec (office).

ABAL, Sam; Papua New Guinea politician; fmr Minister for Provincial Affairs, fmr Minister for Inter-Govt Relations, Minister for Foreign Affairs, Trade and Immigration 2007–10; Deputy Prime Minister 2010–; Acting Prime Minister Dec. 2010–Jan. 2011, April–Aug. 2011; MP for Wabag; mem. Nat. Alliance Party. *Address:* c/o Office of the Prime Minister, POB 639, Waigani, National Capital District, Papua New Guinea.

ABAL MEDINA, Juan Manuel, Jr, PhD; Argentine political scientist and politician; b. 5 May 1968, Buenos Aires; s. of Juan Manuel Abal Medina and Cristina Moldes; ed Univ. of Buenos Aires, Latin American Social Sciences Inst., Mexico City; fmr Lecturer, Univ. of Buenos Aires, Nat. Univ. of Quilmes, Univ. of San Andrés; Dir Nat. Public Admin Inst. 2000–01; Political and Legis. Dir for Mayor of Buenos Aires 2001, Dir of Strategic Planning 2003–05; Under-Sec. of Public Man. and Adviser to Pres. 2005–07, Sec. 2008–11; Communications Sec. Jan.–Dec. 2011; Chief, Cabinet of Ministers 2011–13. *Publications include:* El federalismo electoral argentino 2001, Los partidos políticos: ¿un mal necesario? 2004, Evaluando el desempeño democrático de las instituciones políticas argentinas 2007; numerous articles in political science journals. *Address:* c/o Office of the Cabinet Chief, Avda Julio Argentino Roca 782, C1067ABP Buenos Aires, Argentina (office).

ABALAKIN, Victor Kuz'mich, DPhysMathSc; Russian astronomer; *Adviser, Russian Academy of Sciences;* b. 27 Aug. 1930, Odessa, Ukraine; m.; two c.; ed Odessa State Univ.; jr researcher, Inst. of Geophysics, USSR Acad. of Sciences 1953–55, Inst. for Theoretical Astronomy, USSR Acad. of Sciences 1955–57, Head of Div. 1965–83; Sr Researcher, Odessa Astronomical Observatory 1960–63; Docent, Odessa State Univ. 1963–65; Dir Main Astronomical Observatory, Russian Acad. of Sciences 1983–2000, Adviser 2000–; Corresp. mem. USSR (now Russian) Acad. of Sciences 1987–, Adviser 2000–; mem. Int. Acad. of Ecology, Man and Nature Protection Sciences 1997–; main research in theoretical astronomy, stellar dynamics, history of astronomy; Hon. mem. Russian Acad. of Cosmonautics 1998, Russian Acad. of Natural Sciences; Hon. Citizen of Tucson, Arizona, USA; Medal of the Merits for Fatherland, 2nd class 2006; "For Labour Valour" Medal (USSR) 1976, State Prize (USSR) 1982. *Publications:* seven books including Foundations of Ephemeris Astronomy 1979, Laser Ranging to the Moon 1981; numerous papers. *Leisure interests:* reading classical and modern belles lettres. *Address:* Central (Pulkovo) Astronomical Observatory, Russian Academy of Sciences, 196140 St Petersburg, Pulkovskoye Shosse 65, Bldg 1 (office); 191024 St Petersburg, 162 Nevsky Prospect, Apt 9, Russia (home). *Telephone:* (812) 723-4900 (office); (812) 723-4400 (office); (812) 717-2881 (home). *Fax:* (812) 723-1922 (office); (812) 717-2881 (home). *E-mail:* vicabal@gmail.com (office); vicabal@hotmail.com (office). *Website:* www.gao.spb.ru (office).

ABALKHAIL, Sheikh Mohamed Ali, BA; Saudi Arabian government official and financial executive; b. 30 Oct. 1932, Buraidah; s. of Ali Abdullah Abalkhail and Fatima Abdulaziz Othaim; m. 1966; two s. two d.; ed Cairo Univ., Egypt; began career as Asst Dir of Office of Minister of Communications, later Dir; Dir-Gen. of Inst. of Public Admin; Deputy Minister of Finance and Nat. Econ., then Vice-Minister, Minister of State, Minister for Finance and Nat. Econ. 1975–95; fmr Chair. Riyadh Bank, Riyadh; Chair. Centre for Econ. and Man. Studies; mem. JP Morgan Int. Council; decorations from Belgium, Egypt, France, Niger, Pakistan, Saudi Arabia, Sudan, Germany, Morocco, Spain. *Leisure interests:* reading, sports. *Address:* PO Box 943, Riyadh 11421 (office); PO Box 287, Riyadh 11411, Saudi Arabia. *Telephone:* (1) 478-1722 (office). *Fax:* (1) 478-1904 (office). *E-mail:* mabakhail@sanadco.com (office).

ABAZA, Mohammed Maher, BSc; Egyptian engineer, business executive and fmr politician; *Chairman, MIDTAP Company;* b. 12 March 1930, Sharkia; s. of Muhamed Osman Abazah; m. Ezdehar Abo El-Ela 1955; one s. one d.; ed Cairo Univ. and studies in W Germany and Sweden; engineer, Dept of Hydroelectric Power, Ministry of Public Works 1951–64; several sr positions in Egyptian Electricity Authority 1964–73; First Under-Sec. of State, Ministry of Electricity and Energy 1975–80, Minister of Electricity and Energy 1980–99; Chair. MIDTAP Co., MIDOR Electricity Co., Petrosport Co., Emarat Misr Co.; mem. Bd EMG Co.; Pres. Int. Asscn for Electricity Generation, Transmission and Distribution (Afro-Asian region) 1996–99; mem. numerous nat. and int. scientific cttees; mem. World Energy Council, IEEE, Thomas Alva Edison Foundation, Int. Council on Large Electrical Systems (CIGRE), Int. Conf. on Electricity Distribution (CIRED); The Greatest Nile Medal, Golden Medal of Distinction, Order of the Repub. (First Class, Egypt, France, Poland, Niger), Royal Order of the Polar Star (Grand Cross, Sweden), Grand Cross of the Order of Merit (FRG, Italy), Order of the Grand Cross (Italy), Cross of the Order of Merit (Italy), Grand Cross of the Order of Merit (First Class) (Finland), Order of the State (First Class, Yugoslavia), Order of Merit (Greece), Order of the State (First Class, Syria, Cen. African Repub.). *Publications include:* several articles in trade journals and for int. confs. *Leisure interests:* philately, photography, reading, swimming. *Address:* 22 El Badia Street, Heliopolis, Cairo (office); 8 Taha Hussein Street, Zamalek, Cairo, Egypt (home). *Telephone:* (2) 2918398 (office); (2) 4142028 (office); (2) 7357201 (home). *Fax:* (2) 4147515 (office). *E-mail:* midtap@midtap.com.eg (office).

ABBAS, Mahmud, (Abu Mazen), PhD; Palestinian politician and head of state; *President;* b. 1935, Safad, Galilea; ed Damascus Univ., Syria, Moscow Univ., Russia; civil servant, UAE –1967; co-f. Fatah (largest political party in The Palestine Nat. Liberation Movt), mem. Cen. Cttee 1964–; elected to Palestine Liberation Org. (PLO) Exec. Cttee 1980, Head Pan-Arab and Int. Affairs Dept 1984, Sec.-Gen. PLO Exec. Cttee 1996–2004, Chair. 2004–; Exec. Pres. Palestinian Nat. Authority (PNA) known internationally as Palestinian Authority (PA) 2005–; participated in Middle East Peace Conf., Washington, DC and in Norwegian-mediated peace talks with Israel. *Address:* Office of the President, Ramallah, Palestinian Territories. *E-mail:* fateh@fateh.org. *Website:* www.p-p-o.com; www.fateh.net.

ABBAS, Tan Sri Dato' Shamsul Azhar; Malaysian oil industry executive; *President and CEO, Petroliam Nasional Berhad (PETRONAS);* joined Petronas 1974, served in several sr positions, including Vice-Pres. Oil Business, Vice-Pres. Petrochemicals, Vice-Pres. Exploration (Upstream) and Vice-Pres. Maritime and Logistics, Man. Dir MISC (Petronas subsidiary) –2010, Pres. and CEO Petroliam Nasional Berhad (PETRONAS) 2010–, Acting Chair. 2011–12. *Address:* Petroliam Nasional Berhad (PETRONAS), Tower 1, PETRONAS Twin Towers, Kuala Lumpur City Centre, Kuala Lumpur 50088, Malaysia (office). *Telephone:* (3) 20515000 (office). *Fax:* (3) 20265050 (office). *E-mail:* webmaster@petronas.com.my (office). *Website:* www.petronas.com.my (office).

ABBOTT, Tony, LLB, MA; Australian politician; *Prime Minister;* b. 14 Nov. 1957, London, UK; m. Margaret Abbott; three d.; ed Univ. of Sydney, Univ. of Oxford, UK; began career as journalist and feature writer for The Bulletin and The Australian; Press Sec. and Political Adviser to John Hewson (Leader of the Opposition) 1990–93; Exec. Dir Australians for Constitutional Monarchy 1993–94; mem. House of Reps (Liberal) for Warringah 1994–, Parl. Sec. to Minister for Employment, Educ., Training and Youth Affairs 1996–98, also Leader of the House and Minister assisting the Prime Minister for Public Service 2001–03, Leader of the Opposition 2009–2013, Prime Minister of Australia 2013–; Minister for Employment, Workplace Relations and Small Business 2001, Minister for Health and Ageing 2003–07, Shadow Minister for Families, Community Services, Indigenous Affairs and the Voluntary Sector 2007–09; mem. Liberal Party of Australia, Parl. Leader 2009–. *Publications include:* The Minimal Monarchy 1995, How to Win the Constitutional War 1997. *Address:* Department of the Prime Minister and Cabinet, 1 National Circuit, Barton, ACT 2600, Australia (office). *Telephone:* (2) 6271-5111 (office). *Fax:* (2) 6271-5414 (office). *Website:* www.dpmc.gov.au (office); www.tonyabbott.com.au (office).

ABBOUD, A(lfred) Robert, AB, LLB, MBA; American banker and business executive; *President, A. Robert Abboud and Company;* b. 29 May 1929, Boston, Mass.; s. of Alfred Abboud and Victoria Abboud; m. Joan Grover Abboud 1955; one s. two d.; ed Harvard Coll., Harvard Law School, Harvard Business School; Asst Cashier, Int. Dept, First Nat. Bank of Chicago 1960, Asst Vice-Pres. Int. 1962, Vice-Pres. 1964, Sr Vice-Pres. 1969, Exec. Vice-Pres. 1972, Vice-Chair. 1973, Deputy Chair. of Bd 1974–75, Chair. of Bd 1975–80; Pres., COO and Dir Occidental Petroleum Corpn 1980–84; Pres. A. Robert Abboud and Co. (pvt. investment co.), Fox Grove, Ill. 1984–; Chair. Braeburn Capital Inc. 1984–92; Chair. and CEO First City Bancorp of Tex. Inc., Houston 1988–91, First City Nat. Bank of Houston 1988–91; Co-Chair. and Ind. Lead Dir Ivanhoe Energy Inc., Vancouver 2006–; fmr mem. Bd of Dirs AAR Corpn, Dir Cities Service, ICN Biomedicals, ICN Pharmaceuticals, Inland Steel Co., AMOCO, Hartmarx Corpn, Alberto-Culver Co.; Bronze Star, Purple Heart, US Marine Corps 1952; Baker Scholar, Harvard Business School 1958. *Publications include:* Introduction of US Commercial Paper in Foreign Markets: Premature and Perilous? 1970, A Proposed Course for US Trade and Investment Policies 1971, A Proposal to Help Reverse the Narrowing Balance in the US Balance of Trade 1971, The Outlook for a New Monetary System 1971, Opportunities for Foreign Banks in Singapore 1971, The International Competitiveness of US Banks and the US Economy 1972, Money in the Bank: How Safe Is It? 1988. *Address:* A. Robert Abboud & Co., 960 II Route 22, Suite 212, Fox River Grove, IL 60021 (office); 209 Braeburn Road, Barrington Hills, IL 60010, USA (home). *Telephone:* (847) 639-0101 (office); (847) 658-4808 (home). *Fax:* (847) 639-0233 (office). *E-mail:* araco@mc.net (office).

ABD AL-AZIZ, Muhammad Imhamid; Libyan government official; *Minister of Foreign Affairs and of International Co-operation;* fmr mem. Perm. Mission of Libya to UN, New York; fmr Sr Crime Prevention and Criminal Justice Officer, UN Centre for Int. Crime Prevention, Vienna; Minister of Int. Co-operation 2012–, Deputy Minister of Foreign Affairs –2013, Minister of Foreign Affairs 2013–. *Address:* Ministry of Foreign Affairs and of International Co-operation, Tripoli, Libya (office). *Website:* www.foreign.gov.ly (office).

ABDALLAH MANIRAKIZA, Hon. Tabu, DrEng; Burundian politician; *Minister of Finance and Planning for Economic Development;* b. 6 Oct. 1956; m. Bertille Kabura; three s. one d.; spent several years in exile in Switzerland and Rwanda; returned to Burundi 2006; Dir of Budget and State Control, Ministry of Finance 2006, Minister of Planning 2007, later Sr Adviser to Pres., Minister of Planning and Reconstruction 2010, of Finance and Planning for Econ. Devt 2012–; led team of observers from Int. Conf. on the Great Lakes Region to S Sudan to observe independence referendum 2011; mem. Conseil nat. pour la défense de la démocratie—Forces pour la défense de la démocratie. *Address:* Ministry of Finance, ave des Non-Aligens, BP 1830, Bujumbura, Burundi (office). *Telephone:* 22225142 (office). *Fax:* 22223128 (office). *E-mail:* ta.manirakiza@genie.bi (office). *Website:* www.finances.gov.bi (office).

ABDALLAHI, Sidi Ould Cheikh; Mauritanian politician and fmr head of state; b. 1938, Aleg; m.; three s. one d.; ed William Ponty School, Senegal, Univ. of Dakar, Senegal and Univ. of Grenoble, France; Dir of Planning, Second Plan for the Econ. and Social Devt of Mauritania 1968–71; served in several govt positions including Minister of State for Nat. Economy 1971–78; Econ. Adviser, Kuwait Fund for Arab Econ. Devt, Kuwait 1982–85, Head of Econs and Finance, Niger Div. 1989–2003; Minister of Hydraulics and Energy 1986–87, of Fisheries and Maritime Economy 1987–89; Pres. of Mauritania 2007–08 (ousted in coup).

ABDEL-AZIZ, Hany, BA; Egyptian/Swiss UN official; b. 1946, Cairo; two d.; ed Egyptian Mil. Acad., Univ. of Cairo, American Univ., Cairo; Egyptian Army service 1962–77, left with rank of Col; joined UN as Arabic interpreter at UN Office in

Geneva 1981, later positions included Sr Political Adviser and Second in Command, UN Political Office in Burundi 1993–96, Chief Admin Officer, UN Mission in Chad, Chief, Admin. Services Div., UN Econ. and Social Comm. for W Asia, Head of Central Support Services, UN Office, Geneva, Chief Admin Officer, UN Humanitarian Mission in Iraq, Head of UN Mission in Cen. African Repub., Head of Civil Affairs for Sarajevo, Chief of Staff of Jt UN/African Union Mediation Support Team for Darfur (JMST) –2008, Dir of Mission Support, UN Mission in the Democratic Repub. of the Congo 2008–09, Special Rep. of Sec.-Gen. for Western Sahara 2009–12, also Head of UN Mission for Referendum in Western Sahara –2012. *Address:* Parc Château Banquet No. 6, 1202 Geneva, Switzerland (home). *E-mail:* hany.abdelaziz@hotmail.com.

ABDEL-RAHMAN YOUSSEF, Ali, BSc, MSc, PhD; Egyptian construction engineer, academic and fmr university administrator; ed Cairo Univ., McGill Univ. and Univ. of New Brunswick, Canada,; instructor, Dept of Construction Eng, Cairo Univ. 1974–76, Asst Prof. 1976–81, Assoc. Prof. 1981–86, Prof. of Concrete Construction Design 1986–, Dir of Construction Eng Lab., Faculty of Eng. 1991–, Vice Dean of Educ. and Student Affairs 1995–2001, Dean Faculty of Eng 2001–04, Pres. of Cairo Univ. 2004–08; Chair. Centre for Support of Architectural and Eng Designs; mem. Scientific Cttee Housing and Building Nat. Research Centre; State Prize for Eng Sciences 1985. *Address:* c/o Office of the President, Cairo University, Giza, Egypt (office).

ABDEL-RAZEQ, Omar, PhD; Palestinian economist, academic and government official; b. 3 July 1958, Salfit, West Bank; ed Iowa State Univ., USA; Prof. of Econs, An-Najah Univ., Nablus 1986–93, Head of Econs Dept 1991–93, currently on teaching staff; mem. Islamic Resistance Movt (Hamas: Harakat al-Muqawama al-Islamiyya); mem. Palestinian Legislative Council; Sr Research Fellow, Palestine Econ. Policy Research Inst. 2000–01; Minister of Finance 2006–07. *Address:* Faculty of Economics and Administrative Sciences, An-Najah National University, PO Box 7, Nablus, Palestinian Autonomous Areas. *Website:* eco.najah.edu.

ABDELA'ALI, Fawzi; Libyan politician; fmr militia leader in Misrata; mem. Transitional Nat. Ass. 2011; Minister of the Interior 2011–12. *Address:* c/o Ministry of the Interior, Tripoli, Libya.

ABDELAZIZ, Maged Abdelfattah; Egyptian diplomatist and UN official; *Special Adviser to the Secretary-General on Africa, United Nations;* b. 1954; m.; one d.; ed Ain Shams Univ. School of Law; joined diplomatic service 1979, served in several positions in Ministry of Foreign Affairs including Int. Orgs Div., Legal and Treaties Dept 1979–83 (Head 1987–89), Second and First Sec., Perm. Mission to UN, New York 1983–87, Political Counsellor in charge of Middle East, Arab-Soviet Relations, Int. Orgs and Disarmament, Embassy in Moscow 1989–93, Head, Specialized Agencies Dept, Multilateral Sector, Ministry of Foreign Affairs 1993–95, Political Counsellor, Office of Perm. Rep. to UN, New York 1995–97, Prin. Rep. in all disarmament issues 1997–99, Deputy Perm. Rep. to UN 1997–99, Co-ordinator, Del. during membership on Security Council 1996–97, apptd Rep. in Expert Group, UN Sec.-Gen., UN Register for Conventional Arms 1997, apptd Chair. Disarmament Comm. 1999, Diplomatic Adviser and Official Spokesman of Pres. 1999–2005; Amb. and Perm. Rep. to UN, New York 2005–12; Special Adviser to the Sec.-Gen. on Africa, UN 2012–. *Address:* UN Office of the Special Adviser on Africa, New York, NY 10017, USA (office). *Telephone:* (212) 963-1234 (office). *Fax:* (212) 963-4879 (office). *E-mail:* osaa-info@un.org (office). *Website:* www.un.org/africa/osaa (office).

ABDELKERIM, Mahamat Nour; Chadian government official; trained in French military schools; f. Rally for Democracy and Liberty (RDL) 2005; fmr rebel leader United Front for Democratic Change (FUC), signed peace deal with govt 2006; Minister of Nat. Defence March–Dec. 2007. *Address:* c/o Ministry of National Defence, BP 916, N'Djamena, Chad (office).

ABDESSALEM, Rafik Ben, BA, PhD; Tunisian politician; b. 1968; m. Soumaya Ghannouchi; ed Mohammed V Univ., Rabat, Morocco, Univ. of Westminster, UK; mem. Exec. Office, Union Générale des Etudiants de Tunisie (UGET) 1987–90; in exile in Morocco and later in London during rule of Zine el Abidine Ben Ali; f. Maghreb Center for Research and Translation, London; Chair. London Platform for Dialogue; fmr Visiting Scholar, Oxford Centre for Islamic Studies; Sr Researcher and Head of Research and Studies Office, Al Jazeera Centre for Studies, Doha; Minister of Foreign Affairs 2011–13; mem. Hizb al-Nahdah (Renaissance Party), fmr mem. party bureau in exile, mem. Political Bureau, mem. Exec. Bureau in charge of media 2001–07, mem. Shura council. *Publications include:* La religion, la laïcité et la démocratie, Les États Unis d'Amérique entre la force dure et la force douce, Les réformes islamiques et la modernité; regular contributor to Asharq Al-Awsat (int. Arabic daily newspaper). *Address:* c/o Ministry of Foreign Affairs, ave de la Ligue des états arabes, 1030 Tunis, Tunisia (office).

ABDIC, Fikret 'Babo' (Papa); Bosnia and Herzegovina/Croatian politician and business executive; b. 29 Sept. 1939, Donji Vidovec; Dir Agrokomerc co. 1980s; charged with fraud in Fmr Yugoslavia 1987, convicted, sentenced to two years' imprisonment, acquitted on appeal 1989; Co-Founder (with Alijah Izetbegovic), Party of Democratic Action (PDA); set up autonomous region of W Bosnia in defiance of cen. Govt in Sarajevo 1993, his forces were crushed by Pres. Izetbegovic 1995; fled to Croatia in 1995, f. pvt. food co.; f. political party Democratic People's Union (DNZ) 1996; accused of war crimes by Bosnia 2001; extradition to Bosnia repeatedly refused by Croatian Govt on account of his Croatian citizenship; sentenced by Croatian court to 20 years' imprisonment for war crimes committed during Bosnian war 1993–95 July 2002, reduced on appeal to 15 years' imprisonment, released March 2012; permitted by Bosnian Election Comm. to run for Muslim post in three-man inter-ethnic presidency while still in prison Oct. 2002.

ABDILDIN, Serikbolsyn Abdildayevich, DEcon; Kazakhstani politician; *Leader, Communist Party of Kazakhstan;* b. 25 Nov. 1937, Kyzylkesek, Semipalatinsk; m. Abdildina Laura; one d. one s.; ed Kazakh Nat. Agric. Univ., KasGoz Post-Grad. Coll.; mem. CP of Soviet Union 1964–91; Minister of Agric. 1985–87; mem. CP of Kazakhstan (CPK) 1981–91, apptd First Sec. (Leader) 1994–; Deputy Supreme Council 1985–94, Deputy in Majlis (Nat. Ass.) 1999–2004, First Speaker 1991–94; joined Socialist Party of Kazakhstan (SPK) 1993; unsuccessful cand. in Kazakh Presidential Elections 1999; joined Democratic Choice of

Kazakhstan (DCK—opposition movt) 2001; Deputy Chair. Union of CP 2004–; Prof., Kazakh Nat. Agric. Univ. 1995–. *Publications:* more than 200 scientific publs 1964–2011. *Leisure interests:* fishing, hunting. *Address:* 114, Pushkin Street, Almaty (office); Communist Party of Kazakhstan, Karasai batyr 85/312, Almaty, Kazakhstan (office). *Telephone:* (727) 291-14-00 (office); (727) 265-11-19 (office); (701) 722-42-49 (home). *E-mail:* daptadakz@mail.ru (office). *Website:* www .komparty.kz (office).

ÄBDIQALÏQOVA, Gülşara Nawşaqızı, PhD; Kazakhstani politician; *Deputy Prime Minister;* b. 15 May 1965; ed Dzhambul Technological Inst. of Light and Food Industries; Sr Insp. and Head of Dept, Kyzylorda Regional Dept of Social Security 1987–94; consultant, Cttee of Supreme Council of Repub. of Kazakhstan on social protection of the population 1994–95; worked in Ministry of Labour and Social Protection as Chief of Dept, Deputy Head, Head of Pensions Man., Deputy Dir of Social Welfare Dept, Dir of Dept of Social Security and Social Assistance, Dir of Dept of Pensions and Regulation Incomes 1995–2003; Deputy Minister of Labour and Social Protection 2003–05, 2006–07; Chair. JSC Life Insurance Co.-State Annuity Co. 2005–06; Sec., Ministry of Labour and Social Protection 2007–08; Adviser to Pres. of Kazakhstan 2008–09, 2009–12; Chair. Nat. Comm. for Women, Family and Demographic Policy under Pres. of Kazakhstan 2008–09; Minister of Labour and Social Protection 2009–12; Deputy Prime Minister 2014–. *Address:* Office of the Prime Minister, 010000 Astana, Beibitshilik kosh. 11, Kazakhstan (office). *Website:* www.government.kz (office).

ABDIU, Fehmi, DrIur; Albanian judge and academic; *Dean, Faculty of Law, Illyria University;* b. 5 Jan. 1944, Dibra; m.; two c.; ed Faculty of Law, Tirana Univ., Teachers' Training School, Peshkopi; Judge, Fieri Dist Court 1968–73, Deputy Chief 1974–77, Chief 1977–85; Chief, Tirana Dist Court 1989–90; Judge, Supreme Court 1985–89, Deputy Chief 1990–92; mem. Parl. 1991–98; mem. Constitutional Court 1998–2010, Pres. 1998–2004; currently Dean, Faculty of Law, Illyria Univ., Tirana; Golden Order Naim Frashëri 2004. *Publications include:* The Politic According to the Constitution and Laws, Constitution and the Constitutional Court of the Republic of Albania, The Constitution, the Law and the Justice, Civil Action During Criminal Process. *Address:* Faculty of Law, Illyria University, Rr. "Qemal Stafa" (Ish-Artistike Migjeni), Tirana (office); Bulevard "Zhan D'Ark" Pallati 4, Ap. 1, Kati 9, Albania (home). *Telephone:* (4) 234-1450 (office); (5) 422-8125 (home). *Website:* www.uni-illyria.com (office).

ABDOU MADI, Mohamed; Comoran politician and diplomatist; b. 1956, Mjamaoue; m.; four c.; ed Algeria, Poland; tax insp., Moroni 1988; convicted of fraud, served sentence as a domestic servant; Perm. Sec., CTRAP (org. funded by UNDP to implement reforms in civil service) –1994; Sec.-Gen. Rassemblement pour la Démocratie et le Renouveau (RDR); Prime Minister of the Comoros 1994, also responsible for Public Works; Minister of Justice, Public Affairs, Employment, Professional Training, Admin. Decentralization and Institutional Reform 1998; Adviser, Embassy in Madagascar 2000; joined govt of Anjouan leader Colonel Mohamed Bacar 2007, govt removed from office by combined Comoros and African Union force 2008.

ABDOULAYE DIALLO, Ahmadou, DESS; Malian economist and politician; b. 16 March 1959, Bazi; m.; four c.; ed Inst. polytechnique rural de Katibougou, Centre d'études financières économiques et bancaires, Paris; Head of Dept of Control and Analysis, Malian Office of Livestock and Meat (OMBEVI) and Head of Planning Unit, Ministry of Natural Resources and Livestock 1985–89; Dir of Public Debt, Autonomous Debt Financing Fund (now Directorate-Gen. of Public Debt) 1991–94, tech. adviser to Fund Dir 1994–98; analyst, African Solidarity Fund 1998–2002, Dir of Studies and Projects 2003–05, of Operations 2007–08; econ. adviser to Pres. of Mali 2002; Minister of the Economy, Industry and Commerce (now Industry, Investment and Commerce) 2008–12. *Address:* c/o Ministry of Industry Investment and Commerce, BP 234, Koulouba, Bamako, Mali (office).

ABDOULFATAH CHARIF, Mohamed Bakri Ben, LenD; Comoran lawyer, diplomatist and politician; ed Univ. of Garyounis, Benghazi, Libya; fmr teacher of Arabic; fmr Pres. Tribunal de Première Instance, Fomboni; Sec.-Gen., Ministry of Justice 1992, Pres., Tribunal de Mohéli 1996; took part in drafting of new Constitution 1999; mem. Cour Constitutionelle (Constitutional Court) 2004–06; Amb. to Libya 2006–11; Minister of External Relations and Co-operation, with responsibility for the Diaspora and Francophone and Arab Relations 2011–13. *Address:* c/o Ministry of External Relations and Co-operation, BP 428, Moroni, Comoros.

ABDRASHITOV, Vadim Yusupovich; Russian film director; b. 19 Jan. 1945, Kharkov, Ukraine; s. of Yusup Sh. Abdrashitov and Galina Abdrashitov; m. Natella G. Toidze; one s. one d.; ed Moscow State Inst. of Cinematography (VGIK); mem. Russian Film Acad., Russian Union of Cinematographers; Order of the Fatherland, Fourth Class 2006; RSFSR State Prize 1984, State Prize of the USSR 1991, People's Artist of Russia 1996,. *Films include:* Witness for the Defence (USSR Riga Prize) 1977, The Turning 1978, Foxhunting 1980, The Train Has Stopped 1982, The Parade of the Planets 1984, Plumbum, or a Dangerous Game (Gold Medal at Venice Festival 1987) 1986, The Servant (Alfred Bauer Prize 1989) 1988, Armavir 1991, The Play for a Passenger (Silver Bear Award, Berlin Festival 1995) 1995, Time of the Dancer 1997, Magnetic Storms 2003. *Address:* 119270 Moscow, 3d. Frunzenskaya 9, Apt 211, Russia. *Telephone:* (495) 242-35-54.

ABDRISAEV, Baktybek, PhD; Kyrgyzstani diplomatist, scientist and academic; *Distinguished Visiting Professor, Utah Valley University;* b. 17 April 1958, Bishkek; s. of Dyushen Abdrisaev and Kalicha Jakypova; m. Cholpon Akmatalieva; two c.; ed Bishkek Polytechnical Inst. (now Kyrgyz Tech. Univ.), Inst. of Electronics, Acad. of Sciences of Belarus; Jr Scientific Fellow, Bishkek Polytechnical Inst. 1980–84, Sr Scientific Fellow 1987–88; Scientific Fellow, Inst. of Physics, Acad. of Sciences of Kyrgyz Repub. 1988–91, Sr Scientific Fellow 1991–92; staff expert, Pres.'s Dept of Int. Relations 1992–93, Head of Dept 1993–96; mem. Parl. 1995–2000; Amb. to USA and Canada 1996–2005; currently Distinguished Visiting Prof., Utah Valley Univ., USA; mem. European Acad. of Natural Sciences 2004–, Russian Acad. of Natural Sciences 2005–; Hon. Prof., Int. Univ. of Kyrgyzstan 2006; Union of Youth of Kyrgyzstan Scientific Achievement Award 1992. *Publications include:* Kyrgyzstan's Voice in Washington 2005; more than

100 scientific articles and presentations on applied optics and diplomacy. *Leisure interests:* hiking, table tennis. *Address:* Utah Valley University, Department of History and Political Science, 800 West University Parkway, Orem, UT 84058, USA (office). *Telephone:* (801) 863-8351 (office). *Fax:* (801) 863-7013 (office). *E-mail:* abdrisba@uvu.edu (office). *Website:* www.uvu.edu (office).

ABDUL, Paula; American singer and choreographer; b. 19 June 1962, San Fernando, CA; d. of Harry Abdul and Lorraine Abdul; m. 1st Emilio Estevez 1992 (divorced 1994); m. 2nd Brad Beckerman 1996; ed Van Nuys High School, Northridge Coll. California State Univ.; choreographer, LA Laker basketball cheerleaders; several bands, including Duran Duran, Toto, The Pointer Sisters, ZZ Top; scenes in films Bull Durham, Coming To America, The Waiting Game, The Doors, Touched By Evil, Junior High School; City of Crime video (from film Dragnet); worldwide performances as singer include tours throughout USA, UK, Japan and Far East; f. Co Dance (dance co.); judge, American Idol: The Search for a Superstar (TV series) 2002–09; Rolling Stone Award for Best Female Singer 1989, American Music Awards for Favorite Pop/Rock Female Vocalist 1989, 1992, Billboard Magazine Top Female Pop Album 1990, Grammy Award for Best Music Video (for Opposites Attract) 1991, Starlight Foundation Humanitarian of the Year, Los Angeles 1992. *Choreography include:* pop videos: The Jacksons and Mick Jagger's Torture, George Michael's Monkey, Janet Jackson's Control, Nasty (MTV Video Award for best choreography 1987), When I Think Of You, What Have You Done For Me Lately; television: Dolly Parton Christmas Special, Tracey Ullman Show (Emmy Award for best choreography) 1989. *Recordings include:* albums: Forever Your Girl 1989, Shut Up And Dance (The Dance Mixes) 1990, Spellbound 1991, Head Over Heels 1995, Greatest Hits 2000. *Address:* Third Rail Entertainment, Tri-Star Bldg, 10202 West Washington Avenue, Suite 26, Culver City, CA 90232, USA (office). *Website:* www.paulaabdul.com (office).

ABDUL HADI, Mahdi, PhD; Palestinian research institute director; *Chairman, Palestinian Academic Society for the Study of International Affairs (PASSIA);* ed Bradford Univ., UK; Co-Founder and Ed. Al-Fajr daily newspaper 1972–74; Co-Founder and Gen. Sec. Council for Higher Educ. in the West Bank 1977–80; Founder and Pres. Arab Thought Forum, Jerusalem 1977–81; special adviser to Ministry of Occupied Land Affairs, Amman, Jordan 1985–86; Founder and Chair., Bd of Trustees, Palestinian Academic Soc. for Study of Int. Affairs (PASSIA) 1987–; mem. Arab Thought Forum, Amman 2002; occasional guest lecturer on Palestinian issues at local colls, univs and insts; mem. Jerusalem Arab Council, Palestinian Council for Justice and Peace, Asscn of Palestinian Policy Research Insts; Fellow, Center for Int. Affairs, Harvard Univ. 1985, Salzburg Int. Seminar 1986; mem. Black Sea Univ. Foundation, Bucharest 1990, IISS, London, EuroMeSCo network, Arab Social Science Research Network. *Publications:* Awakening Sleeping Horses 2000; numerous articles, monographs and essays in newspapers and journals. *Address:* The Palestinian Academic Society for the Study of International Affairs, 18, Hatem Al-Ta'i Street, Wadi Al-Joz, POB 19545, Jerusalem, Israel (office). *Telephone:* 2-6264426 (office). *Fax:* 2-6282819 (office). *E-mail:* passia@passia.org (office). *Website:* www.passia.org (office).

ABDUL-JABBAR, Kareem; American basketball coach, writer and fmr professional basketball player; b. (Ferdinand Lewis Alcindor, Jr), 16 April 1947, New York; s. of Lewis Alcindor and Cora Alcindor; ed Power Memorial High School, Univ. of California, Los Angeles; graduated as the leading scorer in UCLA history (2,325 points); played for Nat. Basketball Asscn (NBA) Milwaukee Bucks 1969–75, for NBA Los Angeles Lakers 1975–89; All NBA First Team 1971–74, 1976–77, 1980–81, 1984, 1986; NBA All-Defensive First Team 1974–75, 1979–81; retd from game 1989; Asst Coach Alchesay High School (Whiteriver, AZ) 1999–2000; Asst Coach NBA LA Clippers 2000; Asst Coach NBA Indiana Pacers 2002; Head Coach USBLs Oklahoma Storm 2002; Asst Coach Los Angeles Lakers 2005; NBA career records include: most minutes (57,446), most points (33,387), most field goals made (15,837), most field goals attempted (28,307), most blocks (3,189); first player in NBA history to play 20 seasons; 1,560 games played; 18 NBA All-Star games played; named Cultural Amb. for US 2012; All-City 1963–65, All-American 1963–65, Consensus All-American 1963–65, First Team All-America 1967, 1968, 1969, Nat. Player of the Year 1967, 1969, Nat. Collegiate Athletic Asscn (NCAA) Tournament Most Outstanding Player 1967, 1968, 1969, Naismith Award Winner 1969, NBA Rookie of the Year 1970, NBA Most Valuable Player—MVP 1971, 1972, 1974, 1976, 1977, 1980, NBA Finals MVP 1971, 1975, Sports Illustrated Sportsman of the Year 1985, elected to Basketball's Hall of Fame 1995. *Publications include:* Giant Steps (with Peter Knobler) 1983, Kareem (with Mignon McCarthy) 1990, On the Shoulders of Giants: My Journey Through the Harlem Renaissance (with Raymond Obstfeld) 2007, What Color Is My World? The Lost History of African American Inventors (with Raymond Obstfeld) 2012. *Website:* kareemabduljabbar.com.

ABDUL JALIL, Mustafa Mohammed; Libyan politician and judge; b. 1952, Al Bayda; ed Dept of Shari'a and Law, Arabic Language and Islamic Studies Faculty, Univ. of Libya; apptd Asst to Sec. of Public Prosecutor, Al Bayda, before being apptd a judge in 1978; Pres. Court of Appeals, then Pres. of the Court, Al Bayda 2002–07; Minister of Justice (under Col Gaddafi) 2007–11, resgnd after being sent to Benghazi to negotiate the release of hostages taken by rebels 21 Feb. 2011; Chair. Nat. Transitional Council of Libya March 2011–Aug. 2012. *Address:* c/o National Transitional Council, Benghazi, Libya.

ABDUL-RAHMAN, Tan Sri Datuk Omar, MVD, MRCVS, FASc; Malaysian professor of veterinary pathology and university administrator; *President and CEO, Malaysia University of Science and Technology (MUST);* b. 9 Nov. 1932, Kota Bharu, Kelantan; three c.; ed Sydney and Queensland Univs, Australia and Univ. of Cambridge, UK; Demonstrator in Veterinary Pathology, Queensland Univ. 1959; Veterinary Research Officer, Veterinary Research Inst., Ipoh 1960–67, Sr Research Officer 1967–70, Deputy Dir 1971–72; Foundation Prof. and Dean, Faculty of Veterinary Medicine and Animal Sciences, Universiti Putra Malaysia 1972–78, Prof. of Veterinary Pathology 1982–2001, Deputy Vice-Chancellor 1982–84; apptd Pres. Malaysian Scientific Asscn 1984, currently Adviser; fmr Pres. Asscn of Veterinary Surgeons Malaysia–Singapore; mem. Nat. Council for Scientific Research and Devt, Malaysia, Nat. Comm. for UNESCO, Nat. Devt Planning Cttee of Malaysia 1984; Adviser to Prime Minister on Science and Tech. 1985–2001; Exec. Chair. Venture Capital for Tech. Acquisition 2001–07; currently Pres. and CEO Malaysia Univ. of Science and Tech. (MUST); Founding Chair.

Commonwealth Partnership for Tech. Man. (CPTM); Founding Pres. and Sr Fellow, Malaysian Acad. of Sciences; Pres. Malaysian Asscn of Professional Speakers 2006–; Founding Chair. Malaysian Tech. Devt Corpn, Tech. Park Malaysia Corpn; Founding Jt Chair. Malaysian Industry-Govt Group for High Tech.; Founding Fellow, Islamic Acad. of Sciences; Fellow, Acad. of Sciences for the Third World; mem. Editorial Advisory Bd Tropical Veterinarian (journal) 1983–; Exec. Chair. Kumpulan Modal Perdana Sdn Bhd; mem. Bd of Dirs OSK Ventures Int. Bhd, Green Packet Bhd, Encorp Bhd, Kotra Industries Bhd, Great Wall Plastic Industries Bhd, BCT Technology Bhd; Hon. Fellow, Nat. Acad. of Sciences of Kyrgyz Repub.; Dr hc (Stirling) 1986, (Melbourne), (Guelph), (Bristol), (Queensland); Asean Achievement Award (Science) 1993, Fook Ying Tung South East Asia Prize 1998, Tun Abdul Razak Award (Int. Category) 2000; Darjah Mulia Seri Melaka (state award), Johan Setia Mahkota, Johan Mangku Negara and Panglima Setia Mahkota (fed. awards). *Publications:* over 100 publs on science and tech. *Address:* MUST Ehsan Foundation, Malaysia University of Science and Technology, Unit GL33 (Ground Floor), Block C, Kelana Square, 17, Jalan SS7/26, 47301 Petaling Jaya, Selangor D.E; Malaysian Association of Professional Speakers, c/o Suite 47-4, 4th Floor, PJ Highway Centre, Jalan 51/205, 46050 Petaling Jaya, Selangor, Malaysia. *Telephone:* (3) 78806863 (office). *Fax:* (3) 78806525 (office). *E-mail:* tsomar@must.edu.my (office); info@maps.org.my (home). *Website:* www.must.edu.my (office).

ABDULAI, Yesufu Seyyid Momoh; Nigerian economist and international organization official; b. 19 June 1940, Auchi; s. of Momoh Abdulai and Haijia Fatimah Abdulai; m. Zene Makonnen Abdulai 1982; three s. one d.; ed Mount Allison Univ. and McGill Univ., Canada; taught econs in Canada; Tech. Asst to Exec. Dir (Africa Group I), World Bank Group, Washington, DC 1971–73, Adviser to Exec. Dir 1973–78, Alternate Exec. Dir for Africa Group 1 1978–80, Exec. Dir 1980–82, Vice-Chair. Jt Audit Cttee Exec. Bd 1980–82; Chair. Jt Secr. African Exec. Dirs of World Bank Group and the IMF 1975–77; Man. Dir and CEO Fed. Mortgage Bank of Nigeria 1982–83; Dir-Gen. OPEC Fund for Int. Devt 1983–2003; mem. Prize Cttee, Arab Gulf Programme for UN Devt Orgs (AGFUND) Int. Prize for Pioneering Devt Projects; Grand Decoration of Honour (Austria) 2004. *Leisure interests:* sport, reading, photography, listening to music.

ABDULATIPOV, Ramazan Gadzhimuradovich, DPhilSc; Russian/Dagestan politician, diplomatist and university administrator; *President of Dagestan;* b. 4 Aug. 1946, Guerguta, Dagestan; m.; two s. one d.; ed Dagestan State Univ.; mem. CPSU 1973–91; CP work 1974–76; Sr Teacher, Dagestan Pedagogical Inst. 1975–76; Head of Murmansk Higher School of Marine Eng 1978–87; Head of Sector, Div. of Int. Relations of CPSU Cen. Cttee 1988–90; RSFSR People's Deputy 1990–93, Chair. Council of Nationalities 1990–93; elected to Council of Fed. 1993, Deputy Chair. 1994–96; mem. State Duma 1995–97; Deputy Prime Minister 1997–98, Minister of Nat. Policy 1998–99; Rep. of Saratov Region in Council of Fed. 2000–05; Amb. to Tajikistan 2005–08; Pres. Ass. of Peoples of Russia 1998–; Pres. of Dagestan 2013–; Rector Moscow State Univ. of Culture and Arts; participant in numerous peace-making missions in N Caucasus; Pres. Fed. of UNESCO Clubs in Russia; mem. Russian Acad. of Natural Sciences. *Publications:* Lenin's Policy of Internationalism in USSR, Internationalism and the Spiritual and Moral Development of the Peoples of Dagestan, What is the Essence of Your Being?, Power and Conscience, Nature and Paradoxes of National Consciousness Authority of Sense, Ethnic Question and State Structure of Russia: From Cran Tower to the Kremlin Gates, Inscriptions. *Leisure interests:* painting, aphoristic poetry. *Address:* 367000 Dagestan, Makhachkala, pl. Lenina, Russia (office). *Telephone:* (8722) 67-30-59 (office). *Fax:* (8722) 67-30-60 (home). *Website:* www.president.e-dag.ru (office).

ABDULLA, Ahmed; Maldivian newspaper publisher, fmr politician and fmr diplomatist; *Chairman, Miadhu News;* b. 26 Sept. 1949, Malé; s. of Abdullah Hassan and Hawwa Fulhu; m.; one s. three d.; fmr Amb. to Sri Lanka and India; fmr Minister of Health, of Information, Arts and Culture; Acting Minister of Foreign Affairs 2005; Minister of Environment, Energy and Water 2005–08 (resgnd); mem. Maldivian Democratic Party 2010; Owner and Chair. Miadhu News (newspaper). *Leisure interests:* calligraphy, reading, sports fishing, badminton, swimming. *Address:* G. Mescot, Lonuziyaarai Magu, Malé (home); Miadhu News, G. Mascot, Koimalaa Hingun, Malé 20-02, Maldives (office). *Telephone:* 3322557 (home); 3320700 (office). *Fax:* 3321504 (home); 3320500 (office). *E-mail:* miadhu@dhivehinet.net.mv (office). *Website:* www.miadhu.com.mv (office).

ABDULLAH, Abdullah, DMed; Afghan ophthalmologist and politician; b. 5 Sept. 1960, second dist of Karte Parwan, Kabul; s. of Ghulam Muhayuddine Khan and Siddiqa Muhayuddine Khan; m.; one s. three d.; ed Naderia High School, Faculty of Medicine, Kabul Univ.; completed training in ophthalmology 1983, subsequently served as a specialist at Noor Eye Hosp., Kabul; went to Pakistan during Soviet occupation to care for Afghan refugee families at Sayed Jamal-U-Din Hosp. 1984; joined the Afghan Freedom Fighters 1985, served as caretaker in charge of health affairs for Panjshir Valley resistance front; became an adviser and close companion of Ahmad Shah Massoud; Mujahidin activist, Jamiat-i-Islami group; Sr Spokesman, Defence Ministry 1992–96; Deputy Minister of Foreign Affairs, Northern Alliance 1999, caretaker Minister of Foreign Ministry for the officially recognized govt-in-exile of the Islamic Repub. of Afghanistan from 1999 until the collapse of the Taliban 2001; participated in Future of Afghanistan Govt Talks, Bonn Nov. 2001; Minister of Foreign Affairs, Afghan Interim Authority Dec. 2001–June 2002, Afghan Transitional Authority 2002–04, of Afghanistan 2004–06; Sec.-Gen. Massoud Foundation 2006–09; cand. in presidential election 2009, (withdrew from runoff election Nov. 2009), 2014; f. Coalition for Change and Hope (now National Coalition of Afghanistan) 2009. *Leisure interests:* music, swimming, ping-pong. *Website:* www.nca.af.

ABDULLAH, Burhanuddin, MA; Indonesian economist and fmr central banker; b. 10 July 1947, Garut; ed Padjadjaran Univ. Bandung, Michigan State Univ., USA; joined Bank Indonesia 1979; worked in Credit Dept 1981, later with Econ. Research and Statistics Dept, then Personal Asst to Gov.; joined IMF, Washington, DC 1989, Asst Exec. Dir 1990–93; Head Econ. Co-operation and Int. Trade Div., Indonesia 1993–95; Deputy Dir for Int. Affairs 1995–96; Deputy Dir Econ. Research and Monetary Policy Dept 1996–98; Deputy Gov. Bank Indonesia 2000–03, Gov. 2003–08, also Gov of IMF for Indonesia; Co-ordinating Minister of Econ. Affairs 2001. *Address:* c/o Bank Indonesia, Jalan M. H. Thamrin 2, Jakarta Pusat 10110, Indonesia (office).

ABDULLAH, Farooq, MB; Indian physician and politician; *Minister of New and Renewable Energy;* b. 21 Oct. 1937, Srinagar, Kashmir; s. of Sheikh Mohammad Abdullah and Begum Abdullah; m. Mollie Abdullah 1968; one s. (Omar Farooq Abdullah) three d.; ed S.M.S. Medical Coll., Jaipur, Rajasthan; mem. Lok Sabha (Parl.) 1980–82, for Srinagar constituency 2009–; mem. Jammu and Kashmir Legis. Ass. 1982–90, 1996–2002, Dec. 2008–Feb. 2009; Minister of Health 1983–87, of New and Renewable Energy 2009–; Chief Minister, Jammu and Kashmir 1983–90, 1996–2002, 2002–08; mem. Rajya Sabha (Parl.) 2002–08, Feb.–May 2009; Pres. State Cen. Labour Union, Jammu and Kashmir Nat. Conf.; Chair. Jammu and Kashmir Muslim Auqaf Trust, Sher-i-Kashmir Nat. Medical Inst. Trust, Sher-i-Kashmir Inst. of Medical Sciences; Gen. Sec. Indo-Arab Friendship Soc., Nat. Integration Council; Patron Jammu and Kashmir Nat. Conf.; mem. India Int. Centre; Leader, Jammu and Kashmir Nat. Conf. Parl. Party; Pres. J and K Cricket Asscn; Hon. DLitt. (Aligarh Muslim Univ.); Nat. Solidarity Award 1998, Eminent Personality of the Year, Indian Medical Asscn 1999, Dr B.C. Roy Nat. Award 1999. *Leisure interests:* golf, photography, gardening, music. *Address:* Ministry of New and Renewable Energy, Block 14, CGO Complex, Lodhi Road, New Delhi 110 003 (office); 40, Gupkar Road, Srinagar India (home). *Telephone:* (11) 24361298 (office); (194) 2452540 (home). *Fax:* (11) 24361830 (office); (194) 2452120 (home). *E-mail:* farooq_abdullah@rediffmail.com (home); secymnes@nic.in (office). *Website:* mnes.nic.in (office).

ABDULLAH, Omar Farooq, BCom; Indian politician; *Chief Minister of Jammu and Kashmir;* b. 10 March 1970, Rochford, UK; s. of Farooq Abdullah and Mollie Abdullah; m. Payal Abdullah; two s.; ed Sydenham Coll., Mumbai; Pres. Youth Nat. Conf.; elected to Lok Sabha (Parl.) 1998, re-elected 1999, 2004; Pres. Jammu and Kashmir Nat. Conf. 2002–; mem. Parl. for Srinagar constituency (Nat. Conf. Party) 1998; mem. Cttee of Transport and Tourism, Consultative Cttee, Ministry of Tourism 1998–99; Minister of State for Commerce and Industry 1999–2001, for External Affairs 2001–02; Chief Minister of Jammu and Kashmir 2009–. *Leisure interests:* tennis, skiing, swimming, squash, biking. *Address:* Office of the Chief Minister, Government of Jammu and Kashmir, Civil Secretariat, Jammu/Srinagar, India (office). *Telephone:* (191) 2546466 (office); (194) 2452224 (office). *Fax:* (191) 2545649 (office); (194) 2452120 (office). *Website:* www.jammukashmir.nic.in/govt/welcome.html (office).

ABDULLAH, Yousuf bin al-Alawi bin; Omani government minister and diplomatist; *Minister responsible for Foreign Affairs;* b. 1942, Salalah; s. of Abdullah bin Alawi; ed Egypt, univ. studies in political science, UK; joined Diplomatic Service 1970, Second Sec., Ministry of Foreign Affairs 1972, postings to Cairo and Beirut; Amb. to Lebanon 1973; Under-Sec., Ministry of Foreign Affairs 1974, Minister of State 1982, Minister responsible for Foreign Affairs 1997–; First Grade Sultan Qaboos Decoration, Order of Merit, Egypt, Officier, Légion d'honneur, Grand Decoration of Honour (Austria), Cavaliere Grande Croce (Italy) and other foreign decorations. *Address:* Ministry of Foreign Affairs, PO Box 252, Muscat 112, Oman (office). *Telephone:* 24699453 (office). *Fax:* 24696141 (office). *E-mail:* info@mofa.gov.om (office). *Website:* www.mofa.gov.om (office).

ABDULLAH II IBN AL-HUSSEIN, HM King of Jordan; head of state and army officer; b. 30 Jan. 1962, Amman; s. of the late King Hussein Ibn Talal and of Princess Muna al-Hussein; m. Rania al-Yassin 1993 (Queen Rania); two s. two d.; ed Islamic Educ. Coll., St Edmund's School, Surrey, UK, Deerfield Acad., USA, Sandhurst Mil. Acad. and Univ. of Oxford, UK; succeeded to the throne 7 Feb. 1999; commissioned Second Lt 1981, Reconnaissance Troop Leader 13th/18th Bn Royal Hussars (British Army), FRG and England; rank of First Lt 1984; Platoon Commdr and Co. second-in-command 40th Armoured Brigade, Jordan, Commdr Tank Co. 91st Armoured Brigade 1985–86 (rank of Capt.); Tactics Instructor Helicopter Anti-Tank Wing, 1986–87; undertook advanced studies in int. affairs at School of Foreign Service, Georgetown Univ., Washington, DC 1987–88; Commdr of a co. 17th Tank Bn, 2nd Guards Brigade then Bn second-in-command (rank of Maj.) 1989; attended Command and Staff Coll., Camberley, UK 1990; Armour Rep. Office of the Insp. Gen. 1991, Commdr 2nd Armoured Car Regt, 40th Brigade (rank of Lt Col) 1992; promoted to rank of Col 1993; Deputy Commdr Jordanian Special Forces Jan.–June 1994; promoted to the rank of Brig. 1994 and assumed command of Royal Jordanian Special Forces; Commdr of Special Operations Command 1997–; Pres. Jordan Nat. Football Fed.; Hon. Pres. Int. Tourism Golden Rudder Soc.; Head Nat. Cttee for Tourism and Archaeological Film Production 1997–. *Leisure interests:* car racing, (fmr Jordanian Nat. Rally Racing Champion), water sports, scuba diving, collecting ancient weapons and armaments. *Address:* Royal Hashemite Court, Amman, Jordan. *Website:* www.kingabdullah.jo.

ABDURIXIT, Abdulahat; Chinese politician; b. March 1942, Yining, Xinjiang; ed Xinjiang Eng Coll.; joined CCP 1960; engineer then Vice-Pres. Xinjiang Uygur Autonomous Region Construction Survey and Design Acad., Vice-Dir Xinjiang Uygur Autonomous Region Planning Comm.; Vice-Chair. Xinjiang Uygur Autonomous Region 1965–93; Chair. Xinjiang Uygur Autonomous Region 1993–2003; apptd Vice-Sec. CCP Xinjiang Uygur Autonomous Region Cttee 1993; mem. CCP 15th Cen. Cttee 1997–2002, 16th Cen. Cttee 2002–07, 17th Cen. Cttee 2007–12; Chair. Regional People's Congress, Xinjiang 2003–08; Vice-Chair. 11th CPPCC Nat. Cttee 2008–13.

ABDYKARIMOV, Oralbai; Kazakhstani politician; b. 18 Dec. 1944, Kievka, Karaganda region; m. Abdykarimova Jamal; three s. one d.; ed Alma-Ata Higher CPSU School, Karaganda State Univ.; leading posts in Komsomol and CP organs of Kazakhstan; Deputy Head, then Head of Admin. Office of Pres. of Kazakhstan; Chair. Mazhilis (Parl.); Chair. Higher Disciplinary Council, State Comm. for Fight with Corruption; mem. Senate (Parl.) 1999–, Chair. of Senate 1999–2004, currently Chair. Republican Social Council; Sec. of State and presidential adviser 2004–07; Chair. Nur Otan party public council on fighting corruption 2007; fmr mem. Security Council of Kazakhstan; Order Barys. *Address:* Senat, 010000 Astana, Abay d-ly 33, Parliament House, Kazakhstan (office). *E-mail:* smimazh@parlam.kz. *Website:* www.parlam.kz (office).

ABDYLDAYEV, Erlan Bekeshovich; Kyrgyzstani diplomatist and academic; *Minister of Foreign Affairs;* b. 21 July 1966; m.; one s. one d.; ed Moscow State Inst. of Int. Relations; Asst, Dept of the Socialist Asian Countries, Ministry of Foreign Affairs, USSR 1989, Attaché and Third Sec., Embassy of USSR, later of Russia, in Beijing, People's Repub. of China 1989–94; referent, expert consultant, Int. Dept of the Presidential Admin 1994–97; First Deputy Foreign Minister 1997–2001, Amb. to People's Repub. of China 2001–05 (also accred to Mongolia, Singapore and Thailand); expert, Inst. of Public Policy, Bishkek 2005–; Country Dir for Kyrgyzstan, Inst. for War and Peace Reporting 2007–; Minister of Foreign Affairs 2012–. *Address:* Ministry of Foreign Affairs, 720040 Bishkek, bul. Erkindik 57, Kyrgyzstan (office). *Telephone:* (312) 62-05-45 (office). *Fax:* (312) 66-05-01 (office). *E-mail:* gendep@mfa.gov.kg (office); erlan200521@gmail.com; pressslujba@gmail.com (office). *Website:* www.mfa.kg (office).

ABE, Nobuyasu; Japanese diplomatist, research institute director and fmr UN official; *Director, Center for the Promotion of Disarmament and Non-Proliferation, Japan Institute of International Affairs;* b. 9 Sept. 1945, Akita; m. Akiko Sugawara; two s.; ed Univ. of Tokyo, Amherst Coll., Mass, USA; entered Foreign Service 1967, has held variety of positions in fields of arms control and disarmament; served in Embassy in Washington, DC 1969–71, Pvt. Sec. to Foreign Minister Toshio Kimura 1974, to Kiichi Miyazawa 1974–76, in Perm. Mission to Int. Orgs, Geneva 1977–79, in Embassy in Tel-Aviv 1979–81, Dir of Policy Planning 1984–86, Perm. Mission to UN, New York 1987–90, 1996–97, Embassy in Manila 1990–92, Consul-Gen., Consulate Gen. in Boston 1994–96, Dir-Gen. for Arms Control and Science Affairs 1997–99, Amb. to Int. Orgs, Vienna 1999–2001, to Saudi Arabia 2001–03, to Switzerland 2006–08; UN Under-Sec.-Gen. for Disarmament Affairs, New York 2003–06; currently Dir Center for the Promotion of Disarmament and Non-Proliferation, Japan Inst. of Int. Affairs; serves as Special Asst to the Foreign Minister; mem. UN Sec.-Gen.'s Advisory Bd on Disarmament Matters; mem. Bd of Trustees, UN Inst. for Disarmament Research; mem. Geneva Centre for Security Policy, IISS 1984–, Advisory Bd, Int. Comm. for Nuclear Nonproliferation and Disarmament 2008–10; Int. Fellow, Weatherhead Center for Int. Affairs, Harvard Univ. 1986–87; Visiting Prof., Doshisha Univ. 201–, Akita Int. Univ. 2011–. *Address:* Center for the Promotion of Disarmament and Non-Proliferation, Japan Institute of International Affairs, 3-8-1 Kasumigaseki, Chiyoda-ku, Tokyo 100-0013, Japan (office). *Telephone:* (3) 3503-7558 (office). *Fax:* (3) 3503-7559 (office). *E-mail:* nobuyasu.abe@cpdnp.jp (office). *Website:* www.cpdnp.jp/eng/English/index.htm (office).

ABE, Shinzō, LLB; Japanese politician; *Prime Minister;* s. of the late Shintaro Abe; grandson of the late Nobusuke Kishi; ed Faculty of Law, Seikei Univ., Univ. of Southern California, USA; began career with Kobe Steel Ltd –1982; Exec. Asst to Minister for Foreign Affairs 1982–87; apptd Pvt. Sec. to Chair. of Gen. Council, LDP 1987, Pvt. Sec. to Sec.-Gen. 1987–93, Dir of LDP Social Affairs Div. 1999–2000, Sec.-Gen. 2003–04, Acting Sec.-Gen. 2004, Pres. 2006–07, 2012–; mem. House of Reps (Yamaguchi Pref., 4th Electoral Dist) 1993–, mem. Standing Cttee on Foreign Affairs 1993–99, on Health and Welfare 1999–2000, on Security 1999–2000; Deputy Chief Cabinet Sec. 2000–01, 2001–03, Chief Cabinet Sec. 2005–06, Prime Minister 2006–07 (resgnd), 2012–; ranked by Forbes magazine amongst The World's Most Powerful People (57th) 2013. *Publications include:* Utsukushii Kuni E (Toward a Beautiful Country) 2006. *Address:* Prime Minister's Office, 1-6-1, Nagata-cho, Chiyoda-ku, Tokyo 100-8968 (office); Liberal-Democratic Party, 1-11-23, Nagata-cho, Chiyoda-ku, Tokyo 100-8910, Japan (office). *Telephone:* (3) 3581-2361 (office); (3) 3581-6211 (office). *Fax:* (3) 3581-1910 (office); (3) 5511-8855 (office). *E-mail:* koho@ldp.jimin.or.jp (office). *Website:* www.kantei.go.jp; www.jimin.jp (office).

ABED, Sir Fazle Hasan, Kt, KCMG; Bangladeshi business executive and foundation executive; *Founder and Chairperson, BRAC;* b. 1936; ed Univ. of Dhaka, Univ. of Glasgow, UK; Sr Corp. Exec., Shell Oil, Chittagong early 1970s; left job and went to London, UK to devote himself to Bangladesh's War of Independence; helped initiate campaign called Help Bangladesh to organize funds for the war effort in Bangladesh; returned to newly ind. Bangladesh and est. BRAC (fmrly Bangladesh Rural Advancement Cttee) to rehabilitate returning refugees in a remote area in a northeastern dist of the country 1972, currently Chair.; Chair., Bd of Dirs, BRAC Bank Ltd 2013–; apptd by UN Sec.-Gen. Ban Ki-moon to Eminent Persons Group for Least Developed Countries 2010; Dr hc (Yale Univ.) 2007, (Columbia Univ.) 2008, (Univ. of Oxford) 2009, (Rikkyo Univ.) 2009, (Univ. of Bath) 2010, (Univ. of Manchester) 2012; Ramon Magsaysay Award for Community Leadership 1980, UNICEF's Maurice Pate Award 1992, Olof Palme Award 2001, Schwab Foundation Social Entrepreneurship Award 2002, Gates Award for Global Health 2004, UNDP Mahbub ul Haq Award for Outstanding Contribution in Human Development 2004, Palli Karma Sahayak Foundation Award for Lifetime Achievement in Social Development and Poverty Alleviation 2007, Henry R. Kravis Prize in Leadership 2007, Inaugural Clinton Global Citizen Award 2007, David Rockefeller Bridging Leadership Award 2008, Conrad Hilton Foundation Humanitarian Award 2009, WISE Prize 2011, Open Society Prize 2013. *Address:* BRAC Centre, 75 Mohakhali, Dhaka 1212, Bangladesh (office). *Telephone:* (2) 9881265 (office). *Fax:* (2) 8823542 (office). *E-mail:* info@brac.net (office). *Website:* www.brac.net (office).

ABED DE ZAVALA, Sheila R.; Paraguayan lawyer, environmentalist and politician; *Minister of Justice and Labour;* ed Universidad Nacional de Asunción; Environmental Law & Policy Prof. in the Masters Programme on Environmental Eng, Universidad Nacional de Asunción; Founder and Exec. Dir IDEA (Instituto de Derecho y Economía Ambiental), Asuncion, Paraguay 1996–; past Gen. Co-ordinator Alianza Regional para Políticas de Conservación en América Latina y el Caribe (Regional Alliance for Conservation Policies in Latin America and the Caribbean); mem. Comm. on Environmental Law, Int. Union for Conservation of Nature 2000–, fmr Chair.; Minister of Justice and Labour 2013–; mem. Grupo Zapallar on Trade and Environment (S American coalition of NGOs and individual mems); has represented the Paraguayan Govt before UN Framework Convention on Climate Change; has represented civil society in Biodiversity and Ramsar Conventions. *Publications:* co-author of eight publs. *Address:* Ministry of Justice and Labour, Avda Dr José Gaspar Rodríguez de Francia, esq. Estados Unidos, Asunción, Paraguay (office). *Telephone:* (21) 49-3209 (office). *Fax:* (21) 20-8469 (office). *E-mail:* info@mjt.gov.py (office). *Website:* www.mjt.gov.py (office).

ABEL, Caroline; Seychelles economist and central banker; *Governor, Central Bank of Seychelles;* d. of the late Antoine Abel; ed Univ. of Leeds, Univ. of Glasgow, UK; began career as economist with Social Security Fund; joined Central Bank of Seychelles as Sr Bank Clerk 1994–96, Research Officer, Dept of Research and Statistics 1999, becoming Sr Research Officer and Dir of Research, Head of Div. for

Policy, Market Operations and Statistics 2006–10, Deputy Gov. 2010–11, First Deputy Gov. 2011–12, Gov. Central Bank of Seychelles (first female) 2012–. *Address:* Office of the Governor, Central Bank of Seychelles, Independence Avenue, POB 701, Victoria, Seychelles (office). *Telephone:* 4282000 (office). *Fax:* 4226104 (office). *E-mail:* enquiries@cbs.sc (office). *Website:* www.cbs.sc (office).

ABEL, Edward William, CBE, PhD, DSc; British chemist and academic; *Professor Emeritus of Inorganic Chemistry, University of Exeter;* b. 3 Dec. 1931, Mid-Glamorgan; s. of the late Sydney J. Abel and Donna Maria Grabham; m. Margaret R. Edwards 1960; one s. one d.; ed Bridgend Grammar School, Glamorgan, Univ. Coll. Cardiff and Northern Polytechnic, London; Research Fellow, Imperial Coll. London 1957–59; Lecturer and Reader, Univ. of Bristol 1959–71; Prof. of Inorganic Chem. Univ. of Exeter 1972–97, Deputy Vice-Chancellor 1991–94, now Prof. Emer.; Visiting Prof., Univ. of British Columbia 1970, Univ. of Japan 1971, Tech. Univ. of Brunswick 1973, ANU, Canberra 1990; mem. Council, Royal Soc. of Chem. (RSC) 1978–82, 1983–2002, Pres. RSC 1996–98, Ed.-in-Chief Tutorial Chemistry Texts (10 vols) 1999; Chair. Scientific Affairs Bd, Univ. Grants Cttee 1986–89; Hon. Fellow, Univ. of Cardiff 1999; Hon. DUniv (London Metropolitan Univ.); Hon. DSc (Exeter) 2000, (Univ. of Glamorgan); Tilden Medal, RSC 1981. *Publications:* Organometallic Chemistry Vols 1–25 (ed.) 1970–95, Comprehensive Organometallic Chemistry I (ed.) (nine vols) 1984, II (14 vols) 1995. *Leisure interest:* gardening. *Address:* 1A Rosebarn Avenue, Exeter, Devon, EX4 6DY, England (home). *Telephone:* (1392) 270272 (home). *E-mail:* mea@rosebarn.eclipse.co.uk (home).

ABELA, George, BA, LLB, LLM, PhD; Maltese lawyer, politician and fmr head of state; b. 22 April 1948, Qormi; s. of George Abela and Ludgarda Abela (née Debono); m. Margaret Abela 1976; one s. one d.; ed Univ. of Malta; fmr attorney in pvt. practice, specialising in civil, commercial and industrial law; legal consultant to Gen. Workers' Union 1975–2000; fmr legal adviser to Medical Asscn of Malta; Pres. Qormi FC –1982, Pres. Malta Football Asscn 1982–92; Deputy Leader in charge of Party Affairs, Malta Labour Party 1992–96; legal adviser to Prime Minister of Malta 1996–97; fmr Dir Cen. Bank of Malta; fmr Exec. Dir Bank of Valletta PLC; Pres. of Malta 2009–14. *Address:* c/o Office of the President, The Palace, Valletta VLT, 1190, Malta (office).

ABELE, John E., BS; American medical device industry executive (retd); m. Mary Abele; three c.; ed Amherst Coll.; several exec. positions with medical device firms in 1960s including with Advanced Instruments Inc.; joined Medi-tech 1969 then f. Cooper Scientific 1970 and acquired Medi-tech, Pres. 1970–83, helped develop, manufacture and market first steerable catheter; co-f. (with Peter Nicholas) Boston Scientific Corpn 1979, Chair. 1979–95, Vice-Chair. and Founder, Office of the Chair. 1995–96 (retd); Founder Chair. Argosy Foundation (pvt. family foundation) 1997–; Founding Chair. FIRST (For Inspiration and Recognition of Science and Technology) Foundation 2002–10, Vice-Chair. 2010–; mem. and Hon. Fellow, Soc. of Interventional Radiology. *Address:* c/o FIRST, 200 Bedford Street, Manchester, NH 03101, USA (office). *Website:* www.usfirst.org (office); www.argosyfnd.org.

ABELEV, Garry Israyelevich; Russian immunologist; *Head of Laboratory, N. N. Blokhin Cancer Research Centre, Russian Academy of Medical Sciences;* b. 10 Jan. 1928, Moscow; s. of Israel Abelev and Eugenia Abelev; m. 1st Elfrida Cilart 1949 (died 1996); two s.; m. 2nd Galina Deichman 1999; ed Moscow State Univ.; joined N.F. Gamaleya Inst. of Epidemiology and Microbiology, held several positions including Sr Lab. Technician, Researcher, Head of Lab., Head of Dept 1950–77; Head of Lab. Inst. of Carcinogenesis, N. N. Blokhin Cancer Research Centre 1977–; Prof., Moscow State Univ.; Corresp. mem. USSR (now Russian) Acad. of Sciences 1987–, mem. 2000–; mem. American Acad. of Immunology; conducts research on immunology of tumours, immunochemistry, cell biochemistry; mem. Bd New York Inst. of Cancer, New York Acad. of Sciences; Hon. mem. American Asscn of Immunologists, European Soc. of Cancer Researchers; Gold Medal Cancer Research Inst. (USA) 1975, USSR State Prize 1978, Abbot Prize 1990, Honourable Scientist of Russia 1999, Triumph Prize 2001, Calling Prize 2004. *Publications:* Virusology and Immunology of Cancer 1962, Alpha-Feto-Protein: 25 Years of Study, Tumour Biology 1989, An autobiographical sketch: 50 years in cancer immunochemistry (in 'Comprehensive Biochemistry', ed. G. Semenza) 2007; articles in scientific journals of Russia, Western Europe and USA. *Leisure interests:* music, history of science. *Address:* N.N. Blokhin Cancer Research Centre, Russian Academy of Medical Sciences, 115478 Moscow, Kashirskoye Shosse 24, Russia (office). *Telephone:* (495) 323-59-10 (office). *Fax:* (495) 324-12-05 (office). *E-mail:* abelev@crc.umos.ru (office). *Website:* www.ronc.ru (office); garriabelev.narod.ru (home).

ABERBACH, David, BA, BSc, MLitt, DPhil; British academic; *Professor of Jewish Studies, McGill University;* b. 17 Oct. 1953, London, England; s. of the late Prof. Moshe Aberbach and Rose Aberbach (née Firsht); m. Mimi Skelker 1980; three d.; ed Talmudical Acad. of Baltimore, USA, Univ. Coll., London, Univ. of Oxford, Tavistock Clinic, Open Univ.; fmr Lecturer, Univs of Oxford and Cambridge, Leo Baeck Coll. and Cornell Univ., USA 1982–86; Visiting Asst Prof., McGill Univ., Canada 1986–87, Assoc. Prof., Dept of Jewish Studies 1987–2006, Prof. 2006–; Visiting Prof., Univ. Coll. London 1992–93, 1998, 2001–02, 2008–09; Academic Visitor, Sociology Dept, LSE 1992–93, 1994–98, 2001–03, Govt Dept, LSE 2004, 2006, 2008–10, Humanities Center, Harvard Univ. 2010–12, Weatherhead Center for Int. Affairs and Kennedy Center for Int. Devt, Harvard Univ. 2013; Visiting Sr Fellow, Dept of Int. Devt, LSE 2013–14. *Radio:* broadcasts based on book on charisma (BBC World Service). *Publications include:* At the Handles of the Lock: Themes in the Fiction of S. J. Agnon 1984, Bialik 1988, Surviving Trauma: Loss, Literature and Psychoanalysis 1989, Realism, Caricature and Bias: The Fiction of Mendele Mocher Sefarim 1993, Imperialism and Biblical Prophecy 750–500 BCE 1993, Charisma in Politics, Religion and the Media: Private Trauma, Public Ideals 1996, Revolutionary Hebrew, Empire and Crisis 1998, The Roman-Jewish Wars and Hebrew Cultural Nationalism (co-author) 2000, Major Turning Points in Jewish Intellectual History 2003, C. N. Bialik: Selected Poems (ed.) 2004, Jewish Cultural Nationalism: Origins and Influences 2008, Moshe Aberbach, Jewish Education and History: Continuity, Crisis and Change (ed.) 2009, The European Jews, Patriotism and the Liberal State 1789–1939 2012; articles in British Journal of Sociology, Commentary, Comparative Literature Studies, Ethnic and Racial Studies, Harvard Theological

Review, International History Review, International Journal of Psycho-Analysis, Journal of Modern Jewish Studies, Nations and Nationalism, Polin, TLS and others. *Leisure interests:* cinema, gardening, painting, coastal path hiking. *Address:* Department of Jewish Studies, McGill University, 3438 McTavish, Montreal, PQ H3A 1X9, Canada (office); 32 Ravenshurst Avenue, London, NW4 4EG, England. *Telephone:* (514) 398-5009 (office). *Website:* www.mcgill.ca/jewishstudies/faculty/aberbach (office).

ABERCROMBIE, Neil, BA, MA, PhD; American politician and state governor; *Governor of Hawaii;* b. 26 June 1938, Buffalo, NY; s. of G. Donald Abercrombie and Vera June Abercrombie (née Giersdorf); m. Dr Nancie Ellen Caraway 1981; ed Williamsville High School (now Williamsville South High School), Union Coll., Schenectady, NY, Univ. of Hawaii, Mānoa; variety of jobs when young including as waiter at Chuck's Steak House, Waikiki, locker desk clerk at Cen. YMCA, custodian at Mother Rice Preschool, construction apprentice programme dir; fmr elementary school teacher and coll. lecturer; unsuccessful cand. for Democratic nomination to US Senate 1970; mem. Hawaii State House of Reps 1975–79, Hawaii State Senate 1980–86; mem. US House of Reps, Washington, DC for 1st Congressional Dist of Hawaii 1986–87 (special election), 1991–2010 (resgnd to run in Hawaii gubernatorial election Feb. 2010); mem. Honolulu City Council 1988–90; Gov. of Hawaii 2011–; Democrat. *Publication:* Blood of Patriots (novel with Richard Hoyt) 1996. *Leisure interests:* weightlifting, walking Kanoa, visiting family. *Address:* Executive Chambers, State Capitol, 415 South Beretania Street, Honolulu, HI 96813, USA (office). *Telephone:* (808) 586-0034 (office). *Fax:* (808) 586-0006 (office). *E-mail:* info@neilabercrombie.com. *Website:* governor.hawaii.gov (office); www.neilabercrombie.com.

ABHISIT, Vejjajiva (Mark), BA, MPhil, LLB; Thai economist and politician; *Leader of the Opposition;* b. 3 Aug. 1964, Newcastle-upon-Tyne, England; s. of Dr Athasit Vejjajiva and Dr Sodsai Vejjajiva; m. Dr Pimpen Sakuntabhai; two c.; ed Eton Coll., Univ. of Oxford, UK, Ramkhamhaeng Univ.; fmr Lecturer, Chulachomklao Royal Mil. Acad. and Faculty of Econs, Thammasat Univ.; mem. Parl. (Democrat) for Bangkok 1992–2001, Democrat Party List 2001–06, Democrat Party List Zone 6 2007–; Govt Spokesperson 1992–94, Deputy-Sec. to the Prime Minister for Political Affairs 1994, Chair. House Educ. Affairs Cttee 1995, Cttee to Consider the Nat. Educ. Bill of 1999 1998; Minister to the Prime Minister's Office 2001; Deputy Leader Democrat Party (Prachatipat) 1999, Leader 2005–; Prime Minister 2008–11; Leader of the Opposition 2011–; Kt Grand Cordon of the Most Noble Order of the Crown of Thailand 1998, Kt Grand Cordon (Special Class) of the Most Exalted Order of the White Elephant 1999. *Address:* Democrat Party (Prachatipat), 67 Thanon Setsiri, Samsen Nai, Phyathai, Bangkok 10400, Thailand. *Website:* www.opm.go.th (office); www.democrat.or.th; www.abhisit.org.

ABIL, Iolu Johnson, MBE; Ni-Vanuatu politician and head of state; *President;* b. 1942, Tanna; s. of George Yavinian; ed Onesua High School, Loughborough Int. Co-operative Coll., UK Univ. of the South Pacific, Suva, Fiji; Co-operative Inspector, British Nat. Service, Port Vila 1964; with New Hebrides Co-operative Dept 1964–80; fmr Sec., Ministry of Lands; interim Ombudsman of Vanuatu 2004–05; fmr Chair. Air Vanuatu; Pres. of Vanuatu 2009–; ordained as Elder, Presbyterian Church 1975; mem. Vanuaaku Pati (Our Land Party), fmr Vice-Pres. *Address:* Office of the President, PMB 100, Port Vila, Vanuatu (office). *Telephone:* 23055 (office). *Fax:* 26693 (office).

ABILDAYEV, Bolot; Kyrgyzstani business executive and fmr government official; *General Director, Gazprom Neft Asia;* Minister of Finance 2002–05; Gen. Dir Gazprom Neft Asia 2006–. *Address:* Gazprom, 117997, Moscow, 16 Nametkina Street, V-420, GSP-7, Russia (office). *Telephone:* (495) 719-30-01 (office). *Fax:* (495) 719-83-33 (office). *E-mail:* gazprom@gazprom.ru (office). *Website:* www.gazprom.com (office).

ABILOV, Geldimyrat; Turkmenistani fmr central banker; First Deputy Chair. Cen. Bank of Turkmenistan 2005–06, Chair. 2006–; Rep. of Turkmenistan at World Bank and Asian Devt Bank. *Address:* c/o Central Bank of Turkmenistan, 744000 Aşgabat, ul. Bitarap, Turkmenistan (office). *Telephone:* (12) 38-10-27 (office). *Fax:* (12) 51-08-12 (office). *E-mail:* merkez3@online.tm (office).

ABIRACHED, Robert, DèsSc; French writer and academic; *Professor Emeritus, University of Paris X;* b. 25 Aug. 1930, Beirut, Lebanon; m. Marie-France de Bailliencourt 1974; one s. one d.; ed Lycée Louis-le-Grand and École Normale Supérieure, Paris; Attaché, CNRS 1960–64; Drama Critic, Nouvel Observateur 1964–66; Literary and Drama Critic, La Nouvelle Revue Française 1956–72; Lecturer, later Prof., Univ. of Caen 1969–81; Prof. and Dir Dept of Drama, Univ. of Paris X 1988–99, Prof. Emer. 1999–; Prof., Conservatoire nat. supérieur d'art dramatique 1993–97; Dir Theatre and Exhbns, Ministry of Culture 1981–88; Pres. Int. Festival of Francophones, Limoges 1990–2000; Observatory of Cultural Politics, Grenoble, 1991–2001; Officier, Légion d'honneur; Commdr, Ordre nat. du Mérite; Commdr des Arts et des Lettres; Commdr des Palmes académiques; Prix Sainte-Beuve 1962. *Plays include:* Tu connais la musique? 1972, Giacomo Casanova comédien (in Italian) 1997. *Television includes:* La Consultation, Agnès, Agnès, Le dernier mot 1973. *Publications include:* Casanova ou la dissipation (essay) 1961, l'Emerveillée (novel) 1963, Tu connais la musique? (play) 1971, La crise du personnage dans le théâtre moderne (essay) 1978, Le théâtre et le Prince tome I: L'Embellie 1992, La décentralisation théâtrale (four vols) (ed.) 1992–95, La Théâtre et le Prince tome II: Un système fatigué 2005, Le théâtre en France au XXme siècle (essay and anthology) 2011. *Address:* 4 rue Robert-Turquan, 75016 Paris, France (home). *Telephone:* 1-45-25-24-87 (home). *E-mail:* robert.abirached@orange.fr (home).

ÄBIYEV, Col-Gen. Säfär Axundbala oğlu; Azerbaijani politician and army officer; b. 27 Jan. 1950, Baku, Azerbaijan SSR, USSR; ed Baku Troops Command Acad., Frunze Mil. Acad., Moscow, Russian SFSR; has spent entire professional life in armed forces; served in Azerbaijani Army, attaining rank of Col-Gen.; apptd Chief of Gen. Staff of Azerbaijani Armed Forces and Acting Minister of Defence June 1993, remained as Acting Minister until Aug. 1993, continued to serve as Chief of Gen. Staff until Nov. 1993, reinstated as Minister of Defence 1995–2013; Şöhrät Order 2010. *Address:* c/o Ministry of Defence, 1139 Baku, Azärbaycan pr., Azerbaijan.

ABIZAID, Gen. John; American army officer (retd) and consultant; *Senior Partner, JPA Partners LLC;* m.; three c.; ed US Mil. Acad., West Point, Harvard Univ., Univ. of Jordan, Amman; began career with 82nd Air Airborne Div., Fort Bragg, N Carolina; fmr infantry commdr; led Ranger rifle co. during invasion of Grenada 1983; led 1st infantry div., 504th Parachute Infantry Regt; 66th Commdt US Mil. Acad.; Asst to Chair. of Jt Chiefs of Staff 1993; fmr Dir of Strategic Plans and Policy, Jt Staff, later Dir of the Jt Staff; Deputy Commdr, then Commdr for Combined Forces Command, US Cen. Command 2003–07 (retd); Sr Pnr, JPA Partners LLC (consulting firm), Nov. 2007–; Annenberg Distinguished Visiting Fellow, Hoover Inst., Stanford Univ. 2007; mem. Bd of Dirs RPM International Inc. 2008–; Distinguished Chair of the Combating Terrorism Center, US Military Acad., West Point; Montgomery Fellow, Dartmouth Coll. 2008; mem. Council on Foreign Relations, IISS; Legion of Merit; Defense Distinguished Service Medal, Army Distinguished Service Medal, Bronze Star. *Address:* JPA Partners LLC, PO Box 927, Gardnerville, NV 89410, USA (office). *E-mail:* info@jpapartners.com (office). *Website:* www.jpapartners.com (office).

ABLAZA, Gerardo C., Jr, AB; Philippine telecommunications industry executive; *President and CEO, Manila Water Company, Inc.;* b. 1953; ed De La Salle Univ.; began career at Unilever; several positions at Citibank NA 1983–97 including Country Business Man. for Philippines and Guam 1996–97 and Vice-Pres. Citibank NA Singapore for Consumer Banking; joined Ayala Corpn, assigned to Globe Telecom Inc. as Exec. Vice–Pres. and COO 1997, Pres. and CEO 1998–2009, mem. Man. Cttee, Ayala Corpn, also Sr Man. Dir and Chair. Innove Communications (subsidiary); Pres. and CEO Manila Water Company, Inc. 2010–; mem. Bd of Dirs Bank of The Philippine Islands 2001–; Asia Business Leadership Award and CEO Choice of the Year Award, TNT 2004. *Address:* Manila Water Company, Inc., MWSS Administration Building 489, Katipunan Road, Balara, Quezon City 1105, Philippines (office). *Telephone:* (632) 917-5900 (office). *E-mail:* info@manilawater.com (office). *Website:* www.manilawater.com (office).

ABLYAZOV, Muxtar; Kazakhstani fmr banker and politician; b. 16 May 1963, Galkino, Kazakh SSR, USSR; m. Alma Shalabaeva; two s. two d.; est. Astana Holding (multi-sector pvt. holding co.) 1992; acquired shares in Bank TuranAlem (later known as BTA Bank) 1998; apptd Head of state-owned Kazakhstan Electricity Grid Operating Co. 1997; apptd Minister for Energy, Industry and Trade 1998; co-f. Democratic Choice of Kazakhstan opposition political movt 2001; convicted of "abusing official powers as a minister" and sentenced to six years in prison, released from prison on condition that he renounce politics May 2003; moved to Moscow to rebuild business interests 2003; Chair. BTA Bank 2005–09; accused of money laundering and fraud March 2009, fled to London, UK following issue of an arrest warrant, assets frozen and passport confiscated 2009; Investigative Cttee of Russian Ministry of the Interior also requested a warrant for his arrest on charges of four counts of financial crime; subject of legal proceedings by BTA Bank in the High Court, London to recover assets allegedly misappropriated during his tenure at BTA Bank; lost a legal battle to prevent assets from being subject to a receivership order Oct. 2010; lost a legal battle to have BTA Bank's claims thrown out Feb. 2011; granted asylum in UK July 2011; his extradition requested by Prosecutor Gen.'s Office in Kazakhstan; fled UK after being sentenced to 22 months in jail for contempt of court and for failing to disclose full details about his wealth Feb. 2012; £150m of assets seized and ordered by UK court to pay £1.02bn plus interest Nov. 2012; denied permission by UK Supreme Court to appeal the contempt ruling and prison sentence Feb. 2013; villa in Rome raided by Italian police May 2013, wife and younger daughter taken into custody and deported to Almaty, Kazakhstan on charges of carrying falsified documents; Ablyazov arrested on French Riviera July 2013, ordered by French court to be extradited to Russia or Ukraine to face fraud charges Jan. 2014; *Website:* mukhtarablyazov.org.

ABO AUF, Ezzat; Egyptian actor, fmr doctor and fmr musician; *President, Cairo International Film Festival;* b. 21 Aug. 1948; m. Fatima Abo Auf; one s. one d.; ed Al Azhar Univ. Faculty of Medicine, Cairo; worked as gynaecologist for five years; fmr professional musician, bands include 4M (with four sisters) 1979–91; acting debut in film Ice Cream in Golem 1992; Pres. Cairo Int. Film Festival 2006–, Egyptian Actors Union. *Television:* host of several popular TV shows including talk show Cairo Today (Al Qahira Al Yom). *Films include:* Strawberry War 1992, Traffic Light 1994, Birds of Darkness 1995, Ismailia Back and Forth 1995, Assassination 1996, Searching for Tut Ankh Amun 1996, The Land of Fear 1998, A Woman's Destiny 1999, The Lovers 1999, The Red Book 2000, Let Go 2004, One of the People 2006, Baby Doll's Night 2007, El Zamahlaweya 2008, Bobos 2009, Omar and Salma 2 2009. *Address:* Cairo International Film Festival, c/o Ministry of Culture, 2 Sharia Shagaret ed-Dor, Cairo (Zamalek), Egypt (office). *Website:* www.ciff.org.eg (office).

ĀBOLTIŅA, Solvita; Latvian politician; *Chairman (Speaker), Saeima (Parliament);* b. 19 Feb. 1963, Ogre, Latvian SSR; m.; two c.; ed Rīga Secondary School No. 5, Faculty of Law, Univ. of Latvia; worked for jt stock co. Latvijas kultūrprocess 1979–93; joined Ministry of Foreign Affairs 1993, Sr Officer, Consular Dept 1993–95, Head of Consular and Legal Affairs Div. 1995, Dir Consular Dept 1995–2002; mem. Saeima (Parl.) 2002–, Chair. Legal Affairs Cttee 2002–04, Deputy Chair. (Speaker) of the Saeima 2009–10, Chair. (Speaker) 2010–; legal adviser, Ministry of Foreign Affairs July–Dec. 2004; Minister of Justice 2004–06; mem. Jaunais laiks (New Era) party, Chair. 2008–10; mem. Unity (Vienotība) party, Chair. 2011–. *Address:* Office of the Speaker, Saeima (Parliament), Jekaba iela 11, Rīga 1811 (office); Unity (Vienotība), K. Barona iela 3, Rīga 1050, Latvia. *Telephone:* 6708-7487 (office). *Fax:* 6783-0333 (office). *E-mail:* laura.osleja@saeima .lv (office); birojs@vienotiba.lv (office). *Website:* www.saeima.lv/en/about-saeima/work-of-the-saeima/speaker-2 (office); vienotiba.lv (office).

ABOUMRAD, Daniel Hajj; Mexican telecommunications executive; *CEO, América Móvil;* b. 1966, Mexico City; s.-in-law of Carlos Slim Helú; ed Anáhuac Univ., Dir América Móvil SAB de CV, CEO 2000–; CEO Hulera Euzkadi SAB de CV; mem. Bd of Dirs Carso Global Telecom, América Telecom, Grupo Carso SA de CV, Radiomóvil Dipsa SAB de CV, Telefonos de Mexico (Telmex). *Address:* América Móvil SAB de CV, Lago Alberto 366, Colonia Anáhuac, 11320 México, DF, Mexico (office). *Telephone:* (55) 25813947 (office). *Fax:* (55) 25813948 (office). *E-mail:* info@americamovil.com (office). *Website:* www.americamovil.com (office).

ABOUTRIKA, Mohamed, BPhil; Egyptian professsional footballer; b. 7 Nov. 1978; m.; two c.; ed Cairo Univ.; midfield player; played with Tersana youth team 1990–97, with sr team 1997–2004; striker, Al Ahly Football Club 2004–; mem. Egyptian Nat. Football Team 2001–, tournaments include Confed. of African Football (CAF) African Cup of Nations 2006 (scored winning goal in penalty shootout), CAF Champions League 2006 (top scorer of tournament), FIFA Club World Championship 2006 (top scorer), Egyptian League 2006 (top scorer), African Cup of Nations 2008 (scored winning goal in final); UN World Food Programme Amb. Against Hunger; named Best Player in Egypt 2004, 2005, 2006, 2007, BBC African Footballer of the Year 2008. *Address:* c/o Egyptian Football Association, 5 Gabalaya Street, Gezira El Borg Post Office, Cairo, Egypt (office). *Website:* www .efa.com.eg (office).

ABOUYOUB, Hassan; Moroccan politician and diplomatist; *Ambassador to Italy;* b. 18 May 1952; joined Ministry of Commerce and Industry, then Dir of Int. Trade 1980, Minister of External Trade and Minister of Foreign Investment and Tourism 1990–93; elected mem. Parl. 1993; Amb. to Saudi Arabia 1994–95; Minister of Agric. 1995–97; Amb. responsible for trade negotiations 1998; Amb. to France 1999–2006; apptd Amb.-at-Large and Chief Foreign Policy Adviser to King Mohamed VI of Morocco 2006; directed Morocco's accession to GATT and its trade negotiations with EU, participated in conclusion of Uruguay Round, helped organize Marrakesh Ministerial Conf.; Hon. Chair. SIDA-Entreprises Maroc 2006–; Amb. to Italy 2010–; mem. Bd of Advisors, Global Panel Foundation. *Address:* Embassy of Morocco, Via Lazzaro Spallanzani 8–10, 00161 Rome, Italy (office). *Telephone:* (06) 4402524 (office). *Fax:* (06) 44004458 (office). *E-mail:* sifamaroma@ambasciatadelmarocco.it (office). *Website:* www .ambasciatadelmarocco.it (office).

ABOVA, Tamara Yevgenyevna, DJur; Russian professor of law; *Head, Centre of Civil Studies, Civil Law, Civil and Arbitration Procedure Department, Institute of State and Law, Russian Academy of Sciences;* b. 18 Nov. 1927, Sumy, Ukrainian SSR, USSR; m.; one s.; ed Moscow Inst. of Law; Sr Consultant, USSR Ministry of Transport 1959–64; Sr Researcher 1964, Head of Sector 1987, later Head of Centre of Civil Studies, Civil Law, Civil and Arbitration Procedure Dept, Inst. of State and Law, Russian Acad. of Sciences; Arbitrator, Int. Commercial Arbitration Court, Chamber of Commerce and Industry, Vice-Chair. Arbitrator, Maritime Arbitration Comm. 2006–; mem. Scientific-Consultative Council, Supreme State Arbitration Court of Russian Fed.; Expert Council on Civil Legislation in State Duma (Parl.) of Russian Fed.; participant in USSR and Russian Women's Movt; Honoured Scientist of the Russian Fed. 2006. *Publications:* more than 145 works on civil law, civil procedure, arbitration etc. *Leisure interests:* music, theatre, art exhbns. *Address:* Centre for Civil Studies, IGPRAN, 119991 Moscow, Znamenka str. 10, Russia (office). *Telephone:* (495) 691-17-09 (office). *Fax:* (495) 691-85-74 (office). *E-mail:* igpran@igpran.ru (office).

ABRAHAM, E(dward) Spencer, JD; American consultant and fmr politician; *Chairman and CEO, The Abraham Group LLC;* b. 12 June 1952, East Lansing, Mich.; s. of Eddie Abraham and Juliette Sear Abraham; m. Jane Abraham; three c.; ed Michigan State Univ. and Harvard Law School; attorney, Lansing, Mich. 1980–; Prof., Thomas M. Cooley Law School, Lansing 1981–; Chair. Mich. Republican Party 1983–90; Chair. Mich. Del. Republican Nat. Convention 1984; Chair. Presidential Inaugural Cttee, Mich. 1985; Deputy Chief of Staff to Vice-Pres. Dan Quayle (q.v.) 1991–93; Co-Chair. Nat. Republican Congressional Cttee 1991–93; Counsel to Canfield, Paddock and Stone 1993–94; Senator from Mich. 1995–2001; US Sec. of Energy 2001–04 (resgnd); Founder, Chair. and CEO The Abraham Group LLC (consulting firm), Washington, DC 2004–; Chair. and CEO Abraham & Roetzel LLC; Chair. (non-exec.) AREVA, Inc. 2006–; mem. Bd of Dirs Occidental Petroleum, Ind. Vice-Chair. 2013–; Dir, PBF Energy Inc., NRG Energy, Inc. 2012–; Chair. Advisory Bd Lynx Global Realty Asset Fund Onshore LLC, Uranium Energy Corpn; fmr Dir, GenOn Energy, Inc., ICx Technologies; mem. Bd or Advisory Cttee, Sindicatum Sustainable Resources, C3; Trustee, Churchill Center; Distinguished Visiting Fellow, Hoover Inst., Stanford Univ. –2008, Co-Chair. Cttee for Justice 2005–08; mem. Electricity Advisory Bd (also Sec.) 2001; mem. Mich., American and DC Bar Asscns; Co-founder Federalist Soc. *Publication:* Lights Out!: Ten Myths About (and Real Solutions to) America's Energy Crisis (co-author) 2010. *Address:* The Abraham Group LLC, 600 Fourteenth Street NW, Suite 500, Washington, DC 20005 (office); Areva Inc., 4800 Hampden Lane, Suite 1100, Bethesda, MD 20814, USA (office). *Telephone:* (202) 393-7700 (Abraham Group) (office). *Fax:* (202) 393-7701 (Abraham Group) (office). *Website:* www .abrahamgroupllc.com (office); us.areva.com (office).

ABRAHAM, F(ahrid) Murray; American actor; b. 24 Oct. 1939, Pittsburgh, Pa; m. Kate Hannan 1962; two c.; ed Univ. of Texas; Prof., Brooklyn Coll. 1985–; Dir No Smoking Please, Time & Space Ltd Theatre, New York; numerous Broadway plays, musicals, TV appearances and films; Obie Award (for Uncle Vanya) 1984, Golden Globe Award 1985, Los Angeles Film Critics Award 1985, William Shakespeare Award for Classical Theatre, Shakespeare Theatre Company 2012. *Films include:* Amadeus (Acad. Award 1985) 1985, The Name of the Rose 1987, Russicum 1987, Slipstream, Hard Rain, Personal Choice, Eye of the Widow 1989, An Innocent Man 1990, Mobsters 1991, Bonfire of the Vanities 1991, By The Sword 1992, Last Action Hero 1993, Surviving the Game 1994, Nostradamus 1994, Mighty Aphrodite 1995, Children of the Revolution 1996, Mimic 1997, Star Trek IX 1998, Falcone 1999, Muppets from Space 1999, Finding Forrester 2000, I cavalieri che fecero l'impresa 2001, 13 Ghosts 2001, Joshua 2002, The Bridge of San Luis Rey 2004, And Quietly Flows the Don 2004, Peperoni ripieni e pesci in faccia 2004, A House Divided 2006, The Stone Merchant 2006, Perestroika 2007, Come le formiche 2007, Carnera: The Walking Mountain 2008, Language of the Enemy 2008, Perestroika 2009, Barbarossa: Siege Lord 2009, The Unseen World 2010, September Eleven 1683 2012, Goltzius and the Pelican Company 2012; narrator Herman Melville, Damned in Paradise 1985, OBS 1985,. *Stage appearances:* The Wonderful Ice Cream Suit 1965, The Man in the Glass Booth 1968, 6 Rms Rivvu 1972, Bad Habits 1974, The Ritz 1976, Teibele and Her Demon 1979, Landscape of the Body 1977, The Master and Margarita 1978, King Lear 1981, Frankie and Johnny in the Clair de lune 1987, A Month in the Country 1995. *Television includes:* Dream West 1986, The Betrothed 1989, Largo Desolato 1990, A Season of Giants 1991, The First Circle 1992, Il Caso Dozier 1993, Journey to the Center of the Earth 1993, Larry McMurty's Dead Man's Walk 1996, Color of Justice 1997,

Esther 1999, Noah's Ark 1999, Excellent Cadavers 1999, The Darkling 2000, Dead Lawyers 2004, The Final Inquiry 2006, Shark Swarm 2008, Beauty and the Beast 2012, Homeland (series) 2012. *Address:* c/o IMG Artists, 4111 West Alameda Avenue, Suite 509, Burbank, CA 91505, USA.

ABRAHAM, Ronny; French judge and professor of international law; *Judge, International Court of Justice;* b. 5 Sept. 1951, Alexandria, Egypt; ed Univ. of Paris II, Inst. d'Études Politiques, Ecole Nat. d'Admin, Paris; Prof., Inst. d'Etudes Politiques, Paris –1998; Assoc. Prof., Univ. of Paris X, Nanterre 1997–2003; Assoc. Prof. of Public Int. Law and Human Rights, Univ. of Paris II, Panthéon-Assas 2004–; Admin. Tribunal Judge 1978–85, 1987–88; Asst Dir Office of Legal Affairs, Ministry of Foreign Affairs 1986–87, Dir of Legal Affairs 1998–; Maître des requêtes 1988–2000; Counseiller d'État 2000–; Govt Commr within the judicial system 1989–98; Judge, Int. Court of Justice, The Hague 2005–; Rep. of France to many cases before Int. Court of Justice, European Court of Human Rights, Court of Justice of the EC and int. arbitral tribunals; mem. Cttee of Experts for the Improvement of Procedures for the Protection of Human Rights 1986–98, Chair. 1987–2004; Chair. Jt Consultative Cttee OECD 1994–98; Del. to UN Gen. Ass. 1998–2004; Chair. French Del. to Ass. of States Parties to Rome Statute of Int. Criminal Court 2002–04; Head of French Del. to Cen. Comm. for Navigation of the Rhine 1998–, Chair. 2002–03; mem. Bd Soc. française pout le droit int.; mem. European Group of Public Law. *Publications:* numerous books, papers and articles in professional journals on int. and European law. *Address:* International Court of Justice, Peace Palace, Carnegieplein 2, 2517 KJ, The Hague, The Netherlands (office); Université Panthéon Assas, 12 place Panthéon, 75005 Paris, France (office). *Telephone:* (70) 302-23-23 (The Hague) (office). 1-44-41-57-00 (Paris) (office). *Fax:* (70) 364-99-28 (The Hague) (office). *E-mail:* info@icj-cij.org (office). *Website:* www.icj-cij.org (office); www.u-paris2.fr (office).

ABRAHAMIAN, Hovik A., CandMedSci; Armenian politician; *Prime Minister;* b. 24 Jan. 1958, Mekhchian, Ararat Marz, Armenian SSR, USSR; m.; three c.; ed Yerevan Automobile Road Vocational Coll., Yerevan Inst. of Nat. Economy, trained in burns surgery at Moscow Surgery Inst.; mil. service in Soviet Army 1977–79; Div. Head, Burastan Cognac Factory 1990–91; Dir Artashat Wine and Cognac Factory 1991–95; mem. Republican Party of Armenia, mem. Exec. Bd; mem. Azgayin Zhoghov (Nat. Ass.) first convocation 1995–99, re-elected for Constituency No. 17, Ashtarak 2008–, Chair. (Speaker) 2008–11 (resgnd), 2012–14; Chair. Artashat City Council Exec. Cttee 1995–96; Mayor of Artashat 1996–98; Marzpet (Gov.) of Ararat 1998–2000; Minister of Regional Admin and Urban Devt Co-ordination 2000–01, of Regional Admin 2001–02, of Regional Admin and Infrastructure Co-ordination 2002–05, of Territorial Admin endowed with functions of Co-ordinating Minister 2005–07; mem. Security Council 2005–; Deputy Prime Minister and Minister of Territorial Admin 2007–08; Sec.-Gen. Presidential Staff April–Sept. 2008; election campaign Man., Republican Party of Armenia (HHK) 2011–; Prime Minister 2014–; Chair. Yerevan State Econs Univ. Bd; mem. Yerevan State Univ. Bd; Order of 'Mesrop Mashtots' for services to the Repub. of Artsakh; Anania Shirakatsi Medal, Prime Minister's Commemorative Medal, Marshall Baghramyan Medal, Fridtjof Nansen Commemorative Gold Medal, Golden Medal of the Parl. of Greece, Golden Medal of the Theatrical Figures, IPA CIS Gold Medal, Commemorative Medal of Russian SFS Border Guard Dept in the Repub. of Armenia, First Grade Medal 'For Services Contributed to the Motherland' 2012. *Address:* Office of the Prime Minister, 0010 Yerevan, Hanrapetutyun Hraparak, Govt Bldg 1, Armenia (office). *Telephone:* (10) 51-57-03 (office). *Fax:* (10) 15-10-35 (office). *E-mail:* hotline@gov.am (office). *Website:* www.gov.am (office).

ABRAHAMS, Ivor, RA; British sculptor and painter; b. 10 Jan. 1935, Lancs.; s. of Harry Abrahams and Rachel Kalisky; m. 1st Victoria Taylor 1966 (divorced 1974); one s. (deceased); m. 2nd Evelyne Horvais 1974; one s.; ed Wigan Grammar School, Lancs., St Martin's School of Art and Camberwell School of Art, London; Visiting Lecturer in Sculpture and Drawing, Birmingham Coll. of Art 1960–64, Coventry Coll. of Art 1964–68; Visiting Lecturer, RCA, Slade School of Fine Art and Goldsmith's Coll. of Art 1970–80; Winston Churchill Fellow 1990, Fellow, Royal Soc. of British Sculptors 1994; Visiting Lecturer, RA Schools; Fellow, Royal Soc. of British Sculptors. *Television:* subject of several TV documentaries including Ivor Abrahams/Review BBC 2 1972, Museum of Drawers/Arena produced by Alan Yentob BBC 2 1979. *Publications:* Oxford Garden Sketchbook, Tales & Poems by E. A. Poe (illustrator 20 images), A Philosophical Enquiry into the Sublime and Beautiful Edmund Burke (illustrator 15 images) 1979. *Leisure interests:* books, postcards, golf. *E-mail:* info@ivorabrahams.com (home). *Website:* www .ivorabrahams.com.

ABRAHAMSEN, Egil, MSc, DTech; Norwegian fmr scientist; b. 7 Feb. 1923, Hvaler; s. of Anker Christian Abrahamsen and Aagot Abrahamsen (née Kjoelberg); m. Randi B. Wiborg 1951 (died 2002); one s. two d.; ed Polytechnical Univ. of Norway, Univ. of California, Berkeley, USA, Durham Univ. and Newcastle Univ., UK; Surveyor, Det Norske Veritas 1952–54; Sr Surveyor 1954–57, Prin. Surveyor 1957–75, Deputy Pres. 1967, Pres. 1967–85; Ed. European Shipbuilding 1955–60; Chair. and mem. numerous cttees; Chair. Bd of A/S Veda 1967–70, Bd of Dirs A.S. Computas 1967–83, Norsk Hydro 1985–92, The Abrahamsen Cttee 1984–86; Chair. Norwegian Telecom 1980–95, Royal Caribbean Cruise Line A/S (RCCL) 1985–89, OPAK 1985–2005, I.M. Skaugen 1990–99, Eikland 1990–99, Kosmos 1988–92, IKO Group 1988–92; Innovation 1990–2004; mem. Bd Den Norske Creditbank 1983–88; Kt Commdr, Order of the Lion (Finland) 1983, Commdr, Order of St Olav (Norway) 1987, Chevalier, Légion d'honneur 1987, Ordre nat. du Mérite 1990, and numerous other decorations. *Leisure interests:* skiing, tennis. *Address:* Maaltrostveien 35, 0786 Oslo, Norway (home). *Telephone:* 91-71-40-05 (home); 22-49-18-78. *Fax:* 22-49-93-02. *E-mail:* egiab@online.no.

ABRAHAMSON, Gen. James Alan; American air force officer (retd) and business executive; *Chairman and CEO, StratCom International LLC;* b. 19 May 1933, Williston, ND; s. of Norval S. Abrahamson and Thelma B. Helle; m. Barbara Jean Northcott 1959 (died 1985); one s. one d.; ed Massachusetts Inst. of Tech. and Univ. of Oklahoma; commissioned USAF 1955, Lt-Gen. 1982, Gen. 1987; Flight Instructor, Bryan AF Base, Tex. 1957–59; Spacecraft Project Officer Vela Nuclear Detection Satellite Programme, LAAF Station 1961–64; Fighter Pilot, Tactical Air Command 1964; Astronaut USAF Manned Orbiting Lab. 1967–69; mem. staff, Nat. Aeronautics and Space Council, White House 1969–71; Commdr 4950th Test

Wing USAF 1973–74; Insp. Gen. AF Systems Command 1974–76; Dir F-16 Fighter Programme 1976–80; Deputy Chief of Staff for Systems, Andrews AF Base, Md 1980–81; Assoc. Admin. for Space Transportation System, NASA HQ 1981–84; Dir Strategic Defence Initiative Org. 1984–89; Pres. Transportation Sector, Exec. Vice-Pres. for Devt Hughes Aircraft Co. 1989–92; Chair. Bd Oracle Corpn 1992–95; Lecturer in Astronautics, AIAA 1993; moved to International Air Safety LLC, Washington, DC 1995; Founder and currently Chair. and CEO StratCom International LLC; mem. Nat. Advisory Bd Childhelp USA; numerous awards and medals. *Leisure interests:* sports, music, poetry. *Address:* StratCom International LLC, 20112 Marble Quarry Road, Keedysville, MD 21756-1508, USA (office). *Telephone:* (301) 432-8950 (office). *Fax:* (301) 432-2657 (office). *E-mail:* GenAbe@aol.com.

ABRAMOV, Alexander G., PhD; Russian physicist and business executive; *Chairman, Evraz Group;* b. 1959; ed Moscow Inst. of Physics and Tech.; worked at Inst. of High Temperatures, USSR (now Russian) Acad. of Sciences; f. EvrazMetal (predecessor of Evraz) 1992, mem. Original Group, Chair. and CEO Evraz Group –Jan. 2006, Chair. Jan.–May 2006, mem. (non-exec.) Bd May 2006–08, Chair. Evraz Group 2008–, currently CEO Evraz Invest; Bureau mem. Council of Entrepreneurs, Council of Entrepreneurs set up by Govt of Russian Fed. *Address:* Evraz Group SA, 1 Allée Scheffer, 2520 Luxembourg (office); EvrazHolding OOO, 127006 Moscow, ul. Dolgorukovskaya 15, Bldgs 4 and 5, Russia (office). *Telephone:* (495) 234-46-31 (Moscow) (office). *Fax:* (495) 232-13-59 (Moscow) (office). *E-mail:* info@evraz.com (office). *Website:* www.evraz.com (office).

ABRAMOVIĆ, Marina; Serbian performance artist; b. 30 Nov. 1946, Belgrade, Yugoslavia (now Serbia); ed Acad. of Fine Arts, Belgrade, Acad. of Fine Arts, Zagreb; Lecturer, Acad. of Fine Arts, Novi Sad 1973–75; Prof. for Performance Art, Hochschule für Bildende Kunst, Braunschweig, Germany 1994–2001; now based in New York; f. Marina Abramović Inst. for Preservation of Performance Art, New York; Dr hc (Art Inst. of Chicago) 2004; Hon. Dr of Arts (Univ. of Plymouth, UK) 2009, (Instituto Superior de Arte, Cuba) 2012; Golden Lion, 47th Venice Biennale 1997, Niedersächsicher Kunstpreis 2003, Best Show in a Commercial Gallery Award, Int. Asscn of Art Critics 2003, Austrian Decoration for Science and Art 2008, Cultural Leadership Award, American Fed. of Arts 2011, '13 July' Lifetime Achievement Awards, Podgorica, Montenegro 2012, Berliner Bear 2012. *Address:* c/o Sean Kelly Gallery, 528 West 29th Street, New York, NY 10001-1308, USA. *Telephone:* (212) 239-1181. *Fax:* (212) 239-2467. *E-mail:* contact@mai-hudson.org (office). *Website:* www.marinaabramovicinstitute.com (office).

ABRAMOVICH, Roman Arkadyevich; Russian business executive and politician; b. 24 Aug. 1966, Saratov, Russian SFSR, USSR; s. of Arkadii Nakhimovich Abramovich and Irina Vassilyevna Abramovich; m. 1st Olga Yuryevna Lysova 1987 (divorced 1990); m. 2nd Irina Vyacheslavovna Malandina 1991 (divorced 2007); two s. three d.; partner Dariya 'Dasha' Zhukova; one s. one d.; ed Industrial Inst., Ukhta, Komi, Moscow Gubkin Inst. of Oil and Gas; f. cos Supertechnologiya-Shishmarev, Elita, Petroltrans, GID, NPR 1992–95; Head of Moscow Office, Runicom SA, Switzerland 1993–96; Co-f. (with the late Boris Berezovskii) Jt Stock Co. P.K. Trust 1995; f. cos Mekong, Centurion-M, Agrofert, Multitrust, Oilimpex, Sibreal, Forneft, Servet, Branko, Vektor-A 1995–96; Founder and Dir-Gen. Runicom Ltd, Gibraltar 1997–99; Dir Moscow br., Sibneft 1996–97, Dir Sibneft 1996–2005; acquired major interest in Evraz Group SA (steel and mining cos) 2006; mem. State Duma 1998–2000; Gov. of Chukot Autonomous Okrug 2000–08 (resignation rejected by Pres. Putin 2007, accepted 3 July 2008), Head of Govt 2001–08, Chair. Dist Duma, Chukot Autonomous Okrug 2008–13; Owner, Chelsea Football Club (UK) 2003–; Prin. Owner, Millhouse LLC pvt. investment co.; Order of Honour 2006; named by Ekspert (Russian business magazine) as Person of the Year (jtly) 2003. *Address:* Evraz Group SA, 127006 Moscow, ul. Dolgorukovskaya 15, Buildings 4 and 5, Russia (office). *Telephone:* (495) 232-13-70 (office). *Fax:* (495) 232-13-59 (office). *Website:* www.evraz.com (office).

ABRAMS, Hon. Elliott, BA, MSc (Econ), JD; American lawyer, diplomatist and fmr government official; *Senior Fellow for Middle Eastern Studies, Council on Foreign Relations;* b. 24 Jan. 1948, New York; s. of Joseph Abrams and Mildred Abrams; m. Rachel Abrams (deceased); three c.; ed Harvard Coll., Harvard Law School, London School of Econs, UK; Chief of Staff, Special Counsel for Senator Daniel P. Moynihan 1977–79; Asst Sec. of State for Int. Org. Affairs 1981, for Human Rights and Humanitarian Affairs 1981–85, for Inter-American Affairs 1985–89; Sr Fellow, Hudson Inst. 1990–96; Pres. Ethics and Public Policy Center 1996–2001; mem. US Comm. on Int. Religious Freedom 1999–2001, 2012–14, Chair. 2000–01; Special Asst to Pres. and Sr Dir for Democracy, Human Rights and Int. Operations 2001–02, Special Asst to Pres. and Sr Dir for Near East and North African Affairs 2002–05, Deputy Asst to Pres. and Deputy Nat. Security Adviser for Global Democracy Strategy 2005–09; Sr Fellow for Middle Eastern Studies, Council on Foreign Relations 2009–; mem. US Holocaust Memorial Council 2009–14; mem. bd Nat. Endowment for Democracy 2014–; Grand Cross, Order of the Sun (Peru) 2001; Sec. of State's Distinguished Service Award 1988, Scholar-Statesman Award, Washington Inst. for Near East Policy 2012. *Publications include:* Undue Process: A Story of How Political Differences are Turned into Crimes 1993, Security and Sacrifice: Isolation, Intervention, and American Foreign Policy 1995, Faith or Fear: How Jews Can Survive in a Christian America 1997, Honor Among Nations: Intangible Interests and Foreign Policy 1998, Close Calls: Intervention, Terrorism, Missile Defense, and "Just War" Today 1998, Secularism, Spirituality, and the Future of American Jewry 1999, The Influence of Faith 2001, Democracy – How Direct?: Views from the Founding Era and the Polling Era 2002, Tested By Zion: The Bush Administration and the Israeli–Palestinian Conflict 2013. *Address:* Council on Foreign Relations, 1777 F Street, NW, Washington, DC 20006, USA (office). *Telephone:* (202) 509-8472 (office). *Fax:* (202) 509-8490 (office). *E-mail:* eabrams@cfr.org (office). *Website:* www.cfr.org (office).

ABRAMS, Herbert Leroy, MD; American radiologist and academic; *Professor Emeritus of Radiology, School of Medicine, Stanford University;* b. 16 Aug. 1920, New York; s. of Morris Abrams and Freda Abrams (née Sugarman); m. Marilyn Spitz 1943; one s. one d.; ed Cornell Univ., State Univ. of New York; began medical practice at Stanford Univ., faculty mem., School of Medicine 1951–67, Dir Div. Diagnostic Roentgenology 1961–67, Prof. of Radiology 1962–67; Philip H. Cook Prof. of Radiology, Harvard Univ. 1967–85, Prof. Emer. 1985–, Chair. Dept of

Radiology 1967–80; Radiologist-in-Chief, Peter Bent Brigham Hosp., Boston 1967–80; Chair. Dept of Radiology, Brigham & Women's Hosp., Boston 1981–85; Radiologist-in-Chief, Sidney Farber Cancer Inst., Boston 1974–85; Prof. of Radiology, Stanford Univ. Medical School 1985–90, Prof. Emer. 1990–, also Mem.-in-Residence and Dir Project on Disabled Leadership, Center for Int. Security and Cooperation (CISAC) 1985–; Clinical Prof. Univ. of California Medical School 1986–; Ed.-in-Chief Postgraduate Radiology 1983–99, Cardiovascular and Interventional Radiology 1976–85; R.H. Nimmo Visiting Prof., Univ. of Adelaide 1976; numerous lectureships; mem. Int. Blue Ribbon Panel on Radiation Effects Research Foundation, Hiroshima and Nagasaki; mem. numerous medical asscns; Fellow, Nat. Cancer Inst.; Hon. Fellow, Royal Coll. of Radiology, Royal Coll. of Surgeons (Ireland); Gold Medal, Asscn of Univ. Radiologists 1984, Gold Medal, Radiological Soc. 1995, 2000, Gold Medal, Soc. of Cardiovascular and Interventional Radiology 2000. *Publications include:* Congenital Heart Disease 1965, Coronary Arteriography: A Practical Approach 1983, Ed. Abrams Angiography 1983, The President has been Shot: Confusion, Disability and the 25th Amendment in the Aftermath of the Assassination Attempt on Ronald Reagan 1992, The History of Cardiac Radiology 1996, Health Risks from Exposure to Low Levels of Ionizing Radiation 2004, numerous reports and articles for professional periodicals. *Leisure interests:* English and American literature, tennis, music. *Address:* CISAC, Stanford University, Encina Hall, Stanford, CA 94305-6165 (office); Stanford University School of Medicine, 300 Pasteure Drive, Stanford, CA 94305 (office); 714 Alvarado, Stanford, CA 94305, USA (home). *Telephone:* (650) 725-4873 (office); (415) 723-6258 (office); (415) 424-8552 (home). *Fax:* (650) 723-0089 (office); (415) 725-7296 (office). *E-mail:* hlabrams@stanford.edu (office). *Website:* www -radiology.stanford.edu (office); siis.stanford.edu/people/herbertlabrams (office).

ABRAMS, Norman, AB, JD; American lawyer, academic and university administrator; *Distinguished Professor Emeritus of Law, University of California, Los Angeles;* b. 1933, Chicago, Ill.; ed Univ. of Chicago; Ed.-in-Chief, University of Chicago Law Review while a student; fmr Assoc. in Law, Columbia Univ. Law School; Research Assoc. and Dir Harvard-Brandeis Cooperative Research for Israel's Legal Devt, Harvard Law School –1959; mem. staff, UCLA 1959–, on leave from UCLA serving as Special Asst to US Attorney Gen. in Criminal Div., US Dept of Justice 1966–67, now Distnguished Prof. Emer., UCLA School of Law, teaches and writes on fed. criminal law, anti-terrorism law and evidence, Assoc. Dean of Law School 1989–91, Vice-Chancellor of Academic Personnel 1991–2001, Interim Dean of Law School 2003–04, Acting Chancellor, UCLA 2006–07; Lifetime Distinguished Service Award, UCLA Emeriti Asscn 2012. *Publications include:* Evidence: Cases and Materials (ninth edn, co-author with Berger, Mansfield and Weinstein), Anti-Terrorism and Criminal Enforcement (second edn) 2005, Federal Criminal Law and Its Enforcement (fourth edn, co-author with Beale) 2006. *Address:* UCLA Law School, 385 Charles E. Young Drive East, 1242 Law Building, Los Angeles, CA 90095-1405, USA (office). *Telephone:* (310) 794-4056 (office). *Fax:* (310) 206-6489 (office). *E-mail:* abrams@law.ucla.edu (office). *Website:* www.law .ucla.edu (office).

ABRAMSKY, Dame Jennifer (Jenny), DBE, CBE, BA; British radio producer, editor and broadcasting industry executive; *Chair, Heritage Lottery Fund and National Heritage Memorial Fund;* b. 7 Oct. 1946, d. of the late Chimen Abramsky and Miriam Abramsky (née Nirenstein); m. Alasdair D. MacDuff Liddell 1976 (died 2012); one s. one d.; ed Holland Park School and Univ. of East Anglia; joined BBC Radio as Programme Operations Asst 1969, Producer, The World at One 1973, Ed. PM 1978–81, Producer Radio Four Budget Programmes 1979–86, The World at One 1981–86, Ed. Today programme 1986–87, News and Current Affairs Radio 1987–93, est. Radio Four News FM 1991, Controller BBC Radio Five Live 1993–96, Dir Continuous News Services, BBC (including Radio Five Live, BBC News 24, BBC World Service, BBC News Online, Ceefax) 1996–98, Dir BBC Radio 1998–2000, BBC Radio and Music 2000–06, Head, Audio and Music Group 2006–08, also in charge of BBC Radio Drama and Popular Music TV 2007–08, mem. Exec. Bd; Chair., Heritage Lottery Fund and Nat. Heritage Memorial Fund 2008–; Chair. Univ. of London 2008–; News Int. Visiting Prof. of Broadcast Media, Exeter Coll., Oxford 2002; mem. Econ. and Social Research Council 1992–96, Editorial Bd British Journalism Review 1993–; Vice-Chair. Digital Radio Devt Bureau 2002–08, RAM; mem. Bd of Dirs Hampstead Theatre 2003–, Chair. 2005–; mem. Bd of Govs BFI 2000–06; Gov. Royal Ballet; Trustee, Shakespeare Schools Festival, Central School of Ballet; Radio Acad. Fellowship 1998; Fellow, Central School of Speech and Drama; Hon. Prof., Thames Valley Univ. 1994; Hon. RAM 2002; Hon. MA (Salford) 1997; Dr hc (Westminster), (East Anglia); Hon. DCL (Kent) 2011; Woman of Distinction, Jewish Care 1990, Sony Radio Acad. Award 1995. *Leisure interests:* theatre, music. *Address:* Heritage Lottery Fund, 7 Holbein Place, London, SW1W 8NR, England (office). *Telephone:* (20) 7591-6000 (office). *Fax:* (20) 7591-6001 (office). *E-mail:* enquire@hlf.org.uk (office). *Website:* www.hlf .org.uk (office).

ABRAMSON, Jill Ellen, BA; American newspaper editor; *Executive Editor, New York Times;* b. 1954; d. of Norman L. Abramson and Dovie Abramson; m. Henry Griggs; two c.; ed Harvard Univ.; covered 1976 US presidential election for Time Magazine; Editorial Consultant, The American Lawyer 1976; Ed.-in-Chief Legal Times, Washington, DC 1986–88; Deputy Bureau Chief and investigative reporter, Wall Street Journal 1988–97; joined New York Times 1997, Enterprise Ed., Washington Bureau 1997–99, Washington Ed. 1999–2000, Washington Bureau Chief 2000–03, News Man. Ed. 2003–11, Exec. Ed. 2011–; Nat. Press Club Award 1992, ranked by Forbes magazine amongst The World's 100 Most Powerful Women (12th) 2011, (fifth) 2012, (19th) 2013, and amongst The World's Most Powerful People (64th) 2011, (68th) 2013. *Publications include:* Where They Are Now 1986, Strange Justice (with Jane Mayer) 1994, The Puppy Diaries: Raising a Dog Named Scout 2011. *Address:* New York Times, 620 Eighth Avenue, New York, NY 10018, USA (office). *Telephone:* (212) 556-8000 (office). *E-mail:* managing-editor@nytimes .com (office). *Website:* www.nytimes.com (office).

ABRASZEWSKI, Andrzej, MA, LLD; Polish diplomatist and international organization official; *Member, United Nations Committee on Contributions;* b. 4 Jan. 1938, Paradyz; s. of Antoni Abraszewski and Maria Zaleska; m. Teresa Zagorska; one s.; ed Cen. School for Foreign Service, Warsaw and Copernicus Univ., Toruń; researcher, Polish Inst. for Int. Affairs, Warsaw 1962–71; Sec. Polish Nat. Cttee on the 25th anniversary of the UN 1970; Counsellor to the Minister for

Foreign Affairs, Dept of Int. Orgs, Ministry of Foreign Affairs 1971–83; mem. Polish del. to UN Gen. Ass. 1971–90, with rank of Amb. 2001–, mem. Ad Hoc Working Group on UN's programme and budget machinery 1975, mem. Advisory Cttee on Admin. and Budgetary Questions 1977–82, 2001–09, Vice-Chair. 2006–07, Vice-Chair. Admin. and Budgetary Cttee of Gen. Ass. 1979, Chair. 1982, mem. Cttee on Contribs 1983–88 (Vice-Chair. 1987–88), 2010–, Cttee for Programmes and Co-ordination (Vice-Chair. 1989, Chair. 1990); Asst to Deputy Minister for Foreign Affairs 1984–90; mem. UN Jt Inspection Unit 1991–2000, Vice-Chair. 1993, 1998, Chair. 1994, UN Secr. consultant on results-based management 2011; Prize of the Minister for Foreign Affairs, Prize of the Minister of Finance. *Publications:* various publs on UN affairs, including Reform of the United Nations: a progress report 2000, Financing of the United Nations 2007, paper on results-based management 2011. *Leisure interests:* boating, skiing, swimming. *Address:* United Nations Advisory Committee on Contributions, New York, NY 10017, USA (office); Adriatycka 3, 02-761 Warsaw, Poland (home). *Telephone:* (212) 963-5306 (office). *Fax:* (212) 963-1943 (office). *E-mail:* abraszewski@un.org (office). *Website:* www.polandun.org (office); www.un.org/en/ga/contributions (office).

ABREHE, Berhane, MS; Eritrean civil engineer and politician; *Minister of Finance;* ed Univ. of Illinois, USA; Acting Minister of Land, Water and Environment 1998; Dir of Macroenonomic Policy, Office of the Pres. 1993–2001; Minister of Finance 2001–; mem. Bd of Govs, African Devt Bank Group, Eritrea, Eastern and Southern African Trade and Devt Bank. *Address:* Ministry of Finance, POB 896, Asmara, Eritrea (office). *Telephone:* (1) 118131 (office). *Fax:* (1) 127947 (office).

ABREU, Alcinda António de; Mozambican politician; *Minister of Environmental Co-ordination;* b. 13 Oct. 1953, Nova-Sofala; ed Universidad Eduardo Mondlane, Univs of Johannesburg and London; Deputy Gen. Sec. Organização da Juventude Moçambicana 1977–91; mem. Parl. 1977–94; Minister of Social Welfare Co-ordination 1994–97, of Foreign Affairs and Co-operation 2005–08, of Environmental Affairs (now Minister of Environmental Co-ordination) 2008–; apptd by FRELIMO as mem. Nat. Elections Comms responsible for organizing municipal elections in 1998 and general election 1999; elected to Political Cttee, FRELIMO 2002–. *Address:* Ministry of Environmental Co-ordination, Avda Acordos de Lusaka 2115, CP 2020, Maputo, Mozambique (office). *Telephone:* 21466245 (office). *Fax:* 21465849 (office). *E-mail:* jwkacha@virconn.com (office). *Website:* www.micoa.gov.mz (office).

ABRIAL, Gen. Stéphane; French consultant and fmr air force officer; *Adviser to the Chairman and CEO, Safran;* b. 7 Sept. 1954, Condom-en-Armagnac (Gers); m. Michaela Abrial; two c.; ed École de l'Air, US Air War Coll., Montgomery, Institut des hautes études de défense nationale, Paris; began mil. service 1973, exchange programme in USAF Acad., graduated from French Air Force Acad. 1975, completed pilot training 1976, extensive experience as fighter pilot and operational commdr, served in unit of German Luftwaffe 1981–84, in unit of Greek Air Force 1988, took part in liberation of Kuwait as commdr of French Air Force's 5th Fighter Wing during Operation Desert Storm 1990–91, served at NATO Int. Mil. Staff in Brussels 1996–99, several appointments to pvt. offices of French Prime Minister and Pres., went on to serve as head of French air defence and air operations, Air Force Chief of Staff 2006–09; Supreme Allied Commdr Transformation, NATO 2009–12 (first European apptd permanently as head of a NATO strategic command); Adviser to Jean-Paul Herteman, Chair. and CEO of Safran 2013–; Grand Officier, Légion d'honneur, Officier, Ordre nat. du Mérite, Croix de guerre des théâtres d'opérations extérieures with star, Croix du Combattant, Médaille de l'Aéronautique, Overseas Medal with two bars, Commdr, US Legion of Merit, Verdienstkreuz der Bunderwehr (Silver), German Sports Badge (Mil. version in Bronze), Order of Abdulaziz al Saud (Saudi Arabia) (Superior Class), Kuwait Liberation Medal (Saudi Arabia), Kuwait Liberation Medal (Kuwait), Officer, Order of Aeronautical Merit (Brazil), Santos-Dumont Medal of Merit (Medalha do Mérito Santos Dumont), Brazilian Air Force; Hon. DSc (Old Dominion Univ.) 2011; Distinguished Leadership Award, Atlantic Council 2010. *Address:* Safran, 2 Blvd du Général Martial Valin, 75724 Paris Cedex 15, France (office). *Telephone:* 1-40-60-80-80 (office). *Fax:* 1-40-60-85-01 (office). *Website:* www.safran-group.com (office).

ABRIKOSOV, Alexei Alexeyevich; American (b. Russian) physicist; *Distinguished Scientist, Argonne National Laboratory;* b. 25 June 1928, Moscow, USSR; s. of Aleksei Ivanovich Abrikosov and Fanny Davidovna Vulf; m. Svetlana Yuriyevna Bun'kova 1977; two s. one d.; ed Moscow Univ.; Postgraduate Research Assoc., then Scientist and Sr Scientist, Inst. of Physical Problems, USSR (now Russian) Acad. of Sciences 1948–65; Head of Dept, Landau Inst. of Theoretical Physics, USSR (now Russian) Acad. of Sciences 1965–88, Dir Inst. of High Pressure Physics 1988–91; Distinguished Scientist, Argonne Nat. Lab., USA 1991–; Research Assoc., then Asst Prof. and Prof., Moscow Univ. 1951–68; Prof., Gorky Univ. 1971–72; Prof., Moscow Physical Eng Inst. 1974–75, Chair. Theoretical Physics, Moscow Inst. of Steel and Alloys 1976–91; mem. USSR (now Russian) Acad. of Sciences 1964, American Acad. of Arts and Sciences 1991, NAS 2000; Foreign mem. Royal Soc. 2001; Fellow, American Physics Soc. 1992; Hon. ScD (Moscow) 1955, Hon. DS (Lausanne) 1975, (Bordeaux) 2003, (Loughborough) 2004, (Tsukaba) 2005, (Hong Kong) 2005; Lenin Prize 1966, Fritz London Award 1972, USSR State Prize 1982, Landau Prize 1989, John Bardeen Prize 1991, Nobel Prize in Physics 2003. *Publications:* Quantum Field Theory Methods in Statistical Physics 1962, Introduction to the Theory of Normal Metals 1972, Fundamentals of Metal Theory 1987 and works on plasma physics, quantum electro-dynamics, theory of superconductors, magnetism, astrophysics, quantum liquids and semi-metals. *Leisure interest:* skiing. *Address:* Argonne National Laboratory, 9700 South Cass Avenue, Argonne, IL 60439, USA (office). *Telephone:* (630) 252-5482 (office); (630) 252-6525 (office). *Fax:* (630) 252-7777 (office). *E-mail:* abrikosov@anl.gov (office). *Website:* www.anl.gov (office).

ABRIL, Victoria; Spanish actress; b. (Victoria Mérida Rojas), 14 July 1959, Madrid; m.; two c. *Theatre includes:* Obras de Mihura, Company Tirso de Molina 1977, Viernes, día de libertad, Company L. Prendes 1977, Nuit d'Ivresse, Paris 1986. *Films include:* Obsesión 1975, Robin and Marian 1975, Robin Hood 1975, Caperucita Roja 1975, Cambio de Sexo 1975, La Bien Plantada 1976, Doña Perfecta 1976, Esposa y Amante 1977, La Muchacha de las Bragas de Oro 1979, Asesinato en el Comité Central 1981, La Guerrillera 1981, La Colmena 1982, La

batalla del Porro 1982, Le Bastard 1982, La Lune dans le Caniveau 1982, Sem Sombra de pecado 1982, J'ai Epousé un Ombre 1982, Rio Abajo 1982, Bajo el Signo de Piscis 1983, Le Voyage 1983, Las Bicicletas son para el Verano 1983, L'Addition 1983, Rouge George 1983, La noche más Hermosa 1984, Padre Nuestro 1984, After Dark 1984, L'Addition 1984, La Hora Bruja 1985, Tiempo de Silencio 1985, Max mon Amour 1985, Vado e Torno 1985, El Lute 1987, El Placer de Matar 1987, Barrios Altos 1987, El Juego más Divertido 1987, Ada dans la Jungle 1988, Baton Rouge 1988, Sandino 1989, Atame 1989, A solas Contigo 1990, Amantes 1990, Tie Me Up! Tie Me Down! 1991, High Heels 1992, Lovers (Silver Bear for Best Actress, Berlin Film Festival) 1992, Intruso 1993, Kika 1993, Jimmy Hollywood 1994, Casque Bleu 1994, Nadie Hablará de Nosotras Cuandro Hayamas Muerto (Best Actress, Cannes) 1995, Gazon Maudit 1996, Freedomfighters 1996, La femme du cosmonaute 1998, Between Your Legs 1999, Mon Père, Ma Mère, Mes Frères et Mes Soeurs 1999, 101 Reykjavik 2001, Sin Noticias de Dios 2002, Don't Tempt Me 2003, Incautos 2003, Septimo Dia El 2004, Cause Toujours 2004, Incautos 2004, Escuela de Seduccion 2004, Les gens honnêtes vivent en France 2005, Carne de Neón (short) 2005, Tirante el Blanco (aka The Maidens' Conspiracy) 2006, Les Aristos 2006, El Camino de los Ingleses (aka Summer Rain) 2006, 48 heures par jour 2008, Mejor que nunca 2008, Leur morale… et la nôtre 2008, Solo quiero caminar 2008, Musée haut, musée bas 2008, Man on Asphalt 2012, Mince alors! 2012. *Television includes:* Los libros (series) 1974, La barraca (mini-series) 1979, Estudio 1 (series) 1982, Télévision de chambre: Sous le signe du poisson (film) 1984, La huella del crimen: El crimen del Capitán Sánchez (film) 1985, Los pazos de Ulloa (mini-series) 1985, La mujer de tu vida: La mujer lunática (film) 1990, Riders of the Dawn (series) 1990, X Femmes (series) 2009, Myster Mocky présente (series short) 2009, Le grand restaurant (film) 2010, Clem (series) 2010–12, Les beaux mecs (series) 2011, Hospital Central (series) 2011, La chanson du dimanche (series) 2011. *Address:* c/o Alsira García-Maroto, Gran Via 63–3° izda, 28013 Madrid, Spain.

ABRIL-MARTORELL HERNÁNDEZ, Fernando, BA, BS; Spanish business executive; *CEO, Promotora de Informaciones, SA;* s. of Fernando Abril Martorell; ed Instituto Católico de Administración y Dirección de Empresas-ICADE; began career with JP Morgan; Gen. Man. Corp. Finance, Telefónica SA 1997–99, Pres. Telefónica Publicidad e Información (TPI) 1998–2000, COO Telefónica SA 2000, mem. Bd of Dirs 2000–03, Man. Dir 2001–03; Man. Dir and CEO Grupo Credit Suisse España 2005–10, Sr Adviser 2011; Deputy CEO and CFO Promotora de Informaciones, SA 2010–11, CEO 2012–; mem. Bd of Dirs ENCE Energia y Celulosa SA, Telefonica Brasil SA. *Address:* Promotora de Informaciones, SA, Avda. de los Artesanos 6 Tres Cantos, Madrid 28760, Spain (office). *Telephone:* (91) 3301000 (office). *Website:* www.prisa.com (office).

ABRIL Y CASTELLÓ, HE Cardinal Santos; Spanish ecclesiastic and diplomatist; *Archpriest of the Basilica di Santa Maria Maggiore;* b. 21 Sept. 1935, Alfambra; ed Pontifical Ecclesiastical Acad., Rome; ordained priest, Diocese of Teruel (-Albarracín) 1960; worked in Pakistan, Turkey and Second Section of the Secr. of State in Rome; apptd Titular Archbishop of Tamada 1985; Apostolic Nuncio to Bolivia 1985–89; Apostolic Pro-Nuncio to Cameroon (also accred to Gabon and Equatorial Guinea) 1989–96; Apostolic Nuncio to Yugoslavia 1996–2000, to Argentina 2000–03, to Slovenia 2003–11 (also accred to Bosnia and Herzegovina 2003–05 and Macedonia 2003–11); Vice-Chamberlain of the Apostolic Chamber 2011–; mem. Congregation for Bishops 2011–; Archpriest of the Basilica di Santa Maria Maggiore 2011–; cr. Cardinal (Cardinal-Deacon of San Ponziano) 2012; participated in Papal Conclave 2013. *Address:* Palazzo Apostolico, 00120 Città del Vaticano, Rome, Italy (office). *Telephone:* (06) 69883554 (office); (06) 69886800 (office). *Fax:* (06) 69886817 (office). *E-mail:* sagrestiasmm@org.va (office). *Website:* www.vatican.va/various/basiliche/sm_maggiore/index_en.html (office).

ABSALON, Julien; French mountain biker; b. 16 Aug. 1980, St Amé; m. Emilie; winner World Jr Championships, Mont St Anne 1998, U23 Category, European Championships 2001, 2002; Silver Medal, Elite Category, World Cup 2003; Gold Medal, Cross Country Cycling, Athens Olympics 2004, World Championships, Les Gets 2004, Livigno 2005, Rotorua 2006, Fort William 2007, Beijing Olympics 2008; Silver Medal, European Championships 2005. *Leisure interests:* snowboarding, paragliding, motorcross. *E-mail:* athlet-go@wanadoo.fr. *Website:* www.absalon-julien.com.

ABSE, Dannie, CBE, DLitt, LRCP, MRCS, FRSL; British writer, poet and physician; b. 22 Sept. 1923, Cardiff, Wales; s. of Rudolph Abse and Kate Shepherd; m. Joan Mercer 1951 (died 2005); one s. two d.; ed St Illtyd's Coll. Cardiff, Univ. Coll. Cardiff, King's Coll., London and Westminster Hosp., London; first book of poems published while still a medical student 1948; qualified as doctor 1950; Squadron-Leader RAF 1951–55; doctor in charge of chest clinic at Cen. Medical Establishment, Cleveland Street, London 1954–89; Writer-in-Residence, Princeton Univ., NJ, USA 1973–74; Pres. Poetry Soc. 1979–92; Fellow, Welsh Acad. 1993; Council mem. Royal Soc. of Literature; Hon. Fellow, Univ. of Wales Coll. of Medicine 1999; Hon. DLitt (Univ. of Wales) 1989, (Glamorgan) 1997; Welsh Arts Council Literature Prize 1971, 1987, Henry Foyle Award 1964, Jewish Chronicle Award, Cholmondeley Award 1983, 1985. *Publications include:* poetry: After Every Green Thing 1948, Walking Under Water 1952, Ash on a Young Man's Sleeve 1954, Fire in Heaven 1956, Some Corner of an English Field 1956, Tenants of the House: Poems 1951–1956 1957, Poems, Golders Green 1962, Poems! Dannie Abse: A Selection 1963, Medicine on Trial 1967, Three Questor Plays 1967, A Small Desperation 1968, Demo Sceptre 1969, O. Jones, O. Jones 1970, Selected Poems 1970, Funland and Other Poems 1973, Way Out in the Centre 1981, A Strong Dose of Myself 1983, One-legged on Ice: Poems 1983, Ask the Bloody Horse 1986, Journals From the Ant Heap 1986, White Coat, Purple Coat: Collected Poems 1948–1988 1989, People (contrib.) 1990, Remembrance of Crimes Past: Poems 1986–1989 1990, The View from Row G: Three Plays 1990, Intermittent Journals Seren 1994, On the Evening Road 1994, Selected Poems 1994, Welsh Retrospective 1997, Arcadia, One Mile 1998, Be Seated, Thou: Poems 1989–1998 1999, Encounters Hearing Eye 2001, New and Collected Poems 2002, The Two Roads Taken: A Prose Miscellany 2003, Yellow Bird 2004, Running Late (Roland Mathias Award 2007) 2006, New Selected Poems 1949–2009: Anniversary Collection 2009, Two For Joy – Scenes from Married Life 2010; ed.: Mavericks: An Anthology (co-ed. with Howard Sergeant) 1957, Modern European Verse 1964, Modern Poets in

Focus 1 1971, Modern Poets in Focus 3 1971, Thirteen Poets 1972, Doctors and Patients 1984, Voices in the Gallery: Poems and Pictures (co-ed. with Joan Abse) 1986, The Music Lover's Literary Companion (co-ed. with Joan Abse) 1989, The Hutchinson Book of Post-War British Poets 1989, The Gregory Anthology 1991–93 (co-ed. with A. Stevenson) 1994, Twentieth-Century Anglo-Welsh Poetry 1997, New and Collected Poems 2003, 100 Great Poems of Love and Lust: Homage to Eros (compiler and ed.) 2007, Welsh Retrospective 2008, New Selected Poems 2009, Two for Joy 2010, Speak Old Parrot 2013; fiction: Pythagoras (a play), Ash on a Young Man's Sleeve 1954, Some Corner of an English Field 1956, The View from Row G (three plays) 1990, There Was a Young Man from Cardiff 2001, The Strange Case of Dr Simmonds and Dr Glas 2002, Ash on a Young Man's Sleeve 2006; other: Journals from the Ant Heap 1986, Intermittent Journals 1994, A Welsh Retrospective 1997, Goodbye, Twentieth Century 2001, The Two Roads Taken 2003, The Presence (memoir) (Wales Book of the Year English Language Prize 2008) 2007, Dannie Abse: A Source Book 2009, The Music Lover's Literary Companion (co-compiler) 2009; contribs to BBC and various publs in the UK and USA. *Leisure interests:* chess, supporting Cardiff City Football Club. *Address:* c/o United Agents, 12–26 Lexington Street, London, W1F 0LE (office); 85 Hodford Road, London, NW11 8NH, England (home). *Telephone:* (20) 3214–0884 (office); (20) 8458-1961 (home). *E-mail:* hthompson@unitedagents.co.uk (office). *Website:* www.unitedagents.co.uk (office); www.dannieabse.com.

ABSHIRE, David Manker, PhD; American diplomatist and research institute director; *President and CEO, Center for the Study of the Presidency and Congress;* b. 11 April 1926, Chattanooga, Tenn.; s. of James Ernest Abshire and Phyllis Patten Abshire; m. Carolyn Sample Abshire 1957; one s. four d.; ed Baylor School, Chattanooga, US Mil. Acad., West Point, NY, Georgetown Univ., Washington, DC; co-f. Center for Strategic and Int. Studies, Georgetown Univ. 1962, Exec. Dir 1962–70, Chair. 1973–82, Pres. 1982–83, Vice-Chair. 1999–; Asst Sec. of State for Congressional Relations 1970–73; Perm. Rep. to NATO 1983–87; Special Counsellor to Pres. Jan.–April 1987; Co-ed. Washington Quarterly 1977–83; Chair. US Bd for Int. Broadcasting 1974–77; Dir Nat. Security Group, Transition Office of Pres.-elect Reagan 1980–81; Pres. and CEO Center for the Study of the Presidency and Congress 1999–; Pres. Richard Lounsbery Foundation of New York 2002–; mem. Congressional Cttee on the Org. of Govt for the Conduct of Foreign Policy 1973–75; mem. Bd Procter & Gamble 1987–96, Ogden Corpn, BP American Advisory Bd; mem. Advisory Bd Pres.'s Task Force on US Govt Int. Broadcasting 1991; Order of Crown (Belgium), Commdr Ordre de Léopold (Belgium), Order of the Lion of Finland (1st Class) 1994, Order of the Liberator (Argentina) 1999, Order of Sacred Treasure Gold and Silver Star (Japan) 2001; Pres. Civilian Service Award 1989, Medal of the Pres. of the Italian Repub., Senate, Parl. and Govt, Medal of Diplomatic Merit (Rep. of Korea) 1993, US Mil. Acad. Castle Award 1994, Distinguished Graduate Award, John Carroll Award for Outstanding Service by a Georgetown Univ. Alumnus. *Publications include:* International Broadcasting: A New Dimension of Western Diplomacy 1976, Foreign Policy Makers: President vs. Congress 1979, The Growing Power of Congress 1981, Preventing World War III: A Realistic Grand Strategy 1988, The Global Economy 1990, Putting America's House in Order: The Nation as a Family 1996, Report to the President-Elect 2000: Triumphs and Tragedies of the Modern Presidency 2000. *Leisure interest:* historical literature. *Address:* Center for Study of the Presidency, 1020 19th Street, NW, Suite 250, Washington, DC 20036 (office); 311 South St Asaph Street, Alexandria, VA 22314, USA (home). *Telephone:* (202) 872-9800 (office); (703) 836-2892 (home). *Fax:* (202) 872-9811 (office); (703) 836-2992 (home). *E-mail:* email@thepresidency.org (office). *Website:* www.thepresidency.org (office).

ABU-GHAZALEH, Haifa Shaker, BA, MA, PhD; Jordanian psychologist and politician; m.; one s. two d.; ed Ein Shams Univ., Cairo, Egypt, Univ. of Jordan, Jesuit Univ., Beirut; held several prominent govt positions, including as Adviser to Minister and Gen. Dir for Foreign Relations, Ministry of Educ. 1968–95; Pres. Gen. Fed. of Jordanian Women 1994–96; Regional Project Coordinator for UNIFEM, Regional Programme Dir for Arab States Regional Office, UNIFEM 1996–2007, also served as Arab Region Focal Point for the UN for NGO Forum on Women, Beijing 1995 1993–95; Senator to Upper House of Parl. 2007–10; Gen. Sec. to Family Council for Family Affairs 2007–10; Minister of Tourism and Antiquities 2011; Co-founder Gen. Fed. of Jordanian Women; Founder-mem. Women Workers Asscn 2004; Jordanian Rep. and Exec. mem. Arab Women Org. 2008; Exec. Bd mem. Arab Family Org. 2008; mem. Bd of Trustees, Women Research Centre of Univ. of Jordan 2006; mem. Bd Royal Comm. 'We Are All Jordan-Kalona Al-Ardun' 2006, Nat. Council for Family Affairs 2007, Nat. Cttee for Women's Affairs 2008; mem. ICT Royal Cttee 2006; Int. mem. Sheikh Sebeka Gender Award Foundation; numerous int. and regional women leadership awards, including awards from Omani Ministry of Social Affairs and Gen. Fed. of Jordanian Women, Women Leadership Award, Ministry of Educ. 2001, Women Leadership Award, Ministry of Social Devt (Oman) 2006, UNIFEM Lifetime Achievement Award for Exceptional Services and Commitment 2007, Humanitarian Aid Club 2007, Ministry of Manpower and Migration Award for Egypt 2007, Sheika Sabika Bint Ibrahim Al-Khilkfa Award 2007, UN Econ. and Social Comm. for Western Asia (ESCWA) Award 2007, Teaching Excellent Medal from HM King Abdalla 2009. *Television:* wrote, produced and presented a weekly vocational and educational programme for Jordan TV, also a weekly programme, Window on Modern Education, for Jordan TV. *Publications:* numerous books including Teacher's Guide Book 1982, Student's Guide of the Secondary & Higher Education 1983, General Principles of Social Defense 1983, Information to Education 1984, Counseling & Guidance Guide 1985, Measurement & Education 1985, Teacher's Guide Book for School Health Education (six parts) 1990, Me & My Career (four parts) 1991, Guide Book for Kindergarten Teacher (two parts) 1994, Guide Book for Early Child Development (four parts) 1995, Gender & Development – A Resource Book 1998, Gender and Youth, Training Manual 2005, The Contribution of NGOs to Beijing+10 2005, Al-Kashif in Gender & Development 1999, Arab Women, Beijing and Beyond 2007, CEDAW KIT (UNIFEM) 2007, Team Leader and Expert of CRC Indicators 2009, Arab Women CEDAW+30 2009, CEDAW Indicators 2009; articles have appeared in int. journals including Women for Women International Journal; papers have been presented at numerous int. forums, including several Nat. Women Machineries in the Arab World, Oxford Research Group, Wilton Park Conf. Forum, Govt of Jordan, ABA, UN Foundation, Women for Peace Int. Org., Inst. of Diplomacy, Abu Dhabi, UNESCO, Japanese Univ., Tokyo, American Univ.,

Washington, DC and Finnish Adult Educ. Org. *Address:* Ministry of Tourism and Antiquities, 3rd Circle – Jabal Amman, PO Box 224, Amman 11118, Jordan (office). *Telephone:* (6) 4603360 (office); (6) 5532834 (home); 79-5578678 (mobile). *Fax:* (6) 4648465 (office); (6) 5532938 (home). *E-mail:* haifa.nhdra@gmail.com (home); contacts@mota.gov.jo (office). *Website:* www.mota.gov.jo (office); haifaag .com.

ABU GHAZALEH, Mohammad; Palestinian business executive; *Chairman and CEO, Fresh Del Monte Produce Inc.;* Man. Dir Metico 1967–86; Pres. and CEO United Trading Co. 1986–96; acquired Fresh Del Monte Produce, Inc. 1996, Chair. and CEO 1996–; Chair. and CEO IAT Group, Inc. 1997–2010; Chair. Royal Jordanian Air Acad.; Dir Jordan Kuwait Bank 2004–11, International General Insurance Co. Ltd (fmr Chair.), United Cable Co. Inc., Bank Misr Liban, Amwal Invest. *Address:* Fresh Del Monte Produce, Inc., POB 149222, Coral Gables, FL 33114-9222, USA (office). *Telephone:* (305) 520-8400 (office). *E-mail:* mabu -ghazaleh@freshdelmonte.com (office). *Website:* www.freshdelmonte.com (office).

ABU-GHAZALEH, Talal; Palestinian/Jordanian management consultant and intellectual property expert; *Chairman of the Management Board, Talal Abu-Ghazaleh International;* b. 22 April 1938, Jaffa; m. Nuha Salameh; two s. two d.; ed American Univ. of Beirut; Founder and Chair. Man. Bd Talal Abu-Ghazaleh Int. (TAGI) (mem. firm of Grant Thornton Int.), regional holding group of professional firms operating through 34 offices in Arab World and comprising, among others Talal Abu-Ghazaleh & Co. (TAGCO), Abu-Ghazaleh Consultancy & Co. (AGCOC), Al-Dar Consulting Co. (ADCO), Talal Abu-Ghazaleh Assocs. Ltd (TAGA), Arab Int. Projects Co. (AIPC), The First Projects Man. Co. (FPMC), Talal Abu-Ghazaleh Int. Man. Inc. (TAGIMI), TMP Agents, Arab Bureau for Legal Services (ABLE), Al-Dar Gen. Trading Co. (ADTCO); Chair. Arab Knowledge Man. Soc. (fmrly Arab Man. Soc.) 1989–; Chevalier, Légion d'honneur and decorations from Tunisia, Kuwait, Bahrain and Jordan; Hon. DHumLitt (Canisius Coll. Buffalo, NY) 1988. *Publications:* Taxation in the Arab Countries, The Abu-Ghazaleh English–Arabic Dictionary of Accounting, Trade Mark Laws in the Arab Countries. *Address:* Talal Abu-Ghazaleh International, TAGI House, Queen Noor Street, Shmeisani, Amman; PO Box 921100, Amman 11192, Jordan. *Telephone:* (6) 5669603. *Fax:* (6) 5696284. *E-mail:* tagi@tagi.com. *Website:* www.tagi.com.

ABU-HAMMOUR, Muhammed, MA, PhD; Jordanian economist and government official; b. 1961, Salt; m.; two s. two d.; ed Yarmouk Univ., Univ. of Jordan, Univ. of Surrey, UK; Researcher, Public Finance Div., Cen. Bank of Jordan 1987–91, Chief, External Economy and Balance of Payments Div. 1992–94, Chief, Public Finance Div. 1997–98; Adviser to Minister of Finance 1998–2000, Vice-Chair., Evaluation of Monetary, Financial and Econ. Situations Cttee 1999–; Chair., Fiscal Monitoring Unit 1999, Sec. Gen., Ministry of Finance 2000–03; Minister of Industry and Trade July–Oct. 2003; Minister of Finance 2003–05, 2009–11; Chair. Exec. Privatization Comm. 2005–09; mem. Bd of Dirs Jordan Phosphate Mines Co., Jordan Nat. Bank, The Jordanian Hashemite Fund for Human Devt; fmr mem. Bd of Dirs Jordan Telecom, Royal Jordanian, Arab Bank, Social Security Corpn, Nat. Resources Investment and Devt Corpn, Deposit Insurance Corpn, Jordan Petroleum Refinery Co. Ltd; part-time lecturer to grad. students in Econs, Univ. of Jordan 1998–; Best Minister of Finance of the Year in the Middle East, Euromoney Emerging Markets magazine, Washington, DC 2004. *Publications:* Property Tax in Jordan 1987, Factors Affecting Debt Service Ratio in Jordan 1988, The Impact of Financial Assistance and External Loans on Balance of Payments and Money Supply 1989, The Impact of Budget Deficit on GNP, BOP and Money Supply in Jordan 1990, The Instruments of Islamic Internal Debt 1992, Attracting Foreign Direct Investment in Jordan 1993, Measuring Taxable Capacity and Tax Effort in Jordan 1998. *Address:* c/o Ministry of Finance POB 85, Amman 11118, Jordan.

ABU-JABER, Diana, BA, MA, PhD; Jordanian/American author and academic; *Professor of English, Portland State University;* b. 1960, Syracuse, NY; ed State Univ. of New York, Oswego and Binghamton, Univ. of Windsor, Canada; Visiting Asst Prof. in English, Iowa State Univ. 1990; Asst Prof. of English, Univ. of Oregon 1990–95; Prof. of English, Portland State Univ. 1996–; Nat. Endowment for the Arts Writing Fellowship 1994–96, Int. Writers Nat. Endowment for the Arts Fellowship in Fiction 1996–98, Fulbright Research Award, Amman, Jordan 1996. *Radio:* frequent contrib. to Nat. Public Radio. *Publications:* fiction: Arabian Jazz (Oregon Book Award 1994) 1993, Crescent (PEN Center USA Award for Literary Fiction 2004, Before Columbus Foundation American Book Award 2004, Willamette Writers Northwest Distinguished Author Award 2004) 2003, Origin (Arab-American Book Award 2008, Florida Book Award Bronze Medal 2008) 2007, Birds of Paradise 2011; non-fiction: The Language of Baklava (Northwest Bookseller's Award 2005) 2005; contrib. of short fiction to many journals including Northwest Review, Left Bank, Story, Many Mountains Moving, Kenyon Review, Salt Hill Journal, Middle East Report, Tin House Magazine, Good Housekeeping magazine, Flyway Literary Magazine, Southern Review. *Address:* c/o Miriam Feuerle and Kate Gannon, Lyceum Agency, 915 SE 35th Avenue, #205, Portland, OR 97214, USA (office); c/o Department of English, Neuberger Hall M403, Portland State University, Portland, OR 97207, USA (office). *Telephone:* (503) 467-4622 (office); (503) 267-2918 (office). *Website:* www.lyceumagency.com (office); www.english.pdx .edu (office); www.dianaabujaber.com. *Fax:* (503) 725-3554 (office). *E-mail:* abujaber@pdx.edu (office); abujaber@aol.com.

ABU MAZEN (see ABBAS, Mahmud).

ABU-NIMAH, Hasan; Jordanian diplomatist; *Director, Royal Institute for Inter-Faith Studies;* b. 11 Sept. 1935, Battir, Jerusalem; s. of Abdul Rahim Abu-Nimah and Fatima Othman Oweinah; m. Samira Al-Najjar; three c.; ed Al-Ummah Coll., Bethlehem, American Univ. of Beirut, Birkbeck Coll., London; fmr political commentator, Amman Broadcasting Service and Lecturer, Teacher Training Centre, Ramallah, Jordan; Third Sec., Embassy, Kuwait 1965–67, Second Sec., Embassy, Iraq 1967–70, First Sec. in USA 1970–72, with Foreign Ministry, Amman 1972–73, Counsellor, Embassy, UK 1973–77, Amb. to Belgium (also accred to Netherlands and Luxembourg) 1978–90, to Italy 1990–95; Perm. Rep. to UN 1995–2000; Dir Royal Inst. for Inter-Faith Studies; also currently adviser to Prince El-Hassan bin Talal; contribs to Electronic Intifada and Electronic Iraq (online publs), Green Left Weekly 2003, The Daily Star, Al-Rai; weekly articles in The Jordan Times and Al-Ghad; Order of Grand Cross of Crown of Belgium, Order of Independence of Jordan, Grade I, Order of Al-Kawkab of Jordan, Medal of Pope Paul VI, Order of Grand Cross of Merit, Italy. *Leisure interests:* hunting, reading, researching, writing. *Address:* PO Box 132, Jubeihah, Amman 11941, Jordan (home). *Telephone:* (9626) 461-8051 (office); (9626) 534-1360 (home). *Fax:* (9626) 461-8053 (office). *E-mail:* hasan.abunimah@riifs.org (office); abunimah@nol.com.jo (home).

ABU SULAYMAN, Muna, BA, MA; Saudi Arabian broadcaster; b. 16 May 1973, Philadelphia, Pa, USA; d. of Dr Abdulhamid Abu Sulayman; two d.; ed King Abdulaziz Univ., Int. Islamic Univ. Malaysia, George Mason Univ., USA, King Saud Univ., Riyadh; Lecturer in English Dept, King Saud Univ. 1997–2004; Co-host Kalam Nawaem (Softly Speaking), Middle East Broadcasting Centre 2002–07; Exec. Man. of Strategic Studies and Research Initiatives 2004–06; Exec. Dir and Sec.-Gen. Alwaleed Bin Talal Foundation 2006–12; f. range of fashion accessories; mem. Bd Muslim Women's Fund, Soliya, Meedan Volunteer Dir for Friends of Saudi Arabia Asscn 2004–; mem. Advisory Bd Peaceful Families Project, Gem Schools; mem. Saudi Media Asscn; best known as the first Saudi woman to appear on non-government global TV; Saudi UN Goodwill Amb., UNDP (first Saudi woman) 2005; Goodwill Amb. for UNDP 2005; Young Global Leader, World Econ. Forum 2004, Award for Achievements in Regional and Int. Relations, Middle East Excellence Awards Inst. 2007, named by The Royal Islamic Strategic Studies Centre as one of 500 Most Influential Muslims in the World 2009, Medinge Group Colin Morley Award 2010, ranked by Arabian Business amongst the Power 500: The Worlds's Most Influential Arabs (71st) 2012. *Television includes:* co-host, Kalam Nawaem (Softly Speaking), MBC-TV 2002–07. *Address:* c/o Alwaleed Bin Talal Foundation, PO Box 33, Riyadh 11321, Saudi Arabia. *Telephone:* 5-44244118. *E-mail:* info@munaabusulayman.com. *Website:* www .munaabusulayman.com/home.html.

ABUBAKAR, Gen. Abdulsalami; Nigerian international official, fmr head of state and army officer; b. 13 June 1942, Minna; ed Minna, Bida, Kaduna; joined Nigerian Army 1963, with UN peace-keeping force in Lebanon 1978–79, Chief of Defence Staff and Chair. Jt Chiefs of Staff of the Armed Forces 1993–98, fmrly active in Cttee of W African Chiefs of Staff; Commdr in Chief 1998; Head of Govt of Nigeria 1998–99; apptd UN Special Envoy to Democratic Repub. of the Congo 2000; Head of Commonwealth Observer Mission to Oversee Zimbabwe's Parl. Elections 2000, Mission to Monitor Pres. Elections in Zimbabwe March 2002.

ABUZAYD, Karen Koning; American UN official; *Commissioner, Independent International Commission of Inquiry on the Syrian Arab Republic, United Nations;* b. 21 Aug. 1941, Youngstown, Ohio; m. Abdul Abu Zayd 1969; two c.; ed DePauw Univ., McGill Univ., Canada; fmr Lecturer in Political Science and Islamic Studies, Makerere Univ., Uganda and Juba Univ., Sudan; joined UNHCR 1981, worked on various emergencies across Africa, served as UNHCR Chief of Mission during Bosnian war, Chef du Cabinet to High Commr Sadako Ogata, and Regional Rep. to USA and Caribbean 1981–2000; Deputy Commr-Gen. UNRWA 2000–05, Commr-Gen. 2005–10, Commr, Ind. Int. Comm. of Inquiry on the Syrian Arab Republic, OHCHR, Geneva 2011–; Peace Prize of the UN Asscn in Spain (ANUE) 2011. *Address:* Independent International Commission of Inquiry on the Syrian Arab Republic, Office of the United Nations High Commissioner for Human Rights, Palais des Nations, 1211 Geneva 10, Switzerland (office). *E-mail:* coisyria@ ohchr.org (office). *Website:* www.ohchr.org (office).

ABYKAYEV, Nurtai Abykayevich; Kazakhstani politician and diplomatist; *First Vice-Minister of Foreign Affairs;* b. 15 May 1947, Jambul (now Taraz), Almaty Oblast; m.; three c.; ed S.M. Kirov Ural Polytech. Inst., Alma–Ata (Almaty) Higher CP School; has rank of Amb.; engineer Almaty factory of heavy machine construction 1972–76; CP functionary 1976–88; First Sec. of Cen. Cttee 1988–89; Asst to First Sec. Cen. Cttee CP of Kazakh SSR 1989–90; Head Adm. of Pres. and Prime Minister of Repub. of Kazakhstan, mem. Nat. Security Council 1990–95, Chair. 1999–2000, 2010–; Amb. to UK (also accred to Denmark, Norway and Sweden) 1995–96; First Asst to Pres. of Kazakhstan 1996–99, fmr Head of Presidential Admin; First Deputy Minister of Foreign Affairs 1999; Amb. to Russian Fed. 2002–03, 2007–09; First Vice-Minister of Foreign Affairs 2009–; Chair. of Senate 2004–07. *Address:* National Security Council, Astana, Kazakhstan (office). *Telephone:* (717-2) 32-50-50 (office). *E-mail:* press@knb.kz (office). *Website:* www.knb.kz (office).

ACCARDO, Salvatore; Italian violinist and conductor; b. 26 Sept. 1941, Turin; s. of Vincenzo Accardo and Ines Nea Accardo; m. Resy Corsi 1973; ed Conservatorio S. Pietro a Majella, Naples and Chigiana Acad., Siena; first professional recital 1954; won 1st prize Geneva Competition aged 15 and 1st prize Paganini Competition aged 17; repertoire includes concertos by Bartók, Beethoven, Berg, Brahms, Bruch, Paganini, Penderecki, Prokofiev, Saint-Saëns, Sibelius, Stravinsky and Tchaikovsky; plays with world's leading conductors and orchestras including Amsterdam Concertgebouw, Berlin Philharmonic, Boston Symphony, Chicago Symphony, Cleveland, La Scala, Milan, Santa Cecilia, Rome, BBC Symphony, London Symphony and Philharmonia; also appears as soloist/dir with the English, Scottish and Netherlands Chamber Orchestras; Artistic Dir Naples Festival; Cavaliere di Gran Croce 1982; numerous music prizes include Caecilia Prize (Brussels) and Italian Critics' Prize for recording of the Six Paganini Concertos and Diapuson d'Or for recording of the Sibelius Concerto. *Recordings include:* the Paganini Concertos and Caprices (Deutsche Grammophon), concertos by Beethoven and Brahms, complete works for violin and orchestra by Bruch, concertos by Mendelssohn, Dvořák, Sibelius and Tchaikovsky (Philips/Phonogram). *Publications:* Edn Paganini Sixth Concerto, Paganini: Variations on "Carmagnola". *Leisure interests:* hi-fi, electronics, sport, cooking. *Telephone:* (02) 49434974. *E-mail:* management@salvatoreaccardo.it. *Website:* www .salvatoreaccardo.it.

ACCONCI, Vito Hannibal, MFA; American writer, artist and architect; *Owner, Acconci Studio Inc.;* b. 24 Jan. 1940, Bronx, New York; s. of Amilcar Acconci and Catherine Colombo; ed Holy Cross Coll., Worcester, Mass, Univ. of Iowa; public comms include: The Palladium, New York 1986, Coca Cola Co. Atlanta 1987, St Aubin Park, Detroit 1990, Autry Park, Houston 1990, Embarcadero Promenade, San Francisco 1992, Arvada Art Center, Arvada, Colo 1992, La Fontaine Avenue School, Bronx, New York 1992, Storefront for Art and Architecture, New York 1993, Mur Island, Graz 2003, Roof Like A Liquid Flung Over the Plaza, Tennessee

2004, Open-Book Store, Armory Art Fair, New York 2007; several awards from New York State Council of the Arts 1976, Guggenheim Foundation Fellowship 1979, Nat. Endowment for the Arts, Skowhegan Award 1980. *Leisure interests:* architecture, movies, music. *Address:* Acconci Studio Inc., 20 Jay Street, #215, Brooklyn, New York, NY 11201 (office). *Telephone:* (718) 852-6591 (office). *Fax:* (718) 624-3178 (office). *E-mail:* studio@acconci.com (office). *Website:* (office).

ACCOYER, Bernard; French physician and politician; b. 12 Aug. 1945, Lyon (Rhône); head of clinic, specialising in Oto-Rhino-Laryngology (Ear, Nose and Throat) 1976; Mayor and mem. Municipal Council, Annecy-le-Vieux (Haute-Savoie) 1989–; mem. Conseil Général, Haute-Savoie 1992–98; mem. Assemblée Nationale (Haute-Savoie (1ère)) 1993– (re-elected 1997, 2002, 2007), First Vice-Chair. Union pour un Mouvement Populaire Parl. Group 2002–04, Chair. 2004–07; Pres. Assemblée Nationale 2007–12, mem. Cultural, Family and Social Affairs Cttee. *Address:* 49 Ave. de Genève, 7400 Annecy-le-Vieux; Mairie, 74940 Annecy-le-Vieux, France. *Telephone:* 4-50-23-86-33 (office). *Fax:* 4-50-27-66-90 (office). *E-mail:* bernard.accoyer@wanadoo.fr.

ACEVEDO FLORES, Carlos Gerardo, PhD; Salvadorean central banker and fmr academic; *President, Banco Central de Reserva de El Salvador;* ed Instituto Libre de Filosofía y Ciencias Sociales-Universidad Iberoamericana, Mexico, Vanderbilt Univ., Duke Univ., Boulder Econs Inst., USA; Prof., Dept of Philosophy, Univ. Centroamericana José Simeón Cañas, San Salvador 1984–91, Prof. of Econs 1994, Prof. of Organizational Environment 2007–10; Teaching Asst, Vanderbilt Univ. 1996–98; Sr Analyst, Investigation Dept, Banco Central de Reserva de El Salvador 1998–99, Pres. Banco Central de Reserva de El Salvador 2009–; Prof., Inst. of Business Admin, Instituto Superior de Economía y Administración de Empresas (ISEADE), San Salvador 1999–2010; Prof. of Monetary and Fiscal Policy, School of Econs and Business (ESEN), San Salvador 2000–01; Prof. of Econs and Int. Business Ethics, Universidad Francisco Gavidia, San Salvador 2006–08; Prof. of Econ. Theory, Univ. Dr Jose Matias Delgado, Antiguo Cuscatlán 2007–10; Section Man., Macroeconomics Dept, Fundación Salvadoreña para el Desarrollo Económico y Social (FUSADES) 1999–2004; Deputy Coordinator, Human Devt Report on El Salvador, UNDP 2004–09. *Address:* Office of the President, Banco Central de Reserva de El Salvador, Alameda Juan Pablo II, entre 15 y 17 Avda Norte, Apdo 01-106, San Salvador, El Salvador (office). *Telephone:* 2281-8000 (office). *Fax:* 2281-8011 (office). *E-mail:* info@bcr.gob.sv (office). *Website:* www.bcr.gob.sv (office).

ACHAARI, Mohammad; Moroccan writer; b. 1951, Moulay Idriss Zerhoun; ed Mohammed V Univ.; fmr contrib. to several Moroccan newspapers including Al-Alam, Al Ittihad Al Ichtiraki; mem. Union des Écrivains du Maroc (Moroccan Union of Writers) 1975–, Pres. 1989–96; Sec.-Gen. Syndicat nat. de l'agriculture 1979–84; Bureau Chief, Al Ittihad Al Ichtiraki (daily newspaper) 1983–98; elected mem. Majlis al-Nuab (Parl.) 1997; Minister of Culture 1998, Minister of Culture and of Communications 2000, 2002–07; mem. Union socialiste des forces populaires, mem. Political Bureau; mem. Syndicat nat. de la Presse, Fondation Mohammed V pour la Solidarité. *Publications include:* six collections of poetry, short-story collection; El Jardin de la Soledad/The Garden of Solitude (collected poems in English and Spanish translation) 2005; novels: South of the Soul, The Arch and the Butterfly (co-recipient Int. Prize for Arabic Fiction 2011) 2010.

ACHAKZAI, Mehmood Khan, MSc; Pakistani politician and mechanical engineer; *Governor of Balochistan;* b. 1948, Gulistan, Balochistan; s. of Abdul Samad Khan Achakzai; m.; five c.; ed Univ. of Eng and Tech., Peshawar; Chair. Pakhtoonkhwa Milli Awami Party (Pashtun nationalist party based in Balochistan); mem. Nat. Ass. three times from Qilla Abdullah and also from Quetta; Gov. of Balochistan 2013–; Chair. Pakistan Oppressed Nations Movt; Leader All Parties Democratic Alliance. *Address:* Governor House, Quetta, Balochistan, Pakistan (office). *Telephone:* (81) 9202170 (office). *Fax:* (81) 9202178 (office). *E-mail:* info@ balochistan.gov.pk (office). *Website:* www.balochistan.gov.pk (office).

ACHARYA, Gyan Chandra, BA, MA; Nepalese diplomatist, government official and UN official; *High Representative of the Secretary-General for the Least Developed Countries, Landlocked Developing Countries and Small Island Developing States, United Nations;* b. 20 Nov. 1960, Kathmandu; m.; two c.; ed Tribhuvan Univ.; joined Foreign Service as Section Officer 1983, served in European Div., Ministry of Foreign Affairs 1983–86, Second Sec., Embassy in Cairo 1986–91, served in UN and Int. Orgs Div., Ministry of Foreign Affairs and Office of the Foreign Sec. 1991–95, First Sec./Counsellor, Embassy in Berlin 1995–98, Jt Sec. (Dir-Gen.), Econ. Relations and Coordination Div. April–Sept. 1998, Spokesman of the Ministry of Foreign Affairs and Jt Sec. (Dir-Gen.) Europe-American Div./S Asia and SAARC Div. 1998–2003, Amb. to Switzerland and Perm. Rep. to UN Office and WTO, Geneva 2003–07, Foreign Sec. of Nepal 2007–09, Perm. Rep. to UN, New York 2009–12; Under-Sec.-Gen. and High Rep. of the Sec.-Gen. for the Least Developed Countries, Landlocked Developing Countries and Small Island Developing States, UN 2012–. *Address:* Office of the High Representative for the Least Developed Countries, Landlocked Developing Countries and the Small Island Developing States (UN-OHRLLS), United Nations, Room S-770, New York, NY 10017, USA (office). *Telephone:* (212) 963-7778 (office). *Fax:* (212) 963-5051 (office). *E-mail:* dunn@un.org (office). *Website:* www.unohrlls.org (office).

ACHARYA, Madhu Raman; Nepalese diplomatist and UN official; *Director, United Nations Assistance Mission for Iraq (UNAMI);* b. 24 Feb. 1957, Udavapur; m.; two c.; ed Tribhuvan Univ., Kathmandu; Asst Lecturer, Tribhuvan Univ. 1982–83; Section Officer, Ministry of Home Affairs 1983–90; Asst Sec., Ministry of Finance 1990–93, Under-Sec. of Finance 1993–96; Jt Sec., Ministry of Foreign Affairs 1996–97; Deputy Chief of Mission, New Delhi, India 1997–98; Amb. to Bangladesh 1998–2001; Foreign Sec. 2001–05; Amb. and Perm. Rep. to UN, New York 2005–09, Chair. Fourth Cttee (Special Political and Decolonization) for 61st session of Gen. Ass. 2006; Dir UN Assistance Mission for Iraq (UNAMI) 2010–; participated in several UN missions in Cambodia, S Africa, Liberia in 1990s. *Publications:* several books, including Nepal Culture Shift!: Reinventing Culture in the Himalayan Kingdom 2002. *E-mail:* achouri@un.org (office). *Website:* www .uniraq.org (office).

ACHIDI ACHU, Simon; Cameroonian politician; *Vice-President of the Senate;* b. 1934, Santa Mbu; ed Cameroon Protestant Coll., Bali, Yaoundé Univ., Univ. of

Besançon, France, Nat. School of Magistracy, Yaoundé; worked as agricultural Asst, Cameroon Devt Corpn before entering univ.; fmr interpreter, Presidency, Yaoundé, Chief Accountant, Widikum Council, Pres. N W Prov. Co-operative Union Ltd; Minister-del. in charge of State Reforms 1971; Minister of Justice and Keeper of the Seals 1972–75; worked in pvt. business 1975–88; mem. Parl. (Rassemblement démocratique du peuple camerounais) 1988–92; Prime Minister of Cameroon 1992–96; mem. CPDM; Chair. Société Nationale d'Investissement (Nat. Investment Corpn) 2003; mem. Senate 2013–, Vice-Pres. of Senate 2013–. *Leisure interests:* farming, football. *Address:* Office of the Vice-President, The Senate, Yaoundé, Cameroon (office). *Website:* www.assemblenationale.cm (office).

ACHLEITNER, Paul; Austrian business executive; *Chairman of the Supervisory Board, Deutsche Bank AG;* b. 1956; ed Univ. of St Gallen, Switzerland, Harvard Business School, USA; Man., Strategy Consulting, Bain & Co., Boston, USA 1984–88; Vice-Pres., Mergers and Acquisitions, Goldman Sachs & Co., New York, USA 1988–89, Exec. Dir, Investment Banking, Goldman Sachs International, London, UK 1989–94, Chair. and Partner, (Goldman Sachs Group), Goldman Sachs & Co. OHG, Frankfurt 1994–99; mem. Man. Bd Allianz SE (formely Allianz AG) 2000–12; Chair. Supervisory Bd Deutsche Bank AG 2012–; mem. Supervisory Bd Bayer AG, Daimler AG, RWE AG; mem. Shareholders' Cttee Henkel AG & Co. KGaA. *Address:* Deutsche Bank AG, Taunusanlage 12, 60262 Frankfurt am Main, Germany (office). *Telephone:* (69) 910-00 (office). *Fax:* (69) 910-34225 (office). *E-mail:* info@db.com (office). *Website:* www.db.com (office).

ACHUTHANANDAN, V(elikkakathu) S(ankaran); Indian politician; b. 20 Oct. 1923, Punnapra, Alappuzha, Kerala; s. of Sri. Sankaran and Smt. Accamma; m. K. Vasumathy; one s. one d.; joined State Congress 1938; elected mem. Kerala Legis. Ass. 1967, 1970, 1991, 2001, 2006, mem. for Malampuzha constituency, Palghat Dist 2006–; Leader of Opposition 1992–96, 2001–06; mem. Communist Party of India (CPI) 1940; imprisoned for five and a half years during so-called Freedom Struggle period and went underground for a further four and half years, mem. State Secr. of CPI 1957–, left CPI Nat. Council, formed Communist Party of India (Marxist) CPI(M) 1964, Sec. Kerala CPI(M) 1980–92; apptd mem. Politburo 1985–2009; Chief Minister of Kerala 2006–11. *Leisure interest:* reading. *Address:* Kerala State Committee, AKG Centre, A. Raghavan Road, Thiruvananthapuram 695 034, India (office). *Telephone:* (47) 12305731 (office). *Fax:* (47) 12307141 (office). *E-mail:* cpmkerala@asianetindia.com (office). *Website:* www.cpimkerala.org (office).

ACKEREN, Robert Van; German filmmaker, screenwriter and producer; b. 22 Dec. 1946, Berlin; s. of Max Van Ackeren and Hildegard Van Ackeren; Prof. of TV and Film, Acad. of Media Arts, Cologne; German Film Prize, Ernst Lubitsch Prize, Federal Film Prize (FRG), Max Ophüls Prize, Prix Celuloide, Premio Incontri Int., Prix Cinedecouverte, El Premio Cid, Prix L'âge d'or. *Films:* Einer weiss mehr 1964, Wham 1965, Sticky Fingers 1966, Nou Nou 1967, Ja und Nein 1968, Für immer und ewig 1969, Blondie's No. 1 1971, Küss mich, Fremder 1972, Harlis 1973, Der letzte Schrei 1975, Belcanto 1977, Das andere Lächeln 1978, Die Reinheit des Herzens 1980, Deutschland Privat 1981, Die flambierte Frau 1983, Die Tigerin 1985, Die Venusfalle 1987, Die Wahre Geschichte von Männern und Frauen 1992. *Address:* Kurfürstendamm 132A, 10711 Berlin, Germany (home).

ACKERMAN, F. Duane, BS, MS, MBA; American telecommunications industry executive (retd); *Chairman Emeritus, BellSouth Corporation;* b. 1942, Plant City, Fla; m.; four c.; ed Rollins Coll., Winter Park, Fla, Massachusetts Inst. of Tech.; various posts with BellSouth Group, including Pres. and CEO, BellSouth Telecommunications 1992–95, Vice Chair. and COO, BellSouth Corpn 1995–97, Pres., CEO 1997–98, Chair. and CEO 1998–2006 (retd) 1996–2005, now Chair. Emer.; fmr Chair. Nat. Council on Competitiveness, Georgia Research Alliance; fmr Vice-Chair. Nat. Security Telecommunications Advisory Cttee; mem. Bd of Dirs Home Depot, United Parcel Service of America, Inc. 2007–, Allstate Corpn; mem. Pres.'s Council of Advisors on Science and Tech.; fmr mem. US Homeland Security Advisory Council; Trustee, Rollins Coll.; fmr Gov. Soc. of Sloan Fellows, MIT. *Address:* 1155 Peachtree Street, NE, Suite 2000, Atlanta, GA 30308-7628, USA.

ACKERMAN, Raymond, BCom; South African business executive; *Adviser, Pick n Pay Group;* b. 10 March 1931, Cape Town; s. of Gus Ackerman; m. Wendy Ackerman; four c.; ed Bishops Diocesan Coll., Univ. of KwaZulu-Natal; trainee man., Greatermans Group 1951; f. Pick n Pay Group (retail group) 1967, Chair. 1967–2010, Adviser 2010–; Founder Ackerman Family Educational Trust; Melvin Jones Fellow, Lions Clubs International 1999; Paul Harris Fellow, Rotary International; Dr hc (Rhodes Univ.) 1986, (Univ. of Cape Town) 2001, (Univ. of KwaZulu-Natal) 2009; Outstanding Young South African Award 1965, Business Achiever of the Year, Herald Times 1994, Businessman of the Year Award 1994, Outstanding Business Leadership for Commitment to Improving the Quality of Life in South Africa 1996, Pioneer Award, South Africa Council of Shopping Centres 2001, Woodrow Wilson Centre Award 2008, David Rockefeller Bridging Leadership in Africa Award, Synergos Inst. 2010, Lifetime Achiever Award, Sunday Times, Protea Award, Asscn of Marketers, Humanitarian Award, B'nai B'rith, Man of the Year Award, Millennium Achievement Award, Inst. of Marketing Man. *Publications include:* Hearing Grasshoppers Jump: The Story of Raymond Ackerman (co-author) 2001, A Sprat to Catch a Mackerel: Key Principles to Build Your Business (autobiography) 2010. *Address:* Pick n Pay Group, 101 Rosmead Avenue, Kenilworth, Cape Town, South Africa (office). *Telephone:* (21) 6581000 (office). *Website:* www.picknpay.co.za (office).

ACKERMAN, Valerie (Val) B.; American lawyer, sports executive and fmr basketball player; *President, Board of Directors, USA Basketball;* m. Charlie Rappaport; two d.; ed Univ. of Virginia, UCLA; fmr professional basketball player in France; Assoc. Simpson Thacher and Bartlett (law firm), New York 1986–88; Attorney and Sr Exec. Nat. Basketball Assoc 1988–96; mem. Bd of Dirs USA Basketball 1990–, Pres. 2005–; Founding Pres. Women's Nat. Basketball Assoc 1996–2005; mem. Exec. Cttee Naismith Memorial Basketball Hall of Fame; mem. Bd of Dirs Girls Inc., NYC Sports Devt Corpn; mem. Nat. Bd of Trustees for March of Dimes; Silver Anniversary Award, Nat. Collegiate Athletic Asscn 2006. *Address:* USA Basketball, 5465 Mark Dabling Boulevard, Colorado Springs, CO 80918-3842, USA (office). *Telephone:* (719) 590-4800 (office). *Fax:* (719) 590-4811 (office). *Website:* www.usabasketball.com (office).

ACKERMANN, Haider; Colombian fashion designer; b. 1971, Santa Fé de Bogotá; ed Acad. of Fine Arts, Antwerp, Belgium; enrolled in Acad. of Fine Arts, Antwerp 1994 then worked as an intern at John Galliano's Paris offices; asst to Wim Neels (fmr acad. teacher) and worked on Belgian designer's men's and womenswear collections; presented his first collection in Paris 2001; hired as Head Designer for Ruffo Research, commissioned to design two collections (Spring-Summer and Autumn-Winter 2003) while continuing to produce his own line; signed partnership with fashion group bvba "32" 2005; Swiss Textiles Award 2003. *Address:* bvba "32", Populierenlaan 34, 2020 Antwerp, Belgium (office); c/o Michèle Montagne, 184 rue Saint-Maur, 75010 Paris, France (office). *Telephone:* (3) 830-52-72 (office); 1-42-03-91-00 (office). *Fax:* (3) 830-05-04 (office); 1-42-03-12-22 (office). *E-mail:* info@32.be (office); press@michelemontagne.com (office). *Website:* www.32.be (office); www.haiderackermann.be.

ACKERMANN, Ronny; German professional skier; b. 6 May 1977; winner, Gundersen and Sprint Disciplines, World Cup, Trondheim, Norway 2004; second, Gundersen Discipline, World Cup, Oberhof, Germany 2004; winner Sprint Discipline, World Cup, Ruhpolding, Germany 2005; second, Sprint Discipline, World Cup, Seefeld, Austria 2005; third, Gundersen Discipline 2005; second, Mass Start, World Cup, Sapporo, Japan 2005; winner, Gundersen Discipline, World Ski Championships, Oberstdorf, Germany 2005; third, Sprint Discipline, World Cup, Lahti, Finland 2005; second, Gundersen Discipline, World Cup, Lahti 2005; third, Gundersen Discipline, World Cup, Oslo, Norway 2005; third, Sprint Discipline, World Cup, Oslo 2005; mem. Rhoener WSV Dermbach skiing club. *Address:* c/o Martina Reichel, Deutsche Sport-Marketing GmbH, Schaumainkai 91, 60596 Frankfurt am Main, Germany. *Telephone:* (69) 695801-11 (home). *Fax:* (69) 695801-30 (home). *E-mail:* martina.reichel@dsm-olympia.de. *Website:* www.ronnyackermann.de.

ACKLAND, Joss (Sidney Edmond Jocelyn), CBE; British actor; b. 29 Feb. 1928, London, England; s. of Norman Ackland and Ruth Izod; m. Rosemary Jean Kirkcaldy 1951 (died 2002); two s. (one deceased) five d.; ed Dame Alice Owens School, Cen. School of Speech Training and Dramatic Art; has worked in theatre since 1945; repertory includes Stratford-upon-Avon, Arts Theatre, Buxton, Croydon, The Embassy, Coventry, Oxford, Pitlochry, USA, Yugoslavia, USSR, Ireland; tea planter in Cen. Africa 1954–57; disc jockey in Cape Town 1955–57; mem. Old Vic Theatre Co. 1958–61; Artistic Dir Mermaid Theatre 1961–63; Dir The Plough and the Stars; Amb. for Motor Neurone Disease; mem. Drug Helpline, Amnesty Int; Hon. Fellowship, Central School of Speech and Drama. *Theatre roles include:* Falstaff in Henry IV, Parts I and II, Hook and Darling in Peter Pan, Clarence Darrow in Never the Sinner, Mitch in A Streetcar Named Desire, Brassbound in Captain Brassbound's Conversion, Sir in The Dresser (nat. tour), Petruchio in The Taming of the Shrew (nat. tour), Gaev in The Cherry Orchard, Gus in Hotel in Amsterdam, Sam in Collaborators, Ill in The Visit, Eustace Perrin State in The Madras House, John Tarleton in Misalliance, Weller Martin in The Gin Game, Captain Shotover in Heartbreak House. *West End musical roles include:* Squeezum in Lock Up Your Daughters, Romain Gary in Jean Seburg, Jorrocks in Jorrocks, Frederic in A Little Night Music, Perón in Evita, Captain Hook and Mr Darling in Peter Pan – the Musical. *Films include:* Seven Days to Noon 1949, Crescendo 1969, The House That Dripped Blood, Villain, Great Expectations, The Four Musketeers, Royal Flash, England Made Me, Lady Jane 1984, A Zed and Two Noughts 1985, The Sicilian 1986, To Kill a Priest 1987, White Mischief 1988, Lethal Weapon II, The Hunt for Red October, To Forget Palermo, Tre Colonne in Cronaca 1989, The Object of Beauty, The Sheltering Desert, The Bridge, A Murder of Quality 1990, Voices in the Garden 1992, Georgino, Occhio Pinocchio 1993, Nowhere to Run 1993, The Bible, Miracle on 34th Street, Mad Dogs and Englishmen, A Kid at the Court of King Arthur, Citizen X 1994, Daisies in December, Till the End of Time, Surviving Picasso, Deadly Voyage 1995, Swept from the Sea 1996, Firelight 1997, Game of Mirrors, Son of Sandokan, Milk, Passion of Mind 1998, Mumbo Jumbo 2000, No Good Deed 2001, K19: The Widowmaker 2002, I'll Be There 2002, A Different Loyalty 2004, Asylum 2005, These Foolish Things 2006, How About You... 2007, Flawless 2007, The Boy with Chocolate Fingers (short) 2011, The Stain (short) (voice) 2011, Katherine of Alexandria 2013, Prisoners of the Sun 2013. *Radio roles includes:* Macbeth in Macbeth, The King in The King and I, Honoré Lachailles in Gigi, God in The Little World of Don Camillo, Victor Hugo in Les Misérables, The Dog in Investigations of a Dog, Socrates in The Trial and Death of Socrates 2008, Big Daddy in Cat on a Hot Tin Roof 2008. *Television includes:* The Indian Tales of Rudyard Kipling (series) 1964, Play for Today (series) – The Lie 1970, – The Bankrupt 1972, – Access to the Children 1973, When We Are Married (film) 1987, The Man Who Lived at the Ritz (film) 1991, The Barretts of Wimpole Street (film) 1982, Shadowlands (film) 1985, A Woman Named Jackie (mini-series) 1991, First and Last (film) 1989, They Do It with Mirrors (film) 1991, Deadly Voyage (film) 1996, Tales from the Madhouse (mini-series) – Barabbas 2000, Gioco di specchi (film) 2000, Othello (film) 2001, Lionheart: The Crusade (film) 2003, Henry VIII (film) 2003, Icon (film) 2005, Midsomer Murders (series) – Vixen's Run 2006, Above and Beyond (mini-series) 2006, Moscow Zero, Hogfather (film) 2006, Kingdom (series) 2007, Pinocchio (film) 2008, Crusoe (series) 2008–10. *Publications:* I Must Be in There Somewhere (autobiog.) 1989, My Better Half and Me (with Rosemary Ackland) 2009. *Leisure interests:* writing, painting, reading, 32 grandchildren, 10 great-grandchildren. *Address:* c/o Paul Pearson, 18 Leamore Street, London, W6 0JZ, England (office). *Telephone:* (20) 8748-1478 (office). *E-mail:* joss@converged.net.au (office).

ACKROYD, Norman, CBE, RA, FRCA; British artist; b. 26 March 1938, Leeds; s. of the late Albert Ackroyd and Clara Briggs; m. 1st Sylvia Buckland 1963 (divorced 1975); two d.; m. 2nd Penelope Hughes-Stanton 1978; one s. one d.; ed Cockburn High School, Leeds, Leeds Coll. of Art, Royal Coll. of Art; Tutor in Etching, Cen. School of Art and Design 1965–93; Prof. of Etching, Univ. of Indiana 1970; Professor of Etching, Univ. of the Arts 1994–; comms include: Haringey West Indian Cultural Centre 1986, Lloyds Bank Tech. Centre, London 1990, Tetrapak, Heathrow 1991, Freshfields, London 1992, British Airways, Birmingham Int. Airport—Eurohub 1993, British Embassy, Moscow 2000, Lazard, London 2003, Great Portland Estates, London 2008, Sainsbury Lab., Univ. of Cambridge 2010; elected Royal Academician 1991; Sr Fellow, RCA 2000–; British Int. Print Biennale Prize 1974, 1982, Royal Soc. of Etchers and Engravers 1984, 85, Bronze Medal, Frechen, Germany 1986. *Television includes:* Artists in Print (Etching) 1981, A Prospect of Rivers 1988. *Publications include:* Landscapes and Figures,

Etchings (with William McIllvannry) 1973, The Pictish Coast (with Douglas Dunn) 1988, St Kilda: The Furthest Island 1989, Windrush 1990. *Leisure interests:* British history, archaeology, cricket. *Address:* c/o Zillah Bell Gallery, 15 Kirkgate, Thirsk, North Yorkshire, YO7 1PQ, England. *Website:* www.normanackroyd.com.

ACKROYD, Peter, CBE, MA, FRSL; British writer; b. 5 Oct. 1949, London; s. of Graham Ackroyd and Audrey Whiteside; ed St Benedict's School, Ealing, Clare Coll., Cambridge and Yale Univ., USA; Literary Ed. The Spectator 1973–77, Jt Man. Ed. 1978–82; Chief Book Reviewer, The Times 1986–; Mellon Fellow, Yale Univ.; Hon. Fellow, Clare Coll., Cambridge 2008, Hon. Fellow, RIBA 2009; Hon. DLitt (Univ. of Exeter), (London Guildhall), (City Univ.), (Univ. Coll., London), (Brunel Univ.) 2006. *Play:* The Mystery of Charles Dickens 2000. *Television:* Charles Dickens (BBC 2), Peter Ackroyd's London (BBC 2) 2004, The Romantics (BBC 2) 2006, London Visions (Artsworld) 2007, Peter Ackroyd's Venice (BBC 2) 2009. *Publications include:* fiction: The Great Fire of London 1982, The Last Testament of Oscar Wilde (Somerset Maugham Prize 1984) 1983, Hawksmoor (Whitbread Award for Fiction 1986, Guardian Fiction Award 1986) 1985, Chatterton 1987, First Light 1989, English Music 1992, The House of Doctor Dee 1993, Dan Leno and the Limehouse Golem 1994, Milton in America 1996, The Plato Papers 1999, The Clerkenwell Tales (short stories) 2003, The Lambs of London 2004, The Fall of Troy 2006, The Casebook of Victor Frankenstein 2009, The Canterbury Tales: A Retelling 2009, The Death of King Arthur: The Immortal Legend 2010, Three Brothers 2013; non-fiction: Notes for a New Culture 1976, Dressing Up: Transvestism and Drag: The History of an Obsession 1979, Ezra Pound and His World 1980, T. S. Eliot (RSL W. H. Heinemann Award 1985, Whitbread Award for Biography 1985) 1984, Dickens 1990, Introduction to Dickens 1991, Blake 1995, The Life of Thomas More 1998, London: The Biography 2000, Dickens: Public Life and Private Passion 2002, The Collection 2002, Albion: The Origins of the English Imagination 2002, Illustrated London 2003, The Beginning: Voyages Through Time (juvenile) 2003, Chaucer 2004, Shakespeare: The Biography 2005, Brief Lives – Newton 2006, Thames: Sacred River 2007, Poe: A Life Cut Short 2008, Venice: Pure City 2009, The English Ghost: Spectres through Time 2010, London Under 2011, Foundation: The History of England (Vol. 1) 2011, Wilkie Collins 2012, London: The Concise Biography 2012, Tudors: The History of England from Henry VIII to Elizabeth I 2013; poetry: London Lickpenny 1973, Country Life 1978, The Diversions of Purley 1987. *Address:* c/o Anthony Sheil Associates Ltd, 43 Doughty Street, London, WC1N 2LF, England (office). *Telephone:* (20) 7405-9351 (office).

ACLAND, Sir Antony (Arthur), KG, GCMG, GCVO; British fmr diplomatist; b. 12 March 1930, London; s. of the late Brig. P. B. E. Acland; m. 1st Clare Anne Verdon 1956 (died 1984); two s. one d.; m. 2nd Jennifer McGougan (née Dyke) 1987; ed Eton Coll., Christ Church, Oxford; joined diplomatic service 1953, at Middle East Centre for Arab Studies 1954, served in Dubai 1955, Kuwait 1956, at Foreign Office 1958–62, Asst Pvt. Sec. to Sec. of State 1959–62, mem. UK Mission to UN 1962–66, Head of Chancery, Mission in Geneva 1966–68, at FCO 1968, Head of Arabian Dept 1970–72, Prin. Pvt. Sec. to Foreign and Commonwealth Sec. 1972–75, Amb. to Luxembourg 1975–77, to Spain 1977–79, Deputy Under-Sec. of State 1980–82, Perm. Under-Sec. of State and Head of Diplomatic Service 1982–86, Amb. to USA 1986–91; Provost of Eton 1991–2000; Chancellor, Order of St Michael and St George 1994–2005; Dir Shell Transport and Trading 1991–2000, Booker PLC 1992–99; Chair. Council of the Ditchley Foundation 1991–96, Tidy Britain Group 1991–96 (Pres. 1996–2002); Pres. Exmoor Soc. 2007; Trustee, Nat. Portrait Gallery 1991–99, Esmée Fairbairn Foundation 1991–2005; Hon. DCL (Exeter) 1988, (William and Mary Coll., USA) 1990, (Reading) 1991. *Leisure interests:* country pursuits, reading. *Address:* Staddon Farm, nr Winsford, Minehead, Somerset, TA24 7HY, England (home). *Telephone:* (1643) 831489 (home).

ACOGNY, Germaine; Senegalese/French dancer, choreographer and teacher; *Artistic Director, L'ecole des sables;* b. 1944, Porto Novo, Benin; m. Helmut Vogt; moved to France 1962, returned to Dakar to found pvt. professional dance studio; Dir Mudra Africa Int. Dance School, Dakar 1977–1982; worked in Brussels with Maurice Béjart; dancer, choreographer with Peter Gabriel (q.v.) 1984; first solo performance Sahel 1984; collaborated with drummer Arona N'Diaye to stage Ye'ou, the Awakening 1985; performance at World of Music and Dance Festival 1993; co-f. (with Helmut Vogt) Studio-Ecole-Ballet-Theatre of the Third World, Toulouse, France; f. The School of Sands (L'École des sables maison int. de danse), Toubab Dialaw, Senegal 1995; f. Jant Bi Dance Co.; Artistic Dir Dance Section, Afrique en Creations/AFAA (French Assoc for Artistic Action) 1997–2000; also Artistic Dir Contemporary African Dance Competition; Tchourai Solo 2001–, Fagaala (with Kota Yamazaki) 2004–, organiser annual three-month workshop for African dancers and choreographers; Chevalier, Ordre nat. du Merite, Officier des Arts et des Lettres, Chevalier de L'Ordre Nat. du Lion (Senegal); London Dance and Performance Award for Ye'ou, the Awakening 1991, Bessie Award 2007. *Dance:* Ye'ou The Awakening 1988, Afrique, ce corps memorable 1990, YEWA, Eau Sublime, for dance Biennale Lyon 1994, Le Coq est Mort (The Rooster is Dead) 2001, Tchourai 2001, Fagaala 2004. *Television:* Regard de Femmes, Double Je (Pivot), Ecole des Sables (documentary), Tchourai (documentary). *Publications include:* African Dance 1980, Tchourai 2005. *Address:* Jant-Bi/L'ecole des sables, Toubab Dialaw, BP 22626, Dakar-Ponty (office); Association Jant Bi, BP 22626, 15523 Dakar, Senegal. *Telephone:* (221) 8363619 (office). *Fax:* (221) 8363619 (office). *E-mail:* jant-bi@sentoo.sn (office); jant-bi.acogny@wanadoo.fr (office). *Website:* www.jant-bi-acogny.com (office).

ACOSTA, Carlos, CBE; Cuban/British ballet dancer; b. (Carlos Yunior Acosta Quesada), 2 June 1973, Havana; ed Nat. Ballet School of Cuba; guest appearances with numerous int. ballet cos 1989–91; guest dancer, English Nat. Ballet 1991–92; dancer, Nat. Ballet of Cuba 1992–93; Prin. Dancer, Houston Ballet 1993–; Prin. Guest Artist, The Royal Ballet, London 1998–; Prix de Lausanne Gold Medal 1990, Spanish Vegnale Dance Prix 1990, Grand Prix and Gold Medal, Fourth Annual Ballet Competition, Paris 1990, Grand Prix, Third Juvenile Dance Competition 1991, Dance Fellowship, Princess Grace Foundation (USA) 1995, Int. Critics' Prize Chile, Nat. Dance Awards Best Male Dancer 2004, Outstanding Achievement in Dance, Laurence Olivier Awards 2007, Prix Benois de la Danse 2008. *Performances include:* English Nat. Ballet: Polovtsian Dances from Prince Igor 1991, The Nutcracker 1992, Cinderella 1992; Nat. Ballet of Cuba: Giselle 1994, Don Quixote

1994, Swan Lake 1994; Houston Ballet: The Nutcracker 1993, Swan Lake, La Bayadère, Don Quixote; Royal Ballet: In the middle, somewhat elevated 1998, Raymonda, La Fille mal gardée, Swan Lake, My Brother, My Sisters, Giselle, Rhapsody, Le Corsaire, The Nutcracker 2000, Coppelia 2000, Shadowplay 2000, Don Quixote 2001, Apollo 2002, Tocororo 2003, La Fille mal gardée 2005. *Publication:* No Way Home: A Cuban Dancer's Story (biog.) 2007. *Address:* c/o Carlos Acosta Management, Aviation House, 1–7 Sussex Road, Haywards Heath, West Sussex, RH16 4DZ, England (office). *Telephone:* (1444) 450901 (office). *E-mail:* rupert.rohan@validworldwide.com (office); info@carlosacosta.com (office). *Website:* www.carlosacosta.com.

ACOSTA URQUIDI, Mariclaire, BA; Mexican diplomatist, international organization official and academic; *Visiting Professor on UNESCO Chair in Education and Democracy, School of Human Rights Research;* ed Nat. Autonomous Univ. of Mexico (UNAM), Univ. of Essex, UK; Founding mem. and fmr Pres. Mexican Comm. for the Defence and Promotion of Human Rights; fmr Exec. Dir Mexican Acad. of Human Rights; fmr Under-Sec. for Human Rights and Democracy, Ministry of Foreign Relations; fmr Special Adviser to OAS Sec.-Gen. on Civil Soc. Affairs; currently Americas Dir. Int. Center for Transitional Justice, New York; Visiting Prof. on UNESCO Chair in Educ. and Democracy, School of Human Rights Research, Utrecht, Netherlands 2010–; del. to numerous confs on human rights issues including OHCHR, Geneva 2003; fmr adviser Bd of Social Convergence for Civil Orgs; involved in human rights evaluation projects for int. orgs including Dutch Agency for Int. Co-operation and Ford Foundation. *Address:* School of Human Rights Research, Drift 15, 3512 BR Utrecht, Netherlands (office). *Telephone:* (30) 2538034 (office). *Fax:* (30) 2537168 (office). *E-mail:* rvdm@uu.nl (office). *Website:* www.schoolofhumanrights.org (office).

ACQUAVELLA, William; American art dealer and gallery owner; *Owner, Acquavella Galleries;* s. of the late Nicholas Acquavella (founder of Acquavella Galleries) and of Edythe Acquavella; m. Donna Acquavella; two s. one d.; ed Westminster School, Simsbury, Conn., Washington and Lee Univ., Lexington, Va; began by working for his father at Acquavella Galleries 1960, has sold major paintings and sculpture to pvt. collectors and museums world-wide, gallery has presented exhbns of Claude Monet, Edgar Degas, Paul Cézanne, Alfred Sisley, Pierre-Auguste Renoir, Camille Pissarro, Amedeo Modigliani, Pierre Bonnard, Yves Tanguy, Fernand Léger, Pablo Picasso, Henri Matisse, Robert Rauschenberg, Lyonel Feininger, Alberto Giacometti, Joan Miró, Lucian Freud and James Rosenquist; fmr Pres. Art Dealers Assoc of America; mem. Bd Westminster School. *Leisure interests:* tennis, golf, skiing. *Address:* Acquavella Galleries, Inc., 18 East 79th Street (between Madison and Fifth Avenues), New York, NY 10075, USA (office). *Telephone:* (212) 734-6300 (office). *Fax:* (212) 794-9394 (office). *E-mail:* info@acquavellagalleries.com (office). *Website:* www.acquavellagalleries.com (office).

ACUIL, Awut Deng, BA; South Sudanese politician; *Minister of Gender and Social Development;* b. Tonj; d. of Rek Dinka and Agar Dinka; widowed; seven c.; ed US International Univ., Nairobi, Kenya; refugee in Kenya; mem. Sudanese People's Liberation Movt's negotiating delegation at Intergovernmental Authority on Devt peace talks 2002; Minister of Labour and Public Service 2011, of Gender and Social Development 2013–; co-f. Sudanese Women's Assoc Nairobi, Sudanese Women's Voice for Peace, Sudanese Catholic Bishops Regional Conf.; est. Pankar (peace and good governance grassroots initiative); mem. Inst. for Inclusive Security's Women Waging Peace Network 1999–; InterAction Humanitarian Award 2002, Vital Voices Global Leadership Award 2007. *Address:* Ministry of Gender and Social Development, Ministries Complex, Juba, South Sudan (office).

ACZÉL, János D., PhD, FRSC; Canadian (b. Hungarian) mathematician and academic; *Distinguished Professor Emeritus and Adjunct Professor, Department of Pure Mathematics, University of Waterloo;* b. 26 Dec. 1924, Budapest; s. of Dezső Aczél and Irén Aczél; m. Susan Kende 1946; two d.; ed D. Berzsenyi High School, Univ. of Budapest; teaching asst, Univ. of Budapest 1946–48; Statistician, Metal Workers' Trade Union, Budapest 1948; Asst Prof., Univ. of Szeged 1948–50; Assoc. Prof. and Dept Head, Tech. Univ., Miskolc 1950–52; Dept Head, Assoc. Prof. then Prof., L. Kossuth Univ., Debrecen 1952–65; Prof., Dept of Pure Math., Univ. of Waterloo, Ont., Canada 1965–, Distinguished Prof. 1969–93, Distinguished Prof. Emer. and Adjunct Prof. 1993–; many visiting professorships and fellowships, N America, Europe, Africa, Asia and Australia 1963–; Chair. Int. Symposia on Functional Equations 1962–96, Hon. Chair. 1997–; mem. Canadian Math. Soc., American Math. Soc., New York Acad. of Science; Fellow, Royal Soc. of Canada 1971 (Convener Math. Div. 1974–75, Chair. Acad. of Science Editorial Cttee 1977–78); Foreign Fellow, Hungarian Acad. of Sciences 1990; donor, L. Fejér-J. Aczél Scholarship, Univ. of Waterloo, donor Susan and János Aczél Scholarship; Dr hc (Karlsruhe) 1990, (Graz) 1995, (Katowice) 1996, (Miskolc) 1999, (Debrecen) 2003; M. Beke Award, J. Bolyai Math. Soc. 1961, Award of Hungarian Acad. of Sciences 1962, Cajal Medal, Nat. Research Council of Spain 1988, Kampé de Feriet Award, Int. Conf. on Information Processing and Man. of Uncertainty in Knowledge-Based Systems 2004. *Publications:* more than 300 articles and ten books, including Lectures on Functional Equations and their Applications 1966 (republished 2006), A Short Course on Functional Equations Based upon Recent Applications to the Social and Behavioral Sciences 1987, Functional Equations in Several Variables (with J. Dhombres) 1989, (enlarged Russian trans. 2003); Hon. Ed.-in-Chief Aequationes Math; Ed. Theory and Decision Library, Series B and seven int. mathematical journals. *Leisure interests:* reading, swimming, walking. *Address:* Department of Pure Mathematics, University of Waterloo, Waterloo, ON N2L 3G1, Canada (office). *Telephone:* (519) 888-4567, ext. 36140 (office). *Fax:* (519) 725-0160 (office). *E-mail:* jdaczel@math.uwaterloo.ca (office). *Website:* www.math .uwaterloo.ca (office).

ADABASHYAN, Aleksander Artemovich; Russian scriptwriter, artist and actor; b. 8 March 1945, Moscow; m. Shadrina Yekaterina Igorevna; two d.; ed Moscow (Stroganov) Higher School of Art and Design; began career as art dir working with Nikita Mikhalkov (q.v.). *Films include:* At Home Among Strangers, A Stranger at Home (art dir) 1975, Kinsfolk 1982, Unfinished Piece for Mechanical Piano (scriptwriter/co-scriptwriter) 1997, Five Evenings (actor) 1979, Several Days in the Life of Oblomov 1980, Trans-Siberian Express 1978, The Slave of Love (artistic designer) 1976, Mado, Poste Restante (dir) 1992, The President and His

Niece (actor) 2000. *Address:* Novy Arbat str. 31, Apt 36, 121099 Moscow, Russia. *Telephone:* (495) 205-00-89.

ADACHI, Naoki, LLB; Japanese business executive; *Chairman, Toppan Printing Company Ltd;* ed Chuo Univ.; joined Sales Dept, Toppan Printing Co. Ltd 1962, has held several exec. positions including Man. Dir 1995–97, Sr Man. Dir 1997–98, Vice-Pres. 1998–2000, Pres. and CEO 2000–10, Chair. 2010–. *Address:* Toppan Printing Company Ltd, 1, Kanda Izumi-cho, Chiyoda-ku, Tokyo, 101-0024, Japan (office). *Telephone:* (3) 3835-5111 (office). *Fax:* (3) 3835-0674 (office). *Website:* www .toppan.co.jp (office).

ADADA, Rodolphe; Republic of the Congo politician and diplomatist; *Minister of State for Industrial Development and the Promotion of the Private Sector;* b. 28 April 1946; joined Cen. Cttee of Congolese Labour Party (PCT) 1972; Minister of Mines and Energy 1977–84, of Mines and Oil 1984–89, of Secondary and Higher Educ., in charge of Scientific Research 1989–91, of Foreign Affairs and Cooperation 1997–2007, promoted to rank of Minister of State for Foreign Affairs 2005; elected to Nat. Ass. as PCT cand. in first constituency of Ouenze, 5th arrondissement of Brazzaville 2002–; Jt African Union-UN Special Rep. in Darfur 2007–09; Minister of State for Industrial Devt and the Promotion of the Pvt. Sector 2009–. *Address:* Ministry of Industrial Development and the Promotion of the Private Sector, Centre Administratif, Quartier Plateau, BP 2117, Brazzaville, Republic of the Congo (office). *Telephone:* 281-30-09 (office). *Fax:* 281-06-43 (office).

ADAM, Lt-Gen. Anbaree Abdul Sattar; Maldivian army officer (retd), politician and diplomatist; m. Ihusaana Ahmed; two s. one d.; fmr Dir and Dir-Gen. of Nat. Security, Minister of State for Defence and Nat. Security 1993–96, Chief of Staff of Nat. Security Services (NSS), and Deputy C-in-C of NSS and of Police 1996–2004; first resident High Commr to India (also accred to Nepal and Bhutan) 2004–10; fmr Chair. Air Maldives; Green Diplomatist Award, Diplomatic Endeavour and Action Neology Award, Lifetime Diplomacy Award in the area of Diplomacy and International Relations, Garden Global Leadership Award for Diplomacy, Peace and International Understanding Award, Inst. of UN and UNESCO Studies (IUNUS) 2008.

ADAM, Jean Paul, MA; Seychelles politician; *Minister of Foreign Affairs;* ed Univ. of Manchester, Univ. of Sheffield, UK; worked as language asst, Bordeaux, France 2000; joined Ministry of Foreign Affairs 2001, becoming Protocol Officer and later Second Sec. 2001–05; Dir, Presidential Affairs, Office of the Pres. 2005–06, Dir-Gen. 2006–07, Prin. Sec. 2007–09, Sec. of State in the Office of the Pres. 2009; Minister of Foreign Affairs 2010–; Trustee, Seychelles Univ. Foundation. *Address:* Ministry of Foreign Affairs, Maison Quéau de Quinssy, POB 656, Mont Fleuri, Seychelles (office). *Telephone:* 283500 (office). *Fax:* 224845 (office). *E-mail:* mfapesey@seychelles.net (office). *Website:* www.mfa.gov.sc (office).

ADAM, Sir Kenneth (Ken), Kt, OBE; British film designer; b. (Klaus Hugo Adam), 5 Feb. 1921, Berlin, Germany; ed St Paul's School, London Univ.; moved with family to UK 1934; studied architecture; served six years in RAF in World War II; started film career as draughtsman on set of This Was a Woman 1947; production designer of seven James Bond films; production designer of Goldeneye: Rogue Agent video game 2004. *Films include:* Artistic Dir: The Devil's Pass, Soho Incident, Around the World in Eighty Days; Production Designer: Golden Earrings 1947, Curse of the Demon 1957, Dr No 1962, Woman of Straw 1964, Goldfinger 1964, Dr. Strangelove 1964, Thunderball 1965, Funeral in Berlin 1966, Goodbye Mr Chips 1969, Diamonds Are Forever 1971, Sleuth 1972, The Last of Sheila 1973, Barry Lyndon (Acad. Award) 1975, Patriots, Chitty Chitty Bang Bang, The Spy Who Loved Me 1977, Pennies from Heaven 1981, King David 1985, Agnes of God 1985, Crimes of the Heart 1986, The Deceivers 1988, The Freshman 1990, The Doctor 1991, Company Business 1991, Undercover Blues 1993, Addams Family Values 1993, The Madness of King George (Acad. Award 1994) 1994, Boys on the Side 1995, Bogus 1996, In and Out 1997, The Out-of-Towners 1999, Taking Sides 2001; designed sets for La Fanciulla del West, Royal Opera House, London.

ADAM, Robert, RIBA, FRSA; British architect; *Director, Adam Architecture;* b. 10 April 1948, Hants.; s. of Robert W. Adam and Margaret Adam; m. Sarah J. Chalcraft 1970; one s. one d.; ed Canford School and Regent Street Polytechnic (now Univ. of Westminster); Co-founder Adam Architecture (fmrly Robert Adam Architects) 1986, Dir 2000–; Founder and Chair. Popular Housing Group 1995–; Chair. INTBAU; mem. Planning and Urban Design Group, RIBA 1995–, mem. Council RIBA 1999–, Hon. Sec. 2001–03, Trustee RIBA Trust 2003–; Chair. Faculty of Fine Art, British School at Rome 1993–97 (mem. 1989), Vice-Chair. Council 1997–99; mem. Architecture Club Cttee 1987–, English Heritage London Advisory Group 1996–2002, Dept of the Environment Good Practice Guidance on Design in the Planning System Project Sounding Bd 1997, Comm. for Architecture and the Built Environment 1999–2003; lectures including tours in USA and Russia; Trustee Maria Nobrega Charitable Trust 2003–; contrib. to numerous TV and radio programmes; numerous awards including Bannister Fletcher Prize 1973, Rome Scholarship 1973–74, Commendation, London Borough of Richmond-upon-Thames Conservation and Design Awards Scheme 1991, Winner, Copper Roofing Competition Copper Devt Assoc. 1995, Elmbridge Borough Council Design/Conservation Award 1998, RIBA Southern Region Nat. Housebuilder Design Award, Best Partnership Devt Commendation for 2000, Marsh Country Life Awards 2001, What House? Awards 2013, City of Winchester Trust Award 2013. *Projects:* primary care centre and housing for the elderly, Pulborough, W Sussex, new country houses in Hants., Cambridge, Yorks., S Oxon., Glos., Wilts., Bucks., Dorset; restaurant and display buildings, Nagano Prefecture Japan, roof garden, Daimaru Dept Store, Osaka Japan, new villages for the Duchy of Cornwall, Shepton Mallet and Midsomer Norton, new town centre, Rocester, Staffs., village extension in Trowse, nr Norwich, master plan for St Andrew's Hosp., Northampton, master plan for new dist, Leith Scotland, new co. HQ, Dogmersfield Park, Humanities Library, Univ. of Oxford, new library for Ashmolean Museum, Oxford, Solar House, W Sussex, Millennium Temple Pvt. Estate, Hants., alterations repairs and additions to Heveningham Hall and Park, Suffolk, new offices, Piccadilly, London. *Works in public collections:* V&A Contemporary Furniture Collection (Pembroke table for Alma Furniture Co.), RIBA Drawings Collection Tower of the Orders. *Publications:* Classical Architecture – A Complete Handbook 1990, Buildings by Design 1994; numerous articles in nat. newspapers, magazines and journals. *Leisure interests:* medieval history,

ceramics. *Address:* Adam Architecture, 9 Upper High Street, Winchester, Hants., SO23 8UT, England (office). *Telephone:* (1962) 843843 (office). *Fax:* (1962) 843303 (office). *E-mail:* contact@adamarchitecture.com (office). *Website:* www .adamarchitecture.com (office).

ADAM, Theo; German singer (bass-baritone); b. 1 Aug. 1926, Dresden; s. of Johannes Adam and Lisbeth Adam (née Dernstorf); m. Eleonore Matthes 1949; one s. one d.; ed Gymnasium and Conservatory; engagements with Dresden State Opera 1949, Bayreuth Festival 1952–80, Salzburg Festival 1969, 1970, 1980–89, 1992, 1995; mem. Deutsche Staatsoper, Berlin 1953–; has appeared with Vienna and Munich State Operas since 1967; Pres. of Curatorium Oper, Dresden 1985–; sang at Semper Opera House, Dresden 1985; staged Graun's Cesare e Cleopatra, Berlin State Opera 1992; performed at Royal Festival Hall, London 1994, Berlin Staatsoper 1997; retd from stage 2006; numerous recordings; Österreichischer Kammersänger, Bayerischer Kammersänger; Nat. Prize (First Class) of GDR. *Publications:* Seht, hier ist Tinte, Feder, Papier 1980, Die 100 Rolle, Wie schön ist doch die Musik 1996. *Leisure interest:* swimming. *Address:* Schillerstrasse 14, 01326 Dresden, Germany (home). *Telephone:* (351) 2683997 (home).

ADAMI, Haji Adam; Somali politician; *Minister of Defence, 'Somaliland';* fmr Chair. Somaliland Election Comm.; Minister of Defence, 'Somaliland' 2010–. *Address:* Ministry of Defence, Hargeisa, Somalia (office). *Telephone:* 252-225-3692 (office). *Website:* www.somalilandgov.com (office).

ADAMI, Franco; Italian sculptor; b. 19 Nov. 1933, Pisa; s. of Toscano Adami and Giuseppina Bertoncini; m. Jacqueline Sylvius; one s. two d.; ed Leonardo da Vinci Inst., Pisa, Scuola d'Arte, Cascina and School of Fine Arts, Florence; Sculpture Prize of Cascina 1957, Prix Fernand Dupré for sculpture (France) 1981, Prix Charles Oulmont, Fondation de France 1987. *Leisure interests:* antiques. *Address:* Via del Vicinato 13, Pontestrada, 55045 Piatrasanta, Italy; 250 rue du Faubourg Saint-Antoine, 75012 Paris, France. *Telephone:* (058) 471317. *Fax:* (058) 471317.

ADAMIA, Revaz, PhD; Georgian biologist, politician and fmr diplomatist; *Director, G. Eliava Institute of Bacteriophage, Microbiology and Virology;* b. 20 July 1952, Tbilisi; ed Tbilisi Univ., Moscow School of Political Research of the Council of Europe, Harvard Kennedy School of Governance; Jr Research Asst, Giorgi Eliava Inst. of Microbiology and Virology 1974, Sr Research Asst 1982–88, Head, Lab. of Biotechnology and Genetic Eng 1988–92; mem. Parl. 1992-2002, Chair. Cttee on Defense and Security 1995–2000, Chair. Citizens' Union of Georgia Parl. faction 2000–01; Vice-Pres. Council of Europe Parl. Ass. 2000–01; Perm. Rep. to UN, New York 2002–06, Chair. Disarmament Comm. 2004; Dir G. Eliava Inst. of Bacteriophage, Microbiology and Virology, Tbilisi 2006–; George Soros Award. *Publications:* more than 100 articles on Biochemistry, Molecular Biology, Politics and Int. Relations. *Address:* G. Eliava Institute of Bacteriophage, Microbiology and Virology, 3, Gotua Street, 0160 Tbilisi, Georgia (office). *Telephone:* (32) 38-16-04 (office). *E-mail:* radamia@gmail.com; adamia@pha.ge (office). *Website:* www .eliava-institute.org (office).

ADAMISHIN, Anatoly Leonidovich, CandHistSc; Russian diplomatist, fmr politician and business consultant; *President, Association of Euro-Atlantic Co-operation;* b. 11 Oct. 1934, Kiev, Ukrainian SSR; m. Svetlana Adamishina; one d.; ed Moscow State Univ.; joined diplomatic service 1957, Third, then Second Sec., Embassy in Rome 1959–65, Counsellor in First European Countries Dept, Ministry of Foreign Affairs 1965–71, Counsellor in Dept of Gen. Int. Problems 1973–78, Head of First European Dept 1978–86; Deputy Minister of Foreign Affairs 1986–90, mem. of Collegium, Ministry of Foreign Affairs 1979; mem. State Duma (Parl.) 1993–95, First Deputy Minister 1992–94; Pres. USSR Comm. for UNESCO 1987–90; USSR (now Russian) Amb. to Italy 1990–92, to UK 1994–97; Minister for Co-operation with CIS Countries 1997–98; Vice-Pres. Systema Corpn 1998–2004; currently Pres. Assen of Euro-Atlantic Co-operation; Head of Chair and Prof., Russian Acad. of State Service 1998; mem. Yabloko 2004–; several decorations from USSR, including Red Banner; Grand Cross (Italy) 1992. *Television:* Diplomat's Notes (series) 2003. *Publications:* The Decline and Revival of the Great Power (La Plejade Award, Rome 1995, Best Publication of the Year, International Life, Moscow 2000) 1993, The White Sun of Angola 2001. *Leisure interests:* classical music, opera, tennis. *Address:* Association of Euro-Atlantic Co-operation, 119034 Moscow, 3 ul. Prechistenka (office); Apt 170, 2/1 Kutuzovski, Moscow, Russia (home). *Telephone:* (495) 203-62-71 (office); (495) 243-53-81 (home). *Fax:* (495) 230-22-29 (office); (495) 243-53-81 (home). *E-mail:* aeac@mail .ru (office); adamishin@dialup.ptt.ru (home). *Website:* aeac.narod.ru (office).

ADAMKUS, Valdas; Lithuanian politician and fmr head of state; b. (Voldemaras Adamkavičius, 3 Nov. 1926, Kaunas; m. Alma Adamkienė; ed Munich Univ., Univ. of Ill., Ill. Inst. of Tech.; resistance movt, World War II; left Lithuania; on staff World YMCA, Sec.-Gen. and Chair. Chief Physical Training and Sports Cttee; emigrated to USA 1949; worked in Chicago sports cars factory, draftsman eng co.; f. Academic Sports Club of American Lithuanians 1951; Chair. Bd of Santara Cen. of Lithuanian Students in USA 1957–58; Vice-Chair., Chair. Santara-Sviesa Fed. of Lithuanian Émigrés 1958–67; mem. Bd Lithuanian Community in USA 1961–64; Deputy Chair. Cen. Bd, mem., Chair. American Lithuanian Community; Chair. Org. Cttee World Lithuanian Games 1983; fmr Head Scientific Research Cen. Environment Protection Agency, Admin. for Mid-W Regions Environment Protection Agency, USA, active participation in political life of Lithuania 1993–; Pres. of Lithuania 1998–2002, 2004–09; UNESCO Goodwill Amb. for the Construction of Knowledge Socs 2003–; mem. Club of Madrid; Hon. mem. The Int. Raoul Wallenberg Foundation; Grand Cross of the Order of Falcon (Iceland) 1998, Grand Cross of the Order of St Olof (Norway) 1998, First Class, Order of Yaroslav the Wise (Ukraine) 1998, Collar and Grand Cross of the Order of Mary's Land (Estonia) 1999, Grand Cross of the Order of the Saviour (Greece) 1999, Class Collar and Grand Cross of the Order for Service (Italy) 1999, Order of the White Eagle (Poland) 1999, Grand Cross of the Order for Service (Malta) 1999, Grand Cross of the Order for Service (Hungary) 1999, Grand Cross of the Order of Friendship (Kazakhstan) 2000, Collar and Grand Cross of the Order of Three Stars (Latvia) 2001, Grand Cross, Légion d'honneur 2001, Collar of the Order of the Star of Romania 2001, Order of St Meshrop Mashtots (Armenia) 2002, Collar and Grand Cross of the Order of the White Rose (Finland) 2002, Order of Special Merit (Uzbekistan) 2002, Order of Vytautas the Great with Golden Collar 2003, Golden Collar and Grand Cross of the Order of the White Star (Estonia) 2004, Order of

Isabel the Catholic with Collar (Spain) 2005, Special Class of the Grand Cross of the Order for Service (Germany) 2005, Grand Cross of the Order of Leopold (Belgium) 2006, Grand Cross, Order of the Bath (UK) 2006, First Class of the Order for Merits (Ukraine) 2006, Order 'Mother Theresa' (Albania) 2007, Grand Cordon of the Supreme Order of the Chrysanthemum (Japan) 2007, St George's Victory Order (Georgia) 2007, Grand Cross of the Order of the Lion (Netherlands) 2008, Collar of the Order of the Merit (Chile) 2008, Grand Star of the Decoration for Services to the Repub. 2009, Order of Stara Planina (Bulgaria) 2009; Dr hc (Vilnius) 1989, (Indiana St Joseph Coll.) 1991, (Northwestern Univ.) 1994, (Kaunas, American Catholic Univs) 1998, (Lithuanian Agricultural Univ., Illinois Inst. of Tech.) 1999, (Lev Gumilev Euro-Asian Univ. Kazakhstan) 2000, (De Paul Univ., Chicago, Law Univ. of Lithuania) 2001, (Vytautas Magnus Univ., Lithuania) 2002, (Lithuanian Acad. of Physical Educ.) 2004, (Yerevan State Univ., Armenia, Baku State Univ., Azerbaijan) 2006, (Donetsk Univ., Ukraine) 2006, (Univ. of Notre Dame, USA) 2007, Nicolaus Copernicus Univ., Poland) 2007, Tallinn Univ., Estonia) 2008, (Univ. of Chile) 2008, (Klaipėda Univ.) 2008, John Paul II Catholic Univ., Poland) 2009; ISM Univ. of Man. and Econs) 2009; Pres.'s Award for Distinguished Fed. Civilian Service 1985, Gold Medal, US Environment Protection Agency, US Distinguished Service Award, Int. Environmental Award 1988, St Andrew 'Dialogue of Civilisation' Prize Laureate (Russia) 2002, European of the Year 2007. *Website:* www.adamkus.lt.

ADAMS, Amy; American actress; b. 20 Aug. 1974, Vicenza, Italy; d. of Richard Adams and Kathryn Adams (née Hicken); one d. with Darren Legallo; began performing career as dancer, Boulder's Dinner Theatre and Country Dinner Playhouse, Minneapolis. *Films:* Drop Dead Gorgeous 1999, Psycho Beach Party 2000, The Chromium Hook (short) 2000, Cruel Intentions 2 2000, The Slaughter Rule 2002, Pumpkin 2002, Serving Sara 2002, Catch Me if You Can 2002, The Last Run 2004, Junebug (Nat. Soc. of Film Critics Award for Best Supporting Actress, San Francisco Film Critics Circle Award for Best Supporting Actress, Southeastern Film Critics Asscn Award for Best Supporting Actress) 2005, The Wedding Date 2005, Standing Still 2005, Talladega Nights: The Ballad of Ricky Bobby 2006, Pennies (short) 2006, Tenacious D in The Pick of Destiny 2006, The Ex 2006, Underdog (voice) 2007, Enchanted (Saturn Award for Best Actress) 2007, Charlie Wilson's War 2007, Sunshine Cleaning 2008, Miss Pettigrew Lives for a Day 2008, Doubt 2008, Night at the Museum 2 2009, Julie & Julia 2009, Moonlight Serenade 2009, Leap Year 2010, Love & Distrust 2010, The Fighter (Detroit Film Critics Soc. Award for Best Supporting Actress, Las Vegas Film Critics Soc. Award for Best Supporting Actress) 2010, The Muppets 2011, On the Road 2012, The Master 2012, Trouble with the Curve 2012, Man of Steel 2013, American Hustle (Golden Globe Award for Best Actress in a Motion Picture, Comedy or Musical, Screen Actors Guild Award for Outstanding Performance by a Cast in a Motion Picture 2014) 2013, Lullaby 2014, Big Eyes 2014. *Television:* The Peter Principle (film) 2000, That '70s Show (series) 2000, Charmed (series) 2000, Zoe, Duncan, Jack & Jane (series) 2000, Providence (series) 2000, Buffy the Vampire Slayer (series) 2000, Smallville (series) 2001, The West Wing (series) 2002, King of the Hill (series) 2004, Dr. Vegas (series) 2004, The Office (series) 2005. *Address:* Brillstein-Grey Entertainment, 9150 Wilshire Blvd, Suite 350, Beverly Hills, CA 90212, USA (office). *Telephone:* (310) 275-6135 (office). *Fax:* (310) 275-6180 (office).

ADAMS, Bryan, OC; Canadian/British rock singer, songwriter, musician (guitar) and photographer; b. 5 Nov. 1959, Kingston, Ont.; numerous world-wide tours; 15 Juno Awards, Recording Artist of the Decade, Canada, Grammy Award, American Music Award, Gov.-Gen's Performing Arts Award for Lifetime Artistic Achievement 2010. *Recordings:* albums: Bryan Adams 1980, You Want It You Got It 1981, Cuts Like A Knife 1983, Reckless 1984, Into The Fire 1987, Waking Up The Neighbours 1991, So Far So Good 1992, Live! Live! Live! 1995, 18 'Til I Die 1996, MTV Unplugged 1987, On A Day Like Today 1998, The Best Of Me 2000, Spirit: Stallion of Cimarron (film soundtrack) 2002, Room Service 2004, 11 2008, Bare Bones 2010. *Publications:* Bryan Adams: The Official Biography 1995, Made in Canada (photographs by Bryan Adams). *Address:* The Leighton-Pope Organisation, 8 Glenthorne Mews, 115a Glenthorne Road, Hammersmith, London, W6 0LJ, England (office); 425 Carrall Street, Suite 520, Vancouver, BC V6B 6E3, Canada (office). *Telephone:* (20) 8741-4453 (office). *Fax:* (20) 8741-4289 (office). *E-mail:* info@l-po.com (office); info@bryanadams.com (office). *Website:* www.bryanadams .com.

ADAMS, Gerry; Northern Irish politician and author; *President, Sinn Féin;* b. 6 Oct. 1948, Falls Road, Belfast; s. of the late Gerry Adams, Sr and of Annie Hannaway; m. Colette McCardle 1971; three c.; ed St Mary's Christian Brothers School, Belfast; worked as a barman; Founder-mem. NI Civil Rights Asscn; mem. Belfast Housing Action Cttee; interned in Long Kesh under suspicion of being a terrorist March 1972; released to take part in secret London talks between Sec. of State for NI and Irish Republican Army (IRA) July 1972; re-arrested 1973, attempted to escape from Maze Prison, sentenced to 18 months' imprisonment, released Feb. 1977; charged with membership of Provisional IRA Feb. 1978, freed after seven months because of insufficient evidence for conviction; Vice-Pres. Sinn Féin 1978–83, Pres. 1983–; MP for Belfast West 1983–92, 1997–2011; mem. NI Ass. for Belfast West 1998–2010 (Ass. suspended 11 Feb. 2000 and 14 Oct. 2002); involved in peace negotiations with British Govt 1988–94; TD for Louth 2011–; Thorr Award, Switzerland 1995. *Publications:* Falls Memory 1982, The Politics of Irish Freedom 1986, A Pathway to Peace 1988, Cage 11 (autobiog.) 1990, Who Fears to Speak. . .? 1991 (revised edn 2001), The Street and Other Stories 1993, Selected Writings 1994, Free Ireland: Towards a Lasting Peace 1995, Our Day Will Come (autobiog.) 1996, Before the Dawn (autobiog.) 1996, An Irish Voice 1997, An Irish Journal 2001, Hope and History 2003, A Farther Shore 2005, The New Ireland: A Vision For The Future 2008, An Irish Eye 2007. *Address:* Leinster House, Kildare Street, Dublin 2, Ireland (office). *Telephone:* (1) 6184442 (office). *Fax:* (1) 6184210 (office). *E-mail:* gerry.adams@oireachtas.ie (office). *Website:* www .sinnfein.ie (office).

ADAMS, John Coolidge; American composer and conductor; b. 15 Feb. 1947, Worcester, MA; ed Harvard Univ.; appearances as clarinettist and conductor; Head, Composition Dept, San Francisco Conservatory of Music 1971–81; Adviser on new music, San Francisco Symphony Orchestra 1978–82, Composer-in-Residence 1982–85; conducted Nixon in China at 1988 Edinburgh Festival; Creative Adviser, St Paul Chamber Orchestra, MN 1988–89; The Death of

Klinghoffer premiered at Brussels, Lyon and Vienna 1991 (London premiere at Barbican Hall 2002); I Was Looking at the Ceiling performed at Berkeley, New York, Paris, Edinburgh and Hamburg 1995; Artistic Advisor, Los Angeles Philharmonic Orchestra 2009–; Guggenheim Fellowship 1982, Fellow, BAC&S 2005; Grawemeyer Award for Music Composition 1995, Opera News Award 2008, Nat. Endowment for the Arts Opera Award 2009. *Films:* as composer: Io sono l'amore 2009. *Compositions include:* opera: Nixon in China 1987, The Death of Klinghoffer 1991, I Was Looking at the Ceiling and Then I Saw the Sky 1995; orchestral works: Shaker Loops 1978, Common Tones in Simple Time 1979, Harmonium 1980, Grand Pianola Music 1981–82, Harmonielehre 1984–85, The Chairman Dances 1985, Short Ride in a Fast Machine 1986, Tromba Lontana 1986, Fearful Symmetries 1988, The Wound-Dresser 1989, Eros Piano 1989, El Dorado 1991, Violin Concerto 1993, Gnarly Buttons 1996, A Flowering Tree 2008; chamber and ensemble works: Christian Zeal and Activity 1973, China Gates 1977, Phrygian Gates 1977, Chamber Symphony 1992, John's Book of Alleged Dances 1994, Road Movies 1995, Naïve and Sentimental Music 1998, El Niño 2000, Guide to Strange Places 2001, On the Transmigration of Souls (Pulitzer Prize for Music 2003, Grammy Awards for Best Classical Album, Best Orchestral Performance, Best Classical Contemporary Composition 2005, Classical BRIT Award for Contemporary Music 2005) 2002, Doctor Atomic Symphony (British Composer Award for Best Int. Composition 2009) 2005, The Dharma at Big Sur 2003, My Father Knew Charles Ives (Classical BRIT Award for Contemporary Composer 2007) 2003, Son of Chamber Symphony 2007. *Recording:* Doctor Atomic (Grammy Award for Best Opera Recording 2012). *Publication:* Hallelujah Junction (autobiog.) 2008. *Address:* c/o Jane Brown, Harrison Parrott, 5–6 Albion Court, London, W6 0QT, England (office). *Telephone:* (20) 7229-9166 (office). *Fax:* (20) 7221-5042 (office). *E-mail:* info@harrisonparrott.co.uk (office). *Website:* www.harrisonparrott .co.uk (office); www.earbox.com.

ADAMS, Kirby, MBA; American/Australian steel industry executive; b. Atlanta, Ga; ed Auburn Univ., Univ. of Virginia; Head of Strategy, Armco Inc., Nat. Supply Div., Houston, Tex. 1979–81; series of roles heading operating divs and leading planning, strategy, M&A, and restructuring, including acquisition and spin off of TIMET, NL Industries Inc., Houston and New York City 1981–89; Pres. and CEO Titanium Metals Corpn Inc. (TIMET), Pittsburgh/Denver 1989–95; Pres. and CEO BHP Ltd, Melbourne, Australia 1995–99, Founding Man. Dir and CEO BHP Steel, Melbourne, Australia 2000–02, Pres. BHP Service Cos, Exec. Gen. Man., Corp. Strategy and Business Devt; Sr Man., BlueScope Steel, Melbourne, Australia 2002–07, led BlueScope Steel through demerger from BHP-Billiton and an IPO; CEO Corus Group PLC, UK 2009–10, mem. Exec. Cttee and Bd Tata Steel Europe Ltd and Tata Steel Ltd; mem. Bd Business Council of Australia 2002–07; mem. Int. Iron and Steel Inst. 2000–07 (fmr Chair. and Vice-Chair.); fmr Chair. Titanium Devt Asscn; cr. Indian jt venture with Tata Steel 2006; mem. Bd of Dirs TTR (Trans-Tasman Resources Ltd) 2012–; IISI Silver Medal for steel industry safety leadership. *Leisure interests:* swimming, skiing, physical fitness, travel, architecture. *Fax:* (20) 7717-4455 (office).

ADAMS, Paul Nicholas, BA; British business executive; *Chief Executive, British American Tobacco PLC;* b. 12 March 1953, Manchester; s. of Peter Charles Adams and Joan Adams; m.; one s. two d.; ed Culford School and Ealing Coll.; began career with Shell UK; Marketing Dir Beecham Int. 1983–86; Vice-Pres. of Marketing for Europe, Pepsi-Cola Int. 1986–91; also Man. Dir Pepsi Cola de France and Area Vice-Pres. for Scandinavia; joined British American Tobacco PLC 1991, Regional Dir for Asia Pacific 1991–99, for Europe 1999–2001, Man. Dir 2002–03, Chief Exec. 2004–11; mem. Exec. Cttee Transatlantic Business Dialogue, Trilateral Comm.; Founding mem. Global Business Leaders Alliance Against Counterfeiting. *Leisure interests:* family, theatre, rugby, shooting. *Address:* British American Tobacco PLC, Globe House, 4 Temple Place, London, WC2R 2PG, England (office). *Telephone:* (20) 7845-1936 (office). *Fax:* (20) 7845-2184 (office). *E-mail:* info@bat .com (office). *Website:* www.bat.com (office).

ADAMS, Phillip Andrew, AO, AM, FAHA, FRSA; Australian writer, broadcaster and filmmaker; b. 12 July 1939; m. 1st (divorced); three d.; m. 2nd Patrice Newell; one d.; ed Eltham High School; columnist and critic 1956–; Chair. Film, Radio and TV Bd 1972–75; Founder-mem. Australia Council 1972–75; Vic. Govt Rep., Australian Children's TV Foundation 1981–87; Pres. Vic. Council for Arts 1982–86; Chair. Australian Film Inst. 1975–80, Australian Film Comm. 1983–90, Comm. for the Future 1985–90, Nat. Australia Day Council 1992–96; Foundation Chair., Australian Centre for Social Innovation 2009–; mem. Bd Ausflag 1990–, Cttee for the Centenary of Fed. 1994; worked with Families in Distress 1985–, Montsalvat Artists' Soc. 1986–, CARE Australia 1995–97; Sr ANZAC Fellow 1981; mem. Bd Nat. Museum of Australia 1996–97, Festival of Ideas 1999; mem. Council, Adelaide Festival 1996; Hon. Fellow 2008; Hon. DUniv (Griffith Univ.) 1998, (Univ. of South Australia) 2004; Hon. DLitt (Edith Cowan Univ.) 2003, (Univ. of Sydney), (Macquarie Univ.) 2013; Raymond Longford Award 1981, Australian Arts Award 1987, Australian Humanist of the Year 1987, CSICOP Award for Responsibility in Media (New York) 1996, Australian Republican of the Year 2006, Human Rights and Equal Opportunity Comm. Human Rights Medal 2006. *Films include:* Jack and Jill: A Postscript 1970, The Naked Bunyip 1971, The Adventures of Barry McKenzie 1972, Don's Party 1975, The Getting of Wisdom 1976, Grendel Grendel Grendel 1980, We of the Never Never 1982, Lonely Hearts 1982, Fighting Back 1983. *Radio includes:* Compere, Late Night Live (ABC). *Television includes:* Death and Destiny, Short and Sweet (ABC), Adams' Australia (ABC), The Big Question, Face the Press (SBS). *Publications include:* Adams With Added Enzymes 1970, The Unspeakable Adams 1977, More Unspeakable Adams 1979, The Uncensored Adams 1981, The Inflammable Adams 1983, Adams Versus God 1985, Harold Cazneaux: The Quiet Observer (with H. Ennis) 1994, Classic Columns 1994, The Penguin Book of Australian Jokes (with P. Newell) 1994, The Penguin Book of Jokes from Cyberspace (with P. Newell) 1995, The Big Questions (with P. Davies) 1996, The Penguin Book of More Australian Jokes 1996, Kookaburra 1996, Emperors of the Air 1997, Retreat from Tolerance? 1997, More Big Questions (with P. Davies) 1998, The Penguin Book of Schoolyard Jokes (with P. Newell) 1998, A Billion Voices 1999, The Penguin Book of All New Australian Jokes (with P. Newell) 2000, Adams Ark 2004, Adams vs. God: The Rematch 2007, Backstage Politics 2011, Bedtime Stories 2012, Tales From My 21 Years at RN's Late Night Live 2012. *Leisure* *interests:* archaeology, reading. *Address:* c/o Radio National, ABC, GPO Box 9994, Sydney, NSW 2001, Australia (office). *E-mail:* philadams@ozemail.com.au (home).

ADAMS, Richard George, MA, FRSA, FRSL; British novelist; b. 9 May 1920, Newbury, Berks., England; s. of Dr E. G. B. Adams, FRCS and Lilian Rosa Adams (née Button); m. Barbara Elizabeth Acland 1949; two d.; ed Bradfield Coll., Berks. and Worcester Coll., Oxford; army service 1940–46; Home Civil Service 1948–74; Pres. Royal Soc. for the Prevention of Cruelty to Animals 1980–82; Writer-in-Residence, Univ. of Florida, USA 1975, Hollins Coll., Va, USA 1976; Carnegie Medal 1972, Guardian Award for Children's Fiction 1972, Medal of California Young Readers' Asscn 1977. *Publications include:* Watership Down 1972 (filmed 1974), Shardik 1974, Nature Through the Seasons, The Tyger Voyage 1976, The Plague Dogs 1977 (filmed 1982), The Ship's Cat 1977, Nature Day and Night 1978, The Girl in a Swing 1980 (filmed 1988), The Unbroken Web (The Iron Wolf) 1980, Voyage Through the Antarctic 1982, Maia 1984, The Bureaucats 1985, A Nature Diary 1985, Occasional Poets: anthology (ed. and contrib.) 1986, The Legend of Te Tuna 1986, Traveller 1988, The Day Gone By (autobiography) 1990, Tales From Watership Down 1996, The Outlandish Knight 2000, Daniel 2006, Gentle Footprints 2010. *Leisure interests:* chess, ornithology, folk-song, country pursuits, fly-fishing, travel. *E-mail:* waterbow1920@gmail.com (office).

ADAMS, Robert McCormick, Jr, PhD; American anthropologist and academic; *Adjunct Professor, Department of Anthropology, University of California, San Diego;* b. 23 July 1926, Chicago, Ill.; s. of Robert McCormick Adams and Janet Adams (née Lawrence); m. Ruth Salzman Skinner 1953; one d.; ed Univ. of Chicago; Instructor, Univ. of Chicago 1955–57, Asst Prof. 1957–61, Assoc. Prof. 1961–62, Prof. 1962–84, Dir Oriental Inst. 1962–68, 1981–83, Prof. of Anthropology 1963, Dean of Social Sciences 1970–74, 1979–80, Univ. Provost 1982–84; Sec., Smithsonian Inst. 1984–94; Homewood Prof., Johns Hopkins Univ. 1984; Adjunct Prof., Univ. of Calif., San Diego 1993–; Chair. Ass. of Behavioral and Social Sciences, Nat. Research Council 1973–76; Visiting Prof., Harvard Univ. 1962, 1977, Univ. of California, Berkeley 1963; Annual Prof., Baghdad School, American Schools of Oriental Research 1966–67; Fellow, Inst. for Advanced Study, Berlin 1995–96; conducted field research in Iraq, Iran, Mexico, Saudi Arabia and Syria; Lewis Henry Morgan Prof., Univ. of Rochester 1965; Councillor, NAS 1981 (mem.); mem. American Acad. of Arts and Sciences, American Anthropological Asscn, AAAS, Middle East Studies Asscn, American Philosophical Soc., German Archaeological Inst.; Trustee, Nat. Opinion Research Center 1970–94, Nat. Humanities Center 1976–83, Russell Sage Foundation 1978–91, Santa Fe Inst. 1989–; Great Cross of Vasco Nuñez de Balboa (Panama) 1993; numerous hon. degrees; UCLA Medal 1989, Distinguished Service Award, Soc. for American Archaeology 1996. *Publications:* Land Behind Baghdad: A History of Settlement on the Diyala Plains 1965, The Evolution of Urban Society: Early Mesopotamia and Prehispanic Mexico (with H. J. Nissen) 1966, The Uruk Countryside 1972, Heartland of Cities (with N. J. Smelser and D. J. Treiman) 1981, Behavioral and Social Science Research: A National Resource (two vols) 1982, Paths of Fire 1996. *Leisure interests:* skiing, mountaineering. *Address:* University of California, San Diego, Department of Anthropology, 9500 Gilman Drive, La Jolla, CA 92093-0532 (office); PO Box ZZ, Basalt, CO 81621, USA. *Telephone:* (202) 965-0456 (home); (303) 927-3380 (home). *E-mail:* rmadams@ucsd.edu (office). *Website:* www.anthro.ucsd.edu (office).

ADANI, Gautam S.; Indian business executive; *Executive Chairman, Adani Group;* b. 24 June 1962, Ahmedabad; s. of Shantilal Adani and Shantaben Adani; m. Priti Adani; two s.; ed CN Vidyalay School, Ahmedabad; began career in diamond trade, Mahindra Bros, Mumbai 1978; f. plastics factory, Ahmedabad 1981; f. Adani Group 1988 with interests in commodities trading, power generation, coal mining and agric., currently Exec. Chair.; mem. Bd of Dirs Adani Energy Ltd, Adani Enterprises Ltd, Adani Petronet (Dahej) Port Pvt. Ltd, Adani Welspun Exploration Ltd, Adani Wilmar Ltd, Jain Int. Trade Org. Ltd; Chair. and Man. Dir Mundra Port and Special Econ. Zone Ltd; Excellence in Man. Award 2006. *Leisure interest:* yoga. *Address:* Adani House, Near Mithakhali Six Roads, Navarangpura, Ahmedabad 380 009 (office); Adani House, Plot No 83, Sector 32, Institutional Area, Gurgaon 122 001, India (office). *Telephone:* (79) 25555555 (Ahmedabad) (office). *Fax:* (79) 26565500 (Ahmedabad) (office). *Website:* www.adani.com (office).

ADCOCK, Fleur, OBE, CNZM, MA, FRSL; British writer; b. 10 Feb. 1934, Papakura, New Zealand; d. of Cyril John Adcock and Irene Robinson; m. 1st Alistair Teariki Campbell 1952 (divorced 1958); two s.; m. 2nd Barry Crump 1962 (divorced 1966); ed Victoria Univ., Wellington; Asst Lecturer, Univ. of Otago 1958, Asst Librarian 1959–61; with Alexander Turnbull Library 1962; with FCO 1963–79; freelance writer 1979–; Northern Arts Fellowship in Literature, Newcastle and Durham Univs 1979–81; Eastern Arts Fellowship, Univ. of East Anglia 1984; Writer-in-Residence, Univ. of Adelaide, NZ 1986; mem. Poetry Soc.; Festival of Wellington Poetry Award 1961, NZ State Literary Fund Award 1964, Buckland Award 1967, 1979, Jessie MacKay Award 1968, 1972, Cholmondeley Award 1976, NZ Nat. Book Award 1984, Arts Council Writers' Award 1988. *Publications:* The Eye of the Hurricane 1964, Tigers 1967, High Tide in the Garden 1971, The Scenic Route 1974, The Inner Harbour 1979, Below Loughrigg 1979, The Oxford Book of Contemporary New Zealand Poetry (ed.) 1982, Selected Poems 1983, The Virgin and the Nightingale: Medieval Latin Poems 1983, Hotspur: A Ballad for Music 1986, The Incident Book 1986, The Faber Book of 20th Century Women's Poetry 1987, Orient Express: Poems by Grete Tartler (trans.) 1989, Time Zones 1991, Letters from Darkness: Poems by Daniela Crasnaru (trans.) 1991, High Primas and the Archpoet (ed. and trans.) 1994, The Oxford Book of Creatures (ed. with Jacqueline Simms) 1995, Looking Back 1997, Poems 1960–2000 (Queen's Gold Medal for Poetry 2006) 2000, Dragon Talk 2010, Glass Wings 2013. *Address:* 14 Lincoln Road, London, N2 9DL, England. *Telephone:* (20) 8444-7881.

ADDIS, Richard James, MA; British journalist, newspaper editor, writer and entrepreneur; *Founder and CEO, The Day;* b. 23 Aug. 1956; s. of Richard Thomas Addis and Jane Addis; m. Eunice Minogue 1983 (divorced 2000); one s. two d.; two s. by Helen Slater; ed Rugby School, Downing Coll., Cambridge; Asst Ed. Evening Standard 1985–89; Deputy Ed. Sunday Telegraph 1989–91; Exec. Ed. Daily Mail 1991–95; Ed. Daily Express 1995–98, The Express on Sunday 1996–98; Ed. Mail on Sunday Review 1998–99; Ed. The Globe and Mail, Toronto 1999–2002; Ed. Financial Times Weekend 2002–06; Founder and Man. Dir Shakeup Media, London 2006; Founder and CEO The Day, London 2010–. *Leisure interests:*

dancing, tennis, elementary music-making, mountains. *Telephone:* 7899-968427 (mobile) (office). *E-mail:* richard@theday.co.uk (office). *Website:* www.theday.co.uk (office).

ADDISON, Mark Eric, CB, MA, MBA, PhD; British fmr civil servant; b. 22 Jan. 1951; s. of Sydney Robert James Addison and Prudence Margaret Addison (née Russell); m. Lucinda Clare Booth 1987; ed Marlborough Coll., St John's Coll., Cambridge, City Univ. and Imperial Coll., London; with Dept of Employment 1978–95, Pvt. Sec. to Parl. Under-Sec. of State 1982, Pvt. Sec. to Prime Minister 1985–88; Regional Dir London Training Agency 1988–91, Dir Finance and Resource Man. 1991–94; Dir Safety Policy Health and Safety Exec. 1994–97; Dir Better Regulation Unit, Office of Public Service 1997–98; Chief Exec. Crown Prosecution Service 1998–2001; Dir-Gen. Operations and Service Delivery, Dept for the Environment, Food and Rural Affairs 2001–05, Acting Perm. Sec. 2005, Interim Chief Exec. Rural Payments Agency 2006; Public Appointments Assessor; mem. Advisory Cttee on Business Appointments; Chair. Nursing and Midwifery Council; mem. Which? Council. *Leisure interests:* British motorbikes, our garden and wildflower meadow in Dorset. *Telephone:* 7788-190209 (mobile) (home). *E-mail:* mark@addisonbooth.com (home).

ADDO-KUFUOR, Kwame, MA, BChir, FRCP; Ghanaian politician and physician; b. 14 July 1940, Kumasi, Ashanti Region; ed Achimota School, Univ. Coll. Medical Hosp., London, Univ. of Cambridge and Middlesex Medical School Hosp., UK; worked at several hosps including W Suffolk Gen. Hosp., Edmonds, St Charles Hosp., London, Old Church Hosp., Essex, St Helier Hosp., London 1970s; fmr Medical Dir, Kufuor Clinic, Kumasi; fmr Inspector of Examinations for Final Bachelor of Medicine, Univ. of Ghana Medical School; fmr Chair. of Operations, Prisons Council of Ghana; elected MP (NPP—New Patriotic Party) for Manhyia, served on House Cttee, Health Cttee, Cttee on Selection; Chair. Cabinet Cttee on Governance; fmr Shadow Minister of Health; fmr Acting Minister of Interior; Minister of Defence 2001–07, of Interior 2008–09; Lecturer (part-time), Dept of Medicine, School of Medical Sciences (KNUST); fmr mem. NPP Nat. Council and Chair. Health Cttee; fmr Chair. Jesus Coll. Cambridge UN Students Asscn; fmr Pres. Ghana Medical Asscn; fmr Rep. for W Africa to Confed. of African Medical Asscns; Hon. Sec. Medical Students Asscn, Jesus Coll., Cambridge. *Publications:* Safe Motherhood in the Upper West Region of Ghana (Ed.); several articles in medical journals. *Leisure interests:* music, gardening, football, swimming, watching boxing. *Address:* 95 Obenesu Crescent, East Contonments, Accra, Ghana (home). *Telephone:* (21) 777797 (home). *Fax:* (21) 773951 (home).

ADEANG, David Waiau; Nauruan lawyer and politician; *Minister of Finance, Sustainable Development and Justice;* b. 1969; s. of Kennan Adeang (fmr Pres. of Nauru); MP for Ubenide constituency 2001–, Speaker of Parl. March–April 2008; Minister of Finance May–Aug. 2003, of Foreign Affairs and Justice June–Oct. 2004, of Foreign Affairs and Finance Oct. 2004–07, of Finance, Sustainable Devt and Justice 2013–; Founding mem. Naoero Amo (Nauru First Party). *Address:* Ministry of Finance, Government Offices, Yaren, Nauru (office). *Telephone:* 557-3133. *E-mail:* minister.finance@naurugov.nr.

ADEBAYO, Cornelius Olatunji; Nigerian academic and politician; b. 24 Feb. 1941, Oke-Onigbin, Kwara State; ed Barewa Coll., Zaria, Ahmadu Bello Univ., Zaria, Univ. of Ghana, Legon; Lecturer in English, Univ. of Ife (now Obafemi Awolowo Univ.) 1969–73; Founding Head, Dept of Humanities, Kwara State Coll. of Tech. (now Kwara State Polytechnic) 1973; Commr for Educ., later for Information and Econ. Devt, Kwara State 1975–78; Senator (Unity Party of Nigeria) 1979; Gov. of Kwara State 1983; mem. Nat. Democratic Coalition (NADECO, pro-democracy group) in 1990s, detained in Calabar Prison 1996, in exile in Canada 1996, served as Canada Rep. NADECO-Abroad 1998; Federal Minister of Communications 2003–06, of Works 2006, of Transport 2007, of Defence 2012. *Address:* c/o Ministry of Defence, Ship House, Central Area, Abuja, Nigeria (office).

ADEDEJI, Adebayo, Asiwaju of Ijebu and Olotu'fore of Ijebu-Ode, MPA, PhD; Nigerian economist; *Executive Director, African Centre for Development and Strategic Studies;* b. 21 Dec. 1930, Ijebu-Ode; s. of L. S. Adedeji; m. Susan Aderinola Ogun 1957 (died 2011); eight s. three d.; ed Ijebu-Ode Grammar School, Univ. Coll., Ibadan, Univ. Coll., Leicester and Harvard Univs; Asst Sec., Ministry of Econ. Planning, W Nigeria 1958–61, Prin. Asst Sec., Ministry of Finance, W Nigeria 1962–63; Deputy Dir Inst. of Admin, Univ. of Ife 1963–66, Dir 1967–71; Prof. of Public Admin, Univ. of Ife 1968–71; Nat. Manpower Bd 1967–71; Fed. Commr for Econ. Devt and Reconstruction 1971–75; Chair. Nat. Youth Service Corps 1973–75; UN Under-Sec.-Gen. and Exec. Sec. UN Econ. Comm. for Africa 1975–91, Founder and Exec. Dir African Centre for Devt and Strategic Studies (ACDESS) 1992–; Chair. Senate of UN Inst. for Namibia 1975; Founder and Ed., Quarterly Journal of Administration 1967–75; Fellow, Nigerian Inst. of Man., Nigerian Econ. Soc., African Acad. of Sciences, African Asscn for Public Admin and Man.; Pres. Nigerian Econ. Soc. 1971–72; Pres. African Asscn for Public Admin and Man. 1974–83; Vice-Chair. Asscn of Schools and Inst. of Admin of Int. Inst. of Admin. Sciences 1970–; Head of Commonwealth Observer Group for Kenya's gen. elections Dec. 2002; mem. Advisory Bd on Human Security, UN Trust Fund for Human Security; Hon. DLitt (Ahmadu Bello Univ.); Hon. LLD (Dalhousie Univ., Univ. of Calabar, Univ. of Zambia); Hon. DSc (Obafemi Awolowo Univ.); numerous foreign decorations and awards. *Publications:* A Survey of Highway Development in Western Nigeria 1960, Nigerian Administration and its Political Setting (ed.) 1969, Nigerian Federal Finance: Its Development, Problems and Prospects 1969, Local Government Finance in Nigeria: Problems and Prospects (co-ed.) 1972, Management Problems and Rapid Urbanisation in Nigeria (co-ed.) 1973, The Tanzania Civil Service, A Decade After Independence 1974, Developing Research on African Administration: Some Methodological Issues (co-ed.) 1974, Africa, The Third World and the Search for a New Economic Order 1977, Africa and the New International Economic Order: A Reassessment 1979, The Indigenization of the African Economy 1981, Economic Crisis in Africa: African Perspectives on Development Problems and Potentials (co-ed.) 1985, Towards the Dawn of the Third Millennium and the Beginning of the Twenty-First Century 1986, Towards a Dynamic African Economy: Selected Speeches and Lectures 1975–1986 1989, African Within the World 1993, South Africa and Africa: Within or Apart? 1996, Nigeria: Renewal from the Roots? 1997, Comprehending and Mastering African Conflicts 1999. *Leisure interests:* photography, lawn tennis, golf, walking. *Address:*

African Centre for Development and Strategic Studies, Obafemi Awolowo Way, POB 203, Molipa, Ijebu-Ode, Nigeria (office). *Telephone:* 37-432208 (office); 37-433000 (home). *Fax:* 1-269-1746 (office). *E-mail:* adebayo_adedeji@acdess.org (office).

ADELE, MBE; British singer and songwriter; b. (Adele Laurie Blue Adkins), 5 May 1988, London, England; ed BRIT School for Performing Arts and Tech.; professional solo artist 2008–; tours in UK, USA, Canada; worked with Jim Abiss, Eg White and Mark Ronson; recorded with the Raconteurs, sang with Burt Bacharach at BBC Electric Proms 2008; Critics' Choice Award, BRIT Awards 2008, BRIT Award for Best British Female Solo Artist 2012, Grammy Awards for Best Female Pop Vocal Performance 2008, for Best New Artist 2008, for Record of the Year 2012, for Song of the Year 2012, for Best Pop Solo Performance 2012, for Best Short Form Music Video 2012, for Best Pop Solo Performance 2013, for Best Song Written for Visual Media (for Skyfall) 2014 Songwriter of the Year, Ivor Novello Awards 2012, Ivor Novello Award for Most Performed Work of 2011 (for Rolling in the Deep) 2012, Golden Globe Award for Best Original Song in a Motion Picture (for Skyfall) 2013, Academy Award for Best Original Song (with Paul Epworth) (for Skyfall) 2013. *Television:* Ushi Says: Hi 2001, Saturday Night Live 2008, Ugly Betty 2009. *Recordings include:* albums: 19 2008, 21 (Grammy Awards for Album of the Year 2012, for Best Pop Vocal Album 2012, Mastercard British Album of the Year, BRIT Awards 2012, Billboard Music Award for Top Pop Album 2013) 2011. *Address:* c/o XL Recordings, 1 Codrington Mews, London, W11 2EH, England. *E-mail:* info@septembermanagement.com. *Website:* www.xlrecordings.com; www.adele.tv.

ADELI, Seyed Muhammad Hossein, PhD; Iranian economist, banker and diplomatist; *Chairman and CEO, Ravand Institute for Economic and International Studies;* b. 1952, Ahwaz; m. Khadijeh Aryan; two s. one d.; ed Tehran Business School, Univ. of Tehran, California Coast Univ., USA, Jamia Millia Islamia; temp. Attaché in Canada 1979–80, Dir-Gen. of Econ. Affairs, Ministry of Foreign Affairs 1982–86, Amb. to Japan 1987–89; Gov. Bank Markazi Iran (Cen. Bank of Iran) 1990–95; Amb. to Canada 1995–99, Deputy Minister for Econ. Affairs, Ministry of Foreign Affairs 1999–2004, Amb. to UK 2005; Founder, Chair. and CEO Ravand Inst. for Econ. and Int. Studies (think-tank), Tehran; Chair. Amin Investment Bank 2000–11. *Leisure interest:* reading. *Address:* Ravand Institute for Economic and International Studies, Unit 6-2, 1479 Jam Building, Vali-e Asr Avenue, Tehran, 19668-43116, Iran (office). *Telephone:* (21) 22019734 (office). *Fax:* (21) 22019735 (office). *E-mail:* contact@ravandinstitute.com (office). *Website:* www.ravandinstitute.com (office).

ADELMAN, Irma Glicman, BS, MA, PhD; American economist, academic and international consultant; *Professor Emerita of Economics and Agricultural and Resource Economics, University of California, Berkeley;* b. 14 March 1930, Romania; d. of the late Jacob Max Glicman and Raya Etingon; m. Frank Louis Adelman 1950 (divorced 1979); one s.; ed Univ. of Calif., Berkeley; Asst Prof., Stanford Univ. 1960–62; Assoc. Prof., Johns Hopkins Univ. 1962–66; Prof. of Econs, Northwestern Univ. 1967–72; Sr Economist, Devt Research Centre, IBRD 1971–72; Prof. of Econs, Univ. of Maryland 1972–79; Consultant, US Dept of State 1963–72, IBRD 1968–, ILO, Geneva 1973–; Fellow, Netherlands Inst. of Advanced Study, Cleveringa Chair, Leiden Univ. 1977–78; Prof. of Econs and Agric. and Resource Econs, Univ. of Calif., Berkeley 1979–94, Prof. Emer. 1994–; Vice-Pres. American Econ. Asscn 1979–80, Distinguished Fellow 2004; Fellow, American Acad. of Arts and Sciences, Econometric Soc., Royal Soc. for the Encouragement of the Arts, American Agricultural Econs Asscn; Order of the Bronze Tower (S Korea) 1971. *Publications:* Theories of Economic Growth and Development 1964, Society, Politics and Economic Development (with C. T. Morris) 1967, Economic Growth and Social Equity in Developing Countries (with C. T. Morris) 1973, Income Distribution Planning (with Sherman Robinson) 1978, Comparative Patterns of Economic Development: 1850–1914 (with C. T. Morris) 1988, Village Economies (with J. Edward Taylor) 1996, The Visible and Invisible Hand: The Case of Korea 2002. *Leisure interests:* art, theatre, music. *Address:* Agriculture and Resource Economics Department, 207 Giannini Hall, University of California at Berkeley, Berkeley, CA 94720-3310 (office); 10 Rosemont Avenue, Berkeley, CA 94708, USA (home). *Telephone:* (510) 642-6417 (office); (510) 527-5280 (home). *Fax:* (510) 643-8911. *E-mail:* adelman@are.berkeley.edu (office). *Website:* are.berkeley.edu/~adelman (office).

ADELMAN, Kenneth Lee, PhD; American lobbyist and fmr government official; b. 9 June 1946, Chicago, Ill.; s. of Harry Adelman and Corinne Unger; m. Carol Craigle 1971; two d.; ed Grinnell Coll., Georgetown Univ.; with US Dept of Commerce 1968–70; Special Asst, VISTA, Washington, DC 1970–72; Liaison Officer, AID 1975–76; Asst to Sec. of Defense 1975–77; Sr Political Scientist, Stanford Research Inst., Arlington, Va 1977–81; Amb. and Deputy Rep. to UN, New York 1981–83; Dir Arms Control and Disarmament Agency (ACDA) 1983–88; Vice-Pres. Inst. of Contemporary Studies 1988–; mem. Defense Policy Bd Advisory Cttee; Sr Counselor, Edelman Public Relations, Washington, DC; Co-Founder (with wife) Movers & Shakespeares (consultancy) 1997, currently Vice-Pres.; fmr Exec. Dir USA for Innovation; mem. Exec. Bd Noel Foundation; mem. Advisory Bd Princeton Review; Sec., Bd of Trustees, Freedom House; mem. Bd Shakespeare Theatre, Washington, DC; Instructor in Shakespeare, Georgetown Univ. 1977–79; taught at George Washington Univ.; Co-Host Tech Cen. Station. *Publications:* The Great Universal Embrace 1989, The Defense Revolution (with Norman Augustine) 1990, Shakespeare in Charge: The Bard's Guide to Leading and Succeeding on the Business Stage (with Norman Augustine) 1999, and articles in newspapers, magazines and professional journals. *Address:* Movers and Shakespeares, 4018 North 27th Street, Arlington, VA 22207, USA (office). *Telephone:* (703) 525-0100 (office). *Website:* www.moversandshakespeares.com (office).

ADELSOHN, Ulf, LLB; Swedish politician and business executive; b. 4 Oct. 1941, Stockholm; s. of Oskar Adelsohn and Margareta Adelsohn; m. Lena Liljeroth 1981; one s. one d.; legal adviser, Real Estate Co., Stockholm City 1968–70; Man.'s Asst, Swedish Confed. of Professional Asscns 1970–73; Commr, Street and Traffic Dept, Stockholm City Admin 1973–76; Mayor and Finance Commr 1976–79; Minister for Transport and Communications 1979–81; mem. Riksdagen (Parl.) 1982–88; Leader Moderata Samlingspartiet (Conservative Party) 1981–86; County Gov. of Stockholm 1992–2001; Chair. Luftfartsverket (Civil Aviation Authority)

1992–2002, Skansen (open air museum) 1998–2004; Chair. Swedish Railways 2002–11 (resgnd), Swedish Hotel and Restaurants Asscn 2001; Sr Adviser, Stockholm Chamber of Commerce, Ogilvy; King's Medal of the 12th Dimension with Ribbon of the Order of the Seraphims. *Publications:* Torsten Kreuger, Sanningen på väg (Torsten Kreuger, Truth on its Way) 1972, Kommunalmän: Hur skulle ni göra om det vore era egna pengar? (Local Politicians: What Would You Do If It Was Your Money?) 1978, Ulf Adelsohn Partiledare 1981–86 (Leader of the Party 1981–86) 1987, Priset för ett liv (The Price for a Life) 1991. *Leisure interests:* ice hockey, tennis.

ADEN, Fowsiyo Yusuf Haji; Somali politician; grew up in Somaliland (now self-declared ind. state), also lived in UK; politically active in Somaliland, including run for presidency; f. Nat. Democratic Party (NDP) (later banned); mem. Somaliland House of Reps 2003; following withdrawal of recognition of NDP decided to pursue political career in Somalia rather than Somaliland; Deputy Prime Minister and Minister of Foreign Affairs and Int. Cooperation (first woman) 2012–14. *Address:* c/o Ministry of Foreign Affairs and International Cooperation, 1 Villa Somalia, 2525 Mogadishu, Somalia.

ADENUGA, Mike, BSc, MBA; Nigerian business executive; *Chairman and CEO, Globacom Ltd;* b. 29 April 1953, Ijebu Igbo, Ogun; m.; seven c.; ed Northwestern Univ., Pace Univ., USA; Founder Chair. and CEO Globacom Ltd (mobile telecommunications network) 2003–; Chair. Conoil Plc; Owner, Equitorial Trust Bank Ltd (acquired by Sterling Bank Plc 2011), acquired majority shares in Sterling Bank Plc 2011; Officer, Order of the Niger, Commdr. Order of the Niger. *Leisure interests:* soccer. *Address:* Globacom Ltd., Mike Adenuga Towers, 1 Mike Adenuga Close, Off Adeola Odeku, Victoria Island, Lagos, Nigeria (office). *Telephone:* (805) 0020121 (office). *E-mail:* mikeadenuga@consultant.com. *Website:* www.gloworld.com (office).

ÁDER, János, DrIur; Hungarian politician and head of state; *President;* b. 9 May 1959, Csorna, Győr-Moson-Sopron Co.; m. Anita Herczegh; one s. three d.; ed Révai Miklós Grammar School, Győr, Eötvös Loránd Univ., Budapest; law clerk, Budapest Dist VI Council 1983–84; researcher, Inst. of Sociology, Hungarian Acad. of Sciences 1986–90; joined Fed. of Young Democrats (Fidesz) 1988, mem. Nat. Election Cttee 1989, campaign chief for 1990 parliamentary elections and for both parliamentary and local elections in 1994, Chair. Steering Cttee 1992–93, party Vice-Pres. 1993–2002, Exec. Vice-Pres. 1995–97, 1999–2000, 2001–02, Parl. Group Leader 2002–06; mem. Parl. 1990–98, Deputy Speaker of Nat. Ass. and mem. House Cttee 1997–98, 2006–12, Speaker, Nat. Ass. 1998–2002; mem. European Parl. 2009–12; Pres. of Hungary 2012–. *Leisure interests:* angling, soccer. *Address:* Office of the President, 1014 Budapest, Sándor-Palace, Szent György tér 1–2 (office); Office of the President, 1536 Budapest, Pf. 227, Hungary. *Telephone:* (1) 224-5000 (office). *Fax:* (1) 784-9181 (office). *E-mail:* ugyfelkapu@keh.hu (office). *Website:* keh.hu (office).

ADÈS, Thomas Joseph Edmund, MA, MPhil; British composer, pianist and conductor; b. 1 March 1971, London; s. of Timothy Adès and Dawn Adès; ed Univ. Coll. School, Guildhall School of Music, King's Coll., Cambridge, St John's Coll., Cambridge; solo recitalist with the Composers Ensemble 1992; PLG Young Concert Artists Platform concert at Purcell Room 1993; Composer-in-Assocn, Hallé Orchestra 1993–95; Lecturer, Univ. of Manchester 1993–94; Fellow Commoner in Creative Arts, Trinity Coll., Cambridge 1995–97; Benjamin Britten Prof. of Music, RAM 1997–99; Musical Dir Birmingham Contemporary Music Group 1998–2000; Artistic Dir Aldeburgh Festival 1999–2008; R. and B. Debs Composer Chair., Carnegie Hall, New York 2007–08; conducted the BBC Symphony Orchestra at BBC Proms; Lutine Prize, GSM 1986, winner Paris Rostrum, for best piece by composer under 30 1994, Royal Philharmonic Prize 1997, Elise L. Stoeger Prize 1996, Royal Philharmonic Soc. Award for Large-scale Composition 1997, 2005, Salzburg Easter Festival Prize 1999, Ernst von Siemens Prize 1999, Grawemeyer Prize 2000, Hindemith Prize 2001, ISCM Young Composers Award 2002, Musical America Award for Composer of the Year 2011. *Compositions include:* Five Eliot Landscapes 1990, Chamber Symphony 1990, Catch 1991, Darkness Visible 1992, Under Hamelin Hill 1992, Fool's Rhymes 1992, Still Sorrowing 1993, Life Story 1993, Living Toys 1993, ... but all shall be well 1993, Sonata da Caccia 1994, The Origin of the Harp 1994, Arcadiana 1994, Powder Her Face 1995, Traced Overhead 1995–96, These Premises are Alarmed 1996, Asyla 1997, Concerto Conciso 1997–98, America (A Prophecy) 1999, January Writ 1999, Piano Quintet 2000, Brahms 2001, The Tempest (Olivier Award for outstanding achievement in opera 2005, Royal Philharmonic Soc. award for large-scale composition 2005) 2004, Three Studies from Couperin 2006, Tevot (Royal Philharmonic Soc. Award for large-scale composition) 2007, The Four Quarters (British Composer Award for Best Chamber Music 2012). *Television includes:* Music for the 21st Century: Thomas Adès (Channel 4), Powder her Face (Channel 4). *Address:* c/o Faber Music Ltd, 74–77 Great Russell Street, London, WC1B 3DA, England (office). *Telephone:* (20) 7908-5310 (office). *Fax:* (20) 7908-5339 (office). *E-mail:* information@fabermusic.com (office). *Website:* www.fabermusic.com (office).

ADESIDA, Ilesanmi, BS, MS, PhD, FIEEE; American (b. Nigerian) electrical engineer, academic and university administrator; *Vice Chancellor for Academic Affairs and Provost, University of Illinois at Urbana-Champaign;* ed Univ. of California, Berkeley; worked briefly at Cornell Univ. and then as univ. admin. in Nigeria; joined Faculty, Univ. of Illinois at Urbana-Champaign 1987, currently Donald Biggar Willett Prof. of Eng, Dept of Electrical and Computer Eng, Researcher, Beckman Inst. for Advanced Science and Tech. and at Coordinated Science Lab., also Dir Center for Nanoscale Science and Tech., fmr Dir Micro and Nanotechnology Lab., Interim Dean, Coll. of Eng 2005–06, Dean 2005–12, Vice-Chancellor for Academic Affairs and Provost, Univ. of Illinois 2012–; mem. Bd of Dirs FLUOR Corpn 2007–; mem. Nat. Acad. of Eng, Minerals, Metals and Materials Soc., Materials Research Soc., Soc. for Eng Educ.; Fellow, IEEE, AAAS, American Vacuum Soc., Optical Soc. of America; fmr Pres. IEEE Electron Devices Soc.; attained US citizenship 2002. *Publications:* numerous scientific papers in professional journals on applications of advanced semiconductor processing and in manufacturing of high-speed microelectronic devices and circuits. *Address:* Office of the Provost, University of Illinois, 217 Swanlund Administration Building, 601 East John Street, Champaign, IL 61820, USA (office). *Telephone:* (217) 244-4545 (office). *Fax:* (217) 244-5639 (office). *E-mail:* provost@illinois.edu (office); iadesida@illinois.edu (office). *Website:* mntl.illinois.edu/people/profile.asp?iadesida (office).

ADESINA, Segun, DEd; Nigerian professor of education; *Vice-President, African University Institute;* b. 5 Jan. 1941, Abeokuta, Ogun State; s. of Samuel Adesina and Georgiette Adesina; m. 1968; five c.; ed Loyola Coll., Nigerian Coll. of Arts, Science and Tech., Univ. of Ife and Northern Illinois and Columbia Univs, USA; history tutor, Loyola Coll. 1965–66; Asst Lecturer in Educ., Univ. of Lagos Coll. of Educ. 1967–69, Lecturer 1969–75; Sr Lecturer, Univ. of Lagos Faculty of Educ. 1975–77, Assoc. Prof. 1977–78, Prof. of Educ. 1988–2000, now Dir Inst. of Educ.; fmr Prof. of Educ., Ilorin Univ.; Visiting Prof. and Provost, Univ. of Ife, Adeyemi Coll. of Educ., Ondo 1984–85; Exec. Sec. Nigerian Educational Research Council 1987; Adviser on Educ. UN Office, Geneva 1975–76; consultant, UNESCO, Senegal 1984; Vice-Pres. African Univ. Inst., Imeko, Ogun State 2005–; Fellow, Nigerian Inst. of Admin. Man.; Assoc., Inst. of Personnel Man.; mem. Nigerian Inst. of Man., Presidential Cttee on Brain Drain; Obamoyegun of Ondo; Bajiki of Afon; Okonomo of Imeko. *Publications:* Primary Education in Nigeria: A Book of Readings, Planning and Educational Development in Nigeria (co-ed.) 1978, The Development of Modern Education in Nigeria 1988, Growth Without Development: Nigeria's Educational Experience 1914–2004 2006, Universal Basic Education in Nigeria: Prospects and Challenges 2007. *Leisure interest:* Gospel music. *Address:* PO Box 41, Abeokuta, Nigeria (home). *Telephone:* (803) 5638515 (mobile) (office); (39) 232226 (home); (803) 4388120 (mobile) (home).

ADESOLA, Akin Oludele, MD, MCh, FRCS (Eng), FACS; Nigerian physician and academic; b. 6 Nov. 1930, Aba, Nigeria; s. of Bamgboye F. Adesola and Felicia A. Adesola; m. Oyebola Sodeinde 1959; two d.; ed Abeokuta Grammar School, Univ. of Ibadan, Queen's Univ., Belfast, Royal Coll. of Surgeons of England, Univ. of Rochester, USA; surgical tutor, Queen's Univ. Belfast 1959–61; Sr Buswell Fellow, Univ. of Rochester, New York, USA 1963–64; Prof. of Surgery, Univ. of Lagos 1967–88, Vice-Chancellor 1981–88, Prof. Emer. 2001–; Vice-Chancellor Univ. of Ilorin 1978–81; Pres. W Africa Soc. of Gastroenterology 1967–72, Nigerian Surgical Research Soc. 1975–79, W Africa Coll. of Surgeons 1975–77; Chair. Nat. Orthopaedic Hosps Man. Bd 1977–78, Health Educ. Research and Man. Services 1989, Bd of Trustees W African Coll. of Surgeons 1991, Nat. Cttee on Medical Care and Training 1991; Chair. Asscn of Commonwealth Univs 1984–85, Nat. Bd of Dirs, Leadership for Environment and Development (LEAD) Int. Inc. 1998; mem. Albert Schweitzer Int. Nomination Council 1984–, Commonwealth Expert Group on Distance Educ. 1986–88; Fellow, Nigerian Acad. of Science 1986–; Consultant on Higher Educ. to IBRD 1988, to Canadian Int. Devt Agency 1988; Ed. Nigerian Medical Journal 1970–80; mem. editorial Bd British Journal of Surgery 1968–80; mem. Expert Panel Comm. on Commonwealth Studies, Commonwealth Secr. 1995, Rockefeller Foundation, New York 1996–; Dir Imperial Coll. London, UK 2000–; Hon. LLD (Queen's Univ. Belfast) 1989; Symons Medal for Distinguished Service to Commonwealth Univs 1987, Distinguished Visitor Award, Carnegie Corpn of New York 1988, Adesuyi Prize for Outstanding Contributions to Health in West Africa (West African Health Community) 1993. *Publications:* Coronary Thrombosis: The Influence of Meterological Changes 1960, Hyperparathyroidism and the Alimentary Tract 1960, Adult Intussusception in Western Nigeria 1964, Influence of Vasoactive Agents on Ascites 1965, Chronic Gastritis and Duodenal Ulcer in Nigerians 1974, Endoscopy in Upper Gastrointestinal Disease in Nigerians 1978, Technology in a Developing Economy 1983, The Nigerian University System: Meeting the Challenges of Growth in a Depressed Economy 1991, Anatomy of Service 1997, Nigerian Universities and a Nation in Crisis 1999, The State of Education in Nigeria – An Overview 2000, A Bridge Endowed (autobiography) 2007. *Leisure interests:* golf, swimming, music. *Address:* 1 Ajani Olujare Street, Surulere, POB 51218, Falomo-Ikoyi, Lagos, Nigeria. *Telephone:* (1) 583-4470. *Fax:* (1) 583-4470. *E-mail:* akinadesola@nigol.net.ng (home).

ADEWOYE, Omoniyi, PhD; Nigerian academic and fmr politician; b. 27 Oct. 1939, Inisa, Osun State; s. of the late Chief James Woye and Victoria Fadunke Woye; m. Margaret Titilayo 1967; five d.; ed Kiriji Memorial Coll., Igbajo, Univ. of Ibadan, Univ. of London, UK, Columbia Univ., USA; Lecturer in History, Univ. of Ibadan 1968–75, Sr Lecturer 1975, Prof. of History 1984–2000, Vice-Chancellor 1996–2000, Prof. Emer. 2005–; Commr for Econ. Devt, Western State 1975–76; Commr for Finance and Econ. Devt, Oyo State 1976–77; Fed. Commr for Econ. Devt 1977–79; First Chair. Council of Ministers, Econ. Community of W African States 1977–78; Chair. Council of Ministers, Nigerian–Niger Jt Comm. 1977–78; Consultant to Econ. Comm. for Africa on Econ. Integration in W Africa 1982–83; Hon. Treas. Historical Soc. of Nigeria 1972–77; Woodrow Wilson Dissertation Scholarship (Columbia Univ.) 1967, Afgrad Fellowship (USA) 1964–68; Chair. Bd of Fellows, Osun Anglican Community 2005–; Order of the Federal Republic of Nigeria 2006. *Publications include:* The Legal Profession in Nigeria 1865–1962 1977, The Judicial System in Southern Nigeria 1854–1954 1977, Law and the Management of Change 2003; numerous articles on law and development in Africa. *Leisure interests:* gardening, reading, writing, music. *Address:* University of Ibadan, PO Box 7321, Ibadan, Nigeria. *Telephone:* 806019706 (office); 8042117560 (home). *E-mail:* omoniyiadewoye@yahoo.com.

ADEY, Christopher, FRAM, FRCM, FRWCMD; British conductor; b. 19 Feb. 1943, London; m. Catherine Cave 1964 (divorced 1985); one s.; ed Royal Acad. of Music, London; violinist with Hallé Orchestra 1963–65, London Philharmonic Orchestra 1967–71; Assoc. Conductor, BBC Scottish Symphony Orchestra 1973–76, Ulster Orchestra 1981–83; Conductor and Prof., Royal Coll. of Music (RCM) 1979–92, Dir of Orchestral Studies, RCM Jr Dept 1973–84; Principal Conductor, Nat. Youth Orchestra of Wales 1996–2002; Chief Conductor and Artistic Dir Royal Oman Symphony Orchestra 2000–04; Conductor in Residence, Wells Cathedral School 2001–; also currently Principal Guest Conductor, Orchestra of the Music Makers, Singapore; Hon. Vice-Pres. Welsh Music Guild; Commemorative Medal of Czechoslovakian Govt 1986. *Publication:* Orchestral Performance: A Guide for Conductors and Players 1998. *Address:* Performing Arts, 6 Windmill Street, London, W1T 2IB, England (office); 137 Anson Road, Willesden Green, London, NW2 4AH, England (home). *E-mail:* info@performing-arts.co.uk (office).

ADHANOM GHEBREYESUS, Tewedros, BSc, MSc, PhD; Ethiopian immunologist and politician; *Minister of Foreign Affairs;* m.; four s. one d.; ed Asmara Univ., Univ. of London, Univ. of Nottingham, UK; fmr Head, Tigray Regional Health Bureau; served in various technical posts in Ministry of Health, becoming Minister of State for Health 2004–05, Minister of Health 2005–12; Minister of Foreign Affairs 2012–; Chair. Fourth Conf. of Ministers of Health of the African Union 2009–; fmr Chair. Global Fund Against AIDS, Tuberculosis and Malaria 2009–11, Roll Back Malaria, UNAIDS Programme Coordination Board 2009; Co-Chair. Partnership for Maternal, Newborn and Child Health 2005–09; fmr Chair. Bd of Dirs Addis Ababa Univ.; mem. High Level Taskforce on Innovative Int. Financing for Health Systems 2009; fmr mem. Bd Global Alliance for Vaccines and Immunization; co-f. (with Yale Univ. Global Health Leadership Inst.) Ethiopian Hospital Alliance for Quality 2011; Del. Harvard School of Public Health Forum 2012; American Soc. of Tropical Medicine and Hygiene Young Investigator Award 1999, Ethiopian Public Health Asscn Young Researcher Award 2003, Jimmy and Rosalynn Carter Humanitarian Award 2011, Yale Univ. Stanley T. Woodward Lectureship 2012. *Address:* Ministry of Foreign Affairs, POB 393, Addis Ababa, Ethiopia (office). *Telephone:* (11) 5517345 (office). *Fax:* (11) 5514300 (office). *E-mail:* mfa.addis@telecom.net.et (office). *Website:* www.mfa.gov.et (office).

ADHIKARI, Ram Prashad, MCom; Nepalese banking executive; b. Saping, Kabhrepalanchok; worked in Nepal Rastra Bank for 30 years, worked as Chief Man. at various branch offices as well as in FOREX Div., becoming Exec. Dir Research Dept (retd); Sr Economist, South East Asian Central Banks (SEACEN) Centre, Kuala Lumpur, Malaysia 1997–2000; Chair. Rastriya Banijya Bank, Kathmandu 2009–11, apptd Man. Dir 2011. *Publications include:* Fiscal Consolidation in the SEACEN Countries, Economic Interdependence Among the Asian Countries; has published several articles on foreign exchange, foreign trade, govt finance and monetary policies. *Address:* c/o Office of the Chairman, Rastriya Banijya Bank, Central Office, PO Box 8368, Singha Durbar Plaza, Kathmandu, Nepal.

ADIE, Kathryn (Kate), OBE, BA; British journalist, broadcaster and author; b. 19 Sept. 1945; d. of Babe Dunnett (née Issit) and adopted d. of John Wilfrid Adie and Maud Adie (née Fambely); ed Sunderland Church High School, Univ. of Newcastle; technician and producer BBC Radio 1969–76; reporter BBC TV South 1977–78, BBC TV News 1979–81, corresp. 1982–89, Chief News Corresp. 1989–2003, presenter, From Our Own Correspondent, BBC Radio 4; freelance journalist, broadcaster and TV presenter 2003–; Visiting Fellow, Univ. of Bournemouth 1998–; Hon. Prof., Sunderland Univ. 1995; Hon. Fellow, Royal Holloway, Univ. of London 1996; Freeman of Sunderland 1990; Hon. MA (Bath) 1987, (Newcastle) 1990; Hon. DLitt (City Univ.) 1989, (Loughborough) 1991, (Sunderland) 1993, (Robert Gordon) 1996, (Nottingham) 1998, (Nottingham Trent) 1998; Hon. MUniv (Open Univ.) 1996; Royal Television Soc. News Award 1981, 1987, Monte Carlo Int. News Award 1981, 1990, BAFTA Richard Dimbleby Award 1989. *Publications:* The Kindness of Strangers (autobiog.) 2002, Corsets to Camouflage: Women and War 2003, Nobody's Child: The Lives of Abandoned Children 2005, Into Danger 2008. *Address:* POB 317, Brentford, London, TW8 8WX, England (office). *Telephone:* (20) 8838-2871 (office).

ADIKOESOEMO, Soegiarto; Indonesian business executive; *President Commissioner, AKR Corporindo Tbk;* b. 1938; m.; three c.; Founder AKR Corporindo Tbk, Pres. Dir 1982–92, Pres. Commr 1992–, also Pres. Commr PT Arthakencana Rayatama 1992–, PT Arjuna Utama Kimia 2007–, PT Andahanesa Abadi 2004–, PT AKR Niaga Indonesia 2012–; Chair. and Legal Rep. Khalista (Liuzhou) Chemical Industries Ltd 2004–; Pres. Dir/ Legal Counsel Guangxi (Guigang) AKR Container Port Co. Ltd 2006–, AKR (Guigang) Port Co. Ltd 2006–, AKR (Guigang) Transshipment Port Co. Ltd 2006–, AKR (Guangxi) Coal Trading Co. Ltd 2008–; Vice-Pres. Commr PT Sorini Towa Berlian Corporindo. *Address:* PT AKR Corporindo Tbk, Wisma AKR, Lt 7-8, Jl Panjang No 5, Kebon Jeruk, Jakarta, Indonesia (office). *Telephone:* (21) 5311588 (office). *Website:* www.akr.co.id (office).

ADING, Jack; Marshall Islands accountant and politician; *Minister of Finance;* b. 1 Sept. 1960, Ujelang Atoll; m. Luren Loeak; seven c.; ed Eastern Arizona Coll., USA, Hawaii Pacific Univ.; Accounting Technician, Sr Citizen Program, Marshall Islands Ministry of Social Services 1981–83; Accountant, Marshall Islands Housing Authority 1983–87; Asst to Chief of Housing and Home Improvement, Majuro 1987–89, Chief of Housing and Home Improvement 1989; Accountant, Pacific Resources for Educ. and Learning, Hawaii 1994–2006; Mem. Nitijela (Parl.) from Enewetak/Ujelang 2007–; Minister of Finance 2008–12, 2014–; mem. United People's Party (UPP). *Address:* Ministry of Finance, POB D, Majuro MH 96960, Marshall Islands (office). *Telephone:* (625) 3320 (office). *Fax:* (625) 3607 (office). *E-mail:* secfin@ntamar.net (office).

ADJAYE, David, OBE, MA; British/Tanzanian architect; *Principal, Adjaye Associates;* b. 1966, Dar-es-Salaam, Tanzania; ed Royal Coll. of Art; reformed studio as Adjaye/Associates 2000–; fmr Lecturer at RCA, Visiting Prof., Princeton Prof. School of Architecture, Louis Khan Visiting Prof., Univ. of Pennsylvania, Kenzo Tange Prof. in Architecture, Harvard Grad. School of Design, Unit Tutor, Architectural Asscn, London; Chartered Mem., RIBA; Sr Fellow, Design Futures Council; Hon. Fellow, AIA, Foreign Hon. Mem., American Acad. of Arts and Letters; RIBA First Prize Bronze Medal 1993, Design Miami/ Year of the Artist 2011. *Radio:* hosted BBC Radio programme which featured an interview with Oscar Neimeyer, also interviewed Indian architect Charles Correa 2005. *Television:* co-presented two TV series of Dreamspaces for BBC (six-part series on modern architecture); presented BBC documentary Building Africa: The Architecture of a Continent 2005. *Publications:* Houses: Recycling, Reconfiguring, Rebuilding 2005, Making Public Buildings 2006. *Address:* Adjaye Associates, The Edison, 223–231 Old Marylebone Road, London, NW1 5QT, England (office). *Telephone:* (20) 7258-6140 (office). *Fax:* (20) 7258-6148 (office). *Website:* www.adjaye.com (office).

ADJI, Boukary; Niger economist, banker and politician; Minister of Finance 1983–87; Deputy Gov. Banque Centrale des Etats de l'Afrique de l'Ouest—BCEAO (Cen. Bank of West African States) –1996, 1997–2002; Prime Minister of Niger Jan.–Dec. 1996; Prés. du Conseil d'Admin, Banque Regionale de Solidarite—Niger 2005–. *Address:* Banque Regionale de Solidarite—Niger, Avenue de l'Amitié, BP 10584, Immeuble Marina, Niamey, Niger (office). *Telephone:* 20-73-95-48 (office). *Fax:* 20-73-95-49 (home). *E-mail:* brsniger@groupebrs.com (office). *Website:* www.groupebrs.com/accueil_filiale.php?id=24 (office).

ADKERSON, Richard C., BS, MBA; American business executive; *President and CEO, Freeport-McMoRan Copper & Gold Inc.;* ed Mississippi State Univ., Advanced Man. Program of Harvard Business School; Professional Accounting

Fellow, SEC, Washington, DC and a Presidential Exchange Exec. 1976–78; Pnr and Man. Dir Arthur Andersen & Co. –1989 (headed Worldwide Oil and Gas Industry Practice); joined Freeport-McMoRan 1989, currently Pres. and CEO Freeport-McMoRan Copper & Gold Inc., also Co-Chair. McMoRan Exploration Co. (MMR); Pres. Mississippi State Univ. Foundation Bd of Dirs, Chair. State of the Future capital campaign, mem. University's Advisory Bds for the Coll. of Business and Industry and the Agribusiness Inst.; Chair. Int. Council on Mining and Metals; mem. Exec. Bd Int. Copper Asscn, M.D. Anderson Cancer Center Bd of Visitors, Business Council of New Orleans and the River Region, Devt Bd of Fellowship of Christian Athletes of New Orleans, Bd of New Orleans Police and Justice Foundation, Louisiana State Univ. Ourso Coll. of Business Exec. Bd of Advisors, Xavier Univ. Pres.'s Council, New Orleans Baptist Theological Seminary Foundation Bd; Trustee, The Nat. World War II Museum; Outstanding Accounting Alumnus of Mississippi State Univ. 1989, Outstanding Alumnus of Mississippi State Univ.'s Coll. of Business and Industry 1991, Richard C. Adkerson School of Accountancy est. by Mississippi State Univ. in his honour. *Address:* Freeport-McMoRan Copper & Gold, One North Central Avenue, Phoenix, AZ 85004-4414, USA (office). *Telephone:* (602) 366-8100 (office). *E-mail:* info@fcx.com (office). *Website:* www.fcx.com (office).

ADKISSON, Perry Lee, PhD; American entomologist and academic; *Distinguished Professor of Entomology Emeritus and Chancellor Emeritus, Texas A&M University;* b. 11 March 1929, Hickman, Arkansas; s. of Robert L. Adkisson and Imogene Adkisson (née Perry); m. 1st Frances Rozelle 1956 (died 1995); one d.; m. 2nd Goria Ray 1998; ed Univ. of Arkansas, Kansas State Univ. and Harvard Univ.; Asst Prof. of Entomology Univ. of Missouri 1956–58; Assoc. Prof. of Entomology Texas A&M Univ. 1958–63; Prof. of Entomology 1963–67, Head Dept of Entomology 1967–78, apptd Distinguished Prof. of Entomology 1967, currently Distinguished Prof. Emer., Vice-Pres. for Agric. and Renewable Resources 1978–80, Deputy Chancellor for Agric. 1980–83, Deputy Chancellor 1983–86, Chancellor 1986–91, Chancellor Emer. 1991–, Regent's Prof. 1991–95; Consultant Int. AEC, Vienna 1969–74; Chair. Texas Pesticide Advisory Comm. 1972; mem. Panel on Integrated Pest Control FAO, Rome 1971–78; mem. NAS, Governing Bd Int. Crop Research Inst. for Semi-Arid Tropics 1982–88, Standing Cttee for Int. Plant Protection Congresses 1984–, Texas Science and Tech. Council 1986–88, Advisory Cttee, Export-Import Bank of the US 1987; Alexander Von Humboldt Award 1980, Distinguished Service Award, American Inst. of Biological Sciences 1987, Distinguished Alumni Award (Ark. Univ.) 1990, Wolfe Prize in Agric. 1994–95, World Food Prize 1997, Medallion Alumni Award, Kansas State Univ. 1999 and numerous other awards. *Publications:* Controlling Cotton's Insect Pests: A New System 1982; several papers on insect diapause and other entomological topics. *Leisure interests:* gardening, fishing. *Address:* Texas A&M University, Entomology Department, TAMU 2475, College Station, TX 77843-2475 (office); The Reed House, 1 Reed Drive, College Station, TX 77843, USA (home). *Telephone:* (979) 680-9128 (office); (409) 845-2516 (home). *Website:* insects.tamu.edu (office).

ADLER, Julius, AB, MS, PhD, FAAS; American biologist, biochemist and professor of biochemistry; *Professor Emeritus, Department of Biochemistry, University of Wisconsin;* b. 30 April 1930, Edelfingen, Germany; s. of Adolf Adler and Irma Stern; m. Hildegard Wohl 1963; one s. one d.; ed Harvard Univ., Univ. of Wisconsin; emigrated to USA 1938, naturalized US citizen 1943; Postdoctoral Fellow, Washington Univ., St Louis 1957–59, Stanford Univ. 1959–60; Asst Prof., Depts of Biochemistry and Genetics, Univ. of Wisconsin 1960–63, Assoc. Prof. 1963–66, Prof. 1966–96, Prof. Emer. 1997–, Edwin Bret Hart Prof. 1972; Steenbock Prof. of Microbiological Sciences 1982–92; mem. American Acad. of Arts and Sciences, American Philosophical Soc., NAS, Wisconsin Acad. of Sciences, Arts and Letters; Fellow, American Acad. of Microbiology, Wisconsin Acad. of Sciences, Arts, and Letters 1996; Behring Lecturer, Philips Univ. of Marburg 1989, Hartman-Müller Memorial Lecturer, Univ. of Zürich 1984; Dr hc (Tübingen) 1987, (Regensburg) 1995; Selman A. Waksman Microbiology Award, NAS 1980, Otto-Warburg Medal, German Soc. of Biological Chem. 1986, Hilldale Award, Univ. of Wisconsin 1988, R.H. Wright Award, Simon Fraser Univ. 1988, Abbott-American Soc. for Microbiology Lifetime Achievement Award 1995, William C. Rose Award, American Soc. for Biochemistry and Molecular Biology 1996. *Publications include:* research papers on the behaviour of simple organisms, especially bacteria, research on the behaviour of fruit flies. *Address:* 457C Biochemistry Addition, Department of Biochemistry, 433 Babcock Drive, University of Wisconsin, Madison, WI 53706-1544 (office); 1234 Wellesley Road, Madison, WI 53705, USA (home). *Telephone:* (608) 262-3693 (office). *E-mail:* adler@biochem.wisc.edu (office). *Website:* www.biochem.wisc.edu (office).

ADLERCREUTZ, (Carl) Herman (Thomas), MD, PhD; Finnish clinical chemist and academic; *Professor Emeritus and Head, Institute for Preventative Medicine, Nutrition and Cancer, Folkhälsan Research Centre, Biomedicum, University of Helsinki;* b. 10 April 1932, Helsinki; s. of Erik Adlercreutz and Elisabeth Adlercreutz; m. 1st Marie-Louise Gräsbeck 1956 (divorced 1974); m. 2nd Sirkka T. Neva 1976; one s. two d.; ed Univ. of Helsinki, Folkhälsan Research Centre; specialist training in internal medicine 1961–64; Research Fellow, Hormone Lab. Dept of Obstetrics and Gynaecology, Karolinska Hosp., Stockholm 1958–61; Resident in Internal Medicine, Univ. of Helsinki 1961–64, Acting Asst Prof. of Internal Medicine 1964, Assoc. Prof. of Clinical Chem. 1965–69, Acting Prof. of Clinical Chem. 1967–69, Prof. of Clinical Chem. 1969–97; Chief Physician, Central Lab. Helsinki Univ. Central Hosp. 1965–97; Research Prof., Acad. of Finland 1983–88; Head, Inst. for Preventive Medicine, Nutrition and Cancer, Folkhälsan Research Centre 1997–; mem. 13 foreign socs, numerous editorial bds of journals, Comm. on Health and Science Asscn of European Olympic Cttees 1985–93; Hon. mem. Polish Soc. for Laboratory Diagnostics, Finnish Soc. for Clinical Chem., Finnish Soc. for Nutrition Research; Kt (First Class), Order of the White Rose 1983, Kt of Johanniternorden of the St Johannis vom Spital zu Jerusalem (Germany) 1992; Medal of Japan Foundation for Cancer Research, Tokyo 1984, The Tenth D. R. Edwards Medal 1987, J.W. Runeberg Award 1991, Medal of the Faculty of Medicine, Tartu Univ. (Estonia) 1992, Silver Medal of Univ. of Helsinki 1992, Bronze Paavo Nurmi Memorial Medal (Finland) 1992, Egon Diczfalusy Lecture Medal, Karolinska Inst., Stockholm 2001, Tartu Univ. Faculty of Medicine 60th Anniversary Medal 2007, Finnish Olympic Cttee Medal of Merit 2007, and other awards and distinctions. *Publications:* more than 620 original publs mainly in the fields of steroid hormones, endocrinology, sports medicine, nutrition, phytoestrogens and cancer. *Leisure interests:* gardening, fishing, sport. *Address:* Institute of Clinical Medicine and Folkhälsan Research Centre, Biomedicum, University of Helsinki, PO Box 63, 00014 Helsinki (office); Riskutie 13, 00950 Helsinki, Finland (home). *Telephone:* (9) 19125380 (office); (9) 3250258 (home); 50-5114430 (mobile); (9) 3250327 (home). *Fax:* (9) 19125382 (office); (9) 3250327 (home). *E-mail:* herman.adlercreutz@helsinki.fi (office). *Website:* www.folkhalsan.fi (office).

ADLEŠIĆ, Đurđa; Croatian politician; b. 18 April 1960, Bjelovar; m.; one c.; ed Univ. of Zagreb; mem. Croatian Social Liberal Party (HSLS) 1990–, Vice-Pres. 2000–06, Pres. 2006–; mem. Sabor (Parl.) 1995–, mem. Cttee for Family, Youth and Sports, Cttee for War Veterans, Pres. HSLS Group of Deputies 1998–, Vice-Pres. Sabor 2004–08; Mayor of Bjelovar 2001–08; Deputy Prime Minister 2008–11; cand. in 2005 presidential election; fmr Vice-Pres. Comm. for Determining the Victims of War. *Address:* c/o Office of the Prime Minister, 10000 Zagreb, trg sv. Marka 2, Croatia.

ADLINGTON, Rebecca (Becky), OBE; British swimmer; b. 17 Feb. 1989, Mansfield, Notts.; d. of Steve Adlington and Kay Adlington; ed The Brunts School, Mansfield; began swimming with Sherwood Colliery Swimming Club; selected for Nottinghamshire County Swim Squad (Nova Centurion); European Championships (long course), Budapest 2006: silver medal, 800m freestyle, Budapest 2010: gold medal, 400m freestyle, bronze medal, 4×200m freestyle; World Championships (short course), Manchester 2008: gold medal, 800m freestyle, silver medal, 4×200m freestyle; Olympic Games, Beijing 2008: gold medal, 400m freestyle, 800m freestyle; World Championships (long course), Rome 2009: bronze medal, 400m freestyle, 4×200m freestyle, Shanghai 2011: gold medal, 800m freestyle, silver medal, 400m freestyle; Commonwealth Games, Delhi 2010 (competed for England): gold medal, 400m freestyle, 800m freestyle, bronze medal, 200m freestyle, 4×200m freestyle; Olympic Games, London 2012: bronze medal, 400m freestyle, 800m freestyle; first British swimmer to win two Olympic gold medals since 1908 and GB's most successful Olympic swimmer in 100 years; coach: Bill Furniss; Amb. for the Encephalitis Soc.; retd from all competitive swimming Feb. 2013; named by Sports Journalists' Asscn of GB as Sportswoman of the Year 2008, 2011, voted third in BBC's Sports Personality of the Year Award 2008, Laureus World Sports Awards Breakthrough of the Year Award 2008, Sherwood Swimming Baths in Mansfield renamed the Rebecca Adlington Swimming Centre following refurbishment 2010. *Address:* c/o Graeme Smith, Elite Sports Properties, 3–5 High Pavement, Lace Market, Nottingham, NG1 1HF, England. *Telephone:* (1159) 897355; 7590-206256 (mobile). *Fax:* (1159) 897356. *E-mail:* gsmith@espgb.co.uk. *Website:* www.elitesportsproperties.com.

ADNI, Daniel; Israeli/British pianist; b. 6 Dec. 1951, Haifa; pnr Tessa Isaac; ed High Schools in Haifa and Tel-Aviv, Conservatoire of Music in Paris; first recital in Haifa 1963; professional debut, London 1970; New York debut 1976; has played at most musical centres in the world including UK, Germany, Israel, USA, Japan, South Africa, Switzerland, Norway, Netherlands, Romania, Australia, New Zealand, Finland, Austria; has taught masterclasses including at Dartington Summer School (UK); made over 20 records for EMI-His Master's Voice; First Prize, Paris Conservatoire, First Prize, Young Concert Artists' Auditions, New York. *Leisure interests:* cinema, theatre, bridge, walks, sightseeing. *Address:* c/o 64A Menelik Road, London, NW2 3RH, England (home). *Telephone:* (20) 7794-4075 (home). *Fax:* (20) 7794-4076 (home). *E-mail:* danieladni@waitrose.com.

ADOLFO; American fashion designer; b. (Adolfo F. Sardiña), 15 Feb. 1933, Cardenas, Matanzas, Cuba; ed St Ignacio de Loyola Jesuit School, Havana; served in Cuban Army; apprentice, Cristóbal Balenciaga millinery salon, Paris 1950–52; apprentice millinery designer, Bergdorf Goodman, New York 1953–54; designer Emme (milliners), New York 1954–62; worked as unpaid apprentice, Chanel, New York summers of 1957, 1966; Owner and Head Designer, Adolfo Inc., New York 1962–93; f. Adolfo Enterprises (licensing firm) 1993; Designer, Adolfo Menswear Inc. and Adolfo Scarves Inc., New York 1978; created perfume line for Frances Denny, New York 1979; f. Adolfo F. Sardiña Trust; mem. Council, Fashion Designers of America 1982. *Address:* Adolfo Inc., 60 East 42nd Street, Suite 1138, New York, NY 10165, USA (office). *Telephone:* (212) 682-1977 (office).

ADOUKI, Martin, DJur; Republic of the Congo diplomatist; *Ambassador and Diplomatic Adviser to the President;* b. 8 April 1942, Makoua; ed Bordeaux and Paris Univs and Int. Inst. of Public Admin., Paris; Information Officer for the Group of African, Caribbean and Pacific Countries (ACP) in Brussels and attended negotiations between the ACP and the EEC; fmrly Lecturer in Law at the Marien Ngouabi Univ., Brazzaville and later Special Adviser to the Prime Minister; Perm. Rep. to the UN 1985–94, to UN Security Council 1986–87, Pres. UN Security Council 1986–87, Chair. UN African Group Sept. 1986, Rep. of Chair. of OAU to UN 1986–87, Head Congo Del. to 43rd Session of Gen. Ass. 1988; mem. of the Zone of Peace and Co-operation in the South Atlantic 1988–90, mem. Del. of UN Special Cttee on the Verification of Elections in Namibia 1989, Vice-Pres. UN Gen. Ass. (44th Session) 1989; Observer on the Gen. Elections in Nicaragua Feb. 1990, Head Del. to World Summit for Children Sept. 1990; Chair. 4th Cttee of 45th Session of Gen. Ass. 1990–91; Amb. and Diplomatic Adviser to Pres. 1998–. *Address:* c/o Ministry of Foreign Affairs and Co-operation, BP 2070, Brazzaville, Republic of the Congo.

ADRIANO, Dino, FCCA, FCIM; British business executive; *Trustee, The Sainsbury Archive;* b. 24 April 1943, London, England; s. of Dante Adriano and Yole Adriano; m. Susan Rivett 1996; two d.; ed Strand Grammar School and Highgate Coll.; articled clerk, George W. Spencer & Co., Chartered Accountants 1959–64; joined J. Sainsbury plc 1964, trainee, Accounting Dept 1964–65, Financial Accounts Dept 1965–73, Br. Financial Control Man. 1973–80, Gen. Man. Homebase 1981–86, Area Dir, Sainsbury's Central and Western Area 1986–89, Man. Dir Homebase 1989–95, Chair. 1991–96, Asst Man. Dir J. Sainsbury plc 1995–96, Deputy Chief Exec. 1996–97; Deputy Chair. Shaw's Supermarkets Inc. 1994, Chair. 1994–96; Dir, Giant Food Inc. 1994–96, Laura Ashley plc 1996–98; Chair. Bd Govs, Thames Valley Univ. 2004–09; Trustee, Oxfam 1990–96, 1998–2004, Adviser on Retail Matters 1996–98, 2004–06, Vice-Chair. 2001–04; Trustee, WRVS 2001–07, The Sainsbury Archive 2007–, Sainsbury Veterans Welfare Scheme 2007–; Hon. DUniv (Thames Valley) 2009. *Leisure interests:* opera, music, soccer, cookery. *E-mail:* dino.adriano@lineone.net (office).

ADVANI, Lal Krishna; Indian politician, fmr journalist and social worker; b. 8 Nov. 1927, Karachi (now in Pakistan); s. of Kishinchand Advani and Gyani Advani; m. Kamala Jagtiani 1965; one s. one d.; ed D.G. Nat. Coll., Hyderabad, Sind, Govt Law Coll., Mumbai; joined Rashtriya Swayam Sevak Sangh (RSS, social work org.) 1942, Sec. of Karachi br. 1947; joined Bharatiya Jana Sangh (BJS) 1951, party work in Rajasthan –1958, Sec. Delhi State Jana Sangh 1958–63, Pres. Delhi State Jana Sangh 1970–72, All India Jana Sangh 1973, re-elected 1974, 1975, Bharatiya Janata Party (BJP) 1986–1991, 1993–98; mem. Bharatiya Jana Sangh 1951–77; Vice-Pres. Delhi State Jana Sangh 1965–67; elected mem. Rajya Sabha (Parl.) 1970, 1976, 1982, 1988, 1991, 1998, 1999, 2004, 2009–, Deputy Prime Minister 1999–2004, Leader of Opposition Jan.–April 1980, Lok Sabha 1991–93, 2004–10, mem. Parl. Cttee on Public Undertakings 1972–74, 1981–82, Gen. Purposes Cttee 1980–85, Cttee on Subordinate Legislation 1984–86, 1987–89; Minister for Information and Broadcasting 1977–79, of Kashmir Affairs 1998–99, of Home Affairs 1999–2004, of Coal and Mines (Additional Charge) July–Aug. 2002, of Personnel, Pensions and Public Grievances (Additional Charge) 2003–04; Chair. Delhi Metropolitan Council 1967–70; Gen. Sec. Bharatiya Janata Party 1977–80, 1980–86; Jt Sec. Rajasthan State Jana Sangh 1952–57; mem. Delhi Metropolitan Council 1966–70, Inter-Governmental Conf. on Communication Policies in Asia and Oceania, Kuala Lampur 1977; Indian Del. at UNESCO Gen. Conf. 1978; Leader, Jana Sangh Group in Interim Metropolitan Council 1966–67; Indian Parl. Del. to Strasbourg 1991; mem. Cen. Exec. of BJS 1976; Jt Ed. BJS paper Organizer 1960–67; Outstanding Parliamentarian Award 1999. *Publications include:* A Prisoner's Scrap-Book, The People Betrayed. *Leisure interests:* theatre, cinema, books, sports, music. *Address:* 26 Tughlak Crescent, New Delhi 110 011 (office); 1835/16, Kasturbhai Block, Din Dayal Bhawan, J. P. Chowk, Khanpur, Ahmedabad (home); 30 Prithviraj Raj Road, New Delhi 110 003, India (home). *Telephone:* (11) 23001700 (office); (11) 23794124 (New Delhi) (home). *Fax:* (11) 23001762 (office); (11) 23012791 (office); (11) 23017419 (New Delhi) (home). *E-mail:* advanilk@sansad.nic.in (office). *Website:* www.bjp.org (office); www .lkadvani.in (home).

ADVANI, Pankaj Arjan, BCom; Indian professional snooker player; b. 24 July 1985, Pune, Maharashtra; ed Frank Anthony Public School, Bangalore, Mahaveer Jain Coll., Bangalore; spent early years in Kuwait before moving to Bangalore; trained in snooker by fmr nat. snooker champion Arvind Savur; won Indian Jr Billiards Championship 2000, 2001, 2003, 2005, Indian Jr Snooker Championship 2003, 2005; professional 2003–; won first world championship title at Int. Billiards and Snooker Fed. (IBSF) World Snooker Championship, China 2003; other wins include IBSF World Billiards Championship, Malta 2005, Bangalore 2008, Leeds, UK 2009, Asian Billiards Championship 2005, 2008 (only player to have won title twice), 2009, 2010, 6 Red Snooker Pentangular Team Championship, Bangalore 2008, Australian Open Billiards Championship, Melbourne 2008 (first Indian winner); gold medal, Men's English Billiards, Asian Games, Doha 2006, Guangzhou 2010; bronze medal, Men's English Billiards, Asian Indoor Games, Ho Chi Minh City 2009; Nat. Billiards and Snooker Champion 2009; numerous awards, including Sports Star Sportsperson of the Year 2003, Indo-American Young Achiever's Award 2003, Arjuna Award 2004, Rajeev Gandhi Award 2004, Hero India Sports Award 2004, Bangalore Univ. Sportsperson of the Year 2005, Sports Writers' Asscn of Bangalore Award 2005, Senior Sportsperson of the Year 2005, Vision of India's Int. Indian Award 2005, Rajiv Gandhi Khel Ratna Award 2006, Kempegowda Award, Karnataka 2007, Rajyotsava Award (Karnataka's highest civilian award) 2007, Padma Shri Award 2009. *Address:* c/o Karnataka State Billiards Association, 5/1 Miller Tank Bed Area, Jasma Bhavan Road, Bangalore 560 052, India. *Telephone:* (80) 43223222 (office); (80) 22269970 (office). *Fax:* (80) 22257315 (office). *E-mail:* contact@ksba.in (office); ksba_blr@dataone.in (office). *Website:* www.ksba.in (office).

ADYRKHAYEVA, Svetlana Dzantemirovna; Russian/Ossetian ballerina and ballet teacher; *Director, Svetlana Adyrkhayeva Ballet Studio;* b. 12 May 1938, Khumalag, North Ossetia; d. of Taissya Gougkayeva and Dzantemir Adyrkhayev; m. Alexey Zakalinsky 1966; one d.; ed Leningrad Choreographic School, Theatre Acad. of Russia; danced with Glinka Theatre of Opera and Ballet, Chelyabinsk 1955–58; with Odessa Opera and Ballet 1958–60; dancer at Bolshoi Theatre 1960–88; USSR People's Artist 1984; Dir Svetlana Adyrkhayeva Ballet Studio, Moscow. *Principal parts include:* Odette-Odile, Princess Florine, Woman of the Bronze Mountain (Prokofiev's Stone Flower), Zarema (Asafiev's Fountain of Bakhchisaray), Mehmene Banu (Melikov's Legend of Love), Aegina (Khatchaturyan's Spartacus), Kitri (Minkus's Don Quixote). *Leisure interests:* reading, travelling. *Address:* 121099 Moscow, 1st Smolensky per. 9, Apt. 74, Russia. *Telephone:* (495) 241-13-62.

AEBISCHER, Patrick, MD, DrMed; Swiss medical scientist, academic, university administrator and entrepreneur; *President, École Polytechnique Fédérale de Lausanne;* b. 22 Nov. 1954, Fribourg; s. of Emile Aebischer (known as Yoki) and Joan Aebischer (née O'Boyle); m.; two c.; ed Univs of Geneva and Fribourg; Research Scientist, Asst, Assoc. Prof. of Medical Sciences, Brown Univ., USA 1984–92, Chair. Section of Artificial Organs, Biomaterials and Cellular Tech., Div. of Biology and Medicine 1991; Prof. and Dir Surgical Research Div. and Gene Therapy Centre, Univ. Hosp. of Lausanne 1992–99; Pres. École Polytechnique Fédérale de Lausanne (one of the two Swiss Fed. Insts of Tech.) 2000–; also Prof. of Neurosciences and Head of Neurodegenerative Disease Lab.; f. three start-ups, CytoTherapeutics Inc. 1989, Modex Therapeutics Inc. 1996, Amazentis SA 2007; mem. Bd of Dirs Lonza Group 2008–, Nestlé Health Science 2011–; Fellow, Swiss Nat. Science Foundation 1984–86, Swiss Acad. for the Medical Sciences 1998, American Inst. for Medical and Biological Eng Sciences 2000, Swiss Eng Acad. 2009; Kolff Award (Young Investigator Award, American Soc. for Artificial Internal Organs), New York 1987, Robert Bing Award, Swiss Acad. of Medicine 1994, Pfizer Foundation Award for Clinical Neurosciences 1997. *Publications include:* numerous papers in professional journals on the development of cell and gene transfer approaches for the treatment of neurodegenerative diseases. *Address:* Office of the President, École Polytechnique Fédérale de Lausanne, Centre Est, Station 1, 1015 Lausanne (office); Laboratoire d'étude sur la Neurodégénérescence, École Polytechnique Fédérale de Lausanne, EPFL SV BMI LEN, Bâtiment AI, Station 19, 1015 Lausanne, Switzerland (office). *Telephone:* (2169) 37001 (office); (2169) 39505 (office). *E-mail:* patrick.aebischer@ epfl.ch (office). *Website:* people.epfl.ch/patrick.aebischer (office); len.epfl.ch (office).

AFANASIYEV, Yuri Nikolaevich, DHistSc; Russian historian, academic and politician; b. 5 Sept. 1934, Maina, Ulyanovsk region; m.; two c.; ed Moscow State Univ., Acad. of Social Sciences; mem. CPSU 1956–90; instructor, then sec. Comsomol org. in Krasnoyarsk Region 1957–64, mem. of Comsomol Cen. Cttee 1964–71; Deputy Head of Div. 1971, Lecturer, Higher Comsomol School 1971, Pro-Rector 1972–83; Sr Researcher, Inst. of World History USSR Acad. of Sciences 1983–87; Rector, Moscow Inst. of History and Archives (now Russian Humanitarian Univ.) 1987–; Founder and Rector, Russian State Univ. for the Humanities 1991–2002, Pres. 2003–06; USSR People's Deputy 1989–91, mem. of Interregional Deputies Group, People's Deputy of Russia 1991–92; Co-Chair. Democratic Russia Movt 1991–92. *Publications:* numerous articles and over 10 books on problems of Russian history and contemporary politics including Russia on the Crossroads (three vols) 2000, Dangerous Russia 2001. *E-mail:* afn2007@yandex.ru. *Website:* www.yuri-afanasiev.ru.

AFASH, Mohamed Nagy Ismail ('Gedo'); Egyptian professional footballer; b. 3 Oct. 1984, Damanhur, Beheira; attacking midfielder/striker; started career at Hosh Essa youth centre; played for teams Ala'ab Damanhour 2002–05, Ittihad Alexandria 2005–10, Al-Ahly 2010–; debut with Egyptian Nat. Football Team 2009, took part in African Cup of Nations 2010 (top scorer of the tournament). *Address:* Egyptian Football Association, 5 Gabalaya Street, Gezira El Borg Post Office, Cairo, Egypt (office). *Telephone:* (2) 27351793 (office). *E-mail:* efa_football@ hotmail.com (office). *Website:* www.efa.com.eg (office).

AFEEF, Hassan; Maldivian politician; m. Farhath Afeef; MP for Thaa Atoll, Shadow Home Minister; Leader, Maldivian Democratic Party Parl. Group –2009, currently mem.; Political Adviser to Pres. 2009–10; Minister of Home Affairs 2010–12; fmr mem. Judicial Services Comm. *Address:* Maldivian Democratic Party (MDP), H. Sharaashaa, 2nd Floor, Sosun Magu, Malé 20-059, Maldives (office). *Telephone:* 3340044 (office). *Fax:* 3322960 (office). *E-mail:* secretariat@mdp.org.mv (office); minhab@dhivenhinet.net.mv (office). *Website:* www.mdp.org.mv (office).

AFEWERKI, Issaias; Eritrean head of state; *President;* b. 2 Feb. 1946, Asmara; m. Saba Haile; three c.; trained as engineer; joined Eritrean Liberation Front (ELF) 1966, mil. training in China 1966, Leader of fourth regional area ELF 1968, Gen. Commdr ELF 1969; Founding mem. Eritrean People's Liberation Front (now People's Front for Democracy and Justice—PFDJ 1977), fmr Asst Sec. Gen., Sec. Gen. 1987, currently Leader; Chair. State Council, Nat. Ass.; Sec. Gen. Provisional Govt of Eritrea 1991; assumed power May 1991; elected Pres. of Eritrea by Nat. Ass. 1993–. *Address:* Office of the President, PO Box 257, Asmara, Eritrea (office). *Telephone:* (1) 122132 (office). *Fax:* (1) 125123 (office).

AFFANDI RAJA MOHAMED NOOR, Datuk Raja Mohamed; Malaysian army officer; *Army Chief;* b. 20 June 1957, Kampung Raja, Terengganu State; m. Datin Norlida Abdul Mubin; one s. three d.; ed Officer Cadet School, Port Dickson, mil. insts in Australia and Pakistan; commissioned as Second Lt, Corps of the Royal Malay Regiment (RAMD) 1977, later becoming platoon leader, co. commdr, field commdr, Chief Instructor, Pusasda Army Basic Training Centre, Commanding Officer, 8 RAMD Bn, Mil. Asst to Deputy Chief of Army, Asst Chief of Staff and Chief of Planning and Devt (Div. 2), Chief of Field Office (Army) 2008–09, Armed Forces Chief of Staff 2009–13, Army Chief 2013–; attained rank of Lt-Gen. 2008, Gen. 2013. *Leisure interests:* reading, sports, golf. *Address:* Malaysian Armed Forces Headquarters, Wisma Pertahanan, Wilayah Persekutuan, Kuala Lumpur 50634, Malaysia (office). *Telephone:* (3) 26921333 (office). *Fax:* (3) 26911757 (office). *E-mail:* sk.komlek@mod.gov.my (office). *Website:* www.mafhq.mil.my (office).

AFFLECK, Ben; American actor; b. 15 Aug. 1972, Berkeley; m. Jennifer Garner 2005; two d. *Films include:* School Ties 1992, Buffy the Vampire Slayer, Dazed and Confused, Mallrats 1995, Glory Daze, Office Killer, Chasing Amy 1997, Going All the Way 1997, Good Will Hunting (also screenplay with Matt Damon q.v., Acad. Award and Golden Globe for Best Original Screenplay 1997), Phantoms 1998, Armageddon 1998, Shakespeare in Love 1998, Reindeer Games 1999, Forces of Nature 1999, Dogma 1999, Daddy and Them 1999, The Boiler Room 1999, 200 Cigarettes 1999, Bounce 2000, The Third Wheel (also producer) 2000, Pearl Harbor 2001, The Sum of All Fear 2002, Changing Lanes 2002, Daredevil 2003, Gigli 2003, Paycheck 2003, Jersey Girl 2004, Surviving Christmas 2004, Man About Town 2006, Hollywoodland 2006, Smokin' Aces 2006, Gone Baby Gone (dir, writer and producer) 2007, He's Just Not That Into You 2009, State of Play 2009, Extract 2009, The Company Men 2010, The Town (dir and writer) 2010, Argo (dir Golden Globe Award for Best Dir 2013, Outstanding Directorial Achievement in Feature Film, Directors Guild of America 2013, BAFTA Award for Best Dir 2013) 2012, To the Wonder 2012. *Television includes:* Voyage of the Mimi, Against the Grain, Lifestories: Families in Crisis, Hands of a Stranger, Daddy. *Address:* c/o Grant, Tani Barash & Altman, LL, 9100 Wilshire Blvd, Suite 1000W, Beverly Hills, CA 90212, USA.

AFRIDI, Sahibzada Mohammad Shahid Khan, (Shahid Afridi); Pakistani professional cricketer; b. 1 March 1980, Khyber Agency, Federally Administered Tribal Areas; m.; two d.; allrounder; right-handed batsman; leg-break googly bowler; plays for Karachi 1995–2010, Pakistan 1996–2011 (Capt. 2010–11), Habib Bank Ltd 1997–2009, MCC 2001, Leics. 2001, Derbyshire 2003, Griqualand West 2003–04, Kent 2004, Ireland 2006, Sind 2007–08, Deccan Chargers 2008, South Australia 2009–10, Southern Redbacks 2010, Hants. 2011–, Melbourne Renegades 2011–, Dhaka Gladiators 2011–, Ruhuna Royals 2012, Asia XI, ICC World XI; First-class debut: 1995/96; Test debut: Pakistan v Australia, Karachi 22–26 Oct. 1998; One-Day Int. (ODI) debut: Kenya v Pakistan, Nairobi (Aga) 2 Oct. 1996; T20I debut: England v Pakistan, Bristol 28 Aug. 2006; has played in 27 Tests, taken 48 wickets and scored 1,716 runs (five centuries), highest score 156, average 36.51, best bowling (innings) 5/52, (match) 5/43; has played in 349 ODI matches, taken 348 wickets and scored 7,075 runs (six centuries and 33 fifties), highest score 124, average 23.34, best bowling 6/38; announced temporary retirement from Test cricket April 2006; captained Pakistan in first Test of home series against Australia at Lords July 2010, announced retirement from Test cricket; captained Pakistan to reach semi-final of ICC Cricket World Cup March 2011; known for his aggressive batting style, and currently holds highest career strike rate in history of int. cricket; holds record for fastest one-day century, made in debut innings (101 in 37 balls against Sri Lanka, Nairobi 1996), as well as scoring 32 runs in a single over (second highest scoring over ever in an ODI); hit the first ever 12 in power cricket when he successfully hit the roof 2002; has an ODI strike rate of 113.88 runs per 100 balls, the highest in cricket history 2011; only cricketer to score a half-century and take five wickets on two separate occasions in ODIs; fined Rs3m (£23,800), warned by Chair. of Pakistan Cricket Bd and put on probation for six months for "bringing the game and country into disrepute" following "ball-biting" incident in Perth ODI during tour of Australia March 2010; announced retirement from all forms of int. cricket 30 May 2011, returned to int. cricket Nov. 2011; nickname Boom Boom Afridi; Man of the Series, World Twenty20 2007, named in survey as the most popular cricketer in Pakistan 2007. *Address:* c/o Pakistan Cricket Board, Gaddafi Stadium, Lahore 54600, Pakistan. *Telephone:* (42) 571-7231. *Fax:* (42) 571-1860. *E-mail:* info@pcboard.com.pk. *Website:* www.pcboard.com.pk/home.html.

AGA KHAN IV, HH Prince Shah Karim al-Hussaini, Spiritual Leader and Imam of Ismaili Muslims, KBE, BA; British; b. 13 Dec. 1936, Creux-de-Genthod, Geneva, Switzerland; s. of the late Prince Aly Salomon Khan and of Princess Tajuddawlah Aly Khan (late Viscountess Camrose, née Joan Barbara Yarde-Buller); m. 1st Sarah Frances Croker-Poole (Begum Salimah Aga Khan) 1969 (divorced 1995); two s. one d.; m. 2nd Princess Gabriele zu Leiningen (Begum Inaara Aga Khan) 1998 (separated 2011); one s.; ed Le Rosey, Switzerland, Harvard Univ., USA; became Aga Khan on the death of his grandfather Sir Sultan Mahomed Shah, Aga Khan III, GCSI, GCIE, GCVO 1957; granted title of His Highness by Queen Elizabeth II 1957, of His Royal Highness by the Shah of Iran 1959; Founder and Chair. Aga Khan Foundation 1967, Aga Khan Award for Architecture 1977–, Inst. of Ismaili Studies 1977–, Aga Khan Fund for Econ. Devt, Geneva 1984, Aga Khan Trust for Culture 1988, Aga Khan Agency for Microfinance 2005–; Founder and Chancellor Aga Khan Univ., Pakistan 1983–, Univ. of Central Asia (Tekeli, Kazakhstan, Naryn, Kyrgyzstan and Khorugh, Tajikistan) 2001–; Founder Pres. Yacht Club Costa Smeralda, Sardinia; mem. Royal Yacht Squadron 1982–; Assoc. Foreign mem. Acad. des Beaux-Arts 2008; Foreign mem., Class of Humanities, Lisbon Acad. of Sciences 2009; Hon. Col, 6th Lancers, Pakistani Army 1970; Hon. Citizen of the Town of Kisumu (Kenya) 1981, of Lahore (Pakistan) 1980, of Granada (Spain) 1991, of the City of Samarkand (and Key to the City) 1992, of the Islamic Ummah of Timbuktu (Mali) 2003, of Dar es Salaam (Tanzania) 2005, of the Municipality of Timbuktu 2008; Hon. Prof., Univ. of Osh, Kyrgyzstan 2002; Hon. Fellow, Coll. of Physicians and Surgeons of Pakistan 1985; Hon. FRIBA 1991; Hon. mem. Pakistan Medical Asscn 1981, AIA 1992; Foreign Hon. mem. American Acad. of Arts and Sciences 1996; Hon. Canadian citizenship 2009; Commdr Ordre du Mérite Mauritanien 1960, Grand Croix, Ordre du Prince Henry du Gouvernement Portugais 1960, Ordre Nat. de la Côte d'Ivoire 1965, de la Haute-Volta 1965, Ordre Nat. Malgache 1966, Ordre du Croissant Vert des Comores 1966, Grand Cordon Ordre du Tadj de l'Empire d'Iran 1967, Nishan-i-Imtiaz, Pakistan 1970, Cavaliere di Gran Croce dell'Ordine al Merito della Repubblica (Italy) 1977, Grand Officier de l'Ordre Nat. du Lion (Senegal) 1982, Nishan-e-Pakistan, Pakistan 1983, Grand Cordon of Ouissam-al Arch (Morocco) 1986, Cavaliere del Lavoro (Italy) 1988, Commdr, Légion d'honneur (France) 1990, Gran Cruz de la Orden del Mérito Civil, Spain 1991, Grand Croix, Order of Merit (Portugal) 1998, Order of Friendship (Tajikistan) 1998, Order of Bahrain (First Class) 2003, Hon. CC 2004, Grã-Cruz da Ordem Militar de Cristo (Portugal) 2005, Chief of the Order of the Golden Heart (Kenya) 2007, Grand Cross, Nat. Order of Mali 2008, Grand Mécène (Grand Patron) and Grand Donateur (Grand Donor), Paris 2009, Commdr, Ordre des Arts et des Lettres 2010; Hon. LLD (Peshawar Univ.) 1967, (Univ. of Sind) 1970, (McGill Univ.) 1983, (McMaster Univ.) 1987, (Univ. of Wales) 1993, (Brown Univ.) 1996, (Toronto) 2004, (Nat. Univ. of Ireland) 2008, (Harvard) 2008, (Alberta) 2009; Hon. DLitt (London) 1989; Hon. DHumLitt (American Univ. of Beirut) 2005, (American Univ. in Cairo) 2006; Hon. DD (Cambridge) 2009; Hon. DUniv (Ottawa) 2012; Dr hc (Évora, Portugal) 2006, (Univ. of Sankore, Mali) 2008; Hon. Dr of Sacred Letters (Toronto) 2013; Key to the city of Karachi, Pakistan 1981, The Gold Mercury International 'AD PERSONAM' Award (UK) 1982, Thomas Jefferson Memorial Foundation Medal in Architecture, Univ. of Virginia 1984, AIA Honor Award 1984, La Medalla de Oro del Consejo Superior de Colegios de Arquitectos, Spain 1987, Médaille d'Argent, Acad. d'Architecture, Paris 1991, Huéspéd de Honor de Granada, Spain 1991; Key to the City of Lisbon 1996, Hadrian Award, World Monuments Fund (USA) 1996, Gold Medal, City of Granada (Spain) 1998; Insignia of Honour, Union Int. des Architectes 2001, Archon Award, Int. Nursing Honour Soc. y, Sigma Theta Tau International 2001, State Award of Peace and Progress (Kazakhstan) 2002, Vincent Scully Prize, Nat. Building Museum (USA) 2005, Die Quadriga (Germany) 2005, Andrew Carnegie Medal of Philanthropy (UK) 2005, Key to the City of Ottawa 2005, Tolerance Prize, Evangelical Acad. of Tutzing 2006, Royal Toledo Foundation (Real Fundación de Toledo) Award 2006, 10th annual Peter O'Sullevan Award at the Savoy, London 2006, Honoured Educator of the Repub. of Kazakhstan 2008, Key to the City of Austin, Tex. 2008, Philanthropic Entrepreneur of the Year, Le Nouvel Economiste, Paris 2009, One of The 500 Most Influential Muslims in the World, Royal Islamic Strategic Studies Centre (Jordan) 2009, 2010, 2011, 2012, 2013, ULI J.C. Nichols Prize for Visionaries in Urban Devt, Los Angeles 2011, UCSF Medal, Univ. of California, San Francisco 2011, ITBA Special Recognition Award, Co. Kildare, Ireland 2012, One of The 15 Most Influential Islamic Leaders in the World, blog of Chair. of the public sector of Russia's Muftis Council 2012, David Rockefeller Bridging Leadership Award 2012, One of The 500 Most Powerful People on the Planet, Foreign Policy magazine 2013, Gold Medal, Royal Architectural Inst. of Canada 2013, 2013 North–South Prize of the Council of Europe 2014, Address to the Parl. of Canada 2014. *Leisure interests:* breeding racehorses, yachting, skiing. *Address:* Aiglemont, 60270 Gouvieux, France.

AGAFANGEL, His Eminence (Savvin Alexey Mikhailovich), Metropolitan of Odessa and Izmail, Kand.Theol; Ukrainian Orthodox ecclesiastic; b. 2 Sept. 1938, Burdino, Lipetsk Region; s. of Savvin Mikhail Petrovick and Savvina Marpha Federovna; ed Odessa Seminary, Moscow Theological Acad.; took monastic vows 1965; ordained as archimandrite 1967; Rector Odessa Seminary 1967–75; Bishop of Vinnitsa and Bratslav 1975–81; ordained as Archbishop 1981, Archbishop of Vinnitsa and Bratslav 1981–89; ordained as Metropolitan 1989, Metropolitan of Vinnitsa and Bratslav 1989–92; Metropolitan of Odessa and Izmail 1992–; People's Deputy of Ukraine 1990–94; Rector Odessa Seminary 1993–98; rep. of Russian Orthodox Church in Ukraine; Dr hc (Kiev) 1995; Order of the Holy Cross

(Jerusalem Patriarchate) 1981, Order of Friendship of Peoples 2003; UN Peace Medal 1988, Ukrainian President's Award, 2nd Rank 1999, 1st Rank 2003, Imperial Culture Award, Union of Writers of Russia 2005. *Address:* Monastery of the Dormition, Mayatchny pereulok 6, Odessa 65038, Ukraine (home). *Telephone:* (48) 746-3037 (home).

AGAM, Tan Sri Hasmy, BA, MA; Malaysian diplomatist; *Executive Chairman, Institute of Diplomacy and Foreign Relations, Ministry of Foreign Affairs;* b. 3 Feb. 1944, Malacca; m.; two d.; ed Univ. of Malaya, Kuala Lumpur, Fletcher School of Law and Diplomacy, Tufts Univ., USA; joined Foreign Ministry as Asst Sec. 1968, various positions in Ministry and in missions in Saigon, Washington, DC, Hanoi and London; seconded to Nat. Inst. of Public Admin as Head, Centre for Int. Relations and Diplomacy 1981; Amb. to Libya (also accred to Malta) 1986–88, to France (also accred to Portugal) 1990–92; Alt. Perm. Rep. to UN, Alt. Del. to Security Council 1988–90; Dir-Gen. Relations with ASEAN, Foreign Ministry 1993, Deputy Sec.-Gen. for Int. Orgs and Multilateral Econs 1994–96; Alt. Perm. Rep. to UN 1996–98, apptd Perm. Rep. 1998; mem. Sec.-Gen.'s Advisory Bd on Disarmament Matters; currently Exec. Chair. Institute of Diplomacy and Foreign Relations (IDFR), Ministry of Foreign Affairs; Chair. Human Rights Commission of Malaysia 2010–; Adjunct Prof., Northern Univ. of Malaysia, Int. Islamic Univ. Malaysia, Nat. Univ. of Malaysia; Panglima Setia Mahkota, Panglima Jasa Negara, Darjah Mulia Seri Melaka, Johan Setia Mahkota, Kesatria Mangku Negara. *Address:* Institute of Diplomacy and Foreign Relations, Ministry of Foreign Affairs, Jalan Wisma Putra, 50602 Kuala Lumpur, Malaysia (office). *Telephone:* (3) 21491001 (office). *Fax:* (3) 21445640 (office). *E-mail:* hasmy@idfr.gov.my (office). *Website:* www.idfr.gov.my (office).

AGAM, Yaacov; Israeli artist; b. (Jacob Gipstein), 1928, Rishon Le-zion; m. Clila Agam 1954; two s. one d.; ed Bezalel School of Art, Jerusalem, Atelier d'art abstrait, Paris; travelling retrospective exhbn Paris (Nat. Museum of Modern Art), Amsterdam, Düsseldorf, Tel-Aviv 1972–73. *Publications:* 36 books covering his non-verbal visual learning method (visual alphabet). *Address:* 26 rue Boulard, Paris 75014, France. *Telephone:* 1-43-22-00-88.

AGANBEGYAN, Abel Gezevich; Russian/Armenian economist; b. 8 Oct. 1932, Tbilisi, Georgia; s. of Galina A. Aganbegyan; m. Zoya V. Kupriyanova 1953; one s. one d.; ed Moscow State Econ. Inst.; mem. CPSU 1956–91; Economist, Gen. Econ. Dept, State Cttee for Labour and Wages 1955–61; Head of Lab., Inst. of Econs and Industrial Eng, Siberian Branch of USSR Acad. of Sciences 1961–67, Dir Inst. of Econs and Industrial Eng 1967–85; Prof. of Econs, Novosibirsk State Univ.; Prof. Acad. of Nat. Econ.; Chair. Cttee for Study of Productive Forces and Natural Resources 1965; Rector, Acad. of Nat. Economy 1989–2002; mem. Presidium; Chair. All-Union Club of Managers; Corresp. mem. USSR (now Russian) Acad. of Sciences 1964, mem. 1974, Acad.-Sec., Dept of Econ. 1986–89; Foreign mem. Bulgarian and Hungarian Acads. of Sciences; Corresp. FBA; two Orders of Lenin; Dr. hc (Alicante and Łódź). *Publications:* Wages and Salaries in the USSR 1959, On the Application of Mathematics and Electronic Machinery in Planning 1961, Some Questions of Monopoly Price Theory with Reference to the USA 1961, Economical-Mathematical Analysis of Input-Output Tables in USSR 1968, System of Models of National Economy Planning 1972, Management of the Socialist Enterprises 1979, Management and Efficiency: USSR Economy in 1981–85 1981, Siberia—not by Hearsay (with Z. Ibragimova) 1981, Economic Methods in Planned Management (with D. Kazakevich) 1985, Enterprise: Managing Scientific and Technological Progress (with V. Rechin) 1986; The Challenge: Economics of Perestroika 1987, Moving the Mountain: Inside Perestroika 1989, Measures and Stages of Improving USSR Economy 1991.

AĞAOĞLU, Adalet; Turkish writer; b. 23 Oct. 1929, Ankara; d. of Mustafa Sümer and İsmet Sümer; m. Halim Ağaoğlu 1954; ed Univ. of Ankara; worked for Türkiye Radyo Televizyon Kurumu (TRT) 1953–73; freelance writer 1973–; co-founder Arena Theatre Co.; Hon. PhD (Anadolu Univ.) 1998, Dr hc (Ohio State Univ.) 1998; TDK Theatre Award 1974, Pres. of the Turkish Repub. Grand Prize for Culture and the Arts 1995. *Publications include:* (in Turkish) novels: Lying Down to Die 1973, The Fine Rose of My Mind 1976, A Wedding Night (Sedat Simavi Literature Award 1979, Orhan Kemal Novel Award 1980, Madaralı Novel Award 1980) 1979, The End of Summer 1980, A Few People 1984, Migration Cleansing 1985, No... 1987, Cold in Spirit 1991, A Romantic Viennese Summer (Aydın Doğan Novel Award 1997) 1993; short stories: High Tension (Sait Faik Prize 1975) 1974, The First Sound of Silence 1978, Come On, Let's Go 1982, Ways to Defend Life 1997; essays: Crossing 1986, My Life at Night 1992, Encounters 1993, Other Encounters 1996; plays: Three Play (Prize of Turkish Language Inst.) 1956, Playing Mum and Dad 1964, Bingo 1967, The Crack in The Roof 1969, The Death of a Hero 1973, Cocoons 1973, The Song that Wrote Itself 1977, Plays 1982, Too Far Too Close 1991 (Is Bankasi Grand Award for the Theatre) 1991, The Story of the Wall 1992, The Poem and the Fly 1992. *Leisure interests:* reading, writing. *Address:* Piyasa Cad, Bülbül Sok, 10/5 Ceviz Apt, Büyükdere, Istanbul, Turkey. *Telephone:* (1) 1422636.

AGARWAL, Anil; Indian business executive; *Executive Chairman, Vedanta Resources plc;* b. 2 July 1953, Patna, Bihar; m.; two c.; f. Sterlite Gold Ltd (now Sterlite Industries) 1976; currently Chair. and Man. Dir, Vedanta Resources plc (diversified metals and mining group) after Sterlite acquired Shamsher Sterling, CEO 1979–2005, Exec. Chair. 2005–; mem. Bd of Dirs BALCO, HZL, Vedanta Alumina Ltd; Lifetime Achievement Award, Mining Journal 2009. *Address:* Vedanta House, 75 Nehru Road, Vile Parle (East), Mumbai 400 099, India (office). *Telephone:* (22) 66461000 (office). *Fax:* (22) 66461451 (office). *Website:* www.vedantaresources.com (office).

AGARWAL, Bina, PhD; Indian economist and academic; *Professor of Economics, Institute of Economic Growth, University of Delhi;* b. Jabalpur; ed Univ. of Delhi, Univ. of Cambridge, UK, Delhi School of Econs; Research Assoc., Council for Social Devt 1972–74; Visiting Fellow, Inst. of Devt Studies, Univ. of Sussex, UK 1978–79, Research Fellow, Science Policy Research Unit 1979–80; Assoc. Prof. of Econs, Inst. of Econ. Growth, Univ. of Delhi 1981–88, Prof. 1988–, Head, Population Research Centre 1996–98, 2002–04; Fellow, Bunting Inst., Radcliffe Coll., USA 1989–91; Visiting Prof., Harvard Univ. Cttee on Degrees in Women's Studies 1991–92, First Daniel H.H. Ingalls Visiting Prof. March–Sept. 1999, Visiting Research Fellow, Ash Inst., Kennedy School of Govt 2006–2007, Hon. Visiting Fellow March–Dec. 2008; Visiting Scholar, Inst. for Advanced Study, Princeton

1995; Visiting Prof., School of Natural Resources and Environment, Univ. of Michigan 2003; Visiting Prof., Coll. of Liberal Arts, Univ. of Minnesota May–June 2004, Visiting Prof. and Winton Chair Holder 2004; Global Visiting Prof., New York Univ.; Hirschorn Visiting Prof., Barnard Coll., Columbia Univ. Dec. 2001; Pres. Int. Asscn for Feminist Econs 2004, Vice-Pres. and Bd mem. 1999–2002; Vice-Pres. Int. Econ. Asscn 2002–05; Research Assoc., Council for Social Devt, Delhi, mem. Exec. Cttee 1999–2002; Founder-mem. Ankur (Delhi-based NGO conducting non-formal education in Delhi's slums) 1981; Founder-mem. Exec. Cttee Int. Soc. for Ecological Econs, Delhi 2000–05, Indian Asscn of Women's Studies 1984–86, 1998–2000; mem. Five Year Plans 1988–89, 1996, 2001, 2005–06; mem. Organizing Cttee XI to XIV World Congresses 1995–2004; mem. Bd of Dirs UN Research Inst. for Social Devt 2009–; mem. Research Advisory Cttee on Women's Studies, Indian Council for Social Science Research, New Delhi 1987–89, Research Advisory Cttee on Women and Agricultural Modernisation, Indian Council of Agricultural Research 1987–88, Tech. Mission on Drinking Water and Related Water Man., Ministry of Science and Tech. 1987–89, Expert Group on Structural Adjustment & Women, Commonwealth Secretariat, London 1988–89, Advisory Cttee, Female-Headed Households, Population Council, New York 1989–92, Harvard Centre for Population and Devt Studies 1990–91, Advisory Cttee on Research Priorities for the Educ. of Girls and Women in Africa, African Acad. of Sciences (Kenya) 1992–94; mem. of Advisory Cttee, UNDP Human Devt Report on Poverty 1997, mem. Steering Cttee Int. Union for Conservation of Nature Comm. for Environmental, Econ. and Social Policy 1997–99 (mem. Exec. Cttee 1999–2002), Governing Body of Global Devt Network: 2000–06, Advisory Board Pradan (NGO promoting self-help groups and income generating activities in rural central India) 2000–06, Indo-European Union Round Table 2001–04, Advisory Bd FAO, Rome 2002– (mem. Steering Cttee 2007), Cttee for Devt Policy, UN Econ. and Social Council 2007–, Think Tank of Feminist Economists for 11th Plan 2007; Dr hc (Inst. of Social Studies, The Hague) 2007; Malcolm Adisheshiah Award for distinguished contribs to devt studies 2002, Ramesh Chandra Award for outstanding contribs to agricultural econs 2005, Padma Shri 2008, Leontief Award, Global Devt and Environment Inst., Tufts Univ., USA 2009. *Publications include:* Mechanization in Indian Agriculture 1983, Cold Hearths and Barren Slopes: The Woodfuel Crisis in the Third World 1986, Structures of Patriarchy: State, Community and Household in Modernizing Asia (ed.) 1988, Women, Poverty and Ideology in Asia: Contradictory Pressures, Uneasy Resolutions (co-ed.) 1989, Women and Work in the World Economy 1991, A Field of One's Own: Gender and Land Rights in South Asia 1994 (Ananda Kentish Coomaraswamy Book Prize 1996, Edgar Graham Book Prize 1996, K. H. Batheja Award 1995–96), Psychology, Rationality and Economic Behaviour: Challenging Assumptions (co-ed.) 2005, Capabilities, Freedom and Equality: Amartya Sen's Work from a Gender Perspective (co-ed.) 2006; numerous articles in learned journals on property rights, environment, agricultural technology, poverty, political economy of gender and related topics. *Leisure interests:* writing poetry, painting, reading literature and biography, nature walks, movies. *Address:* Institute of Economic Growth, University Enclave, University of Delhi, Delhi 110 007, India (office). *Telephone:* (11) 27667250 (office); (11) 27667424 (office); (11) 27667101 (office). *Fax:* (11) 27667410 (office); (11) 24353393 (office). *E-mail:* bina@iegindia.org (office); bina_india@yahoo.com. *Website:* www.iegindia.org (office); www.binaagarwal .com.

AGARWAL, Sudarshan, LLB; Indian lawyer and politician (retd); b. 19 June 1931, Ludhiana; m. Usha Agarwal; one s. one d.; Chief Returning Officer, Indian presidential election 1982, 1992; Sec.-Gen. Rajya Sabha 1981–93; Gov. of Uttaranchal (now Uttarakhand) 2003–07, of Sikkim 2007–08; currently involved in community work; participated in several parl. confs and int. goodwill dels worldwide; mem. and Past Pres. Rotary Club of Delhi, Dist Gov. Rotary Int., mem. Bd of Dirs Rotary Int., mem. and Chair. several Rotary Int. Cttees, mem. Nat. Human Rights Comm. 1998–2000, Chair. Rotary Foundation (India) 1992–2002, Trustee Rotary Service to Humanity Awards Trust; Chair. Uttaranchal State Red Cross Soc. and State Child Welfare Council; Pres. Delhi Gymkhana Club 1986–88; Pres. Emer. Rotary Blood Bank & Eye Care Centre; Patron Him Jyoti School, Chief Patron IMA Blood Bank, Dehradun; Hon. DSc (Gurukul Univ., Uttaranchal); Rotary Foundation Citation for Meritorious Service and Rotary Foundation Distinguished Service Award. *Leisure interest:* gardening. *Address:* Rotary Blood Bank, 57 Tughlakabad Institutional Area, New Delhi, 110 062 (office); C-173, Defence Colony, New Delhi, 110 024, India (home). *Telephone:* (11) 29054065 (office); (11) 24332676 (home). *Fax:* (11) 26056333 (office). *E-mail:* sud.agarwal@ gmail.com (home). *Website:* www.rotarybloodbank.org (office); www .himjyotischool.org (office).

AGASSI, Andre; American professional tennis player (retd); b. 29 April 1970, Las Vegas, Nev.; s. of Mike Agassi and Elizabeth Agassi; m. 1st Brooke Shields (q.v.) 1997 (divorced 1999); m. 2nd Steffi Graf (q.v.); one s.; coached from age 13 by Nick Bollettieri, strength coach Gil Reyes; turned professional 1986; semi-finalist, French Open 1988, US Open 1988, 1989; mem. US team that defeated Australia in Davis Cup Final 1990; defeated Stefan Edberg to win inaugural ATP World Championship, Frankfurt 1991; finalist French Open 1990, 1991, US Open 1990, 1995, 2002, Wimbledon 1999; won Wimbledon 1992, US Open 1994, 1999, Canadian Open 1995, Australian Open 1995, 2000, 2001, 2003, French Open 1999; winner Olympic Games tennis tournaments 1996; Asscn of Tennis Professionals World Champion 1990; fifth player to win all four Grand Slam titles; winner of 59 singles titles and one doubles title; retd 2006; f. Andre Agassi Charitable Foundation to help at-risk youth in Las Vegas 1994; f. Agassi Enterprises, Inc. *Publication:* Open (auto-biog.) 2009. *Address:* International Management Group, 1 Erieview Plaza, Suite 1300, Cleveland, OH 44114; Andre Agassi Charitable Foundation, 3960 Howard Hughes Parkway, Suite 750, Las Vegas, NV 89109. USA. *Website:* www.agassifoundation.org.

AGASSI, Shai, BSc; Israeli business executive; b. April 1968, Tel-Aviv; s. of Reuven Agassi; m.; two s.; ed Technion (Israeli Inst. of Tech.); computer programmer, Army Intelligence, Israeli Army; f. QuickSoft (software distribution co.) 1990, Menahel Inc. 1991, TopManage 1992, QuickSoft Media 1994; f. TopTier Software 1992, Chair. 1996–99; Chief Exec. 1999–2001; Chief Exec. SAP Portals (later SAP Markets) 2001–02, mem. Exec. Bd SAP AG, Walldorf 2002–07, Top Tech. Developer 2003, Pres. Product and Tech. Group 2003–07, consultant 2007–; resgnd his position to pursue interests in alternative energy and climate change;

Founder Better Place (fmrly Project Better Place) 2007, CEO 2007–12. *Leisure interests:* reading technology books. *Address:* c/o Better Place, 1070 Arastradero Road, Suite 220, Palo Alto, CA 94304, USA. *E-mail:* information@betterplace.com. *Website:* www.betterplace.com.

AGBOYIBO, (Appolinaire) Yawovi; Togolese politician and lawyer; b. 1943; ed in Togo, Senegal, France and Côte d'Ivoire; fmr Head of Nat. Human Rights Comm.; Leader, Action Cttee for Renewal (CAR) party 1991–2008, Hon. Pres. 2010–, jailed for six months for defaming Togolese Prime Minister Aug. 2001, freed as gesture of appeasement March 2002; cand. in presidential elections 2003, 2010; led inter-Togolese dialogue in Burkina Faso helping to broker agreement to form a power-sharing cabinet Aug. 2006; Prime Minister of Togo Sept. 2006–07. *Address:* Comité d'action pour le Renouveau (CAR), 58 ave du 24 janvier, BP06, Lomé, Togo (office). *Telephone:* 222-05-66 (office). *Fax:* 221-62-54 (office). *E-mail:* yagboyibo@ bibway.com (office).

AGEE, William J., MBA; American business executive; b. 5 Jan. 1938, Boise, Ida; s. of Harold J. Agee and Suzanne Agee; m. 1st Diane Weaver 1957; one s. two d.; m. 2nd Mary Cunningham 1982; one d.; ed Stanford Univ., Boise Junior Coll., Univ. of Idaho, Harvard Univ.; with Boise Cascade Corpn 1963–72; Sr Vice-Pres. and Chief Financial Officer, Bendix Corpn 1972–76, Pres. and COO 1976–77, Chair. and CEO 1977–83, Pres. 1977–79; CEO Semper Enterprises, Inc. (now Semper Pnrs) 1983–; Chair., Pres. and CEO Morrison Knudsen Corpn 1988–95; Dir ASARCO, Equitable Life Assurance Soc. of US, Dow Jones & Co. Inc., Econ. Club of Detroit, Detroit Renaissance Inc., Nat. Council for US–China Trade, Gen. Foods Corpn, Detroit Econ. Growth Corpn 1978–, United Foundation, Nat. Council for US–China Trade; mem. Conf. Bd, Council on Foreign Relations, Business Roundtable, American and other insts of CPAs, Bd of Dirs, Assocs of Harvard Business School 1977, United Negroes Coll. Fund 1977; Chair. Gov.'s Higher Educ. Capital Investment Advisory Cttee, Pres.'s Industrial Advisory Sub-Cttee on Econ. and Trade Policy 1978–79, Advisory Council Cranbrook Educational Community 1978, Trustee 1978; Trustee Urban Inst., Cttee for Econ. Devt 1977, Citizen Research Council, Mich. 1977; numerous hon. degrees. *Leisure interests:* tennis, golf, swimming. *Address:* 1733 Fir Hill, Saint Helena, CA 94574-2356, USA.

AGHILI, Shadmehr; Iranian singer, musician and actor; b. 27 Jan. 1973, Tehran; singer and writer of popular songs. *Film:* Par e Parvaz (also composed soundtrack). *Recordings include:* Bahare Man 1998, Mosaafer 1999, Dehati 2000, Naghmehaye Mashreghi 2001, Pare Parvaz 2002, Khiali Nist 2004, Adam Foroush 2004, Popcorn 2006, Destiny 2009. *E-mail:* Info@shadmehraghili.net. *Website:* www .shadmehraghili.net.

AGIUS, Marcus Ambrose Paul, MA, MBA; British business executive and investment banker; b. 22 July 1946, Walton-on-Thames; s. of the late Alfred Victor Louis Benedict Agius and Ena Eleanora Hueffer; m. Kate Juliette de Rothschild 1971; two d.; ed Univ. of Cambridge, Harvard Business School, USA; grad. trainee with Vickers PLC 1968–70; joined Lazard 1972, Man. Dir 1984–89, Vice-Chair. and Man. Dir Lazard Frères & Co. LLC 1989–2002, Deputy Chair. Lazard LLC 2002–06, Chair. Lazard Bank Ltd 2002–06; mem. Bd of Dirs BAA (British Airports Authority) PLC 1995–2006, Deputy Chair. 1998–2002, Chair. 2002–06; Dir (non-exec.) Barclays PLC 2006–12, Group Chair. 2007–12 (resgnd), Chair. Bd Corp. Governance and Nominations Cttee, Brand and Reputation Cttee, mem. Bd HR and Remuneration Cttee, Exec. Cttee of Institut Int. d'Etudes Bancaires, Takeover Panel; mem. Advisory Council, The CityUK; Sr Ind. Dir (non-exec.) BBC 2006–; Chair. Trustees of The Royal Botanic Gardens, Kew 2004–, British Bankers Asscn 2010; Business Amb., UK Trade and Investment. *Leisure interests:* gardening, shooting, skiing. *Address:* c/o Barclays plc, 1 Churchill Place, Canary Wharf, London, E14 5HP, England.

AGLUKKAQ, The Hon. Leona; Canadian politician; *Minister of the Environment;* b. 28 June 1967; fmr Asst Deputy Minister of Human Resources, Regional Govt of Nunavut; fmr Minister of Health and Social Services and Minister Responsible for Status of Women, Exec. Council of Nunavut; Deputy Clerk, Nunavut Legis. Ass. 2000–02, mem. Legis. Ass. 2004–08; MP for Nunavut 2008–; Minister for Health 2008–13, Minister of Environment, Minister of Canadian Northern Econ. Devt Agency and Minister for Arctic Council 2013–; mem. Conservative Party of Canada. *Address:* Department of Environment, Informathèque, 351 blvd St Joseph, place Vincent-Massey, 8e étage, Gatineau, QC K1A 0H3, Canada (office). *Telephone:* (819) 997-2800 (office). *Fax:* (819) 994-1412 (office). *E-mail:* enviroinfo@ec.gc.ca (office). *Website:* www.ec.gc.ca (office).

AGNELLI, Roger, BEcons; Brazilian mining executive; b. 3 May 1959; ed Fundação Armando Álvares Penteado, São Paulo; began career with Bradesco Group 1981, Exec. Dir Bradesco Bank 1998–2000, Pres. and CEO Bradespar SA 2000–01; Chair. Companhia Vale do Rio Doce (CVRD) 2000–01 (now called Vale), Pres. and CEO 2001–11; Dir Spectra Energy (USA), Duke Energy (USA) 2004–, Suzano Petroquimica SA, Petrobras-Petroleo Brasileiro SA, INCO Ltd 2006–; Dir (non-exec.) Asea Brown Boveri (ABB) 2002–; fmr Counselor, São Paulo Power and Light Co., Companhia Siderurgica Nacional; Vice-Pres. Associação Brasileira da Infraestrutura e Indústrias de Base (ABDIB); mem. Conselho de Desenvolvimento Economico e Social (Econ. and Social Devt Council, CDES); mem. Int. Investments Council for S Africa; mem. Int. Advisory Cttee, NYSENext; O Globo Faz Diferença Award 2007, Latin Trade Bravo Business Leader of the Year 2007, named amongst 100 most influential Brazilians of 2009. *Address:* Office of the Board of Directors, Asea Brown Boveri (ABB), Rua Vinte e Quatro de Fevereiro 126, Bonsucesso, 221040-300 Rio de Janeiro, Brazil (office). *Telephone:* (21) 3868-2090 (office). *Fax:* (21) 3356-9772 (office). *E-mail:* info@abb.com (office). *Website:* www.abb.com (office).

AGNELO, HE Cardinal Geraldo Majella; Brazilian ecclesiastic; *Archbishop Emeritus of São Salvador da Bahia;* b. 19 Oct. 1933, Juiz de Fora; s. of Antônio Agnelo and Silvia Spagnolo Agnelo; ordained priest 1957; elected Bishop of Toledo 1978; Bishop of Londrina 1982; resgnd 1991; Archbishop of São Salvador da Bahía 1999–2011, Archbishop Emer. 2011–; cr. Cardinal (Cardinal-Priest of San Gregorio Magno alla Magliana Nuova) 2001. *Address:* Archdiocese of São Salvador da Bahía, Rua Martin Afonso de Souza 270, 40100–050 Salvador, Bahía (office); Avenida Cardeal da Silva 26, Casa 33, 40220–140 Salvador, Bahía, Brazil (home). *Telephone:* (71) 328-6699 (office); (71) 331-2738 (home). *Fax:* (71) 328-0068 (office); (71) 261-5243 (home). *E-mail:* contato@arquidiocesedesalvador.org.br (office).

AGNEW, Jonathan Geoffrey William, MA; British banker; b. 30 July 1941, Windsor, Berks.; s. of the late Sir Geoffrey William Gerald Agnew and Hon. Doreen Maud Jessel; m. 1st Hon. Agneta Joanna Middleton Campbell 1966 (divorced 1985); one s. two d.; m. 2nd Marie-Claire Dreesmann 1990; one s. one d.; ed Eton Coll. and Trinity Coll., Cambridge; with The Economist 1964–65, IBRD 1965–67; with Hill Samuel & Co. 1967–73, Dir 1971; Morgan Stanley & Co. 1973–82, Man. Dir 1977; with J.G.W. Agnew & Co. 1983–86; Chief Exec. ISRO 1986; with Kleinwort Benson Group PLC 1987–93, Chief Exec. 1989–93; Chair. Limit PLC 1993–2000, Henderson Geared Income & Growth Trust PLC 1995–2003, Gerrard Group PLC 1999–2000, LMS Capital plc 2006–10; Dir and Chair. The Cayenne Trust PLC 2006–, Ashmore Global Opportunities Ltd 2007–13; Dir (non-exec.) Thos. Agnew & Sons Ltd 1969–2008, Thos. Agnew & Sons (Holdings) Ltd 2008–13, Jarvis PLC 2003–04; Dir (non-exec.) Nationwide Building Soc. 1997–2007, Deputy Chair. (non-exec.) 1999–2002, Chair. 2002–07; Dir (non-exec.) Beazley PLC 2002–12, Chair. 2003–12; Dir Soditic Ltd 2001–04; Sr Ind. Dir Rightmove PLC 2006–; mem. Council Lloyd's 1995–98. *Address:* Flat E, 51 Eaton Square, London, SW1W 9BE, England (home). *Telephone:* 7714-243891 (mobile) (office); (20) 7235-7589 (home). *E-mail:* jgwagnew@yahoo.co.uk (home).

AGNEW, (Morland Herbert) Julian, MA; British art dealer; *Chairman, Thomas Agnew & Sons Ltd;* b. 20 Sept. 1943, London, England; s. of the late Sir Geoffrey William Gerald Agnew and Hon. Doreen Maud Jessel, CB, CMG; m. 1st Elizabeth Margaret Moncrieff Mitchell 1973 (divorced 1992); one s. two d.; m. 2nd Victoria Burn Callander 1993 (divorced 2013); one s.; ed Eton Coll., Trinity Coll., Cambridge; joined Thomas Agnew & Sons Ltd 1965, Dir 1968, Man. Dir 1987–92, Chair. 1992–; Pres. British Antique Dealers Asscn 1979–81; Chair. Soc. of London Art Dealers 1986–90; Chair. Friends of the Courtauld Inst. 2002–05, Trustee 2006–; Pres. Evelyn Trust, Cambridge. *Leisure interests:* opera, music, books, golf. *Address:* Thomas Agnew & Sons Ltd, 35 Albemarle Street, London, W1S 4JD (office); Flat 111, Howard House, Dolphin Square, London, SW1V 3PE (home); Egmere Farm House, Egmere, nr Walsingham, Norfolk, England (home). *Telephone:* (20) 7290-9250 (office). *Fax:* (20) 7629-4359 (office). *E-mail:* julianagnew@agnewsgallery.co.uk (office). *Website:* www.agnewsgallery.com (office).

AGNEW, Sir Rudolph (Ion Joseph), Kt, FRSA; British business executive; b. 12 March 1934; s. of Rudolph John Agnew and Pamela Geraldine Agnew (née Campbell); m. Whitney Warren 1980; ed Downside School; Commissioned Officer, 8th King's Royal Irish Hussars 1953–57; joined Consolidated Gold Fields PLC 1957, apptd Exec. Dir 1973, Deputy Chair. 1978–82, Group Chief Exec. 1978–89, Chair. 1983–89, mem. Cttee of Man. Dirs 1986–89; Chief Exec. Amey Roadstone Corpn 1974–78, Chair. 1974–77; Chair. and CEO TVS Entertainment 1990–93; apptd Chair. Stena Int. BV (fmrly Sealink Stena Line) 1990, Federated Aggregates PLC 1991–95, Bona Shipholding Ltd, Bermuda 1993–98, LASMO PLC 1994–2000, Redland PLC 1995–97, Star Mining Corpn 1995–98; Jt Chair. Global Stone Corpn (Canada) 1993–94; Dir (non-exec.) New London PLC 1985–96, Standard Chartered PLC 1988–97, Newmount Mining Corpn, USA 1989–98, Hanson PLC 1989–91; Vice-Pres. Nat. Asscn of Boys Clubs; mem. Council WWF (UK) 1989– (Trustee 1983–89); Fellow, Game Conservancy. *Leisure interest:* shooting. *Address:* 7 Eccleston Street, London, SW1X 9LX, England.

AGON, Jean-Paul; French business executive; *Chairman and CEO, L'Oréal Group;* b. Paris; three c.; ed Hautes Etudes Commerciales; joined L'Oréal Paris Group and worked in sales and marketing 1978–81, Gen. Man. Consumer Products Div., Greece 1981–86, Gen. Man. L'Oréal Paris 1986–89, Int. Man. Dir Luxury Products Div., Biotherm 1989–94, Gen. Man. L'Oréal Germany 1994–97, Man. Dir L'Oréal Group's Asia zone 1997–2001, Pres. and CEO L'Oréal USA 2001–06, CEO L'Oréal 2006–11, Chair. and CEO 2011–. *Address:* L'Oréal SA, 41 rue Martre, 92117 Clichy Cedex, France (office). *Telephone:* 1-47-56-70-00 (office). *Fax:* 1-47-56-80-02 (office). *E-mail:* info@loreal.com (office). *Website:* www.loreal.com (office).

AGOSTINI, Giacomo (Ago); Italian motorcyclist; b. 16 June 1942, Brescia; rode for Morini 1961–64; understudy to Mike Hailwood at MV Augusta 1965, number one rider 1966–73, 1976–77; rode for Yamaha 1974–76; 311 wins; a record 122 Grand Prix wins (54 at 350 cc, 68 at 500 cc); 12 Isle of Man TT wins (350 cc: 1966, 1967, 1968, 1969, 1970, 1972; 500 cc: 1967, 1968, 1969, 1970, 1971, 1972); 18 Italian championship wins; a record 15 World Championship wins (350 cc: 1968, 1969, 1970, 1971, 1972, 1973, 1974; 500 cc: 1966, 1967, 1968, 1969, 1970, 1971, 1972, 1975); shares (with Mike Hailwood) record for most races won in a season (19 in 1970); AMA Motorcycle Hall of Fame 1999, named Grand Prix Legend, Fédération Internationale de Motocyclisme (FIM) 2000. *Website:* www.giacomo-agostini.com.

AGOVAKA, Peter Shanel; Solomon Islands politician; b. 1 Nov. 1959, Bemuta Village, Guadalcanal Prov.; ed North Sydney Inst. of Eng, Australia; fmr Community Affairs Officer, Gold Ridge Mining Ltd; MP for Cen. . Guadalcanal 2006–; Minister for Provincial Govt and Constituency Devt April–May 2006, for Commerce, Industries and Employment 2006–07, of Foreign Affairs 2010–12; Leader, Ind. MPs Jan.–Sept. 2008. *Address:* c/o Ministry of Foreign Affairs and External Trade, POB G10, Honiara, Solomon Islands.

AGRAWAL, Prabhu Lal, PhD; Indian business executive and engineer; b. 22 Oct. 1926, Udaipur, Rajasthan; s. of Tilok Chand Agrawal and Narayan Devi Agrawal; m. Pushpa Devi 1948; one s. one d.; ed Banaras Hindu Univ., Univ. of Sheffield, UK; Asst Prof., Coll. of Mining and Metallurgy, Banaras Hindu Univ. 1947–54, Reader 1954–56; Tech. Officer Rourkela Steel Plant, then Sr Fuel Engineer, then Asst Chief Fuel Engineer, Supt Energy and Economy Dept 1957–65, Chief Supt 1965–66, Asst Gen. Supt 1966–69, Gen. Man. 1971–78; Gen. Supt Alloy Steels Plant 1969–70; Gen. Supt Bokaro Steel Ltd 1970–71; Chair. Steel Authority of India 1978–80; Tech. Adviser, PT Krakatan Steel, Jakarta 1980–86; currently consultant on steel plant operation and man.; Pres. Indian Inst. of Metals 1978, Hon. mem. 1980; mem. Bd of Dirs Secure Meters Ltd; mem. judging panel for Prime Minister's Trophy for Best Operating Integrated Steel Plant 1992–97, 2000–01; Trustee, Sevamandir 1987–; Holkar Fellow, Banaras Hindu Univ.; Bundesverdienstkreuz (1st Class) 1981; Uttar Pradesh Govt Book Prize for Audyogik Indhan, Nat. Metallurgists Day Award 1966, FIE Foundation Award, India 1981, Tata Gold Medal, Indian Inst. of Metals 1981, Platinum Medal, Indian

Inst. of Metals 1993, Lifetime Achievement Award, Govt of India 2005. *Publications include:* Audyogik Indhan, Journey of a Steel Man (autobiog.) 2009; contrib. several tech. papers and reports. *Leisure interests:* reading, social work, walking. *Address:* Narayan Villa, 56-A New Fatehpura, Sukhadia Circle, Udaipur 313 004 (home); Seva Mandir, Old Fatehpura, Udaipur 313 004, India. *Telephone:* (294) 2560380 (office). *Fax:* (294) 2560380 (office). *E-mail:* prabhuagrawal@yahoo.com. *Website:* www.sevamandir.org.

AGRÉ, HE Cardinal Bernard; Côte d'Ivoirian ecclesiastic; *Archbishop Emeritus of Abidjan;* b. 2 March 1926, Monga, Abidjan; ordained priest 1953; Bishop of Man, Côte d'Ivorie 1968–92; Bishop of Yamoussoukro 1992–94; Archbishop of Abidjan 1994–2006 (retd); cr. Cardinal (Cardinal-Priest of S. Giovanni Crisostomo a Monte Sacro Alto) 2001; Commdr de l'Ordre Nat. 1992. *Address:* c/o Archevêché, av. Jean Paul II, 01 BP 1287, Abidjan 01, Côte d'Ivoire (office).

AGRE, Peter C., BA, MD; American physician, molecular biologist and academic; *Director, Johns Hopkins Malaria Research Institute;* b. 1949, Northfield, Minn.; ed Theodore Roosevelt High School, Minneapolis, Augsburg Coll., Minneapolis, Johns Hopkins Univ., Baltimore; Fellow, Univ. of North Carolina 1974–81; Fellow, Depts of Medicine and Cell Biology, Johns Hopkins Univ., Baltimore, Md 1981–2005, Prof. of Biological Chem. 1993–2005; Vice-Chancellor, Science and Tech. of Chem. and Public Policy Studies and Prof. of Cell Biology and Public Policy Studies, Duke Univ. Medical Center 2005–08, mem. Chancellor's Science Advisory Council 2006–07; Prof. and Dir Johns Hopkins Malaria Research Inst. 2008–; mem. NAS 2000–, American Acad. of Arts and Sciences 2003–, AAAS (mem. Bd Dirs, Pres.-Elect 2007–08, Pres. 2009); Founding mem. Scientists and Engineers for America (mem. Bd of Advisors); numerous hon. doctorates; Nobel Prize in Chem. (jt recipient) for his discovery of aquaporins 2003, Distinguished Eagle Scout Award. *Publications include:* numerous specialist papers, including cross-country skiing (has participated in the Vasaloppet ski race). *Address:* E5146 Bloomberg School of Public Health, Baltimore, MD 21205, USA (office). *Telephone:* (443) 287-8745 (office). *Fax:* (410) 955-0105 (office). *E-mail:* malaria@jhsph.edu (office). *Website:* malaria.jhsph.edu (office).

AGREST, Diana, DipArch; American architect and urban designer; *Co-founder and Partner, Agrest and Gandelsonas Architects;* b. 1945, Buenos Aires; m. Mario Gandelsonas; ed Univ. of Buenos Aires, École Pratique des Hautes Etudes and Centre du Recherche d'Urbanisme, Paris, France; Prof., Columbia, Princeton and Yale Univs, USA 1973–96; currently Prof. of Architecture, Cooper Union, New York; Partner (with husband), Agrest and Gandelsonas Architects, New York; f. Diana Agrest Architectural Firm, New York; fmr Fellow, Inst. for Architecture and Urban Studies, New York 1972–84; Design Excellence Award, AIA NY State 2002, Design Excellence Award, AIA New York City 2002, Design Merit Award, Soc. of Registered Architects 2002, Masterwork Award, Municipal Art Soc. 2002, NY State Council on the Arts Grant 2003, AIA Brunner Award Grant 2004. *Architectural and urban design works include:* Melrose Community Center, New York, urban design for Shanghai, People's Repub. of China, plan for West Midtown Manhattan, New York, farm in Sagaponack, NY, house in Sagaponack, farm in Uruguay, Des Moines Vision Plaza, Ia, duplex on Central Park West, Manhattan, house in Majorca, Spain. *Publications include:* A Romance with the City: The Work of Irwin S. Chanin, Architecture from Without: Theoretical Framings for a Critical Perspective, Agrest and Gandelsonas Works (co-author), The Sex of Architecture; articles on architecture in numerous int. publs. *Leisure interest:* film-making. *Address:* Agrest and Gandelsonas Architects, 636 Broadway, Suite 1105, New York, NY 10012 (office); Irwin S. Chanin School of Architecture, Cooper Union, 30 Cooper Square, New York, NY 10003, USA. *Telephone:* (212) 625-3800 (A&G) (office); (212) 353-4100 (Cooper). *Fax:* (212) 965-8830 (A&G) (office); (212) 353-4327 (Cooper). *E-mail:* office@ag-architects.com (office); agrest@cooper.edu. *Website:* www.ag-architects.com (office); www.cooper.edu/architecture.

AGUADO, Victor M., MSc, MEng; Spanish engineer, aviation industry executive and international organization official; b. 9 June 1953; m. Paloma Sierra de Aguado; one s. two d.; ed Polytechnic Univ., Madrid, MIT, USA; student trainee, Lufthansa 1975; Man. of Tech. Standards, Maintenance Airforce Base, Albacete 1977–78; Systems Engineer in civil and mil. air traffic Man., Mitre Corpn, Boston, USA 1978–83; Programme Dir Civil Aviation Authority, Madrid 1983–84; Exec. Adviser to Sec. of State for Aerospace and Telecommunications Affairs 1984–85; Chair. Inter-Govt Task Force on major aerospace programmes 1984–85; Deputy Dir-Gen. in Spanish Admin 1985–88, Dir-Gen. 1988–90; apptd CEO ISDEFE SA Systems Engineering and Consulting Co., Madrid 1990; Air Navigation Commr ICAO, Montréal, Canada, later Pres. of Air Navigation 1996–2000; Dir-Gen. Eurocontrol (European Org. for the Safety of Air Navigation), Brussels 2001–07; Grand Cross of the Aeronautical Order of Merit; Global NavCom '97 Laurel Award. *Address:* c/o Eurocontrol, 96 rue de la Fusée, 1130 Brussels, Belgium.

AGÜERO DE CORRALES, Mireya, LLB, BA; Honduran diplomatist and politician; *Minister of Foreign Affairs;* m. Hector Luis Corrales; four c.; entered Consular Service of Honduras 1981, Foreign Service 1983, various positions including Head, Dept of Int. Politics and Head, Interamerican Affairs Dept within Directorate of Foreign Policy, Dir of Central American Affairs and mem. Advisory Bd for Minister of Foreign Affairs, Vice-Minister of Foreign Affairs 2010–13, Minister of Foreign Affairs 2013–; has participated in numerous forums and negotiation processes within UN, OAS, Central American Integration System and Central America–EU round tables; Area Coordinator for Foreign Policy, Juan Manuel Galvez Centre for Political, Econ. and Social Studies; fmr Campus Dir, Catholic Univ. of Honduras, Prof. of Law 1993; mem. Int. Law Comm. of Bar Asscn of Honduras; Order of Merit, rank of Grand Cross (Chile) 2011, Order of Francisco Morazan, Grade of Grand Cross, Silver Plate 2012. *Address:* Ministry of Foreign Affairs, Centro Cívico Gubernamental, Antigua Casa Presidencial, Blvd Kuwait, Contiguo a la Corte Suprema de Justicia, Tegucigalpa, Honduras (office). *Telephone:* 2230-4156 (office). *Fax:* 2230-5664 (office). *E-mail:* cancilleria.honduras@gmail.com (office). *Website:* www.sre.gob.hn (office).

AGUIAR-BRANCO, José Pedro Correia de; Portuguese lawyer and politician; *Minister of National Defence;* b. 18 July 1957; ed Univ. de Coimbra, Institut d'études politiques de Bordeaux, France; Founding Dir José Pedro Aguiar-Branco & Associados (legal practice) 2003–; mem. Assembleia da República (Parl.) 2005–; Minister of Justice 2004–05, of Nat. Defence 2011–; mem. Partido Social

Democrata (PSD), Chair. PSD Parl. Group 1996–99, 2009–10; mem. Nat. Directorate, Portuguese Asscn of Young Lawyers (APJA) 1987–89, Vice-Pres. 1988–91, Pres. 1991–94; mem. Portuguese Bar Asscn, Pres. Porto Div. 2002–04. *Address:* Ministry of National Defence, Av. Ilha da Madeira 1, 1400-204 Lisbon, Portugal (office). *Telephone:* (21) 3010001 (office). *Fax:* (21) 3020284 (office). *E-mail:* gcrp@sg.mdn.gov.pt (office). *Website:* www.mdn.gov.pt (office).

AGUIAR CUNHA, Paulo Guilherme; Brazilian engineer, academic and business executive; *Chairman, Ultrapar Holdings;* ed Pontificia Universidade Católica do Rio de Janeiro; Prof. of Eng, Pontificia Universidade Católica do Rio de Janeiro and at Fed. Univ. of Rio de Janeiro 1963–66; joined Ultrapar 1967, Vice-Pres. 1973–81, CEO 1981–2007, Chair. Ultrapar Holdings 1998–; mem. Bd of Dirs Monteiro Aranha 1997–; Pres. Brazilian Asscn of Tech. Standards (ABNT), Instituto Brasileiro de Petróleo; fmr Pres. IEDI (Research Inst. for Industrial Devt), currently mem. Bd of Dirs; mem. CMN (Nat. Monetary Council), Bd of BNDESPAR (subsidiary of BNDES), Consulting Bd of Brazilian Chemical Industries Asscn (ABIQUIM), Bd of Superior Council of Economy, Consultative Council for Industry of Federação das Indústrias do Estado de São Paulo (FIESP), Bd of Insper (fmrly IBMEC), IPT (Technological Research Inst.), Bd of Superior Strategic Council of FIESP 2008–. *Address:* Ultrapar Holdings, Avenida Brigadeiro Luiz Antônio 1343, São Paulo 01317-910, Brazil (office). *Telephone:* (11) 3177-7014 (office). *Fax:* (11) 3177-6107 (office). *E-mail:* info@ultra.com.br (office). *Website:* www.ultra.com.br (office).

AGUILAR MARMOLEJO, María de los Dolores, MA, PhD; Mexican international organization executive; *Director General, Inter-American Children's Institute (IIN-OAS);* b. 1966; ed Universidad La Salle, México, Univ. of Santiago de Compostela, Spain; extensive experience as a teacher; has worked with Univ. of Anahuac and Technological Univ. of Mexico; currently Prof. of Basic Educ., with grad. studies in philosophy, Universidad La Salle, México; recognized instructor in workshops and adviser on schoolwork consultancy; lectures on issues of family, children, health, educ., policy and organizational devt, among others; mem. Partido Acción Nacional (Nat. Action Party—PAN) 1984–, cand. for various elective offices at local level; Deputy to Fed. Dist Legis. Ass. 1997–2000; worked for Nat. System for Integral Devt of the Family 2001–08, served as adviser to Directorate-Gen., Deputy Dir Care Unit to the Vulnerable Population and CEO for Child Welfare; participated in design of 'Diagnóstico de la Familia Mexicana' basic tool for the analysis, design and implementation of public policies on the family 2003–05; Dir-Gen. Inter-American Children's Inst. (IIN-OAS) 2008–. *Address:* Inter-American Children's Institute, Avenida 8 de Octubre 2904, Montevideo 11600, Uruguay (office). *Telephone:* (2) 487-2150 (office). *Fax:* (2) 487-3242 (office). *E-mail:* direcciongral@iinoea.org (office). *Website:* www.iin.oea.org (office).

AGUILERA, Christina Maria; American singer; b. 18 Dec. 1980, Staten Island, New York; m. Jordan Bratman 2005 (divorced); one s.; appeared on US Star Search TV talent show aged eight; joined cast of Orlando-based TV show, The New Mickey Mouse Club aged 12; intensive worldwide promotional touring 1997–; solo artist 1998–; coach and judge, The Voice (US TV show) 2011–13; apptd WFP Amb. Against Hunger; Grammy Award for Best New Artist 2000, American Latino Media Arts (ALMA) Award for Best New Entertainer 2000, Billboard Award for Female Vocalist of the Year 2000, Q Award (for Dirrty) 2003, Grammy Awards for Best Female Pop Vocal Performance (for Beautiful) 2004, (for Ain't No Other Man) 2007, MTV Europe Music Award for Best Female Artist 2006, Special Achievement Award, ALMA Awards 2012, George McGovern Leadership Award 2012. *Film:* Burlesque 2010. *Recordings include:* albums: Christina Aguilera 1999, Mi Reflejo (Billboard Latin Music Award for Best Pop Album of the Year 2001) 2000, My Kind Of Christmas 2000, Just Be Free 2001, Stripped 2002, Back to Basics 2006, Bi-On-Ic 2010, Lotus 2012. *Address:* Irving Azoff, Azoff Management, 3500 West Olive Avenue, Suite 600, Burbank, CA 91505, USA (office). *Website:* www .christinaaguilera.com.

AGUILERA, Isabel, MBA; Spanish business executive; *President, General Electric Spain and Portugal;* b. 1961, Seville; two c.; ed Univ. of Seville, Instituto de Empressa, Madrid; studied architecture and urban planning; Dir of Distribution and Marketing Communications Compaq Spain 1985–88; Marketing Man. Hewlett-Packard Spain 1989–95; with Airtel 1995–97; Man. Dir for Spain, Portugal and Italy, Dell Computer SA 1997–2002; COO and mem. Man. Cttee NH Hoteles 2002–06; Man. Dir Google Spain and Portugal 2006–08; Pres. General Electric Spain and Portugal 2008–; mem. Bd of Dirs Indra Sitemas 2006–, Pulsar Technologies, APD; Int. Dir Instituto de Empresa; ranked by Fortune magazine amongst 50 Most Powerful Women in Business outside the US (45th) 2002, ranked 20th by The Financial Times amongst 25 Most Important Women in Business in Europe 2004. *Address:* c/o General Electric Company, 3135 Easton Tpke, Fairfield, CT 06828-0001, USA (office). *Website:* www.ge.com/es (office).

AGUIRRE, Eduardo, Jr, BS; American banker, government official and fmr diplomatist; *Chairman and CEO, Atlantic Partners Group LLC;* b. 30 July 1946, Cuba; m. Maria Teresa Aguirre; one s. one d.; ed Louisiana State Univ., American Bankers Asscn's Nat. Commercial Lending Grad. School; emigrated from Cuba aged 15; apptd to Nat. Comm. for Employment Policy; apptd to State Bar of Tex. as non-attorney Dir 1990; mem. Bd of Regents Univ. of Houston System for a six-year term, Chair. 1996–98; fmr Pres. Int. Pvt. Banking, Bank of America; fmr Vice-Chair. and COO Export-Import Bank of the US (Ex-Im Bank), Acting Chair. for one year; Dir of US Citizenship and Immigration Services, Dept of Homeland Security 2003–05; has served on numerous professional and civic bds, including Tex. Children's Hosp., Tex. Bar Foundation, Operación Pedro Pan Foundation, Bankers Asscn for Finance and Trade, Houston chapters of the American Red Cross and the Salvation Army; Amb. to Spain (also accred to Andorra) 2005–09; Chair. and CEO Atlantic Partners Group LLC 2009–; mem. Bd of Dirs Greater Houston Partnership; mem. Royal Acad. of the Sea 2007–. mem. International Advisory Council, APCO Worldwide; Hon. mem. Foundation for Spanish Royal Acad. of the Sea 2007; Order of Hilal-i-Quaid-i-Azam (Pakistan), Grand Officer, Order of José Matías Delgado (El Salvador), Grand Officer, Order of Christopher Columbus (Dominican Repub.), Grand Cross of the First Class of the Pontifical Equestrian Order of St. Gregory the Great (The Holy See), Order of Isabella the Catholic Grand Cross (Spain); numerous other decorations from Spain, Andorra and Rwanda; Dr hc (Univ. of Connecticut, Univ. of Houston, Universidad Tecnológica de Santiago, Dominican Repub.); Ellis Island Medal of Honor,

Americanism Medal, The Daughters of the American Revolution 2004. *Telephone:* (281) 556-0753. *E-mail:* eaguirre@atlanticpartners.us.

AGUIRRE URIOSTE, Luis Fernando, MSc, PhD; Bolivian biologist, conservationist and academic; *Researcher and Professor, Centre for Biodiversity and Genetics, Universidad Mayor de San Simon;* ed Universidad Mayor de San Andres, La Paz, Antwerp Univ., Belgium; f. Bolivian Bat Conservation Programme of BIOTA (one of four major programmes at Centro de Estudios en Biologia Teorica y Aplicada) to protect bats through educ. and practical habitat conservation throughout Bolivia; currently Researcher and Prof., Centre for Biodiversity and Genetics, Universidad Mayor de San Simon; mem. Scientific Advisory Bd of Bat Conservation International, Network of Educators of Conservation Biology (AMNH), Int. Union for Conservation of Nature Chiropteran Specialist Group; Assoc. Ed. Acta Chiropterologica, Mastozoologia Neotropical, Revista Boliviana de Ecologia, Ecologia en Bolivia; reviewer for several int. scientific journals, including Conservation Biology, Biotropica, Acta Chiropterologica, Ecography, Journal of Tropical Ecology, Journal of Mammalogy; Pres. Asociacion Boliviana de Investigadores de Mamiferos 2005–; Adjunct Researcher, Center for Environmental Research and Conservation, Columbia Univ., New York, USA 2006–; Devt Cooperation Prize, Belgian Cooperation Program 2005, Oliver P. Person Award, American Soc. of Mammalogists 2006, Whitley Award in memory of Daniel Kelly, Rufford Maurice Laing Foundation 2007. *Publications:* more than 30 scientific papers in professional journals. *Address:* Centro de Biodiversidad y Genética, Universidad Mayor de San Simón, Calle Sucre y parque la Torre, Cochabamba, Bolivia (office). *Telephone:* (4) 4231765 (office). *E-mail:* laguirre@fcyt.umss.edu.bo (office). *Website:* www.fcyt.umss.edu.bo/investigacion/biodiversidad (office).

ÁGÚSTSSON, Helgi; Icelandic diplomatist (retd); *Chairman, Save the Children (Iceland);* b. 16 Oct. 1941, Reykjavik; s. of Agúst H. Pétursson and Helga Jóhannesdóttir; m. Hervör Jónasdóttir 1963; three s. one d.; ed Commercial Coll. of Iceland and Univ. of Iceland; joined Ministry for Foreign Affairs 1970; First Sec. and Counsellor, London 1973–77; Dir Defence Div. Ministry for Foreign Affairs and Icelandic Chair. US-Icelandic Defence Council 1979; Minister-Counsellor, Washington, DC 1983–87; Deputy Perm. Sec., Ministry for Foreign Affairs 1987; Amb. to UK (also accred to Ireland, Netherlands and Nigeria) 1989–94; Perm. Sec., Ministry for Foreign Affairs 1995–99; Amb. to Denmark (also accred to Lithuania, Turkey, Israel and Romania) 1998–99, to USA (also accred to Argentina, Brazil, Chile, El Salvador, Guatemala, Mexico and Uruguay) 2002–06; Chief of Protocol, Ministry of Foreign Affairs –2009 (retd); Chair. Save the Children (Iceland) 2009–; fmr Pres. Icelandic Basketball Fed.; Hon. GCVO; Grand Cross, Order of Dannebrog, Kt Commdr of White Rose, Grand Cross of Mérito Civil, Kt Commdr of Pole Star, Grand Cross, Order of the Falcon, Grand Cross Oranje-Nassau Order, Grand Cross Norwegian Service Order, Grand Cross IMR. *Leisure interests:* salmon fishing, music, chess, theatre. *Address:* Save the Children Iceland, Sudurlandsbraut 24, 108 Reykjavík, Iceland (office). *E-mail:* external@simnet.is (home).

AGUT BONSFILLS, Joaquim, BSc, MBA; Spanish media executive; *Director General, CIRSA Gaming Corporation;* ed Univ. Polytécnica de Catalunya, Barcelona, Univ. de Navarra; joined Synthese SA as Dir of Business Devt, Barcelona, Gen. Man. 1980; worked for family-owned co. Agut SA (later acquired by Gen. Electric) 1982; various sr positions with Gen. Electric (GE), including Vice-Pres. and Gen. Man. of Marketing and Sales, Pres. and CEO GE Power Controls, Pres. and CEO GE Nat. Exec. for Spain and Portugal, Chair. Pan European GE Quality Council, Leader of European Corp. Exec. Council (CEC); Chair. Terra Networks –2000; Exec. Chair. Terra Lycos (following merger of Terra and Lycos 2000) 2000–04; Chair. and CEO Endemol Group 2004–06; Dir Gen., CIRSA Gaming Corpn 2006–; Young Businessman of the Year Award 1984. *Address:* CIRSA, Edificio CIRSA, Carretera de Castellar, 298, 08226 Barcelona, Spain (office). *Telephone:* (93) 7396700 (office). *E-mail:* cirsa@cirsa.com (office). *Website:* www.cirsa.com (office).

AGUTTER, Jennifer (Jenny) Ann, OBE; British actress and dancer; b. 20 Dec. 1952, Taunton, Somerset, England; d. of Derek Brodie Agutter and Catherine Agutter (née Lynam); m. Johan Tham 1990; one s.; ed Elmhurst Ballet School; film debut in East of Sudan 1964; has appeared in numerous TV films, dramas and series and on stage with RSC and Nat. Theatre. *Plays include:* The Tempest, Spring Awakening, Hedda Gabler, Betrayal, The Unified Field, Breaking the Code, Love's Labour's Lost, Peter Pan. *Films include:* Ballerina 1964, Gates of Paradise 1967, Star 1968, I Start Counting, The Railway Children 1969, Walkabout, Logan's Run 1975, The Eagle Has Landed, Equus, The Man in the Iron Mask, Riddle of the Sands, Sweet William, The Survivor 1980, An American Werewolf in London 1981, Secret Places 1983, Dark Tower 1987, King of the Wind 1989, Child's Play 2 1991, Freddie as Fro 7 1993, Blue Juice 1995, English Places, English Faces 1996, The Parole Officer 2001, At Dawning 2001, Number One, Longing. Number Two, Regret 2004, Heroes and Villains 2006, Irina Palm 2007, The Magic Door (video) 2007, Intercom (short) 2008, Act of God 2009, Glorious 39 2009, Koda (short) 2009, Burke and Hare 2010, The Mapmaker (short) 2011, Golden Brown 2011, Avengers Assemble 2012, Outside Bet 2012. *Television includes:* Amy 1980, Not a Penny More, Not a Penny Less 1990, The Good Guys, Puss in Boots 1991, Love Hurts 1994, Heartbeat 1994, September 1995, 1996, The Buccaneers 1995, And The Beat Goes On 1996, A Respectable Trade 1997, Bramwell 1998, The Railway Children 2000, Spooks (series) 2002–03, The Inspector Lynley Mysteries (series) – A Cry for Justice 2004, Agatha Christie Marple: 4.50 from Paddington (film) 2004, The Alan Clark Diaries (series) 2004–06, New Tricks (series) 2005, Agatha Christie: Poirot (series) – Taken at the Flood 2006, Diamond Geezer (series) 2007, The Invisibles (series) 2008, Monday Monday (series) 2009, Midsomer Murders (series) – The Creeper 2009, Moving On (series) – Skin Deep 2010, Call the Midwife (series) 2012, True Love (series) – Holly 2012. *Publication includes:* Snap 1983. *Leisure interest:* photography. *Address:* c/o Ken McReddie Associates Ltd, 11 Connaught Place, London, W2 2ET, England. *Telephone:* (20) 7439-1456. *Fax:* (20) 7734-6530. *E-mail:* email@kenmcreddie.com. *Website:* www.kenmcreddie.com; www.jennyagutter.net.

AGYEMAN, Julian, BSc, MA, PhD, FRSA; British environmental social scientist and academic; *Professor, Department of Urban and Environmental Policy and Planning, Tufts University;* b. Beverley, East Yorks., England; ed Durham Univ., Newcastle Univ., Middlesex Univ., Univ. of London; taught geography at a secondary school in Carlisle, Cumbria; Environmental Policy Adviser, Notting Dale Urban Studies Centre, London, later in local govt in the London Boroughs of Lambeth and Islington; consulted and taught environmental policy at London South Bank Univ.; Co-founder Black Environmental Network 1988, Chair. –1994; Co-founder Local Environment: The International Journal of Justice and Sustainability 1996, currently Ed.-in-Chief; ran a consulting firm in London specializing in communicating environmental and sustainable solutions to local govts, not-for-profit orgs and businesses 1992–98; Prof., Dept of Urban and Environmental Policy and Planning, Tufts Univ. 1999–; Visiting Prof., Northumbria Univ., Univ. of South Australia, Adelaide; Contributing Ed., Environment: Science and Policy for Sustainable Development; mem. Editorial Bd, Sustainability: Science, Practice and Policy, Australian Journal of Environmental Education; Series Ed. Just Sustainabilities: Policy, Planning and Practice; Series Co-Ed. Equity, Justice and the Sustainable City; Outstanding Faculty Contrib. to Grad. Studies Award, Tufts Univ. Grad. Student Council 2005. *Publications include:* Local Environmental Policies and Strategies (co-ed.) 1994, People, Plants and Places 1995, Just Sustainabilities: Development in an Unequal World (co-ed.) 2003, Sustainable Communities and the Challenge of Environmental Justice 2005, The New Countryside? Ethnicity, Nation and Exclusion in Contemporary Rural Britain (co-ed.) 2006, Speaking for Ourselves: Environmental Justice in Canada (2009), Environmental Justice in the Former Soviet Union (co-ed.) 2009, Environmental Inequalities Beyond Borders: Local Perspectives on Global Injustices (co-ed.) 2011, Cultivating Food Justice: Race, Class and Sustainability (co-ed.) 2011, Introducing Just Sustainabilities: Policy, Planning and Practice 2013; more than 150 other publs, including book chapters, peer-reviewed articles, published conf. presentations, published reports, book reviews, newspaper articles, op-eds and articles in professional journals and magazines. *Address:* Department of Urban and Environmental Policy and Planning, Tufts University, 97 Talbot Avenue, Medford, MA 02155, USA (office). *Telephone:* (617) 627-3394 (office); (617) 627-4017 (office). *Fax:* (617) 627-3377 (office). *E-mail:* julian.agyeman@tufts.edu (office). *Website:* sites.tufts.edu/julianagyeman (office); julianagyeman.com (office); www.tandfonline.com/toc/cloe20/current (office).

AHADI, Anwar al-Haq, MBA, PhD; Afghan banker, politician and professor of political science; *Minister of Commerce and Industry;* b. 12 Aug. 1951, Jigdalai, Sarobi Dist; s. of Abdul Haq; m. Fatima Gailani; ed Hibibiya High School, American Univ. of Beirut, Lebanon, Northwestern Univ., Chicago, USA; fmr mem. of staff Continental Bank of Chicago; joined Afghan Mellat Party (Afghan Social Democratic Party) 1969, elected to Supreme Council 1987, 1990, Pres. 1995–; Asst Prof. of Political Sciences, Carlton Univ. 1984; Banking Dir, Continental Elona Bank, Chicago 1985–87; Prof. of Political Sciences, Providence Univ. 1987–2002; Gov. Da Afghanistan Bank (Cen. Bank of Afghanistan) 2002–04; Minister of Finance 2004–09, of the Economy 2009, of Commerce and Industry 2009–. *Address:* Ministry of Commerce Darulaman Wat, Kabul, Afghanistan (office). *E-mail:* fawad.it@commerce.gov.af (office). *Website:* www.commerce.gov.af (office).

AHARONOV, Yakir, BSc, PhD; Israeli physicist and academic; *Professor of Theoretical Physics, Department of Physics, Computational Science and Engineering, Schmid College of Science, Chapman University;* b. 1932, Haifa; ed Technion (Israel Inst. of Tech.), Haifa, Univ. of Bristol, UK; Research Assoc., Brandeis Univ., Waltham, Mass, USA 1960–61; Asst Prof., Yeshiva Univ., USA 1961–64, Assoc. Prof. 1964–67, Prof. 1967–73; Prof. of Physics, Tel-Aviv Univ. 1967–73, Prof. Emer. 1973–; Distinguished Prof., Univ. of South Carolina, USA 1973–2006; Prof., George Mason Univ. 2006–08; Prof. of Theoretical Physics, Schmid Coll. of Science, Dept of Physics, Computational Science and Engineering, Chapman Univ., Calif., also James J. Farley Prof. of Natural Philosophy 2008–; Patron, Perimeter Inst. for Theoretical Physics; Chair. in Theoretical Physics, Univ. of South Carolina; Alex Maguy-Glass Chair in Theoretical Physics, Tel-Aviv Univ.; Van Vleck Lecturer, Univ. of Minnesota 2000; Pres. Iyar, Israeli Inst. for Advanced Research; mem. Israeli Nat. Acad. of Science 1990, NAS 1993–; Fellow, American Physical Soc. 1981–; Hon. DSc (Technion – Israel Inst. of Tech.) 1992, (Univ. of South Carolina) 1992, (Univ. of Bristol) 1997; Hon. DUniv (Buenos Aires) 1999; Weizmann Prize in Physics 1984, Rothschild Prize in Physics 1984, Miller Research Professorship Award, Berkeley 1988–89, Israeli Nat. Prize in Physics 1989, Elliot Cresson Medal 1991, Distinguished Scientist Gov. Award, South Carolina 1993, Hewlett-Packard Europhysics Prize 1995, Wolf Prize in Physics (jt recipient) 1998. *Publications:* over 140 papers in learned journals. *Address:* Chapman University, Schmid College of Science, Department of Physics, Computational Science and Engineering, One University Drive, Orange, CA 92866, USA (office). *Telephone:* (714) 289-2052 (office). *Fax:* (714) 289-2041 (office). *E-mail:* aharonov@chapman.edu (office). *Website:* www.chapman.edu (office).

AHERN, Bertie; Irish accountant and politician; b. 12 Sept. 1951, Dublin; s. of Cornelius Ahern and Julia Ahern (née Hourihane); m. Miriam Patricia Kelly 1975 (separated); two d.; ed Rathmines Coll. of Commerce (now Dublin Inst. of Tech.), Univ. Coll., Dublin; TD (Fianna Fáil Party) for Dublin-Finglas 1977–81, Dublin Cen. 1981–, Pres. Fianna Fáil 1994–; mem. Dublin City Council 1978–88, Lord Mayor 1986–87; Asst Chief Whip 1980–81; Fianna Fáil Spokesman on Youth Affairs 1981–82; Govt Chief Whip and Minister of State, Depts of the Taoiseach and of Defence March–Dec. 1982; Opposition Chief Whip 1982–84; Fianna Fáil Front Bench Spokesman on Labour 1984–87; Minister for Labour 1987–91, for Finance 1991–94, for Industry and Commerce Jan. 1993; Tánaiste (Deputy Prime Minister) and Minister for Arts, Culture and the Gaeltacht Nov.–Dec. 1994; Leader of the Opposition 1994–97; Taoiseach (Prime Minister of Ireland) 1997–2008 (resgnd); Pres. European Council Jan.–June 2004; mem. Bd, World Solar Foundation; mem. Agenda Council on Conflict Resolution; Sr Advisor to the Int. Advisory Council of the Harvard Int. Negotiation Program; mem. Bd of Govs IMF 1991–94, World Bank 1991–94; Chair. European Investment Bank 1991–92, Dublin Millennium Cttee 1988; fmr mem. Bd of Govs Univ. Coll. Dublin, Dublin Port and Docks Bd, Eastern Health Bd, Dublin Chamber of Commerce; Hon. Adjunct Prof. of Mediation and Conflict Intervention, School of Business and Law, NUI Maynooth; Grand Cross, Order of Merit with Star and Sash (Germany) 1991. *Publications:* Bertie Ahern: The Autobiography 2009. *Leisure interests:* sports, reading. *Address:* Drumcondra Business Centre, 120 Upper Drumcondra Road, Drumcondra, Dublin 9, Republic of Ireland (office).

AHERN, Dermot, BCL; Irish politician; b. Feb. 1955, Drogheda, Co. Louth; s. of Jeremiah Ahern and Gertrude Alice Ahern (née McGarrity); m. Maeve Coleman; two d.; ed Marist Coll., Dundalk, Univ. Coll., Dublin, Inc. Law Soc. of Ireland; solicitor 1976–; mem. Louth Co. Council 1979–91; mem. Fianna Fáil 1987–; mem. Dáil Éireann for Louth constituency 1987–2011, mem. various parl. cttees; Asst Govt Whip 1988–91; Minister of State at Depts of the Taoiseach and Defence, Govt Chief Whip 1991–92; Minister for Social, Community and Family Affairs 1997–2002, for Communications, Marine and Natural Resources 2002–04, Minister for Foreign Affairs 2004–08, Minister for Justice, Equality and Law Reform 2008–11; mem. British-Irish Parl. Body 1991–97 (Co-Chair. 1993–95). *Address:* c/o Department of Justice, Equality and Law Reform, 94 St Stephen's Green, Dublin 2, Ireland (office).

AHLMARK, Per, BA; Swedish politician, journalist, novelist and poet; *Adviser, Elie Wiesel Foundation for Humanity;* b. 15 Jan. 1939, Stockholm; s. of Prof. Axel Ahlmark; m. 1st (divorced); one s. one d.; m. 2nd Bibi Andersson (q.v.) 1978 (divorced); m. 3rd Lilian Edström; one s.; Leader of Young Liberals 1960–62; columnist for Expressen 1961–95, for Dagens Nyheter 1997–; mem. Parl. 1967–78; Deputy Chair. Swedish-Israeli Friendship Org. 1970–97; mem. Council of Europe 1971–76; mem. Royal Comms. on Literature, Human Rights, etc. in the 1970s; Leader, Folkpartiet (Liberal Party) 1975–78; Deputy Prime Minister and Minister of Labour 1976–78; Deputy Chair. Martin Luther King Fund 1968–73; Chair. Swedish Film Inst. 1978–81; Founder and Deputy Chair. Swedish Comm. Against Antisemitism 1983–95; Adviser to Elie Wiesel Foundation for Humanity, New York 1987–; mem. UN Watch, Geneva 1993–; mem. Acad. Universelle des Cultures, Paris; Fellow, Wissenschaftskolleg zu Berlin 1998–99; Hon. Fellow, Hebrew Univ., Jerusalem 1992; Defender of Jerusalem Award, New York 1986. *Publications include:* Tyranny and the Left 1994, The Open Sore 1997, numerous other political books, essays and numerous articles, three books of poetry, one novel. *Leisure interest:* books. *Address:* Folkungag 61, 11622 Stockholm, Sweden.

AHLSEN, Leopold; German writer; b. 12 Jan. 1927, Munich; s. of Max Alzmann and Margaret; m. Ruth Gehwald 1964; one s. one d.; Gerhart Hauptmann Prize 1955, Schiller-Förderungspreis 1957, Goldener Bildschirm 1968, Silver Nymph of Monte Carlo 1971, Bundesverdienstkreuz and other awards 1990. *Television:* series: The Old Man 1978–89, Cruise of a Globetrotter 1980, Deep Water 1983, From the Loom to a World Power 1983, The Wiesinger 1984, Island of Dreams 1991; movie: Philemon and Baucis 1956, Crime and Punishment 1959, All Power to the Earth 1962, Clothes Make the Man 1963, You Will Die, Sire 1964, The Poor Man Luther 1965, The Ruepp 1965, Berlin Antigone 1968, Boredom 1969, People 1970, Deaths 1971, Pear and Elderberry Shrubs 1971, Fat Eyes - An Idyll of the Small German Town 1972, A Weekend of Alfred Berger 1972, A Selfish Love 1973, Death in Astapovo 1974, The Wittiber 1975, The Hard Trade 1978, The Big Carp Ferdinand and Other Christmas Stories 1978, Defects 1980, François Villon 1981, The Good-Natured Grantler 1982, In This Town Home 1994, The Broken Jug 2003. *Leisure interest:* joinery. *Address:* Waldschulstrasse 58, 81827 Munich, Germany (home). *Telephone:* (89) 4301466 (home). *Fax:* (89) 4301466 (home).

AHLSTRÖM, Krister Harry, BSc, MSc; Finnish business executive; *Senior Adviser and Investing Partner, Desigence Oy;* b. 29 Aug. 1940, Helsinki; s. of Harry F. Ahlström and Asta A. Ahlström (née Seege); m. Anja I. Artto 1974; one s. four d.; ed Helsinki Univ. of Technology; Product Engineer, Gen. Man. and mem. Bd of Man. Oy Wärtsilä Ab 1966–81; Dir and mem. Exec. Bd A. Ahlström Corpn 1981–82, Pres. and CEO 1982–98, Chair. 1998–99; fmr Vice-Chair. StoraEnso; currently Chair. Nordea Securities; currently Sr Adviser and Investing Pnr, Desigence Oy, Helsinki; Chair. Confed. Finnish Employers 1986–92, Fed. of Finnish Metal, Eng and Electrotechnical Industries 1992–96, Orgalime (Organisme de Liaison des Industries Métalliques Européennes) Brussels 1994–96; Chair. Research Inst. of Finnish Economy; mem. Advisory Bd Procuritas AB; mem. Swedish Royal Acad. of Eng Sciences. *Leisure interests:* sailing (world winner 8mR 1975), skiing. *Address:* Desigence Oy, Lemuntie 3-5 B, 00510 Helsinki (office); Kvarnvägen 2A2 00140 Helsinki, Finland (home). *Telephone:* (93) 505280 (office); 500-500788 (mobile) (home). *Fax:* (93) 5052899 (office); (9) 625560 (home). *Website:* www.desigence.com (office).

AHLUWALIA, Montek Singh, BA, MA, MPhil; Indian economist and government official; *Deputy Chairman, Planning Commission;* b. 24 Nov. 1943, New Delhi; s. of Jagmohan Singh and Push J. M. Singh; m. Dr Isher Judge Ahluwalia; two c.; ed Univ. of Delhi, Univ. of Oxford, UK; Economist, World Bank, Washington, DC, USA 1968–71, Deputy Div. Chief, Public Finance Div. 1971–72, Chief of Income Distribution Div., Devt Research Centre 1972–79, Dir Ind. Evaluation Office 2001–04; Econ. Advisor, Dept of Econ. Affairs, Ministry of Finance 1979–85; Additional Sec. to Prime Minister 1985–88, Special Sec. to Prime Minister 1988–90; Sec. of Commerce 1990–91; Sec., Dept of Econ. Affairs, Ministry of Finance 1991–93, Finance Sec. 1993–98; mem. Econ. Advisory Council to Prime Minister 1998–2001; Deputy Chair. Planning Comm. 2004–; several hon. doctorates; Sikh of the Year Award 2008, EDGE Education Personality of the Year Award 2009, Padma Vibhushan. *Publications include:* Re-distribution with Growth: An Approach to Policy (co-author) 1975, Reforming the Global Financial Architecture 2000. *Leisure interest:* playing golf. *Address:* Planning Commission, Yojana Bhavan, Parliament Street, New Delhi 110 001 India (office). *Telephone:* (11) 23096677 (office); (11) 23096688 (office). *Fax:* (11) 23096699 (office). *E-mail:* dch@nic.in (office). *Website:* www.planningcommission.nic.in (office).

AHMAD, Kazi Rakibuddin, BSc, MSc, MBA; Bangladeshi government official; *Chief Election Commissioner;* m.; two d.; ed Univ. of Dhaka, Boston Univ., USA; joined Civil Service of Pakistan in 1960s; took part in War of Independence 1971 as Sub-Divisional Officer, Brahmanbaria; Deputy Sec. and Zonal Admin. Officer under First Bangladesh Govt then Deputy Commr of Comilla; fmr Econ. Minister, Embassy in Tokyo, Jt Sec., Cabinet Div.; Educ. Sec. 2000–03; Parl. Sec. –2003; Chief Election Commr 2012–; Chair. Bangladesh Chemical Industries Corpn, Trading Corpn of Bangladesh; Dir-Gen. NGO Affairs Bureau. *Address:* Election Commission Secretariat, Block 5/6, Sher-e-Bangla Nagar, Dhaka 1207, Bangladesh (office). *Telephone:* (2) 8113601 (office). *Fax:* (2) 8119819 (office). *E-mail:* ecs@bol-online.com (office); becs.info@gmail.com (office). *Website:* www.ecs.gov.bd (office).

AHMAD OF WIMBLEDON, Baron (Life Peer), cr. 2011, of Wimbledon in the London Borough of Merton; **Tariq Ahmad;** British politician and business executive; b. 3 April 1968, London; joined Natwest's Grad. Man. programme 1991, worked in a variety of frontline and strategic roles, including Head of Marketing, Sponsorship and Branding for NatWest's capital markets Div. –2000; worked as part of Exec. Man. team for US-based fund manager Alliance Bernstein 2000–04; joined Sucden Financial, London 2004, served on Exec. Cttee and as Dir of Marketing and Corp. Strategy; Assoc., Inst. of Financial Services; Councillor, Wimbledon, London Borough of Merton 2002–, Cabinet Mem. for Environment and Transport 2006–08, for Community Safety & Engagement 2008–09; Deputy Chair. London Councils' Transport and Environment Cttee 2006–08; Conservative Party Parl. cand. in Croydon North 2005; Vice-Chair. Conservative Party with responsibilities for Cities 2008–10; worked for AMYA nat. youth org. in various nat. roles, including Sec. responsible for Educ. and Training, Health and Sport, as well as Community and Charities, Vice-Pres. 1999–2008; Gov., Wimbledon Park Primary School 2001–06. *Address:* House of Lords, Westminster, London, SW1A 0PW, England (office). *Telephone:* (20) 7219-5353 (office). *E-mail:* ahmadt@ parliament.uk (office). *Website:* www.tariqahmad.com.

AHMADINEJAD, Mahmoud, PhD; Iranian politician and fmr head of state; b. 28 Oct. 1956, Garmsar; ed Iran Univ. of Science and Tech. (IUST); joined Islamic Revolutionary Guards Corps 1986; Prof. of Civil Eng, IUST 1989–; Adviser for Cultural Affairs to Minister of Culture and Higher Educ. 1993; fmr Vice-Gov., then Gov. Maku and Khoy; Gov.–Gen. Ardabil prov. 1993–97; Mayor of Tehran 2003–05; Pres. of Iran 2005–13; interim Minister of Petroleum May–June 2011; mem. Cen. Council, Islamic Soc. of Engineers; mem. Iran Tunnel Soc., Iran Civil Eng Soc. *Publications include:* numerous articles on political, social, cultural and economic topics. *Website:* www.ahmadinejad.ir.

AHMADZAI, Abdullah, BIT; Afghan civil servant; *Deputy Country Representative, The Asia Foundation;* b. 1975, Qarabagh Dist, Kabul Prov.; ed Brains Degree Coll., Peshawar, Pakistan, workshop certificates from Harvard Univ. and Int. Foundation for Electoral Services; actively involved with Afghanistan Constitution Comm. mandated by the 2001 Bonn Agreement to draft a new constitution 2003–04; Kuchies Liaison Officer, Nat. Area Man., Nat. Head of Field Operations, Chief of Operations Counterpart, Chief of Operations, in Jt Election Man. Body and Ind. Election Comm. 2004–06, Chief Electoral Officer and CEO Ind. Election Comm. 2010–13; Sr Nat. Capacity Building Adviser, later Deputy Chief of Party, later Chief of Party, The Asia Foundation 2006–09, Deputy Country Rep. 2013–; Vice-Pres. ASPIRE (Afghanistan Logistic Services co.) 2009; attended numerous workshops in India and UAE on governance. *Address:* The Asia Foundation, PO Box 175, Kabul, Afghanistan (office). *Telephone:* 793-606042 (mobile). *E-mail:* aahmadzai@asiafound.org (office). *Website:* asiafoundation.org (office).

AHMED, Aneesa; Maldivian politician (retd) and organization official; b. 29 Sept. 1949, Malé; divorced; one s. one d.; ed studied nursing in India and Australia; staff nurse, Govt Hosp., Malé 1973–77, Sister-in-Charge 1978–80; mem. People's Special Majlis 1979–85, 1993–97, apptd by Pres. 1997–99, mem. People's Majlis for Mulaku Atoll 1999–2009, Leader Parl. Group Dhivehi Rayyithunge Party 2006–09, Deputy Speaker of People's Majlis 2008–09; Under-Sec., Ministry of Foreign Affairs 1980–81; Asst to Exec. Sec., Pres.'s Office 1981–82, Presidential Aide 1982–89, Sr Presidential Aide 1989–92, Dir-Gen. Foreign Relations, Pres.'s Office 1992–98; Deputy Minister of Women's Affairs and Social Security 1998–2002, Minister of Women's Affairs, Family Devt and Social Security 2002–04, of Health 2004–05, of the Pres.'s Office 2005–08; Founder and Pres. Hope for Women (NGO) 2010–; Humphrey Fellow, Pennsylvania State Univ., USA 1985–86; Int. Women of Courage Award, US Dept of State 2012. *Leisure interests:* reading, walking. *Address:* Hope for Women, 2nd Floor, H. Mialani Sosun Magu, Malé 20069 (office); M Lonuveli, Raiveri Hingun, Malé 20-02, Maldives (home). *Telephone:* 3326566 (home). *E-mail:* hopeforwomenmaldives@gmail.com (office).

AHMED, Azzam al-, BA; Palestinian politician; b. 1947, Jenin; m.; three c.; ed Baghdad Univ., Iraq; Head, Gen. Union of Palestinian Students (GUPS) in Iraq 1971–74, Deputy Head GUPS Exec. Cttee 1974–80; PLO Rep. to Iraq 1979–94; joined Fatah 1989, served in several sr positions, mem. Revolutionary Council 1989; mem. Parl. 1996–, Minister of Public Works 1996–2003, Minister of Telecommunications and IT 2003, Head, Fatah bloc in Palestinian Legis. Council –2007; Deputy Prime Minister March–June 2007. *Address:* c/o Fatah (Harakat at-Tahrir al-Watani al-Filastin—Palestine National Liberation Movement), Gaza, Palestinian Autonomous Areas. *E-mail:* fateh@fateh.net. *Website:* www.fateh.net.

AHMED, Fakhruddin, BA, MA, PhD; Bangladeshi economist, civil servant and fmr central banker; b. 1 May 1940, Munshiganj, British India; s. of Dr Mohiuddin Ahmed and Firoza Akhter Khatun; m. Neena Ahmed; one s.; ed Dhaka Univ., Williams Coll., USA, Princeton Univ., USA; began career as Lecturer in Econs, Dhaka Univ.; served in Civil Service of Pakistan and in Govt of Bangladesh –1978, lastly as Jt Sec., Econ. Relations Div., Ministry of Finance; several sr positions at World Bank, Washington, DC, USA 1978–2001; Gov. Bangladesh Bank 2001–05; Chair. Palli Karma-Sahayak Foundation (apex fund) 2005–07; Hon. Chief Adviser of Caretaker Govt of Bangladesh, in charge of Cabinet Div., of Ministry of Establishment, of Ministry of Home Affairs and of Election Comm. Secr. 2007–08, Hon. Chief Adviser, in charge of Cabinet Div. of Ministry of Establishment and Ministry of Information 2008–09. *Address:* c/o Honourable Chief Adviser's Office, Old Sangshad Bhaban, Tejgaon, Dhaka, Bangladesh.

AHMED, Maj. Hafizuddin; Bangladeshi army officer (retd) and politician; fmr Minister of Water Resources, of Commerce; mem. Standing Cttee and Vice-Pres. Bangladesh Jatiyatabadi Dal (Bangladesh Nationalist Party), apptd Sec.-Gen. of faction Oct. 2007. *Publications include:* Gourobangone 2004, Roktebheja Ekattor 2007. *Address:* Bangladesh Jatiyatabadi Dal, Banani Office, House 23, Road 13, Dhaka, Bangladesh (office). *Telephone:* (2) 8819525 (office). *Fax:* (2) 8813063 (office). *E-mail:* bnpbd@e-fsbd.net (office). *Website:* www.bnpbd.com (office).

AHMED, Jameel Yusuf; Pakistani civil servant and business executive; *Chairman, TPL Direct Insurance Ltd;* b. 10 May 1946, Hyderabad Deccan, India; s. of Yusuf Ahmed and of Amina Yusuf; m.; one s. two d.; ed Karachi Polytechnic Inst.; industrialist in paper cone mfg co. 1969; Founder Citizen Police Liaison Cttee (CPLC) Reporting Cell (est. to restore confidence in police service) 1989, Co-Chief CPLC 1990–96, Chief 1996–2003; currently Chair. TPL Direct Insurance

Ltd; mem. Bd of Govs Karachi Public Transport and Social Educ. Soc. (KPTC) 1999; mem. Advisory Bd Interior Div., Fed. Ministry of the Interior 2000; Hon. Sec. Bd of Govs Al-Murtaza School Network Charitable Trust 1989, Chair. Steering Cttee Professional Devt Centre, Al-Murtaza 2001–; mem. Steering Cttee NGO Resource Centre, Aga Khan Foundation 2001–; Founder and Trustee Panah Women's Shelter 2001–; fmr Chair. All Pakistan Paper Cone Mfrs Asscn; Dir Asia Crime Prevention Foundation, Japan; mem. Advisory Council, Fellowship Fund for Pakistan, Woodrow Wilson International Centre for Scholars 2004–; Sitara-e-Shujaat 1992, Mulla Asghar Memorial Int. Award for Excellence in Educ. 2002. *Address:* Office of the Chairman, TPL Direct Insurance Ltd, 172-B, 2nd Floor, Najeeb Centre, Block-2, P.E.C.H.S., Karachi (office); 37-L/1, Block-6, PECHS, Karachi, Pakistan (home). *Telephone:* (21) 111000301 (office); (21) 4546428 (home). *E-mail:* juchief@hotmail.com (home). *Website:* tplinsurance.com (office).

AHMED, Khurshid, BA, LLB; Pakistani trade union official; *General-Secretary, Pakistan Workers Federation;* b. 13 July 1936, Lahore; s. of Bashid Ahmad Dar and Naseem Ahmed (née Begum); m. Sahaira Nasreen; two s. four d.; active in trade union movt in Pakistan 1956–; Chair. Bukhtiar Memorial Computer Training Centre, Lahore, Faisalabad, Gujranwala and Hyderabad; Vice-Pres. ILO Conf., Geneva 1986; Gen.-Sec. Pakistan Workers Fed. and Pakistan Wapda Hydroelectric Cen. Labour Union; mem. Pakistan Tripartite Cttee, Pakistan Workers Labour Comm., Nat. Industrial Relations Comm.; Sec. and Trustee Bukhtiar Labour Welfare Trust; Ed. Pak Workers, Pakistan Workers journal; elected mem. ILO Governing Body, Geneva since early 1970s; Rep., Int. Workers Group; Sitara Imtaz of Pakistan. *Publications include:* (in Urdu) Trade Union Struggle in Pakistan, Trade Union Struggle of WAPDA Workers, International Labour Organisation, The Challenge of the 21st Century and the Role of the Working Class of Pakistan, Socio-Economic Problems Facing the Working Class of the Country, Responsibility of the Labour Movement of Pakistan; (in English) Dignity of Labour, Journalism on Labour Issues, History of Labour Movement in Pakistan; regular contrib. to nat. press on current labour issues. *Address:* Sadiq Colony, Mumtaz Street, Ghari Shau, Lahore, Pakistan (home). *Telephone:* (42) 6363097 (home). *E-mail:* gs@pwf.org.pk (office). *Website:* www.pwf.org.pk (office).

AHMED, Mahmud Yayale, MA, BA; Nigerian civil servant and government official; b. 15 April 1952, Shira, Bauchi State; s. of Mallam Ahmadu; m.; seven c.; ed Ahmadu Bello Univ., Zaria; began his civil service career in Bauchi State 1977; served as Vice-Prin., Makurdi community secondary school; Deputy Sec., Ministry of Animal Health and Forestry Resources 1982–83; Acting Perm. Sec., Ministry of Rural Devt and Cooperatives 1983–84; based at Ministry of Finance and Econ. Planning 1984–86; joined Fed. Civil Service 1986, served in various posts including Admin. Officer I, Sec. CIPBS, Dir Finance and Accounts, Perm. Sec. and Head of Service of the Fed. 2000–07; Minister of Defence 2007–08; Sec. to the Govt of the Fed. 2008–; fmr mem. Council, Bauchi Coll. of Arts and Science, Coll. of Educ., Azare, Coll. of Legal and Islamic Studies, Misau; Ajiyan Katagum, Akowonio of Idanre Kingdom; Hon. LLD (Abuja), Hon. DLit (Bayero Univ., Kano). *Address:* c/o Office of the Head of State, New Federal Secretariat Complex, Shehu Shagari Way, Central Area District, Abuja, Nigeria (office). *Telephone:* (9) 5233536 (office). *Website:* www.statehouse.gov.ng (office).

AHMED, Lt-Gen. Moeen U.; Bangladeshi army officer (retd); m. Begum Naznin Moeen; one s. one d.; ed Defence Services Command and Staff Coll., Mirpur, US Army Command and Staff Coll., Harvard Univ., Centre for Security Studies of Hawaii, USA; began mil. service 1975, fmr positions include Weapons Training Officer, Platoon Commdr Bangladesh Mil. Acad., Brigade Maj., Infantry Brigade, Grade One Staff Officer, Mil. Operations Directorate, Army HQ, Col Infantry Div., Directing Staff Defence Services Command and Staff Coll., Sr Instructor Army Wing, later Chief Instructor, Commdt School of Infantry and Tactics, Mil. Sec. and Master Gen. of Ordnance, Army HQ, promoted to rank of Lt-Gen. 2005, Chief of Army Staff 2005–09; fmr Defence Adviser, High Comm. in Pakistan; served with UN Assistance Mission for Rwanda (UNAMIR); Force Commdr's Commendation, US Forces Commendation. *Address:* c/o Office of the Chief of Army Staff, Army Headquarters, GS Branch, Dhaka, Bangladesh.

AHMED, Mohamed Ibrahim Youssef; Egyptian politician and fmr police officer; *Minister of the Interior;* b. 1953; fmr Chief of Police for the Dist of Giza in Cairo; Minister of the Interior 2013–. *Address:* Ministry of the Interior, 25 Sharia Sheikh Rihan, Bab el-Louk, Cairo, Egypt (office). *Telephone:* (2) 27955005 (office). *Fax:* (2) 27960682 (office). *E-mail:* center@iscmi.gov.eg (office). *Website:* www .moiegypt.gov.eg (office).

AHMED, Mohamed Jameel, PhD; Maldivian lawyer and politician; *Vice-President;* b. 13 Oct. 1969, Fuvamulah; m. Haulath Faheem; three c.; ed School of Oriental and African Studies, Univ. of London, UK, Int. Islamic Univ., Malaysia; Minister of Justice 2005–07, of Civil Aviation and Telecommunications 2008–09, of Home Affairs 2012–13; running mate of Progressive Party of Maldives presidential cand. Abdullah Yameen 2013; Vice-Pres. of the Maldives 2013–; Founder-mem. New Maldives Group; Sr mem. Japan Int. Co-operation Agency Alumni Soc., Maldives. *Address:* Progressive Party of Maldives, Henveiru, Thema, Malé, Maldives (office); c/o The President's Office, Boduthakurufaanu Magu, Malé 20-05, The Maldives (office). *Telephone:* 3303838 (office). *Fax:* 3330524 (office). *E-mail:* info@ppm.mv (office); info@presidencymaldives.gov.mv (office). *Website:* www.ppm .mv (office); www.presidencymaldives.gov.mv (office).

AHMED, Moudud, MA; Bangladeshi politician and barrister; b. 24 May 1940, Noakhali; s. of the late Bara Moulana; m. Hasna Jasimuddin; two s.; ed Dhaka Univ.; fmr Gen. Sec. East Pakistan House, UK; took active part in struggle for independence, organizing External Publicity Div. of Bangladesh Govt in exile; Ed. Bangladesh (weekly); lawyer, Bangladesh Supreme Court 1972–74; Gen. Sec. Cttee for Civil Liberties Legal Aid 1974; imprisoned during State of Emergency 1974; Head, Bangladesh del. to 32nd Session UN Gen. Ass. 1977; Adviser to Pres. 1977; Minister of Communications 1985–86, Deputy Prime Minister in charge of Ministry of Industries 1986–88, Prime Minister and Minister of Industry 1988–89, Vice-Pres. 1989–90; under house arrest 1990–91, imprisoned Dec. 1991, later released; Minister of Law, Justice and Parl. Affairs 2001–06; Visiting Prof., Elliott School of Int. Affairs, George Washington Univ. 1997; Visiting Fellow, South Asian Inst. of Heidelberg Univ., Harvard Univ. Centre for Int. Affairs, Univ. of Oxford, UK; mem. Elliott School Int. Council. *Publications include:* Bangladesh Contemporary Events and Documents, Bangladesh Constitutional Quest for Autonomy 1979, Bangladesh: Era of Sheikh Mujibur Rahman 1983, Democracy and the Challenge of Development: A Study of Politics and Military Interventions in Bangladesh 1995, South Asia: Crisis of Development – The Case of Bangladesh 2003, Chaloman Itihas. *Address:* Islam Chamber, 9th floor, 125/A, Motijheel C/A, Dhaka 1000, Bangladesh (office). *Telephone:* (2) 9888694 (home).

AHMED, Ougoureh Kifleh; Djibouti politician; b. 1955, Dikhil; Leader Front pour la Restauration de l'Unité et de la Démocratie (FRUD, a splinter group in Afar guerilla movt) 1994, currently Sec.-Gen.; mem. Assemblée Nationale 1997–; Minister of Agric. 1995–97, for the Public Office and Admin. Reforms 1997–99, of Defence 1999–2011; mem. Rassemblement populaire pour le progrès (RPP); Grande Étoile de Djibouti. *Address:* c/o Ministry of Defence, BP 42, Djibouti (office).

AHMED, Salahuddin, BSc, MA, LLM; Bangladeshi lawyer and government official; b. 8 Feb. 1948, Dhaka; ed London School of Econs, UK, Dhaka Univ., Colombia Univ., USA; Asst Prof., Dept of Econs, Dhaka Univ. 1971–77, Asst Prof., Inst. of Business Admin 1980–83; began practising law 1980, lawyer at High Court 1982–2008; Assoc. Counsel, Dr Kamal Hossain & Assocs (law firm), Dhaka –2008; Additional Attorney-Gen. 2007–08, Attorney-Gen. 2008–09; mem. Supreme Court Bar Asscn, Human Rights Bangladesh, South Asian Asscn for Regional Co-operation in Law, Bangladesh Chapter. *Address:* c/o Dr Kamal Hossain & Associates, Chamber Building, 2nd Floor, 122–124 Motijheel CA, Dhaka 1000, Bangladesh.

AHMED, Salehuddin, MA, PhD; Bangladeshi central banker (retd) and academic; *Professor, Business School, BRAC University;* b. 1 Jan. 1949; m.; two c.; ed Dhaka Univ., McMaster Univ., Canada; Lecturer in Econs, Dhaka Univ. 1970; joined civil service and served in various admin. capacities, including in Centre on Integrated Rural Devt for Asia and the Pacific, Dhaka; fmr Dir-Gen. Bangladesh Acad. for Rural Devt, Comilla, Non-Governmental Org. Affairs Bureau of Office of the Prime Minister; Man. Dir Palli Karma Sahayak Foundation (apex funding agency of macro-credit operations in Bangladesh) 1996–2005; Gov. and Chair. Bangladesh Bank (cen. bank) 2005–09; mem. Rating Cttee Credit Rating Agency of Bangladesh Ltd (CRAB); Prof., Business School, North South Univ. 2009–, BRAC Univ. 2009–; Distinguished Alumni Award, McMaster Univ. 2006. *Publications:* more than 60 books, reports and journal articles. *Leisure interests:* listening to music, watching TV movies, travelling. *Address:* Apt 4, Silicon Point, Plot 311, Road 10, Block D, Bashundhara Residential Area, Dhaka 1212, Bangladesh. *Telephone:* (2) 8845340. *E-mail:* asalehuddin@gmail.com. *Website:* www.crab.com.

AHMED, Shahabuddin, MA; Bangladeshi judge and fmr head of state; b. 1930, Pemai of Kendua, Greater Mymensingh Dist; s. of Talukder Risat A. Bhuiyan (deceased); two s. three d.; ed Dhaka Univ., Lahore Civil Service Acad., Univ. of Oxford, UK; joined Civil Service of Pakistan 1954 as Sub-Div. Officer, later Additional Deputy Commr; transferred to Judicial Br. 1960; fmr Additional Dist and Sessions Judge, Dhaka and Barisal; fmr Dist and Sessions Judge, Comilla and Chittagong; fmr Registrar High Court of E Pakistan; elevated to High Court Bench 1972; apptd Judge of Appellate Div., Supreme Court of Bangladesh 1980; Chief Justice 1990, 1991–95; Chair. Labour Appellate Tribunal 1973–74, Bangladesh Red Cross Soc. 1978–82, Comm. of Inquiry into police shootings of students 1983, Nat. Pay Comm. 1984; Vice-Pres. League of Red Cross and Red Crescent Soc., Geneva, Switzerland; Acting Pres. of Bangladesh 1990–91, Pres. 1996–2001; Hon. Master, Hon. Soc. of Gray's Inn, London. *Address:* House Dal Motia, nr Mohammadpur, Dhaka, Bangladesh.

AHMED, Sheikh Sharif Sheikh; Somali politician and fmr head of state; b. 25 July 1964, Middle Shabelle region; m.; two c.; ed Sheikh Sufi Inst., Kordufan Univ., Sudan, Open Univ., Libya; fmr teacher, Juba Secondary School, Mogadishu; elected to head local court in Jowhar 2002, Head of Islamic Courts Union 2002–06; fled to Kenya 2007, returned under UN peace agreements with transitional government 2008; Chair. Alliance for the Re-liberation of Somalia –2009; Pres. of Somalia 2009–12. *Address:* c/o Office of the President, 1 Villa Baidao, 2525 Baydhabo, Somalia.

AHMED, Sufyan, BA, MSc; Ethiopian government official; *Minister of Finance and Economic Development;* b. 1 May 1958; m.; one d.; ed Addis Ababa Univ.; Coll. Instructor 1983–93; Commr, Ethiopian Customs Authority 1993–95; Minister of Finance 1995–2001, Minister of Finance and Econ. Devt 2001–; mem. Bd of Govs, African Development Bank; Chair. Eastern and Southern African Trade and Development Bank (PTA Bank) 2013–; mem. Oromo People's Democratic Org. (OPDO). *Address:* Ministry of Finance and Economic Development, POB 1037, Addis Ababa, Ethiopia (office). *Telephone:* (11) 1552800 (office). *Fax:* (11) 1550118 (office).

AHMED, Syed, MA, PhD; Indian politician; *Governor of Jharkhand;* b. 6 March 1945; s. of Syed Ali Naqi; ed Lucknow Univ., Bombay Univ.; mem. Indian Nat. Congress Party 1977–; mem. All India Congress Cttee (AICC) 2005–, Vice-Pres., AICC Muslim Youth Conf. 1978–90, Vice-Pres. Mumbai Regional Congress Cttee 1995, 2001; elected to Maharashtra Legis. Ass. from 26 Nagpada constituency 1980, 1985, 1990, 1999, 2004, Govt of Maharashtra Minister of State for Environment, Housing, Repairs and Reconstructions, Slum Improvement and Awqaf (Religious Endowments) 1986–88, for Energy, Environment, Textiles, Awqaf and Prohibition Propaganda 1991, Minister for Housing, Slum Improvement, House Repairs and Reconstruction and Awqaf 2001–04; Gov. of Jharkhand 2011–. *Publications:* Pagdandi se Shahar Tak (autobiog.), Maktal se Manzil, Kafas se Chaman, Jange-Azaadi Me Urdu Shayari. *Address:* Office of the Governor, Raj Bhavan, Ranchi, India (office). *Telephone:* (651) 2283469 (office). *Fax:* (651) 2201101 (office). *Website:* rajbhavanjharkhand.nic.in (office).

AHMED, Air Chief Marshal (retd) Tanvir Mehmood, MSc; Pakistani air force officer (retd); b. 1 Feb. 1952; m.; four c.; ed Pakistan Air Force (PAF) Public School, Sargodha, PAF Acad., Risalpur, Turkish Air War Coll. and Nat. Defence Coll., Islamabad; joined Pakistan Air Force (PAF) and took fighter and operational conversion courses, qualified flying instructor and combat commdr on fighter aircraft, commanded Fighter Squadron, F-16s Flg Wing, PAF Base, Sargodha and PAF Acad., Risalpur, Deputy Dir in Operations Br., Personal Staff Officer to two

Air Chiefs, Dir F-16 project, Sr Air Staff Officer at Northern Air Command, Peshawar and Dir-Gen. Air Weapons Complex, Wah, served as Deputy Chief Air Staff Admin and Operations; served in UAE Air Force as fighter instructor pilot; Vice-Chief of Air Staff 2003–06, Chief of Air Staff 2006–09; Sitara-i-Basalat, Sitara-i-Imtiaz (Mil.), Hilal-i-Imtiaz (Mil.), Nishan-e-Imtiaz (Mil.). *Address:* c/o Office of the Chief of Air Staff, Ministry of Defence, Pakistan Secretariat, No. II, Rawalpindi 46000, Pakistan.

AHMED, Vice-Adm. (retd) Zahir Uddin; Bangladeshi naval officer; b. 1957, Kapasia upazilla under Gazipur Dist; s. of the late Shafiuddin Ahmed; m. Shabnam Ahmed; one s. one d.; ed Britannia Royal Naval Coll., Dartmouth, UK, various univ. courses in The Netherlands, Pakistan, China and USA, Defence Services Command and Staff Coll., Dhaka, US Naval War Coll., Newport, RI (class valedictorian), Nat. Defence Coll., Mirpur; joined Bangladesh Navy (BN) as an Officer Cadet 1976; mem. pioneer batch of BN; completed specialization in Navigation and Direction (ND) from Pakistan; first CO frigate BNS Bangabandhu; also commanded BN frigates BNS Umar Farooq, BNS Abu Bakar; served as Cdre Commdg BN Flotilla (COMBAN) and as Cdre Commdg Chittagong (COMCHIT) to command BN Fleet and Chittagong Area Command, respectively; performed duty of Commdt Bangladesh Marine Acad. and Dir Gen. Bangladesh Coast Guard; Chief of the Naval Staff 2009–13; promoted to rank of Vice-Adm. 2009; Chief of the Naval Staff Commendation. *Address:* c/o Ministry of Defence, Gonobhaban Complex, Sher-i-Bangla Nagar, Dhaka 1207, Bangladesh. *E-mail:* modgob@bttb .net.bd.

AHMETI, Ali, (Abaz Gjuka); Macedonian politician; *President, Democratic Union for Integration;* b. 4 Jan. 1959, Zajas, Kičevo municipality; m.; one s. one d.; ed Univ. of Prishtina; political activist as student; imprisoned for taking part in demonstrations by Kosovo Albanians 1981; granted asylum in Switzerland 1986; active in dissident People's Movt of Kosovo throughout 1980s; Founding mem. Kosovo Liberation Army 1996; Co-founder Democratic Union for Integration (Bashkimi Demokratik për Integrim) 1999, Pres. 2002–; elected mem. Parl. 2002; elected Supreme Commdr and Political Rep. of Nat. Liberation Army in Macedonia 2001; formed multi-ethnic coalition Govt with Together for Macedonia coalition 2002–06, and as part of coalition led by Internal Macedonian Revolutionary Org.-Democratic Party for Macedonian Nat. Unity 2008–. *Address:* Democratic Union for Integration (Bashkimi Demokratik për Integrim), 1200 Tetova, Reçicë e vogël, Rruga 170 No. 2 (office); Parliamentary Assembly Buildings, 1000 Skopje, Stojan Andov, 11 Oktomvri bb, Former Yugoslav Republic of Macedonia (office). *Telephone:* (4) 4334398 (office). *Fax:* (4) 4334397 (office). *E-mail:* cabinet@bdi.mk (office). *Website:* www.bdi.org.mk (office).

AHN, Hyun-soo; South Korean short-track speed skater; b. 23 Nov. 1985, Seoul; ed Korea Nat. Sport Univ.; began speed skating at Myungji Elementary School aged eight; debut for S Korea, Olympic Games, Salt Lake City, USA 2002; bronze medal, 500m, World Championships, Beijing 2005; silver medal, 1000m and Overall, World Championships, Montreal 2002, 1000m, Warsaw 2003, 1000m and 5000m Relay, Beijing 2005; gold medal, 5000m Relay, World Championships, Montreal 2002, 1500m, 5000m Relay and Overall 2003, 1000m, 1500m, 5000m Relay and Overall, World Championships, Gothenburg 2004, 1500m and Overall, World Championships, Beijing 2005, 1000m., 1500m. events World Championships, Minneapolis 2006; World Cup ranking: third, 500m and 1000m 2002/03, second, 1500m 2002/03, 500m 2003/05, 1000m and 1500m 2004/05, 1000m 2005/06, first, 1000m and 1500m 2003/04, 500m and 1500m 2005/06, third, Overall 2004/05, second, Overall 2002/03, first, Overall 2003/04, 2005/06; bronze medal, 500m, Olympic Games, Turin 2006; gold medal, 1000m, 1500m and 5000m Relay, Olympic Games, Turin 2006. *Leisure interest:* watching movies. *Address:* c/o Korea Skating Union, Room 412, Olympic Center, 88 Bangyee-Dong, Songpa-Ku, Seoul 138-749, Republic of Korea.

AHO, Esko Tapani, MScS; Finnish business executive and fmr politician; *Executive Vice-President of Corporate Relations and Responsibility, Nokia Corporation;* b. 20 May 1954, Veteli; s. of Kauko Kaleva Aho and Laura Kyllikki (née Harjupatana) Aho; m. Kirsti Hannele Söderkultalahti 1980; two s. one d.; ed Univ. of Helsinki; Chair. Youth Org. of the Centre Party 1974–80, Chair. Finnish Centre Party (KESK) 1990–2002; Political Sec. to Minister of Foreign Affairs 1979–80; Trade Agent, Kannus 1980; mem. Parl. 1983–2003; Prime Minister of Finland 1991–95; unsuccessful cand. for Pres. of Finland 2000; Lecturer, Harvard Univ., USA 2000; Pres. Finnish Nat. Fund for Research and Devt (SITRA) 2004–08; Exec. Vice-Pres. of Corp. Relations and Responsibility, Nokia Corpn 2008–, mem. Exec. Bd 2009–; Vice-Chair. Tech. Industries of Finland 2009–, Liberal Int. 1994–2002, Finnish Olympic Cttee 1997–2000; Chair. Finnish Ski Asscn 1996–2000; mem. Bd of Dirs Fortum Corpn 2006–, Russian Venture Co. 2007–; mem. Club de Madrid, Science and Tech. in Soc. Forum, InterAction Council, Fondation Sophia Antipolis. *Leisure interests:* literature, tennis, theatre. *Address:* Nokia Corporation, Keilalahdentie 2-4, 02150 Espoo, Finland (office). *Telephone:* 7180-08000 (office). *Website:* www.nokia.com (office).

AHOOMEY-ZUNU, Arthème Kwesi Séléagodji, LLM; Togolese lawyer and politician; *Prime Minister;* b. 1 Dec. 1958, Lomé; Admin. Sec., Nat. Comm. on Human Rights 1988–94; mem. Assemblée Nat. (Parl.), mem. Comm. on Human Rights 1994–99; mem. Ind. Nat. Electoral Comm. 1993–2005, Pres. 2000–02; Minister of Territorial Admin 2006–07; Sec. Gen., Presidency of the Repub. 2008–12; Minister of Trade and Pvt. Sector Promotion 2011–12; Prime Minister 2012–; Founder-mem. Convergence Patriotique Panafricaine. *Address:* Office of the Prime Minister, Cité OUA, BP 1161, Lomé, Togo (office). *Telephone:* 22-61-06-23 (office). *Fax:* 22-61-06-87 (office). *E-mail:* pmahoomeyk@yahoo.com (office). *Website:* www.primature.gouv.tg (office).

AHOUSSOU-KOUADIO, Jeannot, LLM; Côte d'Ivoirian lawyer and politician; *Prime Minister and Minister of Justice;* b. 6 March 1951, Raviart, Tie-N'Diekro Dist; m.; six c.; ed Abidjan Univ., Rennes Univ., France; Bureau mem. Mouvement des Etudiants et Elèves de Côte d'Ivoire (MEECI), Lycée Classique de Bouaké 1970, MEECI Faculty of Law 1975–77; Pres. Asscn des Elèves et Etudiants, Didievi 1975–77; Consultant and Trainer, Nat. Inst. of Perm. Devt (INPP) 1979–80; mem. Bar, Abidjan 1981–; Municipal Councillor, Didievi 1985–90; Deputy Mayor, Attécoubé 1990–95; Councillor, city of Abidjan 1995–2000; mem. Econ. and Social Council of Côte d'Ivoire 1999; mem. Assemblée Nationale (Parl.)

for Didievi/Tie-N'Diekro constituency 2000–; Minister of Industry and the Private Sector 2002–05; campaign dir for Henri Konan Bédié during first round of 2010 presidential election, and for Alassane Ouattara during second round; Minister of State, Keeper of the Seals and Minister of Justice 2010–12, Prime Minister and Minister of Justice 2012–; mem. Parti démocratique de la Côte d'Ivoire—Rassemblement démocratique africain, mem. Political Bureau and Deputy Sec.-Gen. for Legal Affairs. *Address:* Office of the Prime Minister, blvd Angoulvant, 01 BP 1533, Abidjan 01, Côte d'Ivoire (office). *Telephone:* 20-31-50-00 (office). *Fax:* 20-22-18-33 (office). *Website:* www.premierministre.ci (office).

AHRENDS, Peter, AADipl, RIBA; British architect (retd); b. 30 April 1933, Berlin, Germany; s. of Steffen Bruno Ahrends and Margarete Marie Sophie Ahrends (née Visino); m. Elizabeth Robertson 1954; two d.; ed King Edward VII School, Johannesburg, Architectural Asscn, London; research into decoration in Islamic Architecture 1956; Visiting Critic and/or External Examiner Kumasi Univ., Architectural Asscn School of Architecture, Nova Scotia Tech. Univ., Univ. of Strathclyde; with Steffen Ahrends & Partners, Johannesburg 1957–58; with Denys Lasdun & Partners 1959–60; with Julian Keable & Partners; teacher, Architectural Asscn School of Architecture 1960–61; f. Ahrends, Burton and Koralek Architects 1961, Partner and Dir 1961–2009 (retd); Visiting Prof., Kingston Polytechnic 1983–84; teacher and conducted workshops Architectural Asscn School of Architecture, Canterbury Art School, Univ. of Edinburgh, Winter School, Edinburgh, Plymouth Polytechnic, Plymouth Art School; Prof., Bartlett School of Architecture and Planning, Univ. Coll. London 1986–89; mem. RIBA, Design Council; Chair. UK Architects Against Apartheid 1988–93; Design Adviser, London Devt Agency; RIBA Good Design in Housing Award 1977, RIBA Architecture Award 1978, 1993, 1996, 1999, Structural Steel Design Award 1980, Structural Steel Design Commendation 1993; RIAI Architecture Award 1999, Gulbenkian Museum of the Year Award 1999, Designs on Democracy Competition Winner. *Publications include:* Ahrends, Burton & Koralek, Architects (monograph) 1991; collaborations: The Architecture of ABK 2002; numerous articles in professional journals. *Leisure interests:* architecture and architecture-related interests. *Address:* c/o ABK Architects Dublin, 34 Lower Leeson Street, Dublin 2, Ireland (office).

AHRENDTS, Angela, BA; American retail executive; *Senior Vice-President, Apple, Inc.;* Pres. Donna Karan International 1989–96; Exec. Vice-Pres. Henri Bendel 1996–98; Vice-Pres. Merchandising and Design, Liz Claiborne Inc. 1998–99, Sr Vice-Pres. Corp. Merchandising and Group Pres. for Modern Brands 1999–2002, Exec. Vice-Pres. 2002–05; Exec. Dir Burberry Group plc 2006–13, CEO 2006–13 (resgnd); Sr Vice-Pres., Retail and Online Stores, Apple, Inc. 2014–; ranked by Forbes magazine amongst The World's 100 Most Powerful Women (66th) 2007, (71st) 2009, (97th) 2010, (58th) 2011, (45th) 2012, (53rd) 2013, ranked by Fortune magazine amongst the 50 Most Powerful Women in Business outside the US (18th) 2007, (27th) 2008, (24th) 2009, (26th) 2010, (21st) 2011–12, ranked by the Financial Times amongst Top 25 Businesswomen in Europe (11th) 2007. *Address:* Apple, 1 Infinite Loop, Cupertino, CA 95014, USA. *Website:* www.apple.com/pr/bios/angela-ahrendts.html (office).

AHRWEILER, Hélène, DenHist, DèsL; French/Greek university professor and administrator; *Professor Emeritus, Sorbonne University;* b. 28 Aug. 1926, Athens, Greece; d. of Nicolas Glykatzi and Calliroe Psaltides; m. Jacques Ahrweiler 1958; one d.; ed Univ. of Athens, Sorbonne Paris; Research Worker CNRS 1955–67, Head of Research 1964–67; apptd Prof., Sorbonne 1967, currently Prof. Emer.; Pres. Univ. de Paris I 1976–81; Rector Acad., Chancellor Univs of Paris 1982–89; Chair. and Pres. Terra Foundation for the Arts, Chicago; Sec.-Gen. Int. Cttee of Historical Sciences 1980–90; Vice-Pres. Conseil d'Orientation du Centre Georges Pompidou 1975–89, Conseil Supérieur de l'Education Nationale 1983–89; Pres. Centre Georges Pompidou 1989–91; Pres. Comité d'Ethique des Sciences, CNRS 1994; Pres. Admin Council, European Cultural Centre of Delphi, Nat. Theatre, Athens; Pres. Asscn Int. Dimitri Chostakovitch; mem. Greek, British, Belgian, German and Bulgarian Acads; Hon. Pres. Asscn of Int. Byzantine Studies; Commdr de la Légion d'honneur, Grand Croix Ordre nat. du Mérite, Commdr des Arts et des Lettres, Officier des Palmes académiques; numerous foreign decorations; Dr hc (London, New York, Belgrade, Harvard, Lima, New Brunswick, Athens Social Science Univ., American Univ. of Paris, Haifa, Thessaloniki, Fribourg, Univ. of Creta). *Publications include:* Byzance et la Mer 1966, Etudes sur les structures administratives et sociales de Byzance 1971, l'Idéologie politique de l'empire byzantin 1975, Byzance: les pays et les territoires 1976, Geographica 1981, The Making of Europe 2000, Les Européens 2001, Why Byzantium 2009, Marathônia and Ethnika 2011; four vols of poetry in Greek; contribs to numerous books. *Leisure interests:* tennis, swimming. *Address:* 28 rue Guynemer, 75006 Paris, France (home). *Telephone:* 1-42-22-98-47 (home). *Fax:* 1-45-44-46-49 (home).

AHSAN, Chaudhry Aitzaz; Pakistani barrister, writer, human rights activist and politician; b. 27 Sept. 1945, Murree, Punjab; ed Aitchison Coll. and Government Coll., Lahore, Univ. of Cambridge, UK; called to the Bar, Gray's Inn, London 1967; came first in Cen. Superior Services examination but refused to join govt service during mil. rule of Gen. Ayub Khan; currently Sr Advocate, Supreme Court; Pres. Supreme Court Bar Asscn; fought cases in defence of Benazir Bhutto 2001 and fmr Prime Minister Nawaz Sharif, successfully represented Chief Justice Iftikhar Mohammad Chaudhry in Supreme Court of Pakistan 2007; began political career 1970s; mem. Pakistan People's Party (PPP); elected to Punjab Ass. and inducted into prov. cabinet, Minister of Information, Planning and Devt 1977 (resgnd); expelled from PPP; became an active leader of Movt for the Restoration of Democracy (MRD) following coup by Gen. Mohammad Zia-ul-Haq, rejoined PPP during martial law period, jailed several times as political prisoner without trial for active participation in MRD movt; mem. Nat. Ass. from Lahore (PPP) 1988–92, 2002– (also from Bahawalnagar in S. Punjab 2002–), mem. Standing Cttee on Interior, Standing Cttee on Public Accounts; elected to Senate 1994, Leader of House and Leader of Opposition 1996–99; Fed. Minister for Law and Justice, Interior, Narcotics Control 1988–90; has been under arrest periodically for involvement in effort to restore Iftikhar Mohammad Chaudhry as Chief Justice of Pakistan following suspension of constitution and removal of Chief Justice Chaudhry from the bench by Pres. Pervez Musharraf 2007; Founder and Vice-Pres. Human Rights Comm. of Pakistan; Asian Human Rights Defender Award, Asian Human Rights Comm., Hong Kong 2008, Award for

Distinction in Int. Law and Affairs, New York State Bar Asscn 2008. *Publications:* The Indus Saga and the Making of Pakistan (also Urdu trans., Sindh Sagar Aur Qyam-e-Pakistan), Divided by Democracy (with Lord Meghnad Desai). *Address:* c/o Pakistan People's Party, 8 Street 19, F-8/2, Islamabad, Pakistan.

AHTISAARI, Martti; Finnish diplomatist and fmr head of state; *Chairman, Crisis Management Initiative;* b. 23 June 1937, Viipuri; s. of Oiva Ahtisaari and Tyyne Ahtisaari; m. Eeva Irmeli Hyvärinen 1968; one s.; ed Univ. of Oulu; joined Finnish Ministry for Foreign Affairs 1965, worked in various positions in Ministry's Bureau for Tech. Cooperation 1965–72, Asst Dir 1971–72; Deputy Dir Ministry for Foreign Affairs, Dept for Int. Devt Co-operation 1972–73; mem. Govt Advisory Cttee on Trade and Industrialisation Affairs of Developing Countries 1971–73; Amb. to Tanzania 1973–76 (also accred to Zambia, Somalia and Mozambique 1975–76); mem. Senate of UN Inst. for Namibia 1975–76; UN Commr for Namibia 1977–81, Special Rep. of Sec.-Gen. for Namibia 1978; Under-Sec. of State in charge of Int. Devt Co-operation, Ministry for Foreign Affairs 1984–86; UN Envoy, Head of operation monitoring Namibia's transition to independence 1989–90, Sr Envoy, participated in peace-making efforts in fmr Yugoslavia 1992–93; Pres. of Finland 1994–2000; EU's Special Envoy on Crisis in Kosovo 1999, Special Envoy of the Sec.-Gen. of the UN for the Future Status Process for Kosovo 2005–08; mem. observer group on Austrian Govt's human rights record 2000; Co-Insp. of IRA arms dumps 2000–01; Head UN fact-finding mission into Israeli operation in Jenin refugee camp 2002; Chair. Int. Crisis Group –2004; mem. Bd War-torn Societies Project Int., Balkan Children and Youth Foundation; mem. Open Soc. Int. Adviser's Group, Exec. Bd of Int. Inst. for Democracy and Electoral Assistance –2003, Jt Advisers' Group Soros Foundations; Chair. Global Action Council of Int. Youth Foundation, Int. Bd WSP Int., founder and Chair. Crisis Man. Initiative, Helsinki 2000–; Co-Chair. EastWest Inst. –2005; Chair. Supervisory Bd Finnish Nat. Opera; mem. Bd of Trustees Averett Univ., Inter Press Service Int. Asscn; mem. Steering Cttee Northern Research Forum; Patron Koeppler Appeal; mem. Bd of Dirs Elcoteq SE, UPM-Kymmene, Naantali Music Festival, EUSTORY; Hon. Chair. Pro Baltica Forum, Advisory Cttee of Eurasia Foundation, Int. Cttee of Vyborg Library; Hon. Trustee, American-Scandinavian Foundation, Hon. AO 2002, Order of the Companion of Oliver Tambo 2004, Golden Medal of Independence (Republic of Kosovo) 2009; Dr hc (Univ. of Oulu) 1989, (Bentley Coll., Waltham, Mass) 1990, (Kasetsart Univ., Bangkok) 1995, (Univ. of Turku) 1995, (Helsinki School of Econs and Business Admin) 1996, (Univ. of Palermo, Argentina) 1997, (Univ. of Helsinki) 1997, 2006, (Univ. of Moscow (MGIMO) 1997, (Kyiv) 1998, (Univ. of Tech., Espoo) 1998, (Univ. of Namibia) 2000, (Columbia Univ.) 2000, (Univ. of Jyväskylä) 2000, (Averett Coll.) 2001, (American Univ., Bulgaria) 2005, (Univ. of Helsinki) 2006, (Univ. of St Gallen) 2007, (Hosei Univ.) 2008, (Univ. Coll. London) 2008, (Univ. of Kuopio) 2010, (Univ. of Eastern Finland) 2010; Franklin D. Roosevelt Four Freedoms Award 2000, Hessen Peace Prize 2000, J. William Fulbright Award for Int. Understanding 2000, European Centre for Common Ground European Peace-builder Award 2003, European Foundation for Culture Euro-Atlantic Bridge Prize 2003, American-Scandinavian Foundation Golden Medal 2006, Friends of the UN Common Humanity Award 2006, Manfred Wörner Medal, German Ministry of Defence 2007, Geuzenmedal, Geuzen Resistance 1940–1945 Foundation 2008, Delta Prize for Global Understanding, Univ. of Georgia and Delta Air Lines 2008, Chair.'s Award of Int. Crisis Group for outstanding contributions to conflict prevention and resolution in Europe, Asia and Africa 2008, Félix Houphouët-Boigny Peace Prize, UNESCO 2008, Nobel Peace Prize 2008, Open Society Prize, Central European Univ. 2009, Arts and Letters Award, Finlandia Foundation 2010. *Leisure interests:* golf, music, reading. *Address:* Crisis Management Initiative, Eteläranta 12, 2nd Floor, 00130 Helsinki, Finland (office). *Telephone:* (9) 4242810 (office). *Fax:* (9) 42428110 (office). *E-mail:* cmi.helsinki@cmi.fi (office). *Website:* www.cmi.fi (office).

AHUJA, Sanjiv, BE, MS; Indian telecommunications industry executive; *Chairman and CEO, Augere Ltd;* b. 1956; ed Delhi Univ., Columbia Univ., USA; various exec. positions at IBM, including head of telecommunications software div. 1990s; fmr Pres. then COO Telcordia Technologies; CEO Comstellar Technologies –2003; COO Orange 2003–04, CEO 2004–07, Chair. Orange UK 2007–08; Chair. and CEO Augere Ltd 2009–; CEO LightSquared Inc. 2010–12, currently Chair.; Founder and Chair. Eaton Telecom Infrastructure; apptd Dir (non-exec.) Telenor SA 2009; fmr Dir (non-exec.) Cadbury Schweppes plc 2006–08; mem. Man. Cttee France Telecom Group; Partner Redwood Venture Partners. *Address:* Augere Ltd, Fifth Floor, 55 Baker Street, London, W1U 8AN, England (office). *Telephone:* (20) 7467-3940 (office). *Fax:* (20) 7467-3941 (office). *E-mail:* enquiries@augereholdings.com (office). *Website:* (office).

AI, Weiwei; Chinese artist and social activist; *Artistic Director, China Art Archive and Warehouse;* b. 1957, Beijing; s. of Ai Qing; m. Lu Qing; ed Beijing Film Acad.; freelance curator, cultural adviser, architect and social critic; Co-founder art group The Stars 1979; Co-founder, with the late Hans van Dijk and Frank Uytterhaegen, loft-gallery China Art Archive and Warehouse (CAAW), Beijing 1998, currently Artistic Dir; collaborated with Swiss firm Herzog de Meuron as architectural consultant for Olympic Stadium ('Bird's Nest') for 2008 Olympic Games in Beijing; outspoken critic of Govt's human rights record; detained by authorities for alleged evasion of taxes and destroying evidence and held in a secret location April 2011, arrest prompted global campaign for his release, released on bail after pleading guilty June 2011; exhibited as part of the German Pavilion at 55th Int. Art Exhbn, Venice Biennale 2013; Lifetime Achievement Award, Chinese Contemporary Art Awards 2008, named "most powerful artist in art world" by ArtReview magazine 2011. *Address:* China Art Archive and Warehouse, PO Box 100102-43, Beijing 100102, People's Republic of China (office). *Telephone:* (10) 84565152 (office). *Fax:* (10) 84565154 (office). *E-mail:* mail@caaw.com.cn (office). *Website:* www.caaw.com.cn (office); aiweiwei.com.

AIBEL, Howard James, BA, DJur; American lawyer, arbitrator, business executive and charitable foundation trustee; b. 24 March 1929, New York; s. of David Aibel and Anne Aibel; m. Katherine W. Webster 1952; three s.; ed Harvard Coll., Harvard Law School; admitted New York Bar 1952, served as Vice-Pres. of Asscn of the Bar of New York City, Chair. Cttee on Fed. Legislation, Assoc. White & Case, New York 1952–57; with Gen. Electric Co. 1957–64, Anti-Trust Litigation Counsel GE 1960–64; Trade Regulation Counsel ITT Corpn, New York 1964–66,

Vice-Pres., Assoc. Gen. Counsel 1966–68, Gen. Counsel 1968–92, Sr Vice-Pres. 1969–87, Exec. Vice-Pres. 1987–94, Chief Legal Officer 1992–94; Pres. Harvard Law School Asscn of New York City 1992–93; Partner, Le Boeuf Lamb Greene & McRae LLP 1994–99, mem. counsel 1999–2001; fmr Trustee, Chair. Advisory Bd School of Law, Bridgeport Univ. 1989–91, Chair. Exec. Cttee Bd of Dirs American Arbitration Asscn 1992–95, Chair. Bd of Dirs 1995–98; Bd of Dirs Alliance of Resident Theaters, New York 1986–, Chair. 1989–2002, Chair. Emer. 2002–; Vice-Chair., Trustee The Fund for Modern Courts 1985–95, Vice-Pres. Harvard Law School Asscn 1994–2002; Vice-Chair. Bd of Trustees, Westport Country Playhouse; mem. American Law Inst., New York State, American Bar Asscn; mem. Bd of Dirs Sheraton Corpn 1982–94, Farrel Corp. 1994–2005; Life Fellow American Bar Foundation; Trustee Int. Bar Asscn Foundation, Lawyers' Cttee for Civil Rights under Law 1991–95; consulting Trustee Nature Centre for Environmental Activities of Westport; Trustee, Sacred Heart Univ., Fairfield, Conn. 2004–10, Trustee Emer. 2010–; Trustee J. H. Geneen Charitable Trust; Commr, Town of Weston Conservation Comm.; Harold S. Geneen Man. Award 1994. *Leisure interests:* theatre, bird study, photography. *Address:* 183 Steep Hill Road, Weston, CT 06883-1924, USA (home). *Telephone:* (203) 227-0738 (home). *E-mail:* howardaibel@mac.com (office); hjaibel@post.harvard.edu (home).

AICHINGER, Ilse; Austrian writer; b. 1 Nov. 1921, Vienna; m. Günter Eich (died 1972); ed Universität Wien; fmrly worked with Inge Scholl at Hochschule für Gestaltung, Ulm; later worked as a reader for S. Fischer (publrs), Frankfurt and Vienna; Förderungspreis des Österreichischen Staatspreises 1952, Preis der Gruppe 47 1952, Literaturpreis der Freien und Hansestadt Bremen 1954, Immermannpreis der Stadt Düsseldorf 1955, Literaturpreis der Bayerischen Akad. 1961, Nyell Sachs-Preis, Dortmund 1971, City of Vienna Literature Prize 1974, Georg Tracke Prize 1979, Petrarca Prize 1982, Belgian Europe Festival Prize 1987, Town of Solothurn Prize 1991, Joseph-Breitbach-Preis 2000. *Publications include:* Die Grössere Hoffnung (novel) 1948, Knöpfe (radio play) 1952, Der Gefesselte (short stories) 1953, Zu keiner Stunde (dialogues) 1957, Besuch im Pfarrhaus (radio play) 1961, Wo ich wohne (stories, dialogues, poems) 1963, Eliza, Eliza (stories) 1965, Nachricht von Tag (stories) 1970, Schlechte Worter 1976, Meine Sprache und Ich Erzählungen 1978, Radio Plays, Selected Poetry and Prose by Ilse Aichinger 1983, Kleist, Moos, Fasane 1987, Collected Works (eight vols) 1991, Film und Verhängnis 2001. *Address:* c/o Fischer Verlag, POB 700480, 60008 Frankfurt, Germany.

AIDA, Takefumi, PhD; Japanese architect and academic; b. 5 June 1937, Tokyo; s. of Takeshi Aida and Chiyo Aida; m. Kazuko Aida 1966; one s. one d.; ed School of Architecture, Waseda Univ., Tokyo; qualified architect 1967; Prof., Shibaura Inst. of Tech., Tokyo 1976–2000, Prof. and Dean Dept of Architecture and Eng 1991–94; major works include: Memorial at Iwo-Jima Island, Tokyo 1983, Toy Block House X, Shibuya, Tokyo 1984, Tokyo War Dead Memorial Park, Bunkyo, Tokyo 1988, Saito Memorial Hall, Shibaura Inst. of Tech., Tokyo 1990, Community Centre, Kawasato 1993, Funeral Hall, Mizuho 1998, Nenseiji Temple 2001; Japan Architects Asscn Annual Prize for Newcomers 1982, 2nd Prize Int. Doll's Houses Competition, UK 1983. *Publications:* Architecture Note, Toy Block Houses 1984, Toy Block House X 1986, Takefumi Aida Buildings and Projects 1990, The Works of Takefumi Aida 1998, The Collected Edition of Takefumi Aida 1998. *Leisure interest:* Shogi. *Address:* 1-3-2 Okubo, Shinjuku-ku, Tokyo 169-0072, Japan (home). *Telephone:* (3) 3205-1585 (home). *Fax:* (3) 3209-7960 (home). *E-mail:* t-aida@kt.rim.or.jp (office).

AIDEED, Hussein; Somali politician; b. 1963; s. of Gen. Mohamed Farah Aideed (died 1996); mem. Habr Gedir clan; m. 1st; m. 2nd 1995; one d.; m. 3rd (divorced); one d.; emigrated to USA 1978, obtained US citizenship; joined US Marine Corps Reserve 1987, attained position of Corporal; translator, US-led peacekeeping force in Somalia 1992; public works clerk, Water Supply and Roads Maintenance Dept, W Covina City Hall, Southern Calif. –1995; returned to Somalia 1995; led reorganization of clan militia and armed conquest of Baidoa 1995; Leader Somali Nat. Alliance 1996–; Co-Chair. Somali Reconciliation and Restoration Council; participated in peace talks on future of Somalia, Nairobi, Kenya 2002; imprisoned in Nairobi on charges of failing to pay debts 2002; Deputy Prime Minister 2004–10; Minister of Internal Affairs 2004–07, of Public Works and Housing 2007–10. *Address:* c/o Ministry of Public Works and Housing, Mogadishu, Somalia (office).

AIDOO, Ama Ata; Ghanaian writer and academic; *Visiting Professor of Africana Studies and Creative Writing, Brown University;* b. Abeadzi Kyiakor, Gold Coast (now Ghana); one d.; Lecturer, Cape Coast Univ. 1970–73; Consultant Prof., Phelps-Stokes Fund Ethnic Studies Program, Washington 1974–75; consultant at univs, acads and research insts in Africa, Europe and USA; Prof. of English, Univ. of Ghana; Minister of Educ. 1982–83; fmr Fellow of Advanced Creative Writing Program, Stanford Univ.; currently Visiting Prof. of Africana Studies and Creative Writing, Brown Univ., also Writer-in-Residence; Chair. African Regional Panel of the Commonwealth Writers' Prize 1990, 1991; fmr mem. Bd of Dirs Ghana Broadcasting Corpn, Arts Council of Ghana, Ghana Medical and Dental Council; Fellow, Inst. for African Studies; Millennium Award for Literary Excellence, Ghana's Excellence Awards Foundation 2005, Woman of Substance Award, African Women's Devt Fund 2005. *Publications include:* novels: Our Sister Killjoy or Reflections from a Black-Eyed Squint 1977, Changes: A Love Story (Commonwealth Writers' Prize for the Africa region 1993) 1991; poetry: Someone Talking to Sometime 1985, Birds and Other Poems; plays: The Dilemma of a Ghost 1965, Anowa 1970, Changes: A Love Story 1991; short stories: No Sweetness Here 1970, The Eagle and The Chicken and Other Stories 1987, The Girl Who Can and Other Stories 1999; numerous contribs to magazines and journals. *Address:* Department of Africana Studies, Brown University, Box 1904, 155 Angell Street, Providence, RI 02912, USA (office). *Telephone:* (401) 863-3137 (office). *Fax:* (401) 863-3559 (office). *E-mail:* Ama_Ata_Aidoo@brown.edu (office). *Website:* www.brown.edu/Departments/Africana_Studies (office).

AIELLO, Danny; American actor; b. 20 June 1933, New York; s. of Daniel Louis Aiello and Frances Pietrocova; m. Sandy Cohen 1955; three s. one d. *Theatre includes:* Lampost Reunion 1975 (Theatre World Award), Gemini 1977 (Obie Award 1977), Hurlyburly 1985. *Films include:* Bang the Drum Slowly 1973, The Godfather II 1976, Once Upon a Time in America 1984, The Purple Rose of Cairo 1985, Moonstruck 1987, Do the Right Thing 1989 (Boston Critics Award, Chicago Critics Award, LA Critics Award, all for Best Supporting Actor), Harlem Nights 1989, Jacob's Ladder 1990, Once Around 1991, Hudson Hawk 1991, The Closer 1991, 29th Street 1991, Mistress 1992, Ruby 1992, The Pickle 1992, The Cemetery Club 1992, The Professional 1994, Prêt-a-Porter 1994, Léon 1994, City Hall 1995, Power of Attorney 1995, Two Days in the Valley 1996, Mojave Moon 1996, Two Much 1996, A Brooklyn State of Mind 1997, Bring Me the Head of Mavis Davis 1998, Wilbur Falls 1998, 18 Shades of Dust 1999, Mambo Cafe 2000, Prince of Central Park 2000, Dinner Rush 2000, Off Key 2001, The Russian Job 2002, Marcus Timberwolf 2002, The Last Request 2002, Mail Order Bride 2003, Zeyda and the Hitman 2004, Brooklyn Lobster 2005, Lucky Number Slevin 2006, The Last Request 2006, The Shoemaker 2006, Stiffs 2010. *Television includes:* The Preppie Murder 1989, A Family of Strangers 1993 (Emmy Award), The Last Don (mini-series) 1997, Dellaventura (series) 1997, The Last Don II (mini-series) 1998. *Music includes:* albums: I Just Wanted To Hear the Words 2004, Live from Atlantic City 2008. *Address:* Tracey Miller and Associates Inc., 2610 Fire Road, Egg Harbor Township, NJ 08234, USA. *Telephone:* (609) 383-2323. *E-mail:* tracey@tmapublicity.com. *Website:* www.dannyaiello.com.

AIGRAIN, Jacques, PhD; Swiss/French business executive; *Chairman, LCH.Clearnet Group Limited;* b. 1954; m., two c.; ed Dauphine Univ., Sorbonne; joined JP Morgan 1981, served as co-head of investment banking client coverage, fmr mem. Man. Cttee; joined Swiss Reinsurance Co. (Swiss Re) as Head, Financial Services Business Group and mem. Exec. Bd Cttee 2001, CEO 2004–09; currently Chair. LCH.Clearnet Group Ltd; mem. Supervisory Bd Deutsche Lufthansa, Swiss International Airlines; mem. Bd of Dirs Resolution; mem. Financial Industry Advisory Bd, Apax Partners LLP. *Address:* Office of the Chairman, LCH.Clearnet Group Limited, Aldgate House, 33 Aldgate High Street, London, EC3N 1EA, England (office). *Telephone:* (20) 7426-7000 (office). *Website:* www.lchclearnet.com (office).

AIKEN, Linda H., PhD, FAAN, FRCN, RN; American nurse, sociologist and academic; *Claire M. Fagin Leadership Professor in Nursing, Professor of Sociology, and Director, Center for Health Outcomes and Policy Research, University of Pennsylvania;* b. 29 July 1943, Roanoke, Va; d. of William Jordan and Betty Philips Harman (née Warner); one s. one d.; ed Univ. of Florida, Univ. of Texas, Univ. of Wisconsin; nurse, Univ. of Florida Medical Center 1964–65, Instructor, Coll. of Nursing 1966–67; Instructor, School of Nursing, Univ. of Missouri 1967–70, Clinical Nurse Specialist 1967–70; Lecturer, School of Nursing, Univ. of Wisconsin 1973–74; Program Officer, Robert Wood Johnson Foundation 1974–76, Dir of Research 1976–79, Asst Vice-Pres. 1979–81, Vice-Pres. 1981–87; Claire M. Fagin Leadership Prof. in Nursing and Prof. of Sociology and Dir Center for Health Outcomes and Policy Research, Univ. of Pennsylvania 1988–; mem. Pres. Clinton's Nat. Health Care Reform Task Force 1993; Commr Physician Payment Review Comm. Nat. Advisory Council, US Agency for Health Care Policy and Research; Assoc. Ed. Journal of Health and Social Behaviour 1979–81; Fellow and Past Pres. American Acad. of Nursing 1978, Inst. of Medecine 1982, Nat. Acad. of Social Insurance 1989; Fellow, American Acad. of Arts and Sciences 1998; numerous awards including Jessie M. Scott Award, American Nurses Asscn 1984, 2002, Nurse Scientist of the Year Award 1991, Distinguished Pathfinder Research Award 2001, Barbara Thoman Curtis Award, Individual Codman Award, Jt Comm. on Accreditation of Healthcare Orgs 2003, Slackler Award for Sustained Nat. Leadership in Health Research 2006, Graham Prize for Health Services Research, Baxter Int. Foundation 2006, Modern Healthcare's 100 Most Powerful People in Healthcare 2004–07 and 25 Top Women in Healthcare, Amb., Research!America's Rogers Soc. for Global Health Research 2009. *Publications:* Nursing in the 1980s: Crises, Challenges, Opportunities (ed.) 1982, Evaluation Studies Review Annual (co-ed. with B. Kehrer) 1985, Applications of Social Science to Clinical Medicine and Health Policy (co-ed. with D. Mechanic) 1986, Charting Nursing's Future (co-ed. with C. Fagin) 1991, Hospital Restructuring in North America and Europe 1997, Advances in Hospital Outcomes Research 1998, Accounting for Variation in Hospital Outcomes: Cross-National Study 1999, International Nursing Migration (co-ed. with P. Pittman and J. Buchan) 2007; contribs to professional journals. *Address:* University of Pennsylvania, Center for Health Outcomes and Policy Research, NEB 332R, 418 Curie Blvd, Philadelphia, PA 19104 (office); 2209 Lombard Street, Philadelphia, PA 19146-1107, USA (home). *Telephone:* (215) 898-5673 (office). *Fax:* (215) 573-2062 (office). *E-mail:* laiken@nursing.upenn.edu (office). *Website:* www.nursing.upenn.edu/chopr (office).

AILES, Roger Eugene, BFA; American television producer and communications executive; *Chairman, Fox Television Stations;* b. 15 May 1940, Warren, OH; s. of Robert Eugene Ailes and Donna Marie Ailes (née Cunningham); m. Elizabeth Tilson 1998; one c.; ed Ohio Univ.; Assoc. Dir KYW-TV, Cleveland 1962–63, Producer and Dir 1963–65; Producer Mike Douglas Show, Westinghouse Broadcasting Corpn, Phila 1965–67, Exec. Producer 1967–68; political and media consultant to presidential campaigns of Richard M. Nixon 1968, Ronald Reagan 1984, and George Bush 1988; resgnd from political consulting 1992; Chair. Ailes Communications Inc., NY 1969–92; Exec. Vice-Pres. TV News Inc. 1975–76; Pres. CNBC, NBC 1993–96; Pres. and Program Host, America's Talking, NBC, NY 1993–96; Chair. and CEO Fox News 1996–, Exec. Ed. FOXnews.com 2000–, Chair. Fox TV Stations 2005–; also Head Twentieth TV; fmr consultant WCBS-TV; Vice-Pres. Conf. Personal Mans; mem. American Fed. of TV and Radio Artists, Dirs Guild of America, Radio and TV News Dirs Asscn; Hon. PhD (Ohio Univ.); Award for Shakespeare Production, Fine Arts Magazine 1964, Emmy Award (twice) for The Mike Douglas Show 1967, 1968, Liberty Bell Award, Advertising Alliance Phila 1971, Commendation Award for Contrib. to Communications, Ohio Univ. 1972, Silver Circle Award, Nat. Acad. TV Arts and Sciences 1999, First Amendment Leadership Award, Radio and TV News Dirs Foundation 2006. *Productions include:* Mother Earth, Broadway Museum (play) 1972, Hot-L Baltimore (play, four Obie Awards 1973) 1973–76, The Last Frontier 1974, Television and the Presidency (Emmy Award) 1984, Fellini: Wizards, Clowns and Honest Liars 1977, Tomorrow: Coast to Coast 1981, The Rush Limbaugh Show 1992–96, A Current Affair, The Maury Povich Show, The Leeza Show, An All-Star Salute to Our Troops 1991. *Publications:* You Are the Message: Secrets of the Master Communicators (co-author with Jon Kraushar) 1987; articles in popular magazines and professional journals. *Address:* Fox News, 1211 Avenue of the Americas, New York, NY 10036, USA (office). *Website:* www.foxnews.com (office).

AILLAGON, Jean Jacques; French politician and cultural official; *President, Château de Versailles;* b. 2 Oct. 1946, Metz; s. of Charles Aillagon and Anne-Marie Louis; two c.; ed Univs of Toulouse and Nanterre; Prof. of History and Geography, Lycée de Tulle 1973–76; Deputy Dir Ecole Nat. Supérieure des Beaux-Arts 1978–82; Admin. Musée Nat. d'Art Moderne (Centre Pompidou) 1982–85; Asst to Dir of Cultural Affairs of City of Paris 1985–88; Del.-Gen. for Cultural Programmes of City of Paris 1988–93; Dir-Gen. Vidéothèque de Paris 1992–93; Dir of Cultural Affairs of City of Paris 1993–96; Pres. Centre Georges Pompidou 1996–2002; Minister of Culture and Communication 2002–04; Pres. and Dir-Gen. TV5 Monde 2005–06; Dir Palazzo Grassi, Venice April–Aug. 2007; Pres. Château de Versailles 2007–; Pres. comm. organizing year 2000 celebrations 1999–2001; Artistic Dir Commissariat for France–Egypt Year 1996–98; Chevalier, Ordre Nat. du Mérite, des Palmes académiques, Légion d'honneur. *Address:* Château de Versailles, RP834, 78008 Versailles Cedex, France (office). *Telephone:* 1-30-83-78-00 (office). *E-mail:* accueil.public@chateauversailles.fr (office). *Website:* www.chateauversailles.fr (office).

AILLERET, François; French government official; *President, École des Neurosciences de Paris-Île-de-France;* b. 7 June 1937; s. of Pierre Ailleret and Denise Nodé-Langlois; m. Chantal Flinois 1963; four c.; ed École Polytechnique, École Nationale des Ponts et Chaussées; served in Algeria and Côte d'Ivoire in early 1960s; various appointments at Paris Airport 1967–80; joined Electricité de France (EdF) 1980, Deputy Dir-Gen. 1987, Dir-Gen. 1994–96, Vice-Pres. 1996, Pres. EdF Int. 1996–2003, Hon. CEO 2003–; Pres. Int. Union of Electricity Producers and Distributors (UNIPEDE) 1997–2000; Admin. Pechiney 1996–2003; currently Pres. Asscn Française de Normalisation (AFNOR) 2002–11; Chair. French Energy Council 1998–2004; mem. Conseil Economique et Social (Nat.) 1999–2010; Pres., Conseil d'Admin, Institut Pasteur 2005–11, École des Neurosciences de Paris-Île-de-France 2011–; Officier, Légion d'honneur; Commdr, Ordre nat. du Mérite; Croix de la Valeur militaire. *Address:* EdF, 151 boulevard Haussmann, 75008 Paris (office); 22 rue Rouelle, 75015 Paris, France (home). *Telephone:* 1-40-42-26-70 (office). Fax: 1-40-42-77-78 (office). *E-mail:* francois.ailleret@edf.fr (office). *Website:* www.paris-neuroscience.fr (office).

AIMÉE, Anouk; French actress; b. (Françoise Dreyfus), 27 April 1932, Paris; d. of Henry Dreyfus and Geneviève Durand; m. 2nd Nico Papatakis 1951; one d.; m. 3rd Pierre Barouh 1966; m. 4th Albert Finney (q.v.) 1970 (divorced 1978); ed Ecole de la rue Milton, Paris, Ecole de Barbezieux, Pensionnat de Bandd, Inst. de Megève and Cours Bauer-Therond; film and TV actress 1955–; Commdr des Arts et des Lettres, Golden Globe Award 1968, Prix Féminin, Cannes. *Theatre includes:* Sud 1954, Love Letters 1990, 1994. *Films include:* Les mauvaises rencontres 1955, Tous peuvent me tuer, Pot bouille and Montparnasse 19 1957, La tête contre les murs 1958, Les drageurs 1959, La dolce vita, Le farceur, Lola, Les amours de Paris, L'imprévu 1960, Quai Notre Dame 1960, Le jugement dernier 1961, Sodome et Gomorrhe 1961, Les grands chemins 1962, Education sentimentale 1962, Huit et demi 1962, Un homme et une femme 1966, Un soir un train 1967, The Appointment 1968, Model Shop 1968, Justine 1968, Si c'était à refaire 1976, Mon premier amour 1978, Salto nel vuoto 1979, La tragédie d'un homme ridicule 1981, Qu'est-ce qui fait courir David? 1982, Le Général de l'armée morte 1983, Vive la vie 1984, Le succès à tout prix 1984, Un homme et une femme: vingt ans déjà 1986, Docteur Norman Bethune 1992, Les Marmottes 1993, Les Cent et une nuits 1995, Prêt-à-porter 1995, Une pour toutes 2000, La Petite prairie aux bouleaux 2003, Ils se marièrent et eurent beaucoup d'enfants 2004, De particulier à particulier 2006. *Television:* Une page d'amour 1979, L'Île bleue 2001, Des voix dans le jardin, Napoléon 2002, Claude Lelouch, on s'aimera (narrator) 2007. *Leisure interests:* reading, life, human rights. *Address:* c/o Artmédia, 20 avenue Rapp, 75007 Paris, France (home).

AINSLEY, John Mark; British singer (tenor); b. 9 July 1953, Crewe, Chesire; s. of John Alwyn Ainsley and Dorothy Sylvia Ainsley (née Anderson); partner William Whitehead; ed Royal Grammar School, Worcester, Magdalen Coll., Oxford; debut in Stravinsky's Mass, Royal Festival Hall 1984; many concert performances from 1985 with Taverner Consort, New London Consort and London Baroque; appearances in Mozart Masses at The Vienna Konzerthaus with Heinz Holliger, Handel's Saul at Göttingen with John Eliot Gardiner, Mozart Requiem under Yehudi Menuhin at Gstaad and Pulcinella at the Barbican under Jeffrey Tate; other concerts with Ulster Orchestra and Bournemouth Sinfonietta; debut in USA at Lincoln Center in Bach's B Minor Mass with Christopher Hogwood 1990; opera debut at the Innsbruck Festival in Scarlatti's Gli Equivoci nel Sembiante, at ENO in the Return of Ulysses 1989; title role in Méhul's Joseph for Dutch Radio, Handel's Acis in Stuttgart and Solomon for Radio France under Leopold Hager; has sung Mozart's Tamino for Opera Northern Ireland and Ferrando for Glyndebourne Touring Opera; sang Ferrando at Glyndebourne 1992, Don Ottavio 1994, Haydn's The Seasons with the London Classical Players; BBC Proms Concerts, London 1993, Stravinsky concert under Andrew Davis at Royal Festival Hall 1997, Monteverdi's Orfeo for Munich Opera Festival 1999, Jupiter in Semele for ENO 1999, Bach's St Matthew Passion at BBC Proms 2002, Skuratov in From the House of the Dead for Amsterdam, Vienna and Aix en Provence Festivals, 2007, Captain Vere in Billy Budd for Frankfurt Opera 2007, Emilio in Partenope for ENO 2008, title role in Idomeneo and Bazajet in Tamerlano for Munich Opera Festival 2008; Grammy Award for Best Opera Recording 1995, Munich Festival Prize 1999, Royal Philharmonic Soc. Singer Award 2007. *Recordings include:* Purcell, Odes (with Trevor Pinnock) 1988, Handel's Nisi Dominus (under Simon Preston) 1989, Handel, Saul 1991, Handel, Acis and Galatea 1993, Blow, Fairest Work of Happy Nature 1993, Great Baroque Arias (with the King's Consort) 1994, Handel, Jephtha 1994, Zelenka, Lamentations of Jeremiah 1994, Finzi, Dies Natalis and Intimations 1996, Warlock, Curlew Capriol Serenade Songs 1997, Mozart, Requiem 1998, Mozart, Songs 1998, Ireland, Songs 1999, Mozart's C Minor Mass (with Christopher Hogwood) 1999, Quilter, Songs 2000, Vaughan Williams, Songs 2000, L'invitation au voyage 2006, Finzi, Intimations of Immortality 2009, Grainger, Jungle Book and Other Choral Works 2011. *Website:* www.askonasholt.com (office).

AINSLIE, Sir Charles Benedict (Ben), Kt, CBE; British sailor; b. 5 Feb. 1977, Macclesfield, Cheshire, England; s. of Roddy Ainslie (skipper of 'Second Life' in first Whitbread Round the World Race 1973–74) and Susan Ainslie; ed Peter Symonds Coll., Winchester, Hants.; began sailing in Restronguet Creek, Cornwall aged eight; competitive results include Laser Radial European Champion 1993, Laser Radial World Champion 1993, Youth World Champion 1995, Laser European Champion 1996, 1998, 1999, 2000, Laser World Champion 1998, 1999, Finn European Champion 2002, 2003, Finn World Champion 2002, 2003, 2004 (first Briton to win three consecutive Finn titles), 2005, 2008, 2012, ISAF Open Match Racing World Championship 2010; four gold medals in successive Olympic Games (Laser Class, Sydney 2000, Finn Class, Athens 2004, Finn Class, Beijing 2008, Finn Class, London 2012), also won silver medal in Laser Class at Atlanta Olympic Games 1996; joined Team New Zealand in late 2004 to compete in America's Cup 2007; announced by British America's Cup Campaign 'Origin' as skipper for 33rd America's Cup challenge in 2009 Sept. 2007; secured fifth world title at Finn Gold Cup in Melbourne 2008 (most successful Finn sailor ever); Hon. mem. Royal Cornwall Yacht Club, Stokes Bay Sailing Club, Restronguet Sailing Club, Hayling Island Sailing Club; Hon. degree in Sports Science (Univ. Coll. of Chichester); British Young Sailor of the Year 1995, British Yachtsman of the Year 1995, 1999, 2000, 2002, Sports Writers' Asscn Best Int. newcomer 1996, Int. Sailing Fed. (ISAF) World Sailor of the Year 1998, 2002. *Leisure interests:* cycling, flying, football, cricket, golf. *E-mail:* jo.grindley@intotheblue.biz. *Website:* www.benainslie.com.

AINSWORTH, Rt Hon Robert (Bob) William; British politician; b. 19 June 1952, Coventry; m. Gloria Ainsworth; two d.; worked for Jaguar Cars, Coventry; held various positions in trade union and Labour movt including Shop Steward, Sec. of Jt Shop Steward Cttee, Sheet Metal Workers Union Br. Pres., Constituency Labour Party Chair.; City Councillor, Coventry 1984–92; MP (Labour) for Coventry North East 1992–, apptd Whip 1995, Lord Commr of HM Treasury (Govt Whip) 1997–2001, Parl. Under-Sec. at Dept for Environment, Transport and the Regions Jan.– June 2001, Home Office Minister with responsibility for Drugs and Organized Crime 2001–03, Govt Deputy Chief Whip 2003–07, Minister for the Armed Forces 2007–09, Sec. of State for Defence 2009–10. *Address:* House of Commons, London, SW1A0AA (office); Bayley House, 22–23 Bayley Lane, Coventry, CV1 5RJ, England (office). *Telephone:* (2476) 226707 (Coventry) (office). *Fax:* (2476) 433401 (Coventry) (office). *E-mail:* smithn@parliament.uk (office).

AIREY, Dawn Elizabeth, MA, FRSA, FRTS; British television executive; *President, CLT-UFA UK TV, RTL Group;* b. 15 Nov. 1960, Preston, Lancs.; one d.; ed Kelly Coll., Girton Coll. Cambridge; with Cen. TV 1985–93; ITV Network Centre 1993–94; Channel 4 1994–96; Channel 5 1996–2002, Chief Exec. 2000–02; Man. Dir Sky Networks 2002–06; CEO Iostar (TV production and distribution co.) April 2007 (resgnd); Dir of Global Content, ITV 2007–08, mem. Bd of Dirs 2008; Chair. and CEO Channel 5 Broadcasting Ltd 2008–10; Pres. CLT-UFA UK TV, RTL Group, London 2010–; Vice-Pres. Royal TV Soc. 2002–; mem. Bd of Dirs (non-exec.) Taylor Nelson Sofres 2007–; Exec. Chair. Media Guardian Edinburgh Int. TV Festival 2001–06; Chair. The Grierson Trust 2010–; mem. Bd Int. Emmy Awards; Olswang Business Woman of the Year 2000. *Leisure interests:* cinema, tennis. *Address:* c/o The Grierson Trust, 28 Sallows Road, Peterborough, PE1 4EU, England (office). *Telephone:* (1733) 891878 (office). *E-mail:* info@griersontrust.org (office). *Website:* www.griersontrust.org (office); clt-ufa.com (office); www.rtlgroup.com (office).

AIRLIE, 13th Earl of; David George Patrick Coke Ogilvy, KT, GCVO, PC, RVO; British business executive; b. 17 May 1926, London; s. of 12th Earl of Airlie, KT, GCVO, MC and Lady Alexandra Marie Bridget Coke; m. Virginia Fortune Ryan 1952; three s. three d.; ed Eton Coll.; Chair. Schroders PLC 1977–84, Ashdown Investment Trust Ltd 1968–84, J. Henry Schroder Bank AG (Switzerland) 1977–84, Baring Stratton Investment Trust PLC 1986–2000; Chair. Gen. Accident Fire and Life Assurance Corpn PLC 1987–97; Dir J. Henry Schroder Wagg & Co. Ltd 1961–84, Schroder, Darling and Co. Holdings Ltd (Australia) 1977–84, Schroders Inc. (USA) 1977–84, Schroder Int. Ltd 1973–84, Scottish & Newcastle Breweries PLC 1969–83; Dir Royal Bank of Scotland Group PLC 1983–93; Lord Chamberlain of the Queen's Household 1984–97; Lord Lt of Angus 1989–2001; Capt.-Gen. of the Royal Co. of Archers 2004–; Chancellor Univ. of Abertay, Dundee 1994–; Chair. Historic Royal Palaces 1998–2002; Pres. Nat. Trust for Scotland 1998–2002; Gov. Nuffield Hosps; Hon. Pres. Scout Asscn in Scotland 1988–2002, JP Angus 1990; Hon. LLD (Dundee) 1990. *Address:* Cortachy Castle, Kirriemuir, Angus, DD8 4LY, Scotland (home); 36 Sloane Court West, London, SW3 4TB, England (home). *Telephone:* (1575) 540231. *Fax:* (1575) 540223 (office). (1575) 540570109. *E-mail:* office@airlieestates.com (office). *Website:* www.airlieestates.com (office).

AITIMOVA, Byrganym Sariyevna; Kazakhstani politician and diplomatist; b. 26 Feb. 1953, West-Kazakhstan region; m.; two c.; ed Ural State Pedagogical Inst., Almaty Inst. of Political Science and Man., Kazakh State Univ.; teacher at public school 1976; fmr Sec., Republican Youth Org.; Deputy Chair. Soviet Children's Fund 1988–90; mem. of Parl. 1990–93; Minister for Youth Affairs, Tourism and Sport 1993–96; Amb. to Israel 1996–2002, to Italy 2002–04; Deputy Prime Minister 2004; Minister of Educ. and Science 2004–07; Perm. Rep. to UN, New York 2007–13. *Address:* Ministry of Foreign Affairs, 10017 Astana, D. Kunaev kosh. 31, Kazakhstan (office). *Telephone:* (7172) 72-05-18 (office). *Fax:* (7172) 72-05-16 (office). *E-mail:* astana@mfa.kz (office). *Website:* www.mfa.kz (office).

AITMATOV, Ilghiz Torokulovich, PhD, DTechSc; Kyrgyzstani geologist; *Director, Institute of Physics and Mechanics of Rocks, Kyrgyz National Academy of Sciences;* b. 8 Feb. 1931, Frunze (now Bishkek); s. of Torokul Aitmatov and Naghima Aitmatova (née Abdulvaliyeva); m. Rosalia Jamankulovna Jenchuraeva 1961; one s. two d.; ed Moscow Inst. of Geological Survey, USSR Acad. of Sciences, Inst. of Mining; foreman, engineer, head anti-avalanche surveillance service, Kyrgyz Geological Dept 1954–57; doctoral studies USSR Acad. of Sciences, Inst. of Mining (Moscow) 1957–60; jr researcher, Head of Lab., Deputy Dir Inst. of Physics and Mechanics of Rocks, Kyrgyz Nat. Acad. of Sciences, Head of Lab. 1960–68, Deputy Dir 1968–79, Dir 1970–88, Pres. 1990–94, Dir 1994–, Academician-Sec., Dept of Physical, Math. and Earth Sciences 1988–90, Pres. Kyrgyz Acad. of Sciences 1990–93; Corresp. mem. Kyrgyz Nat. Acad. of Sciences 1986, mem. 1988-, mem. Political Council, People's Republican Party of Kyrgyzstan 1992–95; mem. Parliament (Supreme Council) of Kyrgyz Repub. 1990–91; mem. Pres. Council 1990–94; mem. Russian Acad. of Mining Sciences, Int. Engineering Acad. and other int. acads.; Kyrgyzstan SSR State Prize 1984, USSR State Prize 1989, Merited Worker of Science of Kyrgyzstan; other medals and awards. *Achievements* *include:* Scientific Discovery Phenomena of Saltatory Release of Residual Stresses in Rocks (co-author) 1998. *Publications:* more than 250 papers on rock and mass geomechanics, including seven monographs, 15 inventions and one scientific discovery. *Address:* 98 ul. Toktoghula, Apartment 9, 720000 Bishkek (home); Institute of Physics and Mechanics of Rocks, National Academy of Sciences, ul. O. Mederova 98, 720035 Bishek, Kyrgyzstan (office). *Telephone:* (312) 54-11-15 (office); (312) 66-21-89 (home). *Fax:* (312) 54-11-17 (office); (312) 68-00-47 (home). *E-mail:* ifmgp@yandex.ru (office); djam@freenet.kg (home).

AIZAWA, Masuo, MSc, BE, DEng, PhD; Japanese research institute director and academic; b. 1942, Yokohama; ed Yokohama Nat. Univ., Grad. School of Science and Eng, Tokyo Inst. of Tech.; Research Assoc., Chemical Resources Lab., Tokyo Inst. of Tech. 1971–80; Assoc. Prof., Inst. of Material Science, Tsukuba Univ. 1980–86; Assoc. Prof., Faculty of Eng, Tokyo Inst. of Tech. 1986, Prof. 1986–94, Dean of Faculty of Bioscience and Biotechnology 1994–96, 1998–2000, Vice-Pres. Tokyo Inst. of Tech. 2000–01, Pres. 2001–07; Advising Prof., Shanghai Jiaotong Univ. 2003–; fmr Pres. Japan Asscn of Nat. Univs 2005–07, Electrochemical Soc. of Japan, Int. Soc. of Molecular Electronics and Biocomputing, Intelligent Materials Forum; fmr Vice-Pres. Chemical Soc. of Japan, Japan Univ. Accreditation Asscn; Exec. mem. Council for Science and Tech. Policy, Cabinet Office 2006–; mem. Science Council of Japan, Cen. Council for Educ.; Chemical Soc. of Japan Award 1997, Electrochemical Soc. Award 2003, 2005, Int. Chemical Sensors Award. *Address:* Council of Science and Technology Policy, Cabinet Office, 3-1-1 Kasumigaseki, Chiyoda-ku, Tokyo 100-8970, Japan (office). *Telephone:* (3) 5253-2111 (office). *Website:* www8.cao.go.jp/cstp/english/policy/index.html (office).

AJAYI, Jacob Festus Ade, PhD; Nigerian historian, academic and writer; b. 26 May 1929, Ikole-Ekiti; s. of the late Chief E. Ade Ajayi and Comfort F. Bolajoko Ajayi; m. Christie Akinleye-Martins 1956; one s. four d.; ed Igbobi Coll. Lagos, Higher Coll. Yaba, Univ. Coll. Ibadan, Univ. Coll. Leicester and King's Coll. London; tutor, Ibadan Boys' High School 1948–49, 1951–52; Fellow, Inst. of Historical Research 1957–58; Lecturer, Sr Lecturer, Univ. of Ibadan 1958–63, Prof. of History 1963–89; Fellow, Center for Advanced Study in the Behavioural Sciences, Stanford Univ. 1970–71; Vice-Chancellor, Univ. of Lagos 1972–78; Pro-Chancellor, Ondo State Univ., Ado-Ekiti 1984–88; mem. UN Univ. Council 1974–80, Chair. 1976–77; Chair. Int. African Inst. 1975–87; mem. Bureau, Asscn of African Univs 1973–80, Vice-Pres. 1976–80; mem. Bureau, Int. Asscn of Univs 1980–90; Pres. Historical Soc. of Nigeria 1972–81; mem. UNESCO scientific cttee for drafting The General History of Africa (Ed. Vol. VI) 1970–93, Council, Nat. Univ. of Lesotho 1976–82, OAU Group of Eminent Persons for Reparation 1992–, editorial Bd Encyclopaedia of Sub-Saharan Africa 1995–; Chair. Nat. Cttee on the UNESCO Slave Routes Project 2003–; mem. Bd of Dirs of SOWSCO 1994–; Corresp. Fellow, Royal Historical Soc., UK; Hon. Fellow, SOAS (Univ. of London) 1994; Bobapitan of Ikole-Ekiti and Onikoyi of Ife 1983; Nigerian Nat. Order of Merit (NNOM) 1986; Officer of the Fed. Repub. (OFR) 2002; Hon. LLD (Leicester) 1975; Hon. DLitt (Birmingham) 1984, (Ondo State Univ.) 1992; Bd of Trustees Nigerian Merit Award 1996, Univ. of Lagos Anniversary Gold Medal 1987, Distinguished Africanist Award, African Studies Asscn of USA 1993. *Publications include:* Milestones in Nigerian History 1962, Yoruba Warfare 1964, Christian Missions in Nigeria, 1841–91: The Making of a New Elite 1965, Cementing Partnership: The Story of WAPCO 1960–90 1990, History and the Nation and other Addresses 1990, History of the Nigerian Society of Engineers 1995, The African Experience with Higher Education 1996, Tradition and Change: Essays of J F Ade Ajayi (ed. Toyin Falola) 2000, A Patriot to the Core: Bishop Ajayi Crowther (with Akinseye-George) 2001, Kayode Eso: The Making of a Judge 2002; ed. or co-ed. of various vols on African history. *Leisure interests:* table tennis, dancing. *Address:* 1, Ojobadan Avenue, Bodija, Ibadan, Nigeria (home). *Telephone:* (2) 8101588 (home). *E-mail:* jadeas@skannet.com.

AJIBOLA, Hon. Prince Bola, LLB; Nigerian lawyer and judge; b. 22 March 1934, Lagos; s. of Oba A. S. Ajibola and Adikatu Ashakun Ajibola; m. Olu Ajibola 1961; three s. two d.; ed Holborn Coll. of Law, London Univ., UK; called to the English Bar (Lincoln's Inn) 1962; Prin. Partner, Bola Ajibola & Co., Lagos, Ikeja, Abeokuta and Kaduna, specializing in commercial law and int. arbitration; fmr Attorney-Gen. and Fed. Minister of Justice; Temporary Pres. UN Gen. Ass., 17th Special Session on Narcotic Drugs 1990; Chair. Task Force for Revision of the Laws of the Fed. 1990, Gen. Council of the Bar, Disciplinary Cttee of the Bar, Advisory Cttee on the Prerogative of Mercy; Founder and Pres. African Concern 1996–; Founder Islamic Movt for Africa 1996; Judge and Vice-Pres. IBRD Tribunal, Washington, DC 1995; Vice-Pres. Inst. of Int. Business Law and Practice, Paris, Int. Contractual Relations Comm., ICC; Chair. Body of Sr Advocates of Nigeria 1986–, Body of Benchers (also life mem.) 1989–90; Nat. Chair. World Peace Through Law Centre; Ed. Nigeria's Treaties in Force 1970–1990, All Nigeria Law Reports 1961–1990; Ed.-in-Chief, Justice; Gen. Ed. Fed. Ministry of Justice Law Review Series (seven vols); Fellow, Chartered Inst. of Arbitrators, Nigerian Inst. of Advanced Legal Studies; mem. Nigerian Bar Asscn (Pres. 1984–85), African Bar Asscn, Int. Bar Asscn, Asscn of World Lawyers, ICC, Commonwealth Law Asscn, World Arbitration Inst., Soc. for the Reform of Criminal Law, Nigerian Inst. of Int. Affairs; mem. Nigerian del. to UN Gen. Ass. 1986, Int. Court of Justice, The Hague 1991–94; mem. Nigeria Police Council, Int. Law Comm., Perm. Court of Arbitration, The Hague, ICC Court of Arbitration, Int. Maritime Arbitration Comm., Paris, Panel of Int. Arbitrators, London Inst. of Arbitrators, Int. Advisory Cttee of World Arbitration Inst., USA; Hon. LLD (Buckingham) 1996; Outstanding Citizen Merit Award, Ogun State of Nigeria 1986. *Publications:* Principles of Arbitration 1980, The Law and Settlement of Commercial Disputes 1984, Law Development and Administration in Nigeria 1987, Integration of the African Continent Through Law 1988, Banking Frauds and Other Financial Malpractices in Nigeria 1989, Women and Children under Nigerian Law 1990, Scheme Relating to Mutual Assistance in Criminal Matters and the Control of Criminal Activities within Africa and numerous other books on other legal topics. *Address:* Bola Ajibola & Co., 52, Allen Avenue, 1st Floor, Ikeja. Lagos, Nigeria (office). *Telephone:* (office). *Fax:* 234-1-2700970 (office). *E-mail:* info@bolaajibolaandco.com (office); bolaajibolaandco@yahoo.com. *Website:* www. bolaajibolaandco.com.

AJODHIA, Jules Rattankoemar; Suriname politician; b. 27 Jan. 1945, Wanica Dist; m. Lucia Kamlawatie Baldew; one s. two d.; ed Univ. of Suriname; Minister of Justice 1988–90; Vice-Pres. 1991–96, 2000–05; currently Vice-Chair. Verenigde

Hervormings Partij (VHP); mem. Nat. Ass. *Address:* Verenigde Hervormings Partij, Mr. J. Lachmonstraat 130, Paramaribo, Suriname (office). *Telephone:* 494497 (office). *Fax:* 434815 (office). *E-mail:* info@vhp.sr (office). *Website:* www.vhp .sr (office).

AJZENBERG-SELOVE, Fay, BS, PhD; American (b. Russian) nuclear physicist and academic; *Professor of Physics Emeritus, University of Pennsylvania;* b. 1926; ed Univ. of Michigan, Univ. of Wisconsin, Columbia Univ., New York; came to USA aged 15 after escaping Nazi takeover of France; carried out post-doctoral research at California Inst. of Tech. (CalTech); Faculty mem. Haverford Coll. 1957–70; fmr Prof. of Physics, Univ. of Pennsylvania, now Prof. of Physics Emer.; Chair. IUPAP Comm. on Nuclear Physics 1978–81; mem. Nuclear Science Advisory Cttee, Dept of Energy/NSF 1977–80; mem. American Physical Soc. (Chair. Div. of Nuclear Physics 1973–74), AAAS (mem. Governing Council 1974–80); Dr hc (Smith Coll.) 1995, (Michigan State Univ.) 1997, (Haverford Coll.) 1999; Guggenheim Fellow 1965–66, Christian and Mary Lindback Foundation Award for Distinguished Teaching 1991, Faye Ajzenberg-Selove Scholarship named in her honour 1998, Nicholson Medal for Humanitarian Service, American Physical Soc. 1999, Distinguished Alumni Fellow Award, Dept of Physics, Univ. of Wisconsin 2001, Nat. Medal of Science 2007. *Achievements include:* organized first session of American Physical Soc. meeting to deal with women in physics, helped found American Physical Soc.'s Cttee on Women in Physics. *Publications:* Nuclear Spectroscopy, Energy Levels of Light Nuclei (five vols) 1986, 1987, 1988, 1990, 1991, A Matter of Choices: Memoirs of a Female Physicist (autobiography) 1994. *Address:* 2N34, David Rittenhouse Laboratory, Department of Physics and Astronomy, University of Pennsylvania, 209 South 33rd Street, Philadelphia, PA 19104-6396, USA (office). *Telephone:* (215) 898-8159 (office); (215) 898-5645 (office). *Fax:* (215) 898-2010 (office). *E-mail:* fay@pobox.upenn.edu (office); fay@physics .upenn.edu (office). *Website:* www.upenn.edu (office).

AKAGAWA, Jiro; Japanese writer; b. 29 Feb. 1948, Fukuoka; m. Fumiko Serita 1973; one d.; ed Toho-gakuen High School; fmr proof-reader for Japan Soc. of Mechanical Engineers; mem. Japanese Mystery Writers' Asscn 1977–; Kadokawa Publishing Book Award 1980. *Publications:* more than 500 works including novels: The School Festival for the Dead 1977, Ghost Train (All Yomimono New Mystery Writers' Prize) 1976, The Deduction of Tortoise-shell Holmes 1978, High School Girl with a Machine Gun 1978, The Requiem Dedicated to the Bad Wife 1980, Virgin Road 1983, Chizuko's Younger Sister 1989, The Ghost Story of the Hitokoizaka-Slope 1995, The Ball at Castle Dracula 2008, Calico Cat Holmes' Tea Party 2008, Yurei Basu Tsua: AI Ni Omakase 1 2011, A Detective Story, Two, Incident in the Bedroom Suburb, Voice From Heaven, Sailor Suit, Machine Gun. *Leisure interests:* classical music, watching movies. *Address:* 40-16-201 Ohyama-cho, Sibuya-ku, Tokyo 151-0065, Japan (home).

AKAIKE, Hirotugu, DSc; Japanese mathematician and academic; *Professor Emeritus, The Institute of Statistical Mathematics;* b. Nov. 1927; ed Tokyo Univ.; joined Inst. of Statistical Math., Tokyo 1952, Head of Second Section, First Div. 1962–73, Dir Fifth Div. 1973–85, Prof. and Dir Dept of Prediction and Control 1985–86, Dir-Gen. Inst. of Statistical Math. 1986–94, Prof. Emer. 1994–; Head of Dept of Statistical Science, Univ. for Advanced Studies 1988–94, Prof. Emer. 1994–; mem. Science Council of Japan 1988–91; Medal with Purple Ribbon 1989, Order of the Sacred Treasure (Gold and Silver Star) 1996; Ishikawa Prize, Union of Japanese Scientists and Engineers 1972, Okochi Prize, Okochi Memorial Foundation 1980, Asahi Prize 1989, Japan Statistical Soc. Prize 1996, Kyoto Prize in Basic Sciences, The Inamori Foundation 2006. *Publications:* Modern Society and Mass Communication, Lectures on Mass Communication, Vol. 5 (with R. Hidaka) 1955, Views on Public Opinion (co-author) 1955, Statistical Analysis and Control of Dynamic Systems (with T. Nakagawa) 1972, Probability and Statistics (co-author) 1985, Special Topics of Statistics (co-author) 1986, Theory of Time Series (co-author) 1988, Statistical Analysis and Control of Dynamic Systems (with T. Nakagawa) 1988, Practice of Time Series Analysis II (co-author) 1995; numerous papers in professional journals. *Address:* The Institute of Statistical Mathematics, 4-6-7 Minami-Azabu, Minato-ku, Tokyo 106-8569, Japan (office). *Telephone:* (3) 3446-1501 (office). *E-mail:* info@ism.ac.jp (office). *Website:* www.ism.ac.jp (office); tswww.ism.ac.jp/kitagawa/HomePage/akaike.html (office).

AKAKA, Daniel Kahikina, BEd, MEd; American politician and fmr teacher; b. 11 Sept. 1924, Honolulu, HI; s. of Kahikina Akaka and Annie Kahoa; m. Mary Mildred Chong 1948; four s. one d.; ed The Kamehameha School for Boys, Univ. of Hawaii; welder, Hawaiian Electric Co. 1942; welder-mechanic, US Army Corps of Engineers 1943–45, on active duty in US Army, including service on Saipan and Tinian 1945–47; schoolteacher, Hawaii 1953–60; Vice-Prin., later Prin. Ewa Beach Elementary School, Honolulu 1960–64; Prin. Pohakea Elementary School 1964–65, Kaneohe Elementary School 1965–68; Dir Hawaii Office of Econ. Opportunity 1971–74; Special Asst, Human Resources Office of the Gov. of Hawaii 1975–76; programme specialist, Hawaii Compensatory Educ. 1978–79, 1985–91; mem. 95th–101st Congresses from 2nd Dist of Hawaii 1977–90; Senator from Hawaii 1990–2013 (retd), Chair. Indian Affairs Cttee, Homeland Security and Governmental Affairs Subcommittee on Oversight of Govt Man., the Fed. Workforce and the Dist of Columbia, mem. Armed Services, Banking, Housing and Urban Affairs and Veterans' Affairs Cttees; Democrat; Founders Lifetime Achievement Award, Univ. of Hawaii Alumni Asscn 1999, Adam Smith Medal, Nat. Council on Econ. Educ. 1999, Chinese Citizen of the Year Si Nan Award, United Chinese Soc. 1999, Outstanding Legislator Award, Asscn of the US Army 2002, Stephen L. Jackstadt Award, Hawaii Council on Econ. Educ. 2003, 19th Annual George Gillispie Congressional Award, Blinded American Veterans Foundation 2004, Endangered Species Award, Conservative Council for Hawaii, on behalf of the Endangered Species Coalition, Earthjustice, Center for Biological Diversity, Nat. Environmental Trust, Natural Resources Defense Council, Nat. Wildlife Fed. and Sierra Club 2005, Adam Smith Award for Excellence in Econ. Educ., Nat. Council on Econ. Educ. 2005, Hawaii's Outstanding Advocate for Children & Youth, State of Hawaii 2005, Medal of Merit as Legislator of the Year, Jewish War Veterans of the USA 2007, Inspirational Leadership Award, Mil. Order of the Purple Heart 2008, Distinguished Community Health Defender Award, Nat. Asscn of Community Health Centers 2009, Congressional Award, Veterans of Foreign Wars 2009, Pinnacle Award, US Pan Asian American Chamber of Commerce 2010, Advocate of the Year Award, Nat. Asscn of State Dirs of Veterans Affairs 2010, Congressional Leadership Award, Nat. Congress of American Indians 2011, Distinguished Public Service Award, American Legion 2011, Col Arthur T. Marix Congressional Leadership Award, Marine Officers Asscn of America 2011, Lifetime Achievement Award, Healthcare Asscn of Hawaii 2011, Public Servant Award, Govt Accountability Project 2011.

AKALAITIS, JoAnne, BA; American theatre director and academic; *Wallace Benjamin Flint and L. May Hawver Flint Professor of Theater, Bard College;* b. 29 June 1932, Chicago; d. of Clement Akalaitis and Estelle Mattis; m. Philip Glass 1965 (divorced 1974); one s. one d.; ed Univ. of Chicago and Stanford Univ. Grad. School; Artistic Dir New York Shakespeare Festival 1991–92; Wallace Benjamin Flint and L. May Hawver Flint Prof. of Theater, Bard Coll. 2003–; Rockefeller Playwright Fellow; Rosamund Gilder Fellow; Guggenheim Fellow 1978; Co-founder Mabou Mines (avant-garde theatre co.), New York 1970; recipient of five Obies for distinguished direction, Edwin Booth Award, Rosamund Gilder Award for Outstanding Achievement in Theatre. *Works directed include:* Beckett's Cascando 1976, Dressed Like an Egg 1977, Dead End Kids 1980, A History of Nuclear Power (writer and dir of play and film), Request Concert (Drama Desk Award) 1981, The Photographer 1983, Beckett's Endgame 1984, Genet's The Balcony 1985, Green Card (writer and dir) 1986, Greg Büchner's Leon & Lena (and Lenz) 1987, Genet's The Screens 1987, Cymbeline 1989, 'Tis Pity She's a Whore 1992, Henry IV (Pts I & II) 1991, Woyzeck 1992, In the Summer House 1993. *Publication:* Green Card. *Leisure interest:* cooking. *Address:* Theater Program, Division of the Arts, Bard College 30 Campus Road, Annandale-on-Hudson, NY 12504-5000, USA. *Telephone:* (845) 758-7936. *E-mail:* akalaiti@bard.edu. *Website:* www.bard.edu/academics/programs/arts.

AKAMATSU, Hirotaka; Japanese politician; b. 3 May 1948, Aichi Pref.; ed Waseda Univ.; began career with Nippon Express 1971; mem. Aichi Prefectural Ass. (three terms) 1979; mem. Social Democratic Party –1996, becoming Sec.-Gen. 1993; mem. House of Reps for Aichi No. 5 constituency 1990–, Chair. several cttees including Cttee on Foreign Affairs 2004–05, mem. Fundamental Nat. Policies Cttee; mem. Democratic Party of Japan 1996–, currently Vice-Pres., Chair. Election Campaign Cttee 2009; Minister of Agric., Forestry and Fisheries 2009–10. *Address:* House of Representatives, 1-7-1 Nagatacho, Chiyoda-ku, Tokyo 100-0014, Japan (office). *Website:* www.shugiin.go.jp (office).

AKAMATSU, Ryoko; Japanese academic, diplomatist and civil servant; *President, Japanese Association of International Women's Rights;* b. 24 Aug. 1929, Osaka; d. of Rinsaku Akamatsu and Asaka Akamatsu; ed Tsuda Coll. and Univ. of Tokyo; joined Ministry of Labour 1955, Dir Women Workers' Div. 1970–72; Dir-Gen. Yamanashi Labour Standard Bureau 1975–78; Counsellor in charge of Women's Affairs, Prime Minister's Office 1978–79; Minister, Perm. Mission to UN, New York 1979–82; Dir-Gen. Women's Bureau, Ministry of Labour 1982–85; Amb. to Uruguay 1986–89; Pres. Japan Inst. of Workers' Evolution 1989–93; Prof., Bunkyo Gakuin Univ. 1992–2003; Minister of Educ., Science, Culture and Sports 1993–94; currently Pres. Japanese Asscn of International Women's Rights; Councillor, Asian Women's Fund; Grand Cordon of the Order of the Rising Sun 2003. *Publications include:* Girls Be Ambitious (autobiography) 1990, Beautiful Uruguay 1990, Enacting Laws of Equal Employment Opportunity for Men and Women 2003. *Leisure interests:* reading, swimming, listening to classical music. *E-mail:* info@jaiwr.org (office). *Website:* www.jaiwr.org (office).

AKASAKA, Kiyotaka, MA; Japanese diplomatist and UN official; *President, Foreign Press Center/Japan;* b. 1948, Osaka; ed Kyoto Univ. and Trinity Coll., Cambridge, UK; joined Foreign Ministry 1971; held several posts at Secr. of GATT 1988–91, WHO 1993–97; Deputy Dir-Gen. Multilateral Co-operation Dept, Ministry of Foreign Affairs 1997–2000; Perm. Rep., UN, New York 2000–01; Consul-Gen. Embassy in Sao Paulo 2001–03; Deputy Sec.-Gen. OECD 2003–07; Under-Sec.-Gen., Dept of Communications and Public Information, UN 2007–12; Pres. Foreign Press Center/Japan 2012–; Rep. to Kyoto Conf. on Climate Change 1997; Vice-Chair. Prep. Cttee World Summit on Sustainable Devt, Johannesburg 2002. *Publications:* The GATT and the Uruguay Round Negotiations; The Cartagena Protocol on Biosafety and numerous journal articles on trade, the environment and sustainable devt. *Address:* Foreign Press Center/Japan, 6F Nippon Press Center Building, 2-2-1, Uchisaiwaicho, Chiyoda-ku, Tokyo, 100-0011, Japan (office). *Telephone:* (3) 3501-3401 (office). *Fax:* (3) 3501-3622 (office). *Website:* fpcj.jp (office).

AKAYEV, Askar Akayevich, DTech; Kyrgyzstani politician and physicist; *Professor of Mathematics, Moscow State University 'M. V. Lomonsov';* b. 10 Nov. 1944, Kyzyl-Bairak Kemin Dist; s. of Akai Tokoyev and Ossel Tokoyeva; m. Mairam Akayeva 1970; two s. two d.; ed Leningrad Inst. of Precise Mechanics and Optics; lecturer; Prof. Frunze (now Bishkek) Politech. Inst. 1972–73, Chair. 1976–86; Prof. Inst. of Precise Mechanics and Optics 1973–76; Head of Science Dept Cen. Cttee Kyrgyz CP 1986–87; mem. CPSU 1981–91 (resgnd); fmr mem. Cen. Cttee Kyrgyz CP, Vice-Pres., Pres. Kirghiz SSR Pres. Kyrgyz SSR Acad. of Sciences 1987–90; fmr mem. CPSU Constitutional Compliance Cttee; fmr mem. USSR Supreme Soviet Cttee on Econ. Reform 1991; Exec. Pres. Kyrgyz SSR 1990, Pres. of Kyrgyzstan 1990–2005; Prof. of Mathematics, Moscow State Univ. 'M. V. Lomonsov' 2005–; Academician, Int. Acad. of Informatization, Canada 1997; Hon. Academician Int. Eng Acad. and of Int. Acad. of Creation 1996; Albert Einstein Award 1999, Devotion to Peace and Good Award, Russia 2000, WIPO Gold Medal 2001, Elizabeth Haub Award for Environmental Diplomacy 2003. *Publications:* Methods of Data Optical Processing 1992, Diplomacy of the Silk Road 1999, The Memorable Decade 2001, Kyrgyz Statehood and National Epos 'Manas' 2002, The Difficult Road to Democracy 2002, more than 80 articles on radiophysics and politics. *Leisure interests:* travelling with the family, mountain skiing, mountaineering. *Address:* Moscow State University 'M. V. Lomonsov', 119992 Moscow, Leninskie Gory, Russia (office). *Telephone:* (095) 939-10-00 (office). *Fax:* (095) 939-01-26 (office). *E-mail:* office@akaev.kg (office); mmf@mech.math.msu.su (office). *Website:* www.msu.ru (office).

AKCHURIN, Renat Suleymanovich, DrMed; Russian cardiovascular surgeon; *Professor and Head, Department of Cardiovascular Surgery, Moscow Institute of Clinical Cardiology;* b. 2 April 1946, Andijan, Uzbekistan; s. of Akchurin Suleyman Safievich and Akchurina Tazkira Kiyamovna; m. Natalya Pavlovna Akchurina; two s.; ed Inst. of Medicine (now Seehenov Acad. of Medicine); gen. practitioner,

polyclinics 1970–73; Ordinator, Jr, Sr Researcher, Inst. of Clinical and Experimental Medicine 1973–84; worked at Baylor Univ., Texas, USA 1984; Surgeon, Prof. and Head of Dept of Cardiovascular Surgery, Moscow Inst. of Clinical Cardiology 1984–; Corresp. mem. Russian Acad. of Medical Sciences 1997, Russian Acad. of Science; Hon. mem. Acad. of Sciences of Tatarstan Repub.; Order of Merit (Russia) 1996, Order of the Commodore (Peru) 2000, Order of the Eagle (Third Class) 1997; USSR State Prize 1982, Russian Fed. State Prize 2001, Russian Govt Prize for research and achievement in the field of surgery 2003. *Achievements include:* performed first heart and lung transplantation operations in USSR; performs about 100 bypass operations a year, performed a bypass operation on Pres. Yeltsin 1996; patented several inventions of medical instruments. *Publications include:* more than 300 scientific papers and articles. *Leisure interests:* music, sports, hunting, cooking. *Address:* Institute of Clinical Cardiology, 121552 Moscow, Cherepkovskaya str. 15A, Russia (office). *Telephone:* (499) 140-93-36 (office); (499) 149-17-08 (office). *E-mail:* rsakchurin@list.ru (office); 3ko@list.ru (office).

AKEIL, Ahmad Abdallah al-; Saudi Arabian banker; Chair. Arab Bank for Econ. Devt in Africa (Banque arabe pour le développement économique en Afrique—BADEA); Chair. SANAD Cooperative Insurance and Reinsurance; mem. Bd of Dirs Arab Nat. Bank. *Address:* Arab Bank for Economic Development in Africa, Sayed Abd ar-Rahman el-Mahdi Street, PO Box 2640, Khartoum 11111, Sudan (office). *Telephone:* (1) 83773646 (office). *Fax:* (1) 83770600 (office). *E-mail:* badea@badea .org (office). *Website:* www.badea.org (office).

AKENSON, Donald Harman, BA, MEd, PhD, DLitt, DHum, FRSA, FRSC, FRHistS; Canadian historian and academic; *Douglas Professor of Canadian and Colonial History, Queen's University, Kingston;* b. 22 May 1941, Minneapolis, Minn.; s. of Donald Nels Akenson and Fern L. Harman Akenson; ed Yale and Harvard Univs; Allston Burr Sr Tutor, Dunster House, Harvard Coll. 1966–67; Assoc. Prof. of History, Queen's Univ., Kingston, Ont. 1970–74, Prof. 1974–, currently Douglas Prof. of Canadian and Colonial History; Beamish Research Prof., Inst. of Irish Studies, Univ. of Liverpool 1998–2002; Guggenheim Fellow 1984–85; Hon. DLitt (McMaster) 1995, (Guelph) 2000; Hon. DHumLitt (Lethbridge) 1996; Hon. LLD (Regina) 2002; Hon. DLH (Queen's Univ. Belfast) 2008, (Victoria Univ., Wellington, NZ) 2010; Chalmers Prize 1985, Landon Prize 1987, Grawemeyer World Peace Prize 1993, Molson Laureate 1996 and many other awards and distinctions. *Publications:* The Irish Education Experiment 1970, The Church of Ireland: Ecclesiastical Reform and Revolution 1800–1885 1971, Education and Enmity: The Control of Schooling in Northern Ireland 1920–50 1973, The United States and Ireland 1973, A Mirror to Kathleen's Face: Education in Independent Ireland 1922–60 1975, Local Poets and Social History: James Orr, Bard of Ballycarry 1977, Between Two Revolutions: Islandmagee, Co. Antrim 1798–1920 1979, A Protestant in Purgatory: Richard Whately: Archbishop of Dublin 1981, The Irish in Ontario: A Study of Rural History 1984, Being Had: Historians, Evidence and the Irish in North America 1985, The Life and Times of Ogle Gowan 1986, Small Differences: Irish Catholics and Irish Protestants, 1815–1921 1988, Half the World from Home: Perspectives on the Irish in New Zealand 1990, Occasional Papers on the Irish in South Africa 1991, God's Peoples: Covenant and Land in South Africa, Israel and Ulster 1992, The Irish Diaspora, A Primer 1993, Conor: A Biography of Conor Cruise O'Brien 1994, If the Irish Ran the World: Montserrat 1630–1730, Surpassing Wonder: The Invention of the Bible and the Talmuds 1998, Saint Saul: A Skeleton Key to the Historical Jesus 2000, Intolerance: The E. Coli of the Human Mind 2004, An Irish History of Civilization (two vols) 2006, Some Family – The Mormons and How Humanity Keeps Track of Itself 2007, Ireland, Sweden and the Great European Migration 1815–1914 2011; novels: The Lazar House Notebooks 1981, Brotherhood Week in Belfast 1984, The Orangeman: The Edgerston Audit 1987, At Face Value: The Life and Times of Eliza McCormack 1990. *Address:* Department of History, Queen's University, Kingston, ON, K7L 3N6, Canada (office). *Telephone:* (613) 533-2150 (office). *E-mail:* 8da8@queensu.ca (office). *Website:* www.queensu.ca/history (office).

AKERLOF, George Arthur, BA, PhD; American economist and academic; *Koshland Professor of Economics, University of California, Berkeley;* b. 17 June 1940, New Haven, Conn.; m. Janet L. Yellen; one s.; ed Massachusetts Inst. Tech., Yale Univ.; Asst Prof., Univ. of Calif., Berkeley 1966–70, Assoc. Prof. 1970–77, Prof. 1977–78, Koshland Prof. 1980–; Visiting Prof., Indian Statistical Inst. 1967–68; Research Assoc., Harvard Univ. 1969; Sr Staff Economist, Pres.'s Council of Econ. Advisers 1973–74; Visiting Research Economist, Special Studies Section, Bd of Govs of the Fed. Reserve System 1977–78; Cassel Prof. with respect to Money and Banking, LSE 1978–80; Sr Fellow, The Brookings Inst. 1994–; Vice-Pres. American Econ. Asscn; mem. Bd of Dirs Nat. Bureau for Economic Research 1997–; Assoc. Ed. several journals on econs; Guggenheim Fellow; Fellow, Econometric Soc., American Acad. of Arts and Sciences, Inst. for Policy Reform; Dr hc (Univ. of Zurich) 2000; Ely Lecturer, American Econ. Asscn 1990, Fisher-Shultz Lecturer, World Congress of the Econometrics Soc. 1995, Harry Johnson Lecturer, Royal Econ. Asscn 1997, Henry George Lecturer, Univ. of Scranton 1998, Gunnar Myrdal Lecturer (Centenary of Birth) 1998, Henry George Lecturer, Williams Coll. 1999, Woodward Lecturer, Univ. of British Columbia 1999, Nobel Prize in Econs 2001 (jt recipient); numerous other awards and prizes. *Publications:* An Economic Theorist's Book of Tales 1984, Animal Spirits: How Human Psychology Drives the Economy, and Why It Matters for Global Capitalism (with Robert Shiller) 2009. *Address:* Department of Economics, 530 Evans Hall, #3880, University of California, Berkeley, CA 94720-3880, USA (office). *Telephone:* (510) 642-5837 (office). *Fax:* (510) 642-6615 (office). *E-mail:* akerlof@econ.berkeley .edu (office). *Website:* elsa.berkeley.edu/~akerlof (office).

AKERMANN, Markus; Swiss business executive; b. 25 Jan. 1947; ed Univ. of St Gallen, Univ. of Sheffield, UK; with Swiss Banking Corpn 1975–78; joined Holcim Ltd 1978, served in posts including Latin America Area Man. 1987, mem. Exec. Cttee 1993–2002, mem. Bd of Dirs and CEO 2002–12 (retd), Dir 2012–, Chair. Man. Bd Holcim Foundation; mem. Bd of Dirs ACC Ltd, India. *Address:* Holcim Group Support Ltd, Hagenholzstrasse 85, 8050 Zurich, Switzerland (office). *Telephone:* (58) 858-58-58 (office). *Fax:* (58) 858-58-59 (office). *E-mail:* info@holcim .com (office). *Website:* www.holcim.com (office).

AKERS-JONES, Sir David, KBE, CMG, JP, MA; British civil servant; b. 14 April 1927; s. of Walter George Jones and Dorothy Jones; m. Jane Spickernell 1951 (died

2002); one s. (deceased) one d.; ed Worthing High School and Brasenose Coll., Oxford; with British India Steam Navigation Co. 1945–49; Malayan Civil Service 1954–57; Hong Kong Civil Service 1957–86, Sec. for New Territories and for Dist Admin, Hong Kong Govt 1973–85, Chief Sec. 1985–86; Acting Gov. Hong Kong 1986–87; Hong Kong Affairs Adviser to China 1993–97; Chair. Nat. Mutual Asia Hong Kong (later AXA China Region) 1988–2001, Hong Kong Housing Authority 1988–93, Global Asset Man. Hong Kong 1988–; Dir Hysan Devt Co. Ltd, The Mingly Corpn Ltd; Vice-Pres. WWF Hong Kong 1995–, Hong Kong Girl Guides; Hon. Pres. Outward Bound Trust (Hong Kong) 1986–; Hon. mem. RICS; Hon. DCL (Kent Univ.) 1987; Hon. LLD (Chinese Univ. of Hong Kong) 1988; Hon. DScS (City Univ., Hong Kong) 1993; Grand Bauhinia Medal (Hong Kong) 2003. *Leisure interests:* painting, gardening, walking and music. *Address:* Flat 1, Floor 25, Bamboo Grove, 80 Kennedy Road, Hong Kong Special Administrative Region, People's Republic of China (home). *Telephone:* (852) 2491-9319 (office); (852) 2491-9319 (home). *Fax:* (852) 2491-1300 (home). *E-mail:* akersjon@pacific.net.hk (home).

AKERSON, Daniel F., BSc (Eng), MSc (Econs); American business executive; *Vice-Chairman and Special Advisor, The Carlyle Group;* ed US Naval Acad., London School of Econs, UK; held several key posts at MCI Communications Corpn 1983–93, including Exec. Vice-Pres. and Chief Financial Officer 1987–90, Pres. and COO 1992–93; Gen. Partner, Forstmann Little & Co. (pvt. equity firm) 1993; Chair. and CEO General Instrument Co. 1993–95; Chair. Nextel Communications, Inc. 1996–2001, CEO 1996–99; Chair. and CEO XO Communications, Inc. 1999–2003; mem. Exec. Cttee, Man. Dir and Head of Global Buyout, The Carlyle Group, Washington, DC 2003–10, Vice-Chair. and Special Advisor 2014–; apptd mem. Bd of Dirs General Motors Co. 2009, CEO 2010–14, Chair. 2011–14; mem. Bd of Dirs US Naval Acad. Foundation, Tsinghua Univ. School and Econs and Man. Advisory Bd, Int. Business Leaders Advisory Council of Shanghai; mem. Business Council; T.C. and Elizabeth Cooke Business Medallion, Coll. of William & Mary 2004, Distinguished Grad. Award, US Naval Acad. 2012. *Address:* The Carlyle Group, 1001 Pennsylvania Avenue, NW, Washington, DC 20004-2505, USA (office). *Telephone:* (202) 729-5626 (office). *Fax:* (202) 347-1818 (office). *Website:* www.carlyle.com (office).

ÅKESSON, Eva, PhD; Swedish professor of chemical physics and university administrator; *Vice-Chancellor, Uppsala University;* b. 30 Dec. 1961, Ängelholm; ed Umeå Univ.; post-doctoral researcher, Univ. of Minnesota, USA; selected as Sr Researcher by Research Council in the field of photochemical reaction mechanisms 1996; Researcher, Lund Univ. from 1996, also worked as a teacher and Dir of Studies, Vice-Rector Lund Univ. 2003–08, with special responsibility for undergraduate educ. and the Bologna Process, acquired Excellent Teaching Practice competence at Faculty of Science 2005, Deputy Vice-Chancellor Lund Univ. 2009–11, with special responsibility for basic and advanced-level studies issues, quality work and related internationalization matters; Rectrix Magnifica (Vice-Chancellor), Uppsala Univ. 2011–; mem. CSN (Cen. Bd for Student Aid), Kristianstad Univ. Coll., Swedish Inst., Nat. Cttee for Chem.; Titular mem. IUPAC Cttee on Chem. Educ. 2005–; Chair. Int. Expert Panels for Evaluating Leadership and Governance of Educ., Univ. of Helsinki 2008, Aalto School of Science 2011. *Publications:* numerous papers in professional journals in the field of femtochemistry, using ultrafast spectroscopy to follow chemical reactions and dynamics. *Address:* Universitetsledningens kansli S:t Olofsg. 10B, Box 256, 751 05 Uppsala, Sweden (office). *Telephone:* (18) 471-33-10 (office). *Fax:* (18) 471-16-40 (office). *E-mail:* rektor@uu.se (office). *Website:* www.uu.se (office).

AKHALAIA, Bachana (Bacho); Georgian lawyer and government official; b. 24 Oct. 1980, Zugdidi; s. of Roland Akhalaia; ed Faculty of Law, Tbilisi State Univ.; Project Co-ordinator, Liberty Inst. (non-govt org.) 2003–04; Deputy Public Defender (Ombudsman) 2004–05; Head of Penitentiary Dept, Ministry of Justice 2005–08; Deputy Minister of Defence 2008–09, Minister of Defence 2009–12, of Internal Affairs July–Sept. 2012; arrested Nov. 2012, accused of exceeding official powers, illegal confinement and torture, acquitted July 2013 but awaiting further trial. *Address:* c/o Ministry of Internal Affairs, 0114 Tbilisi, Gulua 10, Georgia.

AKHMETOV, Danial Kenzhetayevich, BEng, BEcons; Kazakhstani politician; b. 15 June 1954, Pavlodar; m.; two c.; ed Pavlodar Industry Inst.; fmr racing cyclist; fmr Deputy Prime Minister and Minister of Industry, Energy, Transport and Communications; Akim (Gov.) Pavlodar Oblast 1995–97, 2001–03; Akim (Gov.) Northern Kazakhstan Oblast 1997–99; Deputy, then First Deputy Prime Minister 1999–2001; Prime Minister of Kazakhstan 2003–07 (resgnd); Minister of Defence 2007–09. *Address:* c/o Ministry of Defence, 010000 Astana, Beibitshilik 51A, Kazakhstan.

AKHMETOV, Renat Leonidovych, BA; Ukrainian business executive; *President, System Capital Management;* b. 21 Sept. 1966, Donetsk; m. Liliya Smirnova; two s.; ed Donetsk State Univ.; f. Donetsk City Bank; Head, Donetsk Industrial Group (conglomerate of steel and mining cos); Founder, Pres. and prin. shareholder, System Capital Management (holding co. with controlling shares in more than 90 cos); Owner and Pres. Shaktar Donetsk football club 1996–; Deputy (Party of the Regions), Verkhovna Rada (Supreme Council) 2007–12; Founder Foundation for Effective Governance, Kyiv 2007, shut down amid protests against him Jan. 2014; Hon. Citizen of Donetsk 2006; Chevalier of the Miner's Glory Medal, Honoured Worker of Fitness and Sports of Ukraine 1999, Chevalier of Order of Merit (Third Class) 2002, (Second Class) 2004, (First Class) 2006, Sitara-e-Pakistan for Merits to Pakistan 2007, Order of Prince Yaroslav the Wise (Fifth Class) 2010; Donetsk Citizens' Recognition Prize, Donetsk City Council 2008. *Address:* JSC System Capital Management, 83001 Donetsk, Pushkinskiy Business Centre, Maryinska str. 1, Ukraine (office). *Fax:* (62) 381-50-06 (office); (62) 381-50-50 (office). *E-mail:* scm@scm.com.ua (office). *Website:* www.scm.com.ua (office); www.shakhtar.com.

AKHTAR, Muhammad, MSc, PhD, FRS; British/Pakistani biochemist and academic; *Director-General, School of Biological Sciences, University of the Punjab;* b. 23 Feb. 1933, Punjab, India; s. of Muhammad Azeem Chaudhry; m. Monika E. Schürmann 1963; two s.; ed Govt Coll. Sargodha, Govt Coll. Lahore, Univ. of Punjab and Imperial Coll., London; Research Scientist, Research Inst. for Medicine and Chem., Cambridge, Mass, USA 1959–63; Lecturer in Biochemistry, Univ. of Southampton 1963–66, Sr Lecturer 1966–68, Reader 1968–73, Prof.

1973–98, Head, Dept of Biochemistry 1978–93, Chair. School of Biochemical and Physiological Sciences 1983–87, Prof. Emer. of Biochemistry 1998–; Dir Gen. and Prof. (on leave), School of Biological Sciences, Univ. of the Punjab 2002–; Distinguished Nat. Prof., Higher Education Comm., Islamabad 2004–; Chair. School of Biochemical and Physiological Sciences 1983–87, Inst. of Biomolecular Sciences 1989–90; Dir SERC Molecular Recognition Centre 1990–94; Founding Fellow, Third World Acad. of Sciences 1984, Treasurer, mem. Council 1993–97, Vice-Pres. 1997–2003; Foreign Fellow, Pakistan Acad. of Sciences 2000; mem. Council Royal Soc. 1983–85; mem. Biochemical Soc. Cttee 1983–86; Hon. Fellow, Univ. Coll. London 2010; Hon. DSc (Karachi Univ.) 2000; Sitara-I-Imtiaz (Pakistan), Flintoff Medal, Royal Soc. of Chem. 1993, Third World Acad. of Sciences Medal 1996. *Publications:* numerous articles in biochemical and chemical journals. *Address:* Centre for Biological Sciences, University of Southampton, Southampton, SO17 1BJ, England (office); University of the Punjab, Quaid-e-Azam Campus, PO Box 54590, Lahore, Pakistan (office). *Telephone:* (23) 8076-7718 (Southampton) (office); (42) 99231099 (Lahore) (office). *Fax:* (42) 99231101 (Lahore) (office). *E-mail:* ma3@soton.ac.uk (office). *Website:* www.pu.edu.pk (office).

AKHTAR, Shamshad, BA, MA, MSc, PhD; Pakistani economist, international organization official and fmr central banker; *Executive Secretary, Economic and Social Commission for Asia and the Pacific (ESCAP), United Nations;* b. Hyderabad, Sindh Prov.; ed Univ. of Punjab, Quaid-e-Azam Univ., Univ. of Sussex and Paisley Coll. of Tech. (now Univ. of Paisley), UK, Harvard Univ., USA; briefly worked at planning offices in Pakistan at Fed. and Sindh Govt levels; economist, World Bank mission in Pakistan 1980–90; Sr then Prin. Financial Sector Specialist, Asian Devt Bank (ADB) 1990–98; Man. and Coordinator for APEC Finance Ministers' Group 1998–2001, Dir Govt Finance and Trade Div. for East and Cen. Asia Dept, then Deputy Dir Gen. South East Asia Dept 2001–04, Dir Gen. 2004–05; Gov. (first woman) State Bank of Pakistan 2006–09, also Gov. of the IMF for Pakistan; Special Sr Adviser, Office of the Pres. 2009; Vice-Pres., Middle East and North Africa, World Bank 2009–12; Asst Sec.-Gen. for Economic and Social Affairs, UN 2012–; Exec. Sec., ESCAP, UN 2013–; Visiting Fellow, Harvard Univ. Dept of Econs 1987; Best Cen. Bank Gov. in Asia, Emerging Markets newspaper 2007, Cen. Bank Gov. of the Year in Asia, Banker Magazine 2008, named one of Ten Outstanding Asian Women Leaders by Asian Wall Street Journal 2008. *Publications include:* numerous papers on econs and finance. *Address:* UN Economic and Social Commission for Asia and the Pacific (ESCAP), United Nations Building, Rajadamnern Nok Avenue, Bangkok, 10200, Thailand (office). *Telephone:* (2) 288-1234 (office). *Fax:* (2) 288-1000 (office). *Website:* www.unescap.org (office).

AKHTAR, Tasleem, MBBS, DCh, MRCP FRCP; Pakistani paediatrician, medical research officer and academic; *Chief of Research and Academic Advancement, Fatima Memorial College of Medicine and Surgery;* b. 1 Sept. 1944, Village Jhanda, Tehsil Dist; m.; one s. one d.; ed Khyber Medical Coll., Univ. of Peshawar, Royal Coll. of Physicians, London, UK, Royal Coll. of Physicians and Surgeons, Edinburgh, UK; est. Neonatal Unit, Khyber Medical Coll. 1976, Sr Medical Research Officer Pakistan Medical Research Council (PMRC) Research Centre 1979–1980, Research Dir 1980, Exec. Dir PMRC 1994–2004, Chair. 1996–99; currently Chief of Research and Academic Advancement, Fatima Memorial Coll. of Medicine and Surgery, Lahore; Dir Prov. Health Services Acad., Dept of Health, Govt of North-West Frontier Prov. (NWFP) 1999–2000; Gen. Sec. Pakistan Paediatric Asscn, NWFP Br. (PPA–NWFP) 1980–82, 1984–86, Pres. 1982–84, Vice-Pres. PPA Centre 1990; Chief Ed. Pakistan Journal of Medical Research, PMRC; Asst Ed. Pakistan Paediatric Journal, Lahore; mem. Hosp. Monitoring Cttee, Ministry of Health; mem. Governing Bd Nat. Inst. of Health, Islamabad; mem. Bd of Dirs NWFP Health Foundation, The Network for Consumer Protection; mem. Forum on Telemedicine in Pakistan, Tech. Resource Mobilization Unit 2001–02; American Public Health Asscn Award for Most Successful Int. Collaboration 1997. *Address:* Fatima Memorial Hospital, Shadman, Lahore, Pakistan (office). *Telephone:* 111-555-600 (office). *Fax:* 7570586 (office). *E-mail:* tasleem.akhtar@fmsystem.org (office); akhtar_tasleem@hotmail.com (office). *Website:* www.fmsystem.org (office).

AKIHITO, HIM The Emperor of Japan, KG, GCVO; b. 23 Dec. 1933, Tokyo; s. of the late Emperor Hirohito and of Empress Nagako; m. Michiko Shoda 1959; two s. (including HIH Crown Prince Naruhito) one d.; ed Gakushuin schools and Faculty of Politics and Econs, Gakushuin Univ.; official investiture as Crown Prince 1952; succeeded 7 Jan. 1989; crowned 12 Nov. 1990; has undertaken visits to numerous countries and travelled widely throughout Japan; Hon. Pres. or Patron, Asian Games 1958, Int. Sports Games for the Disabled 1964, Eleventh Pacific Science Congress 1966, Japan World Exposition 1970, Int. Skill Contest for the Disabled 1981; mem. Ichthyological Soc. of Japan; Foreign mem. Linnean Soc. of London 1980, Hon. mem. 1986; Research Assoc., Australian Museum; Hon. Sec. Int. Conf. on Indo-Pacific Fish 1985; Hon. mem. Zoological Soc. of London 1992, Research Inst. for Natural Science of Argentina 1997; Collar and Grand Cordon of the Supreme Order of the Chrysanthemum, Grand Cordon of the Order of the Rising Sun with the Paulownia Blossoms (renamed Grand Cordon of The Order of the Paulownia Flowers from 2003), Grand Cordon of the Order of the Sacred Treasure, Order of Culture; Order of the Supreme Sun (Afghanistan), Grand Star, Decoration for Services to the Repub. of Austria, Collar, Order of al-Khalifa (Bahrain), Grand Cordon, Order of Leopold (Belgium), Presidential Order (Botswana), Grand Collar, Order of the Southern Cross (Brazil), Grand Cordon, Order of Valour (Cameroon), Grand Collar, Order of the Merit of Chile, Grand Collar, Order of the Cross of Boyaca (Colombia), Grand Cordon, Nat. Order of the Leopard (Democratic Repub. of the Congo/Zaïre), Grand Cordon, Nat. Order of the Ivory Coast, Order of the White Lion, 1st Class (Civil Div.) with Collar Chain (Czech Repub.), Kt Grand Cross, Order of the Elephant (Denmark) 1953, Grand Collar, Order of the Nile (Egypt), The Collar of the Cross, Order of the Cross of Terra Mariana (Estonia), Grand Collar, Order of Solomon (Ethiopia), Grand Cross with Collar, Order of the White Rose (Finland), Grand Croix, Légion d'honneur, Grand Cross, Special Class, Order of Merit of the FRG, Grand Kt, Order of the Repub. of Gambia, Grand Cross, Order of the Redeemer (Greece), Grand Cross with Chain, Order of Merit of the Repub. of Hungary, Grand Cross with Collar, Order of the Falcon (Iceland), Star of Adipurna, 1st Class (Indonesia), Grand Cross with Cordon, Order of Merit of the Italian Repub., Collar, Order of al-Hussein bin

Ali (Jordan), Order of the Golden Eagle (Kazakhstan), Order of the Golden Heart (Kenya), Collar, Order of Mubarak the Great (Kuwait), Kt Grand Cross with Chain, Order of the Three Stars (Latvia), Kt Grand Band, Order of the Star of Africa (Liberia), Kt Grand Band, Order of the Pioneers of the Repub. (Liberia), Great Grand Cross with Collar, Order of Vytautas the Great (Lithuania), Kt, Order of the Gold Lion of the House of Nassau (Luxembourg), Grand Kt, Order of the Lion (Malawi), Order of the Crown of the Realm (Malaysia), Grand Cordon, Nat. Order of Mali, Grand Collar, Order of the Aztec Eagle (Mexico), Grand Collar, Order of Muhammad (Morocco), Kt, Order of Ojaswi Rajanya (Nepal), Kt Grand Cross, Order of the Netherlands Lion, Grand Cordon, Order of the Fed. Repub. (Nigeria), Grand Cross with Collar, Royal Norwegian Order of St Olav, Order of Oman, Superior Class, Nishan-e-Pakistan, 1st Class, Gold Collar, Order of Manuel Amador Guerrero (Panama), Grand Cross in Brilliants, Order of the Sun (Peru), Chief Kt, Philippine Legion of Honour, Order of the White Eagle (Poland), Grand Collar, Order of St James of the Sword (Portugal), Grand Collar, Order of Prince Henry (Portugal), Collar of Independence (Qatar), Badr Chain (Saudi Arabia), Grand Cordon, Order of the Lion (Senegal), Grand Cross in Gold, Order of Good Hope (South Africa), Kt, Order of the Golden Fleece (Spain), Collar, Order of Charles III (Spain), Kt with Collar, Royal Order of the Seraphim (Sweden), The Most Auspicious Order of the Rajamitrabhorn (Thailand), The Most Illustrious Order of the Royal House of Chakri (Thailand), Order of Prince Yaroslav the Wise, First Class (Ukraine), Collar of the Fed. (UAE), Queen Elizabeth II Coronation Medal, Order of the Yugoslav Star (Yugoslavia); hon. degree from Uppsala Univ., Sweden 2007; Golden Medal of Merit of the Japanese Red Cross, Golden Medal of Hon. mem., King Charles II Medal of the Royal Soc., London; a newly described goby named *Exyrias akihito* in his honour 2005. *Publications:* numerous papers in the journal of the Ichthyological Soc. of Japan and others in the journal Science and the journal Nature. *Leisure interests:* taxonomic study of gobiid fish, natural history and conservation, history, tennis. *Address:* The Imperial Palace, 1-1 Chiyoda, Chiyoda-ku, Tokyo 100, Japan. *Telephone:* (3) 32131111.

AKIKUSA, Naoyuki, BA; Japanese business executive; b. 12 Dec. 1938, Tochigi; m.; two c.; ed Waseda Univ.; joined Fujitsu Ltd as Systems Engineer 1961, Gen. Man., Public Service Systems Eng Div. 1977–86, Group Sr Vice-Pres., System Eng Group 1986–91, mem. Bd of Dirs 1988–08, Sr Vice-Pres. 1991–92, Exec. Vice-Pres. 1992–98, Pres. 1998–2000, Pres. and CEO 2000–03, Chair. and Rep. Dir 2003–08, Sr Adviser 2008–; Corp. Auditor, Advantest Corpn 2005–06, also mem. Bd of Dirs; Vice-Chair. Japan Electronics and Information Tech. Industries Asscn (JEITA) 1998–99, Chair. 1999–2000; Vice-Chair. Communications and Information Network Asscn of Japan (CIAJ) 1998, Bd of Councillors, Japan Fed. of Econ. Orgs (Keidanren) 2000; Co-Chair. Cttee on Trade & Investment, Japan Business Fed. (JBF) 2004–; Corp. Auditor, Fanuc Ltd 2006–; fmr Chair. and CEO LinkCo Inc.; mem. World Econ. Forum, Industrial Re-birth Council. *Leisure interest:* tennis. *Address:* c/o Fujitsu Ltd, Shiodome City Center, 1-5-2 Higashi-Shimbashi, Minato-ku, Tokyo 105-7123, Japan.

AKINKUGBE, Oladipo Olujimi, Atobase of Ife, Babalofin of Ijebu-Igbo, Adingbuwa of Ondo, Ikolaba Balogun Basegun of Ibadan, MD, DPhil, DTM&H, FRCP, FAS, CON; Nigerian professor of medicine; *Professor Emeritus, College of Medicine, University of Ibadan;* b. 17 July 1933, Ondo; s. of the late Chief Odofin David Akinkugbe and Chief (Mrs) Grace Akinkugbe; m. Dr Folasade Dina 1965; two s.; ed Govt Coll., Ibadan, Univ. Coll., Ibadan, Univs of London, Liverpool and Oxford, UK; Lecturer in Medicine, Univ. of Ibadan 1964–66, Sr Lecturer 1966–68, Prof. 1968–95, Prof. Emer. 1996–, Dean of Medicine 1970–74, Chair. of Cttee of Deans 1972–74, mem. Council 1971–74; Visiting Prof. of Medicine, Harvard Univ. 1974–75; Principal, Univ. Coll., Ilorin 1975–77; Vice-Chancellor Univ. of Ilorin 1977–78, Ahmadu Bello Univ. 1978–79; Pro-Chancellor and Chair. Council, Port Harcourt Univ. 1986–90; Pres. Nigerian Asscn of Nephrology 1987–89, Nigerian Hypertension Soc. 1992–95; mem. Scientific Advisory Panel, CIBA Foundation, Council of Int. Soc. of Hypertension, WHO Expert Cttees on Cardiovascular Diseases, Smoking Control, Professional and Tech. Educ. of Medical and Auxiliary Personnel, Sr Consultant 1983–84, WHO Advisory Cttee on Health Research 1990; currently Chair. Premier Medicaid Int.; Visiting Fellow, Balliol Coll., Oxford 1981–82; Visiting Prof. of Medicine, Univ. of Oxford 1981–82; mem. Bd of Trustees, Obafemi Awolowo Foundation, Nigerian Heartcare Foundation 1994–, Chair. 2000– (also mem. Governing Council), Nigerian Educare Trust 1995, The Social Sciences and Reproductive Health Research Network 1996, Ajumogobia Science Foundation; Chair. Bd of Man., Univ. Coll. Hosp., Ibadan 2000–04; Pres. African Heart Network 2001; Founding Pres. Nigerian Soc. for Information, Arts and Culture 2001–; Patron Sickle Cell Asscn of Nigeria; mem. several editorial bds; Fellow, Nigerian Acad. of Science; Hon. Fellow, Univ. of Ibadan 1998; Nigerian Nat. Order of Merit 1997, Commdr, Order of the Niger 1979, Order of the Fed. Repub. of Nigeria 2004, Officier, Ordre Nat. de la République de Côte d'Ivoire; Hon. DSc (Ilorin) 1982, (Fed. Univ. Tech. Akure) 1994, (Port-Harcourt) 1997, (Ogun State Univ.) 1998; Searle Distinguished Research Award 1989, Life Achievement Award, Nigerian Acad. of Science 2004, Boehringer Ingelheim Award, Int. Soc. of Hypertension 2004. *Publications include:* High Blood Pressure in the African 1972, Priorities in National Health Planning (ed.) 1974, Hypertension in Africa (ed.) 1975, Cardiovascular Diseases in Africa (ed.) 1976, Clinical Medicine in the Tropics – Cardiovascular Disease 1986, Nigeria's Health in the 90s (co-ed.) 1996, A Compendium of Clinical Medicine (ed.) 1999; numerous papers on hypertension and renal disease. *Leisure interests:* bird-watching, music, gardening. *Address:* College of Medicine, University of Ibadan, Ibadan, Oyo State (office); The Little Summit, Olubadan Aleshinloye Way, Iyaganku, Ibadan (home); Premier Medicaid International, Olive House N6/53, Fajuyi Road, PO Box 29259, Secretariat Post Office, Adamasingba, Ibadan, Nigeria (office). *Telephone:* (2) 2410052 (office); (3) 7866956 (mobile). *Fax:* (2) 2410052 (office). *E-mail:* p_medicaid@yahoo.co.uk (office); info@premiermedicaid.com.ng (office). *Website:* www.premiermedicaid .com.ng (office).

AKIYA, Einosuke; Japanese religious leader; b. 15 July 1930, Tokyo; s. of Jubei Akiya and Yuki Akiya; m. Akiko Ishida 1957; two s.; ed Waseda Univ.; with Soka Gakkai 1951–, Young Men's Div. Chief 1956–59, Youth Div. Chief 1959–66, Dir 1961–62, Vice-Gen. Dir 1962–67, Gen. Admin. 1967–70, Vice-Pres. 1970–81, Pres. 1981–2006, Chair. Exec. Guidance Conf. 2006–; Ed.-in-Chief Seikyo Shimbun 1968, Rep. Dir 1975–81, Pres. 1987–90, Exec. Adviser 1990–2006; Gen. Dir Soka Gakkai Int. 1981–92, Exec. Counsellor 1992–95, Deputy Pres. 1995–2007,

Counsellor 2007–. *Leisure interests:* reading, music, theatre. *Address:* Soka Gakkai Headquarters, 32 Shinano-machi, Shinjuku-ku, Tokyo 160-8583, Japan (office). *Telephone:* (3) 3353-7111 (office). *Website:* www.sgi.org (office).

AKIYAMA, Kotaro; Japanese newspaper executive; *President, CEO and Representative Director, Asahi Shimbun Company;* Man. Ed. Asahi Shimbun –2005, Pres. and CEO and Rep. Dir The Asahi Shimbun Co. 2005–, Chair. Compliance Cttee 2006–; Ind. Dir TV Asahi Corpn 2006–, NSK (Japanese Newspaper Publrs and Eds Asscn, Chair. –2013); Pres. Mihou Sangyo K.K; Chair. Asahi Shinbun Bunka Zaidan Foundation. *Address:* The Asahi Shimbun Company, 5-3-2 Tsukiji, Chuo-ku, Tokyo 104-8011, Japan (office). *Telephone:* (3) 3545-0131 (office). *Fax:* (3) 3545-8450 (office); (3) 3545-0358 (office). *Website:* www.asahi.com (office).

AKIYAMA, Yoshihisa; Japanese business executive; Chair. Kansai Electric Power Co. –2010, Chair. Kansai Econ. Fed. (Kankeiren); Chair. Kansai Asscn of Corp. Execs 1994–95; Chair. IIS Japan (non-profit making org.), Asscn for Commemorative Events of 1300th Anniversary of Nara Heijo-kyo Capital, Research Inst. of Innovative Tech. for Earth, Osaka Wan Bay Area Kaihatsu Suishin Kiko Foundation, Kinkichiku Chijo Digital Hoso Jikken Jkyogikai; Pres. Akiyama Tosoten, Y.K.; mem. or fmr mem. Bd of Dirs Nippon Life Insurance Co., Japan Airlines Co. Ltd, Japan Productivity Center for Socio-Econ. Devt; Corp. Auditor Japan Airlines Corpn. *Address:* c/o Kansai Electric Power Co., 6-16 Nakanoshima 3-chome, Kita-ku, Osaka 530-8270, Japan.

AKODJÈNOU, Arnauld Antoine, PhD; Benin diplomatist and UN official; *Deputy Special Representative of the Secretary-General, United Nations Operation in Côte d'Ivoire (UNOCI);* b. 27 Oct. 1950; m.; three c.; ed Univ. of Benin, Cotonou, Inst. of Int. Relations of Cameroon, Yaoundé, Grad. Inst. of Int. Studies, Geneva; Political Science Researcher, World Social Prospects Asscn and UNITAR, Geneva 1982–86; Assoc. Social Services Officer, UNHCR, Djibouti 1986–95; Chief of Bureau, Unit of Burundi and Rwanda 1995–97, also various positions in Regional Bureau for Africa, covering Great Lakes, W Africa and Cen. Africa; UNHCR Rep. in Mali 1999–2000, in Sierra Leone 2000–03; Regional Coordinator for Liberia and Côte d'Ivoire, Accra, Ghana 2003; Dir of Emergency and Security Services, UNHCR HQ, Geneva 2003–05; Dir Div. of Operational Services 2005–09; Inspector Gen. UNHCR 2009–11; Deputy Special Rep. of Sec.-Gen., UN Operation in Côte d'Ivoire (UNOCI) 2011–. *Address:* c/o United Nations Operation in Côte d'Ivoire, Hôtel Sebroko, Blvd de la Paix 08, BP 588, Abidjan 08, Côte d'Ivoire (office). *E-mail:* questions_onuci@un.org (office). *Website:* www.un.org/en/peacekeeping/missions/unoci (office).

AKOL AJAWIN, Lam, PhD; South Sudanese engineer and politician; *Leader, Sudan People's Liberation Movement—Democratic Change;* b. 15 July 1950, Dongula; m.; three c.; ed Univ. of Khartoum, Heriot-Watt Univ. and Imperial Coll. London, UK; Teaching Asst, Univ. of Khartoum 1976–80, Lecturer in Chemical Eng 1980–86; Lecturer (part-time), Faculty of Science and Tech., Univ. of Gezira 1982–84; Chair. Port Sudan oil refinery 1985–86; joined Sudan People's Liberation Army (SPLA) 1986, Zonal Commdr of North Upper Nile 1987–88, of Southern Blue Nile 1990–91, Dir SPLM Office of Co-ordination and External Relations 1988–90, SPLA Chief Negotiator in peace talks 1988–91, Chair. SPLM-united 1994–2003; participated in armed rebellion with Dr Riek Machar that split the rebel movt; signed Fashoda Agreement with Sudanese Govt 1997; Minister of Transport 1998–2002; involved in peace process negotiations with ASAP 2003; Minister of Foreign Affairs 2005–07, of Cabinet Affairs 2007; Founder and Leader, Sudan People's Liberation Movt—Democratic Change 2009–. *Publications:* SPLM/SPLA: Inside an African Revolution. *Address:* Sudan People's Liberation Movement—Democratic Change, Juba, South Sudan (office).

AKRAM, Wasim (see WASIM, Akram).

AKSU, Abdülkadir; Turkish politician; *Deputy Chairman, Justice and Development Party (Adalet ve Kalkınma Partisi);* b. 12 Oct. 1944, Diyarbakır; m.; two c.; ed Ankara Univ.; trainee clerk in Diarbekir 1968; Deputy Dist Gov. in Gench, Akchadaa, Doanshehir; Dist Gov. of Kanak 1970; reserve mil. officer in Askale 1971–73; Dist Gov. of Sarakaya 1973–76; Chief of Police, Malatya 1976–77; Gov. of Kahramanmarash 1977–78; Gov. of Rize 1980; Cen. Gov. 1980; Gov. of Gaziantep 1984–87; elected MP (Motherland Party) 1987; Minister of Internal Affairs 1989–91, 2002–07 (resgnd); State Minister for GAP; joined Welfare Party 1996, later Vice-Chair.; joined Justice and Devt Party (Adalet ve Kalkınma Partisi), currently Deputy Chair.; mem. Int. Inst. for Security and Cooperation; Union of Journalists Bureaucrat of the Year 1986, Siyaset Magazine Policy Maker of the Year 2002, Siyaset Magazine Minister of the Year 2002–03. *Address:* Justice and Development Party (Adalet ve Kalkınma Partisi), Söğütözü Caddesi 6, Çankaya, Ankara, Turkey (office). *Telephone:* (312) 2045000 (office). *Fax:* (312) 2045020 (office). *E-mail:* rte@akparti.org.tr (office). *Website:* www.akparti.org.tr (office).

AKSYONOV, Sergei Valeryevich; Ukrainian business executive and politician; *de facto Prime Minister of the 'Republic of Crimea';* b. 26 Nov. 1972, Bălţi, Moldovan SSR, USSR; two c.; moved to Crimea 1989, enrolled in a coll. for Soviet mil. engineers shortly before the collapse of the Soviet Union, refused to swear an oath of allegiance to Ukraine; graduated from Higher Mil.-Political Construction Coll., Simferopol 1993; Deputy Dir Ellada (food products co.) 1993–98; Deputy Dir Asteriks co. 1998–2001; Deputy Dir Eskada co. 2001–14; mem. Russian Community of Crimea 2008–, Civic Active of Crimea 2008–; developed Russian Unity party 2008–09, Leader 2009–; mem. Bd Civil Asset Crimea 2009–; Co-Pres. Co-ordinating Council, For Russian Unity in Crimea! 2009–; Deputy (Russian Unity), Supreme Council of Crimea 2010–; de facto Prime Minister of the self-declared 'Republic of Crimea' Feb. 2014–; warrant for his arrest issued by Shevchenko dist court of Kiev March 2014; put on Canadian, EU and US sanction lists; Head of Crimea's Greco-Roman wrestling org. *Address:* Council of Ministers, 95005 Simferopol, ul. Kirova 13, Crimea, Ukraine (office). *Telephone:* (652) 27-61-65 (office). *Fax:* (652) 24-80-25 (office). *E-mail:* letter@ark.gov.ua (office). *Website:* www.crimea-portal.gov.ua (office).

AKSYUCHITS, Viktor Vladimirovich; Russian politician and Orthodox philosopher; *President, Russian Universities Foundation;* b. 27 Aug. 1949, Vardantsy, Minsk region, USSR (now Belarus); m. 2nd; five c.; ed Riga Navigation School, Moscow State Univ.; served in navy 1969–72; mem. CPSU 1971–78; seasonal worker in Siberia and Far East 1978–88; Founder Orthodox Unity Church; ed

Vybor (journal); Chair. Duma (Bd) of Political Council, Russian Christian Democratic Movt 1990–98; Chair. Orthodox Brotherhood Resurrection 1990–96; People's Deputy of Russia 1990–93; mem. Duma of Russian People's Congress 1992–96; Lecturer, State Acad. of Slavic Culture 1996–2003; adviser to Deputy Prime Minister Boris Nemtsov 1997–98; Chair. Bd of Dirs Orthodox Social Service Foundation 2000–09; Pres. Russian Univs Foundation. *Publications:* seven books on Christian philosophy, theology and philosophy of history, including Cross Grace, Russia's Mission 2009; numerous articles on political science and cultural studies. *Address:* Matveevskaya, 10-2-234, 119517 Moscow, Russia (home). *Telephone:* (985) 991-5669 (home). *E-mail:* aksyu@mail.ru (office).

AKUFO-ADDO, Nano Addo Dankwa, BSc (Econs); Ghanaian politician and lawyer; s. of Edward Akufo-Addo (fmr Chief Justice and Pres. Second Repub.) and Adeline Akufo-Addo; m. Rebecca Akufo-Addo (née Griffiths-Randolph); five c.; ed Lancing Coll., Sussex, UK, Univ. of Ghana, Legon; called to English Bar (Middle Temple) 1971, Ghanaian Bar 1975; Assoc. Counsel, Coudert Freres (US law firm), Paris office, France 1971–75; Jr mem. U. V. Campbell 1975–79; Sr Partner and Co-Founder Prempeh & Co.; Gen. Sec. People's Movt for Freedom and Justice 1977–78;; mem. Gen. Legal Council 1991–96, Gen. Council, Ghana Bar Asscn 1991–96 (Vice-Pres. Greater Accra Regional Br. 1991–96); Founder and first Chair. Ghana Cttee on Human and People's Rights; mem. Nat. Council and Nat. Exec. Cttee, New Patriotic Party (NPP) 1992–2000; mem. Parl. (NPP) for Abuakwa constituency 1996–2000, Chair. NPP Internal Affairs Cttee, NPP Legal and Constitutional Affairs Cttee, Sec. NPP Political Cttee, Sec. NPP Policy Advisory Cttee 1996, Standing Cttee on Subsidiary Legislation 1997–2001; Ranking Minority mem. Parl.'s Select Cttee on Constitutional, Legal and Parl. Affairs 1997–2001; Minister of Foreign Affairs 2000–07; NPP cand. for Pres. of Ghana 2008; Chair. DHL, Ghana Ltd, Kinesec Communications Co. Ltd; Hon. Fellow, Legon Hall, Univ. of Ghana. *Leisure interests:* listening to music, sports. *Address:* c/o New Patriotic Party, C912/2 Duade St, Kokomlemle, POB 3456, Accra-North, Ghana. *E-mail:* npp@africanonline.com.gh.

AKUNIN, Boris; Russian (b. Georgian) writer; b. (Grigory Shalvovich Chkhartishvili), 1956, Georgia; ed Moscow State Univ.; Deputy Ed.-in-Chief Inostrannaya Literatura (magazine) –2000; Ed.-in-Chief, Anthology of Japanese Literature (20 vols); Chair. Exec. Bd Pushkin Library (Soros Foundation). *Publications include:* fiction: Azazel 1998, Winter Queen 1998, Turkish Gambit 1998, Leviathan 1998, The State Counsellor 1999, Jack of Spades 1999, The Seagull 2000, The Coronation 2000, Pelagia and the White Bulldog 2000, Fairy Tales for Idiots 2000, Lover of Death Vol One 2001, Lover of Death Vol Two 2001, Pelagia and the Black Monk 2001, Pelagia and the Red Rooster 2003, The Diamond Chariot 2003, F.M. 2006, Falcon and the Swallow 2009, All the World's a Stage 2009, The Black City 2012; non-fiction: The Writer and Suicide 1999, Cemetery Tales 2004; contrib. to numerous reviews and criticisms, numerous trans of Japanese, American and English literature. *Address:* Poema Press Publications, Zvezdny blvd 23, 129075 Moscow, Russia (office). *Telephone:* (495) 925-42-05 (home). *E-mail:* erikavoronova@mtu-net.ru (office). *Website:* akunin.ru (office).

ALABBAR, Mohammed Ali Rashid, BA; United Arab Emirates government official and business executive; *Chairman, Emaar Properties;* b. 1963; ed Albers School of Business and Econs at Seattle Univ., USA; served as Dir-Gen. Dept of Econ. Devt; Chair. Emaar Properties PJSC (real estate co.) 1997–; Vice-Chair. Dubai Aluminium Co. Ltd (DUBAL) 1992–2003, Dubai World Trade Centre 1992–2002; Chair. Emcredit (first ind. credit information co. in UAE); f. and Chair. Africa Middle East Resources (AMER, mining co.); currently also Sr Aide to Ruler of Dubai and Vice-Pres./Prime Minister of UAE, Sheikh Mohammed bin Rashid al-Maktoum; mem. Dubai Exec. Council; fmr Chair. UAE Golf Asscn (now Emirates Golf Fed.); Dr hc (Seattle Univ.) 2007; Arabian Business Businessman of the Year 2011; named by Golf World magazine amongst the top ten golfing personalities in the world 2012; Arab Bankers' Asscn of N America Achievement Award 2012; ranked by Arabian Business amongst the Power 500: The World's Most Influential Arabs (second) 2009, (fourth) 2010–13. *Address:* Emaar Properties PJSC, PO Box 9440, Dubai (office); Dubai Executive Council, Emirates Towers Building, 20th Floor, Sheikh Zayed Road, 72233 Dubai, United Arab Emirates (office). *Telephone:* (4) 330-2111 (office). *Fax:* (4) 330-2999 (office). *E-mail:* pe@tec.gov.ae (office); info@alabbar.info. *Website:* dubai.ae/en/pages/default.aspx (office); www.alabbar.info; www.emaar.com.

ALAGIAH, George, OBE; British journalist, broadcaster and writer; *Presenter, Six O'Clock News and World News Today, British Broadcasting Corporation (BBC);* b. 22 Nov. 1955, Sri Lanka; m. Frances Robathan; two s.; ed St John's Coll., Portsmouth and Univ. of Durham; family moved to Ghana 1960; worked in print journalism for South Magazine 1982–89; joined the BBC 1989, Leading Foreign Corresp. specializing in Africa and the developing world, BBC's Africa Corresp., Johannesburg 1994–98, Presenter The World News on BBC 4 2002, Presenter BBC Six O'Clock News 2003–, World News Today (rebranded as GMT with George Alagiah 2010) 2006–, BBC World; has interviewed many internationally prominent figures; has contributed to The Guardian, Daily Telegraph, The Independent and Daily Express newspapers; Bd mem. Royal Shakespeare Co.; Patron NAZ Project, Parenting UK 2000–, Fairtrade Foundation 2002–09; Critics' Award and Golden Nymph Award, Monte Carlo TV Festival 1992, Best Int. Report, Royal TV Soc. 1993, Best TV Journalist Award, Amnesty Int. 1994, One World Broadcasting Trust Award 1994, James Cameron Memorial Trust Award 1995, Bayeux Award for War Reporting 1996, Media Personality of the Year, Ethnic Minority Media Awards 1998, BAFTA Award (part of BBC Team) for coverage of Kosovo conflict 2000, Asian Award for Outstanding Achievement in TV 2010. *Publications:* A Passage to Africa 2001, The Day That Shook the World, A Home from Home (autobiography) 2006. *Address:* BBC, Room 1640, Television Centre, Wood Lane, London, W12 7RJ, England (office). *Telephone:* (20) 8743-8000 (office). *Fax:* (20) 8743-7882 (office). *Website:* www.bbc.co.uk (office).

ALAGNA, Roberto; French singer (tenor); b. 7 June 1963, Clichy-sous-Bois; m. 1st (deceased); m. 2nd Angela Gheorghiu 1996; ed studied in Paris, France and Italy; debut as Alfredo in La Traviata, Glyndebourne Touring Opera at Plymouth 1988; Met, New York debut as Rodolfo 1996; appearances worldwide at Covent Garden, London, Monte Carlo, Vienna Staatsoper, Théâtre du Châtelet, Paris, La Scala, Milan, Chicago and at the New York Met; repertoire includes Rodolfo (La Bohème), Edgard (Lucia di Lammermoor), Rigoletto, L'Elisir d'amore, Roméo, Don Carlos, Roberto Devereux, Duke of Mantua, Don Carlos, Alfredo, L'Amico Fritz, La Rondine, Faust; winner Pavarotti Competition 1988, Personalité Musicale de l'Année 1994, Laurence Olivier Award for Outstanding Achievement in Opera 1995, Victor Award for Best Singer 1997; Chevalier, Ordre des Arts et des Lettres. *Recordings include:* Duets and Arias (with Angela Gheorghiu), La Bohème 1996, Don Carlos 1996, La Rondine 1997. *Address:* Theateragentur Dr Germinal Hilbert, Maximilianstrasse 22, 80539 Munich, Germany (office). *Telephone:* (89) 2907470 (office). *Fax:* (89) 29074790 (office). *E-mail:* agentur@hilbert.de (office). *Website:* www.hilbert.de; www.robertoalagna.net/en.

ALAÏA, Azzeddine; French fashion designer; b. Tunis; ed Ecole des Beaux Arts, Tunis; studied sculpture; worked with dressmakers specializing in copies of Parisian haute couture in Tunis and then began making his own designs for pvt. clients in Tunis; moved to Paris 1957; worked briefly at Christian Dior before moving to Guy Laroche workrooms for two seasons; also worked in Paris as cook and housekeeper; began made-to-order dressmaking business in 1960s; set up first atelier in Faubourg Saint Germain 1965–84; first ready-to-wear show, Bergdorf Goodman store, New York 1982; first Azzedine Alaïa boutique opened in Beverly Hills 1983; moved to Marais district of Paris 1984; retrospective exhbn Museum of Modern Art, Bordeaux 1985; Chevalier, Légion d'honneur 2008; named Best Designer of Year by French Ministry of Culture 1985. *Address:* 18 rue de la Verrérie, Paris, France.

ALAINI, Mohsin Ahmed; Yemeni politician and diplomatist; b. 20 Oct. 1932, Bani Bahloul, N Yemen; m. Aziza Abulahom 1962; two s. two d.; ed Faculty of Law, Cairo Univ. and the Sorbonne, Paris; schoolteacher, Aden 1958–60; Int. Confed. of Arab Trade Unions 1960–62; Minister of Foreign Affairs, Yemeni Repub. Sept.–Dec. 1962, 1974–80; Perm. Rep. to UN 1962–65, 1965–66, 1967–69; Minister of Foreign Affairs May–July 1965; Prime Minister Nov.–Dec. 1967, 1974–80; Amb. to USSR 1968–70; Prime Minister, Minister of Foreign Affairs Feb. 1971, 1971–72, 1974–75; Amb. to France Aug.–Sept. 1974, 1975–76, to UK 1973–74, to FRG 1982–84, to USA 1984–97; Perm. Rep. to UN, New York 1980–82; Deputy Chair. Consultative Council 1997–. *Publications include:* Battles and Conspiracies against Yemen 1957, Fifty Years of Mounting Sands (autobiog.) 2000. *Leisure interests:* reading, exercising. *Address:* 8 Wissa Wassif Street, Giza, Cairo, Egypt (home); PO Box 72922, San'a, Yemen. *Telephone:* (1) 441185 (Yemen) (office); (2) 5702423 (Cairo). *Fax:* (2) 5762423 (Cairo) (home).

ALAK, Julio César; Argentine lawyer and politician; *Minister of Justice and Human Rights;* b. 9 Jan. 1958, Benito Juárez; m. three c.; ed Univ. of La Plata; practised as lawyer, La Plata; mem. Partido Justicialista (PJ), Pres. La Plata Br. 1988; Mayor of La Plata 1991–2007; mem. Bd of Dirs Aerolíneas Argentinas and Austral Lineas Aereas 2008–, Pres. 2008–09; Minister of Justice and Human Rights 2009–. *Address:* Ministry of Justice and Human Rights, Sarmiento 329, C1041AAG Buenos Aires, Argentina (office). *Telephone:* (11) 5300-4000 (office). *E-mail:* prensa@jus.gov.ar (office). *Website:* www.jus.gov.ar (office).

ALAKIJA, Folorunsho; Nigerian business executive; *Vice-Chairman, Famfa Oil Limited;* b. 15 July 1951, Lagos; m. Modupe Alakija 1976; four s.; ed Pitman's Central Coll., American Coll. in London, UK; started career as Sec., International Merchant Bank of Nigeria (now defunct); launched fashion label Supreme Stitches; attained Oil Prospecting Licence for Famfa Oil Ltd 1993, currently Vice-Chair.; currently also Man. Dir Rose of Sharon Group (Rose of Sharon Prints and Promotions Ltd, Digital Reality Prints Ltd); Founder-Pres. Rose of Sharon Foundation 2008–; Vice-Chair. Nat. Heritage Council and Endowment for the Arts 2013–; Best Designer in Nigeria 1986. *Publication:* Growing With the Hand That Gives the Rose 2011. *Address:* Famfa Oil Limited, 290A Ajose Adeogun Street, Victoria Island, Lagos, Nigeria (office). *Telephone:* (1) 7747979 (office). *Fax:* (1) 2710933 (office). *E-mail:* admin@famfa.com (office). *Website:* www.famfa.com (office).

ALAM, Mahbub-e, BA, MA, LLB; Bangladeshi lawyer; *Attorney General;* b. 17 Feb. 1949, Mouchhamandra; ed Dhaka Univ., Inst. of Constitutional and Parl. Studies, New Delhi, India, City Law Coll., Dhaka; enrolled as advocate and started practice at Dhaka Court 1973, enrolled on High Court 1975, on Appellate Div. of Supreme Court 1980, as Sr Advocate, Appellate Div., Supreme Court of Bangladesh 1998; Additional Attorney Gen. of Bangladesh 1998–2001, Attorney Gen. 2009–; mem. Bangladesh Supreme Court Bar Asscn, Gen. Sec. 1993–94, Pres. 2005–06; mem. Bangladesh Bar Council 2004–. *Address:* Office of the Attorney General, Bangladesh Supreme Court, Dhaka 2 (office). *Telephone:* (2) 433585 (office). *E-mail:* info@minlaw.gov.bd (office). *Website:* www.minlaw.gov.bd/attornygenarloffice.htm (office).

ALAM, Shah Mahboob Alam, MA; Pakistani civil servant and business executive; ed Karachi Univ., Nat. Inst. of Public Admin, Coll., Lahore; officer of BPS-21, Govt of Pakistan; has served in sr security positions in Sindh and Balochistan; also served on deputation in Ministry of Foreign Affairs for eight years; Dir-Gen. Office of the Nat. Security Adviser to the Prime Minister –2008; apptd Exec. Dir (Security), Oil and Gas Devt Co. Ltd 2008, later CEO and Man. Dir. *Address:* c/o Oil and Gas Development Co. Ltd, OGDCL House, Plot No. 3, Jinnah Avenue, Blue Area, Islamabad, Pakistan.

ALAPAYEV, Marat O.; Kyrgyzstani fmr central banker; m.; two c.; fmr Lecturer, Dept of Political Economy, Osh Pedagogical Teacher Training Coll.; worked as a broker in the securities market; Chair. Bakai Bank 1998–2006; Head, Cttee of Dirs Manas Int. Airport 2005–06; Acting Chair. Nat. Bank of the Kyrgyz Repub. (Kyrgyz Respublikasynyn Uluttuk Banky) April 2006, Chair. 2006. *Address:* c/o Kyrgyz Respublikasynyn Uluttuk Banky, 101 T. Umetaliev str., 720040 Bishkek, Kyrgyzstan (office).

ALARCÓN DE QUESADA, Ricardo; Cuban diplomatist and politician; *President of National Assembly;* b. 21 May 1937; s. of Roberto Alarcón de Quesada; m. Margarita Maza; one d.; ed Univ. de Habana; Head of Student Section, Prov. Office of 26 July Revolutionary Movt 1957–59; Pres. Univ. Students' Fed., Sec. Union of Young Communists; Dir for Regional Affairs (Latin America), Ministry of Foreign Affairs 1962–66; mem. Governing Council of Inst. for Int. Politics, Ministry of Foreign Affairs, Deputy Minister of Foreign Affairs 1978, mem. Tech. Advisory Council 1980; Perm. Rep. of Cuba to the UN 1966–78; Pres. UNDP 1976–77; Alt. mem. Cen. Cttee of CP of Cuba 1980–; mem. Politburo of CP 1992–;

Perm Rep. to UN 1990; Minister of Foreign Affairs 1992–94; Pres. Nat. Ass. of People's Power 1993–. *Address:* Asamblea Nacional del Poder Popular, Havana, Cuba; 42 Street No. 2308 e/23 and 25 Streets, Municipio Playa, Cuba.

ALARCÓN MANTILLA, Luis Fernando, MSc; Colombian politician and engineer; *General Manager, Electrical Interconnection SA-ISA;* b. Aug. 1951, Bucaramanga; m.; ed Univ. of the Andes, Massachusetts Inst. of Tech.; engineer with Mejía Millan y Perry Ltd and Prof. of Civil Eng Univ. of the Andes 1980–83, currently mem. Bd of Dirs; Head of Public Investment Unit, Nat. Dept of Planning 1983–84; Dir-Gen. of Budget, Ministry of Finance and Public Credit 1984–86; economist, Inter-American Devt Bank (IDB), Washington, DC 1986; Vice-Minister, Ministry of Finance and Public Credit 1986–87, Minister of Finance and Public Credit 1987–91; fmr Pres. Flota Mercante Grancolombiana SA, Asscn of Pension Fund Admins and Unemployment, Asofondos of Colombia; Dir-Man., Petrocolombia; CEO Asociación Colombiana de Administradoras de Fondos de Pensiones y Cesantía-Asofondos de Colo; Gen. Man. Electrical Interconnection SA-ISA; also currently Chair. and CEO Grupo Empresarial ISA; Co-Chair. World Econ. Forum on Latin America 2010; mem. of Governing Council for Foreign Trade, Bd of Banco de la República, Nat. Council for Econ. and Social Policy 1997–; Chair. Flota Mercante Grancolombiana; mem. Bd of Dirs Banco de Bogota, Colombia Stock Exchange, Petrocolombia SA, Co. of Electric Energy Transmission Paulista, INTERNEXA, Avianca, Bavaria, Caracol SA, Cafesalud, Valores Bavaria and Caracol TV. *Address:* Electrical Interconnection SA-ISA, Calle 12 Sur No. 18-168, Medellin, Colombia (office). *Telephone:* (4) 325-2270 (office). *Fax:* (4) 317-0848 (office). *E-mail:* isa@isa.com.co (office). *Website:* www.isa.com.co (office).

ALARCON RIVERA, Fabián Ernesto, PhD; Ecuadorean politician; b. 14 April 1947, Quito; s. of Dr Fabián Alarcón Falconi and Maria Antonieta Rivera Larrea; m. Lucía Peña Ochoa 1976; two s. one d.; ed Pontifical Catholic Univ.; councillor, Quito 1969; fmr Prefect of Pinchincha Prov. 1984–88; Pres. of Congress 1991–92, 1995–97; fmr Deputy to Congress (three times), fmr Speaker of Congress (three times); represented Ecuador in Inter-American Congress of Lawyers in Brazil, Puerto Rico and Quito; mem. Patriotic People's Party, American Fed. of Lawyers; Acting Pres. of Ecuador 6–10 Feb. 1997, Pres. of Ecuador 1997–98; arrested on charges of illegally hiring personnel 1999, released 2005; mem. Frente Radical Alfarista, Leader 2002; fmr Pres. Law School Asscn.

ALASANIA, Irakli, LLB; Georgian diplomatist and politician; *Minister of Defence;* b. 21 Dec. 1973, Batumi, Adjara ASSR; s. of the late Gen. Mamia Alasania; m.; two c.; ed Tbilisi State Univ., Georgian Acad. of Security; with Ministry of State Security 1994–98; with Ministry of Foreign Affairs 1998–2001, postings include Embassies in Washington, DC, Ottawa and Mexico City; Head, Directorate for Security Issues, Nat. Security Council 2001–02, Deputy Sec. 2004–05; First Deputy Minister of State Security 2002–04, of Defence March–July 2004; Special Rep. for Abhkazia and Head of Govt, Abkhazia Autonomous Repub. 2005–06, Special Rep. for Abhkazia negotiations 2005–; adviser to Pres. of Georgia on Conflict Resolution 2006; Amb. and Perm. Rep. to UN, New York 2006–08 (resgnd); joined Republican and New Rights parties in an alliance called 'The Alliance for Georgia' Feb. 2009, Chair. 2009–10, Founder and Chair. Our Georgia–Free Democrats (Chveni Sakartvelo—Davisuphali demokratebi) party as part of the alliance July 2009–, alliance cand. in Tbilisi mayoral elections May 2010, announced alliance breaking up June 2010, one of three co-founding parties of Georgian Dream Political Coalition Feb. 2012; Minister of Defence Oct. 2012–. *Address:* Ministry of Defence, 0112 Tbilisi, Gen. Kvinitadze 20 (office); Our Georgia–Free Democrats (Chveni Sakartvelo—Davisuphali demokratebi), 0194 Tbilisi, E. Cherkezishvili 4, Georgia. *Telephone:* (32) 291-04-21 (office); (32) 10-48-83. *Fax:* (32) 291-06-45 (office). *E-mail:* pr@mod.gov.ge (office); contact@ag.ge. *Website:* www.mod.gov.ge (office); www.fd.ge.

ALBA, Jessica Marie; American actress and model; b. 28 April 1981, Pomona, Calif.; d. of Mark Alba and Catherine Alba (née Jensen); m. Cash Warren 2008; two d.; ed David Mamet's Atlantic Theater Co.; took first acting class aged 12, signed by agent 1994; Founder The Honest Company (makes chemical-free products); Choice Actress Teen Choice Award, Saturn Award for Best Actress on Television, ALMA Awar for Breakthrough Actress of the Year 2001, Superstar of Tomorrow, Young Hollywood Awards 2005; named by People Magazine as one of the 50 Most Beautiful People 2005, named to GQ Magazines' 25 Sexiest Women in film of all time. *Films include:* Camp Nowhere 1994, Venus Rising 1995, P.U.N.K.S. (video) 1999, Never Been Kissed 1999, Idle Hands 1999, Paranoid 2000, The Sleeping Dictionary 2003, Honey 2003, Sin City 2005, Fantastic Four 2005, Into the Blue 2005, The Ten 2007, Fantastic 4: Rise of the Silver Surfer (Favourite Female Movie Star, Nickelodeon Kids' Choice Awards 2008) 2007, Good Luck Chuck 2007, Bill 2007, Awake 2007, The Eye 2008, The Love Guru 2008, The Killer Inside Me 2010, Valentine's Day 2010, Machete 2010, An Invisible Sign 2010, Little Fockers 2010, Spy Kids: All the Time in the World in 4D 2011, A.C.O.D. 2013, Escape from Planet Earth (voice) 2013, Machete Kills 2013, Sin City: A Dame to Kill For 2013. *Television includes:* Flipper (series) 1995–98, Dark Angel (series) 2000–02. *Leisure interests:* avid swimmer and PADI-certified scuba diver, playing golf, cooking, Harley Davidson motorcycles. *Address:* c/o Patrick Whitesell, WME Entertainment, 9601 Wilshire Boulevard, Beverly Hills, CA 90210-5213, USA (office).

ALBACETE CARREIRA, Alfonso; Spanish painter; b. 14 March 1950, Málaga; s. of Alfonso Albacete and María Carreira; m. Luisa Gómez 1986; one s. one d.; studied painting, with Juan Bonafé and architecture; studied painting Valencia 1969, then in Paris; first one-man exhbn, Madrid 1972; first exhbn USA, Center for Contemporary Art, Chicago 1989; works included in numerous collections of contemporary art including Chase Manhattan Bank, New York, White House Collection, Washington, Collection Dobe, Zurich, Museo Reina Sofia, Madrid. *Leisure interests:* botany, architecture. *Address:* Vegap, Centro de Madrid, Gran Vía 16, 5 planta, 28013 Madrid, Spain (office); Joaquín Maruía López, 23–7° C, 28015 Madrid, Spain (office). *Telephone:* (91) 5326632 (office); (91) 5491140 (office). *Fax:* (91) 5315398 (office). *E-mail:* infomad@vegap.es (office). *Website:* www.vegap .es (office).

ALBANESE, Thomas (Tom), BS, MS; American mining industry executive; b. 9 Sept. 1957, New Jersey; m. Mary Ross; two d.; ed Univ. of Alaska, Fairbanks, COO Nerco Minerals –1993, Gen. Man. Rio Tinto plc Greens Creek mine (after acquisition of Nerco by Rio Tinto), Admiralty Island, Alaska 1993–95, Group

Exploration Exec., London 1995–98, Vice-Pres. Eng and Tech. Services, Kennecott Utah Copper 1998–2000, CEO Industrial Minerals Group, Rio Tinto 2000–04, CEO Copper Group and Head, Exploration, London 2004, Dir Group Resources, Rio Tinto Group, Melbourne –2006, mem. Bd of Dirs Rio Tinto plc and Rio Tinto Ltd 2006–13, Chief Exec. Rio Tinto Group 2007–13; mem. Bd of Dirs Palabora Mining Co. 2004–06, Ivanhoe Mines 2006–07; mem. Exec. Cttee Int. Copper Asscn 2004–06. *Address:* c/o Rio Tinto plc, 2 Eastbourne Terrace, London, W2 6LG, England; c/o Rio Tinto Ltd, 120 Collins Street, Melbourne, Vic. 3000, Australia. *E-mail:* info@riotinto.com.

ALBAR, Datuk Seri Syed Hamid bin Syed Jaafar; Malaysian politician; *Chairman, Suruhanjaya Pengangkutan Awam Darat (Land Public Transport Commission);* mem. BN-UMNO Party; mem. Parl. for Kota Tinggi; Minister in the Prime Minister's Dept and Minister of Law *c.* 1993; Minister of Defence *c.* 1997; Minister of Foreign Affairs *c.* 1999–2008; Minister of Home Affairs and Internal Security 2008–09; Chair. Land Public Transport Comm. 2010–; *Website:* www.spad .gov.my.

ALBARN, Damon; British singer, musician (keyboards) and songwriter; b. 23 March 1968, Whitechapel, London, England; s. of Hazel Albarn and Keith Albarn; ed Stanway Comprehensive, Colchester, East 15 Drama School, Debden; mem. and lead singer, Blur (fmrly named Seymour) 1989–; live appearances and tours worldwide; Founder-mem. and Musical Dir of 'virtual band', Gorillaz 1998–, collaborating with numerous guest artists; Founder-mem. The Good The Bad and The Queen 2006–; with Blur: BRIT Awards for Best Single, Best Video, Best Album, Best Band 1995, for Outstanding Contrib. to Music 2012, Best Alternative Band, Smash Hits Awards 1994, Best Band and Best Live Act, NME Awards 1995, Best Act in the World Today, Q Awards 1999, Best Band, Best Single (Tender), NME Awards 2000, NME Award for Best Live Event (Blur at Hyde Park) 2010; with Gorillaz: Q Awards for Best Video, for Best Producer 2005, Digital Music Award for Top Online Band, for Best Use of Digital Platforms 2005, MTV Europe Music Award for Best Group Award 2005, Grammy Award for Best Pop Collaboration with Vocals (for Feel Good Inc.) 2006, NME John Peel Music Innovation Award 2006, Ivor Novello Award for Songwriter of the Year 2006, Q Inspiration Award 2007; other: Ivor Novello Awards – Best Songwriters (shared with Noel Gallagher) 1996, PRS for Music Heritage Award 2009, Inspiration Award, MOJO Awards 2009. *Film:* Face 1997. *DVD:* with Gorillaz: Phase One: Celebrity Take Down 2002, Phase Two: Slow Boat to Hades 2006. *Compositions:* wrote film scores for Ravenous (with Michael Nyman) 1998, Ordinary Decent Criminal 1999, 101 Reykjavík (with Einar Örn Benediktsson) 2000; wrote theatre score for Monkey: Journey to the West 2007; wrote libretto and score for opera Dr Dee 2011. *Recordings include:* albums: with Blur: Leisure 1991, Modern Life Is Rubbish 1993, Parklife (Best Album, Q Awards 1994, Best Album, Best Single, Best British Video, BRIT Awards 1995, Best Album, NME Awards 1995) 1994, The Great Escape (Best Album, Q Awards 1995) 1995, Blur 1997, 13 1999, The Best Of Blur 2000, Think Tank (Best Album, Q Awards 2003, Best Album, South Bank Show Awards 2003) 2003, Midlife 2009; with Gorillaz: Gorillaz 2001, G-Sides 2002, Laika Come Home 2002, Demon Days 2005, D-Sides 2007, Plastic Beach 2010, Dr Dee 2012; solo: Mali Music (various contributors) 2002, Democrazy 2003; with The Good The Bad and The Queen: The Good The Bad and The Queen 2007. *Leisure interests:* football, Tae Kwon Do. *Address:* c/o CMO Management International Ltd, Studio 2.6, Shepherds East, Richmond Way, London, W14 0DQ, England (office). *Telephone:* (20) 7316-6969 (office). *Fax:* (20) 7316-6970 (office). *E-mail:* cmoinfo@cmomanagement.co.uk (office). *Website:* www.cmomanagement.co.uk (office); www.blur.co.uk; www.gorillaz.com; www.thegoodthebadandthequeen .com.

ALBEE, Edward Franklin, III; American playwright; b. 12 March 1928, Virginia, VA; adopted s. of Reed Albee and Frances Cotter; ed Lawrenceville and Choate Schools, Washington, DC, Valley Forge Mil. Acad., Trinity Coll., Hartford; Comm. Chair. Brandeis Univ. Creative Arts Awards 1983, 1984; Founder-Pres. The Edward F. Albee Foundation 1967–; Distinguished Prof., Univ. of Houston 1988–2003; mem. Dramatists Guild Council, PEN America, The American Acad., Nat. Inst. of Arts and Letters; Fellow, American Acad. of Arts and Sciences 1972; Dr hc (Bulgarian Nat. Acad. of Theater and Film Arts) 2009; Tony Awards 1963, 1996, 2002, Gold Medal, American Acad. and Inst. of Arts and Letters 1980, inducted into Theater Hall of Fame 1985, Kennedy Center Award 1996, Nat. Medal of Arts 1996, Special Tony Award for Lifetime Achievement 2005. *Plays include:* The Zoo Story (Vernon Rice Award 1960) 1958, The Death of Bessie Smith 1959, The Sandbox 1959, Fam and Yam 1959, The American Dream (Foreign Press Asscn Award 1961) 1960, Who's Afraid of Virginia Woolf? (Drama Critics' Circle Award for Best Play) 1962, stage adaptation of The Ballad of the Sad Café (Carson McCuller) 1963, Tiny Alice 1964, Malcolm (from novel by James Purdy) 1965, A Delicate Balance (Pulitzer Prize 1966) 1966, Everything in the Garden (after a play by Giles Cooper) 1967, Box 1968, Quotations from Chairman Mao Tse-tung 1968, All Over 1971, Seascape (Pulitzer Prize 1975) 1974, Listening 1975, Counting the Ways 1976, The Lady from Dubuque 1977–79, Lolita (adapted from Vladimir Nabokov) 1979, The Man Who Had Three Arms 1981, Finding the Sun 1982, Marriage Play 1986–87, Three Tall Women (Pulitzer Prize 1994) 1990–91, Fragments 1993, The Play About the Baby 1996, The Goat, or, Who is Sylvia? 2000, Occupant 2001, Peter and Jerry (Act 1: Home Life, Act 2: The Zoo Story) 2004, Me, Myself and I 2007, At Home at the Zoo 2009; essays: Stretching My Mind: Essays 1960–2005 2005. *Leisure interest:* collecting art. *Address:* 14 Harrison Street, New York, NY 10013 (office); PO Box 697, Montauk, NY 11954, USA (home). *Telephone:* (212) 226-2020 (office). *Fax:* (212)226-5551 (office). *E-mail:* albee@albeefoundation.org (office); info@albeefoundation.org (office). *Website:* www.albeefoundation.org (office).

ALBERDI, Inés, Doctorado en Ciencias Políticas y Sociología; Spanish sociologist, politician, international organization official and academic; b. 11 Feb. 1948, Seville; m.; one s. one d.; ed Universidad Complutense de Madrid; Asst Prof., Dept of Sociology, Universidad Complutense de Madrid 1971–75, Prof. Encargada 1975–78, Adjunct Prof. 1978, Adjunct Prof. of Sociology 1980–84, Titular Prof. of Sociology 1984–88, 1990–91, Prof. of Sociology 1993–2008; Visiting Scholar, Dept of Sociology, Georgetown Univ., Washington, DC 1978–79, Assoc. Researcher 1988–89; Univ. Prof. of Sociology, Univ. of Saragossa 1991–93; Dir for Research, Centre for Sociological Research 1992–93; Dir Masters programme 'Women's

Studies and Equality Opportunity Policies' organized by School of Doctors and Lawyers in Political Sciences and Sociology and sponsored by Main Directorate of Woman of CAM 1994–96; Deputy in Madrid Ass. 2003–07; Exec. Dir UNIFEM (now UN Women) 2008–10; Adviser for Women in Devt, IDB 1989–90; served as expert for Equal Opportunities Unit of EC on Family and Work and Diversification of Occupational Choices for Women 1998–2000; mem. Bd UN Int. Research and Training Inst. for Advancement of Women (INSTRAW) 1986–89; Eisenhower Fellowship 1998. *Publications include:* Guía didáctica para una orientación no sexista Ministerio de Educación y Ciencia 1988, Estudio Sociológico sobre las viudas en España (second edn; co-author) 1989, La situación social de las viudas en España. Aspectos Cuantitativos (co-author) 1990, Matrimonios y Parejas (co-author) 1994, Informe sobre la situación de la familia en España 1994, Lo personal es político. El movimiento feminista en la transición (co-author) 1996, La nueva familia española 1999, Las mujeres jóvenes en España 2000, Les dones joves à Espanya Fundació 2001, Violencia: Tolerancia Cero (with Luis Rojas Marcos) 2005, Los hombres jóvenes y la paternidad 2007. *Address:* c/o UN Women, 304 East 45th Street, 15th Floor, New York, NY 10017, USA.

ALBERT II, HSH Prince of Monaco (Albert Alexandre Louis Pierre Grimaldi), BA; b. 14 March 1958; s. of the late Prince Rainier III of Monaco and the late Princess Grace (née Kelly); m. Princess Charlene of Monaco (fmr South African swimmer Charlene Wittstock) 2011; ed Albert I High School, Amherst Coll., Mass, USA; ranked as 1st Class Ensign (Sub-Capt.); Pres. Monegasque Del. to Gen. Ass., UN 1993–; Chair. of several sports feds and cttees; Chair. Organizing Cttee, Monte Carlo Int. Television Festival 1988–; Deputy Chair. Princess Grace Foundation of Monaco; named Prince Regent of Monaco 31 March 2005, became Sovereign Prince of Monaco upon death of father Prince Rainier III 6 April 2005, enthroned 12 July 2005; Hon. Pres. Int. Athletic Foundation, Int. Modern Pentathlon Union, World Beach Volleyball, Hon. Citizen of Fort Worth 2000, Hon. Chair. Jeune Chambre Economique, Monaco Aide et Présence, Hon. mem. St Petersburg Naval Ass., Int. Inst. for Human Rights, Hon. Prof. of Int. Studies, Tarrant County Coll., Fort Worth 2000; Grand Cross, Order of Grimaldi 1958, Grand Officier, Nat. Order of the Lion of Senegal 1977, Grand Cross 2012; Grand Cross, Order of Saint-Charles 1979, Kt Grand Cross, Equestrian Order of the Holy Sepulchre of Jerusalem 1983, Grand Officier, Légion d'honneur 1984, Col of the Carabineers 1986, Chevalier, Order of Malta 1989, Grand Officer, Mérite Int. du Sang 1994, Grand Cross, Nat. Order of Merit 1997, Grand Cross, Nat. Order of Niger 1998, Grand Cross of the Jordanian Renaissance (Nahdah Medal) 2000, Grand Collar of the Order of Jose Simeon Cañas (El Salvador) 2002, Grand Cross of the Order of Vasco Núñez de Balboa (Panama) 2002, Grand Cross, Order of the Sun of Peru 2003, Grand Cross, Order Juan Mora Fernandez (Costa Rica) 2003, Order of Stara Planina (Bulgaria) 2004, Kt Grand Cross with Grand Cordon of the Order of Merit of the Italian Repub. 2005, Grand Croix, Légion d'honneur 2006, Grand Prix Humanitaire de France 2007, Commdr, Ordre des Palmes académiques 2009, Kt Grand Cross, Grand Order of King Tomislav (Croatia) 2009, 1st Class decoration of the Order of Stara Planina (Bulgaria) 2011, Grand Cordon of the Supreme Order of the Renaissance (Jordan) 2011, Grand Cordon, Order of Merit (Lebanon) 2011, Grand Officer, Nat. Order of Burkina Faso 2012, Grand Cross, Order of Vytautas the Great (Lithuania) 2012, Grand Cross, Nat. Order of Mali 2012, Order of Merit of the Repub. of Poland (First Class) 2012, Kt Grand Cross,Order of Prince Danilo I, Collar of the Order of Merit of Malta; Dr hc (Pontifical Univ., Maynooth) 1996. *Address:* Palais Princier, BP 518, MC 98015, Monaco. *Website:* www.palais.mc.

ALBERT II, Former King of the Belgians Albert Félix Humbert Théodore Christian Eugéne Marie; b. 6 June 1934, Brussels; s. of King Léopold III and Queen Astrid (fmrly Princess of Sweden); m. Donna Paola Ruffo di Calabria 1959; two s. HM King Philippe I, Prince Laurent, one d. Princess Astrid; fmrly Prince of Liège; succeeded to the throne 9 Aug. 1993, on the death of his brother King Baudouin I, abdicated 21 July 2013 in favour of his son Crown Prince Philippe; Pres. Caisse Générale d'Epargne et de Retraite 1954–92; Pres. Belgian Office of Foreign Trade 1962–93; Pres. Belgian Red Cross 1958–93; Grand Cordon of the Order of Leopold, Grand Master of the Order of Leopold 1993–2012, Order of the African Star, Royal Order of the Lion, Order of the Crown, Order of Leopold II, Great Star of Honour for Services to the Repub. of Austria 1958, Cordon of the Order of Stara Planina (Bulgaria) 2003, GCVO, Grand Cross, Order of the Dannebrog (Denmark), Kt of the Order of the Elephant (Denmark), Collar of the Order of the Cross of Terra Mariana (Estonia) 2008, Grand Cross of the Order of the White Rose (Finland) 2004, Grand Cross, Special Class, Order of Merit of the FRG, Grand Cross, Order of the Redeemer (Greece), Grand Cross with Chain, Order of Merit of the Repub. of Hungary, Civilian Class, Kt of the Collar of the Equestrian Order of the Holy Sepulchre of Jerusalem 1995, Kt Grand Cross of the Order of the Falcon (Iceland) 1979, Kt Grand Cross of the Order of Merit of the Italian Repub. 1973, Kt Grand Cross with Collar of the Order of Merit of the Italian Repub. 1998, Collar of the Order of the Chrysanthemum (Japan), Commdr, Grand Cross with Chain of the Order of Three Stars (Latvia) 2007, Golden Collar of the Order of Vytautas the Great (Lithuania), Kt of the Order of the Gold Lion of the House of Nassau (Luxembourg), Kt Grand Cross of the Order of St Charles (Monaco) 1957, Special Class of the Order of the Mohammedi (Morocco), Kt Grand Cross of the Order of the Netherlands Lion, Kt Grand Cross of the Order of Orange-Nassau, Grand Cross with Collar of the Order of St Olav (Norway), Kt Grand Cross of the Order of the White Eagle (Poland), Grand Cordon of the Mil. Order of Aviz (Portugal) 1985, Grand Collar of the Order of the Infante Dom Henrique 1999, Sash (Collar) of the Order of the Star of Romania 2009, Sash (Collar) of the Order of the Golden Fleece (Spain) 1994, Grand Cross of the Order of Charles III 1977, Kt with Collar of the Order of the Seraphim (Sweden), Bailiff and Kt Grand Cross of Honour and Devotion of the Sovereign Mil. Order of Malta, Kt of the Order of the Golden Fleece (House of Habsburg), Kt of the Order of Saint Michael (House of Bourbon), Kt of the Order of the Most Holy Annunciation, Kt Grand Cross of the Order of Sts Maurice and Lazarus; Dr hc (Catholic Univ. of Leuven, Saint Louis Univ., Baguio City, Ghent Univ., Free Univ. of Brussels, Catholic Univ. of Mons, Polytechnic Faculty of Mons). *Address:* The Royal Palace, Rue Brederode 16, 1000 Brussels, Belgium. *Telephone:* (2) 551-20-20. *Website:* www.monarchie.be.

ALBERTI, Sir (Kurt) George Matthew Mayer, MA, DPhil, FRCP; British physician; *Chairman, King's College Hospital;* b. 27 Sept. 1937, Koblenz, Germany; s. of William Peter Matthew Alberti and Edith Elizabeth Alberti; m.

1st 1964; m. 2nd Stephanie Anne Amiel 1998; three s.; ed Univ. of Oxford; Research Fellow, Harvard Univ. 1966–69; Research Officer, Univ. of Oxford 1969–73; Prof. of Chemical Pathology, Univ. of Southampton 1973–78; Prof. of Clinical Biochemistry and Metabolic Medicine, Univ. of Newcastle 1978–85, Prof. of Medicine 1985–2002, Dean 1995–97; Prof. of Metabolic Medicine, Imperial Coll. London 1999–2002, Sr Research Fellow 2002–, Sr Research Investigator 2002–; Nat. Dir for Emergency Access, Dept of Health 2002–09; Chair. King's Coll. Hospital 2011–, Visiting Prof. 2013–; Dir Research and Devt, Northern and Yorkshire Regional Health Authority 1992–95; Chair. Diabetes UK; Pres. Royal Coll. of Physicians 1997–2002; Fellow, Acad. of Medicine, Singapore, Hong Kong, Coll. of Physicians, Sri Lanka, Thailand, SA; Hon. DMed (Arhus), (Southampton) 2000, (Athens) 2002; Hon. DSc (Cranfield) 2005, (Warwick) 2005. *Publications:* Ed. International Textbook of Diabetes Mellitus 1997 and more than 1,000 papers, reviews and edited books. *Leisure interests:* jogging, hillwalking, crime fiction, opera. *Address:* King's College Hospital, Denmark Hill, London, SE5 9RS (office); 57 Lancaster Avenue, West Norwood, London, SE27 9EL, England (home). *Telephone:* (20) 3299-9000 (office). *Fax:* (20) 3299-3445 (office). *E-mail:* george .alberti@nhs.net.

ALBERTSSON, Per-Åke, BSc, PhD; Swedish biochemist and academic; *Professor of Biochemistry, Lund University;* b. 19 March 1930, Skurup; s. of Albert Olsson and Frideborg Olsson; m. 1st Elisabet Godberg 1955 (divorced 1978); five s. one d.; m. 2nd Charlotte Erlanson 1978; three d.; ed Swedish High School, Ystad and Univs of Lund and Uppsala; Docent, Biochemistry, Univ. of Uppsala 1960, Lecturer 1963–65; Prof. of Biochemistry, Univ. of Umeå 1965–75; Prof. of Biochemistry, Lund Univ. 1975–; Research Zoologist, UCLA 1961–62; Visiting Prof., Stanford Univ. 1972–73, Univ. of Calif., Berkeley 1982–83; mem. Swedish Acad. of Sciences, Swedish Acad. of Eng Sciences, Royal Physiographic Soc. of Lund, Röda Kapellet (symphonic band), City Council of Lund 1991–94; Bd mem. Lunds Energi AB 1994–98, Thylabisco AB 2007–; Gold Medal, Swedish Acad. of Eng Sciences, Gold Medal, Swedish Chemical Soc., Norblad-Ekstrand Medal, Bror Holmberg Medal. *Publications include:* Partition of Cell Particles and Macromolecules 1960 (third edn 1986), Livets uppkomst 1968; more 170 scientific publs in journals. *Leisure interest:* playing music with flute and recorders. *Address:* Lund University, Department of Biochemistry and Structural Biology, Box 124, 22100 Lund, Sweden (office). *Telephone:* (46) 222-8190 (office). *Fax:* (46) 222-4116 (office). *E-mail:* Per-Ake.Albertsson@biochemistry.lu.se (office). *Website:* www.mps.lu.se (office).

ALBERTY, Robert Arnold, BS, MS, PhD, FAAS; American biophysical chemist and academic; *Professor Emeritus of Chemistry, Massachusetts Institute of Technology;* b. 21 June 1921, Winfield, Kan.; s. of Luman H. Alberty and Mattie Alberty (née Arnold); m. Lillian Jane Wind 1944; one s. two d.; ed Lincoln High School, Lincoln, Neb., Univ. of Nebraska and Univ. of Wisconsin; Instructor, Chem. Dept, Univ. of Wis. 1947–48, Asst Prof. 1948–50, Assoc. Prof. 1950–56, Prof. 1956–57, Assoc. Dean of Letters and Science 1962–63, Dean of Grad. School 1963–67; Prof. of Chem., MIT 1967–91, Prof. Emer. 1991–; Dean, School of Science 1967–82; Chair. Comm. on Human Resources, Nat. Research Council 1971–77; Dir Colt Industries 1978–88, Inst. for Defense Analysis 1980–86; Chair. Cttee on Chem. and Public Affairs, ACS 1980; Pres. Physical Chem. Div. IUPAC 1991–93; mem. NAS 1965–, American Acad. of Arts and Sciences 1968–, Inst. of Medicine 1973–; Dr hc (Nebraska) 1967, (Lawrence) 1967; Eli Lilly Award for research in enzyme kinetics 1956. *Publications:* Experimental Physical Chemistry (co-author) 1962, Physical Chemistry (co-author) 2001, Thermodynamics of Biochemical Reactions 2003, Biochemical Thermodynamics: Applications of Mathematica (Methods of Biochemical Analysis) 2006. *Leisure interest:* designing and building a summer cabin. *Address:* Massachusetts Institute of Technology, Room 6-215, 77 Massachusetts Avenue, Cambridge, MA 02139-4307 (office); 931 Massachusetts Avenue, Cambridge, MA 02139-3171, USA (home). *Telephone:* (617) 253-2456 (office). *Fax:* (617) 253-7030 (office). *E-mail:* alberty@mit.edu (office). *Website:* web .mit.edu/chemistry/www/index.html (office).

ALBERY, Tim; British theatre and opera director; b. 20 May 1952, *Plays directed include:* War Crimes 1981, Secret Gardens 1983, Venice Preserv'd 1983, Hedda Gabler 1984, The Princess of Cleves 1985, Mary Stuart 1988, As You Like It 1989, Berenice 1990, Wallenstein 1993, Macbeth 1996, Attempts on Her Life 1997, Nathan the Wise 2004. *Operas directed include:* (for ENO) Billy Budd 1988, Beatrice and Benedict 1990, Peter Grimes 1991, Lohengrin 1993, From the House of the Dead 1997, La Bohème 2000, War and Peace 2001, Boris Godunov 2008; (for Opera North) The Midsummer Marriage 1985, The Trojans 1986, La Finta Giardiniera 1989, Don Giovanni 1991, Don Carlos 1992, Luisa Miller 1995 Così fan tutte 1997, Katya Kabanova 1999, Così fan tutte 2004, One Touch of Venus 2004, 2005, Croesus 2007, Macbeth 2008; (for Welsh Nat. Opera) The Trojans 1987, Nabucco 1995; (for Scottish Opera) The Midsummer Marriage 1988, The Trojans 1990, Fidelio 1994, The King Goes 2003, Don Giovanni 2006; (for Australian Opera) The Marriage of Figaro 1992; (for Netherlands Opera) Benvenuto Cellini 1991, La Wally 1993, Beatrice and Benedict 2001; (for Bayerische Staatsoper) Peter Grimes 1993, Simon Boccanegra 1995, Ariadne Auf Naxos 1996; (for Batignano Festival, Italy) The Turn of the Screw 1983; (for Bregenz Festival, Austria) La Wally 1990; (for Royal Opera House) Cherubin 1994, The Flying Dutchman 2009, Tannhäuser 2010; (for Metropolitan Opera, New York) Midsummer Night's Dream 1996, The Merry Widow 2000; (for Minnesota Opera) Passion 2004; (for Canadian Opera Company, Toronto) Rodelinda 2005, Gotterdammerung 2006, War and Peace 2008; (for Reisopera, Netherlands) Nabucco 2008; (for Luminato Festival, Toronto) The Children's Crusade 2009, Prima Donna 2010; (for Dallas Opera) Otello 2009; (for Sadler's Wells, London) Prima Donna 2010; (for Santa Fe Opera) The Magic Flute 2010. *Address:* c/o Harriet Cruickshank, Cruickshank Cazenove, 97 Old South Lambeth Road, London, SW8 1XU, England (office). *Telephone:* (20) 7735-2933 (office). *Fax:* (20) 7582-6405 (office). *E-mail:* office@cruickshankcazenove.com (office).

ALBRECHT, Ernst Carl Julius, Dr rer. pol; German politician and economist (retd); b. 29 June 1930, Heidelberg; s. of Carl Albrecht, MD and Dr Adda Albrecht (née Berg); m. Dr Heidi Adele Stromeyer 1953; five s. two d.; ed Univs of Tübingen, Cornell, Basle, Bonn; Attaché to Council of Ministers, ECSC 1954; Sec. of Common Market section of Brussels conf. for preparation of Treaties of Rome 1956; CEO to EEC Commr Hans von der Groeben 1958; Deputy Head of Comm. del. at negotiations with Denmark, Ireland, Norway and UK for accession to EEC 1961–63; Dir-Gen. for Competition, EEC Comm. 1967–70; Financial Dir Bahlsens Keksfabrik, biscuit mfrs 1971–76; mem. Landtag (Parl.) for Lower Saxony 1970–90, Minister-Pres. of Lower Saxony 1976–90; personal consultant to Pres. and Prime Minister of Kyrgyzstan 1995–2005; mem. CDU; Grosskreuz der Bundesrepublik Deutschland. *Publication:* Der Staat – Idee und Wirklichkeit (The State – Idea and Reality) 1976–90, Erinnerungen (Memoirs) 1999. *Address:* Am Brink 2B, 31303 Burgdorf, Germany. *Telephone:* (5136) 977900 (office); (5136) 977900 (home). *Fax:* (5136) 977901 (office).

ALBRECHT, Karl; German business executive; b. 20 Feb. 1920, Essen; m.; two c.; served in Army during World War II; Co-f. Albrecht Discount (now ALDI) with brother Theo Albrecht 1948, fmr CEO ALDI Süd, Co-CEO ALDI Group –1994, Chair. 1994–2002. *Leisure interests:* golf, orchids. *Address:* c/o ALDI Group, Eckenbergstrasse 16, Postfach 13 01 110, 45307 Essen, Germany.

ALBRIGHT, Madeleine Korbel, BA, MA, PhD; American diplomatist, international affairs adviser and fmr government official; *Principal, Albright Group LLC;* b. 15 May 1937, Prague, Czechoslovakia; d. of Joseph Korbel and Anna Speeglova; m. Joseph Albright 1959 (divorced 1983); three d.; ed Wellesley Coll. and Columbia Univ.; Prof. of Int. Affairs, Georgetown Univ. 1982–83; Head, Center for Nat. Policy 1985–93; chief legis. asst to Democratic Senator Edmund Muskie 1976–78; mem. Nat. Security Council staff in Carter Admin 1978–81; adviser to Democrat cands Geraldine Ferraro 1984 and Michael Dukakis 1988; Perm. Rep. to UN 1993–97 (first foreign-born holder of this post); Sec. of State 1997–2001 (highest-ranking woman in history of US govt); Co-founder and Prin. The Albright Group LLC 2001–; Chair. Nat. Democratic Inst. for Int. Affairs, Washington, DC 2001–; Chair The PEW Global Attitudes Project; Pres. Truman Scholarship Foundation; mem. Bd NY Stock Exchange; mem. Council on Foreign Relations, American Political Science Asscn, American Asscn for Advancement of Slavic Studies; Presidential Medal of Freedom 2012. *Publications:* Poland: The Role of the Press in Political Change 1983, Madam Secretary: A Memoir 2003, The Mighty and the Almighty: Reflections on Faith, God and World Affairs 2006, Memo to the President Elect 2008, Read My Pins 2009, Prague Winter: A Personal Story of Remembrance and War 1937–1948 2012; numerous articles. *Address:* The Albright Group LLC, 901 15th Street, NW, Suite 1000, Washington, DC 20005, USA (office). *Telephone:* (202) 842-7222 (office). *Fax:* (202) 354-3888 (office). *Website:* www.thealbrightgroupllc.com (office).

ALBUQUERQUE, Maria Luís, MEconSc; Portuguese economist and politician; *Minister of State and of Finance;* b. 1967, Braga; ed Univ. Lusíada, Lisbon, Univ. Técnica de Lisboa; served for several years within Ministry of Finance, including as Sr Adviser, Directorate-Gen. of Treasury and Finance 1996–99, Adviser to Sec. of State for Treasury and Finance 2001, Dir, Dept of Financial Man. 2001–07, Head, Centre for Markets and Treasury Man., Inst. of Treasury and Public Credit 2007–11; Sec. of State for Treasury and Finance 2011–12, Sec. of the Treasury 2012–13, Minister of State and of Finance 2013–; Lecturer, Univ. Lusíada, Inst. of Econs and Man. and Setúbal Univ. Moderna 1991–2006; mem. Partido Social Democrata (PSD). *Address:* Ministry of Finance, Av. Infante D. Henrique 1, 1149-009 Lisbon, Portugal (office). *Telephone:* (21) 8816800 (office). *Fax:* (21) 8816862 (office). *E-mail:* gabinete.ministro@mf.gov.pt (office).

ALBURQUERQUE DE CASTRO, Rafael, DJur; Dominican Republic politician; *Vice-President;* b. 14 June 1940, Santo Domingo; ed Univ. of Santo Domingo, Sorbonne, Université de Paris, France; fmr Minister of Labour; Vice-Pres. of Dominican Repub. 2004–. *Address:* Administrative Secretariat of the Presidency, Palacio Nacional, Avenida México, esq. Dr Delgado, Santo Domingo, DN, Dominican Republic (office). *Telephone:* 686-4771 (office). *Fax:* 688-2100 (office). *E-mail:* prensa@presidencia.gov.do (office). *Website:* www.presidencia.gov.do (office).

ALCHAAR, Mohamed Nedal, PhD; Syrian economist; *Secretary-General, Accounting and Auditing Organisation for Islamic Financial Institutions;* fmr George Washington Univ., USA; fmr Dir of Market Performance Analysis, Fed. Nat. Mortgage Asscn (Fannie Mae), Washington, DC, USA; fmr Vice-Pres. Johnson & Higgins (insurance brokers), Washington, DC; fmr Lecturer, George Washington Univ.; currently Sec.-Gen. Accounting and Auditing Org. for Islamic Financial Insts. *Publications:* numerous books and articles on finance, monetary policy and exchange rate analysis. *Address:* Office of the Secretary-General, Accounting and Auditing Organisation for Islamic Financial Institutions, PO Box 1176, Manama, Bahrain (office). *Telephone:* (17) 244496 (office). *Fax:* (17) 250194 (office). *Website:* www.aaoifi.com (office).

ALCHOURON, Guillermo E.; Argentine farmer, lawyer and fmr politician; b. 4 Nov. 1933; m. María Elina Albin Etchart; two s. three d.; ed Univ. of Buenos Aires; farmer specializing in breeding of Dutch, Argentine and Jersey dairy cattle and milk production at Coronel Brandsen Estate; Pres. Asociación de Criadores de Holando Argentino 1966–69, 1975–77; mem. Bd of Dirs Argentine Rural Soc. 1969–96, Pres. 1984–90; Founder and Pres. Okita Foundation 1991; Pres. Inter-American Confed. of Farmers 1991–97; mem. Argentine Soc. of Jersey Dairy Cattle; Counsellor, Foundation for Latin American Econ. Research 1969; Adviser, Argentine Council for Int. Relations 1987; mem. Parl. (Acción de la República) 1999–2003; mem. Exec. Council, Int. Fed. of Agric. Producers; Gov. World Econ. Forum for Food and Farming Production; Pres. Agric. Soc.; mem. Acción por la República (AR); decorations from Spain, France, USA, Germany and Italy. *Leisure interests:* golf, tennis, cattle raising. *Website:* guillermoalchouron.com.

ALCKMIN, Geraldo José Rodrigues; Brazilian fmr anaesthesiologist and politician; *Governor, São Paulo State Government;* b. 7 Nov. 1952, Pindamonhangaba, São Paulo; m. Maria Lúcia Ribeiro Alckmin; three c.; ed Universidade de Taubaté Medical School; began political career as City Councillor, Pindamonhangaba aged 20, Mayor of Pindamonhangaba 1976–82 (youngest Brazilian mayor); sSate Congressman 1982–86; Fed. Congressman 1983–94, author of Law Project that became the 'Customer Defence Code'; Co-founder Brazilian Social Democracy Party (Partido da Social Democracia Brasileira—PSDB) 1988, Pres. in State of São Paulo 1991–94; Vice-Gov., State of São Paulo 1994–2001, Gov. 2001–06, 2010–, Sec. of Devt 2009–10; PSDB cand. in presidential elections Oct. 2006. *Address:* Governo do Estado de São Paulo, Av. Morumbi, 4500 São Paulo (office); c/o Partido da Social Democracia Brasileria, SGAS, Quadra 607, Edif. Metrópolis, Asa Sul,

70200-670 Brasília DF, Brazil. *Telephone:* (11) 2193-8000 (office); (11) 5078-4545. *Fax:* (11) 2193-8000 (office); (11) 5078-4545. *E-mail:* galckmin@sp.gov.br (office). *Website:* www.saopaulo.sp.gov.br (office); www.psdb-sp.org.br.

ALDA, Alan, BS; American actor; b. 28 Jan. 1936, New York; s. of the late Robert Alda and Joan Browne; m. Arlene Weiss; three d.; ed Fordham Univ.; performed with Second City 1963; Trustee Museum of TV and Radio, Rockefeller Foundation; Presidential Appointee, Nat. Comm. for Observance of Int. Women's Year 1976; Co-Chair. Nat. ERA Countdown Campaign 1982; five Emmy Awards (Best Actor, Best Dir and Best Writer), two Dirs' Guild Awards, Writers' Guild Award, seven People's Choice Awards, Humanitas Award for Writing, elected to TV Acad. Hall of Fame 1994. *Films include:* Gone Are the Days 1963, Paper Lion 1968, The Extraordinary Seaman 1968, The Moonshine War 1970, Jenny 1970, The Mephisto Waltz 1971, To Kill a Clown 1972, California Suite 1978, Same Time Next Year 1978, The Seduction of Joe Tynan (also wrote screenplay) 1979, Crimes and Misdemeanours (D.W. Griffith Award, NY Film Critics' Award) 1989, Whispers in the Dark 1992, And the Band Played On 1993, Manhattan Murder Mystery 1993, White Mile 1994, Canadian Bacon 1995, Everybody Says I Love You 1996, Murder at 1600 1997, Mad City 1997, The Object of My Affection 1998, What Women Want 2000, The Aviator 2004, Resurrecting the Champ 2007, Diminished Capacity 2008, Flash of Genius 2008, Nothing but the Truth 2008, Wanderlust 2011, Tower Heist 2011; actor, dir, writer of The Four Seasons 1981, Sweet Liberty 1986, A New Life 1987, Betsy's Wedding 1990. *Broadway appearances include:* The Owl and the Pussycat, Purlie Victorious, Fair Game for Lovers, The Apple Tree, Our Town (London) 1991, Jake's Women 1992, etc. *TV includes:* The Glass House 1972, M*A*S*H (five Golden Globe Awards) 1972–83, Tune in America 1975, Kill Me If You Can (film) 1977, E.R. 1999, Club Land 2001, The Killing Yard 2001, The West Wing (series) 2004–06, 30 Rock 2009; devised series We'll Get By 1975; Fair Game for Lovers (Theatre World Award); And The Band Played On 1993, White Mile 1994. *Publications include:* Never Have Your Dog Stuffed (memoir) 2006, Things I Overheard While Talking to Myself 2007. *Website:* www.alanalda.com.

ALDER, Berni Julian, PhD; American theoretical physicist; *Professor Emeritus of Applied Science, University of California, Davis;* b. 9 Sept. 1925, Duisburg, Germany; s. of Ludwig Alder and Ottilie Gottschalk; m. Esther Romella Berger 1956; two s. one d.; ed Univ. of California, Berkeley and California Inst. of Tech.; Instructor, Univ. of Calif., Berkeley 1951–54; Theoretical Physicist, Univ. of Calif. Lawrence Livermore Nat. Lab. 1955–93; Prof. of Applied Science, Univ. of California, Davis 1987–93, Prof. Emer. 1993–; NSF Sr Post Doctoral Fellow, Weizman Inst. (Israel) and Univ. of Rome 1963–64; Van der Waals Prof., Univ. of Amsterdam 1971; Guggenheim Fellow, Univ. of Cambridge, UK and Leiden, Netherlands 1954–55; Assoc. Prof., Univ. of Paris 1972; Hinshelwood Prof., Univ. of Oxford 1986; Lorentz Prof., Univ. of Leiden 1990; G.N. Lewis Lecturer 1984, Kistiakowsky Lecturer 1990, Royal Soc. Lecturer 1991, Grad. Lecturer 2000; Ed. Journal of Computational Physics; mem. NAS; Fellow, Japanese Promotion of Science 1989, American Physics Soc.; ACS Hildebrand Award 1985, Berni J. Alder Prize est. by European Physical Soc. 1999, IUPAP Boltzmann Prize 2002, Nat. Medal of Science 2009. *Publications include:* Methods of Computational Physics 1963, many chapters in books and articles in journals. *Leisure interests:* hiking, skiing, gardening. *Address:* Lawrence Livermore National Laboratory, PO Box 808, Livermore, CA 94551-0808 (office); 1245 Contra Costa Drive, El Cerrito, CA 94530, USA (home). *Telephone:* (925) 422-4384 (office); (510) 231-0137 (home). *Fax:* (925) 422-6594 (office). *E-mail:* alder1@llnl.gov (office). *Website:* www.llnl.gov (office).

ALDER, Jens, BSc, MBA; Swiss business executive; *Chairman of the Supervisory Board, RTX Telecom A/S;* b. 1957; ed Swiss Fed. Inst. of Tech. (ETH), Zürich, INSEAD, Fontainebleau, France; trained as electrical engineer; began career with Standard Telephon & Radio AG; various exec. positions Alcatel STR AG, Motor Columbus AG, Alcatel Schweiz AG; Head of Network Services Business Unit and mem. Man. Bd Swisscom AG 1998–99, CEO 1999–2006; Pres. and CEO TDC A/S 2006–08, Adviser 2008; Chair. Supervisory Bd, RTX Telecom A/S 2010–, mobilcom-debitel AG; mem. Bd of Dirs CA Technologies 2011–; Pres. Schweizerische Gesellschaft für Konjunkturforschung; mem. Man. Bd Swiss Information and Telecommunications Tech. Asscn (SICTA), Swiss Employers' Fed. *Leisure interest:* skiing. *Address:* RTX Telecom A/S, Strømmen 6, 9400 Norresundby, Denmark (office). *Website:* www.rtx.dk (office).

ALDERDICE, Baron (Life Peer), cr. 1996, of Knock, in the City of Belfast; **John Thomas Alderdice,** MB, BCh, BAO, FRCPsych, KCFO; British/Irish politician, researcher and psychiatrist (retd); *Convenor, Liberal Democrat Parliamentary Party, House of Lords;* b. 28 March 1955, Lurgan, Co. Antrim, Northern Ireland; s. of the late Rev. David Alderdice and of the late Helena Alderdice (née Shields); m. Joan Margaret (née Hill) 1977; two s. one d.; ed Ballymena Acad., Queen's Univ., Belfast; Royal Coll. of Psychiatrists; Consultant Psychiatrist in Psychotherapy, Eastern Health and Social Services Bd/Belfast Health & Social Care Trust (EHSSB/BH&SCT) 1988–2010; Dir NI Inst. of Human Relations 1991–94; Exec. Medical Dir, S and E Belfast Health and Social Services Trust 1993–97; mem. Alliance Party of NI 1978–2004, mem. Exec. Cttee 1984–98, Chair. Policy Cttee 1985–87, Vice-Chair. 1987, Leader 1987–98; contested Belfast E 1987, 1992, NI European Parl. elections 1989; Councillor, Belfast City Council 1989–97; Leader of Del. to Inter-Party and Inter-Govt Talks on the Future of NI 1991–98; Leader of Del. at Forum for Peace and Reconciliation (Dublin Castle) 1994–96; mem. NI Forum for Political Dialogue 1996–98; Vice-Pres. European Liberal Democrat and Reform Party 1999–2003, Exec. Cttee mem. 1987–2003, Treas. 1995–99; Vice-Pres. Liberal Int. 1992–99, Deputy Pres. 1999–2005, Pres. 2005–09, Chair. Human Rights Cttee 1999–2005; mem. House of Lords 1996–, currently Convenor Liberal Democrat Parliamentary Party; mem. NI Ass. (Belfast E) 1998–2002, Speaker 1998–2004 (Ass. suspended Oct. 2002–May 2007); Commr, Ind. Monitoring Comm. 2003–11; Visiting Prof., Dept of Psychiatry, Univ. of Virginia 2006–10; Sr Research Fellow and Dir, Centre for Resolution of Intractable Conflict, Harris Manchester Coll., Oxford 2012–; Chair. World Fed. of Scientists' Perm. Monitoring Panel on Motivation for Terrorism; Pres. ARTIS (Europe) Ltd, Westminster Pastoral Foundation; Co-Chair. Int. Dialogue Initiative; Vice-Chair. Gulf Policy Forum; Sr Adviser, Conflicts Forum; Adviser, Oxford Research Group; mem. Asscn of Psychoanalytic Psychotherapy, Advisory Bd, Centre for Reform; Trustee, Ulster Museum 1993–97, Nat. Liberal Club 2010– (Chair. Bd of Trustees 2011–); mem.

UK Cttee on Standards in Public Life 2010–; Hon. Lecturer/Sr Lecturer, Faculty of Medicine, Queen's Univ. Belfast 1991–99, Hon. Prof., Faculty of Medicine, Univ. of San Marcos, Lima (Peru) 1999; Hon. DLitt (Univ. of East London) 2008, Hon. LLD (Robert Gordon Univ., Scotland) 2009; W. Averell Harriman Award for Democracy 1998, John F. Kennedy Profiles in Courage Award 1998, Silver Medal of Congress of Peru 1999, Medal of Honour of Peru Coll. of Medicine 1999, Extraordinary Meritorious Service to Psychoanalysis, Int. Psychoanalytical Asscn 2005, Ettore Majorana Erice Prize, World Fed. of Scientists 2005. *Publications include:* articles on psychology of fundamentalism, radicalization, terrorism and violent political conflict. *Leisure interests:* music, singing, gastronomy, travel. *Address:* Harris Manchester College, Mansfield Road, Oxford, OX1 3TD (office); House of Lords, Westminster, London, SW1A 0PW, England (office). *Telephone:* (1865) 618081 (Oxford) (office); (20) 7219-5050 (London) (office). *E-mail:* john.alderdice@hmc.ox .ac.uk (office); alderdicej@parliament.uk (office). *Website:* www.parliament.uk/ biographies/lords/john-alderdice/26850 (office); www.lordalderdice.com.

ALDERS, Hans Gerardus Maria; Dutch politician; *President, EnergieNed;* b. 17 Dec. 1942, Nijmegen; ed vocational school; fmr jr man. in an employment agency; mem. Gelderland Prov. Ass. 1978, Leader Partij van de Arbeid (PvdA) Group 1979; elected mem. Parl. 1982, Sec. PvdA Parl. Group 1987–89; Minister of Housing, Physical Planning and the Environment 1989–94; Commr of the Queen, Prov. of Groningen 1996–2007; Pres. EnergieNed 2007–; also Pres. Supervisory Bd Univ. Medical Center Groningen; mem. Bd of Dirs Lysias Consulting Group, Nat. Foundation Sporttotalisator; mem. Bd of Legal Aid Assistance, Ministry of Justice. *Address:* EnergieNed, PO Box 9042, 6800GD Arnhem, Netherlands (office). *Telephone:* (26) 3569444 (office). *Fax:* (26) 4451347 (office). *E-mail:* secretariaat@ energiened.nl (office). *Website:* www.energiened.nl (office).

ALDINGER, William F., III, BA, JD; American business executive; b. 1947, Brooklyn, New York; s. of William F. Aldinger; four c.; ed Baruch Coll., City Coll., Brooklyn Law School; with US Trust Co. 1969–75; with Citibank Corpn 1975–86; Exec. Vice-Pres. Wells Fargo Bank 1986–92, Vice-Chair. 1992–94; Pres. and CEO Hongkong and Shanghai Banking Corpn (HSBC) (fmrly Household Int.) 1994–96, Chair. and CEO 1996–2005, Pres. and CEO HSBC North America Holdings Inc. 2004–05 (retd); Pres. and CEO Capmark Financial Group 2006–08, Consultant 2008–; mem. Bd of Dirs Children's Memorial Medical Centre, Children's Memorial Hosp., Children's Memorial Foundation, Business Advisory Council, Chicago Urban League, Evanston Northwestern Healthcare; Trustee, Northwestern Univ., J.L. Kellogg Grad. School of Man., Orchestral Asscn, Chicago Symphony Orchestra, Baruch Coll. Fund, Museum of Science and Industry, Chicago; mem. New York Bar, Chicago Club; Dr hc (Baruch Coll.) 2005; inducted into Chicago Business Hall of Fame 2002, Builder Award, Casa Cen.Community 2003, Distinguished Alumnus Award, Baruch Coll. 2004, Adam Smith Business Citizen Medal 2004, Harold H. Hines Award, United Negro Coll. Fund 2004. *Address:* c/o Capmark Financial Group, 116 Welsh Road, Horsham, PA 19044, USA.

ALDISS, Brian Wilson, OBE, FRSL; British writer, critic and actor; b. 18 Aug. 1925, Norfolk; m. 2nd Margaret Manson 1965 (died 1997); two s. two d.; ed Framlingham Coll. and West Buckland School; fmr soldier, draughtsman, bookseller and film critic; Literary Ed. Oxford Mail 1957–69; Pres. British Science Fiction Asscn 1960–65; Jt-Pres. European Science Fiction Cttees 1976–80; Chair. John W. Campbell Memorial Award 1976–77; Chair. Cttee of Man. Soc. of Authors 1977–78; mem. Literature Advisory Panel, Arts Council 1978–80; Chair. Cultural Exchanges Cttee of Authors 1978; Judge, Booker McConnell Prize 1981; Pres. World SF 1982–84; Ed. S.F. Horizons 1964–; Vice-Pres. H. G. Wells Soc., W. Buckland School 1997–; Hon. DLitt 2000; Ditmar Award for World's Best Contemporary Science Fiction Writer 1969, first James Blish Award for Excellence in Criticism 1977, Pilgrim Award 1978, John W. Campbell Award 1983, Kurt Lasswitz Award 1984, IAFA Distinguished Scholarship Award 1986, J. Lloyd Eaton Award 1988, Prix Utopia (France) 1999, Grand Master of Science Fiction 2000. *Opera:* Oedipus on Mars. *Plays (author):* SF Blues, Kindred Blood in Kensington Gore, Monsters of Every Day (Oxford Literary Festival) 2000, Drinks with The Spider King (Florida) 2000; acted in own productions 1985–2002. *Publications:* The Brightfount Diaries 1955, Space, Time & Nathaniel 1957, Non-Stop (Jules Verne Award 1977) 1958, The Male Response 1959, Hothouse (Hugo Award 1962) 1962, The Airs of Earth 1963, The Dark Light Years 1964, Greybeard 1964, Earthworks 1965, Best Science Fiction Stories of Brian W. Aldiss 1965, The Saliva Tree (Nebula Award) 1965, Cities and Stones: A Traveller's Jugoslavia 1966, Report on Probability A 1968, Barefoot in the Head 1969, Intangibles Inc., 1969, A Brian Aldiss Omnibus 1969, The Hand-Reared Boy 1970, The Shape of Further Things 1970, A Soldier Erect 1971, The Moment of Eclipse (British Science Fiction Asscn Award 1972) 1971, Brian Aldiss Omnibus 2 1971, Penguin Science Fiction Omnibus (ed.) 1973, Comic Inferno 1973, Billion Year Spree (III Merit Award 1976) 1973, Frankenstein Unbound (made into film directed by Roger Corman) 1973, The Eighty-Minute Hour 1974, Hell's Cartographers (ed.) 1975, Space Odysseys, Evil Earths, Science Fiction Art 1975, The Malacia Tapestry, Galactic Empires (two vols) 1976, Last Orders, Brothers of the Head 1977, Perilous Planets 1977, A Rude Awakening 1978, Enemies of the System 1978, This World and Nearer Ones 1979, Pile 1979, New Arrivals, Old Encounters 1979, Moreau's Other Island 1980, Life in the West 1980, An Island Called Moreau 1981, Foreign Bodies 1981, Helliconia Spring 1982, Science Fiction Quiz 1983, Helliconia Summer 1983, Seasons in Flight 1984, Helliconia Winter 1985, The Pale Shadow of Science 1985, . . . And the Lurid Glare of the Comet 1986, Trillion Year Spree (Hugo Award 1987) 1986, Ruins 1987, Forgotten Life 1988, Science Fiction Blues 1988, Best SF Stories of Brian W. Aldiss 1988, Cracken at Critical 1989, A Romance of the Equator 1990, Bury My Heart at W. H. Smith's 1990, Dracula Unbound 1991, Remembrance Day 1993, A Tupolev Too Far 1993, Somewhere East of Life 1994, The Detached Retina 1995, At the Caligula Hotel (poems) 1995, The Secret of this Book 1995, Songs from the Steppes of Central Asia 1996, The Twinkling of an Eye 1998, The Squire Quartet (four vols) 1998, When the Feast is Finished 1999, White Mars 1999, Supertoys Last All Summer Long (made into Kubrick–Spielberg film A.I. 2001) 2001, The Cretan Teat 2001, Super-State 2002, Researches and Churches in Serbia 2002, The Dark Sun Rises (poems) 2002, Affairs in Hampden Ferrers 2004, Jocasta 2005, Sanity and the Lady 2005, Cultural Breaks 2006, Harm 2007, A Science Fiction Omnibus (ed) 2007, A Prehistory of Mind 2008, Walcot 2010, Mortal Morning (poetry) 2011, An Exile on Planet Earth 2012, The

Friday Project 2012; contributions: TLS, Nature. *Leisure interests:* the past, the future, obscurity. *Address:* Hambleden, 39 St Andrew's Road, Old Headington, Oxford, OX3 9DL, England. *Telephone:* (1865) 762464. *E-mail:* aldiss.brian@gmail .com. *Website:* www.brianwaldiss.co.uk.

ALDOSHIN, Sergey Mikhailovich, DChem; Russian chemist; *Director, Institute of Problems of Chemical Physics; Vice-President, Russian Academy of Sciences;* b. 1953, Krasny Pochinski, Kadom Dist; ed Rostov State Univ.; Dir, Inst. of Problems of Chemical Physics, Chernogolovka 1997–; Vice-Dir Chernogolovka Br., Moscow State Univ., also Dean of Physical-Chemical Faculty; mem. Presidium, Russian Acad. of Sciences, currently also Vice-Pres.; Gold Medal for Contrib. to World Science and Int. Collaboration 2003, Russian Fed. Govt Award in Science and Eng. *Publications:* numerous scientific papers. *Address:* Institute of Problems of Chemical Physics, 1 Semenov av., 142432 Chernogolovka, Moscow Region, Russia (office). *Telephone:* (495) 993-57-07 (office). *Fax:* (496) 52-25-636 (office). *E-mail:* sma@icp.ac.ru (office). *Website:* www.icp.ac.ru (office).

ALDRIN, (Edwin Eugene) 'Buzz', Jr, DSc; American astronaut, author and scientist; *Chairman, Starcraft Enterprises;* b. 20 Jan. 1930, Montclair, NJ; s. of the late Col Edwin E. Aldrin and Marion Moon; m. 1st (divorced 1978); two s. one d.; m. 2nd Lois Driggs Cannon 1988; ed US Mil. Acad. and Massachusetts Inst. of Tech.; fmr mem. USAF; completed pilot training 1952; flew combat missions during Korean War; later became aerial gunnery instructor, Nellis Air Force Base, Nev.; attended Squadron Officers' School at Air Univ., Maxwell Air Force Base, Ala; later Flight Commdr 36th Tactical Fighter Wing, Bitburg, Germany; completed astronautics studies at MIT 1963; selected by NASA as astronaut 1963; Gemini Target Office, Air Force Space Systems Div., LA, Calif. 1963; later assigned to Manned Spacecraft Center, Houston, Tex.; pilot of backup crew for Gemini IX mission 1966; pilot for Gemini XII 1966; backup command module pilot for Apollo VIII; lunar module pilot for Apollo XI, landed on the moon 20 July 1969; Commdt Aerospace Research Pilot School 1971–72; Scientific Consultant, Beverly Hills Oil Co., LA; Chair. Starcraft Enterprises 1988–, Starcraft Boosters Inc. 1996–, ShareSpace Foundation 1998–, Nat. Space Soc.; Fellow, American Inst. of Aeronautics and Astronautics; retd from USAF 1972; Pres. Research & Eng Consultants Inc. 1972–; consultant to JRW, Jet Propulsion Lab.; Hon. mem. Royal Aeronautical Soc.; several hon. degrees; Medal of Freedom, USA and numerous other awards. *Publications:* First on the Moon: A Voyage with Neil Armstrong (with Michael Collins) 1970, Return to Earth (with Wayne Warga) 1974, Men From Earth (with Malcolm McConnell) 1989, Encounter with Tiber (with John Barnes) 1996, The Return (with John Barnes) 2000, Reaching for the Moon 2005, Magnificent Desolation 2009, Mission to Mars: My Vision for Space Exploration 2013. *Leisure interests:* scuba diving, snow skiing, star gazing. *Address:* 10380 Wilshire Boulevard, Suite 703, Los Angeles, CA 90024, USA (office). *Telephone:* (310) 278-0384 (office); (310) 278-0384 (home). *Fax:* (310) 278-0388 (office); (310) 278-0388 (home). *E-mail:* starbuzz2@aol.com (office). *Website:* www.buzzaldrin .com (office).

ALEKPEROV, Vagit Yusufovich, DEcon; Russian/Azerbaijani business executive; *President, Lukoil;* b. 1 Sept. 1950, Baku, Azerbaijan; m.; one s.; ed Azizbekov Inst. of Oil and Chem., Azerbaijan; worked in oil industry in Azerbaijan and Western Siberia 1968–75; worked as engineer for Kasporneft, Surgutneftegaz, Bashneft cos 1975–84; Dir Kogalymneftegas (oil-extraction co.) 1984–90; Deputy, then First Deputy Minister of Oil and Gas Industry of USSR 1990–91; Chair. Bd Imperial Bank, Petrocommerce Bank; Founder, mem. Bd of Dirs and Pres. OAO Lukoil 1993–, Chair. 1993–2000, currently Chair. Man. Cttee; Deputy Chair. Oil Exporters Union of Russia; Vice-Pres. Int. Oil Consortium; mem. Russian Acad. of Natural Sciences; awarded four orders and eight medals; winner of two Russian Govt prizes. *Publication:* Vertical Integrated Oil Companies in Russia. *Leisure interests:* travel, spending time with family and friends. *Address:* Lukoil, 101000 Moscow, Sretenskii bulv. 11, Russia (office). *Telephone:* (495) 627-44-44 (office). *Fax:* (495) 625-70-16 (office). *E-mail:* pr@lukoil.com (office); DepKadry@lukoil.com (office). *Website:* www.lukoil.com (office).

ALEKSANDROV, Aleksandr Pavlovich, PhD; Russian cosmonaut and pilot; b. 20 Feb. 1943, Moscow; m. Natalia Valentinovna Aleksandrova; one s. one d.; ed Baumann Tech. Inst., Moscow; mem. CPSU 1970; after service in Soviet Army started work with Space Programme 1964–; took part in elaboration of control system of spacecraft, Cosmonaut 1978–; participated in Soyuz-T and Salyut programmes; successfully completed 149-day flight to Salyut-7 orbital station with V. A. Lyakhov 1983 and effected spacewalk, July 1987, with A. Victorenko and M. Fares; joined Yurii Romanenko in space, returned to Earth Dec. 1987; completed 160-day flight on Mir Space Station; Chief, Dept of Crew Training and Extra Vehicular Activity at Energya design and production firm; Chief, NPO Energia Cosmonaut Group 1993–96; Chief, Flight Test Directorate, RKK Energiya im. S.P. Koroleva OAO 1996–2006, currently adviser to Pres.; mem. Extra Vehicular Activity Cttee, IAF 1994–; Academician, Int. Informatization Acad. 1997; Hero of Soviet Union 1983, 1987, Hero of Syria. *Address:* Office of the President, RKK Energiya im. S.P. Koroleva OAO, 141070 Korolev, ul. Lenina 4A, Moskovskaya Oblast (office); 129515 Moscow, Khovanskaya str. 3, 27, Russia. *Telephone:* (495) 513-72-48 (office); (495) 215-56-19 (home). *Fax:* (495) 513-61-38. *Website:* www .energia.ru (office).

ALEKSANDROV, Kiryll Sergeyevich, DPhysMathSc; Russian physicist; b. 9 Jan. 1931, St Petersburg; s. of Sergey Aleksandrov and Ljubov' Aleksandrov; m. Inga Chernjavskaja 1959; one d.; ed Leningrad Electrotech. Inst.; worked as researcher, Inst. of Crystallography; Researcher and Vice-Dir Kirensky Inst. of Physics, Siberian br. of USSR (now Russian) Acad. of Sciences, Krasnoyarsk 1958–83, Dir 1983–2003, currently mem. Scientific Council; Corresp. mem. USSR (now Russian) Acad. of Sciences 1971, mem. 1984, Counsellor 2004–; Chair. Scientific Council on Physics of Segnetoelectrics and Dielectrics, Dept of Gen. Physics and Astronomy, Russian Acad. of Sciences; Vice-Chair. Krasnoyarsk Scientific Centre of Russian Acad. of Sciences; USSR State Prize in Science 1989. *Publications:* Perovskite-like Crystals (co-author) 1997, Perovskites, Modern and Future (co-author) 2004; works in the field of crystal physics, structural phase transitions, physics of materials. *Leisure interests:* numismatics, mushroom hunting. *Address:* L. Kirensky Institute of Physics, 600036 Akademgorodok, Krasnoyarsk, Russia. *Telephone:* (3912) 43-26-35 (office); (3912) 44-41-75 (home).

Fax: (3912) 43-89-23 (home). *E-mail:* kaleks@iph.krasn.ru (office). *Website:* www.kirensky.ru (office).

ALEKSASHENKO, Sergey Vladimirovich, BA, PhD; Russian investment banker, academic and fmr government official; *Director of Macroeconomic Research, Higher School of Economics, National Research University;* b. 23 Dec. 1959, Likino-Dulevo, Moscow Region; m.; two c.; ed Moscow State Univ.; mem. of staff, Moscow Inst. of Econs and Math., USSR Acad. of Sciences 1986–90; leading expert, USSR State Comm. on Econ. Reform; Exec. Dir Inst. of Russian Union of Industrialists and Entrepreneurs 1991–93, Dir-Gen. 1995; Deputy Minister of Finance 1993–95; Pres. Russian Foreign Exchange Market Asscn 1995; Dir-Gen. Expert Univ. RSPP 1995, mem. Scientific Council 1995; First Deputy Chair. Cen. Bank of Russian Fed. 1995–98; Chair. Audit Comm.; Chair. Asscn of Current Stock Exchanges of Russia 1995–; First Deputy Chair. Observation Council Savings Bank 1996–99; Head of Centre of Devt Analytical Group 1999–; Deputy Dir-Gen. Interros (holding co.) 2000–04, Man. Dir 2004; Pres. Antanta Capital Investment Group 2004; Man. Dir and Head of Moscow Rep. Office, Merrill Lynch Investment Bank 2006–08; Dir of Macroeconomic Research, Higher School of Econs, Nat. Research Univ. 2008–; mem. Bd of Dirs OJSC Aeroflot 2008–, Russian National Reserve Bank 2009–; fmr Scholar-in-Residence, Econ. Policy Program, Carnegie Moscow Center; fmr mem. Advisory Council to Chair. of Cen. Bank, Expert Council, Accounts Chamber of Russian Fed.; Hon. Prof., Jilin Univ., China 1997. *Publications include:* Battle for the Rouble, Alma Mater; over 100 publs on fiscal and econ. matters. *Leisure interests:* photography, diving. *Address:* Higher School of Economics, Moscow 109028, Office E 302, 11 Pokrovskiy Bulvar, Russia (office). *Telephone:* (495) 771-3254 (office). *Fax:* (495) 771-3254 (office). *E-mail:* aleksashenko@hse.ru (office). *Website:* www.hse.ru/en (office).

ALEKSEEV, Aleksander Yuryevich; Russian diplomatist and politician; *Permanent Representative, Council of Europe;* b. 20 Aug. 1946, Moscow; m.; one d.; ed Moscow Inst. of Int. Relations; diplomatic posts abroad, including in India and in Ministry of Foreign Affairs of USSR and Russia; Amb. to Pakistan 1993; Dir 3 Asian Dept, Ministry of Foreign Affairs; Perm. Rep. to OSCE 2001–04; Deputy Minister of Foreign Affairs 2004–07; Amb. and Perm. Rep. to Council of Europe, Strasbourg 2007–. *Address:* Permanent Representation of the Russian Federation to the Council of Europe, 75 allée de la Robertsau, 67000 Strasbourg, France (office). *Telephone:* (388) 24-20-15 (office). *Fax:* (388) 24-19-74 (office). *E-mail:* representationpermderussie@wanadoo.fr (office). *Website:* www.coe.mid.ru (office).

ALEKSEEVA, Tatyana Ivanovna, DrSc, PhD; Russian anthropologist, biologist and academic; *Principal Researcher, Research Institute and Museum of Anthropology, Moscow State University;* b. 7 Dec. 1928, Kazan; d. of Ivan Sharabrin and Varvara Majorova; m. Valery Alekseev (deceased); ed Moscow State Univ.; Jr, Sr, Leading, Prin. Researcher, Research Inst. and Museum of Anthropology 1955–; Prin. Researcher, Inst. of Archaeology 1992–; Corresp. mem. USSR (now Russian) Acad. of Sciences 1991, mem. 2000–; research in study of influence of geographical and social medium on aboriginal population; mem. Asscn of Human Biologists; Pres. Russian br. of European Anthropological Asscn; Foreign mem., Montenegro Acad. of Science and Art; Hon. mem. World Org. of Mongolian Studies 1997; Hon. Res., Moscow State Univ. 1997; Order of Friendship 1999; Medal of Moscow 1997. *Publications include:* Origin and Ethnic History of Russian People 1965, Ethnogenesis of East Slavs 1973, Geographical Medium and Biology of Man 1977, Adaptive Processes in Populations of Man 1986, Neolithic Population of the Eastern Europe Forest Zone 1997, Eastern Slavs: Anthropology and Ethnic History 1999, Homo Sungirensis Upper Palaeolithic Man: Ecological and Evolutionary Aspects of the Investigation 2000, Anthropology of Medieval Vlakhs in Comparative Study: on data on Mistikhaly Burial Site 2003. *Leisure interests:* riding, pets. *Address:* Research Institute and Museum of Anthropology, Moscow State University, 125009 Moscow, Mokhovaya str. 11 (office); 119420 Moscow, ul. Profsoyuzhaya 43-1, Apt 125, Russia (home). *Telephone:* (495) 203-35-98 (office); (495) 331-32-73 (home). *Fax:* (495) 203-3554 (office). *E-mail:* homo@antropos.msu.ru (office).

ALEKSEYEV, Sergey Sergeyevich, DJur; Russian lawyer; *Chairman, Council of Research Centre of Private Law;* b. 28 July 1924; m.; two d.; ed Sverdlovsk Inst. of Law; teacher, then Prof. Sverdlovsk (now Yekaterinburg) Inst. of Law 1949–; Dir Inst. of Philosophy and Law, Ural Div. of USSR (now Russian) Acad. of Sciences; Corresp. mem. USSR (now Russian) Acad. of Sciences 1987; USSR People's Deputy 1990–91; Chair. USSR Cttee of Constitutional Inspection 1990–91; Chair. Council of Research Centre of Pvt. Law 1992–; author (with A. Sobchak) of one of projects of Constitution of Russia 1991–92; mem. Presidential Council of Russia 1993–95; USSR State Prize, Merited Worker of Science of Russia. *Publications include:* General Theory of Law (Vols 1–2), 1981–82, Theory of Law: Constitutional Concept 1991, Legal Civil Soc. 1991. *Leisure interests:* tourism, mountain skiing, reading. *Address:* Research Centre of Private Law, Yekaterinburg Branch, 620146 Yekaterinburg, Russia (office). *Telephone:* (3432) 28-89-81 (office).

ALEKSIEVICH, Svetlana; Belarusian journalist and writer; b. 31 May 1948, Minsk, Ukraine; ed Minsk Univ.; worked as journalist on local newspaper in early 1970s; Kurt Tucholsky Prize, Swedish PEN Club, Stockholm 1996, Andrej Sinjavskij Prize, Moscow 1997, Triumph Prize 1998, European Understanding Prize for contrib. to a better understanding among European nations 1998, 'Témoin du Monde', Paris 1999, Erich Maria Remarque Peace Prize (Germany) 2001, Nat. Book Critics' Circle Award, New York 2006, Oxfam Novib PEN Award 2007. *Publications include:* non-fiction: Aposhniya svedki. kniga nedzitsyachyh raskaza? 1985, U voyny ne zhenskoe litso (The War's Unwomanly Face) 1985, Tsinkovye mal'chiki (Zinky Boys: Soviet Voices from a Forgotten War) 1991, Zacharavanyya smertsu (Enchanted with Death) 1993, Poslednie svideteli (The Last Witnesses), Charnobyl'skaya malitva (trans. as Chernobyl Prayer: A Chronicle of the Future) 1997. *Address:* c/o Galina Dursthoff, Marsiliusstr. 70, 50937 Cologne, Germany. *E-mail:* svett_al@hotmail.com; galina@dursthoff.de. *Website:* alexievich.info.

ALEKSISHVILI, Aleksi, MPA; Georgian politician and consultant; *Chairman, Policy and Management Consulting Group;* b. 21 Feb. 1974; m.; one s. one d.; ed Tbilisi State Univ. and Duke Univ., USA; spent five years at Faculty of Econ. Relations, Tbilisi State Univ. 1991–96; fmr Deputy Minister of Finance and First-

Deputy Minister of Finance; Pres. Young Economists Soc. of Georgia 1994–2001; Minister of Econ. Devt 2004–2005; Minister of Finance 2005–07; Gov. for Georgia, IMF and World Bank 2005; mem. Bd of Dirs Nat. Bank of Georgia 2007–08; Chair. UN Comm. on Sustainable Devt 2005–06; Chair. Policy and Management Consulting Group 2007–; PIDP Fellow 2002–04. *Address:* Policy and Management Consulting Group, 57 Uznadze Street, 4th floor, 0102 Tbilisi, Georgia (office). *Telephone:* (322) 92-11-71 (office). *E-mail:* a.aleksishvili@pmcg.ge (office). *Website:* www.pmcg-i.com (office).

ALEMÁN GURDIÁN, Juan Daniel, BLaw&SocSci, DrIntLaw; Guatemalan/Salvadorean (b. Nicaraguan) lawyer, international organization official and academic; *Secretary-General, Central American Integration System (Sistema de la Integración Centroamericana—SICA);* b. 28 Aug. 1956, Leon, Nicaragua; m. Silvia Elizabeth Cáceres Vettorazzi; two s.; ed Universidad Rafael Landívar, Guatemala, Univ. of Navarre, Pamplona, Spain; moved to Guatemala City and became Guatemalan citizen 1973; Pres. Law Students' Asscn 1978–79; participated in summer seminars in Univs of London, UK and Nice, France; began professional career as Tax Dept Man., Peat Marwick & Mitchell (law firm), Guatemala; began career as Univ. Lecturer in Faculty of Law, Universidad Rafael Landívar, later held Chair of Int. Public Law and Business Law; also taught Int. Econ. Law at Inst. of Int. Relations, Universidad Francisco Marroquin, Guatemala, later became its Dir; apptd Adjoint Sec.-Gen. Cen. American Econ. Integration Secr. (SIECA), Guatemala City 1991; left office in SIECA to fill Policy Secr. of Presidency of Repub. of Guatemala; granted incorporation as advocate and notary of Repub. of Nicaragua 1994; moved to San Salvador to serve as Corp. Advocate of SIGMA/Q group (Cen. American co.) 1995, served as Sec., Bd and mem. Strategic Cttee; Visiting Prof. of Business Ethics, Escuela Superior de Negocios (ESEN), El Salvador 2001; granted Salvadorean nationality 2001; authorized to practise as lawyer and notary in El Salvador 2004; Sec.-Gen. Cen. American Integration System (Sistema de la Integración Centroamericana— SICA) 2009–; mem. Chamber of Industry of Guatemala, Training Centre of Guatemala (TAYASAL); Sec., Bd Centre for Nat. Econ. Research of Guatemala (CIEN); Founding mem., Dir and Chair. Cttee of Legal Studies, Salvadoran Foundation for Econ. and Social Devt (FUSADES). *Publications:* regular contrib. to specialized publs. *Address:* Sistema de la Integración Centroamericana (SICA), Boulevard Orden de Malta, No. 470, Urbanización Santa Elena, Antiguo Cuscatlán, El Salvador (office). *Telephone:* 2248-8801 (office). *Fax:* 2248-8899 (office). *E-mail:* info.sgsica@sica.int (office). *Website:* www.sica.int (office); www.sica.int/sgsica (office).

ALEMÁN HEALY, José Miguel, BA, JD; Panamanian lawyer and fmr government official; *Partner, Arias, Alemán & Mora;* b. 8 May 1956; ed Ripon Coll., Wis., Tulane Univ., USA; admitted to Bar 1981; Vice-Pres. Panamanian Bar Asscn 1990–91; Chair. Fourth Annual Lawyers Congress 1990; Vice-Minister of Govt and Justice 1991, Minister of Foreign Affairs 1999–2002; unsuccessful cand. for Pres. (Vision of the Country) 2004; currently Pnr, Arias, Alemán & Mora (law firm); mem. Bd of Dirs Multi Credit Bank Inc., Compañía Nacional de Seguros, SA, Banex Int. SA, Costa Rica. *Address:* Arias, Alemán & Mora, St Georges Bank & Company Building, 16th Floor, POB 0830-1580, Panamá 9, Panama (office). *Telephone:* 270-1011 (office). *Fax:* 270-0174 (office). *E-mail:* jaleman@aramolaw.com (office). *Website:* www.aramolaw.com (office).

ALEMÁN LACAYO, Arnoldo; Nicaraguan lawyer, politician and fmr head of state; b. 23 Jan. 1946, Managua; m. 1st Maria Dolores Cardenal Vargas (died 1989); two s. two d.; m. 2nd Maria Fernanda Flores Lanzas; one s. two d.; ed Nat. Autonomous Univ. of Leon; fmr Leader pro-Somoza Liberal Student Youth Org. during 1960s; served as lawyer 1968–79; imprisoned for alleged counter-revolutionary activity 1980, placed under house arrest 1989; Mayor of Managua 1990; Pres. Fed. of Cen. American Municipalities 1993–95; Leader, Liberal Party Alliance 1996; Pres. of Nicaragua 1997–2001; sentenced to 20 years' imprisonment for corruption Dec. 2003, corruption sentence overturned 2009; Pres. Asociación de Cafetaleros de Managua 1983–90, Unión de Cafetaleros de Nicaragua 1986–90, Federación de Municipios de América Cen. 1992–93, Federación Municipal de Ciudades de Centroamérica 1993–95; Vice-Pres. Unión de Productores Agropecuarios de Nicaragua 1986–90; mem. Consejo Superior de la Empresa Privada 1988–90; Orden Nacional al Mérito, Colombia, Orden de Isabel la Católica, Spain.

ALEMANNO, Gianni, BEng; Italian politician; *Mayor of Rome;* b. 3 March 1958, Bari; m. Isabella Rauti; one s.; ed Univ. of Rome; Prov. Sec., Fronte della Gioventù di Roma 1982; Sec., Movimento Sociale Italiano Youth Div. 1988; fmr mem. Exec. Bd Alleanza Nazionale, becoming Nat. Co-ordinator for Econ. and Social Policy and Vice-Pres., Pres. Rome Div. 2007–; mem. Lazio Regional Council 1990, becoming Vice-Pres. Industrial, Commercial and Trades Comm.; mem. Chamber of Deputies (Parl.) 1994–; Minister of Agric. and Forestry 2001–06; unsuccessful cand. for Mayor of Rome 2006, Mayor of Rome 2008–; Pres. Euro-Mediterranean Conf. on Fisheries and Agric. 2003; Pres. Fondazione Nuova Italia 2006–; f. Area (monthly journal); Dir Aspen Institut Italia; mem. Club alpino italiano; Hon. mem. Kadima World Italia. *Publication:* Intervista sulla destra sociale 2002. *Leisure interest:* mountaineering. *Address:* via Antonio Salandra 18, 00186 Rome (office); Comune di Roma, Via di Campodoglio 1, 00100 Rome; Camera dei Deputati, Palazzo di Montecitorio, 00186 Rome, Italy (office). *Telephone:* (06) 42275000 (office); (06) 0606. *Fax:* (06) 67103590. *Website:* duepuntozero.alemanno.it; www.comune.roma.it.

ALENCHERRY, HE Cardinal George, PhD; Indian ecclesiastic and academic; *Major Archbishop of Ernakulam-Angamaly (Syro-Malabarese);* b. 19 April 1945, Thuruthy, Changanacherry; ed Pontifical Ecclesiastical Seminary of St Joseph, Alwaye, Institut Catholique de Paris, France; ordained priest 1972; served as Sec. of Archeparch of Changanacherry and Asst Pastor of the Cathedral, as well as Dir of Sunday Schools in the archeparchy; apptd Dir of Centre for Catechesis; then directed Pastoral Orientation Centre, Cochin, inter-ritual, of the Kerala Catholic Bishops' Conf.; served as a Prof. of Pastoral Counselling and Systematic Theology, Faculty of Paurastya Vidyapitham, Pontifical Oriental Inst. of Religious Studies, Vadavathoor, Kottayam, and at Pontifical Inst. of Theology and Philosophy, Alwaye; Vicar-Gen. of the archeparchy 1996–97; Bishop of Thuckalay (Syro-Malabarese) 1996–2011, Major Archbishop of Ernakulam-Angamaly (Syro-Malabarese) 2011–; cr. Cardinal (Cardinal-Priest of San Bernardo alle Terme) 2012; Patriarch of Mar Thoma Nasranis and the Gate of All India; participated in

Papal Conclave (one of four cardinal-electors from outside the Latin Church) 2013. *Address:* Major Archbishop's House, PO Box 2580, Broadway, Ernakulam Kochi 682 031, Kerala, India (office). *Telephone:* (484) 2352629 (office); (484) 2352906 (office). *Fax:* (484) 2355010 (office); (484) 2366028 (office). *E-mail:* curia@ernakulamarchdiocese.org (office). *Website:* www.ernakulamarchdiocese.org (office).

ALESHIN, Boris S.; Russian business executive and fmr politician; *General Director, N.E. Zhukovsky Central Aerohydrodynamic Institute;* b. 3 March 1955; ed Moscow Physics and Tech. Inst.; held several positions at Scientific Research Inst. of Automatic Systems, including Lead Engineer, Sr Researcher, Chief of Sector, Chief of Lab., Head of Div. 1982–90; Commercial Dir State Scientific Research Inst. of Aviation Systems 1990–98, Sales Dir 1998–2000; Chair. State Cttee for Standardization and Metrology 2001–03; Deputy Prime Minister responsible for Industrial Policy 2003–04; Chair. Comm. on Export Control of Russian Fed. 2003–04; Head of Rosprom (Fed. Agency for Industry) 2004–07; Pres. and Deputy Chair. AvtoVAZ (Volga Automobile Plant) OAO 2007, Chair. GM-AVTOVAZ Jt Venture 2008–09; currently Gen. Dir N.E. Zhukovsky Central Aerohydrodynamic Inst.; mem. Man. Bd JSCB Novikombank; Assoc. Mem. Russian Acad. of Sciences fmr Chair. Russian-Uzbek Govt Comm.;*Website:* www.tsagi.com.

ALESKEROV, Shamil, PhD; Azerbaijani government official and international organization official; *Secretary-General, Economic Cooperation Organization (ECO);* b. 29 March 1946, Baku; m. Nabinna Alaskarova; two s.; ed Azerbaijan Oil and Chemistry Inst.; Engineer, Sr Engineer, Jr Research Fellow, Azerbaijan Energy Research and Devt Inst., USSR Ministry of Energy, Baku 1968–78; Industrial Devt Officer, Dept for Projects and Program Devt, Secr. UNIDO, Vienna 1981–87; Deputy Dir-Gen., State Foreign Trade Asscn 1988–92; Chief of Div., Dept of Int. Econ. Relations, Ministry of Foreign Affairs 1992–94, Deputy Head 1996–97; Sr Consultant (econ. service), Office of the Pres. 1994–96; Asst to Sec.-Gen. (projects coordinator), Org. of Black Sea Econ. Cooperation 1997–2000; Deputy Sec.-Gen. and Dir, Dept of Energy, Minerals and Environment, ECO 2000–06, Sec.-Gen. ECO 2012–; Amb.-at-Large for energy cooperation and regional econ. orgs, Ministry of Foreign Affairs 2006–09; Deputy Perm. Rep., Perm. Mission to Int. Orgs in Vienna (UN, UNIDO, IAEA, OSCE) 2009–12. *Address:* Economic Cooperation Organization, No. 1, Golbou Alley, Kamranieh Street, Tehran 19519-33114, Iran (office). *Telephone:* (22) 831733 (office). *Fax:* (22) 831732 (office). *E-mail:* Registry@ecosecretariat.org (office). *Website:* www.ecosecretariat.org (office).

ALEXANDER, (Andrew) Lamar, BA, JD; American politician; *Senator from Tennessee;* b. 3 July 1940, Maryville, Tenn.; s. of Andrew Lamar Alexander and Genevra F. Rankin; m. Leslee K. (Honey) Buhler 1969; two s. two d.; ed Vanderbilt and New York Univs; mem. Bar of La. and Tenn.; law clerk to presiding justice, US Court of Appeals (5th Circuit), New Orleans; Assoc., Fowler, Rountree, Fowler & Robertson (law firm), Knoxville 1965; Legis. Asst to Senator Howard Baker, US Senate, Washington, DC 1967–68; Exec. Asst to Bryce Harlow, White House Congressional Liaison Office 1969–70; Pnr, Dearborn & Ewing (law firm), Nashville 1971–78; Gov. of Tenn. 1979–87; Chair. Leadership Inst., Belmont Coll., Nashville 1987–88; Pres. Univ. of Tennessee 1988–90; Sec. of Educ. 1991–93; Counsel, Baker, Donelson, Bearman and Caldwell (law firm) 1993–98; in pvt. legal practice 1999–; Senator from Tenn. 2003–, Chair. Senate Republican Conf. 2007–12; mem. Pres.'s Task Force on Federalism; Chair. Nat. Govs Asscn 1985–86, Pres.'s Comm. on Americans Outdoors 1985–87, Republican Satellite Exchange Network 1993–95; mem. Bd of Dirs Corporate Child Care Inc., Nashville, Martin Marietta Corpn Bethesda, Md; Chair. Republican Neighborhood Meeting 1993; Republican; named by TIME magazine amongst 200 Faces of the Future 1974; numerous awards, including Award of Appreciation, Southern Asscn of Student Financial Aid Admins 2010, Certificate of Appreciation, Citizens for Fort Campbell 2010, Award for Distinguished Public Service, Inst. of Electrical and Electronics Engineers Inc., USA 2010, Spirit of Enterprise Award, US Chamber of Commerce 2010, Corridor Champion Award, Tennessee Valley Corridor 2010, Pres.'s Award, Nat. Music Publrs' Asscn 2010, Distinguished Leadership Award, Nuclear Infrastructure Council 2010, Thomas Jefferson Award, Int. Foodservice Distributors Asscn 2010, Spirit of Enterprise Award, US Chamber of Commerce 2011, Guardian of Small Business Award, Nat. Fed. of Ind. Business 2012. *Publications:* Steps Along the Way 1986, Six Months Off 1988, We Know What We Do 1995. *Leisure interest:* piano. *Address:* 455 Dirksen Senate Office Building, Washington, DC 20510 (office); 3322 West End Avenue, #120, Nashville, TN 37203, USA. *Telephone:* (202) 224-4944 (office); (615) 736-5129. *Fax:* (202) 228-3398 (office); (615) 269-4803. *Website:* alexander.senate.gov (office); www.lamaralexander.com.

ALEXANDER, Anthony J., BS, LLB, JD; American lawyer and business executive; *President and CEO, FirstEnergy Corporation;* b. 1951, Akron, Ohio; m. Becky Alexander; four s.; ed Univ. of Akron, Harvard Univ. Law School, Massachusetts Inst. of Tech.; fmr Dir, COO and Head of UK Operations, Hanson PLC; Exec. Ohio Edison Co. (merged with other utility cos into FirstEnergy Corpn 1997) 1972–89, Vice-Pres., Gen. Counsel 1989–91, Sr Vice-Pres., Gen. Counsel 1991–96, Exec. Vice-Pres., Gen. Counsel 1996–97, currently mem. Bd of Dirs; Exec. Vice-Pres., Gen. Counsel FirstEnergy Corpn 1999–2000, Pres. 2000–01, COO 2001–04, Dir 2002–, Acting CEO 2003–04, Pres. and CEO 2004–; Exec. Vice-Pres. and Gen. Counsel Toledo Edison 1997–2000; Exec. Vice-Pres. and Gen. Counsel Pennsylvania Power Co. 1999–2000, Pres. 2000–, CEO 2004–; Pres. Cleveland Electric Illuminating Co. 2000–, CEO 2004–; Pres. Pennsylvania Electric Co. 2002–, CEO 2004–; Pres. and CEO Metropolitan Edison Co. 2004–; CEO, Pres. and Man. of JCP and Transition Funding LLC 2004–; mem. Bd of Dirs Team NEO, Ohio Electric Utility Inst., Asscn of Edison Illuminating Cos, Inc.; mem. Republican Nat. Cttee's Team 100 2000; apptd to US Energy Dept Transition Team by Pres. George W. Bush 2000; currently Vice-Chair. Greater Akron Chamber; Dir-at-Large Nat. Asscn of Mfrs; Dir Nuclear Energy Inst.; mem. Ohio Business Roundtable; mem. Bd of Trustees Akron Tomorrow, Team NEO; Dr Frank L. Simonetti Distinguished Business Alumni Award, Univ. of Akron. *Address:* FirstEnergy Corporation, 76 South Main Street, Akron, OH 44308, USA (office). *Telephone:* (800) 633-4766 (office). *Fax:* (330) 384-3866 (office). *E-mail:* thowson@firstenergycorp.com (office). *Website:* www.firstenergycorp.com (office).

ALEXANDER, Bill, BA; British theatre director; b. (William Alexander Paterson), 23 Feb. 1948, Hunstanton, Norfolk, England; s. of Bill Paterson and

Rosemary Paterson; m. Juliet Harmer 1978; two d.; ed St Lawrence Coll. Ramsgate and Keele Univ.; began career at Bristol Old Vic directing Shakespeare and the classics and contemporary drama; joined RSC 1977, Assoc. Dir 1978–91, Hon. Assoc. Artistic Dir 1991–; productions for RSC include: Tartuffe, Richard III 1984, Volpone, The Accrington Pals, Clay, Captain Swing, School of Night, A Midsummer Night's Dream, The Merry Wives of Windsor; other theatre work at Nottingham Playhouse, Royal Court Theatre, Victory Theatre, New York and Shakespeare Theatre, Washington, DC; Artistic Dir Birmingham Repertory Co. 1993–2000, productions include: Othello, The Snowman, Macbeth, Dr. Jekyll and Mr. Hyde, The Alchemist, Awake and Sing, The Way of the World, Divine Right, The Merchant of Venice, Old Times, Frozen, Hamlet, The Tempest, The Four Alice Bakers, Jumpers, Nativity (co-author) 1999, Quarantine 2000, Twelfth Night 2000, An Enemy of the People (Theatre Clwyd) 2002, Frozen, Mappa Mundi (Royal Nat. Theatre) 2002, The Importance of Being Ernest (Northampton) 2002, Titus Andronicus (RSC) 2003, King Lear (RSC) 2004, The School of Night (Mark Taper Forum, Los Angeles) 2008, Glamour (Nottingham Playhouse) 2009; Olivier Award for Dir of the Year 1986. *Film:* The Snowman 1998. *Leisure interest:* tennis. *Address:* Rose Cottage, Tunley, Glos., GL7 6LP, England (home). *Telephone:* (1285) 760555 (office). *Fax:* (1285) 760494 (office). *E-mail:* bill2juliet@btinternet.com (office).

ALEXANDER, Brooke, BA; American art dealer and publisher; b. 26 April 1937, Los Angeles; s. of Richard H. Alexander and Marion C. Alexander; m. Carolyn Rankin 1967; two d.; ed Yale Univ.; f. Brooke Alexander Inc. to publish and distribute graphic art 1968, expanded co. 1975; f. Brooke Alexander Editions, opened separate gallery for graphics 1989; partner in Madrid gallery, Galería Weber, Alexander y Cobo 1991–; mem. Governing Bd Yale Univ. Art Gallery 1988–. *Address:* Brooke Alexander Editions, 59 Wooster Street, New York, NY 10012-4349, USA (office). *Telephone:* (212) 925-4338 (office). *Fax:* (212) 941-9565 (office). *E-mail:* info@baeditions.com (office). *Website:* www.baeditions.com (office).

ALEXANDER, Christopher, BS, MS, PhD; British architect, academic, consultant and writer; *Professor in the Graduate School and Professor Emeritus of Architecture, University of California, Berkeley;* b. 4 Oct. 1936, Vienna, Austria; m. Margaret Moore 2008; two d.; ed Oundle, Trinity Coll., Cambridge, Harvard Univ.; fmrly with Center for Cognitive Studies, Harvard Univ., with Jt Center for Urban Studies, Harvard Univ. and MIT 1959–63; Prof. of Architecture, Univ. of Calif., Berkeley 1963, now Prof. Emer., Research Prof. in the Humanities 1965, Prof. in Grad. School, 1998–; Visiting Fellow, Rockefeller Foundation Villa Serbelloni 1965; Founder, Pres., Dir Center for Environmental Structure 1967–; Trustee, Prince of Wales's Inst. for Architecture 1991–97; Chair. Bd of Dirs PatternLanguage.com, Berkeley, Calif. 1999–; Fellow, Harvard Univ. 1961–64, American Acad. of Arts and Sciences 1996; mem. Swedish Royal Acad. 1980–; Best Bldg in Japan Award 1985, Seaside Prize 1994, Nat. Building Museum Vincent Scully Prize 2009, numerous other awards and prizes. *Major works include:* 35 bldgs of New Eishin Univ., Tokyo, Linz Café, Linz, village school, Gujarat, low-cost housing in Mexico and Peru, Shelter for the Homeless, San José, numerous pvt. houses and public bldgs on four continents; Center for Environmental Structure has undertaken around 200 projects, including town and community planning world-wide. *Publications include:* Notes on the Synthesis of Form 1964, The Oregon Experiment 1975, A Pattern Language 1977, The Timeless Way of Building 1979, The Linz Café 1981, A New Theory of Urban Design 1984, The Nature of Order (four vols): The Phenomenon of Life 2001, The Process of Creating Life 2004, The Luminous Ground 2003, A Vision of the Living World 2005; The Battle for the Life and Beauty of the Earth 2012; more than 200 articles in design journals. *Address:* The Center for Environmental Structure, 2701 Shasta Road, Berkeley, CA 94708, USA (office); Meadow Lodge, Binsted, nr Arundel, West Sussex, BN18 0LQ, England (home). *Telephone:* (510) 841-6166 (office). *Website:* www.patternlanguage.com (office); www.livingneighborhoods.org (office).

ALEXANDER, Clifford L., Jr, BA, LLD; American lawyer and fmr government official; *President, Alexander & Associates, Inc.;* b. 21 Sept. 1933, Harlem, New York; s. of Clifford Alexander and Edith Alexander (née McAllister); m. Adele Logan Alexander 1959; one s. one d.; ed Harvard and Yale Univs; practised as lawyer in New York, Pnr, Verner, Liipfert, Bernhard, McPherson and Alexander (law firm); Asst Dist Attorney, New York Co. 1959; Exec. Dir Manhattanville-Hamilton-Grange Neighborhood Conservation Project 1961–62, Harlem Youth Opportunities Unlimited; Foreign Affairs Officer, Nat. Security Council Staff 1963–64; Deputy Special Asst, later Deputy Special Counsel to Pres. Lyndon Johnson 1964–67; Chair. Equal Employment Opportunity Comm. 1967–69 (resgnd); mem. Comm. for Observance of Human Rights 1968; Special Amb. to Swaziland 1968; Pnr, Arnold & Porter (law firm); news commentator and host, Cliff Alexander–Black on White TV programme 1971–74; Prof. of Law, Howard Univ. 1973–74; US Sec. of the Army, Washington, DC 1977–81; Founder-Pres. Alexander & Assocs Inc. 1981–; Adjunct Prof., Georgetown Univ.; Prof., Howard Univ.; Chair. Moody's Corpn –2003; fmr Chair. and CEO Dun & Bradstreet Corpn; mem. Bd of Dirs Mexican-American Legal Defense and Educ. Fund, Dreyfus Third Century Fund Inc., MCI Corpn, Dreyfus Common Stock Fund, Dreyfus Tax Exempt Fund; fmr mem. Bd of Overseers Harvard Univ.; Trustee, Atlanta Univ.; fmr mem. Bd of Govs American Stock Exchange; mem. ABA, DC Bar Asscn, Community and Friends Bd, Kennedy Center; Hon. LLD (Univ. of Maryland, Atlanta Univ., Morgan State Univ., Wake Forest Univ.); Frederick Douglass Award. *Address:* Alexander & Associates, Inc., 400 C Street, NE, Washington, DC 20002-5818 (office); 512 A Street, SE, Washington, DC 20003-1139, USA (home). *Telephone:* (202) 546-0111 (office).

ALEXANDER, Rt Hon. Daniel Grian (Danny), PC, BA (Hons); British politician; *Chief Secretary to the Treasury;* b. 15 May 1972, Edinburgh, Scotland; m. Rebecca Hoar 2005; two d.; ed Lochaber High School, Fort William, St Anne's Coll., Oxford; worked as a press officer for Scottish Liberal Democrats 1993–94; Dir of Communications, European Movt 1996–99; Head of Communications, Britain in Europe 1999–2004; Head of Communications, Cairngorms Nat. Park Authority 2003–05; MP for Inverness, Nairn, Badenoch and Strathspey 2005–; Liberal Democrat Spokesperson for Work and Pensions, especially disabled people 2005–07; Whip 2006–07; Shadow Chancellor of the Duchy of Lancaster (Spokesperson for Social Exclusion) 2007; Shadow Sec. of State for Work and Pensions 2007–08; led Liberal Democrat team in negotiations that resulted in formation of a

Coalition Govt with the Conservative Party May 2010; Sec. of State for Scotland (and provided ministerial support to Deputy Prime Minister) May 2010; Chief Sec. to the Treasury June 2010–; Chief of Staff to Nick Clegg as Leader of the Liberal Democrats 2007–10; Chair. Liberal Democrat Manifesto Group 2007–10; mem. (Select Cttees); Scottish Affairs 2005–08; Liberal Democrat. *Leisure interests:* hill-walking, fishing, cricket, travel, sports of all kinds. *Address:* HM Treasury, 1 Horse Guards Road, London SW1A 2HQ (office); House of Commons, Westminster, London, SW1A 0AA, England; Constituency Office, 45 Huntly Street, Inverness, IV3 5HR, Scotland. *Telephone:* (20) 7270-4558 (HM Treasury) (office); (20) 7219-2300 (Westminster); (1463) 711280 (Inverness). *Fax:* (20) 7270-4861 (HM Treasury) (office); (20) 7219-1438 (Westminster); (1463) 711460 (Inverness). *E-mail:* danny.alexander@hmtreasury.gsi.gov.uk (office); csts.office@hmtreasury.gsi.gov .uk (office). *Website:* www.hm-treasury.gov.uk (office); www.parliament.uk/ biographies/commons/danny-alexander/32109; www.dannyalexander.org.uk.

ALEXANDER, Rt Hon. Douglas Garven, PC, LLB, MA; British solicitor and politician; *Shadow Foreign Secretary;* b. 26 Oct. 1967, Glasgow, Scotland; s. of Douglas N. Alexander; brother of Wendy Alexander MSP; m. Jacqueline Christian; one s. one d.; ed Park Mains High School, Erskine, Lester B. Pearson United World Coll. of the Pacific, Vancouver, Canada, Univ. of Edinburgh, Univ. of Pennsylvania, USA; press steward, Michael Dukakis US presidential campaign and staff mem. of Democratic Senator, USA 1988; Parl. Researcher and speech writer for Gordon Brown MP 1990; qualified as solicitor 1993; unsuccessful cand. in Perth and Kinross by-election 1995, Perth gen. election 1997; MP for Paisley South (following by-election) 1997–2005, for Paisley and Renfrewshire 2005–; Minister for E-Commerce and Competitiveness, Dept of Trade and Industry 2001–02; Minister of State, Cabinet Office 2002–04; Minister for the Cabinet Office and Chancellor of the Duchy of Lancaster 2003–04; Minister of State, Trade, Investment and Foreign Affairs, FCO and Dept of Trade and Industry 2004–05; Minister of State for Europe, FCO 2005–07; Sec. of State for Transport and for Scotland 2006–07, for Int. Devt 2007–10; Shadow Sec. of State for Int. Devt May–Oct. 2010, for Work and Pensions 2010–11, Shadow Foreign Sec. 2011–; mem. Nat. Exec. Cttee, Labour Party; Gen. Election Campaign Coordinator 1999–2001, 2007–. *Address:* House of Commons, Westminster, London, SW1A 0AA (office); 2014 Mile End Mill, Abbey Mill Business Centre, Seedhill Road, Paisley, PA1 1JS, Scotland (office). *Telephone:* (20) 7219-1345 (London) (office); (141) 561-0333 (Paisley) (office). *Fax:* (141) 561-0334 (Paisley) (office). *E-mail:* alexanderd@ parliament.uk (office); dalexander@parliament.uk (office); dalexandermp@talk21 .com (office). *Website:* douglasalexander.org.uk.

ALEXANDER, Héctor, MA, PhD; Panamanian economist, academic and politician; ed Univ. of Panama, Univ. of Chicago and Univ. of St Thomas, Fla, USA, Catholic Univ. of Chile; Prof. of Microeconomics, Analysis and Project Evaluation, Faculty of Econs, Univ. of Panama; Prof. of Accounting and Microeconomics, Panama Canal Coll.; mem. Tech. Comm. for Incentives to Exports, Ministry of Commerce and Industries; Expositor, Seminar on Economy for Journalists, organized by Repub. Nat. Bank 1976; fmr Minister of Planning and Political Economy; fmr Minister for External Relations; fmr Minister of Property and Treasury; fmr Minister in charge of Commerce and Industry; Sub-Gerente, Zona Libre de Colón; Minister of the Economy and Finance 2007–12; Econ. Adviser, Superior Direction, Interoceanica Regional Authority (ARI), Dir of Tech. Planning; mem. of team that negotiated Torrijos-Carter Treaty concerning econ. position of Panama; Finance Minister of the Year/Americas, The Banker magazine 2009. *Address:* c/o Ministry of the Economy and Finance, Edif. Ogawa, Vía España, Apdo 5245, Panamá 5, Panama.

ALEXANDER, Dame Helen Anne, DBE, CBE, MA, MBA; British business executive; *Chairman, Port of London Authority;* b. 10 Feb. 1957; d. of the late Bernard Alexander and Tania Alexander (née Benckendorff); m. Tim Suter 1985; two s. one d.; ed Hertford Coll. Oxford, INSEAD, France; with Gerald Duckworth 1978–79, Faber & Faber 1979–83; joined The Economist Group 1984, Man. Dir Economist Intelligence Unit 1993–96, Group CEO 1997–2008; Sr Adviser, Bain Capital 2008–; Chair. Incisive Media 2009–; Chair. Port of London Authority 2010–; Deputy Pres. CBI 2008, 2011–, Pres. 2009–11; Dir (non-exec.) Northern Foods 1994–2003, British Telecom 1998–2002, Centrica, Rolls-Royce; Chair. Said Business School Advisory Council; Trustee Tate Gallery, WWW Foundation; Gov. St Paul's Girls' School; Hon. Fellow, Hertford Coll., Oxford. *Address:* Port of London Authority, The Lock House, Ranelagh Drive, Twickenham, TW1 1QZ, England (office). *Telephone:* (20) 8843-7210 (office). *Website:* www.pla.co.uk (office).

ALEXANDER, Hon. Jane; American actress, producer and author; b. (Jane Seyferth Quigley), 28 Oct. 1939, Boston, Mass; d. of Thomas Bartlett and Ruth Quigley; m. 1st Robert Alexander 1962 (divorced 1969); one s.; m. 2nd Edwin Sherin 1975; ed Sarah Lawrence Coll., Univ. of Edinburgh, UK; Guest Artist-in-Residence, Oklahoma Arts Inst. 1982; Chair. Nat. Endowment for Arts 1994–97; Francis Eppes Prof., Florida State Univ. 2002–04; mem. Bd of Dirs Women's Action for Nuclear Disarmament 1981–88, Film Forum 1985–90, Nat. Stroke Asscn 1984–91, American Birding Asscn 2007–; mem. Bd of Trustees, Wildlife Conservation Soc. 1997–2007, The MacDowell Colony 1997–2008, Arts International 2000–05; Global Wildlife Amb., Indianapolis Zoo (Indianapolis Prize); Hon. DFA (The Juilliard School) 1994, (North Carolina School of Arts) 1994, (The New School of Social Research) 1996, (Smith Coll.) 1999, (Pa State Univ.) 2000, Hon. PhD (Univ. of Pennsylvania) 1995, (Duke Univ.) 1996, (Coll. of the Atlantic) 2011 and numerous other hon. degrees; Lifetime Achievement Award, Americans for Arts 1999, Harry S. Truman Award for Public Service 1999, Directors' Guild of America Award 2002 and numerous other wards. *Broadway appearances include:* The Great White Hope (Tony Award 1969) 1968–69, Find Your Way Home 1974, Hamlet 1975, The Heiress 1976, Goodbye Fidel 1980, Night of the Iguana 1988, Shadowlands 1990–91, The Visit 1992, The Sisters Rosensweig 1993, Honour 1998. *Other stage appearances include:* Antony and Cleopatra 1981, Hedda Gabler 1981, Approaching Zanzibar 1989, The Cherry Orchard 2000, Mourning Becomes Electra 2002, Rose and Walsh 2003, Chasing Manet 2009, A Moon to Dance By 2010, The Lady from Dubuque 2012. *Films include:* The Great White Hope 1970, All the President's Men 1976, Kramer vs. Kramer 1979, Brubaker 1980, Sweet Country 1986, Glory 1989, The Cider House Rules 1999, Sunshine State 2002, The Ring 2002, Fur: An Imaginary Portrait of Diane Arbus 2006, Feast of Love 2007,

Gigantic 2008, The Unborn 2009, Terminator Salvation 2009, Dream House 2011, Mr. Morgan's Last Love 2012. *Television includes:* Eleanor and Franklin 1976, Playing for Time (Emmy Award 1980) 1980, Kennedy's Children 1981, A Marriage: Georgia O'Keeffe and Alfred Stieglitz 1991, Stay the Night 1992, The Jenifer Estess Story 2001, Carry Me Home 2004, Warm Springs (Emmy Award 2005) 2005, Tell Me You Love Me 2007, The Good Wife (series) 2011, William and Kate – A Royal Romance 2011 and 30 others. *Publications:* The Bluefish Cookbook (with Greta Jacobs) 1979, (co-trans.) The Master Builder (Henrik Ibsen), Command Performance: An Actress in the Theater of Politics 2000. *Leisure interest:* bird watching. *Address:* c/o David Kalodner, WME Entertainment, 1325 Avenue of the Americas, New York, NY 10019, USA (office); c/o Sue Leibman, Barking Dog Entertainment Inc., 609 Greenwich Street, #6, New York, NY 10014-3610, USA (office). *Telephone:* (212) 586-5100 (office); (212) 343-2117 (office). *Fax:* (212) 246-3583 (office). *E-mail:* info@wmeentertainment.com (office); info@ barkingdogentertainment.net (office). *Website:* www.wmeentertainment.com (office); www.barkingdogentertainment.net (office).

ALEXANDER, Jonathan James Graham, DPhil, FBA, FSA; British/American art historian and academic; *Sherman Fairchild Professor Emeritus of Fine Arts, New York University;* b. 20 Aug. 1935, London, England; s. of Arthur Ronald Brown and Frederica Emma Graham; m. 1st Mary Davey 1974 (divorced 1994); one s.; m. 2nd Serita Winthrop 1996 (divorced 2001); ed Magdalen Coll., Oxford; Asst, Dept of Western Manuscripts, Bodleian Library, Oxford 1963–71; Lecturer, History of Art Dept, Univ. of Manchester 1971–73, Reader 1973–87; Prof. of Fine Arts, Inst. of Fine Arts, New York Univ. 1988–2002, Sherman Fairchild Prof. of Fine Arts 2002–11, Emer. 2011–; Lyell Reader in Bibliography, Univ. of Oxford 1982–83; Sandars Lecturer, Univ. of Cambridge 1984–85; Visiting Prof., Univ. Coll. London 1991–92; Fellow, Medieval Acad. of America 1999; John Simon Guggenheim Memorial Foundation Fellowship 1995–96, Distinguished Visiting Fellowship, La Trobe Univ., Melbourne, Australia 1997; Visiting Fellow, All Souls Coll., Oxford 1998; J. Clawson Mills Fellow, Metropolitan Museum of Art, New York 2002; Samuel H. Kress Prof., Center for Advanced Study in the Visual Arts, Nat. Gallery of Art, Washington, DC 2004–05; Panizzi Lectures, British Library, London 2007–08; Hon. Fellow, Pierpont Morgan Library 1995; Prix Minda de Gunzburg 1987. *Publications include:* Illuminated Manuscripts in the Bodleian Library, Oxford (with Otto Pächt) (three vols) 1966, 1970, 1973, Italian Illuminated Manuscripts in the library of Major J. R. Abbey (with A. C. de la Mare) 1969, Norman Illumination at Mont St Michel c. 966–1100 1970, The Master of Mary of Burgundy, A Book of Hours 1970, Italian Renaissance Illuminations 1977, Insular Manuscripts 6th–9th Century 1978, The Decorated Letter 1978, Illuminated Manuscripts in Oxford College Libraries, Age of Chivalry (co-ed.), Art in Plantagenet England 1200–1400 1987, Medieval Illuminators and their Methods of Work 1993, The Painted Page: Italian Renaissance Book Illumination 1450–1550 (ed.) 1994, The Townley Lectionary (introduction) 1997, Studies in Italian Manuscript Illumination 2002; articles in Burlington Magazine, Arte Veneta, Pantheon, Art Bulletin etc. *Leisure interests:* music, gardening. *Address:* Institute of Fine Arts, 1 East 78th Street, New York, NY 10075, USA (office). *Telephone:* (212) 992-5876 (office). *Fax:* (212) 992-5807 (office). *Website:* www.ifa .nyu.edu (office).

ALEXANDER, Meena, BA, PhD; American (b. Indian) poet, writer and academic; *Distinguished Professor of English and Women's Studies, Hunter College and the Graduate School and University Center, City University of New York;* b. 17 Feb. 1951, Allahabad, India; d. of George Alexander and Mary Kuruvilla Alexander; m. David Lelyveld 1979; one s. one d.; ed Univ. of Khartoum, Sudan, Univ. of Nottingham, UK; Lecturer, Univ. of Hyderabad 1977–79, Reader 1979; Asst Prof., Fordham Univ. 1980–87; Asst Prof., Hunter Coll. and the Grad. School and Univ. Center, CUNY 1987–89, Assoc. Prof. 1989–92, Prof. of English 1992–99, Distinguished Prof. of English and Women's Studies 1999–; Visiting Prof., School of the Arts, Columbia Univ. 2005; Poet-in-Residence, Univ. of Hyderabad 2010; mem. Jury, Fifteenth Neustadt Int. Award in Literature 1997–98; mem. Modern Language Asscn, PEN American Center; numerous awards including Altrusa Int. Award 1973, MacDowell Fellow 1993, 1998, Poet-in-Residence, American Coll., Madurai 1994, Artist/Humanist-in-Residence, Intercultural Resource Centre, Columbia Univ. 1995, Int. Writer in Residence, Arts Council of England 1995, Poetry Award, New York State Foundation for the Arts 1999, Poet-in-Residence, Nat. Univ. of Singapore 1999, Imbongi Yesizwe Poetry Int. Award (S Africa) 2002, Hunter Coll. Faculty Fellowship 2002, Fulbright Sr Scholar Award, Mahatma Gandhi Univ., India 2002–03, Bellagio Award, Rockefeller Foundation 2003, Martha Walsh Pulver Residency for a Poet, Yaddo 2005, Fulbright Sr Specialist Award, Elector, American Poet's Corner, Cathedral of St John the Divine, New York 2006–, John Simon Guggenheim Fellowship 2008, Camargo Foundation Fellowship 2008, S Asian Literary Asscn Distinguished Achievement Award in Literature 2009, also awards from Fulbright Foundation, Arts Council of England, Nat. Endowment for the Humanities, American Council of Learned Societies, Nat. Council for Research on Women, New York State Council on the Arts, New York Foundation for the Arts, Ledig-Rowohlt Foundation. *Publications include:* poetry: The Bird's Bright Wing 1976, Stone Roots 1980, House of a Thousand Doors 1988, The Storm: A Poem in Five Parts 1989, Night-Scene: The Garden 1992, River and Bridge 1995, Illiterate Heart (PEN Open Book Award) 2002, Raw Silk 2004, Indian Love Poems (ed.) 2005, Quickly Changing River 2008; poetry and essays: The Shock of Arrival: Reflections on Postcolonial Experience 1996, Poetics of Dislocation 2009; fiction: Nampally Road 1991, Manhattan Music 1997; non-fiction: The Poetic Self: Towards a Phenomenology of Romanticism 1979 (criticism), Women in Romanticism: Mary Wollstonecraft, Dorothy Wordsworth and Mary Shelley 1989, Fault Lines 1993 (new expanded edn 2003); contribs to books, anthologies and periodicals. *Leisure interests:* walking, watching old movies, cooking. *Address:* PhD Program in English, CUNY Graduate Center, 365 Fifth Avenue, New York, NY 10016 (office); English Department, Hunter College, City University of New York, 695 Park Avenue, New York, NY 10065, USA (office). *Telephone:* (212) 772-5164 (office); (212) 772-5200 (office). *Fax:* (212) 772-5411 (office). *E-mail:* malexander@gc.cuny.edu (office). *Website:* web.gc.cuny .edu/English/faculty/alexander.html (office); www.meenaalexander.com.

ALEXANDER, Robert McNeill, CBE, MA, PhD, DSc, FRS; British zoologist and academic; *Professor Emeritus of Zoology, University of Leeds;* b. 7 July 1934, Lisburn, Northern Ireland; s. of Robert Priestley Alexander and Janet Alexander (née McNeill); m. Ann Elizabeth Coulton 1961; one s. one d.; ed Tonbridge School, Univ. of Cambridge; Lecturer, Univ. Coll. of North Wales, Bangor 1958–69; Prof. of Zoology, Univ. of Leeds 1969–99, Prof. Emer. 1999–; Sec., Zoological Soc. of London 1992–99; Vice-Pres. Soc. for Experimental Biology 1993–95, Pres. 1995–97; Pres. Int. Soc. for Vertebrate Morphology 1997–2001; Ed. Proceedings of the Royal Soc. B 1998–2004; mem. Academia Europaea 1996, European Acad. of Sciences 2004; Hon. mem. American Soc. of Zoologists (now Soc. for Integrative and Comparative Biology) 1986, Foreign Hon. mem. American Acad. of Arts and Sciences 2001, Hon. Fellow, Zoological Soc. of London 2003; Hon. DSc (Aberdeen) 2002, Dr hc (Wageningen) 2003; Scientific Medal, Zoological Soc. of London 1969, Linnean Medal for Zoology, Linnean Soc. of London 1979, Muybridge Medal, Int. Soc. for Biomechanics 1991, Borelli Award, American Soc. for Biomechanics 2003. *Publications:* Functional Design in Fishes 1967, Animal Mechanics 1968, Size and Shape 1971, The Chordates 1975, The Invertebrates 1979, Locomotion of Animals 1982, Optima for Animals 1982, Elastic Mechanisms in Animal Movement 1988, Dynamics of Dinosaurs and Other Extinct Giants 1989, Animals 1990, Exploring Biomechanics 1992, The Human Machine 1992, Bones 1994, Energy for Animal Life 1999, Principles of Animal Locomotion 2003, Human Bones 2004; numerous scientific papers. *Leisure interests:* history of biology and history of tableware. *Address:* School of Biology, University of Leeds, Leeds, LS2 9JT (office); 14 Moor Park Mount, Leeds, LS6 4BU, England (home). *E-mail:* r.m.alexander@leeds.ac.uk (office).

ALEXANDER, Wendy, MA, MBA, FRSA; British university administrator and fmr politician; *Associate Dean, Degree Programmes and Career Services, London Business School;* b. 27 June 1963, Glasgow, Scotland; m. Brian Ashcroft; two c.; ed Park Mains High School, Erskine, Pearson Coll., Canada, Univ. of Glasgow, Univ. of Warwick and Institut Européen d'Admin des Affaires (INSEAD), France; fmr consultant with Booz Allen & Hamilton (now Booz & Co.); apptd Special Adviser to Sec. of State for Scotland 1997; MSP (Labour) for Paisley N 1999–2011, Minister for Communities 1999–2000, for Enterprise and Lifelong Learning 2000–01, for Enterprise, Transport and Lifelong Learning 2001–02, Chair. Finance Cttee 2006–07, Chair. Scotland Bill Cttee 2010–11, mem. Economy and Energy Cttee, co-convenor Cross-Party Group in Scottish Parl. for Scottish Economy, Leader, Scottish Labour Party 2007–08 (resgnd); Visiting Prof., Univ. of Strathclyde Business School 2002–12; columnist, Daily Record newspaper 2007; Assoc. Dean, Degree Programmes and Career Services, London Business School 2012–; mem. Royal Soc. for the Protection of Birds, Amnesty International, Aldersgate Group; Scottish Politician of the Year (Channel 4) 2000, Johnnie Walker Award (Scottish Politician of the Year) 2005, Womansphere Global Award honoree 2013; Dr hc (Strathclyde) 2007, (West of Scotland) 2012. *Publications include:* First Ladies of Medicine 1986; contribs to The World is Ill Divided: Women's Work in Scotland 1992, The State and the Nations 1996, The Ethnicity Reader 1997, New Gender Agenda 2000, Chasing the Tartan Tiger 2003, New Wealth for Old Nations (co-ed.) 2003, Donald Dewar, Scotland's First First Minister (ed.) 2005. *Leisure interests:* ornithology, Scottish Islands. *Address:* Office of Degree Programmes and Career Services, London Business School, Regent's Park, London, NW1 4SA, England (office). *Telephone:* (20) 7000-7000 (office). *E-mail:* walexander@london.edu (office). *Website:* www.london.edu (office).

ALEXANDER KARADJORDJEVIC, HRH Crown Prince of Serbia; b. 17 July 1945, London, England; s. of HM King Peter II of Yugoslavia and HRH Princess Alexandra of the Hellenes and Denmark; m. 1st HRH Princess Maria da Gloria of Orléans and Bragança 1972 (divorced 1983); m. 2nd Katherine Batis 1985; three s.; ed Le Rosey, Switzerland, Gordonstoun, Scotland, Culver Mil. Acad., USA, Royal Mil. Acad., UK; commissioned in British Army, 16th/5th The Queen's Royal Lancers, rank of Acting Capt. 1971, British Army Ski Champion 1972; business exec. working in Rio de Janeiro, New York, Chicago and London; in exile from birth, visited Belgrade for the first time Oct. 1991, est. residence in The Royal Palace, Belgrade 2001. *Leisure interests:* skiing, scuba diving, underwater photography, family. *Address:* The Royal Palace, 11040 Belgrade, Serbia (home). *Telephone:* (11) 3064000 (office). *Fax:* (11) 3064040 (office). *E-mail:* office@dvor.rs (office). *Website:* www.royal.rs (office); www.royalfamily.org (office).

ALEXANDRA, HRH Princess (see Ogilvy, HRH Princess Alexandra).

ALEXANDRE, Boniface; Haitian judge and politician; b. 31 July 1936; three c.; fmr lawyer with Cabinet Lamarre; Judge, Supreme Court during 1990s, Chief Justice 2002–04; Acting Pres. 2004–06; currently Lecturer, Port-au-Prince; Hon. Citizen of Lafayette, La, USA 2003.

ALEXEEV, Dmitri Konstantinovich; Russian pianist; *Professor of Piano, Royal College of Music, London;* b. 10 Aug. 1947, Moscow; s. of Konstantin Alekseyev and Gertrude Bolotina; m. Tatiana Sarkisova 1970; one d.; ed Moscow Conservatoire; studied under Dmitri Bashkirov; performs regularly in Russia, in UK and throughout Europe and USA and has toured Japan, Australia etc.; has performed with orchestras including Berlin Philharmonic, Chicago Symphony Orchestra, Philadelphia Orchestra, Royal Concertgebouw Orchestra of Amsterdam, London Symphony Orchestra, London Philharmonic Orchestra, Philharmonia Orchestra, Royal Philharmonic, BBC Symphony Orchestra, Orchestre de Paris, Israel Philharmonic and the Munich Bavarian Radio Orchestra; worked with Ashkenazy, Boulez, Dorati, Gatti, Gergiev, Giulini, Jansons, Muti, Pappano, Rozhdestvensky, Salonen, Svetlanov, Temirkanov, Rostropovich, Lynn Harrell, Yuri Bashmet, Joshua Bell, Nicolai Gedda, Elisabeth Soderstrom and Barbara Hendricks; world premiere of Penderecki's Piano Sextet, Vienna Musikverein 2000, premiere of Penderecki's Piano Concerto under the baton of the composer, Beijing Festival 2002; Artistic Dir Leeds Int. Recital Series 2008–09; Prof. of Piano, Royal Coll. of Music, London 2005–; prizewinner Int. Marguerite Long Competition, Paris 1969, Int. George Enescu Competition, Bucharest 1970, Int. Tchaikovsky Competition, Moscow 1974, 5th Leeds Int. Piano Competition 1975 and other int. competitions; Edison Award (Netherlands) for his recording of the complete Rachmaninov Preludes. *Recordings:* works by Bach, Brahms, Chopin, Grieg, Liszt, Medtner, Prokofiev, Rachmaninov, Schumann, Shostakovich, Scriabin, Glazunov, Gershwin and Hindemith. *Address:* c/o IMG Artists, The Light Box, 111 Power Road, London, W4 5PY, England (office). *Telephone:* (20) 7957-5800 (office). *Fax:* (20) 7957-5801 (office). *E-mail:* artistseurope@imgartists.com (office). *Website:* www.imgartists.com (office).

ALEXEEVA, Ludmilla; Russian human rights activist; *Chairwoman and President, Moscow Helsinki Group;* forced to immigrate to USA in 1977, returned to Russia 1993; co-f. Moscow Helsinki Group, currently Chair. and Pres.; Pres. Int. Helsinki Fed. 1996–2004; mem. Presidential Council on Assistance of Insts of Civil Society and Human Rights; Co-Chair All-Russia Civil Congress; Légion d'Honneur, Commdr's Cross, Germany 2009, Order of the Cross of Terra Mariana III degree (Estonia) 2012; Olof Palme Prize (Jtly) 2004, Human Rights Award, Human Rights First 2005, Andrei Sakharov Prize 2009. *Publications include:* Soviet Dissent 1985. *Address:* Moscow Helsinki Group, 107045 Moscow, Grand Golovin per, Bldg 22, p 1, Russia (office). *Telephone:* (495) 207-60-69 (office). *E-mail:* mhg-main@online.ptt.ru (office). *Website:* www.mhg.ru (office).

ALEXEYEV, Nikolay Gennadyevich; Russian conductor; *Principal Conductor, St Petersburg Philharmonic Orchestra;* b. 1 May 1956, Leningrad; s. of Gennady Nikolayevich Alexeyev and Tamara Andreyevna Alexeyeva; m. Nina Yefimovna Alexeyeva; two s.; ed Glinka Choir School, St Petersburg State Conservatory; Chief Conductor Ulyanovsk Philharmonic Orchestra 1983–2001; Prin. Guest Conductor Zagreb Philharmonic and Estonian Nat. Symphony 1994–97; Artistic Dir and Prin. Conductor Estonian Nat. Symphony Orchestra 2000–10; performs with leading orchestras, Symphony Orchestra, Moscow, Russian Nat. Orchestra, Moscow Philharmonic, tours in Europe, USA, Japan; Assoc. Prin. Conductor St Petersburg Philharmonic Orchestra 2000–, now Prin. Conductor; People's Artist of the Russian Federation 2007; Prize Int. H. von Karajan Music Competition 1982, Int. V. Talikh Competition 1985. *Address:* St Petersburg Philharmonia, Mikhailovskaya str. 2, St Petersburg, Russia (office). *Telephone:* (812) 931-98-71 (office); (812) 271-04-90 (home). *E-mail:* mail@philharmonia.spb.ru (office). *Website:* www.saintpetersburgphilharmonic.com (office).

ALEXIS, Francis, LLM, PhD; Grenadian politician, author and lawyer; *Leader, People's Labour Movement;* b. 3 Oct. 1947, Grenada; s. of John Everest Alexis and Anastasia Omega Alexis; m. Margaret de Bique 1973; three d.; ed Grenada Boys' Secondary School, Univ. of West Indies, Hugh Wooding Law School and Univ. of Cambridge; fmr clerk, Jonas Brown & Hubbards Ltd, Grenada; later civil servant, Grenada; Sr Lecturer in Law and Deputy Dean, Faculty of Law, Univ. of West Indies; barrister-at-law, Grenada; MP 1984–; Minister of Labour, Co-operatives, Social Security and Local Govt 1984–87; Attorney-Gen. and Minister of Legal Affairs and Labour 1987; Opposition MP 1987–90; Founder-mem. and Deputy Leader New Nat. Party 1986, Nat. Democratic Congress 1987–95; Attorney-Gen. and Minister of Legal Affairs and Local Govt 1990–95; Acting Prime Minister on various occasions 1990–95; Leader Govt Business, House of Reps in Parl. 1990–95, Grenada Nat. Del. to Commonwealth Parl. Asscn UK 1986, to Windward Islands Political Union Talks 1991–92, to UN Gen. Ass. 1993, Canada 1994; Father of House of Reps in Parl. 1995–; Founder-mem., Leader Democratic Labour Party, now People's Labour Movement 1995–; Vice-Pres. Grenada Bar Asscn 1997–98, currently Pres. *Publications:* Commonwealth Caribbean Legal Essays 1981, Changing Caribbean Constitutions 1983, H. Aubrey Fraser: Eminent Caribbean Jurist 1985, The Constitution and You 1991; articles in law journals. *Leisure interests:* reading, writing, music. *Address:* Church Street, St George's (office); St Paul's, St George's, Grenada (home). *Telephone:* 440-6743 (office); 440-2378 (home). *Fax:* 440-6591.

ALEXIS, Jacques-Edouard, MSc; Haitian politician and university rector; b. 21 Sept. 1947, Gonaïves; m.; five c.; ed Faculty of Agronomics and Veterinary Medicine, State Univ. of Haïti, Laval Univ.; Prof., Univ. of Quisqueya 1990–, Rector, 1990–96, Co-ordinator, Office of Institutional Devt 2003–05; Minister of Nat. Educ., Youth and Sport 1996–99, of Culture 1997–99, of the Interior and Local Govt 1999–2001; Prime Minister 1998–2001, 2006–08; Pres. Educ. et Société Foundation 2001–.

ALFANO, Angelino; Italian lawyer and politician; *Minister of Interior;* b. 31 Oct. 1970, Agrigento; ed Catholic Univ. of Sacro Cuore, Milan; mem. Sicilian Regional Ass. 1996–2001; Regional Sec., Forza Italia 2005–08, with Popolo della Libertà party 2008–; Minister of Justice 2008–11, Vice-Pres., Council of Ministers April–Sept. 2013, Minister of Interior 2013–. *Address:* Ministry of the Interior, Piazzale del Viminale, Via Agostino Depretis 7, 00184 Rome, Italy (office). *Telephone:* (06) 4651 (office). *Fax:* (06) 46549599 (office). *E-mail:* segreteriaufficiostampa@interno.it (office). *Website:* www.interno.it (office).

ALFARO ESTRIPEAUT, Roberto; Panamanian business executive and fmr diplomatist; m.; five c.; ed George Washington Univ., USA, Inst. of Higher Studies in Admin., Venezuela, Canal Zone Coll., Center for Studies of Insurance Admin.; CEO Financiera de Seguros, SA 1981–97; Gen. Man. Financeria de Seguros SA 1994–97; Pres. Bd of Dirs Aseguradora La Unión 1997–99; Gen. Man. Proexport Int. Devt. Inc. 1998–99; Treasurer Bd of Dirs, Corporación Panameña de Energia SA 1998–99; Vice-Minister of Commerce and Industry, Govt of Panama 1990–91, Minister 1991–94; Amb. to Italy (with concurrent accreditation to Malta) 2000–02, to USA 2003–04; Sr Partner, Interglobal Busisness Brokers; Pres. Asscn of Panamanian Business Execs 2008.

ALFARO MAYKALL, Laura, BA, MA, PhD; Costa Rican economist and politician; *Minister of National Planning and Economic Policy;* ed Universidad de Costa Rica, Pontificia Universidad Católica de Chile, Univ. of California, Los Angeles, USA; Econ. Consultant, Consejeros Económicos y Financieros, San José 1990–92; Asst Prof. of Business Admin, Harvard Business School, USA 1999–2004, Assoc. Prof. 2004–10, Prof. 2010–; Faculty Assoc. Harvard Weatherhead Center for Int. Affairs; Minister of Nat. Planning and Econ. Policy 2010–; Faculty Research Fellow, Nat. Bureau of Econ. Research; Non-resident Fellow, OECD 2009–10; IMF Invited Lecturer May 2010; mem. American Econ. Asscn, Latin America and Caribbean Econ. Asscn; named Young Global Leader by World Econ. Forum 2008. *Publications:* numerous articles in leading academic journals. *Address:* Ministry of National Planning and Economic Policy, De Autos Subarú 200 m al Norte, Barrio Dent, San Pedro de Montes de Oca, Costa Rica (office). *Telephone:* 2281-2700 (office). *Fax:* 2253-6243 (office). *E-mail:* despacho@mideplan.go.cr (office). *Website:* www.mideplan.go.cr (office).

ALFEROV, Zhores Ivanovich, DPhysMathSc; Russian physicist, academic and politician; *Vice-President, St Petersburg Scientific Centre, Russian Academy of Sciences;* b. 15 March 1930, Vitebsk; m.; two c.; ed Leningrad Electrotech. Inst.;

mem. scientific staff, Ioffe Inst. of Physics and Tech., USSR (now Russian) Acad. of Sciences 1953–, Jr Scientist 1953–64, Sr Scientist 1964–67, Head of Lab. 1967–87, Dir 1987–2003, Scientific Dir 2003–06; Chair. Optoelectronics, St Petersburg State Electro Tech. Univ. 1973; Dean of Faculty of Physics and Tech., St Petersburg Tech. Univ. 1988; currently Vice-Pres. Leningrad (now St Petersburg) Scientific Centre, USSR (now Russian) Acad. of Sciences 1990, Rector, Academic Univ., Nanotechnology Research and Educ., Center of the Russian Acad. of Sciences 2009–; mem. Duma (Parl.) 1995–, mem. Cttee of Science and Educ.; Ed.-in-Chief Physics and Technology of Semiconductors, Technical Physics Letters (journal); Corresp. mem. USSR (now Russian) Acad. of Sciences 1972, mem. 1979, Vice-Pres. 1990–; Life Fellow, Franklin Inst., USA 1971; Fellow, Optical Soc. of America, USA 2000; Foreign mem. Polish Acad. of Sciences 1989, Nat. Acad. of Sciences (Belarus) 1995, Nat. Acad. of Sciences (Ukraine) 2000, Korean Acad. of Science and Tech. 1995; Foreign Assoc. Nat. Acad. of Science (USA) 1990; mem. European Acad. of Sciences; Hon. Citizen of St Petersburg; Hon. Prof., Havana Univ., Cuba 1987, State Tech. Univ. 2000, State Electrotechnical Univ. 2001, Moscow State Univ. 2001; Hon. mem. Metrological Acad., St Petersburg 1994, Pakistan Soc. for Semiconductor Science and Tech. 1996; Hon. Academician, Int. Acad. of Refrigeration, St Petersburg 1997; Order of Honour 1959, Nat. Order of the Legion of Honour 2011; numerous hon. degrees including Dr hc (Humanity Univ., St Petersburg) 1998, (Kurchatov Inst., Moscow) 1998, (State Univ., Tomsk) 2008, (Korolev Univ., Samara) 2009, (Tech. Univ., Berlin, Germany) 2009; Stuart Ballantine Gold Medal 1971, Lenin Prize 1972, 1986, Red Banner of Labor 1975, Hewlett-Packard Europhysics Prize 1978, October Revolution 1980, USSR State Prize 1984, Heinrich Welker Medal 1987, A.P. Karpinsky Prize 1989, A.F. Ioffe Prize, Russian Acad. of Sciences 1996, Demidov Prize 1999, Merit for the Fatherland 1999, 2000, 2005, A.S. Popov Medal 2000, Nick Holonyak Jr Award, Optical Soc. of America 2000, Nobel Prize for Physics 2000, Kyoto Prize 2001, V.I. Vernadskiy Award, Nat. Acad. of Sciences (Ukraine) 2001, Golden Plate Award, Acad. of Achievement 2002, Golden Medal, Int. Soc. for Optical Tech. Eng 2002, Global Energy Prize (Russia) 2005. *Achievements include:* inventor of heterotransistor. *Publications:* scientific works on physics and tech. of semiconductors, quantum electronics. *Leisure interest:* history of Second World War. *Address:* St Petersburg Scientific Centre, 199034 St Petersburg, Universitetskaya nab. 5 (office); 194223 St Petersburg, Jacques Duclos str. 8/3-82, Russia (home). *Telephone:* (812) 328-23-11 (office); (812) 297-21-45 (office). *Fax:* (812) 328-37-87 (office); (812) 448-69-98 (office). *E-mail:* zhores_alferov@spbau.ru (office). *Website:* www.spbau.ru (office).

ALFIE, Isaac; Uruguayan economist, academic and politician; b. 27 April 1962; m.; two c.; ed Universidad de la República; fmr Lecturer, Universidad de la República, Universidad ORT, Universidad de Belgrano, Argentina; Dir of Macroeconomic Programming, Ministry of Economy 2000, Macroeconomic Policy Adviser –2003; Minister of Economy and Finance 2003–04; Gov. and Exec. Dir for Uruguay, Inter-American Devt Bank (IDB); Senator (Partido Colorado) 2005–10; currently Prof. of Econs and Public Finance, Universidad de Montevideo, also Assoc. Prof., Dept of Econs, Universidad de la República; Latin American Finance Minister of the Year, Emerging Markets (financial website) 2004. *Address:* Faculty of Business Studies and Economics, Universidad de Montevideo, Dr. Prudencio de Pena 2440, 11100 Montevideo 11600, Uruguay (office). *E-mail:* ialfie@um.edu.uy (office). *Website:* fcee.um.edu.uy (office).

ALGABID, Hamid; Niger lawyer and politician; *Chairman, Rassemblement pour la démocratie et le progrès—Djamaa (RDP);* b. 1941, Tamont; m.; five c.; ed Abidjan Univ.; fmr Minister of State for Planning, Commerce and Transportation; fmr Minister Del. for Finance; Prime Minister of Niger 1983–88; Sec.-Gen. Org. of the Islamic Conf. 1989–96; Chair. Rassemblement pour la démocratie et le progrès—Djamaa (RDP) 1997–; unsuccessful presidential cand. 1999, 2004; mem. Assemblée nationale 1999–; Pres. High Council of Territorial Collectivities (HCCT) 2004–10. *Address:* Rassemblement pour la démocratie et le progrès—Djamaa (RDP), pl. Toumo, Niamey, Niger (office). *Telephone:* 20-74-23-82 (office).

ALHEGELAN, Sheikh Faisal Abdul Aziz; Saudi Arabian diplomatist; b. 7 Oct. 1929, Jeddah; s. of Sheikh Abdul Aziz Al-Hegelan and Fatima Al-Eissa; m. Nouha Tarazi 1961; three s.; ed Faculty of Law, Fouad Univ., Cairo; with Ministry of Foreign Affairs 1952–54, served in Embassy in Washington, DC 1954–58, Chief of Protocol in Ministry 1958–60; Political Adviser to HM King Sa'ud 1960–61; Amb. to Spain 1961–68, to Venezuela and Argentina 1968–75, to Denmark 1975–76, to UK 1976–79, to USA 1979–83, to France 1996–2003; Minister of State and mem. Council of Ministers (Saudi Arabia) April–Sept. 1984, of Health 1984–96; Chair. Bd of Dirs Saudi Red Crescent Soc. 1984–, Saudi Anti-Smoking Soc. 1985–; Chair. Bd of Trustees, Saudi Council for Health Specialties 1992–; Order of King Abdulaziz, Gran Cruz Cordon of King Abdul Aziz, Order of Isabela la Católica (Spain), Gran Cordón, Orden del Libertador (Venezuela), Grande Oficial, Orden Riobranco (Brazil), May Grand Decoration (Argentina); Hon. KBE. *Leisure interests:* bridge, golf.

ALHENDAWI, Ahmad, BA; Jordanian international organization official and UN official; *Envoy of the Secretary-General on Youth, United Nations;* b. 20 May 1984; ed Institut Européen, Al-Balqa Applied Univ.; Youth Policy Adviser to Arab League and Officer, Technical Secr. of the Arab Youth and Sports Ministers' Council 2009–12; apptd Team Leader, World Bank-funded programme to League of Arab States on institutional devt to strengthen Arab policy and participation 2012; Envoy of UN Sec.-Gen. on Youth 2013–; also served as Team Leader for Nat. Youth Policy Project, Iraq, Youth Programme Assoc., UN Population Fund (UNFPA), Iraq, Emergency Programme Officer, Save the Children, Regional Consultant for projects of Danish Youth Council in Middle East and North Africa; Co-founder All Jordan Youth Comm., Youth for Democracy Network, Jordanian Comm. for Democratic (also Head), International Youth Council, New York. *Address:* Office of the Secretary-General, United Nations, New York, NY 10017, USA (office). *Telephone:* (212) 963-1234 (office). *Fax:* (212) 963-4879 (office). *Website:* www.un.org/sg (office).

ALI, Abdiweli Mohamed, BA, MA, PhD; Somali economist and politician; *President, Puntland State of Somalia;* ed Somali Nat. Univ., Vanderbilt Univ., George Mason Univ., Kennedy School of Govt, Harvard Univ., USA; Dir Excise Tax Dept, Ministry of Finance, Mogadishu 1985–86, Asst Dir Research and Statistics 1988–91; Adjunct Prof. of Econs, Northern Virginia Community Coll., Alexandria

1993–98, Teaching Fellow, John F. Kennedy School of Govt, Harvard Univ. 1998–99, Teaching Fellow, Harvard Inst. for Int. Devt 1999; Assoc. Prof. of Econs, Niagara Univ. 2003–11; Deputy Prime Minister and Minister of Planning and Int. Co-operation 2010–11, Prime Minister and Minister of Planning and Int. Co-operation 2011–12; Pres., autonomous Puntland State of Somalia 2014–; fmr consultant to UNDP; Consultant, African Econ. Research Consortium, Nairobi, Kenya 2005–; mem. American Econ. Asscn, Southern Econ. Asscn, Atlantic Econ. Soc., Public Choice Soc., Asscn of Private Enterprise Educ.; Excellence in Research Award, College of Business Administration, Niagara Univ. 2004, 2006, Best Article Award, Atlantic Economic Journal 2002. *Publications:* numerous articles in econ. journals.

ALI, Abdullahi Jama; Somali central banker; currently Gov. Central Bank of Somalia. *Address:* Office of the Governor, Central Bank of Somalia, 1 Villa Somalia, Mogadishu, Somalia (office). *Telephone:* 1) 657733 (office). *Fax:* (1) 215026 (office). *Website:* www.somalbanca.org (office).

ALI, Adel Abdulla, MBA; Bahraini airline industry executive; *Founder and CEO, Air Arabia;* ed Univ. of Manchester, UK, Marlhurst Univ., Oregon, USA; 20-year career with British Airways, including several sr regional posts, becoming Gen. Man. for Middle East and N Africa; Vice-Pres. of Commercial and Customer Service, Gulf Air 2001–03; f. Air Arabia 2003, mem. Bd of Dirs and Group CEO 2003–; Chair. Sharjah Information Systems Assocs, Alpha Sharjah Catering; several awards, including Aviation Business Magazine Airline CEO of the Year 2007, Low Cost Airline CEO of the Year 2007, 2008, 2009, 2010, Best Business Man for the Year 2011, ranked by Arabian Business amongst the Power 500: The World's Most Influential Arabs (8th) 2010, (87th) 2012, (34th) 2013. *Leisure interest:* cooking. *Address:* Air Arabia Head Quarters, Sharjah Freight Center (Cargo), near Sharjah International Airport, PO Box 132, Sharjah, United Arab Emirates (office). *Telephone:* (6) 5088888 (office). *Fax:* (6) 5580244 (office). *E-mail:* contactus@airarabia.com (office). *Website:* www.airarabia.com (office).

ALI, Ahmad Mohamed, BA, MA, PhD; Saudi Arabian development banker; *Chairman of the Board of Executive Directors and President, Islamic Development Bank;* b. 13 April 1934, Medina; s. of Mohamed Ali and Amina Ali; m. Ghada Mahmood Masri 1968; one s. three d.; ed Cairo Univ., Univ. of Michigan and State Univ. of New York, Albany Univ., USA; Dir Scientific and Islamic Inst., Aden 1958–59; Deputy Rector, King Abdul Aziz Univ., Jeddah 1967–72; Deputy Minister of Educ. for Tech. Affairs 1972–75; Pres. Islamic Devt Bank 1975–93, 1995–, currently also Chair. Bd of Exec. Dirs; Sec.-Gen. Muslim World League 1993–95; mem. King Abdul Aziz Univ. Council, King Saud Univ., Oil and Minerals Univ., Islamic Univ., Imam Mohammed Ben Saud Univ.; mem. Admin. Bd Saudi Credit Bank, Saudi Fund for Devt. *Publications:* numerous articles and working papers on Islamic econs, banking and educ. *Leisure interests:* cycling, walking. *Address:* Islamic Development Bank, PO Box 5925, Jeddah 21432, Saudi Arabia (office). *Telephone:* (2) 6361400 (office). *Fax:* (2) 6366871 (office). *E-mail:* idbarchives@isdb .org (office). *Website:* www.isdb.org (office).

ALI, Tan Sri Datuk Ahmad Tajuddin, BSc, PhD; Malaysian engineer; *President, Malaysian Academy of Sciences;* ed Malay Coll. Kuala Kangsar, Universiti Putra Malaysia, King's Coll., Queen Mary Coll., Univ. of London, UK, Harvard Business School, USA; started career as Asst Engineer, Nat. Electricity Bd of Malaya 1973, Sr Research Officer, Tun Ismail Atomic Research Centre 1977–83; Field Expert, IAEA 1985–88; Deputy Dir-Gen., Nuclear Energy Unit of Prime Minister's Dept 1983–89; Dir-Gen., Standards and Industrial Research Inst. of Malaysia 1989–96; Chair. and CEO Tenaga Nasional Berhad 1996–2000; Chair. Energy Comm. of Malaysia 2010–; Pres. Malaysian Acad. of Sciences 2011–; Chair. Gas Malaysia Sdn Bhd 2001–04, UEM Group Berhad 2007–, UEM Land Holdings Berhad 2008–, Malaysian Oxygen Berhad, Malaysian Standards and Accreditation Council; Adjunct Prof., Univ. Utara Malaysia; Fellow, Inst. of Engineers Malaysia, Asean Fed. of Engineering Orgs; mem. Governing Council, Int. Org. for Standardisation, Geneva, Switzerland; Co-Chair. (Industry), Malaysian Industry–Govt Group for High Tech.; mem. Int. Advisory Council, Universiti Tenaga Nasional, APEC Business Advisory Council; mem. Bd of Govs Malay Coll. Kuala Kangsar; Hon. DSc (Universiti Putra Malaysia) 2000, (Universiti Malaysia Terengganu) 2009, Hon. DEng (Universiti Tenaga Nasional) 2008; Inst. of Engineers Malaysia Award for Outstanding Contribution to Engineering Profession 1996, Construction Industry Devt Bd Malaysia Prominent Player Award 2009; awarded Dato' Paduka Mahkota Perlis by Raja of Perlis 1993. *Address:* Akademi Sains Malaysia, 902-4 Jalan Tun Ismail, 50480 Kuala Lumpur, Malaysia (office). *Telephone:* (3) 26949898 (office). *Fax:* (3) 26945858 (office). *E-mail:* admin@akademisains.gov.my (office). *Website:* www.akademisains.gov.my (office).

ALI, Ahmed Thasmeen, BA, MA; Maldivian politician; *President, Dhivehi Rayyithunge Party (DRP—Maldivian People's Party);* b. 1967; ed Univ. of Warwick, UK, American Univ., Cairo, Egypt; mem. Dhivehi Rayyithunge Party (DRP—Maldivian People's Party), Deputy Leader 2008–10, Pres. 2010–; elected mem. People's Majlis (Parl.) for Baa Atoll 1990s, currently for Kendhoo Constituency; fmr Deputy Speaker, Leader of DRP Parl. Group 2009–; fmr Deputy Dir Ministry of Trade and Industry; Minister of Home Affairs 2005–07, of Atolls Devt 2007–08; vice-presidential running mate of Maumoon Abdul Gayoom in presidential election Oct. 2008; Chair. Bd Dirs Dhiraagu 2005–; Regional Rep. CPA; presidential cand. of DRP 2010. *Address:* Dhivehi Rayyithunge Party, Sinamalé 3, Galolhu, Malé, Maldives (office). *Telephone:* 3320456 (office). *Fax:* 3344774 (office). *E-mail:* info@drp.org.mv (office). *Website:* www.drp.org.mv (office).

ALI, Aires Bonifácio; Mozambican politician; b. 6 Dec. 1955; teacher, Frelimo Secondary School, Namaacha –1976; Dir Francisco Manyanga Secondary School, Maputo 1977; Prov. Dir of Educ. and Culture, Nampula 1980–86; Head, Minister of Educ.'s Office 1989–90; Nat. Dir School Social Welfare Programmes 1991–92; Gov. Niassa Prov. 1995–2000, Inhambane Prov. 2000–04; Minister of Educ. and Culture 2005–10; Prime Minister 2010–12. *Address:* c/o Office of the Prime Minister, Praça da Marinha Popular, Maputo, Mozambique.

ALI, Amadou; Cameroonian politician; *Deputy Prime Minister;* Sr Minister in charge of Justice 2000–04; Deputy Prime Minister 2004–; mem. Rassemblement démocratique du peuple camerounais (RDPC). *Address:* c/o Office of the Prime Minister, Yaoundé, Cameroon (office). *Telephone:* 223-8005 (office). *Fax:* 223-5735 (office). *Website:* www.spm.gov.cm (office).

ALI, Anwar, MSc; Pakistani nuclear physicist, academic and administrator; *Research Scientist and Professor of Nuclear Engineering, Pakistan Institute of Engineering and Applied Sciences;* b. Lahore; ed Univ. of Punjab, Govt Coll., Lahore, Univ. of Birmingham, UK; worked as Dir at Dr A.Q. Khan Research Labs (KRL, fmr Eng Research Lab.); joined Pakistan Atomic Energy Comm. (PAEC) as Asst Scientific Officer 1967, mem. (Tech.) PAEC 2001–09, Chair. PAEC 2006–09; Research Scientist and Prof. of Nuclear Eng, Pakistan Inst. of Eng and Applied Sciences 2009–; Sitara-i-Imtiaz 1998, Hilal-e-Imtiaz; Special Commendation from Chief of Army Staff and Chair. Jt Chiefs of Staff Cttee, Pres.'s Medal for Pride of Performance. *Achievements include:* one of pioneers of PAEC's Uranium Enrichment Project-706, Kahuta Research Labs; played key role in formative years of Nat. Defence Complex in developing guidance and control system for Shaheen-I rocket; mem. team of scientists and engineers who carried out nuclear tests at Ras Koh Hills, Chagai region 1998. *Address:* Department of Nuclear Engineering, Pakistan Institute of Engineering and Applied Sciences, PO Nilore, Islamabad, Pakistan (office). *Telephone:* (51) 2207380 (office). *Fax:* (51) 2208070 (office). *E-mail:* webmaster@pieas.edu.pk (office). *Website:* www.pieas.edu.pk (office).

ALI, Datuk Hamidon bin; Malaysian diplomatist and UN official; b. 22 Jan. 1950, Tangkak, Johor; m. Datin Amy Low Abdulah; two s.; ed Monash Univ., Australia, Harvard Univ., USA; worked as Minister Counsellor, Embassy in Tokyo, First Sec., Embassy in Beijing, Second Sec., Embassy in Paris; held several positions at Ministry of Foreign Affairs, including Under-Sec. for Econs, Prin. Asst Sec. for Maritime and the Environment, and Prin. Asst Sec. for the Inspectorate; Under-Sec. I in-charge of multilateral and regional issues, including APEC and Indian Ocean Rim Asscn for Regional Cooperation 1991–96; Perm. Rep. to UN, Geneva 1996–2001, also accred to WTO and UN Conf. on Disarmament; High Commr to Singapore 2001–03; Amb. to Indonesia 2003–05, Perm. Rep. to UN, New York 2005–11; Pres. ECOSOC 2010–11; Chair. UN, Population Award Cttee; fmr Chair. 5th Cttee (Man. and Budgetary) of 62nd Session of UN Gen. Ass.; apptd Vice-Pres. UNICEF 2008; served as Chair. Co-ordinating Bureau of the Non-Aligned Movement and the ASEAN New York Cttee; Vice-Chair. UN Forum on Forests 2006–07; fmr Co-ordinator of the Asian Group on Human Rights; fmr Chair. OIC Group, Group of Representatives of G15, Commonwealth Group of Developing Countries in WTO, Asian Group in UNCTAD, Asia-Pacific Group in ILO; fmr mem. Advisory Bd South-North Development Monitor (published by the Third World Network); chaired the 'Friends of Dr. Supachai' group in run-up to selection of Dr Supachai Panichpakdi as Dir-Gen. of WTO; Commdr, Order of Bernado O'Higgins (Chile) 1994; Darjah Panglima Jasa Negara (PJN) from King of Malaysia (carries the title Datuk), Darjah Kebesaran Setia Mahkota Kelantan Yang Amat Terbilang (SPSK) from Sultan of Kelantan (carries the title Dato), Darjah Yang Mulia Mahkota Johor (DPMJ) from Sultan of Johor (carries the title Dato'), Kesatria Mangku Negara (KMN) from King of Malaysia 1995, Darjah Indera Mahkota Pahang (DIMP) from Sultan of Pahang (carries the title Dato') 2001. *Address:* c/o ECOSOC, United Nations Headquarters, First Avenue at 46th Street, New York, NY 10017, USA.

ALI, Hatem; Syrian actor and film director; b. 1962; fmr Lecturer, Higher Inst. of Dramatic Arts, Damascus; has directed numerous films for cinema and TV, including 30-episode TV drama series El-malek Farouk (King Farouq) 2007. *Films:* as actor: Daerat Al Nar (Circle of Fire), Hegrat Al Qalb Ila Al Qalb, Al Gawareh, Al Ragol S (Mr. S), Abou Kamel; as dir: Al Oshak (The Lovers), Shaghaf (Passion), Silina 2009, Al Layl Al-Tawil (The Long Night) 2009 (Taormina Int. Film Festival Golden Tauro 2009). *Plays:* theatre plays directed: Mat Thalath Marrat (Dead Three Times), Ahl Al Hawa (People of Instincts), Albareha, Alyawm Waghadan (Yesterday, Today and Tomorrow). *Publications:* Mawt Modares Al Tariekh Al Agouz (Death of The Old History Teacher), Hadath Wama Lam Yahdouth (What Happened And What Didn't), Tholatheyet Al Hesar (Blockade trilogy). *Address:* c/o Syrian National Film Organization, Rawda, Damascus, Syria (office). *Telephone:* (11) 3334201 (office). *Website:* www.damascusfest.com (office); www.hatemali.com (office).

ALI, M'Madi Ahamada; Comoran diplomatist and politician; *Chief of Staff to the Presidency in charge of Defence;* fmr Consul, Consulate in Nairobi, Kenya; apptd Minister of Justice and Islamic Affairs 2006; Chief of Staff to the Presidency in charge of Defence 2011–. *Address:* Office of the Head of State, Palais de Beit Salam, BP 521, Moroni, Comoros (office). *Telephone:* 7744808 (office). *Website:* www.beit -salam.km (office).

ALI, Lt-Gen. (retd) Moses, BSc; Ugandan lawyer, politician and fmr army officer; *Third Deputy Prime Minister and Deputy Leader of Government Business;* b. 5 April 1939, Meliaderi, Atabo Parish, Pakele Div., Adjumani Dist; ed Old Kampala Sr Secondary School, Staff Coll. Camberley and Holborn Coll. London, UK; mil. training as Cadet Officer and Paratrooper Instructor; Officer-in-Charge, Uganda Paratrooper School 1969–71, apptd Commdt 1971; elected mem. of Parl. (Adjumani Dist); Minister of Provincial Educ. 1973; Minister of Youth, Culture and Sports –1990; charged with plotting terrorist activities, acquitted 1991, rejoined cabinet 1994; served as Minister of Finance, Second Deputy Prime Minister and Minister of Tourism, Trade and Antiquities; Minister of Internal Affairs 2000; First Deputy Prime Minister and Minister of Disaster Preparedness and Refugees –2006; Third Deputy Prime Minister and Deputy Leader of Govt Business 2011–; Vice-Chair. Nat. Resistance Movt; fmr Chair. W Nile Parl. Group; fmr Gov. African Devt Bank; fmr Chair. Cabinet Econ. Cttee, Islamic Devt Bank of Govs, Fed. of Uganda Football Asscn, Cen. Tender Bd; fmr mem. Nat. Resistance Council, Moyo Dist, Uganda Council, Islamic Univ.; Appointment Cttee of Uganda Parl.; fmr Del. to Constituent Ass. for E Moyo Dist; Distinguished Service Order, Mil. Cross, Operational and Repub. Medal. *Address:* Office of the Deputy Prime Minister, Post Office Bldg, Yusuf Lule Rd, PO Box 341, Kampala (office); National Resistance Movement, PO Box 7778, Kampala, Uganda (office). *Telephone:* (64) 1346295 (office), (64) 1346279 (office). *E-mail:* info@nrm.ug (office). *Website:* www.nrm.ug (office).

ALI, Muhammad; American fmr professional boxer; b. (Cassius Marcellus Clay, Jr), 17 Jan. 1942, Louisville, Ky; s. of Cassius Marcellus Clay Sr and Odessa L. Grady; m. 1st Sonji Roi (divorced 1966); m. 2nd Belinda Boyd (Khalilah Tolaria) 1967 (divorced 1977); m. 3rd Veronica Porche 1977 (divorced 1986); m. 4th Yolanda Williams 1986; two s. seven d.; amateur boxer 1954–60, Olympic Games Light-Heavyweight Champion 1960; turned professional 1960, won World Heavyweight title Feb. 1964, defeating Sonny Liston; adopted name Muhammad Ali 1964; stripped of title after refusing to be drafted into US Army 1967, won case in US Supreme Court and returned to professional boxing 1970; regained World Heavyweight title Oct. 1974, defeating George Foreman in Zaire; lost title to Leon Spinks 1978, regained title from Spinks 1978; 56 victories in 61 fights up to Dec. 1981; lost to Larry Holmes Oct. 1980; mem. of US Black Muslim movt; Special Envoy of Pres. Carter to Africa 1980 (to urge boycott of Olympic Games), of Pres. Bush to Iraq 1990 (prior to Operation Desert Storm); lit Olympic flame, Atlanta 1996; f. Muhammad Ali Center, Louisville, Ky 1997, currently mem. Bd of Dirs; f. Muhammad Ali Enterprises 2006; fmr mem. Peace Corps Advisory Council; numerous awards including Int. Athlete of the Year, United Press 1974, Male Athlete of the Year, Associated Press 1974, Hickok Belt Winner 1974, Athlete of the Century, GQ Magazine, Lifetime Achievement Award, Amnesty Int., Arthur Ashe Courage Award 1997, named Messenger of Peace, UN 1998–2008, Sports Personality of the Year, BBC 1999, Int. Amb. of Jubilee 2000, Presidential Medal of Freedom 2005, Otto Hahn Peace Medal, Germany 2005, Sportsman of the Century, Sports Illustrated, World Sportsman of the Century, World Sports Award, Louisvillian of the Century, Advertising Club of Louisville, Kentuckian of the Century, Essence Award, XNBA Human Spirit Award. *Film appearances include:* The Greatest 1976, Freedom Road (TV) 1978, Freedom Road 1980. *Publications include:* The Greatest: My Own Story (autobiog.) 1975, Healing (with Thomas Hauser) 1996, More Than a Hero (with Hana Ali) 2000, The Soul of a Butterfly: Reflections on Life's Journey (co-author) 2004. *Address:* Muhammad Ali Enterprises LLC, 650 Madison Avenue, 15th Floor, New York, NY 10022, USA. *Telephone:* (212) 407-9173. *Website:* www.ali.com; www.alicenter.org (office).

ALI, Brig.-Gen. Muhammad Nasser Ahmad; Yemeni army officer and government official; *Minister of Defence;* Minister of Defence 2006–. *Address:* Ministry of Defence, POB 4131, San'a, Yemen (office). *Telephone:* (1) 252640 (office). *Fax:* (1) 252375 (office).

ALI, Muhammad Shamsher, MSc, PhD; Bangladeshi physicist, academic and organization official; *President, Bangladesh Academy of Sciences;* b. 9 Nov. 1937, Bheramara, Kushtia; s. of Amir Ali and Rahima Khatun; m. Saqeba Ali; two s.; ed Rajshahi Govt Coll., Univs of Dhaka, Manchester, UK; Scientific Officer, Atomic Energy Comm. 1961–65, Sr Scientific Officer 1965–69, Prin. Scientific Officer 1970–75, Chief Scientific Officer 1976–82; Dir Atomic Energy Centre, Dhaka 1970–78; Prof. of Physics, Univ. of Dhaka 1982–2006; Founder-Vice-Chancellor Bangladesh Open Univ. 1992–96; Founder-Vice-Chancellor, Southeast Univ., Dhaka 2002–10; Vice-Pres. Asscn of Acads of Sciences in Asia 2004–10; mem. Advisory Cttee, Bangladesh Atomic Energy Comm. 1977–87; Sr Assoc., Int. Centre for Theoretical Physics, Trieste; Gen. Sec. Bangladesh Asscn of Scientists and Scientific Professions 1978–81; Dir International Distance Education Accreditation League, Philipines 2011–; Life mem. Asiatic Soc. of Bangladesh, Bangladesh Math. Soc.; mem. New York Acad. of Sciences, Pugwash Group, American Physical Soc., Inter-Acad. Panel on Int. Issues (exec. mem. 2003–09), Fed. of Asian Scientific Acads and Socs, Regional Cttee of Int. Council for Science (Asia and the Pacific) 2006–09, Nat. Council of Science and Tech.; Fellow, Bangladesh Acad. of Sciences (Pres. 2004–), TWAS (The Acad. of Sciences for the Developing World), Islamic Acad. of Sciences (Jordan, mem. Council 1989–94), Bangladesh Physical Soc., Bangla Acad.; Hon. Prof. of Physics, Dhaka Univ. 1973; Hon. mem. World Innovation Foundation 2006, Hon. Fellow; Hari Prasanna Roy Gold Medal, Univ. of Dhaka 1974, Gold Medal, Bangladesh Acad. of Sciences 1985, Third World Network of Scientific Orgs Award 1990, J.C. Bose Gold Medal, Mother Teresa Gold Medal, Khan Bahadur Ahsanullah Gold Medal 2004, Lifetime Achivement Award in Higher Educ. Leadership, Int. Univ. Leadership Colloquium (Malaysia). *Film:* Science Learning at Home: The Hand that Rocks the Cradle Rules the World (documentary) 1985. *Publications include:* as co-author: The Culture of Science in Bangladesh 1983, Poverty and Technology 1986, Scientific Indications in the Holy Quran 1990, Muslim Contributions to Science and Technology 1996, Aladdin's Real Lamp: Science and Technology; more than 70 research papers on nuclear and hypernuclear physics. *Leisure interests:* catching fish, reading poetry and literature, listening to music, travelling. *Address:* Bangladesh Academy of Sciences, National Science and Technology Museum Bhaban, Agargaon, Dhaka 1207, Bangladesh (office). *Telephone:* 1819-253931 (mobile) (office); (2) 9110425 (office); (2) 8628280 (office). *Fax:* (2) 8117049 (office). *E-mail:* office@bas.org.bd (office); bas_bangladesh@yahoo.com (office); msali_37@yahoo.com. *Website:* www.bas.org .bd (office); www.msali.net.bd.

ALI, Mustafa; Syrian sculptor; b. 1956, Lattakia; ed Plastic Arts Centre, Minor Arts Centre, Faculty of Fine Arts, Damascus, Faculty of Fine Arts, Carrara, Italy; known for elegant, monumental sculptures, and widely collected in the Arab world for nearly three decades; mem. Syndicates of Fine Arts, Arab Plastic Artists Union; mem. Higher Cttee for Acquisition, Ministry of Culture; works have been displayed at exhbns in Canada, N Africa, Lebanon, Jordan, Syria and France; works held in Ministry of Culture, Syria, Public Palace, Damascus, Nat. Museum, Syria, Contemporary Art Museum, Syria, Contemporary Art Museum, Jordan, Al Sharjah Museum, UAE, Deir Mar Musa Monastery, Al Nabek; Bronze Prize, Sharjah Biennial 1992, Gold Prize, Lattakia Biennial 1997, Emmar Int. Art Symposium Prize 2007, Winner Arab World Int. Competition 2008, ranked by Arabian Business amongst the Power 500: The Worlds's Most Influential Arabs (97th) 2011–12. *Monuments designed include:* Int. Damascus Fair Tower of Memory, Umayyad Square Monument (with Ihsan Intabi), Syrian Gate in Mediterranean Olympiad, Pari, Italy. *Address:* Mustafa Ali Gallery-Art Foundation, PO Box 14225, Damascus, Syria (office). *Telephone:* (11) 5440236 (office). *Fax:* (11) 5421988 (office). *E-mail:* m-ali@scs-net.org (office).

ALI, Sheikh Razzak, LLB, MA; Bangladeshi politician and diplomatist; b. 1928, Khulna; ed Univ. of Dhaka; fmr reporter and journalist with Daily Pakistan; Asst Ed. 'Enterprise' 1952; Chief Reporter and Commercial Ed. Daily Pakistan Observer 1954–58; practised law in Khulna, lawyer of High Court –1990, 1997–2001; participated in Language Movt 1952, War of Liberation 1971; joined Bangladesh Nat. Party (BNP) 1978, fmr Pres. Khulna Dist BNP, fmr Vice-Chair. BNP Cen. Cttee, fmr mem. BNP Standing Cttee, now mem. LDP; rep. Bangladesh in UN Gen. Ass. 1980; elected mem. Parl. 1970, 1991, 1996; State Minister for Law and Justice 1991; Deputy Speaker of Parl. April–Oct. 1991, Speaker 1991–96; High Commr to UK 2001–02; Pres. and Gen. Sec. Khulna Bar Asscn 1964, 1972; Pres.

Jessore Bar Asscn 1984–86; Founder-Prin. Khulna City Coll.; Founder Khulna Suburban Coll.; Founder-Pres. Khulna Shiromony Eye Hosp. *Address:* c/o Liberal Democratic Party, 102 Park Road, New DOHS, Mohakhali, Dhaka 1206, Bangladesh.

ALI, Dato Paduka Serbinibin Haji; Brunei diplomatist and civil servant; *Ambassador to Belgium;* b. 10 April 1955; m.; four c.; joined Foreign Service early 1980s, with Embassies in Singapore 1982–84, Bangkok 1984–85, Tokyo 1989–92; Asst Dir Protocol and Consular Affairs Dept, Ministry of Foreign Affairs 1985–86, Deputy Dir 1986–89, Deputy Dir Multilateral Econs Dept 1992–96, Dir 1997–98, Dir of Politics (Asia and Pacific Affairs) 1996–97; Deputy Exec. Dir APEC Secr., Singapore Jan.–Dec. 1999, Exec. Dir 1999–2001; Perm. Rep. to UN, New York 2001; Perm. Sec., Ministry of Health *c.* 2007; mem. Del. to Co-ordinators Meeting, Movt of Non-Aligned Countries; attended ministerial-level meetings of OIC, APEC and ASEAN; currently Amb. to Belgium. *Address:* Embassy of Brunei, 238 Avenue F. D. Roosevelt, 1050 Brussels, Belgium (office). *Telephone:* (2) 675-08-78 (office). *Fax:* (2) 672-93-58 (office). *E-mail:* serbini.ali@mfa.gov.bn (office).

ALI, Shahid, BAcc (Hons), MMan, MBA; Maldivian consultant and business executive; *Managing Director, State Trading Organization Plc;* ed Int. Islamic Univ., Malaysia, Australian Nat. Univ.; experienced in business man. finance, investment appraisals and project man. since early 1990s; worked in several projects for multilateral agencies including World Bank, Asian Devt Bank and UNDP; held various Govt positions, including Deputy Dir, Ministry of Finance and Treasury; Man. Dir and Non-Ind. Exec. Dir State Trading Org. Plc 2008–; Sir Roland Wilson Award for Best MBA Student, ANU 2006. *Address:* State Trading Organization Plc, STO Building, Boduthakurufaanu Magu, Maafannu, Malé 20-345, Maldives (office). *Telephone:* 3344333 (office). *Fax:* 3344334 (office). *E-mail:* info@stomaldives.net (office). *Website:* www.stomaldives.com (office).

ALI, Tariq; British (b. Pakistani) political activist and writer; b. 21 Oct. 1943, Lahore, Pakistan; pnr Susan Watkins; one s. two d.; ed Punjab Univ., Univ. of Oxford; Editorial Dir Verso 1999–; mem. editorial bd New Left Review 1982–; mem. Fourth International. *Publications:* fiction: Redemption 1990, Shadows of the Pomegranate Tree 1992, Fear of Mirrors 1998, The Book of Saladin 1999, The Stone Woman 2000, The Illustrious Corpse 2003, A Sultan in Palermo 2005, Night of the Golden Butterfly 2010; non-fiction: The Thoughts of Chairman Harold (compiler) 1967, The New Revolutionaries: A Handbook of the International Radical Left (ed.) 1969, Pakistan: Military Rule or People's Power? 1970, The Coming British Revolution 1972, Chile: Lessons of the Coup: Which Way to Workers' Power? (with Gerry Hedley) 1974, 1968 and After: Inside the Revolution 1978, Trotsky for Beginners 1980, Can Pakistan Survive? 1983, What is Stalinism? (ed.) 1984, The Stalinist Legacy: Its Impact on Twentieth-Century World Politics (ed.) 1984, An Indian Dynasty: The Story of the Nehru-Gandhi Family 1985, Street Fighting Years: An Autobiography of the Sixties 1987, Revolution from Above: Where is the Soviet Union Going? 1988, Moscow Gold (with Howard Brenton) 1990, 1968: Marching in the Streets (with Susan Watkins) 1998, Ugly Rumours (with Howard Brenton) 1998, Masters of the Universe?: NATO's Balkan Crusade (ed.) 2000, The Clash of Fundamentalisms: Crusades, Jihads and Modernity 2002, The Clash of Fundamentalisms: Bush in Babylon: Recolonising Iraq 2003, Rough Music 2005, Conversations with Edward Said 2006, Pirates of the Caribbean: Axis of Hope 2006, The Leopard and the Fox 2007, A Banker for All Seasons: Crooks and Cheats Inc. 2007, The Assassination 2008, The Duel: Pakistan on the Flight Path of American Power 2009, The Protocols of the Elders of Sodom 2009, The Obama Syndrome 2010; contribs to periodicals, including London Review of Books. *Address:* c/o Verso, 6 Meard Street, London, W1F 0EG, England (office). *E-mail:* tariq.ali3@btinternet.com (office). *Website:* www.tariqali.org.

ALI, Zine al Abidine Ben; Tunisian politician and fmr head of state; b. 3 Sept. 1936, Hammam Sousse; m. Leila Ben Ali; three c.; ed as grad. in electronics, Saint-Cyr Mil. Acad., France, Chalons-sur-Marne School of Artillery, France, Special School of Intelligence and Security, USA; Head of Mil. Security 1958–74; Mil. and Naval Attaché, Rabat, Morocco 1974–77; mem. of Cabinet for Minister of Nat. Defence, Dir-Gen. Nat. Security 1977–80; Amb. to Poland 1980–84; Sec. of State for Nat. Security 1984–85, Minister of the Interior 1986–87, Minister of State for the Interior May–Nov. 1987, Pres. of Tunisia 1987–2011 (forced to step down and flee to Saudi Arabia); mem. politbureau of Parti Socialiste Destourien (PSD) 1986, Sec.-Gen. PSD 1986, Chair. Rassemblement Constitutionnel Démocratique (RCD); Order of Merit of Bourguiba, Order of Independence, Order of the Repub., several foreign orders. *Leisure interests:* computers, music, sports.

ALIBEK, Ken, MD, PhD, ScD; American (b. Kazakhstani) industrial biotechnologist and academic; b. (Kanatzhan Alibekov), Kauchuk, Kazakh SSR; s. of Bayzak Alibekov and Rosa Alibekov; m. Lena Yemesheva 1976; four c.; ed Tomsk Medical Inst.; fmr mem. CP; cadet intern in mil. section of Tomsk Medical Inst. 1973; Jr Lt, later Sr Lt in Soviet Army, attained rank of Col 1987; mem. staff E European Scientific Br., Inst. of Applied Biochemistry, Omutninsk, Sr Scientist Siberian Br., Berdsk 1976; Deputy Dir (later Dir) Stepnogorsk Biological Research Centre, Deputy Chief Biopreparat Biosafety Div. 1987, First Deputy Chief 1988, working for Soviet Union's offensive biological weapons programme; Dir Biomash 1990–91; visited American mil. and research sites 1991; defected to USA 1992, debriefed by US mil. on Soviet and Russian biological weapons programme, consultant to NIH and numerous US Govt agencies in fields of industrial tech., medical microbiology, biological weapons defence and biological weapons non-proliferation; currently Pres. and Chief Scientific Officer AFG Biosolutions Inc.; also Founder, Pres. and CEO MaxWell Biocorporation LLC 2006–; Distinguished Prof., George Mason Univ. –2006; Sr Fellow, Centre for Advanced Defense Studies; returned to Astana, Kazakhstan 2010, Prof., Dept of Chem. and Biology, School of Science and Tech., Nazarbayev Univ. 2010–, also Vice-Dean for Research; CEO National Medical Holding JSC, Astana 2013–; Hon. DSc 1988. *Publications include:* Biohazard (autobiog. with Stephen Handelman) 2000, Jane's Chem-Bio Handbook 2002, Biological Weapons 2003, Biological and Chemical Terrorism: A Guide for Healthcare Providers and First Responders 2003, Bioterrorism and Infectious Agents: A New Dilemma for the 21st Century (ed) 2005, New and Evolving Infections of the 21st Century 2009; numerous articles in professional journals. *Address:* School of Science and Technology, Nazarbayev University, 53 Kabanbay batyr Avenue, Astana 010000, Kazakhstan (office). *Telephone:* (717) 2706180 (office). *E-mail:* info@nu.edu.kz (office). *Website:* nu.edu.kz (office).

ALIĆ, Muhidin, LLB; Bosnia and Herzegovina politician; b. 14 Sept. 1960, Šije, Tešanj Prov.; m.; two c.; ed high school in Doboj, Sarajevo Univ.; served in Bosnia and Herzegovina Army, then several positions in police force; fmr Sec. Tešanj Municipal Council; fmr Asst Minister of Justice, Minister of Labour, Social Policy and Refugees, Minister of Interior, Zenica-Doboj Canton Govt; Minister of Internal Affairs, Fed. of Bosnia and Herzegovina 2006–11. *Address:* c/o Minister of Internal Affairs, 71000 Sarajevo, Mehmeda Spahe 7, Bosnia and Herzegovina. *E-mail:* kabinet@fmup.gov.ba.

ALIER, Abel, LLM; South Sudanese politician and judge; b. 1933, Bor Dist, Upper Nile Prov.; s. of Kwai Alier and Anaai Alier; m. Siama Fatma Bilal 1970; one d.; ed Univ. of Khartoum and Yale Univ., USA; fmr advocate; Dist Judge in El Obeid, Wad Medani and Khartoum –1965; participant in Round Table Conf. and mem. Twelve Man Cttee to Study the Southern Problem 1965; mem. Constitution Comms 1966–67, 1968; fmr mem. Law Reform Comm. and Southern Front; Minister of Supply and Internal Trade 1969–70; Minister of Works 1970–71; Minister of Southern Affairs 1971–72; Vice-Pres. of Sudan 1971–82; Minister of Construction and Public Works 1983–85; fmr Chair. Nat. Elections Comm.; mem. Panel of Arbitrators, Perm. Court of Int. Arbitration, The Hague 1988–; apptd head nat. cttee to investigate death of John Garang 2005; Pres. Supreme Exec. Council for the South 1972–78, 1980–81; mem. Political Bureau, Sudanese Socialist Union; mem. Bd of Dirs Industrial Planning Corpn, Nat. Scholarship Bd; Hon. LLD (Khartoum) 1978. *Publications include:* Regional Autonomy for the South 1970, The Visit of President Nyerere to the Southern Region 1974 1975, Peace and Development in the Southern Region 1977, Southern Sudan: Too Many Agreements Dishonoured 1999, Excesses in Human Rights Violations 2002. *Leisure interests:* tennis, athletics, reading, history and literature. *Address:* c/o National Election Commission, Altayef South Kenana Sugar Co., Khartoum, Sudan (office).

ALIERTA IZUEL, César, LLB, MBA; Spanish telecommunications executive; *Executive Chairman and CEO, Telefónica SA;* b. 5 May 1945, Zaragoza; ed Univ. of Zaragoza, Columbia Univ., New York, USA; fmr stockbroker; Gen. Man. Capital Markets Div., Banco Urquijo, Madrid 1970–85; Founder and Chair. Beta Capital 1985–96; Chair. Spanish Financial Analysts' Asscn 1991; Chair. Tabacalera SA 1996–99, Co-Chair. Altadis Group (following merger with French group Seita) 1999–2000; mem. Bd of Dirs Telefónica SA 1997–, Exec. Chair. and CEO 2000–; mem. Bd of Dirs China Unicom, Telecom Italia; Ind. Bd mem., Chair. Remuner-ation Cttee and mem. Nominations Cttee of the Bd of Dirs of International Consolidated Airlines Group (co. resulting from merger of Iberia and British Airways) 2010–; mem. Colombia Business School Bd of Overseers; Chair. Social Bd of UnED (nat. Long Distance Spanish Univ.); Gov. European Foundation for Quality Man.; fmr mem. Bd of Dirs and Standing Cttee Madrid Stock Exchange; charged with insider trading related to sales in 1997 of Tabacalera shares July 2005; The Global Spanish Entrepreneur, Spanish/US Chamber of Commerce in recognition of Telefónica Group's success in joining the New York Dow Jones Global Titans 50 index 2005, Americas Soc. Gold Medal 2010. *Address:* Telefónica SA, Gran Vía 28, 28013 Madrid, Spain (office). *Telephone:* (91) 584-0306 (office). *Fax:* (91) 531-9347 (office). *E-mail:* info@telefonica.com (office). *Website:* www.telefonica.com (office).

ALINGTON, William Hildebrand, MArch; New Zealand architect; b. 18 Nov. 1929, Wellington; s. of Edward Hugh Alington and Beatrice McCrie Alington; m. Margaret Hilda Broadhead 1955; one s. two d.; ed Hutt Valley High School, School of Architecture, Auckland Univ. Coll., School of Architecture Univ. of Illinois; architectural cadet and architect, Head Office Ministry of Works, Wellington 1950–65; architect, London Office of Robert Matthew & Johnson-Marshall 1956–57; Pnr, Gabites & Beard 1965–71, Gabites Toomath Beard Wilson & Pnrs 1971–72, Gabites Alington & Edmondson 1972–79, Gabites Porter & Pnrs 1978–83; Sr Pnr, Alington Group Architects 1984–; Asst Ed. NZIA Journal 1964–69; Pres. Architectural Centre 1970–74; Hon. Lecturer, Victoria Univ. of Wellington School of Architecture 1975–85, Tutor 1986–2003; Vice-Pres. and Br. Chair. New Zealand Inst. of Architects 1977–79, mem. Council 1965–79; mem. Wellington Anglican Diocesan Synod 1972–90. *Publications:* numerous articles in specialist journals. *Leisure interests:* gardening, painting, church government. *Address:* 60 Homewood Crescent, Wellington, New Zealand. *Telephone:* (4) 476-8495. *Fax:* (4) 476-8495 (home). *E-mail:* alington@xtra.co.nz (home).

ALINGUÉ, Jean Bawoyeu; Chadian politician; b. 18 Aug. 1937, N'Djamena; s. of Marc Bawoyeu Alingué and Tabita Poureng; m. Esther Azina 1960; three s. four d.; fmr Pres. of Nat. Ass.; Prime Minister of Chad 1991–92; Minister of Justice and Keeper of the Seals 2008–10, of Posts and Information and Communications Technologies 2010; Chair. Union pour la Démocratie et la République; Presidential Cand. for elections 2001. *Address:* c/o Ministry of Posts and Information and Communications Technologies, BP 154, N'Djamena, Chad (office).

ALIREZA, Abdullah ibn Ahmed Zainal; Saudi Arabian business executive and politician; fmr adviser to Supreme Econ. Council; fmr Chair. Jeddah Chamber of Commerce and Industry; fmr Cabinet Minister without Portfolio; Minister of Commerce and Industry 2008–11; headed team that negotiated Saudi Arabia's to WTO. *Address:* c/o Ministry of Commerce and Industry, POB 1774, Airport Road, Riyadh, Saudi Arabia.

ALIREZA, Yusuf; American business executive; *Executive Director and CEO, Noble Group;* ed Georgetown Univ. School of Foreign Service; joined Goldman Sachs, New York 1992, moved to London 1997, held positions in fixed-income sales and hedge fund sales, Partner 2004, later Head of EMEA Sales and Structuring Efforts –2008, moved to Hong Kong to lead Goldman's Asia Pacific Securities Div. 2008, Co-Pres. Asia (excluding Japan) and mem. Global Man. Cttee –2012; Exec. Dir and CEO Noble Group Ltd, Hong Kong 2012–; mem. Global Bd of Room to Read. *Address:* Noble Group Ltd, 18th Floor, MassMutual Tower, 38 Gloucester Road, Hong Kong Special Administrative Region, People's Republic of China (office). *Telephone:* 2861-3511 (office). *Fax:* 2527-0282 (office). *E-mail:* info@thisisnoble.com (office). *Website:* www.thisisnoble.com (office).

ALITO, Samuel A., Jr, AB, JD; American judge; *Associate Justice, Supreme Court;* b. 1 April 1950, Trenton, NJ; s. of the late Samuel Alito, Sr and of Rose Fradusco; m. Martha-Ann Bomgardner 1985; one s. one d.; ed Princeton Univ. and Yale Law School; law clerk, Third Circuit US Court of Appeals 1976–77; Asst US

Attorney 1977–81; Asst to US Solicitor Gen., Washington, DC 1981–85; Deputy Asst US Attorney Gen. 1985–87; US Attorney, Dist of New Jersey 1987–90; Judge, Third Circuit US Court of Appeals 1990–2005; nominated by Pres. George W. Bush for Assoc. Justice on US Supreme Court Oct. 2005, confirmed 2006; fmr Ed. Yale Law Journal. *Address:* Supreme Court of the United States, 1 First Street, NE, Washington, DC 20543, USA (office). *Telephone:* (202) 479-3211 (office). *Fax:* (202) 479-3021 (office). *Website:* www.supremecourtus.gov (office).

ALIVISATOS, A(rmand) Paul, BSc (Hons), PhD; American chemist and academic; *Professor of Chemistry and Samsung Distinguished Professor in Nanoscience and Nanotechnology Research, University of California, Berkeley;* b. 12 Nov. 1959, Chicago, Ill.; ed Univ. of Chicago, Univ. of California, Berkeley; family moved to Athens, Greece 1970, returned to USA late 1970s; postdoctoral fellow, AT&T Bell Labs 1986–88; mem. Faculty, Univ. of California, Berkeley 1988–, currently Prof. of Chem. and Materials Science & Eng and Samsung Distinguished Prof. in Nanoscience and Nanotechnology Research; Sr mem. Tech. Staff, Lawrence Berkeley Nat. Lab., Dir Materials Sciences Div. 2002–08, Assoc. Lab. Dir for Physical Sciences 2005–08, Deputy Dir Lab. 2008–09, Dir Lab. 2009–; Ed. Nano Letters; mem. NAS 2004, American Acad. of Arts and Sciences 2004; Fellow, American Physical Soc., AAAS; Presidential Young Investigator Award, Alfred P. Sloan Foundation Fellowship, ACS Exxon Solid State Chem. Fellowship, Coblentz Award 1994, Wilson Prize, Harvard Univ., Outstanding Young Investigator Award, Materials Research Soc. 1995, Dept of Energy Award for Sustained Outstanding Research in Materials Chem. 1997, ACS Award in Colloid and Surface Chem. 2004, Rank Prize 2006, Distinguished Alumni Award, Univ. of Chicago 2006, Eni Italgas Prize for Energy and Environment 2006, Ernest Orlando Lawrence Award 2007, Kavli Distinguished Lectureship in Nanoscience, Materials Research Soc. 2008, Linus Pauling Award 2011, Von Hippel Award, Materials Research Soc. 2011, Wolf Foundation Prize in Chem. (shared with Charles Lieber) for his contribs to nanochemistry 2012. *Publications:* numerous papers in professional journals on the structural, thermodynamic, optical and electrical properties of colloidal inorganic nanocrystals. *Address:* D-43A Hildebrand, MC 1460, Department of Chemistry, University of California, Berkeley, CA 94720-1460, USA (office). *Telephone:* (510) 643-7371 (office); 510-642-2148 (Lab.) (office). *Fax:* (510) 642-6911 (office). *E-mail:* alivis@berkeley.edu (office). *Website:* chem .berkeley.edu/faculty/alivisatos (office); www.cchem.berkeley.edu/pagrp (office).

ÄLIYEV, İlhäm Heydar oğlu, BA, PhD; Azerbaijani business executive, politician and head of state; *President;* b. 24 Dec. 1961, Baku, Azerbaijan SSR, USSR; s. of the late Heydar Aliyev, fmr Pres. of Azerbaijan; m. Mehriban Pashayeva; three c.; ed Moscow State Univ. of Int. Relations; lecturer, Moscow State Univ. of Int. Relations 1985–90; engaged in commercial activity in Moscow and İstanbul 1991–94; First Vice-Pres. State Oil Co. of the Azerbaijani Repub. (SOCAR) 1994–2003; mem. Parl. 1995–2003; Deputy Chair. Yeni Azerbaijan (New Azerbaijan) party 1999–2001, First Deputy Chair. 2001–; Prime Minister of Azerbaijan Aug. 2003; Pres. of Azerbaijan Oct. 2003–; Pres. Nat. Olympic Cttee 1997–; Leader Azerbaijani Parl. Del. to Council of Europe Parl. Ass. (PACE) 2001–03; Hon. Prof. L.N. Gumilev Eurasian Nat. Univ., Kazakhstan, Univ. of Nat. and World Economy, Bulgaria, Moscow State Univ. 2008, Belarusian State Univ., Turkmenistan State Univ. named after Makhtumkuli (Turkmenistan); Order of Heydar Äliyev, Order of Şeykülislam (Azerbaijan), Ven. Sergius of Radonezh Order of Russian Orthodox Church (First Degree), Order of Holy Prince Daniel of Moscow, (First Degree), Kt Grand Cross, Order of Three Stars (Latvia), Order of Honour (Georgia) 2003, Order of the Star of Romania 2004, Order of King Abdul Aziz as-Sa'ud (Saudi Arabia) 2005, Grand Croix, Légion d'honneur 2007, Order of Prince Yaroslav The Wise (First Degree) (Ukraine) 2008, Grand Cross, Order of Merit (Poland) 2008, Order of Mubarak Al-Kabeer (Kuwait) 2009, Gold Medal of Greek Parl. 2009, Order of Glory and Honour (First Degree) (Russia) 2010, Order of the Repub. of Serbia 2013, First Class of the Order of State of Repub. of Turkey 2013, Order of Liberty (Ukraine) 2013; Dr hc (Lincoln Univ., USA, Moscow State Univ., Bilkent Univ., Turkey, Nat. Acad. of Taxes, Ukraine, Petroleum and Gas Univ. of Ploieşti, Romania, Kyung Hee Univ., South Korea, Jordan Univ., Corvinus Univ., Hungary, Kyiv Taras Shevchenko Nat. Univ., Ukraine, Baku State Univ., Ankara Univ., Turkey, Çukurova Univ., Turkey); PACE Medal 2004, Ihsan Dogramacı Prize for Int. Relations for Peace (Turkey), included in a 500 Most Influential Muslims of the World book 2009, Supreme Order of the Hall of Fame FILA 'Legend of Sport', Order of Glory of the Int. Confed. of Sport Orgs of CIS countries, Order of Glory 'Great Cordon', Int. Mil. Sport Council. *Address:* Office of the President, 1066 Baku, İstiqlaliyyät küç. 19, Azerbaijan (office). *Telephone:* (12) 492-35-27 (office). *Fax:* (12) 492-35-43 (office). *E-mail:* office@ apparat.gov.az (office). *Website:* www.president.az (office); www.ilham-aliyev.com.

ALIYEV, Mukhu Gimbatovich, PhD; Russian/Dagestan politician; b. 6 Aug. 1940, Tanusi, Dagestan; m.; two c.; ed Dagestan State Univ.; began career as teacher, then Head, Nizhne-Gakvarinskaya Secondary School; Sec., Comsomol Cttee, Dagestan State Univ. 1964–66; First Sec., Makhachkala City Comsomol Cttee 1969–72, Makhachkala Dist CPSU Cttee 1972–85; Bureau Head, Dagestan Div. CPSU Cttee 1985–90; First Sec., Dagestan Repub. CPSU Cttee 1990–91; mem. Supreme Soviet of Dagestan (parl.), Vice-Chair. 1991–95; Chair. Econs Cttee, Repub. of Dagestan 1992–94; Chair. People's Ass., Repub. of Dagestan 1999–2006; Pres. of Dagestan 2006–10; mem. Council of Feds of Russia 1995, Deputy Chair. Cttee on Foreign Affairs 1995–2001; fmr mem. Parl. Ass., CIS and Council of Europe; Labour Red Banner 1976, Badge of Honour 1981, For Services to Motherland, class IV 2000, class III 2005. *Publications:* Dagestan Republic: Priorities of National Policy 1996, Unity and Integrity of Dagestan Republic as a Constitutional Principle 1998, Searching for Consent 2002; numerous articles in magazines and journals. *Address:* 33/1a Korkmasov Street, 367005 Makhachkala, Dagestan, Russia (home). *Telephone:* (8722) 67-04-96 (home).

ÄLIYEV, Natiq Ağäämi oğlu, PhD; Azerbaijani oil industry executive and government official; *Minister of Industry and Energy;* b. 23 Nov. 1947, Baku, Azerbaijan SSR, USSR; ed Azerbaijan State Oil Acad.; began working for Xezerdenizneft state concern 1970; apptd Chief Instructor of Department at Admin of Cen. Cttee of Azerbaijan CP 1984; Dir Econ.-Social Issues Dept 1989–91; apptd Dir of Ipesko rep. office, Baku 1992; concurrently worked as a consultant at State Oil Co. of Azerbaijani Repub. (SOCAR); Chair. Bd of Dirs and Pres. SOCAR 1993–2004; Minister of Industry and Energy 2005–; Chair. State Cttee for Devt of

Azeri-Chirag-Guneshli fields, Bd of Dirs Baku-Tbilisi-Ceyhan (BTC) pipeline; mem. Int. Eng Acad. Moscow 2008; Şöhrät Order, Order of the Glory of Georgia, Chevalier, Légion d'honneur; Merited Engineer Medal. *Publications:* more than 100 scientific publs, articles and books. *Address:* Ministry of Industry and Energy, 1000 Baku, U. Hacibeyov küç. 40, Hökumat House, Azerbaijan (office). *Telephone:* (12) 598-16-75 (office). *Fax:* (12) 598-16-78 (office). *E-mail:* mie@mie.gov.az (office); pressa@mie.gov.az (office). *Website:* www.mie.gov.az (office).

ALKALAJ, Sven, BS, MS; Bosnia and Herzegovina politician, diplomatist and fmr UN official; b. 11 Nov. 1948, Sarajevo; m.; two c.; ed Univ. of Sarajevo, Harvard Business School, USA; Commercial Man., Petrolinvest, Sarajevo 1975–85; Regional Man. for Middle and Far East Energoinvest, Sarajevo 1985–88, Man. Dir Energoinvest, Thailand 1988–94; Amb. to USA 1994–2000, to OAS 2000–04, to Belgium and Head of Perm. Mission to NATO 2004–07; Minister of Foreign Affairs 2007–12; Exec. Sec. UN ECE 2012–14; mem. Party for Bosnia and Herzegovina (SBiH); Silver Badge of Petrolinvest 1994, Sarajevo City Memorial Plaque, for contribs to the City devt, Award of the Centre for Peace, Non-Violence and Human Rights, Sarajevo 2003, Sloboda Award. *Leisure interests:* literature, film, music and the arts, tennis. *Address:* Ministry of Foreign Affairs, 71000 Sarajevo, Musala 2, Bosnia and Herzegovina.

ALKAN, Ali; Turkish judge; *Chief Justice, Supreme Court of Appeals;* b. 9 Feb. 1950, Kızılcahamam, Ankara Prov.; m.; one c.; ed Ankara Univ. Faculty of Law; mil. service as reserve officer, Antalya; began career as judge nominee in Ankara, later serving as judge in Pervari, Çayıralan and Haymana; fmr Judge, Ankara Commercial Court and Chair. Judicial Comm. on Justice; mem. Supreme Court of Appeals 1997–, Pres. 13th Civil Law Chamber of Supreme Court 2009–12, Chief Justice, Supreme Court of Appeals 2012–. *Address:* Office of the Chief Justice, Supreme Court of Appeals, Atatürk Bulvarı No 1, Bakanlıklar, 06658 Ankara, Turkey (office). *Telephone:* (312) 4161000 (office). *E-mail:* iletisim@yargitay.gov.tr (office). *Website:* www.yargitay.gov.tr (office).

ALKATIRI, Mari bin Amude; Timor-Leste politician; *Secretary-General, Frente Revolucionária do Timor Leste Independente (Fretilin);* b. 26 Nov. 1949, Dili; m. Marina Ribeiro; three c.; fmr chartered surveyor; est. Movt for the Liberation of East Timor (Timor-Leste) 1970; Co-Founder and Sec.-Gen. Frente Revolucionário do Timor Leste Independente—Fretilin (Revolutionary Front for an Ind. Timor-Leste) 1974–; lived in political exile, teaching in Mozambique –1999; Minister for Econs in Transitional Admin; Prime Minister of Timor-Leste 2002–06, concurrently Minister for Economy and Devt, then Minister for Devt and the Environment. *Address:* c/o Fretilin, Rua dos Martires da Patria, Dili, Timor-Leste (office). *Telephone:* 3321409 (office). *Website:* fretilin-rdtl.blogspot.com (office).

ALKHANOV, Alu; Russian (Chechen) politician and government official; *Deputy Minister of Justice;* b. 1947, Taldykorgan Prov., Kazakhstan; m.; three c.; ed Transport Police School, Belarus, USSR Interior Ministry Acad.; joined Soviet Militsiya service 1983; served in various positions in Ministry of the Interior, Chechen—Nokchi Repub.; Chief of Transport Police Dept 1995–96, of Shakhty Transport Police, Rostov Region 1997–2000, of Groznyi Transport Police 2000–03; Minister of the Interior, Chechen—Nokchi Repub. 2003–04; Pres. of Chechen—Nokchi Repub. 2004–07; Deputy Minister of Justice 2007–, in charge of penitentiary system 2010–; Order of Courage 1996. *Address:* Ministry of Justice, 119991, GSP-1, Moscow, ulitsa Zhitnaya, Building 14, Russia (office). *Telephone:* (495) 955-59-99 (office). *Fax:* (495) 955-57-79 (office). *Website:* www.minjust.ru (office).

ALLAM, Magdi Cristiano; Italian (b. Egyptian) journalist, editor, author and politician; b. 22 April 1952, Cairo, Egypt; s. of Muhammad Allam and Safeya Allam; m.; two c.; m. 2nd Valentina Colombo; one s.; ed Catholic Coll. of Comboni Sisters, Cairo, Salesian Coll., La Sapienza Univ., Rome; began journalistic career 1978, worked for several Italian publs, including nat. daily newspaper La Repubblica; joined Corriere della Sera 2003, Deputy Dir –2008, currently op-ed. columnist, ad personam Asst Publr and Deputy Ed.; Arab and Islamic affairs commentator; appears frequently on nat. TV news shows; mem. European Parl., Brussels 2009–; f. I Love Italy (political party); co-recipient Dan David Prize, Tel-Aviv Univ. (Israel) 2006, Prix St-Vincent in journalism, Ambrogino the City of Milan, Mass Media Award, American Jewish Cttee. *Publications include:* Vincere la paura (Winning Fear), Diary of Islam 2002, Bin Laden in Italy 2002, Saddam: The Secret History of a Dictator 2003, Kamikaze Made in Europe: Can the West Defeat the Islamic Terrorists? 2004, Overcoming Fear 2005, I Love Italy, but the Italians Love It? 2006, Viva Israel 2007, Thank You Jesus: My Conversion From Islam to Catholicism 2008, Christian Europe Free 2009; numerous other books and articles on relations between Western culture and values and the Islamic world. *Address:* European Parliament, Bât. Altiero Spinelli, 09E202, 60, rue Wiertz, 1047 Brussels, Belgium. *Telephone:* (2) 284-58-83 (office). *Fax:* (2) 284-98-83 (office). *E-mail:* magdicristiano.allam@europarl.europa.eu (office). *Website:* www .ioamolitalia.com (office).

ALLAMAND ZAVALA, Andrés; Chilean lawyer and politician; b. 7 Feb. 1956, Santiago; m. Bárbara Lyon; four c. (one deceased); ed Saint George's Coll., Santiago, Univ. of Chile; f. own legal practice 1980s; f. Movimiento Unión Nacional 1983, becoming Sec.-Gen.; co-f. Renovación Nacional 1987, Sec.-Gen. 1988–90, Pres. 1990–96; mem. Cámara de Diputados (lower house of parl.) for Las Condes, Vitacura y Lo Barnechea Dist 1994–98; mem. Senado (upper house of parl.) for Décima Región Norte 2006–11, Pres. Labour and Social Welfare Cttee 2008; Pres. Instituto Libertad 1996–98; with IDB, Washington, DC 1998–2000; Dean, School of Govt, Univ. Adolfo Ibáñez, Santiago 2002–07; apptd Dir of Devt 2001; Minister of Nat. Defence 2011–12; Sec.-Gen. Unión de Partidos de America Latina 1990–97. *Publications include:* La Travesía del Desierto 1999, La política importa. Democracia y desarrollo en América Latina (co-author) 2003, El Desalojo 2007, La Estrella y el Arco Iris (co-author) 2010. *Address:* c/o Ministry of National Defence, Edif. Diego Portales, 22°, Villavicencio 364, Santiago, Chile.

ALLAN, Sir Alexander (Alex) Claud Stuart, Kt, KCB, MA, MSc; British civil servant; b. 9 Feb. 1951; s. of the late Lord Allan of Kilmahew and of Maureen Catherine Flower Stuart-Clark; m. Katie Christine Clemson 1978 (died 2007); ed Harrow School, Clare Coll., Cambridge, Univ. Coll., London; with HM Customs and Excise 1973–76, HM Treasury 1976–92, Prin. Pvt. Sec. to Chancellor of the Exchequer 1986–89; secondments in Australia 1983–84; Under-Sec. for Int. Finance 1989–90, for Public Expenditure Policy, 1990–92; Prin. Pvt. Sec. to the

Prime Minister 1992–97; High Commr in Australia 1997–2000; e-Envoy, Cabinet Office 1999–2000; Perm. Sec., Dept for Constitutional Affairs, later Ministry of Justice 2004–07; Chair. Jt Intelligence Cttee and Professional Head of Intelligence Analysis, Cabinet Office 2007–11. *Leisure interests:* sailing, Grateful Dead music, cycling, computers, bridge. *E-mail:* alex@whitegum.com (home). *Website:* www .whitegum.com (home).

ALLAN, M. Elyse, BA, MBA; Canadian (b. American) business executive; *President and CEO, General Electric Canada;* m. Don Allan; one s.; ed Dartmouth Coll., Amos Tuck School of Business; began career at General Electric (GE) as consultant in Corp. Marketing Consulting Services group, Bridgeport, Conn. 1984; moved to Canada as Man. Customer Service Program, GE Canada 1988, later Marketing Man. GE Commercial and Industrial Lighting; Dir of Marketing Ont. Hydro; Pres. and CEO Toronto Bd of Trade (first woman) 1995–2004; Pres. and CEO GE Canada 2004–; Chair. Bd of Dirs Providence Healthcare; mem. Nat. Round Table on the Environment and the Economy 2005–; mem. Bd of Dirs Public Policy Forum, Canadian Council of Chief Execs; mem. Bd of Govs Canadian Council on Unity; fmr mem. Bd of Visitors, Rockefeller Centre for Public Policy; Dr hc (Ryerson Univ.) 2005. *Address:* GE Canada, 2300 Meadowvale Blvd, Mississauga, ON L5N 5P9, Canada (office). *Telephone:* (905) 858-6655 (office). *Website:* www.ge.com/can (office).

ALLARD, A. Wayne, DMV; American veterinarian and fmr politician; *Vice-President for Government Relations, American Motorcyclist Association;* b. 2 Dec. 1943, Colorado; s. of Amos W. Allard and S. Jean Stewart; m. Joan Malcolm 1967; two d.; ed Colorado State Univ.; early career as veterinarian, Allard Animal Hosp.; mem. Colo State Senate (Republican) 1982–91, Chair. Health, Environment and Insts Cttee, Chair. Senate Majority Caucus; mem. US House of Reps from 4th Dist, Colo 1991–96, mem. House Agric. Cttee 1991–96, House Small Business Cttee 1991–92, House Interior and Insular Affairs Cttee 1991–92, House Cttee on Cttees 1991–94, House Budget Cttee 1993–96, House Natural Resources Cttee 1993–96, Jt Cttee on Reorganization of Congress 1993–96, Chair. House Sub-Cttee of Agric. Conservation, Forest and Water 1995–96; Senator from Colo 1997–2009 (retd), mem. Banking, Urban Affairs Cttee 1997–2009, Environment and Public Works Cttee 1997–2009, Intelligence Select Cttee 1997–2009, Armed Services Cttee and numerous other cttees; Vice-Pres. for Govt Relations, American Motorcyclist Asscn, Washington, DC 2011–; Founder and Man. Partner, Wayne Allard Assocs, LLC; Founder and CEO Prion Research Inst.; fmr health officer, Loveland, Colo; fmr mem. Regional Advisory Council on Veterinarian Medicine, W Interstate Comm. on Higher Educ., Colo Low-Level Radioactive Waste Advisory Cttee; Chair. United Way; Founding mem. American Veterinary Medical Asscn (AVMA), Colo Veterinarian Medicine Asscn, Larimer Co. Veterinarian Medicine Asscn; mem. Bd Veterinarian Practitioners (Charter mem.), American Animal Hosp. Asscn, Nat. Conf. State Legislatures (Vice-Chair. Human Resources Cttee 1987); mem. Loveland Chamber of Commerce; Fort Collins Lions Club Future Citizen of Tomorrow Award and Scholarship 1962, One of Top Four Colorado 4-H mems in Leadership Guardian Advisory Cttee for NFIB 1963, Honor Alumnus, Colorado State Univ. (CSU) 1990, Honoree, George H. Glover Gallery of Distinguished Faculty and Alumni of CSU 1992, CSU Alumni Charles A. Lory Public Service Award 1999, AMVA Pres.'s Award 1999, George E. Brown, Jr Congressional Honor Award for Leadership in Imaging and Geospatial Information 1999, AVMA Meritorious Service Award 2006. *Address:* American Motorcyclist Association, 101 Constitution Avenue NW, Suite 800W, Washington, DC 20001, USA (office). *Telephone:* (202) 742-4301 (office). *Fax:* (202) 742-4282 (office). *Website:* www .americanmotorcyclist.com (office).

ALLARDT, Erik Anders, MA, PhD; Finnish university chancellor and sociologist; *Professor of Sociology, University of Helsinki;* b. 9 Aug. 1925, Helsinki; s. of Arvid Allardt and Marita Allardt (née Heikel); m. Sagi Nylander 1947; one s. two d.; ed Univ. of Helsinki, Columbia Univ., New York, USA; Prof. of Sociology, Univ. of Helsinki 1958–, Dean of the Faculty of Social Sciences 1969–70; Pres. Acad. of Finland 1986–91; Chancellor of the Åbo Acad. Univ. 1992–94; mem. European Science Foundation Exec. Council 1987–92, Vice-Pres. 1990–92; mem. Bd Scandinavia-Japan Sasakawa Foundation 1987–96; Founder-mem. Academia Europaea 1988–; Fellow, Woodrow Wilson Int. Center for Scholars 1978–79; Visiting Prof. numerous countries and univs; Commdr of the Swedish Order of the Northern Star; Grand Cross Knight, Icelandic Order of the Falcon 1997; Dr hc (Stockholm) 1978, (Åbo Akademi) 1978, (Uppsala) 1984, (Bergen) 1996, (Copenhagen) 2000. *Publications:* (with Rokkan) Mass Politics: Studies in Political Sociology 1970, Att Ha, Att Älska, Att Vara. Om Välfärd i Norden 1975, Implications of the Ethnic Revival in Modern, Industrialized Society 1979, (with Lysgaard and Sørensen) Sociologin i Sverige, vetenskap, miljö och organisation 1988, The History of the Social Sciences in Finland 1997. *Leisure interest:* playing with grandchildren. *Address:* Department of Sociology, PB 18, 00014 University of Helsinki, Helsinki (office); Unionsgatan 45B 40, 00170 Helsinki, Finland (home). *Telephone:* (9) 19123963 (office); (9) 1354550 (home). *Fax:* (9) 19123967 (office). *E-mail:* erik.allardt@helsinki.fi (office).

ALLAWI, Ali Abdel-Amir, SB, MBA; Iraqi business executive, government official and academic; *Visiting Research Professor, Middle East Institute, National University of Singapore;* b. Dec. 1947; ed Massachusetts Inst. of Tech., Harvard Business School, USA; fmr consultant to World Bank and Head, Pan-Arab investment co.; Prof., Univ. of Oxford, UK –2003; Minister of Trade and Minister of Defence, Interim Iraq Governing Council 2003–04, Minister of Finance, Iraqi Transitional Govt 2005–06, then Sr Adviser to Prime Minister of Iraq; Sr Assoc. Mem., St Antony's Coll., Oxford; Sr Fellow, Princeton Univ. 2008–09; Sr Visiting Fellow, Carr Center, Kennedy School of Govt, Harvard Univ. 2009–10; Visiting Research Prof., Middle East Inst., Nat. Univ. of Singapore 2013–; mem. United Iraqi Alliance; Hon. Fellow, Inst. for Arab and Islamic Studies, Exeter Univ., UK; Robert and Joanna Bendetson Global Public Diplomacy Award, Inst. for Global Leadership, Tufts Univ. 2007. *Publications:* The Occupation of Iraq: Winning the War, Losing the Peace 2007, The Crisis of Islamic Civilization 2009. *Address:* Middle East Institute, National University of Singapore, 469A Bukit Timah Road, Tower Block, Level 2, 259770, Singapore (office). *Website:* www.mei.nus.edu.sg (office); www.aliallawi.com.

ALLAWI, Ayad, MSc, DrMed; Iraqi neurologist and politician; b. 1945; ed Baghdad Univ., London Univ., UK; from prominent Shia family in Baghdad; fmr

mem. Ba'ath Party; left Iraq 1971 going first to Beirut then London; survived assassination attempt 1978; formed Iraqi Nat. Accord dissident group 1990, involved in attempted coup against Saddam Hussein 1996; fmr consultant to UNDP, WHO, UNICEF; apptd mem. Iraqi Governing Council 2003, Chair. Security Cttee 2003–04; Interim Prime Minister of Iraq 2004–05; Leader, Iraqi Nat. Movt (Iraqiya) 2010. *Address:* Iraqi National Movement (Iraqiya), Baghdad, Iraq.

ALLÈGRE, Claude Jean, PhD; French professor of earth sciences and politician; *Professor Emeritus, Université Paris Diderot-Paris;* b. 31 March 1937, Paris; s. of Prof. Roger Allègre and Lucette Allègre (née Hugueneq); m. Claude Blanche Simon 1967; three s. one d.; ed Lycées Saint-Maur and Saint-Louis, Faculté des Sciences, Paris; Asst, Univ. de Paris 1962–68; Dir of Lab. of Geochemistry and Cosmochemistry, Univ. de Paris VI and VII 1967–2006, Prof. Emer. 2006–; Asst Physician, Inst. de Physique du Globe 1968–70, Dir 1976–86; Chair-Prof. of Earth Sciences Univ. de Paris VII 1970–2006; joined Socialist Party 1973, mem. Steering Cttee 1987, Exec. Cttee 1990; Prof. of Earth Sciences, MIT 1975–76; Vernadsky Lecturer, Univ. of Moscow 1986; A. D. White Prof.-at-Large, Cornell Univ. 1987–92, USA; Special Adviser to Lionel Jospin 1988–92; mem. European Parl. 1989–94; Regional Councillor, Languedoc-Roussillon 1992; Minister of Nat. Educ., Research and Tech. 1997–2000; science columnist, CPAC, Nat. Ass. 2001–02; Pres. Admin. Council of Bureau de Recherches Géologiques et Minières 1993–97; Foreign mem. NAS, Royal Soc. 2002, Acad. of Sciences of India 2006; mem. Bd of Dirs Ipsos Group 2002; mem. Meteoritical Soc. 1980, American Geophysical Union 1984, Geochemical Soc. and European Assscn for Geochemistry 1990, Institut Universitaire de France 1992, French Acad. of Sciences 1995–, Geological Soc. of America 1998, Institut de Physique du Globe; Hon. mem. American Acad. of Arts and Sciences 1988, European Geosciences Union 1992, European Geophysical Soc. 1992, Trinity Hon. Lecturer, San Antonio, Tex. 1992, Geochemical Soc. of London 1994, Boston Philosophical Soc., Hon. Prof., China Univ. of Geosciences, Beijing 1999; Commdr, Ordre nat. de la Légion d'honneur, Ordre des Palmes Académiques, Grand Cross of Order of Merit (Germany), Commdr, Order of Southern Cross (Brazil); Dr hc (Cardiff Univ.) 1997, (Univ. of Bristol) 1998, (Free Univ. of Brussels) 1998, (Imperial Coll. London) 2001, (Univ. of Rome 3) 2003; Craoford Prize 1986, Goldsmith Medal, Geochemical Soc. of America 1986, Wollaston Medal, Geological Soc. of London 1987, Arthur Day-Gold Medal, Geological Soc. of America 1988, CNRS 1994, William Bowie Medal 1995, Holmes Medal of the European Geosciences Union 1995, Bowie Medal, American Geophysical Union 1995. *Publications include:* L'Ecume de la Terre 1983, De la Pierre à l'Etoile 1985, Les Fureurs de la Terre 1987, Economiser la Planète 1990, Introduction à une Histoire Naturelle 1992, L'Age des Savoires 1993, Ecologie des Villes, Ecologie des Champs 1993, L'Etat de la Planète 1994, La Défaite de Platon 1995, Questions de France 1996, Dieu Face à la Science 1997, Toute Vérité est Bonne à Dire 2000, Vive L'Ecole Libre 2000, Histoires de Terre 2001, Galilée 2002, Géologie isotopique 2005, Le Défi du monde (co-author) 2006, Ma vérité sur la planète 2007, La science et la vie, journal d'un anti-panurge 2008, La Science est le défi du XXIe siècle 2009, L'Imposture climatique 2010. *Address:* Institut de physique du globe, Round 24, BP 89, 4, place Jussieu, 75252 Paris Cedex 05 (office); Université Paris Diderot-Paris, 75205 Paris Cedex 13, France (office). *Telephone:* 1-57-27-57-27 (Institut de physique du globe) (office). *Fax:* 1-44-27-37-52 (Université Paris Diderot-Paris) (office). *Website:* www.academie-sciences.fr (office); www.univ-paris-diderot.fr (office).

ALLÈGRE, Maurice Marie, LenD; French engineer, research co-ordinator and business executive; b. 16 Feb. 1933, Antibes; s. of Guy Allègre and Renée-Lise Bermond; m. Catherine Pierre 1962; one s. one d.; ed Ecole Polytechnique, Ecole Nat. Supérieure des Mines and Ecole Nat. Supérieure du Pétrole et des Moteurs, Faculté de Droit; Engineer, Direction des Carburants, Ministry of Industry 1957–62; Dir Mines de l'Organisme Saharien 1962–64; Tech. Adviser to Ministry of Finance and Econ. Affairs 1965–67; Délégué à l'Informatique and Pres. Inst. de Recherche d'Informatique et d'Automatique 1968–74; Chief of Nickel Mission to New Caledonia 1975; Asst Dir-Gen. Inst. Français du Pétrole 1976–81; Pres. and Dir-Gen. ISIS 1976–81; Pres. FRANLAB, COFLEXIP 1976–81; Pres. Agence Nat. de Valorisation et de la Recherche (ANVAR) 1982–84; Dir Scientific and Tech. Devt, Ministry of Research and Tech. 1982–84; Dir-Gen. Bureau de Recherches Géologiques et Minières 1984–88, Pres. 1988–92; Pres. Agence Nationale pour la Gestion des Déchets Radioactifs (ANDRA—Nat. Agency for Man. of Radioactive Waste) 1993–98; Pres. Sicav Vauban 1998–2000; Pres. AGRER Assscn 1998; int. consultant on energy policy and radioactive waste 1998–; mem. ASPO France; Chevalier, Légion d'honneur, Officier, Ordre nat. du Mérite. *Leisure interests:* photography, skiing, sailing. *Address:* Maurice Allègre Conseils, 85 rue de Sèvres, 75006 Paris; 50 boulevard d'Aguillon, 06600 Antibes, France. *Telephone:* 1-45-44-94-51 (office).

ALLEN, Sir Charles Lamb, Kt, CBE, FRSA, FCMA; British business executive and broadcaster; *Chairman, Global Radio;* b. 4 Jan. 1957; accountant, British Steel 1974–79; Deputy Audit Man. Gallaghers PLC 1979–82; Dir Man. Services Grandmet Int. Services Ltd 1982–85, Group Man. Dir Compass Vending, Grandmet Innovations Ltd 1986–87, Man. Dir Grandmet Int. Services Ltd 1987–88, Man. Dir Compass Group Ltd 1988–91, Chief Exec. Leisure Div., Granada Group 1991–92; Chair. Granada Leisure and Services 1993–2000, CEO LWT (following takeover by Granada) 1994–96 (Chair. 1996), CEO Granada Group PLC 1996–2000, Chair. GMTV 1996–2000, Jt Deputy Chair. Granada Compass PLC 2000, Exec. Chair. Granada PLC 2000–03, CEO ITV PLC (after merger of Granada and Carlton) 2003–07; Chair. Yorkshire Tyne Tees TV 1997–; Chair. M2002 Ltd (Manchester Commonwealth Games); Chair. Global Radio (Heart, Capital, Classic FM, LBC, Gold, XFM, Choice) 2007–; Chair. 2 Sisters food group; Chair. (non-exec.) EMI Music 2009–10, CEO 2010–11; Sr Adviser, Goldman Sachs Capital Partners 2008–; Vice-Chair. London 2012 Ltd (effort to bring 2012 Olympics to London); Dir (non-exec.) Tesco PLC 1999–2010, Endemol 2008–, Virgin Media 2008–, GET A/S 2009–; Hon. DBA (Manchester Metropolitan) 1999, (Salford) 2002. *Leisure interests:* visual and performing arts, int. travel and cultures. *Address:* Global Radio, 30 Leicester Square, London, WC2H 7LA, England (office). *Telephone:* (20) 7766-6000 (office). *Fax:* (20) 7766-6111 (office). *E-mail:* info@thisisglobal.com (office). *Website:* www.thisisglobal.com/radio (office).

ALLEN, Sir Douglas Albert Vivian, GCB (see CROHAM, Baron).

ALLEN, Sir Geoffrey, Kt, PhD, FRS, FREng, FRSC, FInstP, FIM; British polymer scientist and university administrator (retd); b. 29 Oct. 1928, Clay Cross, Derbyshire, England; s. of John James Allen and Marjorie Allen; m. Valerie Frances Duckworth 1972; one d.; ed Clay Cross Tupton Hall Grammar School, Univ. of Leeds; Postdoctoral Fellow, Nat. Research Council, Canada 1952–54; Lecturer, Univ. of Manchester 1955–65, Prof. of Chemical Physics 1965–75; Prof. of Polymer Science, Imperial Coll. of Science and Tech., Univ. of London 1975–76, Prof. of Chemical Tech. 1976–81; Fellow, Imperial Coll. 1986, UMIST 1994; Adviser, Kobe Steel Ltd 1990–2005; Chair. Science Research Council 1977–81; Head of Research, Unilever PLC 1981–90, Dir of Unilever responsible for Research and Eng 1982–90; Dir (non-exec.) Courtaulds 1987–93; Pres. PRI, SCI 1990–92; mem. Nat. Consumer Council 1993–96; Vice-Pres. Royal Soc. 1991–93; Chancellor Univ. of East Anglia 1994–2003; mem. Royal Comm. on Environmental Protection 1994–2000; Pres. Inst. of Materials 1994–95; Visiting Fellow, Robinson Coll., Cambridge 1980–; Fellow, Royal Acad. of Eng; Hon. FCGI, Hon. FIM, Hon. FIChemE; Hon. MSc (Manchester), Hon. DSc (Durham, E Anglia) 1984, (Bath, Bradford, Keele, Loughborough) 1985, (Essex, Leeds) 1986, (Cranfield) 1988, (Surrey) 1989, (North London) 1999, Dr hc (Open Univ.). *Leisure interests:* opera, walking, talking. *Address:* 18 Oxford House, 52 Parkside, London, SW19 5NE, England (home). *Telephone:* (20) 8947-7459 (home). *Fax:* (20) 8879-1959 (home). *E-mail:* sir.geoffrey@tiscali.co.uk.

ALLEN, George, BA, JD; American business executive and fmr politician; *President, George Allen Strategies LLC;* b. 8 March 1952; s. of George Herbert Allen and Henrietta Lumbroso; m. 1st Anne Patrice Rubel 1979 (divorced 1983); m. 2nd Susan Allen (née Brown); three c.; ed Univs of California, Virginia; mem. Va House of Dels 1982–90; mem. US House of Reps, Washington, DC 1991–94; Gov. of Va 1994–98; Senator from Va 2000–07, Chair. Senate High Tech Task Force 2001; currently Pres. George Allen Strategies LLC; f. American Energy Freedom Centre, Chair. –2011; Reagan Ranch Presidential Scholar, Young America's Foundation 2007–, also mem. Bd of Govs; mem. Bd of Dirs Lee Technologies, nanoTox, Hillsdale Group, Xybernaut 1998, Commonwealth Biotechnologies 1998–2006; f. Appalachian School of Law, currently mem. Bd of Trustees; mem. Bd of Advisors Com-Net Ericsson 2000; mem. 'Small b' Business Cttee; Pnr, Business Expansion and Relocation Team, McGuireWoods LLP 1998; Republican; Jefferson Scholar, American Legis. Exchange Council 1998. *Publication:* What Washington Can Learn From the World of Sports 2010. *Address:* George Allen Strategies LLC, 717 Princess Street, Alexandria, VA 22314, USA (office). *Telephone:* (571) 970-4636 (office). *Website:* www.georgeallenstrategies.com (office); www.yaf.org/TheReaganRanch.aspx (office); www.georgeallen.com.

ALLEN, Dame Ingrid Victoria, DBE, DL, MD, DSc, FRCPath, FMedSci, MRIA; British professor of neuropathology; *Professor Emerita, Queen's University, Belfast;* b. 30 July 1932, Belfast; d. of Robert Allen and Doris V. Allen (née Shaw); m. 1st Alan Watson Barnes 1972 (died 1987); m. 2nd John Thompson 1996; ed Ashleigh House School, Belfast, Cheltenham Ladies Coll., Queen's Univ. Belfast; House Officer Royal Victoria Hosp. (RVH), Belfast 1957–58, Sr Registrar 1964–65; Musgrave Research Fellow, Tutor in Pathology, Calvert Research Fellow, Queen's Univ., Belfast (QUB) 1958–64; Sr Lecturer and Consultant in Neuropathology, QUB/RVH 1966–78, Reader and Consultant 1978–79, Prof. Emer. 1997–; Head NI Regional Neuropathology Service 1979–97; mem. MRC 1988–94; Dir for Research and Devt Health and Personal Social Services, NI 1997–2001; Visiting Prof., Univ. of Ulster 1997–; Vice-Pres. Int. Soc. of Neuropathology 1988–92; Fellow, Royal Coll. of Pathologists, Vice-Pres. 1993–96; mem. Cttee on Women in Science and Tech., Office of Public Service and Science; mem. numerous editorial bds; Hon. Fellow, Int. Soc. of Neuropathology 1997. *Publications include:* Greenfield's Neuropathology 1984, McAlpine's Multiple Sclerosis (contrib.) 1990; numerous articles in learned journals on neuropathology, demyelinating diseases, neurovirology, neuro-oncology and biomedical research and devt. *Leisure interests:* reading, sailing, escaping to an island off the NW coast of Ireland. *Address:* Room 113, School of Biology and Biochemistry, Medical Biology Centre, Queen's University Belfast, 97 Lisburn Road, Belfast, BT9 7BL, Northern Ireland (office); 95 Malone Road, Belfast, BT9 6SP, Northern Ireland (home). *Telephone:* (28) 9027-2116 (office); (28) 9066-6662 (home). *Fax:* (28) 9023-6505; (28) 9033-5877 (home). *E-mail:* i.allen@qub.ac.uk (office); ingrid.allen@btinternet.com (home). *Website:* www.qub.ac.uk (office).

ALLEN, Lt-Gen. John R., BSc, MSc, MA; American military officer (retd); b. Fort Belvoir, Va; ed US Naval Acad., Annapolis, Md, Nat. War Coll., Georgetown Univ., Washington, DC; commissioned in US Marine Corps 1976, serving first as Platoon and Rifle Co. Commdr, 2nd Bn, 8th Marines 1976, Operations Officer, 3rd Bn, 4th Marines, Fleet Marine Force 1985; Lecturer, Political Science Dept, US Naval Acad., also Jump Officer and Jump Master 1988; Dir Infantry Officer Course, The Basic School 1990–92, Commdr 1999–2001; Div. G-3 Operations Officer for 2nd Marine Div. 1994, subsequently assumed command of 2nd Bn, 4th Marines (took part in Operation Sea Signal, Caribbean 1994 and Operation Jt Endeavor, Balkans 1995–96); Sr ADC to Commdt of Marine Corps 1996; Deputy Commdt, US Naval Acad. 2001–02, Commdt of Midshipmen in 2002; Prin. Dir for Asian and Pacific Affairs, Office of US Sec. of Defense 2003–06; Deputy Commdg Gen., II Marine Expeditionary Force and Commdg Gen., 2nd Marine Expeditionary Brigade 2006–08 (took part in Operation Iraqi Freedom as Deputy Commdg Gen. of Multi-Nat. Forces West); Deputy Commdr, US Cen. Command, MacDill Air Force Base, Tampa, Fla 2008–11, Acting Commdr June–Aug. 2010; nominated as Special Asst on Afghanistan and Iraq to Chair. of Jt Chiefs of Staff May 2011; Commdr Int. Security Assistance Force (ISAF) and Commdr US Forces Afghanistan (USFOR-A) 2011–13; attained rank of Brig.-Gen. 2003, Maj.-Gen. 2007, Lt-Gen. 2008; fmr term mem. Council on Foreign Relations; numerous mil. awards including Defense Distinguished Service Medal, Legion of Merit with three award stars, Navy and Marine Corps Commendation Medal with three award stars, Global War on Terrorism Service Medal, Nat. Defense Service Medal with two service stars; Meritorious Service Medal (Mongolia), First Class, Gold Medal of the Polish Armed Forces, Order of the Resplendent Banner with Special Cravat (Taiwan). *Address:* c/o Media Operations Center, NATO Headquarters, Blvd Leopold III, 1110 Brussels, Belgium.

ALLEN, John Robert Lawrence, DSc, FRS, FGS, FSA; British geologist, sedimentologist and academic; *Professor Emeritus, University of Reading;* b. 25 Oct. 1932; s. of George Eustace Allen and Alice Josephine (née Formby); m. Jean Mary Wood 1960; four s. one d.; ed St Philip's Grammar School, Birmingham, Univ. of Sheffield; mem. staff, Univ. of Reading 1959–, Prof. of Geology 1972–89, of Sedimentology 1989–93, apptd. Research Prof. Postgrad. Research Inst. for Sedimentology 1993, now Prof. Emer., Visiting Prof. in Archaeology; Assoc. mem. Royal Belgian Acad. of Sciences; Hon. LLD (Sheffield), Hon. DSc (Reading); Lyell Medal, Geological Soc. 1980, David Linton Award, British Geomorphological Research Group 1983, Twenhofel Medal, Soc. of Econ. Paleontologists and Minerologists 1987, G.K. Warren Prize, NAS, USA 1990, Sorby Medal, Int. Asscn of Sedimentologists 1994, Penrose Medal, Geological Soc. of America 1996. *Publications:* Current Ripples 1968, Physical Processes of Sedimentation 1970, Sedimentary Structures 1982, Principles of Physical Sedimentology 1985; numerous contribs. to professional journals. *Leisure interests:* cooking, music, opera, pottery, walking. *Address:* 17C Whiteknights Road, Reading, Berks., RG6 7BY, England (home). *Telephone:* (118) 926-4621 (home); (118) 378-6352 (office). *E-mail:* j.r.l.allen@reading.ac.uk (office).

ALLEN, John Walter, MA, FRSE; British physicist and academic; *Professor Emeritus of Solid State Physics, University of St Andrews;* b. 7 March 1928, Birmingham, England; s. of Walter Allen and Beryl Parsons; m. 1st Mavis Williamson 1956 (died 1972); m. 2nd Hania Szawelska 1981; one s.; ed King Edward's School, Birmingham, Sidney Sussex Coll., Cambridge; RAF Educ. Br. 1949–51; staff scientist, Ericsson Telephones, Nottingham 1951–56; Royal Naval Scientific Service, Services Electronics Research Lab. 1956–68; Visiting Prof., Stanford Univ., USA 1964–66; Tullis Russell Fellow, Univ. of St Andrews 1968–72, Reader in Physics, Dir of Wolfson Inst. of Luminescence 1972–81, Prof. of Solid State Physics 1980–93, Prof. Emer. 1993–; Hon. DSc (St Andrews). *Publications:* some 130 papers in scientific journals including the first account of a practical light-emitting diode 1962. *Leisure interests:* archaeology, traditional dance. *Address:* School of Physics and Astronomy, University of St Andrews, North Haugh, St Andrews, Fife, KY16 9SS (office); 2 Dempster Terrace, St Andrews, Fife, KY16 9QQ, Scotland (home). *Telephone:* (1334) 463029 (office); (1334) 474163 (home). *Fax:* (1334) 463104 (office). *E-mail:* jwa@st-and.ac.uk (office). *Website:* www.st-andrews.ac.uk/physics (office).

ALLEN, Sir Patrick Linton, ON, GCMG, CD, PhD; Jamaican administrator, teacher, ecclesiastic and government official; *Governor-General;* b. 7 Feb. 1951, Portland; s. of Ferdinand Allen and Christina Allen; m.; three c.; ed Moneague Teachers' Coll., Andrews Univ., USA; Prin. Robins Bay Primary School 1976–78, Hillside Primary School 1978–80; ordained Seventh Day Adventist pastor 1989; Asst Registrar, Andrews Univ. 1996–98; Pres. Cen. Jamaica Conf. of Seventh Day Adventists 1998–2000, West Indies Union of Seventh Day Adventists 2000–; Gov.-Gen. of Jamaica 2009–; Chair. Bd of Govs Andrews Memorial Hosp., Adventist Devt and Relief Agency, Book and Nutrition Centre Ltd, West Indies Union Investment Man. Ltd; Dr hc (Northern Caribbean Univ.). *Leisure interests:* badminton, athletics, basketball, cricket. *Address:* Office of the Governor-General, King's House, Hope Road, Kingston 10, Jamaica (office). *Telephone:* 927-6424 (office). *Fax:* 978-6025 (office). *E-mail:* kingshouse@kingshouse.gov.jm (office). *Website:* www.kingshousejamaica.gov.jm (office).

ALLEN, Paul Gardner; American business executive; *Chairman, Vulcan Inc.;* b. 21 Jan. 1953, Seattle, Wash.; s. of Kenneth S. Allen and the late Faye G. Allen; ed Lakeside School, Seattle, Wash. State Univ.; co-f. (with Bill Gates) Microsoft Corpn 1975, Gen. Pnr 1975–77, Vice-Pres. 1977–81, Exec. Vice-Pres. Research and New Product Devt 1981–83; Sr Strategy Advisor 2000–; Founder and Chair. Vulcan Northwest (now Vulcan Inc.) (holding co.) 1986–; f. Asymetrix Corpn 1985, Starwave Corpn 1992; acquired Marcus Cable 1998, Hollywood Entertainment 1998; Founder and Chair. Intervas Research; Owner and Chair. Portland (Ore.) Trail Blazers professional basketball team 1988–, Seattle Seahawks professional football team, Seattle Sounders FC; f. Allen Inst. of Brain Science 2003; sponsor, SpaceShipOne private rocket plane venture 2004; f. Experience Music Project, Seattle, Paul G. Allen Family Foundation Science Fiction Museum and Hall of Fame 2004, Vulcan Productions (ind. film co.); Dir Egghead Discount Software 1983–2000, Darwin Molecular Inc.; fmrly Owner, Chair., Dir Ticketmaster Holdings Group; Life-Time Achievement Award from PC Magazine; inducted into Computer Museum Hall of Fame, Regents' Distinguished Alumnus Award, Washington State Univ. 1999, Special Merit Award, Oregon Sports Award program 2009, listed among 100 Most Influential People in the World, Time Magazine 2007–08. *Album:* Everywhere at Once (Paul Allen and the Underthinkers) 2013. *Publication:* Idea Man 2011. *Address:* Vulcan, Inc., 505 5th Avenue, South, Suite 900, Seattle, WA 98104, USA (office). *Telephone:* (206) 342-2000 (office). *Fax:* (206) 342-3000 (office). *Website:* www.vulcan.com (office); www.paulallen.com.

ALLEN, Richard V.; American academic, international business consultant and fmr government official; *Senior Counselor, APCO Worldwide Inc.;* b. 1 Jan. 1936, Collingswood, NJ; s. of C. Carroll Allen, Sr and Magdalen Buchman; m. Patricia Ann Mason 1957; three s. four d.; ed Notre Dame Univ. and Univ. of Munich; helped found Cen. for Strategic and Int. Studies, Georgetown Univ. 1962; Consultant and fmr Prof., Hoover Inst., Stanford Univ.; with Nat. Security Council 1968–69; mem. Ronald Reagan's staff, campaigns 1976, Bd Govs Ronald Reagan Presidential Foundation 1985; Pres. Richard V. Allen Co., Washington 1982–90, Chair. 1991–; Head Nat. Security Council and Nat. Security Adviser 1981–82; Chair. Fed. Capital Bank 1987; Sr Council for Foreign Policy and Nat. Security Affairs, Repub. Nat. Cttee 1982–88; mem. Bd of Dirs Xsirius Inc. 1991–92; Distinguished Fellow and Chair. Asian Studies Center, The Heritage Foundation 1982; Chair. German-American Tricentennial Foundation 1983; Founding mem. US Nat. Cttee for Pacific Basin 1984; Sr Fellow, Hoover Inst. 1983–; mem. Advisory Bd Catholic Campaign for America 1993–, Nixon Center, Center for Strategic and Int. Studies; mem. Republican Congressional Policy Advisory Bd 1998–, Nat. Security Advisory Group, Defense Policy Bd, Council for Foreign Relations; currently Sr Counselor, APCO Worldwide Inc. (consulting firm), Washington, DC; Order of Diplomatic Merit Ganghwa (Repub. of Korea) 1982; Kt Commdr's Cross (FRG) 1983; Order of Brilliant Star (Repub. of China) 1986; Sovereign Mil. Order of Kts of Malta 1987; hon. degrees (Hanover Coll.) 1981, (Korea Univ.) 1982, Pepperdine

Univ. *Publications:* numerous books on political and economic affairs including Peace or Peaceful Coexistence 1966, Communism and Democracy: Theory and Action 1967. *Address:* APCO Worldwide, 1615 L Street, Suite 900, NW, Washington, DC 20036-5623, USA (office). *Telephone:* (202) 778-1000 (office). *Fax:* (202) 466-6002 (office). *E-mail:* information@apcoworldwide.com (office). *Website:* www.apcoworldwide.com (office).

ALLEN, Samuel R., BA; American business executive; *Chairman and CEO, Deere & Co.;* b. Sumter, SC; ed Purdue Univ., West Lafayette, Ind.; joined Deere & Co. (collectively called John Deere) 1975, worked in Consumer Products Div., Worldwide Construction and Forestry Div., John Deere Power Systems, and Worldwide Agricultural Div., including managing operations in Latin America, China and East Asia, and Australia, has served as a sr officer of co. since 2001, with additional responsibilities in human resources, industrial relations, and John Deere Credit's global operations, Pres., Worldwide Construction and Forestry Div.–June 2009, responsible for global operations of John Deere Power Systems, for Deere's intelligent mobile equipment technologies and for Deere's advanced tech. and eng, mem. Bd of Dirs June 2009–, Pres. and COO Deere & Co. June–Aug. 2009, Pres. and CEO Aug. 2009–10, Chair. and CEO Feb. 2010–; Chair. Council on Competitiveness 2010–; mem. Bd of Dirs Whirlpool Corpn 2010–. *Address:* Deere & Co. World Headquarters, One John Deere Place, Moline, IL 61265, USA (office). *Telephone:* (309) 765-8000 (office). *Fax:* (309) 765-5671 (office). *E-mail:* info@deere .com (office). *Website:* www.deere.com (office).

ALLEN, Sharon; American business executive; *Chairman, Deloitte & Touche USA LLP;* fmrly in charge of Portland office, Deloitte & Touche USA LLP, later mem. Bd of Dirs Deloitte & Touche USA LLP and Man. Pnr, Deloitte US Firms' Pacific Southwest practice, Los Angeles, currently Chair. (first woman) Deloitte & Touche USA LLP, has served on Client Service Standards Task Force, Pnr Admissions Cttee and in many other cttee capacities; mem. Bd of Dirs Los Angeles Area Chamber of Commerce, United Way of Greater Los Angeles, Ind. Colls of Southern Calif., YMCA of Metropolitan Los Angeles; numerous awards for business and community leadership, ranked by Forbes Magazine amongst the 100 Most Powerful Women (96th) 2006, (64th) 2007, (94th) 2008, (98th) 2009. *Address:* Deloitte & Touche USA LLP, 1633 Broadway, New York, NY 10019-6754, USA (office). *Telephone:* (212) 489-1600 (office). *Fax:* (212) 489-1687 (office). *Website:* www.us.deloitte.com (office); www.deloitte.com (office).

ALLÉN, Sture, DPhil; Swedish professor of computational linguistics; *Professor Emeritus of Computational Linguistics, Göteborg University;* b. 31 Dec. 1928, Göteborg; s. of Bror G. Allén and Hanna Johanson; m. Solveig Janson 1954; three c.; ed Univ. of Göteborg; Asst Prof. of Scandinavian Philology, Göteborg Univ. 1965–70, Prof. of Computational Linguistics 1979–93, Pro-Rector 1980–86, Rector 1982, now Prof. Emer.; Assoc. Prof. of Computational Linguistics, Swedish Humanistic Research Council 1970–72, Prof. 1972–79; Perm. Sec. Swedish Acad. 1986–99; mem. Swedish Acad., Royal Soc. of Arts and Sciences of Göteborg, Royal Swedish Acad. of Letters, History and Antiquities, Academia Europaea, Royal Swedish Acad. of Eng. Sciences, Norwegian Acad. of Sciences and Letters, Finnish Soc. of Science and Letters; Corresp. mem. Icelandic Soc. of Sciences; mem. Bd of Dirs Nobel Foundation 1987–99, Trustee 1999–; Hon. mem. Soc. of Swedish Literature in Finland; Medal of King of Sweden in the Ribbon of the Order of Seraphim for Eminent Scientific and Cultural Achievements 1987, Kt Commdr, Order of the White Rose (Finland) 1994, Kt, Order of the Falcon (Iceland) 2007; Dr hc (Swedish Univ. of Abo) 1988; several awards including Gothenburg City Medal (Gold) 1994, Chester Carlson Research Prize 1988, Margit Påhlson Prize 2000, Chalmers Tech. Univ. Medal 2002. *Radio:* From a Linguistic Point of View (series). *Television:* In Plain Swedish (series). *Publications:* author and co-author of numerous textbooks, dictionaries, glossaries, etc. *Leisure interests:* music, sports. *Address:* Swedish Academy, PO Box 2118, 10313 Stockholm (office); Department of Swedish, Göteborg University, PO Box 200, 40530 Göteborg, Sweden (office). *Telephone:* (31) 556102 (office). *Fax:* (31) 551890 (office). *E-mail:* sture.allen@ svenskaakademien.se (home). *Website:* www.svenskaakademien.se (office).

ALLEN, Sir Thomas Boaz, Kt, CBE, MA, FRCM, FRAM; British singer (baritone); *Chancellor, Durham University;* b. 10 Sept. 1944, Seaham Harbour, Co. Durham; s. of Thomas Boaz Allen and Florence Allen; m. 1st Margaret Holley 1968 (divorced 1986); one s.; m. 2nd Jeannie Gordon Lascelles 1988; one step-s. one step-d.; ed Robert Richardson Grammar School, Ryhope, Royal Coll. of Music, London, Univs of Newcastle, Birmingham and Durham; Prin. Baritone, Welsh Nat. Opera 1969–72, Royal Opera House, Covent Garden 1972–78; freelance opera singer 1978–, singing at Glyndebourne Opera 1973, ENO, London Coliseum 1986, La Scala 1987, Chicago Lyric Opera 1990, Royal Albert Hall 2000, London Proms 2002, Royal Opera House, Covent Garden 2003, Metropolitan Opera, New York 2005; Prince Consort Prof., Royal Coll. of Music 1994; Hambro Visiting Prof. of Opera, Univ. of Oxford 2000–01; Pres. British Youth Opera 2000–; Patron Samling Foundation, Music in Hosps, Oxford Lieder Festival, Kathleen Ferrier Awards; Chancellor, Durham Univ. 2011–; performances include: Die Zauberflöte 1973, Le Nozze di Figaro 1974, Così fan tutte 1975, 2010, 2012, Don Giovanni 1977, The Cunning Little Vixen 1977, Simon Boccanegra, Billy Budd, La Bohème, L'Elisir d'Amore, Faust, Albert Herring, Die Fledermaus, La Traviata, A Midsummer Night's Dream, Gianni Schicchi 2008, Der Rosenkavalier 2009–10, Die Meistersinger von Nurnberg 2010, Hansel und Gretel 2010–11, Il turco in Italia 2011, Il barbiere di Siviglia 2011; Albert Herring (as producer) 2002; Dir Così fan tutte, Samling Opera, The Sage, Gateshead 2005, Le nozze di Figaro 2006, Il barbiere di Siviglia 2007, Der Rosenkavalier 2009, Il turco in Italia 2009, Gianni Schicchi 2010; Hon. Fellow, Univ. of Sunderland, Jesus Coll., Oxford; Hon. mem. RAM; Hon. MA (Newcastle) 1984, Hon. DMus (Durham) 1988, (Birmingham) 2007; Queen's Prize 1967, Gulbenkian Fellow 1968, Royal Philharmonic Soc. BBC Radio 3 Listeners' Award 2004, Bayerischer Kammersänger, Bavarian State Opera, Queen's Medal for Music 2013. *Recordings:* numerous including: Duruflé, Requiem and Four Motets 1987, Duparc, Songs 1989, Duruflé and Fauré, Requiems 1998, Songs My Father Taught Me 2002, More Songs My Father Taught Me 2003. *Film:* Mrs Henderson Presents 2005, The Real Don Giovanni 2009. *Publication:* Foreign Parts: A Singer's Journal 1993. *Leisure interests:* painting, drawing, ornithology, golf, fishing.

ALLEN, Tim; American actor and comedian; b. (Timothy Allen Dick), 13 June 1953, Denver; m. 1st Laura Diebel (divorced); one d.; m. 2nd Jane Hadjuk 2006; ed Western Mich. Univ., Univ. of Detroit; fmr creative dir for advertising agency, Detroit; debut as comedian on Showtime Comedy Club All Stars 1988; Favorite Comedy Actor, People's Choice Award 1995, 1997–99. *TV includes:* Home Improvement (series) 1991–99, Tim Allen: Men Are Pigs 1990, Tim Allen Rewrites America (specials), Showtime Comedy Club All-Stars II 1988, Jimmy Neutron: Win, Lose and Kaboom (voice) 2004. *Films include:* Comedy's Dirtiest Dozen, The Santa Clause 1994, Toy Story (voice) 1995, Meet Wally Sparks 1997, Jungle 2 Jungle 1997, For Richer or Poorer 1997, Galaxy Quest 1999, Toy Story 2 (voice) 2000, Buzz Lightyear of Star Command: The Adventure Begins 2000, Who is Cletis Tout? 2001, Joe Somebody 2001, Big Trouble 2002, The Santa Clause 2 2002, Christmas with the Kranks 2004, The Shaggy Dog 2006, Zoom 2006, The Santa Clause 3: The Escape Clause 2006, Wild Hogs 2007, Redbelt 2007, Chimpanzee (narrator) 2012. *Publications:* Don't Stand Too Close to a Naked Man 1994, I'm Not Really Here 1996. *Address:* c/o Messina Baker Entertainment, 955 Carrillo Drive, Suite 100, Los Angeles, CA 90048, USA. *Telephone:* (323) 954-8600.

ALLEN, Woody; American actor, writer, producer and director; b. (Allen Stewart Konigsberg), 1 Dec. 1935, Brooklyn, NY; s. of the late Martin Konigsberg and of Nettie Konigsberg (née Cherry); m. 1st Harlene Rosen 1956 (divorced 1962); m. 2nd Louise Lasser 1966 (divorced 1970); m. 3rd Soon-Yi Previn 1997; two adopted d.; one s. with Mia Farrow (q.v.); ed City Coll. of New York and New York Univ.; made his debut as a performer in 1961 at the Duplex in Greenwich Village; has performed in a variety of nightclubs across the USA; produced the play Don't Drink the Water 1966, Morosco Theater 1966, Broadhurst Theatre 1969; made his Broadway debut as Allan Felix in Play it Again, Sam, which he also wrote; during the 1950s wrote for TV performers Herb Shriner 1953, Sid Caesar 1957, Art Carney 1958–59, Jack Paar and Carol Channing, also wrote for the Tonight Show and the Gary Moore Show; Dr hc (Universitat Pompeu Fabra, Spain) 2007; Laurel Award for Screen Writing Achievement 1987, D.W. Griffith Award 1996, Directors Guild of America Lifetime Achievement Award 1996, San Sebastian Film Festival Donosti a Prize 2004, Cecil B DeMille Award, Golden Globe Awards, Hollywood Foreign Press Association 2013. *Plays include:* Don't Drink the Water 1966, The Floating Lightbulb 1981, Death Defying Acts (one act) 1995. *Opera:* as producer: Gianni Schicchi, Los Angeles Opera 2008. *Films include:* What's New Pussycat? 1965, Casino Royale 1967, What's Up, Tiger Lily? 1967, Take the Money and Run 1969, Bananas 1971, Everything You Always Wanted to Know About Sex 1972, Play it Again, Sam 1972, Sleeper 1973, Love and Death 1976, The Front 1976, Annie Hall (Acad. Awards for Best Dir and Best Writer 1978, BAFTA Film Awards for Best Screenplay and Best Direction 1978) 1977, Interiors 1978, Manhattan (BAFTA Film Award for Best Screenplay – Original 1980) 1979, Stardust Memories 1980, A Midsummer Night's Sex Comedy 1982, Zelig 1983, Broadway Danny Rose (BAFTA Film Award for Best Screenplay – Original 1985) 1984, The Purple Rose of Cairo (BAFTA Film Awards for Best Film and Best Screenplay – Original 1986, Golden Globe Award for Best Screenplay 1986) 1985, Hannah and Her Sisters (BAFTA Film Award for Best Direction 1987, Acad. Award for Best Writing, Screenplay Written Directly for the Screen 1987) 1986, Radio Days 1987, September 1987, Another Woman 1988, Oedipus Wrecks 1989, Crimes and Misdemeanors 1989, Alice 1990, Scenes from a Mall, Shadows and Fog 1991, Husbands and Wives (BAFTA Award Film Award for Best Screenplay – Original 1993) 1992, Manhattan Murder Mystery 1993, Bullets Over Broadway 1995, Mighty Aphrodite 1995, Everyone Says I Love You 1996, Deconstructing Harry 1997, Celebrity 1998, Antz (voice only) 1998, Wild Man Blues 1998, Stuck on You 1998, Company Men 1999, Sweet and Lowdown 1999, Small Town Crooks 2000, The Curse of the Jade Scorpion 2001, Hail Sid Caesar! 2001, Hollywood Ending 2002, Anything Else 2003, Melinda and Melinda 2004, Match Point 2005, Scoop 2006, Cassandra's Dream 2007, Vicky Cristina Barcelona 2008, Whatever Works 2009, You Will Meet a Tall Dark Stranger 2010, Midnight in Paris (Golden Globe Award for Best Screenplay 2012, Acad. Award for Best Writing, Screenplay Written Directly for the Screen 2012) 2011, To Rome With Love 2012, Blue Jasmine 2013, Magic in the Moonlight 2014. *Television:* Sounds from a Town I Love 2001. *Publications include:* Getting Even 1971, Without Feathers 1975, Side Effects 1980, The Complete Prose 1994, Telling Tales (contrib. to charity anthology) 2004, Mere Anarchy 2007, The Insanity Defense 2007; contribs to Playboy and New Yorker. *Leisure interests:* chocolate milk shakes, poker, chess, baseball; also a noted clarinettist. *Address:* 930 Fifth Avenue, New York, NY 10021, USA.

ALLENDE, Isabel; Chilean (b. Peruvian) writer; b. 2 Aug. 1942, Lima, Peru; d. of Tomás Allende and Francisca Llona Barros; m. 1st Miguel Frias 1962; one s. one d.; m. 2nd William Gordon 1988; journalist, Paula women's magazine 1967–74, Mampato children's magazine 1969–74, TV shows and film documentaries 1970–74, El Nacional newspaper, Caracas, Venezuela 1975–84; taught literature at Montclair State Coll., NJ 1985, Univ. of Virginia, Charlottesville 1988, Univ. of California, Berkeley 1989; Goodwill Amb. for Hans Christian Andersen Bicentenary 2004; lecture tours in USA and Europe, speech tours in univs and cols, numerous literature workshops; mem. Academia de Artes y Ciencias, Puerto Rico 1995, Academia de la Lengua, Chile 1989, American Acad. of Arts and Letters 2004; Hon. Citizen of Austin, Tex. USA 1995; Hon. Prof. of Literature, Univ. of Chile 1991; Hon. mem. Acad. of Devt and Peace, Austria 2000; Chevalier, Ordre des Arts et Lettres 1994, Condecoracion Gabriela Mistral (Chile) 1994; Hon. DLitt (New York State Univ.) 1991, (Bates Coll., USA) 1994, (Dominican Coll., USA) 1994, (Columbia Coll., USA) 1996; Hon. DHumLitt (Florida Atlantic Univ.) 1996; Dr hc (Lawrence Univ., USA) 2000, (Mills Coll., USA) 2000, (Illinois Wesleyan Univ.) 2002; Best Novel of the Year (Chile) 1983, Panorama Literario Award (Chile) 1983, Author of the Year (Germany) 1984, Book of the Year (Germany) 1984, Grand Prix d'Evasion Award (France) 1984, Point de Mire Award, Belgian Radio and TV 1985, Best Novel (Mexico) 1985, Author of the Year (Germany) 1986, Quality Paperback Book Club New Voice (USA) 1986, Premio Literario Colima Award (Mexico) 1986, XV Premio Internazionale I Migliori Dell'Anno (Italy) 1987, Mulheres Best Foreign Novel Award (Portugal) 1987, Quimera Libros (Chile) 1987, Book of the Year (Switzerland) 1987, Library Journal's Best Book (USA) 1988, Before Columbus Foundation Award (USA) 1988, Freedom to Write Pen Club (USA) 1991, XLI Bancarella Literary Award (Italy) 1993, Ind. Foreign Fiction Award (UK) 1993, Brandeis Univ. Major Book Collection Award (USA) 1993, Marin Women's Hall of Fame (USA) 1994, Feminist of the Year Award, The Feminist Majority Foundation (USA) 1994, Read About Me Literary Award (USA)

1996, Critics' Choice Award (USA) 1996, Books to Remember Award, American Library Asscn 1996, Gift of HOPE Award, HOPE Educ. and Leadership Fund (USA) 1996, Harold Washington Literary Award, City of Chicago 1996, Malaparte Award, Amici di Capri (Italy) 1998, Donna Città Di Roma Literary Award (Italy) 1998, Dorothy and Lillian Gish Prize (USA) 1998, Sara Lee Frontrunner Award (USA) 1998, GEMS Women of the Year Award (USA) 1999, Donna Dell'Anno 1999 Award (Italy) 1999, Books to Remember, The New York Public Library WILLA Literary Award 2000, Excellence in Int. Literature and Arts Award (USA) 2002, The Celebration of Books Amb. Award (USA) 2002, Int. Women's Forum Award (Mexico) 2002, Nopal Award, Cal Poly Pomona (USA) 2003, Cyril Magnin Lifetime Achievement Award (USA) 2003, Premios Iberoamericano de Letrasjose Donoso (Chile) 2003, Premio Personalidad Distinguida, Universidad del Pacifico (Chile) 2004, Commonwealth Award of Distinguished Service for Literature (USA) 2004, Premio Nacional de Literatura 2010. *Plays:* El Embajador 1971, La balada del medio pelo 1973, Los siete espejos 1974. *Publications:* La casa de los espíritus (novel, trans. as The House of the Spirits) 1982, La gorda de porcelana (juvenile short stories) 1983, De amor y de sombra (novel, trans. as Of Love and Shadows) 1984, Cuentos de Eva Luna (short stories, trans. as Stories of Eva Luna) 1989, El plan infinito (novel, trans. as The Infinite Plan) 1991, Paula (memoir) 1994, Afrodita (trans. as Aphrodite) 1998, Hija de la fortuna (novel, trans. as Daughter of Fortune) 1999, Retrato en sepia (novel, trans. as Portrait in Sepia) 2000, La ciudad de las bestias (juvenile novel, trans. as City of the Beasts) 2002, Mi país inventado (memoir, trans. as My Invented Country) (Latino Literacy Now Award for Best Biography 2004) 2003, El reino del dragón de oro (juvenile novel, trans. as Kingdom of the Golden Dragon) (Latino Literacy Now Award for Best Young Adult Fiction 2003) 2003, El Zorro (novel) 2005, El Bosque de los Pigmeos (juvenile novel, trans. as Forest of the Pygmies) 2005, Inés del alma mía (novel, trans. as Inés of My Soul) 2006, La Suma de los Días (memoirs, trans. as The Sum of Our Days) 2007, La Isla Bajo el Mar (novel, trans. as Island Beneath the Sea) 2009. *Address:* Carmen Balcells, Diagonal 580, Barcelona 21, Spain (office); 116 Caledonia Street, Sausalito, CA 94965, USA (office). *Fax:* (415) 332-4149 (office). *E-mail:* assistant@isabelallende.com (office). *Website:* www.isabelallende.com.

ALLENDE, Jorge Eduardo, PhD; Chilean biochemist, molecular biologist and academic; *Professor of Biochemistry and Molecular Biology, Instituto de Ciencias Biomédicas, University of Chile;* b. 11 Nov. 1934, Cartago, Costa Rica; s. of Octavio Allende and Amparo Rivera; m. Catherine C. Connelly 1961; three s. one d.; ed Louisiana State and Yale Univs, USA; Research Assoc., Lab. of Prof. Fritz Lipmann at Rockefeller Univ. 1961–62; Asst Prof., Dept of Biochemistry, Univ. of Chile 1963–68, Assoc. Prof. 1968–71, Prof. of Biochemistry and Molecular Biology 1972–; Pres. Pan American Assoc of Biochemical Socs 1976; mem. Exec. Cttee Int. Union of Biochemistry 1982–91, Int. Cell Research Org. 1976–; mem. Exec. Bd Int. Council of Scientific Unions 1986–90; Regional Co-ordinator Latin American Network of Biological Sciences 1975–97; mem. UNESCO Int. Scientific Advisory Bd 1996–; Chair. Advisory Comm. on Health Research, Pan-American Health Org. 1999–2003; Co-ordinator Science Educ. Program, Inter-Academy Panel; Foreign Assoc. Inst. of Medicine, NAS 1992, NAS 2001–; Fogarty Scholar-in-Residence, NIH, USA; Founder-mem. Latin American Acad. of Sciences; mem. Chilean Acad. of Sciences, Pres. 1991–94; Fellow, Third World Acad. of Sciences, Vice-Pres. 2004–06; Hon. mem. Chilean Acad. of Medicine; Grand Cross of Scientific Merit (Brazil) 2002; Dr hc (Buenos Aires) 1993; Chilean Nat. Prize in Natural Sciences 1992. *Publications:* more than 140 research articles in learned journals, 25 articles on science policy and science educ. *Leisure interests:* music, reading, swimming. *Address:* Program de Biol. Cel. y Mol., Inst. Cs. Biomed., Facultad de Medicina, Universidad de Chile, Casilla 70086, Santiago 7, Chile (office). *Telephone:* (2) 678-6255 (office). *Fax:* (2) 737-6320 (office). *E-mail:* jallende@abello.dic.uchile.cl (office). *Website:* icbm.cl (office).

ALLERT, Richard (Rick) H., AM, AO; Australian financial executive; *Chairman, Tourism Australia;* ed Kings Coll., Adelaide; Carroll Winter & Co. Chartered Accountants 1959–60; joined Peat Marwick Mitchell & Co. 1960, Pnr 1973–79; Sr Pnr, Allert Heard & Co. Chartered Accountants 1979–89; Chair. Southcorp 1989–2002; apptd Dir Coles Myer Ltd (renamed Coles Group Ltd 2006) 1995, Chair. 2002–07; Chair. Tourism Australia 2007–, AXA Asia Pacific Holdings Ltd, AustralAsia Railway Corpn, Nat. Wine Centre, Aboriginal Foundation of South Australia Inc., Performing Arts Bd, Australia Council; Dir Australian Business Arts Foundation; fmr Chair. Voyages Hotels & Resorts Pty Ltd, Pembroke School Foundation; fmr Nat. Pres. Nat. Heart Foundation of Australia; fmr Deputy Chair. South Australian Devt Council, Adelaide Football Club Ltd; fmr Bd mem. Northern Territory Devt Corpn, Northern Territory Trade Devt Zone, South Australian Oil and Gas Corpn; fmr Commr South Australian Health Comm.; fmr mem. Review of Business Taxation (Ralph Cttee), Singapore Australia Business Alliance Forum; Fellow, Inst. of Chartered Accountants (Australia); Hon. DUniv (Univ. of S Australia) 2000. *Address:* Tourism Australia, GPO Box 2721, Sydney, NSW 1006, Australia (office). *Telephone:* (2) 9360-1111 (office). *Website:* www .tourism.australia.com (office).

ALLEY, Kirstie; American actress; b. 12 Jan. 1951, Wichita, Kan.; m. Parker Stevenson; one s. one d.; ed Univ. of Kansas; People's Choice Award 1998. *Films:* Star Trek II, The Wrath of Khan 1982, One More Chance, Blind Date, Champions 1983, Runaway 1984, Summer School 1987, Look Who's Talking Too 1990, Madhouse 1990, Look Who's Talking Now 1993, David's Mother (TV film) 1994, Village of the Damned 1995, It Takes Two 1995, Sticks and Stones 1996, Nevada 1996, For Richer or Poorer 1997, Deconstructing Harry 1997, Toothless 1997, Drop Dead Gorgeous 1999, The Mao Game 1999, Back By Midnight 2002. *Stage appearances include:* Cat on a Hot Tin Roof, Answers. *Television includes:* Cheers 1987–93, Veronica's Closet 1997, Blonde 2001, Salem Witch Trials (mini-series) 2002, Profoundly Normal 2003, Family Sins 2003, While I Was Gone 2004, Fat Actress (series) 2005, The Minister of Divine 2007, Write & Wrong 2007 and numerous other TV films and series. *Address:* Jason Weinberg and Associates, 122 East 25th Street, 2nd Floor, New York, NY 10010, USA.

ALLEY, Richard B., BSc, MSc, PhD; American geologist and academic; *Evan Pugh Professor of Geosciences, Pennsylvania State University;* b. 1957; ed Ohio State Univ., Univ. of Wisconsin; Postdoctoral Research Asst, Univ. of Wisconsin-Madison 1987–88; Asst Prof., Dept of Geosciences and Coll. of Earth and Mineral Sciences Environment Inst., Pennsylvania State Univ. 1988–92, Assoc. Prof.

1992–96, Prof. 1996–, Evan Pugh Prof. of Geosciences 2000–; three field seasons in Antarctica (geology 1978, glaciology 1984, 1985), eight in Greenland (glaciology 1985, 1989–92, glacial geology 2003 and twice in 2005), three in Alaska (glaciology 1995, 2000, 2002), two in Utah (geology 1979, 1981), one in Wyoming (glacial geology 2008), much work (many months in total) at Nat. Ice Core Lab., Denver, Colo; mem. NAS 2008; Fellow, American Acad. of Arts and Sciences 2010, AAAS, American Geophysical Union, Geological Soc. of America; Dr hc (Univ. of Wisconsin); Faculty Scholar Medal, Pennsylvania State Univ., also Eisenhower Award and Coll. of Earth and Mineral Sciences Wilson Teaching Award, Mitchell Innovative Teaching Award and Faculty Mentoring Award; Heinz Award; Revelle Medal, American Geophysical Union, also Horton Award (Hydrology Section), Emiliani Lecturer (Paleo. Section), Nye Lecturer (Cryospheric Sciences Section) and Bjerknes Lecturer (Atmospheric Sciences Section); Louis Agassiz Medal (Cryospheric Section), European Geosciences Union, Schneider Award for Science Communication, Public Service Award, Geological Soc. of America, also Easterbrook Award of their Quaternary Geology and Geomorphology Section; Award for Outstanding Contrib. to Public Understanding of the Geosciences, American Geological Inst., Distinguished Geographer Award, Pennsylvania Geographical Soc., Sustained Achievement Award, Renewable Natural Resources Foundation, D&L Packard Fellowship, Presidential Young Investigator Award, G. Comer Mentorship, Seligman Crystal, Int. Glaciological Soc. 2005, Tyler Prize for Environmental Achievement 2009, Heinz Award 2012. *Publications include:* Rocking the Parks: Geological Stories of the National Parks 1999, The West Antarctic Ice Sheet: Behavior and Environment (co-ed.) 2001, The Two-Mile Time Machine: Ice Cores, Abrupt Climate Change, and Our Future (Nat. Phi Beta Kappa Science Book Award, Choice Award 2001) 2000, Abrupt Climate Change: Inevitable Surprises (co-author) 2002, Earth: The Operators' Manual 2011; more than 220 papers in scientific journals on glaciology, ice sheet stability and palaeoclimates from ice cores. *Address:* Department of Geosciences, Penn State University, 517B Deike Building, University Park, PA 16802, USA (office). *Telephone:* (814) 863-1700 (office). *Fax:* (814) 863-7823 (office). *E-mail:* rba6@psu .edu (office); ralley@essc.psu.edu (office). *Website:* www.geosc.psu.edu (office).

ALLEYNE, Sir George, Kt, MD, FRCP; Barbadian physician and UN official; *Chancellor, University of the West Indies;* b. 7 Oct. 1932, Barbados; s. of Clinton Alleyne and Eileen Alleyne (née Gaskin); m. Sylvan I. Chen 1958; two s. one d.; ed Harrison Coll., Univ. of the West Indies; Sr Resident, Univ. Hosp. of the West Indies 1963; Research Fellow, Tropical Metabolism Research Unit, Jamaica 1964–72; Prof. of Medicine, Univ. of the W Indies 1972–81, Chair. Dept of Medicine 1976–81; Head Research Unit, Pan American Health Org. 1981–83, Dir Health Programmes 1983–90, Asst Dir 1990–95, Dir 1995–2003, Dir Emer. 2003–; Special Envoy of the UN Sec.-Gen. for HIV/AIDS in the Caribbean 2003–10; Chancellor Univ. of the West Indies 2003–; Order of the Caribbean Community 2001; Hon. DSc (Univ. of the West Indies) 1988. *Publications include:* The Importance of Health: A Caribbean Perspective 1989, Public Health for All 1991, Health and Tourism 1992; over 100 articles in major scientific research journals. *Leisure interests:* gardening, reading. *Address:* Pan American Health Organization, 525 23rd Street, NW, Washington, DC 20037, USA (office). *Telephone:* (202) 974-3057 (office). *Fax:* (202) 974-3677 (office). *E-mail:* alleyned@paho.org (office).

ALLFORD, Simon, BA, DipArch, RIBA; British architect; *Partner, Allford Hall Monaghan Morris;* b. 27 July 1961, London, England; s. of the late David Allford and of Margaret Beryl Allford (née Roebuck); ed Hampstead Comprehensive School, Sheffield Univ., The Bartlett School of Architecture, Univ. Coll. London; with Nicholas Grimshaw 1983–85, BDP 1986–89; Pnr, Allford Hall Monaghan Morris 1989–; Lecturer, Univ. Coll. London 1987–; mem. Architectural Asscn Council 1996–, Hon. Sec. 1991–2001, Hon. Treas. 2001–05; Vice-Pres. RIBA 2005–11; Chair. Architecture Foundation 2013–; Trustee, Architecture Asscn Foundation 2013–; recent projects include The Angel, Tea and Yellow Buildings, Adelaide Wharf, the Saatchi Gallery and Chobham Acad.; currently working on the new Google HQ, The White Collar Factory, 240 Blackfriars, three mixed use projects on Regent Street for the Crown Estate, an academic building for Univ. of Amsterdam, as well as large urban scale projects in London and USA; writer, critic, teacher, judge, adviser, trustee and commentator on architectural subjects; 29 RIBA Awards, eight Housing Design Awards, eight BCI Awards, three BCO Awards, 11 Civic Trust Awards, four AIA Awards, four MIPIM Awards, two WAF Awards, numerous Practice Awards, including Architect's Journal and Building magazine Practice of the Year 2013. *Publications:* manual: The Architecture and Office of Allford Hall Monaghan Morris. *Leisure interests:* architecture, Sheffield Wednesday Football Club. *Address:* Allford Hall Monaghan Morris, 2nd Floor, Block C, Morelands, 5–23 Old Street, London EC1V 9HL (office); 232 Bickenhall Mansions, Bickenhall Street, London, W1U 6BW, England (home). *Telephone:* (20) 7251-5261 (office); (20) 7487-5391 (home). *Fax:* (20) 7251-5123 (office). *E-mail:* sallford@ahmm.co.uk (office). *Website:* www.ahmm.co.uk (office).

ALLI, Baron (Life Peer), cr. 1998, of Norbury in the London Borough of Croydon; **Waheed Alli;** British media executive; b. 16 Nov. 1964; ed Norbury Manor School, Stanley Tech. Coll.; created Planet 24 Productions Ltd (fmrly 24 Hour Productions) with pnr Charlie Parsons, Jt Man. Dir 1992–99; Man. Dir Carlton Productions 1998–2000; Chair. Asos PLC –2012; mem. Bd of Dirs Castaway Television Productions Ltd, BM Creative Management Ltd, Olga TV Ltd, Silvergate Investments Ltd (investment company), Silvergate Retail Ltd, Silvergate Media Ltd, Silvergate PPL Ltd, Silvergate Media Holdings Ltd, Vampire Squid Productions Ltd, Monkey WTB Ltd, Fairytale HD Ltd, QAM Building Management Ltd, Castaway Holdings Ltd; Pres. National Youth Theatre; Vice-Pres. UNICEF UK 2003–; Chancellor, De Montfort Univ. 2006–; Trustee, Crimestoppers, Charley Parsons Foundation; Stonewall Award 2008. *Address:* House of Lords, London, SW1A 0PW, England (office). *Telephone:* (20) 7219-5353 (office). *Fax:* (20) 7219-5979 (office).

ALLIANCE, Baron (Life Peer), cr. 2004, of Manchester in the County of Greater Manchester; **David Alliance,** CBE, CBIM, FRSA; British business executive; b. June 1932, Kashan, Iran; m. (divorced); three c.; first acquisition, Thomas Hoghton (Oswaldtwistle) 1956; acquired Spirella 1968, then Vantona Ltd, 1975 to form Vantona Group 1975; acquired Carrington Viyella to form Vantona Viyella 1983, Nottingham Mfg 1985, Coats Patons to form Coats Viyella 1986; Group Chief Exec. Coats Viyella 1975–90, Chair. 1989–99; Chair. N. Brown Group (mail order firm)

1968–2012 (now mem. Bd of Dirs), Tootal Group PLC 1991–99; Gov. Tel-Aviv Univ. 1989–; Fellow, Royal Soc. for the Encouragement of Arts, Mfrs and Commerce; Fellow, City and Guilds of London Inst.; mem. Prince's Youth Business Trust, Council for Industry and Higher Educ., Univ. of Manchester Foundation, Wiseman Inst.; mem. Liberal-Democrat Party; Hon. Fellow, UMIST, Shenkar Coll. of Textile Tech. and Fashion; Hon. FCGI 1991; Hon. LLD (Manchester) 1989, (Liverpool) 1996; Hon. DSc (Heriot-Watt) 1991;. *Address:* House of Lords, Westminster, London, SW1A 0PW, England.

ALLIES, Bob, MA, DipArch, RIBA, FRSA; British architect and lecturer; *Partner, Allies and Morrison Architects;* b. (Edgar Robin), 5 Sept. 1953, Singapore; s. of Edgar Martyn and Lily Maud; m. Jill Franklin; one s. one d.; ed Reading School, Univ. of Edinburgh; est. Allies and Morrison Architects with Graham Morrison 1983, Partner 1983–; Lecturer, Univ. of Cambridge 1984–88; George Simpson Visiting Prof., Univ. of Edinburgh 1995; Visiting Prof., Univ. of Bath 1996–99; mem. Faculty of Fine Arts, British School of Rome, Italy 1997–2002; Kea Distinguished Visiting Prof., Univ. of Maryland, USA 1999; Chair. The Brick Awards 2009–12, Shape East Design Review Panel 2011–; mem. Council Architectural Asscn 2004–07, CABE Nat. Design Review Panel 2006–, RIBA Awards Group 2009–11, London Mayor's Design Advisory Group 2012–; Rome Scholar in Architecture 1981–82; Medal for Architecture, Edin. Architectural Asscn 1977, Building Awards Architectural Practice of the Year 2004, Building Design Architect of the Year Award 2007, the practice has won 32 RIBA Awards. *Publications include:* Model Futures 1983, Allies and Morrison 1996, Cultivating the City: London Before and After 2012 2009, Allies and Morrison, Vol. 1 2012. *Leisure interest:* contemporary music. *Address:* Allies and Morrison, 85 Southwark Street, London, SE1 0HX (office); 12 Well Road, London, NW3 1LH, England (home). *Telephone:* (20) 7921-0100 (office). *Fax:* (20) 7921-0101 (office). *E-mail:* boballies@alliesandmorrison.com (office). *Website:* www.alliesandmorrison.com (office).

ALLIK, Jüri, PhD; Estonian psychologist and academic; *Professor of Experimental Psychology and Head, Department of Psychology, University of Tartu;* b. 3 March 1949, Tallinn; s. of Karl Allik and Niina Raudsepp; m. Anu Realo; one s. two d.; ed Moscow Univ., Russia, Tampere Univ., Finland; Prof. of Psychophysics, Univ. of Tartu 1992–2002, Dean, Faculty of Social Sciences 1996–2001, Prof. of Experimental Psychology and Head, Dept of Psychology 2002–; Chair. Estonian Science Foundation 2003–09; Pres. Estonian Psychological Asscn 1988–94, Vice-Pres. 1994–2001; Ed. Trames; Assoc. Ed. European Journal of Personality 2004–09; mem. Estonian Acad. of Sciences; Foreign mem. Finnish Acad. of Science and Letters 1997; Order of the White Star, 4th Class (Estonia); Nat. Science Award 1998, 2005. *Publications:* The Five-Factor Model of Personality Across Cultures (co-ed.) 2002; numerous articles in scientific journals on visual perception, comparative study of collectivism vs individualism, the works of Sigmund Freud, and history of psychology. *Address:* Department of Psychology, University of Tartu, Tiigi 78, Tartu 50410, Estonia (office). *Telephone:* (7) 376152 (office). *Fax:* (7) 375900 (office); (7) 376152 (office). *E-mail:* juri.allik@ut.ee (office); jyri@psych.ut.ee (office). *Website:* www.psych.ut.ee/~jyri (office).

ALLIOT-MARIE, Michèle, MA, DenD, DenScPol; French lawyer and politician; b. 10 Sept. 1946, Villeneuve-le-Roi, Val-de-Marne; d. of Bernard Marie and Renée Leyko; m. Michel Alliot (divorced); partner, Patrick Ollier; ed Faculté de Droit et des Sciences Econ. de Paris, Faculté des Lettres de Paris-Sorbonne, Univ. de Paris I; Asst Lecturer, Faculté de Droit et des Sciences Econ. de Paris then at Univ. de Paris I 1970–84, Sr Lecturer in Econs and Man. 1984–; Tech. Adviser to Minister of Social Affairs 1972–73, Adviser to Minister of Overseas Territories 1973–74, to Jr Minister for Tourism March–Sept. 1974, Tech. Adviser to Jr Minister for Univs 1974–76, Chef de Cabinet to Jr Minister for Univs then to Minister for Univs 1976–78; Dir, later Pres.-Dir Gen. UTA-Indemnité 1979–84; adviser on Admin. and Public Service Issues, RPR 1981–84, Asst Sec.-Gen. Legal Advisory Cttee 1984–, mem. Cen. Cttee 1984–, Exec. Cttee 1985–, Nat. Sec. for Educ. and Research 1985–; Deputy for Pyrénées-Atlantiques (RPR) 1986, 1988–93, 1995–2002, 2007–; Sec. of State in charge of schools, Ministry of Educ. 1986–88; Nat. Sec. RPR (Research and Planning) 1988–90, Asst Sec.-Gen. (Foreign Relations) 1990–92; Municipal Councillor for Ciboure 1983–89, for Biarritz 1989–91; mem. European Parl. (UDF-RPR) 1989; Minister for Youth and Sports 1993–95; mem. and First Vice-Pres. Regional Council of Pyrénées-Atlantiques 1995–2001; Mayor of Saint-Jean-de-Luz 1995–2002; Nat. Sec. RPR for Social Affairs 1997–, mem. Political Cttee 1998–, Nat. Sec. in charge of elections 1999–, Pres. RPR 1999–2002; Minister of Defence and Veterans' Affairs 2002–07, of the Interior, Overseas Possessions and Territorial Collectivities 2007–09, of Justice and Keeper of the Seals 2009–10, of Foreign and European Affairs 2010–11 (resgnd); mem. Political Cttee Alliance pour la France 1998; Pres. Comm. for Defence of Rights and Freedoms 1980–, Foundation for Voluntary Orgs –2000 and many current and fmr offices in women's and children's charitable orgs; Commdr de l'Etoile équatoriale (Gabon), de l'Etoile d'Anjouan (Comoros), du Mérite de l'Educ. Nat. (Côte d'Ivoire), Ordre de la République (Egypt), Palmes Magistrales (First Class) (Peru); ranked by Forbes magazine amongst 100 Most Powerful Women (51st) 2005, (57th) 2006, (11th) 2007. *Publications:* L'actionnariat des salariés 1975, La Décision politique: attention une république peut en cacher une autre 1983, La Grande peur des classes moyennes 1996, La République des irresponsables 1999. *Address:* c/o Ministry of Foreign and European Affairs, 37 quai d'Orsay, 75351 Paris Cedex 07, France.

ALLISON, Graham Tillett, Jr, AB, MA, PhD; American academic and government official; *Douglas Dillon Professor of Government and Director, Belfer Center for Science and International Affairs, Harvard University;* b. 23 March 1940, Charlotte, NC; s. of Graham T. Allison, Sr and Virginia Wright; m. Elisabeth K. Smith 1968; ed Davidson Coll., Harvard Univ., Univ. of Oxford, UK; Instructor of Govt, Harvard Univ. 1967–68, Asst Prof. of Govt 1968–70, Assoc. Prof. of Politics 1970–72, Prof. of Politics 1972–93, Assoc. Dean and Chair. Public Policy Program, John F. Kennedy School of Govt 1975–77, Dean and Don K. Price Prof. of Politics 1977–89, Douglas Dillon Prof. of Govt 1989–, Dir Belfer Center for Science and Int. Affairs, John F. Kennedy School of Govt 1994–; Asst Sec. of Defense for Policy and Plans, Dept of Defense, Washington, DC 1993–94; numerous professional appointments; Hon. DPhil (Uppsala Univ.) 1979, Hon. DLaws (Davidson Coll.) 1985, (Univ. of North Carolina, Wilmington) 1992. *Publications include:* Essence of

Decision: Explaining the Cuban Missile Crisis 1971, Sharing International Responsibilities: A Report to the Trilateral Commission 1983; co-author: Hawks, Doves and Owls: An Agenda for Avoiding Nuclear War 1985, Fateful Visions: Avoiding Nuclear Catastrophe 1988, Windows of Opportunity: From Cold War to Peaceful Competition 1989, Window of Opportunity: The Grand Bargain for Democracy in the Soviet Union 1991, Beyond Cold War to Trilateral Cooperation in the Asia-Pacific Region 1992, Avoiding Nuclear Anarchy 1996, America's Achilles Heel: Nuclear, Biological, and Chemical Terrorism and Covert Attack 1998, Catastrophic Terrorism 1998, Realizing Human Rights: Moving from Inspiration to Impact 2000, Nuclear Terrorism: The Ultimate Preventable Catastrophe 2004. *Leisure interests:* fishing, tennis. *Address:* Belfer Center for Science and International Affairs, 79 JFK Street, Cambridge, MA 02138 (office); 69 Pinehurst Road, Belmont, MA 02478-1502, USA (home). *Telephone:* (617) 496-6099 (office). *Fax:* (617) 495-1905 (office). *E-mail:* graham_allison@harvard.edu (office). *Website:* bcsia.ksg.harvard.edu (office).

ALLISON, James Patrick, BS, PhD; American immunologist and academic; *Professor and Chair of Immunology and Executive Director, Immunology Platform, MD Anderson Cancer Center, University of Texas;* b. 7 Aug. 1948, Alice, Tex.; m. Malinda Bell; ed Univ. of Texas; Asst Biochemist and Asst Prof., Univ. of Texas 1977–83, Adjunct Prof. of Zoology 1979–84, Prof. and Chair of Immunology and Exec. Dir, Immunology Platform, MD Anderson Cancer Center 2012–, also Vivian L. Smith Distinguished Chair in Immunology 2013–; Visiting Scholar, Dept of Pathology, Stanford Univ. 1983–84; Prof. of Immunology, Univ. of California, Berkeley 1985–2004, also Dir, Cancer Research Lab. 1985–2004, Interim Head, Div. of Immunology 1987–89, Head, Div. of Immunology 1989–97; David H. Koch Chair of Immunologic Studies, Memorial Sloan-Kettering Cancer Center and Chair., Immunology Program 2004–12, also Dir Ludwig Center for Cancer 2007–12; Investigator, Howard Hughes Medical Inst. 2004–12; Consultant, Becton-Dickinson Immunocytometry Systems, Inc. 1984; mem. Editorial Bd Development Immunology 1989; Reviewing Ed. Science 1985–87; Assoc. Ed. Journal of Immunology 1987, International Immunology 1988; Fellow, AAAS, American Acad. of Microbiology 1997; mem. NAS, American Asscn of Immunologists, American Asscn of Cancer Research, Inst. of Medicine; Breakthrough Prize in Life Sciences 2014, Canada Gairdner Int. Award 2014, Szent-Györgyi Prize for Progress in Cancer Research 2014. *Address:* University of Texas MD Anderson Cancer Center, 1515 Holcombe Boulevard, Houston, TX 77030, USA (office). *Telephone:* (713) 792-2121 (office). *Fax:* (713) 790-1529 (office). *E-mail:* jallison@mdanderson.org (office). *Website:* www.mdanderson.org (office).

ALLISON, Richard Clark, BA, LLB; American judge (retd); b. 10 July 1924, New York; s. of Albert F. Allison and Anice Allison (née Clark); m. Anne Elizabeth Johnston 1950; two s. one d.; ed Univ. of Virginia; called to New York Bar 1948; practised in New York City 1948–52, 1954–55, 1955–; Pnr, Reid & Priest law firm 1961–87; fmr mem. Iran-US Claims Tribunal, The Hague; mem. ABA (Chair. Cttee Latin American Law 1964–68, Int. Law Section 1976–77, Nat. Inst. on Doing Business in Far East 1972, Int. Legal Exchange Program 1981–85), Int. Bar Asscn (Chair. Conf. 1986, Ethics Cttee 1986–88); mem. Soc. Int. des Avocats, Inter-American Bar Asscn, American Foreign Law Asscn, American Arbitration Asscn (Int. Panel), Southwestern Legal Foundation, American Soc. of Int. Law, Council on Foreign Relations, American Bar Foundation, Asscn of Bar of City of New York, Inst. for Transnational Arbitration (Advisory Bd), Raven Soc., SAR, St Andrew's Soc., New York. *Publications:* Protecting Against the Expropriation Risk in Investing Abroad 1988, revised 1998; legal articles. *Address:* 224 Circle Drive, Manhasset, New York, NY 11030, USA (home).

ALLISON, Robert J., Jr, BSc; American petroleum industry executive; *Chairman Emeritus, Anadarko Petroleum Corporation;* b. 1939; m. Carolyn Allison; three c.; ed Kansas Univ.; various sr positions with Amoco Production Co. 1959–73; Vice-Pres. of Operations, Anadarko Production Co. (now Anadarko Petroleum Corpn) 1973–76, mem. Bd of Dirs 1976–, Pres. 1976–79, CEO 1979–2002, Chair. 1986–2005 (resgnd), Chair. Emer. 2005–; mem. Bd of Dirs American Petroleum Inst., US Oil & Gas Asscn; mem. Nat. Petroleum Council, Soc. of Petroleum Engineers, Natural Gas Supply Asscn; Dir Freeport-McMoran Copper & Gold; mem. All-American Wildcatters 1991–, Chair. 1999–2000; Assoc. mem. Univ. Cancer Foundation, Univ. of Texas M. D. Anderson Cancer Center; Trustee United Way of Texas Gulf Coast; Dir Spindletop (fmr Pres. and Chair.); mem. Bd of Dirs N. Harris Montgomery Community Coll. Dist Foundation, Sam Houston Area Council, Boy Scouts of America; Offshore Energy Center Pinnacle Award 2002. *Address:* c/o Board of Directors, Anadarko Petroleum Corporation, 1201 Lake Robbins Drive, The Woodlands, TX 77380, USA (office). *Website:* www.anadarko .com (office).

ALLISON-MADUEKE, Diezani, BSc, MBA; Nigerian architect and government official; *Minister of Petroleum Resources;* b. 6 Dec. 1960, Port Harcourt; m.; ed Howard Univ., Washington, DC, USA, Univ. of Cambridge, UK; fmr Architectural Intern, Charles Szoradi Architects, Washington, DC; fmr Project Engineer, American Interior Builders, Washington, DC; fmr Design Coordinator, Furman Construction Man. Inc., Rockville, Md; fmr Project Man., Facilities Planning and Devt Dept, Howard Univ.; Head of Projects Unit, Shell Petroleum Devt Co. of Nigeria Ltd, Lagos 1993–96; Head of Corporate Issues Man. 1996–2007; Minister of Transportation 2007–08; Minister of Mines and Steel Devt 2008–10; Minister of Petroleum Resources 2010–. *Address:* Ministry of Petroleum Resources, 1st & 2nd Floor, Main Building Federal Secretariat, Shehu Shagrari Way, Abuja, Nigeria (office). *Telephone:* (9) 5230763 (office).

ALLMAND, The Hon. Warren, OC, PC, QC; Canadian academic and fmr politician; *Visiting Scholar, McGill Institute for the Study of Canada, McGill University;* b. 19 Sept. 1932, Montréal; s. of Harold W. Allmand and Rose Irene McMorrow; one s. two d.; ed Loyola High School, Montreal, St Francis Xavier Univ., McGill Univ., Univ. of Paris, France; called to Quebec Bar 1958, Ont. Bar 1976, Yukon and NWT Bars 1976; MP for Montréal-NDG 1965–93, Minister for Indian and Northern Affairs 1976–77, for Consumer and Corp. Affairs 1977–79; Solicitor-Gen. 1972–76; mem. Exec. World Federalists of Canada 1960–65; Int. Pres. Parliamentarians for Global Action 1984–91; Pres. Int. Centre for Human Rights and Democratic Devt 1997–2002; currently Visiting Scholar, McGill Inst. for the Study of Canada; fmr mem. Parliamentarians for East Timor, Parl. Friends of Tibet, Canadian Civil Liberties Asscn; mem. Quebec Bar Asscn, Liberal Party;

Hon. LLD (St Francis Xavier Univ., NS), (St Thomas Univ., NB) 1998; World Peace Award, World Federalists of Canada 1990. *Leisure interests:* ice hockey, long-distance running, skiing, tennis. *Address:* McGill Institute for the Study of Canada, McGill University, 845 Sherbrooke Street West, Montréal, PQ H3A 2T5, Canada (office). *Telephone:* (514) 398-4455 (office). *Fax:* (514) 398-3594 (office). *Website:* www.misc-iecm.mcgill.ca (office).

ALLOTEY, Francis Kofi Ampenyin, DIC, MA, PhD, FRAS, CIIP, FBCS; Ghanaian physicist, mathematician, computer scientist and academic; *Director, Institute of Mathematical Sciences;* b. 9 Aug. 1932, Saltpond; s. of Joseph Allotey and Alice Allotey; m. Asie Mirekua Allotey; four c.; ed Imperial Coll. of Science, Tech. and Medicine and London South Bank Univ., London, UK, Princeton Univ., USA; began academic career at Kwame Nkrumah Univ. of Science and Tech. 1960, Head, Dept of Computer Science 1972, full Prof. of Math. 1973 (first Ghanaian), later Pro-Vice-Chancellor Kwame Nkrumah Univ. of Science and Tech.; currently Dir Inst. of Math. Sciences, Ghana; Chair. Ghana Atomic Energy Comm. 1973–82, Council for Scientific and Industrial Research 1981–97; Gov. IAEA 1994–2000; Visiting Scientist, Int. Centre for Theoretical Physics (ICTP), Trieste, Italy 1967–, Chalmers Univ. of Tech., Gothenberg, Sweden 1970–88; Visiting Prof., Clark Atlanta Univ., Ga, USA 1991, Univ. of Michigan, USA 1992–97; mem. Scientific Council Int. Inst. of Theoretical and Applied Physics, Ames, Ia, USA 1992–2000, High Level Scientific Expert Review Panel for Int. Centre for Science and High Tech., Trieste 1993, UNESCO Physics Action Council 1992–2000, Scientific Council ICTP 1996–, Int. Planning Cttee for World Year of Physics 2005 2002–, Sub-cttee on Tech. Transfer of UN Conf. on New and Renewable Energy Sources; Vice-Pres. Preparatory Cttee UN Conf. for Promotion of Int. Peaceful Uses of Nuclear Energy; Pres. African Physical Soc.; Vice-Pres. IUAP 2011–; Founding Fellow, African Acad. of Sciences 1985, Vice-Pres. (Western Africa) 1985; Fellow, Ghana Acad. of Arts and Sciences 1971 (Pres. 2011–), Third World Acad. of Sciences 1988, British Computer Soc. 1993, Int. Inst. for Information Tech.; Founding Fellow, Ghana Inst. of Physics 1993; Chartered Physicist (UK) 1993; Chartered Information Tech. Professional (UK) 2004; Founder and Patron African Inst. for Math. Sciences, Math. Asscn of Ghana, Computing Asscn of Ghana, Ghana Science Teachers Asscn; Hon. FInstP; Hon. Fellow, Ghana Inst. of Engineers 1993; Order of Volta (Ghana); Hon. DSc from six univs; Prince Philip Gold Medal Award 1973, Nat. Art and Culture Award for Science 1991, Deserving Scientist Award, Ghana Science Asscn 1995, Martin Luther King Jr/Cesar Chevaz/Rosa Parks Visiting Prof. awarded by US Govt and Univ. of Michigan for contribs to physical and math. sciences and int. co-operation in sciences 1997, Ivory Coast Math. Soc. Medal 1998, World Bank/IMF African Club Distinguished Scientist Award 1998, African Math. Union Medal for quality contrib. to math. sciences and for pioneering and promoting math. in Africa 2000, Millennium Excellence Award (Ghana) 2005, honoured by Ghana Govt with special issue postage stamp 2006, Univ. of Maryland Eastern Shore Presidential Award 2009, Ministry of Environment, Science and Tech. Award 2011. *Address:* Institute of Mathematical Sciences, PO Box LG197, Legon-Accra, East Legon, Greater Accra Region 00233, Ghana (office). *Telephone:* (30) 2544102 (office); 27-7404374 (mobile). *E-mail:* fkallotey@gmail.com (office). *Website:* imsghana.org (office).

ALLOUACHE, Merzak; Algerian film director and writer; b. 6 Oct. 1944, Algiers; s. of Omar Allouache and Fatma Allouache; m. Lazib Anissa 1962; one d.; ed Institut des hautes études cinématographiques, Paris, Office de Radiodiffusion-Télévision Française; worked in Nat. Inst. of Cinema, Algiers, later in Inst. of Film, Paris; after return to Algeria worked as Adviser, Ministry of Culture; Silver Prize, Moscow Festival; Tanit d'Or Prize, Carthage 1979. *Films include:* Our Agrarian Revolution (documentary) 1973, Omar Gatlato, Les aventures d'un héros, L'homme qui regardait les fenêtres 1982, Bab El-Oued City 1994, Lumiére et Compagnie 1995, Salut Cousin! 1996, Dans la décapotable 1996, Alger–Beyrouth: Pour Mémoire 1998, Pepe Carvalho: La Solitude du Manager (TV) 1999, À bicyclette (TV) 2001, L'Autre Monde 2001, Chouchou 2003, Bab el seb 2005, Tamanrasset (Premio Signis, Cagliari) 2008, Harragas 2009, Normal! (Best Arab Narrative Film Award, Doha Tribeca Film Festival) 2011, The Repentant 2012. *Publications:* Bab El-Oued (novel) 1994.

ALMAGRO LEMES, Luis Leonardo; Uruguayan lawyer, diplomatist and politician; *Minister of Foreign Affairs;* b. 1 June 1963; ed Univ. de la República, Montevideo; Rep. of Uruguay to UNESCO, Paris 1988; Pres. Int. Co-operation Cttee, Junta Nacional de Prevención del Tráfico Ilícito y Uso Abusivo de Drogas 1989–91; First Sec. (Commerce), Embassy in Iran 1991–96; with Directorate-Gen. for Political Affairs 1996; Nat. Co-ordinator, Grupo de Valdivia 1997–98; Sec., Embassy in Germany 1998–2003; Dir of Int. Affairs, Ministry of Livestock, Agric. and Fishing 2005–07; Amb. to People's Repub. of China 2007–10; Minister of Foreign Affairs 2010–; mem. Movimiento de Participación Popular. *Address:* Ministry of Foreign Affairs, Avda 18 de Julio 1205, 11100 Montevideo, Uruguay (office). *Telephone:* (2) 9022132 (office). *Fax:* (2) 9021349 (office). *E-mail:* webmaster@mrree.gub.uy (office). *Website:* www.mrree.gub.uy (office).

ALMODÓVAR, Pedro; Spanish film director and screenwriter; b. 25 Sept. 1951, Calzada de Calatrava, Ciudad Real, Castilla La Mancha; fronted a rock band; worked at Telefónica for ten years; started career with full-length super-8 films; made 16mm short films 1974–83; f. El Deseo SA (film production co.); Prince of Asturias Award for the Arts 2006. *Films as writer and director:* Film político 1974, Dos putas, o historia de amor que termina en boda 1974, El Sueño, o la estrella 1975, Homenaje 1975, La caída de Sódoma 1975, Blancor 1975, Sea caritativo 1976, Muerte en la carretera 1976, Sexo va, sexo viene 1977, Salomé 1978, ¡Folle...folle... fólleme Tim! 1978, Pepe, Luci, Bom y otras chicas del montón 1980, Laberinto de pasiones 1982, Entre tinieblas 1983, ¿Qué he hecho yo para merecer esto? 1985, Matador 1986, La ley del deseo 1987, Mujeres al borde de un ataque de nervios (Felix award) 1988, ¡Atame! 1990, Tacones lejanos 1991, Kika 1993, La flor de mi secreto 1995, Carne trémula 1997, Todo sobre mi madre (Acad. Award for Best Foreign Language Film) 1999, Hable con ella (BAFTA Award for Best Film not in the English language 2003, Acad. Award for Best Original Screenplay 2003) 2002, La mala educación 2004, Volver (Best Foreign Film Nat. Bd of Review 2006, Goya Award for Best Film, Best Dir 2007, Best Foreign Film, London Film Critics' Circle Awards 2007) 2006, Los abrazos rotos 2009, La piel que habito 2011. *Films as producer:* Laberinto de pasiones 1982, Mujeres al borde de un ataque de nervios 1988, Acción mutante 1993, Mi nombre es sombra (assoc. producer) 1996, Cuernos

de espuma 1996, El Espinazo del diablo 2001, Mi vida sin mí (exec. producer) 2003, La Mala educación 2004, La niña santa 2004, La Vida secreta de las palabras 2005, La Mujer sin Cabeza 2008, El último verano de la Boyita 2009, La piel que habito 2011. *Publications:* Fuego en las entrañas 1982, The Patty Diphusa Stories and Other Writings 1992. *Address:* c/o El Deseo SA, Ruiz Perelló 15, Madrid 28028, Spain (office); Miramax Films, 18 E 48th Street, New York, NY 10017, USA (office).

ALMUNIA AMANN, Joaquín; Spanish economist, politician and international organization official; *Vice-President and Commissioner for Competition, European Commission;* b. 17 June 1948, Bilbao; m.; two c.; ed Univ. of Deusto; Economist, Council Bureau of the Spanish Chambers of Commerce, Brussels 1972–75; Chief Economist, Unión General de Trabajadores (trade union) 1976–79; mem. Parl. 1979–2004, Spokesperson, Socialist Parl. Group 1994–97; mem. Fed. Cttee of the Spanish Socialist Workers' Party (Partido Socialista Obrero Español—PSOE) 1979–, Leader of the PSOE 1997–2000; Minister of Employment and Social Security 1982–86, of Public Admin 1986–91; Socialist cand. for Prime Minister 2000; EU Commr for Econ. and Monetary Affairs 2004–10, Commr for Competition 2010–, EC Vice-Pres. 2010–. *Publication:* Memorias Políticas 2001. *Address:* Rue de la Loi 200, BERL 11/238, 1049 Brussels, Belgium. *Telephone:* (2) 298-09-01 (office). *Fax:* (2) 298-09-97 (office); (2) 298-09-99 (office). *E-mail:* joaquin.almunia@ec.europa.eu (office).

ALOGOSKOUFIS, Georgios; MSc, PhD; Greek economist, academic and politician; b. 17 Oct. 1955, Athens; m. Dika Agapitidou; one s. two d.; ed Univ. of Athens, London School of Econs, UK; Research Assoc., Hellenic Observatory, LSE 1985–2001; Lecturer in Econs, Birkbeck Coll., Univ. of London 1988–92, Reader in Econs 1989–90; Prof. of Econs, Athens Univ. of Econs and Business 1990–; Research Fellow, Centre for Econ. Policy Research, London 1994–98; Counsellor, EC 1989–90, World Bank 1991–92; Pres. Council of Financial Experts (SOE), Ministry of Nat. Economy 1992–93; Pres. Inst. of Econ. Studies 1994–96; elected mem. Parl. 1996, mem. Parl. Cttee for Econ. Relations 1996–2004, Parl. Speaker for Political Economy 1997–2004; Minister of the Economy and Finance 2004–09; mem. Exec. Bd European Econ. Asscn 1994–98; Sayers Prize, Univ. of London 1981. *Publications:* External Constraints on Macroeconomic Policy: The European Experience 1991, The Crisis of Economic Policy 1994, Unemployment: Choices for Europe, Monitoring European Integration 5 1995, La Drachme: du Phoenix à l'euro (Acad. of Athens Prize) 2002, Greece after the Crisis 2009. *Leisure interests:* music, tennis. *E-mail:* athina@alogoskoufis.gr. *Website:* www.alogoskoufis.gr; www.aueb.gr.

ALOIS PHILIPP MARIA, Hereditary Prince, LLM; Liechtenstein royal; *Permanent Representative of the Head of State;* b. 11 June 1968, Zürich, Switzerland; s. of Prince Hans-Adam II and Princess Marie of Liechtenstein; m. HRH Duchess Sophie in Bavaria, Princess of Bavaria, now also Hereditary Princess of Liechtenstein and Countess of Rietberg 1993; three s. one d.; ed Liechtenstein Grammar School, Royal Mil. Acad., Sandhurst, UK, Salzburg Univ., Austria; heir to the throne of Liechtenstein; commissioned Second Lt, Coldstream Guards, Hong Kong and London 1988; swore Oath of Allegiance to Constitution alongside his father 1990; worked for auditing firm, London 1993–96; returned to live in Vaduz and given responsibility for various sections of the royal assets; apptd Perm. Rep. (Regent) for exercising his father's sovereign powers 15 Aug. 2004. *Address:* Fürstenhaus von Liechtenstein, Schloss Vaduz, Vaduz 9490, Liechtenstein (office). *Telephone:* 2381200 (office). *Fax:* 2381201 (office). *E-mail:* office@sfl.li (office). *Website:* www.fuerstenhaus.li (office).

ALOKO, Muhammad Eshaq; Afghan lawyer and government official; *Attorney General;* b. Kandahar; ed Mil. High School and Mil. Acad., Kabul, also studied law and admin in FRG; lived in Germany and worked at Ministry of Justice, Hamburg 1980s to early 2000s; worked as intelligence officer for fmr Pres. Mohammed Daoud Khan; First Deputy Attorney Gen. and Pres. Comm. for Guantanamo Detainees –2008, Attorney Gen. 2008–. *Publications include:* Daud Khan de KGB pa lamunu ke, Jalalabad Naghmey, Puti-e-Tubi, Saharona che Amali Nashu. *Address:* Attorney General's Office, Haji Yaqob Square, Sehrahi Masjid Hanzala, Kabul, Afghanistan (office). *Telephone:* (700) 260440 (mobile) (office). *E-mail:* agadviser@yahoo.com (office). *Website:* www.ago.gov.af (office).

ALOMAR, Raphaël; French banker and business executive; b. 28 July 1941, Tourcoing; s. of Raphaël Alomar and Jeanne Alomar (née Broutin); m. Nicole Labrunie 1964; three s.; ed Sorbonne, Paris, Ecole des Hautes Etudes Commerciales and Ecole Nationale d'Admin (ENA); Sec.-Gen. Etablissements Broutin 1966–69; Adviser to Gen. Man. Société Générale 1969–86; Prof. of Corp. Financial Man., ENA 1974–82, Pres. Alumni Asscn 1984–96; Assoc. Gen. Man. Cie de Navigation Mixte and of Via Banque 1986–93; Gov. Council of Europe Devt Bank 1993–2011; Officier, Légion d'honneur; Commdr Order of Isabella the Catholic; Commdr, Order of the Lion of Finland. *Publication:* Financing Business Development 1981. *Address:* c/o Council of Europe Development Bank, 55 avenue Kléber, 75116 Paris, France.

ALONEFTIS, Andreas P., MBA, ADipC, FAIA; Cypriot business executive and fmr government official; b. 24 Aug. 1945, Nicosia; s. of Polycarpos Aloneftis and Charitini Aloneftis; m. Nedi Georghiades 1967; one s. one d.; ed New York Inst. of Finance Coll. of New York Stock Exchange, Southern Methodist Univ., Harvard Univ., USA, Henley Management Coll. and Univ. of Middlesex, UK; served in Nat. Guard 1964–66; served 16 years in Cyprus Devt Bank; Gen. Man. and Chief Exec. Officer, Cyprus Investment and Securities Corpn Ltd (CISCO) 1982–88; Minister of Defence 1988–93; Gen. Man. ALICO (Cyprus) 1993–95; Man. Dir CYPRIALIFE Ltd 1995–99; Gen. Man. Insurance, Cyprus Popular Bank Group 1999–2003; Chair. and CEO Allied Capital Ltd 2001–; Exec. Vice-Chair. Alliance Reinsurance Co. Ltd 2002–08; Chair. Bd of Govs Cyprus Broadcasting Corpn 2003–06; Business Man./Dir IKOS CIF Ltd 2005–11; currently Assoc. Consultant, Eliades & Partners; Pres. Asscn of Int. Accountants 2007–09; mem. Bd of Dirs Flagstone Alliance Insurance and Reinsurance plc 2008–10; Open Fellowship, Southern Methodist Univ. 1978, Salzburg Seminar Fellow 1984, Paul Harris Fellow; Fulbright Grantee. *Publications:* numerous articles, working papers and monographs. *Leisure interests:* jogging, reading, cinema, travelling. *Address:* 10 Kastellorizo Street, Aglantzia, Nicosia 2108 (home); Eliades & Partners, Frosia House, Corner Evagorou and Menandrou Street 1, 1066 Nicosia, Cyprus.

Telephone: (22) 817970 (home). *Fax:* (22) 817971 (home). *E-mail:* alonefan@cytanet .com.cy (home).

ALONSO DÍAZ, Fernando; Spanish racing driver; b. 29 July 1981, Oviedo, Asturias; s. of José Luis Alonso; m. Raquel del Rosario 2006; ed Santo Angel de la Guarda; began competing on karting circuit at early age, winner of several karting championships at local, regional, national and international levels; first victory came in Pola Liviana 1988; World Jr Karting Champion 1996; moved to open-wheel cars 1999, Spanish Nissan Open Series Champion 1999; Formula One debut at Australian Grand Prix 2001; with Renault team 2002–06, 2008–09, with McLaren team 2007, with Ferrari team 2010–; winner Hungarian Grand Prix 2003, Chinese Grand Prix 2005, San Marino Grand Prix 2005, German Grand Prix 2005, European Grand Prix 2005, French Grand Prix 2005, Bahrain Grand Prix 2005, 2006, Malaysian Grand Prix 2005, 2007, 2012, British Grand Prix 2006, Australian Grand Prix 2006, Canadian Grand Prix 2006, Japanese Grand Prix 2006, Monaco Grand Prix 2006, 2007, Spanish Grand Prix 2006, Singapore Grand Prix 2008, Japanese Grand Prix 2008, Bahrain Grand Prix 2010, German Grand Prix 2010, Italian Grand Prix 2010, Singapore Grand Prix 2010, Korean Grand Prix 2010; winner Formula One Driver's Championship (youngest ever Formula One Champion) 2005, 2006, finished third 2007, second 2010; mem. Bd of Dirs Grand Prix Driver's Asscn; Premio Príncipe de Asturias 2005. *Leisure interests:* cycling, football, tennis. *Address:* c/o Scuderia Ferrari SpA, Via Abetone Inferiore n. 4, 41053 Maranello, Italy (office). *Website:* www.fernandoalonso.com.

ALONSO SUÁREZ, José Antonio, LicenDer; Spanish politician and lawyer; b. 28 March 1960, Léon; m.; one s.; ed Univ. of Léon; defence lawyer, Torrelavega, Santoña and Pamplona 1985–89; Magistrate, Las Palmas de Gran Canaria 1998–89; Judge, Criminal Court then Prov. Higher Court, Madrid 1989; mem. Congreso de los Diputados (Parl.) for Léon; Minister of Interior 2004–06, of Defence 2006–08; mem. Partido Socialista Obrero Español (Socialist Workers' Party), Spokesman in Congress 2008–; Spokesman, Judges for Democracy Asscn 1994–98, Consejo General del Poder Judicial 2001–04. *Address:* Congreso de los Diputados, Calle Floridablanca 1, 28071 Madrid, Spain (office). *Telephone:* (91) 3907260 (office). *Fax:* (91) 3906085 (office). *E-mail:* patricia.soublechero@gps .congreso.es (office). *Website:* www.congreso.es (office).

ALOR KOL, Deng; South Sudanese politician; s. of Deng Majiok; fmr Commdr, Sudan People's Liberation Army (SPLA); attended peace talks in Nairobi 1994; fmr Minister of Cabinet Affairs, Minister of Foreign Affairs 2007, fmr Minister of Regional Co-operation; Minister of Foreign Affairs, Govt of S. Sudan (following independence) 2011, of Cabinet Affairs 2013 (suspended June 2013); mem. Sudan People's Liberation Movt (SPLM). *Address:* c/o Ministry of Cabinet Affairs, Juba, South Sudan (office).

ALOS, Albert, BSc, DrEng; Spanish electronic engineer, academic and fmr university administrator; *Professor Emeritus, Pan-African University;* b. 17 Sept. 1939, Barcelona; ed School of Eng, Univ. of Bilbao; Lecturer in Electrical Eng, Univ. of Ife, Lagos and Ibadan, Nigeria 1967; Co-founder Lagos Business School (now part of Pan-African Univ.) 1991, Dean 1993–2004, Vice-Chancellor Pan-African Univ. 2002–09, now Prof. Emer.; Chair. Ikota Educational Foundation; mem. Vision 2010 Cttee, Editorial Advisory Cttee BusinessDay newspaper; Fellow, Inst. of Dirs, Acad. of Eng; Nat. Univs Comm. Award for Dedication and Exemplary Leadership, Award for vision and contrib. to the foundation of Nigerian Econ. Summit Group, Comm. of Vice-Chancellors Award for leadership role in pvt. univs. *Publication:* The Pains & Gains of Growth: Case Studies on Entrepreneurship. *Address:* Pan-African University, 2 Ahmed Onibudo Street, Victoria Island, Lagos (office); 35 Adeola Hopewell Street, Victoria Island, Lagos, Nigeria (home). *Telephone:* (1) 4616170 (office); (1) 4616173 (home). *E-mail:* aalos@pau.edu.ng (office). *Website:* www.pau.edu.ng (office).

ALPER, Howard, OC, PhD, FRSC; Canadian chemist and academic; *Distinguished University Professor, University of Ottawa;* b. 17 Oct. 1941, Montreal, Quebec; s. of Max Alper and Frema Alper; m. Anne Fairhurst 1966; two d.; ed Sir George Williams Univ., McGill Univ.; NATO Postdoctoral Fellow, Princeton Univ. 1967–68; Asst Prof., State Univ. of New York at Binghamton 1968–71, Assoc. Prof. 1971–74; Assoc. Prof., Univ. of Ottawa 1975–77, Prof. 1977–, Chair. Dept of Chem. 1982–85, 1988–91, 1991–94, Asst Vice-Pres. (Research) 1995–96, Vice-Pres. (Research) 1997–2006, currently Distinguished Univ. Prof.; Pres. RSC 2001–03; Co-Chair. IAP-The Global Network of Science Acads 2006–; Chair. Govt of Canada's Science, Tech. and Innovation Council 2007–, Int. Advisory Bd, Knowledge Economy Network 2011–, Science Advisory Comm., World Econ. Forum; Vice-Chair. RIKEN Advisory Comm. 2008–; Assoc. Fellow, TWAS-Acads of Sciences of the Developing World 2003; Corresp. mem. Mexican Acad. of Sciences 2009; Titular mem. European Acad. of Arts, Sciences and Humanities; Hon. Fellow, Chemical Inst. of Canada, 2006, Chemical Research Soc. of India 2006; Hon. mem. Colombia Acad. of Sciences 2011, Hon. Foreign mem. Chemical Soc. of Japan 2013; Officier, Ordre nat. du Mérite 2002; Chemical Inst. of Canada Inorganic Chem. Award 1980, Catalysis Award 1984, Guggenheim Fellowship 1985–86, Killam Research Fellow 1986–88, Alfred Bader Award in Organic Chem. 1990, Commemorative Medal (125th Anniversary of Canada) 1992, E.W.R. Steacie Award 1993, Urgel-Archambault Prize in Physical Sciences, Math. and Eng (ACFAS) 1996, Chemical Inst. of Canada Medal 1997, Bell Canada Forum Award 1998, Gerhard Herzberg Gold Medal in Science and Eng 2000, Le Seuer Memorial Award 2002, Chemical Inst. of Canada Montreal Medal 2003. *Publications include:* more than 540 papers and more than 32 patents in the area of organometallic chem. and catalysis. *Address:* Department of Chemistry, University of Ottawa, 10 Marie Curie, D'Iorio 402, Ottawa, ON K1N 6N5, Canada (office). *Telephone:* (613) 562-5189 (office). *Fax:* (613) 562-5871 (office). *E-mail:* howard.alper@uottawa.ca (office). *Website:* www.chem.uottawa.ca (office).

ALPERN, Robert J., BS, MD; American nephrologist, academic and university administrator; *Dean, School of Medicine, Yale University;* b. 3 Nov. 1950; m. Patricia Preisig; two c.; ed Northwestern Univ., Univ. of Chicago, Columbia Presbyterian, Univ. of California, San Francisco; intern in internal medicine, Columbia Univ. 1976–77, resident in internal medicine 1977–79; Fellow in Nephrology and Renal Physiology, Univ. of California Cardiovascular Research Inst., San Francisco 1979–82, Asst Prof. of Internal Medicine, Univ. of California, San Francisco 1982; Assoc. Prof., Texas SW Medical Center, Dallas 1987–90, Chief

of Nephrology 1987–98, Prof. of Medicine 1990–2004, Ruth W. and Milton P. Levy Sr Prof. of Molecular Nephrology 1994–2004, also Dean, Texas SW Medical Center 1998–2004; Ensign Prof. of Medicine and Dean, School of Medicine, Yale Univ. 2004–; mem. American Soc. of Clinical Investigation, Asscn of American Physicians, Inst. of Medicine 2007–, American Soc. of Nephrology, Int. Soc. of Nephrology, Soc. of Gen. Physiology, American Physiological Soc., American Heart Asscn; mem. Advisory Council Nat. Inst. of Diabetes and Digestive and Kidney Diseases; mem. Bd of Dirs Abbott Laboratories 2008–; SW Medical Center Outstanding Teaching Award 1999, American Soc. of Nephrology John P. Peters Award 2008. *Publications:* numerous scientific articles and book chapters. *Address:* Office of the Dean, Yale School of Medicine, 333 Cedar Street, New Haven, CT 06510, USA (office). *Telephone:* (203) 785-4672 (office). *E-mail:* Robert .alpern@yale.edu (office). *Website:* www.med.yale.edu/intmed/faculty/alpern.html (office).

ALPERT, Herb; American musician (trumpet), songwriter and record industry executive; b. 31 March 1935, Los Angeles; s. of Louis Alpert and Tillie Goldberg; m. 1st Sharon Mae Lubin 1956 (divorced); two c.; m. 2nd Lani Hall; one d.; ed Univ. of Southern Calif.; co-owner and fmr Pres. Carnival record co., later renamed A&M Record Co., Co-Chair. 1962–94; founder and Co-Chair. Almo Sounds 1994–2002; leader, arranger, own music group, Tijuana Brass 1962–; tours world-wide and numerous concert appearances; f. Herb Alpert Foundation; Lifetime Achievement Award (non-performer), Rock and Roll Hall of Fame Foundation 2005, Nat. Medal of Arts 2012. *Recordings include:* albums: The Lonely Bull 1962, Tijuana Brass 1963, Tijuana Brass Vol. 2 1963, South Of The Border 1964, Whipped Cream & Other Delights 1965, Going Places 1965, What Now My Love 1965, S.R.O. 1966, Sounds Like Us 1967, Herb Alpert's Ninth 1967, Beat Of The Brass 1968, Christmas Album 1968, Warm 1969, The Brass Are Comin' 1969, Summertime 1971, Solid Brass 1972, Four Sider 1973, You Smile, The Song Begins 1974, Coney Island 1975, Just You And Me 1976, Herb Alpert/Hugh Masekela 1978, Rise 1979, Keep Your Eyes On Me 1979, Beyond 1980, Magic Man 1981, Fandango 1982, Blow Your Own Horn 1983, Noche De Amor 1983, Bullish 1984, Wild Romance 1985, Keep Your Eye On Me 1987, Under A Spanish Moon 1988, My Abstract Heart 1989, North On South Street 1991, Midnight Sun 1992, Second Wind 1996, Passion Dance 1997, Colors 1999, Definitive Hits 2001, Lost Treasures 2005, Whipped Cream & Other Delights Rewhipped 2006, Anything Goes (with Lani Hall) 2009, I Feel You (with Lani Hall) 2011, Steppin' Out (Grammy Award for Best Pop Instrumental Album 2014) 2013. *Address:* c/o Herb Alpert Foundation, 1414 Sixth Street, Santa Monica, CA 90401, USA. *Telephone:* (424) 272-7082. *Website:* www .herbalpert.com.

ALPERT, Joseph Stephen, MD; American physician and university administrator; *Professor of Medicine, University of Arizona;* b. 1 Feb. 1942, New Haven, Conn.; s. of Zelly C. Alpert and Beatrice A. Kopsofsky; m. Helle Mathiasen 1965; one s. one d.; ed Yale and Harvard Univs; Instructor in Medicine, Peter Bent Brigham Hosp., Harvard Univ. 1973–74; Lt-Commdr, USN, Dir Coronary Care Unit, San Diego Naval Hosp. and Asst Prof. of Medicine, Univ. of Calif., San Diego 1974–76; Dir Levine Cardiac Unit and Asst Prof. of Medicine, Peter Bent Brigham Hosp. and Harvard Univ. 1976–78; Dir Div. of Cardiovascular Medicine and Prof. of Medicine, Univ. of Massachusetts Medical School 1978–92, Vice-Chair. Medicine Dept 1990–; Budnitz Prof. of Cardiovascular Medicine 1988–92; Prof., Chair. of Medicine Dept, Univ. of Ariz. 1992–; Fulbright Fellow, Copenhagen 1963–64; US Public Health Service Fellow, Harvard and Copenhagen 1966–67; NIH Special Fellow, Harvard 1972–74; Fellow, American Coll. of Physicians, American Coll. of Cardiology (Trustee 1996–2001), American Heart Asscn Clinical Council (Vice-Chair. 1991–92, Chair. 1993–95), American Coll. of Chest Physicians; mem. American Bd of Internal Medicine, Bd of Trustees 2001–03; Ed.-in-Chief, American Journal of Medicine 2005–; Gold Medal of Univ. of Copenhagen and other awards, including Gifted Teacher Award, American Coll. of Cardiology 2004. *Publications include:* The Heart Attack Handbook 1978, Physiopathology of the Cardiovascular System 1984, Modern Coronary Care 1990, Diagnostic Atlas of the Heart 1994, Cardiology for the Primary Care Physician 1998, Valvular Heart Disease 2000; co-author of other books including: Manual of Coronary Care 1978, Manual of Cardiovascular Diagnosis and Therapy; author of more than 400 articles in scientific journals. *Leisure interests:* poetry, music, swimming, cycling, cooking, travel. *Address:* Department of Medicine, 6th Floor, Room 6334, Arizona Health Sciences Center, 1501 North Campbell Avenue, Tucson, AZ 85724-5035 (office); 3440 E Cathedral Rock Circle, Tucson, AZ 85718, USA (home). *Telephone:* (520) 626-6138 (office). *Fax:* (520) 626-6604 (office). *E-mail:* jalpert@u.arizona.edu (office). *Website:* www.deptmedicine.arizona.edu (office).

ALPHANDÉRY, Edmond, DèsSc; French economist, politician and business executive; *Chairman, Centre for European Policy Studies;* b. 2 Sept. 1943, Avignon; ed Inst. d'études politiques de Paris, Univ. of Chicago, USA; Lecturer, Faculty of Law, Univ. d'Aix en Provence and Univ. Paris IX Dauphine 1969–71; Sr Lecturer and Dean of Faculty of Econ. Science, Univ. de Nantes 1972–74; Assoc. Prof., Univ. of Pittsburgh, USA 1975; Prof. of Econs, Univ. of Paris II 1975–93; elected Deputy to Nat. Ass. for Maine and Loire 1978–93, also Vice-Pres. then Pres. Gen. Council of Maine and Loire; mem. Finance Comm., Nat. Ass. 1979–93; Head of Investigatory Mission into European Econ. and Monetary Union 1991; Minister of the Economy 1993–95; Chair. Council of Ministers of the Economy and Finance, EU, Brussels 1995; Chair. Electricité de France (EDF) 1995–98; Founding Pres. Euro 50 Group 1999–; Chair. Supervisory Bd CNP (Caisse Nat. de Prévoyance) Assurances SA 1998–2007, Chair. Bd of Dirs 2007–12; Chair. Centre des Professions Financières –2013, Centre for European Policy Studies, Brussels 2014–; mem. Advisory Bd Banque de France 1996–, RWE 1997–2002, Supervisory Bd Bayernwerk AG 1997–98; Sr Advisor, Nomura Securities France; Dir (non-voting), Crédit Agricole Indosuez (fmrly Calyon) 2002–; Dir, GDF Suez 1967–68; mem. Consultative Cttee A.T. Kearney France 2013–; Fulbright Award 1967–68. *Publications:* Les politiques de stabilisation (co-author) 1974, Cours d'analyse macroéconomique 1976, Analyse monétaire approfondie 1978, 1986 Le piège 1985, La réforme obligée, sous le soleil de l'Euro 2000. *Address:* Compagnie Financière du Lion, 73 boulevard Haussmann, 75008 Paris, France (office). *Telephone:* 1-53-05-31-27 (office). *E-mail:* edmond.alphandery@financieredulion.com (office).

ALSHAMMAR, (Malin) Therese; Swedish swimmer; b. 26 Aug. 1977, Solna Municipality, Stockholm Co.; d. of Krister Alshammar and Britt-Marie Smedh;

won three Olympic medals, 25 World Championship medals and 43 European Championship medals; European Championships (long course), Seville 1997: bronze medal, 50m freestyle, silver medal, 4×100m freestyle, Istanbul 1999: gold medal, 4×100m medley, silver medal, 50m freestyle, 4×100m freestyle, Helsinki 2000: gold medal, 50m freestyle, 100m freestyle, 4×100m freestyle, 4×100m medley, Berlin 2002: gold medal, 50m freestyle, silver medal, 4×100m freestyle, 4×100m medley, Madrid 2004: gold medal, 50m freestyle, Budapest 2006: gold medal, 50m butterfly, silver medal, 50m freestyle, Eindhoven 2008: bronze medal, 50m freestyle, Budapest 2010: gold medal, 50m butterfly, 50m freestyle, silver medal, 4×100m medley, bronze medal, 4×100m freestyle, 100m butterfly; European Championships (short course), Sheffield 1998: silver medal, 50m backstroke, 4×50m medley, Lisbon 1999: gold medal, 50m freestyle, 100m freestyle, 4×50m freestyle, 4×50m medley, Valencia 2000: gold medal, 50m freestyle, 100m freestyle, 4×50m freestyle, 4×50m medley, Antwerp 2001: gold medal, 50m butterfly, 4×50m freestyle, 4×50m medley, silver medal, 50m freestyle, Riesa 2002: gold medal, 4×50m freestyle, 4×50m medley, Trieste 2005: silver medal, 4×50m freestyle, bronze medal, 4×50m medley, Helsinki 2006: gold medal, 50m butterfly, 4×50m freestyle, silver medal, 50m freestyle, 4×50m medley; Olympic Games, Sydney 2000: silver medal, 50m freestyle, 100m freestyle, bronze medal, 4×100m freestyle; World Championships (long course), Fukuoka 2001: silver medal, 50m freestyle, 50m butterfly, Montreal 2005: bronze medal, 50m butterfly, Melbourne 2007: gold medal, 50m butterfly, silver medal, 50m freestyle, Rome 2009: silver medal, 50m freestyle, Shanghai 2011: gold medal, 50m freestyle, silver medal, 50m butterfly; World Championships (short course), Gothenburg 1997: bronze medal, 4×100m freestyle, Hong Kong 1999: bronze medal, 4×100m medley, Athens 2000: gold medal, 50m freestyle, 100m freestyle, 4×100m freestyle, 4×100m medley, Moscow 2002: gold medal, 50m freestyle, 100m freestyle, 4×100m freestyle, 4×100m medley, Indianapolis 2004: silver medal, 4×100m freestyle, bronze medal, 50m freestyle, Shanghai 2006: gold medal, 50m butterfly, silver medal, 50m freestyle, bronze medal, 4×100m freestyle, Dubai 2010: gold medal, 50m butterfly, silver medal, 100m butterfly; personal bests (long course): 50m freestyle 23.88s 2009, 100m freestyle 53.58s 2009, 50m backstroke 29.22s 2005, 50m butterfly 25.07s (world record) 2009, 100m butterfly 57.55s 2010; personal bests (short course): 50m freestyle 23.27s 2009, 100m freestyle 52.17s 2000, 50m backstroke 26.62s 2009, 100m backstroke 57.43s 2009, 50m butterfly 24.46s (world record) 2009, 100m butterfly 55.53s 2010, 100m individual medley 58.51s 2009; clubs: Sundbybergs IK, Stockholmspolisens IF, Järfälla SS −1992, SK Neptun 1993–95, 1996–2008, Helsingborgs SS 1996, Nebraska Cornhuskers 1997–99, Täby Sim 2008−; coach: Johan Wallberg; Female World Cup Overall Winner 2005/06–2007, 2010–11, FINA Swimmer of the Year 2010. *Film appearance:* The Crawl (documentary short) 2004. *Television appearances:* Time Out (series) 2003, M2A – Mission to Athens (series documentary) 2003, Nyhetsmorgon (series) 2008–11, Skavlan (series) 2010. *Address:* c/o Täby Sim, Simhallen, 183 34 Täby, Sweden. *Telephone:* (8) 768-15-44. *E-mail:* kansli@tabysim.se. *Website:* www.tabysim.se.

ALSHAYA, Mohammed Abdul Aziz, BA, MBA; Kuwaiti retail executive; *Executive Chairman, Alshaya Group;* ed Kuwait Univ., Wharton School, Univ. of Pennsylvania, USA; began career working at Mothercare (retailer) in UK for three months; joined Alshaya Group in 1980s, worked in franchise div., then CEO M. H. Alshaya Co. Retail Div. 1990–93, Exec. Chair. 1993–99, CEO Alshaya Group 1999–2002, Exec. Chair. 2002–; Chair. Mabanee (real estate co.); mem. Bd of Trustees Arab Thought Foundation, Mentor Foundation (Int.); mem. Bd of Overseers, Wharton School, Univ. of Pa; mem. Kuwaiti Supreme Council of Planning and Devt; mem. Foreign Direct Investment Council of Turkey; Retail CEO of the Year, CEO Middle East Magazine 2010, ranked by Arabian Business amongst the Power 500: The World's Most Influential Arabs (22nd) 2010, (18th) 2012, (26th) 2013. *Address:* Alshaya Group, PO Box 181, Safat 13002 (office); Alshaya Group, Pepsi Cola Street, behind Mercedes-Benz Garage, Shuwaikh, Kuwait (office). *Telephone:* 22242000 (office). *Fax:* 24842891 (office). *E-mail:* info@alshaya.com (office). *Website:* www.alshaya.com (office).

ALSOP, Marin, MusM; American violinist and conductor; *Music Director, Baltimore Symphony Orchestra;* b. 16 Oct. 1956, New York City; d. of Keith LaMar Alsop and Ruth Alsop (née Condell); m. Kristin Jurkscheit Auden; one s.; ed began piano studies aged two, violin studies aged five; Juilliard Pre-Coll., Yale Univ. and Juilliard School of Music; freelance violinist with New York Symphony Orchestra, Mostly Mozart, New York Chamber Symphony, American Composers Orchestra, several Broadway shows 1976–79; began conducting studies with Carl Bamberger 1979, Harold Farberman 1985; f. String Fever (14-piece swing band) 1981; Founder and Dir Concordia Orchestra 1984–; debut with London Symphony Orchestra 1988; Assoc. Conductor Richmond Symphony 1988; studied with Leonard Bernstein, Seiji Ozawa and Gustav Meier, Tanglewood Music Center 1989; Music Dir Eugene Symphony, Ore. 1989–96, Conductor Laureate 1996–; Music Dir Long Island Philharmonic 1990–96; debut with Philadelphia Orchestra and Los Angeles Philharmonic 1990; Artistic Dir Cabrillo Festival of Contemporary Music 1992–; Music Dir Colorado Symphony, Denver 1993–; debut Schleswig Holstein Music Festival 1993; Creative Conductor Chair. St Louis Symphony Orchestra 1996–98; Prin. Guest Conductor, Royal Scottish Nat. Symphony 1999–; Prin. Guest Conductor, City of London Sinfonia 1999–; Prin. Conductor Bournemouth Symphony Orchestra (first woman to head UK symphony orchestra) 2001–07; guest teacher/artist, Nat. Orchestral Inst. 1991–2001, Oberlin Coll. 1998, Interlochen Center for the Arts 1998, Curtis Inst. 1998; Music Dir Baltimore Symphony Orchestra (first woman to head a major US orchestra) 2007–(15); Music Dir, São Paulo Symphony Orchestra 2012–; Fellow, American Acad. of Arts and Sciences; Hon. DLitt (Gonzaga Univ.) 1995, (Univ. of Minnesota) 2009; Leonard Bernstein Conducting Fellow, Tanglewood Music Festival 1988, 1989, Stokowski Conducting Competition 1988, Koussevitszky Conducting Prize 1989, ASCAP Award for Adventuresome Programming of Contemporary Music 1991, Univ. of Colorado Distinguished Service Award 1997, State of Colorado Gov.'s Award for Excellence in the Arts 1998, Royal Philharmonic Soc. Conducting Award 2003, Gramophone Artist of the Year 2003, Classical BRIT Award for Female Artist of the Year 2005, MacArthur Fellow and Grant 2005, MacArthur Genius Award 2005, Royal Philharmonic Soc. BBC Radio 3 Listeners' Award 2006, Musical America Award for Conductor of the Year 2009. *Achievements:* first woman to conduct the orchestra at La Scala, Concertgebouw Orchestra 2007; est. Orchkids

after-school programme in inner city Baltimore 2008; first woman to conduct Last Night of the BBC Promenade Concerts, London 2013. *Recordings include:* Fever Pitch, Fanfares for the Uncommon Woman, Saint-Saens, Blue Monday, Victory Stride, Fiddle Concerto for Violin and Orchestra, Gorgon, Music of Edward Collins, Too Hot to Handel, Barber Vols I–IV, Passion Wheels, Tchaikovsky Symphony No. 4, Bernstein Chichester Psalms, Brahms cycle with London Philharmonic, Barber cycle with Royal Scottish Nat. Orchestra, John Adams' Nixon in China, Bernstein's Mass. *Address:* c/o Intermusica Artists Management Ltd, Crystal Wharf, 36 Graham Street, London, N1 8GJ, England (office); Opus 3 Artists, 470 Park Avenue South, 9th Floor North, New York, NY 10016, USA (office); BSO 1212, Cathedral Street, Baltimore, MD 21201, USA (office). *Telephone:* (20) 7608-9900 (Intermusica) (office); (212) 584-7568 (Opus 3) (office); (410) 783-8100 (office). *E-mail:* rachel@rachelbowron.com (office); info@opus3artists (office); marinalsop@aol.com (office). *Website:* www.intermusica.co.uk (office); www.opus3artists.com (office); www.marinalsop.com.

ALSOP, William Allen, OBE, DipAA, RA, FRSA; British architect and painter; b. 12 Dec. 1947, Northampton; s. of Francis Alsop and Brenda Hight; m. Sheila Bean 1972; two s. one d.; ed Architectural Asscn; Tutor in Sculpture, Central St Martin's Coll. of Art and Design 1973, Hon. Prof. 1997; Maxwell Fry 1971; worked with Cedric Price 1973–77; Rodrick Ham 1977–79; ARB 1978; RIBA 1978; fmrly in practice with John Lyall; designed a ferry terminal in Hamburg; undertook design work on the Cardiff barrage; Prin., Alsop & Stormer, then Alsop, later SMC Alsop Architects 1979–2009, then consultant; est. own practice, collaborates with Bruce Maclean in producing architectural drawings; Prin. Dir and Chair. Alsop Architects 2001–09; Prin., RMJM 2009–11; Founding Dir, Alsop Lawrie Ltd All Design 2011–; Prof. of Architecture, Technical Univ., Vienna 1996–; Prof. of Architecture, Univ. for the Creative Arts, Canterbury 2013–; Hamburgische Architektenkammer 1992; Chair. Architectural Foundation 2000–07; mem. Design Council 1994–98, Architectural Inst. 1995, Russian Acad. of Art 1995, Urban Renaissance Panel, Yorkshire Forward 2001–03, Int. Design Cttee, Thames Gateway 2004–, Kensington and Chelsea Architectural Advisory Bd 2009–, SADG 1973; Hon. Fellow, Royal Soc. of British Sculptors 1996; Hon. LLD (Leicester) 1996; Hon. DrUniv (Sheffield Hallam) 2001; Hon. DCL (Univ. of East Anglia) 2007; Dr hc (Nottingham Trent) (Sheffield), (Ontario Coll. of Art and Design) 2004, (Univ. of East Anglia) 2007, (Ryerson Univ., Toronto) 2010; Civic Trust Award 2003, Architect's Journal Award 2003, 2004. *Publications include:* City of Objects 1992, William Alsop Buildings and Projects 1992, William Alsop Architect, Four Projects 1993, Will Alsop and Jan Störmer, Architects 1993, Le Grand Bleu-Marseille 1994, Selected and Current Works 1999, Will Alsop, Book 1 2001, Book 2 2002, Supercity 2004. *Leisure interests:* fishing, writing. *Address:* ALL Ltd, 33 Parkgate Road, London, SW11 4NP, England (office). *Telephone:* (20) 7095-0500 (office). *E-mail:* info.london@allworldwide.com (office). *Website:* www.all-worldwide.com (office).

ALSTON, Philip, BComm, LLM, JSD; Australian academic; *Professor of Law, New York University;* b. 23 Jan. 1950, Melbourne; ed Univ. of Melbourne, Univ. of California, Berkeley, USA; Lecturer and Visiting Prof., Harvard Law School 1984–89, 1993; Assoc. Prof. of Int. Law, Fletcher School of Law and Diplomacy, Tufts Univ., Boston 1985–89; Prof. of Law and Foundation Dir, Centre for Int. and Public Law, ANU 1989–95; Helen L. Deroy Visiting Prof. of Law, Univ. of Mich. 1993; Prof. of Int. Law, European Univ. Inst. 1996–2001, Co-Dir Acad. of European Law 1996–2001, Head of Law Dept 1997–98; Visiting Prof., Woodruff Chair of Int. Law, Univ. of Georgia 2000–01; John Norton Pomeroy Prof. of Law, School of Law, New York Univ. 2001–; Chief of Staff to Cabinet Minister, Australia, 1974–75; Human Rights Officer, UN Centre for Human Rights 1978–1984; Sr Legal Adviser to UNICEF 1984–92; Discrimination Commr for ACT 1992–94; rapporteur, UN Cttee on Econ., Social and Cultural Rights 1987–90, Chair. 1991–98; UN Special Rapporteur on Extrajudicial, Summary or Arbitrary Executions 2004–; rapporteur, Meeting of Chairs of UN Human Rights Treaty Bodies, 1988, 1990, 1992, 1997–98, Chair. 1990, 1993, 1997–98; mem. Tech. Advisory Group, UN study on Impact of Armed Conflict on Children 1995–97; ind. expert reporting on effectiveness of UN Human Rights Bodies, reports submitted 1989, 1993, 1997; Co-Ed. Australian Yearbook of Int. Law 1991–96, Ed.-in-Chief European Journal of International Law 1996–; Series Co-Ed. Collected Courses of the Academy of European Law 1998–; mem. editorial and advisory bds of numerous int. journals on law and human rights; Chair. Coordinating Cttee for UN Human Rights Special Procedures 2005–06. *Publications include:* The Future of UN Human Rights Treaty Monitoring (co-ed.) 2000, International Human Rights in Context: Law, Politics, Morals (with H. Steiner) 2000, Peoples' Rights (ed. and contrib.) 2001, Economic and Social Rights: A Bibliography 2005, The United Nations and Human Rights: A Critical Appraisal (ed. and contrib.) 2005, Human Rights and Development (ed.) 2005, Neglected Rights 2006; over 100 articles in journals on law and human rights. *Address:* New York University School of Law, Vanderbilt Hall, 40 Washington Square South, Room 305, New York, NY 10012-1099, USA (office). *Telephone:* (212) 998-6173 (office). *E-mail:* philip.alston@nyu.edu (office). *Website:* www.law.nyu.edu (office).

ALSTON, Hon. Richard Kenneth Robert, BA, BCom, MBA, LLM; Australian diplomatist, politician and business executive; b. 19 Dec. 1941, brother of Philip Alston; m. Margaret Mary Alston; two c.; ed Xavier Coll., Melbourne, Melbourne and Monash Univs; Senator for Vic. 1986–2004; Shadow Minister for Communications 1989–90, for Social Security, Child Care and Retirement Incomes 1990–92, for Social Security, Child Care and Superannuation 1992, for Superannuation and Child Care and Shadow Minister Assisting Leader on Social Policy 1992–93, for Communications and the Arts 1994–96; Minister for Communications and the Arts 1996–2003, for Information Tech. 1998–2003; High Commr to UK 2005–08; Deputy Leader of Opposition in Senate 1993–96, of Govt in Senate 1996–2005; Deputy Chair. Senate Standing Cttee on Legal and Constitutional Affairs 1986, Jt Parl. Cttee on Nat. Crime Authority 1987; mem. Senate Standing Cttee on Finance and Public Admin 1987; State Pres. Liberal Party Vic. Div. 1979–82; mem. Amnesty Int. Parl. Group; Nat. Chair. Australian Council for Overseas Aid 1978–83; Chair. Afghan-Australia Council 1987–90; Fed. Pres. UNA of Australia 1977–79; Gov. Nat. Gallery of Australia Foundation; Adjunct Prof., Faculty of Information Tech., Bond Univ., Queensland; mem. Bell Shakespeare Foundation, Melba Foundation; Fellow, Inst. of Dirs 1983–88. *Leisure interests:* Aboriginal art, modern literature, Oriental rugs, jogging, reading, pumping iron. *Address:* c/o

Department of Foreign Affairs and Trade, R. G. Casey Building, John McEwen Crescent, Barton, ACT 0221, Australia. *Telephone:* (2) 6261-1111.

ALTANKHUYAG, Norovyn; Mongolian politician; *Prime Minister;* b. 1958, Ulaangom, Uvs Prov.; ed Mongolian State Univ., Inst. of Man. Devt, Humboldt Univ., Berlin, Germany; Lecturer, Mongolian State Univ. 1981–91; apptd Sec. MSDP 1990, Vice-Chair. 1994–96, Sec.-Gen. 1999; mem. Mongolian Great Khural 1996–2000, 2001–, Acting Prime Minister Oct. 2009, Chief Deputy Prime Minister –2012, Prime Minister 2012–; Minister of Agric. and Industry April–July 1998, Acting Minister 1998–99; Chair. Songinohayrhan Democratic Party (DP) 2000–01, Sec.-Gen. DP 2001; Deputy Head, Directorate of Govt Affairs Sept. 2004; Minister of Finance and Economy 2004–06. *Address:* Prime Minister's Office, State Palace, Sükhbaataryn Talbai 6, Ulan Bator, Mongolia (office). *Telephone:* (11) 322356 (office). *Fax:* (11) 328329 (office). *Website:* www.pmis.gov.mn (office).

ALTBACH, Philip G., AB, AM, PhD; American academic; *J. Donald Monan Professor of Higher Education, Lynch School of Education, Boston College;* b. 3 May 1941; s. of Milton Altbach and Josephine Huebsch; m. Edith Hoshino 1962; two s.; ed Univ. of Chicago; Lecturer on Educ., Harvard Univ. 1965–67, also Postdoctoral Fellow; Asst Prof., Assoc. Prof., Dept of Educational Policy Studies, Univ. of Wisconsin, Madison 1967–75; Prof., Dept of Educational Org., Admin and Policy, State Univ. of New York, Buffalo 1975, Chair. 1985–88, Dir Comparative Educ. Center 1978–94, Chair. Dept of Social Foundations 1978–82, Adjunct Prof., School of Information and Library Studies 1982, Adjunct Prof., Dept of Sociology 1991; Project Dir NSF study of higher educ. in newly industrializing countries 1988–90; Prof., Lynch School of Educ., Boston Coll. 1994–, J. Donald Monan SJ Prof. of Higher Educ. 1996–, Dir Centre for Int. Higher Educ. 1995–; Chair. Int. Advisory Council, Graduate School of Educ., Shanghai Jiao Tong Univ.; Fulbright Research Prof., Univ. of Bombay 1968; Visiting Prof., Moscow State Univ. 1982, Univ. of Malaya 1983, School of Educ., Stanford Univ. 1988–89, Institut de Sciences Politiques, Paris, Univ. of Mumbai, India; Guest Prof., Inst. of Higher Educ., Peking Univ., China; Onwell Fellow, Univ. of Hong Kong; Sr Scholar, Taiwan Govt; Visiting Fellow, Hoover Inst., Stanford Univ. 1988–89; Fellow, German Academic Exchange Service, Japan Soc. for Promotion of Science; Consultant, Rockefeller Foundation; Sr Assoc. Carnegie Foundation for Advancement of Teaching 1992–96; N American Ed. Higher Education 1996–2004, Educational Policy 1989–2005; Ed. Review of Higher Education 1998–2004; Distinguished Scholar Leader, Fulbright New Century Scholars Programme 2004–06. *Publications include:* Turmoil and Transition: The International Imperative in Higher Education, Comparative Higher Education, Student Politics in America, International Comparison of Academic Salaries: An Exporatory Study (co-author), The Decline of the Guru: The Academic Profession in the Third World (ed), Private Higher Education: A Global Revolution (co-ed) 2005, International Handbook of Higher Education (co-ed) 2006, Higher Education in the New Century: Global Challenges and Innovative Ideas (co-ed) 2007, Tradition and Transition: The International Imperative in Higher Education 2007, World Class Worldwide: Transforming Research Universities in Asia and Latin America (co-ed) 2008, Trends in Global Higher Education: Tracking an Academic Revolution (co-author) 2009, Leadership for World-Class Universities: Challenges for Developing Countries (ed); author or co-author of numerous articles in professional journals etc. *Address:* Boston College, Lynch School of Education, Campion Hall, Room 101, 140 Commonwealth Avenue, Chestnut Hill, MA 02467, USA (office). *Telephone:* (617) 552-4200 (office). *Fax:* (617) 552-0812 (office). *E-mail:* altbach@bc.edu (office). *Website:* www.bc.edu (office).

ALTER, Harvey J., BA, MD; American physician, infectious disease specialist and academic; *Chief, Infectious Disease Section and Associate Director of Research Department, Department of Transfusion Medicine, Warren Magnuson Clinical Center, National Institutes of Health;* ed Univ. of Rochester, NY, Strong Memorial Hosp., Rochester, Nat. Insts of Health, Bethesda, MD, Univ. of Washington Hosp. System, Seattle, Washington, Georgetown Univ. Hosp., Washington, DC; Instructor in Medicine, Georgetown Univ. School of Medicine 1966–68, Asst Prof. of Medicine 1968–69, Clinical Asst Prof. of Medicine 1969–71, Clinical Assoc. Prof. of Medicine 1971–88, Clinical Prof. of Medicine 1988–; Adjunct Prof., Southwest Foundation for Biomedical Research, San Antonio, TX 1986–; on Faculty, Clinical Research Training Program, NIH 1988–, currently Chief, Infectious Disease Section and Assoc. Dir Research Dept, Transfusion Medicine Warren Magnuson Clinical Center; mem. Scientific Advisory Bd Acrometrix Corpn 1999–; ISBT Liason to Int. Consortium for Blood Safety 2000–; mem. Interagency HCV Working Group 2000–, Scientific Advisory Bd Blood Centers of the Pacific 2000–, Scientific Advisory Bd Hepatitis B Foundation 2002–; Ad Hoc Consultant to Food and Drug Admin (FDA) and Blood Products Advisory Comm. 1997–, Review Panel USAID 1998, FDA Cttee on Emerging Infectious Agents 1999–; Assoc. Ed. Transfusion Medicine Reviews 1986–, Journal of Viral Hepatitis 1994–; Section Ed. 'Hepatology Highlights', Hepatology 2001–; mem. NAS 2002–, Inst. of Medicine 2002–, American Fed. for Clinical Research, American Soc. of Hematology, Int. Soc. of Hematology, Int. Soc. of Blood Transfusion, American Asscn of Blood Banks, Mid-Altantic Asscn of Blood Banks, American Asscn for the Study of Liver Diseases, Asscn of American Physicians; Fellow, American Coll. of Physicians, American Soc. of Internal Medicine; Distinguished Service Medal, USPHS 1977, NIH Directors Award 1986, Emily Cooley Award and Lectureship, American Asscn of Blood Banks 1987, Stanley Davidson Lecturer, Royal Coll. of Physicians, Scotland 1990, Karl Lansteiner Award, American Asscn of Blood Banks 1992, Leon Schiff State of Art Lectureship, American Asscn for the Study of Liver Diseases 1996, Emil von Behring Award Lectureship, Int. Soc. of Blood Transfusion 1996, James Blundell Prize, British Blood Transfusion Service 1999, Laboratory Public Service Nat. Leadership Award 1999, Year 2000 World Health Day Award, American Asscn for World Health 2000, Distinguished Scientist Award, Hepatitis B Foundation 2000, Albert Lasker Award for Clinical Medical Research 2000, Scientific Achievement Award, Hepatitis Foundation International 2001, George Hoyt Whipple Award/Lectureship, U. Roch. 2001, Seymour Kalter Lectureship, Southwest Foundation for Biomedical Research 2001, Presidential Award, Int. Soc. for Blood Transfusion 2002, Distinguished Scientist Award, American Liver Foundation 2002. *Publications:* numerous articles in scientific journals. *Address:* National Institutes of Health, Warren G. Magunson Clinical Center, Department of Transfusion Medicine, 10 Center Drive, MSC-1184 Building 10, Room 1C711, Bethesda, MD 20892, USA (office). *Telephone:* (301) 496-

8393 (office). *Fax:* (301) 402-2965 (office). *E-mail:* halter@dtm.cc.nih.gov (office). *Website:* www.cc.nih.gov (office).

ALTHER, Lisa, BA; American writer, academic and journalist; b. (Elisabeth Greene Reed), 23 July 1944, Kingsport, Tenn.; d. of John Shelton Reed and Alice Greene Reed; m. Richard Alther 1966 (divorced); one d.; ed Wellesley Coll.; editorial asst, Atheneum Publrs, New York 1967–68; freelance writer 1968–; Lecturer, St Michael's Coll., Winooski, Vt 1980–81; Prof., East Tennessee State Univ. 1999–2000; Basler Chair, East Tennessee State Univ. *Publications:* Kinflicks 1975, Original Sins 1980, Other Women 1984, Bedrock 1990, Birdman and the Dancer 1993, Five Minutes in Heaven 1995, Kinfolks 2007, Washed in the Blood 2011, Blood Feud 2012, Stormy Weather and Other Stories 2012; contrib. to periodicals. *Address:* c/o Martha Kaplan Agency, 115 West 29th Street, New York, NY 10001, USA (office). *Telephone:* (212) 279-7134 (office). *Fax:* (212) 279-6251 (office). *E-mail:* kaplanagency@sprynet.com (office); lisaalther@lisaalther.com (office). *Website:* www.lisaalther.com.

ALTMAIER, Peter; German politician; *Head of the Federal Chancellery and Federal Minister for Special Tasks;* b. 18 June 1958, Ensdorf, Saar; ed Univ. of the Saarland, Saarbrücken; joined Junge Union (CDU youth org.) 1974, State Chair., Saarland Junge Union 1988–90; joined CDU 1976, District Chair., Saarlouis CDU 2000–08, Deputy State Chair., Saarland CDU 2011–; Research Asst, European Inst., Univ. of the Saarland 1988–90; Civil Servant, European Comm. 1990–94, Gen. Sec., EEC Admin Comm. on Social Security for Migrant Workers 1993–94; mem. Bundestag (Parl.) 1994–, Legal adviser to CDU/CSU Parl. Group 2004–05, First Parl. State Sec., CDU/CSU Parl. Group 2009–12; Parl. State Sec., Fed. Ministry of the Interior 2005–09; Fed. Minister for the Environment, Nature Conservation and Nuclear Safety 2012–13; Head of Fed. Chancellery and Fed. Minister for Special Tasks 2013–; Pres. Europa-Union Deutschland 2006–11. *Address:* Federal Chancellery, Bundeskanzler-Amt, Willy-Brandt Strasse 1, 10557 Berlin, Germany (office). *Telephone:* (30) 40000 (office). *Fax:* (30) 40002357 (office). *E-mail:* internetpost@bpa.bund.de (office). *Website:* www.bundeskanzlerin.de (home); www.peteraltmaier.de.

ALTMAN, Stuart Harold, BBA, MA, PhD; American health policy researcher, economist and academic; *Sol C. Chaikin Professor of National Health Policy, Heller School for Social Policy and Management, Brandeis University;* b. 8 Aug. 1937, Bronx, New York; s. of Sidney Altman and Florence Altman; m. Diane Kleinberg 1959; three d.; ed City Coll. of New York, Univ. of California, Los Angeles; Labor Market Economist, Fed. Reserve Bd 1962–64; Econ. Consultant and Manpower Economist, Office of US Asst Sec. of Defense, Washington, DC 1964–66; Asst Prof. of Econs, Brown Univ. 1966–68, Assoc. Prof. 1968–70; Univ. Fellow and Dir of Health Studies, Urban Inst. 1970–71; Deputy Admin., Office of Health, Cost of Living Council, US Dept of Health, Educ. and Welfare 1973–74, Deputy Asst Sec. for Planning and Evaluation (Health) 1971–76; Visiting Lecturer, Grad. School of Public Policy, Univ. of Calif., Berkeley 1976–77; Sol C. Chaikin Prof. of Nat. Health Policy, Heller School, Brandeis Univ. 1977–, Dean 1977–1992, Co-Chair. Advisory Bd, Schneider Insts for Health Policy, Interim Pres. Brandeis Univ. 1990–91; Chair. Prospective Payment Assessment Comm., US Congress 1984–96, Advisory Bd, Mass Savings Lives Program, Commonwealth Fund 1988–89; Pres. Asscn for Health Services Research 1983–85, Nat. Foundation Health Services Research 1985–86; Chair. Health Industry Forum, Council on Health Care Econs and Policy; Co-Chair. Health Care Task Force for Commonwealth of Mass 2000–04; mem. Bd of Dirs Lincare Holdings Inc. 2001–; mem. NAS Inst. of Medicine 1996–; mem. Bd Robert Wood Johnson Clinical Scholars 1977–83, Beth Israel Hosp., Brookline, Mass 1979–1991, Tufts New England Medical Center 2002–; fmr mem. Pres. Clinton's Health Policy Transition Team; Hon. Fellow, American Coll. of Health Care Execs 1996–97; Dr hc (Brandeis Univ., Rush Univ.); Special Recognition Award, American Asscn of Medical Colls 1996–97, Distinguished Investigator's Award, Acad. Health 2004. *Publications include:* The Growing Physician Surplus: Will it Benefit or Bankrupt the U.S. Health System? 1982, Ambulatory Care: Problems of Cost and Access (with others) 1983, Will the Medicare Prospective Payment System Succeed? Technical Adjustments Can Make the Difference 1986, Competition and Compassion: Conflicting Roles for Public Hospitals 1989, Strategic Choices for a Changing Health Care System 1996, The Future US Healthcare System: Who Will Care for the Poor and Uninsured? 1997, Regulating Managed Care: Theory, Practice and Future Options 1999, America's Health Care SAFETY NET: Intact but Endangered 2000, Policies for an Aging Society 2002. *Leisure interests:* sailing, cross-country skiing, boating, tennis, golf. *Address:* Heller School for Social Policy and Management, Brandeis University, 415 South Street, MS 035, Waltham, MA 02454-9110 (office); 11 Bakers Hill Road, Weston, MA 02493, USA (home). *Telephone:* (781) 736-3803 (office), (781) 891-9144 (home). *E-mail:* altman@brandeis.edu (office). *Website:* heller.brandeis.edu (office).

ALTMANN, Rev. Dr Walter, PhD; Brazilian ecclesiastic and international organization executive; b. 4 Feb. 1944, Porto Alegre; s. of Friedhold Altmann and Ricarda Altmann (née Sättler); m. Madalena Zwetsch Altmann; four d.; ed studied theology in São Leopoldo, Brazil, Buenos Aires, Argentina and Univ. of Hamburg, Germany; parish pastor, Ijui, southern Brazil 1972–74; Prof. of Systematic Theology, Theological Coll., São Leopoldo 1974–2002, 2011–, Head of Theological Coll. 1981–87; Dir Ecumenical Inst. for Postgraduate Studies 1989–94; Pres. Consejo Latinoamericano de Iglesias (Latin American Council of Churches) 1995–2001; Vice-Pres. Evangelical Church of the Lutheran Confession in Brazil 1998–2002, Pres. 2002–10; mem. Council of Lutheran World Fed. 2003–06; Moderator Cen. Cttee, WCC 2006–13; Award of Merit (category: Theological Reflection), Associated Church Press (ACP) 1990. *Publications:* more than ten books, including Der Begriff der Tradition bei Karl Rahner 1974, Luther and Liberation, A Latin American Perspective 1992, Nossa fé e suas razões: O Credo Apostólico – história, mensagem, atualidade 2004, Palavra a seu Tempo 2010, Maravilhoso Presente 2010; 180 articles on Martin Luther, Latin American theology, ethics and ecumenism; hundreds of articles in specialized magazines and reviews in Portuguese, Spanish, German and English, amongst others. *Address:* c/o World Council of Churches, PO Box 2100, 150 route de Ferney, 1211 Geneva 2, Switzerland (office). *E-mail:* walteraltmann@msn.com (office).

ALTON, Roger Martin; British journalist; *Executive Editor, The Times;* b. 20 Dec. 1947, Oxford; s. of the late Reggie Alton and Jeanine Alton; m. (divorced); one d.; ed Clifton Coll., Exeter Coll., Oxford; grad. trainee, Liverpool Post, then Gen. Reporter and Deputy Features Ed. 1969–74; Sub-Ed. News The Guardian 1974–76, Chief Sub-Ed. News 1976–81, Deputy Sports Ed. 1981–85, Arts Ed. 1985–90, Weekend Magazine Ed. 1990–93, Features Ed. 1993–96, Asst Ed. 1996–98, Ed. The Observer (British Press Award for Newspaper of the Year 2007) 1998–2007, The Independent 2008–10; Exec. Ed. The Times 2010–; writes sport column for The Spectator; Editor of the Year, What the Papers Say Awards 2000, GQ Editor of the Year 2005. *Leisure interests:* mountaineering, skiing, films, sports. *Address:* The Times, 1 Pennington Street, London E98 1TT, England (office). *Telephone:* (20) 7782-5000 (office). *Fax:* (20) 7782-5046 (office). *Website:* www.timesonline.co.uk (office).

ALTSCHUL, Stephen F., PhD; American mathematician; *Senior Investigator, Computational Biology Branch, National Center for Biotechnology Information;* b. 28 Feb. 1957; ed Harvard Coll. and Massachusetts Inst. of Tech.; Guest, Rockefeller Univ., New York 1977–78, Guest Investigator 1984–86; NSF Grad. Fellow, MIT 1981–84; Research Asst, Univ. of N Carolina 1986–87; Postdoctoral Fellow, Nat. Inst. of Diabetes, and Digestive and Kidney Diseases/Math. Research Br., Bethesda, MD 1987–89; Staff Fellow, Nat. Library of Medicine/Nat. Center for Biotechnology Information, Bethesda 1989–91, Sr Staff Fellow 1991–94, Sr Investigator, Computational Biology Br. 1994–, Chair. 1996–98; Adjunct Prof., Univ. of Maryland 2002–07; mem. Advisory Bd Genome Biology 1999–2010; Fellow, American Coll. of Medical Informatics 2001; Pehr Edman Award, Int. Asscn for Protein Structure Analysis and Proteomics 2004. *Publications:* numerous articles in scientific journals. *Address:* Computational Biology Branch, National Center for Biotechnology Information, National Library of Medicine, National Institutes of Health, Bethesda, MD 20894, USA (office). *Telephone:* (301) 435-7803 (office). *Fax:* (301) 480-2288 (office). *E-mail:* altschul@ncbi.nlm.nih.gov (office). *Website:* www.ncbi.nlm.nih.gov (office).

ALTYNBAYEV, General Mukhtar; Kazakhstani air force officer; b. 10 Dec. 1945, Karaganda; m. Gulbanu Rahimbaevna Altynbayeva; one s.; ed Karaganda Aviation Centre, Armavir Air Defence Mil. School, G.K. Jukov Air Defence Mil. Acad.; started career as miner, Karaganda 1962–66; graduated pilot school 1964; became pilot-cadet Kinnel-Cherkassy Aviation Training Centre 1965; held various military command positions including Flight Commdr, Squadron Commdr, Deputy Commdr of training regiment 1972–75, apptd Commdr of a fighter's regiment Ural District 1979; Deputy Div. Commdr then Commdr of Air Defence Div., Turkestan Mil. Dist. 1985–88, Commdr of Air Defence Corps 1992; apptd Air Defence Commdr and Deputy Defence Minister 1992, Air Forces Commdr 1993, Minister of Defence 1996, 2001–06, Acting Minister of Defence June 2009. *Address:* c/o Ministry of Defence, Beibitshilik 51a, Astana 473000, Kazakhstan (office).

ALVA, Margaret, BA, BL; Indian lawyer and politician; *Governor of Rajasthan;* b. 14 April 1942, Mangalore, Karnataka; d. of the late Shri P. A. Nazareth and of Elizabeth L. Nazareth; m. Niranjan Alva 1964; three s. one d.; ed Mount Carmel Coll. and Govt Law Coll., Bangalore; Gen. Sec. All India Catholic Univ. Fed. 1961; Jt Sec. Govt Law Coll. Students' Union 1963–64; State Convenor Karnataka Pradesh Congress Women's Front 1972–73, Congress Party (now Indian Nat. Congress) Standing Cttee on Information and Broadcasting 1975–76; MP 1974–2004; elected to Rajya Sabha (Council of States) 1974–98, Deputy Chief Whip Congress Party 1993–95, Gen.-Sec. –2008 (resgnd); Union Minister of State for Parl. Affairs 1984–85, for Youth Affairs, Sports, Women and Child Devt 1985–89, for Personnel, Public Grievances and Pensions 1991 (with additional charge of Parl. Affairs 1993–96); mem. 13th Lok Sabha 1999 (mem. Panel of Chairmen), Cttee on Transport and Tourism 1999–2000, House Cttee 1999–2000, Gen. Purposes Cttee 1999–2000; Chair. Cttee on Empowerment of Women 2000–01; mem. Consultative Cttee, Ministry of Tourism 2000–04; Gov. of Uttarakhand 2009–12, of Rajasthan 2012–; Spokesperson, Congress Parl. Party; Pres. Delhi YWCA 1975–78, World Women Parliamentarians for Peace 1986–88; Founder-Pres. Karuna (NGO working for women and children); mem. Indian Del. to UN Conf., Mexico 1975, UN Gen. Ass. 1976; mem. All India Congress Cttee, Int. Fed. of Women Lawyers, Nat. Children's Bd 1977–78, Nat. Adult Educ. Bd 1978–79, IPU Coordinating Cttee of Women Parliamentarians 2000–; Hon. DLitt (Mysore) 1989; Mahila Siromani Award 1991, Rajiv Gandhi Excellence Award 1991, Dr T.M.A. Pai Foundation Outstanding Konkani Award 1991, Global Leadership Award, Vital Voices Global Partnership 2007. *Leisure interests:* painting, music, drama, travel. *Address:* Office of the Governor, Raj Bhavan, Civil Lines, Jaipur 302 005 (office); 11 Milton Street, Cooke Town, Bangalore 560 001, India (home). *Telephone:* (141) 2228716 (Jaipur) (office); (80) 5469799 (Bangalore) (home). *Fax:* (141) 2228737 (Jaipur) (office).

ALVA CASTRO, Luis; Peruvian politician and economist; b. 17 Feb. 1942, Trujillo; ed Univ. Nacional de Trujillo and Univ. Inca Garcilaso de la Vega; fmr Dir Corporación de Desarrollo Económico y Social de la Libertad; Deputy for Libertad; has held various posts in Partido Aprista Peruano including Sec.-Gen. of Northern Regional Org., mem. Political Comm. and Nat. Sec. for Electoral Matters; Chair. Nat. Planning Comm. of Partido Aprista Peruano; Second Vice-Pres. of Repub. 1985–90, Pres. Council of Ministers (Prime Minister) 1985–90, Minister of Economy and Finance 1985–87, of the Interior 2007–08 (resgnd); re-elected to Congress 2000–11, Pres. of the Congress 2009–10; Pres. Comm. for Integration and Inter-parl. Relations 2001–02; Pres. Econ. Comm. 2001–06; Pres. Andean Parl. Aug.–Dec. 2001, Vice-Pres. 2002–07. *Publications:* La Necesidad del Cambio, Manejo Presupuestal del Perú, En Defensa del Pueblo, Endeudamiento Externo del Perú, Deuda Externa: Un reto para los Latinoamericanos and other books and essays.

ALVAREZ, Aida, BA; American journalist and fmr government official; b. Aguadilla, Puerto Rico; ed Harvard Univ.; fmr news reporter and presenter, Metromedia TV, New York; fmr reporter, New York Post; fmr mem. New York City Charter Revision Comm.; fmr Vice-Pres. New York City Health and Hosps Corpn; investment banker, First Boston Corpn New York, San Francisco 1986–93; Dir Office Fed. Housing Enterprise Oversight 1993–97; Dir US Small Business Admin, Washington, DC 1997–2001; Chair. Latino Community Foundation of San Francisco; mem. Bd of Overseers, Harvard Univ. 2000–; mem. Bd of Dirs UnionBanCal Corpn 2004–, Wal-Mart Stores Inc. 2006–; mem. Diversity Advisory Bd Deloitte & Touche LLP; Trustee Latino Community Foundation; fmr mem. Bd of Dirs Nat. Hispanic Leadership Agenda, New York Community Trust, Nat. Civic

League; fmr Chair. Bd Municipal Assistance Corpn/Victim Services Agency, New York; NY State Chair. Gore Presidential Campaign 1988; Nat. Co-Chair. Women's Cttee Clinton Presidential Campaign 1992; mem. Pres. Econ. Transition Team 1992; official spokeswoman for Senator John Kerry during 2004 US presidential elections; Hon. LLD (Iona Coll.) 1985; Front Page Award 1982, Assoc. Press Award for Excellence 1982.

ALVAREZ, Carlos Alberto, (Chacho); Argentine politician; *Secretary-General, Latin American Integration Association;* b. 26 Dec. 1948, Buenos Aires; m. Liliana Chiernajowsky; one s. three d.; ed Mariano Acosta Coll., Univ. of Buenos Aires; Assessor, Regional Econ. Cttee of Nat. Senate 1983–89; elected Deputy to Nat. Ass. (Partido Justicialista) for Fed. Capital 1989–93, 1997–99; left Partido Justicialista and f. Partido Movimiento por la Democracia y la Justicia Social (MODEJUSO) 1990; f. Frente Grande; Pres. Frente Grande Bloc in Nat. Constitutional Convention 1994; Founder, Leader Frente del País Solidario—FREPASO 1994–; Vice-Pres. of Argentina 1999–2000 (resgnd); Pres. Cttee of Perm. Reps, Mercosur 2005–09; Sec.-Gen. Latin American Integration Asscn 2011–. *Address:* Latin American Integration Association, Cebollatí 1461, Casilla 20.005, 11200 Montevideo, Uruguay (office). *Telephone:* (2) 410-1121 (office). *Fax:* (2) 419-0649 (office). *E-mail:* sgaladi@aladi.org (office). *Website:* www.aladi.org (office).

ALVAREZ, Ralph, BBA; American business executive; *Executive Chairman, Skylark Co. Ltd;* b. 1955, Cuba; ed Univ. of Miami; worked for Burger King Corpn 1977–89, held several exec. positions including Man. Dir Burger King Spain, Pres. Burger King Canada, Regional Vice-Pres. for Florida Region; Corp. Vice-Pres. and Div. Vice-Pres.–Florida, Wendy's International Inc. 1990–94; joined McDonald's 1994, several exec. positions including Pres. McDonald's Mexico, Chief Operations Officer and Pres. Cen. Div., McDonald's USA, Pres. McDonald's N America 2005–06, mem. Bd of Dirs, Pres. and COO McDonald's Corpn 2006–09; Exec. Chair. Skylark Co. Ltd (restaurant chain owner), Tokyo 2013–; mem. Bd of Dirs Eli Lilly and Co. 2009–, Dunkin' Donuts 2012–, Lowes Cos Inc.; serves on Pres.'s Council and Int. Advisory Bd, Univ. of Miami, Fla; fmr Pres. Ronald McDonald House Charities, Mexico; mem. Bd of Trustees, Field Museum, Chicago. *Address:* Office of the Executive Chairman, Skylark Co. Ltd, 1-25-8, Nishikubo, Musashino, Tokyo 180-0013, Japan (office). *Website:* www.skylark.co.jp (office).

ÁLVAREZ MARTÍNEZ, HE Cardinal Francisco, DCL; Spanish ecclesiastic; *Archbishop Emeritus of Toledo;* b. 14 July 1925, Santa Eulalia de Ferroñes; ordained priest 1950; consecrated Bishop of Tarazona 1973; Bishop of Calahorra and La Calzada 1976–89, of Orihuela 1989–95; Archbishop of Toledo 1995–2002, Archbishop Emer. 2002–; Apostolic Admin. of Cuenca 1996; cr. Cardinal-Priest, S. Maria "Regina Pacis" a Monte Verde 2001. *Address:* Archdiocese of Toledo, Arco de Palacio 2, 45002 Toledo, Spain (office). *Telephone:* (25) 224100 (office); (25) 223439 (home). *Fax:* (25) 222639 (office); (25) 222771 (home). *E-mail:* arztoletan@planalfa .es (office). *Website:* www.architoledo.org (office).

ÁLVAREZ RENDUELES, José Ramón, LLM, PhD; Spanish fmr central banker, business executive and university professor; *Chairman and President, Aceralia Corporacion Siderurgica SA;* b. 17 June 1940, Gijón; s. of Ramón Alvarez Medina; m. Eugenia Villar 1964; four s. one d.; State Economist 1964; rank of Full Prof. in Public Finance 1973; Head of Econ. Studies in Planning Comm. 1969; Dir Inst. of Econ. Devt 1973; Tech. Sec.-Gen., Ministry of Finance 1973–75, Under-Sec. for Econ. Affairs 1975–76; Sec. of State for Econ. Affairs 1977–78; Gov. Bank of Spain 1978–84; Chair. COFIR 1988–93, Productos Pirelli 1986–, Peugeot España 1996, Aceralia/ArcelorMittal España SA 1997–; Chair. and Pres. Aceralia Corporacion Siderurgica SA; Pres. Prince of Asturias Foundation 1996–2008; Gran Cruz Mérito Civil, Gran Cruz Isabel la Católica, Legión d'Honneur (France). *Publications:* Valoración actual de la imposición sobre consumo 1971, La Hacienda pública y el medio ambiente 1973. *Leisure interests:* golf, music, literature, lawn tennis. *Address:* SA, Paseo de la Castellano 91, 28046 Madrid (office); Peguerinos 12-F, 28035 Madrid, Spain (home). *E-mail:* aceralia@arcelor.com (office). *Website:* www.aceralia.es (office).

ALWARD, David Nathan, BA, MA; Canadian politician; *Premier of New Brunswick;* b. 2 Dec. 1959, Beverly, Mass, USA; s. of Rev. Ford Alward and Jean Alward; m. Rhonda Alward; two s.; ed Bryan Coll., Dayton, Tenn., USA; civil servant with Fed. Govt 1982–96; self-employed as human resource devt and community devt consultant 1996–99; owned small family cattle farm, Riceville, NB; elected to NB Legis. Ass. for Woodstock electoral dist 1999–, mem. Select Cttee to Review Appointments by Lt-Gov.-in-Council, Select Cttee on Pvt. Passenger Automobile Insurance; NB Minister of Agric., Fisheries and Aquaculture 2003–06; Premier of NB 2010–, also Minister of Intergovernmental Affairs 2010–; mem. Progressive Conservative Party of NB, Leader 2008–. *Address:* Office of the Premier, Centennial Bldg, 670 King Street, POB 6000, Fredericton, NB E3B 5H1, Canada (office). *Telephone:* (506) 453-2144 (office). *Fax:* (506) 453-7407 (office). *E-mail:* premier@gnb.ca (office). *Website:* www2.gnb.ca/content/gnb/en/ departments/premier.html (office).

ALWARD, Peter Andrew Ulrich; British record company executive and classical music consultant; *Intendant and Managing Director, Salzburg Easter Festival;* b. 20 Nov. 1950, London, England; s. of the late Herbert Andrew Alward and Marion Evelyne Schreiber; ed Bryanston School, Guildhall School of Music and Drama; worked for Simrock Music Publrs 1968–70; EMI Records UK 1970–74, European Co-ordinator EMI Classical Div. (Munich) 1975–83, Exec. Producer for all EMI recordings with Herbert von Karajan 1976–89, Man. (UK) Artists and Repertoire 1983, Int. Dir A&R 1985, Vice-Pres. 1989, Sr Vice-Pres. 1997, Pres. EMI Classics 2002–04; mem. Royal Opera House Covent Garden Opera Advisory Bd 1998–99; mem. Bd Trustees Young Concert Artists Trust 1999–2004; mem. Artistic Cttee, Herbert von Karajan Stiftung 2003–10; mem. European Advisory Bd, The Cleveland Orchestra 2009–11; Trustee, Masterclass Media Foundation 2006–; mem. Editorial Advisory Bd, BBC Music 2006–; Dir (non-exec.) Royal Opera House Enterprises 2007–, Opera Rara 2009–11; mem. Kuratorium Salzburg Int. Stiftung Mozarteum 2008–13; consultant, Bavarian Radio Symphony Orchestra 2008–; Jury Pres. ARD Piano Competition Munich 2011; Jury Vice-Pres. Santander Piano Competition 2012; Jury mem. Salzburg Festival/Nestlé Young Conductors Award 2010–; Intendant and Man. Dir Österfestspiele Salzburg (Salzburg Easter Festival) 2010–; Gramophone Special Achievement Award 2004. *Leisure interests:* classical music, painting and sculpture, theatre, books, collecting stage and costume designs, cooking, travelling. *Address:* 24 Midway, Walton-on-Thames, Surrey, KT12 3HZ, England (home). *Telephone:* (1932) 248985 (home). *E-mail:* peter@wotan844.fsnet.co.uk; pa@ofs-sbg.at (office). *Website:* www .osterfestspiele-salzburg.at (office).

ALZAHID, Sheikh; **Issam;** Saudi Arabian business executive; *Chairman, Alzahid Group of Companies;* Chair. Alzahid Group of Companies (f. by Alzahid Family as Alzahid Construction 1951), significant interests in mining, logistics, oil and gas, manufacturing, information technology, foodstuffs, retail and many other sectors. *Address:* Alzahid Group Headquarters, Silver Tower Street, Al-Khobar 31952, Eastern Saudi Arabia (office). *Telephone:* (3) 8656323 (office). *Fax:* (3) 8950948 (office). *E-mail:* chairman@alzahidgroup.com (office). *Website:* www.alzahidgroup .com (office).

AMADI, Capt. Elechi, BSc; Nigerian writer, fmr teacher, fmr army officer and government administrator; b. 12 May 1934, Aluu, Rivers State; s. of Chief Wonuchukwu Amadi and Enwere Amadi; m. 1st Dorah Nwonne Ohale 1957; m. 2nd Priye Iyalla 1991; four s. eight d.; ed Govt Coll. Umuahia, Survey School, Oyo, Univ. Coll. Ibadan, Univ. of Pittsburgh, Brookings Inst., USA; worked as land surveyor, East Regional Govt of Nigeria 1959–60; physics/maths teacher 1960–63; army officer (capt.) 1963–66, with 3rd Marine Commandos during civil war 1968–69, Officer with 14th Brigade, retd with rank of Capt.; Prin. Asa Grammar School 1967–68; Perm. Sec. Rivers State Govt 1973–83, Commr of Educ. 1987–88, of Lands and Housing 1989–90; Writer-in-Residence and Lecturer, Rivers State Coll. of Educ. 1984–85, Dean of Arts 1985–86, Head of Dept of Literature 1991–93; Founder and Dir Elechi Amadi School of Creative Writing 1997–; Chair. Asscn of Nigerian Authors (Rivers State Br.); Fellow, Nigerian Acad. of Educ. 2003–; Chair. Rivers State Scholarships Bd 2008–; mem. Order of Fed. Repub. (Nigeria) 2003; Hon. DSc (Rivers State Univ. of Science and Tech.) 2003. *Publications:* novels: The Concubine 1966, The Great Ponds 1969, The Slave 1977, Estrangement 1987; plays: Isiburu 1973, Peppersoup 1977, The Road to Ibadan 1977, Dancer of Johannesburg 1977, The Woman of Calabar 2002; Sunset in Biafra (war diary) 1973; Ethics in Nigerian Culture (philosophy) 1982; Speaking and Singing (essays and poems) 2003. *Leisure interests:* billiards, playing the piano, writing, reading, music, literary activities. *Address:* PO Box 331, Port Harcourt, Rivers State, Nigeria (home). *Telephone:* (803) 339-8036 (home). *E-mail:* info@elechiamadi.org (office); amadielechi@yahoo.com (home). *Website:* www.elechiamadi.com

AMADOU, Hama; Niger politician; *President, National Assembly;* b. 1950; m.; three c.; ed Ecole nationale d'administration, Niamey, École nationale d'administration, France; started career as regional inspector of customs in Zinder and Maradi 1972–74; Deputy Prefect of Agadez 1978–80, Gen. Secr. Zinder prefecture 1980; fmr Head of Ministry of Information; fmr Man. Dir Niger Broadcasting Bd; fmr Pvt. Sec. to Pres. Seyni Kountche and Pres. Ali Saibou; Prime Minister of Niger 1995–96, 2000–07; Sec.-Gen. Mouvement national pour une société de développement—Nassara 2001–09; arrested on corruption charges 2008, imprisoned and released on health reasons 2009; went into exile in France, returned to Niger 2010; Founder and Pres. Mouvement Démocratique Nigérien (Moden) 2010–; unsuccessful cand. (Moden) for Pres. of Niger 2011; mem. Nat. Ass. (Parl.) 2011–, Pres. Nat. Ass. 2011–. *Address:* Office of the President, National Assembly, pl. de la Concertation, BP 12234, Niamey, Niger (office). *Telephone:* 20-72-27-38 (office). *Fax:* 20-72-43-08 (office). *E-mail:* an@assemblee.ne (office); mdnloumana@gmail.com. *Website:* www.assemblee.ne (office).

AMADUZZI, Luigi, KCVO; Italian diplomatist; b. 22 March 1937, Naples; s. of Aurelio Amaduzzi; m. Giovanna Amaduzzi; one s. one d.; ed Univ. of Rome; joined diplomatic service 1963; Second Sec., London 1967; First Sec., Moscow 1969; First Sec., later Counsellor, Sec.-Gen.'s Office 1972, Head of Office 1983, 1991; Counsellor, Washington, DC 1975; Amb. to Jordan 1985–88, to Romania 1988; apptd Diplomatic Counsellor to the Pres. 1992; Amb. to UK 1999–2004. *Leisure interests:* tennis, painting.

AMAN, Datuk Anifah, BA; Malaysian politician; *Minister of Foreign Affairs;* b. 16 Nov. 1953, Keningau, Sabah; m.; three s.; ed Univ. of Buckingham, UK; Cttee mem., Beaufort Div., Malay Nat. Org. (UMNO) 1991–94, Treasurer 1994–99, Head of Kimanis Div. 2004–; mem. Parl. for Beaufort 1999–; Deputy Minister of Primary Industries 1999–2004, of Plantation Industries and Commodities 2004–08; Minister of Foreign Affairs 2009–; fmr Man. Sabah Football M-League Team; fmr Vice-Pres., Exec. Cttee mem. and Council mem., Football Asscn of Malaysia; fmr Pres. Sabah Football Asscn; Ahli Setia Darjah Kinabalu 1994, Panglima Gemilang Darjah Kinabalu 1998, Darjah Mahkota Pahang 2004; Special Award of Leadership for Sports, Ministry of Culture 1996. *Leisure interests:* football, golf. *Address:* Ministry of Foreign Affairs, Wisma Putra, 1 Jalan Wisma Putra, Presint 2, 62602 Putrajaya, Malaysia (office). *Telephone:* (3) 88874000 (office). *Fax:* (3) 88891717 (office). *E-mail:* webmaster@kln.gov.my (office). *Website:* www.kln.gov .my (office).

AMANI, Michel N'Guessan; Côte d'Ivoirian politician; b. 1957, Messoukro; fmr teacher of history and geography in various secondary schools in Bouaké, Botro and Bodokro; Sec.-Gen. Front Populaire Ivoirien (FPI) for Bouaké 1990–92, Fed.-Sec. for Centre region 1992; Minister of Nat. Educ. 2000–07, of Defence 2007–11. *Address:* c/o Ministry of Defence, Camp Galliéni, côté Bibliothèque nationale, PO Box V241, Abidjan, Côte d'Ivoire (office).

AMANN, Ronald, MSocSc, PhD, FRSA, ACSS; British academic and civil servant (retd); *Professor Emeritus of Comparative Politics, University of Birmingham;* b. 21 Aug. 1943, North Shields; s. of George Amann and Elizabeth Towell; m. Susan Peters 1965; two s. one d.; ed Heaton Grammar School, Newcastle-upon-Tyne and Univ. of Birmingham; Consultant, OECD and Research Assoc. 1965–69; Lecturer, Sr Lecturer in Soviet Science Policy, Univ. of Birmingham 1969–83, Dir Centre for Russian and East European Studies (CREES) 1983–89, Prof. of Comparative Politics 1986–, now Prof. Emer., Dean Faculty of Commerce and Social Science 1989–91, Pro-Vice-Chancellor 1991–94; Chief Exec. and Deputy Chair. Econ. and Social Science Research Council (ESRC) 1994–99; Dir Gen. Centre for Man. and Policy Studies, Cabinet Office 1999–2002; Chair. Centre for Research on Innovation and Competition, Univ. of Manchester; Visiting Fellow, Osteuropa Inst. Munich 1975; Specialist Adviser, House of Commons Select Cttee on Science and Tech. 1976, mem. Steering Cttee, Centre for the Analysis of Risk and Regulation, LSE; Founding Academician, Acad. of Learned Socs. for the Social Services 1999;

ind. mem. West Midlands Police Authority 2007–12. *Publications:* co-author: Science Policy in the USSR 1969, The Technological Level of Soviet Industry 1977, Industrial Innovation in the Soviet Union 1982, Technical Progress and Soviet Economic Development 1986. *Leisure interests:* walking, modern jazz, cricket. *Address:* 26 Spring Road, Edgbaston, Birmingham, B15 2HA, England (home). *Telephone:* (121) 440-6186 (home).

AMANO, Mari; Japanese diplomatist and international organization executive; *Secretary-General, Asian Productivity Organization;* m.; three d.; ed Univ. of Tokyo, Hertford Coll., Oxford, UK; career diplomat for over 30 years in Ministry of Foreign Affairs, posts have included service in Econ. Affairs Bureau, Ministry of Foreign Affairs 1980–84, Embassy in Kuwait 1984–87, Perm. Mission to OECD, Paris 1987–92, Minister at Embassies in Thailand 1994–96, USA 1996–98, Deputy Dir-Gen. in Multilateral Co-operation Dept, Ministry of Foreign Affairs 2000–01, Chief Negotiator for Trade Related Investment Measures in Uruguay Round 2000–03, Consul Gen., Houston, Tex. 2001–04; Deputy Exec. Dir Korean Peninsula Energy Devt Org. (KEDO) Secr. 2004–07; Deputy Sec.-Gen. OECD, in charge of Devt Cluster and Policy Coherence dossier 2007–11; Amb. and Perm. Rep. of Japan to Conf. on Disarmament 2011–13; Sec.-Gen. Asian Productivity Org., Tokyo 2013–. *Address:* Asian Productivity Organization, Leaf Square Hongo Building, 2F 1-24-1 Hongo, Bunkyo-ku, Tokyo 113-0033, Japan (office). *Telephone:* (3) 3830-0411 (office). *Fax:* (3) 5840-5322 (office). *E-mail:* apo@apo-tokyo.org (office). *Website:* www.apo-tokyo.org (office).

AMANO, Yukiya; Japanese diplomatist and international organization official; *Director General, International Atomic Energy Agency;* b. 9 May 1947, Kanagawa Pref.; m.; ed Univ. of Tokyo, Univ. of Franche-Comté, France, Univ. of Nice, France; joined Ministry of Foreign Affairs 1972, postings include embassies in Vientiane, Washington, DC and Brussels, Dir for Research Coordination and Sr Research Fellow, Japan Inst. of Int. Affairs 1988–90, Dir Nuclear Science Div., Ministry of Foreign Affairs 1993–94, also Dir Nuclear Energy Div., Counselor, Japanese Del. to Conf. on Disarmament, Geneva, Switzerland 1994–97, Consul Gen., Marseille, France 1997–99, Deputy Dir-Gen. for Arms Control and Scientific Affairs 1999–2000, Dir-Gen. Disarmament, Nonproliferation and Science Dept 2004–05, Perm. Rep. and Amb. to Int. Orgs, UN, Vienna 2005–09; mem. for Japan, IAEA Bd of Govs 2005–, Chair. IAEA Bd of Govs 2005–06, Dir Gen. IAEA 2009–; Chair. G7 Nuclear Safety Group 2000; Lecturer in Int. Politics, Yamanashi Univ. 1991–92; Fellow, Weatherhead Center for Int. Affairs, Harvard Univ. 2001; Visiting Scholar, Monterey Inst. of Int. Studies, USA 2001–02. *Publications:* Sea Dumping of Liquid Radioactive Waste by Russia 1994; several articles on nuclear non-proliferation and nuclear disarmament. *Address:* Office of the Director General, International Atomic Energy Agency, PO Box 100, Wagramer Strasse 5, 1400 Vienna, Austria (office). *Telephone:* (1) 26000 (office). *Fax:* (1) 26007 (office). *E-mail:* official.mail@iaea.org (office). *Website:* www.iaea.org (office).

AMANPOUR, Christiane, CBE, AB; British journalist and broadcasting correspondent; *Chief International Correspondent, CNN;* b. 12 Jan. 1958, London, England; d. of Mohammad Amanpour and Patricia Amanpour; m. James Rubin 1998; one s.; ed primary school in Tehran, Iran, Holy Cross Convent and New Hall School, UK, Univ. of Rhode Island, USA; radio producer/USA Asst, BBC Radio, London 1980–82; radio reporter, WBRU, Brown Univ., USA 1981–83; electronic graphics designer, WJAR, Providence, RI 1983; Asst, CNN Int. Assignment Desk, Atlanta, Ga 1983, news writer, CNN, Atlanta 1984–86, reporter/producer, CNN, New York 1987–90, Int. Corresp., CNN 1990–94, Sr Int. Corresp. 1994–96, Chief Int. Corresp. 1996–2010, 2011–; also host of nightly foreign affairs programme 'Amanpour'; Anchor, This Week, ABC News 2010–11, Global Affairs Anchor 2011–; mem. Bd of Dirs Cttee to Protect Journalists; Fellow, Soc. of Professional Journalists, American Academy of Arts and Sciences 2010; Hon. Citizen of Sarajevo 2006; Hon. mem. Graduating Class of Harvard Coll. 2010; Hon. Bd mem. Daniel Pearl Foundation; Hon. DHumLitt (Emory Univ.) 1997, (Northwestern Univ.) 2010; Dr hc (Univ. of Rhode Island), (Univ. of Michigan) 2006, (Georgia State Univ.) 2010, (Amherst Coll.) 2012, (Univ. of Southern California) 2012; hon. degree (Smith Coll.); three Dupont-Columbia Awards 1986–96, nine Emmy Awards, Women, Men and Media Breakthrough Award 1991, Livingston Award for Young Journalists 1992, George Polk Award for Television Reporting 1993, 1996, George Foster Peabody Award 1993, named Woman of the Year by New York Chapter of Women in Cable and Telecommunications 1994, Courage in Journalism Award, Int. Women's Media Foundation 1994, Nymphe d'Honneur, Monte Carlo Television Festival 1997, two George Foster Peabody Awards 1998, two News and Documentary Emmy Awards 1999, Univ. of Missouri Honor Award for Distinguished Service to Journalism 1999, Courage in Journalism Award, Worldfest-Houston Int. Film Festival Gold Award, Livingston Award for Young Journalists, Edward R. Murrow Award for Distinguished Achievement in Broadcast Journalism 2002, Goldsmith Career Award for Excellence in Journalism, Kennedy School of Govt, Harvard Univ. 2002, Sigma Chi Award (SDX) for her reports from Goma, Zaïre, WorldFest-Houston Int. Film Festival Gold Award, Int. Emmy, Int. Acad. of Television Arts and Sciences 2005, ranked by Forbes magazine amongst The World's 100 Most Powerful Women (72nd) 2005, (79th) 2006, (74th) 2007, (91st) 2008, (73rd) 2010, (44th) 2011, (53rd) 2012, Persian Woman of the Year 2007, The Fourth Estate Award, Nat. Press Club 2008, Walter Cronkite Award for Excellence in Journalism, Walter Cronkite School of Journalism and Mass Communication 2011. *Leisure interests:* reading, riding, tennis, swimming, sky diving. *Address:* ABC News, 77 West 66th Street, New York, NY 10023, USA (office). *Telephone:* (212) 456-7777 (office). *Fax:* (212) 456-4297 (office). *E-mail:* info@abcnews.go.com (office). *Website:* abcnews.go.com/ThisWeek (office); edition.cnn.com/CNN/ anchors_reporters/amanpour.christiane.html.

AMARASINGHE, Somawansa; Sri Lankan politician; Leader, Janatha Vimukthi Peramuna (People's Liberation Front) –2014, f. 1964, party banned following coup attempt 1971, regained legal status 1977, banned again 1983, regained legal status 1994; fled to London, UK and continued to provide party leadership from abroad, returned to Sri Lanka 2004. *Address:* Janatha Vimukthi Peramuna, 464/20 Pannipitiya Road, Pelawatte, Battaramulla, Colombo, Sri Lanka (office). *Telephone:* (11) 2785612 (office). *Fax:* (11) 2786050 (office). *E-mail:* jvplanka@sltnet.lk (office). *Website:* www.jvpsrilanka.com (office).

AMARATUNGA, John Anthony Emmanuel; Sri Lankan lawyer and politician; *Chief Opposition Whip;* b. 21 May 1940, Colombo; m.; ed Colombo Law Coll.,

Aquinas Coll. of Higher Studies, St Joseph's Coll., Colombo, De Mazenod Coll., Kandana; mem. Parl. for Gampaha (United Nat. Party) 1978–, Chief Opposition Whip 2010–; Minister of State 1989–90, of Prov. Councils 1990, of Home Affairs and Prov. Councils 1993, of Interior and Christian Affairs 2001–04; mem. del. to UN Gen. Ass. 2010. *Address:* Parliament of Sri Lanka, Sri Jayewardenepura Kotte (office); No. 88, Negombo Road, Kandana, Sri Lanka (home). *Telephone:* (11) 2777100 (office). *Fax:* (11) 2777564 (office). *E-mail:* webmaster@parliament.lk (office). *Website:* www.parliament.lk (office).

AMARI, Akira; Japanese politician; *Minister of State for Economic and Fiscal Policy;* b. 27 Aug. 1948, Atsugi, Kanagawa; ed Pref. Sr High School, Atsugi, Keio Univ. Law School; worked for Sony Corpn 1972–74; mem. House of Reps of New Liberal Club for Ninami-Kanto, for Kanagawa Pref. 13th Dist 1983–; subsequently joined LDP, Sr Dir LDP Commerce and Industry Panel 1990–95, Chair. 1995; Parl. Vice-Minister of Int. Trade and Industry 1989; Deputy Sec.-Gen. LDP 1999–2001, Chief Deputy Sec.-Gen. 2001; Minister of Labour 1998–99; Chair. House Budget Cttee 2004–05; Minister of Economy, Trade and Industry 2006–08; Minister of State for Regulatory Reform, Admin. Reform and Civil Service Reform 2008–09; Minister of State for Econ. and Fiscal Policy 2012– also Minister in charge of Econ. Revitalization and Minister in charge of Total Reform of Social Security and Tax; mem. Japan-Korea Parliamentarians' Union, Japan-China Friendship Parliamentarians' Union. *Leisure interest:* collecting antiques. *Address:* Cabinet Office 1-6-1, Nagata-cho, Chiyoda-ku, Tokyo 100-8968 (office); Liberal-Democratic Party (LDP), 1-11-23, Nagata-cho, Chiyoda-ku, Tokyo 100-8910, Japan (office). *Telephone:* (3) 5253-2111 (office); (3) 3581-6211 (office). *E-mail:* koho@ldp.jimin.or.jp (office). *Website:* www.cao.go.jp (office); www.jimin.jp (office); www.amari-akira .com.

AMARJARGAL, Rinchinnyamyn, MEcons; Mongolian politician; m.; one s.; ed Moscow Inst. of Econs, Univ. of Bradford, UK; officer, Cen. Council of Mongolian Trade Unions 1982–83; Lecturer, Mil. Acad. and Tech. Univ. 1983–90; Dir Econs Coll., Ulan Bator 1991–96; MP 1996–99, 2004–; Minister and Acting Minister of External Relations April–Dec. 1998, Prime Minister of Mongolia 1999–2000; fmr mem. Mongolian Nat. Democratic Party Gen. Council; mem. Democratic Party 2000–; f. Amarjargal Foundation 2001; Dr hc (Bradford) 2000. *Address:* c/o Democratic Party, Democratic Party Central Bldg, Sükhbaataryn Talbai 8, Sükhbaatar District, Ulan Bator, Mongolia. *Telephone:* (11) 262055. *Fax:* (11) 312810. *Website:* www.demparty.mn; www.amarjargal.org.

AMARKHIL, Zia ul-Haq; Afghan government official; *Chief Electoral Officer, Independent Election Commission;* Dir Field Operations Dept, Ind. Election Comm. (IEC) –2012, Sec. IEC Secr. and Chief Electoral Officer 2012–. *Address:* Independent Election Commission of Afghanistan, Darlaman Road, close to Ariana Television, Kabul, Afghanistan (office). *Telephone:* 70-0647448 (mobile) (office). *E-mail:* info@iec.org.af (office). *Website:* www.iec.org.af (office).

AMATO, HE Cardinal Angelo, SDB; Italian ecclesiastic and academic; *Prefect of the Congregation for the Causes of Saints;* b. 8 June 1938, Molfetta; ed Salesian high school, Pontifical Salesian Univ., Rome (licenciate in philosophy), Pontifical Gregorian Univ., Rome; entered the Salesians of St John Bosco, after completing novitiate at Salesian high school; ordained a priest 1967; began teaching at Pontifical Salesian Univ. as an asst 1972; Fellow, Ecumenical Patriarchate of Constantinople, Thessaloniki, Greece, at monastery Orthodox Moní Vlatádon, home of Inst. of Patriarchal Patristic Studies 1978–79; spent sabbatical year in Washington, DC, USA studying theology of religions 1988; currently Prof. of Dogmatics at Pontifical Salesian Univ., Dean of Faculty of Theology 1981–87, 1993–97; served as consultor to Congregation for the Doctrine of the Faith and Pontifical Council for Promoting Christian Unity as well as for Congregation for Bishops; Sec. Congregation for the Doctrine of the Faith 2002–08; Titular Archbishop of Sila 2003–; served as a consultor to the Pontifical Councils for Christian Unity and Interreligious Dialogue; mem. Congregation for Divine Worship and the Discipline of the Sacraments; Prefect of the Congregation for the Causes of Saints 2008–; mem. Congregation for the Doctrine of the Faith 2010–; cr. Cardinal (Cardinal-Deacon of S. Maria in Aquiro) 2010;; participated in Papal Conclave 2013. *Address:* Palazzo delle Congregazioni, Piazza Pio XII 10, 00193 Rome, Italy (office). *Telephone:* (06) 69884247 (office). *Fax:* (06) 69881935 (office). *Website:* www.vatican.va/roman_curia/congregations/csaints (office).

AMATO, Giuliano, LLB, LLM; Italian politician, academic and university administrator; *President, Sant'Anna School of Advanced Studies;* b. 13 May 1938, Turin; ed Univ. of Pisa, Sant'Anna School of Advanced Studies, Columbia Univ., USA; Prof. of Italian and Comparative Constitutional Law, Univ. of Rome 1975–97; joined Italian Socialist Party (PSI) 1958, mem. Cen. Cttee 1978–94, Nat. Deputy Sec. 1988–92, Leader –2000, Asst Sec.; mem. Camera dei Deputati for Turin-Novara-Vercelli 1983, 1987–93; Under-Sec. of State, Presidency of Council of Ministers 1983–87, Vice-Pres. Council of Ministers and Minister of the Treasury 1987–89; Deputy Prime Minister of Italy 1987–88, Prime Minister 1992–93, 2000–01; Pres. Italian Antitrust Authority 1994–97; foreign debt negotiator for Albanian Govt 1991–92; Minister for Constitutional Reforms 1998–99; Minister for Treasury 1999–2000; Vice-Pres. EU Special Convention on Pan-European Constitution 2001–06; Senator for Grosseto 2001–06; Minister of Internal Affairs 2006–08; Pres. Sant'Anna School of Advanced Studies 2012–; mem. Partito Democratico 2007–; Foreign Hon. mem. American Acad. of Arts and Sciences 2001. *Publications:* Antitrust and the Bounds of Power 1997, Tornare al Futuro 2001, Dialoghi post-secolari 2006, Un altro mondo è possibile? Parole per capire e per cambiare 2006. *Address:* Office of the President, Sant'Anna School of Advanced Studies, Piazza Martiri della Libertà, 33, 56127 Pisa, Italy (office). *Website:* www .ssup.it (office).

AMATONG, Juanita Dy, BSc, MA; Philippine economist, academic and public finance expert; b. 23 March 1935, Bindoy, Negros Oriental; d. of Eking Dy and Felisa Anuling; m. Ernesto S. Amatong; two s. two d.; ed Silliman Univ., Dumaguete City, Maxwell School of Public Admin and Citizenship, Syracuse Univ. NY, USA; Asst Prof., Silliman Univ. 1961–63; Lecturer, Andres Bonifacio Coll., Zamboanga del Norte, Philippines 1968–71; Sr Financial Analyst, Ministry of Finance 1971–83; Special Asst to Prime Minister 1984–86; economist, IMF, Washington, DC 1985–89; Asst Sec. (Minister) of Finance 1986–95, Under-Sec. (Deputy Minister) of Finance 1992–95, 2001–03, Sec. (Minister) of Finance

2003–05; Exec. Asst Cen. Bank of Philippines (Bangko Sentral ng Pilipinas, BSP) 1984–86, mem. Monetary Bd 2005–11; mem. Faculty, School of Business Man. Educ. and Grad. School Program, Andres Bonifacio Coll. 2013–; Resident Consultant, Govt Myanmar Consultancy 1992; Exec. Dir, Alt. Exec. Dir, Adviser to Exec. Dir World Bank, IFC and Multilateral Investment Guarantee Agency, Washington, DC 1995–98; consultant, Chemonics International 1998–2000; Man. Pnr, Resource and Measures Assoc. Co. 1999–2000; Professorial Lecturer, School of Public Admin, Univ. of the Philippines; mem. Devt Budget Coordinating Cttee, Policy Governing Bd Targeted Interventions for Econ. Reforms and Governance (TIERG) 2004, Policy Advisory Bd Cities Alliance, World Bank (IBRD) 2005; Chair. Bd Trustees, Silliman Univ., Chair. Silliman Univ. Medical Foundation Center Inc.; mem. Bd Trustees Bantay Katarungan (NGO on sentinel of justice) 2000–; Officer, Philippine Legion of Honors 1998; Outstanding Silliman Univ. Alumnus 1977, First Woman Exec. Dir World Bank Group, Philippine Centennial 1998, Living Treasure in the Philippines (Nat. Cttee on the Centennial of Feminist Movement of the Philippines) 2005, Outstanding Negrense in Govt Service (Prov. of Negros Oriental) 2005. *Publications:* Decontrol and its Effects, Taxation of Capital Gains in Developing Countries, The Revenue Importance of Lotteries, The Reconciliation of Government Transaction Statistics: National Accounts, Commission on Audit and Office of Budget and Management Reports 1987, Local Government Fiscal and Financial Management Best Practices (Ed.) 2005. *Leisure interests:* reading, painting, cooking. *Address:* School of Business and Management Education, College Park, Dipolog City 7100 (office); 21 Masambahin Street, Teacher's Village, Dilliman Quezon City 1100, Philippines (home). *Telephone:* (5) 2128462 (office); (2) 9224647 (home). *Website:* www.abcollege.edu.ph (office).

AMATYA, Sushil Chandra; Nepalese politician and diplomatist; *Ambassador to Sri Lanka;* fmr Leader of Communist Party of Nepal (Unified Marxist-Leninist—UML); mem. Constituent Ass. –2009 (resgnd); Amb. to Sri Lanka 2010–. *Address:* Embassy of Nepal, 153 Kynsey Road, Colombo 8, Sri Lanka (office). *Telephone:* (11) 2689657 (office). *Fax:* (11) 2689655 (office). *E-mail:* nepalembassy@eureka.lk (office).

AMBANI, Anil D., MBA; Indian business executive; *Chairman and CEO, Reliance – Anil Dhirubhai Ambani Group;* b. 4 June 1959, Mumbai; s. of the late Dhirubhai Hirachand Ambani and of Kokilaben Dhirubhai Ambani, brother of Mukesh Ambani; m. Tina Ambani; two s.; ed Univ. of Bombay (now Mumbai), Univ. of Pennsylvania, USA; apptd Co-CEO Reliance Industries Ltd 1983, currently Vice-Chair., Man. Dir; mem. Bd of Dirs Reliance Europe Ltd; mem. Bd of Dirs and Vice-Chair. Indian Petrochemicals Corpn Ltd –2005 (resgnd); Chair. and CEO Reliance – Anil Dhirubhai Ambani Group (cr. after division of Reliance Industries Ltd and comprising Reliance Energy, Reliance Capital, and Reliance Infocomm) 2005–; mem. Rajya Sabha (upper house of Parl.) 2004–06; Chair. Bd Govs Nat. Safety Council; mem. Bd of Govs Indian Inst. of Man., Ahmedabad, Indian Inst. of Tech., Kanpur; mem. Bd of Overseers, Wharton School, USA; Business India Businessman of the Year 1997, Indian Alumni Award, Wharton India Econ. Forum 2001, Bombay Man. Asscn Entrepreneur of the Decade Award 2002, MTV Youth Icon of the Year 2003, CEO of the Year, Platts Global Energy Awards 2004, Businessman of the Year, The Times of India 2006, named Third Most Powerful Person in India Today Power List 2009. *Leisure interest:* football. *Address:* Reliance Communications Ltd, I Block, 2nd Floor, Dhirubhai Ambani Knowledge City, Mumbai 400 710, India (office). *Telephone:* (22) 30375522 (office). *Fax:* (22) 30375577 (office). *E-mail:* anil.ambani@relianceada.com (office). *Website:* www.relianceadagroup.com (office).

AMBANI, Mukesh D., BChemEng, MBA; Indian business executive; *Chairman and Managing Director, Reliance Industries Ltd;* b. 19 April 1957, Colony of Aden, Yemen; s. of the late Dhirubhai Hirachand Ambani and of Kokilaben Dhirubhai Ambani, brother of Anil D. Ambani; m. Nita Ambani; two s. one d.; ed Univ. Inst. of Chemical Tech., Mumbai, Stanford Univ., USA; joined family-owned Reliance Industries Ltd (India's largest pvt. co.) 1981, Man. Dir 1986–, Chair. 2002–, Chair. Reliance Retail Ltd, also mem. Bd of Dirs Reliance Europe Ltd (Reliance Energy, Reliance Capital and Reliance Infocomm spun off to brother's co. Anil Dhirubhai Ambani Enterprises 2005), Reliance Infotel Broadband Services Ltd, Reliance Foundation, IMG Reliance Pvt. Ltd; Chair. Indian Petrochemicals Corpn Ltd, FLAG Telecom; Owner Indian Premier League team Mumbai Indians; Chair. Bd of Trustees, Indian Inst. of Software Eng; Chair. Bd of Govs Indian Inst. of Man., Bangalore, Pandit Deendayal Petroleum Univ., Gandhinagar; Co-Chair. India-Russia CEO Council, Japan-India Business Leader's Forum; Vice-Chair. Exec. Cttee World Business Council for Sustainable Devt 2008; mem. Bd of Dirs Bank of America Corpn (first non-American); mem. Prime Minister's Advisory Council on Trade and Industry, Bd Govs of Nat. Council of Applied Econ. Research, Advisory Council of the Indian Banks Asscn, Millennium Devt Goals Advocacy Group constituted by the UN, Foundation Bd of World Econ. Forum, Indo-USA CEOs Forum, Advisory Council for the Grad. School of Business, Stanford Univ., Business Council, McKinsey Advisory Council, Asia Business Council, Advisory Bd of D.E. Shaw India Advisory Services Pvt. Ltd; mem. Advisory Council of the Indian Inst. of Tech., Mumbai, Governing Bd of Public Health Foundation of India; mem. Int. Advisory Bd, Citigroup, Nat. Bd of Kuwait, Brookings; Dr hc (Maharaja Sayajirao Univ.) 2007; Global Leader for Tomorrow, World Econ. Forum, Switzerland 1994, Business India Businessman of the Year Award 1997, Distinguished Alumnus of the Decade, Univ. of Mumbai 1999, Ernst & Young Entrepreneur of the Year Award 2000, rated one of India's Most Admired CEOs in Business Barons-Taylor Nelson Sofres-Mode Survey 2002, Mumbai Man. Asscn Entrepreneur of the Decade Award 2002, ranked first by India Today in The Power List 2003, 2004, Asia Soc. Leadership Award Medal 2004, named 42nd amongst the World's Most Respected Business Leaders 2004, ranked second among the four Indian CEOs featured in a survey conducted by PricewaterhouseCoopers and published in Financial Times, London 2004, World Communication Award for the Most Influential Person in Telecommunications, Total Telecom 2004, chosen by Voice and Data magazine as Telecom Man of the Year 2004, ranked 13th by Fortune magazine in Asia's Power 25 list of The Most Powerful People in Business 2004, ET Business Leader of the Year, The Economic Times (India) 2006, chosen as Businessman of the Year by a public poll in India conducted by NDTV 2007, US-India Business Council Leadership Award for Global Vision 2007, Chitralekha Person of the Year Award, Chief Minister of Gujarat 2008, ranked by Forbes magazine amongst the World's Most Powerful People (44th) 2009, (34th) 2010,

(35th) 2011, (37th) 2012, (38th) 2013, Indian Merchant's Chamber Juran Quality Medal for 2009 2010, Indian Corp. Citizen of the Year, India Leadership Conclave 2009, Dean's Medal, Univ. of Pennsylvania School of Eng and Applied Science 2010, Dwight D. Eisenhower Global Leadership Award, The Business Council for Int. Understanding 2010, ranked by the Harvard Business Review 5th Best Performing CEO in the World in its ranking of the top 50 global CEOs, Entrepreneur of the Decade, All India Management Asscn 2013. *Leisure interests:* movies, cricket. *Address:* Reliance Industries Ltd, Maker Chambers IV, 222, Nariman Point, Mumbai 400 021, India (office). *Telephone:* (22) 22785000 (office). *Fax:* (22) 22870303 (office). *E-mail:* M_Ambani@ril.com (office). *Website:* www.ril .com (office).

AMBARTSUMOV, Yevgeniy Arshakovich, CandHistSc; Russian politician, social scientist, political analyst and journalist; *Professor, Universidad La Salle;* b. 19 Aug. 1929, Moscow; s. of Arshak Ambartsumov and Alexandra Vassilevskaia; m. Nina Ignatovskaia 1978; one s.; ed Moscow Inst. of Int. Relations; with Novoye Vremya 1954–59, Problems of Peace and Socialism 1959–63; Sr Scientific Researcher, Inst. of World Econs and Int. Relations 1956–59, Head of Dept Inst. of World Int. Labour Movt 1966–69; Head of Dept, Inst. of Sociology 1969–73; Head of Dept of Politics, Inst. of Economics of World Socialist System (now Inst. of Int. Economic and Political Studies) 1973–90; Russian People's Deputy 1990–93; Chair. Foreign Affairs Cttee of Russian Supreme Soviet 1992–93; mem. State Duma (Parl.) 1993–94; mem. Presidential Council 1993–95; Amb. to Mexico, also accred to Belize 1994–99; Prof. Universidad La Salle, Mexico 1999–; Order of Aguila Azteca con banda Mexico 1999. *Publications include:* How Socialism Began: Russia under Lenin 1978, NEP: A Modern View 1988, Socialism: Past and Present (ed.) 1990. *Leisure interest:* books. *Address:* Universidad La Salle, Benjamin Franklin 47, Col Condesa, Del. Cuauhtémoc, 06140 México, DF, Mexico. *Telephone:* (55) 26-14-40-79 (Mexico) (home); (495) 332-64-25 (Russia) (home). *Website:* www.ulsa.edu.mx.

AMBARTSUMYAN, Sergey Aleksandrovich, DTech; Armenian scientist and government official; *Counsellor of the Presidium, National Academy of Sciences;* b. 17 March 1922, Alexandrapol (now Gumry); s. of Alexander G. Ambartsumyan and Anna V. Ambartsumyan; m. Seda A. Ambartsumyan 1949; one s. one d.; ed Yerevan Polytechnic Inst.; Dir Inst. of Mechanics and Math. of Armenian SSR 1959–77; Academic Sec., Otdeleniya Physical and Eng Sciences and Math. 1971–74; Rector Yerevan State Univ. 1977–92; Hon. Dir Inst. of Mechanics, Nat. Acad. of Sciences 1993–2006, mem. of Presidium 1971–, Vice-Pres. 1974–77, Counsellor 1991–; USSR People's Deputy 1989–91, mem. Supreme Soviet 1979–91; Prof. Emer., Yerevan Eng Univ.; Academician, Armenian Acad. of Sciences 1964– (Vice-Pres. 1975–77), Int. Acad. of Astronautics 1989, Armenian Eng Acad. 1992, Armenian Philosophy Acad. 1993; mem. Int. Acad. of Sciences, Educ., Industry and Arts 1997, American Soc. of Eng Mechanics, American Soc. of Engineers, Russian Nat. Cttee of Theoretical and Applied Mechanics, Mechanics Union of Armenia; Foreign mem. Russian Acad. of Sciences 2002, Georgian Acad. of Sciences 2013; Hon. Pres. Armenian Acad. of Eng 1997–; Hon. mem. Slovak. Acad. of Sciences, Int. Eng Acad. 1991; Hon. Prof., Peninsula Inst. of Information, Tech. and Business 1998, Yerevan State Architectural and Civil Eng Univ., Inst. of Computer Science and Business Penninsuleya; Hon. Academician, Int. Acad. of Eng, Philosophical Acad. of Armenia; Order of Lenin (Russia), Order of Oct. Revolution (Russia), Order of Red Banner of Labor (Russia), Order of Badge of Honor (Russia), Order of Friendship (Russia), Order of Tigran Mets (Armenia), Order of Mesrop Mashtots and Sahak Partev (Armenia), Order of Mesrop Mashtots (Artsakh); Dr hc (Bratislava) 1984; numerous awards and prizes including Silver and Gold Medals from Int. Eng Acad. *Publications include:* Theory of Anisotropic Shells 1961, Theory of Anisotropic Plates 1967, General Theory of Anisotropic Shells 1974, Magnetoelasticity of Thin Shells and Plates 1977, Different Modulus Theory of Elasticity 1982, Fragments of the Theory of Anisotropic Shells 1990, Some Problems of Electro-magneto-elasticity of Plates 1991, Vibrations and Stability of Current-carrying Elastic Plates 1991, Conductive Plates and Shells in Magnetic Field 1998, Micropolar Theory of Shells and Plates 1999; over 200 articles on mechanics of solids. *Leisure interests:* painting, literature, history. *Address:* Presidium of National Academy of Sciences, 24 Marshal Bagramian Avenue, 0019 Yerevan, Armenia (office). *Telephone:* (10) 520644 (office); (10) 521503 (office); (10) 532050 (home). *Fax:* (10) 569281 (office). *E-mail:* samb@sci.am (office); samb@sd.am. *Website:* www.sci.am (office).

AMBRASEYS, Nicholas, PhD, FICE, FREng; British professor of engineering seismology; *Professor Emeritus, Imperial College London;* b. 19 Jan. 1929, Athens, Greece; s. of Neocles Ambraseys and Cleopatra Ambraseys; m. Xeni Stavrou 1955; ed Nat. Tech. Univ. of Athens and Imperial Coll. of Science and Tech., London; Prof. of Hydrodynamics, Nat. Tech. Univ. of Athens 1963–64; Lecturer in Soil Mechanics, Imperial Coll., London 1965–68, Reader in Eng Seismology 1968–73, Prof. 1973–94, Head of Eng Seismology Section 1969–94, Sr Research Fellow 1995–, Sr Research Investigator 1996–, currently Prof. Emer.; led UN/UNESCO earthquake reconnaissance missions to Yugoslavia, Iran, Turkey, Pakistan, Romania, Algeria, Italy, E Africa, Nicaragua and Cen. Africa 1963–81; mem. UN Advisory Bd for reconstruction of Skopje 1964–69; Chair. British Nat. Cttee for Earthquake Eng, ICE 1966–76; Vice-Pres. European Asscn of Earthquake Eng 1967–75; mem. and Chair. UNESCO Advisory Cttee on Earthquake Risk 1971–81; mem. Academia Europaea 1996; Hon. Fellow, Int. Asscn for Earthquake Eng 1992; Dr hc (Nat. Tech. Univ. Athens) 1993; Busk Medal for Scientific Discovery, Royal Geographical Soc. *Publications:* A History of Persian Earthquakes (with G. Melville) 1982, The Seismicity of Egypt, Arabia and the Red Sea 1994, Seismicity of Turkey 1995, Seismicity of Central America 2000, Seismicity of Iceland 2000 and over 200 papers in scientific and eng journals. *Leisure interests:* historical geography, archaeology, travel. *Address:* Department of Civil Engineering, Imperial College, London, SW7 2BU; 19 Bede House, Manor Fields, London, SW15 3LT, England (home). *Telephone:* (20) 7589-5111 (office); (20) 8788-4219 (home). *Fax:* (20) 7225-2716 (office). *E-mail:* n.ambraseys@ic.ac.uk (office); ambra@otenet.gr (home).

AMBROS, Victor R., PhD; American molecular biologist and academic; *Silverman Professor of Natural Sciences, Program of Molecular Medicine, University of Massachusetts Medical School;* b. 1 Dec. 1953, Hanover, NH; ed Massachusetts Inst. of Tech.; Research Asst, MIT Center for Cancer Research 1975–76, Grad.

Research Asst 1976–79; Chaim Weizmann Postdoctoral Fellow 1979; American Cancer Soc. Postdoctoral Fellow 1980–81; NIH Postdoctoral Fellow 1982–84; Asst Prof., Dept of Cellular and Developmental Biology, Harvard Univ. 1985–88, Assoc. Prof. 1988–92; Assoc. Prof., Biological Sciences, Dartmouth Coll. 1992–96, Prof. 1996–2001, Prof. of Genetics, Dartmouth Medical School 2001–07; Prof., Program in Molecular Medicine, Univ. of Massachusetts Medical School 2008–, currently Silverman Prof. of Natural Sciences, Program of Molecular Medicine, Co-Dir RNA Therapeutics Inst.; mem. NAS 2007; Newcomb Cleveland Prize (co-recipient), AAAS 2003, Gene Knudson Lecturer in Molecular Genetics, Oregon State Univ. 2003, Lewis S. Rosenstiel Award in Basic Medical Science, Brandeis Univ. (co-recipient) 2006, Medal for Outstanding Contribs in the Past 15 Years, Genetics Soc. of America 2006, Jack M. Buchanan Medal, MIT 2006, Benjamin Franklin Medal in Life Sciences (co-recipient) 2008, Albert Lasker Basic Medical Research Award (co-recipient) 2008, Gairdner Foundation Int. Award (co-recipient) 2008, Warren Triennial Prize (co-recipient), Massachusetts Gen. Hosp. 2008, Dickson Prize, Univ. of Pittsburgh 2009, Horwitz Prize, Columbia Univ. (co-recipient) 2009, Massry Award (co-recipient) 2009, Dr Paul Janssen Award for Biomedical Research, Johnson & Johnson (co-recipient) 2012, Keio Medical Science Prize, Keio Univ. (co-recipient) 2013. *Achievements include:* discoverer of first known microRNA. *Publications:* numerous papers in professional journals. *Address:* Program in Molecular Medicine, University of Massachusetts Medical School, Biotech Two, Suite 306, 373 Plantation Street, Worcester, MA 01605, USA (office). *Telephone:* (508) 856-6380 (office). *E-mail:* victor.ambros@umassmed.edu (office). *Website:* www.umassmed.edu/ambroslab/index.aspx (office).

AMBROSE, The Hon. Rona, PC, BA, MA; Canadian politician; *Minister of Health;* b. 15 March 1969, Valley View, Alberta; m. Bruce Ambrose; ed Univs of Victoria and Alberta; fmr political columnist; fmr owner Ambrose Consulting Ltd; fmr Sr Intergovernmental Officer, Int. and Intergovernmental Relations Dept, Govt of Alberta; MP for Edmonton-Spruce Grove 2004–; Sr Intergovernmental Affairs Critic, Conservative Official Opposition 2004, later Int. Trade Critic; Minister of the Environment 2006–07; Pres. of the Queen's Privy Council for Canada, Minister of Intergovernmental Affairs and Minister of Western Econ. Diversification 2007–08, of Labour 2008–10, of Public Works and Govt Services, also for Status of Women 2010–13, of Health 2013–; Vice-Chair. Treasury Bd Cttee 2008–. *Address:* Department of Health, 0900C2, Ottawa, ON K1A 0K9, Canada (office). *Telephone:* (866) 225-0709 (office). *Fax:* (613) 941-5366 (office). *E-mail:* info@hc-sc.gc.ca (office); rona.ambrose.c1a@parl.gc.ca (office). *Website:* www.hc-sc .gc.ca (office); www.ronaambrose.com.

AMELING, Elisabeth (Elly) Sara; Dutch singer; b. 8 Feb. 1938, Rotterdam; m. Arnold W. Beider 1964; ed studied singing with Jo Bollekamp, with Jacoba and Sam Dresden and with Bodi Rapp, studied French art song with Pierre Bernac; recitals in Europe, SA, Japan; debut in USA 1968, annual tours of USA and Canada 1968–, farewell tour 1995; ssng with Concertgebouw Orchestra, New Philharmonic Orchestra, BBC Symphony Orchestra, Berlin Philharmonic, Cincinnati Symphony, San Francisco Symphony, Toronto Symphony, Chicago Symphony; has appeared in Mozart Festival, Washington, DC 1974, Caramoor Festival 1974, Art Song Festival, Princeton, NJ 1974; retired from recital stage in 1990s, now teaches selected masterclasses; Kt Order of Orange-Nassau 1971, Order of the Netherlands Lion 2008; Dr hc (Univ. of BC) 1981, (Westminster Choir Coll., Princeton, NJ) 1985, (Cleveland Inst. of Music) 1986, (Shenandoa Univ.) 1988; First Prize, Concours Int. de Musique, Geneva, Grand Prix du Disque, Edison Prize, Preis der Deutschen Schallplattenkritik, Stereo Review Record of the Year Award. *Recordings include:* Mozart Concert, Handel Concert, Cantatas (Bach), Mörike Lieder (Wolf), Aimez-vous Handel?, Aimez-vous Mozart?, Christmas Oratorio (Bach), Symphony No. 2 (Mahler), Te Deum (Bruckner), Italienisches Liederbuch (Wolf).

AMELIO, William J., BChemEng, MA; American business executive; *President and CEO, CHC Helicopter;* b. 25 Nov. 1957; m. Jamie Amelio; ed Lehigh Univ., Sloan Master's Program at Stanford Univ.; with IBM 1979–96, held several Sr Man. positions, including Gen. Man. of Operations for IBM's Personal Computing Div.; Pres. and CEO Honeywell's transportation and power-systems divs, and Head of turbocharging-systems business at Allied Signal Inc. (predecessor of Honeywell International Inc.) 1997–2000; Exec. Vice-Pres. and COO NCR Corpn's Retail and Financial Group 2000–01; Sr Vice-Pres. Asia-Pacific and Japan, Dell Inc. 2001–05; Pres. and CEO Lenovo Group Ltd 2005–09 (resgnd), special adviser to Bd 2009; Pres. and CEO CHC Helicopter, Richmond, BC, Canada 2010–; Co-f. (with his wife) Caring for Cambodia (through Amelio Foundation). *Address:* CHC Helicopter, 4740 Agar Drive, Richmond, BC V7B 1A3, Canada (office). *Telephone:* (604) 276-7500 (office). *E-mail:* commercial@chc.ca (office). *Website:* www.chc.ca (office).

AMENÁBAR, Alejandro; Spanish/Chilean film director; b. 31 March 1973, Santiago, Chile; ed Complutense Univ., Madrid. *Films:* Head (short film) 1991, Himenóptero (short film) (Best Short Film, Elche Festival, Alicante, Carabanchel Festival, Madrid) 1992, Luna (short film) (Luis García Berlanga Award for Best Script, AICA Award for Best Soundtrack) 1995, Tésis (Thesis) 1996, Abre los Ojos (Open Your Eyes) 1997, The Others 2001, Vanilla Sky (writer) 2001, El Soñador (writer and producer) 2004, Mar adentro (The Sea Inside) (Best Foreign Language Film, Nat. Bd of Review, Best Dir, Best Film, Goya Awards 2005, Best Foreign Film, Ind. Spirit Awards 2005, Grand Prix of Jury, Int. Venice Film Festival 2004, Best Foreign Language Film, Acad. Awards 2005) 2004, Agora (2009),; composer: Al Lado del Atlas (1994), Allanamiento de Morada (1998), La lengua de las mariposas (1999), Nadie conoce a Nadie (1999). *Television:* Un viaje mar adentro 2005. *Website:* www.clubcultura.com/clubcine/clubcineastas/amenabar/index.htm.

AMERASINGHE, Chittharanjan Felix, PhD, LLD; Sri Lankan judge and international lawyer; b. 2 March 1933, Colombo; s. of Samson Felix Amerasinghe, OBE and Mary Victorine Abeyesundere; m. Wimala Nalini Pieris 1964; one s. two d.; ed Royal Coll., Colombo, Trinity Hall, Cambridge, UK, Harvard Univ. Law School, USA; Supervisor in Law, Trinity Hall, Cambridge 1955–57; Jr Exec., Caltex Oil Co., Colombo 1959–61; Lecturer in Law, Univ. of Ceylon 1962–65, Sr Lecturer 1965–68, Reader 1968–69, Prof. of Law 1969–71; Counsel, World Bank 1970–75, Sr Counsel 1975–81, Exec. Sec., World Bank Admin. Tribunal 1981–96; Judge, UN Tribunal, New York 1997–2000, Commonwealth Int. Arbitral Tribunal 1999–2002; Consultant in Int. Law, Govt of Ceylon 1963–70; mem. Ceylon Govt

Comm. on Local Govt 1969; Adjunct Prof. of Int. Law, School of Law, American Univ. 1991–93; mem. Panel of Arbitrators and Conciliators, Law of the Sea Convention, Int. Centre for Settlement of Investment Disputes, Panel of UN Compensation Comm. for Kuwait; Exec. Council mem. American Soc. of Int. Law 1980–83; Assoc. mem. Inst. de Droit Int. 1981–87, mem. 1987–; mem. Int. Law Asscn 1986–; mem. Sr Editorial Bd, Project on Governing Rules of Int. Law, American Soc. of Int. Law; mem. Hon. Cttee Int. Inst. of Human Rights 1968–; mem. Advisory Bd Int. Inst. of Environmental Law 1987–98, Sri Lanka Journal of Int. Law 1989–, Int. Orgs Law Review 2004–; Sr Fellow (Visiting), Trinity Hall, Cambridge 1996–97; Trinity Hall Law Studentship 1956–59, Research Fellowship, Harvard Univ. Law School 1957–58; Hon. Prof. of Int. Law, Univ. of Colombo 1991–94; Henry Arthur Thomas Classical Award, Univ. of Cambridge 1953, Angus Classical Prize 1953, Clement Davies Prize for Law 1955, Major Scholar and Prizeman, Trinity Hall, Cambridge 1953–56, Yorke Prize 1964, Certificate of Merit, American Soc. of Int. Law 1988–89. *Publications:* Some Aspects of the Actio Iniuriarum in Roman-Dutch Law 1966, Defamation and Other Injuries in Roman-Dutch Law 1968, State Responsibility for Injuries to Aliens 1967, Studies in International Law 1969, The Doctrines of Sovereignty and Separation of Powers in the Law of Ceylon 1970, The Law of the International Civil Service (two vols) 1988, Documents on International Administrative Tribunals 1989, Case Law of the World Bank Administrative Tribunal (three vols) 1989, 1991, 1994, Local Remedies in International Law 2003, Principles of the Institutional Law of International Organizations 1996, 2005, Jurisdiction of International Tribunals 2003, Evidence in International Litigation 2005, Diplomatic Protection 2008; articles in leading law and int. law journals. *Leisure interests:* classical and classical jazz music, art, artifacts, philately, photography, walking. *Address:* 6100 Robinwood Road, Bethesda, MD 20817, USA (home). *Telephone:* (301) 229-2766 (home). *Fax:* (301) 229-4151 (home).

AMES, Bruce Nathan, BA, PhD, FAAS; American biochemist and academic; *Professor, Graduate School, Department of Biochemistry and Molecular Biology, University of California, Berkeley;* b. 16 Dec. 1928, New York; s. of Dr M. U. Ames and Dorothy Andres Ames; m. Dr Giovanna Ferro-Luzzi 1960; one s. one d.; ed Cornell Univ. and California Inst. of Tech., Nat. Inst. of Health, Maryland; Postdoctoral Fellow, NIH 1953–54, Biochemist 1954–60; NSF Fellow, Labs of F. C. Crick, Cambridge and F. Jacob, Paris 1961; Chief Section of Microbial Genetics, Lab. of Molecular Biology, NIH 1962–67; Prof. of Biochemistry and Molecular Biology, Univ. of California, Berkeley 1968–, Dir Nat. Inst. of Environmental Health Sciences Centre 1979–, Chair. Dept of Biochemistry 1983–89; Sr Research Scientist, Children's Hosp. Oakland Research Inst. 1968–; Fellow, Acad. of Toxicological Sciences 1992, American Acad. of Microbiology 1992; mem. Nat. Cancer Advisory Bd 1976–82, NAS, American Acad. of Arts and Sciences, American Aging Asscn, AAAS, ACS, American Coll. of Toxicology, American Soc. of Biochemistry and Molecular Biology, American Soc. of Nutritional Sciences, Environmental Mutagen Soc., Gerontological Soc. of America, Mitochondrial Medicine Soc., Molecular Medicine Soc., New York Acad. of Science, Oxygen Soc., Soc. for Free Radical Research, Soc. of Toxicology; Foreign mem. Royal Swedish Acad. of Sciences 1989; Hon. Foreign mem. Japan Cancer Asscn 1987, Hon. mem. Japan Pharmaceutical Soc. 1998; Dr hc (Tufts Univ.) 1987, (Univ. of Bologna) 1989; ACS Eli Lilly Award 1964, Arthur Flemming Award 1966, Rosenstiel Award 1976, Fed. of American Socs. for Experimental Biology Award 1976, Wankel Award 1978, John Scott Medal 1979, Bolton L. Corson Medal 1980, New Brunswick Lectureship Award, American Soc. for Microbiology 1980, Gen. Motors Cancer Research Fund Charles S. Mott Prize 1983, Gairdner Foundation Award 1983, Tyler Prize for Environmental Achievement 1985, ACS Spencer Award 1986, Roger G. Williams Award in Preventive Nutrition 1989, Gold Medal American Inst. of Chemists 1991, Glenn Foundation Prize 1992, shared Japan Prize 1997, Nat. Medal of Science 1998, Linus Pauling Prize for Health Research 2001, Lifetime Achievement Award of American Soc. for Microbiology 2001, Thomas Hunt Morgan Medal, Genetics Soc. of America 2004, M.S. Rose Award, American Soc. for Nutrition/CRN 2008, George C. Marshall Founders Award 2008, elected to Orthomolecular Medicine Hall of Fame 2010, SOT Lifetime Achievement Award 2012. *Achievements include:* invented Ames test which identifies possible carcinogens by studying their mutagenic effect on bacteria. *Publications include:* more than 500 scientific papers in areas of operons, biochemical genetics, histidine biosynthesis, mutagenesis, detection of environmental carcinogens and mutagens, oxygen radicals as a cause of aging and degenerative diseases, anti-carcinogens, micronutrient deficiency. *Address:* Children's Hospital Oakland Research Institute, 5700 Martin Luther King Jr. Way, Oakland, CA 94609-1673 (office); University of California, Berkeley, Department of Biochemistry and Molecular Biology, 142 LSA, Room 3200, Berkeley, CA 94720-3200 (office); 1324 Spruce Street, Berkeley, CA 94709, USA (home). *Telephone:* (510) 450-7625 (office). *Fax:* (510) 597-7128 (office). *E-mail:* bames@chori.org (office). *Website:* mcb.berkeley.edu/site (office); www.bruceames.org (office).

AMES, Roger; Trinidad and Tobago music company executive; *CEO International, Ticketmaster Inc.;* b. 1949; with EMI UK 1975–79; staff A & R Dept, Phonogram, PolyGram UK 1979–83, Chair. and CEO PolyGram UK 1991–94, Group Exec. and Vice-Pres. PolyGram Int. Ltd 1996–99, Pres. PolyGram Music Group 1996–99; Gen. Man. London Records 1983, later Man. Dir, purchased back-catalogue of Factory Records; Pres. Warner Music Int. 1999, Chair. and CEO Warner Music Group 1999–2004; Sr Advisor, Time Warner, EMI Music 2005–07; Pres. EMI Music, North America 2007–08, Pres. EMI Music, UK Jan.–May 2008; CEO Int., Ticketmaster Inc. 2009–; Advisor, Ingenious VCT Funds;. *Address:* Ticketmaster UK, 48 Leicester Square, London, WC2H 7LR, England (office). *Telephone:* (20) 7344-4000 (office). *Fax:* (20) 7915-0411 (office). *Website:* www.ticketmaster.co.uk (office).

AMEY, Julian Nigel Robert, MA; British charitable trust administrator and fmr civil servant; *CEO, Institute of Healthcare Engineering and Estate Management;* b. 19 June 1949; s. of Robert Amey and Diana Amey (née Coles); m. Ann Victoria Brenchley 1972; three d.; ed Wellingborough School, Magdalene Coll., Cambridge; Dir Int. Sales and Marketing Longman Group Ltd 1985–89; Exec. Dir BBC English World Service 1989–94; seconded to Dept of Trade and Industry 1994–96; Dir-Gen. Canning House 1996–2001; Pnr, The English Place 2001–; CEO Chartered Inst. of Building Services Engineers 2001–06, Trinity Coll., London 2006–09, Imperial Soc. of Teachers of Dancing 2009–11, Inst. of Healthcare Eng and Estate Man.

2012–; Chair. Anglo-Chilean Soc.; Gov. Bath Spa Univ.; fmr mem. Ilha da Uniao Samba School. *Publications include:* Spanish Business Directory 1979, Portuguese Business Dictionary 1981. *Leisure interests:* cricket, tennis, travel. *Address:* Institute of Healthcare Engineering and Estate Management, 2 Abingdon House, Cumberland Business Centre, Northumberland Road, Portsmouth, Hants., PO5 1DS, England (office). *Telephone:* (23) 9282-3186 (office). *Fax:* (230 9281-5927 (office). *E-mail:* julian.amey@iheem.org.uk (office). *Website:* www.iheem.org.uk (office).

AMIGO VALLEJO, HE Cardinal Carlos, OFM; Spanish ecclesiastic; *Archbishop Emeritus of Seville;* b. 23 Aug. 1934, Medina de Rioseca, Valladolid; ed Faculty of Medicine, Univ. of Valladolid, Cen. Univ. of Madrid; joined Order of Friars Minor (Franciscans); ordained priest in Rome 1960; provincial of Franciscan Prov. of Santiago 1970; Archbishop of Tangier, Morocco 1973–82; consecrated, Church of San Francisco el Grande, Madrid, 1974; acted as mediator to resolve conflicts in Algeria, Libya, Morocco, Mauritania and Tunisia 1976–82; Metropolitan Archbishop of Seville 1982–2009, Archbishop Emer. 2009–; cr. Cardinal (Cardinal-Priest of Santa Maria in Monserrato degli Spagnoli) 2003; participated in Papal Conclave 2005, 2013; Pres. 5th Centennial of the Evangelization of America 1984, High Bishops of Spain 1993, 1996–, Episcopal Comm. of Missions and Cooperation with Churches 1999, Episcopal Comm. of Spanish Episcopal Conf. 2002; del. to Ordinary Ass. of World Synod of Bishops, Vatican City 1977, 1983, 1994, Gen. Conf. of Latin American Episcopate, Dominican Repub. 1992; mem. Exec. Cttee Spanish Episcopal Conf. 1984, Pontifical Comm. for Latin America 1990, 1995, 2000–, Pontifical Council for Health 2002–, Acads of Buenas Letras, Medicina and Belles Artes of Seville; fmr mem. Nat. Comm. for 5th Centennial, Cttee of Experts of Universal Exhbn; Orden al Mérito de los Padres de la Patria Dominicana (Dominican Repub.) 1995; Hon. PhD (Tech. Univ. of Cibao, Dominican Repub.) 1995, Hon. Academician, Royal Acad. of Veterinary Sciences, Seville; Silver Medal of Repub. of Panama 2000, Gold Medal, Royal Acad. of Veterinary Sciences 2008, Seville. *Address:* Arzobispado de Sevilla, Pza. Virgen de los Reyes s/n, Apartado 6, 41080, Seville, Spain (office). *Website:* www.diocesisdesevilla.org (office).

AMINU, Jibril Muhammed, PhD, FRCP; Nigerian diplomatist, physician and academic; b. 14 Aug. 1939, Song, Adamawa State; m.; nine c.; ed Ahmadu Bello Univ., Univ. of Ibadan; Consultant in Medicine, Sr Lecturer, Sub-Dean of Clinical Studies, Univ. of Ibadan Medical School 1973–75; Exec. Sec., Nat. Univs Comm. 1975–79; Prof. of Medicine, specializing in Cardiology and Hypertension, Univ. of Maiduguri 1979–95, Univ. Vice-Chancellor 1980–85; Visiting Prof. of Medicine, Coll. of Medicine, Howard Univ., Washington, DC 1979–80; Minister of Educ. 1985–89, of Petroleum and Mineral Resources 1989–92; Del. to Nigerian Nat. Constitutional Conf. 1994–95; Amb. to USA 1999–2003; Senator for Adamawa Central (People's Democratic Party) 2003–11, Chair. Senate Cttee on Foreign Affairs; Pres. African Petroleum Producers Asscn 1991, OPEC Conf. 1991–92; Chair. First Meeting of Ministers of Educ. in Sub-Saharan Africa; Vice-Pres. for Africa of Third World Acad. of Sciences Network of Scientific Orgs; Foundation mem. Bd of Trustees, People's Democratic Party of Nigeria 1998; Fellow, Nigerian Acad. of Science 1972, W African Coll. of Physicians 1980, Nigerian Postgraduate Medical Coll. 2004, African Acad. of Science; mem. World Bank Preparatory Cttee on Educ. for All, Jornitien 1990; Ordre National de la Légion d'Honneur 1998, Commdr of the Order (Niger); Hon. DSc (Univ. of Maiduguri) 2005; Bobaselu of The Source 2010. *Publications include:* Quality and Stress in Nigerian Education 1986, Observations 1987. *E-mail:* jubrilaminu@yahoo.com (office).

AMIREDJIBI, Chabua; Georgian writer, editor and politician; b. (Mzechabuk I. Amiredjibi), 18 Nov. 1921, Tbilisi; s. of Irakli Amiredjibi and Maria Nakashidze; m. Tamar Djavakhishvili 1966; four s. (one deceased) two d.; ed Tbilisi State Univ., A. Pushkin Tbilisi Pedagogical Inst.; as student of Tbilisi State Univ. arrested for anti-Soviet activities 1944, sentenced to 25 years' imprisonment in Gulag, released 1959; Dir Advertising-Information Bureau Goskinoprokat 1965–70; Chief Ed. Kino anthology 1970–83; Dir Mematiane documentary film studio 1983–89; mem. Parl. 1992–96; Chair. Defence Fund of Georgia 1992–96; f. PEN Centre of Georgia, Pres. 1994–97, Hon. Chair. 1998–; Publr and Ed.-in-Chief Ganakhlebuli Iveria newspaper 1999–2003; mem. Writers' Union of Georgia 1964–; mem. editorial bds of several journals and newspapers; Honoured Art Worker of Georgia 1987, Order of Honour 1994, Order of King Vakhtang Gorgasili (First Class) 2001; USSR State Prize 1979, Sh. Rustaveli Prize 1994. *Screenplay:* Data Tutashkhia 1979. *Publications:* Road (short stories) 1966, Tales for Children 1966, Data Tutashkhia (novel) 1973, Gora Mborgali (novel) 1994, King George the Excellent (novel) 2003, From the Thoughts 2007. *Leisure interests:* sports, football, basketball. *Address:* 8/45 Tamarashvili Street, 0162 Tbilisi, Georgia (home). *E-mail:* kutsna@posta.ge (office).

AMIS, Martin Louis, BA; British writer; b. 25 Aug. 1949, Oxford; s. of the late Kingsley Amis and of Hilary Bardwell; m. 1st Antonia Phillips 1984 (divorced 1996); two s.; m. 2nd Isabel Fonseca 1998; two d.; ed Exeter Coll., Oxford; Asst Ed., TLS 1971, Fiction and Poetry Ed. TLS 1974–75; Asst Literary Ed., New Statesman 1975–77, Literary Ed. 1977–79; special writer for The Observer newspaper 1980–; Prof., Centre for New Writing, Univ. of Manchester 2007–; Galaxy Nat. Book Award for Outstanding Achievement 2010. *Publications:* fiction: The Rachel Papers (Somerset Maugham Award 1974) 1973, Dead Babies 1975, new edn as Dark Secrets 1977, Success 1978, Other People: A Mystery Story 1981, Money: A Suicide Note 1984, Einstein's Monsters (short stories) 1987, London Fields 1989, Time's Arrow, or, the Nature of the Offence 1991, God's Dice 1995, The Information 1995, Night Train 1997, Heavy Water and Other Stories 1999, Yellow Dog 2003, The Last Days of Muhammad Atta (short stories, novella, essay) 2006, House of Meetings (novella) 2006, The Pregnant Widow 2010, Lionel Asbo 2012; non-fiction: My Oxford (with others) 1977, Invasion of the Space Invaders 1982, The Moronic Inferno and Other Visits to America 1986, Visiting Mrs Nabokov and Other Excursions 1993, Experience: A Memoir (James Tait Black Memorial Prize for Biography 2001) 2000, The War Against Cliché (essays and reviews 1971–2000) 2001, Koba the Dread: Laughter and Twenty Million 2002, The Second Plane 2008; contrib. to many publs. *Leisure interests:* tennis, chess, snooker. *Address:* Wylie Agency (UK) Ltd, 17 Bedford Square, London, WC1B 3JA, England (office). *Telephone:* (20) 7908-5900 (office). *Fax:* (20) 7908-5901 (office). *E-mail:* mail@wylieagency.co.uk (office).

AMISSAH-ARTHUR, Kwesi Bekoe, BSc, MSc; Ghanaian economist, academic, fmr central banker and politician; *Vice-President;* b. 29 April 1951, Cape Coast; m.; two c.; ed Univ. of Ghana, Legon; Research Asst, Inst. of Statistical, Social and Econ. Research, Univ. of Ghana 1974–75, Teaching Asst, Econs Dept 1977–78, Asst Lecturer 1979, Lecturer 1980–88; Lecturer, Dept of Econs, Anambra State Coll. of Educ., Anambra State 1981–83; Special Asst to Provisional Nat. Defence Council Sec. of Finance and Econ. Planning 1983–86, Deputy Sec. for Finance and Econ. Planning 1986–93, Deputy Minister for Finance 1993–97; Consultant for World Bank, The Gambia 1997; Sr Economist, Sigma One Corpn (consultancy) 1998–2000; on assignment for Danish Ministry of Foreign Affairs 2001–02; Gov., Bank of Ghana 2009–12; Vice-Pres. of Ghana 2012–. *Address:* Office of the President, POB 1627, Osu, Accra, Ghana (office). *Telephone:* (30) 2666997 (office). *Website:* www.oop.gov.gh (office).

AMMANN, Karl; Swiss wildlife photographer, journalist, author and conservationist; b. 1948, St Gallen; ed St Gallen Grad. School of Econs, Cornell Univ., USA; moved to Kenya to start work with Intercontinental Hotels 1974, spent six months helping Zaïre Govt organize 'The Rumble in the Jungle' boxing match between George Foreman and Muhammad Ali 1974; moved to Cairo to manage hotel 1978; spent two years in Masai Mara Game Reserve to do research for first photographic title, Cheetah 1980; set up eco-tourism camp in Masai Mara 1983, camp in Virunga Mountains, Rwanda 1986, sold camps to concentrate on photography; Media Asia Advertising Award 1991, BBC Wildlife Photographer of the Year, World in Our Hands Award 1996–2000, Dolly Green Award for Artistic Achievement, Genesis Awards 1997, Chimfunshi Pal award in recognition of his work to raise awareness of plight of chimpanzees 1999, Special Genesis Award for media work in exposing bushmeat crisis 2000, Winner, Landscape and Nature category, American Photo, Special Contest Issue No. 5, a Time Magazine Hero of the Environment 2007, Brigitte Bardot International Genesis Award 2008. *Achievements include:* undertook first investigative expedition in Africa looking into apes orphaned by bushmeat trade 1992; initiated campaign with European Zoo Assoc. leading to a two-million signature petition being presented to European Parl. 1995; has also produced images of a hitherto unknown ape Bili Ape. *Television:* documentary: The Cairo Connection (broadcast on SABC2's 50/50) (Environmental Journalist of the Year, South African Broadcasting Corpn 2008). *Publications:* Cheetah 1984, The Hunters and the Hunted 1989, Die Grossen Menschenaffen (photography) 1992, Masai Mara 1993, Gorillas 1998, Little Bull: Growing Up in Africa's Elephant Kingdom 1998, Orangutan Odyssey (photography) 1999, The Great Apes and Humans (co-author) 2001, Great Ape Odyssey (photography) 2002, Eating Apes (with Dale Peterson) (Science Book of the Year, The Economist and Discovery Magazine) 2003, Consuming Nature (photography) 2005. *E-mail:* karl@karlammann.ch (office). *Website:* www.karlammann.com (office).

AMOAKO, Kingsley Y., BA, MA, PhD; Ghanaian economist; *President, African Center for Economic Transformation;* b. 1947; ed Univ. of Ghana, Univ. of California, Berkeley, USA; with IBRD from the 1970s, Dir Dept of Educ. and Social Policy 1993–95; UN Under-Sec.-Gen. and Exec. Sec. Econ. Comm. for Africa (ECA) 1995–2005; Distinguished African Scholar, Woodrow Wilson Int. Center 2006; Pres. African Center for Econ. Transformation, Accra 2006–; mem. Policy Advisory Bd DATA (debt, AIDS, trade, Africa); Dr hc (Addis Ababa Univ.) 2003, (Kwame Nkrumah Univ. of Science and Tech., Kumasi) 2005. *Address:* African Center for Economic Transformation, 1015 18th Street, NW, Suite 210, Washington, DC 20036-5217, USA (office).

AMON, Angelika, BSc, PhD; Austrian/American molecular and cell biologist and academic; *Professor of Biology and Kathleen and Curtis Marble Professor in Cancer Research, Massachusetts Institute of Technology;* b. 1967, Austria; ed Univ. of Vienna, Research Inst. of Molecular Pathology; Amon Lab began at Whitehead Inst. 1996–99, lab moved to Center for Cancer Research, MIT (now known as David Koch Inst. for Integrative Cancer Research at MIT) 1999–, currently Prof. of Biology and Kathleen and Curtis Marble Prof. in Cancer Research; HHMI Investigator, Howard Hughes Medical Inst. 2000–; mem. NAS 2010; Ernst Jung Prize (co-recipient) 2013. *Publications:* numerous papers in professional journals. *Address:* Koch Institute, Massachusetts Institute of Technology, 77 Massachusetts Avenue, Cambridge, MA 02139, USA (office). *Telephone:* (617) 258-6559 (office). *Fax:* (617) 258-6558 (office). *E-mail:* angelika@mit.edu (office). *Website:* biology.mit.edu/people/angelika_amon (office); amonlab.scripts.mit.edu (office); ki.mit.edu/people/faculty/amon (office).

AMORIM, Celso Luiz Nunes; Brazilian diplomatist and politician; *Minister of Defence;* b. 3 June 1942, Santos, São Paulo; s. of Vicente Matheus Amorim and Beatriz Nunes Amorim; m. Ana Maria Amorim; three s. one d.; ed Rio Branco Inst., Diplomatic Acad. Vienna and London School of Econs; Lecturer in Portuguese, Rio Branco Inst. 1976; Lecturer, Dept of Political Science and Int. Relations, Univ. of Brasília 1977–; Dir-Gen. EMBRAFILME (Brazilian Film Corpn) 1979-1982; Deputy Head of Mission, The Hague 1982–85; Perm. Rep. to UN, GATT and Conf. on Disarmament, Geneva 1991–93 (Pres. 2000), to UN and WTO 1999–2001; Sec. for Int. Affairs, Ministry of Science and Tech. 1987–88; Dir–Gen. for Cultural Affairs, Ministry of Foreign Affairs 1989–90, for Econ. Affairs 1990–91, Sec.-Gen. 1993, Minister of Foreign Affairs 1993–94, 2003–11, of Defence 2011–; Perm. Rep. to UN, New York 1995–99; Amb. to UK 2001–02; Chair. UN Security Council Resolution Sanctions Cttee on Kosovo 1998–99, UN Security Council Panels on Iraq 1999, Governing Body ILO 2000, Council for Trade in Services, WTO 2001; Perm. mem. Dept of Int. Affairs, Inst. of Advanced Studies, Univ. of São Paulo; mem. Canberra Comm. on Elimination of Nuclear Weapons 1966, Int. Task Force on Security Council Peace Enforcement 1997; Foreign Policy Asscn Medal (USA) 1999. *Publications:* several works on political theory, int. relations, cultural policies and subjects connected with science and tech. *Leisure interests:* reading, travel, art, cinema. *Address:* Ministry of Defence, Esplanada dos Ministérios, Bloco Q, 70049-900 Brasília, DF, Brazil (office). *Telephone:* (61) 3312-4000 (office). *Fax:* (61) 3225-4151 (office). *E-mail:* faleconosco@defesa.gov.br (office). *Website:* www.defesa.gov.br (office).

AMOS, Daniel (Dan) Paul, BS; American insurance industry executive; *Chairman and CEO, Aflac Inc.;* b. 13 Aug. 1951, Pensacola, Fla; s. of Paul Amos (Co-founder of Aflac Inc.); ed Univ. of Georgia; joined Aflac Inc. 1973, Sales Dept 1973–83, Pres. 1983–87, COO 1987–90, CEO Aflac Inc. and mem. Bd of Dirs 1990–, Chair. 2001–; mem. Bd of Dirs Synovus Financial Corpn, Southern Co.; mem. Bd of Trustees, Children's Healthcare of Atlanta, House of Mercy of Columbus; fmr mem. Consumer Affairs Advisory Cttee, Securities and Exchange Comm.; fmr Chair. Japan America Soc. of Georgia, Univ. of Georgia Foundation; Dr Martin Luther King Jr Unity Award, Anti-Defamation League's Torch of Liberty Award, named by Institutional Investor magazine as one of America's Best CEOs (insurance category) 2010 (fifth time). *Address:* Aflac Worldwide Headquarters, 1932 Wynnton Road, Columbus, GA 31999, USA (office). *Telephone:* (706) 323-3431 (office); (800) 992-3522 (office). *Fax:* (706) 324-6330 (office). *Website:* www.aflac.com (office).

AMOS, Paul S., II, BEcons, MBA, JD; American business executive; *President, Aflac Inc.;* s. of Daniel P. Amos; ed Duke Univ., Emory Univ., Tulane Univ.; fmrly worked in corp. legal div., Skadden, Arps, Slate, Meagher & Flom (merger and acquisitions firm), Washington, DC; served as state sales coordinator for Aflac's Georgia-North operation, Exec. Vice-Pres. of US Operations 2005–06, COO 2006–07, COO Aflac US 2006–, Pres. Aflac Inc. 2007–, also mem. Bd of Dirs; mem. Bd of Dirs Winship Cancer Center at Emory Univ., Turner School of Business at Columbus State Univ., Make-a-Wish Foundation of Southwest Georgia; mem. Bd of Trustees, Georgia Research Alliance, Bd of Visitors, Duke Univ. Divinity School, Water Contingency Task Force of Gov. Sonny Perdue of Ga. *Address:* Aflac Worldwide Headquarters, 1932 Wynnton Road, Columbus, GA 31999, USA (office). *Telephone:* (706) 323-3431 (office); (800) 992-3522 (office). *Fax:* (706) 324-6330 (office). *E-mail:* info@aflac.com (office). *Website:* www.aflac.com (office).

AMOS, Baroness (Life Peer), cr. 1997, of Brondesbury in the London Borough of Brent; **Valerie Ann Amos,** MA; British politician, diplomatist and UN official; *Under-Secretary-General for Humanitarian Affairs and Emergency Relief Coordinator, United Nations;* b. 13 March 1954, Guyana; d. of E. Michael Amos and Eunice V. Amos; ed Univs of Warwick, Birmingham and East Anglia; Race Relations Adviser, London Borough of Lambeth 1981–83; Women's Adviser, London Borough of Camden 1983–85; Head of Training and Devt, London Borough of Hackney 1985–87, Head of Man. Services 1988–89; Chief Exec. Equal Opportunities Comm. 1989–94; Dir Fraser Bernard 1994–98; Govt Whip 1998–2001; Parl. Under-Sec. of State, FCO 2001–03; Sec. of State for Int. Devt 2003; Leader House of Lords 2003–07; High Commr to Australia 2009–10; Under-Sec.-Gen. for Humanitarian Affairs and Emergency Relief Coordinator, UN, New York 2010–; Commr Fulbright Comm. 2009; Dir Hampstead Theatre 1992–98; Chair. Royal African Soc. 2007–; Deputy Chair. Runnymede Trust 1990–98; Fellow, Centre for Corp. Reputation, Univ. of Oxford 2007–; Dir (non-exec.) Travant Capital Partners 2007–; fmr Dir (non-exec.) Univ. Coll. London Hospitals Trust; fmr Chair. Afiya Trust, Bd of Govs, Royal Coll. of Nursing Inst.; mem. Advisory Cttee Centre for Educ. Devt Appraisal and Research, Univ. of Warwick 1991–98, Gen. Advisory Council BBC, King's Fund Coll. Cttee 1992–98, Council Inst. of Employment Studies 1993–98, Advisory Bd Global Health Group, Univ. of San Francisco; Trustee, Women's Therapy Centre 1989–; fmr Trustee, Inst. of Public Policy Research, VSO; Hon. Prof., Thames Valley Univ. 1995; Hon. LLD (Warwick) 2000, (Staffordshire) 2000, (Manchester) 2001, (Leicester) 2006, (Bradford) 2007, (Birmingham) 2008, (Stirling) 2010. *Leisure interest:* cricket. *Address:* Office for the Co-ordination of Humanitarian Affairs, United Nations Plaza, New York, NY 10017, USA (office). *Telephone:* (212) 963-1234 (office). *Fax:* (212) 963-1312 (office); (212) 963-9489 (office). *E-mail:* ochany@un.org (office). *Website:* ochaonline.un.org (office).

AMOUDI, Sheikh; **Mohammed Hussein Ali Al-;** Saudi Arabian/Ethiopian business executive; *Chairman, Corral Petroleum Holdings;* b. Ethiopia; m. Sofia Saleh Al Amoudi; emigrated to Saudi Arabia became a Saudi citizen 1965; f. construction co. consortium, Mohammed International Development Research and Organization Companies (MIDROC), built nationwide underground oil storage complex 1988, acquired Yanbu Steel 2000; substantial business interests in Ethiopia, also owns oil refineries in Morocco and Sweden; involved also in mining, agriculture, hotels, hospitals, finance, operations and maintenance; holding and operating cos Corral Petroleum Holdings (investment portfolio includes Preem Petroleum, Sweden, Svenska Petroleum & Exploration, SAMIR, Naft Services Co. (Saudi Arabia), Fortuna Holdings (Lebanon) and MIDROC; Order of the Polar Star (Sweden); Hon. PhD (Addis Ababa Univ.); honoured jtly by World Bank and US State Dept for his work in supporting African development 1997, King Saud Univ. Gold Medal from King Abdullah 2009, honoured at 19th Arab Economic Forum Summit in Beirut with special reference to his commitment to sustainable development 2011. *Address:* Corral Petroleum Holdings AB, Sandhamnsgatan 51, 115 90 Stockholm, Sweden (office); MIDROC Head Office, PO Box 12954, Jeddah 21483, Saudi Arabia (office). *Telephone:* (10) 450-10-00 (Stockholm) (office); (2) 650-0111 (Jeddah) (office). *Fax:* (8) 660-90-21 (Stockholm) (office); (2) 657-3149 (Jeddah) (office). *E-mail:* info@preem.se (office); hq@midroc.com (office). *Website:* www.preem.se (office); www.midroc.com (office); www.sheikhmohammedalamoudi.info.

AMOYAL, Pierre Alain Wilfred; French violinist; b. 22 June 1949, Paris; s. of Dr Wilfred Amoyal and Vera Amoyal (née Popravka); m. 2nd Leslie Chabot 1988; ed Cours d'Etat, Vanves, Conservatoire Nat. Supérieur de Musique, Paris, Univ. of Southern Calif., USA; studied with Jascha Heifetz; invited by Sir Georg Solti to perform Berg's violin concerto with Orchestre de Paris 1971 and by Pierre Boulez to perform Schoenberg's Concerto with Orchestre de Paris 1977; recital debut at Carnegie Hall 1985; numerous performances throughout the world with orchestras including Berlin Philharmonic, Vienna Symphony Orchestra, Filarmonica della Scala, Milan, Royal Philharmonic, New Philarmonia, Orchestre Nat. de France, Residentie-Orkest, The Hague; Prof. of Violin, Conservatoire Nat. Supérieur de Musique, Paris 1977–88, Lausanne Conservatory 1987–, Co-founder (with Alexis Weissenberg) and Artistic Dir Lausanne Summer Music Acad. 1991–; f. Camerata of Lausanne 2002, ensemble orchestra of young musicians; Chevalier, Ordre des Arts et des Lettres 1985, Chevalier, Ordre Nat. du Mérite 1995; First Prize, Conservatoire de Versailles 1960, Conservatoire Nat. Supérieur de Musique, Paris 1962, for chamber music, Conservatoire Nat. Supérieur de Musique, Prix Ginette Neveu, Prix Paganini, Prix Enesco 1970, Grand Prix du Disque 1974, 1977, Prix du Rayonnement de la Fondation Vaudoise pour la Promotion et la Création artistique 2002, Prix de Lausanne 2006. *Recordings include:* Symphonie espagnole (Lalo), Violin Concerto (Mendelssohn), Concertos

No. 1 and 2 and Two Sonatas (Prokofiev), Tartini's concertos, Third Concerto, Havanaise and Rondo Capriccioso (Saint-Saëns), Concerto No. 1 (Bruch), Concerto (Glazunov), Sonatas (Fauré), Horn Trio (Brahms), Concertos (Mozart), Concerto (Sibelius), Concerto (Tchaikovsky), Sonatas (Brahms), Concerto (Schoenberg), works of Albert Huybrechts 2009. *Leisure interests:* photography, literature, sport. *Address:* Conservatoire de Lausanne, Haute Ecole de la Musique, Rue de la Grotte 2, 1002 Lausanne, Switzerland (office). *E-mail:* picrrc.amoyal@cdlhem.ch (office). *Website:* www.amoyal.com.

AMR, Mohamed Kamal Ali; Egyptian diplomatist and government official; Counsellor, Embassy in Washington, DC 1990s; fmr Amb. to Saudi Arabia; fmr Perm. Rep. to World Bank; represented Egypt in several African orgs; Minister of Foreign Affairs 2011–13. *Address:* c/o Ministry of Foreign Affairs, Corniche el-Nil, Cairo (Maspiro), Egypt.

AMUDUN, Niyaz; Chinese party and government official; *Chairman, Standing Committee of Xinjiang Uygur Autonomous Regional People's Congress;* b. 1932, Xinjiang Uygur Autonomous Region, Luntai; joined CCP 1953; Sec. CCP Autonomous Prefectural Cttee, Xinjiang Uygur Autonomous Region, Korla 1955–60; mem. CCP Autonomous County Cttee, Secr. Xinjiang Uygur Autonomous Region, Luntai 1960–62; Deputy Dir Commerce Dept, Xinjiang Uygur Autonomous Region 1962–1966, Supply and Marketing Cooperatives 1962–66; Mayor Urumqi City, Xinjiang Uygur Autonomous Region 1966–67; Deputy Sec. CCP Autonomous City Cttee, Urumqi City 1973–78, Sec. 1973–78; Deputy to 4th NPC 1975, Vice-Chair. Ethnic Affairs Cttee 1978–83; Vice-Chair. Govt of Xinjiang Uygur Autonomous Region 1979–83; Chair. Standing Cttee of Xinjiang Uygur Autonomous Region People's Congress 1983–; Deputy Sec. CCP Xinjiang Uygur Autonomous Region Cttee 1985–, Sec. Political Science and Law Cttee 1985–; Chair. Xinjiang Uygur Autonomous Regional 8th People's Congress 1985, Standing Cttee of 7th Xinjiang People's Congress 1989–93, of 8th Xinjiang Uygur Autonomous Regional People's Congress 1993–; Del., 13th CCP Nat. Congress 1987, 15th Nat. Congress 1997–2002; Deputy, 8th NPC 1993–98; mem. Cen. Comm. for Discipline Inspection, CCP Cen. Cttee. *Address:* Standing Committee of Xinjiang Uygur Autonomous Region People's Congress, Urumqi, People's Republic of China.

AMUM OKECH, Pagan; South Sudanese politician; b. Malakal; joined Sudan People's Liberation Army (SPLA) 1983, served as mil. and civilian admin., Malakal, Bahr al-Ghazal, Melut, apptd civilian admin., Kapoeta 1991, fmr commdr SPLM/A operations in eastern Sudan, fmr mem. SPLM negotiating team for CPA (Comprehensive Peace Agreement), Sec.-Gen. SPLM 2005–13 (suspended July 2013); fmr Diplomatic Affairs Adviser to Pres. of Sudan; fmr Sec.-Gen. Nat. Democratic Alliance. *Address:* c/o Sudan People's Liberation Movement, Juba, South Sudan (office). *E-mail:* info@splmtoday.com (office). *Website:* www .splmtoday.com (office).

AMUNUGAMA, Sarath Leelananda Bandara, PhD; Sri Lankan politician, civil servant and newspaper executive; *Senior Minister of International Finance;* b. 10 July 1939; m.; ed Trinity Coll., Kandy, Univ. of Ceylon; fmr govt agent in Kandy Dist; fmr Dir of Information; fmr Perm. Sec. to Ministry of Information and Broadcasting; worked as int. civil servant for UNESCO HQ, Paris, France; fmr Spokesman for People's Alliance (PA); elected MP (United People's Freedom Alliance) for Mahanuwara, Kandy Dist; Minister of Northern Rehabilitation 2000, of Culture 2000, of Finance –2005, of Public Admin and Home Affairs 2005–07, of Enterprise Devt and Investment Promotion 2007–09, of Public Admin and Home Affairs and Deputy Minister of Finance and Planning 2009–10, Sr Minister of Int. Finance 2010–; Chair. The Associated Newspapers of Ceylon Ltd. *Address:* Citizens For Sarath, 50, Kande Veediya, Kandy (office); 50/1 Siripa Road, Colombo 05 (home); Ministry of Finance and Planning Galle Face Secretariat, Colombo 1, Sri Lanka. *Telephone:* (81) 4949580 (office); (77) 3489388 (mobile). *E-mail:* info@ sarathamunugama.com. *Website:* www.sarathamunugama.com (office).

AMUSÁTEGUI DE LA CIERVA, José María; Spanish banker; *Chairman, Banco Vitalicio de Espana SA de Seguros;* b. 12 March 1932, San Roque; s. of Antonio Amusátegui de la Cierva and Dolores Amusátegui de la Cierva; m. 1st Maria Luz; m. 2nd Amalia de León 1988 (divorced); six c.; ed Colegio de Huérfanos de la Armada and Univ. of Madrid; state lawyer, Minister of Finance, Gerona 1959–70; joined Instituto Nacional de Industria 1963, Vice-Chair. 1970; Sec., Bd of Dirs Boada Altos Hornos de Vizcaya 1967; Deputy Chair. Prodinsa 1974; Chair. Catalan Devt Bank 1975, Intelsa 1975–80, Astilleros Españoles 1980; Pres. Spanish Shipyard, Dir Naval Div. 1980; Deputy Chair. Instituto Nacional de Hidrocarburos 1981; Chair. Campsa 1982; Man. Dir and Deputy Chair. Banco Hispano Americano 1985, Chair. 1991–99, also Pres.; Dir Union Fenosa SA 1991–93, Pres. 1993, currently Hon. Chair. and mem. Exec. Cttee; Chair. Banco Cen. Hispano 1992–99; Pres. Banco Vitalicio de Espana SA de Seguros 1993–; Co-Chair. Banco Santander Cen. Hispanoamericano (BSCH, now Banco Santander Cen. Hispano SA) 1999–2002, Hon. Chair. 2002–; Grand Cross of Civil Merit. *Leisure interests:* motorcycling, astronomy, botany. *Address:* Banco Vitalicio de Espana SA de Seguros, Paseo de Gracia, 11, 08007 Barcelona (office); Unión Fenosa, SA, Avenida de San Luis, 77 Madrid, 28033 Madrid, Spain (office). *Telephone:* (93) 4840100 (Barcelona) (office); (91) 5676000 (Madrid) (office). *Fax:* (91) 5718246 (Madrid) (office). *Website:* www.vitalicio.es (office).

AN, Zhendong; Chinese government official and engineer; *Vice-Chairman, Central Committee of the Jiusan Society;* b. 5 Sept. 1930, Tangshan, Hebei Prov.; ed Hebei Engineering Coll. 1951; engineer, Railway Admin, Electric Power Div., Heilongjiang Prov., Qiqihar City 1952–58; engineer, Heilongjiang Silicon Rectifier Factory, Harbin City 1963–67; Engineer, Deputy Factory Dir Harbin Rectifier Equipment Factory 1967–81; Chief Engineer, 2nd Light Industry Bureau 1981–82; joined Jiusan Soc. 1981, Vice-Chair. 6th, 7th, 8th, 9th and 10th Cen. Cttee Jiusan Soc. 1997–; Vice-Gov. Heilongjiang 1983–90; Vice-Chair. Standing Cttee Heilongjiang Prov. People's Congress 1990–93; mem. 6th NPC 1983–88, 7th NPC 1988–93, 8th NPC 1993–98; mem. 9th CPPCC Nat. Cttee, Standing Cttee 1998–2003; Vice-Pres. Chinese Package Soc.; Dir Chinese Industry Econ. Soc.; named Model Worker of Special Grade of Harbin, Model Worker of Heilongjiang Prov. *Achievements include:* inventions include: Signal and Radio Telephone in Railroad Cars 1958, Fire-fighting Automatic System in Cities 1963, Explosion-proof Rectifier Equipment in Coal Mines 1973, Power Factor Electricity Regulator

1976. *Address:* c/o People's Congress Standing Committee of Heilongjiang, Nangang District, Harbin 150001, People's Republic of China.

AN QIYUAN, BEng; Chinese government official and fmr geologist; *Chairman, CPPCC Shaanxi Provincial Committee;* b. 1933, Lingtong Co., Shaanxi Prov.; ed Dept of Geology, Northwest China Univ.; joined CCP 1953; leader geological team of Songliao Petroleum Prospecting Bureau 1958–59; Dir of Oil Mine and Chief, Underground Operation Section of 1st HQ Oil Extracting in Daqing 1964–65; Dir Petroleum Geophysics Prospecting Bureau, Ministry of Petroleum 1973–77; Deputy Dir State Seismological Bureau 1977–80, Dir 1982–88; mem. Standing Cttee CCP Shaanxi Prov. Cttee, Sec. CCP Xian Municipal Cttee 1988; mem. Standing Cttee CPPCC Comm. for Inspecting Discipline 1992–94; Sec. CCP Shaanxi Prov. Cttee 1994–97; Chair. CPPCC Shaanxi Prov. Cttee 1998–; mem. 9th CPPCC Nat. Cttee 1998–2003. *Publications:* Developing Shaanxi Province and Enriching the People by Grasping the Keystone and Fulfilment. *Leisure interest:* reading. *Address:* Shaanxi Provincial Committee, Xian, Shaanxi Province, People's Republic of China. *Telephone:* (29) 85581418 (office); (29) 85581398 (home).

ANAND, Adarsh Sein, LLD; Indian judge; b. 1 Nov. 1936, Jammu, Jammu and Kashmir; ed Jammu and Lucknow Univs, Univ. of London, UK; enrolled as Advocate Bar Council 1964; practised in criminal, constitutional and election law, Punjab and Haryana High Court –1975; apptd Additional Judge, Jammu and Kashmir High Court 1975, Chief Justice 1985–89; Chief Justice Madras High Court 1989–91; Judge, Supreme Court of India 1991–98, Chief Justice 1998–2001; Chair. Nat. Human Rights Comm. 2003–07; Pres. Int. Inst. of Human Rights Soc. 1996; Exec. Chair. Nat. Legal Services Authority (India) 1997; Fellow, Univ. Coll. London 1997; Hon. LLD (Lucknow Univ.) 1996; Hon. DLit (Jammu Univ.) 1999; Padma Vibhushan 2008. *Publication:* The Constitution of Jammu and Kashmir— Its Development and Comments. *Address:* B-29, Sector-14, Noida, 201 301, India (home). *Telephone:* (120) 472292 (home); (120) 516061 (home).

ANANDASANGAREE, Veerasingam; Sri Lankan politician; *President, Tamil United Liberation Front;* b. 15 June 1933, Point Pedro; s. of the late S. Veerasingham and Ratnam; m.; four c.; ed Sri Somaskanda Coll., Christian Coll. Atchuvely, Hartley Coll., Zahira Coll.; teacher, Hindu Coll., Jaffna, Poonakri MMV, Kotelawela GTM School, Ratmalana, Christ King Coll., Ja-Ela 1953–59; Chair. Karaichi Village Council 1965–68, Karaichi Town Council 1968–69; practised as lawyer 1967–83; mem. Ceylon Parl. 1970–83, Sri Lanka Parl. 2000–04; joined All Ceylon Tamil Congress 1966, Youth Front Pres. 1970; joined Tamil United Front (later Tamil United Liberation Front), Propaganda Sec., Tamil United Liberation Front 1976–1983, mem. Politburo 1983–93, Sr Vice-Pres. 1993–2002, Acting Pres. 1998–2001, Pres. 2002–; UNESCO Madanjeet Singh Prize 2006. *Address:* Tamil United Liberation Front, 5/3A Wijayaba Mawatha, Kalubowila, Dehiwala, Colombo, Sri Lanka (office). *Telephone:* (11) 2552372 (office). *E-mail:* tulfsl@yahoo.com (office). *Website:* tamilunitedliberationfront.org (office); anandasangary.com (office).

ANANIASHVILI, Nina Gedevanovna; Georgian/Russian ballet dancer; *Artistic Director, State Ballet of Georgia;* b. 28 March 1963, Tbilisi; d. of Gedevan Ananiashvili and Lia Gogolashvili; m. Gregory Vashadze 1988; one s. one d.; ed State Choreographic Schools of Georgia and Bolshoi Theatre, Moscow; Prima Ballerina, Bolshoi Ballet 1981–, Prin., American Ballet Theater (ABT) 1993–2009; has performed on tour world-wide with New York City Ballet, Royal Ballet, Royal Danish Ballet, Kirov Ballet, Royal Swedish Ballet, Ballet de Monte Carlo, The Munich Ballet, La Scala Ballet, Houston Ballet, Boston Ballet, Tokyo Ballet and others; Prima Ballerina and Artistic Dir, State Ballet of Georgia 2004–, ballets staged include classical works and ballets by Balanchine, Ashton, Bournonville and Kylián; tours to USA 2007/2008/2010, Edinburgh Int. Festival 2008 and Japan 2012; Order for Outstanding Service to Fatherland (Russia) 2000, Order of Honour (Georgia) 2003, Presidential Order of Light (Georgia) 2010, Order of the Star of Italian Solidarity 2011; numerous awards include Grand Prix Int. Ballet Competition, Jackson 1986, People's Artist of Repub. of Georgia and of USSR, State Prize of Russia 1992, State Prize of Georgia 1993, Dance Magazine Award for Outstanding Achievements, USA 2002. *Dance:* over 100 roles including Giselle, Odette/Odile (Swan Lake), Aurora (Sleeping Beauty), Raimonda, Juliet (Romeo and Juliet), Nikya (La Bayadère), Kitri (Don Quixote). *Leisure interests:* antique books, modern painting. *Address:* Tbilisi Opera and Ballet Theatre, 0108 Tbilisi, Rustaveli Ave. 25, Georgia (office); Frunzenskaya nab. 46, Apt. 79, 119270 Moscow, Russia. *E-mail:* ballet@comtv.ru (office). *Website:* www.opera.ge (office).

ANANTHAMURTHY, U. R., MA PhD; Indian academic and writer; b. 21 Dec. 1932, Melige, Karnataka; ed Mysore Univ., Univ. of Birmingham, UK; writer in Kannada; Prof. of English Literature, Mysore Univ. 1970–80; Vice-Chancellor, Mahatma Gandhi Univ., Kottayam 1987–91; Visiting Prof., Univ. of Iowa, USA 1975, Shivaji Univ. 1982, Univ. of Tubingen, Germany 1992, Univ. of Pennsylvania 2000, Cornell Univ. 2001, Univ. of Hyderabad 2001; Ed. and Publr, Rujuvathu 1981; Chair. State Level Cttee on Drug Addiction, Kerala 1988, Review Cttee Indian Inst. of Advanced Study Shimla 1994, Nat. Book Trust 1992–93, Indian Inst. of Social Sciences 1998, Film Inst. of India, Pune 2002; Pres. Sahitya Akademi, Delhi 1993–98; Commonwealth Fellowship (to study in UK 1963–66, Homi Bhabha Fellowship 1972–74; Hon. DLitt (Kendriya uchcha Tibatti Shiksha Samsthanam, Varanasi) 2002, (Rabindra Bharati Univ., Calcutta Univ.) 1995; Poorna Krishna Rao Gold Medal for Highest Rank in MA 1956, Best Story Award—Samskara, Ghatashradda, Bara, Karnataka Film Devt Corpn 1970, 1978, 1989, Fiction Award, Karnataka Sahitya Akademi 1983, Award for Literary Distinction, Govt of Karnataka 1984, Award for Literary Achievement, Karnataka Sahitya Akademi 1984, Rajyothsava Award 1984, Samaj Bhushan Award 1988, Harmony Award 1990, Bharatiya Jnanpith 1994, Masti Award 1994, Padma Bhushan 1998, Bapureddi Puraskaram, Hyderabad 2001, Ganakrishti Award 2002, Keladi Shivappa Nayaka Prashasti, Village Keladi 2002. *Publications include:* novels: Samskara 1966, Bharatipura 1973, Awashte 1986, Bhava 1998, Divya 2001; short stories: Endendhigu Mugiyada Kathe 1955, Prashne 1962, Mouni 1967, Ghata Shradda, Aakaasha Mattu Bekku 1983, Mooru Dashakada Kategalu 1989, Suryana Kudure 1995, Aidu Dashakada Kathegalu 2001; several books of poetry and essays. *Address:* c/o Arvind Kumar Publishers, C1-324, Palam Villas, Palam Vihar, Gurgaon 122 017, India (office). *Telephone:* (124) 4256103 (office). *Fax:* (124) 4256103 (office). *E-mail:* arvind@arvindkumarpublishers.com (office). *Website:* www.arvindkumarpublishers.com (office); www .urananthamurthy.com.

ANASTASE, Roberta Alma; Romanian politician and sociologist; b. 27 March 1976, Ploieşti; ed postgraduate studies in Political Science and European Studies; mem. Democratic Party (now Democratic Liberal Party) 1991–, served in turn as Vice-Pres. Youth Org., mem. Nat. Political Bureau and Head of Prahova Br., currently Exec. Sec. for Int. Relations; mem. Camera Deputaţilor (Chamber of Deputies) for Prahova constituency 2004–07, for 11th Electoral Dist of Prahova (Ploiesti-Vest) 2008–, Chair. (first woman) 2008–12; Observer, European Parl. 2005–07, mem. European Parl. (European People's Party–European Democrats) 2007–08, served as European Parl. Rapporteur for the Black Sea Synergy; represented Romania at Miss Universe competition 1996. *Address:* Camera Deputaţilor (Chamber of Deputies), Palatul Parlamentului, 050563 Bucharest, Palatul Parlamentului, str. Izvor 2–4, Sector 5, Romania (office). *Telephone:* (21) 3160300 (office). *Fax:* (21) 4141111 (office). *E-mail:* roberta.anastase@cdep.ro (office). *Website:* www.cdep.ro (office).

ANASTASIADES, Nikos; Cypriot politician, lawyer and head of state; *President;* b. 1946, Limassol; m. Andri Moustakoudes; two d.; ed Univ. of Athens, Univ. of London, UK; practising lawyer, Limassol 1972–; Dist Sec. Youth Org. of Dimokratikos Synagermos (DISY—Democratic Rally Party) 1976–85 (Pres. 1987–90), Vice-Pres. DISY 1985–86, 1990–93, Parl. Leader DISY 1993–97, Deputy Pres. 1995–97, Pres. 1997–2013; mem. Parl. 1981–2013, Speaker, House of Reps 1996–2001; Pres. of Cyprus 2013–. *Address:* Office of the President, Presidential Palace, Dem. Severis Avenue, 1400 Nicosia (office); Dimokratikos Synagermos, PO Box 25303, 25 Pindarou Street, 1061 Nicosia, Cyprus (office). *Telephone:* 22867400 (office); 22883000 (office). *Fax:* 22753821 (office); 22867594 (office). *E-mail:* president@presidency.gov.cy; disy@disy.org.cy (office). *Website:* www.cyprus.gov .cy (office); www.disy.org.cy (office).

ANAYA, Rudolfo, MA; American academic and author; *Professor Emeritus, University of New Mexico;* b. 30 Oct. 1937, Pastura, NM; s. of Martin Anaya and Rafaelita Mares; m. Patricia Lawless 1966; ed Albuquerque High School, Browning Business School, Univ. of New Mexico; teacher, Albuquerque public schools 1963–70; Dir Counseling Center, Univ. of Albuquerque 1971–73; Lecturer, Univ. Anahuac, Mexico City 1974; Prof., Dept of Language and Literature, Univ. of New Mexico 1974–93, Prof. Emer. 1993–; Founder, Ed. Blue Mesa Review 1989–93; Martin Luther King, Jr/César Chávez, Rosa Parks Visiting Prof., Univ. of Michigan, Ann Arbor 1996; currently Assoc. Ed. The American Book Review; Bd Contributing Ed. The Americas Review; Advisory Ed. Great Plains Quarterly; f. PEN-NM, Teachers of English and Chicano Language Arts 1991; Founder, Pres. NM Rio Grande Writers Asscn; mem. Bd Before Columbus Foundation; mem. Nat. Asscn of Chicano Studies; Hon. DHumLitt (Albuquerque) 1981, (Marycrest Coll.) 1984, (New England) 1992, (Calif. Lutheran Univ.) 1994, (New Hampshire) 1997; Hon. PhD (Santa Fe) 1991; Hon. DLitt (New Hampshire) 1996; recipient of numerous awards, including Nat. Endowment for the Arts Fellowship 1980, NM Gov.'s Award for Excellence and Achievement in Literature 1980, W.K. Kellogg Foundation Fellowship 1983–86, New Mexico Eminent Scholar Award 1989, Rockefeller Foundation Residency Bellagio, Italy 1991, Excellence in the Humanities Award, New Mexico Endowment for the Humanities 1995, Tomás Rivera Mexican American Children's Book Awards 1995, 2000, Distinguished Achievement Award, Western Literature Asscn 1997, Ariz. Adult Authors Award, Arizona Library Asscn 2000, Wallace Stegner Award Center of the American West 2001, Nat. Medal of Arts 2001, Nat. Asscn of Chicano/Chicana Studies Scholar 2002. *Plays:* Billy the Kid, Who Killed Don José?, Matachines, Angie, Ay, Compadre, The Farolitos of Christmas, Bless Me, Ultima 2009. *Publications include:* Bless Me, Ultima (Premio Quinto Sol Award 1971) 1972, Heart of Aztlan 1976, Tortuga 1979 (American Book Award, Before Columbus Foundation 1979), Cuentos: Tales from the Hispanic Southwest (trans.) 1980, The Silence of the Llano (short stories) 1982, The Legend of La Llorona 1984, The Adventures of Juan Chicaspatas (poem) 1985, A Chicano in China 1986, Lord of the Dawn, The Legend of Quetzalcoatl 1987, Alburquerque 1992 (PEN-WEST Fiction Award 1993), The Anaya Reader (anthology) 1994, Zia Summer 1995, The Farolitos of Christmas (children's fiction) 1995, Jalamanta, A Message from the Desert 1996, Rio Grande Fall 1996, Maya's Children (children's fiction) 1997, Descansos: An Interrupted Journey (with Estevan Arellano and Denise Chávez) 1997, Isis in the Heart 1998, Shaman Winter 1999, Farolitos for Abuelo (children's fiction) 1999, My Land Sings 1999, Roadrunner's Dance 2000, Elegy for Cesar Chavez 2000, The Santero's Miracle (children's fiction) 2004, Serafina's Stories 2004, Jemez Spring 2005, The Man who Could Fly and other stories 2006, ChupaCabra and the Roswell UFO (children's fiction) 2008; short stories in literary magazines in USA and internationally; has also edited various collections of short stories. *Leisure interests:* reading, travel, apple orchards. *Address:* 5324 Cañada Vista NW, Albuquerque, NM 87120-2412, USA (home). *Fax:* (505) 899-0014 (home).

ANCRAM, 13th Marquis of Lothian; Michael Andrew Foster Jude Kerr, PC, QC, DL, LLB, MA; British politician; b. 7 July 1945; s. of 12th Marquess of Lothian and Antonella, Marchioness of Lothian; m. Lady Jane Fitzalan-Howard 1975; two d.; ed Ampleforth, Christ Church Coll., Oxford, Univ. of Edinburgh; fmr columnist, Daily Telegraph (Manchester edn); partner in tenanted arable farm; called to Scottish Bar 1970, practised law 1970–79; MP for Berwickshire and East Lothian Feb.–Oct. 1974, for Edinburgh S 1979–87, for Devizes 1992–2010, mem. House of Commons Energy Select Cttee 1979–83; Parl. Under-Sec. of State, Scottish Office 1983–87, Parl. Under-Sec., NI Office 1993–94, Minister of State 1994–97; Shadow Cabinet Spokesman for Constitutional Affairs 1997–98, Shadow Sec. of State for Foreign and Commonwealth Affairs 2001–05, for Int. Affairs 2003–04, for Defence 2005; Vice-Chair. Conservative Party in Scotland 1975–80, Chair. 1980–83, Chair. Conservative Party 1998–2001, Deputy Leader 2001–05; Chair. Northern Corp. Communications 1989–91, Global Strategy Forum 2006–; MEC International Ltd; Dir CSM Parl. Consultants 1998–92; mem. Bd Scottish Homes 1988–90, Intelligence and Security Cttee 2006–10, 2011–; Trustee Mitsubishi UFJ Trust, Oxford Foundation. *Publications:* pamphlets: Still a Conservative 2006, Dancing with Wolves 2008, Farewell to Drift 2010. *Leisure interests:* skiing, fishing, photography, folk-singing. *Address:* House of Lords, London, SW1A 0PW (office); 30 Smith Square, London, SW1P 3HF, England (home). *Telephone:* (20) 7219-5353

(office). *Fax:* (20) 7219-5979 (office). *E-mail:* lothianm@parliament.uk (office); mancram@hotmail.com (home).

ANDERS, Edward, MA, PhD; American professor of chemistry; *Horace B. Horton Professor Emeritus, University of Chicago;* b. 21 June 1926, Liepaja, Latvia; s. of Adolph Alperovitch and Erica Leventals; m. Joan Elizabeth Fleming 1955; one s. one d.; ed Univ. of Munich, Germany, Columbia Univ., USA; Instructor in Chem., Univ. of Ill. at Urbana 1954–55; Asst Prof. of Chem. Univ. of Chicago 1955–60, Assoc. Prof. 1960–62, Prof. 1960–73, Horace B. Horton Prof. of Physical Sciences 1973–91, Prof. Emer. 1991–; Visiting Prof. Calif. Inst. of Tech. 1960, Univ. of Berne 1963–64, 1970, 1978, 1980–81, 1983, 1987–88, 1989–90; Research Assoc. Field Museum of Natural History 1968–91; Fellow American Acad. of Arts and Sciences 1973–; mem. NAS 1974–; Assoc. Royal Astronomical Soc., UK 1974–; Fairchild Distinguished Scholar, Calif. Inst. of Tech. 1992–93; Hon. DChem (Latvian Acad. of Sciences) 2000; Cleveland Prize, AAAS 1959, Smith Medal, NAS 1971, Leonard Medal, Meteoritical Soc. 1974, Goldschmidt Medal, Geochemical Soc. 1990, Kuiper Prize, American Astronomical Soc. 1991, Hess Medal (American Geophysical Union) 1995. *Publications:* over 260 articles in scientific journals. *Leisure interests:* classical music, hiking, photography. *Address:* c/o Department of Chemistry, University of Chicago, 5735 South Ellis Avenue, Chicago IL 60637, USA.

ANDERSEN, Ib; Danish ballet dancer; *Artistic Director, Ballet Arizona;* b. 14 Dec. 1954, Copenhagen; s. of Ingolf Andersen and Anna Andersen; ballet dancer, Royal Danish Ballet 1973–80, Prin. Dancer 1975–80; Prin. Dancer, New York City Ballet 1980–94; Ballet Master, Pittsburgh Ballet Theater 1997; Artistic Dir Ballet Ariz. 2000–; mem. Balanchine Trust; Nijinsky Prize, Gold Medallion of Merit Award, Nat. Soc. of Arts and Letters 2006. *Address:* Ballet Arizona, 3645 East Indian School Road, Phoenix, AZ 85018, USA (office). *Telephone:* (602) 381-0184 (office). *Fax:* (602) 381-0189 (office). *E-mail:* questions@balletaz.org (office). *Website:* www.balletaz.org (office).

ANDERSEN, Nils Smedegaard, MSc; Danish business executive; *Partner and Group CEO, A.P. Møller-Maersk A/S;* b. 8 July 1958, Arhus; ed Arhus Univ.; began career as Sales Dir Tuborg International, becoming Man. Dir of several Carlsberg and Tuborg cos, mem. group man. 1999–2007, CEO Carlsberg A/S 2001–07; mem. Bd Dirs A.P. Møller-Maersk A/S 2005–, Partner and Group CEO 2007–; mem. European Round Table of Industrialists 2001–; Co-Chair. EU-Russia Industrialists' Round Table 2007–; mem. Bd Dirs William Demant Holding A/S, Oticon A/S. *Address:* A.P. Møller-Mærsk A/S, Esplanaden 50, 1098 Copenhagen K, Denmark (office). *Telephone:* 33-63-33-63 (office). *Fax:* 33-63-41-08 (office). *E-mail:* info@ maersk.com (office). *Website:* www.maersk.com (office).

ANDERSEN, Ronald Max, MS, PhD; American sociologist and academic; *Wasserman Professor Emeritus, School of Public Health, University of California, Los Angeles;* b. 15 Feb. 1939, Omaha, Neb.; s. of Max Adolph Andersen and Evangeline Dorothy Andersen (née Wobbe); m. Diane Borella 1965; one d.; ed Univ. of Santa Clara, Purdue Univ.; Research Assoc. Purdue Farm Cardiac Project, Dept of Sociology, Purdue Univ. 1962–63; Assoc. Study Dir Nat. Opinion Research Center, Univ. of Chicago 1963–66, Research Assoc. Center for Health Admin. Studies 1963–77; Instructor, Grad. School of Business, Univ. of Chicago 1966–68, Asst Prof. 1968–72, Asst Prof., Dept of Sociology 1970–72, Assoc. Prof. Grad. School of Business, then Prof. 1974–90, Assoc. Dir Center for Health Admin. Studies 1977–80, Dir Grad. Program in Health Admin. 1980–90; Chair. Editorial Bd Health Administration Press, Chicago 1980–83, 1988–; Wasserman Prof. of Health Services and Prof. of Sociology, UCLA School of Public Health 1991–2006, Chair. Dept of Health Services 1993–96, 2000–03, Wasserman Prof. Emer. 2006–; Fellow, Inst. of Medicine; mem. Royal Soc. of Science, Uppsala; mem. numerous cttees, advisory panels etc.; mem. American Sociological Asscn, American Statistical Asscn, American Public Health Asscn; Hon. doctorate (Purdue Univ.); Baxter Allegiance Prize 1999, Distinguished Investigator Award Asscn for Health Services Research, Leo G. Reeder Award for Distinguished Service to Medical Sociology. *Publications:* author and co-author of numerous books, monographs, book chapters and articles in professional journals. *Address:* UCLA School of Public Health, 650 Charles E. Young Drive South, Los Angeles, CA 90095-1772 (office); 10724 Wilshire Boulevard, Apartment 312, Los Angeles, CA 90024-4453, USA (home). *Telephone:* (310) 206-1810 (office). *Fax:* (310) 825-3317 (office). *E-mail:* randerse@ucla.edu (office). *Website:* www.ph.ucla.edu/hs/andersen.html (office).

ANDERSEN, Torkild, MSc, DPhil; Danish physicist and academic; *Professor Emeritus of Physics, University of Arhus;* b. 19 June 1934, Randers; m. Inger Bloch-Petersen 1957; one s. one d.; ed Tech. Univ., Copenhagen; industrial chemist 1958–59; Asst and Assoc. Prof. of Chem., Univ. of Arhus 1959–71, Prof. of Physics (Atomic Physics) 1971–2001, Prof. Emer. 2001–; Postdoctoral Fellow, Univ. of Cambridge, UK 1961–63, Univ. of Lyon, France 1968; Visiting Prof., Univ. of Colorado, USA 1984–85, Flinders Univ., S Australia 1988, 1994; mem. Bd Carlsberg Foundation 1996–2004; Advisor for Lundbeck Foundation 2005–11; mem. Royal Danish Acad. of Sciences and Letters (Kongelige Danske Videnskabernes Selskab) 1979–; N. Bjerrum Prize 1972, Univ. of Arhus Science Faculty Prize 2006. *Publications:* over 200 scientific contribs to chemistry and physics journals. *Address:* Institute of Physics and Astronomy, University of Arhus, Nordre. Ringgade, 8000 Arhus C (office); 38 Lyngvej, 8600 Silkeborg, Denmark (home). *Telephone:* 87-15-56-83 (office). *Fax:* 86-12-07-40 (office). *E-mail:* fystor@ phys.au.dk (office).

ANDERSON, Bradbury H., BA; American retail executive; b. 1950, Sheridan, Wyo.; m. Janet Anderson; two s.; ed Waldorf Coll., Forest City, Ia, Univ. of Denver; began career as commissioned salesman, Sound of Music Inc. (predecessor to Best Buy), various man. positions, Best Buy Co. Inc. 1973, including Vice-Pres. 1981–86, Exec. Vice-Pres. 1986–91, mem. Bd of Dirs 1986–2010, Pres. and COO 1991–2002, Vice-Chair. 2001–09, CEO 2002–09; mem. Bd of Dirs Best Buy Children's Foundation, Junior Achievement Inc. 2000–, Nat. Junior Achievement, Int. Mass Retail Asscn, Retail Industry Leaders' Asscn, American Film Inst., General Mills Inc. 2007–, Carlson Companies Inc. 2009–; Trustee, Minn. Public Radio Bd; mem. Waldorf Coll. Bd of Regents 1998–, Mayo Clinic, Rochester, NY 2009–, LightHaus Logic Inc. 2012–; mem. Bd of Trustees Minnesota Public Radio; Waldorf Coll. Alumni Distinguished Service Award 1997, Retail Merchandiser

Retail Exec. of the Year 2002. *Leisure interests:* cycling, reading biographies, theatre, music.

ANDERSON, Campbell McCheyne, BEcons; Australian business executive; b. 17 Sept. 1941, Sydney; s. of Allen Taylor Anderson and Ethel Catherine Rundle; m. Sandra Maclean Harper 1965; two s. one d.; ed Armidale School, NSW, Univ. of Sydney; audit clerk, Priestley and Morris 1958–59; with Boral Ltd 1962–69; Gen. Man. then Man. Dir Reef Oil and Basin Oil 1969–72; with Burmah Oil Australia Ltd 1972–73, New York 1973–74, Div. Dir, then Chief Financial Officer, Burmah Oil Trading Ltd, UK 1974–75, Dir 1975–76, Exec. Dir Burmah Oil Co. Ltd 1976–82, Man. Dir Burmah Oil PLC 1982–85; Man. Dir Renison Goldfields Consolidated Ltd 1985, Man. Dir and CEO 1986–93, Dir Consolidated Gold Fields PLC 1985–89; Chair. Ampolex Ltd 1991–96, Dir 1996–97; Man. Dir North Ltd 1994–98; Chair. Energy Resources Australia Ltd 1994–98; Pres. Business Council of Australia 1999–2000; Chair. Southern Pacific Petroleum 2001–07; Pres. Australia/Japan Soc. of Vic. 1995–98; mem. Bd of Dirs Aviva Australia Holdings Ltd 1999–2009, IBJ Bank Australia 1999–2003, Reconciliation Australia 2001–07, ThoroughVisioN 2004–; Assoc., Australian Soc. of Certified Practising Accountants; mem. Sentient Council 2001–. *Leisure interests:* golf, shooting, horse racing, swimming. *Address:* 77 Drumalbyn Road, Bellevue Hill, NSW 2023, Australia. *Telephone:* (4) 1751-2187. *Fax:* (2) 9327-5035.

ANDERSON, Christopher (Chris), BEcons; Australian journalist; b. 9 Dec. 1944; s. of C. F. Anderson and L. A. Anderson; m. Gabriella Douglas 1969; one s. one d.; ed Picton High School, NSW, Univ. of Sydney, Columbia Univ., New York; journalist and political commentator 1962–76; Deputy Ed., later Ed., The Sun-Herald 1976–79; Deputy Ed., later Ed., The Sydney Morning Herald 1980–83, Ed.-in-Chief 1983–88; Man. Dir and Group Ed. Dir John Fairfax Ltd 1987–90, Chief Exec. 1990–91; Man. Ed. Australian Broadcasting Corpn 1993–95; Chief Exec. TV New Zealand Ltd 1995–97; CEO Optus Communications 1997–2004; served as adviser to Packer family on their media interests 2004–09; mem. Bd Austrade 2004–07. *Leisure interests:* cricket, reading.

ANDERSON, Don L., BS, PhD, FAAS; American geophysicist; *Eleanor and John R. McMillan Professor Emeritus of Geophysics, California Institute of Technology;* b. 5 March 1933, Frederick, Md; s. of Richard Andrew and Minola Andrew (née Phares); m. Nancy Lois Ruth 1956; one s. one d.; ed Rensselaer Polytechnic Inst., California Inst. of Tech.; Geophysicist, Chevron Oil Co. 1955–56; Geophysicist, Geophysics Research Directorate, Air Force Cambridge Research Center 1956–58; Geophysicist, Arctic Inst. of North America 1958–60; Research Fellow, Calif. Inst. of Tech. 1962–63, Asst Prof. 1963–64, Assoc. Prof. 1964–68, Prof. 1968–2002, Dir Seismological Lab. 1967–89, Eleanor and John R. McMillan Prof. of Geophysics 1989–2002, Prof. Emer. of Geophysics 2002–; Pres. American Geophysical Union 1988–92; Cloos Memorial Scholar, Johns Hopkins Univ. 1989; H. Burr Steinbach Visiting Scholar, Woods Hole Oceanographic Inst. 1995; Green Scholar, Inst. of Geophysics and Planetary Physics, Univ. of Calif. 1998; Cox Visiting Prof., Stanford Univ. 1998; Ed. Physics of the Earth and Planetary Interiors 1977; Assoc. Ed. Tectonophysics, Physics and Chemistry of the Earth, Journal of Geodynamics; mem. Seismological Soc. of America, Space Science Bd, Geophysics Research Forum (Chair. 1984–86), Bd on Earth Sciences of NAS, Arthur L. Day Award Cttee NAS (Chair. 1989–90), Macelwane Award Cttee (Chair. 1974–75), Bowie Medal Cttee 1984–85 (Chair. 1994–96), Harry Hess Award Cttee 2002–; Fellow, Sloan Foundation 1964–67, American Acad. of Arts and Sciences 1972, NAS 1982, AAAS 1988, American Philosophical Soc. 1990, American Geophysical Union (Pres. 1986–88), Geological Soc. of America, Royal Astronomical Soc.; Guggenheim Fellow 1998; Distinguished Scientists Lecture Series, Trinity Univ. 1995; Hon. Foreign Fellow, European Union of Geosciences 1985; Hon. DSc (Rensselaer Polytechnic Inst.) 2000; Dr hc (Universite de Paris, Institute de Physique du Globe de Paris) 2005; J. B. Macelwane Award, American Geophysical Union 1966, Sr Fulbright-Hays Award (Australia) 1975, AAAS Newcomb Cleveland Prize 1976–77, NASA Distinguished Scientific Achievement Award 1977, Emil Wiechert Medal, German Geophysical Soc. 1986, Arthur L. Day Medal, Geological Soc. of America 1987, Gold Medal, Royal Astronomical Soc. 1988, Bowie Medal, American Geophysical Union 1991, Crafoord Prize, Royal Swedish Acad. of Sciences 1998, Nat. Medal of Science 1998, Guggenheim Fellowship 1998, Distinguished Alumni Award, Baltimore Polytechnic Inst. 2001, Hall of Fame, Rensselaer Polytechnic Inst. 2005. *Address:* Seismological Laboratory, California Institute of Technology, 1200 East California Blvd, MS 252–21, So. Mudd Bldg, Room 370, Pasadena, CA 91125 (office); 669 Alameda Street, Altadena, CA 91001, USA (home). *Telephone:* (626) 395-6901 (office); (626) 564-0715 (home). *Fax:* (626) 564-0715 (office). *E-mail:* dla@gps.caltech.edu. *Website:* www.gps.caltech.edu/~dla (office).

ANDERSON, Donald Thomas, AO, BSc, PhD, DSc, FRS; Australian biologist and academic; *Professor Emeritus of Biology, University of Sydney;* b. 29 Dec. 1931, Eton, Berks., England, UK; s. of Thomas Anderson and Flora Anderson; m. Joanne T. Claridge 1960; one s.; ed Univ. of London, UK, Univ. of Sydney; Lecturer in Zoology, Univ. of Sydney 1958, Sr Lecturer 1963, Reader 1968, Prof. 1972, Challis Prof. of Biology 1984–91, Prof. Emer. 1992–; Visiting Prof., King's Coll., London 1970; Kowalevsky Medal 2001. *Publications:* Embryology and Phylogeny in Annelids and Arthropods 1973, Barnacles 1994, Atlas of Invertebrate Anatomy 1996, Invertebrate Zoology 1998, 2001. *Leisure interests:* photography, gardening. *Address:* 5 Angophora Close, Wamberal, NSW 2260, Australia (home). *Telephone:* (2) 4384-7218 (home). *E-mail:* dtjta@ozemail.com.au (office).

ANDERSON, Gillian, BFA; American actress; b. 9 Aug. 1968, Chicago, Ill.; d. of Edward Anderson and Rosemary Anderson; m. 1st Errol Clyde Klotz (divorced); one d.; m. 2nd Julian Ozanne 2004 (divorced 2006); two s.; ed DePaul Univ., Chicago, Goodman Theater School, Chicago; worked at Nat. Theatre, London; appeared in two off-Broadway productions; Golden Globe Awards 1995, 1997, Screen Actors' Guild Awards 1996, 1997, Emmy Award 1997. *Theatre includes:* Absent Friends (Manhattan Theater Club) (Theater World Award 1991) 1991, The Philanthropist (Along Wharf Theater) 1992, What the Night is For (Comedy Theatre, London, Whatsonstage.com Theatregoers' Choice Best Actress Award 2003) 2002, The Sweetest Swing in Baseball (Royal Court Theatre, London) 2004, A Doll's House (Donmar Warehouse, London) 2009, We Are One: A celebration of tribal peoples (Apollo Theatre, London) 2010. *Films include:* Three at Once 1986, A Matter of Choice 1988, The Turning 1992, Princess Mononoke (voice, English-language version) 1997, Chicago Cab 1998, The X-Files 1998, The Mighty 1998,

Playing By Heart 1998, The House of Mirth 2000, The Mighty Celt 2005, Tristram Shandy: A Cock and Bull Story 2005, The Last King of Scotland 2006, Straightheads 2007, The X Files: I Want to Believe 2008, How to Lose Friends & Alienate People 2008, Boogie Woogie 2009, Johnny Englezovich Reborn 2011, Shadow Dancer 2012, L'enfant d'en haut 2012, Mr. Morgan's Last Love 2012. *Television includes:* Home Fire Burning (film) 1992, The X-Files 1993–2002, When Planes Go Down (film) 1996, Future Fantastic (series presenter, BBC), Bleak House (series, BBC) 2005, Any Human Heart (series) 2010, The Crimson Petal and the White (mini-series) 2011, Moby Dick (series) 2011, Great Expectations (series, BBC) 2011. *Address:* 10100 Santa Monica Blvd, Suite 1300, Los Angeles, CA 90067-4003, USA. *Website:* www.gilliananderson.ws.

ANDERSON, Sir John Anthony, Kt, KBE, FCA; New Zealand banker and business executive; b. 2 Aug. 1945, Wellington; m. Carol M. Anderson 1970; two s. one d.; ed Christ's Coll. and Victoria Univ. of Wellington; with Deloitte Haskins & Sells (chartered accountants), Wellington 1962–69; with Guest & Bell (share-brokers), Melbourne 1969–72; joined South Pacific Merchant Finance Ltd, Wellington 1972, CEO and Dir 1979; Deputy Chief Exec. Nat. Bank of NZ (following merger of Southpac and Nat. Bank) 1988, CEO and Dir 1990–2005; Chair. NZ Merchant Banks Assn 1982–89, Petroleum Corpn of NZ Ltd 1986–88, NZ Bankers Assn 1992, 1999, 2000, NZ Cricket Bd 1995–2008, NZ Sports Foundation Inc. 1999–2002, Television New Zealand 2006–12, Capital and Coast District Health Bd 2007, PGG Wrightson 2010–; mem. Bd of Dirs NZ Steel Ltd 1986–87, Lloyds Merchant Bank (London) 1986–92, Lloyds Bank NZA (Australia) 1989–97; mem. Exec. Bd Int. Cricket Council 1998–2008; Pres. NZ Bankers Inst. 1990–2001; Commr Hawkes Bay Dist Health Bd 2008; fmr NZ Chair. World Wide Fund for Nature; New Zealand Commemoration Medal 1990, Blake Medal 2005. *Leisure interests:* rugby, cricket, golf, bridge. *Address:* 5 Fancourt Street, Karori, Wellington 5, New Zealand (home).

ANDERSON, John Bayard, LLM, JD; American politician; b. 15 Feb. 1922, Rockford, Ill.; s. of E. Albin Anderson and the late Mabel Ring; m. Keke Machakos 1953; one s. four d.; ed Univ. of Illinois, Harvard Law School; admitted to Ill. Bar 1946; practised law, Rockford, Ill. 1946–48, 1950–52, 1955–56; Instructor, Northeastern Univ. Law School 1948–49; State Dept Career Diplomatic Service 1952–55; Winnebago County, Ill., State's Attorney 1956–60; Congressman, 16th Dist, Ill. 1960–80; mem. US House of Reps 1960–79; Chair. House Republican Conf. 1969–79; ind. cand. for US Pres. 1980; Chair. Nat. Unity Party; Pres. and Chair. Center for Voting and Democracy 1993–2008, Chair. Emer. 2008–; Chair. FairVote 1996–2008; Visiting Prof. of Political Science, Brandeis Univ. 1985, Univ. of Mass 1985, Ore. State Univ. 1986, Nova Univ. Center for Study of Law 1987–2002; Pres. and CEO World Federalist Assn 1992–; Lecturer in Political Science, Bryn Mawr Coll. 1985; Visiting Prof. of Law, Washington Coll. of Law of American Univ., Washington, DC 1997; Hon. LLD (Ill., Wheaton Coll., Shimer Coll., Biola Coll., Geneva Coll., North Park Coll., Houghton Coll., Trinity Coll., Rockford Coll.). *Publications:* Between Two Worlds: A Congressman's Choice 1970, Vision and Betrayal in America 1975, Congress and Conscience (ed.) 1970, The American Economy We Need But Won't Get 1984, A Proper Institution: Guaranteeing Televised Presidential Debates 1988. *Leisure interest:* writing occasional commentary or opinion piece on political affairs, lecturing. *Address:* 4120 48th Street, NW, Washington DC 20016, USA (home). *Telephone:* (202) 546-3950 (home). *Fax:* (202) 362-1831 (home). *E-mail:* jbafed@aol.com (home).

ANDERSON, John Duncan, AO, MA; Australian fmr politician; b. 14 Nov. 1956; s. of D. A. Anderson; m. Julia Gillian Robertson 1987; one s. three d.; ed Kings School, Parramatta, St Paul's Coll., Univ. of Sydney; fmr farmer and grazier; MP for Gwydir, NSW 1989–2007; Deputy Leader Nat. Party of Australia 1993–99, Leader 1999–2005; Shadow Minister for Primary Industries 1993–96; Minister for Primary Industries and Energy 1996–98, for Transport and Regional Devt 1997–2005, Deputy Prime Minister 1999–2005 (resgnd). *Leisure interests:* farming, shooting, reading, photography, motoring. *Address:* 206 Conadilly Street, Gunnedah, NSW 2380, Australia (home).

ANDERSON, June, BA; American singer (soprano); b. 30 Dec. 1952, Boston; ed Yale Univ.; opera, concert and oratorio singer; debut with New York City Opera in the Magic Flute 1978, European debut as Semiramide at Rome Opera; performances at most major opera houses in USA and Europe, for companies including Metropolitan Opera, New York, Milwaukee Florentine Opera, San Diego Opera, Seattle Opera, Chicago Lyric Opera, Royal Opera, London, La Scala, Milan, Opéra de Paris, Teatro Colon, Buenos Aires, Gran Teatre del Liceu, Barcelona, Wiener Staatsoper, La Fenice, Venice; has worked with conductors including Leonard Bernstein, James Conlon, Charles Dutoit, Daniele Gatti, James Levine, Zubin Mehta, Riccardo Muti, Seiji Ozawa; Commdr, Ordre des Arts et des Lettres; Bellini d'Oro Prize, Grammy Award for Best Classical Album (for Bernstein: Candide) 1991. *Roles include:* Queen of the Night in The Magic Flute, New York City Opera 1978, title role in Lucia di Lammermoor, Milwaukee Florentine Opera 1982 and Chicago 1990, Gulnara in Il Corsaro, San Diego Opera Verdi Festival 1982, I Puritani, Edmonton Opera 1982–83, title role in Semiramide, Rome Opera 1982–83 and Metropolitan Opera 1990, Rosina in The Barber of Seville, Seattle Opera and Teatro Massimo 1982–83, Cunégonde in Candide 1989, Metropolitan Opera debut as Gilda in Rigoletto 1989, title role in Luisa Miller, La Fenice, Venice 2006; Dialogues des Carmélites at Opéra de Nice and Salome at Opéra Royal de Wallonie 2011, Adams' Nixon in China at Théâtre du Châtelet, Paris 2012; concert and oratorio vocalist: Chicago Pops Orchestra, Handel Festival Kennedy Center, Denver Symphony, St Louis Symphony, Cincinnati Symphony, Maracaibo (Venezuela) Symphony; first Messa di Requiem by Verdi in Paris 2007; concerts/recitals/festivals in Canada, France, Palestine and Israel 2012. *Address:* c/o Hazard Chase, 25 City Road, Cambridge, CB1 1DP, England (office). *E-mail:* info@hazardchase.co.uk (office). *Website:* www.hazardchase.co.uk (office); www.june-anderson.com.

ANDERSON, Laurie P., MFA; American performance artist, musician (keyboards, violin) and writer; b. 5 June 1947, Wayne, Ill.; d. of Arthur T. Anderson and Mary Louise Anderson (née Rowland); m. Lou Reed 2008 (died 2013); ed Columbia Univ., Barnard Coll.; instructor in Art History, City Coll., CUNY 1973–75; freelance critic, Art News, Art Forum; composer and performer in multi-media exhbns; Artist-in-Residence, ZBS Media 1974, NASA 2005–; Distinguished Artist-In-Residence, Experimental Media and Performing Arts Center, Rensselaer

Polytechnic Institute 2012–; Guggenheim Fellow 1983; Dr hc (Art Inst. of Chicago), (Philadelphia Coll. of the Arts); Gish Prize 2007. *Film performances:* Carmen, Personal Service Announcements, Beautiful Red Dress, Talk Normal, Alive From Off Center, What You Mean We?, Language Is A Virus, This Is The Picture, Sharkey's Day, Dear Reader, Home of the Brave (writer, dir, performer) 1986, Puppet Motel (CD-ROM) 1995. *Recordings include:* O Superman 1981, Big Science 1982, United States 1983, Mister Heartbreak 1984, Strange Angels 1989, Bright Red 1994, The Ugly One With The Jewels And Other Stories 1995, Life on a String 2001, Live At Town Hall, New York City 2002, Homeland 2010; film scores: Home Of The Brave 1986, Swimming To Cambodia, Monster In A Box. *Publications include:* The Package 1971, October 1972, Transportation, Transportation 1973, The Rose and the Stone 1974, Notebook 1976, Artifacts at the End of a Decade 1981, Typisch Frac 1981, United States 1984, Empty Places: A Performance 1989, Laurie Anderson's Postcard Book 1990, Stories from the Nerve Bible 1993, Night Life 2007. *Address:* Curtis R. Priem Experimental Media and Performing Arts Center, Rensselaer Polytechnic Institute, 110 8th Street, Troy, NY 12180, USA (office). *Telephone:* (518) 276-3921 (office). *E-mail:* studio@difficultmusic.com (office). *Website:* www.laurieanderson.com (office); empac.rpi.edu (office).

ANDERSON, Michael; British film director; b. 30 Jan. 1920, London; started career as Production Runner, Elstree Studios 1936, Asst Dir 1938; later joined Associated British Pictures. *Films include:* (Co-Dir) Private Angelo (with Peter Ustinov) 1949; (Dir) Waterfront 1950, Hell is Sold Out 1952, Night Was Our Friend, Dial 17, Will Any Gentleman?, The House of The Arrow 1952, The Dam Busters 1954, Around the World in Eighty Days 1956, Yangtse Incident 1957, Chase a Crooked Shadow 1957, Shake Hands with the Devil 1958, Wreck of the Mary Deare 1959–60, All the Fine Young Cannibals 1960, The Naked Edge 1961, Flight from Ashiya (in Japan) 1962, Operation Crossbow 1964, The Quiller Memorandum 1966, The Shoes of The Fisherman 1969, Pope Joan 1970–71, Doc Savage (in Hollywood) 1973, Conduct Unbecoming 1974, Logan's Run (MGM Hollywood) 1975, Orca—Killer Whale 1976, Dominique 1977, Bells 1979–80, Murder by Phone, Second Time Lucky, Separate Vacations, Jeweller's Shop 1989, Millennium, Summer of the Monkeys 1998, The New Adventures of Pinocchio 1999. *Television:* The Martian Chronicles 1980, Sword of Gideon 1986, Young Catherine 1991, The Sea Wolf 1993, Rugged Gold 1994, Captains Courageous 1996, 20,000 Leagues Under the Sea 1997. *Address:* c/o Film Rights Ltd, 113–117 Wardour Street, London, W1C 3TD, England.

ANDERSON, Olive Ruth, BLitt, MA, FRHistS; British historian and academic; *Emerita Professor of History, Queen Mary, University of London;* b. 27 March 1926, Edinburgh; d. of Donald H. F. Gee and Ruth Gee (née Clackson); m. Matthew Smith Anderson 1954 (died 2006); two d.; ed King Edward VI Grammar School, Louth, Lincs., St Hugh's Coll., Oxford; Asst Lecturer in History, Westfield Coll., Univ. of London 1949–56, Lecturer 1958–69, Reader 1969–86, Prof. and Head of Dept 1986–89, Prof. and Deputy Head of Dept, Queen Mary & Westfield Coll. (now Queen Mary) 1989–91, Prof. Emer. and Hon. Research Fellow 1991–, Fellow 1995–; James Ford Special Lecturer, Oxford Univ. 1992; mem. Acad. Council Univ. of London 1989–91 (Exec. Cttee 1990–91); Councillor Royal Historical Soc. 1986–90, Vice-Pres. 1991–95, Hon. Vice-Pres. 2001–; Trustee Theodora Bosanquet Trust 1995–98; mem. Finance Cttee British Fed. of Women Grads Charitable Foundation 1996–99, Grants Cttee 1998–2002. *Publications:* A Liberal State at War 1967, Suicide in Victorian and Edwardian England 1987; regular contrib. to leading journals of historical research 1954–97. *Address:* 45 Cholmeley Crescent, Highgate, London, N6 5EX, England (home).

ANDERSON, Paul G. (Pete), BS; American business executive; *Vice-Chairman and President, INTL FCStone Inc.;* ed Truman Univ.; managed and worked for three cooperative farms in Kan. 1976–87; joined Farmers Commodities Corpn 1987, developed and was Div. Man. Integrated Marketing Program –1995; with FCStone since 1987, Vice-Pres. of Operations 1995–99, Pres. and CEO 1999–2009, Pres. INTL FCStone Inc. (following merger with International Assets Holding Corpn) 2009–, currently also Vice-Chair.; Past Pres. Kansas Cooperative Council; Past Founding Chair. Arthur Capper Cooperative Center, Kansas State Univ.; mem. Bd of Dirs Associated Benefits Corpn; mem. Nat. Council of Farmer Cooperatives, Nat. Feed and Grain Asscn and several other state asscns. *Address:* INTL FCStone Inc., 708 Third Avenue, 15th Floor, New York, NY 10017, USA (office). *Telephone:* (212) 485-3500 (office). *Fax:* (212) 485-3505 (office). *E-mail:* info@intlfcstone.com (office). *Website:* www.intlfcstone.com (office).

ANDERSON, Paul M., BS, MBA; Australian business executive; b. 1 April 1945, USA; m. Kathy Anderson; two d.; ed Univ. of Washington, Stanford Univ., USA; joined Ford Motor Co. 1969, Planning Man. 1972–74; Dir Corp. Planning, Texas Eastern Corpn 1977–80, Pres. Texas Eastern Synfuels Inc. and Project Dir Tri-State Synfuels Co. 1980–82, Vice-Pres. Planning and Eng, Texas Eastern Corpn 1982–85, Sr Vice-Pres. Financial and Diversified Operations 1985–90; Vice-Pres. Finance and Chief Finance Officer Inland Steel Industries Inc. 1990–91; Exec. Vice-Pres., then Pres. Panhandle Eastern Pipe Line Co. 1991–93; Pres. and CEO PanEnergy Corpn 1995–97, Chair. 1997, Dir, Pres., COO Duke Energy Corpn (after merger between Duke Power and PanEnergy Corpn 1997) 1997–98, Chair. and CEO 2003–07; Man. Dir and CEO Broken Hill Pty Co. Ltd (later BHP Ltd, now BHP-Billiton) 1998–2002; mem. Bd of Dirs BAE Systems PLC, Spectra Energy (Chair. 2007–09), BP plc 2010–. *Leisure interest:* motorcycling. *Address:* c/o Board of Directors, BP plc, 1 St. James's Square, London, SW1Y 4PD, England.

ANDERSON, Paul S., BS, PhD; American chemist; b. 3 Feb. 1938, Concord, Vermont; ed Univs of Vermont and New Hampshire; Postdoctoral appointment with Prof. Meinwald at Cornell Univ., NY; joined Merck Sharp & Dohme Research Labs 1964, Sr Research Chemist, Medicinal Chem. Dept 1964–69, Research Fellow 1969–73, Sr Research Fellow 1973–75, Assoc. Dir Medicinal Chem. Dept 1975–79, Sr Dir 1979–80, Exec. Dir 1980–88, Vice-Pres. for Chem. at West Point research facility 1988–94 (retd); worked in DuPont-Merck Pharmaceuticals Co. (became Dupont Pharmaceuticals Co. 1998) 1994–98, Sr Vice-Pres. for Chemical and Physical Sciences 1998–2001, co. acquired by Bristol-Myers Squibb 2001, Vice-Pres. Drug Discovery, Bristol-Myers Squibb 2001–02; Chair. Medicinal Chem. Div., ACS 1987, Gordon Research Conf. on Medicinal Chem. 1991; Pres. ACS 1997; mem. Bd Dirs MDS, Inc., Albany Molecular Research, Inc. 2002–, Chemical Heritage Foundation; Trustee, Gordon Research Confs; mem. Scientific Advisory

Bd Vertex Pharmaceuticals, Inc. 2004–; mem. NIH Study Section on Bioorganic Chem. and Natural Products 1985–88, Chair. 1988–89; fmr mem. NIH Nat. Advisory Gen. Medicinal Sciences Council, Nat. Research Council, Bd on Chemical Sciences and Tech.; Founding mem. Exec. Advisory Council Univ. of Kansas School of Pharmacy; Hon. DSc (Univ. of Vermont, Univ. of Montpelier) 1998; Hon. DChem (Univ. of New Hampshire) 2001; ACS (Philadelphia Section) Award 1992, ACS E. B. Hershberg Award 1995, ACS Award in Industrial Chem. 2001, Perkin Medal, Soc. for Chemical Industry 2002, Nat. Acad. of Sciences Award for Chem. in Service to Soc. 2003, ACS Priestley Medal 2006.

ANDERSON, Paul Thomas; American film director and producer; b. 26 June 1970, Studio City, Calif.; s. of the late Ernie Anderson; partner Maya Rudolph; two d.; ed Montclair Coll. Prep. High School; began career as production Asst on TV films. *Films include:* The Dirk Diggler Story 1988, Cigarettes and Coffee 1993, Hard Eight 1996, Boogie Nights (Boston Soc. of Film Critics Award) 1997, Magnolia (Berlin Film Festival Golden Bear) 1999, Punch-Drunk Love (Cannes Film Festival Best Dir) 2002, Couch (TV) 2003, Blossoms and Blood 2003, There Will Be Blood (Berlin Film Festival Silver Bear for Best Dir) 2007, The Master 2012. *Address:* c/o CAA, 2000 Avenue of the Stars, Los Angeles, CA 90067, USA (office). *Website:* www.ptanderson.info.

ANDERSON, Porter Warren, Jr, BA, MA, PhD; American microbiologist and academic; *Professor Emeritus of Pediatrics, University of Rochester;* b. 1 Jan. 1937, Corinth, Miss.; ed Emory Univ., Harvard Univ.; Research Trainee, Oak Ridge Nat. Lab. 1957; Asst Chemist, Tropical Research Dept, United Fruit Co., Honduras 1959–61; mem. Faculty, Dept of Chem., Stillman Coll., Tuscaloosa, Ala 1966–68; Research Assoc., Children's Hosp. Medical Center, Boston 1968–77; Asst Prof., Harvard Univ. 1972–75, Assoc. Prof. 1975–77; Assoc. . Prof., Dept of Pediatrics and Microbiology, Univ. of Rochester School of Medicine and Dentistry, NY 1977–87, Prof. 1987–95, now Prof. Emer. of Pediatrics; mem. NAS; Albert Lasker Clinical Research Award 1996. *Address:* c/o University of Rochester Medical Center, Department of Pediatrics, 601 Elmwood Avenue, Rochester, NY 14642, USA.

ANDERSON, Reid Bryce; Canadian ballet director; *Artistic Director, The Stuttgart Ballet;* b. 1 April 1949, New Westminster, BC; ed Dolores Kirkwood Acad., Burnaby, Royal Ballet School, London; Prin. Dancer, Stuttgart Ballet 1969–83, Ballet Master 1983–85; Artistic Dir Ballet of British Columbia 1987–89, Nat. Ballet of Canada 1989–96, Stuttgart Ballet 1996–; has staged works for Royal Ballet, Royal Danish Ballet, Ballet of the Teatro alla Scala in Milan, Australian Ballet, Deutsche Staatsoper in Berlin, Hamburg Ballett, Teatro de Colon in Buenos Aires, Boston Ballet, Rome Opera Ballet, Norwegian National Ballet, Nat. Ballet of China, Ballet of the Vienna State Opera, San Francisco Ballet, American Ballet Theater, Opera nationale de Paris Ballet; Bundesverdienstkreuz; John Cranko Prize 1989, 1996, Deutscher Tanzpreis 2006, Dir of the Year, Dance Europe (dance magazine) 2006, Verdienstmedaille of Baden-Wurttemberg 2009. *Address:* Stuttgarter Ballett, Oberer Schlossgarten 6, 70173 Stuttgart, Germany (office). *Telephone:* (711) 2032235 (office). *Fax:* (711) 2032491 (office). *Website:* www.stuttgart-ballet.de (office).

ANDERSON, Richard H., BA, JD; American airline industry executive; *CEO, Delta Air Lines, Inc.;* b. Galveston, Tex.; m. Susan Anderson; ed Univ. of Houston, Clear Lake, South Texas Coll. of Law; joined Continental Airlines 1987, served as Staff Vice-Pres. and Deputy Gen. Counsel; joined Northwest Airlines 1990, served as Sr Vice-Pres., Tech. Operations and Airport Affairs, Exec. Vice-Pres., COO and CEO 2001–04; Exec. Vice-Pres. UnitedHealth Group 2004–07, also served as Pres. Commercial Markets Group; mem. Bd of Dirs and CEO Delta Air Lines, Inc. 2007– (merged with Northwest Airlines 2010); Chair. Airlines for America (fmrly Air Transport Asscn of America), Bd Govs of Int. Air Transport Asscn 2013–; mem. Bd of Dirs Medtronic, Inc., Cargill; Chevalier, Légion d'honneur 2011; Airline Strategy Award for Executive Leadership, Airline Business magazine and Spencer Stuart global exec. search firm 2010, The Sandra Taub Humanitarian Award, Breast Cancer Research Foundation 2011. *Address:* Delta Air Lines Inc., PO Box 20706, 1030 Delta Blvd, Atlanta, GA 30320-6001, USA (office). *Telephone:* (404) 715-2600 (office). *Fax:* (404) 715-5042 (office). *E-mail:* info@delta.com (office). *Website:* www.delta.com (office).

ANDERSON, Robert Geoffrey William, BSc, MA, DPhil, FRSE; British academic and museum director; *Vice-President, Clare Hall, Cambridge;* b. 2 May 1944, London, England; s. of the late Herbert Patrick Anderson and Kathleen Diana Burns; m. 1st Margaret Elizabeth Callis Lea 1973; two s.; m. 2nd Jane Virginia Portal; ed Woodhouse School, London, St John's Coll., Oxford (Casberd Exhibitioner); Asst Keeper, Royal Scottish Museum, Edinburgh 1970–75, Dir 1984–85; Asst Keeper, Science Museum, London 1975–80, Keeper 1980–84; Dir Nat. Museums of Scotland 1985–92; Dir British Museum, London 1992–2002; Curator, School of Advanced Study, Univ. of London 1994–2002, Bd mem. Warburg Inst. 1993–97; currently Vice-Pres. and Fellow, Clare Hall, Cambridge; Pres. British Soc. for the History of Science 1988–90, Scientific Instrument Comm. of the Int. Union of the History and Philosophy of Science 1982–97; Visiting Fellow, Inst. for Advanced Study, Princeton, USA 2002–03, Centre for Research in Arts, Social Sciences and Humanities, Univ. of Cambridge 2003, Churchill Coll. 2003–04, Corpus Christi Coll. 2004–05; mem. Editorial Bd Ambix, Annals of Science, Journal of the History of Collecting; Pres. Asscn of Ind. Libraries 2003–; Chair. Soc. for History of Alchemy and Chem. 2007–; mem. Bd of Dirs Dutch Nat. Science Museum, Boerhaave Museum, Leiden 1995–99; mem. Bd of Visitors, Inst. for Advanced Study in Humanities, Univ. of Edinburgh 1987–2000, Museum of History of Science, Univ. of Oxford 2002–; mem. Int. Acad. of History of Science 2002; Hon. FSA (Scotland) 1991, Hon. Fellow, St John's Coll. Oxford 2002; Commdr, Ordre des Arts et des Lettres 2002; Hon. DSc (Edinburgh) 1995, (Durham) 1998; Dexter Award (ACS) 1986. *Publications include:* The Playfair Collection 1978, Science in India 1982, Science, Medicine and Dissent (ed.) 1987, A New Museum for Scotland (ed.) 1990, Joseph Black: A Bibliography (with G. Fyffe) 1992, Making Instruments Count 1993, The Great Court at the British Museum 2000, Enlightening the British: Knowledge, Discovery and the Museum in the Eighteenth Century (ed.) 2003, The Correspondence of Joseph Black 2012. *Leisure interest:* books. *Address:* Clare Hall, University of Cambridge, Herschel Road, Cambridge, CB3 9AL, England (office). *Telephone:* (1223) 328049 (office). *Website:* www.clarehall.cam.ac.uk (office).

ANDERSON, Sir Roy Malcolm, Kt, PhD, DIC, FRS, FMedSci, FIBiol, ARCS; British scientist, academic and fmr university administrator; *Professor of Infectious Disease Epidemiology, Imperial College London;* b. 12 April 1947, Herts.; s. of James Anderson and Betty Watson-Weatherburn; m. 1st Dr Mary Joan Mitchell 1975 (divorced 1989); m. 2nd Claire Baron 1990; ed Duncombe School, Bengeo, Richard Hale School, Hertford, Imperial Coll., London; IBM Research Fellow, Univ. of Oxford 1971–73; Lecturer, King's Coll., London 1973–77; Lecturer, Imperial Coll. 1977–80, Reader 1980–82, Prof. of Parasite Ecology 1982–93, Head of Dept of Biology 1984–93; Chair. Dept of Infectious Disease Epidemiology, Imperial Coll. Faculty of Medicine, Univ. of London 2000–08, 2009–, Prof. of Infectious Disease Epidemiology 2007–, Rector, Imperial Coll. London 2008–10; Linacre Prof., Univ. of Oxford 1993–2000, Head of Dept of Zoology 1993–98, Dir The Wellcome Trust Centre for the Epidemiology of Infectious Disease 1993–2000; seconded to Ministry of Defence as Chief Scientific Adviser 2003–07; Genentech Visiting Prof., Univ. of Washington, USA 1998; James McLaughlin Visiting Prof., Univ. of Texas, USA 1999; Chair. Infection and Immunity Panel for The Wellcome Trust 1990–92, Terrestrial Life Sciences Cttee, Nat. Environment Research Council, Science Advisory Council, Dept for Environment, Food and Rural Affairs (Defra) 2004–; Council mem. Natural Environment Research Council 1988–91, Advisory Council on Science and Tech. (ACOST) 1989–91, Royal Soc. 1989–92, Zoological Soc. 1988–90; mem. Bd of Dirs AIDS Policy Unit 1988–89, Spongiform Encephalopathy Advisory Cttee 1997–2003; Dir (non-exec.) GlaxoSmithKline 2007–; mem. Science Advisory Bd, Bill and Melinda Gates Foundation 'Grand Challenges in Global Health 1998–2002'; mem. Acad. of Medical Sciences 1998, Academia Europaea 1998; Trustee, The Wellcome Trust 1991–92 (Gov. 1992–2000), Natural History Museum 2008–; Patron Virgin Health Care Foundation; Fellow, Royal Soc. of Tropical Medicine and Hygiene; Fellow, Merton Coll., Oxford 1993–2000; Gov., Inst. of Govt 2008–; Foreign mem. Inst. of Medicine, NAS 2000–, French Acad. of Sciences 2010–; mem. Singapore Nat. Research Foundation, Thailand Science and Tech. Advisory Bd; Hon. FRCPath 1999–, Hon. FRSS 2002–, Hon. MRCP, Hon. Fellow Linacre Coll., Oxford 1997–; Hon. ScD (East Anglia) 1997, (Stirling) 1998, (Aberdeen) 2009; Zoological Soc. Scientific Medal 1982, Huxley Memorial Medal 1983, C.A. Wright Memorial Medal 1986, David Starr Jordan Prize 1986, Chalmers Medal 1988, Weldon Medal 1989, John Grundy Lecture Medal 1990, Frink Medal 1993, Joseph Smadel Lecture and Medal, Infectious Diseases Soc. of America 1994, Distinguished Statistical Ecologist Award 1998. *Publications:* Population Dynamics of Infectious Disease Agents: Theory and Applications (ed.) 1982, Population Biology of Infectious Diseases (co-ed. with R. M. May) 1982, Infectious Diseases of Humans: Dynamics and Control (with R. M. May) 1991. *Leisure interests:* hill walking, croquet, natural history, photography. *Address:* Department of Infectious Disease Epidemiology, Imperial College London, St Mary's Campus, Norfolk Place, London, W2 1PG, England (office). *Telephone:* (20) 7594-3399 (office). *E-mail:* roy.anderson@imperial.ac.uk (office). *Website:* www3.imperial.ac.uk (office).

ANDERSON, Ruth, BA; British professional business services executive; *Vice-Chairman, KPMG LLP;* b. Northern Ireland; ed Univ. of Bradford; joined KPMG LLP (UK unit of KPMG) 1976, apptd Partner 1989, mem. Bd Dirs (first woman on bd of large professional services firm in UK) 1998–2004, Vice-Chair. 2005–. *Leisure interests:* theatre, cinema, gardening. *Address:* KPMG LLP, 8 Salisbury Square, London, EC4Y 8BB, England (office). *Telephone:* (20) 7311-1000 (office). *E-mail:* ruth.anderson@kpmg.co.uk (office). *Website:* www.kpmg.co.uk (office).

ANDERSON, Theodore Wilbur, BS, MA, PhD; American statistician and academic; *Professor Emeritus of Statistics and Economics, Stanford University;* b. 5 June 1918, Minneapolis, Minn.; s. of Theodore Wilbur Anderson and Evelynn Johnson Anderson; m. Dorothy Fisher 1950; one s. two d.; ed North Park Coll., Northwestern Univ., Princeton Univ.; Research Assoc. Cowles Comm. for Research in Econs, Univ. of Chicago 1945–46; Instructor in Math. Statistics, Columbia Univ. 1946–47, Asst Prof. to Prof. 1947–67, Chair. of Dept 1956–60, 1964–65, Dir Office of Naval Research, Dept of Math. Statistics 1950–68; Research Consultant, Cowles Foundation for Research in Econs 1946–60; Guggenheim Fellow, Univs of Stockholm and Cambridge 1947–48; Consultant, RAND Corpn 1949–66; Fellow, Center for Advanced Study in the Behavioral Sciences 1957–58, Visiting Scholar 1972–73, 1980; Visiting Prof. of Statistics, Univ. of Paris 1967–68; Prof. of Statistics and Econs, Stanford Univ. 1967–88, Prin. Investigator NSF Project, Dept of Econs 1969–83, Dept of Statistics 1983–92; Academic Visitor, LSE 1974–75, Univ. of Southern Calif. 1989; Distinguished Scholar, Calif. Inst. of Tech. 1980; S.S Wilks Memorial Lecturer, Princeton Univ. 1983; Prin. Investigator Army Research Office Project, Dept of Statistics 1982–92; Visiting Prof. of Econs, Columbia Univ. 1983–84, New York Univ. 1983–84, Univ. of Moscow; Research Assoc. Naval Postgraduate School 1986–87; Visiting Distinguished Prof. of Norwegian Council for Scientific and Industrial Research, Univ. of Oslo 1989; Academic Visitor, Imperial Coll. of Science and Tech., UK; Pres. Inst. of Math. Statistics 1963; mem. Council; Vice-Pres. American Statistical Soc. 1971–73; Chair. Section U, Statistics, AAAS 1990–91; Sabbaticant, IBM Systems Research Inst. 1984; ed. and fmr ed. of numerous specialist journals; Fellow, Acad. of Arts and Sciences 1974–, AAAS, American Statistical Asscn, Econometric Soc., Inst. of Math. Statistics (mem. of Council), Royal Statistical Soc.; mem. NAS 1976–, Econometric Soc., American Math. Soc., Bernoulli Soc. for Math. Statistics and Probability, Int. Statistical Inst., Psychometric Soc., Indian Statistical Inst., Statistical Soc. of Canada; Foreign mem. Norwegian Acad. of Science and Letters 1994; Hon. DLit (North Park Coll. and Theological Seminary) 1988; Hon. DSc (Northwestern Univ.) 1989; Dr hc (Univ. of Athens)(Univ. of Oslo) 1997; R. A. Fisher Award, Cttee of Pres. of Statistical Socs 1985, Distinguished Alumnus Award, North Park Coll. and Theological Seminary 1987, Samuel S. Wilks Memorial Medal, American Statistical Asscn 1988, Award of Merit, Northwestern Univ. Alumni Asscn 1989, Distinguished Alumnus Award, Minnehaha Acad. 1992. *Publications include:* An Introduction to Multivariate Statistical Analysis 1958, 1984, 2003, The Statistical Analysis of Time Series 1971, A Bibliography of Multivariate Statistical Analysis (with S. D. Gupta and G. Styan) 1972, Introductory Statistical Analysis (with S. Sclove) 1974, An Introduction to the Statistical Analysis of Data (with S. Sclove) 1978, 1986, A Guide to MINITAB for the Statistical Analysis of Data (with B. Eynon) 1986, Collected Papers of T.W. Anderson 1943–85 1990, The New Statistical Analysis of Data (with J.D. Finn) 1996 and some 170 articles in statistical journals. *Leisure interests:* tennis,

swimming, travelling. *Address:* 746 Santa Ynez Street, Stanford, CA 94305-8441, USA (home). *Telephone:* (650) 327-5204 (home).

ANDERSON, Wesley (Wes) Wales; American film director; b. 1 May 1969, Houston, Tex.; ed St John's School, Univ. of Tex.; Best New Filmmaker Award, MTV Movie Awards 1996. *Films:* dir, writer, producer: Bottle Rocket (short) 1994, Bottle Rocket 1996, Rushmore (Best Dir, Ind. Spirit Awards, New Generation Award, LA Film Critics Asscn) 1998, The Royal Tenenbaums 2001, The Life Aquatic with Steve Zissou 2004, The Darjeeling Limited 2007, Fantastic Mr Fox 2009, Moonrise Kingdom 2012, The Grand Budapest Hotel 2014; producer: The Squid and the Whale 2005. *Address:* c/o United Talent Agency Inc., 9560 Wilshire Boulevard, Suite. 500, Beverly Hills, CA 90212, USA (office). *Telephone:* (310) 273-6700 (office). *Website:* www.wesanderson.org.

ANDERSON, Sir (William) Eric (Kinloch), Kt, KT, MA, DLitt, FRSE; British educationalist; b. 27 May 1936, Edinburgh, Scotland; s. of W. J. Kinloch Anderson and Margaret Harper; m. Anne Elizabeth Mason 1960; one s. one d.; ed George Watson's Coll., Univ. of St Andrews, Balliol Coll., Oxford; Asst Master, Fettes Coll., Edinburgh 1960–64, 1966–70, Gordonstoun School 1964–66; Headmaster, Abingdon School 1970–75, Shrewsbury School 1975–80, Eton Coll. 1980–94, Provost 2000–09; Rector, Lincoln Coll. Oxford 1994–2000; mem. Visiting Cttee of Memorial Church, Harvard 2001–07; Trustee, Nat. Heritage Memorial Fund 1996–98 (Chair. 1998–2001), Royal Collection Fund 2000–06, Shakespeare Birthplace Trust 2001–, Abbotsford Trust 2012–; Chair. Cumberland Lodge 1997–2009; Visitor, Harris Manchester Coll., Oxford 2001–; Hon. DLitt (St Andrews, Hull, Siena, Birmingham, Aberdeen). *Publications:* The Journal of Walter Scott (ed.) 1972, The Percy Letters (Vol. IX) 1988, The Sayings of Sir Walter Scott 1995, About Eton 2010; articles and reviews. *Leisure interests:* theatre, golf, fishing. *Address:* The Homestead, Kingham, OX7 6YA, England (office). *E-mail:* anderson1616@btinternet.com (home). *Website:* www.etoncollege.com (office).

ANDERSSON, Bertil, BSc, MSc, PhD, DSc; Swedish biochemist, academic and university administrator; *President, Nanyang Technological University;* ed Umeå Univ., Lund Univ.; apptd Prof. of Biochemistry, Stockholm Univ. 1986, Head of Dept of Biochemistry, then Dean of Faculty of Chemical Sciences 1996–99; Rector (Pres.) Linköping Univ. 1999–2003, Prof. of Biochemistry 2004–; Adjunct Prof., Umeå Univ.; Visiting Prof. and Fellow, Imperial Coll. London, UK; Chief Exec. European Science Foundation, Strasbourg 2004–07; Provost, Nanyang Technological Univ. 2007–11, Pres. 2011–; mem. Nobel Cttee for Chem. (Chair. 1997) 1989–97, Nobel Foundation 2000–06 (also mem. Bd of Trustees); Vice-Pres. Research Advisory Bd European Comm. (EURAB) 2004–07; Chair. Global Alliance of Technological Univs; Swedish Rep. of Fed. of European Biochemical Socs 1988–90; mem. Bd Swedish Agricultural and Forestry Research Council –Chem. 1989–96, Swedish Natural Science Research Council 1991–98; Chair. Swedish Biochemical Soc. 1988–90, Swedish Nat. Cttee for Biochemistry and Molecular Biology 1991–94; mem. Forskningsforum (Forum for Swedish Science) 2001–03; Adviser to Swedish Govt on new research funding mechanisms 2003–04, to Swedish Ministry for Science and Educ. 2003, 2006–09; mem. Bd Kalmar Univ. Coll. 2004–07, Bd Körber Foundation, Hamburg 2005, Governing Bd Singapore Centre on Environmental Life Sciences Eng, Bd Building and Construction Authority, A*STAR Singapore (Govt agency for nat. scientific research and devt); fmr mem. Royal Swedish Acad. of Sciences, Australian Acad. of Sciences, Academia Europaea; Dr hc from several univs, including Hebrew Univ. of Jerusalem, Israel and Univ. of New South Wales, Australia; Wilhelm Exner Medal 2011. *Publications:* more than 300 papers in professional journals on photosynthesis research, biological membranes, protein and membrane purification, light stress in plants, also several articles devoted to popular sciences and science policy. *Address:* Office of the President, Nanyang Technological University, ADM 06-06, 50 Nanyang Avenue, Singapore 639798 (office). *Telephone:* 65148331 (office). *Fax:* 67911604 (office). *E-mail:* bertil.andersson@ntu.edu.sg (office). *Website:* www.ntu.edu.sg (office).

ANDERSSON, Bibi; Swedish actress; b. (Berit Elisabeth Andersson), 11 Nov. 1935; d. of Josef Andersson and Karin Andersson; m. 1st Kjell Grede 1960 (divorced); one d.; m. 2nd Per Ahlmark (q.v.) 1978 (divorced); m. 3rd Gabriel Mora Baeza; ed Terserus Drama School and Royal Dramatic Theatre School, Stockholm; Malmö Theatre 1956–59, Royal Dramatic Theatre, Stockholm 1959–62, 1966–; appearances at Uppsala Theatre 1962–. *Plays include:* Erik XIV 1956, Tre systrar 1961, King John 1961, Le balcon 1961, La grotte 1962, Uncle Vanya 1962, Who's Afraid of Virginia Woolf? 1963, As You Like It 1964, After the Fall 1964–65, The Full Circle 1973, Twelfth Night 1975, The Night of the Tribades 1977, Twelfth Night 1980, Antigone 1981, A Streetcar Named Desire 1981, 1983, L'oiseau bleu 1981, Prisoners of Altona 1982, The Creditors 1984–85, Ett gästabud i Pestens tid 1986, Loner 1994. *Films include:* Sjunde inseglet (The Seventh Seal) 1956, Smultronstället (Wild Strawberries) 1957, Nära livet (The Brink of Life) 1958, Sommarnöje Sökes (Summer House Wanted) 1958, Djävulens öga (Eye of the Devil) 1961, Älskarinnen (The Mistress) 1962, För att inte tala om alla dessa kvinnor (All Those Women) 1964, Juninatt (June Night) 1965, Ön (The Island) 1965, Syskonbädd (My Sister, My Love) 1966, Persona 1966, Duel at Diablo 1966, Story of a Woman 1968, The Girls 1969, The Kremlin Letter 1970, A Passion, The Touch 1971, Scenes from a Marriage 1974, I Never Promised You a Rose Garden, La rivale 1976, An Enemy of the People 1976, Quintet 1979, Svarte Fugler 1982, Berget på månens baksida 1982, The Hill on the Other Side of the Moon 1983, Sista leken 1984, Huomenna 1986, Pobre mariposa 1986, Svart gryning 1987, Babette's Feast 1987, Fordringsägare 1988, Litt et Art 1989, A Passing Season 1992, The Butterfly's Dream 1994, Drømspel 1994, Det blir aldrig som man tänkt sig 2000, Elina: Som om jag inte fanns 2002, När mörkret faller 2006, När: Riket vid vägens slut 2008, The Frost 2009. *Television:* Wallenberg: A Hero's Story 1985, Måsen 1988, The Secret of Nandy 1990, Till Julia 1991, Blank päls och starka tassar 1993, Längtans blåa blomma (miniseries) 1998, The Lost Prince 2003, Return of the Dancing Master 2004.

ANDERSSON, Claes, DMed; Finnish politician, psychiatrist, writer and poet; b. 30 May 1937, Helsinki; s. of Oscar Andersson and Ethel Hjelt; m. Katriina Kuusi 1970; six c.; novelist and poet 1974–; mem. Parl. 1987–99, 2007–08; Minister, Ministry of Educ. 1995–98; fmrly mem. Finnish People's Democratic League 1970–90, mem. Left-Wing Alliance 1990–, Chair. 1990; Chair. Finland's Swedish Union of Writers; Vice-Pres. Information Centre of Finnish Literature 1985–;

Eino-Leino Prize 1985, five times recipient of State Prize of Literature, Bellmanpriset 2007. *Music:* album: Claes Andersson Trio: These Foolish Things - Jazz! 2011. *Publications include:* novels: Bakom bilderna 1972, Den fagraste vår 1976, En mänske börjar likna sin själ 1983, Mina tolv politiska år 2000, Har de sett öknen blomma? 2006, Ottos liv 2011; poetry: Ventil 1962, Som om ingenting hänt 1964, Staden heter Helsingfors 1965, Samhället vi dör i 1967, Det är inte lätt att vara villaägare i dessa tider 1969, Bli, tillsammans 1970, Rumskamrater 1974, Jag har mött dem 1976, Genom sprickorna i vårt ansikte 1977, Trädens sånger 1979, Tillkortakommanden 1981, Under 1984, Det som blev ord i mig 1987, Mina bästa dagar 1987, Som lyser mellan gallren 1989, Huden där den är som tunnasi 1991, Dikter från havets botten 1993, En lycklig mänska 1996, Dessa underbara stränder, förber glidande 2002, Mörkret regnar stjärnor 2002, Det är kallt, det brinner 2004, Tidens framfart 2005, Lust 2008, Mörkrets klarhet 2010, Oton elämä 2011; 20 stage plays and several radio plays and an opera libretto. *Leisure interest:* amateur jazz piano.

ANDERSSON, Göran Bror (Benny); Swedish composer and musician (keyboards); b. 16 Dec. 1946, Stockholm; m. 1st Frida Lyngstad 1978 (divorced 1981); m. 2nd Mona Nörklit 1981; two s. one d.; songwriter with Björn Ulvæus 1966–; duo with Ulvæus as The Hootennanny Singers; partner in production with Ulvæus at Polar Music 1971; mem. pop group, ABBA 1973–82; winner, Eurovision Song Contest 1974; worldwide tours; concerts include Royal Performance, Stockholm 1976, Royal Albert Hall, London 1977, UNICEF concert, New York 1979, Wembley Arena 1979; reunion with ABBA, Swedish TV This Is Your Life 1986; continued writing and producing with Ulvæus 1982–; produced musical Mamma Mia! with Ulvæus, West End, London 1999–; World Music Award for Best Selling Swedish Artist 1993, Ivor Novello Special International Award (with Björn Ulvaeus) 2002. *Films:* ABBA: The Movie 1977, Mamma Mia! 2008. *Compositions include:* ABBA songs (with Ulvaeus); musicals: Chess (with lyrics by Tim Rice) 1983, Mamma Mia! (with Ulvaeus) 1999, Kristina Från Duvemåla (based on Vilhelm Moberg's epic novels, Utvandrarna). *Recordings:* albums: with Ulvaeus: Happiness 1971; with ABBA: Waterloo 1974, ABBA 1976, Greatest Hits 1976, Arrival 1977, The Album 1978, Voulez-Vous 1979, Greatest Hits Vol. 2 1979, Super Trouper 1980, The Visitors 1981, The Singles: The First Ten Years 1982, Thank You For The Music 1983, Absolute ABBA 1988, ABBA Gold 1992, More ABBA Gold 1993, Forever Gold 1998, The Definitive Collection 2001; solo: Story of a Heart 2009; singles include: with ABBA: Ring Ring 1973, Waterloo 1974, Mamma Mia 1975, Dancing Queen 1976, Fernando 1976, Money Money Money 1976, Knowing Me Knowing You 1977, The Name Of The Game 1977, Take A Chance On Me 1978, Summer Night City 1978, Chiquitita 1979, Does Your Mother Know? 1979, Angel Eyes/Voulez-Vous 1979, Gimme Gimme Gimme (A Man After Midnight) 1979, I Have A Dream 1979, The Winner Takes It All 1980, Super Trouper 1980, On And On And On 1981, Lay All Your Love On Me 1981, One Of Us 1981, When All Is Said And Done 1982, Head Over Heels 1982, The Day Before You Came 1982, Under Attack 1982, Thank You For The Music 1983. *Publication:* Mamma Mia! How Can I Resist You? (with Björn Ulvaeus and Judy Craymer) 2006. *Address:* Södra Brobänken 41A, 111 49 Stockholm, Sweden. *Website:* www.abbasite.com.

ANDERSSON, Harriet; Swedish actress; b. 14 Feb. 1932, Stockholm; began career in chorus at Oscars Theatre; subsequently appeared in reviews and then started serious dramatic career at Malmö City Theatre 1953; now appears regularly at Kunigliga Dramatiska Teatern, Stockholm; Swedish Film Asscn plaque. *Films include:* Summer with Monica 1953, Sawdust and Tinsel 1953, Women's Dreams 1955, Dreams of a Summer Night 1955, Through a Glass Darkly (German Film Critics' Grand Prize) 1961, Siska 1962, Dream of Happiness 1963, One Sunday in September 1963, All Those Women 1964, To Love (Best Actress Award, Venice Film Festival) 1964, Loving Couples 1964, For the Sake of Friendship 1965, Vine Bridge 1965, Adventure Starts Here 1965, Stimulantia 1965–66, Rooftree 1966, The Serpent 1966, The Deadly Affair 1967, The Girls 1968, Anna 1970, Cries and Whispers 1972, The Stake, Happy End 1999, Dogville 2003, Bip Bop Bip Bop Bap 2006. *Television includes:* Belinder auktioner 2003, Swedenhielms 2003. *Theatre includes:* Anne Frank in The Diary of Anne Frank, Ophelia in Hamlet, The Beggar's Opera and plays by Chekhov. *Address:* c/o Sandrew Film & Theater AB, Box 5612, 114 86 Stockholm, Sweden.

ANDERSSON, Leif Christer Leander, MD, PhD; Finnish pathologist and academic; *Professor of Pathology, University of Helsinki;* b. 24 March 1944, Esse; s. of Herman Alfons Andersson and Elvi Alina Häll; m. Nea Margareta Gustavson 1971 (died 2003); one s. two d.; ed Univ. of Helsinki; Visiting Investigator, Univ. of Uppsala, Sweden 1975–76, Scripps Clinic and Research Inst., La Jolla, Calif., USA 1989–90; Prof. of Pathology, Univ. of Helsinki 1981–; Research Prof., Finnish Acad. of Science 1987–92; Prof. of Pathology, Karolinska Inst., Stockholm, Sweden 1996–2000, Head of Pathology, Karolinska Hosp. 1997, Foreign Adjunct Prof. 2004–; Head of Diagnostics, Div. of Pathology and Medical Genetics, Helsinki Univ. Hosp. 2002–03; Chair. Finnish Cancer Inst. 2003–11; Pres. Finnish Soc. of Sciences and Letters, Helsinki 2007–10; ERC Panel mem. 2007–; Kt, First Class, Order of the White Rose of Finland 1992, Commdr, Order of the Lion of Finland 2009; Anders Jahres Medical Prize, Univ. of Oslo 1981, Finska Läkaresällskapets Prize 1985, E.J. Nyström Prize, Finnish Soc. of Sciences and Letters 2003, Runeberg Prize 2007, Liv och Hälsa Prize 2012. *Publications:* more than 350 original publs on cell biology, immunology, haematology, oncology and pathology. *Leisure interest:* happy jazz. *Address:* Department of Pathology, Haartman Institute, University of Helsinki, PO Box 21 (Haartmaninkatu 3), 00014 Helsinki, Finland (office). *Telephone:* (9) 1911 (office). *Fax:* (9) 1912-6675 (office). *E-mail:* leif .andersson@helsinki.fi (office). *Website:* www.hi.helsinki.fi/english/about/ pathology.html (office).

ANDO, Hiroyasu; Japanese diplomatist and government official; *President, The Japan Foundation;* b. 22 Nov. 1944, Kanagawa Pref., Tokyo; ed Faculty of Literature, Univ. of Tokyo, studies in USA; joined Ministry of Foreign Affairs 1970, held several posts including Asst Gen. Man. for Econ. Transactions, Sec. of the First Minister, Asst Gen. Man. for Countries of Asia 1986–88, Counsellor, Embassy in London, UK 1991, Dir, Overseas Establishments Div., Ministry of Foreign Affairs 1992–94, Deputy Dir-Gen. Econs Affairs Bureau 1994–96; Pvt. Sec. to Prime Minister 1996; Deputy Dir-Gen. Asian Affairs Bureau, Ministry of Foreign Affairs 1996–99, Envoy Extraordinary and Minister Plenipotentiary, Embassy in Washington, DC 1999–2002, Dir-Gen. Middle Eastern and African Affairs Bureau 2002–03, Consul-Gen. 2003–06, Asst Chief Cabinet Sec. 2006–08, Amb. to Italy (also accred to Albania) 2008–11; Pres. The Japan Foundation 2011–. *Address:* The Japan Foundation, 4-4-1 Yotsuya, Shinjuku-ku, Tokyo 160-0004, Japan (office). *Telephone:* (3) 5369-6051 (office). *Website:* www.jpf.go.jp (office).

ANDO, Tadao; Japanese architect; b. 13 Sept. 1941, Osaka; m. Yumiko Kato 1970; one c.; fmr professional boxer; taught himself architecture by observing bldgs in Africa, America, Europe; Founder and Dir Tadao Ando Architect and Assocs 1969–; Visiting Prof., Columbia, Harvard, Yale Univs, USA; Hon. mem. AIA, American Acad. of Arts and Letters, Royal Acad. of Arts; Gold Medal of Architecture, French Acad., Carlsberg Architecture Prize, Pritzker Prize 1995, Imperial Praemium Prize 1996, RIBA Royal Gold Medal 1997, Gold Medal, American Inst. of Architects 1997, Kyoto Prize 2002, Gold Medal, International Union of Architects 2005. *Works include:* school for Benetton, Northern Italy, the Church of Light, Osaka, Japan, Children's Museum, Hyogo, Japan, Water Temple, Osaka, Rokko Housing nr Osaka. *Publications include:* Tadao Ando 1981, Tadao Ando: Buildings, Project, Writings 1984. *Address:* Tadao Ando Architect and Associates, 5-23 Toyosaki, 2-chome, Kita-ku, Osaka 531, Japan. *Website:* www .tadao-ando.com.

ANDOR, László, MA; Hungarian economist, politician and international organization official; *Commissioner for Employment, Social Affairs and Inclusion, European Commission;* b. 1966, Zalaegerszeg; m. Erika Varsányi; two c.; ed Zrínyi Miklós Gimnázium, Zalaegerszeg, Karl Marx Univ. (now the Corvinus Univ. of Budapest), George Washington Univ., Washington, DC, USA, Univ. of Manchester, UK (British Council Fellow); researcher, Politikatörténeti Intézet (political research inst.); Fellowship, Dept of Political Science, Univ. of Oslo, Norway 1992, Dept of War Studies, King's Coll., London, UK 1995, Netherlands Inst. for Advanced Study in the Humanities and Social Sciences, Wassenaar 2001–02; fmr Visiting Fulbright Scholar, Rutgers Univ., USA; Assoc. Prof., Dept of Econ. Policy, Budapest Univ. of Econ. Sciences, King Sigismund Coll.; mem. econ. policy advisory bd to Prime Minister Ferenc Gyurcsány 2003–05; mem. Bd Econ. Section of Hungarian Socialist Party 2003–; mem. Bd of Dirs EBRD 2005–09; Commr for Employment, Social Affairs and Inclusion, EC, Brussels 2010–; Ed. leftist Hungarian quarterly social science journal, Eszmélet (Consciousness) 1993–; Széchenyi Professorship Grant 2000–03. *Publications include:* Market Failure: Structural Adjustment in Eastern Europe (co-author) 1998, Hungary on the Road to the European Union: Transition in Blue 2000. *Address:* Commissioner for Employment, Social Affairs and Inclusion, European Commission, Rue de la Loi 200, 1049 Brussels, Belgium (office). *Telephone:* (2) 298-17-42 (Spokesperson) (office); (2) 299-11-11 (switchboard) (office). *Fax:* (2) 299-19-70 (office); (2) 295-01-38 (office). *E-mail:* laszlo.andor@ec.europa.eu (office); cab-andor-contact@ec .europa.eu (office). *Website:* ec.europa.eu/commission_2010-2014/andor (office).

ANDOV, Stojan; Macedonian economist and politician; b. 1935; ed Skopje Univ., Belgrade Univ.; Co–Founder and mem. Exec. Bd Liberal Party of Macedonia 1990; Deputy Chair. Repub. Assembly, Exec. Cttee; mem. Union Veche (Parl.) of Yugoslavia; took part in negotiations between Yugoslavia and EC; Amb. of Yugoslavia to Iraq; Del. to Nat. Ass. Repub. of Macedonia 1990–, Chair. 1990–96, Pres. Nat. Ass. 2001; Acting Pres. of Macedonia Oct. 1995–Jan. 1996; Head, Reform Forces of Macedonia-Liberal Party faction, Co-Chair. 1996. *Address:* Sobranje, 1000 Skopje, 11 Oktombri bb, Macedonia (office). *Telephone:* (2) 112255 (office). *Fax:* (2) 237947 (office). *E-mail:* sgjorgi@assembly.gov.uk (office). *Website:* www.assembly.gov.mk/ sobranje.

ANDRÁSFALVY, Bertalan, PhD, DSc; Hungarian politician, ethnographer and academic; *Professor Emeritus, University of Pécs;* b. 17 Nov. 1931, Sopron; s. of Károly Andrásfalvy and Judit Mezey; m. Mária Gere; three s.; ed Budapest Univ. of Arts and Sciences; with Museum of Szekszárd 1955, Transdanubian Research Inst. of the Hungarian Acad. of Sciences 1960–76, Archives of Baranya Co. and Museum of Pécs –1985; Exec., later Dept Head Ethnographic Research Group, Hungarian Acad. of Sciences; Assoc. Prof., Univ. of Pécs 1989–93, Prof. 1993–2001, Prof. Emer. 2001–; mem. Cttee Hungarian Democratic Forum; mem. of Parl. 1990–94; Minister of Culture and Public Educ. 1990–93; Hon. mem. Finnish Literature Soc.; Grand Silver Medal with Ribbon (Austria), Order of Merit Medium Cross with Star (Hungary), Grosse Verdienstkreutz (Germany), Grand Cross of Lion's Order of Knighthood (Finland); Eriksson Prize of the Swedish Royal Acad., István Györffy Memorial Medal of Hungarian Ethnographic Soc. *Publications:* Contrasting Value Orientation of Peasant Communities, Die traditionelle Bewirtschaftung der Überschwemmungsgebiete in Ungarn, European Culture of the Hungarian People, Vom 'Nutzen' der Volkskunst und der Volkskunde, Duna-Drava Nemzeti Park (co-author) 2001, Folyamatok es Fordulopontok (co-author) 2003, Hagyomany es Jovendo: Nepismereti Tanulmanyok 2004. *Leisure interest:* gardening. *Address:* Főutca 26, 7694 Hosszúhetény, Hungary (home). *Telephone:* (72) 490-473 (home). *E-mail:* bercimari@gmail.com (home).

ANDRE, Carl; American sculptor; b. 16 Sept. 1935, Quincy, Mass; s. of George H. Andre and Margaret M. Andre (née Johnson); m. Ana Mendieta 1985 (deceased); ed Phillips Acad.; served in US Army 1955–56; moved to New York 1957; worked as freight brakeman and conductor on Pennsylvania Railroad 1960–64; first public exhbn 1964; numerous public collections in USA and Europe; Fellow, John Simon Guggenheim Memorial Foundation 1984; f. Carl Andre and Mellissa L. Kretschmer Foundation; Roswitha Haftmann Foundation Prize 2011. *Address:* PO Box 100, New York, NY 10276; 300 Mercer Street, Apt 34E, New York, NY 10003-6778, USA. *E-mail:* carlandremelissalkretschmerfound@verizon.net. *Website:* www.carlandre.net.

ANDREA, Pat; Dutch artist; b. 25 June 1942, The Hague; s. of Kees Andrea and Metty Naezer; m. 1st Cecile Hessels 1966 (divorced 1983); m. 2nd Cristina Ruiz Guiñazú 1993; three s. one d.; ed Royal Acad. of Fine Arts, The Hague; paints in figurative style, focusing on personal deformities, people in dramatic situations, sex and violence in suspense; represented in MOMA, New York, Centre Pompidou, Paris and Frissiras Museum, Athens; Prof. Ecole Nat. Supérieur des Beaux Arts, Paris 1998–, Corresp. Académie des Beaux Arts Institut de France; Royal Subsidy for painting 1963, 1972; Jacob Maris Prize 1968. *Films include:* (with Fred Compain) Du crime consideré comme un des Beaux Arts 1981, Journal de Patagonie 1985, (with Marie Binet) L'aventure Pat Andrea 2002, (with Jorge Amat) La puñalada Pat Andrea 2004. *Publications include:* (with H. P. de Boer)

Nederlands gebarenboekje 1979, 2004, (with J. Cortazar) La Puñalada 1982, Pat Andrea: conversations avec Pierre Sterckx 1993. *Address:* 52 avenue F.V.Raspail, 94110 Arcueil, France (office). *Telephone:* (1) 45-47-89-08 (office). *Fax:* (1) 45-47-89-08 (office).

ANDREANI, Jacques; French fmr diplomatist; b. 22 Nov. 1929, Paris; m. 1st Huguette de Fonclare; one s. one d.; m. 2nd Donatella Monterisi 1981; one s. one d.; ed Inst. d'Etudes Politiques, Univ. of Paris and Ecole Nat. d'Admin; Sec. French Embassy, Washington, DC 1955–60, Moscow 1961–64; Ministry of Foreign Affairs 1964–70; Deputy Rep. of France, NATO, Brussels 1970–72; Head, French Del. to CSCE, Helsinki and Geneva 1972–75; Asst Sec. for European Affairs, Ministry of Foreign Affairs 1975–79; Amb. to Egypt 1979–81; Dir of Political Affairs, Ministry of Foreign Affairs 1981–84; Amb. to Italy 1984–88; Chief of Staff, Ministry of Foreign Affairs 1988–89; Amb. to USA 1989–95; Special Asst to Minister of Foreign Affairs 1995–97; Commdr, Légion d'honneur, Ordre nat. du Mérite. *Publication:* L'Amérique et nous 2000. *Leisure interests:* arts, music, golf. *Address:* 40 rue Bonaparte, 75006 Paris, France. *Telephone:* 1-43-26-14-92. *Fax:* 1-43-26-60-82. *E-mail:* jandrean@noos.fr.

ANDREAS, G(lenn) Allen, BA, JD; American business executive (retd); b. 22 June 1943, Cedar Rapids, Ia; s. of Glenn Allen Andreas and Vera Irene Yates; m. Toni Kay Hibma 1964; one s. two d.; ed Valparaiso Univ., Ind., Valparaiso Univ. School of Law; attorney, US Treasury Dept 1969–73; with Legal Dept, Archer Daniels Midland Co. 1973–86, Treasurer 1986–89, Chief Financial Officer of European Operations 1989–94, Vice-Pres. and Counsel to Exec. Cttee 1994–96, mem. Office of CEO 1996–97, Pres. and CEO 1997–99, Chair. and CEO 1999–2006, Chair. 2006–07; mem. World Econ. Forum, Bretton Woods Cttee, Trilateral Comm.; mem. European Advisory Bd, Carlyle Group. *Leisure interest:* golf.

ANDREESSEN, Marc Lowell, BS; American entrepreneur, business executive and software engineer; *Partner, Andreessen Horowitz;* b. 9 July 1971, Cedar Falls, Ia; m. Laura Arrillaga 2006; ed Univ. of Illinois, Urbana-Champaign; raised in New Lisbon, Wis.; undergraduate intern at IBM, Austin, Tex. for one summer; also worked at Nat. Center for Supercomputing Applications, Univ. of Illinois, Urbana-Champaign, co-created, with Eric Bina, Mosaic (first widely-used web browser) 1993; moved to Calif. to work at Enterprise Integration Technologies 1993; Co-founder, with Jim Clark, and Vice-Pres. of Tech., Mosaic Communications Corpn (name later changed to Netscape Communications), distributed the Netscape Navigator web browser 1994, Mosaic source code licensed by Microsoft from Spyglass, Inc. (offshoot of Univ. of Illinois) to create Internet Explorer web browser; Netscape acquired by AOL 1999, Chief Tech. Officer 1999–2001; left Netscape to form Loudcloud (services-based Web hosting co.) 2001, sold hosting business to EDS and renamed Opsware 2003, Chair. 2003–07 (co. bought by Hewlett-Packard 2007); co-f. Ning (provides platform for social-networking websites); investor in Digg (social news website), Plazes, Netvibes, CastTV and Twitter; launched RockMelt browser project 2010; mem. Bd of Dirs Facebook, eBay, Hewlett-Packard, Bump, TinyCo, Mixed Media Labs; fmr mem. Bd of Dirs Open Media Network; Co-founder, with Ben Horowitz, Andreessen Horowitz venture capital firm 2009–, acquired a stake in Skype Ltd 2009, Kno, Inc. (digital education platform co.); one of only six inductees in World Wide Web Hall of Fame announced at first int. Conf. on World Wide Web 1994, featured on the cover of TIME magazine 1996, 1998 and other publs, named to the MIT Technology Review TR100 as one of the top 100 innovators in the world under the age of 35 1999, ranked No. 6 on Vanity Fair's New Establishment List 2011, ranked No. 1 on CNET's most influential investors list 2011, ranked No. 2 on the Forbes Midas List of Tech's Top Investors 2012, named to TIME 100 2012, Queen Elizabeth Prize for Eng (co-recipient) 2013. *Address:* Andreessen Horowitz, 2865 Sand Hill Road, Suite 101, Menlo Park, CA 94025, USA (office). *E-mail:* pmarcablog@gmail.com (office); a16z@theoutcastagency.com (office). *Website:* a16z.com (office); blog .pmarca.com.

ANDREEV, Aleksandr Fyodorovich, DrPhysSc; Russian physicist and academic; *Vice-President, Russian Academy of Sciences;* b. 10 Dec. 1939, Leningrad; s. of Fyodor Andreev and Nina Andreeva; m. Tamara Turok 1960; one d.; ed Moscow Physico-Tech. Inst.; Jr then Sr Researcher 1964–79, Prof. 1979–; Deputy Dir Kapitza Inst. for Physical Problems, USSR Acad. of Sciences 1984–91, Dir 1991–; Corresp. mem. USSR (now Russian) Acad. of Sciences 1981–87, Full mem. 1987, Vice-Pres. 1991–, currently Chair. Research Council on Low-Temperature Physics, mem. Gen. Physics and Astronomy Section, Branch of Physical Sciences; Lorentz Prof., Univ. of Leiden 1992; Ed.-in-Chief Priroda 1993–; Chair. Comm. for State Scientific Stipends; Foreign mem. Finnish Acad. of Science and Letters 2002, Georgian Acad. of Sciences 2002, Polish Acad. of Sciences 2005, National Acad. of Sciences of Ukraine 2008; mem. Scientific Council, Int. Centre of Theoretical Physics 1996–2003; Lomonosov Prize, USSR Acad. of Sciences 1984, Lenin Prize 1986, Carus-Medaille de Deutschen Akad. der Naturforscher Leopoldina, Carus-Preis der Stadt Schweinfurt 1987, Simon Memorial Prize (UK) 1995, Kapitza Gold Medal, Russian Acad. of Sciences 1999, Ind. Prize Triumph 2003, Int. Pomeranchuk Prize 2004, John Bardeen Int. Prize 2006. *Address:* Academy of Sciences, Kapitza Institute for Physical Problems, 119334 Moscow, Kosygin Street 2, Russia (office). *Telephone:* (495) 137-32-48 (office). *Fax:* (495) 651-21-25 (office). *E-mail:* andreev@kapitza.ras .ru (office). *Website:* www.kapitza.ras.ru (office).

ANDREJEVS, Georgs, DMed; Latvian politician, diplomatist, physician and scientist; b. 30 Oct. 1932, Tukums; m. Anita Andrejeva; one s. one d.; ed Latvian Medical Inst.; paramedic, Rīga first aid station 1953–59; Head of Dept, P. Stradiņa Clinic, Rīga 1959–62, Asst 1962–64, teacher 1964–74; Asst Prof., Head Dept of Surgery, Chief Anaesthesiologist and Reanimatologist of Ministry of Health 1962–92; Head of Dept and Prof., Rīga Inst. of Medicine 1974–90; Head of Dept, Latvian Acad. of Medicine 1994–95; Founder Latvijas ceļš (Latvian Way) party 1993; mem. Latvian People's Front; Deputy to Latvian Repub. Supreme Council; Sec. Comm. for Foreign Affairs of Supreme Council; Minister of Foreign Affairs 1992–94; mem. Saima (Parl.) 1993–95; Amb. to Canada 1995–98, to Council of Europe 1998–2004; Chair. Council of Europe Ministers Deputies 2000–01, Council of Europe Cttee of Ministers Working Party on Co-operation between the Council of Europe and the EU 2001–03; mem. European Parl. (Group of the Alliance of Liberals and Democrats for Europe) 2004–09, Vice-Chair. Cttee on the Environment, Public Health and Food Safety, mem. Del. to EU-Armenia, EU-Azerbaijan and EU-Georgia Parl. Cooperation Cttees, Substitute mem. Del. to EU-Croatia Jt Parl. Cttee; mem. Latvian Acad. of Sciences 1995–, European Asscn of Anaesthesiologists 1997–; Fellow, Royal Coll. of Anaesthetists, UK 1995; doyen d'âge, Council of Europe diplomatic corps; Commdr, Order of the Three Stars. *Address:* Akmenu iela 15, 1048 Rīga, Latvia.

ANDREOLI, Kathleen Gainor; American professor of nursing and university administrator; *Dean Emerita, College of Nursing, Rush University;* b. 22 Sept. 1935, Albany, New York; d. of John Edward Gainor and Edmunda Ringelmann Gainor; m. Thomas Eugene Andreoli 1960 (divorced); one s. two d.; ed Georgetown Univ. and Vanderbilt Univ. School of Nursing and Univ. of Alabama School of Nursing, Birmingham; Staff Nurse, Albany Hosp. Medical Center, New York 1957; instructor, various schools of nursing 1957–70; Educational Dir, Physician Asst Program, Dept of Medicine, School of Medicine, Univ. of Alabama 1970–75, subsequently Asst Prof. then Assoc. Prof. of Nursing 1970–79, Prof. of Nursing 1979; Prof. of Nursing, Special Asst to Pres. for Educational Affairs, Univ. of Texas Health Science Center, Houston 1979–82, Vice-Pres. for Educational Services, Interprofessional Educ. and Int. Programs 1983–87; Vice-Pres. Nursing Affairs and John L. and Helen Kellogg Dean of Coll. of Nursing Rush Univ., Chicago 1987–2005, Dean Emer. 2005–; Ed. Heart and Lung, Journal of Total Care 1971; mem. Bd of Dirs American Asscn of Colleges of Nursing 1998–2000; mem. Nat. Advisory Nursing Council V.H.A. 1992, Advisory Bd Robert Wood Johnson Clinic Nursing School Program, Visiting Cttee Vanderbilt Univ. School of Nursing, Editorial/Advisory Bd The Nursing Spectrum 1996–, Advisory Bd Major Diseases: Diabetes Mellitus and Hypertension 1999, numerous other bodies; mem. Inst. of Medicine of NAS, Inst. of Medicine of Chicago; Fellow, American Acad. of Nursing; Founders Award, NC Heart Asscn 1970, Distinguished Alumni Awards, Vanderbilt Univ. and Univ. of Alabama, Birmingham, Sigma Theta Tau Dean's Award 2003, GE Healthcare-American Asscn of Critical Care Nursing Pioneering Spirit Award 2009, Visionary Leadership Award 2010; numerous other awards. *Publications include:* Comprehensive Cardiac Care (co-author) 1983; numerous articles in professional journals. *Leisure interests:* music, art, reading, bicycling, travelling. *Address:* Rush University Medical Center, 600 South Paulina Street, Suite 1080, Chicago, IL 60612-3806 (office); 1212 South Lake Shore Drive, Chicago, IL 60605-2402, USA (home). *Telephone:* (312) 942-7117 (office); (312) 266-8338 (home). *Fax:* (312) 942-3043 (office). *E-mail:* Kathleen_G_Andreoli@rush.edu (office). *Website:* www.rushu.rush.edu/nursing (office).

ANDREOTTI, Lamberto, BA, MA; American pharmaceutical industry executive; *CEO, Bristol-Myers Squibb;* ed Univ. of Rome, Italy, Massachusetts Inst. of Tech.; held various sr roles at Farmitalia Carlo Erba, KABI Pharmacia and then at Pharmacia & Upjohn –1998; Vice-Pres. and Gen. Man., Italy and European Oncology, Bristol-Myers Squibb 1998–2000, Pres., Europe 2000–02, Sr Vice-Pres. and Pres., International 2002–05, Pres. and COO Bristol-Myers Squibb 2005–10, mem. Bd of Dirs 2009–, CEO 2010–. *Address:* Bristol-Myers Squibb, 345 Park Avenue, New York, NY 10154-0037, USA (office). *Telephone:* (212) 546-4000 (office). *Fax:* (212) 546-4020 (office). *E-mail:* info@bms.com (office). *Website:* www .bms.com (office).

ANDRESEN, Brit, MArch; Norwegian architect and academic; *Professor of Architecture, University of Queensland;* ed Univ. of Trondheim; awarded scholarship to study housing in The Netherlands; won competition to co-design Burrell Museum (with John Meunier and Barry Gasson), Glasgow, UK; fmr part-time teacher of architecture, Univ. of Cambridge and Architectural Asscn, UK; currently Prof. of Architecture, Univ. of Queensland, Australia; fmr Visiting Prof., UCLA, USA; Co-founder Andresen O'Gorman Architects (with Peter O'Gorman); Fellow, Royal Australian Inst. of Architects (RAIA); RAIA Gold Medal (first woman to receive medal) 2002. *Architectural works include:* Burrell Museum (Glasgow), Rosebury House (Brisbane), Ocean View House (Mt Mee), Mooloomba House (Point Lookout), Moreton Bay Houses (Wynnum). *Publications include:* articles on architecture in professional journals. *Address:* School of Architecture, University of Queensland, Brisbane, Queensland 4072, Australia (office). *Telephone:* (7) 3365-3780 (office). *E-mail:* b.andresen@uq.edu.au (office).

ANDRETTI, Mario; American business executive and fmr racing driver; b. 28 Feb. 1940, Montona, Italy; s. of Alvise Andretti and Rina Andretti; m. Dee Ann Hoch 1961; two s. one d.; began racing career in Nazareth, Pa aged 19; Indy Car Nat. Champion 1965, 1966, 1969, 1984; winner of Daytona 500 1967; winner of 12 Hours of Sebring 1967, 1970, 1972; winner of Indianapolis 500 1969; USAC Nat. Dirt Track Champion 1974; Formula One World Champion 1978; winner of Int. Race of Champions 1979; all-time Indy Car lap leader (7,587); all-time leader in Indy Car pole positions won (67); oldest race winner in recorded Indy Car history; retd from active driving 1994; Commendatore, Order of Merit; Driver of the Year 1967, 1978, 1984, Driver of the Quarter Century 1992, Driver of the Century 1999–2000, FIA Gold Medal for Motor Sport 2007, Library of Congress Living Legend 2008. *Achievements:* 111 career wins, 52 Indy Car victories (USAC & CART), 12 Formula One victories (FIA), 9 Sprint Car victories (USAC), 9 Midget victories (ARDC, NASCAR & USAC), 7 Formula 5000 victories (SCCA/USAC), 7 World Sports Car victories (FIA), 5 Dirt Track victories (USAC), 4 Three-Quarter Midget victories (ATQMRA), 3 IROC victories, 2 stock car victories (NASCAR & USAC), 1 non-championship race. *Publications:* Mario Andretti: A Driving Passion (biog.), Andretti (biog.). *Leisure interests:* flying ultralight, snowmobiling, tennis, opera. *Telephone:* (248) 335-3535 (office). *Fax:* (248) 335-3352 (office). *E-mail:* jc@ sportsmanagementnetwork.com (office). *Website:* www .sportsmanagementnetwork.com (office); www.marioandretti.com.

ANDREW, Christopher Robert (Rob), MBE, MA; British professional rugby union coach and fmr professional rugby union player; *Director of Operations, Rugby Football Union;* b. 18 Feb. 1963, Richmond, Yorks.; m. Sara Andrew 1989; two d.; ed Univ. of Cambridge; chartered surveyor; fly-half; fmr mem. Middlesbrough, Cambridge Univ., Nottingham, Gordon (Sydney, Australia) clubs; mem. Wasps Club 1987–91, 1992–96, Capt. until 1989–90; with Toulouse 1991–92, Barbarians, Newcastle 1996–; int. debut England versus Romania 1985; Five Nations debut England versus France 1985; Capt. England team, England versus Romania, Bucharest 1989; mem. Grand Slam winning team 1991, 1992; record-holder for drop goals in ints; retd from int. rugby 1995, returned 1997–99; Devt Dir Newcastle Rugby Football Club 1996–2006; Elite Rugby Dir Rugby Football Union 2006–11, Dir of Operations 2011–; fmr Assoc. Dir DTZ Debenham Thorpe; Hon.

Pres. Wooden Spoon. *Publication:* A Game and a Half 1995. *Leisure interests:* gardening, pushing a pram, golf. *Address:* Rugby Football Union, Rugby House, Twickenham Stadium, 200 Whitton Road, Twickenham, Middx, TW2 7BA, England (office). *Telephone:* (871) 222-2120 (office); (871) 222-2003 (office). *E-mail:* media@therfu.com (office). *Website:* www.rfu.com (office).

ANDREWS, Anthony; British actor; b. 1 Dec. 1948, Hampstead, London; m. Georgina Simpson; one s. two d.; ed Royal Masonic School, Herts.; started acting 1967. *TV appearances include:* Doomwatch, Woodstock 1972, A Day Out, Follyfoot, Fortunes of Nigel 1973, The Pallisers, David Copperfield 1974, Upstairs, Downstairs 1975, French Without Tears, The Country Wife, Much Ado About Nothing 1977, Danger UXB 1978, Romeo and Juliet 1979, Brideshead Revisited 1980, Ivanhoe 1982, The Scarlet Pimpernel 1983, Columbo 1988, The Strange Case of Dr. Jekyll and Mr. Hyde 1989, Hands of a Murderer 1990, Lost in Siberia 1990, The Law Lord 1991, Jewels 1992, Ruth Rendell's Heartstones, Mothertime, David Copperfield 2000, Love in a Cold Climate (mini-series) 2001, Cambridge Spies (mini-series) 2003. *Films Include:* The Scarlet Pimpernel, Under the Volcano, A War of the Children, Take Me High 1973, Operation Daybreak 1975, Les Adolescents 1976, The Holcroft Covenant 1986, Second Victory 1987, Woman He Loved 1988, The Lighthorsemen 1988, Hannah's War 1988, Lost in Siberia (also producer) 1990, Haunted (also co-producer) 1995, Last Night 2007. *Plays:* 40 Years On, A Midsummer Night's Dream, Romeo and Juliet, One of Us 1986, Coming into Land 1986, Dragon Variation, Tima and the Conways, My Fair Lady 2003–04, The Woman in White 2005, The Letter 2007.

ANDREWS, John Hamilton, AO, MArch, FTS, RIBA; Australian architect; b. 29 Oct. 1933, Sydney, NSW; s. of the late K. Andrews; m. Rosemary Randall 1958; four s.; ed N Sydney Boys' High School, Univ. of Sydney, Harvard Univ.; in pvt. practice, Toronto, Canada 1962, Sydney 1970–; f. John Andrews Architects (now John Andrews Int. Pty Ltd), Toronto 1962; mem. Staff, Univ. of Toronto School of Architecture 1962–67, Chair. and Prof. of Architecture 1967–69; Chair. Architecture and Design Comm., Australia Council 1980–83, Founding Chair. Design Arts Bd 1983–88; Architectural Juror, Australian Archives Nat. Headquarters Building 1979, Parl. House Competition 1979–80, The Peak, Hong Kong 1983, Hawaii Loa Coll. 1986, Gov. Gen.'s Medals, Canada 1986; Assoc. NZ Inst. of Architects; Foundation mem. Australian Acad. of Design 1990; Fellow, Royal Architectural Inst. of Canada; Life Fellow, Royal Australian Inst. of Architects; mem. Visual Arts Bd, Australia Council 1977–80, Bd mem. 1988–90, RIBA; Hon. FAIA; Hon. DArch (Sydney) 1980; Centennial Medal (Canada) 1967, Massey Medal (Canada) 1967, Arnold Brunner Award, American Acad. of Arts and Letters 1971, American Inst. of Architects Honour Award 1973, Gold Medal, Royal Australian Inst. of Architects 1980, Advance Australia Award 1982, Sulman Medal (Australia) 1983, Design Excellence 25 Year Award, Ontario Asscn of Architecture, Scarborough Coll. 1989. *Publication:* Architecture: A Performing Art 1982. *Leisure interests:* fly fishing, surfing. *Address:* Colleton, Cargo Road, Orange, NSW 2800, Australia (home). *Telephone:* (2) 6365-6223 (office). *Fax:* (2) 6365-6211 (office).

ANDREWS, Dame Julie Elizabeth, DBE; British actress and singer; b. (Julia Wells), 1 Oct. 1935, Walton-on-Thames, Surrey, England; m. 1st Tony Walton 1959 (divorced 1968); one d.; m. 2nd Blake Edwards 1969 (died 2010); one step-s. one step-d. and two adopted d.; ed voice lessons with Lillian Stiles-Allen; first stage appearance aged 12 as singer, London Hippodrome; played in revues and concert tours; debut in Starlight Roof, London Hippodrome 1947; work for UN Devt Fund for Women; three Golden Globe Awards 1964, 1965, Emmy Award 1987, BAFTA Award 1989, Kennedy Center Honor 2001, Screen Actors' Guild Lifetime Achievement Award 2006. *Theatre:* Starlight Roof (London Hippodrome) 1947, Cinderella (London Palladium), The Boy Friend (Broadway) 1954, My Fair Lady 1956–60, Camelot (Broadway) 1960–62, Putting it Together 1993, Victor, Victoria 1995–96. *Films:* Mary Poppins (Academy Award for Best Actress 1964) 1963, The Americanization of Emily 1964, The Sound of Music 1964, Hawaii 1965, Torn Curtain 1966, Thoroughly Modern Millie 1966, Star! 1967, Darling Lili 1970, The Tamarind Seed 1973, 10 1979, Little Miss Marker 1980, S.O.B. 1980, Victor/Victoria 1981, The Man Who Loved Women 1983, That's Life 1986, Duet For One 1986, The Sound of Christmas (TV) 1987, Our Sons (TV) 1991, Relative Values 1999, The Princess Diaries 2001, Shrek 2 (voice) 2004, The Princess Diaries 2: Royal Engagement 2004, The Cat That Looked at a King 2004, Shrek the Third (voice) 2007, Enchanted (voice) 2007, The Tooth Fairy 2010, Shrek Forever After (voice) 2010, Despicable Me (voice) 2010. *TV appearances include:* High Tor 1956, The Julie Andrews Hour 1972–73, Great Performances Live in Concert 1990, The Julie Show (ABC) 1992, Eloise at the Plaza 2003, Eloise at Christmastime 2003. *Recordings:* albums: My Fair Lady (Broadway cast recording) 1956, The Lass With The Delicate Air 1957, Julie Andrews Sings 1958, Rose Marie 1958, Camelot (Broadway cast recording) 1960, Don't Go In The Lion's Cage Tonight 1962, Heartrending Ballads and Raucous Ditties 1962, Julie & Carol at Carnegie Hall (with Carol Burnett) 1962, Mary Poppins (film soundtrack) 1964, The Sound Of Music (film soundtrack) 1965, A Christmas Treasure 1968, Star! 1968, Darling Lili 1969, TV's Fair Julie 1972, The Secret of Christmas 1977, Christmas With Julie Andrews 1982, Love Me Tender 1983, Broadway's Fair Julie 1984, Love Julie 1989, At The Lincoln Center (with Carol Burnett) 1989, The King And I (studio cast) 1992, Broadway: The Music of Richard Rodgers 1994, Here I'll Stay: The Words of Alan Jay Lerner 1996, Nobody Sings It Better 1996. *Publications:* Mandy (as Julie Andrews Edwards) 1972, Last of the Really Great Whangdoodles 1973, The Great American Mousical (as Julie Andrews Edwards, with Emma Walton Hamilton) 2006, Home (autobiog.) 2008. *Leisure interests:* skiing, riding. *Address:* c/o WME Entertainment, 9601 Wilshire Boulevard, 3rd Floor, Beverly Hills, CA 90210, USA (office). *Telephone:* (310) 850-4550 (office); (310) 285-9000 (office). *Fax:* (310) 248-5650 (office); (310) 285-9010 (office). *E-mail:* jcolbert@wmeentertainment.com (office); ndavid@wmeentertainment.com (office). *Website:* www.wma.com (office).

ANDREWS, Nancy Catherine, BS, MS, MD, PhD; American physician, biologist and academic; *Vice-Chancellor and Dean, School of Medicine, Duke University;* b. 29 Nov. 1958, Syracuse, NY; d. of William Shankland Andrews and Virginia Helen Andrews (née Rogers); m. Bernard Mathey-Prevot; one s. one d.; ed Yale Univ., Massachusetts Inst. of Tech., Harvard Medical School; joined faculty of Harvard Univ. Medical School 1991, becoming Leland Fikes Prof. of Pediatrics 2003, George Richards Minot Prof. of Pediatrics 2006, Dean for Basic Sciences and Grad. Studies 2003–07; Investigator, Howard Hughes Medical Inst. 1993–2006; Attending

Physician in Hematology and Oncology, Children's Hosp., Boston 1991–2003; fmr Distinguished Physician, Dana-Farber Cancer Inst., Boston; Vice Chancellor for Academic Affairs and Dean, School of Medicine, Duke Univ. 2007–; Pres. American Soc. of Clinical Investigation 2008–09; mem. NAS Inst. of Medicine 2006–; mem. American Acad. of Arts and Sciences 2007–, Fellow 2006–; Samuel Rosenthal Prize for Excellence in Academic Pediatrics 1998, American Fed. for Medical Research Foundation Outstanding Investigator Award in Basic Science 2000, Soc. for Pediatric Research E. Mead Johnson Award 2002, Harvard Medical School Dean's Leadership Award for Advancement of Women 2004. *Publications include:* over 100 peer-reviewed articles and 23 book chapters. *Address:* Dean's Suite, DUMC 2927, Duke University School of Medicine, Davison Building, 200 Trent Drive, Durham, NC 27710, USA (office). *Telephone:* (919) 684-8111 (office). *Fax:* (919) 684-0208 (office). *E-mail:* nancy.andrews@duke.edu (office). *Website:* medschool.duke.edu (office).

ANDREYCHENKO, Uladzimir Pavlovich; Belarusian agronomist and politician; *Chairman (Speaker), Palata Predstaviteley (House of Representatives);* b. 1949, Maryanovo, Lioznenskiy Dist, Vitebsk Oblast, Belarusian SSR (BSSR), USSR; ed Velikoluk Agricultural Inst., Minsk Higher Party School; early career as technician, Pobeda Sotsializma Agricultural Collective Farm, Verkhnedvinsiy Dist, Vitebsk Oblast 1968; served in Soviet Army 1968–70; agronomist, Lioznenskiy Dist Agricultural Tech. Centre 1970–72; Instructor and Leader, Organizational Dept, Lioznenskiy Dist Cttee Br. Komsomol (Communist Youth League) 1972–74; Instructor, Lioznenskiy Dist Cttee, CP of Belarus 1974–75; Sec., Party Cttee, Akademenki Soviet Farm and Chair. Danukalov Lioznenskiy Collective Farm 1975–81; Sr Agric. Man. Lioznenskiy Dist Exec. Cttee 1981–85, Chair. 1985–87; First Sec., Verkhnedvinskiy Dist Cttee, CP of Belarus 1987–91; Deputy Chair., later Chair., Cttee for Agric. and Supplies, Vitebsk Oblast Exec. Cttee 1991–94, Chair. Vitebsk Oblast Exec. Cttee 1994–2008; Deputy, 12th Supreme Soviet of BSSR (Parl.) 1991–94 (dissolved under new constitution of 1994); mem. first, second and third terms, Soviet Respubliki (Council of the Repub.) 1996–2000, 2000–04, 2004–08, Chair. (Speaker) Palata Predstaviteley (House of Reps) Oct. 2008–; First Deputy Chair. Parl. Ass., Union State of Belarus and Russia 2008–, also mem. Higher State Council of Union Govt; Order of the Fatherland (III Degree, Second Class), Honoured Scholar of Belarusian SSR, Honoured Agricultural Worker of the Repub. of Belarus; Hon. Diplomas of the Supreme Council of BSSR, Nat. Ass. of Belarus, Council of Ministers of Belarus. *Address:* Office of the Chairman, Palata Predstaviteley, 220010 Minsk, vul. Savetskaya 11, Belarus (office). *Telephone:* (17) 222-32-62 (office). *Fax:* (17) 327-37-84 (office). *E-mail:* admin@gov.house.by (office). *Website:* house.gov.by (office).

ANDREYEV, Vladimir Alekseyevich; Russian actor, stage director and academic; *President, Yermolova Theatre;* b. 27 Aug. 1930; m. Natalia Selezneva; one s. one d.; ed State Inst. of Theatre Arts Cinema (GITIS); actor with Yermolova Theatre Moscow 1952–70, Dir 1970–85, 1990–; teaches concurrently at GITIS, Prof. 1978–; Chief Dir of Maly Theatre, Moscow 1985–88; fmr Head, Dept of Acting, Russian Acad. of Theatre Arts (fmr Chair. Drama Faculty); Pres. Vermolova Theatre 2012–; mem. CPSU 1962–92, Int. Acad. of Theatre, Russian Acad. of Theatre Arts; USSR People's Artist 1985; Stanislavsky State Prize 1980, 1993, State Prize of Russia 1990, Govt Prize for Theatre Arts 1994, 2001. *Roles include:* Aleksey in V. Rozov's It's High Time!, Vasilkov in Ostrovsky's Crazy Money, Golubkov in Bulgakov's Flight, Sattarov in Valeyev's I Give You Life, Dorogin in Zorin's Lost Story, Writer in Bunin's Grammar of Love, Nikita in Chekhov's One Big Small Drama. *Productions include:* Vampilov's plays: Last Summer in Chulimsk and The Duck Hunt; Money for Mary (based on a work by V. Rasputin), The Shore (based on Yuriy Bondarev's novel), Uncle Vanya, Three Sisters (Chekhov). *Publications:* I Remember with an Open Heart, One Endless Plot. *Leisure interests* fine art, architecture, football, politics. *Address:* Russian Academy of Theatre Arts, 103888 Moscow, 6, Maly Kislovsky pereulok (office); Tverskaya 9-60, 125009 Moscow, Russia (home). *Telephone:* (495) 691-91-92 (office); (495) 629-48-57 (home). *Fax:* (495) 690-05-97 (office). *E-mail:* yermolova@theatre.ru; info@gitis.net (office). *Website:* www.gitis.net (office); www.ermolova.theatre.ru (office).

ANDRIAMANJATO, Ny Hasina; Malagasy mathematician and politician; *Minister of Posts, Telecommunications and New Technologies;* s. of Richard Andriamanjato; m.; three c.; ed Lomonosov State Univ., Moscow, Russia; mem. Cttee for Econ. and Social Recovery 1992; Minister for Post and Telecommunications 1993–2002; mem. Congress Party for Malagasy Independence; unsuccessful ind. cand. in presidential election Dec. 2006; Gen. Co-ordinator, Admin., Financial, Econ. and Infrastructure and Urban Affairs, Antananarivo Town Hall –2009; apptd Minister of Foreign Affairs (following coup d'état) 2009–10, also Deputy Prime Minister 2009–10 (resgnd); currently Minister of Posts, Telecommunications and New Technologies; voted Man of the Year by Midi Madagasikara magazine 1995, and by Revue de l'Océan Indien 1997. *Leisure interests:* playing the piano. *Address:* Ministry of Posts, Telecommunications and New Technologies pl. de l'Indépendance, Antaninarenina, 101 Antananarivo, Madagascar (office). *Telephone:* (20) 2222902 (office). *Fax:* (20) 2234115 (office). *Website:* www.mtpc.gov.mg (office).

ANDRIEȘ, Andrei, DPhys-MathSc; Moldovan physicist and academic; *Director, Centre of Optoelectronics of the Institute of Applied Physics, Academy of Sciences of Moldova;* b. 24 Oct. 1933, Chișinău (Kishinev); s. of Mihail Andrieș and Maria Andrieș; m. Lidia Vasilievna Klimanova 1959; one s.; ed Kishinev Univ., Ioffe Inst. of Physics and Tech., Leningrad, Moldova State Univ.; Researcher, Inst. of Applied Physics, Acad. of Sciences Moldavian SSR 1962–64, Learning Sec. 1964–71, Head of Lab. Inst. of Applied Physics 1971–2004, Gen. Learning Sec. 1984–89, Dir Centre of Optoelectronics 1993–; Corresp. mem. Presidium of Acad. of Sciences, Moldavian SSR (now Acad. of Sciences of Moldova) 1978–2004, mem. 1984, Pres. 1989–2004, Hon. Pres. 2004–; Co-Pres. Research and Educational Networking Asscn of Moldova 1999, Gen. Dir 2004–; Merited Scientific Researcher 1984; mem. Eng. Acad. of Russian Fed. 1992, New York Acad. of Sciences 1995, Int. Scientific Acad. of Life, the Universe and Nature, Toulouse 1997, World Fed. of Scientists; Hon. Mem. Romanian Acad., American-Romanian Acad. of Arts, Science and Humanities, Cosmonaut's Acad. "Tsiolkovsky"; Order of the Repub. of Moldova 1996; Laureate of Prize C. Miculescu, Romanian Acad. of Sciences 1974, State Prize 1983, 2001, Diploma Man of the Year, American Biographical Inst. 1994,

Merite de L-Invention, Tantae Molis Erat,Bruxelles 1995, 20th Century Award 1995, Int. Man of Year 1994–95, Medaille d-Or avec Mention Pour L-Invention Structures d-impression et methods d-energistrement holographique 1996, Award of Govt of Moldova 2001, Int. Acad. of Rating Tech. and Sociology, Golden Fortune Award 2002, Stanford R. Ovahinsky Award 2005; numerous other decorations and awards. *Publications include:* over 450 works, including five monographs on physics of non-crystalline chalcogenides and new materials for photographic processes; more than 40 patents. *Leisure interests:* reading, travel. *Address:* Centre of Optoelectronics, Institute of Applied Physics, Academy of Sciences of Moldova, Str. Academiei 5, 2028 Chişinău (office); Str. Alexandrescu 13/62, 2008 Chişinău, Moldova (home). *Telephone:* (22) 73-98-05 (office); (22) 75-16-70 (home). *Fax:* (22) 73-81-49 (office); (22) 27-60-14. *E-mail:* andries@asm.md (office); *Website:* www.asm.md (office); www.phys.asm.md (office).

ANDRIKIENĖ, Laima Liucija, DEcon; Lithuanian politician and academic; b. 1 Jan. 1958, Druskininkai; m. (husband deceased); one s.; ed Druskininkai Secondary School, Druskininkai Seven-Year Music School, Vilnius State Univ., Univ. of Manchester, UK; engineer, Computing Centre, Lithuanian Research Inst. of Agricultural Econs 1980–82, Researcher, Sr Researcher 1982–88; British Council Post-Doctoral Fellow, Univ. of Manchester 1988–89; Asst to Deputy Chair. Council of Ministers, Lithuanian SSR 1989–90; Deputy, Supreme Soviet 1990; signatory to Act on Re-establishment of Ind. State of Lithuania 1990; mem. Independence Party 1990–92; mem. Seimas (Parl.) 1992–2000, mem. Foreign Affairs Cttee, Vice-Chair. June–Oct. 2000, European Affairs Cttee 1998–2000; Co-founder Homeland Union Party (Lithuanian Conservatives) 1993, mem. Bd 1993–98; Minister of Trade and Industry 1996, of European Affairs 1996–98; Head, Lithuanian Parl. Del. to Baltic Ass. 1998–2000 (Chair. Presidium 1998–99, 2000); Founder and Chair. Homeland People's Party 1999–2001; mem. Union of the Right 2001–03, Homeland Union 2003–; Chair. Bd Laitenis UAB, Vilnius 2001–03; consultant, Asscn of Lithuanian Chambers of Commerce, Industry and Crafts 2002–; Assoc. Prof., Dept of Political Science, Law Univ. of Lithuania 2002–04, Dir Inst. of EU Policy and Man. 2002–03, Dean Faculty of Public Man. 2003–04; mem. European Parl. (Group of the European People's Party (Christian Democrats) and European Democrats) 2004–, Vice-Chair. Sub-cttee on Human Rights, mem. Cttee on Int. Trade, Del. to Euronest Parl. Ass.; Pew Fellowship Scholar, School of Foreign Service, Georgetown Univ., Washington, DC, USA 1996; Grand Officier, Ordre nat. du Mérite 1997, Cross of Commdr of the Order of the Lithuanian Grand Duke Gediminas 2004; Dr hc (Kingston Univ.) 2007; Independence Medal of Repub. of Lithuania 2000, Medal of the Baltic Ass. 2003, Golden Sign of Honour, Confed. of Lithuanian Industrialists 2008. *Publications include:* more than 60 articles and academic monographs on foreign policy, EU policies and man., interest groups and lobbying, econ. reform, agricultural econs and human rights. *Address:* European Parliament, Bâtiment Altiero Spinelli, ASP 11E153, 60 rue Wiertz, 1047 Brussels, Belgium (office); 8/26 Liejyklos Street, 01120 Vilnius, Lithuania. *Telephone:* (5) 212-2360; 699-05062 (Mobile). *Fax:* (2) 284-9858 (office). *E-mail:* laimaliucija.andrikiene@europarl.europa.eu (office); info@laimaandrikiene.lt. *Website:* www.europarl.europa.eu (office); www.eppgroup.eu; www .laimaandrikiene.lt.

ANDROSCH, Hannes, PhD; Austrian business executive and fmr politician; b. 18 April 1938, Vienna; m. Brigitte Schärf; two d.; ed Hochschule für Welthandel, Vienna; Asst Auditor Fed. Ministry of Finance 1956–66; Sec., Econ. Affairs Section, Socialist Parl. Party 1963–66, Vice-Chair. 1974–85; mem. Nationalrat (Nat. Council) 1967–85; Minister of Finance 1970–81; Vice-Chancellor 1976–81; Chair. and Gen. Man. Creditanstalt-Bankverein 1981–87; Chair. Österreichische Kontrolbank AG 1985–86; Pres. Supervisory Bd Austria Technologie & System-technik AG (A.T. & S.); f. AIC Androsch International Management Consulting GmbH 1989; f. Hannes Androsch Foundation at Austrian Acad. of Sciences 2004; Chief Shareholder, Salinen and Lenzing cos; Grand Gold Medal of Honour; Dr hc (Bratislava School of Law, Slovakia) 2008, (Univ. of New Orleans, USA) 2009, (Univ. of Salzburg) 2011, (Mining Univ. Leoben) 2013. *Address:* AIC Androsch International Management Consulting GmbH, Opernring 1/R/3, 1010 Vienna, Austria (office). *Telephone:* (1) 586-10-54 (office). *Fax:* (1) 586-10-54-30 (office). *E-mail:* office@aic.co.at (office). *Website:* www.androsch.com (office).

ANDRUS, Cecil D.; American business executive, consultant and fmr politician; *of Counsel, Gallatin Public Affairs;* b. 25 Aug. 1931, Hood River, Ore.; s. of Hal S. Andrus and Dorothy Andrus (née Johnson); m. Carol M. May 1949; three d.; ed Oregon State Univ.; served in USN 1951–55; mem. Idaho State Senate 1961–66, 1968–71; State Gen. Man. Paul Revere Life Insurance Co. 1967–70; Gov. of Idaho 1971–77, 1987–95; Chair. Nat. Govs Conf. 1976; US Sec. of Interior, Washington, DC 1977–81; mem. Bd of Dirs Albertson's Inc. 1985–87, 1995–, Coeur d'Alene Mines 1995–, Key Corp. 1996–, Rentrak Corpn; mem. Bd of Trustees Nat. Conservation System Foundation; mem. Bd of Govs Oquirrh Inst.; Chair. Andrus Center for Public Policy, Boise State Univ. 1995–; of Counsel, Gallatin Group (now Gallatin Public Affairs) 1995–; Democrat; Hon. LLD (Gonzaga Univ., Spokane, Wash. 1975, Whitman Coll., Albertson Coll. of Idaho, Oregon State Univ., Univ. of Idaho, Idaho State Univ., Univ. of New Mexico); Conservationist of the Year, Nat. Wildlife Fed. 1980, Ansel Adams Award, Wilderness Soc. 1985, Audubon Medal 1985, Torch of Liberty Award, B'nai B'rith 1991, William Penn Mott Jr Park Leadership Award, Nat. Parks Conservation Asscn 2000. *Publication:* Cecil Andrus: Politics Western Style 1998. *Leisure interests:* hunting, fishing, golf. *Address:* The Gallatin Group, 350 North Ninth Street, Suite 550, Boise, ID 83702, USA (office). *Telephone:* (208) 336-1986 (office). *Fax:* (208) 336-2007 (office). *E-mail:* candrus@gallatinpublicaffairs.com (office). *Website:* www.gallatingroup .com (office).

ANDSNES, Leif Ove; Norwegian pianist; b. 7 April 1970, Stavanger; ed Bergen Music Conservatory; debut, Oslo 1987; British debut with Oslo Philharmonic, Edinburgh Festival 1989; US debut with Cleveland Orchestra under Neeme Järvi 1990; recitals in London, Berlin, Vienna, Amsterdam, New York (Carnegie Hall); performed with Orchestre Nat. de France, Berlin Philharmonic, Chicago Sym-phony, BBC Symphony, London Symphony, LA Philharmonic, Japan Philhar-monic, New York Philharmonic; soloist, Last Night of the Proms 2002; Co-Artistic Dir Risør Music Festival; Commdr Royal Norwegian Order of St Olav 2002; first prize Hindemith Competition, Frankfurt am Main, prizewinner at other int. competitions, Levin Prize (Bergen) 1988, Norwegian Music Critics' Prize 1988,

Grieg Prize (Bergen) 1990, Dorothy B. Chandler Performing Arts Award, Los Angeles 1992, Gilmore Prize 1997, Royal Philharmonic Soc. Instrumentalist Award 2000, Gramophone Award for Best Concerto Recording 2000, for Best Instrumental Recording 2002. *Recordings include:* Rachmaninov Piano Concertos 1 and 2 (Classical BRIT Award for Instrumentalist of the Year 2006, Gramophone Award for Best Concerto Recording 2006) 2005, Horizons (Classical BRIT Award for Instrumentalist of the Year 2007) 2006, Rachmaninov Piano Concertos 3 and 4 2010, Schumann Complete Works for Piano Trio (Gramophone Award for Best Chamber Recording 2012) 2011, also works of Brahms, Chopin, Grieg, Janacek, Liszt, Schumann. *Address:* c/o Kathryn Enticott, IMG Artists, The Light Box, 111 Power Road, London, W4 5PY, England (office). *Telephone:* (20) 7957-5800 (office). *Fax:* (20) 7957-5801 (office). *E-mail:* cclarkson@imgartists.com (office). *Website:* www.imgartists.com (office); www.andsnes.com.

ANEFAL, Sebastian L., BS; Micronesian politician; *Governor of Yap;* b. 21 Jan. 1952, Guror, Gilman, State of Yap; m. Marita Phillip; two s. three d.; ed Yap High School, Sherwood High School, Ore., USA, Univ. of Guam, Agana, Guam, Eastern Ore. State Univ., La Grande, Ore., Micronesian Occupational Coll., Repub. of Palau, Ore. Coll. of Education, Univ. of Hawaii, Ore. State Univ., USA; radio announcer/reporter, WSZA Radio Station, Yap 1970; Asst Dorm Man. Eastern Ore. State Univ. 1972–74; Sec. Educ. for Self-Governmental Task Force 1974; Classroom Instructor in Social Studies, Dept of Educ. 1975–80, Chief of Fed. Programs 1980–82, Chief of Community Outreach Aug.–Dec. 1982, ECIA (US Govt's Educ. Consolidation and Improvement Act of 1981) Chapter I Coordinator July–Sept. 1982, Man. and Support Admin. 1982–87; Public Information Program Coordinator, Office of the Plebiscite Commr, Yap Jan.–June 1982; Convention Sec., Yap Constitutional Convention March–Aug. 1982; Dir Dept of Public Affairs, Yap 1987–88, Dept of Resources and Devt 1988–91, Office of Planning and Budget 1991–95; Special Consultant to Gov. of State of Yap 1991–95, 2007–; Chief of Gilman (Municipality), Yap 1992–2007; Sec. of Dept of Resources and Devt, FSM Nat. Govt 1995–98, Dept of Econ. Affairs 1998–2003, Dept of Foreign Affairs 2003–07; Vice-Chair. Tourist Comm. 1975; mem. Nat. Disaster Control Bd 1976; Chair. Yap SPEA Coordinator, Festival of Arts, Papua New Guinea 1980; Chair. Elementary and Secondary Educ. Act (ESEA) Title IV State Advisory Council, Trust Territory of the Pacific Islands (TTPI) 1980; Chair. UN Day Cttee; Ed. 1981; mem. Old Age Program Advisory Bd 1983, COM Bd of Regents 1984–93, EPA Bd (TTPI/FSM) 1985–87; mem. Bd of Dirs Micronesia Maritime Authority 1989–95; Chair. Bd of Govs Pacific Island Devt Bank 1989–95; Chair. Bd of Nat. Fisheries Corpn 1990–; Vice-Chair. Bd of Dirs Yap Econ. Devt Authority 1990–95; Pres. Yap Fishing Corpn 1990–95; Vice-Pres. Yap Purse Seiners Corpn 1990–95; mem. Bd of Dirs Yap Cooperative Asscn 1990–95, Micronesia Longline Fishing Co. 1990–, FSM Devt Bank 1990–2004; Gov. of Yap 2007–; American Field Service Scholar-ship 1969–72, Trust Territory Social Sciences Scholarship 1972, UNESCO Fellowship in Ethnic Heritage to the Gilbert Islands 1978. *Publications include:* Social Studies Curriculum Guide (ed.) 1980, Tabinaw Rodad (social studies text book) (co-ed.) 1980. *Leisure interests:* spear fishing, hunting, sailing, guitar playing, photography. *Address:* Office of the Governor, POB 39, Colonia, Yap, FM 96943, The Federated States of Micronesia (office).

ANELAY OF ST JOHNS, Baroness (Life Peer), cr. 1996, of St Johns in the County of Surrey; **Rt Hon. Joyce Anne Anelay,** DBE, OBE, PC; British politician; *Lords Chief Whip (Captain of the Honourable Corps of Gentlemen at Arms);* b. (Joyce Anne Clarke), 17 July 1947; m. Richard Anelay QC; ed Enfield County School, Univ. of Bristol; secondary school teacher 1969–74; later worked as a volunteer adviser with the Citizens' Advice Bureau; JP, NW Surrey 1985–97; Opposition Whip in the House of Lords 1997–98; Opposition Spokesperson for Agric. 1997–98, for Culture, Media and Sport 1998–2002, for Home Affairs 1997–98, 2002–07, for Social Security 1997–99, for Legal Affairs 2003–04, Opposition Chief Whip 2007–10; Deputy Speaker of the House of Lords 2008–; Deputy Chair. of Committees 2008–; Govt Chief Whip in the House of Lords (Capt. of the Hon. Corps of Gentlemen at Arms) 2010–; Chair. SE Area Conservative Women's Cttee 1987–90; mem. Nat. Union Exec. Cttee Conservative Party 1987–97, Vice-Chair. SE Area Exec. Cttee 1990–93; Chair. Women's Nat. Cttee 1993–96; Vice-Pres. Nat. Union 1996–97; mem. Social Security Appeal Tribunal 1983–96, Social Security Advisory Cttee for GB and NI 1989–96, Women's Nat. Comm. 1991–94, Child Support Appeal Tribunal 1993–96; Pres. World Travel Market 2003–08; mem. (Conservative) House of Lords 1996–. *Address:* House of Lords, Westminster, London, SW1A 0PW, England (office). *Telephone:* (20) 7219-3132 (office). *Fax:* (20) 7219-6837 (office). *E-mail:* holgovernmentwhips@ parliament.uk (office). *Website:* www.parliament.uk/biographies/lords/joyce -anelay/27108 (office).

ANELL, Lars Evert Roland, MA, MBA; Swedish economist, international organization official and consultant; *Chairman, Swedish Research Council;* b. 23 Oct. 1941, Katrineholm, Sweden; s. of Evert Andersson and Margit Andersson; m. Kerstin Friis 1966; one s. three d.; ed Stockholm School of Econs, Univ. of Stockholm; served in Ministry of Finance 1966–70; Dir for Planning and Research, Ministry for Foreign Affairs 1970–80; Dir-Gen. Swedish Agency for Research Co-operation with Developing Countries 1980–83; Sr Adviser, Prime Minister's Office 1983–86; Perm. Rep. of Sweden to UN orgs in Geneva 1986 and EU; GATT-Uruguay Round Negotiating Group on Intellectual Property Rights 1987–92, GATT Contracting Parties 1991–92, Chair. GATT Council 1990–91; Sr Vice-Pres. AB Volvo 1992–2001, currently Sr Adviser to CEO; Freja Foundation 2001–07; Chair. Stockholm Environment Inst. –2009; Chair. Swedish Research Council 2010–; Chief Negotiator European Spallation Source (ESS) (Europe-wide scientific research facility), Lund 2011–; Chair. UN Intergovernmental Group of Experts on Science and Tech. for Devt 1980–82, UN Cttee on Science and Tech. 1985–86, Int. Org. for Immigration 1991–92, Centre for Int. Youth Exchange 1997–2002, Dag Hammarskjöld Foundation 1997–2005, Bd Univ. of Umeå 1998–2003, UNICE REX-Cttee 2001–05, Swedish Council for Working Life and Social Research 2007–09, MISTRA Research Programme on Trade and Investment 2007, Bd Jönköping Int. Business School 2008, Inst. for Media Research, (Chair. of the Council 2009–); currently Officer, Comm. on Trade and Investment Policy (fmr Chair.), Int. Chamber of Commerce; Bd mem. UN Advisory Group on Financial Flows to Africa 1987–88, UN Research Inst. for Social Devt 1990–96, Swedish Exhibition and Congress Centre 1995–2001, AB Volvo Penta 1997–98, Volvo Aero Corpn 1998–2008, Foundation for Strategic Research 1999–2003. *Publications* *include:* The Other Society 1969, Should Sweden be Asphalted? 1971, Recession, The Western Economies and the Changing World Order 1981, Economic Crises in Theory and Practice 1986. *Address:* Swedish Research Council, PO Box 1035, 101 38 Stockholm (office); Norr Mälarstrand 16, 112 20 Stockholm, Sweden (home). *Telephone:* (8) 546-44-000 (office); (8) 650-64-43 (home). *Fax:* (8) 546-44-180 (office). *E-mail:* lars.anell@vr.se (office); lars@anell.nu. *Website:* www.vr.se (office); europeanspallationsource.se/ (office).

ANFIMOV, Nikolai Appolonovich, PhD; Russian scientist and academic; b. 29 March 1935, Russia; m.; one s.; ed Moscow Inst. of Physics and Tech.; Head of Group, Head of Sector, Research Inst. of Heat Processes 1958–73; Head of Div., Deputy Dir Cen. Research Inst. of Machine Construction 1973–2000, Dir Gen. 2000–09; Chair. Council of Experts, Supreme Certification Comm. on Aviation and Rocket and Space Eng; Deputy Chair. Scientific Council of Russian Security Council; Prof., Moscow Physico-Tech. Inst.; Corresp. mem. Russian Acad. of Sciences 1984, mem. 1997, currently Bureau mem. Branch of Power Industry, Machine Building, Mechanics and Control Processes; mem. Int. Acad. of Astronautics, Russian Acad. of Space, Council on Grants of Pres. of Russia, Russian Foundation for Basic Research, American Inst. of Aeronautics and Astronautics; mem. Editorial Bd Fluid Dynamics; Ed.–in-Chief Kosmonavtika i Raketostroenie; State Prize of Russia, Allan D. Emil Memorial Award 2010, NASA Distinguished Public Service Medal. *Publications include:* Problems of Mechanics and Heat Exchange in Space Tech. 1982, Numerical Modelling in Aerohydrodynamics 1986 and numerous scientific works on heat exchange and heat protection in high-speed, high-temperature regimes, heat regimes of spaceships, radiation gas dynamics. *Leisure interest:* tennis. *Address:* Branch of Power Industry, Machine Building, Mechanics And Control Processes, Russian Academy of Sciences, 119991 Moscow, Leninskii avenue 14, Russia (office). *Telephone:* (495) 938-12-04 (office); (495) 238-40-67 (home). *Fax:* (495) 938-52-34 (office). *E-mail:* anfimov@mcc.rsa.ru (office). *Website:* www.ras.ru (office).

ANGELINI, HE Cardinal Fiorenzo; Italian ecclesiastic; *President Emeritus, Pontifical Council for Pastoral Assistance to Health Care Workers;* b. 1 Aug. 1916, Rome; ed Pontifical Roman Seminary, Pontifical Lateran Univ.; Pontifical Theological Faculty Marianum; ordained priest 1940; Chaplain, Azione Cattolica 1945–59; Master of Pontifical Ceremonies 1947–54; elected Titular Bishop of Messene 1956, consecrated 1956; Auxiliary Bishop of Rome 1977; Pres. Pontifical Council for Pastoral Assistance to Health Care Workers, Roman Curia 1985–96, Pres. Emer. 1996–; apptd Cardinal Deacon of Santo Spirito in Sassia 1991, apptd Cardinal Priest of S. Spirito in Sassia 2002–; f. Italian Catholic Doctors Asscn 1959; mem. Congregation for Evangelization of the Peoples, Papal Council on the Family, Papal Comm. on Latin America. *Address:* c/o Pontifical Council for Pastoral Assistance to Health Care Workers, Via della Conciliazione, 3, 00193 Rome, Italy (office).

ANGELL, Wayne D., PhD; American economist; b. 28 June 1930, Liberal, Kan.; s. of Charlie Francis Angell and Adele Thelma Angell (née Edwards); m.; four c.; ed Univ. of Kansas; Prof., Ottawa Univ. 1956, Dean 1969–72; mem. Kansas House of Reps 1961–67; Dir Fed. Reserve Bank, Kansas City 1979–86; mem. of Fed. Reserve Bd 1986–94; Chief Economist and Sr Man. Dir Bear Sterns & Co. Inc. 1994–2001; with Angell Econs, Arlington Va 2001–; Outstanding Achievement Award, Ottawa Univ. Alumni Asscn 2005. *Leisure interest:* tennis. *Address:* Angell Economics, 1600 North Oak Street, Suite 1915, Arlington, VA 22209, USA (office). *E-mail:* wangell@comcast.net (office).

ANGELOPOULOS-DASKALAKI, Gianna, LLB; Greek business executive, politician and sports administrator; b. 12 Dec. 1955, Heraklion, Crete; m. Theodore Angelopoulos; two s. one d.; ed Aristotelian Univ., Thessaloniki; mem. Athens municipal council; mem. Parl. (New Democracy Party) 1989–90; Vice-Chair. John F. Kennedy School of Govt, Harvard Univ. 1994–; Pres. Athens 2004 Olympic Games Bid Cttee 1998–2000, Athens 2004 Olympic Cttee 2000–04; apptd Ambassador at Large by Greek Govt 1998; mem. Athens Bar Asscn; man. family-owned shipping business; Hellenic Public Radio Phidippides Award 1997, ranked 49th by Fortune magazine amongst 50 Most Powerful Women in Business outside the US 2002, Archbishop Iakovos Leadership 100 Award for Excellence 2008. *Address:* c/o Ministry of Foreign Affairs, 1st Vas. Sofias Avenue, 106 71 Athens, Greece (office).

ANGELOU, Maya; American writer, poet and academic; b. (Marguerite Johnson), 4 April 1928, St Louis, Mo.; d. of Bailey Johnson and Vivian Baxter; one s.; Assoc. Ed. Arab Observer 1961–62; Asst Admin., teacher, School of Music and Drama, Univ. of Ghana 1963–66; Feature Ed. African Review, Accra 1964–66; Reynolds Prof. of American Studies, Wake Forest Univ. 1981–; teacher of modern dance, Rome Opera House, Hambina Theatre, Tel-Aviv; has written several film scores; contrib. to numerous periodicals; Woman of Year in Communication 1976; numerous TV acting appearances; mem. Bd of Govs Maya Angelou Inst. for the Improvement of Child and Family Educ., Winston-Salem State Univ., NC 1998–; distinguished visiting prof. at several univs; mem. various arts orgs; Hon. Amb. to UNICEF 1996–; more than 50 hon. degrees; Horatio Alger Award 1992, Grammy Award Best Spoken Word or Non-Traditional Album 1994, Lifetime Achievement Award for Literature 1999, Presidential Medal for the Arts 2000, Lincoln Medal 2008, Presidential Medal of Freedom 2010, numerous other awards. *Plays:* Cabaret for Freedom 1960, The Least of These 1966, Gettin' Up Stayed On My Mind 1967, Ajax 1974, And Still I Rise 1976, Moon On a Rainbow Shawl (producer) 1988. *Theatre appearances include:* Porgy and Bess 1954–55, Calypso 1957, The Blacks 1960, Mother Courage 1964, Look Away 1973, Roots 1977, How To Make an American Quilt 1995 (feature film 1994). *Films directed include:* Down in the Delta 1998. *Publications include:* I Know Why the Caged Bird Sings 1970, Just Give Me A Cool Drink of Water 'Fore I Die 1971, Georgia, Georgia (screenplay) 1972, Gather Together In My Name 1974, All Day Long (screenplay) 1974, Oh Pray My Wings Are Gonna Fit Me Well 1975, Singin' and Swingin' and Gettin' Merry Like Christmas 1976, And Still I Rise 1976, The Heart of a Woman 1981, Shaker, Why Don't You Sing 1983, All God's Children Need Travelling Shoes 1986, Now Sheba Sings the Song 1987, I Shall Not Be Moved 1990, Gathered Together in My Name 1991, Wouldn't Take Nothing for my Journey Now 1993, Life Doesn't Frighten Me 1993, Collected Poems 1994, My Painted House, My Friendly Chicken and Me 1994, Phenomenal Woman 1995, Kofi and His Magic 1996, Even the Stars Look Lonesome 1997, Making Magic in the World 1998, A Song Flung up to Heaven 2002, Hallelujah! The Welcome Table 2005, Amazing Peace (long poem) (Quill Award for Poetry 2006) 2005, Letter to My Daughter 2008. *Address:* Lordly and Dame Inc., 1344 Main Street, Waltham, MA 02451, USA (office). *Telephone:* (781) 373-3680 (office). *Fax:* (781) 373-3681 (office). *E-mail:* kwheeler@lordly.com (office). *Website:* www.lordly.com (office); www.mayaangelou.com (office).

ANGELOV, Anyu, MA; Bulgarian politician and fmr army officer; b. 22 Dec. 1942, Haskovo; m.; two s.; ed Higher Nat. Mil. Artillery School, G.S. Rakovski Nat. Mil. Acad., Gen. Staff Acad. of the Soviet Armed Forces, Moscow; joined Bulgarian Armed Forces, apptd Lt 1966, Commdr of autonomous platoon 1966–71, Deputy Chief of Dept, Land Forces Air Defence Command 1974–80, Brigade Chief of Staff 1980–82, Brigade Commdr 1984–87, Land Forces Air Defence Chief of Staff 1987–90, Land Forces Air Defence Commdr in Chief 1990–92, Deputy Commdr in Chief of Bulgarian Land Forces 1992–94, rank of Lt-Gen. 1994, Deputy Chief of Gen. Staff of Bulgarian Armed Forces 1994, Defence Attaché, Embassy in London, UK 1997–2000, Commdr, G.S. Rakovski Nat. Mil. Acad. 2000–02, retd from Bulgarian Armed Forces 2002; Dir for Defence Planning, Ministry of Defence 2002, Pres. Centre for Nat. Security Research Foundation –2009, Deputy Minister of Defence 2009–10, Minister of Defence 2010–13; Hon. mem. NATO Defence Coll. Anciens' Asscn; several awards including Order of Merit, Commendation Medal for Meritorious Service under the Colours – First Grade. *Address:* c/o Ministry of Defence, 1090 Sofia, ul. Dyakon Ignatiy 3, Bulgaria.

ANGENOT, Marc, DPhil, DLit, FRSC; Canadian academic; *James McGill Professor Emeritus of Social Discourse Theory, McGill University;* b. 21 Dec. 1941, Brussels, Belgium; s. of Marcel Angenot and Zoé-Martha DeClercq; m. 1st Joséphine Brock 1966 (divorced 1976); one s. one d.; m. 2nd Nadia Khouri 1981; one d.; ed Univ. Libre de Bruxelles; James McGill Prof. of Social Discourse Theory, McGill Univ. 1967–2012, Prof. Emer. 2012–; Assoc. Dir Ecole des Hautes Etudes en Sciences Sociales, France 1985; Northrop Frye Prof. of Literary Theory, Univ. of Toronto 1994; Chaim Perelman Prof. of Rhetoric and Intellectual History, Université Libre de Bruxelles 2012; Vice-Pres. Acad. des Lettres et Sciences Humaines, Royal Soc. of Canada 2001; Chevalier des Palmes académiques; Prix Biguet, Acad. Française 1983, Killam Fellowship, Canada Council 1987, Prix des Sciences Humaines ACFAS (Canada) 1996, Prix Spirale Eva-Le-Grand 1996, Prix André-Laurendeau 1996, Award for High Distinction in Research, McGill Univ. 2001, Prix du Québec 'Léon Gérin' 2005. *Publications include:* Le Roman populaire 1975, Les Champions des femmes 1977, Glossaire pratique de la critique contemporaine 1979, La Parole pamphlétaire 1982, Critique de la raison sémiotique 1985, Le Cru et le faisandé 1986, Le Centenaire de la Révolution 1989, Ce que l'on dit des Juifs en 1889 1989, Mille huit cent quatre-vingt neuf 1989, L'Utopie collectiviste 1993, La Propagande socialiste 1996, Idéologies du ressentiment 1996, Colins et le socialisme rationnel 1999, La critique au service de la Révolution 2000, Religions de l'humanité et sciences de l'histoire 2000, D'où venons-nous, où allons-nous? 2001, L'Antimilitarisme, idéologie et utopie 2003, La démocratie, c'est le mal 2004, Rhétorique de l'anti-socialisme 2004, Le Marxisme dans les Grands récits 2005, Dialogues de sourds: traité de rhétorique antilogique 2008, Vivre dans l'histoire au 20e siècle 2008, Gnose et millénarisme: deux concepts pour le vingtième siècle 2008, En quoi sommes-nous encore pieux? 2009, L'immunité française envers le fascisme 2009, El discurso social 2010. *Address:* Arts Building, 853 Sherbrooke Street West, Montreal, PQ H3A 2T6, Canada (office). *Fax:* (514) 398-8557 (office).

ANGERER, Paul; Austrian conductor, composer and instrumentalist; b. 16 May 1927, Vienna; s. of Otto Angerer and Elisabeth Angerer; m. Anita Rosser 1952; two s. two d.; ed Hochschule für Musik und darstellende Kunst, Vienna; viola player, Vienna Symphony Orchestra 1947, leading solo viola player 1953–57; viola player, Tonhalle Zürich 1948, Suisse Romande Orchestra, Geneva 1949; Dir and Chief Conductor, Chamber Orch. of Wiener Konzerthausgesellschaft 1956–63; composer and conductor, Burgtheater, Vienna and Salzburg and Bregenz festivals 1960–; Perm. Guest Conductor, Orchestra Sinfonica di Bolzano e Trento 'Haydn' 1964–90; First Conductor, Bonn City Theatre 1964–66; Music Dir Ulm Theatre 1966–68; Chief of Opera, Salzburger Landestheater 1967–72; Dir SW German Chamber Orch., Pforzheim 1971–82; Prof. Hochschule, Vienna 1983–92; Moderator ORF 1984–2001, Radio Stephansdom 2001; Leader of Concilium Musicum Vienna; several prizes including Austrian State Prize for Music 1956, Theodor Körner Prize 1958, Vienna Cultural Prize 1983, Cultural Prize of Lower Austria 1987; Nestroy-Ring, City of Vienna 1998; Austrian Order of Honour for Sciences and Arts First Class 2001. *Works include:* orchestral pieces, chamber works, viola and piano concertos, a dramatic cantata, television opera, works for organ, harp, viola, harpsichord, etc.; numerous recordings both as soloist and conductor. *Publications:* Und s'ist alles nicht wahr! Briefe eines Eipeldauers, Mozart auf Reisen: Reisebriefe Leopold Mozarts aus Wien 1762–63, 1767–69, 1773, aus Paris und London 1763, aus Italien 1771–73. *Address:* Esteplatz 3/26, 1030 Vienna, Austria. *Telephone:* (676) 84036244 (mobile). *E-mail:* paulangerer@concilium.at (home).

ANGLADA GONZALEZ, Salvador, BE, MBA; Spanish business executive; ed Instituto de Empresa, Madrid; with Productos Organicos y Minerales and Dow Jones Markets 1990–97; Dir of Banking Sales, Dell Computer 1997, becoming Dir Preferred Accounts Div. and later Dir of Sales and Marketing for Southern Europe –2002; Dir of Sales, Telefónica de Espana 2002–03, Dir of Sales and Marketing 2003; CEO Eurotel Praha 2005–10, mem. Bd of Dirs Ceský Telecom 2005–10, Vice-Pres. Consumer Div. 2006–07, CEO Telefónica O2 Czech Repub. 2007–10. *Address:* c/o Eurotel Praha spol. s.r.o., Vyskočilova 1442/1b, PO Box 70, 14021 Prague 4, Czech Republic.

ANGULA, Nahas Gideon, BEd, MA; Namibian politician; *Minister of Defence;* b. 22 Aug. 1943, Onyaanya; m. Katrina Tangeni Namalenga; four c.; ed Oniipa Boy's School, Engela Boy's School, Ongwediva Training Coll., Oshigambo Jr Secondary School, Nkumbi Int. Coll., Univ. of Zambia, Columbia Univ., New York, Univ. of Manchester, UK; became active in SWAPO 1967, went into exile to Zambia 1967; Sec. for Educ., SWAPO Politburo; returned from exile 1989; Head of Dept, Voter Registration, SWAPO Election Directorate, Windhoek 1989; mem. Constituent Ass. 1989, Nat. Ass. 1990–; Minister of Educ., Sport and Culture 1990–95, of Higher Educ., Training and Employment Creation 1995–2005; nominated as one of three SWAPO presidential cands 2004; Prime Minister of Namibia 2005–12; Minister of Defence 2012–. *Publication:* The African Origin of Civilisation and the Destiny of Africa (co-ed.) 2000. *Address:* Ministry of Defence, PMB 13307,

Windhoek, Namibia (office). *Telephone:* (61) 2049111 (office). *Fax:* (61) 232518 (office). *E-mail:* psecretary@mod.gov.na (office). *Website:* www.mod.gov.na (office).

ANISTON, Jennifer Joanna; American actress, film director and producer; b. 11 Feb. 1969, Sherman Oaks, Calif.; d. of John Aniston and Nancy Dow; m. Brad Pitt (q.v.) 2000 (divorced 2005); ed New York High School of the Performing Arts; gained worldwide recognition for her portrayal of Rachel Green on the TV sitcom Friends 1990s; received a star on the Hollywood Walk of Fame 2012. *Theatre includes:* For Dear Life, Dancing on Checker's Grave. *Films include:* Mac and Me 1988, Leprechaun 1993, Dream for an Insomniac 1996, She's the One 1996, Picture Perfect 1997, 'Til There Was You 1997, The Object of My Affection 1998, The Thin Pink Line 1998, Office Space 1999, The Iron Giant (voice) 1999, Rock Star 2001, The Good Girl 2002, Bruce Almighty 2003, Along Came Polly 2004, Derailed 2005, Rumor Has It... 2005, Friends with Money 2006, The Break-Up 2006, Management 2008, Marley & Me 2008, He's Just Not That Into You 2009, Love Happens 2009, The Bounty Hunter 2010, The Switch 2010, Just Go with It 2011, Horrible Bosses 2011, My Least Favorite Career (video short) 2011, Wanderlust 2012, Unity (documentary) (narrator) 2012. *Television includes:* Molloy (series) 1990, Camp Cucamonga (film) 1990, Ferris Bueller (series) 1990–91, Quantum Leap (series) – Nowhere to Run 1992, The Edge (series) 1992–93, Herman's Head (series) 1992–93, Burke's Law (series) – Who Killed the Beauty Queen? 1994, Muddling Through (series) 1994, Friends (series) (Emmy Award for Best Actress 2002, Golden Globe for Best TV Actress in a Comedy 2003, Screen Actors Guild Award) 1994–2004, The Larry Sanders Show (series) – Conflict of Interest 1995, Partners (series) – Follow the Clams? 1996, Hercules (series) – Hercules and the Dream Date (voice) 1998, South Park (series) – Rainforest Shmainforest (voice) 1999, Freedom: A History of Us (series documentary) – Wake Up America 2003, King of the Hill (series) – Queasy Rider (voice) 2003, Dirt (series) – Ita Missa Est 2007, 30 Rock (series) – The One with the Cast of 'Night Court' 2008, Cougar Town (series) – All Mixed Up 2010, Burning Love (series) 2012. *Address:* c/o Creative Artists Agency, 2000 Avenue of the Stars, Los Angeles, CA 90067, USA (office); 5750 Wilshire Blvd, Los Angeles, CA 90036. *Telephone:* (424) 288-2000 (office). *Fax:* (424) 288-2900 (office). *Website:* www.caa.com (office); www.jenniferaniston.com.

ANKA, Paul, OC; Canadian/American singer, songwriter and actor; b. 30 July 1941, Ottawa, Ont.; m. Marie Ann Alison de Zogheb 1963 (divorced); five d.; numerous TV appearances world-wide, live performances; mem. BMI; Chevalier, Ordre des Arts et des Lettres. *Films:* Girls Town 1959, The Private Lives of Adam and Eve 1960, Look in Any Window 1961, The Longest Day 1962, Captain Ron 1992, Ordinary Magic 1993, Mad Dog Time 1996, 3000 Miles to Graceland 2001. *Television:* The Paul Anka Show (series host) 1982, Perry Mason: The Case of the Maligned Mobster 1991. *Compositions:* theme for The Tonight Show 1962, theme music for films, The Longest Day, No Way Out, Atlantic City, and contrib. of songs to numerous other films; some 900 songs, including It Doesn't Matter Anymore (for Buddy Holly) 1959, My Way (for Frank Sinatra) 1969, She's a Lady (for Tom Jones) 1971, Puppy Love (for Donny Osmond); other songs performed by artists including Elvis Presley, Barbra Streisand, Linda Ronstadt, The Sex Pistols, Nina Simone, Gipsy Kings and Robbie Williams. *Recordings include:* albums: The Fabulous Paul Anka And Others 1956, Paul Anka 1958, My Heart Sings 1959, Paul Anka Sings His Big 15 1959, Vol. II 1962, Vol. III 1962, Paul Anka Swings For Young Lovers 1959, Anka At The Copa 1960, It's Christmas Everywhere 1960, Diana 1962, Young Alive & In Love! 1962, Let's Sit This One Out 1962, Our Man Around the World 1963, Three Great Guys (with Sedaka and Cooke) 1963, Songs I Wish I'd Written 1963, Paul Anka 1964, Paul Anka Italiano 1964, A Casa Nostra 1964, Strictly Nashville 1966, Goodnight My Love 1969, Sincerely 1969, Life Goes On 1969, Paul Anka 70s 1970, Jubilation 1972, My Way 1974, Anka 1974, Feelings 1975, Remember Diana 1975, She's A Lady 1975, Times Of Your Life 1976, The Painter 1977, The Music Man 1977, Listen To Your Heart 1978, Headlines 1979, Both Sides Of Love 1981, Walk A Fine Line 1983, Freedom for the World 1987, Somebody Loves You 1989, Face in the Mirror 1993, After All 1995, Amigos (with others) 1996, A Body Of Work 1998, Rock Swings 2005. *Address:* Paul Anka Productions, 9200 West Sunset Blvd, PH 32, Los Angeles, CA 90069, USA. *E-mail:* paoffice@paulanka.com. *Website:* www.paulanka.com.

ANKUM, Hans (Johan Albert), DJur; Dutch professor of Roman law; *Professor Emeritus of Roman Law, University of Amsterdam;* b. 23 July 1930, Amsterdam; s. of Leendert Ankum and Johanna Ankum (née Van Kuykhof); m. 1st Joke Houwink 1957 (divorced 1970); m. 2nd Pelline van Es 1971; one s. three d.; ed Zaanlands Lyceum, Zaandam, Univ. of Amsterdam, Univ. of Paris; Asst, Roman Law and Juridical Papyrology, Univ. of Amsterdam 1956–60; Lecturer in Roman Law and Legal History, Univ. of Leyden 1960–63, Prof. 1963–69; Prof. of Roman Law, Legal History and Juridical Papyrology, Univ. of Amsterdam 1965–95, Prof. Emer. 1995–; mem. Royal Netherlands Acad. of Arts and Sciences 1986–; Kt, Order of the Dutch Lion 1992; Dr hc (Aix-Marseille) 1985, (Vrije Univ., Brussels) 1986, (Ruhr Universität, Bochum) 1995, (Univ. of Belgrade) 2005, (Charles Univ., Prague) 2008; Winkler Prins Award 1970. *Publications:* De geschiedenis der 'Actio Pauliana' 1962; over 320 books and articles on Roman law and legal history. *Leisure interests:* classical music, history of art, travel. *Address:* Faculty of Law, University of Amsterdam, PO Box 1030, 1000 BA, Amsterdam Oudermanhuispoort 4–6 (office); Zonnebloemlaan 8, 2111 ZG, Aerdenhout, Netherlands (home). *Telephone:* (20) 5253970 (office); (23) 5243036 (home). *Fax:* (20) 5253495 (office).

ANKVAB, Aleksandr Zolotinska-ipa; Georgian (Abkhaz) politician; *President of 'Republic of Abkhazia';* b. 26 Dec. 1952, Sukhumi, Abkhazian ASSR, Georgian SSR, USSR; ed Rostov State Univ.; worked as official of the Lenin Young Communist League (Komsomol) for many years; official in Justice Ministry of Abkhazian ASSR 1975–81; joined Exec. of Cen. Cttee of Georgian CP 1981; Deputy Interior Minister of Georgian SSR 1984–90; became mem. of Abkhazian Supreme Soviet following break-up of Soviet Union and Georgian independence 1991; apptd Interior Minister of Abkhazia's separatist govt during 1992–93 conflict with Georgian Cen. Govt; moved to Moscow and became a successful businessman 1994; returned to Abkhazian politics 2000, set up Aitaira (Revival) movt in opposition to Govt of Pres. Vladislav Ardzinba; announced intention to run for pres. 2004, disqualified on grounds that he could not speak Abkhaz and had not lived long enough in Abkhazia; supported Sergei Bagapsh instead; Prime Minister 2005–10; vice-presidential cand. 2009; Vice-Pres. 'Republic of Abkhazia' Feb. 2010–May 2011, Pres. May 2011–; has survived six assassination attempts since 2005.

Address: Office of the President of 'Republic of Abkhazia', 384900 Sukhumi, nab. Makhajirov 32, Abkhazia, Georgia (office). *Telephone:* (8402) 22-46-22 (office). *Fax:* (8402) 22-71-17 (office). *E-mail:* sukhum-krma@yandex.ru (office).

ANLYAN, William George, BS, MD; American professor of surgery, medical consultant and university administrator; *Chancellor Emeritus, Duke University;* b. 14 Oct. 1925, Alexandria, Egypt; s. of Armand Anlyan and Emmy Anlyan; two s. one d.; ed Yale Univ. and Duke Univ. Hosp.; Instructor in Surgery, Duke Univ. School of Medicine 1950–51, Assoc. 1951–53, Asst Prof. of Surgery 1953–58, Assoc. Prof. 1958–61, Prof. 1961–89, Assoc. Dean 1963–64, Dean 1964–69; Assoc. Provost Duke Univ. 1969, Vice-Pres. for Health Affairs 1969–83, Chancellor for Health Affairs 1983–88, Exec. Vice-Pres. 1987–88, Chancellor 1988–90, Chancellor Emer. 1990–; numerous exec. posts, Asscn of American Medical Colls 1965–, Distinguished Service Mem. 1974–, American Medical Asscn 1971–74, American Surgical Asscn 1964–; mem. Bd of Dirs Asscn for Acad. Health Centers 1971–, Pres. 1974–75; mem. Research Strengthening Group for Special Programme for Research and Training in Tropical Diseases, WHO 1981–85, Chair. Univ. Council's Cttee on Medical Affairs (WHO), Yale Univ. 1987–93; mem. Council Govt-Univ.-Industry Research Roundtable 1984–86; mem. several advisory and research cttees, NC 1965–; Consultant Gen. Surgery, Durham Veterans' Hosp. 1955–73; mem. US dels consulting on health and medical educ., China, Poland, Israel, Egypt, Saudi Arabia, Japan etc.; mem. Bd of Regents Nat. Library of Medicine 1968–71, Chair. 1971–72, Consultant 1972–; mem. Bd of Dirs Wachovia Bank 1970–90, G.D. Searle and Co. 1974–90, Pearle Health Services Inc. 1983–85, NC Inst. of Medicine 1983–, Durham Chamber of Commerce 1988–; mem. Bds of Visitors and Trustees numerous univs; mem. numerous professional socs; mem. Editorial Bd The Pharos 1968–93; Trustee The Duke Endowment 1990–; Hon. DS (Rush Medical Coll.) 1973; Modern Medicine Award for Distinguished Achievement 1974, Gov.'s Award for Distinguished Meritorious Service 1978, Distinguished Surgeon Alumnus, Yale Univ. School of Medicine 1979, The Abraham Flexner Award, Asscn of American Medical Colls 1980, Civic Honor Award, Durham Chamber of Commerce 1981, Award of Merit, Duke Univ. Hosp. and Health Admin Alumni Asscn 1987, Lifetime Achievement Award, Duke Univ. Medical Alumni 1995, Lifetime Achievement Award (for advocacy for medical research), Research America 1997, Distinguished Alumni Service Award, Yale Univ. School of Medicine 1999, Duke Univ. Medal for Distinguished Meritorious Service 2002, N Carolina Award for Science 2002. *Publications:* contrib. and several books; over 100 articles in professional journals on health and surgical topics. *Leisure interests:* piano, tennis. *Address:* Duke University Medical Center, 2200 West Main Street, Suite 400, Durham, NC 27705, USA (office). *Telephone:* (919) 684-3438 (office). *Fax:* (919) 684-3518 (office). *E-mail:* anlya001@mc.duke .edu (office). *Website:* www.mc.duke.edu (office).

ANN-MARGRET; American actress, singer and dancer; b. (Ann-Margret Olsson), 28 April 1941, Stockholm, Sweden; m. Roger Smith 1967; film debut in Pocketful of Miracles 1961; five Golden Globe Awards, three Female Star of the Year Awards. *Films include:* State Fair, Bye Bye Birdie, Once a Thief, The Cincinnati Kid, Stagecoach, Murderer's Row, CC & Co., Carnal Knowledge, RPM, The Train Robbers, Tommy, The Twist, Joseph Andrews, Last Remake of Beau Geste, Magic, Middle Age Crazy, Return of the Soldier, I Ought to Be in Pictures, Looking to Get Out, Twice in a Lifetime, 52 Pick-Up 1987, New Life 1988, Something More, Newsies 1992, Grumpy Old Men 1993, Grumpier Old Men 1995, Any Given Sunday 1999, The Last Producer 2000, A Woman's a Helluva Thing 2000, Interstate 60 2002, Taxi 2004, The Break-Up 2006, The Santa Clause 3: The Escape Clause 2006, The Loss of a Teardrop Diamond 2008. *Television includes:* Who Will Love My Children? 1983, A Streetcar Named Desire 1984, The Two Mrs Grenvilles 1987, Our Sons 1991, Nobody's Children, 1994, Following her Heart, Seduced by Madness: The Diane Borchardt Story 1996, Blue Rodeo 1996, Pamela Hanniman 1999, Happy Face Murders 1999, Perfect Murder, Perfect Town 2000, The Tenth Kingdom 2000, A Place Called Home 2004. *Publication:* (with Todd Gold) Ann-Margret: My Story 1994. *Address:* William Morris Agency, One William Morris Place, Beverly Hills, CA 90212, USA.

ANNADIF, Mahamet Saleh; Chadian politician and international organization official; *African Union Special Representative for Somalia and Head, African Union Mission in Somalia;* b. 25 Dec. 1956, Arada; m. twice; eight c.; with Telecommunications Dept, Office Nat. de Postes et Télécommunications (ONPT) 1981–82, Head of Research 1988–89, Dir-Gen. ONPT 1995–97; Man. Soc. des Télécommunications internationales du Tchad 1990–97; in charge of information and propaganda, Front de libération nationale du Tchad (FROLINAT)/Conseil démocratique révolutionnaire (CDR) 1982–85, Second Vice-Pres. FROLINAT/CDR 1985–88; Sec. of State for Agric. 1989–90; Minister of Foreign Affairs and Cooperation 1997–2003; Dir of Civil Cabinet of Pres. Idriss Deby –2006; Perm. Rep. of African Union to EU, Brussels 2006–11; Sec.-Gen. of the Presidency 2011; African Union Special Rep. for Somalia and Head of African Union Mission in Somalia (AMISOM) 2012–; Commdr Order nat. du Tchad. *Leisure interests:* nature, the countryside. *Address:* African Union Mission for Somalia (AMISOM), PO Box 20182-00200, Nairobi, Kenya (office). *Telephone:* 721-62-05 (office). *Fax:* 721-62-05 (office). *E-mail:* annadifm@africa-union.org (office). *Website:* amisom-au.org (office).

ANNAN, Kofi Atta, GCMG, BA (Econs), MSc; Ghanaian UN official and international organization official; b. 8 April 1938; m. Nane Lagergren; one s. two d.; ed Univ. of Science and Tech., Kumasi, Macalester Coll., St Paul, Minn., USA, Institut des Hautes Etudes Internationales, Geneva, Switzerland, Massachusetts Inst. of Tech., USA; held posts in UN ECA, Addis Ababa, UN, New York, WHO, Geneva 1962–71, Admin. Man. Officer, UN, Geneva 1972–74; Alfred P. Sloan Fellow, MIT 1971–72; Chief Civilian Personnel Officer, UNEF, Cairo 1974; Man. Dir Ghana Tourist Devt Co. 1974–76; Deputy Chief of Staff Services, Office of Personnel Services, Office of UNHCR, Geneva 1976–80, Deputy Dir Div. of Admin. and Head Personnel Service 1980–83; Dir of Admin. Man. Service, then Dir of Budget, Office of Financial Services, UN, New York 1984–87, Asst Sec.-Gen., Office of Human Resources Man. 1987–90; Controller Office of Programme Planning, Budget and Finance 1990–92; Asst Sec.-Gen. Dept of Peace-Keeping Operations 1992–93; Under-Sec.-Gen. 1993–96; UN Special Envoy (a.i.) to Fmr Yugoslavia 1995–96; Sec.-Gen. of UN 1997–2006; Jt Special Envoy of the UN and the League of Arab States on the Syrian crisis Feb.–Aug. 2012; Pres. Kofi Annan

Foundation 2007–; Pres. Global Humanitarian Forum 2007–10; Chair. Alliance for a Green Revolution in Africa (AGRA) 2007–13, Africa Progress Panel 2007–; Chancellor, Univ. of Ghana 2008–; Li Ka Shing Prof., Lee Kuan Yew School of Public Policy, Nat. Univ., Singapore 2009–; Chair., Prize Cttee, Mo Ibrahim Award for Excellence in African Leadership 2007–; apptd Global Fellow, Columbia Univ., USA 2009; Bd mem. UN Foundation, World Econ. Forum, Carnegie Endowment for International Peace, Carnegie Corpn of New York, Club of Madrid, World Org. Against Torture; mem. The Elders; Foreign Hon. mem., American Acad. of Arts and Sciences 2003; Companion of the Order of the Star (Ghana) 2000, Grand Cross with Collar of the Order of the Star (Romania) 2001, Grand Collar of the Order of Liberty (Portugal) 2005, Knight Grand Cross of the Order of the Lion (Netherlands) 2006, Grand Decoration of Honour in Gold with Sash for Services to the Republic of Austria (2007), Grand Cross 1st class of the Order of Merit (Germany) 2008; Dr hc (Univ. of Pennsylvania) 2005, (Universidade Nova de Lisboa) 2005, (George Washington Univ.) 2006, (Univ. of Tokyo) 2006, (Georgetown Univ.) 2006, (King's Coll., London) 2008, (Glasgow Caledonian Univ.) 2011 and several others; Kora All Africa Music Awards in the category of Lifetime Achievement 2000, Philadelphia Liberty Medal 2001, Nobel Peace Prize (jtly with UN) 2001, Profiles in Courage Award, JFK Memorial Museum 2002, James Madison Award, American Whig-Cliosophic Soc. 2002, Freedom Prize, Max Schmidheiny Foundation, Univ. of St Gallen 2003, Zayed Prize 2005, International Achievement Award, Inter Press Service 2006, Olof Palme Prize 2006, Crystal Tiger Award, Princeton Univ. 2006, MacArthur Award 2007, Peace of Westphalia Prize 2008, Gottlieb Duttweiler Prize 2008, Open Soc. Award, CEU Business School Budapest 2008, Reinhard Mohn Prize, Bertelsmann Foundation 2013. *Publication:* Interventions 2012. *Address:* Kofi Annan Foundation, POB 157, 1211 Geneva, Switzerland (office). *Telephone:* 229197520 (office). *Fax:* 229197529 (office). *E-mail:* info@kofiannanfoundation.org (office). *Website:* www.kofiannanfoundation.org (office).

ANNAUD, Jean-Jacques, LèsL; French film director and screenwriter; b. 1 Oct. 1943, Juvisy/Orge; s. of Pierre Annaud and Madeleine Tripoz; m. 1st Monique Rossignol 1970 (divorced 1980); one d.; m. 2nd Laurence Duval 1982; one d.; ed Inst. des Hautes Etudes Cinématographiques and Univ. of Paris, Sorbonne; freelance commercial film dir 1966–75; feature film dir 1975–; mem. Institut de France; Officier des Palmes académiques et du Mérite social, Commdr des Arts et Lettres; Grand Prix Nat. du Cinéma, Grand Prix de l'Acad. Française. *Films include:* Black and White in Colour 1976 (Acad. Award for Best Foreign Film), Hot Head 1979, Quest for Fire (César Award) 1981, The Name of the Rose (César Award), The Bear 1988 (César Award), The Lover 1992, Wings of Courage 1994, Seven Years in Tibet 1997, Enemy at the Gates 2001, Two Brothers 2004, Sa majesté Minor 2007. *Leisure interests:* books, old cameras, world travel. *Address:* c/o Repérage, 10 rue Lincoln, 75008 Paris; 9 rue Guénégaud, 75006 Paris, France (home).

ANNE, HRH The Princess (see Royal, HRH The Princess).

ANNINSKY, Lev Alexandrovich Ivanov, PhD; Russian writer and critic; b. 7 April 1934, Rostov-on-Don; s. of Alexandre Ivanov Anninsky and Anna Alexandrova; m. Alexandra Nikolayevna Ivanova Anninskaya; three d.; ed Moscow State Univ.; freelance literary critic 1956–, cinema critic 1960–, theatre critic 1962–; TV and radio broadcaster 1992–96; mem. Acad. of Russian Literature; Academician, Russian Acad. of Cinema, Russian Acad. of Theatre; jury mem. Yasnaya Polyana Award; fmr Ed. Druzhba Narodov (monthly), Rodina (monthly). *Publications include:* The Core of the Nut: Critical Reviews 1965, Married to the Idea 1971, Literary and Critical Reviews 1977; Hunting for Lev (Lev Tolstoy and Cinematography) 1980, Contacts 1982, Three Heretics: Pisemsky, Melnikov-Pechersky, Leskov 1988, Culture's Tapestry 1991, Elbows and Wings: Literature of the 1980s: Hopes, Reality, Paradoxes 1989, A Ticket to Elysium: Reflections on Theatre Porches 1989, The Sixties Generation 1991, Flying Curtain: Literary-Critical Articles on Georgia 1991, Silver and Black 1997, Bards 1999, Russians plus 2001, numerous titles in Russian, articles on literature, theatre and cinema. *Address:* 119415 Moscow, Udaltsova str. 16, Apt 19, Russia (home). *Telephone:* (495) 131-62-45 (home). *E-mail:* l_anninsky@mtu-net.ru.

ANNOU MALAM, Mamane Badamassi, MEcons, PhD, MBA; Niger economist and politician; ed Centre d'Etudes Financières, Economiques et Bancaires, Paris, France, Univ. of Minnesota-St Paul, USA; Head of Accounts Centre, Ministry of Finance 1981–83, Dir of Public Debt 1983–88; Dir Gen. Crédit du Niger 1988–90; Sec. Gen. at the Presidency 1990–91; Minister of Finance Feb.-Aug. 1991, Minister of Economy and Finance 2010–12; Research Economist, Univ. Arkansas-Fayetteville, USA and Univ. of Guelph, Canada 1999–2006; Prin. Economist, Prov. of Ont., Canada 2006–08; Tech. Dir UNDP Millennium Challenge Account-Niger 2008–10. *Address:* Ministry of the Economy and Finance, BP 389, Niamey, Niger (office).

ANOSOV, Dmitry Victorovich; Russian mathematician and academic; b. 30 Nov. 1936, Moscow; s. of Viktor Yakovlevich Anosov and Nina Konstantinovna Voskresenskaya; m.; one d.; ed Moscow State Univ., Math. Inst., USSR Acad. of Sciences; mem. staff, Steklov Inst. of Math., Russian Acad. of Sciences 1961–, Head of Dept 1997–, also Chair. Dissertation Council, mem. Academic Council; Prof., Dept of Mechanics and Math., Moscow State Univ. 1968; Corresp. mem. Russian Acad. of Sciences 1990, mem. 1992–; Hon. Prof., Moscow State Univ. 1999; Young Mathematician Prize, Moscow Math. Soc. 1965, USSR State Prize 1976, Humboldt Prize 1999, Russian Acad. of Sciences Lyapunov Prize (jtly) 2001. *Address:* Institute of Mathematics, Russian Academy of Sciences, 119991 Moscow, Gubkin str. 8, Russia (office). *Telephone:* (499) 135-22-91 (office). *Fax:* (499) 135-05-55 (office). *E-mail:* anosov@mi.ras.ru (office). *Website:* www.mi.ras.ru (office).

ANSARI, Anousheh, BSc, MSc; Iranian/American engineer and telecommunications industry executive; *CEO, Prodea Systems, Inc;* b. 12 Sept. 1966, Mashhad, Iran; m. Hamid Ansari 1991; ed George Mason Univ., Fairfax, Va, George Washington Univ., Washington, DC; began career as engineer with MCI Telecommunications Corpn, Communications Satellite Corpn (COMSAT); Co-founder and CEO Telecom Technologies, Inc. 1993–2000, merged with Sonus Networks 2000, Gen. Man. and Vice-Pres. Sonus Softswitch Div.; Co-founder Prodea Systems, Inc. 2006, currently CEO; Asscn of Space Explorers, Nat. Soc. of Professional Engineers, IEEE; mem. Advisory Bd Teachers in Space; George Mason Univ. Entrepreneurial Excellence Award, George Washington

Univ. Distinguished Alumni Achievement Award, Ernst & Young Entrepreneur of the Year Award for SW Region, Symons Innovator Award 2009. *Achievements include:* took part as self-funded space tourist in Soyuz TMA-9 mission, spent eight days on Int. Space Station (first Iranian in space) Sept. 2006. *Publication:* My Dream of Stars 2010. *Address:* Prodea Systems, Inc., 6101 West Plano Parkway, Plano, TX 75093, USA (office). *Telephone:* (214) 278-1850 (office). *Fax:* (214) 278-1851 (office). *E-mail:* Anousheh@anoushehansari.com (office). *Website:* www.prodeasystems.com (office); www.anoushehansari.com.

ANSARI, Mohammad Hamid, MA; Indian diplomatist and government official; *Vice-President;* b. 1 April 1937, Calcutta, Bengal, British India (now Kolkata); s. of Mohammad Abdul Aziz Ansari and Aasiya Begum m. Salma Ansari; two s. one d.; ed St Xavier's Coll., Kolkata, Aligarh Muslim Univ.; joined Indian Foreign Service 1961, past positions include Amb. to Saudi Arabia and UAE 1976–79, High Commr to Australia 1985–89, Amb. to Afghanistan 1989–90, to Iran 1990–92, to Saudi Arabia 1995–99; Amb. and Perm. Rep. to UN, New York 1993–95; Vice-Chancellor, Aligarh Muslim Univ. 2000–02; Chair. Nat. Comm. for Minorities 2006–07; Visiting Prof., Centre for West Asian and African Studies, Jawaharlal Nehru Univ. 1999–2000, Acad. of Third World Studies, Jamia Millia Islamia 2003–05; Distinguished Fellow, Observer Research Foundation 2002–06; Chair. Advisory Comm. for Oil Diplomacy, Ministry of Petroleum and Natural Gas 2004–05; Chair. Fifth Statutory Nat. Comm. for Minorities 2006–07; mem. Nat. Security Advisory Bd 2004–06; Vice-Pres. of India 2007–; Chair. Rajya Sabha (Council of States) 2007– (re-elected 2012); Padma Shree 1984. *Publications include:* Iran Today: Twenty-five Years after the Islamic Revolution (ed) 2005, Travelling Through Conflict: Essays on the Politics of West Asia 2008, Teasing Questions: Exploring Disconnects in Contemporary India 2014; numerous articles on West Asian affairs. *Leisure interests:* golf, cricket. *Address:* Vice-President's House, 6 Maulana Azad Road, New Delhi 110 011, India (office). *Telephone:* (11) 23016344 (office). *Fax:* (11) 23016422 (office). *E-mail:* vpindia@nic.in (office). *Website:* vicepresidentofindia.nic.in (office).

ANSCHUTZ, Philip F., BSc; American business executive; *Chairman, Anschutz Corporation;* b. 1939, Russell, Kan.; m. Nancy Anschutz; three c.; ed Univ. of Kansas; f. Anschutz Corpn 1965, Chair. and CEO 1991–; Chair. Southern Pacific Rail Corpn, San Francisco 1988–96; f. Anschutz Entertainment with stakes in LA Kings (professional ice hockey team) 1995–, LA Galaxy (professional soccer team) 1996–, majority owner, Staples Center, LA; Chair. Southern Pacific Rail Corpn 1988–96; Founder, Qwest Communications, Chair. 1993–2006; Owner, San Francisco Examiner newspaper, The Independent (local newspaper), Grant Printing Company, San Francisco 2004—. *Address:* Anschutz Corpn, 555 17th Street, Suite 2400, Denver, CO 80202-3941 (office). *Telephone:* (303) 298-1000 (office). *Fax:* (303) 298-8881 (office).

ANSIP, Andrus; Estonian politician; *Chairman, Estonian Reform Party (Reformierakond);* b. 1 Oct. 1956, Tartu; m. Anu Ansip; three d.; ed Tartu Secondary School No. 5, Tartu State Univ., Univ. of York, Canada, British Council training in Brussels, Dublin and Edinburgh; Sr Engineer, Organic Chem. Chair, Tartu State Univ. 1979–81, Sr Engineer, X-ray Contrast Substances Lab., Coronary and Cardio-surgery Div., Gen. and Molecular Pathology Inst. 1983–87; mil. service in the Baltic Fleet 1981–83; Head of Organizational Dept, Estonian CP, Tartu Dist Cttee, Instructor of Industry Dept 1986–88; Head of Regional Office, Jt Venture Estkompexim 1988–93; Chair. Radio Tartu Ltd 1994–99; Bankruptcy Trustee, Tartu Commercial Bank 1994–98; mem. Bd of Dirs Rahvapank (People's Bank) 1993–95, Fondijuhtide AS 1995–96, Fundmanager Ltd; Chair. Livonia Privatization IF 1995–96; CEO Fondinvesteeringu Maakler AS 1995–96, Investment Fund Broker Ltd; Mayor City of Tartu 1998–2004; Chair. Estonian Reform Party (Reformierakond) 2004–; Minister of Econ. Affairs and Communications 2004–05; Prime Minister 2005–14; mem. Estonian voluntary home guard org. Kaitseliit (Defence League) 2009–; Officer, Nat. Order of Merit (Malta) 2001, Order of the White Star (Third Class) 2005; recognized for his service in fight for Estonian freedom and Estonian national idea by Estonian Cen. Council in Canada 2007, received a copy of the key of the city of Tirana on the occasion of his state visit to Albania 2010. *Address:* Estonian Reform Party (Eesti Reformierakond), Tõnismagi 9, Tallinn 10119, Estonia (office). *Telephone:* 680-8080 (office). *Fax:* 680-8081 (office). *E-mail:* info@reform.ee (office). *Website:* www.reform.ee (office).

ANSTEE, Dame Margaret Joan, DCMG, BSc (Econ), MA (Cantab.); British/Bolivian international organization official, consultant, writer and lecturer; b. 25 June 1926, Writtle, Essex, England; d. of Edward C. Anstee and Anne A. Mills; ed Chelmsford Co. High School for Girls, Newnham Coll. Cambridge and Univ. of London; Lecturer in Spanish, Queen's Univ. Belfast 1947–48; Third Sec., Foreign Office 1948–52; UN Tech. Assistance Bd Manila 1952–54; Spanish Supervisor, Univ. of Cambridge 1955–56; UN Tech. Assistance Bd Colombia 1956–57, Uruguay 1957–59, Bolivia 1960–65; Resident Rep. UNDP, Ethiopia and UNDP Liaison Officer with ECA 1965–67; Sr Econ. Adviser, Office of Prime Minister, London 1967–68; Sr Asst to Commr in charge of study of Capacity of UN Devt System 1968–69; Resident Rep. UNDP Morocco 1969–72, Chile (also UNDP Liaison Officer with ECLAC) 1972–74; Deputy to UN Under-Sec.-Gen. in charge of UN Relief Operation to Bangladesh and Deputy Co-ordinator of UN Emergency Assistance to Zambia 1973; with UNDP, New York 1974–78; Asst Sec.-Gen. of UN (Dept of Tech. Co-operation for Devt) 1978–87; Special Rep. of Sec.-Gen. to Bolivia 1982–92, for co-ordination of earthquake relief assistance to Mexico 1985–87; Under-Sec.-Gen. UN 1987–93, Dir-Gen. of UN office at Vienna, Head of Centre for Social Devt and Humanitarian Affairs 1987–92, Special Rep. of Sec.-Gen. for Angola and Head of Angolan Verification Mission 1992–93; Adviser to UN Sec.-Gen. on peacekeeping, post-conflict peacebuilding and training troops for UN peacekeeping missions 1994; Chair. Advisory Group of Lessons Learned Unit, Dept of Peacekeeping Operations, UN, New York 1996–2002; Co-ordinator of UN Drug Control Related Activities 1987–91, of Int. Co-operation for Chernobyl 1991–92 and for countering impact of burning oil wells in Gulf War 1991–92; Sec.-Gen. 8th UN Congress on Prevention of Crime and Treatment of Offenders Aug. 1990; writer, lecturer, consultant and adviser (ad honorem) to Bolivian Govt 1993–97, 2002–06 and to UN 1993–2001; consultant to UN Dept of Political Affairs on post-conflict peace-building 1996–2001; mem. Advisory Bd UN Studies at Yale Univ. 1994–, Advisory Council Oxford Research Group 1997–, Advisory Bd UN Intellectual History

Project 1999–2010; Trustee, Helpage Int. 1994–97; Patron and Bd mem. British Angola Forum 1998–2010; mem. Pres. Carter's Int. Council for Conflict Resolution 2002–; Vice-Pres. UK/UN Asscn 2002–; mem. Editorial Bd Global Governance 2004–, Strategic Advisory Bd, Durham Global Security Inst., Durham Univ. 2010–; Patron, Peace Direct 2005–; Hon. Fellow, Newnham Coll. Cambridge 1991; Hon. Life Vice-Pres., British Asscn of Former UN Civil Servants 2010–; Commdr Ouissam Alaouite (Morocco) 1972, Dama Gran Cruz Condor of the Andes (Bolivia) 1986, Grosse Goldene Ehrenzeichen am Bande (Austria) 1993, Grand Officer, Order of Bernardo O'Higgins (Chile) 2006; Dr hc (Essex) 1994; Hon. LLD (Westminster) 1996; Hon. DSc (Econ) (London) 1998; Hon. DIur (Cambridge) 2004; Reves Peace Prize, William and Mary Coll., USA 1993, Sir Brian Urquhart Award for Distinguished Service to UN 2011. *Publications:* The Administration of International Development Aid 1969, Gate of the Sun: A Prospect of Bolivia 1970, Africa and the World (co-ed. with R.K.A. Gardiner and C. Patterson) 1970, Desarrollo Diferente para un Pais de Cambios: Salir del Circulo Vicioso de la Riqueza Empobrecedura 1995, Orphan of the Cold War: The Inside Story of the Collapse of the Angolan Peace Process 1992–93 1996, Never Learn to Type: A Woman at the United Nations 2003, The House on the Sacred Lake (and other Bolivian dreams and nightmares) 2009, JB: An Unlikely Spanish Don: The Life and Times of Professor John Brande Trend 2013; numerous articles on UN reforms and peacekeeping, Angola, econ. and social devt. *Leisure interests:* writing, gardening, hill-walking (preferably in the Andes), bird-watching, swimming. *Address:* The Walled Garden, Knill, nr Presteigne, Powys, LD8 2PR, Wales (home); c/o PNUD, Casilla 9072, La Paz, Bolivia (home). *Telephone:* (1544) 267411 (home); (591) 71569987 or 71533742 (Bolivia) (home).

ANSTEY, Caroline, PhD; British international organization official and fmr politician; *Managing Director, World Bank Group;* b. 7 Nov. 1955, London; d. of Edgar Anstey and Daphne Lilly; m. Milton W. Hudson; two s.; ed Univ. of Leeds, Univ. of California, Berkeley, London School of Economics; Political Asst to Prime Minister James Callaghan 1974–79; apptd Consultant in External Affairs, World Bank, Washington, DC 1995, Asst to World Bank Pres. 1996, Country Dir for the Caribbean –2007, Chief of Staff 2007–10, Vice-Pres. of External Affairs 2010–11, Man. Dir World Bank Group 2011–, fmr Dir of Media Relations and Chief Spokesperson; fmr Ed. Analysis (BBC weekly current affairs programme); fmr Secr. mem. InterAction Council. *Address:* Office of the Managing Director, World Bank Group, 1818 H Street, NW, Washington, DC 20433, USA (office). *Telephone:* (202) 473-1000 (office). *Fax:* (202) 477-6391 (office). *Website:* www.worldbank.org (office).

ANTES, Horst; German painter and sculptor; b. 28 Oct. 1936, Heppenheim; s. of Valentin Antes and Erika Antes; m. Dorothea Grossmann 1961; one s. one d.; ed Heppenheim Coll., Akademie der Bildenden Künste, Karlsruhe; worked in Florence, then Rome; Prof., State Acad. of Fine Arts, Karlsruhe 1957–59, Berlin 1984–; teacher, Akademie der Bildenden Künste, Karlsruhe 1965, 1984–2000; Guest Prof., Staatliche Hochschule für Bildende Künste, Berlin 1974; mem. Acad. der Künste, Berlin, now living in Berlin, Karlsruhe and Tuscany, Italy; Pankofer-Preis 1959, Kulturpreis 1959, Villa Romana Prize, Florence 1962, Villa Massimo Prize, Rome 1963, UNESCO Prize, Venice Biennale 1966, Hans-Molfenter-Preis 1989, Kulturpreis (Hesse) 1991, Bienal de Sao Paulo 1991. *Address:* Hohenberg-strasse 11, 76228 Karlsruhe (Wolfartsweier), Germany. *Telephone:* (721) 491621.

ANTHONY, Kenny Davis, LLB, BSc, PhD; Saint Lucia politician; *Prime Minister and Minister of Finance;* b. 8 Jan. 1951; ed Univ. of Birmingham, Univ. of the West Indies; Leader, Saint Lucia Labour Party; Prime Minister of Saint Lucia, Minister of Finance, Planning, Devt, Information and the Civil Service 1997–2001, Prime Minister, Minister of Finance, Int. Financial Services, Econ. Affairs and Information 2001–06, Leader of the Opposition 2006–11, Prime Minister and Minister of Finance 2011–. *Address:* Office of the Prime Minister, Greaham Louisy Administrative Building, 5th Floor, Waterfront, Castries, Saint Lucia (office). *Telephone:* 468-2111 (office). *Fax:* 453-7352 (office). *E-mail:* admin@pm.gov.lc (office). *Website:* www.pm.gov.lc (office).

ANTICH VALERO, José; Spanish journalist and newspaper executive; *Director, La Vanguardia;* b. 23 June 1955, La Seu d'Urgell (Lérida); m.; four c.; ed; writer for Agencia Efe, Barcelona 1977; took part in founding articles of newspaper El Periódico de Catalunya where he started career as political feature writer 1978–82; part of founding team of Catalan edn of El País and worked as political corresp. 1982–94; Chief Political Writer for La Vanguardia 1994–98, coordinator of all political affairs at newpaper 1998–2000, Dir 2000–; VIII Fundación Independiente de Periodismo Camilo José Cela Prize 2004. *Publication:* El Virrey (political study into Jordi Pujol) 1994. *Address:* La Vanguardia, Av. Diagonal 477 pl. 7, 08036 Barcelona, Spain (office). *Telephone:* (93) 4812200 (office). *Fax:* (93) 3185587 (office). *E-mail:* direccio@lavanguardia.es (office). *Website:* www.lavanguardia.es (office).

ANTINORI, Severino, PhD; Italian gynaecologist and embryologist; b. 6 Sept. 1945, Civitella del Tronto; m. Caterina Antinori; two d.; ed Univ. La Sapienza; Perm. Asst in Obstetrics and Gynaecology, Istituto Materno Regina Elena 1973–80, Prin. Asst 1980–82, Dir Reproductive Physiopathology Service 1985–87; at Ospedale Materno Regina Elena 1978–92; specialist in obstetrics and gynaecology, Univ. Cattolica di Roma 1978; Prof., Univ. degli Studi di Pisa 1993–94, Univ. degli Studi G. D'Annunzio, Chieti 1996–97, 1998–99, Univ. degli Studi di Roma 1998–99; fmr Dir Centro RAPRUI (Ricercatori Associati per la Riproduzione Umana); Vice-Pres. Int. Asscn of Pvt. Assisted Reproductive Tech. Clinics and Labs. *Publications include:* numerous articles in medical journals. *Address:* Medical Ristemo, Via Tacitus, 90, 00193 Rome, Italy (office). *Telephone:* (06) 3230171 (office). *Fax:* (06) 3201083 (office). *E-mail:* severino.antinori@tin.it (office). *Website:* www.ristemomedica.com (office).

ANTOINE, Frédéric, PhD; Belgian journalist and academic; *Professor, School of Communication Science, Catholic University of Louvain;* b. 27 Sept. 1955, Uccle, Brussels; s. of Paul Antoine and Suzanne Degavre; m. Christine Masuy; two s. one d.; ed Catholic Univ. of Louvain; journalist, L'Appel 1977, La Libre Belgique 1978–2008; Research Asst, Dept of Communication Science, Catholic Univ. of Louvain 1979, Prof. 1989–; Dir Research Unit on Mediatic Narrative (RECI) 1991–2000, Head of Undergraduate Programme Information and Communication 2006–; News Ed. Radio 1180, Brussels 1979–2009; Prof., Media School IAD,

Louvain-la-Neuve 1981–; Ed. L'Appel 1992–; Invited Prof. Univ. of Namur 2006–; Chair. GRER (Radio Research and Studies Group), France 2010–. *Publications:* On Nous a Changé la Télé 1987, La Télévision à Travers les Programmes 1988, Télévision In: Le Guide des Médias 1989–97; ed. La Médiamorphose d'Alain Vanderbiest 1994; ed. Coupures de Presse 1996, Les Radios et les Télévisions de Belgique 2000, Les Multinationales des Médias 2002, Le Grand Malentendu 2003, Télé-réalité, la réalité si je mens 2008. *Address:* Ruelle de la Lanterne, Magique 14, 1348 Louvain-la-Neuve (office); Magazine L'appel, Rue du beau Mur 45, 4030 Liège (office); Rue Grande 58, 5530 Godinne, Belgium (home). *Telephone:* (1) 47-28-14 (office); (4) 341-10-04 (office); (81) 22-06-62 (home). *Fax:* (1) 47-30-44 (office); (4) 341-10-04 (office). *E-mail:* frederic.antoine@uclouvain.be (office); redacteurenchef@magazine-appel.be (office). *Website:* www.uclouvain.be/comu (office); www.magazine-appel.be (office).

ANTONAKAKIS, Dimitris; Greek architect; b. 22 Dec. 1933, Chania, Crete; m. Maria-Suzana Antonakakis (q.v.) (née Kolokytha) 1961; one s. one d.; ed School of Architecture, Nat. Tech. Univ. of Athens; partnership with Suzana Antonakakis, Athens 1959–; Asst Instructor in Architecture, Nat. Tech. Univ. of Athens 1959–64, Instructor 1964–78, mem. teaching staff 1978–92; Founder and Co-Prin. (with S. Antonakakis) Atelier 66 1965; mem. and Treas. Admin. Cttee, Greek Architectural Asscn 1962–63; Pres. Asscn of Assts and Instructors, Nat. Tech. Univ. 1975–77; Vice-Pres. Cen. Admin. Cttee, Asscn of Assts and Instructors of Greek Univs 1976–77; mem. Int. Design Seminar, Tech. Univ. Delft 1987, Split 1988; Visiting Prof., MIT, USA 1994–99, Nat. Tech. Univ. of Athens 1997–98; Art Dir Centre for Mediterranean Architecture, Crete 1997–; Corresp. mem. Acad. d'Architecture, Paris; Dr hc (Aristotle Univ. of Thessaloniki) 2007; numerous awards and prizes. *Works include:* Archaeological Museum, Chios 1965–66, Hydra Beach Hotel, Hermionis 1965, vertical addition, house in Port Phaliron 1967–72, miners' housing complex, Distomo 1969, apartment bldg, Emm. Benaki 118, Athens 1973–74, Hotel Lyttos, Heraklion, Crete 1973–82, Zannas House, Philopappos Hill, Athens 1980–82, Gen. Hosp., Sitia, Crete 1982, Ionian Bank br., Rhodes 1983, Heraklion, Crete 1987, Faculty of Humanities, Rethymnos, Crete 1982, Tech. Univ. of Crete, Chania 1982, Summer Theatre, Komotini 1989, Traditional Crafts Centre, Ioannina 1990, Museum of Acropolis, Athens 1990, Art Studio, Aegina 1990, office bldg, 342 Syngrou Ave., Athens 1990, Open-air Theatre, Thessaloniki 1995–96, Pissas House, Heraklion, Crete 1997, Rehabilitation of ancient Agora area, Athens 1997, Museum of Science and Technology, Patras 1999, Kallithea and Ano Patisia railway stations, Athens 2001–02, Kolonaki Square, Athens 2004; several pvt. houses. *Publications:* Le Corbusier Une Petite Maison (trans.) 1998; numerous architectural articles. *Address:* Atelier 66, Emm. Benaki 118, Athens 114-73, Greece (office). *Telephone:* (210) 3300323 (office). *Fax:* (210) 3801160 (office). *E-mail:* a66@otenet.gr (office). *Website:* www .a66architects.com (office).

ANTONAKAKIS-KOLOKYTHA, Maria-Suzana; Greek architect; b. 25 June 1935, Athens; m. Dimitris Antonakakis (q.v.) 1961; one s. one d.; ed School of Architecture, Nat. Tech. Univ., Athens; partnership with Dimitris Antonakakis, Athens 1959–; Founder and Co-Prin. (with Dimitris Antonakakis) Atelier 66 1965; mem. Admin. Cttee Greek Architects Asscn 1971–72; Pres. Dept of Architecture, Tech. Chamber of Greece 1982–83; mem. Int. Design Seminar, Tech. Univ. Delft 1987, Split 1988; mem. Greek Secr., Int. Union of Architects (UIA) 1985–2002; newspaper columnist 1998–; Dr hc (Aristotle Univ. of Thessaloniki) 2007; numerous awards and prizes. *Works include:* Archaeological Museum, Chios 1965–66, Hydra Beach Hotel, Hermionis 1965, vertical additions, House in Port Phaliron 1967–72, miners' housing complex, Distomo 1969, apartment bldg, Emm. Benaki 118, Athens 1973–74, Hotel Lyttos, Heraklion, Crete 1973–82, Zannas House, Philopappos Hill, Athens 1980–82, Gen. Hosp. Sitia, Crete 1982, Ionian Bank branch, Rhodes 1983, Heraklion, Crete 1987, Summer Theatre, Komotini 1989, Art Studio, Aegina 1990, office bldg, 342 Syngrou Ave, Athens 1990, Traditional Crafts Centre, Ioannina 1990, Museum of Acropolis, Athens 1990, Open-air Theatre, Thessaloniki 1995-96, Pissas House, Heraklion, Crete 1997, rehabilitation of ancient Agora area, Athens 1997, Museum of Science and Technology, Patras 1999, Kallithea and Ano Patisia railway stations, Athens 2001–02, New Acropolis Museum, Athens 2001, Kolonaki Square, Athens 2004; several pvt. and holiday houses. *Publications:* numerous architectural articles; trans. Entretien (Le Corbusier) 1971. *Address:* Atelier 66, Emm. Benaki 118, Athens 114-73, Greece (office). *Telephone:* (210) 3300323 (office). *Fax:* (210) 3801160 (office). *E-mail:* a66@otenet.gr (office). *Website:* www.a66architects.com (office).

ANTONAKOPOULOS, Gen. Georgios, LLB; Greek army officer; b. 5 Jan. 1943, Patra, Peloponnisos; s. of Antonios Antonakopoulos; m.; two c.; ed Aristotle Univ. of Thessaloniki, Hellenic Nat. Defence Coll., Hellenic Higher Army War Coll.; began career in Hellenic Armed Forces 1967, held positions successively as Artillery Battery Commdr, Instructor Artillery Schools, Staff Officer Infantry Div., Staff Officer Intelligence Div., Commdr Artillery Battalion, Commdr Field Artillery Command, Chief of Staff Mechanized Div., Dir 1st Staff Office Hellenic Army Gen. Staff, Brigade Commdg Gen., Dir Operation Br. Hellenic Army Gen. Staff, Commdg Gen. XII Mechanized Infantry Div., Commdg Gen. D'Army Corps, Chief of Hellenic Army Gen. Staff, Chief of Hellenic Nat. Defence Gen. Staff 2002–05; Medal for Mil. Valour Class A and B, Chief of Hellenic Army Gen. Staff Commendation Medal, Star of Merit and Honour, Army Meritorious Command Commendation Medal Class A, Staff Officer Service Commendation Medal Class A, Golden Cross of the Order of Honour, Knight Commdr's Cross of Order of the Phoenix, Knight Commdr's Cross of Order of Honour.

ANTONELLI, HE Cardinal Ennio, DPhil; Italian ecclesiastic and academic; *President Emeritus, Pontifical Council for the Family;* b. 18 Nov. 1936, Todi; ed Seminary of Todi, Pontifical Regional Seminary of Assisi, Pontifical Higher Seminary of Rome, Pontifical Lateran Univ., Rome, State Univ. of Perugia; ordained priest, Diocese of Todi 1960; Prof. of Theology, Vice-Rector, then Rector, Seminary of Perugia; Prof. of Theology, Regional Seminary of Assisi; Prof. of Art History, Superior Insts of Assisi and Deruta; Bishop of Gubbio 1982–88; Metropolitan Archbishop of Perugia-Città della Pieve 1988–95; Sec.-Gen. Italian Episcopal Conf. 1995–2001; del. to Special Ass. for Europe, World Synod of Bishops, Vatican City 1999; Archbishop of Florence 2001–08, Archbishop Emer. 2008–; cr. Cardinal (Cardinal-Priest of Sant'Andrea delle Fratte) 2003; participated in Papal Conclave 2005, 2013; Pres. Pontifical Council for the Family 2008–12, Pres. Emer. 2012–; mem. Pontifical Council for the Pastoral Care of Migrants and Itinerants 2011–. *Address:* Pontifical Council for the Family, Piazza di San Calisto 16, 00153 Rome, Italy (office). *Telephone:* (06) 69887243 (office). *Fax:* (06) 69887272 (office). *E-mail:* pcf@family.va (office). *Website:* www.vatican.va/roman_curia/pontifical_councils/family/index.htm (office); www.familia.va (office).

ANTONESCU, George Crin Laurenţiu (Crin); Romanian teacher and politician; *President, National Liberal Party (Partidul Naţional Liberal);* b. 21 Sept. 1959, Tulcea; m. 1st Aurelia Antonescu (died 2004); one d.; m. 2nd Adina Vălean 2009; ed Univ. of Bucharest; worked as history teacher in Soleşti, Vaslui Co. 1985; later returned to Tulcea, continuing his academic activity in Niculiţel –1989; worked as curator for Tulcea Museum of History and Archaeology 1989–90; joined Nat. Liberal Party (Partidul Naţional Liberal—PNL) 1990, elected Vice-Pres. 1995, Pres. 2009–; mem. Chamber of Deputies 1996–2008, Leader PNL Parl. Group 2005–08; Minister of Youth and Sports 1997–2000; mem. Senate 2008–, Vice-Pres. of Senate 2008–09, Pres. 2012–14 (resgnd); unsuccessful presidential cand. 2009; Acting Pres. of Romania (following suspension of Traian Băsescu) 10 July–27 Aug. 2012. *Address:* National Liberal Party (Partidul Naţional Liberal), 011866 Bucharest, Blvd Aviatorilor 86 (office); Senatul Romaniei (The Senate), 050711 Bucharest 5, Calea 13 Septembrie 1–3, Romania (office). *Telephone:* (21) 2310795 (PNL) (office); (21) 3113532 (Senate) (office). *Fax:* (21) 2310796 (PNL) (office). *E-mail:* presedinte@pnl.ro (office). *Website:* www.pnl.ro (office); www.senat.ro (office); www.crinantonescu.ro.

ANTONICHEVA, Anna; Russian ballet dancer; *Principal Dancer, Bolshoi Theatre Ballet Company;* b. 1973, Baku, Azerbaijan; ed Moscow Academic School of Choreography; joined Bolshoi Theatre Ballet Co. 1991, now Prin. Dancer; coached by Marina Kondratieva and Ekaterina Maximova; Transcaucasian Competition of Ballet Artists 1988, Merited Artist of the Russian Fed. 1998, Gold Medal, Int. Ballet Competition, Jackson, Miss. 1998, Soul of Dance Prize (Up-and-Coming-Star nomination), Ballet magazine 1999, People's Artist of the Russian Fed. 2008. *Ballet:* leading and solo parts include Shirin (The Legend of Love), Odette-Odile and Swan Princess (Swan Lake), Giselle and Myrtha (Giselle), Juliet (Romeo and Juliet), Phrygia (Spartacus), Aurora and Princess Florine (Sleeping Beauty), Kitri and Dulcinea (Don Quixote), Nikiya (La Bayadere), ballet soloist (Symphony in C), Sylph (Chopiniana), Hero (Love for Love), Concert number (Carnival in Venice), Diana and Concert number (Esmeralda), Concert numbers (Listening into the Music by Mozart, Tango, Taming the Fire (S. Bobrov's version)), Esmeralda (Notre-Dame de Paris), Raymonda (Raymonda), ballet soloist (Agon). *Address:* The State Academic Bolshoi Theatre of Russia, Teatralnaya Pl. 1, Moscow, Russia (office). *E-mail:* pr@bolshoi.ru (office); support@bolshoi.net. *Website:* www.bolshoi.ru/en/theatre/ballet_troupe/soloists (office).

ANTONIO, Joseph Philippe, LLB; Haitian politician and diplomatist; b. 22 July 1939, Saint-Marc; six c.; ed Port-au-Prince Univ., Ecole Normale Supérieure, Univ. of Geneva, Switzerland; Prof. Nouveau Collège Bird, Haiti 1966–71; Dir-Co-ordinator Haitian Centre of Research and Documentation 1978–91; Chargé d'affaires, UN, New York 1991–94, Perm. Rep. 1995, 1998; Chargé d'affaires, Embassy in Germany 1992–94; Minister of Foreign Affairs and Religion 2001–04. *Address:* c/o Ministry of Foreign Affairs and Religion, boulevard Harry S. Truman, Cité de l'Exposition, Port-au-Prince, Haiti (office).

ANTONOVA, Irina Aleksandrovna; Russian museum researcher; *Director, Pushkin Museum of Fine Arts;* b. 20 March 1922, Moscow; ed Moscow State Univ.; worked in Pushkin Museum of Fine Arts 1945–, Sr Researcher 1945–61, Dir 1961–; organizer of numerous exhbns and regular exchange with museums of Europe and America; f. together with Sviatoslav Richter Festival of Arts December Nights accompanied by art shows 1981–; Vice-Pres. Int. Council of Museums 1980–92, Hon. mem. 1992–; mem. Russian Acad. of Educ. 1989; Corresp. mem. San-Fernando Acad., Madrid; Commdr des Arts et Lettres; State Prize 1995. *Publications:* more than 60 articles on problems of museum man., art of Italian Renaissance, contemporary painting. *Leisure interests:* swimming, cars, music, ballet. *Address:* A. S. Pushkin Museum of Fine Arts, 121019 Moscow, Volkhonka str. 12, Russia. *Telephone:* (495) 203-46-76 (office). *E-mail:* Finearts@gmii.museum.ru (office). *Website:* www.museum.ru/gmii (office).

ANTONSSON, Markús Örn; Icelandic diplomatist; b. 25 May 1943; m. Steinunn Armannsdóttir; two c.; ed Reykjavík Coll., exchange student in USA; part-time journalist and photographer, Morgunbladid (daily) 1961–65; trained in broadcasting journalism and TV production in UK and Sweden; reporter, newspresenter and programme producer, RUV TV 1965–70, Dir-Gen. Nat. Broadcasting Service, RUV TV and Radio 1985–91, Dir RUV Radio Div. 1995–98, Dir-Gen. RUV TV and Radio 1998–2005; mem. Broadcasting Council 1979–85, Chair. 1983–85; City Councillor, Reykjavík 1970–85, mem. Exec. Cttee Reykjavík City Council and Chair. several other cttees, Pres. City Council 1983–85, Chair. City Council Exec. Cttee and Leader of Independence Party Councillors' Group; Mayor of Reykjavík 1991–94; Amb. to Canada 2005–08; Dir Icelandic National Heritage Centre, Reykjavík 2008–; mem. Bd Atlantic Alliance Asscn of Young Political Leaders 1971–75, Man. of Eurimages, European Film Fund 1994–99, Icelandic Symphony Orchestra 1995–98, Icelandic Nat. League 1997–2003 (Pres. 1998–2003); Ed. business and travel magazines with Frjálst framtak publishing house 1972–83; mem. Rotary 1983–, Jt-Ed. Rotary Norden (regional magazine for Rotary in the five Nordic countries) 1996–; mem. Exec. Cttee and Advisory Council European Cultural Foundation, Amsterdam 1994–.

ANTONY, Arackaparambil Kurian, BA, BL; Indian politician; *Minister of Defence;* b. 28 Dec. 1940, Cherthala, Alappuzha Dist, Kerala; s. of Arackaparambil Kurian Pillai and Aleyamma; m. Elizabeth Antony; two s.; ed Maharajas Coll., Govt Law Coll., Ernakulam; Chief Minister of Kerala 1977–78, 1995–96, 2001–04; mem. Rajya Sabha (Parl.) from Kerala 1985–95, 2005–; Minister of Civil Supplies, Consumer Affairs and Public Distribution 1993–95; Leader of Opposition, Kerala Legis. Ass. 1996–2001; Minister of Defence 2006–; Chair. Disciplinary Cttee of All India Congress Cttee. *Address:* Ministry of Defence, 104 South Block, New Delhi 110 011 (office); Anjanam, Easwara Vilasam Rd, Thiruvananthapuram 695 014, India (home). *Telephone:* (11) 23019030 (office); (11) 23012286 (office); (11) 23019474 (office). *Fax:* (11) 23015403 (office). *E-mail:* ak.antony@sansad.nic.in (office); akantony@antony.com (home). *Website:* www.mod.nic.in (office).

ANTUNOVIĆ, Željka, MD; Croatian physician and politician; *Deputy President, Social Democratic Party of Croatia (Socijaldemokratska partija hrvatske);* b. 1955, Virovitica; m.; two c.; ed Univ. of Zagreb, Harvard Univ., USA; Head of Finance Section, Sljeme Meat Industry 1980–84; head of finance, housing utilities co., Zagreb 1984–93; Councillor, City of Zagreb Ass. 1993–95, 1997–98; mem. Main Cttee of Social Democratic Party (Socijaldemokratska partija hrvatske—SDP) 1994–95, 1995–, City Cttee of SDP, Zagreb 1997–98, currently Deputy Pres.; mem. Parl. (Croatian Nat. Sabor) 1995–99, 2003–, Pres. Parl. Cttee for Families, Youth and Sport 2005–, mem. Cttee on Equal Opportunities for Women and Men; Pres. Social Democratic Forum of Women in SDP 1995–99; Deputy Prime Minister in charge of Social Affairs 2000–03; Minister of Defence 2002–03; Ed. Accounting and Finance magazine, Croatian Asscn of Accountants and Finance Employees 1993–95. *Address:* Social Democratic Party of Croatia (Socijaldemokratska partija hrvatske), 10000 Zagreb, Iblerov trg 9; Croatian National Parliament, Hrvatski Sabor Trg Svetog Marka 6–7, 1000 Zagreb, Croatia (office). *Telephone:* (1) 4552658 (SDP). *Fax:* (1) 4552842 (SDP). *E-mail:* sdp@sdp.hr. *Website:* www.sdp.hr; www.sabor.hr.

ANUSZKIEWICZ, Richard Joseph, BS, MFA; American artist; b. 23 May 1930, Erie, Pa; s. of Adam Jacob Anuszkiewicz and Victoria Jankowski; m. Sarah Feeney 1960; one s. two d.; ed Cleveland Inst. of Art, Yale Univ., Kent State Univ.; moved to New York City 1957; Conservator, Metropolitan Museum of Art 1957–58; Silver Designer Tiffany and Co. 1958–59; teacher, Cooper Union, New York 1963–65; Artist-in-Residence, Dartmouth Coll. 1967, Univ. of Wis. 1968, Cornell Univ. 1968, Kent State Univ. 1968, Charles Foley Gallery, Columbus 1988, Newark Museum 1990, Center for Arts, Vero Beach, Fla 1993; represented in collections at Museum of Modern Art, Whitney Museum of American Art, Albright-Knox Art Gallery, Butler Art Inst., Yale Art Gallery, Chicago Art Inst., Fogg Art Museum, Corcoran Gallery of Art, Harvard Univ., Chicago Museum of Contemporary Art, Cleveland Museum of Art, Columbus Museum of Art, Denver Museum of Art, Blanton Museum of Art, Univ. of Texas, Boca Raton Museum of Art, Guggenheim Museum, New York, Hokkaido Museum of Modern Art, Metropolitan Museum of Art, Philadelphia Museum of Art, Wadsworth Atheneum, Hartford; Charles of the Ritz Oil Painting Award 1963, Silvermine Guild Award 1964, Cleveland Arts Prize 1977, Childe Hassam Fund Purchase Award 1980, 1988, New York State Art Teachers Asscn Award 1994, Emil and Dines Carlson Award 1995, New Jersey Pride Award 1996, Lee Krasner Award 2000, Lorenzo the Magnificent Award, Florence Int. Biennale of Contemporary Art 2005. *Publications include:* Anuszkiewicz: OpArt 1999; several articles in learned journals. *Address:* c/o D. Wigmore Fine Art, 730 Fifth Avenue, Suite 602, New York, NY 10019, USA.

ANWAR, Yaseen, BA, BSc (Econs); Pakistani central banker; *Governor, State Bank of Pakistan;* ed Aitcheson Coll., Lahore, Grammar School, Karachi, Karachi American School, Wharton School of Business at Univ. of Pennsylvania, USA; trained at JPMorgan Chase, New York, USA 1973–75; Asst Man., Paris/London, Bank of America 1976–79, Asst Man., Cairo, Egypt 1979–81, Asst Vice-Pres., New York 1982–84, Vice-Pres. and Section Head for Global Export Finance Group and Middle East 1984–91; Vice-Pres. Merrill Lynch & Co., New York/London 1992–2001; Dir (Pvt. Banking), Riggs and Co., London, UK 2001–03; Exec. Vice-Pres. Kraken Financial Group, London 2003–07; Deputy Gov. State Bank of Pakistan 2007–10, Acting Gov. June–Sept. 2010, Gov. 2011–; Dir (non-exec.) United Nat. Bank Ltd (UK) 2001–06; Founder and Pres. Pakistan Bankers Asscn, UK 1997–99; fmr mem. Arab Bankers Asscn, UK; fmr Exec. Dir American Turkish Soc., New York; fmr Dir on US-Pakistan Econ. Council, on American Middle East Business Asscn; fmr mem. Council on Foreign Relations. *Address:* State Bank of Pakistan, Central Directorate, I.I. Chundrigar Road, Karachi 2, Pakistan (office). *E-mail:* info@sbp.org.pk (office). *Website:* www.sbp.org.pk (office).

ANWAR, Yusuf, SE, MA, LLM, PhD; Indonesian economist, government official and diplomatist; b. Tasikmalaya, West Java; ed Padjajaran Univ., Vanderbilt Univ., USA; Pres. and CEO Danareksa Securities and Investment 1992–93; fmr Chair. Jakarta Initiative; Sec.-Gen. Ministry of Finance 1993–95, Chair. Education and Training Agency 1995–98, Chair. Capital Market Supervisory Agency 1998–2000, Minister of Finance and State Enterprises Devt 2004–05; Exec. Dir Asian Devt Bank 2000–04; Amb. to Japan 2006–10.

ANWAR, Zainah; Malaysian writer and activist; b. Johor; d. of Tan Sri Haji Anwar bin Abdul Malik and Saodah bte Abdullah; ed MARA Inst. of Tech., Shah Alam, Fletcher School of Law and Diplomacy, Tufts Univ., Boston Univ., USA; began career as journalist, New Straits Times; Sr Analyst, Inst. of Strategic and Int. Studies (think-tank), Kuala Lumpur 1986–91; fmr Chief Programme Officer, Political Affairs Div., Commonwealth Secr., London; worked for 20 years with Sisters in Islam (non-govt org.) promoting rights of Muslim women, finishing as Exec. Dir; Founding mem. Musawah (lobby group for equality and justice in Muslim families); fmr mem. Human Rights Comm. of Malaysia. *Publication:* Islamic Revivalism in Malaysia: Dakwah Among the Students. *Address:* Sisters in Islam, No. 7, Jalan 6/10, 46000 Petaling Jaya, Selangor, Malaysia (office). *Telephone:* (603) 7785-6121 (office). *E-mail:* sistersinislam@pd.jaring.my (office). *Website:* www.sistersinislam.org.my (office).

ANYAOKU, Eleazar Chukwuemeka (Emeka), Ndichie Chief Adazie of Obosi, Ugwumba of Idemili, CON, BA, FRSA; Nigerian diplomatist and international organization official; b. 18 Jan. 1933, Obosi; s. of the late Emmanuel Chukwuemeka Anyaoku, Ononukpo of Okpuno Ire and Cecilia Adiba (née Ogbogu); m. Ebunola Olubunmi Solanke 1962; three s. one d.; ed Merchants of Light School, Oba, Univ. of Ibadan, Univ. of London, UK; Commonwealth Devt Corpn, London and Lagos 1959–62; joined Nigerian Diplomatic Service 1962, mem. Nigerian Perm. Mission to UN, New York 1963–66; seconded to Commonwealth Secr., Asst Dir Int. Affairs Div. 1966–71, Dir 1971–75, Asst Sec.-Gen. of the Commonwealth 1975–77, elected Deputy Sec.-Gen. (Political) Dec. 1977, re-elected, 1984, Sec.-Gen. 1990–2000; Minister of External Affairs, Nigeria Nov.–Dec. 1983; Sec., Review Cttee on mem. Commonwealth Intergovernmental Orgs June–Aug. 1966; Commonwealth Observer Team for Gibraltar Referendum Aug.–Sept. 1967; mem. Anguilla Comm., West Indies Jan.–Sept. 1970; Deputy Conf. Sec., meeting of Commonwealth Heads of Govt, London 1969, Singapore 1971, Conf. Sec., Ottawa 1973, Kingston, Jamaica 1975; Leader, Commonwealth Mission to Mozambique 1975; Commonwealth Observer, Zimbabwe Talks, Geneva Oct.–Dec. 1976; accompanied Commonwealth Eminent Persons Group (EPG) SA 1986; Vice-Pres.

Royal Commonwealth Soc. 1975–2000, Pres. 2000–; mem. Council of Overseas Devt Inst. 1979–90, Council of the Selly Oak Colleges, Birmingham 1980–86, Council, Save the Children Fund 1984–90, Council of IISS, London 1987–93, Int. Bd of United World Colleges 1994–2000, World Comm. on Forests and Sustainable Devt 1995–98; Pres. Royal Africa Soc. 2000–; Chair. Presidential Advisory Council on Int. Relations (Nigeria) 2000–; Int. Pres. WWF (World Wide Fund for Nature) 2002–09; Freedom of City of London 1998; Hon. Fellow, Inst. of Educ., London 1994, Coll. of Preceptors 1998; Hon. mem. Club of Rome 1992; Commdr of the Order of the Niger (Nigeria) 1982; Order of the Trinity Cross (Trinidad and Tobago) 1999; Hon. GCVO 2000; Hon. DLitt (Ibadan) 1990, (Buckingham) 1994, (Zimbabwe) 1999, (UDFD Sokoto) 2001, (Rhodes, SA) 2001, (UNILORIN) 2002; Hon. DPhil (Ahmadu Bello) 1991; Hon. LLD (Nigeria) 1991, (Aberdeen) 1992, (Reading) 1992, (Bristol) 1993, (Oxford Brookes) 1993, (Birmingham) 1993, (Leeds) 1994, (South Bank, London) 1994, (New Brunswick, Canada) 1995, (North London) 1995, (Liverpool) 1997, (London) 1997, (Nottingham) 1998, (Trinity Coll. Dublin) 1999, (UNIZIK) 2001; Dr hc (Bradford) 1995; Livingston Medal, Royal Scottish Geographical Soc. 1996. *Publications:* The Missing Headlines (vol. of speeches) 1997, essays in various publs. *Leisure interests:* tennis, athletics, swimming, reading. *Address:* Orimili, Okpuno Ire, Obosi, Anambra State, Nigeria.

ANYIM, Anyim Pius, LLM; Nigerian lawyer and government official; b. 19 Feb. 1961, Ishiagu, Ebonyi State; s. of Chief Anyim Ivo Osita and Agnes Anyim; m. Chioma Blessing; two s. one d.; ed Imo State (now Abia State) Univ., Okigwe, Univ. of Jos, Jos; called to Nigerian Bar 1989; Legal Adviser, Directorate of Social Mobilisation (MAMSER) HQ, Abuja 1989–92; Head of Protection Dept Nat. Comm. for Refugees HQ, Abuja 1992–97; fmr Registrar, Refugee Appeal Bd; Senator 1999–2003, Speaker of Senate 2000–03; Fellow, Nigerian Environmental Soc., Inst. of Purchasing and Supply Man.; Grand Patron Abuja Chapter, Soc. for Int. Devt; mem. People's Democratic Party, Nigerian Bar Asscn; Grand Commdr, Order of Niger, Nat. Productivity Order of Merit Award; Hon. DPA (Fed. Univ. of Agric., Umudike, Abia State), Hon. DD (Baptist Seminary and Theological Inst., Ogbomoso, Oyo State); Distinguished Service Award, Nigerian Foundation Inc., USA and other awards. *Leisure interests:* farming, swimming, reading. *Address:* Legislators Quarters, Apo Mansion, Abuja, Nigeria (home). *Telephone:* (9) 2310009 (home). *Fax:* (9) 3143660 (home).

ANZAI, Yuichiro, BEng, MEng, PhD; Japanese engineer, academic and university administrator; *President, Japan Society for the Promotion of Science;* ed Keio Univ.; Instructor, Dept of Admin Eng, Faculty of Eng, Keio Univ. 1971–79, Asst Prof. 1979–85, Prof., Dept of Electrical Eng, Faculty of Science and Tech. 1988–96, Prof., Center for Computer Science, Grad. School of Science and Tech. 1989–2000, Chair. Grad. School of Science and Tech. and Dean of Faculty of Science and Tech. 1993–2001, Prof., Dept of Information and Computer Science 1996–, Prof., School of Open and Environmental Systems, Grad. School of Science and Tech. 2000–, Pres. Keio Univ. 2001–09; Postdoctoral Research Fellow, Dept of Psychology and Computer Science, Carnegie-Mellon Univ., Pittsburgh, USA, 1976–78, Visiting Asst Prof., Dept of Psychology 1981–82; Assoc. Prof., Dept of Behavioral Science, Faculty of Letters, Hokkaido Univ. 1985–88; Visiting Prof., McGill Univ., Canada 1990; Pres. Japan Soc. for the Promotion of Science 2011–, Japan Asscn of Pvt. Colls and Univs 2003, Fed. of Japanese Pvt. Colls and Univs Asscns 2003; Chair. Fed. of All Japan Pvt. Schools Asscns 2003; Gen. Man. 'Biosimulation' Leading Project, Ministry of Educ., Culture, Sports, Science and Tech.; Chair. Sub-div. on Cen. Council for Educ.; mem. Science Council of Japan, Admin. Council Univ. of Tsukuba, Council of Univ. Man., Tohoku Univ., Strategic Council on Intellectual Property, Cabinet Office; mem. Council for Univ. Establishment and School Corpn, Ministry of Educ., Culture, Sports, Science and Tech.; Exec. Dir Research Org. of Information and Systems, Governing Bd Japan Asscn for Philosophy of Science; Vice-Chair. Asscn of Pacific Rim Univs (Vice-Chair. Steering Cttee); Pres. Information Processing Soc. of Japan; fmr Pres. Japanese Cognitive Science Soc.; fmr mem. Council Bd Japan Soc. for Philosophy of Science, Council Bd Japan Soc. for Neuroscience; fmr Dir The Soc. of Instrument and Control Engineers, Japan Soc. for Eng Educ.; mem. Bd of Dirs Daiichi Sankyo Co Ltd, Sony Corpn 2011–12; fmr mem. Life Science Cttee Council for Science and Tech., Informatics Cttee Council for Science and Tech.; Commdr, Ordre des Palmes académiques 2005; Dr hc (Ecole Centrale de Nantes, France) 2007; Best Tech. Paper Award, Soc. for Instrumental and Control Engineers 1972, Best Paper Award, Information Processing Soc. of Japan 1988, Achievement Award, Japanese Soc. for Artificial Intelligence 2001. *Address:* Office of the President, Japan Society for the Promotion of Science, Kojimachi Business Center Building, 5-3-1 Kojimachi, Chiyoda-ku, Tokyo 102-0083, Japan (office). *Website:* www.jsps.go.jp (office).

ANZUETO GIRÓN, Col Ulises Noé; Guatemalan army officer and politician; *Minister of National Defence;* b. 1959; over 30 years of army service, becoming Col in Kaibiles special forces div.; Dir Instituto Adolfo V. Hall, Chiquimula –2011; Minister of Nat. Defence 2011–. *Address:* Ministry of National Defence, Antiguas Instalaciones de la Escuela Politécnica, Avda La Reforma 1-45, Zona 10, Guatemala City, Guatemala (office). *Telephone:* 2269-4924 (office). *Fax:* 2360-9919 (office). *E-mail:* dip@mindef.mil.gt (office). *Website:* www.mindef.mil.gt (office).

AOKI, Satoshi; Japanese motor company executive; joined Honda Motor Co. Ltd 1969, Gen. Man. Finance Div. for Business Man. Operations 1994–98, Rep. Dir 1995–, Chief Financial Officer and Exec. Vice-Pres. 1995–, COO for Business Man. Operations 1999–2000, Man. Dir 1998–2000, Sr Man. Dir 2000–04, Compliance Officer 2004–05, Head of US operations 2005–07, Chair. Honda Motor Co. Ltd 2007–10; mem. Bd of Dirs and Chair. Japan Automobile Mfrs Asscn 2008–. *Address:* c/o Honda Motor Co. Ltd, 2-1-1 Minami-Aoyama, Minato-ku, Tokyo 107-8556, Japan. *E-mail:* info@honda.com.

AOUN, Gen. Michel; Lebanese politician and fmr army officer; *President, Free Patriotic Movement Party;* b. 18 Feb. 1935, Haret Hreik; m. Nadia El Chami; three d.; attended Christian school, Beirut; enrolled in mil. school 1955; trained as artilleryman; training courses in Châlons-sur-Marne, France 1958–59, Fort Seale, USA 1966, Ecole Supérieure de Guerre, France 1978–80; became Brigade Gen. 1984; C-in-C of Army 1984; following abandoned presidential elections of Sept. 1988, outgoing Pres. Gemayel named him prime minister of interim mil. admin; evicted from Baabda Presidential Palace by Syrian forces, refuge in French Embassy 1990–91, in exile in France 1991; returned to Lebanon May 2005, elected

mem. Parl. (Majlis Al-Nawab) 2005–09, re-elected 2009–; Head of Change and Reform Parl. Bloc 2005–; Pres. Free Patriotic Movt Party; Memorial Medal of 31 Dec. 1961, Lebanese Silver Order of Merit, War Medals (four times), Nat. Cedar Medal, Kt, Lebanese Order of Merit (Second Rank), Purple Heart Medal, Lebanese Order of Merit (First Rank), Nat. Cedar Medal, rank of Officer, Nat. Cedar Medal, rank of Grand Officer, Distinction of the Gen. C-in-C of the Army (six times), Commendations of the C-in-C of the Army (three times), Commdr, Légion d'honneur 1986, Great Sash, Nat. Order of the Cedar 1988. *Publication:* Une Certaine Vision du Liban 2007. *Address:* Street 17th, Rabieh, Lebanon (office). *E-mail:* claudineaoun@gmail.com (office). *Website:* www.parliament.gov.lb; www.tayyar.org (office).

APEL, Karl-Otto, DPhil; German academic; *Professor Emeritus of Philosophy, University of Frankfurt am Main;* b. 15 March 1922, Düsseldorf; s. of Otto Apel and Elisabeth Gerritzen; m. Judith Jahn 1953; three d.; ed Univs of Bonn and Mainz; Prof. of Philosophy, Univ. of Kiel 1962–69, Univ. of Saarbrücken 1969–72, Univ. of Frankfurt am Main 1972–90, Prof. Emer. 1990–; many hon. degrees; Galileo Galilei Int. Prize 1988, F. Nietzsche Int. Prize 1989. *Publications include:* Idee der Sprache in der Tradition des Humanismus 1963, Transformation der Philosophie (translated as Towards a Transformation of Philosophy 1980) 1973, Der Denkweg von C. Peirce (translated as Charles Peirce: From Pragmatism to Pragmaticism 1981) 1975, Die Erklären: Verstehen-Kontroverse in transzendentalpragmatischer Sicht (translated as Understanding and Explanation: A Transcendental-Pragmatic Perspective 1984) 1979, Diskurs und Verantwortung 1988, Towards a Transcendental Semiotics (selected essays) 1994, Ethics and the Theory of Rationality (selected essays) 1996, Auseinandersetzungen 1998, From a Transcendental-Semiotic Point of View 1998, The Response of Discourse Ethics 2001, Diskursethik und Diskursanthropologie (co-author) 2002, Paradigmen der Ersten Philosophie 2011. *Leisure interest:* history of art. *Address:* Am Schillertempel 6, 65527 Niedernhausen, Germany (home). *Telephone:* (6127) 2170 (home). *E-mail:* karl-otto.apel@online.de (home). *Website:* www.karl-otto-apel.de.

APELOIG, Yitzhak, BSc, MSc, PhD; Israeli chemist and research institute administrator; *Professor of Chemistry, Technion—Israel Institute of Technology;* b. 1 Sept. 1944, Buchara, Uzbekistan; m. Zipora Zaltzberg; two s.; ed Hebrew Univ. of Jerusalem; family emigrated to Israel 1947; Postdoctoral Research Fellow, Princeton Univ., USA 1974–76; joined Faculty of Chem., Technion—Israel Inst. of Tech. 1976, Full Prof. 1988–, Chair incumbent 1993–, Dean, Faculty of Chem. 1995–99, Pres. Technion 2001–09; Visiting DAAD (Deutscher Akademischer Austausch Dienst—German Academic Exchange Service) Fellow and Prof., Universität Erlangen-Nornberg 1979, 1985, 1992; Visiting Prof., Tel-Aviv Univ. 1983, 1986, Cornell Univ., USA 1983–84; Louis Klein Visiting Professorship in Australian Univs 1986; Visiting DAAD Prof., Technische Universität Berlin 1985, 1991; Visiting JSPS (Japan Soc. for the Promotion of Science) Prof., Kyushu Univ. 1991, Sendai Univ. 1999; Visiting Alexander von Humboldt Prof. 1994, Technische Universität Berlin and Universität Ulm 1997; Visiting Prof., Univ. of Utah, USA 2000; Co-founder and Co-Dir Lise Meitner Center for Computational Chem. 1996–; Chair. Asscn of Univ. Pres in Israel 2004; Chair. IUPAC Conf. on Physical Organic Chem., Haifa 1990, Fourth World Congress of Theoretically Oriented Chemists, Jerusalem 1996, Symposium on Frontiers in Electronic Structure Calculations, Haifa 1998; mem. Acting Bd Israel Chemical Soc.; mem. Editorial Bds Journal of the Chemical Society, Perkin Transactions II, Progress in Physical Organic Chemistry, Journal of Computational Chemistry, Theoretical Chemical Accounts, Silicon Chemistry, Molecules; Hon. Foreign mem. American Acad. of Arts and Sciences 2010; Dr hc (Tech. Univ. of Berlin) 2006; Pres.'s Prize for Distinction in Chem. Studies, Hebrew Univ., Jerusalem, Yashinski Prize for Distinguished PhD Thesis, Hebrew Univ. 1974, Bat-Sheba de Rothschild Fellow 1977–78, Technion Award for Academic Excellence 1988, Henri Gutwirth Prize for Excellence in Research, Technion 1991, 1993, Sr Scientist Exchange Fellow (Italy) 1993, granted a Minerva Center in Computational Quantum Chem. 1996, Distinguished Teacher Award, Technion Student Asscn 1986, 1993, 1997, JSPS Sr Visiting Prof. Award 1991, 1999, Alexander von Humboldt–Lise Meitner Sr Research Award 1994–99, 2010, Coulson Lecturer, Univ. of Georgia, USA 2002, Israel Chemical Soc. Prize 2002, Wacker Silicone Award 2007, Fredric Stanely Kipping Award in Silicon Chem., ACS 2010. *Publications include:* more than 190 publs in int. scientific journals on organosilicon chem., computational chem., mechanistic organic chem., reactive intermediates; co-ed four books (with Z. Rappoport) on Chemistry of Organic Silicon Compounds, one book (with Z. Rappoport) on Chemistry of Organic Germanium, Tin and Lead Compounds and two special journal issues dedicated to computational chem. *Address:* Department of Chemistry, Technion—Israel Institute of Technology, Technion City, Haifa 32000, Israel (office). *Telephone:* (4) 8293721 (office). *Fax:* (4) 8294601 (office). *E-mail:* apeloig@tx.technion.ac.il (office). *Website:* www.admin.technion.ac.il/ApeloigYitzhak (office).

APICELLA, Lorenzo Franco, BA, DipArch, RIBA, AIA, FRSA; Italian architect and designer; *Partner, Pentagram Design Ltd;* b. 4 Feb. 1957, Ravello; s. of Belfiore Carmine Apicella and Carmina Apicella (née Nolli); one d.; ed Univ. of Nottingham, Canterbury Coll. of Art, Royal Coll. of Art, UK; Asst Architect, Skidmore Owings & Merill, Houston, Tex., USA 1981; Project Architect, CZWG Architects, London 1982; Consultant Architect, Visiting Lecturer, Canterbury Coll. of Art 1983–86; Head of Architecture Interiors and Exhbn Design, Imagination, London 1986–89, f. Apicella Assocs Architecture & Design, London 1989; Partner, Pentagram Design Ltd, London and San Francisco 1998–; fmr External Examiner, Oxford Brookes School of Architecture, UCE Birmingham School of Design, Royal Coll. of Art, London; mem. RIBA, AIA, RSA; Design Week Annual Awards Winner 1990, 1991, Designers Minerva Award 1993, RIBA Award 1999, Aluminium Imagination Awards 1993, 1997, IDSA Award 2001, Art Directors Club 80th Annual Awards 2001. *Address:* Pentagram Design SF, 220 Montgomery Street, Suite 865, San Francisco, CA 94104, USA (office). *Telephone:* (415) 398-4063 (office). *E-mail:* apicella@pentagram.com (office). *Website:* www.pentagram.com (office).

APOTHEKER, Léo, BA; German business executive; *Vice-Chairman of the Supervisory Board, Schneider Electric SA;* b. 18 Sept. 1953, Aachen; ed Hebrew Univ., Jerusalem, Israel; began career at SAP 1988, worked in a variety of positions, mem. Exec. Bd 2002–10, served as Head of North American operations, Pres. of Global Customer Solutions and Operations, Deputy CEO and Co-CEO,

CEO SW Europe Region –1999, Pres. SAP EMEA (Europe, Middle East and Africa) 1999–2002, CEO and Founder SAP France and SAP Belgium, CEO SAP –2010; Founding Pres. and COO ECsoft BV (European venture capital start-up) 1992–94; mem. Bd of Dirs, Pres. and CEO Hewlett-Packard 2010–11; also held exec. positions at ABP Partners, McCormack & Dodge Europe, S.W.I.F.T. and Altex GmbH; Vice-Chair. Supervisory Bd Schneider Electric SA; Chair. KMD (Denmark) 2012–; mem. Bd of Dirs GT Nexus; Ind. Dir Steria 2012–; mem. Bd PlaNet Finance (non-profit org.); Chevalier, Légion d'honneur 2007. *Address:* Schneider Electric SA, 35 rue Joseph Monier, 92500 Rueil Malmaison, France (office). *Telephone:* 1-41-29-70-00 (office). *Fax:* 1-41-29-71-00 (office). *E-mail:* info@schneider-electric .com (office). *Website:* www.schneider-electric.com (office).

APPIAH, Kwame Anthony, PhD; American (b. British) academic and writer; *Professor of Philosophy and Law, New York University;* b. (Kwame Anthony Akroma-Ampim Kusi Appiah), 8 May 1954, London, England, UK; s. of Joe Appiah and Peggy Appiah; m. Henry David Finder; ed Ullenwod Manor School for Boys, Port Regis and Bryanston School, UK, Univ. of Cambridge, UK; raised in Ghana; taught at Univ. of Ghana; has held position as Lecturer or Prof. of Philosophy and/ or Prof. of African Studies and African-American Studies at Univ. of Cambridge, Yale Univ., Cornell Univ., Duke Univ., Harvard Univ. 1991–2002; Laurance S. Rockefeller Univ. Prof. of Philosophy and Univ. Center for Human Values, Princeton Univ. 2002–13; Prof. of Philosophy and Law, New York Univ. 2014–; Juror, Neustadt Prize, Univ. of Oklahoma 2001; mem. American Philosophical Soc. 2001, American Acad. of Arts and Letters 2008; Hon. DLitt (Richmond) 2000, (Colgate) 2003, (Bard Coll.) 2004, (Fairleigh Dickinson) 2006, (Swarthmore Coll.) 2006, (Dickinson Coll.) 2008, (Columbia) 2009, (The New School) 2009; Hon. LLD (Colby Coll.) 2010, (Harvard) 2012; Hon. DHum (Berea Coll.) 2010, (Occidental Coll.) 2012, (Pennsylvania) 2013; Annisfield-Wolf Book Award 1993, Herskovits Award, African Studies Asscn 1993, Annual Book Award, N American Soc. for Social Philosophy 1996, Ralph J. Bunche Award, American Political Science Asscn 1997, Gustavus Myers Center Award 1997, Phi Beta Kappa Speaker, Harvard Commencement 2000, Tanner Lecturer, Univ. of California, San Diego and Univ. of Cambridge 2001, Morehouse Coll. Candle in the Dark Award in Educ. 2003, Arthur Ross Book Award, Council on Foreign Relations 2007, Joseph B. and Toby Gittler Prize 2008, Book Award, NJ Council of Humanities 2011, Nat. Humanities Medal 2011. *Publications include:* Assertion and Conditionals 1985, For Truth in Semantics 1986, Necessary Questions: An Introduction to Philosophy 1989, Avenging Angel (novel) 1991, In My Father's House: Africa in the Philosophy of Culture (essays) (Annisfield-Wolf Book Award 1993, African Studies Asscn Herskovits Award 1993) 1992, Nobody Likes Letitia (novel) 1994, Color Consciousness: The Political Morality of Race (with Amy Gutman) (North American Soc. for Social Philosophy Annual Book Award) 1996, The Ethics of Identity 2005, Cosmopolitanism: Ethics in a World of Strangers (Council on Foreign Relations Arthur Ross Award) 2006, Experiments in Ethics 2007, Mi Cosmopolitismo 2008, The Politics of Culture, the Politics of Identity 2008, The Honor Code: How Moral Revolutions Happen 2010, Lines of Descent 2014; editor: Early African-American Classics 1990; co-editor with Henry Louis Gates, Jr: Critical Perspectives Past and Present (series) 1993–, The Dictionary of Global Culture 1996, Africana: The Encyclopedia of African and African American Experience 1999; with Peggy Appiah: Bu Me Bé: The Proverbs of the Akan; with Martin Bunzl: Buying Freedom 2007. *Leisure interest:* gardening. *Address:* Department of Philosophy, New York University, 5 Washington Place, New York, NY 10003, USA (office). *Telephone:* (212) 998-7864 (office). *Fax:* (212) 995-4179 (office). *E-mail:* anthony.appiah@nyu .edu (office); anthony.appiah@gmail.com (home). *Website:* philosophy.fas.nyu.edu/ page/home (office); www.appiah.net (home).

APPLEBY, Malcolm Arthur; British artist; b. 6 Jan. 1946, Beckenham, Kent; s. of James William Appleby and Marjory Stokes; m. Philippa Swann; one d.; ed Hawes Down Co. Secondary Modern School, Beckenham School of Art, Ravensbourne Coll. of Art, Cen. School of Arts and Crafts, Sir John Cass School of Art, Royal Coll. of Art; started career as engraver 1968; Littledale Scholar 1969, Liveryman Worshipful Co. of Goldsmiths 1991; Founder-mem. and Chair. British Art Postage Stamp Soc.; fmr Chair. Crathes, Drumoak and Durris Community Council; mem. Hand Engravers Asscn, British Art Medal Soc., Soc. for Protection of Ancient Buildings; represented in collections at Birmingham City Art Gallery, Victoria and Albert Museum, London, Worshipful Co. of Goldsmiths, London, Royal Armouries, Contemporary Art Soc., London, British Museum, London, Fitzwilliam Museum, Cambridge, East Midland Arts, Aberdeen Art Gallery and Museums, Perth Art Gallery and Museum, Royal Museum, Edinburgh, Huntarian Art Gallery, Univ. of Glasgow, Nat. Maritime Museum, Finland, Aland Maritime Museum, Finland, Adelaide Maritime Museum, Australia; Hon. mem. Strathtay and Grandtully SWRI; Hon. DLitt (Heriot-Watt Univ.) 2006; Gold Medal, Silver Award, Annual Goldsmiths Craft and Design Awards. *Leisure interests:* garden, work, family. *Address:* Hand Engravers Association, POB 60239, London, EC1P 1QQ, England (office); Aultbeag, Grandtully, Perthshire, PH15 2QU, Scotland (home). *Telephone:* (75) 0046-2910 (office); (1887) 840484 (home). *Fax:* (1887) 840785 (home). *E-mail:* info@handengravers.co.uk (office); swapp@dircon.co.uk (home). *Website:* www.handengravers.co.uk (office).

APPY, Bernard; Brazilian economist, banking executive and consultant; ed Faculty of Econs, Univ. of São Paolo, Universidade Estadual de Campinas; fmr Prof. of Econs, Pontificia Universidade Catolica do Sao Paolo (PUC-SP), Unicamp; Partner, Luciano Coutinho & Assocs (consultancy) 1995–2002, Dir Public Policy & Taxation 2011–; joined Ministry of Finance 1994, served as Sec. for Econ. Policies 2005–06, 2007–08, Deputy Minister of Finance 2003–05, 2006–07; Econ. Adviser to Pres. of Brazil 2008; Chair. Banco do Brasil SA –2009; Dir Strategy and Planning at BM&FBOVESPA –2011; fmr mem. Bd of Dirs The Brazilian Devt Bank (BNDES); Member of the Fiscal Council Vale SA 2006–. *Address:* LCA, Rua Desembargador Paulo Passaláqua, 308 Pacaembu, 01248-010 São Paulo SP, Brazil (office). *Telephone:* (11) 3879-3700 (office). *E-mail:* contato@lcaconsultores.com.br (office). *Website:* www.lcaconsultores.com.br (office).

APTED, Michael David, CMG; British film director; b. 10 Feb. 1941, Aylesbury, Bucks.; m. 1st (divorced); two s.; m. 2nd Dana Stevens; one s.; ed Downing Coll., Cambridge; started career as researcher, Granada TV 1963, then worked as investigative reporter for World in Action; feature film dir 1970s–; Pres. Directors Guild of America 2003–09. *Films include:* The Triple Echo 1972, Stardust 1975,

The Squeeze 1977, Agatha 1979, The Coal Miner's Daughter 1980, Continental Divide 1981, PTangYang Kipperbang, Gorky Park 1983, Firstborn 1984, Critical Condition, Gorillas in the Mist 1988, Class Action 1990, Incident at Oglala, Thunderheart 1992, Blink 1993, Moving the Mountain 1993, Nell 1994, Extreme Measures 1996, Inspirations 1997, Me and Isaac Newton 1999, The World Is Not Enough 1999, Enigma 2001, Enough 2002, Lipstick 2002, Amazing Grace 2006, The Chronicles of Narnia: The Voyage of the Dawn Treader 2010, Chasing Mavericks 2012. *Television includes:* (dir) episodes of Coronation Street, comedy series The Lovers, children's series Folly Foot, Another Sunday and Sweet F.A., Kisses at Fifty, Poor Girl, Jack Point, Up documentary series including 28 Up and 35 Up, 42: Forty-two Up 1998, Always Outnumbered 1998, Nathan Dixon 1999, Married in America 2002, Rome (series, Dirs Guild of America Best Director of Dramatic Series 2006) 2005, 49 Up 2005, Married in America 2 2006. *Publications:* 7 Up 1999. *Address:* United Agents, 12–26 Lexington Street, London, W1F 0LE, England (office). *Telephone:* (20) 3214-0800 (office). *Fax:* (20) 3214-0801 (office). *E-mail:* info@unitedagents.co.uk (office). *Website:* unitedagents.co.uk (office).

AQUINO, Benigno Simeon 'Noynoy' Cojuangco, III, AB (Econs); Philippine politician and head of state; *President;* b. 8 Feb. 1960; only s. of the late Senator Benigno 'Ninoy' Aquino, Jr (assassinated 1983) and fmr Pres. Corazon Aquino; brother of Kris Aquino (TV host and actress); ed Ateneo de Manila Univ.; joined family in Boston, USA in exile following univ.; brief tenure as mem. of Philippine Business for Social Progress 1983; retail sales supervisor and youth promotions asst for Nike Philippines 1985–86; later an asst for advertising and promotion for Mondragon Philippines; Vice-Pres. family-owned Intra-Strata Assurance Corpn 1986; wounded by rebel soldiers led by Gregorio Honasan in failed coup attempt during his mother's presidency 28 Aug. 1987; worked for Cen. Azucarera de Tarlac sugar refinery owned by Cojuangco clan 1993; Rep. for 2nd Dist of Tarlac Prov., House of Reps 1998–2007 (re-elected 2001, 2004), mem. several parl. cttees, Deputy Speaker of House of Reps 2004–06; elected to Senate of 14th Congress under banner of Genuine Opposition (GO— coalition of several parties, including own Liberal Party) 2007–; Sec.-Gen. Liberal Party of the Philippines 1999–2002, 2004–06, Vice-Pres. for Luzon 2002–04, Vice-Chair. Liberal Party of the Philippines 2006–; Pres. of the Philippines 2010–. *Leisure interests:* shooting, billiards, listening to mellow, bossa nova and OPM (Original Pinoy Music). *Address:* Office of the President, New Exec. Bldg, Malacañang Palace Compound, J. P. Laurel St, San Miguel, Metro Manila, Philippines (office). *Telephone:* (2) 7356201 (office). *Fax:* (2) 9293968 (office). *E-mail:* opnet@ops.gov.ph (office). *Website:* www.op.gov.ph (office); www.noynoy.ph.

ARABY, Nabil El-, LLB, LLM, JSD; Egyptian lawyer, diplomatist, international organization official, government official and judge; *Secretary-General, League of Arab States;* b. 15 March 1935, Cairo; m.; two s. one d.; ed Cairo Univ., New York Univ. Law School, USA; fmr Rep. of Egypt to various UN bodies, including Gen. Ass., Security Council, ECOSOC, Comm. on Human Rights, Conf. on Disarmament; Legal Adviser to Egyptian del. to UN Middle East Peace Conf., Geneva 1973–75; Dir Legal and Treaties Dept, Ministry of Foreign Affairs 1976–78, 1983–87; Amb. to India 1981–83; led Egyptian del. to Taba talks 1986–89; Deputy Perm. Rep. to UN, New York 1978–81, Perm. Rep. 1991–99; Perm. Rep., UN Office at Geneva 1987–91; apptd by ICC as Arbitrator in a dispute concerning Suez Canal 1989; Judge, Judicial Tribunal of Org. of Arab Petroleum Exporting Countries (OAPEC) 1990–; Visiting Scholar, Robert F. Wagner Grad. School of Public Service, New York Univ. 1992–93; apptd Partner, Zaki Hashem and Partners, Cairo 1998, currently Sr Partner; Commr UN Compensation Comm., Geneva 1999–2001; Pres. Ordinary Arbitration Div., Court of Arbitration for Sport; Dir Regional Cairo Centre for Int. Commercial Arbitration 2008–; Minister of Foreign Affairs March–June 2011; Sec.-Gen. League of Arab States 2011–; fmr chair. numerous UN cttees and working groups; mem. Governing Bd Stockholm Int. Peace Research Inst. 2000–10, Egyptian Bar Asscn; mem. Int. Law Comm. 1994–2001, Int. Court of Justice 2001–06, Perm. Court of Arbitration 2005–; Kt of Italian Repub. 1962, Order of the Repub. (Egypt) 1976. *Publications include:* several articles on UN Charter, peacekeeping and various int. issues. *Leisure interest:* tennis. *Address:* League of Arab States, PO Box 11642, Arab League Building, Tahrir Square, Cairo 11211, Egypt (office). *Telephone:* (2) 575-0511 (office). *Fax:* (2) 574-0331 (office). *Website:* www.arableagueonline.org (office).

ARAD, Ron; British designer and architect; b. 24 April 1951, Tel-Aviv, Israel; ed Jerusalem Acad. of Art and Architectural Asscn; Founder One Off Ltd 1981–94, Ron Arad Assocs 1989–; Prof. of Product Design, Hochschule, Vienna 1994–97; Prof. of Design Product, RCA 1997–2009; Oribe Art and Design Award, Japan 2001, Giò Ponti Int. Design Award, Denver, CO 2001, Barcelona Primavera Int. Award for Design 2001, Architektur & Wohnen Designer of the Year 2004. *Leisure interests:* tennis, ping-pong. *Address:* Arad Associates, 62 Chalk Farm Road, London, NW1 8AN, England (office). *Telephone:* (20) 7284-4963 (office). *Fax:* (20) 7379-0499 (office). *E-mail:* info@ronarad.com (office). *Website:* www.ronarad.co.uk (office).

ARAGALL GARRIGA, Giacomo Jaime; Spanish singer (tenor); b. 6 June 1939, Barcelona; s. of Ramon Aragall and Paola Garriga; m. Luisa Aragall 1964; three s.; winner of int. competition in Busseto; has sung in several opera productions at Verona 1965, Covent Garden 1968, Metropolitan Opera 1968, San Francisco 1973, Budapest, Venice, Genoa, Palermo, Parma, Modena, Naples, Rome and Turin; Founder-Pres. Concurso Internacional de Canto Jaume Aragall 1994–; Peseta de Oro and Medalla de Plata for appearing at 1992 Olympics, Barcelona, Medalla de Oro de Bellas Artes 1992. *Operas include:* Gerusalemme 1963, L'amico Fritz, Esclarmonde 1974, Joan Sutherland 1975, Donizetti's Caterina Cornaro, Lucia di Lammermoor, Madama Butterfly, La Favorita, La Traviata, Werther, Faust, Tosca, Manon, Don Carlo, Adriana Lecouvreur, Un Ballo in Maschera and Simon Boccanegra. *Address:* Concurso Internacional de Canto Jaume Aragall, Sra. Silvia Gasset, C/ Rocafort, 39-1st 2nd, 08015 Barcelona, Spain (office). *Telephone:* (60) 9423896 (office). *Fax:* (93) 2893871 (office). *Website:* www.concursaragall.com (office).

ARAI, Jun; Japanese business executive; *President and Representative Director, Showa Shell Sekiyu K.K.;* b. 28 Feb. 1959; joined Shell Sekiyu K.K. 1983 (acquired by Showa Oil Co. Ltd to form Showa Shell Sekiyu K.K. 1985), Man., Man. Information System 1999–2001, Man., Treasury 2001–02, Gen. Man., Man. Information Service 2002–04, Gen. Man., Finance and Accounting 2004–05,

Exec. Officer and Gen. Man., Finance and Accounting 2005–06, Dir, Finance and Accounting 2006–07, Man. Dir 2007–08, Acting Pres. and Rep. Dir Showa Shell Sekiyu K.K. Aug.–Nov. 2008, Pres. and Rep. Dir Nov. 2008–. *Address:* Showa Shell Sekiyu K.K., Daiba Frontier Building, 2-3-2, Daiba, Minato-ku, Tokyo 135-8074, Japan (office). *Telephone:* (3) 5531-5591 (office). *Fax:* (3) 5531-5598 (office). *E-mail:* info@showa-shell.co.jp (office). *Website:* www.showa-shell.co.jp (office).

ARAIZA ANDRADE, Francisco José; Mexican singer (tenor) and teacher; *Director, International Hugo Wolf Akademie;* b. 4 Oct. 1950, Mexico City; s. of José Araiza and Guadalupe Andrade; m. 1st Vivian Jaffray (divorced); one s. one d.; m. 2nd Ethery Inasaridse; one s. one d.; ed Univ. of Mexico City and Nat. School of Music, Mexico City and Munich Acads of Music; first engagement as lyric tenor in Karlsruhe, Germany 1974; debut as Ferrando in Così fan Tutte 1975; debut at Zurich Opera House with Almaviva 1976, perm. mem. 1978–; has performed at major opera houses in London, Paris, Munich, Berlin, Madrid, Barcelona, Milan, Parma, New York, Chicago, San Francisco, Tokyo as well as in concerts or recitals; named Kammersänger by Vienna State Opera 1988; has participated in festivals of Salzburg (debut under von Karajan 1980), Hohenems, Bayreuth, Edinburgh, Pesaro, Verona, Macerata, Aix-en-Provence, Orange, Garmisch; Prof., Stuttgart Musikhochschule 2003–, Int. Opernstudio IOS, Zurich 2005–; Dir Int. Hugo Wolf Akad. 2007–09; Bertelsmann Neue Stimmen (Jury and Master-classes) 1998–; Artist-in-Residence, Boston Univ. Coll. of Fine Arts 2013; Deutscher Schallplattenpreis, Orphée d'Or, Mozart Medal, Univ. of Mexico City, Otello d'Oro, Goldener Merkur, Best Performer Award, Munich 1996, Dr A. Ortiz Tirado Medal (Sonora, Mexico) 2008, Gold Medal, Instituto Nacional de Bellas Artes y Literatura y la Compañía Nacional de Opera Mexico City for lifetime achievement 2011. *Films include:* videos: Manon, Faust, La Cenerentola (two), Falstaff, Die Entführung aus dem Serail, Don Giovanni, Die Schöpfung, Recital Tokio, Die Zauberflöte (two), Così fan tutte, Mozart Gala Verona 1 & 2, Bach Magnificat, Francisco Araiza – I am a Romantic, Fast ein Gentleman (TV film), Schumann's Dichterliebe, Schubert's Winterreise. *Television includes:* Melodien zum Muttertag 2000, Gala der Europahilfe 2000, Kein Schöner Land 2000, Zauber der Musik mit André Rieu 2002, Sternstunden der Musik 2003. *Recordings include:* The Magic Flute, Faust, Das Lied von der Erde, Die schöne Müllerin, Der Freischütz, Maria Stuarda, Don Pasquale, Die Schöpfung, Mozart Requiem, Don Giovanni, Idomeneo, Rossini's Messa di Gloria, 200 Jahre La Fenice, Die Winterreise, La Bohème, Berlioz' Requiem, Verdi, No Limits from Mozart to Wagner 2013. *Address:* c/o Opern-Agentur und Artists' Mgt Lewin, Tal 15, 80331 Munich, Germany (office). *Telephone:* (89) 29161662 (office). *Fax:* (89) 29161667 (office). *E-mail:* tschaidse@opern-agentur.com (office); faraiza@aol.com. *Website:* www.opern-agentur.de (office); www.franciscoaraiza.com.

ARAKAWA, Shoshi, BA; Japanese business executive; *Advisor, Bridgestone Corporation;* b. 8 April 1944; ed Tokyo Univ.; joined Bridgestone Tire Co. 1968, Man. Exec. Secretarial Office 1988–91, Gen. Man. F21 Planning and Promotion Project Group 1991–92, Man. Dir Bridgestone Tire Co. Thailand 1992–97, mem. Bd of Dirs 1997–, Gen. Man. China Dept 1997–2001, Dir Asia and Oceania Div. 1998–2001, CEO and Chair. Bridgestone/Firestone Europe SA 2001–06, Chair., Pres., CEO and Rep. Dir Bridgestone Corpn 2006–12, Chair. 2012–13, Advisor 2013–, also served as Chief Risk-Management Officer; Commdr, Order of Leopold (Belgium) 2009. *Address:* Bridgestone Corpn, 10-1, Kyobashi 1-chome, Chuo-ku, Tokyo 104-8340, Japan (office). *Telephone:* (3) 3567-0111 (office). *Fax:* (3) 3535-2553 (office). *E-mail:* info@bridgestone.co.jp (office). *Website:* www.bridgestone.co.jp (office).

ARAKI, Minoru S. (Sam), BS, MS; American aeronautics engineer (retd); b. 12 July 1931, Saratoga, Calif.; ed Stanford Univ.; joined Lockheed Missiles & Space Co. in 1958 as Sr Scientist, held numerous positions including Asst Chief Engineer, Devt 1975–76, Dir Systems Eng 1976–78, Dir Advanced Systems, Space Systems Division (SSD) 1978–83, Vice-Pres. Space Systems Div., Vice-Pres. and Program Man. Milstar programs 1983, Vice-Pres. and Asst Gen. Man. SSD 1985–87, Pres. and Gen. Man. SSD 1987–88, also a Vice-Pres. of Lockheed Corpn, Exec. Vice-Pres. Lockheed's Missiles and Space Systems Group 1988–95, Pres. Lockheed Martin Missiles & Space Co. 1995–2007 (retd); currently Founder, CEO and Pres. ST-Infonox, Inc.; Chair. ECOPIA Farms (organic farming co.); mem. Nat. Acad. of Eng; Fellow, American Astronautical Soc.; AIAA Von Braun Award for Excellence in Space Program Man. 2004, Charles Stark Draper Prize, Nat. Acad. of Eng (co-recipient) 2005, named a Pioneer of Nat. Reconnaissance by Nat. Reconnaissance Office, Distinguished Lifetime Achievement Award, Chinese Inst. of Engineers–USA 2007. *Address:* ECOPIA Farms, 1520 Dell Avenue, Campbell, CA 95008, USA. *Telephone:* (408) 871-9091. *E-mail:* webinfo@ecopiafarms.com. *Website:* www.ecopiafarms.com.

ARAM I (KESHISHIAN), His Holiness, Catholicos of Cilicia, MDiv, STM, PhD; Lebanese ecclesiastic; *President, Middle East Council of Churches;* b. 8 March 1947, Beirut; ed Seminary of the Armenian Apostolic Church, Antelias, Ecumenical Inst. of Bossey, Switzerland, Near East School of Theology, Beirut, American Univ. of Beirut, Fordham Univ., New York, USA; ordained priest 1968; apptd Rep. for Ecumenical Relations, Catholicosate of the See of Cilicia of Armenian Apostolic Church 1972, Catholicos 1995–; named to WCC Faith and Order Comm. 1975; locum tenens of diocese of Lebanon 1978; Primate 1979; ordained Bishop 1980; elected to Cen. Cttee of WCC 1983, youngest person and first Orthodox to be elected Moderator of Cen. Cttee of WCC 1991–2005; Founder-mem. Middle East Council of Churches 1974, Pres. 2007–; Founder-mem. Oriental Orthodox-Eastern Orthodox Theological Dialogue, Oriental Orthodox-Reformed Theological Dialogue, Orthodox-Evangelical Dialogue; Hon. Pres. World Religions for Peace, World Religions Museum Foundation, Hon. mem. Pro-Oriente Catholic Ecumenical Foundation, Vienna, Austria; numerous decorations from states, churches and orgs. *Publications include:* Nerses the Gracious: Theologian and Ecumenist 1974, The Witness of the Armenian Church in a Diaspora Situation 1978, The True Image of the Armenian Church 1979, With the Will of Re-Building 1983, With the People 2007, Conciliar Fellowship: A Common Goal 1991, Orthodox Perspectives on Mission 1992, Towards the 1700th Anniversary of the Christianization of Armenia 1996, The Challenge to be a Church in a Changing World 1997, Jesus Christ: The Son of God – the Son of Man 1999, Church, Nation and Homeland 1999, In search of Ecumenical Vision 2000, L'eglise Face aux Grands défis 2000, The Armenian Church Beyond the 1700th Anniversary 2002, The

Mission of Faith 2003, Justice, Paix, Réconciliation 2003, The Christian Witness at the Crossroads in the Middle East 2004, Der Zor: A National Sanctuary 2005, The Dignity of Serving 2005, For a Church Beyond Its Walls 2006, Pour un Monde Transformé 2006, To Enrich Life with Values 2010, A Journey of Faith, Hope and Vision 2011, Taking the Church to the People 2011. *Address:* Catholicosate of Cilicia, PO Box 70317, Antelias, Lebanon (office). *Telephone:* (4) 410001 (office); (4) 410003 (office). *Fax:* (4) 419724 (office). *E-mail:* info@armenianorthodoxchurch.org (office). *Website:* www.armenianorthodoxchurch.org (office).

ARAMBURUZABALA LARREGUI, María Asunción; Mexican business executive; *President and CEO, Tresalia Capital;* b. 2 May 1963, Mexico City; d. of Pablo Aramburuzabala Ocaranza; granddaughter of Felix Aramburuzabala, Co-founder of Mexican brewery Grupo Modelo; m. 1st Paulo Patricio Zapata Navarro 1982 (divorced) 1997; two c.; m. 2nd Amb. Antonio O. Garza, Jr 2005 (divorced 2010); ed Instituto Tecnológico Autónomo de México (ITAM); worked as accountant at Mexican securities firm; Partner, Vice-Chair. and mem. Exec. Cttee Grupo Modelo SA de CV (brewing co.) 1996–; Vice-Chair. and mem. Exec. Cttee Grupo Televisa SA 2000–; Pres. and CEO Tresalia Capital SA de CV; Vice-Chair. DIFA; Chair. Tresalia Educación; Chair. Siemens Mexico (first woman) 2003–06; mem. Mexican Stock Exchange Bd (first woman) 2003–06; mem. Bd of Dirs Grupo Financiero Banamex-Accival, SA de CV, Banco Nacional de Mexico, SA, America Movil, SA de CV, Empresas ICA, Aeromexico, BCBA Impulse, KIO Networks, GA&A Group; mem. New York Stock Exchange Advisory Cttee; mem. ITAM's Business School Advisory Cttee, David Rockefeller Center for Latin American Studies at Harvard Univ. Advisory Bd, Advisory Bd Ministry of Educ., Ministry of the Economy Advisory Bd for Int. Business Trade; The Leading Women Entrepreneurs of the World, Star Group 1998, Private Sector Professional Merit Award, ITAM's Alumni Asscn 2003, The Golden Plate Award, Acad. of Achievement 2004, 2000 Women of the Year, Mexican Expansion Magazine, Mont Blanc Businesswoman Award 2004, Women's Medal, Anahuac Univ. 2005, among others, ranked by Fortune magazine amongst the 50 Most Powerful Women in Business outside the US (14th) 2002, (13th) 2003, (11th) 2004, (14th) 2005–06, (26th) 2007, (28th) 2008, (26th) 2009, (41st) 2010, ranked by Forbes magazine amongst The World's 100 Most Powerful Women (78th) 2004, (53rd) 2005. *Address:* Grupo Televisa SA, 2000 Avenida Vasco De Quiroga Santa Fe, 01210 Mexico City, DF, Mexico (office). *Telephone:* (55) 5261-2000 (office). *Fax:* (55) 5261-2494 (office). *Website:* www.televisa.com (office).

ARANA SEVILLA, Mario, PhD; Nicaraguan government official and fmr central banker; *Executive Director, Nicaraguan Foundation for Economic and Social Development (FUNIDES);* ed Univ. of Texas, USA; Minister of Devt, Industry and Commerce 2002–04, of Finance and Public Credit 2005–06; Pres., Central Bank of Nicaragua 2006–07, fmr Gov. for Nicaragua IMF, World Bank and IDB, Int. Finance Corpn; currently Exec. Dir Nicaraguan Foundation for Econ. and Social Devt (FUNIDES), Managua; Past Fellow, Centre on Pacific Economies, Grad. School of Int. Relations and Pacific Studies; Coordinator, Presidential Comm. on Competitiveness; mem. Bd of Dirs Ram Power Corp. 2007–. *Address:* Office of the Executive Director, Nicaraguan Foundation for Economic and Social Development (FUNIDES), Discover Business Center, 2nd Floor in front of Club Terraza, Villa Fontana, Managua, Nicaragua (office). *Telephone:* 2270-6490 (office). *E-mail:* info@funides.com (office). *Website:* www.funides.com (office).

ARANDA, Julieta, MFA; Mexican artist and editor; b. 1975, Mexico City; ed Columbia Univ. School of the Arts, New York; lives and works in Berlin and New York; with Anton Vidokle and Brian Kuan Wood, began a set of projects related to their interests, including an art collective (e-flux), a school (unitednationsplaza; Night School), an archive (e-flux video rental; Martha Rosler Library); co-f., with Anton Vidokle, a time bank for artists, curators, writers and others in the arts to exchange their time and skills 2008, has nearly 4,000 members and operates branches in The Hague, Moscow, Berlin, Frankfurt and other cities. *Address:* e-flux, 311 East Broadway, New York, NY 10002, USA. *E-mail:* info@e-flux .com (office). *Website:* www.e-flux.com (office).

ARANGIO-RUIZ, Gaetano; Italian professor of law; b. 10 July 1919, Milan; s. of Vincenzo Arangio-Ruiz and Ester Mauri Arangio-Ruiz; ed Univ. of Naples; Prof. of Int. Law, Univ. of Camerino 1952–54, Univ. of Padua 1955–67, Univ. of Bologna 1968–74; Prof. of Int. Law, Univ. of Rome 1974–, now Prof. Emer.; mem. Iran-United States Claims Tribunal, The Hague 1989–; Visiting Prof., Virginia Univ. Law School 1965, European Cen., Johns Hopkins School of Advanced Int. Studies 1967–75; Lecturer, Hague Acad. of Int. Law 1962, 1972, 1977, 1984; mem. UN Int. Law Comm. 1985–96; Special Rapporteur on State Responsibility 1987–96; mem. Int. Law Inst.; Dr hc (Univ. Panthéon-Assas, Paris II, France) 1997; Giuseppe Capograssi Prize 1990, Scanno Law Prize 2001. *Publications include:* Rapporti contrattuali fra Stati e organizzazione internazionale 1950, Gli enti soggetti 1951, Sula dinamica della base sociale 1954, The Normative Role of the UN General Assembly (Hague Rec.) Vol. III 1972, Human Rights and Non-Intervention in the Helsinki Final Act (Hague Rec.) Vol. IV 1977, The UN Declaration on Friendly Relations and the System of the Sources of International Law 1979, le Domaine réservé, General Course in International Law (Hague Rec.) Vol. V 1990, Non-Appearance Before the International Court of Justice (report to the Int. Law Inst.) International Law Institute Yearbook 1991, On the Nature of the International Personality on the Holy See, Revue Belge de Droit International 1996/2, On the Security Council's 'Law-Making', Rivista di Diritto Internazionale 2000, Dualism Revisited: International Law and Interindividual Law, Rivista di Diritto Internazionale 2003, Article 39 of the ILC First-Reading Articles on State Responsibility, *ibidem*, The ICJ Statute, The Charter and Forms of Legality Review of Security Council Decisions, Liber Amicorum Cassese 2003, Customary Law, on the theory of 'spontaneous' international custom, Droit du Pouvoir, Pouvoir du Droit 2007, International Law and Interindividual Law: New Perspectives on the Divide Between National and International Law (co-eds J. Nijman and A. Nollkaemper) 2007, La Persona Internazionale dello Stato 2008. *Address:* c/o Iran-United States Claims Tribunal, Parkweg 13, 2585 JH The Hague, Netherlands (office); Corso Trieste 51, interno 4, 00198 Rome, Italy (home). *Telephone:* (70) 3520064 (office); (06) 8559720 (home); (70) 3551371 (Netherlands) (home); (0564) 819200 (Italy) (home). *Fax:* (70) 3502456 (office). *E-mail:* damekklaassen@iusct.nl (office).

ARANGO, Jeronimo; Mexican (b. Spanish) retail executive; b. 1926, Spain; f. Bodega Aurrera discount stores 1958, through Cifra Group entered into jt venture with Wal-Mart Stores in early 1990s and co. renamed Wal-Mart de México (later Walmex), fmr Chair. and CEO, also mem. Bd of Dirs Wal-Mart (now Walmart) 1997; owner of luxury resort in Acapulco, Mexico.

ARÁOZ ESPARZA, Ántero Flores; Peruvian lawyer, politician and academic; b. 28 Feb. 1942, Lima; ed Pontifical Catholic Univ. of Peru, Univ. of the Pacific, Nat. Univ. of San Marcos, Lima; Prof., Faculty of Law, Univ. of Lima, Faculty of Law, Univ. of St Martín de Porres, Inst. of Govt, Univ. of St Martín de Porres; visiting prof. at numerous univs; Expository Pres. Peruvian Inst. of Humanistic Studies; Dir Estudio Flores-Aráoz & Asociados S.C. de R.L.; Vice-Pres. Sociedad de Beneficencia Pública de Lima 1980–85; Vice-Pres. and Pres. Caja de Ahorros de Lima (Savings Bank of Lima) 1980–85; Pres. Lotteries of Lima and Callao 1980–85; Metropolitan Regidor of Lima 1987–89, Dir Caja Municipal de Crédito Popular; Nat. Deputy 1990–92, mem. Constituent Congress 1993–95, Congressman of the Repub. 1995–, re-elected 2000, 2001, 2006, fmr mem. Consultative Comm., Ministry of Integration, Consultative Comm., Sec. of State of Integration, Consultative Comm. of Integration, Ministry of Industries, Tourism and Integration; mem. Consultative Cttee, Constitutional Comm. of Congress 2006–07, Consultative Comm., Ministry of Justice, Pres. Congress of the Repub. 2004–05, Pres. Constitutional Comm. Regulation of the Congress of the Repub. 2005–06; Minister of Defence 2007–08 (resgnd); Rep. of Peru before the OAS 2007; Vice-Pres. Cttee against the Territory of the OAS 2007; mem. Peruvian Del. to Socio-Econ. Advisory Cttee (CAES) of Cartagena Agreement for several years; mem. and Pres. Partido Popular Cristiano –2007; mem. Unidad Nacional (Nat. Unity); columnist in various media; Hon. Prof. at several univs; Gran Cruz de la Orden José Gregorio Paz Soldán, Decoration 'Hipólito Unanue', Gran Cruz del Congreso de la República, Gran Cruz de la Orden del Sol; decorations from Colombia, Chile, Russian Fed. and Morocco; decorations of Peruvian Navy, Air Force, Nat. Police; Dr hc from several univs. *Publication:* Autoritarismo o Democracia 2006. *Address:* Unidad Nacional, Calle Ricardo Palma 1111, Miraflores, Lima, Peru (office). *Telephone:* (1) 2242773 (office).

ARÁOZ FERNÁNDEZ, Mercedes Rosalba, BEcons, MA; Peruvian economist and politician; b. 5 Aug. 1961, Lima; ed Universidad del Pacífico, Lima, Univ. of Miami, USA; Peruvian Co-ordinator on Competition Policies, (APEC) 1998; Exec. Co-ordinator, Andean Project for Competitiveness (jt project between Universidad del Pacífico, Harvard Univ. and Andean Devt Fund) 2000–01; fmr Assoc. Prof. of Int. Economy, Universidad del Pacífico, also mem. Universidad del Pacífico Research Center; Exec. Dir Nat. Council for Competitiveness 2005–06; Minister of Foreign Commerce and Tourism 2006–09, of Production July–Dec. 2009, of Economy and Finance Dec. 2009–10. *Address:* c/o Ministry of Economy and Finance, Jirón Junín 339, 4°, Circado de Lima, Lima 1, Peru (office).

ARASKOG, Rand Vincent; American business executive; b. 30 Oct. 1931, Fergus Falls, Minn.; s. of Randolph Victor Araskog and Hildred Mathilda Araskog; m. Jessie Marie Gustafson 1956; one s. two d.; ed US Mil. Acad., West Point and Harvard Univ.; Special Asst to Dir US Dept of Defense, Washington, DC 1954–59; Dir of Marketing, Aeronautical Div., Honeywell Inc., Minneapolis 1960–66; Vice-Pres. ITT, Group Exec. ITT Aerospace Electronics, Components and Energy Group, Nutley, NJ 1971–76, Pres. 1979–85, CEO ITT Corpn, New York 1979–80, Chair. 1980–98, also Dir, Chair., Pres. and CEO ITT Holdings Inc., New York, 1995–98, mem. Bd of Dirs ITT Industries 1980–98, ITT Educational Services Inc. 1994–2004, Chair., CEO and Pres. Starwood Hotels and Resorts Worldwide Inc. (subsidiary); Prin., RVA Investments 1998–; mem. Bd of Dirs Int. Steel Group, Inc., Arcelor Mittal USA Inc. 2004–, Cablevision Systems Corpn 2005–, CSC Holdings, LLC 2005–, Palm Beach Civic Asscn; Chair. Nat. Security Telecommunications Advisory Cttee 1982–84; Trustee, New York Zoological Soc., Salk Inst. for Biological Studies; mem. Bd of Govs Aerospace Industries Asscn, Exec. Council, Air Force Asscn; mem. Business Council, Business Roundtable, Trilateral Comm.; Officier, Légion d'honneur 1987, Grand Officer Order of Merit (Italy), Order Gen. Bernardo O'Higgins (Chile); Hon. DHumLitt (Hofstra Univ.) 1990. *Publications include:* Dawn Raiders and White Knights: The Inside Story of a Corporation Under Siege 1989, ITT Wars 1999; numerous articles. *Address:* 320 El Vedado Road, Palm Beach, FL 33480, USA.

ARAÚJO, María Consuelo; Colombian politician; b. 1971, Cesar Prov.; m.; one c.; ed Externado Univ. of Colombia, Columbia Univ., New York, Univ. of Milan, Sorbonne, Paris; teaching asst, Externado Univ. of Colombia; Vice-Minister's Asst, Ministry of Law and Justice; Foreign Trade Adviser, Agricultural and Rural Devt Ministry; President's Asst, Communications Dept Chief, Housing Programme Dir, Rural and Industrial Bank; Commercial Dir Bermudez y Valenzuela Finance Co.; Botanic Garden Dir, Bogota; Recreation and Sports Inst. Dir, Bogota; Minister of Culture 2002–06, of Foreign Affairs 2006–07 (resgnd); mem. Bd of Dirs Bogota Aqueduct and Sewer Enterprise, Nat. Network of Botanical Gardens, Recreational and Sportive Local Inst., Capital Channel, Inst. for Childhood Protection; Ciudad de Bogota Civil Meritory Order. *Leisure interests:* music, film. *Address:* c/o Ministry of Foreign Affairs, Palacio de San Carlos, Calle 10a, No 5-51, Bogotá, DC, Colombia (office).

ARAÚJO PERDOMO, Fernando, DEng; Colombian politician and engineer; b. 1955, Cartagena; s. of Alberto Araújo Merlano and Judith Perdomo; m.; four s.; ed Javeriana Pontifical Univ.; Gen. Man. Empresas Públicas de Cartagena 1983–84; Dir Gen. Inmuebles Nacional 'MOPT' 1985–86; fmr Prof. of Engineering, Jorge Tadeo Lozano Univ., Univ. of Cartagena; Minister of Devt 1998–2000; captured and held hostage by Revolutionary Armed Forces of Colombia (FARC) 2000–06; Minister of Foreign Affairs 2007–08; unsuccessful cand. in Cartagena mayoral elections 1998; fmr Pres. Colombian Chamber of Construction (CAMACOL); fmr mem. Bd of Dirs El Universal (magazine), Hotel Las Américas Beach Resort. *Leisure interests:* sport, reading. *Address:* c/o Ministry of Foreign Affairs, Palacio de San Carlos, Calle 10a, No 5-51, Bogotá, DC, Colombia (office).

ARBASINO, Alberto; Italian author, essayist and critic; b. 22 Jan. 1930, Voghera; ed Univ. of Milan; Ed. Italo Calvino 1957–59; began literary career writing reports for the weekly Il Mondo from Paris and London; also worked for newspapers Il Giorno and later Il Corriere della sera; has collaborated with la Repubblica 1975–; mem. Group 63; hosted programme Match on RAI2 1977, Che

tempo che fa by Fabio Fazio 2006; Deputy, Italian Parl. (elected as ind. for Italian Republican Party) 1983–87; Cavaliere di Gran Croce Ordine al Merito della Repubblica Italiana 1995, Commdr des Arts et des Lettres 2010. *Publications include:* Le piccole vacanze 1957, L'Anonimo lombardo 1959, Parigi o cara 1960, Fratelli d'Italia 1963, La narcisata – La controra 1964, Grazie per le magnifiche rose 1966, La maleducazione teatrale 1966, Off-Off 1968, Super Eliogabalo 1969, Sessanta posizioni 1971, I Turchi 1971, Certi romanzi – La Belle Epoque per le scuole 1977, Il principe costante 1972, La bella di Lodi 1972, Amate Sponde (con Mario Missiroli) 1974, La narcisata 1975, Un paese senza 1980, Matine 1983, Il meraviglioso, anzi 1985, Lettere da Londra 1997, Passeggiando tra i draghi addormentati 1997, Paesaggi italiani con zombi 1998, Le muse a Los Angeles 2000, Rap! 2001, Marescialle e libertini 2004, Dall'Ellade a Bisanzio 2006, L'Ingegnere in blu 2008, La vita bassa 2008, Romanzi e Racconti 2009, 2010; contrib. to L'illustrazione italiana, Officina, Il Mondo, Tempo presente, Il Verri, Espresso, il Giorno, la Repubblica. *Address:* Gruppo Editoriale L'Espresso, Div. La Repubblica, Via C. Colombo 90, 00147 Rome, Italy (office). *Telephone:* (06) 49822499 (office). *Fax:* (06) 49822651 (office). *E-mail:* segreteria_cultura@repubblica.it (office). *Website:* www.repubblica.it (office).

ARBER, Werner; Swiss microbiologist and academic; *President, Pontifical Academy of Sciences;* b. 1929, Gränichen, Aargau; m.; two c.; ed Aargau Gymnasium, Eidgenössische Technische Hochschule, Zürich and Univ. of Geneva; Asst at Lab. of Biophysics, Univ. of Geneva 1953–58, 1960–62, Dozent, then Extraordinary Prof. of Molecular Genetics 1962–70; Research Assoc., Dept of Microbiology, Univ. of Southern California, USA 1958–59; Visiting Investigator, Dept of Molecular Biology, Univ. of California, Berkeley 1970–71; Prof. of Microbiology, Univ. of Basel 1971–96, Rector 1986–88; Pres. Int. Council of Scientific Unions (ICSU) 1996–99; Pres. Pontifical Acad. of Sciences 2010–; Nobel Prize for Physiology or Medicine (jtly) 1978. *Address:* The Pontifical Academy of Sciences, Casina Pio IV, 00120 Vatican City, Italy (office). *Telephone:* (06) 83451 (office). *Fax:* (06) 85218 (office). *E-mail:* pas@pas.va (office). *Website:* www .casinapioiv.va (office).

ARBHABHIRAMA, Anat, PhD; Thai scientist and business executive; *Adviser to the Board of Directors, Bangkok Mass Transit System Public Company, Ltd.;* b. 13 Jan. 1938, Bangkok; s. of Arun Arbhabhirama and Pathumporn Arbhabhirama; m. Mrs Benjarata 1966; three s.; ed Chulalongkorn Univ., Bangkok, Asian Inst. of Tech., Bangkok, Colorado State Univ.; Vice-Pres. for Acad. Affairs and Provost, Asian Inst. of Tech. 1979–80; Deputy Minister of Agric. and Co-operatives 1980, Minister 1980–81; Head, Regional Research and Devt Center, Asian Inst. of Tech. 1981–84; Pres. Thailand Devt Research Inst. 1984–87; Chair. Intergovernmental Council of the Int. Hydrological Programme, UNESCO 1984–88; Gov. Petroleum Authority of Thailand 1987; Chair. PTT Exploration and Production Co. Ltd 1988, The Aromatics Co. Ltd (Thailand) 1990; mem. Bd of Dirs BTS Group Holdings Public Co. Ltd –2009; fmr mem. Bd of Dirs and currently Adviser to Bd Bangkok Mass Transit System Public Co. Ltd; mem. Council of Trustees and Bd of Dirs Thailand Devt Research Inst., Petroleum Inst. of Thailand; Companion (Fourth Class) of Most Admirable Order of Direkgunabhorn 2003; Outstanding Researcher of the Year 1987. *Publications include:* Thailand: Natural Resources Profile 1988, numerous articles and papers on water resources and hydraulics. *Leisure interests:* golf, jogging, chess. *Address:* c/o Board of Directors, Bangkok Mass Transit System Public Company Ltd, 1000 Phahonyothin Road, Chom Phon, Chatuchak, Bangkok 10900, Thailand.

ARBIA, Silvana, LLD; Italian judge; b. 19 Nov. 1952, Senise; ed Univ. of Padua, prosecutor and judge in Venice, Rome and Milan Courts of Appeal 1979–; mem. Italian Del., Diplomatic Conf. on drafting statute of Int. Criminal Court, Rome 1998; Judge, Supreme Court and Court of Cassation of Italy 1999; Sr Trial Attorney, Int. Criminal Tribunal for Rwanda 1999, becoming Acting Chief of Prosecutions and Chief of Prosecutions; Registrar, Int. Criminal Court, The Hague 2008–13; mem. Advisory Bd, Forum for International Criminal and Humanitarian Law; Paul Harris Fellow, Rotary Int.; Premio Nicola Sole 2011. *Publications include:* Mentre il Mondo, Stava a Guardare 2011; several essays and books on human rights and children's rights. *Address:* Forum for International Criminal and Humanitarian Law, 100 Avenue des Saisons, 1050, Brussels, Belgium (office). *Telephone:* (2) 6393911 (office). *E-mail:* info@fichl.org (office). *Website:* www.fichl .org (office).

ARBOUR, Louise, CC, BA, LLL; Canadian judge (retd), international organization official and fmr UN official; *President, International Crisis Group;* b. 10 Feb. 1947, Montréal; one s. two d.; ed Collège Regina Assumpta, Montréal, Université de Montréal; articling, Legal Dept, City of Montréal 1970; called to Québec Bar 1971, Ont. Bar 1977; law clerk, Supreme Court of Canada 1971–72; Research Officer, Law Reform Comm. and mem. Criminal Procedure Project 1972; Lecturer in Criminal Procedure, Osgoode Hall Law School, York Univ., Toronto 1974, Asst Prof. 1975, Assoc. Prof. 1977–87, Assoc. Dean July–Dec. 1987; called to Bar, Ont. 1977; Judge, Supreme Court of Ont. (High Court of Justice) 1987–90; Judge, Court of Appeal for Ont. 1990–96; apptd by Order-in-Council as Commr to conduct inquiry into certain events at Prisons for Women, Kingston April 1995; Chief Prosecutor, Int. Criminal Tribunals for Fmr Yugoslavia and Rwanda, The Hague 1996–99; Puisne Judge, Supreme Court of Canada 1999–2004; UN High Commr for Human Rights 2004–08; Pres. Int. Crisis Group 2009–; Vice-Pres. Canadian Civil Liberties Asscn –1987; Lifetime mem. l'Asscn des jurists d'expression française de l'Ontario 1992–, Int. Council, Inst. for Global Legal Studies, Washington Univ. School of Law, Saint Louis, Mo. 2001; mem. Advisory Bd International Journal of Constitutional Law 2001–; mem. Bd of Eds Journal of International Criminal Justice 2003–; Hon. Prof., Univ. of Warwick, UK 1999–2004; Hon. mem. American Soc. of Int. Law 2000, Golden Key Nat. Honour Soc. 2000; Hon. Bencher Gray's Inn, London, England 2001; Hon. Fellow, American Coll. of Trial Lawyers 2003; Grande Officière, Ordre national du Québec 2009, Order of National Merit, Grand Cross class (Columbia) 2010, Commdr, Ordre national de la Légion d'honneur 2010; Hon. LLD (York) 1995, (Law Soc. of Upper Canada, New Brunswick, Laurentian Univ., Université du Québec à Montréal) 1999, (Université Libre de Bruxelles, Univ. of Victoria, Kingston Royal Mil. Coll., Chicago-Kent Coll. of Law, Université de Montréal, McMaster Univ., Univ. of Western Ontario, Univ. of Toronto, Univ. of Glasgow, Queen's Univ., Carleton Univ.), (Mount Saint Vincent Univ., Univ. of King's Coll., Université de

Moncton, Memorial Univ., St John's, Newfoundland, Windsor Univ., Concordia Univ., Univ. of British Columbia) 2001, (Lakehead Univ.) 2002, (Université de Picardie Jules Verne, St Francis Xavier Univ., Antigonish, NS) 2003; Hon. DUniv (Ottawa) 1997; Médaille de l'Université de Montréal 1995, Achievement Award, Women's Law Asscn, Toronto 1996, G. Arthur Martin Award, Criminal Lawyers' Asscn 1998, First Recipient Toronto 1999 Medal of Honour, Int. Asscn of Prosecutors 1998, Medal of Honour, Int. Asscn of Prosecutors 1999, Médaille du Mérite, Institut de recherches cliniques de Montréal 1999, Fondation Louise Weiss Prize, Paris 1999, Second Annual Service to Humanity Award, Pennsylvania Bar Foundation 2000, Franklin and Eleanor Roosevelt Four Freedoms Medal (Freedom from Fear), Roosevelt Study Centre, Middleburg, Netherlands 2000, Women of Distinction Award, Toronto Hadassah-Wizo 2000, Peace Award, World Federalists of Canada 2000, Lord Reading Law Soc.'s Human Rights Award 2000, Wolfgang Freidman Memorial Award, Columbia Law School 2000, Eid-ul-Adha Award, Asscn of Progressive Muslims of Ontario 2000, Médaille du Barreau du Québec 2001, Nat. Achievement Award, Jewish Women Int. of Canada 2001, Stefan A. Riesenfeld Symposium Award, Berkeley Journal of International Law 2002, McGill Centre for Research and Teaching on Women Person of the Year 2002 Award 2002, 2002 Year Award, Prix de la Fondation Justice dans le Monde de l'Union internationale des Magistrats 2002, Médaille de la Faculté de droit de l'Université de Montréal 2003, inducted into Int. Hall of Fame – International Women's Forum 2003, Médaille 125e anniversaire, Faculté de droit, Asscn des diplômés en droit, Université de Montréal 2003, North-South Prize, Council of Europe (co-winner) 2011. *Publications:* numerous articles on criminal procedure, human rights, civil liberties and gender issues. *Address:* International Crisis Group, 149 Avenue Louise, Level 24, 1050 Brussels, Belgium (office). *Telephone:* (2) 502-90-38 (office). *Fax:* (2) 502-50-38 (office). *E-mail:* brussels@crisisgroup.org (office). *Website:* www.crisisgroup.org (office).

ARBUZOV, Serhiy Hennadiyovych, PhD; Ukrainian economist, central banker and government official; b. 24 March 1976, Donetsk; s. of Valentina Arbuzova; m. Iryna Arbuzova; ed Donetsk State Univ.; began career as Economist, later Head of Div. and Head of Office, Donetsk br., PrivatBank, becoming Dir Konstantyniv Br., PrivatBank; Chair. Donechchyna Bank (renamed UkrBiznes-Bank) 2003–04; Chair. Supervisory Bd Ukreximbank 2010; Deputy Gov. Nat. Bank of Ukraine (Natsionalny Bank Ukrainy) Sept.–Dec. 2010, Gov. Dec. 2010–12; mem. Our Ukraine 2005–10, Party of Regions 2010–; First Deputy Prime Minister 2012–14; Acting Prime Minister Jan.–Feb. 2014 (dismissed). *Address:* c/o Office of the Cabinet of Ministers, 01008 Kyiv, vul. M. Hrushevskoho 12/2, Ukraine. *E-mail:* web@kmu.gov.ua.

ARCAND, Denys, CC; Canadian film director and film producer; b. 25 June 1941, Deschambault, Québec; m. Denise Robert; ed Univ. of Montreal; worked at Office Nat. du Film 1962–65; Vice-Pres. Asscn des Réalisateurs et Réalisatrices de films du Québec; mem. Royal Canadian Acad. of Arts; Ordre national de la Légion d'honneur, Commander de l'Ordre des Arts et des Lettres. *Films include:* Seul ou avec d'autres (co-dir) 1962, Champlain (short) 1963, Les Montrealistes (short) 1964, La Route de l'Ouest (short) 1965, Montreal, un jour d'été and Parcs atlantiques (shorts) 1966, Volleyball 1967, On est au coton (documentary) 1970, Québec: Dupléssis et après 1970, La maudite galette 1971, Réjeanne Padovani 1972, Gina 1974, La lutte des travailleurs d'hôpitaux (short) 1975, Le confort et l'indifférence 1980 (Best Film Prize, Quebec Film Critics' Asscn 1982), Empire Inc. (TV) 1982, Le crime d'Ovide Plouffe 1984, Le déclin de l'empire américain (Canadian Genie Awards, Int. Critics Prize, Cannes Film Festival) 1986, Jésus de Montréal 1989 (Canadian Genie Awards, Cannes Jury Prize 1989), Love and Human Remains 1993, Poverty and Other Delights, Stardom 2001, The Invasions of the Barbarian (Cannes Best Screenplay, Critics' Choice Award, Best Foreign Language Film 2004, Acad. Award, Best Foreign Language Film 2004, César Awards 2004) 2003, The Age of Ignorance 2007,. *Television:* Duplessis (writer) 1978, Adam & Eve (series, writer) 2012. *Plays:* Les Lettres de la religieuse portuguaise 1989.

ARCE CATACORA, Luis Alberto, MSc; Bolivian government official; *Minister of Economy and Public Finance;* b. 28 Sept. 1963, La Paz; m.; three c.; ed Universidad Mayor de San Andrés, Univ. of Warwick, UK; with Cen. Bank of Bolivia 1988–2006; fmr consultant Natsuky Co., Nacida Co., Centro de Estudios para el Desarrollo Laboral y Agrario, Sistema Contable Computarizado; Minister of Economy and Public Finance 2006–. *Publications include:* numerous journal articles. *Address:* Ministry of Economy and Public Finance, Edif. Palacio de Comunicaciones, 19°, CP 3744, La Paz, Bolivia (office). *Telephone:* (2) 220-3434 (office). *Fax:* (2) 235-9955 (office). *E-mail:* ministro_web@economiayfinanzas.gob.bo (office). *Website:* www.economiayfinanzas.gob.bo (office).

ARCHER, David, BS, PhD; American oceanographer and academic; *Professor, Department of the Geophysical Sciences, University of Chicago;* b. 15 Sept. 1960; ed Indiana Univ., Univ. of Washington; Asst Prof. of Geophysical Sciences, Univ. of Chicago 1993–97, Adjunct Prof. of Environmental Sciences 1996–, Assoc. Prof. of Geophysical Sciences 1997–2001, Full Prof. of Geophysical Sciences 2001–; Lamont Fellow Postdoctoral Fellowship, Lamont Doherty Earth Observatory, Columbia Univ., New York 1990–92, Postdoctoral Research Scientist 1992–93, Adjunct Prof. 1994–; Contributing Ed. realclimate.org (climate science blog site). *Publications:* Global Warming: Understanding the Forecast 1992, The Long Thaw: How Humans are Changing the Next 100,000 Years of Earth's Climate 2008; more than 70 scientific papers in professional journals on the global carbon cycle and its relation to global climate, with special focus on ocean sedimentary processes. *Address:* HGS 419, Department of the Geophysical Sciences, 5734 South Ellis Avenue, University of Chicago, Chicago, IL 60637, USA (office). *Telephone:* (773) 702-0823 (office). *Fax:* (773) 702-9505 (office). *E-mail:* d-archer@uchicago.edu (office). *Website:* geosci.uchicago.edu (office).

ARCHER, Marco Shearer, LLB, MBA; Cayman Islands lawyer, statistician and politician; *Minister of Finance and Economic Development;* m. Tammy Archer; two d.; ed Barry Univ., USA, Univ. of Liverpool, UK, Coll. of Law, London, UK, Univ. of Miami, USA; began career with Statistics Office 1989 (merged with Econs Unit to become Econs and Statistics Office); Project Man. for govt-wide financial reform projects including Integrated Resources Information Systems (IRIS) 1998, Financial Management Initiative (FMI) 1999; held various posts within the Portfolio of Finance and Econ. Devt (PFED), becoming Sr Asst Sec. 2003, later Sr Statistician

responsible for econ. and business statistics programme; called to the bar 2008; fmr attorney-at-law with Mourant Ozannes (offshore law firm); mem. Legis. Assembly for Georgetown; Minister of Finance and Econ. Devt 2013–; Founding Dir Generation NOW (mentoring group and think-tank) 2007–13; mem. Cayman Islands Bar Asscn; mem. Peoples' Progressive Movement. *Address:* Government Administration Bldg, Elgin Avenue, George Town, Grand Cayman, Cayman Islands (office). *Telephone:* 244-2458 (office). *Fax:* 945-1746 (office). *E-mail:* tedc@gov.ky (office).

ARCHER, Dame Mary Doreen, DBE, MA, PhD, CChem, FRSC, CSci; British chemist and hospital administrator; b. 22 Dec. 1944, Ewell, Surrey; d. of the late Harold Norman Weeden and the late Doreen Weeden (née Cox); m. Jeffrey Howard Archer (now Baron Archer of Weston-super-Mare q.v.) 1966; two s.; ed Cheltenham Ladies' Coll., St Anne's Coll. Oxford, Imperial Coll. London; Jr Research Fellow, St Hilda's Coll. Oxford 1968–71; temporary Lecturer in Chem., Somerville Coll. Oxford 1971–72; Research Fellow, Royal Inst. of GB 1972–76; Lector in Chem., Trinity Coll. Cambridge 1976–86; Fellow and Coll. Lecturer in Chem., Newnham Coll. Cambridge 1976–86; Sr Academic Fellow, De Montfort Univ. 1990–; Visiting Prof., Dept of Biochemistry, Imperial Coll. London 1991–2000, Visiting Prof., Centre for Energy Policy and Tech. 2001–03; Visitor, Univ. of Herts. 1993–2004; Trustee Science Museum 1990–2000, Cambridge Foundation 1997–2004; mem. Council, Royal Inst. 1984–85, 1999–2001, Cheltenham Ladies' Coll. 1991–2000, UK Stem Cell Fed. 2005–; Chair Nat. Energy Foundation 1990–2000, Pres. 2000–; mem. Bd of Dirs Anglia TV Group 1987–95, Mid Anglia Radio 1988–94, Cambridge & Newmarket FM Radio (now Heart) 1988–97; Dir, Cambridge Univ. Hosps NHS Foundation Trust 1992–, Vice-Chair. 1999–2002, Chair. 2002–12; Chair. East of England Stem Cell Network 2004–08; Convenor UK Univ. Hosps Chairs Group 2008–12; mem. Council of Lloyd's 1989–92; Pres. Guild of Church Musicians 1989–, UK Solar Energy Soc. 2001–; Hon. Patron, Prostate Action 2010; Hon. DSc (Hertfordshire) 1994; Energy Inst. Melchett Medal 2002, Inst. of Chem. of Ireland Eva Philbin Award 2007. *Publications:* Rupert Brooke and The Old Vicarage, Grantchester 1989, Clean Energy from Photovoltaics (co-ed.) 2001, Molecular to Global Photosynthesis (co-ed.) 2004, Transformation and Change: the 1702 Chair of Chemistry at Cambridge (co-ed.) 2004, The Story of The Old Vicarage, Grantchester 2004, Solar Photon Conversion in Nanostructured and Photoelectrochemical Systems (co-ed.) 2008; contribs to chemical journals. *Leisure interests:* reading, writing, singing. *Address:* The Old Vicarage, Grantchester, Cambridge, CB3 9ND, England (home). *Telephone:* (1223) 840213 (home).

ARCHER, Robyn, AO, BA, DipEd; Australian singer, performer and writer; b. 18 June 1948, Adelaide, S Australia; d. of the late Clifford Charles Smith and Mary Louisa Wohling; ed Enfield High School, Adelaide Univ.; singer 1952–; recorded ten albums including Brecht, Weill and Eisler repertoire; has toured world-wide in recital, concert and cabaret performances; has sung with Australian and Adelaide Chamber Orchestras, Adelaide, Melbourne and Tasmanian Symphony Orchestras; numerous TV appearances in Australia and UK; has written over 100 songs; writing for theatre includes Songs from Sideshow Alley, The Pack of Women (also Dir), Cut & Thrust Cabaret (also Dir), Café Fledermaus, See Ya Next Century, Ningali, A Star is Torn, Comes a Cropper; writing for TV includes The One That Got Away; also writes for radio; Artistic Counsel Belvoir Street Theatre 1986; Artistic Dir Nat. Festival of Australian Theatre 1993–95, Adelaide Festival 1998, 2000, Melbourne Int. Festival of Arts 2002–04; Artistic Adviser Australia Day, Hanover Festival EXPO 2000; Creative Consultant Melbourne Museum 1995–98; Creator and Inaugural Artistic Dir, Ten Days on the Island, Tasmania 2001–05; Artistic Dir Liverpool Capital of Culture Festival 2004; Chair. Community Cultural Devt Bd, Australia Council 1993–95; Commonwealth Appointee to Centenary of Fed. Advisory Cttee 1994; mem. Bd Dirs Int. Soc. of Performing Arts, Council Victorian Coll. of the Arts, Adelaide Festival Centre Trust; Trustee, Don Dunstan Foundation; Artistic Dir The Light in Winter (Federation Square, Melbourne) 2009; currently artistic adviser to Govts of S Australia and Western Australia; Patron Australian Art Orchestra, Arts Law Centre, Australian Script Centre, Brink Productions, Globalism Inst.; fmr mem. Bd Helpmann Acad.; fmr Patron Nat. Affiliation of Arts Educators; Inaugural Amb. Adelaide Festival Centre Trust; Amb. Adelaide Football Club; Chevalier des Arts et des Lettres 2000, Federation Medal 2001, Officer of the Crown (Belgium) 2008; Hon. DUniv (Flinders); Sydney Critics' Circle Award 1980, Henry Lawson Award 1980, Australian Creative Fellowship 1991–93, Australian Record Industry Award for Best Soundtrack for Pack of Women 1986, for Best Children's Album for Mrs Bottle 1989, Exec. Woman of the Year, Australian Women's Network 1998, S Australia Arts and Culture Award 1998, 2000, Int. Citation of Merit, Int. Soc. of Performing Arts, New York 2006. *Performance roles include:* Annie I in The Seven Deadly Sins 1974, 1993, Jenny in The Threepenny Opera 1976, Brecht Compilations, Never the Twain, To Those Born Later, Sung and Unsung, Brecht & Co, Pierrot Lunaire, Out of the East, Mrs Peachum in The Threepenny Opera 1999. *One-woman shows include:* Tonight Lola Blau (Australian tour), A Star is Torn (two Australian tours, Theatre Royal, Stratford East and Wyndham's Theatre, London West End). *Theatre directed:* The Pack of Women (Australian tour), Cut and Thrust Cabaret (London), Scandals (Australian tour), On Parliament Hill (Sydney), ABC (Sydney), Akwanso Fly South (Adelaide Festival and Australian tour), Mayday (Darwin and Hobart), Labour of Love (Darwin and Hobart), Le Chat Noir (Brisbane and Canberra), The Bridge (Perth), Accidental Death of an Anarchist (Adelaide and Sydney), Boy Hamlet (Brisbane), January (Tim Finn/Dorothy Porter), Toughnut Cabaret (Pittsburgh) 2009. *Publications include:* The Robyn Archer Songbook 1980, Mrs Bottle Burps 1983, The Pack of Women 1986, A Star is Torn 1986; for theatre: Kold Komfort Kaffee 1977, The Pack of Women 1981, Cut & Thrust Cabaret 1984, Songs from Sideshow Alley 1986, Il Magnifico 1987, Akwanso Fly South 1988, Poor Johanna 1983, The Hanging of Minnie Thwaites 1983, A Star is Torn 1979, Scandals 1985, Ningali 1992, Architektin 2008; contrib. to The All Australian HaHa Book 1983, Australia Fair 1984, Mrs Bottle's Absolutely Blurtingly Beautiful World-Beating Burp 1990, Cafe Fledermaus 1990, Penguin Anthology of Contemporary Australian Women's Writing 1991, Loaves and Fishes 1991, Hope and Fear 1995, The Myth of the Mainstream 2004, Australian Greats 2008, Essentially Creative (Griffith Review) 2009. *Address:* c/o Rick Raftos Management, Box 445, Paddington, NSW 2021, Australia (office). *Telephone:* (2) 9281-9622 (office). *Fax:* (2) 9212-7100 (office). *Website:* www.robynarcher.com.au (home).

ARCHER OF WESTON-SUPER-MARE, Baron (Life Peer), cr. 1992, of Mark in the County of Somerset; **Jeffrey Howard Archer;** British writer and fmr politician; b. 15 April 1940, London, England; s. of William Archer and Lola Archer (née Cook); m. Mary Doreen Archer (q.v.) (née Weeden) 1966; two s.; ed Wellington School, Brasenose Coll., Oxford; mem. GLC for Havering 1966–70; MP for Louth (Conservative) 1969–74; Deputy Chair. Conservative Party 1985–86; mem. House of Lords 1992–. *Plays:* Beyond Reasonable Doubt 1987, Exclusive 1989, The Accused (writer and actor) 2000. *Film:* Bridget Jones's Diary (as himself) 2001. *Publications include:* Not a Penny More, Not a Penny Less 1975, Shall We Tell the President? 1977, Kane and Abel 1979, A Quiver Full of Arrows 1980, The First Miracle (with Craigie Aitchison) 1980, The Prodigal Daughter 1982, First Among Equals 1984, A Matter of Honour 1985, A Twist in the Tale (short stories) 1988, As The Crow Flies 1991, Honour Among Thieves 1993, Twelve Red Herrings (short stories) 1994, The Fourth Estate 1996, The Collected Short Stories 1997, The Eleventh Commandment 1998, To Cut a Long Story Short (short stories) 2000, Sons of Fortune 2002, A Prison Diary Vols I and II 2002, A Prison Diary Vol. III 2004, False Impression 2005, Cat O' Nine Tales (short stories) 2006, The Gospel According to Judas 2007, A Prisoner of Birth (Prix Polar Int. Prize 2009) 2008, Paths of Glory (Prix Relay du roman d'evasion 2010) 2009, 30th Anniversary revised edn of Kane and Abel 2009, And Thereby Hangs a Tale (short stories) 2010, Only Time Will Tell 2011, The Sins of the Father 2012, Best Kept Secret 2013, Be Careful What You Wish For 2014. *Leisure interests:* theatre, cricket, auctioneering. *Address:* 93 Albert Embankment, London, SE1 7TY, England (office). *E-mail:* questions@jeffreyarcher.co.uk (office). *Website:* www.jeffreyarcher.com (home).

ARCULUS, Sir Ronald, KCMG, KCVO, MA, FBIM; British fmr diplomatist; b. 11 Feb. 1923, Birmingham; s. of the late Cecil Arculus, MC and Ethel Lilian Arculus; m. Sheila Mary Faux 1953; one s. one d.; ed Solihull School, Exeter Coll., Oxford and Imperial Defence Coll.; served in Fourth Queen's Own Hussars 1942–45 (attained rank of Capt.); Foreign Office 1947; San Francisco 1948–50; La Paz 1950; Ankara 1953–56; Foreign Office 1957–60; First Sec. (Commercial), Washington, DC 1961–65; Dir of Trade Devt, New York 1965–68; Imperial Defence Coll. 1969; Head to Science and Tech. Dept, FCO 1970–73; Minister (Econ.), Paris 1973–77; Amb. to Law of Sea Conf. 1977–79; Amb. to Italy 1979–83; Special Adviser to Govt on Channel Tunnel trains 1987–88; Dir Glaxo PLC 1983–91, consultant 1992–95; Chair. Kensington Soc. 1999–2001, Pres. 2001–11; Dir of Appeals, King's Medical Research Trust 1984–88; Trustee, Glaxo Trustees Ltd 1988–93; Gov. British Inst., Florence 1984–93; consultant, London and Continental Bankers Ltd 1985–90, Trusthouse Forte 1983–86; Freeman of the City of London; Hon. Fellow, Exeter Coll., Oxford 1989. *Leisure interests:* travel, fine arts, music, antiques. *Address:* 20 Kensington Court Gardens, London, W8 5QF, England (home). *Telephone:* (20) 7938-1594 (home).

ARDALAN, Nader, BArch, MArch; American architect and planner; *President, Ardalan Associates LLC;* b. 9 March 1939, Tehran, Iran; s. of Abbas Gholi Ardalan and Faranguis Davar Ardalan; m. 1st Laleh Bakhtiar 1962 (divorced 1976); one s. two d.; m. 2nd Shahla Ganji 1977; one s.; ed New Rochelle High School, Carnegie-Mellon Univ., Harvard Univ. Grad. School of Design; designer, S.O.M. 1962–64; Chief Architect, Nat. Iranian Oil Co. 1964–66; Design Partner, Aziz Farmanfarmaian & Assocs 1966–72; Man. Dir Mandala Collaborative Tehran/Boston 1972–79; Prof. of Design, Tehran Univ. Faculty of Fine Arts 1972–77; Founder-Pres. Nader Ardalan Assocs LLC 1979–; Prin. Jung/Brannen Assocs Inc., Boston 1983–94; Man. Prin. Jung/Brannen Assocs Inc., Abu Dhabi 1992; Sr Vice-Pres. and Dir of Design KEO International Consultants 1994–2006; Pres. Ardalan Associates LLC 2006–; Research Fellow, Harvard Center for Middle East Studies 2006–10; Sr Research Assoc. and Sr Ed. Gulf Encyclopedia for Sustainable Urbanism, Grad. School of Design, Harvard Univ. 2011–, Convener of Urbanism, Spirituality and Well Being Harvard Symposium; Visiting Prof., Harvard Univ. Grad. School of Design 1977–78, 1981–83, Yale Univ. 1977, MIT 1980; Founding mem. Steering Cttee, Aga Khan Award 1976–80; collections exhibited at Venice Biennale; Exhibitor, Smithsonian's Cooper-Hewitt Museum, New York; Perm. Collection, Avery Library, Columbia Univ.; Int. Jury Pres., Saudi Aramco Cultural Center; King Fahd Award 1987; design awards: ADMA OPCO HQ, Information Tech. Coll., UAE Univ., Al Ain, UAE. *Radio:* interview on sustainable design, Nat. Public Radio. *Television:* interviewed by Dan Rather on Power to the People. *Publications include:* Sense of Unity 1972, Masjid Al Haram Mecca 1975, Habitat Bill of Rights 1976, Pardisan, Environmental Park 1976, Blessed Jerusalem 1985, New Arab Urbanism 2010 (Persian) Gulf Sustainable Urbanism 2012; articles in leading professional journals. *Leisure interests:* study of sacred architecture, photography, swimming, hunting. *Address:* Ardalan Associates LLC, PO Box 590548, Newton Center, Newton, MA 02459 (office); 59 Beverly Road, Chestnut Hill, MA 02467, USA (home). *Telephone:* (617) 232-2698 (office). *E-mail:* nader.ardalan@gmail.com (office); nardalan@gsd.harvard.ac (office). *Website:* www.ardalanassociates.com (office).

ARDANT, Fanny; French actress; b. 22 March 1949, Monte Carlo; d. of Lt-Col Jean Ardant and Jacqueline Lecoq; three c.; Grand Prix Nat., Ministry of Culture. *Films include:* Les Chiens 1979, Les uns et les autres 1981, The Woman Next Door 1981, Life is a Novel, Confidentially Yours 1983, Benevenuta 1983, Desire, Swann in Love 1984, Love Unto Death, Les Enragés, L'Eté prochain 1986, Family Business 1986, Affabulazione, Melo, The Family 1987, La Paltoquet, Three Sisters, Australia 1989, Pleure pas my love, Adventure of Catherine C., Afraid of the Dark 1991, Rien que des mensonges, La Femme du déserteur, Amok, Colonel Chabert 1994, Beyond the Clouds 1995, Ridicule 1996, Pédale douce (César Award for Best Actress) 1996, Elizabeth 1998, La Débondade 1999, Le Fils du Français 1999, Le Dîner et le Libertin 2000, Callas Forever 2002, 8 Femmes 2002, Nathalie 2003, L'odore del Sangue 2004, El Año del diluvio 2004, Paris, je t'aime 2006, Roman de gare 2007, The Secrets 2007, Hello Goodbye 2008, Cendres et sang (Ashes and Blood) 2009, Visage 2009. *Theatre includes:* Polyeucte, Esther, The Mayor of Santiago, Electra, Tête d'Or. *Leisure interest:* music (piano).

ARDEBERG, Arne Lennart, PhD; Swedish astronomer and academic; *Professor, Lund Observatory;* b. 10 Nov. 1940, Malmö; s. of Kurt Ardeberg and Elly Ardeberg; m. Margareta Vinberg 1969; one s. two d.; ed Lund Univ.; staff astronomer, Lund Observatory 1965–69, Prof. 1973–79, Dir Lund Observatory 1984–1998, 2004–07; Prof., Lund Univ. 1980–, Vice-Dean, Faculty of Science

1984–87, Dean 1987–98, Pro-Vice-Chancellor 1998–2002; staff astronomer, European Southern Observatory (ESO), La Silla, Chile 1969–73, Assoc. Astronomical Dir 1979–81, responsible for ESO VLT Site Investigation, Northern Chile 1982–87, Dir ESO 1981–84, Chair. ESO Site Evaluation Cttee 1984–89, ESO Scientific-Tech. Cttee 1987–92, ESO Site Selection Cttee 1988–91; Dir Nordic Optical Telescope Scientific Asscn 1984–95; Chair. European Telescope Consortium Euro50 2001–04; Deputy Project Man. European Extremely Large Telescope 2004–; mem. Royal Physiographical Soc. (Sweden) 1980–, Royal Swedish Acad. of Sciences 1983– (Chair. Astronomy and Space Research Bd), Royal Soc. of Sciences (Sweden) 1986–, Swedish Nat. Research Working Policy Group, Jt European ELT Exec. Cttee; Deputy Project Leader Jt European Design Study Project; Wallmark Prize, Royal Swedish Acad. of Sciences 1977. *Publications include:* 250 publs in int. journals and books on astronomy, physics and related technology. *Leisure interests:* mountaineering, forestry, literature. *Address:* Lund Observatory, Room B 256, Box 43, 221 00 Lund (office); Blåmesvägen 2, 247 35 Södra Sandby, Sweden (home). *Telephone:* (46) 222-72-90 (office); (46) 46-570-16 (home). *Fax:* (46) 222-46-14 (office). *E-mail:* arne@astro.lu.se (office). *Website:* www.astro.lu.se (office).

ARDEN, Rt Hon. Dame Mary (Howarth), DBE, PC, MA, LLM; British judge; *Lady Justice of Appeal;* b. 23 Jan. 1947; d. of the late Lt-Col E. C. Arden and of M. M. Arden (née Smith); m. Sir Jonathan Hugh Mance 1973; one s. two d.; ed Huyton Coll., Girton Coll., Cambridge, Harvard Law School, USA; called to the Bar, Gray's Inn 1971; admitted to Lincoln's Inn 1973, Bencher 1994; QC 1986; Dept of Trade and Industry Inspector Rotaprint PLC 1988–91; Attorney Gen. Duchy of Lancaster 1991–93; Judge of High Court of Justice, Chancery Div. 1993–2000; Chair. Law Comm. 1996–99; Lady Justice of Appeal 2000–; Bar mem. Law Soc.'s Standing Cttee on Company Law 1976–; mem. Financial Law Panel 1993–2000, Steering Group, Company Law Review 1998–2001; Fellow, Girton Coll. Cambridge; Hon. Fellow, Liverpool John Moores Univ. 2006; Hon. DUniv (Essex) 1997; Hon. LLD (Liverpool) 1998, (Warwick) 1999, (Royal Holloway and Bedford New Coll., London) 1999, (Nottingham) 2002; The Times Woman of Achievement Lifetime Award in 1997. *Publications:* Buckley On The Companies Acts (Jt Gen. Ed.) 2000; contrib. to numerous books, articles in legal journals. *Leisure interests:* reading, swimming. *Address:* Royal Courts of Justice, Strand, London, WC2A 2LL, England. *Telephone:* (20) 7947-6402 (office). *Fax:* (20) 7947-7201 (office).

ARDITI, Pierre; French actor; b. (Pierre Marie Denis Arditi), 1 Dec. 1944, Paris; s. of Georges Arditi; Chevalier, Légion d'honneur 2002, Ordre nat. du Mérite 1994, Officier 2005. *Theatre includes:* L'aide mémoire 1993, Art 1994, En attendant Godot 1996, Le mari, la femme et l'amant 1997, Rever peut-être 1998, L'école des femmes 2001–02, Joyeuses Paques 2001–02, Mathilde 2003, Lunes de miel 2004, La danse de l'albatros 2006, Faisons un rêve 2007, 2008–09, 2010, L'idée fixe 2007, Elle est là 2008, Tailleur pour dames 2008, Les fausses confidences 2009, L'éloignement 2009, Sentiments provisoires 2009, La vérité 2011, Moi, je crois pas 2012, Comme s'il en pleuvait 2012. *Films include:* Last Leap 1970, Alyse and Chloe 1970, Le funambule 1974, Rape of Love 1978, My American Uncle 1980, Pile ou face 1980, Nestor Burma, Shock Detective 1982, Life Is a Bed of Roses 1983, Jusqu'à la nuit 1983, Swann in Love (voice) 1984, Femmes de personne 1984, Love Unto Death 1984, The Children 1985, Farewell to Fred 1985, Strictement personnel 1985, À coeur perdu (short) 1985, Follow My Gaze 1986, Mélo (César Award for Best Actor in a Supporting Role 1987) 1986, L'état de grâce 1986, Triple sec (short) 1986, Poker 1987, La petite allumeuse 1987, Agent trouble 1987, Flag 1987, De guerre lasse 1987, La passerelle 1988, Natalia 1988, Bonjour l'angoisse 1988, Vanille fraise 1989, Radio Corbeau 1989, Le pont du silence (short) (voice) 1990, The Pleasure of Love 1991, Les clés du paradis 1991, L'ombre 1992, The Little Apocalypse 1993, Smoking/No Smoking (César Award for Best Actor 1994) 1993, The Horseman on the Roof 1995, Beaumarchais (voice, uncredited) 1996, Unpredictable Nature of the River 1996, Hommes, femmes, mode d'emploi 1996, Messieurs les enfants 1997, Same Old Song 1997, Chance or Coincidence 1998, Un chat dans la gorge 1999, A Monkey's Tale (voice) 1999, La fausse suivante 2000, Actors 2000, Le dernier plan 2000, Le voeu (short) (voice) 2002, The Mystery of the Yellow Room 2003, Not on the Lips 2003, The Car Keys 2003, Why (Not) Brazil? 2004, The First Time I Turned Twenty 2004, Victoire 2004, One Stays, the Other Leaves 2005, Le courage d'aimer 2005, Le parfum de la dame en noir 2005, Nos amis les Terriens (voice) 2006, Private Fears in Public Places 2006, Le grand appartement 2006, Coup de sang 2006, The Great Alibi 2008, Tu peux garder un secret? 2008, Musée haut, musée bas 2008, Le code a changé 2009, Je vais te manquer 2009, Park Benches 2009, Bambou 2009, Together Is Too Much 2010, Je ne vous oublierai jamais 2010, Roses à crédit 2010, Streamfield, les carnets noirs 2010, Granny's Funeral 2012, You Ain't Seen Nothin' Yet 2012, La fleur de l'âge 2012; numerous TV films and series. *Address:* c/o Anna Morin, VMA, 20 avenue Rapp, 75007 Paris, France (office). *Telephone:* 1-43-17-37-06 (office). *E-mail:* a.morin@vma.fr (office). *Website:* www.vma.fr (office).

ARDITO BARLETTA, Nicolás, PhD, MS; Panamanian politician and economist; b. 21 Aug. 1938, Aguadulce, Coclé; s. of Nicolás Ardito Barletta and Leticia de Ardito Barletta; m. María Consuelo de Ardito Barletta; two s. one d.; ed Univ. of Chicago and North Carolina State Univ., USA; Cabinet mem. and Dir Planning 1968–70; Dir Econ. Affairs OAS 1970–73; Minister of Planning 1973–78; Negotiator of econ. aspects of Panama Canal Treaties 1976–77; Vice-Pres. World Bank for Latin America and Caribbean 1978–84; Founder and first Pres. Latin American Export Bank (BLADEX) 1978; Pres. Latin American Econ. System (SELA) Constituent Ass.; Pres. of Panama 1984–85; Gen. Dir of Int. Centre for Econ. Growth 1986–95; Dir Autoridad de la Región Interoceanía 1995–2000; Chair. Asesores Estrategicos; mem. Bd of Dirs of several corpns, banks and policy insts including Superintendencia de Bancos 2006–(14). *Publications:* numerous publications on econ. and social devt issues. *Leisure interests:* tennis and music. *Address:* PO Box 0830, 00378 Panamá 9, Panama. *Telephone:* 264-6675. *Fax:* 223-6488. *E-mail:* asesores@cwpanama.net.

AREF, Mohammad Reza, BS, BEng, MS, PhD; Iranian electronics engineer, politician and academic; *Professor, Department of Electrical Engineering, Sharif University of Technology;* b. 1951, Yazd; ed Univ. of Tehran, Stanford Univ., USA; politically active as student, supporter of Ayatollah Khomeini, arrested by secret police 1963; mem. of Muslim students org. during stay in US, subsequently head of that org.; has held a number of govt posts including Minister of Posts, Telegraphs and Telecommunications, Deputy Minister of Culture and Higher Educ. in charge of Student Affairs 1981–82 and Adviseor to Minister of Culture and Higher Educ., Deputy to Minister of Science, Research and Tech. 1981–84, Deputy to Minister of Science, Research and Tech. 1989–91; Deputy to Man. Dir Telecom Co. 1980–1981; Faculty mem. Isfahan Univ. of Tech. 1982–95; Chancellor Univ. of Tehran 1994–97; Minister of Information, Communication and Tech. 1997–2000; First Vice-Pres. of Iran 2001–05; Prof., Electrical Engineering Dept, Sharif Univ. of Tech. 1995–; Pres. Iranian Soc. of Cryptology 2000–, Iranian Command and Intelligence Soc. 2007–, Foundation for Advancement of Science and Tech. 2007–; Bd BARAN Foundation 2005–; mem. Expediency Discernment Council of System 2003–, Supreme Cultural Revolution Council 2002–, Acad. of Sciences 2007–; cand. in 2013 presidential election (withdrew); First Prize, Nat. Math. Competition 1959, Isfahan Tech. Univ. Scholarship. *Address:* Department of Electrical Engineering, Sharif University of Technology, POB 11365-8639, Tehran, Iran (office). *Telephone:* (21) 6005419 (office); (61) 63935 (office). *Fax:* (21) 6012983 (office). *E-mail:* aref@sharif.edu (office). *Website:* ee.sharif.edu/~aref (office).

ARENAS DE MESA, Alberto, DEcon; Chilean economist, academic and politician; *Minister of Finance;* b. 5 Oct. 1965; ed Univ. of Chile, Univ. of Pittsburgh, USA; Economist, Research Dept, Banco Sud Americano, Santiago 1989–90; Adviser, Ministry of Finance and Budget 1990–93; Graduate Research Asst, Univ. of Pittsburgh 1993–96, Teaching Fellow, Dept of Econs 1996–97; Prof., Dept of Econs, Georgetown Univ.-ILADES, Santiago 1999–2003; Head of Research Dept, Directorate of Budget, Ministry of Finance 1997–2000, Asst, Rationalization and Public Service 2000–06, Dir of Budget 2006–10, Minister of Finance 2014–; Asst Prof. and Researcher, Microdata Center, Dept of Econs, Univ. of Chile 2010; Dir Channel 13 (TV) 2010–; mem. (Dir) Parl. Appropriations Resolution Council 2010. *Address:* Ministry of Finance, Teatinos 120, 12°, Santiago, Chile (office). *Telephone:* (2) 2828-2000 (office). *Website:* www.minhda.cl (office).

ARENDARSKI, Andrzej, PhD; Polish politician, business executive and academic; *President, National Chamber of Commerce (Poland);* b. 15 Nov. 1949, Warsaw; m. Agnieszka Łypacewicz; three s. one d.; ed Univ. of Warsaw; teacher, East Dembowski Secondary School, Warsaw 1972–73, Inst. of Philosophy and Sociology of Polish Acad. of Sciences, Warsaw 1973–75; mem. Solidarity Trade Union 1980–; Ed.-in-Chief, underground journal Zeszyty Edukacji Narodowej 1981–82; co-f. Agric.-Industrial Soc., Konin 1988; mem. Soc. for Econ. and Econ. Action, Warsaw 1988; co-f. Social Movt for Econ. Initiatives SPRING 1988; Deputy to Sejm (Parl.) 1989–93; mem. Liberal Democratic Congress (KLD) 1989–94, Deputy Chair. KLD 1989–94, mem. KLD Political Council 1991–94, then Chair.; Chair. Democratic Party 2002–06; Pres. Polish Chamber of Commerce 1990–; Minister of Foreign Econ. Co-operation 1992–93; Chair. Polish-Ukrainian Chamber of Commerce 1996; Sec.-Gen. Polish Asscn Industry, Commerce and Finance 1997; Chair. Polish-American Small Business Consultation Fund; CEO Tel-Emergo, Telephony Service Providers. *Publications:* contribs to underground journals 1981–89; co-author: Polska lat 80-tych: Analiza stanu obecnego i perspektywy rozwoju sytuacji politycznej w Polsce 1984, Stan środowiska przyrodniczego 1984. *Leisure interests:* travel, sailing, art of cooking. *Address:* Krajowa Izba Gospodarcza, ul. Trębacka 4, 00-074 Warsaw, Poland. *Telephone:* (22) 630-96-00 (office). *Fax:* (22) 827-46-73 (office). *E-mail:* aarendarski@kig.pl (office). *Website:* www.kig.pl/english/index.htm (office); arendarski.blogbank.pl.

ARENS, Moshe; Israeli aeronautics engineer, politician, academic and diplomatist; b. 7 Dec. 1925, Kovno, Lithuania; ed Massachusetts Inst. of Tech., California Inst. of Tech., USA; Assoc. Prof. of Aeronautical Eng, Technion (Israel Inst. of Tech.), Haifa; Deputy Dir Israel Aircraft Industries, Lod; mem. Knesset (Likud) 1973–82, 1984–99, mem. Knesset Finance Cttee 1973; Amb. to USA 1982–83; Minister of Defence 1983–84, 1999, without Portfolio –1987, of Foreign Affairs 1988–90, of Defence 1990–92; Adviser to Prime Minister 2001; currently Chair. International Board of Governors, Ariel Univ. Center of Samaria; Chair. Teuzah Fund (venture capital fund); Fellow, Institute for Zionist Strategies; Assoc. Fellow, AIAA,; Israel Defence Prize 1971. *Publications:* Broken Covenant 1994, Flags Over the Warsaw Ghetto 2011, several books on propulsion and flight mechanics. *Address:* Office of the Chairman, Teuzah Fund, PO Box 25266, Haifa 31250, Israel. *E-mail:* teuza@teuzafund.com. *Website:* www.teuza.co.il.

ARGENTO, Asia; Italian actress, singer, model and film director; b. (Aria Asia Anna Maria Vittoria Rossa Argento), 20 Sept. 1975, Rome; d. of Dario Argento and Daria Nicolodi; great-granddaughter of composer Alfredo Casella; one d. with Marco Castoldi; m. Michele Civetta 2008; one s.; published book of poems aged eight; began acting aged nine, playing small part in film Sogni e bisogni by Sergio Citti; also had a small part in Demons 2 (written and produced by her father) 1986 and its unofficial sequel, La chiesa (The Church) 1989; began appearing in English-language films, including B. Monkey and New Rose Hotel 1998, French-language films, including La Reine Margot 1994; made first foray into directing in short films Prospettive and A ritroso 1994; directed a documentary on her father 1996, and second on Abel Ferrara (Rome Film Festival Award) 1998; directed and wrote her first full-length film, Scarlet Diva, co-produced by her father 2000; has modelled for and endorses the brand 'Miss Sixty'; contributed a video diary 'Don't Bother To Knock' to Nick Knight's website, SHOWstudio Oct. 2006; appeared in Placebo's music video for 'This Picture'; appeared on Brian Molko (frontman of Placebo) cover version of 'Je t'aime. . . moi non plus'; has been part of Tiger Man's project Femina 2009; featured on the song 'Life Ain't Enough for You', released as a single along with B-side 'Il Mio Stomaco É Il Piu Violento de Tutta Italia'; mem. jury, Cannes Film Festival 2009. *Films include:* Dèmoni 2: L'incubo ritorna 1986, Palombella Rossa 1988, La chiesa (The Church) 1989, Red Lob 1989, Zoo 1990, Close Friends 1992, Condannato a nozze 1993, Trauma 1993, Perdiamoci di vista! (David di Donatello for Best Actress 1994), La Reine Margot 1994, DeGenerazione (also writer and dir) 1995, The Stendhal Syndrome 1996, Il cielo è sempre più blu 1996, Compagna di viaggio (Travelling Companion) (David di Donatello for Best Actress 1996, Grolla d'oro Award 1996) 1996, Viola bacia tutti 1998, New Rose Hotel 1998, B. Monkey 1998, The Phantom of the Opera 1998, La tua lingua sul mio cuore (short) (also writer and dir) 1999, Scarlet Diva (also writer and dir) 2000, Loredania (short) (also writer, dir, creative producer and supervising producer) 2000, L'assenzio (also writer and dir) 2001, Love Bites 2001, La sirène rouge (The Red Siren) 2002, xXx 2002, Ginostra 2002, The Keeper 2004, The Heart Is Deceitful Above All Things (also writer and dir) 2004, Last Days 2005, Cindy: The Doll Is Mine (short) 2005, Land of the Dead 2005, Live Freaky Die Freaky (voice) 2006, Sean Lennon's Friendly Fire 2006, Marie Antoinette 2006, Transylvania 2006, Boarding Gate 2007, Go Go Tales 2007, Désengagement 2007, Une vieille maîtresse (aka The Last Mistress) 2007, Mother of Tears 2007, De la guerre (On War) 2008, Coin Locker Babies 2008, Diamond 13 2009, King Shot 2010, Gli sfiorati 2011, Baciato dalla fortuna 2011; as dir: Abel/Asia (documentary short) 1998, La scomparsa (short) (also producer) 2000, Lest We Forget: The Video Collection (video (s)AINT, Marilyn Manson music video) 2004. *Television includes:* Sogni e bisogni (mini-series) 1985, Turno di notte (series) 1987, Les Misérables (mini-series) 2000, Milady (film) 2004. *Publications:* I Love You Kirk (novel) 1999; several stories for magazines including Dynamo, L'Espresso, Sette and Village. *E-mail:* infoaria_23@yahoo.it (office). *Website:* www.asiargento.it (office).

ARGERICH, Martha; Argentine pianist; b. 5 June 1941, Buenos Aires; ed studied with V. Scaramuzzo, Friedrich Gulda, Nikita Magaloff, Madeleine Lipatti and Arturo Benedetti Michelangeli; debut Buenos Aires 1949; London debut 1964; soloist with leading orchestras and conductors worldwide; debut at BBC London Proms (Schumann Concerto) 2000; as chamber musician, has toured Europe, USA and Japan with Gidon Kremer and Mischa Maisky; numerous recordings including most of repertoire for four hands and for two pianos with Nelson Freire, Stephen Bishop-Kovacevich, Nicolas Economou and Alexandre Rabinovitch; performances at Lockenhaus, Munich Piano Summer, Lucerne and Salzburg Festivals; Artistic Dir, Beppu Festival, Japan 1998–; pres. jury, Int. Martha Argerich Piano Competition 1999–; cr. Martha Argerich Presents Project, to bring together young players and renowned artists to play rarely performed compositions and masterpieces of the repertoire; Accademica di Santa Cecilia di Roma 1997, Commdr, Ordre des Arts et des Lettres 2004, Order of the Rising Sun, Gold Rays with Rosette, Japan 2005; First Prize Busoni Contest and Geneva Int. Music Competition 1957, Int. Chopin Competition, Warsaw 1965, Prix Caecilia 1991, Diapason d'Or 1992, Edison Award 1993, Tokyo Record Academy Award 1995, CD Compact Award 1997, Musical America Musician of the Year 2001, Praemium Imperiale Award (Japan) 2005, Gramophone Awards Artist of the Year, three Grammy Awards. *Recordings include:* works by Brahms, Rachmaninov, Ravel and Schubert (with Nelson Freire) 2009, Argerich plays Chopin 2010, Argerich Lugano Concertos 2002–2010 (four CDs) 2012, Brahms & Schumann (with Bashmet Maisky) 2012. *Address:* Agence Artistique Jacques Thelen, 15 Avenue Montaigne, 75008 Paris, France (office). *Telephone:* 1-56-89-32-00 (office). *Fax:* 1-56-89-32-01 (office). *E-mail:* jthelen@wanadoo.fr (office); info@marthaargerichpresents.com (office). *Website:* jacquesthelen.com (office); www.marthaargerichpresents.com (office).

ARGUETA, Manlio; Salvadorean writer and librarian; b. 24 Nov. 1935, San Miguel; lived in exile in Costa Rica for many years since 1973; Dir Biblioteca Nacional de El Salvador 1996. *Publications:* En el costado de la luz (poetry) 1968, Un hombre por la patria 1968, El valle de las Hamacas 1977, Caperucita en la zona roja 1977, Un día en la vida (Univ. of Cen. America Prize) 1980, Cuscatlán (novel) 1987, Milagro de la Paz (novel) 1996, Siglo de O(g)ro 1997. *Address:* Biblioteca Nacional, 4ta Calle Oriente y Avda Mons. Oscar A. Romero #124, San Salvador, El Salvador (office). *Telephone:* 2221-2099 (office). *Fax:* 2221-8847 (office). *Website:* www.binaes.gob.sv (office).

ARGUETA ANTILLÓN, José Luis (Lucho); Salvadorean economist, academic and university administrator; *Member, Administrative Council, Faculty of Economics, University of El Salvador;* b. 16 July 1932, El Salvador; s. of Tomás Antillón and Andrea Argueta; m. María Luz Márquez 1956; four s. two d.; ed Univ. of El Salvador, Univ. of Chile, Universidad del Païs Vasco; Prof., Univ. of El Salvador 1964–67, Sec., Faculty of Econ. Sciences 1967–69, Prof., Faculty of Investigative Econs 1974–78, Dir 1985–86, Asst to Acting Rector 1979–80, Dir, Inst. of Econs Research, Rector 1985–90, Sec. for Postgraduates 1993–99, Investigator, Faculty of Econs 2000–, mem. Gen. Ass., mem. Admin. Council, Faculty of Econs 2013–; Prof. and Researcher, Cen. American Univ. 1980–85; Scholar, Universidad del Païs Vasco 1991–92, Investigator, Faculty of Econs 2001–07, mem. Gen. Ass. 2009–13; Dr hc (Univ. of Simón Bolívar, Colombia) 1987; Economist of the Year 1985, Distinguished Economist (several times). *Publications include:* Manual de Contabilidad Nacional 1967, La Economía Salvadoreana—Algunos Elementos de Análisis 1984, La Reedición de Reforma Universitaria de Córdoba—Una Necesidad Histórica 1989, Efectos Fiscales del CAFTA, Agenda para la Integración de Centroamèrica, Problemas de Población Educación y Desarrollo. *Leisure interest:* sport. *Address:* Universidad de El Salvador, Facultad de Ciencias Económicas, Ciudad Universitaria, Final Av. Héroes y Mártires del 30 de Julio, San Salvador, El Salvador (office). *Telephone:* 2225-8930 (office). *E-mail:* antillon@navegante.com.sv (office); antillon_luis@yahoo.com (home).

ARGUETA DE BARILLAS, Marisol; Salvadorean lawyer and diplomatist; *Senior Director and Head of Latin America, World Economic Forum;* b. 1968; m. Carlos R. Barillas; three d.; ed Univ. of Oxford, UK, New York Univ., USA; fmr Asst Prof. of Constitutional Law and Political Law, El Salvador; Alt. Rep. to UN, New York 1990–97, Minister Counsellor, Embassy in Washington, DC 1997–99, Gen. Dir of Foreign Policy, Ministry for Foreign Affairs –2004, Adviser to Minister of Foreign Affairs 2004–08, Minister of Foreign Affairs 2008–09; Sr Dir and Head of Latin America, World Econ. Forum 2010–; fmr Vice-Pres. OAS Nat. Authorities Meeting for the World Economy; Co-founder Vital Voices – El Salvador; mem. Bd of Dirs Hogares CREA-El Salvador, Salvadorean Foundation for the Elderly, Int. Inst. for Women; mem. Oxford Union Soc. *Address:* c/o World Economic Forum USA, 3 East 54th Street, 18th Floor, New York, NY 10022, USA. *Website:* www.weforum.org.

ARGUS, Donald (Don) Robert, AC; Australian banker and business executive; b. 1 Aug. 1938, Bundaberg; s. of Dudley Francis Argus and Evelyn Argus; m. Patricia Anne Argus 1961; three d.; ed Royal Melbourne Inst. of Tech., Harvard Univ.; Chief Man. Corp. Lending, Nat. Australia Bank Ltd 1983, then Gen. Man. Credit Bureau, then Gen. Man. Group Strategic Devt, then Exec. Dir and COO, Man. Dir, CEO 1990–99; Dir Broken Hill Pty Co. Ltd (BHP Ltd) 1996–2009, Chair. 1999–2009, Chair. BHP Billiton Ltd, BHP Billiton Plc 2001–09; Chair. Brambles Industries Ltd 1999–2008; Chair. Australian Bankers Asscn 1992–94; Dir Southcorp Ltd 1999–, Australian Foundation Investment Co. Ltd 1999–; mem. Bank of America/ Merrill Lynch Global Advisory Council 2013–, Int. Advisory

Council, Allianz AG 2000–, Int. Advisory Cttee, New York Stock Exchange Bd of Dirs 2005–; conducted review of Australian cricket team 2011. *Leisure interests:* hockey, golf, reading.

ARGYROS, George L.; American business executive and diplomatist; *Chairman Emeritus and Treasurer, Horatio Alger Association of Distinguished Americans Inc.;* b. 1937, Detroit; m. Julia Argyros; three c.; ed Chapman Univ.; Founder Pnr, Westar Capital, Chair. 1976–2001; Co-owner AirCal 1981–87; Owner Seattle Mariners professional baseball team 1981–89; Pres. and CEO Horatio Alger Asscn of Distinguished Americans Inc. 1995–98, Chair. 1998–2000, currently Treas. and Chair. Emer.; Chair. and CEO Arnel and Affiliates CA –2001; Amb. to Spain and Andorra 2001–04; Founder-Chair. Nixon Center, Washington, DC; Chair. Bd of Dirs Beckman Foundation; fmr Chair. Richard Nixon Library and Birthplace Foundation, Orange County Council Boy Scouts of America; mem. Bd Fed. Home Loan Mortgage Corpn (FreddieMac) 1990–93, US Chamber of Commerce, M.D. Anderson Cancer Center; fmr Bd Chair. Orange Co. Council Boy Scouts of America; fmr mem. Bd of Dirs Rockwell Int. Corpn, First American Corpn, DST Systems Inc., Newhall Land and Farming Co., Tecstar, Doskocil Manufacturing Co., Igloo Products Corp., Harper Leather Goods Inc., Verteq Inc.; mem. Bd of Trustees, Chapman Univ. 2001–, California Inst. of Tech. (fmr Vice-Chair. Business and Finance Cttee), Center for Strategic and Int. Studies, Washington, DC, Library of Congress Open World Leadership Center; Counselor Layalina Productions Inc.; apptd Archon Mother Church of Constantinople, Greek Orthodox Church, Order of St Andrew 2005; mem. Advisory Cttee for Trade Policy and Negotiations USA Trade Rep. –1990; Hon. DHumLitt (Chapman Univ.) 2005, Hon. DIur (Pepperdine Univ.) 1997; Horatio Alger Award of Distinguished Americans 1993, Ellis Island Medal of Honor 2001. *Address:* Horatio Alger Association of Distinguished Americans Inc., 99 Canal Center Plaza, Suite 320, Alexandria, VA 22314, USA (office). *Telephone:* (703) 684-9444 (office). *Fax:* (703) 548-3822 (office). *Website:* www.horatioalger.org (office).

ARHABI, Abd al-Karim Ismail al-, MA; Yemeni politician; b. 1947, Alssadah, Ibb Prov.; ed Martin Luther Univ., Germany, academic and field training in USA, Germany and UK; worked in pvt. sector 1977–79; Gen. Dir Industrial Estate Authority 1979–81; Man. Dir Yemeni Industrial Bank 1981–94; Head of Small Enterprise Devt Unit 1994; est. and was Man. Dir Social Fund for Devt 1996; Minister of Social Affairs and Labour 2001–06; Deputy Prime Minister for Econ. Affairs and Minister of Planning and Int. Cooperation 2006–12. *Address:* c/o Ministry of Planning and International Cooperation, PO Box 175, San'a, Yemen.

ARHAR, France, BA, MA, PhD; Slovenian business executive and fmr central banker; *Chairman of the Managing Board, UniCredit Banka Slovenija d.d.;* b. 24 April 1948, Ljubljana; ed Univ. of Ljubljana; joined Nat. Bank of Slovenia 1971, Head of Section 1974–76, Asst Gen. Man. Int. Div. 1976–78, Gen. Man. Int. Div. and Asst Gov. 1978–88; trainee, Linklaters & Paines Pnrs, London, UK 1979, Hessische Landesbank Frankfurt 1982; Gen. Man. Corp. Finance LHB Int. Handelsbank, Frankfurt 1988–91; Gov. Bank of Slovenia 1991–2001; Chair. Man. Bd Vzajemna (pvt. health insurer) 2001–03, Bank Austria Creditanstalt d.d. Ljubljana (now UniCredit Banka Slovenija d.d.) 2003–; Asst Prof. of Int. Econ. Law, Faculty of Law, Univ. of Ljubljana 1988, Asst Prof. of Int. Finance and Int. Financial Law 2005; Pres. Ethics Cttee of the Int. Forum for Scientific Research in Pharmaceutical Use, Slovenian Cttee for Negotiations on Succession by the Vienna Agreement, Council of Slovene Nat. Theatre, Ljubljana; Deputy Pres. Supervisory Bd, Bank Asscn of Slovenia; mem. Man. Cttee, Univ. of Ljubljana, mem. Council of the Faculty of Econs; mem. Govt Strategic Council on the Economy; mem. ILO, Geneva. *Publications include:* three books on foreign trade, int. finance and int. econ. law and over 80 articles. *Address:* UniCredit Banka Slovenija d.d., Smartinska 140, Ljubljana, 1000, Slovenia (office). *Telephone:* (1) 5876600 (office). *Website:* www.unicreditbank.si (office).

ARIARAJAH, Wesley, BSc, BD, ThM, MPhil, PhD; Sri Lankan ecclesiastic and academic; *Professor of Ecumenical Theology, Drew University;* b. 2 Dec. 1941, Jaffna; s. of Ponniah David Seevaratnam and Grace Annalukshmi (née Sinnapu); m. Christine Shyamala Chinniah 1974; three d.; ed Madras Christian Coll., India, United Theological Coll., Bangalore, India, Princeton Seminary, NJ, USA, Univ. of London, UK; ordained in Methodist Church; Minister, Methodist Church of Sri Lanka, Jaffna 1966–68; Lecturer, Theological Coll. Lanka, Pilimatalawa 1969–71; Chair. North and East Dist, Methodist Church, Jaffna 1974–81; mem. staff WCC programme on Dialogue with People of Living Faiths, Geneva 1981–83, Dir 1983–93, Deputy Sec.-Gen. WCC 1993–97; Prof. of Ecumenical Theology, Drew Univ., NJ 1997–; delivered Sixth Lambeth Interfaith Lecture 1987. *Publications include:* Dialogue 1980, The Bible and People of Other Faiths 1985, Hindus and Christians: A Century of Protestant Ecumenical Thought 1991, Gospel and Culture, An Ongoing Discussion in the Ecumenical Movement 1994, Did I Betray the Gospel? The Letters of Paul and the Place of Women 1996, Not Without My Neighbour: Issues in Interfaith Dialogue 1999, Axis of Peace: Christian Faith in Times of Violence and War 2004; contrib. articles to specialist journals. *Leisure interest:* reading. *Address:* Seminary Hall, School of Theology, Drew University, Madison, NJ 07940 (office); 34B Loantaka Way, Madison, NJ 07940, USA (home). *Telephone:* (973) 408-3979 (office); (973) 360-9296 (home). *Fax:* (973) 408-3808 (office). *E-mail:* wariaraj@drew.edu (office); ariarajah@hotmail.com (home). *Website:* www.drew.edu (office).

ARIAS, Ileana, BA, MA, PhD; American clinical psychologist and health official; *Principal Deputy Director, Centers for Disease Control and Prevention;* ed Barnard Coll., State Univ. of New York at Stony Brook; began career as Research Assoc., SUNY, Stony Brook; Asst Prof., later Dir of Clinical Training and Prof. of Clinical Psychology, Univ. of Georgia –2000; joined Centers for Disease Control and Prevention (CDC) and Agency for Toxic Substances and Disease Registry 2000, currently Prin. Deputy Dir CDC; Acting Dir Nat. Center for Injury Prevention and Control 2004–05, Dir 2005; mem. editorial bd Journal of Aggression, Maltreatment, and Trauma, Review of Aggression and Violent Behavior, Violence and Victims; reviewer for 11 professional journals; mem. Advisory Bd Psychiatric and Forensic Doctor of Nursing Program, Univ. of Tennessee Health Science Center Coll. of Nursing, Nat. Safety Council, Univ. of Maryland Center for Risk Communication Research, European Center for Injury Prevention; mem. Defense Task Force on Sexual Assault in the Mil. Services. *Address:* Office of the Principal Deputy Director, Centers for Disease Control and Prevention, 1600 Clifton Rd,

Atlanta, GA 3033, USA (office). *E-mail:* cdcinfo@cdc.gov (office). *Website:* www.cdc .gov (office).

ARIAS, Inocencio F.; Spanish civil servant and diplomatist; b. 20 April 1940; m.; three c.; joined diplomatic service 1967, Dir of Diplomatic Information Office, Ministry of Foreign Affairs 1980–82, 1985–88, 1996–97, Under-Sec., Ministry of Foreign Affairs 1988–91; State Sec. for Int. Co-operation for Iberoamerican Affairs 1991–93; Gen. Dir Real Madrid 1993–95; Perm. Rep. to UN, New York 1998–2004; Consul Gen., Los Angeles, Calif. –2010 (retd); fmr Prof. of Int. Relations, Univ. Complutense, Univ. Carlos III, Madrid; 30 Spanish and foreign decorations. *Publications include:* numerous papers and contribs; Confesiones de un diplomático, Tres Mitos del Real Madrid.

ARIAS SÁNCHEZ, Oscar, PhD; Costa Rican politician, academic and fmr head of state; b. 13 Sept. 1940, Heredia; s. of Juan Rafael Arias Trejos and Líllyan Sánchez Cortes; m. Margarita Penón; one s. one d.; m.; ed Univ. of Costa Rica, Univ. of Essex, UK; Prof., School of Political Sciences, Univ. of Costa Rica 1969–72; Financial Adviser to Pres. of Repub. 1970–72; Minister of Nat. Planning and Econs Policy 1972–77; Int. Sec. Liberación Nacional Party 1975, Gen. Sec. 1979–83, 1983; Congressman in Legis. Ass. 1978–82; Pres. of Costa Rica 1986–90, 2006–10; f. Arias Foundation for Peace and Human Progress 1988; mem. Bd Cen. Bank 1972–77, Vice-Pres. 1970–72; ad hoc Comm. mem. Heredia's Nat. Bank 1972–75; mem. Bd Tech. Inst. 1974–77; mem. Rector's Nat. Council 1974–77; mem. Bd Int. Univ. Exchange Fund, Geneva 1976; mem. North–South Roundtable 1977; has participated in numerous int. meetings and socialist conventions; instrumental in formulating the Cen. American Peace Agreement 1986–87; approx. 50 hon. degrees; Nobel Peace Prize 1987, Martin Luther King Award 1987, Príncipe de Asturias Award 1988, shared Philadelphia Liberty Medal 1991, Albert Schweitzer Prize for Humanitarianism, and other awards. *Publications:* Pressure Groups in Costa Rica 1970 (Essay's Nat. Award 1971), Who Governs in Costa Rica? 1976, Latin American Democracy, Independence and Society 1977, Roads for Costa Rica's Development 1977, New Ways for Costa Rican Development 1980 and many articles in newspapers and in nat. and foreign magazines. *Address:* Arias Foundation for Peace and Human Progress, Costado suroeste de la Plaza de Democracia, sobre Avenida 2A, San José, Costa Rica. *Website:* www.arias.or.cr.

ARIAS SÁNCHEZ, Rodrigo, LLM; Costa Rican lawyer and politician; b. 1946, San Francisco de Heredia; s. of Juan Rafael Arias Trejos and Lillyam Sánchez Cortés; brother of Oscar Arias Sánchez; ed Univ. of Costa Rica, Univ. of Pennsylvania, USA; Prof. of Commercial Law, Univ. of Costa Rica 1971–73; attorney, then legal adviser, Dir and Vice-Pres. Bolsa Nacional de Valores 1971–85, Man. 1997–2003; Chair. Ingenio Taboga SA 1974–; Pres. Municipality of Heredia 1974–86; Minister of the Presidency 1986–99, 2006–10;*Website:* www .rodrigoarias.com.

ARIDJIS, Homero; Mexican author, poet and diplomatist; b. 6 April 1940, Contepec, Michoacán; m. Betty Ferber 1965, two d.; ed Autonomous Univ. of Mexico 1961; lecturer in Mexican literature at univs in USA; Cultural Attaché, Embassy in Netherlands 1972, later Amb. to Switzerland and the Netherlands; Man. Cultural Inst., Michoacán, Dir Festival Int. de Poesia 1981, 1982, 1987; f. Review Correspondencias; Chief Ed. Dialogos; Visiting Prof., Univ. of Indiana and New York Univ.; Poet-in-Residence, Columbia Univ. Translation Center, New York; co-f. Pres. Grupo de los Cien 1985 (100 internationally renowned artists and intellectuals active in environmental affairs); Nichols Chair in the Humanities and the Public Sphere, Univ. of Calif. at Irvine; Pres. International PEN 1997–2003, Pres. Emer. 2003–09; fmr Amb. to UNESCO; Guggenheim Fellow 1966–67, 1979–80; Hon. DHumLitt (Indiana) 1993; Global 500 Award 1987, Novedades Novela Prize 1988, Grinzane Cavour Prize for Best Foreign Fiction 1992, Prix Roger Caillois, France 1997, Presea Generalisimo José María Morelos, City of Morelia 1998, Environmentalist of the Year Award, Latin Trade Magazine 1999, John Hay Award, Orion Soc. 2000, Forces for Nature Award, National Resources Defense Council 2001, Green Cross Millennium Award for Int. Environmental Leadership, Global Green 2002. *Publications include:* poetry: Los ojos desdoblados 1960, Antes del reino 1963, Ajedrez-Navegaciones 1969, Los espacios azules 1969 (Blue Spaces 1974), Quemar las naves 1975, Vivir para ver 1977, Construir la muerte 1982, Obra poética 1960–86 1987, Imágenes para el fin del milenio 1990, Nueva expulsión del paraíso 1990, El poeta en peligro de extinción 1992, Tiempo de ángeles 1994, Ojos de otro mirar 1998 (Eyes to See Otherwise: Selected Poems of Homero Aridjis 2002), El ojo de la ballena 2001; prose: La tumba de Filidor 1961, Mirándola adentro 1964, Perséfone 1967 (Persephone 1986), El poeta niño 1971, Noche de independencia 1978, Espectáculo del año dos mil 1981, Playa nudista y otros relatos 1982, 1492 vida y tiempos de Juan Cabezón de Castilla 1985, El último Adán 1986, Memorias del nuevo mundo 1988, Gran teatro del fin del mundo 1989, La leyenda de los soles 1993, El Señor de los últimos días: Visiones del año dos mil 1994, ¿En quién piensas cuando haces el amor? 1996, Apocalipsis con figuras 1997, La montaña de las mariposas 2000, El silencio de Orlando 2000, La zona del silencio 2002, El hombre que amaba el Sol 2005.

ARIE, Thomas Harry David, CBE, MA, BM, DPM, FRCP, FFPH; British psychiatrist and academic; *Professor Emeritus of Health Care of the Elderly, University of Nottingham;* b. 9 Aug. 1933, Prague, Czechoslovakia; s. of Dr O. M. Arie and H. Arie; m. Eleanor Aitken 1963; one s. two d.; ed Balliol Coll., Oxford; Sr Lecturer in Social Medicine, London Hosp. Medical Coll. 1962–74; Consultant Psychiatrist for Old People, Goodmayes Hosp. 1969–77; Foundation Prof. and Head, Dept of Health Care of the Elderly, Univ. of Nottingham 1977–95, Prof. Emer. 1995–; Visiting Prof., NZ Geriatrics Soc. 1980, Univ. of the Negev, Israel 1988, UCLA, USA 1991, Univ. of Keele 1997; Consultant Psychiatrist to the Nottingham Hosps 1977–95; Vice-Pres. Royal Coll. of Psychiatrists 1984–86, Chair. Specialist Section on Old Age 1981–86, Hon. Fellow 2001; Chair. Geriatric Psychiatry Section, World Psychiatric Asscn 1989–93; mem. Standing Medical Advisory Cttee for the Nat. Health Service 1980–84, Cttee on the Review of Medicines 1981–91, Registrar Gen.'s Medical Advisory Cttee 1990–94; Gov., Centre for Policy on Ageing 1992–98; Vice-Chair. Royal Surgical Aid Soc. (AgeCare) 1995–2007, Vice-Pres. 2008; Fellow, Faculty of Public Health; Dhole-Eddlestone Memorial Prize, British Geriatrics Soc. 1996; Lifetime Award, Int. Psychogeriatric Asscn 1999, Founders' Medal, British Geriatrics Soc. 2005, Lifetime Award, Old Age Faculty, Royal Coll. of Psychiatrists 2012. *Publications:* Health Care of the Elderly (ed.) 1981, Recent Advances in Psychogeriatrics (Vol. 1)

1985, (Vol. 2) 1992; papers on care of the aged, old age psychiatry, epidemiology and educ. *Address:* Cromwell House, West Church Street, Kenninghall, Norfolk, NR16 2EN, England.

ARIFI, Teuta, BA, MA, PhD; Macedonian (ethnic Albanian) philologist and politician; *Mayor of Tetovo;* b. 19 Oct. 1969, Tetovo; m.; two c.; ed Univ. of Prishtina, Kosovo, SS. Cyril and Methodius Univ., Skopje; Fellow, Women's Leadership Inst., Santa Fe, NM, USA 1992; Fellow and Researcher, CORE Inst. on OSCE Studies, Univ. of Hamburg 1999–2001; Asst Prof. of History of Albanian Literature, Faculty of Philology, SS. Cyril and Methodius Univ. 1997–; Assoc. Prof. of Multicultural Issues, Teacher Training Faculty, SEE Univ., Tetovo 2001–, Dean of the Teacher Training Faculty 2001–06, mem. Jt Bd SEE Univ. 2001–; Vice-Pres. Democratic Union for Integration 2002–; mem. Parl. 2002–11, Head of Foreign Policy Cttee, mem. Parl. Del. in Parl. Ass. of Council of Europe, Head of Parl. Del. at North Atlantic Council, Head of Cttee on Culture 2006–11, Head of Foreign Policy Cttee; Deputy Prime Minister, responsible for European Integration 2011–13; Mayor of Tetovo 2013–; Vice-Chair. Group of Specialists of the Council of Europe on positive actions in the field of equality between women and men 1998–2000; adviser to Ministry of Foreign Affairs and Head of the Unit for OSCE and other int. orgs within the Ministry 1996–97; mem. Macedonian Del. at OSCE Conf. in Vienna, Working Group 2, Human Dimension Nov. 1996, at 4th World Conf. on Women, Beijing, Working Group 2 1995–96; mem. OSCE team for monitoring of parl. elections in Albania May 1996; mem. Bd Soros Open Society Inst. in Macedonia 1995–96; Sec. Gen. Cttee in Macedonia, Helsinki Civil Ass. 1992–94; mem. of initial group for the foundation of Helsinki Cttee for Human Rights in Macedonia 1994, initial group for the foundation of the League of Albanian Women in Macedonia 1992; responsible for the page of the political weekly KOHA in Prishtina dedicated to women 1991–92; Rep. of Steering Cttee of experts on equality between women and men in the Council of Europe, Strasbourg 1995–2000, mem. Bureau of the Steering Cttee on Equality 1996–2000; mem. Bd, Centre for Multiculture and Understanding, Skopje 1997–99; radio commentator, South European Dept, Radio Deutsche Welle, Cologne 1992–2002; mem. research team on the work of OSCE High Commr for Minorities, Peace Inst., Univ. of Hamburg 1999–2001, Advisory Bd, Research Team of the situation of minorities in South Europe, CEI-Budapest 1998–2000; columnist, Dnevnik (Daily) 2006–. *Publications:* Gjeografia mie (My Geography) (poetry) 1996, Feminizmi ekzisten-cialist (Existential Feminism) (study) 1997, Ucestvoto na zenite vo sovremenite trendovi vo Republika Makedonija (Women's Participation in Contemporary Trends in the Republic of Macedonia) (study) 1997, Shatë ditë magjike (Seven Magical Days) (novel) 1998. *Address:* Municipality of Tetovo, Dervish Cara, NN, 1200 Tetovo, Former Yugoslav Republic of Macedonia. *Telephone:* (44) 335499. *Fax:* (44) 339420. *E-mail:* cabinet@tetova.gov.mk. *Website:* www.tetova.gov.mk.

ARIGONI, Duilio, DScTech; Swiss chemist and academic; *Professor Emeritus of Organic Chemistry, Swiss Federal Institute of Technology (ETH);* b. 6 Dec. 1928, Lugano; s. of Bernardino Arigoni and Emma Arigoni (née Bernasconi); m. Carla Diener 1958 (died 1998); two s. one d.; ed Swiss Fed. Inst. of Tech. (ETH), Zürich; Lecturer in Organic Chem., ETH Zürich 1961–62, Assoc. Prof. 1962–67, Prof. 1967–96, Prof. Emer. 1996–; Visiting Prof., Harvard Univ., USA 1969, 1983, Technion, Haifa, Israel 1970, Univ. of Cambridge 1981; Prof.-at-Large, Cornell Univ. 1980–87, Univ. of Innsbruck, Austria 2003; mem. Deutsche Akad. der Naturforscher Leopoldina 1976, Academia Europaea, London 1989, Accad. Nazionale delle Scienze, Rome 1991, European Acad. of Sciences, Brussels 2004; Foreign mem. Royal Soc., London 1991; Foreign Assoc. NAS, Washington, DC 1998, Acad. des Sciences, Paris 2005; Hon. FRSC 1978, Hon. mem. French Chem. Soc. 1976, Italian Chem. Soc. 1981, American Acad. of Arts and Sciences 1988; Dr hc (Université de Paris-Sud) 1982; Davy Medal, Royal Soc., London 1983, R.A. Welch Award, Welch Foundation, USA 1985, ACS Arthur C. Cope Award 1986, Wolf Prize, Israel 1989, Marcel Benoist Prize, Switzerland 1992 and other prizes and awards. *Publications:* over 200 publs in scientific journals. *Leisure interest:* music, especially Bach, Mozart. *Address:* Laboratorium für Organische Chemie, ETH Hönggerberg, HCI H307, Wolfgang-Pauli-Strasse 10, 8093 Zürich (office); Im Glockenacker 42, 8053 Zürich, Switzerland (home). *Telephone:* (44) 632-2891 (office); (44) 381-1383 (home). *Fax:* (44) 632-1154 (office). *E-mail:* arigoni@org .chem.ethz.ch (office); duilio.arigoni@org.chem.ethz.ch (office). *Website:* www.chab .ethz.ch/forschung/loc/index_EN (office).

ARIMA, Akito, CBE, BSc, MSc, DSc; Japanese scientist and academic; *President and Chair of the Board of Trustees, International Human Frontier Science Program Organization;* b. 13 Sept. 1930, Osaka; s. of Johji Arima and Kazuko Arima; m. Hiroko Aota 1957; one s. one d.; ed Musashi Koto Gakko Coll., Univ. of Tokyo; Research Assoc. Inst. for Nuclear Studies, Univ. of Tokyo 1956, Lecturer, Dept of Physics 1960, Assoc. Prof. 1964, Prof. of Physics, Faculty of Science 1975, Dir Computer Centre 1981–87, Councillor 1983–87, Dean, Faculty of Science 1985–87, Vice-Pres. 1987–89, Pres. 1989–93, Prof. Emer. 1993; Visiting Prof., Rutgers and Princeton Univs 1967–68, State Univ. of New York, Stony Brook 1968, USA 1971–73; Prof., Hosei Univ. April-Sept. 1993; Scientific Counsellor Ministry of Educ. 1993–98; Pres. Inst. of Physical and Chemical Research (RIKEN) 1993–98; Chair. Cen. Council for Educ. 1995–98; Minister of Educ. Science, Sports and Culture 1998–99; Minister of State for Science and Tech. Jan.-Oct. 1999; Chair. Japan Science Foundation 2000–; Dir Science Museum 2004–; Pres. and Chair. Bd of Trustees, Int. Human Frontier Science Program Org. 2009–; Deputy Chair. Council for Relocation of Diet and other orgs 1996–98; mem. Science Council of Japan 1985–94, Admin. Reform Council 1996–98, House of Councillors 1998–2004; Hon. Prof., Univ. of Science and Tech., China 1992, Peking Univ., China 1998; Das Grosse Verdienstkreuz (Germany) 1990, Order of Orange Nassau (Netherlands) 1991, au grade d'Officier dans l'ordre nat. de la Légion d'Honneur 1998, Grand Cordon of the Order of the Rising Sun (Japan); Hon. DSc (Univ. of Glasgow) 1979, Dr hc (Drexel Univ., USA) 1992, (Chung Yuan Christian Univ., Taiwan) 1992, (State Univ. of New York, USA) 1994, (Univ. of Groningen, Netherlands) 1994, (Univ. of Birmingham, UK) 1996, (Univ. of Surrey, UK) 1999, (Weizmann Inst. of Science, Israel) 1999, (Univ. of Stellenbosch, South Africa) 1999, (Univ. of Arizona, USA) 2000; Nishina Memorial Prize 1978, Humboldt Prize 1987, John Price Wetherill Medal, Franklin Inst., USA 1990, Bonner Prize, American Physical Soc. 1993, Japan Acad. Prize 1993. *Publications include:* Interacting Boson Model 1987, Einstein's Century: Akito Arima's Haiku 2001. *Leisure interests:* Haiku, calligraphy, reading. *Address:* International Human

Frontier Science Program Organization, 12 quai Saint-Jean, BP 10034, 67080 Strasbourg Cedex, France; Science Museum, 2-1 Kitanomaru-koen, Chiyoda-ku, Tokyo 102-0091, Japan (office). *Telephone:* (3) 3212-8544 (office). *Fax:* (3) 3212-8443 (office). *E-mail:* akito_arima@sangiin.go.jp (office). *Website:* www.hfsp.org; www.jsf.or.jp.

ARINZE, HE Cardinal Francis A., DD, STL; Nigerian ecclesiastic; *Prefect of Congregation Emeritus for Divine Worship and the Discipline of the Sacraments;* b. 1 Nov. 1932, Eziowelle, Onitsha; s. of Joseph Arinze Nwankwu and Bernadette M. Arinze; ed Bigard Memorial Seminary, Nigeria, Urban Univ., Rome and Univ. of London; ordained 1958; consecrated Bishop (Titular Church of Fissiana) 1965; Archbishop of Onitsha 1967; cr. Cardinal 1985; Pres. Pontifical Council for Inter-Religious Dialogue 1984–2002; Prefect of Congregation for Divine Worship and the Discipline of the Sacraments 2002–08, Emer. 2009–; Hon. PhD (Univ. of Nigeria) 1986; Hon. LLD (Catholic Univ. of America) 1998; Hon. DD (Wake Forest Univ., USA) 1999, (Univ. of Our Lady of the Lake, USA) 2003; Hon. DH (Univ. of Santo Tomas, Philippines) 2001, DD hc (Christendom Coll., VA) 2004. *Publications:* Partnership in Education 1965, Sacrifice in Ibo Religion 1970, Answering God's Call 1983, Alone With God 1986, Church in Dialogue 1990, Meeting Other Believers 1997, Brücken Bauen 2000, The Holy Eucharist 2001, Religions for Peace 2002, Trust in Divine Providence 2003, God's Invisible Hand 2003. *Leisure interests:* tennis, reading. *Address:* Congregation for Divine Worship and the Discipline of the Sacraments, Palazzo delle Congregazioni, Piazza Pio XII 10, 00193 Rome, Italy (home). *Telephone:* (06) 69884316 (home). *Fax:* (06) 69883499 (home). *E-mail:* cultdiv@ccdds.va (home). *Website:* www.vatican.va/roman_curia/congregations/ccdds (home).

ARISMENDI CHUMACERO, Elizabeth; Bolivian lawyer, judge and politician; *Minister of the Legal Defence of State;* ed Universidad Tomás Frias, Potosi; fmr Lecturer, Ilustre Colegio Departamental de Abogados de Potosí; fmr judge; Minister of the Legal Defence of State 2011–. *Address:* Ministry of the Legal Defence of State, Edif. Hansa, 4°, Avda Mariscal Santa Cruz, La Paz, Bolivia (office). *Telephone:* (2) 211-8454 (office). *Fax:* (2) 211-8454 (office). *E-mail:* mdle@defensalegal.gob.bo (office). *Website:* www.defensalegal.gob.bo (office).

ARISMUNANDAR, Wiranto, MSc; Indonesian mechanical engineer, academic and politician; *Professor of Mechanical Engineering, Institut Teknologi Bandung;* b. 19 Nov. 1933, Semarang; s. of Raden Arismunandar and Raden Roro Sri Wuryan; m. Nyi Raden Sekarningrum Wirakusumah; three s. three d.; ed Univ. of Indonesia, Purdue and Stanford Univs, USA; Research Assoc., Dept of Mechanical Eng, Stanford Univ. 1961–62; training in rocket propulsion, Japan 1965; Vice-Chair. Indonesian Nat. Inst. of Aeronautics and Space 1978–89; Prof. of Mechanical Eng, Inst. of Tech., Bandung 1973–, Pres. 1988–97; Minister of Educ. and Culture 1998; Sr Scientist, Indonesian Agency for the Assessment and Application of Tech.; technological adviser, Indonesian Aircraft Industry 1979–; Consultant, Indonesian Nat. Atomic Energy Agency; Chair. Patent Appeal Cttee, Ministry of Justice; currently Fellow, Islamic Acad. of Sciences; mem. People's Consultative Council 1992–97, Consultative Bd Indonesian Islamic Council, Nat. Energy Cttee, World Energy Conf., Nat. Telecommunication Council, Indonesian Nat. Cttee; mem. Indonesian Nat. Research Council, AIAA, Indonesian Aeronaut-ics and Astronautics Inst., Soc. of Automotive Engineers of Indonesia (Founding mem.) and many other nat. and int. eng bodies; Chief Ed. Teknology magazine; Satyalancana Dwidya Sistha Medal of Merit 1968, 1983, 1989, 1992, Satyalancana Karya Satya (First Class) 1990, Satyalancana Karya Satya for 30 years' service, Bintang Jasa Utama 1998. *Publications:* 13 books and more than 100 papers. *Leisure interests:* sport, photography. *Address:* Institut Teknologi Bandung, Department of Mechanical Engineering, Faculty of Industrial Technology, Ganesa 10, Bandung 40132 (office); Bukit Dago Utara I/6, Bandung 40135, Indonesia (home). *Telephone:* (22) 2534118 (office); (22) 2503558 (home). *Fax:* (22) 2534212 (office); (22) 2503558 (home). *E-mail:* wiranto@lmbsp.ms.itb.ac.id (office). *Website:* lmbsp.ms.itb.ac.id (office).

ARISMUNANDAR, Lt-Gen. Wismoyo; Indonesian army officer (retd); b. 10 Feb. 1940, Bondowoso, East Java; ed Mil. Acad.; brother-in-law of fmr Pres. Suharto; Danjen Kopassus 1983–85, Trikora Mil. Commdr 1983–85, Kostrad 1990–93, Commdr Jakarta Strategic Reserve Command, fmr Army Deputy Chief, Chief of Army Staff 1993–95; Chair. KONI (Nat. Sports Cttee) 1995; mem. Bd of Trustees, All Indonesian Billiards Sports Asscn, Fed. of Sports Karate-do Indonesia. *Address:* c/o Board of Trustees, All Indonesian Billiards Sports Association, Doors VII Main Stadium, Bung Karno, Senayan, Jakarta 10270, Indonesia (office).

ARISTIDE, Jean Bertrand, PhD; Haitian academic, fmr ecclesiastic and fmr head of state; b. 15 July 1953, Salut; m. Mildred Trouillot 1996; one d.; ed Univ. of South Africa; Roman Catholic priest; expelled from Salesian Order 1988; resgnd from priesthood Nov. 1994; Pres. of Haiti Feb.–Oct. 1991, 1993–96, 2001–04; in exile in Caracas, Venezuela Oct. 1991; returned Oct. 1993 after resignation of junta; f. La Fanmi Lavalas party 1996; fled to Africa following civil unrest Feb. 2004; Hon. Research Fellow in African Languages, Univ. of SA 2004; returned to Haiti 2011. *Publications:* Haiti and the New World Order 1995, Dignity 1996, Eyes of the Heart 2000. *Website:* www.hayti.net.

ARITON, Ion; Romanian economist and politician; b. 15 Feb. 1956, Piteşti; ed Univ. of Timisoara, Lucian Blaga Univ. of Sibiu; Commercial Dir SC Petrom SA, Sibiu 1993–2000, Dir Gen. Sibiu Br. 2000–01; Exec. Dir SC Intermedia, Sibiu 2003–04; Financial Man. referent, CSU Sibiu, Lucian Blaga Univ. of Sibiu 2004–05; Prefect of Sibiu Co. 2005–07; Government Insp. 2007–08; mem. Senatul (Senate) 2008–10, Chair. Cttee on Budget, Finance, Banking Activity and Capital Market; Minister of the Economy, Trade and the Business Environment 2010–12; mem. Democratic Liberal Party (Partidul Democrat Liberal—PD-L), Chair. PD-L Sibiu Br. 2008–; Kt, Order of the Star of Romania 2007; Prize for Excellence 2006. *Address:* c/o Ministry of the Economy, Trade and the Business Environment, 010096 Bucharest 1, Calea Victoriei 152, Romania. *E-mail:* ion.ariton@gmail.com.

ARKIN, Alan Wolf; American actor, director and author; b. 26 March 1934; s. of David Arkin and Beatrice Arkin; m. 2nd Barbara Dana; one s.; m. 3rd Suzanne Newlander; two s. from first marriage; ed Los Angeles City Coll., Los Angeles State Coll., Bennington Coll.; made professional theatre debut with the Compass Players, St Louis 1959; later joined Second City group, Chicago 1960; made New York debut at Royal, in revue From the Second City 1961; played David Kolvitz in

Enter Laughing 1963–64 (Tony Award 1963), appeared in revue A View Under The Bridge 1964, Harry Berline in Luv. *Films include:* Enter Laughing (New York Film Critics Theatre World Award 1964) 1964, The Russians Are Coming, The Russians Are Coming (Golden Globe Award) 1966, Women Times Seven 1967, Wait Until Dark 1967, Inspector Clouseau 1968, The Heart is a Lonely Hunter 1968, Popi 1969, Catch-22 1970, Little Murders (also Dir) 1971, Last of the Red Hot Lovers 1972, Freebie and the Bean 1974, Rafferty and the Gold Dust Twins 1975, Hearts of the West (Best Supporting Actor Award) 1975, The In-Laws 1979, The Magician of Lublin 1979, Simon 1980, Chu Chu and the Philly Flash 1981, Improper Channels (Canadian Acad. Award) 1981, The Last Unicorn 1982, Joshua Then and Now (Canadian Acad. Award) 1985, Coupe de Ville 1989, Havana 1990, Edward Scissorhands 1990, The Rocketeer 1990, Glengarry Glen Ross 1992, Indian Summer 1993, So I Married an Axe Murderer 1993, Steal Big, Steal Little 1995, Mother Night 1995, Grosse Point Blank 1997, Gattaca 1998, The Slums of Beverly Hills 1998, Jakob the Liar 1999, Arigo 2000, America's Sweethearts 2001, Thirteen Conversations About One Thing 2001, Counting Sheep 2002, Noel 2004, Eros 2004, The Novice 2004, Firewall 2006, Little Miss Sunshine (Screen Actors' Guild Award for Outstanding Performance by a Cast 2007, BAFTA Award for Best Supporting Actor 2007, Acad. Award for Best Supporting Actor 2007) 2006, The Santa Clause 3: The Escape Clause 2006, Raising Flagg 2006, Rendition 2007, Get Smart 2008, Marley & Me 2008, City Island 2009, The Private Lives of Pippa Lee 2009, Argo 2012, Stand Up Guys 2012. *TV appearances include:* The Love Song of Barney Kempinski 1966, The Other Side of Hell 1978, The Defection of Simas Kudirka 1978, Captain Kangaroo, A Deadly Business 1986, Escape from Sobibor, Necessary Parties, Cooperstown, Taking the Heat, Doomsday Gun, Varian's War 2001, The Pentagon Papers 2003, And Starring Pancho Villa as Himself 2003, Noel 2004. *Theatre includes:* dir: Eh? at the Circle in the Square, 1966, Hail Scrawdyke 1966, Little Murders, 1969, White House Murder Case 1970, The Sunshine Boys, Eh? 1972, Molly 1973, Joan Lorraine 1974, Power Plays (also wrote and directed), Promenade Theatre 1998, The Sorrows of Stephen, Room Service. *Publications:* Tony's Hard Work Day, The Lemming Condition, Halfway Through the Door, The Clearing 1986, Some Fine Grampa! 1995, One Present from Flekmans 1998, Cassie Loves Beethoven 1999, An Improvised Life: A Memoir 2011. *Address:* c/o The Endeavor Agency, 9601 Wilshire Blvd, 10th Floor, Beverly Hills, CA 90212, USA (office). *Telephone:* (310) 248-2000 (office). *Fax:* (310) 248-2020 (office).

ARLACCHI, (Giuseppe) Pino; Italian sociologist, academic, international organization official and politician; b. 21 Feb. 1951, Gioia Tauro, Reggio Calabria; m.; two c.; ed Univ. of Florence 1988–94; apptd Prof. of Sociology, Univ. of Sassari 1994; elected to Chamber of Deputies 1994–95, to Senate 1995–97; Vice-Pres. Parl. Comm. on the Mafia; UN Under-Sec.-Gen. and Dir-Gen. UN, Vienna 1997–2002; Exec. Dir UN Office for Drug Control and Crime Prevention 1997–2002; Prof. of Sociology, School of Political Science, Univ. of Sassari 1998–; MEP 2009–, Vice Chair. Del. for Relations with Afghanistan, mem. Cttee on Foreign Affairs; mem. Hon. Cttee of the Foundation for Dialogue among Civilizations; Pres. Int. Asscn for the Study of Organized Crime 1984–87; Hon. Pres. Giovanni Falcone Foundation 1992–2000; Fellow, Ford Foundation; adviser to Govt of China about security for 2008 Beijing Olympic Games. *Publications:* numerous publs on int. organized crime. *Leisure interest:* sailing. *Address:* European Parliament, Bât. Altiero Spinelli, 09G309 60, rue Wiertz, 1047 Brussels, Belgium (office). *Telephone:* (2) 284-56-06 (office). *Fax:* (2) 284-96-06 (office). *E-mail:* pino.arlacchi@europarl.europa.eu (office); pino@pinoarlacchi.it. *Website:* www.pinoarlacchi.it.

ARLMAN, Paul, MA; Dutch international civil servant and trade association administrator; *President, Transparency International (Dutch Chapter);* b. 11 July 1946, Bussum; s. of Evert Arlman and Corrie Jacobs; m. Kieke Wijs 1971; one s. one d.; ed Hilversum Grammar School, Rotterdam Econ. Univ., Peace Research Inst., Groningen and Nice European Inst., France; served in the Treasury, The Hague 1970–74; Treasury Rep. Embassy in Washington, DC 1974–78; Div. Chief, Treasury, The Hague 1978–81; Dir and Deputy Asst Sec. Int. Affairs 1981–86; Dir Int. Affairs Amsterdam Exchanges 1997–98; Chair. Industry Advisory Cttee to European Parl. Financial Services Forum 2001–03; Chair. Plan Int. 2005–; Pres. Transparency Int. (Dutch Chapter) 2006–; Sec.-Gen. Amsterdam Stock Exchange 1991–96 (Chair. Trading Markets Cttee), Fed. European Securities Exchanges 1998–2005; mem. Bd of Dirs EIB 1981–86, (Chair. Policy Cttee 1983–84), World Bank Group 1986, IBRD, IDA, IFC, MIGA 1986–90, Multilateral Agency for Investment Guarantees (Chair. Audit Cttee) 1988; Founder mem. European Corp. Governance Inst. 2002–08; mem. Bd European Capital Market Inst., Peters Cttee on Corp. Governance, Bd Int. Corp. Govt Inst. *Leisure interests:* literature, tennis, skiing, outdoor sports. *Address:* Transparency International (Dutch Chapter), Benoordenhoutseweg 23, 2596 BA The Hague (office); Jan van Nassaustraat 33, 2596 BM The Hague, Netherlands (home). *Telephone:* (70) 3142452 (office); (70) 3244938 (home). *Fax:* (70) 3240458 (home). *E-mail:* communicatie@transparency .nl (office); paul@arlman.com (home). *Website:* www.transparency.nl (office).

ARMACOST, Michael Hayden, MA, PhD; American diplomatist and government official; *Shorenstein Distinguished Fellow, Asia Pacific Research Center, Institute for International Studies, Stanford University;* b. 15 April 1937, Cleveland, Ohio; s. of George H. Armacost and Verda Gay Armacost (née Hayden); brother of Samuel Henry Armacost (q.v.); m. Roberta June Bray 1959; three s.; ed Carleton Coll., Friedrich Wilhelms Univ., Columbia Univ.; Assoc. Prof. of Govt, Pomona Coll., Claremont, Calif. 1962–70; Wig Distinguished Prof. 1966; Special Asst to Amb., Embassy in Tokyo 1972–74; mem. Policy Planning, Staff Dept, Washington, DC 1974–77; Sr Staff mem., Nat. Security Council, Washington, DC 1977–78; Deputy Asst Sec. Defense, Int. Security Affairs 1978–79, Principal Deputy Asst Sec., E Asian and Pacific Affairs 1980–81, Amb. to Philippines 1982–84, Under-Sec. for Political Affairs 1984–89, Amb. to Japan 1989–93; Pres. Brookings Inst., Washington, DC 1995–2002; Shorenstein Distinguished Fellow, Asia Pacific Research Center, Stanford Inst. for Int. Studies 2002–; mem. Council on Foreign Relations; Visiting Prof. of Int. Relations, Int. Christian Univ., Tokyo 1968–69; Grand Cordon, Order of the Rising Sun (Japan); Dr hc (Carleton Coll., Pomona Coll., Denison Univ., Washington Coll., Univ. of Maryland, American Univ., Alaska Pacific Univ., S Dakota School of Mines, Hamyang Univ., Univ. of the City of Manila); Superior Honour Award, State Dept 1976; Distinguished Civilian Service Award, Defence Dept 1980; Presidential Distinguished Service Award; Sec. of State Distinguished Service Award. *Publications:* The Politics of

Weapons Innovation 1969, The Foreign Relations of United States 1969, Friends or Rivals 1996, America's Alliances in Northeast Asia 2004. *Leisure interests:* reading, music, golf. *Address:* Asia Pacific Research Center, Stanford University, Encina Hall, Room E301, Stanford, CA 94305-6055, USA (office). *Telephone:* (650) 724-4002 (office). *Fax:* (650) 723-6530 (office). *E-mail:* armacost@stanford.edu (office). *Website:* fsi.stanford.edu/people/michaelharmacost (office).

ARMACOST, Samuel Henry, BA, MBA; American business executive; *Chairman Emeritus, SRI International;* b. March 1939, Newport News, Va; brother of Michael Hayden Armacost (q.v.); m. Mary Jane Armacost 1962; two d.; ed Denison Univ., Granville, Ohio, Stanford Univ.; joined Bank of America as credit trainee 1961, London branch 1969–71; Advisor Office of Monetary Affairs (exec. exchange programme) 1971–72; Head Europe, Middle East and Africa Div., London 1977–79; Cashier Bank of America and Treasurer of its Holding Co. Bank-America Corpn 1979–80; Pres. and CEO Bank of America and Bank-America Corpn 1981–86, Chair. and CEO 1986 (resgnd); Investment Banker Merrill Lynch and Co. 1987; Man. Dir Merrill Lynch Capital Markets 1987–1990; Man. Dir Weiss, Peck & Greer LLC 1990–98; Chair. SRI Int. (fmrly Stanford Research Inst.) 1998–2010, currently Chair. Emer.; mem. Bd of Dirs ChevronTexaco Corpn 2001–, Callaway Golf Co., The James Irvine Foundation, Del Monte Foods Co., Scios Inc., Exponent Inc., Sarnoff Corpn, Bay Area Council; mem. Exec. Bd Bay Area Science Infrastructure Consortium (BASIC); fmr mem. Advisory Council, California Acad. of Sciences. *Address:* c/o SRI International, 333 Ravenswood Avenue, Menlo Park, CA 94025-3493, USA (office).

ARMANI, Giorgio; Italian fashion designer and business executive; *Chairman, President and CEO, Giorgio Armani SpA;* b. 11 July 1934, Piacenza; s. of the late Ugo Armani and of Maria Raimondi; ed Univ. of Milan; worked in mil. hospital –1957; window dresser, then Asst Buyer, La Rinascente, Milan 1957–64; Designer and Product Developer Hitman (menswear co. of Cerruti Group) 1964–70; freelance designer for several firms 1970; f. Giorgio Armani SpA with Sergio Galeotti 1975, achieved particular success with unconstructed jackets of mannish cut for women, trademarks also in babywear, underwear, accessories, perfume; appeared on cover of Time 1982; Patron Sydney Theatre Co.; Grand'Ufficiale dell'ordine al merito 1986, Gran Cavaliere 1987; Dr hc (RCA, London) 1991, (Univ. of the Arts, London) 2006, (Polytechnic Univ., Milan) 2007; Neiman-Marcus Award 1979, Cutty Sark Award 1980, 1981, 1984, 1986, 1987, (First Designer Laureate 1985), Ambrogino d'Oro, Milan 1982, Int. Designer Award, Council of Fashion Designers of America 1983, L'Occhio d'Oro 1984, 1986, 1987, 1988, L'Occhiolino d'Oro 1984, 1986, 1987, 1988, Time-Life Achievement Award 1987, Cristobal Balenciaga Award 1988, Woolmark Award, New York 1989, 1992, Senken Award, Japan 1989, Award from People for the Ethical Treatment of Animals, USA 1990, Fiorino d'Oro, Florence, for promoting Made in Italy image 1992, Hon. Nomination from Brera Acad., Milan 1993, Aguja de Oro Award, Spain, for Best Int. Designer 1993, Telva Triunfador Award, Madrid, for Best Designer of the Year 1993. *Leisure interests:* cinema, music, books. *Address:* Giorgio Armani SpA, Via Borgonuovo 21, 20121 Milan, Italy (office); Giorgio Armani SpA, 650 Fifth Avenue, New York, NY 10019, USA (office). *Telephone:* (02) 801481 (Italy) (office). *Fax:* (02) 46461914 (Italy) (office). *Website:* www.giorgioarmani.com (office).

ARMATRADING, Joan, MBE, BA; British singer and songwriter; b. 9 Dec. 1950, St Kitts, West Indies; d. of Amos Ezekiel Armatrading and Beryl Madge Benjamin; ed Open Univ.; moved to Birmingham, UK 1958; began professional career in collaboration with lyric-writer Pam Nestor 1972; tours worldwide; Hon. Fellow, John Moores Univ. 2000, Univ. of Northampton 2003; Hon. DLitt (Aston Univ.) 2006; Hon. DMus (Birmingham) 2002, (Royal Scottish Acad. of Music and Drama) 2008, (Open Univ.) 2013 BASCA Gold Badge Award 2011, Lifetime Achievement Award, British Folk Festival 2012. *Recordings include:* albums: Whatever's For Us 1973, Back To The Night 1975, Joan Armatrading 1976, Show Some Emotion 1977, Me Myself I 1980, Walk Under Ladders 1981, The Key 1983, Secret Secrets 1985, The Shouting Stage 1988, Hearts and Flowers 1990, The Very Best of 1991, Square the Circle 1992, What's Inside 1995, Lovers Speak 2003, Into the Blues 2007, This Charming Life 2010, Live at Royal Albert Hall 2011, Starlight 2012. *Leisure interests:* British comics, vintage cars. *Address:* 72 New Bond Street, London, W1S 1RR, England (office). *Website:* www.joanarmatrading.com (office).

ARMEY, Richard (Dick) Keith, BA, MA, PhD; American economist, consultant and fmr politician; b. 7 July 1940, Cando, ND; s. of Glen Armey and Marion Gutschlag; m. Susan Byrd; four s. one d.; ed Jamestown Coll., ND and Univs of N Dakota and Oklahoma; mem. Faculty of Econs, Univ. of Montana 1964–65; Asst Prof., West Texas State Univ. 1967–68, Austin Coll. 1968–72; Assoc. Prof., North Texas State Univ. 1972–77, Chair. Dept of Econs 1977–83; mem. US House of Reps from 26th Tex. Dist 1985–2002 (retd), Majority Leader 1995–2002; Sr Policy Adviser and Co-Chair. Homeland Security Task Force, DLA Piper Rudnick Gray Cary 2003–09 (resgnd); Chair. Freedom Works Inc., Washington, DC –2012 (resgnd); Republican; Hon. Patron, Univ. of Dublin Philosophical Soc. 2008. *Publications:* Price Theory 1977, The Freedom Revolution 1995, The Flat Tax 1996, Armey's Axioms 2003, Give Us Liberty: A Tea Party Manifesto (with Matt Kibbe) 2010. *Address:* c/o Freedom Works, 600 Pennsylvania Avenue, NW, North Building, Suite 700, Washington, DC 20004, USA.

ARMFIELD, Diana Maxwell, RA, RWS, CSIA; British painter; b. 11 June 1920, Ringwood, Hants.; d. of Joseph Harold Armfield and Gertrude Mary Uttley; m. Bernard Dunstan 1949; three s. (one deceased); ed Bedales School, Bournemouth Art School, Slade School of Art, Cen. School of Arts and Crafts, London; teacher, Byam Shaw School of Art 1959–80; Artist in Residence, Perth, Australia 1985, Jackson, Wyoming, USA 1989; Assoc. RA 1989–1991, full mem. 1991–; mem. Royal Soc. of Painters in Watercolours (ARWS) 1977–, Royal Watercolour Soc. (RWS) 1983–; Hon. mem. New English Art Club, Pastel Soc., RA 1989–; Hon. retd mem. Royal Cambrian Acad., Royal West of England Acad.; Hunting Finalist Prize 1980, 1981. *Publications:* Painting in Oils, Drawing, The Art of Diana Armfield 1995. *Leisure interests:* music, gardening. *Address:* 10 High Park Road, Kew, Richmond, Surrey, TW9 4BH, England; Llwynhir, Parc, Bala, Gwynedd, LL23 7YU, Wales. *Telephone:* (20) 8876-6633 (Richmond) (home); (1678) 540289 (Gwynedd) (home). *Fax:* (20) 8876-6633 (Richmond) (home).

ARMITAGE, Richard Lee; American fmr diplomatist; *President, Armitage International LC;* b. 1945; ed US Naval Acad.; US naval officer, served in Viet Nam

–1973; with US Defense Attache Office, Saigon 1973–75; consultant to Pentagon 1975, posted Tehran, Iran –1976; worked in private sector 1976–78; Admin. Asst to Kan. Senator Robert Dole 1978–80; Sr Advisor, Interim Foreign Policy Advisory Bd 1980; Deputy Asst Sec. of Defense, E Asia and Pacific Affairs 1981–83, Asst Sec. of Defense, Int. Security Affairs 1983–89; Presidential Special Negotiator, Philippines Mil. Bases Agreement and Special Mediator for Water, Middle East 1989–92; Special Emissary to King Hussein, Jordan 1991; Coordinator, Emergency Humanitarian Assistance 1992; Dir, assistance to new independent states (NIS), fmr Soviet Union 1992–93; Pres. Armitage Associates LLC 1993–2001; Deputy Sec. of State 2001–05; Pres. Armitage Int. LC 2005–; mem. Bd of Dirs ManTech Int. Corpn 2005–, ConocoPhillips Co. 2006–, Transcutaneous Technologies Inc. (TTI) 2006–; mem. Bd of Trustees Center for Strategic and Int. Studies (CSIS); Distinguished Public Service (four times), Outstanding Public Service, State Dept Distinguished Honor Award, numerous US mil. decorations, decorations from govts of Thailand, Repub. of Korea, Bahrain, Pakistan; Dept of Defense Medal, Sec. of Defense Medal, Presidential Citizens Medal. *Address:* Armitage International LC, 2300 Clarendon Blvd, Suite 601, Arlington, VA 22201-3392, USA (office). *Telephone:* (703) 248-0344 (office). *Fax:* (703) 248-0166 (office). *Website:* www.armitageinternational.com (office).

ARMITT, Sir John Alexander, Kt, KBE, CBE, FREng, FICE; British civil engineer, transport industry executive and construction industry executive; *Chairman, Olympic Delivery Authority;* b. 2 Feb. 1946, London, England; m. Mavis Sage 1969 (divorced); one s. one d.; ed Portsmouth Northern Grammar School, Portsmouth Coll. of Tech.; civil engineer, John Laing Construction Co. 1963–93, Chair. Int. and Civil Eng Divs 1987–93; CEO Union Railways 1993–97, oversaw devt of high-speed Channel Tunnel Rail Link; CEO Costain plc (eng and construction group) 1997–2001; CEO Railtrack PLC 2001–02, Network Rail 2002–07; Chair. UK Eng and Physical Sciences Research Council (EPSRC) 2007–12, Olympic Delivery Authority 2007–; Dir (non-exec.) Berkeley Group 2007–; mem. Advisory Bd Siemens plc 2009–, PWC 2007–; Dr hc (Birmingham), (Portsmouth), (Warwick), (Reading). *Address:* Olympic Delivery Authority, One Churchill Place, Canary Wharf, London, E14 5LN, England (office). *Telephone:* (20) 3023-6768 (office). *E-mail:* john.armitt@london2012.com (office). *Website:* www.london2012.com/about-us/the-people-delivering-the-games/the-olympic-delivery-authority (office).

ARMSTRONG, Billie Joe; American singer and musician (guitar); b. 17 Feb. 1972, San Pablo, Calif.; m. Adrienne Nesser 1994; two s.; Founding mem., Sweet Children, renamed Green Day 1989–; numerous tours and television appearances; side projects include Pinhead Gunpowder, Screeching Weasel, The Network and Foxboro Hot Tubs; Australian MTV Awards for Best Group 2005, for Best Rock Video (for American Idiot) 2005, MTV Award for Best Rock Video, Best Group Video (both for Boulevard of Broken Dreams), Best Group, MTV Viewer's Choice Award 2005, Kerrang! Awards for Best Band on the Planet, Best Live Act 2005, NME Award for Best Video (for American Idiot) 2005, MTV Europe Music Awards for Best Rock Act 2005, 2009, 2013, Billboard 200 Album Group of the Year 2005, Billboard Music Awards for Pop Group of the Year, for Hot 100 Group of the Year, for Rock Artist of the Year, for Rock Song of the Year (for Boulevard of Broken Dreams), for Modern Rock Artist of the Year 2005, Grammy Award for Record of the Year (for Boulevard of Broken Dreams) 2006, BRIT Award for Best Int. Group 2006, ASCAP Awards for Creative Voice, and for Song of the Year (for Boulevard of Broken Dreams) 2006, American Music Award for Favorite Rock Artist 2009. *Recordings include:* albums: with Green Day: 39/Smooth 1990, Kerplunk 1991, Dookie 1994, Insomniac 1994, Nimrod 1997, Warning 2000, International Superhits (compilation) 2001, Shenanigans 2002, American Idiot (Grammy Award for Best Rock Album 2005, MTV Europe Music Award for Best Album 2005, American Music Award for Favorite Pop/Rock Album 2005, BRIT Award for Best Int. Album 2006) 2004, 21st Century Breakdown (Grammy Award for Best Rock Album 2010) 2009, ¡Uno! 2012, ¡Dos! 2012, ¡Tres! 2012; with The Network: Money Money 2020 2003; with Foxboro Hot Tubs: Stop Drop and Roll!!! 2008. *E-mail:* info@greenday.com (office). *Website:* www.greenday.com.

ARMSTRONG, C. Michael, BS; American business executive; b. 18 Oct. 1938, Detroit, Mich.; s. of Charles H. Armstrong and Zora Jean Armstrong (née Brooks); m. Anne Gossett 1961; three d.; ed Miami Univ., Dartmouth Inst.; joined IBM Corpn 1961, Dir Systems Man. Marketing Div. 1975–76, Vice-Pres. Market Operations East 1976–78, Pres. Data Processing Div. 1978–80, Vice-Pres. Plans and Controls, Data Processing Product Group 1980–84, Asst Group Exec. 1980–83, Group Exec. 1983–92, Sr Vice-Pres. 1984–92, fmrly Pres. IBM Corpn Europe, Pres. and Dir Gen. World Trade (Europe, Middle East, Africa) 1987–89; Chair. World Trade Corpn 1989–92; Chair., CEO Hughes Aircraft Co. 1992–93, Hughes Electronics Corpn 1993; Chair., CEO AT&T 1997–2002; Chair. Comcast Corpn 2002–04; Chair. Bd of Trustees, Johns Hopkins Medicine 2005–; Chair. Pres.'s Export Council 1994; Visiting Prof. of Practice of Man., MIT Sloan School of Man.; Chair. FCC Network Reliability and Inter-Operability Council 1999; Dir HCA Inc. 2004–10; mem. Bd of Dirs Citigroup 1989–2010, IHS, Inc. 2003–; mem. Supervisory Bd Thyssen-Bornemisza Group, Council on Foreign Relations, Nat. Security Telecommunications Advisory Cttee, Defence Policy Advisory Cttee on Trade (DPACT); Sr Advisor, SV Investment Partners, Tudor Venture Capital; mem. Bd of Trustees of Carnegie Hall, The Johns Hopkins Univ.; Hon. LLD (Pepperdine Univ.) 1997, (Loyola Marymount Univ.) 1998. *Address:* SV Investment Partners, 1133 Avenue of the Americas, 31st Floor, New York, NY 10036, USA (office). *Website:* www.svip.com (office).

ARMSTRONG, Clay M., BA, MD; American physiologist and academic; *Professor Emeritus of Physiology, School of Medicine, University of Pennsylvania;* ed Rice Univ., Houston, Tex., Washington Univ. School of Medicine, St Louis, Mo.; Intern, Univ. of Chicago Clinics 1960–61; Multiple Sclerosis Soc. Research Fellowship, Neurology Dept, Washington Univ. School of Medicine, St Louis 1961; Research Assoc. NIH 1961–64; Asst Prof. of Physiology, Duke Univ. 1966–69; Assoc. Prof., Univ. of Rochester, NY 1969–75, Prof. of Physiology, Univ. of Rochester School of Medicine 1974–75; Prof. of Physiology, Univ. of Pennsylvania School of Medicine 1976, currently Prof. Emer.; Trustee, Marine Biological Lab., Woods Hole, MA 1980–93; mem. Neurosciences Grad. Group; mem. NAS, Biophysical Soc., Soc. of Gen. Physiologists (Pres. 1985–86), Physiological Study Section, American Physiological Soc. 1975–79 (Chair. 1979), Inst. of Medicine 1996; mem. Editorial

Bd Journal of General Physiology 1976–, Journal of Neurophysiology 1980–84; Hon. Research Assoc., Univ. Coll., London, UK 1964–66; Scholarship, Washington Univ. School of Medicine 1956–60, Teacher of the Year, Freshman Medical Class, Univ. of Rochester 1973, K.S. Cole Award, Biophysical Soc. 1975, Bowditch Lecturer, American Physiological Soc. 1975, Distinguished Lecturer, Soc. of Gen. Physiologists, IUPAB Meeting 1986, Distinguished Alumnus, Rice Univ. 1995, Louisa Gross Horwitz Prize 1996 (co-recipient), Albert Lasker Award for Basic Medical Research 1999, John Scott Award 2000, Gairdner Foundation Int. Award 2001, Jacob Javits Neuroscience Research Award, NIH. *Publications include:* numerous articles in scientific journals. *Address:* University of Pennsylvania, Department of Physiology, B701 Richards Building, 3700 Hamilton Walk, Philadelphia, PA 19104-6085, USA (office). *Telephone:* (215) 898-7816 (office). *Fax:* (215) 573-5851 (office). *E-mail:* carmstro@mail.med.upenn.edu (office). *Website:* www.med.upenn.edu (office).

ARMSTRONG, David John, BA; Australian journalist and media executive; b. 25 Nov. 1947, Sydney; s. of Allan E. Armstrong and Mary P. Armstrong; m. Deborah Bailey 1980 (deceased); two d.; ed Marist Brothers High School, Parramatta, Univ. of NSW; Ed. The Bulletin 1985–86; Deputy Ed. The Daily Telegraph 1988–89; Ed. The Australian 1989–92, Ed.-in-Chief 1996–2002; Ed. The Canberra Times 1992–93; Ed. South China Morning Post, Hong Kong 1993–94, Ed.-in-Chief 1994–96; Ed.-in-Chief, South China Morning Post 2003–05, mem. Bd Dirs Post Publishing 2004–09, Pres. and COO 2005–08, mem. Exec. Cttee 2006–08, currently Adviser to Sr Man.; mem. Bd Dirs HFP-Post 2006–09; mem. Asian Bd Int. News Media Asscn 2006–; Australian Centenary Medal 2003. *Leisure interests:* reading, golf. *Address:* c/o Bangkok Post Building, 136 Na Ranong Road, off Sunthorn Kosa Road, Klong Toey, Bangkok 10110, Thailand.

ARMSTRONG, David Malet, AO, BA, BPhil, PhD, FAHA, FBA; Australian academic and writer; *Professor Emeritus of Philosophy, University of Sydney;* b. 8 July 1926, Melbourne, Vic.; s. of Cdre J. M. Armstrong and Philippa Suzanne Marett; m. Jennifer Mary de Bohun Clark 1982; ed Dragon School, Oxford, UK, Geelong Grammar School, Sydney Univ., Exeter Coll., Oxford, Univ. of Melbourne; Asst Lecturer in Philosophy, Birkbeck Coll., London, UK 1954–55; Lecturer, Sr Lecturer in Philosophy, Univ. of Melbourne 1956–63; Challis Prof. of Philosophy, Univ. of Sydney 1964–91, Prof. Emer. 1992–; mem. Bd Quadrant magazine; mem. US Acad. of Arts and Science; Hon. DLitt (Nottingham). *Publications:* Berkeley's Theory of Vision 1961, Perception and the Physical World 1961, Bodily Sensations 1962, A Materialist Theory of the Mind 1968, Belief, Truth and Knowledge 1973, Universals and Scientific Realism 1978, The Nature of the Mind and Other Essays 1983, What is a Law of Nature? 1983, Consciousness and Causality (with Norman Malcolm) 1984, A Combinatorial Theory of Possibility 1989, Universals: An Opinionated Instruction 1989, Dispositions: A Debate (with C. B. Martin and U. T. Place) 1996, A World of States of Affairs 1997, The Mind-Body Problem: An Opinionated Introduction 1999, Truth and Truthmakers 2004, Sketch for a Systematic Metaphysics 2010; contribs to scholarly books and journals. *Leisure interest:* genealogy. *Address:* 206 Glebe Point Road, Glebe, NSW 2037, Australia (home). *Telephone:* (2) 9660-1435 (home). *Fax:* (2) 9660-8846 (home). *E-mail:* armo.dm@gmail.com (office).

ARMSTRONG, Dido Florian Cloud de Bounevialle (see Dido).

ARMSTRONG, Fraser Andrew, BSc, PhD, FRS; British chemist and academic; *Professor of Chemistry and Fellow of St John's College, University of Oxford;* b. Cambridge; ed Univ. of Leeds; Royal Soc. Univ. Research Fellowship, Univ. of Oxford 1983–89, Prof. of Chem. and Fellow of St John's Coll. 1993–; mem. Chem. Faculty, Univ. of California, Irvine 1989–93; Pres. Soc. of Biological Inorganic Chem. 2004–06; European Medal for Biological Inorganic Chem. 1998, RSC Award for Inorganic Biochemistry 2000, Carbon Trust Academic Innovation Award (co-recipient) 2003, Max-Planck 'Frontiers in Biological Chem.' Award 2004, RSC Medal for Interdisciplinary Chem. 2006, RSC Joseph Chatt Award 2010, Davy Medal, Royal Soc. 2012, RSC Barker Award 2012. *Publications:* numerous papers in professional journals on biological redox chemistry. *Address:* Department of Chemistry, University of Oxford, South Parks Road, Oxford, OX1 3QR, England (office). *Telephone:* (1865) 272647 (office); (1865) 287182 (St John's) (office). *E-mail:* fraser.armstrong@chem.ox.ac.uk (office). *Website:* armstrong.chem.ox.ac.uk (office).

ARMSTRONG, Gillian May, AM; Australian film director; b. 18 Dec. 1950, Melbourne; d. of Raleigh Edward Armstrong and Patricia May Armstrong; m.; two d.; ed Swinburne Art Coll., Nat. Australian Film & TV School, Sydney; mem. Dirs' Guild of America, Acad. of Motion Picture Arts and Sciences; Patron Sydney Film Festival, Flickerfest Short Film Festival, Nat. Gallery of Victoria; Companion of the Australian Rotary Health Research Fund; Hon. Doctorate in Film (Swinburne Univ.) 1998, Hon. DLitt (Univ. of NSW) 2000; numerous awards including Women in Hollywood Icon Award 1988, Dorothy Arzner Directing Award, USA 1993. *Feature films include:* The Singer and The Dancer 1976, My Brilliant Career (Best Film and Best Dir, Australian Film Inst. Awards, Best First Feature British Film Critics Award) 1979, Starstruck 1982, Mrs Soffel 1984, High Tide (Best Film, Houston Film Festival, Grand Prix Festival Int. de Creteil, France) 1987, Fires Within 1990, The Last Days of Chez Nous 1991, Little Women 1995, Oscar and Lucinda 1997, Charlotte Gray 2001, Unfolding Florence 2005, Death Defying Acts 2006, Love Lust and Lies 2010. *Address:* c/o HLA Management, PO Box 1536, Strawberry Hills, NSW 2012, Australia (office). *Telephone:* (2) 9549-3000 (office). *Fax:* (2) 9310-4113 (office). *E-mail:* hla@hlamgt.com.au (office). *Website:* www.hlamgt.com.au (office).

ARMSTRONG, Greg L., BS, CPA; American oil executive; *Chairman and CEO, Plains All American Pipeline LP;* ed Southeastern Oklahoma State Univ.; joined Plains Resources 1981, Corp. Sec. 1981–88, Vice-Pres. and Chief Financial Officer (CFO) 1984–91, Treas. 1984–97, Sr Vice-Pres. and CFO 1991–92, Exec. Vice-Pres. and CFO June–Oct. 1992, Pres. and COO Oct.–Dec. 1992, Pres., CEO and Dir 1992–2001, Chair. and CEO Plains All American Pipeline LP 2001–; mem. Bd Dirs Petroleum Club of Houston, Varco Int. Inc. 2004–; mem. Texas SE Regional Bd Trustees, IPAA. *Address:* Plains All American Pipeline LP, 333 Clay Street, Suite 1600, Houston, TX 77002, USA (office). *Telephone:* (713) 646-4100 (office). *Fax:* (713) 646-4572 (office). *E-mail:* info@paalp.com (office). *Website:* www.paalp.com (office).

ARMSTRONG, Lance Edward; American fmr professional cyclist; b. (Lance Edward Gunderson), 18 Sept. 1971, Plano, Tex.; s. of Eddie Charles Gunderson and Linda Gayle (née Mooneyham); adopted s. of Terry Keith Armstrong; m. Kristin Richard 1998 (divorced 2003); one s. twin d.; US Nat. Amateur Champion 1991; mem. US Olympic team 1992, 1996, 2000 (bronze medal); mem. Motorol team 1992–96, Cofidis team 1999, US Postal Service Pro Cycling Team 1998–2004, Discovery Channel 2005, Astana 2009, Team RadioShack 2010–11; winner of numerous races, including US Pro Championship, World Championships 1993, Clasica San Sebastian, Tour Du Pont 1995, Tour Du Pont 1996, Tour de Luxembourg 1998, Tour de Suisse 2001, Criterium du Dauphine Libere 2002, Criterium du Dauphine Libere 2003, Tour de France 1999–2005 (first to win seven Tours); survived testicular cancer 1996; Founder and Chair. Lance Armstrong Foundation (Livestrong) 1996–2012; retd from competitive racing after completion of 2005 Tour de France; came out of retirement and joined Astana team 2008; charged by US Anti-Doping Agency (USADA) with having used illicit performance-enhancing drugs June 2012, announced lifetime ban from competition as well as the stripping of all his titles since 1 Aug. 1998 Aug. 2012, USADA findings accepted by Int. Cycling Union and confirmed the lifetime ban and the stripping of all titles Oct. 2012; Hon. DHumLitt (Tufts Univ.) 2006; Triathlon magazine's Rookie of the Year 1988, VeloNews magazine's North American Male Cyclist of the Year 1993, 1995, 1996, 1998, 1999, 2002, 2005, Union Cycliste Internationale: World Number 1 Ranked Elite Men's Cyclist 1996, US Olympic Cttee SportsMan of the Year 1999, 2001, 2002, 2003, Vélo d'Or Award, Velo magazine in France 1999, 2000, 2001, 2003, 2004, Mendrisio d'Or Award in Switzerland 1999, Premio Coppi-Bici d'Oro Trophy, Fausto Coppi Foundation in conjunction with La Gazzetta dello Sport 1999, 2000, ESPN/Intersport's ARETE Award for Courage in Sport (Professional Div.) 1999, ABC's Wide World of Sports Athlete of the Year 1999, World's Most Outstanding Athlete Award, Mildred 'Babe' Didrikson Zaharias Courage Award, US Sports Acad. 1999, Jesse Owens International Trophy 2000, Prince of Asturias Award in Sports 2000, Laureus World Sports Award for Comeback of the Year 2000, ESPY Award for Best Comeback Athlete 2000, VeloNews magazine's International Cyclist of the Year 2000, 2001, 2003, 2004, William Hill Sports Book of the Year: It's Not About the Bike: My Journey Back to Life 2000, Associated Press Male Athlete of the Year 2002, 2003, 2004, 2005, Presidential Delegation to XIX Olympic Winter Games 2002, Sports Illustrated magazine's Sportsman of the Year 2002, Reuters Sportsman of the Year 2003, Sports Ethics Fellows, Inst. for Int. Sport 2003, Laureus World Sports Award for Sportsman of the Year 2003, BBC Sports Personality of the Year Overseas Personality Award 2003, ESPY Award for Best Male Athlete 2003, 2004, 2005, 2006, Trophee de L'Acad. des Sport (France) 2004, Marca Legend Award, Marca (Spanish sports daily in Madrid) 2004, ESPY Award for GMC Professional Grade Play Award 2005, Favorite Athlete Award, Nickelodeon Kids' Choice Awards 2006, Pace car driver for the Indianapolis 500 2006, asteroid 1994 JE9 named 12373 Lancearmstrong in his honour. *Publications:* It's Not About the Bike, The Lance Armstrong Performance Programme, Every Second Counts (with Sally Jenkins) 2003. *Address:* c/o Capital Sports & Entertainment, 300 West 6th Street, Suite 2150, Austin, TX 78701 (office); c/o Livestrong, 2201 East Sixth Street, Austin, TX 78702, USA. *Telephone:* (855) 220-7777. *E-mail:* livestrong@livestrong.org. *Website:* www.livestrong.org; www.lancearmstrong.com.

ARMSTRONG, Robin Louis, BA, PhD, FRSC; Canadian physicist and academic; *Professor Emeritus of Physics, University of Toronto;* b. 14 May 1935, Galt, Ont.; s. of Robert Dockstader Armstrong and Beatrice Jenny Armstrong (née Grill); m. Karen Elisabeth Hansen 1960; two s.; ed Univ. of Toronto and Univ. of Oxford, UK; RSC Rutherford Memorial Fellowship 1961; Asst Prof. of Physics, Univ. of Toronto 1962–68, Assoc. Prof. 1968–71, Prof. 1971–90, Adjunct Prof. 1990–99, Prof. Emer. 1999–; Assoc. Chair. Physics, Univ. of Toronto 1969–74, Chair. 1974–82, Dean Faculty of Arts and Science 1982–90, Adjunct Prof. 1990–99; Visitante Distinguido, Univ. of Córdoba, Argentina 1989; Pres. and Prof. of Physics, Univ. of New Brunswick 1990–96; Adviser to Pres., Wilfrid Laurier Univ. 1997–2000; Pres. Canadian Inst. for Neutron Scattering 1986–89, Canadian Asscn of Physicists 1990–91; Dir Canadian Inst. for Advanced Research 1981–82, Huntsman Marine Lab. 1983–87; mem. Research Council of Canadian Inst. for Advanced Research 1982–2000, Natural Science and Eng Research Council of Canada (NSERC) 1991–97 (mem. Exec. 1992–97, Vice-Pres. 1994–97), Bd of Dirs Canadian Arthritis Network (Chair. 2004–), Research and Devt Advisory Panel, Atomic Energy of Canada Ltd 1999–2012 (Vice-Chair. 2004–05, Chair. 2006–07); Exec. Dir College Univ. Consortium Council 2006–08; Hon. DSc (Univ. of New Brunswick) 2001; Herzberg Medal 1973, Medal of Achievement (Canadian Asscn of Physicists) 1990, Commemorative Medal for 125th Anniversary of Canadian Confed. 1992, Preston High School Hall of Fame 2007. *Publications include:* over 180 research articles on condensed matter physics in numerous journals. *Leisure interests:* golf, gardening. *Address:* Room MP311, University of Toronto, Department of Physics, 60 St George Street, Toronto, ON M5S 1A7, Canada (home). *Telephone:* (416) 978-2940 (office). *E-mail:* r.armstrong35@gmail.com (office); robinl.armstrong@sympatico.ca. *Website:* www.physics.utoronto.ca (office).

ARMSTRONG, Sheila Ann, FRAM; British singer (soprano); b. 13 Aug. 1942, Ashington, Northumberland; d. of William R. Armstrong and Janet Armstrong; m. David E. Cooper 1980 (divorced 1999); ed Hirst Park Girls' School, Ashington and Royal Acad. of Music, London; sang Despina in Cosi fan tutte at Sadler's Wells 1965, Belinda in Dido and Aeneas, Glyndebourne 1966, Mozart's Pamina and Zerlina and Fiorella in Rossini's Il Turco in Italia, Glyndebourne; sang in the premiere of John McCabe's Notturni ed Alba at Three Choirs Festival 1970; New York debut with New York Philharmonic 1971; sang with Los Angeles Philharmonic under Mehta; Covent Garden debut as Marzelline in Fidelio 1973; sang Donizetti's Norina and Mozart's Donna Elvira for Scottish Nat. Opera; concert engagements included Messiah at the Concertgebouw, tour of the Far East with the Bach Choir; numerous recordings; fmr Pres. Kathleen Ferrier Soc.; fmr Trustee, Kathleen Ferrier Award; Fellow, Hatfield Coll., Durham Univ. 1992; mem. Royal Philharmonic Soc.; Hon. MA (Newcastle); Hon. DMus (Durham) 1991; Mozart Prize 1965, Kathleen Ferrier Memorial Award 1965. *Recordings include:* Samson, Dido and Aeneas, Mozart's Requiem, Carmina Burana, Elgar's Apostles, The Pilgrim's Progress, Cantatas by Bach, Haydn's Stabat Mater, Beethoven's Ninth Symphony, Mahler's 2nd and 4th, Spring Symphony, Child of Our Time, Semele, Fauré Requiem, Rachmaninov's The Bells, Grieg's Peer Gynt Suite,

Schubert's Lazarus, Holst's The Mystic Trumpeter, Messiah Highlights, Don Giovanni Highlights, Britten's Spring Symphony, Strauss' Four Last Songs with Royal Philharmonic, Elgar's Oratorios, Vaughan Williams' Sea Symphony and Hugh the Drover, Mozart Arias (with Barry Tuckwell). *Leisure interests:* collecting keys, interior decoration and design, flower-arranging, sewing, gardening and garden design, travel.

ARMSTRONG, Tim, BS; American business executive; *Chairman and CEO, AOL Inc.;* ed Lawrence Acad., Connecticut Coll.; started career by co-founding and running newspaper in Boston; joined International Data Group (IDG) Inc. to launch I-Way (consumer internet magazine); fmr Dir of Integrated Sales and Marketing, Starwave/Disney ABC/ESPN Internet Ventures; fmr Vice-Pres. of Sales and Strategic Partnerships, Snowball.com; Vice-Pres. for Advertising and Sales, Google Inc. 2000, Pres. North America 2007–08, Pres. Americas Operation and Sr Vice-Pres. Advertising Sales and Operations, Google Inc.–09; Chair. and CEO AOL LLC (div. of Time Warner Inc.), Dulles, Va 2009, Chair. and CEO AOL Inc., New York 2009–; Dir Interactive Advertising Bureau, Advertising Council, Advertising Research Foundation. *Address:* Office of the Chairman, AOL LLC, 22000 AOL Way, Dulles, VA 20166, USA (office). *Telephone:* (703) 265-1000 (office). *Website:* corp.aol.com (office).

ARMSTRONG-JONES, Baron (see Snowdon, Earl of).

ARMSTRONG OF HILL TOP, Baroness (Life Peer), cr. 2010, of Crook in the County of Durham; **Hilary Jane Armstrong,** PC, BSc; British politician; b. 30 Nov. 1945, Sunderland; d. of the late Rt Hon Ernest Armstrong and Hannah P. Armstrong (née Lamb); m. Paul D. Corrigan 1992; ed Monkwearmouth Comprehensive School, Sunderland, West Ham Coll. of Tech., Univ. of Birmingham; mem. Labour Party 1960–; teacher with VSO, Murray Girls' High School, PO Mwatate, Kenya 1967–69; social worker, Newcastle City Social Services Dept 1970–73; community worker, Southwick Neighbourhood Action Project, Sunderland 1973–75; Lecturer in Community and Youth Work, Sunderland Polytechnic (now Univ. of Sunderland) 1975–86; Councillor, Durham City Council 1985–87; MP (Labour) for Durham NW 1987–2010; Frontbench Spokesperson on Educ. (under-fives, primary and special educ.) 1988–92, on Treasury Affairs 1994–95; Parl. Pvt. Sec. to Leader of the Opposition 1992–94; mem. Nat. Exec. Labour Party 1992–97; Minister of State Dept of Environment, Transport and the Regions 1997–2001; Parl. Sec. to HM Treasury and Govt Chief Whip 2001–06; Cabinet Office Minister, Minister for Social Exclusion and Chancellor of the Duchy of Lancaster 2006–07; fmr Vice-Pres. Nat. Children's Homes; fmr mem. British Council; fmr mem. Bd VSO; fmr mem. Manufacturing Science Finance (MSF) Union. *Leisure interests:* reading, theatre, watching football. *Address:* North House, 17 North Terrace, Crook, Co. Durham, DL15 9AZ, England (home). *Telephone:* (1388) 767065 (home). *Fax:* (1388) 767923 (home).

ARMSTRONG OF ILMINSTER, Baron (Life Peer), cr. 1988, of Ashill in the County of Somerset; **Robert Temple Armstrong,** GCB, CVO, MA; British fmr civil servant; b. 30 March 1927, Oxford; s. of Sir Thomas Armstrong and of Lady Armstrong (née Draper); m. 1st Serena Mary Benedicta Chance 1953 (divorced 1985); two d.; m. 2nd (Mary) Patricia Carlow 1985; ed Eton Coll. and Christ Church, Oxford; Asst Prin. Treasury 1950–55, Pvt. Sec. to Econ. Sec. 1953–54; Pvt. Sec. to Chancellor of the Exchequer (Rt Hon. R. A. Butler) 1954–55; Prin. Treasury 1955–64; Asst Sec. Cabinet Office 1964–66; Asst Sec. Treasury 1966–68; Prin. Pvt. Sec. to Chancellor of the Exchequer (Rt Hon. Roy Jenkins) 1968; Under-Sec. Treasury 1968–70; Prin. Pvt. Sec. to the Prime Minister 1970–75; Deputy Under-Sec. of State, Home Office 1975–77, Perm. Under-Sec. of State 1977–79; Sec. of the Cabinet 1979–87; Perm. Sec. Man. and Personnel Office 1981–87; Head, Home Civil Service 1981–87; Chair. Biotechnology Investments Ltd 1989–2000; Chair. Forensic Investigative Assocs PLC 1997–2003; Chair. Hestercombe Gardens Trust 1995–2005, Bd of Govs Royal Northern Coll. of Music 2000–05; Sec. Radcliffe Cttee on Monetary System 1957–59; Sec. to the Dirs, Royal Opera House, Covent Garden 1968–87, Dir 1988–93; Dir Bristol and West Bldg Soc. 1988–97 (Chair. 1993–97), Bank of Ireland and other cos; Chair. Bd of Trustees, Victoria and Albert Museum 1988–98; mem. Rhodes Trust 1975–97; Fellow, Eton Coll. 1979–94; Chancellor, Univ. of Hull 1994–2006; Pres. The Literary Soc. 2004–; Trustee, Leeds Castle Foundation 1987– (Chair. 2001–); Hon. Student, Christ Church 1985; Hon. Bencher, Inner Temple 1986; Hon. LLD. *Leisure interest:* music. *Address:* House of Lords, Westminster, London, SW1A 0PW, England (office). *Telephone:* (20) 7219-4983 (office). *Fax:* (20) 7219-1259 (office).

ARNAOUD ALI, Idriss; Djibouti politician; *President, National Assembly;* b. 25 Dec. 1945, Ali-Sabieh; m.; four c.; Chief Admin. and Labour Relations, Head of External Relations, Dept, Head Admin. and Financial Service 1982–85; Deputy Dir Gen., Chief of Admin. and Financial Dir, Air Djibouti 1985, Acting Exec. 1986–90, Man. Dir 1990–91; Tech. Advisor to Minister of Nat. Educ. 1992–97; elected to Nat. Ass. 1997, Pres. (Speaker) 2003–; Sec.-Gen. Rassemblement pour le Progrès 1997–; fmr Pres. Perm. Comm., Nat. Ass.; fmr mem. Defense Comm. *Address:* National Assembly, BP 138, pl. Lagarde, Djibouti, Djibouti (office). *Telephone:* 350172 (office). *Website:* www.assemblee-nationale.dj (office).

ÁRNASON, Kristinn F., LLM; Icelandic diplomatist and international organization official; *Secretary–General, EFTA;* b. 5 Jan. 1954, Reykjavík; m.; three c.; ed Univ. of Iceland, Univ. of Exeter, UK, Univ. of Oslo, Norway; solicitor in pvt. attorney's office 1979–80, 1982, for Fed. of Employees 1983–85; First Sec. Ministry of Foreign Affairs (MFA) 1985–87; Deputy Perm. Rep. to Int. Orgs, Geneva 1987–92; Chief Negotiator and Spokesman on Fisheries, MFA 1992–94, Dir for External Trade 1994–98; apptd Amb. 1997; Amb. to Slovakia and Poland 1999–2002, to Norway and Czech Repub. 1999–2003, to Egypt 2000–03; Dir Defence Dept, MFA 2003–05; Amb. and Perm. Rep. to Int. Orgs, Geneva 2006–12; Sec.-Gen. European Free Trade Asscn (EFTA) 2012–; *Address:* European Free Trade Asscn, 9-11, rue de Varembé, 1211 Geneva 20, Switzerland (office). *Telephone:* 22-332-26-00 (home). *Fax:* 22-332-26-77 (office). *E-mail:* mail.gva@efta.int (office). *Website:* www.efta.int (office).

ARNAULT, Bernard; French business executive and art collector; *Chairman and CEO, LVMH;* b. 5 March 1949, Roubaix (Nord); s. of Jean Arnault and Marie-Jo Arnault (née Savinel); m. 1st Anne Dewavrin 1973 (divorced 1990); two c.; m. 2nd Hélène Mercier 1991; three s.; ed Ecole Polytechnique; joined Ferret-Savinel (family construction co.) 1971, Pres. 1978–84; lived in USA 1981–84; took over

Boussac Saint-Frères (parent co. of Dior) 1985; CEO LVMH (luxury goods group which includes Louis Vuitton bags, Moët et Chandon champagne, Parfums Christian Dior, Hennessy and Hine cognac) 1989–, Chair. 1992–, Chair. Christian Dior SA; Pres. Bd of Dirs Montaigne 1997–; Owner Phillips auction house 1999– (merged with Bonhams & Brooks 2001); fmr Dir Diageo; through holding co. Financière Agache owns fashion houses Dior, Lacroix and Céline and dept store Bon Marché; Commdr, Légion d'honneur 2007, Officier, Ordre nat. du Mérite; ranked by Forbes magazine amongst The World's Most Powerful People (52nd) 2009, (43rd) 2010, (55th) 2011, (56th) 2012, (54th) 2013. *Publication:* La Passion créative 2000. *Leisure interests:* music, tennis. *Address:* 11 rue François 1er, 75008 Paris; LVMH, 22 avenue Montaigne, 75008 Paris, France (office). *Telephone:* 1-44-13-22-22 (office). *Fax:* 1-44-13-22-23 (office). *E-mail:* info@lvmh.com (office). *Website:* www.lvmh.com (office).

ARNETT, Emerson James, QC, BA, LLM; Canadian lawyer and business executive; b. 29 Sept. 1938, Winnipeg, Man.; s. of Emerson Lloyd Arnett and Elsie Audrey Rhind; m. Edith Alexandra Palk 1964; four c.; ed Univ. of Man., Harvard Univ.; worked in civil litigation section, Dept of Justice, Ottawa 1964–65; Assoc. Pitblado and Hoskin (law firm), Winnipeg 1965–66; Asst to Exec. Vice-Pres. Vickers and Benson Advertising, Toronto 1966–67; Assoc./Pnr, Davies, Ward and Beck (law firm), Toronto 1968–73; Pnr, Stikeman, Elliott (law firm), Toronto 1973–97, Resident Pnr, Washington, DC 1993–96; Pres. and CEO Molson Inc. 1997–2000; mem. Bd of Dirs Mirabaud Asset Man. (Canada) Inc. 2002–. *Publications include:* Doing Business (co-ed.); numerous law review and newspaper articles and conf. papers. *Leisure interests:* shooting, skiing, hiking, reading. *Address:* c/o Board of Directors, Mirabaud Asset Management (Canada) Inc., 161 Bay Street, Suite 2706, Toronto, ON M5J 2S1, Canada.

ARNETT, Peter; New Zealand/American journalist and television reporter; b. 13 Nov. 1934, Riverton, New Zealand; m. Nina Nguyen 1964 (divorced 1983); two c.; ed Waitaki Coll., Oamaru, New Zealand; with Associated Press (AP) 1960–; war corresp. in Viet Nam, Middle East, Nicaragua, El Salvador and Afghanistan; special writer for AP, New York; worked with Cable News Network (CNN) 1981–99; served as corresp. in Moscow for two years; later nat. security reporter, Washington, DC; CNN corresp. Baghdad 1991; Chief Foreign Corresp. Foreign-TV.com, New York 1998, then reporter MSNBC, fired for making unauthorized remarks to state-run Iraqi TV 2003, then reporter in Iraq for Daily Mirror (UK newspaper); also worked for Nat. Geographic, Global Vision magazines; Visiting Prof., Cheung Kong School of Journalism and Communication, Shantou Univ., China 2007, currently Prof.; Officer of the Order of Merit (New Zealand) 2006; Pulitzer Prize 1966, George Foster Peabody Award, Golden Cable ACE Award. *Publication:* Live from the Battlefield 1994. *Leisure interests:* collector of books and oriental statuary. *Address:* Cheung Kong School of Journalism and Communication, Shantou University, 243 Daxue Road, Shantou 515063, People's Republic of China (office). *Telephone:* (54) 82902305 (office). *Fax:* (54) 82510505 (office). *Website:* www.stu.edu.cn (office).

ARNOLD, Frances Hamilton, BS, PhD; American chemical engineer and academic; *Dick and Barbara Dickinson Professor of Chemical Engineering, Bioengineering and Biochemistry and Director, Donna and Benjamin M. Rosen Bioengineering Center, California Institute of Technology;* b. 25 July 1956, Edgewood, Pa; d. of William Howard Arnold; m.; three s.; ed Princeton Univ., Univ. of California, Berkeley; Postdoctoral Researcher in Chem., Univ. of California, Berkeley 1985–86; Postdoctoral Researcher in Chem., California Inst. of Tech. 1986, now Dick and Barbara Dickinson Prof. of Chemical Eng, Bioengineering and Biochemistry and Dir Donna and Benjamin M. Rosen Bioengineering Center; mem. Advisory Bd, Joint BioEnergy Inst., Packard Fellowships in Science and Eng; mem. Pres.'s Advisory Council, King Abdullah Univ. of Science and Tech.; mem. judging panel, Queen Elizabeth Prize for Eng 2013; mem. Nat. Acad. of Eng 2000, Inst. of Medicine of Nat. Acads 2004, NAS 2008, American Acad. of Arts and Sciences 2011; Fellow, American Inst. for Medical and Biological Eng 2001, American Acad. of Microbiology 2009, AAAS 2010; Dr hc (Stockholm) 2013; AIChE Professional Progress Award 2000, Sir Robert Price Lecturer, CSIRO, Melbourne 2003, ACS David Perlman Lecture Award in Biochemical Tech. 2003, Carothers Award, ACS Delaware Div. 2003, ACS Francis P. Garvan-John M. Olin Medal 2005, AIChE Food, Pharmaceuticals and Bioengineering Div. Award 2005, Excellence in Science Award, Fed. of American Socs for Experimental Biology 2007, Enzyme Eng Award 2007, Cruickshank Lecturer, Gordon Research Confs 2008, Linnaeus Lecturer, Uppsala Univ. 2008, Charles Stark Draper Prize 2011, Nat. Medal of Tech. and Innovation 2011, Emanuel Merck Lecturer in Chem. 2013, ENI Prize in Renewable and Nonconventional Energy 2013. *Publications:* numerous papers in professional journals. *Address:* 228B Spalding, Chemical Engineering, California Institute of Technology, MC 210-41, Pasadena, CA 91125, USA (office). *Telephone:* (626) 395-4162 (office). *Fax:* (626) 568-8743 (office). *E-mail:* frances@cheme.caltech.edu (office). *Website:* www.che.caltech.edu (office).

ARNOLD, Hans Redlef, PhD; German fmr diplomatist, writer and academic; *Lecturer, Academy of Political Science, Munich;* b. 14 Aug. 1923, Munich; s. of Karl Arnold and Anne-Dora Volquardsen; m. Karin Baroness von Egloffstein 1954; three c.; ed Univ. of Munich; joined Foreign Service, FRG; served Embassy in Paris 1952–55, Foreign Office, Bonn 1955–57, Embassy in Washington, DC 1957–61, Foreign Office 1961–68, sometime head of Foreign Minister Willy Brandt's office; Amb. to the Netherlands 1968–72; Head, Cultural Dept, Foreign Office 1972–77; Amb. to Italy 1977–81; Insp.-Gen. German Foreign Service 1981–82; Amb. and Perm. Rep. to UN and Int. Orgs, Geneva 1982–86; Lecturer, Acad. of Political Science, Munich; several nat. and foreign decorations. *Publications include:* Cultural Export as Policy? 1976, Foreign Cultural Policy 1980, The March (co-author) 1990, Europe on the Decline? 1993, Germany's Power 1995, Europe To Be Thought Anew: Why and How Further Unification? 1999, Security for Europe (co-ed.) 2002, How Much Unification Does Europe Need? 2004; regular contribs to periodicals and newspapers. *Address:* 83083 Riedering-Heft, Germany (home). *Telephone:* (8032) 5255 (home). *E-mail:* hans.arnold@gmx.net.

ARNOLD, Luqman, BSc; British business executive and banker; b. April 1950, Calcutta, India; m.; one s.; ed Oundle School, Univ. of London; with Mfrs Hanover Corpn, London, Hong Kong and Singapore 1976–82; with First Nat. Bank (Dallas), Singapore and London 1972–76; with Credit Suisse First Boston, London and

Tokyo 1982–92, responsible for Asia Pacific origination, Private Placements, Cen. and Eastern Europe, later Head of Investment Banking, New Business, mem. Operating Cttee; sabbatical year (research into drivers and outlook for cross-border institutional investment flows) 1992–93; Global Head of Investment Banking, Paribas Capital Markets, Banque Paribas, London 1993–95, Group Head of Business Devt, Paris 1995–96; CEO Asia Pacific UBS AG, Singapore and Tokyo 1996–98, COO, London 1998–99, Chief Financial Officer and Head of Corp. Centre, Zurich 1999–2001, Pres. and Chair., Exec. Bd, Zurich 2001; CEO Abbey National 2002–04; Chair. (also co-founder) Olivant Advisers Ltd 2006–20; Dir and Co-founder Cartesius SA 2010–; Chair. Bd of Trustees Design Museum; Trustee, Architecture Foundation; Sr Advisor to Chair. of Grupo Santander; fmr Pnr Corsair Capital LLC; mem. Devt Council, Univ. of the Arts London; fmr mem. FSA Practitioner Panel, FSA Financial Capability Steering Group, British Bankers' Asscn Council, Asscn of British Insurers' Bd, European Securities Forum. *Leisure interest:* opera.

ARNOLD, Roseanne (see Roseanne).

ARNON, Ruth, PhD; Israeli immunologist and academic; *Paul Ehrlich Professor of Immunology, Weizmann Institute of Science;* b. 1 June 1933, Tel-Aviv; m. Uriel Arnon; one s. one d.; ed Hebrew Univ., Jerusalem, Weizmann Inst. of Science, Rehovot; Visiting Scientist, Rockefeller Inst., New York, USA 1960–62, Univ. of Washington, Seattle, USA 1968–69; Assoc. Prof., Weizmann Inst. of Science 1971, Head, Dept of Chemical Immunology 1973–74, 1975–78, Prof. 1975, now Paul Ehrlich Prof. of Immunology, Dir MacArthur Center for Parasitology 1984–89, Dean, Faculty of Biology 1985–93, Vice-Pres. 1988–93, Vice-Pres. for Int. Scientific Relations 1995–97; Visiting Scientist, UCLA 1977–78, Institut Pasteur, Paris, France 1983, 1998, Walter and Eliza Hall Inst., Melbourne, Australia 1994, Imperial Cancer Research Fund, London, UK 1995, Rockefeller Foundation's Bellagio Conf. and Study Center, Lake Como, Italy 1995; Sec.-Gen. Int. Union of Immunological Socs 1989–93; Pres. European Fed. of Immunological Socs 1983–86; mem. Steering Cttee WHO Task Force on Immunological Methods for Fertility Control 1972–77, European Molecular Biology Orgs (EMBO); mem. Israel Acad. of Sciences and Humanities 1990– (Chair. Science Div. 1995–2001), Vice-Pres. 2004–; Adviser for Science to Pres. of Israel 2001–06; Foreign mem. American Philosophical Soc. 2009–; Pres. Israel Acad. of Sciences and Humanities 2010–; Chevalier de la Légion d'honneur 1994; Dr hc (Beer Sheba Univ.) 2001, (Tel-Hai Univ.) 2008; Robert Koch Prize in Medical Sciences (Germany) 1979, Jimenez Diaz Award (Spain) 1986, Fogarty Scholarship, NIH, USA 1996, 1997–98, Wolf Prize 1998, Rothschild Prize 1998, Israel Prize in Medical Research 2001. *Publications include:* more than 400 articles, chapters and books on immunology and biochemistry. *Address:* Department of Immunology, Wolfson Building, 431A, Weizmann Institute of Science, 76100 Rehovot, Israel (office). *Telephone:* (8) 934-4017 (office). *Fax:* (8) 946-9712 (office). *E-mail:* ruth.arnon@weizmann.ac.il (office). *Website:* www.weizmann.ac.il (office).

ARNOUL, Françoise; French actress; b. (Françoise Gautsch), 9 June 1931, Constantine, Algeria; d. of Gen. Arnoul Gautsch and Jeanne Gradwohl; m. Georges Cravenne (divorced); ed Lycée de Rabat, Lycée Molière, Paris and Paris Conservatoire; Chevalier de la Légion d'honneur; Officier des Arts et Lettres. *Films include:* L'Épave 1949, Nous irons à Paris 1950, La maison Bonnadieu 1951, La plus belle fille du monde 1951, Le désir et l'amour 1952, Les compagnons de la nuit 1953, Les amants du Tage 1955, French-Cancan 1955, Des gens sans importance 1955, Thérèse Etienne 1958, La chatte 1958, Asphalte 1958, La bête à l'affût 1959, Le bal des espions 1960, La chatte sort ses griffes 1960, La morte-saison des amours 1960, Les Parisiennes 1962, Le Congrès s'amuse 1966, Le Dimanche de la vie 1967, spáñolas en Paris 1970, Van der Valk 1972, Dialogue d'exiles 1975, Dernière sortie avant Roissy 1977, Ronde de Nuit 1984, Nuit Docile 1987, Voir L'Éléphant 1989, Années campagne, Les 1992, Les Cent et une nuits de Simon Cinéma 1995, Temps de chien 1996, Post coïtum animal triste 1997, Photo de famille 2000, Merci pour le geste 2000; theatre debut in Les Justes (Camus), Versailles 1966. *Television includes:* La Guêpe 1965, Le Petit théâtre de Jean Renoir 1970, Van der Valk und das Mädchen 1972, La Mort d'un enfant 1974, Lockruf des Goldes (mini-series) 1975, L'Automate 1981, Les Brus 1981, Mon enfant, ma mère 1981, Vivre ma vie 1982, L' Amour s'invente 1982, Un garçon de France 1985, L'Herbe rouge 1985, La Garçonne 1988, L'Étrange histoire d'Émilie Albert 1989, Héloïse 1991, Billard à l'étage 1996, Une pension de charme 1997, L'Alambic 1998, Duval: Un mort de trop 2001, Le voyageur de la Toussaint 2007. *Leisure interest:* dancing. *Address:* 53 rue Censier, 75005 Paris, France (home).

ARNOULT, Érik, (Érik Orsenna), DèsScEcon, PhD; French civil servant and writer; b. 22 March 1947, Paris; s. of Claude Arnoult and Janine Arnoult (née Bodé); m. 2nd Catherine Clavier; one s. one d.; m. 3rd Isabelle de Saint Aubin; ed École Saint-Jean de Béthune, Versailles, Institut d'Études Politiques, Paris, Univ. of Paris I, London School of Econs; Lecturer, Inst. d'Études Politiques, Paris 1975–80, École Normale Supérieure 1977–81; Literary Ed., Editions Ramsay 1977–81; Sr Lecturer, Université de Paris I 1978–81; Tech. Adviser to Ministry of Co-operation and Devt 1981–83, to Minister of Foreign Affairs 1990–92; Cultural Adviser to Pres. of Repub. 1983–90; Maître des Requêtes, Conseil d'État 1985–, Sr mem. 2000–; Pres. Centre Int. de la Mer 1991–, École Nat. Supérieure du Paysage 1995–; Vice-Pres. Cytale Soc. 2000–03; mem. Foundation for World Agric. and Rural Life 2006–, Acad. française 1998. *Film screenplay:* Indochine (co-writer) (Acad. Award for Best Foreign Film). *Publications include:* Loyola's blues 1974, Espace national et déséquilibre monétaire 1977, La vie comme à Lausanne 1977 (Prix Roger Nimier) 1988, Grand amour 1993, Histoire du monde en neuf guitares 1996, Deux étés (novel) 1996, Longtemps (novel) 1998, Portrait d'un homme heureux, André Le Nôtre 1613–1700 2000, La grammaire est une chanson douce 2001, Madame Bâ 2003, Les chevaliers du Subjonctif 2004, Portrait du Gulf Stream 2005, Voyage aux pays du coton (Prix du livre d'économie, Second Prize, Lettre Ulysses Award) 2006, La révolte des accents 2007, L'avenir de l'eau 2009, Et si on dansait? 2009, L'Entreprise des Indes (The Indies Enterprise) 2010, Princesse Histamine 2010. *Leisure interest:* yachting. *Address:* Conseil d'État, 1 place du Palais Royal, 75001 Paris (office); 8 passage Sigaud, 75013 Paris, France (home). *Website:* www.erik-orsenna.com.

ARONOFSKY, Darren; American film director and producer; b. 12 Feb. 1969, Brooklyn, New York; s. of Abraham Aronofsky and Charlotte Aronofsky; one s.

with Rachel Weisz; ed Harvard Univ.; f. Protozoa Pictures (production co.). *Films directed:* Pi (also writer and producer) (Sundance Film Festival Best Dir 1999) 1998, Requiem for a Dream (also writer) 2000, Below (producer and writer) 2002, The Fountain (also writer) 2006, The Wrestler (also producer) (Venice Film Festival Golden Lion 2007) 2008, Black Swan (San Francisco Film Critics Circle Awards Best Dir 2010) 2010. *Address:* c/o Protozoa Pictures, 104 North 7th St, Brooklyn, NY 11211-3020, USA. *Telephone:* (718) 388-5280. *Fax:* (718) 388-5425. *Website:* www.protozoa.com; www.darrenaronofsky.com (office).

ARORA, Sunil, MA; Indian government official and airline industry executive; *Principal Secretary to Government, Industries, State Enterprises and NRI;* b. 13 April 1956; Sec. to Chief Minister, Rajasthan; Sec. (Policy and Planning) 1993–98; Dir Dept of Econ. Affairs (Banking Div.), Govt of India 1999; Jt Sec., Ministry of Civil Aviation 1999–2002; Chair. and Man. Dir Indian Airlines 2002–05; Man. Dir Air India 1 Aug.–21 Dec. 2003; Prin. Sec. to Chief Minister, Govt, Information and Public Relations Dept, Rajasthan 2005–08; Prin. Sec. to Govt, Industries, State Enterprises and NRI 2009–; Chair. Rajasthan State Industrial Devt and Investment Corpn Ltd 2008–09; Chair. RIICO Jaipur 2009–. *Address:* Rajasthan State Industrial Development & Investment Corporation Ltd, Udyog Bhawan, Tilak Marg, Jaipur 302 005, India (office). *Telephone:* (141) 5113200 (office). *E-mail:* chairman@riico.co.in (office). *Website:* www.riico.com (office).

ARP, Fredrik, BS; Swedish business executive; *Chairman, Qioptiq;* b. 1953, Köping; m. Suzanne Arp; four c.; ed Univ. of Lund; salesman Tarkett France, Swedish Match Group, later Div. Man. for Flooring; with Tyre Div., Trelleborg Group 1985, Vice-Pres. 1996; Pres. and CEO PLM (now Rexam) 1996–99; Pres. and CEO Trelleborg AB 1999–2005; Pres. and CEO Volvo Car Corpn 2005–08; Chair. Qioptiq 2010–; Sr Adviser for Nordic region, Candover 2009–; mem. Bd of Dirs Hilding Anders SACC–NY; fmr Chair. Thule AB, Hilding Anders; Hon. DEcon (Univ. of Lund, Sweden). *Leisure interests:* golf, skiing. *Address:* Qioptiq, 25 avenue, Pierre de Coubertin, 75647 Paris Cedex 13, France (office). *Telephone:* 1-44-16-01-10 (office). *Fax:* 1-44-16-01-11 (office). *Website:* www.qioptiq.com (office).

ARPEY, Gerard J., BBA, MBA; American airline industry executive; *Partner, Emerald Creek Group, LLC;* b. 26 July 1958; m. Lisa Walsh 1980s; two s. one d.; ed Univ. of Texas, Austin; joined American Airlines 1982, Financial Analyst 1982–83, Sr Financial Analyst 1983–85, Man. Financial Analysis 1985–87, Dir Airline Profitability Analysis 1987–88, Man. Dir Financial Analysis 1988, Man. Dir Financial Planning 1988–89, Vice-Pres. Financial Planning and Analysis 1989–92, Sr Vice-Pres. Planning 1992–95, Sr Vice-Pres. Finance and Planning and Chief Financial Officer 1995–99, Exec. Vice-Pres., Operations 2000–02, Pres. and COO 2002–03, mem. Bd of Dirs and Pres. AMR Corpn and American Airlines Inc. 2003–10, CEO 2003–11, Chair. 2004–11; Partner, Emerald Creek Group, LLC 2011–; mem. Bd of Dirs S. C. Johnson & Son, Inc.; Dir Dallas Museum of Art; mem. The Business Council, Advisory Council McCombs School of Business at Univ. of Texas. *Leisure interest:* private pilot (holds a FAA Multi-Engine Instrument Pilot Rating). *Address:* Emerald Creek Group, LLC, 8901 Gaylord Drive, Suite 200, Houston, TX 77024, USA (office). *Telephone:* (713) 468-4050 (office). *E-mail:* gerard .arpey@emeraldcreek.com (office). *Website:* www.emeraldcreek.com/Gerard.html (office).

ARQUETTE, Patricia; American actress; b. 8 April 1968; d. of Lewis Arquette and Mardi Arquette; m. 1st Nicolas Cage (q.v.) 1995 (divorced); m. 2nd Thomas Jane 2006; one s. one d. *Films:* Pretty Smart 1986, A Nightmare on Elm Street 3: Dream Warriors 1987, Time Out 1988, Far North 1988, The Indian Runner 1991, Prayer of the Rollerboys 1991, Ethan Frome 1993, Trouble Bound 1993, Inside Monkey Zetterland 1993, True Romance 1993, Holy Matrimony 1994, Ed Wood 1994, Beyond Rangoon 1995, Infinity 1995, Flirting with Disaster 1996, The Secret Agent 1996, Lost Highway 1997, Nightwatch 1998, In the Boom Boom Room 1999, Goodbye Lover 1999, Stigmata 1999, Bringing out the Dead 1999, Little Nicky 2000, Human Nature 2001, Holes 2003, Tiptoes 2003, Deeper than Deep 2003, Fast Food Nation 2006, Girl in Progress 2012. *TV includes:* Daddy 1987, Dillinger 1991, Wildflower 1991, Betrayed by Love 1994, Toby's Story 1998, The Hi-Lo Country 1998, The Badge 2002, Medium (series) (Emmy Award for Best Actress in a Drama 2005) 2005–09. *Address:* c/o U.T.A., 9560 Wilshire Boulevard, 5th Floor, Beverly Hills, CA 90212, USA.

ARQUETTE, Rosanna; American actress; b. 10 Aug. 1959, New York; d. of Lewis Arquette and Mardi Arquette; m. 1st (divorced); m. 2nd James N. Howard (divorced); m. 3rd. John Sidel 1993; f. Flower Child Productions. *Films include:* Gorp 1980, S.O.B. 1981, Off the Wall 1983, The Aviator 1985, Desperately Seeking Susan 1985, 8 Million Ways to Die 1986, After Hours 1986, Nobody's Fool 1986, The Big Blue 1988, Life Lessons, Black Rainbow 1989; Wendy Cracked a Walnut 1989, Sweet Revenge 1990, Baby, It's You 1990, Flight of the Intruder 1990, The Linguini Incident 1992, Fathers and Sons 1992, Nowhere to Run 1993, Pulp Fiction 1994, Search and Destroy 1995, Crash 1996, Liar 1997, Gone Fishin' 1997, Buffalo '66 1997, Palmer's Pick Up 1998, I'm Losing You 1998, Homeslice 1998, Floating Away 1998, Hope Floats 1998, Fait Accompli 1998, Sugar Town 1999, Palmer's Pick Up 1999, Pigeonholed 1999, Interview with a Dead Man 1999, The Whole Nine Yards 2000, Too Much Flesh 2000, Things Behind the Sun 2001, Big Bad Love 2001, Good Advice 2001, Diary of a Sex Addict 2001, Gilded Stones 2004, Dead Cool 2004, Max and Grace 2005, Iowa 2005, Kids in America 2005, Welcome to California 2005, I-See-You.Com 2006, Ball Don't Lie 2008, Growing Op 2008, The Divide 2012. *TV films include:* Harvest Home, The Wall, The Long Way Home, The Executioner's Song, One Cooks, the Other Doesn't, The Parade, Survival Guide, A Family Tree, Promised a Miracle, Sweet Revenge, Separation, The Wrong Man, Nowhere to Hide, I Know What You Did, The Law and Mr. Lee 2003, Rush of Fear 2003, The L Word (series) 2004–07, What About Brian (series) 2006–07. *Address:* c/o Abrams Artists Agency, 9200 Sunset Blvd, 11th Floor, Los Angeles, CA 90069, USA (office).

ARRABAL, Fernando; Spanish writer; b. 11 Aug. 1932, Melilla; s. of Fernando Arrabal and Carmen Terán González; m. Luce Moreau 1958; one s. one d; ed Univ. of Madrid; political prisoner in Spain 1967; Founder Panique Movt with Topor, Jodorowsky, others; Officier, Ordre des Arts et des Lettres 1984, Chevalier, Légion d'honneur 2005; Superdotado Award 1942, Ford Foundation Award 1959, Grand Prix du Théâtre 1967, Grand Prix Humour Noir 1968, Obie Award 1976, Premio Nadal (Spain) 1983, World's Theater Prize 1984, Medalla de Oro de Bellas Artes

(Spain) 1989, Prix du Théâtre (Acad. Française) 1993, Prix Int. Vladimir Nabokov 1994, Premio de Ensayo Espasa 1994, Grand Prix Soc. des Gens de Lettres 1996, Grand Prix de la Méditerranée 1996, Medal of Centre for French Civilization and Culture, New York 1997, Prix de la Francophonie 1998, Premio Mariano de Cavia 1998, Prix Alessandro Manzoni di Poesia 1999, Premio Nacional de las Letras, Premio Eninci Cine y Literatura 2000, Premio Nacional de Teatro 2001, Premio Ercilla Teatro 2001. *Publications include:* plays: numerous plays including Le cimetière des voitures, Guernica, Le grand cérémonial, L'architecte et l'Empereur d'Assyrie, Les plus des délices, Et ils passèrent des menottes aux fleurs, Le ciel et la merde, Bella ciao, La Tour de Babel, L'extravagante réussite de Jésus-Christ, Karl Marx et William Shakespeare, Les délices de la chair, La traversée de l'empire, Luly, Cielito, Fando et Lis, Lettre d'amour; novels: Baal Babylone 1959, L'enterrement de la sardine 1962, Fêtes et rites de la confusion 1965, La tour prends garde, La reverdie, La vierge rouge, Bréviaire d'amour d'un halterophile, L'extravagante croisade d'un castrat amoureux 1991, La tueuse du jardin d'hiver 1994, El Mono 1994, Le Funambule de Dieu 1998, Ceremonia por un teniente abandonado 1998, Porté disparu 2000, Champagne pour tous 2002, Como un paraíso de locos 2008; poetry includes: La pierre de la folie 1963, 100 sonnets 1966, Humbles paradis 1983, Liberté couleur de femme 1993, Arrabalesques 1994, Passion, Passions 1997, Le Frénétique du Spasme 1997; essays: numerous, including Le Panique, Le New York d'Arrabal, Lettre au Général Franco, Greco 1970, Lettre à Fidel Castro 1983, Goya-Dali 1992, La Dudosa Luz del Día 1994. *Films:* directed and written: Viva la Muerte, J'irai comme un cheval fou, L'arbre de Guernica, L'odyssée de la Pacific, Le cimetière des voitures, Adieu Babylone!, J.-L. Borges (Una Vida de Poesía) 1998. *Leisure interest:* chess. *Address:* 22 rue Jouffroy d'Abbans, Paris 75017, France (home). *Fax:* 1-42-67-01-26 (home). *E-mail:* fernando.arrabal@orange.fr (home); arrabalf@gmail.com (home). *Website:* www .arrabal.org.

ARRAYED, Jawad Salim al-, BA, LLB; Bahraini politician; *Deputy Prime Minister;* b. 23 Sept. 1940; ed Cairo Univ., Leeds Univ., UK; Public Prosecution Dir 1969–71; Minister of Labour and Social Affairs 1971–73; Minister of State for Cabinet Affairs 1973–82; Minister of Health and Chair. Environmental Protection Cttee 1982–95, Minister of State 1995–99; Minister of State for Municipalities and Environmental Affairs 1999–2002; Minister of Justice 2002–05; Advisor to Prime Minister on Legal Affairs 2005–06; Deputy Prime Minister 2006–; mem. Hon. Soc. of Gray's Inn; mem. al-Wifaq party. *Address:* c/o Office of the Prime Minister, POB 2088, Government House, Government Rd, Manama, Bahrain.

ARREAZA MONSERRAT, Jorge Alberto; Venezuelan politician; *Vice-President and Minister of Science and Technology;* b. 1973; m. Rosa Virginia Chávez Colmenares (daughter of fmr Pres. of Venezuela Hugo Chávez); two c.; ed Universidad Central de Venezuela, Univ. of Cambridge, UK; fmr journalist; fmr Lecturer, Universidad Central de Venezuela; fmr presenter and interviewer on several public TV stations in Venezuela, including as host of TV series Diálogo abierto; Pres. Fundayacucho (student grant org.) 2005–10; Deputy Minister of Science and Tech. 2010–11, Minister 2011–; Vice-Pres. of Venezuela 2013–; mem. Partido Socialista Unido de Venezuela. *Address:* Palacio de Miraflores, final Avda Urdaneta, esq. de Bolero, Caracas, Venezuela (office). *Telephone:* (212) 806-3111 (office). *Fax:* (212) 806-3229 (office). *E-mail:* dggcomunicacional@presidencia.gob .ve (office). *Website:* www.presidencia.gob.ve (office).

ARROW, Kenneth Joseph, BS, MA, PhD; American economist and academic; *Professor Emeritus of Economics and Operations Research, Stanford University;* b. 23 Aug. 1921, New York, NY; s. of Harry I. Arrow and Lillian Arrow; m. Selma Schweitzer 1947; two s.; ed The City College, Columbia Univ.; Capt. in USAF 1942–46; Research Assoc., Cowles Comm. for Research in Econ., Univ. of Chicago 1947–49; Asst Prof., then Assoc. Prof., then Prof. of Econs, Statistics and Operations Research, Stanford Univ. 1949–68, Prof. of Econs and Operations Research 1979–91, Prof. Emer. 1991–; Prof. of Econs, Harvard Univ. 1968–79; mem. NAS, American Acad. of Arts and Sciences, American Philosophical Soc., Finnish Acad. of Sciences, British Acad., Inst. of Medicine, Pontifical Acad. of Social Sciences; Pres. Int. Soc. for Inventory Research 1983–90, Int. Econ. Asscn, Econometric Soc., American Econ. Asscn, Soc. for Social Choice and Welfare; Dir various cos; Order of the Rising Sun (Japan); Hon. LLD (City Univ., Univ. of Chicago, Washington Univ., Univ. of Pennsylvania, Ben-Gurion Univ., Harvard Univ., Univ. of Cyprus, Univ. of Buenos Aires), Hon. Dr of Social and Econ. Sciences (Vienna), Hon. ScD (Columbia Univ.) 1973, Hon. DSocSci (Yale) 1974, Hon. LLD (Hebrew Univ. Jerusalem) 1975, Hon. DPolSci (Helsinki) 1976, Hon. DLitt (Cambridge) 1985, (Harvard) 1999, Hon. DUniv (Uppsala) 1995, Hon. PhD (Univ. of Tel-Aviv) 2001, Dr hc (Univ. René Descartes) 1974, (Univ. Aix-Marseille III) 1985, (Univ. of Cyprus) 2000; Nobel Memorial Prize in Econ. Science 1972, John Bates Clark Medal, Von Neumann Prize, Medal of Univ. of Paris 1998, Nat. Medal of Science 2006, Lippincott Award 2011. *Publications include:* Social Choice and Individual Values 1951, 1963, Studies in the Mathematical Theory of Inventory and Production (with S. Karlin and H. Scarf) 1958, Studies in Linear and Nonlinear Programming (with L. Hurwicz and H. Uzawa) 1958, A Time Series Analysis of Inter-industry Demands (with M. Hoffenberg) 1959, Public Investment, The Rate of Return and Optimal Fiscal Policy (with M. Kurz) 1970, Essays in the Theory of Risk-Bearing 1971, General Competitive Analysis (with F. H. Hahn) 1971, The Limits of Organization 1973, Studies in Resource Allocation Processes (with L. Hurwicz) 1977, Collected Papers 1983–85, Social Choice and Multi-criterion Decision Making (with H. Raynaud) 1985; more than 240 articles in learned journals. *Leisure interests:* walking, music. *Address:* Room 342, Landau Economics, Department of Economics, Stanford University, Stanford, CA 94305-6072 (office); 620 Sand Hill Road, Apartment 406C, Palo Alto, CA 94304, USA (home). *Telephone:* (650) 327-3957 (office). *Fax:* (650) 326-1702 (office). *E-mail:* arrow@stanford.edu (office). *Website:* economics.stanford.edu/faculty/arrow (office).

ARROYO, Mary T. K., BSc, PhD, FLS, FRSNZ; New Zealand biologist and academic; *Director, Institute of Ecology and Biodiversity;* b. (Mary Therese Kalin), 12 Nov. 1944, New Plymouth; d. of Alexander Meinrod Kalin and Shiela Frances Hurley; m. Manuel Patricio Arroyo; one s.; ed Univ. of Canterbury, Christchurch, New Zealand, Univ. of California, Berkeley, USA; Postdoctoral Research Fellow, with Dr Peter Raven, residing in New York Botanical Garden 1971–72; Full Prof. of Biology, Universidad de Chile, Dir Inst. of Ecology and Biodiversity; Head of Ind.

Scientific Comm. of the Rio Condor Project (jt collaboration between Chilean scientific community and Chilean forestry industry); her studies led to designation of the central Chilean biodiversity hotspot and a better understanding of the conservation values of protected areas of central Chile; 68,000 hectares of the Condor River drainage basin have been protected; has worked extensively on pollination mechanisms, plant breeding systems and flower longevity in the Chilean Andes; Corresp. mem. Botanical Soc. of America 1995, NAS 1999, Chilean Acad. of Sciences 2003; mem. Third World Acad. of Sciences (now TWAS, The World Acad. of Sciences) 2004; Condecoración al Mérito 'Amanda Labarca' 1996; Percival Memorial Prize in Botany, Univ. of Canterbury 1966, Premio Cultural 'Angel Faivovich' 1982, Guggenheim Fellow 1984, Cátedra Presidencial en Ciencias, 1997–99, Medalla Rectoral, Universidad de Chile 1998, Premio Fundación BBVA a la Investigación a la Biología de la Conservación 2004, Volvo Environment Prize (Sweden) 2005, Chilean Nat. Science Prize in Natural Sciences 2010. *Publications:* numerous papers on reproductive systems of plants, studies of complete communities and conservation. *Leisure interests:* hiking, biking, reading. *Address:* Institute of Ecology and Biodiversity, University of Chile, Castilla 653, Santiago, Chile (office). *Telephone:* (2) 2715464 (office). *E-mail:* southern@uchile.cl (office). *Website:* www.ieb-chile.cl (office).

ARRUKBAN, Abdulaziz bin Mohamed; Saudi Arabian UN official and fmr transport executive; *Special Humanitarian Envoy, United Nations;* b. 1959; ed coll. in Georgia, USA; began career working in transport sector in USA; moved back to Riyadh as COO of one of Saudi Arabia's largest transportation cos; Special Amb., UN World Food Programme 2005–07, UN Special Humanitarian Envoy 2007–. *Address:* Office of the Secretary-General, UN Headquarters, First Avenue at 46th Street, New York, NY 10017, USA (office). *Website:* www.un.org (office).

ARSALA, Hedayat Amin, PhD; Afghan economist and politician; b. 12 Jan. 1942, nephew of Pir Gailani (leader of Qadiriyyah Sufi order); m.; three c.; ed high school in Kabul, George Washington Univ., USA; ethnic Pashtun descended from Jabar Khel tribe; foreign language trainer for three consecutive Peace Corps training programmes in USA; started his professional career at World Bank Youth Professional Program 1969, held various econ. and sr operational posts 1969–87; returned to Afghanistan to join Afghan resistance to Soviet occupation 1987–89, served as Sr Adviser and mem. Afghan Mujahideen Unity Council; Minister of Finance, Transitional Govt of Afghanistan 1989–92; Minister of Foreign Affairs 1993–96; Sr mem. Exec. Council of Loya Jirga (traditional council of Afghan tribal leaders) 1998–; played key role in Intra-Afghan Bonn Conf. following fall of the Taliban regime 2001; apptd Vice-Chair. and Minister of Finance of the interim admin 2001; named one of four Vice-Pres, Transitional Islamic State of Afghanistan 2001–04, Chair. Ind. Civil Services Admin Reform Comm., adviser to Cen. Statistics Office and Afghan Econ. Cooperation Cttee; mem. Afghan Nat. Security Council; Minister of Commerce and Sr Presidential Adviser 2004–06, Sr Minister in the Cabinet 2006–10, currently Sr Adviser to Pres.; apptd Chair. Govt Co-ordination Cttee 2008; Co-Chair. Jt Co-ordination and Monitoring Bd 2008; cand. in presidential elections 2009, 2014; Dr hc (Southern Illinois Univ., USA) 2008. *E-mail:* arsalapressoffice@gmail.com. *Website:* hedayatamin-arsala.com.

ARSENIS, Gerasimos; Greek economist and politician; b. 1931, Cephalonia; m. Louka Katseli; three s. one d.; ed Univ. of Athens, Massachusetts Inst. of Tech.; economist, UN Secr. 1960–64; Dir Dept of Econ. Studies, OECD Research Centre 1964–67; Sr Economist, UNCTAD 1967–74, Dir 1974, Ind. Expert to Ministerial Cttee on Reform of Int. Monetary System (later IMF Interim Cttee) 1974–80; Gov. Bank of Greece 1981–84; Minister of Nat. Economy 1982–85, of Finance and Nat. Economy 1984–85, of Merchant Marine June–July 1985, of Defence 1993–96, of Nat. Educ. and Religious Affairs 1996–2000; expelled from PASOK 1986; f. Democratic Initiative Group 1987, Leader 1987–89; returned to PASOK 1989, mem. Exec. Bureau 1990–; Pres. Athens Devt and Governance Inst. 2005–06, mem. Bd of Dirs 2009–; Pres. Hellenic-Russian Soc. 2008; mem. UN Cttee of Devt Planning 1982–92; mem. Parl. for Athens Dist 1990–. *Address:* 23 Sina Street, 106 801 Athens, Greece (office). *Telephone:* (21) 03644558 (office). *Fax:* (21) 03603558 (office). *E-mail:* garsenis@otenet.gr (office). *Website:* www.garsenis.gr (office).

ARTÉS-GÓMEZ, Mariano; Spanish academic; *Professor and Director of Mechanics Department, Universidad Nacional de Educación a Distancia;* b. 5 March 1947, Murcia; s. of Mariano Artés and Elisa Gómez; m. María José Caselles 1973; three s.; ed Universidad Politécnica de Madrid, Int. Centre for Theoretical Physics, Trieste; Asst Prof. of Mechanics, Universidad Politécnica de Madrid 1971–78, Assoc. Prof. 1979–80; Prof. Universidad de Oviedo 1980–81; Prof. and Dir of Dept of Mechanics, Universidad Nacional de Educación a Distancia 1981–, Vice-Rector for Research 1986, Dean of Faculty of Industrial Eng 1987, Rector 1987–96; mem. Asocs Española de Informática y Automática, Asocs Española de Ingeniería Mecánica, Soc. for Research into Higher Educ. (UK); Premio Citema 1975, Premio Extraordinario de Doctorado 1977, Laurel de Murcia 1987. *Publications include:* El Papel Instrumental de la Informática en el Proceso Educativo 1975, Dinámica de Sistemas 1979, Mecánica 1982, numerous articles on informatics in educ. and applied mechanics. *Leisure interests:* music, reading. *Address:* Universidad Nacional de Educación a Distancia, Ciudad Universitaria, Department of Mechanics, Industrial Engineering School, Juan del Rosal 12, 28040 Madrid, Spain (office). *Telephone:* (1) 3986433 (office). *Fax:* (1) 3986536 (office). *E-mail:* mberrocal@pas.uned.es (office). *Website:* www.uned.es (office).

ARTHUIS, Jean Raymond Francis Marcel; French politician; b. 7 Oct. 1944, Saint-Martin du Bois, Maine-et-Loire; s. of Raymond Arthuis and Marthe Cotin; m. Brigitte Lafont 1971; one s. one d.; ed Coll. Saint-Michel, Château-Gontier, Ecole Supérieure de Commerce, Nantes and Inst. d'Etudes Politiques, Paris; chartered accountant, Paris 1971–86; Mayor of Château-Gontier 1971–2001; mem. Conseil, Gen., Mayenne, Château-Gontier canton 1976–, Pres. 1992–; Senator from Mayenne (Centrist Group) 1983–86, 1988–95, 2011–; Sec. of State, Ministry of Social Affairs and Employment 1986–87, Ministry of Economy, Finance and Privatization 1987–88; Spokesman on Budget in Senate 1992–95; Minister of Econ. Devt and Planning May–Aug. 1995, of Econ. and Finance 1995–97; Vice-Pres. Force Démocrate (fmrly Centre des démocrates sociaux) 1995–; Vice-Pres. Nouvelle Union pour la Démocratie Française (UDF) 1998; Pres. Union centriste du Sénat 1998–2002, Financial Comm. in Senate 2002–11; Chevalier du Mérite agricole, Commdr, Ordre du Mérite (Germany). *Publications:* Justice sinistrée, Démocratie en danger (co-author) 1991, Les Délocalisations et l'emploi 1993, Dans

les coulisses de Bercy, Le Cinquième pouvoir 1998, Mondialisation, la France à Contre Emploi 2007, SOS Finances Publiques, osons les vraies réformes 2011, La France peut s'en sortir (co-author) 2011. *Address:* Sénat, Palais du Luxembourg, 75291 Paris Cedex 06 (office); Conseil général de la Mayenne, 39 rue Mazagran, BP 1429, 53014 Laval Cedex (office); 8 rue René Homo, 53200 Château-Gontier, France (home).

ARTHUR, James Greig, PhD, FRS, FRSC; Canadian mathematician and academic; *University Professor, Department of Mathematics, University of Toronto;* b. 18 May 1944, Hamilton; s. of John G. Arthur and Katherine Arthur (née Scott); m. Dorothy P. Helm 1972; two s.; ed Univ. of Toronto, Yale Univ.; Instructor, Princeton Univ. 1970–72; Asst Prof., Yale Univ. 1972–76; Prof., Duke Univ. 1976–79; Prof. of Math., Univ. of Toronto 1979–87, Univ. Prof. 1987–; Sloan Fellow 1975–77, Stracie Memorial Fellowship 1982–84; Vice-Pres. American Math. Soc. 1999–2001, Pres. 2005–07; Fellow, Royal Soc. of Canada 1980, Royal Soc. (UK) 1992; Guggenheim Fellowship 2000; Dr hc (Univ. of Ottawa) 2002; Synge Award in Math. 1987, Henry Marshall Tory Medal 1997, Canadian Gold Medal for Science and Eng 1999, Wilbur Lucius Cross Medal, Grad. School of Yale Univ. 2000, Killam Prize 2004. *Publications:* numerous scientific papers and articles. *Leisure interests:* tennis, squash, golf. *Address:* Department of Mathematics, University of Toronto, Toronto, ON M5S 3G3 (office); 23 Woodlawn Avenue West, Toronto, ON M4V 1G6, Canada (home). *Telephone:* (416) 978-4524 (office). *E-mail:* arthur@math.toronto.edu (office). *Website:* www.math.toronto.edu (office).

ARTHUR, Michael James Paul, MB BS, MD, FRCP, FMedSci, FRSA; British physician, academic and university administrator; *President and Provost, University College London;* b. 3 Aug. 1954, Purley, Surrey; m. Elizabeth S. McCaughey 1979; one s. two d.; ed Burnt Mill School, Harlow, Essex, Univ. of Southampton, Univ. of California, San Francisco, USA; Fogarty Int. Travelling Fellowship, Univ. of California, San Francisco 1988–90; Research Fellow and Lecturer in Medicine, Univ. of Southampton 1982–89, Sr Lecturer 1989–92, Prof. of Medicine 1992–2004, Dir of Research 1995–98, Head of the School of Medicine 1998–2003, Dean of the Faculty of Medicine, Health and Life Sciences 2003–04; Vice-Chancellor Univ. of Leeds 2004–13; Pres. and Provost Univ. Coll. London 2013–; US/UK Fulbright Commr 2008–; mem. Council of MRC 2008–; Chair. Worldwide Univs Network, Cell and Molecular Panel of the Wellcome Trust 2003–04, Nat. Steering Group for Nat. Student Survey 2005–08, Russell Group of Univs 2009–12, Advisory Group for Nat. Specialised Services (NHS) 2010–; mem. Higher Educ. Funding Council for England (HEFCE)'s Research Assessment Exercise panel for hospital-based medicine 2001, HEFCE's Strategic Research Cttee 2003–05, Dept of Health's Advisory Group on Hepatitis 1998–2004; Pres. British Asscn for the Study of the Liver 2001–03; Chair. Bd of Trustees, British Liver Trust 2003–06, Vice-Pres. 2007–; Council mem. Council for Industry and Higher Educ. 2012–; mem. Bd Opera North 2006–; fmr mem. Editorial Bd Journal of Hepatology, Comparative Hepatology, Gut and Clinics in Gastroenterology; American Liver Foundation Research Prize 1987, Linacre Medal, Royal Coll. of Physicians, London 1994, Fulbright Distinguished Scholar Award to conduct cell biology research at Mount Sinai School of Medicine, New York City 2002. *Publications:* numerous papers in professional journals. *Leisure interest:* sailing. *Address:* President and Provost's Office, University College London, Gower Street, London, WC1E 6BT, England (office). *Telephone:* (20) 7679-7234 (office). *Fax:* (20) 7388-5412 (office). *E-mail:* michael.arthur@ucl.ac.uk (office). *Website:* www.ucl.ac.uk/provost (office).

ARTHUR, Rt Hon. Owen, PC; Barbadian politician and economist; b. 17 Oct. 1949; m. Beverley Jeanne Batchelor 1978; ed Harrison Coll., Univ. of the West Indies, Cave Hill, Univ. of the West Indies, Mona; Research Asst, Univ. of the West Indies, Jamaica 1973; Asst Econ. Planner, Chief Econ. Planner Nat. Planning Agency, Jamaica 1974–79; Dir of Econs, Jamaica Bauxite Inst. 1979–81; Chief Project Analyst, Ministry of Finance, Barbados 1981–83; lecturer Dept of Man., Univ. of the West Indies, Cave Hill 1986, Resident Fellow 1993; Senator 1983–84; Parl. Sec. Ministry of Finance 1985–86; mem. Barbados Labour Party (BLP), Chair. 1993–96; Prime Minister of Barbados, Minister of Defence and Security, Finance and Econ. Affairs and for the Civil Service Sept. 1994–2008. *Publications:* The Commercialisation of Technology in Jamaica 1979, Energy and Mineral Resource Development in the Jamaican Bauxite Industry 1981, The IMF and Economic Stabilisation Policies in Barbados 1984. *Leisure interests:* gardening, cooking. *Address:* Barbados Labour Party, Grantley Adams House, 111 Roebuck Street, Bridgetown, Barbados (office). *Telephone:* 429-1990 (office). *Fax:* 427-8792. *E-mail:* will99@caribsurf.com (office). *Website:* labourparty.wordpress.com (office).

ARTHURS, Harry William, OC, OOnt, BA, LLM, FRSC, FBA; Canadian professor of law and political science; *University Professor Emeritus and President Emeritus, York University;* b. 9 May 1935, Toronto, Ont.; s. of Leon Arthurs and Ellen H. Arthurs (née Dworkin); m. Penelope Geraldine Ann Milnes 1974; two s.; ed Univ. of Toronto, Harvard Univ., USA; Asst, Assoc. then full Prof. of Law, Osgoode Hall Law School, York Univ., Ont. 1961–95, Dean of Law School 1972–77, Pres. York Univ. 1985–92, Pres. Emer. 1992–, Univ. Prof. 1995–2005, Univ. Prof. Emer. 2005–; Assoc., Canada Inst. of Advanced Research 1995–98; mediator and arbitrator in labour disputes 1962–85; author, lecturer 1961–; Bencher, Law Soc. of Upper Canada 1979–83; mem. Econ. Council of Canada 1978–81; Chair. Consultative Group, Research and Educ. in Law 1980–84; Chair. Council of Ont. Univs 1987–89; Commr to Review Federal Labour Standards 2004–06; Chair. Ontario Expert Comm. on Pensions 2006–08, Ontario Workplace Safety and Insurance Bd, Funding Review 2010–12; Order of Ontario; Hon. LLD (Sherbrooke, McGill, Brock, Montreal, Toronto, York, Simon Fraser Univs, Law Soc. of Upper Canada), Hon. DLitt (Lethbridge), Hon. DCL (Windsor); Killam Prize for Social Sciences, Canada Council 2002, Bora Laskin Prize for contribs to Labour Law 2002, ILO Decent Work Research Prize (co-winner) 2008, Lifetime Achievement Award, Labour Law Research Network 2013. *Publications:* Industrial Relations and Labour Law in Canada (co-author) 1984, Law and Learning (Report on Legal Research and Education in Canada) 1984, Without the Law: Administrative Justice and Legal Pluralism in Nineteenth Century England 1985, Fairness at Work (Report on Federal Labour Standards) 2006, A Fine Balance (Report on Pensions) 2008, Fair Funding (report on Workplace Insurance) 2012, Rethinking Workplace Regulation: Beyond the Standard Contract of Employment (co-author) 2013. *Address:* Osgoode Law School, York University, 4700 Keele Street, North York, ON M3J 1P3 (office); 11 Hillcrest Park, Toronto, ON M4X 1E8, Canada (home). *Telephone:* (416) 736-5407 (office). *Fax:* (416) 736-5736 (office). *E-mail:* harthurs@osgoode.yorku.ca (office).

ARTHUS-BERTRAND, Yann Marie; French photographer; b. 13 March 1946, Paris; s. of Claude Arthus-Bertrand and Jeanne Arthus-Bertrand (née Schildge); m. 2nd Anne Thual 1984; three s.; early career as asst dir and actor 1963–66; worked on wildlife reserve, Allier River 1966–76; balloon pilot, Masai Mara Reserve, Kenya 1976–78; f. Altitude agency (aerial photographs) 1991, cr. Earth from Above project 1995, Six Billion Others project 2003, Good Planet 2005; Good Will Amb., UNEP 2009–; elected Académie des Beaux-Arts 2006; Officier, Légion d'Honneur; Earth Champion Prize 2009. *Publications:* more than 60 books of photographs including Lions 1981, Three Days in France 1989, La terre vue du ciel (The Earth from Above) 1999 (updated annually), 365 jours pour réfléchir sur la terre 2000 (updated annually), Etre Photographe 2003, Agenda Chevaux 2005, Bestiaux 2006. *Address:* Altitude, Domaine de Longchamp, Carrefour de Longchamp, 75116 Paris, France (office). *E-mail:* yannab@club-internet.fr (office). *Website:* www.yannarthusbertrand.com.

ARTIN, Michael, AB, MA, PhD; American mathematician and academic; *Professor Emeritus of Mathematics, Massachusetts Institute of Technology;* b. 28 June 1934, Hamburg, Germany; s. of Emil Artin and Natalia (Natascha) Naumovna Jasny; ed Princeton and Harvard Univs, USA; spent time at Institut des Hautes Etudes Scientifiques, France, contributing to SGA4 vols of Séminaire de géométrie algébrique in early 1960s; Benjamin Peirce Lecturer, Harvard Univ. 1960–63; joined MIT Math. Faculty 1963, apptd Prof. 1966, Norbert Wiener Prof. 1988–93, now Prof. Emer., Chair. Pure Math. 1982–83, Chair. Undergraduate Cttee 1994–97, 1997–98; mem. NAS; Foreign mem. Royal Netherlands Soc. of Sciences; Fellow, American Acad. of Arts and Sciences 1969, AAAS, Soc. for Industrial and Applied Math., American Math. Soc. (Pres. 1990–92); Hon. mem. Moscow Math. Soc.; Dr hc (Antwerp), (Hamburg); MIT Undergraduate Teaching Prize and Educational and Grad. Advising Award, Leroy P. Steele Prize for Lifetime Achievement, American Math. Soc. 2002, Harvard Grad. School of Arts & Sciences Centennial Medal 2005, Wolf Prize in Math. (co-recipient) 2013. *Publications:* numerous papers in professional journals. *Address:* Department of Mathematics, Massachusetts Institute of Technology, Room E18-312, 77 Massachusetts Avenue, Cambridge, MA 02139-4307, USA (office). *Telephone:* (617) 253-3689 (office). *E-mail:* artin@math.mit.edu (office). *Website:* math.mit.edu (office).

ARTUCIO RODRIGUEZ, Alejandro, DJur, DScS; Uruguayan diplomatist; b. 22 Aug. 1934; m.; two c.; ed Univ. of the Republic; Chief Counsel and Commr, Int. Comm. of Jurists, Geneva 1985–2005; Amb. and Perm. Rep. to UN, New York 2004–06, to UN, Geneva 2007–09; Special Rapporteur on Equatorial Guinea, UN High Comm. on Human Rights 1993–99; Chief Counsel for Human Rights, UN Verification Mission in Guatemala (MINUGUA) 1997; fmr mem. Governing Council, Inst. of Legal and Social Studies, Uruguay, Governing Council, Asscn for Prevention of Torture, Geneva, Advice Council, Int. Service for Human Rights, Geneva, Int. Consulting Council, Legal and Social Studies Centre, Argentina. *Address:* Ministry of Foreign Affairs, Palacio Santos, Avda 18 de Julio 1205, 11100 Montevideo, Uruguay (office). *Telephone:* (2) 9021010 (office). *Fax:* (2) 9021349 (office). *E-mail:* webmaster@mrree.gub.uy (office). *Website:* www.mrree.gub.uy (office).

ARTZT, Alice Josephine, BA; American classical guitarist, writer and teacher; b. 16 March 1943, Philadelphia, Pa; d. of Maurice Gustav Artzt and Harriett Green Artzt; m. Bruce B. Lawton, Jr; ed Columbia Univ. and studied composition with Darius Milhaud and guitar with Julian Bream, Ida Presti and Alexandre Lagoya; taught guitar at Mannes Coll. of Music, New York 1966–69, Trenton State Univ. 1977–80; worldwide tours as soloist 1969–94; f. Alice Artzt Guitar Trio (with M. Rutscho and R. Burley) 1989; toured in duo with R. Burley; fmr mem. Bd of Dirs Guitar Foundation of America (Chair. 1986–89); several Critics' Choice Awards. *Recordings include:* Bach and His Friends, Guitar Music by Fernando Sor, Guitar Music by Francisco Tarrega, 20th Century Guitar Music, English Guitar Music, The Music of Manuel Ponce, The Glory of the Guitar, Virtuoso Romantic Guitar, Musical Tributes, Variations, Passacaglias and Chaconnes, American Music of the Stage and Screen, Alice Artzt Classic Guitar, Alice Artzt Plays Original Works. *Publications:* The Art of Practicing, The International GFA Guitarists' Cookbook (ed.), Rhythmic Mastery 1997; numerous articles in guitar and music periodicals. *Leisure interests:* hi-fi, travel, Chaplin movies. *Address:* 51 Hawthorne Avenue, Princeton, NJ 08540, USA. *Telephone:* (609) 921-6629. *E-mail:* guitartzt@aol.com. *Website:* guitartzt.com.

ARTZT, Edwin Lewis, BJ; American business executive; b. 15 April 1930, New York; s. of William Artzt and Ida Artzt; m. Ruth N. Martin 1950; one s. four d.; ed Univ. of Oregon; Account Exec. Glasser Gailey Advertising Agency, Los Angeles 1952–53; joined Proctor & Gamble Co., Cincinnati 1953, Brand Man. Advertising Dept 1956–58, Assoc. Brand Promotion Man. 1958–60, Brand Promotion Man. 1960, 1962–65, Copy Man. 1960–62, Advertisement Man. Paper Products Div. 1965–68, Man. Products Food Div. 1968–69, Vice-Pres. 1969, Vice-Pres., Acting Man. Coffee Div. 1970, Vice-Pres., Group Exec. 1970–75, Dir 1972–75, 1980–95, Group Vice-Pres. Procter & Gamble Co., Europe, Belgium 1975–80, Pres. Procter & Gamble Int. 1980–89, Chair., CEO 1995–99, Vice-Chair. Procter & Gamble Co. 1980–89, Chair. 1989–95, CEO 1995–99; mem. Bd of Dirs Delta Airlines 1990–2002, American Express Co. 1991–2002, GTE (now Verizon) 1992–2002, Barilla G.E.R. SpA 1995–98, Spalding Sports and Barilla SpA, Italy, Juvenile Diabetes Foundation; Trustee, Cttee for Econ. Devt; Sr Adviser, Kohlberg, Kravis, Roberts and Co. 2001–08, Gabelli Group Capital Partners Inc. 2003–08; fmr mem. Business Council, Presidential Advisory Cttees on Trade Policy and Negotiations, Council on Foreign Relations; Martin Luther King, Jr Salute to Greatness Award 1995, Leadership Conf. on Civil Rights Pvt. Sector Leadership Award 1995. *Address:* 9495 Whitegate Lane, Cincinnati, OH 45243, USA (home).

ARULKUMARAN, Sir Sabaratnam, Kt, MD, PhD, FRCS, MRCOG; British (b. Sri Lankan) obstetrician and gynaecologist and academic; *President, International Federation of Obstetrics and Gynaecology;* ed Univ. of Ceylon; has been in clinical practice since 1972; began career as Lecturer, rising to Prof. and Head of Dept Obstetrics and Gynaecology, Nat. Univ. of Singapore 1982–97; Foundation Prof. at Derby as part of Univ. of Nottingham, UK 1997–2001; Dir (non-exec.) Southern Derbyshire Acute Hosp. NHS Trust 1997–2001; Prof. and Head of Obstetrics and

Gynaecology, St George's Univ. of London, UK 2001–; Deputy Sec.-Gen. Asia & Oceanic Fed. 1989–97; Treas. and later Sec.-Gen. Int. Fed. of Obstetrics & Gynaecology 1997–2006, Pres. 2012–; Vice-Pres. Royal Coll. of Obstetricians and Gynaecologists 2005–07, Pres. 2009–10; Ed.-in-Chief Best Practice & Research in Clinical Obstetrics and Gynaecology 1998–; Hon. Fellow of American, S African, Indian, Sri Lankan, Pakistan, Australia and New Zealand Colls of Obstetricians and Gynaecologists; Hon. mem. German, S African, Malaysian and Canadian Socs of Obstetrics and Gynaecology; Dr hc (Univ. of Athens). *Publications include:* 24 books as author or ed., 150 book chapters and 240 articles in professional journals. *Address:* Section of Obstetrics & Gynaecology, Division of Clinical Developmental Sciences, St George's University of London, Cranmer Terrace, London SW17 0RE, England (office). *Telephone:* (20) 8725-5956 (office). *Fax:* (20) 8725-5958 (office). *E-mail:* sarulkum@sgul.ac.uk (office). *Website:* www.sgul.ac.uk (office); www.figo .org.

ARUNGA, June, LLB; Kenyan journalist and film company executive; *Founder and President, Open Quest Media LLC;* b. 1981; ed Univ. of Buckingham, UK, Univ. of Nairobi; Founder and Pres. Open Quest Media LLC (film and TV production co.), New York, USA 2006–; Vice-Pres. New Liberty Films LLC; Assoc. Ed. AfricanLiberty.org; mem. Bd of Advisors Global Envison (USA), The Inter-Region Econ. Network (Kenya), Grassroot Free Markets (Hawaii), The Bastiat Soc., Charleston, SC; mem. Creative Council, Moving Pictures Inst., New York; H.B. Earhart Grad. Fellow of Law; Sr Fellow, Istituto Bruno Leoni, Milan, Italy; Fellow, IMANI Center for Policy and Educ., Int. Policy Network, London, UK; honoured by Clutch magazine as one of 21 International Women of Power 2008. *Television:* writer/host of The Devil's Footpath (BBC TV) 2004, co-presenter/subject of Africa: Who is to Blame? (BBC World TV) 2005, writer/producer of Africa's Ultimate Resource (Victory Studios) 2005, The Cell-Phone Revolution in Kenya (BBC Newsnight mini-documentary) 2007. *Publication:* The Cell-Phone Revolution in Kenya (co-author) 2007. *Address:* Open Quest Media LLC, 119 W 72nd Street (No. 158), New York, NY 10023, USA (office). *Telephone:* (206) 719-6485 (office). *E-mail:* junearunga@openquestmedia.com (office). *Website:* www .openquestmedia.com (office); junearunga.typepad.com/openquest/2007/10/index .html (office).

ARVIND, B.Tech, MS, PhD; Indian computer scientist and academic; *Johnson Professor of Computer Science and Engineering, Massachusetts Institute of Technology;* b. (Arvind Mithal), 1947, Lucknow, Uttar Pradesh; m. Gita Mithal; two s.; ed Indian Inst. of Tech., Kanpur, Univ. of Minnesota, USA; Asst Prof. of Information and Computer Science, Univ. of California, Irvine, USA 1974–78; Lecturer, Indian Inst. of Tech., Kanpur 1977–78, N. Rama Rao Chair, Dept of Computer Science and Eng 1998–99; joined MIT 1978, currently Johnson Prof. of Computer Science and Eng, also mem. Computer Science and Artificial Intelligence Lab. (CSAIL); f. Sandburst Corpn (semiconductor co.) 2002; Co-f. Bluespec Inc. 2003, currently Dir; mem. Editorial Bd several journals including Journal of Parallel and Distributed Computing, Journal of Functional Programming; Fujitsu Visiting Prof., Univ. of Tokyo 1992–93; Chief Technical Adviser, UN-sponsored Knowledge Based Computer Systems Project, India 1986–92; Gen. Chair. ICS05 (Int. Conf. on Supercomputing), Cambridge, Mass 2005; Fellow, IEEE 1994, Nat. Acad. of Eng 2008; mem. American Asscn of Arts and Sciences 2012–; IEEE Charles Babbage Outstanding Scientist Award 1994, Distinguished Alumnus Award, Indian Inst. of Tech., Kanpur 1999, Alumni Award, Univ. of Minnesota 2001, Outstanding Achievement Award, Univ. of Minnesota 2008, IEEE Harry Goode Memorial Award 2012. *Publications include:* Implicit Parallel Programming in pH (co-author) 2001, Operation-Centric Hardware Descriptions and Synthesis (co-author) 2004, Rate Guarantees and Overload Protection in Input-Queued Switches (co-author) 2004, Modular Scheduling of Guarded Atomic Actions (co-author) 2004, High-Level Synthesis: An Essential Ingredient for Designing Complex ASICs (co-author) 2004. *Address:* The Stata Center, MIT, 32 Vassar Street, 32-G866, Cambridge, MA 02139, USA (office). *Telephone:* (617) 253-6090 (office). *Fax:* (617) 253-6652 (office). *E-mail:* arvind@mit.edu (office); arvind@ csail.mit.edu (office). *Website:* www.csail.mit.edu (office); csg.csail.mit.edu/Users/ arvind (home).

ARYAL, Krishna Raj, MEd, MA; Nepalese politician, educationist and diplomatist; b. Dec. 1928, Kathmandu; m. Shanta Laxmi 1956; one s.; ed Durbar High School, Tri-Chandra Coll., Allahabad Univ., India, Univ. of Oregon, USA; Lecturer, Nat. Teachers' Training Centre 1954–56; Prof. Coll. of Educ., Dir Publs Govt Educ. Devt Project 1956–59; Founder, Admin. and Prin. Shri Ratna Rajya Laxmi Girls' Coll. 1961–71; Asst Minister of Educ. 1971–72, of State 1972–73, Minister 1973–75, of Foreign Affairs 1975–79; Amb. to France (also accred to Spain, Italy, Portugal and Israel) and Perm. Del. to UNESCO 1980–84; Chair. Asian Group and mem. Bureau UNESCO 1982–83; mem. Raj Sabha 1985–90, Rastriya Panchayat (unicameral legis.) 1986–90; Chair. Brahmacharya Ashram; Ed. Education Quarterly 1956–59, Nabin Shikshya 1956–59; fmr Sec. Cricket Asscn of Nepal; Exec. mem. World Hindu Fed.; Gorakha Dakhinbahu (1st Class), Grand Cordon of Yugoslav Star, Order of the Rising Sun, 1st Class (Japan), Grand Officier, Order Nat. du Mérite (France), Order of Civil Merit, 1st Class (Spain) and other decorations. *Publications include:* Education for the Development of Nepal 1970, Monarchy in the Making of Nepal 1975, The Science of Education. *Address:* 17/93 Gaihiri Dhara, Kathmandu, Nepal (home).

ARYSTANBEKOVA, Akmaral Khaidarovna, PhD, DSc; Kazakhstani politician and diplomatist; *Ambassador-at-Large, Ministry of Foreign Affairs;* b. 12 May 1948, Alma-Ata (now Almaty); d. of Khaidar Arystanbvekov and Sharbanu Bekmanovna Nurmuhamedova; ed Kazak State Univ.; mem. Staff Dept of Chem., Kazak State Univ. 1975–78; Chief of Dept and Sec. Cen. State Cttee, Kazak Komsomol 1978–83; mem. Supreme Council Kazakstan 1985–90, Presidium 1987–90; Minister of Foreign Affairs 1989–91; Rep. of Kazakhstan at Perm. Mission of the fmr USSR 1991–92; Perm. Rep. and Amb., Perm. Mission of Kazakstan to UN 1992–99; Amb. to France 1999–2003; currently Amb.-at-Large, Ministry of Foreign Affairs; Deputy Chair. Kazak Friendship Soc. 1983–84; Chair. Presidium Kazakh Soc. for Friendship and Cultural Relations with Foreign Countries 1984–89; Medal of Supreme Soviet of USSR 1970, 1981, Kurmat Order 1996. *Publications:* United Nations and Kazakhstan 2002, Kazakhstan in the UN: History and Perspectives 2004, Globalization 2007; numerous contribs to periodicals. *Leisure interests:* classical music, piano. *Address:* Ministry of Foreign Affairs,

010000 Astana, Beibitshilik 11 (office); 050000, Almaty, Aiteke-Bi, 65, Kazakhstan (home). *Telephone:* (7172) 32-76-69 (office); (7272) 72-07-40 (home). *Fax:* (7172) 32-76-67 (home); (7272) 72-01-03 (home). *E-mail:* mta_almaty@mail.ru (home). *Website:* www.mfa.kz (office).

ARZÚ IRIGOYEN, Alvaro Enrique, BS; Guatemalan politician; b. 14 March 1946, Guatemala City; m. 1st Silvia García Granados; three c.; m. 2nd Patricia Escobar Dalton; two c.; ed Univ. of Rafael, Landívar; Dir Guatemalan Tourist Inst. 1978–81; Mayor of Guatemala City 1986–90, 2004–07; unsuccessful presidential cand. 1990; Sec. Gen. Partido de Avanzada Nacional (PAN) 1991–95; Minister of Foreign Relations 1991; Pres. 1996–2000; Del. to Cen. American Parl. 2000–04; fmr squash nat. champion; Grand Cross of the Order of San Carlos (Colombia); Dr hc (St Paul Univ., Chicago) 1998; Prince of Asturias and Int. Cooperation Award 1997, Feliz Houphout Boigny Prize (UNESCO), Galardón Monseñor Leonidas Proaño Award, Latin American Asscn for Human Rights. *Leisure interests:* soccer, swimming, cycling, golf, horse riding. *Address:* c/o Partido de Avanzada Nacional (PAN),18-28 3rd Avenue 10th Zone 14, Guatemala City, Guatemala.

ARZUMANYAN, Aleksander Robertovich, BS, MS; Armenian politician and diplomatist; b. 24 Dec. 1959, Yerevan; m.; two c.; ed People's Friendship Univ., Russia, Yerevan State Univ.; Eng Yerevan Research Inst. of Automatic Systems of City Man. 1985–88; Dir Information Cen. Armenian Nat. Movt 1989–90; Asst Chair. of Supreme Council of Armenia 1990–91; Rep. to N America 1991–92; Chargé d'affaires to USA 1992–93; Perm. Rep. to UN 1992–96; rank of Amb. 1992; Minister of Foreign Affairs 1996–98; Chief Advisor to Pres. Armagrobank 1998–2000; Pres. Exec. Council Armenian Nat. Movt 2000–02; Founder-mem. Armenian-Turkish Reconciliation Comm. 2001–; Chair. Regional Group for Eastern Europe 1992–96; participated in and headed del. to int. meetings; elected Deputy Chair. 49th Gen. UN Ass., concurrently mem. Gen. Cttee, UN, Appellation Cttee on resolutions of Admin. Court, UN 1994. *Address:* c/o Ministry of Foreign Affairs, Republic Sq., Govt Bldg 2, 0010 Yerevan, Armenia.

ASAAD, Reem Mohammad, BChem, MBA; Saudi Arabian financial adviser, lecturer, writer and women's rights advocate; b. Egypt; m.; two d.; ed King Abdulaziz Univ., Jeddah, Northeastern Univ., Boston, USA; had accounting experience in family's healthcare business –2001; worked as investment analyst at Nat. Commercial Bank 2001–08; teaches banking and finance at Dar Al-Hekma Women's Coll. 2008–; began appearing on regional financial TV talking about financial markets and econ. affairs 2005; launched a campaign calling for better employment opportunities for women and improved consumer rights, the 'Lingerie Campaign'; ranked by Arabian Business amongst the Power 500: The Worlds's Most Influential Arabs (third) 2012. *Publications:* has written and published numerous econ. articles in the Saudi press. *Leisure interests:* swimming, reading, languages, discovering new talents. *Telephone:* 506646701 (mobile). *E-mail:* askreemasaad@gmail.com (office). *Website:* www.askreem.com; reemasaad .blogspot.co.uk.

ASADA, Teruo; Japanese business executive; *Chairman, Marubeni Corporation;* joined Marubeni Corpn in 1972, has held several exec. positions, including Man. Exec. Officer, Chief Information Officer, Sr Man. Exec. Dir and Dir, mem. Bd of Dirs 2005–, Pres., CEO and Rep. Dir Marubeni Corpn 2008–13, Chair. 2013–. *Address:* Marubeni Corpn, 42 Ohtemachi 1-chome, Chiyoda-ku, Tokyo 100-8088, Japan (office). *Telephone:* (3) 3282-2111 (office). *Fax:* (3) 3282-4241 (office). *E-mail:* info@marubeni.com (office). *Website:* www.marubeni.com (office).

ÄSÄDOV, Oktay Sabir oğlu; Azerbaijani engineer and politician; *Chairman, Milli Mäclis (National Assembly);* b. 3 Jan. 1955, Şaharcik village, Qafan Dist, Azerbaijan SSR, USSR; m.; two c.; ed Azerbaijan Chem. Inst.; Asst Man. then Man., Baku Air Conditioning Factory 1976–79; Sr Engineer, Azerbaijan Special Installation and Construction Co. 1979–81; Sr Engineer, Azärbaycantexqurash-dirma 1981–83, Head of Dept No. 1 1983–89; CEO Santexqurashdirma Industrial Union 1989–96; Pres. Absheron Regional Jt Stock Water Co. 1996–2004; Pres. Azersu Jt Stock Co. 2004–05; mem. New Azerbaijan Party 1999–; Deputy, Milli Mäclis (Nat. Ass.) 2000–, Chair. 2005–; Head of Azerbaijani del. to Inter-Parl. Ass. of CIS and to Parl. Ass. of Turkic-speaking Countries (TÜRKPA); mem. Political Council of New Azerbaijan Party; mem. Int. Water Asscn. *Address:* Milli Mäclis (National Assembly), 1152 Baku, Parliament pr. 1, Azerbaijan. *Telephone:* (12) 510-87-86 (office). *Fax:* (12) 493-49-43 (office). *E-mail:* international@meclis .gov.az (office); azmm@meclis.gov.az (office). *Website:* www.meclis.gov.az (office).

ASAMOAH, Obed Y., JSD; Ghanaian politician and lawyer; b. 6 Feb. 1936, Likpe Bala, Volta Region; s. of William Asamoah and Monica Asamoah; m. Yvonne Wood 1964; two s. one d.; ed Achimota Secondary School, Woolwich Polytechnic, London, King's Coll. London and Columbia Univ., New York; called to the Bar, Middle Temple, London 1960; upon return to Ghana practised as solicitor and advocate of Supreme Court of Ghana; Lecturer, Faculty of Law, Univ. of Ghana, Legon 1965–69; fmr Chair. Bd of Dirs of Ghana Film Industry Corpn, Ghana Bauxite Co.; mem. Constituent Ass. which drafted Constitution for Second Repub. of Ghana 1969; elected to Parl. (Nat. Alliance of Liberals) 1969; mem. Constituent Ass. which drafted third Republican Constitution 1979; Gen. Sec. United Nat. Convention 1979, All People's Party 1981; Minister of Foreign Affairs 1982–97; Attorney-Gen. and Minister of Justice 1993–2001; Chair. Nat. Democratic Congress 2002–05; mem. Ghana Bar Asscn; has served on several int. and public orgs; Patron Democratic Freedom Party 2006–12; Order of the Star of Ghana 2001. *Publications include:* The Legal Significance of the Declaration of the General Assembly of the United Nations 1967; articles in legal journals. *Leisure interests:* reading, farming. *Address:* PO Box 14581, Accra, Ghana (home). *Telephone:* (302) 335414 (home); (20) 811-99-11 (mobile). *E-mail:* obed@obedasamoah.org.

ASANKOJOEVA, Zina Mukaevna; Kyrgyzstani banker; *Chair, National Bank of the Kyrgyz Republic;* b. 1965; ed Kyrgyz State Univ.; Deputy Chief Accountant, State Bank of the USSR 1988–92, Dir of Accounting, Chief Accountant 1992–94; Head of Finance and Credit Policy for Govt Office 1994–97; Head of Financial Sector and Monetary Policy in Office of the Prime Minister 1997–2005, Head of Finance Dept 2005–07, Head of Dept responsible for examination of govt decisions 2007–10; Head, Finance and Credit Policy Dept, Presidential Admin Aug.–Dec. 2010; Deputy Chair., Nat. Bank of the Kyrgyz Repub. (central bank) Jan.–June 2011, Chair. June 2011–. *Address:* National Bank of the Kyrgyz Republic, 720040 Bishkek, Umetaliyeva 101, Kyrgyzstan (office). *Telephone:* (312) 66-90-08 (office)

Fax: (312) 61-07-30 (office). *E-mail:* mail@nbkr.kg (office). *Website:* www.nbkr.kg (office).

ASANO, Tadanobu; Japanese actor; b. 27 Nov. 1973, Yokohama-shi, Kanagawa. *Films include:* Ichi the Killer 2001, Zatoichi 2003, Last Life in the Universe (Upstream Prize for Best Actor, Venice Film Festival 2004) 2003, Mongol 2007, Thor 2011, Battleship 2012, Thor: The Dark World 2013, 47 Ronin 2013. *Address:* c/o Anore Inc., 9F Ochiai-Harajuku Bldg, 6-17-15 Jingumae Shibuya-ku, Tokyo, 150-0001, Japan (office). *Telephone:* (3) 5468-6606 (office). *Fax:* (3) 5468-6607 (office). *E-mail:* anore@ya2.so-net.ne.jp (office). *Website:* www.anore.co.jp/artist/actor/asano (office).

ASANTE, Samuel Kwadwo Boaten, LLM, JSD; Ghanaian lawyer and international legal consultant; *Chairman, Ghana Arbitration Centre;* b. 11 May 1933, Asokore; s. of Daniel Y. Asante and Mary Baafi; m. Philomena Margaret Aidoo 1961; two s. three d.; ed Achimota School, Univs of Nottingham and London, UK and Yale Univ. Law School, USA; State Attorney in the Ministry of Justice of Ghana 1960–61; Lecturer in Law and Acting Head of Law Dept, Univ. of Ghana 1961–65; Lecturer, Univ. of Leeds, UK 1965–66; Attorney, World Bank, Washington, DC 1966–69; Adjunct Prof. of Law, Howard Univ. Law School, Washington, DC 1967–69; Solicitor-Gen. of Ghana 1969–74; mem. Arbitration Panel, Int. Cen. for Settlement of Investment Disputes, Washington, DC 1971–; Chair. Public Agreements Review Cttee of Ghana 1972–77; Deputy Attorney-Gen. of Ghana 1974–77; Chief Legal Adviser, UN Comm. on Transnational Corpns, New York 1977–83, Dir 1983–92; Chair. Cttee of Experts on Ghana Constitution 1991; Dir UN Legal Advisory Services for Devt 1992–93; Dir Int. Third World Legal Studies Asscn, New York; installed as Paramount Chief of Asante-Asokore, Ashanti, Ghana 1995–; Chair. Ghana Public Utilities Regulatory Comm. 1997–2002, Ghana Arbitration Centre 1997–; mem. Bd of Dirs Int. Devt Law Inst., Rome; Taylor Lecturer, Lagos Univ. 1978; consultant, Commonwealth Secr., African Devt Bank, UNITAR; guest lecturer, numerous univs and insts worldwide; Guest Fellow, Berkeley Coll., Yale Univ. 1964–65; fmr Sterling, Fulbright and Aggrey Fellow; Fellow, World Acad. of Arts and Sciences 1975, Ghana Acad. of Arts and Sciences 1976 (Pres. 2002–); Visiting Fellow, Clare Hall, Cambridge, UK 1978–79, Life mem.; Visiting Prof., Temple Univ. Law School, Philadelphia 1976; Patron Int. Centre for Public Law, Inst. of Advanced Legal Studies, Univ. of London; mem. Int. Bar Asscn, Exec. Council, American Soc. of Int. Law 1979, Gen. Legal Council, Ghana, Advisory Bd, Foreign Investment Law Journal-ICSID Review, Int. Court of Arbitration of ICC 1993–2002 and of several other int. arbitral panels; Ghana Book Award. *Publications:* Property Law and Social Goals in Ghana 1976, Transnational Investment Law and National Development 1979 and various articles in law journals. *Leisure interests:* tennis, golf, reading biographies. *Address:* S. K. B. Asante & Associates, PO Box GP 18615, Accra, Ghana (office). *Telephone:* (21) 678973 (office); (21) 678776 (office). *Fax:* (21) 678776 (office). *E-mail:* drskba@ghana.com (office).

ASARTA CUEVAS, Maj.-Gen. Alberto, BA, MA; Spanish army officer and UN official; b. 1951, Zaragoza; m. Clara Eugenia Pedraza; one s. one d.; ed Army Staff Coll., Argentine Nat. Defence School, completed mil. courses in various insts, including US Naval Postgraduate School and NATO School, Germany; commissioned as Infantry Officer 1975; platoon and co. commdr in paratrooper forces, Spanish Legion and 'Canarias 50' Infantry Regt; also taught at Paratrooper Training School; held command appointments up to level of Armoured Brigade Commdr; Mil. Information Officer with UN Observer Group in Cen. America (ONUCA) 1991; assigned to Eurocorps HQ, Strasbourg, France 1993; served in NATO Stabilization Force (SFOR) in Bosnia and Herzegovina 1997, 2001–02; Commdr Infantry Mechanised Regt 'Castilla 16' in Iraq 2003–05; Sector East Commdr, UN Interim Force in Lebanon (UNIFIL) 2008–09, Head of Mission and Force Commdr, UNIFIL 2009–12; promoted to rank of Maj.-Gen. 2009; Adviser to Chief of Staff of Spanish Army –2010. *Address:* c/o Ministry of Defence, Paseo de la Castellana 109, 28071 Madrid, Spain.

ASASHORYU AKINORI; Mongolian fmr sumo wrestler; b. (Dolgorsuren Dagvadorj), 27 Sept. 1980, Ulan Bator; m. (divorced 2009); one s. one d.; debut in 1999; Sekitori title 2000, Makuuchi title 2001, Ozeki title 2002; first victory in Nov. 2002 in only 24th tournament (joint quickest victory in Sumo history); became 68th wrestler to reach Yokozuna level (highest rank) March 2003 (first non-Japanese or non-American to reach Yokozuna level), Yokozuna 2004–07; career record includes 25 Makuuchi titles, 1 Makushita title, 1 Sandanme title, 1 Jonidian title; retd 2010; Sansho Award, three Fighting Spirit prizes, numerous Outstanding Performance awards.

ASBAR, Ali Ahmad Said, (Adonis), PhD; Syrian poet and academic; b. 1930, Kassabin, nr Latakia; two d.; ed Univ. of Damascus, Univ. of St Joseph, Beirut; Prof. of Arabic Literature, Lebanese Univ., Beirut 1971–85; PhD Adviser, Univ. of St Joseph, Beirut 1971–85; Visiting Lecturer, Collège de France, Paris 1983, Georgetown Univ., Washington, DC 1985; Assoc. Prof. of Arab Poetry, Univ. of Geneva 1989–95; mem. Acad. Stéphane Mallarmé, Paris, Haut Conseil de Réflexion du Collège Int. de Philosophie, Paris; Officier, Ordre des Arts et des Lettres 1993; Prix des Amis du Livre, Beirut 1968, Syria-Lebanon Award, Int. Poetry Forum 1971, Nat. Prize for Poetry, Lebanon 1974, Grand Prix des Biennales Internationales de la Poésie de Liège, Belgium 1986, Prix Jean Malrieu-Etranger, Marseille 1991, Feronia-Cita di Fiano, Rome 1993, Nazim Hikmat Prize, Istanbul 1994, Prix Méditerranée-Etranger, France 1995, Bjørnson Prize 2007, Goethe Prize 2011. *Publications include:* Songs of Mihyar, the Damascene 1961, The Book of Changes and Migration to the Regions of Day and Night 1965, A Time Between Ashes and Roses 1970, Introduction to Arab Poetry 1971, A Tomb for New York 1971, The Blood of Adonis 1971, Singular in the Form of Plural 1974, Further Songs of Mihyar, the Damascene 1975, The Shock of Modernity 1978, The Book of Five Poems 1980, Manifesto of Modernity 1980, Transformations of the Lover 1982, Mémoire du Vent 1991, La Prière et L'Épée 1992, Soleils Seconds 1994, The Pages of Day and Night 2001, Chants de Mihyar le Damascène 2002, If Only the Sea Could Sleep 2003, Commencement du Corps, Fin de l'Océan 2004, Histoire qui se Déchire sue le Corps d'une Femme 2008, Selected Poems 2010. *Address:* 1 sq Henri Regnault, 92400 Courbevoie, France (home).

ÅSBRINK, Erik, BSc, BA, MBA; Swedish business executive and fmr politician; b. 1 Feb. 1947, Stockholm; s. of Per Åsbrink; m. Anne-Marie Lindgren; three c.; ed

Univ. of Stockholm, Stockholm School of Econs; worked at Inst. for Soviet and E European Econ. Affairs 1972; Nat. Inst. of Econ. Research 1972–74; Ministry of Finance 1974–76; Ministry of the Budget 1976–78; Research Sec., parl. group of Social Democratic Party (SDP) 1978–82; Under-Sec. of State, Ministry of Finance 1982–90; Deputy Minister for Fiscal and Financial Affairs, Ministry of Finance 1990–91, Minister of Finance 1996–99; Man. Dir Vasakronan AB 1993–96; mem. of Parl. 1998–99; Chair. Comm. on Business Confidence (govt comm.); Chair. Lantbrukskredit AB 1983–85, State Housing Finance Corpn 1984–85, Governing Bd Sveriges Riksbank 1985–90, Sparbanken Första 1992, Confortia AB 1993, Swedish Bond Promotion 1993, Bd of Forsakringsbolaget SPP 2000, Budo and Martial Arts Fed. 2000–05; Chair. Exec. Bd Stockholm School; Vice-Chair. Systembolaget AB 1986–90; Dir Gen. Building Soc. 1991; Int. Adviser, Goldman Sachs 2011–; mem. Bd Nat. Pension Insurance Fund 1982–90, AB Vin & Sprit AB (Swedish Wine and Spirits Corpn) 1986–90, 1993–, AB Trav & Galopp 1989–90, Sparbanken Sverige AB 1991–93, ABB Investment Man. 1993–, SkandiaBanken 1994–, Swedish Concert Hall Foundation 1995–, SNS, Centre for Business and Policy Studies 1995–; mem. Fiscal Policy Council. *Address:* c/o Goldman Sachs & Co., 200 West Street, New York, NY 10282, USA (office).

ASCHBACHER, Michael George, BS, PhD; American mathematician and academic; *Shaler Arthur Hanisch Professor of Mathematics, California Institute of Technology;* b. 8 April 1944, Little Rock, Ark.; ed California Inst. of Tech., Univ. of Wisconsin; joined faculty of California Inst. of Tech. 1970, Full Prof. 1976–, currently Shaler Arthur Hanisch Prof. of Math.; Fellow, American Acad. of Arts and Sciences 1992; mem. Inst. for Advanced Study, Princeton 1978–79; Cole Prize in Algebra, American Math. Soc. 1980, Royal Swedish Acad. of Sciences Rolf Schock Prize 2011, AMS Leroy P. Steele Prize for Mathematical Exposition 2012, Wolf Prize in Math. (shared with Luis Caffarelli) 2012. *Publications:* Finite Group Theory, Sporadic Groups, 3-Transposition Groups, The Finite Simple Groups and Their Classification, Overgroups of Sylow Subgroups in Sporadic Groups, The Classification of Quasithin Groups. I Structure of Strongly Quasithin K-groups, Mathematical Surveys and Monographs 111 (with Stephen D. Smith) 2004, The Classification of Quasithin Groups. II Main Theorems: The Classification of Simple QTKE-groups, Mathematical Surveys and Monographs 112 (with Stephen D. Smith) 2004; numerous papers in professional journals on finite groups, algebraic groups and combinatorics. *Address:* California Institute of Technology, Mathematics 253-37, Pasadena, CA 91125, USA (office). *Telephone:* (626) 395-4364 (office). *Fax:* (626) 585-1728 (office). *E-mail:* asch@caltech.edu (office). *Website:* www.math.caltech.edu/people/asch.html (office).

ASFARI, Ayman; Syrian (b. Syrian) business executive; *Group CEO, Petrofac Ltd;* b. 8 Aug. 1958; m.; four s.; ed Aleppo Coll., Syria; began career as construction site engineer in Oman, later becoming Man. Dir of civil and mechanical construction co.; acquired Petrofac 2001, est. Petrofac Int., becoming CEO –2002, Group CEO Petrofac Ltd 2002–; mem. Bd of Trustees, American Univ. of Beirut; Ernst & Young UK Entrepreneur of the Year 2010. *Leisure interests:* golf, skiing. *Address:* Petrofac International, 4th Floor, 117 Jermyn Street, London, SW1Y 6HH, England (office). *Telephone:* (20) 7811-4900 (office). *Fax:* (20) 7811-4901 (office). *Website:* www.petrofac.com (office).

ASGHAR, Muhammad, LLB, DPhil (Oxon.); French (b. Pakistani) physicist and academic; *Professor, Laboratoire de Physique Subatomique et de Cosmologie;* b. 7 June 1936, Pakistan; s. of Muhammad Fazal and Bibi Fazal; m.; one c.; ed Univ. of Punjab, Univ. of Oxford, UK; with Pakistan Inst. of Tech., Nilore, also worked at atomic energy research stations at Harwell, UK and Saclay, France; Assoc. Prof., Univ. of Bordeaux 1968–71; physicist, Inst. Laue-Langevin (ILL), Grenoble 1971–78, CCR Euratom, Ispra 1978–80, Centre d'Etudes Nucléaires, Grenoble 1980–81; Prof. of Physics, Houari Boumedienne Univ., Algiers 1981–94, Laboratoire de Physique Subatomique et de Cosmologie, Grenoble 1994–; field of research: low-energy nuclear physics and fundamental physics, specialist in nuclear fission and nuclear energy, has coordinated int. teams in major experiments at high flux nuclear reactor, ILL, Grenoble; Fellow, Islamic Acad. of Sciences 1998. *Publications include:* more than 200 research papers. *Leisure interest:* writing poetry in English, French and Persian. *Address:* Laboratoire de Physique Subatomique et de Cosmologie, 53 avenue des Martyrs, 38026 Grenoble (office); 12 rue des Aberlles, 38240 Meylan, France (home). *Telephone:* (4) 76-28-40-00 (office); (4) 76-18-00-22 (home). *Fax:* (4) 76-28-40-04 (office). *E-mail:* masgharfr@yahoo.fr (office).

ÁSGRÍMSSON, Halldór; Icelandic politician; *Secretary General, Nordic Council of Ministers;* b. 8 Sept. 1947, Vopnafjördur; s. of Ásgrímur Halldórsson and Gudrún Ingólfsdóttir; m. Sigurjóna Sigurdardóttir; three d.; ed Co-operative's Commercial Coll. and commerce univs in Bergen and Copenhagen; Certified Public Accountant 1970; Lecturer in Auditing and Accounting, Univ. of Iceland 1973–75; mem. Parl. 1974–78, 1979–; mem. Bd Cen. Bank of Iceland 1976–83, Chair. 1981–83; mem. Nordic Council 1977–78, 1979–83, 1991–95, Chair. 1982–83, Chair. Icelandic Del. 1982–83, mem. Presidium 1991–94, Chair. Liberal Group 1992–94; Minister of Fisheries 1983–91, of Nordic Co-operation 1985–87, 1995, of Justice and Ecclesiastical Affairs 1988–89, of Foreign Affairs and External Trade 1995–2004; Prime Minister and Minister of the Statistical Bureau of Iceland 2004–06 (resgnd); Vice-Chair. Framsóknarflokkurinn (Progressive Party) 1980–94, Chair. 1994–2006; Vice-Pres. Liberal Int. 1994–99; Sec.-Gen. Nordic Council of Ministers 2007–; Kt of Order of Falcon of Iceland. *Address:* Nordic Council of Ministers, Store Strandstraede 18, 1255 Copenhagen K, Denmark (office). *Telephone:* 33-96-03-22 (office). *E-mail:* ha@norden.org (office). *Website:* www.norden.org (office).

ASH, Sir Eric Albert, Kt, CBE, PhD, FRS, FCGI, FIEE, FIEEE, FInstP, FREng; British professor of physical electronics; *Consultant, TCE Ltd;* b. 31 Jan. 1928, Berlin, Germany; s. of Walter Ash and Dorothea Ash (née Schwarz); m. Clare Babb 1954; five d.; ed Univ. Coll. School and Imperial Coll., London; Research Fellow, Stanford Univ. 1952–54; Research Asst, Queen Mary Coll., London 1954–55; Research Engineer, Standard Telecommunications Labs Ltd 1955–63; Sr Lecturer, Univ. Coll. London 1963–65, Reader 1965–67, Prof. of Electrical Eng 1967–80, Pender Prof. and Head, Dept of Electronic and Electrical Eng 1980–85, Prof. of Electrical Eng 1993–97, Prof. Emer. 1997–; Rector, Imperial Coll. London 1985–93; Dir (non-exec.) British Telecom 1987–93, Student Loans Co. PLC 1994–; Consultant, TCE Ltd; Chair. BBC Science Advisory Cttee 1987–; Chair. of Council, Vice-Pres. Royal Inst. 1995– (fmr Sec., Man.); Treasurer, Royal Soc. 1997–2002;

Trustee, Science Museum 1987–93, Wolfson Foundation 1988–; Foreign mem. Nat. Acad. of Eng, Russian Acad. of Sciences; Chevalier, Ordre nat. du Mérite 1990; hon. degrees from Univs of Aston, Leicester, Edinburgh, New York Polytechnic, INPG Grenoble, Westminster, Sussex, Glasgow and Surrey and Chinese Univ. of Hong Kong; Faraday Medal of the IEE 1980, Royal Medal of the Royal Soc. 1986. *Publications:* papers on topics of physical electronics in various engineering and physics journals. *Leisure interests:* music, writing. *Address:* 11 Ripplevale Grove, London, N1 1HS, England. *Telephone:* (20) 7607-4989. *Fax:* (20) 7700-7446. *E-mail:* eric_ash99@yahoo.co.uk.

ASHANTI; American hip-hop and R&B singer, songwriter and actress; b. (Ashanti Douglas), 13 Oct. 1980, Glen Cove, New York; d. of Ken-Kaide Thomas Douglas and Tina Douglas; signed record deal when 14 years old; guest vocalist with artists, including Big Punisher, Ja Rule, J. Lo, Big Pun, Fat Joe, Notorious B.I.G.; solo artist 2002–; Music of Black Origin (MOBO) Award for Best R&B Act 2002, American Music Awards for Best New Pop/Rock Artist, Best New Hip Hop/R&B Artist 2003, Nat. Asscn for the Advancement of Colored People (NAACP) Image Award, Comet Award, Teen Choice Award, Nickelodeon's Kid Choice Award. *Television appearances:* Polly (musical film), American Dreams (one episode) 2002, Buffy the Vampire Slayer (one episode) 2003, The Muppets' Wizard of Oz (TV film) 2005. *Film appearances:* Bride & Prejudice 2004, Coach Carter 2005, John Tucker Must Die 2006, Resident Evil: Extinction 2007. *Recordings include:* albums: Ashanti 2002 (Grammy Award for Best Contemporary R&B Album 2003), Foolish/Unfoolish: Reflections on Love 2002, Chapter II 2003, Ashanti's Christmas 2003, Concrete Rose 2004, The Declaration 2008. *Website:* www.ashantimusic.net.

ASHBERY, John Lawrence, MA; American poet, author, critic and academic; *Charles P. Stevenson, Jr Professor of Languages and Literature, Bard College;* b. 28 July 1927, Rochester, NY; s. of Chester F. Ashbery and Helen L. Ashbery; ed Deerfield Acad., Mass, Harvard, Columbia and New York Univs; asst, Literature Dept, Brooklyn (NY) Public Library 1949; copywriter, Oxford Univ. Press, New York 1951–54, McGraw-Hill Book Co. 1954–55; went to France as a Fulbright Scholar 1955–56, 1956–57, lived there 1958–65; Art Critic, Int. edn New York Herald-Tribune, Paris 1960–65; Co-Ed. Locus Solus, Lans-en-Vercors, France 1960–62, Art and Literature, Paris 1964–67; Art Critic, Art International, Lugano 1961–63, New York Magazine 1978–80, Newsweek 1980–85; Paris corresp. Art News, Paris New York 1964–65, Exec. Ed. 1965–72; Prof. of English and Co-Dir MFA Program in Creative Writing, Brooklyn Coll., NY (CUNY) 1974–90, Distinguished Prof. 1980–90, Distinguished Prof. Emer. 1990–; Poetry Ed. Partisan Review, New York 1976–80; Charles Eliot Norton Prof. of Poetry, Harvard Univ. 1989–90; Charles P. Stevenson, Jr Prof. of Languages and Literature, Bard Coll., Annandale-on-Hudson, NY 1990–; Chancellor Acad. of American Poets 1988–99; Leader, Fondation d'Art de La Napoule 1989; Poet Laureate, New York State 2001–03, MtvU (to promote poetry in US universities) 2007–; mem. American Acad. of Arts and Letters 1980–, American Acad. of Arts and Sciences 1983–; works translated into more than 20 languages; Chevalier des Arts et Lettres 1993, Officier, Légion d'honneur 2002; Hon. DLitt (Southampton Coll. of Long Island Univ.) 1979, (Univ. of Rochester, NY) 1994, (Harvard Univ.) 2001; recipient of numerous awards, grants and honours, including two Guggenheim Fellowships 1967, 1973, MacArthur Fellow 1985–90, Horst Bienek Prize for Poetry (Bavarian Acad. of Fine Arts) 1991, Ruth Lilly Prize for Poetry 1992, Antonio Fraternelli Int. Prize for Poetry (Accad. Nazionale dei Lincei, Rome) 1992, Robert Frost Medal (Poetry Soc. of America) 1995, Grand Prix de Biennales Internationales de Poésie (Brussels) 1996, Gold Medal for Poetry (American Acad. of Arts and Letters) 1997, Bingham Poetry Prize 1998, Walt Whitman Citation of Merit (State of New York and New York State Writers' Inst.) 2000, Signet Soc. Medal for Achievement in the Arts 2001, Wallace Stevens Award (Acad. of American Poets) 2001. *Plays:* The Heroes 1952, The Compromise 1956, The Philosopher 1963, Three Plays 1978. *Publications include:* poetry: Turandot and Other Poems 1953, Some Trees 1956, The Tennis Court Oath 1962, Rivers and Mountains 1966, The Double Dream of Spring 1970, Three Poems 1972, The Vermont Notebook 1975, Self-Portrait in a Convex Mirror (Pulitzer Prize 1975, Nat. Book Award 1975, Nat. Book Critics' Circle Award 1975) 1975, Houseboat Days 1979, As We Know 1979, Shadow Train 1981, A Wave 1984, Selected Poems 1985, April Galleons 1987, Flow Chart 1991, Hotel Lautréamont 1992, And the Stars Were Shining 1994, Can You Hear, Bird 1995, Wakefulness 1998, Girls on the Run 1999, Your Name Here 2000, As Umbrellas Follow Rain 2001, Chinese Whispers 2002, Where Shall I Wander 2005, Notes from the Air: Selected Later Poems (Griffin Prize for Poetry 2008) 2007, Planisphere 2009, Quick Question 2012; novel: A Nest of Ninnies (with J. Schuyler) 1969; essays and criticism: Fairfield Porter 1983, R. B. Kitaj (with others) 1983, Reported Sightings: Art Chronicles 1957–1987 1989, Other Traditions (The Charles Eliot Norton Lectures at Harvard) 2000; numerous translations from French including works by Raymond Roussel, Max Jacob, Alfred Jarry, Antonin Artaud and Pierre Martory, including Every Question but One 1990, The Landscape is behind the Door 1994. *Address:* c/o George Borchardt Inc., 136 East 57th Street, New York, NY 10022-2707; Bard College, Department of Languages and Literature, PO Box 5000, Annandale-on-Hudson, NY 12504-5000, USA (office). *Telephone:* (845) 758-7290 (office). *Website:* www.bard.edu/academics/programs/langlit (office).

ASHBURTON, 7th Baron, cr. 1835; **John Francis Harcourt Baring,** Kt, KG, KCVO, MA, DL, FIB; British merchant banker; b. 2 Nov. 1928, London, England; s. of 6th Baron Ashburton and Hon. Doris Mary Therese Harcourt; m. 1st Susan Mary Renwick 1955 (divorced 1984); two s. two d.; m. 2nd Sarah Crewe 1987; ed Eton Coll. and Trinity Coll., Oxford; Chair. Barings PLC 1985–89 (Dir (non-exec.) 1989–94), Baring Bros & Co. Ltd 1974–89 (a Man. Dir 1955–74); Dir Trafford Park Estates Ltd 1964–77; Royal Insurance Co. Ltd 1964–82 (Deputy Chair. 1975–82); Dir Outwich Investment Trust Ltd 1965–86 (Chair. 1968–86), British Petroleum Co. 1982–95 (Chair. 1992–95), Dunlop Holdings 1981–84, Bank of England 1983–91, Baring Stratton Investment Trust PLC 1986–98 (Chair. 1986–98), Jaguar PLC 1989–91; mem. British Transport Docks Bd 1966–71; Vice-Pres. British Bankers Asscn 1977–81; mem. Pres.'s Cttee CBI 1976–79, Gen. Council CBI 1976–80; Chair. Accepting Houses Cttee 1977–81, NEDC Cttee on Finance for Industry 1980–87; Pres. Overseas Bankers Club 1977–78; Rhodes Trustee 1970–79, Chair. 1987–98; Trustee, Nat. Gallery 1981–87; Trustee and Hon. Treas. Police Foundation 1989–2001; mem. Exec. Cttee Nat. Art Collections Fund 1989–99; mem. Council Baring Foundation 1971–98, Chair. 1987–98; mem.

Southampton Univ. Devt Trust 1986–96 (Chair. 1989–96); mem. Winchester Cathedral Trust 1989– (Chair. 1993–2006); Lord Warden of the Stannaries, Duchy of Cornwall 1990–94, Receiver-Gen. 1974–90; High Steward Winchester Cathedral 1991–; DL Hants. 1994–; Fellow, Eton Coll. 1982–97; Hon. Fellow, Hertford Coll., Oxford 1976, Trinity Coll., Oxford 1989; Dr hc (Southampton) 2007. *Address:* Lake House, Northington, Alresford, Hants., SO24 9TG, England (office). *Telephone:* (1962) 738728 (office). *E-mail:* johnashburton@btconnect.com (office).

ASHBY, Michael Farries, CBE, PhD, FRS, FREng; British professor of engineering materials; *Royal Society Research Professor and Principal Investigator, Engineering Design Centre, University of Cambridge;* b. 20 Nov. 1935; s. of Lord Ashby and Elizabeth Helen Farries; m. Maureen Stewart 1962; two s. one d.; ed Campbell Coll., Belfast, Queens' Coll., Cambridge; Asst, Univ. of Göttingen, FRG 1962–65; Asst Prof., Harvard Univ., USA 1965–69, Prof. of Metallurgy 1969–73; Prof. of Eng Materials, Univ. of Cambridge 1973–89, Royal Soc. Research Prof., Dept of Eng 1989–; currently Royal Acad. Visiting Prof., RCA, London; Ed. Acta Metallurgica 1974–96, Progress in Materials Science 1995–; mem. Akad. der Wissenschaften zu Göttingen 1985–, American Acad. of Arts and Sciences 1993–; Foreign mem. US Nat. Acad. of Eng 1990; Fellow Royal Swedish Acad. of Eng Sciences 1985–, Inst. of Metals, UK 1991; Hon. Life mem. Soc. Francaise de Materiaux 1990, Materials Research Soc. of India 1990, Materials Research Soc. of the USA 1990; Hon. MA (Harvard) 1969; Dr hc (Leuven) 1990, (Royal Inst. of Tech., Stockholm) 1995, (Tech. Univ. of Lisbon) 1996; L.B. Pfeil Medal, Metals Soc. 1975, Rosenheim Medal, Metals Soc. 1979, Mehl Medal, American Soc. for Metals 1983, Amourers and Brasiers Medal, Royal Soc. 1985, A.A. Griffiths Medal, Metals Soc. 1985, Acta Metallurgica Gold Medal 1986, Hume-Rothery Award, American Soc. for Metals 1988, Paul Bergsoe Medal, Danish Metallurgical Soc. 1989, Materials Medal, Soc. Francaise de Materiaux 1990, Hatfield Memorial Lecturer, Royal Soc. of Great Britain 1992, Von Hippel Award, Materials Research Soc. of the USA 1992, Gold Medal, Fed. of European Materials Socs 1993, Luigi Losana Medal, Associazione Italiana di Metallurgia 1993, Campbell Lecturer, American Soc. for Metals 1994, The Körber Prize 1996, Platinum Medal, Inst. of Materials, London 1998, Hirsch Lecturer, Univ. of Oxford 1998, A. Cemal Eringen Medal, SES, USA 1999. *Publications:* Deformation Mechanism Maps 1982, Engineering Materials (Vol. 1) 1989, (Vol. 2) 1996, Cellular Solids 1997, Materials Selection in Design (2nd edn) 1999, Materials and Design – The Art and Science of Product Design 2002, Materials and the Environment 2009. *Leisure interests:* music, design, watercolour painting. *Address:* University of Cambridge, Department of Engineering, Trumpington Street, Cambridge, CB2 1PZ (office); 51 Maids Causeway, Cambridge, CB5 8DE, England (home). *Telephone:* (1223) 303015 (home); (1223) 332635 (home). *Fax:* (1223) 332662 (home). *E-mail:* mfa2@eng.cam.ac.uk (office). *Website:* www-edc.eng.cam.ac.uk (office).

ASHCROFT, Andrew (Andy) Richard; British business executive, consultant and fmr diplomatist; b. 28 May 1961, Almondsbury, Glos.; s. of Ivor John Ashcroft and Amy Joan Ashcroft (née Hiscock); m. Anna Danielewicz; one step-d.; ed Millfield School, Somerset; joined Diplomatic Service, overseas assignments included Commercial Sec., Embassy in Muscat, Oman, various positions at Embassy in Tel-Aviv, Pvt. Sec. to Minister of Foreign Affairs 1992–96, First Sec., High Comm. in Harare 1996–99, Head of Caribbean Section, FCO 1999–2002, Amb. to Dominican Repub. and Haiti 2002–06; currently Man. Dir Ambassador Communications (consultancy); Bd mem. New Forest Business Partnership; currently Jt Pnr, Koolskools Ethical School Clothing; Jt Pnr, FAIR4DR (consultancy); fmr mem. Nat. Youth Brass Band. *Leisure interests:* music (piano/singing), golf. *Address:* Ambassador Communications, 103 The Meadows, Lyndhurst, Hants., SO43 7EJ, England (office). *Telephone:* (23) 8028-3223 (office); 7757-978898 (mobile). *E-mail:* arashcroft@btinternet.com (office); andy@koolskools.co.uk (office); andy@ambassadorcommunications.co.uk (office). *Website:* www.ambassadorcommunications.co.uk (office); www.koolskools.co.uk (office).

ASHCROFT, Frances Mary, BA, PhD, ScD, FRS, FMedSci; British physiologist and academic; *Royal Society GlaxoSmithKline Research Professor of Physiology, University of Oxford;* b. 15 Feb. 1952; d. of John Ashcroft and Kathleen Ashcroft; ed Talbot Heath School, Bournemouth, Girton Coll., Cambridge; MRC Training Fellow in Physiology, Univ. of Leicester 1978–82; Demonstrator in Physiology, Univ. of Oxford 1982–85, EPA Cephalosporin Jr Research Fellow, Linacre Coll. 1983–85, Royal Soc. Univ. Research Fellow in Physiology 1985–90, Lecturer in Physiology, Christ Church 1986–87, Trinity Coll. 1988–89 (Sr Research Fellow 1992–); Tutorial Fellow in Medicine, St Hilda's Coll. 1990–91, Univ. Lecturer in Physiology 1990–96, Prof. of Physiology 1996–2001, Royal Soc. GlaxoSmithKline Research Prof. 2001–, Dir, Oxford Centre for Gene Function; mem. European Molecular Biology Org.; Dr hc (Open Univ.) 2003, (Univ. of Leicester) 2007; Frank Smart Prize, Univ. of Cambridge 1974, Andrew Culworth Memorial Prize 1990, G.B. Morgagni Young Investigator Award 1991, G.L. Brown Prize Lecturer, Yale Univ. 1997, Peter Curran Lecturer 1999, Charter Award, Inst. of Biology 2004, Walter B. Cannon Award, American Physiological Soc. 2007, L'Oréal-UNESCO For Women in Science Award (Europe) for her discovery of an ATP-sensitive potassium channel linking glucose metabolism and insulin secretion and its role in neonatal diabetes 2012, Croonian Lecturer, The Royal Soc. 2012. *Television:* appeared (as a diner) on Masterchef, along with several other Fellows of the Royal Soc. 2011. *Publications include:* Insulin-Molecular Biology to Pathology (co-author) 1992, Ion Channels and Disease 2000, Life at the Extremes: The Science of Survival 2000, and numerous articles in scientific journals. *Leisure interests:* reading, walking, writing, sailing. *Address:* Department of Physiology, Anatomy and Genetics, Sherrington Building, Parks Road, Oxford, OX1 3PT, England (office). *Telephone:* (1865) 285810 (office). *Fax:* (1865) 285812 (office). *E-mail:* frances.ashcroft@dpag.ox.ac.uk (office). *Website:* www.dpag.ox.ac.uk/team/a-g/frances-ashcroft (office); oxion.dpag.ox.ac.uk (office).

ASHCROFT, John David, JD; American lobbyist and fmr politician; *Chairman, Ashcroft Group LLC;* b. 9 May 1942, Chicago; m. Janet Else; two s. one d.; ed Yale Univ. and Univ. of Chicago; admitted, Missouri State Bar, Supreme Court Bar; Instructor of Business Law SW Missouri State Univ. 1967–72; legal practice, Springfield, Mo. until 1973; State Auditor, Missouri 1973–75, Asst Attorney-Gen. 1975–77, Attorney-Gen. 1976–85; Gov. of Missouri 1985–93; Senator from Missouri 1995–2001; Attorney Gen. 2001–04 (resgnd); f. Ashcroft Group, LLC (lobbying firm) 2005; Distinguished Prof. of Law and Govt, Pat Robertson's Regent Univ.; apptd mem. of Faculty, Regent Univ. 2006; Chair. Republican Gov.'s Asscn 1989–90, Nat. Asscn of Attorneys Gen. 1991, Nat. Gov.'s Asscn 1991–92; Chair. Advisory Cttee, Order; Chair. Bd of Advisers, Innova Holdings; mem. Federalist Soc.; mem. Advisory Bd, Russian-American Christian Univ., Ceelox, Dulles Research LLC, D2C Solutions; recordings as gospel singer. *Publications:* College Law for Business (with Janet Elise), It's the Law 1979, Never Again 2006. *Address:* The Ashcroft Group, LLC, 1399 New York Avenue, NW, Suite 950, Washington, DC 20005, USA (office). *Telephone:* (202) 942-0202 (office). *Fax:* (202) 942-0216 (office). *E-mail:* info@ashcroftgroupllc.com (office). *Website:* www.ashcroftgroupllc.com (office).

ASHCROFT, Baron (Life Peer), cr. 2000, of Chichester in the County of West Sussex; **Michael Anthony Ashcroft,** Kt, KCMG, PC; Belizean/British business executive and diplomatist; b. 4 March 1946; s. of Frederic Parker Ashcroft and Mary Lavinia Long; m. 1st Wendy Mahoney 1972 (divorced 1984); two s. one d.; m. 2nd Susi Anstey 1986; ed King Edward VI Grammar School, Norwich, Royal Grammar School, High Wycombe, Mid-Essex Tech. Coll., Chelmsford; varied business interests in public and private cos in UK, USA and the Caribbean; Chair. BB Holdings, later BCB Holdings 1987–2010; fmr Chair. Hawley Group, ADT Ltd; Dir, Tyco International 1984–2002; Amb. from Belize to the UN 1998–2000; Party Treas., Conservative Party 1998–2001, a Deputy Chair. Conservative and Unionist Party 2005–10; Treas. Int. Democratic Union 2007–; Sr Ind. Advisor on Sovereign Base Areas, Cyprus 2011; Founder and Chair. Crimestoppers Trust 1988–; Chair. Ashcroft Tech. Acad. (fmrly ADT Coll.) 1991–; Chancellor, Anglia Ruskin Univ. 2001–; Pres. and Trustee, West India Cttee 2011–; Trustee, Cleveland Clinic 2004–, Imperial War Museum Foundation 2010, Imperial War Museum; Vice-Patron Intelligence Corps Museum 2009–; apptd UK Govt Special Rep. for Veterans' Transition, working with all depts to ensure mil. personnel receive the support they need when making the transition to civilian life 2012. *Publications include:* Smell the Coffee: A Wake Up Call to the Conservative Party 2005, Dirty Politics, Dirty Times 2005, Victoria Cross Heroes 2006, Special Forces Heroes 2008, George Cross Heroes 2010, Minority Verdict: The Conservative Party, the Voters and the 2010 Election 2010, Heroes of the Skies 2012. *Leisure interests:* researching the Victoria Cross, entertaining friends, trying something new, messing about in boats. *Address:* House of Lords, Westminster, London, SW1A 0PW, England (office). *Telephone:* (20) 7219-3000 (office). *Website:* www.lordashcroft.com.

ASHDOWN OF NORTON SUB-HAMDON, Baron (Life Peer), cr. 2001, of Norton Sub-Hamdon in the County of Somerset; **Jeremy John Durham (Paddy) Ashdown,** GCMG, KBE, PC; British politician; b. 27 Feb. 1941, Delhi, India; s. of John W. R. D. Ashdown and Lois A. Ashdown; m. Jane Courtenay 1961; one s. one d.; ed Bedford School; served in Royal Marines 1959–71, rank of Capt.; joined Diplomatic Service, First Sec. Mission to UN, Geneva 1971–76; Commercial Man.'s Dept, Westland Group 1976–78; Sr Man., Morlands Ltd 1978–81; employee, Dorset Co. Council 1982–83; Parl. Spokesman for Trade and Industry 1983–86; Liberal/SDP Alliance Spokesman on Education and Science 1987; Liberal MP for Yeovil 1983–88, Liberal Democrat MP for Yeovil 1988–2001; Leader Liberal Democrats 1988–99; UN Int. High Rep. to Bosnia and Herzegovina 2002–06. *Publications:* Citizen's Britain: A Radical Agenda for the 1990s 1989, Beyond Westminster 1994, The Ashdown Diaries 1988–1997 2000, The Ashdown Diaries Vol. II 1997–1999 2001, Swords and Ploughshares 2007, A Fortunate Life 2009. *Leisure interests:* walking, gardening, wine making. *Address:* House of Lords, Westminster, London, SW1A 0PW, England (office). *Telephone:* (20) 7219-3000 (office). *Fax:* (20) 7219-5979 (office).

ASHER, Jane; British actress, food industry executive and writer; b. 5 April 1946, London, England; d. of the late Richard A. J. Asher and of Margaret Eliot; m. Gerald Scarfe (q.v.); two s. one d.; ed North Bridge House, Miss Lambert's Parents' Nat. Educational Union; has appeared in numerous films, on TV and the London stage and has written several best-selling books; Proprietor Jane Asher Party Cakes Shop and Sugarcraft 1990–; designer, consultant for Sainsbury's cakes 1992–99; Pres. Nat. Autistic Soc., Arthritis Care, Parkinson's UK; spokesperson and consultant to Heinz Frozen Desserts 1999–2001; Cookware and Gift Food Designer for Debenhams 1998–2005; creator of Home Baking Mixes for Victoria Foods 1999–; Hon. LLD. *Plays include:* Henceforward…, School for Scandal 1990, Making It Better 1992, The Shallow End 1997, Things We Do for Love 1998, House and Garden 2000, What the Butler Saw 2001, Festen 2004, The World's Biggest Diamond 2005, Bedroom Farce 2009, Reluctant Debutant 2011, The Importance of Being Earnest 2011, Farewell to the Theatre 2011. *Films include:* Greengage Summer, Masque of the Red Death, Alfie 1966, Deep End, Henry the Eighth and his Six Wives 1970, Success is the Best Revenge, Dreamchild, Paris By Night 1988, Tirante el Blanco 2006, Death at a Funeral 2007. *Television includes:* Closing Numbers 1994, The Choir 1995, Good Living 1997, Crossroads 2003, Miss Marple 2004, New Tricks 2005, Holby City 2007, The Old Guys 2009, 2010, Waterloo Road 2011, Dancing on the Edge 2012. *Publications include:* The Moppy Stories 1987, Keep Your Baby Safe 1988, Calendar of Cakes 1989, Eats for Treats 1990, Time to Play 1993, Jane Asher's Book of Cake Decorating Ideas 1993; novels: The Longing 1996, The Question 1998, Losing It 2002, Cakes for Fun 2005, Beautiful Baking 2007. *Leisure interests:* reading, Times crossword. *Address:* c/o United Agents, 12–26 Lexington Street, London, W1F 0LE, England (office); 24 Cale Street, London, SW3 3QU, England. *Telephone:* (20) 3214-0800 (office). *Fax:* (20) 3214-0801 (office). *E-mail:* info@unitedagents.co.uk (office). *Website:* www.unitedagents.co.uk (office).

ASHFIELD, The Hon. Keith, PC; Canadian business executive and politician; b. 28 March 1952, Fredericton; s. the late Jack Ashfield and of Nora Locke; m. Judy Ashfield; two c.; ed Univ. of New Brunswick; mem. New Brunswick Legis. Ass. 1996–2008, Deputy Speaker 1999–2003, Provincial Minister of Natural Resources 2003–06; MP for Fredericton 2008–; Minister of State (Atlantic Canada Opportunities Agency) 2008–10, Minister of Nat. Revenue, Minister of the Atlantic Canada Opportunities Agency and Minister for the Atlantic Gateway 2010–11, Minister of Fisheries 2011–13; mem. Conservative Party of Canada. *Address:* Conservative Party of Canada, 130 Albert Street, Suite 1204, Ottawa, ON K1P 5G4 Canada (office). *Telephone:* (613) 755-2000 (office). *Fax:* (613) 755-2001 (office). *Website:* www.conservative.ca (office).

ASHIDA, Akimitsu; Japanese business executive; *Chairman Executive Officer, Mitsui OSK Lines;* joined Mitsui OSK Lines Ltd 1967, positions held include Dir 1st Regular Line, Dir of Planning, Man. Dir, Sr Man. Dir, Sr Man. Exec. Officer, Vice-Pres., Exec. Vice-Pres., Pres. and Dir, Rep. Dir and Exec. Pres. 2005–10, Chair. Exec. Officer 2010–. *Address:* Mitsui OSK Lines Ltd, 1-1 Toranomon, 2-chome, Tokyo 105-8688, Japan (office). *Telephone:* (3) 3587-6224 (office). *Fax:* (3) 3587-7734 (office). *E-mail:* info@mol.co.jp (office). *Website:* www.mol.co.jp (office).

ASHIDA, Jun; Japanese fashion designer; *Chairman, Jun Ashida Company Ltd;* b. 21 Aug. 1930; s. of Sadao Ashida and Ritsuko Ashida; m. Tomoko Tomita 1960; two d.; ed Tokyo High School; studied under Jun-ichi Nakahara 1948–52; consultant designer to Takashimaya Dept Store 1960; est. Jun Ashida Co. Ltd and Jun Ashida label 1963, Pres. 1963–13, Chair. 2014–; exclusive designer to HIH Crown Princess (now Empress) Michiko 1966–76, designs for several mems of Imperial family; presented first collection in Paris 1977; launched Miss Ashida and Jun Ashida for Men labels 1985–86; opened shop Jun Ashida in Paris 1989; designed uniforms for Japanese Pavilion, Expo World Fair, Seville 1992, All Nippon Airways, Fuji Xerox, Imperial Hotel, Nomura Securities, Idemitsu Kosan, Tokyo Kaijo, Japanese team at Olympic Games, Atlanta 1996; mem. Postal Service Council of Ministry of Posts and Telecommunications; Japanese Hans Christian Andersen Goodwill Amb. 2005; Purple Ribbon Medal 1991, Officier, Ordre nat. du Mérite 2000, Officer, Order of Merit (Italy) 2002, Order of the Rising Sun, Gold Rays with Neck Ribbon 2006, Officier, Ordre nat. du Mérite (Luxembourg) 2006, Officier, Ordre des Arts et des Lettres 2010; FEC Award (Japan) 1971. *Publications include:* Young Man (essays) 1986, Jun Ashida, 30 Years of Design 1993, Patches of Unshaven Beard 1998, A Time for Reflection 2010, The Road Less Taken 2011; articles on fashion and lifestyle in daily newspapers. *Leisure interests:* tennis, golf. *Address:* 1-3-3 Aobadai, Meguro-ku, Tokyo 153-8521, Japan (office). *Telephone:* (3) 3463-8631 (office). *Fax:* (3) 3463-9638 (office). *E-mail:* secretary@jun-ashida.co.jp (office). *Website:* www.jun-ashida.co.jp (office).

ASHIRU, Olugbenga Ayodeji, BA; Nigerian diplomatist; b. 27 Aug. 1948, Ijebu-Ode, Ogun State; s. of Simeon Adeyemi Ashiru and Janet Solabomi Ashiru; m. Omokehinde Dina 1976; four s.; ed Univ. of Lagos; joined diplomatic service as Third Sec., Ministry of Foreign Affairs (MFA) 1972, Asst Sec., Africa Dept 1972–74, First Sec., Embassy in Tokyo 1974–77, Counsellor (Capital Projects) MFA 1977–79, Sr Counsellor, Embassy in Stockholm 1979–82, Sr Counsellor and Acting Head of American Affairs Dept, MFA 1982–84, Chargé d'Affaires to Cen. African Repub. 1984–85, Minister Plenipotentiary, High Comm. in London 1985–88, Deputy Dir European Affairs Dept, MFA 1988–91, Amb. to North Korea 1991–99, Dir (Regions), MFA 1999–2005, High Commr to South Africa (also accred to Lesotho and Swaziland) 2005; Minister of Foreign Affairs 2011–13; Order of the Repub. (North Korea) 1997, Commdr, Ordre Nat. de Mérite 1999, Nat. Honour Award of the Federal Repub. of Nigeria. *Address:* c/o Ministry of Foreign Affairs, Sir Tafawa Balewa House, Federal Secretariat, PMB 130, Abuja, Nigerian (office).

ASHKENASI, Shmuel; American violinist; b. 11 Jan. 1940, Tel-Aviv, Israel; m. Mihaela Ionescu Ashkenasi; two s.; ed Musical Acad. of Tel-Aviv, Curtis Inst. of Music, Philadelphia; concert violinist since 1962; First Violinist, Vermeer String Quartet; Prof. of Music and Artist-in-Residence, Univ. of Northern Illinois 1969–2007; also taught at Roosevelt Univ., Chicago and Musikhochschcule Lübeck, Germany; mem. performance faculty, Curtis Inst. of Music 2007–; has collaborated with Rudolf Serkin, Thomas Hampson, Murray Perahia, Peter Serkin, Menahem Pressler; First Prize, Merriweather Post Contest, Washington, DC 1958, Finalist, Queen Elizabeth Competition, Brussels 1959, Second Prize, Tchaikovsky Competition, Moscow 1962. *Leisure interests:* tennis, chess. *Address:* Curtis Institute of Music, 1726 Locust Street, Philadelphia, PA 19103, USA (office). *Telephone:* (215) 893-5252 (office). *Fax:* (215) 893-9065 (office). *Website:* www.curtis.edu (office).

ASHKENAZY, Vladimir; Icelandic (b. Russian) pianist and conductor; *Principal Conductor and Artistic Adviser, Sydney Symphony Orchestra;* b. 6 July 1937, Gorky, USSR; s. of David Ashkenazy and Evstolia Ashkenazy (née Plotnova); m. Thorunn Sofia Johannsdóttir 1961; two s. three d.; ed Cen. Music School, Moscow and Moscow Conservatoire; Prin. Guest Conductor, Philharmonia 1982–83; Music Dir Royal Philharmonic Orchestra 1987–94, Deutsches Symphonie-Orchester Berlin (fmrly Berlin Radio Symphony) 1989–99; Chief Conductor Czech Philharmonic Orchestra 1998–2003; Music Dir EUYO (European Union Youth Orchestra) 2002–; Music Dir NHK Symphony, Tokyo 2004–07; apptd Artist Laureate, Royal Liverpool Philharmonic Orchestra during Liverpool's tenure as European City of Culture 2008; Principal Conductor and Artistic Adviser, Sydney Symphony Orchestra 2009–(14); Hon. RAM; Icelandic Order of the Falcon; Hon. DMus (Nottingham) 1995; Second Prize, Int. Chopin Competition, Warsaw 1955, Gold Medal, Queen Elizabeth Int. Piano Competition, Brussels 1956, Jt Winner (with John Ogdon) Int. Tchaikovsky Piano Competition, Moscow 1962, Grammy Award for Best Instrumental Soloist Performance (with orchestra) for Prokofiev's Piano Concertos Nos 2 and 3 2010. *Publication:* Beyond Frontiers (with Jasper Parrott) 1985. *Address:* Harrison Parrott, 5–6 Albion Court, London, W6 0QT, England (office). *Telephone:* (20) 7229-9166 (office). *Fax:* (20) 7221-5042 (office). *E-mail:* info@harrisonparrott.co.uk (office). *Website:* www.harrisonparrott.com (office).

ASHMAWY, Muhammad Saïd al-, BA; Egyptian lawyer, writer and academic; b. 1 Dec. 1932; ed Cairo Univ.; Asst of Dist Attorney, Alexandria 1954, Dist Attorney 1956; Judge 1961; Chief Prosecutor, Cairo 1973; Counsellor of State for Legislation 1977; Chief Justice High Criminal Court, Cairo 1985; mem. Faculty, Cairo Univ. School of Law. *Publications:* Roots of Islamic Law 1979, Political Islam 1987, Islamic Caliphate 1990, Religion for the Future 1992, Veil and Tradition in Islam 1995, The Conflict between Arabs and Israel 1997, Reason in Islam 1998, Book of Ethics 1999, Egyptian Roots of Judaism 2001, Clash of Nations 2002. *Leisure interests:* music, driving, tennis. *Address:* 9 Gezira al-Wosta Street, Zamalek, Cairo 11211, Egypt (home). *Telephone:* (2) 735-2060 (home). *Fax:* (2) 735-2060 (home). *E-mail:* ashmawy2@hotmail.com (home).

ASHRAF, Raja Pervaiz, BA; Pakistani politician; b. 26 Dec. 1950, Sanghar, Sindh; m.; two s. two d.; ed Univ. of Sindh; worked in agric. before entering politics; mem. Nat. Ass.; Fed. Minister for Water and Power 2008–11; Prime Minister 2012–13; Sr Leader Pakistan People's Party (PPP), fmr Sec.-Gen. *Address:* c/o Office of the Prime Minister's Secretariat, Cabinet Secretariat, Cabinet Division, Islamabad, Pakistan.

ASHRAFUL, Mohammad, (Ashraful Matin); Bangladeshi professional cricketer; b. 7 July 1984, Dhaka; right-handed batsman; right-arm offbreak and leg-break bowler; plays for Dhaka Metropolis 2000–01, Dhaka Div. 2001–, Bangladesh 2001– (Capt. 2007–09), Mohammedan Sporting Club 2008–, Mumbai Indians 2009, Asia XI; First-class debut: 2000/01; Test debut: Sri Lanka v Bangladesh, Colombo (SSC) 6–8 Sept. 2001; One-Day Int. (ODI) debut: Zimbabwe v Bangladesh, Bulawayo 11 April 2001; T20I debut: Kenya v Bangladesh, Nairobi (Gym) 1 Sept. 2007; youngest player to score a test century (144 runs against Sri Lanka) in an int. match aged 17, Sept. 2001. *Address:* c/o Bangladesh Cricket Board, Sher-e-Bangla National Cricket Stadium, Mirpur, Dhaka 1216, Bangladesh. *E-mail:* pd@tigercricket.com. *Website:* www.tigercricket.com.

ASHRAWI, Hanan Daoud Khalil, BA, MA, PhD; Palestinian politician, organization executive and academic; *Media Director and Spokesperson, League of Arab States;* b. 8 Oct. 1946, Ramallah (then part of British Mandate of Palestine); d. of Daoud Mikhail (a founder of Palestinian Liberation Org.—PLO) and Wadi'a Ass'ad; m. Emile Ashrawi; two d.; ed American Univ. of Beirut, Univ. of Virginia, USA; joined mainstream PLO Fatah faction; Prof. of English Literature, Birzeit Univ., West Bank 1973–90, mem. Faculty 1973–95, Chair. English Dept 1973–78, 1981–84, Dean of Faculty of Arts 1986–90; activist, Palestinian Women's Movt 1974–; f. Birzeit Univ. Legal Aid Cttee/Human Rights Action Project 1974; joined Intifada Political Cttee 1988, served on its Diplomatic Cttee 1988–93; official spokeswoman for Palestinian Del. to Middle East peace process 1991–93, mem. Leadership/Guidance Cttee and Exec. Cttee of del.; mem. Advisory Cttee Palestinian Del. at Madrid Peace Conf. on Middle East; mem. Palestinian Ind. Comm. for Palestinian Repub., Head 1993–95; Founder and Commr Gen. Palestinian Ind. Comm. for Citizens' Rights 1993–95; mem. Palestinian Legis. Council 1996– (re-elected on a nat. list, The Third Way 2006); Palestinian Authority Minister of Higher Educ. and Research 1996–98 (resgnd in protest against political corruption); f. MIFTAH (Palestinian Initiative for the Promotion of Global Dialogue and Democracy) 1998; currently Human Rights Commr (semi-official ombudsman) and mem. Palestinian Council; Media Dir and Spokesperson Arab League 2001–; mem. Exec. Cttee Palestine Liberation Org.; Trustee, Inst. for Palestine Studies; Dr hc (American Univ. of Beirut) 2008, (Earlham Coll., Smith Coll.); Olof Palme Prize 2002, Sydney Peace Prize 2003, ranked 96th by Forbes magazine amongst The 100 Most Powerful Women 2004. *Publications include:* numerous poems, short stories and papers and articles on Palestinian culture, literature and politics, including Anthology of Palestinian Literature (ed., The Modern Palestinian Short Story: An Introduction to Practical Criticism, Contemporary Palestinian Literature under Occupation, Contemporary Palestinian Poetry and Fiction, Literary Translation: Theory and Practice; A Passion for Peace 1994, This Side of Peace: A Personal Account (memoirs) 1995. *Address:* Arab League, PO Box 11642, Arab League Building, Tahrir Square, Cairo, Egypt (office). *Telephone:* (2) 5750511 (office). *Fax:* (2) 5775726 (office). *Website:* www .arableagueonline.org (office); www.miftah.org (office).

ASHTON OF UPHOLLAND, Baroness (Life Peer), cr. 1999, of St Albans in the County of Hertfordshire; **Catherine Margaret Ashton,** PC, BSc; British economist, politician and European Union official; *High Representative of the Union for Foreign Affairs and Security Policy and Vice-President of the European Commission, European Union;* b. 20 March 1956, Upholland, Lancs., England; d. of Harold Ashton and Clare Ashton; m. Peter Kellner 1988; one s. one d. three step-c.; ed Upholland Grammar School, Billinge Higher End, Lancs., Wigan Mining and Tech. Coll., Wigan, Bedford Coll., London (now part of Royal Holloway, Univ. of London); Admin. Sec., Campaign for Nuclear Disarmament 1977–79; Man. Coverdale Org. 1979–81; Dir of Public Affairs, Business in the Community 1983–89; policy adviser 1989–98; Chair. Hertfordshire Health Authority 1998–2001; Parl. Under-Sec. of State and Govt Spokesperson, Dept for Educ. and Skills 2001–04, Early Years and School Standards 2001–02, Early Years and Childcare 2002, Sure Start (also Dept for Work and Pensions) 2002–04; Govt Spokesperson for Children 2003; Parl. Under-Sec. of State and Govt Spokesperson, Dept for Constitutional Affairs/Ministry of Justice 2004–07, Leader House of Lords and Lord Pres. of the Council 2007–08, on leave of absence 2010–; Commr for Trade, EC 2008–09, High Rep. of the Union for Foreign Affairs and Security Policy, EU 2009–, also first Vice-Pres. EC 2010–; hon. degree from Univ. of East London 2005; House Magazine Minister of the Year 2005, Channel 4 Peer of the Year 2005, Stonewall Politician of the Year 2006, assessed by Woman's Hour on BBC Radio 4 as one of the 100 most powerful women in the UK 2013. *Address:* BERL 12, 200 rue de la Loi-Wetstraat, 1049 Brussels, Belgium (office). *Telephone:* (2) 298-85-90 (office). *Fax:* (2) 298-86-57 (office). *E-mail:* COMM-SPP-HRVP-ASHTON@ec .europa.eu (office). *Website:* www.eeas.europa.eu/ashton (office); www.parliament .uk/biographies/lords/baroness-ashton-of-upholland/2500.

ASHWORTH, Sir John Michael, Kt, PhD, DSc; British biologist and academic; b. 27 Nov. 1938, Luton, Beds., England; s. of Jack Ashworth and Mary Ousman; m. 1st Ann Knight 1963 (died 1985); one s. three d.; m. 2nd Auriol Stevens 1988; ed Exeter Coll., Oxford, Univ. of Leicester, Brandeis Univ. and Univ. of California, San Diego, USA; Harkness Fellow, Commonwealth Fund, New York, NY 1965–67; Lecturer, Biochemistry Dept, Univ. of Leicester 1967–71, Reader 1971–73; Prof., Biology Dept, Univ. of Essex 1973–79; Chief Scientist, Cen. Policy Review Staff, Cabinet Office 1976–81; Under-Sec. Cabinet Office 1979–81; Vice-Chancellor, Univ. of Salford 1981–89; Dir LSE and Political Science 1990–96; Chair. Bd Nat. Computer Centre 1983–91, Nat. Accreditation Council for Certification Bodies 1984–88, British Library 1996–2001; mem. Bd Granada TV 1987–89, Dir Granada Group 1990–2002; Dir J. Sainsbury 1993–96, Strategic Health Authority, NE London 2002–03; mem. Council, Inst. of Cancer Research (ICR) 1998–2007, Fellow, ICR 2007; Chair. Barts and the London Nat. Health Service (NHS) Trust 2003–07; Dir (non-exec.) Colchester Hosp. Univ. Foundation NHS Trust; Hon. Fellow, Exeter Coll., Oxford 1983, LSE 1997; Hon. DSc (Salford) 1991, (City Univ.) 2005, (Essex) 2011; Hon. LLD (Leicester) 2005; Colworth Medal of Biochemical Soc. 1972. *Publications:* ed.: Outline Studies in Biology; author: Cell Differentiation 1973, The Slime Moulds (with J. Dee) 1976; more than 100 papers on biological, biochemical and educational topics in scientific journals. *Leisure interest:* sailing. *Address:* Garden House, Wivenhoe, Essex, CO7 9DB, England. *Telephone:* (1206) 822256. *Fax:* (1206) 822256. *E-mail:* john@ashworthstevens.net.

ASIM, Mohamed, BA, MA, PhD; Maldivian diplomatist; *Additional Secretary, Ministry of Foreign Affairs;* b. 1960; m. Mariyam Ali Manik; one s. one d.; ed American Univ. of Beirut, Lebanon, California State Univ., Sacramento, USA, Australian Nat. Univ., Canberra, Australia; early govt career as Admin. Officer, Ministry of Educ. 1982; Personnel Services Officer, Pres.'s Office 1983, then Sr Research Officer, Int. Div.; Presidential Aide 1990–92; Dir Employment Affairs 1992–96, Dir-Gen. 1996–99; Dir-Gen. Public Service Div. of Pres.'s Office 1999–2004; High Commr to Sri Lanka 2004–07, to UK 2007–08; Additional Sec., Ministry of Foreign Affairs 2008–; Pres. Colombo Plan Council 2004–; Grad. Asst, School of Business and Public Admin, Calif. State Univ. 1983–85; taught professional short courses in human resources man. at ANU, Canberra 1996–98; represented Maldives at numerous confs including Commonwealth Meeting of Small States, Windhoek, Namibia 1995, Third Asia Pacific Conf. on Public Admin, Katmandu, Nepal 1991; mem. Maldives del. to Commonwealth Heads of States and Govts Meeting, Kuala Lumpur, Malaysia 1989. *Address:* Ministry of Foreign Affairs, Boduthakurufaanu Magu, Malé 20-077, Maldives (office). *Telephone:* 3323400 (office). *Fax:* 3323841 (office). *E-mail:* admin@foreign.gov.mv (office). *Website:* www.foreign.gov.mv (office).

ASJES, Ivar Onno Odwin, MEconSc; Curaçao politician; *Prime Minister;* b. 16 Sept. 1970, Rotterdam, Netherlands; ed Erasmus Univ.; mem. Island Council and Commr of Finance, Island Govt of Curaçao Sept.–Oct. 2010 (council discontinued following dissolution of Netherlands Antilles); mem. Staten (Parl.) of Curaçao 2010–13; Prime Minister 2013–; Leader, Pueblo Soberano party. *Address:* Office of the Prime Minister, Fort Amsterdam 17, Willemstad, Curaçao (office). *Telephone:* (9) 463-0495 (office). *Fax:* (9) 461-7199 (office). *Website:* www.pueblosoberano.org (office).

ASLAKHANOV, Col-Gen. Aslanbek Akhmedovich, CandJur; Chechen politician; b. 11 March 1947, Novye Atagi; m.; two c.; ed Kharkov State Pedagogical Inst., Acad. of USSR; teacher Moscow Mining Inst. 1965–67; numerous positions in USSR Ministry of Internal Affairs 1967–, investigator, then Head of Dept, then Sr Inspector, then Deputy Head, then Head of Div., Chief Inspector Organizational Dept 1981–89; head of successful operation to end hijacking of an aircraft in N Caucasus 1989; Pres. All-Russian Asscn of Security Veterans and Courts; mem. Soviet of Nationalities, USSR Supreme Soviet 1989–91; elected to State Duma (Parl.) 2000, representing Chechen Repub.; Adviser to Pres. Putin 2003–; mem. Fed. Council for Omsk region 2008–; numerous awards. *Leisure interests:* freestyle wrestling, sport. *Address:* State Duma, 103265 Moscow, Okhotny Ryad 1, Russia. *Telephone:* (495) 292-02-04.

ASNER, Edward (Ed) American actor and film producer; b. 15 Nov. 1929, Kansas City; m. 1st Nancy Sykes 1957; three c.; m. 2nd Cindy Gilmore 1998; one s. with Carol Jean Vogelman; ed Univ. of Chicago; film and TV actor 1961–; Pres. Screen Actors Guild 1981–85; f. Quince Productions, Inc. (production co.); seven Emmy Awards, five Golden Globe Awards, Ralph Morgan Award, Screen Actors Guild 2000, Lifetime Achievement Award 2002. *Film appearances include:* Fort Apache the Bronx 1981, JFK 1991, The Golem 1995, Hard Rain 1998, The Batchelor 1999, Above Suspicion 2000, Mars and Beyond 2000, The Animal 2001, The Confidence Game (also co-producer) 2001, Academy Boyz 2001, Fair Play 2002, The Commission 2003, Missing Brendan 2003, Elf 2003, Crab Orchard 2006, All In 2005, Sleeping Dogs Lie 2005, Ways of the Flesh 2006, Hard Four 2007, Channels 2008, Gigantic 2008, So Others May Live 2008, The Raft 2009; numerous TV film appearances. *Films produced:* Payback (TV) 1997, A Vision of Murder: The Story of Donielle (TV) (exec. producer) 2000. *TV series include:* The Mary Tyler Moore Show (as Lou Grant) (five Emmy Awards) 1970–77, Lou Grant (as Lou Grant) 1977–82, Witch 2006, Studio 60 on the Sunset Strip 2006–07. *Address:* Quince Production, Inc., 12400 Ventura Blvd., #371, Studio City, CA 91604.

ASO, Taro; Japanese politician; *Deputy Prime Minister;* b. 20 Sept. 1940; m.; two c.; ed Gakushuin Univ., Stanford Univ., USA and London School of Econs, UK; joined Aso Cement Co. Ltd 1966, Pres. 1973–79; mem. House of Reps for Fukuoka Prefecture 8th Dist 1979–; Parl. Vice-Minister, Ministry of Educ., Science and Sports 1988; Chair. Standing Cttee on Foreign Affairs 1991; Minister of State for Econ. Planning 1996; mem. Judge Indictment Cttee 1998; apptd Minister of State for Econ. and Fiscal Policy 2001–03; Minister for Public Man., Home Affairs, Posts and Telecommunications 2003–05, of Foreign Affairs 2005–07; Prime Minister 2008–09; Deputy Prime Minister 2012–, also Minister of Finance, Minister of State for Financial Services, Minister in charge of Overcoming Deflation and Counting Yen Appreciation; Dir Educ. Div., LDP Policy Research Council 1990, Dir Foreign Affairs Div. 1992, Deputy Sec.-Gen. LDP 1993, Deputy Chair. Policy Research Council 1999, Dir-Gen. LDP Treasury Bureau 2000, Chair. Policy Research Council 2001, Sec.-Gen. 2007, 2008, Pres. 2008–09; mem. Japan Olympic Shooting Team, Montréal 1976; Pres. Japan Jr Chamber of Commerce 1978. *Address:* Ministry of Finance, 3-1-1, Kasumigaseki, Chiyoda-ku, Tokyo 100-8940 (office); Liberal-Democratic Party (Jiyu-Minshuto), 1-11-23, Nagata-cho, Chiyoda-ku, Tokyo 100-8910, Japan (office). *Telephone:* (3) 3581-4111 (office); (3) 3581-6211 (office). *Fax:* (3) 5251-2667 (office); (3) 3581-1910 (office). *E-mail:* info@mof.go.jp (office); koho@ldp.jimin.or.jp (office). *Website:* www.mof.go.jp (office); www.jimin.jp (office).

ASPECT, Alain, PhD; French physicist and academic; *Augustin Fresnel Professor, Institut d'Optique;* b. 15 June 1947, Agen, Lot-et-Garonne, Aquitaine; m. Annie Aspect; two c.; ed École Normale Supérieure de Cachan, Orsay Univ.; Asst Lecturer, Orsay Univ. 1969–71; teacher, Yaoundé, Cameroon 1971–74; Lecturer, École Normale Supérieure, Cachan 1974–85; Scientist, Collège de France, Paris 1985–92; Augustin Fresnel Prof., Institut d'Optique and Prof. (part-time) École Polytechnique, Palaiseau 1992–, also CNRS Distinguished Scientist Emer. and Research Dir Emer. Laboratoire Charles Fabry and mem. Atom Optics Group; mem. Prime Minister's Higher Council for Science and Tech.; mem. Académie des Sciences 2002; Foreign Assoc. NAS 2008, Austrian Acad. of Sciences 2009; Fellow, Optical Soc. of America 2002, American Physical Soc. 2005, European Optical Soc. 2006; Chevalier, Légion d'honneur; Officier, Ordre nat. du Mérite; Commdr des Palmes académiques; Dr hc (Ecole Polytechnique, Montreal) 2006, (Univ. of Montreal) 2006, (ANU) 2008, (Heriot-Watt Univ.) 2008, (Univ. of Glasgow) 2010, (Technion Univ.) 2011; numerous awards including Académie des Sciences Prix Servan 1983, US Commonwealth Award for Science and Invention 1985, Société Française de Physique and Inst. of Physics Holweck Prize 1991, Max Born Award,

Optical Soc. of America 1999, Humboldt-Gay Lussac Prize 1999, CNRS Gold Medal 2005, European Physical Soc. Quantum Electronics Prize 2009, Wolf Prize in Physics (with John F. Clauser and Anton Zeilinger) 2010, Herbert Walther Award, Optical Soc. of America and Deutsche Physikalische Gesellschaft 2011, Albert Einstein Medal, Albert Einstein Soc. 2012, Ives Medal/Quinn Prize, Optical Soc. of America 2013, Tommasoni Prize, Univ. of Rome 'La Sapienza' 2013. *Achievements include:* best known for Bell test experiments, laser cooling of atoms and experiments with Bose-Einstein Condensates. *Publications:* Lévy Statistics and Laser Cooling: How Rare Events Bring Atoms to Rest (co-author) 2002, Demain la Physique (co-author) 2004, An Introduction to Quantum Optics: From the Semiclassical Approach to Quantized Light (co-author) 2010; around 200 articles in int. journals. *Address:* Laboratoire Charles Fabry, Institut d'Optique, 2 Avenue Fresnel, 91127 Palaiseau, France (office). *Telephone:* 1-64-53-31-03 (office). *Fax:* 1-64-53-31-18 (office). *E-mail:* alain.aspect@institutoptique.fr (office). *Website:* www.lcf.institutoptique.fr (office).

ASSAD, Asma al-, BSc; Syrian state official and investment banker; *First Lady;* b. (Asma Fawaz al-Akhras), 11 Aug. 1975, Acton, London, England, UK; d. of Dr Fawaz Akhras and Sahar Akhras; m. Bashar al-Assad 2000; two s. one d.; ed Queen's Coll. secondary school, London and King's Coll., London; economist, Hedge Fund Man., Deutsche Bank, London 1996–97; Investment Banker, Mergers and Acquisitions for Biotechnology Cos, JP Morgan, London, New York, Paris 1998–2000; First Lady of Syria 2001–, state visits to Tunisia, Spain, Morocco, France, Italy, Qatar, UK, The Vatican; represented Syria in talks with Bank of England concerning Syrian econ. reform, London 2002, with UNESCO concerning educ. and literacy, with Arab Women's Org. on the improvement of women's status in the Arab world; Founder and Chair. The Syria Trust for Devt 2001; introduced and championed rights for the disabled in Syria, including comprehensive legislation; hosted numerous int. confs, including the Women in Business Conf. (largest ever gathering of business women in Middle East) 2002; Chair. AAMAL (Syrian Org. for the Disabled) 2006–; mem. World Links Arab Region Advisory Council, Higher Council in Arab Women's Org.; Patron Syrian Comm. for Family Affairs, Damascus Arab Capital of Culture (UNESCO) 2008; Patron Transformation of Nat. Museums and Cultural Heritage Sites; Hon. Chair. Special Olympics, Syria; Hon. PhD (La Sapienza Univ., Rome) 2004; Arab First Lady of the Year 2008, Italian Presidency Gold Medal of the Year 2008, named by Arabian Business amongst Power 100: World's Most Influential Arabs (61st) 2009. *Leisure interest:* horse riding, skiing, cycling. *Address:* Office of HE Mrs al-Assad, Rawda Square, Damascus, Syria (office). *Telephone:* (11) 2231112 (office). *Fax:* (11) 3345801 (office). *E-mail:* fares.kallas@mopa.gov.sy (office).

ASSAD, Lt-Gen. Bashar al-; Syrian ophthalmologist, army officer and head of state; *President;* b. 11 Sept. 1965, Damascus; s. of the late Hafiz al-Assad (Pres. of Syria 1971–2000) and Anissa Makhlouf; m. Asmaa al-Akhras 2001; three s.; ed Al-Huria High School, Damascus, Univ. of Damascus Faculty of Medicine, also studied ophthalmology at Western Eye Hosp., London, UK, Homs Mil. Acad., Damascus; completed ophthalmology residency training in Tishreen Mil. Hosp., Damascus; recalled from studies in London to join Syrian army following death of his brother in a car accident 1994; Capt., Medical Corps 1994, fmr commdr armoured div., Syrian Armed Forces, rank of Col 1999; apptd Leader of Ba'ath Party and C-in-C of Armed Forces following death of his father 2000–; Pres. of Syria 2000– (confirmed as pres. by an unopposed referendum); Regional Sec. Ba'ath Party; fmr Head Syrian Computer Soc. (introduced the Internet to Syria 2001). *Leisure interest:* surfing the net. *Address:* Office of the President, Raouda Palace, Damascus, Syria (office). *Telephone:* (11) 2231112 (Raouda Palace); (11) 2233600 (Al-Shaeb Palace); (11) 3734535 (Teshreen Palace).

ASSAF, Ibrahim ibn Abd al-Aziz al-, PhD; Saudi Arabian politician and economist; *Minister of Finance;* b. 28 Jan. 1949, Ayoun Al-Jawa, Qassim; m.; four c.; ed King Saud Univ. Riyadh, Univ. of Denver, Colo State Univ., USA; Teaching Asst King Abdulaziz Mil. Acad. (KAMA) Riyadh 1971–82, Asst Prof. 1982–86, Head Dept of Admin. Sciences 1982–86; Visiting Lecturer Staff's Acad. 1982–83; Econ. Adviser Saudi Fund for Devt 1982–86; Alt. Exec. Dir IMF Saudi Arabia, Washington, DC 1986–89; Exec. Dir World Bank Saudi Arabia, Washington, DC 1989–95; Minister of Finance and Nat. Economy 1996–; Chair. Bd, Public Investment Fund, Pension and Retirement Fund, Saudi Fund Devt, Real Estate Devt Fund; Gov. for Saudi Arabia, Islamic Devt Bank, World Bank Group, IMF, Arab Funds and Financial Insts.; mem. Bd Supreme Econ. Council, Higher Advisory Council for Petroleum and Minerals, Saudi Arabian Oil Company (SAUDI ARAMCO), Gen. Investment Authority, Supreme Tourism Authority, Higher Council Islamic Affairs, Higher Council for Unives, Civil Service Council, Manpower Council, Mil. Service Council, Higher Council for Civil Defense, Saudi Econ. Asscn. *Address:* Ministry of Finance, Airport Road, Riyadh, 11177, Saudi Arabia (office). *Telephone:* (1) 405-0000 (office). *Fax:* (1) 401-0583 (office). *E-mail:* Minister@mof.gov.sa. *Website:* www.mof.gov.sa.

ASSANGE, Julian Paul; Australian journalist, computer programmer and activist; *Editor-in-Chief and Spokesperson, WikiLeaks;* b. 3 July 1971, Townsville, Queensland; one s.; ed Univ. of Melbourne; previously a physics and math. student, computer hacker and programmer before taking on current role as mem. Bd, Ed.-in-Chief and Spokesperson for WikiLeaks (unpaid volunteer); represented Univ. of Melbourne at Australian Nat. Physics Competition 2005; mem. International Subversives (hacker group), pleaded guilty to 24 charges of hacking 1992; took refuge in and eventually granted political asylum in Ecuadorean Embassy, London while awaiting extradition to Sweden to answer charges of sexual assault Aug. 2012; winner, Amnesty International Media Award (New Media) 2009 (for exposing extrajudicial assassinations in Kenya The Cry of Blood – Extra Judicial Killings and Disappearances investigation) 2009, winner, Economist Index on Censorship Award 2008, Sam Adams Award, Sam Adams Assocs for Integrity in Intelligence 2010, voted 23rd by New Statesman magazine amongst The World's 50 Most Influential Figures 2010, named by Utne Reader magazine as one of the 25 Visionaries Who Are Changing Your World 2010, ranked 68th by Forbes magazine amongst The World's Most Powerful People 2010. *Address:* WikiLeaks, Box 4080, Australia Post Office – University of Melbourne Branch, Melbourne, Vic. 3052, Australia (office). *E-mail:* info@wikileaks.org (office). *Website:* www.wikileaks.org (office).

ASSELBORN, Jean; Luxembourg politician; *Minister of Foreign Affairs and Immigration;* b. 27 April 1949, Steinfort; m. Sylvie Asselborn-Huber 1980; two d.; ed Athénée de Luxembourg and Univ. of Nancy; left school to work for Uniroyal Labs 1967; became involved in trade-union movt, elected to post of Youth Rep. of Fed. of Luxembourg Workers (Lëtzebuerger Aarbechterverband, precursor to current OGB-L or Ind. Fed. of Trade Unions of Luxembourg); joined civil admin of Luxembourg City 1968–69; returned to Steinfort to serve in local admin 1969; Admin. Inter-municipal Hosp., Steinfort 1976; Mayor of Steinfort 1982–2004; elected to Luxembourg Parl. 1984–, Head, Parl. Group of Luxembourg Socialist Workers' Party (LSAP) 1989, Chair. LSAP 1997–2004, Vice-Pres. Luxembourg Parl. 1999–2004, mem. Cttee of the Regions of the EU; Vice-Pres. European Socialist Party 2000–04; Deputy Prime Minister 2004–13; Minister for Foreign Affairs and Immigration 2004–. *Address:* Ministry of Foreign Affairs and Immigration, Hôtel St Maximin, 5 rue Notre-Dame, 2240 Luxembourg, Luxembourg (office). *Telephone:* 247-82-301 (office). *Fax:* 22-31-44 (office). *E-mail:* officielle.boite@mae.etat.lu (office). *Website:* www.mae.lu (office).

ASSI, Lamia Mari; Syrian politician and diplomatist; *Minister of Tourism;* b. 27 Dec. 1955; m.; Vice-Minister of Finance 2002–06; Amb. to Malaysia 2006–10; Minister of Economy and Trade 2010–11 (resgnd with rest of cabinet at Pres.'s request following popular protests), Minister of Tourism 2011–. *Address:* Ministry of Tourism, BP 6642, rue Barada, Damascus, Syria (office). *Telephone:* (11) 2210122 (office). *Fax:* (11) 2242636 (office). *E-mail:* min-tourism@mail.sy (office). *Website:* www.syriatourism.org (office).

ASSOWEH, Ali Farah; Djibouti politician; *Minister of Justice and Penal Affairs;* b. 1965; Minister of Economy, Finance and Planning, in charge of Privatization 2005; Gov. for Djibouti IMF, World Bank, Int. Finance Corpn, Islamic Devt Bank 2005; currently Minister of Justice and Penal Affairs, in charge of Human Rights. *Address:* Ministry of Justice and Penal Affairs, BP 12i, Djibouti, Djibouti (office). *Telephone:* 351506 (office). *Fax:* 354012 (office).

ASTAKHOV, Pavel Alekseyevich, LLB, LLM, PhD; Russian barrister; *Children Rights Commissioner for the President;* b. 8 Sept. 1966, Moscow; m. Astakhova Svetlana; three s.; ed Higher KGB School, Univ. of Pittsburgh, USA; legal adviser, pvt. practice 1989–; has worked in Spain, France, USA, Greece, Czech Repub. –1990; Founder, Head Advocates' Group, P. Astakhov 1990–; Rep., Int. Business Centre, Moscow 1990–; currently Chair. Moscow City Bar Asscn; Children Rights Commr for the Pres. 2009–; mem. Moscow City Collegiate of Advocates; mem. Moscow City Bar 1994–, Lawyers Bar of Moscow City 2002–, Paris Barrister Asscn 2005–; mem. Moscow Barrister Chamber; mem. Expert Advisory Council for Chair. of Accounts Chamber; mem. European (Brussels) Court of Arbitration and Mediation; mem. Arbitration Tribunal for Russian Union of Industrialists and Entrepreneurs; mem. Public Chamber Comm. for Communications, Information Policy; est. Pravo TV (production group); Prof., TGP faculty, Moscow MVD Univ.; Honourable Lawyer of Russia Medal 2001, Femida Award 2004, Person of the Year 2005. *Television includes:* Chas Suda 2003, Defence. *Radio:* Barrister Defence Methods. *Publications include:* Pravopisnye istiny ili levosudie dlja vseh 2000, Chas Suda 2003, Legal Truths or Left Judgment for Everyone, Counter Actions Against Raider Acquisitions, Your Lawyer P.Astakhov series, Raider 2007, Mayor. *Leisure interests:* travelling, hunting, writing, diving. *Address:* c/o Office of the President, 103132 Moscow, Staraya pl. 4, Russia. *E-mail:* pavel@astakhov.ru. *Website:* www.astakhov.ru.

ASTORI, Danilo; Uruguayan economist and politician; *Vice-President;* b. 1940, Montevideo; m.; four c.; ed Univ. of the Repub., Montevideo; econs researcher in govt agric. agencies and econ. consultant to UN agencies 1961–89; consultant to Head of Frente Amplio party 1984; f. Asamblea Uruguay party 1994; elected as Senator 1995–2000, re-elected 2000–05; Minister of Economy and Finance 2005–08; Vice-Pres. 2010–. *Address:* 2121 Asamblea Uruguay, Frente Amplio, Carlos Quijano, 1273 Montevideo, Uruguay (office). *E-mail:* info@2121.org.uy (office). *Website:* www.2121.org.uy (office).

ÅSTRÖM, Jan, MSc; Swedish business executive; b. 21 March 1956; m. Marana Makela; two c.; ed Royal Swedish Inst. of Tech. Stockholm; Paper Mill Man. Modo Paper, Husum Mill 1989–93; Man. Dir Svenska Cellulosa Aktiebolaget (SCA) Packaging 1993–96, Business Group Pres. SCA Fine Paper, Germany 1996–99; Pres. and CEO Modo Paper AB, Stockholm 1999–2000; Exec. Vice-Pres. and Deputy CEO SCA 2000–02, Pres. and CEO 2002–07; currently Owner Boxen Media; Environmental Man. of the Year 2004. *Address:* Boxen Media AB, Path of Love 10, 13934 Gustavsberg, Sweden (office). *Telephone:* (70) 5590145 (mobile). *E-mail:* jan@boxenmendia.se (office). *Website:* www.boxenmedia.se (office).

ASTRUC, Alexandre, LèsL; French film director, writer and journalist; b. 13 July 1923, Paris; s. of Marcel Astruc and Huguette Haendel; m. Elyette Helies 1983; ed Lycée de Saint-Germain-en-Laye, Lycée Henri IV and Faculté des Lettres, Paris; journalist and film critic 1945–; film dir 1952–; TV reporter for Radio Luxembourg 1969–72; film critic, Paris Match 1970–72; contributor to Figaro-Dimanche 1977–; Chevalier, Légion d'honneur; Officier, Ordre nat. du Mérite; Commdr des Arts et des Lettres; various film prizes and other awards. *Films directed include:* Le rideau cramoisi 1952, Les mauvaises rencontres 1955, Une vie 1958, La proie pour l'ombre 1960, Education sentimentale 1961, Evariste galois 1965, La longue marche 1966, Flammes sur l'Adriatique 1968, Sartre par lui-même 1976; also TV films and series. *Publications:* Les vacances 1945, La tête la première, Ciel de cendres 1975, Le serpent jaune 1976, Quand la chouette s'envole 1978, Le permissionnaire 1982, Le roman de Descartes 1989, De la caméra au stylo 1992, L'autre versant de la colline 1993, Evariste Galois 1994, Le montreur d'ombres 1996, La France au coeur 2000, Un rose en hiver 2006, Les secrets de Mademoiselle Fechtenbaum 2008. *Leisure interests:* mathematics, literature. *Address:* 168 rue de Grenelle, 75007 Paris, France (home). *Telephone:* 6-24-60-87-81 (home).

ASTURIAS, HRH The Prince of; Felipe de Borbón, (Prince of Girona, Prince of Viana, Duke of Montblanc, Count of Cervera, Lord of Balaguer), LLB, MA; Spanish; b. 30 Jan. 1968, Madrid; s. of King Juan Carlos I and Queen Sofia of Spain; m. Letizia Ortiz Rocasolano 2004; two d.; ed Santa Maria de los Rosales, Madrid, Lakefield Coll., Canada, Gen. Mil. Acad., Zaragoza, Naval Coll., Marin, Air Force Gen. Acad., San Javier, Madrid Autonomous Univ., Georgetown Univ., USA; heir to the throne; received dispatches as Infantry Lt, Sub-Lt and Lt of the

Air Arm 1989, holds mil. ranks of Commdr of the General Land Army Corps (Infantry), Lt Commdr in the General Navy and Commdr of the General Air Force; qualified helicopter pilot; numerous official visits to countries in Europe, Latin America, Middle East, Asia and Australasia 1995–; named Eminent Person for UN Int. Year of Volunteers 2001; mem. Olympic sailing team, Barcelona 1992; established Prince of Asturias Foundation; Hon. Pres. Codespa Foundation, Asscn of European Journalists, Spain. *Address:* c/o The Royal Household of HM the King, La Zarzuela Palace, Madrid, Spain (office). *Website:* www.casareal.es.

ASYLMURATOVA, Altynai; Kazakhstani ballerina and artistic director; *Artistic Director, Vaganova Ballet Academy;* b. 1962, Alma-Ata (now Almaty); m. Konstantin Zaklinsky; one d.; ed Vaganova Ballet School, Leningrad (now St Petersburg); dancer with Kirov (now Mariinsky) Ballet 1980, then Prin. Dancer; numerous foreign tours including Paris 1982, USA, Canada 1987; Artistic Dir Vaganova Ballet Acad, St. Petersburg 2000–; Honoured Artist of Russia 1983, Baltika Prize 1998, Golden Sophit 1999, People's Artist of Russia 2001. *Roles include:* Odette/Odile in Swan Lake, Shirin in Legend of Love, Kitzi in Don Quixote, Aurora in Sleeping Beauty, Nike in Boyaderka, Giselle. *Address:* Vaganova Ballet Academy, 2 Rossi Street, St Petersburg 191023, Russia (office). *Fax:* (812) 315-53-90 (office). *E-mail:* umo@vaganova.ru (office). *Website:* www .vaganova.ru (office).

ATABAY, Zia; American (b. Iranian) media entrepreneur; *CEO, National Iranian Television;* m. Parvin; fmr singer; first hit record aged 18; fmr exec. and Gen. Man. CBS Records, Tehran; moved to Europe 1980, lived in Sweden, Spain and England; settled in Los Angeles 1986; talk show host, cable TV late 1990s; Founder-Pres. and CEO, Nat. Iranian TV (NITV) 2000–. *Address:* National Iranian Television (NITV), 21050 Erwin Street, Woodland Hills, CA 91367, USA (office). *Telephone:* (818) 716-0000 (office). *Fax:* (818) 716-0023 (office). *E-mail:* zia@nitv.tv (office). *Website:* www.nitv.tv (office).

ATAKHANOV, Shamil Yesenjanovich; Kyrgyzstani politician; b. 22 July 1948, Uzgen, Osh Oblast; ed Frunze (now Bishkek) Polytechnical Inst., USSR Ministry of Internal Affairs Acad. and Moscow State Inst. of Int. Relations (MGIMO) Int. Business School, Moscow, Russian SFSR; electrical engineer 1971–72; served in Soviet Army 1972–73; worked in Komsomol and CP posts in Kyrgyz SSR 1973–84; head of dept for combating organized crime, Ministry of Internal Affairs, Kyrgyz SSR 1986–87; head of admin in trade-financial orgs of Frunze State Municipal Enterprise 1987–88; Deputy Head, then Acting Head of Internal Affairs section, Frunze City; Gen. Dir of 'Inter-Bishkek' jt venture 1991–2005, 2005–10; First Deputy Mayor of Bishkek May–Aug. 2005; Deputy Prime Minister 2010–13 (resgnd); Acting Sec. of Defence Council 2011–13; Chair. State Cttee for Nat. Security 2011–13; mem. Social Democratic Party of Kyrgyzstan (SDPK—Kyrgyzstandyn Sotsial-Demokratiyalyk Partiyasy). *Address:* Social Democratic Party of Kyrgyzstan (Kyrgyzstandyn Sotsial-Demokratiyalyk Partiyasy), 720000 Bishkek, Shabdan Batyr 46D, Kyrgyzstan (office). *Telephone:* (312) 53-16-84 (office). *Fax:* (312) 53-16-87 (office). *E-mail:* sdpkkenesh@gmail.com (office). *Website:* www.sdpk.kg (office).

ATALLAH, Walid; Lebanese fashion designer; b. Beirut; ed Univ. of Chicago, USA; showed first collection in Dubai 1996; first US show at Couture Fashion Week, New York 2009; house now has brs in Al Ain (UAE), Qatar, Lebanon, Saudi Arabia and Libya; best known for evening and bridal designs, often incorporating diamonds, precious gems and Swarovski crystals; launched W pret-à-porter line; mem. Advisory Bd Dubai Fashion Week; French Asscn of Fashion Designers Excellence in Int. Design Award. *Address:* Al Maktoum Rd, POB 22855, Deira, Dubai, United Arab Emirates (office). *Telephone:* (4) 2226172 (office). *Fax:* (4) 2226706 (office). *E-mail:* info@walid-atallah.com (office). *Website:* www.walid -atallah.com (office).

ATAMAN, Kutluğ, MFA; Turkish artist and film director; b. 1961, Istanbul; ed Univ. of California, Los Angeles, USA; works held in major int. collections including MoMA New York, Tate Modern, London, Thyssen-Bornemisza Art Contemporary, Vienna, Dimitris Daskalopoulos Collection, Athens, Carnegie Museum, Pittsburgh; art works have been shown at Venice Biennale 1999, Documenta 2002, biennials in Istanbul 1997, 2003 and 2007, Berlin 2001, Sao Paulo 2002 and 2010; f. Inst. for the Readjustment of Clocks (contemporary art production and exhibition org.); Chair. Jury, Istanbul Int. Film Festival 2009; Carnegie Prize, Carnegie Museum of Art, Pittsburgh 2004, European Cultural Fund 'Routes' Princess Margriet Award for cultural diversity 2011. *Films:* Serpent's Tale (Karanlık Sular) (Turkish Film Critics Asscn Best Film, Dir and Screenplay, Istanbul Int. Film Festival, Ankara Int. Festival Jury Prize) 1994, Lola+Bilidikid (New Festival Best Film Prize, New York, Berlin Festival Jury Special Prize) 1998, 2 Girls (Best Dir and Best Film prizes at Ankara and Antalya Film Festivals, Best Film, Asian Film Festival, India) 2005, Journey to the Moon 2009. *Address:* c/o Galeri Manâ, Kemankeş Mahallesi Ali, Paşa Değirmeni Sokak, no 16–18, Beyoğlu 34425 Istanbul, Turkey (office). *Telephone:* (212) 259-22-25 (office). *Website:* www.saatleriayarlamaenstitusu.com (office).

ATAMBAYEV, Almazbek Sharshenovich; Kyrgyzstani engineer, politician and head of state; *President;* b. 17 Sept. 1956, Alamudun, Chui Oblast; ed Moscow Inst. of Man.; engineer with Kyrgyz SSR Ministry of Communications 1980–81; Sr Engineer with DU-4, Frunze (now Bishkek) 1981–83; held position in Presidium of Supreme Soviet, Kyrgyz SSR 1983–87; Deputy Chair. Exec. Cttee Pervomaisky Dist Council of People's Deputies, Frunze 1987–89; Founder and Head, Forum (business firm) 1989; Deputy in Jogorku Kenesh (Parl.) 1995–2000; Gen.-Dep. Kyrgyzavtomash 1997–99; Chair. Social Democratic Party of Kyrgyzstan 1999–; unsuccessful presidential cand. 2000; Minister of Industry, Trade and Tourism 2005–06 (resgnd); Co-Chair. Opposition For Reforms movt 2006; Prime Minister March–Nov. 2007, 2010–11; Acting First Deputy Chair. of Interim Govt 2010; Pres. of Kyrgyzstan 2011–; Dank Medal 1999. *Address:* Office of the President, 720003 Bishkek, pr. Chui 205, Kyrgyzstan (office). *Telephone:* (312) 63-89-20 (office). *E-mail:* ps@adm.gov.kg (office). *Website:* www.president.kg (office).

ATANASIU, Teodor; Romanian politician; b. 23 Sept. 1962, Cugir, Alba Co.; m. 1st Maria Atanasiu (divorced 2005); m. 2nd Laura Maria Bisboaca; one d.; ed Faculty of Mechanics, Cluj-Napoca Polytechnic, Open Univ. Business School; engineer, U.M. Cugir 1987–95, Chief of Workshop 1995–96, Dir 1997–2001; joined Nat. Liberal Party (PNL) 1990, Sec. Liberal Cugir 1990–92, Pres. Liberal Cugir

98

1992–93, Pres. Alba County PNL chapter 1993–, Vice-Pres. PNL 2006–08, mem. Perm. Cen. Bureau 2001–02, 2005–06, Exec. Cttee 2005–; Councillor, Cugir Local Council 1992–96, Alba Co. Council 1996–2004 (Pres. of Council –2004); Parl. Expert, Chamber of Deputies 2001–04; Minister of Nat. Defence 2004–06 (resgnd); Dir APA-CTTA SA, Alba Iulia 1996–97, FPS (State Devt Fund), Bucharest 1997–2000; Head Authority for State Assets Recovery –2008; Deputy Dir-Gen., SC Cugir SA 1997–2001; Man. Palplast Sibiu SA 2001–04, B&M Direct Consulting Cugir 2003–04; mem. Chamber of Deputies, Alba County 2008–09. *Address:* National Liberal Party (NLP) (Partidul Național Liberal) (PNL), 70112 Bucharest, Bd. Aviatorilor 86, Sector 1, Romania (office). *Telephone:* (21) 2310795 (office). *Fax:* (21) 2310796 (office). *E-mail:* dre@pnl.ro (office). *Website:* www.pnl.ro (office).

ATANASOF, Alfredo; Argentine politician; b. 24 Nov. 1949; official, Gen. Confed. of Labour; Minister of Labour, Employment and Social Affairs; Chief Cabinet of Ministers 2002–03; Nat. Deputy for Buenos Aires 2009–; currently Pres. Comm. for Foreign Affairs, Chamber of Deputies; mem. Gremios Solidarios Group. *Address:* Cámara de Diputados, Av. Rivadavia 1864, C1033AAU Buenos Aires, Argentina (office). *Telephone:* (11) 6310-7100 (office). *E-mail:* aatanasof@diputados.gov.ar (office). *Website:* www.diputados.gov.ar (office).

ATANGANA MEBARA, Jean-Marie; Cameroonian politician; b. 27 March 1954; Minister of Higher Educ. 1997–2002; Pres. Int. Inst. of Admin. Sciences 2001–04; Minister of State and Sec.-Gen. Presidency of Cameroon 2002–06; Minister of State and Minister of External Relations 2006–07; arrested for embezzlement of public funds 2008. *Address:* c/o Ministry of External Relations, Yaoundé, Cameroon.

ATAYEVA, Aksoltan Toreevna; Turkmenistani diplomatist, politician and medical practitioner; *Permanent Representative, United Nations;* b. 6 Nov. 1944, Ashgabat; m. Tchary Pirmoukhamedov 1969; one s. one d.; ed Turkmenistan State Medical Inst., Ashgabat; doctor, Hosp. Number 1, Ashgabat 1968–79, Asst to Chief Doctor 1979–80; Vice-Dir Regional Health Dept, Ashgabat 1980–85; Vice-Minister of Health 1985–90, Minister 1990–94; Minister of Social Security 1994–95; Amb. and Perm. Rep. to UN, New York 1995–; mem. Democratic Party 1992–, Khalk Maslakhaty (Supreme People's Council of Turkmenistan) 1993–; Pres. Trade Unions of Turkmenistan 1994–95; Hon. Assoc. of Int. Acad. of Computer Sciences and Systems, Kiev, Ukraine 1993; Neutrality Order, Gairat Medal 1992, Medal for Love of Motherland 1996, Order of Gurbansoltan Eje 1997, Order of Bitaraplyk 1999, Order for the Great of Independent Turkmenistan; Hon. DrMed (Russian Scientific Research Inst. for Social Hygiene and Health Care Man.). *Publications include:* 108 publs and two monographs on health and maternity care. *Leisure interests:* books, arts, sports. *Address:* Permanent Mission of Turkmenistan to United Nations, 866 United Nations Plaza, Suite 424, New York, NY 10017, USA (office). *Telephone:* (212) 486-8908 (office). *Fax:* (212) 486-2521 (office). *E-mail:* turkmenistan@un.int (office). *Website:* www.un.int/wcm/content/site/turkmenistan (office).

ATHEL, Saleh Abdul Rahman al-, BSc, MSc, PhD; Saudi Arabian professor of mechanical engineering and university president; b. 1940, Al-Rus; m.; several c.; ed Stanford Univ., Univ. of Texas, USA; joined teaching staff of King Saud Univ., Vice-Dean, Coll. of Eng 1974–75, Dean 1975–76, Vice-Pres. for Grad. Studies and Research 1976–84; Pres. King Abdulaziz City for Science and Tech., Riyadh 1984–2004; Fellow, Islamic World Acad. of Sciences (Vice-Pres. 1986–90); mem. American Soc. of Mechanical Engineers, UN World Comm. on Environment and Devt, UN Advisory Cttee on Science and Tech. for Devt; mem. ASME, Saudi Working Cttee for Educ. Policy, Scientific Cttee Pio Manza Int. Research Centre; fmr mem. Exec. Cttee Org. for Islamic Co-operation Ministerial Cttee of Scientific and Tech. Co-operation. *Publications:* a book on eng structures, trans of three books, more than 50 articles. *Address:* Islamic World Academy of Sciences, 17 Djibouti Street, Sixth Circle, PO Box 830036, Amman, 11183, Jordan (office). *Telephone:* (55) 23385 (office). *Fax:* (55) 11803 (office). *E-mail:* ias@go.com.jo (office); secretariat@ias-worldwide.org (office). *Website:* www.ias-worldwide.org (office).

ATHERTON, David, OBE, MA, LRAM, LTCL, LGSM; English conductor; *Conductor Laureate, Hong Kong Philharmonic Orchestra;* b. 3 Jan. 1944, Blackpool, Lancs.; s. of Robert Atherton and Lavinia Atherton; m. 1st Ann Gianetta Drake 1970; one s. two d.; m. 2nd Eleanor Ann Roth 2012; ed Univ. of Cambridge; Répétiteur, Royal Opera House 1967–68, Resident Conductor 1968–79; Co-founder and Artistic Dir London Sinfonietta 1968–73, 1989–91; youngest-ever conductor at Royal Opera House and Henry Wood Promenade Concerts, London 1968; debut, Royal Festival Hall, London 1969, La Scala, Milan 1976, San Francisco Opera 1978, Metropolitan Opera, New York 1984; has conducted performances in Europe, Middle East, Far East, Australasia, N America 1970–; Artistic Dir and Conductor, London Stravinsky Festival 1979–82, Ravel/Varèse Festival 1983–84; Prin. Conductor and Artistic Adviser, Royal Liverpool Philharmonic Orchestra 1980–83, Prin. Guest Conductor 1983–86; Music Dir and Prin. Conductor, San Diego Symphony Orchestra 1980–87; Prin. Guest Conductor, BBC Symphony Orchestra 1985–89; Music Dir and Prin. Conductor, Hong Kong Philharmonic Orchestra 1989–2000, Conductor Laureate 2000–; Founder and Artistic Dir Mainly Mozart Festival, Southern Calif. and Northern Mexico 1989–2013; Prin. Guest Conductor, BBC Nat. Orchestra of Wales 1994–97; Co-founder, Pres. and Artistic Dir Global Music Network 1998–2002; Conductor of the Year Award, Composers' Guild of GB 1971, Edison Award 1973, Grand Prix du Disque Award 1977, Koussevitzky Award 1981, Int. Record Critics' Award 1982, Prix Caecilia 1982. *Publications:* The Complete Instrumental and Chamber Music of Arnold Schoenberg and Roberto Gerhard (ed.) 1973, Pandora and Don Quixote Suites by Roberto Gerhard (ed.) 1973; contrib. to The Musical Companion 1978, The New Grove Dictionary 1981. *Leisure interests:* travel, films, theatre, computers. *Address:* c/o Alison Nethsingha, Askonas Holt, Lincoln House, 300 High Holborn, London, WC1V 7JH, England (office). *Telephone:* (20) 7400-1743 (office). *Fax:* (20) 7400-1799 (office). *E-mail:* alison.nethsingha@askonasholt.co.uk (office). *Website:* www.askonasholt.co.uk (office).

ATHERTON, Michael Andrew, OBE; British broadcaster, journalist, author and fmr professional cricketer; *Cricket Correspondent, The Times;* b. 23 March 1968, Newton Heath, Manchester, Lancs.; s. of Alan Atherton and Wendy Atherton; ed Manchester Grammar School and Downing Coll., Cambridge; right-

hand opening batsman; leg spin bowler; played for Cambridge Univ. 1987–89 (Capt. 1988–89), Lancs. 1987–2001, MCC 1987–90; England Test debut against Australia 1989; toured Australia 1990–91, 1994–95 (Capt.); ODI debut against India 1990, 54 ints (43 as Capt.) to 20 Aug. 1998; toured SA 1995–96, Zimbabwe and NZ 1996–97, West Indies 1998; mem. team touring Australia 1998–99, SA 1999–2000, Pakistan and Sri Lanka 2000–01 (retd); played in 115 Tests, took 2 wickets and scored 7,728 runs (16 centuries), highest score 185 not out, average 37.69, best bowling (innings) 1/20, (match) 1/20; ODIs: 54 matches, scored 1,791 runs, average 35.11, highest score 127; First-class: 336 matches 21,929 runs, average 40.83, highest score 268 not out, best bowling (innings) 6/78; fmr journalist, Sunday Telegraph; Cricket Corresp., The Times 2008–; cricket commentator for Channel 4 TV 2002–05; worked as a commentator for BBC Radio and Talksport on test matches outside England 2002–05; mem. Sky Sports commentary team 2005–; often performs as post-match master of ceremonies for ints in England, presenting awards and interviewing players; nicknames, Athers, Cockroach, Dread, Iron Mike, FEC; Jack Hobbs Memorial Award as the Outstanding Schoolboy Cricketer at under-15 level 1983, Wisden Cricketer of the Year 1991, Cornhill Player of the Year 1994, Sports Journalist of the Year, British Press Awards 2010, Sports Writer of the Year, Sports Journalists Asscn 2011. *Publications:* A Test of Cricket 1995, Opening Up (autobiography) 2002, Gambling: A Story of Triumph and Disaster 2006, Atherton's Ashes 2009. *Leisure interests:* decent novels, good movies, food, wine, travel, most sports, music. *Address:* The Times, 1 Virginia Street, London, E98 1XY, England (office); c/o Sky Sports, British Sky Broadcasting Ltd, Grant Way, Isleworth, TW7 5QD, England (office). *Telephone:* (20) 7782-5000 (The Times) (office). *E-mail:* contact@mikeatherton.co.uk. *Website:* www.timesonline.co.uk/tol/sport/cricket (office); www.mikeatherton.co.uk.

ATHFIELD, Ian Charles; New Zealand architect; *Director, Athfield Architects Limited;* b. 15 July 1940, Christchurch; s. of Charles Leonard Athfield and Ella Agnes Taylor; m. Nancy Clare Cookson 1962; two s.; ed Christchurch Boys High School, Auckland Univ. School of Architecture; Prin. of Structon Group Architects, Wellington 1965–68; Dir Athfield Architects Ltd (own practice) 1968–; Professional Teaching Fellowship, Victoria Univ. of Wellington 1987–88; Pres. New Zealand Inst. of Architects (NZIA) 2006–08, New Zealand APEC Architect 2006–, NZIA Architectural Amb. to Christchurch following 2010 and 2011 earthquakes; Dir Auckland Property Enterprise Bd; mem. New Zealand Historic Places Trust Bd; Companion, New Zealand Order of Merit; Univ of Auckland Alumni Fellow, NZIA Fellow; Hon. DLitt (Victoria Univ. of Wellington) 2000; Wellington Architectural Centre Award for Most Significant Architect 1946–2006, AAA Award 1968, 1972, NZIA Silver Medal 1970, Bronze Medal 1975, New Zealand Tourist and Publicity Design Award 1975, Int. Design Competition for Housing, Manila, Philippines 1976, Design Competition for Low Cost Housing, Fiji (jt winner) 1978, Gold Medal 1982, 2004, AAA Monier Design Award 1983, NZIA Nat. Design Award 1984, 1985, 1986, 1987, 1988, 1989, 1993, 1997, 1998, 1999, 2003, 2006, 2007, 2008, 2009, Environmental Design Award 1986, New Zealand Wool Bd Award 1987, 1991, New Zealand Commemoration Medal 1990, Jt Supreme Award 2003, 2007, Nat. Design Award 2009, 2010, 2012, 2013, New Zealand Designers Inst. Black Pin Award 2013, New Zealand Arts Foundation Icon Award 2013. *Television include:* Today Tonight, TVNZ 1980, Ian Athfield, TVNZ 1989, Deconstructing Athfield, TVNZ 2004. *Films include:* Architect Athfield, New Zealand Film Unit 1977, Architect of Dreams: Ian Athfield, Messenger Films 2008, Erik Mootz En Nouvelle Zelande, The New Explorers, France 2013. *Publications include:* Architecture: an Involvement 1963, The Architecture of Self-Help Communities 1978, Joyful Architecture 1980. *Leisure interests:* building, gardening. *Address:* 105 Amritsar Street, PO Box 3364, Wellington 6035, New Zealand (office). *Telephone:* (4) 499-1727 (office). *Fax:* (4) 499-1960 (office). *E-mail:* ath@athfieldarchitects.co.nz (office). *Website:* www.athfieldarchitects.co.nz (office).

ATILIO BENÍTEZ PARADA, Gen. José; Salvadorean army officer and government official; *Minister of National Defence;* fmr Insp.-Gen. of Armed Forces, also Commdr, Logistics Support Command of the Armed Forces and Commdr, Artillery Brigade; veteran of missions to Iraq including as Commdr, Cuscatlan Bn, Ninth Contingent in Iraq; Deputy Minister of Nat. Defence –2011, Minister 2011–. *Address:* Ministry of National Defence, Alameda Dr Manuel E. Araújo, Km 5, Carretera a Santa Tecla, San Salvador, El Salvador (office). *Telephone:* 2250-0100 (office). *E-mail:* fuerzaarmada@faes.gob.sv (office). *Website:* www.fuerzaarmada.gob.sv (office).

ATIQUR RAHMAN, A. K. M., BSc, MSc; Bangladeshi economist, diplomatist and academic; *High Commissioner to Malaysia;* b. 31 Dec. 1954; m.; ed National Defence College, Dhaka,; fought during war of independence in 1971; Asst Sec. then Sr Asst Sec., Ministry of Foreign Affairs 1986–91, Dir 1997–2001, Dir-Gen. 2001–03, 2005–06; Second Sec. then First Sec., Embassy in Rome 1991–94; Counsellor, Embassy in Dakar 1994–97; Consul Gen., Consulate Gen. in Hong Kong 2003–05; Amb. to Bhutan 2006–09; High Commr to Malaysia 2009–; fmr Assoc. Prof., later Prof. and Chair. Dept of Econs, North South Univ., Dhaka, Head of Inst. of Devt, Environmental and Strategic Studies; fmrly with Centre for Studies in Int. Relations and Devt, Kolkata; Vice-Pres. Mercantile Bank Ltd. *Leisure interests:* music, reading, gardening, writing. *Address:* Bangladesh High Commission, Block 1, Lorong Damai 7, Jalan Damai, 55000 Kuala Lumpur, Malaysia (office). *Telephone:* (3) 21487940 (office). *Fax:* (3) 21413381 (office). *E-mail:* bddoot@streamyx.com (office); akmatiq@northsouth.edu (office). *Website:* www.bangladesh-highcomkl.com (office).

ATIYAH, Sir Michael Francis, Kt, OM, MA, PhD, ScD, FRS, FRSE; British mathematician and academic; b. 22 April 1929, London; s. of Edward Selim Atiyah and Jean Atiyah (née Levens); m. Lily Brown 1955; three s.; ed Victoria Coll., Egypt, Manchester Grammar School and Trinity Coll. Cambridge; Research Fellow, Trinity Coll., Cambridge 1954–58, Hon. Fellow 1976, Master 1990–97, Fellow 1997–; Fellow, Pembroke Coll., Cambridge 1958–61 (Hon. Fellow 1983), Univ. Lecturer 1957–61; Reader, Oxford Univ. and Fellow St Catherine's Coll., Oxford 1961–63, Hon. Fellow 1991; Savilian Prof. of Geometry, Univ. of Oxford and Fellow, New Coll., Oxford 1963–69, Hon. Fellow 1999; Prof. of Mathematics, Inst. for Advanced Study, Princeton, NJ 1969–72; Royal Soc. Research Prof., Oxford Univ. 1973–90, Fellow, St Catherine's Coll., Oxford 1973–90; Dir Isaac Newton Inst. of Math. Sciences, Cambridge 1990–96; Chancellor Univ. of Leicester

1995–2005; Pres. Royal Soc. of Edinburgh 2005–08; Pres. London Math. Soc. 1974–76, Pres. Math. Asscn 1981; mem. Science and Eng Research Council 1984–89; Pres. Pugwash Confs 1997–2002; mem. Council Royal Soc. 1984–85, Pres. 1990–95; Fellow American Math. Soc. 2012; Foreign mem. American Acad. of Arts and Sciences, Swedish Acad. of Sciences, Leopoldina Acad. (Germany), NAS, Acad. des Sciences (France), Royal Irish Acad., Third World Acad. of Science, Indian Nat. Science Acad., Australian Acad. of Sciences, Chinese Acad. of Sciences, American Philosophical Soc., Ukrainian Acad. of Sciences, Russian Acad. of Sciences, Georgian Acad. of Sciences, Venezuelan Acad. of Sciences, Accad. Nazionale dei Lincei, Royal Spanish Acad. of Sciences, Norwegian Acad. of Science and Letters; Hon. Prof., Univ. of Edinburgh 1997–; Hon. Fellow, Darwin Coll., Cambridge 1992, Hon. FREng 1993, Hon. Faculty of Actuaries 1999, Univ. of Wales Swansea 1999; Commdr Order of the Cedars, Gold Order of Merit, Lebanon, Order of Andreas Bello (Venezuela), Grand Officier, Legion d'honneur; Hon. DSc (Bonn, Warwick, Durham, St Andrew's, Dublin, Chicago, Edinburgh, Cambridge, Essex, London, Sussex, Ghent, Reading, Helsinki, Leicester, Rutgers, Salamanca, Montreal, Waterloo, Wales, Queen's-Kingston, Keele, Birmingham, Lebanon, Open, Brown, Oxford, Prague, Chinese, Hong Kong, Heriot-Watt, York Univs, American Univ. of Beirut, Scuola Normale Pisa, Polytechnic Univ. of Catalonia); Dr hc (UMIST) 1996, (Hong Kong Univ. of Science and Tech.) 2012; Fields Medal, Int. Congress of Mathematicians, Moscow 1966, Royal Medal of Royal Soc. 1968, De Morgan Medal, London Math. Soc. 1980, Copley Medal of Royal Soc. 1988, Feltrinelli Prize, Accad. Nazionale dei Lincei 1981, King Faisal Int. Prize for Science 1987, Benjamin Franklin Medal, American Philosophical Soc., Nehru Medal, Indian Nat. Science Acad., Abel Prize, Norwegian Acad. of Sciences (jtly with Isadore Singer) 2004, Grande Medaille, Acad. des sciences (France). *Publications:* K-Theory 1966, Commutative Algebra 1969, Geometry and Dynamics of Magnetic Monopoles 1988, Collected Works (five vols) 1988, vol. 6 2005, The Geometry and Physics of Knots 1990. *Leisure interests:* gardening, music. *Address:* University of Edinburgh, Room 6319, School of Mathematics, Mayfield Road, Edinburgh, EH9 3JZ (office); 3/8 West Grange Gardens, Edinburgh, EH9 2RA, Scotland (home). *Telephone:* (131) 650-6018 (office); (131) 667-0898 (home). *E-mail:* m.atiyah@ed.ac.uk (home). *Website:* www.maths.ed.ac.uk (office).

ATKINS, Dame Eileen June, DBE; British actress; b. 16 June 1934; d. of Arthur Thomas Atkins and of the late Annie Ellen Elkins; m. Bill Shepherd; ed Latymer Grammar School, Edmonton and Guildhall School of Music and Drama; Hon. DLitt; Evening Standard Award for best film script 1999; OFFIE Award for Best Actress 2013; numerous other awards in the USA. *Stage appearances include:* Twelfth Night, Richard III, The Tempest 1962, The Killing of Sister George (Best Actress, Evening Standard Awards) 1965, The Cocktail Party 1968, Vivat! Vivat Regina! (Variety Award) 1970, Suzanne Andler, As You Like It 1973, St Joan 1977, Passion Play 1981, Medea 1986, The Winter's Tale, Cymbeline (Laurence Olivier Award for Best Actress) 1988, Mountain Language 1988, A Room of One's Own (New York Drama Critics Circle Special Citation) 1989, Exclusive 1989, The Night of the Iguana 1992, Vita and Virginia 1993, Indiscretions 1995, John Gabriel Borkman 1996, A Delicate Balance (Evening Standard Award for Best Actress 1997) 1997, The Unexpected Man (Laurence Olivier Award for Best Actress) 1998, 2000–01, Honor (Laurence Olivier Award) 2003, The Retreat from Moscow 2003–2004, There Came a Gypsy Riding 2007, The Sea 2008, The Female of the Species 2008, All That Fall 2013. *Films include:* Equus 1974, The Dresser 1984, Let Him Have It 1990, Wolf 1994, Cold Comfort Farm 1995, Jack and Sarah 1995, The Avengers 1998, Women Talking Dirty 1999, Gosford Park 2002, The Hours 2003, Cold Mountain 2003, Vanity Fair 2004, Ask the Dust 2006, Scenes of a Sexual Nature 2006, Evening 2007, Wild Target 2008, Last Chance Harvey 2008, Robin Hood 2010, Beautiful Creatures 2013. *Radio work includes:* adaptation of To the Lighthouse 2000, Restless 2009. *TV appearances include:* The Duchess of Malfi, Sons and Lovers, Smiley's People, Nelly's Version, The Burston Rebellion, Breaking Up, The Vision, Mrs Pankhurst in In My Defence (series) 1990, A Room of One's Own 1990, The Lost Language of Cranes 1993, The Maitlands 1993, Talking Heads 2 1998, Madame Bovary 2000, The Sleeper 2000, Wit 2001, Bertie and Elizabeth 2001, The Lives of Animals 2002, Cranford (BAFTA for Best Actress, Emmy Award for Best Supporting Actress) 2007, Waking the Dead 2007, Ballet Shoes 2007, Psychoville (series) 2009–11, Upstairs Downstairs (series) 2010, Poirot: Murder on the Orient Express 2010, Doc Martin (series) 2011, 2013, The Scapegoat 2012. *Play:* as writer: Vita and Virginia. *Co-creator:* Upstairs Downstairs, The House of Eliott TV series. *Adaptation:* Mrs Dalloway (Evening Standard Film Award) 1999. *Leisure interests:* books, cats. *Address:* c/o Paul Lyon Maris, ICM, Oxford House, 76 Oxford Street, London, W1D 1BS, England (office); 2 The Moorings, Strand on the Green, Chiswick, London, W4 3PG, England. *Telephone:* (20) 7636-6565 (office); (20) 8994-6577. *Fax:* (20) 7323-0101 (office). *E-mail:* billshepherd@billshepherdproductions.com.

ATKINSON, Sir Anthony Barnes (Tony), Kt, MA, FBA; British economist and academic; *Fellow, Nuffield College, University of Oxford;* b. 4 Sept. 1944, Caerleon; m. Judith Mary Mandeville 1965; two s. one d.; ed Cranbrook School, Kent and Churchill Coll., Cambridge; Prof. of Econs, Univ. of Essex 1970–76; Head, Dept of Political Economy, Univ. Coll. London 1976–79; Prof. of Econs, LSE 1980–92, currently Centennial Prof.; Prof. of Political Economy, Univ. of Cambridge, Fellow, Churchill Coll. 1992–94; Warden, Nuffield Coll. Oxford 1994–2005, currently Fellow; Ed. Journal of Public Economics 1972–97; mem. Royal Comm. on Distribution of Income and Wealth 1978–79, Retail Prices Index Advisory Cttee 1984–90, Pension Law Review Cttee 1992–93, Conseil d'Analyse Economique 1997–2001, European Statistics Governance Advisory Bd 2009–; Fellow, St John's Coll., Cambridge 1967–70, Econometric Soc. 1974– (Pres. 1988); Vice-Pres. British Acad. 1988–90; Pres. of the European Econ. Asscn 1989, Int. Econ. Asscn 1989–92, Royal Econ. Soc. 1995–98; Founding Mem. Academia Europaea 1988–; Hon. mem. American Econ. Asscn 1985; Hon. Fellow, LSE 2004; Chevalier Légion d'honneur 2001; Hon. Dr rer. pol (Univ. of Frankfurt); Dr hc (Lausanne) 1988, (Liège) 1989, (Athens Univ. of Econs) 1991, (Univ. of Stirling) 1992, (Univ. of Edin.) 1994, (Ecole Normale Supérieure, Paris) 1995, (Essex) 1995, (Bologna) 1995, (South Bank Univ.) 1996, (Louvain La Neuve) 1996, (Nottingham) 2000, (London Metropolitan) 2002, (Ghent) 2004, (Antwerp) 2004, (European Univ. Inst.) 2004, (Molise) 2006, (Marseille) 2010; UAP Prix Scientifique 1986, Frank E. Seidman Distinguished Award in Political Economy 1995, A.SK Social Science Prize 2007. *Publications:* Poverty in Britain and the Reform of Social Security 1969, Unequal Shares 1972,

The Economics of Inequality 1975, Distribution of Personal Wealth in Britain (with A. Harrison) 1978, Lectures on Public Economics (with J. E. Stiglitz) 1980, Social Justice and Public Policy 1983, Parents and Children (with A. Maynard and C. Trinder), Poverty and Social Security 1989, Economic Transformation in Eastern Europe and the Distribution of Income (with J. M. Micklewright) 1992, Public Economics in Action 1995, Incomes and the Welfare State 1996, Poverty in Europe 1998, The Economic Consequences of Rolling Back the Welfare State 1999, Social Indicators (jtly) 2002. *Leisure interest:* sailing. *Address:* Nuffield College, Oxford, OX1 1NF (office); 93 Hamilton Road, Oxford, OX2 7QA, England (home). *Telephone:* (1865) 278520 (office); (1865) 513373 (home). *E-mail:* tony.atkinson@nuffield.ox.ac.uk (office).

ATKINSON, Conrad, NDD, ATD, ADF, Cert RAS (Hons); American (b. British) artist and academic; *Professor Emeritus of Art, University of California, Davis;* b. 15 June 1940, Cleator Moor, Cumbria; m. Margaret Harrison 1967; two d.; ed Whitehaven Grammar School, Carlisle and Liverpool Colls of Art and Royal Acad. Schools, London; Granada Fellow in Fine Art 1967–68; Churchill Fellow in Fine Art 1972; Fellow in Fine Art, Northern Arts 1974–76; Lecturer, Slade School of Fine Art 1976–79; Visual Art Adviser to GLC 1982–86; Power Lecturer, Univ. of Sydney, Australia 1983; Artist-in-Residence, London Borough of Lewisham 1984–86, Edin. Univ. 1986–87; Adviser, Visual Arts Policy, Labour Party 1985–86; Adviser, California Arts Council; Distinguished Visiting Prof., Courtauld Inst., London; Prof. Emer. of Art, Univ. of California, Davis; Hon. Fellow, Univ. of Cumbria. *Leisure interest:* rock and roll music. *Address:* c/o Ronald Feldman Gallery, 31 Mercer Street, New York, NY 10013, USA; The Cottage, Boustead Hill, Carlisle, Cumbria, CA5 6AA, England (home). *Telephone:* (1228) 576463 (home). *E-mail:* cratkinson@ucdavis.edu (office). *Website:* www.conradatkinson.com

ATKINSON, Sir Frederick John, Kt, KCB, MA; British economist; b. 7 Dec. 1919, London; s. of George E. Atkinson and Elizabeth S. Cooper; m. Margaret Grace Gibson 1947; two d.; ed Jesus Coll., Oxford Univ.; Lecturer, Jesus and Trinity Colls, Oxford 1947–49; Econ. Adviser, Cabinet Office 1949–51, at Embassy, Washington, DC 1951–54 and at Treasury 1955–69; Chief Econ. Adviser, Dept of Trade and Industry 1970–73; Asst Sec.-Gen. OECD 1973–75; Deputy Sec. to Chief Econ. Adviser, Dept of Energy 1975–77; Chief Econ. Adviser, Treasury 1977–79; Hon. Fellow, Jesus Coll., Oxford 1979–. *Publication:* (jt author) Oil and the British Economy 1983. *Leisure interest:* reading. *Address:* 26 Lee Terrace, Blackheath, London, SE3 9TZ; Tickner Cottage, Church Lane, Aldington, Kent, TN25 7EG, England. *Telephone:* (20) 8852-1040; (1233) 720514.

ATKINSON, Harry Hindmarsh, BSc, MSc, PhD (Cantab); British physicist; b. 5 Aug. 1929, Wellington, New Zealand; s. of the late Harry Temple Atkinson and Constance Hindmarsh Atkinson (née Shields); m. Anne Judith Barrett 1958; two s. one d.; ed Canterbury Univ. Coll., NZ, Cornell Univ., Corpus Christi Coll. and Cavendish Lab., Univ. of Cambridge; Asst Lecturer in Physics, Canterbury Univ. Coll., NZ 1952–53; Research Asst, Cornell Univ., USA 1954–55; Sr Research Fellow, AERE, Harwell 1958–61; Head, General Physics Group, Rutherford Lab. 1961–69; Staff Chief Scientific Adviser to UK Govt, Cabinet Office 1969–72; Head, Astronomy, Space and Radio Div., Science Research Council 1972–78, Under-Sec. and Dir Astronomy, Space and Nuclear Physics 1983–86; Under-Sec. and Dir of Science, Science and Eng Research Council 1988–92, Under-Sec. and Dir (Special Responsibilities) 1988–92, Consultant 1992–; Chief Scientist (part-time), UK Loss Prevention Council 1990–98; Consultant North Comm. on Future of Oxford Univ. 1995–97; Chair. Anglo-Dutch Astronomy Cttee 1981–88, Steering Cttee, Inst. Laue Langevin, Grenoble 1984–88; UK Del. Council, European Space Agency 1973–87, Vice-Chair. 1981–84, Chair. 1984–87; UK Del. Intergovernmental Panel on High Energy Physics 1983–91, Council of European Synchrotron Radiation Facility 1986–88; Assessor, Univ. Grants Cttee 1987–89, consultant 1995–97; UK mem. S African Astronomical Observatory Cttee 1979–83, Anglo-Australian Telescope Bd 1979–88; mem. Working Group on Int. Collaboration, Cabinet Office 1989, NI Cttee of Univ. Funding Council 1989–93; Co-ordinator Australia, NZ, UK Science Collaboration 1989–94; Chair. Govt Task Force on Potentially Hazardous Near Earth Objects 2000; mem. Advisory Council on Science and Tech. (ACOST)'s Working Group on Int. Collaboration, Cabinet Office 1989, European Science Foundation Working Group on Near Earth Objects 2001; Consultant to Hong Kong Govt's Univ. Grants Cttee 1993–95, Univ. of Oxford's Comm. on the Future of the Univ. 1995–96; Trustee, Trans-Antarctic Asscn 1993–. *Address:* Atkinson Associates, Bampton, Oxon., OX18 2JN, England (home).

ATKINSON, Kate, MBE, BA; British writer and playwright; b. 1951, York, England; m. (divorced); two d.; ed Univ. of Dundee; fmrly home help, teacher and short story writer for women's magazines; writer 1988–; Woman's Own Short Story Competition 1986, Ian St James Award 1993, E.M. Forster Award, American Acad. of Arts and Letters 1997. *Plays include:* Nice 1996, Abandonment 2000. *Publications include:* Behind the Scences at the Museum (novel) (Whitbread First Novel award and Book of the Year 1996, Boeker Prize, SA, Livre Book of the Year, France) 1995, Human Croquet (novel) 1997, Emotionally Weird (novel) 2001, Not the End of the World (short stories) 2002, Case Histories (novel) 2004, One Good Turn (novel) 2006, When Will There be Good News? (British Book Award for Best Read of the Year 2009) 2008, Started Early, Took My Dog 2010, Life After Life (Costa Novel Award and South Bank Sky Arts Literature Prize) 2013; contrib. of short stories to Daily Telegraph, BBC 2, BBC Radio 4, Daily Express, Daily Mail, Scotsman. *Address:* c/o Transworld Publishers Ltd, 61–63 Uxbridge Road, London, W5 5SA, England. *Website:* www.booksattransworld.co.uk; www.kateatkinson.co.uk.

ATKINSON, Roger, BA, PhD; British environmental scientist and academic; *Professor Emeritus of Atmospheric Chemistry, University of California, Riverside;* ed Univ. of Cambridge; Post-doctoral Researcher, Nat. Research Council of Canada, Ottawa 1969–71; York Univ. Centre for Research in Experimental Space Science, Downsview, Ont. 1971–72; Asst Research Chemist, Statewide Air Pollution Research Center, Univ. of California, Riverside 1972–76, Assoc. Research Chemist 1976–78, 1980–81, Research Chemist 1981, Prof. of Environmental Science and Chem. 1990, Assoc. Dir Dept of Environmental Sciences 1990–92, Interim Dir 1993–96, Dir 1996–2005, now Prof. Emer. of Atmospheric Chem.; Sr Scientist, Shell Research Ltd, Thornton Research Centre, Chester 1978–79; Sr Scientific Adviser, Environmental Research and Technology Inc., Westlake Village, Calif. 1979–80; mem. ACS, American Geophysical Union, AAAS.

Publications: numerous specialist publs on atmospheric chem. *Address:* Air Pollution Research Center, University of California, Riverside, Fawcett Laboratory 123, Riverside, CA 92521-0312, USA (office). *Telephone:* (951) 827-4191 (office). *E-mail:* roger.atkinson@ucr.edu (office). *Website:* www.chem.ucr.edu (office).

ATKINSON, Rowan Sebastian, CBE, MSc; British actor and writer; b. 6 Jan. 1955, Consett, Co. Durham, England; s. of the late Eric Atkinson and of Ella Atkinson; m. Sunetra Sastry 1990; one s. one d.; ed Durham Cathedral Choristers' School, St Bees School and Univs of Newcastle and Oxford; stage appearances include: Beyond a Joke, Hampstead 1978, Oxford Univ. revues at Edinburgh Fringe, one-man show, London 1981, The Nerd 1985, The New Revue 1986, The Sneeze 1988, Oliver! 2008–09, Quartermaine's Terms 2013. *Films:* Never Say Never Again 1983, The Tall Guy 1989, The Appointments of Dennis Jennings 1989, The Witches 1990, Four Weddings and a Funeral 1994, Hot Shots – Part Deux 1994, Bean: The Ultimate Disaster Movie 1997, Blackadder – Back and Forth 2000, Maybe Baby 2000, Rat Race 2002, Scooby Doo 2002, Johnny English 2003, Love Actually 2003, Mickey's PhilharMagic (voice) 2003, Keeping Mum 2005, Mr. Bean's Holiday 2007, Johnny English Reborn 2011. *Television includes:* Not the Nine O'Clock News 1979–82, Blackadder 1983, Blackadder II 1985, Blackadder the Third 1987, Blackadder Goes Forth 1989, Mr Bean (13 episodes) 1990–96, Rowan Atkinson on Location in Boston 1993, Full Throttle 1994, The Thin Blue Line 1995–96, Bean 1997, The Jubilee Girl 2002. *Leisure interests:* motor cars, motor sport. *Address:* c/o PBJ Management Ltd, 22 Rathbone Street, London, W1T 1LA, England (office). *Telephone:* (20) 7054-5950 (office). *Fax:* (20) 7287-1191 (office). *E-mail:* general@pbjmgt.co.uk (office).

ATMAR, Mohammad Hanif, BA, MA; Afghan politician; b. 1968, Laghman Prov.; s. of Mohammad Asef Atmar; ed Univ. of York, UK; adviser to aid agencies in Afghanistan and Pakistan 1992–94; Program Man. Norwegian Cttee for Afghanistan 1994–2000; Deputy Dir-Gen. Int. Rescue Cttee 2000–02; Minister of Rural Rehabilitation and Devt 2002–06, of Educ. 2006–08, of Interior Affairs 2008–10. *Publications include:* Development of Non-Governmental Organizations in Developing Countries, From Rhetoric to Reality, Humanitarian Aid, War and Peace in Afghanistan: What to Learn?, Politics and Humanitarian Aid in Afghanistan and Its Aftermath for the People of Afghanistan, Afghanistan or a Stray War in Afghanistan.

ATNAFU, Teklewold, BSc, MSc; Ethiopian politician and central banker; *Governor, National Bank of Ethiopia;* began career with Building Construction Authority; fmr Prof., Addis Ababa Univ.; Gov. Nat. Bank of Ethiopia (central bank) 1998–; mem. House of People's Reps (Parl.) for Boloso Sore constituency 2005; mem. Southern Ethiopian Peoples' Democratic Movt. *Address:* Office of the Governor, National Bank of Ethiopia, Sudan Avenue, POB 5558, Addis Ababa, Ethiopia (office). *Telephone:* (11) 5517438 (office). *Fax:* (11) 5514588 (office). *E-mail:* nbe.gov@ethionet.et (office). *Website:* www.nbe.gov.et (office).

ATRASH, Muhammad al-, PhD; Syrian banker, politician and international organization official; b. 13 Nov. 1934, Tartous; s. of Hassan Sayed al-Atrash and Aziza Sayed al-Atrash; m. Felicia al-Atrash 1958; two s. one d.; ed American Univ., Beirut, Lebanon, American Univ., USA, London School of Econs, UK; joined Cen. Bank of Syria 1963, Research Dept 1963, Head of Credit Dept 1966–70; Alt. Exec. Dir IMF 1970–73; Deputy Gov. Cen. Bank of Syria 1974; Exec. Dir IBRD 1974–76, IMF 1976–78; Del. to Second Cttee of UN Gen. Ass., to UNCTAD and other int. econ. confs 1963–70; part-time Lecturer, Univ. of Damascus 1963–70; mem. Deputies of IMF Interim Cttee of the Bd of Govs on Reform of Int. Monetary System 1972–74; Assoc. mem. IMF Interim Cttee 1974–76, ex officio mem. 1976–78; Minister of Economy and Foreign Trade 1980–82; Minister of Finance 2001–03. *Publications:* articles in Al-Abhath (Quarterly of the American Univ. of Beirut) 1963, 1964, 1966; several articles on int. political economy, regional econs, Arab–Israeli conflict etc. *Leisure interests:* swimming, walking, reading books on history and literature.

ATTALI, Bernard; French business executive; *Senior Adviser, TPG Capital;* b. 1 Nov. 1943, Algiers; s. of the late Simon Attali and Fernande Abecassis; twin brother of Jacques Attali (q.v.); m. Hélène Scebat 1974; one d.; ed Lycée Gauthier, Algiers, Lycée Janson-de-Sailly, Paris, Faculté de Droit, Paris, Inst. d'Etudes Politiques, Paris and Ecole Nat. d'Admin; auditeur, Cour des Comptes 1968, adviser 1974; on secondment to Commissariat Général du Plan d'Equipement et de la Productivité 1972–74; Délégation à l'Aménagement du Térritoire et à l'Action Regionale (Datar) 1974–80, 1981–84; Finance Dir Soc. Club Meditérranée 1980–81; Pres. Regional Cttee of EEC 1981–84; Pres. Groupe des Assurances Nationales 1984–86; Pres. Banque pour l'Industrie Française 1984–86; Adviser on European Affairs, Commercial Union Assurance 1986–88, Chair. Air France 1988–93; Pres. Supervisory Council, Sociétés Epargne de France 1986–88, Commercial Union Lard 1986–88; Pres. Euroberlin 1988, Union de Transports Aériens 1990, Asscn des Transporteurs Aériens Européens 1991; Vice-Pres. Supervisory Bd BIGT 1995; Admin. Aérospatiale 1989, Air Inter 1990; Chief Adviser, Revenue Court 1991–93; Chair. Supervisory Bd Banque Arjil (part of Lagadère) 1994; Chair. Bankers Trust Co. France 1996–99; Vice-Pres. Investment Banking in Europe Div., Deutsche Bank 1999–2000; currently Sr Adviser, TPG Capital; mem. European Bd Orrick Rambaud Martel, Bd Air Canada, Bd Baccarat; Commdr, Légion d'honneur; Commdr, Ordre nat. du Mérite. *Publication:* Les Guerres du Ciel 1994. *Address:* TPG, 6, rue Christophe Colomb, 75008 Paris (office). *E-mail:* contact@bernardattali.com; battali@tpg.com (office). *Website:* www.bernardattali.com; www.tpg.com (office).

ATTALI, Jacques; French international bank official and writer; *President, Attali et Associés;* b. 1 Nov. 1943, Algiers; s. of Simon Attali and of Fernande Abecassis; twin brother of Bernard Attali (q.v.); m. Elisabeth Allain 1981; one s. one d.; ed Ecole Polytechnique, Inst. d'Etudes Politiques de Paris, Ecoles des Mines de Paris, Ecole Nat. d'Admin; started career as mining engineer, then Lecturer in Econs, Ecole Polytechnique; Auditeur, Council of State; Adviser to the Pres. 1981–91; State Councillor 1989–91; Pres. EBRD, London 1991–93; Pres. Attali et Associés (ACA) 1994–; mem. Council of State 1981–90, 1993–; Admin. KeeBoo 2000–; Pres. Attali Comm. (est. to evaluate means of liberalising econ. growth in France) 2007–; columnist for L'Express magazine; Dr hc (Univ. of Kent, Univ. of Haifa). *Publications include:* Analyse économique de la vie politique 1972, Modèles

politiques 1973, Anti-économique (with Marc Guillaume) 1974, La parole et l'outil 1975, Bruits, Essai sur l'économie politique de la musique 1976, La nouvelle économie française 1977, L'ordre cannibale 1979, Les trois mondes 1981, Histoires du temps 1982, La figure de Fraser 1984, Un homme d'influence 1985, Au propre et au Figuré 1988, La vie éternelle (novel) 1989, Millennium: Winners and Losers in the Coming World Order 1991, 1492 1991, Verbatim (Tome I) 1993, Europe(s) 1994, Verbatim (Tome II) 1995, Economie de l'Apocalypse 1995, Tome III 1996, Chemins de Sagesse 1996, Au delà de nulle part 1997, Dictionnaire du XXIe siècle 1998, Les portes du int 1999, La femme du menteur 1999 (novel), Fraternités 1999, Blaise Pascal ou le génie français 2000, Bruits 2001, Nouv'Elles 2002 (novel), L'homme nomade 2003, La Confrérie des Eveillés 2004 (novel), Karl Marx ou l'esprit du Monde 2004, Une brève histoire de l'avenir 2007, La crise, et après? 2008. *Address:* Attali et Associés 5 Avenue de Messine, 75008 Paris, France (office). *Telephone:* 1-53-57-38-38 (office). *Website:* www.attali.com/en (office).

ATTALIDES, Michalis A., BSc (Econ.), PhD; Cypriot sociologist, academic, university administrator and diplomatist; *Rector, University of Nicosia;* b. 1941; m.; two c.; ed London School of Econs, UK and Princeton Univ., USA; Lecturer in Sociology, Univ. of Leicester 1966–68; sociologist, Cyprus Town and Country Planning Project 1968–70; counterpart of UNESCO expert, Social Research Centre, Cyprus 1971, 1973–74; mil. service 1972; Guest Lecturer Otto Suhr Inst., Free Univ. of Berlin 1974–75; journalist 1975–76; worked in Int. Relations Service, House of Reps of Cyprus 1977–89, Dir 1979–89; Amb. and Dir of Political Affairs Division B (Cyprus question), Ministry of Foreign Affairs 1989–91; Amb. of Cyprus to France (also accred to Morocco, Portugal and Spain) 1991–95, Amb. to Belgium (also accred to Luxembourg) and Perm. Del. of Cyprus to EU 1995–98, High Commr to UK 1998–2000; Perm. Sec., Ministry of Foreign Affairs 2000–01; Rep. of Govt of Cyprus to European Convention 2002–03; Dean, School of Humanities, Social Sciences and Law, InterCollege, Nicosia 2003–06, Rector 2006–07; Rector, Univ. of Nicosia 2007–; Chair. Cyprus Rectors' Conf. 2011–13; Jean Monnet Chair. and Personam in Diplomacy and Politics of European Integration 2011–14; Grand Officier, Ordre nat. du Mérite. *Publications:* Social Change and Urbanization in Cyprus: A Study of Nicosia 1971, Cyprus: Nationalism and International Politics 1980, Cyprus: State, Society and International Environment (in Greek) 2009; articles on Cyprus, Greece, Turkey and EU. *E-mail:* attalides.m@cytanet.com.cy; attalides.m@unic.ac.cy (office). *Address:* PO Box 24005, 1700 Nicosia (office); 8 Sachtouris Street, 1080 Nicosia, Cyprus (home). *Telephone:* (22) 841572 (office); (22) 680808 (home). *Website:* www.unic.ac.cy (office).

ATTALLAH, Naim Ibrahim, FRSA; British publisher and financial adviser; *Chairman, Namara Group;* b. 1 May 1931, Haifa, Palestine; s. of Ibrahim Attallah and Genevieve Attallah; m. Maria Nykolyn 1957; one s.; ed Coll. des Frères, Haifa and Battersea Polytechnic, London; Propr Quartet Books 1976–, Women's Press 1977–, Robin Clark 1980–, Pipeline Books 1978–2000, The Literary Review 1981–2001, The Wire 1984–2000, Acad. Club 1989–96, The Oldie 1991–2001; Group Chief Exec. Asprey PLC 1992–96, Deputy Chair. Asprey (Bond Street) 1992–98; Man. Dir Mappin and Webb 1990–95; Exec. Dir Garrard 1990–95; Chair. Namara Group of cos 1973–, launched Parfums Namara 1985, Avant L'Amour and Après L'Amour 1985, Naïdor 1987, L'Amour de Namara 1990; Hon. MA (Surrey) 1993; Retail Personality of the Year, UK Jewellery Awards 1993. *Films produced:* The Slipper and the Rose (with David Frost) 1975, Brimstone and Treacle (Exec. Producer) 1982 and several TV documentaries. *Theatre:* Happy End (Co-Presenter) 1975, The Beastly Beatitudes of Balthazar B. (Presenter and Producer) 1981, Trafford Tanzi (Co-Producer) 1982. *Publications:* Women 1987, Singular Encounters 1990, Of a Certain Age 1992, More of a Certain Age 1993, Speaking for the Oldie 1994, A Timeless Passion 1995, Tara and Claire (novel) 1996, Asking Questions 1996, A Woman a Week 1998, In Conversation with Naim Attalah 1998, Insights 1999, Dialogues 2001, The Old Ladies of Nazareth 2004, The Boy in England (memoir) 2005, In Touch with His Roots: a Second Memoir 2006, Fulfilment & Betrayal 2007. *Leisure interests:* classical music, opera, theatre, cinema, photography and fine arts. *Address:* 25 Shepherd Market, London, W1J 7PP, England (home). *Telephone:* (20) 7499-2901 (home). *Fax:* (20) 7499-2914 (home). *E-mail:* nattallah@aol.com (office).

ATTANASIO, Paul; American screenwriter; m. Katie Jacobs; one d.; ed Harvard Univ., Harvard Law School; began career as a journalist; film critic for Washington Post 1984–87. *Films include:* Quiz Show 1994, Disclosure 1994, Donnie Brasco 1997, Sphere 1998, The Sum of All Fears 2002, The Good German 2006. *TV includes:* Doctor, Doctor 1989, Homicide: Life on the Street 1993, Gideon's Crossing (also producer) 2000, R.U.S./H. (also producer) 2002, House (exec. producer) 2004–12. *Address:* c/o CAA, 2000 Avenue of the Stars, Los Angeles, CA 90067, USA.

ATTAR, Najah al-, PhD; Syrian academic, politician and writer; *Second Vice-President, responsible for Cultural Policy;* b. 12 Dec. 1933, Damascus; sister of Issam al-Attar (leader of Damascus Faction of Syrian Muslim Brotherhood who has lived in exile in Aachen, Germany since 1970s); m. Dr Majed Al-Azmeh; one s. one d.; ed Damascus Univ., Univ. of Edinburgh, UK; schoolteacher in Damascus 1960–62; Dir of Composition and Literature Translation, Ministry of Culture 1962, Minister of Culture and Nat. Guidance (first woman minister) 1976–2000, served as spokeswoman for Syrian Govt early 1980s, co-f. Nat. Symphonic Orchestra 1995, initiated construction of Syrian Opera House; Dir Centre for the Dialogue of Civilisations 2002–06; mem. Bd Kalamoun Univ., Dayr Atiya 2003–; Pres. Bd of Trustees, Syrian Virtual Univ. 2003–; Second Vice-Pres. of Syria (first woman and first non-Baath Party mem.), responsible for Cultural Policy 2006–; Friendship Among People's Order (USSR), Polish Culture Order, Grand Officier, Ordre nat. du Mérite 1983, Commdr, Légion d'honneur 1992, Order of Great Lady, Malta Kts, Order of Holy Cross (Poland) 1999, Order of Holy Treasure of Grand Sash (Japan) 2002, Medallion of Honour (Chile) 2004, Order of Katrina the Great, Acad. of Security, Defence and Law (Russian Fed.) 2007. *Publications:* For Us To Be or Not To Be (two vols), The Literature of War, Who Remembers Those Days?, A Diary, Life's Questions, Coloured Words, The Revolutionary Fabric Between March and November, Spain, Hemingway and the Bulls; weekly newspaper and magazine columns; numerous articles. *Address:* c/o Office of the President, Damascus, Syria (office). *Telephone:* (11) 3323023 (office). *Fax:* (11) 3341404 (office). *E-mail:* center -cs@mail.sy (office).

ATTENBOROUGH, Sir David Frederick, Kt, OM, CH, CVO, CBE, MA, FRS; British broadcaster, naturalist and writer; b. 8 May 1926, London; s. of the late Frederick Attenborough and of Mary Attenborough; brother of Lord Attenborough (q.v.); m. Jane Elizabeth Ebsworth Oriel 1950 (died 1997); one s. one d.; ed Wyggeston Grammar School, Leicester and Clare Coll., Cambridge; served with RN 1947–49; editorial asst in publishing house 1949–52; with BBC Television 1952–73, Producer of zoological, archaeological, travel, political and other programmes 1952–64, Controller BBC 2 1964–68, Dir of Programmes, TV 1969–73; writer, presenter BBC series: Tribal Eye 1976, Wildlife on One, annually 1977–2004, Life on Earth 1979, The Living Planet 1984, The First Eden 1987, Lost World, Vanished Lives 1989, The Trials of Life 1990, Life in the Freezer 1993, The Private Life of Plants 1995, The Life of Birds 1998, State of the Planet 2000, The Blue Planet (narrator) 2001, The Life of Mammals 2002, Life in Cold Blood 2008, Charles Darwin and the Tree of Life (writer) 2009, First Life (writer) 2010, Frozen Planet 2011, Kingdom of Plants 3D 2012; Huw Wheldon Memorial Lecturer, RTS 1987; Pres. BAAS 1990–91, Royal Soc. for Nature Conservation 1991–96; mem. Nature Conservancy Council 1975–82; Fellow, Soc. of Film and Television Arts 1980; Int. Trustee, World Wild Life Fund 1979–86; Trustee, British Museum 1980–2000, Science Museum 1984–87, Royal Botanical Gardens, Kew 1986–92; Hon. Fellow, Clare Coll., Cambridge 1980, UMIST 1980, Inst. of Biology; Order of Merit; Hon. DLitt (Leicester, London, Birmingham, City); Hon. DSc (Liverpool, Ulster, Sussex, Bath, Durham, Keele, Heriot-Watt, Bradford, Nottingham); Hon. LLD (Bristol, Glasgow) 1977; Hon. DUniv (Open Univ.) 1980, (Essex) 1987, Antwerp 1993; Dr hc (Edin.) 1994; Special Award, Guild of TV Producers 1961, Silver Medal, Royal TV Soc. 1966, Silver Medal, Zoological Soc. of London 1966, Desmond Davis Award, Soc. of Film and TV Arts 1970, UNESCO Kalinga Prize 1982, Medallist, Acad. of Natural Sciences, Philadelphia 1982, Founders Gold Medal, Royal Geographical Soc. 1985, Int. Emmy Award 1985, Encyclopedia Britannica Award 1987, Kew Award 1996, Edin. Medal, Edin. Science Festival 1998, BP Natural World Book Prize 1998, Faraday Prize, Royal Soc. 2003, Int. Documentary Asscn Career Achievement Award 2003, Raffles Medal, Zoological Soc. of London 2004, Caird Medal, Nat. Maritime Museum 2004, British Book Awards Lifetime Achievement Award 2004. *Publications:* Zoo Quest to Guiana 1956, Zoo Quest for a Dragon 1957, Zoo Quest in Paraguay 1959, Quest in Paradise 1960, Zoo Quest to Madagascar 1961, Quest under Capricorn 1963, The Tribal Eye 1976, Life on Earth 1979, The Zoo Quest Expeditions 1982, The Living Planet 1984, The First Eden, The Mediterranean World and Man 1987, The Trials of Life 1990, The Private Life of Plants 1994, The Life of Birds (BP Natural World Book Prize) 1998, The Life of Mammals 2002, Life on Air (memoirs) 2002, Life in the Undergrowth 2005, Life in Cold Blood 2008, Life Stories 2009, Frozen Planet 2011. *Leisure interests:* music, tribal art, natural history. *Address:* 5 Park Road, Richmond, Surrey, TW10 6NS, England. *Website:* www.davidattenborough.co.uk.

ATTENBOROUGH, Hon. Michael John, CBE, BA (Hons); British fmr theatre director; b. 13 Feb. 1950, London, England; s. of Richard Attenborough (Baron Attenborough of Richmond) (q.v.) and Sheila Sim; m. 1st Jane Seymour 1971 (divorced); m. 2nd Karen Lewis 1984; two s.; ed Westminster School, Univ. of Sussex; Assoc. Dir, Mercury Theatre, Colchester 1972–74, Leeds Playhouse 1974–79, Young Vic Theatre 1979; Artistic Dir, Palace Theatre, Watford 1980–84, Hampstead Theatre 1984–89; Exec. Producer/Prin. Assoc. Dir, RSC 1990–2002; Artistic Dir, Almeida Theatre 2002–13; freelance dir 2013–; mem. Council Royal Acad. of Dramatic Art for 17 years; Hon. Prof. of English, Univ. of Sussex; Hon. DLitt (Sussex) 2005, (Leicester) 2009; Award for Excellence, Int. Theatre Inst. 2012. *Productions include:* RSC: The Herbal Bed, Romeo and Juliet, Othello, Pentecost, Henry IV Parts 1 and 2, Almeida Theatre: Measure For Measure, The Knot of the Heart, Reasons To Be Pretty, Filumena, King Lear, Enemies, Big White Fog, The Late Henry Moss.

ATTENBOROUGH, Baron (Life Peer), cr. 1993, of Richmond-upon-Thames in the London Borough of Richmond-upon-Thames; **Richard (Samuel) Attenborough**, Kt, CBE; British actor, producer and director; b. 29 Aug. 1923; s. of the late Frederick Attenborough and of Mary Attenborough; brother of Sir David Attenborough (q.v.); m. Sheila Beryl Grant Sim 1945; one s. (Michael Attenborough (q.v.)), two d.; ed Wyggeston Grammar School, Leicester, Royal Acad. of Dramatic Art, London; first stage appearance as Richard Miller in Ah! Wilderness, Palmers Green 1941; West End debut in Awake and Sing 1942; first film appearance In Which We Serve 1942; joined RAF 1943; seconded to RAF Film Unit for Journey Together 1944, demobilised 1946; returned to stage 1949; formed Beaver Films with Bryan Forbes 1959, Allied Film Makers 1960; Goodwill Amb. for UNICEF 1987–; mem. British Actors' Equity Asscn Council 1949–73, Cinematograph Films Council 1967–73, Arts Council of GB 1970–73; Chair. Actors' Charitable Trust 1956–88 (Pres. 1988–), Combined Theatrical Charities Appeals Council 1964–88 (Pres. 1988–), BAFTA 1969–70 (Vice-Pres. 1971–94), Royal Acad. of Dramatic Arts 1970 (mem. Council 1963–), Capital Radio 1972–92 (Life Pres. 1992–), Help a London Child 1975–, UK Trustees Waterford-Kamhlaba School, Swaziland 1976– (Gov. 1987–), Duke of York's Theatre 1979–92, BFI 1981–92, Goldcrest Films and Television 1982–87, Cttee of Inquiry into the Arts and Disabled People 1983–85, Channel Four TV 1987–92 (Deputy Chair. 1980–86), British Screen Advisory Council 1987–96, European Script Fund 1988–96 (Hon. Pres. 1996); Gov. Nat. Film School 1970–81, Motability 1977–; Pres. Muscular Dystrophy Group of GB 1971– (Vice-Pres. 1962–71), The Gandhi Foundation 1983–, Brighton Festival 1984–95, British Film Year 1984–86, Arts for Health 1989–, Gardner Centre for the Arts, Sussex Univ. 1990– (Patron 1969–82); Dir Young Vic 1974–84, Chelsea Football Club 1969–82; Trustee Tate Gallery 1976–82, 1994–96, Tate Foundation 1986–, Foundation for Sport and the Arts 1991–; Patron Kingsley Hall Community Centre 1982–, RA Centre for Disability and the Arts, Leicester 1990–; Pro-Chancellor Sussex Univ. 1970–98, Chancellor 1998–2008; Fellow, King's Coll. London 1993, BAFTA; Freeman of Leicester 1990; Hon. Fellow, BFI 1992, Nat. Film and TV School 2001; Commdr des Arts et Lettres; Chevalier, Légion d'honneur; Hon. DLitt (Leicester) 1970, (Kent) 1981, (Sussex) 1987; Hon. DCL (Newcastle) 1974; Hon. LLD (Dickinson, Penn.) 1983; Evening Standard Film Award for 40 Years' Service to British Cinema 1983, Martin Luther King, Jr Peace Prize 1983, Padma Bhushan, India 1983, European Film Awards Award of Merit 1988, Shakespeare Prize for Outstanding Contrib. to European Culture 1992, Dilys Powell Award 1995, Patricia Rothermere Award, Evening Standard Theatre Awards 2004. *Stage appearances include:* The Little Foxes 1942,

Brighton Rock 1943, The Way Back Home (Home of the Brave) 1949, To Dorothy a Son 1965, Sweet Madness 1952, The Mousetrap 1952–54, Double Image 1956–57, The Rape of the Belt 1957–58. *Film appearances include:* School for Secrets, The Man Within, Dancing with Crime, Brighton Rock, London Belongs to Me, The Guinea Pig, The Lost People, Boys in Brown, Morning Departure, Hell is Sold Out, The Magic Box, Gift Horse, Father's Doing Fine, Eight O'Clock Walk, The Ship that Died of Shame, Private's Progress, The Baby and the Battleship, Brothers in Law, The Scamp, Dunkirk, The Man Upstairs, Sea of Sand, Danger Within, I'm All Right Jack, Jet Storm, S.O.S. Pacific, The Angry Silence (also co-prod.) 1959, The League of Gentlemen 1960, Only Two Can Play, All Night Long 1961, The Dock Brief, The Great Escape 1962, Seance on a Wet Afternoon (also prod., Best Actor, San Sebastian Film Festival and British Film Acad.), The Third Secret 1963, Guns at Batasi (Best Actor, British Film Acad.) 1964, The Flight of the Phoenix 1965, The Sand Pebbles (Hollywood Golden Globe) 1966, Dr. Doolittle (Hollywood Golden Globe), The Bliss of Mrs. Blossom 1967, Only When I Larf 1968, The Last Grenade, A Severed Head, David Copperfield, Loot 1969, 10 Rillington Place 1970, And Then There Were None, Rosebud, Brannigan, Conduct Unbecoming 1974, The Chess Players 1977, The Human Factor 1979, Jurassic Park 1992, Miracle on 34th Street 1994, The Lost World: Jurassic Park 1997, Elizabeth 1998, Puckoon 2002, Closing the Ring 2007. *Produced:* Whistle Down the Wind 1961, The L-Shaped Room 1962. *Directed:* Young Winston (Hollywood Golden Globe) 1972, A Bridge Too Far (Evening News Best Drama Award) 1976, Magic 1978, A Chorus Line 1985, Grey Owl 2000, Closing the Ring 2004. *Produced and directed:* Oh! What a Lovely War (16 int. Awards), Gandhi (eight Oscars, five BAFTA Awards, five Hollywood Golden Globes, Dirs Guild of America Award for Outstanding Directorial Achievement) 1980–81, Cry Freedom (Berlinale Kamera, BFI Award for Tech. Achievement) 1987, Chaplin 1992, Shadowlands 1993 (Alexander Korda Award for Outstanding British Film of the Year, BAFTA), In Love and War 1997, Grey Owl 2000. *Publications:* In Search of Gandhi 1982, Richard Attenborough's Chorus Line (with Diana Carter) 1986, Cry Freedom, A Pictorial Record 1987, Entirely Up To You (autobiog., co-author) 2007. *Leisure interests:* music, collecting art, watching football. *Address:* Old Friars, Richmond Green, Richmond, Surrey, TW9 1NQ, England.

ATTERSEE, Christian Ludwig; Austrian artist; b. 28 Aug. 1940, Pressburg; s. of Christian Ludwig and Susanne Ludwig; ed Akad. für Angewandte Kunst, Vienna; has worked as an artist since 1963; more than 400 solo exhbns in USA, Germany, France, Netherlands, Italy, Austria, Switzerland, including Venice Biennale 1984; Prof., Universität für angewandte Kunst, Vienna 1990–; Austrian Cross of Honour for Science and Art 1st Class 2005; Grand Austrian State Prize 1997, Lovis Corinth Prize of the Künstlergilde Esslingen, Germany 2004. *Publications:* Attersee Werksquer 1962–82, Attersee, Biennale Venedig 1984. *Leisure interest:* sailing. *Address:* Atelier/Archiv Attersee, Tuchlauben 17/4/7, 1010 Vienna, Austria. *E-mail:* attersee@utanet.at. *Website:* www.attersee -christian-ludwig.com.

ATTIYA, Abdul Rahman bin Hamad Al-, BA; Qatari diplomatist and international organization official; b. 15 April 1950, Doha; m.; two s. four d.; ed Univ. of Miami, USA; joined Ministry of Foreign Affairs 1972; Consul-Gen. in Geneva, Switzerland 1974–81, Perm. Rep. to UN and other Int. Orgs, Geneva 1975–81; Perm. Rep. to FAO, Rome 1975–81; Amb. to Saudi Arabia (also accred to Yemen and Djibouti) 1981–84; Amb. to OIC 1981–84; Perm. Repub. to UNESCO 1984–90; Amb. to France (also accred to Italy and Greece) 1984–92; Alt. Gov. IFAD 1985–92; Deputy Minister, Ministry Foreign Affairs 1988–2002; Sec.-Gen. of the Cooperation Council for the Arab States of the Gulf 2002–11; Legion of Merit (Italy) 1992, Chevalier, Légion d'honneur 1993; Independence Medal 2005, Unity Medal 2006, Diamond Medal 2010. *Leisure interests:* reading, exercising. *Address:* c/o Co-operation Council for the Arab States of the Gulf, PO Box 7153, Riyadh 11462, Saudi Arabia. *E-mail:* Alattiyah50@hotmail.com.

ATTIYA, Khalid bin Muhammad al-, LLB, PhD; Qatari politician and fmr lawyer; *Minister of Foreign Affairs;* b. 9 March 1967; m.; ed King Faisal Air Acad., Saudi Arabia, Arab Univ. of Beirut, Lebanon, Cairo Univ., Egypt; fighter pilot, Qatar Emiri Air Force 1987–95; f. own law firm 1995, pvt. legal practice 1995–2008; Minister of State for Int. Cooperation 2008–11, Acting Minister of Business and Trade 2009, Minister of State for Foreign Affairs and mem. Council of Ministers 2011, Minister of Foreign Affairs 2013–; Chair. Nat. Cttee for Human Rights 2003–08; Chair. Qatar Exchange 2009; Chair. Exec. Cttee Qatari Diar (property investment co.) 2009; Deputy Chair. Supreme Council for Information and Communication Tech. 2009, Qatar Financial Centre 2009; mem. Bd of Trustees Arab Democracy Foundation 2007–. *Address:* Ministry of Foreign Affairs, POB 250, Doha, Qatar (office). *Telephone:* 44334334 (office). *Fax:* 44324131 (office). *E-mail:* webmaster@mofa.gov.qa (office). *Website:* www.mofa.gov.qa (office).

ATTIYAH, Abdullah bin Hamad al-, BA; Qatari government official; *Second Deputy Premier and Chairman of the Emiri Diwan;* b. 1952, Qatar; m.; six c.; ed Univ. of Alexandria, Egypt; joined Ministry of Finance and Petroleum 1972, Head Dept of Int. and Public Affairs 1973–86, Dir Office of Minister 1986–89; Dir Office of Minister of Interior and Acting Minister of Finance and Petroleum 1989–92; Minister of Energy and Industry 1992–99, 2001–11, of Energy, Industry, Electricity and Water 1999–2000, Second Deputy Premier 2003–, also Chair. Emiri Diwan; Chair. State Planning Council 1998; Deputy Chair. Q-Tel 1987–95; Chair. Gulf Helicopters 1975–; mem. Bd of Dirs Gulf Airways Corpn 1986–2002; Man. Dir and Chair. of Bd Qatar Petrol Co. 1992–; fmr Head Al-Sadd Sports Club; Chair. Qatar Amateur Radio Asscn 1992–, Qatar Gen. Electricity and Water Corpn 1999–. *Leisure interests:* reading, fishing, amateur radio, football, travelling. *Website:* www.diwan.gov.qa (office).

ATTRIDGE, Harold W., PhD; American academic; *Sterling Professor of Divinity, Yale Divinity School;* b. Nov. 1946; ed Boston Coll., Cambridge Univ., UK, Hebrew Univ. of Jerusalem, Israel, Harvard Univ.; Asst Prof. of New Testament, Perkins School of Theology, Southern Methodist Univ. 1977–82, Assoc. Prof. of New Testament 1982–85; Assoc. Prof., Dept of Theology, Univ. of Notre Dame 1985–87, Prof., Dept of Theology 1988–97, Dean, Coll. of Arts and Letters 1991–97; Prof. of New Testament, Yale Univ. Divinity School 1997, Dean 1991–97, now Sterling Prof. of Divinity; mem. Soc. of Biblical Literature 1969–, Chair. SW Region Progam 1980–81, mem. Annual Meeting Program Cttee 1985–88, Cttee on Research and Publs 1990–93, Devt Cttee 1995– (Vice-Pres. 2000), Finance Cttee 2001– (Pres.

2001); mem. Catholic Biblical Asscn 1974–, Int. Asscn for Coptic Studies 1975–, American Philosophical Asscn 1976–, Soc. for New Testament Studies 1981–; mem. Editorial Bd Catholic Biblical Quarterly 1983–90, Journal of Biblical Literature 1982–87, 1996–2001, Hermeneia Commentary Series 1984–; Editorial Consultant, Harvard Theological Review 1978–90; Ed., Soc. of Biblical Literature, Texts and Trans: Pseudepgrapha Series 1979–85, Early Christian Literature Series 1990–95; Nat. Endowment for the Humanities Summer Research Stipend 1982; John Simon Guggenheim Fellowship 1983–84. *Publications:* The Testament of Job 1974, The Syrian Goddess 1976, The Interpretation of Biblical History in the Antiquitates Judaicae of Flavius Josephus 1976, First-Century Cynicism in the Epistles of Heraclitus 1976, Philo of Byblos, The Phoenician History 1981, Nag Hammdi Codex I (The Jung Codex) 1985, Hebrews: A Commentary on the Epistle to the Hebrews 1989; numerous articles; ed. of eleven books. *Address:* Yale Divinity School, 409 Prospect Street, New Haven, CT 06511, USA (office). *Telephone:* (203) 432-5304 (office). *E-mail:* harold.attridge@yale.edu (office). *Website:* www.yale.edu/divinity (office).

ATWAN, Abdel Bari, MA; British (b. Palestinian) journalist and editor; *Editor, Al Quds Al Arabi; b.* 1950, Deir al-Balah, Gaza; *s.* of Muhammad Atwan and Zilfa Atwan; *m.* 1984; three c.; ed Cairo Univ., Egypt, School of Oriental and African Studies, London Univ., UK; began career as journalist in Libya 1974; later worked for newspapers al-Madina and Asharq al-Awsat in Saudi Arabia; Founding Ed. Al Quds Al Arabi (pan–Arabian daily newspaper), London 1989–; frequent appearances in TV debates on CNN, Al Jazeera English, Channel 4 News; also regular lecturer worldwide and contributor to int. confs. *Publications:* The Secret History of al-Qa'ida 2007, A Country of Words (memoir) 2007. *Address:* Alquds Alarabi, 164-166 King Street, London, W6 0QU, England (office). *Telephone:* (20) 8741-8008 (office). *E-mail:* abatwan@googlemail.com (office). *Website:* www.abdelbariatwan.com (office); www.alquds.co.uk (office).

ATWOOD, Margaret Eleanor, CC, AM, FRSC; Canadian writer; *b.* 18 Nov. 1939, Ottawa, Ont.; *m.* Graeme Gibson; one d.; ed Victoria Coll., Univ. of Toronto, Radcliffe Coll. and Harvard Univ., USA; Lecturer in English, Univ. of British Columbia, Vancouver 1964–65; Instructor in English, Sir George Williams Univ., Montreal 1967–68, Univ. of Alberta 1969–70; Asst Prof. of English, York Univ., Toronto 1971; Writer-in-Residence, Univ. of Toronto 1972–73, Maquarie Univ., Australia 1987, Trinity Univ., San Antonio, Tex. 1989; Berg Chair, New York Univ. 1986; Pres. Writers' Union of Canada 1981–82, International PEN (Canadian Centre—English Speaking) 1984–86; MFA Hon. Chair, Univ. of Alabama, Tuscaloosa 1985, Foreign Hon. mem. American Acad. of Arts and Sciences 1988; Order of Ont. 1990, 125th Anniversary of Canadian Confederation Commemorative Medal 1992, Chevalier, Ordre des Arts et des Lettres 1994, Order of Literary Merit (Norway) 1996, Markets Initiative Order of the Forest 2006; Hon. DLitt (Trent) 1973, (Concordia) 1980, (Smith Coll., Mass) 1982, (Toronto) 1983, (Mount Holyoke) 1985, (Waterloo) 1985, (Guelph) 1985, (Oxford) 1998, (Ontario Coll. of Art and Design) 2009; Hon. LLD (Queen's Univ.) 1974, Dr hc (Victoria Coll.) 1987, (Université de Montréal) 1991, (Leeds) 1994, (McMaster) 1996, (Lakehead) 1998, (Oxford) 1998, (Cambridge) 2001, (Algoma) 2001, (Harvard) 2004, (Sorbonne Nouvelle) 2005, (Literary and Historical Soc., Univ. Coll. Dublin) 2005, (Ontario Coll. of Art and Design) 2009, (Nat. Univ. of Ireland) 2011, (Ryerson Univ.) 2012, (Royal Mil. Coll.) 2012; E.J. Pratt Medal 1961, Pres.'s Medal, Univ. of Western Ontario 1965, First Prize, Centennial Comm. Poetry Competition 1967, Union Poetry Prize, Chicago 1969, Bess Hoskins Prize for Poetry, Chicago 1974, City of Toronto Book Award 1977, Canadian Bookseller's Asscn Award 1977, Periodical Distributors of Canada Short Fiction Award 1977, St Lawrence Award for Fiction 1978, Radcliffe Grad. Medal 1980, Molson Award 1981, Guggenheim Fellowship 1981, Welsh Arts Council Int. Writer's Prize 1982, Ida Nudel Humanitarian Award 1986, Toronto Arts Award 1986, Los Angeles Times Fiction Award 1986, Arthur C. Clarke Award for Best Science Fiction 1987, Commonwealth Literary Prize (regional winner) 1987, 1994, Silver Medal for Best Article of the Year, Council for Advancement and Support of Educ. 1987, Humanist of the Year Award 1987, YWCA Women of Distinction Award 1988, First Prize, Nat. Magazine Award for Environmental Journalism 1988, Canadian Booksellers Asscn Author of the Year 1989, 1996, Harvard Univ. Centennial Medal 1990, John Hughes Prize, Welsh Devt Bd 1992, Commemorative Medal for the 125th Anniversary of Canadian Confed. 1992, Best Local Author, NOW Magazine Readers' Poll 1995, 1997, 1998, 1999, 2000, 2003, 2004, Nat. Arts Club Medal of Honor for Literature 1997, London Literature Award 1999, Int. Crime Writers' Asscn Dashiell Hammett Award 2001, Canadian Booksellers Asscn People's Choice Award 2001, Radcliffe Medal 2003, Harold Washington Literary Award 2003, Edinburgh Int. Book Festival Enlightenment Award 2005, Chicago Tribune Literary Prize 2005, Premio Príncipe de Asturias, Spain 2008, Dan David Prize 2010, Crystal Award, World Econ. Forum 2010, Sun Life Financial Arts & Communications Award: Canada's Most Powerful Women Top 100 2011, Canadian Booksellers' Lifetime Achievement Award 2012, Nashville Public Library Foundation Literary Award 2012. *Play:* The Penelopiad – The Play 2007. *Radio script:* The Trumpets of Summer (CBC Radio) 1964. *Television screenplays include:* The Servant Girl (CBC) 1974, Snowbird 1981, Heaven on Earth (with Peter Pearson) 1986. *Recordings include:* The Poetry and Voice of Margaret Atwood 1977, Margaret Atwood Reads From A Handmaid's Tale, Margaret Atwood Reads Unearthing Suite 1985, audio edns of her novels. *Publications include:* poetry: Double Persephone 1961, The Circle Game (Gov.-Gen.'s Award 1966) 1964, Kaleidoscopes Baroque 1965, Talismans for Children 1965, Speeches for Doctor Frankenstein 1966, The Animals in That Country 1968, The Journals of Susanna Moodie 1970, Procedures for Underground 1970, Power Politics 1971, You are Happy 1974, Marsh, Hawk 1977, Two-Headed Poems 1978, True Stories 1981, Notes Towards a Poem That Can Never Be Written 1981, Snake Poems 1983, Interlunar 1984, Selected Poems II: Poems Selected and New 1976–1986 1986, Selected Poems 1966–1984 1990, Margaret Atwood Poems 1965–1975 1991, Morning in the Burned House (Trillium Award for Excellence in Ontario Writing) 1995, The Door 2007; fiction: The Edible Woman 1969, Surfacing 1972, Lady Oracle 1976, Dancing Girls (short stories) 1977, Life Before Man 1979, Bodily Harm 1981, Encounters with the Element Man 1982, Murder in the Dark (short stories) 1983, Bluebeard's Egg (short stories) (Periodical Distributors of Canada/ Foundation for The Advancement of Canadian Letters Book of the Year Award) 1983, Unearthing Suite 1983, The Handmaid's Tale (Gov.-Gen.'s Award 1986)

1985, Cat's Eye (Torgi Talking Book—CNIB 1989, City of Toronto Book Award 1989, Coles Book of the Year 1989, Foundation for the Advancement of Canadian Letters/Periodical Marketers of Canada Book of the Year 1989) 1988, Wilderness Tips (short stories) (Govt of Ont. Trillium Award (with Jane Urquhart) for Excellence in Ontario Writing 1992, Periodical Marketers of Canada Book of the Year Award 1992) 1991, Good Bones (short stories) 1992, The Robber Bride (Canadian Authors' Asscn Novel of the Year 1993, Trillium Award for Excellence in Ontario Writing 1994, Commonwealth Writers' Prize for the Canadian and Caribbean Region 1994, Sunday Times Award for Literary Excellence 1994, Swedish Humour Asscn's Int. Humorous Writer Award 1995) 1993, Bones and Murder 1995, The Labrador Fiasco 1996, Alias Grace (Giller Prize 1996, Premio Mondello 1997, Salon Magazine Best Fiction of the Year 1997) 1996, The Blind Assassin (Booker Prize 2000) 2000, Oryx and Crake 2003, Telling Tales (contrib. to charity anthology) 2004, Bottle 2004, The Penelopiad 2005, The Tent (short stories) 2006, Moral Disorder (short stories) 2006, The Year of the Flood 2009, MaddAddam: A Novel 2013, Stone Mattress (short stories) 2014; juvenile: Up in the Tree 1978, 2006, Anna's Pet 1980, For the Birds 1990, Princess Prunella and the Purple Peanut 1995, Rude Ramsay and the Roaring Radishes 2003, Bashful Bob and Doleful Dorinda 2004, Wandering Wenda 2011; non-fiction: Survival: A Thematic Guide to Canadian Literature 1972, Days of the Rebels 1815–1840 1977, Second Words: Selected Critical Prose 1982, Strange Things: The Malevolent North in Canadian Literature 1995, Negotiating with the Dead: A Writer on Writing 2002, Moving Targets: Writing With Intent 1982–2004 2004, Curious Pursuits: Occasional Writing 2005, Writing with Intent: Essays, Reviews, Personal Prose 1983–2005 2005, Payback: Debt and the Shadow Side of Wealth (Libris Award for Best Non-Fiction Book 2009) 2008, In Other Worlds: SF and the Human Imagination 2011; editor: The New Oxford Book of Canadian Verse in English (ed.) 1982, The Oxford Book of Canadian Short Stories in English (with Robert Weaver) 1986, The Canlit Foodbook 1987, The Best American Short Stories (with Shannon Ravenel) 1989, The New Oxford Book of Canadian Short Stories in English (with Robert Weaver) 1995; reviews and critical articles have appeared in Canadian Literature, Maclean's, Saturday Night, This Magazine, New York Times Book Review, Globe and Mail, National Post, The Nation, Books In Canada, Washington Post, Harvard Educational Review, and many others; works have been translated into many languages, including French, German, Italian, Urdu, Estonian, Romanian, Serbo-Croat, Catalan, Turkish, Russian, Finnish, Dutch, Danish, Norwegian, Swedish, Portuguese, Greek, Polish, Japanese, Icelandic, Spanish, Hebrew. *Address:* c/o McClelland & Stewart Ltd, 1 Toronto Street, Suite 300, Toronto, ON M5C 2V6, Canada (office). *Telephone:* (416) 364-4449 (office). *Fax:* (416) 957-1587 (office). *E-mail:* publicity@mcclelland.com (office). *Website:* www.mcclelland.com (office); www.margaretatwood.ca.

ATZMON, Moshe; Israeli conductor; *b.* (Miklos Groszberger), 30 July 1931, Budapest, Hungary; *m.* 1954; two d.; ed Tel-Aviv Acad. of Music, Jerusalem Acad. of Music, Guildhall School of Music, UK; left Hungary for Israel 1944; played the horn professionally in various orchestras for several years; has conducted in Israel, England, Australia, Germany, Sweden, Norway, Switzerland, Spain, Finland, Italy, Austria, Turkey and USA; Chief Conductor, Sydney Symphony Orchestra 1969–71; Chief Conductor, North German Radio Symphony Orchestra 1972–74; Musical Dir Basel Symphony Orchestra 1972–86; Chief Conductor Tokyo Metropolitan Orchestra 1979–83, Nagoya Philharmonic Orchestra 1987–92, Conductor Laureate 1992–; Musical Dir Dortmund Opera House and Philharmonic Orchestra 1991–93; second prize Dimitri Mitropoulos Competition for Conductors, New York 1963, Leonard Bernstein Prize 1963, First Prize, Int. Conductors Competition, Liverpool, England 1964. *Leisure interests:* reading, travelling. *Address:* Artists Management Company srl unipersonale, Piazza R. Simoni, 1E, 37122 Verona, Italy (office); Patrick Garvey Management, 40 North Parade, York, YO30 7AB, England (office). *E-mail:* panozzo@amcmusic.com (office); patrick@patrickgarvey.com (office). *Website:* www.amcmusic.com/en/artists/biography/moshe-atzmon (office); www.patrickgarvey.com (office).

AUBERGER, Bernard, Ing Civil, LenD; French banker; *b.* 5 Dec. 1937, Gennevilliers; *s.* of Paul Auberger and Jeanne Auberger (née Geny); *m.* Christine Baraduc 1963; three s. one d.; ed Ecole des Mines, Paris, Inst. d'Etudes Politiques, Paris, Ecole Nat. d'Admin, Paris; Investigating Officer, French Ministry of Finance 1966–70; Adviser to Gen. Man. Crédit Nat., Paris 1970–72; Financial Attaché, Embassy in New York 1972–74; Dir of Cabinet for Under-Sec. for Finance 1974; attached to Industrial Relations Cttee 1974–75; Dir Production and Trade, Ministry of Agric. 1975–80; Cen. Man. Société Générale 1983–86; Gen. Man. Caisse Nat. de Crédit Agricole 1986–88; Insp. Gen. of Finances 1988; Advisor to Pres. of Paluel-Marmont 1990; Pres. Cortal Bank 1991–98, Banque Directe 1994–2001; Vice-Pres., Dir-Gen. Crédit du Nord 1993–94, Chair., CEO 1994–95; Pres. Asscn Opéra Comique-Salle Favart 1994–2001; Dir Compagnie Bancaire 1991–98, Banque Paribas 1994–97; Judge, Tribunal de Commerce de Paris 1998–2012; mem. Econ. and Social Council 1982–84; Officier, Ordre nat. du Mérite, Chevalier du Mérite agricole, Officier, Légion d'honneur. *Leisure interest:* opera. *Address:* 193 Boulevard St Germain, 75007 Paris, France (home). *Telephone:* 1-45-48-94-11 (home).

AUBERT, Guy, PhD; French scientist and academic; *Scientific Advisor, Commissariat a l'Energie Atomique; b.* 9 May 1938, Les Costes, Hautes-Alpes; *s.* of Gontran Aubert and Marguerite Vincent; *m.* 1st 1962; two d.; *m.* 2nd 1998; ed Ecole normale supérieure de Saint-Cloud; Research Assoc. Lab. d'Electrostatique et de Physique du Metal, CNRS, Grenoble; Titular Prof. Univ., Scientifique et Médicale de Grenoble 1970, Vice-Pres. in Charge of Research 1981–84; Scientific Del. of CNRS for Rhône-Alpes region 1981–83; Dir Ecole Normale Supérieure de Lyon 1985–94; Dir-Gen. CNRS 1994–97; Extraordinary mem. Conseil d'Etat 1997–2000; Dir-Gen. CNED 2000–03; Scientific Advisor to Commissariat a l'Energie Atomique 2003–; mem. French Physics Soc.; Officier, Légion d'honneur, Ordre nat. du Mérite; Commdr des Palmes académiques; Chevalier du Mérite agricole. *Publications:* papers in scientific journals and several patents. *Leisure interests:* skiing, tennis. *Address:* Université de Poitiers, Présidence, 15 rue de l'Hôtel Dieu, 86034 Poitiers Cedex (office); 34T, rue des Feuillants, 86000 Poitiers, France (home). *Telephone:* (5) 49-45-43-39 (office). *Fax:* (5) 49-36-62-34 (office). *E-mail:* guy.aubert@ext.univ-poitiers.fr (office).

AUBOUIN, Jean Armand, DèsSc; French academic; b. 5 May 1928, Evreux; s. of Jean Aubouin and Yvonne Joubin; m. Françoise Delpouget 1953; two d.; ed Lycées Buffon and St-Louis, Ecole Normale Supérieure (St-Cloud) and Univ. of Paris; Lecturer, Univ. of Paris 1952–61, Prof. 1961–90 (Univ. Pierre et Marie Curie from 1969), now Prof. Emer.; mem. Acad. of Sciences, Inst. of France 1981–, Vice-Pres. 1986–88, Pres. 1989–90; mem. Univ. Consultative Cttee 1967–73, Nat. Cttee CNRS 1976–84; Pres. Soc. Géologique de France 1976, Cttee de Télédétection du CNES (Centre National d'Etudes spatiales) 1974–78, 23rd Int. Geological Congress 1980, Cttee Geological Map of the World 1984–92, Scientific Advisory Bds of GPF (Géologie profonde de la France) program 1982–86, Bureau de Recherches Géologiques et Minières 1982–91, Inst. Français de Recherche pour l'Exploitation de la Mer 1985–90; mem. Scientific Advisory Bds Planning Cttee Int. Programme of Ocean Drilling 1980–84, Fondation de France 1984–87 Inst. Français du Pétrole 1985–91; mem. Bd of Dirs Office de Recherche Scientifique d'Outre-mer 1984–88, Bureau de Recherche Géologique et Minières 1989–92, Inst. Océanographique, Paris and Monaco 1994– (Pres. Comité Perfectionnement 1992–); mem. Conseil Supérieur Recherche et Technologie 1983–87; Pres. French Cttee of Int. Decade for the Reduction of Natural Disasters 1990–93; mem. Advisory Bd Parc Naturel du Verdun 1996–2000; Founder and mem. Acad. des Technologies 2000–; Admin. Chancellery Acad. de Nice 1996–, Acad. de Paris 2000–04; Foreign mem. Accad. dei Lincei, Italy 1974–, USSR (now Russia) Acad. of Sciences 1976–, Acad. of Athens, Greece 1980–, Academia Europaea 1988–, Acad. of Zagreb, Croatia 1990–, Acad. Royale Sciences, Arts et Lettres de Belgique 1994–, Deutsche Akad. der Naturforscher Leopoldina 1995–, Acad. de la Latinité 2000–; Hon. mem. Geological Soc. of London 1976–, Soc. Physique Histoire Naturelle (Geneva) 1990–, Geological Soc. of Greece 2001–; Hon. Fellow, Geological Soc. of America 1980–; Chevalier, Ordre des Palmes académiques 1965, Ordre Nat. du Mérite 1981, Légion d'honneur 1989; Dr hc (Athens) 1992; CNRS Medal 1959, Prix Viquesnel de la Soc. Géologique de France 1962, Prix Charles Jacob Acad. des Sciences 1976, Museo de la Plata Medal 1977, Argentina, Dumont Medal, Soc. Géologique de Belgique 1977, Ville de Paris Medal 1980, Gaudry Prize, Soc. Géologique de France 1990, Gold Medal, Acad. Royale des Sciences de Belgique 1990. *Publications:* Géologie de la Grèce septentrionale 1959, Geosynclines 1965, Manuel de Cartographie (co-ed.) 1970, Précis de Géologie (co-ed., four vols) 1968–79, approx. 400 scientific articles. *Leisure interests:* reading, mountain walking and swimming at sea. *Address:* c/o Académie des technologies, Grand Palais des Champs Elysées, Porte C, Avenue Franklin D. Roosevelt, 75008 Paris, France (office). *E-mail:* jean.aubouin@academie-technologies.fr (office).

AUBRY, Martine Louise Marie; French politician; *First Secretary, Socialist Party;* b. (Martine Delors), 8 Aug. 1950, Paris; d. of Jacques Delors (q.v.) and Marie Lephaille; m. 1st Xavier Aubry; one d.; m. 2nd Jean Louis Brochon 2004; ed Lycée Paul-Valéry, Pantheon-Assas Paris II Univ., Univ. of Paris 1 Pantheon-Sorbonne, Institut Saint-Pierre-Fourier, Faculté de Droit, Paris, Institut des Sciences Sociales du Travail, Institut d'Etudes Politiques, Paris and Ecole Nat. d'Admin, Strasbourg; Ministry of Labour 1975–79; Instructor, Ecole Nat. d'Admin 1978; Dir of preparations for econ. competition for admin. of Univ. Paris-Dauphine 1978; civil admin., Conseil d'Etat 1980–81; Deputy Dir Pvt. Office of Minister of Labour 1981; special assignment for Minister of Social Affairs and Nat. Solidarity 1983–84; Dir of Labour Relations, Ministry of Labour 1984–87; Maître des Requêtes, Conseil d'Etat 1987; Deputy Dir-Gen. Pechiney 1989–91; Minister of Labour, Employment and Professional Training 1991–93; Pres. FACE 1993–97; First Asst Mayor of Lille 1995–2001, Mayor 2001–; Vice-Pres. Lille Urban Council 1995–; mem. Nat. Ass. for Nord region (Socialist Party) 1997–2002; Minister of Employment and Social Affairs 1997–2000; Nat. Sec. Socialist Party (Parti socialiste—PS) 2000–05, First Sec. 2008–, joined Reformer (think tank) 2000; mem. club Le Siècle; Int. Press Prize, Le Trombinoscope 1999. *Publications include:* Pratique de la fonction personnel: le management des ressources humaines (co-author) 1982, Le Choix d'Agir 1994, Carnet de route d'un maire de banlieue: entre innovations et tempêtes 1995, Petit dictionnaire pour lutter contre l'extrême droite (co-author) 1995, Il est grand temps 1997, C'est quoi la solidarité? 2002, Muscler sa conscience du bonheur en trente jours 2004, Quel projet pour la gauche? 2004, Une vision pour espérer, une volonté pour transformer 2004, Agir contre les discriminations 2006, Et si on se retrouvait... 2008. *Leisure interests:* tennis, skiing. *Address:* Parti socialiste, 10 rue de Solférino, 75333 Paris Cedex 07 (office); Mairie, BP 667, 59033 Lille Cedex France. *Telephone:* 1-45-56-77-00 (office). *Fax:* 1-47-05-15-78 (office). *E-mail:* infosp@parti-socialiste.fr (office). *Website:* www.parti-socialiste.fr/l-equipe/martine-aubry (office).

AUCOIN, Louis M., BA, JD; American lawyer and UN official; *Deputy Special Representative of the Secretary-General for Operations and Rule of Law, United Nations Mission in Liberia (UNMIL);* b. 26 Jan. 1950; ed Coll. of Holy Cross, Worcester, Boston Coll. Law School; numerous academic positions including Fulbright Lecturer, Sorbonne Law Dept, Assoc. Prof., Inst. of Comparative Law, Lecturer in Comparative Law, Int. Human Rights and Trial Advocacy, Boston Univ. School of Law 1984–2000; adviser on drafting new constitutions in Cambodia 1993, E Timor 2001–02, Rwanda 2001–03, Kosovo 2007–08; Legal Adviser to Haiti's Minister for Justice 1997–98; Acting Head of Judicial Affairs, UN Transitional Authority in E Timor (UNTAET) 2000; Program Officer in Rule of Law Program, US Inst. of Peace 2000–03; US Supreme Court Fellow 2001–02; Prin. Foreign Adviser to Haitian Parl. on reform of Criminal Code and Code of Criminal Procedure 2003–06; Academic Dir Master of Law Programme in Int. Law, Fletcher School of Law, Tufts Univ., Medford, Mass –2011; Deputy Special Rep. of Sec.-Gen. for Operations and Rule of Law, UN Mission in Liberia (UNMIL) 2011–. *Publications include:* The French Constitution 2003, Constitution-Making, Peace-Building and National Reconciliation 2004, The Role of Informal Justice Systems in Fostering the Rule of Law in Post Conflict Countries 2005, Improving Transitional Justice: an Assessment of Progress in the Former Yugoslav States (co-author) 2006. *Address:* United Nations Mission in Liberia (UNMIL) Headquarters, Pan African Plaza, Tubman Boulevard, 1st Street, Monrovia, Liberia (office); United Nations Mission in Liberia (UNMIL), PO Box 4677, Grand Central Station, New York, NY 10163-4677, USA (office). *Telephone:* (5) 314000 (Monrovia) (office); (212) 963-9925 (New York) (office). *Fax:* (212) 963-9924 (New York) (office). *Website:* unmil.unmissions.org (office).

AUDIBET, Marc; French fashion designer; b. 1955, Boulogne-sur-Seine; celebrated in fashion world for his research into stretch fabrics and their use in garments without hooks, eyes, buttons or zippers, expertise acquired while working as an assistant to Emanuel Ungaro in 1972, and then as designer for Pierre Balmain, Madame Gres and Nino Cerruti; presented first collection in 1975; took over design at house of Christian Aujard 1977–81; designed for Basile and Laure Biagiotti 1981–84; continued with own label until 1988 when he designed for Parallel; collaborated with Azzedine Alaia to work closely with Du Pont on project to mix Lycra with fabrics such as satin and silk 1984, became textile adviser to Du Pont and helped create and launch single and two-way stretch fabrics made from Du Pont's Lycra; has continued to design and create seamless garments made from Lycra mixed with a wide range of other fabrics such as cotton, silk, linen and wool; also designed for Hermes 1990s; designed nine collections for Prada 1990–96; worked as consultant for Italian house of Trussardi; designer for Salvatore Ferragamo 2000–02; Artistic Adviser to Vionnet 2007–08;*Website:* www .marcaudibet.com.

AUDRAIN, Paul André Marie; French business executive; b. 17 May 1945, Chambéry, Savoie; s. of Jean Audrain and Margueritte Gubian; m. Danièle Pons 1967; two s.; ed Lycée d'Etat de Chambéry, Lycée du Parc Lyon, Ecole Supérieure des Sciences Economiques et Commerciales, Paris; Engineer, IBM France 1969–70; Financial and Admin. Dir Aiglon, Angers 1970–74; Financial Dir Christian Dior 1974–79, then Sec.-Gen., Financial and Admin. Dir 1979–84, Chair. and CEO 1984–85, Pres. 1985–86; Int. Dir Financière Agache 1986–87; Chair. and CEO Christian Lacroix 1987–88, Pierre Balmain 1988–89; CEO Société Crillon 1990–93, Int. Consulting & Licensing; Chevalier, Ordre nat. du Mérite 1985. *Address:* 27 rue du Phare, Port Navalo, 56640 Arzon (home); 20 boulevard du Montparnasse, 75015 Paris, France (home). *Telephone:* (6) 87-78-46-15 (office); (2) 97-53-85-45 (home). *E-mail:* paulaudrain@wanadoo.fr (home).

AUDRAN, Stéphane (see Dacheville, Colette).

AUERBACH, Frank Helmuth; British (b. German) artist; b. 29 April 1931, Berlin, Germany; s. of Max Auerbach and Charlotte Auerbach; m. Julia Wolstenholme 1958; one s.; ed St Martin's School of Art, London, Royal Coll. of Art; works in public collections in UK, Australia, Brazil, USA, Mexico, Israel, SA, Canada; Silver Medal for Painting, Royal Coll. of Art. *Address:* c/o Marlborough Fine Art, 6 Albemarle Street, London, W1S 4BY, England.

AUGUST, Bille; Danish film director; b. 9 Nov. 1948; ed Christer Stroholm School of Photography, Stockholm, Danish Film School; worked as cameraman on Homewards at Night, Manrape, The Grass is Singing, Love, before making first feature film 1978; Hans Christian Andersen Prize 2003. *Television includes:* The World is So Big, So Big, May, Three Days with Magnus, Buster's World (series), episode of The Young Indiana Jones, Detaljer. *Feature films:* In My Life 1978, Zappa 1983, Twist and Shout 1986, Pelle the Conqueror 1989 (Oscar for Best Foreign Film, Palme d'Or, Cannes Film Festival, Golden Ram, Stockholm, Golden Globe, LA), The Best Intentions 1991, The House of the Spirits, Smilla's Feeling for Snow, A Song for Martin 2001, Return to Sender 2004, Goodbye Bafana 2007.

AUGUSTINE, Norman Ralph, BSc, MSc, FIEEE; American aerospace industry executive; b. 27 July 1935, Denver, Colo; s. of Ralph Harvey Augustine and Freda Irene Augustine (née Immenga); m. Margareta Engman 1962; two c.; ed Princeton Univ.; Research Asst, Princeton Univ. 1957–58; Program Man., Chief Engineer Douglas Aircraft Co. Inc., Santa Monica, Calif. 1958–65; Asst Dir of Defense Research and Eng, Office of US Sec. for Defense, Washington, DC 1965–70; Vice-Pres. Advanced Systems, Missiles and Space Co., LTV Aerospace Corpn, Dallas 1970–73; Asst Sec. of the Army, The Pentagon, Washington, DC 1965–70, Under-Sec. 1973–75; Vice-Pres. Operations, Martin Marietta Aerospace Corpn, Bethesda, Md 1977–82, Pres. Martin Marietta Denver Aerospace Co. 1982–85, Sr Vice-Pres. Information Systems 1985, Pres. COO 1986–87, Vice-Chair. and CEO 1987–88, Chair. and CEO 1988–95; Pres. Lockheed Martin 1995–96, Pres. CEO 1996–97, Chair. –1997, Chair. Exec. Cttee, Bd of Dirs 1997–98; Chair. NASA Space Systems and Tech. Advisory Bd 1985–89, American Red Cross 1992–2001, Review of US Human Space Flight Plans Cttee 2009, US Antarctic Program Blue Ribbon Panel 2011–12; fmr Chair. Nat. Acad. of Eng (NAE) Council, now Chair. Nat. Acads Philanthropy Council; mem. NATO Group of Experts on Air Defence 1966–70, NASA Research and Tech. Advisory Council 1973–75; mem. Bd of Dirs Phillips Petroleum Co. (now ConocoPhillips), Procter & Gamble Co., Black and Decker Corpn; fmr mem. Bd of Dirs Riggs Nat. Bank Corpn; Prof., Princeton Univ. 1997–99; Fellow, AIAA, IEEE, American Acad. of Arts and Sciences, Royal Aeronautical Soc., American Astronautical Soc.; mem. United States Energy Security Council, Int. Acad. of Astronautics, New York Acad. of Sciences, Nat. Acad. of Eng; fmr Pres. Boy Scouts of America; 18 hon. degrees including Hon. DEng (Princeton) 2007; Distinguished Service Medal, Dept of Defense five times, Goddard Medal, AIAA 1988, Nat. Eng Award, American Asscn of Eng Socs 1991, Nat. Medal of Tech. 1997, AAAS Philip Hauge Abelson Prize 2005, Public Welfare Medal, Nat. Acad. of Sciences 2006, Harold W. McGraw, Jr. Prize in Educ. 2006, Bower Award for Business Leadership 2007. *Publications:* Augustine's Laws, The Defense Revolution (co-author) 1990, Augustine's Travels 1997, Shakespeare in Charge: The Bard's Guide to Leading and Succeeding on the Business Stage (with K. Adelman) 2001.

AUGUSZTINOVICS, Maria, PhD, DEconSci; Hungarian economist and academic; *Consultant, Institute of Economics, Hungarian Academy of Sciences;* b. 12 Feb. 1930, Budapest; m. Gabor Fekecs; one s.; ed Budapest Univ. of Econs; at Ministry of Finance 1955–61; at Nat. Planning Bureau 1961–84; Sr Research Adviser, Inst. of Econs, Hungarian Acad. of Sciences 1984–2000 (retd), Consultant 2000–; Prof. of Econs, Budapest Univ. of Econs (now Corvinus Univ.) 1986, now Hon. Prof.; Visiting Prof., Univ. of Michigan, USA 1969; lecturing tour at several univs in India and Bangladesh 1975; Visiting Research Fellow, Int. Inst. for Applied Systems Analysis, Laxenburg, Austria 1982; Visiting Prof., Wesleyan Univ., Conn., USA 1988, La Trobe Univ., Melbourne, Australia 1993; Sec. Cttee of Econs, Hungarian Acad. of Sciences 1958–78, Vice-Chair. 1993–; mem. UN Cttee for Devt Policy (Vice-Chair.) 1978–84, Council of Habilitations, Budapest Univ. of Econs 1994–, Council of European Soc. for Population Econs 1996–; Vice-Chair. Hungarian Asscn of Economists 1995–; mem. Editorial Bd Journal of Policy Modeling, Acta Oeconomica, Közgazdasági Szemle; Fellow, Econometric Soc. 1976–. *Publications:* numerous articles on macroeconomic aspects and models of the human life-cycle (over-lapping generations, life-cycle theory, human capital), economic demography, pension econs. *Address:* Institute of Economics, Hungarian Academy of Sciences, Budaörsi út 45 1112 Budapest, Hungary (office). *Telephone:* (1) 816-4253 (office); (23) 344-226 (home). *Fax:* (1) 816-3136 (office); (23) 344-226 (home). *E-mail:* auguszti@econ.core.hu (office). *Website:* econ.core.hu/english/inst/auguszti.html (office).

AUKIN, David, BA, FRSA; British theatre, film and television producer; b. 12 Feb. 1942, Harrow; s. of Charles Aukin and Regina Aukin; m. Nancy Meckler 1969; two s.; ed St Paul's School, London and St Edmund Hall, Oxford; Co-founder Foco Novo and Jt Stock Theatre cos and admin. producer for various fringe theatre groups 1970–75; Admin. Dir Hampstead Theatre 1975–79, Dir 1979–84; Dir Leicester Haymarket Theatre 1984–86; Exec. Dir Royal Nat. Theatre of Great Britain 1986–90; Pres. Soc. of West End Theatres 1988–90; Head of Drama, Channel 4 TV 1990–97, Head of Film 1997–98; Jt Chief Exec. HAL Films 1998–2000; Producer and Man. Dir David Aukin Productions Ltd 2001–. *Films produced include:* Mansfield Park 1998, Elephant Juice 1999, About Adam 2000, The Hamburg Cell 2004, Mrs. Henderson Presents 2005. *Address:* c/o Act Productions Ltd, 20–22 Stukeley Street, London WC2B 5LR, England (office). *E-mail:* info@actproductions.co.uk (office). *Website:* actproductions.co.uk (office).

AULETTA ARMENISE, Giampiero, BEcons; Italian banking executive; *CEO, Unione di Banche Italiane SpA;* b. 1957, Rome; m.; three c.; ed Univ. of Rome, La Sapienza; with Bonifiche Siele Finanziaria Group 1978–98; Head of Analyses, Planning and Investments Dept, then Head of Financial Control and Risk Monitoring Dept, Banco Ambrosiano Veneto 1995–98, Man. Planning, Investments and Financial Control Sector, Banca Intesa 1998–2002; CEO Banca Popolare Commercio e Industria 2002–03, Banche Popolari Unite Group 2003–07, Unione di Banche Italiane SpA 2007–, mem. Bd of Dirs Banca Popolare di Bergamo SpA, Banca Popolare Commercio e Industria SpA, Banca Popolare di Ancona SpA, Banca Carime SpA, Centrobanca SpA, Banco di Brescia SpA. *Address:* Unione di Banche Italiane SpA, Piazza Vittorio Veneto 8, 24122 Bergamo, Italy (office). *Telephone:* (035) 392111 (office). *Website:* www.ubibanca.it (office).

AUMANN, Robert John, BS, SM, PhD; Israeli/American mathematician, economist and academic; *Professor Emeritus, The Hebrew University of Jerusalem;* b. 8 June 1930, Frankfurt am Main, Germany; s. of Siegmund Aumann and Miriam Aumann (née Landau); m.; five c.; ed City Coll. of New York, Massachusetts Inst. of Tech., USA; Instructor, Dept of Math., Hebrew Univ. of Jerusalem 1956–58, Lecturer 1958–61, Sr Lecturer 1961–64, Assoc. Prof. 1964–68, Prof. 1968–2000, Prof. Emer. 2001–, Fellow, Inst. for Advanced Studies 1979–80, mem. Center for the Study of Rationality 1991–; Research Assoc., Princeton Univ. 1960–61; Visiting Prof., Yale Univ. 1964–65, Univ. of California, Berkeley 1971, 1985–86, Univ. Catholique de Louvain, Belgium 1972, 1978, 1984, Stanford Univ. 1975–76, 1980–81, New York Univ. 1997; External Prof. (part-time), Tel-Aviv Univ. 1969–93; Prof. (part-time), Center for Game Theory in Econs, Stony Brook Univ. 1986–89, 1991–2013; Visiting Scholar, Cowles Foundation for Research in Econs, Yale Univ. 1989; Nemmers Prof. of Econs, Northwestern Univ. 1999–2000; Assoc. Ed. Journal of Economic Theory 1974–79, Econometrica 1975–78, Journal of the European Mathematical Society 2000–; mem. Editorial Bd International Journal of Game Theory 1971–, Journal of Mathematical Economics 1974–, SIAM Journal on Applied Mathematics 1976–80, Games and Economic Behavior 1989–; Pres. Israel Math. Union 1990–92, Game Theory Soc. 1998–2003; mem. Inst. for Math., Univ. of Minn. 1984, Math. Sciences Research Inst., Berkeley 1985–86, Fellow, Econometric Soc. 1966–, mem. Council 1977–82, Exec. Cttee 1982–85; mem. NAS 1985, Israel Acad. of Sciences and Humanities 1989; Corresp. FBA 1995; Corresp. mem. Royal Acad. of Financial Science and Econs (Spain) 2011; Foreign Hon. mem. American Acad. of Arts and Sciences 1974, Hon. mem. American Econ. Asscn 1993–; Dr hc (Univ. of Bonn) 1988, (Univ. Catholique de Louvain) 1989, (Univ. of Chicago) 1992, (CUNY) 2006, (Bar Ilan Univ.) 2006; Israel Prize in Econs 1994, Lanchester Prize in Operations Research 1995, Erwin Plein Nemmers Prize in Econs, Northwestern Univ. 1998, EMET Prize in Econs, Prime Minister of Israel 2002, Von Neumann Prize in Operations Research 2005, Nobel Memorial Prize in Econs 2005. *Publications:* Values of Non-atomic Games (with L. S. Shapley) 1974, Lectures on Game Theory 1989, Repeated Games with Incomplete Information (with M. Maschler) 1995, Collected Papers 2000, Handbook of Game Theory with Economic Applications (co-ed) 1992, 1994, 2002; numerous articles in professional journals and conf. papers on game theory, econ. theory and theory of choice. *Leisure interests:* skiing, hiking, cooking, Talmud study. *Address:* Center for the Study of Rationality, The Hebrew University, 91904 Jerusalem, Israel (office). *Telephone:* (2) 6586254 (office). *Fax:* (2) 6513681 (office). *E-mail:* nobel@huji.ac.il (office). *Website:* www.ma.huji.ac.il/raumann (office); www.ratio.huji.ac.il (office).

AUMONT, Jacques; French author and professor of film aesthetics; *Director of Studies, Ecole des hautes études en sciences sociales;* b. 1942, Avignon; m. Lyang Kim; two c.; ed École polytechnique, École nationale supérieure des télécommunications; began career as engineer, ORTF (nat. broadcasting co.) 1965–70; film reviewer, Les Cahiers du cinéma 1967–74; Dir Editions de l'Etoile 1970–74; Lecturer in Cinema, Univ. of Paris III 1970–, later Prof. of Film Aesthetics; Dir of Studies, Ecole des hautes études en sciences socials (EHESS) 1995–; mem. of various film festival juries and selection cttees; visiting lecturer at numerous foreign establishments, including Berkeley, Madison, Iowa City, Nijmegen, Lisbon; Chevalier des Palmes académiques. *Publications include:* Montage Eisenstein 1979, Esthétique du film (co-author) 1983, L'analyse des films (co-author) 1988, L'oeil interminable 1989, L'image 1990, Du visage au cinéma 1992, A quoi pensent les films 1997, De l'ésthetique au présent 1998, Dictionnaire critique et théorique du cinéma (co-author) 2001, Ingmar Bergman 2003, Matière d'images 2005; over 200 reviews in periodicals. *Leisure interests:* piano/chamber music. *Address:* Université Paris-3, 13 rue Santeuil, 75005 Paris, France (office). *Telephone:* 1-45-87-42-38 (office). *Fax:* 1-45-87-48-94 (office). *E-mail:* aumont@ehess.fr (office). *Website:* www.ehess.fr (office).

AUNG SAN SUU KYI, BA; Myanma politician; *Chairperson and General Secretary, National League for Democracy;* b. 19 June 1945, Rangoon; d. of the late Aung San and Khin Kyi; m. Michael Aris 1972 (died 1999); two s.; ed St Francis Convent, Methodist English High School, Lady Shri Ram Coll., Delhi Univ., St Hugh's Coll., Oxford; Asst Sec. Advisory Cttee on Admin. and Budgetary

Questions UN Secr., New York 1969–71; Resident Officer, Ministry of Foreign Affairs, Bhutan 1972; Visiting Scholar Centre for SE Asian Studies, Kyoto Univ., Japan 1985–86; Fellow, Indian Inst. of Advanced Studies 1987; Co-founder and Gen. Sec. Nat. League for Democracy 1988 (expelled from party), reinstated as Gen. Sec. 1995, Chair. 2013–; returned from UK 1988, under house arrest 1989–95, house arrest lifted July 1995, placed under de facto house arrest Sept. 2000, released unconditionally May 2002, arrested following Depayin massacre 30 May 2003, held in secret detention for over three months before being returned to house arrest, house arrest extended by one year 25 May 2007, mil. junta extended her house arrest another year 27 May 2008, release date set by court ruling Aug. 2009, released from house arrest 13 Nov. 2010; elected to Parl. 2012; Freeman, City of Dublin, Ireland 1999, Hon. mem. Bd Council Int. Inst. for Democracy and Electoral Assistance 2003, Hon. Canadian citizenship 2007, Hon. Pres. LSE Students' Union 2007, Freeman, City of Glasgow, Scotland 2009; Hon. AC 1996; numerous hon. degrees, including Hon. LLD (Memorial Univ. of Newfoundland) 2004, (Colgate Univ.) 2008, (Univ. of Ulster) 2009; Thorolf Rafto Memorial Prize 1990, Sakharov Prize 1990, European Parl. Human Rights Prize 1991, Nobel Peace Prize 1991, Simón Bolívar Int. Prize 1992, Liberal Int. Prize for Freedom 1995, Jawaharlal Nehru Award for Int. Understanding 1995, Freedom Award of Int. Rescue Cttee 1995, Presidential Medal of Freedom 2000, UNESCO Madanjeet Singh Prize for the Promotion of Tolerance and Non-Violence 2002, Free Spirit Prize, Freedom Forum USA 2003, Gwangju Prize for Human Rights 2004, ranked by Forbes magazine amongst The World's 100 Most Powerful Women (45th) 2004, (15th) 2005, (47th) 2006, (71st) 2007, (38th) 2008, (26th) 2011, (19th) 2012, (29th) 2013, Olof Palme Prize 2005, Freedom from Fear Award 2006, US Congressional Gold Medal 2008, Premi Internacional Catalunya 2008, Mahatma Gandhi Int. Award for Peace and Reconciliation 2009, Amb. of Conscience Award, Amnesty International 2009, Int. Bhagwan Mahavir World Peace Award 2012. *Publications:* Tibetan Studies in Honour of Hugh Richardson (co-ed.) 1979, Aung San 1984, Burma (Let's Visit Series) 1985, Nepal (Let's Visit Series) 1985, Bhutan (Let's Visit Series) 1986, Burma and India: Some Aspects of Intellectual Life Under Colonialism 1990, Aung San (Leaders of Asia Series) 1990, Aung San of Burma: A Biographical Portrait by His Daughter 1991, Freedom from Fear 1991, Towards a True Refuge 1993, Burma's Revolution of the Spirit: The Struggle for Democratic Freedom and Dignity (co-author) 1994, Freedom from Fear and Other Writings (co-author) 1995, Letter to Daniel: Despatches from the Heart by Fergal Keane (foreword by Aung San Suu Kyi) 1996, The Voice of Hope (with Alan Clements) 1998 (revised edn 2008), Letters from Burma (with Fergal Keane) 1998, Der Weg zur Freiheit (with U Kyi Maung and U Tin O) 1999. *Address:* c/o National League for Democracy, 97B West Shwegondine Road, Bahan Township, Yangon, Myanmar. *Website:* www.dassk.com.

AURAKZAI, Lt-Gen. (retd) Ali Mohammad Jan; Pakistani army officer (retd) and government administrator; b. 1 Dec. 1947; s. of Haji Khial Din and Naze Gul Aurakzai; m. Mujahida Khanum; three s. one d.; ed Peshawar Univ., Balochistan Univ.; fmr Commdr 11th Corps, Peshawar; fmr Adjutant-Gen. of Gen. HQ; Gov. of North-West Frontier Prov. 2006–08 (resgnd); Sitara-e-Basalat 1999, Hilal-e-Imtiaz (Mil.) 2000, Hilal-e-Imtiaz (Civil) 2004. *Leisure interests:* music, hunting. *Address:* House #2, Street 2, Sector 2, DHA Phase 1, Morgah, Islamabad, Pakistan (home). *Telephone:* (51) 5788298 (home). *E-mail:* ali.aurakzai@hotmail.com (office).

AURESCU, Bogdan Lucian, PhD; Romanian lawyer, diplomatist and politician; *Secretary of State for Strategic Affairs, Ministry of Foreign Affairs;* b. 9 Sept. 1973, Bucharest; ed Univ. of Bucharest, Institut Franco-Roumain du Droit des Affaires et Cooperation Internationale, Bucharest, The Hague Acad. of Int. Law, Nat. Defence Coll. of Romania; Attaché, Int. Law and Treaties Dept, Ministry of Foreign Affairs 1996–98, Counsellor, Office of the Minister 1998–99, Deputy Dir Int. Law and Treaties Dept 1999, Dir 2000–01, Dir Office of the Minister 1999, Dir Gen. Dept for Legal Affairs 2001, Under-Sec. of State for Legal Affairs 2003–04, Sec. of State for European Affairs 2004–05, for Strategic Affairs 2009–; Univ. Asst 2002, Lecturer in law 2004; Rep. of Romanian Govt at European Court of Human Rights 2003–04; Visiting Prof., Faculty of Law, Univ. of Hamburg, Germany 2006; Ed.-in-Chief, Romanian Journal of International Law; mem. Romanian Asscn for Int. Law and Int. Relations 1996–; Kt, Ordinul Naţional Serviciul Credincios 2002, Ordinul Meritul Diplomatic 2007. *Publications include:* Contemporary International Law (co-author) 2000, The New Sovereignty: Between Legal Reality and Political Necessity in the Contemporary International System 2003, The System of International Jurisdictions 2005. *Address:* Ministry of Foreign Affairs, 011822 Bucharest, Al. Alexandru 31, Romania (office). *Telephone:* (21) 3192169 (office). *Fax:* (21) 3192153 (office). *E-mail:* mae@mae.ro (office). *Website:* www.mae.ro (office).

AUSHEV, Lt-Gen. Ruslan Sultanovich; Russian/Ingush politician; b. 29 Oct. 1954, Volodarskoye, Kokchetav Region, USSR (now Kazakhstan); s. of Sultan Aushev and Tamara Aushev; m. Aza Ausheva 1983; two s. two d.; ed Ordzhonikidze Gen. Troops School, M. Frunze Mil. Acad.; Commdr motorized infantry co., then platoon 1975–80; Chief of HQ, then Commdr motorized Bn in Afghanistan 1980–82; Chief of Regt HQ in Afghanistan 1985–87; Commdr motorized infantry regt, then Deputy Commdr motorized infantry div. Far East Command 1987–91; at Council of Heads of Govts of CIS countries 1991–92; USSR People's Deputy 1989–91; Head of Admin in newly formed Ingush Repub. Nov.–Dec. 1992; Pres. Repub. of Ingushetiya 1993–2001 (resgnd); mem. Fed. Council of Russia 1993–2000, Rep. of Ingushetiya to Fed. Council 2002–03; fmr Chair. Political Council, Rossiiskaya Partiya Mira (Russian Party of Peace); Hero of Soviet Union (Gold Star). *Leisure interest:* football.

AUST, Stefan; German journalist and writer; b. 1 July 1946, Stade; m. Ulrike Meinhof; Ed. Concrete magazine 1966–69; staff mem. NDR TV 1970–72; journalist Panorama (political magazine) 1972–86; Chief Ed. Der Spiegel TV 1988–94, Ed.-in-Chief Der Spiegel 1994–2008; Man. Dir Der Spiegel TV GmbH 1995–; fmr TV host with talkshow Talk in the Tower, currently Host Spiegel-TV; Goldenen Kamera 2005. *Publications include:* Kennwort 100 Blumen – Verwicklung des Verfassungsschutzes in den Mordfall Ulrich Schmücker 1980, Brokdorf: Symbol Einer Politischen Wende 1981, Der Baader Meinhof Komplex 1985, Stammheim (film script) 1986, Werner Mauss – Ein Deutscher Agent 1988, Der Pirat: Die Drogenkarriere des Jan C. 1990, Die Flucht: Über die Vertreibung der Deutschen aus dem Osten 2002, Der Lockvogel. 2002, Irak: Geschichte eines modernen Krieges 2003, Die Gegenwart der Vergangenheit: Der lange Schatten des Dritten Reichs 2004, Wettlauf um die Welt: Die Globalisierung und wir 2007, Deutschland, Deutschland: Expedition durch die Wendezeit 2011. *Address:* Der Spiegel, Brandstwiete 19/Ost-West-Strasse 23, 20457 Hamburg, Germany (office). *Telephone:* (40) 30070 (office). *Fax:* (40) 30072247 (office). *E-mail:* spiegel@spiegel.de (office). *Website:* www.spiegel.de (office).

AUSTEN, K(arl) Frank, MD; American professor of medicine; *Astra Zeneca Professor of Respiratory and Inflammatory Diseases, Department of Medicine, Brigham and Women's Hospital;* b. 14 March 1928, Akron, Ohio; s. of Karl Arnstein and Bertle J. Arnstein; m. Jocelyn Chapman 1959; two s. two d.; ed Amherst Coll. and Harvard Medical School; Intern in Medicine, Mass. Gen. Hosp. 1954–55, Asst Resident 1955–56, Sr Resident 1958–59, Chief Resident 1961–62, Asst in Medicine 1962–63, Asst Physician 1963–66; Capt., US Army Medical Corps, Walter Reed Army Inst. of Research 1956–58; U.S.P.H.S. Postdoctoral Research Fellow, Nat. Inst. for Medical Research, Mill Hill, London, UK 1959–61; Physician-in-Chief, Robert B. Brigham Hosp. Boston 1966–80; Physician, Peter Bent Brigham Hosp. Boston 1966–80; Chair. Dept Rheumatology and Immunology, Brigham and Women's Hosp., Boston 1980–95, Dir Inflammation and Allergic Diseases Research Section, Div. of Rheumatology and Immunology 1995, now Astra Zeneca Professor of Respiratory and Inflammatory Diseases; Asst in Medicine, Harvard Medical School 1961, Instr. 1962, Assoc. 1962–64, Asst Prof. 1965–66, Assoc. Prof. 1966–68, Prof. 1969–72, Theodore Bevier Bayles Prof. of Medicine 1972–; Pres. Int. Soc. of Immunopharmacology 1994; mem. numerous professional orgs; recipient of numerous prizes and awards. *Publications:* numerous publications on immunology, etc. *Leisure interests:* skiing, jogging, gardening. *Address:* Department of Medicine, Brigham and Women's Hospital, Smith Building, Room 638, One Jimmy Fund Way, Boston, MA 02115, USA (office). *Telephone:* (617) 525-1300 (office). *Fax:* (617) 525-1310 (office). *Website:* dms.hms.harvard.edu/immunology (office).

AUSTER, Paul, BA, MA; American writer, poet and film director; b. 3 Feb. 1947, Newark, NJ; s. of the late Sam Auster and Queenie Auster; m. 1st Lydia Davis 1974 (divorced 1982); one s.; m. 2nd Siri Hustvedt 1982; one d.; ed Columbia High School, NJ, Columbia Coll., New York, Columbia Univ., New York; worked as census taker; oil tanker utility man. on the Esso Florence; moved to Paris, France 1971, returned to USA 1974; worked as translator; Lecturer in Creative Writing and Translation, Princeton Univ. 1986–90; juror, Cannes Film Festival 1997; mem. PEN (fmr Sec. and Vice-Pres. PEN American Center); Nat. Endowment for the Arts fellowships 1979, 1985; Prix Médicis Etranger 1993, Prince of Asturias Prize for Literature 2006, Premio di Napoli 2011; Commandeur, Ordre des Arts et des Lettres. *Films:* screenplays: Smoke 1995, Blue in the Face (co-dir) 1995, Lulu on the Bridge (also dir) 1998, The Inner Life of Martin Frost (also dir) 2007. *Publications:* fiction: City of Glass 1985, Ghosts 1986, The Locked Room 1986, In the Country of Last Things 1987, Moon Palace 1989, The Music of Chance 1990, Leviathan 1992, Mr Vertigo 1994, Timbuktu 1999, The Book of Illusions 2002, Oracle Night 2003, The Brooklyn Follies 2005, Travels in the Scriptorium 2006, Man in the Dark 2008, Invisible 2009, Sunset Park 2010; non-fiction: White Spaces 1980, The Invention of Solitude 1982, The Art of Hunger 1982, Hand to Mouth (memoir) 1989, The Red Notebook 1995, Why Write? 1996, Translations 1996, Collected Prose 2003, Winter Journal 2012; poetry: Unearth 1974, Wall Writing 1976, Fragments From Cold 1977, Facing the Music 1980, Disappearances: Selected Poems 1988, Collected Poems 2003; editor: The Random House Book of Twentieth-Century French Poetry 1982, True Tales of American Life 2001, Samuel Beckett: The Grove Centenary Edn 2006. *Address:* Carol Mann Agency, 55 Fifth Avenue, New York, NY 10003, USA (office). *Website:* www.paulauster.co.uk.

AUSTRIAN, Neil R.; American business executive; b. 1940; fmr CEO Doyle, Dane, Bernbach (advertising co.); Chair. and CEO Showtime/The Movie Channel –1987; Man. Dir Dillon, Read & Co. 1987–91; Pres. and COO Nat. Football League (NFL) 1991–99; mem. Bd of Dirs Office Depot Inc. 1998–, CEO and Interim Chair. 2004–05; mem. Bd of Dirs DirecTV Group 2003–, Viking Office Products 1988–98; mem. Advisory Bd Mid-Ocean Pnrs. *Address:* c/o Board of Directors, Office Depot Inc., 2200 Old Germantown Road, Delray Beach, FL 33445, USA (office).

AUTEUIL, Daniel; French actor; b. 24 Oct. 1950, Algeria; s. of Henri Auteil and Yvonne Auteil; m. Aude Ambroggi 2006; two d. (one with Emmanuelle Béart q.v.); worked in musical comedies in Paris; screen debut in L'Agression 1974; stage appearances include Le Garçon d'Appartement 1980; Chevalier des Arts et des Lettres. *Films include:* Attention les Yeux 1975, La Nuit Saint-Germain des Près 1976, L'Amour Violé 1976, Monsieur Papa 1977, Les Héros n'ont pas Froid aux Oreilles 1978, A Nous Deux 1979, Bête Mais Discipliné 1979, Les Sous-Doués 1980, Clara et les Chics Types 1980, Les Hommes Préfèrent les Grosses 1981, Les Sous-Doués en Vacances 1981, T'empêches Tout le Monde de Dormir 1981, Pour Cent Briques t'as Plus Rien 1981, Que les Gros Salaires Lèvent le Doigt 1982, P'tit Con 1983, Les Fauves 1983, Palace 1983, L'Arbalete 1984, L'Amour en Douce 1984, Jean de Florette (César for Best Actor 1986) 1985, Manon des Sources (César for Best Actor 1986, Best Actor Award, Cannes Film Festival) 1985, Le Paltoquet 1986, Quelques Jours Avec Moi 1988, Romuald and Juliette 1989, Lacenaire 1989, Ma Vie Est Un Enfer 1991, Un Coeur en Hiver 1992, Ma Saison Préférée 1992, Quelques Jours Avec Moi, L'Elegant Criminel, Tout Ça Pour Ça 1993, La Séparation 1994, La Reine Margot 1994, Ma Saison Préférée 1994, The Eighth Day 1996, Les Voleurs 1998, La Fille sur le Pont, The Lost Son 1999, La Veuve de Saint Pierre 2000, Sade 2000, Le Placard 2001, L'Adversaire 2002, Aprés vous 2003, Pourquoi (pas) le Brésil 2004, 36 Quai des Orfèvres 2004, L'Un reste, l'autre part 2005, Caché 2005, Peindre ou faire l'amour 2005, La Doublure 2006, L'Entente cordiale 2006, Mon meilleur ami 2006, N (Io e Napoleone) 2006, Dialogue avec mon jardinier 2007, La personne aux deux personnes 2008, Je l'aimais 2009, Donnant, donnant 2010, La fille du puisatier (also director) (The Well Digger's Daughter) 2011. *Address:* c/o Artmédia, 20 avenue Rapp, 75007 Paris, France (office).

AVAKOV, Arsen Borysovych; Ukrainian engineer and politician; *Interim Minister of Internal Affairs;* b. 2 Jan. 1964, Baku, Azerbaijan SSR, USSR; m.; one s.; ed Kharkiv Polytechnic Inst.; lab. asst, Chair for Automated Control Systems, Kharkiv Polytechnic Inst. 1981–82; engineer, All-Union Scientific-Research Inst. on Water Protection (Kharkiv) 1987–90; Founder and Head of Supervisory Bd, Investor JSC 1990–2005, Basis Commercial Bank 1992–2005;

elected mem. Exec. Cttee, Kharkiv City Council 2002; apptd Head of Kharkiv Regional State Admin 2005; Deputy of Kharkiv Regional Council 2006–10, mem. Standing Cttee on Budgetary Issues 2006–10, Deputy of Kharkiv Regional Council 2010–12, mem. Standing Cttee on Science, Educ., Culture, Historical Heritage, Intellectual Wealth and Nat. Minorities 2010; withdrew from Our Ukraine party 2010; mem. Fatherland United Opposition (Batkivshchyna Obyednana Opozytsiya) 2010–, accepted offer from Yulia Tymoshenko to become Chair. of regional org. (Bloc Yulia Tymoshenko); charged with illegally transferring land Jan. 2012, put on Interpol int. wanted list March 2012, detained in Frosinone, Italy late March 2012, placed under house arrest by Italian court as a preventive measure April 2012; mem. Verkhovna Rada (Parl.) Oct. 2012–; restriction measures and arrest warrant cancelled by a court ruling Dec. 2012; Interim Minister of Internal Affairs 2014–; Pres. Supervisory Bd, Renaissance Charity Foundation, Kharkiv Regional Charitable Org.; Head of Kharkiv Regional Div. of Nat. Olympic Cttee 2005–10; Co-founder Marianna Avakova Fund; Co-Chair. Star Bridge Int. Science Fiction Festival Organizing Cttee; Founder Producing Foundation of Arsen Avakov. *Publications:* a monograph, 12 scientific papers and several essays on political and social issues. *Address:* Ministry of Internal Affairs, 10124 Kyiv, vul. Ak. Bohomoltsya 10, Ukraine (office). *Telephone:* (44) 256-03-33 (office). *Fax:* (44) 256-16-33 (office). *E-mail:* mail@centrmia.gov.ua (office). *Website:* mvs.gov.ua (office); www.avakov.com.

AVDEYEV, Aleksander Alekseyevich; Russian politician and diplomatist; *Ambassador to the Holy See;* b. 8 Sept. 1946, Kremenchug, Poltava Region, Ukrainian SSR; m.; one s.; ed Moscow State Inst. of Int. Relations; diplomatic service with USSR Ministry of Foreign Affairs since 1968, Second, then First Sec., USSR Embassy in Paris 1977–85, Head of Sector, First European Dept, USSR Ministry of Foreign Affairs 1985–87, USSR Amb. to Luxembourg 1987–90, First Deputy Head, First European Dept, Ministry of Foreign Affairs 1990–91, USSR Deputy Minister of Foreign Affairs 1991–92, Amb. at Large, Russian Ministry of Foreign Affairs 1992, Amb. to Bulgaria 1992–96, Deputy Minister of Foreign Affairs 1996–98, First Deputy Minister 1998–2002, Amb. to France 2002–08 (also accred to Monaco 2007–08); Minister of Culture 2008–12; Amb. to Holy See 2012–; Order of Honour, Order of Friendship. *Address:* Embassy of Russia, Via della Conciliazione 10, 00193 Rome, Italy (office). *Telephone:* (06) 6877078 (office). *Fax:* (06) 6877168 (office). *E-mail:* russsede@libero.it (office).

AVEN, Peter Olegovich, PhD; Russian economist; *Chairman, Alfa Banking Group;* b. 16 March 1955, Moscow; s. of Oleg I. Aven; m.; two c.; ed Moscow State Univ.; researcher, All-Union Inst. for Systems Studies, USSR (now Russian) Acad. of Sciences 1981–88; Int. Inst. of Applied System Analysis, Laxenburg, Austria 1989–91, First Deputy Minister of Foreign Affairs, Chair. Cttee of Foreign Econ. Relations 1991–92; Russian Minister of Foreign Econ. Relations Feb.–Dec. 1992; mem. State Duma 1993–94; Pres. and Deputy Chair. Alfa Bank 1994–2011, Chair. Alfastrakhovaniye (Alfa Insurance) 2007–; Chair. STS Television 1998, Golden Telecom Inc. 2001–; Co-Chair. CTC Media; mem. Bd Competitiveness and Entrepreneurship Council, Bolshoi Theatre; Trustee Russian Econ. School, Nat. Asscn for Nat. Financial Reporting Standards; lectures internationally on econ. devts in Russia; several int. awards, named Russia's Most Admired Exec. in the Financial Services by Institutional Investor magazine 2004. *Publications:* The International Economy 2003; numerous books, scientific papers and articles on econ. and trade issues and reform of the rural economy. *Leisure interests:* the arts, theatre, collecting early 20th century Russian art. *Address:* Alfa Bank, 107078 Moscow, 27 Kalanchevskaya st, Russia (office). *Telephone:* (495) 620-91-91 (office). *Fax:* (495) 974-24-56 (office). *E-mail:* mail@alfabank.ru (office). *Website:* www.alfabank.ru (office).

AVERCHENKO, Vladimir Alexandrovich, CandEcon; Russian politician and engineer; b. 23 July 1950, Belaya Kalitva, Rostov Region; m.; three c.; ed Novocherkassk Polytech. Inst., New York Univ.; army service 1969–71; on staff Belokalitvinsky City CPSU Cttee 1975–80; constructor major industrial sites Rostov Region; Head of Itominstroi, then Promstroi Rostov Region 1980–89; Deputy Chair. Novocherkassk City Exec. Cttee 1989–91; First Vice-Maj. Novocherkassk 1991–98; Deputy Gov., Minister of Econ., Int. and Foreign Relations, Rostov Region 1998–99; concurrently Head Econ. Council Asscn of Social-Econ. Devt N Caucasus; Deputy State Duma, People's Deputies Group 1999; Head Del. of Fed. Ass. in Parl. Ass. of Black Sea Econ. Co-operation (PACHES); Deputy Chair. State Duma 2000–03; Dir Fed. Agency for Construction and Housing Economy 2004–05; state awards and int. Award for contrib. to devt of free market relations between Russia and CIS countries 1994. *Publications:* numerous publs, eight books on man., investment policy, ecology. *Leisure interests:* chess, basketball, collecting figurines of lions, collecting coins. *Address:* c/o State Duma, 103265 Moscow, Okhotny Ryad 1, Russia (office). *Telephone:* (495) 292-84-40 (office). *Fax:* (495) 292-52-23 (office).

AVERY, Bryan Robert, MA, DipArch, RIBA; British architect and designer; *Principal, Avery Associates Architects;* b. 2 Jan. 1944, Aston Tirrold, Berks., England; one d.; ed Brockenhurst Co. High School, Leicester Coll. of Art and Univ. of Essex; specialised in component devt and industrialized bldg techniques 1967–69; studied history and theory of architecture, Univ. of Essex 1969–70; worked in various architect practices 1970–78; Founder and Prin. Avery Assocs 1978–; Minerva Award for Nat. Film Theatre, UNESCO Award for Advanced Tech. Housing; awards for Museum of the Moving Image: PA Award for Innovation 1988, Civic Trust Award 1989; City Heritage Award for Plantation House 1992; awards for No. 1 Neathouse Place: Aluminium Imagination Architectural Awards 1997, British Construction Industry Award 1997, Glassex Award 1997, Westminster Soc.'s Award 1997, Nat. Lighting Design Awards 1997, British Council for Offices Award 1998, Civic Trust Commendation 1998, British Inst. of Architectural Technologists 1999, Millennium Products Award 1999; awards for BFI London IMAX Cinema: Millennium Products Award 1999, FX Int. Interior Design Awards 1999, British Construction Industry Awards 1999, Comedia Creative City Award for Urban Innovation 2000, Civic Trust Award 2000, Nat. Drywall Awards 2001; awards for Royal Acad. of Dramatic Art: Camden Design Award Commendation 2001, ADAPT Trust Access Award 2001, RIBA Award 2001, Civic Trust Commendation 2002, British Inst. of Architectural Technologists Commended Award 2002, Open Award for Tech. Excellence in Architectural Tech. 2002, United States Inst. of Theater Technicians Merit Award 2003, Building Quality Awards

Excellence in Inclusive Design Award 2003; Best New Permanent Gallery Award for London Transport Museum 2008, Chicago Athenaeum Int. Architecture Award for Old Bailey 2010, Civic Trust Award commendation for Old Bailey 2010, RICS East Midlands Award for Repton School 2012, CIAT Award for Repton School 2012, RIBA East Midlands Bldg of the Year Award for Repton School 2013. *Artistic achievements:* major bldgs completed include Museum of the Moving Image, London 1987–88, Nat. Film Theatre foyers and bookshop 1989, No. 1 Neathouse Place 1997, IMAX Cinema for the British Film Inst. 1999, Royal Acad. of Dramatic Art (RADA) 2000, regeneration of London Transport Museum 2007; Concert Hall for Oakham School; Rutland 2007; Repton School Theatre Derby 2011; major design and research projects include Advanced Tech. Housing Project, Wilderness City Project and Ecological Beacons Project, Kolkata New Town, India. *Publications include:* numerous articles in the UK and abroad. *Leisure interests:* film, theatre, country walking. *Address:* Avery Associates Architects, 270 Vauxhall Bridge Road, London, SW1V 1BB, England (office). *Telephone:* (20) 7233-6262 (office). *Fax:* (20) 7233-5182 (office). *E-mail:* enquiries@avery-architects.co.uk (office). *Website:* www.avery-architects.co.uk (office).

AVICE, Edwige, LèsL; French consultant and fmr politician; b. 13 April 1945, Nevers; d. of Edmond Bertrand and Hélène Guyot; m. Etienne Avice 1970; ed Cours Fénelon, Nevers, Lycée Pothier, Orléans, Univ. of Paris; worked for Nat. Cttee for Housing Improvement 1970; Int. Dept, Crédit Lyonnais 1970–73; on staff of Dir-Gen. of Paris Hosps 1973–78; Pres. Asscn Démocratique des Français de l'Etranger 1991–93; mem. Parti Socialiste (PS) 1972, mem. Exec. Bureau 1977, Nat. Secr. 1987–94, PS Nat. Del. for Nat. Service; mem. Nat. Ass. 1978–81, 1986–88; Minister-Del. for Free Time, Youth and Sports 1981–84; Sec. of State attached to the Minister of Defence 1984–86; Minister-Del. attached to the Minister for Foreign Affairs 1988–91; Minister of Co-operation and Devt 1991–93; Conseillère de Paris 1983–88; Pres. and Dir-Gen. Financière de Brienne 1993–2005, Chair Brienne Council and Finance 1993–2005; currently Assoc. Dir BIPE (econ. consultancy); Pres. Int. Defence Council 1999–2003. *Publication:* Terre d'élection 1993. *Leisure interests:* travelling, music, swimming, walking, fencing. *Address:* BIPE, Le Vivaldi, 11/13 rue René Jacques, 92138 Issy-les-Moulineaux Cedex, France (office). *Telephone:* 1-70-37-23-23 (office). *Fax:* 1-70-37-23-00 (office). *E-mail:* contact@bipe.fr (office). *Website:* www.bipe.com (office).

ÁVILA, Rodrigo, BEng, BA; Salvadorean police officer and politician; b. 25 June 1965, San Salvador; three d.; ed North Carolina State Univ. and Gainesville Coll., Ga, USA, courses in police specialization at FBI Acad. and police admin at Texas A&M Univ., USA; rose through ranks of police force to serve as Deputy Chief of Police Operations Feb.–June 1994, Chief of Police 1994–99, 2006–08; Deputy Head of Alianza Republicana Nacionalista (ARENA) Bench in Congress 2000–03; cand. in mayoral elections for Santa Tecla 2003; Deputy Minister for Security 2003–06; ARENA party cand. for Pres. of El Salvador 2008. *Address:* c/o Alianza Republicana Nacionalista (ARENA), Prolongación Calle Arce 2423, entre 45 y 47 Avda Norte, San Salvador, El Salvador.

AVILA VILLEGAS, Eruviel, LLB, LLM; Mexican lawyer and politician; *Governor, State of Mexico;* b. 1 May 1969, Ecatepec de Morelos; m. (divorced); four c.; ed Universidad Tecnológica de México, Nat. Autonomous Univ. of Mexico; fmr teacher, Universidad Tecnológica de México; Sec., Ecatepec de Morelos City Council 1994–96; mem. Congreso de la Unión (Parl.) 1997–2000, 2006–09; Mayor of Ecatepec 2003–06, 2009–11; Gov. State of Mexico 2011–; Pres. Federación Nacional de Municipios de México (Nat. Fed. of Municipalities of Mexico); mem. Partido Revolucionario Institucional (PRI), Pres. PRI Edomex 2006. *Publications:* La Creación de la Corte Constitucional del Estado de México 2003. *Address:* Office of the Governor, State of Mexico, 50000 Toluca, Mexico (office). *Website:* www .eruviel.com.mx.

AVILDSEN, John Guilbert; American film director, cinematographer and editor; b. 21 Dec. 1935, Ill.; s. of Clarence John Avildsen and Ivy Avildsen (née Guilbert); m. Tracy Brooks Swope 1987; two s. one d.; ed New York Univ.; Advertising Man. Vespa Motor Scooters 1959; served in US Army 1959–61; Asst Dir Greenwich Village Story 1961; worked as asst cameraman and production man.; with Muller, Jordan & Herrick Industrial Films 1965–67; mem. Dirs Guild of America, Motion Picture Photographers Union, Motion Picture Eds Union, Writers Guild of America. *Films include:* Turn On to Love 1967, Sweet Dreams 1968, Guess What We Learned in School Today 1969, Joe 1970, Cry Uncle 1971, Save the Tiger 1972, Inaugural Ball 1973, W.W. and the Dixie Dancekings 1974, Rocky (Acad. Award for Best Dir) 1976, Slow Dancing in the Big City 1978, The Formula 1980, Neighbors 1981, Traveling Hopefully 1982, A Night in Heaven 1983, The Karate Kid 1984, Happy New Year 1985, The Karate Kid II 1986, For Keeps 1987, The Karate Kid III 1989, Lean on Me (Image Award, Nat. Asscn for the Advancement of Colored People) 1989, Rocky V 1990, The Power of One 1992, 8 Seconds 1994, A Fine and Private Place 1998. *Television:* From No House to Options House (Emmy Award).

AVINERI, Shlomo; Israeli political scientist and academic; *Professor Emeritus of Political Science, Hebrew University of Jerusalem;* b. 20 Aug. 1933, Bielsko, Poland; s. of Michael Avineri and Erna Groner; m. Dvora Nadler 1957; one d.; ed Shalva Secondary School, Tel-Aviv, Hebrew Univ., Jerusalem and London School of Econs; has lived in Israel since 1939; Prof. of Political Science, Hebrew Univ. Jerusalem 1971–, now Emer., Dir Eshkol Research Inst. 1971–74, Dean of Faculty of Social Sciences 1974–76; Dir-Gen. Ministry of Foreign Affairs 1976–77; Dir Inst. for European Studies, Hebrew Univ. 1997–; visiting appointments at Yale Univ. 1966–67, Wesleyan Univ., Middletown, Conn. 1971–72, Research School of Social Sciences, ANU 1972, Cornell Univ. 1973, Univ. of California 1979, Queen's Coll., New York 1989, Univ. of Oxford 1989; mem. Int. Inst. of Philosophy 1980–; Fellow, Woodrow Wilson Center, Washington, DC 1983–84; Visiting Prof., Cardozo School of Law, New York 1996–97, 2000–01, Brookings Inst., Washington, DC 1991, Cen. European Univ., Budapest 1994, Northwestern Univ., Evanston 1997, Carnegie Endowment for Int. Peace, Washington, DC 2000–01; mem. Israel Acad. of Sciences and Humanities; Fellow, Collegium Budapest 2002; Freedom Medal, Senate of the Czech Repub. 2008; Commdr, Star of Italian Order of Solidarity 2009; Dr hc (Weizmann Inst. of Science) 2010; British Council Scholarship 1961, Rubin Prize in the Social Sciences 1968, Naphtali Prize for Study of Hegel 1977, Present Tense Award for Study of Zionism 1982, Carlyle Lecturer, Univ. of Oxford 1989, Israel Prize 1996, Life Award, Israel Political Science Asscn 2005. *Publications:*

The Social and Political Thought of Karl Marx 1968, Karl Marx on Colonialism and Modernization 1968, Israel and the Palestinians 1971, Marx's Socialism 1972, Hegel's Theory of the Modern State 1973, Varieties of Marxism 1977, The Making of Modern Zionism 1981, Moses Hess – Prophet of Communism and Zionism 1985, Arlosoroff – A Political Biography 1989, Communitarianism and Individualism (co-author) 1992, Herzl's Diaries 1998, Identity and Integration 1999, The Law of Religious Identity (co-author) 1999, Identities in Transformation 2002, Herzl: Theodor Herzl and the Foundation of the Jewish State 2013. *Address:* Faculty of Social Sciences, Hebrew University of Jerusalem, Mount Scopus, Jerusalem 91905 (office); 10 Hagedud Ha-ivri Street, Jerusalem 92345, Israel (home). *Telephone:* (2) 588-3009 (office); (2) 563-0862 (home). *Fax:* (2) 588-1333 (office). *E-mail:* shlomo .avineri@huji.ac.il (office); euroavi@mscc.huji.ac.il (office). *Website:* politics.huji.ac .il (office).

AVNET, Jonathan (Jon) Michael, BA; American film industry executive and film director; b. 17 Nov. 1949, Brooklyn, New York; m. Barbara Brody; one s. two d.; ed Sarah Lawrence Coll., Univ. of Pennsylvania, Conservatory for Advanced Film Studies; Reader, United Artists, LA 1974; Dir of Creative Affairs, Sequoia Pictures, LA 1975–77; Pres. Tisch/Avnet Productions, LA 1977–85; Chair. Avnet/Kerner Co., LA 1985–; Pres. Allied Communications Inc.; Trustee LA Co. Opera; Fellow, American Film Inst.; mem. Dirs Guild of America, Writers Guild of America, Acad. of Motion Pictures Arts and Sciences. *Films:* Dir and Producer: Fried Green Tomatoes at the Whistle Stop Cafe (three Golden Globes), The War, Up Close and Personal, George of the Jungle, 88 Minutes 2007, Righteous Kill 2008; Producer, Exec. Producer: Risky Business, Men Don't Leave, Less than Zero, When a Man Loves a Woman, Mighty Ducks, Deal of the Century, Miami Rhapsody, Three Musketeers; Exec. Producer: The Burning Bed, Silence of the Heart, Heatwave (four Cable Ace Awards, including Best Picture), Do You Know the Muffin Man, No Other Love, Steal This Movie. *Television includes:* Call to Glory (series) 1984–85, Between Two Women (film) 1986, Uprising (film) 2001, Bunker Hill (film) 2009, Pleading Guilty (film) 2010, Have a Little Faith (film) 2011, Jan (series) 2013, Justified (series) 2010–13, Lauren (series) 2013. *Leisure interests:* basketball, skiing, biking.

AVOKA, Cletus, LLB; Ghanaian politician and lawyer; ed Univ. of Ghana; Chair. Public Tribunal for Northern Ghana 1983–84; mem. Parl. (Nat. Democratic Congress) for Bawku W 1992–2005; Minister of State 1995–97, Minister of Lands and Forestry 1997, of Environment, Science and Tech. 1998, of the Interior 2009–11; worked in pvt. legal practice, Accra 2005–09. *Address:* c/o Ministry of the Interior, POB M42, Accra, Ghana (office).

AVRAMOPOULOS, Dimitris, LLB; Greek politician and fmr diplomatist; *Minister of National Defence;* b. 6 June 1953, Athens; s. of Lambros Avramopoulos and Helene Avramopoulos; m. Vivian Avramopoulos; two s.; ed Univ. of Athens, Boston Univ., USA, Univ. Libre de Bruxelles, Belgium, Diplomatic Acad. of Ministry of Foreign Affairs; served in diplomatic service 1981–93, postings included Consul in Liège, Belgium 1983–88, Consul-Gen., Geneva 1992, Dir of Diplomatic Office of Prime Minister Konstantinos Mitsotakis 1993; mem. Vouli (Parl.) (New Democracy) for Athens A Electoral Dist 1993–94, 2004–11; Mayor of Athens 1995–2002; Minister of Tourism Devt 2004–06, of Health and Social Solidarity 2006, 2007–09, of Nat. Defence 2011–12, 2013–, of Foreign Affairs 2012–13; mem. New Democracy party 1993–95, 2004–, mem. Cen. Cttee 1993–95, Vice-Pres. 2010–; Visiting Fellow, Kennedy School of Govt, Harvard Univ., USA 2003; Hon. Prof., Moscow State Acad. of Technological Sciences 2002, Peking Univ., Beijing 2002; numerous awards and decorations from several countries; Dr hc (Adelphi Univ., New York) 1995, (Deree Coll., Athens) 1997, (Drexel Univ., Philadelphia) 2000, (Kingston Univ.) 2000. *Address:* Ministry of National Defence, Odos Mesogeion 227–231, Holargos, 154 51 Athens, Greece (office). *Telephone:* (210) 6598100 (office). *Fax:* (210) 6443832 (office). *E-mail:* minister@mod.mil.gr (office). *Website:* www.mod.mil.gr (office).

AVRIL, Pierre; French academic; *Professor Emeritus, University of Paris;* b. 18 Nov. 1930, Pau; s. of Stanislas Avril and Geneviève Camion; m. Marie-Louise Hillion 1959; one s.; Asst, Pierre Mendès France 1955–62, Ed.-in-Chief Cahiers de la République 1960–62; Sub-Ed., Soc. Gen. de Presse 1962–69; Prof., Faculté de Droit de Poitiers 1972–79, Univ. de Paris X 1979–88, Inst. d'études politiques 1982–97, Univ. de Paris II 1988–99; mem. Conseil supérieur de la magistrature 1998–2002; Pres. Comm. de réflexion sur le statut pénal du Président de la République 2002; mem. Comité scientifique de la Comm. Nat. des archives constitutionnelles 2002–12; Hon. Pres., Association Française de Droit Constitutionnel 2005. *Publications:* Le Régime politique de la Vᵉ République 1964, Un président pour quoi faire? 1965, Essais sur les partis politiques 1990, La Vᵉ République – histoire politique et constitutionnelle 1994, Les conventions de la Constitution 1997, Droit parlementaire (with others) 2010. *Address:* 48 rue Gay-Lussac, 75005 Paris, France (home). *Telephone:* 1-43-26-36-43 (home).

AVRIL, Brig.-Gen. Prosper; Haitian politician and army officer; ed Mil. Acad., Haiti and Univ. of Haiti Law School; fmr adviser to deposed Pres. Jean-Claude Duvalier; adviser to mil.-civilian junta headed by Gen. Namphy (q.v.) and mem. Nat. Governing Council 1986; Commdr Presidential Guard 1988; major participant in June 1988 coup which overthrew civilian Govt of Leslie Manigat; leader of coup which deposed regime of Gen. Namphy Sept. 1988; Pres. of Haiti 1988–90.

AWAD, Nihad; American organization official; *Executive Director, Council on American-Islamic Relations;* b. Jordan; ed Univ. of Minnesota; began career at Univ. of Minnesota Medical Center; fmr Public Relations Dir Islamic Asscn for Palestine; Exec. Dir Council on American-Islamic Relations, Washington, DC 1994–; mem. Vice-Pres. Al Gore's Civil Rights Advisory Panel, White House Comm. on Aviation Safety and Security 1997; mem. American Muslim Political Co-ordinating Cttee 2000. *Address:* Council on American-Islamic Relations, 453 New Jersey Avenue, SE, Washington, DC 20003, USA (office). *Telephone:* (202) 488-8787 (office). *Fax:* (202) 488-0833 (office). *E-mail:* info@cair.com (office). *Website:* www.cair.com (office).

AWADALLAH, Bassem I, PhD; Jordanian business executive and fmr government official; b. 1964; ed Georgetown Univ., USA, London School of Econs, UK; worked in investment banking in UK 1986–91; Econ. Sec. to Prime Minister of Jordan 1992–96, Econ. Adviser 1996–99; Dir Econ. Dept, Royal Hashemite Court 1999–2001; Minister of Planning and Int. Co-operation 2001–Feb. 2005; Minister of Finance April–June 2005; Dir Office of His Majesty King Abdullah II of Jordan 2006–07, Chief of the Royal Hashemite Court 2007–08 (resgnd); Founder and CEO Tomoh Advisory (consultancy), Dubai; fmr Vice-Chair. Bd of Trustees King Abdullah I Fund for Devt; mem. Bd of Dirs Al Baraka Banking Group; Trustee Dubai School of Govt; Lee Kuan Yew Fellow 2005; Al Kawkab and Al Istiqlal Decorations of the First Order of the Hashemite Kingdom of Jordan; Al Hussein Medal for Distinguished Service, Royal Hashemite Award for Distinguished Service 1995, named Young Global Leader by World Econ. Forum 2009.

AWORI, Arthur Moody; Kenyan politician and business executive; b. 5 Dec. 1927, Butere; s. of Jeremiah Awori and Maria Awori; m.; ed Chartered Inst. of Secretaries; MP for Funyula constituency 1983–; numerous posts as Asst Minister under Pres. Daniel arap Moi, including Asst Minister for Educ.; left Kanu Party late 2002 to join new Narc alliance; Minister of Home Affairs 2002–05, Vice-Pres. 2003–05; fmr Chair. Western Province Kanu MPs Parl. Group; Chair. Francis Da Gama Rose Group 1981–; Dir East Africa Building Soc., Akiba Bank Ltd, Mercantile Life and General Insurance Co. Ltd, Macmillan Publrs Kenya Ltd, Securicor Security Services Ltd; Founding Chair. Asscn for the Physically Disabled of Kenya; Propr of Gulumwoyo Ltd, Western Sunrise Properties Ltd, Mocian Ltd, Rose Mareba Ltd, Mareba Enterprises Ltd; Sec. to the Bd of East African Industries (EAI); Elder of the Burning Spear. *Leisure interests:* tennis, swimming. *Address:* National Office, Association for the Physically Disabled of Kenya, PO Box 46747, Nairobi 00100, Kenya (office). *E-mail:* nat@apdk.org (office).

AXEL, Richard, MD; American biochemist and academic; *Professor of Biochemistry and Molecular Biophysics, Columbia University;* b. 1946; ed Columbia Coll., Johns Hopkins Univ. School of Medicine; began academic career as Fellow, Columbia Univ. Inst. of Cancer and Nat. Inst. of Health; currently Prof. of Biochemistry and Molecular Biophysics, Columbia Univ. and Prof. of Pathology, Columbia Univ. Coll. of Physicians and Surgeons; Investigator, Howard Hughes Medical Inst. (HHMI); mem. NAS, American Philosophical Soc., American Acad. of Arts and Sciences; Eli Lilly Award in biological chemistry, Richard Lounsberry Award, NAS, Bristol-Myers Squibb Award for distinguished achievement in neuroscience research, Gairdner Foundation Int. Award, Nobel Prize in Physiology or Medicine (jtly with Linda B. Buck, q.v.) 2004. *Address:* Columbia University Medical Center, Room 1014, 701 West 168 Street, New York, NY 10032 (office); Howard Hughes Medical Institute, 4000 Jones Bridge Road, Chevy Chase, MD 20815-6789, USA (office). *Telephone:* (212) 305-6915 (office); (301) 215-8500 (office). *Fax:* (212) 923-7249 (office). *E-mail:* ra27@columbia.edu (office). *Website:* cpmcnet.columbia.edu/dept/gsas/biochem/faculty/axel.html (office); cpmcnet .columbia.edu/dept/neurobeh/axel (office); www.hhmi.org (office).

AXELROD, David M., BA; American political consultant and fmr government official; b. 22 Feb. 1953, New York City; m. Susan Landau 1979; ed Univ. of Chicago; reporter and columnist, Chicago Tribune newspaper 1977–84; Communications Man. then Co-Dir Paul Simon's US Senate campaign in Illinois 1984; Founding Pnr, Axelrod & Assocs (political consultancy firm, now AKP&D Message and Media) 1985–; worked on mayoral campaigns of Harold Washington, Dennis Archer, Michael R. White, Anthony A. Williams, Lee P. Brown and John F. Street; worked with John Edwards' Presidential campaign team and Barack Obama's Senate campaign 2004; consultant for gubernatorial campaigns of Eliot Spitzer in New York and Deval Patrick in Massachusetts 2006; chief political advisor to Rahm Emanuel in US House of Reps election 2006; chief strategist and media advisor for Barack Obama's presidential campaign 2007–08; Sr Advisor to Pres. of USA, The White House 2009–11, Sr Strategist for Pres. Barack Obama's re-election campaign 2011–12; Sr Political Analyst, NBC News and MSNBC 2013–. *Address:* . *Website:* www.nbcnews.com

AXFORD, David Norman, MA, MSc, PhD, CEng, FIEE, FRMetS; British meteorologist (retd); b. 14 June 1934, London, England; s. of Norman Axford and Joy A. Axford (née Williams); m. 1st Elizabeth A. Stiles 1962 (divorced 1980); one s. two d.; m. 2nd Diana R. J. Bufton 1980; three step-s. one step-d.; ed Merchant Taylors School, Plymouth Coll., St John's Coll., Cambridge, Univ. of Southampton, Kellogg Coll., Oxford (Diploma and Advanced Diploma in English Local History, Dept of Continuing Educ., Univ. of Oxford); Scientific Officer, Kew Observatory 1960–62; Sr Scientific Officer, various RAF stations 1962–68; Prin. Scientific Officer, Meteorological Research Flight, Royal Aircraft Establishment, Farnborough 1968–76; Asst Dir (SPSO) Operation Instrumentation Branch 1976–80, Asst Dir (SPSO), Telecommunications 1980–82; Deputy Dir Observational Services 1982–84; Dir of Services and Deputy to Dir-Gen. Meteorological Office 1984–89; Pres. N Atlantic Ocean Station Bd 1982–85; Chair. Cttee of Operational World Weather Watch System Evaluations – N Atlantic (CONA) 1985–89; Deputy Sec.-Gen. World Meteorological Org., Geneva 1989–95, Special Exec. Adviser to Sec.-Gen. Jan.–May 1995; Consultant Meteorologist 1995–; Consultant to Earthwatch Europe, Oxford 1996–2000; Chair. of Trustees, Stanford-in-the-Vale Public Purposes Charity 2000–02, Clerk/Corresp. 2002–; Hon. Sec., Royal Meteorological Soc. 1983–88, Vice-Pres. 1989–91, Chair. Accreditation Bd 1999–2004, Sec., Special Group on Observations and Instruments 1999–2001; Trustee, Thames Valley Hospice, Windsor 1996–98; mem. Exec. Cttee British Asscn of Former UN Civil Servants 1996–2004, Vice-Chair. 1998, Chair. 1999–2004, 2009–10, Vice-Pres. 2004–; Chartered Meteorologist of Royal Meteorological Soc. 1994–; Vice-Pres. and Treas. European Meteorological Soc. 2002–05; Chair. Stanford-in-the-Vale Local History Soc. 2004–11; Trustee, Friends of the Ridgeway 2008–, Stanford-in-the-Vale Village Hall Man. Cttee 2010–; Groves Award 1972. *Publications include:* articles in professional journals and local history magazine The Stanfordian. *Leisure interests:* home and garden, food and wine, Tibetan terrier, 12 grandchildren, one great-grandson, local and family history. *Address:* Honey End, 14 Ock Meadow, Stanford-in-the-Vale, Oxon., SN7 8LN, England (home). *Telephone:* (1367) 718480 (home).

AXMEDBAYEV, Maj.-Gen. Adxam Akramovich; Uzbekistani army officer and government official; *Minister of Internal Affairs;* First Deputy Minister of Internal Affairs –2013, Minister of Internal Affairs 2013–. *Address:* Ministry of Internal Affairs, 100029 Tashkent, Yu. Rajaby ko'ch. 1, Uzbekistan (office). *Telephone:* (71) 139-73-36 (office). *Fax:* (71) 133-89-34 (office). *E-mail:* info@mvd.uz (home). *Website:* www.mvd.uz (office).

AXMETOV, Serik Niğmetulı, DEcon; Kazakhstani metallurgist and politician; *Minister of Defence;* b. 25 June 1958, Qarağandi Oblast; m.; two c.; ed Technical Univ. of Qarağandi, Russian Acad. of Man.; started career at Qarağandi Metallurgical Plant, becoming Head, Foreign Econ. Relations Dept; worked in Komsomol (Communist Party youth movt) and CP bodies, becoming First Sec., Qarağandi regional Komsomol Cttee 1983–90; engaged in business 1993–95; Pres. Ken Dala (Cen. Kazakhstan commodity exchange) 1995–2001; Akim (Gov.) Temirtaw city 2001–03; fmr first Deputy Akim of Astana; Head, State Inspection for Admin. Supervision and Personnel Policies, Kazakhstan Presidential Admin 1998–2001; Chair. Atameken (Nat. Union of Entrepreneurs and Employers) 2005; Minister of Transport and Communications 2006–09; Deputy Prime Minister 2009; Akim of Qarağandi oblast 2009–12; First Deputy Prime Minister Jan.–Sept. 2012, Prime Minister Sept. 2012–14 (resgnd); Minister of Defence 2014–; Order of Parasat (Nobility), Kurmet Medal of Honour 2005, 10 years of Astana Medal 2008. *Address:* Ministry of Defence, 010000 Astana, Soljagaw, AEA, 2-ui Barlyk kukyktar korgalgan, Kazakhstan (office). *Telephone:* (7172) 72-14-11 (office). *Fax:* (7172) 50-41-97 (office). *E-mail:* pressa@mod.gov.kz (office). *Website:* www .mod.gov.kz (office).

AX:SON JOHNSON, Antonia, BA, MA; Swedish business executive; *Chairman, Axel Johnson Group;* b. 6 Sept. 1943, New York City, USA; d. of Axel Ax:son Johnson, Jr and Antonia de Souza; m. Göran Ennerfelt; four c.; ed Radcliffe Coll., USA, Univ. of Stockholm; succeeded father as Chair. of family-owned A. Johnson & Co. (now Axel Johnson Group) 1982–, group has interests in energy, telecommunications and real estate, holds 45% share of Axfood AB (one of largest food operations in Scandinavia), mem. Bd of Dirs AxFast AB, Axfood AB, Mekonomen AB, Nordstjernan AB, NCC AB, Axel and Margaret Ax:son Johnson Foundation, and others; mem. City Council Täby Municipality; mem. Liberal Party; Chair. Dressage Cttee, Swedish Equestrian Fed. 2001–08; mem. numerous Swedish charities, including World Childhood Foundation; Hon. DCL (Bishop's Univ., Canada), Hon. DHumLitt (Middlebury Coll. of Vermont); ranked by Forbes magazine amongst The World's 100 Most Powerful Women (65th) 2004, (61st) 2005, (71st) 2006, (69th) 2007, ranked by the Financial Times amongst the Top 25 Businesswomen in Europe (fourth) 2005–06, (third) 2007, ranked by Fortune magazine amongst the 50 Most Powerful Women in Business outside the US (21st) 2008, (22nd) 2009, (24th) 2010. *Leisure interest:* avid horsewoman. *Address:* Axel Johnson AB, Villagatan 6, PO Box 26008, 100 41 Stockholm, Sweden (office). *Telephone:* (8) 7016100 (office). *Fax:* (8) 213026 (office). *Website:* www.axeljohnson .se (office); www.axeljohnson.com (office).

AXWORTHY, Lloyd, BA, MA, PhD, OM, OC; Canadian academic administrator and fmr politician; *President and Vice-Chancellor, University of Winnipeg;* b. 21 Dec. 1939; s. of Norman Joseph Axworthy and Gwen Jane Axworthy; m. Denise Ommaney 1984; two s. one d.; ed United Coll. (now Univ. of Winnipeg), Princeton Univ., USA; Asst Prof. of Political Science, Univ. of Winnipeg 1964–79, Dir Inst. of Urban Studies 1970–79, Pres. and Vice-Chancellor 2004–; mem. Man. Legis. 1973–79; mem. House of Commons 1979–; MP for Winnipeg Fort-Garry 1979–88, for Winnipeg South-Centre 1988–2000; Minister of Employment and Immigration 1980–83, Minister responsible for Status of Women 1980–81; Minister of Transport 1983–84; Minister of Human Resources Devt and Minister of Western Econ. Diversification 1993–96, of Foreign Affairs 1996–2000; UN Special Envoy to Ethiopia and Eritrea 2004–; Dir and CEO Liu Centre for the Study of Global Issues, Univ. of British Columbia 2001–04; Pres. World Federalist Movt–Inst. for Global Policy 2004–; Chair. Human Security Centre for UN Univ. for Peace, State of the World Forum, Comm. on Globalization; mem. Cttee High Level Comm. for the Empowerment of the Poor, UNDP 2005–; Head, OAS Electoral Observation Mission to Peru 2006; mem. Bd Univ. of Winnipeg Foundatioo, MacArthur Foundation, Human Rights Watch (Chair. Advisory Board For Americas Watch), Lester B. Pearson Coll., Univ. of the Arctic, Pacific Council on Int. Policy, Churchill Gateway Devt Corpn; mem. Advisory Bd Port of Churchill, Ethical Globalization Initiative; mem. Liberal Party; Hon. Fellow, American Acad. of Arts and Sciences, Hon. Chair. Canadian Landmine Foundation; mem. Order of Canada, Order of Manitoba; Dr hc (Queen's, Lakehead, Victoria, Denver, Niagara, Winnipeg, Dalhousie, Guelph); Peace Award, North-South Inst., Senator Patrick J. Leahy Award, Vietnam Veterans of America Foundation, Madison Medal, Princeton Univ., CARE Int. Humanitarian Award. *Publication:* Navigating a New World: Canada's Global Future 2003. *Leisure interest:* golf. *Address:* President's Office, University of Winnipeg, 3W02, 515 Portage Avenue, Winnipeg, Manitoba, R3B 2E9, Canada (office). *Telephone:* (204) 786-9214 (office). *Fax:* (204) 786-1693 (office). *E-mail:* president@uwinnipeg.ca (office). *Website:* www.uwinnipeg.ca/ index/admin-president (office).

AXWORTHY, Thomas Sidney, OC, BA (Hons), MA, PhD; Canadian civil servant, political scientist, writer, philanthropist and academic; *President and CEO, Walter & Duncan Gordon Foundation;* b. 23 May 1947, Winnipeg, Man.; m.; two c.; ed Univ. of Winnipeg, Queen's Univ., Kingston, Ont.; began career in public policy as a research asst to Task Force on Structure of the Canadian Economy 1967; served as asst to Minister of Housing and Urban Affairs, then Minister of Nat. Revenue, before joining Prime Minister's office as Sr Policy Adviser; Prin. Sec. to Prime Minister Pierre Trudeau 1981–84, key strategist on repatriation of the Constitution and the Charter of Rights and Freedoms; Chair. Arctic Advisory Steering Group, Walter & Duncan Gordon Foundation 1989–96 (worked on creation of the Arctic Council), Renewal Comm. of the Liberal Party of Canada 2006, Advisory Panel on the Creation of a Canadian Democracy Promotion Agency 2009; taught at Inst. of Politics, Kennedy School of Govt, Harvard Univ. 1984–85, Visiting Mackenzie King Chair of Canadian Studies 1985–86, subsequently taught for many years at the Kennedy School; Chair. Centre for the Study of Democracy, School of Policy Studies, Queen's Univ. 2003–09, currently Distinguished Sr Fellow, Munk School of Global Affairs; Sr Fellow, Massey Coll.; career in philanthropy began with appointment to the CRB Foundation 1986, initiated Heritage Minutes and Nat. Heritage Fairs Programs; worked at Historica Foundation of Canada 1999–2005; mem. Bd, then Chair. Asia Pacific Foundation of Canada 2001–06; Pres. and CEO Walter & Duncan Gordon Foundation 2009–; has worked extensively with the InterAction Council of Fmr Heads of State and Govt, co-drafted, with theologian Hans Kung, A Universal Declaration of Human Responsibility 1997, Sec.-Gen. InterAction Council 2011; frequent commentator on public and nat. issues; Hon. LLD (Wilfrid Laurier Univ.) 2003; Public Affairs Asscn

Award of Distinction, Public Affairs Asscn of Canada 2008, Diamond Jubilee Medal 2012. *Publications:* Politics of Innovation 1972, Our American Cousins (ed.) 1987, Marching to a Different Drummer: An Essay on the Liberals & Conservatives in Convention (with Martin Goldfarb) 1988, Towards a Just Society: The Trudeau Years (co-ed) ed. 1990, Searching for the New Liberalism: Perspectives, Policies, Prospects (co-ed.) 2003, Bridging the Divide: Religious Dialogue and Universal Ethics (co-ed.) 2008; contrib. of specialist articles to various academic journals, magazines and newspapers, especially the opinion pages of the Toronto Star, Globe and Mail and the National Post. *Address:* Walter & Duncan Gordon Foundation, Suite 400, 11 Church Street, Toronto, ON M5E 1W1, Canada (office). *Telephone:* (416) 601-4116 (office). *E-mail:* taxworthy@gordonfn.org (office); interact@vega.ocn.ne.jp (office). *Website:* www.interactioncouncil.org (office); gordonfoundation.ca (office).

AYAD, Jelloul, MEconSc; Tunisian economist and politician; b. 6 Feb. 1951, Khniss; m.; three c.; ed Univ. of Tunis, Univ. of Maryland, USA; joined Citibank 1980 as Man., Tunisian operations, becoming Vice-Pres. Citicorp 1987, Dir Gen., Corp. Bank Div., UAE 1988, Man. Dir Citibank Maghreb, Casablanca and Citicorp/Citibank Country Corp. Officer for Morocco 1990–95, Sr Banker, Europe, Africa and Middle East Finance Div., Citicorp International Ltd, London 1996–98; joined Banque marocaine du commerce extérieur (BMCE), in charge of corp. and business banking 1998, Chair. Gen. Man. Cttee, BMCE 2002, Gen. Man., Corp. and Investment Div. and Deputy Dir Gen. 2004, Vice-Pres. London br. 2010; Minister of Finance Jan.–Dec. 2011; fmr Vice-Pres. Supervisory Council, RMA Watanya (insurance co.), Morocco; Pres. American Chamber of Commerce, Casablanca 1993–95, now Hon. Pres.; fmr Vice-Pres. Euromed Forum; mem. Morocco–American Council for Trade and Investment. *Musical compositions:* composer of classical symphonies, which have been performed in Tunisia and Morocco; symphonies include Magador, Hannibal Barca, Parfum de Jasmin. *Address:* c/o Ministry of Finance, pl. du Gouvernement, La Kasbah, 1008 Tunis, Tunisia (office).

AYALA, Francisco Jose, BS, MA, PhD; American (naturalized) biologist, geneticist and academic; *Donald Bren Professor of Biological Sciences and University Professor, University of California, Irvine;* b. 12 March 1934, Madrid, Spain; s. of Francisco Ayala and Soledad Ayala (née Pereda); m. Hana Lostakova 1985; two s. (by previous m.); ed Univ. of Madrid, Columbia Univ., New York; Research Assoc. Rockefeller Univ., New York 1964–65, Asst Prof. 1967–71; Asst Prof., Providence Coll., RI 1965–67; Assoc. Prof., later Prof. of Genetics, Univ. of California, Davis 1971–87, Dir Inst. of Ecology 1977–81, Assoc. Dean of Environmental Studies 1977–81; Distinguished Prof. of Biology, Univ. of California, Irvine 1987–89, Donald Bren Prof. of Biological Sciences 1989–, Univ. Prof. 2003–; Pres. AAAS 1994–95; Pres.-Elect Sigma Xi, The Scientific Research Soc. 2003–04, Pres. 2004–05; mem. NAS, American Acad. of Arts and Sciences, American Philosophical Soc. (Pres. Cttee of Advisers on Science and Tech. 1994–2001); Dr hc (León, Spain) 1982, (Madrid) 1986, (Barcelona) 1986, (Athens) 1991, (Vigo, Spain) 1996, (Valencia) 1999, (Bologna) 2000, (Vladivostok) 2002, (Masaryk, Czech Repub.) 2003, (Las Islas Baleares) 2006, (Padua) 2006, (Nacional de La Plata) 2007, (Salamanca) 2007, (Warsaw) 2009, (Buenos Aires) 2009, (Pais Vasco) 2010, (South Bohemia, Czech Repub.) 2010, (Ohio State) 2010, (Nacional de Chile) 2010, (Macao) 2011, (Int. Univ. of Menéndez Pelayo, Spain) 2013; US Nat. Medal of Science 2001, Templeton Prize 2010. *Publications:* Studies in the Philosophy of Biology 1974, Molecular Evolution 1976, Evolution 1977, Evolving: The Theory and Processes of Organic Evolution 1979, Population and Evolutionary Genetics 1982, Modern Genetics 1984, Darwin and Intelligent Design 2006, Darwin's Gift to Science and Religion 2007, Human Evolution: Trails from the Past 2007, Contemporary Debates in Philosophy of Biology 2010, Am I a Monkey? The Big Questions: Evolution 2012, and more than 1,100 scientific articles. *Leisure interests:* travel, reading, collecting fine art. *Address:* Department of Ecology and Evolutionary Biology, University of California, Irvine, CA 92697 (office); 2 Locke Court, Irvine, CA 92617, USA (home). *Telephone:* (949) 824-8293 (office). *Fax:* (949) 824-2474 (office). *E-mail:* fjayala@uci.edu (office). *Website:* www.faculty.uci.edu/profile.cfm?faculty_id=2134 (office).

AYALA-LASSO, José; Ecuadorean lawyer, diplomatist and international civil servant; b. 29 Jan. 1932, Quito; m.; four c.; ed Pontificia Universidad Católica del Ecuador, Universidad Cen. del Ecuador, Université Catholique de Louvain, Belgium; several foreign service postings including at embassies in Tokyo, Seoul, Beijing, Rome, Minister of Foreign Affairs 1977, 1997–99, fmr Amb. to Belgium, Luxembourg, Peru, EEC; Lecturer, Int. Law Inst., Universidad Cen. del Ecuador; Deputy Legal Sec., Perm Comm. for the South Pacific, Perm. Rep. to UN, New York 1989–94, Chair. Security Council Cttee concerning Fmr Yugoslavia 1991, Chair. working group to establish post of High Commr for Human Rights 1993, UN High Commr for Human Rights 1994–97, Amb. to Holy See 1999–2002; Grand Cross, Nat. Order of Merit (Ecuador); numerous decorations from Japan, Belgium, Brazil, etc. *Address:* c/o Ministry of Foreign Affairs, Avda 10 de Agosto y Carrión, Quito, Ecuador.

AYALES ESNA, Edgar, BA, MPhil; Costa Rican economist and government official; b. 1950, Curridabat; m.; two c.; ed Univ. of Costa Rica, Univ. of Kent at Canterbury, UK; fmr Exec. Dir Inter-American Devt Bank, Alt. Exec. Dir World Bank and Adviser to Gov., Central Bank of Costa Rica; fmr Chief of Financial Insts Div., Statistics Dept, IMF, Washington, DC, becoming Deputy Dir Statistics Dept 1983–2012; Minister of Finance 2012–14. *Address:* c/o Ministry of Finance, Edif. Antiguo Banco Anglo, Avda 2a, Calle 3a, San José, Costa Rica (office).

AYALON, Adm. (retd) Ami, MA; Israeli politician and naval officer (retd); *Founding Director, The People's Voice;* b. 1945, Kibbutz Ma'agan; ed Bar-Ilan Univ., Naval War Coll., Newport, RI and Harvard Univ., USA; drafted into Flotilla 13 elite commando unit, Israeli Navy, commissioned officer, participated in hundreds of secret missions, served with distinction in Six Day and Yom Kippur wars, Commdr Israeli Navy 1992–96 (retd); Dir Shin-Beit (Israeli internal security service) 1996–2000; Co-Founding Dir The People's Voice (with Sari Nusseibeh—civil org. advocating two states for Israel and Palestine secured through non-violent means) 2000–; mem. Labour Party 2004–; Ribbon of Valour, Medal of Supreme Bravery, Quality Govt Kt Award. *Address:* The People's Voice, Ramat Gan, Israel. *Telephone:* 3-7538888. *Fax:* 3-7538887. *E-mail:* mifkad@mifkad.org.il. *Website:* www.mikkad.org.il.

AYALON, Daniel (Danny), BA, MBA; Israeli fmr diplomatist; *Co-Chairman, Nefesh B'Nefesh;* b. 1955, Tel-Aviv; m. Anne Ayalon; two d.; ed Tel-Aviv Univ., Bowling Green State Univ., USA; fmr Capt. Armored Corps, Israel Defense Forces; sr finance exec. before joining Foreign Service; Deputy Chief of Mission, Panama 1991–92, Dir Bureau of Israel's Amb. to UN, New York 1993–97, Deputy Foreign Policy Adviser to fmr Prime Ministers Ehud Barak and Benjamin Netanyahu 1997–2001, Chief Foreign Policy Adviser to Prime Minister Ariel Sharon 2002, Amb. to USA 2002–06; Co-Chair. Nefesh B'Nefesh, Jerusalem 2006–. *Address:* Nefesh B'Nefesh, Beit Ofer, 5 Nachum Hefzadi, Jerusalem, 95484, Israel (office). *Fax:* (2) 6595701 (office). *E-mail:* dayalon@nbn.org.il (office). *Website:* www.nbn .org.il (office); www.dannyayalon.com.

AYARI, Chédli, LenD, DèsSc(Econ), PhD; Tunisian economist, diplomatist, politician and central bank governor; *Governor, Banque Centrale de Tunisie;* b. 24 Aug. 1933, Tunis; s. of Sadok Chedly and Fatouma Chedly; m. Elaine Vatteau 1959; three c.; ed Collège Sadiki and Inst. de Hautes Etudes, Sorbonne, Paris; with Société Tunisienne de Banque 1958; Asst Faculté de Droit et des Sciences Economiques et Politiques, Tunis 1959; Econ. Counsellor, Perm. Mission of Tunis at UN 1960–64; Exec. Dir IBRD 1964–65; Dean, Faculté de Droit, Tunis 1965–67; Dir CERES 1967–69; Sec. of State in charge of Plan 1969–70; Minister of Nat. Educ., Youth and Sport 1970–71; Amb. to Belgium Feb.–March 1972; Minister of Nat. Economy 1972–74, of Planning 1974–75; Chair. of Bd and Gen. Man. Arab Bank for Econ. Devt in Africa 1975; Gov. Banque Centrale de Tunisie 2012–; Prof. of Economics, Agrégé de Sciences Economiques, Tunis, currently Prof. Emer.; Assoc. Prof. Univ. of Aix-Marseilles 1989–; mem. UN Cttee of Planning for Devt; currently Vice Pres., Nat. Consultative Counsel on Scientific Research and Tech.; Sr Assoc., Econ. Research Forum, Cairo; Grand Officier Légion d'honneur, Grand Cordon, Ordre de la République; Dr hc (Aix-Marseilles) 1972. *Publications:* Les Enjeux méditerranéens 1992, La Méditerranée economique 1992; books and articles on econ. and monetary problems. *Leisure interest:* music. *Address:* Banque Centrale de Tunisie, 25 rue Hédi Nouira, BP 777, 1080 Tunis (office); Rue Tanit, Gammarth, La Marsa, Tunis, Tunisia (home). *Telephone:* (71) 340-588 (office). *Fax:* (71) 354-214 (office). *E-mail:* boc@bct.gov.tn (office). *Website:* www.bct.gov.tn (office).

AYASSOR, Adji Othèth, LLD; Togolese lawyer and politician; *Minister of the Economy and Finance;* b. 1952; m.; four c.; ed Univ. of Bordeaux, France, Univ. of Wisconsin, USA; fmr Prof. of Law, Lomé Univ.; fmr Prof., École nationale d'administration (ENA), Lomé; int. consultant and expert on educ.; mem. Nat. Assembly (Parl.) for Doufelgou Pref.; Dir-Gen. Ministry of Educ. 1990–2006; Sec.-Gen. Cabinet Office 2006–07; Minister of the Economy and Finance 2007–. *Address:* Ministry of the Economy and Finance, CASEF, Avenue Sarakawa, BP 387, Lomé, Togo (office). *Telephone:* 22-21-35-54 (office). *Fax:* 22-21-09-05 (office). *E-mail:* eco@republicoftogo.com (office). *Website:* www.finances.gouv.tg (office).

AYCKBOURN, Sir Alan, Kt, CBE, FRSA; British playwright and theatre director; b. 12 April 1939, London, England; s. of Horace Ayckbourn and Irene Maud Ayckbourn (née Worley); m. 1st Christine Helen Roland 1959 (divorced 1997); two s.; m. 2nd Heather Elizabeth Stoney 1997; ed Haileybury; on leaving school went straight into the theatre as stage manager and actor with various repertory cos in England; Founder-mem. Victoria Theatre Co., Stoke on Trent 1962–64; Drama Producer, BBC Radio 1964–70; Artistic Dir Stephen Joseph Theatre, Scarborough 1972–2009; Prof. of Contemporary Theatre, Univ. of Oxford 1992; Hon. Fellow, Bretton Hall Coll. 1982, Cardiff Univ. 1995; Hon. Prof., Univ. of Hull 2007; Hon. DLitt (Hull) 1981, (Keele, Leeds) 1987, (Bradford) 1994, (York St John) 2011; Hon. DUniv (York) 1992, (Open Univ.) 1998, (Manchester) 2003; Variety Club of GB Playwright of the Year 1974, Lifetime Achievement Award, Writers' Guild of GB 1993, John Ederyn Hughes Rural Wales Award for Literature 1993, Birmingham Press Club Personality of the Year Award 1993, Yorkshire Man of the Year 1994, Montblanc de la Culture Award for Europe 1994, Sunday Times Award for Literary Excellence 2001, Variety Club of GB Lifetime Achievement Award 2004, Yorkshire Arts and Entertainment Personality Award, Yorkshire Awards 2005, Soc. of West End Theatre's Special Award (Olivier) 2009, inducted into Hall of Fame for Achievements in American Theatre 2009, Laurence Olivier Awards Special Award 2009, Critics' Circle Award for Services to the Arts 2010, Special Tony Award for Lifetime Achievement in the Theatre 2010. *Plays:* Mr Whatnot 1963, Relatively Speaking 1965, How the Other Half Loves 1969, Ernie's Incredible Illucinations 1969, Family Circles 1970, Time and Time Again 1971, Absurd Person Singular (Evening Standard Award for Best New Comedy 1973) 1972, The Norman Conquests (Evening Standard Award for Best New Play 1974, Plays and Players Award for Best New Play 1974, New York Drama Critics' Circle Special Citation 1999, Outer Critics' Circle Award for Outstanding Revival 2009, Drama Desk Award for Outstanding Revival 2009, Tony Award for Best Revival of a Play 2010) 1973, Jeeves (book and lyrics for Andrew Lloyd Webber musical) 1975 (rewritten as By Jeeves – TMA Regional Theatre Awards for Best Musical 1996), Absent Friends 1974, Confusions 1974, Bedroom Farce 1975, Just Between Ourselves (Evening Standard Award for Best New Play 1977) 1976, Ten Times Table 1977, Joking Apart (Co-winner Plays and Players Award for Best New Comedy 1979) 1978, Family Circles 1978, Sisterly Feelings 1979, Taking Steps 1979, Suburban Strains (musical play with music by Paul Todd) 1980, Season's Greetings 1980, Me, Myself & I (with Paul Todd) 1981, Way Upstream 1981, Intimate Exchanges 1982, It Could Be Any One Of Us 1983, A Chorus of Disapproval (London Evening Standard Award, Olivier Award and DRAMA Award for Best Comedy 1985) 1984 (film 1988), Woman in Mind 1985, A Small Family Business (London Evening Standard Award for Best New Play 1987) 1987, Henceforward (London Evening Standard Award for Best Comedy 1989) 1987, A View from the Bridge (Plays and Players Director of the Year Award) 1987, Man of the Moment (Evening Standard Best Comedy Award 1990) 1988, Mr A's Amazing Maze Plays (TMA/Martini Regional Theatre Award for Best Show for Children and Young People 1993) 1988, The Revengers' Comedies 1989, Invisible Friends 1989, Body Language 1990, This Is Where We Came In 1990, Callisto 5 1990 (rewritten as Callisto 7 1999), Wildest Dreams 1991, My Very Own Story 1991, Henceforward… (Drama-Logue Critic Award) 1991, Time of My Life 1992, Dreams From a Summer House (with music by John Pattison) 1992, Communicating Doors (Writers' Guild of GB Award for Best West End Play 1996, Moliere for Best Comedy 1997) 1994, Haunting Julia 1994, A Word from Our Sponsor (with music by John Pattison) 1995, The Champion of Paribanou 1996, Things We Do For Love

(Lloyds Pvt. Banking Playwright of the Year Award 1997, Moliere for Best Comedy 2003) 1997, Comic Potential 1998, The Boy Who Fell into a Book 1998, House & Garden 1999, Whenever (with music by Denis King) 2000, Damsels in Distress (trilogy: GamePlan, FlatSpin, RolePlay) 2001, Snake in the Grass 2002, The Jollies 2002, Sugar Daddies 2003, Orvin – Champion of Champions (with music by Denis King) 2003, My Sister Sadie 2003, Drowning on Dry Land 2004, Private Fears in Public Places 2004, Miss Yesterday 2004, Improbable Fiction 2005, The Girl Who Lost Her Voice 2005, If I Were You 2006, Life and Beth 2008, Awaking Beauty 2008, My Wonderful Day 2009, Life of Riley 2010, Dear Uncle (adaptation of Checkov's Uncle Vanya) 2011, Neighbourhood Watch 2011, Surprises 2012, Arrivals & Departures 2013, Farcicals (pair of one-act plays) 2013; as director: A View from the Bridge (Plays and Players Director of the Year Award) 1987; has directed all world premieres of own plays since 1967, including 32 London premieres, and more than 200 plays by other writers. *Publications:* fiction: majority of plays have been published; non-fiction: Conversations with Ayckbourn (with I. Watson) 1981, The Crafty Art of Playmaking 2002. *Leisure interests:* music, cricket. *Address:* c/o Casarotto Ramsay & Associates Ltd, Waverley House, 7–12 Noel Street, London, W1F 8GQ, England (office). *Telephone:* (20) 7287-4450 (office). *Fax:* (20) 7287-9128 (office). *E-mail:* info@casarotto.uk.com (office). *Website:* www.casarotto.uk.com (office); www.alanayckbourn.net (home).

AYER, Ramani, BS, DEng, PhD; American insurance industry executive; ed Indian Inst. of Tech., Drexel Univ.; joined The Hartford Financial Services Group Inc. 1973, Asst Sec. and Staff Asst to Chair. 1979, Vice-Pres. HartRe (subsidiary) 1983, Pres. Hartford Specialty Co. 1986, Sr Vice-Pres. The Hartford 1989, Exec. Vice-Pres. 1990, apptd mem. Bd of Dirs 1991, COO 1991–97, Chair., Pres. and CEO 1997–2007, Chair. and CEO 2007–09, also Chair. Hartford Life; Chair. Hartford Healthcare; Vice-Chair. Connecticut Council of Education Reform; mem. Bd of Dirs XL Group plc, David Lynch Foundation. *Address:* c/o Hartford Healthcare, 1 State Street, Hartford, CT 06103, USA.

AYÉVA, Zarifou; Togolese politician; b. 22 April 1942, Sokode; m.; ed Collège Moderne de Sokodé, Lycée Classique de COCODI, Abidjan, Univ. of Mons, Belgium; Financial Dir SGGG, Lomé 1969–73, Head of Sales Dept 1973–85; Lecturer, Univ. of Lomé 1975–77; Asst Gen. Dir Société Nlle de Sidérurgie 1977–79, Gen. Dir 1979–82; Minister of Commerce and Transport 1978, of Information 1979; Dir CODIS 1983–, STOP-FEU-TOGO 1986–; Minister of State, Minister of Foreign Affairs and African Integration 2005–07; Pres. Parti pour la démocratie et le renouveau (PDR) 1991. *Address:* Parti pour la démocratie et le renouveau (PDR), Lomé, Togo (office).

AYISSI, Henri Eyebe, PhD; Cameroonian politician; ed Nat. Advanced School of Admin and Magistracy; Minister of Urban Affairs 1990–92; Inspector of Gen. Affairs, Ministry of Higher Educ. 1998; fmr mem. Nat. Census Comm. and Inspector-Gen. of elections; State Minister for External Relations 2007–11. *Address:* c/o Ministry of External Relations, Yaoundé, Cameroon (office).

AYKROYD, Daniel (Dan) Edward; American (b. Canadian) actor; b. 1 July 1952, Ottawa, Canada; s. of Peter Hugh Aykroyd and Lorraine Gougeon Aykroyd; m. 1st Maureen Lewis 1974 (divorced); three s.; m. 2nd Donna Dixon 1984; two d.; ed Carleton Univ., Ottawa; started as a stand-up comedian; worked on Saturday Night Live ensemble TV show (NBC) 1975–79; cr. and performed as The Blues Brothers (with the late John Belushi); Emmy Award 1976–77. *Films include:* 1941 1979, Mr. Mike's Mondo Video 1979, The Blues Brothers (also screenwriter) 1980, Neighbors 1981, Doctor Detroit 1983, Trading Places 1983, Twilight Zone 1983, Ghostbusters 1984, Nothing Lasts Forever 1984, Into the Night 1985, Spies Like Us (also screenwriter) 1985, Dragnet (co-screenwriter) 1987, Caddyshack II 1988, The Great Outdoors 1988, My Stepmother is an Alien 1988, Ghostbusters II 1989, Driving Miss Daisy 1990, My Girl, Loose Canons, Valkemania, Nothing But Trouble 1991, Coneheads 1993, My Girl II 1994, North, Casper (also co-screenwriter) 1995, Sergeant Bilko (also co-screenwriter) 1996, Grosse Pointe Blank (also co-screenwriter) 1997, Blues Brothers 2000 1997, The Arrow 1997, Susan's Plan 1998 (also dir and screenwriter), Antz (voice) 1999, Diamonds (also dir and screenwriter) 1999, The House of Mirth 2000, Stardom 2000, The Loser 2000, The Devil and Daniel Webster 2001, Pearl Harbor 2001, Evolution 2001, Crossroads 2002, The Curse of the Jade Scorpion 2002, Unconditional Love 2002, Bright Young Things 2003, 50 First Dates 2004, Intern Academy 2004, Christmas with the Kranks 2004, I Now Pronounce You Chuck and Larry 2007, The Campaign 2012. *Albums include:* Briefcase Full of Blues, Made in America, The Blues Brothers, Best of the Blues Brothers. *Address:* c/o Fred Specktor, CAA, 9830 Wilshire Boulevard, Beverly Hills, CA 90212; 9200 Sunset Boulevard, #428, Los Angeles, CA 90069, USA (office).

AYKUT, Imren; Turkish organization official and fmr politician; *President, ÇESAV—Çevre Eğitim Sağlık ve Sosyal Yardımlaşma Vakfı;* b. 1941, Adana; s. of Şevket Şadi and Rahime Aykut; ed Istanbul Univ., Univ. of Oxford, UK; fmr man. of trades unions; industrial relations expert in Turkish glass industries; fmr Sec.-Gen. Paper Industry Employers' Union; mem. Constitutional Ass. 1981; Deputy, Nat. Ass. 1983–; Minister of Labour and Social Security 1987–91; Govt Spokesperson 1991; Vice-Chair. Inter-Parl. Union Turkish Group 1994–95; State Minister by Premier Minister (Women and Family Affairs) 1996; Minister of Environment 1997–99; Pres. Turkish Inter-Parl. Group 1991; currently Pres. ÇESAV—Çevre Eğitim Sağlık ve Sosyal Yardımlaşma Vakfı (Environment, Educ., Health and Social Solidarity Foundation); mem. Anavatan Partisi (Motherland Party); Order of Isabella Catolica of Spain 1993, Order Grand Cruz Medallion (Chile) 1996; Economist of the Year 1988, chosen one of 100 Most Successful Women of the Century, World Assocn of Women's Clubs 1994. *Publications:* numerous articles and research papers. *Leisure interests:* hand-made carpets, antiquities. *Address:* ÇESAV, Meşrutiyet Caddesi, Bayındır 2, Sokak No 59/6, 06620 Kızılay, Ankara, Turkey (office). *Telephone:* (312) 4174925 (office). *Fax:* (312) 4252432 (office). *E-mail:* cesav@cesav.org.tr (office). *Website:* www.cesav.org.tr (office).

AYLING, Robert (Bob) John; British business executive; b. 3 Aug. 1946; m. Julia Crallan 1972; two s. one d.; ed King's Coll. School, Wimbledon; joined Elborne, Mitchell & Co. 1968; legal adviser on British accession to the EC 1973–75, Head of Dept of Trade Aviation Law br. 1978 (responsible for parl. bill that led to privatization of British Airways), Under-Sec. for EC, int. trade,

competition issues 1981; with British Shipbuilders 1975; joined British Airways (legal and govt affairs) 1985, Co. Sec. 1987, organized legal arrangements concerning BA's privatization 1987 and BA's acquisition of British Caledonian 1988, Dir Human Resources 1988, Dir Marketing and Operations 1991, Group Man. Dir 1993–95, CEO 1996–2000; Dir (non-exec.) Holidaybreak 2003, Chair. 2003–09; Dir (non-exec.) Royal & SunAlliance Insurance Group PLC 1993–2004; Dir (non-exec.) Welsh Water (Dwr Cymru Cyfyngedig) 2008–13, Chair. 2010–13; Chair. Dyson Ltd 2010–, HM Courts and Tribunals Service 2011–; Gov. King's Coll. School 1996; Hon. LLD (Brunel) 1996. *Address:* Office of the Chairman, Dyson Ltd, Tetbury Hill, Malmesbury, Wilts., SN16 0RP, England. *Website:* www .dyson.co.uk; www.justice.gov.uk.

AYLWIN AZÓCAR, Patricio; Chilean lawyer, university professor, consultant and fmr head of state; b. 26 Nov. 1918, Viña del Mar; s. of Miguel Aylwin G. and Laura Azócar; m. Leonor Oyarzun Ivanovic 1948; five c.; ed Universidad de Chile; Senator 1965–73, Pres. of Senate 1971–72; Pres. Christian Democrat party (PDC) 1973, 1987–91, Vice-Pres. 1982–89; leader of opposition coalition rejecting Gen. Augusto Pinochet in nat. plebiscite Oct. 1988; opposition coalition cand. 1989; PDC cand. for Pres. 1989; Pres. of Chile 1990–94; Pres. Corporación Justicia y Democracia; mem. Club of Madrid; Hon. Pres. World Democratic Conf. 1997; awarded hon. doctorate degrees from univs in Australia, Canada, Colombia, France, Italy, Japan, Portugal, Spain, and USA and from seven Chilean univs; North-South Prize, Council of Europe 1997, J. William Fulbright Prize for Int. Understanding 1998. *Publications include:* El Juicio Arbitral 1943, La Transición Chilena: Discursos escogidos Marzo 1990–92, Crecimiento con Equidad: Discursos escogidos 1992–94, Justicia, Democracia y Desarrollo: Conferencias y discursos 1994–95.

AYNSLEY-GREEN, Sir Albert, Kt, MA, MBBS, DPhil, MRCS, FRCP, FRCPE, FRCPCH, FMedSci, FRSA; British paediatrician and writer; *Director, Aynsley-Green Consulting;* b. 30 May 1943; m. Rosemary Boucher 1967; two d.; ed Glyn Grammar School, Epsom and Univs of London and Oxford; House Officer, Guy's Hosp. London, St Luke's Hosp. Guildford, Radcliffe Infirmary, Oxford and Royal Postgraduate Medical School, Hammersmith 1967–70; Wellcome Research Fellow, Radcliffe Infirmary 1970–72, Clinical Lecturer in Internal Medicine 1972–73, Sr House Officer and Registrar in Paediatrics (also John Radcliffe Hosp.) 1973–74; European Science Exchange Fellowship, Univ. Children's Hosp. Zürich 1974–75; Clinical Lecturer in Paediatrics, Univ. of Oxford 1975–78, Univ. Lecturer 1978–83; Prof. of Child Health and Head of Dept, Univ. of Newcastle-upon-Tyne 1984–93; Nuffield Prof. of Child Health, Univ. of London 1993–; Dir of Clinical Research and Devt, Great Ormond St Hosp. and Inst. of Child Health, London 1993–2003; Chair. Nat. Children's Taskforce and Nat. Clinical Dir for Children, Dept of Health 2001–05; Children's Commr for England 2005–10; Founder and Dir Aynsley-Green Consulting 2010–; six hon. doctorates; numerous nat. and int. esteem indicators. *Publications:* papers on child health, childhood and government policy for children. *Leisure interests:* family, walking, music, photography. *Address:* Old Parsonage, Harnham, Salisbury, Hants., SP2 8LE, England. *Telephone:* 7500-338353 (mobile). *E-mail:* al@aynsley-green.com (office). *Website:* www.aynsley -green.com.

AYONG, Most Rev. James Simon, BTheol; Papua New Guinea ecclesiastic; b. 3 Sept. 1944, Kumbun, West New Britain Prov.; s. of Julius Ayong and Margaret Ayong; m. Gawali Ayong 1967; two d. (one deceased); Local Govt Officer 1964–70, 1974–76; Prin. Newton Theological Coll. 1989–93; Archbishop of Papua New Guinea and Bishop of Diocese of Aipo Rongo 1995–2009 (retd); Primate of Anglican Prov. of Papua New Guinea 1996. *Leisure interest:* watching football. *Address:* Kumbun Village, PO Box 806, Kimbe, West New Britain, Papua New Guinea (home).

AYOTTE, Kelly A., BA, JD; American lawyer and politician; *Senator from New Hampshire;* b. 27 June 1968, Nashua, NH; m. Joseph Daley; one s. one d.; ed Nashua High School, Pennsylvania State Univ., Villanova Univ. School of Law; admitted to the Bar of NH and Me; Ed. Environmental Law Journal, Villanova Univ. School of Law; clerked for Hon. Sherman D. Horton, Assoc. Justice of NH Supreme Court 1993–94; Assoc., McLane, Graf, Raulerson & Middleton (law firm) 1994–98; Asst Attorney Gen., Homicide Unit, NH 1998–2000, Sr Asst Attorney Gen. and Chief, Homicide Unit 2000–02, Deputy Attorney Gen. of NH 2003–04, Attorney Gen. 2004–09; Legal Counsel to Gov. Craig Benson 2003; Senator from NH 2011– (youngest female Senator), mem. Select Cttee on Aging 2011–, Commerce, Science and Transportation Cttee 2011–, Small Business and Entrepreneurship Cttee 2011–; mem. New Hampshire Bar Asscn, Maine Bar Asscn; Republican; Kirby Award, New Hampshire Bar Foundation 2004, named Citizen of the Year, New Hampshire Union Leader 2008. *Address:* 144 Russell Senate Office Building, Washington, DC 20510, USA (office). *Telephone:* (202) 224-3324 (office). *Fax:* (202) 224-4952 (office). *Website:* ayotte.senate.gov (office).

AYRAULT, Jean-Marc; French politician; b. 25 Jan. 1950, Maulévrier (Maine-et-Loire); s. of Joseph Ayrault and Georgette Uzenot; m. Brigitte Terrien; two c.; ed Lycée Colbert, Cholet, Univ. of Nantes, spent a term in Würzburg, Germany, graduate teaching diploma; probationary teaching year at Rezé, Nantes; worked as a German language teacher in Saint-Herblain 1973–86; youth mem. of a movement of young Christians in rural areas; joined Parti socialiste (PS—Socialist Party) after Épinay Congress 1971, affiliated to Jean Poperen's faction, mem. PS Nat. Cttee 1979–81, Exec. 1981–; mem. Gen. Council of Loire-Atlantique département 1976–82, Mayor of Saint-Herblain (suburb of Nantes) 1977–89 (youngest mayor of a French city of more than 30,000 inhabitants), Mayor of Nantes 1989–2012; Deputy for Loire Atlantique in Nat. Ass. 1986–, Pres. Socialist Parl. group 1997–; Pres. Urban Community of Nantes Métropole 2002–; Prime Minister of France 2012–14. *Address:* 47 place de Preux, BP 50351, 44800 Saint-Herblain, France. *Telephone:* 2-40-43-13-18. *Fax:* (office). *Website:* jmayrault.fr.

AYRE, Richard James, BA; British journalist; *Trustee, British Broadcasting Corporation;* b. 1 Aug. 1949, Newcastle-upon-Tyne, England; s. of Thomas Henry Ayre and Beth Carson; partner Guy Douglas Burch; ed Univ. Coll., Durham; Pres. Durham Univ. Students' Union 1969–70; producer and reporter, BBC NI 1973–76, Home News Ed., TV News 1979–84, Head of BBC Westminster 1989–92, Controller of Editorial Policy 1993–96, Deputy Chief Exec., BBC News 1996–2000; Chair. Asian & Afro-Carribean Reporters' Trust 1997–2000; mem.

Bd Food Standards Agency 2000–07; Freedom of Information Adjudicator, Law Soc. 2001–; Chair. Article 19 2002–05; Civil Service Commr 2005–06; Bd mem. for England, Ofcom Content Bd 2006–10; Chair. Dairy Partnership 2008–10; mem. Bd BBC Trust 2010–; Benton Fellow, Univ. of Chicago, USA 1984–85. *Address:* 88 Cumberland Mills, London, E14 3BJ, England (home). *E-mail:* richardayre@ whats2hide.com (office).

AYUB, Alfredo Elías, BS, MBA; Mexican civil servant and energy industry executive; b. 13 Jan. 1950, Mexico City; ed Anáhuac Univ., Harvard Univ., USA; has held numerous public sector posts including Exec. Co-ordinator of Urban Devt, Secr. of Public Works and Dir, Nat. Fund for Social Activities; worked for nine years at Secr. of Energy, Mines and Govt-controlled Industry holding positions on Coordinating Comm. of Advisors to Sec., Under-Secr. of Mines and Basic Industry, Under-Secr. of Energy; fmr CEO and Pres. Airports and Auxiliary Services; Gen. Dir Comisión Federal de Electricidad 1999–2011; Dir, Azteca Acquisition Corpn 2011–; active in family's real-estate business; fmr Dir School of Eng, Anáhuac Univ.; fmr Chair. Devt Bd, Anáhuac Univ., Mexico Foundation, Harvard Univ. *Address:* Azteca Acquisition Corporation, 421 North Beverly Drive, Suite 300, Beverly Hills, CA 90210, USA (office); c/o Comisión Federal de Electricidad, Rio Rodano 14, Col. Cuauhtemoc, México DF 06598, Mexico. *Telephone:* (310) 553-7009 (office).

AYUSHEYEV, Pandito Hambo Lama Damba Badmayevich; Russian Buddhist leader; b. 1963, Russia; abbot in Buddhist monastery Baldan Braybun 1995; elected Head of Buddhists of Russia (Khambo Lama) at conf. of Buddhist clergy, Ulan-Ude 1995–; Shiretuy Buddhist datsan Baldan-Braybun; mem. Presidium of the Interreligious Council of Russia 1998–, Presidium of the Interreligious Council of the CIS 2004–, Council for Co-operation with Religious Union Under the Pres. of the Russian Fed.; Vice-Pres. Asian Buddhist Conf. for Peace. *Address:* c/o Buddist Centre, Petrovsky blvd., 17/1, Suite 35, 103051 Moscow, Russia (office). *Telephone:* (495) 925-16-81 (office).

AYUSO GARCÍA, Joaquín, BEng; Spanish business executive; *Second Vice-Chairman and Executive Member of Board of Directors, Ferrovial SA;* b. 1955, Madrid; ed Univ. Politécnica de Madrid; joined Ferrovial as Site Engineer 1982, becoming Project Supervisor, Group Man., Area Man. and Regional Man., CEO Ferrovial Agromán 1999–2002, CEO Grupo Ferrovial (now Ferrovial SA) and Ferrovial Infraestructuras 2002–09, currently Second Vice-Chair. and Exec. Mem. of Bd of Dirs; fmr First Vice-Chair. Cintra Concesiones de Infraestructuras de Transporte SA; Dir BAA PLC 2006–07; fmr Dir Budimex SA, Poland; Madrid Inst. of Civil Engineers Medal of Honour 2006. *Website:* www.ferrovial.com.

AZA, Alberto; Spanish diplomatist; b. 22 May 1937, Tetuán, Morocco; s. of Alberto Aza and Marcela Arias; m. María Eulalia Custodio Martí 1963; two s. four d.; ed Univ. of Oviedo and Madrid; joined Diplomatic Service 1965, served in Libreville, Algiers, Rome, Madrid; Dir Cabt. of Prime Minister of Spain 1977–83; Chief Dir OAS, Latin America Dept, Ministry of Foreign Affairs 1983; Minister Counsellor, Lisbon 1983–85; Amb. to OAS, Washington, DC 1985–89 (also acred to Belize); Amb. to Mexico 1990–92, to UK 1992–99; Gen. Dir O.I.D. 2000–02; Head of the Spanish Royal Household 2002–12; Perm. Advisor of State and Pres., Council of State 2012–; Gran Cruz del Mérito Civil 1979; Gran Cruz de la Order del Mérito Naval 1996; Hon. DLitt (Portsmouth) 1997. *Leisure interests:* golf, fishing, walking. *Address:* Council of State, Mayor 79, 28013 Madrid, Spain (office). *Telephone:* (91) 5166262 (office). *Fax:* (91) 5166244 (office). *E-mail:* tramitaciones@ consejo-estado.es (office). *Website:* www.consejo-estado.es (office).

AZAD, Ghulam Nabi, MSc; Indian politician; *Minister of Health and Family Welfare;* b. 7 March 1949, Soti village, Bhadarwah, Doda Dist, Jammu and Kashmir; s. of Rahamatullah and Basa Begum; m. Shrimati Shameem Dev Azad 1980; one s. one d; ed Kashmir Univ.; began political career in 1973; mem. Lok Sabha (Parl.) 1980–89; Union Deputy Minister of Law, Justice and Co. Affairs 1982–83, of Information and Broadcasting 1983–84, Union Minister of State of Parl. Affairs 1984–86, of Home Affairs 1986, Union Minister of State, Ministry of Food and Civil Supplies 1986–87; mem. Rajya Sabha (Parl.) 1990–; Union Minister of Parl. Affairs 1991–93, of Civil Aviation and Tourism 1993–96, of Parl. Affairs, Civil Aviation and Tourism 1995–96, of Parl. Affairs and Minister of Urban Devt 2004–05; Chief Minister of Jammu and Kashmir 2005–08; Minister of Health and Family Welfare 2009–; Chair. Youth Services Cttee IX Asian Games 1982, also mem. Special Organizing Cttee; Chair. Rajghat Samadhi Cttee 2004–05; Block Sec., Congress Cttee, Blessa 1973–75; Pres. Congress Cttee, Doda Dist 1977; Pres. All India Muslim Youth Conf. 1978–81; Pres. Jammu and Kashmir Pradesh Congress Cttee; Gen. Sec. All India Congress Cttee 1987 (re-elected as Gen. Sec. nine times); mem. Cttee on Public Undertakings 1980–82. *Leisure interests:* gardening, meeting people and cultural activities, secularism and national integration. *Address:* Ministry of Health and Family Welfare, Nirman Bhavan, Maulana Azad Road, New Delhi, 110 011 (office); House No. 58, New Rehari, Jammu Jogi Gate, Gujjar Nagar, Jammu (home); 5, South Avenue Lane, New Delhi India (home). *Telephone:* (11) 23061647 (office); (11) 23792052 (New Delhi) (home); (11) 23792944 (New Delhi) (home). *Fax:* (11) 23061647 (office). *E-mail:* azadg@sansad.nic.in (office). *Website:* www.mohfw.nic.in (office).

AZALI, Col. Assoumani; Comoran politician and fmr head of state; Chief of Staff, Comoran Armed Forces –1999; seized power in coup d'état April 1999; Head of State of the Comoros and C-in-C of the Armed Forces 1999–2002, Fed. Pres. of the Union of the Comoros 2002–06.

AZAM, Ghulam; Bangladeshi politician and professor; b. 7 Nov. 1922, Dhaka; s. of Mawlana Ghulam Kabir and Sayeda Ashrafunnisa; m. Sayeda Afifa Khatun; six s.; joined Tablig Jamaat 1950, Ameer (Leader) Rangpur Dist 1952–54; joined Tamaddin Majlis 1952, Chair. Rangpur Dist 1952–54; joined Jamaat-e-Islami 1954, Sec.-Gen. 1957–1967, Ameer 1967–1971, Ameer Jamaat-e-Islami Bangladesh 1971–2000; arrested by Int. Crimes Tribunal for genocide and war crimes 2012.

AZARENKA, Victoria (Vika); Belarusian professional tennis player; b. (Viktoriya Fiodorovna Azarenka), 31 July 1989, Minsk, Byelorussian SSR, USSR; plays right-handed (two-handed backhand); turned professional 2003; jr highlights include Grand Slam singles titles at Australian Open 2005, US Open 2005, Grand Slam doubles titles at Wimbledon (with Govortsova) 2004, (with

Szavay) 2005, French Open (with Szavay) 2005; winner, ITF/Petange, Luxembourg 2005, Miami 2009, Memphis 2009, Brisbane 2009, Stanford 2010, Moscow 2010, Miami 2011, Marbella 2011, Qatar Total Open, Doha 2013; winner, Women's Doubles, ITF/Ramat Hasharon, Israel (with Govortsova) 2003, ITF/Tucson (with Poutchek) 2005, Tashkent (with Poutchek) 2006, ITF/Las Vegas (with Poutchek) 2007, Indian Wells (with Zvonareva) 2009, Memphis (with Wozniacki) 2009, Cincinnati (with Kirilenko) 2010, Madrid (with Kirilenko) 2011; gold medal, Mixed Doubles (with Max Mirnyi), Olympic Games, London 2012, bronze medal, Women's Singles 2012; Grand Slam Singles results: fourth round, US Open 2007, quarterfinalist, French Open 2009, 2011, Australian Open 2010, semi-finalist, Wimbledon 2011, 2012, French Open 2013, finalist, US Open 2012, 2013, winner, Australian Open 2012, 2013; Grand Slam Doubles results: finalist, Australian Open 2008, 2011, quarterfinalist, Wimbledon 2008, finalist, French Open 2009; Grand Slam Mixed Doubles results: winner US Open (with Mirnyi) 2007, Roland Garros (with Bob Bryan) 2008, finalist, Australian 2007; mem. Federation Cup Team for Belarus 2005, 2007, 2009, Belarusian Olympic Team 2008; ranked World No. 1 30 Jan. 2012; ITF Jr Girls World Champion 2005. *Address:* Lagardère Unlimited, 16-18 rue du Dôme, Boulogne-Billancourt, 92100 Paris, France (office). *Telephone:* 1-74-31-72-08 (office). *E-mail:* jtobias@lagardere-unlimited.com (office). *Website:* www.lagardere-unlimited.com (office); www.vikaazarenkatennis.com.

AZARNOFF, Daniel Lester, MS, MD; American physician, academic and business executive; *President, D.L. Azarnoff Associates;* b. 4 Aug. 1926, Brooklyn, New York; s. of Samuel J. Azarnoff and Kate Azarnoff; m. Joanne Stokes 1951; two s. one d.; ed Rutgers Univ., Univ. of Kansas School of Medicine; Instructor in Anatomy, Univ. of Kansas 1949–50, Research Fellow 1950–52, Intern 1955–56, Nat. Heart Inst. Resident Research Fellow 1956–58, Asst Prof. of Medicine 1962–64, Assoc. Prof. 1964–68, Dir Clinical Pharmacology Study Unit 1964–68, Assoc. Prof. of Pharmacology 1965–68, Prof. of Medicine and Pharmacology 1968, Dir Clinical Pharmacology-Toxicology Center 1967–68, Distinguished Prof. 1973–78, Clinical Prof. of Medicine 1982–; Asst Prof. of Medicine, St Louis Univ. 1960–62; Visiting Scientist, Fulbright Scholar, Karolinska Inst., Stockholm, Sweden 1968; Clinical Prof. of Pathology and Prof. of Pharmacology, Northwestern Univ. 1978–85; Prof. of Medicine, Univ. of Kansas Coll. of Health Sciences 1984, Stanford Univ. School of Medicine 1998–2002; Sr Vice-Pres. Clinical Regulatory Affairs, Cellegy Pharmaceuticals 1999–2006; Sr Vice-Pres. Worldwide Research and Devt, G. D. Searle & Co., Chicago 1978, Pres. Searle Research and Devt, Skokie, Ill. 1979–85; Pres. D.L. Azarnoff Assocs, Inc. 1987–; mem. Bd of Dirs De Novo Inc. 1994–95, Oread Inc. 1994–98 (Chair. 1998–), Entropin Inc. 1997–2000; mem. Editorial Bd Drug Investigation 1989–2002; Chair. Cttee on Problems of Drug Safety, NAS 1972–76; consultant to numerous govt agencies; mem. Nat. Comm. on Orphan Diseases, Dept of Health and Human Services; mem. Bd of Dirs Oread Laboratories Inc. 1993; Ed. Review of Drug Interactions 1974–77, Yearbook of Drug Therapy 1977–79; Series Ed. Monographs in Clinical Pharmacology 1977–84; Fellow, American Coll. of Physicians, New York Acad. of Scientists; mem. American Soc. of Clinical Nutrition, American Nutrition Inst., American Fed. of Clinical Research, British Pharmacological Soc., Royal Soc. for the Promotion of Health, Inst. of Medicine (NAS), insts of medicine of nat. acads; Distinguished Prof. of Medicine and Pharmacology, Univ. Kansas Medical Center; Burroughs Wellcome Scholar 1964, Markle Scholar 1963–68, Ciba Award for gerontological research 1958, Rector's Medal, Univ. of Helsinki 1968, Oscar B. Hunter Award, American Soc. for Clinical Pharmacology and Therapeutics, Distinguished Alumni Award, Univ. of Kansas School Medicine, Nathanial T. Kwit Memorial Service Award, American Coll. of Clinical Pharmacology. *Publications:* more than 175 publs in scientific and medical journals. *Address:* 610 Edgewood Drive, Rio Vista, CA 94571, USA (office). *Telephone:* (707) 374-2715 (office). *Fax:* (765) 374-2716 (office). *E-mail:* dan@azarnoffassociates.com (office). *Website:* www.azarnoffassociates.com (office).

AZAROV, Mykola Yanovych, PhD; Ukrainian geologist, economist and politician; b. (Nikolai Yanovich Pakhlo), 17 Dec. 1947, Kaluga, Russian SFSR, USSR; s. of Yan Robertovich Pakhlo and Yekaterina Kvasnikova; m. Lyudmyla Azarova; one s.; ed M. Lomonosov Moscow State Univ.; Lab. Man. and Head of Dept, Moscow Research Design Coal Inst. 1976–84; Deputy Dir Ukrainian State Research and Design Inst. of Mining Geology, Geomechanics and Mine Survey, Coal Ministry 1984–95; Chief of State Tax Admin 1996–2002; First Deputy Prime Minister and Minister of Finance 2002–05, 2006–07; apptd Chair. Political Council, Party of the Regions 2003; Acting Prime Minister 7–28 Dec. 2004, 5–24 Jan. 2005; Prime Minister 2010–14 (resgnd following riots and Euromaidan protests), fled to Austria then to Russia; mem. Nat. Acad. of Sciences of Ukraine 1997–; Honoured Economist of Ukraine 1997. *Publications:* numerous books and articles on geology and taxation. *Leisure interests:* reading, painting. *Address:* c/o Office of the Cabinet of Ministers, 01008 Kyiv, vul. M. Hrushevskoho 12/2; Party of the Regions (Partiya Rehioniv), 01021 Kyiv, vul. Lypska 10, Ukraine (office). *Website:* www.partyofregions.org.ua (office).

AZCUNA, Adolfo, AB, LLB; Philippine lawyer; b. 16 Feb. 1939; s. of Felipe Azcuna and Carmen Sevilla; m. Maria Asuncion Aunario 1968; one s. three d.; ed Ateneo de Manila and Univ. of Salzburg, Austria; elected Del. 1971 Constitutional Convention 1971–73; mem. Constitutional Comm. 1986–87; Press Sec. 1989; Presidential Legal Counsel 1987–90, Presidential Spokesman 1989–90; Pres. Manila Hotel 1997–98; Partner, Azcuna, Yorac, Sarmiento, Arroyo & Chua Law Offices 1992–2002; Corazon Aquino Fellowship, Harvard Univ. 1990 (deferred); Assoc. Justice, Supreme Court of the Philippines 2002–09; Chancellor Philippine Judicial Acad. 2009. *Publications include:* Doing Business in the Philippines, Foreign Judgment Enforcement in the Philippines, Asian Conflict of Law, The Philippine Writ of Amparo, The Aquino Presidency: Destiny with Valor and Grace, International Humanitarian Law: A Field Guide to the Basics, The Writ of Amparo – A New Constitutional Remedy in the Philippines. *Leisure interests:* reading, biking, photography. *Address:* Philippine Judicial Academy, 3/F Centennial Building, Supreme Court, P. Faura Street, Ermita, Manila (office); 140 CRM Avenue, Las Pinas, Metro Manila, Philippines (home). *Telephone:* (2) 552-9514 (office); 801-1685 (home). *Fax:* (2) 552-9621 (office). *E-mail:* philja@sc.judiciary.gov.ph (office). *Website:* www.philja.supremecourt.gov.ph (office).

AZÉMA, Jean, BEng; French agricultural engineer and insurance executive; *CEO, Groupama SA;* b. 1953; ed Ecole Supérieure d'Agriculture de Purpan, Centre Nat. d'Etudes Supérieures de Sécurité; various positions within Groupe Groupama, including Man. Caisse Régionale des Pyrénées Orientales 1975–78, Caisse Régionale de l'Allier 1979–86, Finance Dir Groupama Cie 1987–95, later Dir of Investment, Consolidation and Insurance, Groupama, Man. Dir Groupama Sud-Ouest 1996–98, Groupama Sud 1998–2000, CEO Caisse Centrale Groupama 2000–04, CEO Groupama SA, Féd. Nat. Groupama, Groupama Holding 2004–; Chair. Féd. Française des Soc. d'Assurance Mutuelles 2001–08; Dir Mediobanca, Véolia Environnement, Société Générale, Bolloré. *Address:* Groupama SA, 8–10 rue d'Astorg, 75383 Paris Cedex 08, France (office). *Telephone:* 1-44-56-77-77 (office). *E-mail:* relations.exterieures@groupama.com (office). *Website:* www .groupama.fr (office).

AZESKI, Branko; Macedonian business executive; *President, Managing Board, Economic Chamber of Macedonia;* b. 31 Jan. 1962, Ohrid; fmr Gen. Man. Alexandar Palace Hotel; Founder and Owner, Hit Plus DOOEL, Skopje; Pres. Man. Bd Econ. Chamber of Macedonia 2005–; Pres. Asscn of Balkan Chambers 2005–. *Address:* Economic Chamber of Macedonia, Str. Dimitrie Cupovski 13, 1000 Skopje, Macedonia (office). *Telephone:* (2) 3244000 (office). *Fax:* (2) 3244088 (office). *E-mail:* ic@ic.mchamber.org.mk (office). *Website:* www.mchamber.org.mk (office).

AZHARI, Yasmina, BA; Syrian business executive; *Owner and General Manager, Mira Trading LLC;* b. 19 June 1961, Lattakia; one s. one d.; ed Tishreen Univ.; Partner and Vice-Pres. Trade Coordination Office (shipping agency representing Maersk Line in Syria) 1979–; Rep. of Dutch org. PUM 1999; Head of Lattakia Business Women Cttee 2002–; mem. British Syrian Soc. 2002–, local rep. in Lattakia and Tartous; Founder Mawred (non-governmental org. (NGO) for modernizing and activating women's role in econ. devt) 2003, elected rep. of Mawred in the western region, Pres. Mawred 2006–; est. environmental non-governmental cttee for protecting Slounfeh and Kassab forests 2006; Pres. Bashaer Al Nour NGO for care of children affected by autism and Down syndrome 2006–; Head of Bd, Al Dalfin housing society, Lattakia 2008; Founder Mira Trading LLC 2010, Al Yam LLC (import and export) 2011; mem. Bd of Admin, Lattakia Chamber of Commerce and Industry (first woman) 2005–; mem. Arab Business Women Council representing Syria 2006; mem. Bd Syrian Business Council 2007, Bd UN Global Compact Advisory Council in Syria 2008; mem. Advisory Bd, Bank Audi, Syria 2005; mem. Bd Tartous Port Co. (first woman) 2009; mem. Admin. Bd, Syrian Dutch Business Council 2010, Syrian Chinese Business Council 2010, OECD 2010, Syrian Indian Business Council 2010; Hon. Consul of the Netherlands, Lattakia & Tartous 1999–; Kt, Order of the Netherlands Lion 2009; listed by Forbes Economic Magazine amongst the 50 Most Powerful Women in the Arab World 2006, 2008, listed by Arabian Business Magazine amongst the 100 Women Who Made a Change in the Arab World 2011–13, chosen by CEO Middle East amongst the 100 Most Powerful Women in the Arab World 2011, Ernst & Young World Entrepreneur of the Year Winner for Syria 2011. *Address:* Trade Coordination Office, Al-Mutanabi Street, Lattakia (office); Mira Trading llc, Qudssya Main Square, Damascus, Syria (office). *Telephone:* (41) 235183 (Lattakia) (office); (41) 235184 (Lattakia) (office). *Fax:* (41) 235189 (Lattakia) (office); (41) 235190 (Lattakia) (office). *E-mail:* yasmina .azhari@gmail.com (office). *Website:* www.maerskline.com (office); www.mirallc .com (office).

AZIMI, Abdul Salam, PhD; Afghan judge, politician and academic; *Chief Justice of the Supreme Court (Stera Mahkama);* b. 1937, Now Bahar, Farah Prov.; ed Kabul Univ., Al-Azhar University, Egypt, George Washington Univ., USA; Head of Scientific and Research Centre, Univ. of Neb. in Afghanistan 1986–99; Minister of Educ. 2001–03; mem. Constitutional Comm. to draft a new Afghan Constitution (primary drafter) 2002–03, Vice-Chair. Constitutional Review Comm. 2003; 2006; legal adviser to Pres. Hamid Karzai and Dir of Legal and Judicial Bd of Office of the Pres. 2004–06; Chief Justice of the Supreme Court (Stera Mahkama) 2006–. *Address:* Supreme Court of Afghanistan (Stera Mahkama), Kabul, Afghanistan (office). *Website:* supremecourt.gov.af.

AZIMI, Capt. Jahed; Afghan airline industry executive; fmr pilot, Ariana Afghan Airlines, Pres. 2002–05; fmr CEO Kam Airlines; CEO East Horizon Airlines 2011–; fmr Deputy Minister in charge of Admin, Ministry of Transport. *E-mail:* info@ flyeasthorizon.com. *Website:* flyeasthorizon.com.

AZIMOV, Rustam Sodiqovich, PhD; Uzbekistani economist and politician; *First Deputy Prime Minister, Minister of Finance, responsible for Macroeconomic Development, Structural Economic Transformation and Integrated Regional Development;* b. 20 Sept. 1958, Tashkent; ed Tashkent State Univ., Tashkent Inst. of Agricultural Engineers; Economist, Yulius Fuchik collective farm; Chief Economist of agricultural amalgamation in Jizzax; Chair. Ipak July Uzbek Bank for Innovation –1991, Nat. Bank for Foreign Econ. Activity 1991–98; mem. Oly Majlis (Supreme Ass.) 1994–; Minister of Finance 1998–2000, 2005; Deputy Prime Minister and Minister of Macroeconomics and Statistics 2000–02; Deputy Prime Minister and Economy Minister 2002–05; Minister of Foreign Econ. Relations July–Nov. 2005; Deputy Prime Minister, responsible for the Econ. sector and Foreign Econ. Relations 2005–10, First Deputy Prime Minister, Minister of Finance, responsible for Macroeconomic Devt, Structural Economic Transformation and Integrated Regional Devt 2010–; Uzbekistan Del. to Asian Devt Bank; fmr Lecturer in Econs, Tashkent State Univ.; Gov., EBRD, London. *Publications:* numerous articles on econs. *Address:* Ministry of Finance, 100008 Tashkent, Mustaqillik maydoni 5, Uzbekistan (office). *Telephone:* (71) 233-70-73 (office). *Fax:* (71) 244-56-43 (office). *E-mail:* iyuldashev@mf.uz (office). *Website:* www.mf.uz (office).

AZINGER, Paul William; American professional golfer; b. 6 Jan. 1960, Holyoke, Mass.; m. Toni Azinger; two d.; ed Brevard Jr Coll. and Florida State Univ.; started playing golf aged five; turned professional 1981; won Phoenix Open 1987, Herz Bay Hill Classic 1988, Canon Greater Hartford Open 1989, MONY Tournament of Champions 1990, AT&T Pebble Beach Nat. Pro-Am 1991, TOUR Championship 1992, BMW Int. Open 1990, 1992, Memorial Tournament, New England Classic, PGA Championship, Inverness 1993; GWAA Ben Hogan Trophy 1995; mem. US Ryder Cup Team 1989, 1991, 1993, 2002, Capt. 2008; mem. Pres. 's Cup 1994, 2000; broadcasting debut as reporter for NBC, 1995 Ryder Cup; golf analyst, American

Broadcasting Corpn (ABC) Sports 2005–; PGA Tour Player of the Year 1987, Ben Hogan Award 1995. *Publications:* Zinger 1995, Cracking the Code: The Winning Ryder Cup Strategy: Make it Work for You 2010. *Leisure interest:* fishing. *Website:* www.paulazinger.com.

AZIZ, Tan Sri Paduka Rafidah, MEcons; Malaysian academic and politician; b. 4 Nov. 1943, Selama Perak; m. Mohammed Basir bin Ahmad; three c.; ed Univ. of Malaya; held several positions at Univ. of Malaya 1966–76, including tutor, Asst Lecturer, Lecturer and Chair. Rural Devt Div., Faculty of Econs; mem. Parl. 1986–; Deputy Minister of Finance 1977–80; Minister of Public Enterprise 1980–88, of Int. Trade and Industry 1987–2008; mem. UMNO, mem. Supreme Council 1975–, Chair. Women's Wing 1999–2009; Ahli Mangku Negara, Datuk Paduka Mahkota Selangor. *Leisure interests:* reading, decoration, music, squash. *Address:* United Malays National Organization (Pertubuhan Kebangsaan Melayu Bersatu), Menara Dato' Onn, 38th Floor, Jalan Tun Ismail, 50480 Kuala Lumpur, Malaysia. *Telephone:* (3) 40429511. *Fax:* (3) 40412358. *E-mail:* email@umno.net .my. *Website:* www.umno-online.com.

AZIZ, Sartaj; Pakistani economist, politician and fmr international organization official; *Adviser to the Prime Minister on National Security and Foreign Affairs;* b. 7 Feb. 1929; ed Punjab Univ., Harvard Univ., USA; joined Ministry of Finance as civil servant 1952, becoming Jt Sec., Plan Coordination, Planning Comm. 1967–71; Dir of Commodities and Trade Div., FAO, Rome 1971–74, Deputy Sec.-Gen. World Food Conf. 1974, Deputy Exec. Dir World Food Council 1975–77, Asst Pres. Policy and Planning, IFAD 1977–84; Minister of State for Food and Agric. 1984–88, Minister of Finance 1990–93, 1997–98, of Foreign Affairs 1998–99, Adviser to the Prime Minister on Nat. Security and Foreign Affairs 2013–; mem. Senate 1985–89; Vice-Chancellor, Beaconhouse Nat. Univ., Lahore 2004–; Sitara-e-Khidmat 1967. *Publications:* Rural Development: Learning from China 1978, Between Dreams and Realities: Some Milestones in Pakistan's History 2009. *Address:* Ministry of Foreign Affairs, Constitution Avenue, Islamabad, Pakistan (office). *Telephone:* (51) 9210335 (office). *Fax:* (51) 9207600 (office). *Website:* www.mofa.gov.pk (office).

AZIZ, Shaukat, BSc, MBA; Pakistani politician and banker; b. 6 March 1949, Karachi; m.; three c.; ed Gordon Coll., Rawalpindi, Pakistan Business School Inst. of Business Admin, Karachi, Univ. of Karachi; various posts with Citibank including Head of Corp. and Investment Banking, Asia Pacific Region, Head of Corp. and Investment Banking for Cen. and Eastern Europe, Middle East and Africa, Corp. Planning Officer, Citicorp, Man. Dir, Saudi American Bank, Global Head, Pvt. Banking, Vice-Pres. 1969–99; Minister of Finance and Revenue, Econ. Affairs and Statistics and of Planning and Econ. Devt 1999–2004; mem. Senate 2002–04; Prime Minister of Pakistan and Minister of Finance and Revenue, Econ. Affairs and Statistics 2004–07; Bd mem. Millennium and Copthorne Hotels PLC, Blackstone Group; apptd Financial Adviser to Indian businessman Lakshmi Mittal 2010. *Leisure interests:* golf, music, art. *Address:* c/o Office of the Prime Minister's Secretariat, Constitution Avenue, Cabinet Division, Cabinet Block, Islamabad, Pakistan.

AZIZ, Ungku Abdul, DEcons; Malaysian academic and university administrator; b. 28 Jan. 1922, London, UK; m. Sharifah Azah Aziz; one d.; ed Raffles Coll. and Univ. of Malaya in Singapore, Waseda Univ., Tokyo, Johore State Civil Service; Lecturer in Econs, Univ. of Malaya in Singapore –1952; Head, Dept of Econs, Univ. of Malaya, Kuala Lumpur 1952–61, Dean of Faculty 1961–65, Vice-Chancellor 1968–88, Royal Prof. of Econs 1978; Pres. Nat. Co-operative Movement (ANGKASA) 1971, Asscn of SE Asian Institutions of Higher Learning (ASAIHL) 1973–75; Chair. Asscn of Commonwealth Univs 1974–75, Malaysian Nat. Council for ASAIHL, Malaysian Examinations Council 1980; mem. UN Univ. Council; Corresp. mem. of Advisory Bd, Modern Asian Studies 1973–75; mem. Econ. Asscn of Malaysia, Int. Asscn of Agricultural Economists, Jt Advisory Cttee of FAO, UNESCO and ILO; mem. Nat. Consultative Council and Nat. Unity Advisory Council, Govt of Malaysia; mem. numerous cttees and orgs; Fellow, World Acad. of Arts and Sciences 1965–; Ordre des Arts et Lettres (France) 1965; Hon. DHumLitt (Univ. of Pittsburgh); Hon. EdD (Chulalongkorn Univ., Thailand) 1977; Hon. DJur (Waseda Univ., Japan) 1982; Hon. DLitt (Univ. of Warwick) 1982; Hon. DIur (Univ. of Strathclyde) 1986, (Utara Univ., Malaysia) 1988; Hon. DEcon (Kebangsaan Univ., Malaysia) 1986; Hon. LLD (Buckingham) 1987; Tun Abdul Razak Foundation Award 1978, Japan Foundation Award 1981; Special Award, Muslim Pilgrim Savings Fund Bd 1988; Grand Cordon of the Order of the Sacred Treasure, Emperor of Japan 1989; ASEAN Achievement Award (Educ.) 1992, Int. Academic Prize (City of Fukoka) 1993, Tokoh Ekonomi Melayu 2005, Anugerah Melayu Terbilang 2005, National Academic Award 2006. *Leisure interests:* jogging, reading and photography.

AZMAT, Ali; Pakistani musician; b. 1970, Lahore; ed Ashfield Business School, Sydney, Australia; began musical career in band Jupiters, Lahore 1991; Founder-mem. Junoon (with Salman Ahmad and Brian O'Connell) 1991–, banned by Pakistani authorities for criticism of govt corruption early 1990s; upon invitation of UN Sec.-Gen., Kofi Annan, performed at UN Gen. Ass. (first band to play at Gen. Ass.); tours throughout Asia, N America, Middle East and Europe; Jazbe-e-Junoon selected as official song of cricket world cup, hosted by Pakistan 1996; simultaneous solo career 2002–; Channel V Music Award for International Group 1998, UNESCO Award for Outstanding Achievement in Music and Peace 1999, BBC Asia Award 1999. *Film music:* Paap (directed by Pooja Bhatt), Jism-2 2012. *Recordings include:* albums: with Junoon: Junoon 1990, Talaash 1993, Inquilaab 1995, Khashmakash 1996, Azaadi 1997, Parvaaz 1999, Andaz 2001, The Millennium Edition (compilation) 2000, Daur-e-Junoon 2002, Dewaar 2003; solo: Social Circus 2005, Klashinfolk 2008, Josh-E-Junoon 2010, Bum Phatta 2011, Chalta Mein Jaaon 2011; singles: with Junoon: Jazbe-e-Junoon 1996, Saeein, Ehtesaab 1996, Sayonee 1997, Taara jala. *Address:* Junoon Inc., 210 Old Tappan Road, Tappan, NY 10983, USA (office). *E-mail:* alishan@aliazmat.com (office); info@ junoon.com (office). *Website:* www.junoon.com (office).

AZMI, Shabana, BA; Indian actress, politician and human rights activist; b. 18 Sept. 1951, Hyderabad; d. of Kaifi Azmi and Shaukat Kaifi; m. Javed Akhtar 1984; ed St Xavier's Coll. Mumbai, Film and TV Inst., Pune; mem. Rajya Sabha (Upper House of Parl.) 1997–2003; speaker on women's rights and communication in USA; campaigner on social justice issues; Chair. Nivara Hakk Suraksha Samiti (campaigning org. for upgrading of slum dwellings); Chair. Children's Film Soc.

1992–94; Goodwill Amb. UN Population Fund (UNFPA) 1998–; Chair. of Jury Montréal and Cairo Int. Film Festivals; mem. Nat. Integration Council, Advisory Council Endowment Campaign for Chair. in Indian Studies, Columbia Univ.; Visiting Prof., Univ. of Michigan, USA; Dr hc (Leeds Metropolitan Univ., UK) 2007; Soviet Land Nehru Award 1985, Padma Shri Award 1988, Rajiv Gandhi Award for Excellence in Secularism 1994, Yash Bhartiya Award for promoting women's issues, Govt of Uttar Pradesh 1988, King Chevaz Award, Univ. of Michigan, Martin Luther King Professorship Award, Univ. of Michigan 2002, Gandhi Foundation Int. Peace Award 2006, Crystal Award, World Econ. Forum 2006, Lifetime Achievement Award, Filmfare 2006, Pres.'s Memorial Award for Nat. Integration 2007, Global Leadership Award, Int. Indian Film Acad., Macao 2009. *Plays include:* Nora (Singapore Repertory Theatre), The Waiting Room (Nat. Theatre, London), Sufaid Kundali, Tumhari Amrita, Emma in Betrayal (Singapore Repertory Theatre), Shaukat Kaifi in Kaifi Aur Main, Manjula and Malini Sharma in Broken Images. *Films include:* nearly 150 films including Ankur (Nat. Award for Best Actress) 1974, Nishant 1976, Swami (Filmfare Award) 1977, Shatranj Ke Khiladi 1977, Junoon 1978, Amardeep 1979, Sparsh 1980, Masoom 1983, Arth (Nat. Award) 1983, Mandi 1983, Doosri Dulhan 1983, Khandhar (Nat. Award) 1984, Paar (Nat. Award) 1985, Libaas (Int. Best Actress Award, N Korea 1993) 1988, Bhavna (Filmfare Award) 1984, Madame Sousatzka 1988, Bengali Night 1988, City of Joy 1992, The Journey, Son of the Pink Panther 1993, Patang (Best Actress Award, Taormina Art Festival Italy) 1994, Fire (Silver Hugo Award for Best Actress, Chicago Int. Film Festival), (Outstanding Actress in a Feature Film, LA Outfest) 1996, Saaz 1997, Godmother (Nat. Award, Bengal Film Journalists' Asscn Awards) 1999, Hari-Bhari: Fertility 2000, Makdee 2002, Tehzeeb (Zee Cine Award) 2003, Lakshya 2004, Morning Raga 2004 (Star Screen Award) 2005, 15 Park Avenue 2005, Waterborne 2005, Umrao Jaan 2006, Honeymoon Travels Pvt. Ltd 2007, Loins of Punjab Presents 2007, Sorry Bhai! 2008, It's a Wonderful Afterlife 2010, Kalpvriksh 2011, A Decent Arrangement 2011, Matru Ki Bijlee Ka Mandola 2012. *Television:* Anupama (Hindi serial). *Leisure interests:* reading, singing. *Address:* 702 Sagar Samrat, Green Fields, Juhu, Mumbai 400 049, India (home). *Telephone:* (22) 26200066 (home). *Fax:* (22) 26202602 (office). *E-mail:* azmishabana@gmail.com (office).

AZNAN, Syed Jaafar, MBA, PhD; Malaysian civil servant and banker; b. 1947; m.; three c.; ed Univ. of Malaya, Wharton School, USA, Henley Man. Coll./Brunel Univ., UK; civil servant in Malaysia holding several sr positions in various ministries 1970–97; Vice-Pres. Trade and Policy, Islamic Devt Bank, Jeddah, Saudia Arabia 1997–2009; Dir Bank Pembangunan Malaysia Berhad 2010–; Chair. Perbadanan Kemajuan Ekonomi Islam Negeri Perak; mem. Council Majlis Agama Islam dan Adat Melayu Perak;. *Address:* c/o Bank Pembangunan Malaysia Berhad (16562-K), Menara Bank Pembangunan Bandar Wawasan, N0 1016, Jalan Sultan Ismail, 50250 Kuala Lumpur, Malaysia (office).

AZNAR LÓPEZ, José María; Spanish politician and academic; *President, FAES Fundación para el Análisis y los Estudios Sociales;* b. 1953, Madrid; m. Ana Botella; two s. one d.; ed Universidad Complutense; fmr tax inspector; fmr Chief Exec. Castile-Leon region; joined Rioja br. Alianza Popular 1978, Deputy Sec.-Gen. and mem. Cortes (Parl.) 1982; Premier Castilla y León Autonomous Region 1987; Pres. Partido Popular (PP, fmrly Alianza Popular) 1990–2004, now Hon. Chair.; Prime Minister of Spain and Pres. of the Council 1996–2004; currently Pres. FAES Fundación para el Análisis y los Estudios Sociales, Madrid; Distinguished Scholar in the Practice of Global Leadership, Georgetown Univ., Washington, DC 2004–; Vice-Pres. European Democratic Union; Pres. Int. Democratic Centre 2001; Chair. Friends of Israel Initiative; mem. Bd of Dirs News Corpn 2006–; Distinguished Fellow, School of Advanced Int. Studies, Johns Hopkins Univ. (Chair. Atlantic Basin Initiative)· mem. Int. Advisory Bd Atlantic Council (Co-Chair. Transatlantic Task Force on Latin America); mem. Int. Advisory Bd Barrick Gold Corpn; Sr Advisor to Global Bd, DLA Piper; Hon. Prof., Universidad de Ciencias Aplicadas, Perú 2006; Dr hc (Sophia Univ., Tokyo) 1997, (Florida International Univ.) 1998, (Bar-Ilan Univ., Israel) 2005, (Universidad Andrés Bello, Chile) 2006, (Universidad Francisco Marroquín, Guatemala) 2006, (Università Cattolica Sacro Cuore, Milán) 2007, (Universidad Cardenal Herrera CEU) 2009, (Universidad San Ignacio de Loyola, Perú) 2009, (Ilia Chavchavadze Univ., Georgia) 2009, (Universidad San Antonio) 2010, (Universidad de las Américas, Ecuador) 2011; Pres.'s Medal, Georgetown Univ. 2004. *Publication:* Ocho años de gobierno: una visión personal de España 2004. *Address:* FAES Fundación para el Análisis y los Estudios Sociales, C/Juan Bravo, 3C, 7°, 28006 Madrid, Spain (office); Mortara Center for International Studies, Edmund A. Walsh School of Foreign Service, Georgetown University, ICC, Suite 304, 37th and O Streets, NW, Washington, DC 20057, USA (office). *Telephone:* (91) 5766857 (office). *Fax:* (91) 5754695 (office). *E-mail:* presidencia@fundacionfaes.org (office); atencion@pp.es (office). *Website:* www.fundacionfaes.org (office); www.georgetown.edu/sfs/mortara (office); www.pp .es (office).

AZNAVOUR, Charles; French/Armenian film actor, singer and diplomatist; *Armenian Ambassador to Switzerland;* b. (Shahnour Vaghenag Aznavourian), 22 May 1924; m. 1st Micheline Rugel 1946; m. 2nd Evelyne Plessis 1955; m. 3rd Ulla Thorsel 1967; five c.; ed Ecole Centrale de T.S.F., Centre de Spectacle, Paris; with Jean Dasté Company 1941; Man. Dir French-Music 1965–; Roving UNESCO Amb. to Armenia 1995–; Hon. Pres. Belgrade Film Festival 2003; numerous song recitals in Europe and USA; film music includes: Soupe au lait, L'île du bout du monde, Ces dames préfèrent le mambo, Le cercle vicieux, De quoi tu te mêles Daniela, Douce violence, Les Parisiennes; also author and singer of numerous songs; composer of operetta Monsieur Carnaval 1965, Douchka 1973; Armenian Amb. to Switzerland and Amb. and Perm. Rep. of Armenia to UN, Geneva 2009–; Commdr, Légion d'honneur 2004, Commdr des Arts et des Lettres; Dr hc (Univ. of Montréal) 2009; several prizes including Grand Prix nat. de la chanson 1986, César d'honneur 1997, Time Magazine Entertainer of the Century 1998, Molière amical 1999, MIDEM Lifetime Achievement Award 2009, Grigor Lusavorich Award (Nagorno-Karabakh Republic) 2009. *Recordings include:* albums: Jazznavour 1998, Aznavour 2000, Colore ma vie 2007, Tú pintas mi vida 2008, Charles Aznavour et ses amis au Palais Garnier 2008. *Films and television include:* La tête contre les murs 1959, Tirez sur le pianiste 1960, Un taxi pour Tobrouk, Le testament

d'Orphée, Le diable et les dix commandements, Haute-infidélité 1964, La métamorphose des cloportes 1965, Paris au mois d'août 1966, Le facteur s'en va-t-en guerre 1966, Candy 1969, Les intrus 1973, Sky Riders, Intervention Delta, Folies bourgeoises, Dix petits nègres 1976, The Twist 1976, The Tin Drum 1979, Qu'est-ce qui a fait courir David? 1982, Les fantômes du chapelier 1982, La montagne magique 1983, Vive la vie 1984, Mangeclous 1988, Il Maestro 1992, Les Années Campagne 1992, Pondichéry Dernier Comptoir des Indes 1996, Les Mômes 1999, Judaicaë I 2000, Laguna 2001, Angelina (TV) 2002, Passage du bac (TV) 2002, Ararat 2002, Le Père Goriot 2004, Emmenez-moi 2005. *Leisure interest:* photography. *Address:* Embassy of Armenia, Avenue du Mail 28, 1205 Geneva, Switzerland (office). *Telephone:* (22) 320-11-00 (office). *Fax:* (22) 320-61-48 (office). *E-mail:* mission.armenia@bluewin.ch (office). *Website:* www.switzerland.mfa.am (office); www.charlesaznavour-lesite.fr.

AZOUR, Jihad, MS, PhD; Lebanese economist and government official; b. 4 May 1964, Sir Denniye; m. Roula Rizk; ed Assad Univ., Univ. of Paris, IEP Paris, France, Harvard Univ., USA; with McKinsey, Lebanon 1989–93; Program Man. and Advisor to Dir Gen. Asscn d'Economie Financière 1993–94; Man. Pnr, AM&F Consulting 1996–98; consultant to IMF and Booz Allen 2005; Prof., American Univ. Beirut; Dir UNDP/World Bank project 1999–2005; Adviser to Ministry of Finance 1999–2004; Minister of Finance 2005–08. *Address:* c/o Ministry of Finance, 4e étage, Immeuble MOF, place Riad es-Solh, Beirut, Lebanon (office).

AZRIELI, David Joshua, CM, CQ, BA, MArch; Canadian designer, architect and philanthropist; *Director, Canpro Investments Ltd;* b. 10 May 1922, Makow, Poland; m. Stephanie Azrieli; four c.; ed Technion Univ., Haifa, Israel, Carleton Univ.; escaped Poland 1939, journeyed secretly through Russia and Cen. Asia 1940–41, sought exile in Palestine 1942; studied architecture in Haifa; served in Israeli Defence and Air Forces 1948; emmigrated to Montreal, Canada 1954; Founding Dir Canpro Investments Ltd, Montreal 1958–, working in commercial real estate markets in Canada, USA and Middle East, designing, developing and building skyscrapers, shopping malls and office towers; est. Azrieli Foundation 1989, David Arzieli Fellowship, Concordia Univ.; donated funds to est. David Arzieli School of Architecture, Tel Aviv Univ. 1994 and David J. Arzieli Pavilion, Theatre and Inst. of Grad. Studies in Architecture, Carleton Univ. 2002; Chevalier Ordre Nat. du Québec 1998; Dr hc (Concordia, Yeshiva, Technion, Tel Aviv and Carleton Univs); Prime Minister's Jubilee Award (Israel) 1998, Jerusalem Prize, Commemorative Medal on Canada's 125th Anniversary, Golden Jubilee Medal. *Architectural designs include:* Tel Aviv Enclosed Shopping Mall (first in Israel) 1986, Les Promenades de l'Outaouais, Gatineau, Quebec, Azrieli Centre, Tel Aviv 1998. *Address:* Canpro Investments Ltd, 1010 rue Sainte-Catherine Ouest, Montreal, PQ H3BA 4S3, Canada (office). *Website:* www.canpro.ca (office).

AŽUBALIS, Audronius; Lithuanian journalist and politician; b. 17 Jan. 1958, Vilnius; m. Loreta Ažubalienė; two d.; ed Antanas Vienuolis Secondary School, Vilnius, Vilnius State Univ., World Press Inst., Macalester Coll., USA; various positions in journalism and publishing 1979–88, including Lithuanian State Cttee of Publishing Houses, Polygraph Enterprises and Book Trade, Scientific Methodological Culture Centre of Lithuania, State Cttee for TV and Radio Broadcasting, Lithuanian Cinema Rental Bureau; corresp., Atgimimas (weekly newspaper) 1989–90; Spokesman for Chair. of Supreme Council (Reconstituent Seimas) 1990–92, Head of Seimas Information and Analysis Centre 1991–93; f. Lithuania's first private relations consultancy 1993, Chair. 1993–96; mem. Seimas (Parl.) 1996–2000, 2008–10, apptd Chair. Cttee on Foreign Affairs 2004, Deputy Chair. Cttee on European Affairs; Dir-Gen. Translation, Documentation and Information Centre, Govt Chancellery 2001–04; Minister of Foreign Affairs 2010–12; Pres. Lithuania-GB Chamber of Commerce 1998–2000; mem. Homeland Union—Lithuanian Conservatives (now Homeland Union—Lithuanian Christian Democrats) 1998–; Pres. Nat. Magazine Publrs Asscn 2001–03; Third Degree, Order of Merit (Ukraine) 2007; 13th Jan. Commemorative Medal 1999, Commemorative Badge of Lithuania's admission to NATO 2003. *Leisure interests:* reading historical themes, homestead farm work, fishing. *Address:* Homeland Union—Lithuanian Christian Democrats, L. Stuokos-Gucevičiaus g. 11, Vilnius 01122, Lithuania (office). *Telephone:* (5) 212-1657 (office). *Fax:* (5) 278-4722 (office). *E-mail:* sekretoriatas@tsajunga.lt (office). *Website:* www.tsajunga.lt (office).

AZUMA, Takamitsu, JIA, DArch; Japanese architect; b. 20 Sept. 1933, Osaka; s. of Yoshimatsu Azuma and Yoshiko Azuma (née Ikeda); m. Setsuko Nakaoka 1957; one d.; ed Osaka Univ.; designer, Ministry of Postal Service, Osaka 1957–60; Chief Designer, Junzo Sakakura Architect & Assocs, Osaka 1960–63; Tokyo 1963–67; Prin. Takamitsu Azuma Architect & Assocs, Tokyo 1968–85; Instructor, Univ. of Art and Design 1976–78, Tokyo Denki Univ. 1980–82, Tokyo Univ. 1983–85; Instructor, Osaka Univ. 1981–85, Prof. 1985–97, Prof. Emer. 1997–; Instructor, Osaka Art Univ. 1985–87; Architect, Azuma Architects and Assocs 1985–97; Prof., Chiba Inst. of Tech. 1997–; mem. Architectural Inst. of Japan; Visiting Prof., School of Architecture, Washington Univ., St Louis, USA 1985; 1st Prize Kinki Br., Inst. of Architects Competition 1957; Architectural Inst. of Japan Architectural Design Prize 1995. *Publications:* Revaluation of the Residence 1971, On the Japanese Architectural Space 1981, Philosophy of Living in the City 1983, Device from Architecture 1986, Space Analysis of the Urban Residence 1986, White Book about Tower House 1987, On Urban Housing 1997. *Leisure interests:* travelling, reading, computing. *Address:* Azuma Architects & Associates, 3-6-1 Minami-Aoyama Minato-ku, Tokyo 107-0016 (office); 3-39-4 Jingumae, Shibuya-ku, Tokyo 150-0001, Japan (home). *Telephone:* (3) 3403-5593 (office); (3) 3404-0805 (home).

AZUMI, Jun; Japanese lawyer and politician; *Deputy Secretary-General, Democratic Party of Japan;* b. 17 Jan. 1962, Oshika Dist, Miyagi Pref.; m.; two s.; ed Waseda Univ.; began career as political reporter for NHK (Japan Broadcasting Corpn) 1985–93; mem. House of Reps for Miyagi No. 5 Dist 1993–; apptd Chair. Security Cttee, Democratic Party of Japan 2009, Parl. Affairs Cttee 2011, Deputy Sec.-Gen. 2012–; Sr Vice-Minister of Defence 2010, Minister of Finance 2011–12. *Address:* Democratic Party of Japan, 1-11-1, Nagata-cho, Chiyoda-ku, Tokyo 100-0014, Japan (office). *Telephone:* (3) 3595-9988 (office). *Fax:* (3) 3595-9988 (office). *E-mail:* dpjenews@dpj.or.jp (office). *Website:* www.dpj.or.jp (office).

B

BÂ, Amadou; Senegalese politician; *Minister of the Economy and Finance;* b. 1961, Dakar; m.; three c.; ed Ecole nat. d'admin et de magistrature (Enam), Univ. Cheikh Anta Diop (UCAD); has held numerous positions in Ministry of the Economy and Finance, including Controller of Insurance, Dept of Insurance 1992–94, Head of Training, Centre Ouest Africain de Formation et d'Etudes Bancaires (part of Banque centrale des Etats de l'Afrique de l'Ouest) 1995–2000, Auditor, Audit and Verification Dept 2000–02, Dir of Taxes 2004–06, Dir-Gen. of Taxation 2006–13, Minister of the Economy and Finance 2013–. *Address:* Ministry of the Economy and Finance, rue René Ndiaye, BP 4017, Dakar, Senegal (office). *Telephone:* 33-889-2100 (office). *Fax:* 33-822-4195 (office). *E-mail:* i_diouf@minfinances.sn (office). *Website:* www.finances.gouv.sn (office).

BA, Amadou Lamine, MSc, PhD; Senegalese development consultant and diplomatist; m. Oulimata Ba; ed Ecole des Cadres Ruraux, Ohio State Univ., USA; Dir Regional Educ. Centre, Crop Protection Directorate (Direction de la Protection des Végétaux/DPV), Dakar 1980–82; consultant in int. devt, USAID-Washington, in The Gambia 1981, in Guinea-Bissau 1981, in Niamey 1983; Research Asst, Coll. of Agric., Ohio State Univ., Columbus 1988–93, Researcher and Asst Prof. 1997–99; Consultant and Visiting Scholar, Dept of Int. Studies, Univ. of Vermont 1993; consultant in int. devt 1993–97; Jt Leader, Human Rights, Democracy and New Leadership in Africa (HDNA) 1995–97; mem. Exec. Bd US-Africa Inst. 1997–99; Prof. of Science, Bunker Hill Coll., Boston, Mass 1999–; Amb. to USA 2002–10; mem. Forum des Citoyens pour l'Alternance, Asscn des Professeurs de Sciences, Int. Soc. of Quality Assurance; Key to City of Baton Rouge, La 2006. *Publications:* Integrated Pest Management and International Agriculture Development Policies: A Case Study of the United States and Africa 1993, Global Issues in Pesticides Regulation 1999. *Address:* c/o Ministry of Foreign Affairs. place de l'Indépendance, BP 4044, Dakar, Senegal (office).

BAALBAKI, Ayman, DEA; Lebanese artist; b. 1975, Odeissé; ed Inst. des Beaux Arts, Lebanese Univ., Beirut, Univ. Paris VIII, Ecole nat. supérieure des Arts Décoratifs, Paris; works include oil paintings and installations; chosen to take part in The Future of a Promise (first pan-Arab exhbn of contemporary art), 2011 Venice Biennale; mem. Asscn des Artistes libanais; Silver Medal (painting), Jeux de la Francophonie, Niger 2005. *Address:* c/o Agial Art Gallery, 63 Abdul Aziz Street, Hamra District, Beirut, Lebanon (office). *Telephone:* (1) 1345213 (office). *Website:* www.radisnoir.com/ayman (office).

BABACAN, Ali, MBA, BSc; Turkish politician; *Deputy Prime Minister and State Minister in charge of coordination of the Economy;* b. 1967, Ankara; m.; two c.; ed Middle East Tech. Univ., Ankara, Northwestern Univ., USA; worked at QRM, Inc., Chicago, Ill. 1992–94; chief adviser to Mayor of Ankara 1994; ran family-owned textile co. 1994–2002; mem. of Grand Nat. Ass., representing Ankara 2002–; Minister of State for Economy 2002–05; Chief Negotiator in accession talks with EU 2005–; Minister of Foreign Affairs 2007–09; Deputy Prime Minister and Minister of State in charge of coordination of the Economy 2009–; Co-founder and Bd mem. AKP (Adalet ve Kalkınma Partisi/Justice and Devt Party). *Address:* Deputy Prime Ministers' Office, Başbakan yard. ve Devlet Bakanı, Bakanlıklar, Ankara, Turkey (office). *Telephone:* (312) 4191621 (office). *Fax:* (312) 4191547 (office).

BABAEV, Agadzhan Geldyevich, DrGeogSc; Turkmenistani geographer and academic; b. 10 May 1929, Mary; s. of Geldy Babaev and Ogulbek Babaevai; m. Dunyagozel Palvanova 1951; two s. six d.; ed State Pedagogical Inst., Ashkhabad (now Ashgabat), Turkmenistan State Univ.; Head, Geography Dept, Turkmenistan State Univ. 1952–59; Deputy Dir Desert Research Inst., Turkmenistan Acad. of Sciences 1959–60, Dir 1960–99; Chair. Scientific Council for Desert Problems 1967–; Ed.-in-Chief Problems of Desert Devt 1967–; Dir Turkmenistan Research and Training Centre on Desertification Control for ESCAP; Deputy to USSR Supreme Soviet 1979–89; Chair. Turkmenistan Soc. for Chinese-Soviet Friendship; mem. Turkmenistan Acad. of Sciences, Pres. 1975–86, 1989–93; Corresp. mem. USSR (now Russian) Acad. of Sciences 1976; Academician, Islamic Acad. of Sciences 1996–; Vice-Pres. Turkmens of the World Humanitarian Asscn; Deputy, Turkmenistan Parl.; USSR State Prize 1981, Academician Karpinskii Medal 1990, Jerald Piel Medal 1992. *Publications:* 12 monographs, 329 articles for professional journals. *Address:* 113 Kosaev Street, Ashgabat 744020, Turkmenistan (home). *Telephone:* (12) 34-26-24 (home).

BABANGIDA, Maj.-Gen. Ibrahim Badamasi; Nigerian army officer (retd) and fmr head of state; b. 17 Aug. 1941, Minna; m. Maryam King 1969 (died 2009); two s. two d.; ed Niger provincial secondary school, Bida, Kaduna Mil. Training Coll. and Indian Mil. Acad.; commissioned 1963, Lt 1966; training with RAC, UK 1966; CO during Biafran Civil War; Co Commdr and Instructor, Nigerian Defence Acad. 1970–72; rank of Maj. then Lt-Col Armoured Corps 1974; trained at US Army Armoury School 1974; promoted to Maj.-Gen., Dir of Army Duties and Plans 1983; took part in overthrow of Pres. Shehu Shagari 1983; mem. Supreme Mil. Council and Chief Army Staff 1983–85; Pres. of Nigeria following coup overthrowing Maj.-Gen. Muhammadu Buhari 1985–93; Pres. Police Council 1989; Minister of Defence Dec. 1989–90; Hon. GCB 1989. *Publications:* Civil and Military Relationship, The Nigerian Experience 1979, Defence Policy within the Framework of National Planning 1985.

BABANOV, Omurbek Toktogulovich; Kyrgyzstani politician and business executive; *Leader, Republic Political Party (Respublika);* b. 20 May 1970, Chimkent village, Kara-Burinskii dist, Talas Oblast, Kyrgyz SSR, USSR; ed Timiryazev Moscow Agricultural Acad., Acad. of Nat. Economy at Govt of the Russian Fed., Higher Coll. of Financial Man., Moscow, Kyrgyz State Judicial Acad. at Govt of the Kyrgyz Repub.; served in Soviet Army in GDR 1988–89; rep. of Shymkentnefteosintez (Chimkent Oil Refinery) Co. in Kyrgyz Repub. –1999; Dir, Arlan LLP, Taras, Kazakhstan 1995–98; Deputy Gen. Dir Munai Co., Bishkek 1999–2000; Pres. Kyrgyzkhlopok (Kyrgyz Cotton) Co., Jalal-Abad 2000–04; Chief Rep., Petro Kazakhstan Oil Products in Kyrgyz Repub., Bishkek 2002–05; mem. Bd of Dirs Munai Myrza Invest Co. 2004–05, Chair. 2008, 2009–10; Adviser to Chair. of Kommerchiskii bank-Kyrgyzstan Jan.–Oct. 2010; Deputy in Zhogorku

Kenesh (Parl.) 2005–07, Nov. 2010, rep. of Karabuurinsky Electoral Dist No. 56, mem. Parl. Cttee for Int. Affairs and Interparliamentary Communications, Social and Religious Orgs, mem. El Birimdigi factions of deputies, Head of Deputy Group for Friendship of the Zhogorku Kenesh with the Parl. of the Russian Fed., Turkey and Kazakhstan, mem. Perm. Comm. for Econs and Finances of the Interparliamentary Ass. of the mem. states of the CIS, mem. working group for the preparation of constitutional amendments, Head of pre-election team of Social Democratic Party of Kyrgyzstan (SDPK) Oct. 2007; First Deputy Prime Minister (expelled from SDPK in consequence) Jan.–Oct. 2009; participant and Co-Chair. Ak-niet Movt April–June 2010; Founder and Chair. Republic Political Party (Respublika) 2010–; First Deputy Prime Minister Dec. 2010–Sept. 2011 (suspended from office at his own request April–May 2011), Acting Prime Minister Sept.–Nov., 1–23 Dec. 2011, Prime Minister 23 Dec. 2011–1 Sept. 2012 (resgnd); Businessman of the Year in Kyrgyzstan 2004. *Address:* Republic Political Party (Respublika), 720000 Bishkek, Toktogula 126, Kyrgyzstan (office). *Telephone:* (312) 66-31-21 (office). *E-mail:* pr@republic.kg (office). *Website:* www.republic.kg (office).

BABAR, Alamgir; Pakistani diplomatist; fmr Deputy Perm. Rep., later Acting Perm. Rep. to UN, New York; Dir-Gen. (Americas), Ministry of Foreign Affairs –2005; High Commr to Bangladesh 2005–10. *Address:* Ministry of Foreign Affairs, Constitution Avenue, Islamabad, Pakistan (office). *Telephone:* (51) 9210335 (office). *Fax:* (51) 9207600 (office). *Website:* www.mofa.gov.pk (office).

BABBAR, Raj; Indian politician, actor and filmmaker; b. 23 June 1952, Agra Dist, Uttar Pradesh; s. of Kaushal Kumar and Shobha Rani; m. 1st Nadira Babbar 1975; m. 2nd Smita Patil (died 1986); two s. one d.; ed Nat. School of Drama, New Delhi; mem. Rajya Sabha 1994–99, mem. Home Affairs Cttee, Rules Cttee, Consultative Cttee, Ministry of Civil Aviation; mem. Lok Sabha 1999–, mem. Defence Cttee, Environment Cttee, Transport, Tourism and Culture Cttee 1999–2000, 2004, Petitions Cttee; mem. Personnel, Public Grievances, Law & Justice 2007–; Pres. Jan Morcha party 2006–; Yash Bharti Award, Uttar Pradesh Govt, Punjabi Male Actor of the Millennium, Punjabi American Festival 2000. *Films include:* Shaheed Uddham Singh 2000, LoC Kargil 2003, Kyaa Dil Ne Kahaa 2002, The Legend of Bhagat Singh 2002, Talaash 2003, Sheen 2004, Police Force: An Inside Story 2004, Shikaar 2004, Yaaran Naal Baharaan 2005, Bunty Aur Babli 2005, Ek Dhun Banaras Kee 2006, Corporate 2006, UNNS: Love Forever 2006, Ek Jind Ek Jaan 2006, Sirf Romance: Love by Chance 2007, Aap Kaa Surroor: The Moviee 2007, Fashion 2008. *Address:* 20 Mahadev Road, New Delhi 110 001 (home); Nepathay 20, Gulmohar Road, J.V.P.D. Scheme, Mumbai 400 049 India (home). *Telephone:* (11) 23352728 (New Delhi) (office); (22) 26282819 (Mumbai) (home). *Fax:* (11) 23352728 (New Delhi) (office); (22) 26248868 (Mumbai) (home). *E-mail:* rajbabbars@yahoo.in. *Website:* loksabha.nic.in (office).

BABBITT, Bruce Edward, LLB; American lawyer, business executive and fmr politician; b. 27 July 1938; m. Hattie Coons; two c.; ed Univ. of Notre Dame, Univ. of Newcastle, UK, Harvard Univ. Law School; Attorney-Gen. Ariz. 1975–78; Gov. of Ariz. 1978–87; Pnr, Steptoe & Johnson, Phoenix; US Sec. of Interior 1993–2001; Sec. of Counsel, Environmental Dept, Latham & Watkins LLP (law firm) 2001; Pres. Raintree Ventures (investment firm), Washington, DC; Chair. World Wildlife Fund 2006, now Dir Emer.; Chair. Nat. Groundwater Policy Forum 1984; Pres. League of Conservation Voters; Marshall Scholar 1960–62; Democrat; Thomas Jefferson Award, Nat. Wildlife Fed. 1981, Special Conservation Award 1983. *Publications:* Color and Light: The Southwest Canvases of Louis Akin 1973, Grand Canyon: An Anthology 1978, Cities in the Wilderness: A New Look at Land Use in America 2005. *Address:* Raintree Ventures, 5169 Watson Street, NW, Washington, DC 20016, USA (office).

BABENKO, Hector; Argentine filmmaker; b. 7 Feb. 1946, Buenos Aires; eight years in Europe as writer, house painter, door-to-door salesman, film extra etc.; moved to Brazil 1969; Best Foreign Film Award for Pixote (New York Film Critics). *Films:* as writer, dir, producer: Fabuloso Fittipaldi, O 1973, O Rei Da Noite 1976, Pixote 1980, Corazón iluminado 1996, Carandiru 2003; as writer, dir: Lucio Flavio–Passageiro da Agonia 1978, At Play in the Fields of the Lord 1991; as dir, producer: Kiss of the Spider Woman 1985; as producer: Besame Mucho 1987; as dir: Ironweed 1987, El pasado 2007.

BABESHKO, Vladimir A.; Russian physicist and university official; b. 30 May 1941; m.; two d.; ed Rostov State Univ.; with Rostov Univ. 1966–82, fmr Asst. Prof., Deputy Dir; Rector, Kuban State Univ. 1982–2008; Chair. Russian S Branch, Int. Acad. of Higher Educ. Sciences; mem. Council for Sciences, Tech. and Educ. under Pres. of Russian Fed. 2004–; Academician, Russian Acad. of Sciences 1997–; Order of People's Friendship 1986; Lenin Komsomol Prize 1977, Vavilov Medal 1990, State Award of Russian Fed. in the Field of Science and Eng 2001, Hero of Labour of Kuban Medal 2003, Rector of the Year Hon. Breastplate 2004, 2005, Distinguished Citizen of Krasnodar. *Publications:* author or co-author of more than 300 scientific publs, including five monographs. *Address:* c/o Office of the Rector, Kuban State University, 350040 Krasnodar, 149 Libknekhta str., Russia.

BABICH, Mikhail Viktorovich; Russian politician; *Presidential Representative to the Volga Federal Okrug;* b. 28 May 1969; m.; two c.; ed Ryazan Higher Mil. School of Communications, Moscow Inst. of Econ. Man. and Law, State Acad. of Man.; sr officer in airborne troops 1990–94; worked in pvt. sector 1995–99; Deputy Dir-Gen. Fed. Agency for Food Market Regulation, Ministry of Agric.; fmr Deputy Gov. Moscow Region, forced to resign following accusations of misappropriating US humanitarian aid; First Deputy Gov. Ivanovskaya Region 2001–02; Chair. of Republican Govt (Prime Minister) of Chechnya Nov. 2002–Jan. 2003 (resgnd); mem. State Duma Dec. 2003–, Deputy Chair. Defence Cttee; Asst to Minister of Econ. Devt 2003–; Presidential Rep. to Volga Fed. Okrug 2011–; Dir of election staff, Vladimir Oblast regional branch, United Russia (Yedinaya Rossiya) party; Order of Friendship 2006. *Address:* Office of the Presidential Representative, 603082 Nizhnii Novgorod, Kreml, kor. 1, Russia (office). *Telephone:* (831) 431-47-65 (office); (831) 431-46-54; (831) 431-46-61. *Fax:* (831) 431-47-51 (office). *Website:* www.pfo.ru (office).

BABIŠ, Andrej; Czech business executive and politician; *Deputy Prime Minister and Minister of Finance;* b. 2 Sept. 1954, Bratislava; s. of Štefan Babiš and Andriana Babišová; four c.; ed gymnasium in Bratislava, Univ. of Economics; worked as employee of Slovak Communist-controlled int. trade co. Petrimex in Morocco; returned to Czechoslovakia after Velvet Revolution and resided in Czech Repub. following dissolution of Czechoslovakia; Owner and CEO Agrofert from 1993; Founder and Leader, ANO 2011 – Akce nespokojených občanů (Yes 2011 – Action of Dissatisfied Citizens) 2011–; Deputy Prime Minister and Minister of Finance 2014–. *Address:* Ministry of Finance, Letenská 15, 118 00 Prague 1, Czech Republic (office). *Telephone:* (2) 57041111 (office). *Fax:* (2) 57042788 (office). *E-mail:* podatelna@mfcr.cz (office). *Website:* www.mfcr.cz (office).

BABIUC, Victor, PhD; Romanian politician and lawyer; b. 3 April 1938, Răchiţi Commune, Botoşani Co.; s. of Victor Babiuc and Olga Babiuc; m. Lucia Babiuc 1978; one d.; ed Law School of Bucharest, Romanian Acad. for Econ. Studies, Univ. of Bucharest; juridical counsellor, judge in Braşov; Chief Juridical Counsel Ministry of Foreign Trade, Sr Researcher at the World Economy Inst. 1977–90; mem. House of Deputies 1992–2000; Minister of Justice 1990–91, Minister of the Interior 1991–92; Minister of Nat. Defence 1996–98, Minister of State, Minister of Nat. Defence 1998–2000; mem. Chamber of Deputies for Brasov Ward 2000–04; mem. Democratic Party (PD) 1992–2000, Vice Pres. 1995–2000; mem. Nat. Liberal Party 2000–; Chair. Commercial Arbitration Court, Chamber of Commerce and Industry of Romania (CCIR) 1993–2008, Pres. CCIR 2005–07; Prof. of Int. Trade Law, Acad. of Econ. Studies of Bucharest 1992–; Chair. Cttee for Investigation into Corruption and Cases of Abuse and for Petitions of the Chamber of Deputies 1992–96; mem. Panel of Arbitrators of American Arbitration Asscn, Moscow, Sofia, Abu Dhabi, Warsaw, New Delhi, Cairo 1991–; mem. Cen. European Acad. of Science and Art 2004–; mem. National Liberal Party. *Publications:* over 200 publications mainly in the field of econ. legislation and int. trade law. *Leisure interests:* theatre, walking, reading books on politics, history, memoirs. *Address:* Individual Office Attorney, Bd. Hristo Botev, MR 3, Apartment, Sector 3, Bucharest (office); Bd Libertatii No. 20, Sector 5, Bucharest, Romania (home). *Telephone:* (4021) 3147722 (office); (4021) 3147788 (office); (4021) 3143732 (home). *Fax:* (4021) 3147799 (office). *Website:* babiuc.victor@yahoo.com (office).

BABURIN, Sergei Nikolaevich, LLD, JSD; Russian politician, academic and university administrator; *Rector, Russian State Trade and Economics University;* b. 31 Jan. 1959, Semipalatinsk; s. of Nikolay Baburin and Valentina Baburina; m. Tatiana Nikolaevna Baburina; four s.; ed Omsk State Univ., Leningrad State Univ.; mem. CPSU 1981–91; mil. service in Afghanistan 1982–83; worked as lawyer; lecturer, Dean of Law Faculty, Omsk Univ. 1988–90, Professor of Law 1999–; People's Deputy of RSFSR (now Russia); mem. Supreme Soviet 1990–93; mem. Constitutional Comm. 1991; Co-Chair. Exec. Bd of All Russian Peoples' Union 1991; Co-Chair. Nat. Salvation Front 1992–; mem. State Duma (Parl.) 1995–99, Deputy Chair. 1996–99, 2000–03, 2003–07; Rector, Russian State Trade and Economics Univ. 2002–04, 2007–; Chair. All Russian People's Union 1994–2001; Deputy Chair. Parl. Ass. Union of Russia and Belarus 1996–2000; Pres. Inst. of Nat. Reform Strategy 2000; Deputy Dir for Research, Russian Acad. of Sciences (Inst. of Social and Political Research) 2001; Chair. Bd Inter-regional Collegium of Advocates of Businessmen and Citizens' Interactions 2001–02; Leader People's Will—Party of National Rebirth (Narodnaya volya—Partiya natsionalnogo vozrozhdeniya) 2001; Co-Chair. Exec. Council, Motherland–National-Patriotic Union electoral block (Rodina–Narodno-patrioticheskii soyuz). *Publications:* Russian Way: Selected Speeches and Essays 1990–95 1995, Russian Way: Losses and Acquisitions 1997, Territory of State: Law and Geopolitical Problems 1997. *Address:* Office of the Rector, Russian State Trade and Economics University, 125993 Moscow, ul. Smolnaya 36, Russia (office). *E-mail:* rsute.perm.ru (office).

BACA DE LA COLINA, Susana; Peruvian singer; b. Chortillos, Lima; m. Ricardo Pereira; formed experimental group combining poetry and song; took part in int. Agua Dulce Festival in Lima; with husband f. Instituto Negrocontinuo 1992; first US performance in Brooklyn 1995; one US and six European tours; Minister of Culture July–Dec. 2011; Pres. OAS Comm. of Culture 2011–13; Order of Arts and Letters (France), Order of Merit of the Repub. of Peru. *Albums include:* Susana Baca 1997, Del Fuego y del Agua 1999, Eco de Sombras 2000, Lamento Negro (early Cuban recordings, Latin Grammy Award for Best Folk Album) 2001, Espiritu Vivo 2002, Travesias 2006, Cantos de Adoración 2010, Afrodiaspora 2011. *Publication:* The Cultural Importance of Black Peruvians (co-author with Richard Pereira) 1992. *Address:* c/o Iris Musique, 5 Passage St-Sebastien, 75011 Paris, France. *Telephone:* (1) 4769933 (office). *Website:* www.luakabop.com/susana_baca.

BACALL, Lauren; American actress; b. 16 Sept. 1924, New York; m. 1st Humphrey Bogart 1945 (died 1957); 2nd Jason Robards 1961 (divorced); two s. one d.; fmr model; Commdr des Arts et des Lettres 1995; Hon. Acad. Award 2009. *Films include:* Two Guys from Milwaukee 1946, To Have and Have Not, The Big Sleep, Confidential Agent, Dark Passage, Key Largo, Young Man with a Horn, Bright Leaf, How to Marry a Millionaire, Woman's World, The Cobweb, Blood Alley, Written on the Wind, Designing Woman, The Gift of Love, Flame over India, Sex and the Single Girl, Harper, Shock Treatment 1964, Murder on the Orient Express 1974, The Shootist 1976, Health 1980, The Fan 1981, Appointment with Death 1988, Mr North 1988, Tree of Hands 1989, A Star For Two 1990, Misery 1990, All I Want for Christmas 1991, A Foreign Field 1993, The Portrait 1993, Prêt à Porter 1995, Le Jour et la Nuit 1996, The Mirror Has Two Faces (Golden Globe 1996, Screen Actors' Guild Award), My Fellow Americans, Day and Night, Diamonds, The Venice Project, Presence of Mind, Dogville 2003, The Limit 2003, Birth 2004, Manderlay 2005, These Foolish Things 2006, The Walker 2007. *Plays:* Goodbye Charlie 1960, Cactus Flower 1966, Applause 1970 (Tony Award, Best Actress in a Musical 1970) (London 1972), Wonderful Town 1977, Woman of the Year 1981 (Tony Award 1981), Sweet Bird of Youth (London) 1985, The Visit (Chichester, UK), Waiting in the Wings. *Publications:* Lauren Bacall By Myself 1978, Lauren Bacall Now 1994, By Myself and Then Some 2005. *Address:* c/o Johnnie Planco, William Morris Agency, 1325 Avenue of the Americas, New York, NY 10019, USA.

BACH, Thomas; German lawyer, business executive, sports administrator and international organization official; *President, International Olympic Committee;* b. 29 Dec. 1953, Wurzburg, Franconia; fmr fencer, won gold medal in team foil fencing event at Summer Olympics, Montreal 1976, World Champion, Buenos Aires 1977; mem. IOC 1991, Chair. Legal Comm. and Head of Anti-Doping

investigations, mem. Exec. Bd 1996–2000, Vice-Pres. 2000–04, 2006–13, Pres. IOC 2013–; Pres. German Olympic Cttee; mem. Supervisory Bd FIFA 2006 World Cup Organizing Cttee; Chair. Bd of Trustees, FIFA Women's World Cup, Germany 2011 Organizing Cttee; Head of Munich's bid for the 2018 Winter Olympics. *Address:* International Olympic Committee, Château de Vidy, 1007 Lausanne, Switzerland (office). *Telephone:* (21) 6216111 (office). *Fax:* (21) 6216216 (office). *Website:* www.olympic.org (office).

BACH NUÑEZ, Jaume, PhD; Spanish architect; *PhD Professor, Technical Superior University of Architecture, Barcelona;* b. 4 April 1943, Sabadell; s. of Miquel Bach and Josefa Nuñez; m. Carmen Triadó Tur 1978; two s.; ed Tech. Superior Univ. of Architecture, Barcelona (ETSAB); architect, ETSAB 1969, tutor 1972–, currently PhD Prof.; in partnership with Gabriel Mora Gramunt (q.v.), Bach/Mora Architects 1976–98; f. Bach Arquitectes (with son Eugeni) 1998–; Tutor, Int. Lab. of Architecture and Urban Design, Urbino, Italy 1978; Visiting Prof., Univ. of Dublin 1993, Univ. of Hanover 1994; has lectured and shown work in Spain, Germany, Austria, France, Netherlands, Italy, Slovenia, UK, Ireland, Finland, Portugal, Romania, USA, Argentina, Mexico, Venezuela, Chile and Japan; Hon. Mem. Caracas Contemporary Art Museum Foundation; Hon. PhD (Polytechnic Univ. of Barcelona) 1991; various professional awards including eight FAD Prizes and four Brunel Commendations; two ASCER Ceramics Prizes, Bonaplata Award. *Works include:* UAB Bellaterra Station 1984, Urban Design Superblock, Olympic Village 1986, Auditorium Reina Sofia, Madrid 1987, Cellar Raventós i Blanc 1988, Health Clinic Corachán 1990, Palau Macaya (la Caixa) 1991, Telephone Exchange, Olympic Village, Barcelona 1992, Operating Railway Center FGC 1995, Multicomplex Fleming, Barcelona 1999, social housing, Gavà 2000, Tarragona sea front 2000, Landscape Office bldg, Sant Cugat del Vallés 2003, Casa 4C, Barcelona 2003, Tibet House, Barcelona 2004, Liturgical adaptation for Parma Cathedral, Italy (First Prize, Int. Invited Competition 2005) 2005, Landscape Office bldg, Barcelona, Sant Cugat del Valles, Barcelona 2005, Apartment block Casp 74, Barcelona 2009, HQ of Banc Sabadell, Sant Cugat del Valles 2012. *Publications include:* Junge Architekten in Europa (co-author) 1983, Young Spanish Architecture (co-author) 1985, Bach/Mora, Contemporary Architectural Catalogues 1987, Bach – Mora, Architects 1996, Architecture Guide Spain 1920–2000 1998, Twentieth-Century Architecture Spain 2000, Landscape Office Building 2003; numerous magazine articles. *Address:* c/o Hercegovina 24-27, 08006 Barcelona, Spain (office). *Telephone:* (93) 200-29-11 (office). *Fax:* (93) 200-29-98 (office). *E-mail:* j.bach@coac.es (office). *Website:* www.bacharquitectes.com (office).

BACHA, Edmar Lisboa, PhD; Brazilian economist; *Director, Institute of Political and Economic Studies, Casa das Garças;* b. 14 Feb. 1942, Lambari, Minas Gerais; s. of Felicio Bacha and Maria de Jesus Lisboa Bacha; m. Maria Laura Cavalcanti; ed Fed. Univ. of Minas Gerais, Yale Univ., USA; Research Assoc., MIT, Cambridge, Mass, USA 1968–69; Prof. of Econs, Vargas Foundation, Rio de Janeiro 1970–71, Univ. of Brasília 1972–78, Catholic Univ. of Rio de Janeiro 1979–93, Fed. Univ. of Rio de Janeiro 1993–97; Pres. Statistical Office of Brazil, Rio de Janeiro 1985–86; Econ. Adviser to Brazilian Govt 1993; Pres. Nat. Devt Bank, Rio de Janeiro 1995; Senior Consultant, Banco Itaú BBA 1996–2010; Visiting Prof., Harvard Univ. 1975, Columbia Univ. 1983, Yale Univ. 1984, Univ. of Calif., Berkeley 1988, Univ. of Stanford 1989; Founder and Dir Inst. of Political and Econ. Studies, Casa das Garças 2003–; Pres. Nat. Asscn of Investment Banks (ANDIB) 2000–03; mem. Exec. Cttee, Int. Econ. Asscn, Paris 1987–92, Cttee for Devt Planning, UN, New York 1987–94, Int. Consultative Cttee Yale Univ. 1999–, Consultative Cttee, BrazilFoundation, Rio de Janeiro 2001–, Consultative Cttee Faculdade Pitágoras, Belo Horizonte 2001–, Admin. Cttee Companhia Siderúrgica Nacional (CSN) 2001–03, Admin. Cttee, Banco Itaú BBA 2003–09; Hon. mem. Latin American and Caribbean Econ. Asscn (LACEA) 1998–; Grand Officer, Ordem do Cruzeiro do Sul 1995. *Publications:* numerous books and articles including Mitos de uma Decada 1976, Models of Growth and Distribution for Brazil 1980, El Milagro y la Crisis 1986, Social Change in Brazil 1986, Recessão ou Crescimento 1987, Requirements for Growth Resumption in Latin America 1993. *Address:* Institute of Political and Economic Studies, Casa das Garças, Avenida Padre Leonel Franca, Rio de Janeiro, 22451-000, Brazil (office). *Telephone:* (21) 2512-6166 (office). *E-mail:* iepecdg@iepecdg.com (office). *Website:* www.iepecdg.com (office).

BACHARACH, Burt; American composer, arranger, conductor and musician (piano); b. 12 May 1928, Kansas City, MO; m. 1st Paula Stewart 1953 (divorced 1958); m. 2nd Angie Dickinson 1965 (divorced 1980), one d. (deceased); m. 3rd Carole Bayer Sager 1982 (divorced 1990), one s.; m. 4th Jane Hansen 1993, two c.; ed McGill Univ., Montréal, Music Acad. West, Santa Barbara; jazz musician 1940s; accompanist, arranger, conductor for various artists, including Vic Damone, Marlene Dietrich, Joel Gray, Steve Lawrence; writer of songs, film music and stage musicals; regular collaborations with Hal David 1962–70, Carole Bayer Sager from 1981; Cue Magazine Entertainer of the Year (with Hal David) 1969, three Acad. Awards, four Grammy Awards, two Emmy Awards, one Tony Award, Royal Swedish Acad. of Music Polar Music Prize 2001, Gershwin Prize for Popular Song (with Hal David), US Library of Congress 2012. *Film appearance:* Magic of Marlene (TV) 1965. *Film scores:* What's New, Pussycat? 1965, After the Fox 1966, On the Flipside 1966, Casino Royale 1967, Butch Cassidy and the Sundance Kid 1969, Lost Horizon 1973, Arthur 1981, Night Shift 1982, Arthur 2 On the Rocks 1988, Grace of My Heart 1996, My Best Friend's Wedding 1997. *Compositions include:* Promises, Promises (musical) 1969; with Hal David: The Story of My Life, Magic Moments, Tower of Strength, Wives and Lovers, 24 Hours From Tulsa, What The World Needs Now Is Love, Walk On By, Trains and Boats and Planes, Do You Know The Way To San Jose?, Alfie, Anyone Who Had A Heart, There's Always Something There To Remind Me, Make It Easy On Yourself, What's New Pussycat?, This Guy's In Love With You, Raindrops Keep Fallin' On My Head, Close To You; with Carole Bayer Sager: Making Love, Heartlight, That's What Friends Are For, On My Own; with Carole Bayer Sager, Peter Allen and Christopher Cross: Arthur's Theme. *Recordings include:* albums: Searching Wind 1958, Brigitte Bardot 1961, Move It On The Backbeat (with The Backbeats) 1961, Saturday Sunshine 1963, Don't Go Breaking My Heart 1965, Hit Maker! 1965, The Man 1965, Nikki 1966, Alfie 1967, Reach Out 1967, The Bell That Couldn't Jingle 1968, I'll Never Fall In Love Again 1969, Make It Easy On Yourself 1969, All Kinds of People 1971, Burt Bacharach 1971, Portrait In Music 1971, Living Together 1973, Saturday Sunshine 1973, Futures 1977, Painted from Memory 1998, One

Amazing Night 1998, Isley Meets Bacharach – Here I Am (with Ronald Isley) 2003, At This Time (Grammy Award for Best Pop Instrumental Album 2006) 2005. *Address:* c/o Sony BMG, 550 Madison Avenue, New York, NY 10022, USA.

BACHCHAN, Amitabh, BSc; Indian actor, singer and television presenter; b. 11 Oct. 1942, Allahabad, Uttar Pradesh; s. of Harivansh Rai and Teji Bachchan; m. Jaya Bachchan; one s. one d.; ed Sherwood Coll. Nainital, Delhi Univ.; mem. Lok Sabha (Parl.) 1984–87; re-launched film co. AB Corpn 2003; Goodwill Amb. for UNICEF 2003–; Hon. Citizen, Deauville, France 2003–; Chevalier, Ordre nat. de la Légion d'honneur 2006; Dr hc (Jhansi Univ.) 2004, (Delhi Univ.) 2006, (De Montfort Univ., UK) 2006, (Leeds Metropolitan Univ.) 2007, (Queensland Univ. of Tech., Australia) 2009; Avadh Samman, Govt of UP 1980, Padma Shri 1984, Greatest Star of the Millennium (result of BBC online poll) 1999, Special Hon. Award, Int. Indian Film Acad. Awards 2000, Star of the Century Award, Alexandria Int. Film Festival 2001, Yash Bharati Samman, Govt of UP 1995, Padma Bhushan 2001, named Most Powerful Actor in Bollywood, Forbes magazine 2001, Dayawati Modi Award 2002, Kishore Kumar Award, Madhya Pradesh Govt 2002, Raj Kapoor Award, Govt of Maharashtra 2002, Living Legend Award, Fed. of Indian Chambers of Commerce and Industry 2004, Shyam Sunder Dyay Kishan Munshi Lifetime Achievement Award 2004, Deenanath Mangeshkar Award 2005, Special Award, Mumbai Acad. of Moving Image Int. Film 2007, Visit London Special Award for Outstanding Achievement 2007, Crystal Award, World Econ. Forum 2009, Asian Film Cultural Award 2009, Life OK Screen Lifetime Achievement Award 2014; numerous other nat. and int. awards. *Films include:* Saat Hindustani (Nat. Award 1970) 1969, Anand (Filmfare Award) 1971, Parwaana 1971, Bombay to Goa 1972, Zanjeer 1973, Namak Haraam (Filmfare Award) 1973, Abhimaan 1973, Majboor 1974, Deewar 1975, Sholay 1975, Chupke Chupke 1975, Kabhi Kabhie 1976, Imaan Dharam 1977, Amar Akbar Anthony (Filmfare Award) 1977, Don (Filmfare Award) 1978, Kasme Vaade 1978, Mr. Natwarlal 1979, Jurmana 1979, Ram Balram 1980, Shaan 1980, Barsaat Ki Ek Raat 1980, Manzil 1981, Lawaaris 1981, Silsila 1981, Nammak Halal 1982, Shakti 1982, Coolie 1983, Mahaan 1983, Sharaabi 1984, Mard 1985, Aakhree Raasta 1986, Kaun Jeeta Kaun Hara 1987, Shahenshah 1988, Jadugar 1989, Agneepath (Nat. Award 1991) 1990, Hum (Filmfare Award) 1991, Ajooba 1991, Khuda Gawah 1992, Insaniyat 1994, Bade Miyan Chote Miyan 1998, Tumhare Liye 1999, Sooryavansham 1999, Mohabbatein (IIFA 2001, Filmfare Award) 2000, Aks (Filmfare Award) 2001, Kabhi Khushi Kabhi Gham 2001, Kaante 2002, Baghban 2003, Khakee 2004, Veer-Zaara 2004, Ab Tumhare Hawale Watan Saathiyo 2004, Waqt 2005, Sarkar 2005, Black 2005 (Nat. Award, Filmfare Award) 2006, Kabhi Alvida Naa Kehna (Never Say Goodbye) 2006, Eklavya – The Royal Guard 2007, Nishabd 2007, Zamaanat 2007, Cheeni Kum 2007, The Last Lear (Stardust Award) 2008, Paa 2009, Rann 2009, Teen Patti 2010, The Great Gatsby 2013. *Television:* presenter, Kaun Banega Crorepati? (Who Wants To Be A Millionaire?). *Address:* Pratiksha, 10th Road, JVPD Scheme, Mumbai, 400 049, India (home). *Telephone:* (22) 6207579 (home); (22) 6206162 (home).

BACHELET JERIA, (Verónica) Michelle, MD; Chilean physician, politician, UN official and head of state; *President;* b. 29 Sept. 1951, Santiago; d. of Gen. Aire Alberto Bachelet (died 1974) and Angela Jeria; m. Jorge Leopoldo Dávalos Cartes; three c.; ed Universidad de Chile, Inter-American Coll. of Defense, Washington, DC, USA; placed in Villa Grimaldi and Cuatro Alamos detention centres for father's resistance to Pinochet regime 1975; lived in Australia, then Germany 1975–80; trained as medical surgeon and epidemiologist, Universidad de Chile; Head of Medical Dept, PIDEE (NGO assisting the children of victims of the military regime); consultant to Panamerican Health Org. and WHO 1990; mem. Cen. Cttee Socialist Party 1995–, Political Cttee 1998–; Adviser to Under-Sec. of Health 1994–97, to Ministry of Defence 1998–99; Minister of Health 2000–02, of Nat. Defence (first woman in position) 2002–04; Pres. of Chile (first woman) 2006–10, 2014–; f. think-tank Fundación Dialoga 2010–; mem. Club of Madrid; Under-Sec.-Gen. for Gender Equality and the Empowerment of Women, UN, New York 2010–13; Knight Grand Cross of the Order of Merit (Italy) 2007, Order of Vytautas the Great with Golden Chain (Lithuania) 2008, Companion of the Order of Australia 2012; Dr hc (Univ. of Brasilia) 2004, (Universidad de San Carlos de Guatemala) 2007, (Univ. of Essex) 2008, (Pompeu Fabra Univ.) 2010, (Nat. Univ. of Córdoba) 2010, (Catholic Univ. of Córdoba) 2010, (Universidad Internacional Menéndez Pelay) 2010, (Universidad Autónoma de Santo Domingo) 2010, (Univ. of Paris III: Sorbonne Nouvelle) 2010, (Columbia Univ.) 2012; ranked by Forbes magazine amongst 100 Most Powerful Women (17th) 2006, (27th) 2007, (25th) 2008, (22nd) 2009; World Jewish Congress Shalom Award 2008, Washington Office on Latin America Human Rights Award 2010, Eisenhower Medal for Leadership and Service 2012. *Address:* Office of the President, Palacio de La Moneda, Santiago, Chile (office). *Telephone:* (2) 6904000 (office). *Website:* www.gob.cl (office); michellebachelet.cl.

BACHELIER, Bernard, French agronomist; b. 27 July 1950, Levallois-Perret; s. of Pierre Bachelier and Claire Pardon; ed Inst. Nat. Agronomique, Paris-Grignon; worked in Africa for several years; Del. for Africa and Indian Ocean, Centre de Coopération Internationale en Recherche Agronomique pour le Développement (Cirad), Paris 1988–90; Pres. Cirad Centre, Montpellier 1993; Head of Devt Research, Ministry of Educ. and Research 1993–96; Dir-Gen. Cirad 1996–2002; Chair., Council of Admin., Centre Nat. d'Etudes Agronomiques des Régions Chaudes (CNEARC) 1998–2003; advisor to minister in charge of Research and New Tech. 2002–04, to Minister for Research and Higher Educ. 2005; Dir Fondation pour l'agriculture et la ruralité dans le monde (FARM) 2006, now mem. Bd of Dirs; mem. Council for European and Int. Prospective Analysis of Agric. and Food (COPEIAA); Chevalier, Ordre nat. du Mérite, Ordre du Mérite agricole. *Address:* 9 rue Thérèse, 75001 Paris, France (home).

BACHELOT-NARQUIN, Roselyne, PharmD; French pharmacist and politician; b. 24 Dec. 1946, Nevers (Nièvre); d. of Jean Narquin and Yvette Narquin (née Le Dû); m. Jacques Bachelot; one c.; Gen. Councillor, Maine-et-Loire 1982–88; mem. Regional Council, Pays de la Loire 1982–88, Vice-Pres. 2001–04; elected Deputy for Maine-et-Loire 1988–; mem. RPR, Sec.-Gen. 1989–92, 2001–, Del. for the Status of Women 1992–93, for Labour and Social Exclusion 1995–97, Sec.-Gen. for Labour 1998–2001, mem. Political Bureau RPR; Reporter-Gen. Observatoire de la parité 1995–98; Pres. Nat. Consultative Council for Handicapped Persons 1996–; mem. European Parl. 2004–07; Minister of Ecology and Sustainable Devt 2002–04,

of Health, Youth and Sports 2007–10, for Solidarity and Social Cohesion 2010–12. *Publications include:* Les Maires: fête ou défaite? 2001. *Address:* c/o Union pour un Mouvement Populaire (UMP), TSA 41557, 75901 Paris, Cedex 15, France (office). *Telephone:* 1-40-76-60-00 (office). *E-mail:* webmaster@u-m-p.org (office). *Website:* www.u-m-p.org (office).

BACHER, Aron ('Ali'), MB BCh; South African sports administrator and fmr cricketer; *Chairman, Right to Care;* b. 24 May 1942, Johannesburg, Gauteng; s. of Kopel Bacher and Rose Bacher; m. Shira Ruth Teeger 1965; one s. two d.; ed King Edward VII High School and Univ. of the Witwatersrand, Johannesburg; right-hand batsman; played for Transvaal 1959–74 (Capt. 1963–74); 12 tests for S Africa 1965–70, four (all won) as Capt. against Australia 1970; scored 7,894 First-Class runs (18 centuries); toured England 1965; intern, Baragwanath and Natalspruit Hosps; pvt. practice, Rosebank, Johannesburg 1970–79; Man. Dir Delta Distributors (Pty) Ltd 1979–81; Man. Dir The Transvaal Cricket Council 1981–86; Man. Dir The South African Cricket Union 1986–91, United Cricket Bd of South Africa 1991–2000; mem. Exec. Bd, Int. Cricket Council (ICC) 1997–2000, Exec. Dir 2003 ICC Cricket World Cup 2001–03; South African Sports Award Admin. 1991; Pres. Sports Award Admin. (Cricket) 1997; Exec. Dir Wits Foundation 2003–06; Chair. Seniors' Finance 2007, Right to Care 2008–; Alexander Forbes Community Trust 2012–; Dr hc (Rhodes Univ.) 1998, Hon. Legum Doctoris (Witwatersrand) 2001; South African Sports Merit Award 1972, 1991, Paul Harris Fellow Award 1989, Jack Cheetham Memorial Award 1990, Int. Jewish Sports Hall of Fame 1991, Da Vinci Laureate Award for Social Architecture 2013. *Leisure interest:* jogging. *Address:* PO Box 55041, Northlands 2116, South Africa (office). *Telephone:* (11) 276-8871 (office); (11) 783-1263 (home); 83-2128008 (mobile) (home). *E-mail:* ali .bacher@righttocare.org (office). *Website:* www.righttocare.org (office).

BACHIRI, Mohamed, MBA; Moroccan administrator, engineer and business executive; *CEO, HP Construction Company;* b. 14 July 1948, Berkane; s. of Mimoun Bachiri and Aïcha Ouadi; m. Badia Khelfaoui 1972; three c.; ed Ecole Mohammedie d'Ingénieurs, Rabat, Ecole Nationale des Ponts et Chaussées, Paris, France; qualified civil engineer; responsible for public works, Berkane and Nador Provs. 1969; Asst Dir Moroccan Ports 1978; Regional Dir of Public Works, Marrakesh 1983; Dir Nat. Vocational Training 1984; Insp. Gen. Council of Public Works 1991–95; CEO Drapor Port Dredging Co. 1995–2008; CEO HP Construction Co. 2009–; Founder and Chair. Investment GID Group 1991; Founding Pres. Public Works Foundation; Founder and Dir Al Handassa Lwatania Eng journal 1981; mem. Bd of Dirs Cen. Dredging Asscn (CEDA), Chair. CEDA–African Section; Royal Decoration of Chevalier for Merit and Knighthood 1998; trophée d'Ingénieur Créateur. *Publications:* Drainage and Environment (ed.), Reference Dredging and Environment; articles and editorials in Al Handassa Lwatania, contrib. to other professional journals. *Leisure interest:* golf. *Address:* 3 Avenue Ma Al Aynine, Agdal, Rabat, Morocco (home). *Telephone:* (37) 77-46-24 (home). *Fax:* (37) 68-14-94 (home). *E-mail:* bachiri@iam.net.ma (home).

BACHMANN, John William, AB, MBA; American business executive; *Senior Partner, Edward D. Jones & Co., LP;* b. 16 Nov. 1938, Centralia, Ill.; s. of George Adam Bachmann and Helen Bachmann (née Johnston); m. Katharine I. Butler; one s. one d.; ed Wabash Coll., Crawfordsville, Ind., Northwestern Univ.; broker, Edward Jones, St Louis 1962–63, investment rep. 1963–70, Gen. Pnr 1970–80, Man. Pnr 1980–2003, Sr Pnr 2004–; mem. Bd of Dirs Trans World Airlines 1996–2001, American Airlines Inc., Monsanto Co.; Trustee Wabash Coll. 1980–, Washington Univ.; fmr mem. Bd of Dirs US Chamber of Commerce, Washington, DC 1995–, Chair. 2004–05, Chair. Exec. Cttee 2005–06; Campaign Chair. United Way of Greater St. Louis 2002; Chair. St Louis Regional Chamber and Growth Association 2000–02; Chair. Bd of Visitors Drucker Center, Claremont (Calif.) Grad. School 1987; fmr Chair. Arts and Educ. Council of Greater St Louis, St Louis Symphony Orchestra; fmr Commr St Louis Art Museum; mem. Nat. Asscn of Securities Dealers (fmr district Chair.), Securities Industry Asscn (Chair. 1976–79), Securities Industry Foundation for Econ. Educ. (Chair. of Trustees 1988–92); Hon. LLD (Wabash Coll.) 1990, (Univ. of Missouri, St Louis) 2003, (Westminster Coll.) 2005. *Address:* Edward D. Jones & Co., LP, 12555 Manchester Road, St Louis, MO 63131, USA (office). *Telephone:* (314) 515-2626 (office). *Fax:* (314) 515-2622 (office). *E-mail:* john.bachmann@edwardjones.com (office). *Website:* www.edwardjones.com (office).

BACHMANN, Michele Marie, BA, LLM, JD; American lawyer and politician; b. 6 April 1956, Waterloo, Ia; d. of David John Amble and Jean Amble (née Johnson); m. Dr Marcus Bachmann 1978; two s. three d.; ed Anoka High School, Winona State Univ., O.W. Coburn School of Law at Oral Roberts Univ., Coll. of William and Mary Law School; following graduation, spent time working on a kibbutz in Israel 1974; worked as research asst on John Eidsmoe's 1987 book, Christianity and the Constitution; tax attorney, Internal Revenue Service 1988–93; mem. Minnesota State Senate from 56th Dist 2001–03, from 52nd Dist 2003–07, Asst Minority Leader in charge of Policy for Senate Republican Caucus 2004–05; mem. US House of Reps for 6th Congressional Dist of Minn. (first Republican woman to represent the state in Congress) 2007–; founder of House Tea Party Caucus 2010; cand. for Republican 2012 presidential nomination June 2011, withdrew Jan. 2012; owns (with her husband) Bachmann & Assocs (counselling practice); Republican; ranked by Forbes magazine amongst The World's 100 Most Powerful Women (22nd) 2011. *Publication:* Core of Conviction (autobiog.) 2011. *Address:* 103 Cannon HOB, Washington, DC 20515, USA (office). *Telephone:* (202) 225-2331 (office). *Fax:* (202) 225-6475 (office). *Website:* bachmann.house.gov (office); www.michelebachmann .com.

BACHYNSKI, Morrel Paul, PhD, FRSC, FIEEE, FAPS; Canadian physicist; *President and CEO, MPB Technologies Inc.;* b. 19 July 1930, Bienfait, Sask.; s. of Nick Bachynski and Karolina Bachynski; m. Slava Krkovic 1959; two c.; ed Univ. of Saskatchewan, McGill Univ.; mem. Scientific Staff, RCA Ltd 1955–58, Dir Microwave Physics Lab. 1958–65; Dir Research 1965–75, Vice-Pres. Research and Devt 1975–76; Pres. and CEO MPB Techs Inc. 1977–; mem. Canadian Asscn of Physicists (Pres. 1968), Asscn of Scientific, Eng and Tech. Community of Canada (Pres. 1974–75), Nat. Research Council of Canada (Chair. on Fusion 1977–87), Science Council of Canada; Fellow, Canadian Aeronautics and Space Inst., American Physical Soc., Canadian Acad. of Eng (Pres. 2003–04); Hon. mem. Eng Inst. of Canada; Hon. LLD (Waterloo) 1993, (Concordia) 1997; Hon. DSc (McGill) 1994; Prix Scientifique du Québec 1974, Canada Enterprise Award 1977, Queen's

Silver Jubilee Medal 1977, Canadian Asscn of Physicists Medal 1984, Canadian Research Man. Asscn Award 1988, Prix PME (Québec) 1988, Canada Award for Business Excellence-Entrepreneurship 1989, 1990, Prix ADRIQ 1991, Canadian Asscn of Physicists Medal for Industrial and Applied Physics 1995, Prix du Québec – Lionel Boulet 2001, RSC Thomas W. Eadie Medal 2004. *Publications:* The Particle Kinetics of Plasmas (co-author) 1968; more than 90 publs in scientific and eng journals. *Leisure interest:* tennis. *Address:* 78 Thurlow Road, Montreal, PQ H3X 3G9, Canada (home). *Telephone:* (514) 694-8751 (office); (514) 481-2359 (home). *Fax:* (514) 695-7492 (office). *E-mail:* m.p.bachynski@mpbc.ca (office). *Website:* www.mpbc.ca (office).

BACKE, John David, MBA; American communications industry executive; b. 5 July 1932, Akron, Ohio; s. of John and Ella A. Backe (née Enyedy); m. Katherine Elliott 1955; one s. one d.; ed Miami Univ., Xavier Univ.; various eng, financial and marketing positions at General Electric Co. 1957–66; Vice-Pres. and Dir of Marketing, Silver Burdett Co. 1966–68, Pres. 1968–69; Exec. Vice-Pres. General Learning Corpn 1969, Pres. and CEO 1969–73; Pres. of Publishing Group, CBS Inc. 1973–76, of CBS Inc. (also CEO) 1976–80, Dir of Business Marketing, Corpn of New York 1978; Pres. and CEO Tomorrow Entertainment 1981–84, Chair. 1984; Chair. Cinema Products, Los Angeles 1992–; Founder, Chair. and CEO Backe Group Inc. 1984–; Chair. Station WRGB Schenectady, NY 1983–; Chair. Station WLNS Lansing, Mich. 1984; Chair. Station WKBT Lacrosse, Wis.; Chair. Dorchester Publ Co. Inc., NY 1984; Chair. Kingswood Advertising 1988; Station WDKY-TV, Lexington 1985–93; Gulfshore Publ Co., Naples 1986–; Gulfstream Newspapers, Pompano 1987–; Andrews Communications, Westtown, Pa 1987–; Atlantic Publs, Accomac, Va 1989–; Special Del. to UNESCO Conf. on publishing for Arabic-speaking countries 1972; mem. Nat. Advisory Cttee for Illinois Univ. Inst. for Aviation; Hon. LLD (Miami and Xavier); Cable Ace Award 1988, Oxford Cup, Beta Theta Pi 2005. *Leisure interest:* multi-engine piloting. *Address:* The Backe Group, 11 West Avenue Suite 103, Wayne, PA 19087-3224, USA. *Telephone:* (610) 995-9244. *Fax:* (610) 995-9274.

BACKÈS, Sonia, MEng; New Caledonian trade unionist and politician; *Minister of Budget, Finance, Tax and Digital Economy;* b. (Sonia Dos Santos), 21 May 1976, Nouméa; m.; two s.; ed Univ. of Grenoble, Inst. Nat. Polytechnique, Grenoble, Switzerland; mem. Rassemblement pour la Calédonie dans la République (renamed Rassemblement-UMP) 1994–2006, 2009–; trade unionist, Syndicat des fonctionnaires de catégorie A—Confédération générale des cadres (SFA—CGC), Sec. Gen. 2004–06; Pres., UTCFE—CGC (Union territoriale de la Confédération française de l'encadrement—Confédération générale des cadres) 2006–08; Minister of Education 2009–11, of Energy, Audiovisual Communication, Higher Education and Research 2011–, of Budget, Finance, Tax and Digital Economy 2011–. *Address:* Artillerie 8, Route des Artifices, BP M2, 98849 Nouméa Cedex, New Caledonia (office). *Telephone:* 24-65-65 (office). *Website:* soniabackes.over-blog.com.

BAČKIS, HE Cardinal Audrys Juozas, BPhil, LTh, DCL; Lithuanian ecclesiastic; *Archbishop of Vilnius;* b. 1 Feb. 1937, Kaunas; ed Inst. Catholique, Paris, Pontifical Gregorian Univ., Rome, Pontifical Lateran Univ., Rome; ordained priest 1961; served in Holy See diplomatic corps in The Philippines 1964–65, Costa Rica 1966–68, Turkey 1969–70, Nigeria 1971–73; with Vatican Secr. of State 1974–88; Titular Archbishop of Meta and Apostolic Pro-Nuncio to Netherlands 1988–91; Archbishop of Vilnius 1991–; cr. Cardinal (Cardinal-Priest of Natività di Nostro Signore Gesù Cristo a Via Gallia) 2001; participated in Papal Conclave 2005, 2013; Grande Oficial da Ordem Militar de Cristo (Portugal) 1981, Grosse Verdienstkreuz mit Stern (Germany) 1982, Grand Officier, Order of the Phoenix (Greece) 1982, Grand Officier, Ordre Nat. Honneur et Mérite (Haiti) 1984, Officier, Légion d'honneur 1984, Gran Oficial, Orden al Merito por Servicios Distinguidos (Peru) 1985, Grande Ufficiale, Ordine al Merito della Repubblica Italiana 1985, Gran Oficial, Orden de Manuel Amado Guerrero (Panama) 1985, Commdr, Ordre Gran-Ducal de la Couronne de Chêne (Luxembourg) 1988, Commendator cum nomismate (Ordo equester S. Sepulcri Hierosolymitani) 1990, Groot Kruis in de Orde van Oranje-Nassau (Netherlands) 1992, Commdr, Royal Norwegian Order of Merit 1998, Order of Grand Duke Gediminas (Second Degree) 2000, Order of Vytautas the Great Grand Cross 2003; Dr hc (Vilnius Pedagogical Univ.) 1997, (Krakow Pontifical Theological Acad.) 2003. *Address:* Vilnius Archdiocesan Curia, Šventaragio 4, 01122 Vilnius, Lithuania (office). *Telephone:* (5) 2123653 (office); (5) 2123413 (home). *Fax:* (5) 2122807 (office). *E-mail:* curia@vilnensis.lt (office). *Website:* www.vilnius.lcn.lt (office).

BACKLEY, Steve, OBE; British consultant and fmr professional athlete; b. 12 Feb. 1969, Sidcup, Kent; s. of John Backley and Pauline Hogg; javelin thrower; coached by Mike Trower; Commonwealth record-holder 1992 (91.46m); Gold Medal European Jr Championships 1987; Silver Medal World Jr Championships 1988; Gold Medal European Cup 1989, 1997, Bronze Medal 1995; Gold Medal World Student Games 1989, 1991; Gold Medal World Cup 1989, 1994, 1998; Gold Medal Commonwealth Games 1990, 1994, 2002, Silver Medal 1998; Gold Medal European Championships 1990, 1994, 1998, 2002; Bronze Medal Olympic Games 1992, Silver Medal 1996, 2000; Silver Medal World Championships 1995, 1997; retd 2004; Prin. Javelin Business Strategies 2006; Partner, BlackleyBlack (consultancy); Athlete of the Year, UK Athletics 2000. *Publication:* The Winning Mind. *E-mail:* info@BackleyBlack.com. *Website:* www.stevebackley.com; www.backleyblack.com.

BÄCKSTRÖM, Urban, PhD; Swedish banker; *Chief Executive, Confederation of Swedish Enterprise;* b. 25 May 1954, Sollefteå; s. of Sven-Ake Bäckström and Maj-Britt Filipsson; m. Ewa Hintze 1978; one s. one d.; ed Stockholm Univ. and Stockholm School of Econs; Research Asst Inst. for Int. Econ. Studies, Stockholm 1978–80; First Sec. Int. Dept Ministry of Foreign Affairs 1980–82; Chief Economist, Moderate Party 1982–83, 1986–89; Under-Sec. of State, Ministry of Finance 1991–93; Gov. Sveriges Riksbank (Swedish Cen. Bank) 1994–2002; Bd mem. Bank for Int. Settlements 1994–2002, Chair. and Pres. 1999–2002; CEO Skandia Liv 2002–05; CEO Confed. of Swedish Enterprise 2005–. *Address:* Confederation of Swedish Enterprise, Storgatan 19 11482 Stockholm, Sweden (office). *Telephone:* (8) 553 430 00 (office). *Fax:* (8) 553 430 99 (office). *Website:* www.svensktnaringsliv.se (office).

BACKUS, George Edward, SM, PhD, FRAS, FRSA, FAGU; American theoretical geophysicist and academic; *Research Professor Emeritus of Geophysics, University of California, San Diego;* b. 24 May 1930, Chicago, Ill.; s. of the late Milo Morlan Backus and of Dora Backus (née Mendenhall); m. 1st Elizabeth E Allen 1961; two s. one d.; m. 2nd Marianne McDonald 1971; m. 3rd Varda Peller 1977; ed Thornton Township High School, Harvey, Ill. and Univ. of Chicago; Asst Examiner, Univ. of Chicago 1949–50; Jr Mathematician, Inst. for Air Weapons Research, Univ. of Chicago 1950–54; Physicist, Project Matterhorn, Princeton Univ. 1957–58; Asst Prof. of Math., MIT 1958–60; Assoc. Prof. of Geophysics, Univ. of California, La Jolla 1960–62, Prof. 1962–94, Research Prof. 1994–99, Prof. Emer. 1999–; mem. Scientific Advisory Cttee to NASA on Jt NASA/CNES Magnetic Satellites; Co.-Chair. Int. Working Group on Magnetic Field Satellites 1983–92; mem. Visiting Cttee, Inst. de Physique du Globe de Paris (IPGP) 1987; Guggenheim Fellowship 1963, 1971; mem. NAS; Foreign mem. Acad. des Sciences de l'Institut de France; Fellow, American Geophysical Union; Dr hc (IPGP) 1995; Gold Medal, Royal Astronomical Soc. 1986, John Adam Fleming Medal, American Geophysical Union 1986. *Publications:* numerous scientific works 1958–. *Leisure interests:* hiking, swimming, history, reading, skiing. *Address:* Munk Lab 331, Institute of Geophysics and Planetary Physics, Scripps Institution of Oceanography, University of California San Diego, La Jolla, CA 92093-0225 (office); 9362 La Jolla Farms Road, La Jolla, CA 92037, USA (home). *Telephone:* (858) 534-2468 (office); (858) 455-8972 (home). *Fax:* (858) 534-8090 (office). *Website:* www.igpp.ucsd.edu (office); www-mpl.ucsd.edu/cg/people/gbackus.html (office).

BACON, Kevin; American actor; b. 8 July 1958, Philadelphia, Pa; m. Kyra Sedgwick; one s. one d.; ed Manning Street Actor's Theatre; mem. Bacon Brothers band. *Stage appearances include:* Getting On 1978, Glad Tidyings 1979–80, Mary Barnes 1980, Album 1980, Forty-Deuce 1981, Flux 1982, Poor Little Lambs 1982, Slab Boys 1983, Men Without Dates 1985, Loot 1986, Road, Spike Heels. *Film appearances include:* National Lampoon's Animal House 1978, Starting Over 1979, Hero at Large 1980, Friday the 13th 1980, Only When I Laugh 1981, Diner 1982, Footloose 1984, Quicksilver 1985, White Water Summer 1987, Planes, Trains and Automobiles 1987, End of the Line 1988, She's Having a Baby 1988, Criminal Law 1989, The Big Picture 1989, Tremors 1990, Flatliners 1990, Queens Logic 1991, He Said/She Said 1991, Pyrates 1991, JFK 1992, A Few Good Men 1992, The Air Up There 1994, The River Wild 1994, Murder in the First 1995, Apollo 13 1995, Sleepers 1996, Telling Lies in America 1997, Picture Perfect 1997, Digging to China 1997, Wild Things 1998, My Dog Skip 1999, The Hollow Man 1999, Stir of Echoes 1999, Novocaine 2000, We Married Margo 2000, 24 Hours 2001, Trapped 2002, In the Cut 2003, Mystic River 2003, The Woodsman 2004, Cavedweller 2004, Loverboy 2005, Beauty Shop 2005, Where the Truth Lies 2005, The Air I Breathe 2007, Death Sentence 2007, Rails and Ties 2007, Saving Angelo 2007, Frost/Nixon 2008, My One and Only 2009, Beyond All Boundaries (voice) 2009, X Men First Class 2011, Crazy, Stupid, Love 2011, Jayne Mansfield's Car 2012. *Television appearances include:* The Gift 1979, Enormous Changes at the Last Minute 1982, The Demon Murder Case 1983, The Tender Age, Lemon Sky, Frasier (voice), Happy Birthday Elizabeth: A Celebration of Life 1997, Taking Chance (Golden Globe for Best Performance by an Actor in a Mini-series or Motion Picture made for Television 2010) 2009. *Address:* c/o Frank Frattaroli, WME, 9601 Wilshire Blvd, Beverly Hills, CA 90210, USA. *Website:* www.baconbros.com.

BACONSCHI, Teodor, PhD; Romanian diplomatist and politician; b. 14 Feb. 1963, Bucharest; m.; two c.; ed Bucharest Theological Univ. Inst., New Europe Coll., Bucharest, Université de Paris IV-Sorbonne, France; post-doctoral studies as Fellow of New Europe Coll. of Bucharest 1996; began career as Dir, Anastasia Publr, Bucharest; fmr Ed.-in-Chief Spiritual Life (TV series); fmr adviser with Ministry of Culture; fmr Ed. Biblical and Mission Inst. Publishing Office, Romanian Orthodox Church; joined diplomatic service, becoming Amb. to The Holy See (also accred to San Marino and with the Sovereign Mil. Order of Malta) 1999–2001, Dir-Gen. Ministry of Foreign Affairs 2001, Amb. to Portugal 2002–04, State Sec. for Global Affairs, Ministry of Foreign Affairs 2005–06; Adviser to Pres. on political affairs 2006–07; Amb. to France (also accred to Monaco and Andorra) 2007–09, Minister of Foreign Affairs 2009–12 (dismissed); Affiliate mem. Int. Asscn of Patristic Studies (AIEP), Paris; Founding mem. Reflection Group for the Renewal of the Church, Bucharest; mem. New Europe Coll., Bucharest, Social Dialogue Group, Bucharest; Grand Cross, Order of Pius IX (Holy See), Grand Officer, Order of St Agatha (San Marino), Officer, Nat. Order of the Faithful Service (Romania), Grand Officer, Order of the Star of Italian Solidarity, Grand Officer, Nat. Order of Merit (Portugal). *Publications:* more than ten books in French and Romanian, including Jacob and the Angel – 45 Hypostases of the Religious Dimension 1996, The Temptation of Goodness – Essays on the Urban Dimension of Faith 1999, The Power of Schism – A Portrait of European Christianity 2001. *Address:* c/o Ministry of Foreign Affairs, 011822 Bucharest, Al. Alexandru 31, Romania.

BACQUIER, Gabriel; French singer (baritone); b. 17 May 1924, Béziers; s. of Augustin Bacquier and Fernande Severac; m. 1st Simone Teisseire 1943; one s.; m. 2nd Mauricette Bénard 1958; one s.; ed Paris Conservatoire; debut at Théâtre Royal de la Monnaie, Brussels 1953; joined Opéra de Paris 1956; debut at Carnegie Hall 1960, Metropolitan Opera, New York 1961; has appeared at the Vienna State Opera, Covent Garden, La Scala, Opéra de Paris and most leading opera houses; repertoire includes Otello, Don Giovanni, Pelléas et Mélisande, Damnation de Faust, Tosca, Falstaff; retired from stage in 1994; taught at Paris Conservatoire and Acad. de Musique de Monaco; several recordings; Prix nat. du disque français 1964; Chevalier, Légion d'honneur; Officier, Ordre nat. du Mérite; Commdr des Arts et des Lettres; Médaille de Vermeil, Paris, Victoires de la Musique 1985. *Films include:* La Grande Récré, Falstaff. *Leisure interests:* painting, drawing. *Address:* c/o OIA, 16 avenue Franklin D. Roosevelt, 75008 Paris, France (home).

BADA, Hajime, MSc; Japanese business executive; *President and CEO, JFE Holdings, Inc.;* ed Tokyo Univ.; joined Kawasaki Steel Corpn 1973, held positions as Man. Chiba Works Steelmaking Shop No. 1, Man. Mizushima Works Steelmaking Shop No. 2, Steel Business Planning Man., Gen. Man. Steel Business Planning Dept and Gen. Man. Corpn Planning Dept, mem. Bd of Dirs JFE Holdings, Inc. and JFE Steel Corpn (subsidiary), Dir California Steel Industries Inc. 1998–, Sr Vice-Pres. JFE Steel Corpn –2005, Pres., CEO and Rep. Dir 2005–10, Pres. and CEO JFE Holdings, Inc. 2010–. *Address:* JFE Holdings Inc., 2-

2-3 Uchisaiwaicho, Chiyoda-ku, Tokyo 100-0011, Japan (office). *Telephone:* (3) 3597-4321 (office). *E-mail:* info@jfe-holdings.co.jp (office). *Website:* www.jfe -holdings.co.jp (office).

BADAL, Parkash Singh, BA; Indian agriculturist and politician; *Chief Minister of Punjab;* b. 8 Dec. 1927, Abulkhurana, Punjab; s. of the late Raghuraj Singh and Sundri Kaur; m. Surinder Kaur; one s. one d.; entered politics 1947, first elected to Punjab Vidhan Sabha (Legis. Ass.) 1957, re-elected 1969; mem. and fmr Pres. Shiromani Akali Dal party; fmr mem. Shiromani Gurdwara Prabandhak Cttee; elected to Ass. 1957, re-elected 1969; Minister for Community Devt Panchayati Raj, Animal Husbandry, Dairying and Fisheries 1969–70; Chief Minister of Punjab 1970–71, 1977–80, 1997–2002, 2007–; imprisoned during State of Emergency 1975–77; elected to Lok Sabha (Parl.) 1977; Minister for Agric. 1977; elected Leader of Opposition, Punjab Vidhan Sabha (Legis. Ass.) 1972, 1980, 2002; imprisoned on corruption charges Dec. 2003; Chair. Punjab Arts Council; mem. Nankana Sahib Educational Trust, Ludhiana. *Leisure interest:* social service. *Address:* Office of the Chief Minister, Govt of Punjab, 45, Sector 2, Chandigarh (office); Room No.1, Floor 2, Punjab Civil Secr., Chandigarh, India (office). *Telephone:* (172) 740737 (home); (172) 2740325 (office); (172) 2743463 (office). *Fax:* (172) 2740769 (office). *E-mail:* cm@punjabmail.gov.in (office). *Website:* punjabgovt .nic.in (office).

BADAWI, Tun Abdullah Bin Haji Ahmad, BA; Malaysian politician; b. 26 Nov. 1939, Pulau Pinang; m. Datin Endon bint Datuk Mahmud (died 2005); ed Univ. of Malaya; Asst Sec., Public Service Dept 1964; Asst Sec., MAGERAN 1969; Asst Sec., Nat. Security Council 1971; Dir (Youth), Ministry of Sport, Youth and Cultural 1971–74, Deputy Sec.-Gen. 1974–78; Minister without Portfolio, Prime Minister's Dept 1982; Minister of Educ. 1984–86, of Defence 1986–87; mem. UMNO Supreme Council 1982–, Vice-Pres. 1984; Minister of Foreign Affairs 1991; Deputy Prime Minister and Minister of Home Affairs 1998–2003, Prime Minister and Minister of Finance 2003–09 (resgnd). *Address:* c/o United Malays National Organization (Pertubuhan Kebangsaan Melayu Bersatu), Menara Dato' Onn, 38th Floor, Jalan Tun Ismail, 50480 Kuala Lumpur, Malaysia (office).

BADAWI, Zeinab Mohammed-Khair, MA; British (b. Sudanese) journalist and broadcaster; b. 3 Oct. 1959; d. of Mohammed-Khair El Badawi and Asia Malik; m. David Antony Crook 1991; two s. two d.; ed Hornsey School for Girls, St Hilda's Coll. Oxford and Univ. of London; presenter and journalist, current affairs and documentaries on Yorkshire TV 1982–86; current affairs reporter, BBC TV 1987–88; newscaster and journalist, ITN Channel Four News 1988, co-presenter Channel Four News with Jon Snow 1989–98; joined BBC 1998, worked in radio presenting The World Tonight (Radio 4) and BBC World's Newshour, presenter, The World (BBC Four) 2005–07, World News Today 2007–; Vice-Pres. UN Int. Asscn; Chair. Article 19 Int. Org. for Freedom of Speech; Chair. Africa Medical Partnership Fund; Advisor Foreign Policy Centre; mem. Bd British Council; Trustee, BBC World Service Trust, Nat. Portrait Gallery, British Council, Centre for Contemporary British History; mem. jury for Diageo Africa Business Reporting Award. *Publications include:* numerous articles. *Leisure interests:* languages, opera, family, reading. *Website:* www.bbc.co.uk/bbcfour.

BADHAM, John Macdonald, BA, MFA; American (b. British) film director; b. 25 Aug. 1939, Luton, England; s. of Henry Lee Badham and Mary Iola Hewitt; m. Julia Laughlin 1992; one d.; ed Yale Univ., Yale Drama School; joined Universal Studio as mailroom employee, then tour guide, subsequently Casting Dir and Assoc. Producer; Pres. Great American Picture Show; Chair. Bd JMB Films Inc.; Founder and Pres. Badham Co., Calif. 1975–; currently Prof. and Head of Directing Program, Graduate Conservatory of Motion Pictures, Chapman Univ., Orange, Calif.; George Pal Award. *Films include:* The Bingo Long Travelling All-Stars and Motor Kings, Saturday Night Fever 1977, Dracula (Best Horror Film Award, Acad. of Science Fiction, Fantasy and Horror Films) 1979, Whose Life Is It Anyway? (San Rafael Grand Prize) 1981, War Games (Best Dir, Science Fiction/Fantasy Acad.) 1983, Stakeout (also exec. producer) 1987, Disorganized Crime (exec. producer only), Bird on a Wire 1989, The Hard Way 1990, Point of No Return 1993, Another Stakeout (also exec. producer) 1993, Drop Zone (also exec. producer) 1994, Nick of Time (also producer) 1995, Incognito 1997, Brother's Keeper 2002. *Television includes:* The Impatient Heart (Christopher Award 1971), Isn't It Shocking? 1973, The Law, The Gun (Southern Calif. Motion Picture Council Award 1974), Reflections of Murder 1973, The Godchild 1974, The Keegans, Sorrow Floats 1998, Floating Away 1998, The Jack Bull 1999, Footsteps 2003, Evel Knievel 2004,; several series episodes. *Publication:* I'll Be In My Trailer: The Creative Wars Between Directors and Actors 2006. *Address:* MKS 352, Dodge College of Film and Media Arts, Chapman University, One University Drive, Orange, CA 92866, USA. *Website:* www.johnbadham.com (office).

BADI, Mohammed, MVD; Egyptian professor of veterinary medicine and religious leader; b. 7 Aug. 1943, El-Mahalla el-Koubra; m. Samia Alshenawy; four c. (one deceased); ed Cairo Univ.; Lecturer, Faculty of Veterinary Medicine, Assiut Univ. 1965; imprisoned 1965–74; Asst Teacher, Univ. of Zagazig 1977–79, Teacher 1979–83, Asst Prof. 1983; Expert, Veterinary Inst., Sana'a, Yemen 1982–86; Prof. of Veterinary Medicine, Beni Suef Univ. 1987, also Chair., Dept of Pathology, Faculty of Veterinary Medicine 1990; mem. Muslim Brotherhood (Al-Ikhwan al-Muslimun), mem. Admin. Office, El-Mahalla el-Koubra 1975, mem. Admin. Office, Beni Suef 1986, Admin. Official, Beni Suef 1990, Educ. Official 1994, mem. Exec. Guidance Bureau 1996, mem. Int. Guidance Bureau 2007, Supreme Guide (leader) Muslim Brotherhood 2010–13; arrested by Egyptian authorities 2013;*Website:* www.ikhwanonline.com (office).

BADINTER, Élisabeth; French author, historian, academic and business executive; *Non-Executive Chairperson, Publicis Omnicom Group;* b. 5 March 1944, Boulogne-Billancourt (Hauts-de-Seine); d. of Marcel Bleustein-Blanchet (founder of Publicis Groupe); m. Robert Badinter 1966; two s. one d.; Prof. of Philosophy, École Polytechnique, Paris; Chair. (non-exec.) Publicis Omnicom Group 2014–; Commdr, Order of Cultural Merit (Monaco) 2011; named by Marianne news magazine as one of France's "most influential intellectuals" 2010. *Publications include:* L'Amour en plus: histoire de l'amour maternel (XVIIe–XXe siècle) 1981, Les Goncourt: Romanciers et historiens des femmes, La Femme au XVIIe siècle d'Edmond et Jules de Goncourt (foreword) 1981, Émilie, Emilie, L'ambition féminine au XVIIIe siècle 1983, Les Remontrances de Malesherbes

(1771–1775) 1985, L'Un est l'autre 1986, Condorcet. Un intellectuel en politique 1988, Correspondance inédite de Condorcet et Madame Suard (1771–1791) 1988, Madame d'Épinay, Histoire de Madame de Montbrillant ou les Contreconfessions (foreword) 1989, Thomas, Diderot, Madame d'Épinay: Qu'est-ce qu'une femme? (foreword) 1989, Condorcet, Prudhomme, Guyomar: Paroles d'hommes (1790–1793) 1989, XY, de l'identité masculine 1992, Madame du Châtelet, Discours sur le bonheur (foreword) 1997, Les Passions intellectuelles, Vol. 1: Désirs de gloire (1735–1751) 1999, Vol. 2: L'exigence de dignité (1751–1762) 2002, Vol. 3: Volonté Pouvoir (1762–1778) 2007, Simone de Beauvoir, Marguerite Yourcenar, Nathalie Sarraute (co-author) 2002, Fausse route 2003, Dead End Feminism 2006 (translated from Fausse route by Julia Borossa), Madame du Châtelet, Madame d'Épinay: Ou l'Ambition féminine au XVIIIe siècle 2006, Le conflit, la femme et la mère 2010, The Conflict: How Modern Motherhood Undermines the Status of Women 2012 (translated from Le Conflit by Adriana Hunter). *Address:* Publicis Omnicom Group, 133 avenue des Champs Elysées, 75008 Paris, France (office). *Telephone:* 1-44-43-70-00 (office). *Fax:* 1-44-43-75-25 (office). *E-mail:* contact@publicisgroupe.com (office). *Website:* www.publicisgroupe .com (office).

BADINTER, Robert, AM, LLD; French lawyer and professor of law; *President, Court of Conciliation and Arbitration, Organization for Security and Co-operation in Europe;* b. 30 March 1928, Paris; s. of Simon Badinter and Charlotte Rosenberg; m. 1st Anne Vernon 1957; m. 2nd Elisabeth Bleustein-Blanchet 1966; two s. one d.; ed Univ. of Paris, Columbia Univ., New York; Lawyer, Paris Court of Appeal 1951; Prof. of Law, Paris I (Sorbonne) 1974–81; Minister of Justice and Keeper of the Seals 1981–86; Pres. Constitutional Council 1986–95; Pres. Court of Conciliation and Arbitration, OSCE 1995–; Senator (Hauts de Seine) 1995–2011. *Play:* C.3.3., Paris 1995. *Publications:* L'exécution 1973, Liberté, libertés 1976, Condorcet (with Elisabeth Badinter) 1988, Libres et égaux: L'émancipation des juifs sous la révolution française 1989, La prison républicaine 1992, C.3.3. 1995, Un antisémitisme ordinaire: Vichy et les avocats juifs 1940–44 1997, L'abolition 2000, Une Constitution européenne 2002, Le plus grand bien 2004, Contre la peine de mort 2006. *Address:* Court of Conciliation and Arbitration within the OSCE, 266 route de Lausanne, PO Box 20, 1292 Chambesy, Geneva, Switzerland (office); 38 rue Guynemer, 75006 Paris, France (home). *Telephone:* 1-45-49-04-59 (home). *Fax:* 1-45-44-87-47 (home). *E-mail:* cca.osce@bluewin.ch (office); r.badinter@senat.fr (office). *Website:* www.osce.org (office); www.senat.fr (office).

BADRAN, Adnan, PhD; Jordanian politician, university president and international organization official; *Chairman, National Centre for Human Rights;* m.; several c.; ed Oklahoma State Univ., Michigan State Univ., USA; Prof. of Science and Dean Faculty of Science, Univ. of Jordan 1971–76; Pres. Yarmouk Univ. 1976–86; Asst Dir Gen. for Science, UNESCO 1990–93, Deputy Dir Gen. 1993–98; fmr Minister of Agric. and Minister of Educ.; Pres. Philadelphia Univ., Jordan –2005; Prime Minister and Minister of Defence April–Nov. 2005 (resgnd); Senator and Chair. Senate Cttee on Educ. Science, Culture and Media; Pres. Petra Univ.; Chair. Nat. Center for Human Rights, Jordan 2008–; fmr Sec.-Gen. Higher Council for Science and Tech.; Sec.-Gen. and Fellow, Third World Acad. of Sciences; mem. Arab Thought Forum 1978–, World Affairs Council 1980–, Inst. of Biological Sciences, AAAS 1993–; Fellow, Islamic Acad. of Sciences, mem. Council and Treas. 1999–; Dr hc (Sung Kyuakwan Univ., Seoul); Al-Nahda Medal (Jordan), Al-Yarmouk Medal (Jordan), Istilal Medal (Jordan) 1995, Alfonso X Medal (Spain). *Publications include:* author and ed. of over 18 books and 90 research papers in the fields of botany, economic devt, educ. and int. co-operation. *Address:* National Centre for Human Rights, PO Box 5503, Amman 11183 (office); PO Box 477, Amman 11941, Jordan (home). *Telephone:* (6) 5931256 (office); (6) 5161880 (home). *Fax:* (6) 5930072 (office); (6) 5165285 (home). *E-mail:* mail@nchr.org.jo (home); abadran@wanadoo.com (home). *Website:* www.nchr.org.jo (office).

BADRAN, Ibrahim, BSc, PhD; Jordanian government official, foundation director and academic; *Adviser to the President for International Relations and Scientific Centres, Philadelphia University;* b. 19 July 1939, Nablus, Palestine; m.; four c.; ed Univs. of Cairo and London; Lecturer in Electrical Eng, Univ. of Libya, Tripoli 1970–74; Chief Engineer and Head, Electricity Section, Consultancy and Architecture, Ministry of Planning, Baghdad 1974–76; Dir of Planning and Dir of Standards and Specifications, Jordan Electricity Authority 1978–80; Dir of Energy, Ministry of Trade and Industry 1980–84; Sec.-Gen. (Under-Sec.) Ministry of Industry and Trade 1984–85; Sec.-Gen. Ministry of Energy and Natural Resources 1985–90; Adviser to Prime Minister 1991–94; Co-ordinator-Gen. of Peace Process, Ministry of Foreign Affairs 1994–95; Exec. Dir Noor Al-Hussein Foundation 1995–97; Supervisor, Human Rights Unit, Prime Minister's Office; Asst Pres. Philadelphia Univ. 1999–, Dean of Faculty of Eng 2000–07, currently Adviser to Pres. for Int. Relations and Scientific Centres; Minister of Education 2009–10; mem. Arab Language Acad.; Chair. Bd of Dirs Jordan Glass Co. 1985–87, Commercial Centers Cooperation-Jordan 1984–85, 1990–91; mem. Bd of Dirs Jordan Atomic Energy; mem. Bd Consultance Albayan Magazine; fmr Dir Jordanian Petroleum Refinery, Jordanian Phosphate Co., Jordan Valley Authority, Jordan Water Authority, Jordan Electricity Authority, Jordan Natural Resources Authority, Industrial Bank of Jordan etc.; mem. Royal Advisory for Educ.; mem. Higher Council for Family Affairs; Gov. for Jordan, IAEA 1982–90; writes weekly column in Aldustou (daily newspaper); Al Istiqlal Decoration of the 1st Order 1990; Hussein Gold Medal for Scientific Distinctions, State Appreciation Award for Human Sciences and Arab Thoughts 2000. *Publications:* Study on the Arab Mind, On Progress and History in the Arab World, Science and Technology in the Arab World, Culture Decline, National Strategy for Societal Culture 2004, Renaissance and Survival 2005, Engineering and Engineers 2007, Entrepreneurship 2012, and other books on aspects of science, tech., nuclear energy, natural resources and devt in the Arab world; two theoretical plays. *Leisure interests:* farming, reading, writing, travelling. *Address:* Office of the President, Philadelphia University, PO Box 1, Amman 19392 (office); 29 Ali Thyabat Street, Tla'a Al Ali, Amman, Jordan (home). *Telephone:* (2) 6374444 (office); (2) 5347777 (home). *Fax:* (2) 6374370 (office); (2) 5344448 (home). *E-mail:* i.badran@philadelphia.edu.jo (office); ebrbadran2@gmail.com (home). *Website:* www.philadelphia.edu.jo (office).

BADRÉ, Bertrand, MA; French business executive and international organization official; *Managing Director and Chief Financial Officer, World Bank Group;* b. 10 May 1968; s. of Denis Badré; m. Vanessa Du Merle 1995; four c.; ed Hautes études commerciales de Paris, Institut d'Etudes Politiques de Paris, Université Paris Sorbonne (Paris IV), Ecole nationale d'Administration; Asst Group Controller, BFI-Ibexsa 1989–91; Inspecteur des Finances 1995–99; seconded to World Bank, Togo 1997; Asst Dir Lazard 1999–2000, Vice-Pres. 2000–02, Man. Dir 2004–07; Deputy Personal Rep. of Pres. Chirac for Africa for the G8 2003; Chief Financial Officer, Crédit Agricole 2007–11; Group Chief Financial Officer Société Générale 2012–13; Man. Dir and Chief Financial Officer, World Bank Group, Washington, DC 2013–; mem. Bd of Dirs Haulotte Group 2005–, Sofiouest 2008–; mem. global panel on 'Financing Water for All' 2002; mem. Supervisory Bd Eurazeo 2010–12. *Address:* World Bank Group, 1818 H Street NW, Washington, DC 20433, USA (office). *Telephone:* (202) 473-1000 (office). *Fax:* (202) 473-1000 (office). *Website:* www.worldbank.org (office).

BADRI, Muhammad bin, BSc, PhD; Malaysian chemist and academic; *Dean and Professor, Faculty of Science and Environmental Studies, Universiti Putra Malaysia;* b. May 1943; ed St Francis Xavier Univ., USA, Dalhousie Univ., Canada; teacher 1965–72; Lecturer, Universiti Putra Malaysia 1972–75, Assoc. Prof. 1976–84, Dean and Prof., Faculty of Science and Environmental Studies 1984–; mem. Council of Malaysia Inst. of Chem. 1980–84, Nat. Asscn of Science and Math. Educ., Malaysian Rubber Producers Council, ACS 1984, Bd Rubber Research Inst. of Malaysia, Environmental Quality Council, Ministry of Science, Malaysia; mem. Malaysian del. to IUPAC Comm. on High Temperature and Solid State Chem.; mem. ACS 1984; Founding Fellow, Islamic Acad. of Sciences 1986, Acad. of Sciences, Malaysia 1996. *Address:* Universiti Putra Malaysia, 43400 Serdang, Selangor Darul Ehsan, Malaysia (office). *Telephone:* (3) 89486101 (office). *Fax:* (3) 89483244 (office).

BADURA-SKODA, Paul; Austrian pianist; b. 6 Oct. 1927, Vienna; s. of Ludwig Badura and Margarete Badura (née Winter); m. Eva Badura-Skoda (née Halfar); two s. two d.; ed Realgymnasium courses in conducting and piano, Konservatorium der Stadt Wien and Edwin Fischer's masterclass in Lucerne; regular concerts since 1948; tours world-wide as soloist and with leading orchestras; conductor of chamber orchestra 1960–; yearly master classes fmrly in Edin., Salzburg and Vienna Festival 1958–63; Artist in Residence, Univ. of Wisconsin, master classes in Madison, Wis. 1966–71; recorded more than 200 LP records and CDs, including complete Beethoven, Mozart and Schubert sonatas; Austrian Cross of Honour for Science and Arts (First Order) 1976, Bösendorfer-Ring 1978, Chevalier, Légion d'honneur 1992, Commdr des Arts et des Lettres 1997, Grosses Silbernes Ehrenzeichen mit dem Stern der Republik Österreich 2007, Goldenes Ehrenzeichen für die Verdienste um das Land Wien 2007; Dr hc (Mannheim) 2006, (Kraków) 2013; First Prize, Austrian Music Competition 1947. *Compositions:* Mass in D, Cadenzas to Piano, Flute and Violin Concertos by Mozart and Haydn, completion of five unfinished Piano Sonatas by Schubert 1976 and of unfinished Larghetto and Allegro for 2 Pianos by Mozart, Elégie pour Piano 1980, Sonatine Romantique for Violin and Piano 1994, Sonate romantique for Flute (or Violin) and Piano. *Publications:* Die Klaviersonaten von Beethoven (with Jörg Demus) 1970, Interpreting Bach at the Keyboard 1993, Interpreting Mozart on the Keyboard (with Eva Badura-Skoda) (second edn) 2008; Editions of Schubert, Mozart, Chopin; numerous articles. *Leisure interest:* chess. *Address:* c/o 3116 Live Oak Street, Dallas, TX 75204, USA. *Website:* www.badura-skoda.com.

BAE, Jung Choong; South Korean insurance industry executive; ed Korea Univ.; joined Dongbang Life (now Samsung Life Insurance) 1969, with Samsung Fire and Marine Insurance 1995–98, returned to Samsung Life Insurance 1999 as Exec. Vice-Pres. and Rep. Dir, Pres. and CEO 2000–06, also mem. restructuring cttee of Samsung Group and non-standing Dir Hana Bank and Samsung Investment Trust and Securities Co.; honoured by Korea Man. Asscn three times for leadership in customer service. *Address:* c/o Samsung Life Insurance, Samsung Life Insurance Building, 150 Taepyung-ro 2–ga, Chung-gu, Seoul 100–716 Republic of Korea (office).

BAEZ, Joan Chandos; American folk singer; b. 9 Jan. 1941, Staten Island, NY; d. of Albert V. Baez and Joan Baez (née Bridge); m. David Harris 1968 (divorced 1973); one s.; ed School of Fine and Applied Arts, Boston Univ.; began career as singer in coffee houses, appeared at Ballad Room, Club 47 1958–68, Gate of Horn, Chicago 1958, Newport, RI, Folk Festival 1959–69, Town Hall and Carnegie Hall, New York 1962, 1967, 1968; gave concerts in black colls in southern USA 1963; toured Europe and USA 1960s–90s, Democratic Repub. of Viet Nam 1972, Australia 1985; recordings with Vanguard Records 1960–72, A & M Record Co. 1972–76, Portrait Records 1977–80, Gold Castle Records 1987–89, Virgin Records 1990–93, Guardian Records 1995–, Grapevine Label Records 1995–; awarded eight gold albums, one gold single; many TV appearances; began refusing payment of war taxes 1964; detained for civil disobedience opposing conscription 1967; speaking tour of USA and Canada for draft resistance 1967–68; Founder and Vice-Pres. Inst. for Study of Non-Violence (now called Resource Center for Non-Violence) 1965–; Founder Humanitas Int. Human Rights Comm. 1979–92; Chevalier, Légion d'honneur; Gandhi Memorial Int. Foundation Award 1988. *Recordings include:* albums: Joan Baez 1960, Joan Baez, Vol. 2 1961, In Concert, part 2 1963, 5 1964, Farewell Angelina 1965, Noel 1966, Joan 1967, Baptism 1968, Any Day Now 1968, David's Album 1969, One Day At A Time 1969, First Ten Years 1970, Carry It On (soundtrack) 1971, Ballad Book 1972, Come From The Shadows 1972, Where Are You Now My Son? 1973, Hits, Greatest and Others 1973, Gracias A La Vida 1974, Contemporary Ballad Book 1974, Diamonds and Rust 1975, From Every Stage 1976, Gulf Winds 1976, Blowin' Away 1977, Best Of 1977, Honest Lullaby 1979, Very Early Joan 1982, Recently 1987, Diamonds and Rust In The Bullring 1989, Speaking Of Dreams 1989, Play Me Backwards 1992, Rare Live and Classic 1993, Ring Them Bells 1995, Gone from Danger 1997, Dreams 1997, Best Of... 1997, 20th Century Masters: The Millennium 1999, Dark Chords on a Big Guitar 2003, Bowery Songs 2005, Day After Tomorrow 2008, How Sweet the Sound 2009. *Publications include:* Joan Baez Songbook 1964, Daybreak 1968, Coming Out (with David Harris) 1971, And Then I Wrote... (songbook) 1979, A nd a Voice to Sing With 1987. *Address:* Diamonds and Rust Productions, PO Box 1026, Menlo Park, CA 94026-1026, USA. *Telephone:* (650) 328-0266. *Fax:* (650) 328-0845. *E-mail:* jbwebpages@aol.com. *Website:* www.joanbaez.com.

BAGABANDI, Natsagiin, PhD, ScD; Mongolian politician; b. 22 April 1950, Zavkhan Prov.; s. of Mendiin Natsag and Rashjamtsiin Dogoo; m. Azadsurengiin Oyunbileg 1971; one s. one d.; ed Refrigeration Jr Coll., Leningrad (now St

Petersburg), USSR, Food Tech. Inst. of USSR, Odessa, Acad. of Social Science, Moscow, USSR; machine operator, mechanic and engineer, Ulan Bator City Brewery and Distillery 1972–75; Chief of Dept Mongolian People's Revolutionary Party's (MPRP) Cttee of Tuv Aimag 1980–84; Chief of Div., Div. Adviser Cen. Cttee of MPRP 1987–90; Sec., Deputy Chair. Cen. Cttee of MPRP 1990–92, Chair. Feb.– June 1997; mem. of State Great Hural, Chair. 1992–96; Pres. of Mongolia and C-in-C of the Armed Forces 1997–2005; Hon. Prof., Mongolian Socio-Econ. Inst. 'Explorer XXI'; 70th Anniversary Order of the People's Revolution 1991, 'Golden Star' Olympic Order 1997, Academician Title 'Bilguun Nomch', Mongolian Nomadic Civilization Acad. and 'Ikh-Zasag' Univ. 2000, 'Peace' Order of Russian Fed. 2000, Order of Chinggis Khaan 2000; Dr hc (Nat. Food Tech. Acad. of Odessa, Ukraine) 1995, (Seng-Shui Univ., Japan) 1998, (Ankara Univ., Turkey) 1998, (Alma-Ata Univ., Kazakhstan) 1998, (Mongolian Admin Acad.) 1999, (Mongolian 'Otgontenger' Univ.) 2001, (Mongolian Defense Univ.) 2001, (Sougan Univ., S Korea) 2001, (Mongolian Science and Tech. Univ.) 2002, (Soka Univ., Japan), (Tokyo Univ. of Agric.), (Indiana Univ., USA) 2005, (Hokuriku Univ., Japan) 2007; Sukhbaatar Fund Prize 1996, Peter the Great Int. Prize 2001. *Publications include:* Mongolian Behaviour 1992, The President: Thought and Recommendation Before the New Century 1998, The President: Policy and Objectives Before the New Century 1998, Policy and Mind of the President 2000, Significance of Restoration and Tradition to the Development 2000, Mongolian Intelligence 2001, Policy and Diligence of the President 2001, Thought and Ideas of the President 2001, XXI Century Will Test You 2001, New Era and New Objectives of Mongolian Buddhist Religion 2001, Let Us Respect and Admire Elders 2001, Children, Youths and the President 2001, Multi-Sided National Security 2001, New Century: Adore Consent and Friendship, Develop the Country 2003, New Century: Meaning of Self-reliance upon Globalization, and Globalization upon Self-reliance 2004, New Century: Meaning of Cherishing the Democracy 2005, Policy and Activity of President of Mongolia N. Bagabandi 2005. *Leisure interests:* reading, fishing. *Address:* c/o Mr Ayursaikhan Tumurbaatar, Secretary to Former President N. Bagabandi, State Palace, Ulan Bator 12, Mongolia (office). *E-mail:* ayursaikhan@yahoo.com (office).

BAGÃO FÉLIX, António; Portuguese politician and economist; b. 9 April 1948, Aveiro; ed Inst. of Economic and Financial Sciences, INSEAD, France; Financial Dir Companhia de Seguros Mundial 1973–76; Dir Bank of Commerce and Industry 1985–87; Sec. of State for Work and Professional Training 1987, Sec. of State for Social Security 1987–91; Dir Bank of Portugal 1992–93, Vice Gov. 1993–94; Dir Gen. Portuguese Commercial Bank 1994–2002; Minister of Social Security and Employment 2002–04; Minister of Finance 2004–05; currently Visiting Prof., Univ. Lusíada; Chair. Supervisory Bd Bank Against Hunger 1997–2002; consultant to Portuguese Episcopal Conference for Social Affairs and Ethics 2001–; mem. Bd of Dirs Asscn for Econ. and Social Devt. *Publications include:* several books and articles for numerous journals, newspapers and magazines. *Address:* Av. Almirante Gago Coutinho, 92, 1700-031 Lisbon, Portugal (home).

BAGAYEV, Sergei Nikolayevich; Russian physicist and research institute director; *Director, Institute of Laser Physics, Russian Academy of Sciences (Siberia);* b. 9 Sept. 1941; m.; one s.; ed Novosibirsk State Univ.; Jr, Sr Researcher, Head of Lab., Inst. of Physics of Semiconductors, Siberian Br., USSR Acad. of Sciences 1965–78, Head of Lab., Head of Div., Deputy Dir Inst. of Thermal Physics, Siberian Br., USSR Acad. of Sciences 1978–91, Deputy Dir Inst. of Laser Physics, Siberian Br., Russian Acad. of Sciences 1991–92, Dir 1992–; Corresp. mem. USSR (now Russian) Acad. of Sciences 1990, Academician 1993–; research in non-linear laser spectroscopy of superhigh resolution, laser frequency standards, physics and their applications in precision physical experiments; Order of Friendship 1999, Chevalier, Légion d'honneur 2004, Medal of the Order 'For Services to the Motherland' 2006; State Prize of Russian Fed. 1998, V. A. Koptyug Prize, SBRAS/Belarus Nat. Acad. of Sciences 1999. *Publications include:* Laser Frequency Standards 1986, Single-frequency Intracavity Doubled Yb:YAG Ring Laser 2005, Investigation of Transcapillary Exchange by the Laser Method 2005, and numerous articles. *Address:* Institute of Laser Physics, Siberian Branch of Russian Academy of Sciences, Prosp. Lavrentyev 13/3, 630090 Novosibirsk, Russia (office). *Telephone:* (383) 333-24-89 (office). *Fax:* (383) 333-20-67 (office). *E-mail:* bagayev@laser.nsc.ru (office). *Website:* www.laser.nsc.ru (office).

BAGAZA, Col Jean-Baptiste; Burundian army officer and politician; *Leader, Parti pour le redressement national (PARENA);* b. 29 Aug. 1946, Rutovu, Bururi Prov.; m. Fausta Bagaza; four c.; ed Ecole des Cadets, Brussels and the Belgian Mil. School; fmr Asst to Gen. Ndabemeye; Chief of Staff of Armed Forces, with rank of Lt-Col; led coup to overthrow Pres. Micombero Nov. 1976; Pres. of Repub. of Burundi 1976–87, also Minister of Defence; Pres. Union pour le progrès national (UPRONA) 1976–87; promoted to Col 1977; currently Leader Parti pour le redressement national (PARENA). *Leisure interest:* sports. *Address:* Parti pour le redressement national (PARENA), Bujumbura, Burundi.

BAGEL-TRAH, Simone, Dr rer. nat; German microbiologist and business executive; *Chairwoman of the Supervisory Board and Shareholders' Committee, Henkel KGaA;* b. 10 Jan. 1969, Düsseldorf; m.; two c.; ed Univ. of Bonn; consultant, Project Man. for Verein für angewandte Mikrobiologie (Asscn of Applied Microbiology) 1998–2000, Co-ordination of industrial projects for Pharmaceutical Microbiology Dept, Bonn Univ. 1998–2000; Pnr and Dir Antiinfectives Intelligence Gesellschaft für klinisch mikrobiologische Forschung und Kommunikation mbH (Clinical Microbiological Research & Communication) 2000–; mem. Shareholders' Cttee Henkel KGaA 2005–08, mem. Supervisory Bd and Vice-Chair. Shareholders' Cttee Henkel AG & Co. KGaA 2008–09, Vice-Chair. Supervisory Bd Henkel Management AG 2008–09, Chair. Supervisory Bd and Shareholders' Cttee 2009–; mem. Advisory Bd HSBC Trinkaus & Burkhardt AG; mem. Rotary Düsseldorf, Bd of Trustees Düsseldorf Business School, Bd of Trustees Stiftung Schloss und Park Benrath (Benrath Castle and Park Foundation), Bd of Trustees Dr Konrad Henkel Foundation, Bd of Trustees Jost Henkel Foundation, Bd of Heinrich Heine Univ., Düsseldorf. *Address:* Henkel AG & Co. KGaA, Henkelstrasse 67, Düsseldorf 40191, Germany (office). *Telephone:* (211) 797-0 (office). *Fax:* (211) 7982484 (office). *E-mail:* info@henkel.com (office). *Website:* www.henkel.com (office).

BAGGE, Sverre Hakon, PhD; Norwegian historian and academic; *Professor and Head, Centre for Medieval Studies, University of Bergen;* b. 7 Aug. 1942, Bergen; s. of Sverre Olsen and Gunvor Bagge; m. Guro Mette Skrove; two s. one d.; Lecturer,

Univ. of Bergen 1973, Sr Lecturer 1974, Prof. 1991–, Prof., Head Centre for Medieval Studies 2002–; Brage Prize, Clara Lachmann's Prize, Jarl Gallén Prize for Medieval Studies, Univ. of Helsinki 2004, Møbius Prize from Norwegian Research Council 2008. *Publications*: The Political Thought of the King's Mirror 1987, Society and Politics in Snorri Sturluson's Heimskringla 1991, From Gang Leader to the Lord's Anointed 1996, Kings, Politics, and the Right Order of World in German Historiography c. 950–1150, From Viking Stronghold to Christian Kingdom, State Formation in Norway c. 900-1350 2010. *Address*: Center for Medieval Studies, University of Bergen, PO Box 7800, Villaveien 1A, 5020 Bergen (office); Moldbakken 13, 5035 Bergen, Norway (home). *Telephone*: 55-58-23-25 (office). *Fax*: 55-58-80-90 (office). *E-mail*: sverre.bagge@cms.uib.no (office). *Website*: www.uib.no/cms (office).

BAGGIO, Roberto; Italian fmr professional footballer; b. 18 Feb. 1967, Caldogno, Veneto; s. of Fiorindo Baggio and Matilde Baggio; m. Andreina Fabbri; two d.; second striker; with Vicenza 1982–85, Fiorentina 1985–90, Juventus 1990–95, Milan 1995–97, Bologna 1997–98, Inter Milan 1998–2000, Brescia 2000–04, 488 appearances, 318 career goals; played for Italian Nat. Team in 1990 (third place), 1994 (second place) and 1998 World Cups; only Italian player ever to score in three World Cups (nine goals); made 56 appearances and scored 27 goals for Italy; apptd Goodwill Amb. for FAO 2002; U-23 European Footballer of the Year 1990, UEFA Cup Winners' Cup Top Scorer 1990–91, FIFA World Player of the Year 1993, European Footballer of the Year 1993, Platinum Football Award, TV Sorrisi and Canzoni 1992, Onze D'Or by French Magazine Onze Mondial 1993, Bravo Award with Fiorentina 1990, Golden Guerin with Vicenza 1985, Golden Guerin with AC Milan 1996, Golden Guerin with Brescia 2001, Azzuri Team of the Century 2000, FIFA Dream Team of All Time 2002, Most Loved Player Award via Internet Polls 2001, Most Loved Player Award at Italian Oscars 2002, Giuseppe Prisco Award 2004, The Champions Promenade – Golden Foot 2003, Peace Summit Award 2010. *Publication*: Una porta nel cielo (autobiography) 2001. *Leisure interests*: hunting, music. *Address*: Via Bazoli 10, 25127 Brescia, Italy (office). *Telephone*: (30) 241075 (office). *Fax*: (30) 2410787 (office). *E-mail*: info@bresciacalcio.it (office). *Website*: www.bresciacalcio.it (office); www.robertobaggio.com (home).

BAGHDASARIAN, Artur, DJur; Armenian politician; b. 8 Nov. 1968, Yerevan; m.; two c.; ed Yerevan State Univ.; army service 1988–89; Corresp., Head of Dept Avangard newspaper 1989–93; mem. Nat. Ass. 1995–, Chair. 2003–06; Chair. Council on State and Legal Affairs 1998–; Leader Orinats Yerkir party 1998–; Chair. French Univ. of Armenia 2000–; Chair. European Regional Acad. in the Caucasus 2002–. *Publications*: several scientific monographs and articles. *Address*: c/o National Assembly of the Republic of Armenia, Marshal Bagramian St 19, 375095 Yerevan, Armenia (office). *E-mail*: abagdasaryan@parliament.am (office). *Website*: www.parliament.am (office).

BAGIS, Egemen, MPA, BBA; Turkish politician; b. 23 April 1970, Bingol; m. Beyhan N. Bagis; two c.; ed Baruch Coll., City Univ. of New York, USA; elected to Nat. Ass. for Istanbul 2002–; Foreign Policy Adviser to Prime Minister 2002–09, Minister for EU Affairs and Chief Negotiator 2009–13; mem. AK Party (Justice and Devt Party), serves as Deputy Chair. for Foreign Affairs; Chair. NATO Parl. Ass. on Transatlantic Relations; Chair. Turkey–USA Inter-Parl. Friendship Caucus; Chair. Advisory Cttee, Istanbul 2010 European Capital of Culture Initiative; Founding Patron, Istanbul Modern Museum, Santral Museum of Art and Industry; fmr Pres. Fed. of Turkish-American Asscns; Hon. mem. Bd of Dirs Siirt Solidarity Foundation. *Address*: Turkish Grand National Assembly, A Blok, Alt Zemin, 3. Banko, No. 3, Bakanliklar, 06543 Ankara, Turkey (office). *Telephone*: (312) 4205908 (office). *Fax*: (312) 4206947 (office). *E-mail*: egemen@egemenbagis .com (office). *Website*: www.egemenbagis.com (office).

BAGLAY, Marat Viktorovich, DJur, DHist; Russian lawyer; b. 13 March 1931, Baku, Azerbaijan; m.; three d.; ed Rostov State Univ., Inst. of State and Law; Researcher, Inst. of State and Law 1957–62; Prof., Moscow Inst. of Int. Relations 1962–95; Head of Dept, Inst. of Int. Workers' Movt Acad. of Sciences 1967–77; Pro-Rector and Prof., Acad. of Labour and Social Relations 1977–95; judge, Constitutional Court of Russian Fed. 1996–2003, Chair. 1997–2003; Corresp. mem. Russian Acad. of Sciences 1997–; mem. Bureau, European Comm. for Democracy Through Law 2005–; Hon. LLD (Baku Univ., Rostov-on-Don Univ., Odessa Nat. Acad. of Law); Merited Scientist of Russia. *Publications include*: Way to Freedom, Constitutional Law of Russian Federation, numerous books and articles.

BAGNASCO, HE Cardinal Angelo; Italian ecclesiastic; *Archbishop of Genoa;* b. 14 Jan. 1943, Pontevico; ed Univ. of Genoa; ordained priest, Genoa 1966; served as Prof. of Metaphysics and Atheism, Theological Faculty of Northern Italy, also led archdiocesan liturgical and catechesis offices; fmr diocesan rep. to FUCI (Italian Catholic Fed. of Univ. Students); Bishop of Pesaro 1998–2000, Archbishop of Pesaro 2000–03; Archbishop of the Mil. Ordinariate of Italy 2003–06; Archbishop of Genoa 2006–; cr. Cardinal (Cardinal-Priest of Gran Madre di Dio) 2007; participated in Papal Conclave 2013; has held several posts within Italian Episcopal Conf. (CEI) 2001–, including Pres. Admin. Bd of newspaper Avvenire and Sec. for Schools and Univs 2001–, Pres. CEI 2007–. *Address*: Arcivescovado, Piazza Matteotti 4, 16123 Genoa, Italy (office). *Telephone*: (010) 27-001 (office). *Fax*: (010) 27-00-220 (office). *E-mail*: info@diocesi.genova.it (office). *Website*: www .diocesi.genova.it (office).

BAGRATIAN, Hrant Araratovich, PhD; Armenian economist and politician; b. 18 Oct. 1958, Yerevan; m.; one s.; ed Yerevan Inst. of Nat. Econ., Inst. of Economy of Armenian Acad. of Sciences; Jr researcher, then Sr researcher, Inst. of Econs, Armenian Acad. of Sciences 1982–90; First Deputy Chair. Council of Ministers of Armenian SSR, Chair. State Cttee on Econs 1990; Vice-Prime Minister and Minister of Econs Repub. of Armenia 1991–93; Prime Minister of Armenia 1993–96; Adviser to IMF 1996–97; Deputy Head and Dir Human Resources, Yerevan Brandy Factory 1998–2006; Founder and Leader, Liberty (Azatutiun) Party; cand. in presidential election Feb. 2013. *Publications include*: several books and articles.

BAGRI, Baron (Life Peer), cr. 1997, of Regents Park in the City of Westminster; **Raj Kumar Bagri,** CBE; British commodities executive; *Chairman, Minmetco;* b. 24 Aug. 1930; m. 1954; one s. one d.; joined a metals business in Calcutta 1946; moved into int. metals trading 1949; set up UK br. office of an Indian co. 1959; f. own company in UK, Metdist Ltd, which became London Metal Exchange (LME)

ring dealing mem. 1970, currently Chair. Minmetco (holding co. of Metdist Group of Cos); joined LME's Man. Cttee 1973, apptd. Dir of LME 1983, Vice-Chair. 1990, Chair. 1993–2002, Hon. Pres. 2003–06; Hon. Fellow, London Business School 2004; Hon. DSc (City Univ.) 1999, (Nottingham) 2000. *Leisure interest*: cricket. *Address*: Metdist Enterprises Ltd, 80 Cannon Street, London, EC4N 6EJ, England (office). *Telephone*: (20) 7280-0000 (office). *Fax*: (20) 7606-6650 (office). *E-mail*: vmanning@metdist.com (office).

BAGSHAWE, Kenneth Dawson, CBE, MD, FRCP, FRCR, FRCOG, FRS; British physician and medical oncologist; *Professor Emeritus of Medical Oncology, Charing Cross Hospital Medical School;* b. 17 Aug. 1925, Marple, Cheshire; s. of Harry Bagshawe and Gladys Bagshawe; m. 1st Ann A. Kelly 1946 (divorced 1976, died 2000); m. 2nd Sylvia D. Lawler (née Corben) 1977 (died 1996); one s. one d.; m. 3rd Surinder Kanta Sharma 1998; ed Harrow Co. School, London School of Econs and St Mary's Hosp. Medical School, Univ. of London; served in RN 1943–46; Research Fellow, Johns Hopkins Hosp., USA 1955–56; Sr Registrar, St Mary's Hosp. 1956–60; Sr Lecturer in Medicine, Charing Cross Hosp. Medical School 1961–63; Consultant Physician and Dir Dept of Medical Oncology 1961–90, Prof. of Medical Oncology 1974–90, Prof. Emer. 1990–; Chair. Enzacta Scientific Co. Ltd 1998–2000; Chair. Council Cancer Research Campaign 1988–90; Pres. Asscn of Cancer Physicians 1986–93, British Asscn for Cancer Research 1990–94; Fellow, Royal Coll. of Radiologists; Hamilton Fairley Lectureship 1989; Hon. DSc (Bradford) 1990; Krug Award for Excellence in Medicine 1980; Edgar Gentilli Prize, Royal Coll. of Obstetricians and Gynaecologists 1980, Galen Medal, London Soc. of Apothecaries 1993. *Achievements include*: invented cytotoxic drug therapy. *Publications*: Choriocarcinoma 1969, Medical Oncology 1976, Germ Cell Tumours 1983, Antibody Directed Prodrug Therapy 1987 and articles in professional journals. *Leisure interests*: travel, walking, photography, music, art. *Address*: 115 George Street, London, W1H T5A, England (home). *Telephone*: (20) 7262-6033 (home). *E-mail*: kbagshawe@googlemail.com (home).

BAH, Amadou Lamarana; Guinean diplomatist and government official; b. 1950, Pita; ed Univ. of Havana, Cuba; Lecturer in Hispanic Culture and Civilisation, Gamal Abdel Nasser Univ., Conakry 1974–77; Press Attaché, Office of Pres. 1977–80; First Sec., Embassy in Havana 1980–83, Embassy in Monrovia 1986–87, Embassy in Abidjan 1987–91, First Counsellor, Embassy in Paris 1991–96, Counsellor, Embassy in Lagos 1996–98, Dir Immunities and Privileges Div., Ministry of Foreign Affairs, Co-operation, African Integration and Guineans Abroad 1998–2008, Minister of Foreign Affairs, Co-operation, African Integration and Guineans Abroad 2008. *Leisure interests*: reading, jogging. *Address*: c/o Ministry of Foreign Affairs, Co-operation, African Integration and Guineans Abroad, face au Port, ex-Primature, BP 2519, Conakry, Guinea (office).

BAHADIAN, Adhemar Gabriel; Brazilian diplomatist; b. 22 Oct. 1940, Rio de Janeiro; s. of Aziz Bahadian and Gracinda Gabriel Bahadian; ed Università Gama Filho, Istituto Rio Branco; joined Ministry of Foreign Affairs 1967, Head Int. Commerce Div. 1987, Chief of Cabinet, Secr.-Gen. for Foreign Affairs 1994, Asst Sec.-Gen. 1995; First Sec., Perm. Mission to UN, Geneva 1976, Counsellor 1980, Minister Counsellor 1990, Alt. Perm. Rep. 2000; Consul-Gen. in Buenos Aires 2002; Amb. to Italy 2005–09; fmr chief FTAA (Free Trade Area of the Americas) negotiator; mem. Bd of Dirs TIM Participacoes SA 2010–; Gran Croce, Ordine del Rio Branco 1994, Grande Ufficiale, Ordine al Merito Navale 1994, Grande Ufficiale, Ordine al Merito Militare 1995, Grande Ufficiale, Ordine al Merito dell'Aeronautica 1996, Commdr Legion d'Honneur (France) 1996, Ordine Francisco de Miranda (Venezuela) 1997, Cavalieri di Gran Croce (Italy) 1997, Gran Croce, Ordine di Bernardo O'Higgins (Chile) 1998, and other decorations from Germany, Finland, Portugal. *Address*: c/o Board of Directors, TIM Participacoes SA, Avenida das Américas Rio de Janeiro, Rio de Janeiro 22640-102, Brazil.

BAHAR, Shaikha Khalid al-, BA, MBA; Kuwaiti banking executive; *CEO–Kuwait, National Bank of Kuwait;* ed Kuwait Univ., Harvard Business School, Stanford Univ., Duke Univ., USA; fmr Chair. Al Watany Bank of Egypt; Group Gen. Man., Corp. Banking, Nat. Bank of Kuwait 2003–08, Deputy CEO Nat. Bank of Kuwait 2008–10, CEO– Kuwait 2012–, Vice-Chair. NBK Capital (bank's investment arm); Chair. Nat. Bank of Kuwait (Lebanon) 2005–; mem. Bd of Dirs International Bank of Qatar, Zain Group 2005–; ranked by Arabian Business amongst the 100 Most Powerful Arab Woman (15th) 2011, (eighth) 2012, ranked by Forbes magazine amongst The World's 100 Most Powerful Women (85th) 2012. *Address*: National Bank of Kuwait, PO Box 95 Safat, Abdullah Al Ahmad Street, 13001 Kuwait City, Kuwait (office). *Telephone*: 22422011 (office). *Fax*: 22462469 (office). *E-mail*: info@nbk.com (office). *Website*: www.nbk.com (office).

BAHARNA, Husain Mohammad al-, PhD; Bahraini lawyer and politician; b. 5 Dec. 1932, Manama; s. of Mohammad Makki Al-Baharna and Zahra Sayed Mahmood; m.; three s. two d.; ed Baghdad Law Coll., Iraq, London Univ. and Cambridge Univ., UK; mem. English Bar (Lincoln's Inn) and Bahraini Bar; Legal Adviser, Ministry of Foreign Affairs, Kuwait 1962–64; Legal Adviser and Analyst Arab Gulf Affairs, Arabian-American Oil Co., Saudi Arabia 1965–68; Legal Adviser, Dept of Foreign Affairs, Bahrain 1969–70; Legal Adviser to the State and mem. Council of State, Pres. Legal Cttee 1970–71; Minister of State for Legal Affairs 1971; mem. Del. of Bahrain to Sixth (Legal) Cttee UN Gen. Ass. 1986, UN Int. Law Comm., Geneva 1987, Del. of Bahrain to Summit of Heads of State of Gulf Co-operation Council 1991; fmr legal adviser and del. to numerous int. confs and summit meetings; Chair. Del. of Bahrain to UN Preparatory Comm. for Int. Sea Bed Authority and Int. Tribunal for Law of the Sea 1983; mem. Cttee of Experts on Control of Transnational and Int. Criminality and for the establishment of the Int. Criminal Court, Siracusa, Italy 1990; Council mem. Centre for Islamic and Middle East Law, SOAS, London Univ.; Editorial Bd Arab Law Quarterly; Hon. mem. Euro-Arab Forum for Arbitration and Business Law, Paris; mem. British Inst. of Int. and Comparative Law, American Soc. of Int. Law, Int. Law Asscn, Egyptian Soc. of Int. Law; Assoc. mem. Int. Comm. of Jurists, Int. Law Comm., UN; Arab Historian Medal (Union of Arab Historians) 1986. *Publications*: The Legal Status of the Arab Gulf States 1968, Legal and Constitutional Systems of the Arabian Gulf States (in Arabic) 1975, The Arabian Gulf States – Their Legal and Political Status and their International Problems 1975; articles in learned journals. *Leisure interest*: reading. *Address*: Dr Husain M al-Baharna & Associates, PO Box 10407,

120

Manama, Bahrain (office). *Telephone:* 17533773 (office). *Fax:* 17535242 (office). *E-mail:* hbaharna@batelco.com.bh (office).

BAHÇELI, Devlet, DEcon; Turkish politician and academic; *Leader, Nationalist Action Party (MHP);* b. 1948, Osmaniye; ed Ankara Econ. and Commercial Sciences Acad., Gazi Univ. Social Sciences Inst.; Sec.-Gen. Turkish Nat. Students Fed. 1970–71; instructor, Ankara Econ. and Commercial Sciences Acad., mem. Faculty of Econ. and Admin. Sciences, Gazi Univ. 1972–87; mem. Parl. 2007–; Sec.-Gen. Nationalist Action Party (MHP) 1987, Leader 1997–; Deputy Prime Minister and State Minister 1999–2002; Founder mem. and Pres. Financiers and Economists Asscn. *Address:* Milliyetçi Hareket Partisi (Nationalist Action Party), Ceyhun Atif Kansu Cad. 128, Balgat, Ankara, Turkey (office). *Telephone:* (312) 4725555 (office). *Fax:* (312) 4731544 (office). *E-mail:* bilgi@mhp.org.tr (office). *Website:* www.mhp.org.tr (office).

BAHIDDHA-NUKARA, Parnpree, LLB, MPA, PhD; Thai politician, government official and company chairman; *Independent Director and Chairman, PTT Public Co. Ltd;* ed Chulalongkorn Univ., Univ. of Southern California and Claremont Graduate Univ., USA, certifications from Thailand Energy Acad. and Judicial Training Inst. at King Prajadhipok's Inst.; mem. Pheu Thai Party, Deputy Leader 2008–10; served as Thailand Trade Rep. 2005, Vice-Minister for Commerce, Vice-Minister for Industry, Adviser to Prime Minister, Adviser to Deputy Prime Minister, Thailand's Chief Negotiator for Thailand-India Free Trade Agreement (FTA), Thailand-BIMST-EC FTA, Chair. Cttee on Investment and Trade Promotion under FTA, Chair. Public Warehouse Org., Chair. Bangkok Fashion City; Ind. Dir and Chair. PTT Public Co. Ltd 2013–. *Address:* PTT Public Co. Ltd, 555 Vibhavadi Rangsit Road, Chatuchak, Bangkok 10900, Thailand (office). *Telephone:* (2) 537-2000 (office). *Fax:* (2) 537-3499 (office). *E-mail:* info@pttplc.com (office). *Website:* www.pttplc.com (office).

BAHK, Jae-wan, BA, MPP, PhD; South Korean politician; ed Seoul Nat. Univ., Harvard Univ., USA; Asst Dir, Bd of Audit and Inspection, Seoul 1983–92; Deputy Dir, Ministry of Finance 1992–94; Asst Chief Sec. to Pres. for Policy Planning, Office of the Pres. 1994–96; Prof., Graduate School of Governance, Sungkyunkwan Univ. 2004–; mem. Nat. Ass. (Grand Nat. Party) 2004–08; Head, Task Force for Govt Restructuring & Regulatory Reform, Presidential Transition Cttee 2007–08; Sr Sec. to Pres. for Political Affairs Feb.–June 2008, for State Affairs Planning 2008–10; Minister of Employment and Labour 2010–11, of Strategy and Finance 2011–13; Chair. Policy Coordination Cttee, Citizens' Coalition for Econ. Justice; mem. Grand Nat. Party (renamed Saenuri Party, New Frontier Party 2012). *Address:* c/o Ministry of Strategy and Finance, Govt Complex II, 88, Gwanmunro, Gwacheon City 427-725, Gyeonggi Province, South Korea (office).

BAHMANI, Mahmoud, PhD; Iranian economist and central banker; *Governor, Central Bank of Iran;* b. 1947, Karaj, Alborz Prov.; 17 years as lecturer, Islamic Azad Univ. and Inst. of Banking and Man.; various Sr Man. roles with Bank Melli Iran, including Vice-Pres. of Finance; Gov. Central Bank of Iran 2008–. *Address:* Office of the Governor, Central Bank of Iran, POB 15875-7177, 144 Mirdamad Blvd, Tehran, Iran (office). *Telephone:* (21) 29954855 (office). *Fax:* (21) 29954780 (office). *E-mail:* g.secdept@cbi.ir (office). *Website:* www.cbi.ir (office).

BAHNASSI, Afif, MA, PhD; Syrian academic; b. 17 April 1928, Damascus; m. 1st Hiba Wadi 1962 (died 1966); m. 2nd Maysoun Jazairi 1971; four s. one d.; ed Univ. of Syria, Univ. of Paris (Sorbonne), France; Dir Fine Arts Dept 1959–71; Dir Gen. of Antiquities and Museums of Syria 1972–88; mem. Arab Writers' Union 1967–; Chair. Fine Arts Asscn of Syria 1968; fmr mem. Governing Bd, IRCICA, Org. of the Islamic Conf. Research Centre for Islamic History, Art and Culture; Prof. of History of Art and Architecture, Univ. of Damascus 1988, now Prof. Emer.; co-designer of Martyr Monument 1991, October Monument 1998; Commdr des Arts and des Lettres; First Prize in Islamic Architecture 1991, ICO Award, Jeddah; numerous other awards and medals. *Publications:* General History of Arts and Architecture 1962, L'Esthétique de l'art arabe 1979, Arabic Modern Art 1979, Damascus 1981, L'Art et l'Orientalisme 1983, En Syrie 1986, The Ancient Syria 1987, The Great Mosque of Damascus 1988, Arab Architecture 1994, Dictionnaire d'architecture 1994, Dictionnaire des termes de calligraphie, The Great Mosque of San'a 1996, Aesthetics of al Tawhidi 1997, Criticism of Art 1997, Modernism and Postmodernism 1997, Islamic Tiles 1997, Arab Calligraphy 1997, Interlocution in Islamic Art 2000, Encyclopédie de l'architecture islamique 2002, Formation of Damascus 2002, Damascus – Capital of Umayyad Dynasty 2002. *Leisure interests:* painting, sculpture. *E-mail:* info@afif-bahnassi.com. *Website:* afif-bahnassi.com.

BAHR, Egon; German journalist and government official; b. 18 March 1922, Treffurt; s. of Charles Bahr and Hedwig Bahr; m. Dorothea Grob 1945; one s. one d.; journalist 1945–, contrib., Die Neue Zeitung 1948–59, Das Tagesspiegel 1950; Chief Commentator RIAS (Rundfunk im amerikanischen Sektor Berlins) 1950–60; Dir Press and Information Office of Berlin 1960–66; promoted to rank of Amb. in diplomatic service 1967; Dir of Planning Staff, Diplomatic Service 1967–68; Ministerial Dir 1968–69; State Sec., Bundeskanzleramt and Plenipotentiary of the Fed. Govt in Berlin 1969–72; mem. Bundestag (SPD) 1972–90; Fed. Minister without Portfolio attached to Fed. Chancellor's Office 1972–74, for Overseas Devt Aid (Econ. Co-operation) 1974–76; Dir Institut für Friedensforschung und Sicherheitspolitik, Univ. of Hamburg 1984–94; mem. PEN 1974–, Ind. Comm. on Disarmament and Security 1980; Bundesverdienstkreuz 1973, Grosses Bundesverdienstkreuz, Theodor-Heuss-Preis 1976, Gustav-Heinemann-Bürgerpreis 1982, Verdienstorden (North Rhine-Westphalia) 2010; Göttingen Peace Prize 2008, Willy Brandt Prize, Norwegian-German Willy Brandt Foundation 2011, Steiger Award 2011. *Publications:* Was wird aus den Deutschen? 1982, Zum Europäischen Frieden 1988, Zu meiner Zeit 1996, Deutsche Interessen 1998, Nationalstaat: Überholt und unentbehrlich 1999. *Address:* Ollenhauerstrasse 1, 53113 Bonn, Germany.

BAHUGUNA, Vijay, BA, LLB; Indian politician and lawyer; b. 28 Feb. 1947, Allahabad, UP; s. of Hemwati Nandan Bahuguna and Kamla Bahuguna; m. Sudha Bahuguna 1969; two s. one d.; ed Univ. of Allahabad; started career as Advocate, Allahabad High Court, later Judge; Judge, Bombay (now Mumbai) High Court –1998; Vice-Chair. Planning Comm., Uttarakhand 2002–07; mem. Lok Sabha (lower house of parl.) (mem. Indian Nat. Congress) 2007–, mem. Consultative Cttee, Ministry of Power, Standing Cttee on Defence, Cttee on Public Accounts, Cttee on Health and Family Welfare, Cttee on Ethics, Cttee on Offices of Profit;

Chief Minister of Uttarakhand 2012–14 (resgnd); worked at Perm. Mission, UN Gen. Ass., New York in support of perm. seat for India in Security Council 2008. *Leisure interests:* reading, travelling, golf. *Address:* D 13, Sector 1, Defence Colony, Dehradun, 248 001, India (home). *Telephone:* (135) 2666660 (home).

BAI, Chunli, PhD; Chinese chemist and academic; *President, Chinese Academy of Sciences;* b. 26 Sept. 1953, Liaoning; s. of Bai Fuxin and Li Fengyun; m. Li Chunfang 1981; one s.; ed Peking Univ., Inst. of Chem., Chinese Acad. of Sciences; Research Asst, Changchun Inst. of Applied Chem., Chinese Acad. of Sciences (CAS) 1978, Research Assoc., Inst. of Chem. 1981–85; Visiting Research Assoc., Calif. Inst. of Tech., USA 1985–87; Assoc. Prof. and Dir Study Group on Scanning Tunnelling Microscopy (STM), Inst. of Chem., CAS 1987–89, Prof. 1989–, Deputy Dir 1992–96, Vice-Pres. CAS 1996–2004, Exec. Vice-Pres. 2004–11, Pres. 2011–, Academician 1997–; Dir Nat. Centre of Nanoscience 2004–; Visiting Prof., Inst. for Materials Research, Tohoku Univ., Japan 1991–92; Vice-Pres. China Material Research Soc. 2000–, China Asscn for Science and Tech. 2001–; Sec.-Gen. and mem. Exec. Council Chinese Chemical Soc. 1994–98, Pres. 1999–; Vice-Pres. All-China Youth Fed. 1995–2000; Pres. China Young Scientists' Asscn 1996–; mem. Editorial Advisory Bd Journal of the American Chemical Society, Angewandte Chemie, Advances in Materials; mem. 8th CPPCC Nat. Cttee 1993–98; Alt. mem. 15th CCP Cen. Cttee 1997–2002, 16th CCP Cen. Cttee 2002–07, 17th CCP Cen. Cttee 2007–12, mem. 18th CCP Cen. Cttee 2012–; Fellow, Third World Acad. of Sciences 1997–; Foreign mem. Mongolian Acad. of Sciences 2005–, NAS (USA) 2006–; Outstanding Young Scholar, Hong Kong Qiu Shi Science and Tech. Foundation 1995, Ho Leung Ho Lee Prize; numerous prizes and awards. *Publications:* 10 books and more than 250 papers in scientific journals. *Address:* Chinese Academy of Sciences, 52 San Li He Road, Beijing 100864, People's Republic of China (office). *Telephone:* (10) 68597606 (office). *Fax:* (10) 68512458 (office). *E-mail:* clbai@cashq.ac.cn (office).

BAI, Donglu, PhD; Chinese professor of medicinal chemistry; *Professor and Director, Shanghai Institute of Materia Medica, Chinese Academy of Sciences;* b. 8 Feb. 1936, Dinghai Co., Zhejiang Prov.; s. of Bai Daxi and Zhang Yunxiao; m. Ni Zhifang 1969; one d.; ed Shanghai First Medical Coll., Czechoslovak Acad. of Sciences, Prague; Prof. and Dir, Shanghai Inst. of Materia Medica, Chinese Acad. of Sciences; Science and Tech. Progress Award, Nat. Natural Science Prize of China 2000. *Publications include:* three monographs and more than 160 papers in scientific journals. *Leisure interest:* stamp collecting. *Address:* Shanghai Institute of Materia Medica, 555 Zuchongzhi Road, Zhangjiang 201203, People's Republic of China (office). *Telephone:* (21) 50805896 (office). *Fax:* (21) 50805896 (office). *E-mail:* dlbai@mail.shcnc.ac.cn (office). *Website:* www.simm.ac.cn (office).

BAI, Enpei; Chinese politician; b. Sept. 1946, Qingjian Co., Shaanxi Prov.; ed Northwest Tech. Univ. 1965; sent to do manual labour (Ind. Div. Farm, Shaanxi Prov. Mil. Command) 1970–73; joined CCP 1973; Deputy Dir and Dir Yan'an Diesel Engine Plant, Shaanxi Prov. 1974–83, Deputy Sec. CCP Party Cttee 1974–83; Vice-Sec. CCP Yan'an Prefectural Cttee 1983–90; Sec. CCP Yan'an Prefectural Cttee 1985; Alt. mem. 13th CCP Cen. Cttee 1987–92, 14th CCP Cen. Cttee 1992–97, mem. 15th CCP Cen. Cttee 1997–2002, mem. 16th CCP Cen. Cttee 2002–07, mem. 17th CCP Cen. Cttee 2007–12; Head CCP Inner Mongolia Autonomous Regional Cttee, Org. Dept 1990–93, mem. CCP Inner Mongolia Autonomous Regional Cttee Standing Committee 1990–93, Deputy Sec. Inner Mongolia Autonomous Regional Cttee 1993–97; Vice-Sec. CCP Qinghai Prov. Cttee 1997–99, Sec. 1999–2001; Acting Gov. Qinghai Prov. 1997–1998, Gov. 1998–99; Chair. Qinghai Prov. People's Congress 2000–01; Sec. CCP Yunnan Prov. Cttee 2001–11, mem. Standing Cttee 2001–. *Address:* c/o Chinese Communist Party Yunnan Provincial Committee, Kunming, Yunnan Province, People's Republic of China.

BAI, Keming; Chinese journalist and party official; b. Oct. 1943, Jingbian, Shaanxi Prov.; s. of Bai Jian; ed Harbin Mil. Eng Inst.; joined CCP 1975; worker, Metallurgy and Geology Bureau, Harbin City, Heilongjiang Prov. 1968–70; Teacher Harbin Shipbuilding Inst. 1970–73, National Defence Industry Cttee, Shaanxi Prov. 1973–78; Deputy Div. Chief, Gen. Office, Ministry of Educ. 1978–86, Vice Div. Chief then Deputy Dir 1986–89; Head Educ. Science, Culture and Public Health Group, Research Office of the State Council 1989–93; Sec.-Gen. Propaganda Dept of CCP Cen. Cttee 1993, Deputy Head 1993–2000; Del. 15th CCP Nat. Congress 1997–2002; Deputy Dir CCP Cen. Cttee Gen. Office 2000–01; Pres. CCP Cen. Cttee People's Daily (newspaper) 2000–01; Sec. CCP Hainan Prov. Cttee and Chair. Hainan People's Congress 2001–02; Sec. CCP Prov. Cttee, Hebei Prov. 2002–07; mem. 16th CCP Cen. Cttee 2002–07; Vice-Chair. China Asscn for Educ., Science, Culture and Public Health, Nat. People's Congress 2007–08, Chair. 2008–13. *Address:* National People's Congress, Beijing, People's Republic of China (office). *Website:* npc.people.com.cn (office).

BAI, Lichen; Chinese politician; b. 1941, Lingyuan, Liaoning Prov.; ed Shenyang Agricultural Coll.; technician, Yingkou Agricultural Coll., Agricultural Machinery Inst., Yingkou, Liaoning Prov. 1964–68; joined CCP 1971; clerk, CCP City Cttee Org. Dept, Yingkou 1972–80, Deputy Section Chief Personnel Supervision Bureau 1972–80, Deputy Sec. then Sec. CCP City Cttee, Yingkou 1980–83, Mayor of Yingkou 1983–84; Sec. CCP City Cttee, Panjin City, Liaoning Prov. 1984–85; mem. Standing Cttee CCP Liaoning Prov. Cttee 1985–87; Asst to Gov. Liaoning Prov. 1984–85, Vice-Gov. 1985–86; mem. 13th Cen. Cttee CCP 1987–92, 14th Cen. Cttee CCP 1992–97, 15th Cen. Cttee 1997–2002, 16th Cen. Cttee 2002–07, 17th Cen. Cttee 2007–; Vice-Chair., Acting Chair. and Chair. Ningxia Hui Autonomous Regional People's Govt 1987–97; Deputy Sec. CCP Regional Cttee 1988–97; Sec. CCP Leading Party Group, All-China Fed. of Supply and Marketing Co-operatives 1997–99, Pres. Second Council 1999–2002; Vice-Chair. 9th Nat. Cttee of CPPCC 1998–2003, 10th Nat. Cttee of CPPCC 2003–08, 11th Nat. Cttee of CPPCC 2008–2013. *Address:* c/o National Committee of the Chinese People's Political Consultative Conference, 23 Taiping Qiao Street, Beijing, People's Republic of China.

BAI, Shuxian; Chinese ballerina; *Deputy Chairperson, China Dramatists' Association;* b. 1939; ed Beijing Coll. of Dancing; Prin. Dancer, Cen. Ballet Co. 1958, Dir 1984–90; mem. 5th Nat. Cttee CPPCC 1978–82, 6th Nat. Cttee 1983–87, 7th Nat. Cttee 1988–92, 8th Nat. Cttee 1993–97; Vice-Dir Beijing Ballet 1980–; Performing Artist, Longjiang Opera; Perm. mem. China Dancers' Asscn, Chair.

1992–; Vice-Chair. China Fed. of Literary and Art Circles 1996–; Deputy Chair. China Dramatists' Asscn; First Grade Dancer of the Nation, Chinese Opera Plum Blossom Award, Shanghai Theatrical Festival White Magnolia Prize. *Films:* Absurd Baoyu (Grand Wenhua Prize), The Legend of Hua Mulan (Grand Wenhua Prize, Huabiao Prize, Expert's Golden Rooster Prize) 1994, Saga of Mulan 2004. *Performances include:* Swan Lake, Giselle, The Fountain of Bakhchisarai, The Emerald, Sylvia, Red Women Army, Song of Yimeng, Song of Jiaoyang, The Trilogy, Shuangsuo Mountain. *Address:* Longjiang Opera, No 114, Ashihe Street, Nangong, 150001 Harbin, Heilongjiang Province, People's Republic of China.

BAIBOLOV, Lt-Gen. Kubatbek; Kyrgyzstani politician; b. 2 Jan. 1952; m.; two s. six d.; fmr Col, KGB and Head of Intelligence Dept 1991–92; Deputy, Parl. 1995–2007, Speaker 2004–05; Chair. constituent asse. responsible for drafting new Kyrgyz constitution 2006; lived in self-exile in USA 2008–10; First Deputy Chair. Kyrgyz State Cttee for Nat. Security –2010; apptd Commdt, Jalal-Abad Oblast after ethnic clashes 2010; Minister of Internal Affairs June–Sept. 2010; Prosecutor-Gen. 2010–11; Founder and Co-Chair. Union of Democratic Forces 2005; Leader, Kyrgyz Parliamentarians Against Corruption 2005; joined For Reforms! (opposition movt) 2006. *Address:* c/o Office of the Prosecutor-General, 720040 Bishkek, Kyrgyzstan (office).

BAIGUTTIYEV, Zhenishbek S.; Kyrgyzstani politician; b. 9 May 1966, Bishkek; ed Kyrgyz State Univ.; served in Soviet Army Service 1985–87; Chair. Tolubay Bank 1996; Minister of Econ. Regulation 2009. *Address:* c/o Ministry of Economic Regulation, 720003 Bishkek, Kyrgyzstan (office).

BAILEY, David, CBE, FRPS, FSIAD, FCSD; British photographer and film director; b. 2 Jan. 1938, London, England; s. of Herbert William Bailey and Gladys Agnes Bailey; m. 1st Rosemary Bramble 1960; m. 2nd Catherine Deneuve 1965 (divorced 1972); m. 3rd Marie Helvin 1975 (divorced 1985); m. 4th Catherine Dyer 1986; two s. one d.; self-taught; photographer for Vogue, UK, USA, France, Italy and advertising photography 1959–; Dir Commercials 1966–, TV documentaries 1968–; photographer for Harpers and Queen 1999; directed and produced TV film Who Dealt? 1993; documentary: Models Close Up 1998; Dir feature film The Intruder 1999; Dr hc (Bradford) 2001; V&A Award for Outstanding Achievement in Fashion, British Fashion Awards 2004. *Publications:* Box of Pinups 1964, Goodbye Baby and Amen 1969, Warhol 1974, Beady Minces 1974, Mixed Moments 1976, Trouble and Strife 1980, NW1 1982, Black and White Memories 1983, Nudes 1981–84 1984, Imagine 1985, The Naked Eye: Great Photographs of the Nude (with Martin Harrison) 1988, If We Shadows 1992, The Lady is a Tramp 1995, Rock & Roll Heroes 1997, Archive One 1999, Chasing Rainbows 2001, Bailey's Democracy 2005, Pictures that Mark Can Do 2007, Fotographie Portfolio Stern 2007, Is That So Kid 2008, 8 Minutes 2009, EYE 2009, Flowers, Skulls and Contacts 2010, British Heroes in Afghanistan 2010, Delhi Dilemma 2012. *Leisure interests:* photography, aviculture, travel, painting. *E-mail:* studio@camera-eye.co .uk (office).

BAILEY, Donovan; Canadian marketing consultant and fmr athlete; b. 16 Dec. 1967, Manchester, Jamaica; s. of George Donovan and Icilda Donovan; one d. by Michelle Mullin; ed Sheridan Coll.; grew up in Jamaica and emigrated to Canada 1981; mem. Canada's winning 4×100m team, Commonwealth Games 1994, Olympic Games 1996; world indoor record-holder for 50m 1996; Canadian 100m record-holder 1995, 1996; world, Commonwealth and Olympic 100m record-holder 1996; retd from athletics 2001; Pres. and CEO DBX Sport Management; f. Donovan Bailey Fund to assist Canadian amateur athletes; Founder and Chair. Tranz4M 2003; Amb. of Goodwill for Canadian Fed. Govt; mem. Bd of Dirs Big Brothers and Sisters of Canada, ParticipAction Canada, Circle of Champions, Merge Inc.; Sprinter of the Decade, Track and Field News 1998, inducted into Canada's Sports Hall of Fame 2004. *Website:* www.donovanbailey.com.

BAILEY, Jerry; American professional jockey (retd) and television analyst; b. 29 Aug. 1957, Dallas; s. of James Bailey; m. Suzee; one s.; thoroughbred racing jockey 1974–2006, began career with win at Sunland Park, New Mexico 1974 (Fetch); moved to New York 1982; winner Gulfstream Park Handicap 1990, 1995 (Cigar), 1996, 1997, 1998; 14 Breeders' Cup titles, including Breeders' Cup Classic 1991 (Black Tie Affair), 1993 (Arcangues), 1994 (Concern), (Cigar) 1995, (Saint Liam) 2005, Breeders' Cup Mile (Six Perfections) 2003; winner Belmont 1991 (Hansel); winner Preakness Stakes 1991 (Hansel), 2000 (Red Bullet); winner Hollywood Gold Cup Handicap 1992, 1995 (Cigar), 1998, 1999; winner Woodward Stakes 1992, 1995 (Cigar), 1996 (Cigar), 1998; winner Kentucky Derby 1993 (Sea Hero), 1996 (Grindstone); winner Travers Stakes 1993 (Sea Hero); winner Oaklawn Park Handicap, Pimlico Special, Jockey Club Gold Cup, Don Handicap 1995 (Cigar); winner Massachussets Handicap 1995 (Cigar), 1996 (Cigar), 1998 (Skip Away); winner Dubai World Cup 1996 (Cigar), 1997 (Singspiel), 2001 (Captain Steve); Saratoga riding title 1994, 1995, 1996, 1997, 2000; 16 straight victories on Cigar 1995–96; seven winners on one card, Florida Derby Day 1995; North America's leading money-winning rider 1995–1997 and 2001, 2002; first rider to win more than $20 million in one season (2001); retd 2006 with 5,892 career wins; currently TV analyst for ABC and ESPN; Nat. Pres. Jockeys' Guild 1996–96; George Woolf Memorial Jockey Award 1992, Mike Venezia Award (New York Racing Assn) 1993, Eclipse Award for Outstanding Jockey 1995, 1996, 1997, 2000, 2001, 2002, 2003, elected to racing's Hall of Fame 1995, Broward Co. Sports Hall of Fame 2006. *Publication:* Against the Odds: Riding for My Life 2005. *E-mail:* info@jerrybailey .com.

BAILEY, Michael (Mike) J.; British business executive; *Chairman and CEO, TrustHouse Services Group;* s. of Sidney William Bailey and Joyce Mary Bailey; m. Michelle Bailey; two d.; ed Southend Culinary School, Westminster Coll., London; Food Service Man., Gardner Merchant 1961, later becoming Man. Dir, Pres., US subsidiary 1985–91; Exec. Vice-Pres. Nutrition Man. Services 1991–93; joined Compass Group PLC 1993, Group Devt Dir 1993–94, CEO N American Div. 1994–99, Group CEO 1999–2006; Co-founder TrustHouse Services Group 2008, currently Chair. and CEO–; Fellow, Hotel and Catering Int. Man. Assn. *Address:* TrustHouse Services Group, 2201 Water Ridge Parkway, Suite 320, Charlotte, NC 28217, USA (office). *Telephone:* (704) 424-1071 (office). *Fax:* (704) 424-1074 (office). *Website:* www.trusthouseservices.com (office).

BAILEY, Norman A., PhD; American economist, academic and government official; *President, Institute for Global Economic Growth;* ed Oberlin Coll. and

Columbia Univ.; fmr economist, Mobil Oil Co.; f. Overseas Equity Inc. (later Bailey, Tondu, Warwick & Co., Inc.), Pres. 1980–84; fmr Prof. of Econs, CUNY; Prof., Center for Strategic and Int. Studies 1980–81; Dir Cttee for Monetary Research and Educ. 1980–81; Sr Dir of Econ. Affairs, Nat. Security Council 1981–83; Special Asst to Pres. Ronald Reagan 1983–89; Pres. Norman A. Bailey Inc. 1984–; Sr Fellow, Potomac Foundation, Inc. 2003–06; Adjunct Prof., Inst. of World Politics, Washington, DC 2003–06, currently Consultant Economist; Mission Man. for Cuba and Venezuela, Office of the Dir of Nat. Intelligence 2006–07; President, Institute for Global Economic Growth; Kt Royal Order of Our Lady of the Conception of Vila Vicosa (Portugal); Nat. Security Award, Cold War Commemorative Medal, Medal of the Pan American Soc. *Publications:* The Strategic Plan that Won the Cold War 1999; numerous articles in professional journals. *Address:* Institute for Global Economic Growth, 2944 Hunter Mill Road, Suite 204, Oakton, VA 22124, USA (office). *Telephone:* (703) 553-3700 (office). *Website:* www.igeg.org (office).

BAILEY, Paul, FRSL; British writer; b. (Peter Harry Bailey), 16 Feb. 1937; s. of Arthur Oswald Bailey and Helen Maud Burgess; ed Sir Walter St John's School, London; actor 1956–64, appearing in The Sport of My Mad Mother 1958 and Epitaph for George Dillon 1958; Literary Fellow at Univs of Newcastle and Durham 1972–74; Bicentennial Fellowship 1976; Visiting Lecturer in English Literature, North Dakota State Univ. 1977–79; Somerset Maugham Award 1968, E.M. Forster Award 1978, George Orwell Memorial Prize 1978. *Publications:* At the Jerusalem (Author's Club First Novel Award, Somerset Maugham Award 1968) 1967, Trespasses 1970, A Distant Likeness 1973, Peter Smart's Confessions 1977, Old Soldiers 1980, An English Madam 1982, Gabriel's Lament 1986, An Immaculate Mistake (autobiography) 1990, Hearth and Home 1990, Sugar Cane 1993, The Oxford Book of London (ed.) 1995, First Love (ed.) 1997, Kitty and Virgil 1998, The Stately Homo: A Celebration of the Life of Quentin Crisp (ed.) 2000, Three Queer Lives: An Alternative Biography of Naomi Jacob, Fred Barnes and Arthur Marshall 2001, Uncle Rudolf (novel) 2002, A Dog's Life 2003, Chapman's Odyssey 2011; numerous newspaper articles. *Leisure interests:* visiting churches, opera, watching tennis. *Address:* Rogers, Coleridge and White Ltd., 20 Powis Mews, London W11 1JN, England (office); 2/79 Davisville Road, London, W12 9SH, England (home). *Telephone:* (20) 7221-3717 (office); (20) 8248-2127 (home). *Fax:* (20) 7229-9084 (office). *E-mail:* info@rcwlitagency.com (office). *Website:* www .rcwlitagency.com (office).

BAILEY, Sly; British publishing and media executive; b. (Sylvia Grice), 24 Jan. 1962, London; d. of Thomas Lewis and Sylvia Grice (née Bantick); m. Peter Bailey 1998; ed St Saviours and St Olaves Grammar School for Girls; telephone sales exec. at The Guardian 1984–87; Advertisement Sales Man., The Independent 1987–89; moved to IPC Magazines 1989, Advertising Sales Exec. 1994, mem. Bd of Dirs 1994–2003, Man. Dir TX 1997, CEO 1999–2003; mem. Bd of Dirs and CEO Trinity Mirror PLC 2003–12; Dir (non-exec.) Littlewoods PLC April–Sept. 2002, EMI 2004– (Sr Ind. Dir 2007–); mem. Ind. Panel on BBC Charter Review 2004; Dir The Press Assocn; Pres. NewstrAid Benevolent Soc.; Dr hc (Univ. of East London) 2005; Periodical Publrs Asscn Marcus Morris Award for Outstanding Contrib. to Publishing Industry 2002, named as one of 50 Most Powerful Women in Britain by Management Today 2002, named as one of Britain's Most Influential Women by Daily Mail 2003, ranked amongst top 20 of MediaGuardian's 100 Most Influential Figures in Media 2003, ranked by Fortune magazine amongst 50 Most Powerful Women in Business outside the US (23rd) 2003, (23rd) 2004, (33rd) 2005, (45th) 2006, ranked by the Financial Times amongst Top 25 Businesswomen in Europe (12th) 2005, (18th) 2006, (25th) 2007. *Leisure interest:* family. *Address:* c/o Trinity Mirror PLC, 1 Canada Square, Canary Wharf, London, E14 5AP, England.

BAILIE, Robert Ernest (Roy), OBE; British business executive; *Chairman, The Baird Group;* b. 2 June 1943; s. of Robert Bailie and Rosetta Bailie; ed Harvard Business School, USA; joined W&G Baird (later The Baird Group) 1965, Man. Dir 1972, Dir 1977–, Chair. 1982–; Chair. CBI, NI 1992–94, NI Tourist Bd 1996–2002, 105.8 FM 2005–; Vice-Pres. British Printing Industries Fed. 1997–99, Pres. 1999–2001; Dir Graphic Plates Ltd 1977–, MSO Ltd 1984–; Dir (non-exec.) Blackstaff Press Ltd 1995–, UTV 1997–, Court, Bank of England 1998–2003, Court, Bank of Ireland 1999–2005, Corporate Document Services Ltd 2000–; Chair. Northern Ireland Opera 2010–, National Trust (NI) 2010–. *Leisure interests:* golf, sailing, walking. *Address:* 60 Ballymena Road, Doagh, Ballyclare, Co. Antrim, BT39 0QR, Northern Ireland (home). *Telephone:* (28) 9446-6107 (office); (28) 9334-0383 (home). *Fax:* (28) 9446-6266 (office). *E-mail:* roy.bailie@ thebairdgroup.co.uk (office). *Website:* www.thebairdgroup.co.uk (office).

BAILLIE, A. Charles, Jr, OC, BA, MBA, DJur; Canadian fmr banker; b. 20 Dec. 1939, Orillia, Ont.; s. of Charles Baillie and Jean G. Baillie; m. Marilyn J. Michener 1965; three s. one d.; ed Trinity Coll., Univ. of Toronto, Harvard Business School, USA, Queen's Univ.; joined The Toronto Dominion Bank 1964, Vice-Pres. and Gen. Man., USA Div. 1979, Sr Vice-Pres. 1981, Exec. Vice-Pres., Corp. and Investment Banking Group 1984, Vice-Chair. 1992, Pres. The Toronto Dominion Bank 1995, CEO 1997–2002, Chair. 1998–2003 (retd); Chancellor, Queen's Univ. 2002–08, Chancellor Emer. 2008–; fmr Pres. Art Gallery of Ont.; mem. Bd of Dirs Telus Corpn 2003–, Canadian Nat. Railway Co. 2003–, Dana Corpn, Ballard Power Systems, George Weston Ltd; Chair. Campaign 2000, United Way of Greater Toronto; Chair. Capital Campaign, Shaw Festival; Campaign Co-Chair. Nature Conservancy; Campaign Hon. Chair. Sir Sam Steele Art Gallery; Vice-Chair. Exec. Cttee Business Council on Nat. Issues; mem. Corpn and Hon. Cabinet, Trinity Coll.; Fellow, Inst. of Canadian Bankers 1967; Hon. LLD (Queen's Univ.) 2000. *Leisure interests:* birdwatching, travelling, collecting antiquarian books.

BAILLY, Jean-Paul, MSc; French engineer and business executive; b. 29 Nov. 1946, Hénin-Beaumont (Pas-de-Calais); s. of Jean Bailly and Hélène Bailly (née Viénot); m. Michèle Moulard 1972; two s.; ed Lycées d'Oujda, Morocco, Louis-le-Grand and Ecole polytechnique, Paris, Massachusetts Inst. of Tech., USA; engineer, Regie Autonome des Transports Parisiens (RATP) 1970, Chief Consultant SOFRETU for Mexico City Metro 1978–81, Sr Engineer 1981–88, Personnel Dir 1989, Jt Dir-Gen. 1990–94, Pres. and Dir-Gen. 1994–97; Pres. Int. Union of Public Transport (UITP) 1997–2001; Chair., Pres. and CEO La Poste 2002–13, Chair. Supervisory Bd La Banque Postale 2006–13; Pres. French Section, Centre européen des entreprises à participation publique (CEEP) 1998–2001, Int. Post Corpn 2006–; mem. Supervisory Bd La Banque Postale Asset Management,

Sogeposte; mem. Bd of Dirs CNP Assurances SA 2007–, GDF Suez 2008–12, Accor SA 2009–, Edenred 2010–, Gaz de France SA, SF2 and Systar SA, Sofipost, Geopost, Xelian, SF 12, Efipost, Poste Immo, Sopassure, The Jean-Jacques Laffont-Toulouse School of Econs Foundation, Fondation du Collège de France, Groupement des Commerçants du Grand Var intercompany partnership; mem. Conseil Economique, Social et Environnemental (Econ., Social and Environmental Advisory Cttee) 1995–; Officier, Légion d'honneur, Ordre nat. du Mérite; Pitney Bowes Industry Leadership Award, World Mail Awards, London 2007. *Leisure interest:* tennis. *Address:* c/o La Poste, 44 boulevard de Vaugirard, 75757 Paris Cedex 15, France. *E-mail:* jean-paul.bailly@laposte.fr.

BAILY, Martin Neil, PhD; American economist and fmr government official; *Senior Fellow, Brookings Institution;* b. 13 Jan. 1945, Exeter, England; s. of the late Theodore Baily and Joyce Baily; m. Vickie Lyn Baily (née Hyde) 1986; two s. two d.; ed King Edward's School, Birmingham, Christ's Coll., Cambridge, Massachusetts Inst. of Tech.; teaching positions at MIT and Yale Univ. 1972–79; Sr Fellow, Brookings Inst. 1979–94, 1996–99; Prof. of Econs, Univ. of Maryland 1989–94; mem. Council of Econ. Advisers 1994–96 during Clinton administration, Chair. and mem. of the Cabinet 1999–2001; Prin. McKinsey and Co. 1996–99, Sr Advisor 2002–; Sr Fellow, Peterson Inst., Washington, DC 2001–07; Sr Fellow, Brookings Inst., Washington, DC 2007–, also Bernard L. Schwartz Chair in Econ. Policy Devt and Dir Business and Public Policy Initiative; Sr Dir Albright Stonebridge Group; Co-Chair. Bipartisan Policy Center Financial Reform Initiative; mem. Bd of Dirs The Phoenix Companies; mem. Squam Lake Group (financial economists); Prizewinner in Econs, Christ's Coll., Cambridge 1967. *Publications:* Macroeconomics, Financial Markets and the International Sector 1994, Efficiency in Manufacturing (Brookings Papers) 1995, Economic Report of the President: 2000, Transforming the European Economy (co-author) 2004. *Leisure interests:* squash, music, travel. *Address:* Brookings Institution, 1775 Massachusetts Avenue, NW, Washington, DC 20036, USA (office). *Website:* www.brookings.edu (office).

BAILYN, Bernard, PhD; American historian, author and academic; *Professor Emeritus of History, Harvard University;* b. 10 Sept. 1922, Hartford, Conn.; s. of Charles Manuel Bailyn and Esther Schloss; m. Lotte Lazarsfeld 1952; two s.; ed Williams Coll. and Harvard Univ.; mem. Faculty, Harvard Univ. 1953–, Prof. of History 1961–66, Winthrop Prof. of History 1966–81, Adams Univ. Prof. 1981–93, Prof. Emer. 1993–, James Duncan Phillips Prof. in Early American History 1991–93, Prof. Emer. 1993–; Dir Charles Warren Center for Studies in American History 1983–94; Pitt Prof. of American Hist., Cambridge Univ. 1986–87; Dir Int. Seminar on History of Atlantic World 1995–; Ed.-in-Chief John Harvard Library 1962–70; Co-Ed. Perspectives in American History (journal) 1967–77, 1984–86; mem. American Historical Assen (Pres. 1981), American Acad. of Arts and Sciences, Nat. Acad. of Educ., American Philosophical Soc.; Foreign mem. Russian Acad. of Sciences, Academia Europaea, Mexican Acad. of History and Geography; Sr Fellow, Soc. of Fellows; Hon. Fellow Christ's Coll., Cambridge Univ.; Corresp. Fellow, British Acad. 1989, Royal Historial Soc.; Trustee, Inst. of Advanced Study, Princeton 1989–94; Trevelyan Lecturer, Cambridge Univ. 1971; Jefferson Lecturer, Nat. Endowment for the Humanities 1998; 15 hon. degrees; Robert H. Lord Award, Emmanuel Coll. 1967, Pulitzer Prize for History 1968, 1987, Thomas Jefferson Medal 1993, Henry Allen Moe Prize, American Philosophical Soc. 1994, Foreign Policy Assen Medal 1998; Catton Prize, Soc. American Historians 2000, Nat. Humanities Medal 2010, Samuel Eliot Morison Award 2011. *Publications include:* The New England Merchants in the 17th Century 1955, Massachusetts Shipping 1697–1714: A Statistical Study (jtly) 1959, Education in the Forming of American Society 1960, Pamphlets of the American Revolution 1750–1776, Vol. I (ed.) (Faculty Prize, Harvard Univ. Press) 1965, The Apologia of Robert Keayne (ed.) 1965, The Ideological Origins of the American Revolution (Pulitzer and Bancroft Prizes 1968) 1967, The Origins of American Politics 1968, The Intellectual Migration 1930–1960 (co-ed.) 1969, Law in American History (co-ed.) 1972, The Ordeal of Thomas Hutchinson (Nat. Book Award 1975) 1974, The Great Republic (co-author) 1977, The Press and the American Revolution (co-ed.) 1980, The Peopling of British North America 1986, Voyagers to the West (Pulitzer Prize 1986) 1986, Faces of Revolution 1990, Strangers Within the Realm (co-ed.) 1991, The Debate on the Constitution (two vols, ed.) 1993, On the Teaching and Writing of History 1994, To Begin the World Anew: The Genius and Ambiguities of the American Founders 2003, Atlantic History 2005, The Barbarous Years 2012. *Address:* Department of History, Harvard University, Cambridge, MA 02138 (office); 170 Clifton Street, Belmont, MA 02478-2604, USA (home). *Website:* fas -www.harvard.edu/~atlantic/bailyn.html (home).

BAIN, Neville Clifford, MCom, LLD, FCA, CMA, FCIS, FIOD; British company director and consultant; *Chairman, Institute of Directors;* b. 14 July 1940, Dunedin, NZ; s. of Charles Alexander Bain and Gertrude Mae Bain (née Howe); m. Anne Patricia Bain (née Kemp); one s. one d. one step-d.; ed King's High School, Dunedin, Otago Univ., Dunedin, NZ; trainee insp. Inland Revenue, NZ 1957–59; Cost Accountant then Finance Dir Cadbury Schweppes, NZ 1960–75, Commercial Dir and Group Finance Dir Cadbury Schweppes, SA 1975–80, Group Strategy Dir, apptd to Main Bd Cadbury Schweppes PLC 1980–83, Man. Dir Cadbury UK 1983–86, Worldwide Man. Dir Group Confectionery 1986–89, Deputy CEO and Finance Dir Cadbury Schweppes PLC 1989–90, Chief Exec. Coats Viyella PLC 1990–97; Chair. Hogg Robinson PLC 1997–2006, SHL 1998– (Dir 1997–), The Post Office 1998–2001; Chair. Gartmore Split Capital Opportunities Trust 1999–2001; Chair. of Trustees, Hogg Robinson Group Pension Fund 2007–; Chair. Scottish and Newcastle Pension Plan Ltd 2007–; currently Chair. Inst. of Dirs, London; Deputy Chair. McDowell Alcobevs Ltd (India) 2003–10; Dir and Chair. Audit Cttee Biocon Ltd (India) 2000–; Dir United Breweries Ltd (India) 2003–05; Dir (non-exec.) Safeway PLC 1993–2000, Scottish & Newcastle PLC 1997–, Gartmore Scotland Investment Trust PLC 1991–2001; mem. Council for Excellence in Man. and Leadership; Trustee, Nat. Centre for Social Research 2002–09. *Publications:* Successful Management 1995, Winning Ways through Corporate Governance (with D. Band) 1996, The People Advantage (with Bill Mabey) 1999, The Effective Director 2007, The Effective Board (with Roger Barker) 2010. *Leisure interests:* sport, walking, music. *Address:* High Trees, Cavendish Road, St. Georges Hill, Weybridge, Surrey, KT13 0JX (home); Institute of Directors, 116 Pall Mall, London, SW1Y 5ED, England (office). *Telephone:* (1932) 856451 (home); (20) 7766-8866 (office). *Fax:* (1932) 830899 (home); (20) 7766-8833 (office). *E-mail:*

bainneville@yahoo.co.uk (home); enquiries@iod.com (office). *Website:* www.iod.com (office).

BAINDURASHVILI, Kakha, MA; Georgian politician; *Chairman of the Supervisory Board, Georgian Post;* b. 26 Sept. 1978, Tbilisi; ed Tbilisi State Univ., Williams Coll., Williamstown, USA; ed., Prime-News news agency, Tbilisi 1999–2000; consultant, UNDP 2002–04; adviser to the Prime Minister 2004–05; Head of Investment Monitoring Unit, Ministry of Finance 2000–02, Chair. Tax Dept 2006–07, First Deputy Minister of Finance 2007–09, Minister of Finance 2009–11; Chair. Supervisory Bd state-owned Georgian Post 2011–; Gov. for Georgia and Vice-Chair. Bd of Govs Asian Devt Bank. *Address:* Office of the Chairman of the Supervisory Board, Georgian Post, c/o #1 Post Office, 0101 Tbilisi, 3 Khudadov Street, Georgia (office). *Telephone:* (32) 296-60-07 (office). *E-mail:* k.baindurashvili@georgianpost.ge (office). *Website:* www.georgianpost.ge (office).

BAINIMARAMA, Cdre (retd) Josaia Voreqe, (Frank Bainimarama), OStJ; Fijian fmr military officer; *Prime Minister and Minister for Finance;* b. 27 April 1954, Kiuva, Tailevu Province; m. Maria Makitalena; six c.; ed Maris Brothers High School, numerous mil. courses and insts; enlisted in Fiji Navy as Ordinary Seaman 1975, commissioned as Ensign 1977, Navigation Officer Aug. 1978, Sub-Lt Nov. 1978, Exec. Officer HMFS Kiro 1979, Commdr HMFS Kikau 1982–84, HMFS Kula 1984–86, Lt Commdr 1986, served with Multinational Force and Observers in Sinai 1986–87, CO and Commdr Fiji Navy 1988, promoted to Capt. 1994, Chief of Staff 1997–99, Cdre and Commdr of Armed Forces 1999–14; Head, Interim Mil. Govt of Fiji May–July 2000; Acting Pres. of Fiji (after mil. overthrow of govt of Prime Minister Laisenia Qarase) Dec. 2006–07, Prime Minister Jan. 2007–, also Minister of Home Affairs, Immigration and Information 2007–, Minister of Finance 2008–; fmr Chair. Fiji Rugby Union; Meritorious Service Decoration, Peacekeeping Medal, General Service Medal, Fiji Republic Medal, 25 Anniversary Medal. *Address:* Office of the Prime Minister, PO Box 2353, New Government Buildings, Suva, Fiji (office). *Telephone:* 3211201 (office). *Fax:* 3306034 (office). *E-mail:* pmsoffice@connect.com.fi (office). *Website:* www.fiji.gov.fj (office).

BAINWOL, Mitch, BA, MBA; American business executive; *President and CEO, Alliance of Automobile Manufacturers;* b. 1959; m. Susan Bainwol; three c.; ed Georgetown Univ., Rice Univ.; fmr Budget Analyst, Pres. Ronald Reagan's Office of Management and Budget, Chief of Staff Senator Connie Mack (R-FL); Leadership Staff Dir Senate 1993–97; Chief of Staff Republican Nat. Cttee 1998; lobbyist Clark & Weinstock 1999; Leader The Bainwol Group 2002–; Chair. and CEO Recording Industry Assen of America (RIAA) 2003–11; Pres. and CEO Alliance of Automobile Manufacturers 2011–; mem. Bd of Bd of Dirs Nat. Fatherhood Initiative, Bryce Harlow Foundation. *Address:* Alliance of Automobile Manufacturers, 1401 Eye Street, NW, Suite 900, Washington, DC 20005, USA (office). *Telephone:* (202) 326-5500 (office). *Website:* www.autoalliance.org (office).

BAIR, Sheila Colleen, BA, JD; American academic, author and fmr banking official; *Senior Advisor, Pew Charitable Trusts;* b. 3 April 1954, Wichita, Kan.; d. of Albert Bair and Clara Bair (née Brenneman); m. Scott P. Cooper; one s. one d.; ed Univ. of Kansas, Univ. of Kansas School of Law; called to the Bar, Kan. 1979; Teaching Fellow, Univ. of Arkansas School of Law 1978–79; Advisor, Kan. State Dept of Health 1979–81; Research Dir, Deputy Counsel and Counsel to Senate Majority Leader Robert Dole 1981–88; Of Counsel, Kutak, Rock & Campbell (law firm) 1986–87; Legis. Counsel, New York Stock Exchange, Washington, DC 1988–91, Sr Vice-Pres. for Govt Relations 1995–2000; Commr US Commodity Futures Trading Comm. 1991–95, Acting Chair. 1993; Asst Sec. for Financial Insts, US Dept of the Treasury 2001–02; Dean's Prof. of Financial Regulatory Policy, Isenberg School of Man., Univ. of Massachusetts-Amherst 2002–06; Chair. Fed. Deposit Insurance Corpn 2006–11; Sr Advisor, Pew Charitable Trusts 2011–; mem. Insurance Marketplace Standards Assen, Women in Housing and Finance, Center for Responsible Lending, NASD Ahead-of-the-Curve Advisory Cttee, Mass Savings Makes Cents, ABA, Exchequer Club, Soc. of Children's Book Writers and Illustrators; The Treasury Medal 2002, Distinguished Achievement Award, Assen of Educ. Publrs 2005, Personal Service Feature of the Year, Author of the Month Award, Highlights Magazine for Children 2002, 2003, 2004, ranked by Forbes magazine amongst The World's 100 Most Powerful Women (second) 2008, (second) 2009, (15th) 2010, chosen by Time magazine amongst the 100 Most Influential People in the World 2009. *Publications:* Rock, Brock, and the Savings Shock 2006, Isabel's Car Wash 2008. *Address:* Pew Charitable Trusts, 901 E Street, NW, Washington, DC 20004-2008, USA (office). *Telephone:* (202) 552-2000 (office). *Fax:* (202) 552-2299 (office). *E-mail:* info@pewtrusts.org (office). *Website:* www .pewtrusts.org (office).

BAIRD, Hon. John Russell (Rusty), PC, BA; Canadian politician; *Minister of Foreign Affairs;* b. 26 May 1969, Ottawa, Ont.; ed Queen's Univ., Kingston, Ont.; Pres. youth wing of Ont. Progressive Conservative Party late 1980s; worked on political staff of Perrin Beatty, Fed. Minister of Nat. Defence, and through subsequent cabinet shifts early 1990s; worked as a lobbyist in Ottawa 1993–95; MPP (Conservative Party of Canada) for Nepean, Legis. Ass. of Ont. 1995–99, for Nepean—Carleton 1999–2005, Parl. Asst to Minister of Labour 1995–97, Parl. Asst to Chair. Man. Bd of Cabinet April–Nov. 1997, Parl. Asst to Minister of Finance Nov. 1997–99, Minister of Community and Social Services and Minister responsible for Francophone Affairs 1999–2002, Minister responsible for Children 2001–02, Chief Govt Whip and Assoc. Minister for Francophone Affairs April–Aug. 2002, Minister for Energy Aug. 2002–03, Leader of Govt in Ont. Legislature 2003, Official Opposition Critic for Finance, Culture, Francophone Affairs, Intergovernmental Affairs and Health 2003–05; Co-Chair. Ont. Conservative Party for fed. elections 2004; left prov. politics to campaign for Fed. House of Commons 2005; MP for Ottawa West-Nepean 2006–, Leader of the Govt in House of Commons 2010–11; Pres. Treasury Bd 2006–07, also held ministerial responsibilities for Harbourfront Centre and Toronto Waterfront Revitalization Corpn; Minister of the Environment 2007–08, of Transport, Infrastructure and Communities 2008–10, of the Environment 2010–11, of Foreign Affairs 2011–; mem. Royal Canadian Legion (Bell's Corners Br.); Life mem. Assen for Community Living; Hon. mem. Nepean Kiwanis. *Address:* Foreign Affairs and International Trade Canada, Lester B. Pearson Bldg, 125 Sussex Drive, Ottawa, ON K1A 0G2, Canada (office). *Telephone:* (613) 944-4000 (office). *Fax:* (613) 996-9709 (office). *E-mail:* enqserv@international.gc.ca (office); bairdj@parl.gc.ca (office). *Website:* www.international.gc.ca (office); www .johnbaird.com.

BAIRD, Nicholas Graham Faraday (Nick), CMG, CVO; British diplomatist and business executive; *Group Corporate Affairs Director, Centrica plc*; b. 15 May 1962; m. Caroline; one s. two d.; Third, later Second Sec. (Chancery), Kuwait 1986–89, First Sec. (Econ./Finance), UK Representation to EU, Brussels 1989–93, Pvt. Sec. to Parl. Under-Sec. of State, FCO 1993–95, Head of Amsterdam IGC Unit, EU Dept (Internal) 1995–97, Deputy Head of Mission, Muscat 1997–98, Counsellor (Justice and Home Affairs), UK Representation to EU, Brussels 1998–2002, Head of EU Dept (Internal) 2002–03, on secondment to Immigration and Nationality Directorate at Home Office as Dir of Int. Delivery 2003–04, as Sr Policy Dir 2004–06, Amb. to Turkey 2006–09, Dir Gen. for Europe and Globalization, FCO 2009–11, Chief Exec. UK Trade & Investment 2011–13; Group Corp. Affairs Dir, Centrica plc 2014–. *Address:* Centrica plc, Millstream, Maidenhead Road, Windsor, Berks., SL4 5GD, England (office). *Telephone:* (1753) 494000 (office). *Fax:* (1753) 494001 (office). *E-mail:* info@centrica.com (office). *Website:* www .centrica.com (office).

BAIS, Ramesh; Indian agriculturalist and politician; b. 2 Aug. 1948, Raipur, Chhattisgarh; s. of the late Khomlal Bais and Kejabai Bais; m. Rambai Bais; one s. two d.; ed B.S.E., Bhopal, Madhya Pradesh; Councillor, Raipur Municipal Corpn 1978–83; mem. Madhya Pradesh Legis. Ass. 1980–84, mem. Estimates Cttee 1980–82, Library Cttee 1982–84; elected mem. Lok Sabha (Parl.) 1989, re-elected 1996, 1998, 2004, 2009; Union Minister of State for Steel and Mines 1998–99, for Information and Broadcasting 2000–03, for Ministry of Mines 2003–04, for Environment and Forests Jan.–May 2004; mem. Pradesh Mantri Bharatiya Janata Party (BJP), Madhya Pradesh 1982–88, Vice-Pres. 1989–90, 1994–96, mem. BJP Nat. Exec. 1993–; Chair. Seed and Agricultural Devt Corpn of Madhya Pradesh 1992–93; Pres. Chhattisgarh Archery Olympic Asscn. *Leisure interests:* woodcrafting, painting, interior decoration, gardening. *Address:* C-1/8, Tilak Lane, New Delhi 110 001 (home); 9 Ravi Nagar, Raipur 492 001 India (home). *Telephone:* (11) 23782730 (home); (11) 23389305 (home); (0771) 2423000 (Raipur) (home). *Fax:* (11) 23389305 (home); (0771) 2423000 (Raipur) (home). *Website:* www.india.gov.in (office); loksabha.nic.in (office).

BAJAJ, Rahul, BA, LLB, MBA; Indian automobile industry executive; *Chairman, Bajaj Group*; b. 10 June 1938, Bengal Presidency, British India (now Kolkata); s. of Kamalnayan Bajaj and Savitri Bajaj; m. Rupa Bajaj 1961; two s. one d.; ed St Stephen's Coll., Delhi, Govt Law Coll., Bombay (now Mumbai), Harvard Univ., USA; Dir Bajaj Group 1956–60, CEO 1968, Chair. and Man. Dir 1972–2008, Chair. 2008–; Dir Devt Council for Automobiles and Allied Industries 1975–77, Maharashtra Scooters Ltd 1975–2006, Indian Airlines 1986–89, Tech. Devt Advisory Group 1991; Pres. Asscn of Indian Automobile Mfrs 1976–78, Mahratta Chamber of Commerce and Industries 1983–85, Confed. of Indian Industry 1979–80, 1999–2000; Vice-Chair., Chair. and Dir Mukand Group 1994–2007; apptd Chair. Bd of Govs Indian Inst. of Tech., Mumbai 2003; elected to Rajya Sabha (Parl.) 2006; fmr Co-Chair. Commonwealth Business Council; mem. Exec. Cttee Confed. of Eng Industry 1978 (Pres. 1979–80), Governing Council, Automotive Research Asscn of India 1972, Devt Council for Automobiles and Allied Industries 1987, World Econ. Forum Advisory Council 1984, Prince of Wales Int. Business Leaders Forum 1992, Indo-German Consultative Group 1992, Soc. of Indian Automobile Mfrs; mem. Global Advisory Bd, Indian School of Business, Harvard Business School, Int. Advisory Cttee, NYSE Euronext, Int. Advisory Council, Brookings Inst.; Dr hc (Indian Inst. of Tech., Roorkee) 2005, (Rani Durgavati Vishwa Vidyalaya) 2005; Man of the Year Award, Nat. Inst. of Quality Assurance 1975, Business Man of the Year Award, Business India Magazine 1985, Bombay Man. Asscn Award 1990, Rashtrabhushan Award 1996, Lokmanya Tilak Award 2000, Padma Bhushan 2001, Jeevan Sadhana Gaurav Puraskar, Pune Univ. 2002, Economic Times Life Time Achievement Award 2004, Ernst & Young Life Time Achievement Award 2004, Alumni Achievement Award, Harvard Business School 2005, Marathwada Mitra Puraskar, Marathwada Lok Vikas Manch 2006, JRD Tata Corp. Leadership Award, All India Man. Asscn 2007. *Address:* Bajaj Auto Ltd., Akurdi, Pune 411 035 (office); 4, Meena Bagh, New Delhi 110 002, India (home). *Telephone:* (20) 27472851 (office); (20) 27476151 (office); (11) 23795255 (home). *Fax:* (11) 23795055 (home). *E-mail:* rahulbajaj@bajajauto.co.in (office); rahul.bajaj@sansad.nic.in (office). *Website:* www.bajajauto.com (office).

BAJNAI, (György) Gordon; Hungarian economist, business executive and politician; *Leader, Together 2014*; b. 5 March 1968, Szeged; m. (separated); two c. and two c. with current partner; ed Budapest Univ. of Econ. Sciences; with Creditum (financial consulting co.) 1991–93; consultant, EUROCORP Int. Finance plc 1993–94; Dir Corp. Finance and Equity Capital Market Div., CA IB Securities plc 1995–2000; CEO Wallis PLC 2000–05, mem. Bd of Dirs 2000–06, Vice-Pres. 2006; Pres. Budapest Airport Inc. 2005; Govt Commr for Devt Policy 2006–07; Minister of Local Govt and Regional Devt 2007–08, of Nat. Devt and Economy 2008–09; Prime Minister 2009–10; f. Patriotism and Progress Public Policy Foundation (Haza és Haladás Közpolitikai Alapítvány) 2011; Leader of Together 2014 (Együtt 2014, officially Together – Party for a New Era (Együtt – A Korszakváltók Pártja)) 2012–; Adjunct Prof. of Int. and Public Affairs, Columbia Univ., New York, USA 2011; Chair. Budapest Airport PLC 2006; mem. Bd of Dirs Danubius Radio 1998–99, Graboplast PLC 2001–04, Rába PLC 2003–05; mem. Investment Cttee Equinox Pvt. Equity Fund 1999; mem. Supervisory Bd Zwack Inc. 2003–06; mem. Econ. Council, Budapest Univ. of Econ. Sciences 2006; Officer's Cross, Order of Merit 2006; Pro Universitate 1994, voted one of the 30 most promising Cen.-Eastern European business execs by Central European Business Review 1999, Young Manager of the Year, Nat. Asscn of Managers 2003. *Leisure interests:* football (plays as goalkeeper for Építők SK football club, Footballer of the Year 2001). *Address:* Haza és Haladás Közpolitikai Alapítvány (Patriotism and Progress Public Policy Foundation), 1037 Budapest, Seregély u. 3–5 (office); Together 2014 (Együtt 2014), 1122 Budapest, Városmajor utca 48/b, Hungary. *Telephone:* (1) 880-3038 (office); (1) 919-1414. *Fax:* (1) 880-3039 (office). *E-mail:* info@hazaeshaladas.org (office). *Website:* www.hazaeshaladas.org (office); www .egyutt2014.hu.

BAJO, Lamin Kaba; Gambian politician and diplomatist; *Minister of the Interior*; b. 10 Nov. 1964, Brikama; m. Mariama Jarju-Bajo; several c.; joined gendarmerie 1984, rose to position of commdr in mil. police 1989, subsequently Deputy Commdr Mobile Gendarmerie; served as Presidential Guard at State House before coup of 22 July 1994; apptd Commr Western Div. 1994; mem. Armed Forces Provisional Ruling Council 1995; Minister for Interior and Religious Affairs 1995–98, served in Ministry of Youth and Sports 1997 and Ministry for Local Govt and Lands 1998; Amb. to Saudi Arabia 2002–05, Perm. Rep. to OIC; Sec. of State for Foreign Affairs 2005–06; Amb. to Iran 2007–09, to Qatar 2009; Minister of Fisheries, Water Resources and Religious Affairs 2010–11, of Fisheries, Water Resources and Nat. Ass. Matters 2011–12, of the Interior 2012–; Gen. Service Medal, Long Service and Good Conduct Medal, Order of the Repub. of The Gambia, Al Noot (Libya). *Leisure interests:* jogging, watching and listening to world and current affairs, watching sports, farming, reading. *Address:* Ministry of the Interior, 5 J. R. Forster Street, Banjul, The Gambia (office). *Telephone:* 4223277 (office). *Fax:* 4201320 (office). *E-mail:* info@moi.gov.gm (office). *Website:* www.moi.gov.gm (office).

BAKA, András B., JSD, PhD; Hungarian judge and professor of law; b. 11 Dec. 1952, Budapest; ed St Stephen's High School, Budapest and Eötvös Loránd Univ., Budapest; Research Fellow, Comparative Law Dept, Inst. for Legal and Admin. Sciences of Hungarian Acad. of Sciences 1978–82, Sr Research Fellow, Constitutional and Admin. Dept 1982–90; Prof. of Constitutional Law, Budapest School of Public Admin. 1990–; Dir-Gen. and Pres. Bd Budapest School of Public Admin. 1990–; mem. Parl. and Sec., Human Rights Comm. of Hungarian Parl. 1990–91; Judge, European Court of Human Rights 1991–2008, Section Vice-Pres. 2000–08; Chief Justice, Supreme Court 2009–11; Pres. Network of the Presidents of the Supreme Judicial Courts of the EU –2011, Hon. Pres. 2011–; Visiting Prof., Brown Univ. 1986, Univ. of Virginia 1987, Univ. of Calif., Berkeley 1987, Columbia Univ. 1987; Prof., Santa Clara Univ. School of Law, Inst. of Int. and Comparative Law, Santa Clara, Calif. 1991; Hon. Pres. Scientist Award, Hungarian Acad. of Sciences 1988. *Publications:* several publs on minority rights. *Address:* c/o Network of the Presidents of the Supreme Courts of the European Union, 5 quai de l'Horloge, 75001 Paris, France.

BAKANI, Loi Martin, BEcons, MEconSc; Papua New Guinea economist and central banker; *Governor, Bank of Papua New Guinea*; b. 12 Aug. 1963, Kulungi village, Talasea; m.; three c.; ed Univ. of Papua New Guinea, Univ. of Wollongong, Australia; joined Bank of Papua New Guinea as Research Officer, Monetary and Banking Div. of Econs Dept 1985, Head of Econs Dept and Chief Econ. Adviser for the Bank 1998–2005, Deputy Gov. 2005–09, Gov. 2009–; mem. Papua New Guinea Inst. of Dirs, Australian Econ. Soc., Papua New Guinea Econ. Soc. *Leisure interests:* rugby, sightseeing, travel. *Address:* Office of the Governor, Bank of Papua New Guinea, POB 121, Port Moresby 121, Papua New Guinea (office). *Telephone:* 3227200 (office). *Fax:* 3211617 (office). *E-mail:* info@bankpng.gov.pg (office). *Website:* www.bankpng.gov.pg (office).

BAKATIN, Vadim Viktorovich; Russian politician (retd); b. 6 Nov. 1937, Kiselevsk, Kemerovo Dist; s. of Victor Aleksandrovich Bakatin and Nina Afanasievna Bakatina; m. Ludmila Antonovna Bakatina; two s.; ed Novosibirsk Construction Eng Inst., Acad. of Social Sciences; supervisor, chief engineer, Dir of construction works 1960–71; mem. CPSU 1964–91; chief engineer of housing construction combine, Kemerovo 1971–73; Second Sec., Kemerovo City Cttee 1973–75; Sec., Kemerovo Dist Cttee 1977–83; Insp., CPSU Cen. Cttee 1985; First Sec. Kirov Dist Cttee 1985–87; mem. CPSU Cen. Cttee 1986–90; First Sec., Kemerovo Dist Cttee 1987–88; USSR Minister of Internal Affairs 1988–90; mem. Presidential Council Jan.–Nov. 1990; Head of KGB Aug.–Dec. 1991, Interrepublican Security Service 1991–92; Vice-Pres. and Dir Dept of Political and Int. Relations, Reforma Fund 1992–98; mem. Bd of Dirs Vostok Capital, mem. Advisory Cttee, Baring Vostok Capital Partners. *Publication:* The Deliverance from the KGB 1992. *Leisure interests:* painting, reading, tennis. *Address:* Baring Vostok Capital Partners, 123056, Moscow, Gasheka str. 7, Bldg 1, Ducat Place II, Suite 750, Russia (office). *Telephone:* (495) 967-13-07 (home). *Fax:* (495) 967-13-08 (office). *E-mail:* info@bvcp.ru (office). *Website:* www.bvcp.ru (office).

BAKAYOKO, Youssouf; Côte d'Ivoirian politician and diplomatist; *President, Electoral Commission*; b. 9 April 1943, Bouaké; began diplomatic career 1973; Counsellor, Perm. Mission of Côte d'Ivoire to EU and Int. Orgs in Geneva 1973–83; Minister of Foreign Affairs 2006–10; Pres. Electoral Comm. 2010–. *Address:* Commission électorale indépendant, 08 BP 2648, Abidjan, Côte d'Ivoire (office). *Telephone:* 21-30-58-01 (office). *Website:* www.ceici.org (office).

BAKER, Akbar al-, BEcons; Qatari airline industry executive; *CEO, Qatar Airways*; b. 1960, Doha; ed studied in India; worked at Civil Aviation Directorate –1997; joined Qatar Airways 1997, CEO 1997–, also CEO Qatar Airways Holidays, Qatar Aviation Services, Qatar Duty Free Co., Doha Int. Airport, Qatar Distribution Co., Qatar Aircraft Catering Co.; Chair. Qatar Tourism Authority 2004; mem. Bd Govs IATA; ranked by Arabian Business amongst its Power 500: The World's Most Influential Arabs (29th) 2010, (33rd) 2012, (24th) 2013. *Address:* Qatar Airways, PO Box 22550, Qatar Airways Tower, Airport Road, Doha, Qatar (office). *Telephone:* 4496666 (office). *Fax:* 4621792 (office). *E-mail:* infodesk@qatarairways.com (office). *Website:* www.qatarairways.com (office).

BAKER, Alan, PhD, FRS; British mathematician and academic; *Professor Emeritus of Pure Mathematics, University of Cambridge*; b. 19 Aug. 1939, London, England; s. of Barnet Baker and Bessie Baker; ed Stratford Grammar School, Univ. Coll., London, Trinity Coll., Cambridge; Fellow, Trinity Coll., Cambridge 1964–, Research Fellow 1964–68, Dir of Studies in Math. 1968–74; Prof. of Pure Math., Univ. of Cambridge 1974–2006, Prof. Emer. 2006–; Visiting Prof., Stanford Univ. 1974 and other univs in USA, Univ. of Hong Kong 1988, 1999; Guest Prof., ETH, Zurich 1989; mem. Academia Europaea 1998; Foreign Fellow, Indian Nat. Science Acad. 1980, Nat. Acad. of Sciences India 1993; Hon. Fellow, Univ. Coll. London 1979; Hon. mem. Hungarian Acad. of Sciences 2001; Dr hc (Univ. Louis Pasteur, Strasbourg) 1998; Fields Medal 1970, Adams Prize 1972. *Publications:* Transcendental Number Theory 1975, A Concise Introduction to the Theory of Numbers 1984, New Advances in Transcendence Theory (ed.) 1988, Logarithmic Forms and Diophantine Geometry (with G. Wüstholz) 2007, A Comprehensive Course in Number Theory 2012; papers in mathematical journals. *Leisure interests:* travel, theatre. *Address:* Centre for Mathematical Sciences, Wilberforce Road, Cambridge, CB3 0WB (office); Trinity College, Cambridge, CB2 1TQ, England (home). *Telephone:* (1223) 338400 (office). *Fax:* (1223) 338564 (office). *E-mail:* a.baker@dpmms.cam.ac.uk (office). *Website:* www.dpmms.cam.ac.uk/people/a.baker (office).

BAKER, Howard Henry, Jr, LLB; American diplomatist, attorney and fmr politician; b. 15 Nov. 1925, Huntsville, Tenn.; s. of Howard H. Baker and Dora Ladd; m. 1st Joy Dirksen 1951 (died 1993); one s. one d.; m. 2nd Nancy Kassebaum 1996; ed The McCallie School, Chattanooga, Univ. of the South, Tulane Univ. of New Orleans and Univ. of Tennessee Coll. of Law; served in USN 1943–46; Pnr, Baker, Worthington, Barnett & Crossley 1949–66; Senator from Tennessee 1967–85, Minority Leader 1977–81, Majority Leader 1981–85, Co-Chair. US Senate Watergate Cttee 1973–74; Pnr, Baker, Worthington, Crossley, Stansberry & Woolf 1985–87, 1988–95, Baker, Donelson, Bearman & Caldwell, Washington, DC 1995–; mem. law firm Vinson and Elkins 1985–87; White House Chief of Staff to Pres. Ronald Reagan 1987–88; Amb. to Japan 2001–05; del. to UN 1976; mem. Pres.'s Foreign Intelligence Advisory Bd 1985–87, 1988–90; Int. Councillor, Center for Strategic and Int. Studies 1991–; mem. Bd The Forum for Int. Policy 1993–, Museum of Appalachia Foundation, Maureen and Mike Mansfield Foundation, Forum of International Policy; Co-founder Bipartisan Policy Center 2007; mem. Int. Advisory Bd Citigroup; mem. Council on Foreign Relations 1973–, Inst. of Foreign Affairs 1992–, Washington Inst. of Foreign Affairs; Republican; Order of the Rising Sun (Japan) 2008; several hon. degrees; Jefferson Award for Greatest Public Service Performed by an Elected or Appointed Official 1982, Presidential Medal of Freedom 1984, American Soc. of Photographers Award 1993, United States Capitol Historical Soc. Freedom Award 2008, American Lawyer Magazine Lifetime Achievement Award 2008. *Publications:* No Margin for Error 1980, Howard Baker's Washington 1982, Big South Fork Country 1993, Scott's Gulf 2000. *Leisure interests:* photography, tennis. *Address:* c/o Baker, Donelson, Bearman & Caldwell & Berkowitz, One Courthouse Square, Huntsville, TN 37756, USA.

BAKER, James Addison, III, LLB; American lawyer and fmr government official; *Senior Partner, Baker Botts LLP;* b. 28 April 1930, Texas; s. of James A. Baker, Jr and Bonner Means; m. Susan Garrett 1973; eight c.; ed Princeton Univ. and Univ. of Texas Law School; served in US Marine Corps 1952–54; with law firm Andrews, Kurth, Campbell and Jones, Houston, Tex. 1957–75; Under-Sec. of Commerce under Pres. Ford 1975; Nat. Chair. Ford's presidential campaign 1976; Campaign Dir for George Bush in primary campaign 1980, later joined Reagan campaign; White House Chief of Staff and on Nat. Security Council 1981–85; Trustee, Woodrow Wilson Int. Center for Scholars, Smithsonian Inst. 1977–; Sec. of the Treasury 1985–88, Sec. of State 1989–92; White House Chief of Staff and Sr Counsellor 1992–93; Gov. Rice Univ. 1993; Sr Pnr, Baker Botts LLP 1993–; also currently Sr Counselor, The Carlyle Group; *Personal Envoy of UN Sec.-Gen.*, UN Mission for the Referendum in Western Sahara (MINURSO) 1997–2004 (resgnd); apptd special envoy on Middle East debt by US Pres. George W. Bush 2003; mem. Bd of Dirs Howard Hughes Medical Inst.; Hon. Chair. James A. Baker III Inst. for Public Policy, Rice Univ.; Co-Chair. Iraq Study Group, US Inst. of Peace 2006–07; currently Co-Chair. Nat. War Powers Comm. *Publications:* The Politics of Diplomacy 1995, Work Hard, Study . . . and Keep Out of Politics! Adventures and Lessons from an Unexpected Public Life 2006. *Leisure interests:* jogging, tennis, hunting. *Address:* Baker Botts LLP, One Shell Plaza, 910 Louisiana Street, Houston, TX 77002-4995, USA (office). *Telephone:* (713) 229-1234 (office). *Fax:* (713) 229-1522 (office). *E-mail:* james.baker@bakerbotts.com (office). *Website:* www.bakerbotts.com (office).

BAKER, Dame Janet Abbott, CH, DBE, CBE, FRSA; British singer (mezzo-soprano); b. 21 Aug. 1933, Hatfield, Yorks.; d. of Robert Abbott Baker and May Baker (née Pollard); m. James Keith Shelley 1957; ed York Coll. for Girls and Wintringham School, Grimsby; Pres. London Sinfonia 1986–; Chancellor Univ. of York 1991–2004; Trustee, Foundation for Sport and the Arts 1991–; mem. Munster Trust; Hon. Fellow, St Anne's Coll., Oxford 1975, Downing Coll., Cambridge 1985; Hon. DMus (Birmingham) 1968, (Leicester) 1974, (London) 1974, (Hull) 1975, (Oxford) 1975, (Leeds) 1980, (Lancaster) 1983, (York) 1984, (Cambridge) 1984, Hon. LLD (Aberdeen) 1980, Hon. DLitt (Bradford) 1983; Commdr des Arts et des Lettres; Daily Mail Kathleen Ferrier Memorial Prize 1956, Queen's Prize, Royal Coll. of Music 1959, Hamburg Shakespeare Prize, Hamburg 1971, Grand Prix, French Nat. Acad. of Lyric Recordings 1975, Léonie Sonning Prize (Denmark) 1979, Gold Medal of Royal Philharmonic Soc. 1990, Inc. Soc. of Musicians' Distinguished Music Award 2008, Gramophone Award for Lifetime Achievement 2011. *Publication:* Full Circle (autobiog.) 1982. *Leisure interests:* walking, reading. *Address:* Foundation for Sport and the Arts, Walton House, 55 Charnock Road, Walton, Liverpool, L67 1AA, England (office). *Telephone:* (15) 1259-5505 (office). *Fax:* (15) 1230-0664 (office). *E-mail:* contact@thefsa.net (office). *Website:* www.thefsa.net (office).

BAKER, Rt Rev. John Austin, MA, MLitt, DD; British ecclesiastic; *Emeritus Fellow, Corpus Christi College, Oxford;* b. 11 Jan. 1928, Birmingham, England; s. of George Austin Baker and Grace Edna Baker; m. Gillian Mary Leach 1974; ed Marlborough Coll., Oriel Coll., Oxford and Cuddesdon Theological Coll.; ordained 1954; Official Fellow, Chaplain and Lecturer in Divinity, Corpus Christi Coll., Oxford 1959–73; Lecturer in Theology, Brasenose and Lincoln Colls, Oxford; Dorrance Visiting Prof., Trinity Coll., Hartford, Conn., USA 1967; Canon of Westminster 1973–82; Visiting Prof., King's Coll., London 1974–76; Sub-Dean of Westminster and Lector Theologiae 1978–82; Rector of St Margaret's, Westminster 1978–82; Chaplain to Speaker of House of Commons 1978–82; Bishop of Salisbury 1982–93; mem. Church of England Doctrine Comm. 1967–81, 1984–87, Chair. 1985–87; mem. Standing Comm., WCC Faith and Order Comm. 1983–87; Emer. Fellow, Corpus Christi Coll., Oxford 1977–. *Publications include:* The Foolishness of God 1970, Travels in Oudamovia 1976, The Whole Family of God 1981, The Faith of a Christian 1996; numerous theological articles and trans. *Leisure interest:* music. *Address:* 4 Mede Villas, Kingsgate Road, Winchester, Hants., SO23 9QQ, England. *Telephone:* (1962) 861388. *E-mail:* johnjillb@talktalk.net (office).

BAKER, Sir John Hamilton, Kt, QC, PhD, LLD, FBA, FRHistS; British legal historian; *Emeritus Downing Professor of the Laws of England, University of Cambridge;* b. 10 April 1944, Sheffield; s. of Kenneth Lee Vincent Baker and Marjorie Bagshaw; m. 1st Veronica Margaret Lloyd 1968 (divorced 1997); two d.; m. 2nd Fiona Rosalind Holdsworth (née Cantlay) 2002 (died 2005); m. 3rd Elisabeth Maria Cornelia Faber (née van Houts) 2010; ed King Edward VI Grammar School, Chelmsford and Univ. Coll. London; Asst Lecturer in Law, Univ.

Coll. London 1965–67, Lecturer 1967–70; Barrister Inner Temple, London 1966; Librarian, Squire Law Library, Cambridge 1971–73; Lecturer in Law, Univ. of Cambridge 1973–83, Reader in English Legal History 1983–88, Prof. 1988–98, Downing Prof. of the Laws of England 1998–2011, currently Emer. Downing Prof., Fellow of St Catharine's Coll. 1971– (Pres. 2004–07), Hon. Fellow 2012–; Visiting Prof., New York Univ. School of Law 1988–2010; Corresp. Fellow, American Soc. for Legal History 1992; Visiting Fellow, All Souls Coll. Oxford 1995; Jt Literary Dir Selden Soc. 1981–90, Literary Dir 1991–2011; Fellow of Univ. Coll. London 1991; Hon. Bencher, Inner Temple, London 1988, Gray's Inn 2013; Hon. Fellow, Soc. for Advanced Legal Studies 1998; Hon. Foreign mem. American Acad. of Arts and Sciences 2001; Hon. LLD (Chicago) 1991; Yorke Prize (Cambridge) 1975, Ames Prize (Harvard Law School) 1985. *Publications:* An Introduction to English Legal History 1971, The Reports of Sir John Spelman 1977, Manual of Law French 1979, The Order of Serjeants at Law 1984, English Legal MSS in the USA (Part I) 1985, The Legal Profession and the Common Law 1986, Sources of English Legal History (with S. F. C. Milsom) 1986, The Notebook of Sir John Port 1987, Readings and Moots at the Inns of Court 1990, English Legal MSS in the USA (Part II) 1990, Cases from the Lost Notebooks of Sir James Dyer 1994, Catalogue of English Legal MSS in Cambridge University Library 1996, Spelman's Reading on Quo Warranto 1997, Monuments of Endless Labours 1998, Caryll's Reports 1999, The Common Law Tradition 2000, The Law's Two Bodies 2001, Readers and Readings 2001, Oxford History of the Laws of England (Vol. VI) 2003, Reports from the Time of Henry VIII 2003–04, An Inner Temple Miscellany 2004, The Men of Court 2012, Collected Papers on English Legal History 2013. *Address:* St Catharine's College, Cambridge, CB2 1RL, England.

BAKER, Sir John William, Kt, CBE, BA; British business executive; *Chairman, Maersk Company Ltd;* b. 5 Dec. 1937; s. of Reginald Baker and Wilhelmina Baker; m. 1st Pauline Moore 1962; one s.; m. 2nd Gillian Bullen; ed Harrow Weald Co. Grammar School and Oriel Coll., Oxford; served army 1959–61, Ministry of Transport 1961–70, Dept of Environment 1970–74; Deputy CEO Housing Corpn 1974–78; Sec. Cen. Electricity Generating Bd 1979–80, Bd mem. 1980–89, Jt Man. Dir 1986–89; CEO Nat. Power PLC 1990–95, Chair. 1995–97; Dir (non-exec.) Royal Insurance (now Royal and Sun Alliance Insurance Group) 1995–2002, Deputy Chair. 2002–03; Dir (non-exec.) The Maersk Co. Ltd 1996–, currently Chair.; Deputy Chair. Medeva PLC 1996–2000, Celltech Group 2000–03; Int. Business Council mem. AP Möller; Chair. Renewable Energy Holdings Plc –2013, Groundwork Foundation 1995–99, World Energy Council Exec. Ass. 1995–98, ENO 1996–2001; Chair. *Governing* Body, Holland Park School; Dir Kingston Theatre Trust; mem. Associated Bd, Royal Schools of Music 2000–; mem. Sr Salaries Review Bd 2000–, Chair. 2002–. *Leisure interests:* tennis, bridge, music, theatre. *Address:* The Maersk Company Ltd, Maersk House, Braham Street, London, E1 8EP, England (office). *Telephone:* (20) 7712-5000 (office). *Fax:* (20) 7712-5100 (office). *Website:* www.maersk.co.uk (office).

BAKER, Baron (Life Peer), cr. 1997, of Dorking in the County of Surrey; **Kenneth Wilfred Baker**, PC, CH; British politician and writer; b. 3 Nov. 1934, Newport, Wales; s. of the late W. M. Baker; m. Mary Elizabeth Gray-Muir 1963; one s. two d.; ed St Paul's School and Magdalen Coll., Oxford; nat. service 1953–55; served Twickenham Borough Council 1960–62; as Conservative cand. contested Poplar 1964, Acton 1966; Conservative MP for Acton 1968–70, St Marylebone 1970–83, Mole Valley 1983–97; Parl. Sec. Civil Service Dept 1972–74, Parl. Pvt. Sec. to Leader of Opposition 1974–75; Minister of State and Minister for Information Tech., Dept of Trade and Industry 1981–84; Sec. of State for the Environment 1985–86, for Educ. and Science 1986–89; Chancellor of the Duchy of Lancaster and Chair. Conservative Party 1989–90; Sec. of State for the Home Dept 1990–92; mem. Public Accounts Cttee 1969–70; mem. Exec. 1922 Cttee 1978–81; Chair. Hansard Soc. 1978–81, MTT PLC 1996–97, Business Serve PLC, Northern Edge Ltd, Museum of British History, Belmont Press (London) Ltd, Monstermob, Teather & Greenwood 2003–; Pres. Royal London Soc. for the Blind; Sec. Gen. UN Conf. of Parliamentarians on World Population and Devt 1978; Chair. (non-exec.) Teather & Greenwood PLC, Monstermob, Business Serve; Dir (non-exec.) Hanson 1992–, Stanley Leisure PLC; Chair. Information Cttee, House of Lords 2002–; Companion of Honour 1997. *Publications:* I Have No Gun But I Can Spit 1980, London Lines (ed.) 1982, The Faber Book of English History in Verse (ed.) 1988, The Faber Book of English Parodies (ed.) 1990, Unauthorized Versions (ed.) 1990, The Faber Book of Conservatism (ed.) 1993, The Turbulent Years: My Life in Politics 1993, The Prime Ministers: An Irreverent Political History in Cartoons 1995, The Kings and Queens: An Irreverent Cartoon History of the British Monarchy 1995, The Faber Book of War Poetry (ed.) 1996, Children's English History in Verse (ed.) 2000, The Faber Book of Landscape Poetry (ed.) 2000, George III: A Life in Caricature 2007. *Leisure interests:* collecting books, political cartoons. *Address:* House of Lords, Westminster, London, SW1A 0PW, England (office). *Telephone:* (20) 7219-3000 (office).

BAKER, Meredith Attwell, BA, LLB; American lawyer, business executive and fmr government official; *Senior Vice-President of Government Affairs, NBCUniversal;* b. 5 July 1968, Houston, Tex.; d. of Kirby Attwell; m. James Addison (Jamie) Baker IV 2006; four step-d.; ed Washington & Lee Univ., Lexington, Va, Univ. of Houston; worked in Legis. Affairs Office of US Dept of State, Washington, DC 1990–92; worked at US Court of Appeals Fifth Circuit in Houston and with DeLange and Hudspeth, LLP (law firm); Dir of Congressional Affairs, Cellular Telecommunications Industry Asscn 1998–2000; Sr Counsel, Covad Communications 2000–02; participated in the George W. Bush presidential campaign 2000; served briefly as Vice-Pres. Williams Mullen Strategies (lobbying firm) 2004; political appointee as Sr Advisor to Nat. Telecommunications and Information Admin 2004, named a Deputy Asst Sec. of Commerce by Pres. George W. Bush 2007, Acting Asst Sec. of Commerce for Communications and Information and Acting Admin. Nat. Telecommunications and Information Admin 2007–09; also served as Acting Assoc. Admin. for Office of Int. Affairs and on detail to Office of Science and Tech. Policy, The White House; apptd by Pres. Barack Obama as mem. Fed. Communications Comm. 2009–11; Sr Vice-Pres. of Govt Affairs, NBCUniversal (following merger with Comcast), Washington, DC 2011–; mem. Texas State Bar. *Address:* NBCUniversal Media LLC, 30 Rockefeller Plaza, New York, NY 10112, USA (office). *Telephone:* (212) 664-4444 (office). *Fax:* (212) 664-4085 (office). *E-mail:* info@nbcuni.com (office). *Website:* www.nbcuni.com (office); www.comcast.com (office).

BAKER, Raymond, CBE, PhD, FRS; British research scientist and academic (retd); b. 1 Nov. 1936, Ilkeston, Derbyshire, England; s. of Alfred Baker and May Golds; m. Marian Slater 1960; one s. two d.; ed Ilkeston Grammar School and Univ. of Leicester; Postdoctoral Fellow, UCLA, USA 1962–64; Lecturer in Organic Chem., Univ. of Southampton 1964–72, Sr Lecturer 1972–74, Reader 1974–77, Prof. 1977–84; Dir Wolfson Unit of Chemical Entomology 1976–84; Dir of Medicinal Chem. Merck Sharp Dohme Research Labs 1984–89, Exec. Dir 1989–96; Chief Exec. Biotechnology and Biological Sciences Research Council 1996–2001; Visiting Prof., Univ. of Edinburgh 1988–96, Univ. of Leicester 1990–93; Hon. DSc (Nottingham Trent) 1990, (Aston) 1997, (Leicester) 1998, (St Andrews) 1998, (Southampton) 1999; RSC Prize for Medicinal Chem. 1991, Hugo Muller Medal for Chem. associated with Biology 1992. *Publications:* Mechanism in Organic Chemistry 1971; over 300 articles in professional journals. *Leisure interests:* golf, gardening, travel. *Address:* Angeston Court, Uley, Dursley, Glos., GL11 5AL, England.

BAKER, Richard; British retail executive; b. 6 Aug. 1962; ed Univ. of Cambridge; began career at MG Rover Group; various positions with Mars Inc. in UK, including roles in Nat. Account Man., Marketing and Head of Sales for UK Multiples 1986–1995; COO and Marketing Officer Asda Group Ltd 1995–2003; CEO Boots Group PLC 2003–06, CEO Alliance Boots PLC (after merger with Alliance Unichem) 2006–07; Operating Pnr, Advent Int. 2009–, Chair. DFS group 2010–; Chair. Virgin Active 2007–, Europ. Dir., Groupe Aeroplan; mem. Bd of Dirs (non-exec.) Whitbread PLC. *Address:* Advent International, 111 Buckingham Palace Road, London, SW1W 0SR, England (office). *Telephone:* (20) 7333-0800 (office). *Fax:* (20) 7333-0801 (office). *E-mail:* news@adventinternational .com (office). *Website:* www.adventinternational.com (office); www.aeroplan.com (office).

BAKER, Richard Douglas James, OBE, MA; British broadcaster and author; b. 15 June 1925; s. of Albert Baker and Jane I. Baker; m. Margaret C. Martin 1961; two s.; ed Kilburn Grammar School and Peterhouse, Cambridge; served in RN 1943–46; actor 1948; teacher 1949; BBC Third Programme announcer 1950–53, BBC TV newsreader 1954–82, commentator for State Occasion Outside Broadcasts 1967–70, TV introductions to Promenade concerts 1960–95, panellist, Face the Music (BBC 2) 1966–79, presenter, Omnibus (BBC TV) 1983 presenter of various other shows on BBC Radio including Start the Week 1970–87, These You Have Loved 1972–77, Baker's Dozen 1978–87, Mainly for Pleasure 1986–92, Comparing Notes 1987–95; presenter, Classic Countdown for Classic FM radio 1995–97, Sound Stories Radio 3 1998–2000, Melodies for You 1999–2003, Your Hundred Best Tunes 2003–; mem. Broadcasting Standards Council 1988–93; Hon. Fellow, London Coll. of Music; Hon. FRCM; Hon. mem. Royal Liverpool Philharmonic Soc.; Hon. LLD (Strathclyde) 1979, (Aberdeen) 1983; TV Newscaster of the Year (Radio Industries Club), 1972, 1974, 1979, BBC Radio Personality of the Year (Variety Club of GB) 1984, Sony Gold Award for Radio 1996. *Publications:* Here is the News (broadcasts) 1966, The Terror of Tobermory 1972, The Magic of Music 1975, Dry Ginger 1977, Richard Baker's Music Guide 1979, Mozart 1982, London, A Theme with Variations 1989, Richard Baker's Companion to Music 1993, Franz Schubert 1997, The Classical Music Quiz Book (compilation) 2006. *Leisure interests:* gardening, music. *Address:* c/o Stephanie Williams Artists, 9 Central Chambers, Wood Street, Stratford upon Avon, CV37 6JQ, England (office).

BAKER, Russell Wayne, BA, DLitt; American journalist and author; b. 14 Aug. 1925, London Co., Va; s. of Benjamin R. Baker and Lucy E. Robinson; m. Miriam E. Nash 1950; two s. one d.; ed Johns Hopkins Univ.; served USNR 1943–45; with Baltimore Sun 1947–64; mem. Washington Bureau, New York Times 1954–62, author-columnist, editorial page 1962–98; Fellow, American Acad., Inst. of Arts and Letters 1993; several hon. degrees; Pulitzer Prize for distinguished commentary 1979, and other awards. *Television:* Masterpiece Theatre (host) 1993–2004. *Publications:* American in Washington 1961, No Cause for Panic 1964, All Things Considered 1965, Our Next President 1968, Poor Russell's Almanac 1972, The Upside Down Man 1977, Home Again, Home Again 1979, So This is Depravity 1980, Growing Up (Pulitzer Prize) 1982, The Rescue of Miss Yaskell and Other Pipe Dreams 1983, The Good Times (memories) 1989, There's a Country in My Cellar 1990, Russell Baker's Book of American Humor 1993, Looking Back 2004; contrib. to The New York Times Magazine, Sports Illustrated, Saturday Evening Post, McCalls.

BAKER, (Winifred) Mitchell, AB, JD; American software development executive; *Chairperson, Mozilla Foundation;* b. 7 June 1957, Berkeley, Calif.; d. of Theodore Baker and Anne Baker; m. Casey Dunn; one s.; ed Univ. of California, Berkeley, Boalt Hall School of Law; Corp. and Intellectual Property Assoc., Fenwick & West LLP 1990–93; Assoc. Gen. Counsel, Sun Microsystems 1993–94; Assoc. Gen. Counsel, Netscape Communications Corpn 1994–99; joined Mozilla.org 1998, Gen. Man. (officially known as Chief Lizard Wrangler) Mozilla project 1999–, involved in open-source software devt, creators of Mozilla Firefox and Mozilla Thunderbird, Pres. Mozilla Foundation 2003–05, Chair. 2008–, CEO Mozilla Corpn 2005–08; mem. Bd of Dirs Open Source Applications Foundation 2002–. *Address:* Mozilla Foundation, 1981 Landings Drive, Building K, Mountain View, CA 94043-0801, USA (office). *Telephone:* (650) 903-0800 (office). *Fax:* (650) 903-0875 (office). *E-mail:* mitchell@mozilla.org (office). *Website:* www.mozilla.org/ foundation (office); www.mozilla.com (office); blog.lizardwrangler.com (office).

BAKEWELL, Baroness (Life Peer), cr. 2011, of Stockport in the County of Greater Manchester; **Joan Dawson Bakewell,** DBE, MA; British broadcaster and author; b. 16 April 1933, Stockport, Cheshire (now Greater Manchester), England; d. of John Rowlands and Rose Bland; m. 1st Michael Bakewell 1955 (divorced 1972); one s. one d.; m. 2nd Jack Emery 1975 (divorced 2001); ed Stockport High School for Girls and Newnham Coll., Cambridge; TV Critic, The Times 1978–81, columnist, Sunday Times 1988–90; columnist ('Just Seventy'), The Guardian 2003; began fortnightly column in Times2 section of The Times 2008; currently has a weekly column in The Independent; Assoc. Newnham Coll., Cambridge 1980–91, Assoc. Fellow 1984–87; Council mem. Aldeburgh Foundation 1985–99; Gov. BFI 1994–99, Chair. 2000–02; Govt-apptd Voice of Older People 2008–10; Chair. and Trustee, Shared Experience theatre co.; mem. (Labour) House of Lords 2011–; Dr hc (Royal Holloway London, Queen Margaret's Edinburgh, Chester, Lancaster, Univ. of the Arts London, Essex, Stafford, Open Univ.); Dimbleby Award, BAFTA 1995, Journalist of the Year, Stonewall Awards 2009. *Radio includes:* Artist of the

Week 1998–99, The Brains Trust 1999–, Belief (BBC Radio 3) 2000–, Saturday Live (BBC Radio 4), Inside the Ethics Committee (BBC Radio 4). *Television includes:* Sunday Break 1962, Home at 4.30 (writer and producer) 1964, Meeting Point, The Second Sex 1964, Late Night Line Up 1965–72, 2008, The Youthful Eye 1968, Moviemakers at the National Film Theatre 1971, Film 72, Film 73, Holiday 74, 75, 76, 77, 78 (series), Reports Action (series) 1976–78, Arts UK: OK? 1980, Heart of the Matter (BBC 1) 1988–2000, My Generation 2000, One Foot in the Past 2000, Taboo (series) 2001, Daily Politics (BBC 1), Permissive Night (BBC Parliament) 2008, GMTV's Sunday programme, Panorama (BBC 1) 2010, 2012. *Publications:* The New Priesthood: British Television Today (co-author) 1970, A Fine and Private Place (co-author) 1977, The Complete Traveller 1977, The Heart of the Heart of the Matter 1996, The Centre of the Bed: An Autobiography 2004, selection of her interviews for radio series Belief published 2005, The View from Here: Life at 70 2007, All the Nice Girls (novel) 2009, She's Leaving Home (novel) 2011; contribs to journals. *Leisure interests:* theatre, travel, cinema. *Address:* c/o Knight Ayton Management, 35 Great James Street, London, WC1N 3HB, England (office); House of Lords, Westminster, London, SW1A 0PW, England. *Telephone:* (20) 7831-4400 (office); (20) 7219-5353 (House of Lords). *Fax:* (20) 7831-4455 (office). *E-mail:* info@knightayton.co.uk (office). *Website:* knightayton.co.uk (office).

BAKHIT, Maj.-Gen. (retd) Marouf al-, PhD; Jordanian government official and military officer (retd); b. 1947; ed Univ. of Jordan, Univ. of Southern California, USA, Univ. of London, UK, Royal Jordanian Mil. Coll.; served with Jordan Armed Forces 1964–1999, positions included Dir of Studies, Devt, and Procurement and Personnel Affairs; fmr Prof. of Political Science and Vice-Pres. for Mil. Affairs, Muta Univ.; fmr Amb. to Turkey, Israel; fmr Nat. Security Chief; Prime Minister and Minister of Defence 2005–07, Feb.–Oct. 2011 (resgnd); apptd Senator 2009, currently Chair. Senate Foreign Affairs Cttee; 14 Jordanian medals. *Address:* Majlis al-Aayan (Assembly of Senators), House of Parliament, Amman 11118, Jordan (office). *E-mail:* info@senate.jo (office). *Website:* www.senate.jo (office).

BAKHRESA, Said Salim Awadh; Tanzanian business executive; *Chairman, Bakhresa Group of Companies;* b. 1949, Zanzibar; m.; two c.; opened shoe repair shop in Dar es Salaam 1968, restaurant 1973, bakery and ice cream parlour 1975; est. Bakhresa Group of Cos 1983, currently Chair. *Address:* Bakhresa Group of Companies, PO Box 2517, Dar Es Salaam, Tanzania (office). *Telephone:* (22) 2861116 (office). *Fax:* (22) 2861140 (office). *E-mail:* azam@raha.com (office). *Website:* www.bakhresa.com (office).

BAKIYEV, Kurmanbek Saliyevich; Kyrgyzstani politician, engineer and fmr head of state; b. 1 Aug. 1949, Masadan (now Teyyit), Suzdak Dist, Jalal-Abad; s. of Sali Bakiyev; m. Tatyana Vasilyevna Bakiyeva; two s.; ed Kuibyshev (now Samara) Polytechnic Inst., Russia; trained as electrical engineer 1972; served in Soviet Armed Forces 1974–86; electrical engineer, Maslennikov Plant, Kuibyshev (now Samara, Russia) 1976–79; Sr Engineer, Head of VTs, then Deputy Chief Engineer, Jalal-Abad Electrical Factory 1979–85; Dir Profil Plant, Kok-Yangak 1985–90; First Sec. CP Kok-Yangak City Council 1990; Deputy Chair. Jalal-Abad Council of People's Deputies 1991–92; Head of Toguz-Torou Regional Admin 1992–94; Deputy Chair. State Property Fund 1994–95; First Deputy Head, then Head Jalal-Abad State Admin and Gov. of Jalal-Abad Oblast 1995–97; Gov. of Chui Oblast 1997–2000; Prime Minister of Kyrgyzstan 2000–02, Acting Prime Minister March–June 2005; mem. Jogorku Kenesh (Parl.) 2003–05; Acting Pres. of Kyrgyzstan March–Aug. 2005, Pres. Aug. 2005–April 2010 (forced to flee the capital during a popular uprising; went into exile in Belarus still insisting he was legitimate head of state); Leader, Bright Road People's Party (Ak Jol) 2007, 2009– (in exile 2010–); reported by news agency that he was granted citizenship of Belarus in 2010 Feb. 2012; sentenced by a Kyrgyz court in absentia to 24 years' imprisonment for abuse of power Feb. 2013, also being tried for organizing mass killings and ordering troops to fire on unarmed protesters.

BAKKER, M. Peter; Dutch business executive; *Chairman of the Management Board and CEO, TNT NV;* b. 1961; began career with TS Seeds Holding BV 1984–91; joined PTT Post (later TPG Post) 1991, Finance Dir Parcels Business Unit 1993–95, Dir of Marketing and Sales, PTT Post Logistics 1995–96, Financial Control Dir, TPG Post 1996, mem. Bd of Man. 1997–98, Chief Financial Officer and mem. Bd of Man. TPG NV (cr. following demerger of PTT Post from Royal PTT Nederland NV) 1998–2001, Chair. Man. Bd and CEO TNT NV 2001–; fmr Chair. Dutch Cttee on Labour Market Participation; fmr mem. Dutch Cttee Kapitaalmarkt; mem. Advisory Bd World Press Photo; mem. Advisory Council Royal Bank of Scotland NV; mem. Moving the World Foundation; Industry Leadership Award 2009. *Address:* TNT NV, Neptunusstraat 41–63, 2132 JA Hoofddorp, Netherlands (office). *Telephone:* (20) 500-6000 (office). *Fax:* (20) 500-7000 (office). *Website:* www .tpg.nl (office).

BAKO ARIFARI, Nassirou; Benin social scientist and politician; *Minister of Foreign Affairs, African Integration, Francophone Affairs and Beninois Abroad;* b. 30 Oct. 1962, Karimama; m.; six c.; ed Univ. of Bayreuth, Univ. of Cologne, Germany, Institut des Hautes Etudes en Sciences Sociales, France; Assoc., Institut für Ethnologie und Afrikastudien, Mainz, Germany in 1990s; fmr Dean of Sociology, Univ. d'Abomey-Calavi, Cotonou; Founder and Dir Laboratoire d'Etudes et de Recherches sur les Dynamiques Sociales et le Développement Local (LASDEL) (research inst.) –2009; mem. Assemblée Nationale 2009–10, mem. cttees on Culture, Educ., Social Affairs and Employment; Gen. Supervisor, Commission politique de supervision 2010–11; Minister of Foreign Affairs, African Integration, Francophone Affairs and Beninois Abroad 2011–; mem. Union pour la Relève; Coordinator G13 (political alliance). *Publications:* author of several academic publications. *Address:* Ministry of Foreign Affairs, African Integration, Francophone Affairs and Beninois Abroad, Zone Résidentielle, route de l'Aéroport, 06 BP 318, Cotonou, Benin (office). *Telephone:* 21-30-09-06 (office). *Fax:* 21-38-19-70 (office). *E-mail:* infos@maebenin.bj (office). *Website:* www.maebenin.bj (office).

BAKOYANNIS, Dora; Greek politician; b. (Theodora Mitsotaki), 6 May 1954, Athens; d. of Constantine Mitsotakis (fmr Prime Minister) and Marika Yannoukou; m. 1st Pavlos Bakoyannis 1974 (assassinated 1989); one s. one d.; m. 2nd Isidoros Kouvelos 1998; ed German School of Athens and Paris, France, Univ. of Munich, Germany, Univ. of Athens; family fled to Paris to escape mil. dictatorship that ruled Greece 1967–74; worked at Ministry of Econ. Co-ordination and later Ministry of Foreign Affairs 1974–84; Chief of Staff, New Democratic Party 1984–1990; elected Deputy for Evrytania 1990, re-elected three times and later moved candidacy to central Athens; served as Under-Sec. of State 1990, later as Minister of Culture 1992–93; apptd shadow Foreign and Defence Minister 2000; Mayor of Athens (first woman) 2003–06; Minister of Foreign Affairs (first woman) 2006–09; Chairperson-in-Office OSCE Jan.–Oct. 2009; Int. Leadership Award, Women's Int. Center 1992, Fontana di Roma Award, 14th Int. Symposium 1993, World Mayor Award 2005, ranked by Forbes Magazine amongst 100 Most Powerful Women (66th) 2006, (67th) 2007, (78th) 2008, Emperor Maximilian Award-European Award for Regional Policy and Local Govt, Prov. of Tyrol and the City of Innsbruck 2008. *Address:* D. Aeropagitou 3, 117 42 Athens, Greece. *Telephone:* (210) 9249487. *E-mail:* politikografeio@dorabak.gr. *Website:* www.dorabak.gr.

BAKRADZE, David, PhD, MPA; Georgian physicist and politician; *Minority Leader, Sakartvelos Parlamenti (Georgian Parliament);* b. 1 July 1972, Tbilisi; m. Maka Metreveli; two d.; ed Georgian Tech. Univ., Georgian-American Inst. of Public Admin, Swiss Int. Relations Univ. Seminars (SIRUS), Geneva, G. Marshall European Center for Security Studies, Garmisch-Partenkirchen, Germany, NATO Defense Coll., Rome, Italy, Japanese Inst. of Political Sciences, Tokyo, Galilee Coll., Tivon, Israel, Nat. Defence Coll., Stockholm, Sweden, Int. Law Enforcement Acad., Budapest, Hungary; First Class State Counsellor; holds diplomatic rank of Chief Minister Counsellor; Deputy Head of Disarmament and Arms Control Div., Politico-Mil. Dept, Ministry of Foreign Affairs 1996–98, Head of Disarmament and Arms Control Div. 1998–2000, Deputy Dir Politico-Mil. Dept 2000–02, Head, Service for Security Issues, Nat. Security Council of Georgia 2002–03, Dir Dept for Int. Security and Conflict Man. 2003–04, Dir Dept for Political Security 2004; mem. Sakartvelos Parlamenti (Georgian Parl.) 2004–, Chair. Cttee on European Integration 2004–07, Chair. Sakartvelos Parlamenti 2008–12, Minority Leader 2012–, Chair. Standing Del. to European Parl., Co-Chair. EU-Georgia Parl. Co-operation Cttee, mem. numerous dels; State Minister on Conflict Resolution Issues 2007–08; Minister of Foreign Affairs Feb.–May 2008; mem. United Nat. Movt (UNM) Party, named as UNM cand. for Oct. 2013 presidential election July 2013, finished second Oct. 2013; Commdr's Cross, Order of Merit (Poland) 2010, St George's Cross 2013; numerous awards, including Special Prize of Pres. of Georgia for Academic Excellence to the Best Student of Inst. of Public Admin 1996, NATO/EAPC Research Fellowship 1998, Swiss Leadership Award in Int. Relations, Special Award of Grad. Inst. of Int. Studies, Geneva 2005. *Address:* Sakartvelos Parlamenti, 4600 Kutaisi, Abashidze 26, Georgia (office). *Telephone:* (32) 228-91-56 (office). *Fax:* (32) 299-93-86 (office). *E-mail:* contact@parliament.ge (office). *Website:* www.parliament.ge (office).

BAKRIE, Aburizal, BEng; Indonesian business executive and politician; *President and Chairman, Partai Golongan Karya (Golkar);* b. 15 Nov. 1946, Lampung; m.; three c.; ed Bandung Inst. of Tech.; Chair. Grup Bakrie & Bros; Pres. ASEAN Business Forum 1991–95; Chair. Indonesian Chamber of Commerce and Industry (Kadin) 1994–2004, now adviser; major shareholder in Bank Nusa, May Bank Nusa International, PT Daya Sarana Pratama and other cos; f. Indonesian Young Entrepreneurs Org. 1972; adviser, Indonesia-Australia Business Council, Jakarta; Co-ordinating Minister for the Economy, Finance and Industry 2004–05, Co-ordinating Minister for the People's Welfare 2005–09; Pres. and Chair. Partai Golongan Karya (Golkar) 2009–. *Address:* Partai Golongan Karya (Golkar), Jalan Anggrek Nellimurni, Jakarta 11480, Indonesia (office). *Telephone:* (21) 5302222 (office). *Fax:* (21) 5303380 (office). *E-mail:* info@golkar.or.id (office). *Website:* www.golkar.or.id (office).

BALA-GAYE, Mousa G., BA; Gambian politician; b. 13 Aug. 1946; ed Legon Univ., Univ. of Manchester, UK, IMF Inst.; Asst Sec., Ministry of Works and Communications 1971–73; Sec., Public Service Comm. 1973; Asst Sec., Ministry of Local Govt and Lands 1973; Sr Asst, Ministry of Finance and Trade 1976–79, Under-Sec. 1979–80, Deputy Perm. Sec. 1980–82, Perm. Sec. 1982–86; Exec. Dir African Devt Bank, Abidjan, Côte D'Ivoire 1986–89; Perm. Sec., Office of the Pres. 1989–90; Man. Dir Heron Ltd 1990; Chair. and Man. Dir Afri-Swiss Travel Ltd 1993; Vice-Chair. First Int. Bank Ltd 1999, Acting Chair. 2002; Alt. Dir Senegambia Beach Hotel 2000; Vice-Chair. Int. Trust Insurance Co. Ltd 2000; Sec. of State for Finance and Econ. Affairs 2003–05, for Foreign Affairs March–Oct. 2005, for Trade, Industry and Employment Oct.–Nov. 2005, for Finance and Econ. Affairs Nov. 2005–09; fmr mem. Bd Dirs Cen. Bank of The Gambia, Gambia Produce Marketing Bd, Social Security and Housing Finance Corpn, Gambia Nat. Insurance Corpn; del. to numerous int. and multilateral confs and meetings of IMF, World Bank, OPEC Fund, the Commonwealth; Alt. Gov. African Devt Bank, Islamic Devt Bank, World Bank.

BĂLĂIŢĂ, George; Romanian writer; b. 17 April 1935, Bacău; s. of Gheorghe Bălăiţă and Constantina Popa Bălăiţă; m. Lucia Gavril 1959; one s.; ed Coll. of Philology; Ed. of cultural review Ateneu (Bacău) 1964–78; Dir Cartea Românească publishing house, Bucharest 1982–90, Ed.-in-Chief Arc 1991–97; Dir Copyro (soc. for defending authors' rights) 1997–; Fulbright stipendiate 1980; Prize of the Romanian Writers' Union 1975, Prize of the Romanian Acad. 1978, Award of Bucharest Writers' Assocn 1994, Opera Omnia Award, Writers' Assocn 2004, Nat. Prize, Romanian Writers' Union 2008. *Publications:* novels: Lumea în două zile (The World in Two Days) 1975, Ucenicul neascultător (The Disobedient Apprentice) 1978; essays: A Provincial's Nights 1984, Gulliver in No Man's Land (essays) 1994, Câinele în lesă (Dog on a Leash) (interviews and essays) 2004. *Leisure interests:* music, the arts, his pet dog. *Address:* 115 Victoriei Road, Bucharest (office); 62 Căderea Bastiliei (Copyro), Bucharest; 24–26 Blvd, Lascăr Catargiu, Bucharest, Romania (home). *Telephone:* (1) 3142251 (office); (1) 3171154 (home). *Fax:* (1) 3142251 (office).

BALAKRISHNAN, Arun, BE; Indian chemical engineer and oil industry executive; ed Govt Coll. of Eng, Indian Inst. of Man.; spent five years as Dir of Planning with Oil Coordination Cttee; several positions in Marketing, Corp. and Human Resources, Hindustan Petroleum Corpn Ltd, Dir Human Resources –2007, Chair. and Man. Dir 2007–10 (retd); Chair. Scientific Advisory Cttee for Hydrocarbons, Centre for High Technology, Ministry of Petroleum and Natural Gas 2010–; Fellow, All India Man. Asscn; Scroll of Honour, Inst. of Engineers (India). *Address:* C – 122, 12th Floor, Trinity Tower, DLF Phase – V, Gurgaon 122 002, India. *Website:* www.cht.in/scientific_advisory_committee.php.

BALAKRISHNAN, K(onakuppakatil) G(opinathan), BSc, LLM; Indian lawyer and judge; b. 12 May 1945, Thalayolaparambu, Kottayam, Kerala; s. of Gopinathan; m. Nirmala Balakrishnan; ed Maharaja Coll., Ernakulam, Maharaja Law Coll., Ernakulam; enrolled as advocate of Kerala Bar Council 1968; practised civil and criminal law in Ernakulam; apptd a Munsif in Kerala Judicial Service 1973, later resgnd and resumed practice as advocate in Kerala High Court; judge, Kerala High Court 1985–97, Gujarat High Court 1997–98; Chief Justice of High Court of Gujarat 1998–99, of High Court of Judicature, Madras 1999; Judge, Supreme Court 2000–07, Chief Justice of India 2007–10; Chair. National Human Rights Comm. 2010–; mem. Lincoln's Inn, England; several hon. degrees, including Dr hc (Kurukshetra Univ.), (Univ. of Gulbarga), (Univ. of Kerala), (Univ. of Bangalore), (Mahatma Gandhi Univ.), (Kottayam, Kerala), (Andhra Pradesh Univ.); Sri V K Krishna Menon Award. *Address:* Office of the Chairman, National Human Rights Commission, Manav Adhikar Bhawan Block-C, GPO Complex, INA, New Delhi 110 023, India (office). *E-mail:* covdnhrc@nic.in (office). *Website:* nhrc.nic.in (office).

BALANKIN, Alexander Sergeevich, MSc, PhD, DSc; Mexican/Russian scientist and academic; *Professor, National Polytechnic Institute of Mexico;* b. 3 March 1958, Moscow, Russia; ed Moscow Eng Physics Inst.; served as mem. Council of the Union (fmr USSR) for the Physics of Materials Resistance and Fracture (Russia) 1991–92; Full Prof., Monterrey Inst. of Tech. and Higher Educ., Mexico City 1992–97; joined Dept of Electromechanical Eng, Nat. Polytechnic Inst. (IPN) 1997, cr. Lab. of Fracture Mechanics; fmr mem. Advisory Council in Science and Tech. to the Presidency of Mexico; fmr Counsellor of Membership Cttee of Nat. Researcher System; Adviser, Mexican Petroleum Inst., Mexican Transport Inst.; consultant, Mexican Nat. Petroleum Co. (PEMEX); f. Nat. Interdisciplinary Research Group Fractal Mechanics (jt venture between industry and academia) 1998; cr. Inter-university Lab. Fractal Analysis of Complex Systems; mem. Mexican Acad. of Sciences 1998; Fellow, Nat. Researcher System 1998; State Prize of Russian Ministry of Defence 1990, Prize of Acad. of Sciences of USSR 1991, Pleiades Publishing Inc. Prize 1996, First Place Romulo Garza Prize for Research and Technological Devt in Mexico 1996, Nat. Prize of Arts and Sciences in Tech. and Design 2002, Nat. Prize in Financial Research 2004, Lazaro Cardenas' Gold Medal (highest award for Science and Tech. achievements), Pres. of Mexican Repub. 2005, UNESCO Science Prize 2005, Juchimán de Plata Award 2009. *Publications:* five books and more than 120 scientific papers in professional journals on fractal solid mechanics, probabilistic fracture mechanics, fluid flow through porous media mechanics and their eng applications. *Address:* Instituto Politécnico Nacional, CP 07738, Mexico City, DF, Mexico (office). *Telephone:* (55) 5729-6000 (office). *E-mail:* info@ipn.mx (office). *Website:* www.ipn.mx (office).

BALARAM, Padmanabhan, MSc, PhD; Indian research institute director and molecular biophysicist; *Director, Indian Institute of Science;* b. 1949; ed Fergusson Coll., Pune Univ., Indian Inst. of Tech., Carnegie-Mellon Univ., USA; postdoctoral researcher, Dept of Chem., Harvard Univ., USA; Lecturer, Indian Inst. of Science 1973–77, Asst Prof. 1977–82, Assoc. Prof. 1982–85, Prof. 1986–, Astra Prof. of Biological Sciences 1997–2000, Chair. Molecular Biophysics Unit 1995–2000, Chair. Div. of Biological Sciences 2000–05, Dir Indian Inst. of Science 2005–; Ed., Current Science; Assoc. Ed. Indian Journal of Chemical Educ. 1977–82; mem. Editorial Bd Proceedings of the Indian Academy of Sciences, Chemical Sciences 1980–83, Proceedings of the Indian Nat. Science Acad., Section B 1985–90, Indian Journal of Biochemistry and Biophysics 1989–91, Indian Journal of Chemistry Section B 1985–91, Int. Journal of Peptide and Protein Research 1984–97, Journal of Peptide Research 1997, Protein Eng, Design and Selection 2004, Biopolymers (Peptide Science) 2004; mem. Editorial Cttee Current Science 1991–94, Ed. Current Science 1995–; mem. Editorial Advisory Bd Chem Biochem: A European Journal of Chemical Biology 2000–; Fellow, Indian Acad. of Sciences, Indian Nat. Science Acad., Third World Acad. of Sciences; Young Scientist Medal, Indian Nat. Science Acad. 1977, Shanti Swaroop Bhatnagar Award, Indian Science Congress Asscn 1986, G D Birla Award 1994, Distinguished Alumnus Award, Indian Inst. of Tech., Kanpur 2000, Padma Shri 2002, Third World Acad. of Sciences Award in Chem., Padma Bhushan 2014. *Publications include:* ed one book and wrote more than 380 publs on structural biology, protein eng and design. *Address:* Indian Institute of Science, Bangalore 560 012, India (office). *Telephone:* (80) 23600690 (office); (80) 22932222 (office). *Fax:* (80) 23600936 (office). *E-mail:* diroff@admin.iisc.ernet.in (office); pb@mbu.iisc.ernet.in (office). *Website:* www.iisc.ernet.in (office).

BALASSA, Sándor, DLA; Hungarian composer; b. 20 Jan. 1935, Budapest; s. of János Balassa and Eszter Bora; m. Marianna Orosz; one s. one d.; ed Budapest Conservatory and Music Acad. of Budapest, studied composition under Endre Szervánszky; began career as a mechanic; entered Budapest Conservatory at age 17; Music Dir, Hungarian Radio 1964–80; Asst Prof., later Lecturer, Music Acad. of Budapest 1981–93, Univ. Prof. 1993–96; Erkel Prize 1972, Critics' Prize, Hungarian Radio 1972, 1974, Listeners' Prize, Hungarian Radio 1976, Distinction for Best Work of the Year, Paris Int. Tribune of Composers 1972, Merited Artist of the Hungarian People's Repub. 1978, Kossuth Prize 1983, Bartók-Pásztory Prize 1988, 1999, Excellent Artist of the Hungarian People's Repub. 1989. *Compositions include:* vocal: Eight Songs from Street Rottenbiller 1957, Two Songs to Poems by Dezső Kosztolányi 1957, Two Songs to Poems by Attila József 1958, Five Choruses (for children's choir) 1967, Legenda 1967, Antinomia 1968, Summer Night (for female choir) 1968, Requiem for Lajos Kassák 1969, Cantata Y 1970, Motetta 1973, Tresses 1979, Kyrie (for female choir) 1981, Madaras énekek (for children's choir) 1984, The Third Planet, opera-cantata 1986, Bánatomtól szabadulnék (for female choir) 1988, Oldott kéve (for mixed choir) 1992, Kelet népe (for children's choir) 1992, Damjanich's prayer (for mixed choir) 1993, Chant of Orphans (for mixed choir) 1995, Capriccio (for female choir) 1996, Spring Song, Autumn Song (for female choir) 1997, Woodcutter (for male choir) 1998, Moon-gesang and Sun-anthem (for male choir) 1998, Winter cantata (for children's chorus and string orchestra) 1999, Christmas (for mixed choir) 1999, Secrets of Heart (for solo tenor and string orchestra) 2002, Songs from Sümegvár Street 2003, A Gólyához (for mixed choir) 2003, Three songs to poems by Albert Wass 2003, Cry in December 2005; opera: Az áljön kivül 1976, The Third Planet 1986, Karl and Anna 1992, Földindulás 2001, Erderschütterung; instrumental: Dimensioni 1966, Quartetto per percussioni 1969, Xenia 1970, Tabulae 1972, The Last Shepherd 1978, Quintet for Brass 1979, The Flowers of Hajta 1984, Divertimento for two cimbaloms 1992, Sonatina for harp 1993, Little Garland (trio for flute, viola and harp) 1994, Five Brothers (piano) 1994, Jánosnapi muzsika (solo violin) 1994, Vonósnégyes (string quartet) 1995, Bells of Nyirbátor (for twelve brass instruments) 1996, Sonatina for Piano 1996, Preludes and Fantasia for Organ 1996, Duets (for flute and harp) 1998, Pastoral and Rondo (for violin and horn) 1998, Eight Movements for two clarinets 2001, Sonatina II (for piano) 2003, Párosító Hegedüduók (Duet for violins) 2003, Xenia II (nonetto) 2004, Letters from a Reservation (for Cimbalom) 2004, Greeting to Viola (for solo viola) 2004, Three Movements for Cello 2005, Ha szól a Tárogató 2006, Eszterlánc Duets (for flute and violin 2006, Fantasia for Piano 2006, Four Pieces for Cimbalom 2006, Trio I for Strings 2006, Müvész utca II/a 2007, Obne Doom-Doom 2007, Trio II for Strings 2008; orchestral: Violin Concerto 1965, Lupercalia 1971, Iris 1972, Chant of Glarus 1978, The Island of Everlasting Youth 1979, Calls and Cries 1980, A Daydreamer's Diary 1983, Three Phantasias 1984, Little Grape and Little Fish 1987, Tündér Ilona 1992, Prince Csaba (for string orchestra) 1993, Bölcske Concerto (for string orchestra) 1993, Dances of Mucsa 1994, Sons of the Sun 1995, Four Portraits 1996, Number 301 Parcel 1997, Pécs Concerto 1998, Hungarian Coronation Music 1998, Hun's Valley (Val d'Anniviers) 1999, Double Concerto (for oboe, horn and string orchestra) 2000, Fantasy (for harp and string orchestra) 2002, Flowers of October 2003, Gödöllő Concerto (for guitar orchestra) 2003, Excursion to the Sun Mountain (for string orchestra) 2003, Concerto (for trumpet) 2004, Szeged concerto (for string orchestra) 2005, Summer Music (for flute and string orchestra) 2005, Civisek Városa 2005, Journeys in Bihar 2005, Lovagi erények dícsérete 2007, Overture and Scenes (for string orchestra) 2007. *Recordings include:* Karl and Anna 2003, Pécs Concerto 2003, Violin Concerto No. 3 2006, The Third Planet 2006, The Man Outside 2007, Journeys in Bihar Country 2008, Works for String Orchestra 2010. *Leisure interest:* nature. *Address:* str. 18 Sümegvár, 1118 Budapest, Hungary (home). *Telephone:* (1) 319-7049 (home). *E-mail:* sandor@balassa.hu (home).

BALAYAN, Roman Gurgenovich; Armenian film director; b. 15 April 1941, Nagorno-Karabak Autonomous Region; m. Natalia Balayan; two s.; ed Yerevan Inst. of Theatrical Arts, Kiev Theatre Inst., USSR; State Prize 1987. *Films include:* The Romashkin Effect, 1973, Kashtanka 1976, Biryuk (Morose) 1977, The Kiss 1983, Dream and Waking Flights 1983, Keep Me Safe, My Talisman (Tulip Award, Int. Istanbul Film Festival 1987) 1985, Police Spy 1988, Lady Macbeth of Mtcensk 1989, Two Moons, Three Suns 1998 (dir and writer), Letniy Dozhd 2002 (producer), The Night is Bright 2004, Birds of Paradise 2008. *TV:* Who's Afraid of Virginia Woolf 1992, The Tale of the First Love 1995. *Address:* 125212 Moscow, Leningradsky Prosp. 33, Apt. 70, Russia. *Telephone:* (495) 159-99-74.

BALAZS, Artur Krzysztof, MEng; Polish politician, trade union official and farmer; b. 3 Jan. 1952, Ełk; s. of Adam Balazs and Irena Balazs; m. Jolanta Balazs 1973; three d.; ed Agricultural Acad., Szczecin; worked in agric. service of Communal Office, Kołczewo 1974–76; own farm in Łuskowo 1976–; mem. Polish United Workers' Party (PZPR) 1975–81; active in Agric. Solidarity Independent Self-governing Trade Union 1980–81, participant 1st Nat. Congress of Solidarity of Pvt. Farmers Trade Union, Warsaw 1980; participant agric. strikes and co-signatory agreements in Ustrzyki, Rzeszów and Bydgoszcz 1981; mem. All-Poland Founding Cttee of Solidarity of Private Farmers Trade Union, mem. Comm. for Realization of Rzeszów-Ustrzyki Agreements; interned Dec. 1981–Dec. 1982; mem. Presidium of Solidarity Provisional Nat. Council of Farmers 1987; mem. Interfactory Strike Cttee Szczecin 1988; mem. Civic Cttee attached to Lech Wałęsa, Chair. of Solidarity Trade Union 1988–91; participant Round Table debates, mem. group for union pluralism and team for agric. matters Feb.–April 1989; mem. Episcopate Comm. for the Pastoral Care of Farmers 1989–; Deputy to Sejm (Parl.) 1989–93, 1997–; mem. Solidarity Election Action Parl. Club 1997–; Chair. Sejm Cttee for Admin. and Internal Affairs 1992–93; Vice-Chair. Christian Peasant Party 1990–94, 1995–97, Chair. 1994–95; mem. Nat. Bd Conservative Peasant Party (SKL) 1997–, Vice-Chair. 1998–99, Chair. 2000–02, Chair. Conservative Party–New Poland Movt (SKL–RNP) 2002–; Chair. European Fund for the Devt of Polish Villages 1990–; Minister, mem. Council of Ministers 1989–90, Minister without Portfolio 1991–92; mem. Senate 1995–97; mem. Cttee for Agric.; Minister of Agric. and Rural Devt 1999–2002. *Leisure interests:* press, politics.

BALÁZS, Péter, PhD, Dr (Habil), DrSci; Hungarian economist, diplomatist, politician and academic; b. 5 Dec. 1941, Kecskemét; ed Budapest School of Econs; early position as economist, Elektroimpex (trading co.) 1963–68; Desk Officer, later Dir Ministry of Foreign Trade 1969–82; Counsellor, Embassy in Brussels 1982–87; served in Prime Minister's Office 1987–88, responsible for int. econ. orgs; Dir-Gen. Ministry of Int. Econ. Relations 1988–92; Perm. State Sec., Ministry of Industry and Trade 1992–93; Amb. to Denmark 1994–96, to Germany 1997–2000; Prof., Budapest Univ. of Econs and Public Admin 2000–02, Corvinus Univ. 2002–, Faculty of Int. and European Studies, Cen. European Univ. 2005–; State Sec. for Integration and External Econ. Relations, Ministry of Foreign Affairs 2002–03; Perm. Rep. to EU 2003–04, EU Commr (without Portfolio) May–Nov. 2004; Minister of Foreign Affairs 2009–10; Ed. Európa Fórum Budapest; Founding mem. ECSA Hungary, Hungarian Foreign Affairs Soc., European Movt Hungary; mem. Union of Hungarian Economists; Dr hc (Hungarian Acad. of Sciences). *Publications include:* Legal and Theoretical Questions of the Implementation of the Europe Agreement (co-ed.) 1995, The External Relations of the EU and Hungary 1996, European Unification and Modernisation 2001, Foreign Policy of the European Union and the Development of Relations Between Hungary and the EU 2002. *Address:* Nador u. 11.Room: 604, Central European University, 1051 Budapest, Hungary (office). *Telephone:* (1) 327-3000 (office). *E-mail:* balazsp@ceu .hu (office). *Website:* www.ceu.hu (office).

BALBINOT, Sergio, MBA; Italian business executive; *Joint Managing Director, Assicurazioni Generali SpA;* b. 8 Sept. 1958, Tarvisio (Udine); m.; one s. one d.; began career with business scholarship, EC, Brussels; joined Assicurazioni Generali as graduate trainee, Munich 1983, positions in Trieste, later Zurich 1989, Paris 1992, returned to HQ, Trieste 1995, Gen. Man., Generali Group 2000, Jt Man. Dir 2002–, mem. Supervisory Bd Generali Investments SpA; Vice-Chair. and Dir of several Austrian, Chinese, French, Israeli, Dutch, Spanish, US and German cos, including Generali España Holding Entidades de Seguros SA, Generali Holding Vienna AG, Generali France SA, Generali China Life Insurance Co. Ltd, Graafschap Holland Participatie Maatschappij NV, Generali Deutschland Holding AG, Generali España –SA de Seguros y Reaseguros, Future Generali India Insurance Co. Ltd and Future Generali India Life Insurance Co. Ltd; mem. Supervisory Bd Commerzbank AG; Chair. Generali PPF Holding BV; Pres. Insurance Europe (European insurance and reinsurance federation) 2011–; mem. Bd Geneva Asscn; mem. European Financial Services Round Table, Pan European Insurance Forum. *Address:* Assicurazioni Generali SpA, Piazza Duca degli Abruzzi 2, 34132 Trieste, Italy (office). *Telephone:* (40) 6711 (office). *Fax:* (40) 671600 (office). *E-mail:* info@generali.com (office). *Website:* www.generali.com (office).

BALBUS, Steven A., BS, PhD; American astronomer, astrophysicist and academic; *Savilian Professor of Astronomy, University of Oxford;* b. 23 Nov. 1953, Philadelphia, Pa; ed William Penn Charter School, Massachusetts Inst. of Tech., Univ. of California, Berkeley; held postdoctoral appointments at Princeton Univ., MIT and Univ. of Virginia 1985; Professeur des Universités, Physics Dept, École Normale Supérieure de Paris 2004–12; Savilian Prof. of Astronomy, Univ. of Oxford and Professorial Fellow, New Coll., Oxford 2012–; Bohdan Paczynski Visitor and Spitzer Lecturer, Princeton Univ. 2011; Visiting Miller Prof., Univ. of California at Berkeley 2012; Wolfson Research Merit Award, awarded a Chaire d'excellence by French Ministry of Higher Educ. 2004, Shaw Prize in Astronomy (co-recipient) 2013. *Publications:* numerous papers in professional journals on astrophysical fluid dynamics, especially the behaviour of magnetized gases. *Address:* Denys Wilkinson Building, Keble Road, Oxford, OX1 3RH, England (office). *Telephone:* (1865) 273639 (office). *E-mail:* steven.balbus@astro.ox.ac.uk (office). *Website:* www2.physics.ox.ac.uk (office).

BALCEROWICZ, Leszek, MBA, DEconSc; Polish politician, economist, academic and fmr central banker; *Head, Department of Comparative International Studies, Warsaw School of Economics;* b. 19 Jan. 1947, Lipno; s. of Wacław Balcerowicz and Barbara Balcerowicz; m. 1977; two s. one d.; ed Cen. School of Planning and Statistics, Warsaw, St John's Univ., New York; on staff, Cen. School of Planning and Statistics (now Warsaw School of Econs), Warsaw 1970–, Inst. of Int. Econ. Relations 1970–80; Head, Research Team attached to Econ. Devt Inst. 1978–81, Scientific Sec. Econ. Devt Inst. 1980–; Prof. and Head, Dept of Comparative Int. Studies, Warsaw School of Econs 1992–; mem. Polish United Workers' Party (PZPR) 1969–81; consultant, Network of Solidarity Ind. Self-governing Trade Union 1981–84; Deputy Prime Minister and Minister of Finance 1989–91, 1997–2000; Leader, Freedom Union (UW) 1995–2000; Pres. Nat. Bank of Poland 2001–07; Deputy to Sejm (Parl.) 1997–2000; fmr mem. Council of Econ. Advisers to Pres. Wałesa; Head of Inst. for Comparative Int. Studies, Warsaw School of Econs 1993–; Chair. Council of Centre for Social and Econ. Research, Warsaw 1992–2000, Bruegel, Brussels (think tank) 2008–12; mem. Polish Econ. Soc. 1970–, Vice-Chair. Gen. Bd 1981–82; mem. Polish Sociological Soc. 1983–, Warsaw Civic Cttee Solidarity 1989, Group of Thirty Consultative Group on Int. Econ. and Monetary Affairs, Inc., Washington, DC, Distinguished Assocs of the Int. Atlantic Econ. Soc. 2006–, Group of Trustees, Inst. of Int. Finance 2006–, Bd Peterson Inst., Washington, DC; Corresp. mem. History and Philosophy Class of Polish Acad. of Arts and Sciences 2006; numerous hon. degrees including Dr hc (Univ. of Aix-en-Provence, France) 1993, (Univ. of Sussex, UK) 1994, (De Paul Univ. of Chicago, USA) 1996, (Univ. of Szczecin, Poland) 1998, (Staffordshire Univ., UK) 1998, (Nikolaj Kopernik Univ. of Toruń, Poland) 1998, (Univ. of Dundee, UK) 1998, (Univ. of Econs, Bratislava, Slovakia) 1999, (Viadrina European Univ., Frankfurt (Oder), Germany) 2001, (Univ. of the Pacific, Lima, Peru, 'Alexandru Ioan Cuza' Univ., Iasi, Romania) 2002, (Gerhard Mercator Univ., Duisburg, Germany) 2004, (Karol Adamiecki Univ. of Econs, Katowice) 2006, (Poznań Univ. of Econs) 2006, (Wroclaw Univ. of Econs) 2006, (Univ. of Gdańsk) 2006, (Warsaw School of Econs) 2007, (Univ. of Warsaw) 2008, (Univ. of New South Wales, Australia) 2008, (Babeş-Bolyai Univ., Romania) 2009, (Acad. of Economic Studies of Moldova) 2010, 9Burgas Prof. Assen Zlatarov Univ., Bulgaria) 2010, (Russian Presidential Acad. of Nat. Economy and Public Admin) 2011, (Higher School of Economics, Russia) 2011, (Central Connecticut State Univ., USA) 2011; Awards of Minister of Science, Higher Educ. and Tech. 1978, 1980, 1981, Ludwig Erhard Prize, Ludwig Erhard Foundation (Germany) 1992, Euromoney Finance Minister of the Year 1998, Transatlantic Leadership Award, European Inst. of Washington 1999, Cen. European Award for Finance Minister of the Year 1999, Friedrich von Hayek Prize (Germany) 2001, Carl Bertelsman Prize 2001, Fasel Foundation Prize for Merits for the Social Market Economy 2002, European Cen. Banker of the Year, The Banker magazine 2004, Emerging Markets Award for Emerging Europe's Cen. Bank Gov. of the Year 2004. *Publications include:* Socialism, Capitalism, Transformation 1995, Freedom and Development: The Economics of the Free Market (in Polish) 1995, Post-communist Transition: Some Lessons 2002, Toward a Limited State 2003; numerous scientific works on int. econ. relations and problems of econ. systems. *Leisure interests:* basketball, detective stories. *Address:* Warsaw School of Economics, Aleja Niepodległości 162, 02-554 Warsaw, Poland (office). *Telephone:* (22) 5649345 (office). *Fax:* (22) 5649833 (office). *E-mail:* kmsp@sgh.waw.pl (office). *Website:* www.sgh.waw.pl (office); www .balcerowicz.pl.

BALČYTIS, Zigmantas; Lithuanian economist and politician; b. 16 Nov. 1953, Juodziai, Zemaiciu Naumiestis Co., Silute Dist; m. Severina Balčytienė; one s. one d.; ed Faculty of Finance and Accounting, Vilnius Univ.; Engineer, Planning and Design Bureau, Ministry of Food Industry 1976–78; Young Communist League 1978–84; Deputy Dir Lithuanian Nat. Philharmonic 1984–89; Man. of Trade Union Affairs and Dir of Training Centre 1989–91; Dir Vilnius Asphalt and Concrete Factory 1992–94; Deputy Gov. Vilnius Co. 1994–96; First Deputy Dir of Lithuanian–Hungarian Jt Venture Lithun 1996–2000; mem. Vilnius City Council 1994; Deputy Gov. Vilnius Dist 1994–96; Minister of Transport and Communications 2001–05; mem. Siemas 2004–09; Minister of Finance and Gov. of EIB for Lithuania 2005–07 (resgnd); Acting Prime Minister June–July 2006; mem. Social Democratic Party; mem. Parl. Ass. of Council of Europe 2008–09; mem. European Parl. 2009–; f. Padèkime kitiems (Let's help others) Foundation 2003; Order of the Cross of the Gunner (Lithuania), Order of the Great Cross (Spain), (Portugal), Order of Merit (Lithuania); Medal of Afanasij Nikitin, Commemorative Medal of 750th Anniversary of King Mindaugas' Coronation. *Leisure interests:* hunting, tennis. *Address:* European Parliament, Bât. Altiero Spinelli, 13G146 60, rue Wiertz, Brussels, Belgium (office); Ž. Liauksmino g. 3/8, Vilnius 01101, Lithuania (office). *E-mail:* info@balcytis.lt (office). *Website:* www.balcytis.lt (office).

BALDACCI, John Elias, BA; American politician; b. 30 Jan. 1955, Bangor, Me; m. Karen Weston; one s.; ed Bangor High School, Univ. of Maine; worked in family restaurant Momma Baldacci's, Bangor; mem. Bangor City Council 1978–81; mem. Me State Senate 1982–94; mem. US House of Reps from Second Dist of Me, Washington, DC 1995–2003; Gov. of Me 2003–11; hired by Under-Sec. of Defense Clifford L. Stanley to study mil. health care 2011–12; Democrat; Nat. Energy Assistance Dirs Asscn Award 1997, Small Business Assistance Award, NASA, Big M Award, Me State Soc., Washington, DC 2000. *Leisure interest:* holds technician class amateur radio licence with call sign KB1NXP. *Address:* 1400 Defense, Pentagon, Washington, DC 20301-1400 (office); c/o Office of the Governor, 1 State House Station, Augusta, ME 04333, USA. *Telephone:* (703) 571-3343 (office). *Website:* www.defense.gov (office); www.mhs.osd.mil (office).

BALDAUF, Sari Maritta, MSc, DSc; Finnish business executive; b. 10 Aug. 1955, Kotka; ed Helsinki School of Econs and Business Admin; Researcher, Finland Int. Business Operations project, Helsinki School of Econs and Business Admin 1977–78; Training Officer, Finnish Inst. of Exports 1979–80; Market Man. Falcon Communications, Abu Dhabi 1981–82; Planning Man. Nokia Corpn 1983–85, Vice-Pres. Corp. Planning, Nokia Electronics 1985–86, Asst Vice-Pres. Business Devt and Venture Capital, Nokia, New York 1986–87, Vice-Pres. Business Devt, Telenokia 1987–88, Pres. Cellular Systems, Nokia Telecommunications 1988–96, mem. Group Exec. Bd Nokia Corpn 1994, Exec. Vice-Pres. Nokia APAC 1997–98, Pres. Nokia Networks 1998–2003, Exec. Vice-Pres. and Gen. Man. of Networks 2004–05; mem. Bd of Dirs F-Secure Corpn 2006–, YIT Corpn 2006–, Int. Youth Foundation 2000–, Foundation for Econ. Educ. 2002–, SanomaWSOY 2003–, Hewlett-Packard Co. 2006–, CapMan 2007–, Finland-China Trade Assen 1997–99, Tech. Research Centre of Finland 1998–2001; Chair. Savonlinna Opera Festival; mem. Nat. Cttee for the Information Soc. Issues 1996–2003, Finnish Acad. of Tech., Consultative Cttee of Sibelius Acad. Support Foundation 2003–; mem. Int. Advisory Bd Instituto de Empresa (business school) 2007–; Knight, 1st Class of the Order of the White Rose of Finland 1996; Hon. DTech (Helsinki Univ. of Tech.); ranked by Fortune magazine amongst 50 Most Powerful Women in Business outside the US (14th) 2003, (12th) 2004. *Leisure interest:* classical music, hiking, skiing, spending time with family and friends at her country house. *Address:* c/o Board of Directors, Savonlinna Opera Festival Office, Olavinkatu 27, 57130 Savonlinna, Finland (office).

BALDELLI, HE Cardinal Fortunato; Italian ecclesiastic and diplomatist; b. 6 Aug. 1935, Valfabbrica; ordained priest, Diocese of Assisi-Nocera Umbra-Gualdo Tadino, Italy 1961; joined diplomatic service of the Holy See 1966, worked in Cuba and Egypt, career continued at Secr. of State and the Council for Public Affairs of the Church and the Council of Europe in Strasbourg, as a special envoy with a perm. observer of the Holy See; Titular Archbishop of Mevania 1983–; Apostolic Del. to Angola 1983–85; Apostolic Pro-Nuncio to São Tomé and Príncipe 1985–91; Apostolic Nuncio to Dominican Repub. 1991–94, to Peru 1994–99, to France 1999–2009; Major Penitentiary of the Apostolic Penitentiary 2009–12, Major Penitentiary Emer. 2012–; mem. Congregation for the Causes of Saints 2011–, Secr. of State (second section) 2011–; cr. Cardinal (Cardinal-Deacon of S. Anselmo all'Aventino) 20 Nov. 2010. *Address:* c/o Paenitentiaria Apostolica, Palazzo della Cancelleria 1, 00186 Rome, Italy (office). *Telephone:* (06) 69887526 (office); (06) 69887523 (office). *Fax:* (06) 69887557 (office). *E-mail:* info@penitenzieria.va (office). *Website:* www.vatican.va/roman_curia/tribunals/apost_penit (office); www .penitenzieria.va (office).

BALDESCHWIELER, John Dickson, PhD; American chemist and academic; *J. Stanley Johnson Professor and Professor of Chemistry, Emeritus, California Institute of Technology;* b. 14 Nov. 1933, Elizabeth, NJ; s. of Emile L. Baldeschwieler and Isobel M. Dickson; m. Marlene Konnar 1991; two s. one d. from previous m.; ed Cornell Univ. and Univ. of California, Berkeley; Asst Prof., Harvard Univ. 1962–65; Assoc. Prof., Stanford Univ. 1965–67, Prof. of Chem. 1967–73; Deputy Dir Office of Science and Tech., The White House, Washington, DC 1971–73; Prof. of Chem., Calif. Inst. of Tech. 1973, then J. Stanley Johnson Prof., now Prof. Emer., Chair., Div. of Chem. and Chem. Eng 1973–78; Founder and Chair. Vestar Research Inc. 1981–; Founder and fmr Dir Combion Inc.; fmr Chair. Acad. Cttee on Commercial Aviation Security; fmr advisor to US Fed. Aviation Admin; Alfred P. Sloan Foundation Fellow 1962–65; Fellow, NAS, American Acad. of Arts, American Philosophical Soc.; ACS Award in Pure Chem. 1967, William H. Nichols Award 1990, Nat. Medal of Science 2000, ACS Award for Creative Invention 2001, Othmer Gold Medal, Chemical Heritage Foundation 2003. *Publications:* numerous articles in professional journals. *Leisure interests:* hiking, skiing, photography, music, travel. *Address:* Division of Chemistry and Chemical Engineering, 232 Noyes, Mail Code 127-72, California Institute of Technology, Pasadena, CA 91125 (office); PO Box 50065, Pasadena, CA 91115-0065, USA (home). *Telephone:* (626) 395-6088 (office). *Fax:* (626) 568-0402 (office). *E-mail:* jb@caltech.edu (office). *Website:* www.cce.caltech.edu (office).

BALDESSARI, John, MA; American artist and academic; b. 17 June 1931, National City, Calif.; ed San Diego State Univ., Univ. of California, Berkeley, Univ. of California, Los Angeles, Otis Art Inst., Los Angeles, Chouinard Art Inst., Los Angeles; teacher, Calif. Inst. of the Arts, Valencia 1970–1988; Prof. of Art, UCLA 1996–2007; Los Angeles Inst. for the Humanities Fellow, Univ. of Southern Calif. 2002; Guggenheim Fellowship 1988; Hon. DFA (Otis Art Inst. of Parsons School of Design of the New School of Social Research) 2000, (San Diego State Univ.) 2003, (Calif. State Univ.) 2003; Oscar Kokoschka Prize (Austria) 1996, Gov. of Calif.'s Award for Lifetime Achievement in the Visual Arts 1997, Spectrum-International Award for Photography, Foundation of Lower Saxony, Germany 1999, Coll. Art Asscns' Lifetime Achievement Award 1999, Artist Space, New York 2000, Best Web-Based Original Art, AICA USA Best Show Awards 2002, 2nd Place, Best Show Commercial Gallery National for exhibit at Margo Leavin Gallery, US Art Critics Asscn 2003, Americans for the Arts Lifetime Achievement Award, New York 2005, honoured by Rolex Mentor and Protégé Arts Initiative, New York 2005, BACA Int. 2008, Golden Lion for Lifetime Achievement, La Biennale di Venezia 2009. *Publications:* Throwing a Ball to Get Three Melodies and Fifteen Chords 1975, Close-Cropped Tales 1981, The Life and Opinions of Tristam Shandy (39 photo-collage illustrations for the novel by Laurence Sterne) 1988, The Telephone Book (With Pearls) 1988, Lamb (co-author) 1989, Zorro (Two Gestures and One Mark) 1998, The Metaphor Problem Again (co-author) 1999, Brown and Green and

Other Parables 2001; numerous articles and reviews. *Address:* c/o John Baldessari, 626½ Vernon Avenue, Venice, CA 90291, USA. *E-mail:* john@baldessari.org (office). *Website:* www.baldessari.org.

BALDING, Clare, OBE; British television presenter, writer, broadcaster and amateur jockey (retd); b. 29 Jan. 1971, Kingsclere, Hants., England; d. of Ian Balding and Emma Balding (née Hastings-Bass); civil partner Alice Arnold 2006–; ed Downe House, Berks., Newnham Coll., Cambridge; amateur flat jockey 1988–93, Champion Lady Rider 1990; Pres. Cambridge Union Soc. 1992; trainee with BBC Nat. Radio 1994, worked on 5 Live, Radio 1, Radio 2 and Radio 4; debut as TV presenter introducing highlights of Royal Ascot 1995, became BBC's lead horse racing presenter 1997, covered Grand National 1998–2012, for Channel 4 2013–, anchored coverage of Cheltenham Festival March 2013; has worked on five Summer Olympic Games, four Paralympic Games and four Winter Olympic Games; continues to present Horse Racing for Channel 4; has also presented a wide range of sporting and other events; host, Ramblings (BBC Radio 4) 1999–; worked on Britain's Hidden Heritage and Countryfile 2011–12; presented Sport and the British for BBC Radio 4 2012; regular presenter of Good Morning Sunday (BBC Radio 2) 2012–; presenter of Britain's Brightest on BBC TV 2013; has written regular columns for The Observer, Evening Standard, The Sporting Life; Patron British Thyroid Foundation 2010–; mem. of several BAFTA Award-winning programmes, Best Sports Presenter, Royal Television Soc. (RTS) Television Sport Awards 2003, Racing Journalist of the Year Award 2003, RTS Presenter of the Year Award for her coverage of the London 2012 Olympic and Paralympic Games, Sports Presenter of the Year, TRIC Awards, Special Achievement Award, Women in Film and Television Awards for her work on the Olympics and Paralympics, also honoured with awards from Attitude Magazine, Red Magazine, Tatler and the Horserace Writers' Asscn, British Sports Journalism Award for Sports Broadcaster of the Year (BBC and Channel 4), Sports Journalists' Asscn 2012, Award for Sports Presenter, Television and Radio Industries Club Awards 2013, Special BAFTA Award 2013, assessed as being one of the 100 most powerful women in the UK by BBC Radio 4's Woman's Hour 2013. *Publication:* My Animals and Other Family (autobiog.) (Biography/Autobiography of the Year, Nat. Book Awards) 2012. *Address:* c/o David Phillips, James Grant Group Ltd, 94 Strand on the Green, Chiswick, London, W4 3NN, England (office). *E-mail:* david@jamesgrant.co.uk (office). *Website:* www.clarebalding.co.uk.

BALDINI, Stefano; Italian long distance runner; b. 25 May 1971, Castelnovo di Sotto; m. Virna De Angeli; one d.; competes in 5,000m., 10,000m. and marathon events; holds nat. record for marathon; winner World Half Marathon 1996; Gold Medal Marathon, European Championships 1998, 2006, Athens Olympics 2004; Bronze Medal Marathon, World Athletics Championships Edmonton 2001, Paris 2003; Commendatore, Ordine al Merito della Repubblica Italiana 2004. *Publications:* Con le ali ai piedi 2005, Quelli che corrono 2007, Maratona per tutti 2009. *Website:* www.stefanobaldini.net (home).

BALDWIN, Alexander (Alec) Rae, III; American actor; b. 3 April 1958, Masapequa, NY; s. of Alexander Rae Baldwin, Jr and Carol Baldwin (née Martineau); m. Kim Basinger (q.v.) 1993 (divorced 2002); one d.; ed George Washington and New York Univs, Lee Strasberg Theater Inst.; also studied with Mira Rostova and Elaine Aiken; mem. Screen Actors' Guild, American Fed. of TV and Radio Artists, Actors Equity Asscn; mem. Bd of Dirs People for the American Way, New York Philharmonic 2011–. *Stage appearances include:* Loot (Theatre World Award 1986) 1986, Serious Money 1988, Prelude to a Kiss 1990, A Streetcar Named Desire 1992. *Film appearances include:* Forever Lulu 1987, She's Having a Baby 1987, Beetlejuice 1988, Married to the Mob 1988, Talk Radio 1988, Working Girl 1988, Great Balls of Fire 1989, The Hunt for Red October 1990, Miami Blues 1990, Alice 1990, The Marrying Man 1991, Prelude to a Kiss 1992, Glengarry Glen Ross 1992, Malice 1993, The Getaway 1994, The Shadow 1994, Heaven's Prisoners 1995, Looking for Richard 1996, The Juror 1996, Ghosts of Mississippi 1996, Bookworm 1997, The Edge 1997, Thick as Thieves 1998, Outside Providence 1998, Mercury Rising 1998 (also producer), The Confession 1999, Notting Hill 1999, Thomas and the Magic Railroad 2000, State and Main 2000, Pearl Harbor 2001, Cats and Dogs (voice) 2001, Final Fantasy: The Spirit's Within 2001, The Royal Tenenbaums 2001, The Devil and Daniel Webster 2001, Path to War 2002, Dr Seuss' The Cat in the Hat 2003, The Cooler 2003, Along Came Polly 2004, The Last Shot 2004, The Aviator 2004, Elizabethtown 2005, Fun with Dick and Jane 2005, Mini's First Time 2006, The Departed 2006, Running with Scissors 2006, The Good Shepherd 2006, Suburban Girl 2007, Brooklyn Rules 2007, Lymelife 2008, My Best Friend's Girl 2008, Madagascar: Escape 2 Africa (voice) 2008, My Sister's Keeper 2009, It's Complicated 2009, AmeriQua 2011, Rock of Ages 2012, Rise of the Guardians 2012. *TV appearances include:* The Doctors 1980–82, Cutter to Houston 1982, Knot's Landing 1984–85, Love on the Run 1985, A Dress Gray 1986, The Alamo: 13 Days to Glory 1986, Sweet Revenge 1990, Nuremberg 2000, Path to War 2002, Second Nature 2002, Dreams and Giants 2003, Thomas and Friends: The Best of Gordon 2004, 30 Rock (series) (Golden Globe Award for Best Actor in a Musical or Comedy TV Series 2007, 2009, Screen Actors' Guild Award for Outstanding Performance by a Male Actor in a Comedy Series 2007, 2008, Emmy Award for Outstanding Lead Actor in a Comedy Series 2009, Golden Globe Award for Best Actor in a Musical or Comedy TV Series 2010) 2006–, The Marriage Ref 2010. *Publication:* A Promise to Ourselves: A Journey through Fatherhood and Divorce (with Mark Tabb) 2008. *Website:* www.alecbaldwin.com.

BALDWIN, Sir Jack Edward, Kt, PhD, FRS; British chemist and academic; *Professor, Chemistry Research Laboratory, University of Oxford;* b. 8 Aug. 1938, London; s. of Frederick C. Baldwin and Olive F. Headland; m. Christine L. Franchi 1977; ed Lewes Co. Grammar School and Imperial Coll., London; Asst Lecturer in Chem., Imperial Coll. London 1963–66, Lecturer 1966; Asst Prof., Pennsylvania State Univ. 1967, Assoc. Prof. 1969; Assoc. Prof. of Chem., MIT 1970–72, Prof. 1972–78; Waynflete Prof. of Chem., Univ. of Oxford 1978–2003, now Prof., Chemistry Research Lab., Head, Dyson Perrins Lab. 1978–2003, Dir Oxford Centre for Molecular Studies, Fellow, Magdalen Coll. 1978–; Daniell Prof. of Chem., King's Coll., London 1972; Hon. DSc (Warwick) 1988, (Strathclyde) 1988; Corday Morgan Medal, Chem. Soc. 1975, Karrer Medal, Univ. of Zürich 1984, Dr P. Janssen Prize (Belgium) 1988, Davy Medal, Royal Soc. 1993, Leverhulm Medal, Royal Soc. 1999, Kitasako Medal 2000. *Publications:* papers in organic and bio-organic chem. in Journal of the American Chemical Society, Journal of the

Chemical Society and Nature. *Leisure interests:* British motorbikes, gardening. *Address:* Chemistry Research Laboratory, University of Oxford, Mansfield Road, Oxford, OX1 3TA, England (office). *Telephone:* (1865) 275670 (office). *E-mail:* jack .baldwin@chemistry.oxford.ac.uk (office). *Website:* www.chem.ox.ac.uk/ researchguide/jbaldwin.html (office).

BALDWIN, Peter Jeremy, BEE, BA; Australian fmr politician; b. 12 April 1951, Aldershot, UK; ed Univ. of Sydney, Macquarie Univ.; fmr engineer and computer programmer; mem. NSW State Parl. (Upper House) 1976–82; mem. House of Reps (Australian Labor Party) for Sydney 1983–98, mem. Parl. Cttee on Foreign Affairs, Defence and Trade 1987–90, House of Reps Standing Cttee on Industry, Science and Tech. 1987–90; Minister for Higher Educ. and Employment Services and Minister Assisting Treasurer 1990–93; Minister for Social Security 1993–96; apptd Shadow Minister for Finance 1997; Co-founder DebateGraph (web-based collaborative tool). *Address:* Level 3, 10 Mallet Street, Camperdown, NSW 2050, Australia. *Website:* debategraph.org.

BALDWIN, Tammy Suzanne Green, BA, JD; American lawyer and politician; *Senator from Wisconsin;* b. 11 Feb. 1962, Madison, Wis.; d. of Joseph Edward Baldwin and Pamela Baldwin (née Green); partner Lauren Azar 1995–2010; ed Madison West High School, Smith Coll., Univ. of Wisconsin, Madison; practised law 1989–92; elected to Dane Co. Bd of Supervisors 1986–94; mem. Wisconsin State Ass. from 78th Dist 1993–99, Chair. Educ. Cttee, Criminal Justice Cttee; mem. US House of Reps for the 2nd Congressional Dist of Wis. 1999–2013, mem. Cttee on Energy and Commerce; Senator from Wisconsin 2013–; Democrat. *Address:* United States Senate, Washington, DC 20510, USA (office). *Telephone:* (202) 224-3121 (office). *Website:* www.senate.gov (office); www.tammybaldwin .com.

BALE, Christian; British actor; b. 30 Jan. 1974, Haverfordwest, Pembrokeshire, Wales; m. Sandra Blažić; one d. *Films include:* Mio min Mio (aka The Land of Faraway) 1987, Empire of the Sun 1987, Henry V 1989, Newsies 1992, Swing Kids 1993, Prince of Jutland 1994, Little Women 1994, Pocahontas 1995, The Portrait of a Lady 1996, The Secret Agent 1996, Metroland 1997, Velvet Goldmine 1998, All the Little Animals 1998, A Midsummer Night's Dream 1999, American Psycho 2000, Shaft 2000, Captain Corelli's Mandolin 2001, Laurel Canyon 2002, Reign of Fire 2002, Equilibrium 2002, The Machinist 2004, Hauru no ugoku shiro (aka Howl's Moving Castle; voice: English version) 2004, Batman Begins 2005, The New World 2005, Rescue Dawn 2006, Harsh Times 2006, The Prestige 2006, I'm Not There 2007, 3:10 to Yuma 2007, The Dark Knight 2008, Terminator Salvation 2009, Public Enemies 2009, The Fighter (Nat. Bd of Review Award for Best Supporting Actor, New York Film Critics Online Best Supporting Actor, Washington, DC Area Film Critics Asscn Award for Best Supporting Actor, Golden Globe Award for Best Supporting Actor 2011, Academy Award for Actor in a Supporting Role 2011) 2010, The Flowers of War 2011, The Dark Knight Rises 2012, American Hustle 2013. *Television includes:* Anastasia: The Mystery of Anna 1986, Heart of the Country (mini-series) 1987, Treasure Island 1990, A Murder of Quality 1991, Mary, Mother of Jesus 1999, Nyhetsmorgon (episode) 2009. *Address:* c/o WME Entertainment, 9601 Wilshire Blvd, Beverly Hills, CA 90210, USA (office). *Telephone:* (310) 285-9000 (office). *Fax:* (310) 285-9010 (office). *Website:* www.wma.com (office).

BALE, Gareth Frank; Welsh professional football player; b. 16 July 1989, Cardiff; s. of Frank Bale and Debbie Bale; partner Emma Rhys-Jones; one d.; ed Whitchurch High School, Cardiff; winger; youth career at Southampton, playing at left back 2005–06 (won Premier Academy League 2005–06); has played for Southampton 2006–07 (40 appearances, 5 goals), Tottenham Hotspur 2007–13 (146 appearances, 42 goals) (runner-up, League Cup 2009), Real Madrid 2013– (winners, Copa del Rey 2014); played for Wales U17 2005–06 (7 appearances, 1 goal), Wales U19 2006 (1 appearance, 1 goal), Wales U21 2006–08 (4 appearances, 2 goals), Wales 2006– (44 appearances, 12 goals); BBC Wales Carwyn James Junior Sportsman of the Year 2006, Football League Championship PFA Team of the Year 2006–07, Football League Young Player of the Year 2007, FAW Young Player of the Year 2007, FA Cup Player of the Round (5th Round) 2009–10, Tottenham Hotspur Young Player of the Year 2009–10, 2010–11, Wales Player of the Year Award 2010, 2011, BBC Wales Sports Personality of the Year 2010, Premier League PFA Team of the Year 2010–11, 2011–12, 2012–13, PFA Players' Player of the Year 2010–11, 2012–13, Premier League Player of the Month April 2010, Jan. 2012, Feb. 2013, UEFA Team of the Year 2011, FWA Footballer of the Year 2012–13, PFA Young Player of the Year 2012–13, UEFA Team of the Year 2011, 2013. *Address:* c/o FC Real Madrid, Estadio Santiago Bernabéu, Paseo de la Castellana 104, Madrid, Spain. *E-mail:* info@realmadrid.com. *Website:* www .realmadrid.com.

BALESTRINI, Nanni; Italian poet, author and artist; b. 2 July 1935, Milan; mem. group of poets called Novissimi and co-founder of Gruppo 63 in Palermo 1963; one of prin. eds of literary magazine Il Verri; co-editor (with Alfredo Giuliani) Quindici magazine 1966–68; has organized numerous confs and exhbns; also a figurative artist, exhibiting in many galleries in Italy and abroad, and at Venice Biennale in 1993. *Publications include:* poetry: Come si agisce 1963, Ma noi facciamone un'altra 1966, Le ballate della signorina Richmond 1977, Blackout 1980, Ipocalisse 1986, Il ritorno della signorina 1987, Osservazioni sul volo degli uccelli, poesie 1954–56 1988, The Unseen 1989, Il pubblico del labirinto 1992, Estremi rimedi 1995, Le avventure complete della signorina 1999, Elettra, operapoesia 2001, Sfinimondo 2003, Sconnessioni 2008, Blackout e altro 2009, Lo sventramento della storia 2009, Caosmogonia 2010; novels: Tristano 1964, Vogliamo tutto 1971, La violenza illustrata 1976, Gli invisibili 1987, L'editore 1989, I furiosi 1994, Una mattina ci siam svegliati 1995, La Grande Rivolta (comprising Vogliamo tutto, Gli invisibili, L'editore) 1999, Sandokan, storia di camorra 2004, Liberamilano seguito da Una mattina ci siam svegliati 2011; other works: Gruppo 63. Il romanzo sperimentale 1965, L'Opera di Pechino (with Letizia Paolozzi) 1966, L'orda d'oro (with Primo Moroni) 1988, Paladino 2002, Parma 1922 (radio drama) 2002, Con gli occhi del linguaggio 2006, Les yeux invisibles 2008, Qualcosaper tutti 2010; contrib. to many periodicals and journals. *E-mail:* info@ nannibalestrini.it (office). *Website:* www.nannibalestrini.it (office).

BALGIMBAYEV, Nurlan Utebovich; Kazakhstani engineer and politician; *Adviser to the President;* b. 20 Nov. 1947, Atyrau; ed Kazakh Polytechnic Inst.,

Univ. of Massachusetts, Boston, USA; Chief Engineer, Embaneft and Aktyubinskneft 1979–86; Deputy Head of Main Directorate on Oil Production, USSR Ministry of Oil and Gas Industry 1986–92; with Chevron Corpn in USA 1993–94; Minister of Petroleum and Gas Industry 1994–97; Pres. Kazakhoil Co. (now KazMunayGas) March–Oct. 1997, 1999–2002; Prime Minister of Kazakhstan 1997–99; Pres. Kazakhstan Oil Investment Co. 2002–07; Adviser to Pres. of Kazakhstan 2007–, Special Rep. for Issues of Exploiting the Caspian Sea Resources 2008–; Order of Barys (II degree). *Address:* Office of the President, 010000 Astana, Beibitshilik kosh. 11, Kazakhstan. *Telephone:* (7172) 32-13-99. *Fax:* (7172) 32-61-72. *E-mail:* egov@nitec.kz. *Website:* www.akorda.kz.

BALIBAR, Jeanne; French actress; b. 13 April 1968, Paris; d. of Etienne Balibar and Françoise Balibar; pnr, Mathieu Amalric; two s.; ed Univ. de Paris I. *Plays:* Dom Juan (Avignon) 1993, Le Square, Les Bonnes, La Glycine, Clitandre (Comédie Française), Macbeth 1997, Penthesilea 1997, Uncle Vanya (Paris) 2003, Le cadavre vivant (Paris) 2003, Le Soulier de Satin (Paris) 2003. *Films:* La Sentinelle 1992, Un dimanche à Paris 1994, Comment je me suis disputé ... (ma vie sexuelle) 1996, J'ai horreur d'amour 1997, Trois ponts sur la rivière 1999, Sade 2000, Comédie d'innocence 2000, Va savoir 2001, Avec tout mon amour 2001, Intimisto 2001, Une affaire privée 2002, Saltimbank 2003, Code 46 2003, Toutes ces belles promesses 2003, Clean 2004, Mademoiselle Y 2006, Call Me Agostino 2006, J'aurais voulu être un danseur 2007, Ne touchez pas la hache 2007. *Recordings include:* Paramour 2003. *Address:* Zelig, 57 rue de Turbigo, 75003 Paris, France (office).

BALKENENDE, Jan Pieter, MA, LLM, PhD, DIur; Dutch politician and academic; *Professor of Governance, Institutions and Internationalisation, Erasmus University;* b. 7 May 1956, Kapelle; m. Dr Bianca Hoogendijk; one d.; ed Free Univ. of Amsterdam; Legal Affairs Policy Officer, Netherlands Univs Council 1982–84; mem. Amstelveen Municipal Council 1982–98, Leader, Council Christen-Democratisch Appèl (CDA) Group 1994–98; Prof. of Econs, Free Univ. of Amsterdam 1993–2002; mem. staff, Policy Inst. of the CDA 1984–98; mem. Parl. 1998–2002, Parl. Leader CDA 2001, Party Leader –2010 (resgnd); Prime Minister of the Netherlands 2002–10, also Minister of Gen. Affairs 2002–10; Prof. of Governance, Insts and Internationalisation, Erasmus Univ., Rotterdam 2010–; Partner, Ernst and Young 2011–; Grand Crosses from Netherlands, Luxembourg, Jordan, Germany, Brazil, Ghana, Sweden, Chile; Dr hc (Károli Gáspár Reformed Univ., Budapest) 2005, (Keio Univ., Tokyo) 2009, (Yonsei Univ., Seoul) 2010; Abraham Kuyper Prize, Perceptive, 2004, Foreign Policy Asscn Award, New York 2008, Benelux-Europa Prize 2008, Nordrhein-Westphalen Staatspreis 2009, Rus Prix 2010. *Publications include:* numerous articles on liberal individualism and communitarianism in Dutch society. *Address:* Erasmus School of Economics, Erasmus Univ., PO Box 1738, 3000 DR, Rotterdam (office); c/o Christen-Democratisch Appèl (CDA), Dr Kuyperstraat 5, PO Box 30453, 2500 GL The Hague, Netherlands. *Telephone:* (10) 884078716 (office). *Fax:* (10) 884078933 (office). *E-mail:* amalia.angel.rodriguez@nl.ey.com (office). *Website:* www.ese.eur .nl (office); www.ey.com (office).

BALKHEYOUR, Khalid Ahmed; Saudi Arabian engineer and international organization executive; *President and CEO, Arab Satellite Communications Organization (ARABSAT);* fmr Vice-Pres. Lucent Technologies (Saudi Arabia); fmr Dir of Int. Relations, Saudi Telecommunications Co.; currently Pres. and CEO Arab Satellite Communications Org. (ARABSAT). *Address:* Arab Satellite Communications Organization (ARABSAT), Diplomatic Quarter, Alfazari Square, Abdulla Bin Huthafa Al Sahmy Street, Public Pension Agency Complex, Riyadh 11431, Saudi Arabia (office). *Telephone:* (1) 4820000 (office). *Fax:* (1) 4887999 (office). *E-mail:* infot@arabsat.com (office). *Website:* www.arabsat.com (office).

BALL, Anthony (Tony), MBA; British media industry executive; b. 18 Dec. 1955; ed Kingston Univ.; with Thames TV 1976–88; fmr sports broadcaster for Trans World Int.; with BSB Sport 1988–91; with Int. Man. Group 1991–93; with BSkyB 1993–95; with Fox/Liberty Network 1995–99; Exec. Dir British Sky Broadcasting (BSkyB) 1999–2004; mem. Bd of Dirs Kabel Deutschland 2005–, Chair. Supervisory Bd 2010–; Dir (non-exec.) Marks & Spencer PLC 2000–02, Grupo Corporativo ONO 2006–, BT Plc 2009–; mem. Supervisory Bd ProSiebenSat.1 Media 2004–; Chair. Ingenious Media Active Capital 2006–08; Sr Advisor, Providence Equity Partners 2012–; Fellow, Royal Television Soc. *Address:* Kabel Deutschland GmbH, Betastrasse 6–8, 85774 Unterfoehring, Germany (office). *Website:* www .kabeldeutschland.com (office).

BALL, Sir Christopher John Elinger, (John Elinger), Kt, MA, FRSA; British academic (retd); b. 22 April 1935, London; s. of the late Lawrence Elinger Ball and Christine Florence Mary (née Howe) Ball; m. Wendy Ruth Colyer 1958; three s. three d.; ed St George's School, Harpenden, Merton Coll., Oxford; Second Lt in Parachute Regt 1955–56; Lecturer in English Language, Merton Coll., Oxford 1960–61; Lecturer in Comparative Linguistics, SOAS, Univ. of London 1961–64; Fellow and Tutor in English Language, Lincoln Coll., Oxford 1964–69, Bursar 1972–79, Warden, Keble Coll., Oxford 1980–88; Jt Founding Ed. Toronto Dictionary of Old English 1970; mem. General Bd of the Faculties 1979–82, Hebdomadal Council 1985–89, Council and Exec., Templeton Coll., Oxford 1981–92, Editorial Bd, Oxford Review of Educ. 1984–96, CNAA 1982–88; Chair. Bd of Nat. Advisory Body for Public Sector Higher Educ. in England 1982–88, Univ. of Oxford English Bd 1977–79, Jt Standing Cttee for Linguistics 1979–83, Conf. of Colls. Fees Cttee 1979–85, Higher Educ. Information Services Trust 1987–90; Sec., Linguistics Asscn GB 1964–67; Publications Sec., Philological Soc. 1969–75; Gov. St George's School, Harpenden 1985–89, Centre for Medieval Studies, Oxford 1987, Brathay Hall Trust 1988–91, Manchester Polytechnic 1989–91; Founding Fellow in Kellogg Forum for Continuing Education, Univ. of Oxford 1988–89, RSA Fellow in Continuing Educ. 1990–92, Dir of Learning 1992–97; Founding Chair. Nat. Advisory Council for Careers and Educational Guidance (NACCEG); Pres. Nat. Campaign for Learning 1995–97, Patron 1998–; Chancellor Univ. of Derby 1995–2003; Founding Chair. The Talent Foundation 1999–2004; Chair. Global Univ. Alliance 2000–; Millennium Fellow, Auckland Univ. of Tech., NZ 2000; Vice-Pres. Autistica 2010–; Chair. DownsEd Int. 2010–; Hon. Fellow, Lincoln Coll., Oxford 1981, Merton Coll., Oxford 1987, Keble Coll., Oxford 1989, Manchester Polytechnic 1988, Polytechnic of Cen. London 1991, Auckland Univ. of Tech., NZ 1992, North East Wales Inst. 1996, Oxford Brookes Univ. 2007; Hon. DLitt (CNAA) 1989; Hon. DUniv (Univ. of N London) 1993, (Open

Univ.) 2002, (Univ. of Derby) 2003; Hon. DEd (Greenwich Univ.) 1994. *Publications:* Fitness for Purpose 1985, Aim Higher 1989, Higher Education into the 1990s (co-ed.) 1989, More Means Different 1990, Learning Pays 1991, Sharks and Splashes!: The Future of Education and Employment 1991, Profitable Learning 1992, Start Right 1994; poetry (as John Elinger): Still Life 2008, Operatic Interludes 2008, That Sweet City (with Katherine Shock) 2013; various contribs to philological, linguistic and educ. journals. *Address:* 45 Richmond Road, Oxford, OX1 2JJ, England (home). *Telephone:* (1865) 310800 (home).

BALL, Sir John Macleod, Kt, BA (Hons), DPhil, FRS, FRSE; British mathematician and academic; *Sedleian Professor of Natural Philosophy and Director of the Oxford Centre for Nonlinear Partial Differential Equations, University of Oxford;* b. 19 May 1948, Farnham, Surrey; m.; three c.; ed Mill Hill School, London, St John's Coll., Cambridge, Univ. of Sussex; SRC Postdoctoral Fellow, Heriot-Watt Univ. 1972–74, on leave to Lefschetz Center for Dynamical Systems, Brown Univ., USA 1972–74, Lecturer in Math., Heriot-Watt Univ. 1974–78, Reader in Mathematics 1978–82, Science and Eng Research Council Sr Fellow 1980–85, Prof. of Applied Analysis 1982–96, Hon. Prof. 1998–; Sedleian Prof. of Natural Philosophy and Dir Oxford Centre for Nonlinear Partial Differential Equations, Univ. of Oxford 1996–, Fellow, The Queen's Coll.; Visiting Prof., Univ. of California, Berkeley 1979–80, Inst. for Advanced Study, Princeton 1993–94 (mem. 2002–03), Tata Inst. of Fundamental Research, Bangalore 2001, Univ. of Montpellier II 2003, Univ. of Chile, Santiago 2004, Université Pierre et Marie Curie, Paris 2009; mem. Exec. Bd, Int. Council for Science; Chair. Isaac Newton Inst. Scientific Steering Cttee; mem. Conseil Scientifique du CNRS, Conseil Scientifique d'Electricité de France; Council mem. Eng and Physical Sciences Research Council 1994–99; Pres. Edinburgh Math. Soc. 1989–90, London Math. Soc. 1996–98; fmr Pres. Int. Math. Union; Chief Ed. (with R. D. James) Archive for Rational Mechanics and Analysis; Ed. Oxford Mathematical Monographs, Oxford Lecture Series in Mathematics and its Applications; Consulting Ed. World Scientific Series in Applied Analysis; mem. Editorial Bd, Analyse Nonlinéaire, Annali di Matematica Pura ed Applicata, Applicable Analysis, Calculus of Variations and Partial Differential Equations, Control, Optimization and Calculus of Variations, Dynamics and Differential Equations, Journal of Differential Equations, Mathematics in Action, Journal de Mathématiques Pures et Appliquées, Mathematical Methods and Models in Applied Science, Tbilisi Mathematical, Unione Matematica Italiana Lecture Notes Series Journal; mem. Academia Europaea 2008; Associé Etranger, Acad. des Sciences 2000; Foreign mem. Istituto Lombardo 2005, Norwegian Acad. of Science and Letters 2007; Fellow, Inst. of Math. and its Applications 2003; Hon. mem. Edinburgh Math. Soc. 2008; Dr hc (École Polytechnique Fédérale de Lausanne); Hon. DSc (Heriot-Watt) 1998, (Sussex) 2000, (Univ. of Montpellier II) 2003, (Edinburgh) 2005; Whittaker Prize, Edinburgh Math. Soc. 1981, Keith Prize, Royal Soc. of Edinburgh 1990, Naylor Prize in Applied Math., London Math. Soc. 1995, Theodore Von Karman Prize, Soc. of Industrial and Applied Math. 1999, David Crighton Medal, Inst. of Math. and its Applications and London Math. Soc. 2003, Royal Medal, Royal Soc. of Edinburgh 2006, Sylvester Medal, Royal Soc. 2009. *Publications:* numerous papers in professional journals. *Address:* Room S1.17, Mathematical Institute, University of Oxford, Andrew Wiles Building, Radcliffe Observatory Quarter, Woodstock Road, Oxford, OX2 6GG, England (office). *Telephone:* (1865) 615110 (office). *E-mail:* john.ball@maths.ox.ac.uk (office). *Website:* www.maths.ox.ac.uk (office).

BALL, Michael Ashley; British singer; b. 27 June 1962, Bromsgrove; s. of Anthony George Ball and Ruth Parry Ball (née Davies); pnr Cathy McGowan; ed Plymouth Coll., Farnham Sixth Form Coll., Guildford School of Acting; numerous nat. and int. concert tours; co-founder and patron Research into Ovarian Cancer; Dr hc (Univ. of Plymouth); Variety Club of Great Britain Most Promising Artiste Award 1989, The Variety Club Best Recording Artiste 1998, Theatregoers Club of Great Britain Most Popular Musical Actor 1999. *Theatre appearances include:* Judas/John the Baptist in Godspell (debut), Aberystwyth 1984, Frederick in The Pirates of Penzance, Manchester Opera House 1984, Marius in Les Misérables, London 1985–86, Raoul in The Phantom of the Opera, London 1987–88, Alex in Aspects of Love, London 1989–90, New York (debut) 1990, Giorgio in Passion, London 1996, Alone Together (part of Divas Season), London 2001, Caractacus Potts in Chitty Chitty Bang Bang, London 2002–04, The Woman in White 2005, Hairspray (Olivier Award for Best Actor in a Musical) 2008, Sweeney Todd - The Demon Barber of Fleet Street (Olivier Award for Best Actor in a Musical) 2012. *Film:* England My England 1995. *Television:* own TV series 'Michael Ball' 1993, 1994, Royal Variety performances, Michael Ball in Concert (video) 1997, Michael Ball at Christmas 1999; represented UK in Eurovision Song Contest 1992, An Evening with Michael Ball 1998, Lord Lloyd Webber's 50th Birthday 1998, BBC Radio 2 series Sunday Night with Michael Ball 2014. *Recordings include:* albums: Rage of the Heart 1987, Michael Ball 1992, Always 1993, One Careful Owner 1994, The Best of Michael Ball 1994, First Love 1996, Michael Ball - The Musicals 1996, Michael Ball - The Movies 1998, Christmas 1999, Live at the Royal Albert Hall 1999, This Time It's Personal 2000, Centre Stage 2001, Music 2005, One Voice 2006, Back to Bacharach 2007, Past and Present 2009, Songs of Love 2009, Encore 2010, Heroes 2011, Both Sides Now 2013; stage show cast recordings include Les Miserables 1986, Aspects of Love 1989, West Side Story 1993, Passion 1996, Chitty Chitty Bang Bang 2002, Sweeney Todd: The Demon Barber of Fleet Street 2012. *Leisure interests:* collecting graphic novels and single malt whiskies, country walking, music, theatre, cooking. *Address:* c/o Phil Bowdery, Live Nation (Music) UK Ltd, Regent Arcade House, 19-25 Argyll Street, London, W1F 7TS, England (office). *Telephone:* (20) 7009-3333 (office). *Fax:* (20) 7009-3211 (office). *E-mail:* sarah.donovan@livenation.co.uk (office); mbe@michaelball.co.uk (office). *Website:* www.livenation.co.uk (office); www.michaelball.co.uk; www.mbfc.co.uk (office).

BALL, Sir (Robert) James, Kt, MA, PhD, CBIM, FIAM; British economist and academic; *Professor Emeritus of Economics, London Business School;* b. 15 July 1933, Saffron Walden; s. of Arnold James Hector Ball; m. 1st Patricia Mary Hart Davies 1954 (divorced 1970); one s. (deceased 2); one d. (deceased); m. 2nd Lindsay Jackson (née Wonnacott) 1970; one step-s.; ed St Marylebone Grammar School, Queen's Coll., Oxford, Univ. of Pennsylvania, USA; RAF 1952–54; Research Officer, Univ. of Oxford Inst. of Statistics 1957–58; IBM Fellow, Univ. of Pennsylvania 1958–60; Lecturer, Univ. of Manchester 1960–63, Sr Lecturer 1963–65; Prof. of Econs, London Business School 1984–98, Prof. Emer. 1998–, Deputy Prin. 1971–72, Prin. 1972–84; Dir Barclays Bank Trust Co. Ltd 1973–86,

Tube Investments 1974–84, IBM UK Holdings Ltd 1979–95, IBM UK Pensions Trust 1994; Chair. Legal and General Group PLC. 1980–94, Royal Bank of Canada Holdings (UK) Ltd 1995–98; Dir LASMO 1988–94, Royal Bank of Canada 1990–98; Vice-Pres. Chartered Inst. of Marketing 1991–94; mem. Council British-N American Cttee 1985–98, Research Asscn 1985–, Marshall Aid Commemoration Comm. 1987–94; Econ. Adviser, Touche Ross & Co. 1984–95; Trustee Foulkes Foundation 1984–, Civic Trust 1986–91, The Economist 1987–99, ReAction Trust 1991–93; mem. Advisory Bd IBM UK Ltd 1995–98; Freeman of City of London 1987; Hon. DSc (Aston) 1987; Hon. DSocSc (Manchester) 1988. *Publications:* An Economic Model of the United Kingdom 1961, Inflation and the Theory of Money 1964, Inflation (ed.) 1969, The International Linkage of National Economic Models (ed.) 1972, Money and Employment 1982, The Economics of Wealth Creation (ed.) 1992, The British Economy at the Crossroads 1998, articles in professional journals. *Leisure interests:* chess, fishing, gardening. *Address:* London Business School, Sussex Place, Regent's Park, London, NW1 4SA, England (office). *Telephone:* (20) 7000-8419 (office). *Fax:* (20) 7000-7001 (office). *E-mail:* jball@london.edu (office). *Website:* www.london.edu/economics (office).

BALLANTYNE, Sir Frederick Nathaniel, Kt, GCMG, MD, DrSci; Saint Vincent and the Grenadines cardiologist and government official; *Governor-General;* b. 5 July 1936, Layou; m. Sally Ann Ballantyne; ed Howard Univ. and Syracuse Univ. School of Medicine, USA; fmr Chief of Medicine, Kingstown General Hosp.; fmr Chief Medical Officer for Saint Vincent; Gov.-Gen. St Vincent and the Grenadines 2002–. *Address:* Office of the Governor-General, Government House, Old Montrose, Kingstown, Saint Vincent and the Grenadines (office). *Telephone:* 456-1401 (office). *Fax:* 457-9710 (office). *E-mail:* govthouse@vincysurf .com (office).

BALLARD, Mark, MA; British consultant, university administrator and fmr politician; *Assistant Director for Policy, Barnardo's Scotland;* b. 27 June 1971, Leeds; m. Heather Stacey; one s.; ed Univ. of Edinburgh; with European Youth Forest Action 1994–98; Ed. Reforesting Scotland (journal) 1998–2001; MSP (Green Party) for Lothians 2003–07, mem. Parl. Finance Cttee; fmr consultant for several charities and social enterprises on business devt, promotion and lobbying; Rector Univ. of Edinburgh 2006–09; Communications Man. Scottish Council for Voluntary Orgs 2007; currently Asst Dir of Policy, Barnardo's Scotland; Ed.-in-Chief Bright Green (website); mem. Editorial Bd Scottish Left Review; mem. Friends of the Earth, Sustrans, Campaign for Nuclear Disarmament, Democratic Left Scotland, Reforesting Scotland, Water of Leith Conservation Trust. *Address:* Barnardo's Scotland, 111 Oxgangs Road, North Edinburgh, EH14 1ED, Scotland (office). *Telephone:* (131) 314-6611 (office). *Website:* www.barnardos.org.uk (office); www.brightgreenscotland.org.

BALLARD, Robert D., PhD; American oceanographer; *President, Institute for Exploration;* b. 30 June 1942, Wichita, Kan.; Barbara Earle Ballard; two s. one d.; ed Univs of California, Southern California, Hawaii and Rhode Island; 2nd Lt, US Army Intelligence 1965–67, later transferred to USN 1967–70; served with USN during Vietnam War, Consultant, Deputy Chief of Naval Operations for Submarine Warfare 1984–90, Consultant, Nat. Research Council, Marine Bd Comm. 1984–87, Commdr USNR 1987–2001; Research Assoc. Woods Hole Oceanographic Inst., Cape Cod, Mass. 1969–74, Asst Scientist 1974–76, Assoc. Scientist 1976–83, Sr Scientist 1983–, Founder Deep Submergence Laboratory 1983–, Dir Center for Marine Exploration 1989–95, Emer. 1997–; Visiting Scholar, Stanford Univ. 1979–80, Consulting Prof. 1980–81; Founder and Chair. Jason Foundation for Educ. 1989–; Founder Inst. for Exploration, Mystic, Conn. 1995–, Pres. 1997–; Founder and Pres. Immersion Inst. 2001–; Prof. of Oceanography, URI 2002–; has led or participated in over 100 deep-sea expeditions including discoveries of German battleship Bismarck, RMS Titanic 1985, warships from lost fleet of Guadalcanal, the Lusitania, Roman ships off coast of Tunisia 1997, USS Yorktown 1998; expeditions included first manned exploration of Mid-ocean Ridge, discovery of warm water springs and their fauna in Galapagos Rift, first discovery of polymetallic sulphides; has participated in numerous educ. programmes with major TV networks in Europe, Japan and USA, hosted Nat. Geographic Explorer show 1989–91; Founder Inst. for Archaeological Oceanography, Graduate School of Oceanography, Univ. of Rhode Island 2003; Hon. Dir Explorers Club 1988–; Hon. Dir Sigma Pi Sigma, Physics Soc. 1996–; Dr hc (Clark Univ.) 1986, (Univ. of Rhode Island) 1986, (Southeastern Massachusetts Univ.) 1986, (Long Island Univ.) 1987, (Univ. of Bath, UK) 1988, (Tufts Univ.) 1990, (Lenoir-Rhyne Coll.) 1991, (Skidmore Coll.) 1992, (Worcester Polytechnic Inst.) 1992, (Bridgewater State Coll.) 1993, (Lehigh Univ.) 1993, (Maine Maritime Acad.) 1994, (Massachusetts Maritime Acad.) 1994, (Univ. of Wisconsin) 2000, (Univ. of Hartford) 2001, (Univ. of Delaware) 2001; Distinguished Mil. Grad., US Army 1967, Newcomb-Cleveland Award, American Asscn for the Advancement of Science 1981, Nat. Geographic Soc. Centennial Award 1988, American Geological Inst. Award 1990, USN Robert Dexter Conrad Award 1992, The Kilby Award 1994, Explorers Medal, Explorers Club 1995, Nat. Geographic Soc. Hubbard Medal 1996, USN Memorial Foundation Lone Sailor Award 1996, NII Award for Best Internet Site for Education 1996, American Geophysical Union 'Excellence in Geophysical Education' Award 1997, Commonwealth Award 2000, Lindbergh Award 2001, The Navy League Award Robert M. Thompson Award for Outstanding Leadership 2001, Nat. Humanities Medal 2003; numerous other awards and prizes. *Films:* Secrets of the Titanic (Int. Film Festival Award) 1987, Search for Battleship Bismarck (Emmy Award for Best Documentary) 1990, Last Voyage of the Lusitania (Emmy Award for Best Documentary) 1994. *Publications:* Photographic Atlas of the Mid-Atlantic Ridge 1977, The Discovery of the Titanic (with Rick Archbold) (New York Times and The Times No. 1 Best Seller 1987) 1987, The Discovery of the Bismarck (New York Times and The Times No. 1 Best Seller 1990) 1990, Bright Shark (novel) 1992, The Lost Ships of Guadalcanal (with Rick Archbold) 1993, Explorations (autobiography) 1995, Exploring the Lusitania (with Spencer Dunmore) 1995, Lost Liners (with Rick Archbold) 1997, Return to Midway 1999, The Water's Edge 1999, Eternal Darkness: A Personal History of Deep-Sea Exploration (with Will Hively) 2000, Graveyards of the Pacific 2001, Adventures in Ocean Exploration 2001; non-fiction for children: Exploring the Titanic (Virginia State Reading Asscn Young Readers Award 1993) 1988, The Lost Wreck of the Isis 1990, Exploring the Bismarck 1991, Explorer 1992, Ghost Liners 1998; Deep Sea Explorer (CD-ROM) 1999; has also published more than 57 articles in scientific journals and numerous popular articles. *Leisure interest:* family. *Address:* Institute for Exploration, 55

Coogan Boulevard, Mystic, CT 06355, USA (office). *Telephone:* (860) 572-5955 ext. 602 (office). *E-mail:* lbradt@ife.org (office). *Website:* www.ife.org (office).

BALLARD, Shari L.; American business executive; *Enterprise Executive Vice-President and President, International, Best Buy Company Inc.;* b. Mich.; joined Best Buy 1993, has held several positions including Asst Store Man., Gen. Store Man., Vice-Pres. and Sr Vice-Pres., Exec. Vice-Pres., Human Resources and Legal 2004–07, Exec. Vice-Pres., Retail Channel Man. 2007–10, Exec. Vice-Pres. and Pres., Americas 2010–12, Enterprise Exec. Vice-Pres. and Pres., International 2012–; mem. Bd of Trustees, Univ. of Minnesota Foundation, mem. Exec. Cttee, Human Resources Cttee; ranked by Fortune magazine amongst the 50 Most Powerful Women in Business in the US (48th) 2010, (46th) 2011. *Address:* Best Buy Company Inc., 7601 Penn Avenue South, Richfield, MN 55423, USA (office). *Telephone:* (612) 291-1000 (office). *Fax:* (612) 292-4001 (office). *E-mail:* info@ bestbuy.com (office). *Website:* www.bestbuy.com (office).

BALLE, Francis, DèsSc, PhD; French academic; *Professor, Université de Paris II – Panthéon-Assas;* b. 15 June 1939, Fourmies; s. of Marcel Balle and Madeleine (née Leprohon) Balle; m. Marie Derieux 1972; three d.; ed Inst. d'Etudes Politiques, Univ. de Paris-Sorbonne; philosophy teacher, Ecole Normale d'Oran 1963–65; Asst Lecturer, Faculté des Lettres, Ecole de Journalisme, Algiers 1965–67, Univ. de Paris-Sorbonne 1967–70, Univ. René Descartes, Univ. Paris VI 1970–72; Lecturer, Univ. de Paris II – Panthéon-Assass 1972, Prof. 1978–; Vice-Chancellor Universités de Paris 1986–89; Visiting Prof., Stanford Univ. 1981–83; Pres. statistical Cttee for TV action outside France 1997–; Dir Inst. Français de Presse 1976–86, Inst. de Recherche et d'Etudes sur la Communication 1986–; mem. Conseil Supérieur de l'Audiovisuel 1989–93; Dir Information and New Technologies at Ministry of Nat. Educ. 1993–95, of Scientific Information, Tech. and of Libraries 1995–; Dir French Media Inst. 1997; mem. Conseil d'administration de Radio France 2004–, mem. Fulbright Comm.; Founding Ed. Le Revue Européenne des Médias; Chevalier, Légion d'honneur 1998, Commandeur 2007, Officier, Palmes académiques; Prize of Acad. des Sciences Morales et Politiques 1995;. *Publications:* Médias et Sociétés 1980, 2013, The Media Revolution in America and Western Europe 1984, Les nouveaux médias (with Gerard Eymery) 1987, Et si la Presse n'existait pas 1987, La Télévision 1987, Le Mandarin et le marchand 1995, Dictionnaire des médias 1998, Les Médias 2000, Dictionnaire du Web 2002, Les médias, PUF, Que sais-je? 2012, Lexique d'information communication 2006. *Leisure interests:* music, painting. *Address:* Université Panthéon-Assas (Paris II), I.R.E.C., 92 rue d'Assas, 75006 Paris (office); 18 rue Greuze, 75116 Paris, France (home). *Telephone:* 1-43-26-15-66 (office); 1-47-27-78-31 (also fax) (home). *Fax:* 1-43-26-15-78. *E-mail:* balle@u-paris2.fr (office); francisballe@gmail .com (home). *Website:* www.u-paris2.fr (office).

BALLIN, Ernst Hirsch (see Hirsch Ballin, Ernst).

BALLMER, Steven (Steve) Anthony, BA; American software industry executive; b. 24 March 1956, Detroit, Mich.; m. Connie Ballmer; three c.; ed Detroit Country Day School, Harvard Univ., Stanford Univ. Grad. School of Business; while a student, managed football team, worked on Harvard Crimson newspaper and univ. literary magazine; fmr accountant; Asst Product Man. Procter & Gamble, Vice-Pres. Marketing; Sr Vice-Pres. Systems Software, Microsoft Corpn, Redmond, Wash. 1980–92, Exec. Vice-Pres. Sales and Support, Pres. 1998, CEO 2000–14; Dir Accenture 2001–06, Gen. Partner, Accenture SCA 2001; mem. Bd of Dirs Detroit Country Day School; Chevalier, Légion d'honneur; ranked by Forbes magazine amongst The World's Most Powerful People (46th) 2012. *Leisure interests:* exercise, basketball. *Address:* c/o Microsoft Corporation, 1 Microsoft Way, Redmond, WA 98052-8300, USA.

BALLS, Edward Michael (Ed); British economist and politician; *Shadow Chancellor of the Exchequer;* b. 25 Feb. 1967, Norwich, Norfolk, England; s. of Prof. Michael Balls and Carolyn J. Balls; m. Yvette Cooper MP 1998; one s. two d.; ed Nottingham High School, Keble Coll., Oxford, John F. Kennedy School of Govt, Harvard Univ., USA; Teaching Fellow, Dept of Econs, Harvard Univ. 1989–90; fmr Research Asst, Nat. Bureau of Econ. Research, USA; econs leader writer, Financial Times 1990–94; econs columnist, The Guardian 1994–97; Econ. Adviser to Gordon Brown 1990–97; Chief Econ. Adviser to HM Treasury 1999–2004; Research Fellow, Smith Inst. 2004–05; Labour MP for Normanton 2005–10, for Morley and Outwood 2010–; Econ. Sec. to the Treasury 2006–07; Sec. of State for Children, Schools and Family 2007–10; Shadow Educ. Sec. 2010–11; unsuccessful cand. in Labour Party leadership election Sept. 2010; Shadow Chancellor of the Exchequer 2011–; Ed. European Economic Policy 1994–97; mem. Transport and Gen. Workers' Union, Unison, Co-operative Party; Hon. LLD (Nottingham) 2003; Young Financial Journalist of the Year, Wincott Foundation 1992. *Publication:* Reforming Britain's Economic and Financial Policy (co-ed.) 2001, Microeconomic Reform in Britain: Delivering Opportunities for All (co-ed.) 2004. *Address:* House of Commons, Westminster, London, SW1A 0AA, England (office). *Telephone:* (20) 7219-4115 (office). *Fax:* (20) 7219-3398 (office). *E-mail:* ballse@parliament.uk (office). *Website:* www.edballs.co.uk (office).

BALMER, Jean-François; Swiss actor; b. 18 April 1946, Valangin; ed Conservatoire d'Art Dramatique de Paris; has worked extensively in French cinema, TV and stage productions since early 1970s; played Pres. George Pompidou in the TV film Death of a President 2011. *Theatre includes:* Henri IV, Le Bien-Aimé, Théâtre des Mathurins 2010. *Films include:* Nothing to Report 1973, Le mouton enragé 1974, The Mouth Agape (scenes deleted) 1974, The Night Caller 1975, Le petit Marcel 1976, The Castaways of Turtle Island 1976, La menace 1977, Mountain Pass 1978, L'adolescente 1979, Les égouts du paradis 1979, Ils sont grands, ces petits 1979, Cop or Hood 1979, Rien ne va plus 1979, Neige 1981, Strange Affair 1981, Bluff (short) 1982, The Good Soldier 1982, Le quart d'heure américain 1982, L'africain 1983, Swann in Love 1984, Polar 1984, Les fauves 1984, Le sang des autres 1984, Folie suisse 1985, Urgence 1985, Le transfuge 1985, L'amour ou presque 1985, Golden Eighties 1986, La dernière image 1986, La révolution française 1989, Bal perdu 1990, Madame Bovary 1991, La fenêtre 1992, Diên Biên Phú 1992, Sam suffit 1992, Desencuentros 1992, Vent d'est 1993, Mauvais garçon 1993, Rocking Poponguine 1994, La lumière des étoiles mortes 1994, Le livre de cristal 1994, Ma soeur chinoise 1994, Lou n'a pas dit non (voice) 1994, XY, drôle de conception 1996, Beaumarchais 1996, Rien ne va plus 1997, Time Regained 1999, La dilettante 1999, T'aime 2000, The King's Daughters 2000, Charming Fellow

2001, Belphégor – Le fantôme du Louvre 2001, That Day 2003, Ripoux 3 2003, L'ivresse du pouvoir 2006, A Winter in Paris 2006, Elephant Tales (voice) 2006, Le grand appartement 2006, Lucifer et moi 2008, Tokyo! 2008, The Valley 2009, Lucky Luke 2009, Mumu 2010, Celles qui aimaient Richard Wagner 2011, Equinox 2011, Dead Europe 2012, Dans la maison 2012. *Television includes:* films: Bonheur, impair et passe 1977, Le chandelier 1977, La vie séparée 1979, Une page d'amour 1980, Les amours du mal-aimé 1980, Le mariage de Figaro 1981, Concierto barroco 1982, Par ordre du Roy (segment 'Madame Tiquet') 1983, Le roi de la Chine 1984, Le scénario défendu 1984, Visa pour nulle part 1985, En attendant Godot 1989, L'enveloppe 1991, Spender: The French Collection 1993, Le misanthrope 1994, Le héron (also dir) 1995, La pitié du diable 1996, Le propre de l'homme 1996, Le dernier chant 1996, Parfum de famille 1997, Le censeur du lycée d'Epinal 1997, La vérité est un vilain défaut 1997, Aventurier malgré lui 1997, Meurtres sans risque 1998, Deutschlandspiel 2000, Bien agités! 2004, Pierre et Jean 2004, Novecento 2006, Henry Dunant: Red on the Cross 2006, La française doit voter 2007, L'affaire Sacha Guitry 2007, Clémentine 2008, Beauregard 2009, Chateaubriand 2010, Colère 2010, La joie de vivre 2011, Mort d'un président 2011, Territoire de mensonges (film) 2011, L'infiltré 2011; series: Gil Blas de Santillane 1974, Le petit théâtre d'Antenne 2 1980–81, Les poneys sauvages (mini-series) 1983, Cinéma 16 1983, Espionne et tais-toi (seven episodes) 1988, Médecins des hommes 1988, L'or du diable (mini-series) 1989, Antoine Rives, juge du terrorisme 1993, Spender 1993, Christmas Special – The French Collection 1993, Arithmétique appliquée et impertinente 1995, Louise et les marchés (mini-series) 1998, Boulevard du Palais 1999–2012. *Address:* c/o Rosalie Cimino, UBBA, 6 rue de Braque, 75003 Paris, France (office). *Telephone:* 1-44-54-26-40 (office). *Fax:* 1-44-54-08-44 (office). *E-mail:* info@ubba.eu (office). *Website:* www.ubba.eu (office).

BALOCH, Abdul Malik, MB BS; Pakistani ophthalmologist and politician; *Chief Minister of Balochistan;* b. Turbat Dist, Balochistan; s. of Haji Abdul Salam Hoth; ed Ata Shad Degree Coll., Turbat, Bolan Medical Coll., Quetta; began political career with Baloch Student Org.; est. Balochistan Nat. Movt 1988; won Balochistan Nat. Ass. (BNM) seat 1988; Prov. Health Minister in Nawab Akbar Khan Bugti's cabinet; Prov. Educ. Minister 1993; merged with political followers of Mir Ghaus Bakhsh Bizenjo in BNM and became the National Party 2004; elected a Senator 2006, Chair. Functional Cttee on Problems of Less Developed Areas, mem. Standing Cttee on Minorities Affairs, Standing Cttee on Ports and Shipping, Standing Cttee on Food and Agric.; Pres. National Party 2008–; Chief Minister of Balochistan (first non-tribal leader) 2013–. *Address:* Office of the Chief Minister, Quetta, Balochistan, Pakistan (office). *Telephone:* (2161) 2069 (office). *Fax:* (2161) 2069 (office). *E-mail:* cm@balochistan.gov.pk (office). *Website:* www.balochistan .gov.pk (office).

BALOHA, Viktor Ivanovich; Ukrainian politician; b. 15 June 1963, Zavydovo, Mukachev dist, Transcarpathian Oblast; ed Lviv Trade and Econ. Inst.; fmr commodities researcher; Chair. Admin Transcarpathian Oblast 1999–2001, Feb.–Sept. 2005; mem. Our Ukraine party; mem. Verkhovna Rada (Parl.) 2002–05, 2012–; Mayor of Mukachevo 2004–06; Minister of Emergency Situations 2005–06, 2010–12; Chief of the Presidential Secr. 2006–09. *Address:* Verkhovna Rada, 01008 Kyiv, vul. M. Hrushevskoho 5, Ukraine (office). *Telephone:* (44) 255-21-15 (office). *Fax:* (44) 253-32-17 (office). *E-mail:* umz@rada.gov.ua (office). *Website:* www.rada.gov.ua (office).

BALOI, Oldemiro; Mozambican economist, business executive and politician; *Minister of Foreign Affairs and Co-operation;* Deputy Minister of Co-operation early 1990s; Minister of Industry and Trade and Tourism 1995–2000; active in pvt. business since leaving politics, notably as mem. Bd of Dirs and of Exec. Bd Millennium-BIM (Int. Bank of Mozambique); Minister of Foreign Affairs and Co-operation 2008–. *Address:* Ministry of Foreign Affairs and Co-operation, Av. Julius Nyerere 4, CP 2787, Maputo, Mozambique (office). *Telephone:* 21490222 (office). *Fax:* 21494070 (office). *E-mail:* minec@zebra.uem.mz (office).

BALSAI, István, DIur; Hungarian politician and judge; *Member, Constitutional Court;* b. 5 April 1947, Miskolc; s. of József Balsai and Mária Szalontai; m. Ilona Schmidt; two s.; chemical lab. asst 1966; on staff, Faculty of Political and Legal Sciences, Eötvös Loránd Univ., Budapest 1967–72; worked as attorney, Budapest; mem. Hungarian Democratic Forum 1988; mem. Parl. 1990–2011, Pres. Cttee for Employment and Labour, mem. Cttee on Constitution and Justice, Second Vice-Pres. Hungarian Nat. Council; Minister of Justice 1990–94; Leader of Legal Cabinet of Magyar Demokrata Fórum (Hungarian Democratic Forum)—MDF Parl. Group, 1994–98, Group Leader of MDF 1998–2002; mem. European Parl. (Group of the European People's Party (Christian Democrats) and European Democrats) May–July 2004, mem. Cttee on Constitutional Affairs, Cttee on Petitions; mem. Constitutional Court of Hungary 2011–; Founding mem. Asscn of Christian Intellectuals 1989–. *Leisure interest:* folk architecture. *Address:* Constitutional Court (Alkotmánybíróság), 1015 Budapest, Donáti u. 35–45, Hungary (office). *Telephone:* (1) 488-3100 (office). *Fax:* (1) 488-3187 (office). *E-mail:* balsai@ mkab.hu (office). *Website:* www.mkab.hu (office).

BALSEMÃO, Francisco Pinto (see Pinto Balsemão).

BALSILLIE, James Laurence (Jim), CA, BCom, MBA; Canadian electronics industry executive; b. 3 Feb. 1961, Seaforth, Ont.; m. Heidi Balsillie; ed Peterborough Collegiate and Vocational School, Trinity Coll. at Univ. of Toronto, Harvard Grad. Business School, USA; trained as accountant and held various positions at Ernst & Young, Toronto, including Sr Assoc., Strategy Consulting Group and Sr Accountant, Entrepreneurial Services Group; Exec. Vice-Pres. and mem. Bd of Dirs Sutherland-Schultz Ltd, Kitchener, Ont. –1992; mem. Bd of Dirs and Chair. Research In Motion Ltd (name changed to BlackBerry 2013) (designer and mfr of wireless products including BlackBerry email device), Waterloo, Ont. 1992–2007, Co-Chair. and Co-CEO 1992–2012 (resgnd); f. Centre for Int. Governance Innovation (research inst.) 2002, currently Chair.; f. Balsillie School of Int. Affairs 2008; apptd to UN Sec.-Gen.'s High-level Panel on Global Sustainability 2010; Chair. Canadian Int. Council 2007; Dir Ont. Mfg Council 2008; Fellow, Ont. Inst. of Chartered Accountants 2003; numerous hon. doctorate degrees; inducted into Business Hall of Fame 2009. *Leisure interest:* triathlete. *Address:* c/o Board of Directors, BlackBerry, 295 Phillip Street, Waterloo, ON N2L 3W8, Canada.

BALTIMORE, David, PhD; American biologist and university administrator; *Robert A. Millikan Professor of Biology, California Institute of Technology;* b. 7 March 1938, New York, NY; s. of Richard Baltimore and Gertrude Lipschitz; m. Alice Huang 1968; one d.; ed Swarthmore Coll., Rockefeller Univ.; Postdoctoral Fellow, MIT 1963–64, Albert Einstein Coll. of Medicine, New York 1964–65; Research Assoc., Salk Inst., La Jolla, Calif. 1965–68; Assoc. Prof., MIT 1968–72, Prof. of Microbiology 1972–95, Ivan R. Cottrell Prof. of Molecular Biology and Immunology 1994–97, Inst. Prof. 1995–97; American Cancer Soc. Prof. of Microbiology 1973–83, 1994–97; Dir Whitehead Inst. for Biomedical Research 1982–90; Pres. Rockefeller Univ. 1990–91, Prof. 1990–94; Pres. Calif. Inst. of Tech. 1997–2006, Pres. Emer. 2006–, currently Robert A. Millikan Prof. of Biology; Fellow, AAAS (Pres. 2007); mem. NIH Advisory Council on AIDS Research, Chair. Vaccine Cttee 1997–2002, NAS, Inst. of Medicine; Foreign mem. The Royal Soc.; Eli Lilly Award in Microbiology and Immunology 1971, US Steel Foundation Award in Molecular Biology 1974, Nobel Prize in Physiology or Medicine (jt recipient) 1975, Nat. Medal of Science 1999, Warren Alpert Foundation Prize 2000, American Medical Asscn Scientific Achievement Award 2002. *Publications:* more than 600 scientific articles. *Leisure interests:* fly fishing, skiing. *Address:* California Institute of Technology, MC 147-75, 1200 East California Boulevard, Pasadena, CA 91125-3100, USA (office). *Telephone:* (626) 395-3581 (office). *Fax:* (626) 585-9495 (office). *E-mail:* baltimo@caltech.edu (office). *Website:* biology .caltech.edu/Members/Baltimore (office).

BALTSA, Agnes; Greek singer (mezzo-soprano); b. Lefkas; ed Acad. of Music, Athens and in Munich (Maria Callas Scholarship); opera debut as Cherubino, Frankfurt 1968; debut at Vienna State Opera as Octavian 1970, Salzburg Festival 1970, La Scala, Milan (Dorabella) 1976, Paris Opera and Covent Garden, London (Cherubino) 1976, Metropolitan Opera, New York (Octavian) 1980; mem. Deutsche Oper Berlin 1973–; performs at all maj. opera houses in world, and has given concerts in Europe, USA and Japan with Karajan, Böhm, Bernstein, Muti and others; sang Elektra at Opernhaus Zurich, Théâtre du Capitole, Toulouse, Deutsche Oper Berlin, Bayerische Staatsoper, Staatsoper Munich and Wiener Staatsoper 2009–12, also several lieder concerts; Österreichische Kammersängerin 1980, Deutscher Schallplattenpreis 1983, Prix Prestige Lyrique (French Ministry of Culture) 1984. *Leisure interests:* swimming, fashion. *Address:* c/o Management Rita Schültz, Rütistr 52, 8044 Zurich-Gockhausen, Switzerland.

BALUYEVSKII, Col-Gen. Yurii Nikolayevich; Russian army officer and government official; *Deputy Secretary, Security Council of Russian Federation;* b. 9 Jan. 1947, Trubavets, Drohobych Raion, Lviv Oblast, Ukrainian SSR; ed Leningrad (now St Petersburg) Higher Mil. Command School of Gen. Army, M. Frunze Mil. Acad., Mil. Acad. of Gen. Staff; infantry officer 1970–82; Sr Officer, Operator, and Head of Group Chief Operation Dept of Gen. Staff; First Deputy Commdr of Group, Russian Forces in Caucasus; Deputy Head, Chief Operation Dept of Gen. Staff 1982–2001, First Deputy Chief of Gen. Staff 2001–04, Chief and First Deputy Minister of Defence 2004–08; apptd to Security Council of Russian Fed. 2004, Deputy Sec. 2008–; Order for Service to Motherland in Armed Forces, Order of Audacity; nine medals. *Address:* Security Council of Russian Federation, Moscow, Ipatyevsky per. 4/10, entr. 6, Russia (office). *Telephone:* (495) 206-35-96 (office). *Website:* www.scrf.gov.ru (office).

BALZANI, Vincenzo, Laurea in Chimica cum laude; Italian chemist and academic; *Professor of Chemistry, University of Bologna;* b. 15 Nov. 1936, Forlimpopoli; m. Carla Balzani; six c.; ed Univ. of Bologna; Asst Prof., Univ. of Bologna 1963–68, Assoc. Prof. 1969–73, Prof. of Chem. 1973–, Chair. Doctorate in Chem. Science 2002–, also Dir Center for the Photochemcail Conversion of Solar Energy 1981–; Asst Prof., Univ. of Ferrara 1968–89; Dir Italian Nat. Research Council /Photochemistry and Radiation Chem. Inst. (FRAE) 1977–88; Visiting Prof., Hebrew Univ. of Jerusalem Energy Research Center, Israel 1979; Visiting Prof., Univ. of Strasbourg, France 1990; Dir NATO Science Forum, Taormina 1991; Visiting Prof., Univ. of Leuven, Belgium 1991; Dir ICS School of Photochemistry, Trieste 1993; Visiting Prof., Univ. of Bordeaux, France 1994; mem. Editorial Bd several journals including Nanotechnology 1994–2000, Chemistry European Journal 1995–, Chemical Society Reviews 1997–98, ChemPhysChem 2000–, Tetrahedron 2003–, Comptes Rendus Chimie 2004–, Topics in Current Chemistry 2005–, Small 2005–, ChemSusChem 2008–; mem. Academia Europaea, European Photochemical Asscn, Societa Chimica Italiana; Fellow, AAAS, Royal Soc. of Chem., Accademia Nazionale delle Scienze dei XL, Accademia Nazionale dei Lincei; Grande Ufficiale dell'Ordine al Merito della Repubblica Italiana 2006; Dr hc (Univ. of Fribourg) 1989; Univ. of Bologna Miriam Borsari Medal 1960, Italian Chemical Soc. Cannizzaro Gold Medal 1988, Accademia Nazionale dei Lincei Chem. Award 1992, Porter Medal 2000, French Chem. Soc. Prix Franco-Italien 2002, Premio al Merito, Camera di Commercio, Industria e Agricoltura della Provincia di Forli-Cesena 2003, Quilico Gold Medal, Italian Chemical Soc. 2006, Blaise Pascal Medal, European Acad. of Sciences 2009. *Leisure interest:* football. *Address:* Dipartimento di Chimica, Università di Bologna, Via Selmi 2, 40126 Bologna, Italy (office). *Telephone:* (01) 209-9560 (office). *Fax:* (01) 209-9456 (office). *E-mail:* vincenzo.balzani@unibo.it (office). *Website:* www.ciam.unibo.it/photochem/balzani.html (office).

BAMBANG YUDHOYONO, Lt-Gen. Susilo, MA; Indonesian politician and head of state; *President;* b. 1949, East Java; m. Ani Herrawati; two s.; ed Indonesian Mil. Acad. and Webster Univ., USA; participated in Operation Seroja (invasion of Timor Leste) and commanded Dili-based Battalion 744 1970s; spent much of mil. career with Kostrad airborne units; mil. training in USA and Europe 1980s–90s; lectured at Army Staff Command Coll. (Seskoad) 1980s; worked in territorial commands in Jakarta and S. Sumatra (Pangdam II/Sriwijaya) mid 1990s; Chief Mil. Observer in Bosnia 1995–96; Chief of the Armed Forces Social and Political Affairs Staff (Kassospol Abri) (renamed Chief of Territorial Affairs (Kaster) Nov. 1998) 1997–2000; retd from active mil. service 2000; Minister of Mines 1999–2000; Co-ordinating Minister for Political Affairs, Security and Social Welfare 2000–04 (resgnd); Pres. of Indonesia 2004–; UNPKF Medal; Mil. Service medals include Bintang Dharma, Bintang Mahaputera Adipurna, Bintang Republik Indonesia Adipurna. *Address:* Office of the President, Instant Merdeka, Jakarta 10110, Indonesia (office). *Telephone:* (21) 3840946 (office). *Website:* www .presidensby.info (office).

BAMERT, Matthias; Swiss conductor and composer; b. 5 July 1942, Ersigen; m. Susan Exline 1969; one s. one d.; ed studied in Bern and Paris, studied composition with Jean Rivier and Pierre Boulez; asst conductor to Leopold Stokowski 1970–71; Resident Conductor Cleveland Orchestra 1971–78; Music Dir Swiss Radio Orchestra, Basel 1977–83; Prin. Guest Conductor Scottish Nat. Orchestra 1985–90; Dir Musica Nova Festival, Glasgow 1985–90, Lucerne Festival 1992–98; Music Dir London Mozart Players 1993–2000; has appeared with Orchestre de Paris, Rotterdam Philharmonic, Cleveland Orchestra, Pittsburgh Symphony, Montreal Symphony, Royal Philharmonic Orchestra, London, London Philharmonic Orchestra, BBC Philharmonic, City of Birmingham Symphony Orchestra and at BBC Promenade Concerts, London; has toured worldwide; Prin. Conductor and Artistic Adviser Malaysian Philharmonic Orchestra 2005–08; George Szell Memorial Award 1971. *Compositions include:* Concertino for English horn, string orchestra and piano 1966, Septuria Lunaris for orchestra 1970, Rheology for string orchestra 1970, Mantrajana for orchestra 1971, Once Upon an Orchestra for narrator, 12 dancers and orchestra 1975, Ol-Okun for string orchestra 1976, Keepsake for orchestra 1979, Circus Parade for narrator and orchestra 1979. *Address:* MusicVine Performing Arts and Wine Consulting, 2576 Broadway, Suite 239, New York, NY 10025, USA (office). *E-mail:* info@ musicvinearts.com (office). *Website:* www.musicvinearts.com (office).

BAMFORD, Baron (Life Peer), cr. 2013, of Daylesford in the County of Gloucestershire and of Wootton in the County of Staffordshire; **Anthony (Paul) Bamford;** British business executive; *Chairman, J C Bamford Excavators Ltd (JCB);* b. 23 Oct. 1945; s. of the late Joseph Cyril Bamford and of Marjorie Griffin; m. Carole Gray Whitt 1974; two s. one d.; ed Ampleforth Coll., Grenoble Univ.; joined JCB 1962, Chair. and Man. Dir 1975–; Dir Tarmac 1987–94; Pres. Midlands Industrial Council, Staffs. Agricultural Soc. 1987–88, Burton-upon-Trent Conservative Asscn 1987–90; Pres.'s Cttee CBI 1986–88; mem. Design Council 1987–89; DL Staffs., High Sheriff Staffs. 1985–86; Trustee Bamford Charitable Foundation, Sir Anthony Bamford Charitable Foundation, Daylesford Foundation; Chevalier, Ordre nat. du Mérite 1989, Commendatore della Repubblica Italiana 1989; Hon. MEng (Birmingham) 1987; DUniv (Keele) 1988; Hon. DSc (Cranfield) 1994; Hon. DBA (Robert Gordon Univ., Aberdeen) 1996; Hon. DTech (Staffordshire) 1998, (Loughborough) 2002; Young Exporter of the Year (UK) 1972, Young Businessman of the Year (UK) 1979, Top Exporter of the Year (UK) 1995, IAgrE Award of Merit 2008. *Leisure interests:* farming, gardening, collecting vintage Ferraris. *Address:* House of Lords, London, SW1A 0PW; JCB World Headquarters, Rocester, Uttoxeter, Staffs., ST14 5JP, England (office). *Website:* www.jcb.co.uk (office).

BAMFORD-ADDO, Rt Hon. Joyce Adeline; Ghanaian lawyer, judge and politician; b. 26 March 1937, Accra; five c.; called to English Bar 1961, Ghana Bar 1963; practised law 1961–63; Asst State Attorney 1963–65, State Attorney 1965–70, Sr State Attorney 1970–73, Prin. Attorney 1973–76, Chief State Attorney 1976–86, Dir of Public Prosecutions 1986–91; Justice, Supreme Court 1991–2004 (retd); Speaker of Parl. (first woman) 2009–13; Ghana Rep. to UN Comm. on the Status of Women 1990, 1991; fmr mem. Ghana Law Reform Comm., Legal Aid Bd, Gen. Legal Council. *Address:* c/o Office of the Speaker, Parliament House, Accra, Ghana. *E-mail:* clerk@parliament.gh.

BAN, Ki-moon, BA, MPA; South Korean politician, diplomatist and UN official; *Secretary-General, United Nations;* b. 13 June 1944, Eumseong, North Chungcheong; m. Yoo Soon-taek; one s. two d.; ed Seoul Nat. Univ., Kennedy School of Govt, Harvard Univ., USA; early assignments at Embassy in New Delhi, two terms at Embassy in Washington, DC, First Sec., Perm. Observer Mission to UN, New York; fmr Dir UN Div.; Amb. to Austria, also Chair. Preparatory Comm. for the Comprehensive Nuclear Test Ban Treaty Org. (CTBTO) 1999; Dir-Gen. of American Affairs 1990–92; Vice-Chair. South-North Jt Nuclear Control Comm. 1992; Deputy Minister for Policy Planning 1995–96; Nat. Security Adviser to the Pres. 1996–2000; Chef-de-Cabinet to Pres. of UN Gen. Ass. 2001; Vice-Minister 2000, then Foreign Policy Adviser to the Pres.; Minister of Foreign Affairs and Trade 2004–06; Sec.-Gen.-designate UN Oct.–Dec. 2006, Sec.-Gen. 2007–; Order of Service Merit 1975, 1986, 2006, Grand Decoration of Honour (Austria) 2001, Grand Cross of Rio Blanco (Brazil) 2002, Gran Cruz del Sol (Peru) 2006, Grand'Croix, Ordre Nat. (Burkina Faso) 2008, Grand Officier, Ordre Nat. (Côte d'Ivoire); Dr hc (Seoul Nat. Univ.) 2008, Hon. LLD (Univ. of the Philippines Coll. of Law) 2008; James A. Van Fleet Award, Korea Soc., New York 2005, ranked by Forbes magazine amongst The World's Most Powerful People (41st) 2010, (38th) 2011, (30th) 2012, (32nd) 2013. *Address:* Office of the Secretary-General, United Nations, New York, NY 10017, USA (office). *Telephone:* (212) 963-1234 (office). *Fax:* (212) 963-4879 (office). *Website:* www.un.org/sg (office).

BAN, Shigeru, BArch; Japanese architect and academic; *Director, Shigeru Ban Architects;* b. 5 Aug. 1957, Tokyo; ed Southern Calif. Inst. of Architecture and Cooper Union, New York, USA; worked for Arata Isozaki, Tokyo 1982–83; est. Shigeru Ban Architects, Tokyo 1985; Consultant, UNHCR 1995; est. Voluntary Architects Network 1995; Adjunct Prof. of Architecture, Tokohama Nat. Univ. 1995–99, Nihon Univ. 1996–2000; Visiting Prof., Columbia Univ., New York 2000; Prof. of Architecture, Keio Univ. 2001–08; Visiting Prof., Harvard Univ. Grad. School of Design 2010–; mem. jury for Pritzker Architecture Prize 2006–09; Hon. Fellow, Royal Architectural Inst. of Canada 2005; Ordre nat. de la Légion d'honneur 2009, Ordre des Arts et des Lettres 2010; Dr hc (Tech. Univ. of Munich) 2009; Third Kansai Architect Grand Prize, Japan Inst. of Architecture 1996, Japan Inst. of Architecture Best Young Architect of the Year 1997, 18th Tohoku Architecture Prize, Architectural Inst. of Japan 1998, Interior Magazine Best Designer of the Year 2000, World Architecture Awards Best Architecture of the Year in Europe 2001, Matsui Gengo Award 2001, World Architectural Awards Best House of the Year 2002, Grande Medaille d'Or, Academie d' Architecture 2004, Thomas Jefferson Medal in Architecture, Univ. of Virginia 2005, Arnold W. Brunner Memorial Prize in Architecture 2005, Grand Prize of AIJ 2009, Pritzker Architecture Prize 2014. *Architectural works include:* Paper Arbor 1989, House of Double Roof 1993, MDS Gallery 1994, Curtain Wall House 1995, Furniture House 1995, Paper Church 1995, Paper Loghouse 1995, Tazawako Station 1997, Wall-less House 1997, 9 Square Grid House 1997, Hanegi Forest 1997, Paper Dome 1998, Ivy Structure House 1998, Japan Pavilion for Expo 2000 Hanover 2000, A Paper Arch, Museum of Modern Art Courtyard, New York 2000, GC Osaka Bldg 2000, Naked House 2000, Day-Care Center 2001, Gymnasium 2001, Paper Art Museum 2002,

Paper Theater 2003, Paper Dome 2003, Paris Temporary Structure 2004, Paper House 2005, Singapore Bienale Pavilion 2006, Paper Bridge 2007, Paper Tea House 2008, Paper Dome Taiwan 2008, Paper Tower 2009, Quinta Botanica 2009. *Publications include:* Shigeru Ban 1997, Ban Shigeru 1998, Paper Tube Architecture from Kobe to Rwanda 1998, Shigeru Ban—Projects in Progress 1999, Shigeru Ban 2001, Shigeru Ban 2003, Shigeru Ban 2008. *Address:* Shigeru Ban Architects, 5-2-4 Matsubara Ban Building, First Floor, Setagaya, Tokyo 156-0043, Japan (office). *Telephone:* (3) 3324-6760 (office). *Fax:* (3) 3324-6789 (office). *E-mail:* SBA@ tokyo.email.ne.jp (office); Tokyo@ShigeruBanArchitects.com (office). *Website:* www.dnp.co.jp/millennium/SB/VAN.html (office); www.shigerubanarchitects .com.

BANDA, Etta Elizabeth; Malawi nurse and politician; Chair., WHO Global Advisory Group on Nursing and Midwifery, Geneva, Switzerland 2000; mem. Democratic Progressive Party (DPP); MP for Nkhata Bay South 2009–, Minister of Foreign Affairs 2009–11. *Address:* c/o Ministry of Foreign Affairs, POB 30315, Lilongwe 3, Malawi.

BANDA, Joyce, BA; Malawi politician, business executive and head of state; *President;* b. 1952, Malemia, Zomba; m. 1st Roy Kachale, three c.; m. 2nd Richard Banda, two c.; early career working as sec.; mem. Parl. for Zomba-Malosa constituency –2009; Minister of Foreign Affairs and Int. Co-operation 2006–09; Vice-Pres. of Malawi 2009–12, Pres. 2012–; fmr mem. United Democratic Front; mem. Democratic Progressive Party (DPP) 2004–10; Founder-mem. and Pres. People's Party 2011–; Chair. Malawi Housing Corpn; mem. Bd Malawi Entrepreneurs Devt Inst., Malawi Polytechnic; Founder and Chair. Nat. Asscn of Business Women 1989, now Exec. Dir; f. Hunger Project, Young Emerging Leader's Network, Joyce Banda Foundation; numerous awards, including Africa Prize for Leadership 1997, 100 Heroines Award 1998, ranked by Forbes magazine amongst The World's 100 Most Powerful Women (71st) 2012, (47th) 2013. *Address:* Office of the President and Cabinet, Private Bag 301, Capital City, Lilongwe 3, Malawi (office). *Telephone:* 1789311 (office). *Fax:* 1788456 (office). *Website:* www.malawi .gov.mw/opc/opc.htm (office).

BANDA, Rupia Bwezani; Zambian diplomatist, politician, business executive and fmr head of state; b. 13 Feb. 1937, Gwenda, Southern Rhodesia (now Zimbabwe); m. Hope Mwansa Makulu 1966; five s.; ed Munali Secondary School, Univ. of Ethiopia, Univ. of Lund, Sweden, Wolfson Coll., Cambridge, UK; UNIP rep. in Europe 1960 to 1964; Amb. to UAR 1965–67, to USA 1967–70; Exec. Chair. Rural Devt Corpn and Gen. Man. Nat. Marketing Bd of Zambia 1970–74; Perm. Rep. to UN, New York 1974–75, Chair. UN Council on Namibia; Minister of Foreign Affairs 1975–76; fmr MP for Munali for many years; Vice-Pres. of Zambia 2006–08, Pres. 2008–11; fmr Chair. Chipoza Holdings, Robert Hudson Ltd, Allenwest and Chiparamba Enterprise.

BANDARA, Dixon Déla; Sri Lankan politician and diplomatist; *High Commissioner to the Maldives;* ed Thurston Coll.; Gov. Sabaragamuwa Prov. –2008, Northern Prov. 2008–09; High Commr to the Maldives 2009–; mem. Advisory Bd Thurston Coll. Old Boys' Union. *Address:* High Commission of Sri Lanka, 1st Floor, H. Haifa Building, Bodufungadu Magu, Malé, The Maldives (office). *Telephone:* 3322845 (office). *Fax:* 3321652 (office). *E-mail:* highcom@dhivehinet .net.mv (office). *Website:* www.slhcmaldives.com (office).

BANDARANAYAKE, Shirani, LLB, PhD; Sri Lankan lawyer, academic and judge; b. April 1958, Kurunagala; d. of Wilson Bandaranayake and Flora Bandaranayake; m. Pradeepa Kariyawasam; one s.; ed Univ. of Colombo, Univ. of London, England; Visiting Lecturer, Faculty of Law, Univ. of Colombo 1981, Head 1987–92, Dean 1992, Assoc. Prof. of Law 1993; Attorney-at-Law, Supreme Court 1983, apptd Judge 1996, Chief Justice 2011–13; Founder and Co-ordinator Kotalawala Defence Acad. (now Gen. Sir John Kotelawala Defence Univ.); mem. Faculty of Humanities and Social Sciences, Open Univ. of Sri Lanka; mem. Postgraduate Inst. of Man., Univ. of Sri Jayawardenapura; mem. Judges Inst., Judicial Service Comm., Human Rights Task Force, Council of Legal Educ., Law Comm. of Sri Lanka, Nat. Task Force on Forestry Legislation, Working Cttee for Law and Computers, Expert Working Cttee on Banking and Law, Nat. Task Force on Environmental Law; mem. Bd of Govs International Jurists Org., India; Commonwealth Open Scholarship 1983, Chevening Scholarship 1989, British Council Award 1990, British Council Assert Award 1993, 1994, Fulbright-Hays Fellowship 1996, Woman of Achievement Award 1998, District 306 C, International Lions Club 2004, Int. Women's Day Award 2007.

BANDERAS, Antonio; Spanish film actor; b. 10 Aug. 1960, Málaga; s. of José Domínguez and Anna Banderas; m. 1st Ana Banderas; m. 2nd Melanie Griffith 1996; one d.; ed School of Dramatic Art; began acting aged 14; performed with Nat. Theatre, Madrid for six years. *Films include:* Labyrinth of Passion 1982, El Señor Galíndez 1984, El Caso Almería 1984, The Stilts, 27 Hours, Matador 1986, Law of Desire 1987, Women on the Verge of a Nervous Breakdown 1988, Tie Me Up! Tie Me Down! 1989, The House of Spirits, Interview with the Vampire, The Mambo Kings 1992, Philadelphia 1993, Love and Shadow, Miami Rhapsody, Young Mussolini, Return of Mariaolu, Assassins, Desperado 1995, Evita 1996, The Mask of Zorro 1997, Never Talk to Strangers, Crazy in Alabama (dir), The 13th Warrior, White River Kid (producer)1999, Dancing in the Dark 2000, Malaga Burning (dir) 2000, The Body 2000, Forever Lulu (producer) 2000, Spy Kids 2001, Femme Fatale 2002, Frida 2003, Once Upon a Time in Mexico 2003, Imagining Argentina 2003, Shrek II 2004, The Legend of Zorro 2005, Take the Lead 2006, El Camino de los Ingleses (Summer Rain, Dir) 2006, Bordertown 2007, Shrek the Third (voice) 2007, Missing Lynx (producer) 2008, My Mom's New Boyfriend 2008, The Other Man 2008, Thick as Thieves 2009, The Big Bang 2010, Shrek Forever After (voice) 2010, You Will Meet A Tall Dark Stranger 2010, La piel que habito (The Skin I Live In) 2011, Puss in Boots (voice) 2011, Black Gold 2011, Haywire 2011, Ruby Sparks 2012. *Television:* And Starring Pancho Villa as Himself 2003. *Address:* c/o CAA, 2000 Avenue of the Stars, Los Angeles, CA 90067, USA; Agents Associés, 201 rue du Faubourg Saint-Honoré, 75008 Paris, France.

BANDIĆ, Milan; Croatian politician; *Mayor of Zagreb;* b. 22 Nov. 1955, Bandiĉa Brig, nr Grude, Bosnia and Herzegovina; s. of Jozo Bandić and Blagica Bandić (née Tomić); m. Vesna Bandić (divorced 1996); one d.; ed Antun Branko Simić High School Grude, Univ. of Zagreb; worked for Ledo Co. 1980–83; worked in Municipality of Pešćenica 1989–90; joined League of Communists of Croatia

(reformed as Social Democratic Party—SDP of Croatia 1990); mem. Zagreb City Council 1995–, Leader of Zagreb SDP 1997, Mayor of Zagreb 2000–02, 2005–; Rep. in House of Reps of Croatian Parl. 2000–, Vice-Pres. Parl. Cttee for Internal Policy and Nat. Security; mem. SDP 2000–09, unsuccessful cand. for party pres. 2007, expelled from party Nov. 2009; unsuccessful presidential cand. Jan. 2010; Citizen of Honour of Srebrenica 2009. *Leisure interest:* distance running. *Address:* The Mayor's Office, Zagreb, trg Stjepana Radića, Croatia (office). *Telephone:* (1) 6101111 (office). *Fax:* (1) 6101313 (office). *E-mail:* uprava@zagreb.hr (office). *Website:* www.zagreb.hr (office).

BANDIER, Martin, BA, LLD; American lawyer and entertainment business executive; *Chairman and CEO, Sony/ATV Music Publishing;* b. 21 July 1941, New York, NY; m. Dorothy Bandier; three c.; ed Syracuse Univ., Brooklyn Law School; began career with law firm in Manhattan; joined legal dept at LeFrank Organisation, becoming Sr Vice-Pres.; Co-f. Entertainment Co. 1975, Entertainment Music Co. 1985, SBK Entertainment World 1987; Vice-Chair. Thorn EMI 1989–91, CEO EMI Music Publishing 1991–2007, Chair. 1992–2007, mem. Bd of Dirs EMI Group plc 1998–2006; Chair. and CEO, Sony/ATV Music Publishing LLC 2007–; mem. Bd of Dirs United Jewish Appeal, City of Hope, Songwriter's Hall of Fame, Nat. Music Publrs' Asscn, Rock and Roll Hall of Fame; Trustee, T.J. Martell Foundation, Syracuse Univ.; mem. Metropolitan New York Advisory Bd, Nat. Acad. of Recording Arts and Sciences; Abe Olman Publisher Award 1990, Arents Award 1994, Patron of the Arts Award, Songwriters Hall of Fame 2003. *Leisure interests:* playing the piano, golf. *Address:* Sony/ATV Music Publishing LLC, 550 Madison Avenue, Fifth Floor, New York, NY 10022, USA (office). *Telephone:* (212) 833-8000 (office). *Fax:* (212) 833-5552 (office). *E-mail:* info@sonyatv.com (office). *Website:* www.sonyatv.com (office).

BANDLER, John William, PhD, DSc (Eng), FIEE, FIEEE, FEIC, FCAE, FRSC; Canadian professor of electrical and computer engineering; *Professor Emeritus, McMaster University;* b. 9 Nov. 1941, Jerusalem; m. 3rd Beth Budd 1990; two d.; ed Imperial Coll. London; Mullard Research Labs, Redhill, Surrey 1966; Univ. of Manitoba 1967–69; McMaster Univ. 1969, Prof. 1974, Prof. Emer. 2000–; Chair. Dept of Electrical Eng, McMaster Univ. 1978–79, Dean of Faculty 1979–81, Dir of Research, Simulation Optimization Systems Research Lab. 1983–; Pres. Optimization Systems Assocs Inc. 1983–97, Bandler Corpn 1997–; ARFTG Automated Measurements Career Award for Automated Microwave Techniques 1994, IEEE Microwave Theory and Techniques Soc. Microwave Application Award 2004, IEEE Canada A.G.L. McNaughton Gold Medal 2012. *Publications:* more than 470 papers in journals and books and book chapters. *Address:* Department of Electrical and Computer Engineering, McMaster University, Hamilton, Ont., L8S 4K1, Canada (office). *Telephone:* (905) 525-9140 (office). *Fax:* (905) 521-2922 (office). *Website:* www.sos.mcmaster.ca (office).

BANDURA, Albert, PhD; Canadian psychologist and academic; *David Starr Jordan Professor Emeritus of Social Science in Psychology, Stanford University;* b. 4 Dec. 1925, Mundare, Alberta; m. Ginny Bandura; two d.; ed University of British Columbia, Univ. of Iowa, USA; Instructor then Prof. of Psychology, Stanford Univ., USA 1953, then David Starr Jordan Prof. of Social Science in Psychology, now Prof. Emer.; Chair. Dept of Psychology 1976–77; Fellow, Center for Advanced Study in the Behavioral Sciences 1969–70; Sir Walter Scott Distinguished Visiting Prof., Univ. of New South Wales, Australia 1988; mem. Bd of Scientific Affairs, American Psychological Asscn 1968–70, mem. Credentials Cttee (Div. 7) 1970, mem. Bd of Convention Affairs 1973, Pres. and Chair. Bd of Dirs 1974, Chair. Council of Reps 1974, Chair. Cttee on Constitutional Issues 1975, Chair. Election Cttee 1975, mem. Comm. on Org. 1978–82; mem. Inst. of Medicine, NAS 1989; Trustee, American Psychological Foundation 1975–82; mem. Western Psychological Asscn 1979–82, Chair. Bd of Dirs 1980, Pres. 1980; mem. US Nat. Cttee for the Int. Union of Psychological Sciences 1985–93, Cttee on Int. Affairs of Soc. for Research in Child Devt 1991–95; Series Ed. on Social Learning Theory 1970–; mem. Editorial Bd Journal of Personality and Social Psychology 1963–77, Journal of Experimental Social Psychology 1967–77, Journal of Experimental Child Psychology 1967–82, Behaviour Research and Therapy 1963–, Journal of Applied Behavior Analysis 1968–72, 1975–78, 1980–81, Behavior Therapy 1970–73, 1989–91, 1992–, Personality: An International Journal 1970–72, Journal of Behavior Therapy and Experimental Psychiatry 1970–, Child Development 1971–77, Journal of Abnormal Psychology 1973, Aggression: An International Interdisciplinary Journal 1974–82, Cognitive Therapy and Research 1977–79, 1982–, Journal of Mental Imagery 1978–, Clinical Behavior Therapy Review 1979–81, Gestalt Therapy: An International Multidisciplinary Journal 1979–, Review of Personality and Social Psychology 1979–85, 1999–2002, Humboldt Journal of Social Relations 1979–, Psychological Review 1980–82, 1999–2004, Journal of Cognitive Psychotherapy 1986–, Behaviour Change 1985–95, Journal of Anxiety Disorders 1986–91, British Journal of Clinical Psychology 1987–, Annual Review of Psychology 1987–91, Anxiety Stress and Coping 1988–, Psychological Inquiry 1989–2002, Applied and Preventive Psychology: Current Scientific Perspectives 1991–, Medienpsychologie 1990–2000, Applied Psychology: An International Review 1993–, Social Behavior and Personality: An International Journal 1992–, Media Psychology 1998–, Journal of Social and Clinical Psychology 2002–, International Journal of Clinical and Health Psychology 2005–; Special Research Fellowship, Nat. Inst. of Mental Health 1969; Guggenheim Fellow 1972; Fellow, American Acad. of Arts and Sciences 1980, Japan Soc. for the Promotion of Science 1982; Hon. Pres. Canadian Psychological Asscn 1999, Hon. Fellow, World Innovation Foundation 2004; Dr hc (Univ. of British Columbia) 1979, (Univ. of Lethbridge) 1983, (Univ. of New Brunswick) 1985, (State Univ. of New York) 1987, (Univ. of Waterloo) 1990, (Freie Universität Berlin) 1990, (Univ. of Salamanca) 1992, (Indiana Univ.) 1993, (Univ. of Rome) 1994, (Leiden Univ.) 1995, (Alfred Univ.) 1995, (Pennsylvania State Univ.) 1999, (Grad. School and Univ. Center, City Univ. of New York) 2002, (Universität Jaume I) 2002, (Univ. of Athens) 2003, (Univ. of Catania) 2004; Distinguished Scientist Award (Div. 12), American Psychological Asscn 1972, Distinguished Scientific Achievement Award, Calif. Psychological Asscn, 1973, Distinguished Contrib. Award, Int. Soc. for Research on Aggression 1980, Distinguished Scientific Contribs Award, American Psychological Asscn 1980, Distinguished Scientist Award, Soc. of Behavioral Medicine, William James Award, American Psychological Soc. 1989, Distinguished Lifetime Contribs Award, Calif. Psychological Asscn 1998, Thorndike Award for Distinguished Contribs of Psychology to Educ., American Psychological Asscn 1999, Lifetime

Achievement Award, Asscn for the Advancement of Behavior Therapy 2001, Healthtrac Award for Distinguished Contributions to Health Promotion 2002, Lifetime Achievement Award, Western Psychological Asscn 2003, McGovern Medal for Distinguished Contribution to Health Promotion Science 2004, James McKeen Cattell Award, American Psychological Soc. 2004, Outstanding Lifetime Contribution to Psychology, American Psychological Asscn 2004, Distinguished Achievement Alumni Award, Univ. of Iowa 2005, Distinguished Lifetime Achievement Award, American Acad. of Health Behavior 2006, Gold Medal Award for Distinguished Lifetime Contribs to the Advancement of Psychology, American Psychological Foundation 2006, Everett M. Rogers Award 2007, Grawemeyer Award 2008. *Publications:* Adolescent Aggression (co-author) 1959, Social Learning and Personality Development (co-author) 1963, Principles of Behavior Modification 1969, Psychological Modeling: Conflicting Theories (ed.) 1971, Aggression: Social Learning Analysis 1973, Social Learning Theory 1977, Social Foundations of Thought and Action: A Social Cognitive Theory 1986, Self-efficacy in Changing Societies (ed.) 1995, Self-efficacy: The Exercise of Control 1997; numerous articles in scientific journals. *Address:* Department of Psychology, Jordan Hall, Bldg 420, 450 Serra Mall, Stanford University, Stanford, CA 94305-2130, USA (office). *Telephone:* (650) 725-2409 (office). *Fax:* (650) 725-5699 (office). *E-mail:* bandura@psych.stanford.edu (office). *Website:* www-psych.stanford.edu (office).

BANERJEE, Mamata, BEd, LLB, MA; Indian politician; *Chief Minister of West Bengal;* b. 5 Jan. 1955, Hazra, Calcutta (now Kolkata); d. of Shri Promileswar and Gayetri Banerjee; ed Sikshayatan Coll., Jogesh Chandra Choudhury Coll. of Law, Univ. of Calcutta; Gen. Sec. Mahila Congress (I), W Bengal 1970–80; Sec. Dist Congress Cttee, Calcutta S 1978–81; mem. Lok Sabha (House of the People, Parl.) 1984, 1991–, mem. Consultative Cttee, Ministry of Human Resource Devt 1987–93, of Home Affairs 1987–88, 1993–96, 1996–97, 1998–99, 2006–, of Industries 2001–03, mem. Gen. Purposes Cttee 1998–99, 2001–, Chair. Cttee on Railways 1998–99, Cttee on Personnel, Public Grievances, Law & Justice 2004–; Union Minister of State, Human Resource Devt, Dept of Youth Affairs and Sports, and Women and Child Devt 1991–93, of Railways 1999–2001, 2009–, Minister without Portfolio 2003–04, of Coal and Mines 2004; Leader, All India Trinamool Congress Parl. Party 1999–; Chief Minister of W Bengal 2011–; Gen. Sec. and mem. Nat. Council, All India Youth Congress (I) Cttee 1985–87, Pres. Youth Congress (W Bengal) 1990; mem. Exec. Cttee Congress Parl. Party 1988–, Pradesh Congress Cttee 1989–; Sec. W Bengal TUC 1981–87. *Publications include:* Upalabdhi, Janatar Darbare, Maa, Pallabi, Manabik, Struggle for Existence, Motherland, Crocodile Island, Trinamool, Sishu Sathi, Anubhuti, Abishasya, Janmaini, Ekantee, Ashubho Shanket, Jago Banglaa, Ganotantre Lazza, Anoson Keno, Andolaner Katha, Soroni, Langoli, Maa-Mati-Manush, Ajab Chora, Ek Guchho Bhavana, Struggle for Existence, Smile, Dark Horizon, Slaughter of Democracy, Nandi Ma. *Leisure interests:* music, writing, painting. *Address:* Ministry of Railways, Rail Bhavan, Raisina Road, New Delhi 110 001 (office); All India Trinamool Congress, 125-D, Parliament House, New Delhi 110 001 (office); 5, Ashoka Road, New Delhi 110 001 (home); 30B Harish Chatterjee St, Kolkata 700 026, India (home); C-4, M. S. Flats, B. K. S. Marg, New Delhi 110 001 (home). *Telephone:* (11) 23386645 (Ministry) (office); (11) 24540881 (Parl.) (office); (33) 24753000 (Kolkata) (home); (11) 23722975 (home). *Fax:* (11) 23387333 (Ministry) (office); (33) 24540880 (Kolkata) (home). *E-mail:* secyrb@rb.railnet.gov.in (office); mamata.sansad@sansad.nic.in (home). *Website:* www.indianrailways.gov.in (office); www.trinamoolcongress.com (office).

BANFIELD, Jillian (Jill) Fiona, BSc, MSc, PhD; Australian scientist and academic; *Professor of Earth and Planetary Science, University of California, Berkeley;* b. 18 Aug. 1959, Armidale, NSW; d. of James E. Banfield and Eve Banfield; m. Perry Smith; two s. one d.; ed Australian Nat. Univ., Johns Hopkins Univ., USA; exploration geologist, Western Mining Corpn 1982–83; Asst Prof., Dept of Geology and Geophysics, Univ. of Wisconsin 1990–95, Assoc. Prof. 1995–99, Prof. 1999–2001, Dept of Chem. 1998–2001; Prof. Dept of Earth and Planetary Science, Univ. of California, Berkeley 2001–, Prof. Dept of Environmental Science, Policy and Man. 2001–, Researcher and mem. geochemistry group, Lawrence Berkeley Nat. Lab.; Assoc. Prof., Mineralogical Inst., Univ. of Tokyo 1996–97, Prof. 1998; John D. and Catherine T. MacArthur Foundation Fellow 1999–2004; John Simon Guggenheim Foundation Fellowship 2000; Distinguished Lecturer, Mineralogical Soc. of America 1994–95, Fellow 1997–; Gast Lecturer, Geochemical Soc. 2000, NSF Earth Science Week Lecturer (Inaugural) 2000, Rosenqvist Lecturer, Norway 2005, Pioneer Lecturer, Clay Minerals Soc. 2005; mem. NAS Bd on Earth Sciences and Resources 2002–05; mem. Mineralogical Soc. of America, Councilor 1997–99, Chair. Roebling Award Cttee 1998, Chair. Mid Career Award Cttee 1998–99, Assoc. Ed. American Mineralogist, Journal of the Mineralogical Society of America 1997–2000; mem. US Dept of Energy, Basic Energy Sciences Geoscience Advisory Cttee; mem. American Soc. for Microbiology; mem. Clay Minerals Soc., Councilor, Student Awards Cttee, Bailey Award Cttee 2000; Geological Soc. of Australia Prize 1978, Award for Outstanding Research, US Dept of Energy 1995, Mineralogical Soc. of America Award 1997, D.A. Brown Medal, ANU 1999, Dana Medal, Mineralogical Soc. of America 2010, Benjamin Franklin Medal in Earth and Environmental Science, Franklin Inst. 2011, L'Oréal-UNESCO Women in Science Award (North America) 2011, and several other prizes and awards. *Publications:* numerous scientific papers. *Address:* Department of Environmental Science, Policy and Management, 130 Mulford Hall #3114, University of California, Berkeley, CA 94720, USA (office). *Telephone:* (510) 643-2155 (office); (510) 642-3804 (Lab.) (office); (510) 642-5438 (home). *Fax:* (510) 643-9980 (office). *E-mail:* jbanfield@berkeley.edu (office); jill@nature.berkeley.edu (office). *Website:* ourenvironment.berkeley.edu/people_profiles/jill-banfield (office); geomicrobiology.berkeley.edu (office).

BANGA, Manvinder Singh, BSc, MBA; Indian business executive; *Senior Advisor, Clayton, Dubilier & Rice, LLC;* b. 31 Oct. 1954, Shimla; s. of Jaswant Banga and Harbhajan Singh Banga; m. Kamini Banga; two s.; ed Indian Inst. of Tech., Delhi, Indian Inst. of Man., Ahmedabad; joined Hindustan Lever Ltd 1977, served in various sales and marketing roles including Head of Personal Products, Chair. and Exec. Dir Soaps and Detergents Div. 1995–98, Sr Vice-Pres. Hair and Oral Care Divs 1998–2000, Chair. and Man. Dir Hindustan Unilever Ltd (fmrly Hindustan Lever Ltd) 2000–04, Business Group Pres. Home and Personal Care Asia, Unilever PLC and Chair. Hindustan Unilever 2004–05, Pres. Foods,

Unilever PLC 2005–08, Pres. Foods, Home and Personal Care, Unilever PLC 2008–10; Sr Advisor, Clayton Dubilier & Rice LLP 2010–; apptd mem. Bd of Dirs Maruti Suzuki India Ltd 2003, Marks and Spencer Group plc, Thomson Reuters; mem. Bd of Govs Indian Inst. of Man. Ahmedabad, Indian School of Business Hyderabad, Prime Minister of India's Council of Trade and Industry, Wharton Asia and Int. Bd, World Pres Org.; Charter Mem. Indus Entrepreneur; Gold Medal, Indian Inst. of Tech. Delhi, Indian Inst. of Man. Ahmedabad; Padma Bhushan 2010. *Leisure interest:* golf. *Address:* Clayton Dubilier & Rice, LLP, Cleveland House 33 King Street, London, SW1Y 6RJ, UK (office). *Telephone:* (20) 7747-3800 (office). *Fax:* (20) 7747-3801 (office). *Website:* www.cdr-inc.com (office).

BANGA-BOTHY, Léonie Mbazoa, LLM; Central African Republic lawyer and politician; Dir Legal Affairs and Litigation Dept, Ministry of Foreign Affairs 2011; Minister of Foreign Affairs, African Integration, Francophony and Central Africans Abroad 2013–14; Pres. Central African Repub. Br., Avocats sans Frontières. *Address:* c/o Ministry of Foreign Affairs, African Integration, Francophony and Central Africans Abroad, Bangui, Central African Republic (office).

BANGEMANN, Martin, DJur; German lawyer, telecommunications industry executive and fmr politician; b. 15 Nov. 1934, Wanzleben; s. of Martin Bangemann and Lotte Telge; m. Renate Bauer 1962; three s. two d.; ed secondary school, Emden and Univs of Tübingen and Munich; mem. Freie Demokratische Partei (FDP) 1963–, Deputy 1969, mem. Regional Exec. Baden-Württemberg FDP 1973–78 (resgnd), mem. Nat. Exec. 1969– (resgnd as Gen. Sec. 1975), Chair. FDP 1985–88; mem. Bundestag 1972–80, 1987–88, European Parl. 1979–84; Minister of Finance 1984–88; EEC (now EU) Commr for Internal Market, Industry, Relations with European Parl. 1989–92, for Industrial Affairs and Tech. 1993–95, for Industrial Affairs, Information and Telecommunications Technologies 1995–99, a Vice-Pres. 1993–95; Dir Telefonica, Madrid 1999, mem. Advisory Bd 2000–05; Fed. Cross of Merit with Star. *Leisure interests:* philosophy, horticulture.

BANGURA, Zainab Hawa, BA; Sierra Leonean human rights activist, politician and UN official; *Special Representative of the Secretary-General on Sexual Violence in Conflict, United Nations;* b. (Zainab Sesay), 18 Dec. 1959, Yonibana Chiefdom, Tonkolili Dist, Northern Prov.; apptd Asst Reinsurance Man. Nat. Insurance Co. 1983; f. Women Organized for a Morally Enlightened Nation (WOMEN) 1995, Nat. Accountability Group 2001; Co-f. Campaign for Good Governance 1996, Movt for Progress (political party promoting good governance and empowerment of women, youth and the disabled) 2002, nominated Nat. Chair.; contested as only female cand. in presidential elections 2002; Chief Civil Affairs Officer to UN Mission in Liberia; Minister of Foreign Affairs and Int. Co-operation 2007–10, of Health and Sanitation 2010–12; Special Rep. of the Sec.-Gen. on Sexual Violence in Conflict, UN 2012–; Assoc. and Fellow, Chartered Insurance Inst. (UK) 1991–; fmr Reagan-Fascell Democracy Fellow, The Nat. Endowment for Democracy; mem. Steering Cttee World Movt for Democracy; African Int. Award of Merit for Leadership 1999, New York Lawyers Cttee for Human Rights Human Rights Award 2000, A. Philip Randolph Inst. Bayard Rustin Humanitarian Award 2002, Nat. Endowment for Democracy Award, Washington, DC 2006. *Address:* Office of the Secretary-General, United Nations, New York, NY 10017, USA (office). *Telephone:* (212) 963-1234 (office). *Fax:* (212) 963-4879 (office). *Website:* www.un.org/sg (office).

BANHAM, Sir John Michael Middlecott, Kt, MA, LLD, DL; British business executive; b. 22 Aug. 1940, Torquay, Devon; s. of the late Terence Middlecott Banham and of Belinda Joan Banham CBE; m. Frances Favell 1965; one s. two d.; ed Charterhouse, Queens' Coll., Cambridge; with HM Foreign Service 1962–64; Dir of Marketing, Wallcoverings Div., Reed Int. 1965–69; with McKinsey & Co. Inc. 1969, Assoc. 1969–75, Prin. 1975–80, Dir 1980–83; Controller Audit Comm. for Local Authorities in England and Wales 1983–87; Dir-Gen. CBI March 1987–92; Chair. WestCountry TV Ltd 1992–95, John Labatt Ltd (now Interbrew Ltd) 1992–95, ECI Ventures LLP 1992–2005, Local Govt Comm. for England 1992–95, Tarmac PLC 1992–2000, Kingfisher 1996–2000, Whitbread PLC 2000–06, Geest PLC 2002–06, Johnson Matthey PLC 2006–11, Sultan Scientific Ltd 2008–; Sr Non-executive Dir Invesco Ltd; Dir Cyclacel Ltd, Nat. Westminster Bank 1992–98, Nat. Power PLC 1992–98, Amvescap PLC; Man. Trustee Nuffield Foundation 1988–97, ShelterBox 2011–12 (resgnd); Hon. Treas. Cancer Research Campaign 1991–2002; DL Cornwall 1999; Hon. LLD (Bath) 1987; Hon. DSc (Loughborough) 1989, (Exeter) 1993, (Strathclyde) 1995. *Publications:* Future of the British Car Industry 1975, Realising the Promise of a National Health Service 1977, The Anatomy of Change 1994 and numerous reports for Audit Comm. on educ., social services, housing, etc. 1984–87 and on the economy, skill training, infrastructure and urban regeneration for the CBI 1987–. *Leisure interests:* gardening, walking, music. *Address:* Penberth, St Buryan, nr Penzance, Cornwall, England. *Fax:* (1736) 810-722 (home). *E-mail:* frances@peaver.plus.com (home).

BANI, Father John Bennett; Ni-Vanuatu politician and fmr head of state; b. 4 July 1941, Pentecost; Dir of Rural Devt, Youth and Sport Vanua'aku Parti 1979–80; Pres. of Vanuatu March 1999–2004; fmr mem. Union of Moderate Parties.

BANISADR, Abolhassan; Iranian economist and politician; b. 22 March 1933, Hamadan; s. of the Ayatollah Seyed Nasrollah Banisadr; m. Ozra Banisadr; one s. two d.; ed Univ. of Paris (Sorbonne) and Univ. of Tehran; supporter of Mossadeq (Prime Minister of Iran 1951–53); joined underground anti-Shah movt 1953; imprisoned after riots over Shah's land reforms 1963; in exile in Paris 1963–79; taught at the Sorbonne; close assoc. of the Ayatollah Ruhollah Khomeini and returned to Iran after overthrow of Shah; Minister of Econ. and Financial Affairs 1979–80; Acting Foreign Minister 1979 (resgnd); Pres. of Iran and C-in-C of the Armed Forces 1980–81; mem. Supervisory Bd of Cen. Bank of Iran 1979; mem. Revolutionary Council 1979–81 (Pres. 1980–81); overthrown in 'creeping coup' June 1981, fled to France 1981, subsequently formed Nat. Council of Resistance to oppose the Govt (in alliance with Massoud Rajavi, Leader of Mujaheddin Kalq and Abdel-Rahman Ghassemlov, Leader of Democratic Party of Kurdistan, Nat. Democratic Front and other resistance groups), Chair. 1981–84; opposed decision of Rajavi about collaborating with Saddam Hussein which consequently ended his alliance with Council of Nat. Resistance. *Publications:* Oil and Violence (with Paul Vielle) 1974, The Economy of Tawhid 1975, Cult of Personality 1978, Women in

Shahnameh 1979, Equilibriums 1979, Relationship Between Spirituality and Materialism 1979, Principles and Precepts of Islamic Government 1981, L'espérance trahie 1982, My Turn to Speak: Iran, the Revolution, and Secret Deals with the U.S. 1991, Human Rights in Islam and the Guiding Principles of Islamic Law 2003, Free Intellect 2005, Social Justice 2009, A Critique of Contrast and Contradiction in Syllogistic Logic 2010; numerous articles and pamphlets on philosophy, theology, economics and politics. *Address:* 5 rue General Pershing, 78000 Versailles, France. *Telephone:* 1-39-54-45-26; 1-39-54-01-47. *E-mail:* ab_banisadr@yahoo.de. *Website:* www.banisadr.com.fr.

BANJADE, Yagyamurti; Nepalese lawyer and government official; Attorney-Gen. of Nepal 2006–08; mem. Nepal Law Soc.. *E-mail:* ybanjade@ntc.net.np.

BANJO, Ladipo Ayodeji, CON, PhD; Nigerian linguist, academic and university administrator; *Vice-Chancellor, Ajayi Crowther University;* b. 2 May 1934, Ijebu-Igbo, Ogun State; s. of the late Ven Banjo. and S. A. Banjo; m. Alice Mbamali; two s. two d.; ed Nigerian Coll. of Arts, Science and Tech., Univs of Glasgow and Leeds, UK, Univ. of California, Los Angeles, USA, Univ. of Ibadan; Educ. Officer W Nigeria 1960–64 (Sr Educ. Officer Jan.–Oct. 1966); Lecturer, Dept of English, Univ. of Ibadan 1966–71, Sr Lecturer 1971–73, Reader and Acting Head 1973–75, Prof. 1975–97, Prof. Emer. 1997–, Dean Faculty of Arts 1977–79, Chair. Cttee of Deans 1978–79, Deputy Vice-Chancellor 1981–84, Vice-Chancellor 1984–91; fmr Pro-Chancellor, Univ. of Port Harcourt; Pro-Chancellor, Univ. of Ilorin; currently Vice-Chancellor Ajayi Crowther Univ., Oyo; Dir Reading Centre 1970–72 (Co-Dir 1966–70); Chair. Int. Panel on English Language, West African Examination Council 1979–85, Advisory Cttee Nat. Language Centre 1980–85; Pres. West African Modern Languages Asscn 1981–; Vice-Pres. Int. Fed. of Languages and Literatures 1985–89, Yoruba Studies Asscn 1979–82; J. P. Oyo State 1986–; Dir Spectrum Books 1997, Blackwell Safari 1997; Pres. and Fellow, Nigerian Acad. of Letters 2000–; Chair. Cttee of Vice-Chancellors 1989–90, Chair. Cttee of Pro-Chancellors of Nigerian Univs 2000–04; Commander of the Order of the Niger 2001. *Publications:* Oral English 1971, Letter Writing 1973, Effective Use of English 1976, Developmental English 1985, New Englishes: A West African Perspective (ed. with A. Bamgbose and A. Thomas) 1995, Making a Virtue of Necessity: An Overview of the English Language in Nigeria 1996, In the Saddle: A Vice-Chancellor's Story 1997. *Leisure interests:* music, photography, reading. *Address:* Office of the Vice-Chancellor, Ajayi Crowther University, Oyo, Oyo State, Nigeria (office). *Website:* www.acu.edu.ng (office).

BANKS, Charles A., BA; American business executive; b. Greensboro, NC; m.; three c.; ed San Bernardino High School, Calif., Hempstead High School, NY, Brown Univ.; served in USN 1962–64, attained rank of Lt, served in US Naval Reserve 1964–69; joined Peebles Supply Div., Ferguson Enterprises 1967, becoming Gen. Man., Ferguson Herndon and later Regional Man., Southeast Region, Sr Exec. Vice-Pres. Ferguson Enterprises 1987–89, Pres. 1992–2001; mem. Bd of Dirs Wolseley PLC 1992, Group CEO 2001–06 (retd); Pnr, Clayton, Dubilier & Rice (pvt. equity investment firm) 2006–10 (retd); currently Exec. Advisor, Gryphon Investors; Chair. VWR Int.; mem. Bd of Dirs William and Mary Business School Foundation 1989 (Chair. 1992–2001), mem. Bd of Visitors 2006–, currently Vice Rector of the Coll. and Vice-Chair. Exec. Cttee; mem. Bd of Dirs TowneBank/Peninsula; mem. Bd of Regents, Harris Manchester Coll., Univ. of Oxford, UK; Hon. DrSc (Christopher Newport Univ.); T.C. and Elizabeth Clarke Medallion, William and Mary Business School Foundation 2006. *Leisure interests:* travelling with family, golf, wines. *Address:* Gryphon Investors, One Market Plaza, Steuart Tower, 24th Floor, San Francisco, CA 94105, USA (office). *Website:* www.gryphon-inv.com (office).

BANKS, Jeff, CBE, DArts, FRSA; British fashion designer; b. (Jeffrey Tatham-Banks), 17 March 1943, Ebbw Vale, Gwent, S Wales; m. 1st Sandie Shaw 1967 (divorced); one d.; m. 2nd Sue Mann; ed Brockley County Grammar School, Camberwell School of Art, Cen. St Martin's Coll. of Art and Design, Parsons The New School for Design, New York, USA; studied interior design and textiles; opened Clobber boutique in London 1964, launched own fashion label 1969, opened first stand-alone Jeff Banks shop in London, as well as retail outlets in 22 dept stores, including Harrods and Harvey Nichols 1975; co-launched fashion chain Warehouse late 1970s, taken over by retail chain Sears; continued to work as freelance designer of both men's and women's clothing, jewellery and home furnishings; started fashion design studio in partnership with Richard Carnill, HQ Design 1989; cr. homeware range Ports Of Call 1994; cr. own corp. clothing co., Incorporatewear 1996, produces clothing for Barclays Bank plc, My Travel, Nationwide Building Society, BAA, Abbey National, Swinton Building Society, Bradford & Bingley Building Society, Thompson Holidays, Local Authority Dinner Ladies, Stagecoach, Boots, Butlins, J Sainsbury plc (Jeff & Co shops 2000–04, Jeff & Co brand now part of Matalan portfolio), Guide Asscn, England football team, London's 2012 Olympics bid; launched first of stand-alone Jeff Banks retail concept 2006, nine shops by 2008; Visiting Lecturer, Cen. St Martin's, Harrow School of Art, Univ. of Middlesex, Univ. of Northumbria, Univ. of Kingston, Croydon Art School, Bournemouth School of Art, London Coll. of Fashion, Swire School of Fashion, Hong Kong, La Salle School of Fashion, Shanghai; External Examiner, John Moores Univ., Liverpool, Brighton Univ., Univ. of Cen. Lancashire, Cen. St Martin's, Harrow School of Art (now Westminster Univ.), Univ. of Northumbria, RCA, Surrey Inst.; mem. Council CNAA 1978; formed charity Graduate Fashion Week 1990; Chair. Royal Soc. Fashion Medal Awards Scheme 1992–2002; Pres. Chartered Soc. of Designers 2002; co-hosted with Mary Quant The Clothes Show Expo, Hong Kong 1996; cr. Chartered Soc. of Designers Awards Medal for Fashion, DR Ind. Retailer of the Year Awards 1988, Prima Retailer of the Year Awards (in conjunction with National Magazines) 1991 (also Chair. judging panel and host of event); Fellow, Chartered Soc. of Designers 1978; hon. degrees from Univs of Lancaster, East London, Newcastle & Northumbria, Westminster, Univ. Coll. for the Creative Arts; British Designer of the Year 1980, 1982, British Coat Designer of the Year 1981, British Retailer of the Year 1984, Drapers Lifetime Achievement Award 2007. *Television includes:* presenter, with Selina Scott and Caryn Franklin, The Clothes Show (BBC TV) 1986–95; cr. Clothes Show Live (BBC TV) 1988; cr. and presented more than 120 episodes of The Style Challenge (BBC TV) 1997–98. *Address:* Incorporatewear, Edison Road, Hams Hall, National Distribution Park, Coleshill, B46 1DA, England (office). *Telephone:* (844) 257-0530 (office). *Fax:* (844) 257-0591 (office). *E-mail:* website@hqdesign.co

.uk (office). *Website:* www.jeffbanks.co.uk (office); www.incorporatewear.co.uk (office).

BANKS, Russell, BA; American writer; b. 28 March 1940, Barnstead, NH; s. of Earl Banks and Florence Banks; m. 1st Darlene Bennett (divorced 1962); one d.; m. 2nd Mary Gunst (divorced 1977); three d.; m. 3rd Kathy Walton (divorced 1988); m. 4th Chase Twichell; ed Colgate Univ. and Univ. of North Carolina; fmr teacher of creative writing at Emerson Coll. Boston, Univ. of NH at Durham, Univ. of Ala, New England Coll.; teacher of creative writing, Princeton Univ. 1982–97; Pres. Parl. Int. des Écrivains 2001–; Best American Short Stories Awards 1971, 1985, Fels Award for Fiction 1974, O. Henry Awards 1975, St Lawrence Award for Fiction 1976, Guggenheim Fellowship 1976, Nat. Endowment for the Arts Fellowships 1977, 1983, John Dos Passos Award 1985, American Acad. of Arts and Letters Award 1985. *Publications include:* poetry: Waiting to Freeze 1967, 30/6 1969, Snow: Meditations of a Cautious Man in Winter 1974; novels: Family Life 1975, Hamilton Stark 1978, The Book of Jamaica 1980, The Relation of My Imprisonment 1984, Continental Drift 1985, Affliction 1989, The Sweet Hereafter 1991, Rule of the Bone 1995, Cloudsplitter 1998, The Angel on the Roof 2000, The Darling 2004, The Reserve 2008, Outer Banks 2008, Lost Memory of Skin 2011; collected short stories: Searching for Survivors 1975, The New World 1978, Trailerpark 1981, Success Stories 1986; contrib. short stories to magazines and periodicals, including New York Times Book Review, Washington Post, American Review, Vanity Fair, Antaeus, Partisan Review, New England Review, Fiction International, Boston Globe Magazine. *Address:* Steven Barclay Agency, 12 Western Avenue, Petaluma, CA 94952, USA (office); 1000 Park Avenue, New York, NY 10028, USA. *Telephone:* (707) 773-0654 (office). *Fax:* (707) 778-1868 (office). *Website:* www.barclayagency.com (office).

BANKS, Tyra; American model; b. 4 Dec. 1973; d. of Carolyn London; ed Immaculate Heart High School; has modelled since 1991 for Karl Lagerfeld (q.v.), Yves St Laurent, Oscar De La Renta (q.v.), Chanel etc.; featured on covers of Elle, GQ, Sports Illustrated, German Cosmopolitan, Spanish Vogue, Scene, Arena; retd from modelling 2005; f. TYInc. *Video appearances include:* Too Funky by George Michael (q.v.), Black or White by Michael Jackson (q.v.), Love Thing by Tina Turner (q.v.). *Film appearances include:* Black or White 1991, Higher Learning 1995, A Woman Like That 1997, Love Stinks 1999, Love & Basketball 2000, Coyote Ugly 2000, Halloween: Resurrection 2002, Eight Crazy Nights (voice) 2002. *Television appearances include:* Inferno 1992, The Apartment Complex 1999, Life-Size 2000, Felicity 2000; exec. producer America's Next Top Model 2003–; exec. producer and host The Tyra Banks Show (talk show) 2005–10. *Publication:* Tyra's Beauty Inside and Out 1998. *Address:* c/o IMG Models, 304 Park Avenue South, 12th Floor, New York, NY 10010, USA. *Telephone:* (212) 253-8884. *Fax:* (212) 253-8883. *Website:* tyrashow.warnerbros.com.

BANKS, Victor Franklin, MA; Anguillan politician; *Leader, Anguilla United Front;* b. 8 Nov. 1947, The Valley; m. Cerise Banks; three c.; ed The Valley Secondary School, Coll. of the Virgin Islands, St Thomas and New School, New York, USA; teacher, The Valley Secondary School 1964–68; Man. Shipping Dept, SARAND, Inc., New York 1974–80; Gov. Liaison Officer, Anguilla 1980–81; Deputy to House of Ass. (Anguilla People's Party) for Valley North 1981–84, Deputy (Anguilla Democratic Party) for Valley South 1985–; Minister of Social Services 1981–84; Leader Anguilla Democratic Party 1985–2000, Anguilla United Front (AUF) 2000–; Minister of Finance, Econ. Devt, Investment and Commerce 2002–10; Pres. Banx Professional Services Ltd 1981–. *Leisure interests:* community work, counselling, political educ.; volleyball, squash, handball, duck shooting. *Address:* c/o Anguilla United Front (AUF), The Valley, Anguilla (office). *Telephone:* (264) 497-2451 (office). *Website:* www.unitedfront.ai (office).

BANNISTER, (Richard) Matthew, LLB; British radio presenter and fmr broadcasting executive; b. 16 March 1957, Sheffield, Yorks., England; s. of the late Richard Neville Bannister and of Olga Margaret Bannister; m. 1st Amanda Gerrard Walker 1984 (died 1988); one d.; m. 2nd Shelagh Margaret Macleod 1989 (died 2005); one s.; m. 3rd Katherine Jane Hood 2007; ed King Edward VII School, Sheffield, Univ. of Nottingham; Presenter, BBC Radio Nottingham 1978–81; Reporter/Presenter Capital Radio, London 1981–83, Deputy Head News and Talks 1985–87, Head 1987–88; with Newsbeat, BBC Radio 1 1983–85; Man. Ed. BBC Greater London Radio 1988–91, Project Co-ordinator, BBC Charter Renewal 1991–93, Controller BBC Radio 1 1993–98, Dir BBC Radio 1996–98, Chief Exec. of Production BBC 1999–2000; Dir Marketing and Communications, BBC 2000; Chair. Trust the DJ 2001; fmr Presenter BBC Radio 5 Live, currently Presenter of Outlook on BBC World Service and Last Word on BBC Radio 4; mem. Bd Chichester Festival Theatre 1999–2005; Fellow, Radio Acad.; Hon. DLitt (Nottingham) 2011. *Publications include:* articles in The Times. *Leisure interests:* rock music, theatre, collecting P.G. Wodehouse first edns. *Address:* c/o Knight Ayton Management, 35 Great James Street, London, WC1N 3HB, England (office). *Telephone:* (20) 7831-4400 (office). *E-mail:* info@knightayton.co.uk (office). *Website:* www.knightayton.co.uk (office).

BANNISTER, Sir Roger G., Kt, CBE, DM, FRCP; British consultant physician, neurologist, university administrator and fmr athlete; b. 23 March 1929, London; s. of the late Ralph Bannister and of Alice Bannister; m. Moyra Elver Jacobsson 1955; two s. two d.; ed City of Bath Boys' School, Univ. Coll. School, Exeter and Merton Colls, Oxford, St Mary's Hosp. Medical School, London; winner, Oxford and Cambridge Mile 1947–50; Pres. Oxford Univ. Athletic Club 1948; British Mile Champion 1951, 1953, 1954; world record one mile 1954, first sub-four minute mile 1954; Master, Pembroke College, Oxford 1985–93; Hon. Consultant Neurologist, St Mary's Hosp. Medical School, Nat. Hosp. for Neurology and Neurosurgery, London (non-exec. Dir 1992–96), London and Oxford Dist and Region; Chair. St Mary's Hosp. Devt Trust, Govt Working Group on Sport in the Univs 1995–97, Clinical Autonomic Research Soc. 1982–84; mem. Physiological Soc., Medical Research Soc. Asscn of British Neurologists; Fellow, Imperial College; Trustee, Leeds Castle Foundation 1988–2005; St Mary's Hosp. Medical School Devt Trust 1994–2006; Hon. Fellow, UMIST 1974, Exeter Coll., Oxford 1980, Merton Coll., Oxford 1986, Harris Manchester Coll., Oxford 2007, Brunel Univ. 2008; Hon. LLD (Liverpool) 1972; Hon. DSc (Sheffield) 1978, (Grinnell) 1984, (Bath) 1984, (Rochester) 1986, (Williams) 1987; Hon. MD (Pavia) 1986; Hon. DL (Univ. of Victoria, Canada) 1994, (Univ. of Wales, Cardiff) 1995, (Loughborough) 1996, (Univ. of East Anglia) 1997; Dr hc (Jyväskylä, Finland); Hans-Heinrich Siegbert Prize 1977. *Publications:* The

First Four Minutes (aka Four Minute Mile) 1955, Brain and Bannister's Clinical Neurology (ed.) 1992, Autonomic Failure (co-ed.) 1993; various medical articles on physiology and neurology. *Address:* 21 Bardwell Road, Oxford, OX2 6SV, England. *Telephone:* (1865) 511413.

BANNON, John Charles, AO, BA, LLB; Australian fmr politician; b. 7 May 1943; s. of C. Bannon and Joyce Marion Bannon; m. 1st Robyn Layton 1968 (divorced); one d.; m. 2nd Angela Bannon 1982; ed St Peter's Coll., Univ. of Adelaide; Industrial Advocate, AWU 1969–73; Adviser to Commonwealth Minister of Labour and Immigration 1973–75; Asst Dir S Australian Dept of Labour and Industry 1975–77; mem. House Ass. 1977–93; Minister for Community Devt, Minister for Local Govt, Minister for Recreation and Sport 1978–79; Leader of the Opposition 1979–82; Premier and Treasurer of S Australia, Minister of State Devt and Minister for the Arts 1982–85; Premier and Treasurer of S Australia and Minister for the Arts 1985–89; Premier and Treasurer of S Australia 1982–92; Nat. Pres. Australian Labour Party 1988–91; Dir Australian Broadcasting Corpn 1994–2000, Adelaide Symphony Orchestra Bd 1997–; mem. Council Constitutional Centenary Foundation 1995– (Chair. 1996–); Master St Mark's Coll., Adelaide 2000–; Ed. The New Federalist (Nat. Journal of Australian Fed. History) 1998. *Publications:* The Crucial Colony 1994, Supreme Federalist: The Political Life of Sir John Downer 2009; articles, monographs on Fed./State relations. *Leisure interests:* running, gardening. *Address:* PO Box 323, Rundle Mall, Adelaide, South Australia 5000, Australia.

BANNY, Charles Konan; Côte d'Ivoirian fmr central banker and economist; b. 11 Nov. 1942, Divo; m.; four c.; ed Ecole Supérieure des Sciences Economiques et Commerciales, Paris; served as Chargé de Mission, Stabilisation and Support Fund of Agric. Product Prices; Deputy Sec.-Gen. Inter-African Coffee Org., Paris 1970, Sec.-Gen. 1971; Dir of Admin. and Social Affairs, Cen. Bank of West African States (BCEAO) 1976, later Cen. Dir of Securities, Investment, Borrowing and Lending, then Cen. Dir of Research, apptd Nat. Dir BCEAO for Côte d'Ivoire 1983, Gov. BCEAO 1994–2007; interim Prime Minister of Côte d'Ivoire 2005–07. *Address:* c/o Parti démocratique de la Côte d'Ivoire—Rassemblement démocratique africain, 05 BP 36, Abidjan 05, Côte d'Ivoire (office).

BANSAL, Brij Mohan, BTech, DIIT; Indian oil industry executive; ed Indian Inst. of Tech., Delhi; mem. Bd of Dirs Indian Oil Corpn Ltd (IndianOil) 2005–, briefly headed IndianOil's Research and Devt function, Dir of Planning and Business Devt 2005–11, Dir of Human Resources –2010, Chair. Indian Oil Corpn Ltd 2010–11, also Chair. of IndianOil's subsidiaries: Chennai Petroleum Corpn Ltd (CPCL), IndianOil Mauritius Ltd (IOML), IOT Infrastructure & Energy Services Ltd (Jt Venture of IndianOil and Oiltanking GmbH); fmr mem. Bd Bongaigaon Refinery & Petrochemicals Ltd (now merged with IndianOil), Petronet LNG Ltd, Engineers India Ltd, Lubrizol India Pvt. Ltd; fmr Chair. IndianOil Technologies Ltd (subsidiary of IndianOil), Green Gas Ltd (Jt Venture of IndianOil and GAIL (India) Ltd), IndianOil Petronas Pvt. Ltd (Jt Venture of IndianOil and Petroliam Nasional Berhad (Petronas), Malaysia); first Chair. India Chapter of Int. DME (Di-Methyl Ether) Assocn (IDA), USA; Chair. Emer. Bio-Diesel Assocn of India. *Address:* c/o Indian Oil Corpn Ltd, Corporate Office, 3079/3, J. B. Tito Marg, Sadiq Nagar, New Delhi 110 049, India.

BANSAL, Pawan Kumar, BSc, LLB; Indian lawyer and politician; *Minister of Railways;* b. 16 July 1948, Sunam, Sangrur Dist, Punjab; s. of Piara Lal Aggarwal (Tapa Wale) and Rukmani Devi; m. Madhu Bansal; two s.; ed Yadavindra Public School, Patiala, Govt Coll., Chandigarh, Punjab Univ., Chandigarh; Gen.-Sec. Chandigarh Territorial Youth Congress 1976–78, Pres. 1982; Gen.-Sec. Punjab Pradesh Youth Congress 1978–82, Pres. 1982–83; elected to Rajya Sabha (upper house of Parl.) 1984–90, mem. Rajya Sabha Panel of Vice-Chairmen 1985–87, Whip, Congress (I) Parl. Party, Rajya Sabha 1989–90; elected to 10th Lok Sabha (lower house of Parl.) for Chandigarh constituency 1991, Whip, Congress (I) Parl. Party, Lok Sabha 1992–96, re-elected to 13th Lok Sabha 1999–2004, 14th Lok Sabha 2004–09, 15th Lok Sabha 2009–; Pres. Chandigarh Territorial Congress Cttee 1997–98; Sec. All India Congress Cttee 1999; Treas. Indian Parl. Group 2004–09; Minister of State for Expenditure, Banking and Insurance, Ministry of Finance 2006–09, Minister of State for Parl. Affairs 2008–09, Union Cabinet Minister for Parl. Affairs 2009–12, for Water Resources 2009–11, for Science and Tech. and Earth Sciences Jan.–July 2011, for Parl. Affairs and Water Resources 2011–12, Minister of Railways 2012–; mem. Indian parl. dels to numerous countries. *Address:* Ministry of Railways, Rail Bhavan, Raisina Road, New Delhi 110 001, India (office). *Telephone:* (11) 23386645 (office). *Fax:* (11) 23387333 (office). *E-mail:* secyrb@rb.railnet.gov.in (office). *Website:* www.indianrailways.gov .in (office).

BANVILLE, John; Irish writer; b. 8 Dec. 1945, Wexford; m. Janet Dunham; two s.; ed St Peter's Coll., Wexford; fmrly night copy ed., The Irish Times, Literary Ed. 1988–99, Chief Literary Critic and Assoc. Literary Ed. 1999–2002; Lannan Foundation Award 1998, Franz Kafka Prize 2011, Irish PEN Award for Outstanding Achievement in Irish Literature 2013. *Film script:* The Last September 1998. *Plays:* The Broken Jug (after Kleist) 1994, God's Gift (after Kleist's 'Amphitryon') 2000. *Publications include:* novels: Nightspawn 1971, Birchwood 1973, Dr Copernicus 1976, Kepler 1983, The Newton Letter 1985, Mefisto 1987, The Book of Evidence (Guinness Peat Aviation Prize 1989) 1989, Ghosts 1993, Athena 1995, The Untouchable 1996, Eclipse 2000, Shroud 2003, The Sea (Man Booker Prize 2005, Irish Novel of the Year 2005) 2005, The Infinities 2009; as Benjamin Black: Christine Falls 2006, The Silver Swan 2007, The Lemur 2008, Elegy for April 2010, A Death in Summer 2011, Ancient Light 2012, Vengeance 2012; non-fiction: Prague Pictures: Portraits of a City 2003; short stories: Imagined Lives: Portraits of Unknown People 2011; contribs to New York Review of Books, Irish Times, Guardian, New Republic. *Address:* c/o Ed Victor Ltd, 6 Bayley Street, Bedford Square, London, WC1B 3HE, England (office). *Telephone:* (20) 7304-4100 (office). *Fax:* (20) 7304-4111 (office).

BAO, Xuding; Chinese government official and business executive; *President, China International Engineering Consulting Corporation;* b. Feb. 1939, Wuxi City, Jiangsu Prov.; ed Shenyang School of Machine Industry, CCP Cen. Party School; joined CCP 1961; Deputy Dir then Dir City Machine Building Industry Bureau, Sichuan Prov. 1986; Dir Sichuan Prov. Econ. Planning Comm. 1986; Vice-Minister of Machine Building and Electronics Industries 1990–93; Vice-Minister of Machine

Building Industry 1993–96, Minister 1996–98; Vice-Minister State Devt and Reform Comm. 1998–99; Deputy Sec. CCP Municipal Cttee, Chongqing 1999; Deputy Mayor of Chongqing 1999–2000, Mayor 2000–02; Pres. China Int. Engineering Consulting Corpn 2002–; mem. 15th CCP Cen. Cttee 1997–2002; mem. 10th CPPCC Nat. Cttee 2003–08. *Address:* China International Engineering Consulting Corporation, 32 Che Gong Zhuang Xilu, 100044 Beijing, People's Republic of China. *E-mail:* ciecc@ciecc.com.cn. *Website:* www.ciecc.com.cn.

BAPTISTA NETO, Clovis José; Brazilian engineer and international organization executive; *Executive Secretary, Inter-American Telecommunication Commission (Comisión Interamericana de Telecomunicaciones—CITEL);* ed Pontifical Catholic University of Rio de Janeiro; held several sr positions with EMBRATEL (telecommunications operator) 1974–95; held several key positions with Ministry of Communications; fmr Head of Int. Affairs, Brazilian Telecommunications Regulatory Agency, ANATEL; currently Exec. Sec. Inter-American Telecommunication Comm. (Comisión Interamericana de Telecomunicaciones—CITEL), Washington, DC 2000–; participant in confs and int. meetings of ITU, CITEL and WTO, among others; represents OAS at Hemispheric Advisory Bd Inst. for Connectivity in the Americas (Govt-supported Canadian org.). *Address:* Inter-American Telecommunication Commission (CITEL), 1889 F Street, NW, Washington, DC 20006, USA (office). *Telephone:* (202) 458-3004 (office). *Fax:* (202) 458-6854 (office). *E-mail:* citel@oas.org (office). *Website:* www.citel.oas.org (office).

BAPTISTE, Alva Romanus, MSc; St Lucia politician and fmr transport official; *Minister for Foreign Affairs, International Trade and Civil Aviation;* ed Cranfield Univ., UK; Air Traffic Control Asst 1985–86, Air Traffic Control Officer 1988–97, Asst Airport Man., Hewanorra Int. Airport 2001–02, with St Lucia Air and Sea Ports Authority 1985–2002, Civil Aviation Officer, Ministry of Civil Aviation 2003–05; mem. House of Ass. for Laborie constituency 2006–; Minister for Foreign Affairs, Int. Trade and Civil Aviation 2011–; mem. St Lucia Labour Party. *Address:* Ministry of Foreign Affairs, International Trade and Civil Aviation, Conway Business Centre, 7th Floor, Waterfront, Castries, St Lucia (office). *Telephone:* 468-4501 (office). *Fax:* 452-7427 (office). *E-mail:* foreign@candw.lc (office).

BAQUET, Dean Paul; American journalist and editor; *Assistant Managing Editor and Washington Bureau Chief, New York Times;* b. 21 Sept. 1956, New Orleans; s. of Edward Joseph Baquet and Myrtle Baquet (née Romano); m. Dylan Landis 1986; one s.; ed Columbia Univ., New York; investigative reporter, New Orleans 1978–84; investigative reporter, Chicago Tribune 1984–87, Chief Investigative Reporter 1987–90; investigative reporter, New York Times 1990–92, Projects Ed. 1992–95, Deputy Metropolitan Ed. 1995, Nat. Ed. 1995–2000, Asst Man. Ed. and Washington Bureau Chief 2007–; Man. Ed. Los Angeles Times 2000–05, Ed. 2005–06; mem. Bd of Dirs Cttee to Protect Journalists; Pulitzer Prize for Investigative Reporting 1988. *Address:* New York Times, 1627 Eye Street, NW, 7th Floor, Washington, DC 20006, USA (office). *Telephone:* (202) 862-0300 (office). *Fax:* (202) 862-0340 (office). *Website:* www.nytimes.com (office).

BAR-ON, Ronnie; Israeli lawyer and politician; b. 2 June 1948, Tel-Aviv; m.; three c.; ed Hebrew Univ., Jerusalem; completed mil. service with rank of Lt-Col, served as judge, Mil. Court of Appeals in Judea, Samaria, Gaza; mem. Cen. Cttee of Israel Bar 1995–2003, also served as mem. Jerusalem Regional Cttee of Israel Bar, Council for Admin. Courts, Advisory Comm. to Govt Cos Authority, Public Defenders Comm.; mem. Knesset (Likud and Kadima) 2003–11; Minister of Nat. Infrastructures and Minister of Science and Tech., January–May 2006, of the Interior 2006–07, of Finance 2007–09; mem. Bd of Dirs Alrov (Israel) Ltd 2013–.

BARADEI, Mohammad Mostafa el-, BL, DEA, PhD; Egyptian lawyer, diplomatist, international organization official and politician; b. 17 June 1942, Cairo; s. of Mostafa el-Baradei; m. Aida el-Kachef; one s. one d.; ed Univ. of Cairo, Grad. Inst. of Int. Studies, Geneva, Switzerland, New York Univ., USA; with Egyptian Ministry of Foreign Affairs, Dept of Int. Orgs 1964–67; mem. Perm. Mission to UN, New York 1967–71; Sr Fellow, Center for Int. Studies, New York Univ. 1973–74; Special Asst to Foreign Minister, Ministry of Foreign Affairs 1974–78; mem. Perm. Mission to UN, Geneva and Alt. Rep. Cttee on Disarmament 1978–80; Sr Fellow and Dir Int. Law and Orgs Programme, UN Inst. for Training and Research, New York 1980–84; Adjunct Prof. of Int. Law, New York Univ. 1981–87; Rep. of Dir-Gen. of IAEA to UN, New York 1984–87, Legal Adviser, then Dir Legal Div., IAEA, Vienna 1987–91, Dir of External Relations 1991–93, Asst Dir-Gen. for External Relations 1993–97, Dir-Gen. IAEA 1997–2009 (three terms); f. Nat. Assocn for Change (political reform movt) 2010–; co-f. Dustour (Constitution) Party 2012; Acting Vice-Pres. of Egypt July–Aug. 2013 (resgnd); mem. Int. Law Assocn, American Soc., of Int. Law, Nuclear Law Assocn; Hon. Patron Trinity's Univ. Philosophical Soc. 2006; Greatest Nile Collar (highest Egyptian civilian decoration), Order of Francisc Skorina (Belarus), Order of Friendship of Peoples (Belarus), Decoration for Services to the Repub. of Austria (Grand Decoration in Gold with Sash) 2009, Order of Merit of the FRG (Grand Cross with Star and Sash) 2010; Dr hc (New York Univ., Univ. of Maryland, American Univ., Cairo, Free Mediterranean Univ. (LUM), Bari, Italy, Soka Univ. of Japan, Tsinghua Univ., Beijing, Polytechnic Univ., Bucharest, Universidad Politecnica de Madrid, Konkuk Univ., Seoul, Univ. of Florence, Univ. of Buenos Aires, Nat. Univ. of Cuyo, Argentina, Amherst Coll., Cairo Univ.); Nobel Peace Prize (jt winner with IAEA) 2005, Franklin D. Roosevelt Four Freedoms Award 2006, James Park Morton Interfaith Award, Golden Plate Award, American Acad. of Achievement, Jit Trainor Award, Georgetown Univ., Human Security Award, Muslim Public Affairs Council, Prix de la Fondation, Crans Montana Forum, El Athir Award (Algeria's highest nat. distinction), Golden Dove of Peace Prize, Pres. of Italy, Award for Distinguished Contrib. to the Peaceful Worldwide Use of Nuclear Tech., World Nuclear Assocn 2007, Mostar Int. Peace Award, Mostar Center for Peace and Multiethnic Cooperation 2007, Peacebuilding Award, EastWest Inst. 2008, Int. Seville NODO Prize for Peace, Security and Inter-Cultural Dialogue 2008, Indira Gandhi Prize for Peace, Disarmament and Devt 2009, Delta Prize for Global Understanding, sponsored by Univ. of Georgia and Delta Airlines 2009. *Publications:* The International Law Commission: The Need for a New Direction 1981, Model Rules for Disaster Relief Operations 1982, The Role of International Atomic Energy Agency Safeguards in the Evolution of the Non-Proliferation Regime 1991, The International Law of Nuclear Energy 1993, On Compliance with Nuclear Non-Proliferation Obligations (Security Dialogue) 1996; articles in int. law journals.

Address: c/o Presidential Palace, Abdeen, Cairo, Egypt. *E-mail:* info@presidency .gov.eg.

BARAK, Lt-Gen. Ehud; Israeli politician, fmr army officer and business executive; b. 12 Feb. 1942, Israel; s. of Israel Brog and Esther Brog; m. Nava Cohen; three d.; ed Hebrew Univ. Jerusalem and Stanford Univ. Calif.; enlisted in Israeli Defence Force (IDF) 1959; grad. Infantry Officers' course 1962; commando course, France 1963; Armoured Corps Co. Commdrs' course 1968; various command roles; also served in operations br. of Gen. Staff; active service in Six Day War 1967 and Yom Kippur War 1973; Commdr Tank Commdrs' course 1974; Head, Gen. Staff Planning Dept 1982–83; Dir IDF Mil. Intelligence 1983–86; Commdr Cen. Command 1986–87; Deputy Chief of Gen. Staff Israeli Defence Force 1987–91, Chief of Gen. Staff 1991–94; Minister of Interior July–Nov. 1995, of Foreign Affairs 1995–1996; Chair. Israel Labour Party 1997–2001, 2007–11; f. breakaway party Ha'atzmaut (Independence) Jan. 2011–; Prime Minister of Israel 1999–2001; Deputy Prime Minister and Minister of Defence 2007–13; mem. Knesset (Parl.) and of Parl. Security and Foreign Affairs Cttee 1996; Chair. Barak & Assocs LLC; most decorated soldier in history of IDF. *Leisure interest:* playing the piano. *Address:* c/o Ministry of Defence, Kaplan Street, Hakirya, Tel-Aviv 67659, Israel.

BARAKA, Nizar, PhD; Moroccan economist and government official; b. 1964, Rabat; m. Radia el-Fassi; ed Univ. of Aix-Marseille, France; held sr teaching positions at Faculty of Law, Econs and Social Sciences, Univ. Mohammed V, Rabat; joined Ministry of Finance 1996, Head, Econ. Watch Service, Financial Research and Forecasts Unit 1998, Div. Head, Econ. Policy and Macro-Economic Analysis 2006, Deputy Dir, Financial Research and Forecasts Unit, Ministry of Finance and Privatization, Minister-del. to Prime Minister in charge of Econ. and Gen. Affairs 2010–12, Minister of Economy and Finance 2012–13; mem. Parti de l'Istiqlal. *Address:* Parti de l'Istiqlal, 4 avenue Ibn Toumert, Bab el-Had, 50020 Rabat, Morocco (office). *Telephone:* (53) 7730951 (office). *Fax:* (53) 7725417 (office). *E-mail:* p.istiqlal2009@hotmail.com (office). *Website:* www.partistiqlal.org (office).

BARAKAUSKAS, Dailis Alfonsas; Lithuanian politician; *Minister of the Interior;* b. 29 June 1952, Geručiai, Pakruojis Dist; m.; two c.; ed Vilnius Secondary School, Pakruojis Dist, Kaunas Polytechnic Inst. (now the Kaunas Univ. of Tech.), Vilnius Univ., Harvard Inst. for Int. Devt, USA, study programmes in Sweden, Germany, the Netherlands, UK, Denmark and Canada; Head of Shift, Head of Programming Bureau, Deputy Chief Engineer, Head of Foreign Relations and Marketing Service, Siauliai Machine Tools Enterprise 1975–92; Dir Siauliai Regional Chamber of Commerce and Industry 1992–96, Dir Gen. Siauliai Chamber of Commerce, Industry and Crafts 1996–2000; elected to Siauliai City Council 1997, 2000, mem. Bd and Chair. Investment and Zokniai Devt Cttee; mem. Seimas (Parl.) 2000–04, 2006–12, mem. Cttee on Econs 2000–02, later Cttee on Legal Affairs, Chair. Group for Interparliamentary Relations with UK 2000–04, Deputy Chair. Petitions Comm. 2000–04, mem. Cttee of Foreign Affairs 2006–12, mem./ Deputy Chair. Cttee of European Affairs 2006–12, Chair. Group for Interparliamentary Relations with Sri Lanka 2008–12; Minister of Communications 2001; Dir Econ.-Social Research and Training Centre 2005–06; Minister of the Interior 2012–; mem. and mem. Bd Liberal Union of Lithuania 1992–2000, Deputy Chair. 1996–99; mem. and Deputy Chair. Liberal Democratic Party (Party Order and Justice) 2002–, Adviser to the Chair. of Party Order and Justice 2004–08, Deputy Chair. Party Order and Justice 2012–; participated in re-establishment of Rotary International in Lithuania; First Pres. Siauliai Rotary Club 1992; mem. Bd of Experts, Baltic-American Partnership Fund 1998–2000; Hon. Consul of Sri Lanka in Lithuania Feb.–Nov. 2008; Commemorative Badge to mark Lithuania's invitation to NATO 2003. *Publications:* Nuomonių sankryžos (Crossroads of Opinions) 2008; more than 150 articles on economic, social and political topics. *Leisure interests:* gardening, fishing, history of Lithuanian art. *Address:* Ministry of the Interior, Sventaragio 2, Vilnius 01510 (office); Pergalès g. 8-201, Vilnius, Lithuania. *Telephone:* (5) 271-7200 (office); (5) 271-7130 (office). *Fax:* (5) 271-8551 (office). *E-mail:* dailis.alfonsas.barakauskas@vrm.lt (office); bendrasisd@vrm.lt (office); korespondencija@vrm.lt (office). *Website:* www.vrm.lt (office).

BARAMIDZE, Giorgi; Georgian politician and engineer; *Deputy Chairman, Sakartvelos Parlamenti (Georgian Parliament);* b. 5 Jan. 1968, Tbilisi; m. Eka Jafaridze; one d.; ed Polytechnic Inst. of Georgia, George C. Marshall Center for European Security Studies, Germany; Founding mem. Green Party of Georgia 1990; commanded state centre responsible for the search for the missing and for freeing prisoners during war in Abkhazia 1992–93; Chair. Comm. for the Protection of Human Rights and Nat. Minorities 1992–94; mem. Sakartvelos Parlamenti (Georgian Parl.) 1992–, Chair. Anti-Corruption Comm. 1996–98, Defence and Security Cttee 2000–03, a Deputy Chair. of the Parl. 2012–; Founding mem. Citizens' Union of Georgia 1995, Chair. Parl. Group 1996–98; Research Assoc., Georgetown Univ., Washington, DC, USA 1998–99; Minister of Internal Affairs 2003–04, of Defence June–Dec. 2004; State Minister, responsible for European and Euro-Atlantic Integration 2004–12, also Deputy Prime Minister 2006–12; Cross of Commdr, Order for Merits to Lithuania 2006. *Address:* Parliament of Georgia, 4600 Kutaisi, Abashidze 26, Georgia (office). *Telephone:* (32) 228-90-53 (office). *E-mail:* contact@parliament.ge (office). *Website:* www .parliament.ge (office).

BARAŃCZAK, Stanisław, PhD; Polish poet, translator, literary critic and academic; *Alfred Jurzykowski Professor of Polish Language and Literature, Harvard University;* b. 13 Nov. 1946, Poznań; m.; one s. one d.; ed Adam Mickiewicz Univ., Poznań; on staff, Nurt magazine, Poznań 1967–71; Asst Lecturer, later Prof., Adam Mickiewicz Univ. 1969–80; Co-Founder Committee for the Defence of the Workers (and of clandestine quarterly Zapis) 1976; in the USA 1981–; Prof. of Slavic Languages and Literatures, Harvard Univ. 1981–84, Alfred Jurzykowski Prof. of Polish Language and Literature 1984–; Co-Founder and Co-Ed. Zeszyty Literackie, Paris 1983–; Assoc. Ed. The Polish Review 1986–87, Ed.-in-Chief 1987–90; mem. American Asscn for Polish-Jewish Studies, American Asscn for Advancement of Slavic Studies, PEN Polish Center, Polish Inst. of Arts and Sciences in America, Polish Writers' Asscn, Union of Polish Authors, Union of Polish Writers Abroad; Chivalric Cross of the Order of Polonia Restituta 1991; Alfred Jurzykowski Foundation Literary Award 1980, Guggenheim Fellowship 1989, Terrence Des Pres Poetry Prize 1989, Special Diploma for Lifetime Achievement in Promoting Polish Culture Abroad, Polish Minister of

Foreign Affairs 1993, Co-Winner PEN Best Trans. Award 1996, Award for Lifetime Achievement, Wrocław Silesius Poetry Awards 2009. *Publications:* poetry collections: Korekta twarzy (Face Correction) 1968, Jednym tchem (In One breath) 1970, Dziennik poranny (Morning Diary) 1972, Sztuczne oddychanie (Breathing Underwater) 1974, Ja wiem, że to niesłuszne (I know That It's Wrong) 1977, Atlantyda (Atlantis) 1986, Widokówka z tego świata (A Postcard from This World) 1988, The Weight of the Body 1989, Podróż zimowa (Winter Journey) 1994, Zimy i podroze (Winter and Journeys) 1997, Chirurgiczna precyzja (Surgical Precision) (Nike Prize 1999) 1998, Wiersze zebrane 2006; criticism includes: Ironia i Harmonia (Irony and Harmony) 1973, Etyka i poetyka (Ethics and Poetry) 1979, Przed i po (Before and After) 1988, Tablica z Macondo (Board from Macondo) 1990, Ocalone w tłumaczeniu (Saved in Translation) 1992, Fioletowa krowa (Violet Cow) 1993, Poezja i duch h uogólnienia. Wybor esejow 1970–1995 (Poetry and the Spirit of Generalization: Selected Essays) 1996; essays: Breathing Under Water and Other East European Essays 1990; numerous trans of English, American and Russian poetry and of William Shakespeare, including A Fugitive From Utopia: The Poetry of Zbigniew Herbert 1987, The Weight of the Body: Selected Poems 1989, Panorama der polnischen Literatur des 20. Jahrhunderts (in German) 1997, Polnische Lyrik aus 100 Jahren (in German) 1997; regular contrib. to Teksty Drugie. *Address:* Department of Slavic Languages and Literatures, Barker Center 374, 12 Quincy Street, Cambridge, MA 02138, USA (office). *Telephone:* (617) 495-4065 (office). *Fax:* (617) 496-4466 (office). *E-mail:* abarancz@fas.harvard.edu (office). *Website:* www.fas.harvard.edu/~slavic (office).

BARBA, Eugenio, MA; Italian theatre director; *Director, International School of Theatre Anthropology;* b. 29 Oct. 1936, Brindisi; s. of Emanuele Barba and Vera Gaeta; m. Judith Patricia Howard Jones 1965; two s.; ed Univ. of Oslo, Theatre School, Warsaw and Jerzy Grotowski's Theatre Lab. Opole; Founder and Dir Odin Teatret (Interscandinavian Theatre Lab.) 1964–; more than 72 productions 1965–; Founder and Dir Int. School of Theatre Anthropology 1979–; mem. Bd of Advisers, Int. Cttee Théâtre des Nations 1975–80; adviser, Danish Ministry of Culture 1981–82; UNESCO adviser, Centro de Estudios Teatrales, Museo de Arte Moderno, Bogotá 1983; adviser, Centre of Theatre Exchanges, Rio de Janeiro 1987–; mem. Bd of Advisers, Int. Comparative Literature Assn 1998; lectures regularly at univs, theatre schools, etc.; Order of the Dannebrog (Denmark); Dr hc (Århus) 1988, (Ayacucho) 1998, (Bologna) 1998, (Havana) 2002, (Warsaw) 2003, (Plymouth) 2005, (Hong Kong) 2006, (Buenos Aires) 2008, (Tallinn) 2009, (Cluj-Napoca) 2012; Danish Acad. Award 1980, Mexican Theatre Critics' Prize 1984, Diego Fabbri Prize 1986, Pirandello Int. Prize 1996, Reconnaissance de Mérite Scientifique (Montreal) 1999, Sonning Prize 2000, Gold Gloria Artis Medal 2009, Atahualpa del Cioppo (Uruguay) 2013. *Publications include:* In Search of a Lost Theatre 1965, The Floating Islands 1978, Il Brecht dell' Odin 1981, La Corsa dei Contrari 1981, Beyond the Floating Islands 1985, The Dilated Body 1985, Anatomie de l'Acteur (with N. Savarese) 1988, Brechts Aske, Oxyrhincus Evangeliet (two plays) 1986, The Secret Art of the Performer 1990, The Paper Canoe 1992, Theatre – Solitude, Craft, Revolt 1996, Land of Ashes and Diamonds 1999, Arar el cielo 2002, Burning the House 2009, La conquista della differenza 2012; numerous articles, essays etc. *Address:* International School of Theatre Anthropology, Odin Teatret, Box 1283, 7500 Holstebro, Denmark (office). *Telephone:* 97-42-47-77 (office). *Fax:* 97-41-04-82 (office). *E-mail:* odin@odinteatret.dk (office). *Website:* www.odinteatret.dk (office).

BARBARIN, HE Cardinal Philippe Xavier Ignace, MA, PhD; French ecclesiastic; *Archbishop of Lyon;* b. 17 Oct. 1950, Rabat, Morocco; ed Sorbonne, Paris and Institut Catholique, Paris; ordained priest of Créteil 1977; priest in parishes of Notre-Dame d'Alfortville and Notre-Dame de Vincennes 1977–85, St Hilaire de la Varenne 1985–90; asst, Parish of St François de Sales, d'Adamville, St-Maur; Chaplain of St-Maur secondary school 1985–90; Pastor of St Léger Parish, Boissy St Léger 1991–94; Fidei donum priest and Prof. of Theology, Sr Seminary of Vohitsoa, Fianarantsoa, Madagascar 1994–98; Pastor, Bry-sur-Marne, Créteil; Bishop of Moulins 1998; Archbishop of Metropolitan See of Lyon and Primate of Gaul 2002–; cr. Cardinal (Cardinal-Priest of Santissima Trinità al Monte Pincio) 2003; participated in Papal Conclave 2005, 2013; Chevalier, Légion d'honneur 2002. *Address:* Archdiocese of Lyon, 1 Place de Fourviere, 69321 Lyon, Cedex 05, France (office). *Telephone:* (4) 72-38-80-90 (office). *Fax:* (4) 78-36-06-00 (office). *E-mail:* archeveche.de.lyon@wanadoo.fr (office). *Website:* catholique-lyon .cef.fr (office).

BARBENEL, Joseph Cyril, BDS, BSc, MSc, PhD, FInstP, FSBiol, FRSE, FIPEM, FEAMBES; British bioengineer and academic; *Professor Emeritus, University of Strathclyde;* b. 2 Jan. 1937, London, England; s. of Tobias Barbenel and Sarah Barbenel; m. Lesley Mary Hyde Jowett 1964; two s. one d.; ed Hackney Downs Grammar School, London, London Hosp. Dental School, Univ. of London, Queen's Coll., Univ. of St Andrews, Univ. of Strathclyde, Glasgow; Dental House Surgeon, London Hosp. 1960; Royal Army Dental Corps 1960–62; gen. dental practice, London 1963; Lecturer, Dental Prosthetics, Univ. of Dundee 1967–69; Lecturer, Univ. of Strathclyde 1970, Sr Lecturer, Bioengineering Unit 1970–82, Reader 1982–85, Prof. 1985–2001, Head Dept 1992–98, Vice-Dean (Research) Faculty of Eng 1997–2001, Prof. Emer. 2001–; Consulting Prof., Chongqing Univ., China 1986–; Co-Chair. Constitution and Bylaws Cttee, Int. Fed. of Medical and Biological Eng; mem. Eng Advisory Bd, Inst. of Physics and Eng in Medicine; Founding Fellow and mem. Exec. Bd, European Alliance for Medical and Biological Eng Sciences; Nuffield Foundation Award 1963–66, Pres.'s Medal, Soc. of Cosmetic Scientists 1994, European Pressure Ulcer Advisory Panel Lifetime Achievement Award 2002. *Publications include:* Clinical Aspects of Blood Rheology (with Lowe and Forbes) 1981, Pressure Sores (with Lowe and Forbes) 1983, Blood Flow in Artificial Organs and Cardiovascular Prostheses (co-ed.) 1988, Blood Flow in the Brain (co-ed.) 1988; 115 papers in professional journals. *Leisure interests:* music, theatre, reading. *Address:* Royal College Building, University of Strathclyde, Glasgow, G1 1XW (office); 151 Maxwell Drive, Glasgow, G41 5AE, Scotland (home). *Telephone:* (141) 427-0765 (home). *E-mail:* jcbarbenel@btinternet.com; j.c .barbenel@strath.ac.uk (office).

BARBER, Sir Brendan Paul, Kt, BA (Hons); British trade union official; b. 3 April 1951, Southport, Lancs., England; m Mary Gray; two d.; ed St Mary's Coll., Sefton, City Univ., London; taught in Ghana with VSO; Pres. Students' Union, City Univ., London; worked for Ceramics, Glass and Mineral Products Industrial

Training Bd; joined Org. and Industrial Relations Dept, TUC 1975, Head Dept 1987–93, Head Press and Information Dept 1979–87, Deputy Gen. Sec. TUC 1993–2003, Gen. Sec. 2003–12; mem. Council of Advisory, Conciliation and Arbitration Service (ACAS) 1995–2004; mem. Court of Bank of England 2003–; Hon. DSc (City Univ., London) 2007. *Leisure interest:* Everton Football Club. *Address:* c/o TUC, Congress House, Great Russell Street, London, WC1B 3LS, England. *E-mail:* info@tuc.org.uk.

BARBER, Eunice; French athlete; b. 17 Nov. 1974, Freetown, Sierra Leone; d. of Margaret Barber; heptathlete/long jumper; personal best: heptathlon 6,889 points (Arles, June 2005), long jump 7.05m (Monaco, June 2003); African record holder heptathlon 6,416 points 1996; Sierra Leone record holder at 100m, high jump, long jump, shot put, javelin, heptathlon; became French citizen 1999; winner, African Championships long jump 1995, European Cup heptathlon 1999, Meeting International d'Arles 1999, 2003, Decastar Talence heptathlon 1999, IAAF World Combined Events Challenge 1999, runner up 2005, World Championships heptathlon 1999, 1995 (fourth place), 2003 (runner-up), 2005 (runner up), Hypo-Meeting Götzis heptathlon 2000, 2001, European Cup long jump 2003, World Championships long jump 2003, 2005 (third place); fifth place, Olympic Games heptathlon 2000; sixth place, World Indoor Championships pentathlon 1997; coach Bob Kersee. *Leisure interests:* fashion, cinema, music, singing, travelling. *Address:* c/o Fédération Française d'Athlétisme, 33 avenue Pierre de Coubertin, 75013 Paris, France. *Telephone:* 1-53-80-74-91. *Fax:* 1-53-80-74-97. *E-mail:* contact_barber@athleteline.com (office). *Website:* www.barber-eunice.com.

BARBER, Lionel, BA; British journalist; *Editor, Financial Times;* b. 1955, London; m.; two c.; ed Univ. of Oxford; journalist, The Scotsman 1978–81; Business Corresp., The Times (London) 1981–85; Washington Corresp. and US Ed. Financial Times 1986–92, Brussels bureau chief 1992–98, News Ed. 1998–2000, Ed. Continental European Edn 2000–02, US Man. Ed. 2002–05, Ed. Financial Times 2005–; Visiting Fellow, European Univ. Inst., Florence, Italy 1996; mem. Bd of Dirs Int. Center for Journalists; mem. Bd of Trustees Tate Gallery; Woodrow Wilson Foundation Fellow 1991, Eliot-Winant Fellow, British-American-Canadian Foundation 1994; Laurence Stern Fellowship, Washington Post 1985. *Publications include:* Price of Truth: Story of the Reuters Millions (with John Lawrenson) 1984, Not With Honour: Inside the Westland Scandal (co-author) 1986, Britain and the New European Agenda 1998. *Leisure interests:* watching rugby, cycling, reading American presidential biographies, listening to opera. *Address:* Financial Times, One Southwark Bridge, London, SE1 9HL, England (office). *Telephone:* (20) 7873-4222 (office). *Fax:* (20) 7873-3924 (office). *Website:* www.ft.com (office).

BARBERIS, Alessandro; Italian business executive; *President, EUROCHAMBRES;* b. 28 Aug. 1937, Turin; m.; three c.; ed Polytechnic Univ. of Turin; trained as engineer; joined Fiat SpA 1964, Dir 1972, Dir Fmb (Fiat Group in Latin America), Brazil 1976–78, Head of Metalworks 1978–1982, Dir-Gen. Magneti Marelli 1982–93, Dir of Industrial Co-ordination Fiat Auto 1993–96, COO 2002, CEO Dec. 2002, then Vice-Chair. Feb.–May 2003; Dir-Gen. Isituto Bancario San Paulo di Torino 1996–97; Pres. Piaggio & C. SpA 1997–2002, Unione Industriale di Pisa 1998–2001, ANCMA (construction asscn) 1999–2001, Confindustria Toscana 1999–2003, Chamber of Commerce of Industry Crafts and Agric. of Torino 2004–, EUROCHAMBRES (asscn of European chambers of commerce), Brussels 2010–; Pres. Infocamere 2008–, Chair. 2010–; Chair. CDC Point SpA 2001; Vice-Pres. Unioncamere Italiana 2006–09, Piemonte Agency for Investments, Export and Tourism 2007–, Int. Chamber of Commerce 2008–; mem. Gen. Council World Fed. of Chambers of Commerce 2011–; mem. Bd of Dirs Polytechnic of Turin 2013–. *Address:* EUROCHAMBRES, Avenue des Arts, 19 A/D, 1000 Brussels, Belgium (office). *Telephone:* (2) 282-08-50 (office). *Fax:* (2) 230-00-38 (office). *E-mail:* eurochambres@eurochambres.eu (office). *Website:* www.eurochambres.eu (office).

BARBIZET, Patricia Marie Marguerite; French business executive; *Director-General and CEO, Artémis Group;* b. 17 April 1955, Paris; d. of Philippe Dussart and Monique Cartier; m. Jean Barbizet 1979; one d.; ed Ecole Supérieure de Commerce de Paris; Man. Asst Renault Véhicules Industriels 1977–79, Int. Treas. 1979–82, Group Treas. 1977–84; Financial Dir Renault Crédit Int. 1984–89; Financial Dir Groupe Pinault 1988–90, Deputy Dir-Gen. in charge of Finance and Communication 1990–92, Dir-Gen. Financière Pinault 1992–, Chair. Pinault-Printemps-Redoute (owner of Gucci) and Pres. PPR (new name since 2005) Group Supervisory Bd 2002–; Admin., Dir-Gen. and CEO Artémis Group 1992–; Chair. Société Nouvelle du Théâtre Marigny; Dir Christie's Int. PLC, TF1 (also Chair. Audit Cttee), Fnac SA; Pres. French Asscn for Co. Treasurers (AFTE) 1989–92, now Hon. Pres.; mem. Supervisory Bd Gucci Group NV (Netherlands), Yves Saint Laurent Couture; Perm. Rep. of Artémis on Bd of Dirs of Agefi, Bouygues, Sebdo le Point; mem. Man. Bd Château Latour; mem. Bd of Dirs Total SA 2008–, Air France; apptd to head Investment Cttee of Strategic Investment Fund (subsidiary of Caisse des Depots et Consignations) 2008; Officier, Légion d'honneur; Commdr, Ordre nat. du Mérite 2002; ranked by Fortune magazine amongst the 50 Most Powerful Women in Business outside the US (sixth) 2001–02, (15th) 2003, (16th) 2004, (18th) 2005, (19th) 2006, (22nd) 2007, (16th) 2008–09, (13th) 2010–11, (20th) 2012. *Leisure interests:* literature, music. *Address:* Artémis, 12 rue François 1er, 75008 Paris (office); 10 rue du Dragon, 75006 Paris, France (home). *Telephone:* 1-44-11-20-52 (office). *Fax:* 1-44-11-20-18 (office). *Website:* international.pprgroup.com (office).

BARBOSA, Marcia C. B., PhD; Brazilian physicist and academic; *Professor, Institute of Physics, Federal University of Rio Grande do Sul;* b. Rio de Janeiro; ed Colégio Marechal Rondon, Canoas, Rio Grande do Sul, Universidade Federal do Rio Grande do Sul (UFRGS), Porto Alegre; Postdoctoral Researcher, Univ. of Maryland, USA for two years; currently Prof. of Physics, UFRGS, Dir Instituto de Física 2008–; fmr Chair. IUPAP Working Group on Women in Physics, Vice-Pres. Union of Pure and Applied Physics 2008; Nicholson Medal, American Physical Soc. 2009, Laureate for Latin America, L'Oréal-UNESCO Awards for Women in Science 2013. *Publications:* numerous papers in professional journals. *Address:* Instituto de Física, Federal University of Rio Grande do Sul, CP15051, 91501-970 Porto Alegre, Brazil (office). *Telephone:* (51) 33086516 (office). *Fax:* (51) 33087286 (office). *E-mail:* marcia.barbosa@ufrgs.br (office). *Website:* www.if.ufrgs.br/~barbosa (office).

BARBOSA, Rubens Antonio, MA; Brazilian diplomatist and business consultant; *President, Rubens Barbosa & Associados;* b. 13 June 1938, São Paulo; m. Maria Ignez Correa da Costa 1969; one s. one d.; ed Univ. of São Paulo, Brazilian Foreign Service Acad. and London School of Econs, UK; Exec. Sec. Brazilian Trade Comm. with socialist countries of Eastern Europe 1976–84; Chief of Staff, Ministry of Foreign Affairs 1985–87; Under-Sec.-Gen. for Multilateral and Special Political Affairs 1986; Sec. for Int. Affairs, Ministry of the Economy 1987–88; Amb. and Perm. Rep. to Latin American Integration Asscn (ALADI) 1988–91; Pres. Cttee of Reps ALADI 1991–92; Under-Sec.-Gen. for Trade, Regional Integration and Econ. Affairs, Ministry of Foreign Affairs 1991–93; Co-ordinator, Brazilian section of Mercosul (Southern Cone Common Market) 1991–93; Amb. to UK 1994–99, to USA 1999–2004; currently Head of Council on Foreign Trade of Fed. of Industries of the State of São Paulo (FIESP); Pres. Rubens Barbosa & Associados (consultancy); Sr Dir Albright Stonebridge Group; Publisher, Interesse Nacional (politics and econs journal); Hon. LVO, Hon. GCVO, Grand Cross, Order of Rio Branco, Commdr, Légion d'honneur, decorations from Argentina, Mexico and Italy. *Publications:* América Latina em Perspectiva: Integração Regional da Retórica à Realidade 1991; Panorama: Visto de Londres 1998, The Mercosur Codes 2000, O Brasil dos Brasilianistas, um Guia dos Estudos sobre o Brasil nos Estados Unidos (1945–2000) 2002, O Dissenso de Washington 2011, National Interest and Vision of the Future 2012; essays and articles in newspapers and magazines. *Leisure interests:* classical music, tennis. *Address:* Avenida Brigadeiro Faria Lima 2413, Sobreloja-Conj. B, CEP 01452-000 São Paulo, Brazil (office). *Telephone:* (11) 3039-6330 (office). *Fax:* (11) 3039-6334 (office). *E-mail:* rubarbosa@terra.com.br (home). *Website:* www.rbarbosaconsult.com.br (office).

BARBOSA FILHO, Nelson Henrique, BEcons, MEcons, PhD; Brazilian economist, academic, government official and banking executive; *Chairman, Banco do Brasil SA;* ed Fed. Univ. of Rio de Janeiro, The New School for Social Research (later New School Univ., now The New School), New York, USA; Substitute Prof., Fluminense Fed. Univ. 1993–94; Asst Prof., Candido Mendes Univ. 1997; Adjunct Prof., Grad. Faculty, New School Univ. 1999–2002, Researcher, Center for Econ. Policy Analysis 1998–2001, Asst Dir 2001–02; Asst Prof., Saint Francis Coll., New York 2000–01; Adjunct Prof., Inst. of Econs, Fed. Univ. of Rio de Janeiro 2002–, Prof. of Macroeconomics and Public Finance; Analyst, Cen. Bank of Brazil, Rio de Janeiro Police Force 1994–97; Deputy Chief Econ. Advisor, Ministry of Planning, Budget and Man. 2003; Advisor to Pres. of Banco Nacional de Desenvolvimento Economico e Social (BNDES—Brazilian Devt Bank) 2005–06; Asst Sec. for Macroeconomic Policy and Analysis Survey, Ministry of Finance 2006–07, Sec. 2008–10, Sec. of Econ. Monitoring 2007–08, Exec. Sec. Ministry of Finance 2011–; Chair. Banco do Brasil SA 2009–; mem. Bd of Dirs EPE-Empresa de Pesquisa Energetica 2007–09, Brasilcap 2010–11, Brasilve culos 2011–, Vale SA 2011–. *Address:* Banco do Brasil SA, SBS Qd. 01 Bloco C, Edificio Sede III, 24º Andar, 70073-901 Brasília, DF, Brazil (office). *Telephone:* (61) 3310-3400 (office); (61) 3310-5920 (office). *Fax:* (61) 3310-3735 (office). *E-mail:* presidencia@bb.com.br (office). *Website:* www.bb.com.br (office).

BARBOSA GOMES, Joaquim Benedito, LLB, DJur; Brazilian judge; *President, Supremo Tribunal Federal;* b. 7 Oct. 1954, Paracatu; one c.; ed Univ. of Brasilia, Univ. of Paris II, France; began career as janitor at electoral tribunal, Brasilia; fmr worker at congressional printing press; served in Chancellery, Embassy in Helsinki 1976–79; Counsel, Fed. Service of Data Processing, Serpro 1979–84; Chief Legal Counsel, Ministry of Health 1985–88; Dist Attorney, Rio de Janeiro 1988–2003; Judge, Supreme Fed. Tribunal 2003–12, Vice-Pres. April–Nov. 2012, President 2012–; Visiting Scholar, Human Rights Inst., Columbia Univ. School of Law, New York 1999–2000; Visiting Scholar, UCLA School of Law 2002–03; Fellow, Conselho Nacional de Desenvolvimento Científico e Tecnológico (CNPq) 1988–1992, Ford Foundation 1999–2000, Fulbright Foundation 2002–03. *Publications include:* La Cour Suprême dans le Système Politique Brésilien 1994, Bibliothèque et de Science Politique constitutionnelle 2001, Affirmative Action and Constitutional Principle Equality 2001, Law as an Instrument of Social Transformation 2001, The US Experience 2001. *Address:* Supreme Federal Tribunal, Praça dos Tres Poderes, 70175 Brasilia, Brazil (office). *Telephone:* (61) 3217-3000 (office). *Fax:* (61) 3217-4412 (office). *Website:* www.stf.jus.br (office).

BARBOSA PEQUENO, Ovídio Manuel; São Tomé and Príncipe journalist, politician and diplomatist; b. 5 Nov. 1954; m.; ed Pacific Western Univ., Inst. of Tech. of New York, USA; joined diplomatic service, overseas assignments included First Sec., Perm. Mission to UN, New York 1983–90; Sr Ed. Voice of America, Washington, DC 1990–99, headed Angola Bureau 1998–99; returned to diplomatic service and served as Amb. to Taiwan 1999–2004, Minister of Foreign Affairs and Co-operation 2004–06 (resgnd), 2007–08, Perm. Rep. to UN, New York and Amb. to USA (also accred to Canada and Brazil) 2006–07, 2009–12. *Address:* Ministry of Foreign Affairs, Co-operation and Communities, Avda 12 de Julho, CP 111, São Tomé, São Tomé e Príncipe (office). *Telephone:* 2222309 (office). *Fax:* 2223237 (office). *E-mail:* minecoop@cstome.net (office). *Website:* www.mnecc.gov.st (office).

BARBOT, Ivan, BA, LèsL; French police commissioner and government official; b. 5 Jan. 1937, Ploeuc; s. of Pierre Barbot and Anne Barbot (née Le Calvez); m. Roselyne de Lestrange 1971; three c.; ed Lycée de Saint-Brieuc, Univ. of Paris; Prin. Pvt. Sec. to Chief Commr, Tarn-et-Garonne 1961; Prin. Pvt. Sec., later Dir of Staff to Chief Commr, Haute-Savoie 1962; Dir of Staff, Paris Region Pref. 1967; Deputy Chief Commr, Etampes 1969; Deputy Chief Commr without portfolio, Official Rep. to the Cabinet 1974; Tech. Adviser to Minister of the Interior 1974–77; Sec.-Gen. Seine-Saint-Denis 1977–82; Chief Commr and Supt, Dept de la Charente 1982–85, du Var 1985–87; Dir-Gen. Police Nat. 1987–89; Pres. Interpol 1988–92; Prefect Poitou-Charentes 1989, Vienne 1989–91; with Prime Minister's office, responsible for security 1991–92; Pres. Admin. Council of French concessionary co. for the construction and exploitation of the road tunnel under Mont-Blanc 1992–94; Chair. and CEO OFEMA (French Office of Aeronautics Equipment) 1993–97, Chair. and CEO SOFEMA (formed after merger with SOFMA) 1997–2004; currently Consultant; Commdr de la Légion d'honneur, du Mérite agricole, Commdr, Ordre nat. du Mérite, Chavalier des Palmes académiques, des Arts et des Lettres. *Address:* 10 place de Séoul, 75014 Paris, France. *E-mail:* ibarbotconseil@wanadoo.fr (office).

BARBOUR, Haley Reeves, JD; American state official; b. 22 Oct. 1947, Yazoo City, Miss.; s. of the late Jeptha F. Barbour Jr and LeFlore Johnson; m. Marsha

Dickson 1971; two s.; ed Univ. of Mississippi Law School; field rep., Miss. Republican Party 1968, Deputy Exec. Dir 1972–73, Exec. Dir 1973–76; Regional Technician, Bureau of Census 1969–70; Exec. Dir Southern Asscn of Republican State Chairmen 1973–76; Southeastern Campaign Dir Pres. Ford Cttee 1976; Chair. 3rd Congressional Dist Cttee Miss. 1976–84; Republican nominee for US Senator from Miss. 1982; Municipal Judge, Yazoo City 1980–81, City Attorney 1981–85; Co-founder, Chair. and CEO Barbour Griffith & Rogers LLC (lobbying firm), Washington, DC 1991–99; Founder Nat. Policy Forum 1993; Chair. Republican Nat. Cttee 1993–97; Gov. of Miss. 2004–12; Chair. Republican Govs Asscn 2009; fmr mem. Bd of Dirs Deposit Guarranty Corpn, Amtrak, Mobil Telecommunications Technologies Inc.; Deacon, First Presbyterian Church of Yazoo City; Hon. Patron, Univ. Philosophical Soc., Trinity Coll., Dublin 2009; Gulf Guardian Award, US Environmental Protection Agency. *Publication:* Agenda for America 1996. *Address:* c/o Office of the Governor, POB 139, Jackson, MS 39205, USA.

BARBUT, Monique, MA (Econs), MPhil (Econs); French international organization official; *Special Adviser to the CEO, Agence francaise de developpement;* b. 22 Aug. 1956; m.; three c.; ed Univ. of Paris I, Grad. Inst. of Int. Studies, IHE, Paris II; several internships in banking, including three months at Volksbank, Zürich, Switzerland 1979; Program Man. Saint-Denis La Réunion, Caisse Centrale de Cooperation Economique 1981–84, Head of Dept of sector-based policies and retrospective evaluation 1984–89, in charge of all public credit and housing cos in French Overseas Depts 1990, at Ministry of Cooperation and Devt 1990–93, in charge of Secr. of French Global Environment Fund (inter-ministerial field) 1994–96; Deputy Dir French Overseas Depts and Territories and Dir Div. in charge of Devt inside same Dept, Agence Française de Développement (AFD) 1996–2000, Exec. Dir at AFD, in charge of all activities in French Overseas Depts and Territories, and responsible for all programmes for Pacific, Indian, Caribbean Ocean Islands 2000–02, Special Adviser to the CEO 2012–; Dir Div. of Tech., Industry and Econs, UNEP 2003–06; Chair. and CEO Global Environment Facility 2006–12; currently Councillor, World Future Council; mem. French Govt Del., Earth Summit, Rio de Janeiro, Brazil 1992. *Address:* Agence francaise de developpement, 5 Rue Roland Barthes, 75598 Paris, Cedex 12 (office); 1 rue Frédéric Bastiat, 75008 Paris, France (home). *Telephone:* 1-53-44-31-31 (office); 1-42-89-42-33 (home). *Fax:* 1-44-87-99-39 (office). *E-mail:* site@afd.fr (office). *Website:* www.afd.fr (office).

BARBUY, Beatriz Leonor Silveira, PhD; Brazilian astrophysicist and academic; *Professor, Institute of Astronomy, Geophysics and Atmospheric Sciences, University of São Paulo;* b. 1950; ed Univ. of Paris, France; currently Prof. at Inst. of Astronomy, Geophysics and Atmospheric Sciences, Univ. of São Paulo; Pres. Sociedade Astronômica Brasileira 1992–94; Brazilian Rep. for NSF's Gemini Project through Asscn of Univs for Research in Astronomy 1998–2002; Vice-Pres. Int. Astronomical Union (IAU), Co-Chair. triennial Gen. Ass. of IAU, Rio de Janeiro 2009, mem. Finance Cttee of IAU 2009–12; Vice-Co-ordinator Instituto Nacional de Ciência e Tecnologia de Astrofísica, Ministry of Science and Tech. 2009–12; mem. Haut Comité Scientifique de l'Observatoire de Paris 2010–14, Aura Cttee for Gemini AOC-G 2011–14, Council of the Int. Inst. of Physics, MCTI/Universidade de Natal; mem. Academia Brasileira de Ciência 2001, TWAS, The World Acad. of Sciences 2007; Foreign Assoc., Acad. des sciences (France) 2005; Hon. FRAS 2010; Comendador, Ordem Nacional do Mérito Científico 2005, Grã-Cruz 2010; Officier, Ordre nat. du Mérite 2011; Trieste Science Prize in Earth, Space, Ocean and Atmospheric Sciences (co-recipient) 2008, L'OREAL-UNESCO Award for Women in Science (Latin America) 2009, described by Epoca magazine as "one of the 100 most influential Brazilians" 2009, Prêmio Scopus, Elsevier-Capes 2010. *Publications:* 12 books edited; more than 210 papers in scientific journals on the evolution of the chemical composition of the stars. *Address:* Instituto de Astronomia, Geofísica e Ciências Atmosféricas, Universidade de São Paulo, Rua de Matão 1226, Cidade Universitária, São Paulo 05508-090, Brazil (office). *Telephone:* (11) 3091-2810 (office). *Fax:* (11) 3091-2860 (office). *E-mail:* b.barbuy@iag.usp.br (office). *Website:* www.astro.iag.usp.br/~barbuy (office).

BÁRCENA IBARRA, Alicia, BSc, MSc, MPA; Mexican biologist and UN official; *Executive Secretary, United Nations Economic Commission for Latin America and the Caribbean;* b. 5 March 1952; ed Universidad Nacional Autónoma de Mexico (UNAM), Harvard Univ., USA, Instituto Miguel Angel, Mexico; Research Asst, UNAM 1975–76, Assoc. Prof. of Botany, UNAM (Universidad Autónoma Metropolitana) 1976–78; Researcher on Ethnobotany, Instituto Nacional sobre Recursos Bióticos 1978–80; Regional Exec. Dir/Research Coordinator Instituto Nacional de Investigaciones sobre Recursos 1980–82; Under-Sec. of Ecology (Vice-Minister), Secretaría de Desarrollo Urbano y Ecología—SEDUE), Ministry of Urban Devt and Ecology 1982–86; consultant, IDB Aug.–Nov. 1987; Pres. Cultura Ecológica, Civil Soc. Org. in Mexico 1987–88; Dir Gen. Nat. Inst. of Fisheries, SEPESCA (Secretaría de Pesca) 1988-90; Prin. Officer, Programme Unit II, UN Conf. on Environment and Devt, Geneva, Switzerland 1990–92; Exec. Dir Earth Council Foundation, San Jose, Costa Rica 1992–95; Programme Coordinator Global Environmental Citizenship Programme, UNEP 1996–97; Chief Tech. Adviser on Environment and Devt, seconded by UNEP, Regional Bureau for Latin America and the Caribbean, UNDP 1998–99; Chief, Div. of Sustainable Devt and Human Settlements, ECLAC 1999–2003, Deputy Exec. Sec. 2003–06; Deputy Chef de Cabinet, UN, New York Feb.–March 2006, Acting Chef de Cabinet March 2006–07, Under-Sec.-Gen. for Man. 2007–08; Exec. Sec. ECLAC 2008–. *Publications:* The Millenium Development Goals: A Latin American and Caribbean Perspective 2005; numerous articles in professional journals. *Address:* Economic Commission for Latin America and the Caribbean, Casilla de Correo 179-D, Av. Dag Hammarskjöld, 3477 Vitacura, Santiago, Chile (office). *Telephone:* (2) 471-2000 (office). *Fax:* (2) 208-0252 (office). *E-mail:* secretaria.se@cepal.org (office). *Website:* www.eclac.org (office).

BARCLAY, H(ugh) Douglas, BA, JD; American attorney, business executive and fmr diplomatist; *Of Counsel, Hiscock & Barclay, LLP;* b. 5 July 1932, Pulaski, NY; m. Sara J. 'Dee Dee' Seiter; two s. three d.; ed Yale Univ. and Syracuse Univ.; Pnr, Hiscock & Barclay, NY 1961–2003; various positions, NY State Senate 1965–84, including Chair. Codes Cttee, Select Task Force on Court Reorganization, Senate Republican (Majority) Conf.; several sr advisory positions at KeyCorp 1971–89; fmr Chair. Panthus Corpn, QMP Enterprises Inc., Eagle Media Inc.;

Amb. to El Salvador 2003–06; Of Counsel, Hiscock & Barclay, LLP 2007–; fmr mem. Bd of Dirs Overseas Private Investment Corpn, Mohawk Airlines, Syracuse China, Giant Portland & Masonry Cement Co., Coradian Corpn, Empire Airlines Inc., Excelsior Insurance Co.; fmr mem. New York State Econ. Devt Power Allocation Bd; fmr Overseer, Nelson A. Rockefeller Inst. of Govt, State Univ. of New York; Trustee, Syracuse Univ. 1979–2003, Chair. Bd of Trustees 1992–98; fmr Trustee, New York Racing Asscn, Clarkson Univ.; Noble Amigo de El Salvador (El Salvadorian Nat. Congress) 2006,Orden Nacional Jose Matias Delgado en el Grado de Gran Cruze de Plata (El Salvador) 2007; several hon. doctorates; law library at Syracuse Univ. Coll. of Law is named in his honour; numerous prestigious academic awards. *Address:* Hiscock & Barclay, LLP, One Park Place, 300 South State Street, Syracuse, NY 13202, USA (office). *Telephone:* (315) 425-2738 (office). *Fax:* (315) 425-8550 (office). *E-mail:* dbarclay@hblaw.com (office). *Website:* www.hblaw.com (office).

BARCO ISAKSON, Carolina, BSc, MBA; Colombian politician and city planner; b. Boston, Mass, USA; d. of fmr Pres. of Colombia, Virgilio Barco; ed Wellesley Coll., Harvard Univ. and Massachusetts Inst. of Tech., USA, Université Libre de Bruxelles, Belgium, Instituto de Empresa, Madrid, Spain; Tech. Consultant and Researcher, OMPU, Caracas, Venezuela 1976, Head of Special Studies, Metropolitan Planning Office 1977–78; Co-Dir Study of Revitalization of Bogotá, Nat. Planning Dept, City Planning Dept and Fonade 1985; Head of Program to Recover City Centre, Office of the Mayor, Bogotá 1986–88; Coordinator Project to Strengthen Regional Culture, UNDP 1989–90; Int. Cooperation Adviser to Ministry of Devt 1992; Coordinator Project to Support City Housing, Ministry of Devt 1993–95; Adviser to La Candelaria Corpn 1995; Coordinator Study of City Planning for Ciudadela Usme Project 1996; Researcher Coordinator, Universidad de los Andes 1996; Head, Tech. Assistance Project, Fondo Nacional del Ahorro 1996; Dir Study on Environmental Man., Ministry of Environment 1997; Adviser to Strategic Plan for Bogotá 2000, Office of the Mayor 1997; Coordinator, Study on Treatment of Bogotá Land, City Planning Dept 1988, Study of Occupation Trends, Office of Gov. of Cundinamarca 1988; Dir of City Planning, Bogotá 1999–2002; Minister of Foreign Affairs 2002–06; Amb. to USA 2006–10; mem. Bd of Dirs Lincoln Inst.; Hon. mem. Sociedad Colombiana de Arquitectos 2002; Carlos Martínez Prize for Architecture, Bogotá 1996. *Publications include:* Diagnosis of Central Caracas 1977, The Recovery of City Centers: Operating Plan for Central Bogotá (co-author, 27 vols) 1986, Zoning Plan for Central Bogota (co-author) 1988, Land Use Guidelines for Bogotá and the Sabana (co-author) 2000; numerous articles and working papers on land use, city zoning regulations, cultural policy and governance. *Address:* Ministry of Foreign Affairs, Palacio de San Carlos, Calle 10, No 5-51, Bogotá, DC, Colombia.

BARD, Allen J., BS, MA, PhD; American chemist and academic; *Norman Hackerman-Welch Regents Chair in Chemistry, University of Texas;* b. 18 Dec. 1933, New York; m. Frances Segal 1957; one s. one d.; ed City Coll. of New York and Harvard Univ.; Thayer Scholarship 1955–56; NSF Postdoctoral Fellowship 1956–58; joined staff of Univ. of Texas, Austin 1958, Prof. of Chem. 1967–, Jack S. Josey Prof. 1980–82, Norman Hackerman Prof. 1982–85, Norman Hackerman-Welch Regents Chair in Chem. 1985–; consultant to several labs including E.I. duPont, Texas Instruments and several govt agencies; Vice-Chair. Nat. Research Council; Ed.-in-Chief Journal of American Chemical Society 1982–2001; Chair. NAS Chemical Section 1996–; mem. editorial bd of numerous journals; Gov. Weizmann Inst. 1995–; mem. NAS 1982, ACS, Electrochemical Soc.; Dr hc (Paris) 1986, (Weizmann Inst.); Ward Medal in Chem. 1955, ACS Harrison Howe Award 1980, Electrochemical Soc. Carl Wagner Memorial Award 1981, Royal Australian Chem. Inst. Bruno Breyer Memorial Medal 1984, ACS Fisher Award in Analytical Chem. 1984, Soc. of Electroanalytical Chem. Charles N. Reilley Award, 1984, New York Acad. of Sciences Award in Math. and Physical Sciences 1986, ACS Willard Gibbs Award 1987, Electrochemical Soc. Olin-Palladium Award 1987, Univ. of Cincinnati Oesper Award 1989, NAS Chemistry Award 1998, Linus Pauling Award 1998, Pittsburgh Analytical Chem. Award 2001, ACS Priestley Medal 2002, Welch Award 2004, Wolf Prize in Chem. 2008, SURA Distinguished Scientist Award 2009. *Publications include:* Chemical Equilibrium 1966, Electrochemical Methods (with L. R. Faulkner) 1980, Integrated Chemical Systems: A Chemical Approach to Nanotechnology 1994, approx. 850 papers and book chapters; Ed. Electroanalytical Chemistry (23 vols) 1966–, The Encyclopedia of the Electrochemistry of the Elements, 16 vols 1973–83, Encyclopedia of Electrochemistry (11 vols) 2002–07. *Address:* Chemistry and Biochemistry Department, University of Texas at Austin, 1 University Station A5300, Austin, TX 78712-0165, USA (office). *Telephone:* (512) 471-3761 (office). *Fax:* (512) 471-0088 (office). *E-mail:* ajbard@mail.utexas.edu (office). *Website:* www.cm.utexas.edu/allen_bard (office); bard.cm.utexas.edu (office).

BARDACH, Hannes, PhD; Austrian engineer, business executive and fmr academic; *CEO, Frequentis AG;* b. 24 March 1952, Vienna; ed Vienna Univ. of Tech., Vienna Univ. of Econs and Business Admin, SMP Man. Programme at St Gallen, Switzerland, Man. of Corp. Growth Exec. Program at Stanford Univ., USA; fmr Asst Prof., Inst. for Computer Sciences, Vienna and Univ. Lecturer on microprocessor technologies; began professional career as tech. consultant for system eng in the field of microprocessors, worked for several high-tech cos in Austria and Germany; f. own eng and tech. consulting office in Vienna 1979; Man. Dir Frequentis 1983, Owner 1986, retained ownership following change to legal form of a public co. 2007, currently CEO of co. designs and manufactures integrated voice- and data-switching systems and other products for air traffic control, air defence, C3I and public safety markets; mem. Supervisory Bd Austrian Research Promotion Agency 2004–; Hon. Dr techn. 2006; First Prize for EU Export Award 1995, Chair.'s Citation of Merit, US Air Traffic Control Asscn 1999, Wilhelm Exner Medal, Austrian Asscn for SME (Oesterreichischer Gewerbeverein—OGV) (jtly) 2006. *Publications:* several papers in professional journals on computer science; European and US technology patents for 'Method of and Apparatus for Transmission of Data'. *Address:* Frequentis AG, Innovationsstraße 1, 1100 Vienna, Austria (office). *Telephone:* (1) 81150-0 (office). *Fax:* (1) 81150-5009 (office). *E-mail:* info@frequentis.com (office). *Website:* www.frequentis.com (office).

BARDEM, Javier; Spanish actor; b. 1 March 1969, Las Palmas, Gran Canaria; m. Penélope Cruz 2010; one s.. *Films include:* Jamón, Jamón 1992, Huidos 1992, El Amante bilingüe 1993, Huevos de oro 1993, Días contados 1994, El Detective y la muerte 1994, La Teta y la luna 1995, Boca a boca 1995, La Madre 1995, Más que amor, frenesí 1996, El Amor perjudica seriamente la salud 1997, Airbag 1997, Carne trémula 1997, Perdita Durango 1997, Los Lobos de Washington 1999, Segunda piel 2000, Before Night Falls 2000 (Best Actor Prize, Venice Film Festival 2000), The Dancer Upstairs 2002, Los Lunes al Sol 2002, Collateral 2004, The Three Ages of the Crime 2004, Mar Adentro (The Sea Inside) (Best Actor, Goya Awards 2005) 2004, Goya's Ghosts 2006, No Country for Old Men (Golden Globe for Best Supporting Actor 2008, Outstanding Performance by a Male Actor in a Supporting Role, Screen Actors Guild 2008, Acad. Award for Best Supporting Actor 2008) 2007, Love in the Time of Cholera 2007, Vicky Cristina Barcelona 2008, Biutiful (Best Actor, Cannes Film Festival 2010) 2010, Eat Pray Love 2010, Skyfall 2012, To the Wonder 2012. *Address:* c/o WME, 9601 Wilshire Blvd., 10th Floor, Beverly Hills, CA 90210, USA.

BARDER, Sir Brian Leon, KCMG, BA; British diplomatist (retd); b. 20 June 1934, Bristol; s. of Harry Barder and Vivien Young; m. Jane M. Cornwell 1958; one s. two d.; ed Sherborne School, St Catharine's Coll., Cambridge; Nat. Service 1952–54; Colonial Office 1957–64; First Sec., Perm. Mission to UN, New York 1964–68, at FCO 1968–70, First Sec., Embassy in Moscow 1971–73, Counsellor, Canberra 1973–77; at Canadian Nat. Defence Coll. 1977–78; Head of Southern Africa Dept, FCO 1978–82, Amb. to Ethiopia 1982–86, to Poland 1986–88, High Commr to Nigeria and Amb. (non-resident) to Benin 1988–91, High Commr to Australia 1991–94; Commonwealth Election Monitor, Namibia Elections 1994; Know How Fund Diplomatic Training Consultant 1996; mem. Bd of Man. Royal Hosp. for Neurodisability 1996–2003, English-Speaking Union Cttee for Speech and Debate 1996–2009, Special Immigration Appeals Comm. 1998–2004; Hon. Visiting Fellow, Dept of Politics and Int. Relations, Univ. of Leicester 2006–. *Leisure interests:* politics, classical music, cycling, the internet, polemical blogging, writing to newspapers. *Address:* 20 Victoria Mews, London, SW18 3PY, England (home). *Telephone:* (20) 8355-8394 (home). *E-mail:* brianbarder@compuserve.com (home). *Website:* www.barder.com/ephems (home).

BARDHAN, Ardhendu Bhushan, MA, LLB; Indian politician and trade union official; b. 25 Sept. 1925, Sylhet (now in Bangladesh); s. of Hemendra Kumar and Sarala Bala; one s. one d.; mem. Maharashtra State Legis. Ass. 1957–62; Gen.-Sec. Communist Party of India 1996–2012. *Address:* Ajoy Bhavan, 15 Com. Indrajit Gupta Marg, New Delhi 110 002, India (home).

BARDIN, Garry Yakovlevich; Russian film director; b. 11 Sept. 1941, Orenburg; m.; one s.; ed Studio-School of Moscow Art Theatre; actor, Moscow Gogol Drama Theatre; Stage Dir Moscow Puppet Theatre; animation film dir in studio Soyuzmultfilm 1975–90; also scriptwriter; Founder, Pres. and Artistic Dir Animated Film Studio Stayer 1991–; Diplomas, Moscow Int. Film Festival, Bilbao Int. Film Festival, Spain, Tampere Int. Film Festival, Finland, Hon. Diploma Krakow Int. Film Festival, Poland, TV Prize, Rennes Int. Film Festival, France, Jury Prizes, Los Angeles Film Festival, USA, Hiroshima Int. Film Festival, Japan, Grand Prix Ruan Int. Film Festival, Annecy Int. Film Festival, France, Golden Dove Prize, Leipzig Int. Film Festival, Germany, Golden Palm Branch Prize, Cannes Film Festival, France, Nika Prize of Russian Acad. of Cinematic Arts (three times), State Prize of Russian Fed. 1999, Golden Prize, New York Int. Film Festival, USA. *Films include:* Dostat do neba (Reach the Sky) 1975, Veselaya karusel (Happy Carousel) (TV) 1976, Letuchiy korabl (Flying Ship) 1979, Pif-paf, oy-oy-oy! 1980, Prezhde my byli ptitsami (We Were Birds Before) 1982, Konflikt (Conflict) 1983, Break! 1985, Banket 1986, Vykrutasy 1988, Seryi volk & Krasnaya Shapochka (aka Grey Wolf and Little Red Riding Hood) 1990, The Coiling Prankster 1990, Chucha (Choo Choo) 1997, Adagio 2000, Chucha 2 (Choo Choo 2) 2002, Chucha 3 (Choo Choo 3) 2005. *Address:* Animated Film Studio Stayer, 107143 Moscow, Otkrytoye shosse 28, korp.6A (office); 119021 Moscow, Lev Tolstoy str. 3, apt. 11, Russia (home). *Telephone:* (495) 167-01-54 (office); (495) 246-45-86 (home). *Fax:* (495) 292-85-11 (office); (495) 167-01-54 (home). *E-mail:* garry@bardin.ru (office). *Website:* www.bardin.ru (office).

BARDOT, Brigitte; French actress; b. 28 Sept. 1934, Paris; d. of Louis Bardot and Anne-Marie (Mücel); m. 1st Roger Vadim (died 2000); m. 2nd Jacques Charrier; one s.; m. 3rd Gunther Sachs 1966 (divorced 1969, died 2011); m. 4th Bernard d'Ormale 1992; ed Paris Conservatoire; stage and film career 1952–; Founder and Pres. Fondation Brigitte Bardot; Chevalier, Légion d'honneur 1985; Étoile de Cristal from Acad. of Cinema 1966. *Recordings include:* Behind Brigitte Bardot 1960; albums include: Brigitte Bardot Sings 1963, Special Bardot 1968. *Films include:* Les dents longues (uncredited) 1952, Manina: la fille sans voile 1952, Le trou normand 1952, Le portrait de son père 1953, Un acte d'amour 1953, Tradita 1954, Si Versailles m'était conté (uncredited) 1954, Le fils de Caroline chérie 1955, Futures vedettes 1955, Doctor at Sea 1955, Les grandes manoeuvres 1955, La lumière d'en face 1955, Mi figlio Nerone 1956, Cette sacrée gamine 1956, La mariée est trop belle 1956, Helen of Troy 1956, Et Dieu... créa la femme 1956, En effeuillant la marguerite 1956, Une parisienne 1957, Les bijoutiers du clair de lune 1958, En cas de malheur 1958, La femme et le pantin 1959, Babette s'en va-t-en guerre 1959, Voulez-vous danser avec moi? 1959, Le testament d'Orphée, ou ne me demandez pas pourquoi! (uncredited) 1960, L'affaire d'une nuit (uncredited) 1960, La bride sur le cou 1961, Amours célèbres 1961, Vie privée 1962, Le repos du guerrier 1962, Le mépris 1963, Une ravissante idiote 1964, Viva Maria! 1965, Masculin, féminin: 15 faits précis (uncredited) 1966, A coeur joie 1967, Histoires extraordinaires 1968, Shalako 1968, L'ours et la poupée 1969, Les femmes 1969, Les novices 1970, Boulevard du rhum 1971, Les pétroleuses 1971, Don Juan ou Si Don Juan était une femme... 1973, L'Histoire très bonne et très joyeuse de Colinot trousse-chemise 1973. *Television:* Étoiles et toiles – L'érotisme au cinéma (episode) 1983. *Publications include:* Initiales BB 1996 (Prix Paul Léautaud 1996) 1996, Le Carré de Pluton 1999, Un Cri Dans Le Silence 2003, Pourquoi? 2006. *Address:* Fondation Brigitte Bardot, 28 rue Vineuse, 75116 Paris, France (home). *Telephone:* 1-45-05-14-60. *Fax:* 1-45-05-14-80. *E-mail:* fbb@fondationbrigittebardot.fr (office). *Website:* www.fondationbrigittebardot.fr (office).

BAREIRO SPAINI, Gen. (retd) Luis Nicanor; Paraguayan military officer and politician; fmr Commdr Cadets Corps, Mil. Acad., Commdr Army Artillery Corps, Commdr Army Mil. Inst.; fmr Dir Inst. of High Strategic Studies, Ministry of Defence; fmr Dir Inspectorate Gen., Armed Forces; Minister of Defence 2008–12. *Address:* c/o Ministry of National Defence, Avda Mariscal López y Vice-Presidente Sánchez, Asunción, Paraguay (office).

BAREKZAI, Shukria, (Dawi); Afghan journalist, editor and politician; *Editor-in-Chief, Ayina-e Zan;* b. 1972, Kabul; m.; three d.; ed Univ. of Kabul; organized and funded secret women's schools during Taliban regime; mem. Afghanistan's Constitutional Reviewing Comm. 2001; Founder and Ed.-in-Chief Ayina-e Zan (Women's Mirror) weekly newspaper 2002–; f. Asia Women Org. 2002; mem. Parl. 2005–; Int. Ed. of the Year Award, Worldpress.org 2005. *Address:* Ayina-e Zan (Women Mirror), House 186, St 12, Wazir Akbar Khan, Kabul, Afghanistan (office). *Telephone:* (70) 281864. *E-mail:* womensmirror@hotmail.com; women .mirror@gmail.com; shukriabarakzai@yahoo.com. *Website:* shukriabarakzai.net.

BARENBLATT, Grigory Isaakovich, MA, PhD, ScD; Russian mathematician and academic; *Professor-in-Residence, Department of Mathematics, University of California, Berkeley;* b. 10 July 1927, Moscow; s. of Isaak Grigorievich Barenblatt and Nadezhda Veniaminovna Kagan; m. Iraida Nikolaevna Kochina 1952; two d.; ed Moscow Univ., Univ. of Cambridge, UK; Research Scientist, Inst. of Petroleum, USSR Acad. of Sciences, Moscow 1953–61; Prof. and Head, Dept of Mechanics of Solids, Inst. of Mechanics, Moscow Univ. 1961–75; Head, Theoretical Dept, Inst. of Oceanology, USSR Acad. of Sciences 1975–92; G.I. Taylor Prof. of Fluid Mechanics, Univ. of Cambridge 1992–94, Prof. Emer. 1994–; Prof. of Math., Univ. of Calif. at Berkeley 1997–; Foreign mem. American Acad. of Arts and Sciences 1975, Royal Soc. 2000; Fellow, Gonville and Caius Coll., Cambridge 1994–99, Hon. Fellow 1999–; Foreign Assoc. Nat. Acad. of Eng 1992, NAS 1997; mem. Academia Europaea 1993; Hon. DTech (Royal Inst. of Tech., Stockholm) 1989, Hon. D Civil Eng (Turin Polytechnic Inst.) 2005; Laureate, Panetti Gold Medal and Prize 1995, G.I. Taylor Medal, American Soc. of Eng Sciences 1999, J.C. Maxwell Prize, Int. Congress on Industrial and Applied Math. 1999, Accad. Dei Lincei Lagrange Medal 1995, S. P. Timoshenko Medal, American Soc. of Civil Engineers 2005. *Publications:* Similarity, Self-Similarity and Intermediate Asymptotics 1979, Dimensional Analysis 1987, Theory of Fluid Flows in Porous Media (jtly) 1990, Scaling, Self-Similarity and Intermediate Asymptotics 1996, Scaling 2003, Self-similar Phenomena, Dimensional Analysis and Scaling 2009; articles in scientific journals. *Leisure interest:* historical reading. *Address:* Department of Mathematics, 735 Evans Hall, University of California, Berkeley, CA 94720-3840 (office); 1800 Spruce Street, Apt 102, Berkeley, CA 94709-1836, USA (home). *Telephone:* (510) 642-4162 (office); (510) 849-0155 (home). *Fax:* (510) 642-8204 (office). *E-mail:* gibar@math.berkeley.edu (office). *Website:* math.berkeley.edu/~gibar (office).

BARENBOIM, Daniel, FRCM; Israeli/Palestinian pianist and conductor; *Music Director, La Scala, Milan;* b. 16 Nov. 1942, Buenos Aires, Argentina; s. of Prof. Enrique Barenboim and Aida Barenboim (née Schuster); m. 1st Jacqueline du Pré 1967 (died 1987); m. 2nd Elena Bashkirova 1988; two s.; studied piano with his father and other musical subjects with Nadia Boulanger, Edwin Fischer and Igor Markevitch; debut in Buenos Aires aged seven; played Bach D Minor Concerto with orchestra at Salzburg Mozarteum aged nine; has played in Europe regularly 1954–; yearly tours of USA 1957–; has toured Japan, Australia and S America; has played with or conducted London Philharmonic, Philharmonia Orchestra, London Symphony Orchestra, Royal Philharmonic, Chicago Symphony Orchestra, New York Philharmonic, Philadelphia Orchestra, Israel Philharmonic, Vienna Philharmonic, Berlin Philharmonic; frequently tours with English Chamber Orchestra and with them records for EMI (projects include complete Mozart Piano Concertos and late Symphonies); other recording projects include complete Beethoven Sonatas and Beethoven Concertos (with New Philharmonia Orchestra conducted by Klemperer); has appeared in series of masterclasses on BBC TV; presented Festival of Summer Music on South Bank, London 1968, 1969; leading role in Brighton Festival 1967–69; appears regularly at Edinburgh Festival; conductor, Edinburgh Festival Opera 1973; Music Dir Orchestre de Paris 1975–89, Chicago Symphony Orchestra 1991–2006, Hon. Conductor 2006–; Gen. Music Dir Deutsche Staatsoper, Berlin 1992– (Chief Conductor for Life Staatskapelle Berlin 2000–); projects with the late Edward Said, the West-Eastern Divan Workshop (Orchestra) 1999–, and the Barenboim-Said Foundation (which promotes music and co-operation through projects targeted at young Arabs and Israelis); Charles Eliot Norton Prof., Harvard Univ. 2006; Maestro Scaligero, La Scala, Milan 2006–11, Music Dir 2011–; debut with Metropolitan Opera 2008; Commdr, Légion d'honneur 2007, Grand Officer 2011, Hon. KBE 2011; Hon. DMus (Manchester) 1997, (Oxford) 2007; Beethoven Medal 1958, Paderewski Medal 1963, Beethoven Soc. Medal 1982, Prix de la Tolérance, Protestant Acad. of Tutzing 2002, Premio Príncipe de Asturias 2002, Grammy Award (for recording of Wagner's Tannhäuser) 2003, Wilhelm Furtwängler Prize (with Staatskapelle Berlin) 2003, Wolf Foundation Prize in Arts 2004, chosen to deliver Reith Lectures 2006, Zwickau Robert Schumann Prize 2006, Conductor of the Year, ECHO Klassik Awards 2006, Ernst von Siemens Prize 2006, Hessischer Peace Prize 2006, Goethe Medal 2007, Praemium Imperiale 2007, Royal Philharmonic Soc. Gold Medal 2008, Otto Hahn Peace Medal 2010, Edison Award for Lifetime Achievement 2011, ECHO Klassik Award for Lifetime Achievement 2012. *Publications:* A Life in Music (jtly) 1991, Parallels and Paradoxes (with Edward W. Said) 2003, La Musica Sveglia il Tempo 2007, Everything is Connected 2008. *Address:* Opus 3 Artists, 470 Park Avenue South, 9th Floor North, New York, NY 10016, USA (office); c/o Daniel Barenboim Secretariat, 29 rue de la Coulouvrenière, 1204 Geneva, Switzerland (office). *Telephone:* (212) 584-7500 (office). *Fax:* (646) 300-8200 (office). *E-mail:* info@opus3artists.com (office); danielbarenboim@hotmail.com. *Website:* www.opus3artists.com (office); www.danielbarenboim.com.

BARFIELD, Julia, MBE, RIBA, FRSA; British architect; *Director, Marks Barfield Architects;* b. 15 Nov. 1952; d. of Arnold Robert Barfield and Iolanthe Mary Barfield; m. David Joseph Marks (q.v.) 1981; one s. two d.; ed Godolphin and Latymer School, London, Architectural Asscn School of Architecture, London; spent year out designing for Barriadas, Lima, Peru 1975; Co-founder Tetra Ltd 1978–79, Richard Rogers Partnership 1979–81, Foster Assocs 1981–88; co-f. Marks Barfield Architects with David Marks (q.v.) 1989–, London Eye Co. (formally Millennium Wheel Co.) to realize London Eye project 1994–2005; lectures include RA 2000, 2001, RIBA 2000, The Prince's Foundation Urban Villages Forum 2000, Royal Inst. 2001, Cooper-Hewitt Nat. Design Museum, New York 2001, Univ. of Virginia 2006, 'G-Maggiube Summit', Beijing 2011; Civic Trust/RIBA Awards Assessor; Vice-Pres. Architectural Assocn School of Architecture; mem. Lambeth Democracy Comm. 2000–01, Nat. Design Review Cttee, Comm. for Architecture and the Built Environment (CABE) 2001–06, Architectural Assocn Council 2000–06, Council of Guys and St Thomas' Hosp. for five years; Gov. Godolphin &

Latymer School; RIBA Awards for Architecture 2000, 2004, 2006, 2007, 2008 2009, 2010, London First Millennium Award 2000, Royal Inst. of Chartered Surveyors Award 2000, AIA Design Award 2000, Prince Philip Designers Prize 2000, Pride of Britain Award for Innovation 2001, Design Week Special Award 2001, D&AD Awards, Silver and Gold 2001, 2004, Blueprint Award 2001, Architectural Practice of the Year 2001, Civic Trust Award 2002, 2006, 2008, 2009, Queen's Award for Enterprise (for Innovation) 2003, Coolbrands 2003–05, BDI Excellence in Architecture Award 2005, People's Choice Award 2008, Arts Fund Prize 2008, Structural Steel Design Award 2009, BD Architect of the Year Award 2009. *Publications:* Eye: The Story Behind the London Eye, Gentle Landmarks. *Leisure interests:* family, travel, art, film, current affairs, social responsibility. *Address:* Marks Barfield Architects, 50 Bromells Road, London, SW4 0BG, England (office). *Telephone:* (20) 7501-0180 (office). *Fax:* (20) 7498-7103 (office). *E-mail:* jbarfield@ marksbarfield.com (office). *Website:* www.marksbarfield.com (office).

BARFOOT, Joan Louise, BA; Canadian novelist and journalist; b. 17 May 1946, Owen Sound, Ont.; d. of Robert Barfoot and Helen MacKinnon; ed Univ. of Western Ontario; reporter, Religion Ed. Windsor Star 1967–69; feature and news writer, Mirror Publications, Toronto 1969–73, Toronto Sunday Sun 1973–75; with London Free Press 1976–79, 1980–94; has taught both journalism and creative writing at Univ. of Western Ontario and creative writing through Humber Coll.; juror, Books in Canada First Novel Award 1987; mem. Writers' Union of Canada, PEN Canada; Books in Canada First Novel Award 1978, Marian Engel Award 1992. *Publications:* Abra 1978, Dancing in the Dark 1982, Duet for Three 1985, Family News 1989, Plain Jane 1992, Charlotte and Claudia Keeping in Touch 1994, Some Things about Flying 1997, Getting Over Edgar 1999, Critical Injuries 2001, Luck 2005, Exit Lines 2008. *E-mail:* jbarfoot@sympatico.ca (home). *Website:* www3.sympatico.ca/jbarfoot (home).

BARGHOUTHI, Mustafa, MD, MSc; Palestinian politician, human rights activist and physician; *Member, Palestinian Legislative Council;* b. 15 Jan. 1954, Jerusalem; ed trained as medical doctor in fmr Soviet Union, post-graduate training in Jerusalem and Stanford Univ., Calif., USA; lectured at Harvard, John Hopkins and Stanford Univs, also at IISS and Chatham House, London, UK, Brookings Inst., USA, Sydney Inst., Australia; est. Palestinian Medical Relief Soc. 1979, currently Pres.; Co-founder Health, Devt, Information and Policy Inst., Ramallah, Grassroots Int. Protection for the Palestinian People; del. to Madrid Peace negotiations 1991; fmr mem. steering cttee of tech. cttee that prepared establishment of various Palestinian ministries; Co-founder and Sec. Palestinian Nat. Initiative (Mubadara); twice arrested for speaking out against Israeli blockade of Occupied Territories Jan. 2002; presidential cand. (ind.) in Palestinian Authority elections Jan. 2005; mem. Palestinian Legis. Council 2006–; Ordine Della Stella Della Solidartietá Italiana 2007, Chevalier, Légion d'honneur 2010. *Publications:* author or co-author of books and research on health development; numerous articles on civil society, democracy issues and the political situation in Palestine; Our Story (DVD). *Address:* PO Box 51483, Jerusalem, Israel (office). *Telephone:* 59-9201528 (mobile) (office). *Fax:* 2-2969993 (office). *E-mail:* mustafa@ hdip.org (home).

BARGHOUTI, Marwan Haseeb, MA; Palestinian resistance leader; b. 6 June 1959, Kobar, Ramallah; m. Fadwa Bargouthi; three s. one d.; ed Bir Zeit Univ.; joined Fatah Movt aged 15; imprisoned for involvement in an intifada (uprising) 1976; placed under admin. detention without charges for six months 1985; deported to Jordan by Israeli authorities for allegedly inciting struggle against occupation 1987; returned to W Bank, Pres. student body, Bir Zeit Univ.; served in PLO in Tunis, cen. liaison officer between PLO and Fatah; helped organize political aspects of the first Intifada 1987; mem. Revolutionary Council of Fatah 1989, Sec.-Gen. in W Bank; returned to Ramallah under Oslo Accords 1994; mem. Palestinian Legis. Council (PLC) 1996–, mem. Legal Cttee, Political Cttee, Chair. Parl. Cttee with French Parl.; participated in outbreak of second Intifada in W Bank and Gaza 2000; sponsor of Tanzim (Fatah's operation dept); arrested by Israeli armed forces during incursion into Ramallah April 2002, accused of being the leader of the al-Aqsa Martyrs Brigade, indicted on terrorism charges Aug. 2002; detained by Israel in Maskoubieh Prison, W Jerusalem, trial at Israeli court commenced Sept. 2002, found guilty of organizing suicide attacks which led to five deaths May 2004, given five consecutive life sentences June 2004; Founder and Head, Al-Mustaqbal 2005. *E-mail:* fateh@fateh.org. *Website:* www.fateh.org.

BARGMANN, Cornelia (Cori) Isabella, BS, PhD; American geneticist, neuroscientist and academic; *Torsten N. Wiesel Professor and Director, Lulu and Anthony Wang Laboratory of Neural Circuits and Behavior, The Rockefeller University;* b. 1961, Athens, Ga; d. of Rolf Bargman; m. 1st Michael J. Finney; m. 2nd Richard Axel; ed Univ. of Georgia, Massachusetts Inst. of Tech.; Postdoctoral Fellow, MIT –1991; mem. Faculty, Univ. of California, San Francisco 1991–2004; Torsten N. Wiesel Prof., The Rockefeller Univ., New York 2004–, Dir Lulu and Anthony Wang Lab. of Neural Circuits and Behavior, Co-Dir Shelby White and Leon Levy Center for Mind, Brain and Behavior; Investigator, Howard Hughes Medical Inst. 1995–; mem. NAS 2003, American Philosophical Soc.; Fellow, American Acad. of Arts and Sciences 2002; Lucille P. Markey Award 1990–95, Searle Scholar Award 1992–95, Taskago Prize, W. Alden Spencer Award, Charles Judson Herick Award, Dargut and Milena Kemali Int. Prize for Research in Basic and Clinical Neurosciences 2004, Richard Lounsbery Award, NAS and Acad. des sciences 2009, Biotechnology Achievement Award, Dart/New York Univ. 2012, Kavli Prize in Neuroscience 2012, Breakthrough Prize in Life Sciences (co-recipient) 2013. *Publications:* numerous papers in professional journals. *Address:* The Rockefeller University, 1230 York Avenue, New York, NY 10065, USA (office). *Telephone:* (212) 327-8000 (office). *Fax:* (212) 327-7974 (office). *E-mail:* cori .bargmann@rockefeller.edu (office). *Website:* www.rockefeller.edu/research/ faculty/labheads/CoriBargmann (office).

BARI, Air Marshal Muhammad Enamul; Bangladeshi air force officer; *Chief of Air Staff;* b. 1960, Dhaka; m. Mary Enam; one s. two d.; ed Flying Instructor Course, UK, Jt Air War Course, India, Defence Services Command and Staff Coll., Command and Staff Coll., Indonesia, Air Force Command Coll., China, Nat. Defense Univ., USA; joined Bangladesh Air Force (BAF) as a flight cadet 1978, commissioned in Gen. Duties (Pilot) Br. 1981, joined operational fighter squadron of BAF and served in almost all fighter squadrons in various appointments, has flown FUJI-200, AA-5A, PT-6, T-37B, FOUGA, FT-5, FT-6, F-6 and A-5IIIA fighter

aircraft, also a Qualified Flying Instructor and carried out extensive instructional flying in various fixed-wing trainers and fighter aircraft, logged more than 2,000 flying hours, commanded the Trendsetters (25 Squadron, BAF), also commanded the Avengers (21 Squadron), subsequently commanded two BAF bases at Chittagong and Jessore, also served as a Directing Staff in Defence Services Command and Staff Coll., Mirpur and Deputy Commdt of BAF Acad., staff assignments have included Dir of Air Operations and Dir of Air Training at Air HQ and Dir of Training at Armed Forces Div., served in two Prin. Staff Officer positions at Air HQ level as Asst Chief of Air Staff for five years, Asst Chief of Air Staff (Operations and Training) followed by Asst Chief of Air Staff (Admin) 2009–12, Chief of Air Staff 2012–; Fellow, Nat. Defence Coll., Mirpur; Maj. Gen. Theodore Antonelli Award for Industry Study Excellence, Nat. Defense Univ. (USA) 2006. *Address:* Directorate of Communication & Electronics, Air Force Headquarters, Dhaka Cantonment, Bangladesh (office). *Telephone:* (2) 8753420 (office). *Fax:* (2) 8751931 (office). *E-mail:* dce@baf.mil.bd (office). *Website:* www.baf .mil.bd (office).

BARIANI, Didier, DèsSc; French politician; *Vice-President, Union Pour la Démocratie Française;* b. 16 Oct. 1943, Bellerive sur Allier; m. Chantal Maufroy (divorced); two c.; ed Inst. d'Etudes Politiques de Paris; Chargé de Mission, then Dept Head, Conseil Nat. du Patronat Français 1969–74; Dir, later Chair. Bd of Dirs, Centre de Perfectionnement et de Recherche des Relations Publiques 1974–79; Prin. Pvt. Sec. to Sec. of State for Environment, Ministry of Quality of Life June–Oct. 1974, to Sec. of State in charge of Public Admin, Prime Minister's Office 1974–76; Lecturer, Inst. d'Etudes Politiques de Paris 1975–79; Pres. Paris Fed. of Parti Radical Socialiste (PRS) 1973–78; Sec.-Gen. of Party 1977–79, UDF Deputy for Paris 20th Arrondissement 1978–81, Vice-Pres. UDF Group in Nat. Ass. 1978–81, Exec. Vice-Pres. 1994–97, Nat. Vice-Pres. UDF 1979–83, 1995–97, Pres. UDF, Paris 1999–2002; Pres. PRS 1979–83; mem. Steering Cttee, Exec. Cttee PRS 1971; mem. UDF Nat. Council 1978; Paris Councillor 1983, mem. Perm. Comm., Conseil de Paris; Pres. and Dir-Gen. Saemar Saint-Blaise 1983–2001; Mayor 20th Arrondissement, Paris 1983–95, Deputy Mayor of Paris 1983–2001; Sec. of State, Ministry of Foreign Affairs 1986–88; Pres. Parti Radical 1979–83; Nat. Del. of UDF (relations with int. orgs) 1988–92; Man. Soc. INFORG (Information, Communication et Organisation) 1977; Pres. Parti Radical Fédération Régionale de l'Ile de France 1988–; Exec. Vice-Pres. (in Nat. Ass.) UDF 1994–97, 1999–, Pres. UDF, Paris Council 1999–; Jt Sec.-Gen. responsible for UDF's relations with int. insts 1992–96; mem. Nat. Ass. 1993–97, Vice-Pres. 1995–97; mem. Comm. for Foreign Affairs 1993–97; Titular Judge High Court of Justice 1995–97; Pres. France-Israel Friendship Group 1993–97; Adviser to Mayor of Paris 1995–2001; Co-Producer UDF/RPR Project 'Gouverner ensemble' 1986, 'Projet UDF/RPR pour la France' 1993; Hon. Pres. Parti Radical, Paris Football Club; Chevalier Légion d'honneur, Officier Ordre nat. du Mérite. *Publication:* Les immigrés: pour ou contre la France? 1985, Manifeste des Radicaux (jtly) 1995, Manifestement Radical (jtly) 1996. *Leisure interests:* football, skiing, tennis. *Address:* Groupe UDF-9, Hôtel de Ville de Paris, 75196 Paris RP, France. *Telephone:* 1-42-76-51-27 (office). *Fax:* 1-42-76-64-57 (office). *E-mail:* didier .bariani@paris.fr (office). *Website:* www.paris.fr (office); www.udf.org (office).

BARICCO, Alessandro; Italian writer and playwright; b. 25 Jan. 1958, Turin; music critic, La Repubblica; cultural correspondent, La Stampa; co-founder La Scuola Holden (narrative skills workshop) 1994; collaboration with French band, Air, to produce backing music for City 2003; Assoc. Fandango Libri Publishing House 2005–; several literary prizes. *Television:* L'amore è un dardo 1993, Pickwick, del leggere e dello scrivere 1994, Totem. Letture, suoni, lezioni 1998–2001. *Plays:* Novecento 1994, Davila Roa 1996, Partita Spagnola 2003. *Film:* Lezione 21 2008. *Publications:* novels: Castelli di rabbia (trans. as Lands of Glass) (Premio Selezione Campiello, Prix Médicis étranger) 1991, Oceano Mare (trans. as Ocean Sea) (Premio Viareggio) 1993, Novecento. Un Monologo 1994, Seta (trans. as Silk) 1996, City 1999, Senza sangue (trans. as Without Blood) 2002, Omero, Iliade 2004, Questa Storia 2005, Emmaus 2009, Mr Gwyn 2011; non-fiction: Il Genio in fuga 1988, L'anima di Hegel e le mucche del Wisconsin 1992, Barnum (collection of articles) 1995, Barnum 2 (collection of articles) 1998, Next 2002, I Barbari 2006. *Address:* Fandango Libri, viale Gorizia 19, 00198, Rome, Italy (office).

BARING, Arnulf Martin, LLD; German academic; b. 8 May 1932, Dresden; s. of Martin Baring and Gertrud Stolze; m.; three d. one s.; ed Univs of Hamburg, Berlin, Freiburg, Columbia Univ., NY, USA, Freie Univ. Berlin, Inst. of Admin. Science, Speyer and Fondation Nat. des Sciences Politiques, Paris; Lecturer, Inst. for Public and Admin. Law, Freie Univ. Berlin 1956–58, in Political Science and Int. Relations 1966–68, Univ. Lecturer, Faculty of Econ. and Social Sciences 1968, Prof. of Political Science, Otto-Suhr-Inst. and John F. Kennedy Inst. 1969–, of Contemporary History and Int. Relations, Dept of History 1976–98 (retd); Research Assoc., Center for Int. Affairs, Harvard Univ. 1968–69; Political Ed. Westdeutscher Rundfunk 1962–64; Guest Prof. Stiftung für Wissenschaft und Politik, Ebenhausen, Sr Research Assoc., Inst. for East-West Security Studies, New York, Fellow, Wilson Int. Center for Scholars, Washington, DC 1986–88; mem. Inst. for Advanced Study, Princeton, NJ 1992–93; Fellow, St Antony's Coll., Oxford 1993–94. *Publications include:* Charles de Gaulle: Grosse und Grenzen (with Christian Tautil) 1963, Aussenpolitik in Adenauers Kanzlerdemokratie 1969, Sehr verehrter Herr Bundeskanzler, Heinrich von Brentano im Briefwechsel mit Konrad Adenauer 1949–64, 1974, Zwei zaghafte Riesen? Deutschland und Japan nach 1945 (co-ed.) 1977, Machtwechsel, Die Ära Brandt-Scheel 1982, Unser neuer Grössenwahn, Deutschland zwischen Ost und West 1988, Deutschland, was nun? 1991, Scheitert Deutschland? 1997, Es lebe die Republik, es lebe Deutschland! 1999; contrib. to Frankfurter Allgemeine Zeitung, Westdeutscher und Norddeutscher Rundfunk, Sender Freies Berlin. *Leisure interests:* travel, rambling. *Address:* Ahrenshooper Zeile 64, 14129 Berlin, Germany. *E-mail:* anfragen@ arnulf-baring.de. *Website:* www.arnulf-baring.de.

BARING, Hon. Sir John Francis Harcourt (see Ashburton, Baron).

BARKAT, Nir, BSc; Israeli business executive and politician; *Mayor of Jerusalem;* b. 1959, Jerusalem; m. Beverly Barkat; three d.; ed Hebrew Univ.; served as paratrooper in Israel Defence Forces 1977–83; Co-founder BRM Group (antivirus software co.) 1988, BRM Capital 2000; Co-founder Snunit (nonprofit org. for promotion of use of computer software in elementary educ.); Co-founder Israel

142

Venture Network 2001; Founder Jerusalem Will Succeed party 2003; unsuccessful candidate for Mayor of Jerusalem 2003; mem. Jerusalem City Council 2003–08; Mayor of Jerusalem 2008–; fmr Chair. BackWeb and Checkpoint. *Address:* Jerusalem Municipality, Information Unit, 1 Safra Square, Jerusalem 91007, Israel (office). *Telephone:* 2-6296910 (office). *Website:* www.jerusalem.muni.il/model (office).

BARKER, Graeme W. W., PhD, FBA, FSA; British archaeologist and academic; *Disney Professor of Archaeology and Director, McDonald Institute for Archaeological Research, University of Cambridge;* b. 23 Oct. 1946; ed St John's Coll., Cambridge; Lecturer in Prehistoric Archaeology, Univ. of Sheffield 1972–84; Dir British School at Rome 1984–88; Prof. of Archaeology and Head, School of Archaeology and Ancient History, Univ. of Leicester 1988–2004, Founding Grad. Dean 2000–03, apptd one of three Pro-Vice-Chancellors 2003; Disney Prof. of Archaeology and Dir McDonald Inst. for Archaeological Research, Univ. of Cambridge 2004–, Professorial Fellow, St John's Coll., Cambridge; has conducted fieldwork in UK, Italy, Libya, Jordan, Mozambique and Borneo; mem. British Acad.'s Review Cttee of the British Schools and Insts Abroad, British Acad.'s Bd for Acad.-Sponsored Insts and Socs; mem. several editorial panels, including Cambridge University Press 'Manuals in Archaeology', Leicester Univ. Press, Journal of Mediterranean Archaeology; Pres. Prehistoric Soc.; Dan David Prize (jtly) 2005. *Publications:* more than 20 books, including A Mediterranean Valley: Landscape Archaeology as Annales History in the Biferno Valley 1995 (Italian trans. 2001), The Biferno Valley Survey: The Archaeological and Geomorphological Record 1995, Farming the Desert: The UNESCO Libyan Valleys Archaeological Survey (two vols) 1996, Archaeology and Desertification: The Wadi Faynan Landscape Survey 2006; more than 200 papers on subsistence archaeology, forager-farmer transitions, Mediterranean landscape history, desertification, and rainforest foraging and farming. *Address:* Department of Archaeology, University of Cambridge, Downing Street, Cambridge, CB2 3DZ, England (office). *Telephone:* (1223) 339284 (office). *Fax:* (1223) 333536 (office); (1223) 339285 (office). *E-mail:* gb314@cam.ac.uk (office); director.pa@mcdonald.cam.ac.uk (office). *Website:* www.arch.cam.ac.uk (office); www.mcdonald.cam.ac.uk (office).

BARKER, Patricia (Pat) Margaret, CBE, BSc (Econ), FRSL; British author; b. 8 May 1943, Thornaby-on-Tees; m. David Barker 1978; one s., one d.; ed London School of Econs; taught in colls of further educ. 1965–70; Patron New Writing North; mem. Soc. of Authors, PEN; Hon. Fellow, LSE 1998; Hon. MLitt (Teesside) 1993; Hon. DLitt (Napier) 1996, (Durham) 1998, (Hertfordshire) 1998, (London) 2002; Dr hc (Open Univ.) 1997; Fawcett Prize 1983, Guardian Prize for Fiction 1993, Northern Electric Special Arts Award 1994. *Publications include:* novels: Union Street 1982, Blow Your House Down 1984, The Century's Daughter 1986 (retitled Liza's England 1996), The Man Who Wasn't There 1989; trilogy of First World War novels: Regeneration 1991, The Eye in the Door 1993, The Ghost Road (Booker Prize 1995) 1995, Toby's Room 2012; Another World 1998, Border Crossing 2001, Double Vision 2003, Life Class 2007. *Address:* 10 The Avenue, Durham, DH1 4ED, England.

BARKER, The Hon. Richard (Rick); New Zealand politician; b. 27 Oct. 1951, Greymouth; m.; three c.; ed Greymouth High School, Otago Univ.; various jobs including shop assistant, bartender, storeworker, farmhand, driver, factory worker, quarrier; Nat. Sec. Service Workers' Union; Exec. mem. Council of Trade Unions; Labour Party MP for Hastings 1993–2011, Asst Speaker 2008–11; Minister of Customs 2002–05, for the Community and Voluntary Sector 2004–05, for Courts 2003–08, of Internal Affairs, of Civil Defence, of Veterans' Affairs 2005–08; Trustee, Nga Tukimata O Kahungunu; Chair. Hawke's Bay Work Trust; Patron SPELD (Specific Learning Disabilities Federation), Deerstalkers Asscn, Schizophrenics Soc. *Address:* c/o New Zealand Labour Party, Parliament Buildings, Wellington, New Zealand.

BARKIN, Ellen; American actress; b. 16 April 1955, New York; m. 1st Gabriel Byrne 1988 (divorced 1999); two c.; m. 2nd Ronald Perelman 2000 (divorced 2006); ed City Univ. of New York and Hunter Coll. *Films:* Diner 1982, Daniel 1983, Tender Mercies 1983, Eddie and the Cruisers 1983, The Adventures of Buckaroo Banzai 1984, Harry and Son 1984, Enormous Changes at the Last Minute 1985, Down by Law 1986, The Big Easy 1987, Siesta 1987, Sea of Love 1989, Johnny Handsome, Switch, Man Trouble 1992, Mac 1993, This Boy's Life 1993, Into the West 1993, Bad Company 1995, Wild Bill 1995, Mad Dog Time 1996, The Fan 1996, Fear and Loathing in Las Vegas, Popcorn, Drop Dead Gorgeous, The White River Kid 1999, Crime and Punishment in Suburbia 2000, Mercy 2000, Someone Like You 2001, Palindromes 2005, Trust the Man 2005, Ocean's Thirteen 2007, Brooklyn's Finest 2009, Happy Tears 2009, Twelve 2010, The Chameleon 2010, Shit Year 2010, Rogues Gallery 2010, Another Happy Day 2011, Very Good Girls 2013. *Stage appearances include:* Shout Across the River 1980, Killings on the Last Line 1980, Extremities 1982, Eden Court, The Normal Heart (Tony Award for Best Featured Actress in a Play 2011) 2011. *TV appearances include:* Search for Tomorrow, Kent State 1981, We're Fighting Back 1981, Terrible Joe Moran 1984, Before Women Had Wings 1998 (Emmy Award), A Mann's World (film) 2011, The New Normal (series) 2012–13. *Address:* c/o CAA, 9830 Wilshire Boulevard, Beverly Hills, CA 90212, USA (office).

BARLOW, Sir Frank, Kt, CBE; British business executive; b. 25 March 1930; s. of John Barlow and Isabella Barlow; m. Constance Patricia Ginns 1950 (died 2000); one s. two d.; ed Barrow Grammar School, Cumbria; with Nigerian Electricity Supply Corpn 1952–59; worked for Daily Times, Nigeria 1960–62; Man. Dir Ghana Graphic 1962–63, Barbados Advocate 1963, Trinidad Mirror Newspapers 1963–64, Daily Mirror 1964–67, King & Hutchings 1967–75; Dir and Gen. Man. Westminster Press 1975–83; CEO Westminster Press Group 1985–90; Dir Economist 1983–99; CEO Financial Times Group 1983–99 (Chair. 1993–96); Man. Dir Pearson PLC 1990–96; Chair. BSkyB 1991–95, Logica PLC 1995–2002; Pres. Les Echos, Paris 1988–90; Dir Elsevier UK 1991–94; Chair. Lottery Products Ltd 1997–; Dir Press Asscn 1985–93; fmr Chair. Printers' Charitable Corpn; Dir Royal Philharmonic Orchestra 1988–93; mem. Bd of Dirs Soc. Européenne des Satellites SA 2000–. *Leisure interests:* golf, fell walking, angling.

BÄRLUND, Kaj-Ole Johannes, MSc(Econ); Finnish politician and international organization official; b. 9 Nov. 1945, Porvoo; s. of Elis Bärlund and Meri Bärlund; m. Eeva-Kaisa Oksama 1972; one s. one d.; journalist, Finnish Broadcasting Co.

1967–71; Public Relations Officer, Cen. Org. of Finnish Trade Unions 1971–72; Legis. Sec. Ministry of Justice 1972–79; mem. Parl. 1979–91; Chair. Porvoo City Bd 1979–87, 2009–12 Nat. Cttee on Natural Resources 1979–83; Chair. Swedish Labour Union of Finland 1983–90; mem. Nordic Council, Vice-Chair. Nordic Council Social and Environment Cttee 1983–87; mem. Exec. Bd Finnish Broadcasting Co. 1982–83, Neste Oy 1983–90; Chair. Bureau of the Montreal Protocol 1989–90; Chair. UN/ECE Cttee on Environmental Policy 1991–95; Minister of the Environment 1987–91; Dir-Gen. Nat. Bd of Waters and the Environment 1990–95; Dir-Gen. Finnish Environment Inst. 1995–2001; Dir Environment and Human Settlements Div. (later Environment, Housing and Land Man. Div.) UN ECE 1995–2008; Chair. Consumers' Union of Finland 1983–90, Peoples of Finland and Russia Friendship Soc. 1991–95, Union of the Pulmonary Disabled in Finland 1993–95; mem. Party Exec., Finnish Social Democratic Party 1984–91, Chair. Environmental Working Group 1981–87; State Publicity Prize (Finland) 1972. *Publications include:* Miksi Ei EEC 1971, Palkat Paketissa 1972. *Leisure interests:* tennis, cross-country skiing, literature, roller skating. *Address:* Sorsatie 4, 06100 Porvoo, Finland (home). *Telephone:* 405284844 (mobile). *E-mail:* kaj.barlund@pp.inet.fi (office).

BARMANBEK, İmre, BSc; Turkish business executive; *Deputy Chairperson, Doğan Holding;* b. 1942; ed Ankara Univ.; began career as asst tax auditor, Bd of Accountancy Specialists, Ministry of Finance, later Chief Accountant Specialist –1977; fmr State Planning Specialist, State Planning Org.; mem. Tax Appeals Comm. –1977; Chief Financial Officer, jt venture co. formed between Koç and Doğus Akü Industry Inc., later Gen. Man.; Chief Financial Officer, Doğan Group of Companies Holding Inc., mem. Exec. Bd 1999–, CEO 1999–2003, Deputy Chair. 2003–; mem. Turkish Industrialists and Businessmen's Asscn (TÜSİAD); Best Woman Manager of the Year (Turkey) 1999, ranked by Fortune magazine amongst 50 Most Powerful Women in Business outside the US (33rd) 2001, (22nd) 2002, (21st) 2003, (22nd) 2004, (23rd) 2005, (39th) 2006, (43rd) 2007, ranked by Forbes magazine amongst 100 Most Powerful Women (100th) 2006, (88th) 2007. *Address:* Office of the Deputy Chairperson, Doğan Şirketler Grubu Holding A.Ş., Oymacı Sok., 51 Altunizade, Üsküdar, 34662 Istanbul, Turkey (office). *Telephone:* (216) 556-9000 (office). *Fax:* (216) 556-9398 (office). *Website:* www.doganholding.com.tr (office).

BARNABY, Charles Frank, BSc, MSc, PhD; British physicist; *Consultant Emeritus, Oxford Research Group;* b. 27 Sept. 1927, Andover, Hants.; s. of Charles H. Barnaby and Lilian Sainsbury; m. Wendy Elizabeth Field 1972; one s. one d.; ed Andover Grammar School and Univ. of London; Physicist, UK Atomic Energy Authority 1950–57; mem. Sr Scientific Staff, MRC, Univ. Coll. Medical School 1957–68; Exec. Sec. Pugwash Confs on Science and World Affairs 1968–70; Dir Stockholm Int. Peace Research Inst. (SIPRI) 1971–81; Prof. of Peace Studies, Free Univ., Amsterdam 1981–85; Dir and Scientific Adviser, World Disarmament Campaign (UK) 1982–; fmr Consultant, Oxford Research Group, currently Consultant Emer.; Ed. Int. Journal of Human Rights; Hon. DSc (Frei Univ., Amsterdam) 1982, (Southampton) 1996, (Bradford) 2007. *Publications:* Man and the Atom 1971, Preventing the Spread of Nuclear Weapons (ed.) 1971, Anti-ballistic Missile Systems (co-ed.) 1971, Disarmament and Arms Control 1973, Nuclear Energy 1975, The Nuclear Age 1976, Prospects for Peace 1980, Future Warfare (co-author and ed.) 1983, Space Weapons 1984, Star Wars Brought Down to Earth 1986, The Automated Battlefield 1986, The Invisible Bomb 1989, The Gaia Peace Atlas 1989, The Role and Control of Weapons in the 1990s 1992, How Nuclear Weapons Spread 1993, Instruments of Terror 1997, How to Build a Nuclear Bomb and Other Weapons of Mass Destruction 2003, The Future of Terror 2007; articles in scientific journals. *Leisure interest:* natural history. *Address:* Brandreth, Chilbolton, Stockbridge, Hants., SO20 6HW, England (home). *Telephone:* (1264) 860423 (home). *Fax:* (1264) 860868 (home). *E-mail:* frank.barnaby@btinternet.com (home).

BARNALA, Surjit Singh, LLB; Indian politician; b. 21 Oct. 1925, Ateli, Haryana; s. of Nar Singh and Jasmer Kaur; m. Surjit Kaur 1954; three s. one d.; ed Univ. of Lucknow; participated in Quit India Movement 1942; practised law in Dist Court, Barnala; Shiromani Akali Dal MP for Barnala 1967–77; Educ. Minister of Punjab 1969–71; MP from Sangrur 1977; Union Minister for Agric., Irrigation and Food, Janata Govt 1977–80; elected Pres. Shiromani Akali Dal 1985; Chief Minister of Punjab 1985–87; Gov. of Tamil Nadu 1990–91, 2004–11, of Uttaranchal 2000–03, of Andhra Pradesh 2003–04, Acting Gov. of Orissa 2003–04; Minister of Chemicals and Fertilizers 1998–99, of Food 1998–2001; Admin. of Puducherry 2009–; has represented India at UN, FAO and other int. orgs. *Publications include:* Story of an Escape 1996, My Other Two Daughters 2007. *Leisure interests:* painting, reading, writing, ecology, charity work. *Address:* c/o Governor's Secretariat, Raj Bhavan, Chennai 600 022, India.

BARNARD, Eric Albert, PhD, FRS; British biochemist and academic; *Visiting Professor of Pharmacology, University of Cambridge;* b. 2 July 1929, London; m. Penelope J. Hennessy 1956; two s. two d.; ed Davenant Foundation School, King's Coll., Univ. of London; Nuffield Foundation Fellow, King's Coll. 1956–59, Asst Lecturer 1959–60, Lecturer 1960–64; Assoc. Prof. of Biochemical Pharmacology, State Univ. of New York 1964–65, Prof. of Biochemistry 1965–76, Head Biochemistry Dept 1969–76; Rank Prof. of Physiological Biochemistry, Imperial Coll. of Science and Tech., London 1976–85, Chair. Div. of Life Sciences 1977–85, Head Dept of Biochemistry 1979–85; Dir MRC Molecular Neurobiology Unit, Cambridge 1985–92; Dir Molecular Neurobiology Unit, Prof. of Neurobiology, Royal Free Hosp. School of Medicine, London Univ. 1992–; Rockefeller Fellow, Univ. of Calif., Berkeley 1960–61; Guggenheim Fellow, MRC Lab. of Molecular Biology, Cambridge 1971; Visiting Prof., Univ. of Marburg, FRG 1965, Tokyo Univ. 1993; Visiting Scientist, Inst. Pasteur, France 1973; Ed.-in-Chief Receptors and Channels 1993–; Visiting Prof. Dept of Pharmacology, Cambridge Univ. 1999–; mem. American Soc. of Biological Chemists, Int. Soc. of Neurochemistry; cttee mem. MRC; foreign mem. Polish Acad. of Sciences 2000; mem. editorial bd four scientific journals; Josiah Macy Faculty Scholar Award, USA 1975, Medal of Polish Acad. of Sciences 1980, Ciba Medal and Prize 1985, Eastman Kodak Award (USA) 1988, Erspamer Int. Award for Neuroscience 1991, Eli Lilly Prize for European Neuroscience 1998, Thudichum Prize for Molecular Neuroscience 2007. *Publications:* ed. eight scientific books; numerous papers in learned journals. *Leisure interest:* the pursuit of good claret. *Address:* Department of Pharmacology,

University of Cambridge, Tennis Court Road, Cambridge, CB2 1PD, England (office). *Telephone:* (1223) 847876 (office). *E-mail:* eb247@cam.ac.uk (office). *Website:* www.phar.cam.ac.uk/research (office).

BARNARD, Lukas Daniël (Niel), MA, DPhil; South African intelligence officer and academic; b. 14 June 1949, Otjiwarongo; s. of Nicolaas Evehardus Barnard and Magdalena Catharina Beukes; m. Engela Brand 1971; three s.; ed Otjiwarongo High School, Univ. of Orange Free State; Sr Lecturer, Univ. of OFS 1976, Prof. and Head, Dept of Political Science 1978; Dir-Gen. Nat. Intelligence Service (fmrly Dept of Nat. Security) 1980–91, Head of Constitutional Devt Service 1992; Dir-Gen. Prov. Admin of Prov. of the Western Cape 2001; S African Police Star for Outstanding Service 1985, Order of the Star of S Africa (Class 1), Gold 1987, Nat. Intelligence Service Decoration for Outstanding Leadership, Gold Nat. Intelligence Service Medal for Distinguished Service, Senior Service Award, Gold (CDS) 1992. *Publications:* one book, 26 articles in popular and technical scientific journals. *Leisure interest:* tennis.

BARNDORFF-NIELSEN, Ole Eiler, mag.scient., ScD; Danish mathematician, statistician and academic; *Professor, Department of Mathematics, Arhus University;* b. (Ole Eiler Nielsen), 18 March 1935, Copenhagen; s. of Niels Eiler Nielsen and Edith Barndorff; m. Bente Jensen-Storch 1956; two s. one d.; ed Univ. of Copenhagen, Arhus Univ.; Prof. of Math. Statistics, Inst. of Math., Arhus Univ. 1973–, Scientific Dir Math. Centre 1995–97, MaPhySto (Centre for Math. Physics and Stochastics) 1998–2003; invited visitor to univs in Europe, Australia, Brazil, Japan, Mexico, USA; Pres. Bernoulli Soc. for Math. Statistics and Probability 1993–95; Chair. European Research Centres on Math. (ERCOM), European Math. Soc. 1997–2002; Ed. Int. Statistical Review 1981–87; Ed.-in-Chief Bernoulli 1994–2000; Co-Ed. Journal of the European Mathematical Society 1998–2011; mem. Royal Danish Acad. of Sciences and Letters 1980, Academia Europaea 1990; Assoc., Inst. of Advanced Studies, Tech. Univ. of Munich; Fellow, World Innovation Foundation 2004; Corresp. Fellow, Royal Soc. of Edinburgh; Hon. Fellow, Royal Statistical Soc., Hon. mem. Danish Soc. for Theoretical Statistics, Int. Statistical Inst.; Dr hc (Univ. Paul Sabatier, Toulouse) 1993, (Katholieke Univ. Leuven) 1999; Humboldt Research Award 2001, Faculty of Science Prize, Arhus Univ. 2010. *Film:* Blown Sands. *Publications includes:* six monographs, nine edited collected works, approx. 275 scientific papers. *Leisure interests:* biographies, opera, tennis, bridge. *Address:* Department of Mathematics, Arhus University, Ny Munkegade 118, 8000 Arhus (office); Dalvangen 48, 8270 Højbjerg, Denmark (home). *Telephone:* 23-38-20-69. *E-mail:* oebn@imf.au.dk (home). *Website:* math.au.dk/en (office).

BARNER, Andreas, PhD, MD; German business executive; *Chairman of the Board of Managing Directors, Boehringer Ingelheim GmbH;* ed Univ. of Freiburg, Swiss Fed. Inst. of Tech.; began career at Ciba-Geigy AG (Novartis), Basle, Switzerland in Cen. Function of Research and Medical Dept, later Head of Devt Indication Area for Inflammatory, Bone and Allergy Diseases within Research and Devt Dept –1992; joined Boehringer Ingelheim GmbH 1992, later Head of Corp. Medical Dept, later Corp. Medical Dir responsible for global clinical research, drug regulatory affairs, information and biometry, and drug safety, currently Chair. and mem. Bd of Man. Dirs, responsible for Corp. Bd Div. Pharma-Research, Devt and Medicine; Chair. German Asscn of Research-based Pharmaceutical Cos (VFA); Deputy Chair. Nat. Genome Research Network Steering Cttee; mem. Advisory Bd NGN Capital, EFPIA R&D Dirs Group, Advisory Bd to Univ. of Mainz, Bd of Trustees German Chemical Industry Fund. *Address:* Boehringer Ingelheim, Binger Str. 173, 55216 Ingelheim, Germany (office). *Telephone:* (6132) 77-0 (office). *Fax:* (6132) 72-92300 (office). *E-mail:* webmaster@boehringer-ingelheim .com (office). *Website:* www.boehringer-ingelheim.com (office).

BARNES, Christopher Richard, CM, BSc, PhD, FRSC, PGeol; Canadian (b. British) geologist and academic; *Professor Emeritus, University of Victoria;* b. 20 April 1940, Nottingham, England; m. Susan M. Miller 1961; three d.; ed Univ. of Birmingham, UK, Univ. of Ottawa; NATO Research Fellow, Univ. of Wales, Swansea 1964–65; Asst Prof., Earth Sciences Dept, Univ. of Waterloo 1965–70, Assoc. Prof. 1970–76, Prof. and Chair. 1976–81, Biology Dept 1973–81, Sr Research Fellow, Univ. of Southampton, UK 1971–72; Univ. of Cambridge 1980–81; Prof. and Head, Memorial Univ. of Newfoundland 1981–87; Acting Dir Centre for Earth Resources Research 1984–87; Dir-Gen. Sedimentary and Marine Geosciences, Geological Survey of Canada 1987–89; Dir Centre for Earth and Ocean Research, Univ. of Victoria 1989–2000, Dir School of Earth and Ocean Sciences 1991–2002, Dir Neptune Canada 2001–11, Prof. Emer. 2002–; Pres. Canadian Geoscience Council 1979, Geological Asscn of Canada 1983–84, Acad. of Sciences, RSC 1990–93; Commr American Comm. of Stratigraphic Nomenclature 1973–75; Chair. Council of Chairs of Canadian Earth Science Departments 1983–85, 1995–97, 1997–99; mem. Earth Science Grants Selection Cttee, Natural Sciences and Eng Research Council of Canada 1977–80, Chair. 1979–80, Group Chair. Earth Sciences 1987–90, Group Chair. Interdisciplinary 1988–90; mem. Canadian Nat. Cttee and Int. Exec. Cttee, Int. Ocean Drilling Program 1987–89; mem. Bd of Dirs Canadian Geological Foundation 1991–96; mem. Science Council of BC 1991–95, Atomic Energy Control Bd 1996–2000, Canadian Nuclear Safety Comm. 1996–2010; mem. ITU/WMO/UNESCO-IOC Jt Task Force to investigate the potential of using submarine telecommunications cables for ocean and climate monitoring and disaster warning 2012–; mem. Acad. of Sciences, Cordoba, Argentina 2003; Order of Canada 1996; Hon. DSc (Waterloo) 2007; Past-Pres.'s Medal, Geological Asscn of Canada 1977, Geological Asscn of Canada Nat. Lecturer 1978, Bancroft Award, Royal Soc. of Canada 1982, J. Willis Ambrose Medal, Geological Asscn of Canada 1991, Queen's Golden Jubilee Medal 2002, Elkanah Billings Medal, Geological Asscn of Canada 2005, Pander Soc. Medal 2009, Logan Medal, Geological Asscn of Canada 2010, Brady Medal, The Micropalaeontology Soc. 2010, Queen's Diamond Jubilee Medal 2012. *Publications:* more than 140 refereed publs in scientific journals; more than 40 other scientific publs; more than 240 published conf. abstracts. *Address:* School of Earth and Ocean Sciences, University of Victoria, PO Box 1700, Victoria, BC V8W 2Y2, Canada (office). *Telephone:* (250) 721-8847 (office). *Fax:* (250) 721-6200 (office). *E-mail:* crbarnes@uvic.ca (office). *Website:* web.uvic.ca/~crbarnes (office).

BARNES, Jonathan, FBA, FAAS; British academic (retd); b. 26 Dec. 1942, Much Wenlock, Salop., England; s. of the late A. L. Barnes and K. M. Barnes; m. Jennifer Mary Postgate 1964; two d.; ed City of London School, Balliol Coll., Oxford; Lecturer in Philosophy, Exeter Coll., Oxford 1967–68, Fellow, Oriel Coll., Oxford 1968–78, Balliol Coll., Oxford 1978–94; Prof. of Ancient Philosophy, Univ. of Oxford 1989–94, Univ. of Geneva 1994–2002, Univ. of Paris IV-Sorbonne 2003–06; visiting posts at Univ. of Chicago 1966–67, Inst. for Advanced Study, Princeton 1972, Univ. of Mass 1973, Univ. of Tex. 1981, Wissenschaftskolleg zu Berlin 1985, Univ. of Alberta 1986, Univ. of Zurich 1987, Istituto Italiano per la Storia della Filosofia 1989, 1994, 1999, Ecole Normale Supérieure, Paris 1996, Scuola Normale di Pisa 2002; mem. L'Acad. scientifique, Geneva, Aristotelian Soc., Mind Asscn; Hon. Fellow, Oriel Coll., Oxford 2008–, Hon. Citizen of Velia 2010; Dr hc (Université de Genève) 2010, (Humboldt Univ. of Berlin) 2012; Condorcet Medal 1996, John Locke Lecturer, Univ. of Oxford 2004. *Publications:* The Ontological Argument 1972, Aristotle's Posterior Analytics 1975, The Presocratic Philosophers 1979, Doubt and Dogmatism (with M. F. Burnyeat and M. Schofield) 1980, Aristotle 1982, Science and Speculation (with J. Brunschwig and M. F. Burnyeat) 1982, The Complete Works of Aristotle 1984, The Modes of Scepticism (with J. Annas) 1985, Early Greek Philosophy 1987, Matter and Metaphysics (with M. Mignucci 1988, Philosophia Togata (with M. Griffin) Vol. I 1989, Vol. II 1997, The Toils of Scepticism 1991, Sextus Empiricus: Outlines of Scepticisim (with J. Annas) 1994, The Cambridge Companion to Aristotle 1995, Logic and the Imperial Stoa 1997, The Cambridge History of Hellenistic Philosophy (with K. Algra, J. Mansfield and M. Schofield) 1999, Porphyry: Introduction 2003, Coffee with Aristotle 2008, Zenone e l'infinito 2009, Method and Metaphysics 2011, Logical Matters 2012. *Address:* Les Charmilles, 36200 Ceaulmont; 12 boulevard Arago, 75013 Paris, France. *E-mail:* jonathanbarnes@wanadoo.fr.

BARNES, Julian Patrick, (Dan Kavanagh, Basil Seal), BA; British writer; b. 19 Jan. 1946, Leicester; m. Pat Kavanagh (died 2008); ed City of London School, Magdalen Coll., Oxford; lexicographer, Oxford English Dictionary Supplement 1969–72; Asst Literary Ed. New Statesman 1977–79, reviewer 1977–81, TV critic 1979–82; Contributing Ed. New Review, London 1977–78; Deputy Literary Ed. Sunday Times, London 1979–81; TV Critic, The Observer 1982–86; Hon. Fellow, Magdalen Coll., Oxford 1996–; E. M. Forster Award, US Acad. of Arts and Letters 1986, Gutenberg Prize 1987, Grinzane Cavour Prize, Italy 1988, Shakespeare Prize, Germany 1993, Austrian State Prize for European Literature 2004, David Cohen Prize for Literature 2011; Chevalier, Ordre des Arts et des Lettres 1988, Officier, Ordre des Arts et des Lettres 1995, Commdr, Ordre des Arts et des Lettres 2004. *Publications:* Metroland (Somerset Maugham Award 1981) 1980, Before She Met Me 1982, Flaubert's Parrot (Geoffrey Faber Memorial Prize, Prix Médicis 1986) 1984, Staring at the Sun 1986, A History of the World in $10\frac{1}{2}$ Chapters 1989, Talking it Over (Prix Femina Etranger 1992) 1991, The Porcupine 1992, Letters From London 1990–95 (articles) 1995, Cross Channel (short stories) 1996, England, England 1998, Love, etc. 2000, Something to Declare (essays) 2002, In the Land of Pain, by Alphonse Daudet (ed. and trans.) 2002, The Lemon Table (short stories) 2004, The Pedant in the Kitchen 2004, Arthur & George 2005, Nothing to be Frightened Of 2008, Pulse 2011, The Sense of an Ending (Man Booker Prize 2011) 2011, Levels of Life 2013; as Dan Kavanagh: Duffy 1980, Fiddle City 1981, Putting the Boot In 1985, Going to the Dogs 1987. *Address:* United Agents, 12–26 Lexington Street, London, W1F 0LE, England (office). *Telephone:* (20) 3214-0800 (office). *Fax:* (20) 3214-0801 (office). *E-mail:* info@unitedagents.co .uk (office). *Website:* unitedagents.co.uk (office); www.julianbarnes.com.

BARNES, Peter John, MA, DM, DSc, FRCP, FMedSci, FRS; British medical scientist and academic; *Professor and Head of Thoracic Medicine, National Heart and Lung Institute, Imperial College London;* b. 29 Oct. 1946, Birmingham, England; s. of the late John Barnes and Eileen Barnes; m. Olivia Harvard-Watts 1976; three s.; ed Leamington Coll., Univ. of Cambridge, Univ. of Oxford Clinical School; medical positions at Oxford, Brompton Hosp., Nat. Hosp., Univ. Coll. Hosp. 1972–78; Sr Registrar, Hammersmith Hosp. 1979–82; Sr Lecturer, Consultant Physician, Royal Postgrad. Medical School 1982–85 (MRC Research Fellow 1978–79); Prof. of Clinical Pharmacology, Cardiothoracic Inst. 1985–87, of Thoracic Medicine, Nat. Heart and Lung Inst. 1987–; Hon. Consultant Physician, Royal Brompton Hosp. 1987–; MRC Travelling Fellow, Cardiovascular Research Inst., San Francisco 1981–82; Pres. European Respiratory Soc.; hon. medical degrees from Univs of Ferrara, Athens, Tampere and Leuven; numerous awards. *Publications:* Asthma: Basic Mechanics and Clinical Management, The Lung: Scientific Foundations 1991, Pharmacology of the Respiratory Tract 1993, Conquering Asthma 1994, Molecular Biology of Lung Disease 1994, Asthma (two vols) 1997, Airway Disease 2003, An Atlas of COPD 2004, New Drugs and Targets for Asthma and COPD 2010. *Leisure interests:* ethnic art, foreign travel, gardening. *Address:* Airway Disease Section, National Heart and Lung Institute (Imperial College), Dovehouse Street, London, SW3 6LY (office); 44 Woodsome Road, London, NW5 1RZ, England (home). *Telephone:* (20) 7351-8174 (office); (20) 7485-6582 (home). *Fax:* (20) 7351-5675 (office). *E-mail:* p.j.barnes@imperial.ac.uk (office). *Website:* www1.imperial.ac.uk/medicine (office).

BARNETT, Correlli Douglas, CBE, MA; British historian; *Fellow, Churchill College, Cambridge;* b. 28 June 1927, Norbury, Surrey; s. of Douglas A. Barnett and Kathleen M. Barnett; m. Ruth Murby 1950; two d.; ed Trinity School, Croydon and Exeter Coll. Oxford; Intelligence Corps 1945–48; North Thames Gas Bd 1952–57; public relations 1957–63; Keeper of Archives, Churchill Coll. Cambridge 1977–95; Defence Lecturer, Univ. of Cambridge 1980–83; Fellow, Churchill Coll., Cambridge 1977–; mem. Council, Royal United Services Inst. for Defence Studies 1973–85; mem. Cttee London Library 1977–79, 1982–84; Winston Churchill Memorial Lecturer, Switzerland 1982; Hon. DSc (Cranfield Univ.) 1993; Hon. Fellow, City and Guilds of London Inst. 2003; Screenwriters' Guild Award for Best British TV Documentary (The Great War) 1964; FRSL Award for Britain and Her Army 1971; Chesney Gold Medal Royal United Services Inst. for Defence Studies 1991. *Television includes:* The Great War (BBC TV) 1964, The Lost Peace (BBC TV) 1966, The Commanders (BBC TV) 1972. *Publications:* The Hump Organisation 1957, The Channel Tunnel (with Humphrey Slater) 1958, The Desert Generals 1960, The Swordbearers 1963, Britain and Her Army 1970, The Collapse of British Power 1972, Marlborough 1974, Bonaparte 1978, The Great War 1979, The Audit of War 1986, Hitler's Generals 1989, Engage the Enemy More Closely 1991 (Yorkshire Post Book of the Year Award 1991), The Lost Victory: British Dreams, British Realities 1945–1950 1995, The Verdict of Peace: Britain Between Her Yesterday and the Future 2001, The Lords of War: Supreme Leadership from Lincoln to Churchill 2012. *Leisure interests:* gardening, interior decorating, eating, idling, mole-hunting. *Address:* Catbridge House, East Carleton, Norwich, Norfolk,

NR14 8JX, England (home). *Telephone:* (1508) 570410 (home). *Fax:* (1508) 570410 (home).

BARNETT, Baron (Life Peer), cr. 1983, of Heywood and Royton in Greater Manchester; **Joel Barnett,** PC, JP; British politician and accountant; b. 14 Oct. 1923; s. of Louis Barnett and Ettie Barnett; m. Lilian Goldstone 1949; one d.; ed Derby Street Jewish School, Manchester Central High School; Certified Accountant 1974; Sr Partner in accountancy practice, Manchester 1953–74, 1979–80; served Royal Army Service Corps and British Mil. Govt in Germany; mem. Borough Council, Prestwich, Lancs. 1956–59; Labour cand. for Runcorn Div. of Cheshire 1959; MP for Heywood and Royton Div. of Lancashire 1964–83, mem. House of Commons Public Accounts Cttee 1965–71, Chair. 1979–83; mem. Public Expenditure Cttee 1971–74, Select. Cttee on Tax Credits 1973–74; Vice-Chair. Parl. Labour Party Econ. and Finance Group 1966–67, Chair. 1967–70, 1972–74; Opposition Spokesman on Treas. Matters 1974–79, Chief Sec. to the Treas. 1974–79, mem. Cabinet 1977–79; mem. Hallé Cttee 1982–93; Vice-Chair. Bd of Govs, BBC 1986–93; Chair. Mercury Recycling Group Ltd, British Screen Finance Ltd 1985–95, Hansard Soc. for Parl. Govt 1984–95; Pres. Royal Inst. of Public Admin. 1989–92, Children's Medical Charity Trust PLC; Hon. Fellow, Birkbeck Coll., London Univ. 1992; Trustee, Victoria and Albert Museum 1984–96, Open Univ. Foundation 1995–, Global Warming Policy Foundation; Gov. Birkbeck Coll., Hon. Fellow 2002; Hon. Treas. Manchester Fabian Soc. 1953–65; Hon. Visiting Fellow, Univ. of Strathclyde 1980–83; Hon. LLD (Strathclyde) 1983. *Publication:* Inside the Treasury 1982. *Leisure interests:* walking, conversation, reading, good food. *Address:* House of Lords, London, SW1A 0PW (office); 7 Hillingdon Road, Whitefield, Manchester, M45 7QQ, Lancs. England. *Telephone:* (20) 7219-5353 (House of Lords) (office); (161) 766-3634 (Manchester). *Fax:* (20) 7219-5979 (House of Lords) (office). *E-mail:* barnettj@parliament.uk (office).

BARNETT, Mickey D., BBA, JD; American lawyer, politician and government official; *Chairman of the Board of Governors, United States Postal Service;* m. Janet Barnett; one s. one d.; ed Eastern New Mexico Univ., George Washington Univ. Nat. Law Center; mem. Bar Asscn of State of NM, US Court of Appeals 10th Circuit, US Supreme Court; currently Man. Partner, Barnett Law Firm, Albuquerque, NM; Legis. Asst to Senator Pete Domenici 1972–76; NM State Senator 1980–84; mem. Appellate Nominating Comm. for NM Supreme Court and Court of Appeals 1995–2002; apptd Gov. of US Postal Service (USPS) by Pres. George W. Bush 2006–, Vice-Chair. Bd of Govs 2011–12, Chair. 2012–, mem. Audit and Finance Cttee; mem. Federalist Soc. *Address:* United States Postal Service, 475 L'Enfant Plaza, SW, Washington, DC 20260-0010, USA (office). *Telephone:* (202) 268-2500 (office). *Fax:* (202) 268-4860 (office). *E-mail:* pmgceo@usps.gov (office). *Website:* www.usps.com (office).

BARNETT, Peter Leonard, AM; Australian journalist, broadcaster and administrator; *Company Chairman, Light Technologies Pty Ltd;* b. 13 Feb. 1941, Albany, Western Australia; s. of Leonard Stewart and Ruby Barnett; m. Siti Nuraini Jatim 1970; one s.; ed Guildford Grammar School, Western Australia, Univ. of Western Australia; Canberra Rep. and Columnist, The Western Australian 1953–57; SE Asia Corresp., Australian Broadcasting Comm. 1961, 1963, 1964, Jakarta Rep. 1962, New York and UN Corresp. 1964–67, Washington Corresp. 1967–70; News Ed. Radio Australia, Melbourne 1971–72, Washington Corresp. 1972–80, Controller, Melbourne 1980–84, Dir 1984–89; Exec. Dir Australian Broadcasting Corpn 1984–89; fmrly Exec. Dir Media Centre, Islamic Council of Victoria; currently Cu. Chair., Light Technologies Pty Ltd; convenor, Melbourne City Circle; mem. editorial Bd Dialogue/Asia Pacific; Australia Award 1988. *Publication:* Foreign Correspondence 2001. *Leisure interests:* swimming, literature, musical composition. *Address:* Light Technologies Pty Ltd, 50 Market Street, Melbourne 3000 (office); 66/46 Lansell Road, Toorak, Vic. 3142, Australia (home). *Telephone:* (3) 9649-7770 (office); (3) 9827-5979 (home). *E-mail:* peter@lighttechnologies.com.au (office); plsnb@netspace.net.au (home).

BARNEVIK, Percy Nils, MBA; Swedish business executive; *Chairman, Hand in Hand International;* b. 13 Feb. 1941, Simrishamn; s. of Einar Barnevik and Anna Barnevik; m. Aina Orvarsson 1963; two s. one d.; ed Gothenburg School of Econs, Stanford Univ., USA; Man. Corp. Devt, Group Controller, Sandvik AB 1969–74, Pres. US subsidiary 1975–79, Exec. Vice-Pres. parent co. 1979–80, Chair. Sandvik AB 1983; Pres. and Chief Exec. ASEA AB, Västerås 1980–87; Pres. and CEO ABB Ltd 1988–96, Chair. 1996–2001; Dir Skanska 1986–92, Chair. 1992–97; Chair. Investor AB 1997–2002, AstraZeneca PLC 1999–2005; mem. Bd of Dirs General Motors Corpn 1996–2009, Du Pont Co. 1991–98; Adviser, Hand in Hand India (charity) 2000–, also Chair. Hand in Hand International; Fellow, Royal Acad. of Eng 1998; mem. of numerous professional orgs; recipient of several hon. degrees and numerous awards. *Address:* Hand in Hand International, Kungsgatan 36, 111 35 Stockholm, Sweden. *Telephone:* (8) 716-58-90. *Fax:* (8) 716-90-35. *Website:* www .hihinternational.org.

BARNEY, Matthew, BA; American film director, actor, artist and sculptor; b. 25 March 1967, San Francisco, Calif.; s. of Marsha Gibney; m. Mary Farley (divorced); pnr Björk; one d.; ed Capital High School, Yale Univ.; Europa 2000 Prize, 45th Venice Biennale 1996, Guggenheim Museum Hugo Boss Award 1996, James D. Phelan Art Award in Video, Bay Area Video Coalition, San Francisco Foundation 1999, Glen Dimplex Award, Irish Museum of Modern Art, Dublin 2001, Kaiser Ring Award 2007. *Films include:* Cremaster 4 1995, Cremaster 1 1996, Cremaster 5 1997, March of the Anal Sadistic Warrior 1998, Cremaster 2 1999, Cremaster 3 2002, De Lama Lamina 2005, Drawing Restraint 9 2005, Destricted 2006, Matthew Barney: No Restraint (documentary) 2007. *Address:* c/o Regen Projects, 633 North Almont Drive, Los Angeles, CA 90069, USA. *Website:* www.cremaster .net.

BARNIER, Michel; French politician and international organization official; *Commissioner for Internal Market and Services, European Commission;* b. 9 Jan. 1951, l'Isère; m.; three c.; ed Ecole Supérieure de Commerce, Paris; Pvt. Office of the Ministers for the Environment, Youth and Sport and for Trade and Craft Industries 1973–78; Departmental Councillor for Savoie 1973; mem. Nat. Ass. for Savoie 1978–93; Chair. Departmental Council of Savoie 1982; Co-Pres. Organizing Cttee for XVIth Olympic Games, Albertville and Savoie 1987–92; Minister of the Environment 1993–95; Minister of State for European Affairs 1995–97; Senator for Savoie 1997; Chair. French Asscn of Council of European Municipalities and

Regions 1997; Pres. Senate Del. for the EU 1998; EU Commr for Regional Policy and Institutional Reform 1999–2004, Special Adviser to EU Pres. Barroso 2006–07, Commr for Internal Market and Services, EC 2010–; Minister of Foreign Affairs 2004–05, for Agric. and Fisheries 2007–10; Chevalier, Légion d'honneur. *Publications:* Vive la politique 1985, Le défi écologique, chacun pour tous 1990, L'Atlas des risques majeurs 1992, Vers une mer inconnue 1994. *Leisure interest:* skiing. *Address:* European Commissioner for Internal Market and Services, European Commission, BERL 12/181, 1049 Brussels, Belgium (office). *Telephone:* (2) 298-17-51 (office). *Fax:* (2) 292-13-47 (office). *E-mail:* Michel.Barnier@ec.europa .eu (office). *Website:* ec.europa.eu/commission_2010-2014/barnier (office); www .michelbarnier.eu.

BARNSLEY, Victoria, OBE, BA, MA; British publisher; b. 4 March 1954; d. of the late Thomas E. Barnsley and Margaret Gwyneth Barnsley (née Llewellin); m. Nicholas Howard 1992; one d. one step-s.; ed Loughborough High School, Beech Lawn Tutorial Coll., Univ. of Edinburgh, Univ. Coll. London, Univ. of York; with Junction Books 1980–83; Founder, Chair. and CEO Fourth Estate 1984–2000; CEO HarperCollins UK 2000–13, also for Australia, New Zealand, India and South Africa 2008–13, CEO HarperCollins UK and International –2013; Trustee, Tate Gallery 1999–; Dir Tate Enterprises Ltd 1998–; council mem. Publishers Asscn 2001–, Vice-Pres. 2009–10, Pres. 2010–11. *Address:* c/o HarperCollins, 77–85 Fulham Palace Road, London, W6 8JB, England.

BAROIN, François, MA; French lawyer and politician; *Mayor of Troyes;* b. 21 June 1965, Paris; m. 1st Valérie Broquisse 1991 (divorced 2006); m. 2nd Michèle Laroque Baroin; three c.; ed Pantheon-Assas Paris II Univ., Inst. of Higher Man. Studies (ISG), Paris; town councillor for Nogent-sur-Seine, Aube 1989; Deputy for Aube (Union for a Popular Movement—UMP), Assemblée Nationale 1993–95, 1997–2005, 2007–10; Mayor of Troyes 1995–; Sec. of State and Govt Spokesperson 1995–97; Pres. Town Community Council (Mayor) of Troyes 2001–; barrister in pvt. law firm, Paris 2001–; Vice-Pres. Nat. Ass. 2002–05; Spokesperson for UMP 2003; Minister of Overseas Territories 2005–07, Minister of the Interior, Internal Security and Local Freedoms March–May 2007, Minister of the Budget, Public Accounts and State Reform 2010–11, also Govt Spokesperson 2010–12, Minister of the Economy, Finance and Industry 2011–12; mem. Dawn 1993–95, 1997–2005, 2007–10. *Leisure interests:* hunting, fishing, reading, chess, sports. *Address:* Hôtel de ville, Place Alexandre Israël, BP 767, 10026 Troyes Cedex, France (office). *Telephone:* (3) 25-42-33-33 (office). *Fax:* (3) 25-73-47-43 (office). *E-mail:* francoisbaroin3@aol.com. *Website:* www.ville-troyes.fr (office).

BARON, Franklin Andrew Merrifield; Dominican business executive, politician and diplomatist; *Managing Director, Paramount Printers Ltd & The Chronicle Company;* b. 19 Jan. 1923, Dominica; s. of Alexander Baron and O. M. Baron; m. Sybil Eva McIntyre 1973; ed Dominica Grammar School, St Mary's Acad.; Man. A.A. Baron & Co. 1939–45, Pnr 1945–78, sole owner 1987–; mem. Dominica Legis. and Exec. Councils 1954–60; rep. of Dominica to Fed. Talks 1956–60; Founder and Political Leader, Dominica United People's Party 1957–66; Minister of Trade and Production 1956–60; Chief Minister and Minister of Finance 1960–61; Man. Dir Franklyn Hotels Ltd 1970–75; Man. Sisserou Hotel 1975–76; Chair. Dominica Tourist Bd 1970–72, Dominica Electricity Services 1983–91, Nat. Commercial Bank of Dominica 1986–90, Fort Young Hotel Co. Ltd 1986–, New Chronicle Newspaper 1990–96, Paramount Printers Ltd 1992 (currently Man. Dir); Man. Dir The Chronicle Co., Propr The Chronicle 1996–; Adviser, Barclays Bank Int. 1976–84; non-resident Amb. to USA 1982–95; Perm. non-resident Rep. to UN and to OAS 1982–95, Chair. OAS 1985, 1993; non-resident High Commr to UK 1986–92; mem. Industrial Devt Corpn 1984–88; Dominica Award of Honour. *Leisure interests:* gardening, reading. *Address:* 14 Cork Street, PO Box 57, Roseau (office); Wallhouse, Loubiere, Roseau (office); Syb Bar Aerie, Champs Fleurs, Eggleston, Dominica (home). *Telephone:* 4480415 (office); 4488151 (home). *Fax:* 4480047 (office). *E-mail:* thechronicle@cwdom.dm (office); paramount@cwdom.dm (office).

BARON, Martin, BA, MBA; American journalist and publishing executive; *Executive Editor, The Washington Post;* b. Tampa, Fla; ed Lehigh Univ.; state reporter, business writer The Miami Herald 1976–79; joined Los Angeles Times 1979, apptd Business Ed. 1983, Asst . Man. Ed. for 'Column One' 1991, Ed. Orange Co. Edn 1993; joined The New York Times 1996, Assoc. Man. Ed. responsible for night-time news operations 1997–99; Exec. Ed. The Miami Herald 1999–2001; Ed. The Boston Globe 2001–2012; Exec. Ed. The Washington Post 2012–; Pulitzer Prize 2001, Ed. of the Year, Editor & Publisher Magazine 2002. *Address:* The Washington Post, 1150 15th Street, NW, Washington, DC 20071, USA (office). *Telephone:* (202) 334-6000 (office). *Website:* www.washingtonpost.com (office).

BARON COHEN, Sacha; British actor and screenwriter; b. 13 Oct. 1971, London; m. Isla Fisher 2010; two c.; ed Christ's Coll., Cambridge; f. Four By Two Films (production co.) 2009. *Films include:* Punch 1996, The Jolly Boys' Last Stand 2000, Ali G Indahouse 2002, Spyz 2003, Madagascar (voice) 2005, Talladega Nights: The Ballad of Ricky Bobby 2006, Borat: Cultural Learnings of America for Make Benefit Glorious Nation of Kazakhstan (Best Actor, Los Angeles Film Critics Asscn, Toronto Film Critics Asscn 2006, London Evening Standard Peter Sellers Award for Best Comedy 2007) 2006, Sweeney Todd: The Demon Barber of Fleet Street 2007, Madagascar: Escape 2 Africa (voice) 2008, Brüno 2009, Hugo 2011, The Dictator 2012, Les Misérables 2012, Anchorman 2: The Legend Continues 2013. *Television includes:* Jack and Jeremy's Police 4 1995, Live from the Lighthouse 1998, Comedy Nation 1998, The 11 O'Clock Show 1998–99, Ali G's Alternative Christmas Message 1999, Da Ali G Show (series) 2000–04, Curb Your Enthusiasm (episode) 2005, Night of Too Many Stars: An Overbooked Event for Autism Education 2006, Friday Night with Jonathan Ross (episode as Borat Sagdiyev) 2006, Saturday Night Live (episode as Borat Sagdiyev) 2006, Late Show with David Letterman (episode as Borat Sagdiyev) 2006, Reel Comedy: Borat Moviefilms Special Preview 2006, The Daily Show (episode as Borat Sagdiyev) 2006, The Tonight Show with Jay Leno (episode as Borat Sagdiyev) 2006, Howard Stern on Demand (episode as Borat Sagdiyev) 2006, Jensen! (episode,) 2006, Comic Relief 2007: The Big One 2007, El hormiguero (episode) 2009. *Publication:* Borat: Touristic Guidings to Glorious Nation of Kazakhstan (as Borat Sagdiyev) 2007. *Address:* Four By Two Films, 9100 Wilshire Blvd, Suite 1000 West, Beverly Hills, CA 90212 (office); c/o Jimmy Miller, 10th Floor, 9200 Sunset Blvd, Los Angeles, CA 90069 (office); c/o William Morris Endeavor Entertainment, 9601 Wilshire Blvd,

10th Floor, Beverly Hills, CA 90212, USA (office). *Telephone:* (310) 248-2000 (WME Entertainment) (office). *Fax:* (310) 248-2020 (WME Entertainment) (office).

BARÓN CRESPO, Enrique; Spanish lawyer and politician; b. 1944, Madrid; m.; one s.; ed Calasancio de las Escuelas Pías Coll., Instituto Católico de Dirección de Empresas, Ecole Supérieure des Sciences Economiques et Commerciales, Paris; fmr Prof. of Agrarian Econs, INEA, Valladolid, Prof. of Econ. Structures, Universidad Complutense of Madrid 1966–70; practised as human rights lawyer before Tribunal of Public Order 1970–74; ran legal and econ. consultancy with Agapito Ramos; mem. Convergencia Socialista and Federación de Partidos Socialistas (FPS); negotiated electoral coalition of FPS with the Partido Socialista Obrero Español (PSOE); mem. Congress of Deputies 1977–87, PSOE Spokesman for Econ. Affairs, Public Finance and the Budget 1977–82; Minister of Transport and Tourism 1982–85; mem. European Parl. 1986–, Pres. 1989–92, Party of European Socialists Group Chair. 1999–2004, Cttee on Foreign Affairs 1992–95; Pres. International Yehudi Menuhin Foundation; mem. Bd of Dirs Dali Foundation, Istituto per l'Opera e la Poesía di Verona. *Publications:* Population and Hunger in the World, Europa 92, Europe at the Dawn of the Millennium. *Leisure interests:* jazz, painting, walking, skiing. *Address:* Parlement Européen, ASP 6H 263, rue Wiertz 60, 1047 Brussels, Belgium. *Telephone:* (2) 284-5490 (office). *Fax:* (2) 284-9490 (office).

BAROUD, Ziad S.; Lebanese lawyer and politician; b. 1970; s. of Salim Baroud and Antoinette Baroud; m. Linda Karam; one s. one d; ed St Joseph Univ., Beirut; admitted to Bar 1993; Lecturer on Public Law, Labour Law and Educational Law, St Joseph Univ., Beirut 1995–, also mem. Bd, Law Faculty; Lecturer on Institutional Law, Finance Inst. 2000–, Univ. St Esprit, Kaslik 2001–; Founding mem. Democratic Renewal Movt 2001; Founding Pnr, HBDT (law firm) 2003–; Research Assoc., Lebanese Centre for Policy Studies; Minister of the Interior and Municipalities 2008–11; Sec. Gen. Lebanese Asscn for Democratic Elections 2004–05; mem. Nat. Council for a New Electoral Law; Legal Consultant to UNDP, UNESCO, UNEP; mem. Beirut Bar Asscn 1993–. *Address:* c/o Ministry of the Interior and Municipalities, Grand Sérail, place Riad es-Solh, Beirut, Lebanon (office).

BARQUÍN DURÁN, Edgar Baltazar; Guatemalan accountant and central banker; *President, Banco de Guatemala;* ed Universidad San Carlos de Guatemala, Centro de Estudios Monetarios Latinoamericanos (CEMLA), Mexico, Univ. of Hartford, USA; Head, Credit Dept, Banco de Occidente SA 1979–82; Head, Investment Dept, Credomatic Latinoamericana 1982–83; Inspector, later Supervisor and Dir, Superintendencia de Bancos (regulatory body) 1985–2005; Man. Grupo Financiero de Occidente (financial risk group) 2005; fmr Dir of Technical Coordination, Banco de Guatemala (central bank), currently Pres. *Address:* Office of the President, Banco de Guatemala, 7a Avda 22-01, Zona 1, Apdo 365, Guatemala City, Guatemala (office). *Telephone:* 2429-6000 (office). *Fax:* 2253-4035 (office). *E-mail:* webmaster@banguat.gob.gt (office). *Website:* www.banguat.gob.gt (office).

BARR, Roseanne (see Roseanne).

BARR, William Pelham, MA, JD; American lawyer, business executive and fmr government official; b. 23 May 1950, New York; s. of Donald Barr and Mary Ahern; m. Christine Moynihan 1973; three d.; ed Columbia Univ., George Washington Univ.; staff officer in CIA, Washington, DC 1973–77; barrister 1977–78; law clerk to US Circuit Judge 1977–78, Assoc., Shaw, Pittman, Potts & Trowbridge (law firm), Washington, DC 1978–82, 1983–84, Pnr 1985–89, 1993–; Deputy Asst Dir Domestic Staff Policy, The White House, Washington, DC 1982–83; Asst Attorney Gen., Office of Legal Counsel, US Dept of Justice, Washington, DC 1989–91, Attorney Gen. US 1991–93; Exec. Vice-Pres. and Gen. Counsel, GTE Corpn (now Verizon Communications Inc.), Washington, DC 1994–2008 (retd); Counsel, Kirkland & Ellis LLP Jan.–July 2009; mem. Bd of Dirs Time Warner Inc. 2009–, Dominion Resources, Inc., Selected Funds, Holcim US; mem. Virginia State Bar Asscn, DC Bar Asscn; mem. Bd of Visitors, Coll. of William & Mary 1997–2005. *Leisure interest:* music. *Address:* c/o Board of Directors, Time Warner, Inc., One Time Warner Center, New York, NY 10019-8016, USA.

BARRA, Mary T., BS (ElecEng), MBA; American automotive industry executive; *CEO, General Motors Company;* b. 24 Dec. 1961, Royal Oak, Mich.; m.; two c.; ed Kettering Univ., Stanford Grad. School of Business (GM fellowship); began career with General Motors Co. (GM), Detroit, as a General Motors Inst. (Kettering Univ.) co-op student at Pontiac Motor Div. 1980, held numerous senior positions in manufacturing, including Exec. Dir, Vehicle Manufacturing Eng 2004–08, Vice-Pres., Global Manufacturing Eng 2008–09, Vice-Pres., Global Human Resources 2009–11, mem. Bd of Dirs 2011–, Sr Vice-Pres., Global Product Devt 2011–13, CEO 2014–; mem. Bd of Dirs General Dynamics, Inforum Center For Leadership; mem. Bd of Trustees Kettering Univ.; Key Exec. for Stanford Univ.; ranked by Forbes magazine amongst The World's 100 Most Powerful Women (76th) 2011, (41st) 2012, (35th) 2013, ranked by Fortune magazine amongst the 50 Most Powerful Women in Business in the US (27th) 2012. *Address:* General Motors Company, PO Box 33170, Detroit, MI 48232-5170, USA (office). *Telephone:* (313) 556-5000 (office). *E-mail:* info@gm.com (office). *Website:* www.gm.com (office).

BARRA, Ornella; Italian business executive and pharmacist; *Chief Executive, Pharmaceutical Wholesale Division, Alliance Boots;* b. nr Genoa; ed Univ. of Genoa; started as pharmacist, first managing and then establishing own pharmacy; f. pharmaceutical wholesaler Di Pharma 1984, taken over by Alleanza Salute Italia 1986, apptd Man. Dir 1986, mem. Bd of Dirs Alliance Santé France 1990–, Chair. Alleanza Salute Italia (now Alliance Healthcare Italia) 1994, Exec. Dir Alliance UniChem Bd following merger of Alliance Santé with UniChem to form Alliance UniChem Group 1997, mem. Bd of Dirs Safa Galenica (Spain) 1998, Chair. Alliance UniChem Farmaceutica (Portugal) 1999–2005, Chair. Safa Galenica (now Alliance Healthcare Espana) and mem. Bd Alliance UniChem Farmaceutica (now Alliance Healthcare Portugal) 2005–06, Alliance Boots formed following merger of Alliance UniChem Plc with Boots Group Plc 2006, mem. Bd of Dirs following acquisition of the Group by Stefano Pessina and Kohlberg Kravis Roberts (AB Acquisitions) 2007–, Chief Exec. Pharmaceutical Wholesale Div., Alliance Boots 2009–, Chair. Alliance Boots Social Responsibilities Cttee 2009–, also responsible for Boots International; f. European Pharmacists Forum 1999; Special Prof., School of Pharmacy, Univ. of Nottingham, UK; ranked by Fortune

magazine amongst the 50 Most Powerful Women in Business outside the US (ninth) 2010–11, (12th) 2012. *Address:* Alliance Boots GmbH, Baarerstrasse 94, 6300 Zug, Switzerland (office). *Telephone:* (41) 727-7575 (office). *E-mail:* enquiries@allianceboots.com (office). *Website:* www.allianceboots.com (office); www.ornellabarra.com (office).

BARRAK, Saad Hamad al-, BSc, MSc, PhD; Kuwaiti engineer and business executive; *Chairman, ILA Group;* ed Ohio and Harvard Univs, USA, Univ. of London, UK; fmr Chair. IT Soft, Cairo, Arab Telecom; Dir (non-exec.) Arab Man. Asscn, Cairo; Man. Dir International Turnkey Systems –2002; Deputy Chair. and Man. Dir (CEO) MTC (renamed Zain 2007) 2002–10, mem. Exec. Bd Celtel International; Chair. ILA Group (consultancy firm) 2012–, est. ILA Advanced Technology SAE in Cairo; fmr Vice-Chair. Social Devt Office, Amiri Diwan, Kuwait; E-businessman of the Year Award 2003, Middle East CEO of the Year Award in the Information Communication Tech. sector 2005, Outstanding Contribution to Business Award, CEO Middle East Awards 2012, ranked by Arabian Business amongst the Power 500: The Worlds's Most Influential Arabs (369th) 2011, (82nd) 2012. *Publication:* A Passion for Adventure: Turning Zain into a Telecom Giant 2012. *Address:* ILA Group, 33 Ibrahim Abo El Naga Street, Nasr City, Cairo, Egypt (office). *Telephone:* (2) 271-6215 (office). *Fax:* (2) 271-6286 (office). *E-mail:* info@ila-group.com (office). *Website:* www.ila-group.com (office).

BARRASSO, John Anthony, III, BS, MD; American orthopaedic surgeon and politician; *Senator from Wyoming;* b. 21 July 1952, Reading, Pa; m. 1st Linda Nix (divorced); m. 2nd Bobbi Brown; three c.; ed Georgetown Univ.; orthopedic surgeon in pvt. practice, Casper, Wyo.; ran unsuccessfully for Republican nomination for Senator 1996, elected to Wyo. State Senate 2002, re-elected 2006, served as Chair. Transportation, Highways and Mil. Affairs Cttee, mem. Labor, Health and Social Services Cttee, Select Cttee on Legis. Tech., Dept of Health Advisory Council; apptd Senator from Wyo. (upon death of Senator Craig Thomas) 2007–, won a special election to fill the remaining four years of Thomas's term 2008, Chair. Senate Republican Policy Cttee, Senate Western Caucus, mem. Energy and Natural Resources Cttee, Environment and Public Works Cttee, Indian Affairs Cttee, Senate Foreign Relations Cttee; Chief of Staff Wyo. Medical Center; State Pres. Wyo. Medical Soc.; Pres. Nat. Asscn of Physician Broadcasters; mem. American Medical Asscn Council of Ethics and Judicial Affairs; physician for Professional Rodeo Cowboys' Asscn; mem. Bd of Dirs Presidential Classroom; mem. Casper Chamber of Commerce, Casper Rotary Club; Republican; Wyo. Physician of the Year, Wyo. Nat. Guard Medal of Excellence, Veterans of Foreign Wars Legislative Service Award. *Publications:* Keeping Wyoming Healthy, Caring for Wyoming's Seniors newspaper columns. *Address:* 307 Dirksen Senate Office Building, Washington, DC 20510 (office); 100 East B Street, Suite 2201, PO Box 22201, Casper, WY 82602, USA (office). *Telephone:* (202) 224-6441 (DC) (office); (307) 261-6413 (Casper) (office). *Fax:* (202) 224-1724 (office). *Website:* barrasso .senate.gov (office).

BARRAULT, Marie-Christine; French actress; b. 21 March 1944, Paris; d. of Max-Henri Barrault and Marthe Valmier; m. 1st Daniel Toscan de Plantier (divorced); one s. one d.; m. 2nd Roger Vadim 1990 (died 2000); ed Conservatoire national d'art dramatique; Officier, ordre des Arts et des Lettres, Officier, Legion d'honneur. *Theatre includes:* Andorra, Othon, Un couple pour l'hiver, Travail à domicile, Conversation chez les Stein sur Monsieur de Goethe absent, Dylan, cet animal étrange, Partage du midi, L'Etrange intermède, Même heure l'année prochaine, Enfin seuls!, La Cerisaie, Le bonheur des autres, Qui a peur de Virginia Woolf?, La mènagerie de verre, Barrage contre le pacifique. *Films include:* Ma nuit chez Maude 1966, Le distrait 1970, Cousin, cousine 1975 (Prix Louis Delluc), Du côté des tennis 1976, L'état sauvage 1978, Femme entre chien et loup 1978, Ma chérie 1979, Stardust Memories 1980, L'amour trop fort 1981, Un amour en Allemagne 1983, Les mots pour le dire 1983, Un amour de Swann 1984, Pianoforte 1985, Le jupon rouge 1987, Adieu je t'aime 1988, Sanguines 1988, Prisonnières 1988, Un été d'orage 1989, Dames galantes 1990, L'amour nécessaire 1991, Bonsoir 1994, C'est la tangente que je préfère 1997, La dilettante 1999, Azzurro 2000, Berlin Niagara 2000, Les amants de Mogador 2002, L'empreinte de l'ange 2004. *Musical:* L'homme rêvé 2000. *Television includes:* Marie Curie (series; Nymphe d'argent, Monte Carlo TV Festival 1991, 7 d'Or for best comedienne 1991), Le vieil ours et l'enfant 2001, Garonne (mini-series) 2002, Le don fait à Catchaires 2003, La deuxième vérité 2003, Rêves en France 2003, Droit d'asile 2003, Saint-Germain ou La négociation 2003, L'empreinte de l'ange 2004, Parlez-moi d'amour 2005, Ange de feu (mini-series) 2006. *Publication:* Le Cheval dans la pierre 1999. *Address:* c/o Babette Pouget, 10 avenue George V, 75008 Paris, France.

BARRÉ-SINOUSSI, Françoise Claire, DèsSc; French scientist; *Director, Retroviral Infections Unit, Institut Pasteur;* b. 30 July 1947, Paris; d. of Roger Sinoussi and Jeanine Fau; m. Jean-Claude Barré 1978; ed Lycée Bergson, Faculty of Science, Paris VII and Paris VI; Research Asst, Inst. nat. de la Santé et de la recherche médicale (Inserm) 1975–80, Researcher 1980–86, Dir of Research 1986–; Head of Lab., Biology of Retroviruses Unit, Inst. Pasteur 1988–92, Dir Retroviral Infections Unit 1993–; Co-Chair. UN Panel on AIDS Prevention; Pres. Int. AIDS Soc. 2012– (mem. Governing Council 2006–); Chevalier, Ordre nat. du Mérite; Officier, Légion d'honneur 2006, Grand Officer 2013; Hon. DSc (Tulane Univ.) 2009; Prize of Fondation Körber pour la promotion de la Science européenne 1986, Prize of Acad. de médecine 1988, King Faisal Int. Prize for Medicine 1993, Prix du Rayonnement Français 2003, Nobel Prize in Physiology or Medicine (jtly) 2008; inducted into Women in Tech. Int. Hall of Fame 2006, Georgia Research Alliance Pioneer Award 2011. *Publications include:* more than 200 scientific publs including co-author of publ. in Science that first reported discovery of a retrovirus later named HIV 1983. *Leisure interests:* theatre, reading. *Address:* Régulation des Infections Rétrovirales, Institut Pasteur, 25–28 rue du Docteur Roux, 75724 Paris Cedex 15, France (office). *Telephone:* 1-45-68-87-33 (office). *Fax:* 1-45-68-89-57 (office). *E-mail:* francoise.barre-sinoussi@pasteur.fr (office). *Website:* www.pasteur .fr/ip/easysite/pasteur/en/research/scientific-departments/virology/regulation-of -retroviral-infections/regulation-of-retroviral-infections (office).

BARREIRO, Magdalena, PhD; Ecuadorean academic and government official; b. 1954; ed Escuela Politécnica del Ejército, Massachusetts Inst. of Tech. Sloan School of Man., Illinois Inst. of Tech.; Financial Sector Coordinator, Cen. Bank of Ecuador 1992–96; Econ. and Financial Adviser, Nat. Council for State Modernization and Privatization 1997–98; Prof. of Finance, Universidad San Francisco de

Quito 2000–05; apptd Deputy Minister for Economy and Finance 2005, Minister of Economy and Finance Aug.–Dec. 2005; currently local partner (Ecuador), GlobalSource Partners, also ind. consultant. *Address:* GlobalSource Partners, 708 Third Avenue, 18th Floor Suite 1801, New York, NY 10017, USA (office). *Telephone:* (212) 317-8015 (office). *Fax:* (212) 317-8318 (office). *E-mail:* info@globalsourcepartners.com (office). *Website:* www.globalsourcepartners.com (office).

BARRERA, Marco Antonio; Mexican boxer; b. 17 Jan. 1974, Iztacalco; m.; one s.; professional flyweight boxing debut age 15; known as 'Baby-Faced Assassin'; winner Super Flyweight Title, Mexico 1992, NABF Super Flyweight Title 1993, WBO Super Bantamweight Title 1995, 1998, Ring Featherweight Title, WBC Super Featherweight Title 2004, 2005, 2006, IBF World Junior Lightweight Title 2005; 74 fights, 66 wins, seven losses, 43 knockouts; commentator ESPN Deportes' weekly boxing show Golpe a Golpe 2009–;*Website:* www.marcobarrera.com.

BARRERA DE IRIMO, Antonio; Spanish business executive and politician; b. 4 Jan. 1929, Ribadeo; ed Univs of Deusto and Valladolid; Prof. of Public Finance, Univ. of Deusto and Central Univ. of Madrid; Pres. Telefónica 1964–73; Vice-Pres. of Spain and Minister of Finance 1973–74; fmr Chair. Sema Group PLC; Chair. Bull International from 2002, Bull (Spain) SA; fmr Chair. Pechiney and Générale des Eaux; fmr mem. Bd Banco Hispano Americano. *Publication:* Teoria General de la Urbanizacion Volumen III 1971. *Address:* c/o Bull (España) SA, Paseo de las Doce Estrellas 2, Campo de las Naciones, 28042 Madrid, Spain. *E-mail:* info@bull.es.

BARRETO OTAZÚ, César Amado, MA; Paraguayan economist and politician; ed Universidad Nacional de Asunción, Pontificia Universidad Católica de Chile; with Entidad Binacional Itaipú 1988–94; Econ. Adviser, Nat. Econ. Equipment, Ministry of Finance 1997–98; Product Man., Cash Man. and Trade, Citibank NA, Paraguay Br. 1998–2000; Founding Pnr, Macroanálisis Consultora 1999; Project Man., Hutchison Telecom Paraguay SA Jan.–Oct. 2001, Gen. Man. 2001–02, Exec. Dir 2002–05; Exec. Dir Devt in Democracy 2004–05; Pres. Directory and Gen. Man. Agencia Financiera de Desarrollo 2005–07; Minister of Finance 2007–08; fmr Prof. of Int. Economy and Master's Programme in Economy and Finances, Universidad Católica de Asunción. *Address:* c/o Ministry of Finance, Sede Central: Chile 252, 1220 Asunción, Paraguay (office).

BARRETT, Colleen C.; American airline industry executive; *President Emeritus, Southwest Airlines Co.;* b. 14 Sept. 1944, Bellows Falls, Vt; m. (divorced); one s.; ed Becker Jr Coll., Worcester, Mass; Exec. Asst to Herb Kelleher (Southwest Airlines founder) at his law firm –1978; joined Southwest Airlines Co. 1978, Corp. Sec. 1978–2008, Vice-Pres. Admin 1986–90, Exec. Vice-Pres. Customer Services 1990–2001, Pres. 2001–08; mem. Bd of Dirs Better Business Bureau of Metropolitan Dallas Inc. 2002–, JCPenney Co. Inc. 2004–; mem. Advisory Bd Ken Blanchard Coll. of Business 2006–; Trustee, Becker Coll. 2006–; mem. Int. Women's Forum 1985–, Dallas Forum 1990–; mem. Hon. Bd of Advisors, Nat. Soc. of High School Scholars 2003–; numerous awards and honours including The Most Powerful Woman in Travel, Travel Agent Magazine, Top Women Execs, Women's Enterprise 1999, Tex. Business Woman of the Year, Tex. Women's Chamber of Commerce 2001, America's Most Powerful Business Women, Fortune Magazine 2001, Kupfer Distinguished Exec. Award 2002, Women's Leadership Exchange Compass Award 2002, Best Managers, BusinessWeek 2002, 50 Most Powerful Women in Business, Fortune Magazine 2002, 2003, Distinguished Women's Award, Northwood Univ. 2003, ranked by Forbes magazine amongst 100 Most Powerful Women 2004–07, Horatio Alger Award 2005. *Address:* c/o Southwest Airlines, PO Box 36647-ICR, Dallas, TX 75235-1647, USA (office).

BARRETT, Craig R., BS, MS, PhD; American computer industry executive; b. 29 Aug. 1939, San Francisco, Calif.; m. Barbara Barrett; one s. one d.; ed Stanford Univ.; Assoc. Prof., Dept of Materials Science and Eng, Stanford Univ. 1964–74; NATO Postdoctoral Fellowship, Nat. Physical Lab., England 1964–65; Fulbright Fellowship, Tech. Univ. of Denmark 1972; joined Intel Corpn as a Tech. devt man. 1974, Vice-Pres. 1984–87, Sr Vice-Pres. 1987–90, Exec. Vice-Pres. 1990–92, mem. Bd Dirs 1992–, COO 1993–97, Pres. 1997–2005, CEO 1998–2005, Chair. 2005–09; Chair. UN Global Alliance for Information and Communication Technologies and Devt –2009; Co-Chair. Business Coalition for Student Achievement, Nat. Innovation Initiative Leadership Council, Achieve, Inc.; Pres. and Chair. BASIS School, Inc.; apptd to Pres.'s Advisory Cttee for Trade Policy and Negotiations and to American Health Information Community; apptd by Pres. Obama as one of pvt. sector leaders for a nat. educ. science, tech., eng and math. (STEM) initiative now known as Change The Equation 2010; apptd by Pres. of Russian Fed. as Int. Co-Chair. to lead the Bd of the Fund for Devt of the Center for Elaboration and Commercialization of New Technologies; fmr mem. Nat. Govs' Asscn Task Force on Innovation America, Nat. Infrastructure Advisory Council, Cttee on Scientific Communication and Nat. Security, US-Brazil CEO Forum; mem. Bd Dirs Society for Science and the Public, Dossia, Nat. Forest Foundation (Vice-Chair.), Science Foundation Arizona; fmr mem. Bd Dirs US Semiconductor Industry Asscn, Nat. Action Council for Minorities in Eng, TechNet; mem. Bd of Trustees US Council for Int. Business, Advisory Bd Clinton Global Initiative Educ., Advisory Bd Peter G. Peterson Foundation, Arizona Commerce Authority Bd, faculty of Thunderbird School of Global Man.; mem. and fmr Chair. Nat. Acad. of Eng; Hon. Chair. Irish Tech. Leadership Group; Hardy Gold Medal, American Inst. of Mining and Metallurgical Engineers. *Publications:* Principles of Engineering Materials; more than 40 tech. papers on the influence of the microstructure of materials. *Leisure interests:* hiking, skiing, horse riding, cycling, fly-fishing. *Address:* c/o Intel Corporation, 2200 Mission College Boulevard, Santa Clara, CA 95052-1537, USA. *E-mail:* info@intel.com.

BARRETT, George S., BA, MBA; American business executive; *Chairman and CEO, Cardinal Health Inc.;* ed Brown Univ., New York Univ.; served in various positions with NMC Laboratories 1981–91, served as Pres. from 1988 through its acquisition by Alpharma Inc., Pres. Barre National (subsidiary of Alpharma Inc.) 1991–94, Pres. Alpharma's US pharmaceutical group 1994–97; Pres. and CEO Diad Research (tech. start-up based at Johns Hopkins School of Medicine) 1997–98; Pres. Teva USA 1998–2005, Pres. and CEO Teva North America and Group Vice-Pres. (North America) 2005–06, Pres. and CEO Teva North America and Exec. Vice-Pres. (Global Pharmaceutical Markets) and mem. Office of the CEO

of Teva Pharmaceutical Industries Ltd 2006–08; Vice-Chair. Cardinal Health Inc. and CEO Healthcare Supply Chain Services Jan.–Aug. 2009, Chair. and CEO Cardinal Health Inc. Aug. 2009–; mem. Bd of Dirs IVAX Corpn 2006–; mem. Business Advisory Bd Cera Products, Inc.; mem. Bd and fmr Chair. Generic Pharmaceutical Industry Asscn; mem. Bd American Foundation for Pharmaceutical Educ., Univ. of Maryland School of Pharmacy; Distinguished Alumni Award of Excellence in Global Business, New York Univ. Stern School of Business, Ellis Island Medal of Honor. *Address:* Cardinal Health Inc., 7000 Cardinal Place, Dublin, OH 43017, USA (office). *Telephone:* (614) 757-5000 (office). *Fax:* (614) 757-8871 (office). *E-mail:* info@cardinal.com (office). *Website:* www.cardinal.com (office).

BARRETT, Matthew W., OC, LLD; Irish/Canadian banker; b. 20 Sept. 1944, Co. Kerry, Ireland; m. 1st Irene Korsak (divorced 1995); m. 2nd Anne-Marie Sten 1997; four c.; ed Harvard Business School; joined Bank of Montreal, London, UK 1962; moved to Canada 1967; Vice-Pres. Man. Services, Bank of Montreal 1978, Vice-Pres. BC Div. 1979, Sr Vice-Pres. Eastern and Northern Ont. 1980, Sr Vice-Pres. and Deputy Gen. Man. Int. Banking Group 1981, Sr Vice-Pres. and Deputy Group Exec. Treasury Group 1984, Exec. Vice-Pres. and Group Exec. Personal Banking 1985, Pres. and COO 1987, CEO 1989–99, Chair. 1990–99; Group CEO Barclays plc 1999–2004, Chair. 2004–06; mem. Bd of Dirs Harry Winston Diamond Corpn 2008–, Goldman Sachs Bank USA 2009–, Samuel, Son & Co. Ltd 2009–, Samuel Manu-Tech Inc. 2009–; Trustee, First Canadian Mortgage Fund; fmr Gov. London Business School; mem. Int. Advisory Bd Bank of Kuwait; Hon. Dir Bank of Montreal; Hon. LLD (St Mary's Univ., Halifax, NS, York Univ., Ont., Concordia Univ., Univ. of Waterloo, Acadia Univ.); Hon. DCL (Bishop's Univ.) 1993; Canadian Catalyst Prize, Canada's Outstanding CEO of the Year 1995, Harvard Business School Alumni Achievement Award 1997, Communicator of the Year Award, British Asscn of Communicators in Business 2001. *Leisure interests:* fly-fishing, tennis, reading.

BARRIE, George Napier, BA, LLD; South African professor of law and advocate; *Special Professor, Faculty of Law and Researcher, Centre for the Study of International Law in Africa, University of Johannesburg;* b. 10 Sept. 1940, Pietersburg; m. Marie Howell 1970; two s. one d.; ed Pretoria Univ., Univ. of South Africa and Univ. Coll., London, UK; State Advocate, Supreme Court 1964–69; Sr Law Adviser, Dept of Foreign Affairs 1970–80; Prof. of Int. and Constitutional Law, Rand Afrikaans Univ. 1981–, Dean Faculty of Law 2001–04; Visiting Prof., Free Univ. of Brussels 1992; Leader of S African del. to numerous int. confs; mem. S African del. to Int. Bar Asscn Conf. 1984, Nat. Council on Correctional Services 1996–; Special Prof., Faculty of Law and Researcher, Centre for Study of Int. Law in Africa, Univ. of Johannesburg 2005–. *Publications include:* Topical International Law 1979, Self-Determination in Modern International Law 1995 and numerous works and articles on int. and constitutional law; co-author: Nuclear Non-Proliferation: The Why and the Wherefore 1985, Constitutions of Southern Africa 1985, Law of South Africa 1986, Law of the Sea 1987, Bill of Rights Compendium 1996, Managing African Conflicts 2000. *Leisure interests:* long distance running, long distance cycling. *Address:* Faculty of Law, University of Johannesburg, PO Box 524, Auckland Park, Johannesburg 2006, South Africa (office). *Telephone:* (11) 7044376 (home). *Fax:* (11) 5592027 (office); (11) 7044376 (home). *E-mail:* barriegm@telkomsa.net. *Website:* www.uj.ac.za (office).

BARRINGTON, Edward John, BA, MA; Irish civil servant and diplomatist; b. 26 July 1949, Dublin; m. Clare O'Brien 1972; one s.; ed Univ. Coll. Dublin; Third Sec. Dept of Foreign Affairs, EC Div. 1971–73, First Sec. 1973–75, First Sec. EC Perm. Rep. Office, Brussels 1975–80, First Sec. Press Section, HQ Aug.–Dec. 1980, Counsellor Political Div., HQ 1980–85, Asst Sec.-Gen. Admin. Div., HQ 1985–89, Asst Sec.-Gen. EC Div., HQ 1989–91, Asst Sec.-Gen. Political Div. and Political Dir, HQ 1991–95, Deputy Sec. 1995; Amb. to UK 1995–2001; currently Hon. Prof., Research Inst. for Irish and Scottish Studies, Univ. of Aberdeen, UK; Visiting Research Fellow, Inst. for British-Irish Studies, Univ. Coll. Dublin; Hon. DUniv (Univ. of North London) 2001. *Leisure interests:* cinema, hiking, jazz, theatre. *Address:* Sun Villa, Mauritius Town, Rosslare Strand, Co. Wexford, Ireland (home). *Telephone:* (53) 32880 (home).

BARRINGTON, Sir Nicholas John, KCMG, CVO, MA, FRSA; British diplomatist; b. 23 July 1934; s. of the late Eric A. Barrington and Mildred Bill; ed Repton School and Clare Coll., Cambridge; joined HM Diplomatic Service 1957, served in Kabul 1959, UK Del. to European Communities, Brussels 1963, Rawalpindi 1965, Tokyo 1972–75, Cairo 1978–81, Minister and Head, British Interests Section, Tehran 1981–83, Extra Amb. to UN, New York 1983; Coordinator for G7 London Summit 1984; Asst Under-Sec. of State, FCO 1984–87, Amb. to Pakistan 1987–89, High Commr 1989–94, also Amb. (non-resident) to Afghanistan 1994; Trustee, Ancient India and Iran Trust, Cambridge 1992–; served on various bodies linking Britain with Asia and Christianity with Islam; Hon. Fellow, Clare Coll. Cambridge 1992; Order of the Sacred Treasure, Japan 1975. *Publications:* A Passage to Nuristan 2005; memoirs: Envoy 2013, Nicholas Meets Barrington 2013. *Leisure interests:* theatre, drawing, prosopography, Persian poetry. *Address:* 2 Banhams Close, Cambridge, CB4 1HX, England (home). *Telephone:* (1223) 360802 (home).

BARRINGTON-WARD, Rt Rev. Simon, KCMG, BA, MA; British ecclesiastic; *Assistant Bishop of Ely;* b. 27 May 1930, London; s. of Robert McGowan Barrington-Ward and Margaret A. Radice; m. Dr Jean Caverill Taylor 1963; two d.; ed Eton Coll., Magdalene Coll. Cambridge and Westcott House, Cambridge; ordained, diocese of Ely 1956; Chaplain, Magdalene Coll. Cambridge 1956–60; Lecturer, Ibadan Univ. Nigeria 1960–63; Fellow and Dean of Chapel, Magdalene Coll. Cambridge 1963–69, Hon. Fellow 1991–; Hon. Asst Chaplain 1999–; Prin., Church Missionary Soc. Coll., Selly Oak, Birmingham 1969–74; Gen. Sec. Church Missionary Soc. 1974–85; Canon, Derby Cathedral 1975–85; Chaplain to HM The Queen 1983–85; Bishop of Coventry 1985–97; Chair. Int. and Devt Affairs Cttee, Gen. Synod of Church of England 1986–96; Prelate to the Most Distinguished Order of St Michael and St George 1989–2005; Asst Bishop of Ely 1997–; Hon. Fellow, Magdalene Coll. Cambridge 1977–; Hon. Asst Chaplain 1999–; Hon. DD (Wycliffe Coll. Toronto) 1983, Hon. DLitt (Warwick Univ.) 1988, Dr hc (Anglia-Ruskin Univ., Cambridge) 2008. *Publications:* Love Will Out 1988, Christianity Today 1988, The Weight of Glory 1991, Why God? 1993, The Jesus Prayer 1996, Praying the Jesus Prayer Together 2001, revised edn 2008); articles and book chapters. *Leisure interests:* hill walking, music, cycling, calligraphy. *Address:* 4

Searle Street, Cambridge, CB4 3DB, England (home). *Telephone:* (1223) 740460 (home). *E-mail:* sb292@cam.ac.uk (home).

BARRIOS DE CHAMORRO, Violeta; Nicaraguan politician, publisher and fmr head of state; *President, Fundación Violeta Chamorro;* b. 18 Oct. 1929, Rivas; m. Pedro Joaquín Chamorro (died 1978) 1950; two s. two d.; ed Our Lady of the Lake Catholic School, San Antonio and Blackstone Coll., USA; mem. and Dir Sociedad Interamericana de Prensa 1978–89, Prensa Freedom Comm. 1978–89; Pres. and Dir-Gen. La Prensa (daily newspaper) 1978–89; Nat. Opposition Union cand. for Pres. 1989–90; Pres. of Nicaragua 1990–97, also Minister of Nat. Defence 1990; Founder and Pres. Fundación Violeta Chamorro; Grand Cross of the Order of Isabel la Católica (Spain) 1991, Grand Collar of the Order of the Aztec Eagle (Mexico) 1993, Grand Cross of the Order of Merit (Germany) 1996; six hon. degrees including Hon. LLD (American Univ., Washington, DC) 1997; Hon. DH (Catholic Univ. of Nicaragua Redemptores Mater) 1995; Dr hc (American Univ., Managua) 1998, (Univ. for Peace, Costa Rica) 1999; numerous nat. and int. awards including Louis Lyon Prize, Harvard Univ. 1986, American Soc. Gold Ensign Award 1990, Int. Rescue Cttee Freedom Award 1990, Int. Peace Asscn Woman for Peace Award 1990, Pan-American Devt Foundation Inter-american Leadership Award 1991, Lutheran Univ. of Calif. Thomas Wade Landry Award 1991, The Path to Peace Foundation Award 1997. *Publication:* Dreams of the Heart (autobiog.) 1996. *Address:* Fundación Violeta Chamorro, Plaza España, Edificio Málaga, Módulo B-9, Managua, Nicaragua (office). *Telephone:* (2) 68-6500 (office). *Fax:* (2) 68-6502 (office). *E-mail:* violetabch@ibw.com.ni (office). *Website:* www.violetachamorro.org.ni (office).

BARRO, Robert Joseph, PhD; American economist and academic; *Paul M. Warburg Professor of Economics, Harvard University;* b. 28 Sept. 1944, New York; m. Rachel McCleary; four c.; ed Harvard Univ., California Inst. of Tech.; Asst Prof., Brown Univ. 1968–72, Assoc. Prof. of Econs 1972–73; Visiting Assoc. Prof., Univ. of Chicago 1972–73, Assoc. Prof. 1973–75, Prof. of Econs 1982–84; Prof., Univ. of Rochester 1975–78, John Munro Prof. of Econs 1978–82, Distinguished Prof. of Arts and Sciences 1984–87; Prof. of Econs, Harvard Univ. 1987–95, Robert C. Waggoner Prof. 1995–2004, Paul M. Warburg Prof. of Economics 2004–; Research Assoc., Nat. Bureau of Economic Research 1978–; Fellow, Hoover Inst., Stanford Univ. 1977–78, 1989–90, 1993–94, Sr Fellow 1995–; Visiting Prof., UCLA 1986; Viewpoint Columnist, Business Week magazine 1998–2006; Co-Ed. Quarterly Journal of Economics 2004–; Academic Advisor, New York Fed. Reserve Bank 2006–; Pres. Western Econ. Asscn 2002–05; Vice-Pres. American Econ. Asscn 1998; mem. Mont Pelerin Soc. 1990–; Hoover Inst. Nat. Fellowship 1977–78; John Simon Guggenheim Memorial Fellowship 1982–83; Fellow, Econometric Soc. 1980–; mem. American Acad. of Arts and Sciences 1988–; Houblon-Norman Fellow, Bank of England 1994–95; Hon. Prof., Wuhan Univ. 2003, Seoul National Univ. 2003, Tsinghua Univ. 2005; Hon. Dean, China Econs and Man. Acad., Cen. Univ. of Beijing 2006; Dr hc (Universidad Francisco Marroquin); Frank Paish Lecturer, Meeting of Royal Econ. Soc., Oxford, 1985; Henry Thornton Lecturer, City Univ. Business School, London 1987; Horowitz Lecturer, Israel 1988; Lionel Robbins Lecturer, LSE 1996;. *Publications include:* Money, Employment and Inflation (co-author) 1976, The Impact of Social Security on Private Savings: Evidence from the US Time Series 1978, Money, Expectations, and Business Cycles 1981, Macroeconomics 1984, Macroeconomic Policy 1990, European Macroeconomics (co-author) 1994, Canadian Macroeconomics (co-author) 1994, Economic Growth (co-author) 1995, Getting it Right: Markets and Choice in a Free Society 1996, Determinants of Economic Growth: A Cross-Country Empirical Study 1997, Currency Unions (co-ed.) 2001, Nothing Is Sacred: Economic Ideas for the New Millennium 2002, Macroeconomics: A Modern Approach 2008; numerous articles in journals. *Address:* Department of Economics, Harvard University, Cambridge, MA 02138 (office); 183 Kings Grant Road, Weston, MA 02493, USA (home). *Telephone:* (617) 495-3203 (office); (781) 894-8184 (home). *Fax:* (617) 496-8629 (office); (781) 894-4521 (home). *E-mail:* rbarro@harvard.edu (office). *Website:* www.economics.harvard.edu (office).

BARRON, Sir Donald James, Kt, DL, BCom, CA; British fmr business executive; b. 17 March 1921, Edinburgh; s. of Albert Gibson Barron and Elizabeth Macdonald; m. Gillian Mary Saville 1956; three s. two d.; ed George Heriot's School, Edinburgh, Univ. of Edinburgh; served with King's Own Scottish Borderers 1941–45; joined Rowntree & Co. Ltd 1952, Dir 1961, Vice-Chair. 1965; Chair. Rowntree Mackintosh Ltd 1966–81; Vice-Chair. Midland Bank PLC 1981–82 (Dir 1972–87), Chair. 1982–87; mem. Bd of Banking Supervision 1987–89; Dir Canada Life Assurance Co., Toronto 1980–96; Vice-Chair. Canada Life Assurance Co. of Great Britain 1983–91, Chair. 1991–94 (Dir 1980–96); Dir Canada Life Unit Trust Mans 1980–96 (Chair. 1982), 3i Group PLC 1980–91; mem. Council of CBI 1966–81, Soc. Science Research Council 1971–72, Univ. Grants Cttee 1972–81, Council Inst. of Chartered Accountants of Scotland 1980–81, Council of British Inst. of Man. 1979–80; Trustee, Joseph Rowntree Foundation 1966–73, 1975–96, Chair. 1981–96; mem. NEDC 1983–85; Dir Clydesdale Bank 1986–87; Gov. London Business School 1982–89; Treas. Univ. of York 1966–72, Pro-Chancellor 1982–94; Chair. York Millennium Bridge Trust 1998–2002; Dr hc (Loughborough) 1982, (Heriot-Watt) 1983, (CNAA) 1983, (Edinburgh) 1984, (Nottingham) 1985, (York) 1986. *Leisure interests:* golf, tennis, travelling, gardening. *Address:* Greenfield, Sim Balk Lane, Bishopthorpe, York, YO23 2QH, England (home). *Telephone:* (1904) 705675 (home). *Fax:* (1904) 700183 (home).

BARRON, Eric J., BS, MS, PhD; American geologist, oceanographer, academic and university administrator; *President, Florida State University;* b. 26 Oct. 1951, Lafayette, Ind.; m. Molly Barron; two c.; ed Florida State Univ., Univ. of Miami; Cray Supercomputing Fellowship, Nat. Center for Atmospheric Research, Boulder, Colo 1976, Postdoctoral Research Fellow 1980, Scientist, Climate Section 1981–85, Dir 2008–10; Assoc. Prof., Univ. of Miami 1985–86; Dir Earth System Science Center and Assoc. Prof. of Geosciences, Pennsylvania State Univ. 1986–89, Prof. of Geosciences 1989–2006, Dir Earth and Mineral Sciences Environment Inst. 1998–2003, Distinguished Prof. of Geosciences 1999–2006, Dean, Coll. of Earth and Mineral Sciences 2002–06, Trustee, Univ. Corpn for Atmospheric Research 2002–06; Jackson Chair in Earth Science and Dean, Jackson School of Geosciences, Univ. of Texas at Austin 2006–10; Dir National Center for Atmospheric Research, Boulder, Colo 2008–10; Pres. Florida State Univ. 2010–; mem. Bd of Govs Jt Oceanographic Insts, Inc. 2003–; Ed.-in-Chief Palaeogeo-

graphy, Palaeoclimatology, Palaeoecology 1985–91, Earth Interactions (electronic journal) 1995–99; Ed. Global and Planetary Change 1988–96; Assoc. Ed. Journal of Climate 1989–95; mem. Editorial Bd Geology 1982–89, Palaeogeography, Palaeoclimatology, Palaeoecology 1984–85, 1992–, Geotimes 1994–96, Consequences 1994–2000, Global Change Encyclopedia 1998; Chair. Nat. Research Council (NRC) Climate Research Cttee 1990–96, Co-Chair. Bd on Atmospheric Sciences 1997–99, Chair. 1999; mem. NRC Cttee on Global Change Research, Assessment of NASA Post-2000 Plans, Climate Change Science, Human Dimensions of Global Change, Panel on Grand Environmental Challenges, Cttee on Tools for Tracking Chemical, Biological, and Nuclear Releases in the Atmosphere: Implications for Homeland Security; fmr Chair. Science Exec. Cttee for NASA's Earth Observing System and NASA's Earth Science and Applications Advisory Cttee, US Global Change Research Program Forum on Climate Modeling, Allocation Panel for the Interagency Climate Simulation Lab., US Nat. Cttee for PAGES, NSF Earth System History Panel; mem. American Geophysical Union (Chair. Selection Cttee, Ed. Paleoceanography, Biogeochemical Cycles 1995, 1997) 1991; Fellow, American Geophysical Union, American Meteorological Soc. 1995, AAAS 2004, Geological Soc. of America; Fellow, Nat. Inst. for Environmental Science, Univ. of Cambridge, UK 2002; Texaco Fellow 1975–77, Outstanding Student Award, Miami Geological Soc. 1977–78, Koczy Fellowship (most outstanding student in last year of study) 1979–80, Smith Prize (most creative dissertation) 1980, Excellence of Presentation Award, Soc. of Econ. Paleontologists and Mineralogists 1988, Hon. Mention for Excellence of Presentation Award, Soc. of Econ. Paleontologists and Mineralogists 1989, Wilson Research Award, Coll. of Earth and Mineral Sciences, Pennsylvania State Univ. 1992, Provost Award for Collaborative Instruction and Curricular Innovations 1992, 1993, Excellence of Presentation Award, Soc. of Sedimentary Geology (SEPM) 1993, American Geophysical Union Fellow 1993, Hon. Mention for Excellence of Presentation (Poster), American Asscn of Petroleum Geologists 1993, Distinguished Lecturer, American Asscn of Petroleum Geologist 1997, Wilson Teaching Award, Coll. of Earth and Mineral Sciences 1999, NASA Outstanding Earth Science Educ. Product (Discover Earth: Earth-as-a-System) 1999, NASA Group Achievement Award for Research Strategy for the Earth Science Enterprise 2001, Frontiers in Geophysics Lecturer, American Geophysical Union 2002, NASA Distinguished Public Service Medal 2003. *Publications:* numerous scientific papers in professional journals on climatology, numerical modelling and Earth history. *Address:* Office of the President, Florida State University, Tallahassee, FL 32306-1470, USA (office). *Telephone:* (850) 644-1085 (office). *Fax:* (850) 644-9936 (office). *E-mail:* ebarron@fsu.edu (office). *Website:* www.president.fsu.edu (office).

BARROS, Rui Duarte; Guinea-Bissau economist and politician; *Prime Minister;* b. 1964; Minister of Employment and Civil Service 2001, of Economy and Finance 2002; Commr responsible for Dept of Admin. and Financial Affairs, Union Economique et Monétaire Ouest Africain (UEMOA) 2006–08, for Dept of Social and Cultural Devt 2008–09, Acting Pres. of UEMOA 2009; Prime Minister (in interim govt following coup) 2012–; Conselho Africano e Malgaxe para o Ensino Superior (CAMES) Ordem Internacional das Palmas Académicas. *Address:* Office of the Prime Minister, Av. dos Combatentes da Liberdade da Pátria, CP 137, Bissau, Guinea-Bissau (office). *Telephone:* 3211308 (office). *Fax:* 3201671 (office).

BARROT, Jacques, LenD; French politician; *Member, Constitutional Council of France;* b. 3 Feb. 1937, Yssingeaux, Haute-Loire; s. of Noël Barrot and Marthe Pivot; one s. two d.; ed Coll. d'Yssingeaux and Faculté de Droit, Paris and Inst. d'Etudes Politiques, Paris; Deputy to Nat. Ass. (Union Centriste) 1967–74, 1978, (Union pour la Démocratie Française) 1981–95, 1997–2002, (UMP) 2002–03, Pres. UMP Group 2002–04; Councillor, Haute-Loire Regional Council 1966–2004, Pres. 1976–2004; Sec. of State, Ministry of Equipment 1974–78; Minister of Commerce and Working Classes 1978–79, of Health and Social Security 1979–81; Pres. Conseil-Gen. Haute-Loire 1976–2004; Mayor of Yssingeaux 1989–2001; Minister of Labour, Social Dialogue and Participation 1995–97, EU Commissioner for Regional Policy and Institutional Reform 2004, for Transport 2004–08, for Justice, Freedom and Security 2008–10; Pres. Nat. Union for Environmental Improvement 1991–93; mem. Fondatems du "Dialogue et Initiations", Constitutional Council of France 2010–. *Publications:* Les Pierres de l'avenir 1978, Notre contrat pour l'alternance 2002, L'Europe n'est pas ce que vous croyez 2007. *Leisure interest:* mountain sports. *Address:* Rue de la Loi 200, 1049 Brussels, Belgium (office); 2 Rue de l'Ecole de Mars, 92200 Neuilly-sur-Seine, France (home). *Telephone:* (2) 299-11-11 (office); 1-40-15-30-08. *Fax:* (2) 295-01-38 (office); 1-40-20-93-27. *E-mail:* jacques.barrot@conseil-constitutionel.fr (office). *Website:* europa.eu (office).

BARROW, Dean Oliver, MA, LLM; Belizean politician; *Prime Minister and Minister of Finance;* b. 2 March 1951, Belize City; ed Univ. of West Indies and Center for Advanced Int. Studies, Univ. of Miami, USA; elected (United Democratic Party—UDP) to Belize City Council 1983; elected to Nat. Ass. (UDP) for Queen Square Div. 1984–89; Deputy Leader UDP 1990, currently Leader; Minister of Foreign Affairs and Econ. Devt 1984–86; Attorney-Gen. 1986–89; apptd Deputy Prime Minister, Minister of Foreign Affairs and Econ. Devt and Attorney-Gen. 1993, also Minister of Nat. Security, Immigration and Nationality Matters 1995; Prime Minister 2008–, Minister of Finance 2008–; Pnr, Barrow and Williams (law firm). *Address:* Office of the Prime Minister, Sir Edney Cain Building, Belmopan (office); United Democratic Party, South End Bel-China Bridge, POB 1898, Belize City, Belize (office). *Telephone:* 822-2345 (office); 227-2576 (office). *Fax:* 822-3323 (office); 227-6441 (office). *E-mail:* primeministerbelize@btl.net (office); info@udp.org.bz (office). *Website:* www.udp.org.bz (office).

BARROW, John David, BSc, DPhil, FRS, FRAS, CPhys, FInstP, FRSA; British astrophysicist and academic; *Professor of Mathematical Sciences, University of Cambridge;* b. 29 Nov. 1952, London, England; s. of the late Walter Henry Barrow and Lois Miriam Barrow (née Tucker); m. Elizabeth Mary East 1975; two s. one d.; ed Van Mildert Coll., Durham Univ., Magdalen Coll., Oxford; Lindemann Fellow, Astronomy Dept, Univ. of California, Berkeley 1977–78, Miller Fellow, Physics Dept 1980–81; Jr Research Lecturer, Christ Church Coll. and Astrophysics Dept, Univ. of Oxford 1977–80; Lecturer, Astronomy Centre, Univ. of Sussex 1981, later Sr Lecturer, Prof. 1989–99, Dir Astronomy Centre 1995–99; Prof. of Math. Sciences, Univ. of Cambridge 1999–, Fellow, Clare Hall 1999– (Vice-Pres. 2004–07), Gresham Prof. of Astronomy 2003–07, Gresham Prof. Emer. of

Astronomy, Gresham Coll. 2007–08, Gresham Prof. of Geometry 2008–12, Fellow, Gresham Coll. 2012–; Gordon Godfrey Visiting Prof., Univ. of New South Wales 2000, 2003; First Eastern Visiting Cambridge Prof. (China and Hong Kong) 2005; Li Ka Shing Foundation Visiting Scholar (China and Hong Kong) 2006; Dir Millennium Math. Project 1999–; Pres. British Science Asscn (Physics and Astronomy Section) 2008–09, (Math. Section) 2011–12; mem. Int. Soc. for Science and Religion 2002, Academia Europaea 2009; Titular mem. L'Acad. Internationale de Philosophie des Sciences 2009; Nuffield Fellow 1986–87, Leverhulme Royal Soc. Fellow 1992–93, PPARC Sr Fellow 1994–99; Hon. Prof., Nanjing Univ. 2005–; Hon. Citizen, Louisville, Ky 2006; Hon. DSc (Hertfordshire) 1999, (Szczecin) 2007, (Durham) 2008, (Sussex) 2010, (South Wales) 2014; numerous awards, including Gifford Lecturer, Univ. of Glasgow 1988, Samuel Locker Prize 1989, Collingwood Lecture, Durham 1990, Spinoza Lecturer, Amsterdam 1993, George Darwin Lecturer, Royal Astronomical Soc. 1993, Elizabeth Spreadbury Lecturer, Univ. Coll. London 1993, Templeton Award 1995, Robert Boyle Memorial Lecturer, Oxford 1996, RSA Lecturer 1999, Kelvin Medal 1999, Tyndall Lecturer, Bristol 2001, Darwin Lecturer, Cambridge 2001, Whitrow Lecturer, Royal Astronomical Soc. 2002, Brasher Lecturer, Kingston 2002, Italgas Prize 2003, Hubert James Lecturer, Purdue 2004, Von Weizsäcker Lecturer, Hamburg 2004, McCrea Centenary Lecturer, Sussex 2004, Wood Memorial Lecturer, Newcastle 2005, Lacchini Prize 2005, Hamilton Lecturer, Dublin 2005, Queen's Anniversary Prize 2005, Templeton Prize 2006, Knight Lecturer, Bath 2006, Boyle Lecturer, St Mary-le-Bow 2007, Roscoe Lecturer, Liverpool 2007, Kallen Lecturer, Lund 2007, John D. Barrow Drama Room named in his honour at Cranbrook School, Kent 2007, Phillips Lecturer, Cardiff 2008, Si-Wei Lecturer, Nat. Chengchi Univ. 2008, Sciama Lecturer, Oxford and Trieste 2008, Faraday Medal, Royal Soc., London 2008, Faraday Prize Lecturer, Royal Soc., London 2009, Kelvin Medal and Prize, Inst. of Physics, London 2009, Gresham Prize, Gresham Coll., London 2009, Premio Oriente Science Prize, Colletti Foundation 2010, Merck-Serono Prize for Science and Literature, Merck-Serono 2011, Christopher Zeeman Medal, London Math. Soc. and IMA 2011, Antico Pignolo Prize 2012. *Play:* Infinities (Italian Theatre Prize, Premi Ubu 2002, Italgas Prize 2003) 2002, 2003, 2008. *Publications include:* The Left Hand of Creation 1983, L'Homme et le Cosmos 1984, The Anthropic Cosmological Principle 1986, The World Within the World 1988, Theories of Everything 1991, Perche il Mondo è Matematico? 1992, Pi in the Sky 1992, The Origin of the Universe 1994, The Artful Universe 1995, Impossibility 1998, Between Inner Space and Outer Space 1999, The Universe That Discovered Itself 2000, The Book of Nothing 2000, The Constants of Nature 2002, Science and Ultimate Reality (ed.) 2003, The Infinite Book 2005, The Artful Universe Expanded 2005, New Theories of Everything 2007, Cosmic Imagery 2008, 100 Essential Things You Didn't Know You Didn't Know 2008, The Book of Universes 2011, One Hundred Essential Things You Didn't Know You Didn't Know About Sport 2012. *Leisure interests:* athletics, books, theatre, writing. *Address:* Centre for Mathematical Sciences, University of Cambridge, Wilberforce Road, Cambridge, CB3 0WA, England (office). *Telephone:* (1223) 766696 (office). *Fax:* (1223) 765900 (office); (1223) 309509 (home). *E-mail:* j.d.barrow@damtp.cam.ac.uk (office). *Website:* www.damtp.cam.ac.uk/user/jdb34 (office).

BARRY, Edward William, BA; American publishing executive; b. 24 Nov. 1937, Stamford, Conn.; s. of Edward Barry and Elizabeth Cosgrove; m. Barbara H. Walker 1963; one s. one d.; ed Univ. of Connecticut; Pres. The Free Press, New York 1972–82, Oxford Univ. Press Inc., New York 1982–2000; Sr Vice-Pres. Macmillan Publishing Co., New York 1973–82; mem. Exec. Council, Professional and Scholarly Publications 1993; mem. Advisory Bd Pace Univ. Grad. Program in Publishing 1990–; mem. Bd of Dirs Asscn of American Publrs 1995; Trustee, Columbia Univ. Press 2000–; Hon. LittD (Univ. of Oxford) 2000. *Address:* 266 Old Poverty Road, Southbury, CT 06488-1769, USA (home). *Telephone:* (203) 267-7854 (home).

BARRY, Nancy Marie, BA, MBA; American banking executive; *President, NBA Enterprise Solutions to Poverty;* b. 1949; ed Stanford Univ., Harvard Business School; joined World Bank 1975, various sr positions including Head of Global Industry Devt Div., Chair. Donor's Cttee on Small and Medium Enterprises, Founding mem. CGAP Policy Advisory Group; Pres. Women's World Banking 1990–2006, mem. Bd of Trustees 1981–; Social Entrepreneur in Residence, Harvard Business School 2006, advisor to Social Cos and Poverty initiative; f. Nancy Barry Assocs (NBA) 2006–, Founder and Pres. NBA Enterprise Solutions to Poverty 2006–; Chair. Donald A. Strauss Foundation; mem. Council on Foreign Relations; Founding mem. Advisory Bd Harvard Business School Social Enterprise Initiative; mem. Asia Soc. Asian Social Issues Cttee; Outstanding Women in Finance and Consulting, HBS Women's Student Asscn 2001, Forbes Exec. Women's Summit Trailblazer Award 2002, Kellogg-McKinsey Award for Distinguished Leadership 2004, ranked by Forbes magazine amongst 100 Most Powerful Women (98th) 2004, (98th) 2005. *Address:* c/o Advisory Board, Social Enterprise Initiative, Loeb House, 3rd Floor, Soldiers Field, Boston, MA 02163, USA (office). *Telephone:* (617) 495-6421 (office). *Fax:* (617) 496-7416 (office). *Website:* www.hbs .edu/socialenterprise (office).

BARRYMORE, Drew; American film actress and producer; b. 22 Feb. 1975, Los Angeles; d. of the late John Barrymore, Jr and of Jaid Barrymore; m. 1st Jeremy Thomas 1994 (divorced); m. 2nd Tom Green 2001 (divorced 2001); appeared in dog food commercial 1976; film debut in TV movie Suddenly Love 1978; f. Flower Films (production co.); apptd Amb. for Hunger, WFP 2007. *Films include:* Altered States 1980, E.T.: The Extra-Terrestrial 1982, Irreconcilable Differences 1984, Firestarter 1984, Cat's Eye 1985, See You In The Morning 1988, Far From Home 1989, Motorama 1991, Guncrazy 1992, Poison Ivy 1992, Beyond Control: The Amy Fisher Story 1992, No Place to Hide 1993, Doppelganger 1993, Wayne's World 2 1993, Bad Girls 1994, Inside the Goldmine 1994, Boys On The Side 1995, Batman Forever 1995, Mad Love 1995, Scream 1996, Everyone Says I Love You 1996, All She Wanted 1997, Best Men 1997, Never Been Kissed (also producer) 1998, Home Fries 1998, The Wedding Singer 1998, Ever After 1998, Titan A.E. (voice) 2000, Charlie's Angels (also producer) 2000, Donnie Darko (also producer) 2001, Riding in Cars With Boys 2001, Confessions of a Dangerous Mind 2002, Duplex (also producer) 2003, So Love Returns (also producer) 2003, Charlie's Angels: Full Throttle (also producer) 2003, Fifty First Dates 2004, Fever Pitch 2005, The Perfect Catch 2005, Music and Lyrics 2006, Lucky You 2007, He's Just Not That Into You 2009, Whip It (also dir) 2009, Everybody's Fine 2009, Going the Distance 2010, Big Miracle 2012.

Television includes: Grey Gardens (Golden Globe for Best Performance by an Actress in a Mini-series or Motion Picture made for TV 2010, Screen Actors Guild Award) 2009). *Address:* c/o Creative Artists Agency, 2000 Avenue of the Stars, Los Angeles, CA 90067, USA (office).

BARSALOU, Yves; French banking executive and wine producer; *Chairman, Crédit Foncier de Monaco;* b. 18 Sept. 1932, Bizanet; s. of Marcell Barsalou and Marie-Louise Salvan; m. Claire-Marie Vié 1955; two s.; ed Ecoles de Carcassonne et Narbonne; mem. Dept Centre of Young Farmers 1957–67; Pres. Caisse Locale de Crédit Agricole de Narbonne 1974–; mem. Cen. Cttee, then Vice-Pres. Caisse nat. du Crédit agricole (CNCA) 1981–88, Pres. 1988–2000, Chair. CNCA 1989; Vice-Pres. Fed. Nationale du Crédit Agricole (FNCA) 1992–2000; mem. Plenary Comm., Fed. nat. du Crédit agricole 1975–77, Dir 1977–81, Pres. 1982–92; Vice-Pres., Pres. Fed. Int. du Crédit Agricole (CiCa) 1993–2001; Vice-Pres. Bd Crédit Agricole Indosuez 1996–2001; Chair. Crédit Foncier de Monaco 1999–; mem. Bd of Dirs Elf Aquitaine Group 1994–, TotalFinaElf 2000–03; fmr mem. Bd of Dirs Total SA, Banco Espirito Santo SA; Hon. Chair. Credit Agricole; Commdr, Légion d'honneur, Mérite agricole. *Address:* Domaines Barsalou, 14, rue Jean-Jacques Rousseau, 11200 Bizanet, France; Crédit Foncier de Monaco, 11 Boulevard Albert 1er 98012 Monaco (office). *Telephone:* 93-10-20-00 (office). *Fax:* 93-10-23-50 (office). *E-mail:* contact@cfm.mc (office). *Website:* www.cfm.mc (office); domainesbarsalou.com.

BARSHCHEVSKY, Mikhail Yuryevich, LLD; Russian lawyer and government official; *Representative of the Government of the Russian Federation to the Constitutional Court, the Supreme Court and the Supreme Arbitration Court;* b. 27 Dec. 1955, Moscow; m. Olga Barkalova; one d.; ed Moscow State Law Acad., All-Union Inst. of Law; legal consultant in Moscow butter factory 1973–79; Sr Legal Consultant, Dept of Trade, Reutov Town 1979–80; Founder, Head Moscow Lawyers 1991–, (Barshevsky and Partners Co. 1993–), defended Obshchaya Gazeta newspaper 1993, Oblik TV Co. 1997; TV arbiter, What? Where? When? 1997–; Prof., State Acad. of Law, Moscow State Jurists' Acad.; Govt Rep., Constitutional Court, Supreme Court, Higher Arbitration Court 2001–; Chair. Moscow Inst. of Econs, Politics and Law; Chair. High Council for the Civilian Power Party; Pres. Moscow International Business Asscn 2012–; mem. Moscow City Bar 1980–; mem. Bd All Russian Co-ordination Council for Public-Political Union, Moscow Region 1999–; mem. Russian Acad. of Natural Sciences, Russian Acad. of Lawyers, Moscow Collegiate of Advocates 1980–2001; Advocate of Honour, Plevako Gold Medal 2000. *Publications:* seven books and over 100 legal publs. *Leisure interests:* theatre, chess, travelling. *Address:* Krasnopresnenskaya emb. 2, 103274 Moscow, Russia (office). *Telephone:* (495) 205-40-51 (office); (495) 605-53-29 (office). *Fax:* (495) 205-65-25 (office); (495) 605-52-43 (office). *E-mail:* duty_press@ aprf.gov.ru (office). *Website:* www.government.ru (office).

BARSHEFSKY, Charlene, BA, JD; American lawyer and fmr government official; *Senior International Partner, Wilmer Cutler Pickering LLP;* ed Univ. of Wisconsin; Pnr, Steptoe & Johnson (law firm), Washington, DC 1975–93; Deputy US Trade Rep. 1993–96, Acting US Trade Rep. April–Nov. 1996, US Trade Rep. 1997–2001; Sr Int. Pnr, Wilmer Cutler Pickering LLP (law firm) 2001–; mem. Bd American Express 2001–, Estée Lauder Cos 2001–, Idenix Pharmaceuticals Inc. 2002–, Starwood Hotels & Resorts Worldwide Inc. 2001–, Intel Corpn 2004–. *Address:* Wilmer Cutler Pickering LLP, 2445 M Street, NW, Washington, DC 20037, USA. *Telephone:* (202) 663-6000 (office). *Fax:* (202) 663-6363 (office). *Website:* www.wilmer.com (office).

BARSKIY, Maxim; Russian business executive; *CEO, Matra Petroleum;* ed Leningrad State Univ., Univ. of California, Berkeley, USA; held series of trading and investment banking positions at Troika Dialog (investment co.) during late 1990s; performed duties of Corp. Devt Dir at Cityline, Man. Dir at Salford Continental Inc. (investment fund) and Sr Investment Dir at Finartis 2000–04; mem. Bd of Dirs West Siberian Resources Ltd 2004, Man. Dir 2004–08, worked as Gen. Dir for WSR Invest –2008; Investment Dir at rep. office of Alltech Investments Ltd 2009; Exec. Vice-Pres., Strategy and New Business Devt, TNK-BP May–Dec. 2009, Deputy CEO TNK-BP 2009–11; mem. Bd of Dirs and CEO Matra Petroleum plc 2012–. *Address:* Matra Petroleum plc, 101 Finsbury Pavement, London, EC2A 1RS, England (office). *Telephone:* (20) 3116-6555 (office). *Fax:* (20) 3116-6558 (office). *E-mail:* info@matrapetroleum.com (office). *Website:* www.matrapetroleum.com (office).

BARSTOW, Dame Josephine Clare, DBE, CBE, BA; British singer; b. 27 Sept. 1940, Sheffield, Yorks., England; d. of Harold Barstow and Clara Barstow; m. 1st Terry Hands 1964 (divorced 1968); m. 2nd Ande Anderson 1969 (died 1996); ed Univ. of Birmingham; taught English in London area for two years; debut in operatic profession with Opera for All 1964; for short time company mem. Welsh Nat. Opera, then ENO; now freelance singer in all nat. opera houses in UK and in Paris, Vienna, Salzburg, Zürich, Geneva, Turin, Florence, Cologne, Munich, Berlin, USSR, Chicago, San Francisco, New York, Houston and many other American opera houses; Hon. DMus (Birmingham, Kingston, Sheffield, Sheffield Hallam, Leeds, Hull); Fidelio Medal. *Chief roles:* Violetta in La Traviata, Leonora in Forza del Destino, Elisabeth in Don Carlos, Lady Macbeth, Amelia in Ballo in Maschera, Attila, Leonore in Fidelio, Sieglinde, Senta, Arabella, Salome, Octavian, The Marschallin, Chrysothemis, Amelia, Tosca, Mimi, Minnie, Musetta, Manon Lescaut, Emilia Marty, Jenůfa, Katya Kabanova, Medea, Renata in The Fiery Angel, Katerina Ismailova, Kostelnicka in Jenůfa, Marie in Wozzeck, Gloriana, Lady Billows in Albert Herring; world premieres of Tippett, Henze and Penderecki. *Television films:* Macbeth 1972, Idomeneo 1974, Un ballo in maschera 1989, Gloriana 2000, Owen Wingrave 2001. *Recordings include:* Verdi Recital Record with ENO Orchestra and Mark Elder, Amelia with Herbert von Karajan, Anna Maurant in Street Scene, Kate in Kiss Me Kate, Four Finales, Gloriana, Albert Herring, Wozzeck, Carmelites. *Leisure interests:* farming (cattle), breeding Arabian horses, gardening. *Address:* c/o Musichall Ltd, Oast House, Crouch's Farm, Hollow Lane, East Hoathly, BN8 6QX, England (office). *E-mail:* info@ musichall.uk.com (office). *Website:* www.musichall.uk.com (office).

BART, Hon. Delano Frank, LLB; Saint Christopher and Nevis lawyer, politician and international organization official; *Permanent Representative, United Nations;* b. 28 Oct. 1952; ed Basseterre Sr School, Matthew Bolton Tech. Coll., Birmingham and Queen Mary Coll. and Inns of Court School, London, UK; teacher, Molineux All Age School 1970–72; mem. Lincoln's Inn, London 1976; part-time Lecturer in Law, Coll. of Distributive Justice, London 1977–79; admitted to Bar of England and Wales 1977, of Anguilla 1984, of Saint Christopher and Nevis 1984, of Antigua and Barbuda 1989; in pvt. practice from Chambers, The Temple, London 1977–95, appeared in variety of criminal and civil rights cases; Asst Counsel to Comm. of Inquiry, Bahamas 1993–94; Legal Rep. of Govt 1995–2001; mem. Legal Affairs Cttee Org. of Eastern Caribbean States 1995–; various positions with Caribbean Community and Common Market (CARICOM) 1995–, including mem. Legal Affairs Cttee, Attorney-Gen. to Caribbean Asscn of Regulators of Int. Business (CARIB), mem. Del. to Heads of Govt Meetings, Barbados, Bahamas, Canada; Head Del. to Defence Ministerial of the Americas Meetings 1995, 1996, 1998, 2000; head numerous other govt dels including Commonwealth Law Ministers Conf., Malaysia; Attorney-Gen. and Minister of Justice and Legal Affairs 2001–04, Minister of Justice 2006–06; Amb. and Perm. Rep. to UN, New York 2006–; Del. to Talks on Drafting Saint Christopher and Nevis Constitution 1982; fmr Exec. mem. Soc. of Black Lawyers in England and Wales. *Leisure interests:* music, art, reading, swimming. *Address:* Permanent Mission of Saint Christopher and Nevis to the United Nations, 414 East 75th Street, 5th Floor, New York, NY 10021, USA (office); #45 Horizon Villa, Frigate Bay, Basseterre, Saint Christopher and Nevis (home). *Telephone:* (212) 535-1234 (office); (869) 465-3581 (home). *Fax:* (212) 535-6854 (office). *E-mail:* sknmission@aol.com (office). *Website:* www.stkittsnevis.org (office).

BARTÁK, Martin, MD; Czech neurosurgeon and politician; b. 14 Feb. 1967, Prague; m.; ed High School Voděradská, Prague, Charles Univ., Prague, postgraduate studies at Harvard Univ., USA, Univ. of Oxford, UK, Hanover Univ., Germany; neurosurgeon, 'Na Homolce' Hosp., Prague 1992–96, 1996–2006, Radcliffe Infirmary, Oxford, UK 1996; Adviser to Vice-Chair. of Civic Democratic Party (ODS) Petr Nečas, for security and defence issues 2000–06; Adviser to Chair. of Defence and Security Cttee, Chamber of Deputies (Parl.) 2002–06; First Deputy Minister of Defence 2006–09; Deputy Prime Minister and Minister of Defence 2009–10; Deputy Minister of Finance 2010–11; on trial for corruption, Prague Municipal Court, Jan. 2014. *Leisure interests:* sports, literature, music.

BARTELS, Lt-Gen. Knud; Danish military officer; *Chief of Defence;* b. 8 April 1952, Copenhagen; m. Inge Vansteenkiste; ed Royal Danish Army Acad., Ecole Supérieure de Guerre, Paris, US Army War Coll.; promoted to First Lt 1977, Capt. 1982, Major 1987, Lt-Col 1992, Col 1996, Brig. 2001, Maj.-Gen. 2001, Lt-Gen. 2006, Gen. 2009; regimental service 1977–80, UN Forces Cyprus 1980–81; Jr Army and Jt Staff Course 1981–82; Instructor in tactics, Army Combat School 1982–84, Instructor in tactics/operations, Royal Danish Defence Coll. 1986–87, 1988–90, Dir Army Command and Gen. Staff Course 1994–96; Co. Commdr, 2nd Armoured Bn Zealand Life Regt 1987–88, Staff Officer Danish Defence Command 1990–92, Commdg Officer 1st Bn Slesvig Foot Regt 1992–93, Commdr 3rd Jutland Brigade 1996–97, ACOS Plans Danish Defence Command 1997–99, Gen. Officer Commdg Danish Div. 2004–06; Sr Nat. Rep. KFOR/MNB (N) 1999, Dir for Operations, NATO Int. Mil. Staff 2000–04, Deputy Mil. Rep., NATO 2001, Gen. Officer Commanding Div. 2004–06, Mil. Rep., NATO, EU 2006–09; Chief of Defence 2009–; Commdr Order of Dannebrog, Ordre national du Mérite, Chevalier, Légion d'honneur; 25 Years Good Service Medal, UN Peacekeeping Force in Cyprus Medal, NATO KFOR Medal. *Address:* Ministry of Defence, Holmens Kanal 42, 1060 Copenhagen K, Denmark (office). *Telephone:* 33-92-33-20 (office). *Fax:* 33-32-06-55 (office). *E-mail:* fmn@fmn.dk (office). *Website:* www.fmn.dk (office).

BARTENSTEIN, Martin, PhD; Austrian politician and business executive; *Managing Director, Gerot Lannach Holding GmbH Ltd;* b. 3 June 1953, Graz; m. Ilse Bartenstein; five c.; ed Akademisches Gymnasium, Miami Univ., OH, USA, Karl Franzens Univ., Graz; joined Lannacher Heilmittel GmbH (family-owned pharmaceutical co.) 1978, Man. Dir 1980–86; Chief Exec. Genericon Pharma GesmbH 1986–90; mem. Bd of Dirs Pharmavit AG, Budapest 1990; Chair. Asscn of Young Austrian Industrialists 1988; mem. Austrian People's Party (Österreichische Volkspartei—ÖVP), Party Spokesman on Industry 1991; Deputy Regional Chair. Styrian People's Party 1991; mem. Nationalrat (ÖVP) 1991–; State Sec., Fed. Ministry for Public Economy and Transport 1994; Minister for the Environment 1995, for Environment, Youth and Family Affairs 1996, for Econ. Affairs and Labour 2000–08; Chair. Cancer Relief Fund for the Children of Styria 1998–92, Austrian Cancer Relief Fund for Children 1993–; Pres. Österreichischen Basketballbundesliga 2002–; Man. Dir Gerot Lannach Holding GmbH 2009–; Hon. Pres. Austrian Children's Cancer Aid Soc. 2009. *Address:* Parlamentsklub der ÖVP, Dr.-Karl-Renner-Ring 3, 1017 Vienna, Austria (office). *Telephone:* (1) 401-10-0 (office). *E-mail:* martin.bartenstein@parlament.gv.at (office). *Website:* www.parlament.gv.at (office).

BARTH, Else M.; Norwegian/Dutch professor of logic and analytical philosophy; b. 3 Aug. 1928, Strinda, Norway; m. Hendrik A. J. F. Misset 1953; ed Univs of Oslo, Trondheim, Amsterdam and Leyden; Reader in Logic, Utrecht Univ. 1971–77; Prof. of Analytical Philosophy, Groningen Univ. 1977–87, of Logic and Analytical Philosophy 1987–; Pres. Evert Willem Beth Foundation 1976; mem. Royal Netherlands Acad. of Arts and Sciences, Norwegian Acad. of Sciences. *Publications:* The Logic of the Articles in Traditional Philosophy. A Contribution to the Study of Conceptual Structures 1974, Perspectives on Analytic Philosophy, in Mededelingen der Koninklijke Nederlandse Akad. van Wetenschappen, afd. Letterkunde, Nieuwe Reeks 1979, From Axiom to Dialogue – A Philosophical Study of Logics and Argumentation (with E. C. W. Krabbe) 1982, Argumentation: Approaches to Theory Formation. Containing the Contributions to the Groningen Conference on the Theory of Argumentation, October 1978 (ed., with J. L. Martens) 1982, Problems, Functions and Semantic Roles – A Pragmatist's Analysis of Montague's Theory of Sentence Meaning (co-ed. with R. T. P. Wiche) 1986; numerous contribs to learned journals and published lectures. *Leisure interests:* music, cultural and political philosophy, literature, skiing. *Address:* Nachtegaallaan 26, 2224 JH Katwijk aan Zee (home); Filosofisch Instituut, University of Groningen, Westersingel 19, 9718 CA Groningen (office); Kamperfoelieweg 16, 9765 HK Paterswolde, Netherlands. *Telephone:* (50) 636146 (office); (5907) 4315 (Paterswolde); (1718) 13353 (Katwijk aan Zee).

BARTH, John M.; American business executive; b. 1946; ed Carnegie-Mellon Univ., Gannon Univ., Northwestern Univ. Inst. for Man.; joined Johnson Controls Inc. 1969, various man. positions including Dir Johnson Controls Automotive Systems Group 1990, mem. Bd of Dirs 1997–2007, Pres. and COO 1998, CEO 2002,

Chair. 2004–07; fmr Chair. Nat. Minority Supplier Devt Council; mem. Bd of Dirs Handleman Co. 1995–2003, Covisint Corpn; Leadership Award, Nat. Minority Supplier Devt Council 2006. *Address:* c/o Johnson Controls Inc., 5757 North Green Bay Avenue, POB 591, Milwaukee, WI 53201, USA (office).

BARTH, John Simmons, MA; American novelist and academic; *Professor Emeritus in the Writing Seminars, Johns Hopkins University;* b. 27 May 1930, Cambridge, Md; s. of John J. Barth and Georgia Simmons; m. 1st Harriette Anne Strickland 1950 (divorced 1969); two s. one d.; m. 2nd Shelly Rosenberg 1970; ed Johns Hopkins Univ.; Instructor, Pennsylvania State Univ. 1953, Assoc. Prof. until 1965; Prof. of English, State Univ. of New York at Buffalo 1965–73, Johns Hopkins Univ. 1973–91, Prof. Emer. in the Writing Seminars 1991–; Rockefeller Foundation Grant; mem., American Acad. of Arts and Letters 1974, Fellow, American Acad. of Arts and Sciences 1974; Hon. LittD (Univ. of Maryland) 1969, (Salisbury Univ.) 1975; Hon. DHL (Pennsylvania State Univ.) 1996, (Western Maryland Coll.) 1973, (Towson Univ.) 1981, (Univ. of Colorado) 2009; Laurea hc in Letter (Univ. Macerata, Italy) 1990; Hon. LittD (Colby Coll.) 2007; Brandeis Univ. Citation in Literature, Nat. Acad. of Arts and Letters Award, Nat. Book Award 1973, F. Scott Fitzgerald Award 1997, President's Medal, Johns Hopkins Univ. 1997, PEN/Malamud Award 1998, Lifetime Achievement Award, Lannan Foundation 1998, Lifetime Achievement in Letters Award, Enoch Pratt Soc. 1999, Roozi Rozegari (Iranian literature prize) 2008. *Publications:* The Floating Opera 1956, The End of the Road 1958, The Sot-Weed Factor 1960, Giles Goat-Boy 1966; Lost in the Funhouse (stories) 1968, Chimera 1972, Letters 1979, Sabbatical 1982, The Friday Book (essays) 1984, The Tidewater Tales: A Novel 1987, The Last Voyage of Somebody the Sailor 1991, Once Upon a Time 1994, On with the Story (stories) 1996, Coming Soon!!! (novel) 2001, The Book of Ten Nights and a Night (stories) 2004, Three Roads Meet (novella) 2005, The Development (stories) 2008, Every Third Thought: A Novel in Five Seasons 2011. *Address:* The Writing Seminars, 135 Gilman Hall, Johns Hopkins University, 3400 North Charles Street, Baltimore, MD 21218, USA (office). *Telephone:* (410) 167-563 (office). *Website:* www.jhu.edu/writsem (office).

BARTH, (Thomas) Fredrik (Weybye), MA, PhD; Norwegian social anthropologist and academic; *Professor Emeritus of Anthropology, Boston University;* b. 22 Dec. 1928, Leipzig, Germany; s. of Prof. Tom Barth and Randi Barth; m. Unni Wikan 1972; one s.; ed Berg School, Oslo, Univ. of Chicago, USA, Univ. of Cambridge, UK; Research Fellow in Social Anthropology, Univ. of Oslo 1953–61; Prof. of Social Anthropology, Univ. of Bergen 1961–72, Univ. of Oslo 1973–86; Research Fellow, Ministry of Educ. and Science 1987–; Prof. of Anthropology, Boston Univ., USA –2008 (retd), now Prof. Emer.; Visiting Prof., Columbia Univ. 1960, Univ. of Khartoum 1963–64, Yale Univ. 1972, Johns Hopkins Univ. 1977, Univ. of Calif., Berkeley 1980, CUNY 1987, Emory Univ. 1989–96, Harvard Univ. 1996–97; mem. Norwegian Acad. of Science and Letters;; Hon. Life Fellow, Royal Anthropological Inst. 1968; Hon. Life mem. Int. Union of Anthropological and Ethnological Sciences 1993; Foreign Hon. Mem. American Acad. of Arts and Sciences in 1997; Dr hc (Memorial Univ., Canada) 1988, (Univ. of Edin.) 1996, (Univ. of Aarhus) 2003; Retzius Gold Medal, Royal Swedish Soc. 1988, Lifetime Achievement Award, IUAES Comm. on Nomadic Peoples 1998; Sir James Frazer Memorial Lecturer, Cambridge 1983; Sir Thomas Huxley Memorial Lecturer, London 1989. *Publications:* Political Leadership Among Swat Pathans 1959, Nomads of South Persia 1961, Models of Social Organization 1964, Ethnic Groups and Boundaries 1969, Ritual and Knowledge among the Baktaman of New Guinea 1975, Selected Essays 1981, Sohar 1983, The Last Wali of Swat 1985, Cosmologies in the Making 1987, Balinese Worlds 1993. *Leisure interests:* travel, art. *Address:* Rödkleivfaret 16, 0788 Oslo, Norway. *Telephone:* (47) 22-147483. *Fax:* (47) 22-145748.

BARTHOLOMEOS I, Patriarch, DCnL; Turkish ecclesiastic; *Archbishop of Constantinople (New Rome) and Ecumenical Patriarch;* b. 29 Feb. 1940, Hagioi Theodoroi, Island of Imvros; s. of Christos Archondonis and Merope Archondonis; ed Theological School of Halki, Pontifical Oriental Inst., Rome, Ecumenical Inst. Bossey, Switzerland and Univ. of Munich; mil. service 1961–63; ordained deacon 1961, priest 1969; Asst Dean, Theological School of Halki 1968; elevated to rank of Archimandrite 1970; Admin. Pvt. Patriarchal Office of Ecumenical Patriarch Dimitrios 1972–90; Metropolitan, See of Philadelphia, Asia Minor 1973; mem. Holy and Sacred Synod 1974; Metropolitan of Chalcedon 1990–91; Archbishop of Constantinople (New Rome) and Ecumenical Patriarch 1991–; Founding mem. and Vice-Pres. Soc. of Canon Law of the Oriental Churches; mem. Exec. and Cen. Cttees, WCC 1991–; Fellow, Orthodox Acad. of Crete, Greece; Hon. mem. Pro-Oriente Foundation, Vienna; Dr hc (Athens), (Holy Cross Orthodox School of Theology, Brookline, Mass) and from numerous other univs; US Congressional Gold Medal 1997, Sophie Foundation Award 2002, Binding Foundation Award 2002. *Address:* Chief Secretariat of the Holy and Sacred Synod of the Ecumenical Patriarchate, Greek Orthodox Church, Rum Ortodoks Patrikhanesi, 34220 Fener-Haliç, Istanbul, Turkey (office). *Telephone:* (212) 5319671 (office). *Fax:* (212) 5316533 (office). *E-mail:* patriarchate@ec-patr.org (office). *Website:* www.patriarchate.org (office).

BARTKUS, Gintautas; Lithuanian lawyer, academic and fmr government official; *Managing Partner, Baltic Legal Solutions Lithuania;* b. 30 June 1966, m.; two c.; ed Vilnius State Univ., Helsinki Univ., Jean Moulin Univ., Lyon, France; Adviser to Dir Dept of Nat. Lithuanian Govt 1990–92; Visiting Prof., John Marshall Law School, Chicago, USA 1993–96; Founder and Pnr, Law Co. Lideika, Petrauskas, Valiunas and Pnrs 1990–2000; Minister of Justice 2000–01; Managing Partner, Advocate, Baltic Legal Solutions Lithuania; mem. Working Group for Drafting the Civil Code of Lithuania 1992–2000; Asst Prof., Vilnius Univ. 1989–; mem. EC Advisory Group on Corp. Governance and Co. Law 2005–; Arbitrator, Vilnius Court of Commercial Arbitration; mem. Lithuanian Bar Asscn. *Address:* Baltic Legal Solutions Lithuania, Subačiaus 7, 01302 Vilnius, Lithuania (office). *Telephone:* (5) 274-24-10 (office). *E-mail:* Gintautas.Bartkus@lt.blslawfirm.com (office). *Website:* www.blslawfirm.com (office).

BARTLETT, Jennifer, BA, BFA, MFA; American artist; b. 14 March 1941, Long Beach, Calif.; ed Mills Coll., Oakland, Calif., Yale Univ. School of Art and Architecture; taught art at Univ. of Connecticut 1964–72, School of Visual Arts, New York 1972–77; first New York exhbn, Alan Saret's SoHo gallery 1970; numerous public commissions; Harris Prize, Art Inst. of Chicago 1976, Award of

American Acad. and Inst. of Arts and Letters 1983, American Inst. of Architects Award 1987. *Address:* 134 Charles Street, New York, NY 10014, USA (office). *Website:* www.richardgraygallery.com.

BARTLETT, John Vernon, CBE, MA, FICE; British fmr consulting engineer; b. 18 June 1927, London; s. of Vernon F. Bartlett and Olga Bartlett (née Testrup); m. Gillian Hoffman 1951; four s.; ed Stowe School, Trinity Coll., Cambridge; engineer, John Mowlem & Co., Ltd 1951–57; joined Mott Hay & Anderson (now Mott MacDonald Group) 1957, Pnr 1966, Chair. 1973–88, Consultant 1988–95; Chair. British Tunnelling Soc. 1977–79; Pres. Inst. of Civil Engineers 1982–83; mem. Governing Body Imperial Coll. London 1991–95; Master Worshipful Co. of Engineers 1992–93; Founder, Bartlett Library, Nat. Maritime Museum Cornwall 2002; Fellow, Royal Acad. of Engineering; Telford Gold Medals 1971, 1973, S.G. Brown Medal, Royal Soc. 1973. *Publications include:* Tunnels: Planning, Design and Construction (with T.M. Megaw) 1981, Ships of North Cornwall 1996; various professional papers. *Leisure interests:* sailing, maritime history. *Address:* 6 Cottenham Park Road, Wimbledon, London, SW20 0RZ, England (home). *Telephone:* (20) 8946-9576 (home).

BARTOLI, Cecilia; Italian singer (coloratura mezzo-soprano) and recitalist; b. 4 June 1966, Rome; d. of Pietro Angelo Bartoli and Silvana Bazzoni; ed Accademia di Santa Cecilia, Rome; professional career began with TV appearance aged 19; US debut in recital at Mostly Mozart Festival, New York 1990; Paris debut as Cherubino in The Marriage of Figaro, Opéra de Paris Bastille 1990–91; debut, La Scala, Milan in Rossini's Le Comte Ory 1990–91 season; appeared as Dorabella in Così fan tutte, Maggio Musicale, Florence 1991; debut with Montreal Symphony Orchestra and Philadelphia Orchestra 1990–91 season; recitals in collaboration with pianist András Schiff since 1990; appeared in Marriage of Figaro and Così fan tutte conducted by Daniel Barenboim in Chicago Feb. 1992; debut at Salzburg Festival 1992; appeared in recital at Rossini bicentenary celebration at Lincoln Center, New York 1992; has appeared with many leading conductors including Herbert von Karajan, Claudio Abbado, Riccardo Chailly, Myung-Whun Chung, William Christie, Charles Dutoit, Adam Fischer, Nikolaus Harnoncourt, Christopher Hogwood, James Levine, Sir Neville Marriner, Zubin Mehta, Riccardo Muti, Giuseppe Sinopoli and Sir George Solti; particularly associated with the operas of Mozart and Rossini; highlights of the 2000–01 season included Cenerentola in Munich, Così fan tutte and Don Giovanni in Zurich, concert performances of Haydn's Orfeo with Hogwood in Birmingham, Amsterdam, Bremen and Paris, orchestral appearances with Harnoncourt and the Berlin Philharmonic in Berlin, Barenboim and the Chicago Symphony in Chicago and New York, Boulez and the London Symphony Orchestra in London and Amsterdam, Chailly and the Concertgebouw Orchestra in Amsterdam, all-Vivaldi concerts with the Giardino Armonico in Merano, Zurich, Paris, Lindau, Liechtenstein, New York, Vancouver, Los Angeles and San Francisco, baroque music concerts with the Akademie für Alte Musik in Oslo, Goteborg, Stockholm, Helsinki and Vienna; Artistic Dir, Salzburg Whitsun Festival 2012–; Hon. mem. RAM 2005; Chevalier, Ordre des Arts et des Lettres; two Grammy Awards for Best Classical Vocal Album 1994, Deutsche Schallplatten Preis, La Stella d'Oro, Italy, Caecilia Award, Belgium, Diapason d'Or, France, Best Opera Recording of the Year for La Cenerentola, Japan, Classical BRIT Award for Female Artist of the Year 2004, Echo Klassik Award for Female Singer of the Year 2008, Sonning Music Prize 2009. *Recordings include:* albums: Rossini Arias, Rossini Songs, Mozart Arias, Rossini Heroines, Chants d'amour, If You Love Me 1992, Mozart Portraits 1995, An Italian Songbook 1997, Cecilia Bartoli – Live Vivaldi Album 1999, Cecilia & Bryn, Il Turco in Italia, Mitridate, Rinaldo, Armida in Italy, The Salieri Album, The Vivaldi Album, Gluck Italian Arias, Opera proibito 2005, Maria (Gramophone Award for Best Recital 2008) 2007, Sacrificium (Grammy Award for Best Classical Vocal Performance 2011) 2009. *Address:* MusicArt Management AG, PO Box 123, 8702 Zollikon-Zürich, Switzerland (office). *Website:* www.ceciliabartolionline.com.

BARTON, Jacqueline K., AB, PhD; American chemist and academic; *Arthur and Marian Hanisch Memorial Professor of Chemistry, California Institute of Technology;* b. 7 May 1952, New York, NY; d. of William Kapelman and Claudine Kapelman (née Gutchen); m. Prof. Peter Brendan Dervan 1990; ed Barnard Coll. and Columbia Univ., New York; Visiting Research Assoc., Dept of Biophysics, Bell Labs 1979; Postdoctoral Fellow, Bell Labs and Yale Univ. 1980; Asst Prof. of Chem. and Biochemistry, Hunter Coll., CUNY 1980–82; returned to Columbia Univ. 1983, Assoc. Prof. of Chem. and Biological Sciences 1985–86, Prof. 1986–89; Prof., California Inst. of Tech. 1989–, currently Arthur and Marian Hanisch Memorial Prof. of Chem., Chair. Div. of Chem. and Chemical Eng 2009–; mem. NSF Chem. Advisory Cttee 1985–88, NIH Metallobiochemistry Study Section 1986–90 (Chair. 1988–90); mem. Bd of Dirs Dow Chemical Co. 1993–, currently Chair. Environment, Health and Safety Cttee and mem. Governance and Compensation Cttees; Fellow, American Acad. of Arts and Sciences 1991, American Philosophical Soc. 2000, NAS 2002; fmr Fellow, Sloan Foundation; fmr NSF Presidential Young Investigator; Hon. DSc (Knox Coll.) 1991, (Williams Coll.) 1992, (New Jersey Inst. of Tech.) 1993, (Kenyon Coll.) 1994, (Lawrence Univ.) 1994, (Skidmore Coll.) 1997, (Yale Univ.) 2005, (Columbia Univ.) 2010; NSF Predoctoral Fellow 1975–78, NIH Postdoctoral Fellow 1979–80, Harold Lamport Award, New York Acad. of Sciences 1984, NSF Alan T. Waterman Award 1985, Camille and Henry Dreyfus Teacher-Scholar 1986–91, ACS Award in Pure Chem. 1988, ACS Eli Lilly Award in Biological Chem. 1987, ACS Baekeland Medal 1991, Fresenius Award 1986, Univ. Medal, Barnard Coll. 1990 and Columbia Univ. 1992, MacArthur Foundation Fellowship 1991, ACS Garvan Medal 1992, ACS Tolman Medal 1994, Mayor of New York's Award in Science and Tech. 1988, Havinga Medal 1995, Paul Karrer Medal 1996, ACS Nichols Medal 1997, Weizmann Women and Science Award 1998, ACS Ronald Breslow Award in Biomimetic Chem. 2003, named an Outstanding Dir by ODX 2006, Willard Gibbs Award, Chicago Section of ACS 2006, ACS Cotton Medal 2007, ACS Pauling Medal 2007, Nat. Medal of Science 2010. *Publications:* more than 250 publs in scientific journals on the application of transition metal complexes as tools to probe recognition and reactions of double helical DNA. *Address:* Department of Chemistry, M/C 127-72, California Institute of Technology, 1200 East California Blvd, Pasadena, CA 91125-7200, USA (office). *Telephone:* (626) 395-6070 (office). *Fax:* (626) 577-4976 (office). *E-mail:* jkbarton@caltech.edu (office). *Website:* www.its.caltech.edu/~jkbgrp (office).

BARTON, Rev. John, MA, DPhil, DLitt, FBA; British academic; *Oriel and Laing Professor of the Interpretation of Holy Scripture, Oriel College, University of Oxford;* b. 17 June 1948, London, England; s. of Bernard A. Barton and Gwendolyn H. Barton; m. Mary Burn 1973; one d.; ed Latymer Upper School, London and Keble Coll. Oxford; Jr Research Fellow, Merton Coll. Oxford 1973–74; Univ. Lecturer in Theology, Univ. of Oxford 1974–89, Reader in Biblical Studies 1989–91; Fellow, St Cross Coll. Oxford 1974–91; Oriel and Laing Prof. of the Interpretation of Holy Scripture and Fellow, Oriel Coll. Oxford 1991–; Canon Theologian of Winchester Cathedral 1991–2003; mem. Norwegian Acad. of Arts and Sciences 2008; Hon. DrTheol (Bonn) 1998. *Publications:* Amos's Oracles Against the Nations 1980, Reading the Old Testament 1984, Oracles of God 1986, People of the Book? 1988, Love Unknown 1990, What is the Bible? 1991, Isaiah 1–39 1995, The Spirit and the Letter 1997, Making the Christian Bible 1997, Ethics and the Old Testament 1998, The Cambridge Companion to Biblical Interpretation 1998, Oxford Bible Commentary 2001, Joel and Obadiah 2001, The Biblical World 2003, Understanding Old Testament Ethics 2003, The Original Story (with J. Bowden) 2004, Living Belief 2005, The Nature of Biblical Criticism 2007, The Old Testament: Canon, Literature, Theology 2007. *Address:* Oriel College, Oxford, OX1 4EW, England (office). *Telephone:* (1865) 276537 (office). *E-mail:* john.barton@oriel.ox.ac.uk (office). *Website:* www.oriel.ox.ac.uk (office).

BARTON, John Bernard Adie, CBE, MA; British theatre director; b. 26 Nov. 1928, London; s. of Sir Harold Montagu Barton and Lady Joyce Barton (née Wale); m. Anne Righter 1968; ed Eton Coll. and King's Coll., Cambridge; Drama Lecturer, Univ. of Calif., Berkeley 1953–54; Fellow, King's Coll., Cambridge 1954–59; Asst Dir (to Peter Hall) RSC 1959, Assoc. Dir 1964–91, Advisory Dir 1991–; Sam Wanamaker Award 2001. *Productions for RSC include:* The Wars of the Roses (adapted, edited, co-directed) 1963, Love's Labour's Lost 1965, 1978, All's Well That Ends Well, Julius Caesar, Troilus and Cressida 1968–69, Twelfth Night, When Thou Art King 1969–70, Othello, Richard II, Henry V 1971, Richard II 1973, Dr. Faustus, King John (co-dir) 1974–75, Much Ado About Nothing, Troilus and Cressida, The Winter's Tale, King Lear, A Midsummer Night's Dream, Pillars of the Community 1976, The Way of the World 1978, The Merchant of Venice, Love's Labour's Lost 1978, The Greeks 1980, Hamlet 1980, Merchant of Venice, Two Gentlemen of Verona 1981, Titus Andronicus 1981, La Ronde 1982, Life's a Dream 1984, The Devils 1984, Waste 1985, Dream Play 1985, The Rover 1986, The Three Sisters 1988, Coriolanus 1989, Peer Gynt 1994, 1995, Cain 1995; also School for Scandal, London 1983, For Triumph Apollo 1983, The Vikings 1983; for Nat. Theatre, Oslo: Peer Gynt 1990, Measure for Measure, As You Like It 1991–92; The War That Still Goes On 1991, Tantalus, Denver Center Theater Co. 2000. *Television productions:* Playing Shakespeare 1982, Mallory's Morte d'Arthur 1983, The War That Never Ends (scriptwriter) 1991. *Publications:* The Hollow Crown 1962, The Wars of the Roses 1970, The Greeks 1981, Playing Shakespeare 1982, Tantalus 2000. *Leisure interests:* travel, chess, work. *Address:* c/o Casarotto Marsh Ltd, Waverley House, 7-12 Noel Street, London, W1F 8GQ; 14 De Walden Court, 85 New Cavendish Street, London, W1W 6XD, England (home).

BARTON, Nicholas Hamilton (Nick), PhD, FRS, FRSE; British biologist and academic; *Professor, Institute of Science and Technology Austria;* ed Univ. of East Anglia; Demonstrator, Dept of Genetics, Univ. of Cambridge 1980–82; Lecturer, Dept of Genetics and Biometry, Univ. Coll. London 1982–90; mem. staff, Univ. of Edinburgh 1990, Prof. of Evolutionary Biology 1994–2008, currently Visiting Prof., Inst. of Evolutionary Biology; Prof., Inst. of Science and Tech. Austria (IST Austria), Klosterneuburg, Austria 2008–; Handling Ed. Evolution (text book) 2008–11; mem. Editorial Bd Public Library of Science 2003; David Starr Jordan Prize 1994, Pres.'s Award, American Soc. of Naturalists 1998, Wolfson Merit Award 2005, Darwin Medal, Royal Soc. 2006, Darwin-Wallace Medal and Award (co-recipient), Linnean Soc. 2008. *Publications:* numerous scientific papers in professional journals on hybrid zones, speciation and multi-locus evolution, and on understanding the evolution of traits which depend on interactions between large numbers of genes. *Address:* Institute of Science and Technology Austria (IST Austria), Am Campus 1 A, 3400 Klosterneuburg, Austria (office); Room 126, Ashworth Labs, School of Biological Sciences, University of Edinburgh, Michael Swann Building, King's Buildings, Mayfield Road, Edinburgh, EH9 3JR, Scotland. *E-mail:* nick.barton@ist.ac.at (office); n.barton@ed.ac.uk (office). *Website:* ist.ac.at/research-groups-pages/barton-group (office).

BARTOV, Omer, DPhil; Israeli/American historian and academic; *John P. Birkelund Distinguished Professor of European History, Brown University;* ed Univ. of Oxford, UK; fmrly at Rutgers Univ.; currently John P. Birkelund Distinguished Prof. of European History and Prof. of History, Brown Univ.; Visiting Fellow, Davis Center, Princeton Univ.; Jr Fellow, Soc. of Fellows, Harvard Univ.; mem. American Acad. of Arts and Sciences; Fellow, Nat. Endowment for the Humanities (NEH), Alexander von Humboldt Foundation, Radcliffe Inst. for Advanced Study, Harvard Univ. 2002–03, American Acad., Berlin 2007; Guggenheim Fellow 2003–04; NEH Fellowship 2008–09; Center for Advanced Holocaust Studies at US Holocaust Memorial Museum Fellowship 2012–13. *Publications include:* The Eastern Front 1941–45: German Troops and the Barbarisation of Warfare 1985, Hitler's Army 1991, Murder in Our Midst (Fraenkel Prize in Contemporary History) 1996, Mirrors of Destruction 2000; Ed.: The Holocaust: Origins, Implementation, Aftermath 2000; Co-Ed.: In God's Name: Genocide and Religion in the Twentieth Century 2001, Germany's War and the Holocaust 2003, The Crimes of War: Guilt and Denial in the Twentieth Century 2002, The "Jew" in Cinema 2005, Erased: Vanishing Traces of Jewish Galicia in Present-Day Ukraine 2007; numerous book chapters, articles and reviews in several languages. *Address:* Brown University, Department of History, Peter Green House, 79 Brown Street, Box N, Providence, RI 02912, USA (office). *Telephone:* (401) 863-1375 (office). *Fax:* (401) 863-1040 (office). *E-mail:* Omer_Bartov@brown.edu (office). *Website:* www.brown.edu (office).

BARTUMEU CASSANY, Jaume; Andorran lawyer and politician; b. 10 Nov. 1954, Andorra la Vella; m. Carme Garcia Puy; two s.; ed Univ. of Barcelona, Spain, Univ. of Toulouse, France; legal practice, Andorra la Vella 1982–; Minister of Finance, Commerce and Industry 1990–92; mem. Andorran Del. to European Council 1995–2001, 2004–08, Vice-Pres. Human Rights Sub-Comm. 2004, Pres. Sub-Comm. on Crime Problems and the Fight against Terrorism 2005–; Founding mem. Partit Socialdemòcrata (Social Democratic Party) 2000, First Sec. 2000–04;

Leader of the Opposition, Consell Gen. 2005–09, Cap del Govern (Head of Govt) 2009–11; mem. Andorran Bar Council 1986–89; mem. Exec. Cttee Int. Asscn of Young Lawyers 1987–90. *Address:* c/o Office of the Head of Government, Govern d'Andorra, Carrer Prat de la Creu 62–64, Edif. Administratiu, Andorra la Vella AD500, Andorra (office). *Website:* www.jaumebartumeu.com.

BARTZ, Carol Ann, BA; American business executive; b. 29 Aug. 1948; m. Bill Marr; two s. one d.; ed Univ. of Wisconsin; fmr Man. Product Line and Sales, Digital Equipment Corpn and 3M Corpn; various roles with Sun Microsystems rising to Exec. Officer 1983–92; mem. Bd of Dirs and Chair., Pres. and CEO Autodesk, Inc. 1992–2006, Exec. Chair. 2006–09; mem. Bd of Dirs and CEO Yahoo! Inc. 2009–11, Pres. 2009–11; mem. Bd of Dirs BEA Systems, Cisco Systems, Network Appliance, TechNet, Foundation for the Nat. Medals of Science and Tech., New York Stock Exchange; mem. Pres. Bush's Council of Advisors on Science and Tech.; Hon. DHumLitt (New Jersey Inst. of Tech.), Hon. DSc (Worcester Polytechnic Inst.), Hon. DLitt (Williams Woods Univ.); numerous awards including Soc. of Manufacturing Engineers Donald C. Burnham Manufacturing Man. Award 1994, Women in Tech. Int. Hall of Fame 1997, Ernst & Young's Master Entrepreneur of the Year Award 2001, Ada Lovelace Award, Asscn for Women in Computing 2003, Avatar Award for Women of Excellence, Nat. Asscn of Female Execs 2003, named by San Francisco Business Times amongst the 100 Most Influential Women in Business 2004, named by Business Week in Women in Technology List 2004, ranked by Forbes magazine amongst The World's 100 Most Powerful Women (90th) 2004, (86th) 2005, (12th) 2009, (42nd) 2010, (37th) 2011, ranked by Fortune magazine amongst 50 Most Powerful Women in Business in the US (31st) 2005, (eighth) 2009, (tenth) 2010, named by The Wall Street Journal as one of 50 Women to Watch 2005, named by Barron's amongst The World's 30 Most Respected CEOs 2005. *Leisure interests:* golf, tennis, gardening. *Address:* c/o Yahoo! Inc., 701 1st Avenue, Sunnyvale, CA 94089, USA.

BARYSHNIKOV, Mikhail (Misha); Russian/American ballet dancer; *Artistic Director, Baryshnikov Arts Center;* b. 28 Jan. 1948, Riga, Latvia; s. of Nikolay Baryshnikov and Aleksandra (née Kisselov) Baryshnikova; one d.; ed Riga Ballet School and Kirov Ballet School, Leningrad; mem. Kirov Ballet Co. 1969–74; guest artist with many leading ballet cos including American Ballet Theater, Nat. Ballet of Canada, Royal Ballet, Hamburg Ballet, FRG, Ballet Victoria, Australia, Stuttgart Ballet, FRG, Alvin Ailey Co., USA 1974–; joined New York City Ballet Co. 1978, resgnd 1979; Artistic Dir, American Ballet Theater 1980–89; Co-Founder (with Mark Morris) and Dir White Oak Dance Project 1990–2002; Founder and Artistic Dir, Baryshnikov Arts Center, New York 2005–; Fellow, American Acad. of Arts and Sciences 1999; Officer, nat. Légion d'honneur 2010; Dr hc (Northwestern Univ.) 2013; Gold Medal, Varna Competition, Bulgaria 1966, First Int. Ballet Competition, Moscow, USSR 1968, Nijinsky Prize, First Int. Ballet Competition, Paris Acad. de Danse 1968, Kennedy Center Honors, Nat. Medal of Honor 2000, Jerome Robbins Award 2005, Commonwealth Award, Vilcek Prize in Dance 2012. *Ballets (world premières):* Vestris 1969, Medea 1975, Push Comes to Shove 1976, Hamlet Connotations 1976, Other Dances 1976, Pas de Duke 1976, La Dame De Pique 1978, L'Après-midi d'un Faune 1978, Santa Fe Saga 1978, Opus 19 1979, Rhapsody 1980. *Films:* The Turning Point 1977, White Nights 1985, Giselle 1987, Dancers 1987, Dinosaurs 1991. *Television:* appeared in episodes of Sex and the City 2003–04. *Choreography:* Nutcracker 1976, Don Quixote 1978, Cinderella 1984. *Publications:* Baryshnikov at Work 1977, Moments in Time 2005. *Address:* Baryshnikov Arts Center, 450 West 37th Street, Suite 501, New York, NY 10018, USA (office). *Telephone:* (646) 731-3200 (office). *Fax:* (646) 731-3207 (office). *E-mail:* info@bacnyc.org (office). *Website:* www.bacnyc.org (office).

BARZANI, Masoud; Iraqi (Kurdish) politician; *President, Kurdistan Region and Leader, Kurdistan Democratic Party;* b. 16 Aug. 1946, Mahabad, Iran; s. of Mustafa Barzani, founder of Kurdistan Democratic Party (KDP); m.; five s. three d.; ed Tehran Univ.; father forced to flee to USSR 1946, returned to Iraq following overthrow of Iraqi monarchy in 1958; reunited with his father, family returned to their home village of Barzan; KDP launched armed struggle to defend Kurdish people 1961, joined Peshmerga forces 1962; participated in del. that signed autonomy agreement with Govt in Baghdad March 1970; engaged in renewed Kurdish armed struggle 1970s; succeeded his father as Pres. of KDP 1979–; led KDP in establishing a govt in Iraqi Kurdistan with PUK; mem. Iraqi Governing Council following invasion of Iraq 2003, Pres. Council April 2004; elected first Pres. Kurdistan Region in Iraq by Kurdistan Nat. Ass. June 2005–; Italian Atlantic Cttee Atlantic Award 2011. *Publication:* Mustafa Barzani and the Kurdish Liberation Movement (with Ahmed Ferhani) (three vols in Arabic; first vol. also in English and Turkish). *Leisure interests:* reading and football. *Address:* Office of the President, Kurdistan Regional Government, Erbil, Iraq. *E-mail:* info@krg .org (office); party@kdp.se (office). *Website:* www.krg.org; www.kdp.se (office).

BARZANI, Nechirvan Idris; Iraqi (Kurdish) politician; b. 21 Sept. 1966, Barzan, southern Kurdistan; grandson of Mustafa Barzani, founder of Kurdistan Democratic Party (KDP), nephew of Masoud Barzani, Pres. of Kurdistan Region; m. Nabila Barzani; two c.; ed Tehran Univ.; family forced to flee to Iran 1975; often accompanied his father and sr Kurdistan Democratic Party (KDP) mem. Idris Barzani on his missions abroad; political science studies in Tehran cut short due to sudden death of his father 1987; took up active role in Kurdish politics, working in KDP youth orgs, rose rapidly through ranks of KDP; first elected to leadership of KDP in 1989, re-elected 1999; participated in negotiations with Iraqi Govt following Gulf War 1991; Deputy Prime Minister of KDP's controlled region in Iraqi Kurdistan 1996–99, Prime Minister 1999–2006, first Prime Minister of unified Govt of Kurdistan Region 2006–09. *Leisure interest:* Kurdish and Persian poetry. *Address:* c/o Office of the Prime Minister, Council of Ministers Building, Kurdistan Regional Government, Erbil, Iraq.

BARZEL, Amnon, MSc; Israeli art writer, critic, consultant and museum director; b. 5 July 1935, Tel -Aviv; m. Shafrira Glikson 1956; one s. one d.; ed Hebrew Univ., Jerusalem, Sorbonne, Paris; Lecturer, Avni Inst., Univ. of Haifa; Founding Ed. Painting and Sculpture 1971; Art Consultant for City of Tel-Aviv 1975–76; Curator, Biennale of Venice, Italy 1976–78, 1980, Two Environments, Forte Belvedere, Florence and Castle of Prato, Italy 1978, São Paulo Biennale, Brazil 1985; Founding Curator Contemporary Art Meetings, Tel Hai, Israel

1980–83, Villa Celle Art Spaces Collection, Giuliano Gori, Prato, Italy 1981–82; Founding Dir Centre of Contemporary Art Luigi Pecci, Prato, Italy 1986, Dir School for Curators 1991; Artistic Dir European Sculpture City (UNESCO), Turku, Finland 1992–95, Premio Mercedes Benz for Contemporary Art, Monte Firidolfi 1997, Artostrada 1998; Dir Berlin Jewish Museum 1994–97; Consultant, Leube Foundation, Gartenau, Salzburg 1985; Consultant for creation of Museum of Contemporary Art, Florence 1989; fmr Consultant, Phoenix Int. Art Collection; mem. Curatorial Cttee for Int. Sculpture Center, Washington, DC 1990. *Publications include:* Isaac Frenel 1973, Dani Karavan 1978, Art in Israel 1986, Europe Now 1988, Julian Schnabel 1989, Enzo Cucchi 1989, Contemporary Russian Artists (co-ed.) 1990, Der Wettbewerb für das 'Denkmal für die ermordeten Juden Europas': Eine Streitschrift (co-author) 1995, Hermann Pedit: Arbeiten 1954-1997 (co-author) 1997, Leben Im Wartesaal: Exil in Shanghai, 1938-1947 (co-author) 1997, Massimo Lippi: L'albero Della Vita (co-author) 2001, Light Art: Targetti Light Art Collection 2006, Hans Hartung: In the Beginning There Was Lightning/ In Principio Era Il Fulmine (co-author) 2007. *Leisure interests:* poetry, holy contemporary philosophy. *Address:* Via Giovanni Prati, 26, 50124 Florence, Italy (home). *Telephone:* (55) 220098 (home).

BAS, Philippe; French politician; b. 20 July 1958, Paris; ed Inst. of Political Studies, Nat. School of Man., Paris; mem. Council of State 1987–92; Advisor to Minister of Social Affairs, Health and Towns and to Minister of State for Health 1993–94; Asst Dir, Cabinet of Minister of Social Affairs, Health and Towns 1994–95; Dir, Cabinet of Minister of Employment and Social Affairs 1995–97; Social Affairs Advisor to Pres. of France 1997–2000; Asst Sec.-Gen., Cabinet of Pres. 2000–02, Sec.-Gen. 2002–07; Minister of Health and Social Protection March–May 2007; Vice-Pres. Gen. Council of La Mancha; Chair. French Office for Immigration and Integration, Ministry of Immigration, Integration, Nat. Identity and Shared Devt 2007–; Ordre national de la Légion d'honneur 2009. *Film appearance:* The Assault 2010. *Publications:* L'Afrique Australe dans la Tourmente (with Denis Tersen) 1988. *Address:* Ministry of Immigration, Integration, National Identity and Shared Development, 101 rue de Grenelle, 75700 Paris, France (office). *Telephone:* 1-77-72-61-00 (office). *Website:* www.immigration.gouv .fr (office).

BASANT ROI, Rameswurlall, GCSK, MA (Econs); Mauritian fmr central banker; b. 17 Aug. 1946; ed Dehli School of Econs, Univ. of Delhi, India; joined Bank of Mauritius 1976, Research Officer 1976–84, Asst Dir Dept of Research 1984–87, Dir 1987–98, Gov. 1998–2007; Grand Commdr of the Order of the Star and Key of the Indian Ocean 2004. *Publications include:* several papers on econs including Monetary Policy Making in Mauritius (co-author with Maxwell Fry) 1995. *Address:* 15 Couvent de Lorette, Vacoas, Mauritius (home).

BAŞÇI, Erdem, BSc, MBA, MA, PhD; Turkish economist and central banker; *Governor, Central Bank of the Republic of Turkey;* b. 9 Aug. 1966, Ankara; m.; ed TED Ankara Coll., Middle East Tech. Univ., Bilkent Univ., Johns Hopkins Univ., USA; Teaching Asst, Dept of Man., Bilkent Univ. 1988–89, Research Asst, Dept of Econs 1989–95, Asst Prof. 1996–; Deputy Gov. Türkiye Cumhuriyet Merkez Bankası AŞ (Central Bank of the Repub. of Turkey) 2008–11, Gov. 2011–; Hon. Visiting Fellow, Univ. of York, UK 1999; mem. Econometric Soc., Royal Econ. Soc. *Address:* Office of the Governor, Türkiye Cumhuriyet Merkez Bankası AŞ, İstiklal Cad. 10 Ulus, 06100 Ankara, Turkey (office). *Telephone:* (312) 5075000 (office). *Fax:* (312) 5075640 (office). *E-mail:* iletisimbilgi@tcmb.gov.tr (office). *Website:* www.tcmb.gov.tr (office).

BASELITZ, Georg; German artist; b. (Hans-Georg Bruno Kern), 23 Jan. 1938, Deutschbaselitz, Saxony; m. Elke Kretzschmar 1962; two s.; ed Gymnasium, Kamenz, Kunstakad. E. Berlin and Akad. der Künste, W. Berlin; Instructor, Staatliche Akad. der Bildenden Kunste, Karlsruhe 1977–78, Prof. 1978–83; Prof. Hochschule der Kunste, Berlin 1983–2003; mem. Acad. of the Arts, Berlin 1984–92, Bavarian Acad. of Fine Arts 2009–; works in numerous public collections; Hon. mem., Royal Acad. of Art (UK) 1999, Hon. Citizen, town of Imperia, Italy 2006; Commdr de l'Ordre des Arts et Lettres 2002; Hon. Prof. (Acad. of Fine Art, Krakow) 2000, (Accademia di Belle Arti, Florence) 2004; Kaiserring Prize, Goslar 1986, Rhenus Art Prize, Mönchen-Gladbach 1999, Julio González Prize, Valencia 2001, Niedersächsischer Staaspreis 2003, Praemium Imperial, Japan 2004, Decoration for Science and Art, Vienna, Austria 2005, B.Z. Culture Prize 2008, Cologne Fine Art Award of the Asscn of German Galleries and Editions 2009. *Publications:* books, pamphlets, manifestos and articles. *Address:* Schloss Derneburg, 31188 Holle, Germany (office). *Website:* www.georgbaselitz.com.

BĂSESCU, Traian; Romanian politician, head of state and fmr naval officer; *President;* b. 4 Nov. 1951, Basarabi, Constanța Co.; s. of the late Dumitru Băsescu and Elena Băsescu; m. Maria Băsescu; two d.; ed Inst. of Civil Marine Mircea cel Bătrân and Norwegian Acad.; Officer Grades III, II and I, Romanian Navy 1976–81, Capt., Merchant Navy 1981–87; Head of Navrom Agency, Antwerp, Belgium 1987–89; Gen. Dir State Inspectorate of Civil Navigation, Ministry of Transportation 1989–90, Under-Sec. of State and Head of Naval Transportation Dept 1990–91, Minister of Transport 1991–92, 1996–2000; mem. Democratic Party (PD), Pres. 2001–04; mem. Chamber of Deputies 1992–96, 1996–2000; Vice-Pres. Chamber of Deputies Comm. for Industry and Services 1992–96; investigated for corruption and fraud 1996; Dir electoral campaign for Petre Roman (pres. cand.) 1996; Co-Pres. Justice and Truth Alliance (DA) 2003–; Mayor of Bucharest 2000–04; Pres. of Romania 2004– (suspended from post 20 April–23 May 2007, 6 July–27 Aug. 2012); Collar of the Order of the Cross of Terra Mariana (Estonia), First Class with Chain of the Order of the Three Stars (Latvia), Order of the Republic (Moldova), Order of the White Eagle (Poland), Grand Cross, Order of Saint-Charles (Monaco) 2009. *Address:* Office of the President, 060116 Bucharest, Palatul Cotroceni, Str. Geniului 1–3, Sector 5, Romania (office). *Telephone:* (21) 4100581 (office). *Fax:* (21) 4103858 (office). *E-mail:* presedinte@basescu.ro (home); presedinte@presidency.ro (office). *Website:* www.basescu.ro (home); www .presidency.ro (office).

BASHA, Lulzim Xhelal, LLM; Albanian lawyer and politician; *Mayor of Tirana;* b. 12 June 1974, Tirana; m. Aurela Isufi; one c.; ed Utrecht Univ., Netherlands; worked for Int. Criminal Tribunal for the fmr Yugoslavia and was mem. war crimes investigation team of Serbian forces in Kosovo 1998–99; Legal Adviser, Justice Dept, UN Mission in Kosovo (UNMIK) 2000–01, Deputy Chief of Cabinet of

Dir of Justice Dept 2001–02, Special Adviser for Transition, Justice Dept 2002–05; mem. Democratic Party of Albania (Partia Demokratike e Shqipërisë, PDSh) 2005–, Co-ordinator Cttee for Policy Orientation 2005–, Nat. Council 2005–, mem. Presidency 2005–, Leader 2013–, Spokesman of Gen. Election Campaign May–July 2005; mem. Parl. 2005–, Minister of Public Works, Transport and Telecommunications 2005–07, of Foreign Affairs 2007–09, of the Interior 2009–11; Mayor of Tirana 2011–; Freedom of the City of London 2013. *Address:* Office of the Mayor, Municipality of Tirana, Blvd Dëshmorët e Kombit, Tirana, Albania (office). *Telephone:* (4) 2253053 (office); (4) 2229100 (office). *Fax:* (4) 2228430 (office). *E-mail:* e-mayor@tirana.gov.al (office); info@tirana.gov.al (office). *Website:* www.tirana.gov.al (office); lulzimbasha.al.

BASHIR, Maria; Afghan lawyer and government official; *Chief Prosecutor General, Herat Province;* b. 1970; m.; one s., one d.; ed Kabul Univ.; criminal investigator in prosecutor's office 1994–95, 2001–; Chief Prosecutor Gen. Herat Prov. (first woman) 2006–; Int. Women of Courage Award, US State Dept 2011. *Address:* Attorney-General's Office, Herat, Afghanistan (office). *Website:* www.ago.gov.af (office).

BASHIR, Marie Roslyn, AC, CVO, MBS; Australian state governor and professor of psychiatry; *Governor of New South Wales;* b. Narrandera; d. of M. Bashir; m. Sir Nicholas Shehadie 1957; three c.; ed Sydney Girls High School, Univ. of Sydney; elected to Coll. Council 1959, Hon. Sec. 1960, Chair. 1982–90, life mem. Coll. Union 1969–; fmr teacher Univs of Sydney and New South Wales; Foundation Dir, Rivendell Child Adolescent and Family Service 1972–87; Dir Community Health Services, Cen. Sydney 1987–93; Clinical Prof. of Psychiatry, Univ. of Sydney 1993–2001; Consultant to NSW Juvenile Justice Facilities 1993–2000; Area Dir of Mental Health Services, Cen. Sydney 1994–2001; Sr Consultant to Aboriginal Medical Service, Redfern and Kempsey 1996–2001; Gov. of NSW 2001–; Chancellor Univ. of Sydney 2007–; Co-Chair. NSW Mental Health Strategy for Aboriginal People; Fellow, Royal Australian and New Zealand Coll. of Psychiatrists 1971–; mem. Amnesty International, Nat. Trust, NSW Camellia Research Soc., Tandanya Nat. Aboriginal Cultural Centre; Patron Sydney Symphony and Opera Australia; Patron New South Wales Branch, Order of Australia Asscn; mem. numerous univ. cttees, medical research bodies, mental health bds; involved in establishment of post grad. medical training in psychiatry in Viet Nam and other medical educ. visits to Laos and Cambodia; named Mother of the Year NSW 1971. *Publications include:* research papers and publs on child, adolescent, refugee and Aboriginal mental health issues. *Leisure interests:* int. affairs, Australian history, early Australian antique furniture, classical music, opera, Aboriginal art, growing camellias. *Address:* Office of the Governor, Macquarie Street, Sydney, NSW 2000 (office); Order of Australia Association, Old Parliament House, King George Terrace, Parkes, ACT 2600, Australia (office). *Telephone:* (2) 6273-0322 (Parkes) (office). *E-mail:* oaasecretariat@ozemail.com.au (office). *Website:* www.parliament.nsw.gov.au (office); www.theorderofaustralia.asn.au (office).

BASHIR, Lt-Gen. Omar Hassan Ahmad al-; Sudanese army officer and head of state; *President and Prime Minister;* b. 1 Jan. 1944, Hoshe Bannaga, Anglo-Egyptian Sudan; ed Sudan Mil. Acad., Egyptian Mil. Acad., Cairo; fought in Egyptian army during 1973 war with Israel; career army officer rising to rank of Brig., then Lt-Gen.; overthrew Govt of Sadiq al-Mahdi in coup 30 June 1989; Chair. Revolutionary Command Council for Nat. Salvation 1989–; Minister of Defence 1989–93; Pres. and Prime Minister of Sudan 1993–; Pres. National Congress Party; Chair. Ass. Intergovernmental Authority on Devt 2000–01; charged with genocide by Int. Criminal Court (ICC) 14 July 2008, warrant issued for his arrest on two counts of war crimes and five counts of crimes against humanity in Darfur (first ICC warrant for a serving head of state) 4 March 2009. *Address:* Office of the President, Khartoum, Sudan (office). *Website:* www.presidency.gov.sd (office).

BASHIR, Salah ed-Din al-, MA, PhD; Jordanian lawyer, academic and politician; b. 1966; ed Univ. of Jordan, Harvard Law School, USA, McGill Univ., Canada; Adjunct Prof. of Law, Univ. of Jordan 1996–, Dir Centre for Strategic Studies 1999; fmr Minister of Industry and Trade, fmr Minister of State for Cabinet Affairs, fmr Minister of Justice; Minister of Foreign Affairs 2007–09; Man. Pnr, Abu Ghazaleh Legal Services; mem. Econ. Consultative Council 1999; Founder and Sr Man. Pnr, Int. Business Legal Assocs (IBLAW); Co-Chair. Jordanian–American Comm. for Educational Exchange. *Address:* IBLAW, Rabiyeh, Sequilia Street, Salem Centre, 1st Floor, PO Box 9028, Amman 11191, Jordan (office). *E-mail:* sbashir@iblaw.com.jo (office). *Website:* www.iblaw.com.jo (office).

BASHKIROV, Dmitri Aleksandrovich; Russian pianist and academic; *Professor Titular, Escuela Superior de Música Reina Sofía;* b. 1 Nov. 1931, Tbilisi, Georgia; s. of Alexandr Bashkirov and Ester Ramendik; m. Natalya Bashkirova 1987; one s.; one s. from second marriage; one d. from a previous marriage; ed Moscow P.I. Tchaikovsky State Conservatory; studied in Tbilisi under A. Virsaladze, Moscow State Conservatory under A. Goldenweiser; concerts since 1955 in more than 30 countries; participated in Wiener Festwochen, Verbier, Switzerland, Helsinki, Granada, Ruhr Piano Fest, Germany and other festivals; repertoire includes works by Mozart, Schumann, Brahms, Debussy, Prokofiev; Moscow State Conservatory 1957, Prof. 1976–90; mem. jury numerous int. competitions; Prof. classes Acad. Mozarteum Salzburg, Sibelius Acad. Helsinki, Acad. of Music Jerusalem, Paris National Conservatory and others in London, Vienna, New York, Los Angeles, Lisbon, Stockholm; Prof. Internat. Acad. di Musica, Como, Italy 1992–; fmr Prof. Moscow Conservatory; Chair. Piano Dept Queen Sofia Higher School of Music, Madrid 1991–, now Titular Prof.; taught at Conservatory of The Hague 2008; Hon. Prof., Schanchaj Conservatorium; Grand Prix M. Long Int. Competition (Paris) 1955, People's Artist of Russia, Hon. R. Schumann Medal (Zwickau, Germany) 1970, Hon. Medal, Univ. Autónoma de Madrid, Hon. Prix Ruhr pianisten festivals. *Music:* more than 30 recordings on various labels, including Melodia, RCD, EMI, Erato and Harmonia Mundi. *Address:* San Antonio 17, Pozaelo, Madrid, Spain (home); Studencheskaja 31, app. 74, Moscow, Russia (home). *Telephone:* (91) 3511060 (office); (95) 2493741 (home). *Fax:* (91) 3570788 (office); (95) 2493741 (home). *Website:* www.escuelasuperiordemusicareinasofia.es (office).

BASHMACHNIKOV, Vladimir Fedorovich, DEcon; Russian politician; b. 27 March 1937; m.; three d.; ed Urals State Univ.; worker, deputy chair. kolkhoz, Sverdlovsk Region 1959–62; teacher, docent, Prof., Urals State Univ. 1962–65; Founder All-Russian Inst. of Labour (now All-Russian Inst. of Econ. and Man. in Agric.) 1964–72, Deputy Dir 1972–84; consultant, Econ. Dept, Cen. Cttee CPSU 1984–89; mem. Cttee on Land Reform Cen. Cttee CPSU 1989–91; active participant in movt for privatization of land; mem. State Duma; mem. faction Our Home Russia; mem. Cttee on Agrarian Problems 1995–; Pres. Asscn of Farmers' and Agric. Co-operatives of Russia 1991–2005; Chair. Union of Land-Owners of Russia 1994; mem. Co-ordination Council, Round Table Business of Russia. *Publications:* over 150 books and articles on org. of labour in agric. *Address:* c/o Association of Farmers' and Agricultural Co-operatives of Russia, 107139 Moscow, Orlikov per 3, Suite 405, Russia (office).

BASHMET, Yuri Abramovich; Russian violist and conductor; *Founder and Artistic Director, Moscow Soloists;* b. 24 Jan. 1953, Rostov-on-Don; m. Natalia Bashmet; one d.; ed Moscow State Conservatory; concerts since 1975; gave recitals and played with maj. orchestras of Europe, America and Asia; played in chamber ensembles with Sviatoslav Richter, Vladimir Spivakov, Victor Tretyakov and others; restored chamber repertoire for viola, commissioned and was first performer of music by contemporary composers, including concertos by Alfred Schnittke, Giya Kancheli, Aleksandr Tchaikovsky; first viola player to give solo recitals at leading concert halls including Tchaikovsky Hall, Moscow, Concertgebouw, Amsterdam, La Scala, Milan, Suntory Hall, Tokyo; Founder and Artistic Dir Chamber Orchestra Soloists of Moscow 1989–; founder, Artistic Dir and conductor, Moscow Soloists 1992–; Artistic Dir and Chief Conductor Young Russian Symphony Orchestra 2002–; f. Yuri Bashmet Int. Competition for Young Viola Players 1994–; Artistic Dir Dec. Nights Festival, Moscow 1998–; Founder and Artistic Dir Elba Music Festival 1998–; f. Yu. Bashmet Viola Competition, Moscow 1999–; f. Int. Foundation to award Shostakovich Prize annually; prize winner of int. competitions in Budapest 1975, Munich 1976; People's Artist of Russia 1986, State Prize of Russia 1993, Sonning Prize (Denmark) 1995, Russian Biographic Soc. Man. of the Year 2000, Olympus Nat. Award 2003. *Address:* International Classical Artists, The Tower Building, 11 York Road, London SE1 7NX, England (office); Briyusov per. 7, Apt. 16, 103009 Moscow, Russia (home). *Telephone:* (20) 7902-0520 (office); (095) 561-66-96 (office); (495) 229-73-25 (home). *Fax:* (20) 7902-0530 (office). *E-mail:* info@icartists.co.uk (office). *Website:* www.icartists.co.uk (office); www.yuribashmet.com.

BASILASHVILI, Oleg Valeriyanovich; Russian actor; b. 26 Sept. 1934, Moscow; m. Galina Mshanskaya; two d.; ed Moscow Art Theatre; debut at Leningrad Theatre of Lenin's Komsomol 1956–59; leading actor, Leningrad (now St Petersburg) Bolshoi Drama Theatre of Tovstonogov 1959–; several leading roles, including Gayev (The Cherry Orchard), Voynitsky (Uncle Vanya), Khlestakov (The Government Inspector); active participant of democratic movt since end of 1980s, People's Deputy of Russia 1990–93; Hon. mem. Russian Acad. of Arts; Order of Friendship 1994, Order Merit to Fatherland Fourth Degree 2004, Order of Radiance (Georgia) 2010; People's Actor of Russia 1977, State Prize of Russia 1978, USSR People's Actor 1984, Laureat Golden Soffit 1997. *Films include:* Alive Corpse 1969, Business Love Affair 1977, Autumn Marathon 1979, Railway Station for Two 1983, The Promised Heaven 1991, The Prophecy 1992, The Ticket in the Red Theatre 1994, Heads and Tails 1995, The Romanovs: An Imperial Family 2000, Poisons or the World History of Poisoning 2001, Idiot (TV) 2003; Dorogaya Masha Berezina 2004, The Master and Margarita (TV) 2005, Sonka – Zolotaya Ruchka (Sonka – Golden Pen) 2006; numerous TV productions. *Address:* Borodinskaya str. 13, Apt 58, 196180 St Petersburg, Russia (home). *Telephone:* 113-55-56 (home).

BASIN, Yefim Vladimirovich, DEcon; Russian engineer, business executive and fmr politician; *CEO, Inzhtransstroi Corporation;* b. 3 Jan. 1940, Khislovichi, Tambov Region; m.; one s. and one d.; ed Belarus Inst. of Transport Eng, Acad. of Nat. Econs; Master, Chief Engineer, Head, Yaroslavl Construction Dept 1962–69; Deputy Man., Chief Engineer, Gortransstroi, Gorky (now Nizhny Novgorod) 1969–72; Head Construction Dept, Pechorstroi 1972–78; First Deputy Head Glavbamstroi 1980–86; USSR Deputy Minister of Transport Construction; Head, Glavbamstroi and Bamtransstroi production cos 1986–90; Deputy, State Duma of RSFSR; mem. Supreme Soviet; Chair. Cttee on Construction, Architecture and Housing 1990–92; Chair. State Cttee on Problems of Architecture and Construction 1992–94; Minister of Construction 1994–97; Chair. State Cttee on Construction Policy 1997–98; First Deputy Head, Complex of Perspective Construction, then Head, Dept of Construction Devt, Moscow Govt May–Oct. 1998; Chair. State Cttee on Construction, Architecture and Housing Policy 1998–99; First Vice-Pres. Inzhtransstroi Corpn 1999, currently CEO; Pres. Nostroi (Nat. Asscn of Builders) 2009–; mem. La Spinetta One Liter Club; Hero of Socialist Labour 1990, Merited Constructor of Russian Fed. 1998, State Prize of Russian Fed. 1998. *Leisure interests:* hunting, tennis, tourism. *Address:* Inzhtransstroi Corporation, 107217 Moscow, Sadovaya-Spasskaya str. 21/1, Russia. *Telephone:* (495) 777-79-04 (office). *Fax:* (495) 777-73-78 (office). *E-mail:* nzm@transstroy.ru (office).

BASINDWAH, Mohammed Salim; Yemeni politician; *Prime Minister;* b. Jan. 1935, Aden; Founder-mem. People's Socialist Party 1962; fmr political adviser to leadership council; Minister of Social Affairs, Labour and Youth 1974, Minister of Devt and Chair. Central Planning Org. 1976, Minister of Information and Culture 1978, Minister of Foreign Affairs (first govt following reunification of N and S Yemen) 1993–94, Minister of Information and political adviser to Pres. Saleh 1994–95, Prime Minister of Yemen 2011–; mem. Shura (consultative council) 1988; fmr mem. Gen. People's Congress; Chair. Nat. Opposition Council. *Address:* Office of the Prime Minister, San'a, Yemen (office).

BASINGER, Kim; American actress; b. 8 Dec. 1953, Athens, Ga; d. of Don Basinger; m. 1st Ron Britton 1980 (divorced 1990); m. 2nd Alec Baldwin (q.v.) 1993 (divorced 2002); one d.; model 1971–76; first TV role 1976; f. Skyfish Productions (film production co.). *Films include:* Hard Country 1981, Mother Lode 1982, Never Say Never Again 1982, The Man Who Loved Women 1983, The Natural 1984, 9½ Weeks 1985, Fool for Love 1985, No Mercy 1986, Batman 1989, The Marrying Man 1990, Too Hot to Handle 1991, Final Analysis 1992, Cool World 1992, The Real McCoy 1993, Getaway 1994, Wayne's World II 1994, Pret-a-Porter 1994, LA Confidential (Acad. Award and Golden Globe for Best Supporting Actress 1998)

1997, Bless the Child 2000, I Dreamed of Africa 2000, People I Know 2002, 8 Mile 2003, Elvis Has Left the Building 2004, Cellular 2004, The Door in the Floor 2004, The Sentinel 2006, Even Money 2006, The Burning Plain 2008, While She Was Out 2008, The Informers 2009, Charlie St. Cloud 2010. *Address:* CAA, 9830 Wilshire Boulevard, Beverly Hills, CA 90212; c/o Judy Hofflund, Hofflund Polone, 9465 Wilshire Boulevard, Suite 820, Beverly Hills, CA 90212; Skyfish Productions, 725 Arizona Avenue, Suite 100, Santa Monica, CA 90401, USA.

BAŠKA, Jaroslav; Slovak politician; *Governor, Trenčín Region;* b. 5 April 1975, Považská Bystrica; m.; three c.; ed Electro-Technical Faculty, Univ. of Žilina; Matador Púchov 1998–2000; Project Man. for information systems 1999–2000; Asst Dir for Econs 2001–02; mem. Parl. (Smer-Sociálna demokracia) 2002–06, 2010–, mem. Perm. Del. to Parl. Ass. of Council of Europe 2002–06; Mayor of Doňiany 2003–06; State Sec., Ministry of Defence 2006–08, Minister of Defence 2008–10; Gov. Trenčín Region 2013–. *Address:* Trenčín Regional Administration, K dolnej stanici 7282/20A, 911 01 Trenčín, Slovakia (office). *Telephone:* (32) 6555-811 (office). *Fax:* (32) 6555-909 (office). *E-mail:* info@tsk.sk (office). *Website:* www.tsk.sk (office).

BASRI, Muhammad Chatib, PhD; Indonesian economist and politician; *Minister of Finance;* b. 22 Aug. 1965, Jakarta; ed Univ. of Indonesia, Australian Nat. Univ.; Chair. Inst. for Econ. and Social Research 2005–09; mem. Advisory Team to Indonesian Nat. Team on Trade Negotiation 2005–12; Deputy Minister of Finance for G-20 2006–09; Special Adviser to Minister of Finance 2006–10; 'Sherpa' to Pres. of Indonesia for G-20 meeting, Washington, DC Nov. 2008; Co-founder and Sr Partner, CReco Research Inst. (econ. consulting firm), Jakarta 2010–12; Vice-Chair. Nat. Econ. Cttee of Pres. of Indonesia 2010–12; Chair. Indonesian Investment Coordinating Bd 2012–; Minister of Finance 2013–; Sr Lecturer, Dept of Econs, Univ. of Indonesia 1992–; ind. mem. IMF Asia Pacific Regional Advisory Group; mem. Davos High Level Trade Experts Group 2010–11; ind. Dir (non-exec.) Axiata Group Bhd 2010–12; fmr mem. Regional Advisory Bd, Toyota Motor Asia Pacific; fmr consultant for World Bank, Asian Development Bank, USAID, AUSAID, OECD and UNCTAD. *Publications:* author of numerous papers in int. journals; contributor to various leading nat. newspapers and magazines. *Address:* Ministry of Finance, Jalan Lapangan Banteng Timur 2–4, Jakarta 10710, Indonesia (office). *Telephone:* (21) 3841067 (office). *Fax:* (21) 3808395 (office). *E-mail:* helpdesk@depkeu.go.id (office). *Website:* www.depkeu.go.id (office); chatibbasri.net.

BASS, Ronald (Ron); American songwriter and screenwriter; b. 26 March 1942, Los Angeles, Calif.; ed Yale Univ., Harvard Law School; began career as entertainment lawyer. *Films include:* screenplays: Code Name: Emerald, Black Widow, Gardens of Stone, Rain Man (Acad. Award for Best Original Screenplay) 1988, Sleeping with the Enemy, The Joy Luck Club, When a Man Loves a Woman 1994, Dangerous Minds 1995, Waiting to Exhale, My Best Friend's Wedding 1997, What Dreams May Come 1998, Stepmom 1998, Entrapment 1999, Snow Falling on Cedars 1999, Passion of Mind 1999, The Lazarus Child (exec. prod.) 2004, Mozart and the Whale 2005, Just Like Heaven 2005, Amelia 2009. *Television includes:* Dangerous Minds (series), Moloney. *Publications include:* novels: The Perfect Thief 1978, Lime's Crisis 1982, The Emerald Illusion 1984. *Address:* c/o Beth Swofford, Creative Artists Agency, 2000 Avenue of the Stars, Los Angeles, CA 90067, USA (office).

BASSET, Lytta, DTheol; Swiss theologian, writer and academic; *Professor and Vice-Dean, Faculty of Theology, University of Neuchâtel;* m.; three c.; ed Univs of Strasbourg and Geneva; missionary work in India, Iran, Djibouti, French Polynesia and USA 1970–; fmr Lecturer in Philosophy and Theology, Faculty of Theology, Univ. of Lausanne; currently Prof. and Vice-Dean, Faculty of Theology, University of Neuchâtel. *Publications include:* Le pardon original 1995, La joie impregnable 1998, Moi, je ne juge personne 1998, Guérir du malheur 1999, Le pouvoir de pardonner 1999, Culpabilité 2000, La fermeture à l'amour 2000, Histoire et Herméneutique 2002, Sainte colère 2002; numerous articles and essays on Protestant theology. *Address:* University of Neuchâtel, Faculty of Theology, Faubourg de l'Hôpital 41, 2000 Neuchâtel, Switzerland (office). *Telephone:* 327181907 (office). *E-mail:* Lytta.Basset@unine.ch (office). *Website:* www2.unine.ch/theol (office).

BASSETT, Angela; American actress; b. 16 Aug. 1958, New York; ed Yale School of Drama. *Theatre includes:* Colored People's Time 1982, Antigone, Black Girl, The Mystery Plays 1984–85, The Painful Adventures of Pericles, Prince of Tyre 1986–87, Joe Turner's Come and Gone 1986–87, Ma Rainey's Black Bottom, King Henry IV (Part I) 1987. *Films include:* F/X 1986, Kindergarten Cop 1990, Boyz 'N the Hood 1991, City of Hope 1991, Critters 4, Innocent Blood 1992, Malcolm X 1992, Passion Fish 1992, What's Love Got to Do with It 1993 (Golden Globe Award Best Actress 1994), Strange Days 1995, Panther 1995, Waiting to Exhale 1995, A Vampire in Brooklyn 1995, Contact 1997, How Stella Got Her Groove Back 1998, Music of the Heart 1999, Supernova 2000, Boesman and Lena 2000, The Score 2001, Sunshine State 2002, Masked and Anonymous 2003, The Lazarus Child 2004, Mr 3000 2004, Akeelah and the Bee 2005, Time Bomb 2006, Meet the Robinsons (voice) 2007, Olympus Has Fallen 2013. *TV films include:* Line of Fire: The Morris Dees Story 1991, The Jacksons: An American Dream 1992, A Century of Women 1994. *Address:* c/o The Gersh Agency, 9465 Wilshire Boulevard, 6th Floor, Beverly Hills, CA 90212, USA (office).

BASSEY, Dame Shirley Veronica, DBE; British popular singer; b. 8 Jan. 1937, Tiger Bay, Cardiff, Wales; d. of Henry Bassey and Eliza Bassey (née Mendi); one d.; m. 1st Kenneth Hume 1961 (divorced 1965; deceased); m. 2nd Sergio Novak 1971 (divorced 1981); one d. (deceased) one adopted s.; sang at Astor Club, London; signed up for Such is Life by impresario Jack Hylton 1955; started making records 1956; appeared in cabaret in New York 1961; Artist for Peace, UNESCO 2000; Int. Amb., Variety Club 2001; Chevalier, Légion d'honneur 2010; numerous awards, including 20 Gold Discs and 14 Silver Discs for sales in UK, Netherlands, France, Sweden and other countries; Best Female Singer (TV Times) 1972, 1973, (Music Week) 1974, Best Female Entertainer (American Guild of Variety Artists) 1976, Britannia Award for Best Female Singer 1977. *Film:* La Passione 1996. *Albums include:* Born to Sing the Blues 1958, And I Love You So 1972, Magic is You 1978, I Am What I Am 1984, Sassy Bassey 1985, New York, New York 1991, Great Shirley Bassey 1999, Thank You For the Years 2003, Get the Party Started 2007, The

Performance 2009. *Singles include:* Banana Boat Song, As I Love You, Kiss Me Honey Honey Kiss Me, As Long As He Needs Me, theme song for film Goldfinger 1964, Diamonds Are Forever 1971. *Address:* 31 Avenue Princesse Grace, 98000 MC, Monaco (office). *E-mail:* burnmycandle@monaco.mc (office). *Website:* www.dameshirleybassey.com.

BASSIL, Gebran, BE, MSc; Lebanese politician; *Minister of Foreign Affairs and Emigrants;* b. 21 June 1970, Batroun; m. Chantale Michel Aoun; three c.; ed American Univ. of Beirut; began career by founding co. that built residential projects and renovated old houses; Minister of Telecommunications 2008–09, of Energy and Water 2011–14, of Foreign Affairs and Emigrants 2014–; mem. Free Patriotic Movt, Lebanese Red Cross, Rotary Club, Lebanon Green. *Address:* Ministry of Foreign Affairs and Emigrants, al-Sultana Bldg, al-Jnah, Sultan Ibrahim, Beirut, Lebanon (office). *Telephone:* (1) 840767 (office). *Fax:* (1) 840924 (office). *E-mail:* director@emigrants.gov.lb (office). *Website:* www.emigrants.gov.lb (office); gebranbassil.com.

BASSIOUNI, Muhammad Abd al-Aziz; Egyptian diplomatist; b. 31 July 1937, Cairo; s. of Abdel Aziz Bassiouny; m. Nagwa Elsabouny; one s. one d.; ed Egyptian Mil. Acad.; served in Egyptian Army 1956–80; mem. teaching staff, Mil. Acad. 1959–66; Mil. Attaché to Syria 1968–76, Liaison Officer between Egyptian and Syrian Commands, War of Oct. 1973; Brig.-Gen. in Egyptian Army 1978; Mil. Attaché to Iran 1978–80; joined Foreign Service 1980; Counsellor, then Minister Plenipotentiary, Embassy, Tel-Aviv 1980, Amb. to Israel 1986–2000; participated in all Egyptian-Israeli talks on normalization of relations and on Taba dispute; twelve mil. decorations from Egyptian Army; High Medal of Honour for Bravery with rank of Kt, Syria; Dr hc (Ben Gurion Univ., Israel) 1995. *Publications:* several articles on Egyptian-Israeli relations, the peace process and the Taba talks. *Leisure interests:* sport, reading. *Address:* c/o Ministry of Foreign Affairs, Corniche en-Nil, Cairo, Egypt (office).

BASSLER, Bonnie Lynn, BS, PhD; American biochemist, molecular biologist and academic; *Squibb Professor in Molecular Biology, Endowed Chair, Princeton University;* b. 1962, Chicago, Ill.; ed Univ. of California, Davis, Johns Hopkins Univ.; raised in Danville, Calif.; Prof., Princeton Univ. 1994–, Squibb Prof. in Molecular Biology, Endowed Chair 2007–, Director, Council on Science and Tech.; mem. NAS 2006, USA Science & Eng Festival's Nifty Fifty (group of the most influential scientists and engineers in USA dedicated to re-invigorating the interest of young people in science and eng); Fellow, American Acad. of Microbiology 2002, AAAS 2004, American Acad. of Arts and Sciences 2007; hon. degree (Swarthmore Coll.) 2010; MacArthur Fellowship 2002, Theobald Smith Soc. Waksman Award 2003, Thomas Edison Patent Award, Medical Technology, New Jersey R and D Council 2004, Inventor of the Year, New York Intellectual Property Lawyers Asscn 2004, Eli Lilly & Co. Research Award, American Soc. for Microbiology 2006, Pres.'s Distinguished Teaching Award, Princeton Univ. 2008, World Cultural Council Award for Scientific Merit 2008, Wiley Prize in Biomedical Sciences 2009, NAS Richard Lounsbery Award 2011, L'Oréal-UNESCO For Women in Science Award (N America) (for discovering the chemical signals and mechanisms bacteria use to communicate and coordinate group behaviours) 2012. *Publications:* numerous papers in professional journals. *Address:* Department of Molecular Biology, Princeton University, 119 Lewis Thomas Laboratory, Washington Road, Princeton, NJ 08544-1014, USA (office). *Telephone:* (609) 258-2857 (office), (609) 258-2864 (Lab.) (office). *Fax:* (609) 258-3980 (office). *E-mail:* bbassler@princeton.edu (office). *Website:* molbio.princeton.edu/faculty/molbio-faculty/31-bassler (office).

BASSOLE, Bazomboué Léandre, MA; Burkinabè diplomatist and UN official; b. 21 Sept. 1946, Koudougou; s. of the late Bassole Baourla and of Kanki Eyombie; m. Louise Ouedraogo 1975; four s. one d.; ed Higher Educ. Centre, Ouagadougou, Univ. of Bordeaux and Int. Inst. for Public Admin., Paris; Counsellor, State Protocol Dept, Legal Affairs and Claims Dept and Int. Co-operation Dept of Ministry of Foreign Affairs 1975–76, Dir for Admin. and Consular Affairs 1976–77; Second Counsellor, later First Counsellor, Upper Volta Embassy, Paris 1977–81; First Counsellor, Perm. Mission of Upper Volta to the UN, New York 1981–82, Chargé d'affaires 1982–83, Perm. Rep. of Upper Volta (now Burkina Faso) to the UN 1983–86; Amb. to USA March–Aug. 1986; Minister of External Affairs and Co-operation 1986–87; Amb. to Canada 1988–91, to Côte d'Ivoire 1991–2001; currently with office of UN Special Rep. for West Africa (UNOWA). *Leisure interests:* classical music, soccer, cycling, swimming, movies. *Address:* United Nations Office for West Africa, Lot 14, Ouest Almadies, Dakar, Sénégal (office). *Telephone:* 33-869-8585 (office). *Fax:* 33-820-4638 (office). *E-mail:* bassolel@un.org (office). *Website:* www.un.org/unowa (office).

BASSOLÉ, Djibril Yipènè; Burkinabé government official and UN official; *Minister of Foreign Affairs and Regional Co-operation;* b. 30 Nov. 1957, Nouna; ed Collège Charles Luanga de Nouna, Prytanée Militaire de Kadiogo, Université de Ouagadougou, Acad. Royale Militaire de Meknès, Ecole Nationale de la Gendarmerie, Abidjan, Côte d'Ivoire, Ecole Supérieure de la Gendarmerie, Maisons Alfort, France; served as Commdt, Gendarmerie Nationale (nat. police force) 1983–95, served in various sr positions including Chef d'Etat-Major (head of police force) 1997–99; Minister-Del. for Security 1999–2000, Minister for Security 2000–07, Minister of Foreign Affairs and Regional Co-operation 2007–08, 2011–; Jt UN-African Union Chief Mediator for Darfur 2008–11; Officier et Commdr de l'Ordre Nat. de Burkina Faso, Médaille d'honneur Militaire, Médaille d'honneur de la Police, Officier de l'Ordre Nat. du Lion (Senegal), Commdr de l'Ordre du Mérite du Niger, Commdr de l'Ordre du Mérite du Gabon, Officier de l'Ordre Nat. du Mérite. *Address:* Ministry of Foreign Affairs and Regional Co-operation, rue 988, blvd du Faso, 03 BP 7038, Ouagadougou 03, Burkina Faso (office). *Telephone:* 50-32-47-34 (office). *Fax:* 50-30-87-92 (office). *E-mail:* webmaster.mae@mae.gov.bf (office). *Website:* www.mae.gov.bf (office).

BASTARRECHE SAGÜES, Carlos, LLB; Spanish diplomatist and academic; *Ambassador to France;* b. 1950, Madrid; m. Rosalía Gómez-Pineda Goizueta; four c.; entered diplomatic corps 1976, served at Embassy in Bucharest 1976–79, Sec., Conf. for Spanish Accession to EU, Perm. Mission of Spain to EU, Brussels 1979–84, Adviser to Sec. of State for EU Affairs, Madrid 1984–85, Asst Dir-Gen. for EU Co-ordination, Secr. of State for EU Affairs 1986–90, Dir-Gen. of Legal and Institutional Co-ordination 1990–91, Asst Perm. Rep. to EU 1991–96, Sec.-Gen. of

Foreign Political and EU Affairs 1996–2000, Sec.-Gen. of European Affairs 2000–02, Amb. and Perm. Rep. to EU 2002–10, Amb. to France 2010–; Prof. of Community Affairs, Escuela Diplomatica. *Address:* Embassy of Spain, 22, avenue Marceau, 75381 Paris Cedex 08, France (office). *Telephone:* 1-44-43-18-00 (office). *Fax:* 1-47-23-59-55 (office); 1-47-20-56-69 (office). *E-mail:* emb.paris@maec.es (office). *Website:* www.maec.es/subwebs/Embajadas/Paris/es/home/Paginas/home_paris.aspx (office).

BASTIAN, Edward H., BBA, CPA; American business executive; *President, Delta Air Lines, Inc.;* b. 1957; m. Anna Bastian; four c.; ed St Bonaventure Univ.; fmr Partner, Price Waterhouse, New York, becoming Strategic Planning Partner; fmr Vice-Pres. Finance and Controller Frito-Lay International, becoming Vice-Pres. of Business Processes Re-engineering, later Vice-Pres. of Finance, PepsiCo International (parent co.); Vice-Pres. of Finance and Controller, Delta Air Lines, Inc. 1998–2000, Sr Vice-Pres. 2000–05, Chief Financial Officer 2005–09, Pres. 2007–, Pres. and CEO NWA (wholly owned subsidiary) 2008–09; Sr Vice-Pres. and Chief Financial Officer Acuity Brands June–July 2005; mem. Int. Bd of Dirs Habitat for Humanity, Woodruff Arts Center, Atlanta. *Address:* Delta Air Lines Inc., PO Box 20706, 1030 Delta Blvd, Atlanta, GA 30320-6001, USA (office). *Telephone:* (404) 715-2600 (office). *Fax:* (404) 715-5042 (office). *E-mail:* info@delta.com (office). *Website:* www.delta.com (office).

BASTOS, Márcio Thomaz de, LLB; Brazilian lawyer and politician; *Chairman, Instituto Innovare;* b. 30 July 1935, Cruzeiro, São Paulo; m. Maria Leonor de Castro Bastos; one s. one d.; ed Univ. of São Paulo; criminal lawyer 1957–, involved in over 700 cases including acting for the prosecution of Chico Mendes, Lindomar Castilho and Pimenta Neves; Minister of Justice 2003–07; Co-founder Action for the Citizenship Movt, Inst. of Defense of the Right of Defense; fmr Pres. Ordem dos Advogados do Brasil (Brazil bar asscn); Chair. Instituto Innovare 2009–. *Address:* Instituto Innovare, rua. Barão de Lucena, no. 20, casa, Botafogo, RJ, 22260-020 Brasília, DF, Brazil (office). *Website:* www.premioinnovare.com.br (office).

BAT-ÜÜL, Erdeniin; Mongolian politician; *Mayor of Ulaanbaatar;* b. 1 July 1957, Ulan Bator; m. B. Delgertuja 1977; two s. one d.; teacher, First Constructing Tech. Training School, Ulan Bator 1981–82, secondary school, Höbsögöl Prov. 1982–85; scientist, Observatory of Acad. of Sciences 1985–89; Founder-mem. Mongolian Democratic Union, mem. Gen. Co-ordinating Council 1989–, Gen. Co-ordinator Political Consultative Centre 1990–; elected Deputy to Great People's Hural 1990, 1996, 2004, 2008; mem. Political Consultative Centre of Mongolian Democratic Party 1992–; mem. Gen. Council and Dir Political Inst. of Mongolian Nat. Democratic Party 1992, Regional Sec. 1993, Gen. Sec. and Presidium of Co-ordinating Council of Mongolian Democratic Union 1993–96; Mayor of Ulaanbaatar 2012–. *Address:* Mongolian National Democratic Party, Ulan Bator (office); Suchbaatar District 1-40,000, 62-1-4 Ulan Bator, Mongolia (home). *Telephone:* 372810 (office); 321105 (home). *Fax:* 372810.

BATALOV, Aleksey Vladimirovich; Russian actor and film director; b. 20 Nov. 1928, Moscow; m. Gitana Azkad'yevna Leonchenko 1963; two d.; ed Moscow Arts Theatre Studio; actor with Cen. Theatre of Soviet Army 1950–53; with Moscow Art Academic Theatre 1953–60; film debut 1954; Dean, Actors Studio, Moscow State Film Inst. VGIK 1975–2005; Order of Lenin; People's Artist of USSR 1976, Hero of Socialist Labour 1989, Lifetime Achievement Nika Award 2002, State Prize of the Russian Fed. 2005. *Films include:* as actor: Zoya 1944, Aleksei Zhurbin in A Large Family 1954, Sasha in The Rumyantsev Case 1956, Boris in The Cranes Are Flying 1957, Gusev in Nine Days in One Year 1962, Pavel Vlasov in Mother 1964, Gurov in The Lady with the Lap-dog 1965, Golubkin in The Flight 1971, Georgi Ivanovich in Moscow Does Not Believe in Tears 1980, Rokovyye Yaytsa 1996; as director: The Overcoat 1960, The Three Fat Men 1966, The Living Corpse 1969, The Flight 1971, The Gambler 1973. *Publication:* Fate and Craftsmanship 1984. *Address:* Serafimovicha 2, Apt. 91, 109072 Moscow, Russia (home). *Telephone:* (495) 238-16-29 (home).

BATALOV, Andrei Yevgenyevich; Russian ballet dancer; b. 22 April 1974, Izhevsk, Udmurt Repub., Russia; ed Vaganova Acad. of Russian Ballet; Prin. Dancer, Maly Theatre of Opera and Ballet 1992–94; joined Mariinsky Theatre 1994, Prin. Dancer 1996–; Prin. Dancer, Danish Royal Theatre of Opera and Ballet (Danish Royal Ballet) 2000–02; Int. Ballet Competition, Nagoya, Japan, First Prize and Gold Medal 1996, Int. Ballet Competition, Budapest, Second Prize and Silver Medal 1996, Int. Ballet Competition, Perm, First Prize and Gold Medal, The Mikhail Baryshnikov Prize 1996, Int. Ballet Competition, Paris, First Prize and Gold Medal 1996, VIII Int. Ballet Competition, Moscow, Grand Prix 1997, Honoured Artist of Russia 2010. *Roles in ballets include:* James (La Sylphide), Blue Bird (Sleeping Beauty), Prince (Nutcracker), Peasants' Pas de Deux (Giselle), Clown (Legend of Love), Bozhok and Solor (La Bayadère), Basil (Don Quixote), Ali (Le Corsaire), Golden Slave (Sheherazada), Lescaut (Manon Lescaut), Ondine (Matteo), The Prodigal Son (Prodigal Son), Pas de Deux (Diana and Acteon). *Address:* Mariinsky Theatre, 1 Teatralnaya Square, St. Petersburg, Russia. *Website:* www.mariinsky.ru.

BATBAYAR, Bat-Erdeniin, BSc; Mongolian scientist, publisher and fmr politician; *General Director, Nepko Publishing Co.;* b. 1955, Arkhangai Prov.; ed Mongolian State Univ., Imperial Coll., Univ. of London, UK; Researcher, Microbiological Research and Production Centre 1981–91; teacher at secondary school, Hentii Prov. 1982–84; scientist, Inst. of Microbiology 1984–; Founding mem. Democratic Socialist Movt; Founding mem. Mongolian Social Democratic Party, Chair. 1990–94 (resgnd); mem. State Great Hural 1996–2000; Minister of Finance 1998–99 (resgnd); Foreign Policy Adviser to Prime Minister 2004–05; Founder and Gen. Dir Nepko Publishing Co. 2006–; mem. Advisory Bd World Growth Mongolia. *Publications include:* Don't Forget. Otherwise, We'll Be Doomed 1989, History of Mongolia (State Award 2009) 1996. *E-mail:* info@nepko.mn (office). *Website:* www.nepko.mn (office).

BATBOLD, Sükhbaataryn; Mongolian business executive and politician; *Chairman, Mongolian People's Party;* b. 1963, Ulan Bator; ed Univ. of Moscow, Russia, Diplomacy Acad. of Moscow, London School of Business, England; Adviser, Ministry of Econ. Foreign Relations 1986–88, Head, Mongol Impex Cooperative (export co.) 1988–92; Dir-Gen., Altai Trading LLC 1992–2000; mem. Parl. 2004–; Vice-Minister of Foreign Affairs 2000–04, Minister of Trade and Industry 2004–06, of External Affairs 2008–09, Prime Minister 2009–12; Chair. Mongolian People's

Party 2010–; fmr Chair. Mongolian Devt Strategy Inst. *Address:* Mongolian People's Party, Independence Palace, Ulan Bator, Mongolia (office). *Telephone:* (77) 444167 (office). *E-mail:* contact@mpp.mn (office). *Website:* www.mpp.mn (office).

BATCHELOR, Paul John; Australian financial services executive; *Partner, DB Capital Partners Ltd;* b. 22 Sept. 1950, Sydney; s. of John Eastley Batchelor and Patricia Fay Batchelor (née Smith); m. Therese Batchelor 1974; three s.; Pnr, Touche Ross & Co. 1981–85; Financial Dir Nat. Mutual Royal Bank 1985–87; Exec. Dir of Operations Westmax 1987–89; Dir Retail Asia Man. 1993–96; Group Chief Financial Officer and Group Exec. Australasia Fiji Colonial Mutual Assurance Soc. Ltd 1995–97; Chief Financial Officer AMP Ltd Group 1997–99, Man. Dir and CEO 1999–2002; fmr CEO Home Credit & Finance Bank, Russia; Prin. Yorkway Partners; currently Pnr, DB Capital Partners Ltd; mem. Bd of Dirs Jardine CMG Life Holdings Ltd 1994–, Colonial Mutual Funds 1993–, Colonial Mutual Funds Man. Ltd 1993–, Colonial Investment Man. Ltd 1993–, Colonial State Bank 1995–, Jacques Martin Pty Ltd 1993–; fmr Chair. Henderson Asset Management PLC, GIO Insurance Ltd; mem. Business Council of Australia, Financial Sector Advisory Council, Investment Advisory Cttee, Australian Olympic Foundation; Fellow, Inst. of Charted Accountants. *Address:* DB Capital Partners Ltd, 701 Hong Kong House, 17–19 Wellington Street, Central, Hong Kong Special Administrative Region, People's Republic of China (office). *Telephone:* (2) 81999252 (office); (2) 8005-0335 (Australia) (office). *E-mail:* paul.batchelor@dbcapital-partners.com (office). *Website:* www.dbcapital-partners.com (office).

BATE, (Andrew) Jonathan, CBE, PhD, FBA, FRSL; British academic; *Professor of Shakespeare and Renaissance Literature, University of Warwick;* b. 26 June 1958, Sevenoaks, Kent, England; s. of Ronald Montagu Bate and Sylvia Helen Bate; m. 1st Hilary Gaskin 1984 (divorced 1995); m. 2nd Paula Jayne Byrne 1996; two s. one d.; ed St Catharine's Coll., Cambridge; Harkness Fellow, Harvard Univ. 1980–81; Research Fellow, St Catharine's Coll., Cambridge 1983–85, Hon. Fellow 2000–; Fellow, Trinity Hall, Cambridge, Lecturer 1985–90; King Alfred Prof. of English Literature, Univ. of Liverpool 1991–2003; Prof. of Shakespeare and Renaissance Literature, Univ. of Warwick 2003–; Research Reader, British Acad. 1994–96; Leverhulme Personal Research Prof. 1999–2004; Gov. Bd RSC, Ed. Shakespeare Edition; Hon. Fellow, St Catharine's Coll., Cambridge; Calvin & Rose Hoffman Prize 1996, NAMI NY Book Award 2003. *Radio:* features and reviews for BBC Radio 3 and Radio 4. *Television:* South Bank Show and other arts programmes. *Publications:* Shakespeare and the English Romantic Imagination 1986, Charles Lamb: Essays of Elia (ed.) 1987, Shakespearean Constitutions: Politics, Theatre, Criticism 1730–1830 1989, Romantic Ecology: Wordsworth and the Environmental Tradition 1991, The Romantics on Shakespeare (ed.) 1992, Shakespeare and Ovid 1993, The Arden Shakespeare: Titus Andronicus (ed.) 1995, Shakespeare: An Illustrated Stage History (ed.) 1996, The Genius of Shakespeare 1997, The Cure for Love (novel) 1998, The Song of the Earth 2000, John Clare: A Biography (Hawthornden Prize 2003, James Tait Black Memorial Prize 2004) 2003, I Am: The Selected Poetry of John Clare (ed.) 2003, Andrew Marvell: Complete Poems (ed.) 2005, William Shakespeare: Complete Works (ed.) 2007, Soul of the Age: The Life, Mind and World of William Shakespeare 2008. *Leisure interests:* gardening, tennis, walking, opera, home. *Address:* c/o Wylie Agency Ltd, 17 Bedford Square, London, WC1B 3JA, England (office); Department of English, Room H513, University of Warwick, Coventry, CV4 7AL, England (office). *E-mail:* j.bate@warwick.ac.uk (office). *Website:* www2.warwick.ac.uk/fac/arts/english (office).

BATE, Jennifer Lucy, OBE, BA, FRCO, FRSA, LRAM, ARCM; British organist; b. 11 Nov. 1944, London; d. of Horace Alfred Bate and Dorothy Marjorie Bate; ed Univ. of Bristol; Shaw Librarian, LSE 1966–69; full-time concert career 1969–; has performed world-wide; has organized several teaching programmes; collaboration with Olivier Messiaen 1975–92; designed portable pipe organ with N.P. Mander Ltd 1984 and a prototype computer organ 1987; gives masterclasses world-wide and lectures on a wide range of musical subjects; mem. Inc. Soc. of Musicians, British Music Soc. (Vice-Pres.), Royal Philharmonic Soc., Royal Soc. of Arts; North London Festival (Vice-Pres.); hon. Italian citizenship for services to music 1996; Hon. DMus (Bristol) 2007; F.J. Read Prize, Royal Coll. of Organists, Young Musician 1972, voted Personnalité de l'Année, France 1989, one of the Women of the Year, UK 1990–97, Grand Prix du Disque (Messiaen), Diapason d'Or, Prix de Répertoire, France, Preis der deutschen Schallplattenkritik, Germany and MRA Award for 18th century series From Stanley to Wesley. *Compositions include:* Toccata on a Theme of Martin Shaw, Introduction and Variations on an Old French Carol, Four Reflections, Homage to 1685: Four Studies, The Spinning Wheel, Lament, An English Canon, Variations on a Gregorian Theme, Suite on 'Veni Creator Spiritus'. *Recordings include:* Complete Works of Messiaen, Complete Works of Franck, An English Choice, Virtuoso French Organ Music, Panufnik: Metasinfonia, Vivaldi Double and Triple Concertos, Jennifer Bate and Friends, Jennifer Bate Plays Vierne, From Stanley to Wesley on period instruments, Reflections: The Organ Music of Jennifer Bate, Samuel Wesley Organ Music, The Wesleys and their Contemporaries, Complete Works of Felix Mendelssohn, Complete Organ Works of Peter Dickinson. *Television:* South Bank Show on Messiaen, La Nativité du Seigneur (Channel 4). *Publications include:* Grove's Dictionary of Music and Musicians, Organist's Review. *Leisure interests:* cooking, theatre, philately, gardening. *Address:* c/o Andrew Roberts, 28 Oakenbrow, Sway, Lymington, Hampshire, SO41 6DY, England (office); 35 Collingwood Avenue, Muswell Hill, London, N10 3EH, England (office). *Telephone:* (1590) 682060 (office); (20) 8883-3811 (office). *E-mail:* andrewlroberts@btinternet.com (office); jenniferbate@classical-artists.com (office). *Fax:* (20) 8444-3695 (office). *Website:* www.classical-artists.com/jbate.

BATEMAN, Barry Richard James, BA; British investment services industry executive; *Vice-Chairman, Fidelity International Investment Advisors (UK) Ltd;* b. 21 June 1945; m. Christine Bateman; one s.; ed Univ. of Exeter; investment analyst, Hoare Govett 1967–72, Research Dir 1972–75; Marketing Dir Datastream 1975–81; Sr Marketing Dir Fidelity Int. Man. Ltd 1981–86, Man. Dir Fidelity Investment Ltd 1986–97, Pres. Fidelity Int. Ltd 1991–2001, Vice-Chair. Fidelity International Investment Advisors (UK) Ltd 2001–; Chair. Unit Trust Asscn 1991–93; mem. Bd of Dirs Colt Group 1996–2007, Chair. (non-exec.) 2003–07; mem. Bd of Dirs Investment Management Asscn; mem. Advisory Bd Univ. of

Exeter. *Address:* Fidelity International Ltd, Oakhill House, 130 Tonbridge Road, Hildenborough, Tonbridge, Kent, TN11 9DZ, England (home). *Telephone:* (1732) 361144 (home). *Fax:* (1732) 777441 (office). *Website:* www.fidelity-international.com (office).

BATEMAN, Robert McLellan, OC, BA, RCA; Canadian artist; b. 24 May 1930, Toronto; s. of Joseph W. Bateman and Anne Bateman (née McLellan); m. 1st Suzanne Bowerman 1960; two s. one d.; m. 2nd Birgit Freybe 1975; two s.; ed Forest Hill Collegiate Inst., Toronto, Univ. of Toronto, Ontario Coll. of Educ.; high school art teacher for 20 years; began full-time painting 1976, numerous museum exhbns since 1969, including the Smithsonian Inst. 1987, Nat. Museum of Wildlife Art, Jackson, Wyo. 1997, Everard Read Gallery, Johannesburg 2000, Retrospective Tours, 2002-03, 2008-09, Gerald Peters Gallery, Santa Fe 2004, Robert Bateman in Russia 2009–10; Hon. Dir Kenya Wildlife Fund, EcoJustice Canada, Hon. Chair. Harmony Foundation, Bateman Foundation, Hon. Fellow, Royal Canadian Geographical Soc., Hon. Life mem. Audubon Soc., Canadian Wildlife Fed., Sierra Club, Fed. of Canadian Artists 1983–, Royal Canadian Acad. of Arts; Order of British Columbia 2001; Hon. DFA, Hon. DLitt, Hon. DSc, Hon. LLD; Queen Elizabeth II Silver Jubilee Medal 1977, Soc. of Animal Artists Award of Excellence 1979, 1980, 1981, 1986, 1990, Master Artist, Leigh Yawkey Woodson Art Museum 1982, Member of Honour Award, World Wildlife Fund 1985, Lescarbot Award, Canadian Govt 1992, Rachel Carson Award 1996, Golden Plate Award, American Acad. of Achievement 1998, One of 20th Century's 100 Champions of Conservation, US Nat. Audubon Soc. 1998, Rungius Medal 2001, Pres.'s Medal, Sir Edmund Hillary Foundation of Canada 2005, Human Rights Defender Award, Amnesty International 2007, Royal Canadian Geographical Soc. Gold Medal 2013 and numerous other awards. *Publications include:* with Ramsay Derry: The Art of Robert Bateman 1981, The World of Robert Bateman 1984; with Rick Archbold: Robert Bateman: An Artist in Nature 1990, Robert Bateman: Natural Worlds 1996, Safari 1998, Thinking Like a Mountain 2000; with Kathryn Dean: Birds 2002; with Ian Coutts: Backyard Birds 2005; with Nancy Kovacs: Birds of Prey 2007, Polar Worlds 2008, Vanishing Habitats 2010, New Works 2010, Hope & Wild Apples 2012. *Address:* PO Box 115, Fulford Harbour, Salt Spring Island, BC V8K 2P2, Canada (office). *E-mail:* rb@gulfislands.com (office). *Website:* www.robertbateman.ca (office); www.batemancentre.ca (office).

BATENIN, Vyacheslav Mikhailovich, DrPhys-MathSc; Russian physicist and academic; *Deputy Director, Joint Institute of High Temperatures (IVTAN), Russian Academy of Sciences;* b. 12 March 1939; m.; one s.; ed Moscow Energy Inst.; Engineer, then Sr Engineer, Jt Inst. of High Temperatures, USSR (now Russian) Acad. of Sciences 1962–, Dir 1986–2006, Deputy Dir 2007–; Ed.-in-Chief High Temperature 1986–2002; Corresp. mem. Russian Acad. of Sciences 1987–. *Publications include:* works on physics of gas explosion and low-temperature plasma, problems of applied superconductivity and magnetic hydrodynamics, unconventional energy sources. *Leisure interests:* tennis, travelling. *Address:* Joint Institute for High Temperatures RAS (IVTAN), 125412 Moscow, Izhorskaya str. 13/19, Russia (office). *Telephone:* (495)485-23-11 (office); (495) 331-32-52 (home). *Fax:* (495) 485-99-22 (office).

BATES, Kathy, BFA; American actress; b. 28 June 1948, Memphis, Tenn.; d. of Langdon Doyle Bates and Bertye Kathleen Talbert; m. Tony Campisi 1991; ed White Station High School, Southern Methodist Univ.; singing waitress Catskill mountains, cashier Museum of Modern Art, Manhattan; Dr hc (Southern Methodist Univ.) 2002; Mary Pickford Award, Int. Press Acad. 2007. *Theatre work includes:* Varieties 1976, Crimes of the Heart 1979 (won Pulitzer Prize 1981), The Art of Dining 1979, Goodbye Fidel 1980, Chocolate Cake 1980, Extremities 1980, The Fifth of July 1981, Come Back to the 5 & Dime Jimmy Dean, Jimmy Dean 1982, 'night, Mother 1983 (Outer Critics Circle Award), Days and Nights Within 1985, Rain of Terror 1985, Deadfall 1985, Curse of the Starving Class 1985, Frankie and Johnny in the Clair de Lune 1987 (Obie Award), The Road to Mecca 1988. *Films include:* Taking Off 1971, Straight Time 1978, Summer Heat 1987, Arthur 2 on the Rocks 1988, High Stakes 1989, Dick Tracy 1990, White Palace 1990, Men Don't Leave 1990, Misery 1990 (Acad. Award for Best Actress 1991, Golden Globe Award from Hollywood Foreign Press Asscn), Prelude to a Kiss 1991, At Play in the Fields of the Lord 1991, The Road to Mecca 1991, Fried Green Tomatoes at the Whistle Stop Café 1991, Used People 1992, A Home of Our Own 1993, North 1994, Curse of the Starving Class 1994, Diabolique 1996, The War at Home 1996, Primary Colors 1998, Swept from the Sea 1998, Titanic 1998, A Civil Action 1999, Dash and Lilly 1999, My Life as a Dog 1999, Bruno 2000, Rat Race 2001, American Outlaws 2001, About Schmidt 2002, Love Liza 2002, Evelyn 2003, The Tulse Luper Suitcases: The Moab Story 2003, The Ingrate 2004, Little Black Book 2004, Around the World in 80 Days 2004, The Bridge of San Luis Rey 2004, Rumor Has It 2005, Charlotte's Web (voice) 2006, Bee Movie (voice) 2007, Fred Claus 2007, Christmas Is Here Again (voice) 2007, P.S., I Love You 2007, The Golden Compass 2007, The Family That Preys 2008, The Day the Earth Stood Still 2008, Revolutionary Road 2008, Chéri 2009, Personal Effects 2009, Valentine's Day 2010, A Little Bit of Heaven 2011, You May Not Kiss the Bride 2011, Midnight in Paris 2011, Cadaver (short) 2012. *TV films include:* Johnny Bull, Uncommon Knowledge, No Place like Home, One for Sorrow—Two for Joy, Signs of Life, Murder Ordained, Straight Time, Hostages, The West Side Waltz 1995, The Late Shift (Golden Globe 1997) 1996, Annie 1999, My Sister's Keeper 2002. *Television includes:* Alice (mini-series) 2009, The Office (series) 2010–11, Harry's Law (series) 2011–12, Two and a Half Men (series) (Emmy Award for Best Guest Actress in a Comedy 2012) 2012. *Address:* c/o The Harry Walker Agency Inc., 355 Lexington Avenue, 21st Floor, New York, NY 10017, USA (office). *Telephone:* (646) 227-4900 (office). *E-mail:* info@harrywalker.com (office). *Website:* www.harrywalker.com (office); www.mskathybates.com.

BATESON, (Paul) Patrick (Gordon), PhD, FRS; British ethologist and academic; *Professor Emeritus of Ethology, University of Cambridge;* b. 31 March 1938, Chinnor Hill, Oxon.; s. of Richard Gordon Bateson and Solvi Helene Berg; m. Dusha Matthews 1963; two d.; ed Westminster School, King's Coll., Univ. of Cambridge; Stanford Medical Centre, Univ. of Calif.; Jr Research Fellow, King's Coll. Cambridge 1964–68, Sr Research Fellow 1968–69, Official Fellow 1969–84, Professorial Fellow 1984–88, Provost 1988–2003, Life Fellow 2003–; Sr Asst in Research Sub-Dept of Animal Behaviour, Univ. of Cambridge 1965–69, Dir 1976–80, Lecturer in Zoology 1969–78, Reader in Sub-Dept of Animal Behaviour

1978–84, Prof. of Ethology 1984–2005, Prof. Emer. 2005–; Visiting Miller Prof., Univ. of California 1986; Niko Tinbergen Lecturer, Asscn for the Study of Animal Behaviour 1989, Pres. 1977–80; Fellow, Inst. for Advanced Study Indiana Univ. 1991; Storer Lecturer, Univ. of California 1992; Pres. Zoological Soc. of London 2004–; mem. Council Museums and Galleries Comm. 1995–2000; Trustee, Inst. for Public Policy Research 1988–95; Biological Sec., Vice-Pres. Royal Soc. 1998–2003; Foreign mem. American Philosophical Soc. 2006–; Rutherford Lecturer, Auckland 2007; Hon. Fellow, Zoological Soc. of London 2002; Dr hc (St Andrews Univ.) 2001; Scientific Medal, Zoological Soc. of London 1976, Asscn for Study of Animal Behaviour Medal 2001. *Publications:* Defended to Death (co-author) 1983, Perspectives in Ethology (ten vols; co-ed.) 1973–93, Growing Points in Ethology (co-ed.) 1976, Mate Choice (co-ed.) 1983, Measuring Behaviour (co-author) 1986, The Domestic Cat: The Biology of its Behaviour (co-ed.) 1988, The Development and Integration of Behaviour (co-ed.) 1991, Behavioural Mechanisms in Evolutionary Perspective (co-author) 1992, Design for a Life: How Behaviour Develops (co-author) 1999, Biologia del comportomento. Il Mondo dei Viventi 2000 (co-ed.), Plasticity, Robustness, Development and Evolution (co-author). *Address:* Sub-Department of Animal Behaviour, Department of Zoology, University of Cambridge, Madingley, Cambridge, CB3 8AA (office); The Old Rectory, Rectory Street, Halesworth, Suffolk, IP19 8BL, England (home). *Telephone:* (1223) 331338 (office); (1954) 210301 (office); (1986) 873182 (home). *Fax:* (1223) 336676 (office). *E-mail:* ppgb@cam.ac.uk (office). *Website:* www.zoo.cam.ac.uk/zoostaff/bateson (office).

BATISTA, Eike Fuhrken; Brazilian entrepreneur and philanthropist; *Chairman and CEO, OGX;* b. 3 Nov. 1956, Governador Valadares, Minas Gerais; s. of Eliezer Batista da Silva, fmr head of mining co. Vale (Companhia Vale do Rio Doce); m. Luma de Oliveira 1991 (divorced 2004); two s.; ed Univ. of Aachen, Germany; childhood in Brazil, lived in Geneva, Switzerland, Düsseldorf, Germany, and Brussels, Belgium with his family during early teens; as a student, sold door-to-door insurance policies to earn own living; moved back to Brazil to begin a gold and trading co. in the Amazon 1980; worked as intermediary between producers in Amazonia and buyers in Brazil and Europe; set up first mechanized alluvial gold plant in Amazonia 1980s; then joined Canadian mining firm TVX Gold Inc., served as Chair., Pres. and CEO, sold stake in co. for $1 billion 2000; reinvested in several businesses, including mining; large portion of wealth made from OGX (oil and gas exploration co.) f. in 2007, currently Chair. and CEO, also CEO EBX, Chair. MMX (mining), MPX (energy); Chair. EBX Investimentos Group, Rio de Janeiro since 1980s; other cos founded include LLX (logistics), OSX, Mr Lam (Chinese restaurant), Porto de Peruíbe 2004–08; ranked 58th by Forbes magazine amongst The World's Most Powerful People 2010. *Achievements include:* completed 220 nautical miles between Santos and Rio de Janeiro in three hours, 1 minute and 47 seconds, and broke record of crossing on machine 'Spirit of Brazil' 2006. *Leisure interests:* running, swimming, speed boats. *Address:* OGX Petróleo e Gás Participações S/A, Do Flamengo 154, 4° E 5° Andar - Parte Rio de Janeiro, Rio de Janeiro 22210-030, Brazil (office). *Telephone:* (21) 25555200 (office). *Fax:* (21) 25555202 (office). *E-mail:* info@ogx.com.br (office). *Website:* www.ogx.com.br (office); www.eikebatista.com.br.

BÁTIZ CAMPBELL, Enrique; Mexican conductor; *Chief Conductor, Symphonic Orchestra of Guanajuato;* b. 4 May 1942, Mexico City, DF; s. of José Luis Bátiz and María Elena Campbell; m. 1st Eva María Zuk 1965 (divorced 1983); one s. one d.; m. 2nd Elena Campbell Lombardo; ed Centro Universitario México, Southern Methodist Univ., Dallas, Tex., USA, Juilliard School, New York, Warsaw Conservatoire, Poland; founder and Prin. Conductor, Orquesta Sinfónica del Estado de México 1971–83, 1990; Artistic Dir, Orquesta Filarmónica de la Ciudad de México 1983–90; Prin. Guest Conductor, Royal Philharmonic Orchestra, London 1984–; Chief Conductor, Symphonic Orchestra of Guanajuato 2005–; Guest Conductor with 130 orchestras; Order of Rio Branco (Brazil) 1986; Distinguished Artist of the Year, Mexican Union of Theatrical and Musical Broadcasters 1971, 1981, 1983, 1996, Mozart Medal, Domecq Cultural Inst. 1991, Sor Juana Ines de la Cruz Award for Arts and Letters 1994, State of Mexico Prize 1995. *Leisure interest:* swimming. *Address:* Cerrada Rancho de los Colorines No. 11, Col Huipulco Tabla del Llano, Código Postal 14380, Zona Postal 22, México, DF, Mexico.

BATKHUYAG, Jamyandorjiin, MA, PhD; Mongolian economist and politician; b. 1964; ed Univ. of Colorado at Denver, USA; fmr Lecturer, Mongolian Nat. Univ. and Higher Polytechnic; fmr Sr Adviser on Econ. Policy to Prime Minister; fmr Learned Sec. and Dir Inst. of Finance and Econs; mem. Great Khural (Parl.) 2004–; Minister of Defence 2007–08; mem. Nat. New Party.

BATLLE IBÁÑEZ, Jorge Luis, LLD; Uruguayan fmr head of state; b. 25 Oct. 1927; m. Mercedes Menafra; one s. one d.; ed Universidad de la República; journalist 1946–76; mem. Parl. (Partido Colorado) 1959–63, 1963–67; blacklisted by mil. Govt, frequently arrested 1973–84; Senator Partido Colorado 1985–90, 1995–99; co-author constitutional reform project 1996; Pres. of Uruguay 2000–05.

BATTEN, Alan Henry, PhD, DSc, FRSC; Canadian (b. British) astronomer; b. 21 Jan. 1933, Whitstable, Kent, England; s. of George Cuthbert Batten and Gladys Batten (née Greenwood); m. 1st Lois Eleanor Dewis 1958 (died 2010); one s. one d.; m. 2nd Erica Frances Dodd 2011; ed Wolverhampton Grammar School, Univs of St Andrews and Manchester; Research Asst, Univ. of Manchester and Jr Tutor, St Anselm Hall of Residence 1958–59; Post-doctoral Fellow, Dominion Astrophysical Observatory, Victoria, BC, Canada 1959–61, staff mem. 1961–91, Sr Research Officer 1976–91, Guest Worker 1991–2011; Visiting Erskine Fellow, Univ. of Canterbury, NZ 1995; Vice-Pres. Astronomical Soc. of Pacific 1966–68; Pres. Canadian Astronomical Soc. 1974–76, Royal Astronomical Soc. of Canada 1977–78 (Hon. Pres. 1994–98), Comm. 30 of Int. Astronomical Union 1976–79, Comm. 42 1982–85; Vice-Pres. Int. Astronomical Union 1985–91; mem. Advisory Council, Centre for Studies in Religion and Society, Univ. of Victoria 1993–2002 (Chair. 1997–2000), 2006–12, mem. Editorial Bd, Journal of Astronomical History and Heritage 1998–, Sessional Lecturer in History 2003–04; mem. Craigdarroch Research Awards Cttee, Univ. of Victoria 2004–06; Queen's Silver Jubilee Medal 1977. *Publications include:* The Determination of Radial Velocities and their Applications (co-ed.) 1967, Extended Atmospheres and Circumstellar Matter in Close Binary Systems (ed.) 1973, Binary and Multiple Systems of Stars 1973, Resolute and Undertaking Characters: The Lives of Wilhelm and Otto Struve 1988, Algols (ed.) 1989, Astronomy for Developing Countries (ed.) 2001, Our

Enigmatic Universe: One Astronomer's Reflections on the Human Condition 2011; nearly 200 scientific papers. *Leisure interest:* campanology. *Address:* 2594 Sinclair Road, Victoria, BC V8N 1B9, Canada.

BATTERSBY, Sir Alan Rushton, Kt, PhD, DSc, ScD, FRS; British chemist and academic; *Professor Emeritus, University of Cambridge;* b. 4 March 1925, Leigh; s. of William Battersby and Hilda Battersby; m. Margaret Ruth Hart 1949 (died 1997); two s.; ed Leigh Grammar School, Univ. of Manchester, St Andrews Univ.; Lecturer in Chem., St Andrews Univ. 1948–53, Univ. of Bristol 1954–62; Prof. of Organic Chem., Univ. of Liverpool 1962–69, Univ. of Cambridge 1969–92, Prof. Emer. 1992–; Baker Lectureship, Cornell Univ. 1984, Robert Robinson Lectureship 1985, Marvel Lectureship, Illinois, USA 1989, Gilman Lectureship, Iowa, USA 1989, Kurt Alder Lectureship, Univ. of Cologne, Germany 1991, Romanes Lectureship, Univ. of Edin. 1993, Univ. Lectureship, Ottawa 1993, William Dauben Lectureship, Univ. of Calif., Berkeley, USA 1994, Alexander Cruickshank Lectureship, Gordon Confs, USA 1994, Linus Pauling Distinguished Lectureship, Ore. State, USA 1996, IAP Lectureship, Columbia, USA 1999; Hon. LLD (St Andrew's) 1977; Hon. DSc (Rockefeller) 1977, (Sheffield) 1986, (Bristol) 1994, (Liverpool) 1996; Corday-Morgan Medal and Prize 1961, Tilden Lectureship and Medal 1963, Hugo Müller Lectureship and Medal 1972, Flintoff Medal 1975, Paul Karrer Medal 1977, Davy Medal 1977, Max Tishler Award and Lectureship (Harvard) 1978, W von Hofmann Award and Lectureship 1979, Medal for Chemistry of Natural Products 1979, Pedlar Lectureship and Medal 1980, Roger Adams Award and Medal, ACS 1983, Davy Medal, Royal Soc. 1984, Havinga Medal 1984, Longstaff Medal 1984, Royal Medal 1984, Antonio Feltrinelli Int. Prize for Chem., Accad. Nazionale dei Lincei, Italy 1986, Varro Tyler Award, Purdue, USA 1987, Medal of Soc. Royale de Chimie, Belgium 1987, Adolf Windaus Medal and Lectureship German Chemical Soc. 1987, Wolf Foundation Chemistry Prize 1989, Arun Guthikonda Award and Lectureship, Columbia Univ., USA 1991, W. von Hofmann Memorial Medal 1992, Tetrahedron Prize 1995, Hans-Herloff Inhoffen Medal and Prize, Germany 1997, Robert A. Welch Award, USA 2000, Copley Medal, Royal Soc. 2000, Robert B. Woodward Career Award, USA 2004. *Publications:* numerous papers in the major chemical journals. *Leisure interests:* trout fishing, camping, hiking, gardening, classical music. *Address:* c/o University Chemical Laboratory, Lensfield Road, Cambridge, CB2 1EW (office); 20 Barrow Road, Cambridge, CB2 2AS, England (home). *Telephone:* (1223) 336400 (office); (1223) 363799 (home). *Fax:* (1223) 336362.

BATTISTON, Giuseppe; Italian actor; b. 22 July 1968, Udine. *Films include:* Italia–Germania 4–3 (Italy–Germany 4–3) 1990, Un'Anima divisa in due (A Soul Split in Two) 1993, Le acrobate (The Acrobat) 1997, Il più lungo giorno 1998, Pane e tulipani (Bread and Tulips) (David di Donatello Award for Best Supporting Actor 2000, Ciak d'Oro for Best Supporting Actor 2000) 2000, Guarda il cielo: Stella, Sonia, Silvia (Watch the Sky: Stella, Sonia, Silvia) 2000, Chiedimi se sono felice (Ask Me If I'm Happy) 2000, La forza del passato (The Power of the Past) 2002, Nemmeno in un sogno 2002, Un aldo qualunque 2002, Agata e la tempesta (Agata and the Storm) 2004, L'Uomo perfetto 2005, La bestia nel cuore (The Beast in the Heart; aka Don't Tell (UK)) 2005, La tigre e la neve (The Tiger and the Snow) 2005, Apnea 2005, Non prendere impegni stasera 2006, Uno su due (One Out of Two) 2006, A casa nostra (Our Country) 2006, La fine del mare 2007, Non pensarci (Don't Think About It) 2007, Giorni e nuvole (Days and Clouds) 2007, La giusta distanza (The Right Distance) 2007, Le pere di Adamo (voice) 2007, Amore, bugie e calcetto 2008, We Can Do That 2008, The Hush 2009, Come Undone 2010, The Passion 2010, Notizie degli scavi 2010, Unlikely Revolutionaries 2010, Make a Fake 2011, Shun Li and the Poet 2011, Bar Sport 2011, The Commander and the Stork 2012. *Television includes:* L'Avvocato (episode La prova del fuoco) 2003, Al di là delle frontiere (mini-series) 2004, Una famiglia in giallo (mini-series) 2005, La notte breve 2006, A Mother's Ray of Hope 2008, The Collegno Amnesiac 2009, Non pensarci, la serie (series) 2009, Tutti pazzi per amore (series) 2010, The Swing Girls 2010.

BATTLE, Kathleen Deanna, MMus; American singer (soprano); b. Portsmouth, OH; d. of Ollie Layne Battle and Grady Battle; ed Coll.-Conservatory of Music, Univ. of Cincinnati; professional debut in Brahms Requiem, Cincinnati May Festival, then Spoleto Festival, Italy 1972; debut with Metropolitan Opera, New York as shepherd in Wagner's Tannhäuser 1977; regular guest with orchestras of New York, Chicago, Boston, Philadelphia, Cleveland, LA, San Francisco, Vienna, Paris and Berlin, at Salzburg, Tanglewood and other festivals and at the major opera houses including Metropolitan, New York, Covent Garden, London, Paris and Vienna; season 1985–86 appearances included Sophie in Der Rosenkavalier and Susanna in Figaro, Metropolitan New York, US premiere parts of Messiaen's St Francis of Assisi with Boston Symphony Orchestra and recitals USA and in Toronto, Paris, Vienna and Florence; season 1986–87 appearances included Zerbinetta in Ariadne auf Naxos and Adina in L'Elisir d'amore, Metropolitan New York and recitals in Japan, London, Salzburg and Vienna; Dr hc (Cincinnati and Westminster Choir Coll., Princeton), Grammy Award 1987, 1988. *Recordings include:* Brahms Requiem and Songs, Mozart Requiem, Don Giovanni, Seraglio and concert arias, Verdi's Un Ballo in Maschera and Berg's Lulu Suite, New Year's Eve Gala, Vienna, Best of Kathleen Battle 2004. *Leisure interests:* gardening, cooking, sewing, piano, dance. *Address:* c/o Columbia Artists Management Inc., 1790 Broadway, New York, NY 10019-1412, USA (office). *Telephone:* (212) 841-9500 (office). *Fax:* (212) 841-9744 (office). *E-mail:* info@cami.com (office). *Website:* www.cami.com (office).

BATTS, Warren Leighton, BS, MBA; American business executive and academic; *Adjunct Professor of Strategic Management, Booth School of Business, University of Chicago;* b. 4 Sept. 1932, Norfolk, Va; s. of John Leighton Batts and Allie Belle Batts (née Johnson); m. Eloise Pitts 1957; one d.; ed Georgia Inst. of Tech., Harvard Business School; with Kendall Co. 1963–64; Exec. Vice-Pres. Fashion Devt Co. 1964–66; Vice-Pres., Douglas Williams Assocs 1966–67; Founder, Triangle Corpn 1967, Pres. and Chief Exec. Officer 1967–71; Vice-Pres. Mead Corpn 1971–73, Pres. 1973–80, CEO 1978–80; Pres. Dart Industries 1980–81, Pres. Dart & Kraft 1981–86; Chair. Premark Int. Inc. 1986–97, CEO 1986–96; Chair., CEO Tupperware Corpn 1996–97; now Adjunct Prof. of Strategic Man., Booth School of Business, Univ. of Chicago; Chair. Cook County Health & Hospital System; Life Trustee Northwestern Univ.; fmr Chair. now Life Dir Children's Memorial Hospital, Chicago; Dir of the Year Award, Nat. Asscn of Corp. Dirs 2006.

Address: Booth School of Business, University of Chicago, 5807 South Woodlawn Avenue, Chicago, IL 60637, USA (office). *Telephone:* (312) 867-0417 (office). *Fax:* (312) 867-0800 (office). *E-mail:* fwbatts@chicagobooth.edu (office). *Website:* www.chicagobooth.edu (office).

BATUMUBWIRA, Antoinette, MA; Burundian corporate communications executive and government official; *Head of External Relations and Communication Unit, African Development Bank Group;* m. Jean-Marie Ngendahayo; two d.; ed Univ. of Bordeaux III, France; emigrated to Finland as refugee 2003; journalist, La voix de la Révolution du Burundi 1979–81; Information Officer, UN Information Center, Bujumbura, Burundi 1981–95; Head of Public Relations and Communications, ICO Global Communications 1997–99; Head of Communications, Office of Resident Coordinator, UN, Comoros 1999–2000; consultant responsible for organization of African Regional Conference on the Information Society, UN, Comoros 2002; Head, Center for Planning, Employment and Economic Development for Southern Finland, Helsinki 2003–04; Minister of External Relations and Int. Co-operation 2005–09; Head of External Relations and Communication Unit, African Development Bank Group 2009–. *Publications:* The Route Towards Integration: The Share of Everyone 2004. *Address:* External Relations and Communication Unit, African Development Bank Group, 15 Avenue du Ghana, PO Box 323-1002, Tunis-Belvedère, Tunisia (office). *E-mail:* afdb@afdb.org (office). *Website:* www.afdb.org (office).

BATURIN, Yuri Mikhailovich, DJur; Russian politician, cosmonaut, lawyer and journalist; *Director, S.I.Vavilov Institute of the History of Science and Technology, Russian Academy of Sciences;* b. 12 June 1949, Moscow; m.; one d.; ed Moscow Inst. of Physics and Tech., All-Union Inst. of Law, Moscow State Univ. School of Journalism, Mil. Acad. of Gen. Staff; worked in research production union Energia 1973–80; Inst. of State and Law USSR (now Russian) Acad. of Sciences 1980–91; Research Scholar, Kennan Inst. for Advanced Russian Studies, The Woodrow Wilson Center, Washington, DC, USA 1991; on staff of Pres. Mikhail Gorbachev Admin 1991; mem. Pres.'s Council 1993, Asst to Pres. on legal problems 1993–94, on Nat. Security Problems 1994–96, mem. Council on Personnel Policy of Pres. 1994–97; Sec., Defence Council of Russian Fed. 1996–97; Asst to Pres., Chair. Cttee for Mil. Ranks and Posts 1995–97; currently Dir S.I.Vavilov Inst. of the History of Science and Technology, Russian Acad. of Sciences; columnist, Novaya Gazeta newspaper 1997–; cosmonaut and test pilot of the Cosmonaut Corps 1998–2009, Deputy Commr 2000–09, participated in space flight to Mir Station Aug. 1998, second space flight to Int. Space Station 2001; Prof. of Computer Law, Moscow Inst. of Eng and Physics; Prof., Moscow Inst. of Physics and Tech.; Prof., School of Journalism, Moscow Univ., Pres. of the School, Media Law and Policy Center; Chair. Center for Anti-Corruption Research and Initiative Transparency Int. 2000–; Union of Journalists Prize 1990, Award for Outstanding Contribution to Mass-Media Law 1997, Themis Award 1998. *Films:* documentaries: Tuch-and-go in Space 1997, Ladder to Heaven 2000. *Publications:* drafts of the laws on the freedom of the press of the USSR 1989 and of Russia 1991, Problems of Computer Law 1991. *Address:* Institute for the History of Science and Technology, Moscow 103012, Staropansky 1/5, Russia (office). *Telephone:* (495) 988-22-80 (office). *Website:* www.ihst.ru (office).

BAUCHARD, Denis M(ichel) B(ertrand), MA; French diplomatist; *Senior Fellow, Institut français des relations internationales;* b. 20 Sept. 1936, Paris; s. of Charles Bauchard and Marguerite Duhamel; m. Geneviève Lanoë 1961; two s. two d.; ed Sciences Po, Paris, Ecole nat. d'admin; Civil Admin., Ministry of Finance 1964–66, 1968–74; Financial Attaché, Near and Middle East, Embassy in Beirut 1966–68; Asst to Minister 1974–76; Financial Counsellor, Perm. Mission to UN, New York 1977–81, Deputy Asst Sec., Ministry of Foreign Affairs 1981–85, Asst Sec. 1986–89, Amb. to Jordan 1989–93, Asst Sec., Ministry of Foreign Affairs (N Africa and Middle East) 1993–96, Chief of Staff to Minister of Foreign Affairs 1996–97, Amb. to Canada 1998–2001; Pres. Institut du Monde Arabe 2002–04; Consultant and Sr Fellow, Institut français de relations internationales 2004–; Officier, Légion d'honneur, Ordre nat. du Mérite. *Publications:* Le jeu mondial des pétroliers 1970, Economie financière des collectivités locales 1972, La démocratie est-elle soluble dans l'islam? 2007, Le nouveau monde arabe 2012; many articles and policy papers on the Middle East. *Address:* Institut français des relations internationales, 27 rue de la Procession, 75015 Paris (office); 91 rue de Rennes, 75006 Paris, France (home). *Telephone:* 1-40-61-60-00 (office); 1-45-44-18-05 (home); 6-19-35-44-46 (home). *E-mail:* bauchard@ifri.org (office); denis.bauchard@wanadoo.fr (home). *Website:* www.ifri.org (office).

BAUCHEREL, Jean-Luc; French farmer and insurance industry executive; *Chairman, Groupama SA;* joined Groupama SA 1975, Dir Morbihan Mutual 1975–78, mem. Exec. Bd 1978–, mem. Bd of Dirs Groupama Bretagne 1992–, Vice-Chair. 1996–2000, Chair. 2000–05, Chair. Groupama Loire-Bretagne 2002–, Chair. Fédération Nationale Groupama and Groupama SA 2004–, also Dir Groupama Holding, mem. Supervisory Bd Groupama SA –2003 (Vice-Chair. –2003, Vice-Chair. Bd –2004), Supervisory Bd Groupama Assurances et Services –2003, Bd of Dirs Groupama Plus Ultra –2004, Supervisory Bd Groupama International –2003 (Dir –2006), Supervisory Bd Groupama Banque –2005; Chair. Supervisory Bd Groupama Vie –2003, Chair. Bd of Dirs –2004; Chair. Supervisory Bd Gan Prévoyance –2003; mem. Supervisory Bd Gan Assurances Vie –2003; Dir, Gan Patrimoine –2004, Minster Insurance Co. Ltd –2004. *Address:* Groupama SA, 8–10 rue d'Astorg, 75383 Paris Cedex 08, France (office). *Telephone:* 1-44-56-77-77 (office). *E-mail:* relations.exterieures@groupama.com (office). *Website:* www.groupama.com (office); www.groupama.fr (office).

BAUCUS, Max S., LLB; American lawyer, politician and diplomatist; *Ambassador to China;* b. 11 Dec. 1941, Helena, Mont.; m. 1st Ann Geraciomo (divorced 1982); one s.; m. 2nd Wanda Minge 1983; ed Helena High School, Stanford Univ. and Stanford Law School; staff attorney, Civil Aeronautics Bd, Washington, DC 1967–69; legal staff, SEC, Washington, DC 1969–71, Legal Asst to SEC Chair. 1970–71; in pvt. law practice in Missoula, Mont. 1971; Attorney, George and Baucus (law firm) 1971; Acting Exec. Dir Mont. Constitutional Convention; elected to Montana State Legislature 1972; served two terms for Mont. Western Dist in US House of Reps, Washington, DC, mem. House Appropriations Cttee and Deputy Whip; Senator from Montana 1979–2014, Chair. Senate Int. Trade Sub-cttee of Finance, Senate Environment and Public Works Cttee, Senate Agric. and Intelligence Cttee, Finance Cttee 2001; Amb. to People's

Repub. of China 2014–. *Leisure interests:* hunting, fishing, hiking. *Address:* US Embassy, 55 An Jia Lou Lu, Beijing 100600, People's Republic of China (office). *Telephone:* (10) 85313000 (office). *Fax:* (10) 85314200 (office). *E-mail:* beijingwebmaster@state.gov (office). *Website:* beijing.usembassy-china.org.cn (office).

BAUDIN, Ronald; Haitian politician; fmr Pres. CMO-HOPE (trade comm.); Sec. Gen. Office of the Prime Minister –2009; fmr Dir Gen. Ministry of the Economy and Finance, Minister of Economy and Finance 2009–11. *Address:* c/o Ministry of the Economy and Finance, Palais des Ministères, rue Monseigneur Guilloux, Port-au-Prince, Haiti (office).

BAUDO, Serge; French conductor; b. 16 July 1927, Marseille; s. of Etienne Baudo and Geneviève Tortelier; m. Madeleine Reties 1947; one s. one d.; ed Conservatoire nat. supérieur de musique, Paris; Music Dir Radio Nice 1957–59; Conductor, Paris Opera Orchestra 1962–66; titular Conductor and Orchestral Dir a.i. Orchestre de Paris 1968–70; Music Dir Opéra de Lyon 1969–71, Orchestre Nat. de Lyon 1971–87; Prin. Conductor, Orchestra della Svizzera Italiana 1997–2000; Prin. Conductor, Orchestre Symphonique de Prague 2001–06; has conducted many of world's leading orchestras; Founder, Berlioz Festival, Lyon 1979–89; Officier Légion d'honneur, Ordre des Arts et Lettres, Chevalier Ordre nat. du Mérite; numerous prix du disque and other awards. *Films:* music for Le Monde sans Soleil 1964. *Address:* Les Hauts du Ferra, 2901 Chemin Charré, 13600 Ceyreste, France (home).

BAUDOUIN, Jean-Louis, BA, BCL, PhD; Canadian lawyer, professor of law and fmr judge; *Partner, Fasken Martineau DuMoulin LLP;* b. 8 Aug. 1938, Boulogne, France; s. of Louis Baudouin and Marguerite Guerin; m. Christianne Dubreuil; four d.; ed Univ. of Paris, McGill Univ., Montreal; admitted to Bar of Québec 1959; Prof. of Law, Univ. of Montreal 1962–89, Assoc. Prof. of Law 1989–; Commr, Law Reform Comm. of Canada 1976–78, Vice-Chair. 1978–80; Judge, Court of Appeal, Québec 1989–2009; currently Partner, Fasken Martineau DuMoulin LLP (law firm), Montreal; Ed. Civil Law Quarterly Review 1968–89, Supreme Court Law Review 1982–89, Canadian Bar Review 1983–89; Pres. Asscn Henri Capitant (Québec chapter) 1973–; Pres. Asscn of Law Teachers of Quebec 1974–75; mem. RSC 1979; Dr hc (Sherbrooke) 1990, (Paris) 1994, (Namur) 1998, (Ottawa) 2001, (McGill) 2007, (Université de Lyon III) 2009; Henri Capitant Medal 1973, 1986, 2004, Médaille du Bureau de Québec 1988, Award of Excellence, Quebec Bar 1988, Yves Pélicier Award, Int. Acad. of Law and Mental Health 2001, Canadian Bar Asscn Ramon John Hnatyshyn Award 2004. *Publications include:* Les Obligations 1970–2004, La Responsabilité Civile 1973–2013, Le Secret Professionnel 1964, Produire l'Homme: de quel Droit? 1987, Ethique de la Mort, Droit à la Mort 1992. *Leisure interests:* skiing, fishing, wine-tasting. *Address:* Fasken Martineau DuMoulin LLP, The Stock Exchange Tower, PO Box 242, Suite 3700, 800 Victoria Square, Montreal, PQ H4Z 1E9 (office); 875 Antonine Maillet, Montreal, PQ H2V 2Y6, Canada (home). *Telephone:* (514) 270-1884 (home); (514) 397-5299 (office). *Fax:* (514) 397-7600 (office). *E-mail:* jbaudouin@fasken.com (office). *Website:* www.fasken.com (office).

BAUGH, Kenneth Leigh O'Neill, MD; Jamaican politician and physician; b. Montego Bay, St James; m. Vilma Baugh; two s. one d.; ed Univ. of West Indies, Royal Coll. of Surgeons; MP for NW St James 1980–89, currently for St Catherine West Central; fmr Deputy Leader of the Opposition; fmr Minister of Health; Shadow Minister for Health and Environment –2007; Deputy Prime Minister and Minister of Foreign Affairs and Foreign Trade 2007–12; mem. Jamaica Labour Party (currently Chair.). *Leisure interests:* art, drawing, swimming. *Address:* c/o Office of the Deputy Prime Minister, 1 Devon Road, Kingston 10, Jamaica.

BAULCOMBE, Sir David Charles, Kt, BSc, PhD, FRS, FMedSci; British botanist and academic; *Regius Professor of Botany, Royal Society Research Professor and Head of Department of Plant Sciences, University of Cambridge;* m.; four c.; ed Univs of Leeds and Edinburgh; Post-doctoral Fellow, McGill Univ., Montreal, Canada 1977–78, Univ. of Georgia, Athens, USA 1978–80; Higher Scientific Officer, Plant Breeding Inst., Cambridge 1980–86, Prin. Scientific Officer 1986–88; joined The Sainsbury Lab., Norwich 1988, Sr Research Scientist and Head of Lab. 1990–93, 1999–2003; Prof., Univ. of East Anglia 2002–07; Regius Prof. of Botany, Royal Soc. Research Prof. and Head of Dept of Plant Sciences, Univ. of Cambridge 2007–, Fellow, Trinity Coll., Cambridge 2009; mem. Editorial Bd The Plant Journal 1991–, Virology 1996–, Physiological and Molecular Plant Pathology 1999–, EMBO Reports 1999–, EMBO Journal (also Sr Adviser) 2005–, Genome Biology 2005–; mem. Scientific Advisory Bd, Nat. Inst. for Biological Sciences, Beijing 2006–09, Nat. Inst. of Chemical Physics and Biophysics, Tallinn, Science Foundation Ireland 2004–07; Panel mem. Health and Safety Exec. Scientific Advisory Cttee on Genetic Modification (Contained Use) 2004–07; Pres. Int. Soc. of Plant Molecular Biology 2003–04; mem. European Molecular Biology Org. 1997, Academia Europaea 2002; Foreign Assoc. mem. NAS 2005; Hon. Prof., Univ. of East Anglia 1998–2002; Dr hc (Wageningen Univ.) 2008; numerous awards including Prix des Cerealiers de France for work on hormonally regulated genes of cereals 1990, Kumho Science Int. Award in Plant Molecular Biology and Biotechnology, Kumho Cultural Foundation (S Korea) 2002, Ruth Allen Award, American Phytopathology Soc. 2002, Wiley Prize in Biomedical Science, Wiley Foundation, Rockefeller Univ. (co-recipient) 2003, M.W. Beijerinck Virology Prize, Royal Netherlands Acad. of Arts and Sciences 2004, Royal Medal, Royal Soc. 2006, Benjamin Franklin Medal in Life Science (co-recipient) 2008, Albert Lasker Basic Medical Research Award (co-recipient) 2008, Harvey Prize in Science and Tech. 2009, Wolf Prize in Agric. 2010. *Publications:* numerous scientific papers in professional journals. *Leisure interests:* music, sailing, hill walking. *Address:* Department of Plant Sciences, University of Cambridge, Downing Street, Cambridge, CB2 3EA, England (office). *Telephone:* (1223) 339386 (office). *Fax:* (1223) 333953 (office). *E-mail:* david.baulcombe@plantsci.cam.ac.uk (office). *Website:* www.plantsci.cam.ac.uk/directory/baulcombe-david (office).

BAULIEU, Etienne-Emile, DenM, DèsSc; French physician, biochemist and academic; *Chairman, Institut Professor Baulieu;* b. 12 Dec. 1926, Strasbourg; s. of Léon Blum and Thérèse Lion; m. Yolande Compagnon 1947; one s. two d.; ed Lycée Pasteur, Neuilly-sur-Seine, Faculté de Médecine and Faculté des Sciences, Paris; Intern, Paris Hosps. 1951–55; Chef de Clinique, Faculté de Médecine, Paris 1955–57, Assoc. Prof. of Biochemistry 1958; Visiting Scientist, Dept of Obstetrics,

Gynaecology and Biochemistry, Columbia Univ. New York 1961–62; Dir Research Inst. 33, Hormones Lab., Inst. Nat. de la Santé et de la Recherche Médicale (INSERM) 1963–97; Prof. of Biochemistry, Faculté de Médecine de Bicêtre, Univ. Paris-Sud 1970; Prof. at Collège de France 1993, a chair. 1994, now Hon. Prof.; Consultant, Roussel Uclaf; Founder and Chair. Institut Prof. Baulieu 2008–; mem. Editorial Bds several French and int. journals; mem. and Past Pres. INSERM, Fondation pour la Recherche Médicale Française; Pres. Société Française d'Endocrinologie 1975; Vice-Pres. Acad. of Sciences 2000–02, Pres. 2003–; mem. Organizing Cttee Karolinska Symposia on Reproductive Endocrinology, NCI-INSERM Cancer and Hormones Programme (Past French Scientific Chair.), fmr mem. Scientific Advisory Bd WHO Special Programme in Human Reproduction; mem. Endocrine Soc., USA 1966–, Royal Soc. of Medicine, London 1972–, Inst. de France (Acad. des Sciences) 1982– (Vice-Pres. 2000–02, Pres. 2003–04), New York Acad. of Sciences 1985–; Foreign Assoc. mem. NAS 1990–; mem. Nat. Consultative Ethics Cttee for Life Sciences and Health 1996–; mem. Expert Advisory Panel, Int. Fed. of Gynaecology and Obstetrics (FIGO) 1997–; Mem. Emer. Academia Europaea 1997–; developed RU486 abortion pill and anti-aging pill from human hormone, DeHydroEpiAndrosterone (more commonly known as DHEA); Hon. mem. American Physiological Soc. 1993, Acad. Nationale de Médecine 2002; Chevalier Ordre nat. du Mérite 1967; Officier Ordre du Mérite du Gabon 1979; Commdr Légion d'honneur 1990, Grand Officier de la Légion d'honneur 2003; Dr hc (Ghent) 1991, (Tufts) 1991, (Karolinska Inst.) 1994, (Worcs. Foundation, Shrewsbury) 1994; Reichstein Award, Int. Soc. of Endocrinology 1972, Grand Prix Scientifique 1989 de la Ville de Paris 1974, First European Medallist of Soc. of Endocrinology (GB) 1985, Albert & Mary Lasker Clinical Research Award 1989, American Acad. of Achievement Golden Plate Award 1990, Premio Minerva, Rome 1990, Christopher Columbus Discovery Award in Biomedical Research (Genoa and NIH) 1992, Nat. Award, American Asscn for Clinical Chem. 1992, Grand Prix Scientifique, Fondation pour la Recherche Médicale, Paris 1994, Ken Myer Medal (Australia) 2000, Int. Acad. of Humanism Laureat 2002, Charles H. Sawyer Distinguished Lecture 2003 and numerous other prizes and awards. *Publications:* The Antiprogestin Steroid Ru 486 and Human Fertility Control 1985, Génération pilule 1989, Hormones 1990, The Abortion Pill: Ru-486: A Woman's Choice 1991, Contraception: Constraint or Freedom?; numerous specialist papers. *Address:* Institute Professor Baulieu, Pincus Building, 80 rue du Général Leclerc, Le Kremlin Bicêtre, 94276 Paris Cedex, France (office). *Website:* www.institut-baulieu.org (office).

BAUM, Bernard René, MSc, PhD, FRSC; Canadian agricultural research scientist; *Principal Research Scientist, Eastern Cereal and Oilseed Research Centre, Agriculture and Agri-Food Canada;* b. 14 Feb. 1937, Paris, France; s. of Kurt Baum and Marta Berl; m. Danielle Habib 1961; one d.; ed Hebrew Univ., Jerusalem; Research Scientist, Plant Research Inst., Dept of Agric., Ottawa, Canada 1966–74; Sr Research Scientist, Biosystematics Research Inst., Agriculture and Agri-Food Canada, Ottawa 1974–80, Prin. Research Scientist, Biosystematics Research Centre 1980–90, Prin. Research Scientist, Centre for Land and Biological Resources Research 1990–95, Eastern Cereal and Oilseed Research Centre 1996–; Section Chief, Cultivated Crops Section 1973–77, Section Head, Vascular Plants Section 1982–87, Acting Dir, Geostrategy Div., Devt Policy Directorate 1981–82; mem. Acad. of Sciences (RSC) 1981, Botanical Soc. of America, Soc. Botanique de France, Int. Asscn for Plant Taxonomy and other socs; Founder-mem. Hennig Soc.; George Lawson Medal, Canadian Botanical Asscn 1979. *Publications:* Material of an International Oat Register 1973, Oats: Wild and Cultivated. A Monograph of the Genus Avena 1977, The Genus Tamarix 1978, Barley Register 1985, Triticale Register; more than 330 scientific publs. *Leisure interests:* swimming long distance, running 10k, pilates, classical music. *Address:* Eastern Cereal and Oilseed Research Centre, Agriculture Canada, Central Experimental Farm, 960 Carling Avenue, Ottawa, ON K1A 0C6, Canada (office). *Telephone:* (613) 759-1821 (office). *Fax:* (613) 759-1701 (office). *E-mail:* bernard.baum@agr.gc.ca (office); baumbd@sympatico.ca (home). *Website:* www.agr.gc.ca (office).

BAUM, HE Cardinal William Wakefield, STD, STL; American ecclesiastic; b. 21 Nov. 1926, Dallas, Tex.; s. of Harold E. White and Mary Leona White (née Hayes), step-father Jerome B. Baum; ed Kenrick Seminary, St Louis and Univ. of St Thomas Aquinas, Italy; ordained to priesthood 1951; Assoc. Pastor, St Aloysius, St Therese's and St Peter's parishes, Kan. City, Mo. 1951–56; Instructor and Prof., Avila Coll., Kan. City 1954–56; 1958–63; Admin. St Cyril's Parish, Sugar Creek, Mo. 1960–61; Hon. Chaplain of His Holiness the Pope 1961; Peritus (Expert Adviser), Second Vatican Council 1962–65; First Exec. Dir Bishops' Comm. for Ecumenical and Interreligious Affairs, Washington, DC 1964–67, Chair. 1972; mem. Jt Working Group of Reps of Catholic Church and World Council of Churches 1965–69; mem. Mixed Comm. of Reps of Catholic Church and Lutheran World Fed. 1965–66; Chancellor, Diocese of Kan. City, St Joseph 1967–70; Hon. Prelate of His Holiness the Pope 1968; Pastor, St James Parish, Kan. City 1968–70; Bishop, Diocese of Springfield-Cape Girardeau 1970–73; mem. Synod of Bishops 1971; Archbishop of Washington 1973–80; Chancellor of the Catholic Univ. 1973–80; cr. Cardinal 1976; Prefect, Sacred Congregation for Catholic Educ. 1980–91; Major Penitentiary of Apostolic Penitentiary, Roman Curia 1990–2001 retd), Major Penitentiary Emer. of Apostolic Penitentiary 2001–; Perm. Observer-Consultant for Vatican Secr. for Promoting Christian Unity; Chair. USCC-NCCB Doctrine Cttee, Cttee for Pastoral Research and Practices; mem. Secr. for Non-Christians; Hon. DD (Muhlenberg Coll., Allentown, Pa 1967, Georgetown Univ., Wash., St John's Univ., Brooklyn, NY). *Publications:* The Teaching of HE Cardinal Cajetan on the Sacrifice of the Mass 1958, Considerations Toward the Theology on the Presbyterate 1961. *Leisure interests:* reading, music. *Address:* c/o Apostolic Penitentiary, Palazzo della Cancelleria 1, 00186 Rome, Italy. *Telephone:* (06) 69887526. *Fax:* (06) 69887557.

BAUMAN, Robert Patten, BA, MBA; American business executive; b. 27 March 1931, Cleveland, Ohio; s. of John Nevan Bauman, Jr and Lucille Miller Patten; m. Patricia Hughes Jones 1961; one s. one d.; ed Ohio Wesleyan Univ., Harvard Business School; fmr officer in USAF; joined Gen. Foods Corpn 1958, Corp. Vice-Pres. 1968, Group Vice-Pres. 1970, Exec. Vice-Pres. and Corp. Dir 1972–81; Dir Avco Corpn 1980, Chair. and CEO 1981–85; Vice-Chair. and Dir Textron Inc. 1985–86; Chair. and Chief Exec. Beecham Group 1986–89, CEO SmithKline Beecham 1989–94; Chair. British Aerospace PLC 1994–98, BTR PLC, London

1998–99; mem. Bd of Dirs Russell Reynolds Assocs, Bolero International Ltd; fmr mem. Bd of Dirs BTR plc, CIGNA Corpn, Hathaway Holdings, Inc., Morgan Stanley Dean Witter, Union Pacific Corpn, Cap Cities/ABC Inc., Bolero.net, Reuters; Trustee, Ohio Wesleyan Univ.; Hon. Fellow, London Business School. *Publication:* Plants as Pets 1982, From Promise to Performance 1997. *Leisure interests:* growing orchids, paddle tennis, jogging, tennis, photography, golf, sailing. *Address:* c/o Board of Directors, Russell Reynolds Associates, 200 Park Avenue, Suite 2300, New York, NY 10166-0002, USA (office).

BAUMAN, Zygmunt, MA, PhD; British academic and writer; *Professor Emeritus of Sociology, University of Leeds;* b. 19 Nov. 1925, Poznań, Poland; s. of Maurycy Bauman and Zofia Bauman (née Cohn); m. Janina Bauman (née Lewinson) 1948 (died 2009); three d.; ed Univ. of Warsaw; held Chair of Gen. Sociology, Univ. of Warsaw 1964–68, Prof. Emer. 1968–; Prof. of Sociology, Tel-Aviv Univ., Israel 1968–71; Prof. of Sociology, Univ. of Leeds 1971–91, Prof. Emer. 1991–; mem. British Sociological Asscn, Polish Sociological Asscn; Krzyż Walecznych (Poland) 1945; Dr hc (Oslo) 1997, (Lapland) 1999, (Uppsala) 2000, (Prague) 2001, (Copenhagen) 2001, (Sofia) 2001, (West of England) 2002, (London) 2003, (Leeds) 2004, (Gotenburg) 2005, (Leeds, Metropolitan) 2007, (Kaunas) 2008, (New School, New York) 2008, (Aberdeen) 2009, (Copenhagen Business School) 2009; Amalfi Prize for Sociology and Social Sciences 1989, Theodor W. Adorno Prize 1998, Príncipe de Asturias Prize (jtly) 2010. *Publications:* Culture as Praxis 1972, Hermeneutics and Social Science 1977, Memories of Class 1982, Legislators and Interpreters 1987, Modernity and the Holocaust 1989, Modernity and Ambivalence 1990, Intimations of Postmodernity 1991, Thinking Sociologically 1991, Mortality, Immortality and Other Life Strategies 1992, Postmodern Ethics 1993, Life in Fragments 1995, Postmodernity and Its Discontents 1996, Globalization: The Human Consequences 1998, Work, Consumerism and the New Poor 1998, In Search of Politics 1999, Liquid Modernity 2000, Individualized Society 2000, Community: Seeking Safety in an Uncertain World 2001, Society Under Siege 2002, Liquid Love: On the Frailty of Human Bonds 2003, Wasted Lives: Modernity and its Outcasts 2003, Europe: An Unfinished Adventure 2004, Liquid Life 2005, Liquid – Modern Fears 2006, Has Ethics a Chance in a Society of Consumers? 2008, The Art of Life 2008, Living on Borrowed Time 2009, 44 Letters from the Liquid Modern World 2010, Collateral Damage: Social Inequalities in a Global Age 2011, Culture in a Liquid Modern World 2011, This is Not a Diary 2012; contrib. to scholarly journals and general periodicals. *Leisure interest:* photography. *Address:* 1 Lawnswood Gardens, Leeds, LS16 6HF, England. *E-mail:* janzygbau@aol.com. *Website:* baumaninstitute.leeds.ac.uk.

BAUMANN, Herbert Karl Wilhelm; German composer and conductor; b. 31 July 1925, Berlin; s. of Wilhelm Baumann and Elfriede Baumann (née Bade); m. Marianne Brose 1951; two s.; ed Berlin Classical High School, Schillergymnasium and Int. Music Inst.; Conductor, Tchaikovsky Symphony Orchestra 1947; Composer and Conductor, Deutsches Theater, Berlin 1947–53, Staatliche Berliner Bühnen: Schillertheater and Schloss-parktheater 1953–70, Bayerisches Staatsschauspiel: Residenztheater, Munich 1971–79; freelance composer 1979–; mem. GEMA for 50 years; Mem. of Honour, BDZ 1990; Bundesverdienstkreuz 1998; Diploma of Honour Salsomaggiore (Italy) 1981; Silbernes Ehrenzeichen GDBA 1979. *Works include:* stage music for more than 500 plays, 40 TV plays and the ballets Alice in Wonderland and Rumpelstiltskin, music for radio, cinema and television, orchestral, chamber and choir works, several suites for plucked instruments, music for strings, music for wind instruments, three concertos and works for organ. *Films include:* Das Jahrhundert des Kindes, Die Stadt von Morgen, Menschen in der Stadt, König Fußball, Timpi Tox und Ali Bum, Berlin Sketchbook. *Leisure interests:* reading, especially books on fine arts. *Address:* Weitlstrasse 66, Apt 2049, 80935 Munich, Germany (home). *Telephone:* (89) 38582049 (home). *Fax:* (89) 38582049 (home). *E-mail:* hkwbau@augustinum.net (home). *Website:* www.komponisten.net/baumann.

BAUMANN, Karl-Hermann, Dipl.-Kfm, Dr.rer.oec; German business executive; b. 22 July 1935, Dortmund; Asst, Dept of Business Admin, Univ. of Saarland, Saarbrücken 1964–70; joined Siemens AG 1970, various positions in Corp. Finance Div. 1970–78, Sr Vice-Pres. Siemens Capital Corpn, NY and Siemens Corpn, Iselin, NJ, USA 1978–83, Head of Corp. Financial Accounting Div., Munich 1983–84, Vice-Pres. Siemens AG 1984–88, apptd to Bd of Man. 1987, apptd mem. Exec. Cttee 1988, Head of Corp. Finance 1988–98, Chair. Supervisory Bd Siemens AG 1998–2005; mem. Supervisory Bds Allianz AG 1998–2001, Bayer Schering Pharma AG (fmrly Schering AG) 1994–2009, Deutsche Bank AG 1998–2005, E.ON AG 1998–2008, Linde AG 1998–2008, MG Technologies AG 1998–2003, Thyssen Krupp AG 1998–2005.

BAUMEISTER, Wolfgang, Dr rer. nat (Habil.); German biochemist and academic; *Professor and Head of Department of Structural Biology, Max Planck Institute of Biochemistry;* b. 1946, Wesseling; ed Univs of Münster, Bonn and Düsseldorf; worked at Cavendish Lab., Cambridge, UK 1970s, Lecturer in Biophysics 1978–83; Prof., Univs of Düsseldorf and Munich; Group Leader, Max Planck Inst. of Biochemistry, Martinsried 1983–88, Dir and Head of Dept of Structural Biology 1988–; mem. several acads, including American Acad. of Arts and Sciences; Hon. Prof. of Physics, Tech. Univ. of Munich; Otto Warburg Medal, Schleiden Medal, Louis Jeantet Prize for Medicine, Stein and Moore Award, Harvey Prize in Science and Tech., Technion – Israel Inst. of Tech. 2005. *Publications:* numerous scientific papers in professional journals on cellular protein quality control. *Address:* Department of Molecular Structural Biology, Max Planck Institute of Biochemistry, Am Klopferspitz 18, 82152 Martinsried, Germany (office). *Telephone:* (89) 8578-2642 (office); (89) 8578-2387 (office). *Fax:* (89) 8578-2641 (office); (89) 8578-3557 (office). *E-mail:* baumeist@biochem.mpg.de (office). *Website:* www.biochem.mpg.de/baumeister (office).

BAUMOL, William Jack, PhD; American economist, academic and consultant; *Academic Director and Professor of Economics, New York University;* b. 26 Feb. 1922, New York; s. of Solomon Baumol and Lillian Baumol; m. Hilda Missel 1941; one s. one d.; ed Coll. of City of New York, Univ. of London, UK; jr economist, US Dept of Agric. 1942–43, 1946; Asst Lecturer, London School of Econs 1947–49; Asst Prof., Dept of Econs, Princeton Univ. 1949–52, Prof. of Econs 1952–92, Prof. Emer. and Sr Research Economist 1992–; Prof. of Econs, New York Univ. 1971–, Dir C.V. Starr Center for Applied Econs 1983–2000, Harold Price Prof. of Entrepreneurship and Academic Dir, Berkley Center for Entrepreneurship & Innovation 2005–;

Pres. Eastern Econ. Asscn 1978–79, Asscn of Environmental and Resource Economists 1979, American Econ. Asscn 1981, Atlantic Econ. Soc. 1985; mem. NAS, Accademia Nazionale de Lincei, Rome 2001; Hon. Fellow, LSE; Hon. Prof. Univ. of Belgrano 1996; Dr hc (Princeton Univ. Joseph D. Green Prof.) 1968, (Stockholm School of Econs) 1971, (Univ. of Basel) 1973, (Univ. of Lille) 1997; numerous awards including Frank E. Seidman Award, Political Econ. 1987, Henry H. Villand Research Award 1997, Int. Award for Entrepreneurship and Small Business Research, Swedish Foundation for Small Business Research and Swedish Business Devt Agency 2003, Antonio Feltrinelli Int. Prize for Econ. and Social Sciences, Accademia Nazionale dei Lincei, Rome, Italy 2005, Wellington Award, Inst. of Industrial Engineers 2005, Lifetime Achievement to Scholarship, Research Inst. for Social Sciences, Univ. of Tampere, Finland 2007. *Publications:* more than 40 books including: Economic Dynamics 1951, Business Behavior, Value and Growth 1959, Economic Theory and Operations Analysis 1961, Performing Arts: The Economic Dilemma (with W. G. Bowen) 1966, Theory of Environmental Policy (with W. E. Oates) 1975, Economics, Environmental Policy and the Quality of Life (with W. E. Oates and S. A. Batey Blackman) 1979, Economics: Principles and Policy (with A. S. Blinder) 1979, Productivity Growth and US Competitiveness (co-ed. with K. McLennan) 1985, Superfairness: Applications and Theory 1986 (Best Book in Business, Man. and Econs, Asscn of American Publishers), Productivity and American Leadership: The Long View (with S. A. Batey Blackman and E. N. Wolff) 1989, The Information Economy and the Implications of Unbalanced Growth (with L. Osberg and E. N. Wolff) 1989, Perfect Markets and Easy Virtue: Business Ethics and the Invisible Hand (co-author) 1991, Toward Competition in Local Telephony (with G. Sidak) 1994, Convergence of Productivity: Cross-National Studies and Historical Evidence (with R. R. Nelson and E. N. Wolff) 1994, Assessing Educational Practices: The Contribution of Economics (with W. E. Becker) 1995, Baumol's Cost Disease: The Arts and Other victims (co-ed. R. Towse) 1997, Global Trade and Conflicting National Interests 2000, Welfare Economics (with C. A. Wilson) 2001, The Free-Market Innovation Machine: Analyzing the Growth Miracle of Capitalism 2002, Downsizing in America: Reality, Causes, and Consequences (with A. S. Blinder and E. N. Wolff) 2003, Growth, Industrial Organization and Economic Generalities 2003; 500 articles in professional journals. *Leisure interests:* woodcarving, painting (traditional & computer). *Address:* Berkley Center for Entrepreneurship & Innovation, Stern School of Business, New York University, Room 7-98, 44 West Fourth Street, New York, NY 10012-1126, USA (office). *Telephone:* (212) 998-8943 (office). *Fax:* (212) 995-4211 (office). *E-mail:* william.baumol@nyu.edu (office). *Website:* pages.stern.nyu.edu/~wbaumol (office).

BAVIN, Rt Rev. Dom Timothy John, MA; British monk; *Oblate Master, Alton Abbey;* b. 17 Sept. 1935, Northwood; s. of Edward Bavin and Marjorie Bavin; ed St George School, Windsor, Brighton Coll., Worcester Coll., Univ. of Oxford, Cuddesdon Coll.; Asst Priest, St Alban's Cathedral, Pretoria 1961–64, Chaplain 1964–69; Asst Priest, Uckfield, Sussex 1969–71; Vicar, Church of the Good Shepherd, Brighton 1971–73; Dean of Johannesburg 1973–74, Bishop 1974–84; Bishop of Portsmouth, England 1985–95, Hon. Asst Bishop 2012–; Hon. Asst Bishop, Diocese of Winchester 2013–; Monk, Order of St Benedict, Alton Abbey 1996–, Oblate Master 2011–; mem. Oratory of the Good Shepherd 1987–95; Hon. Fellow, Royal School of Church Music 1991. *Publications:* Deacons in the Ministry of the Church 1986, In Tune with Heaven (ed.) 1992. *Leisure interests:* music, walking, gardening. *Address:* Alton Abbey, Alton, Hants., GU34 4AP, England.

BAXTER, Glen; British artist; b. 4 March 1944, Leeds; s. of the late Charles Baxter and of Florence Baxter; m. Carole Agis; one s. one d.; ed Cockburn Grammar School, Leeds and Leeds Coll. of Art; has exhibited drawings in New York, San Francisco, Venice, Amsterdam, Lille, Munich, Tokyo and Paris and represented UK at Sydney Biennale 1986, Adelaide Festival 1992, Hôtel Furkablick (Switzerland) 1993; major retrospectives at Musée de l'Abbaye Sainte-Croix, Les Sables d'Olonne, France 1987, 'Une Ame en Tourment', Centre nat. de l'art imprimé Chatou, Paris; illustrated Charlie Malarkey and the Belly Button Machine 1986; tapestry commissioned by French Govt to commemorate 8th centenary of death of Richard the Lion-Heart. *Publications:* Atlas 1979, The Impending Gleam 1981, His Life: The Years of Struggle 1983, Jodhpurs in the Quantocks 1986, Welcome to the Weird World of Glen Baxter 1989, The Billiard Table Murders, A Gladys Babbington Morton Mystery 1990, Glen Baxter Returns to Normal 1992, The Collected Blurtings of Baxter 1993, The Further Blurtings of Baxter 1994, The Wonder Book of Sex 1995, Glen Baxter's Gourmet Guide 1997, Blizzards of Tweed 1999, Podium 2000, The Unhinged World of Glen Baxter 2002, Trundling Grunts 2002, Loomings Over the Suet 2004, Le Monde de Glen Baxter 2009, Ominous Stains 2009. *Leisure interests:* marquetry, snood retrieval. *E-mail:* glenbaxter@mac.com. *Website:* www.glenbaxter.com (home).

BAXTER, Rodney James, ScD, GradDip (Theol), FRS, FAA; Australian (b. British) mathematical physicist and academic; *Professor Emeritus, Australian National University;* b. 8 Feb. 1940, London, England; s. of Thomas J. Baxter and Florence Baxter; m. Elizabeth A. Phillips 1968; one s. one d.; ed Bancroft's School, Essex, Trinity Coll., Cambridge and Australian Nat. Univ.; Reservoir Engineer, Iraq Petroleum Co. 1964–65; Research Fellow, ANU 1965–68, Fellow 1971–81, Prof., Dept of Theoretical Physics, Research School of Physical Sciences 1981–, jtly with School of Math. Sciences 1989–, now Emer. and Visiting Fellow; Asst Prof., MIT, USA 1968–70; Royal Soc. Research Prof., Univ. of Cambridge 1992; Pawsey Medal, Australian Acad. of Science 1975, IUPAP Boltzmann Medal 1980, Thomas Ranken Lyle Medal, Australian Acad. of Science 1983, Dannie Heineman Prize, American Physical Soc. 1987, Harrie Massey Medal and Prize, Australian Inst. of Physics/Inst. of Physics (UK) 1994, Centenary Medal, Australian Govt 2003, Onsager Prize, American Physical Soc. 2006, Lars Onsager Lecture and Medal, Norwegian Univ. of Science and Tech. 2006, Royal Medal, Royal Soc. 2013. *Publication:* Exactly Solved Models in Statistical Mechanics 1982, contrib. to professional journals. *Leisure interest:* theatre. *Address:* Centre for Mathematics and Its Applications, Mathematical Sciences Institute, Building 27, Australian National University, Canberra, ACT 0200, Australia. *Telephone:* (2) 6125-3511. *Fax:* (2) 6125-5549.

BAY, Michael Benjamin; American film director and producer; b. 17 Feb. 1965, Los Angeles, Calif.; adopted s. of Jim Bay and Harriet Bay; ed Crossroads School, Santa Monica, Wesleyan Univ., Art Center Coll. of Design, Pasadena; interned with George Lucas aged 15; began working at Propaganda Films, directing commercials for Nike, Reebok, Coca-Cola, Budweiser and Miller Lite and cr. music videos for Tina Turner, Meat Loaf, Lionel Richie, Wilson Phillips, Donny Osmond and The Divinyls; directed Goodby, Silverstein & Partners Got Milk? advertisement campaign for the California Milk Processors Bd 1993, campaign now resides in perm. collection of Museum of Modern Art, New York; gained attention of producers Jerry Bruckheimer and Don Simpson, and as a result directed his first feature-length film, Bad Boys 1995; Co-founder The Institute, aka The Inst. for the Devt of Enhanced Perceptual Awareness; Co-Chair. and part Owner of Digital Domain digital effects house; Co-owner Platinum Dunes production house; Clio Award for first nat. commercial for the Red Cross 1992, Grand Prix Clio for Commercial of the Year for his Got Milk/Aaron Burr commercial, Gold Lion for The Best Beer campaign for Miller Lite, as well as the Silver for Got Milk, Cannes Film Festival, Commercial Dir of the Year, Dirs Guild of America 1995. *Films directed:* Play That Funky Music (video short) (segment 'I Love You') 1990, Playboy: Kerri Kendall – September 1990 Video Centerfold (video documentary) 1990, Great White: My... My... My... the Video Collection (video 'Call It Rock 'N' Roll') 1991, Shadows and Light: From a Different View (video documentary short) 1992, Meat Loaf: Bat Out of Hell II – Picture Show (music videos) 1994, Bad Boys 1995, The Rock (Best Action Scene, MTV Movie Awards) 1996, Armageddon 1998, Pearl Harbor (Best Action Scene, MTV Movie Awards) 2001, Bad Boys II (also actor) (Best Action Scene, MTV Movie Awards) 2003, The Lionel Richie Collection (video documentary) ('Do It to Me') 2003, The Island 2005, Transformers (also exec. producer) (MTV Movie Awards: Best Movie and Best Summer Movie You Haven't Seen Yet) 2007, Transformers: Revenge of the Fallen (also exec. producer) 2009, Transformers: Dark of the Moon (also exec. producer) 2011, Pain and Gain (also producer) 2013. *Film roles in:* Mystery Men 1999, Coyote Ugly 2000, Zigs 2001. *Films produced:* The Texas Chainsaw Massacre 2003, The Amityville Horror 2005, The Island 2005, Pissed 2005, The Texas Chainsaw Massacre: The Beginning, 2006, The Hitcher 2007, Their War (video documentary) (exec. producer) 2007, Our World (video documentary) (exec. producer) 2007, From Script, to Sand: The Skorponok Desert Attack (video documentary short) (exec. producer) 2007, Horsemen 2009, The Unborn 2009, Friday the 13th 2009, A Nightmare on Elm Street 2010, I Am Number Four 2011, Uncharted Territory: NASA's Future Then and Now (video documentary short) (exec. producer) 2012, Above and Beyond: Exploring Dark of the Moon (video documentary) (exec. producer) 2012, Vigilandia 2013. *Television includes:* Miami Vice (series) 1986, Vengeance: The Story of Tony Cimo (film) 1986. *Address:* Bay Films, 2110 Broadway, Santa Monica, CA 90404 (office); The Institute for the Development of Enhanced Perceptual Awareness, 804-A Hampton Drive, Venice, CA 90291, USA. *E-mail:* info@theinstitute.tv. *Website:* www.theinstitute.tv; www.michaelbay.com.

BAYAR, Sanjaagiin (Sanjiin); Mongolian politician, diplomatist and journalist; b. 1956, Ulan Bator; ed Moscow State Univ., USSR; fmr officer, Ulan Bator City Ass. and Nairamdal Dist Office 1978–79; officer, Gen. HQ Nat. Defence Army 1979–83; journalist and ed., Novosti Mongolii newspaper, Chief Ed. and Gen. Ed. Montsame news agency 1983–88; Deputy Head of Admin Agency, Mongolian Radio TV 1988–90; mem. Nat. Congress 1990–92; Head, Strategy and Research Centre, Ministry of Defence 1992–97; Chief of Staff, Office of the Pres. 1997–2001; Amb. to Russian Fed. 2001–05; Gen. Sec. Mongolian People's Revolutionary Party 2005–07, Chair. 2007–; Prime Minister of Mongolia 2007–09 (resgnd). *Address:* Mongolian People's Revolutionary Party, Sukhbaatar District, UB-14191, Ulan Bator, Mongolia (office). *Telephone:* 50067805 (office). *Fax:* 50067805 (office). *E-mail:* contact@mprp.mn (office). *Website:* www.mprp.mn (office).

BAYARTSAIKHAN, Nadmidyn; Mongolian academic and politician; b. 27 Jan. 1971, Ulan Bator; m.; two c.; fmr Lecturer and Prof.; mem. Parl., fmr Chair. Standing Cttee on Budget; Minister of Finance 2006–07; mem. Mongolian People's Party (MPP); fmr Pres. Nat. Asscn of Mongolian Agricultural Cooperatives.

BAYÉ, Jules, MSc; Niger government official; *Minister of the Economy and Finance;* b. 1 Sept. 1945, Barra; ed Univ. Paris–Dauphine, Ecole Nat. des Douanes, Neuilly, France; Head of Audit and Verification, Customs Directorate-Gen. Jan.– May 1974, Deputy Dir-Gen. of Customs 1974–86; Dir-Gen. of Taxation 1986–88, 1993–96, 1999–2000; with Ministry of Finance, in charge of relations with Communauté Economique de l'Afrique de l'Ouest (CEAO)/Communauté Economique des Etats de l'Afrique de l'Ouest (CEDEAO)/Conseil de Coopération Douanière (CCD) 1988–89, Financial Controller, CEDEAO, Lagos 1989–93, Technical Adviser, Ministry of Finance 1996–99; with West African Econ. and Monetary Union 2000–01; Minister of the Economy and Finance 2012–; mem. numerous cttees including nat. CEAO/CEDEAO cttees; fmr Chair. Société Nationale des Transports Nigériens. *Address:* Ministry of the Economy and Finance, BP 389, Niamey, Niger (office). *Telephone:* 20-72-23-74 (office). *Fax:* 20-73-59-34 (office). *Website:* www.mef-niger.org (office).

BAYE, Nathalie; French actress; b. 6 July 1948, Mainneville; d. of Claude Baye and Denise Coustet; one d. by Johnny Hallyday; ed Conservatoire nat. d'art dramatique de Paris; Femme en or—Trophée Whirlpool 2000. *Stage appearances include:* Galapages 1972, Liola 1973, Les trois soeurs 1978, Adriana Monti 1986, Les fausses confidences 1993, La parisienne 1995. *Films include:* Two People 1972, La nuit américaine 1973, La gueule ouverte 1974, La Gifle 1974, Un jour la fête 1974, Le voyage de noces 1975, Le plein de super 1976, Mado 1976, L'homme qui aimait les femmes 1977, Monsieur Papa 1977, La communion solennelle 1977, La chambre verte 1978, Mon premier amour 1978, La mémoire courte 1978, Sauve qui peut 1979, Je vais craquer 1979, Une semaine de vacances 1980, Provinciale 1980, Beau-père, Une étrange affaire, L'ombre rouge 1981, Le retour de Martin Guerre 1981, La balance (César for Best Actress 1983) 1982, J'ai épousé une ombre 1982, Notre histoire 1983, Rive droite, rive gauche 1984, Détective 1984, Le neveu de Beethoven 1985, Lune de Miel 1985, De guerre lasse 1987, En toute innocence 1988, La Baule-les-Pins 1990, Un week-end sur deux 1990, The Man Inside 1990, L'Affaire Wallraff 1991, La Voix 1992, Mensonges 1993, La machine 1994, Les soldats de l'espérance 1994, Enfants da salud 1996, Si je t'aime... prends garde à toi 1998, Food of Love 1998, Paparazzi 1998, Vénus beauté 1999, Une liaison pornographique 1999, Ça ira mieux demain 2000, Selon Matthieu, Barnie et ses petites contrariétés 2001, Absolument fabuleux 2001, Catch Me If You Can 2002, La Fleur du mal 2003, Les Sentiments 2003, France Boutique 2003, Une vie à t'attendre 2004, L'un reste, l'autre part 2005, Le Petit Lieutenant (César Award for

Best Actress 2006) 2005, Ne le dis à personne 2006, Mon fils à moi 2006. *Address:* c/o Artmédia, 20 avenue Rapp, 75007 Paris, France (office).

BAYER, Oswald; German ecclesiastic and professor of theology; b. 30 Sept. 1939, Nagold; s. of Emil Bayer and Hermine Bayer; m. Eva Bayer 1966 (deceased 1993); ed Tübingen, Bonn and Rome, Italy; Vicar, Evangelische Landeskirche, Württemberg 1964; Asst Univ. of Tübingen 1965–68; Evangelical Stift, Tübingen 1968–71; Pastor, Tübingen 1972–74; Prof. of Systematic Theology, Univ. of Bochum 1974–79, Univ. of Tübingen 1979–2005, Dir Inst. of Christian Ethics 1979–95; Ed. Zeitschrift für Systematische Theologie und Religionsphilosophie 1986–2006. *Publications:* numerous books and essays on theological and philosophical issues. *Address:* Kurhausstr. 138, 53773 Tübingen (home). *Telephone:* (2242) 918951 (home). *E-mail:* bayer@unitybox.de (home).

BAYERO, Alhaji Ado; Nigerian university administrator and fmr diplomatist; *Emir of Kano;* b. 25 July 1930, Kano; s. of Alhaji Abdullahi Bayer, Emir of Kano; m. Halimatu Sadiya; ed Kano Middle School and School for Arabic Studies; clerk, Bank of West Africa 1947–49; mem. Northern House of Ass. 1955–57; Chief of Kano Native Authority Police 1957–62; Amb. to Senegal 1962–63; 13th Emir of Kano 1963–; Chancellor, Univ. of Nigeria, Nsukka, E Nigeria 1966–75, Univ. of Ibadan 1975–85. *Leisure interests:* photography, riding, reading. *Address:* c/o Office of the Chancellor, University of Ibadan, Ibadan, Nigeria.

BAYH, Birch Evans (Evan), III, BS, JD; American lawyer, politician and broadcaster; *Partner, McGuireWoods LLP;* b. 26 Dec. 1955, Shirkieville, Ind.; s. of Birch Evans Bayh Jr and Marvella Hern; m. Susan Bayh; twin s.; ed Indiana Univ., Univ. of Virginia; Sec. of State of Ind. 1987–89; Gov. of Ind. 1989–97; Partner, Baker & Daniel Assocs (law firm), Indianapolis 1997; Lecturer, Indiana Univ. Kelley School of Business 1997–98; Senator from Ind. 1999–2011 (retd); Partner, McGuireWoods LLP law firm, Washington, DC 2011–; Chair. Democratic Leadership Council 2001–05; f. Moderate Dems Working Group; mem. Bd of Dirs Nat. Endowment for Democracy; Sr Advisor, Apollo Global Management, New York; contrib., Fox News 2011–; Democrat; Dr hc (Golden Gate Univ. School of Law). *Publications include:* From Father to Son: A Private Life in the Public Eye 2003. *Address:* McGuireWoods LLP, 2001 K Street NW, Suite 400, Washington, DC 20006-1040 (office); 10 West Market Street, Suite 1650, Indianapolis, IN 46204-2934, USA. *Telephone:* (202) 828-2818 (office). *Fax:* (202) 828-3331 (office). *E-mail:* ebayh@mcguirewoods.com (office). *Website:* www.mcguirewoods.com (office).

BAYI, Filbert, BSc (Educ.); Tanzanian sports administrator and fmr athlete; *Secretary-General, National Olympic Committee;* b. (Habiye), 22 June 1953, Karatu, Arusha Region; s. of the late Sanka Bayi and Magdalena Qwaray; m. Anna Lyimo 1977; two s. two d.; ed Univ. of Texas at El Paso, USA; joined Air Transport Battalion (TPDF), Dar es Salaam; middle distance runner; beat Tanzanian Nat. Champion over 1,500m, Dar es Salaam 1972; 1,500m Gold Medal Nat. Championships, Dar es Salaam 1972, All African Games, Lagos, Nigeria (record time) 1973; first competed Europe June 1973; 1,500m Gold Medal (and world record), Commonwealth Games, Christchurch, New Zealand 1974; 1,500m Gold Medal, All African Games, Algiers, Algeria 1978; 1,500m Silver Medal Commonwealth Games, Edmonton, Canada 1978; 3,000m Steeplechase Silver Medal, Olympic Games, Moscow, USSR 1980; Athletic Nat. Coach; Army Chief Coach ATHL; Sec. TAAA Tech. Cttee, Tanzania Olympic Cttee; mem. TAAA Exec. Cttee, IAAF Tech. Cttee; IAAF Athletic Coaching Lecturer; Nat. Chief Instructor and Athletic Coach; IOC Nat. Course Dir; Exec. mem. Nat. Olympic Cttee, Sec.-Gen. Nat. Olympic Cttee 2002–; Gen. Chair. Bd of Dirs Filbert Bayi Nursery, Primary and Secondary School, Filbert Bayi Foundation; United Repub. of Tanzania Medal 1995. *Leisure interests:* reading, sports, watching TV, talking to children. *Address:* Filbert Bayi Nursery and Primary School—Kimara, Morogoro Road, PO Box 60240, Dar es Salaam, Tanzania. *Telephone:* (22) 2420635 (office); (22) 2420634 (home). *Fax:* (22) 2420178 (office); (22) 2420178 (home). *E-mail:* filbertbayischools@yahoo.com (office); fsbayi@yahoo.com (home). *Website:* www .filbertbayischools.org.

BAYKAM, Bedri; Turkish painter, writer and politician; b. 26 April 1957, Ankara; s. of Suphi Baykam and Mutahhar Baykam; m. Sibel Yağci; one s.; ed French Lycée, Istanbul, Univ. of Paris I (Panthéon-Sorbonne), France, California Coll. of Arts and Crafts, USA; numerous solo exhbns Paris, Brussels, Rome, New York, Istanbul, Munich, Stockholm, Helsinki, London 1963–99; mem. Cen. Bd CHP (Republican Party of the People) 1995–98; f. Piramid Publishing 1998; Founder, The Patriotic Movement 2005; Painter of the Year, Nokta magazine 1987, 1989, 1990, 1996–97, Best Artist and Best Performance, Art Jonction, Cannes 1994. *Major art works include:* The Prostitute's Room 1981, The Painting 1985, This Has Been Done Before 1987, Livart 1994, The Years of 68 1997, Curatorial Schizophrenia 2005. *Publications include:* The Brain of Paint (Boyanin Beyni) 1990, Monkey's Right to Paint 1994, Mustafa Kemal's on Duty Now 1994, Secular Turkey Without Concession 1995, Fleeting Moments, Enduring Delights 1996, His Eyes Always Rest on Us 1997, The Color of the Era 1997, The Years of 68 (Vols 1 and 2) 1998–99, I'm Nothing but I'm Everything 1999, The Last Condottiere of the Millennium, Che 2000, The Bone 2000 (English trans. 2005), The Millennium Crack 2002, End of the Empire of Fear 2004. *Leisure interests:* tennis, football, music, pool. *Address:* Piramid Publishing, Feridiye Cad 23- 25 Taksim, Istanbul (office); Palanga Cad 33/23, Ortaköy, Istanbul 80480, Turkey (home). *Telephone:* (212) 2973120 (office); (212) 2580809 (home). *E-mail:* bedri .baykam@gmail.com (office). *Website:* www.bedribaykam.com; www.piramidsanat.com (office).

BAYLE, Abdirahman Ducaale, PhD; Somali economist and politician; *Minister of Foreign Affairs and International Co-operation;* b. Awdal region; ed Univ. of Wisconsin, USA; taught econs, statistics and finance at univs in Saudi Arabia and USA; fmr Finance Officer with African Devt Bank, Tunisia, becoming Head, Dept of Agric. and Agro-Industry; Minister of Foreign Affairs and Int. Co-operation 2014–; mem. Bd of Trustees, African Fertilizer and Agribusiness Partnership. *Address:* Ministry of Foreign Affairs and International Co-operation, 1 Villa Somalia, 2525 Mogadishu, Somalia (office). *Telephone:* (5) 424640 (office). *Fax:* (5) 424640 (office). *Website:* www.mfa.somaligov.net (office).

BAYLEY, John Oliver, MA, FBA, CBE, FRSL; British writer and professor of English; b. 27 March 1925; s. of F. J. Bayley; m. 1st (Jean) Iris Murdoch 1956 (died

1999); m. 2nd Audi Villers 2000; ed Eton Coll., New Coll., Oxford; served in army 1943–47; mem. St Antony's and Magdalen Colls, Oxford 1951–55; Fellow and Tutor in English, New Coll., Oxford 1955–74; Warton Prof. of English Literature and Fellow, St Catherine's Coll., Oxford 1974–92; Heinemann Literary Award. *Publications:* In Another Country (novel) 1954, The Romantic Survival: A Study in Poetic Evolution 1956, The Characters of Love 1961, Tolstoy and the Novel 1966, Keats and Reality 1969, Pushkin: A Comparative Commentary 1971, The Uses of Division: Unity and Disharmony in Literature 1976, An Essay on Hardy 1978, Shakespeare and Tragedy 1981, The Order of Battle at Trafalgar 1987, The Short Story: Henry James to Elizabeth Bowen 1988, Tolstoy and the Novel 1988, Housman's Poems 1992, Alice (novel) 1994, The Queer Captain (novel) 1995, George's Lair (novel) 1996, The Red Hat (novel) 1997, Iris and the Friends: A Year of Memories 1998, Elegy for Iris: A Memoir (1999) 1999, Widower's House 2001, Hand Luggage – An Anthology 2001, The Power of Delight – A Lifetime in Literature: Essays 1962–2002 2005; The Wings of the Dove (by Henry James) (ed.). *Address:* c/o St Catherine's College, Manor Road, Oxford, OX1 3UJ, England.

BAYLEY, Stephen Paul, MA; British design consultant, writer, exhibition organiser and museum administrator; b. 13 Oct. 1951, Cardiff, Wales; s. of the late Donald Bayley and Anne Bayley; m. Flo Fothergill 1981; one s. one d.; ed Quarry Bank School, Liverpool, Univ. of Manchester, Univ. of Liverpool School of Architecture; Lecturer in History of Art, Open Univ. 1974–76, Univ. of Kent 1976–80; Dir Conran Foundation 1981–89; Dir Boilerhouse Project, Victoria and Albert Museum, London 1982–86; Founding Dir then Chief Exec. Design Museum 1986–89; Creative Dir New Millennium Experience Co. 1997–98 (resgnd); lectured throughout the UK and abroad; Hon. Fellow, Univ. of Wales Inst., Cardiff 2007; Hon. FRIBA 2008; Chevalier des Arts et des Lettres 1990; Periodical Publrs Asscn Magazine Columnist of the Year 1995. *Publications include:* In Good Shape 1979, The Albert Memorial 1981, Harley Earl and the Dream Machine 1983, Conran Directory of Design 1985, Sex, Drink and Fast Cars 1986, Commerce and Culture 1989, Taste 1991, General Knowledge 1996, Labour Camp 1998, Moving Objects (ed.) 1999, General Knowledge 2000, Sex: An Intimate History (ed.) 2001, Dictionary of Idiocy 2003, Life's a Pitch 2007, Design: Intelligence Made Visible 2007, Cars 2008, Woman as Design 2009, La Dolce Vita 2011, Ugly – The Aesthetics of Everything 2012. *Leisure interests:* travel-related services, solitary sports, books. *Address:* 23 Ganton Street, London, W1F 9BW, England (office). *Telephone:* (20) 7287-5888 (office). *E-mail:* guru@stephenbayley.com.

BAYLY LETTS, Jaime; Peruvian journalist, writer and broadcaster; b. 19 Feb. 1965, Lima; s. of Jaime Bayly Llona and Doris Letts; m. Sandra Masías; two d.; ed Inmaculado Corazón, Markham Coll., Lima, Colegio San Agustín de Lima, Pontificia Universidad Católica del Perú; began career as columnist for La Prensa (newspaper) 1980; 1996, anchor, 24-hour news network CBS Telenoticias 1996–2000; fmr political corresp., TV series Pulso, Canal 5; fmr presenter 1,990 en America; presenter, El Francotirador (TV show) 2006–10; presenter, Bayly (chat show), Mega TV, Miami, Nuestra Tele Noticias (NTN) 24; columnist, The Miami Herald, Peru 21; GLAAD Visibility Award, USA 2007. *Publications include:* novels: No se lo digas a nadie (Don't Tell Anyone) 1994, Yo amo a mi mami (I Love my Mummy) 2000, Y de Repente, Un Ángel (Suddenly, an Angel) 2005, El Cojo y el Loco (The Crippled and the Crazy) 2009, Morirás mañana: El Escritor Sale a Matar (You Will Die Tomorrow: The Writer Goes On to Kill) 2010, Morirás mañana 2: El misterio de Alma Rossi 2011, Morirás mañana 3: Escupirán sobre mi tumba 2012.

BAYM, Gordon Alan, AM, PhD, FAAS; American physicist and academic; *Professor of Physics, University of Illinois;* b. 1 July 1935, New York; s. of Louis Baym and Lillian Baym; two s. two d.; ed Cornell Univ., Harvard Univ.; Fellow, Universitetets Institut for Teoretisk Fysik, Copenhagen 1960–62; Lecturer, Univ. of Calif., Berkeley 1962–63; Prof. of Physics, Univ. of Ill., Urbana 1963–; Visiting Prof., Univs of Tokyo and Kyoto 1968, Nordita, Copenhagen 1970, 1976, Niels Bohr Inst. 1976–, Univ. of Nagoya 1979; Visiting Scientist, Academia Sinica, Beijing 1979; mem. Advisory Bd Inst. of Theoretical Physics, Santa Barbara, Calif. 1978–83; mem. Sub-cttee on Theoretical Physics, NSF 1980–81, Physics Advisory Cttee 1982–85; mem. Nuclear Science Advisory Cttee, Dept of Energy/NSF 1982–86; mem. Editorial Bd Procs. NAS 1986–92; Fellow, American Acad. of Arts and Sciences, American Physical Soc.; Research Fellow, Alfred P. Sloan Foundation 1965–68; NSF Postdoctoral Fellow 1960–62; Trustee, Assoc. Univs Inc. 1986–90; Assoc. Ed. Nuclear Physics; mem. American Astronomical Soc., Int. Astronomical Union, NAS (fmr Chair. Physics Section), American Philosophical Soc.; Sr US Scientist Award, Alexander von Humboldt Foundation 1983, Hans A. Bethe Prize, American Physical Soc. 2002, Lars Onsager Prize (jtly), American Physical Soc. 2008. *Publications:* Quantum Statistical Mechanics (jt author) 1962, Lectures on Quantum Mechanics 1969, Neutron Stars 1970, Neutron Stars and the Properties of Matter at High Density 1977, Landau Fermi-Liquid Theory (jt author) 1991. *Leisure interests:* photography, mountains. *Address:* 337c Loomis Laboratory, University of Illinois, 1110 West Green Street, Urbana, IL 61801, USA (office). *Telephone:* (217) 333-4363 (office). *Fax:* (217) 244-7559 (office); (217) 333-9819. *E-mail:* gbaym@illinois.edu (office). *Website:* physics.illinois.edu (office).

BAYMENOV, Alixan Mukhamedyevich; Kazakhstani politician; b. 25 March 1959, Qarağandi; held numerous govt posts including Head of Presidential Admin 1998–99; Minister of Labour and Social Security 2000–01; Co-founder Democratic Choice of Kazakhstan party 2001; Co-founder and Chair. Bright Road—Democratic Party of Kazakhstan (Ak Jol) 2002–12; unsuccessful presidential cand. 2005. *Address:* Bright Road—Democratic Party of Kazakhstan (Ak Jol), 010000 Astana, Imanov 18/7, Kazakhstan (office). *Telephone:* (7172) 20-05-85 (office). *Fax:* (7172) 21-37-50 (office). *E-mail:* akzholpress@mail.ru (office). *Website:* www.akzhol.kz (office).

BAYNE, Sir Nicholas Peter, KCMG, MA, DPhil; British diplomatist (retd); *Fellow, International Trade Policy Unit, London School of Economics;* b. 15 Feb. 1937, London; s. of the late Capt. Ronald Bayne, RN and of Elizabeth Bayne (née Ashcroft); m. Diana Wilde 1961; three s. (one deceased); ed Eton Coll. and Christ Church, Oxford; joined HM Diplomatic Service 1961; served in Manila 1963–66, Bonn 1969–72; seconded to HM Treasury 1974–75; Financial Counsellor, Paris 1975–79; Head of Econ. Relations Dept, FCO 1979–82; Royal Inst. of Int. Affairs 1982–83; Amb. to Zaïre (also accred to Congo, Rwanda, Burundi) 1983–84; Amb. and Perm. Rep. to OECD, Paris 1985–88; Deputy Under-Sec. of State, FCO 1988–92; High Commr in Canada 1992–96; Fellow, Int. Trade Policy Unit, LSE

1997–. *Publications:* Hanging Together: The Seven-Power Summits (with R. Putnam) 1984, Hanging In There: The G7 and G8 Summit in Maturity and Renewal 2000, The Grey Wares of North-West Anatolia and their Relations to the Early Greek Settlements 2000, The New Economic Diplomacy (with S. Woolcock) 2003, Staying Together: The G8 Summit Confronts the 21st Century 2005, Economic Diplomat 2010. *Leisure interests:* reading, sightseeing. *Address:* 2 Chetwynd House, Hampton Court, Surrey, KT8 9BS, England.

BAYONA, Juan Antonio; Spanish film director; b. 1975, Barcelona; ed Cinema and Audiovisual School of Catalonia (ESCAC); began career directing commercials and pop videos for Spanish musical groups, including OBK, Hevia, Ella Baila Sola and Camela. *Films include:* Mis vacaciones (short) (also writer) 1999, Diminutos del calvario (short) (segment 'Muerte') 2001, El hombre Esponja (short) (also writer and exec. producer) 2002, Sonorama (video) (as J. A. Bayona) 2004, 10 años con Camela (video) 2004, Lo echamos a suertes (video short) (segment 'Cómo repartimos los amigos') 2005, Tierra de Hevia (music video) 2005, The Orphanage (as J. A. Bayona) 2007, The Impossible 2012; actor: Spanish Movie (as J. A. Bayona) 2009. *Address:* c/o Creative Artists Agency, 2000 Avenue of the Stars, Los Angeles, CA 90067, USA (office). *Telephone:* (424) 288-2000 (office). *Fax:* (424) 288-2900 (office). *Website:* www.caa.com (office).

BAYROU, François; French politician; *President, Mouvement démocrate;* b. 25 May 1951, Bordères, Basses-Pyrénées; s. of Calixte Bayrou and Emma Sarthou; m. Elisabeth Perlant; three s. three d.; ed Lycée de Nay-Bourdettes, Lycée Montaigne, Bordeaux and Univ. of Bordeaux III; fmr school teacher; Prof., Pau 1974–79; special attachment to Office of Minister of Agric. 1979; Ed.-in-Chief, Démocratie Moderne (weekly) 1980–91; Nat. Sec. Centre des Démocrates Sociaux (now Force démocrate) 1980–86, Deputy Sec.-Gen. 1986–94, Pres. 1994–97 (then merged into Nouvelle UDF then into Union pour la Démocratie Française (UDF), Gen. Del. (UDF) 1989–91, Sec. Gen. 1991–94, Pres. 1998–2007; Pres. Mouvement démocrate 2007–; Conseiller Gen. Pau 1982–93, 2008–; Pres. Conseil Gen. des Pyrénées-Atlantiques 1992–2001; Conseiller Régional, Aquitaine 1982–86; Town Councillor, Pau 1988–92; Adviser to Pierre Pflimlin (Pres. of Ass. of EC) 1984–86; Deputy to Nat. Ass. 1986–93, 1997–99, 2002–12; Minister of Nat. Educ. 1993–95, also of Higher Educ., Research and Professional Training 1995–97; mem. European Parl. 1999–2002; presidential cand. 2002, 2007, 2012. *Publications include:* La Décennie des mal-appris 1990, Le roi libre 1994, Henri IV, le roi libre 1994, le Droit au sens 1996, Saint-louis 1997, Henri IV 1998, L'Edit de Nantes 1998, Hors des sentiers battus 1999, Relève 2001, Oui : Plaidoyer pour la Constitution européenne 2005, Au nom du Tier-Etat 2006. *Leisure interests:* raising horses, literature. *Address:* 34 Rue Henri Faisans, 64000 Pau (office); Mouvement Démocrate, 133 Bis Rue de l'Université, 75007 Paris (office); 27 rue Duboué, 64000 Pau, France (home). *Telephone:* 5-59-30-61-91 (office); 1-53-59-20-00 (office). *E-mail:* f.bayrou@udf.org (office); fbayrou@assemblee-nationale.fr (office). *Website:* www.bayrou.fr.

BAZALGETTE, Sir Peter Lytton (Baz), Kt, FRTS; British television producer; b. 22 May 1953, Romney Marsh, Kent, England; great-great-grandson of Victorian civil engineer Sir Joseph Bazalgette; m. Hilary Newiss; two c.; ed Dulwich Coll., London, Fitzwilliam Coll., Cambridge; joined BBC News graduate news training scheme, subsequently chosen by Esther Rantzen as researcher on That's Life! from 1977; reporter for BBC for Man Alive; joined Epic video production co.; responsible for producing the Food and Drink programme; formed own co. Bazal Productions 1987, Man. Dir 1987–89, cr. Ready Steady Cook (BBC 2), Can't Cook Won't Cook (BBC 1), Changing Rooms (BBC 2), Ground Force (BBC 1), formats sold to 30 countries, co. acquired by Broadcast Communications 1990, latter acquired by Endemol, Chair. Endemol UK 2002–07, Creative Dir of Endemol Group worldwide 2005–07, adviser 2007; Pres. Royal Television Soc.; Dir (non-exec.), Dept of Culture Media & Sport; consultant to two of Sony's TV divs in UK; Chair. MirriAd; Deputy Chair. ENO (Trustee 2004–), Crossness Engines Trust; Vice-Chair. British Acad. of Gastronomes 1993–; Dir (non-exec.) Base79, Nutopia, Victoria Real, Zeppotron, Channel 4 2001–04, YouGov.com 2005–; mem. Advisory Bd BBH; fmr mem. Bd Channel 4; Deputy Chair. Nat. Film & Television School 2002–; Trustee, Debate Mate; Ind. Producer of the Year, Broadcast Production Awards 1997, McTaggart Lecturer, Edinburgh Int. TV Festival 1998, Hat Trick Pioneer Award Indies 1998, Indi-vidual Award for Outstanding Personal Contrib. to the Ind. Sector 2000, Weldon Lecturer, Royal Television Soc. (RTS) 2001, RTS Judges' Award 2003, BAFTA Fellowship 2000. *Television includes:* Food and Drink (series documentary) (producer) 1988, Southern Italian Feast (series documentary) (exec. producer) 1998, Big Brother and Beyond: The Royal Television Society Huw Wheldon Memorial Lecture 2001, Tabloid Tales (series documentary) 2003, Faking It (series) (judge) 2003, Happy Birthday BBC Two (documentary) 2004, Who Killed Saturday Night TV ? (documentary) 2004, HARDtalk Extra (series) 2005, The 50 Greatest Documentaries (documentary) 2005, This Week (series) 2006–07, Channel 4 at 25 (documentary) 2007, TV Is Dead? (mini-series documentary) 2007, How TV Changed Britain (series documentary) 2008, The Money Programme (series documentary) 2009, The TV Show (series documentary) 2009, The Noughties… Was That It? (documentary) 2009, History of Now: The Story of the Noughties (series documentary) 2010, The Review Show (series) – British TV Special 2011. *Publications:* B.B.C. Cook: Your Practical Guide to Safe Food (with D. Edwards) 1989, The Food Revolution (with Tom Sanders) 1991, You Don't Have to Diet (with T. A. B. Sanders) 1994, Entertaining with Food and Drink (with Michael Barry and Jilly Goolden) 1995, Billion Dollar Game: How 3 Men Risked it All and Changed the Face of TV 2005. *Leisure interests:* gluttony, cricket. *Address:* c/o Endemol UK, Shepherd's Building Central, Charecroft Way, Shepherd's Bush, London, W14 0EE, England (office). *Website:* www.endemoluk.com (office).

BAŽANT, Zdeněk Pavel, CE, PhD, Docent (habil.); American (b. Czech) engineer, physicist and academic; *McCormick Institute Professor and Walter P. Murphy Professor of Civil and Environmental Engineering, Mechanical Engineering and Material Science and Engineering, Robert R. McCormick School of Engineering and Applied Science, Northwestern University;* b. 10 Dec. 1937, Prague, Czechoslovakia; ed Czech Tech. Univ. (ČVUT), Czechoslovak (now Czech) Acad. of Sciences, Charles Univ., Prague; worked as bridge engineer for state consulting firm Dopravoprojekt, Prague; Visiting Researcher, Centre Experimental de Recherches et d'Études du Bâtiment et des Travaux Publics, France 1966; appointments at Univ. of Toronto, Canada and Univ. of California, Berkeley, USA; remained in USA following Russian invasion of Czechoslovakia 1968; Assoc. Prof.

of Civil Eng, Northwestern Univ. 1969–73, Prof. 1973–, Dir, Center for Geomaterials 1981–87, currently McCormick Inst. Prof. and Walter P. Murphy Prof. of Civil and Environmental Eng, Mechanical Eng and Material Science and Eng; mem. Nat. Acad. of Eng 1996, NAS 2002; Fellow, American Acad. of Arts and Sciences 2008; Founding Pres. IA-FraMCoS, IA-ConCreep; Past Pres. Soc. of Eng Science; Hon. mem. ASCE, ASME, ACI, IA-FRAMCOS; Dr hc (CVUT) 1991, (Karlsruhe Inst. of Tech.) 1997, (Univ. of Colorado, Boulder) 2000, (Politecnico di Milano) 2001, (INSA de Lyon) 2004, (Vienna Univ. of Tech.) 2005, (Ohio State Univ.) 2011; winner Czechoslovak Math. Olympics 1955, ASME Timoshenko, Nadai and Warner Medals, ASCE von Karman, Newmark, Biot and Croes Medals and Life Achievement Award, SES Prager Medal, RILEM L'Hermite Medal, Wilhelm Exner Medal, Austrian Asscn for SME (Oesterreichischer Gewerbeverein—OGV) (jtly) 2008, Torroja Medal, Madrid, American Ceramic Soc. Roy Award, Solin Medal, Bazant Medal (Prague), Stodola Medal (Slovakia), IACMAG Outstanding Contrib. Award, ICOSSAR Lecture Award, SEAOI Meritorious Paper Award, Best Eng Book of the Year (SAP). *Achievements include:* developed a new method to analyse fracturing and cracking in concrete structures. *Publications:* Creep of Concrete in Structural Analysis (monograph, in Czech) 1966, Stability of Structures: Elastic, Inelastic, Fracture and Damage Theories (with L. Cedolin) 1991, Concrete at High Temperatures: Material Properties and Mathematical Models (with M. F. Kaplan) 1996, Fracture and Size Effect in Concrete and Other Quasibrittle Materials (with J. Planas) 1998, Inelastic Analysis of Structures (with M. Jirásek) 2002, Scaling of Structural Strength 2002; several book chapters and more than 550 research papers in peer-reviewed journals. *Leisure interests:* music, skiing, tennis, history. *Address:* Department of Civil and Environmental Engineering, Robert R. McCormick School of Engineering and Applied Science, Northwestern University, 2145 Sheridan Road, #A135, Evanston, IL 60208-3109, USA (office). *Telephone:* (847) 491-4025 (office). *Fax:* (847) 491-4011 (office). *E-mail:* z-bazant@northwestern.edu (office). *Website:* www.mccormick .northwestern.edu (office); www.civil.northwestern.edu (office).

BAZER, Fuller W., MSc, PhD; American biologist and academic; *Regents Fellow, O.D. Butler Chair in Animal Science, Associate Vice-President for Research and Associate Dean for Agricultural and Life Sciences, Texas A&M University;* b. 1938, Shreveport, La; ed Centenary Coll. of Louisiana, Louisiana State Univ., North Carolina State Univ.; Grad. Research Prof. in Animal Science, NC State Univ., then Research Prof. in Paediatrics, Univ. of Fla 1968–92; joined Faculty of Biosciences, Tex. A&M Univ. 1992, currently holds several positions including Regents Fellow, Prof. and O.D. Butler Chair in Animal Science, Assoc. Vice-Pres. for Research and Exec. Assoc. Dean for Agricultural and Life Sciences and Dir Centre for Animal Biotechnology, Inst. of Biosciences and Tech. (Dir IBT 1994–2001); fmr Pres. and Ed.-in-Chief, Biology of Reproduction Journal, Soc. for the Study of Reproduction (SSR); Assoc. Dir Tex. Agricultural Experimental Station 2001–04; co-f. Gordon Research Conf. on Reproductive Tract Biology 1972; Fellow, AAAS; mem. Bd of Dirs Texas Soc. for Biomedical Research 2005–; mem. Texas Dept of Agric.-Texas Israel Exchange/Binational Agricultural Research and Devt Program Jt Advisory Cttee 2004–; Dr hc (Univ. of Guelph) 2004; L.E. Casida Award for Grad. Educ., American Soc. of Animal Science Physiology and Endocrinology, distinguished service awards from Soc. for the Study of Reproduction Research, Biotechnology 94, Distinguished Achievement in Agric. Award, Gamma Sigma Delta 1996, Alexander von Humboldt Research Award in Agric. 2000, Tex. A&M Vice-Chancellor for Agric. Award in Excellence for Research 2000, inducted into Byrd Alumni Hall of Fame 2002, Wolf Prize for Agric. 2003, SSR Research Award, SSR Distinguished Award, SSR Carl G. Hartman Award 2004, Distinguished Professor Award, Texas A&M Univ. 2004, Vice-Chancellor for Agric. Award for Team Research in Uterine Biology and Pregnancy 2006, Soc. for Research and Fertility Distinguished Research Award 2007, SSR Trainee Mentoring Award 2009. *Publications:* Endocrinology of Pregnancy (Ed.) 1998; numerous articles in professional journals. *Address:* Department of Animal Science, 442 D Kleberg, Mail Stop 2471, Texas A&M University, College Station, TX 77843-2471, USA (office). *Telephone:* (979) 862-2659 (office). *Fax:* (979) 862-2662 (office). *E-mail:* fbazer@cvm.tamu.edu (office). *Website:* animalscience.tamu .edu (office); cerh.tamu.edu (office); www.ibt.tamhsc.edu.

BAZHANOV, Evgeny Petrovich, CSc, MA, PhD, DHist; Russian diplomatist, political scientist, historian and writer; *Rector, Diplomatic Academy of the Ministry of Foreign Affairs;* b. 6 Nov. 1946, Lvov, Ukraine; s. of Petr Bazhanov and Anna Bazhanova; m. Natalia Bazhanova 1968; ed Nanyang Univ., Singapore, Moscow Inst. of Int. Relations, Inst. of the Far East, Diplomatic Acad., Inst. of Oriental Studies; Political Officer, Ministry of Foreign Affairs, USSR 1970–72; Vice-Consul, USSR Gen. Consulate, San Francisco 1973–79; Political Counsellor, USSR Embassy in Beijing 1981–85; Adviser on foreign policy to USSR Pres. Mikhail Gorbachev 1985–91; Dir Inst. for Contemporary Int. Studies, Moscow 1991–2006; Vice-Rector for Research and Int. Affairs, Diplomatic Acad. of the Ministry of Foreign Affairs 1991–2011, Rector 2011–; Chair. Dissertation Council, Diplomatic Acad., Moscow 1992–; Chair. Editorial Bd 1992; Chair. Advisory Bd Ministry of Educ. 1994–; Examination Cttee, Friendship Univ., Moscow 2000–; mem. Exec. Cttee Asscn for Dialogue and Co-operation in Asian-Pacific Region 1991–, Nat. Cttee on Security 1996–, Council on Foreign Policy 2001–; mem. Int. Ecological Acad., Acad. of Humanitarian Research, American Acad. of Political Sciences, Asscn of Russian Sinologists 1986–, Russian Acad. of Humanities, World Ecological Acad., Political Science Asscn, Asscn of Asian Studies; Hon. Prof., People's Univ. of China; Dr hc (Bishkek Univ.) 2009; Best Journalist Award, New Times Magazine 1987, Distinguished Scholar of the Russian Fed. 1997. *Publications:* 40 books and over 1,000 articles and book chapters on world affairs, internal and foreign policy of Russia, China, USA, North Korea, Europe, Middle East and Southeast Asia. *Address:* Diplomatic Academy of the Ministry of Foreign Affairs, Moscow 119992, Ostozhenka 53/2 (office); 121165 Moscow, 30 Kutuzovsky Av. #462, Russia (home). *Telephone:* (499) 940-13-55 (office); (495) 249-15-60 (home). *Fax:* (499) 244-18-78 (office). *E-mail:* info.rector@dipacademy.ru (office). *Website:* www.dipacademy.ru (office).

BAZIN, Henry; Haitian economist, academic and fmr government official; ed State Univ. of Haiti, Univ. of Paris, France; taught econs at Ecole Nationale d'Administration, Mali 1962–68; held various positions at UN Econ. Comm. for Africa, Addis Ababa, Ethiopia, including Dir Div. of Int. Trade and Finance and Dir of Econ. Cooperation 1974–85; Sr Econ. Adviser and Dir UNDP Regional

Programme for Africa, New York 1986–91; Technical Adviser to Prime Minister Marc Bazin 1992; Minister of Finance, Minister of Economy and Finance 2004–06; Prof. of Econs, Quisqueya Univ. 2006–. *Address:* Université Quisqueya, 218 Avenue Jean-Paul II, Haut de Turgeau, Port-au-Prince, Haiti (office). *Website:* www.uniq.edu (office).

BAZOLI, Giovanni; Italian lawyer, academic and banking executive; *Chairman of the Supervisory Board, Intesa Sanpaolo SpA;* b. 18 Dec. 1932, Brescia; Prof. of Law, Faculty of Econs, Univ. Cattolica di Milano –2001, Prof. of Admin. Law and Insts of Public Law –2003; Chair. Banca Intesa SpA 1982–2006, Chair. Supervisory Bd Sanpaolo IMI (following merger between Banca Intesa and Sanpaolo) 2007–, Chair. Supervisory Bd Intesa Sanpaolo SpA 2010–; apptd Dir Fondazione Giorgio Cini 1987, Chair. 1999–; Chair. Fondazione Giorgio Cini, Mittel SpA; fmr Chair. Istituto Studi Direzionale SpA; Deputy Chair. Banca Lombarda, Editrice La Scuola SpA; mem. Bd of Dirs Banco di Brescia, ABI Associazione Bancaria Italiana (mem. Exec. Cttee), Alleanza Assicurazione SpA, FAI Fondo per l'Ambiente Italiano, Ente Bresciano Istruzione Superiore; mem. Supervisory Bd UBI Banca SpA; mem. Gen. Advisory Bd Assonime, Exec. Cttee Istituto Paolo VI, Congregazione dei Conservatori di Biblioteca Ambrosiana; Cavaliere del Lavoro 2000, Cavaliere di Gran Croce 2002, Officier, Légion d'honneur 2002; Dr hc (Università degli Studi di Macerata) 1997, (Università degli Studi di Udine) 2001. *Address:* Intesa Sanpaolo SpA, Piazza San Carlo 156, 10121 Turin, Italy (office). *Telephone:* (011) 5551 (office). *E-mail:* info@sanpaoloimi.comt (office). *Website:* www.intestasanpaolo.com (office).

BAZZAZ, Saad al-, MA; Iraqi journalist and broadcaster; *Editor-in-Chief, Al-Zaman (Time);* b. 18 April 1952, Mosul; ed Univ. of Baghdad, Arab League Inst. for Research and Studies, Univ. of Exeter, UK; Dir Iraqi TV Second Channel 1974–79; Dir Iraqi Cultural Centre, London 1979–84; Gen. Man. Nat. House for Printing and Distribution, Baghdad 1984–86; Gen. Man. Iraq News Agency 1986–88; Gen. Dir Iraqi TV and Radio 1988–90; Ed.-in-Chief, Al-Jammhoria 1990–92; left Iraq Oct. 1992; Founder and Ed.-in-Chief, Al-Zaman (Time), London 1997–2003, Baghdad 2003–; Owner Al Sharqiya satellite channel 2004–. *Publications include:* Alhijrat (Migrations) 1972, Searching for the Sea Birds 1976, Future of the Boy and the Girl 1980, Future of Radio Broadcasts 1980, The Secret War 1987, The Scorpion 1987, At 6:30 Hours: Secrets of FAO Battle 1988, A War Gives Birth to Another 1992, Ashes of War 1995, The Generals are the Last to Know 1996, Kurds in Iraqi Question 1996. *Address:* Al-Zaman (Time), Baghdad, Iraq. *Telephone:* (1) 717-7587. *E-mail:* postmaster@azzaman.com. *Website:* www.azzaman.com; www .alsharqiya.com.

BBUMBA, Syda, BComm, MBA; Ugandan politician; *Minister of Gender, Labour and Social Affairs;* b. 7 Jan. 1952; m.; Commr, Interim Electoral Comm. 1996; mem. Parl. 1996–; Minister of State for Dept of Econ. Monitoring, Office of the Pres. 1996–99; Minister of Energy and Mineral Devt 1999–2006, of Gender, Labour and Social Services 2006–09, of Finance 2009–11, of Gender, Labour and Social Affairs 2011–; mem. Nat. Resistance Movt. *Address:* Ministry of Gender, Labour and Social Affairs, Plot 2, Lumumba Avenue, Simbamanyo House, POB 7136, Kampala, Uganda (office). *Telephone:* (41) 347854 (office). *Fax:* (41) 256374 (office). *E-mail:* ps@mglsd.go.ug (office); www.mglsd.go.ug (office).

BEACH, David Hugh, PhD, FRS, FMedSci; British molecular biologist and academic; *Professor of Stem Cell Biology, Barts and The London School of Medicine and Dentistry, Queen Mary, University of London;* b. 18 May 1954, London; s. of Gen. Sir Hugh Beach and Estelle Beach; ed Winchester Coll., Peterhouse, Cambridge, Univ. of Miami, USA; Postdoctoral Fellow, Univ. of Sussex 1978–82; Postdoctoral Fellow, Cold Spring Harbor Lab., NY 1982–83, Jr then Sr Staff Investigator 1984–89, Tenured Scientist 1992– (Sr Staff Scientist 1989–97, Adjunct Investigator 1997–2000); Investigator, Howard Hughes Medical Inst. 1990–97; Adjunct Assoc. Prof., State Univ. of NY at Stony Brook 1990–97; f. Mitotix Inc. 1992; Founder and Pres. Genetica Inc. 1996–; fmr Hugh and Catherine Stevenson Prof. of Cancer Biology, Univ. Coll. London; currently Prof. of Stem Cell Biology, Barts and The London School of Medicine and Dentistry, Queen Mary, Univ. of London; Eli Lilly Research Award 1994, Bristol-Myers Squibb Award 2000, Raymond Bourgine Award 2001. *Publications:* numerous papers in scientific journals. *Address:* Barts and The London School of Medicine and Dentistry, Turner Street, London, E1 2AD (office); 15 Springalls Wharf, 25 Bermondsey Wall West, London, SE16 4TL, England (home). *Telephone:* (20) 7882-3004 (office). *E-mail:* dhbeach@btinternet.com (home). *Website:* www.qmul.ac.uk (office).

BEALE, Graham; British chartered accountant and business executive; *Chief Executive, Nationwide Building Society;* one s. one d.; ed Coll., Univ.; joined Nationwide Building Society 1985, held several sr and gen. man. positions, including Man. Dir of a wholly owned property co. and Divisional Dir of Commercial Lending, mem. Bd of Dirs and Group Finance Dir 2003–07, Chief Exec. 2007–; Dir (non-exec.) Visa Europe Ltd, Visa Europe Services. *Address:* Nationwide Building Society, Pipers Way, Swindon, Wilts., SN38 1NW, England (office). *Telephone:* (1793) 656789 (office). *Fax:* (1793) 455341 (office). *E-mail:* info@ nationwide.co.uk (office). *Website:* www.nationwide.co.uk (office).

BEALES, Derek Edward Dawson, BA, PhD, LittD, FBA; British historian and academic; *Professor Emeritus of Modern History, Sidney Sussex College, Cambridge;* b. 12 June 1931, Felixstowe, Suffolk, England; s. of Edward Beales and Dorothy K. Dawson; m. Sara J. Ledbury 1964; one s. one d.; ed Bishop's Stortford Coll. and Sidney Sussex Coll., Cambridge; Research Fellow, Sidney Sussex Coll., Cambridge 1955–58, Fellow 1955–, Asst Lecturer in History, Univ. of Cambridge 1962–65, Lecturer 1965–80, Prof. of Modern History 1980–97, Prof. Emer. 1997–; Stenton Lecturer, Univ. of Reading 1992, Birkbeck Lecturer, Trinity Coll., Cambridge 1993; Recurring Visiting Prof., Cen. European Univ., Budapest 1995–; Ed. Historical Journal 1971–75; mem. Standing Cttee for Humanities, European Science Foundation 1994–99; Leverhulme 2000, Emer., Fellowship 2001–03; Prince Consort Prize, Univ. of Cambridge 1960, Henry Paolucci/Walter Bagehot Prize, Intercollegiate Studies Inst., Wilmington, Del. 2004. *Publications:* England and Italy 1859–60 1961, From Castlereagh to Gladstone 1969, History and Biography 1981, History, Society and the Churches (with G. Best) 1985, Joseph II, Vol. I: In the Shadow of Maria Theresa 1987, Mozart and the Habsburgs 1993, Sidney Sussex Quatercentenary Essays (with H. B. Nisbet) 1996, The

Risorgimento and the Unification of Italy (second edn with E. Biagini) 2002, Prosperity and Plunder: European Catholic Monasteries in the Age of Revolution 2003, Enlightenment and Reform in the 18th Century 2005, Joseph II, Vol. II: Against the World 2009. *Leisure interests:* music, walking, bridge. *Address:* Sidney Sussex College, Cambridge, CB2 3HU, England (office). *Telephone:* (1223) 338833 (office). *E-mail:* derek@beales.ws (home).

BEALL, Donald Ray, BS, MBA; American business executive; *Partner, Dartbrook Partners LLC;* b. 29 Nov. 1938, Beaumont, Calif.; s. of Ray C. Beall and Margaret Beall (née Murray); m. Joan Frances Lange 1961; two s.; ed San Jose State Coll. and Univ. of Pittsburgh; various financial and management positions, Ford Motor Co., Newport Beach, Calif., Philadelphia and Palo Alto, Calif. 1961–68; Exec. Dir Corporate Financial Planning, Rockwell Int., El Segundo, Calif. 1968–69, Exec. Vice-Pres. Electronics Group 1969–71; Exec. Vice-Pres. Collins Radio Co., Dallas 1971–74; Pres. Collins Radio Group, Dallas, Rockwell Int. 1974–76, Pres. Electronics Operations 1976–77, Exec. Vice-Pres. 1977–79; Pres. Rockwell Int. (now Rockwell Collins) 1979–88, COO 1979–88, Chair. and CEO 1988–98 (CEO 1988–97), Chair. Exec. Cttee 1998, mem. Bd Dirs 2001, Chair. 2001–02, Chair. Emer. 2002–; mem. Pres.'s Export Council 1981–85; Chair. Beall Family Foundation; Pnr, Dartbrook Partners LLC (family investment partnership); mem. Foundation Bd of Trustees Univ. of Calif., Irvine 1988–; mem. Bd of Dirs Conexant Systems, Proctor & Gamble, Skyworks Solutions 2002–05, Mindspeed Technologies, Inc. 2003–07; Overseer, Hoover Inst.; Trustee, Calif. Inst. of Tech., Naval Postgraduate School Foundation; mem. Business Council; Founding mem. New Majority, Orange Co.; Fellow, American Inst. of Aeronautics and Astronautics; Sword of Life Award, American Cancer Soc. 1989, Horatio Alger Award 1998. *Leisure interests:* tennis, boating. *Address:* Dartbrook Partners, 5 Civic Plaza, #320, Newport Beach, CA 92660, USA (office). *E-mail:* beallfoundation@gmail.com. *Website:* www.beallfoundation.com.

BEAN, Charles Richard, PhD; British economist and banker; *Deputy Governor, Bank of England;* b. 16 Sept. 1953, Basildon, Essex, England; s. of Charles Ernest Bean and Mary Bean; m. Elizabeth Nan Callender-Bean; ed Brentwood School, Emmanuel Coll., Cambridge, Massachusetts Inst. of Tech., USA; Econ. Asst, Short-Term Forecasting Div., HM Treasury 1975–79; Econ. Adviser, Monetary Policy Div. 1981–82; Lecturer in Econs, LSE 1982–86, Reader 1986–90, Prof. 1990–2000, Deputy Dir Centre for Econ. Performance 1990–94, Head of Econs Dept 1999–2000; Visiting Prof., Stanford Univ. 1990, Reserve Bank of Australia 1999; mem. Monetary Policy Cttee, Bank of England 2000–, Exec. Dir and Chief Economist 2000–08, Deputy Gov., Monetary Policy 2008–, mem. Financial Policy Cttee 2011–; Pres. Royal Econ. Soc. 2013–(15). *Address:* Bank of England, Threadneedle Street, London, EC2R 8AH, England (office). *Telephone:* (20) 7601-4999 (office). *Fax:* (20) 7601-3047 (office). *Website:* www.bankofengland.co.uk (office).

BEAN, Sean; British actor; b. 17 April 1958, Sheffield, Yorks., England; ed Royal Acad. of Dramatic Art, London; professional debut as Tybalt in Romeo and Juliet, Watermill Theatre, Newbury. *Stage appearances include:* The Last Days of Mankind and Der Rosenkavalier at Citizens' Theatre, Glasgow, Lederer in Deathwatch, Young Vic Studio, Who Knew Mackenzie? and Gone, Theatre Upstairs, Royal Court, Starvling in Midsummer Night's Dream and Romeo in Romeo and Juliet, RSC, Stratford-upon-Avon 1986, Captain Spencer in The Fair Maid of the West, RSC, London, Macbeth in Macbeth, Albery Theatre, London 2002. *Films include:* Winter Flight 1984, Samson and Delilah 1985, Caravaggio 1986, Stormy Monday 1988, War Requiem 1989, How to Get Ahead in Advertising 1989, Windprints 1990, The Field 1990, In the Border Country 1991, Prince 1991, Patriot Games 1992, Shopping 1994, Black Beauty 1994, Goldeneye 1995, When Saturday Comes 1996, Anna Karenina 1997, Airborne 1998, Ronin 1998, Bravo Two Zero 1999, Essex Boys 2000, Don't Say a Word 2001, The Lord of the Rings: The Fellowship of the Ring 2001, Tom and Thomas 2002, The Lord of the Rings: The Two Towers 2002, Equilibrium 2002, The Big Empty 2003, The Lord of the Rings: The Return of the King 2003, Troy 2004, National Treasure 2004, North Country 2005, The Dark 2005, The Island 2005, Flightplan 2005, Silent Hill 2006, The Hitcher 2007, Outlaw 2007, Far North 2007, Red Riding: In the Year of Our Lord 1974 2009, Red Riding: In the Year of Our Lord 1983 2009, Drumhead (short) (voice) 2009, Percy Jackson & the Lightning Thief 2010, Ca$h 2010, Black Death 2010, Death Race 2 (video) 2010, Age of Heroes 2011, Mirror Mirror: The Untold Adventures of Snow White 2012, Cleanskin 2012, Soldiers of Fortune 2012, Silent Hill: Revelation 3D 2012. *Radio work:* A Kind of Loving, The True Story of Martin Guerre, Saturday Night and Sunday Morning. *TV appearances include:* Lorna Doone 1990, Small Zones 1990, Wedded 1990, My Kingdom for a Horse (series) 1991, Clarissa 1991, Tell Me That You Love Me 1991, Fool's Gold: The Story of the Brink's-Mat Robbery 1992, Sharpe's Rifles 1993 (also several Sharpe episodes in subsequent years), Lady Chatterley 1993, A Woman's Guide to Adultery 1993, Scarlett (mini-series) 1994, Jacob 1994, Extremely Dangerous 1999, Henry VIII 2003, Pride (voice) 2004, Faceless (film) 2006, Sharpe's Challenge (film) 2006, Sharpe's Peril (film) 2008, Crusoe (series) 2008–10, The Lost Future (film) 2010, Game of Thrones (series) 2011, Missing (series) 2012. *Address:* c/o ICM Ltd, Oxford House, 76 Oxford Street, London, W1D 1BS, England (office). *Telephone:* (20) 7636-6565 (office). *Fax:* (20) 7323-0101 (office).

BEARPARK, Andrew, CBE, BSc; British security industry executive and fmr international organization official; ed Univ. of London; with UK Overseas Devt Admin. (ODA) responsible for Devt programmes in Asia and Africa 1973–86, Head of Information and Emergency Aid Dept, responsible for programmes in Bosnia, Rwanda, N Iraq and Somalia 1991–97, Press Sec. to ODA Minister Baroness Chalker 1991–95; Pvt. Sec. to Prime Minister Margaret Thatcher 1986–89, responsible for Home Affairs, then Parl. Affairs, Chief of Staff to Lady Thatcher 1990–91; UN Deputy High Rep. for Reconstruction and Return Task Force, Sarajevo 1998–2000; Deputy Special Rep. for Reconstruction and Econ. Devt, UN Interim Admin. Mission in Kosovo 2000–03; fmr Dir of Reconstruction, Coalition Provisional Authority, Baghdad; fmr Vice-Pres. Special Projects, Olive Group LLC (pvt. security firm); Punchline (public relations consultancy) 1989; Founder and Dir Post Conflict People (consultancy); Dir-Gen. then Hon. Dir-Gen. British Asscn of Private Security Cos; Trustee, CARE International (UK). *Address:* Post Conflict People, PO Box 276, Cirencester, Gloucestershire, GL7 9ER, England (office).

Telephone: (20) 3355-7789 (office). *E-mail:* enquiries@postconflictpeople.org (office). *Website:* www.postconflictpeople.org (office).

BÉART, Emmanuelle; French actress; b. 14 Aug. 1965, Gassin; d. of Guy Béart (q.v.) and Geneviève Galéa; one d. with Daniel Auteuil (q.v.); began acting career with appearance as a child in Demain les Momes 1978. *Films:* Un Amour Interdit, L'Enfant Trouvé 1983, L'Amour en Douce 1984, Manon des Sources 1985, Date with an Angel 1987, A Gauche en Sortant de l'Ascenseur 1988, Les Enfants du Désordre 1989, Capitaine Fracasse 1990, La Belle Noiseuse 1991, J'Embrasse Pas 1991, Un Coeur en Hiver 1991, Ruptures 1992, L'Enfer 1993, Mission Impossible 1995, Nelly and M. Arnaud 1995, Time Regained 1999, Les Destinées Sentimentales 2000, La Repetition 2001, 8 Femmes 2002, Strayed 2003, Histoire de Marie et Julien 2003, Nathalie 2003, À boire 2004, D'Artagnan et les trois mousquetaires 2005, Un fil à la patte 2005, L'Enfer 2005, A Crime 2006, Le Héros de la famille 2006, Les Témoins 2007, Mes Stars et moi 2008, Nous trois 2010, Ça commence par la fin 2010, Bye Bye Blondie 2011, Pirate TV 2012, Par exemple, Electre 2013.

BÉART, Guy; French singer, composer, engineer and author; b. 16 July 1930, Cairo, Egypt; s. of David Behart-Hasson and Amélia Taral; one s. one d. (Emmanuelle Béart); ed Lycée Henri IV, Paris and Ecole Nat. des Ponts et des Chaussées; music transcriber, Prof. of Math., then Eng 1952–57; subsequently made debut in cabaret in Paris; composed songs for Zizi Jeanmaire, Juliette Greco, Patachou, Maurice Chevalier, etc.; recitalist in various Paris theatres and music-halls; composer of more than 200 songs, also film music (including L'Eau vive, Pierrot la tendresse and La Gamberge); author and producer of TV series Bienvenue 1966–72; Chevalier, Légion d'honneur, Officier, Ordre Nat. du Mérite, Commdr des Arts et des Lettres; Grand Prix, Acad. du Disque 1957, Grand Prix du Disque, Acad. Charles Cros 1965, Grand Prix de la chanson Sacem 1987, Prix Balzac 1987, Grand Médaille de la Chanson Française (Académie Française) 1994. *Recordings:* albums: Vive la Rose 1966, V'La L'Joli Vent 1973, Le meilleur des choses 2010. *Publications:* Couleurs et colères du temps 1976, L'Espérance folle 1987, Il est temps 1995. *Leisure interest:* chess. *Address:* Editions Temporel, 2 rue du Marquis de Morès, 92380 Garches, France (office).

BEASLEY, David Muldrow, JD; American consultant and fmr politician; *Chairman, Center for Global Strategies, Ltd;* b. 26 Feb. 1957, Lamar, SC; s. of Richard L. Beasley and Jacqueline A. Blackwell; m. Mary Wood Payne; two s., two d.; ed Clemson Univ. and Univ. of South Carolina; practising attorney Beasley, Ervin & Warr; Rep. for SC State, Dist 56 1979–92; Majority Leader, SC House of Reps 1987; Gov. of S. Carolina 1995–99; Fellow, Inst. of Politics, Kennedy School of Govt, Harvard Univ. 1999; Prin. Bingham Consulting Group 1999–2001; mem. Bd of Trustees, Francis Marion Coll. 1988-91, Univ. of South Carolina 1990–91; unsuccessful campaign for US Senate 2004; fmr Chair. Nat. Advisory Cttee on Rural Health and Human Services, US Dept of Health and Human Services; currently Chair. Center for Global Strategies, Ltd, Columbia, SC; mem. Bd of Trustees, Francis Marion Coll. 1988–91; mem. Bd of Trustees, Univ. of South Carolina 1990–91; Republican; Dr hc (Univ. of South Carolina, The Citadel, Charleston Southern Univ., Regent Univ., Medical Univ. of South Carolina, Coll. of Charleston, Bob Jones Univ., Newberry Coll.); American Swiss Foundation Friendship Award 1996, John F. Kennedy Profile in Courage Award 2003. *Address:* 4813 North Governor Williams Highway, Society Hill, SC 29593, USA. *Website:* www.centerforglobalstrategies.org.

BEATH, John Arnott, MA, MPhil, FRSE, FRSA; British economist and academic; *Secretary-General, Royal Economic Society;* b. 15 June 1944, Thurso, Caithness, Scotland; s. of James Beath and Marion McKendrick Beath (née Spence); m. Monika Schröder 1980; ed Hillhead High School, Glasgow, Univs of St Andrews, London, Pennsylvania and Cambridge; Thouron Scholar, Univ. of Pennsylvania 1968–71, Fels Fellow 1971–72; Research Officer, Univ. of Cambridge 1972–79, Fellow, Downing Coll. 1978–79; Lecturer, then Sr Lecturer, Univ. of Bristol 1979–91; Prof. of Econs, Univ. of St Andrews 1991–2009, currently Prof. Emer., also Head, School of Social Sciences 1997–2003; Chair. Econ. Research Inst. of Northern Ireland 2003–09; mem. Doctors' and Dentists' Review Body 2003–09; Sec.-Gen. Royal Economic Soc. 2008–; Chair. Training and Skills Cttee 2009–, mem. Council; mem. Prison Service Pay Review Body 2010–, Competition Appeal Tribunal 2011–; Thouron Scholar. *Publications include:* Economic Theory of Product Differentiation. *Leisure interests:* gardening, golf, walking. *Address:* Royal Economic Society, School of Economics and Finance, University of St Andrews, St Andrews, Fife, KY16 9AL, Scotland (office). *Telephone:* (1334) 462421 (office). *Fax:* (1334) 462444 (office). *E-mail:* jab@st-and.ac.uk (office). *Website:* www.st-andrews .ac.uk/economics (office).

BEATRIX WILHELMINA ARMGARD, HRH Princess; b. 31 Jan. 1938, Baarn; d. of Queen Juliana (died 2004) and Bernhard, Prince of the Netherlands; m. Claus George Willem Otto Frederik Geert Jonkheer von Amsberg 10 March 1966 (died 2002); children: Willem-Alexander Claus George Ferdinand, King of The Netherlands, b. 27 April 1967; Prince Johan Friso Bernhard Christiaan David, b. 25 Sept. 1968; Prince Constantijn Christof Frederik Aschwin, b. 11 Oct. 1969; ed Baarn Grammar School, Leiden State Univ.; succeeded to the throne on abdication of her mother 30 April 1980; Queen of The Netherlands 1980–2013, abdicated 30 April 2013; Hon. KG; ranked 35th by Forbes magazine amongst 100 Most Powerful Women 2004. *Leisure interests:* sculpting, riding, sailing. *Address:* Noordeinde Palace, Postbus 30412, 2500 The Hague, Netherlands. *Website:* www .koninklijkhuis.nl/english.

BEATSON, Sir Jack, Kt, QC, DCL, LLD, FBA; British judge; *Judge, Court of Appeal;* b. 3 Nov. 1948, Haifa, Israel; s. of the late John James Beatson and Miriam White; m. Charlotte H. Christie-Miller 1973; one s. (deceased) one d.; ed Whittingehame Coll. Brighton and Brasenose Coll., Oxford; Lecturer in Law, Univ. of Bristol 1972–73; Fellow and Tutor in Law, Merton Coll. Oxford 1973–93, Hon. Fellow 1997–, Hon. Fellow, Brasenose Coll. 2009–; Rouse Ball Prof. of Law, Univ. of Cambridge 1993–2003, Chair. Faculty of Law 2001–03, Fellow, St John's Coll., Cambridge 1994–2003, Hon. Fellow 2005–; Dir Centre for Public Law, Cambridge 1997–2001; QC 1998; Deputy High Court Judge 2000–03, Justice of the High Court, Queen's Bench Div. 2003–13; Judge of the Court of Appeal 2013–; Visiting Prof., Osgoode Hall Law School, Toronto, Canada 1979, Univ. of Virginia Law School, USA 1980, 1983; Distinguished Visiting Prof., Univ. of Toronto 2000; Sr Visiting Fellow, Nat. Univ. of Singapore 1987; Visiting Fellow, Univ. of Western

Australia 1988; Law Commr for England and Wales 1989–94; Recorder of Crown Court 1994–2003; Pres. British Acad. of Forensic Science 2007–09; mem. Competition Comm. 1995–2001; Bencher, Inner Temple. *Publications:* Administrative Law: Cases and Materials (second edn with M. Matthews 1989), The Use and Abuse of Restitution 1991, Chitty on Contracts (co-ed., 28th edn) 1999, Good Faith and Fault in Contract Law 1995, European Public Law (co-ed.) 1998, Anson's Law of Contract (29th edn 2010), Human Rights: The 1998 Act and the European Convention (with S. Grosz and P. Duffy), Unjustified Enrichment: Cases, Materials and Texts (co-ed.) 2003, Jurists Uprooted: German Speaking Émigré Lawyers in Twentieth Century Britain (co-ed.) 2004, Human Rights: Judicial Protection in the UK (co-author) 2009. *Leisure interest:* attempting to relax. *Address:* Royal Courts of Justice, Strand, London, WC2A 2LL, England (office).

BEATTIE, Ann, MA; American writer and academic; *Edgar Allan Poe Professor of Literature and Creative Writing, University of Virginia;* b. 8 Sept. 1947, Washington; d. of James Beattie and Charlotte Crosby; m. Lincoln Perry; ed American Univ., Univ. of Connecticut; Visiting Asst Prof., Univ. of Virginia, Charlottesville 1976–77, Visiting Writer 1980; Briggs Copeland Lecturer in English, Harvard Univ. 1977; Guggenheim Fellow 1977; currently Edgar Allan Poe Prof. of Literature and Creative Writing, Univ. of Virginia; mem. American Acad. of Arts and Letters, PEN, Authors' Guild; Hon. LHD (American Univ.); Award in Literature, American Acad. of Arts and Letters 1980, PEN/Bernard Malamud Award (co-recipient) 2000. *Publications:* Chilly Scenes of Winter 1976, Distortions 1976, Secrets and Surprises 1979, Falling in Place 1990, Jacklighting 1981, The Burning House 1982, Love Always 1985, Where You'll Find Me 1986, Alex Katz (art criticism) 1987, Picturing Will 1990, What Was Mine (story collection) 1991, My Life Starring Dara Falcon 1997, Park City: New and Selected Stories 1998, Perfect Recall 2001, The Doctor's House 2002, Follies 2005, Walks with Men 2010, The New Yorker Stories 2010, Mrs. Nixon: A Novelist Imagines a Life 2011. *Address:* Department of English, University of Virginia, 219 Bryan Hall, PO Box 400121, Charlottesville, VA 22904-4121 (office); c/o Scribner, Simon & Schuster, 1230 Avenue of the Americas, New York, NY 10020, USA. *Website:* www .engl.virginia.edu (office).

BEATTY, (Henry) Warren; American actor; b. 30 March 1937, Richmond, Virginia; s. of Ira Beatty and Kathlyn Maclean; brother of Shirley Maclaine (q.v.); m. Annette Bening (q.v.) 1992; one s. three d.; ed Stella Adler Theatre School; Fellow, BAFTA 2002; Hon. Chair. Stella Adler School of Acting 2004; Commdr Ordre des Arts et des Lettres; Irving Thalberg Special Acad. Award 2000, recipient of Kennedy Center Honors 2004, Golden Globe Cecil B DeMille Award 2007, American Film Inst. Life Achievement Award 2008. *Film appearances include:* Splendor in the Grass 1961, Roman Spring of Mrs. Stone 1961, All Fall Down 1962, Lilith, 1965, Mickey One 1965, Promise Her Anything 1966, Kaleidoscope 1966, Bonnie and Clyde 1967, The Only Game in Town 1969, McCabe and Mrs. Miller 1971, Dollars 1972, The Parallax View 1974, Shampoo (producer and co-screenwriter) 1975, The Fortune 1976, Heaven Can Wait (producer, co-dir and co-screenwriter) 1978, Reds (producer, dir, Acad. Award for Best Dir 1981) 1981, Ishtar 1987, Dick Tracy 1989, Bugsy 1991, Love Affair, Bulworth (also dir) 1998, Town and Country 2001, Dean Tavoularis: The Magician of Hollywood (documentary) 2003, One Bright Shining Moment (documentary) 2005. *Theatre roles include:* A Loss of Roses 1960. *TV includes:* Studio One and Playhouse 90, A Salute to Dustin Hoffman 1999. *Address:* c/o Risa Gertner, CAA, 9830 Wilshire Boulevard, Beverly Hills, CA 90212-1825, USA (office). *Telephone:* (310) 288-4545 (office). *Fax:* (310) 288-4800 (office). *Website:* www.caa.com (office).

BEATTY, Hon. Perrin, BA; Canadian business executive and fmr politician; *President and CEO, Canadian Chamber of Commerce;* b. 1 June 1950, Toronto; s. of George Ernest Beatty and Martha Beatty (née Perrin); m. Julia Kenny 1974; two s. (one deceased); ed Upper Canada Coll., Univ. of Western Ont.; Special Asst to Minister of Health, Prov. of Ont.; mem. House of Commons 1972–93; Minister of State for Treasury Bd 1979; Minister of Nat. Revenue 1984–85; Solicitor-Gen. for Canada 1985–86, Acting Solicitor-Gen. 1989; Minister of Defence 1986–89, of Nat. Health and Welfare 1989–91, of Communications 1991–93, of External Affairs 1993; Pres. and CEO CBC 1995–2000, Canadian Mfrs & Exporters 1999–2007, Canadian Chamber of Commerce 2007–; Chancellor, Univ. of Ontario Inst. of Tech. 2008–; mem. Special Jt Cttee on Constitution 1978, Chair. Progressive Conservative Caucus Cttee on Supply and Services, Spokesperson on Communications; Co-Chair. of Standing Jt Cttee on Regulations and Other Statutory Instruments; Caucus spokesperson on Revenue Canada; Chair. of Caucus Cttee on Fed. Prov. Relations and of Progressive Conservative Task Force on Revenue Canada 1983. *Leisure interests:* music, travel, technology and reading. *Address:* Canadian Chamber of Commerce, 360 Albert Street, Suite 420, Ottawa, ON K1R 7X7, Canada (office). *Telephone:* (613) 238-4000 (office). *Fax:* (613) 238-7643 (office). *E-mail:* info@chamber.ca (office). *Website:* www.chamber.ca (office).

BEAUCE, Thierry Martin de, LenD; French government official; b. 14 Feb. 1943, Lyon; s. of Bertrand Martin de Beauce and Simone de Beauce (née de la Verpillere); m. Diana Segard (divorced); two d.; ed Univ. of Paris and Ecole Nat. d'Admin; Civil Admin., Ministry of Cultural Affairs 1968–69; seconded to Office of Prime Minister 1969–73; Tech. Adviser, Pvt. Office of Pres. of Nat. Ass. 1974; seconded to Econ. Affairs Directorate, Ministry of Foreign Affairs 1974–76; Cultural Counsellor, Japan 1976–78; Second Counsellor, Morocco 1978–80; Vice-Pres. for Int. Affairs Société Elf Aquitaine 1981–86; Dir-Gen. of Cultural, Scientific and Tech. Relations, Ministry of Foreign Affairs 1986–87; State Sec. attached to Minister of Foreign Affairs 1988–91; Adviser to the Pres. for African Affairs 1991–94; Vice-Pres. of Conf. for Yugoslavia 1992; Amb. to Indonesia 1995–97; Special Adviser to Chair. and CEO for Int. Affairs, Vivendi Universal (became Vivendi 2006) 1997–2000, fmr Sr Exec. Vice-Pres. for Int. Affairs, Vivendi Environnement; Pres. MEDEF Int. for Middle East 1998–; Deputy Pres. Assen of Democrats 1989–; Chevalier, Légion d'honneur. *Publications:* Les raisons dangereuses (essay) 1975, Un homme ordinaire (novel) 1978, L'Ile absolue (essay) 1979, Le désir de guerre 1980, La chute de Tanger (novel) 1984, Nouveau discours sur l'universalité de la langue française 1988, Le livre d'Esther 1989, La République de France 1991, La nonchalence de Dieu 1995, L'archipel des épices 1998, L'absent de Marrakech 2006. *Address:* 45 rue de Richelieu, 75001 Paris, France (home).

BEAUDET, Alain, MD, PhD, FRSC; Canadian physician, neuroscientist and research administrator; *President, Canadian Institutes of Health Research;* b. 21 Sept. 1947, Montréal, Québec; m. Nathalie Beaudet; one s.; ed Univ. of Montreal; Postdoctoral Research, Centre d'études nucléaires, Saclay, France 1977–79, Univ. of Zürich Brain Research Inst., Switzerland 1979–80; Researcher, Montréal Neurological Inst. 1980, becoming Assoc. Dir of Research 1985–92; Head of Neurobiology Group, McGill Univ., Montréal 1988–96, becoming Prof. of Neurosciences; Pres. Canadian Asscn for Neuroscience 1995–97, Canadian Insts of Health Research 2008–; Pres. and CEO Fonds de la recherche en santé du Québec 2004–08; Fellow, Canadian Acad. of Health Sciences 2007; Officier, Ordre des Palmes académiques 2007; Chevalier, Ordre nat. du Québec 2011; Dr hc (Univ. Pierre et Marie Curie, France) 2007, (Univ. of Sherbrooke) 2013; Prix Adrien-Pouliot, Asscn francophone pour le savoir 2004, Lifetime Achievement Award, Montreal Neurological Inst. 2005, Genesis Prize, BioQuebec 2008. *Publications:* more than 200 publs in professional journals. *Address:* Office of the President, Canadian Institutes of Health Research, 160 Elgin Street, 9th Floor, Ottawa, ON K1A 0W9, Canada (office). *Telephone:* (613) 941-2672 (office). *Fax:* (613) 954-1800 (office). *E-mail:* alain.beaudet@cihr-irsc.gc.ca (office). *Website:* www.cihr-irsc.gc.ca (office).

BEAUDOIN, Laurent Robert, CC, CMG, BA, MComm, CA, FCA; Canadian financial executive; *Chairman, Bombardier Inc.;* b. 13 May 1938, Laurier Station, PQ; son-in-law of Joseph Armand Bombardier; m.; one s.; ed St-Anne Coll., NS, Univ. of Sherbrooke, PQ; began career with Beaudoin, Morin, Dufresne & Assocs Chartered Accountants 1961–63; Comptroller, Bombardier Ltd 1963–64, Gen. Man. 1964–66, Pres. 1966–79, Chair. and CEO 1979–99, Chair. Bd and Exec. Cttee Bombardier Inc. 1999–, CEO 2004–08, Chair. Bombardier Recreational Products Inc. 2003–Chair. Regroupement Économie et Constitution 1991; mem. Advisory Bd Lazard Canada 2000–, Carlyle Group (Canada) 2001–; mem. Bd of Dirs Championnat des Amériques 2003; Fellow, Ordre des comptables agréés du Québec 1989; Officier, Ordre Nat. du Québec 1990, Golden Emblem of Merit, Prov. Govt of Upper Austria 1999, Grosse silberne Ehrenzeichen mit Stern (Austria) 2009; Hon. PhD (Montreal), (York); Hon. DBA (Sherbrooke); Hon. DEcon (St-Anne); Hon. DCL (Bishop's Univ.); Hon. DJur (Toronto), (McGill); Hon. DEng (Carleton); numerous awards including mem. Canadian Business Hall of Fame, Canadian Business Leader Award, Univ. of Alberta 1991, CEO of the Year, The Financial Post 1991, Laureate Award in Aeronautics/Propulsion, Aviation Week & Space Tech. Magazine 1993, CD Home Award, Canadian Aeronautics and Space Inst. 1995, Canadian Business Leadership Award, Harvard Business Club of Toronto 1996, Prix de Carrière, Conseil du Patronat du Québec 1997, Int. Distinguished Entrepreneur Award, Univ. of Man. 1998, Lifetime Achievement Award, Ernst and Young Entrepreneur of the Year Program in Québec 2000, Aguila Azteca Award from Pres. of Mexico 2005, Canadian Youth Business Foundation Lifetime Achievement Award 2006, Woodrow Wilson Award for Corp. Citizenship, Canada Inst. of the Woodrow Wilson Int. Center for Scholars, Washington, DC 2007, Int. Michael Smurfit Business Achievement Award, The Ireland Chamber (USA) 2008, Best Global Business Award, Canada China Business Council, Beijing 2008. *Address:* Bombardier Inc., 800 René-Lévesque Boulevard West, Montréal, PQ H3B 1YB, Canada (office). *Telephone:* (514) 861-9481 (office). *Fax:* (514) 861-7053 (office). *E-mail:* piero.scaramuzzi@defence .bombardier.com (office). *Website:* www.bombardier.com (office).

BEAUDOIN, Pierre; Canadian business executive; *President and CEO, Bombardier Inc.;* ed Brébeuf Coll., McGill Univ.; worked as Canadian Customer Service Man. for BIC Sport Inc.; helped organize Marine Products Div. of Bombardier 1985, Vice-Pres. Product Devt for Sea-Doo/Ski-Doo (following fusion of marine products and snowmobile divs Oct. 1990) 1990–92, Exec. Vice-Pres. Sea-Doo/Ski-Doo Div., Bombardier Inc. 1992–94, Pres. 1994–96, Pres. and COO Bombardier Recreational Products 1996–2001, also responsible for Bombardier-Rotax, Pres. Bombardier Aerospace, Business Aircraft Feb.–Oct. 2001, mem. Bd of Dirs, Pres. and COO Oct. 2001–04, Exec. Vice-Pres. Bombardier Inc. 2004–08, Pres. and CEO 2008–; mem. Bd of Dirs Power Corporation of Canada. *Address:* Bombardier Inc., 800 René-Lévesque Boulevard West, Montréal, PQ H3B 1YB, Canada (office). *Telephone:* (514) 861-9481 (office). *Fax:* (514) 861-7053 (office). *E-mail:* piero .scaramuzzi@defence.bombardier.com (office). *Website:* www.bombardier.com (office).

BEAUMONT, (John) Michael, OBE, BSc, DLC (Hons), CEng; British engineer (retd); *Seigneur of Sark;* b. 20 Dec. 1927, Egypt; s. of the late Lionel Beaumont and Enid Beaumont (née Ripley); m. Diana La Trobe-Bateman 1956; two s.; ed Loughborough Coll.; Chief Stress Engineer, Beagle Aircraft 1965–69, Chief Tech. Engineer 1969–70; Sr Engineer, Guided Weapons, Filton 1970–74; inherited Fief of Sark 1974. *Leisure interests:* theatre, music, gardening. *Address:* La Seigneurie de Sark, Channel Islands, GY9 0SF (office). *Telephone:* (1481) 832017 (office). *E-mail:* seigneur@gov.sark.gg (office). *Website:* www.gov.sark.gg (office).

BEAUMONT, Lady Mary Rose, BA (Hons); British art historian, academic, teacher and writer; b. (Mary Rose Wauchope), 6 June 1932, Petersfield, Hants., England; d. of Charles Edward Wauchope and Elaine Mary Armstrong-Jones; m. Lord Beaumont of Whitley, The Rev. Timothy Wentworth Beaumont 1955 (died 2008); one s. (one s. deceased) two d.; ed Prior's Field School, Godalming, Surrey, Courtauld Inst. of Fine Art, Univ. of London; f. Centre for the Study of Modern Art, Inst. of Contemporary Arts (ICA) 1972; art critic for Art Review 1978–96; Lecturer in Modern Art for Christies' Educ. 1978–2001; Exhbn curator for British Council in E Europe and Far East 1983–87; Exhbn Curator The Human Touch, Fischer Fine Art Gallery 1986, The Dark Side of the Moon, Rhodes Gallery 1990, Three Scottish Artists, Pamela Auchincloss Gallery, New York 1990; Picker Fellow, Kingston Polytechnic 1986–87; Lecturer in Humanities, Dept City & Guilds School of Art 1996–2008; mem. Exec. Cttee of Contemporary Art Soc. 1979–89, Advisory Cttee Govt Art Collection 1994–2001; Hon. Fellow, Royal Soc. of British Sculptors. *Publications include:* An American Passion: The Susan Kasen Summer and Robert D. Summer Collection of Contemporary British Painting (contrib. artists' profiles) 1995, Open Studio: Derek Healey 1997, Jean MacAlpine: Intervals in Light 1998, Carole Hodgson 1999, George Kyriacou 1999, Jock McFadyen: A Book About a Painter (contrib.) 2000, New European Artists Vol. I (contrib.) 2000, Albert Irvin: The Complete Prints 2010, The MacGuffin (catalogue essay with Anna McNay) 2011. *Leisure interests:* reading novels, listening to opera. *Address:* 40 Elms Road,

London, SW4 9EX, England (home). *Telephone:* (20) 7498-8664 (home). *Website:* www.cityandguildsartschool.ac.uk (office).

BEAZLEY, Hon. Kim Christian, AC, BA, MA, MPhil; Australian politician and diplomatist; *Ambassador to USA*; b. 14 Dec. 1948, Perth, Western Australia; s. of Kim Edward Beazley and Betty Judge; m. 1st Mary Beazley 1974 (divorced 1989); two d.; m. 2nd Susie Annus 1990; one d.; ed Hollywood Sr High School, Perth, Univ. of Western Australia, Balliol Coll., Oxford, UK; fmr Lecturer in Social and Political Theory, Murdoch Univ. Perth; MP for Swan 1980–96, for Brand 1996–2007; Minister for Aviation 1983–84, for Defence 1984–90, for Transport and Communications 1990–91, of Finance 1991, 1993–96, of Employment, Education and Training 1991–93; Deputy Prime Minister 1995–96; Special Minister of State 1983–84; Leader of the House 1988–96; Leader of Australian Labor Party 1996–2001, 2005–06; Winthrop Prof., Dept of Politics and Int. Relations, Univ. of Western Australia 2007–; Chancellor ANU 2008–09; Amb. to USA 2010–; mem. Council of Advisors, US Studies Centre, Univ. of Sydney; Rhodes Scholarship, Univ. of Western Australia 1973. *Leisure interests:* reading, swimming, watching cricket. *Address:* Embassy of Australia, 1601 Massachusetts Avenue NW, Washington, DC 20036-2273, USA (office). *Telephone:* (202) 797-3000 (office). *Fax:* (202) 797-3168 (office). (202) 797-3331 (office). *E-mail:* library.washington@dfat.gov.au (office). *Website:* www.usa.embassy.gov.au (office).

BEBA, Ümran, BEng MBA; Turkish business executive; *President, Asia Pacific, PepsiCo;* ed Bosphorus Univ.; pursued marketing career at Colgate-Palmolive; began career with PepsiCo when she joined Frito Lay 1994, served in various roles including human resources, sales and marketing, Gen. Man. PepsiCo South East Europe Region 2001–10, Pres. PepsiCo Asia Pacific 2010–; ranked by Fortune magazine amongst the 50 Most Powerful Women in Business outside the US (23rd) 2010, (25th) 2011, (42nd) 2012. *Address:* PepsiCo Asia Pacific, 20th Floor, Caroline Center, 28 Yun Ping Road, Causeway Bay, Hong Kong Special Administrative Region, People's Repub. of China (office). *Telephone:* 2839-0288 (office). *E-mail:* huw.gilbert@pepsico.com (office). *Website:* www.pepsico.com (office); www.pepsiworld.com (office).

BÉBÉAR, Claude; French business executive; *Honorary Chairman, AXA Group;* b. 29 July 1935, Issac; s. of André Bébéar and Simone Bébéar (née Veyssière); m. Catherine Dessagne 1957; one s. two d.; ed Lycées de Périgueux and St Louis, Paris, Ecole Polytechnique, Paris; joined Ancienne Mutuelle (renamed Mutuelles Unies 1978) 1958, CEO 1975–82; Chair. and CEO AXA Group 1982–2000, currently Hon. Chair.; mem. Bd of Dirs Schneider Electric SA 1986–2013, BNP Paribas 2012–, Vivendi 2012– (mem. Supervisory Bd 2005–); Founder and Chair. Institut Montaigne 2001–; Hon. Pres. Inst. des Actuaires Français 1989–, Hon. Chairman IMS-entreprendre pour la Cité; Grand Officier, Légion d'honneur, Officier, Ordre nat. du Mérite. *Publications include:* Le courage de réformer 2002, Ils vont tuer le capitalisme 2003, Réformer par temps de crise 2012. *Address:* AXA Group, 25 avenue Matignon, 75008 Paris, France (office). *Telephone:* 1-40-75-58-00 (office). *Fax:* 1-40-75-57-50 (office). *Website:* www.axa.com (office).

BEBIĆ, Luka; Croatian agricultural engineer and politician; b. 21 Aug. 1937, Desne-Kula Norinska; m.; two c.; ed Faculty of Agric., Sarajevo; mem. Croatian Democratic Union (Hrvatska demokratska zajednica—HDZ) 1989–; mem. Sabor (Parl.) since Croatia's independence, Deputy Speaker, Parl., mem. and Vice-Chair. Cttee for Consideration and Political System, Chair. Club of Reps of HDZ 2003–08, Pres. (Speaker) of Sabor 2008–11; Minister of Defence July–Sept. 1991. *Address:* Sabor, 10000 Zagreb, trg sv. Marka 6–7, Croatia (office). *Telephone:* (1) 4569444 (office); (1) 6303544 (office). *Fax:* (1) 1 6303010 (office). *E-mail:* marija.dujic@sabor .hr (office); sabor@sabor.hr (office). *Website:* www.sabor.hr (office).

BEBLAWI, Hazem Abdel Aziz al-, LLB, PhD; Egyptian economist, academic and politician; b. 17 Oct. 1936, Cairo; m.; ed Cairo Univ., Univ. of Grenoble, France, Univ. of Paris 1 Pantheon-Sorbonne; Asst Prof., Assoc. Prof., then Prof., Univ. of Alexandria 1965–80, now Prof. Emer. of Econs; Sr Economist, Arab Fund for Econ. and Social Devt 1974–79; Man., Econs Dept, Industrial Bank of Kuwait 1980–83; Chair. and CEO Export Devt Bank of Egypt 1983–95; Under-Sec. Gen. and Exec. Sec., UN Econ. and Social Comm. for Western Asia (ESCWA) 1995–2000; Adviser, Arab Monetary Fund, Abu Dhabi 2001–11; Founding mem. Egyptian Social Democratic Party following Egyptian revolution Jan.–Feb. 2011; Deputy Prime Minister for Econ. Affairs and Minister of Finance July–Dec. 2011; Acting Prime Minister of Egypt 2013–14; columnist, Al-Ahram newspaper; Chevalier, Légion d'honneur 1992, Commdr, Order of Leopold II (Belgium) 1992, Grand Officier, Nat. Order of the Cedar (Lebanon) 2000. *Publications include:* L'Interdependance Agriculture – Industrie et le Développement Economique: le cas de l'Égypte, 1968, The Arab Gulf Economy in a Turbulent Age 1984, The Rentier State (co-author) 1987, Arba Shohour Fi Qafas Al Hokouma (Four Months in the Government's Cage) 2012; numerous articles on money and banking, int. trade, finance, and devt. *Address:* Egyptian Social Democratic Party, Mahmoud Bassiouni Street 16, second round Abdel Moneim Riad Square Downtown, Cairo, Egypt (office). *Telephone:* (2) 25772515 (office). *Fax:* (2) 25772512 (office). *E-mail:* info@egysdp.com (office); feedback@hazembeblawi.com. *Website:* www.egysdp.com (office); hazembeblawi.com.

BECCARI, Luca; San Marino politician; *Co-Captain Regent;* b. 29 Oct. 1974; m. Anna Beccari; one s.; joined Banca Centrale della Repubblica di San Marino 1997, becoming Co-ordinator, Finance Dept 2005–06, 2008–12; mem. Consiglio Grande e Generale (Parl.) 2012–, mem. Finance Cttee; Co-Captain Regent 2014–; mem. Partito Democratico Cristiano Sammarinese 1993–, mem. Cen. Cttee 2010–. *Leisure interests:* kitesurfing, windsurfing, cinema. *Address:* Office of the Captains Regent, Palazzo Begni, Contrada Omerelli, 47890 San Marino (office). *Website:* www.sanmarino.sm (office).

BECH NIELSEN, Brian, PhD; Danish physicist, academic and university administrator; *Rector, Aarhus University;* b. Holstebro, West Jutland; Prof. of Experimental Solid State Physics and Head of Dept of Physics and Astronomy, Aarhus Univ. 2007–, co-operated with iNANO (univ.'s centre for nanotechnology research), Dean of Faculty of Science and Tech. –2013, Rector Aarhus Univ. 2013–; served on several bds of dirs; mem. Royal Danish Acad. of Sciences and Letters. *Publications:* numerous papers in professional journals on semiconductor materials. *Address:* Rector's Office, Aarhus University, Room 224, Building 1430, Nordre Ringgade 1, 8000 Aarhus C, Denmark (office). *Telephone:* 87-15-20-25 (office); 23-

38-23-49 (mobile). *E-mail:* rector@au.dk (office). *Website:* pure.au.dk/portal/en/ rektor@au.dk (office).

BECHERER, Hans Walter, MBA; American business executive; b. 19 April 1935, Detroit, Mich.; s. of Max Becherer and Mariele Specht; m. Michele Beigbeder 1959; one s. (deceased) one d.; ed Trinity Coll., Hartford, Conn. and Univ. of Munich, Germany, Harvard Univ.; Exec. Asst, Office of Chair. Deere & Co., Moline, Ill. 1966–69; Gen. Man. John Deere Export, Manuninheim, Germany 1969–73, Dir Export Marketing, Deere & Co., Moline, Ill., USA 1973–77, Vice-Pres. 1977–83, Sr Vice-Pres. 1983–86, Exec. Vice-Pres. 1986–87, Pres. 1987–90, COO 1987–89, CEO 1989–2000, Chair. 1990–2000; mem. Bd of Dirs Schering-Plough Corpn 1989–2009, Honeywell International Inc. 1991–2005, Chase Manhattan Corpn and Chase Manhattan Bank (now JPMorgan Chase & Co.) 1998–2006; fmr mem. Bd of Dirs Allied Signal Inc.; mem. The Business Roundtable 1989–, Chase Manhattan Bank Int. Advisory Cttee 1990–98, The Business Council 1992–; Trustee, Cttee for Econ. Devt 1990; Junior Achievement US Business Hall of Fame 2004.

BECHTEL, Marie-Françoise; French jurist; *Conseiller d'Etat;* b. 19 March 1946, Coarraze, Basses Pyrénées; d. of Gaston Cassiau and Marie Cassiau (née Sahores); one s. one d.; ed Univ. de Paris-Sorbonne, Ecole Nat. d'Admin.; secondary school teacher 1972–75; civil servant at Ecole Nat. d'Admin. 1978–80; Officer, Council of State 1980–84, Counsel 1984–85, Sr mem. 1996–; Adviser to Minister of Justice 1992–93, to Minister of the Interior 1999–2000; Dir Ecole Nat. Admin. 2000–02; Tech. Adviser to Minister of Nat. Educ. 1984–86; Sr Lecturer, Inst. d'Etudes Politiques 1983–87; Vice-Pres. UN Cttee of Experts on Admin. Reforms 2002–06, mem. 2006–; Vice-Pres. Fondation Res Publica; mem. Int. Civil Service Comm., UN Gen. Ass. 2011–. *Publications include:* contribs to Revue Française d'administration publique on institutions, organization, justice, civil rights etc. 1983–99, to "Ofer dire non", Fayard, Pais 2005; Rapport général du Comité pour la révision de la Constitution 1993. *Leisure interest:* modern art. *Address:* Conseil d'Etat, place du Palais Royal, 75001 Paris (office); 29 boulevard Edgard Quinet, 75014 Paris, France (home). *Telephone:* 1-40-20-87-80 (office). *Fax:* 1-43-20-59-53 (home). *E-mail:* marie-francoise.bechtel@conseil-etat.fr (office). *Website:* www .conseil-etat.fr (office).

BECK, Aaron T., MD; American psychotherapist and academic; *Professor Emeritus of Psychiatry, University of Pennsylvania;* b. 18 July 1921, Providence, RI; m.; four c.; ed Brown Univ., Yale Univ. Medical School; fmr Assoc. Ed. Brown Daily Herald; Resident in Pathology, RI Hosp. 1946; Resident in Neurology, Cushing Veterans Admin Hosp., Framingham, Mass; Fellow, Austin Riggs Center, Stockbridge; Asst Chief of Neuropsychiatry, Valley Forge Army Hosp.; joined Dept of Psychiatry, Univ. of Pennsylvania 1954, currently Prof. Emer. of Psychiatry; developed field of cognitive behaviour therapy research; funded research investigations of psychopathology of depression, suicide, anxiety disorders, alcoholism, drug addiction and personality disorders 1959–; f. Beck Inst. for Cognitive Therapy and Research; fmr Visiting Scientist, Medical Research Council, Oxford, Visiting Fellow, Wolfson Coll., Visiting Prof., Harvard, Yale and Columbia Univs; mem. Inst. of Medicine, NAS; consultant or mem. several review panels, Nat. Inst. of Mental Health; served on editorial bds of several professional journals; Hon. DMedSc (Brown Univ.), Hon. DHumLitt (Assumption Coll.); Brown Univ.: Francis Wayland Scholarship, Bennet Essay Award, Gaston Prize for Oratory; MERIT Award, Nat. Inst. of Mental Health, American Psychiatric Asscn Research Award, Sarnat Award, Inst. of Medicine, Albert Lasker Clinical Medical Research Award 2006. *Publications:* more than 550 articles and author or co-author of 23 books. *Address:* Aaron T. Beck Psychopathology Research Center, 3535 Market Street, Room 2032, Philadelphia, PA 19104-3309, USA (office). *Fax:* (215) 573-3717 (office). *E-mail:* abeck@mail.med.upenn.edu (office). *Website:* www.med.upenn .edu/suicide/beck (office); www.beckinstitute.org (office).

BECK, Rev. Brian Edgar, MA, DD; British ecclesiastic; b. 27 Sept. 1933, London; s. of A. G. Beck and C. A. Beck; m. Margaret Ludlow 1958; three d.; ed City of London School, Corpus Christi Coll., Cambridge and Wesley House, Cambridge; Asst Tutor, Handsworth Coll. 1957–59; ordained Methodist Minister 1960; Circuit Minister, Suffolk 1959–62; St Paul's United Theological Coll., Limuru, Kenya 1962–68; Tutor Wesley House, Cambridge 1968–80, Prin. 1980–84; Sec. Methodist Conf. of GB 1984–98, Pres. 1993–94; Co.-Chair. Oxford Inst. of Methodist Theological Studies 1976–2002; Sec. E African Church Union Consultation Worship and Liturgy Cttee 1963–68; mem. World Methodist Council 1966–71, 1981–98; Visiting Prof., Wesley Theological Seminary, Washington, DC 1999. *Publications:* Reading the New Testament Today 1977, Christian Character in the Gospel of Luke 1989, Gospel Insights 1998; Exploring Methodism's Heritage 2004; (contrib. to) Christian Belief, A Catholic-Methodist Statement 1970, Unity the Next Step? 1972, Suffering and Martyrdom in the New Testament 1981, Community-Unity-Communion 1998, Rethinking Wesley's Theology 1998, Managing the Church? 2000, Apostolicity and Unity 2002, Reflections on Ministry 2004, Unmasking Methodist Theology 2004, A Thankful Heart and a Discerning Mind 2010, The Ashgate Research Companion to World Methodism 2013, and articles in theological journals. *Leisure interests:* walking, cross-stitch, DIY. *Address:* 26 Hurrell Road, Cambridge, CB4 3RH, England (home). *Telephone:* (1223) 312260 (home).

BECK, Sir (Edgar) Philip, Kt, MA; British business executive; b. 9 Aug. 1934; s. of the late Sir Edgar Charles Beck and of Mary Agnes Sorapure; m. 1st Thomasina Joanna Jeal 1957 (divorced); two s.; m. 2nd Bridget Alexandra Heathcoat Amory 1991; ed Jesus Coll., Cambridge; Chair. John Mowlem and Co. PLC 1979–95 (Dir 1963–95), Railtrack 1999–2001; fmr Dir numerous assoc. cos; Chair. Fed. of Civil Eng. Contractors 1982–83; Dir (non-exec.) Invensys PLC 1991– (Interim Chair. 1998, Deputy Chair. 1998–99), Delta PLC 1994–2004, Yorks. Electricity Group PLC 1995–97, Railtrack Group 1999–2001 (non-exec. Dir 1995–2001). *Leisure interest:* sailing. *Address:* Lower Park House, Westholme, Pilton, Somerset, BA4 4EN, England (home). *Telephone:* (1749) 899491 (home). *E-mail:* philipbeck98@aol .com (home).

BECK, John C., MD, CM, MACP, FRCP; American/Canadian professor of medicine; *Director Emeritus, Multicampus Program in Geriatrics and Gerontology, University of California, Los Angeles;* b. 4 Jan. 1924, Audubon, Ia; s. of Wilhelm Beck and Marie Beck; one s.; ed McGill Univ.; Physician-in-Chief, Royal

Victoria Hosp., Montreal, Canada 1964–74, Sr Physician, Dept of Medicine 1974–81; Prof. of Medicine, Univ. of Calif., San Francisco 1974–79; Visiting Prof., UCLA 1978–79, Dir Multicampus Div. of Geriatric Medicine, School of Medicine, UCLA 1979–93, Prof. of Medicine 1979– (now Emer.), Dir Multicampus Program in Geriatrics and Gerontology 1987–93, Dir Emer. 1993–; numerous other professional appointments; Hon. PhD (Ben-Gurion Univ., Israel) 1981, Hon. DSc (McGill Univ., Canada) 1994; Ronald V. Christie Award, Canadian Asscn of Profs of Medicine 1987, Duncan Graham Award, Royal Coll. of Physicians and Surgeons 1990, Distinguished Service Recognition Award, Asscn for Gerontology in Higher Educ. 2001, Donald P. Kent Award, Gerontological Soc. of America 2001, Philips Award, American Coll. of Physicians/American Soc. of Internal Medicine 2003, Chaikin Oration, Australian Acad. of Technological Sciences and Eng 2004. *Publications:* more than 300 articles in professional journals and book chapters. *Address:* 1562 Casale Road, Pacific Palisades, CA 90272, USA (home). *Telephone:* (310) 459-5927 (office). *Fax:* (310) 454-1944 (office). *E-mail:* egebjcb@ucla.edu (office).

BECK, Kurt; German politician; b. 5 Feb. 1949, Bad Bergzabern; m. Roswitha Beck 1968; one s.; apprenticeship as mechanic, specializing in electronics; mem. ÖTV (Public Employees' Union) 1969; mem. SPD 1972–; mem. Rhineland-Palatinate State Ass. 1979–, Whip of SPD Parl. Group 1985–91, Chair. 1991–94; Chair. Rhineland-Palatinate SPD 1993–, Deputy Chair. SPD Party (Germany) 2003–06, Chair. 2006–08; Minister-Pres. of Rhineland-Palatinate 1994–2013; Chair. Bundesrat 2000–01; Mayor of Steinfeld 1989–94; Chair. Broadcasting Comm. of Fed. States' Minister-Pres.'s 1994–; responsible for cultural matters under German-French co-operation agreement 1999–2002; Chair. Bd Dirs Zweites Deutsches Fernsehen (ZDF) 1999–; Order of Merit, Grand Officier, Légion d'Honneur; Dr hc (Francis Marion Univ.).

BECKE, Axel Dieter, PhD, FRSC, FRS; German chemist and academic; *Canada Council Killam Research Fellow and Killam Chair in Computational Science, Dalhousie University;* b. 6 Oct. 1953, Esslingen; ed Queen's Univ., McMaster Univ., Canada; NSERC Postdoctoral Fellow, Dalhousie Univ., Halifax, NS 1981–83, E.B. Eastburn Postdoctoral Fellow 1983–84, Canada Council Killam Research Fellow and Killam Chair in Computational Science 2006–; NSERC Univ. Research Fellow, Queen's Univ., Kingston, Ont. 1984–94, Prof. of Chem. 1994–2006; mem. Int. Acad. of Quantum Molecular Science; Fellow, Chemical Inst. of Canada, World Asscn of Theoretically Oriented Chemists; Medal of Int. Acad. of Quantum Molecular Science 1991, Noranda Lecture Award, Canadian Soc. for Chem. 1994, Prize for Excellence in Research, Queen's Univ. 1999, Schroedinger Medal, World Asscn of Theoretically Oriented Chemists 2000. *Publications:* more than 50 articles in scientific journals. *Address:* Department of Chemistry, Dalhousie University, 6274 Coburg Road, PO Box 15000, Halifax, NS B3H 4R2, Canada (office). *Telephone:* (902) 494-2986 (office). *Fax:* (902) 494-1310 (office). *E-mail:* axel.becke@dal.ca (office). *Website:* chemistry.dal.ca (office).

BECKENBAUER, Franz Anton; German sports administrator and professional football manager; b. 11 Sept. 1945, Munich; s. of the late Franz Beckenbauer Sr and of Antonia Beckenbauer; m. three times, including to Brigitte Wittmann; five c.; ed Northern Coll. of Insurance Studies; sweeper; played for Bayern Munich 1959–64 (youth team), 1964–77 (sr team), New York Cosmos 1977–80, 1983, Hamburg 1980–82 football clubs, West Germany B 1965, West Germany 1965–77 (Capt. 1972–77, 103 appearances, 14 goals); won West German Cup (with Bayern Munich) 1966, 1967, 1969, 1971, West German Championship 1972, 1974, European Cup Winners 1967, European Cup 1974–76, World Club Championship 1976; won European Nations Cup (with West German Nat. Team) 1972, World Cup (only man to have won the World Cup both as Capt. and man.) 1974; won North American Championship (with New York Cosmos) 1977, 1978–80; retd 1984; Man. West German Nat. Team 1984–90; briefly coach for Marseilles; Pres. FC Bayern Munich 1994–2002, Chair. Advisory Bd 2002–; apptd Vice-Pres. Deutscher Fussball-Bund 1998, currently Rep. for Int. Tasks; Pres. 2006 World Cup Organizing Cttee; f. Franz Beckenbauer Foundation 1982; Adviser, Mitsubishi Mrawa Football Club 1992–; mem. Exec. Cttee, FIFA 2007–; Bundesverdienstkreuz, Bayerischer Verdienstorden 1982; West German Footballer of the Year 1966, 1968, 1974, 1976, FIFA World Cup Young Player of the Tournament 1966, FIFA World Cup Team of the Tournament 1966, 1970, 1974, European Football Championships Team of the Tournament 1972, 1976, European Footballer of the Year 1972, 1976, Winner, World Soccer Magazine of the Year 1972, 1976, Order of FIFA 1984, one of FIFA World Cup Winning Managers 1990, UEFA Cup Winning Coach 1995–96, IFFHS The Universal Genius of World Football 2007, Marca Leyenda 2012, FIFA Presidential Award 2012, UEFA Pres.'s Award 2013. *Publication:* Einer wie ich (Someone like Me) 1975, Franz Beckenbauer's Soccer Power 1978. *Address:* Deutscher Fußball-Bund e.V. (DFB), Hermann-Neuberger-Haus, Otto-Fleck-Schneise 6, 60528 Frankfurt am Main, Germany (office); Fédération Internationale de Football Association, FIFA-Strasse 20, PO Box 8044 Zurich, Switzerland (office). *Telephone:* (69) 67-88-0 (Frankfurt) (office); (43) 222-77-77 (Zurich) (office). *Fax:* (69) 67-88-266 (Frankfurt) (office); (43) 222-78-78 (Zurich) (office). *E-mail:* info@dfb.de (office); info@fifa.com (office). *Website:* www.dfb.de (office); www.fifa.com (office).

BECKER, Boris; German tennis coach and fmr professional tennis player; b. 22 Nov. 1967, Leimen, nr Heidelberg; s. of the late Karl-Heinz Becker and of Elvira Becker; m. 1st Barbara Feltus (divorced 2001); two s. one d.; m. 2nd Sharlely Becker 2009; one s.; started playing tennis aged three, later joined Blau-Weiss Club, Leimen; won West German Jr Championship 1983; subsequently runner-up US Jr Championship; turned professional and coached by Ion Tiriac from 1984; quarter-finalist, Australian Championship, Winner Young Masters Tournament, Birmingham, England 1985, Grand Prix Tournament, Queen's 1985; won Men's Singles Championship, Wimbledon 1985 (youngest ever winner and finalist; beat Kevin Curren); also won 1986, 1989, finalist 1988, 1990, 1991, 1995; finalist, Benson and Hedges Championship, Wembley, London 1985; Masters Champion 1988, finalist 1989; US Open Champion 1989; Semi-finalist French Open 1989; Winner Davis Cup for Germany 1989, Australian Open Championships 1991, 1996, IBM/ATP Tour Championship 1992, 1995, Grand Slam Cup 1996; named World Champion 1991, 64 career titles (49 singles, 15 doubles); Gold Medal (with Michael Stich), Olympic Games, Barcelona 1992; retd from professional tennis 1999; mem. Bd Bayern Munich Football Club 2001–; Co-founder Boris Becker &

Co., Völkl GmbH; Partner, DaimlerChrysler; owner of three car dealerships; Chair. Laureus Sports for Good Foundation 2002–, Tennis Masters Hamburg Rothenbaum; commentator for BBC TV –2013, Premiere channel (Germany); Head Coach, Novak Djokovic 2014; columnist, The Times, Handelsblatt (Germany), Blick (Switzerland); Founder Cleven-Becker-Stiftung; Amb. for German AIDS Foundation, for Youwin.com (online betting co.); mem. Bd Elton John AIDS Foundation; convicted of tax evasion, given a two-year suspended sentence Oct. 2002; Hon. Citizen of Leimen 1986; Sportsman of the Year 1985. *Publication:* The Player (autobiog.) 2004. *Leisure interests:* football, basketball, chess, backgammon. *Address:* Boris Becker & Co., Grafenauweg 4, 6300 Zug, Switzerland (office). *Telephone:* (41) 724-65-11 (office). *Fax:* (41) 724-65-05 (office). *Website:* borisbeckertennis.com.

BECKER, Gert O.; German business executive; b. 21 Aug. 1933, Kronberg; s. of Otto Becker and Henriette Becker (née Syring); m. Margrit Bruns 1960; one s. one d.; ed Akad. für Welthandel, Frankfurt; with Sales Dept, Degussa, Frankfurt 1956, with rep. office in Tehran, Iran 1960, with subsidiary in São Paulo, Brazil 1963, Div. Man., Frankfurt 1966, Dir 1971, Man. Dir Degussa, Frankfurt 1977–96, Chair. Supervisory Bd 1996–2001; fmr Pres. and CEO; Pres. Asscn of Chemical Industries 1994–95; fmr Chair. Supervisory Bd Bilfinger Berger Industrial Services AG, then Hon. Chair. *Leisure interests:* literature, book collecting, golf. *Address:* c/o Bilfinger Berger Industrial Services, Gneisenaustr. 15, 80992 Munich, Germany.

BECKER, HE Cardinal Karl Josef, SJ; German ecclesiastic, theologian and academic; *Cardinal-Deacon of San Giuliano Martire;* b. 18 April 1928, Cologne; professed mem. of Soc. of Jesus 1948, ordained priest 1958; consultor for Congregation for the Doctrine of the Faith 1977–; taught at Gregorian Univ., Rome; participated in doctrinal discussions between Soc. of St Pius X and Holy See 2009; cr. Cardinal (non-voting) (Cardinal-Deacon of San Giuliano Martire) 2012. *Address:* Congregation for the Doctrine of the Faith, Palazzo del Sant'Uffizio, Piazza del S. Uffizio 11, 00193 Rome, Italy (office). *Telephone:* (06) 69883357 (office). *Fax:* (06) 69883409 (office). *E-mail:* cdf@cfaith.va (office). *Website:* www.vatican.va/roman_curia/congregations/cfaith (office).

BECKER, Thomas; American business executive and consultant; Man. American Express Co. 1998–2000, Dir 2000–01; Vice-Pres. and Sr Strategy Man. Treasury Services New Business Devt Group, J.P. Morgan 2005–07; CEO Thom Browne (fashion co.), New York 2007–09; Founding Prin. BSI-NYC 2009–; Prin. Becker Harris and Co. (man. consultancy), New York 2010–. *Address:* Becker Harris & Co., 154 Grand Street, New York, NY 10013, USA (office). *Telephone:* (917) 727 1242 (office). *E-mail:* hello@beckerharris.com (office). *Website:* www.beckerharris.com (office).

BECKERS, Pierre-Olivier, MA, MBA; Belgian retail executive; *President and CEO, Delhaize Group;* b. 1960; ed IAG Louvain-La-Neuve, Harvard Business School, USA; began working in food retail industry as store manager for bakery chain in Belgium 1982; joined Delhaize Group 1983, positions include store man., buyer, Dir of Purchasing, mem. Exec. Cttee 1990–, later Exec. Vice-Pres. responsible for int. activities, Dir Delhaize Group 1995–, Pres. and CEO 1999–, Chair. Delhaize America 2002–; Co-Chair. Consumer Good Forum –2010; Dir Food Marketing Inst., CIES – The Food Business Forum (Chair. 2002–04); Pres. Belgian Olympic Interfederal Cttee 2004–13; mem. IOC 2012–; mem. Bd Guberna, The Corporate Governance Cttee, Belgian Comm. on Corp. Governance –2010; Manager of the Year, Trends/Tendances magazine 2000. *Address:* Delhaize Group SA, Rue Osseghemstraat 53, 1080 Brussels, Belgium (office). *Telephone:* (2) 412-22-11 (office). *Fax:* (2) 412-22-22 (office). *E-mail:* info@delhaizegroup.com (office). *Website:* www.delhaizegroup.com (office).

BECKETT, Rt Hon. Dame Margaret Mary, DBE, PC; British politician; b. 15 Jan. 1943, Ashton-under-Lyne, Lancs.; d. of Cyril Jackson and Winifred Jackson; m. Leo Beckett 1979; two step-s.; ed Notre Dame High School, Manchester and Norwich, Manchester Coll. of Science and Tech., John Dalton Polytechnic; eng apprentice (metallurgy), Associated Electrical Industries Ltd, Manchester, subsequently Experimental Officer, Univ. of Manchester; Sec. Trades Council and Labour Party 1968–70; researcher (Industrial Policy), Labour Party HQ 1970–74; Political Adviser to Minister of Overseas Devt Feb.–Oct. 1974; MP (Labour) for Lincoln 1974–79, for Derby S 1983–; Parl. Pvt. Sec., Minister for Overseas Devt 1974–75; Asst Govt Whip 1975–76; Minister, Dept of Educ. 1976–79; Prin. Researcher, Granada TV 1979–83; Opposition Spokeswoman with responsibility for Social Security 1984–89; Shadow Chief Sec. 1989–92; Shadow Leader of House, Campaigns Co-ordinator, Deputy Leader of Opposition 1992–94, Leader of Opposition May–July 1994; Shadow Sec. of State for Health 1994–95; Shadow Pres. Bd of Trade 1995–97, Pres. Bd of Trade and Sec. of State for Trade and Industry 1997–98; Pres. of Council and Leader House of Commons 1998–2001; Sec. of State for Environment, Food and Rural Affairs 2001–06, for Foreign and Commonwealth Affairs 2006–07; Chair. Intelligence and Security Cttee 2008; Minister of State for Housing and Planning, Dept for Communities and Local Govt 2008–09; Ministerial visits and trade missions to USA, Japan, Mexico, Netherlands, Australia, Paris, Brussels, Singapore, China, Hong Kong and Pakistan, India 1997–2001; mem. Labour Party 1963–, Nat. Exec. Cttee 1980–81, 1985–86, 1988–97, Transport & General Workers Union 1964–, T&GWU Parl. Labour Party Group; mem. Nat. Union of Journalists, BECTU, Fabian Soc., Anti-Apartheid Movt, Tribune Group, Socialist Educ. Cttee, Labour Women's Action Cttee, Derby Co-op Party, Socialist Environment & Resources Asscn, Amnesty Int., Council of St George's Coll., Windsor 1976–82; PC 1993–; Hon. Pres. Labour Friends of India; ranked 29th by Forbes magazine amongst 100 Most Powerful Women 2006. *Publications:* Vision for Growth – A New Industrial Strategy for Britain 1996, Renewing the NHS 1995, relevant sections of Labour's Programme 1972, 1973, The Nationalisation of Shipbuilding, Ship Repair and Marine Engineering, The National Enterprise Board, The Need for Consumer Protection. *Leisure interests:* cooking, reading, caravanning. *Address:* House of Commons, Westminster, London, SW1A 2NE, England (office). *Telephone:* (20) 7219-3000 (office); (1332) 345636 (constituency office) (office). *Fax:* (20) 7944-4101 (office); www.parliament.uk (office).

BECKETT, Wendy, (Sister Wendy), MA; British art writer and nun; b. 25 Feb. 1930, Johannesburg, SA; ed Univ. of Oxford; mem. Sacred Heart teaching order, currently living in solitude on the grounds of a Carmelite Monastery. *Television:* several series for BBC and Public Broadcasting Service including Sister Wendy's Grand Tour 1997, Sister Wendy's Story of Painting 1997. *Publications:* A Thousand Masterpieces, The Story of Painting, Meditations, My Favourite Things, Sister Wendy's American Collection 2000, Living the Lord's Prayer (with Rowan Williams) 2007. *Address:* Toby Eady Associates Ltd, Third Floor, 9 Orme Court, London, W2 4RL, England. *Telephone:* (20) 7792-0092 (office). *Fax:* (20) 7792-0879 (office). *E-mail:* toby@tobyeady.demon.co.uk (office). *Website:* www .tobyeadyassociates.co.uk (office).

BECKHAM, David Robert Joseph, OBE; British professional footballer; b. 2 May 1975, Leytonstone, London, England; m. Victoria Beckham (née Adams) (q.v.) 1999; three s. one d.; youth played with Brimsdown Rovers, Tottenham Hotspur 1987–91, Manchester United 1991–93; sr career with Manchester United 1993–2003 (team debut 1992), on loan to Preston North End 1995, League debut 1995, 386 appearances for Manchester United, 80 goals; player with Real Madrid 2003–07, with Los Angeles Galaxy (Major League Soccer, USA) (Capt. 2007–08) 2007–12, on loan to AC Milan 2009, 2010, with Paris Saint-Germain 2013 (retd); nine caps for England Under-21s 1994–96, rep. England 1996–2009 (115 caps, 17 goals), Capt. 2000–06; Football Assc'n Youth Cup medal, six Premiership medals, two Football Assc'n Cup medals, European Cup medal, Intercontinental Cup medal, four Community Shield winner medals; Supercopa de España medal 2003, La Liga medal (both with Real Madrid) 2006–07; Western Conference medal (with LA Galaxy) 2009, helped LA Galaxy to a 1–0 win over Houston Dynamo in MLS Cup final 2011, helped them retain championship with 3–1 win over Houston Dynamo 2012; only English player, and 21st player regardless of nationality, to score in three World Cups, and only fifth player in World Cup history to score twice from a direct free kick; first England player ever to collect two red cards and first England capt. to be sent off; UNICEF Goodwill Amb. 2005–; involved in promoting London's successful bid for the 2012 Olympic Games and in Opening Ceremony of the Olympic Games in Stratford, East London 27 July 2012; announced retirement from professional football 16 May 2013; f. David Beckham Acad. football school, London and Los Angeles, Calif.; Bobby Charlton Skills Award 1987, Sir Matt Busby Player of the Year 1996–97, Professional Football Assc'n Young Player of the Year 1996–97, Sky Football Personality of the Year 1997, FIFA World Cup Team of the Tournament 1998, UEFA Club Player of the Year 1999, Premier League 10 Seasons Awards 1992/93–2001/02: Overall Team of the Decade, Goal of the Decade (17 Aug. 1996), BBC Sports Personality of the Year 2001, FIFA 100, England Player of the Year 2003, ESPY Award – Best Male Soccer Player 2004, ranked 15th by Forbes magazine on The Celebrity 100 2007, ranked No. 1 by Arena magazine on list of the 40 most influential men under the age of 40 in the UK 2007, ESPY Award – Best MLS Player 2008, English Football Hall of Fame 2008, Britain's Greatest Ambassador, 100 Greatest Britons Awards, Time 100 2008, BBC Sports Personality of the Year Lifetime Achievement Award 2010, MLS Comeback Player of the Year Award 2011, Major League Soccer Best XI 2011, ESPY Award for Best MLS Player 2011, Do Something Athlete Award 2011. *Films:* cameo appearance with Zinedine Zidane and Raúl in Goal!: The Dream Begins 2005, appears in sequels Goal! 2: Living the Dream…, Goal! 3: Taking on the World (DVD) 2009. *Publications:* David Beckham: My Side 2002, David Beckham: My World (with Dean Freeman) 2001, Beckham: Both Feet on the Ground (with Tom Watt) 2003. *Address:* c/o Simon Fuller, 19 Entertainment, Unit 33 Ransomes Dock Business Centre, 35–37 Parkgate Road, London, SW11 4NP, England (office); c/o Paris Saint-Germain Football Club, 24 rue du Commandant Guilbaud, 75781 Paris Cedex 16, France (office). *E-mail:* press@psg.fr (office). *Website:* www.psg.fr (office); www.davidbeckham.com.

BECKHAM, Victoria Caroline; British singer, model, actress, fashion designer and business executive; b. 17 April 1974, Harlow, Essex, England; d. of Tony Adams and Jackie Adams; m. David Beckham (q.v.) 1999; three s. one d.; ed St Mary's High School, Cheshunt, Herts., Jason Theatre School, Laine Arts Theatre Coll.; mem. Touch, later renamed The Spice Girls 1993–2001, as 'Posh Spice', reunion tour 2007–08; solo artist 2000–; launched her dvb Denim collection in New York 2007, also unveiled new eye-wear range, launched Intimately Beckham perfume 2007, debut cosmetics line V-Sculpt launched in Tokyo 2008; the face of Marc Jacobs for his Spring collection 2008; own fashion collection debuted during New York Fashion Week at the Waldorf Hotel 2008; appeared on covers of British Vogue April 2008, Indian Vogue Nov. 2008, Russian Vogue Feb. 2009; guest judge, Project Runway 2008, Germany's Next Topmodel 2009, American Idol 2010; two Ivor Novello songwriting awards 1997, Smash Hits Award for Best Band 1997, BRIT Awards for Best Single (for Wannabe) 1997, for Best Video (for Say You'll Be There) 1997, for Best Performance of the last 30 years 2010, three American Music Awards 1998, Special BRIT Award for Int. Sales 1998, Glamour Magazine Awards for Woman of the Year and for Entrepreneur of the Year 2007. *Films:* Spiceworld: The Movie 1997, Ugly Betty (episode, A Nice Day for a Posh Wedding) 2007, Spongebob Squarepants (voice of Queen Amphitrite) 2010; documentaries: Victoria's Secrets 2000, Being Victoria Beckham 2002, The Real Beckhams 2003, Full Length & Fabulous, Victoria Beckham: Coming to America 2007. *Recordings include:* albums: with The Spice Girls: Spice 1996, Spiceworld 1997, Forever 2000, Greatest Hits 2007; solo: Victoria Beckham 2001, Not Such An Innocent Girl 2004. *Publications:* Learning to Fly (autobiog.) 2001, That Extra Half an Inch 2006. *Leisure interests:* shopping. *Address:* c/o 19 Entertainment, Unit 33, Ransomes Dock, 35–37 Parkgate, London, SW11 4NP, England (office). *Website:* www .victoriabeckham.com.

BECKINSALE, Kate; British actress; b. 26 July 1973; d. of the late Richard Beckinsale and of Judy Loe; m. (with Michael Sheen); m. Len Wiseman 2004; ed Godolphin and Latymer School, London and New Coll., Oxford. *Films:* Much Ado About Nothing 1993, Prince of Jutland 1994, Uncovered 1994, Haunted 1995, Marie-Louise ou la permission 1995, Shooting Fish 1997, The Last Days of Disco (London Critics Circle Supporting Actress Award 1999) 1998, Brokedown Palace 1999, The Golden Bowl 2000, Pearl Harbor 2001, Serendipity 2001, Laurel Canyon 2002, Underworld 2003, Tiptoes 2003, Van Helsing 2004, The Aviator 2004, Underworld Evolution 2005, Click 2006, Snow Angels 2007, Vacancy 2007, Winged Creatures 2008, Nothing But the Truth 2008, Underworld: Rise of the Lycans 2009, Whiteout 2009, Everybody's Fine 2009, Contraband 2012, Underworld: Awakening 2012, Total Recall 2012, Happy Holidays, Katherine Sloane 2012. *Play:* The Seagull 1995. *Television:* Devices and Desires (series) 1991, One Against the

Wind 1991, Rachel's Dream 1992, Cold Comfort Farm 1994, Emma 1996, Alice Through the Looking Glass 1998. *Address:* International Creative Management, Oxford House, 76 Oxford Street, London, W1N 0AX, England (office). *Telephone:* (20) 7636-6565 (office).

BECKMANN, David; American economist and pastor; *President, Bread for the World;* ed Yale Univ., Christ Seminary, London School of Econs, UK; worked at World Bank 1976–91; Pres. Bread for the World 1991–, Bread for the World Inst.; Founder and Pres. Alliance to End Hunger; Co-Chair. Modernizing Foreign Assistance Network; fmr mem. Bd InterAction, Partnership to Cut Hunger and Poverty in Africa, ONE Campaign, Nat. Anti-Hunger Orgs, UN Millennium Hunger Task Force; serves as Lutheran pastor; six hon. doctorates; World Food Prize (co-recipient) 2010. *Publications include:* Transforming the Politics of Hunger and Grace at the Table: Ending Hunger in God's World, Exodus from Hunger: We Are Called to Change the Politics of Hunger; numerous articles. *Address:* Bread for the World, 425 3rd Street, SW, Suite 1200, Washington, DC 20024, USA (office). *Telephone:* (202) 639-9400 (office). *Fax:* (202) 639-9401 (office). *E-mail:* bread@bread.org (office); institute@bread.org (office). *Website:* www.bread .org (office).

BECKSTROM, Rod Allen, BA, MBA; American business executive and international organization official; *President and CEO, Internet Corporation for Assigned Names and Numbers;* ed Stanford Univ.; Chair. Privada Inc. 1999–2001; Co-founder CATS Software Inc. (later sold to Misys PLC); Chair. and Chief Catalyst Twiki.net 2007; Dir Nat. Cybersecurity Center, Dept of Homeland Security 2008–09 (resgnd); Pres. and CEO Internet Corpn for Assigned Names and Numbers (ICANN) 2009–; Co-founder Global Peace Network, Mergent Systems; Chair. Council of Pres. of Associated Students, Stanford Univ.; Fulbright Scholar, Univ. of St Gallen, Switzerland; Trustee, Environmental Defense Fund, Jamii Bora Trust. *Publication:* The Starfish and the Spider: The Unstoppable Power of Leaderless Organizations (co-author) 2008. *Address:* Internet Corporation for Assigned Names and Numbers, 4676 Admiralty Way, Suite 330, Marina del Rey, CA 90292-6601, USA (office). *Telephone:* (310) 823-9358 (office). *Fax:* (310) 823-8649 (office). *Website:* www.icann.org (office); www.beckstrom.com.

BECTON, Henry P., Jr; American broadcast executive; b. 16 Oct. 1943; ed Yale Univ., Harvard Univ.; joined WGBH as producer 1970, Program Manager for Cultural Affairs 1974–78, Vice-Pres. and Gen. Man. 1978–99, Pres, WGBH Educational Foundation 1984–2007, Vice-Chair. 2008–; fmr mem. Bd of Dirs PBS, Becton, Dickinson & Co.; Founding Dir American Documentary, Inc.; Trustee, Boston Museum of Science; mem. Bd of Overseers New England Aquarium. *Address:* WGBH Educational Foundation, One Guest Street, Boston, MA 02135, USA.

BEDDALL, David; Australian (b. British) politician and business executive; *Chairman, GPS Online Solutions;* b. 27 Nov. 1948, Manchester, England; s. of G. A. Beddall; m. Helen Beddall; one d.; two s. from previous m.; mem. staff,Commonwealth Banking Corpn 1967–78; Loans Officer, Australian Guarantee Corpn Ltd 1978–83; commercial finance consultant 1979–83; mem. House of Reps for Fadden, Queensland 1983, for Rankin 1984–98; Minister for Small Business and Customs 1990–93, for Communications 1993, for Resources 1993–96; Chair. Jt Standing Cttee on Foreign Affairs and Defence 1984–87, House of Reps Standing Cttee on Industry, Science and Tech. 1987–93; Chair. GPS Online Ltd (now GPS Online Solutions) 1999–; Pres. Australian Franchisees Assc'n Inc. *Address:* GPS Online Solutions, Centenary Technology Park, 532 Seventeen Mile Rocks Road, Sinnamon Park, Brisbane, Qld 4073 (office); Inala Plaza, Corsair Avenue, Inala, Qld 4077, Australia. *Telephone:* (7) 3725-5400 (office). *Fax:* (7) 3376-6702 (office). *E-mail:* enquiries@gpsonline.com.au (office). *Website:* www.gpsonline .com.au (office).

BEDFORD, Steuart John Rudolf, BA, FRCO, FRAM; British conductor; b. 31 July 1939, London; s. of L. H. Bedford and Lesley Bedford (née Duff); m. 1st Norma Burrowes 1969 (divorced 1980); m. 2nd Celia Harding 1980; two d.; ed Lancing Coll., Sussex, Univ. of Oxford, Royal Acad. of Music; operatic training as repetiteur, Asst Conductor, Glyndebourne Festival 1965–67; English Opera Group (later English Music Theatre), Aldeburgh and London 1967–73; Co-Artistic Dir, English Musical Theatre 1976–80, Artistic Dir English Sinfonia 1981–90, Artistic Dir (also Exec. Artistic Dir) Aldeburgh Festival 1987–98; freelance conductor, numerous performances with ENO, Welsh Nat. Opera, Metropolitan Opera, New York (operas include Death in Venice, The Marriage of Figaro), Royal Danish Opera; also at Royal Opera House, Covent Garden (operas include Owen Wingrave, Death in Venice, Così fan tutte) Santa Fe Opera, Teatro Colón, Buenos Aires, Lyon, Garsington Opera, Opéra de Toulon, San Diego Opera, Boston Lyric Opera, Ópera Theatre of St Louis etc.; conductor for Orchestre Philharmonique de Montpellier, Mahler Chamber Orchestra, Southern Sinfonia; Medal of the Worshipful Co. of Musicians. *Recordings include:* Death in Venice, Phaedra, Beggar's Opera, Collins Britten series. *Film:* Peter Grimes. *Leisure interests:* golf, skiing. *Address:* c/o Harrison Parrott, 5–6 Albion Court, London, W6 0QT, England (office). *Telephone:* (20) 7229-9166 (office). *E-mail:* info@harrisonparrott.co.uk (office). *Website:* www.harrisonparrott.com (office).

BEDI, Bishan Singh, BA; Indian fmr professional cricketer; b. 25 Sept. 1946, Amritsar; s. of the late Gyan Singh Bedi and Rajinder Kaur Bedi; m. 1st Glenith Jill Bedi 1969; one s. one d.; m. 2nd Inderjit Bedi 1980; ed Punjab Univ.; fmr employee, Steel Authority of India, New Delhi; slow left-arm bowler; played for Northern Punjab 1961–62 to 1966–67, Delhi 1968–69 to 1980–81, Northants. 1972–77; played in 67 Tests for India (1967/68–79), 22 as Capt. 1975–79, taking 266 wickets (average 28.71) and scored 656 runs (highest score 50 not out); took 1,560 first-class wickets; toured England 1971, 1974, 1976 and 1975 (World Cup); coach, Indian cricket team 1990–; fmr nat. selector; Hon. Life mem. MCC 1981; Padma Shri Award 1969, Arjuna Award 1971. *Leisure interests:* reading, photography, swimming, letter writing. *Address:* Ispat Bhawan, Lodhi Road, New Delhi 110 003, India.

BEDI, Kiran; Indian police professional (retd); *General Secretary, Navjyoti;* b. 9 June 1949, Amritsar; d. of Prakash Peshawaria and Prem Peshawaria; m. Brij Bedi; one d.; ed Sacred Heart School, Amritsar, Govt Coll. for Women, Amritsar, Punjab Univ., Chandigarh, Delhi Univ., Indian Inst. of Tech., Delhi; Lecturer, Khalsa College for Women, Amritsar 1970–72; joined Indian Police Service 1972, held various assignments including Dist Police, Delhi Traffic Police, Special Traffic, Goa, Narcotics Control Bureau; fmr Deputy Insp.-Gen., Mizoram; fmr Insp.-Gen. of Prisons, of Tihar Jails, Delhi; fmr Special Sec. to Lt Gov. of Delhi; fmr Jt Commr, Delhi Police; fmr Insp.-Gen. of Police, Chandigarh; fmr Jt Commr of Police (Training), Delhi; UN Civilian Police Adviser 2003; fmr Dir Gen. Bureau of Police Research and Devt, Ministry of Home Affairs; f. website www.saferindia.com 2007; Founder and Gen. Sec. Navjyoti (residential community-based therapeutic treatment centre) 1987; Founder and Chair. India Vision Foundation 1994–; Host and presiding judge on TV series Aap Ki Kachehri; Jawaharlal Nehru Fellowship; Dr hc (Guru Nanak Dev Univ.), Hon. LLD CUNY School of Law 2005; Pres.'s Gallantry Award 1979, Women of the Year Award 1980, Asia Region Award for Drug Prevention and Control 1991, Int. Org. of Good Templars Asia-Region Award, Ramon Magsaysay Peace Award for Govt Service 1994, Mahila Shiromani Award 1995, Father Machismo Humanitarian Award 1995, Lion of the Year Award 1995, Joseph Beuys Foundation Award for Holistic and Innovative Man. Award 1997, Asscns of Christian Colls and Univs Int. Award 1998, Pride of India Award, American Fed. of Muslims from India 1999, Serge Sotiroff Memorial Award (for Navjyoti Centre) 1999, State Award (for Navjyoti Centre), Indian Inst. of Tech. Alumni Asscn Award 2000, Western Soc. of Criminology 1999 Gitchoff Award 2001, Blue Drop Group Man. Cultural and Artistic Asscn (Italy) Woman of the Year Award 2002, Chinmoy Award for Welfare Policing 2003, Power of the Dedicated Professional Award, Univ. of South Florida and Fed. of Indian Americans 2003, FICCI Award 2005, Mother Teresa Award for Social Justice 2005, Transformative Leadership in Indian Police Service 2006, Baba Farid Award 2007, Zee Astitva Award 2007, Public Service Excellence Award 2007, Amity Woman Achiever for Social Justice 2007, Suryadatta Nat. Award 2007, Lifetime Achievement Award, Bank of Baroda 2008, Indian Soc. of Criminology Award 2008, Pride of Punjab Award 2008, Indo–American Award 2009, Certificate of Recognition, City of LA 2009, Women Excellence Award Aaaj Tak 2009, Kalpana Chawla Excellence Award 2010. *Film:* Real Salute 2001. *Achievements include:* fmr Nat. Jr, Sr and Asian tennis champion. *Publications include:* It's Always Possible (autobiography) 1998; Government@net (jtly with Sandeep Srivastava); writes a fortnightly column 'What Went Wrong' in The Times of India and Navbharat Times (compilation of 37 of these articles published in book form, also Hindi trans. Galti Kiski). *Leisure interest:* community work. *Address:* India Vision Foundation, 56 Uday Park (Basement), New Delhi 110 049 India. *Telephone:* (11) 26525741. *E-mail:* kiran@saferindia.com. *Website:* www.saferindia.com/kiranbedi; www .indiavisionfoundation.org; www.kiranbedi.com; www.navjyoti.org.in.

BÉDIÉ, Henri Konan, LenD; Côte d'Ivoirian politician; *President, Parti démocratique de la Côte d'Ivoire—Rassemblement démocratique africain (PDCI—RDA);* b. 1934, Dadiekro; m. Henriette Koinzan Bomo 1958; two s. two d.; ed Univ. of Poitiers; Asst Dir Caisse de Sécurité de la Côte d'Ivoire 1959–60; Counsellor, Embassy in Washington, DC March–Aug. 1960; mem. Perm. Mission to UN 1960; Chargé d'affaires a.i., Embassy in Washington, DC Aug.–Dec. 1960; Amb. to USA 1960–66; Minister-Del. for Econ. and Financial Affairs 1966–68; Minister of Economy and Finance 1968–75; Special Adviser, IFC 1976–80; re-elected Deputy, Nat. Ass. 1980; Pres. Nat. Ass. 1980, re-elected 1985, 1986; mem. Political Bureau, Parti démocratique de la Côte d'Ivoire—Rassemblement démocratique africain (PDCI—RDA), Pres. 1994, 2002–; Pres. Office Africain et Malgache de la Propriété Industrielle; Pres. of Côte d'Ivoire 1993–99 (overthrown in coup d'état), in exile in France, returned to Côte d'Ivoire 2005. *Address:* Parti démocratique de la Côte d'Ivoire—Rassemblement démocratique africain (PDCI—RDA), 05 BP 36, Abidjan 05, Côte d'Ivoire (office). *E-mail:* sg@pdcirda.org (office). *Website:* www.pdcirda.org (office).

BEDJAOUI, Mohammed; Algerian judge and diplomatist; b. 21 Sept. 1929, Sidi-Bel-Abbès; s. of Benali Bedjaoui and Fatima Oukili; m. Leila Francis 1962; two d.; ed Univ. of Grenoble and Institut d'Etudes Politiques, Grenoble; Lawyer, Court of Appeal, Grenoble 1951; research worker at CNRS, Paris 1955; Legal Counsellor of the Arab League in Geneva 1959–62; Legal Counsellor Provisional Republican Govt of Algeria in Exile 1958–61; Dir Office of the Pres. of Nat. Constituent Ass. 1962; mem. Del. to UN 1957, 1962, 1977, 1978–82; Sec.-Gen. Council of Ministers, Algiers 1962–63; Pres. Soc. Nat. des Chemins de Fer Algériens (SNCFA) 1964; Dean of the Faculty of Law, Algiers Univ. 1964; Minister of Justice and Keeper of the Seals 1964–70; mem., special reporter, Int. Law Comm. 1965–82; Amb. to France 1970–79; Perm. Rep. to UNESCO 1971–79, to UN, New York 1979–82; Vice-Pres. UN Council on Namibia 1979–82; mem. UN Comm. of Inquiry (Iran) 1980; Pres. Group of 77 1981–82; Judge Int. Court of Justice 1982–2001 (Pres. 1994–97); Pres. Algerian Constitutional Council 2002–05; Minister of State for Foreign Affairs 2005–07; fmr Pres. African Soc. of Int. and Comparative Law; Head of Algerian Del. to UN Conf. on Law of the Sea 1976–80; mem. Int. Inst. of Law; Commr Int. Comm. Against the Death Penalty; Ordre du Mérite Alaouite (Morocco), Order of the Repub. (Egypt), Commdr Légion d'honneur, Ordre de la Résistance (Algeria). *Publications:* International Civil Service 1956, Fonction publique internationale et influences nationales 1958, La révolution algérienne et le droit 1961, Succession d'états 1970, Terra nullius, droits historiques et autodétermination 1975, Non-alignment et droit international 1976, Pour un nouvel ordre économique international 1979, Droit international: bilan et perspectives 1992. *Address:* 39 rue des Pins, Hydra, Algiers, Algeria.

BEDNARSKI, Krzysztof; Polish sculptor, performer and graphic designer; b. 25 July 1953, Kraków; m. Marina Fabbri; two s.; ed Acad. of Fine Arts, Warsaw; worked for Laboratorium Theatre of Jerzy Grotowski, Wrocław 1976–82; Artist-in-Residence, OMI Foundation, New York 1995; Guest Teacher, studio of Prof. Grzegorz Kowalski, Sculpture Dept, Acad. of Fine Arts, Warsaw 1996–97; Artist-in-Residence, Art Foundation by Daniel Spoerri 'The Garden', Tuscany, Italy 1998–99; contrib. to European project 'Global Village Garden' (Germany) 2002–03; has participated in more than 300 exhbns world-wide; Grant from Leube Foundation, Salzburg, Austria 2003, K. Kobro Award, Łódź 2004, 'Exit-New Art in Poland' Award 2004. *Works include:* created series of posters for productions including Vigil 1976–77, Project Mountain 1977, Project Earth 1977–79, Human Tree 1979, and others; installations such as Total Portrait of Karl Marx 1978 (realised in many versions up to 1999, such as The Collected Works of Karl Marx 1988), In Memory of Jan Szeliga 1980, sculptures such as Victoria Victoria 1983, Moby Dick (Best Polish Sculpture 1987) 1987, The Xram Lrak Burial Mound 1988, Moby Dick – Mask 1989, La Rivoluzione siamo Noi 1989, Finite Column 1991,

Unsichtbar 1993, Missing Lenin's Hand 1995; monument of Federico Fellini, Rimini designed 1994, tomb of Krzysztof Kieślowski, Warsaw 1997, Vision & Prayer 1998–; artwork in Light Art Collection, Targetti Group, Florence, Italy 2005; works in numerous collections in Poland, Italy and elsewhere. *Publications include:* Linda Nochlin, The Body in Pieces, The Fragment as a Metaphor of Modernity 1994, Moby Dick Museum of Art 1994, Dictionary of Contemporary Artists 2001, Achille Bonito-Oliva, Oggetti di turno. Dall'arte alla critica 1997, Stownik Sztuki xx wieku 1998, L'arte come forma di difesa 2010. *Address:* Via Dei Banchi Vecchi 134, 00-186 Rome, Italy (home); ul. Nowowiejska 28/55, 010–02 Warsaw, Poland (home). *Telephone:* 3486529476 (Italy; mobile) (office); 504653975 (Poland; mobile) (office); (06) 6896068 (home). *E-mail:* kmbednarski@gmail.com. *Website:* www.bednarski.art.pl (office).

BEDNORZ, George, PhD; German physicist; b. 16 May 1950, North-Rhine Westphalia; s. of Anton Bednorz and Elisabeth Bednorz; ed Univ. of Münster, Swiss Federal Inst. of Tech.; with IBM Research Lab., Rüschlikon, Zürich 1982–; Fellow, IBM 1987; Marcel Benoist Prize (jtly) 1986, Nobel Prize for Physics (jtly) 1987, Fritz London Memorial Award (jtly) 1987, Dannie Heineman Prize (jtly) 1987, Robert Wichard Pohl Prize (jtly) 1987, Otto Klung Prize 1987, Viktor Mortiz Goldschmidt Prize 1987, Hewlett-Packard Europhysics Prize 1988, APS Int. Prize for Materials Research (jtly) 1988, Minnie Rosen Award 1988. *Address:* IBM Zürich Research Laboratory, Säumerstrasse 4, 8803 Rüschlikon, Zürich, Switzerland (office). *Telephone:* 447248111 (office). *Fax:* 447248911 (office). *E-mail:* iho@zurich.ibm.com (office). *Website:* www.zurich.ibm.com (office).

BEEBE, Michael Dale (Mike), BA, JD; American lawyer, politician and state governor; *Governor of Arkansas;* b. 28 Dec. 1946, Amagon, Jackson Co., Ark.; m. Ginger Beebe; three c.; ed Newport High School, Arkansas State Univ., Univ. of Arkansas at Fayetteville; family lived in Detroit, St Louis, Chicago, Houston and Alamagordo, NM before moving back to Ark.; served in US Army Reserve; practised law in Searcy, Ark. for 10 years after graduating from law school; Ark. State Senator 1983–2002; Ark. Attorney Gen. 2003–06; Gov. of Arkansas 2007–; Democrat. *Address:* Office of the Governor, Room 250, State Capitol, Little Rock, AR 72201 (office); Washington Office of the Governor, State of Arkansas, 400 North Capitol Street NW, Suite 365, Washington, DC 20001, USA (office). *Telephone:* (501) 682-2345 (Little Rock) (office); (202) 220-1340 (DC) (office). *Fax:* (501) 682-1382 (Little Rock) (office); (202) 220-1344 (DC) (office). *Website:* governor.arkansas .gov (office); mikebeebe.com.

BEEBEEJAUN, Ahmed Rashid, FRCP; Mauritian politician; *Deputy Prime Minister and Minister of Energy and Public Utilities;* b. 22 Dec. 1934; m.; ed Univ. of Birmingham, UK; Child Health Consultant 1971–93; mem. Mouvement Militant Mauricien (MMM) 1993–97; mem. Mauritius Labour Party 2000–, Deputy Leader –2004; mem. Nat. Ass. 2005–; Deputy Prime Minister 2005–, Minister of Public Infrastructure, Land Transport and Shipping 2005–08, of Energy and Public Utilities 2008–. *Leisure interests:* music, theatre. *Address:* Ministry of Energy and Public Utilities, Air Mauritius Centre, 10th Floor, John F. Kennedy St, Port Louis, Mauritius (office). *Telephone:* 211-0049 (office). *Fax:* 208-6497 (office). *E-mail:* mpu@mail.gov.mu (office). *Website:* www.gov.mu/portal/site/mpusite (office).

BEEBY, Thomas Hall; American architect and academic; *Chairman Emeritus, Hammond Beeby Rupert Ainge;* b. 12 Oct. 1941, Oak Park, Ill.; m. 1st Marcia D. Greenlease 1960 (divorced 1973); one s. one d.; m. 2nd Kirsten Peltzer 1975; two s.; ed Lower Merion High School, Ardmore, Pa, Gresham's School, Holt (UK), Cornell and Yale Univs; Assoc., C.F. Murphy Associates, Chicago 1965–71; Pnr, Hammond Beeby & Associates, Chicago 1971–76; Pnr and Dir of Design, Hammond Beeby & Babka (now Hammond Beeby Rupert Ainge—HBRA), Chicago 1976, now Chair. Emer.; Assoc. Prof., Dept of Architecture, Illinois Inst. of Tech., Chicago 1973–80; Dir School of Architecture, Univ. of Ill. at Chicago 1980–85; Dean and Prof., School of Architecture, Yale Univ. 1985–91, Adjunct Prof. 1992–; mem. Advisory Bd Dept of Architecture, Illinois Inst. of Tech. 1993–, Trustee 1997–; contributor to numerous exhbns of architecture and design in USA and Europe including Venice Biennale 1980; Distinguished Building Award, American Inst. of Architects, Chicago Chapter (numerous times); Nat. Design Award 1984, 1987, 1989, 1991, 1993, Driehaus Award, Univ. of Notre Dame 2013. *Publications:* articles in professional journals. *Address:* Hammond Beeby Rupert Ainge Inc., 372 West Ontario Street, 2nd Floor, Chicago, IL 60654, USA (office). *Telephone:* (312) 527-3200 (office). *Fax:* (312) 527-1256 (office). *E-mail:* tbeeby@hbra-arch.com (office); info@hbra-arch.com (office). *Website:* www.hbra-arch.com (office).

BEERING, Steven Claus, MD; American physician, academic and university administrator; *President Emeritus, Purdue University;* b. 20 Aug. 1932, Berlin, Germany; s. of Steven Beering and Alice Friedrichs Beering; m. Jane Pickering 1956; three s.; ed Univ. of Pittsburgh; Prof. of Medicine, Indiana Univ. School of Medicine 1969, Asst Dean 1969–70, Assoc. Dean 1970–74, Dean 1974–83, Dir Indiana Univ. Medical Center 1974–83; Pres. Purdue Univ. and Purdue Univ. Research Foundation 1983–2000, Pres. Emer. 2000–; Hon. ScD (Indiana) 1988, Hon. LLD; numerous awards and prizes. *Publications:* numerous articles in professional journals. *Leisure interests:* music, photography, reading, travel. *Address:* Purdue University, Purdue Memorial Union, Room 218, West Lafayette, IN 47906-3584 (office); 10487 Windemere Drive, Carmel, IN 46032, USA (home). *Telephone:* (765) 496-7555 (office); (317) 581-1414 (home). *Fax:* (765) 496-7561 (office). *E-mail:* scb@purdue.edu (office); sbeering@indy.rr.com (home). *Website:* www.purdue.edu (office).

BEEVOR, Antony, FRSL; British historian, writer and academic; b. 14 Dec. 1946, London, England; s. of John Grosvenor Beevor and Carinthia Jane Beevor (née Waterfield); m. Artemis Cooper 1986; one s. one d.; ed Winchester Coll., Grenoble Univ., Royal Mil. Acad. Sandhurst; Exec. Council French Theatre Season 1997; Lees-Knowles Lecturer, Univ. of Cambridge 2002–03; Visiting Prof., Birkbeck Coll., London 2002–, Univ. of Kent 2010–; Boeing Visiting Fellow, Australian War Memorial 2012; Cttee mem. Soc. of Authors 2001–05 (Chair. 2003–05), mem. of Council 2005–; mem. Steering Cttee Samuel Johnson Prize 2004–, Cttee Waterloo 200 2012–; judge, British Acad. Book Prize 2004, David Cohen Prize 2004; mem. Anglo Hellenic League, Friends of the British Libraries, London Library; Chevalier des Arts et des Lettres 1997, Order of Cross of Terra Mariana (Estonia) 2008; Hon. DLitt (Kent) 2004, (Bath) 2010. *Publications include:* The Spanish Civil

War 1982, The Enchantment of Christina Von Retzen (novel) 1988, Inside the British Army 1990, Crete: The Battle and the Resistance (Runciman Award 1992) 1991, Paris After the Liberation 1944–49 (with Aretmis Cooper) 1994, Stalingrad (Samuel Johnson Prize for Non-Fiction 1999, Wolfson Prize for History 1999, Hawthornden Prize 1999) 1998, Berlin: The Downfall 1945 (Longman-History Today Trustees' Award 2003) 2002, The Mystery of Olga Chekhova 2004, A Writer at War: Vasily Grossman with the Red Army 1941–1945 (co-ed.) 2005, The Battle for Spain – The Spanish Civil War 1936–39 (Premio Vanguardia 2005) 2005, D-Day – The Battle for Normandy (Prix Henry Malherbe, Duke of Westminster Medal for Military Literature, Royal United Services Inst. 2010) 2009, The Second World War 2012; contribs to New York Review of Books, New York Times, Washington Post, TLS, Times, Telegraph, Independent, Spectator, Guardian. *Address:* c/o Andrew Nurnberg Associates, 20–23 Greville Street, London, EC1N 8SS, England (office). *Telephone:* (20) 3327-0400 (office). *Fax:* (20) 7430-0801 (office). *E-mail:* contact@andrewnurnberg.com (office). *Website:* www .andrewnurnberg.com (office); www.antonybeevor.com.

BEFFA, Jean-Louis Guy Henri; French business executive; *Honorary Chairman, Compagnie de Saint-Gobain;* b. 11 Aug. 1941, Nice; s. of Edmond Beffa and Marguerite Feursinger; m. Marie-Madeleine Brunel-Grasset 1967; two s. one d.; ed Lycée Masséna, Nice, École Nat. Supérieure des Mines and Inst. d'Études Politiques, Paris; mining engineer, Clermont-Ferrand 1967, motor fuel man. 1967–74, head of refinery service 1970–73, Asst to Dir 1973–74, Chief Mining Eng 1974; Dir of Planning, Pont-à-Mousson (subsidiary of Saint-Gobain Group) 1975–77, Dir-Gen. 1978, Pres. Dir-Gen. 1979–82, Deputy Dir (Pipelines) Saint-Gobain-Pont-à-Mousson 1978, Dir 1979–82, Dir-Gen. Compagnie de Saint-Gobain 1982–86, CEO 1982, Chair. and CEO 1986–2007, Chair. 2007–10, Hon. Chair. 2010–, apptd Chair. Saint-Gobain Centre for Econ. Research 2000, currently Co-Chair. Centre Cournot pour la Recherche en Économie; Pres. Inst. de L'Histoire de L'Industrie (Idni) 1992–98; Pres. Supervisory Bd Poliet 1996–; Vice-Pres. Compagnie Générale des Eaux 1998–; Vice-Pres. Admin. Bd BNP Paribas 2000–; mem. Int. Consultative Cttee, Chase Manhattan Bank 1986–, AT&T 1987; mem. Admin. Council Ecole Polytechnique 1993–; Admin. Banque Nat. de Paris, Cie Gen. des Eaux, Cie de Suez et de Petrofina; Sr Advisor, Lazard, Chair. Lazard Asia Investment Banking; mem. Bd of Dirs GDF-Suez, Groupe Bruxelles Lambert, Le Monde SA; mem. Supervisory Bd Siemens AG; Chair. Asscn pour le Rayonnement de l'Opéra nat. de Paris; Grand Officier, Légion d'honneur; Officier, Ordre nat. du Mérite, des Arts et des Lettres; Commdr du Mérite (FRG); CBE (UK) (Foreign mem.). *Leisure interests:* swimming, golf. *Address:* Compagnie de Saint-Gobain, Les Miroirs, 18 avenue d'Alsace, 92096 Paris la Défense Cedex, France (office). *Telephone:* 1-47-62-30-00 (office). *Fax:* 1-47-78-45-03 (office). *E-mail:* info@saint -gobain.com (office). *Website:* www.saint-gobain.com (office).

BEG, Gen. (retd) Mirza Aslam, BA, MSc; Pakistani army officer (retd) and politician; b. 2 Aug. 1931, Azamgarh, Uttar Pradesh, India; s. of Mirza Murtuza Beg; m.; one s. two d.; ed Shibli Coll., Azamgarh, Aligarh Univ., India, Command and Staff Coll., Quetta and Nat. Defence Coll., Quaid-Azam Univ., Rawalpindi; commissioned 1952; served in Baluch (Infantry) Regt; joined Special Service Group (Commandos) 1961; Brig. Maj. of an Infantry Brigade during India–Pakistan war 1965; Lt-Col 1969; in command, Infantry Bn, India–Pakistan war 1971; Brig. in command of Infantry Brigade 1974; Maj.-Gen. in command of Infantry Div. 1978; Chief of Gen. Staff 1980–85; Lt-Gen. 1984; Corps Commdr 1985; Gen. and Vice-Chief of Army Staff 1987; Chief of Army Staff 1987–91; Chair. FRIENDS Foundation, Pakistan; Founder, Pres. and Chair. Awami Qiyadat Party; Sitara-e-Basalat 1981, Hilal-e-Imtiaz (Mil.) 1982, Nishan-e-Imtiaz (Mil.) 1988, Tongil (First Class) Medal (S Korea) 1988, US Legion of Merit 1989, Bintang Yudha Dharm (Indonesia) 1990, Kt Grand Cross (First Class) (Thailand) 1991. *Publications:* articles in journals and nat. and int. newspapers. *Address:* House No. 9-City Villas, Near High Court Building, Rawalpindi (office); No. 1, National Park Road, Rawalpindi, Pakistan (home). *Telephone:* (51) 3029533 (office); (51) 5567637 (home). *Fax:* (51) 5521219 (home). *E-mail:* friendsfoundation@live.co.uk (office). *Website:* www.friends.org.pk (office).

BEGG, David, MPhil, PhD, FRSE; British economist and academic; *Principal of Business School and Professor of Economics, Imperial College London;* b. 1951; ed Univ. of Cambridge, Univ. of Oxford, Massachusetts Inst. of Tech., USA; Fellow and Lecturer, Worcester Coll., Univ. of Oxford 1976–86; Research Fellow, Centre for Econ. Policy Research 1983–; Prof. of Econs, Birkbeck Coll., Univ. of London 1986–2003; Prin. of Business School and Prof. of Econs, Imperial Coll., London 2003–; Econ. Policy Adviser to Bank of England 1986–, also Adviser on monetary policy to IMF, HM Treasury; commissioned to provide econs training to Govt of Czechoslavakia 1991, to Nat. Bank of Hungary 1998–99; Chair. Begg Comm. 1999–2005; fmr Research Dir, Centre for Econ. Forecasting, London Business School; mem. Bellagio Group 1999–, Keynes Seminar (convened quarterly by UK Chancellor of the Exchequer) 1999–; mem. HM Treasury Academic Panel 1981–96; mem. Research Awards Advisory Cttee, Leverhulme Trust 1986–93; Founding Man. Ed. Economic Policy 1984–2000. *Publications include:* The Rational Expectations Revolution in Macroeconomics, Economics 2000, Foundations of Economics 2002, The Making of Monetary Union 2005, Emu: Getting The Endgame Right 2005. *Address:* Office of the Principal, Business School, Imperial College, South Kensington Campus, London, SW7 2AZ, England (office). *Telephone:* (20) 7594-9100 (office). *Fax:* (20) 7823-7685 (office). *E-mail:* d.begg@imperial.ac.uk (office). *Website:* www3.imperial.ac.uk/business-school (office).

BEGGS, Jean Duthie, CBE, PhD, FRS, FRSE; British molecular biologist and academic; *Royal Society Darwin Trust Research Professor, University of Edinburgh;* b. 16 April 1950, Glasgow, Scotland; d. of William Renfrew Lancaster and Jean Crawford Lancaster (née Duthie); m. Ian Beggs 1972; two s.; ed Univ. of Glasgow; Postdoctoral Fellow, Dept of Molecular Biology, Univ. of Edinburgh 1974–77; Plant Breeding Inst., Cambridge 1977–79; Beit Memorial Fellow for Medical Research 1976–79; Lecturer in Biochemistry, Imperial Coll., London 1979–85; Univ. Research Fellow, Dept of Molecular Biology, Univ. of Edinburgh 1985–89; Professorial Research Fellow 1994–99, Prof. of Molecular Biology 1999–, Royal Soc. Darwin Trust Research Prof. 2005–; Vice-Pres. Royal Soc. of Edinburgh 2009–; Chancellor's Award, Univ. of Edinburgh, Royal Soc. Gabor Medal 2003, UK Biochemical Soc. Novartis Medal 2004. *Leisure interests:* walking, dogs, scuba diving. *Address:* Wellcome Trust Centre for Cell Biology, University of Edinburgh,

King's Buildings, Mayfield Road, Edinburgh, EH9 3JR, Scotland (office). *Telephone:* (131) 650-5351 (office). *E-mail:* j.beggs@ed.ac.uk (office). *Website:* www.wcb .ed.ac.uk/beggs (office); beggs.bio.ed.ac.uk (office).

BEGICH, Mark P.; American politician; *Senator from Alaska;* b. 31 March 1962, Anchorage, Alaska; s. of the late Nick Begich and of Pegge Begich; m. Deborah Bonito 1990; one s.; ed Steller Secondary School,; mem. Anchorage Ass. 1988–98, Chair. 1996–98; Mayor of Anchorage 2003–09; Senator from Alaska 2009–, Chair. Commerce Cttee's Subcommittee on Oceans, Atmosphere, Fisheries and Coast Guard, Senate Democratic Steering and Outreach Cttee; Owner, Carson Hot Springs Resort, Carson City, Nev., also owner of vending machine and property rental cos in Anchorage; mem. Bd of Dirs Boys and Girls Club, Spirit of Youth Foundation, Family Resource Center; mem. Air Force Asscn, Nat. Rifle Asscn; fmr Chair. Alaska Student Loan Corpn; f. Making a Difference Program for first time juvenile offenders; Democrat; named Friend of Educ. by Anchorage Educ. Asscn, voted Alaska's top state official by municipal officials 1997, 2004. *Leisure interests:* spending time with family, reading, travelling. *Address:* 111 Russell Senate Office Building, Washington, DC 20510, USA (office). *Telephone:* (202) 224-3004 (office). *Fax:* (202) 224-2354 (office). *Website:* begich.senate.gov (office).

BEGLEY, Charlene T., BS; American business executive; *President and CEO, GE Home & Business Solutions;* m.; three d.; ed Univ. of Vermont; began her career at General Electric (GE) 1988, held a variety of leadership roles including Vice-Pres. Operations, GE Capital Mortgage Services, Quality Leader, GE Transportation Systems 1995, Chief Financial Officer 1997, Dir of Finance, GE Plastics-Europe 1998–99, Vice-Pres. Corp. Audit Staff 1999, Pres. and CEO GE Fanuc Automation North America, Inc. 2001–03, Pres. and CEO Transportation Systems (fmrly known as GE Transportation Rail) of GEFS (Suisse) AG (div. of General Electric Co.) 2003–05, Pres. and CEO SABIC Innovative Plastics (fmrly GE Plastics Inc.) of General Electric Co. 2005–07 (first woman Sr Vice-Pres. in GE history), Pres. and CEO GE Enterprise Solutions 2007–10, Pres. and CEO GE Home & Business Solutions 2010–, also Sr Vice-Pres. and Chief Information Officer, GE; spent a year as Acting CEO Casablanca Fan Co.; mem. Bd of Dirs Nat. Asscn of Mfrs; serves on World Econ. Forum's Young Global Leaders, Business Advisory Council of Univ. of Vermont; ranked by Fortune magazine amongst the 50 Most Powerful Women in Business in the US (20th) 2005, (22nd) 2006, (26th) 2007–08, (27th) 2009, (20th) 2010–11, (29th) 2012, ranked by Forbes magazine amongst The World's 100 Most Powerful Women (96th) 2009. *Address:* GE Enterprise Solutions, 1 Plastics Avenue, Pittsfield, MA 01201-3662, USA (office). *Telephone:* (413) 448-7110 (office). *E-mail:* Christopher.Tessier@ge.com (office). *Website:* www.ge.com (office).

BEGLITIS, Panagiotis (Panos); Greek diplomatist and politician; b. 1957, Velo, Corinthia; m. Maria Gargali; one s. one d.; ed Nat. Kapodistrian Univ. of Athens, Univ. of Paris (Sorbonne), France; joined diplomatic service 1987, with Hellenic Perm. Del. to EU, Brussels 1992–96, Dir of Information Service and Spokesman, Ministry of Foreign Affairs 1999–2004; MEP (Panhellenic Socialist Movt, PASOK) 2004–07, Vice-Chair., Del. to EU–Turkey Jt Parl. Cttee, mem. European Parl. Foreign Affairs Cttee, Euro-Mediterranean Parl. Ass.; mem. Vouli (Parl.) for Corinthia 2007–; Alt. Minister of Nat. Defence 2009–11, Minister of Nat. Defence 2011. *Address:* Politburo Of Corinth, Cyprus 82, mezzanine, 20100, Corinth, Greece (office). *E-mail:* panos.beglitis@gmail.com (office). *Website:* www.beglitis.gr.

BÉGUIN, Bernard, LèsL; Swiss journalist; b. 14 Feb. 1923, Sion, Valais; s. of Bernard Béguin and Clemence Welten; m. Antoinette Waelbroeck 1948; two s. two d.; ed Geneva High School, Geneva Univ. and Graduate Inst. of Int. Studies; Swiss Sec. World Student Relief 1945–46; corresp. at UN European Headquarters; Journal de Genève 1946–70, Foreign Ed. 1947, Ed.-in-Chief 1959–70; Diplomatic Commentator, Swiss Broadcasting System 1954–59, Swiss TV 1959–70; Head of Programmes, Swiss French-speaking TV 1970–73; Deputy Dir Radio and TV 1973–86; Cen. Pres. Swiss Press Asscn 1958–60, Hon. mem. 1974–; Visiting Prof. in Professional Ethics, Univ. of Neuchâtel 1984–88; Pres. Swiss Press Council 1985–90; Pres. Swiss Ind. Authority on Complaints concerning Broadcasting Programmes 1991–92; consultant with UNESCO (assessment of the media environment), Belarus 1994; mem. Fed. Comm. on Cartels 1964–80; mem. Bd, Swiss Telegraphic Agency 1968–71. *Publication:* Journaliste, qui t'a fait roi? Les médias entre droit et liberté 1988. *Leisure interests:* sailing, camping. *Address:* 41 avenue de Budé, 1202 Geneva 1, Switzerland (home). *Telephone:* (22) 733-75-30 (home). *Fax:* (22) 733-75-30 (home). *E-mail:* beguinb@worldcom.ch (home).

BEHBEHANI, Kazem, PhD, FRCPath; Kuwaiti international organization official; *Envoy, World Health Organization;* ed Univs of Liverpool and London, UK; fmr Deputy Dir Gen. Kuwait Inst. for Scientific Research; Prof. Kuwait Medical Faculty; Vice-Rector for Research, Kuwait Univ.; Programme Man., Special Programme for Research and Training, Tropical Diseases, WHO 1991–94, Dir of Tropical Diseases 1994–99, Dir Eastern Mediterranean Liaison Office and in charge of Resource Mobilization for the Eastern Mediterranean Region 1999–2003, Asst Dir Gen. WHO 2003–05, now Envoy; Visiting Prof./Scholar, Harvard Medical School, USA, currently Co-Chair. Scientific Advisory Bd for the Environment and Public Health; mem. British Soc. of Parasitology, American Soc. for Tropical Medicine and Hygiene, Electron Microscopy Soc. of America and European Acad. of Arts, Science and the Humanities; Fellow Islamic Acad. of Sciences; Award for Research in Medicine, Kuwait Foundation for the Advancement of Sciences. *Publications:* a book on science and tech. and more than 100 scientific papers. *Address:* Kuwait Mission, Geneva, Switzerland (office). *Telephone:* (22) 918-01-00 (office). *E-mail:* albader@kuwaitmission.ch (office). *Website:* www .kazembehbehani.com.

BEHMEN, Alija, BBA, MBA, PhD (Econ.); Bosnia and Herzegovina economist, academic and politician; b. 25 Dec. 1940, Split, Croatia; m.; two s.; ed Faculty of Econs, Univ. of Sarajevo; worked at Inst. of Econs, Sarajevo; mem. staff, Railways Enterprise ŽTO Sarajevo, Deputy Pres., Pres. Exec. Bd 1970–78; Pres. Exec. Bd INTERSPED 1978–80; Assoc. Prof., Faculty of Transportation and Communications, Univ. of Sarajevo 1980–; mem. Ass. of Sarajevo Canton 1998–2000; Deputy Chair. Parl. of Bosnia and Herzegovina 1998–2001; Prime Minister of the Fed. of Bosnia and Herzegovina 2001–03; mem. House of Reps 2006–09; Mayor of Sarajevo 2008–13; Vice-Pres. Social Democratic Party and mem. of its Presidency; Order of Labour with Golden Wreath (Socialist Fed. Repub. of Yugoslavia) 1989;

Certificate of Merit of SFRY Railways (15th April Award) 1986, Best Mayor of Central and South Europe 2011. *Publications:* Materials and Goods in Transport: Classification, Standardization Identification; Management of Quality. *Leisure interest:* historiography. *Address:* Mehmeda Spahe 6, 71000, Sarajevo, Bosnia and Herzegovina (home). *Telephone:* (33) 201444 (home).

BEHNISCH, Stefan, Dipl.Ing; German architect; *Principal Partner, Behnisch Architekten;* b. 1 June 1957, Stuttgart; s. of Günter Behnisch; m. Petra Behnisch; two s.; with Behnisch & Pnr 1987–; f. Buero Innenstadt 1989, Prin. 1990–, co. became ind. 1991, later renamed Behnisch Architekten; teaches at various univs; also Visiting Prof. at several American univs and External Examiner at several European univs; frequent lecturer at architectural symposia in Germany and abroad; Hon. FAIA 2008; awards include several RIBA awards, Architectural Record/Business Week Awards, Trophée Sommet de la terre et bâtiment (France) 2002, Environmental Champion Award (USA) 2004, Global Award for Sustainable Architecture 2007, Chicago Athenaeum Good Design Award (People Category) 2009. *Projects include:* numerous residential buildings in Germany, USA and several other countries, as well as office buildings, museums, laboratories, healthcare buildings, etc including Swimming Pool Complex Grünauer Welle, Leipzig, Oceaneum-German Oceanographic Museum, Stralsund, WIPO HQ, Geneva, Marco-Polo-Tower, Hamburg, Genzyme Center, Cambridge, Mass, Harvard Univ. Allston Science Complex, Allston/Boston, John and Frances Angelos Law Center, Univ. of Baltimore, Office Building for Comune di Ravenna, Italy. *Address:* Behnisch Architekten, Rotebühlstraße 163, 70197 Stuttgart (office); Blumenstraße 17, 80331, Munich, Germany (office); 125 Kingston Street, Boston, MA 02111, USA (office). *Telephone:* (711) 607720 (Stuttgart) (office); (89) 85630980 (Munich) (office); (617) 375-9380 (Boston) (office). *Fax:* (711) 6077299 (Stuttgart) (office); (617) 348-2114 (Boston) (office). *E-mail:* buero@behnisch.com (office); bamuc@behnisch.com (office); bueroboston@behnisch.com (office). *Website:* www.behnisch.com (office).

BEHRMAN, Richard Elliot, MD, JD; American professor of pediatrics and consultant; *Executive Director, Non-Profit Healthcare and Educational Consultants to Medical Institutions;* b. 13 Dec. 1931, Philadelphia, Pa; s. of Robert Behrman and Vivian Keegan; m. Ann Nelson 1954; one s. three d.; ed Amherst Coll., Harvard Univ., Univ. of Rochester and Johns Hopkins Univ.; Oregon Regional Primate Research Center and Univ. of Oregon Medical School 1965–68; Prof. of Pediatrics and Dir Neonatal Intensive Care Unit and Nurseries, Univ. of Illinois Coll. of Medicine 1968–71; Prof. and Chair. Dept of Pediatrics and Dir Babies Hospital, Columbia Univ. Coll. of Physicians and Surgeons 1971–76; Prof. and Chair. Dept of Pediatrics and Dir Dept of Pediatrics, Rainbow Babies and Children's Hosp. Case Western Reserve Univ. School of Medicine 1976–82; Dean, School of Medicine, Case Western Reserve Univ. 1980–89, Vice-Pres. Medical Affairs 1987–89; Dir Center for Future of Children, David and Lucile Packard Foundation 1989–99; Clinical Prof., Stanford Univ. and UCSF 1989; Chair. Lucile Packard Foundation for Children 1997–99, Sr Vice-Pres. Medical Affairs 1999–2002; Exec. Chair. Fed. of Pediatric Orgs 2002; currently Exec. Dir Non-Profit Healthcare and Educational Consultants to Medical Insts, Santa Barbara, Calif.; Ed.-in-Chief Nelson Textbook of Pediatrics 1980–2006; mem. Bd of Dirs, UCSF Stanford Health Care 1997, Children's Hospices and Palliative Care Coalition, Teddy Bear Cancer Foundation 2007–; mem. Inst. Medicine, NAS; mem. Medical Advisory Bd iMetrikus, Inc.; Fellow, American Acad. of Pediatrics; Hon. DSc (Medical Coll., Wis.) 2000. *Publications:* The Future of Children (ed.) 1990–, Essentials of Paediatrics (Ed.) 2002, Nelson Textbook of Paediatrics (Ed.) 2003. *Leisure interests:* running, hiking, reading. *Address:* c/o Board of Directors, Children's Hospices and Palliative Care Coalition, 65 Nielson Street, #108, Watsonville, CA 95076, USA. *Telephone:* (805) 565-2953 (office); (805) 729-1266 (mobile). *E-mail:* behrmannon-profitconsult@nphec.org. *Website:* www.nphec.org.

BEHURIA, Sarthak, BA, MBA; Indian oil industry executive; b. 2 March 1952, Chatrapur, Orissa; s. of Nrusingha Behuria and Suvarnalata Behuria; one s. one d.; ed St Stephen's Coll., Delhi, Indian Inst. of Man., Ahmedabad; trainee with Burmah-Shell (later renamed Bharat Petroleum Corpn Ltd) 1973; held various positions including Dir of Operations, Oil Co-ordination Cttee, Exec. Dir of Sales 1995–98, Dir of Marketing 1998–2002, Chair. and Man. Dir 2002–05; Chair. Indian Oil Corpn Ltd 2005–10, also fmr Chair. (part-time) group cos Chennai Petroleum Corpn Ltd, Bongaigaon Refinery & Petrochemicals Ltd; fmr Head of Indian Oiltanking Ltd (jt venture); Chair. Petroleum Fed. of India (PetroFed) 2003, now Hon. Chair.; Chair. Standing Conf. of Public Enterprises (SCOPE) 2006–, Council of Indian Employers; First Vice-Pres. (representing Asia) World LPGas Asscn 2006–08, Pres. 2008–; Hon. Fellow, Energy Inst. (UK); named by Upstream journal amongst the 10 Most Influential Oilmen in India, Udyog Ratna Award, Progress, Harmony and Devt Chamber of Commerce and Industry 2006, SCOPE Award for Excellence and Outstanding Contrib. to Public Sector Man. (Individual Category) 2006–07. *Address:* c/o Indian Oil Corporation Ltd, 3079/3, JB Tito Marg, Sadiq Nagar, New Delhi 110 049, India. *Telephone:* (11) 26851524 (home). *Fax:* (11) 26511410 (home).

BEHZAD, Mohamed Ben Yousef, BBA, MS (Econ); Qatari economist and international organization executive; *Director-General, Arab Industrial Development and Mining Organization;* b. 30 June 1954, Doha; ed Cairo Univ., Egypt, California State Polytechnic Univ., Pomona, USA; Econs Researcher, Econs Dept, Qatar Petroleum 1979–88, Economist and Planning Engineer, Tech. Dept 1988–89, Planning Dept 1989–91; Planning Economist, Industrial Studies Dept, Gulf Org. for Industrial Consulting, Qatar 1992–93; Sr Economist and Head of Econ. Planning Dept, Supreme Council for Planning Doha Jan.–Oct. 1994; Financial Economist, OPEC, Vienna, Austria 1994–2006; Dir-Gen. Arab Industrial Devt and Mining Org. 2006–. *Address:* Arab Industrial Development and Mining Organization, rue France, Zanagat al-Khatawat, PO Box 8019, Rabat, Agdal, Morocco (office). *Telephone:* (37) 274500 (office). *Fax:* (37) 772188 (office). *E-mail:* aidmo@aidmo.org (office). *Website:* www.aidmo.org (office).

BEILIN, Yossi, PhD; Israeli politician; b. 1948, Israel; m.; two c.; ed Tel-Aviv Univ.; fmr journalist and mem. Editorial Bd of Davar; Spokesman for Labour Party 1977–84; Cabinet Sec. 1984–86; Dir Gen. for Political Affairs of Foreign Ministry 1986–88; mem. Knesset 1988–99, 2004–08, mem. Foreign Affairs and Defence, Immigration and Absorption and Constitution, Law and Justice Cttees 1990–92, Foreign Affairs and Defence, Constitution, Law and Justice, Advance-

ment of the Status of Women Cttees 1996–99; Deputy Minister of Finance 1988–90; Deputy Minister of Foreign Affairs 1992–95; Minister of Econs and Planning July–Nov. 1995; Minister without Portfolio 1995–96; Minister of Justice 1999–2001; Founder and Leader Meretz-Yahad (Social Democratic) Party 2002–04, Chair. 2004–08; founded 'Beilink', a business consultancy company; Chevalier, Légion d'honneur 2009; Dr hc (Univ. of Paris 13); Int. Activist Award, The Gleitsman Foundation 1999, Seligmann Prize 2004. *Publications:* Sons in the Shadow of their Fathers, The Price of Unity, Industry in Israel, Touching Peace, His Brother's Keeper, Israel, A Concise Political History, Touching Peace 1997, The Manual for Leaving Lebanon 1998, From Socialism to Social Liberalism 1999, His Brother's Keeper 2000, Manual for a Wounded Dove 2001, The Path to Geneva: The Quest for a Permanent Agreement. *Telephone:* (2) 747786 (office). *E-mail:* beilin@myparty.org.il (office).

BEINEIX, Jean-Jacques; French film director; b. 8 Oct. 1946, Paris; several films as Asst Dir 1970–77; Founder Cargo Films; numerous prizes and awards at film festivals. *Films include:* Le Chien de Monsieur Michel 1971, Diva 1981, La Lune dans le caniveau (The Moon in the Gutter) 1983, 37.2° le matin (Betty Blue) 1986, Roselyne and the Lions 1989, IP5 1992, Mortel Transfert 2001, Loft Paradoxe (TV) 2002. *Publications:* Diva 1991, L'île aux pachydermes 1992. *Address:* Cargo Films, 12-16 Villa Saint-Michel, 75018 Paris, France (office). *Telephone:* 1-53-34-13-80 (office). *Fax:* 1-53-34-13-81 (office). *E-mail:* cargo@cargofilms.com (office). *Website:* www.cargofilms.com (office).

BEIT-ARIÉ, Malachi, MA, MLS, PhD; Israeli palaeographer and academic; *Ludwig Jesselson Professor Emeritus of Codicology and Palaeography, Hebrew University of Jerusalem;* b. 20 May 1937, Petah-Tiqva; s. of Meir Beit-Arié and Esther Beit-Arié (née Elpiner); one s. two d.; ed Hebrew Univ., Jerusalem; Dir Hebrew Palaeography Project, Israel Acad. of Sciences and Humanities 1965, Inst. of Microfilmed Hebrew Manuscripts 1970–78; Sr Lecturer in Codicology and Palaeography, Hebrew Univ. of Jerusalem 1975–78, Assoc. Prof. 1979–83, Prof. 1984, then Ludwig Jesselson Professor of Codicology and Palaeography, Prof. Emer. 2005–; Dir Nat. and Univ. Library 1979–90; Chair. Int. Advisory Council Jewish Nat. Library 1991; Visiting Fellow, Wolfson Coll., Oxford 1984–85; Visiting Researcher, IRHT (CNRS) Paris 1991; Visiting Scholar, Harvard Univ. 1992; Fellow, Center for Advanced Judaic Studies, Univ. of Pennsylvania 1996, 1999–2000; Anne Frank Award for poetry 1961. *Publications:* These Streets, Those Mountains (lyrics) 1963, The Hills of Jerusalem and All the Pain (poems) 1967, Manuscrits médiévaux en caractères hébraiques (with C. Sirat), Parts I–III 1972–86, Hebrew Codicology 1977, The Only Dated Medieval MS Written in England 1985, Medieval Specimens of Hebrew Scripts 1987, The Makings of the Medieval Hebrew Book 1993, Hebrew Manuscripts of East and West: Towards Comparative Codicology 1993, Catalogue of the Hebrew MSS in the Bodleian Library (Supplement) 1994, Codices Lebraicis litteris exarati quo tempore scripti fuerint exhibentes I–II (with C. Sirat and M. Glatzer) 1997–99, Hebrew Manuscripts in the Biblioteca Palatina in Parma (with B. Richler) 2001. *Leisure interest:* classical music. *Address:* The Hebrew University, Mt Scopus, Jerusalem 91905 (office); PO Box 34165, Jerusalem 91341 (office); 11C Alkalai Street, Jerusalem 92223, Israel (home). *Telephone:* 2-5619270 (office); 2-5633940 (home). *E-mail:* beitarie@vms.huji.ac.il (office). *Website:* www.huji.ac.il (office).

BEJO, Bérénice; Argentine/French actress; b. 7 July 1976, Buenos Aires, Argentina; d. of Miguel Bejo and Silvia Bejo; m. Michel Hazanavicius; two c.; moved from Argentina to France aged three; est. film and TV career in France mid-1990s; US film debut 2001. *Plays:* L'Opera De Quat'Sous. *Films include:* Les soeurs Hamlet 1996, Meilleur espoir feminin 2000, Passionnément 2000 A Knight's Tale 2001, 24 Hours in the Life of a Woman 2002, Like an Airplane 2002, Sem Ela 2003, The Great Role 2003, Cavalcade 2005, OSS 117: Cairo, Nest of Spies 2006, 13 m² 2007, The House 2007, Modern Love 2008, Bouquet final 2008, L'Enfer d'Henri-Georges Clouzot 2009, Prey (La Traque) 2010, The Artist (César Award for Best Actress 2011, Capri Actress Award 2011, Hollywood Film Festival Spotlight Award 2011, Romy Schneider Award 2012 Best Actress Lumiere Award 2011, Best Supporting Actress Award, Phoenix Film Critics Soc. 2012, Best Supporting Actress Award, St Louis Gateway Film Critics Asscn 2012) 2011, Brave (voice) 2012, Populaire 2012, The Scapegoat (Au Bonheur des Ogres) 2013, Le Passé 2013. *Television includes:* Le juge est une femme 1997, Un et un font six 1997–99, Alliés 1998, La Famille Sapajou (film) 1999, Sauvetage 2000, Koan 2001 Dissonnances 2002, Nuages (film) 2005, Sa raison d'être (film) 2008. *Address:* c/o Adéquat Talent Agency, 108 rue Réaumur, 75002 Paris, France (office); c/o MIAM Communication Agency, 39 rue de Rome, 75008 Paris, France. *Telephone:* 1-42-80-00-42 (office); 1-55-50-22-22 (office). *Fax:* 1-42-80-00-43 (office). *E-mail:* agence@agence -adequat.com (office); n.iund@miamcom.com (office). *Website:* www.agence -adequat.com (office); www.miamcom.com/berenicebejo (office).

BEKELE, Kenenisa; Ethiopian athlete; b. 13 June 1982, Bekoji; ran first competitive race aged 15; set world jr record for 3,000m 2001; won long and short races at World Cross Country Championships 2002, became first to repeat in consecutive years 2003, won both events again 2004; primarily competes in 5,000m and 10,000m events; won Golden League 5,000m in Oslo 2003; gold medal 10,000m, bronze medal 10,000m World Championships 2003; gold medal 10,000m, silver medal 5,000m Olympic Games, Athens 2004; gold medal 10,000m, gold medal 5,000m Olympic Games, Beijing 2008; gold medal 10,000m World Championships 2009; holds world records at 5,000m (set in Hengelo, Netherlands 2004) and 10,000m (set in Ostrava, Czech Repub. 2004); based in Njimegen, Netherlands; Goodwill Amb. for UNICEF 2004–; Int. Asscn of Athletics Feds World Athlete of the Year 2004. *Address:* PO Box 3241, Addis Ababa, Ethiopia. *Website:* www.ethiosports.com.

BEKENOV, Sunatilla Xusanovich; Uzbekistani politician; Head of the Exec. Admin of the Cabinet of Ministers and Deputy Finance Minister 2006–09, Minister of the Economy 2009–10. *Address:* c/o Ministry of the Economy, 100003 Tashkent, O'zbekiston shoh ko'ch. 45A, Uzbekistan.

BEKENSTEIN, Jacob David, BS, MS, MS, PhD; Israeli/American theoretical physicist and academic; *Polak Professor of Theoretical Physics, Hebrew University of Jerusalem;* b. 1 May 1947, Mexico City, Mexico; s. of Joseph Bekenstein and Esther Bekenstein; m. Bilha Bekenstein; three c.; ed Polytechnic Inst. of Brooklyn, Princeton Univ.; Postdoctoral Fellow, Center for Relativity, Univ. of Texas, Austin

1972–74; Sr Lecturer, Dept of Physics, Ben Gurion Univ. 1974–76, Assoc. Prof. 1976–78, Full Prof. 1978–90, Robert and Jean Arnow Chair in Astrophysics 1983–90; Prof., Racah Inst. of Physics, Hebrew Univ. of Jerusalem 1990–, Polak Prof. of Theoretical Physics 1993–; Visiting Prof. at numerous int. univs, including Univ. of Wisconsin, Milwaukee 1980, Aspen Center for Physics 1983, 1993, Center for Astrophysics, Harvard Univ. 1985, Inst. of Astronomy, Cambridge, UK 1988, Univ. of California, Santa Barbara 1992–93, Swiss Fed. Polytechnic Inst., Zurich 1995, 1996, Imperial Coll., London 2005, Inst. for Advanced Study, Princeton (IBM Einstein Fellow) 2009–10; mem. Int. Astronomical Union 1979, Israel Acad. of Sciences and Humanities 1997, World Jewish Acad. of Sciences 2003, Int. Soc. for Gen. Relativity and Gravitation; Ernst David Bergmann Prize for Science 1977, Landau Prize for Research in Physics 1981, Rothschild Prize in the Physical Sciences 1988, Israel Prize in Physics 2005, Weizmann Prize in the Exact Sciences, Tel-Aviv Municipality 2011, Wolf Prize in Physics 2012. *Publications include:* Buchi neri, Comunicazione, Energia 2001, Of Gravity, Black Holes and Information 2006, Albert Einstein Memorial Lectures (co-ed.) 2012; numerous book chapters and papers in peer-reviewed journals on black hole thermodynamics and other aspects of the connections between information and gravitation. *Address:* Racah Institute of Physics, Hebrew University of Jerusalem, Givat Ram, Jerusalem 91904, Israel (office). *Telephone:* 2-6584374 (office); 2-6585512 (office); 2-6584605 (office). *Fax:* 2-5611519 (office). *E-mail:* bekenste@phys.huji.ac.il (office). *Website:* www.phys.huji.ac.il/~bekenste (office).

BEKKER, Koos, LLB, MBA; South African business executive; *Group CEO, Naspers Ltd;* b. 14 Dec. 1952, Potchefstroom; m. Karen Roos; two c.; ed Stellenbosch Univ., Univ. of Witwatersrand, Columbia Univ., USA; CEO M-Net Ltd 1984–91; CEO Myriad International Holdings (MIH) Group, Netherlands 1991–97, mem. Bd of Dirs 1998–; Founder-Dir MTN Group Ltd 1992–98; Group CEO Naspers Ltd 1997–, currently also mem. Bd of Dirs; Commr Global Information Infrastructure Comm. 1990–97; Dir Local Organising Cttee 2010 FIFA World Cup 2004–10; mem. Bd of Dirs MultiChoice Africa (Pty) Ltd 1984–, NetHold 1995–97, Media24 1997–, Tencent Holdings Ltd 2012–, MIH B.V., MIH (Mauritius) Ltd, MultiChoice South Africa Holdings, Nasboek, SuperSport International; Dr hc (Univ. of Stellenbosch); Best Entrepreneur (South Africa) Award, Ernst & Young 2006, Lifetime Achievement Award, Business Times. *Address:* Naspers Ltd, 40 Heerengracht, Cape Town 8001, South Africa (office). *Telephone:* (21) 4062121 (office). *Website:* www.naspers.com (office).

BEKRI, Tahar, PhD; Tunisian poet; *Lecturer, University of Paris X-Nanterre;* b. 7 July 1951, Gabès; m. Annick Le Thoër 1987; ed Univ. of Tunisia, Sorbonne, Univ. of Paris; Lecturer, Univ. of Paris X-Nanterre; mem. Soc. des Gens de Lettres de France, Maison des Ecrivains; Officier, Mérite Culturel, Tunisia 1993; Prix Tunisie-France 2006. *Recordings:* album: Si la musique doit mourir 2011. *Publications:* Poèmes bilingues 1978, Exils 1979, Le laboureur du soleil 1983, Les lignes sont des arbres 1984, Le chant du roi errant 1985, Malek Haddad 1986, Le coeur rompu aux océans 1988, Poèmes à Selma 1989, La sève des jours 1991, Les chapelets d'attache 1993, Littératures de Tunisie et du Maghreb 1994, Les songes impatients 1997, Journal de neige et de feu 1997, Le pêcheur de lunes 1998, Inconnues (translated as Unknown Seasons) 1999, De la littérature tunisienne et maghrébine 1999, Marcher sur l'oubli 2000, L'horizon incendié 2002, La brûlante rumeur de la mer 2004, Le vent sans abri 2005, Dernières nouvelles de l'été 2005, Si la musique doit mourir 2006, Le livre du souvenir 2007, Les Dits du fleuve 2009, Salam Gaza 2010, Je te nomme Tunisie 2011, Au souvenir de Yunus Emre 2012, Poésie de Palestine 2013; contrib. to various publs. *Address:* 32 rue Pierre Nicole, 75005 Paris, France (home). *Telephone:* 1-43-29-33-39 (home). *Fax:* 1-43-29-33-39 (home); 1-40-97-71-51 (office). *E-mail:* taharbekri@wanadoo.fr (home); tahar.bekri@u_paris10.fr (office). *Website:* tahar.bekri.free.fr.

BEL, Jean-Pierre, MA; French lawyer and politician; *President of the Senate;* b. 30 Dec. 1951, Lavaur (Tarn); m. 1st 1985 (divorced 2001); two d.; m. 2nd 2009; one d.; ed Lycée Berthelot and Univ. of Social Sciences, Toulouse (diplôme d'études approfondies de droit public); head of a resort at Font-Romeu and dir of a tourist office 1977–82; active in Ligue communiste révolutionnaire until 1978, then moved to Mijanès; Mayor of Mijanès 1983–95; joined the Parti Socialiste 1983; Regional Councillor, Midi-Pyrenees 1992; technical adviser to Minister of Relations with Parl. 1997–98; elected to Gen. Council of Ariège in neighbouring canton of Lavelanet 1998–2001; Mayor of Lavelanet 2001–08; elected Senator (Parti Socialiste) from Ariège (Midi-Pyrénées) 1998, re-elected 2008, Sec. of the Senate 2001–04, Pres. of Socialist Group in Senate 2004–11, Socialist cand. for post of Pres. of the Senate 2008, Pres. of the Senate (first Socialist) 2011–, Chair. France-Spain Group; mem. Conseil nat. de la montagne 1998–2001; joined Nat. Council of Parti Socialiste 1993, served in nat. office –2003, Nat. Sec. of Fed. 1994–97, Nat. Sec. of Elections –1998, Nat. Sec. to First Sec. 1997–2007; Chair. Asscn of Mayors and Elected Officials of Ariège 2001; mem. Office of the Asscn of Mayors of France 2001–06. *Address:* Palais du Luxembourg, 75291 Paris Cedex 06, France (office). *Telephone:* 1-42-34-36-77 (office). *Fax:* 1-42-34-20-94 (office). *E-mail:* bel1.jean -pierre@wanadoo.fr (office); presidence@senat.fr (office). *Website:* www.senat.fr (office).

BELAFONTE, Harry; American singer; b. 1 March 1927, New York; s. of Harold George Belafonte Sr and Malvene Love Wright; m. 1st Marguerite Byrd 1948; m. 2nd Julie Robinson 1957; one s. three d.; ed George Washington High School, New York; in Jamaica 1935–39; service with US Navy 1943–45; student, American Negro Theater, then at Manhattan New School for Social Research Dramatic Workshop 1946–48; first engagement at the Vanguard, Greenwich Village; European tours 1958, 1976, 1981, 1983, 1988; Pres. Belafonte Enterprises Inc.; Goodwill Amb. for UNICEF 1987; Host of Nelson Mandela Birthday Concert, Wembley, UK 1988; concerts in USA, Europe 1989, Canada 1990, USA and Canada 1991, N America, Europe and Far East 1996; mem. Bd NY State Martin Luther King Jr Inst. for Nonviolence 1989–; mem. Bd of Trustees, Inst. for Policy Studies; Hon. DHumLitt (Park Coll., Mo.) 1968, Hon. Dr Arts, New School of Social Research, New York 1968, Hon. DCL (Newcastle) 1997, numerous other hon. doctorates; Grammy Award 1985, Kennedy Center Honors 1989, Golden Acord Award, Bronx Community Coll. 1989, Mandela Courage Award 1990, Nat. Medal of the Arts 1994, New York Arts and Business Council Award 1997, Award of Excellence, Ronald McDonald House Charities 2000, Grammy Lifetime Achievement Award 2000, Distinguished American Award, John F. Kennedy Library,

Boston 2002, BET Humanitarian Award 2006, Andrew Goodman Foundation Lifetime Achievement Award 2011. *Achievements include:* RCA album Calypso made him the first artist in industry history to sell over one million LPs. *Films include:* Bright Road 1953, Carmen Jones 1954, Island in the Sun 1957, The World, the Flesh and the Devil 1959, Odds Against Tomorrow 1959, The Angel Levine 1970, Buck and the Preacher 1972, Uptown Saturday Night 1974, White Man's Burden 1995, Kansas City 1996, Bobby 2006, Motherland 2009, Sing Your Song 2011. *Publication:* My Song: A Memoir 2011. *Leisure interests:* photography, water skiing, recording. *Address:* c/o William Morris Endeavor Entertainment LLC, 9601 Wilshire Blvd, Suite 3, Beverly Hills, CA 90210-5219, USA.

BELAIZ, Tayeb, LenD; Algerian politician and fmr judge; *Minister of the Interior;* b. 21 Aug. 1948, Maghnia; ed Univ. of Oran; early positions at Ministry of the Interior; fmr judge and Pres. of the Chamber, Court of Oran, also fmr Pres. Court of Saida, Court of Sidi-Bel-Abbès and adviser to Supreme Court Judge; Minister of Labour and Social Security 2002–03, Minister of Justice and Attorney-Gen. 2003–12, Minister of the Interior 2013–; mem. Nat. Comm. for Judicial Reform 1999. *Address:* Ministry of the Interior and Local Authorities, 18 rue Docteur Saâdane, Algiers, Algeria (office). *Telephone:* (21) 73-76-81 (office). *Fax:* (21) 73-61-54 (office).

BÉLANGER, Gerard, MA, MSocSc, RSC; Canadian economist and academic; *Professor of Economics, Université Laval;* b. 23 Oct. 1940, St Hyacinthe; s. of Georges Bélanger and Cécile Girard; one d.; ed Princeton and Laval Univs; Prof., Dept of Econs, Laval Univ. 1967–, Prof. of Econs 1977–; Research Co-ordinator, Howe Inst., Montreal 1977–79; mem. Task Force on Urbanization, Govt of Québec 1974–76; Sec. Acad. of Letters and Social Sciences, RSC 1985–88; Woodrow Wilson Fellow; Doug Purvis Memorial Prize 2008. *Publications:* The Price of Health 1972, Le financement municipal au Québec 1976, Taxes and Expenditures in Québec and Ontario 1978, Le prix du transport au Québec 1978, L'économie du secteur public 1981, Croissance du Secteur Public et Fédéralisme 1988, L'Économique de la santé et l'État providence 2005. *Address:* Department of Economics, Pavillon J.-A.-DeSève, local 2256, Université Laval, Québec, PQ G1V 0A6, Canada (office). *Telephone:* (418) 656-5363 (office); (418) 681-3075 (home). *Fax:* (418) 656-2707 (office). *E-mail:* gebe@ecn.ulaval.ca (office); gerard.belanger@ecn.ulaval.ca (office). *Website:* www.ulaval.ca/Al/bienvenueanglais.html (office).

BÉLAVAL, Philippe Marie, LLM; French library executive and civil servant; *Chief of Heritage, Ministry of Culture and Communication;* b. 21 Aug. 1955, Toulouse; s. of Jacques Bélaval and Marie-Thérèse Bélaval (née Chazarenc); ed Faculté des Sciences Sociales de Toulouse, Inst. d'études politiques de Toulouse; trainee at École nationale d'admin. 1977–79, auditor 1979; technical adviser Conseil d'Etat 1983–84, counsel 1984, rep. of Sec. of State for Budget and Consumption 1984–86; Asst Dir Office of Minister of Public Affairs and Admin. Reform 1988–89, Dir 1989–90; Dir-Gen. Théâtre nationale de l'Opéra de Paris 1990–92; Dir-Gen. Bibliothèque nationale de France 1994–98; Dir-Gen. Archives de France 1998–2000; Pres. Admin. Council Groupe vocal de France 1985–90; Pres. Cour administrative d'appel, Bordeaux 2001–04, Pres. Cour administrative d'appel de Versailles 2004–08; Chair. Nat. Heritage Inst. 2008–; Chief of Heritage, Ministry of Culture and Communication 2010–; Council of State 1996; Pres. Supreme Council and Literary Property Artistic; mem. Admin. Council of École des chartes; Sr Lecturer, Inst. d'études politiques de Paris; Chevalier Légion d'honneur, Chevalier Ordre nat. du Mérite, Commdr des Arts et des Lettres. *Address:* Ministry of Culture and Communication, 3 rue de Valois, 75001 Paris, France (office). *Telephone:* 1-40-15-80-00 (office). *Fax:* 1-40-15-81-72 (office). *E-mail:* point.culture@culture.fr (office). *Website:* www.culture.gouv.fr (office).

BELCHIOR, Miriam, MA; Brazilian academic and politician; *Minister of Planning, Budget and Administration;* b. 5 Feb. 1958, Santo André; m. Celso Daniel (deceased); ed Fundacao Getulio Vargas, São Paulo, Universidade Estadual de Campinas; Sec. of Admin and Modernization, municipality of Santo André (São Paulo) 1997–2000, Sec. for Social Inclusion and Housing 2001–02; Prof., Univ. São Marcos 1999–2002; Prof., Foundation for Research and Devt 2001–08; joined transition staff of Pres. Lula da Silva 2002, Special Adviser to Pres. Lula 2003–04; General Coordinator, Growth Acceleration Programme 2010; Minister of Planning, Budget and Admin 2011–; Dir Eletrobras; mem. Partido dos Trabalhadore. *Address:* Ministry of Planning, Budget and Administration, Esplanada dos Ministérios, Bloco K, 7º andar, 70040-906, Brasília DF Brazil (office). *Telephone:* (61) 2020-4102 (office). *Fax:* (61) 2020-5009 (office). *E-mail:* ministro@planejamento.gov.br (office). *Website:* www.planejamento.gov.br (office).

BELDA, Alain J. P., BBA; French business executive; *Managing Director, Warburg Pincus LLC;* b. 1943; ed Universidade Mackenzie, Brazil; joined Aluminum Co. of America 1969, Pres. Alcoa Aluminio SA, Brazil 1979–94, Vice-Pres. Alcoa (Latin America) 1982–91, Pres. 1991–94, Exec. Vice-Pres., Alcoa Inc. 1994–95, Vice-Chair. 1995–97, Exec. Dir 1998–, Pres. and COO 1997–99, Pres. and CEO 1999–2001, Chair. and CEO 2001–08, Chair. 2008–09; Man. Dir Warburg Pincus LLC 2009–, leads firm's investment efforts in Latin America; Dir Banco Indusval & Partners, International Business Machines, Omega Energia Renovavel SA, Renault SA 2009–; Co-Chair. Brazil Project Advisory Bd at The Woodrow Wilson Int. Center for Scholars; mem. The Business Council, Business Roundtable, Cttee to Encourage Corp. Philanthropy, World Business Council for Sustainable Devt, World Econ. Forum, Int. Business Council; Trustee, Ford Foundation, The Conference Bd, Brown Univ. Corpn. *Address:* Warburg Pincus do Brasil Ltda., Av. Brig. Faria Lima 2277 - 9º andar, Jd.Paulistano, 01451-001 São Paulo SP, Brazil (office). *Telephone:* (11) 3096-3500 (office). *Fax:* (11) 3096-3509 (office). *E-mail:* info@warburgpincus.com (office). *Website:* www.warburgpincus.com (office).

BELÉN ELGOYHEN, Ana, PhD; Argentine geneticist and academic; *Senior Associate Professor, Department of Pharmacology, Faculty of Medicine, University of Buenos Aires;* Sr Assoc. Prof., Dept of Pharmacology, Faculty of Medicine, Univ. of Buenos Aires; Ind. Researcher, Consejo Nacional de Investigaciones Científicas y Técnicas (CONICET); Howard Hughes Medical Inst. Int. Scholar; Laureate for Latin America, L'Oréal-UNESCO Awards for Women in Science 2008. *Publications:* numerous papers in professional journals. *Address:* INGEBI, Vuelta de Obligado 2490, C1428ADN, Buenos Aires, Argentina (office). *Telephone:* (11) 4783-2871 (office). *Fax:* (11) 4786-8578 (office). *E-mail:* elgoyhen@dna.uba.ar (office). *Website:* www.ingebi-conicet.gov.ar/dr_anabelen.php (office).

BELENKOV, Yuri N., Dr Med.; Russian neurophysiologist and university administrator; *Vice-Rector, Lomonosov Moscow State University;* b. 9 Feb. 1948, Leningrad; s. of Nikita Yu. Belenkov and Marina T. Koval; m. Natalia V. Belenkova; one s.; ed Leningrad State Univ.; held several posts at Myasnikov Inst. of Cardiology 1975–91, including Jr Researcher, Sr Researcher, Head of Lab., Deputy Dir, Dir 1991–2008; Head of Fed. Agency for Health and Social Devt 2006–08; currently Vice-Rector, Lomonosov Moscow State Univ.; fmr Chief Cardiologist of Russian Ministry of Public Health; Ed.-in-Chief Kardiologya; mem. Editorial Bd International Journal of Medical Practice, Circulation, European Journal of Heart Failure; mem. Presidium Russian Soc. of Cardiologists; Corresp. mem. Russian Acad. of Medical Sciences 1993–99, Full mem. 1999–; Corresp. mem. Russian Acad. of Sciences 2000–; Hon. mem. Acad. of Medicine of Colombia 1989; Order of Friendship of People 1988, Order of Honour 1998, Order for Service to the Fatherland (third degree); Lenin Komsomol Prize 1978, USSR State Prize 1980, 1989, RF Government Prize 2003. *Achievements include:* was the first to introduce to USSR echocardiography in 1973 and cardiovascular MRI in 1983. *Publications include:* more than 600 scientific papers on ultrasonic diagnostics, magnetic resonance tomography and cardiology; 18 monographs, including Ultrasound Diagnostics in cardiology 1981, Practical Echocardiography 1982, Clinical Application of Magnetic Resonance Tomography 1996, Magnetic Resonance Tomography of Heart and Vessels 1997, Primary Lung Hypertension 1999, Principles of Rational Treatment of Cardiac Insufficiency 2000. *Leisure interests:* driving, classical music, jazz, sports. *Address:* Lomonosov Moscow State University, Moscow 119991, GSP-1, Leninskie Gory, Russia (office). *Telephone:* (495) 939-10-00 (office). *Fax:* (495) 939-01-26 (office). *E-mail:* info@rector.msu.ru (office). *Website:* www.msu.ru (office).

BELICHICK, William (Bill) Stephen, BEcons; American football coach; *Head Coach, New England Patriots;* b. 16 April 1952, Nashville, Tenn.; s. of Steve Belichick; m. Debby Clarke (divorced 2006); two s. one d.; ed Annapolis High School, Phillips Acad., Andover, Mass, Wesleyan Univ., Middletown, Conn.; raised in Annapolis, Md; Special Asst to Head Coach Ted Marchibroda, Baltimore Colts 1975–76; Asst Special Teams Coach, Tight Ends and Receivers Coach, Detroit Lions 1976–78; Asst Special Teams Coach and Asst to Defensive Coordinator Joe Collier, Denver Broncos 1978–79; Defensive Asst and Special Teams Coach, New York Giants 1979–86, Defensive Coordinator 1986–90; Head Coach, Cleveland Browns 1991–95; Asst Head Coach and Defensive Asst, New England Patriots 1996, Head Coach 2000–; Asst Head Coach and Defensive Backs Coach, New York Jets 1997–99; only head coach in league history to win three Super Bowl championships in a four-year span 2001, 2003, 2004; inducted into Annapolis High School Hall of Fame, AP Nat. Football League Coach of the Year 2003, 2007, 2010, named one of 100 Most Powerful and Influential People in the World, Time Magazine 2004. *Address:* New England Patriots, 1 Patriot Place, Foxborough, MA 02035-1388, USA (office). *Telephone:* (508) 543-8200 (office). *Fax:* (508) 543-0285 (office). *Website:* www.patriots.com (office).

BELINGA-EBOUTOU, Martin, Cameroonian diplomatist, government official and international organization official; *Director, Civil Cabinet of the Presidency;* b. 17 Feb. 1940, Nkilzok; m.; six c.; ed Catholic Univ., Lavanium-Kinshasa, Univ. of Paris; joined Ministry of Foreign Affairs 1968, Chargé d'Affaires, Congo 1970–74, Chief, Regional Orgs Unit 1974–85, Head Econ. Mission of Cameroon, Paris, Rome, Tunis, Rabat 1985–89; Dir then Chief of State Protocol, Office of Pres. 1989–97, Dir Civil Cabinet 1996–97, 2009–; Perm. Rep. to UN, New York and Geneva and Amb. to Jamaica 1998–2007; Pres. ECOSOC 2001, Pres. UN Security Council Oct. 2002, Chair. Third Cttee of Gen. Ass. (Social, Humanitarian and Cultural Cttee) 2003; Special Adviser to Pres. of Cameroon 2007–09; Assoc. Prof., Inst. of Int. Relations 1974–76. *Address:* Office of the President, Palais de l'Unité, Yaoundé, Cameroon (office). *Telephone:* 2223-4025 (office).

BELIZ, Gustavo, LLD; Argentine politician and academic; b. 7 Jan. 1962, Buenos Aires; m. Mary Florence Meritello; three s. one d.; ed Univ. of Buenos Aires, London School of Econs, UK; sports journalist, El Gráfico magazine 1979–85; political journalist and head of editorial dept, La Razón 1985–89; sec. of public functions to the presidency and speechwriter for Pres. Carlos Menem 1989–93, Minister of the Interior 1992–93; consultant and researcher, ECLAC 1994–95; Prof., School of Information Sciences, Universidad Austral 1995–2001; pvt. consultant and researcher 1996–97; f. Nueva Dirigencia (political party) 1996; legislator, Ciudad Autónomica de Buenos Aires 1996–2003, Senator and Head of City Govt 1999–2003; Research Assoc., Inst. of Altos Estudios Empresariales,Universidad Austral 2000–01; Assoc. Prof., Southern Univ. 2001; Minister of Justice, Human Rights and Internal Security 2003–04 (resgnd); currently Perm. Staff Inter-American Devt Bank; fmr Pres. Nat. Inst. of Public Admin; fmr mem. Bd of Dirs Latin American Council for Devt Research; chosen as one of 10 outstanding young talents in Argentina, Cámara Junior de Buenos Aires 1992. *Address:* Inter-American Development Bank, Casilla de correo Nº 181, Sucursal 1, Buenos Aires, Argentina. *Telephone:* (11) 4320-1800 (office). *E-mail:* BIDArgentina@iadb.org (office). *Website:* www.iadb.org (office).

BELKA, Marek Marian, MA, PhD; Polish politician, economist, academic, UN official and central banker; *President, National Bank of Poland;* b. 9 Jan. 1952, Łódź; m.; two c.; ed Łódź Univ., Univ. of Chicago, USA, London School of Econs, UK; Master of Econs and Sociology Faculty, Łódź Univ. 1972, Asst Prof., then Prof. of Econs 1973–96; Visiting Scholar, Columbia Univ. (Fulbright Foundation), USA 1978–79; American Council of Scholarly Socs, Univ. of Chicago 1985–86; LSE 1990; Asst Prof., Inst. of Econs, Polish Acad. of Sciences (PAN) 1986–97, Dir 1993–97; adviser and consultant Finance Ministry, Privatisation Ministry and Cen. Planning Office 1990–96; Deputy Chair. Govt Council of Socio-Econ. Strategy 1994–96; Econ. Adviser to the Pres. of Poland 1996–97, 1997–2001; consultant to World Bank 1990–96; adviser to JP Morgan Chase; Deputy Prime Minister and Minister of Finance 1997, 2001–02; Head Coalition Council for Int. Co-ordination in Iraq 2003; Dir in charge of econ. policy, Coalition Provisional Authority 2003–04; Prime Minister of Poland 2004–05; Exec. Sec. UN ECE 2005–08; Dir European Dept, IMF 2008–10; Pres. Nat. Bank of Poland (central bank) 2010–; Hon. mem. Int. Raoul Wallenberg Foundation; elected to Polish Economy Hall of Fame 2013. *Publications:* about a dozen books and more than 100 articles in Polish and foreign press on anti-inflation policy in developed countries, the Milton Friedman socio-economic doctrine and macro-economic policy in transition

periods. *Leisure interests:* travelling, basketball, music. *Address:* Narodowy Bank Polski – NBP (National Bank of Poland), 00-919 Warsaw, ul. Świętokrzyska 11/21, PO Box 1011, Poland (office). *Telephone:* (22) 6531000 (office). *Fax:* (22) 6208518 (office). *E-mail:* listy@nbp.pl (office). *Website:* www.nbp.pl (office).

BELKEZIZ, Abdelouahed, DrIur; Moroccan international organization official, lawyer, diplomatist and university administrator; *President, University of Mohammed V Agdal;* b. 5 July 1939, Marrakesh; ed Sidi Mohammed Coll., Marrakesh, Faculty of Law, Rabat, Univ. of Rennes, France; Dean Faculty of Juridical, Econ. and Social Sciences, Moroccan Univ., Rabat 1966, Hassan II Univ., Casablanca 1985, Univ. of Ibn Tofail, Kenitra 1992, Univ. Muhammad V, Rabat 1997–2000; Pres. High Studies Reform Comm. 1969; mem. Perm. Royal Comm. for Judicial Reforms, Trade Codification, Penal and Civil Procedures 1971; Juridical Adviser, Moroccan Del. to UN 1976–77; Amb. to Iraq 1977–79; Minister of Information 1979–81, of Information, Youth and Sports 1981–83, of Foreign Affairs 1983–85; Pres. Exec. Cttee of Islamic World Univs Fed., Council of Maghreb Univs 1997–2000; Chair. Nat. Conf. of Moroccan Univ. Deans 1997–2000; Sec.-Gen. OIC 2001–04; currently Pres. Univ. of Mohammed V Agdal; mem. Moroccan Award Comm. for Social Sciences 1968–74, Nat. Council for Youth and Future 1985; mem. American Asscn of Comparative Law 1970–; King Abdulaziz Decoration of the Second Rank 1979, Great Spanish Civil Merit Cordon 1979, Commdr of the Civil Div., Order of the British Empire 1980, Great Officer of the Merit Order, Senegal 1981, Grand Officier, Ordre nat. du Mérite 1983, Great Cross of the Order of Rio Branco, Brazil 1984, Commdr of the Throne Order 1994. *Address:* Office of the President, University of Mohammed V Agdal, BP 554, Ave des Nations Unies, Agdal, Rabat, Morocco (office). *Telephone:* 37-27-27-50 (office). *Fax:* 37-67-14-01 (office). *E-mail:* presidence@um5a.ac.ma (office). *Website:* www .um5a.ac.ma (office).

BELKHADEM, Abdelaziz; Algerian politician; *Minister of State and Personal Representative to the Head of State;* b. 8 Nov. 1945, Aflou; Deputy Dir of Int. Relations, Office of the Pres. 1972–77; Rapporteur, Planning and Finance Comm. 1978–87; mem. Front de Libération Nationale (FLN) 1977–, mem. Bureau Politique 1991–97, currently Sec.-Gen.; Deputy for Sougueur to Assemblée Populaire Nationale (APN) 1977–92, Vice-Pres. 1988–90, Pres. 1990–91, Pres. Educ., Training and Scientific Research Comm. 1987; Minister of State for Foreign Affairs 2000–05; Minister of State and Special Rep. of the Pres. 2005–06; Prime Minister 2006–08; Minister of State and Personal Rep. to Head of State 2008–. *Address:* Front de libération nationale (FLN), 7 rue du Stade, 16405, Hydra, Algiers, Algeria (office). *Telephone:* (21) 69-42-81 (office). *Fax:* (21) 69-47-07 (office). *E-mail:* contact@pfln.dz (office). *Website:* www.pfln.dz (office).

BELL, Edward; British publisher; *Partner, Bell Lomax Moreton Agency;* b. 2 Aug. 1949; s. of Eddie Bell and Jean Bell; m. Junette Bannatyne 1969; one s. two d.; ed Airdrie High School; with Hodder & Stoughton 1970–85; Man. Dir Collins Gen. Div. 1985–89; launched Harper Paperbacks in USA 1989; Deputy Chief Exec., HarperCollins UK 1990–91, Chief Exec. 1991–92, Chair. 1992–2000; Chair. HarperCollins India 1994–2000; Dir (non-exec.) Haynes Publishing 2001–09, Sr Ind. non-exec. Dir 2009–; Dir (non-exec.) Be Cogent Ltd, Management Diagnostics Ltd; Chair. (non-exec.) OAG Worldwide Ltd 2001; Pnr, Bell Lomax Moreton Agency 2002–. *Leisure interests:* golf, supporting Arsenal, collecting old books. *Address:* The Bell Lomax Moreton Agency, James House, 1 Babmaes Street, London, SW1Y 6HF, England (office). *Telephone:* (20) 7930-4447 (office). *Fax:* (20) 7925-0118 (office). *E-mail:* eddie@bell-lomax.co.uk.

BELL, Geoffrey Lakin, BSc (Econ); British international banker; *President, Geoffrey Bell & Co. Ltd;* b. 8 Nov. 1939, Grimsby, Lincs.; s. of the late Walter Lakin Bell and of Anne Bell; m. Joan Rosine Abel 1973; one d.; ed Grimsby Tech. High School, London School of Econs; HM Treasury 1961–63; Visiting Scholar, Fed. Reserve System, Fed. Reserve Bank of St Louis 1963–64; HM Treasury and Lecturer, LSE 1964–66; adviser, British Embassy, Washington, DC 1966–69; joined J. Henry Schroder Wagg and Co. Ltd 1969, Asst to Chair. 1969–72; Dir and Exec. Vice-Pres. Schroder Int. Ltd; Dir Schroder Bermuda Ltd; Founder, Exec. Sec. and mem. Bd of Dirs Group of Thirty Consultative Group on Int. Econ. and Monetary Affairs, Inc., Washington, DC 1978–; Pres. Geoffrey Bell & Co. Ltd 1982–; Chair. Guinness Mahon Holdings 1987–93; mem. Court of Govs LSE 1994–; fmr financial adviser to Cen. Bank of Venezuela, currently financial adviser to Govt of Barbados and Govt of Jamaica; Companion of Honour of Barbados. *Publications include:* The Euro-Dollar Market and the International Financial System 1973 (translated into French and Japanese); contrib. The Times, International Herald Tribune and numerous academic and other publs. *Address:* 780 Third Avenue, 7th Floor, New York, NY 10017-2024, USA (office). *Telephone:* (212) 888-3700 (office). *E-mail:* geoffrey.bell@verizon.net (home). *Website:* www.group30 .org.

BELL, Graeme I., PhD; Canadian biologist and academic; *Louis Block Distinguished Service Professor, Departments of Medicine and Human Genetics, University of Chicago;* b. Victoria, BC; ed Univ. of Calgary, Alberta, Univ. of California, San Francisco, USA; Postgraduate Research Biochemist, Dept of Biochemistry and Biophysics, Univ. of California, San Francisco 1977–78, Asst Research Biochemist 1978–81, Asst Adjunct Prof. 1981–84, Asst Adjunct Prof., Metabolic Research Unit 1984–86; also worked as Sr Scientist, Chiron Corpn 1981–86; Assoc. Prof., Dept of Biochemistry and Molecular Biology, Univ. of Chicago 1986–90, Assoc. Prof., Dept of Medicine 1987–90, Prof., Depts of Biochemistry and Molecular Biology, and Medicine 1990–94, Louis Block Prof., Depts of Biochemistry and Molecular Biology, and Medicine 1994–98, Louis Block Distinguished Service Prof., Depts of Medicine and Human Genetics 1998–; Assoc. Investigator, Howard Hughes Medical Inst., Chevy Chase, Md 1986–90, Investigator 1990–; mem. NAS 1998, Inst. of Medicine 1998; Fellow, American Acad. of Arts and Sciences 2008; Hon. Foreign mem. La Sociedad Artina de Diabetes 2000; Elliot P. Joslin Research and Devt Award, American Diabetes Asscn (ADA) 1980–82, Rolf Luft Award, Swedish Medical Soc. 1989, Mary Jane Kugel Award, Juvenile Diabetes Foundation Int. (JDFI) 1989, Outstanding Scientific Achievement Award by an Investigator (Lilly Award), ADA 1990, William C. Stadie Award, Greater Philadelphia Affiliate of ADA 1990, Distinguished Alumni Award, Univ. of Calgary 1991, Gerold and Kayla Grodsky Basic Research Scientist Award, JDFI 1995, Naomi Berrie Award for Outstanding Achievement in Diabetes Research, Columbia Univ., New York 2000, Benjamin F. Stapleton, Jr Lecturer,

Univ. of Colorado Health Science Center 2002, J. Allyn Taylor Int. Prize in Medicine for Diabetes 2002. *Address:* University of Chicago, 5841 S Maryland Avenue, MC1027, Chicago, IL 60637-1027, USA (office). *Telephone:* (773) 702-9116 (office). *Fax:* (773) 702-9237 (office). *E-mail:* g-bell@uchicago.edu (office). *Website:* drtc.bsd.uchicago.edu (office); gbell.bsd.uchicago.edu (office).

BELL, John Anthony, OBE, AO; Australian theatre director and actor; *Artistic Director, The Bell Shakespeare Company;* b. 1 Nov. 1940, Newcastle, NSW; s. of Albert Bell and Joyce Feeney; m. Anna Volska 1965; two d.; ed Maitland Marist Brothers High School, NSW and Univ. of Sydney; actor with Old Tote Theatre Co. 1963–64, with RSC, UK 1964–69; Co-founder Nimrod Theatre Co. 1970–85; Founder and Artistic Dir Bell Shakespeare Co. 1990–; roles include King Lear, Macbeth, Shylock, Malvolio and Richard III, Prospero; Hon. DLitt (Newcastle) 1994, (Sydney) 1996, (NSW) 2006; Australia Nat. Living Treasure, Nat. Trust of Australia 1997, Dame Elisabeth Murdoch Cultural Leadership Award, Australian Business Arts Foundation 2003. *Publications include:* The Time of My Life (autobiog.) 2002, On Shakespeare 2011. *Leisure interests:* reading, music, painting. *Address:* The Bell Shakespeare Company, PO Box 10, Millers Point, Sydney NSW 2000, Australia (office). *Telephone:* (2) 8298-9000 (office). *Fax:* (2) 9241-4643 (office). *E-mail:* mail@bellshakespeare.com.au (office). *Website:* www .bellshakespeare.com.au (office).

BELL, Sir John Irving, Kt, DM, PMedSci, FRS, FRCP; Canadian medical scientist and academic; *Regius Professor of Medicine, University of Oxford;* b. 1 July 1952; ed Ridley Coll., Univ. of Alberta, Magdalen Coll., Oxford; Clinical Fellow, Dept of Medicine, Stanford Univ., Calif. 1982–87; Wellcome Sr Clinical Fellow and Hon. Consultant, Radcliffe Hosp., Oxford 1987–89, Lecturer, Nuffield Dept of Clinical Medicine, Oxford Univ. 1989–92, Nuffield Prof. of Clinical Medicine 1992–2002, Regius Prof. of Medicine 2002–, Emer. Fellow, Magdalen Coll.; f. Wellcome Trust Centre for Human Genetics 1993; Founder Fellow, Acad. of Medical Sciences 1998 (Pres. 2006–11); Chair. Office for the Strategic Coordination of Health Research (OSCHR) 2006–, Oxford Health Alliance, GMEC Management Company Ltd, Human Genome Strategy Group; mem. Bd of Dirs Roche AG 2001–, Genentech 2009–, Oxford Biomedical Research Centre 2009–, Gray Laboratory Cancer Research Trust, Edward Jenner Inst. for Vaccine Research, Isis Innovation Ltd, Oxagen Ltd, 459-Plus; mem. Bill and Melinda Gates Foundation Scientific Advisory Cttee, Scientific Advisory Bd AstraZeneca 1997–2000, Scientific Advisory Bd Roche Palo Alto 1998–; Trustee, Rhodes Trust, Oxford Lotus Fund; fmr mem. Oxford Univ. Council, MRC Council; Hon. Fellow, Royal Acad. of Eng. *Address:* The Offices of the Regius Professor, Level 4, Academic Centre, John Radcliffe Hospital, Headley Way, Headington, Oxford, OX3 9DU, England (office). *Telephone:* (1865) 221340 (office). *Fax:* (1865) 220993 (office). *E-mail:* regius@medsci.ox .ac.uk (office). *Website:* www.medsci.ox.ac.uk (office).

BELL, Joshua; American violinist; b. 9 Dec. 1967, Indiana; ed Indiana Univ.; youngest guest soloist at a Philadelphia Orchestra Subscription concert 1982; European tour with St Louis Symphony 1985; German tour with Indianapolis Symphony 1987; European tour with Dallas Symphony 1997; European tours with Nat. Symphony Orchestra 2002, Minnesota Orchestra 2003; guest soloist with numerous orchestras in USA, Canada, Europe; has also appeared in USA and Europe as a recitalist; played premiere of violin concerto by Nicholas Maw, written for him, with Philharmonia Orchestra 1993; Music Dir, Acad. of St Martin in the Fields 2011–; Visiting Prof. at RAM, London; Artistic Partner, St Paul Chamber Orchestra; Gramophone Award for Best Concerto Recording 1998 (for Barber Concerto), Mercury Music Award 2000, Acad. Award for Best Soundtrack (for Red Violin), Grammy Award 2001, Avery Fisher Prize 2007, named Young Global Leader by World Econ. Forum 2007, Musical America Award for Instrumentalist of the Year 2010. *Recordings:* Mendelssohn and Bruch concertos with the Academy of St Martin-in-the-Fields and Sir Neville Marriner, Tchaikovsky and Wieniawski concertos with the Cleveland Orchestra and Vladimir Ashkenazy, recital album of Brahms, Paganini, Sarasate and Wieniawski with Samuel Sanders, Lalo Symphonie Espagnole and Saint-Saëns Concerto with Montreal Symphony Orchestra and Charles Dutoit, Franck, Fauré and Debussy, Chausson Concerto for violin, piano and string quartet with Thibaudet and Isserlis, Poème with Royal Philharmonic Orchestra and Andrew Litton, Mozart Concertos Nos 3 and 5 with the English Chamber Orchestra and Peter Maag, Prokofiev violin concertos with Montréal Symphony Orchestra and Charles Dutoit, Barber and Walton concertos and Bloch Baal Shem with Baltimore Symphony Orchestra and David Zinman, recital disc with Olli Mustonen, Gershwin Fantasy with London Symphony Orchestra and John Williams, Short Trip Home with Edgar Meyer, The Red Violin film soundtrack with Philharmonia Orchestra, Sibelius Goldmark Concertos with Los Angeles Philharmonic Orchestra and Esa-Pekka Salonen, Maw Concerto for violin with London Philharmonic Orchestra and Roger Norrington, Bernstein Serenade and West Side Story Suite with Philharmonia Orchestra and David Zinman, Beethoven and Mendelssohn concertos with Camerata Salzburg and Sir Roger Norrington, Irish film soundtrack, Romance of the Violin 2003, Tchaikovsky Violin Concerto 2005, Voice of the Violin 2006, The Red Violin Concerto 2007, Vivaldi: The Four Seasons 2008, At Home with my Friends 2009, French Impressions with Jeremy Denk (ECHO Klassik Award for Chamber Music Recording of the Year/Strings – 19th Century) 2012. *Leisure interests:* chess, computers, golf. *Address:* c/o Elizabeth Sobol Gomez, IMG Artists, Carnegie Hall Tower, 152 West 57th Street, 5th Floor, New York, NY 10019, USA (office). *Telephone:* (212) 994-3541 (office). *Fax:* (212) 994-3550 (office). *E-mail:* esobol -gomez@imgartists.com (office); heidi@joshuabell.com (office); jb@joshuabell.com (office). *Website:* www.imgartists.com (office); www.joshuabell.com (office).

BELL, Marian, CBE, MA, MSc; British economist; *Director, Alpha Economics;* b. 28 Oct. 1957, London, England; d. of Joseph Denis Milburn Bell and Wilhelmenia Maxwell Bell (née Miller); m. Richard Adkin; two d.; ed Hertford Coll., Oxford, Birkbeck Coll. London; Econ. Adviser, HM Treasury 1989–91; Sr Treasury Economist, Head of Research, Treasury and Capital Markets, Royal Bank of Scotland 1991–2000; consultant, Alpha Economics 2000–02, currently Dir; External Mem. Monetary Policy Cttee, Bank of England 2002–05; Dir (non-exec.), Emerging Health Threats Forum 2006–12; mem. Fiscal Policy Panel, States of Guernsey 2007–11, Int. Advisory Council, Zurich Insurance Group 2007–; Gov. Contemporary Dance Trust, The Place 2005–, Vice-Chair. 2008–. *Leisure interests:* contemporary dance, art. *E-mail:* Assist.bell@btinternet.com (office).

BELL, Martin, OBE, MA; British broadcaster and politician; *Humanitarian Ambassador, United Nations International Children's Emergency Fund (UNICEF);* b. 31 Aug. 1938; s. of the late Adrian Bell and Marjorie Bell (née Gibson); m. 1st Nelly Gourdon 1971 (divorced); two d.; m. 2nd Rebecca Sobel 1985 (divorced 1993); m. 3rd Fiona Goddard 1998; ed The Leys School, Cambridge, King's Coll., Cambridge; joined BBC 1962, news Asst, Norwich 1962–64, gen. reporter, London and overseas 1964–76, Diplomatic Corresp. 1976–77, Chief N American Corresp. 1977–89, Berlin Corresp. BBC TV News 1989–93, Vienna Corresp. 1993–94, Foreign Affairs Corresp. 1994–96, Special Corresp., Nine O'Clock News 1997; has reported from over 70 countries and has covered wars in Vietnam, Middle East 1967, 1973, Angola, Rhodesia, Biafra, El Salvador, Gulf 1991, Nicaragua, Croatia, Bosnia; MP (Ind.) for Tatton 1997–2001; Humanitarian Amb. for UNICEF 2001–; Dr hc (Derby) 1996; Hon. MA (E Anglia) 1997, (Aberdeen) 1998; Royal TV Soc. Reporter of the Year 1976, 1992, TV and Radio Industries Club Newscaster of the Year 1995, Inst. of Public Relations Pres.'s Medal 1996. *Publications:* In Harm's Way 1995, An Accidental MP 2000, Through Gates of Fire 2003, The Truth That Sticks: New Labour's Breach of Trust 2007. *Address:* 71 Denman Drive, London, NW11 6RA, England (home).

BELL, Baron (Life Peer), cr. 1998, of Belgravia in the City of Westminster; **Timothy John Leigh Bell,** FIPA; British public relations executive; b. 18 Oct. 1941; s. of Arthur Leigh Bell and Greta Mary Bell (née Findlay); m. Virginia Wallis Hornbrook 1988; one s. one d.; ed Queen Elizabeth's Grammar School, Barnet, Herts.; with ABC Television 1959–61, Colman Prentis & Varley 1961–63, Hobson Bates 1963–66, Geers Gross 1966–70; Man. Dir Saatchi & Saatchi 1970–75, Chair. and Man. Dir Saatchi & Saatchi Compton 1975–85; Group Chief Exec. Lowe Howard-Spink Campbell Ewald 1985–87, Deputy Chair. Lowe Howard-Spink & Bell PLC 1987–89; Chair. Lowe-Bell Communications 1987–89, Chime Communications 1994–; f. Lowe-Bell Govt Relations 1993–; arranged man. buy-out of Lowe-Bell Communications 1989; Special Adviser to Chair. Nat. Coal Bd 1984–86; mem. South Bank Bd 1985–86; Chair. Charity Projects 1984–93, Pres. 1993–; Dir Centre for Policy Studies; mem. Industry Cttee SCF, Public Relations Cttee Greater London Fund for the Blind 1979–86, Council Royal Opera House 1982–85, Public Affairs Cttee, Worldwide Fund for Nature 1985–88; Creative Leaders' Network Gov. British Film Inst. 1983–86. *Leisure interests:* golf, politics. *Address:* House of Lords, London, SW1A 0PW (office); Chime Communications PLC, 14 Curzon Street, London, W1J 5HN, England (office). *Telephone:* (20) 7219-5353 (House of Lords) (office). *Fax:* (20) 7219-5979 (House of Lords) (office). *Website:* www.chimeplc.com (office).

BELL BURNELL, Dame S(usan) Jocelyn, DBE, CBE, PhD, FRS, FRSE; British astrophysicist, academic and fmr univ. administrator; *Visiting Professor, University of Oxford;* b. 15 July 1943, Belfast, Northern Ireland; d. of (George) Philip Bell and (Margaret) Allison Bell (née Kennedy); m. (divorced); one s.; ed Univs of Glasgow and Cambridge; Lecturer, Univ. of Southampton 1968–73; part-time with Mullard Space Lab., Univ. Coll. London 1974–82; part-time with Royal Observatory, Edin. 1982–91; Chair. Physics Dept, Open Univ. 1991–99; Dean of Science, Univ. of Bath 2001–04; Visiting Prof. for Distinguished Teaching, Princeton Univ., USA 1999–2000; Visiting Prof., Univ. of Oxford 2004–; Pres. Royal Astronomical Soc. 2002–04; Pres. Inst. of Physics 2008–10; Pro-Chancellor Trinity Coll. Dublin 2013–; Foreign Assoc., NAS 2005; frequent speaker and radio and TV broadcaster on science, on being a woman in science, on astronomy and poetry and on science and religion; Hon. Fellow, New Hall, Cambridge 1996, British Science Asscn 2006, Singapore Inst. of Physics 2008, European Physical Soc. 2010, Science Museum London 2010, Glyndwr Univ. 2011, Inst. of Physics 2012, Distinguished Fellow, Inst. of Advance Studies, Ewha Univ. 2006, Hon. Prin., No 35 School, Beijing 2012, Hon. mem. Royal Irish Acad. 2012, Hon. Prof., Xinjiang Astronomical Observatory 2013; 27 hon. doctorates, including Univs of Cambridge, London, Michigan and Harvard; Joseph Black Medal and Cowie Book Prize, Univ. of Glasgow 1962, Michelson Medal, Franklin Inst., USA 1973, J. Robert Oppenheimer Memorial Prize, Center for Theoretical Studies, Fla 1978, Beatrice M. Tinsley Prize, American Astronomical Soc. (first recipient) 1987, Herschel Medal, Royal Astronomical Soc., London 1989, Edinburgh Medal 1999, Magellanic Premium, American Philosophical Soc. 2000, Joseph Priestly Award, Dickinson Coll., Pa 2002, Robinson Medal, Armagh Observatory 2004, Kelvin Medal 2007, Royal Soc. Faraday Award 2010, Grote Reber Medal 2011, Sven Berggren Prize, Royal Physiographic Soc. (Sweden) 2012, assessed by Woman's Hour (BBC Radio 4) as one of the 100 most powerful women in the UK 2013. *Achievements include:* discovered the first four pulsars. *Radio:* Scientific Life 2011. *Television:* Beautiful Minds 2010. *Publications:* three books, including Broken for Life 1989, Dark Matter: Poems of Space (co-ed.) 2008; three book chapters, approx. 70 scientific papers and 35 Quaker publs. *Leisure interests:* popularizing astronomy, walking, Quaker activities, listening to choral music, gardening. *Address:* University of Oxford, Astrophysics, Denys Wilkinson Building, Keble Road, Oxford, OX1 3RH, England (office). *Telephone:* (1865) 273306 (office). *Fax:* (1865) 273390 (office).

BELL LEMUS, Gustavo; Colombian academic, journalist and fmr politician; *Director, El Heraldo;* b. 1 Feb. 1957, Barranquilla; m. Maria Mercedes de la Espriella; one d.; ed Javeriana Univ. of Bogotá, Andes Univ. and Univ. of Oxford, UK; fmr Prof., Univ. del Norte e del Atlantico; fmr Man. Nat. Industrial Asscn (Andi), Barranquilla; fmr Gov. of Atlantico; Vice-Pres. of Colombia 1998–2002; Minister of Nat. Defence 2001–02; Dir El Heraldo (newspaper), Barranquilla, Atlantico. *Address:* c/o El Heraldo, Calle 53b, No 46–25, Barranquilla, Atlántico, Colombia (office). *Telephone:* (5) 371-5000 (office). *Fax:* (5) 371-5091 (office). *Website:* (office).

BELLAMY, Carol, JD; American lawyer and international organization official; *Chairman, International Baccalaureate;* b. 1942, Plainfield, NJ; ed Gettysburg Coll., New York Univ.; Peace Corps Volunteer, Guatemala 1963–65; Assoc., Cravath, Swaine & Moore, New York 1968–71; spent 13 years as elected public official including term as mem. New York State Senate 1973–77; Pres. New York City Council (first woman) 1978–85; Prin., Morgan Stanley and Co. 1986–90; Man. Dir Bear Stearns & Co. 1990–93; Prin. Morgan Stanley & Co. New York; Dir Peace Corps, Washington, DC 1993–95; Exec. Dir UNICEF 1995–2005; Pres. School for Int. Training and CEO World Learning 2005–09; Chair. Bd of Dirs Fair Labor Foundation 2007; Chair. Global Partnership for Education 2009–13; Chair. Bd of

Govs International Baccalaureate 2009–; Chair. Alliance for Ethical International Recruitment Practices; mem. Advisory Bd Innovative Finance Foundation 2012–; fmr Fellow, Inst. of Politics, Kennedy School of Govt, Harvard Univ.; Hon. mem. Phi Alpha Alpha, the US Nat. Honor Soc. for Accomplishment and Scholarship in Public Affairs and Admin; Chevalier, Légion d'Honneur 2009; Hon. LHD (Bates Coll.) 2003; ranked 95th by Forbes magazine amongst 100 Most Powerful Women 2004. *Address:* International Baccalaureate, Route des Morillons 15, Grand-Saconnex, Geneva 1218, Switzerland (office). *E-mail:* ibhq@ibo.org (office). *Website:* www.ibo.org (office).

BELLAMY, Sir Christopher (William), Kt, MA, QC; British barrister and consultant; *Senior Consultant, Linklaters;* b. 25 April 1946, Waddesdon, Bucks.; s. of the late William Albert Bellamy and Vyvienne Hilda Bellamy (née Meyrick); m. Deirdre Patricia Turner; one s. two d.; ed Tonbridge School, Brasenose Coll., Oxford; called to the Bar, Middle Temple 1968 (Bencher 1994), in full-time practice 1970–92, QC 1986, Asst Recorder 1989–92; Judge of Court of First Instance of the EC 1992–99; Pres. of Appeal Tribunals, Competition Comm. (now Competition Appeal Tribunal) 1999–2007; Deputy High Court Judge 2000–; Judge of Employment Appeal Tribunal 2000–07; mem. Council, British Inst. of Int. and Comparative Law 2000–06, Advisory Bd 2007–; Recorder, Crown Court 2001–07; Sr Consultant, Linklaters, London (law firm) 2007–, Chair. Global Competition Practice 2011–; Gov. Ravensbourne Coll. of Design and Communication 1988–92. *Publication:* European Community Law of Competition (6th edn) (ed. P. Roth and V. Rose) 2007. *Leisure interests:* family life, walking, history. *Address:* Linklaters, 1 Silk Street, London, EC2Y 8HA, England (office). *Telephone:* (20) 7456-3457 (office). *E-mail:* christopher.bellamy@linklaters.com (office). *Website:* www.linklaters.com (office).

BELLAMY, David James, OBE, PhD, CBiol, FIBiol; British botanist, writer, broadcaster and environmental organization administrator; b. 18 Jan. 1933, London; s. of Thomas Bellamy and Winifred Green; m. Rosemary Froy 1959; two s. three d.; ed Sutton County Grammar School, Chelsea Coll. of Science and Tech., Bedford Coll., Univ. of London; Lecturer, then Sr Lecturer, Dept of Botany, Univ. of Durham 1960–80, Hon. Prof. of Adult and Continuing Educ. 1980–82; Visiting Prof., Massey Univ., NZ 1988–89; Special Prof. of Botany, Univ. of Nottingham 1987–; TV and radio presenter and scriptwriter; Founder Dir Conservation Foundation; Pres. WATCH 1982, Youth Hostels Asscn 1983, Population Concern 1988–, Nat. Asscn of Environmental Educ. 1989–, Plantlife 1990–2005, Wildlife Trust's Partnership 1996–2005, British Inst. of Cleaning Science 1997–, Council Zoological Soc. of London 1991–94, BH&HPA 2000–, Camping and Caravanning Club 2002–; Vice-Pres. BTCV, Fauna and Flora International, Marine Conservation Soc., Australian Marine Conservation Soc.; Chair. Int. Cttee for the Tourism for Tomorrow Awards; Dir David Bellamy Assocs (environmental consultants) 1988–97, Bellamy & Nevard Environmental Consultants 2003–; Trustee, Living Landscape Trust, World Land Trust 1992–2002; Patron Project AWARE Foundation, The Space Theatre, Dundee, Te Pua O Whirinaki Regeneration Trust, NZ; Hon. Fellow, Chartered Inst. of Water and Environmental Man.; Hon. FLS; Hon. Prof., Central Queensland Univ.; Hon. mem. BSES Expeditions; Dutch Order of the Golden Ark 1989; Hon. DSc (Bournemouth); Hon. DUniv; Dr hc (CNAA) 1990; UNEP Global 500 Award 1990, Busk Medal, Royal Geographical Soc., Duke of Edinburgh's Award for Underwater Research, BAFTA Richard Dimbleby Award, BSAC Diver of the Year Award. *Television series include:* Life in Our Sea 1970, Bellamy on Botany 1973, Bellamy's Britain 1975, Bellamy's Europe 1977, Botanic Man 1978, Up a Gum Tree 1980, Backyard Safari 1981, The Great Seasons 1982, Bellamy's New World 1983, End of the Rainbow Show 1986, S.W.A.L.L.O.W. 1986, Turning the Tide 1986, Bellamy's Bugle 1986, 1987, 1988, Bellamy on Top of the World 1987, Bellamy's Journey to the Centre of the World 1987, Bellamy's Bird's Eye View 1989, Wheat Today What Tomorrow? 1989, Moa's Ark 1990, Bellamy Rides Again 1992, Blooming Bellamy 1993, 1994, Routes of Wisdom 1993, The Peak 1994, Bellamy's Border Raids 1996, Westwatch 1997, A Welsh Herbal 1998, Salt Solutions 1999, The Challenge 1999. *Publications include:* more than 45 books, including Bellamy on Botany 1972, Peatlands 1974, Bellamy's Britain 1974, Life Giving Sea 1975, Green Worlds 1975, The World of Plants 1975, Bellamy's Europe 1976, Botanic Action 1978, Botanic Man 1978, Half of Paradise 1979, Forces of Life 1979, Bellamy's Backyard Safari 1981, The Great Seasons (with Sheila Mackie, illustrator) 1981, Il Libro Verde 1981, Discovering the Countryside with David Bellamy (Vols I, II) 1982, (Vols III, IV) 1983, The Mouse Book 1983, Bellamy's New World 1983, The Queen's Hidden Garden 1984, Bellamy's Bugle 1986, Bellamy's Ireland 1986, Turning the Tide 1986, Bellamy's Changing Countryside (four vols) 1987, England's Last Wilderness 1989, England's Lost Wilderness 1990, Wetlands 1990, Wilderness Britain 1990, How Green Are You? 1991, Tomorrow's Earth 1992, World Medicine: Plants, Patients and People 1992, Blooming Bellamy 1993, Trees of the World 1993, Poo, You and the Poteroo's Loo 1997, Bellamy's Changing Countryside 1998, The Glorious Trees of Great Britain 2002, Jolly Green Giant (autobiog.) 2002, A Natural Life (autobiog.) 2002, The Bellamy Herbal 2003, Conflicts in the Countryside: The New Battle for Britain 2005, and books connected with TV series; Consultant Ed. and contrib. for series published by Hamlyn in conjunction with Royal Soc. for Nature Conservation: Coastal Walks 1982, Woodland Walks 1982, Waterside Walks 1983, Grassland Walks 1983. *Leisure interests:* children and ballet. *Address:* The Mill House, Bedburn, Bishop Auckland, Co. Durham, DL13 3NN, England (home).

BELLENS, Didier; Belgian media executive; *CEO, Belgacom SA;* b. 9 June 1955; m.; two c.; ed Ecole de Commerce Solvay, Univ. Libre de Bruxelles; Deputy Gen. Man. Pargesa Holding SA, Geneva –1992; Man. Dir Groupe Bruxelles Lambert SA, Brussels 1992–2000; CEO CLT-UFA, Luxembourg 2000 (merged with Pearson TV to become RTL Group 2000); CEO RTL Group (owns 24 TV and 17 radio stations), Luxembourg 2000–03; CEO Belgacom SA, Brussels 2003–. *Leisure interests:* hikes in the Libyan desert, Morocco and Namibia. *Address:* Belgacom, Boulevard Roi Albert II 27, 1030 Brussels, Belgium (office). *Telephone:* (2) 202-69-30 (office). *Fax:* (2) 217-99-66 (office). *E-mail:* about@belgacom.be (office). *Website:* www.belgacom.be (office).

BELLERIVE, Jean-Max; Haitian economist and politician; b. 1958, Port-au-Prince; electoral co-ordinator for municipal and presidential elections, Ouest Dept 1999–2000; has held positions in govt under six different prime ministers 1990–; Chief of Staff to Prime Minister Jean-Marie Chérestal 2001–02; mem. staff of

Prime Minister Yvon Neptune 2002–04; Minister of Planning and External Co-operation –2009; Prime Minister 2009–11 (resgnd). *Address:* c/o Office of the Prime Minister, Villa d'Accueil, Delmas 60, Musseau, Port-au-Prince, Haiti.

BELLINGHAM, Alastair John, CBE, FRCP, FRCPE, FRCPath; British professor of haematology; b. 27 March 1938, London; m. 1st Valerie Jill Morford 1963 (died 1997); three s.; m. 2nd Julia d'Q. Willott 2002; ed Tiffin Boys' School, Univ. Coll. Hosp. Medical School, London; Sr Lecturer, Hon. Consultant Haematology Dept, Univ. Coll. Hosp. Medical School 1971; Prof. of Haematology, Univ. of Liverpool 1974, King's Coll., London 1984–97; Pres. British Soc. for Haematology 1992–93, Royal Coll. of Pathologists 1993–96; Chair. Nat. Health Service Information Authority 1999–2005. *Publications:* numerous publs on red cell physiology and biochemistry, inherited red cell abnormalities, sickle cell disease. *Leisure interests:* photography, wine and viticulture. *Address:* Broadstones, The Street, Teffont Magna, Salisbury, Wilts., SP3 5QP, England (home). *Telephone:* (1722) 716267 (home). *E-mail:* savage@teffont.freeservcer.co.uk (home).

BELLINI, Mario; Italian architect, designer and academic; *CEO, Mario Bellini Architects S.r.l.;* b. 1 Feb. 1935, Milan; ed Politecnico di Milano; Dir of Design, La Rinascente 1961–63; Prof., Istituto Superiore del Disegno Industriale 1962–65; Chief Design Consultant, Olivetti 1963–91; Prof., Domus Acad. 1986–91; fmr Visiting Prof., Royal Coll. of Art, London; Ed. Domus 1986–91; CEO Mario Bellini Architects S.r.l. 1980–; has designed projects including Tokyo Design Centre, Sakurada Dori Dist, Exhbn Centre in Villa Erba on Lake Como, Natuzzi America HQ, Trade Fair in Essen, Germany, Nat. Gallery of Victoria, Melbourne, HQ of Deutsche Bank, Frankfurt, Verona Forum complex, Museum of the History of Bologna, Museum of Islamic Art, The Louvre, Paris, Milan Convention Centre, Milan Trade Fair (Portello); current projects include Cultural Centre, Turin, renovation and restyling of Pinacoteca di Brera, Milan, Science and Tech. Park, Genoa; numerous exhbns in Italy and abroad; works in perm. collections, including 25 works at Museum of Modern Art, New York; numerous talks world-wide; Medaglia d'Oro, Pres. of Italy 2004; Ambrogino d'oro, Municipality of Milan 2011; Compasso d'Oro 1962, 1964, 1970, 1979, 1981, 1984, 2001. *Address:* Mario Bellini Architects S.r.l., Piazza Arcole 4, 20143 Milan, Italy (office). *Telephone:* (2) 5815191 (office). *Fax:* (2) 58113466 (office). *E-mail:* info@mariobellini.com (office). *Website:* www.mariobellini.com (office).

BELLO, Col (retd) Sani; Nigerian business executive, diplomatist and fmr army officer; *Chairman, Amni International Petroleum Development Company Limited;* b. 27 Nov. 1942, Kontagora, Niger State; m.; three c.; ed Bida Govt Coll., Royal Mil. Acad., Sandhurst, UK; joined Army as Cadet 1962, held various posts including Co. Commdr, Asst Quarter Master-Gen. 3rd Marine Commando Div., ADC to Supreme Commdr, Deputy Adjutant-Gen. of the Army, 1st Nigerian Principal Staff Officer, Armed Forces Command and Staff Coll.; Mil. Gov. old Kano State 1975–78, retd 1979; High Commr to Zimbabwe 1984–86; Founder-Chair. Amni International Petroleum Devt Co. Ltd; currently also Chair. MH Healthcare Ltd, Sani Bello Foundation; Vice-Chair. MTN Nigeria Communications Ltd 1999–; fmr Chair. Niger State Green Revolution, Niger State Nat. Youth Service Corps, Niger State Polytechnic School Bd, Niger State Science and Technical School Bd, Nigerian Table Tennis Fed., Continental Merchant Bank Plc, Globe Re-Insurance Plc, Law, Union and Rock Insurance Plc, Broadbank Nigeria Ltd; mem. Bd of Dirs Dantata and Sawoe Construction Co. Ltd 1991–, Equatel Communication Ltd 2006–; fmr Pres. Nat. Asscn of Indigenous Petroleum Explorers in Nigeria. *Address:* Amni International Petroleum Development Company Limited, Plot 1377, Tiamiyu Savage Street, Victoria Island, Lagos, Nigeria (office). *Telephone:* (1) 7404679 (office). *Fax:* (1) 4613904 (office). *Website:* www.amnipetroleum.com (office).

BELLOCH JULBE, Juan Alberto; Spanish politician; *Mayor of Zaragoza;* b. 3 Feb. 1950, Mora de Rubielos (Teruel); m. Mari Cruz Soriano; one s.; ed Univ. of Barcelona; mem. Democratic Justice; Founder Assan of Judges for Democracy, Assan des Magistrats Européens pour la démocratie et les libertés; Founder and Pres. Assan for the Human Rights of the Basque Country; Judge, La Gomera, Berga Vic y Alcoy from 1975; Magistrate and Pres. Court of Justice of Biscay 1981–90; mem. Gen. Council of Judiciary 1990–93; Minister of Justice 1993–96, of the Interior 1994–96; Senator 1999–2003; Mayor of Zaragoza 2003–; Pres. European Forum for Urban Security 2007–10. *Address:* c/o PSOE, Ferraz 68 y 70, 28008 Madrid, Spain. *Telephone:* (91) 5820444. *Fax:* (91) 5820422. *E-mail:* juanalbertobelloch@zaragoza.es.

BELLOCHIO, Marco; Italian director, actor, writer and producer; b. 9 Nov. 1939, Piacenza, Emilia-Romagna; retrospective at Locarno Int. Film Festival 1998; mem. Jury, Venice Film Festival 1999, Cannes Film Festival 2007; Bronze Leopard for his complete works, Locarno Int. Film Festival 1976, Jury Distinction for his artistic contrib. to the art of cinema, Montréal World Film Festival 1988, Silver St George for Contrib. to World Cinema, Moscow Int. Film Festival 1999, Career Award (Cinema), Flaiano Int. Prizes 2002, Pietro Bianchi Award, Venice Film Festival 2006, Sergei Parajanov Lifetime Achievement Award, Yerevan Int. Film Festival 2006. *Film roles in:* Francesco d'Assisi (Francis of Assisi) 1966, Sbatti il mostro in prima pagina (Slap the Monster on Page One) 1972, Pianeta Venere (Planet Venus) 1974, Salò o le 120 giornate di Sodoma (Salo, or the 120 Days of Sodom) (voice; uncredited) 1975, Vacanze in Val Trebbia (Vacation in Val Tribbia) 1980, L'ora di religione (Il sensio di mia madre) (The Religion Hour (My Mother's Smile)) 2002, Buongiorno, notte (Good Morning, Night) (uncredited) 2003. *Films directed:* Ginepro fatto uomo 1962, La colpa e la pena 1965, I pugni in tasca (Fists in the Pocket) (Silver Sail, Locarno Int. Film Festival 1965, Silver Ribbon for Best Original Story, Italian Nat. Syndicate of Film Journalists 1966) 1965, La Cina è vicina (China is Near) (FIPRESCI Prize and Special Jury Prize, Venice Film Festival 1967, Silver Ribbon for Best Original Story, Italian Nat. Syndicate of Film Journalists 1968) 1967, Amore e rabbia (Love and Anger; segment 'Discutiamo, discutiamo') 1969, Nel nome del padre (In the Name of the Father) 1972, Sbatti il mostro in prima pagina (Slap the Monster on Page One) 1972, Matti da slegare (Fit to be Untied) (OCIC Award and FIPRESCI Prize – Recommendation, Berlin Int. Film Festival 1975) 1975, Marcia trionfale (Victory March) 1976, Vacanze in Val Trebbia (Vacation in Val Tribbia) 1980, Salto nel vuoto (Leap into the Void) (David di Donatello Award for Best Dir 1980) 1980, Gli occhi, la bocca (Those Eyes, That Mouth) 1982, Enrico IV (Henry IV) 1984, Il diavolo in corpo (Devil in the Flesh) 1986, La visione del Sabba 1988, La condanna (The Conviction) (Silver Berlin Bear, Berlin Int. Film Festival 1991) 1991, Il sogno della farfalla (The Butterfly's Dream) 1994, Sogni infranti (Broken Dreams) 1995, Elena 1997, Il Principe di Homburg (The Prince of Homburg) 1997, La religione della storia 1998, La balia (The Nanny) 1999, L'Affresco 2000, Un altro mondo è possibile (Another World is Possible) 2001, L'ora di religione (Il sorriso di mia madre) (The Religion Hour (My Mother's Smile)) (also producer) (Prize of the Ecumenical Jury – Special Mention, Cannes Film Festival 2002, Best Film, Flaiano Film Festival 2002, Silver Ribbon for Best Dir, Italian Nat. Syndicate of Film Journalists 2002) 2002, Buongiorno, notte (Good Morning, Night) (also producer) (FIPRESCI Prize, European Film Awards 2003, CinemAvvenire Award for Best Film, Little Golden Lion Award and Outstanding Individual Contrib. Award, Venice Film Festival 2003) 2003, Il regista di matrimoni (The Wedding Director) (also producer) 2006, Sorelle 2006, Vincere 2009, Sorelle Mai 2010, Dormant Beauty 2012. *Television:* Il gabbiano 1977, La macchina cinema (The Cinema Machine, USA) (FIPRESCI Prize, Berlin Int. Film Festival 1979) 1979, L'uomo dal fiore in bocca 1992, ...Addio del passato... (also producer) 2002.

BELLON, Pierre; French business executive; *Chairman, Sodexo SA;* b. 24 Jan. 1930, Marseille; m.; four c.; ed École des Hautes Études Commerciales; began career with family's ship chandlery business, Marseille 1950s; Asst Man. Soc. d'Exploitations Hôtelières, Aériennes et Terrestres 1958, later Man. Dir, Chair. and CEO; f. Sodexho SA, food and management services co., Marseille 1966 (renamed Sodexho Alliance SA 1997, renamed Sodexo SA 2008), CEO 1966–2005, Chair. 1974–; Chair. and CEO Bellon SA (family holding co. that controls Sodexo) 1988–, Chair. Man. Bd 1996–2002, Chair. Supervisory Bd 2002–; joined Bureau Francis Lefebvre law firm 1991, Chair. Man. Bd –2004; mem. Bd Lafarge Ciments –2010; mem. Supervisory Bd ELS (Éditions Lefebvre Sarrut) –2010; Nat. Pres. Nat. Centre for Young Business Leaders (fmrly the Centre for Young Employers) 1968–70; Pres. Nat. Fed. of Hotel and Restaurant Chains 1972–75; mem. Exec. Council of CNPF (French employers' fed.) 1976–, Vice-Chair. CNPF (now known as MEDEF) 1980–2005; Founder Asscn Progrès du Man. 1986; currently Chair. and CEO ANSA (French Nat. Asscn of Jt Stock Cos); mem. Econ. and Social Council 1969–79, Conseil des Prélèvements Obligatoires (French Tax and Social Charges Bd); Commdr, Légion d'honneur, Ordre nat. du Mérite, Chevalier, Ordre du Mérite Agricole, Commdr, Order of Rio Branco (Brazil); French Inst. Alliance Française (FIAF) Pilier d'Or 2007. *Publication:* I Have Had a Lot of Fun (The Sodexo Story). *Address:* Sodexo SA, 255 quai de la Bataille de Stalingrad, 92130 Issy-les-Moulineaux, France (office). *Telephone:* 1-57-75-82-03 (office). *Fax:* 1-57-75-80-01 (office). *E-mail:* noelle.robillard@sodexo.com (office). *Website:* www.sodexo.com (office).

BELLUCCI, Monica; Italian fashion model and actress; b. 30 Sept. 1964, Città di Castello, Perugia; m. Vincent Cassel 1999; two d.; ed Univ. of Perugia; model Elite Model Man., Milan 1988–90, appeared in advertising campaigns for Dolce & Gabbana; began taking acting lessons 1989; debut in TV film Vita Coi Figli (Life With the Sons) 1990. *Films include:* Briganti 1990, La riffa 1991, Bram Stoker's Dracula 1992, Ostinato destino 1992, I mitici 1994, Palla di neve 1995, Il cielo è sempre più blu 1995, L'appartement 1996, Come mi vuoi 1996, Dobermann 1997, Mauvais genre 1997, L'ultimo capodanno dell'umanità (Best Actress, Globo d'Oro) 1998, A los que aman 1998, Méditerranées 1998, Comme un poisson hors de l'eau 1999, Under Suspicion 2000, Franck Spadone 2000, Malèna 2000, Il patto dei lupi 2000, Astérix et Obélix: Mission Cléopâtre 2001, Irreversible 2002, Ricordati di me 2002, The Matrix Reloaded 2003, Tears of the Sun 2003, She Hate Me 2004, The Passion of the Christ 2004, The Brothers Grimm 2005, Combien tu m'aimes? 2005, Sheitan 2006, N (Io e Napoleone) 2006, Le Concile de pierre 2006, Manuale d'amore 2 (Capitoli successivi) 2007, Shoot 'Em Up 2007, Le Deuxième Souffle 2007, Sanguepazzo 2008, L'Uomo che ama 2008, The Private Lives of Pippa Lee 2009, The Whistleblower 2010, The Ages of Love 2011, Un été brûlant 2011, Rhino Season 2012, Des gens qui s'embrassent 2013. *Address:* c/o Carol Levi, Via G. Pisanelli 2, 00196 Rome, Italy (office); Agence Intertalent, 5 rue Clement-Marot, Paris 75008, France (office).

BELMONDO, Jean-Paul; French actor; b. 9 April 1933, Neuilly-sur-Seine; s. of Paul Belmondo and Madeleine Rainaud-Richard; m. 1st Elodie Constantin 1953 (divorced 1967); m. 2nd Natty Belmondo 2002 (divorced 2008); one s. two d. (one deceased); ed Ecole Alsacienne, Paris, Cours Pascal and Conservatoire nat. d'art dramatique; started career on the stage; mainly film actor since 1957; Pres. French Union of Actors 1963–66; Pres. Annabel Productions 1981–; Dir Théâtre des Variétés 1991; Officier Légion d'honneur, Chevalier, Ordre nat. du Mérite 1986, des Arts et des Lettres; Prix Citron 1972, Career Achievement Award, Los Angeles Film Critics Asscn 2010. *Plays acted in include:* L'hôtel du libre-échange, Oscar, Trésor-Party, Médée, La mégère apprivoisée, Kean 1987, Cyrano de Bergerac 1990, Tailleur pour Dames 1993, La Puce à l'oreille 1996, Frédérick ou le boulevard du crime 1998. *Films acted in include:* Sois belle et tais-toi, A pied, à cheval et en voiture, les Tricheurs, Charlotte et son Jules, Drôle de dimanche 1958, Les Copains du dimanche, Mademoiselle Ange, A double tour, Classe tous risques, Au bout de souffle, L'Amour, La Novice, La Ciociara, Moderato Cantabile, Léon Morin Prêtre, Le Doulos 1962, Dragées au poivre, L'Aîné des Ferchaux, Peau de banane, 100,000 dollars au soleil 1963, Two Women, The Man From Rio, Echappement libre 1964, Les tribulations d'un Chinois en Chine, Pierrot le Fou 1965, Paris, brûle-t-il? 1966, Le Voleur 1966, Casino Royale 1967, The Brain 1969, La Sirène du Mississippi 1969, Un Homme qui me plaît 1970, Borsalino 1970, The Burglars 1972, La Scoumoune 1972, L'Héritier 1972, Le Magnifique 1973, Stavisky 1974, Peur sur la ville 1975, L'Incorrigible 1975, L'Alpageur, Le corps de mon ennemi 1976, L'Animal 1977, Flic ou Voyou 1979, L'As de as (also produced) 1982, Le Marginal 1983, Joyeuses Pâques, Les Morfalous 1984, Hold-up 1985, Le Solitaire 1987, Itinéraire d'un enfant gâté (César for Best Actor 1988), L'Inconnu dans la Maison 1992, Les Cent et une Nuits 1995, Les Misérables 1995, Désiré 1996, Une chance sur deux 1998, Peut-être 1999, Les Acteurs 2000, Amazone 2000, L'Aîné des Ferchaux (TV) 2001, Down in the Boondocks 2008, A Man and His Dog 2009. *Publication:* 30 Ans et 25 Films (autobiog.) 1963. *Leisure interests:* boxing, football. *Address:* Artmédia, 20 avenue Rapp, 75007 Paris, France (office).

BELNAP, Nuel, PhD; American philosopher and academic; *Alan Ross Anderson Distinguished Professor of Philosophy, University of Pittsburgh;* b. 1 May 1930, Evanston, Ill.; s. of Nuel Dinsmore and Elizabeth Belnap (née Dafter); m. 1st Joan Gohde 1953; m. 2nd Gillian Hirth 1982; four c.; m. 3rd Birgit Herbeck 1997; ed Univ. of Illinois, Yale Univ.; instructor in Philosophy, then Asst Prof., Yale Univ.

1958–63; Assoc. Prof. of Philosophy, Univ. of Pittsburgh 1963–66, Prof. 1966–, Alan Ross Anderson Distinguished Prof. of Philosophy 1984–, Prof. of Sociology 1967–80, of History and Philosophy of Science 1971, of Intelligent Systems 1988–93, Fellow, Center for Philosophy of Science; Visiting Prof. of Philosophy, Univ. of Calif., Irvine 1973; Visiting Fellow, ANU 1976; Visiting Oscar R. Ewing Prof. of Philosophy, Indiana Univ. 1977, 1978, 1979; Visiting Leibniz-Prof., Zentrum für Höhere Studien 1996; mem. several editorial bds; Sterling Jr Fellow 1955–56; Fulbright Fellow 1957–58; Morse Research Fellow 1962–63; Guggenheim Fellow 1975–76; Fellow, Center for Advanced Studies in Behavioral Science 1982–83; Hon. DPhil (Leipzig) 2000. *Publications:* Computer Programs Bindex Tester 1976; The Logic of Questions and Answers (co-author) 1976, Entailment: The Logic of Relevance and Necessity (co-author) (Vol. I) 1975, (Vol. II) 1992, The Revision Theory of Truth (co-author) 1993, Facing the Future: Agents and Choices in Our Indeterministic World (co-author) 2001. *Address:* Department of Philosophy, University of Pittsburgh, Fifth Avenue, Pittsburgh, PA 15260 (office); 5803 Ferree Street, Pittsburgh, PA 15217, USA (home). *Telephone:* (412) 624-5777 (office), (412) 521-3897 (home). *Fax:* (412) 624-5377 (office). *E-mail:* belnap@pitt.edu (office). *Website:* www.pitt.edu/~belnap (office).

BELO-OSAGIE, Hakeem, MA, MBA; Nigerian petroleum economist, lawyer and business executive; *Chairman, Emerging Markets Telecommunication Services Ltd (Etisalat Nigeria);* b. 1955; s. of the late Tiamiyu Bello-Osagie; m.; ed King's Coll., Oxford, King's Coll., Cambridge, UK, Harvard Business School, USA; worked as Special Asst to Nigerian Minister of Petroleum and Energy; also worked in Petrochemicals Div., Nigerian Nat. Petroleum Corpn –1986 (resgnd); est. CTIC (energy consultancy firm) 1986; f. First Securities Discounts House Ltd 1992; currently Chair. Emerging Markets Telecommunication Services Ltd (Etisalat Nigeria); also Chair. United Bank for Africa Plc –2004, Abuja Investment Co. –2012, Chocolate City Group 2012–; mem. Bd of Dirs Metis Capital Partners Ltd, Timbuktu Media; mem. Global Advisory Council, African Leadership Acad.; Leadership Excellence Award, Africa Business Club of Harvard Business School 2012. *Address:* Emerging Markets Telecommunication Services Ltd. (Etisalat Nigeria), Plot 19, Zone L, Banana Island Foreshore Estate, Federal Government Layout, Ikoyi, Lagos, Nigeria (office). *Telephone:* (9) 0000200 (office). *Fax:* (9) 0000201 (office). *Website:* www.etisalat.com.ng (office).

BĚLOBRÁDEK, Pavel, MVDr, MPA, PhD; Czech veterinary physician and politician; *Deputy Prime Minister and Minister of Science, Research and Innovation;* b. 25 Dec. 1976, Náchod; m.; c.; ed Veterinary and Pharmaceutical Univ., Brno, CEVRO Inst., Liberal Conservative Acad.; obtained 1st level attestation at Czech State Veterinary Admin 2003; veterinary inspector, Regional Veterinary Service for Hradec Králové 2001–09; mem. Christian and Democratic Union – Czechoslovak People's Party (KDU-CSL) 2004–, mem. Local Org. Cttee, Náchod 2004, mem. Regional Cttee, Hradec Králové region 2005, Vice-Chair. Dist Cttee, Náchod 2007–09, Chair. 2008–09, Pres. Dist Cttee 2009, mem. KV PKV KDU-CSL, Pardubice Region 2009–10, mem. Bureau of KV KDU-CSL, Hradec Králové region 2010, Chair. KDU-CSL 2010–; mem. Young Christian Democrats (MKD) 2005–, Vice-Pres. 2008–09; Rep. of City of Náchod 2010; mem. Parl. for the Hradec Králové region 2012–; Deputy Prime Minister for Science, Research and Innovation 2014–, Chair. Research, and Innovation Council. *Leisure interests:* home and garden, nature, history, literature, art. *Address:* Office of the Government, náb. E. Beneše 4, 118 01 Prague 1 (office); Palác Charitas, Karlovo nám. 5, 128 01 Prague 2, Czech Republic. *Telephone:* (2) 24002111 (office); (2) 26205111; 73-1603880 (mobile). *Fax:* (2) 57531283 (office). *E-mail:* posta@vlada.cz (office); predseda@kdu.cz (office). *Website:* www.vlada.cz (office).

BĚLOHLÁVEK, Jiří, Czech musician and conductor; *Chief Conductor, Czech Philharmonic Orchestra;* b. 24 Feb. 1946, Prague; m. Anna Fejérová 1971; two d.; ed Acad. of Performing Arts, Prague with Sergiu Celibidache; Conductor Orchestra Puellarum Pragensis (chamber orchestra), Prague 1967–72; Asst Conductor Czech Philharmonic Orchestra 1970–71, Conductor 1981–90, Prin. Conductor and Music Dir 1990–92, Music Dir and Chief Conductor 2012–; Conductor Brno State Philharmonic Orchestra 1971–77; Chief Conductor Prague Symphony Orchestra 1977–90; Conductor Int. Philharmonic Youth Orchestra, Prague 1987–89; Founder and Music Dir Prague Philharmonia 1994–2005; Prin. Guest Conductor BBC Symphony Orchestra 1995–2000, Chief Conductor 2006–12, Conductor Laureate 2012–; Prof., Acad. of Music, Prague 1995–; Prin. Guest Conductor Nat. Theatre Prague 1998; guest appearances with numerous orchestras, including USSR State Symphony Orchestra, BBC Philharmonic, BBC Nat. Orchestra of Wales, Scottish Nat. Orchestra, Royal Liverpool Philharmonic, City of Birmingham Symphony, Berlin Philharmonic, Vienna Symphony Orchestra, Leipzig Gewandhaus, Stockholm Philharmonic, Bavarian Radio Orchestra, Dresden Philharmonic, Deutsche Kammerphilharmonie, Tonhalle Orchestra Zürich, New York Philharmonic, Boston Symphony Orchestra, St Louis Orchestra, Washington Nat. Orchestra, Montreal Symphony Orchestra, NHK Philharmonic Tokyo; Hon. CBE 2012; Supraphon Prize 1977, Artist of Merit 1986, Supraphon Golden Disc 1986, 1987, 1994, 1999, Diapason d'Or 1992, Barclay Theatre Award 2000, Medal for Merit, Prague 2001. *Recordings include:* with BBC Symphony Orchestra: The Excursions of Mr Broucek (Gramophone Award for Best Opera Recording 2009) 2008, Martinů The 6 Symphonies (Gramophone Award for Best Orchestral Recording 2012) 2011, Josef Suk: Prague/A Summer's Tale (Gramophone Award for Best Orchestral Recording 2013) 2012. *Leisure interests:* gardening, hiking. *Address:* Czech Philharmonic Orchestra, Alsovo nabrezi 12, 110 00, Prague 1, Czech Republic (office); c/o BBC Symphony Orchestra, BBC Maida Vale Studios, Delaware Road, London, W9 2LG, England (office). *Telephone:* 227059221 (office); (20) 7765-2956 (office). *Fax:* 227059246 (office); (20) 7286-3251 (office). *E-mail:* info@cfmail.cz (office); bbcso@bbc.co.uk (office). *Website:* www.ceskafilharmonie.cz/en; www.bbc.co.uk/orchestras/symphonyorchestra (office); www.jiribelohlavek.com.

BELOTSERKOVSKY, Oleg Mikhailovich, PhD; Russian mathematician; *Honorary Director, Institute for Computer-Aided Design, Russian Academy of Sciences;* b. 29 Aug. 1925, Livni, Orlov Region; m.; two c.; ed Lomonosov Moscow State Univ.; Sr Researcher, Applied Math. Div. and Computing Centre, USSR (now Russian) Acad. of Sciences 1953–76, Head of Computer Centre 1976; Rector, Moscow Inst. of Physics and Tech. 1962–87; Corresp. mem. USSR (now Russian) Acad. of Sciences 1972–79, mem. 1979–, Chair. Scientific Council on Cybernetics; Dir Inst. of Computer-Aided Design 1987, now Hon. Dir; Dir Computer Simulation

Center, Central Aerohydrodynamic Inst. 2012–; mem. Int. Acad. of Astronautic Fed.; Order of the Red Banner of Labour 1965, 1975, 1981, Order of the October Revolution 1971, Order of Lenin 1985, Order of Merit to the Fatherland (3rd Degree) 1999; N. Zhukovsky Prize and Gold Medal for the Best Work on the Theory of Aviation 1962, Lenin Prize 1966, S. Korolev Medal 1978, S. I. Vavilov Medal. *Publications include:* Flow Past Blunt in Supersonic Flow—Theoretical and Experimental Results 1967, Numerical Methods in Fluid Dynamics 1976, The 'Coarse-Particle' Method in Gas Dynamics 1982, Numerical Modelling in Mechanics of Continuous Media 1984, Computational Mechanics: Contemporary Problems and Results 1991, Mathematical Modelling of Myocardial Infarction 1993, Computational Experiment in Turbulence: From Order to Chaos 1997, Turbulence and Instabilities 1999, Modern Solution Methods for Nonlinear Multidimensional Problems: Mathematics, Mechanics, Turbulence 2000. *Leisure interests:* tennis, swimming. *Address:* Computer Simulation Center, Central Aerohydrodynamic Institute (TsAGI), 140180 Moscow, 1 Zhukovsky Street, Russia (office). *Website:* www.tsagi.ru (office).

BELSHAW, Cyril Shirley, PhD, FRSC; Canadian anthropologist, writer and publisher; b. 3 Dec. 1921, Waddington, NZ; s. of Horace Belshaw and Marion L. S. Belshaw (née McHardie); m. Betty J. Sweetman 1943 (deceased); one s. one d.; ed Auckland Univ. Coll. and Victoria Coll., Wellington (Univ. of New Zealand), London School of Econs; Dist Officer and Deputy Commr for Western Pacific, British Solomon Islands 1943–46; Sr Research Fellow, ANU 1950–53; Prof., Univ. of British Columbia 1953–86, Prof. Emer. 1986–; Dir Regional Training Centre for UN Fellows, Vancouver 1961–62; Ed. Current Anthropology 1974–84; mem. numerous UNESCO comms, working parties and consultancy groups; Pres. Int. Union of Anthropological and Ethnological Sciences 1978–83, XIth Int. Congress of Anthropological and Ethnological Sciences 1983; Exec. American Anthropological Assoc. 1969–70; Chair. Standing Cttee Social Sciences and Humanities Pacific Science Asscn 1968–76; Ed. The Anthroglobe Journal 1998–2000, 2004–06; Propr Webzines of Vancouver 2000–; Man. Ed. Adam's Vancouver Dining Guide 1997–2007, www.anthropologising.ca 2001–08; Hon. Life Fellow, Royal Anthropological Inst., Pacific Science Asscn, Asscn for the Social Anthropology of Oceania, Hon. Life mem. Royal Anthropological Inst. 1978, Pacific Science Asscn 1981; World Utopian Champion 2005. *Publications include:* Island Administration in the South West Pacific 1950, Changing Melanesia 1954, In Search of Wealth 1955, The Great Village 1957, The Indians of British Columbia (with others) 1958, Under the Ivi Tree 1964, Anatomy of a University 1964, Traditional Exchange and Modern Markets 1965, The Conditions of Social Performance 1970, Towers Besieged 1974, The Sorcerer's Apprentice 1976, The Complete Good Dining Guide to Restaurants in Greater Vancouver 1984, Choosing Our Destiny 2006, Remuera: Memories of a New Zealand Boy Between the Wars 2009, Bumps on a Long Road: Essays from an Anthropologist's Memory 2009, Fixing the World 2010, Just Do It! Manifesto for the New Age 2012. *Leisure interests:* gardening, photography, travel, restaurants. *Address:* Suite 2901, 969 Richards Street, Vancouver, BC V6B 1A8, Canada (home). *Telephone:* (604) 739-8130 (home). *E-mail:* cyril@anthropologising.ca. *Website:* www.anthropologising.ca (home).

BELTRATTI, Andrea, PhD; Italian economist, academic and business executive; *Chairman of the Management Board, Intesa Sanpaolo SpA;* b. 9 Feb. 1959, Turin; ed Univ. of Turin, Yale Univ., USA; Full Prof., Luigi Bocconi Univ., Milan 2003–, teaches Financial Econs and Equity Portfolio Man., Dir of the Degree in Econs, Statistics and Social Sciences (CLE) and of the Degree in Econs and Social Sciences (DES) 2000 –04, Vice-Rector Undergraduate Dept 2004–08; Scientific Coordinator, Foundation BSI-Gamma, Lugano 1997–2010; Chair. Man. Bd Intesa Sanpaolo SpA 2010–; mem. School Council of PhD in Econs, Bocconi Univ. 2001–05, Comm. for Univ. and Teaching Legislation and for PhDs of the Società Italiana degli Economisti 2005–07; mem. Editorial Bd Geneva Paper on Risk and Insurance – Issues and Practice 2009–. *Address:* Intesa Sanpaolo SpA, Piazza San Carlo 156, 10121 Turin, Italy (office). *Telephone:* (011) 5551 (office). *Fax:* (011) 5557007 (office). *E-mail:* info@intesasanpaolo.com (office). *Website:* www.group.intesasanpaolo.com (office).

BELY, Mikhail Mikhailovich; Russian diplomatist; m.; two d.; ed Moscow State Inst. of Int. Relations, Nanyang Univ., Singapore; fmr Dir First Dept of Asia-Pacific Region, Ministry of Foreign Affairs, served as Attaché, Embassy in Singapore, First Sec. Embassy in Beijing 1994–99, Counsellor, Perm. Mission to the UN, New York 1999–2004, Amb. to Singapore, Indonesia, Timor Leste, Papua New Guinea, Kiribati 2004–07, to Japan 2007–12. *Address:* Ministry of Foreign Affairs, 119200 Moscow, Smolenskaya-Sennaya pl. 32/34, Russia (office). *Telephone:* (495) 244-16-06 (office). *Fax:* (495) 230-21-30 (office). *E-mail:* ministry@mid.ru (office). *Website:* www.mid.ru (office).

BELZA, Svyatoslav Igorevich, BA; Russian literary and music critic; b. 26 April 1942, Chelyabinsk; s. of Igor Belza and Zoya Gulinskaya; divorced; two s.; ed Moscow State Univ.; Researcher, Inst. of World Literature USSR (now Russian) Acad. of Sciences 1965–; Founder and reviewer TV programme Music on TV 1988–97, Man. and Artistic Dir 1995–97; works as literary critic and TV broadcaster; mem. Union of Russian Journalists 1971, Russian Union of Writers 1975, Union of Russian Theatre Workers 1999; mem. Acad. of Russian TV 1994–; Hon. mem. Russian Acad. of Arts 2008–; Officer Cross of Merit (Poland) 1998, Order of St Nicholas (Ukraine) 1998, Order of Friendship 2001; Merited Master of Arts of Russia 1994, of Ukraine 2004, Golden Sign of Honour 1999, Irina Arkhipova Foundation Prize 2001, Prize of Moscow 2002, People's Artist of Russia 2006. *Publications include:* Homo legens 1983, 1990 and over 300 literary works and reviews. *Leisure interests:* reading, travel. *Address:* 119311 Moscow, Stroiteley str. 4, korp. 7, Apt 9, Russia (home). *Telephone:* (495) 930-36-61 (home). *Fax:* (495) 930-36-61 (home).

BEM, Pavel, MD; Czech physician and politician; b. 18 July 1963; m. Radmila Bem; two s.; ed Faculty of Medicine, Charles Univ., Prague and post-grad. studies in psychiatry, Johns Hopkins Univ., Baltimore, Florida State Univ. and Univ. of California, San Diego, USA, Mediterranean Inst. for Research and Training in Physiotherapy and Psychiatry, Italy; specialized in psychiatry working with drug addicts; House Officer, Psychiatric Clinic Kosmonosy, Mlada Boleslav 1987; House Officer, Detoxification Ward, Psychiatric Clinic, Charles Univ. 1988–90, Chief Psychiatrist, Outpatient Treatment Centre for Drug Addicts, Faculty Hosp. 1990–91; Man. Dir Filia Foundation for the Support of Mentally Disabled and

Drug Dependent Persons 1992–94; Dir and Chief Psychiatrist (Outreach Programme), Contact Centre, Prague 1994; Sec.-Gen. (Anti-Drug Policy Implementation), Nat. Drug Comm., Office of Govt of Czech Repub. 1994–95, Exec. Sec. (Coordination of entire Drug Policy), Nat. Drug Comm., Cabinet of Prime Minister 1997–98; Adviser on Law Enforcement Aspects and Legislation to Minister of the Interior 1996; mem. Civic Democratic Party (ODS) 1998–, Deputy Leader 2006–08, Chair. 2008–10; Mayor of Municipal Dist of Prague 6 1998–2002, Mayor of Prague 2002–10; mem. Parl. 2010–; mem. Exec. Bd Soc. of Addictive Disorders of Czech Medical Asscn; mem. Advisory Bd to Ministry of Health on Drug Matters 1993–95; mem. Soc. for Psychotherapy and Family Therapy of Czech Medical Asscn, Chamber of Physicians of Czech Repub., Int. Council on Alcohol and Addiction, Euro – Methwork. *Publications:* Risks of HIV Transmission among IVDU's in the Czech Republic, Minimum Standards and Criteria of Effective Primary Prevention, Methodological Guidelines for School Based Primary Prevention – Manual, Teaching the Teachers Didactics, Risk Behaviour Among Drug Users in Prague, Extent of Substance Abuse in the Czech Republic, Drugs and AIDS – Parents' Guide, Methodological Guide for Community Based Prevention, Organization and Management of Drug Problems at Local Level, The Minimum Criteria for Workers in the Prevention and Treatment of Drug Addiction, Methodology for Primary Prevention in Primary and Secondary Schools (co-author), Rapid Assessment of the Extent of Drug Abuse in the Republic (co-author). *Leisure interests:* hiking, cycling, tennis, diving, classical music, rock, jazz, travel. *Address:* Chamber of Deputies (Poslanecká sněmovna), Sněmovní 4, 118 26 Prague 1, Czech Republic (office). *Telephone:* 257172017 (office). *E-mail:* bemp@psp.cz (office). *Website:* www.pavelbem.cz (office).

BEMBAMBA, Lucien Marie-Noël; Burkinabè economist and politician; *Minister of the Economy and Finance;* b. 8 Jan. 1957; m.; three c.; Finance Admin. Cen. Bank of West African States 1982–93; Gen.-Dir Treasury and Public Accounting Dept, Ministry of Economy and Finance 1993–2007, Del. in Charge of the Budget 2007–08, Minister of Economy and Finance 2008–; Alt. Gov. IMF 2006; Chair. Nat. Public Debt Cttee 2006. *Address:* Ministry of the Economy and Finance, 03 BP 7050, Ouagadougou, Burkina Faso (office). *Telephone:* 50-32-42-11 (office). *Fax:* 50-31-27-15 (office). *Website:* www.finances.gov.bf (office).

BEMENT, Arden L., Jr, DrIng; American organization official, engineer and academic; *David A. Ross Distinguished Professor of Nuclear Engineering and Director of the Global Policy Research Institute, Purdue University;* b. 22 May 1932, Pittsburgh, Pa; ed Colorado School of Mines, Univ. of Idaho, Univ. of Michigan; Sr Research Assoc., Gen. Electric Co. 1954–65; Man. of Fuels and Materials Dept and Metallurgy Research Dept, Battelle Northwest Labs 1965–70; Prof. of Nuclear Materials, MIT 1970–76; Dir Office of Materials Science, Defense Advanced Research Projects Agency (DARPA) 1976–79; Deputy Under-Sec. of Defense for Research and Eng, Dept of Defense 1979–80; Vice-Pres. of Tech. Resources and of Science and Tech., TRW Inc. 1980–92; Dir Midwest Superconductivity Consortium and Basil S. Turner Distinguished Prof. of Eng, Purdue Univ. 1993–98, Head of School of Engineering and David A. Ross Distinguished Prof. of Nuclear Eng 1998–2001, 2010–, Founding Dir Global Policy Research Inst. 2010–, Chief Global Affairs Officer 2010–; Dir Nat. Inst. of Standards and Tech. (NIST) Dept of Commerce 2001–04; Acting Dir NSF 2004, Dir 2004–10; with US Nat. Science Board 1990–94, Head NIST's Advanced Tech. Program Advisory Cttee 1999, with US Nat. Comm. for UNESCO, and Vice-Coordinator of Natural Sciences and Eng Cttee 2004, with G-8 Heads of Research Councils 2004; has given over 100 invited lectures and presentations; Lt Col (retd) Corps of Engineers US Army Reserve; mem. Nat. Acad. of Eng; Fellow, AAAS, American Inst. of Chemists, American Nuclear Soc., ASM Int., American Acad. of Arts and Sciences; Trustee, Skolkovo Inst. of Science and Tech.; Hon. Prof., Chinese Acad. of Sciences Graduate School 2011; Order of the Rising Sun, Gold and Silver Star (Japan) 2009, Chevalier, Ordre nat. de la Légion d'honneur 2011; Hon. PhD (Cleveland State Univ.) 1989, (Case Western Reserve Univ.) 2000, (Colorado School of Mines) 2004; Distinguished Civilian Service Medal of the Dept of Defense, American Nuclear Soc. Outstanding Achievement Award 2004, Washington Acad. of Science Award for Distinguished Career in Science 2006, American Chemical Soc. Public Service Award 2006, Navigator Award, Potomac Inst. for Policy Study 2010. *Publications:* materials sciences and engineering courses; books and monographs on chemistry, engineering, and metals and alloys; reports of the Atomic Energy Comm.; research articles in prof. journals; science policy articles in trade journals. *Leisure interests:* philately, history, biography. *Address:* College of Engineering, Purdue University, Neil Armstrong Hall of Engineering, 701 West Stadium Avenue, West Lafayette, IN 47907, USA (office). *Telephone:* (765) 496-6713 (office). *E-mail:* bement@purdue.edu (office). *Website:* engineering.purdue.edu/Engr (office).

BEN ACHOUR, Mohamed al Aziz, DHist; Tunisian historian and international organization official; b. 5 Jan. 1951, La Marsa; ed Univ. of Tunis, Univ. of Paris (Sorbonne); Councillor, Tunis Municipal Council 1995–2000; Vice-Mayor of Tunis and City Man. of the Medina (UNESCO World Heritage Site) 2000–05; Minister of Culture and Nat. Heritage 2004–08; Dir-Gen. Arab League Educational, Cultural and Scientific Org. 2009–13; Keeper, Sidi Bou Saïd historical site; Head Researcher, Museum of Tunisian Contemporary and Modern History Ksar Said Castle project; Conservator, Centre for Arts and Popular Culture, Nat. Heritage Inst.; Grand Officier, Ordre de la République de Tunisie, Commdr, Ordre du 7 Novembre (Tunisia), Ordre des Arts et des Lettres, Chevalier, Ordre Nat. du Mérite de la République française, Officier, Ordre des Palmes académiques; Aga Khan Award for Architecture, Lahore 1980, Prize of the Foundation, Crans Montana Forum, Baku 2012. *Publications include:* La mosquée-université de la Zitouna 1992, Les décorations tunisiennes d'époque husseinite 1994, Le Bardo, palais des beys de Tunis 2000, La cour du bey de Tunis 2003, Zaouïas et confréries 2004.

BEN-AMI, Shlomo, BA, MA, PhD; Israeli academic and fmr politician; *Vice-President, Toledo International Centre for Peace;* b. 1943, Morocco; m.; three c.; ed Tel-Aviv Univ., Univ. of Oxford, UK; Visiting Fellow, St Antony's Coll., Oxford 1980–82; Head, Grad. School of History, Tel-Aviv Univ. 1982–86, Elias Sourasky Chair for Spanish and Latin American Studies.1986–, Founder and Head, Curiel Center for Int. Studies 1993–96; Amb. to Spain 1987–91; mem. Knesset 1996–2001; Head of Israel Del. to the Multilateral Talks on Refugees, Ottawa

1992; participated at the Camp David Summit for Israel and Palestine Peace 2000; leader of Israel Del. at the Taba Peace Talks 2001; fmr mem. Foreign Affairs and Defense Cttee; Minister of Public Security 1999–2001; Minister of Foreign Affairs 2000–01; currently Vice-Pres. Toledo International Centre for Peace (TICpax), Spain; mem. Bd of Dirs Int. Crisis Group 2006–. *Publications include:* Quel avenir pour Israel? 2001, A Front Without a Rearguard: A Voyage to the Boundaries of the Peace Process 2004, Scars of War, Wounds of Peace. The Arab-Israeli Tragedy 2006. *Address:* Toledo International Centre for Peace, Felipe IV, 5 Bajo Izq., 28014 Madrid, Spain (office). *Telephone:* (91) 5237452 (office). *Fax:* (91) 5219313 (office). *E-mail:* toledopax@toledopax.org (office). *Website:* www.toledopax.org (office).

BEN-DAVID, Zadok; British-Israeli sculptor; b. 1949, Bayhan, Yemen; s. of Moshe Ben-David and Hana Ben-David; ed Bezalel Acad. of Art and Design, Jerusalem, Univ. of Reading, St Martin's School of Art, London; Sculpture Teacher at St Martin's School of Art 1977–82, Ravensbourne Coll. of Art and Design, Bromley 1982–85; first solo show at Air Gallery, London 1980; Tel-Aviv Museum Prize for Sculpture 2005, Grande Prémio, XIV Biennial Internacional de Arte de Vila Nova de Cerveira, Portugal 2007. *Publications:* (catalogues) Zadok Ben-David 1987, The Israeli Pavilion: The Venice Biennale 1988, De Circasia et al. 2007. *Address:* 65 Warwick Avenue, London, W9 2PP, England (home). *Telephone:* (20) 7266-0536 (home); (20) 7328-6857 (office). *Fax:* (20) 7328-3892 (home); (20) 7328-6857 (office). *E-mail:* zadokbd@yahoo.com (home); zadokstudio@gmail.com (office). *Website:* www.zadokbendavid.com (home).

BEN-ELIEZER, Benjamin (Fuad); Israeli politician and army officer; b. 12 Feb. 1936, Basra, Iraq; s. of Saleh and Farha; m.; five c.; ed Israel Nat. Defence Coll.; emigrated to Israel 1949; career officer Israel Defence Forces (IDF), Commdr Six Day War 1967, served on IDF Mil. Mission to Singapore 1970–73, Commdr Yom Kippur War 1973, First CO Southern Lebanon 1977–78, Commdr Judea and Samaria 1978–81; Govt Co-ordinator of Activities in the Administered Areas 1983–84; Minister of Housing and Construction 1992–96; mem. Knesset 1984–, served on Foreign Affairs Cttee 1988–92; mem. Israel Labour Party, Chair. –2002; Deputy Prime Minister and Minister of Communications 1999–2001, Minister of Defence 2001–02, of Nat. Infrastructure 2006–09, of Industry, Trade and Labour 2009–11. *Address:* c/o Ministry of Industry, Trade and Labour, 5 Bank of Israel Street, Jerusalem 91009, Israel.

BEN HAMMOUDA, Hakim, DEcon; Tunisian economist and government official; *Minister of the Economy and Finance;* b. 7 Aug. 1961; ed Univ. de Grenoble, France; Consultant, UNDP 1997–2000; Dept Dir, Council for Devt of Social Research in Africa, Dakar 1997–2000; Dir, ECA office in Central Africa, Yaoundé 2001–03, Dir, Trade and Regional Integration Div., Addis Ababa 2003–06, Chief Economist and Dir, Trade, Finance and Econ. Devt Div. 2006–08; Dir Inst. for Training and Technical Cooperation, WTO 2008–11; Special Adviser to Pres. of ADB 2011–14; Minister of Economy and Finance 2014–; regular lecturer on int. econs and devt econs at several univs including Institut d'Etudes et de Recherches Economiques et Sociales, Paris 1988–90, Univ. de Grenoble 1987–90, 1993–95. *Publications:* more than 25 books on econs and more than 40 articles in int. journals. *Address:* Ministry of Finance, place du Gouvernement, La Kasbah, 1008 Tunis, Tunisia (office). *Telephone:* (71) 571-888 (office). *Fax:* (71) 572-390 (office). *E-mail:* pcontenu@finances.gov.tn (office). *Website:* www.portail .finances.gov.tn (office).

BEN JELLOUN, Tahar; Moroccan writer and poet; b. 1 Dec. 1944, Fès; m. Aicha Ben Jelloun 1986; two s. two d.; ed Lycée Regnault de Tanger, Faculté de Lettres, Mohammed-V Univ., Rabat and Univ. of Paris; worked as a prof. in Morocco, teaching philosophy first in Tetouan and then in Casablanca; emigrated to France 1971; columnist, Le Monde 1973–, La Repubblica (Italy) and La Vanguardia (Spain); mem. Conseil supérieur de la langue française; UN Goodwill Amb. for Human Rights; Dr hc (Montréal); Chevalier des Arts et des Lettres 1983, Chevalier de la Légion d'honneur 1988, Grand Croix 2008; Prix de l'Amitié Franco-Arabe 1976, Médaille du Mérite Nat. (Morocco), Prix Goncourt 1987, Prix des Hemisphere 1991, UN Global Tolerance Award 1998, Prix Ulysse 2005, Special Prize for "peace and friendship between people" at Lazio between Europe and the Mediterranean Festival 2006, Prix de la ville Catania 2009, Argana Int. Poetry Award 2010, Erich Maria Remarque Peace Prize 2011, Prix de la Fondation Crans Montana 2011. *Publications include:* fiction: Harrouda 1973, La Réclusion solitaire 1976 (trans. as Solitaire 1988), Moha le fou, Moha le sage 1978, La Prière de l'absent 1980, Muha al-ma'twah, Muha al-hakim 1982, L'Ecrivain public 1983, L'Enfant de sable 1985 (trans. as The Sand Child 1987), La Nuit sacrée 1987 (trans. as The Sacred Night 1989), Jour de silence à Tanger 1990 (trans. as Silent Day in Tangier 1991), Les Yeux baissés 1991, L'Ange aveugle 1992, L'Homme rompu 1994, Corruption 1995, Le Premier amour est toujours le dernier 1995, Les Raisins de la galère 1995, La Soudure fraternelle 1995, La Nuit de l'erreur 1997, L'Auberge des pauvres 1999, Labyrinthe des Sentiments 1999, Cette aveuglante absence de lumière (trans. as This Blinding Absence of Light) (Int. IMPAC Dublin Literary Award 2004) 2001, Amours sorcières 2003, La Belle au bois dormant 2004, Le Dernier Ami (trans. as The Last Friend) 2004, Partir 2005, L'ecole perdue 2006, Yemma 2007, Sur ma mère 2008, Au pays 2009, Leaving Tangier 2009, A Palace in the Old Village 2010; poetry: Hommes sous linceul de silence 1970, Cicatrice du soleil 1972, Le Discours du chameau 1974, La Mémoire future: Anthologie de la nouvelle poésie du Maroc 1976, Les Amandiers sont morts de leurs blessures 1976, A l'insu du souvenir 1980, Sahara 1987, La Remontée des cendres 1991, Poésie Complète (1966–95) 1995, The Rising of the Ashes 2010; plays: Chronique d'une solitude 1976, Entretien avec Monsieur Said Hammadi, ouvrier algérien 1982, La Fiancée de l'eau 1984; non-fiction: La Plus haute des solitudes: Misère sexuelle d'émigrés nord-africains 1977, Haut Atlas: L'Exil de pierres 1982, Hospitalité française: Racisme et immigration maghrebine 1984, Marseille, comme un matin d'insomnie 1986, Giacometti 1991, Le Racisme expliqué à ma fille 1998, L'islam expliqué aux enfants 2002. *Address:* c/o Editions Gallimard, 5 rue Sébastien-Bottin, 75328 Paris Cedex 07, France. *E-mail:* tbjweb@gmail.com (office). *Website:* www.taharbenjelloun.org.

BEN-NATAN, Asher; Israeli diplomatist; b. 15 Feb. 1921, Vienna, Austria; s. of Nahum Natan and Berta Natan; m. Erika (Rut) Frucht 1940; one s. one d.; ed Z. P. Hayut Hebrew Coll., Vienna and Institut des Hautes Etudes Internationales, Geneva; Co-Founder and mem. Kibbutz Mederot-Zeraim 1938–44, latterly Sec. and Treas.; Political Dept, Jewish Agency 1944–45; on mission to Europe to organize rescue of Jews and illegal immigration to Palestine: attached to office of Head of Jewish Agency 1945–47; Ministry of Foreign Affairs 1948–51; studies in Geneva 1951–53; Govt Rep. on Bd of Red Sea Inkodeh Co. 1953–56, Gen. Man. 1955–56; Rep. of Ministry of Defence in Europe 1956–58; Dir-Gen. Ministry of Defence 1959–65; Amb. to FRG 1965–70, to France 1970–75; Political Adviser to Minister of Defence 1975–78; Adviser to Prime Minister on Special Affairs 1985; Amb. on Special Mission 1993; Chair. Ben-Gurion Foundation 1983; Pres. Israel-German Asscn 1973; Officier Légion d'honneur, Commdr Ordre nat. (Ivory Coast), Commdr Ordre de l'Etoile équatoriale (Gabon), Grosses Bundesverdienstorden (Germany) 2000; Grosses Verdienstkreuz mit Mand (Germany); Dr hc (Ben Gurion Univ.) 1990; Hon. DPhil (Ben Gurion Univ.) 1997; Louis Waiss Peace Prize 1974, Heinz Galinski Prize (Berlin) 1992. *Publications:* Briefe an den Botschafter 1970, Dialogue avec des Allemands 1973, Die Chuzpe zu Leben 2004, Broecken Baden aber Nicht Vergessen 2004, Die Bricha 2005, The Audacity To Live (autobiog.) 2007. *Address:* 89 Haim Levanon Street, Tel-Aviv 69345, Israel (home). *Telephone:* (3) 641-3398 (home). *E-mail:* asherbn@u13.net (home).

BEN YAHIA, Habib; Tunisian politician; *Secretary General, Arab Maghreb Union;* b. 30 July 1938, Tunis; m. Naget Ben Yahia; one s. one d.; ed Univ. of Tunis, Columbia Univ., New York, USA; fmr Dir African Div., Ministry of Foreign Affairs, then Dir Econ. Co-operation with US Div.; fmr Econ. Counsellor, Embassies in Paris and Washington, DC; fmr Chief of Staff, Ministry of Foreign Affairs; Amb. to UAE, Japan and Belgium –1981, apptd Amb. to USA 1981; Minister of Foreign Affairs 1991–97, of Defence and Foreign Affairs 1999–2004; Sec. Gen. Arab Maghreb Union 2006–. *Address:* Union du Maghreb Arabe, 14 Rue Zalagh Agdal, Rabat, Morocco (office). *Telephone:* (3) 7671274 (office); (3) 7671280 (office). *Fax:* (3) 7671253 (office). *E-mail:* sg.uma@maghrebarabe.org (office). *Website:* www .maghrebarabe.org (office).

BENACHENHOU, Abdellatif; Algerian economist and government official; fmr financial consultant; worked for UNESCO; fmr econ. consultant for World Bank and UNEP; fmr chief consultant for Mediterranean Comm. on Sustainable Devt Working Group on Trade and Environment; Minister of Finance 1999–2001, 2003–05, currently econ. adviser to Pres. of Algeria. *Address:* c/o Office of the President, Présidence de la République, el-Mouradia, Algiers, Algeria. *Telephone:* (21) 69-15-15. *Fax:* (21) 69-15-95. *Website:* www.el-mouradia.dz.

BENAÏSSA, Muhammad, BA; Moroccan politician; b. 3 Jan. 1937, Asilah; m. Laila Hajoun-Benaissa; five c.; ed Univ. of Minnesota, Columbia Univ., USA; Press Attaché, Perm. Mission of Morocco to UN, New York 1964–65; Information Officer, UN Dept of Information, 1965–67; Regional Information Adviser, FAO, Rome 1967–71, Head of Devt Support Communication 1971–73, Asst to Dir of Information 1973–74, Dir of Information Div. 1974–76; Asst Sec.-Gen. of UN, World Food Conf. 1975; elected to City Council of Asilah 1976–83, elected Mayor 1992, then Pres. City Council of Asilah; Founder and Chair. Asilah Forum Foundation; Co-Founder Moussem Cultural International Asikah (arts festival) 1978; mem. Moroccan Parl. 1977–83; Co-Founder and Exec. mem. Moroccan Social Democratic Party (Rassemblement Nat. des Independents) 1978; consultant, UNDP, IFAD, UNFPA 1978–85; Chief Ed. Al-Mithak Al-Watani and Al-Maghrab publs 1980–85; Amb. to USA 1993–99; Minister of Foreign Affairs and Co-operation 1999–2007; Dr hc (Univ. of Minnesota) 2007. *Publications include:* Grains de Peau 1974. *Address:* Asilah Forum Foundation, Hassan II Centre, Asilah, Morocco (office). *Website:* www.assilah.net (office).

BÉNASSY, Jean-Pascal, PhD; French economist and researcher; *Director of Research, Centre National de la Recherche Scientifique;* b. 30 Dec. 1948, Paris; s. of Jean Bénassy and Jeannine Bénassy; ed Ecole Normale Supérieure, Paris, Univ. of California, Berkeley, USA; Research Assoc., CEPREMAP 1973–, Dir of Research, CNRS 1981–; Dir Laboratoire d'Economie Politique, Ecole Normale Supérieure 1984–88; Dept of Econs Ecole Polytechnique 1987–2002; Fellow, Econometric Soc. 1981, mem. Council 1990–92; Guido Zerilli Marimo Prize, Acad. des Sciences Morales et Politiques 1990. *Publications:* The Economics of Market Disequilibrium 1982, Macroéconomie et théorie du déséquilibre 1984, Macroeconomics: An Introduction to the Non-Walrasian Approach 1986, Macroeconomics and Imperfect Competition 1995, The Macroeconomics of Imperfect Competition and Nonclearing Markets: A Dynamic General Equilibrium Approach 2002, Imperfect Competition, Nonclearing Markets and Business Cycles 2006, Money, Interest and Policy 2007, Macroeconomic Theory 2011; numerous articles in specialized journals. *Address:* CEPREMAP-ENS, 48 boulevard Jourdan, Bâtiment E, 75014 Paris, France (office). *Telephone:* 1-43-13-63-38 (office). *E-mail:* benassy@pse.ens.fr (office).

BENATAR, Pat; American singer; b. (Pat Andrejewski), 1953, Brooklyn, New York; m. Neil Giraldo; one c.; Grammy Awards for Best Female Rock Vocal Performance 1981, 1982, 1983, 1984. *Recordings include:* albums: In the Heat of the Night 1979, Crimes of Passion 1980, Precious Time 1981, Get Nervous 1982, Live From Earth 1983, Tropico 1984, Seven the Hard Way 1985, Wide Awake in Dreamland 1988, Best Shots 1989, True Love 1991, Gravity's Rainbow 1993, All Fired Up: The Very Best of Pat Benatar 1994, Best of Pat Benatar Vols 1 and 2 2001, Christmas In America 2001, Go 2003. *Publication:* Between a Heart and a Rock Place 2010. *Website:* benatargiraldo.com.

BENAUD, Richard (Richie), OBE; Australian sports commentator and fmr cricketer; b. 6 Oct. 1930, Penrith, NSW; s. of Louis Richard and Irene Benaud; m. Daphne Elizabeth Surfleet 1967; two s. by previous marriage; ed Parramatta High School; right-hand middle-order batsman and right-arm leg-break and googly bowler; played for NSW 1948/49–63/64 (Capt. 1958/59–63); played in 63 Tests for Australia 1951/52–63/64, 28 as Capt. (1958/59–61, 1961–63/64), scoring 2,201 runs (average 24.45) including 3 hundreds, taking 248 wickets (average 27.03); first to score 2,000 runs and take 200 wickets in Tests; scored 11,719 runs (23 hundreds) and took 945 wickets in first-class cricket; toured England 1953, 1956, 1961; int. sports consultant; TV Commentator, BBC 1960–99, Channel Nine 1977–, Channel 4 1999–2005; Wisden Cricketer of the Year 1962. *Publications include:* Way of Cricket 1960, Tale of Two Tests 1962, Spin Me a Spinner 1963, The New Champions 1965, Willow Patterns 1972, Benaud on Reflection 1984, The Appeal of Cricket 1995, Anything But … An Autobiography 1998, My Spin on Cricket 2005, Over But Not Out 2010. *Leisure interest:* golf. *Address:* 19/178 Beach Street, Coogee, NSW 2034, Australia (home). *Telephone:* (2) 9664-1124 (home).

BENAVIDES FERREYROS, Ismael Alberto, MBA; Peruvian politician and fmr banker; b. 10 May 1945, Lima; s. of Ismael Benavides de la Quintana; ed Univ. of California, Berkeley, USA; Minister of Fisheries 1984–85; mem. Congreso for Ica constituency 1990–92 (parl. dissolved); Dir and Gen. Man. Banco Internacional del Perú (Interbank) 1994–2007; spent time during mid-1990s with family business producing traditional Huamaní pisco (brandy); Minister of Agric. 2007–08, of Economy and Finance 2010–11; fmr adviser to World Bank; fmr Pres. Asociación de Bancos, Cámara de Comercio Peruano-Chilena. *Address:* c/o Ministry of Economy and Finance, Jirón Junín 319, 4°, Circado de Lima, Lima 1, Peru (office).

BENAVIDES GANOZA, Roque, BS, MBA; Peruvian business executive; *President and CEO, Compañía de Minas Buenaventura SAA;* b. 1954; s. of Alberto Benavides de la Quintana; ed Pontificia Universidad Catolica del Peru, Henley Business School, Harvard Business School, USA, Univ. of Oxford, UK; served in various exec. positions at Compañía de Minas Buenaventura SAA 1978–85, Chief Financial Officer 1985–2000, Pres. and CEO 2000–, mem. Bd of Dirs 2004–; Chair. Nat. Asscn of Minerals, Petroleum and Energy 1993–95; Pres. Nat. Confed. of Pvt. Business Insts (Confiep) 1999–2001; Vice-Chair. World Gold Council 2001, Silver Inst. 2007; mem. Bd of Dirs Banco de Crédito, Cementos Lima. *Address:* Compañía de Minas Buenaventura SAA, Avenida Carlos Villarán 790, Santa Catalina, La Victoria, Lima 13, Peru (office). *Telephone:* (1) 4192500 (office). *Fax:* (1) 4716522 (office). *E-mail:* recursos@buenaventura.com.pe (office). *Website:* www.buenaventura.com.pe (office).

BENBITOUR, Ahmed, MBA, PhD; Algerian economist, academic and fmr politician; b. 20 June 1946, Ghardaia; m.; four c.; ed Univ. of Algiers, Univ. of Montreal, Canada; fmr CEO Nat. Co. of Studies and Processing, Nat. Co. of Juice and Tinned Fruits of Algeria; fmr Prof. of Business Man.; fmr mem. Parl., Chair.Econ. and Finance Comm. at Council of the Nation (Senate); fmr consultant at World Bank and IMF; fmr Minister of Finance, of Energy, of Treasury; Prime Minister of Algeria 1999–2000; currently Lecturer, African Inst. for Econ. Devt and Planning, Dakar, Senegal. *Publications:* several publs on econ. reforms and finance. *Address:* African Institute for Economic Development and Planning, POBox 3186, 18524 Dakar, Senegal (office). *Telephone:* 823-10-20 (office). *Fax:* 822-29-64 (office). *E-mail:* idep@unidep.org (office). *Website:* www.unidep.org (office).

BENDER, Sir Brian Geoffrey, Kt, KCB, PhD; British civil servant (retd); *Chairman, London Metal Exchange;* b. 25 Feb. 1949, Sheffield; s. of the late Prof. Arnold Eric Bender; m. Penelope Clark 1974; one s. one d.; ed Imperial Coll., London; joined Dept of Trade and Industry 1973; Pvt. Sec. to Sec. of State for Trade 1976–77; First Sec., Office of Perm. Rep. to EC 1977–82; Prin., Dept of Trade and Industry 1982–84; Counsellor, Office of Perm. Rep. to EC 1985–89; UnderSec. and Deputy Head of European Secr., Cabinet Office 1990–93; Head of Regulation Devt Div., Dept of Trade and Industry 1993–94; Deputy Sec. and Head of European Secr., Cabinet Office 1994–98; Head of Public Service Delivery, Cabinet Office 1998–99; Perm. Sec. Cabinet Office 1999–2000, Ministry of Agric., Fisheries and Food 2000–01, Dept for Environment, Food and Rural Affairs 2001–05, Dept of Trade and Industry 2005–07, Perm. Sec., Dept for Business, Enterprise and Regulatory Reform 2007–09 (retd); Chair. London Metal Exchange 2010–; Chair. Honda European Communication and Consultation Group; Dir (non-exec.) Financial Reporting Council 2014–; Bd Mentor, Criticaleye; Sr Adviser, MHP Communications; Adviser to the Bd BSI Group 2009–12; mem. Offshore Advisory Cttee of Mainstream Renewable Power; Trustee Lloyds Register Foundation 2013–; Gov. Dulwich Coll. *Address:* London Metal Exchange, 56 Leadenhall Street, London, EC3A 2DX, England (office). *Telephone:* (20) 7264-5555 (office). *Website:* www.lme.com (office).

BENDINE, Aldemir, BA, MBA; Brazilian business executive; *Vice-Chairman and President, Banco do Brasil SA;* fmr Br. Man., Banco do Brasil SA, then Exec. Man. Directory of Retail, then Exec. Sec. Bd of Officers, then Vice-Pres. of Retail and Distribution, mem. Exec. Bd 2006–, Vice-Pres. of Credit and Debt Cards and New Business on Retail Services –2009, Vice-Chair. and Pres. (CEO) Banco do Brasil SA 2009–; Exec. Dir Federação de Bancos Brasileiros (Febraban); mem. Bd of Dirs and CEO Brazilian Asscn of Business Cards and Services (ABECS); Chair. Visa Vale – CBSS; CEO BB Administradora de Cartoes, BB Administradora de Consorcios. *Address:* Banco do Brasil SA, SBS Qd. 01 Bloco C, Edificio Sede III, 24° Andar, 70073-901 Brasília, DF, Brazil (office). *Telephone:* (61) 3310-3400 (office); (61) 3310-5920 (office). *Fax:* (61) 3310-3735 (office). *E-mail:* presidencia@bb.com.br (office). *Website:* www.bb.com.br (office).

BENDTSEN, Bendt; Danish politician; b. 25 March 1954, Odense; m. Kirsten Bendtsen; three c.; ed agricultural school, Danish Police Acad.; farm hand 1971–75; Police Inspector, Odense 1980–84. Detective Inspector 1984–99, Vice-Chair. Odense Criminal Police Asscn 1986–94; mem. Odense City Council 1990–99; parl. cand. (Conservative People's Party) 1990, 1992, 2001; substitute mem. Parl. April 1994, mem. Parl. Sept. 1994–2008, Deputy Prime Minister 2001–08; Leader, Conservative Party and Conservative Group in Danish Parl. 1999–2008 (resgnd); Minister for Econ. and Business Affairs 2001–08 (resgnd), Minister for Nordic Cooperation 2001–02; mem. Internal Market Council 2001–08 (Chair. 2002), Vice-Chair. Globalisation Council 2005–06; mem. European Parl. (European People's Party) 2009–; Commdr, Order of the Dannebrog 2002, Commdr 1st Degree, Order of the Dannebrog 2008, Grand Cross of the Order of the Crown (Belgium) 2002, Grand Cross of the Order of Merit (Germany) 2002, Commdr Grand Cross of the Royal Swedish Order of the Northern Star 2007, Grand Cross (Brazil) 2007, Order of the Aztec Eagle (Mexico) 2009; Schuman Medal from European Parliament's PPE-DE Group 2003. *Leisure interests:* hunting, playing golf, driving a motorcycle. *Address:* European Parliament, Bât. Altiero Spinelli 10E116, 60, rue Wiertz, 1047 Brussels, Belgium (office). *Telephone:* (2) 284-51-25 (office). *E-mail:* bendt.bendtsen@europarl.europa.eu (office). *Website:* www.konservative.dk/Personer/B/Bendt-Bendtsen (office).

BENDUKIDZE, Kakha Avtandilovich, BSc; Georgian business executive and fmr government official; b. 20 April 1956, Tbilisi; ed Tbilisi State Univ., Lomonosov State Univ., Moscow, Russia; Sr Lab. Asst and Scientific Research Asst, USSR Acad. of Sciences Inst. of Biochemistry and Physiology of Microorganisms 1981–85; Head, Molecular Genetics Lab., Scientific Research Inst. of Biotechnology 1985–92; f. Bioprocess Asscn 1988, Dir 1990–92; Chair. Bd of Dirs Promtorgbank (Industrial and Trade Bank) 1992–93; Chief Dir NIPEK (Nat. Oil Investment

Corpn) 1993–95; co-f. Russian Business Round Table 1993; Chair. Uralmash-Izhora Group 1995–98, CEO 1998–2004; fmr Head of AtomStroyExport; Prof., Higher School of Econs, Moscow 2002; Minister of Econ. Devt June–Dec. 2004, State Minister, responsible for Econ. Reforms Dec. 2004–2007; Head, Chancellery of the Govt 2008–09; f. Linnaeus Capital Partners, B.V. (private equity fund) 2009; Founder and Chair. Bd of Trustees Free Univ. of Tbilisi. *Address:* Linnaeus Capital Partners, B.V., Haaksbergweg 39, 1101BP Amsterdam Zuidoost, Netherlands. *Website:* linnaeuscp.com.

BENEDICT XVI, His Holiness Pope (Joseph Alois Ratzinger); German ecclesiastic; b. 16 April 1927, Marktl am Inn, Bavaria; s. of Joseph Ratzinger and Maria Peintner; ed Univ. of Munich; ordained Chaplain 1951; Prof. of Theology, Freising 1958, Bonn 1959–63, Münster 1963–66, Tübingen 1966–69, Regensburg 1969; co-f. Communio (theological journal) 1972; apptd Archbishop of Munich-Freising 1977–82; cr. Cardinal of Munich by Pope Paul VI 1977; Cardinal Bishop of the Episcopal See of Velletri-Segni 1993; fmr Chair. Bavarian Bishops' Conf.; Prefect, Sacred Congregation for the Doctrine of the Faith 1981–2005; Vice-Dean Coll. of Cardinals 1998–2002, Dean 2002–05; Titular Bishop of Ostia 2002; presided over funeral of Pope John Paul II and the Conclave which elected him April 2005; elected Pope and Bishop of Rome 2005–13 (resgnd), Pope Emer. 2013–; Pres. Int. Theological Comm., Pontifical Biblical Comm.; mem. of the Congregations for the Oriental Churches, for the Divine Worship and the Discipline of the Sacrament, for the Bishops, for the Evangelization of Reapers, for Catholic Educ.; mem. Pontifical Council for the Promotion of Christian Unity; Dr hc (Navarra) 1998, numerous other hon. doctorates; ranked by Forbes magazine amongst The World's Most Powerful People (11th) 2009, (fifth) 2010, (seventh) 2011, (fifth) 2012. *Publications:* books and articles on theological matters including Without Roots (with Marcello Pera) 2006. *Address:* c/o Palazzo Apostolico Vaticano, 00120 Città del Vaticano, Rome, Italy. *Website:* www.vatican.va.

BENEDIKTSSON, Bjarni, LLM; Icelandic lawyer and politician; *Minister of Finance and Economic Affairs;* b. 26 Jan. 1970; m. Þóra Margrét Baldvinsdóttir; four c.; ed Univ. of Iceland, Univ. of Miami, USA; Deputy Dist Commr, Keflavik 1995; private legal practice with own law firm 1999–2003; Chair. BNT hf (bank) and N1 (retail and service co.) 2005–08; mem. Althingi (parl.) for SW Constituency 2003–, mem. Budget Cttee 2003–07, Foreign Affairs Cttee 2005–13 (Chair. 2007–09), mem. Icelandic del. to WEU Assembly 2003–05 (Chair. 2003–05), to EFTA and EEA Parl. Cttees 2005–09 (Vice-Chair. 2007–09), to Nordic Council 2009–12, mem. EU–Iceland Jt Parl. Cttee 2010–13; Minister of Finance and Econ. Affairs 2013–; mem. Independence Party (IP), Chair. 2009–. *Leisure interests:* football and fishing. *Address:* Ministry of Finance and Economic Affairs, Arnarhvoli við Lindargötu, 150 Reykjavík, Iceland (office). *Telephone:* 5459200 (office). *Fax:* 5459299 (office). *E-mail:* postur@fjr.is (office). *Website:* www.fjarmalaraduneyti.is (office).

BENEGAL, Shyam, MA; Indian film director and screenwriter; b. 14 Dec. 1934, Aliwal, Hyderabad; m. Neera Benegal; ed Osmania Univ., Film and TV Inst. of India Pune; advertising copywriter and dir of more than 620 advertising shorts for Lintas Agency, Bombay 1960–66; Dir Indian Nat. Film Devt Corpn 1980; Chair. Film and TV Inst. of India during 1980–83, 1989–92; mem. Nat. Integration Council 1986–89, Nat. Council of Arts; Chair. Academic Council Whistling Woods Int.; Advisor, Partners for Urban Knowledge, Action and Research; Trustee India Foundation for the Arts; Homi Bhabha Fellowship 1970; Dr hc (Calcutta) 2012; Padma Shri 1976, Sovietland Nehru Award 1989, Padma Bhushan 1991, Indira Gandhi Award 2004, Dadasaheb Phalke Award 2006. *Films:* Dir: Gher Betha Ganga 1962, Close to Nature 1967, A Child of the Streets 1967, Indian Youth: An Exploration 1968, Flower Garden 1969, Quest for a Nation 1970, The Pulsating Giant 1971, Raga and Melody 1972, Power to the People 1972, Suhani Sadak 1973, Violence: What Price? Who Pays? 1974, The Quiet Revolution 1974, Bal Sansar 1974, Hero 1975, Charandas Chor 1975, Nishaant (Nat. Film Award 1976) 1975, Bhumika (Nat. Film Award 1978) 1976, Manthan (Nat. Film Award 1977) 1976, Kondura 1978, Pashu Palan 1979, Jawaharlal Nehru (Nat. Film Award 1984) 1982, Satyajit Ray (Nat. Film Award 1985) 1982, Arohan (Nat. Film Award 1982) 1982, Mandi 1983, Vardan 1985, Festival of India 1985, Nature Symphony 1990, Antarnaad 1991, Suraj Ka Satvan Ghoda (Nat. Film Award 1993) 1993, Mammo (Nat. Film Award 1995) 1994, Sardari Begum (Nat. Film Award 1997)1996, The Making of the Mahatma (Nat. Film Award 1996) 1996, Hari-Bhari 2000, Zubeidaa (Nat. Film Award 2001) 2001, Bose: The Forgotten Hero (Nat. Film Award 2005) 2004, Welcome to Sajjanpur 2008, Well Done Abba 2009; Writer: Ankur (Nat. Film Award 1975) 1974, Manthan 1976, Bhumika 1976, Junoon (Nat. Film Award 1979) 1978, Anugraham 1978, Kalyug (Golden Prize 1981, Filmfare Award 1982) 1980, Mandi 1983, Trikal 1985; Producer: Susman 1987, Powaqqatsi 1988, Sardari Begum 1996, Welcome to Sajjanpur 2008, Well Done Abba 2009. *Television:* Yatra 1986, Katha Saagar 1986, TV mini-series—Bharat Ek Khoj 1988, Amravati ki Kahaniyan. *Address:* India Foundation for the Arts, 'Apurva' Ground Floor, No 259, 4th Cross, Raj Mahal Vilas IInd Stage, IInd Block, Bangalore 560 094, India. *Telephone:* (80) 23414681; 9820290888 (home). *Fax:* (80) 23412683. *E-mail:* contactus@indiaifa.org (office). *Website:* www.indiaifa.org (office).

BENETTON, Alessandro, BS, MBA; Italian business executive; *Chairman, Benetton Group;* b. 2 March 1964, Treviso; s. of Luciano Benetton (q.v.) and Maria Teresa Benetton; m. Deborah Compagnoni; three c.; ed Boston Univ., Harvard Business School, USA; early position as Analyst, Global Finance Dept, Goldman Sachs, London; Chair. Benetton Formula Ltd 1988–98; Founder, Chair. and Man. Dir. 21 Investimenti SpA (investment bank) 1992–; mem. Bd of Dirs Benetton Group 2004–, Exec. Deputy Chair. 2008–12, Chair. 2012–; mem. Bd of Dirs Edizione Holding SpA, Autogrill SpA, Permasteelisa SpA, Industrie Zignago Santa Margherita SpA, Sirti SpA; Chair. 21 Pnrs S.G.R. SpA, 21 Investimenti Pnrs SpA; Vice Chair. Nordest Marchant SpA; Sole Dir. Saibot S.r.l.; mem. Supervisory Bd 21 Centrale Pnrs SA; mem. Advisory Cttee Robert Bosch Internationale Beteiligungen; mem. Council, Confindustria; Entrepreneur of the Year, Ernst & Young 2011. *Address:* Benetton Group Headquarters, Villa Minelli, 31050 Ponzano, Treviso (office); 21 Investimenti SpA, Via G. Felissent, 90, 31100 Treviso, Italy (office). *Telephone:* (0422) 316611 (office). *Fax:* (0422) 316600 (office). *E-mail:* info@21investimenti.it (office). *Website:* www.benettongroup.com (office); www.21investimenti.it (office); www.alessandrobenetton.com.

BENETTON, Carlo; Italian business executive; b. 26 Dec. 1943; four c.; Co-founder (with brothers) Benetton Group 1965, responsible for production, Deputy Chair. Benetton Group 1978–, also Deputy Chair. Edizione Holding and Edizione S.r.l.; Chair. Maccarese SpA. *Address:* Benetton Group SpA, Villa Minelli 1, 31050 Ponzano, Treviso, Italy (office). *Telephone:* (422) 519111 (office). *Fax:* (422) 969501 (office). *E-mail:* info@benetton.it (office). *Website:* www.benettongroup.com (office).

BENETTON, Luciano; Italian business executive; b. 13 May 1935, Treviso; s. of Leone Benetton and Rosa Benetton; m. Maria-Teresa Benetton (separated); four c.; Co-founder (with three brothers) Benetton 1963, Chair. Benetton Group SpA 1965–2012; mem. Bd of Dirs Edizione Holding (family-owned financial holding co.), Atlantia SpA, Autogrill SpA; mem. Italian Senate 1992–94; Hon. MBA (Instituto de Empresa, Madrid) 1992, Hon. JD (Boston Univ.) 1994, Hon. Laurea in Economia Aziendale (Università ca' Foscari di Venezia) 1995; Civiltà Veneta 1986, Premio Creatività 1992. *Address:* c/o Benetton Group SpA, Via Minelli, 31050 Ponzano (Treviso), Italy. *Website:* www.benettongroup.com.

BENGOA ALBIZU, Vicente, BSc; Dominican Republic economist; *Secretary of State for Finance;* ed Univ. of Chile; Prof. of Econs and Public Finance, Univ. of Santo Domingo 1973–94, Dir Econs Dept, Technological Inst. 1978–82; Superintendent of Banking 1997–2000; Deputy in Nat. Ass. 1982–86; Sec. of State for Finance 2004–. *Address:* Secretariat of State for Finance, Avenida México 45, esq. Leopoldo Navarro, Apdo. 1478, Santo Domingo, DN, Dominican Republic (office). *Telephone:* 687-5131 (office). *Fax:* 682-0498 (office). *E-mail:* webmaster@finanzas.gov.do (office). *Website:* www.finanzas.gov.do (office).

BENGSTON, Billy Al, (Moon Doggie, Moondoggy, Moontang, Two Moons); American artist and designer; b. 7 June 1934, Dodge City, Kan.; m. Wendy Al; one d.; ed Los Angeles City Coll., Calif. Coll. of Arts and Crafts, Oakland and Otis Art Inst.; instructor, Chouinard Art Inst. Los Angeles 1961; Lecturer, UCLA 1962–63; Guest Artist, Univ. of Oklahoma 1967; Guest Prof., Univ. of Colorado 1969; Guest Lecturer, Univ. of California, Irvine 1973; Dir Pelican Club Productions Los Angeles 1981–84; Exec. Dir Westfall Arts 1995–98; numerous solo exhbns; works in numerous public collections including Museum of Modern Art, New York, Whitney Museum of American Art, New York, Solomon R. Guggenheim Museum, New York, San Francisco Museum of Art, The Beaubourg, Paris; Tamarind Fellow 1968, 1982, 1987; Guggenheim Fellowship 1975; Nat. Foundation for the Arts Grant 1967; various comms and other awards. *Publications:* contribs to Art in America, Art Forum, Paris Review. *Address:* 110 Mildred Avenue, Venice, CA 90291, USA (office). *Telephone:* (310) 822-2201 (office). *E-mail:* artiststudio@billyalbengston.com (office). *Website:* www.billyalbengston.com (office).

BENGU, Sibusiso Mandlenkosi Emmanuel, PhD; South African politician, diplomatist and academic; b. 8 May 1934, Kranskop, Natal; s. of Rev. Jackonia Bengu and Augusta Bengu; m. Ethel Funeka 1961; one s. four d.; ed Univ. of Geneva; Founder and Prin. Dlangezwa High School 1968–76; Publicity Sec., Natal African Teachers' Asscn 1969–71; Dir Students' Advisory Services, Univ. of Zululand 1977–78; Exec. Sec. for Research and Social Action, Lutheran World Fed., Geneva 1978–91; Rector and Vice-Chancellor Univ. of Fort Hare 1991–94, Head of History Writing Project 2004; Minister of Educ. Govt of Nat. Unity 1994–99; Pres. Intergovernmental Cttee, Ministers of Educ. of Africa (MINEDAF) 1998–99; Amb. to Germany 2000–04; First Gen. Sec. Inkatha Freedom Party, now mem. ANC; Trustee, African Centre for Constructive Resolution of Disputes; Hon. Fellowship of the Coll. of Perceptors (Manchester Univ.) 1997; Hon. DD (Wartburg Theological Seminary, Dubuque Univ.) 1986, Hon. LLD (California State Univ.) 1996, Hon. PhD in Political Science (Univ. of Fort Hare) 2001, Dr hc (Univ. of Kwazulu-Natal) 2009; Gamaliel Chair for Peace and Justice, Lutheran Campus Ministry, Univ. of Wisconsin in Milwaukee 1985; Distinguished Int. Educator Award, American Council of Education 1975. *Publications:* African Cultural Identity and International Relations 1975, Chasing Gods Not our Own 1975, Mirror or Model. *Leisure interests:* listening to music, watching sports, reading, research.

BENHABIB, Seyla, MA, PhD; American political scientist, philosopher and academic; *Eugene Meyer Professor of Political Science and Professor of Philosophy, Yale University;* b. 9 Sept. 1950, Istanbul, Turkey; of Sephardic Jewish parentage; m. James A. Sleeper; one d.; ed American Coll. for Girls, Istanbul, Brandeis and Yale Univs, USA; Prof. of Philosophy and Political Science, New School for Social Research 1991–93; Prof., Dept of Govt and Sr Research Fellow, Center for European Studies, Harvard Univ. 1993–2000, Chair., Program in Social Studies 1996–2000; Ed.-in-Chief Constellations: An International Journal of Critical and Democratic Theory 1993–97; Visiting Sr Fellow, Institut für Wissenschaft vom Menschen, Vienna, Austria 1996; Eugene Meyer Prof. of Political Science and Prof. of Philosophy, Yale Univ. 2000–, Dir, Program in Ethics, Politics and Econs 2002–08; Baruch de Spinoza Distinguished Professorship, Univ. of Amsterdam 2000; Pres. American Philosophical Asscn 2007; Russell Sage Foundation Fellow 2000–01; Sr Research Fellow, Wissenschaftskolleg, Berlin 2009; Dr hc (Univ. of Utrecht) 2004, (Univ. of Valencia) 2010; Seeley Lecturer, Cambridge 2002, Tanner Lecturer, Berkeley 2004, Ernst Bloch Prize 2009, Guggenheim Fellow 2012, Fellow, Straus Center for Advanced Legal Studies, New York Univ. Law School Spring 2012, Leopold Lucas Prize 2012. *Publications include:* Critique, Norm and Utopia: A Study of the Foundations of Critical Theory 1986, Situating the Self: Gender, Community and Postmodernism in Contemporary Ethics 1992, The Reluctant Modernism of Hannah Arendt 1996, Feminist Contentions: A Philosophical Exchange 1996; (as ed.): Feminism as Critique: Essays on the Politics of Gender in Late-Capitalist Societies 1987, The Communicative Ethics Controversy (co-ed. with Fred Dallmayr) 1990, On Max Horkheimer (co-ed. with Wolfgang Bonss and John McCole) 1993, The Philosophical Discourses of Modernity (ed. with M. Passerin d'Entreves) 1996, Democracy and Difference: Changing Boundaries of the Political 1996, Transformation of Citizenship – Dilemmas of the Nation-State in the Era of Globalization 2000, The Claims of Culture – Equality and Diversity in the Global Era 2002, The Rights of Others: The John Seeley Lectures (Ralph Bunche Award, American Political Science Asscn 2005, North American Soc. for Social Philosophy Best Book Award 2005) 2004, Another Cosmopolitanism, with Responses by Jeremy Waldron, Bonnie Honig and Will Kymlicka, Mobility and ImmobilityL Gender, Borders and Citizenship (ed. with Judith Resnik) 2010; (trans.): Hegel's Ontology and the Theory of Historicity by Herbert Marcuse 1987; more than 110 articles on social and political thought,

feminist theory and the history of modern political theory. *Address:* Room 225, Department of Political Science, Yale University, PO Box 208301, 115 Rosenkranz Hall, New Haven, CT 06520-8301, USA (office). *Telephone:* (203) 432-5246 (office). *Fax:* (203) 432-6196 (office). *E-mail:* seyla.benhabib@yale.edu (office). *Website:* www.yale.edu/polisci/people/sbenhabib.html (office).

BENHAMOUDA, Boualem, DIur; Algerian politician and lexicographer; b. 8 March 1933, Cherchell; m.; two s. one d.; ed Algiers Univ.; served with Army of Nat. Liberation 1956–62; mem. Parl. 1962–65; Minister of Ex-Combatants 1965–70, of Justice 1970–77, of Public Works 1977–80, of the Interior 1980–82, of Finance 1982–86; responsible for Inst. of Global Studies of Strategy 1986–90; mem. Political Bureau of Nat. Liberation Front (FLN) 1979–, Chair. FLN Cttee on Educ. Training and Culture 1979–80, Gen. Sec. FLN 1995–2001, currently mem. Cen. Cttee; Medal of Liberation. *Publications:* The Keys of Arabic Language 1991, The Arabic Origin of Some Spanish Words 1991, The Democratic Practice of Power (Between Theory and Reality) 1992, Spanish-Arabic Pocket Dictionary 1993, The Arabic Origin of About 1000 French Words, General French-Arabic Dictionary 1996, General Arabic-French Dictionary 2000, 2001, Citizenship and Power 2006, Read and Understand The Coran 2006. *Leisure interests:* reading, studying, cultural travel, philosophy, science, languages. *Address:* Siege du Parti du FLN, Rue du Stade, Hydra, Algiers (office); 5 Rue de Frère Ennouch, El-Biar, Algiers, Algeria (home). *Telephone:* (21) 694701 (office). *Fax:* (21) 923538 (home).

BENICHOU, Alain; French engineer and business executive; *President, IBM France;* b. 9 July 1959, Oran, Algeria; ed Supélec, Paris; joined IBM as Client, Univ. 1984, has held several man. positions in Europe and USA, including as Dir French Gen. Business Div. and Dir Operations, Global SMB, Vice-Pres. IBM Global Services 2001, Vice-Pres. Distribution Sector, Europe Middle East and Africa 2002, Vice-Pres. Gen. Business, Northeast Europe 2005–07, Gen. Man. Global Distribution Sector, IBM Corpn 2007–10, Pres. IBM France 2010–. *Address:* IBM France, Centre Relations Clients, 110 boulevard de la Salle, 45760 Boigny-sur-Bionne, France (office). *Telephone:* (2) 38-55-77-77 (office). *Fax:* (2) 38-86-17-27 (office). *E-mail:* frmail@uk.ibm.com (office). *Website:* www.ibm.com/fr (office); www.ibm.com/planetwide/fr (office).

BENIGNI, Roberto Remigio; Italian actor, director and writer; b. 27 Oct. 1952, Misericordia, Tuscany; s. of Remigio Benigni and Isolina Papini; m. Nicoletta Braschi 1991; ed Instituto Tecnico Commericale Datini di Prato; Cavaliere di Gran Croce OMRI; Dr hc (Ben-Gurion Univ.) 1999, (Univ. of Bologna) 2002, (Univ. Vita-Salute San Raffaele) 2003, (Univ. of Malta) 2008. *Films include:* Belingua ti voglio bene (actor, writer) 1977, Down by Law (actor) 1986, Tutto Benigni (actor, writer) 1986, Johnny Stecchino (dir, actor, writer) 1992, Night on Earth (actor) 1992, Son of the Pink Panther (acted) 1993, Mostro (dir, actor, writer), Life is Beautiful (dir, actor, writer, Acad. Award for Best Actor and Best Foreign Film) 1998, Asterisk and Obelisk (actor) 1998, Pinocchio 2002, Coffee and Cigarettes 2003, The Tiger and the Snow (dir, actor) 2006, To Rome with Love (actor) 2012. *Publications include:* E l'alluce fu monologhi e gags 1996.

BENING, Annette; American actress; b. 29 May 1958, Topeka, Kan.; m. 1st Steven White (divorced); m. 2nd Warren Beatty (q.v.) 1992; four c.; ed San Francisco State Univ.; stage appearances in works by Ibsen, Chekhov and Shakespeare in San Diego and San Francisco; other stage roles in Coastal Disturbances, The Great Outdoors; European Achievement in World Cinema Award 2000. *Films:* The Great Outdoors 1988, Valmont 1989, Postcards from the Edge 1990, The Grifters 1990, Guilty by Suspicion 1991, Regarding Henry 1991, Bugsy 1991, Love Affair 1994, Richard III 1995, The American President 1995, Mars Attacks! 1996, The Siege 1998, In Dreams 1999, American Beauty 1999, What Planet Are You From? 2000, Open Range 2003, Being Julia (Best Actress Award, Nat. Bd of Review, Best Actress in a Musical or Comedy, Golden Globe Awards 2005) 2004, Running with Scissors 2006, The Women 2008, Mother and Child 2009, The Kids Are All Right (Hollywood Award for Best Actress 2010, Golden Globe Award for Best Actress in a Comedy or Musical 2011) 2010. *Television includes:* Mrs Harris (film) 2005. *Address:* c/o Kevin Huvane, CAA, 2000 Avenue of the Stars, Los Angeles, CA 90067, USA (office). *Telephone:* (424) 288-2000 (office). *Fax:* (424) 288-2900 (office). *Website:* www.caa.com (office).

BENIZRI, Shlomo; Israeli politician; b. 1961, Haifa; m.; seven c.; army service; ordained as a rabbi at Or Hachaim Talmudic Coll., Jerusalem; fmr Head of Talmudic Coll.; mem. Knesset 1992–2008; mem. Finance and Anti-Drug Abuse Cttees 1992–96; fmr Head of Shas Knesset Faction; Deputy Minister of Health 1996–99, Minister of Health 1999–2001; Minister of Labour and Social Welfare 2001–02; convicted of accepting bribes and breaching the public trust April 2008, sentenced to four years' imprisonment. *Publication:* The Sky is Talking (astrology). *Leisure interests:* sports, computers, nature.

BENJAMIN, George William John, CBE; British composer, conductor, pianist and teacher; b. 31 Jan. 1960, London; s. of William Benjamin and Susan Benjamin (née Bendon); civil partner Michael Waldman; ed Westminster School, Paris Conservatoire, King's Coll., Cambridge, Institut de recherche et coordination acoustique/musique, Paris; first London orchestral performance, BBC Proms 1980; Prince Consort Prof. of Composition, Royal Coll. of Music, London 1984–2001; Henry Purcell Prof. of Composition, King's Coll. London 2001–; has conducted widely in GB, Europe, USA, Australia and Far East; Prin. Guest Artist, Hallé Orchestra 1993–96; operatic conducting debut: Pelléas et Mélisande, La Monnaie, Brussels 1999; Carte Blanche at Opéra Bastille, Paris 1992; Founding Artistic Dir Wet Ink Festival, San Francisco Symphony Orchestra 1992, Meltdown Festival, South Bank 1993; Featured Composer, 75th Salzburg Festival 1995, Tanglewood Festival 1999, 2000, 2003, Deutsches Symphonie Orchester 2004–05, Strasbourg Musica Festival 2005, Spanish Nat. Orchestra 2005, Festival d'Automne, Paris 2006, Lucerne Festival 2008, Project San Francisco 2010; London Symphony Orchestra Retrospective 'By George', Barbican, London 2002–03; Artistic Consultant, BBC Sounding the Century 1996–99; Music Dir Ojai Music Festival, Calif. 2010; mem. Bavarian Acad. of Fine Arts 2000; Hon. RAM, Hon. RCM, Hon. GSMD, Hon. mem. Royal Philharmonic Soc.; Chevalier, Ordre des Arts et des Lettres 1996; Lili Boulanger Award, USA 1985, Koussevitzky Int. Record Award 1987, Grand Prix du Disque de l'Académie Charles Cros 1987, Gramophone Contemporary Award 1990, Edison Award 1998, Schönberg Prize, Deutsche Sinfonie Berlin 2002; Royal Philharmonic Soc. Award 2003, 2004. *Publications:* orchestral works:

Ringed by the Flat Horizon 1980, A Mind of Winter 1981, At First Light 1982, Jubilation 1985, Antara 1987, Sudden Time 1993, Three Inventions for Chamber Orchestra 1995, Sometime Voices 1996, Palimpsests 2002, Dance Figures 2004, Duet for piano and orchestra 2008; chamber music: Piano Sonata 1978, Octet 1978, Flight 1979, Sortilèges 1981, Three Studies for Piano 1985, Upon Silence 1990, Viola, Viola 1997, Shadowlines for solo piano 2001, Three Miniatures for violin 2001, Olicantus 2002, Piano Figures 2004; stage works: Into the Little Hill (Royal Philharmonic Soc. Award for Best Large-Scale Composition 2009) 2006, Written on Skin 2012. *Address:* c/o Faber Music, 74–77 Great Russell Street, London, WC1B 3DA, England (office). *Telephone:* (20) 7908-5310 (office). *Fax:* (20) 7908-5339 (office). *E-mail:* information@fabermusic.com (office). *Website:* www.fabermusic.com (office).

BENJAMIN, John Oponjo; Sierra Leonean economist and politician; *National Chairman, Sierra Leone People's Party;* b. 29 Nov. 1952, Segbwema; Chief Sec. of State, Nat. Provisional Ruling Council (NPRC) 1992; Sec.-Gen. NPRC Govt 1993; Interim Chair. Nat. Unity Party 1997; Minister of Finance 2005–07; currently Nat. Chair. Sierra Leone People's Party; Exec. Dir African Information Tech. Holdings. *Address:* Sierra Leone People's Party, 15 Wallace Johnson St, Freetown, Sierra Leone (office). *Telephone:* (22) 2256341 (office). *E-mail:* info@slpp.ws (office). *Website:* www.slpp.ws (office).

BENJAMIN, Raymond; French international civil aviation official; *Secretary General, International Civil Aviation Organization;* responsible for negotiating bilateral air transport agreements on behalf of French Civil Aviation Authority 1976–77; Air Transport Officer, European Civil Aviation Conf. 1977–82, Deputy Sec. 1982–83, Exec. Sec. 1983–89; Chief of Aviation Security Br., ICAO 1994–2007, also served as Sec. Aviation Security Panel and Group of Experts for the Detection of Plastic Explosives 1989–94, Sec. Gen. ICAO 2009–; Special Adviser to Jt Aviation Authorities Training Org. (JAA/TO) and to European Aviation Security Training Inst. 2007–. *Address:* International Civil Aviation Organization, 999 University Street, Montréal, PQ H3C 5H7, Canada (office). *Telephone:* (514) 954-8220 (office). *Fax:* (514) 954-6376 (office). *E-mail:* icaohq@icao.int (office); ray.benjamin@hotmail.com (home). *Website:* www.icao.int (office).

BENJAMIN, Regina Marcia, BS, MD, MBA; American physician; *Surgeon General;* b. 26 Oct. 1956, Mobile, Ala; ed Morehouse School of Medicine, Xavier Univ., New Orleans, Univ. of Alabama, Birmingham, Tulane Univ., New Orleans; intern and resident in family practice at Medical Center of Cen. Georgia; Founder and CEO Bayou La Batre Rural Health Clinic, Ala 1990–; Surgeon Gen. of USA 2009–; fmr Assoc. Dean for Rural Health, Coll. of Medicine, Univ. of South Alabama, Mobile; Pres. Medical Asscn of the State of Alabama 2002–03; mem. Bd of Trustees, American Medical Asscn (first physician under age 40 and first African-American woman) 1995; Diplomate of American Bd of Family Practice; apptd to Clinical Lab. Improvement Act Cttee and to Council of Grad. Medical Educ., US Dept of Health and Human Services; mem. numerous bds and cttees, including Kaiser Comm. on Medicaid and the Uninsured, Catholic Health East, Medical Asscn of the State of Alabama, Alabama Bd of Medical Examiners, Alabama State Cttee of Public Health, Mobile Co. Medical Soc., Alabama Rural Health Asscn, Leadership Alabama, Mobile Area Red Cross, Mercy Medical, Mobile Chamber of Commerce, United Way of Mobile, and Deep South Girl Scout Council; mem. Step 3 Cttee; has served as Vice-Pres. of Gov.'s Comm. on Aging; fmr mem. Gov.'s Health Care Reform Task Force, Gov.'s Task Force on Children's Health; Fellow, American Acad. of Family Physicians; fmr Kellogg Nat. Fellow; fmr Rockefeller Next Generation Leader; US recipient of Nelson Mandela Award for Health and Human Rights 1998, named by TIME magazine as one of the "Nation's 50 Future Leaders Age 40 and Under" 1998, chosen by CBS This Morning as "Woman of the Year" 1998, chosen by People Magazine as "Woman of the Year" 1998, Nat. Caring Award 2000, awarded Papal Cross Pro Ecclesia et Pontifice by Pope Benedict XVI 2006, named by U.S. News & World Report as one of "America's Best Leaders" 2008, one of 25 recipients of the $500,000 Genius Awards, John D. and Catherine T. MacArthur Foundation 2008. *Address:* Office of the Surgeon General, 5600 Fishers Lane, Room 18-66, Rockville, MD 20857 (office); Bayou Clinic, 13833 Tapia Lane, Bayou La Batre, AL 36509, USA. *Telephone:* (301) 443-4000 (office); (251) 824-4985. *Fax:* (301) 443-3574 (office); (251) 626-2200. *E-mail:* info@surgeongeneral.gov (office); info@bayouclinic.org. *Website:* www.surgeongeneral.gov (office); www.bayouclinic.org.

BENJELLOUN, Othman; Moroccan business executive; *Chairman and CEO, BMCE Bank;* b. 1931, Casablanca; s. of Haj Abbas Benjelloun; m. Leila Meziane; one s. one d.; ed Ecole Polytechnique de Lausanne; acquired Royale Marocaine d'Assurances (RMA) 1988, est. RMA Watanya; Chair. and CEO BMCE Bank 1995–; acquired Al Wataniya (insurance co.) 1998; Chair. Meditelecom 2005–; Pres. Finance.com Groupe, Professional Asscn of Banks in Morocco, Union of Maghreb Banks; World Union of Arab Bankers, currently also Deputy Chair. for Overseas Region; fmr Chair. US Moroccan Trade Investment Council; mem. Arab Thought Foundation, Global Philanthropist Circle, Synergos Inst., New York, USA; Chancellor, Al Akhawayn Univ., Ifrane 1998–2004; Adviser, Centre for Strategic International Studies, USA; Officier de l'Ordre du Trône du Royame du Maroc, Commdr, Royal Order of the Polar Star (Sweden), Nat. Order of the Lion (Senegal); Arab Banker of the Year 2007. *Address:* BMCE Bank, Avenue Hassan Ii 140, Casablanca, Morocco (office). *Telephone:* (52) 2200325 (office). *Website:* www.bmcebank.ma (office).

BENKIRANE, Abdelilah, BSc; Moroccan politician; *Prime Minister;* b. 4 April 1954, Rabat; m.; six c.; ed Univ. Mohammed V-Agdal, Rabat; began career as teacher, Ecole normale supérieure de l'enseignement technique, Rabat; mem. Chabiba Islamiya (Islamist group) 1976; f. Al Jamaa Al Islamiya 1981 (renamed Réforme et Renouveau 1992); mem. Parl. for Salé constituency 1997–; Leader of the Opposition 2008–11; Prime Minister 2011–; mem. Mouvement populaire démocratique constitutionnel, renamed Parti de la justice et du développement (PJD) 1998, PJD Sec.-Gen. 2008–. *Address:* Office of the Prime Minister, Palais Royal, Touarga, Rabat, Morocco (office). *Telephone:* (53) 7219400 (office). *Fax:* (53) 7768656 (office). *E-mail:* courrier@pm.gov.ma (office). *Website:* www.pm.gov.ma (office).

BENKOVIC, Stephen J., BS, PhD; American chemist and academic; *Eberly Chair in Chemistry, Pennsylvania State University;* b. Orange, NJ; ed Lehigh

Univ., Cornell Univ., Univ. of California, Santa Barbara; Post-Doctoral Research Assoc., Univ. of Calif., Santa Barbara 1964–65; joined Dept of Chemistry, Pennsylvania State Univ. 1965, Prof. of Chem. 1970, Evan Pugh Prof. 1977–, Eberly Chair in Chemistry 1986–; Scientific Pnr, RhO Ventures; co-founder Anacor Pharmaceuticals, mem. Bd of Dirs 2000–; Head of Scientific Advisory Bd, Glaxo SmithKline; mem. NAS 1985–, Inst. of Medicine 1994–, American Philosophical Soc. 2002–; Fellow, American Acad. of Arts and Sciences 1984; Guggenheim Fellowship; Alfred P. Sloan Fellowship; Hon. DSc (Lehigh Univ.) 1995; NIH Career Devt Award, Pfizer Award 1977, Gowland Hopkins Award 1986, Arthur C. Scope Scolar Award 1988, Repligen Award 1989, Alfred Bader Award 1995, Chemical Pioneer Award, American Inst. of Chemists, Christian B. Afinsen Award 2000, Nakanishi Prize 2005, Benjamin Franklin Medal 2009, Ralph F. Hirschmann Award 2010. *Address:* Department of Chemistry, 104 Chemistry Building, Pennsylvania State University, University Park, PA 16802, USA (office). *Telephone:* (814) 865-2882 (office). *Fax:* (814) 865-2973 (office). *E-mail:* sjb1@psu.edu (office). *Website:* www.psu.edu/profs/benkovic.html (office); research.chem.psu.edu/sjbgroup (office).

BENMAKHLOUF, Alexandre; French lawyer; b. 9 Sept. 1939, Oran, Algeria; s. of Tahar Benmakhlouf and Sylviane Jan; m. Gabrielle Steinmann 1965; one s. one d.; ed Institut d'Etudes Politiques; Deputy Public Prosecutor, Meaux 1970, Versailles 1972; seconded to Chancellery 1974–84; Pres. Nanterre Magistrates' Court 1984–86; Deputy Sec.-Gen. Professional Asscn of Magistrates 1984–86; Adviser to Prime Minister Jacques Chirac 1986–89; Legal Adviser to Jacques Chirac, Mayor of Paris 1989–91; Pres. Court of Appeal, Versailles 1991–93; Dir of Civil Affairs and Dir of Cabinet of Guardian of the Seal, Ministry of Justice 1993–96; Attorney-Gen., Court of Appeal 1996–97, Solicitor-Gen. 1997–2000, First Counsel for the Prosecution 2001–07, Hon. First Counsel 2007–; Chevalier Légion d'honneur, Ordre des Palmes académiques. *Leisure interests:* reading, travelling, cinema. *Address:* c/o Cour de Cassation, 5 quai de l'Horloge, 75055 Paris RP, France (office).

BENMOSCHE, Robert (Bob) H., BA; American insurance industry executive; *President and CEO, American International Group (AIG), Inc.;* b. Brooklyn, NY; ed Alfred Univ.; in US Army Signal Corps 1966–68, attained rank of Lt; with Chase Manhattan Bank 1976–79, Vice-Pres. of Tech. 1979–82; joined Paine Webber 1982, Sr Vice-Pres. of Marketing 1984–86, Chief Financial Officer, Retail Div. 1986–87, Dir Securities Operations 1988, responsible for tech. org. 1990, for human resources 1992, later Exec. Vice-Pres. and mem. Bd of Dirs –1995; Exec. Vice-Pres. MetLife Inc. 1995–97, Exec. Vice-Pres. for Individual Business 1996, Pres. and COO 1997–98, Dir Metropolitan Life Insurance Co. 1997, Metlife Inc. 1999–2005, Chair., Pres. and CEO Metropolitan Life Insurance Co. 1998–2006, Chair. MetLife Inc. 1999–2006 (retd); mem. Bd of Dirs, Pres. and CEO American International Group (AIG), Inc. 2009–; Dir Nat. Securities Clearing Corpn 1990–94, Chicago Stock Exchange 1994–95, Crédit Suisse Group 2002–, New England Financial, New York Philharmonic, Alfred Univ.; mem. Int. Business Leaders' Advisory Council for Mayor of Beijing 2002–. *Address:* American International Group, Inc., 180 Maiden Lane, New York, NY 10038, USA (office). *Telephone:* (212) 770-7000 (office). *Fax:* (212) 509-9705 (office). *E-mail:* AnswerCenter@AIG.com (office). *Website:* www.aigcorporate.com (office).

BENN, Rt Hon. Hilary James Wedgwood, BA; British politician; *Shadow Secretary of State for Communities and Local Government;* b. 26 Nov. 1953, Hammersmith, London, England; s. of the late Tony Benn and Caroline Benn; m. 1st Rosalind Retey (died 1979); m. 2nd Sally Christina Clark 1982; three s. one d.; ed Holland Park School, London, Univ. of Sussex, Brighton; Research Officer, ASTMS, rose to become Head of Policy for Manufacturing, Science and Finance (MSF, trade union); Council Deputy Leader and Chair of Educ. in Ealing, W London 1986–90; Labour cand. for Ealing N in Gen. Elections 1983, 1987; Special Adviser to David Blunkett MP, Sec. of State for Educ. and Employment 1997–99; MP (Labour) for Leeds Cen. 1999–, fmr mem. Environment, Transport and Regions Select Cttee, mem. House of Commons Comm. 2010–; with Dept for Int. Devt 2001–02; Home Office Minister 2002–03; unsuccessful cand. for Deputy Leadership of Labour Party June 2007; Sec. of State for Int. Devt 2003–07, for Environment, Food and Rural Affairs 2007–10; Shadow Sec. of State for Environment, Food and Rural Affairs May–Oct. 2010; Shadow Leader of the House of Commons Oct. 2010–11; Shadow Sec. of State for Communities and Local Govt 2011–; Patron, Holbeck Elderly Aid, Leeds, Faith Together, Leeds, Caring Together, Woodhouse and Little London. *Leisure interests:* gardening, watching sport. *Address:* House of Commons, Westminster, London, SW1A 0AA (office); Leeds Central Parliamentary Office, 2 Blenheim Terrace, Leeds, W Yorks., LS2 9JG, England (office). *Telephone:* (20) 7219-5770 (London) (office); (113) 244-1097 (Leeds) (office). *E-mail:* hilary.benn.mp@parliament.uk (office); boxj@parliament.uk (office). *Website:* www.hilarybenn.org.

BENNACK, Frank Anthony, Jr; American publishing executive; *Vice-Chairman of the Board and CEO, Hearst Corporation;* b. 12 Feb. 1933, San Antonio; s. of Frank Bennack and Lula Connally; m. Luella Smith 1951; five d.; ed Univ. of Maryland and St Mary's Univ.; advertising account exec. San Antonio Light 1950–53, 1956–58, Advertising Man. 1961–65, Asst Publr 1965–67, Publr 1967–74; Gen. Man. (newspapers), Hearst Corpn New York 1974–76, Exec. Vice-Pres. and COO 1975–78, Pres. and CEO 1978–2002, Vice-Chair. Bd 2002–, Chair. Exec. Cttee 2002–08, Chair. Hearst-Argyle Television 2008–, CEO 2008–; Chair. Museum of TV and Radio, NY City 1991–; Pres. Tex. Daily Newspaper Asscn 1973–; mem. Bd of Dirs J.P. Morgan Chase & Co., Wyeth, Polo Ralph Lauren Corpn, Metropolitan Opera of New York; Dir, Vice-Chair. Lincoln Center for the Performing Arts; Dir Newspaper Asscn of American (fmrly American Newspaper Publrs Asscn), Chair. 1992–93; Gov., Vice-Chair. New York Presbyterian Hosp.; mem. Bd of Dirs Mfrs Hanover Trust Co., New York; mem. American Acad. of Arts and Sciences 2007–. *Address:* Hearst Corporation, Hearst Tower, 12th Floor, 300 West 57th Street, New York, NY 10019, USA (office). *Telephone:* (212) 649-4190 (office). *Fax:* (212) 649-2108 (office). *E-mail:* hearstnewspapers@hearst.com (office). *Website:* www.hearstcorp.com (office).

BENNET, Douglas J., Jr, PhD; American fmr government official and fmr academic administrator; b. 23 June 1938, Orange, NJ; s. of Douglas Bennet and Phoebe Bennet; m. 1st Susanne Klejman 1959 (divorced 1995); m. 2nd Midge Bowen Ramsey 1996; two s. one d.; ed Wesleyan Univ., Middletown, Conn., Univ.

of California, Berkeley and Harvard Univ.; Asst to Econ. Adviser (Dr C. E. Lindblom), Agency for Int. Devt, New Delhi, India 1963–64; Special Asst to Amb. Chester Bowles, Embassy in New Delhi 1964–66; Asst to US Vice-Pres. Hubert Humphrey 1967–69; Admin. Asst to US Senator T. F. Eagleton 1969–73, to US Senator A. Ribicoff 1973–74; Staff Dir Senate Budget Cttee 1974–77; Asst Sec. of State for Congressional Relations, Dept of State 1977–79; Admin. US Agency for Int. Devt 1979–81; Pres. Roosevelt Center for American Policy Studies 1981–83; Pres. and CEO Nat. Public Radio (NPR) 1983–93; Asst Sec. of State for Int. Organizational Affairs, Dept of State 1993–95; Pres. Wesleyan Univ. 1995–2007; mem. Council of Foreign Relations, North South Round Table, Soc. for Int. Devt, Carnegie Endowment Study on Organizing Int. Financial Co-operation in 1980s, Rockfall Foundation, AIAA; mem. Bd of Dirs Overseas Educ. Fund, KTI Corpn, Salzburg Seminar, Middlesex Co. Chamber of Commerce; Hon. DrIur (Wesleyan Univ.) 1994, (Trinity Coll.) 2008. *Publications:* articles in newspapers and journals. *Leisure interests:* sailing, skiing. *Address:* c/o Office of the President, Wesleyan University, 269 High Street, Middletown, CT 06459, USA (office).

BENNET, Michael Farrand, BA, JD; American lawyer, politician, college administrator and media executive; *Senator from Colorado;* b. 28 Nov. 1964, New Delhi, India; s. of Douglas J. Bennet and Susanne Christine Bennet (née Klejman); m. Susan Daggett 1997; three d.; ed Wesleyan Univ., Yale Law School; worked for Ohio Gov. Richard Celeste 1988–90; Ed.-in-Chief The Yale Law Journal; worked as law clerk 4th Circuit Court of Appeals; later Counsel to US Deputy Attorney Gen. during Clinton Admin; Man. Dir Anschutz Investment Co. 1997–2003; Chief of Staff to Mayor of Denver, John Hickenlooper 2003–05; Supt of Denver Public Schools 2005–09; apptd to US Senate 2009, Senator from Colorado 2010–, mem. Cttee on Agric., Nutrition and Forestry, Cttee on Health, Educ., Labor and Pensions, Cttee on Banking, Housing and Urban Affairs, Special Cttee on Aging; Democrat; listed by TIME magazine amongst the nation's 11 leading educational activists 2011. *Address:* 458 Russell Senate Office Building, Washington, DC 20510, USA (office). *Telephone:* (202) 224-5852 (office). *Website:* bennet.senate.gov (office).

BENNETT, Alan, BA; British playwright and actor; b. 9 May 1934, Leeds; s. of Walter Bennett and Lilian Mary Peel; ed Leeds Modern School, Exeter Coll., Oxford; Jr Lecturer, Modern History, Magdalen Coll., Oxford 1960–62; co-author and actor Beyond the Fringe, Edin. 1960, London 1961, New York 1962; Trustee Nat. Gallery 1993–98; Hon. Fellow, Royal Acad. 2000; Hon. Fellow, Exeter Coll., Oxford; Freeman of Leeds 2004; Hon. DLitt (Leeds); Evening Standard Award 1961, 1969, Hawthornden Prize 1988, two Olivier Awards 1993, Evening Standard Film Award 1996, Lifetime Achievement Award, British Book Awards 2003, Evening Standard Best Play Award 2004, Olivier Award for outstanding contribution to British theatre 2005, British Book Awards Reader's Digest Author of the Year 2006, Bodley Medal 2008. *Plays:* On the Margin (TV series, author and actor) 1966, Forty Years On (author and actor) 1968, Getting On 1971, Habeas Corpus 1973, The Old Country 1977, Enjoy 1980, Kafka's Dick 1986, Single Spies 1988, The Wind in the Willows (adapted for Nat. Theatre) 1990, The Madness of George III 1991, The Lady in the Van 1999, The History Boys (Royal Nat. Theatre, London) (Evening Standard Award for Best Play 2004, Critics Circle Theatre Award for Best New Play 2005, Olivier Award for Best New Play 2005, New York Drama Critics' Circle Play of the Year 2006, Drama Desk Award for Best Play 2006, Tony Award for Best Play 2006) 2004, The Habit of Art 2009, People 2012, Untold Stories 2012. *Radio:* The Last of the Sun 2004, Denmark Hill 2013. *Television scripts:* A Day Out (film) 1972, Sunset Across the Bay (TV film) 1975, A Little Outing, A Visit from Miss Prothero (plays) 1977, Doris and Doreen, The Old Crowd, Me! I'm Afraid of Virginia Woolf, All Day on the Sands, Afternoon Off, One Fine Day 1978–79, Intensive Care, Our Winnie, A Woman of No Importance, Rolling Home, Marks, Say Something Happened, An Englishman Abroad 1982, The Insurance Man 1986, Talking Heads (Olivier Award) 1992, 102 Boulevard Haussmann 1991, A Question of Attribution 1991, Talking Heads 2 1998. *Films:* A Private Function 1984, Prick Up Your Ears 1987, The Madness of King George 1994, The History Boys 2006. *Television documentaries:* Dinner at Noon 1988, Poetry in Motion 1990, Portrait or Bust 1994, The Abbey 1995, Telling Tales 1999. *Publications:* Beyond the Fringe (with Peter Cook, Jonathan Miller and Dudley Moore) 1962, Forty Years On 1969, Getting On 1972, Habeas Corpus 1973, The Old Country 1978, Enjoy 1980, Office Suite 1981, Objects of Affection 1982, The Writer in Disguise 1985, Two Kafka Plays 1987, Talking Heads 1988, Single Spies 1989, Poetry in Motion 1990, The Lady in the Van 1991, The Wind in the Willows (adaptation) 1991, The Madness of George III 1992, Writing Home (autobiog.) 1994, Diaries 1997, The Clothes They Stood Up In 1998, Talking Heads 2 1998, The Complete Talking Heads 1998, A Box of Alan Bennett 2000, Father, Father! Burning Bright 2000, The Laying on of Hands 2001, The History Boys 2004, Untold Stories 2005, The Uncommon Reader 2007, Smut (short stories) 2011; regular contrib. to London Review of Books. *Address:* Chatto & Linnit, World's End Studios, 132–134 Lots Road, London, SW10 0RJ, England (office). *Telephone:* (20) 7349-7722 (office).

BENNETT, Brian Maurice, BA; British fmr diplomatist; *Administrator, The Humphrey Richardson Taylor Charitable Trust;* b. 1 April 1948, Portsmouth, Hants., England; s. of Valentine Bennett and Dorothy Bennett; m.; three s.; ed Univ. of Sheffield; joined FCO 1971, Desk Officer, Western Orgs Dept 1971–73, Desk Officer, Personnel Policy Dept 1979–83, Desk Officer, Man. Review 1992–94, Desk Officer, Cen. European Dept 1994–97, Deputy Head, Personnel Services Dept 2001–02; Third Sec., Information, Prague, Czechoslovakia 1973–76; Third Sec., Chancery, Helsinki, Finland 1977–79; Second Sec., Commercial, Bridgetown, Barbados 1983–86; Second, later First, Sec., UK Del. to Mutual and Balanced Force Reductions Talks, Vienna, Austria 1986–88; First Sec., The Hague, Netherlands 1988–92; Deputy Head of Mission, Tunis, Tunisia 1997–2000; Amb. to Belarus 2003–07; Admin. The Humphrey Richardson Taylor Charitable Trust 2008–. *Publication:* The Last Dictatorship in Europe: Belarus under Lukashenko 2011. *Leisure interests:* walking, singing, writing. *Address:* Humphrey Richardson Taylor Charitable Trust, 28 Chipstead Station Parade, Coulsdon, Surrey, CR5 3TF, England (office). *Telephone:* (1737) 557546 (office). *E-mail:* hrtaylortrust@btconnect.com (office). *Website:* www.hrtaylortrust.org.uk (office).

BENNETT, Charles Henry, BS, PhD; American physicist and computer scientist; *IBM Fellow, Thomas J. Watson Research Center, International Business*

Machines; b. 1943, New York, NY; s. of Boyd Bennett and Anne Bennett (née Wolfe); m. Theodora M. Bennett; three c.; ed Croton-Harmon High School, Brandeis and Harvard Univs; Researcher, Argonne Nat. Lab. 1971–73; joined IBM Research 1972, currently an IBM Fellow, Thomas J. Watson Research Center; Visiting Prof. of Computer Science, Boston Univ. 1983–85; mem. NAS; Fellow, American Physical Soc.; Harvey Prize, Technion, Israel (co-recipient) 2008. *Achievements include:* co-discovered 'quantum teleportation' 1993, helped found the quantitative theory of entanglement and introduced several techniques for faithful transmission of classical and quantum information through noisy channels 1995–97. *Publications:* numerous papers in professional journals; six US patents. *Leisure interests:* photography, music. *Address:* Thomas J. Watson Research Center, 1101 Kitchawan Road, Yorktown Heights, NY 10598, USA (office). *Telephone:* (914) 945-3118 (office). *Fax:* (914) 945-2141 (office). *E-mail:* bennetcatus@ibm.com (office). *Website:* www.watson.ibm.com (office).

BENNETT, Charles L., BS, PhD; American astronomer and academic; *Alumni Centennial Professor of Physics and Astronomy and Gilman Scholar, Johns Hopkins University;* b. Nov. 1956; ed Univ. of Maryland, Carnegie Inst. of Washington, Massachusetts Inst. of Tech.; astrophysicist, NASA Goddard Space Flight Center (GSFC) 1984–2004, Acting Head, Infrared Astrophysics Br. April–Aug. 1993, April–Aug. 1994, Head 1994–2000, Sr Scientist for Experimental Cosmology 2004; Prof., Johns Hopkins Univ. 2005–, Alumni Centennial Prof. of Physics and Astronomy and Gilman Scholar 2011–; fmr Deputy Prin. Investigator, Differential Microwave Radiometers (DMR) instrument and mem. Science Team of Cosmic Background Explorer (COBE) mission; Leader and Prin. Investigator, Wilkinson Microwave Anisotropy Probe mission; mem. American Acad. of Arts and Sciences 2004, NAS 2005, American Astronomical Soc., American Inst. of Physics, Int. Astronomical Union; Fellow, American Physical Soc. 1999, AAAS 2004; numerous awards including NASA Outstanding Performance 1985, 1994, NASA Exceptional Scientific Achievement Medal for COBE 1992, GSFC Group Award for MAP Proposal 1996, NASA/GSFC Performance Award 1996, 1998, 2002, Popular Science 'Best of What's New' Award in Aviation and Space for WMAP 2001, ISI Highly Cited Researchers 2002, Sr Scientist for Experimental Cosmology 2002, NASA/GSFC Center of Excellence Group Achievement Award for MAP 2002, NASA/GSFC Group Achievement Award for MAP 2002, Distinguished Alumnus of the Year, Univ. of Maryland 2003, John C. Lindsay Memorial Award for Space Science 2003, NASA Outstanding Leadership Medal 2003, NASA Performance Award 2003, Science Magazine Breakthrough of the Year for WMAP/Sloan proof of Dark Energy 2003, NASA Group Achievement Award to WMAP Science Team 2004, Rotary Nat. Award for Space Achievement Mid-Career Stellar Award 2005, NAS Henry Draper Medal 2005, Gruber Foundation Cosmology Prize (as mem. COBE Team) 2006, Harvey Prize, Technion – Israel Inst. of Tech. 2006, NAS Comstock Prize in Physics 2009, Shaw Prize (co-recipient) 2010, Gruber Cosmology Prize (co-recipient with WMAP team) 2012, Karl G. Jansky Prize Lecturer 2013. *Publications:* After The First Three Minutes, AIP Conference Proceedings 222 (co-author) 1991, Dark Matter, AIP Conference Procedings 336 (co-author) 1995; more than 150 scientific papers in professional journals. *Address:* Bloomberg 209, Department of Physics and Astronomy, The Johns Hopkins University, 3400 North Charles Street, Baltimore, MD 21218-2686, USA (office). *Telephone:* (410) 516-6177 (office). *Fax:* (410) 516-7239 (office). *E-mail:* cbennett@jhu.edu (office). *Website:* physics-astronomy.jhu.edu/directory/charles-l-bennett (office); cosmos .pha.jhu.edu/bennett (office).

BENNETT, Hywel Thomas; British actor and director; b. 8 April 1944, Garnant, S. Wales; s. of Gorden Bennett and Sarah Gwen Lewis; m. 1st Cathy McGowan 1967 (divorced 1988); one d.; m. 2nd Sandra Layne Fulford 1998; ed Henry Thornton Grammar School, Clapham, London and Royal Acad. of Dramatic Art; London stage debut as Ophelia in Youth Theatre's Hamlet, Queen's Theatre 1959; played in repertory, Salisbury and Leatherhead 1965; Fellow, Welsh Coll. of Music & Drama; Hon. Fellow, Univ. of Wales, Cardiff 1997. *Stage roles include:* Puck in A Midsummer Night's Dream, Edinburgh Festival 1967; Prince Hal in Henry IV (Parts I and II), Mermaid 1970; Antony in Julius Caesar, Young Vic 1972; Stanley in The Birthday Party, Gardner Cen., Brighton 1973; Hamlet (touring S. Africa) 1974; Danny in Night Must Fall, Sherman, Cardiff 1974 and Shaw, 1975; Jimmy Porter in Look Back in Anger, Belgrade, Coventry 1974; Konstantin in the Seagull (on tour), Birmingham Repertory Co. 1974, Otherwise Engaged, Comedy Theatre 1978, Terra Nova, Chichester 1979, The Case of the Oily Levantine, Her Majesty's 1980, She Stoops to Conquer, Nat. Theatre 1984–85; Andrey in Elijah Moshinksy's production of The Three Sisters, Albery Theatre 1987, Treasure Island 1990; has directed several plays including Rosencrantz and Guildenstern are Dead, Leatherhead 1975, A Man for All Seasons, Birmingham 1976, I Have Been Here Before, Sherman Theatre, Cardiff 1976, Otherwise Engaged, Library Theatre, Manchester 1978, What the Butler Saw, Theatre of Wales, Cardiff 1980, Fly Away Home (also producer), Hammersmith 1983. *Films include:* The Family Way 1966, Twisted Nerve 1968, The Virgin Soldiers 1969, Loot 1970, Percy 1971, Alice in Wonderland 1972, Endless Night 1972, Murder Elite, War Zone, Frankie and Johnnie 1985, The Twilight Zone, Checkpoint Chiswick, Age Unknown, Married to Malcolm 1997, Misery Harbour 1998, Nasty Neighbours, Vatel, Jesus and Mary 2000, One for the Road 2003. *Radio:* No Telegrams No Thunder, Dialogues on a Broken Sphere, Dracula, Witness for the Prosecution, Night Must Fall. *TV appearances include:* Romeo and Juliet, The Idiot, Unman, Wittering and Zigo, A Month in the Country, Malice Aforethought (serial), Shelley (two series), Tinker, Tailor, Soldier, Spy (serial) 1979, Coming Out, Pennies From Heaven, Artemis '81, The Critic, The Consultant, Absent Friends, Checkpoint Chiswick, The Secret Agent, A Mind to Kill, Casualty, Virtual Murder, The Other Side of Paradise, Trust Me, Frontiers, Karaoke, Harpur and Isles, Hospital, Neverwhere, Dirty Work, Eastenders 2003, The Second Quest 2004, The Final Quest 2004; many voice-overs and narrations; radio plays. *Leisure interests:* fishing, cooking, golf, painting, walking, swimming, reading and solitude. *Address:* c/o Gavin Barker, 2D Wimpole Street, London W1G 0EB, England.

BENNETT, Jana Eve, OBE, BA, MSc, FRTS; British broadcasting executive; *President, BBC Worldwide Networks and Global iPlayer;* b. Cooperstown, NY, USA; d. of Gordon Willard Bennett and Elizabeth Bennett (née Cushing); m. Richard Clemmow 1996; one s. one d.; ed Bognor Comprehensive School, St Anne's Coll., Oxford, London School of Econs; News trainee, BBC 1979, fmrly Asst Producer The Money Programme, Producer Newsnight, Producer/Dir Panorama,

Series Producer Antenna, Ed. Horizon, Head of BBC Science; Dir of Production and Deputy Chief Exec. BBC 1997–99, Dir of TV 2002–06, mem. Exec. Bd BBC 2004–, mem. Bd BBC Worldwide 2006–09, Comic Relief (Trustee), Dir BBC Vision (in charge of BBC TV, BBC Films and BBC Productions) 2006–11, Pres. BBC Worldwide Networks and Global iPlayer 2011–; Exec. Vice-Pres. Learning Channel, US Discovery Communications Inc. 1999–2002; mem. Bd UKTV 2006–; mem. Exec. Cttee, Int. Acad. of Television Arts and Sciences 2010–; mem. BAFTA, Advisory Cttee Natural History Museum, Univ. of Oxford; Gov. RSC; Golden Nymph Award (Panorama), BAFTA, Emmy, Prix Italia (Horizon). *Publication:* The Disappeared: Argentina's Dirty War 1986 (co-author). *Leisure interests:* skiing, family, world music, travel, mountains, guitar. *Address:* BBC Worldwide, Media Centre, 201 Wood Lane, London, W12 7TQ, England (office). *Telephone:* (20) 8433-3391 (office). *Fax:* (20) 8433-3513 (office). *E-mail:* jana.bennett@bbc.com (office). *Website:* www.bbc.com (office).

BENNETT, Martin Arthur, PhD, DSc, FRS, FAA, FRSC; British/Australian chemist and academic; *Professor Emeritus, Australian National University;* b. 11 Aug. 1935, Harrow, Middx, England; s. of Arthur Edward Charles Bennett and Dorothy Ivy Bennett; m. Rae Elizabeth Mathews 1964; two s.; ed Haberdashers' Aske's Hampstead School, Imperial Coll. of Science and Tech., London; Postdoctoral Fellow, Univ. of Southern California 1960–61; Turner and Newall Fellow, Univ. Coll. London 1961–63, Lecturer 1963–67; Fellow, Research School of Chemistry, ANU 1967–70, Sr Fellow 1970–79, Professorial Fellow 1979–91, Prof. 1991–2000, Prof. Emer. 2001–; Adjunct Prof., Royal Melbourne Inst. of Tech. Univ. 2000–; various professorial and visiting fellowships in Canada, Germany, USA, NZ and Japan; mem. Int. Advisory Bd for Dictionary of Organometallic Compounds 1984 and Dictionary of Inorganic Compounds 1988; Corresp. mem. Bavarian Acad. of Sciences 2005; H.G. Smith Medal, Royal Australian Chem. Inst. 1977, RSC Award 1981, G.J. Burrows Award, Royal Australian Chem. Inst. 1987, Nyholm Medal, RSC 1991, Max Planck Soc. Research Award 1994. *Publications:* chapters on ruthenium in Comprehensive Organometallic Chemistry; over 280 papers in journals. *Leisure interests:* golf, reading, foreign languages. *Address:* Research School of Chemistry, Australian National University, Canberra, ACT 0200 (office); 21 Black Street, Yarralumla, ACT 2600, Australia (home). *Telephone:* (2) 6125-3639 (office); (2) 6282-4154 (home). *Fax:* (2) 6125-3216 (office). *E-mail:* bennett@rsc.anu.edu.au (office). *Website:* rsc.anu.edu.au/index.php (office).

BENNETT, Maxwell Richard, AO, BEng, DSc, FAA; Australian physiologist and academic; *Professor of Neuroscience and Head, Neurobiology Laboratory, University of Sydney;* b. 19 Feb. 1939, Melbourne; s. of Herman Adler Bennett (Bercovici) and Ivy G. Arthur; m. Gillian R. Bennett 1965; one s. one d.; ed Christian Brothers Coll., St Kilda, Melbourne and Univ. of Melbourne; John & Alan Gilmour Research Fellow, Univ. of Melbourne 1965; Lecturer in Physiology, Univ. of Sydney 1969, Reader 1973, Prof. of Physiology 1982–2000, Dir Neurobiology Research Centre 1982–90, Prof. of Neuroscience 2000–, also Head, Neurobiology Laboratory, Founder and Dir Brain and Mind Research Inst. 2003–; Convener, Sydney Inst. of Biomedical Research 1995; Founder Fed. Australian Scientific and Tech. Socs 1985; Co-Founder Australian Neural Networks Soc. 1990; Pres. Australian Neuroscience Soc. 1989–92; Pres. Int. Soc. for Autonomic Neuroscience 2001–03; First Univ. Chair., Univ. of Sydney 2000; Fellow, Australian Acad. of Science 1981–; Dir Neuroscience Australia 2002, Brain Foundation 2004, Brain and Mind Research Foundation 2004; mem. Bd of Dirs Australian Brain Foundation 2004–; Sr Adviser Templeton Foundation 2009–; Ed. Journal of the Autonomic Nervous System 1997–, Neuroscience News 1997–, Progress in Neurobiology 1997–, NeuroReport 2001–04, Purinergic Mechanisms 2005–; mem. Council of Mental Health Research Inst. 2003, Mental Health Council of Australia; mem. Council Int. Brain Research Org. 1989–91; Opening Plenary Lecture, World Congress of Neuroscience 1995, Goddard Research Prize Nat. Heart Foundation 1996, Ramaciotti Medal for Excellence in Biomedical Research 1996, Renenessin Research Prize Nat. Heart Foundation 1998, Almigren Research Prize, Nat. Heart Foundation 1999, Burnet Medal and Lecture Australian Acad. of Science 1999, Neuroscience Distinguished Achievement Medallion 2001, Ophthalmologica Internationalis Award 2002, Tall Poppy for Excellence in Science Prize 2002, Centenary Medal 2003. *Publications:* Autonomic Neuromuscular Transmission 1972, Development of Neuromuscular Synapses 1983, Optimising Research and Development 1985, The Idea of Consciousness 1997, History of the Synapse 2001, Philosophical Foundations of Neuroscience 2003, Neuroscience and Philosophy: Brain, Mind, and Language (co-author) 2006, History of Cognitive Neuroscience (co-author) 2008; 350 papers on neuroscience. *Leisure interests:* history and philosophy of science, science policy. *Address:* Department of Physiology, Anderson Stuart Building F13, University of Sydney, Sydney, NSW 2006, Australia (office). *Telephone:* (2) 9351-2034 (office). *E-mail:* info.centre@sydney.edu.au (office). *Website:* www.physiol.usyd.edu.au/research/labs/nrc (office).

BENNETT, Michael Vander Laan, BS, DPhil; American neuroscientist and academic; *Sylvia and Robert S. Olnick Professor of Neuroscience and Distinguished Professor, Albert Einstein College of Medicine;* b. 7 Jan. 1931, Madison, Wis.; s. of Martin Toscan Bennett and Cornelia Vander Laan Bennett; m. 1st Ruth Berman 1963 (divorced 1993); one s. one d.; m. 2nd Ruth Suzanne Zukin 1998; ed Yale Univ., Univ. of Oxford, UK; research worker, Dept of Neurology, Coll. of Physicians and Surgeons, Columbia Univ. 1957–58, Research Assoc. 1958–59; Asst Prof. of Neurology, Columbia Univ. 1959–61, Assoc. Prof. 1961–66; Prof. of Anatomy, Albert Einstein Coll. of Medicine, Yeshiva Univ., NY 1967–74, Co-Dir Neurobiology Course, Marine Biological Lab. 1970–74, Prof. of Neuroscience 1974–, Dir Div. of Cellular Neurobiology 1974–, Chair. Dept of Neuroscience 1982–96, Sylvia and Robert S. Olnick Prof. 1986–, also Distinguished Prof., Dominick P. Purpura Dept of Neuroscience; mem. Editorial Bds Brain Research 1975–, Journal of Cell Biology 1983–85, Journal of Neurobiology 1969–95 (Assoc. Ed. 1979–93), Journal of Neurocytology 1980–82, Journal of Neuroscience (Section Ed. 1981–85); mem. NAS 1982, American Asscn of Anatomists, American Physiological Soc., American Soc. for Cell Biology, American Soc. of Zoologists, Biophysical Soc., Soc. for Neuroscience, Soc. of Gen. Physiologists; Fellow, Nat. Neurological Research Foundation 1958–60, New York Acad. of Sciences, AAAS; Rhodes Scholar 1952; Sr Research Fellowship, NIH 1960–62. *Publications:* more than 300 papers in scholarly books and journals. *Leisure interests:* running, hiking, skiing and scuba. *Address:* Albert Einstein College of Medicine, Department of

Neuroscience, 1300 Morris Park Avenue, Bronx, NY 10461, USA (office). *Telephone:* (718) 430-2536 (office). *Fax:* (718) 430-8932 (office). *E-mail:* mbennett@aecom.yu.edu (office). *Website:* www.aecom.yu.edu/phd/facProfile.asp?id=8219&k= (office).

BENNETT, Natalie Louise, BAgricSci (Hons), BA (Hons), MA; British (b. Australian) politician; *Leader, Green Party of England and Wales;* b. 10 Feb. 1966, Sydney, NSW, Australia; ed MLC School, Burwood, NSW, Univ. of Sydney, Univ. of New England (Australia), Univ. of Leicester; began career in journalism at Eastern Riverina Observer, Henty, NSW, then worked for Cootamundra Herald and Northern Daily Leader, Tamworth; spent two years as Australian Volunteer Abroad working in Office of the Nat. Comm. of Women's Affairs; worked as Chief Foreign Sub-Ed. for Bangkok Post newspaper; began writing for Guardian newpaper's 'Comment is Free' section 2006, Deputy Ed. The Guardian Weekly –2007, Ed. 2007–12; joined the Green Party 2006, cand. in Camden Council election for Regent's Park Ward 2006, for Somerstown Ward 2010, Internal Communications Coordinator on Nat. Exec. of the Green Party 2006–10, selected to stand for parl. seat of Holborn and St Pancras 2010, cand. in London Ass. elections on London-wide list for Green Party 2012; Leader, Green Party of England and Wales 2012–; Chair. Camden Green Party 2011–; Founding Chair. Green Party Women 2008–; Founder Carnival of Feminists; Editorial Bd Convenor, Green World 2010–12; books ed. on Blogcritics.org; Trustee, Fawcett Soc. *Publications include:* Thailand Country Study: Best Practice Guide on Sustainable Action Against Child Labour (ed.) 1998, Women's Health and Development, Country Profile Thailand (ed.); contrib. to The Independent, The Times. *Address:* National Green Party Office, Development House, 56–64 Leonard Street, London, EC2A 4LT, England (office). *Telephone:* (20) 7549-0310 (office). *E-mail:* natalie.bennett@greenparty.org.uk (office). *Website:* www.greenparty.org.uk (office); nataliebennett.co.uk.

BENNETT, Tony, MusD; American singer and entertainer; b. (Anthony Dominick Benedetto), 3 Aug. 1926, Astoria; s. of John Benedetto and Anna Suraci; m. 1st Patricia Beech 1952 (divorced 1971); two c.; m. 2nd Sandra Grant 1971 (divorced 1984); two d.; m. 3rd Susan Crow 2007; ed American Theatre Wing, NY and Univ. of Berkeley; frequent appearances on TV and in concert; owner and recording artist with Improv Records; paintings exhibited at Butler Inst. of American Art, Youngstown, Ohio 1994; f. Frank Sinatra School of the Arts 2001; Grammy Award for Best Traditional Pop Vocal Performer 1998, Kennedy Center Honor 2005, Billboard Century Award 2006, Nat. Endowment for the Arts Jazz Masters Award 2006, Grammy Award for Best Pop Collaboration with Vocals (with Stevie Wonder) 2007, Ronnie Scott Lifetime Achievement Award 2007, inducted into New Jersey Hall of Fame 2011. *Recordings include:* The Art of Excellence 1986, Bennett/Berlin 1988, Astoria: Portrait of the Artist 1990, Perfectly Frank (Grammy Award for Best Traditional Vocal Performance) 1992, Steppin' Out (Grammy Award for Best Traditional Pop Vocal) 1993, The Essence of Tony Bennett 1993, MTV Unplugged (Grammy Award for Album of the Year, Best Traditional Pop Vocal) 1994, Here's to the Ladies 1995, The Playground 1998, Cool (Grammy Award) 1999, The Ultimate Tony 2000, A Wonderful World (with kd lang) (Grammy Award for Best Traditional Pop Vocal Album 2004) 2003, The Art of Romance (Grammy Award for Best Traditional Pop Vocal Album 2006) 2005, Duets: An American Classic (Grammy Award for Best Traditional Pop Vocal Album 2007) 2006, Tony Bennett Sings the Ultimate American Songbook, Vol. 1 2007, A Swingin Christmas 2008, Body and Soul (Grammy Award for Pop Duo/Group Performance with the late Amy Winehouse 2012) 2011, Duets II (Grammy Award for Traditional Pop Vocal Album 2012) 2011. *Publication:* The Good Life: The Autobiography of Tony Bennett. *Address:* 130 West 57th Street, Apartment 9D, New York, NY 10019, USA. *Website:* www.tonybennett.com.

BENNOUNA, Mohamed, DIntLaw; Moroccan diplomatist, academic, lawyer and international judge; *Judge, International Court of Justice;* b. 29 April 1943, Marrakech; m.; three c.; ed Univ. of Nancy, Sorbonne Univ., Paris, France and The Hague Acad. of Int. Law, Netherlands; Prof. of Public Law and Political Science, Univ. of the Sorbonne, Paris 1972–75; Prof., Faculty of Law, Mohammed V Univ. of Rabat and Casablanca 1975–79, Dean 1979–85; Dir-Gen. Arab World Inst. 1991–98; Judge, Int. Criminal Tribunal for the fmr Yugoslavia 1998–2001; Perm. Rep. of Morocco to UN, New York 1985–89, 2001–05; Judge, Int. Court of Justice, The Hague 2006–, Judge ad hoc for dispute between Benin and Niger 2002; Chair. UN Compensation Comm., Geneva 1992–95, Group of 77 and China, UN 2003; mem. UNESCO Int. Panel on Democracy and Devt 1997–, UNESCO World Comm. on Ethics of Scientific Knowledge and Tech. (COMEST) 2002–, UNESCO Int. Bioethics Cttee 1992–98, UN Int. Law Comm., Geneva 1992–95; Chevalier, Légion d'honneur; Nat. Prize for Culture, Morocco, Medal for Culture, Yemen. *Publications:* numerous books, essays and articles on int. law. *Address:* International Court of Justice, Peace Palace, Carnegieplein 2, 2517 KJ, The Hague, The Netherlands (office). *Telephone:* (70) 302-23-23 (office). *Fax:* (70) 302-24-09 (office). *E-mail:* info@icj-cij.org (office). *Website:* www.icj-cij.org (office).

BENOIST, Gilles, LenD; French insurance industry executive; b. 1947; ed Institut d'Etudes Politiques, Ecole Nat. d'Admin; began his career with French Interior Ministry, first as Dir Office of the Prefect of Oise Dept 1974–76, then Sec. Gen. Ariège Dept 1976–78; Prin. Pvt. Sec. to Dir Gen. of Local Authorities at Ministry of the Interior 1978–81, Prin. Pvt. Sec. to Minister of the Economy, Finance and Budget 1981–83; Public Auditor, Cour des Comptes (Court of State Auditors) 1983, served successively as rapporteur on Budget and Finance Disciplinary Court and rapporteur to MODAC governmental org. project, seconded to Caisse des Dépôts et Consignations as adviser to Deputy CEO 1987, mem. Exec. Bd and Corp. Sec. Crédit Local de France, promoted to Sr Public Auditor at Cour des Comptes 1989–91, Dir of Cen. Services, Caisse des Dépôts et Consignations 1991–95, mem. Exec. Cttee 1993–98, Group Corp. Sec. and Dir of Human Resources, Caisse des Dépôts Group 1995–96, Chief Advisor, Cour des Comptes 1996–98; Pres. Exec. Bd and CEO CNP Assurances 1998–2012, mem. Bd of Dirs 2007–12; mem. Bd of Dirs Dexia, Suez Environnement 2008–; Pres. Fédération française des sociétés anonymes d'assurance; Officier, Légion d'honneur. *Address:* Suez Environnement, 1 rue d'Astorg, 75383 Paris Cedex 08, France (office). *Telephone:* 1-58-18-50-00 (office). *Fax:* 1-58-18-50-50 (office). *E-mail:* suez_env.pressoffice@suez-env.com (office). *Website:* www.suez-environnement.com (office).

BENOMAR, Jamal, MA, PhD; Moroccan diplomatist and UN official; *Special Adviser to the Secretary-General on Yemen, United Nations;* b. April 1957; ed Univ. of Rabat, Univ. of Paris (Sorbonne), Univ. of London, UK; imprisoned in Morocco after opposing govt 1976–83; Lecturer and Assoc. Researcher, Univ. of Paris VII 1983–86; Africa Research Specialist, Int. Secr., Amnesty International, London 1987–91; Dir of Human Rights Program, Carter Center, Emory Univ., USA 1991–94; Head of Technical Cooperation Branch, UN Office of High Commr for Human Rights; worked in UNDP in various capacities 1994–, including as Head of Technical Cooperation Branch, Office of High Commr for Human Rights, as Sr Adviser on Governance and Rule of Law in Conflict and Post-Conflict Countries, as Head, Conflict Prevention and Peacebuilding Unit, as Special Adviser –2006; Envoy of UN Sec.-Gen. in Afghanistan and Iraq, to facilitate Nat. Dialogue Conf. 2004; Dir Office of UN Sec.-Gen., establishing Peacebuilding Comm. and Peacebuilding Support Office 2006; Dir Rule of Law Unit, Office of UN Sec.-Gen. 2008–11; Special Adviser to UN Sec.-Gen. on Yemen 2011–. *Address:* United Nations Headquarters, 760 United Nations Plaza, New York, NY 10017, USA (office). *Telephone:* (212) 963-5012 (office). *Fax:* (212) 963-7055 (office). *E-mail:* ecu@un.org (office). *Website:* www.un.org (office).

BENSON, Bruce D., BSc; American business executive and university administrator; *President, University of Colorado;* b. 4 Aug. 1938, Chicago; m. Marcy Benson; three c.; ed Univ. of Colorado; f. Benson Mineral Group 1965; Chair. Colo Comm. on Higher Educ. 1986–89; Chair. Colo Republican Party 1987–93, 2002–03; Chair. Gov.'s Blue Ribbon Panel for Higher Educ. for 21st Century 2001–03; Chair. Metropolitan State Coll. Bd of Trustees 2002–07; Pres. Univ. of Colorado 2008–, also Exec. in Residence and Prof. Attendant, Univ. of Colorado Business School; fmr mem. Bd of Dirs US Exploration Inc., American Land Lease Corpn, Asset Investors Corpn; mem. Smith Coll. Bd of Trustees 1990–95; Hon. DHumLitt (Colo) 2004 Univ. of Colorado Medal 1999, Ira C. Rothgerber Award 2003. *Address:* Office of the President, University of Colorado, 1800 Grant Street, Suite 800, Denver, CO 80203, USA. *Telephone:* (303) 860-5600 (office). *Fax:* (303) 860-5610 (office). *E-mail:* bdbenson2000@yahoo.com; OfficeofthePresident@cu.edu (office). *Website:* www.cu.edu (office).

BENSON, Sir Christopher John, Kt, FRICS, JP, DL; British business executive and chartered surveyor; b. 20 July 1933, Wheaton Aston; s. of Charles Woodburn Benson and Catherine Clara Bishton; m. Margaret Josephine Bundy 1960; two s.; ed Worcester Cathedral King's School, Thames Nautical Training Coll. HMS Worcester; Midshipman RNR 1949–52; Sub-Lt RNVR 1952–53; worked as chartered surveyor and agricultural auctioneer 1953–64; Dir Arndale Devts Ltd 1965–69; Chair. Dolphin Devts Ltd 1969–71, Dolphin Farms Ltd 1969–, Dolphin Property (Man.) Ltd 1969–; Asst Man. Dir The Law Land Co. Ltd 1972–74; Dir Sun Alliance and London Insurance Group 1978–84, Chair. Sun Alliance Insurance Group PLC 1993–96 (Dir 1988, Vice-Chair. 1991, Deputy Chair. 1992), Chair. Royal and Sun Alliance Insurance Group PLC 1996–97; Adviser to British Petroleum Pension Fund 1979–84, Cathedral PLC; Underwriting Mem. of Lloyd's 1979–97; mem. Council CBI 1979–97; Pres. British Property Fed. 1981–83; Dir House of Fraser PLC 1982–86; Chair. London Docklands Devt Corpn 1984–88; Chair. Reedpack Ltd 1989–90; Man. Dir MEPC PLC 1976–88, Chair. 1988–93; Chair. Housing Corpn; Chair. Boots Co. PLC 1990–94 (Dir 1989); Chair. Costain Group PLC 1993–96; Chair. Funding Agency for Schools 1994–97; Deputy Chair. Thorn Lighting Group PLC 1994–98; Chair. Albright and Wilson PLC 1995–; Chair. Devt Bd Macmillan Cancer Relief 1995–2001, Cross London Rail Links 2001–05, Stratford (East London) Renaissance Partnerships 2009–13, Salisbury Vision 2009–13; Gov. Inns of Court School of Law 1996–2000, Prin. 2000–02; Pres. London Chamber of Commerce and Industry 2000–02, Nat. Deaf Children's Soc. 1995–; Vice-Pres. RSA 1992–97; High Sheriff of Wilts. 2002–03; mem. Advisory Bd Hawkpoint Partners Ltd 1999–2001; Master Co. of Watermen and Lightermen of the River Thames 2004–05; Chair. and Trustee Coram Family 2005–12; Liveryman of Hon. Co. of Air Pilots; Lay Canon, Salisbury Cathedral; Chair. Britain-Australia Soc. Educ. Trust 2012–; Trustee, Magna Carta Trust, Salisbury Cathedral, Marine Soc. and Sea Cadets 2002– (Hon. Vice-Pres.); Patron Changing Faces; Friend, Royal Coll. of Physicians; numerous other public and charitable interests; Hon. Vice-Pres. Nat. Fed. of Housing Asscns 1994–; Hon. Fellow, Wolfson Coll. Cambridge 1990, Chartered Inst. of Bldg 1992–, Royal Coll. of Pathologists 1992–, Southampton Univ.; Hon. Bencher Hon. Soc. of Middle Temple 1984–; Hon. DSc (City), (Bradford). *Leisure interests:* opera, ballet, farming in Wiltshire, flying, swimming. *Address:* Pauls Dene House, Castle Road, Salisbury, SP1 3RY (home); Flat 2, 50 South Audley Street, London, W1K 2QE, England (home). *Telephone:* (20) 7629-2398 (office). *Fax:* (20) 7493-1334 (office); (1722) 336980 (home). *E-mail:* sircjbenson@btconnect.com (office).

BENSON, George; American musician (guitar) and singer; b. 22 March 1943, Pittsburgh, Pa; session musician in Pittsburgh; guitarist with Brother Jack McDuff; session work with Herbie Hancock, Wes Montgomery 1966; solo artist 1966–; regular world-wide tours, concerts and festivals; Grammy Awards for Best R&B Instrumental 1976, 1980, Record of the Year 1976, Best Pop Instrumental 1976, 1984, Best R&B Male Vocal Performance 1978, 1980, Best Jazz Vocal Performance 1980, Best Jazz Instrumental Performance 1991, Grammy Award for Best Pop Instrumental Performance (for Mornin') 2007, for Best Traditional R&B Vocal Performance (for God Bless the Child) 2007. *Recordings include:* albums: It's Uptown 1966, Benson Burner 1966, Giblet Gravy 1967, Tell It Like It Is 1969, The Other Side Of Abbey Road 1970, Beyond The Blue Horizon 1972, Good King Bad 1973, Bad Benson 1974, Supership 1975, Breezin' 1976, Benson And Farrell (with Joe Farrell) 1976, George Benson In Concert: Carnegie Hall 1977, In Flight 1977, Weekend In LA 1978, Livin' Inside Your Love 1979, Give Me The Night 1981, George Benson Collection 1981, In Your Eyes 1983, 20/20 1985, The Love Songs 1985, While The City Sleeps 1986, Collaboration 1987, Twice The Love 1988, Tenderly 1989, Big Boss Band 1990, Midnight Moods: The Love Collection 1991, Love Remembers 1993, The Most Exciting New Guitarist On The Jazz 1994, Take Five 1995, Live and Smokin' 1995, California Dreamin' 1996, That's Right 1996, Lil' Darlin' 1996, Talkin' Verve 1997, Essentials 1998, Standing Together 1998, Masquerade 1998, Masquerade Is Over 1999, Love And Jazz 1999, Live At Casa Caribe 2000, Absolute Benson 2000, All Blues 2001, Irreplaceable 2004, Givin' It Up 2006, Songs and Stories 2009, Guitar Man 2011, Inspiration: A Tribute to Nat King Cole 2013. *Address:* c/o Rick Gonzalez, Apropos Management & Marketing, 365 Avenida de los Arboles, Suite 220, Thousand Oaks, CA 91360, USA (office).

E-mail: rick@aproposmanagement.com (office). *Website:* www.georgebenson.com (office).

BENSOUDA, Fatou B., LLM; Gambian lawyer and fmr government official; *Chief Prosecutor, International Criminal Court;* b. 31 Jan. 1961, Banjul; m.; two c.; ed Univ. of Ife, Nigeria, Nigeria Law School, Int. Maritime Law Inst., Malta; various roles with state prosecution service, including Public Prosecutor, Sr State Counsel and Prin. State Counsel 1987–93, Deputy Dir of Public Prosecutions 1993–97, Solicitor-Gen. and Legal Sec. 1997–98, Attorney-Gen. and Sec. of State (Minister of Justice) 1998–2000; served in pvt legal practice, Ya Sadi, Bensouda and Co. Chambers, Banjul 2000–02; Gen. Man. Int. Bank for Commerce (Gambia) Ltd Jan.–May 2002; Legal Adviser and Trial Attorney, Int. Criminal Tribunal for Rwanda, becoming Sr Legal Adviser and Head of Legal Advisory Unit, Tanzania 2002–04; Deputy Prosecutor in charge of Prosecutions Div., Int. Criminal Court (ICC) 2004–12, Chief Prosecutor 2012–; Visiting Lecturer, Univ. of Turin, Italy, Kennesaw State Univ., USA; mem. Int. Asscn of Prosecutors, Gambian Bar Asscn, Nigerian Bar Asscn; mem. Int. Advisory Council, Int. Bd of Maritime Healthcare 2000–, Professional Women's Advisory Bd 2000–, Advisory Bd African Centre For Democracy and Human Rights Studies 1998–2000; mem. Bd of Govs The Gambia High School 1992–95; Int. Jurists Award, Int. Comm. of Jurists 2009, World Peace Through Law Award, Whitney Harris World Law Inst., Washington Univ. in St Louis, USA 2011. *Achievements include:* first int. maritime law expert in The Gambia. *Address:* International Criminal Court, Maanweg 174, 2516 AB, The Hague, Netherlands (office). *Telephone:* (70) 5158515 (office). *Fax:* (70) 5158555 (office). *Website:* www.icc-cpi.int (office).

BENTALL, Richard, BSc, MClinPsychol, MA, PhD; British psychologist and academic; *Professor of Clinical Psychology, School of Psychology, Bangor University;* b. 1956, Sheffield, Yorks.; partner Aisling; one s. one d.; ed Uppingham School, Rutland, High Storrs School, Sheffield, Univ. Coll. of North Wales, Bangor, Univ. of Liverpool and Univ. Coll., Swansea; worked as forensic clinical psychologist in Nat. Health Service 1986; Lecturer, Univ. of Liverpool 1986–94, Prof. of Clinical Psychology 1994–99, later Prof., Inst. of Psychology, Health and Society; Prof. of Experimental Clinical Psychology, Univ. of Manchester 1999, now holds Chair in Experimental Psychology; currently Prof. of Clinical Psychology, School of Psychology, Bangor Univ.; Fellow, British Psychological Soc.; May Davidson Award, British Psychological Soc. 1989, British Psychological Society Book Award 2005. *Publications:* Sensory Deception: A Scientific Analysis of Hallucination (co-author) 1988, Reconstructing Schizophrenia (co-author) 1992, Madness Explained: Psychosis and Human Nature 2003, Doctoring the Mind: Is Our Current Treatment of Mental Illness Really Any Good? 2009; numerous book chapters and articles in scientific journals on psychiatric classification and methodology in psychopathology, cognitive-behavioural therapy, subjective appraisal of neuroleptic drugs and the treatment of chronic fatigue syndrome. *Address:* School of Psychology, Bangor University, Adeilad Brigantia, Penrallt Road, Bangor, Gwynedd, LL57 2AS, Wales (office). *Telephone:* (1248) 383624 (office). *Fax:* (1248) 382599 (office). *E-mail:* richard.bentall@bangor.ac.uk (office). *Website:* www.bangor.ac.uk/psychology (office).

BENTÉGEAT, Gen. Henri; French army officer and diplomatist; *Chairman, Military Committee, European Union;* b. 27 May 1946, Talence; m.; four c.; ed Mil. Acad. of St Cyr, Institut d'Études Politiques de Paris; jr officer in French Armed Forces, serving in Germany, Senegal, France and Djibouti 1968–73; as field grade officer, served in Army Public Information Service, Chief Operations of 9th Marine Div., Commdr Marine Infantry and Armoured Bn 1988–90; Asst Defence Attaché, Embassy in Washington, DC 1990–92; Asst to Chief of Mil. Staff of Pres. of Repub. 1993–96; Commdr French Forces in West Indies 1996–98; Asst to Dir for Strategic Affairs, Ministry of Defence 1998–99; Chief of Mil. Staff of Pres. of Repub. 1999–2002; Chief of Defence Staff 2002–06; Chair. EU Mil. Cttee 2006–; apptd Maj.-Gen. 1998, Lt-Gen. 1999, Gen. 2001; Commandeur, Ordre nat. du Mérit, Grand officier, Légion d'honneur 2006. *Leisure interest:* reading. *Address:* EU Military Committee, rue de la loi 175, 1048 Brussels, Belgium (office). *Telephone:* 22-81-96-92 (office). *Fax:* 22-81-59-28 (office). *Website:* www.consilium.europa.eu (office).

BENTHAM, Richard Walker, BA, LLB, FRSA; British professor of law and barrister; *Professor Emeritus, University of Dundee;* b. 26 June 1930; s. of Richard H. Bentham and Ellen W. Fisher; m. Stella W. Matthews 1955; one d.; ed Trinity Coll., Dublin and Middle Temple, London; called to Bar 1955; Lecturer in Law, Univ. of Tasmania 1955–57, Univ. of Sydney 1957–61; Legal Dept British Petroleum Co. PLC 1961–83, Deputy Legal Adviser 1979–83; Prof. of Petroleum and Mineral Law and Dir Centre for Petroleum and Mineral Law Studies, Univ. of Dundee 1983–90, Prof. Emer. 1991–; Russian Petroleum Legislation Project (Univ. of Houston, World Bank, ODA) 1991–96; mem. Council ICC Inst. of Int. Business Law and Practice 1988–95; British nominated mem. panel arbitrators IEA Dispute Settlement Centre; mem. Bd Scottish Council for Int. Arbitration 1988–98; mem. Int. Law Asscn, Int. Bar Asscn; Julian Prize, Trinity Coll. Dublin 1952. *Publications:* publications in learned journals in the UK and overseas. *Leisure interests:* cricket, military history. *Address:* Earlham, 41 Trumlands Road, St Marychurch, Torquay, Devon, TQ1 4RN, England. *Telephone:* (1803) 314315. *Fax:* (1803) 314315.

BENTLEY, Gerald Eades, Jr, DPhil, DLitt, FRSC; American/Canadian fmr professor of English; b. 23 Aug. 1930, Chicago, Ill.; s. of Gerald Eades Bentley and Esther Felt Bentley; m. Elizabeth Budd 1952; two d.; ed Princeton Univ. and Univ. of Oxford, UK; Instructor, Dept of English, Univ. of Chicago 1956–60; Asst, later full Prof. of English, Univ. of Toronto, Canada 1960–96; Fulbright Lecturer, Univ. of Algiers, Algeria 1967–68, Univ. of Poona, India 1975–76, Fudan Univ. Shanghai, People's Repub. of China 1982–83; Visiting Fellow, Univ. Coll., Swansea, UK 1985, Univ. of Hyderabad, India 1988, Fudan Univ. 1988; Guggenheim Fellow, London 1958–59; Fellow of Canada Council and successor Social Science and Humanities Research Council of Canada 1963–64, 1970–71, 1977–78, 1984–85, 1991–94, 1995–98; Harold White Fellow, Nat. Library of Australia 1989, Connaught Fellow 1991–92; Rockefeller Research Fellow, Bellagio, Italy 1991; Prof. and Visiting Research Fellow, Princeton Univ. 1992, Merton Coll., Oxford 1993, Hatfield Coll., Durham 1996; Visiting Lecturer, Australian Defence Force Acad. 1997; Co-Founder Conf. on Editorial Problems 1964–, Occasional Chair.; Jenkins Award for Bibliography 1978. *Publications* *include:* William Blake (ed.), Vala, or The Four Zoas 1963, The Early Engravings of Flaxman's Classical Designs 1964, A Blake Bibliography (with M. K. Nurmi) 1964, William Blake's Tiriel (ed.) 1967, Blake Records 1969, William Blake's America (ed.) 1974, William Blake's Europe (ed.) 1975, William Blake: The Critical Heritage 1975, A Bibliography of George Cumberland 1975, Editing Eighteenth Century Novels (ed.) 1975, William Blake's Writings (two vols) (ed.) 1978, Blake Books 1977, William Blake's Works in Conventional Typography (ed.) 1984, Blake Records Supplement 1988, George Cumberland, the Captive of the Castle of Sennaar (ed.) 1991, Blake Studies in Japan 1994, Blake Books Supplement 1995, The Stranger from Paradise: A Biography of William Blake 2001, Blake Records (2nd edn), Paul Mellon Centre for studies in British Art 2004, William Blake: Selected Poems (ed.) 2006, William Blake's Conversations 2008, William Blake and His Circle (online) 2013. *Leisure interest:* travel. *Address:* 246 MacPherson Avenue, Toronto, ON M4V 1A2, Canada (home); Dutch Boys Landing, Mears, MI 49436, USA (May–Sept.) (home). *Telephone:* (416) 922-5613 (home).

BENTLEY, Robert Julian, BS, MD; American dermatologist, business executive, politician and state governor; *Governor of Alabama;* b. 3 Feb. 1943, Columbiana, Shelby Co., Ala; s. of David Harford Bentley and Mattie Boyd Bentley (née Vick); m. Martha 'Dianne' Jones 1965; four s.; ed Shelby Co. High School, Univ. of Alabama, Tuscaloosa, Univ. of Alabama School of Medicine; internship, Carraway Methodist Hosp., Birmingham 1968–69; joined USAF as Capt. 1969–75, served as gen. medical officer at Pope Air Force Base, Fayetteville, NC; residency in dermatology, Univ. of Alabama 1974; dermatology practice in Tuscaloosa 1974–98; mem. (Republican) Alabama House of Reps for 63rd Dist 2002–10; Gov. of Alabama 2011–; f. several small businesses, including Alabama Dermatology Assocs (currently Pres.); fmr mem. State Advisory Bd for Sexually Transmitted Diseases; Founder and fmr Pres. Alabama Dermatology Soc.; mem. American Acad. of Dermatology, Medical Asscn of Ala, American Legion, Veterans of Foreign Wars (Life); mem. Bd of Trustees, Judson Coll., Marion, Ala, Alabama Medical Educ. Consortium (co-founder); Deacon and Sunday School Teacher, First Baptist Church, Tuscaloosa, Chair. Bd of Deacons four times, mem. Youth for Christ Advisory Bd, Family Counseling Advisory Bd; Republican; named to Best Doctors in America, Statesmanship Award, Christian Coalition of Alabama 2010. *Address:* Office of the Governor, State Capitol, 600 Dexter Avenue, Suite N104, Montgomery, AL 36130-2751, USA (office). *Telephone:* (334) 242-7100 (office). *Fax:* (334) 353-0004 (office). *Website:* governor.alabama.gov (office).

BENTON, Fletcher Chapman, II, BFA; American artist, painter, sculptor and academic; b. 25 Feb. 1931, Jackson, Ohio; m. Roberta Lee 1964; one s. one d.; ed Miami Univ.; mem. Faculty, Calif. Coll. of Arts and Crafts 1959, San Francisco Art Inst. 1964–67; Prof. of Art, Calif. State Univ., San Jose 1967–86; Hon. DFA (Miami Univ.) 1993, (Columbus Univ. of Rio Grande, Rio Grande, Ohio) 1994; American Acad. of Arts and Letters Award for Distinguished Service to the Arts 1979, President's Scholar Award, Calif. State Univ. San José 1980, San Francisco Arts Comm. Award of Honor for Outstanding Achievement in Sculpture 1982; Lifetime Achievement Award in Contemporary Sculpture, Int. Sculpture Center 2008, Distinguished Artist Alumni Award, School of Fine Arts and Dept of Art, Miami Univ. 2012. *Address:* Fletcher Benton Studio, 250 Dore Street, San Francisco, CA 94103, USA. *E-mail:* bstudio@penn.com (office). *Website:* www.fletcherbenton.com (office).

BENTON, Peter Faulkner, MA, CCMI; British science and economic consultant (retd); b. 6 Oct. 1934, London, England; s. of S. Faulkner Benton and Hilda Benton; m. Ruth S. Cobb 1959; two s. three d.; ed Oundle School, Queens' Coll. Cambridge; jr man. positions in Unilever, Shell Chemicals and Berger, Jenson and Nicholson 1959–64; consultant, McKinsey & Co., London and Chicago 1964–71; Dir Gallaher Ltd 1971–77, also Chair. subsidiaries; Man. Dir Post Office Telecommunications 1978–81; Deputy Chair. British Telecom 1981–83; Special Adviser to EEC 1983–84; Chair. European Practice, Nolan, Norton & Co. 1984–87, Enfield Dist Health Authority 1986–92; Vice-Pres. European Council of Man. 1989–92; Dir Singer & Friedlander Ltd 1983–89, Tandata Holdings PLC 1983–89, Turing Inst. 1985–95, Woodside Communications Ltd 1995–96; Dir Gen. British Inst. of Man. 1987–92; Chair. Enterprise Support Group 1993–96; Chair. Visiting Group Inst. for Systems, Eng and Informatics, Italy 1993–94, Visiting Group Inst. for Systems, Informatics and Safety, Italy 1996–99; Adviser to Arthur Andersen 1992–98; mem. Int. Advisory Bd for Science and Tech. to Govt of Portugal 1996–2002, Industrial Devt Advisory Bd (DTI) 1988–94; Adviser to Stern Stewart Inc. 1995–2001; gave lectures at Univ. of Pennsylvania 2002–05; mem. Exec. Cttee Athenaeum 1997–2002; Chair. Ditchley Conf. on Information Tech. 1980, North London Hospice 1985–89, World Bank Confs on Catastrophe 1988, 1989, Chair. Delhi Conf. on Indian Infrastructure 1998; Adam Smith Lecturer 1991; Pres. Highgate Literary and Scientific Inst. 1981–88; Treas. Harington Scheme, London 1983–93; Gov. Molecule Theatre, London 1985–91; Ind. mem. British Library Advisory Council 1988–93; IEE Award 1994. *Achievements include:* led reorganization of UK gas industry 1966–71. *Publication:* Riding the Whirlwind 1990. *Leisure interests:* reading, conversation, sailing, early music. *Address:* Northgate House, Highgate Hill, London, N6 5HD (home); Dolphins, Polruan-by-Fowey, Cornwall, PL23 1PP, England (home). *Telephone:* (20) 8341-1122 (London) (home).

BENYON, Margaret, MBE, PhD, BFA; British/Australian artist; b. 29 April 1940, Birmingham; m. William Rodwell 1974; one s. one d.; ed Kenya High School, Slade School of Fine Art, Univ. Coll. London, Royal Coll. of Art, London; Visiting Tutor, Coventry Coll. of Art 1966–68, Trent Polytechnic, Nottingham 1968–71; Holography Unit, RCA 1985–89; Fellow in Fine Art, Univ. of Nottingham 1968–71; Leverhulme Sr Art Fellow, Univ. of Strathclyde 1971–73; Co-ordinator Graphic Investigation, Canberra School of Art, Australia 1977–80; Creative Arts Fellow ANU, Canberra 1978; Artist-in-Residence, Museum of Holography, New York 1981, Center for Holographic Arts, New York 1999; Hon. Professorial Visiting Fellow, Coll. of Fine Arts, Univ. of NSW, Australia 2006–09; pioneered holography as an art medium 1968; works in public collections including Australian Nat. Gallery, Nat. Gallery of Vic., Australia, MIT Museum Boston, USA, Calouste Gulbenkian Foundation, Portugal, Victoria and Albert Museum, London; over 100 exhbns to date, including London, Vienna, New York, Frankfurt, Lisbon, Madrid, Nagoya, Liverpool, Bradford, Berlin, Boston, Tokyo, Australia; Hon. FRPS 2001; Audrey Mellon Prize 1964, Carnegie Trust Award 1972, Kodak Photographic Bursary 1982, Calouste Gulbenkian Holography Award 1982, Agfa 'Best of

Exhibition' Award (USA) 1985, Shearwater Foundation Holography Award (USA) 1987, Lifetime Achievement Award, Art in Holography International Symposium (UK) 1996, Shearwater Foundation Holography Purchase Award (USA) 2002. *Publications:* articles in more than 100 publs. *Address:* 18 Burra Close, Mount Colah, NSW 2079, Australia (office). *E-mail:* mbenyon@optusnet.com.au (office). *Website:* www.mbenyon.com (office).

BENZ, Edward J., Jr, MD, MA; American professor of medicine, paediatrics and pathology, physician and hospital administrator; *President and CEO, Dana-Farber Cancer Institute, Harvard University;* b. 22 May 1946, Pittsburgh; m. Margaret A. Vettese; one s. one d.; ed Allentown Cen. Catholic High School, Princeton Univ., Harvard Medical School, Yale Univ.; research fellowships at Princeton and Boston Univs 1967–71; Jr Asst Health Services Officer, US Public Health Service, NJH, NHLBI 1972–73, Sr Asst Surgeon 1973–75; intern, Peter Bent Brigham Hosp., Boston 1973–74, Asst Resident Physician 1974–75; Clinical Fellow, Harvard Medical School 1973–75; Fellow in Medicine (Hematology), Children's Hosp. Medical Center, Boston 1974–75; Research Assoc., Molecular Hematology Br. NHLBI, NIH, Bethesda, Md 1975–78; Fellow in Hematology, Yale Univ. School of Medicine 1978–80, Asst Prof. of Medicine, Hematology Section, Dept of Internal Medicine, Yale Univ. School of Medicine 1979–82, Assoc. Prof. of Medicine 1982–84, Assoc. Prof. of Human Genetics (Jt) 1983–87, Assoc. Prof. of Internal Medicine 1984–87, Prof. of Internal Medicine and Genetics 1987–93, Chief of Hematology Section, Dept of Internal Medicine 1987–93, Assoc. Chair. for Academic Affairs 1988–90, Vice-Chair. 1990–93, Assoc. Attending in Medicine Yale-New Haven Hosp. 1979–81, Attending Physician 1981–93; Jack D. Myers Prof. and Chair. Dept of Medicine, Univ. of Pittsburgh School of Medicine 1993–95, Prof. of Molecular Genetics and Biochemistry (Jt) 1993–95; Adjunct Prof. of Biological Sciences, Carnegie Mellon Univ., Pittsburgh 1993–95; Chief of Medicine Service, Univ. of Pittsburgh Medical Center 1993–95; Sir William Osler Prof. and Dir Dept of Medicine, Johns Hopkins Univ. School of Medicine 1995–2000, Prof. of Molecular Biology and Genetics 1995–2000, Physician-in-Chief Johns Hopkins Hosp. 1995–2000; Richard and Susan Smith Prof. of Medicine, Prof. of Pediatrics, Prof. of Pathology, Faculty Dean for Oncology, Harvard Medical School 2000–, Pres. and CEO Dana-Farber Cancer Inst., Harvard Univ. 2000–, CEO Dana-Farber/Partners Cancer Care 2000–, Dir Dana-Farber/Harvard Cancer Center, mem. Governing Bd Dana-Farber/Children's Center; Chair. Red Cells and Hemoglobin Sub-cttee, American Soc. of Hematology 1983, 1989, Molecular Genetics Educ. Panel 1984–87, Hematology I Study Section, NIH Research 1993–95; Pres. American Soc. of Clinical Investigation 1992, Scientific Affairs Cttee 1992, Educ. Program 1994; mem. Exec. Cttee American Soc. of Hematology 1994–, (Vice-Pres. 1998, Pres. 2000); mem. Scientific Advisory Bd Inst. of Molecular Medicine, Univ. of Oxford 1998, Cardiokine, Inc.; mem. AAAS Asscn of American Physicians, Inst. of Medicine; mem. Editorial Bd American Journal of Hematology 1985–, International Journal of Hematology, Tokyo 1990–99, American Journal of Medicine 1994–; Adviser in Medicine, Oxford University Press 1994–; Consulting Ed. Journal of Clinical Investigation 1998–; Assoc. Ed. New England Journal of Medicine 2001–; Fellow, American Asscn of Physicians 1992; Basil O'Connor Award, March of Dimes, Nat. Foundation 1980, NIH Research Career Devt Award 1982, Scientific Research Award, American Asscn of Blood Banks 1986, Inst. of Medicine Award and other awards. *Publications:* Molecular Genetics (Methods in Hematology series) (ed.) 1989, Hematology: Principles and Practice (jt ed.) 1990, Oxford Textbook of Medicine (co-ed.) 1997 and around 200 articles in professional journals. *Leisure interests:* tennis, reading, travel, hiking. *Address:* Office of the President, Dana-Farber Cancer Institute, Room D1628, 44 Binney Street, Boston, MA 02115 (office); 28 Chestnut Hill Terrace, Chestnut Hill, MA 02467, USA (home). *Telephone:* (617) 632-4266 (office); (617) 916-5345 (home). *Fax:* (617) 632-2161 (office); (617) 916-5681 (home). *E-mail:* edward_benz@dfci .harvard.edu (office); ebenz@comcast.net (home). *Website:* www.dana-farber.org (office).

BENZI, Roberto; Italian/French conductor; b. 12 Dec. 1937, Marseille, France; s. of the late Giuseppe Benzi and the late Maria Pastorino; m. Jane Rhodes 1966; ed Univ. of Paris (Sorbonne), France; studied conducting with Andre Cluytens; debut as conductor, France 1948; tours in Europe and S America 1949–52; opera conducting debut 1954; conducted Carmen, Paris Opera 1959, Faust, Met 1971–72; guest conductor Europe, Japan, China, Israel, Mexico, Canada, USA, S Africa and main music festivals; Music Dir Bordeaux-Aquitaine Orchestra 1973–87, Arnhem Philharmonic 1989–98, Dutch Nat. Youth Orchestra 1991–96; Chevalier, Légion d'honneur, Ordre Nat. du Mérite, Ordre des Palmes Académiques, Order of Orange-Nassau. *Publications:* orchestrations of Brahms op. 23 Schumann Variations 1970, Brahms op. 24 Variations and Fugue on a theme by Handel 1973, Rossini Prélude, Thème et Variations 1978, Erik Satie Je te veux, valse 1987. *Leisure interests:* wildlife, astronomy, cycling. *Address:* 12 Villa Ste-Foy, 92200 Neuilly-sur-Seine, France (home). *Telephone:* 1-46-24-27-85 (home). *Fax:* 1-46-24-55-73 (home). *Website:* robertobenzi.com.

BÉRARD, Jean-Luc; French business executive; *Human Resources Director, Safran;* b. 4 Dec. 1958; m.; two c.; began career as lawyer Groupement des Industries Métallurgiques d'Île de France 1983–86; Dir Groupe Esys-Montenay (Compagnie Générale des Eaux) 1986–92; Human Resources Dir Union Nationale pour l'Emploi dans l'Industrie et le Commerce (UNEDIC) (nat. unemployment insurance scheme) 1992–99, Dir-Gen. 2007–10; Human Resources Dir, Compagnie Air Liberté 1999–2000; Human Resources Dir, CEGETEL, Groupe Vivendi 2000–01; Human Resources Dir, Groupe AOM Air Liberté 2001; Labour Relations Dir Snecma Moteurs 2002–07; Human Resources Dir Safran 2010–. *Address:* Safran, 2, bd du Général Martial Valin, 75724 Paris Cedex 15, France (office). *Telephone:* 1-40-60-80-80 (office). *Fax:* 1-40-60-85-01 (office). *Website:* www.safran -group.com (office).

BERARDI, Antonio, BA; British fashion designer; b. 21 Dec. 1968, Grantham; ed Cen. St Martin's School of Art and Design; career launched when graduation collection was purchased by Liberty and A la Mode; first Spring/Summer own label collection also bought by Liberty and A la Mode 1995; designs featured in New Generation catwalk promotion sponsored by Marks and Spencer 1996; joined Italian Mfrs Givuesse 1996; launched Autumn/Winter label 1997; apptd design consultant Ruffo leather and suede mfrs 1997; Best New Designer, VHI Awards (USA) 1997. *Telephone:* (20) 7938-5007 (London) (office); (2) 87338749 (office).

E-mail: annika@tcs-uk.net (office); info@antonioberardi.com (office). *Address:* Show-Room Gibo-Co SpA, via Orobia 34, 20139 Milan, Italy (office); St Martin's House, 59 St Martin's Lane, London, WC2N 4JS, England. *Fax:* (2) 4801497 (office) . *Website:* www.antonioberardi.com.

BERARDI, Fabio, BSc; San Marino geologist and politician; b. 26 May 1959, Borgo Maggiore; m. Emanuele Bollini; two s.; ed Liceo Classico, Univ. of Bologna; began career with Sotecsa SA (Studio di Geologia Tecnica), San Marino 1984–86; mem. Council Borgo Maggiore 1984–89, 1995–98; Consultant, Studio Geotecnico Italiano, Milan 1986–89; pvt. practice as geologist 1989–95; Co-ordinator Dept of Territory, Environment and Agric. 1995–98; Pres. Admin. Council Azienda Autonoma di Stato per i Servizi Pubblici 1997–98; mem. Consiglio Grande Generale (Parl.) 1998–, Sec. of State for Territory, Environment and Agric. 2001–03, for Foreign and Political Affairs and Econ. Planning 2003–06, for Tourism and Relations with the Azienda Autonoma di Stato per i Servizi Pubblici (AASS) 2008–13; mem. Partito Socialista Sammarinese (PSS), mem. PSS Secr. 1999–; fmr Pres. Order of San Marino Geologists. *Address:* c/o Secretariat of State for Tourism, Palazzo del Turismo, Contrada Omagnano, 47890 San Marino, San Marino (office).

BERCA, Gabriel; Romanian politician; b. 6 Dec. 1968; m.; one c.; ed Polytechnic Univ. of Bucharest, Nat. Inst. of Admin (INA), Ecole Nat. d'Admin, Paris, France, Univ. 'Gheorghe Asachi', Iaşi; Design Engineer, Industrial Valves SA SC 1995–2000; Dir of Marketing, Monitor Bacau 2000–01; Dir of Sales, SC Prod Cressus SA 2001–04; Adviser to Gen. Dir of SC CET SA Oct.–Nov. 2004; Dir Public Social Services, Municipality of Bacau June–Sept. 2004; Prefect, Pref., Bacau Co. 2005–08; Sec. Gen. of Govt March–Sept. 2008; Sec. of State, SGG Sept. 2008–11; Minister of Admin and the Interior 2012; Vice-Pres. Bacau Br., Red Cross 2007–; mem. Bd responsible for the North-East, Asscn of Prefects and Deputy Prefects of Romania 2007–; mem. competition for recruitment of sr civil servants 2008–; Hon. mem. academic community 'George Bacovia' 2005, Senate's 'George Bacovia' 2005. *Address:* c/o Ministry of Administration and the Interior, 010086 Bucharest 1, Piaţa Revoluţiei 1A, Romania. *E-mail:* gabriel.berca@gov.ro (office).

BERDIYEV, Maj.-Gen. Qobul Raimovich; Uzbekistani army officer and government official; *Minister of Defence;* Deputy Minister of Defence and Commdr, SW Special Mil. Dist–Sept. 2008, Minister of Defence Sept. 2008–. *Address:* Ministry of Defence, 100000 Tashkent, Ak. Abdullaev ko'ch. 100, Uzbekistan (office). *Telephone:* (71) 269-82-43 (office). *Fax:* (71) 269-82-28 (office).

BERDYMUHAMEDOV, Gurbanguly Myalikgulyyevich, PhD; Turkmenistani politician, head of state and fmr dentist; *President and Chairman of the Government;* b. 29 June 1957, Babarab, Ahal Prov.; ed Turkmen State Medical Inst.; mem. Dentistry Faculty, Turkmen State Medical Inst. 1979–97, Assoc. Prof. and Dean 1995–97; Head of Dentistry Centre, Ministry of Health 1995–97; Minister of Health 1997–2001; Deputy Prime Minister 2001–07; Acting Pres. (following death of Saparmyrat Niyazov) 2006–07, Pres. and Chair. of the Govt 2007–; Chair. Nat. Olympic Cttee 2007–; Second Chair. Democratic Party of Turkmenistan 2006–13 (Acting Chair. 2006–07); Ind. 2013–. *Address:* Office of the President and the Council of Ministers, 744000 Aşgabat, Galkynyş köç. 20, Turkmenistan (office). *Telephone:* (12) 35-45-34 (office). *Fax:* (12) 35-51-12 (office). *E-mail:* nt@online.tm (office). *Website:* www.turkmenistan.gov.tm (office).

BERDYYEV, Yilym; Turkmenistani politician; *Minister of National Security;* b. Baharly dist, Ahal Velayat; ed Turkmenistani Agricultural Univ.; worked in Man. Cttee of Nat. Security in Ahal Velayat 1995–2003; Sr Insp. in State Service for Registration of Foreign Citizens, Deputy Head of Dept in Aşgabat City, then Deputy Head of State Service for Registration of Foreign Citizens 2003–06, Chair. State Service for Registration of Foreign Citizens and Head of Analytical Dept of Law Enforcement and Mil. Organs of the Presidential Apparatus 2006–08; Head of State Migration Service May–June 2008, of State Customs Service 2008–09; Minister of Defence and Sec. of State Security Council 2009–11; Minister of Nat. Security 2011–. *Address:* Ministry of National Security, 744000 Aşgabat, Magtymguly Şaýoly 93, Turkmenistan (office). *Telephone:* (12) 39-71-58 (office).

BEREND, T. Ivan, PhD, DEcon; American (b. Hungarian) economic historian and academic; *Professor of History, University of California, Los Angeles;* b. 11 Dec. 1930, Budapest, Hungary; s. of Mihály Berend and Elvira Gellei; two d.; ed Univ. of Economics and Eötvös Loránd Univ. of Sciences, Faculty of Philosophy, Budapest; Asst Lecturer, Karl Marx Univ. of Economics 1953, Sr Lecturer 1960, Prof. of Econ. History 1964–, Head of Dept 1967–85, Rector 1973–79; Prof. of History, UCLA 1990–, Dir Center for European and Eurasian Studies 1993–2005, Chair. European Studies Interdepartmental Program 2008–10; Gen. Sec. Hungarian Historical Soc. 1966–72, Pres. 1975–79; Corresp. mem. Hungarian Acad. of Sciences 1973–79, mem. 1979–, Pres. 1985–90; Fellowship, Ford Foundation, New York 1966–67; Visiting Fellow, St Antony's Coll. Oxford, UK 1972–73, All Souls Coll. Oxford 1980; Visiting Prof., Univ. of California, Berkeley 1978; Fellow, Woodrow Wilson Int. Center for Scholars, Washington, DC 1982–83; Co-Chair. Inst. for East-West Security Studies 1986; mem. Exec. Cttee of Int. Econ. History Soc. 1982–86, Vice-Pres. 1986–1994; First Vice-Pres. Int. Cttee of Historical Sciences 1990–95, Pres. 1995–2000; Corresp. mem. Royal Historical Soc. 1981, Academia Europaea 1987, Bulgarian Acad. of Sciences 1988, British Acad. 1989, Austrian Acad. of Sciences 1989, Czechoslovak Acad. of Sciences 1989; Hon. mem. Portuguese Asscn of Int. Relations 1996; Hon. DLitt (St John's Univ., New York) 1986, (Glasgow) 1990, (Janus Pannonius Univ., Pécs) 1994; Kossuth Prize 1961, State Prize 1985, Konstantin Jireček Gold Medal, Suedosteuropa Gesellschaft 2005. *Publications:* (with György Ránki): Magyarország gyáripara 1900–1914 1955, Magyarország gyáripara a II. világháboru elött és a háboru idöszakában 1933–1944 1958, Magyarország a fasiszta Németország "életterében" 1960, Magyarország gazdasága az I. világháboru után 1919–1929 1966, Economic Development in East-Central Europe in the 19th and 20th Centuries 1974, Hungary—A Century of Economic Development, Underdevelopment and Economic Growth, The European Periphery and Industrialization 1780–1914 1982, The Hungarian Economy in the Twentieth Century 1985, The European Economy in the Nineteenth Century 1987; (as sole author): Ujjáépités és a nagytöke elleni harc Magyarországon 1945–1948 1962, Gazdaságpolitika az elsö ötéves terv meginditásakor 1948–1950 1964, Öt elöadás gazdaságról és oktatásról 1978, Napjaink a történelemben 1980, Válságos évtizedek 1982, Gazdasági utkeresés

1983, The Crisis Zone of Europe 1986, Szocializmus és reform 1986, The Hungarian Economic Reforms 1990, Central and Eastern Europe 1944–93 – Detour from the Periphery to the Periphery 1996, Decades of Crisis: Central and Eastern Europe Before World War II 1998, History Derailed: Central and Eastern Europe in the 'Long' 19th Century 2003, An Economic History of 20th Century Europe 2006, From the Soviet Bloc to the European Union: The Economic and Social Transformation of Central and Eastern Europe since 1973 2009, History in My Life – A Memoir in Three Eras 2009, Europe Since 1980 2010. *Leisure interests:* walking, swimming. *Address:* Department of History, UCLA, 6265 Bunche Hall, Box 951473, Los Angeles, CA 90095-1473, USA (office). *Telephone:* (310) 825-1178 (office). *Fax:* (310) 206-3556 (office); (310) 247-9844 (home). *E-mail:* iberend@history.ucla.edu (office). *Website:* www.history.ucla.edu/berend (office).

BERENDT, John, BA; American writer and journalist; b. (John Lawrence Berendt), 5 Dec. 1939, Syracuse, NY; s. of Ralph Berendt and Carol Berendt (née Descher); ed Nottingham High School, Syracuse, NY and Harvard Univ., Cambridge, Mass; Assoc. Ed. Esquire 1961–69, columnist 1982–94; Ed. New York magazine 1977–79; freelance writer 1979–; mem. PEN, The Century Asscn. *Publications:* Midnight in the Garden of Good and Evil (Southern Book Award for Non-fiction) 1994, The City of Falling Angels 2005. *Address:* c/o Suzanne Gluck, William Morris Agency, 1325 Avenue of the Americas, New York, NY 10019, USA (office); c/o Hodder & Stoughton, 338 Euston Road, London, NW1 3BH, England. *Telephone:* (212) 903-1169 (office); (20) 7873-6000. *E-mail:* sgluck@wmeentertainment.com (office).

BÉRENGER, Paul Raymond, BA; Mauritian politician; b. 26 March 1945, Quatre Bornes; m. Arline Perrier 1971; one s. one d.; ed Collège du Saint Esprit, Univ. of Wales, UK, Univ. of Paris (Sorbonne), France; Gen. Sec. Mouvement Militant Mauricien 1969–82, Leader 1983–2013; MP 1976–87, 1991–; Minister of Finance 1982–83, of Foreign Affairs 1991; Deputy Prime Minister and Minister of Foreign Affairs and Int. and Regional Co-operation 1995; Deputy Prime Minister and Minister of Finance Sept. 2000–03; Prime Minister, Minister of Defence and Home Affairs and of External Communications Sept. 2003–05; Gov. IMF, African Devt Bank/African Devt Fund. *Leisure interests:* reading, swimming. *Address:* c/o Mouvement Militant Mauricien, 21 Poudrière Street, Port Louis, Mauritius.

BERENGER, Tom; American actor; b. (Thomas Michael Moore), 31 May 1950, Chicago, Ill.; m. 1st Barbara Wilson 1976 (divorced 1984); m. 2nd Lisa Williams 1986 (divorced 1997); m. 3rd Patricia Alvaran 1998; one s. five d.; ed Univ. of Missouri; stage appearances in regional theatre and off-Broadway including The Rose Tattoo, Electra, A Streetcar Named Desire, End as a Man. *Films include:* Beyond the Door 1975, Sentinel, Looking for Mr Goodbar, In Praise of Older Women, Butch and Sundance: The Early Days, The Dogs of War, The Big Chill, Eddie and the Cruisers, Fear City, Firstborn, Rustler's Rhapsody, Platoon, Someone to Watch Over Me, Shoot to Kill, Betrayed, Last Rites, Major League, Love at Large, The Field, Shattered, Chasers, Sniper 1993, Sliver 1993, Major League 2 1994, Last of the Dogmen 1994, Gettysburg 1994, The Substitute 1996, An Occasional Hell 1996, The Gingerbread Man 1997, Takedown 2000, One Man's Hero (also producer) 1999, Diplomatic Siege 1999, A Murder of Crows 1999, The Hollywood Sign 2000, Fear of Flying 2000, Training Day 2001, Watchtower 2001, Eye See You 2001, D-Tox 2002, Sniper 2 2002, Sniper 3 2004, The Christmas Miracle of Jonathan Toomey 2007, Stiletto 2008, Charlie Valentine 2009, Breaking Point 2009, Silent Venom (video) 2009, Smokin' Aces 2: Assassins' Ball (video) 2010, Sinners & Saints 2010, Last Will 2010, Firedog 2010, Inception 2010, Faster 2010, War Flowers 2011, Last Will 2012, Quad 2013. *Television includes:* One Life to Live (series), Johnny We Hardly Knew Ye, Flesh and Blood, If Tomorrow Comes, Johnson County War 2002, Junction Boys 2002, Sniper 2 2002, Peacemakers 2003, Capital City 2004, The Detective 2005, Into the West (miniseries) 2005, Amy Coyne 2006, Nightmares and Dreamscapes: From the Stories of Stephen King (miniseries) 2006, October Road (series) 2006–07, Desperate Hours: An Amber Alert (film) 2008, XIII: The Series (series) 2011, Hatfields & McCoys (mini-series) (Emmy Award for Supporting Actor in a Miniseries or Movie 2012) 2012. *Address:* c/o ICM, 10250 Constellation Boulevard, Los Angeles, CA 90067, USA.

BERENGO GARDIN, Gianni; Italian photographer; b. 10 Oct. 1930, Santa Margherita Ligure; s. of Alberto Berengo Gardin and Carmen Maffei Berengo Gardin; m. Caterina Stiffoni 1957; one s. one d.; began working as photographer 1954; has lived and worked in Switzerland, Rome, Venice; living in Milan 1965–; photographs originally published by Il Mondo magazine, now published by major magazines in Italy and world-wide; photographs in perm. collections of Museum of Modern Art, New York, Bibliothèque Nationale Paris, Eastman House, Rochester, NY, Musée de l'Elysée, Lausanne, Museum of Aesthetic Art, Beijing, Maison Européene de la Photographie, Paris; Mois de la Photo Brassaï Award, Paris 1990, Leica Oskar Barnack Award, Arles 1995, Oscar Goldoni Award 1998, Werner Biscof Award 2006, Award for Lifetime Achievement, Lucie Awards 2008. *Publications:* over 210 photographic books. *Leisure interests:* photography, farming, his little dog Nina. *Address:* Via S. Michele del Carso 21, 20144 Milan, Italy (home). *Telephone:* (02) 4692877. *Fax:* (02) 4692877.

BERESFORD, Bruce; Australian film director; b. 16 Aug. 1940, Sydney; s. of Leslie Beresford and Lona Beresford; m. 1st Rhoisin Beresford 1965; two s. one d.; m. 2nd Virginia Duigan 1989; one d.; ed Univ. of Sydney; worked in advertising; worked for Australian Broadcasting Comm.; went to England 1961; worked in odd jobs including teaching; film ed. Nigeria 1964–66; Sec. to British Film Inst.'s Production Bd 1966–71. *Films directed:* The Adventures of Barry Mackenzie 1972, Barry Mackenzie Holds His Own 1974, Side by Side 1975, Don's Party (Australian Film Inst. Award 1976) 1976, The Getting of Wisdom 1977, Money Movers 1979, Breaker Morant (Australian Film Inst. Award 1980) 1980, Puberty Blues 1981, The Club 1981, Tender Mercies 1983, King David 1984, Crimes of the Heart 1986, Fringe Dwellers 1986, Aria (segment) 1987, Her Alibi 1988, Driving Miss Daisy 1989 (Acad. Award Best Film 1990), Mr. Johnson 1990, Black Robe (Canadian Film Acad. Awards 1990) 1990, Rich in Love 1993, A Good Man in Africa 1993, Silent Fall 1994, The Last Dance 1995, Paradise Road 1996, Double Jeopardy 1998, Rigoletto (opera) 2000, Bride of the Wind 2001, Evelyn 2002, The Contract 2006, Mao's Last Dancer 2009, Peace, Love and Misunderstanding 2011. *Television includes:* And Starring Pancho Villa as Himself 2003, Orpheus 2006. *Publications include:* Josh Hartnett Definitely Wants to Do This: True Stories from a Life in the Screen Trade 2007. *Address:* c/o Anthony A. Williams, P.O. Box 1379, Darlinghurst, NSW 2010, Australia. *Website:* bruceberesford.org (office).

BEREZOVSKY, Boris Vadimovich; Russian pianist; b. 4 Jan. 1969, Moscow; three c.; ed Moscow Conservatoire; London début Wigmore Hall 1988; appeared with Soviet Festival Orchestra, London 1990; recitals in New York, Washington, London, Amsterdam, Salzburg, Moscow, Leningrad, Tokyo, Osaka, etc.; appearances with orchestras including Philharmonia, New York Philharmonic, Philadelphia Orchestra, NDR Hamburg and Danish Nat. Radio Symphony Orchestra; winner Prize of Hope competition, City of Ufa 1985, Gold Medal, Int. Tchaikovsky Piano Competition, Moscow 1990. *Recordings:* numerous recordings including Chopin Godowsky Etudes 2005. *Website:* www.askonasholt.co.uk/artists/instrumentalists/piano/boris-berezovsky.

BERG, Christian, DPhil; Danish mathematician and academic; *Professor of Mathematics, University of Copenhagen;* b. 2 June 1944, Haarslev; m. Margrete Vergmann 1967; one s. one d.; ed Univ. of Copenhagen; Assoc. Prof., Univ. of Copenhagen 1972, Prof. of Math. 1978–, Chair. Math. Dept 1996–97, Dir Inst. for Math. Sciences 1997–2002; Pres. Danish Mathematical Soc. 1994–98; mem. Danish Natural Sciences Research Council 1985–92, Royal Danish Acad. of Sciences and Letters 1982– (Vice-Pres. 1999–2005); Univ. of Copenhagen Gold Medal 1970. *Publications:* research monographs: Potential Theory on Locally Compact Abelian Groups (with Forst) 1975, Harmonic Analysis on Semigroups (with Christensen and Ressel) 1984, research papers on potential theory and mathematical analysis. *Address:* Department of Mathematical Sciences, Universitetsparken 5, 2100 Copenhagen Ø, Denmark (office). *Telephone:* 35-32-07-25 (office). *Fax:* 35-32-95-55 (office). *E-mail:* berg@math.ku.dk (office). *Website:* www.math.ku.dk/~berg (office).

BERG, Eivinn; Norwegian diplomatist; b. 31 July 1931, Oslo; s. of Morten Berg and Ester Christoffersen; m. Unni Berg 1957; one s. two d.; ed Norwegian Coll. of Econs and Business Admin., Bergen; entered Foreign Service 1957, Attaché and Vice-Consul, Washington, DC and Chicago, USA 1957–60, with Ministry of Foreign Affairs 1960–63, 1968–70, First Sec., Norwegian Perm. Del. to EFTA/GATT, UN Office, Geneva 1963–66, Head of Dept, EFTA 1966–68, Counsellor, Embassy in Brussels and Mission to EEC 1970–73; Dir Int. Affairs, Norwegian Shipowners Asscn, Oslo 1973–78; Deputy Dir-Gen. Ministry of Foreign Affairs, Dept of External Econ. Affairs 1978–80, Dir-Gen. 1980–81, State Sec., Ministry of Foreign Affairs 1984–88, Amb. and Perm. Rep. of Norway to NATO, Brussels 1984–89, to European Union 1989–96; Chief Negotiator, European Economic Area 1990–92, for proposed accession of Norway to EU 1993–94, for Schengen Agreement 1995–96; Sr Adviser on int. and European affairs to Statoil, Norske Skog, Statkraft; Commdr, Order of the Crown (Belgium) 1974, Commdr, Henrique Infante (Portugal) 1980, Caballero Gran Cruz al Mérito Civil (Spain) 1982, Grand Lion Order of the Lion (Finland) 1983, Grand Officier, Order nat. du Mérite 1984, Commdr, Royal Order of St Olav 1987. *Leisure interests:* golf, sailing, mountain hiking. *Address:* Aasstubben 64, 0381 Oslo, Norway (home). *Telephone:* 22-52-50-08 (home). *Fax:* 22-52-51-88 (home). *E-mail:* eivinnbe@online.no (office).

BERG, Jeffrey (Jeff) Spencer, MA; American arts management agent; *Chairman and CEO, International Creative Management, Inc.;* b. 26 May 1947, LA; m. Denise Lura 1981; ed Univ. of California, Berkeley, Univ. of Southern California; fmrly Head of Literature Div., Creative Management Assocs, fmrly Vice-Pres.; Vice-Pres. Motion Picture Dept, Int. Creative Man. Inc. 1975–80, Pres. 1980–85, Chair. and CEO 1985–; fmr Co-Chair. California's Council on Information Technology; mem. Bd of Dirs Oracle Corpn 1997–, Leapfrog Enterprises, Inc., Josephson International Inc., Marshall McLuhan Center of Global Communication; Pres. Letters and Science Exec. Bd Univ. of Calif., Berkeley; Trustee, UCLA Anderson School of Man. *Address:* International Creative Management Inc., 10250 Constellation Boulevard, Los Angeles, CA 90067, USA (office). *Telephone:* (310) 550-4000 (office). *Fax:* (310) 550-4100 (office). *Website:* www.icmtalent.com (office).

BERG, Paul, PhD, FAAS; American biochemist and academic; *Professor Emeritus, Department of Biochemistry, Stanford University;* b. 30 June 1926, New York; s. of Harry Berg and Sarah Brodsky; m. Mildred Levy 1947; one s.; ed Pennsylvania State Univ. and Case Western Reserve Univ.; Postdoctoral Fellow, Copenhagen Univ., Denmark 1952–53; Postdoctoral Fellow, Wash. Univ., St Louis, Mo. 1953–54; Scholar in Cancer Research 1954–57; Asst to Assoc. Prof. of Microbiology 1955–59; Prof. of Biochemistry, Stanford Univ. School of Medicine 1959, Willson Prof. of Biochemistry 1970–94, Chair. of Dept 1969–74, Dir Beckman Center for Molecular and Genetic Medicine 1985–2001, Robert W.and Vivian K. Cahill Prof. of Cancer Research 1994–2000, Prof. Emer., Dept of Biochemistry 2000–; Dir Nat. Biomedical Research Foundation 1994–; Pres. American Soc. of Biological Chemists 1974–75; Chair. Nat. Advisory Cttee Human Genome Project 1990–92; Chair. Scientific Advisory Bd Beckman Foundation; currently Chair. Bd of Advisory Scientists, Whitehead Inst., MIT; Sr Post-Doctoral Fellow, NSF 1961–68; Non-resident Fellow, Salk Inst. 1973–83; Foreign mem. Académie des Sciences, France 1981, Royal Soc., London 1992; mem. Inst. of Medicine, NAS; Hon. mem. Alpha Omega Alpha Honor Medical Soc. 1992; Dr hc (Washington Univ.) 1986, (Pennsylvania State Univ.) 1995; Eli Lilly Prize in Biochemistry 1959, Calif. Scientist of the Year 1963, V. D. Mattia Award 1972, Nobel Prize for Chem. (jtly) 1980, Nat. Medal of Science 1983 and other awards and prizes. *Publications:* Genes and Genomes 1991, Dealing with Genes. The Language of Heredity 1992, Exploring Genetic Mechanisms 1997. *Leisure interests:* travel, art and sports. *Address:* c/o Stanford University School of Medicine, Department of Biochemistry, MC: 5307, Beckman Center, B400, 279 West Campus Drive, Stanford, CA 94305, USA (office). *Website:* berg-emeritusprofessor.stanford.edu (office).

BERGANT, Boris; Slovenian journalist and broadcasting executive; *Senior Consultant, European Broadcasting Union;* b. 19 April 1948, Maribor; s. of Evgen Bergant and Marija Bergant; m. Verena Bergant 1969; one s.; ed Univ. of Ljubljana, Kenyon Coll., USA; fmrly Ed. Foreign Affairs, Ed.-in-Chief of News TV Slovenia; fmr radio journalist; fmr Deputy Dir-Gen., Int. Relations and Programme Cooperation, RTV Slovenia, Deputy Dir-Gen. RTV Slovenia 1992–2006, Adviser to Dir-Gen. for Int. Relations and Projects 2006; mem. Asscn of Journalists of Slovenia (Pres. 1987–91); CIRCOM Regional (Pres. 1990–92, Sec.-Gen. 1993–); mem. Admin. Council, European Broadcasting Union (EBU) 1990–92, 1996–, Vice-Chair. TV Programme Cttee 1993–98, mem. Radio Cttee 1993, Vice-Pres. EBU 1999–2009, Sr Consultant 2012–; Pres. South East Europe Media Org. (SEEMO), Vienna 2009–12; mem. European Inst. for the Media; Tomšičeva Nagrada Prize for Best Journalistic Achievement in Slovenia, Awards at Monte Carlo, New York and Leipzig TV festivals. *Leisure interests:* tennis, golf. *Address:* BorBER Media Activities, Abramova ulica 8, 1000 Ljubljana (office); Abramova Ulica 8, 1000 Ljubljana, Slovenia (home). *Telephone:* 41-641877 (mobile) (office); (1) 256-15-58 (home). *Fax:* (1) 256-15-59 (home). *E-mail:* boris.bergant@borber.si (office); bergantb@siol.net (home).

BERGANZA, Teresa; Spanish singer (mezzo-soprano); b. 16 March 1933, Madrid; d. of Guillermo Berganza and Ascensión Berganza; m. 1st Felix Lavilla 1957; one s. two d.; m. 2nd José Rifa 1986; debut in Aix-en-Provence 1957, in UK at Glyndebourne 1958; has sung at La Scala, Milan, Opera Rome, Metropolitan, New York, Chicago Opera House, San Francisco Opera, Covent Garden, etc.; has appeared at festivals in Edinburgh, the Netherlands, Glyndebourne; concerts in France, Belgium, the Netherlands, Italy, Germany, Spain, Austria, Portugal, Scandinavia, Israel, Mexico, Buenos Aires, USA, Canada, etc.; appeared as Rosina in Il Barbiere di Siviglia, Covent Garden 1967; sung Carmen, at opening ceremony of Expo 92, Seville, also at opening ceremonies of Barcelona Olympics 1992; mem. Real Academia de Bellas Artes de San Fernando, Spanish Royal Acad. of Arts 1994; Grande Cruz, Isabel la Católica, Commdr, Ordre des Arts et des Lettres; Premio Lucrezia Arana, Premio Extraordinario del Conservatorio de Madrid, Harriet Cohen Award, Int. Critic Award 1988, Grand Prix du Disque (six times), Grand Prix Rossini. *Films include:* The Barber of Seville 1972, Don Giovanni 1979, Werther 1980, Carmen 1980. *Publication:* Flor de Soledad y Silencio 1984. *Leisure interests:* art, music, reading. *Address:* c/o Javier Lavilla, Apartado 118, 28200 San Lorenzo del Escorial, Madrid, Spain (office). *Telephone:* (67) 0237485 (office). *Fax:* (67) 0237489 (office). *E-mail:* info@teresaberganza.com (office). *Website:* www.teresaberganza.com.

BERGARA DUQUE, Mario Esteban, MEconSc, PhD; Uruguayan economist, accountant and central banker; *Minister of Economy and Finance;* b. 4 May 1965, Montevideo; ed Univ. de la República Oriental del Uruguay, Univ. of California, Berkeley, USA; began career with Banco de la República Oriental del Uruguay; Head, Dept of Econ. Studies, Banco Central del Uruguay 1998–2001, Pres. 2008–13; Vice-Minister of Economy and Finance 2005–08, Minister of Economy and Finance 2013–; mem. Bd Communication Services Regulatory Agency 2001–05; fmr Prof., Univ. of the Repub. and Univ. ORT Uruguay; fmr mem. Partido Comunista de Uruguay. *Address:* Ministry of Economy and Finance, Colonia 1089, 3°, 11100 Montevideo, Uruguay (office). *Telephone:* (2) 7122910 (office). *Fax:* (2) 7122919 (office). *E-mail:* seprimef@mef.gub.uy (office). *Website:* www.mef.gub.uy (office).

BERGARECHE BUSQUET, Santiago, LicenDer; Spanish business executive; *Non-Executive Chairman, Compañía Española de Petróleos SA (CEPSA);* ed Univ. of Deusto, Bilbao; held several man. positions until becoming Gen. Man. and mem. Exec. Man. Cttee BBVA, apptd Chair. Metrovacesa; Chair. Agromán (following acquisition by Ferrovial Group), later Chair. Ferrovial, subsequently CEO, currently ind. Vice-Chair. Ferrovial Group, mem. Bd of Dirs Gamesa and Vocento and Chair. (non-exec.) Dinamia Ferrovial Group; Chair. (non-exec.) Compañía Española de Petróleos SA (CEPSA) 2008–. *Address:* Compañía Española de Petróleos SA, Campo de las Naciones, Avenida del Partenón 12, 28042 Madrid, Spain (office). *Telephone:* (91) 3376000 (office). *Fax:* (91) 7211613 (office). *E-mail:* webcepsa@cepsa.com (office). *Website:* www.cepsa.com (office).

BERGÉ, Pierre Vital Georges; French business executive; *CEO, Fondation Pierre Bergé Yves Saint Laurent;* b. 14 Nov. 1930, l'Île d'Oléron; s. of Pierre Bergé and Christiane Bergé (née Sicard); ed Lycée Eugène-Fromentin, La Rochelle; Dir and Ed.-in-Chief La Patrie Mondiale 1949–61; Co-founder and Dir-Gen. Yves Saint Laurent 1961, Pres. 1971–2002, Pres. Dir-Gen. Yves Saint Laurent of America Inc., New York 1971–2002, Pres., Dir-Gen. Yves Saint Laurent Parfums (merged with Elf-Sanofi) 1987–93; co-f. and CEO Fondation Pierre Bergé Yves Saint Laurent 2002–; Pres. Pierre Bergé & Associés; became majority shareholder of Le Monde group and apptd Pres. of Supervisory Cttee 2010; Chair. Asscn of Theatres of the Paris Opera 1988–94, Hon. Pres. 1994–; Pres. Chambre Syndicale du Prêt-à-Porter des Couturiers et des Créateurs de Mode 1988–93; Goodwill Amb. for UNESCO 1993; Dir Lundis Musicaux de l'Athénée 1977; Admin., Cttee for the Devt and Promotion of Textile and Design, Fondation Cartier Parsons School of Design 1985–, Pres. 1991–; Pres. Inst. Français de la Mode 1985–; Pres. Asscn des Amis de l'Institut François Mitterrand 1999–, Médiathèque Musicale Mahler 2000–; Commdr, Légion d'honneur, des Arts et des Lettres, Officier, Ordre Nat. du mérite, Order of Orange-Nassau (Netherlands). *Publications include:* Bernard Buffet 1957, Liberté, j'écris ton nom 1991, l'Affaire Clovis 1996, l'Inventaire Mitterrand 2001, Les jours s'en vont je demeure 2003, Album Cocteau 2006, Lettres à Yves 2010. *Leisure interest:* modern art. *Address:* Pierre Bergé & Associés, 92, avenue d'Iéna, 75116 Paris; Fondation Pierre Bergé Yves Saint Laurent, 5 avenue Marceau, 75116 Paris (office); 5 rue Bonaparte, 75006 Paris, France (home). *E-mail:* p.berge@fondation-pb-ysl.net (office). *Website:* www.fondation-pb-ysl.net (office); www.pba-auctions.com (office).

BERGEN, André, MEconSc; Belgian banking executive; b. 1950, Sint-Truiden; ed Univ. of Louvain; joined Econs Research Dept, Kredietbank NV 1977, Foreign Exchange and Treasury Dept, Kredietbank, NY 1979; with Foreign Exchange Advisory Service, Chemical Bank, NY 1980–82; joined Generale Bank, Belgium 1982, mem. Exec. Cttee, Generale (Fortis) Bank 1993–2000; Vice-Pres., Chief Financial and Admin. Officer, Agfa-Gevaert NV, Belgium 2000–01, Deputy Chair. Man. Bd 2001–03; CEO KBC Bank 2003–09, Deputy CEO KBC Group 2003–05, Man. Dir and Deputy CEO 2005–06, Pres. Exec. Cttee, Exec. Dir and Group CEO KBC Group 2006–09, mem. Agenda Cttee, Nomination Cttee, mem. Bd Dirs KBC Bank, KBC Insurance; mem. Bd Dirs NYSE Euronext NV; mem. Flemish Architecture Inst. *Address:* c/o NYSE Euronext NV, Beursplein 5, 1000 GD, Amsterdam, The Netherlands (office). *Telephone:* (20) 550-4444 (office). *Fax:* (20) 550-4900 (office). *Website:* www.nyse.com (office).

BERGEN, Candice Patricia; American actress and photojournalist; b. 9 May 1946, Beverly Hills; d. of Edgar Bergen and Frances Bergen (née Westerman); m. 1st Louis Malle 1980 (died 1995); one d.; m. 2nd Marshall Rose 2000; ed Westlake School for Girls, Univ. of Pennsylvania; photojournalist work has appeared in

Vogue, Cosmopolitan, Life and Esquire. *Films include:* The Group 1966, The Sand Pebbles 1966, The Day the Fish Came Out 1967, Vivre Pour Vivre 1967, The Magus 1968, Getting Straight 1970, Soldier Blue 1970, The Adventurers 1970, Carnal Knowledge 1971, The Hunting Party 1971, T. R. Baskin 1972, 11 Harrowhouse 1974, Bite the Bullet 1975, The Wind and the Lion 1976, The Domino Principle 1977, A Night Full of Rain 1977, Oliver's Story, 1978, Starting Over 1979, Rich and Famous 1981, Gandhi 1982, Stick 1985, Au Revoir les Enfants (Co-Dir) 1987, Miss Congeniality 2000, Sweet Home Alabama 2002, View from the Top 2003, The In-Laws 2003, Sex and the City 2008, The Women 2008, Bride Wars 2009, The Romantics 2010. *Television appearances include:* Murphy Brown (series) (Emmy Award 1989, 1990) 1988–98, Mary and Tim 1996, Footsteps 2003, Boston Legal (series) 2005–07, House (series) 2011. *Publications:* The Freezer (in Best Short Plays of 1968), Knock Wood (autobiog.) 1984. *Address:* c/o WME, 9601 Wilshire Blvd, Beverly Hills, CA 90210, USA.

BERGEN SCHMIDT, Ernst Ferdinand; Paraguayan government official and business executive; b. 5 Oct. 1963, Colonia Fernheim (Chaco paraguayo); m. Lucía Ruth Giesbrecht; three c.; has held positions with Tecnoservice SAECA, Inverfin SAECA, Century System SRL, IMAG SRL, Mercotec SRL; fmr Pres. Récord Electric; Minister of Industry and Commerce –2005, of Finance 2005–07, Econ. Adviser to Pres. of Paraguay 2007–. *Address:* Office of the President, Asunción, Paraguay.

BERGER, Albert, LLB; German lawyer and university administrator; *Chancellor, Technische Universität München (TUM);* b. 1962, Munich; ed Ludwig-Maximilians-Universität, Munich; civil servant, Legal Div., Munich Regional High Court 1989–92; Lecturer, Deutsche Privat Finanzakademie AG 1991–92; Prof. of Public Law, Inst. of Law, Armed Forces Univ., Munich 1992–93; lawyer in Personnel and Org. Div., Technischen Universität München (TUM) 1994–95, Head of Personnel Div. 1995–98, Admin Dir Weihenstephan Life and Food Sciences Centre 1998–2003, Chancellor Technische Universität München (TUM) 2006–; Chancellor Rosenheim Univ. of Applied Science 2003–06; Deputy Nat. . Spokesman, Kanzlerinnen und Kanzler der Universitäten Deutschlands 2009–12, Nat. Spokesman 2012–. *Address:* Office of the Chancellor, Technische Universität München, Arcisstrasse 21, 80333 Munich, Germany (office). *Telephone:* (89) 289-01 (office). *Fax:* (89) 289-22000 (office). *E-mail:* eckenweber@zv.tum.de (office). *Website:* portal.mytum.de (office).

BERGER, Geneviève, PhD, MD; French physician, medical researcher and academic; *Chief Research and Development Officer, Unilever PLC;* b. 1955, Moselle; ed Ecole Normale Supérieure, Cachan, Univ. of Paris VI-Pierre et Marie Curie, Univ. of Paris V-René Descartes; mem. Scientific Bd Dept of Eng, CNRS 1991–98, Scientific Sec., Treatment and Drugs, Design and Resources Section, CNRS Nat. Cttee Scientific Research 1991–95, Chair. 1995–98, Founder and Researcher Parametric Imaging Lab. 1991–, Dir 1991–2000; Dir-Gen. CNRS 2000–03; Prof. and Hosp. MD, Univ. of Paris VI-Pierre et Marie Curie 1996–2008; Head, Dept Biophysics and Nuclear Medicine, Hôtel-Dieu Hosp. 1997–2000; Dir Dept of Bio-Eng, Drugs and Agri-Food, Ministry of Educ., Research and Tech. 1998–2000; Pres. Consultative Cttee Tech. Devt 1999–2000; Pres. Bd of Dirs CNRS Diffusion Soc. 2000–03, INIST-Diffusion Soc. 2000–03, FIST Soc. 2000–03; Prof. and Hosp. Practitioner, La Pitié-Salpétrière Teaching Hosp. 2003–08; Chair. Health Advisory Group, EC 2006–08; Non-exec. mem. Bd of Dirs Unilever PLC 2007–08, Chief Research and Devt Officer 2008–; Dir (non-exec.) Smith & Nephew 2010–; mem. Tech. Programme Cttee IEEE 1990–2008, Conseil de l'ordre des Palmes académiques 2000, French Research Inst. for Sea Exploitation 2000; Govt Commr Office of Geological and Mining Research 2000; Chair. Health Advisory Bd for Commr of Research, EU 2006–08; mem. Bd of Dirs Commissariat à l'Energie Atomique 2000, French Research Inst. for Sea Exploitation 2000, Ecole Normale Supérieure, Cachan 2000–03; Hon. Fellow, American Inst. of Ultrasound in Medicine 2006; Chevalier, Légion d'honneur 1988, Commdr des Palmes académiques 2000; Gold Medal, Univ. of Paris V-René Descartes 1985, CNRS Silver Medal 1994, Yves Rocard Prize, French Physics Soc. 1997, Pan-European Grand Prix for Innovation Award 2001, ranked by Fortune magazine amongst the 50 Most Powerful Women in Business outside the US (30th) 2010. *Address:* Unilever PLC, Unilever House, 100 Victoria Embankment, London, EC4Y 0DY, England (office). *Telephone:* (20) 7822-5252 (office). *Fax:* (20) 7822-5951 (office). *Website:* www .unilever.com (office).

BERGER, Helmut; Austrian actor; b. 29 May 1944, Bad Ischl; ed Feldkirk Coll., Univ. of Perugia, Italy; first film role in Luchino Visconti's Le Streghe 1966. *Films include:* The Young Tigers 1968, The Damned 1069, Do You Know What Stalin Did To Women?, The Garden of the Finzi-Continis 1970, The Picture of Dorian Gray, A Butterfly with Bloody Wings 1971, The Greedy Ones, The Strange Love Affair, Ludwig 1972, Ash Wednesday 1973, Conversation Piece 1974, The Romantic Englishwoman 1975, Orders to Kill 1975, Madame Kitty 1976, Merry-Go-Round, Code Name: Emerald 1985, The Glass Heaven, Faceless 1988, The Betrothed, The Godfather Part III 1990, Once Arizona, Still Waters, Unter den Palmen 1999, Die Haupter Meiner, Honey Baby 2004, Damals warst du still 2005, Blutsfreundschaft 2008, Iron Cross 2010, Mörderschwestern 2011, The Devil's Violinist 2013. *Publication:* Ich (autobiog.) 1998.

BERGER, John; British author and art critic; b. 5 Nov. 1926, London; s. of the late S. J. D. Berger and Miriam Berger (née Branson); ed Cen. School of Art and Chelsea School of Art, London; began career as painter and teacher of drawing; exhbns at Wildenstein, Redfern and Leicester Galleries, London; Art Critic Tribune, New Statesman; Visiting Fellow BFI 1990–; numerous TV appearances including Monitor, two series for Granada; Scenario: La Salamandre (with Alain Tanner), Le Milieu du Monde, Jonas (New York Critics Prize for Best Scenario of Year 1976); George Orwell Memorial Prize 1977, Golden PEN Award 2009. *Plays:* The Three Lives of Lucy Cabrol (with Simon McBurney) 1994, Isabelle (with Nella Bielski) 1998. *Radio:* Will It Be A Likeness? 1996. *Publications:* fiction: A Painter of Our Time 1958, The Foot of Clive 1962, Corker's Freedom 1964, G (Booker Prize, James Tait Black Memorial Prize) 1972, Pig Earth 1979, Once in Europa 1989, Lilac and Flag 1991, To The Wedding 1995, Photocopies 1996, King: A Street Story 1999, Here is Where we Meet 2005, From A to X: A Story in Letters 2008; theatre: Question of Geography (with Nella Bielski) 1984 (staged in Marseille, Paris and by RSC, Stratford), Francisco Goya's Last Portrait (with Nella Bielski) 1989, I Send You This Cadmium Red (with John Christie) 2000; non-fiction: Marcel Frishman

1958, Permanent Red 1960, The Success and Failure of Picasso 1965, A Fortunate Man: The Story of a Country Doctor (with J. Mohr) 1967, Art and Revolution, Moments of Cubism and Other Essays 1969, The Look of Things, Ways of Seeing 1972, The Seventh Man 1975 (Prize for Best Reportage, Union of Journalists and Writers, Paris 1977), About Looking 1980, Another Way of Telling (with J. Mohr) 1982, And Our Faces, My Heart, Brief as Photos 1984, The White Bird 1985 (USA as The Sense of Sight 1985), Keeping a Rendezvous (essays and poems) 1992, Titian: Nymph and Shepherd (with Katya Berger) 1996, Steps Towards a Small Theory of the Visible 1996, The Shape of a Pocket 2001, John Berger Selected Essays (ed. by Geoff Dyer) 2001, Hold Everything Dear: Dispatches on Survival and Resistance 2008; poetry: Pages of the Wound: Poems, Drawings, Photographs 1956–96 1996; translations: (with A. Bostock): Poems on the Theatre by B. Brecht 1960, Return to My Native Land by Aimé Césaire 1969; Oranges for the Son of Alexander Levy by Nella Bielski (with Lisa Appignanesi) 1982. *Address:* Quincy, Mieussy, 74440 Taninges, France (home). *Telephone:* 4-50-43-03-36 (home).

BERGER, Samuel R. (Sandy), BA, JD; American lawyer and fmr government official; *Chairman, Albright Stonebridge Group;* b. 28 Oct. 1945, Sharon, Conn.; m. Susan Berger; three c.; ed Cornell Univ., Harvard Univ. Law School; called to the Bar, Washington, DC 1971; Legis. Asst to Senator Harold E. Hughes (Ia) 1971–72, Congressman Joseph Resnick (NY); Special Asst to New York Mayor John V. Lindsay 1972; Deputy Dir Policy Planning Staff, US Dept of State, Washington, DC 1977–80; Partner, Hogan & Hartson 1981–97; Asst Dir Nat. Security Presidential Transitional Team 1992; Deputy Asst to Pres. for Nat. Security Affairs 1993–96, Asst 1996–97, Nat. Security Advisor 1997–2001; currently Chair. Albright Stonebridge Group (fmrly Stonebridge International LLC); mem. Bd of Dirs World Food Program US, CDC Development Solutions; fmr Sr Advisor, Lehman Brothers; Int. Strategic Advisor, Hogan and Hartson; mem. Int. Advisory Council of Brookings Doha Center, Advisory Bd of America Abroad Media; Trustee, International Crisis Group. *Publications:* Dollar Harvest 1971; numerous articles on int. affairs. *Address:* Albright Stonebridge Group, 1101 New York Avenue, NW, Suite 900, Washington, DC 20005, USA (office). *Telephone:* (202) 842-7222 (office). *Fax:* (202) 370-3599 (office). *Website:* www.albrightstonebridge .com (office).

BERGER, Thomas Louis, BA; American writer; b. 20 July 1924, Cincinnati, Ohio; s. of Thomas C. Berger and Mildred Berger; m. Jeanne Redpath 1950; ed Univ. of Cincinnati and Columbia Univ. Grad. School; mil. service 1943–46; Assoc. Ed., Popular Science Monthly 1952–53; Distinguished Visiting Prof., Southampton Univ. 1975–76; Visiting Lecturer, Yale Univ. 1981, 1982; Regents Lecturer, Univ. of Calif., Davis 1982; Dial Fellow 1962; Hon. LittD (Long Island) 1986; Rosenthal Award, Nat. Inst. of Arts and Letters 1965, Western Heritage Award 1965, Ohiona Book Award 1982. *Play:* Other People 1970. *Publications include:* Crazy in Berlin 1958, Reinhart in Love 1962, Little Big Man 1964, Killing Time 1967, Vital Parts 1970, Regiment of Women 1973, Sneaky People 1975, Who is Teddy Villanova? 1977, Arthur Rex 1978, Neighbors 1980, Reinhart's Women 1981, The Feud 1983, Nowhere 1985, Being Invisible 1987, The Houseguest 1988, Changing the Past 1989, Orrie's Story 1990, Meeting Evil 1992, Robert Crews 1994, Suspects 1996, The Return of Little Big Man 1999, Best Friends 2003, Adventures of the Artificial Woman 2004. *Leisure interest:* cooking. *Address:* Don Congdon Associates, 156 Fifth Avenue, Suite 625, New York, NY 10010-7002 (office); 80 Rive Road, Nyack, NY 10960-4902, USA (home). *Telephone:* (212) 645-1229 (office). *Fax:* (212) 727-2688 (office). *E-mail:* doncongdon@aol.com (office).

BERGER PERDOMO, Oscar José Rafael, LLD; Guatemalan business executive, lawyer, politician and fmr head of state; b. 11 Aug. 1946, Guatemala City; m. Wendy Widmann 1967; three s. two d.; ed Liceo Javier, Univ. Rafael Landívar; Founder-mem. Partido de Avanzada Nacional (PAN) 1984; Councillor, Guatemala City 1984–89, Mayor 1990–99; fmr Pres. Federación de Municipios de Centroamérica y Panamá, Pres. Asociación Nacional de Municipalidades 1991–93, Pres. Federación de Municipios del Istmo Centroamericano 1996–97; defeated in presidential elections 1999; left PAN 1999, rejoined 2002, selected as PAN presidential cand. Nov. 2002, won primary elections at head of Gran Alianza Nacional (Gana) Nov. 2003, President 2003–08; Order of Leopold II (Belgium) 1992, Légion d'honneur 2000. *Address:* c/o Partido de Avanzada Nacional (PAN), 7a Avda 10–38, Zona 9 Guatemala City, Guatemala.

BERGGREN, Bo Erik Gunnar; Swedish business executive; b. 11 Aug. 1936, Falun; s. of Tage Berggren and Elsa Höglund; m. Gunbritt Haglund 1962; two s. two d.; ed Royal Inst. of Tech.; metallurgical research and Devt, STORA Kopparbergs Bergslags AB (now STORA), Domnarvet 1962–68, Mill Man., Söderfors 1968–74, Exec. Vice-Pres., Falun 1975–78, Pres. 1984–92, CEO 1984–94, apptd Chair. Bd STORA Stockholm 1995–98; Pres. Incentive AB, Stockholm 1978–84; mem. Prime Minister's Special Industry Advisory Cttee 1994–; Chair. Astra; fmr Chair. SAS (Sweden), SAS (Sverige) AB; Vice-Chair. Investor, Fed. of Swedish Industries, Skandinaviska Enskilda Banken; mem. Bd Telefonaktiebolaget L. M. Ericsson, Danisco A/S, Royal Inst. of Tech.; fmr mem. Bd of Dirs Marcus Wallenberg Prize; mem. Int. Council J. P. Morgan & Co. Inc., Robert Bosch Internationale Beteiligungen Advisory Cttee, Royal Swedish Acad. of Eng Sciences, of Forestry and Agric.; Dr hc (Royal Inst. of Tech., Stockholm) (Dalhousie Univ.) 1996; King's Medal 12th Dimension with Ribbon of Order of the Seraphim 1987. *Leisure interests:* the arts, family, music. *Address:* Granvägen 14, 791 37, Falun, Sweden.

BERGGREN, Thommy; Swedish actor; b. 12 Aug. 1937, Mölndal; ed The Pickwick Club (pvt. dramatic school), Atelierteatern, Stockholm and Gothenburg Theatre; with Gothenburg Theatre 1959–63, Royal Dramatic Theatre, Stockholm 1963. *Plays include:* Gengangaren (Ibsen) 1962, Romeo and Juliet 1962, Chembalo 1962, Who's Afraid of Virginia Woolf? 1964. *Films include:* Pärlemor 1961, Barnvagnen (The Pram) 1962, Kvarteret Korpen (Ravens End) 1963, En söndag i september (A Sunday in September) 1963, Karlek 65 (Love 65) 1965, Elvira Madigan 1967, The Black Palm Trees 1969, The Ballad of Joe Hill 1971, Kristoffers hus 1979, Brusten himmel 1982, Berget på månens baksida (A Hill on the Dark Side of the Moon) 1983, La Sposa americana (The American Bride) 1986, Söndagsbarn 1992, Stora och små män 1995, Glasblåsarns barn 1998, Kontorstid 2003.

BERGKAMP, Dennis Nicolaas Maria; Dutch football manager and coach and fmr professional footballer; b. 10 May 1969, Amsterdam; m. Henrita Ruizendaal; one s. one d.; second striker; played for Ajax Amsterdam youth team 1981–86, sr team 1986–93, Inter Milan 1993–95, Arsenal, London, UK 1995–206, Premiership winner 1998, 2002, 2004, Football Asscn (FA) Cup winner 1998, 2002, 2003, 2005, Community Shield winner 1998, 1999, 2002, 2004; player for Holland 1990–2000, made 79 appearances and scored 37 goals, fmr all-time leading scorer; fourth place, FIFA World Cup 1998; began fast-track coaching diploma for fmr Dutch int. footballers 2008, because of his aviophobia, he will study under Arsène Wenger in London; undertook trainee role at Ajax, Asst Coach 2008–; signed contract with Koninklijke Nederlandse Voetbal Bond as Team Man. for newly formed Netherlands B team 2008; Dutch Talent of the Year 1990, Eredivisie Top Scorer 1991, 1992, 1993, UEFA Euro 1992 Team of the Tournament, UEFA Euro 1992 Top Scorer, Dutch Player of the Year 1992, 1993, UEFA Cup Top Scorer 1994, European Footballer of the Year: third place 1992, second place 1993, English PFA Players' Player of the Year 1998, English Football Writers' Player of the Year 1998, English PFA Team of the Year 1998, FIFA World Cup All-Star Team 1998, English Goal of the Season 1997–98, 2001–02, Arsenal FC Player of the Year 1998, FIFA Player of the Year: third place 1993, 1997, FA Premier League Player of the Month Aug. 1997, Sept. 1997, March 2002, Feb. 2004, inducted into English Football Hall of Fame (first and currently only Dutch player to receive this honour) 2007, FIFA 100, Unitar Dean's List Award 2008–09, selected by Pelé as one of the FIFA 125 greatest living players. *Leisure interests:* snooker, golf, reading, films, basketball. *Address:* AFC Ajax, Arena Boulevard 29, 1101 AX Amsterdam Zuidoost, The Netherlands. *Telephone:* (548) 377666. *E-mail:* ajax@oad.nl. *Website:* www.ajax.nl.

BERGKAMP, Ger, MA, PhD; Dutch environmental scientist, hydrologist and international organization official; *Executive Director, International Water Association;* ed Univ. of Amsterdam; has worked in environmental sciences, hydrology, irrigation and drainage, and soil and water conservation throughout Latin America, the Mediterranean, Africa and S and SE Asia and at int. level since late 1980s; Freshwater Man. Adviser, Wetlands and Water Resources Programme, Int. Union for Conservation of Nature (IUCN—The World Conservation Union) 1997–2008; Gen. Dir World Water Council 2008–13; Exec. Dir International Water Asscn 2013–. *Address:* International Water Association, Alliance House, 12 Caxton Street, London, SW1H 0QS, England (office). *Telephone:* (20) 7654-5500 (office). *Fax:* (20) 7654-5555 (office). *E-mail:* water@iwahq.org (office). *Website:* www.iwahq.org (office).

BERGMAN, Robert George, BS, PhD; American chemist and academic; *Gerald E. K. Branch Distinguished Professor, University of California, Berkeley;* b. 23 May 1942, Chicago, Ill.; ed Carleton Coll., Univ. of Wisconsin; NATO Fellow, Columbia Univ. 1966–67; Noyes Research Instructor, California Inst. of Tech. 1967–69, Asst Prof. 1969–71, Assoc. Prof. 1971–73, Prof. 1973–77; Prof. of Chem., Univ. of California, Berkeley 1977–, Gerald E. K. Branch Distinguished Prof. 2002–, Vice-Chair. Dept of Chem. 1985–87, Asst Dean, Coll. of Chem. 1987–91, 1996, 2004–06; mem. Chemical Sciences Div., Lawrence Berkeley Nat. Lab.; mem. Editorial Bd Journal of Organic Chemistry 1980–83, 1996–98, Organometallics 1981–84, 1992–95, Chemical Reviews 1981–84, International Journal of Chemical Kinetics 1986–89, Journal of the American Chemical Society 1990–95, Organic Letters 1999–; mem. NAS 1984, American Acad. of Arts and Sciences 1984; NIH Predoctoral Fellowship, Alfred P. Sloan Fellowship 1969, Camille and Henry Dreyfus Foundation Teacher-Scholar Award 1970, California Inst. of Tech. Student Government Award for Excellence in Teaching 1978, ACS Award in Organometallic Chem. 1986, ACS Arthur C. Cope Scholar Award 1987, E.O. Lawrence Award in Chem., US Dept of Energy 1994, ACS Arthur C. Cope Award 1996, Edward Leete Award for Teaching and Research in Organic Chem. 2001, Dept of Chem. Teaching Award, Univ. of California, Berkeley 2002, ACS James Flack Norris Award in Physical Organic Chem. 2003, Award for Excellence in Tech. Transfer, Lawrence Berkeley Nat. Lab. 2005, NAS Award in Chemical Sciences 2007, T.W. Richards Medal, Northeastern Section of ACS 2008, RSC Sir Edward Frankland Prize Lectureship 2008, Chancellor's Award for Public Service, Univ. of California, Berkeley 2008–09, 2011–12, Willard Gibbs Award, ACS Chicago Section 2011. *Publications:* numerous research papers in professional journals. *Address:* Department of Chemistry, University of California, Berkeley, 419 Latimer Hall, Berkeley, CA 94720-1460, USA (office). *Telephone:* (510) 642-2156 (office). *Fax:* (510) 642-7714 (office). *E-mail:* rbergman@berkeley.edu (office). *Website:* www.cchem.berkeley.edu/rgbgrp (office).

BERGMANN, Barbara Rose, MA, PhD; American economist and academic; *Professor Emerita of Economics, American University;* b. 20 July 1927, New York; d. of Martin Berman and Nellie Wallenstein; m. Fred H. Bergmann 1965; one s. one d.; ed Cornell and Harvard Univs; economist, US Bureau of Statistics, New York 1949–53, New York Metropolitan Regional Study 1957–61; Instructor, Harvard Univ. 1958–61; Sr Research Assoc., Harvard Econ. Research Project 1960–61; Sr Staff Economist, Council of Econ. Advisers, Washington, DC 1961–62; Assoc. Prof., Brandeis Univ. 1962–64; mem. sr staff, Brookings Inst. Washington, DC 1963–65; Sr Econ. Adviser, AID, Washington, DC 1966–67; Prof. of Econs, Univ. of Maryland College Park 1971–88; Distinguished Prof. of Econs, American Univ. Washington, DC 1988–97, Prof. Emer. 1997–; Vice-Pres. American Econ. Asscn 1976; columnist on econ. affairs New York Times 1981–82, Los Angeles Times 1983–; Pres. American Asscn of Univ. Profs 1990–92, Int. Asscn for Feminist Economists 1999; Hon. PhD (De Montford Univ., UK) 1996, (Muhlenberg Coll.) 2000; Carolyn Shaw Bell Award 2004. *Publications:* Projection of a Metropolis (co-author) 1961, The Impact of Highway Investment on Development (co-author), A Microsimulated Transactions Model of the U.S. Economy (co-author) 1985, The Economic Emergence of Women 1986, Saving Our Children from Poverty: What the United States Can Learn From France 1995, In Defense of Affirmative Action 1996, Is Social Security Broke? A Cartoon Guide to the Issues 1999, America's Child Care Problem: The Way Out (co-author) 2002. *E-mail:* bberg@american.edu (office). *Website:* www.american.edu/cas/econ/faculty/bergmann.htm (office).

BERGNER, Christoph, DrAgrar; German politician; *Parliamentary Under-Secretary of State, Federal Ministry of the Interior;* b. 24 Nov. 1948, Zwickau; m.; three c.; ed Univs of Jena and Halle; mem. CDU without office in fmr GDR 1971; Research Asst Inst. of Biochemistry of Plants, Univ. of Halle 1974–90; mem. Landtag (State Parl.) of Saxony-Anhalt 1990–2002; Vice-Chair. Saxony-Anhalt CDU Asscn 1991–94; Chair. CDU Parl. Party in Landtag 1991–93, 1994–2001; Minister-Pres. of Saxony-Anhalt 1993–94; mem. Bundestag (Fed. Ass.) 2002–; Parl. Under-Sec. of State, Fed. Ministry of the Interior 2005–; Fed. Commr for Matters Related to Repatriates and Nat. Minorities 2006–; Pres. Sports Association Hall; mem. Inst. for Economic Research. *Address:* Deutscher Bundestag, Platz der Republik, 11011 Berlin, Germany (office). *Telephone:* (30) 22773775 (office). *E-mail:* christoph.bergner@bundestag.de (office). *Website:* www.bergner.de.

BERGSTEN, C. Fred, MA, PhD; American economist and research institute director; *Senior Fellow and Director Emeritus, Peterson Institute for International Economics;* b. 23 April 1941, New York, NY; s. of Dr Carl Bergsten and Halkaline Bergsten; m. Virginia W. Bergsten; one s.; ed Cen. Methodist Coll., Fletcher School of Law and Diplomacy, Tufts Univ.; Asst for Int. Econ. Affairs, US Nat. Security Council 1969–71; Asst Sec. for Int. Econ. Affairs, US Treasury, Washington, DC 1977–81; Dir Inst. for Int. Econs (now Peterson Inst. for Int. Econs) 1981–2012, Sr Fellow and Dir Emer. 2012–; Chair. Competitiveness Policy Council 1991–95, Asia-Pacific Econ. Co-operation Eminent Persons Group 1993–95; mem. President's Advisory Cttee on Trade Policy and Negotiations; mem. Advisory Cttee to the Export-Import Bank; Global Advisor to Pres. of Repub. of Korea 2009; Co-Chair. Private Sector Advisory Group to United States–India Trade Policy Forum; Sr Fellow, Council on Foreign Relations 1967–68, Brookings Inst. 1972–76, Carnegie Endowment for Int. Peace 1981; Hon. Fellow, Chinese Acad. of Social Sciences 1997; Chevalier Légion d'honneur 1985, Order of the Polar Star (Sweden) 2013; Dept of State Meritorious Honor Award 1965, Dept of Treasury Exceptional Service Award 1981, Distinguished Alumnus Award, Fletcher School of Law and Diplomacy, Tufts Univ. 2010. *Publications include:* America in the World Economy: A Strategy for the 1990s 1988, Pacific Dynamism and the International Economic System (with M. Noland) 1993, Reconcilable Differences? United States-Japan Economic Conflict (with M. Noland) 1993, The Dilemmas of the Dollar (second edn) 1996, Global Economic Leadership and the Group of Seven 1996; Whither APEC? The Progress to Date and Agenda for the Future 1997, No More Bashing: Building a New Japan-United States Economic Relationship 2001, The Korean Diaspora in the World Economy 2003, Dollar Overvaluation and the World Economy 2003, Dollar Adjustment: How Far? Against What? 2004, The United States and the World Economy (ed.) 2005, China: The Balance Sheet 2006; numerous other books and journal articles. *Leisure interests:* photography, basketball, snorkelling. *Address:* Peterson Institute for International Economics, 1750 Massachusetts Avenue, NW, Washington, DC 20036-1903 (office); 4106 Sleepy Hollow Road, Annandale, VA 22003, USA (home). *Telephone:* (202) 328-9000 (office); (703) 256-3802 (home). *Fax:* (202) 659-3225 (office). *E-mail:* kstewart@piie.com (office). *Website:* www.iie.com (office).

BERGSTRÖM, Lars, PhD; Swedish academic; *Professor Emeritus of Practical Philosophy, Stockholm University;* b. 17 July 1935, Stockholm; m. Ulla von Heland 1960; one s.; ed Stockholm Univ.; Assoc. Prof., Lecturer in Philosophy, Stockholm Univ. 1967–74; Prof. of Practical Philosophy, Uppsala Univ. 1974–87; Prof. of Practical Philosophy, Stockholm Univ. 1987–2001, Prof. Emer. 2001–; mem. Royal Swedish Acad. of Sciences 1998–. *Publications:* The Alternatives and Consequences of Actions 1966, Objektivitet 1972, Grundbok i Värdeteori 1990, Döden, Livet och Verkligheten 2004. *Leisure interests:* music, tennis. *Address:* Department of Philosophy, Stockholm University, 106 91 Stockholm (office); Telegrafgränd 1B, 111 30 Stockholm, Sweden (home). *Telephone:* (8) 164209 (office); (8) 6698899 (home). *E-mail:* lars.bergstrom@philosophy.su.se (office). *Website:* www.philosophy.su.se/personal/bergstrom.htm (office).

BERISHA, Kolë; Kosovo politician; b. 26 Oct. 1947, Doberdol; m.; two c.; fmr high school teacher in Klina; fmrly Sec., Democratic League of Kosovo (LDK), Vice-Pres. 1998–; Pres., Ass. of Kosovo 2006–07; mem. Parl. Group of LDK, Cttee for Rules of Procedure of Ass. *Address:* Kodra e Diellit, Rruga Sali Nivica, 10000 Priština; c/o Office for Media and Publications, Assembly of Kosovo, Rruga Nëna Terezë, Kosovo, 10000 Priština, Serbia. *Telephone:* (38) 211186.

BERISHA, Sali, PhD; Albanian cardiologist, academic and politician; b. 15 Oct. 1944, Viçidol, Tropojë Dist, Kukës Co.; m. Liri Ramaj; one s. one d.; ed Univ. of Tirana and studies in Paris, France; worked as cardiologist in Tirana Cardiology Clinic; taught at Univ. of Tirana 1980–90; fmr mem. Albanian Workers' Party; co-f. Democratic Party of Albania (Partia Demokratike e Shqipërisë), Leader 1991–92, 1997–2013; mem. Kuvendi Popullor (People's Ass.) 1991–; Pres. of Albania 1992–97 (re-elected Feb. 1997, resgnd July 1997); Prime Minister 2005–13; mem. Nat. Medical Research Cttee, European Cttee on Medical Scientific Research 1968–; Hon. mem. Nat. Raoul Wallenberg Foundation. *Publications:* has published several textbooks and scientific articles on cardiology; numerous political articles in newspapers and magazines. *Address:* c/o Office of the Prime Minister, Office of the Council of Ministers, Bulevardi Dëshmorët e Kombit, Tirana, Albania.

BERIZIKY, Omer; Malagasy politician and fmr diplomatist; b. 9 Sept. 1950, Vohemar; fmr Prof. of History, Univ. of Madagascar, Ambohitsaina; Amb. to Belgium and Perm. Rep. to EU, Brussels 1995–2006; Prime Minister 2011–14; also Acting Minister of Environment and Forests; mem. Libéralisme économique et action démocratique pour la reconstruction nationale (LEADER/Fanilo). *Address:* c/o Office of the Prime Minister, BP 248, Palais dEtat Mahazoarivo, 101 Antananarivo, Madagascar.

BERKELEY, Michael Fitzhardinge, CBE, FRAM, FRWCMD; British composer; b. 29 May 1948, London, England; s. of the late Sir Lennox Berkeley and Elizabeth Freda Berkeley (née Bernstein); m. Deborah Jane Coltman-Rogers 1979; one d.; ed Westminster Cathedral Choir School, The Oratory School, Royal Acad. of Music; writer on music and arts for the Observer, Vogue and The Listener 1970–75; presents music programmes (including Proms) for BBC TV 1975–; BBC Radio 3 announcer 1974–79; Dir Britten-Pears Foundation 1996–; mem. Exec. Cttee Asscn of Professional Composers 1982–84, Cen. Music Advisory Cttee, BBC 1986–90; Music Panel Adviser to Arts Council 1986–90; Visiting Prof. Huddersfield Univ. (fmrly Polytechnic) 1991–94; Artistic Dir Cheltenham Int. Festival 1995–2005; Co-Dir Spitalfields Festival 1994–97; Dir Royal Opera House, Covent Garden 1996–2000 (mem. 1994–98, Chair. Opera Bd 1998); Chair. Bd of Govs Royal Ballet 2003–; Composer-in-Asscn BBC Nat. Orchestra of Wales, Welsh Coll. of Music and Drama 2002–; has also composed music for film, TV and radio; The

Guinness Prize for Composition 1977, Silver Medal, Worshipful Co. of Musicians 2003. *Major works include:* Meditations for Strings, Oboe Concerto, Fantasia Concertante, Gregorian Variations (orchestra), For The Savage Messiah (piano quintet), Or Shall We Die? (oratorio to text by Ian McEwan), 4 String quartets, Piano Trio, Songs of Awakening Love, Entertaining Master Punch, Clarinet Concerto, Speaking Silence, Baa Baa Black Sheep (opera), Jane Eyre (opera), Viola Concerto, Catch Me If You Can (chamber), Dark Sleep (keyboard), Tristessa (orchestra), The Garden of Earthly Delights (orchestra), Magnetic Field (string quartet), Winter Fragments, Secret Garden (orchestra), Odd Man Out, Entertaining Master Punch, Abstract Mirror (string quartet), Gethsemane (for tenor and ensemble), For You (opera, libretto by Ian McEwan), Gabriel's Lament for orchestra, Piano Quintet, Atonement (opera, libretto by Craig Raine), Collision (electro-acoustic and visual installation, collaboration with artist Kevin Laycock) 2009, Three Rilke Sonnets (written for the Nash Ensemble and soprano Claire Booth) 2011, Hollow Fires (song cycle for baritone and piano setting texts by Housman and Hardy) 2011. *Radio:* presenter Private Passions (BBC Radio 3). *Publication:* The Music Pack 1994; numerous articles in newspapers and magazines. *Leisure interests:* walking, farming, reading, contemporary painting. *Address:* c/o Oxford University Press, Repertoire Promotion Department, Great Clarendon Street, Oxford, OX2 6DP, England (office). *E-mail:* repertoire .promotion.uk@oup.com (office). *Website:* ukcatalogue.oup.com/category/music/ composers/berkeley.do (office); www.michaelberkeley.co.uk.

BERKMAN, Lisa, BA, MS, PhD; American epidemiologist and academic; *Thomas D. Cabot Professor of Public Policy and of Epidemiology and Director, Harvard Center for Population and Development Studies, Harvard University;* ed Northwestern Univ., Evanston, Ill., Univ. of California, Berkeley; Lecturer, Dept of Epidemiology and Int. Health, School of Medicine, Univ. of California, San Francisco 1977–78; Research Specialist in Epidemiology, Human Population Lab., Calif. State Dept of Health, Berkeley 1977–78; Asst Prof., Dept of Epidemiology and Public Health and Inst. for Social and Policy Studies, Yale School of Medicine 1979–83, Assoc. Prof. 1983–85, Assoc. Prof. with tenure 1986–92, Prof. 1992–95, Head of Div. of Health Policy and Resources 1988–91, Head of Div. of Chronic Disease/Epidemiology 1991–95; Florence Sprague Norman and Laura Smart Norman Prof., Health and Social Behavior and Epidemiology, Harvard School of Public Health 1995–2001, Chair. Health and Social Behavior 1995–2003, Dir Center for Society and Health, Harvard Univ. 1997–99, Chair. 1999–, Thomas D. Cabot Prof. of Public Policy 2001–, Chair. Society, Human Devt and Health, Harvard School of Public Health 2003–08, Dir Harvard Center for Population and Devt Studies 2007–; Researcher, Unit 136, Institut Nat. de la Santé et de la Recherche Médicale (INSERM), Paris, France 1993–94, Visiting Prof., Unit 88 1994–; Hon. Sr Lecturer, Dept of Community Medicine, Univ. Coll. London and Middlesex Hosp., London, UK; Pres. Soc. for Epidemiological Research 2002; Chair. Bd of Scientific Counselors, Nat. Inst. of Aging 2005–08; mem. American Epidemiological Soc. 1991, Inst. of Medicine 2001, US Health and Retirement Study Advisory Bd, SHARE Advisory Bd, ELSA Advisory Bd, Macarthur Foundation Aging Soc. Network; Foreign mem. Academia Europaea; Regents of Univ. of California Fellowship, Univ. of California, Berkeley 1974–75, NIMH Mental Health Epidemiology Training Grant, Univ. of California, Berkeley 1975–77, Grossman Endowment for Doctoral Research, Univ. of California, Berkeley 1975–77, Sr Fulbright Scholar, London 1985–86, Alumna of the Year Award School of Public Health, Univ. of California, Berkeley 1997. *Publications:* Health and Ways of Living (with L. Breslow) 1983, Social Epidemiology (co-ed. with I. Kawachi) 2000, Neighborhoods and Health (co-ed. with I. Kawachi) 2003; numerous book chapters and more than 200 papers in peer-reviewed journals. *Address:* Department of Society, Human Development and Health, Harvard School of Public Health, 9 Bow Street, Cambridge, MA 02138, USA (office). *Telephone:* (617) 495-8498 (office). *E-mail:* lberkman@hsph.harvard.edu (office). *Website:* www.hsph.harvard.edu (office).

BERKOFF, Steven; British actor, writer and director; b. 3 Aug. 1937, Stepney, London; s. of Alfred Berkoff and Pauline Berkoff; m. 1st Alison Minto 1970; m. 2nd Shelley Lee 1976 (divorced); ed Hackney Downs Grammar School, Webber-Douglas School of Drama. *Films include:* Octopussy, First Blood 2, Beverly Hills Cop, Absolute Beginners, War and Remembrance (TV) 1988, The Krays 1990, Decadence 1994, Rancid Aluminium 2000, Head in the Clouds 2004, Brides 2004, Forest of the Gods 2005. *Plays / Productions include:* Agamemnon (London) 1973, The House of Usher 1974, The Trial 1974, East 1978, Hamlet 1980, 2001, Greek 1980, Decadence 1981, Agamemnon (USA) 1984, Harry's Xmas 1985, Kvetch 1986, 1991 (Evening Standard Award for Comedy of the Year 1991), Sink the Belgrano 1987, Coriolanus 1988, Metamorphosis 1988, Salome 1989, The Trial 1991, Brighton Beach Scumbags 1994; Dir West (London) 1983, Acapulco (LA) 1990, One Man (London) 1993, Coriolanus 1996, Mermaid 1996, Massage (LA and Edinburgh) 1997, Shakespeare's Villains 1998, Messiah 2000 (London 2003), Dir Sit and Shiver (Los Angeles) 2004, Dir Richard II (Ludlow Festival) 2005, Sit and Shiver (London) 2006, Biblical Tales (London) 2010. *Publications:* America 1988, I am Hamlet 1989, A Prisoner in Rio 1989, The Theatre of Steven Berkoff (photographic) 1992, Coriolanus in Deutschland 1992, Overview (collected essays) 1994, Free Association (autobiog.) 1996, Graft: Tales of an Actor 1998, Shopping in the Santa Monica Mall, Ritual in Blood, Messiah 2000 (Glasgow Herald Golden Angel Award, Edinburgh Festival Fringe First), Oedipus 2000, The Secret Love Life of Ophelia 2001 (Glasgow Herald Golden Angel Award), Tough Acts 2003, My Life in Food 2008. *Leisure interests:* photography, travelling, table tennis, eating. *Address:* East Productions, 1 Keepier Wharf, 12 Narrow Street, London, E14 8DH, England (office). *Telephone:* (20) 7790-6313 (office). *Fax:* (20) 7790-1752 (office). *E-mail:* eastproductions@stevenberkoff.com (office). *Website:* www.stevenberkoff .com.

BERKOWITZ, Richard Lee, MD; American physician, endocrinologist, geneticist, obstetrician and gynaecologist and academic; *Professor of Obstetrics and Gynecology, Columbia Medical Center, Columbia University;* ed New York Univ. School of Medicine, Yale Univ. School of Medicine; Internship, Kings County Medical Center; Residency, Cornell Medical Center, New York Hosp. 1971; served for 18 years as Chair. Dept of Obstetrics and Gynecology, Mount Sinai School of Medicine and Dir Div. of Maternal-Fetal Medicine; currently Prof. of Obstetrics and Gynecology, Columbia Medical School, Columbia Univ., New York; affiliated with New York-Presbyterian Hosp./Columbia Univ., apptd Dir of Resident Educ.

2005, currently Dir of Quality Assurance; King Faisal Int. Prize for Medicine (co-recipient) 2012. *Publications:* author or editor of more than 35 books and book chapters; more than 200 papers in peer-reviewed journals. *Address:* Columbia Ob/ Gyn Midtown, 51 West 51st Street, Suite 320, New York, NY 10019, USA (office). *Telephone:* (212) 326-8951 (office). *Fax:* (212) 326-5610 (office). *E-mail:* info@www .columbiaobgyn.org (office). *Website:* www.columbiaobgyn.org (office).

BERLIJN, Maj.-Gen. (retd) Dick L.; Dutch fmr military officer; b. 18 March 1950, Amsterdam; m. Elly M. A. Hermelink; two s.; ed Royal Mil. Acad., Breda, Air Force Staff Coll.; served as Operations Officer, later Commdr, Transition and Conversion Div., Leeuwarden Air Base 1983–85; Supervisor, Fighter Weapon Instruction Training, Denmark 1987; Head, Fighter Weapons Br., Tactical Air Command 1988; Head of Operations and Training, Royal Netherlands Air Force Staff 1991–92, Head, Fighter Operations Div. 1994, Deputy Chief (Operations) and Air Commodore 1995; Chief of Flying Operations, Twenthe Air Base 1992; Commdr first F-16 detachment to Italy 1993; apptd Commdr Tactical Air Force, rank Maj.-Gen. 1998; Commdr-in-Chief Royal Netherlands Air Force 2000–04; Chief of the Defence Staff 2004–08; mem. Supervisory Bd Thales Nederland 2008–, fonds slachtofferhulp 2008–; mem. Foundation Bd Foundation naNOcancer 2010–; Sr Bd Advisor Deloitte Nederland 2008–, mem. Bd of Dirs; mem. Int. Advisory Bd Royal Ten Cate 2010–; mem. Bd of Advisors Subsolar Energy 2011–; Legion of Merit (USA), Légion d'honneur; Long Service Medal, NATO Medal, Multinational Peace Operations Medal. *Address:* Deloitte Nederland, chenkkade 47, POB 90721, 2509 LS The Hague, Netherlands (office). *E-mail:* dberlijn@deloitte.nl (office). *Website:* www.deloitte.com/view/nl_NL/nl/index.htm (office).

BERLUSCONI, Marina Elvira; Italian business executive; *Chairman, Fininvest SpA;* b. (Maria Elvira Berlusconi), 10 Aug. 1966, Milan; d. of Silvio Berlusconi and Carla Elvira Lucia Dall'Oglio; m. 2nd Maurizio Vanadia; two s. (one from previous m.); worked in London boutique aged 18; Deputy Chair. Fininvest SpA 1996–2005, Chair. 2005–; Chair. Arnoldo Mondadori SpA (Italy's largest publishing co.) 2003–; mem. Bd Dirs Mediaset SpA 1995–, Medusa Film 1995–2007 (Pres. 2001–02), 21 Investimenti SpA 2000–07, Mediobanca SpA 2008–; ranked by Fortune magazine amongst the 50 Most Powerful Women in Business outside the US (ninth) 2001–02, (seventh) 2003, (ninth) 2004, (sixth) 2005, (seventh) 2006–07, (eighth) 2008, (tenth) 2009, (12th) 2010–11, (24th) 2012, ranked by Forbes magazine amongst The World's 100 Most Powerful Women (36th) 2004, (74th) 2005, (42nd) 2006, (33rd) 2007, (34th) 2008, (33rd) 2009, (48th) 2010. *Address:* Fininvest SpA, Via Paleocapa 3, 20121 Milan, Italy (office). *Telephone:* (02) 85411 (office). *Website:* www.fininvest.it (office); www.mondadori.it (office).

BERLUSCONI, Silvio; Italian politician and business executive; b. 29 Sept. 1936, Milan; s. of Luigi Berlusconi and Rosa Bossi; m. 1st; one d. one s.; m. 2nd Veronica Lari; three c.; ed Univ. of Milan; started building and property devt business aged 26; f. Elinord construction co. 1962; built up Fininvest, major conglomerate with interests in commercial TV, printed media, publishing, advertising, insurance and financial services, retailing and football; worked on Milan 2 Housing project 1969; Canale 5 network began broadcasting 1980; bought Italia 1 TV network 1983, Rete 4 TV network 1984; took stake in La Cinq commercial TV network 1985, Chain, Cinema 5 (largest in Italy); bought Estudios Roma 1986; Milan AC Football Club 1986; La Standa (Italy's largest Dept store chain) 1988; Chair. Arnoldo Mondadori Editore SpA Jan.–July 1990, (half-share) 1991; Founder and Pres. Forza Italia political movt 1993, began full-time political career 1994, declaring he had stepped down from exec. posts in Fininvest, owned 51% of Mediaset (Italy's largest pvt. TV network operator) through Fininvest, reduced stake by one-third 2005; led Forza Italia to win general elections in alliance with Lega Nord and Alleanza Nazionale parties 1994; Prime Minister of Italy April–Dec. 1994, 2001–06, 2008–11 (resgnd), also Minister of Foreign Affairs 2002; Founder and Pres. Casa delle Libertà (House of Freedoms) 2002–07, replaced by Popolo della Libertà 2007–13, relaunched Forza Italia 2013, current leader; Pres. EU Council July–Sept. 2003; mem. European Parl. 1999; convicted of fraud by an Italian court for tax evasion and sentenced to four years in prison, shortened to one year Oct. 2012, sentence confirmed by Court of Appeals May 2013, by Court of Cassation Aug. 2013, ordered by Tribunale di sorveglianza in Milan to serve sentence through part-time community service in a home for elderly people April 2014; convicted of paying for sex with an underage prostitute and of abusing his office June 2013, sentenced to seven years in prison and banned from public office for life; mem. Senate March–Nov. 2013 (expelled); Ordine al Merito del Lavoro 1977, Kt Grand Cross, Order of the Star of Romania 2002, Kt Grand Cross, Order of Merit of the Repub. of Poland 2002, Hon. Companion of Honour of the Nat. Order of Merit (Malta) 2004, Grand Officer, Order of the Three Stars (Latvia) 2005, Al-Fateh Medal (Libya) 2009, Mem. (First Class), Order of Abdulaziz al Saud (Saudi Arabia) 2009, Kt Grand Cross, Sacred Mil. Constantinian Order of St George; ranked by Forbes magazine amongst The World's Most Powerful People (12th) 2009, (14th) 2010, (21st) 2011. *Recording:* Meglio'ne Canzone (album) 2003. *Website:* www.forzasilvio.it.

BERMAN, Gail, BA; American media executive; b. 17 Aug. 1956, Long Island, NY; m. Bill Masters; two c.; ed Univ. of Maryland Coll. of Arts and Humanities; co-produced with Susan Rose first US production of Andrew Lloyd Webber's Joseph and the Amazing Technicolour Dreamcoat, Broadway, New York 1982–83; Supervisor Original Production, HBO's Comedy Channel (precursor of Comedy Central) late 1980s; Head of Sandollar Television, Southern Calif. early 1990s; Founder-Pres. and Partner, Regency Television Inc. 1998–2000; Pres. of Entertainment, Fox Broadcasting Co. 2000–05; Pres. Paramount Pictures Corp 2005–07; Co-owner and Co-founder BermanBraun LLC 2007–; mem. Bd of Trustees, Univ. of Maryland 2010; mem. Advisory Bd, Carsey-Wolf Center; ranked by Fortune magazine amongst 50 Most Powerful Women in Business in the US (25th) 2003, (25th) 2004, named No. 5 on Power 100 List, Women in Entertainment Report 2003, Women in Film Lucy Award 2003, Brandon Tartikoff Legacy Award, Nat. Asscn of Television Production Execs, Exec. of the Year, Caucus for Television Producers, Writers and Directors 2005, 2006, She Made It honoree, Paley Center for Media, ranked by Forbes magazine amongst The World's 100 Most Powerful Women (49th) 2004, (69th) 2005, (90th) 2006. *Plays produced:* Almost an Eagle 1982, Hurlyburly 1984, Blood Knot (co-producer) 1985–86, The Nerd 1987–88. *Television:* co-producer: Joseph and the Amazing Technicolor Dreamcoat, Hurlyburly by David Rabe 1984, Athol Fugard's Blood Knot 1985, The

Nerd 1987; exec. producer: Someone Like Me 1994, All-American Girl 1994, Social Studies 1997, Buffy the Vampire Slayer 1997, Angel 1999, Firefly 2002, HBO Presents Hazelle, American Idol, 24, That 70s Show, House, Arrested Development, Bones, Family Guy. *Address:* Carsey-Wolf Center, 4435 Social Sciences and Media Studies, University of California, Santa Barbara, CA 93106-4010, USA (office). *Telephone:* (805) 893-4637 (Carsey-Wolf Center) (office); (310) 255-7272 (BermanBraun LLC) (office). *Fax:* (805) 893-2467 (Carsey-Wolf Center) (office); (310) 255-7058 (BermanBraun LLC) (office). *E-mail:* info@bermanbraun.com (office). *Website:* www.carseywolf.ucsb.edu (office); www.bermanbraun.com (office).

BERMAN, Jason (Jay); American music industry executive; fmr rep. for Warner Music, Recording Industry Asscn of America (RIAA) Bd –1987, Pres. RIAA 1987–92, Chair. 1992–98; Chair. and CEO Int. Federation for the Phonographic Industry (IFPI) 1998–2004; est. anti-piracy consultancy, Berman Rosen Global Strategies; US Special Counsel for Trade to President Clinton 1998; Bd mem. Loudeye Corpn. *Address:* c/o Loudeye Corpn 1130 Rainier Avenue, South Seattle, WA 98144, USA.

BERMÚDEZ AMADO, Brig. Gen. Francisco; Guatemalan military officer, government official and diplomatist; fmr Brig. Gen., Guatemalan Armed Forces; Minister of Nat. Defence 2006–07; Amb. to Taiwan 2007. *Address:* c/o Ministry of National Defence, Antiguas Instalaciones de la Escuela Politécnica, Avda La Reforma 1-45, Zona 10, Guatemala City, Guatemala.

BERMÚDEZ MERIZALDE, Jaime, PhD; Colombian lawyer, politician and diplomatist; *President, MBA Lazard Colombia;* b. 1966, Bogotá; m.; two c.; ed Univ. de los Andes, Univ. of Oxford, UK; with Human Rights Advisory Office 1991–93; Adviser to Minister of Foreign Affairs 1993–94, also coordinator Neighborhood Commissions; pvt. communications consultant –2002; Dir Asociación Primero Colombia (political asscn) 2002–06; communications adviser during presidential election campaign of Alvaro Uribe 2002, Presidential Adviser in Communications 2002–06; Amb. to Argentina 2006–07; Minister of Foreign Affairs 2008–10; Pres. MBA Lazard Colombia 2010–; served as UN observer during South African presidential elections 1994. *Address:* MBA Lazard Colombia, Carrera 7 N° 71 - 21 Torre B Of. 908, Bogotá, DC Colombia (office). *Website:* www.mba-lazard.com.

BERNABÈ, Franco; Italian business executive; *Chairman and CEO, Telecom Italia SpA;* b. 18 Sept. 1948, Vipiteno/Sterzing (Bozen); s. of Bruno Bernabè and Clara Frigerio; m. Maria Grazia Curtetto; one s. one d.; ed Univ. of Turin; postgraduate fellow, Einaudi Foundation and Prof. of Econs, Univ. of Turin 1973; Sr Economist, Dept of Econs and Statistics, OECD, Paris 1976–78; Chief Economist, FIAT, Turin 1978–83; Asst to Chair. ENI SpA 1983–86, Head of Corp. Planning, Financial Control and Corp. Devt 1986–92, CEO ENI SpA 1992–98; Chair. Telecom Italia SpA 1998–99, 2011–, CEO 2007–, Pres. Telecom Italia Foundation 2012–; f. FB Group (investment co.) 1999, Vice-Chair. Rothschild Europe (following merger of financial advisory activities of FB Group with Rothschild Group) 2004–; Ind. Dir (non-exec.) PetroChina 2000–; fmr mem. Bd of Dirs Fiat, TPG-TNT; Chair. GSMA (int. org. of mobile operators); apptd by Prime Minister as special rep. of Italian Govt for the reconstruction of Kosovo 1999; Chair. La Biennale di Venezia 2001–03, Mart (Italian museum of modern art) 2004–; mem. European Roundtable; Co-Pres. Italy-Brazil Business Council; Vice-Pres. Rome Industrialist and Enterprises Asscn with special responsibility for innovation and broadband; mem. Advisory Bd of Observatoire Méditérranéen de l'Énergie; fmr mem. Advisory Bd Council on Foreign Relations, Bd Peres Center for Peace; Cavaliere del Lavoro 2011. *Publications include:* Financial Structure and Economic Policy in Italy 1975, Labour Market and Unemployment (with A. Boltho) 1982, Industrial Policies and Industrialization: The Case of the Automobile Industry 1982. *Address:* Telecom Italia SpA, Piazza degli Affari 2, 20123 Milan, Italy (office). *Telephone:* (02) 85951 (office). *Fax:* (02) 85954018 (office). *E-mail:* info@telecomitalia.it (office). *Website:* www.telecomitalia.it (office).

BERNANKE, Ben Shalom, PhD; American economist, academic, banking executive and fmr government official; b. 13 Dec. 1953, Augusta, Ga; m. Anna Bernanke; two c.; ed J.V. Martin Junior High, Dillon High School (class valedictorian), Harvard Univ., Massachusetts Inst. of Tech.; taught at Stanford Grad. School of Business 1979–85; Prof. of Econs and Public Affairs, Princeton Univ. 1985–96, Howard Harrison and Gabrielle Snyder Beck Prof. of Econs and Public Affairs and Chair. Econs Dept 1996–2002; fmr Dir Monetary Econs Program, Nat. Bureau of Econ. Research (NBER), fmr mem. Business Cycling Dating Cttee; mem. Bd of Govs, Fed. Reserve System –2005, Chair. 2006–13; Chair. Pres.'s Council of Econ. Advisers 2005–06; fmr mem. Montgomery Township Bd of Educ.; Fellow, Econometric Soc. 1997, American Acad. of Arts and Sciences; Guggenheim Fellowship, Sloan Fellowship; Distinguished Leadership in Govt Award, Columbia Business School 2008, ranked by Forbes magazine amongst The World's Most Powerful People (fourth) 2009, (eighth) 2010–11, (sixth) 2012, (seventh) 2013, TIME magazine Person of the Year 2009. *Publications include:* Principles of Microeconomics (co-author), Principles of Economics (co-author), Macroeconomics (co-author) 2001, Essays on the Great Depression 2005, Inflation Targeting: Lessons from the International Experience (co-author) 2005, Principles of Macro Economics (co-author) 2007; numerous articles. *Address:* c/o Board of Governors of the Federal Reserve, 20th Street and Constitution Avenue, NW, Washington, DC 20551, USA.

BERNARD, Claire Marie Anne; French violinist; b. 31 March 1947, Rouen; d. of Yvan Bernard and Marie Chouquet; ed Conservatoire Régional de Musique, Rouen and Conservatoire Nat. Supérieur de Musique (CNSM), Paris; began professional career as solo violinist 1965; mem. jury, Tchaikovsky Int. Competition, Moscow 1974; Prof. of Violin at state-run conservatoires and music schools in France; Asst at Conservatoire nat. supérieur de musique, Lyon 1990–; mem. contemporary music ensemble Les Temps Modernes 1993–; Prof. CNR, CNSM; recordings include works by Khatchaturian, Prokofiev, Barber, Milhaud, Mozart, Haydn, Sarasate, Leclair, Gaviniès, Telemann and Vivaldi; Chevalier, Ordre nat. du Mérite; First Prize George Enesco Int. Competition 1964 and other awards and prizes. *Leisure interests:* painting, gymnastics, swimming. *Address:* 53 rue Rabelais, 69003 Lyon, France (home). *Telephone:* 6-69-45-53-07 (mobile). *E-mail:* bernard-claire16@bbox.fr (home).

BERNARD, Daniel; French business executive; *Chairman, Kingfisher plc;* b. 18 Feb. 1946; s. of Paul Bernard and Simone Bernard (née Doise); m. Chantal Leduc 1968; one s. two d.; ed Lycée Camille Desmoulins, Cateau, Lycee Faidherbe, Lille, École des Hautes Etudes Commerciales (HEC), Univ. of Paris; worked with Delcev Industries 1969–71, Socam Miniprix 1971–75, Ruche Picarde 1975–80; Dir Mammouth and Delta hypermarket chains 1976–81; Man. Dir Metro France 1981–89, mem. Bd of Dirs Metro International (Switzerland) 1989–92; CEO Carrefour SA 1992–98, Chair. and CEO 1998–2005; Deputy Chair. Kingfisher plc 2006–09, Chair. 2009–; Founder and Pres. Provestis (investment co.); mem. Bd of Dirs Alcatel-Lucent (fmrly Alcatel) 1997–, Cap Gemini 2005–; Sr Advisor, Towerbrook Capital Partners 2010–; Pres. HEC Foundation; Chevalier, Légion d'honneur; Officier, Ordre nat. du Mérite. *Leisure interests:* mountains, skiing, opera. *Address:* Kingfisher plc, 3 Sheldon Square, Paddington, London, W2 6PX, England (office); Provestis, 14 rue de Marignan, 75008 Paris, France (office). *Telephone:* (20) 7644-8008 (office). *Fax:* (20) 7644-1001 (office). *Website:* www.kingfisher.co.uk (office).

BERNARD, Desiree Patricia, LLB; Guyanese attorney-at-law and judge; *Judge, Caribbean Court of Justice;* b. 2 March 1939, Georgetown; d. of William Bernard and Maude Bernard; one d.; ed Bishops' High School, Georgetown, Univ. of London, UK; solicitor 1963–1979; Commr of Oaths and Notary Public 1976; admitted to English Roll of Solicitors 1977; magistrate 1979–80; Judge (first woman), High Court of Guyana 1980–92; Justice of Appeal 1992–96; Chief Justice (first woman) 1996–2001; Chancellor of the Judiciary (first woman) 2001–05; Judge of the Caribbean Court of Justice (first woman) 2005–; Founding Pres. Guyana Asscn of Women Lawyers; Founding mem. Conf. on the Affairs and Status of Women in Guyana; Sec. Caribbean Women's Asscn (CARIWA) 1970–74; Pres. Org. of Commonwealth Bar Asscn 1976; mem. and Chair. Caribbean Steering Cttee for Women's Affairs 1978; Rapporteur UN Cttee for Convention on Elimination of All Forms of Discrimination Against Women (CEDAW) 1982–84, Chair. 1985–89, mem. 1982–98; Chair. Georgetown Legal Aid Clinic 1994, Family Matters and Maintenance Cttee 1996–97; Chancellor of Anglican Diocese 1994; mem. Commonwealth Magistrates and Judges Asscn, Int. Asscn of Women Judges, Commonwealth Lawyers Asscn; involved in writing laws on equal rights of women and children, property rights of women, discrimination and domestic violence; Cacique Crown of Honour 1985, Order of Roraima 2002; Hon. LLD (Univ. of the West Indies) 2007; Univ. of Guyana Award for Achievements in Law 1989, Caribbean Women's Asscn Award 1991, Guild of Grads of Univ. of the West Indies Award, New York Chapter 1992, Bishops' High School Alumni Achievement Award 1999, Caribbean Bar Asscn Award 2001, CARICOM Triennial Award for Women 2005. *Leisure interests:* travel, cricket, promoting women's rights. *Address:* Caribbean Court of Justice, 134 Henry Street, PO Box 1768; Port-of-Spain (office); 9 Barbados Road, Federation Park, Port-of-Spain, Trinidad & Tobago (home). *Telephone:* 623-2225 (office); 622-3588 (home). *Fax:* 622-4814 (home). *E-mail:* dbernard@caribbeancourtofjustice.org (office). *Website:* www.caribbeancourtofjustice.org (office).

BERNAUER, David W., BPharm; American pharmaceutical industry executive (retd); b. 1944; m. Mary Bernauer; three c.; ed North Dakota State Univ.; joined Walgreen Co. in 1966, Dist Man. 1979–87, Regional Vice-Pres. 1987–90, Vice-Pres. and Treasurer 1990–92, Vice-Pres. of Purchasing 1992–95, Vice-Pres. 1995, Sr Vice-Pres. 1996–99, Pres. and COO 1999–2002, CEO 2002–06, Chair. 2003–07; mem. Bd of Dirs Nat. Asscn of Chain Drug Stores (now Vice-Chair.), Office Depot 2004–, Students in Free Enterprise, Lowe's Companies Inc. 2007–; mem. Bd of Trustees, Field Museum, Chicago; Co-Chair. North Dakota State Univ. Coll. of Pharmacy Devt Fund; Hon. DPharm (North Dakota State Univ.) 2000; North Dakota State Univ. Distinguished Alumni Award 1999. *Address:* c/o Board of Directors, Office Depot, 6600 North Military Trail, Boca Raton, FL 33496, USA (office).

BERNERD, Elliott; British property developer; *Executive Chairman, Chelsfield Partners LLP;* b. 23 May 1945, London; s. of the late Geoffrey Bernerd and of Trudie Malawer (née Melzack); m. 1st Susan Elizabeth Lynton 1968 (divorced 1989); two d.; m. 2nd Sonia Ramsay (née Ramalho) 1992; Co-founder and Exec. Chair. Chelsfield PLC (now Chelsfield Pnrs) 1987–, Chair. Duelguide PLC (after taking Chelsfied PLC pvt.) 2004–; Chair. and CEO Michael Laurie & Partners; Co-founder Stockley PLC; Chair. London Philharmonic Trust 1987–94, Wentworth Group Holdings Ltd 1990–, South Bank Foundation 1996–2002, South Bank Bd Ltd 1998–2002, CancerBACUP Benefactor's Scheme 2003–; Chair. of Trustees, Facial Surgery Research Foundation; mem. Bd of Dirs Investment Property Databank (IPD) 2005–; Hon. FRIBA. *Leisure interests:* tennis, skiing. *Address:* Chelsfield Partners LLP, 67 Brook Street, London, W1K 4NJ, England (office). *Telephone:* (20) 7290-2388 (office). *E-mail:* ebernerd@chelsfield.com (office). *Website:* www.chelsfield.com (office).

BERNERS-LEE, Sir Timothy John, Kt, OM, KBE, OBE, BA, FRS, FREng; British computer scientist and academic; *Senior Research Scientist and Director of World Wide Web Consortium, Laboratory for Computer Science and Artificial Intelligence, Massachusetts Institute of Technology;* b. 8 June 1955, London; s. of Conway Berners-Lee and Mary Lee Woods; ed Emanuel School, London, Queen's Coll., Oxford; with Plessey Telecommunications Ltd 1976–78; software engineer, D.G. Nash Ltd 1978; consultant software engineer CERN June–Dec. 1980, fellowship to work on distributed real-time systems for scientific data acquisition and system control 1984; with Image Computer Systems Ltd, responsible for tech. design 1981–84; began work on global hypertext project (now known as World Wide Web) 1989, launched within CERN 1990, on Internet 1991; joined Lab. for Computer Science (now Lab. for Computer Science and Artificial Intelligence), MIT 1994–, currently Sr Research Scientist and Dir World Wide Web Consortium; 3Com Founders Chair 1999–; Dir World Wide Web Foundation 2009–; Pres. Open Data Inst. 2012–; helped launch the Alliance for Affordable Internet (A4AI) 2013; mem. NAS 2009; Fellow, IEEE 2008; Distinguished Fellow, British Computer Soc.; Hon. FIEE; Sultan Qaboos Order for Culture, Science and Arts (First Class) (Oman) 2012; Hon. DFA (Parsons School of Design, New York) 1996; Hon. DSc (Southampton) 1996, (Oxford) 2001, (Port Elizabeth) 2002, (Lancaster) 2004, (Harvard) 2011, (St Andrews) 2013; Hon. DUniv (Essex) 1998, (Southern Cross) 1998; Dr hc (Universidad Politécnica de Madrid) 2009, (Vriji Universiteit Amsterdam) 2009; one of only six members of the World Wide Web Hall of Fame

1994, Young Innovator of the Year, Kilby Foundation 1995, Software Systems Award, Asscn for Computing Machinery (ACM) (co-recipient) 1995, ACM Kobayashi Award 1996, IEEE Computer Soc. Wallace McDowell Award 1996, Computers and Communication Award (co-recipient) 1996, Duddell Medal, Inst. of Physics 1997, Charles Babbage Award 1998, Mountbatten Medal, Nat. Electronics Council 1998, Royal Soc. Royal C Medal 2000, Greatest Briton Award 2004, Millennium Tech. Prize 2004, Charles Stark Draper Prize 2007, Lovelace Medal, British Computer Soc. 2007, D&AD Pres.'s Award 2007, BITC Award for Excellence 2008, Pathfinder Award, Kennedy School of Govt, Harvard Univ. 2008, IEEE/RSE Wolfson James Clerk Maxwell Award 2008, Lifetime Achievement Award, Webby Awards 2009, one of first three recipients of the Mikhail Gorbachev Award for "The Man Who Changed the World" 2011, inducted into IEEE Intelligent Systems' AI's Hall of Fame 2011, inducted into Internet Hall of Fame by the Internet Soc. 2012, honoured as the "Inventor of the World Wide Web" during the Summer Olympic Games opening ceremony, London 2012, Queen Elizabeth Prize for Eng (co-recipient) 2013 and numerous other awards. *Publications:* Weaving the Web: The Original Design and Ultimate Destiny of the World Wide Web by its Inventor 1999; several articles in professional journals. *Address:* Laboratory for Computer Science and Artificial Intelligence, Massachusetts Institute of Technology, Stata Center, Building 32, 32 Vassar Street, Cambridge, MA 02139, USA (office). *Telephone:* (617) 253-5702 (office). *Fax:* (617) 258-5999 (office). *E-mail:* timbl@w3.org (office). *Website:* www.w3.org (office).

BERNES, Thomas Anthony, BA; Canadian international organization official; *Distinguished Fellow, Centre for International Governance Innovation;* b. 21 March 1946, Winnipeg; m. Ann Boyd 1974 (divorced 1997); one s. one d.; ed Univ. of Manitoba; Dir Gen. Trade Policy, Dept of Industry, Trade and Commerce 1981–82, Economic Policy Planning Secr. 1982–83; Head Gen. Trade Policy Div., OECD 1983–85; Dir GATT Affairs, Dept of Foreign Affairs and Int. Trade, Govt of Canada 1985–87; Dir Internal Econ. Relations, Dept of Finance 1987–88, Gen. Dir Int. Trade and Finance Br. 1988–91, Exec. Dir Coordinating Secr. on Canadian Unity, Office of the Deputy Minister 1991–92, Asst Deputy Minister, Int. Trade and Finance Br. 1992–95; G7 Finance Deputy 1995–96; Alt. Gov. for Canada, IMF, Asia Devt Bank, African Devt Bank and IDB 1996; Dir Canadian Export Devt Corpn 1996; Exec. Dir IMF 1996–2001; Exec. Sec., Devt Cttee of Int. Bank for Reconstruction and Devt (World Bank) and IMF 2001–05, Dir Int. Evaluation Office, IMF 2005–09; Exec. Dir Centre for Int. Governance Innovation 2009–12, Distinguished Fellow 2012–; mem. Governing Bd INET 2011–13; Bd mem. New Rules For Global Finance 2013–. *Address:* Centre for International Governance Innovation, 57 Erb Street West, Waterloo, ON N2L 6C2, Canada (office). *Telephone:* (202) 250-3426 (office). *E-mail:* tbernes@cigionline.org (office). *Website:* www.cigionline.org (office).

BERNHARD, Sandra; American actress, comedienne and singer; b. 6 June 1955, Flint, Mich.; d. of Jerome Bernhard and Jeanette Bernhard; stand-up comedienne in nightclubs in Beverly Hills 1974–78; Dir HGOCo initiative, Houston Grand Opera 2007–. *Films include:* Cheech and Chong's Nice Dreams 1981, The King of Comedy 1983 (Nat. Soc. Film Critics Award), The House of God 1984, Sesame Street Presents: Follow That Bird 1985, Track 29 1988, Hudson Hawk 1991, Truth or Dare 1991, Inside Monkey Zetterland 1992, Dallas Doll 1994, Museum of Love 1996, The Apocalypse 1997, Plump Fiction 1997, Lover Girl 1997, Exposé 1998, An Alan Smithee Film: Burn Hollywood Burn 1998, Somewhere in the City 1998, Wrongfully Accused 1998, I Woke Up Early the Day I Died 1998, Hercules: Zero to Hero (voice) 1999, Dinner Rush 2000, Playing Mona Lisa 2000, Zoolander 2001, The Third Date 2003, The Easter Egg Adventure (voice) 2004, Twenty Dollar Drinks 2006, Dare 2009. *Stage appearances (solo):* Without You I'm Nothing 1988, Giving Till It Hurts 1992, I'm Still Here...Damn It! 1998, Everything Bad and Beautiful 2006. *TV appearances:* Without You I'm Nothing 1990, Roseanne (series) 1991–97, Sandra Bernhard: I'm Still Here... Damn It! 1999, The Sandra Bernhard Experience 2001, Silver Lake 2004, The L Word (series) 2005. *Recordings:* albums: I'm Your Woman (co-author 8 songs) 1985, Without You I'm Nothing 1989, Excuses For Bad Behavior (Part One) 1991. *Publications include:* Confessions of a Pretty Lady 1988, Love Love and Love 1993, May I Kiss You on the Lips, Miss Sandra? 1998. *Telephone:* (516) 303-6019. *E-mail:* kennethhartung@comcast.net. *Website:* www.sandrabernhard.com.

BERNHARD, Wolfgang, MSc, MBA, PhD; German automobile industry executive; b. (Wolfgang Ayerle), 3 Sept. 1960, Böhen, Landkreis Unterallgäu; ed Maristenkolleg, Mindelheim, Tech. Univ. of Darmstadt, Columbia Univ., USA, Johann Wolfgang Goethe Univ.; Man. Consultant, Mercedes-Benz AG 1990–92, Project Man. 1992–94, Man. for S-Class Ass., Sindelfingen Plant 1994–99, CEO Mercedes-AMG GmbH 1999–2000; Deputy mem. of Man. Daimler-Chrysler AG 2000–02, mem. 2002–04, COO Chrysler Group 2000–04, mem. Bd of Man. Daimler AG (Daimler Trucks) 2010–; mem. Bd of Man. and Chair. Volkswagen AG 2005–07; adviser, Cerberus Capital Management LP 2007. *Address:* c/o Board of Management, Daimler AG, 70546 Stuttgart, Germany (office). *Website:* www .daimler.com (office).

BERNIER, The Hon. Maxime, BCom; Canadian politician and lawyer; *Minister of State for Small Business, Tourism and Agriculture;* b. 18 Jan. 1963, Beauce; s. of Gilles Bernier and Doris Bernier; ed Univ. of Québec, Univ. of Ottawa; called to Québec Bar 1990; fmr Legis. Asst Office of the Deputy Premier of Quebec; Vice-Pres. Standard Life of Canada 2003–05; Man. Corp. and Int. Relations, Comm. des valeurs mobilières du Québec 2003–05; MP 2006–, Minister of Industry 2006–07, of Foreign Affairs 2007–08 (resgnd); Minister of State for Small Business and Tourism 2011–, Minister of State for Agriculture 2013–; mem. Conservative Party of Canada; fmr mem. Bd of Dirs Montreal Econ. Inst. *Address:* Conservative Party of Canada, 130 Albert Street, Suite 1204, Ottawa, ON K1P 5G4, Canada (office). *Telephone:* (613) 755-2000 (office). *Fax:* (613) 755-2001 (office). *Website:* www .conservative.ca (office).

BERNIK, France, PhD; Slovenian academic; b. 13 May 1927, Ljubljana; s. of Franc Bernik and Cecilija Bernik (née Smole); m. Marija Kanc 1956; one d.; ed Univ. of Ljubljana; teaching asst in Slovene literature, Univ. of Ljubljana 1951–57; Ed., Sec. Slovenska Matica, Ljubljana 1961–71; affiliated with Slovenian Acad. of Sciences and Arts Research Centre 1972–99; Scientific Adviser Inst. for Slovene Literature and Literary Sciences 1977–99, Assoc. mem. 1983, mem. 1987, Pres. Slovenian Acad. of Sciences and Arts 1992–2002; mem. Senator Academia

Scientiarum et Artium Europaea, Salzburg 1993; mem. Croatian Acad. of Sciences and Arts 1994, Int. Acad. of Energy 1997, Sankt Peterburg 1995, L'Accad. del Mediterraneo, Napoli 1999; mem. Akademie der Wissenschaften zu Göttingen 2003, Liebniz Sozietät der Wissenschaften zu Berlin 2003; Hon. mem. Slovenian Acad. of Sciences and Arts 2003, Hon. Citizen (Ljubljana) 2005, Hon. Senator, European Acad. of Sciences and Arts, Salzburg 2010; Eques commendator Ordinis sancti Gregorii Magni 1997, Golden Hon. Decoration of Freedom of Repub. of Slovenia 1997, Maréchal Ordre de Saint Fortunat 2001; Dr hc (Maribor) 2000; Int. Cultural Diploma of Honour 1996, Zois Award of Repub. of Slovenia 1999, Grand Award of Excellence and Mastery 2005, Austrian Medal for Sciences and Arts I 2010. *Publications include:* The Lyrics of Simon Jenko 1962, Fran Levec (1846–1916) 1965, Cankar's Early Prose 1976, Simon Jenko 1979, Problems of Slovene Literature 1980, Typology of Cankar's Prose 1983, Ivan Cankar: A Monograph Study 1987, Slovene War Prose 1941–80 (with Marjan Dolgan) 1988, Studies on Slovene Poetry 1993, Slowenische Literatur im europäischen Kontext 1993, Ivan Cankar: Ein slowenischer Schriftsteller des europäischen Symbolismus 1997, Horizons of Slovenian Literature 1999, Spektrum creativity 2004, Simon Jenko 2004, Slovenian Academy of Arts and Sciences: From 1992 to 2002 2005, Ivan Cankar 2006, Chronicle of My Life (I–II) 2012; Ed.-in-Chief Collected Works of Slovene Poets and Writers 1981–2010. *Address:* Zidovska 1, 1000 Ljubljana, Slovenia (home). *Telephone:* (1) 4706151 (office); (1) 4250365 (home). *Fax:* (1) 4253423 (office). *E-mail:* ana.batic@sasu.si (office).

BERNINI, Giorgio, LLM, SJD; Italian lawyer, politician and university lecturer; b. 9 Nov. 1928, Bologna; ed Univ. of Bologna, Univ. of Michigan Law School, USA; Prof., Univ. of Ferrara 1964–66, Univ. of Padua 1966–70; Prof. in Commercial Law, Univ. of Bologna; fmr adviser to EC (now EU) and Italian Govt on questions of int. commercial law, customs tariffs and tech. transfer; mem. Camera dei deputati (Forza Italia) 1994–96; Minister for Foreign Trade 1994–95; Sr Pnr, Studio Bernini e Associati; Pres. Asscn for the Teaching and Study of Arbitration and Int. Trade Law; mem. Exec. Cttee Italian Arbitration Asscn; fmr Chair. Int. Council for Commercial Arbitration, currently Hon. Pres. and mem. Advisory Bd; Cavalier, Grand'croix; Dean's Medal, New York Law School. *Publications:* articles in specialized journals and in daily newspapers. *Address:* Studio Bernini e Associati, via Mascarella 94–96, 40126 Bologna, Italy (office). *Telephone:* (05) 1240788 (office). *Fax:* (05) 1240131 (office). *E-mail:* info@berninistudiolegale.it (office). *Website:* www.studioberninieassociati.it (office).

BERNSTEIN, Carl, LLD; American journalist and author; b. 14 Feb. 1944, Washington; s. of Alfred Bernstein and Sylvia Walker; m. 2nd Nora Ephron 1976 (divorced); two s.; m. 3rd Christine Bernstein; ed Univ. of Maryland and Boston Univ.; copyboy, reporter, Washington Star 1960–65; reporter, Elizabeth (NJ) Journal 1965–66, Washington Post 1966–77; Washington bureau chief, ABC 1979–81; corresp. ABC News, New York 1981–84; Corresp. and contrib. Time Magazine 1990–91; Visiting Prof., New York Univ. 1992–93; Exec. Vice-Pres. and Exec. Dir Voter.com –2001; contributing ed. Vanity Fair 1997–; frequent political commentator on network TV; fmr rock and music critic for Washington Post; Drew Pearson Prize for investigative reporting of Watergate 1972, George Polk Memorial Award and other awards for journalism. *Publications include:* All the President's Men (with Bob Woodward) (Pulitzer Prize 1977) 1974, The Final Days (with Bob Woodward) 1976, Loyalties: A Son's Memoir 1989, His Holiness: John Paul II and the Hidden History of Our Time (with Marco Politi) 1996, A Woman in Charge: the Life of Hillary Rodham Clinton 2007; numerous articles in The New Republic, Rolling Stone, The New York Times, Newsweek and Der Spiegel. *Address:* c/o Knopf Publishing/Author Mail, 1745 Broadway, New York, NY 10019, USA (office). *Website:* www.carlbernstein.com.

BERNSTEIN, David Alan, CBE; British chartered accountant, business executive and sports administrator; b. 22 May 1943, St Helens, Lancs., England; fmr Chair. French Connection Group Plc; mem. Bd Manchester City Football Club 1994–2003, Chair. 1998–2003; mem. Bd of Dirs Wembley Stadium Ltd 2003–, Chair. 2008–; Chair. The Football Asscn 2011–13; mem. Bd of Dirs several public cos, including French Connection Group Plc, Ted Baker Plc, Blacks Leisure Plc (Chair. 1996–), Carluccio's (restaurant chain); Pres. Nat. Asscn of Disabled Supporters. *Address:* c/o The Football Association, Wembley Stadium, PO Box 1966, London, SW1P 9EQ, England.

BERNSTEIN, Nils, MSc; Danish government official and central banker; *Chairman, Danmarks Nationalbank;* b. 4 Jan. 1943; m. Ulla Agenfeld 1964; ed Univ. of Copenhagen; Sec., Ministry of Finance 1970–75; First Sec., Financial Affairs, Embassy in Washington, DC 1975–77; Private Sec. to Minister of Finance 1978–79, Head, Dept of Budget, Ministry of Finance 1980–83, Perm. Sec., Dept of Man. 1984–86; Perm. Sec., Ministry of Agric. 1986–94, Ministry of Agric. and Fisheries 1994–96, Perm. Sec., Prime Minister's Office 1996–2005; Sec. of The Queen in Council 1996–2005; Gov. by Royal Appointment and Chair. Bd of Govs, Danmarks Nationalbank (central bank) 2005–; mem. Gen. Council, European Central Bank 2005–; Chair. Kongeriget Danmarks Fiskeribank (Danish Fisheries' Bank) 1995–96, Dansk-Færøsk Kulturfond (Danish-Faroese Cultural Foundation) and Dansk-Grønlandsk Kulturfond (Danish-Greenlandic Cultural Foundation) 1996–2005; mem. Bd of Dirs Landbrugslotteriet (lottery) 1988–2005, GiroBank A/ S 1995–96, Den Kgl. Grønlandsfond (Royal Greenland Foundation) 1996–2005, North Atlantic House Foundation 2002–05, Dansk Ekspeditionsfond (Danish Expedition Foundation) 2004–05. *Address:* Danmarks Nationalbank, Havnegade 5, 1093 Copenhagen K, Denmark (office). *Telephone:* 33-63-63-63 (office). *E-mail:* nationalbanken@nationalbanken.dk (office). *Website:* www.nationalbanken.dk (office).

BERNSTEIN, Robert Louis; American publisher; b. 5 Jan. 1923, New York, NY; s. of Alfred Bernstein and Sylvia Bernstein; m. Helen Walter 1950; three s.; ed Harvard Univ.; US Army Air Force 1943–46; with Simon & Schuster (book publrs) 1946–57, Gen. Sales Man. 1950–57; Random House Inc. 1958–61, Vice-Pres. (Sales) 1961–63, First Vice-Pres. 1963–65, Pres. and CEO 1966–89, Chair. 1975–89; Publr at Large, Adviser John Wiley & Sons Inc. 1991–98; Vice-Chair. Asscn of American Publrs 1970–72, Chair. 1972–73; Chair. Asscn of American Publrs Cttee on Soviet-American Publishing Relations 1973–74, on Int. Freedom to Publish 1975; Chair. US Helsinki Watch Cttee, New York, 1979–92, Founding Chair. 1992; Chair. Fund for Free Expression 1975–90, Founding Chair. 1990; Founding Chair. Human Rights Watch 1975–, now Emer. Bd Mem.; Co-Chair.

Human Rights in China 1999–; fmr mem. Council on Foreign Relations, Nat. Advisory Cttee Amnesty Int.; mem. Americas Watch, Asia Watch, Middle East Watch, Africa Watch, Advisory Cttee Carter-Menil Human Rights Foundation, Advisory Bd Robert F. Kennedy Foundation Human Rights Award, Int. Liberal Education Bd Bard Coll.; Vice-Pres. Bd of Dirs Aaron Diamond Foundation, The Century Asscn; Hon. LLD (New School for Social Research) 1991, (Swarthmore Coll.) 1997; Hon. DHumLitt (Bard Coll.) 1998, (Hofstra) 1998, (Tougaloo Coll.) 2000, (Bates Coll.) 2000, (Yale) 2003; Human Rights Award (Lawyers' Cttee for Human Rights) 1987, Spirit of Liberty Award for the American Way 1989, Barnard Medal of Distinction, Barnard Coll. 1990, Liberty Award, Brandeis Univ. 1994, Eleanor Roosevelt Human Rights Award 1998, and other awards. *Leisure interests:* skiing, tennis, swimming. *Address:* 277 Park Avenue, 49th Floor, New York, NY 10172-0003, USA (office). *E-mail:* r.l.bernstein@att.net (office).

BERNSTEN, Thorbjørn; Norwegian trade union official and politician; b. 13 April 1935, Oslo; s. of the late Hans Berntsen Bertrand and Anna Mathilde Halvorsen; m. Adda Bernsten; ed Tech. Coll., Officers' Training School; with Nylands Shipyard 1951–66; Information Sec. Norwegian Union of Iron and Metalworkers, Leader 1965–66; Leader, Akers mek. Verksted AS 1962–64; Chair., later Deputy Chair. Oslo Municipal Consultative Cttee for Trade and Industry 1969–83; Deputy Chair. Labour Party 1989; Minister of the Environment 1990–97; mem. Cttee of Reps Oslo Labour Party 1962 (Chair. 1976–82); mem. Storting (Parl.) 1977–97, mem. Standing Cttee on Local Govt and the Environment 1973–86 (Chair. 1989–90); Norwegian Air Award 2004.

BERRESFORD, Susan Vail; American foundation executive; b. 1943, New York, NY; ed The Brearley School, Vassar Coll., Radcliffe Coll.; Program Officer, Neighborhood Youth Corps 1965–67; Manpower Career Devt Agency 1967–68; Project Asst Div. of Nat. Affairs, Ford Foundation 1970–72, Program Officer 1972–80, Officer in charge of Women's Programs 1980–81, Vice-Pres. US and Int. Affairs Programs 1981, Vice-Pres. Program Div. in charge of Worldwide Programming, then Exec. Vice-Pres. and COO, Pres. and mem. Bd of Trustees 1996–2007; Visiting Philanthropist, New York Community Trust 2008–; fmr mem. Bd of Dirs Council on Foundations, Chase Manhattan Bank, Chase Manhattan Corpn, Hermine and Robert Popper Foundation; mem. American Acad. Arts and Sciences, Council on Foreign Relations, N American Cttee Trilateral Comm.; Leadership for Equity and Diversity (LEAD) Award 1997, ranked by Forbes magazine amongst 100 Most Powerful Women (72nd) 2004, (93rd) 2005, (77th) 2006, Work Life Legacy Award 2005. *Address:* New York Community Trust, 909 Third Avenue, 22nd Floor, New York, NY 10022, USA (office). *Telephone:* (212) 686-0010 (office). *Website:* www.nycommunitytrust.org (office).

BERRI, Nabih, BA, LLM; Lebanese lawyer and politician; *President, Majlis al-Nuab;* b. 28 Jan. 1938, Freetown, Sierra Leone; s. of Mustaha Berri; m. 1st; six c.; m. 2nd; ed Ecole de la Sagesse, Beirut, Lebanese Univ., Faculté de Droit, Sorbonne, Paris, France; Pres. Nat. Fed. of Lebanese Students (UNUL), Sorbonne, Paris 1963; lawyer, Court of Appeals, Beirut 1963; joined resistance movt of Imam Moussa Al-Sadr against Israeli occupation of S Lebanon 1975; Head of Amal Movt (militia) 1984–; Minister of Justice 1984–88; Minister of Hydraulic & Electric Resources and of Housing & Cooperatives 1989–90; Minister of State May–Oct. 1992; Pres. Majlis al-Nuab (Nat. Ass.) 1992–. *Address:* Majlis al-Nuab, Place de l'Etoile, Beirut, Lebanon (office). *Telephone:* (1) 982047 (office). *Fax:* (1) 982059 (office). *E-mail:* nberri@lp.gov.lb (office). *Website:* www.lp.gov.lb (office).

BERRIDGE, Baroness (Life Peer), cr. 2011, of the Vale of Catmose in the County of Rutland; **Elizabeth Berridge,** MA (Cantab.); British barrister; b. Oakham, Rutland, England; ed Vale of Catmose Coll., Oakham Rutland Sixth Form Coll., Emmanuel Coll., Cambridge, Inns of Court, School of Law, London; fmr personal injury barrister in King's Chambers, Manchester; Parl. cand. for Stockport in Gen. Election 2005; mem. Jt Cttee on Human Rights, Advisory Council, Foundation for Relief and Reconciliation in the Middle East (charity), Dir and Trustee, Kainos (prisons charity), More than Gold (charity), British Future, Thinktank; Dir, Conservative Christian Fellowship (allied with British Conservative Party) 2005–11, Patron 2011–; Hon. LLB. *Leisure interests:* swimming, Ghana, Church. *Address:* House of Lords, Westminster, London, SW1A 0PW, England (office). *Telephone:* (20) 7183-9905 (office). *Fax:* (20) 7219-5979 (office). *E-mail:* walls@parliament.uk (office). *Website:* www.parliament.uk/biographies/lords/elizabeth-berridge/37710 (office); www.baronessberridge.com.

BERRIDGE, Sir Michael (John), Kt, PhD, FRS; British biologist and academic; *Emeritus Babraham Fellow, Babraham Institute;* b. 22 Oct. 1938, Gatooma, Rhodesia (now Zimbabwe); s. of George Kirton Berridge and Stella Elaine Hards; m. Susan Graham Winter 1965; one s. one d.; ed Univ. Coll. of Rhodesia and Nyasaland, Univ. of Cambridge, UK; Post-doctoral Fellow, Univ. of Virginia, USA 1965–66; Postdoctoral Fellow, Case Western Reserve Univ., USA 1966–67, Research Assoc. 1967–69; Sr Scientific Officer, Unit of Invertebrate Chem. and Physiology, Univ. of Cambridge 1969–72, Prin. Scientific Officer 1972–78, Sr Prin. Scientific Officer, Unit of Insect Neurophysiology and Pharmacology 1978–90, Hon. Prof. of Cell Signalling 1994–, Fellow, Trinity Coll. 1972–; Deputy Chief Scientific Officer, Lab. of Molecular Signalling, Babraham Inst., Cambridge 1990–, Head of Signalling Programme 1996–2003, Emer. Fellow 2003–; mem. numerous editorial bds, including Biochemical Journal 1987–, Journal of Endocrinology 1989–, Molecular Biology of the Cell 1989–, Advances in Second Messenger and Phosphoprotein Research 1990–, Journal of Basic and Clinical Physiology and Pharmacology 1990–, Journal of Experimental Biology 1993–; Advisory Ed. BioEssays 1994–; mem. Scientific Advisory Bd Venetian Inst. for Molecular Medicine 2013–; Gov. Strangeways Research Lab. 1987–98; Trustee, Isaac Newton Trust 1991–2000; Foreign Corresp., Acad. Royale de Médecine de Belgique 1994–; mem. Soc. of Gen. Physiologists, Academia Europaea 1989, European Molecular Biology Org. 1991, Acad. of Medical Sciences 1998, NAS 1999, American Philosophical Soc. 2007; Hon. mem. American Physiological Soc. 1992, Biochemical Soc. 2004, European Calcium Soc. 2006, Japanese Biochemical Soc.; Hon. Life mem. Soc. for Experimental Biology 1995; Foreign Hon. mem. American Acad. of Arts and Science 1999; Hon. Fellow, Gonville and Caius Coll. Cambridge 1998, Inst. of Biology 2000; Dr hc (Limburgs Universitaire Centrum, Belgium) 1993, (Univ. of Liverpool) 2007; numerous prizes, awards and medals including Feldberg Prize 1984, King Faisal Int. Prize in Science 1986, Louis Jeantet Prize in Medicine 1986, William Bate Hardy Prize, Cambridge Philosophical Soc. 1987, Gairdner

Foundation Int. Award 1988, Baly Medal, Royal Coll. of Physicians 1989, Albert Lasker Basic Medical Research Award 1989, Dale Medal, Soc. for Endocrinology 1990, Royal Medal, Royal Soc. 1991, Dr H. P. Heineken Prize for Biochemistry and Biophysics 1994, Wolf Foundation Prize in Medicine, (Israel, jtly) 1995, Massry Prize 1996, Ernst Schering Prize 1999, Shaw Prize in Life Science and Medicine 2005. *Publications:* more than 100 scientific papers. *Leisure interests:* gardening, golf. *Address:* The Babraham Institute, Babraham Research Campus, Cambridge, CB22 3AT, England (office). *Telephone:* (1223) 496621 (office). *E-mail:* michael.berridge@babraham.ac.uk (office). *Website:* www.babraham.ac.uk.

BERROU, Claude, MEng; French electrical engineer and academic; *Professor, Electronics Department, Télécom Bretagne;* b. 23 Sept. 1951, Penmarc'h; ed Institut Nat. Polytechnique de Grenoble; joined École Nationale Supérieure des Télécommunications de Bretagne (now Télécom Bretagne) 1978, currently Prof., Electronics Dept; mem. Acad. des sciences 2007; Fellow, IEEE 2008; Chevalier, Légion d'honneur; SEE Médaille Ampère 1997, IEEE (Information Theory) Golden Jubilee Award for Technological Innovation 1998, IEEE Richard W. Hamming Medal 2003, Grand Prix France Télécom de l'Acad. des sciences 2005, Marconi Prize, Marconi Foundation 2005. *Achievements include:* co-inventor with Alain Glavieux in 1991 (and Punya Thitimajshima who developed later similar methods published in a doctorate thesis when he was a student in the same research lab) of groundbreaking quasi-optimal error-correcting coding scheme called Turbo codes. *Publications:* Codage de canal – des bases théoriques aux turbocodes (Channel encoding – from theoretical grounds to turbocodes; co-author) 2005, Codes et turbocodes (Codes and turbocodes; co-author) 2007; several book chapters and more than 80 scientific papers in professional journals on algorithm/silicon interaction, electronics and digital communications at large, error correction codes, turbo codes and iterative processing, soft-in/soft-out (probabilistic) decoders; author or co-author of 12 registered patents. *Address:* Télécom Bretagne, CS 83818, 29238 Brest Cedex 3, France (office). *Telephone:* (2) 29-00-13-06 (office). *Fax:* (2) 29-00-11-84 (office). *E-mail:* claude.berrou@telecom-bretagne.eu (office). *Website:* www.telecom-bretagne.eu (office); perso.enst-bretagne.fr/claudeberrou (office).

BERRUGA FILLOY, Enrique, BA, MA; Mexican diplomatist, business executive and writer; *Vice-President of Corporate Affairs and Communication, Grupo Modelo;* ed El Colegio de México, Johns Hopkins Univ., USA, Instituto Tecnológico Autónomo de México; began career in Foreign Service 1984, Press Attaché, Embassy in Washington, DC 1986–89, Sec., Political Affairs, Embassy in London 1989–90, Chargé d'affaires ad hoc, Embassy in Dublin 1991, Sec. Gen., Mexican Comm. UNESCO 1993, Chief of Staff to Minister of Foreign Affairs 1993–97; Dir–Gen. Int. Affairs Div., Ministry of Educ. 1994; Personal Rep. of Pres. of Mexico for Reform of UN 1995–97; Amb. to Costa Rica 1997–99; Exec. Dir Mexican Inst. Int. Cooperation 1999–2000; Undersecretary of Foreign Affairs 2000–03; Perm. Rep. to UN, New York 2003–07; Vice-Pres. of Corp. Affairs and Communication, Grupo Modelo 2007–; columnist, El Universal (daily newspaper). *Publications include:* novels: Destino los Pinos 1982, El Martes del Silencio 1995, Propiedad Ajena 2000 (translated as Foreign Property 2003); numerous articles and papers. *Address:* Grupo Modelo, Campos Elíseos #400, 8th Floor, Colonia Lomas de Chapultepec 11000 México DF, Mexico (office). *Telephone:* (55) 5283-3600 (office). *Fax:* (55) 5280-6718 (office). *Website:* www.gmodelo.com.mx (office).

BERRUIEN, Nuri, BA, PhD; Libyan oil industry executive; *Chairman, National Oil Corporation;* b. 1946; ed Texas A&M Univ., USA; Gen. Man. of Production, Eng and Operation, Arabian Gulf Oil Co. (Agoco), Benghazi 1983–90, also mem. Bd 1983–90; Sr Eng Adviser and mem. Bd Teknica Ltd, London 1990–93; Chair. state-owned Nat. Oil Corpn, Tripoli 2011–. *Address:* National Oil Corporation, Bashier Sadawi Street, POB 2655, Tripoli, Libya (office). *Telephone:* (21) 3337141 (office). *Website:* en.noclibya.com.ly (office).

BERRUTI, Azucena; Uruguayan lawyer, human rights advocate and politician; b. 1929; Sec.-Gen. City Admin of Montevideo 1980s; mem. Partido del Sol (PS); Minister of Nat. Defence 2005–08. *Address:* c/o Ministry of National Defence, Edif. General Artigas, Avda 8 de Octubre 2628, Montevideo, Uruguay.

BERRY, Brian Joe Lobley, BSc, MA, PhD, FRGS, FBA, FAICP; American/British geographer, academic, political economist and policy analyst; *Lloyd Viel Berkner Regental Professor and Dean of the School of Economic, Political and Policy Sciences, University of Texas at Dallas;* b. 16 Feb. 1934, Sedgley, Staffs., England; s. of Joe Berry and Gwendoline Alice Berry (née Lobley); m. Janet E. Shapley 1958; one s. two d.; ed Univ. Coll., London and Univ. of Washington; Asst Prof., then Prof., Univ. of Chicago 1958–76; Faculty mem. Brookings Inst. 1966–76; Prof., Harvard Univ. 1976–81; Prof. and Dean, School of Urban and Public Affairs, Carnegie Mellon Univ. 1981–86; Prof., Univ. of Tex. at Dallas 1986–, Lloyd Viel Berkner Regental Prof. and Prof. of Political Economy 1991, currently Dean of the School of Econ., Political and Policy Sciences; mem. NAS (mem. Council 1999–2002), Asscn of American Geographers (Pres. 1978–79), American Inst. of Certified Planners, Regional Science Asscn Int.; Founding mem. Acad. of Medicine, Eng and Science of Texas; Fellow, American Inst. of Certified Planners, NAS, Univ. Coll. London 1983, American Acad. of Arts and Sciences, AAAS, Texas Acad. of Medicine, Eng and Science, Weimar School of Land Econs, Inst. of British Geographers; Hon. AM (Harvard) 1976; Anderson Medal, Asscn of American Geographers 1987, Victoria Medal, Royal Geographical Soc. 1988, Rockefeller Prize 1991, Lauréat, Prix Int. de Géographie Vautrin Lud 2005, and others. *Publications:* several books and more than 500 articles and other professional pubs. *Leisure interests:* family history, genealogy, travel, pseud-onymous novelist. *Address:* School of Economic, Political and Policy Sciences, GR31, University of Texas-Dallas, PO Box 83-0688, Richardson, TX 75083 (office); 2404 Forest Court, McKinney, TX 75070, USA (home). *Telephone:* (972) 569-7173 (office); (972) 562-1058 (home). *Fax:* (972) 883-6297 (office); (972) 562-1058 (home). *E-mail:* brian.berry@utdallas.edu (office). *Website:* brianjlberry.com (office).

BERRY, (Charles Edward Anderson) Chuck; American singer and composer; b. 18 Oct. 1926, St Louis; m. Thermetta Suggs 1948; four c.; plays guitar, saxophone, piano; concert and TV appearances 1955–; inducted into Int. Hall of Fame, Nashville Songwriters Asscn 1982, Grammy Award for Life Achievement 1984, inducted into Rock and Roll Hall of Fame 1985, Broadcast Music, Inc. (BMI) Icon Award 2002, Polar Music Prize 2014. *Albums include:* After School Sessions

1958, One Dozen Berrys 1958, New Juke Box Hits 1960, Chuck Berry 1960, More Chuck Berry 1960, On Stage 1960, You Can Never Tell 1964, Greatest Hits 1964, Two Great Guitars 1964, Chuck Berry in London 1965, Fresh Berrys 1965, St Louis to Liverpool 1966, Golden Hits 1967, At the Fillmore 1967, Medley 1967, In Memphis 1967, Concerto in B Goods 1969, Home Again 1971, The London Sessions 1972, Golden Decade 1972, St Louis to Frisco to Memphis 1972, Let the Good Times Roll 1973, Golden Decade (Vol. II) 1973, (Vol. V) 1974, Bio 1973, Back in the USA 1973, I'm a Rocker 1975, Chuck Berry 75 1975, Motorvatin' 1976, Rockit 1979, Chess Masters 1983, The Chess Box 1989, Missing Berries 1990, Rarities 1990, On the Blues Side 1993, Anthology 2000. *Films include:* Go, Johnny Go, Rock, Rock, Rock 1956, Jazz on a Summer's Day 1960, Let the Good Times Roll 1973, Hail! Hail! Rock 'n' Roll 1987. *Publication:* Chuck Berry: The Autobiography 1987. *Website:* www.chuckberry.com.

BERRY, Halle; American actress and model; b. 14 Aug. 1966, Cleveland, Ohio; d. of Jerome Berry and Judith Berry (née Hawkins); m. 1st David Justice 1993 (divorced 1996); m. 2nd Eric Benet 2001 (divorced 2005); partner Gabriel Aubry 2005–10; m. 3rd Olivier Martinez 2013; one s. one d.; ed Cuyahoga Community Coll.; began competing in formal beauty contests 1980s, won title Miss Ohio 1986; mem. Nat. Breast Cancer Coalition; Harvard Foundation for Intercultural and Race Relations Award. *Films include:* Strictly Business 1991, Jungle Fever 1991, The Last Boy Scout 1991, Boomerang 1992, Father Hood 1993, Alex Haley's Queen 1993, The Program 1993, The Flintstones 1994, Losing Isaiah 1995, The Rich Man's Wife 1996, Executive Decision 1996, Race the Sun 1996, Girl 6 1996, B.A.P.S. 1997, Why Do Fools Fall in Love 1998, The Wedding 1998, Bulworth 1998, Victims of Fashion 1999, Ringside 1999, Introducing Dorothy Dandridge (also producer) (Golden Globe for Best Actress, Screen Actors' Guild Award) 1999, X-Men 2000, Swordfish 2001, Monster's Ball (Acad. Award for Best Actress 2002) 2001, James Bond: Die Another Day (Nat. Asscn for the Advancement of Colored People–NAACP Award for Best Supporting Actress 2003) 2002, X-Men 2 2003, Gothika 2003, Catwoman 2004 (BET Award for Best Actress 2004), Robots (voice) 2005, X-Men: The Last Stand 2006 (People's Choice Award for Favorite Female Action Hero 2007), Perfect Stranger 2007, Things We Lost in the Fire 2007, Frankie and Alice 2010 (Nat. Asscn for the Advancement of Colored People–NAACP Award for Outstanding Actress in Motion Picture 2011), Dark Tide 2011, New Year's Eve 2011, Cloud Atlas 2012, The Call 2013 (Teen Choice Award for Movie Actress: Drama 2013). *Television:* TV debut with sitcom Living Dolls 1989, Knots Landing 1991–92, Their Eyes Were Watching God 2005. *Address:* c/o Vincent Cirrincione Associates, 8721 Sunset Blvd, Suite 205, Los Angeles, CA 90069 (office); c/o ICM, 8942 Wilshire Blvd, Beverly Hills, CA 90211, USA (office). *E-mail:* info@vincentcirrincione.com (office).

BERRY, L(eonard) Michael; Canadian diplomatist; b. 28 Sept. 1937, Bolton, UK; s. of Leonard Berry and Margaret Berry (née Wynne); m. 1st Linda Kathleen Randal 1963 (deceased); one s. two d.; m. 2nd Anna Sumanti Gill 2002; ed McGill Univ.; joined Dept of External Affairs 1964, served in Berlin 1966–68 and London 1971–75, High Commr to Singapore 1979–82, Amb. to OECD 1988–91, High Commr to Australia 1991–95, Canadian Special Co-ordinator for the Reconstruction of Fmr Yugoslavia 1995–97, Diplomat-in-Residence, Malaspina Univ., BC 1997–99; Int. Adviser, Berry Assocs 1999–; mem. Bd of Dirs Port of Nanaimo Authority 2002–05, Pacific Pilotage Authority 2005–, British Columbia Centre for Int. Educ. *Leisure interests:* skiing, golf, cricket, music, investment. *Address:* 541 St Andrew's Road, Qualicum Beach, BC V9K 1L5, Canada. *Telephone:* (250) 752-9360 (home). *Fax:* (250) 752-9360 (home).

BERRY, Mary Frances, PhD; American lawyer, historian and academic; *Geraldine R. Segal Professor of American Social Thought and Professor of History, University of Pennsylvania;* b. 17 Feb. 1938, Nashville, Tenn.; d. of George Ford and Frances Southall; ed Howard Univ., Univ. of Michigan; Asst Prof. of History, Cen. Mich. Univ. 1966–68; Asst Prof. Eastern Mich. Univ. 1968–69, Assoc. Prof. 1969–70; Acting Dir Afro-American Studies, Univ. of Md 1970–72, Dir 1972–74, Acting Chair. Div. of Behavioural and Social Sciences 1973–74; Provost 1973–76; Prof. of Law, Univ. of Colo 1976–80, Chancellor 1976–77; Asst Sec. for Educ. US Dept of Health, Educ. and Welfare 1977–80; Prof. of History and Law, Howard Univ., Washington 1980–; Geraldine R. Segal Prof. of American Social Thought and Prof. of History, Univ. of Pa 1987–; Vice-Chair. US Comm. on Civil Rights 1980–82, Chair. 1982–2004; mem. Advisory Bd Feminist Press 1980–, Inst. for Higher Educ. Law and Governance, Univ. of Houston; Fellow, Soc. of American Historians, Nat. Acad. of Public Admin; mem. Council UN Univ. 1986–; numerous awards and hon. degrees. *Publications:* Black Resistance/White Law 1971, Military Necessity and Civil Rights Policy 1977, Stability, Security and Continuity, Mr Justice Burton and Decision-Making in the Supreme Court 1945–58 1978, Long Memory: The Black Experience in America 1982 (jtly), The Pig Farmer's Daughter and Other Tales of American Justice: Episodes of Racism and Sexism in the Courts from 1865 to the Present 1999, And Justice for All: The United States Commission on Civil Rights and the Continuing Struggle for Freedom in America 2009, Power in Words: The Stories Behind Barack Obama's Speeches, from the State House to the White House 9with Josh Gottheimer) 2010. *Address:* Department of History, University of Pennsylvania, 208 College Hall, Philadelphia, PA 19104-6379, USA (office). *Telephone:* (215) 898-9587 (office). *E-mail:* mfberry@sas.upenn.edu (office); mfb@maryfrancesberry.com. *Website:* www.maryfrancesberry.com.

BERRY, Sir Michael Victor, Kt, BSc, PhD, FRS, FRSA; British physicist and academic; *Melville Wills Professor Emeritus of Physics, Bristol University;* b. 14 March 1941, Surrey; ed Univ. of Exeter, Univ. of St Andrews; Dept of Scientific and Industrial Research Fellow, Dept of Physics, Bristol Univ. 1965–67, Lecturer 1967–74, Reader in Physics 1974–79, Prof. of Physics 1979–88, Royal Soc. Research Prof. 1988–, Melville Wills Prof. of Physics, now Prof. Emer.; visiting lecturer at numerous int. univs; mem. Council BAAS 2002–; mem. Bd of Govs, Weizmann Inst., Israel 2000–; Ed. Proceedings of the Royal Society 2006–; mem. Editorial Bd several journals including Journal of Physics A 1994–; mem. Royal Soc. of Sciences, Uppsala 1986–, European Acad. 1989–, Indian Acad. of Sciences 1990–, London Mathematical Soc. 1995–; foreign mem. NAS (USA) 1995–, Royal Netherlands Acad. of Arts and Sciences 2000–; Fellow, Royal Inst. 1983–; Hon. Prof., Wuhan Univ. 1994, Hon. Fellow, Inst. of Physics 1999–; DSc hc (Trinity Coll. Dublin) 1996, (Open Univ.) 1997, (St Andrews Univ.) 1998, (Univ. of Warwick)

1998, (Univ. of Ulm) 2001, (Weizmann Inst.) 2003; Inst. of Physics Maxwell Medal 1978, American Physical Soc. Julius Edgar Lilienfeld Prize 1990, Inst. of Physics Paul Dirac Medal 1990, Royal Soc. Royal Medal 1990, London Mathematical Soc. Naylor Prize 1993, Louis-Vuitton Moët-Hennessey 'Science for Art' Prize 1994, Hewlett-Packard Europhysics Prize 1995, Int. Centre for Theoretical Physics (Trieste) Dirac Medal 1996, Russian Acad. of Sciences Kapitsa Medal 1997, Wolf Prize in Physics 1998, Ig Nobel Prize in Physics 2000, Norwegian Tech. Univ. (Trondheim) Onsager Medal 2001, Novartis/Daily Telegraph Visions of Science Prize 2002, Polya Prize, London Mathematical Soc. 2005, Chancellor's Medal, Bristol Univ. 2005. *Publications:* over 400 research papers. *Address:* H H Wills Physics Laboratory, Royal Fort, Tyndall Avenue, Bristol BS8 1TL, England (office). *Telephone:* (117) 928-8778 (office). *Fax:* (117) 925-5624 (office). *Website:* michaelberryphysics.wordpress.com (office).

BERRY, Richard Stephen, AM, PhD, FAAS, FRSC; American chemist and academic; *James Franck Distinguished Service Professor Emeritus of Chemistry, University of Chicago;* b. 9 April 1931, Denver, Colo; s. of Morris Berry and Ethel (Alpert) Berry; m. Carla Lamport Friedman 1955; one s. two d.; ed Harvard Univ.; Instructor, Univ. of Mich. 1957–60; Asst Prof. Yale Univ. 1960–64; Assoc. Prof. Univ. of Chicago 1964–67, Prof. Dept of Chem., James Franck Inst. 1967–89, James Franck Distinguished Service Prof. 1989–, now Prof. Emer.; Gaest Prof. Univ. of Copenhagen 1967, 1979; consultant, Los Alamos Science Lab. 1973–2003, Argonne Nat. Lab. 1976–2006; Visiting Prof., Univ. de Paris-Sud 1979–80; Hinshelwood Lecturer, Oxford 1980; Chair., Numerical Data Advisory Bd, National Research Council 1978–84; Newton Abraham Prof., Oxford Univ., England 1986–87; mem. Visiting Comm. of Applied Physics, Harvard Univ. 1977–81; mem. NAS (Home Sec. 1999–2003); mem. numerous cttees and orgs; Foreign mem. Royal Danish Acad. of Sciences; Fellow, American Acad. of Arts and Sciences (Vice-Pres. 1995–98), American Philosophical Soc. 2011; Dr hc (Romanian Medical Soc.) 2009; MacArthur Prize Fellow 1983, Alexander von Humboldt Preistraeger 1993, J. Heyrosky Medal 1997, inducted into East High School Alumni Heritage Hall, Denver, Colo 2010. *Publications:* (with L. Gaines and T. V. Long II) TOSCA: The Social Costs of Coal and Nuclear Power 1979, (with S. A. Rice and J. Ross) Physical Chemistry 1980, Understanding Energy: Energy, Entropy and Thermodynamics for Everyman 1991, (with others) Optimization Methods in Finite Time Thermodynamics 1999, Phase Changes in Simple Systems (with B. M. Smirnov) 2008; approx. 540 scientific papers in specialist journals. *Leisure interests:* music, skiing, hiking and climbing, photography, fly-fishing. *Address:* Department of Chemistry, SCL 101, University of Chicago, 5735 South Ellis Avenue, Chicago, IL 60637 (office); 5317 South University Avenue, Chicago, IL 60615, USA (home). *Telephone:* (773) 702-7021 (office). *Fax:* (773) 834-4049 (office). *E-mail:* berry@uchicago.edu (office). *Website:* berrygroup.uchicago.edu (office); chemistry.uchicago.edu/faculty/faculty/person/member/r-stephen-berry.html (office).

BERRY, Wendell, MA; American writer; b. 5 Aug. 1934, Henry County, Ky; m. Tanya Amyx 1957; one s. one d.; ed Univ. of Kentucky; mem. Faculty, Univ. of Kentucky 1964–77, 1987, Distinguished Prof. of English 1971–72. *Publications include:* novels: Nathan Coulter 1962, A Place on Earth 1967, The Memory of Old Jack 1974, Remembering 1988, The Discovery of Kentucky 1991, Fidelity 1992, A Consent 1993, Watch With Me 1994, A World Lost 1996, Jayber Crow 2001, Hannah Coulter 2004, Whitefoot 2009; short stories: The Wild Birds 1986; poetry: The Broken Ground 1964, Openings 1968, Findings 1969, Farming: A Handbook 1970, The Country of Marriage 1973, Clearing 1977, A Part 1980, The Wheel 1982, Collected Poems 1985, Sabbaths 1987, Sayings and Doings and an Eastward Look 1990, Entries 1994, The Farm 1995, A Timbered Choir: The Sabbath Poems 1979–1997 1999, Given 2005, The Mad Farmer Poems 2008, Leavings 2009, A Place in Time: Twenty Stories of the Port William Membership 2012; essays: The Long-Legged House 1969, The Hidden Wound 1970, The Unforseen Wilderness 1971, A Continuous Harmony 1972, The Unsettling of America 1977, Recollected Essays 1965–80 1981, The Gift of Good Land 1981, Standing by Words 1985, Standing on Earth 1991, Sex, Economy, Freedom and Community 1993, Another Turn of the Crank 1995, Life is a Miracle: An Essay Against Modern Superstition 2000, Citizenship Papers 2005, The Way of Ignorance 2006, Imagination in Place 2010, The Poetry of William Carlos Williams of Rutherford 2011; co-ed. Meeting the Expectations of the Land 1985, Home Economics 1987, What Are People For? 1990, Harland Hubbard: Life and Work 1990, Standing on Earth 1991. *Address:* 2803 Oak Ridge Road, Vanceburg, KY 41179-8447, USA (home). *Telephone:* (606) 796-2937 (home). *Website:* www.wendellberrybooks.com.

BERSANI, Pier Luigi; Italian politician; b. 29 Sept. 1951, Bettola, Emilia-Romagna; s. of Giuseppe Bersani; m. Daniela Ferrari; two d.; ed Univ. of Bologna; began career as teacher; Pres. of Emilia-Romagna Region 1994–96; Minister of Industry, Commerce and Craftsmanship 1996–99, of Transport and Navigation 1999–2001, of Econ. Devt 2006–08; mem. Chamber of Deputies (Camera dei Deputati) for Emilia-Romagna 2001–04, 2006–; mem. European Parl. (Socialist Group) 2004–06; mem. Partito Democratico 2007–, Nat. Sec. 2009–13; Chair. Nuova Romea Soc. 2002–07. *Publication:* Per una buona ragione 2011. *Address:* Partito Democratico, Via Sant'Andrea delle Fratte 16, 00187 Rome, Italy (office). *Telephone:* (06) 695321 (office). *E-mail:* redazione@partitodemocratico.it (office). *Website:* www.partitodemocratico.it (office); www.bersanisegretario.it.

BERSELLINI, Anita, PhD; French physicist, academic and university administrator; *Full Professor, Exceptional Class, Université Paris-Sud XI;* b. 10 Jan. 1943, Nice; d. of Sosthène Bersellini and Anna Migliore; m. Henri Marchal; one d.; ed Université Paris-Sud XI; researcher, Laboratoire d'Infrarouge, Université Paris-Sud XI 1965–76, Lecturer, 1966–76, Asst Prof. 1976–87, Full Prof. 2nd Class 1987–91, Head NFI Optronics Eng Degree 1991–2000, Full Prof. 1st Class 1992–99, Full Prof., Exceptional Class 1999–, Vice-Pres. 1998–2004, Pres. 2004–09; Researcher, Laboratoire de Photophysique Moléculaire, CNRS 1977–2008; Sec. of State responsible for the Paris region 2009–; Chevalier, Légion d'honneur 2008. *Publications:* contrib. to over 50 journals. *Leisure interests:* African art, modern art, music. *Address:* Université Paris Sud XI, Campus d'Orsay, Bât. 300, 91405 Orsay, France (office). *Telephone:* 6-07060762 (mobile); 6-46014753 (mobile). *E-mail:* anita.bersellini@u-psud.fr (office). *Website:* www.u-psud.fr (office).

BERSET, Alain, Dr.oec; Swiss politician; *Member, Federal Council and Head, Federal Department of Home Affairs;* b. 9 April 1972, Freiburg; m. Muriel Zeender; three c.; ed Neuenburg Univ.; asst and researcher, Research Inst. for Regional Econ. Devt, Univ. of Neuchâtel 1996–2000; Visiting Researcher, Inst. for Econ. Research, Hamburg 2000–01; Strategic Adviser, Canton of Neuchâtel Dept of Econ. Affairs 2001–04; pvt. practice as strategy and communications consultant 2006–11; mem. Ständerat/Conseil des Etats (Council of States) for Fribourg 2003–11, Pres. 2008–09, Vice-Pres. Socialist Group 2005–11, mem. Finance Cttee, Econ. Affairs and Taxation Cttee, Law Cttee; mem. Fed. Council 2011–, Head, Fed. Dept of Home Affairs 2012–. *Address:* Federal Department of Home Affairs, Schwanengasse 2, 3003 Bern, Switzerland (office). *Telephone:* (31) 3228041 (office). *Fax:* (31) 3227901 (office). *E-mail:* info@gs-edi.admin.ch (office). *Website:* www.edi .admin.ch (office).

BERSON, Jerome Abraham, BS, MA, PhD; American chemist and academic; *Sterling Professor Emeritus of Chemistry, Yale University;* b. 10 May 1924, Sanford, Fla; s. of Joseph Berson and Rebecca Bernicker Berson; m. Bella Zevitovsky 1946; two s. one d.; ed City Coll. of New York, Columbia and Harvard Univs; NRC Postdoctoral Fellow, Harvard Univ. 1949–50; Asst Prof., Univ. of Southern Calif. 1950–53, Assoc. Prof. 1953–58, Prof. 1958–63; Prof., Univ. of Wis. 1963–69; Prof., Yale Univ. 1969–79, Chair. Dept of Chem., 1971–74, Irénée duPont Prof. 1979–92, Sterling Prof. of Chemistry 1992–94, Sterling Prof. Emer. 1994–, Dir Div. of Physical Sciences and Eng 1983–90; Sherman Fairchild Distinguished Scholar, California Inst. of Tech. 1974–75; Nat. Research Council Postdoctoral Fellow; mem. NAS; Fellow, American Acad. of Arts and Sciences; ACS (Calif. Section) Award 1963, James Flack Norris Award in Physical Organic Chem. 1978, Sr US Scientist Award, Alexander von Humboldt Foundation 1980, Townsend Harris Medal 1984, William H. Nichols Medal 1985, Roger Adams Award 1987, NIH Merit Award 1989, Arthur C. Cope Scholar Award 1992, Oesper Award 1998, Literature Prize, German Chemical Industry Asscn 2000. *Publications:* Chemical Creativity 1999, Chemical Discovery and the Logicians' Program: A Problematic Pairing 2003; scientific papers on organic chem. published mostly in Journal of the American Chemical Society; papers on history and philosophy of science. *Leisure interest:* piano performance. *Address:* Department of Chemistry, Yale University, Box 208107, New Haven, CT 06520-8107 (office); 200 Leeder Hill Drive, Apt 205, Hamden CT 06517, USA (home). *Telephone:* (203) 230-0154 (home). *E-mail:* jerome .berson@yale.edu (office). *Website:* www.chem.yale.edu/faculty/berson.html (office).

BERTARELLI, Ernesto, BA, MBA; Swiss entrepreneur; b. 22 Sept. 1965, Rome, Italy; m. Kirsty Roper; three c.; ed Babson Coll., Boston, Harvard Business School, USA; began career with Serono SA (family-owned biotechnology co.) 1985, several positions in Sales and Marketing 1985–90, Deputy CEO 1990–95, Vice-Chair. Bd of Dirs 1991–2006, CEO and Chair. Exec. Cttee 1996–2006 (Serono acquired by Merck 2006); Chair. Waypoint Group; f. Ares Life Sciences (investment co.) 2008, Northill Capital 2010; mem. Bd of Dirs UBS 2002–09; mem. Strategic Advisory Bd, École Polytéchnique Fédérale de Lausanne (EPFL); Pres. Fondation Bertarelli; collaborating with Univ. of Geneva and EPFL to create Campus Biotech SA biotech centre, Geneva 2012–; f. Team Alinghi (yachting syndicate) 2000; Légion d'Honneur, Cavaliere di Gran Croce; Hon. Dr of Marine Science (Plymouth Univ.) 2013; five times winner Bol d'Or (Lake Geneva) 1997, 2000, 2001, 2002, 2003, winner 12-Metre and Farr 40 Championships 2001, winner America's Cup with Alinghi 2003, 2007; Paolo Venanzangeli Sailing Award 2008. *Leisure interest:* yachting. *E-mail:* enquiries@waypointcapital.net. *Website:* www.waypointcapital .net; www.bertarelli.com/en.

BERTELLO, HE Cardinal Giuseppe, DCL; Italian ecclesiastic and diplomatist; *President, Governorate of Vatican City State;* b. 1 Oct. 1942, Foglizzo; ed Pontifical Ecclesiastical Acad., Rome; ordained priest 1966; entered diplomatic service of the Holy See 1971, served in Apostolic Nunciatures of Sudan, Turkey and Venezuela; apptd Titular Archbishop of Urbs Salvia 1987; Apostolic Pro-Nuncio to Benin (also accred to Ghana and Togo) 1987–91; Apostolic Nuncio to Rwanda 1991–95, to Perm. Mission of the Holy See at UN Office, Geneva 1995–97, Perm. Observer of Holy See to UN Office, Geneva and to WTO 1997–2000, Apostolic Nuncio to Mexico 2000–07, to Italy (also accred to San Marino) 2007–11; Pres. Governorate of Vatican City State 2011–; Pres. Pontifical Comm. for Vatican City State 2011–; cr. Cardinal (Cardinal-Deacon of Santi Vito, Modesto e Crescenzia) 2012; participated in Papal Conclave 2013. *Address:* Governorate of Vatican City State, Palazzo Apostolico Vaticano, 00120 Città del Vaticano, Rome, Italy (office). *E-mail:* info@vatican.va (office). *Website:* www.vatican.va/ vatican_city_state (office).

BERTHELOT, Yves M.; French statistician, economist and international organization official; *President, World Organisation Against Torture;* b. 15 Sept. 1937, Paris; m. Dosithée Yeatman 1961; three s. one d.; ed Ecole Polytechnique and Ecole Nationale de la Statistique et de l'Admin Economique; Dir of Studies in the Ministry of Planning, Côte d'Ivoire 1965–68; Chief of the Study of Enterprises Div., then Chief of Service of Programmes of Institut Nat. de la Statistique et des Etudes Economiques 1971–75; Chief, Service des Etudes et Questions Int., Ministry of Cooperation 1976–78; Dir of Research, Devt Centre of OECD, Paris 1978–81; Dir CEPII (Prospective Studies and Int. Information Centre) 1981–85; Deputy Sec.-Gen. of UNCTAD 1985–93; Exec. Sec. UN Econ. Comm. for Europe 1993–2000; Vice-Pres. Fondation Européenne pour le Développement durable des Régions 1996–; Pres. Comité Français de Solidarité Internationale 2002–, Développement et Civilisations—Lebret-Irfed 2005, World Org. Against Torture; Officier, Ordre nat. du Mérite, Ordre Nat. (Côte d'Ivoire), Chevalier, Légion d'honneur. *Publications:* numerous articles on economics. *Leisure interests:* sailing, skiing. *Address:* World Organisation Against Torture, PO Box 21, 8 rue du Vieux-Billard, Geneva 8, Switzerland (office); Développement et Civilisations—Lebret-Irfed, 49 rue de la Glacière, 75013 Paris (office); 3 rue Auguste Comte, 75006 Paris, France (home); Comité Français de Solidarité Internationale, 32 rue Le Peletier, 75009 Paris (office). *E-mail:* berthelotyd@wanadoo.fr (home). *Website:* www.lebret-irfed.org (office).

BERTHOIN, Georges Paul, LenD, LèsL; French civil servant; b. 17 May 1925, Nérac; s. of Jean Berthoin and Germaine Mourgnot; m. 1st Anne W. Whittlesey (deceased); m. 2nd Pamela Jenkins 1965 (deceased); two s. four d.; ed Univ. of Grenoble, Ecole des Sciences Politiques, Univ. of Paris, Harvard Univ., USA and

McGill Univ., Canada; Pvt. Sec. to Minister of Finance 1948–50; Head of Staff, Prefecture of Alsace-Lorraine-Champagne 1950–52; Prin. Pvt. Sec. M. Jean Monnet, Pres. of ECSC 1952–55; Counsellor for Information, ECSC 1955–56; Deputy Chief Rep. of ECSC in UK 1956; Acting Chief Rep. of Comm. of EEC 1967–68, Deputy Chief Rep. 1968–71, Chief Rep. 1971–73; Exec. mem. Trilateral Comm. 1973–75, European Chair. 1975–92, Hon. Chair. 1993–; Int. Chair of European Movement 1978–81; Dir Int. Peace Acad., New York; Bd mem. Aspen-Berlin Inst.; mem. Int. Advisory Bd Johns Hopkins Univ., Bologna, Nine Wise Men Group on Africa; Aspen Inst. Distinguished Fellow; Hon. Chair. Jean Monnet Asscn; Officier, Légion d'honneur 2006, Médaille Militaire, Croix de Guerre, Médaille de la Résistance. *Leisure interests:* art, theatre, walking, collecting objects. *Address:* 67 avenue Niel, 75017 Paris, France (home).

BERTINI, Hon. Catherine Ann, BA; American international organization official and academic; *Professor of Public Administration, Maxwell School of Citizenship and Public Affairs, Syracuse University;* b. 30 March 1950, Syracuse, New York; d. of Fulvio Bertini and Ann Vino Bertini; ed Cortland High School, NY, State Univ. of New York at Albany; Youth Dir, New York Republican State Cttee 1971–74, Republican Nat. Cttee 1975–76; Man., Public Policy, Container Corpn of America 1977–87; Dir Office of Family Assistance, US Dept of Health and Human Services 1987–89; Acting Asst Sec., US Dept of Health and Human Services 1989, Asst Sec. US Dept of Agric. 1989–92; Exec. Dir World Food Programme of UN, Rome 1992–2002; mem. UN Sec.-Gen.'s Panel of High-Level Personalities on African Devt 1992–95; UN Sec.-Gen.'s Special Envoy on Drought in the Horn of Africa 2000–01; UN Sec.-Gen.'s Personal Humanitarian Envoy to Middle East 2002; Chair. UN System Standing Cttee on Nutrition 2002–06; UN Under-Sec.-Gen. for Man. 2002–05; Prof. of Public Admin, Maxwell School of Citizenship and Public Affairs, Syracuse Univ. 2005–; Fellow, Inst. of Politics, Harvard Univ. 1986; Commr Ill. State Scholarship Comm. 1979–84, Ill. Human Rights Comm. 1985–87; Towsley Foundation Policy Maker in Residence, Gerald R. Ford School of Public Policy, Univ. of Michigan 2002; Sr Fellow, Bill & Melinda Gates Foundation 2007–; Order of Merit (Italy) 2002; Hon. DSc (McGill Univ., Montreal) 1997, (Pine Major Coll.) 2000; Hon. DHL (State Univ. of New York, Cortland) 1999, (American Univ., Rome) 2001, (Loyola Univ., Chicago) 2002, (Dakota Wesleyan Univ., Mitchell, SDak) 2003; (Univ. of S Carolina, Spartanburg) 2003, (Colgate Univ.) 2004, Dr hc (Slovak Agricultural Univ., Nitra) 1999, Hon. DPS (John Cabot Univ., Rome) 2001; Leadership in Human Services Award, American Public Welfare Asscn 1990, Excellence in Public Service Award, American Acad. of Pediatrics 1991, Leadership Award, Nat. Asscn of WIC Dirs 1992, Quality of Life Award, Auburn School of Human Sciences 1996, Building World Citizenship Award, World Asscn of Girl Guides/Scouts 2001, Prize of Excellence, Asscn of African Journalists 2002, World Food Prize Laureate 2003, Univ. of Albany Medallion 2002, Leadership Award, Chicago Council on Foreign Relations 2004, Life Time Achievement in Child Nutrition Award, School Nutrition Asscn 2007. *Leisure interest:* music, including playing clarinet. *Address:* Department of Public Administration, 355 Eggers Hall, The Maxwell School of Syracuse University, Syracuse, NY 13244, USA (office). *Telephone:* (315) 443-1341 (office). *Fax:* (315) 443-9085 (office). *E-mail:* cbertini@ maxwell.syr.edu (office). *Website:* www.maxwell.syr.edu (office).

BERTINOTTI, Fausto; Italian politician; b. 22 March 1940, Milan; joined Gen. Confed. of Italian Labour 1964, Regional Sec. in Piedmont 1975–85; joined Italian Communist Party (PCI) 1972, left to join Partito della Rifondazione Comunista (PRC) (Party of Communist Refoundation), Nat. Sec. 1994–2006; mem. Camera dei Deputati 1994–2004, Pres. Camera dei Deputati 2006–08; Dir Rivista Binestrale Alternative il Socialism; mem. European Parl. 1999–2006. *Publications:* La camera dei lavori 1987, Verso la democrazia autoritaria 1991, Tutti i colori del rosso 1995, Le due sinistre (co-author) 1997, Pensare il '68 (co-author) 1998, Le idee che non muoiono (co-author) 2000, Per una pace infinita (co-author) 2002, Analisi collettiva (co-author) 2004, Non violenza – Le ragioni del pacifismo 2004, Il ragazzo con la maglietta a strisee 2005, La città degli uomini: Cinque riflessioni in un mondo che cambia 2007, Devi augurarti che la strada sia lunga 2009, L'Europa delle passioni forti (co-author), Io ci provo (co-author). *Address:* Alternative per il socialismo, Via della Consulta, 1, 00184 Rome, Italy (office). *E-mail:* posta@ alternativeperilsocialismo.it (office). *Website:* www.alternativeperilsocialismo.it (office).

BERTMAN, Dmitry Aleksandrovich; Russian theatre director; *Artistic Director, Helikon Opera Theatre;* b. 17 Oct. 1967, Moscow; s. of Alexander Bertman and Ludmila Zhumaeva; ed Lunacharsky State Inst. of Theatre Arts, Russian Acad. of Theatre Arts; started career as Dir in theatres in Moscow, Tver, Odessa, Syktyvkar; Founder and Artistic Dir Helikon Opera Theatre, Moscow 1990–; has also directed productions abroad, including in Vienna and Klagenfurt, Austria; Prof., Russian Acad. of Theatre Arts 1996–; teaches masterclasses on acting, Bern Opera Studio 1994–; mem. Council of Culture 2012–; The Maltese Cross (Malta) 2003, Count of Sovereign Military and Hospitaller Order of St. John of Jerusalem (Rhodes) 2003, Officier des Palmes Academiques 2003, Order of Santa Maria Land (Estonia) 2008, Order of Friendship; Honored Art Worker of Russia 1997, People's Artist of Russia 2005, Golden Mask Nat. Prize 1998, 1999, 2001. *Stage productions include:* Lady Macbeth of Mtsensk, Eugene Onegin, La Traviata, Falstaff, Aida, The Rake's Progress, Lulu, Peter the Great. *Address:* Helikon Opera, 103009 Moscow, B. Nikitskaya str. 19, Russia (office). *Telephone:* (495) 290-28-88 (office). *Fax:* (495) 291-13-23 (office). *E-mail:* helikon@helikon.ru (office). *Website:* www .helikon.ru (office); www.bertman.ru.

BERTOLINI, Mark T., BS, MBA; American business executive; *Chairman, President and CEO, Aetna Inc.;* b. 1957; ed Wayne State Univ., Cornell Univ.; COO, later CEO SelectCare Inc. 1992–95; fmr Exec. Vice-Pres. NYLCare Health Plans; Exec. Vice-Pres. Cigna HealthCare 2000–02, Sr Vice-Pres., Regional & Middle Market 2002–03; joined Aetna Inc. 2003, Head of Specialty Products 2003–05, Sr Vice-Pres. Specialty Group 2005, Sr Vice-Pres. Regional Business 2005–06, Exec. Vice-Pres. Regional Business 2006–07, Exec. Vice-Pres. and Head of Business Operations 2007, Pres. Aetna Inc. 2007–, CEO 2010–, Chair. 2011–; Chair. Operations Cttee, Asscn of Health Insurance Plans; mem. Bd Dirs US-China Business Council, Hole in the Wall Gang Camp, FIDELCO, Univ. of Connecticut Health Center; elected the first straight ally Bd mem. Nat. Gay and Lesbian Chamber of Commerce 2009–; mem. Advisory Bd Cornell Univ. School of Human Ecology; Nat. Gay and Lesbian Chamber of Commerce Healthcare

Leadership Award 2007, honoured for his leadership by Nat. Italian American Foundation, Outward Bound, Nat. Kidney Registry, Out & Equal Workplace Advocates, Quinnipiac Univ. Business School, Wayne State Univ. School of Business amongst others. *Address:* Aetna Inc., 151 Farmington Avenue, Hartford, CT 06156, USA (office). *Telephone:* (860) 273-0123 (office). *Fax:* (860) 273-3971 (office). *E-mail:* info@aetna.com (office). *Website:* www.aetna.com (office).

BERTOLUCCI, Bernardo; Italian film director; b. 16 March 1940, Parma; s. of the late Attilio Bertolucci and Ninetta Giovanardi; m. 1st Adriana Asti (divorced); m. 2nd Clare Peploe 1978; ed Univ. of Rome; worked with Pier Paolo Pasolini on Accattone; Fellow, British Film Inst.; Dr hc (Turin) 2000; European Film Award 1988, nine Acad. Awards, Hon. Golden Lion Award, Venice Film Festival 2007, Hon. Palme d'Or, Cannes Film Festival 2011. *Films directed:* La Commare Secca 1962, Prima della Rivoluzione 1964, Agonia in Aurore e Rabbia 1967, Partner 1968, La Strategia del Ragno 1970, Il Conformista 1970, Last Tango in Paris 1972, 1900 1976, La Luna 1979, Tragedy of a Ridiculous Man 1981, The Last Emperor (Acad. Awards 1988 for Best Dir and Best Screenwriter) 1987, The Sheltering Sky 1989, Little Buddha 1993, Stealing Beauty 1995, I Dance Alone 1996, Besieged (Globo D'Oro Award for Best Film 1999) 1998, Ten Minutes Older: The Cello (segment) 2002, The Dreamers 2003. *Publications:* In cerca del mistero (poems) 1962 (Viareggio Prize 1962), Paradiso e inferno (poems) 1999. *Address:* c/o Carol Levi and Co., 2 Via Pisanelli, 00196 Rome, Italy.

BERTONE, HE Cardinal Tarcisio Pietro Evasio, DCnL; Italian ecclesiastic and professor of canon law; *Camerlengo of the Holy Roman Church;* b. 2 Dec. 1934, Romano Canavese; ed Oratorio di Valdocco, Turin, Salesian novitiate of Monte Oliveto, Pinerolo, Pontifical Salesian Athenaeum (now Univ.), Rome; entered Soc. of St Francis and St John (Salesian Order); made religious profession 1950; ordained priest by Albino Mensa, Bishop of Ivrea 1960; Prof. of Special Moral Theology, Pontifical Salesian Univ. 1967, Dir of Theologians 1974–76, Prof. of Canon Law 1976–91, Dean Faculty of Canon Law 1979–85, Vice-Rector 1987–89, apptd Rector 1989; Guest Prof. of Public Ecclesiastical Law, Pontifical Lateran Univ. 1978; collaborated in drafting revision of Code of Canon Law; Archbishop of Vercelli 1991–95; Sec. of Congregation of Doctrine of Faith 1995–2002; entrusted with publ. of third secret of Fatima by Pope John Paul II 2000; Archbishop of Genoa 2002–06; cr. Cardinal (Cardinal Priest of Santa Maria Auxiliatrice in via Tuscolana) 2003, Cardinal-Bishop of Frascati 2008; participated in Papal Conclave 2005, 2013; Sec. of State, Roman Curia 2006–13; Camerlengo of the Holy Roman Church 2007–; consultant to several dicasteries of Roman Curia; served temporarily as Admin. of Holy See and Acting head of state of Vatican City state from resignation of Benedict XVI in Feb. 2013 until election of Pope Francis in March 2013; Hon. PhD (Catholic Univ. of Salta, Argentina) 2005. *Address:* Office of the Camerlengo, 00120, Cittá del Vaticano, Italy (office). *Telephone:* (06) 69883913 (office). *Fax:* (06) 69885255 (office). *Website:* www.vatican.va/roman_curia/uffici/camera_apostolica/documents/rc_camera-apostolica_20060606_organico_it .html#top (office).

BERTOZZI, Carolyn R., AB, PhD; American chemist and academic; *T.Z. and Irmgard Chu Distinguished Professor of Chemistry and Professor of Molecular and Cell Biology, University of California, Berkeley;* b. 10 Oct. 1966, Boston, Mass; d. of William Bertozzi; ed Harvard Univ., Univ. of California, Berkeley; postdoctoral work in cellular immunology at Univ. of California, San Francisco 1993–96; mem. Faculty, Univ. of California, Berkeley 1996–, currently T.Z. and Irmgard Chu Distinguished Prof. of Chem. and Prof. of Molecular and Cell Biology; Investigator, Howard Hughes Medical Inst.; Sr Faculty Scientist, Lawrence Berkeley Nat. Lab.; mem. NAS 2005, American Acad. of Arts and Sciences 2003, German Acad. of Sciences Leopoldina 2008, Inst. of Medicine 2011; Fellow, AAAS 2002; Danforth Teaching Award 1987, New England American Inst. of Chemists Award 1988, Thomas T. Hoopes Undergraduate Thesis Prize 1988, Outstanding Grad. Student Instructor Awards 1989, 1990, Camille and Henry Dreyfus New Faculty Award 1995, Bruce Mahan Teaching Award 1992, Exxon Educ. Fund Young Investigator Award 1996, Pew Scholars Award in the Biomedical Sciences 1996, Burroughs Wellcome New Investigator Award in Pharmacology 1997, Alfred P. Sloan Research Fellow 1997, ACS Horace S. Isbell Award in Carbohydrate Chem. 1997, Office of Naval Research Young Investigator Award 1998, Research Corpn Research Innovation Award 1998, Glaxo Wellcome Scholar 1998, Prytanean Faculty Award 1998, Beckman Young Investigator Award 1998, Joel H. Hildebrand Chair in Chem. 1998–2000, ACS Arthur C. Cope Scholar Award 1999, Camille Dreyfus Teacher-Scholar Award 1999, MacArthur Foundation Award 1999, Presidential Early Career Award in Science and Eng 2000, Dept of Chem. Teaching Award, Univ. of California, Berkeley 2000, Merck Academic Devt Program Award 2000, ACS Award in Pure Chem. 2001, Distinguished Teaching Award, Univ. of California, Berkeley 2001, Donald Sterling Noyce Prize for Excellence in Undergraduate Teaching 2001, Irving Sigal Young Investigator Award of Protein Soc. 2002, Iota Sigma Pi Agnes Fay Morgan Research Award 2004, Havinga Medal, Univ. of Leiden 2005, Ernst Schering Prize 2007, GLBT Scientist of the Year Award, Nat. Org. of Gay and Lesbian Scientists and Tech. Professionals 2007, Li Ka Shing Women in Science Award 2008, Roy L. Whistler Int. Award in Carbohydrate Chem. 2008, Willard Gibbs Medal, ACS Chicago Local Section 2008, W.H. Nichols Award 2009, Harrison Howe Award 2009, Albert Hofmann Medal, Univ. of Zurich 2009, Lemelson-MIT Prize 2010, Bio-organic Chem. Award, RSC Organic Div. 2010, Tetrahedron Young Investigator Award for Bio-organic and Medicinal Chem. 2011, Emanuel Merck Lectureship 2011, Heinrich Wieland Prize 2012. *Publications:* Glycochemistry: Principles, Synthesis and Applications (co-ed.) 2001, Essentials of Glycobiology (second edn, co-ed.) 2009; more than 290 papers in scientific journals. *Address:* 820 Latimer Hall, Department of Chemistry, B84 Hildebrand Hall #1460, University of California, Berkeley, CA 94720-1460, USA (office). *Telephone:* (510) 643-1682 (office). *Fax:* (510) 643-2628 (office). *E-mail:* crb@berkeley.edu (office). *Website:* chem.berkeley .edu (office); www.cchem.berkeley.edu/crbgrp/bio.htm (office).

BERTRAND, Xavier, PhD; French politician; *Mayor of Saint-Quentin;* b. 21 March 1965, Châlons-sur-Marne, Marne; m. Emmanuelle Gontier; three c.; mem. Union pour un Mouvement Populaire, Sec.-Gen. March–Dec. 2008, 2009–; Deputy Mayor of Saint-Quentin, Aisne 1995–2010, Mayor 2010–; Deputy in Nat. Ass. for Aisne 2002–04, 2007, 2009–10; Sec. of State for Health Insurance, Ministry of Health and Social Welfare 2004–05; Minister of Health and Social Protection

2005–07 (resgnd), for Labour, Labour Relations and Solidarity 2007–09, of Labour, Employment and Health 2010–12; Spokesman for Nicolas Sarkozy's presidential campaign 2007. *Address:* Hôtel de ville, 02100 Saint-Quentin, Aisne, France (office). *Telephone:* (3) 23-06-90-00 (office). *E-mail:* mairie@ville-saint -quentin.fr (office). *Website:* www.ville-saintquentin.fr (office).

BERTRANOU, Armando Victorio, PhD; Argentine academic; *President, National Agency for the Promotion of Science and Technology;* b. 14 May 1942, Mendoza; s. of Pablo Luis Bertranou and Susana Angélica Saligari; m. Clara Alicia Jalif 1965; two s. two d.; ed Universidad Nacional de Cuyo, Univ. of California, Davis; Titular Prof., Faculty of Agricultural Sciences, Universidad Nacional de Cuyo, fmr Rector; fmr Dir-Gen. Fund for Scientific and Technological Research, Nat. Scientific and Technological Research; fmr Chair. Nat. Council of Scientific and Technical Research; fmr Chair. Nat. Inst. of Science and Tech. Basins, Ministry of Natural Resources and Sustainable Devt; Pres. Nat. Agency for Promotion of Science and Tech. 2009–; mem. Bd of Dirs Nat. Water Inst., Center for Econs, Law and Water Man., Nat. Parks Admin. *Publications:* numerous articles and papers on irrigation and water man. *Leisure interests:* aerobics, rugby, rowing. *Address:* National Agency for Promotion of Science and Technology, Ministry of Science, Technology and Productive Innovation, Avda Córdoba 831, C1054AAH Buenos Aires, Argentina (office). *Telephone:* (11) 4891-8300 (office). *Fax:* (11) 4312-8364 (office). *E-mail:* contacto@mincyt.gov.ar (office). *Website:* www .agencia.mincyt.gob.ar (office).

BĒRZIŅŠ, Andris; Latvian politician, business executive and head of state; *President;* b. 10 Dec. 1944, Nītaure, Latvian SSR, USSR; m. Dace Seisuma 2011; ed First Middle School of Sigulda, Rīga Polytechnical Inst., Latvian State Univ.; became a radio engineer at 'Elektrons' factory, worked his way up to Dir; apptd Deputy Minister of Municipal Services of Latvian SSR 1988; elected to Valmiera Dist Council (Soviet) of People's Deputies 1989–93, apptd Chair. Exec. Comm.; elected to Supreme Council of Latvian SSR representing Valmiera 1990; joined Latvian Popular Front faction in Supreme Council; Chair. Privatization Fund of Bank of Latvia 1993; Pres. Latvijas Unibanka (jt-stock co.) 1993–2004; also owned numerous real-estate properties; worked as adviser to Pres. of SEB; mem. Bd several jt-stock cos, including Valmiera stikla šķiedra (Valmiera Fibreglass) and Lode; returned to politics when he ran unsuccessfully for Mayor of Riga as Leader of Union of Greens and Farmers party list 2005; Pres. Latvian Chamber of Industry and Commerce 2006–10; Chair. Latvenergo –2009; elected Deputy of the Saeima (Union of Greens and Farmers) 2010; Pres. of Latvia 2011–; Patron European Acad. of Science and Art 2013–; Hon. mem. Rīga Tech. Univ. 2012, Univ. of Latvia 2012; Commemorative badge for participants in the 1991 barricades 1996, Commdr, Order of the Three Stars 2000, Cross of Recognition (First Class) 2011, Order of Viesturs (First Class) 2011, Order of the Three Stars (First Class) with Chain 2011. *Address:* Chancery of the President, Pils lauk. 3, Rīga 1900, Latvia (office). *Telephone:* 6709-2106 (office). *Fax:* 6709-2157 (office). *E-mail:* prese@president.lv (office). *Website:* www.president.lv (office).

BĒRZIŅŠ, Andris; Latvian historian and politician; b. 4 Aug. 1951, Riga; m.; two c.; ed Latvian State Univ.; teacher and admin. in several schools 1975–82; Head, Div. of Personnel Training Cttee for Vocational and Tech. Training 1982–86; Head, Div. State Cttee for Labour and Social Affairs 1986–90; Head, Div., Deputy Dir Welfare Dept Ministry of Econs 1990–92; Deputy Minister, concurrently Head, Labour Dept Ministry of Welfare 1992–93; State Minister of Labour 1993–94; Deputy Prime Minister, Minister of Welfare 1994–95; Minister of Labour 1995–97; Chair. Riga City Council 1997–2000; Prime Minister of Latvia 2000–02; Chair. Latvian Way (Latvijas ceļš) 2000; strategic consultant for UNDP, Latvia 2004; currently mem. Saeima (Parl.). *Address:* Saeima (Parliament), Jekaba iela 11, Riga 1811, Latvia (office). *Telephone:* 6708-7111 (office). *Fax:* 6708-7100 (office). *E-mail:* Berzins.Andris@saeima.lv (office). *Website:* www.saeima.lv (office).

BESCH, Werner Walter, DPhil; German professor of German; *Professor Emeritus, University of Bonn;* b. 4 May 1928, Erdmannsweiler, Black Forest; s. of Matthias Besch and Elisabeth Besch (née Fuss); m. Katharina Müller 1957; one s. two d.; Prof. of German Language and Early German Literature, Ruhr Univ., Bochum 1965–70, Univ. of Bonn 1970–93, Prof. Emer. 1993–; Rector, Univ. of Bonn 1981–83, Pro-Rector 1983–85; mem. Scientific Bd, Inst. für Deutsche Sprache, Mannheim 1976–93; mem. Nordrhein-Westfälische Akad. der Wissenschaften; mem. Publishing Cttee on writings of Martin Bucers, Heidelberg Akademie 1968–2008; mem. Rat für Deutsche Rechtschreibung 2004–10; Corresp. mem. Heidelberg Akad. der Wissenschaften, Inst. of Germanic Studies, Univ. of London; Hon. mem. Gesellschaft Ungarischer Germanisten 2005; Wolfgang Paul Medaille, Univ. of Bonn, Hon. mem Internationale Gesellschaft für Dialektologie des Deutschen 2003. *Publications include :* Lautgeographie und Lautgeschichte im obersten Neckar-u. Donaugebiet 1961, Sprachlandschaften und Sprachausgleich im 15. Jahrhundert 1967, Dialekt/Hochsprache-Kontrastiv 1977, Handbuch Dialektologie 1983, 1984 (co-ed.), Handbuch Sprachgeschichte 1985, (2nd edn) (co-ed.) 1998–2004, Duzen, Siezen, Titulieren. Zur Anrede im Deutschen heute und gestern (2nd edn) 1998, Zur Rolle Luthers in der deutschen Sprachgeschichte 1999, Grundlagen der Germanistik (co-ed.) 1989–2007, Deutsche Sprache im Wandel 2003, Deutscher Bibelwortschatz in der frühen Neuzeit, Auswahl-Abwahl-Veralten 2008, Geschichte der deutschen Sprache: Längsschnitte, Zeitstufen, linguistische Studien 2009; various essays and articles. *Address:* Römerstrasse 118, Apt 2512, 53117 Bonn, Germany (home).

BESHEAR, Steven (Steve) Lynn; American lawyer, politician, business executive and state governor; *Governor of Kentucky;* b. 21 Sept. 1944, Dawson Springs, Hopkins Co., Ky; s. of Orlando Russell Beshear and Mary Elizabeth Beshear (née Joiner); m. Jane Beshear; two s.; ed Dawson Springs High School, Univ. of Kentucky; elected Pres. Student Body during his third undergraduate year; served in US Army Reserve 1969–75, intelligence analyst, also carried out certain Judge Advocate Gen. duties; elected to Kentucky House of Reps for 76th Dist 1974–79; Attorney Gen. of Kentucky 1980–81, Lt Gov. 1983–87, cr. and headed Kentucky Tomorrow Comm.; cand. in election for Gov. of Kentucky 1987; practised law in Lexington, Kentucky, sr exec. of multi-state law firm; was the Democratic nominee for US Senate 1996; Gov. of Kentucky 2007–; mem. Commerce Lexington, Inc., Kentucky Horse Park Foundation, God's Pantry Food Bank, Bluegrass Tomorrow, Kentucky World Trade Center, Univ. of Kentucky Coll. of Law Visiting Cttee; Democrat. *Address:* 700 Capital Avenue, Suite 100, Frankfort, KY 40601 (office);

Washington Office of the Governor, Commonwealth of Kentucky, 444 North Capitol Street, Suite 224, Washington, DC 20001, USA (office). *Telephone:* (502) 564-2611 (Frankfort) (office); (202) 220-1350 (DC) (office). *Fax:* (502) 564-2517 (Frankfort) (office); (502) 564-0437 (Frankfort) (office); (202) 220-1359 (DC) (office). *E-mail:* info@stevebeshear.com (office); info@governor.ky.gov (office). *Website:* governor.ky.gov (office); www.stevebeshear.com (office).

BESIMI, Fatmir, PhD; Macedonian politician; *Deputy Prime Minister, responsible for European Integration;* b. 18 Nov. 1975, Tetovo; m. Albertina Besimi; one d.; ed Kiril Pejčinovik Gymnasium, Tetovo, Faculty of Econs, SS. Cyril and Methodius Univ., Skopje, Staffordshire Univ., Stoke-on-Trent, UK, postgraduate studies at Univ. of South-Eastern Europe, Tetovo; foreign exchange work, br. office of Stopanska Banka AD, Tetovo Jan.–July 2000; researcher and analyst, Nat. Bank of the Repub. of Macedonia 2001–02, Vice-Gov. 2003–04; Man., PE for Airport Services-Makedonija 2002–03; Minister of the Economy 2004–06, 2008–11; Economist, World Bank, Prishtina, Kosovo 2007–08; Minister of Defence 2011–13; Deputy Prime Minister, responsible for European Integration Feb. 2013–; Lecturer, State Univ., Tetovo 1999–2008, Univ. Riinvest, Prishtina 2007; part-time mem. of staff, Doctoral Programme, Staffordshire Univ., UK 2010–; Guest Lecturer, Harvard Univ., Georgetown Univ., Johns Hopkins Univ. and Univ. of Vermont, USA. *Publications:* two books in English and several professional and academic articles in the fields of economics and politics published in English, Albanian and Macedonian in journals in Macedonia and abroad. *Address:* Office of the Prime Minister, 1000 Skopje, Ilindenska bb 2, Former Yugoslav Republic of Macedonia (office). *Telephone:* (2) 3118022 (office). *Fax:* (2) 3112561 (office). *E-mail:* primeminister@primeminister.gov.mk (office). *Website:* www.vlada.mk (office).

BESSÉ, Albert; Central African Republic politician; fmr Chargé de Mission des Banques et Institutions Financières, Ministry of Finance and Budget, Minister of Finance and the Budget 2009–11; Gen. Treas. CIDEL (Center for Integrated Devt of Ethics and Leadership). *Address:* c/o Ministry of Finance and the Budget, BP 696, Bangui, Central African Republic (office).

BESSER, Gordon Michael, MB, MD, DSc, FRCP, FMedSci; British physician, endocrinologist and professor of medicine (retd); *Consultant Endocrinologist, The London Clinic Centre for Endocrinology;* b. 22 Jan. 1936, London, England; ed Medical Coll. of St Bartholomew's Hosp., Univ. of London; Sr Lecturer in Medicine, St Bartholomew's Hosp. Medical Coll. 1970–74, Head of Endocrinology and Hon. Consultant Physician 1970–95, Prof. of Endocrinology 1974–92, Prof. of Medicine 1992–2001; Prof. of Medicine and Head of Endocrinology, St Bartholomew's and Royal London School of Medicine and Dentistry 1995–2001, Prof. Emer. 2001–; Civilian Consultant in Endocrinology, RN 1989–97, to the Triservice Medical Service 1997–2004; Visiting Consultant Endocrinologist to Govt of Malta 1989–2002; Chief Exec. Barts NHS Trust 1992–94; Consultant Endocrinologist, The London Clinic Centre for Endocrinology 2001–; Fellow, Queen Mary Univ. of London 2005; Lecturer to Royal Coll. of Physicians: Goulstonian 1974, Lumlean 1993, Simms 1999, Soc. for Endocrinology, Hon. Fellow, Royal Soc. of Medicine 2007; Hon. MD (Turin) 1985; Jubilee Medalist and Lecturer 2002, William Julius Mickle Fellowship for the Advancement of Medical Science, Univ. of London 1976, Medal of Soc. for Endocrinology 1978, Clinical Endocrinology Prize 1986, Medal of European Neuroendocrinology Asscn 1999. *Publications:* Clinical Endocrinology 1984, DeGroot's Endocrinology (section ed.) 1985, 26 textbooks in gen. medicine and endocrinology and over 500 articles in journals of basic and clinical endocrinology and medicine. *Leisure interests:* early Chinese ceramics, modern European art, physical fitness, opera, ballet. *Address:* The London Clinic Centre for Endocrinology, 5 Devonshire Place, London, W1G 5HL (office); Department of Endocrinology, St Bartholomew's & Royal London School of Medicine, London, EC1A 7BE, England (office). *Telephone:* (20) 7935-4444 (office); (20) 7034-6215 (office). *Fax:* (20) 7616-7791 (office). *E-mail:* endo@thelondonclinic.co.uk (office).

BESSHO, Yoshiki; Japanese business executive; *Chairman and Executive Officer, Suzuken Company Ltd;* began career at The Bank of Tokyo-Mitsubishi UFJ Ltd; joined Suzuken Co. Ltd 1970, served successivley as Man. Dir, Sr Man. Dir, Pres., Exec. Pres. and Dir, Rep. Dir, Chair. and Exec. Officer Suzuken Co. Ltd 2007–. *Address:* Suzuken Co. Ltd, 8 Higashi Kataha-machi, Higashi-ku, Nagoya, Aichi 461-8701, Japan (office). *Telephone:* (52) 961-2331 (office). *E-mail:* info@suzuken.co.jp (office). *Website:* www.suzuken.co.jp (office).

BESSMERTNYKH, Alexander Alexandrovich, CandJurSc; Russian politician and diplomatist; *President, International Foreign Policy Association;* b. 10 Nov. 1933, Biisk; s. of Alexander Bessmertnykh and Maria Bessmertnykh; m.; one s. one d.; ed Moscow State Inst. of Int. Relations; joined Diplomatic Service 1957, served at Embassy in Washington, DC 1970–83; fmr arms control negotiator; First Deputy Foreign Minister (with special responsibility for N America and the Middle East) 1987–90, Deputy 1986; Amb. to USA 1990–91; Minister of Foreign Affairs Jan.–Aug. 1991; mem. CP Cen. Cttee 1990–91; Head of Policy Analysis Centre Soviet (now Russian) Foreign Policy Asscn 1991–92; Pres. Int. Foreign Policy Asscn 1992–, Chair. World Council of Fmr Foreign Ministers 1993–; Dir Gen. Ass. for Int. Business and Political Connections 2011–; Chair. Supervisory Bd Advanced Tech. Research Programs Foundation; Prof. Moscow Univ.; mem. Acad. of Social Sciences of Russian Fed.; Corresp. mem. Chilean Acad. of Social and Political Sciences; Order of Friendship of Peoples, Order of Peter the Great, Order of Lomonosov; Badge of Honour, various medals. *Publications:* numerous articles on foreign policy, diplomacy and military strategy. *Leisure interests:* literature, classical music, tennis. *Address:* International Foreign Policy Association, 105064 Moscow, Yakovo-Apostolski per. 10, Russia (office). *Telephone:* (495) 917-25-14 (office); (495) 917-15-85 (office). *Fax:* (495) 917-19-13 (office). *E-mail:* fpa@forpolicy .ru (office). *Website:* fpamoscow.org.

BESSON, Luc; French film director, producer and screenwriter; b. 18 March 1959, Paris; s. of Claude Besson and Danièle Plane; m. 1st Anne Parillaud (divorced); m. 2nd Milla Jovovich 1997 (divorced 1999); m. 3rd Virginie Silla 2004; one s. four d.; worked as asst on films in Paris and Hollywood; First Asst for several advertising films; two features (Homme libre and Les Bidasses aux grandes manoeuvres) and four shorts; f. Les Films du Loup (now Leeloo Productions) 1982; Co-founder and Chair. EuropaCorp 1999–. *Films include:* L'Avant dernier 1981, Le Dernier Combat 1983, Subway 1985, The Big Blue 1988, Nikita (Italian Nat.

Syndicate of Film Journalists Silver Ribbon for Best Dir, Foreign Film 1990) 1990, Atlantis 1991, Leon 1994, The Fifth Element (Cesar Award for Best Dir 1997) 1997, The Messenger: The Story of Joan of Arc 1999, Angel-A 2006, Arthur and the Invisibles 2006, Taken 2008, District 13: Ultimatum 2009, From Paris with Love 2010, Les aventures extraordinaires d'Adèle Blanc-Sec 2010, Arthur 3: The War of the Two Worlds 2010, The Lady 2011, Colombiana (screenplay) 2011, Taken 2 2012. *Publications:* Arthur and the Minimoys (juvenile) 2005, Arthur and the War of the Two Worlds. *Address:* Leeloo Productions, 53 rue Boissée, 91540 Mennecy (office); c/o CBC, 11 rue de la Croix Boissée, 91540 Mennecy, France. *Telephone:* 1-44-71-94-94 (Europacorp) (office). *E-mail:* lucbesson@luc-besson.com (office); contact@europacorp.com (office). *Website:* luc-besson.com (office); www.europacorp -corporate.com (office).

BESTUZHEV-LADA, Igor Vassilyevich, PhD, DHist; Russian sociologist and historian; *Chairman, Russian Pedagogical Society;* b. 12 Jan. 1927, Lada, Penza Region; m.; one s. one d.; ed Inst. of Int. Relations, Inst. of History; researcher, Inst. of History, USSR (now Russian) Acad. of Sciences 1950–66; Head of Dept of Social Forecasting, Inst. of Sociology, USSR (now Russian) Acad. of Riinvces 1967–2000, Prof. Emer. 2001–; Prof., Moscow State Univ. 1969–2000; Academician Sec., Russian Acad. of Education 1993–2002; Pres. Russian Future Studies Acad. 1997–; Vice Pres. Future Research Cttee, Soviet Sociological Asscn 1967–91, Int. Sociological Asscn 1970–96; Pres. Moscow Humanitarian Prognostic Univ. 2000–; Chair. Presidium Russian Pedagogical Soc. 1989–; Co-founder World Future Studies Fed. 1984; Hon. Pres. Int. Future Research Acad. 1999–, Hon. mem. World Future Studies Fed. 1984; Order of St Daniel 1998, Order of Friendship 2003, Order of Honour 2007. *Publications include:* Exploratory Social Forecasting, Normative Social Forecasting, Forecasting Grounding Social Innovations, Alternative Civilization, Anthology of Classics in Future Studies 1952–82, Memories, Vols 1–5, 2004, Short Russian Encyclopedia of Future Studies 2006, Too Short History of Earth and Mankind 2007, My Goddamned Russia – History of 8 Dictatures from Rurik to Stalin 2007, From Colossus to Collapse and Backwards 2008. *Leisure interests:* classic literature, book design. *Address:* Shipilovsky proezd 49/1, Apartment 364, 115551 Moscow, Russia (home). *Telephone:* (495) 343-08-52 (home). *E-mail:* pedobsh@online.ru; mail@pedobsh.ru. *Website:* www.pedobsh.ru.

BETANCOURT DE GARCÍA, Edmeé; Venezuelan politician and fmr central banker; ed Univ. of Carabobo, Univ. Simón Bolívar; Administrative Vice Chancellor, Univ. of Carabobo 1988–92; Vice-Minister of Labour 2000–02; Minister of Light Industry and Trade 2005–07; Rep. to Comm. of Comunidad Andina 2005; Vice-Chancellor of Social Affairs, Univ. Nacional Experimental Politécnica de la Fuerza Armada (Unefa) 2006–09; Pres. Banco de Desarrollo Económico y Social de Venezuela (Bandes) 2010; Minister of Commerce 2011; Rep. of Venezuela to FAO 2011; Pres. and Chair. Banco Central de Venezuela 2013. *Address:* c/o Banco Central de Venezuela, Avda Urdaneta, esq. de Carmelitas, Caracas 1010, Venezuela.

BETANCUR CUARTAS, Belisario; Colombian politician, lawyer and fmr head of state; *President, Fundación Santillana;* b. 4 Feb. 1923, Amagá, Antioquia; s. of Rosendo Betancur and Ana Otilia Cuartos; m. Rosa Helena Alvarez; one s. two d.; ed Univ. Bolivariana de Medellín; founder of the Tercer Mundo publishing company; mem. House of Reps, later Senator; Conservative Party presidential cand. 1962, 1970, 1978; Minister of Labour 1963; Amb. to Spain 1974; Pres. of Colombia 1982–86; Founder Tercer Mundo publishing co.; currently Pres. Fundación Santillana para Iberoamérica, Colombia; Hon. Mem. Bd of Dirs Due Process of Law Foundation; mem. Club of Rome (currently Vice-Pres. for Latin America), Club of Madrid, Colombian Academies of History, Jurisprudence and Language; Founder-mem. Pontifical Acad. of Social Sciences 1994–; Dr hc (Georgetown, Colorado); Prince of Asturias Peace Award (Spain). *Address:* Fundación Santillana, calle 80, No 9-75, Apartado Aéreo 3974, Santa Fe de Bogotá, Colombia (office). *Website:* www.fundacionsantillana.org (office).

BÉTEILLE, André Marie, MSc, PhD; Indian sociologist and academic; *Professor Emeritus, Delhi School of Economics;* b. 30 Sept. 1934, Chandannagore; s. of the late Maurice Béteille and Renuka Béteille (née Mukherjee); m. Esha Ghoshal; two d.; ed Univs of Calcutta and Delhi; Research Assoc. Indian Statistical Inst. 1958–59; Lecturer in Sociology, Delhi School of Econs 1959–64, Reader 1964–72, Prof. 1972–99, Prof. Emer. 1999–; fmr teacher, Univ. of Oxford, Univ. of Cambridge, Univ. of Chicago, LSE; mem. Nat. Knowledge Comm. 2005–06 (resgnd); Nat. Research Prof. 2007–; fmr Chair. Indian Council of Social Science Research (ICSSR); Chancellor, North-Eastern Hill Univ., Shillong; Chair. Centre for Studies in Social Sciences, Kolkata; Corresp. Fellow, British Acad. 1992; Trustee Sameeksha Trust, Nat. Foundation for India, New India Foundation; Hon. Fellow, Royal Anthropological Inst. 2002; Hon. DSc (Vidyasagar Univ.) 2004, Hon. DLitt (Kolkata) 2006; Padma Bhushan Award 2005. *Publications:* Caste, Class and Power: Changing Patterns of Stratification in a Tanjore Village 1965, Castes: Old and New, Essays in Social Structure and Social Stratification 1969, Studies in Agrarian Social Structure 1974, Six Essays in Comparative Sociology 1974, Inequality Among Men 1977, The Idea of Natural Inequality and Other Essays 1983, Society and Politics in India: Essays in a Comparative Perspective 1991, Antinomies of Society: Essays on Ideologies and Institutions 2000, Chronicles of Our Time 2000, Sociology: Essays on Approach and Method 2002, Equality and Universality: Essays in Social and Political Theory 2003, Anti-Utopia: Essential Writings of André Béteille (ed. by Dipankar Gupta) 2005, Ideology and Social Science 2006, Marxism and Class Analysis 2007; numerous articles in professional journals. *Address:* 69 Jor Bagh, New Delhi 110 003, India (home). *Telephone:* (11) 24645172 (home).

BETHENOD, Martin; French journalist, art dealer and gallery director; *Director, Palazzo Grassi and Punta della Dogana, Venice;* b. 1966; journalist, Connaissance des arts, then with Vogue; began career as special adviser to Jean-Jacques Aillagon, Dir of École nationale supérieure des beaux-arts; then worked at Vidéothèque de Paris; Chief of Staff to Jean-Jacques Aillagon 1996–98; Dir Pompidou Centre, Dir of Publs 1998–2001; delegated to the Visual Arts at Ministry of Culture and communication 2003–04; Commr Gen. Foire Internationale d'Art Contemporain (FIAC—Int. Contemporary Art Fair), Paris 2004–10; Dir Palazzo Grassi and Punta della Dogana owned by François Pinault in Venice, Italy 2010–; Chevalier, Ordre nat. du Mérite 2007. *Address:* Palazzo Grassi, Campo San Samuele 3231, 30124 Venice, Italy (office). *Telephone:* (041) 2401353 (office). *Fax:*

(041) 2401338 (office). *E-mail:* palazzograssi@palazzograssi.it (office). *Website:* www.palazzograssi.it (office).

BETHKE, Siegfried, PhD; German physicist and academic; *Managing Director, Max-Planck-Institute for Physics;* b. 15 April 1954, Ludwigshafen; ed Univ. of Heidelberg; Asst. Univ. of Heidelberg 1983–86; Feodor-Lynen Fellow, Univ. of Calif., Berkeley Lab., USA 1988–89; Prof. of Physics, Rheinisch-Westfälische Technische Hochschule, Aachen 1993–96; Dir Max-Planck-Inst. for Physics, Munich 1999–, Man. Dir 2000–; Heisenberg Fellow, CERN, Geneva 1989–93; Co-Ed. European Physical Journal C 1994–; mem. numerous specialist cttees including High Energy Physics Referee Bd, Ministry of Science, Research, Tech. and Educ. 1995–2002; mem. Editorial Bd, Journal of Physics G 1997–2002; Chair. CERN LHC (Large Hadron Collider) Computing Review 2000–01; Chair. ATLAS Collaboration Bd 2004–05, Deputy Chair. 2003–06; mem. German Physical Soc.; Scientific mem. Max-Planck Soc. 1999–; mem. Deutsches Elektronen Synchroton (German Synchrotron Research Centre, DESY) Scientific Council, Hamburg 2000–, Chair. 2002–05; Hon. Prof., Technische Universität München; Gottfried Wilhelm Leibniz Prize 1995. *Publications:* numerous specialist publs. *Address:* Max-Planck-Institute for Physics, Foehringer Ring 6, Room 219, 80805 Munich, Germany (office). *Telephone:* (89) 32354-381 (office). *Fax:* (89) 32354-305 (office). *E-mail:* bethke@mppmu.mpg.de (office). *Website:* www.mpg.de (office); www .mppmu.mpg.de/common/members/bethke.html (office).

BETORI, HE Cardinal Giuseppe, LicTheol, DSacredScript; Italian ecclesiastic and academic; *Archbishop of Florence;* b. 25 Feb. 1947, Foligno; ed Pontifical Gregorian Univ. and a doctorate in Sacred Scripture at the Pontifical Biblical Inst.; ordained priest, Diocese of Foligno 1970; fmr Prof. of Anthropology and Biblical Exegesis; Dean of the Theological Inst. of Assisi; apptd Titular Bishop of Falerone 2001; Sec.-Gen. Italian Episcopal Conf. 2001–08; Archbishop of Florence 2008–; cr. Cardinal (Cardinal-Priest of San Marcello) 2012; mem. Pontifical Council for Culture 2011–; participated in Papal Conclave 2013. *Address:* Arcivescovado, Piazza S. Giovanni 3, 50129 Florence, Italy (office). *Telephone:* (055) 271071 (office). *Fax:* (055) 2710741 (office). *E-mail:* info@diocesifirenze.it (office). *Website:* www.diocesifirenze.it (office).

BETRIAN, Stanley Mario; Curaçao politician; b. 1 Nov. 1951; ed HTS Eindhoven, Netherlands, Catholic Univ. of Nijmegen; Exec. Vice-Pres. Central Bank of the Netherlands Antilles 1983–92; Lt-Gov. of Curaçao (whilst still part of Netherlands Antilles) 1992–94; Chair. Curaçao Social and Econ. Council (SER) –2012; Prime Minister of Curaçao and Minister of Gen. Affairs, of Justice, and of Traffic, Transport and Spatial Planning and Energy Sept.–Dec. 2012; fmr Chair. Foundation for Privatization Implementation (StIP), Antillean Co-Financing Org. *Address:* c/o Office of the Prime Minister, Fort Amsterdam 17, Willemstad, Curaçao.

BETT, Sir Michael, Kt, CBE, MA; British fmr business executive; b. 18 Jan. 1935; s. of Arthur Bett OBE and Nina Daniells; m. Christine Angela Reid 1959; one s. two d.; ed Aldenham School, Pembroke Coll., Cambridge; Dir Industrial Relations, Engineering Employers Fed. 1970–72; Personnel Dir General Electric Co. Ltd 1972–77; Personnel Dir BBC 1977–81; Bd mem. for Personnel British Telecom (BT) 1981–84, Corp. Dir, Personnel and Corp. Services 1984–85, Man. Dir Local Communications Services 1985–87, Man. Dir UK Communications 1987–88, Man. Dir BT UK 1988–91, Exec. Deputy Chair. 1991–94, Dir (non-exec.) 1994–96; Pres. Chartered Inst. of Personnel and Devt 1992–98; Chair. Nurses' Pay Review Body 1990–95, Cellnet Group 1991–99, Save the Children Fund 1992–97, Social Security Advisory Cttee 1993–95, Review of Armed Forces' Manpower and Pay 1994–95, Chair. Inspectorate of the Security Industry 1994–2000, One World Broadcasting Trust, 1996–2002, English Shakespeare Company International 1997–2000, Nat. Security Inspectorate 2000–07; Pro-Chancellor, Aston Univ. 1993–2003, Chancellor 2004–11; First Commr for the Civil Service 1995–2000, Pensions Protection Investment Accreditation Bd 2000–06, Pace Micro Technology PLC 2000–06, J2C PLC 2000–02; mem. Bd of Dirs English Shakespeare Co. 1988–95; mem. Advisory Bd Tribold 2005–06; mem. Campaign Bd, New Marlowe Theatre, Canterbury; Hon. Fellow, Pembroke Coll., Cambridge 2004; Hon. DSc (Aston) 1996, Hon. DUniv (Kent) 2013, Hon. DBA (Liverpool John Moores) 2013, (IMCB). *Leisure interests:* theatre, music, gardening, cooking.

BETTEL, Xavier, DEA; Luxembourg lawyer and politician; *Prime Minister;* b. 3 March 1973, Luxembourg-Ville; ed Univ. Nancy 2, France, Aristotle Univ., Greece; several years' practice as lawyer; four years as host, Sonndes em 8 (weekly talk show), T.TV TV network early 2000s; elected to Luxembourg-Ville communal council 1999, Mayor of Luxembourg-Ville 2011–13; mem. Chamber of Deputies (Parl.) 1999–2011; Prime Minister, and Minister of State, of Communications and Media and of Religious Affairs 2013–; mem. Demokratesch Partei, Leader 2013–. *Address:* Office of the Prime Minister, 4 rue de la Congrégation, 1352 Luxembourg, Luxembourg (office). *Telephone:* 247-82101 (office). *Fax:* 46-17-20 (office). *E-mail:* ministere.etat@me.etat.lu (office). *Website:* www.gouvernement.lu (office).

BETTENCOURT, Liliane; French business executive; *President, Fondation Bettencourt Schueller;* b. 21 Oct. 1922; d. of Eugène Schueller (founder of L'Oréal); m. André Bettencourt 1950; one d.; inherited L'Oréal fortune from her father 1957, prin. shareholder, Chair. Man. and Remuneration Cttee, L'Oréal; Founder and Pres. Bettencourt Schueller Foundation 1987–; ranked by Forbes magazine amongst 100 Most Powerful Women (79th) 2004, (39th) 2005. *Leisure interest:* wine. *Address:* Fondation Bettencourt Schueller, 16 Place Vendôme, 75001 Paris, France (office). *Website:* www.fondationbs.org (office); www.loreal.com (office).

BETTENCOURT SANTOS, Humberto, (Humbertona); Cape Verde business executive and fmr diplomatist; *Chairman, Cabo Verde Telecom SA;* b. 17 Feb. 1940, Santo Antão Island; s. of Severino Santos and Inacia Bettencourt; m.; two c.; ed Catholic Univ. of Louvain, Belgium, Licencié en Sciences Économiques Appliquées; mem. del. in negotiations on colonial dispute with Portugal 1975; elected Deputy to Nat. Ass. 1975, re-elected 1980; Dir-Gen. Fisheries 1975–82; Amb. to EC and to Nordic and Benelux countries 1982–87; Perm. Rep. of Cape Verde to UN 1987–91; mem. Nat. Comm. on Law of the Sea 1979–82; int. consultant; dir of pvt. computer training centre; pvt. consultant in econ. and fisheries for FAO and UNDP 1991; Dist Gov. Rotary International 2006–07; currently Chair. Cabo Verde Telecom SA; Hon. Consul of the Netherlands for the Cape Verde Islands; Hon. Consul of Belgium; Chevalier, Order of Orange Nassau

(Netherlands) 2010. *Recordings:* six LPs and CDs under Humbertona label. *Leisure interests:* music (guitar), tennis, golf. *Address:* Rua Cabo Verde Telecom, Várzea, CP 220, Praia, Santiago, Cape Verde (office). *Telephone:* 2609200 (office). *Fax:* 2619935 (office). *E-mail:* humbertona@hotmail.com (office); humberto .bettencourt@cvt.cv. *Website:* www.cvtelecom.cv (office).

BETTINI, Paolo; Italian road cyclist; b. 1 April 1974, Cecina; m. Monica Orlandini 2000; one d.; Tuscany Prov. Champion 1994; professional debut 1997; mem. Nat. Team, World Championships, Valkenburg 1998; winner Liège-Bastogne-Liège 2000, 2002, Championship of Zürich 2001, 2005, Milan-San Remo 2003, HEW Cyclassics 2003, Clásica de San Sebastián 2003, Tour of Lombardy 2005, 2006; Silver Medal World Championships, Lisbon 2001; winner Union Cycliste Internationale (UCI) World Cup 2002–04; Gold Medal Road Race, Athens Olympics 2004; first in UCI Ranking 2003, second 2004; winner Tirreno-Adriatico 2004; winner World Road Race Championships 2006, 2007; fmrly with Mapei-Quick Step cycling team (now Quick Step-Innergetic Cycling Team); coach of Italian national cycling team 2010–;*Website:* www.federciclismo.it.

BEUTLER, Bruce Alan, MD; American geneticist and academic; *Regental Professor and Director, Center for the Genetics of Host Defense, University of Texas Southwestern Medical Center;* b. 29 Dec. 1957, Chicago, Ill.; s. of Ernest Beutler and Brondelle May Fleisher; m. Barbara Lanzl 1979 (divorced 1988); three s.; ed Pritzker School of Medicine, Univ. of Texas Southwestern Medical Center, Rockefeller Univ.; Postdoctoral Fellow, The Rockefeller Univ. 1983–85, Asst Prof. 1985, Assoc. Physician, The Rockefeller Univ. Hosp. 1984–86; Asst Prof., Dept of Internal Medicine, Univ. of Texas Southwestern Medical Center, Dallas 1986, Dir Center for the Genetics of Host Defense and Regental Prof. 2011–, also Raymond and Ellen Willie Distinguished Chair in Cancer Research; Asst Investigator, Howard Hughes Medical Inst., Md 1986–90, Assoc. Prof. and Assoc. Investigator 1990–96, Prof. 1996; Prof., Dept of Immunology, Scripps Research Inst., La Jolla, Calif. 2000–11, Chair. Dept of Genetics 2007–11; mem. NAS, Asscn of American Physicians, American Soc. for Clinical Investigation; Assoc. mem. European Molecular Biology Org.; MD hc (Technical Univ. of Munich) 2007; Robert Koch Foundation Robert Koch Prize (with Jules Hoffmann and Shizuo Akira) 2004, US Cancer Research Inst. William B. Coley Award (with Shizuo Akira) 2006, Balzan Prize for Innate Immunity (with Jules Hoffmann) 2007, Will Rogers Inst. Annual Prize for Research 2009, Albany Medical Center Prize (with Charles Dinarello and Ralph Steinman) 2009, Shaw Prize (with Jules Hoffmann and Ruslan Medzhitov) 2011, Nobel Prize in Physiology or Medicine (with Jules Hoffmann and Ralph Steinman) 2011. *Publications include:* more than 300 papers and reviews. *Leisure interests:* hiking, listening to music. *Address:* Beutler Lab, UT Southwestern Medical Center, 5323 Harry Hines Blvd, Dallas, TX 75390-8505, USA (office). *Telephone:* (214) 648-5838 (office). *E-mail:* bruce.beutler@ utsouthwestern.edu (office). *Website:* www.utsouthwestern.edu/labs/beutler (office).

BEVAN, Tim, CBE; British film producer; *Co-Chairman, Working Title Films;* b. 1958, Queenstown, NZ; m. 1st Joely Richardson (q.v.) 1992; one d.; m. 2nd Amy Gadney; one s. one d.; began career as a runner for John Cleese's Video Arts; f. Aldabra (music video production co.) with Sarah Radclyffe; formed Working Title Films (film production co.) with Eric Fellner (q.v.) 1984, now Co-Chair.; Chair. UK Film Council 2009–; Empire Film Award for outstanding contribution to British cinema (jtly) 2005, six Academy Awards, 26 Bafta Awards, Michael Balcon Award for Outstanding Contrib. to British Cinema, Alexander Walker Award for Film, Tribute Award, Gotham Ind. Film Awards. *Films include:* My Beautiful Laundrette 1985, Personal Services 1987, Wish You Were Here, Caravaggio, Pascali's Island, The Tall Guy 1989, The Rachel Papers, Hidden Agenda, Dakota Road, Map of the Human Heart 1993, Bob Roberts, Posse 1993, Romeo is Bleeding 1993, The Hudsucker Proxy 1994, Four Weddings and a Funeral 1994, Dead Man Walking 1995, Elizabeth 1998, Notting Hill 1999, High Fidelity 2000, Fargo, O Brother, Where Art Thou? 2000, Captain Corelli's Mandolin 2001, The Big Lebowski, Plunkett & Macleane 1999, The Man Who Cried 2000, Bridget Jones' Diary 2001, Man Who Wasn't There, Long Time Dead 2002, 40 Days and 40 Nights 2002, Ali G. Indahouse 2002, About a Boy 2002, The Guru 2002, My Little Eye 2002, Thirteen 2003, Shape of Things, Ned Kelly 2003, Johnny English 2003, The Italian Job 2003, Gettin' Square 2003, Love Actually 2003, Shaun of the Dead 2004, The Calcium Kid 2004, Thunderbirds 2004, Wimbledon 2004, Bridget Jones: The Edge of Reason 2004, Mickybo and Me, United 93 (Best British Producer, London Film Critics' Circle Awards 2007) 2006, Hot Fuzz 2007, The Boat that Rocked 2008, Wild Child 2008, Burn After Reading 2008, Frost/Nixon 2008, The Boat that Rocked 2009, The Soloist 2009, State of Play 2009, A Serious Man 2009, Nanny McPhee and the Big Bang 2010, Green Zone 2010. *TV includes:* Tales of the City, The Borrowers, High Fidelity. *Address:* Working Title Films, 26 Aybrook Street, London, W1U 4AN, England (office). *Telephone:* (20) 7307-3000 (office). *Fax:* (20) 7307-3001 (office). *Website:* www.workingtitlefilms.com (office).

BEVAN, Sir Timothy (Hugh), Kt; British banker; b. 24 May 1927, London; s. of the late Hugh Bevan and Pleasance Bevan (née Scrutton); m. Pamela Murray (née Smith) 1952; two s. two d.; ed Eton Coll.; called to the Bar, Middle Temple 1950; joined Barclays Bank Ltd (now Barclays Bank PLC) 1950, Dir 1966–93, Vice-Chair. 1968–73, Deputy Chair. 1973–81, Chair. 1981–87; Dir Barclays Int. Ltd 1971; Dir BET Public Ltd Co. 1987–92, Chair. 1988–91; Dir Foreign and Colonial Investment Trust PLC 1988–98 (Deputy Chair. 1993–98); fmr Dir Soc. Financière Européenne 1967, Commercial Union Assurance Co. Ltd, Union Discount Co. of London Ltd; Chair. Cttee of London Clearing Bankers 1983–85; Chair. City Communications Centre 1982–83. *Leisure interests:* sailing, gardening.

BEVANDA, Vjekoslav; Bosnia and Herzegovina politician; *Chairman of the Council of Ministers (Prime Minister);* b. 13 May 1956; ed Univ. of Mostar; worked in aeroplane factory 'SOKO', Mostar 1979–89; with APRO bank, Mostar 1990–93; fmrly with Eurosped Group Zagreb (mem. EG Man.); Dir, Nord Adria Trieste, Italy, Nord Adria Wien, Austria 1993–99; with Euro Center, Split 2000–01; Dir Commerce Bank, Sarajevo 2001–07; mem. Croatian Democratic Union of Bosnia and Herzegovina; Deputy Prime Minister and Minister of Finance, Bosnia and Herzegovina 2007–11; Chair. Council of Ministers (Prime Minister) 2012–. *Address:* Office of the Chairman of the Council of Ministers, 71000 Sarajevo, trg Bosne i Hercegovine 1, Bosnia and Herzegovina (office). *Telephone:* (33) 282611 (office). *Fax:* (33) 282613 (office). *E-mail:* predsjedatelj@vijeceministara.gov.ba (office). *Website:* www.vijeceministara.gov.ba (office).

BEWKES, Jeffrey (Jeff) L., BA, MBA; American broadcasting executive; *Chairman and CEO, Time Warner Inc.;* b. 25 May 1952, Paterson, NJ; s. of Eugene Garrett Bewkes, Jr; m. Margaret (Peggy) Brim; one c.; ed Yale Univ., Stanford Univ. Grad. School of Business; early career as Operations Dir Sonoma Vineyards, Calif.; Accountant Officer, Citibank, New York 1984–86; Exec. Vice-Pres. and Chief Financial Officer Home Box Office Inc. 1986–91, Pres. and COO 1991–95, Chair. and CEO 1995–2002; Chair. Entertainment and Network Group, AOL Time Warner Inc. (now Time Warner Inc.) 2002–05, Pres. Time Warner Inc. 2005–08, also COO 2005–07, mem. Bd of Dirs 2007–, CEO 2008–, Chair. 2009–; mem. Bd of Dirs Nixon Center; mem. Advisory Bd Stanford Univ. Grad. School of Business, American Museum of Natural History, Museum of Television and Radio, The Creative Coalition, Paley Center for Media; Trustee, Yale Univ., Museum of the Moving Image; mem. Council on Foreign Relations. *Address:* Time Warner Inc., 1 Time Warner Center, New York, NY 10019, USA (office). *Telephone:* (212) 484-8000 (office). *Fax:* (212) 489-6183 (office). *E-mail:* info@timewarner.com (office). *Website:* www.timewarner.com (office).

BEWLEY, Thomas Henry, MA, MD, FRCP, FRCPI; Irish consultant psychiatrist; *Consultant Emeritus, St Thomas' Hospital;* b. 8 July 1926, Dublin; s. of Geoffrey Bewley and Victoria Jane Wilson; m. Beulah Knox 1955; one s. four d.; ed St Columba's Coll., Dublin, Trinity Coll., Dublin; trained at St Patrick's Hosp., Dublin, Maudsley Hosp., London and Univ. of Cincinnati, USA; Consultant Psychiatrist, Tooting Bec and St Thomas' Hosps, London 1961–88, currently Consultant Emer., St Thomas' Hosp.; mem. Standing Advisory Cttee on Drug Dependence 1966–71, Advisory Council on Misuse of Drugs 1972–84; Consultant Adviser on Drug Dependence to Dept of Health and Social Security 1972–81; Consultant WHO 1969–78; Hon. Sr Lecturer, St George's Hosp. Medical School, Univ. of London 1974–96; Pres. Royal Coll. of Psychiatrists 1984–87 (Dean 1977–82); Jt Founder and mem. Council, Inst. for the Study of Drug Dependence 1967–96; Hon. CBE, Hon. MD. *Publications include:* Handbook for Inceptors and Trainees in Psychiatry 1976, Madness to Mental Illness 2008; papers on drug dependence, medical manpower and side effects of drugs. *Address:* 4 Grosvenor Gardens Mews North, London, SW1W 0JP, England. *Telephone:* (20) 7730-9592. *E-mail:* thomasbewley@waitrose.com.

BEXELL, Göran Bertil David, PhD; Swedish academic and fmr university administrator; *Professor of Ethics, Lund University;* b. 24 Dec. 1943, Högsby; Prof. of Ethics, Dept of Theology, Lund Univ. 1990–, Dean, Theology Faculty 1997–99, Vice-Chancellor Lund Univ. 2003–08; Ed. Svensk Teologisk Kvartalskrift 1990–97; fmr Pres. Asscn of Swedish Higher Educ. *Publications:* Teologisk etik: en introduktion (co-author), Universal Ethics: Perspectives and Proposals from Scandinavian Scholars (co-ed. with Dan-Erik Andersson) 2002, Academic Values S?show the Way 2011. *Address:* Department of Theology, Lund University, PO Box 117, 221 00 Lund, Sweden (office). *Telephone:* (222) 00-00 (office). *Fax:* (222) 47-20 (office). *E-mail:* Goran.Bexell@rektor.lu.se (office). *Website:* www.lu.se (office).

BEYENE, Tekie, BA; Eritrean fmr central banker; b. 15 June 1941, Asmara; m. Maaza Haile; ed Univ. of Asmara; fmr Gov. Bank of Eritrea; mem. Bd of Govs IMF 2007. *Publications:* contribs to magazine Hewyet (Recovery). *Leisure interest:* writing. *Address:* Tiro Alvolo Street 702, No. 14–16, Asmara, Eritrea (home). *Telephone:* (1) 184351 (home).

BEYNON, John David Emrys, PhD; British professor of electronics and college principal; b. 11 March 1939, Risca, Gwent, Wales; s. of John Emrys Beynon and Elvira Beynon; m. Hazel Janet Hurley 1964; two s. one d.; ed Univ. of Wales and Univ. of Southampton; Scientific Officer, Radio Research Station, Slough 1962–64; Lecturer, Sr Lecturer, then Reader, Univ. of Southampton 1964–67; Prof. of Electronics, Univ. of Wales Inst. of Science and Tech., Cardiff 1977–79; Head of Dept of Electronic and Electrical Eng, Univ. of Surrey 1979–83, Pro Vice-Chancellor 1983–87, Sr Pro Vice-Chancellor 1987–90; Prin., King's Coll., London 1990–92, Fellow 1990; Fellow, Royal Acad. of Engineering; Hon. Fellow, Univ. Coll. of Swansea 1990; mem. British Library Advisory Council 1994–99, Ind. TV Comm. 1995–2000; Chair. Westminster Christian Council 1999–2000; Sec., Bloomsbury Central Baptist Church, London 2000–14. *Publications include:* Charge-coupled Devices and Their Applications (with D. R. Lamb) 1980; papers on plasma physics, semi-conductor devices and integrated circuits and eng educ. *Leisure interests:* music, photography, travel. *Address:* Chalkdene, 13 Great Quarry, Guildford, GU1 3XN, England (home). *Telephone:* (1483) 503458 (home).

BEYNON, John Herbert, BSc, DSc, CChem, FRSC, CPhys, FInstP, CSci, FRS; British chemist and academic (retd); *Professor Emeritus, University of Wales;* b. 29 Dec. 1923, Ystalyfera, Wales; s. of Leslie Ewart Beynon and Phyllis Beynon (née Gibbon); m. Yvonne Lilian Fryer 1947 (died 2009); Scientific Officer, Tank Armament Research 1943–47; Man. and Sr Research Assoc., Physical Chem. Research, ICI Dyestuffs Div. 1952–74; Prof. of Chem. and Dir Mass Spectrometry Center, Purdue Univ., USA 1969–75; Assoc. Prof. of Molecular Sciences, Univ. of Warwick 1972–74; Visiting Prof., Univ. of Essex 1982–; Univ. Prof. and Royal Soc. Research Prof., Univ. of Wales, Swansea 1974–86, Research Prof. 1987–, Prof. Emer. 1991–; Chair. Science Curriculum Devt Cttee, Cttee for Wales 1983–88; Pres. Asscn for Science Educ., Wales 1985–86; Ed. Int. Journal of Mass Spectrometry and Ion Processes 1983–85; Founder and Ed.-in-Chief Rapid Communications in Mass Spectrometry 1987–97; mem. Editorial Bd Organic Mass Spectrometry 1967–88, 1992–94, Int. Journal of Mass Spectrometry and Ion Processes 1967–97, Mass Spectrometry Reviews 1984–2003, Biological Mass Spectrometry 1992–94, J. Mass Spectrometry 1995–; Chair. Swansea Sports Club 1988–92; Dir Swansea Cricket and Football Club 1991–92; Founder Pres. European Mass Spectrometry Soc. 1993–96; Assoc. Inst. Jožef Stefan, Yugoslavia; Fellow, Univ. of Wales Swansea 1988–; Hon. mem. mass spectrometry socs of Japan, China, Italy and Yugoslavia; Hon. Fellow, Serbian Chem. Soc. 1982–; Hon. DSc (Purdue Univ., USA) 1995, (Babeş-Bolyai Univ., Romania) 1997; 3M-Boomer Award 1965, Hasler Award for Spectroscopy 1979, Jan Marc Marci Medal 1984, Gold Medal of the Int. Mass Spectrometry Soc. 1985, Frank H. Field and Joe L. Franklin Award of the American Chemical Soc. 1987, Aston Medal of British Mass Spectrometry Soc. 1990, Gold Medal, Italian Chemical Soc. 1992. *Publications:* 10 books and over 400 scientific papers. *Leisure interests:* photography, golf, rugby.

Address: Brynfield Manor Nursing Home, Room 48, 42 Brynfield Road, Langland, Swansea, SA3 4SX, Wales (home). *Telephone:* (1792) 363180 (home).

BEYONCÉ; American singer, songwriter, actress and producer; b. (Beyoncé Giselle Knowles), 4 Sept. 1981, Houston, Tex.; d. of Mathew Knowles and Tina Knowles; m. Jay-Z (Shawn Carter) 2008; one d.; Founding mem. GirlsTyme (with Kelly Rowland, later joined by LaTavia Roberson and LeToya Luckett), group renamed Something Fresh, then The Dolls before settling on Destiny's Child 1989–2005; numerous live performances, tours; solo artist 2001–; est. clothing label Touch of Couture; Amb. for World Humanitarian Day campaign 2012; (with Destiny's Child) Billboard Award for Artist of the Year, Group of the Year, Hot 100 Singles Artist of the Year, Hot 100 Group of the Year 2000, NAACP Image Award for Outstanding Duo or Group (for Say My Name) 2001, MTV Video Award for Best R&B Video (for Say My Name) 2001, American Music Award for Favorite Soul/R&B Group 2001, Soul Train Sammy Davis Jr Award for Entertainer of the Year 2001, American Music Award for Favorite Pop/Rock Band, Duo or Group 2002, BRIT Award for Best Int. Group 2002, MOBO Award for Best Gospel Act 2002, World Music Award for World's Best Pop Group 2005, Lady of Soul Award for Best Group Single (for Soldier) 2005, American Music Award for Favorite Soul/R & B Band, Duo or Group 2005; (solo) Billboard Awards for New Female Artist of the Year, New R&B Artist, Hot 200 Female Artist 2003, Female R&B/Hip Hop Artist of the Year 2006, Female Artist of the Decade 2009, Radio Artist of the Decade 2009, Millennium Award 2011, BRIT Awards for Best Int. Female Solo Artist 2004, Billboard R&B/Hip Hop Awards for Top Female Artist, New Artist 2004, Grammy Awards for Best R&B Song, Best R&B Performance by a Duo or Group with Vocal (for Say My Name) 2001, for Best R&B Performance by a Duo or Group with Vocals (for Survivor) 2002, for Best R&B Song, Best Rap/Sung Collaboration (for Crazy in Love, with Jay-Z) 2004, for best R&B performance by a duo or group (for The Closer I Get To You, with Luther Vandross) 2004, for Best Female R&B Vocal Performance (for Dangerously In Love) 2004, (for Single Ladies) 2010, for Best R&B Performance by a Duo or Group with Vocals (for So Amazing, with Stevie Wonder) 2006, for Song of the Year (for Single Ladies) 2010, for Best Female Pop Vocal Performance (for Halo) 2010, for Best Traditional R&B Vocal Performance (for At Last) 2010, for Best R&B Song (for Single Ladies) 2010, for Best Traditional R&B Performance (for Love on Top) 2013, Billboard Music Award for R&B/Hip-Hop Group of the Year 2005, MOBO Awards for Best Song and Best Video (both for Deja Vu), for Best Int. Female 2006, Soul Train Award for Best Single by a Female (for Irreplaceable) 2007, for Best Dance Performance (for Run the World (Girls)) 2011, BET Award for Best R&B Female 2007, for Video of the Year (for Irreplaceable) 2007, MTV Video Music Award for Best Collaboration (for Beautiful Liar with Shakira) 2007, MTV Europe Music Awards for Best Female 2009, for Best Song (for Halo) 2009, for Best Live Act 2013, American Music Award for Favorite Female Soul/Rhythm and Blues Artist 2009, named to VH1's list of the 100 Greatest Artists of All Time 2010, ranked by Forbes magazine amongst The World's 100 Most Powerful Women (ninth) 2010, (18th) 2011, (32nd) 2012, (17th) 2013, ranked third on VH1's 100 Greatest Women in Music 2012, Writing Award, New York Asscn of Black Journalists 2012. *Recordings include:* albums: with Destiny's Child: Destiny's Child 1998, The Writing's On The Wall 1999, Survivor (American Music Award for Favorite Pop/Rock Album 2002) 2001, Eight Days Of Christmas 2001, Destiny Fulfilled (Lady of Soul Award for Best Group Album 2005, American Music Award for Favorite Soul/R&B Album 2005) 2004; solo: Soul Survivors 2002, Dangerously in Love (Grammy Award for Best Contemporary R&B Album 2004) 2003, Live At Wembley 2004, B-Day (Grammy Award for Best Contemporary R&B Album 2007) 2006, I Am… Sasha Fierce (Grammy Award for Best Contemporary R&B Album 2010) 2008, 4 2011, Beyoncé 2013. *Films include:* Austin Powers in Goldmember 2002, The Fighting Temptations 2003, The Pink Panther 2006, Dreamgirls 2006, Cadillac Records (also exec. producer) 2008, Obsessed (also exec. producer) 2009, Epic (voice) 2013. *Television includes:* Carmen: A Hip Hopera (film) 2001, Wow! Wow! Wubbzy! (series) 2009, Robins (series) 2010. *Address:* c/o Music World Entertainment, 1505 Hadley Street, Houston, TX 77002-8927, USA (office). *Telephone:* (713) 772-5175 (office). *Website:* musicworldent.com (office); www.beyonceonline.com; www.destinyschild.com.

BEYRER, Markus J.; Austrian diplomatist and business executive; *Director General, BUSINESSEUROPE;* b. 19 Aug. 1965, St Pölten; m. Petra Beyrer; one s. one d.; ed Univ. of Vienna, Vienna Univ. of Econs and Business Admin, postgraduate studies of European Law at Danube Univ., Krems Stanford Exec. Program, Grad. School of Business, Stanford Univ.; mem. EU Expert Team (EU Cadet), Dept for European Integration and Trade Policy, Austrian Fed. Econ. Chamber 1992–94; Stage in European EC, Directorate Gen. XI (Environment) Spring 1994; Attaché for Industrial and Commercial Affairs, Perm. Rep. of Austria to EU 1994–96; Expert for European and Int. Affairs, Dept for Environmental Policy, Austrian Fed. Econ. Chamber 1996–99; Sr Econ. Adviser to Fed. Vice-Chancellor and Fed. Minister for Foreign Affairs, then to Austrian Fed. Chancellor 1999–2002; Dir for Econ. Affairs, Austrian Fed. Econ. Chamber 2002–04; Dir Gen. Fed. of Austrian Industries (IV) 2004–11; CEO Österreichische Industrieholding AG (ÖIAG) 2011–12; Chair. Supervisory Bd OMV Group 2011–12, Österreichische Post AG 2011–12, Telekom Austria AG 2011–12, APK Pensionskasse AG 2011–12; Dir (non-exec.) Austrian Cen. Bank (Österreichische Nationalbank) 2008–; Vice-Chair. Supervisory Bd Raiffeisen Holding Niederösterreich, Vienna (financial expert in Audit Cttee) 2006–11; mem. Exec. Cttee BUSINESSEUROPE 2004–11, Dir Gen. 2012–; mem. Supervisory Bd G4S Security Services AG 2007–11, Siemens AG Österreich 2010–11. *Address:* BUSINESSEUROPE a.i.s.b.l., Avenue de Cortenbergh 168, 1000 Brussels, Belgium (office). *Telephone:* (2) 237-65-11 (office). *Fax:* (2) 231-14-45 (office). *E-mail:* main@businesseurope.eu (office). *Website:* www.businesseurope.eu (office).

BEZHUASHVILI, Gela, LLM, LLM, MPA; Georgian politician, diplomatist and lawyer; *Director, Georgian Intelligence Service;* b. 1 March 1967, Tetritskaro Region; m.; two s. one d.; ed Kiev State Univ., Ukraine, Southern Methodist Univ. Law School and John F. Kennedy School of Govt, Harvard Univ., USA; positions at Ministry of Foreign Affairs including Second Sec. of Int. Law Problems Div., Deputy Head of Dept then Deputy Head of Int. Law Bd 1991–93; Envoy, Embassy in Kazakhstan 1993–96; Dir Int. Law Dept 1997–2000; Deputy Minister of Defence 2000–04, Minister of Defence 2004; Asst to Pres. of Georgia on Nat. Security Issues and Sec. Nat. Security Council 2004–05; Minister of Foreign Affairs 2005–08; Head of Special Service, Intelligence Service 2008–; mem. Cttee on Int. Law, Cttee

Against Corruption and Sub-Cttee on Protection of Nat. Minorities, European Council; Rep. of Georgia, Baku-Tbilisi-Ceyhan Law Documentation Package 1999–2000; Order of Merit, First Class (Ukraine) 2006, Order of Maarjamaa Rist III Class 2007; winner Edmund Muskie Fellowship Program (USA) 1995. *Publications:* International Law Aspects of the Foreign Policy of Georgia 2003; articles in professional journals of int. law, nat. minorities and self-determination. *Address:* Georgian Intelligence Service, 4 Kekelidze Street, Tbilisi, Georgia (office). *Telephone:* (32) 228-4101 (office). *Fax:* (32) 228-4102 (office). *E-mail:* dir .int@fiss.gov.ge (office). *Website:* www.gis.gov.ge (office).

BEZOS, Jeffrey (Jeff) Preston, BS; American online retail executive; *Chairman, President and CEO, Amazon.com, Inc.;* b. 12 Jan. 1964, Albuquerque, NM; m. Mackenzie Bezos; two s.; ed Miami Palmetto Senior High School, Princeton Univ.; worked on Wall Street in computer science field; later worked on building a network for int. trade for Fitel; with Bankers Trust Co. 1988–90; joined D. E. Shaw & Co. 1990, Sr Vice-Pres. 1992–94; f. Amazon.com Inc., Seattle, Wash. 1994, Chair., Pres. and CEO 1995–; f. Blue Origin LLC (human spaceflight startup co.) 2000; f. Bezos Expeditions (investment co.); acquired Washington Post newspaper 2013; Dr hc in Science and Tech. (Carnegie Mellon Univ.) 2008; Silver Knight Award 1982, TIME magazine Person of the Year 1999, selected by U.S. News & World Report as one of America's Best Leaders 2008, ranked by Forbes magazine amongst The World's Most Powerful People (66th) 2010, (40th) 2011, (27th) 2012, (15th) 2013. *Address:* Amazon.com Inc., 410 Terry Avenue North, Seattle, WA 98109-5210, USA (office). *Telephone:* (206) 266-1000 (office). *Fax:* (206) 266-1821 (office). *Website:* www.amazon.com (office); www.blueorigin.com (office).

BEZUIDENHOUT, Kristian; South African pianist, fortepianist and harpsichordist; b. 1979; ed studied at Eastman School of Music, Rochester, NY with Rebecca Penneys, Malcolm Bilson and Paul O'Dette; moved with family from South Africa to Queensland, Australia 1988; gained int. recognition at age 21 after winning first prize and also audience prize, Bruges Fortepiano Competition 2001; frequent guest artist with several ensembles including Freiburg Baroque Orchestra, Orchestra of the 18th Century, Concerto Köln, Chamber Orchestra of Europe, Collegium Vocale Ghent, Handel and Haydn Soc.; has performed with artists such as Frans Brüggen, Pieter Wispelwey, Daniel Hope, Viktoria Mullova and Christopher Hogwood; regular Lied recitals with Carolyn Sampson, Mark Padmore and Jan Kobow; performs regularly with baroque violinist Petra Müllejans; appearances at early music festivals of Barcelona, Boston, Bruges, Innsbruck, St Petersburg, Venice and Utrecht, Saintes Festival, La Roque d'Anthéron, Chopin Festival Warsaw, Musikfest Bremen, Tanglewood Festival, Mostly Mozart Lincoln Center; Erwin Bodky Prize 2007. *Recordings include:* Schubert Die schöne Müllerin 2005, Mozart: Sonatas for Fortepiano and Violin 2009, Mozart Complete Keyboard Music Vol. I (Diapason Découverte Award, Caecilia Prize) 2010, Vol. II 2011, Schumann Dichterliebe (with Mark Padmore) (Edison Award) 2010, Beethoven Violin Sonatas (with Viktoria Mullova) (Int. Classical Music Award for Best Chamber Music Recording 2011) 2010, Mozart Sturm und Drang 2011. *Address:* Interartists Management Klinkhamer van der Vliet, Willemsparkweg 114, 1071 HN Amsterdam, Netherlands (office). *Telephone:* (20) 6754061 (office). *Fax:* (20) 6754771 (office). *E-mail:* stephan.brekelmans@ky -artists.nl (office). *Website:* kristianbezuidenhout.com (office).

BHABHA, Homi K., MA, DPhil; Indian writer and academic; *Anne F. Rothenberg Professor of the Humanities, Harvard University;* b. 1949; ed Univ. of Bombay (now Mumbai), Christ Church Coll. Univ. of Oxford, UK; Tutor, Wadham Coll., St Anne's Coll., Oxford, 1976–78; Lecturer in Creative Writing, Warwick Univ. 1977–78; Reader in English Literature, Sussex Univ. 1978–94; Visiting Scholar, Brown Univ. 1987, SUNY Stonybrook 1990, Univs of Pennsylvania and Queensland, Australia 1991, Princeton Univ. 1992, Dartmouth Coll. 1993; Distinguished Prof., Univ. of Edmonton, Canada 1992; Mellon Prof., Tulane Univ., New Orleans 1994; Prof. of English Literature, Univ. of Chicago 1994, Chester D. Tripp Distinguished Prof. in the Humanities 1996–2000; Chair. Program in History and Literature, Harvard Univ. 2001–04, Anne F. Rothenberg Prof. of English and American Literature and Language, Harvard Univ. 2001–06, Anne F. Rothenberg Prof. of the Humanities 2006–, Dir Humanities Center 2005–; Distinguished Visiting Prof., Univ. Coll. London 2004–; Faculty Advisor, World Econ. Forum, Davos; Fellow, Wissenschaftskolleg zu Berlin 2001–2002; British Council Scholarship 1976, Violet Vaughan-Morgan Grad. Fellowship Univ. of Oxford; Asian American Inst. Milestone Award 2000. *Publications include:* Nation and Narration (ed.) 1990, The Location of Culture 1993, Die Bhagavadgita 1997, Anish Kapoor (co-author) 1998, Die Verortung der Kultur 2000, Cosmopolitanism (ed.) 2002, Habitations of Modernity: Essays in the Wake of Subaltern Studies 2002, Edward Said: Continuing the Conversation (ed.) 2005, Without Boundary (co-author) 2006, The Urgency of Theory 2008; numerous essays and articles in professional journals. *Address:* Humanities Center, Harvard University, 12 Quincy Street, Barker Center 134, Cambridge, MA 02138, USA (office). *Telephone:* (617) 495-0739 (office). *Fax:* (617) 495-0730 (office). *E-mail:* hbhabha@fas.harvard.edu (office). *Website:* www.aaas.fas.harvard.edu (office).

BHADESHIA, Harshad Kumar Dharamshi Hansraj, BSc, PhD, FRS, FREng, FInstP, FIM, CEng, CPhys; British metallurgist and academic; *Tata Steel Professor of Metallurgy, University of Cambridge;* b. 27 Nov. 1953, Nairobi, Kenya; s. of Dharamshi Hansraj Bhadeshia and Narmda Dharamshi Bhadeshia; m. 1978 (divorced 1992); two d.; ed City of London Polytechnic, Univ. of Cambridge; Science Research Council Research Fellow, Univ. of Cambridge, UK 1979–81, Demonstrator 1981–85, Lecturer 1985–94, Reader in Physical Metallurgy 1994–99, Prof. of Physical Metallurgy 1999, Tata Steel Prof. of Metallurgy 2008–; Distinguished Adjunct Prof., Grad. Inst. of Ferrous Tech., POSTECH, South Korea 2005; Vice-Pres. Industrial Trust; mem. European Acad. of Sciences; Founding Ed. Science and Technology of Welding and Joining 1996–; mem. Editorial Bd Australasian Journal of Welding 2000–, Material Transactions of JIM 2000–, Science and Technology of Advanced Materials 2001–, Materials Science and Technology 2002–, Current Opinion: Solid-State and Materials Science 2002–; Fellow, Darwin Coll., Cambridge 1985–, Inst. of Materials 1998–; Foreign Fellow, Indian Nat. Acad. of Eng 2004–; Royal Charter Prize 1976, Pfeil Medal and Prize 1979, 1991, Larke Medal 1992, Hume-Rothery Prize 1992, Rosenhain Medal and Prize 1994, CBMM Charles-Hatchett Medal and Award, Brazil, 1996, Royal Soc. Armourers and Brasiers' Co. Award 1997, Medal and Rose Bowl 2000, Reaumur

Medal 2001, 5th Tendolkar Memorial Lecture India 2002, 37th John Player Memorial Lecture 2002, Brooker Medal 2003, Sawamura Award 2003, Comfort A. Adams Award Lecture 2004, 52nd Hatfield Lecture 2004, 17th Hume-Rothery Lecture 2005. *Publications include:* Geometry of Crystals 1987, Bainite in Steels 1992, (jtly) Steels 1995. *Leisure interests:* television, squash. *Address:* Department of Materials Science and Metallurgy, Phase Transformations and Complex Properties Research Group, University of Cambridge, Pembroke Street, Cambridge, CB2 3QZ (office); 57 Barrons Way, Comberton, Cambridge, CB3 7EQ, England (home). *Telephone:* (1223) 334301 (office). *Fax:* (1223) 334567 (office). *E-mail:* hkdb@cam.ac.uk (office); hkdb@postech.ac.kr (office). *Website:* (office).

BHAGWANDAS, Rana, LLB, LLM, MA; Pakistani judge (retd); *Chairman, Federal Public Service Commission;* b. 20 Dec. 1942, Naseerabad, Larkana Dist (now Qamber Shahdadkot Dist), Sindh; called to the Bar 1965, practised law 1965–67; joined Pakistani Judicial System 1967, later became a sessions judge, subsequently judge of Sindh High Court 1994, apptd to superior judiciary 1999, appointment challenged by a constitutional petition, subsequently rejected, claiming that only Muslims can be apptd to superior judiciary; Judge of Supreme Court 2000–08, served as Acting Chief Justice 2005 (first Hindu and second non-Muslim to serve in this post); Chair. Fed. Public Service Comm. 2009–; honoured with 'Siropa' (robe of honour) during visit to Harimandir Sahib, Amritsar, India 2005. *Address:* Office of the Chairman, Federal Public Service Commission, F-5/1 Aga Khan Road, Islamabad, Pakistan. *Telephone:* (51) 9205075. *Fax:* (51) 9210783. *E-mail:* fpsc@fpsc.gov.pk. *Website:* www.fpsc.gov.pk (office).

BHAI, Aziz Mohammad; Bangladeshi business executive; *Chairman, Ambee Pharmaceuticals Limited;* b. Kanpur, India; Founding Chair. Ambee Pharmaceuticals Ltd 1976–; fmr Pres. Dhaka Chamber of Commerce and Industry, Aga Khan Supreme Council for Bangladesh; mem. Rotary Club. *Address:* Ambee Pharmaceuticals Ltd, House 1, Road 71, Gulshan 2, Dhaka 1212, Bangladesh (office). *Telephone:* (2) 8813991 (office). *Fax:* (2) 8827777 (office). *E-mail:* info@ ambeepharma.com (office). *Website:* www.ambeepharma.com (office).

BHALLA, Bhupinder S.; Indian civil servant and government official; *Administrator of Dadra and Nagar Haveli and of Daman and Diu;* ed Univ. of Georgia, USA, Indian Inst. of Man.; Admin. Service Officer, posted to Goa 1992–94, Daman and Diu, Dadra and Nagar Haveli 1994–97, Jt Sec. (L&B), Delhi Govt 1997–2000, Sec. (IT) and Chief Electoral Officer, Govt of Goa 2002–04, Dir of Econ. Affairs (Banking Div.) 2004–08, Counsellor (Econ.) Econ. Wing, Embassy in Washington, DC 2008–11, Sec. (Health, Revenue, Educ., IT), Andaman and Nicobar Islands 2011–12, Admin. of Dadra and Nagar Haveli (DNH) Aug. 2012– and of Daman and Diu (DD) Sept. 2012–. *Address:* Office of the Administration of Dadra and Nagar Haveli, Administrator's Bungalow, Moti Daman, Daman, 396 210, India (office). *Telephone:* (260) 2642777 (DNH) (office); (260) 2230700 (DD) (office). *Fax:* (260) 2642702 (DNH) (office); (260) 2230775 (DD) (office). *E-mail:* administrator@dnh .nic.in (office); admr-dadranagar@nic.in (office). *Website:* dnh.nic.in (office); www .daman.nic.in (office).

BHANDARE, Murlidhar Chandrakant, BSc, LLB; Indian lawyer and politician; b. 10 Dec. 1928, Bombay (now Mumbai); s. of Chandrakant Laxmikant Bhandare and Sunanda Bhandare; m.; one s. one d.; Sr Advocate in Supreme Court of India, Pres. Supreme Court Bar Asscn 1986–88; mem. Rajya Sabha 1980–94; Gov. of Orissa 2007–13; Chair. UN Sub-Comm. for Prevention of Discrimination and Protection of Minorities 1984–89, UNESCO's Appeals Body 1990–2003, Indira Gandhi Nat. Integration Award Cttee; active in supporting empowerment of women and protection of rights of children and physically handicapped. *Publications include:* The World of Gender Justice (ed.); articles on law, human rights, population control, gender parity and justice published in leading magazines and journals. *Address:* c/o Raj Bhavan, Bhubaneswar, India (office).

BHANDARI, Bidya Devi; Nepalese politician; *Vice-Chairman, Communist Party of Nepal (Unified Marxist-Leninist);* b. June 1961, Ambote, Bhojpur dist; d. of Ram Bahadur Pandey; m. Madan Bhandari 1982 (died 1993); ed Bhojpur Campus, Mahendra Morang Campus, Biratnagar; mem. All Nepal National Free Student Union during student years; elected to House of Reps 1994; Minister for Population and Environment 1997; mem. All Nepalese Women's Asscn (ANWA) 1980–, fmr Pres. Biratnagar chapter, Morang dist and Koshi zone, then Chair. ANWA 1998; detained and held in custody following public protests against monarchy 2005, released 2006; Minister of Defence 2009–11; currently Vice-Chair. Communist Party of Nepal (Unified Marxist-Leninist); Patron Madan Bhandari Study and Research Centre. *Address:* Communist Party of Nepal (Unified Marxist-Leninist), Madan Nagar, Balkhu, POB 5471, Kathmandu, Nepal (office). *Telephone:* (1) 4278081 (office). *Fax:* (1) 4278084 (office). *E-mail:* uml@ntc.net.np (office). *Website:* www.cpnuml.org (office).

BHANDARI, Sarat Singh; Nepalese politician; *Minister of Defence;* b. Mahottari Dist; fmr Minister for Health, for Culture and for Tourism and Civil Aviation; Minister of Defence 2011–; fmr mem. Nepali Congress Party; currently mem. Madhesi Jana Adhikar Forum Nepal (Madhesi People's Rights Forum Nepal). *Address:* Ministry of Defence, Singha Durbar, Kathmandu, Nepal (office). *Telephone:* (1) 4211289 (office). *Fax:* (1) 4211294 (office). *E-mail:* mod@mos.com .np (office). *Website:* www.mod.gov.np (office).

BHARDWAJ, Hans Raj, LLB, MA; Indian politician and lawyer; *Governor of Karnataka;* b. 17 May 1937, Haryana; s. of Jagan Nath Prasad Sharma and Sarti Devi; m. Prafulata Bhardwaj 1960; one s. two d.; ed B.M. Coll., Shimla, Agra Univ. and Panjab Univ., Chandigarh; mem. Nat. Exec., Indian Youth Congress 1957; Public Prosecutor, Delhi High Court 1972–77; Sr Standing Counsel for UP, Supreme Court of India 1980–82; mem. Rajya Sabha (Parl.) for Haryana 1982–2006, Leader Parl. Del. to Repub. of Korea 1989; mem. Cttee of Privileges, Rajya Sabha (Parl.) 1996–2004, of Home Affairs Cttee 1998–2004, Advisory Council, Delhi Devt Cttee 2000–04, Business Advisory Cttee 2002–04; Minister of State for Law and Justice 1984–89, 1992–96; Sr Vice-Pres. Inst. of Constitutional and Parl. Studies, New Delhi 1988–90; Minister of State for Planning and Programme Implementation 1991–92; Minister of Law and Justice 2004–09; Gov. of Karnataka 2009–, additional charge of Kerala 2012–13; mem. Bar Asscn of India, Legal Affairs Cttee for Asian Games 1982, Indo-US Sub-Comm. for Educ. and Culture 1982–84, Law Asia, Int. Law Asscn, United Int. Advocates; Hon. Chair., Int. Centre for Alternative Dispute Resolution; Dr hc (Kurukshetra Univ.).

Publications include: Law, Lawyers and Judges, Soul of India, Crime, Criminal Justice and Human Rights. *Leisure interests:* gardening and farming. *Address:* Raj Bhavan, Raj Bhavan Road, Bangalore 560 001 (office); E-7/19, Charimili, Bhopal, Madhya Pradesh, India (home). *Telephone:* (80) 22254102 (office). *Fax:* (80) 22258150 (office). *E-mail:* rbblr@vsnl.com (office). *Website:* www.rajbhavan.kar.nic .in (office); www.kar.nic.in/kla/governor.htm (office).

BHARGAVA, Manjul, AB, PhD; Canadian mathematician and academic; *Professor of Mathematics, Princeton University;* b. 1974, Hamilton, Ont.; ed Harvard Univ., Princeton Univ.; grew up in Long Island, NY; with Nat. Security Agency, summer 1994; Duluth Summer Research Program, summer 1995; Center for Communications Research, Princeton, summer 1996; AT&T Labs Research, Florham Park, NJ, summer 1997; Clay Research Fellowship (first recipient), Clay Math. Inst., Cambridge, Mass 2000–05; Visiting Mathematician, Princeton Univ. 2001–02; Visiting Asst Prof., Harvard Univ., spring 2003; Prof. of Math., Princeton Univ. (hired at rank of full prof. with tenure just two years after finishing grad. school) 2003–; fmr Co-Pres. Harvard Math Club; Winner of NY State Science Talent Search 1992, Detur Prize for Outstanding Academic Achievement, Harvard Univ. 1993, Derek Bok Award for Excellence in Teaching, Harvard Univ. 1993, 1994, 1995, Hoopes Prize for Excellence in Scholarly Work and Research, Harvard Univ. 1996, Hertz Foundation Grad. Fellowship in Math. 1996–2000, AMS-MAA-SIAM Frank and Brennie Morgan Prize 1997, named one of Popular Science Magazine's "Brilliant 10" 2002, Hasse Prize for Exposition, Math. Asscn of America 2003, Packard Foundation Fellowship in Science and Eng 2004, Leonard M. and Eleanor B. Blumenthal Award for the Advancement of Research in Pure Math. 2005, Clay Research Award, Clay Math. Inst. (co-recipient) 2005, SASTRA Ramanujan Prize (co-recipient) 2005, MS Frank Nelson Cole Prize in Number Theory, American Math. Soc. 2008, Fermat Prize 2011, Simons Investigator Award 2012, Infosys Prize 2012. *Achievements include:* 13 new Gauss composition laws, including quartic and quintic degree cases; proof of 15 theorem, including extension of theorem to other number sets such as prime numbers; proof of 290 theorem; novel generalization of factorial function, resolving decades-old conjecture by George Pólya. *Publications:* several papers in professional journals on algebraic number theory, combinatorics and representation theory. *Leisure interests:* tabla player (studied under Zakir Hussain), linguistics and its various connections to math. and music. *Address:* 1206 Fine Hall, Department of Mathematics, Princeton University, Princeton, NJ 08544, USA (office). *Telephone:* (609) 258-4192 (office). *Fax:* (609) 258-1367 (office). *E-mail:* bhargava@math .princeton.edu (office). *Website:* www.math.princeton.edu (office).

BHARGAVA, Pushpa Mittra, PhD; Indian scientist, writer and consultant; b. 22 Feb. 1928, Ajmer, Rajasthan; s. of Dr Ram Chandra Bhargava and Gayatri Devi Bhargava; m. Edith Manorama Patrick 1958; one s. one d.; ed Univ. of Lucknow; Lecturer, Dept of Chem., Osmania Univ., Hyderabad, then mem. staff Cen. Labs Hyderabad; Post-doctoral Fellow, Univ. of Madison 1953–56; at Nat. Inst. for Medical Research, UK 1957–58; joined Regional Research Lab. (now Indian Inst. of Chemical Tech.) 1958–77; Founder, Centre for Cellular and Molecular Biology, Hyderabad, Dir 1977–90; Council of Scientific and Industrial Research Distinguished Fellow 1990–93; Visiting Prof., Collège de France, Paris; Scientific adviser in several industries; has worked by invitation at McArdle Lab. for Cancer Research, USA, Nat. Inst. for Medical Research, UK, Institut du Radium, France, Max-Planck Institut für Biophysikalische Chemie, Germany; Vice-Chair. Nat. Knowledge Comm. –2008; Founder Guha Research Conf.; Founder-mem. Soc. for Study of Reproduction (USA); Past-Pres. Soc. of Biological Chemists; Treas. Int. Union for Science Communicators; Fellow, Indian Nat. Science Acad., Indian Acad. of Sciences, Nat. Acad. of Sciences (India), Nat. Acad. of Medical Sciences (India), World Acad. of Arts and Sciences, Indian Acad. of Social Sciences; Corresp. mem. American Asscn for Cancer Research and other bodies; mem. Nat. Security Advisory Bd 2006–; Life Fellow, Clare Hall, Cambridge, UK; Légion d'honneur 1998; Hon. DSc (Univ. of Burdwan); numerous prizes and awards, including Nat. Citizens Award 1988; Padma Bhushan 1986, Lifetime Achievement Award, BioSpectrum Awards 2007. *Publications include:* several books, including Proteins of Seminal Plasma 1989, The Saga of Indian Science Since Independence 2003, Angels, Devils and Science, A Collection of Articles on Scientific Temper (with Chandana Chakrabarti) 2007; numerous articles. *Leisure interests:* fine arts, reading, current affairs, sports, music, films, photography. *Address:* Anveshna, Furqan Cottage, 12-13-100 Lane 1, Street No. 3, Tarnaka, Hyderabad 500 017 (office); 12-5-27 Vijayapuri, Tarnaka, Hyderabad 500 017, India (home). *Telephone:* (40) 27017789 (office); (40) 27003517 (home). *Fax:* (40) 27017857 (office). *E-mail:* pmb1928@yahoo.co.in (office); bhargava.pm@gmail.com (home).

BHARTIA, Shobhana; Indian newspaper executive; *Chairperson and Editorial Director, The Hindustan Times;* b. 4 Jan. 1957, Calcutta (now Kolkata); d. of the late Dr Krishna Kumar Birla and Manorama Devi; m. Shyam Sunder Bhartia 1974; two s.; ed Loreto House, Calcutta; Exec. Dir The Hindustan Times Ltd 1986, Chair. and Editorial Dir 2008–; Chair. HT Vision Ltd 1990–; nominated to Rajya Sabha (Parl.) 2006, Pres. FICCI (women's org.); Chair. and Treas. Bd of Govs Delhi Coll. of Arts and Commerce 1988–90; Chair. Bd of Govs Shyama Prasad Mukherjee Coll. (for Women) 1992; mem. Bd of Dirs Press Trust of India Ltd 1987– (Chair.), Indian Airlines Ltd, New Delhi 1988–90, Air Travel Bureau Pvt. Ltd 1989, Shri Mata Vaishno Devi Shrine, Katra 1991, Hero Honda Ltd; Chair. Endeavor India; Deputy Chair. Exec. Cttee, Audit Bureau of Circulations; Pro-Chancellor, Birla Inst. of Tech. and Science, Pilani; Leader of dels to Australia, NZ, the Philippines and to World Congress of Women Conf. (Moscow, fmr USSR) 1987–88; mem. Bd North Regional Bd of Reserve Bank of India; mem. Exec. Cttee Indian Newspaper Soc. and Commonwealth Press Union, London; mem. Apex Cttee of Commonwealth Games 2010, Governing Council, India Habitat Centre, Alliance of Civilizations Bd of Govs., Nat. Inst. of Fashion Tech., Indian Public School Society (The Doon School); Trustee, Indira Gandhi Memorial Trust, Bhartiya Vidya Bhavan; Int. Cultural Devt Award 1989, Mahila Shiromani Award 1990, Lok Shri Award, Inst. of Econ. Studies 1990, Vijaya Shri Award, Int. Friendship Soc. of India 1991, Nat. Press India Award 1992, Nat. Unity Award 1993, Global Leader for Tomorrow, World Econ. Forum 1996, Outstanding Businesswoman Award, PHD Chamber of Commerce & Industry, Punjab, Haryana, Delhi Chamber of Commerce and Industry 2001, Padma Shri 2005, Ernst and Young Entrepreneur of the Year Award 2005, Business Woman Award, The Economic Times Awards for Corp. Excellence 2007, ranked by Fortune magazine amongst the 50 Most Powerful Women in Business outside the US (34th) 2008, (43rd) 2009, (44th) 2010. *Leisure interests:* reading, music. *Address:* Hindustan Times House, 18–20 Kasturba Gandhi Marg, New Delhi, 110 001 (office); HT Media Ltd, Park Centra Building, 7th Floor, Sector-30, Delhi–Jaipur Highway, Gurgaon 122 001, India (office). *Telephone:* (11) 23361234 (office); (124) 3954700 (office); (11) 6830260 (home). *Fax:* (11) 66561270 (office). *E-mail:* feedback@hindustantimes.com (office). *Website:* www.hindustantimes.com (office); www.htmedia.in (office).

BHATIA, Mick, BSc, PhD; Canadian biologist and academic; *Director and Senior Scientist, Stem Cell and Cancer Research Institute, McMaster University;* b. 1970; ed McMaster Univ., Univ. of Guelph; worked for Dept of Human Biology, Univ. of Guelph; Postdoctoral Fellow, Hosp. for Sick Children, Univ. of Toronto; Canadian Research Chair and Dir Krembil Centre for Stem Cell Biology, Robarts Research Inst., Univ. of Western Ont., London 2003–05; currently Prof. of Biochemistry and Biomedical Sciences, Assoc. Mem. Dept of Pathology and Molecular Medicine, McMaster Univ., Hamilton, Dir and Sr Scientist, McMaster Stem Cell and Cancer Research Inst., also Dir and Sr Scientist, DeGroote Chair in Stem Cell and Cancer Biology 2006–; Postdoctoral Fellowship, Nat. Cancer Inst. of Canada 1995–97; Canada Research Chair in Stem Cell Biology and Regenerative Medicine (Tier 2) 2002–05, Canada Research Chair in Human Stem Cell Biology (Tier 1) 2006–11; Krembil Foundation Research Chair in Stem Cell Biology and Regenerative Medicine 2003–05; mem. Medical Review Panel, Gairdner Foundation; Annual Trainee Award, American Soc. of Dermatology 1997, Young Scientist Scholarship Award, Medical Research Council 1999–2002, Premiers' Research Excellence Award, Ministry of Energy, Science and Tech. 2000–05, Univ. of Guelph Alumni Medal of Achivement 2008, Molecular and Cellular Biology Award, Canadian Soc. for Biochemistry 2009, McMaster University Innovator of the Year 2011, Queen's Diamond Jubilee Medal 2012, CBMTG 2013 Till and McCulloch Award 2013. *Publications:* numerous articles in professional journals. *Address:* Michael G. DeGroote Centre for Learning and Discovery, 1280 Main Street West, Hamilton, ON L8S 4K1, Canada (office). *Telephone:* (905) 525-9140 (office). *Fax:* (905) 522-7772 (office). *E-mail:* mbhatia@mcmaster.ca (office). *Website:* sccri.mcmaster.ca/ bhatia_mick.html (office); sccri.mcmaster.ca/bhatia_lab.html.

BHATIA, Raghunanthanlal, LLB; Indian politician; b. 3 July 1921, Amritsar, Punjab; s. of the late Arooramal Bhatia and Lal Devi Bhatia; m. Sarala Bhatia; one s. one d.; ed Univ. of the Punjab; fmr Pres. Students' Union; mem. Lok Sabha for Amritsar Constituency 1972, 1980–99, mem. Select Cttee for Amendment of the Constitution 1992, several consultative parl. cttees, including Ministry of Home Affairs, Educ., Railways, Information and Broadcasting, Law and Justice and Company Affairs, leader or mem. del. of AICC to People's Repub. of China, USSR, Poland, Bulgaria, Czechoslovakia, USA, Cambodia, Viet Nam, Afghanistan, Japan, UK; Pres. Punjab Pradesh Congress Cttee 1982–84; Union Minister of State for External Affairs July 1992; Gov. of Kerala 2004–08, of Bihar 2008–09; mem. Exec. Cttee Congress Parl. Party 1975–77, India Council for Cultural Relations 1983–84; Gen. Sec. All India Congress Cttee 1991; Chair. Cttee on Petitions 1983, India Bulgaria Friendship Soc., India GDR Friendship Asscn 1983–90; Co-Chair. All India Peace and Solidarity Org. 1981–83; Vice-Pres. Friends of the Soviet Union 1983–84; mem. Local Body of Amritsar for nine years; represented India as a del. to UN, del. to 7th NAM Summit, Delhi 1983, Commonwealth Heads of Govt Meeting, New Delhi 1983, 6th SAARC Summit, Colombo 1991, 5th Meeting of Coordinating Countries of the Action Programme for Econ. Cooperation of Non-aligned Countries, Delhi 1986. *Leisure interests:* reading, gardening. *Address:* 44 Kamalpushpa, Congress Nagar, Amravati 444 601, India (office). *Telephone:* (612) 2226207 (office).

BHATIA, Sabeer, BSc, MS; Indian/American internet services industry executive and entrepreneur; b. 30 Dec. 1968, Chandigarh; s. of Baldev Bhatia and Daman Bhatia; m. Tania Sharma 2008; ed Birla Inst. of Tech. and Science, Pilani, California Inst. of Tech. and Stanford Univ., USA; Systems Integrator, Apple Computers; joined Firepower Systems Inc. 1994, co-founded Hotmail Corpn 1995, launched pioneering web-based email service Hotmail (with Jack Smith), sold to Microsoft 1997; worked for Microsoft 1998–99; f. Arzoo.com 1999, relaunched as travel portal 2006; launched Blogeverywhere.com 2006; Entrepreneur of the Year, Draper Fisher Jurvetson 1998, named among Elite 100, Upside Magazine, TR100 Award, MIT, listed among ten most successful entrepreneurs by San Jose Mercury News and POV magazine 1998, named among People to Watch in Int. Business, Time Magazine 2002. *Address:* Arzoo.com, Samruddhi Venture Park, 5th Floor, MIDC Central Road, Andhei East, Mumbai 400 093, India (office). *Telephone:* (22) 67134444 (office). *Fax:* (22) 28316680 (office). *Website:* www.arzoo.com (office).

BHATT, Om Prakash, BSc, MA; Indian fmr central banker; b. 7 March 1951; joined State Bank of India (SBI) as probationary officer 1972, held several positions including Scheme Co-ordinator of br. computerization at Cen. Office of SBI, Regional Man. with Jaipur Zone, Gen. Man. with Lucknow Zone and Chief Gen. Man. with North Zone, Man. Dir State Bank of Travancore, Man. Dir and Group Exec. SBI April–Oct. 2006, Chair. 2006–11; Chair. Banking and Financial Insts Cttee, Fed. of Indian Chambers of Commerce and Industry, Indian Banks' Asscn 2010–11; Ind. Dir Hindustan Unilever Ltd 2011–; mem. Bd of Dirs EXIM Bank and GIC, Indian Council for Research on International Econ. Relations; mem. Xavier Labour Relations Inst. of Banking Personnel Selection, Inst. for Devt and Research in Banking Tech., Khadi and Village Industries Comm., Nat. Co-operative Devt Corpn; Banker of the Year, Business Standard 2006–07, CNN-IBN Businessman of the Year 2007, Transformational Leader Award 2007, Best Executive Award 2008. *Address:* c/o Board of Directors, Hindustan Unilever Limited, Unilever House, B. D. Sawant Marg, Chakala, Andheri East, Mumbai 400 099, India.

BHATTACHARYA, Buddhadev, BA; Indian politician; b. 1 March 1944, Kolkata; s. of Nepal Chandra Bhattacharya; m. Meera Bhattacharya; one d.; ed Sailendra Sarkar Vidyalaya and Presidency Coll., Kolkata; mem. Communist Party of India—Marxist Secr., Cen. Cttee, mem. of Politbureu –2008; Minister-in-Charge, W Bengal Information and Public Relations Dept 1977–82, Dept of Information and Cultural Affairs 1987–99, Dept of Local Govt, Dept of Urban Devt and Metropolitan Devt 1987–91, Dept of Information and Cultural Affairs 1991–93, 1994, 1996, Dept of Urban Devt and Municipal Affairs 1991–93, Dept of Home Affairs and Dept of Information Tech. 1996–99, Deputy Chief Minister of West Bengal 1999–2000, Chief Minister 2000–11. *Publication:* collection of poems and plays. *Leisure interests:* cricket, travelling. *Address:* West Bengal State Committee, 31, Alimuddin Street Muzaffar Ahmad Bhawan, Kolkata 700 016, India (office). *Telephone:* (33) 22176633 (office). *Fax:* (33) 22640721 (office). *E-mail:* wbcpim@gmail.com (office). *Website:* www.cpimwb.org.in (office).

BHATTACHARYA, Tara Shankar, MSc; Indian banking executive; ed Jadavpur Univ., Kolkata, Saha Inst. of Nuclear Physics, Jamnalal Bajaj Inst. of Man., Mumbai; fmr State Bank of India, Mumbai, held various positions, including Head Retail Banking, Marketing and Product Devt Dept and Gen. Man., Chandigarh, Deputy Man. Dir State Bank of India 2004–05, Man. Dir 2005–08, Acting Chair. and Group Exec. for Corp. Banking 2006–08; Advisor, Ernst & Young Pvt. Ltd, Mumbai; Dir, Infrastructure Leasing & Financial Services Ltd, Sayaji Hotels Ltd, Nuclear Power Corpn of India Limited 2008–, Jagson Airlines Ltd 2010–; Ind. Dir JSL Stainless Ltd 2009–, Abhijeet Power Ltd 2010–; Ind. Dir (non-exec.) Surya Roshni Ltd 2011–; Additional Dir, AGS Transact Technologies Ltd 2010–11; Certified Assoc. Indian Inst. of Bankers. *Address:* Sayaji Hotels Ltd, H/1, Scheme No. 54, Vijay Nagar, Indore 452 010, Madhya Pradesh, India (office). *Telephone:* (731) 4006666 (office). *Fax:* (731) 4003131 (office). *E-mail:* mail@sayajiindore.com. *Website:* www.sayajihotels.com (office).

BHATTACHARYYA, S. K.; Indian banking executive; ed St Stephen's Coll.; joined State Bank of India (SBI) 1972; positions include Man. Dir SBI Int. (Mauritius) Ltd, Chief Gen. Man. Hyderabad Circle, Deputy Gen. Man. (Vigilance), Chennai Circle; Man. Dir State Bank of Bikaner & Jaipur –2007, Man. Dir and Chief Credit and Risk Officer, SBI 2007–10; Dir, Dabur India Ltd. *Address:* Dabur India Ltd, Kaushambi, Ghaziabad 201 010, Uttar Pradesh, India (office). *Telephone:* (120) 3982000 (office). *E-mail:* info@dabur.com (office). *Website:* www.dabur.com (office).

BHATTARAI, Baburam, BArch (Hons), PhD; Nepalese politician, academic and fmr guerrilla leader; b. 26 May 1954, Belbas, Khoplang VDC of Gorkha Dist; ed Amar Jyoti Janata Secondary School, Luintel, Gorkha (also known as Luintel School), Tribhuvan Univ., Chandigarh Coll. of Architecture, Jawaharlal Nehru Univ., New Delhi, India; became politically active during student days in India; f. All India Nepalese Students Asscn 1977; became active in CP of Nepal (Masal), Spokesperson of United Nat. People's Movt during uprising 1990, broke away with others from CPN (Masal) 1991; joined CP of Nepal (Unity Centre) 1991, became head of Samyukta Janamorcha Nepal (United People's Front Nepal, political front of CP of Nepal (Unity Centre) in Parl.), sided with hardline section (which later took name CPN(M)) when CPN (UC) split in 1994, became leader of parallel SJM led by Maoists; became known throughout Nepal after start of Nepalese People's War; fmr commdr of rebel army; Head of Int. Dept of the party for a time and Convener of United Revolutionary People's Council, Nepal; Sr mem. Standing Cttee of Politburo, Unified Communist Party of Nepal (Maoist); elected to Constituent Ass. from Gorkha 2008; Minister of Finance 2008–09; Prime Minister 2011–13. *Publications include:* Nepal: A Marxist View 1996, Politico-Economic Rationale of People's War in Nepal 1998, The Nature of Underdevelopment and Regional Structure of Nepal: A Marxist Analysis 2003, Nepal! krantika adharharu (in Nepali) 2004, Monarchy vs. Democracy: The Epic Fight in Nepal 2005; numerous articles in nat. and int. journals and newspapers. *Telephone:* (1) 4211096. *E-mail:* press@baburambhattarai.com. *Website:* baburambhattarai.com.

BHATTARAI, Bijaya Nath, BCom, MCom, MA (Econs); Nepalese fmr central banker; b. 9 Nov. 1949; m.; two c.; ed Tribhuvan Univ., Vanderbilt Univ., USA; Asst Research Officer, Research Dept, Nepal Rastra Bank (Cen. Bank) 1972–81, Research Officer 1981–92, Econ. Advisor 1992–95, Chief Controller, Foreign Exchange Dept 1995–98, Chief Accountant, Accounts and Expenditure Dept 1998–2000, Deputy Gov. and mem. Bd of Dirs 2000–05, Gov. and Chair. 2005–07 (suspended on charges of corruption, won protracted legal battle and was subsequently reinstated) 2009–10; Chair. Asian Clearing Union 2005–; fmr Chair. Rural Self-Reliance Fund; fmr mem. Bd of Dirs Environment Protection Fund, Nepal Inter-modal Transport Devt Bd, Poverty Alleviation Fund, Nepal Bangladesh Bank 1993–97, Agricultural Devt Bank 1998–2000. *Publications:* articles and contribs to various bank publs. *Address:* Kha-1, 964 Kalimati, Kathmandu 4, Nepal (home). *Telephone:* (1) 4271148 (home); (1) 4271829 (home).

BHAVE, Chandrasekhar Bhaskar, BE; Indian economist and government official; *Chairman, Securities and Exchange Board of India;* b. Nagpur; started career in Admin. Service 1975; Additional Industries Commr for Maharasthra 1989–92; fmr Under-Sec., Ministry of Finance; Deputy Sec. Ministry of Petroleum 1984–89; Sr Exec. Dir Securities and Exchange Bd of India 1992–96, Chair. 2008–; fmr Chair. and Man. Dir Nat. Securities Depository Ltd; mem. Bd of Dirs CMC (now part of Tata Group), Avaya Global Connect. *Address:* Securities and Exchange Board of India, Plot No.C4-A, G Block, Bandra Kurla Complex, Bandra (East), Mumbai 400 051, India (office). *Telephone:* (22) 26449000 (office); (22) 40459000 (office). *Fax:* (22) 26449016 (office). *E-mail:* sebi@sebi.gov.in (office). *Website:* chairman@sebi.gov.in; www.sebi.gov.in (office).

BHAVSAR, Natvar, BA, AM, MFA; American (b. Indian) artist; b. 7 April 1934, Gothava, Gujarat; s. of Prahladji Bhavsar and Babuben Bhavsar; m. Janet Brosious Bhavsar; three c.; ed Gujarat Univ., Univ. of Pennyslvania School of Design, USA; art instructor, Seth School of Fine Arts, Ahmedabad, Gujarat 1957–62; Prof., Univ. of Rhode Island, USA 1967–69; work in public collections including: Australian Nat. Gallery, Boston Museum of Fine Arts, Solomon R. Guggenheim Museum, Metropolitan Museum of Art, MIT, Philadelphia Museum of Art; work in numerous pvt. collections; John D. Rockefeller 3rd Fund Fellowship 1965–66, John Simon Guggenheim Fellowship 1975–76, Aspen Inst. Fellowship 1980, 1983; Vishva Gurjari, Gujarat, India 1987, Cultural Reader, World Econ. Forum 2000, 2002,. *Publication:* Monogram 1998. *Leisure interests:* travel, reading, music, dance. *Address:* 131 Greene Street, New York, NY 10012, USA. *Telephone:* (212) 674-1293. *E-mail:* info@NatvarBhavsar.com. *Website:* www.natvarbhavsar.com.

BHEENICK, Rundheersing; Mauritian economist, central banker and fmr politician; *Governor, Bank of Mauritius;* b. 1944; ed Merton Coll., Oxford, UK; Lecturer in Devt Econs, Univ. of Mauritius 1968–69; Economist, Prime Minister's Office 1969–70; Industrial Devt Officer, UNIDO, Vienna 1970–74; with Ministry of Econ. Planning and Devt 1974–95, becoming Sec. for Aid Coordination, Deputy Dir and Dir-Gen.; mem. Nat. Assembly (Parl.) 1995–2000; Minister of Finance

1995–96, of Econ. Devt, Productivity and Regional Cooperation 1997–2000; Prin. Consultant, Development Associates 2001–07; Gov. Bank of Mauritius (central bank) 2007–; Chair., Council of Ministers, Indian Ocean Rim Asscn for Regional Co-operation 1997–99, COMESA 2000, ADB/EU/IMF/World Bank-sponsored Cross-Border Initiative (subsequently Regional Integration Facilitation Forum) 1997–2000, Commonwealth Partnership Tech. Man. Finance Working Group 2001–06; Hon. Prof. of Political Economy, Univ. of Mauritius 1989. *Address:* Office of the Governor, Bank of Mauritius, Sir William Newton Street, POB 29, Port Louis, Mauritius (office). *Telephone:* 202-3800 (office). *Fax:* 208-9204 (office). *E-mail:* governor.office@bom.intnet.mu (office). *Website:* www.bom.mu (office).

BHIROMBHAKDI, Chamnong; Thai business executive; *Chairman, Singha Corporation;* b. 1928; s. of Boonrawd Sreshthaputra and Khunying Lamai; m. Khunying Supachari; three c.; Chair. Singha Corpn (Boon Rawd Brewery); mem. Bd of Dirs Bangkok Glass Industry Co., Ltd.; Founder Skeet and Trap Shooting Asscn of Thailand. *Address:* Boon Rawd Brewery, 999 Samsen Road, Dusit, Bangkok 10300, Thailand (office). *Telephone:* (2) 242-4000 (office). *Fax:* (2) 669-2089 (office). *E-mail:* pr_relations@boonrawd.co.th (office). *Website:* www.boonrawd.co.th (office).

BHOSLE, Asha; Indian singer, composer and restaurateur; b. 8 Sept. 1933, Sangli, Maharashtra; d. of Dinanath Mangeshkar; m. 1st Ganpatrao Bhosle (divorced); m. 2nd Rahul Dev Burman 1980 (died 1994); two s. one d.; Indian film playback singer; has recorded over 12,000 songs in 18 languages; first film Chunaria 1948; first solo in Raat Ki Rani 1949; sang in styles influenced by Latin American and American Big Band Jazz; worked extensively with Kishore Kumar 1970s; owns restaurants in several cities world-wide; Dr hc (Univ. of Amravati), (Univ. of Jalgaon); Filmfare Award 1967, 1968, 1971, 1972, 1973, 1974, 1977, 1996, Nat. Award 1981, 1986, Nightingale of Asia 1987, Lata Mangeshkar Award, Madhya Pradesh Govt 1989, Maharashtra Govt 1999, Filmfare Special Award, Rangeela Re 1996, Screen Videocon Award 1997, MTV Contribution to Music Award 1997, five Channel V Awards, Singer of the Millennium, Dubai 2000, Kolhapuri Bhushan Award 2000, Sangli Bhushan Award 2000, Omega Excellence Lifetime Achievement Award 2000, Filmfare Lifetime Achievement Award 2001, Dada Saheb Phalke Award 2001, Dayawati Modi Award 2001, BBC Mega Mela Lifetime Achievement Award 2002, Swaralaya Yesudas Award 2003, Living Legend Award, Fed. of Indian Chamber of Commerce and Industry 2004, MTV Immies 2005, Padma Vibhushan 2008, Freddie Mercury Award. *Recordings include:* albums (soundtracks): Dus Lakh 1967, Shikhar 1968, Hare Rama Hare Krishna 1972, Naina 1973, Pran Jaye Par Vachan Na Jaye 1974, Don 1977, Umrao Jaan 1981, Ijazat 1986, Dilwale Dulhania Le Jayeng 1995, Rangeela 1996; solo: Songs of My Soul – Rare and Classic Vols 1 and 2 2001, You've Stolen My Heart (with the Kronos Quartet) 2005, 75 Years of Asha 2008. *Film:* Mai (as actress) 2013. *Leisure interest:* cooking. *Address:* 1st Floor, Prabhu Kunj Apartment, Pedder Road, Mumbai 400 026, India (home). *Telephone:* (22) 64938070. *E-mail:* info@ashasrestaurants.com. *Website:* www.ashasrestaurants.com.

BHOWMIK, Neem Chandra; Bangladeshi diplomatist, physicist and academic; fmr Prof. and Chair. Dept of Applied Physics, Electronics and Communication Eng, Dhaka Univ., Dir Renewable Energy Research Centre; has worked in India, UK, Germany, Italy and Thailand –2009; Amb. to Nepal 2009–12; Pres. Bangladesh Muktijodha Foundation, Bangladesh Puja Udjapan Parishad; Gen. Sec. Bangladesh Hindu Bouddha Christian Oikya Parishad (protects the rights of minority groups in Bangladesh); participated in World Renewable Energy Congress; UNESCO Young Scientist Award 1988.

BHUIYAN, Lt Gen. Iqbal Karim; Bangladeshi military officer; *Chief of Army Staff;* b. 2 June 1957, Comilla; m. Tahmina Yasmin; one s. two d.; ed Bangladesh Mil. Acad., Defence Services Command and Staff Coll., Command and Gen. Staff Coll., USA; commissioned into Bangladeshi Army 1976, later attained rank of Lt Gen., held numerous positions including UN Force Commdr during deployment of Bangladeshi peacekeepers, Commdr, Ghatail Div. and Chittagong Div., GOC, 9th Infantry Div., Savar, Chief of Gen. Staff of Army, Quartermaster Gen. of the Army –2012, Chief of Army Staff 2012–, also served as Platoon Commdr, Bangladesh Mil. Acad., Directing Staff, Defence Services Command and Staff Coll., Commdt, School of Infantry and Tactics, Defence Services Command and Staff Coll.; fmr Commdr, Sector-4, UN Mission in Sierra Leone; Liberation of Kuwait Medal. *Address:* Army Headquarters, GS Branch, IT Directorate, Dhaka, Bangladesh (office). *Telephone:* 8871234 (office). *Fax:* 8712388 (office). *E-mail:* itdte@army.mil.bd (office). *Website:* www.army.mil.bd (office).

BHUMIBOL ADULYADEJ, HM King of Thailand (King Rama IX); b. 5 Dec. 1927, Cambridge, Mass., USA; youngest s. of Their Royal Highnesses Prince and Princess Mahidol of Songkla; m. Mom Rajawongse Sirikit Kitiyakara 1950; one s., Crown Prince Maha Vajiralongkorn, b. 28 July 1952; three d., Princess Ubol Ratana, b. 5 April 1951, Princess Maha Chakri Sirindhorn, b. 2 April 1955, Princess Chulabhorn, b. 4 July 1957; ed Bangkok and Lausanne, Switzerland; succeeded his brother, King Ananda Mahidol, 9 June 1946; formal coronation 5 May 1950. *Address:* Chitralada Villa, Bangkok, Thailand.

BHUPATHI, Mahesh Shrinivas; Indian tennis player; b. 7 June 1974, Chennai; s. of C.G. Krishna Bhupathi and Mira Bhupathi; m. 1st Shvetha Jaishankar 2002 (divorced 2009); m. 2nd Lara Dutta 2011; one d.; ed Univ. of Mississippi, USA; NCAA doubles championship in 1995, French Open (mixed doubles) 1997, (men's doubles) 1999, 2001, US Open (mixed doubles) 1999, 2005, (men's doubles) 2002, Wimbledon 1999, (mixed doubles) 2002, 2005, Asian Games (men's doubles), Doha 2006, Australian Open (mixed doubles) 2006, 2009, Canada Masters (men's doubles) 2007, Commonwealth Games (silver medal), Delhi 2010, French Open (mixed doubles) 2012, Paris Masters (men's doubles) 2012; Founder-Man. Dir Globosport; mem. Indian Davis Cup team 1995–; Arjuna Award 1995, Padma Shri 2001. *Address:* Globosport, 130, 1st Floor, 2nd Cross, Amarjyoti Layout, Off Intermediate Ring Road, Domlur, Bangalore 560 071, India (office). *Telephone:* (80) 41154214 (office). *Fax:* (80) 41154403 (office). *E-mail:* info@globosportworld.com (office). *Website:* www.globosportworld.com (office).

BHUTTO, Fatima Murtaza, BA, MA; Pakistani writer; b. 29 May 1982, Kabul, Afghanistan; d. of Murtaza Bhutto and Fauzia Fasihudin Bhutto; grand-d. of Zulfikar Ali Bhutto (fmr Prime Minister of Pakistan); niece of Benazir Bhutto; ed Columbia Univ., USA, SOAS, Univ. of London, UK; fmr columnist, Jang (Urdu daily newspaper), The News (sister publ.); currently writes columns for The Daily Beast, The New Statesman, The Guardian, The Caravan Magazine. *Publications include:* Whispers in the Desert (poetry) 1997, 8.50 a.m. 8 October 2005 2006, Songs of Blood and Sword: A Daughter's Memoir 2010, The Shadow of the Crescent Moon 2013. *Address:* 70 Clifton Road, Old Clifton, Karachi, Pakistan. *Website:* www.fatimabhutto.com.pk.

BHUTTO ZARDARI, Bilawal; Pakistani politician; *Co-Chairman, Pakistan People's Party;* b. 21 Sept. 1988; s. of Asif Ali Zardari and the late Benazir Bhutto, fmr Prime Minister; grandson of fmr Prime Minister Zulfiqar Ali Bhutto; ed Karachi Grammar School, Froebels Int. School, Islamabad, Rashid School for Boys, Dubai, Univ. of Oxford, UK; has spent most of his life outside Pakistan, travelling with his mother who went into self-imposed exile in 1999, moving between London and Dubai; fmr Vice-Pres. Student Council, Rashid School for Boys, Dubai; Co-Chair. (with his father) Pakistan People's Party following assassination of his mother Benazir Bhutto Dec. 2007–. *Leisure interests:* cricket, shooting, horse-riding, black belt in Taekwondo. *Address:* Pakistan People's Party, 8 Street 19, F-8/2, Islamabad Karachi, Pakistan (office). *Telephone:* (51) 2255264 (office). *Fax:* (51) 2282741 (office). *E-mail:* ppp@comsats.net.pk (office). *Website:* www.ppp.org.pk (office).

BIALYSTOK, Ellen, PhD, FRSC; Canadian psychologist and academic; *Distinguished Research Professor of Psychology, York University;* ed Univ. of Toronto; currently Distinguished Research Prof. of Psychology, York Univ.; Assoc. Scientist, Rotman Research Inst. of the Baycrest Centre for Geriatric Care; Killam Research Fellowship, Walter Gordon Research Fellowship, Dean's Award for Outstanding Research, Language Learning Distinguished Scholar in Residence, York Univ., Killam Prize in Social Sciences, Canada Council for the Arts 2010. *Publications:* Spatial cognition: The Structure and Development of the Mental Representation of Spatial Relations (with D. R. Olson) 1983, Communication Strategies: A Psychological Analysis of Second-Language Use 1990, Language Processing in Bilingual Children (ed.) 1991, In Other Words: The Psychology and Science of Second Language Acquisition (with K. Hakuta) 1994, Bilingualism in Development: Language, Literacy, and Cognition 2001, Lifespan Cognition: Mechanisms of Change (co-ed.) 2006, Language Acquisition and Bilingualism: Special Issue of Applied Psycholinguistics (co-ed.) 2007; more than 100 scientific papers in journals and books. *Address:* Department of Psychology, Faculty of Health, Behavioural Sciences Building, 234 York University, 4700 Keele Street, Toronto, ON M3J 1P3, Canada (office). *Telephone:* (416) 736-2100 (ext. 66109) (office). *E-mail:* ellenb@yorku.ca (office). *Website:* www.yorku.ca/coglab (office).

BIANCHERI, Franck; Monegasque government official and business executive; *CEO, Monaco QD International Hotels and Resorts;* m.; two c.; ed Ecole Supérieure de Commerce de Paris; Diplôme d'Expertise Comptable Supérieure (chartered accountancy qualification); Franco-German and British Chambers of Commerce Diplomas; Man. Boulogne-Billancourt Group, Credit Lyonnais 1983–90, responsible for product line for small- and medium-sized firms, Marcel Sembat Agency 1983–90, Channel Man. for product line for cos, Boulogne-Billancourt 1985–88; Dir Aeronautic Dept, Faugère & Jutheau/Groupe Marsh & McLennan 1990–95; Dir Gen. Dept of Finance and the Economy, Principality of Monaco 1995–2000, Rep. Dept of Finance and the Economy within Asscns Sportel and Festival de Télévision de Monte-Carlo 1995–2000; Govt Counsellor for Finance and the Economy 2000–05; Official Rep. to Cabinet of HSH the Prince while retaining the functions of Govt Counsellor for Finance and the Economy 2003–05; Govt Counsellor for External Relations and Int. Econ. and Financial Dossiers 2010–; CEO Monaco QD Hotels and Resorts Management 2010–; Dir Cube Infrastructure Fund at Natixis Environnement and Infrastructures, VisuRay Plc.

BIANCHI, Andrés, MA, PhD; Chilean diplomatist and banking executive; b. 12 Sept. 1935, Valdivia; m. Lily Urdinola; two s. one d.; ed Univ. of Chile, Yale Univ., USA; Dir Int. Labor Office Regional Employment Program of Latin America and the Caribbean 1971–73; Visiting Research Assoc. Woodrow Wilson School of Public and Int. Affairs, Princeton Univ. 1973–75; Visiting Prof. Center for Latin American Devt Studies, Boston Univ. 1978; Dir Econ. Devt Div., UN Econ. Comm. for Latin America and the Caribbean 1981–88, Deputy Exec. Sec 1988–89; Gov. Cen. Bank of Chile 1989–91; Chair. Credit Lyonnais Chile 1992–96, Dresdner Banque Nationale de Paris, Chile 1996–2000; mem. External Advisory Group, Latin America and Caribbean Regional Office, World Bank 1994–2000; mem. Pres. of Chile's Nat. Savings Comm. 1997–98; Amb. to USA 2000–06; fmr adviser to cen. banks of Bolivia, Colombia, Mexico and Venezuela. *Leisure interests:* tennis, travel, classical music.

BIANCHI, Tancredi; Italian banker and professor of banking economics; b. 1928, Caravaggio; ed Bocconi Univ.; Lecturer, "Ca Foscari", Venice 1959–64; Full Prof., Univ. of Rome "La Sapienza" 1964–68; Prof. of Banking Econs, Bocconi Univ., Milan 1979, now Prof. Emer.; Exec. Vice-Chair., CEO then Chair. Credito Bergamasco 1981–89; Chair. Italian Private Banking Asscn 1982–2003; Chair. Italian Banking Asscn 1991–98, now Hon. Chair.; fmr Chair. Centrobanca, Fondo Immobiliare Polis.

BIANCO, Jean-Louis; French civil servant and politician; *President, Observatoire de la laïcité;* b. 12 Jan. 1943, Neuilly-sur-Seine; s. of Louis Bianco and Gabrielle Bianco (née Vandries); m. Martine Letoublon 1971; three s.; ed Lycée Janson-de-Sailly and Inst. d'études politiques, Paris; auditor, Conseil d'Etat 1971; Official Rep. Groupe central des villes nouvelles 1973–74; attached to Ministry of Health 1976–79; Counsel, Conseil d'Etat 1976; Official Rep. Syndicat intercommunal de Devt Durance-Bléone 1979–81; Official Rep. to the advisers of the Pres. 1981; Sec.-Gen. to the Pres. 1982–91; Minister of Social Affairs and Integration 1991–92, of Equipment, Transport and Housing 1992–93; mem. Regional Council of Alpes-de-Haute-Provence 1992–2012, Pres. 1998–2012; Mayor of Digne-les-Bains (Alpes de Haute Provence) 1995–2001; Deputy from Alpes de Haute-Provence (Socialist) June 1997–2012; Pres. François Mitterrand Inst. 1999–2002; Pres. High Council for Int. Co-operation 1999–2002; campaign dir for Ségolène Royal during Presidential elections 2007; Pres. Observatoire de la laïcité 2013–; Chevalier, ordre nat. de la Légion d'honneur 2001. *E-mail:* secretariat.laicite@pm .gouv.fr. *Website:* www.gouvernement.fr/gouvernement/observatoire-de-la-laicite.

BIAOU, Rogatien, (Assika Oyinlola), CEPE, BEPC, DUEG, DEA; Benin (b. Niger) politician and diplomatist; b. 19 May 1952, Niamey, Niger; s. of the late

Joseph Yaï Biaou and of Jeanette Thiakou Afouda; m. Justine Kaoui Atioukpe 1987; four c.; ed Cours Secondaire Protestant de Cotonou, Lycée Mathieu Bouké de Parakou, Nat. Univ. of Benin, Abomey-Calavi, Centre de Formation Admin. et de Perfectionnement, Cotonou, Institut Int. d'Admin Publique (IIAP), Paris, France, Institut des Nations Unies pour la Formation et le Recherche (UNITAR); Université Libre de Bruxelles, Brussels, Belgium; Asst to Gen. Man., Ministry of Higher Educ. and Scientific Research 1980–82; Head of France Div., Direction Europe, Ministry of Foreign Affairs and Cooperation 1982–85, Head of Service, Western European Countries 1985–87, Head of Service, African Countries S of the Sahara, Direction Africa and Arab Countries 1987–90; First Counsellor, Perm. Mission of Benin to UN, New York 1990–93, Minister Counsellor 1993–97; Amb. and Deputy Dir of Cabinet, Ministry of Foreign Affairs 1997–98, Amb. and Dir of Europe Dept 1998–2000, Amb. and Sec.-Gen., Ministry of Foreign Affairs and African Integration 2000–03, Minister for Foreign Affairs and African Integration 2003–06; mem. Cabinet, Ministry of Foreign Affairs 2006–; Chevalier de l'Ordre Nat. du Bénin. *Publications:* Les Moyens de Communication de Masse et La Politique d'Information au Benin 1980, La Grève de la Faim en Ulster: Conséquences Biologiques et Politiques 1981, Essai d'Analyse du Code de la Citoyenneté de la CEDEAO 1982, An X du Plan d'Action de Lagos 1990, The Challenge of Poverty Eradication in Africa 1996; numerous articles on politics, econs and devt issues. *Leisure interests:* literature, Scrabble, music, sport, cinema. *Address:* 03 BP 2752, Cotonou (home); c/o Zone Résidentielle, route de l'Aéroport, BP 318, Cotonou 06, Benin (office). *Telephone:* 21-36-08-96 (home); 90-94-80-93 (home). *E-mail:* rogasbiaou@yahoo.fr (home).

BICHARD, Baron (Life Peer), cr. 2010, of Nailsworth in the County of Gloucestershire; **Michael (George) Bichard,** KCB, LLB, MScS, FIPD, CCMI, FRSA; British civil servant; b. 31 Jan. 1947, Southampton; s. of the late George Bichard and Nora Reeves; m. Gillian Bichard; ed Univ. of Manchester, Univ. of Birmingham; articled clerk, solicitor, Sr Solicitor Reading Borough Council 1969–73; Co. Liaison Officer, Berks. Co. Council 1973–77; Head of Chief Exec.'s Office, Lambeth Borough Council 1977–80; Chief Exec. Brent Borough Council 1980–86, Glos. Co. Council 1986–90, Social Security Benefits Agency 1990–95; Jt Perm. Sec. Dept for Educ. and Employment July–Dec. 1995, Perm. Sec. 1996–2002; Rector, The London Inst. (now Univ. of the Arts London) 2001; Chair. Social Care Inst. For Excellence, Mentora Trust, Rathbone Training Ltd 2001–08, RSe Consulting 2003–08, ARTIS, 2003–08, Legal Services Comm. 2005–08; mem. Econ. and Social Research Council 1989–92, Prince's Trust Volunteers Nat. Bd 1992–97; mem. ESRC 1989–92; Fellow, Chartered Inst. of Personnel and Devt, Birmingham Inst. of Local Govt Studies; mem. NESTA Creative Pioneer Programme Cttee; Gov. Henley Man. Coll. 2002; mem. Bd of Companions, Inst. of Man.; mem. Guild of Educators; apptd by UK Home Office to chair Soham/ Bichard Inquiry Jan. 2004; Ed. Solace Foundation, Chair. Film Club 2006–, The Design Council 2008–; Exec. Dir Inst. for Govt 2008–10; Vice-Pres. Local Govt Asscn; Adviser, Cronin Management Consultants, Ten Lifestyle Management Ltd; Trustee Globe Theatre, River and Rowing Museum; Hon. Fellow, Inst. of Local Govt Studies (Birmingham Univ.); Hon. DUniv (Leeds Metropolitan) 1992, (Middlesex) 2001; Hon. LLD (Birmingham) 1999; Dr hc (Bradford) 2004, (Solent). *Address:* House of Lords, London, SW1A 0PW, England (office). *Telephone:* (20) 7219-5353 (office). *Fax:* (20) 7219-5979 (office).

BICHIR, Demián; Mexican actor; b. (Demián Bichir Nájera), 1 Aug. 1963, Mexico City; s. of Alejandro Bichir and Maricruz Nájera; m. Lisset Gutierrez 2001 (divorced), one d. *Television includes:* Rina 1977, Vivir enamorada 1982, Cuando los hijos se van 1983, Los años felices 1984, Guadalupe 1984, El rincón de los prodigios 1988, Lazos de amor 1996, Nada personal 1996, Demasiado corazón 1998, In the Time of the Butterflies 2001, La otra mitad del sol 2005, Sombreros 2005, Capadocia 2008, Weeds 2008–10. *Films include:* Choices of the Heart 1983, Viaje al paraiso 1985, Astucia 1986, Hotel Colonial 1987, The Penitent 1988, Rojo amanecer 1989, Marea suave 1992, Miroslava 1993, La vida conyugal 1993, Hasta morir (Silver Ariel Award for Best Actor 1995) 1994, Ya la hicimos 1994, Pruebas de amor 1994, Nadie hablará de nosotras cuando hayamos muerto 1995, Salón México 1996, Solo 1996, Perdita Durango 1997, Luces de la noche 1998, Cilantro y perejil 1998, Santitos 1999, Sexo, pudor y lágrimas 1999, Ave Maria 1999, Cerebro 2000, Todo el poder 2000, La toma de la embajada 2000, Sin noticias de Dios 2001, Dark Cities 2002, Heartbreak Hospital 2002, Bendito infierno 2002 (MTV Movie Awards-Mexico Special Award for Best Bichir in a Movie 2003) 2003, Hipnos 2004, Zapata: Amor en rebeldia 2004, American Visa 2007, Fuera del cielo 2007, Enemigos intimos 2008, Che: Parts One and Two 2008, The Runway 2010, Hidalgo – La historia jamás contada (also co-producer) 2010, A Better Life 2011, Foreverland 2011, El sueño de Iván 2011, Savages 2012. *Address:* c/o Carlos Carreras, APA Talent and Literary Agency, 405 South Beverly Drive, Beverly Hills, CA 90212, USA.

BIČKAUSKAS, Egidijus; Lithuanian politician and lawyer; b. 29 May 1955, Prienai; m. Jurate Bičkauskienė; ed Vilnius Univ.; investigator, special cases investigator, Procurator Gen.'s Office 1978–89; joined People's Front Movt Sajudis 1988; Deputy of USSR Supreme Soviet 1989–90; elected to Parl. Restoration Seimas of Repub. of Lithuania 1990–92, signatory of the Lithuanian Repub. Independence Restoration Act 1990; Head Lithuanian diplomatic mission to Moscow 1990–96; mem. Parl. (Seimas) of Repub. of Lithuania, Deputy Chair. 1992–96, head of faction of Centre Party in Seimas of Lithuania 1996–2000; Vice-Chair. Presidium of Baltic Ass. *Address:* Laury 35, 2046 Vilnius, Lithuania (home). *Telephone:* (3702) 225493 (home); (8698) 88761 (home). *E-mail:* info@ bickauskas.lt (home). *Website:* www.bickauskas.lt (home).

BIDAYA, Thanong, MA, PhD; Thai business executive, academic and fmr government official; b. 28 July 1947, Supanburi Prov.; ed Yokohama Nat. Univ., Japan, Northwestern Univ., USA; Pres. Thai Military Bank Public Co. 1988–99, currently Chair. Advisory Bd, TMB Asset Management; fmr positions include Commercial Union Insurance (Thailand) Co., N.C.C. Man. and Devt Co.; fmr Dean Assumption Univ., Business Admin Dept, Nat. Inst. of Devt Admin, fmr Dean Grad School Business MBA Program, also Distinguished Prof.; Chair. Thai Airways Int. Public Co. 2002–05; Minister of Finance 1997, 2005–06, Chair. Nat. Econ. and Social Devt Bd 2001–05, Vice-Chair. Council of Econ. Advisers to Prime Minister 2001–05; Thai Trade Rep. 2001–02; Minister of Commerce 2005; Visiting Prof., Int. Grad. School of Social Sciences, Yokohama Nat. Univ. 2007; Chair. Thai

Tap Water Supply PLC 2009–, MSIG Insurance; mem. Bd of Counsellors, Asia Mezzanine Capital Advisers Ltd, Hong Kong; Hon. mem. Suphanburi Chamber of Commerce, Hon. Chair. TMB Asset Management Co. Ltd, Hon. Chair. Charoensin Group of Co.; Commdr (Third Class) of the Most Noble Order of the Crown of Thailand 1991, Kt Grand Cross (First Class) of the Most Exalted Order of the White Elephant 1997, Kt Grand Cordon (First Class) of the Most Noble Order of the Crown of Thailand 2003, Grand Cordon of the Order of the Rising Sun (Japan) 2005, Kt Grand Cordon (Special Class) of the Most Exalted Order of the White Elephant 2005, Officier, Ordre national du Mérite 2005; Dr hc (Yokohama Nat. Univ.) 2004. *Address:* c/o Board of Counsellors, Asia Mezzanine Capital Advisers Ltd, 3205 Alexandra House, 16-20 Chater Road, Hong Kong Special Administrative Region, People's Republic of China.

BIDDISS, Michael Denis, MA, PhD, FRHistS, FHA; British academic and writer; *Professor Emeritus of History, University of Reading;* b. 15 April 1942, Farnborough, Kent; s. of Daniel Biddiss and Eileen Biddiss (née Jones); m. Ruth Margaret Cartwright 1967; four d.; ed Queens' Coll., Cambridge, Centre des Hautes Etudes Européennes, Univ. of Strasbourg, France; Fellow in History, Downing Coll., Cambridge and Dir of Studies in History, Social and Political Sciences 1966–73; Lecturer, then Reader in History, Univ. of Leicester 1973–79; Prof. of History, Univ. of Reading 1979–2004, Prof. Emer. 2004–, Dean, Faculty of Letters and Social Sciences 1982–85; Visiting Prof., Univ. of Victoria, Canada 1973, Univ. of Cape Town, South Africa 1976, 1978, Univ. of Cairo, Egypt 1985, Monash Univ., Australia 1989, Univ. of Nanjing, China 1997; Chair. History at the Univs Defence Group 1984–87; mem. Council, The Historical Assen 1985– (Pres. 1991–94), Vice-Pres. Royal Historical Soc. 1995–99 (mem. Council 1988–92); Lister Lecturer, BAAS 1975; Hon. Fellow, Faculty of the History of Medicine (Pres. 1994–98), Soc. of Apothecaries 1986–; several awards from Soc. of Apothecaries of London including Osler Medal 1989, Locke Medal 1996, Thomas Sydenham Medal 2000, Master's Medal 2009. *Publications:* Father of Racist Ideology 1970, Gobineau: Selected Political Writings (ed.) 1970, Disease and History (co-author) 1972, The Age of the Masses 1977, Images of Race (ed.) 1979, Thatcherism (co-ed.) 1987, The Nuremberg Trial and the Third Reich (co-author) 1992, The Uses and Abuses of Antiquity (co-ed.) 1999, The Humanities in the New Millennium (co-ed.) 2000, Themes in Modern European History 1890–1945 (co-ed.) 2008, The Wiley-Blackwell Dictionary of Modern European History since 1789 (co-author) 2010. *Leisure interests:* cricket, music and opera, mountain walking, art, travel. *E-mail:* m.d.biddiss@reading.ac.uk (office).

BIDDLE, Martin, OBE, MA, FBA, FSA; British archaeologist and academic; *Emeritus Professor of Medieval Archaeology, University of Oxford;* b. 4 June 1937, North Harrow, Middx; s. of Reginald Samuel Biddle and Gwladys Florence Biddle (née Baker); m. Birthe Kjølbye 1966; two d. and two d. by previous m.; ed Merchant Taylors' School and Pembroke Coll., Cambridge; Asst Insp. of Ancient Monuments, Ministry of Public Building and Works 1961–63; Lecturer in Medieval Archaeology, Univ. of Exeter 1963–67; Visiting Fellow, All Souls Coll. Oxford 1967–68; Dir Winchester Research Unit. 1968–; Dir Univ. Museum and Prof. of Anthropology and History of Art, Univ. of Pa 1977–81; Lecturer of The House, Christ Church, Oxford 1983–86; Astor Sr Research Fellow in Medieval Archaeology, Hertford Coll. Oxford 1989–2002; Prof. of Medieval Archaeology, Univ. of Oxford 1997–2002, Emer. Prof. 2002–, Emer. Fellow, Hertford Coll. 2002–; Dir excavations and investigations at Nonsuch Palace 1959–60, Winchester 1961–71, Repton 1974–88, 1993, St Alban's Abbey 1978, 1982–84, 1991, 1994–95, Holy Sepulchre, Jerusalem 1989–90, 1992, 1993, 1998, Qasr Ibrim, Egypt 1990, 1992, 1995, 2000; archaeological consultant to Canterbury Cathedral, St Alban's Abbey, Eurotunnel, etc.; mem. Royal Comm. on Historical Monuments for England 1984–95; Trevelyan Lecturer, Univ. of Cambridge 1991; Pres. Soc. for Medieval Archaeology 1995–98; Chair. Historic Towns Trust; Hon. Fellow, Pembroke Coll., Cambridge, 2006–; Frend Medal, Soc. of Antiquaries (with Birthe Kjølbye-Biddle) 1986. *Publications:* The Future of London's Past (with C. Heighway) 1973, Winchester in the Early Middle Ages (with others) 1976, The History of the King's Works, Vol. IV, Part 2 (with others) 1982, King Arthur's Round Table 2000, Object and Economy in Medieval Winchester 1990, The Tomb of Christ 1999, King Arthur's Round Table 2000, The Church of the Holy Sepulchre 2000, Nonsuch Palace: The Material Culture of a Noble Restoration Household 2005; papers in learned journals. *Leisure interests:* travel, especially Hellenic travel, architecture, Renaissance art. *Address:* Hertford College, Oxford, OX1 3BW (office); Knight Ayton Management, 114 St. Martin's Lane, London, WC2N 4BE (office); 19 Hamilton Road, Oxford, OX2 7PY, England (home). *Telephone:* (1865) 513056 (home); (1865) 559017 (office). *Fax:* (1865) 559017 (home); (1865) 559017 (office). *E-mail:* martin.biddle@hertford.ox.ac.uk (office). *Website:* winchesterstudies.org.uk (office).

BIDEN, Joseph (Joe) Robinette, Jr, JD; American lawyer, politician and academic; *Vice-President;* b. 20 Nov. 1942, Scranton, Pa; s. of Joseph R. Biden and Jean F. Biden; m. 1st Neilia Hunter (deceased); two s. one d. (deceased); m. 2nd Jill Tracy Jacobs 1977; one d.; ed Univ. of Delaware, Syracuse Univ. Coll. of Law; Trial Attorney in the Public Defender's Office, Del. 1968; Founder Biden & Walsh Law Firm, Wilmington 1968–72; mem. New Castle Co. Council 1970–72; Senator from Delaware 1972–2008, mem. Foreign Relations Cttee (fmr Chair.), Judiciary Cttee (Chair. 1987–95), Chair. Senate Caucus on Int. Narcotics Control, Co-Chair. Senate NATO Observer Group, Senate Nat. Security Working Group, Congressional Fireman's Caucus, Congressional Int. Anti-Piracy Caucus, mem. Democratic Steering and Coordinating Cttee, Nat. Guard Caucus, Senate Auto Caucus, Senate Biotechnology Caucus, Congressional Port Security Caucus, Congressional Air Force Caucus; fmr Vice-Chair. NATO Parl. Ass.; unsuccessful cand. for Democratic nomination for US Pres. 2007; Vice-Pres. of the US 2009–; Adjunct Prof., Widener Univ. School of Law 1991–; mem. Del. Bar Assn, ABA, American Trial Lawyers Assn; Democrat. *Leisure interests:* sports, history, public speaking, American architecture. *Address:* Office of the Vice-President, Eisenhower Executive Office Building, 1650 Pennsylvania Avenue, NW, Washington, DC 20502, USA (office). *Telephone:* (202) 456-1414 (office). *Fax:* (202) 456-2461 (office). *Website:* www.whitehouse.gov/administration/vice_president_biden (office).

BIDWELL, Charles Edward, PhD, FAAS; American sociologist and academic; *William Claude Reavis Professor Emeritus of Sociology, University of Chicago;* b. 24 Jan. 1932, Chicago, Ill.; s. of Charles L. Bidwell and Eugenia Campbell Bidwell; m. Helen Claxton Lewis 1959; one s.; ed Univ. of Chicago; Lecturer in Sociology,

Harvard Univ. 1959–61; Assoc. Prof., Univ. of Chicago 1965–70, Prof. of Educ. and Sociology 1970–85, Reavis Prof. of Educ. and Sociology 1985–2001, Prof. Emer. 2001–, Chair. Dept of Educ. 1978–88, Chair. Dept of Sociology 1988–94, Dir Ogburn-Stouffer Center 1988–94; mem. Nat. Acad. of Educ., Sociological Research Asscn; Fellow, American Educational Research Asscn 2009–; Guggenheim Fellow 1971–72, Willard Waller Award for a Career of Distinguished Scholarship 2007, Norman Maclean Faculty Award for Excellence in Teaching 2012. *Publications include:* The School as a Formal Organization, in Handbook of Organizations (Ed. J. March) 1965, The Organization and its Ecosystem (with J. D. Kasarda) 1985, The Collegial Focus: Teaching Fields, Colleague Relationships, and Instructional Practice in American High Schools in Sociology of Education (with J. Yasumoto) 1999. *Leisure interests:* skiing and reading. *Address:* 5760 South Harper Avenue, Chicago, IL 60637 (home); Department of Sociology, 5848 South University Avenue, Chicago, IL 60637, USA (office). *Telephone:* (773) 702-0388 (office). *Fax:* (773) 702-4617 (office). *E-mail:* cbidwell@uchicago.edu (office).

BIEBER, Justin; Canadian singer; b. (Justin Drew Bieber), 1 March 1994, London, Ont.; s. of Jeremy Bieber and Pattie Mallette; discovered by Scooter Braun after posting videos of his performances on YouTube 2008, came to the attention of Usher who signed him to a recording contract; professional solo artist 2009–; tours: Urban Behavior Tour 2009, My World Tour 2010–11; Queen Elizabeth II Diamond Jubilee Medal 2012; numerous awards including: TRL Award for Best Int. Act 2010, Teen Choice Awards for Best Male Artist, for Best Breakout Male Artist 2010, MTV Video Music Awards for Best New Artist 2010, for Best Male Video (U Smile) 2011, MTV Europe Music Awards for Best Male 2010, 2011, 2012, 2013, for Best Push Act 2010, for Best Pop Act 2011, 2012, for Best World Stage Performance 2012, Young Hollywood Awards Newcomer of the Year 2010, American Music Awards for Artist of the Year 2010, 2012, for Favorite Pop/Rock Male Artist 2010, 2012, for T-Mobile Breakthrough Artist 2010, BRIT Award for Best Int. Breakthrough Act 2011, Juno Fan Choice Awards 2011, 2012, Billboard Music Awards for Top New Artist 2011, for Top Social Artist 2011, 2012, for Top Streaming Artist 2011, for Top Digital Media Artist 2011, Billboard Music Awards for Top Male Artist 2013, for Top Social Artist 2013. *Recordings:* albums: My World 2.0 (Teen Choice Award for Best Pop Album 2010, American Music Award for Favorite Pop/Rock Album 2010, Billboard Music Award for Top Pop Album 2011, Juno Award for Pop Album of the Year 2011) 2009, Under the Mistletoe 2011, Believe (American Music Award for Favorite Pop/Rock Album 2012) 2012, Complete My Journals 2013. *Website:* www.justinbiebermusic.com.

BIEDENKOPF, Kurt Hans, DJur; German politician and lawyer; b. 28 Jan. 1930, Ludwigshafen; s. of Wilhelm Biedenkopf and Agathe Biedenkopf (née Schmidt); m. Ingrid Ries 1979; Prof. of Law, Ruhr Univ., Bochum 1964–70, Rector 1967–69; Chair. Govt Comm. on Co-determination 1968–70; Gen. Sec. Christian Democratic Party (CDU) 1973–77, Vice-Pres. 1977–83, Pres. CDU Regional Asscn, North Rhine-Westphalia 1980–84; mem. Bundestag 1976–80, 1987–90; Prime Minister of Saxony 1990–2002; Pres. Dresden International Univ. 2003–05, Hon. Pres. 2006–; Chair. Kuratorium Trust of Devt and Peace; Research Prof., Wissenschaftszentrum Berlin für Sozialforschung 2011–; Chair. Bd of Trustees, Global School of Governance, Hertie Stiftung 2003–10, Hon. Chair. 2010–; mem. Bd Inst. for Econ. and Social Policy, Bonn 1977; mem. Bd German Nat. Trust; mem. Landtag of North Rhine-Westphalia 1980–88; mem. Senate Max Planck Gesellschaft; Hon. DrJur (Davidson Coll.) 1974, (Georgetown) 1978, (New School for Social Research) 1993, (Katholic Univ., Brussels) 1994. *Publications:* Vertragliche Wettbewerbsbeschränkung und Wirtschaftsverfassung 1958, Grenzen der Tarifautonomie 1964, Fortschritt in Freiheit 1974, Die programmierte Krise–Alternativen zur staatlichen Schuldenpolitik 1979, Die neue Sicht der Dinge 1985, Zeitsignale–Parteienlandschaft im Umbruch 1989, Einheit und Erneuerung 1994, Ordnungspolitik in einer Zeit des Umbruchs 1998, Ein deutsches Tagebuch 1989–90 2000. *Leisure interests:* skiing, sailing. *Address:* Biedenkopf Rechtsanwälte, Ferdinandplatz 1, 01069 Dresden, Germany. *Website:* www.biedenkopf-kurt.de.

BIEGMAN, Nicolaas H., PhD; Dutch historian, diplomatist and writer; b. 23 Sept. 1936, Apeldoorn; s. of Nicolaas Biegman and Aukje de Boer; m. Mirjana Cibilic; two s.; ed Univ. of Leiden; Lecturer in Turkish and Persian, Univ. of Leiden 1960–62; various posts in Netherlands Foreign Service 1963–84, including postings in Australia and Tanzania, Amb. to Egypt 1984–88, Dir-Gen. for Int. Co-operation, Ministry of Foreign Affairs 1988–92, Perm. Rep. to UN, New York 1992–97, Perm. Rep. to NATO 1998–2001 (retd); Sr Civilian Rep. of NATO in Macedonia, Skopje 2002–04; Chair. Bd of Trustees East West Parl. Practice Project, Amsterdam; fmr mem. Bd of Dirs Int. Peace Acad.; Order of The Netherlands Lion, Order of Merit, UAR. *Publications include:* The Turco-Ragusan Relationship 1967, Egypt-Moulids, Saints, Sufis 1990, Egypt's Sideshows 1992, An Island of Bliss 1993, Mainly Manhattan 1997, God's Lovers 2006, Oil Wrestlers 2009, Living Sufism 2009, Whipped Cream and Other Delights of Amsterdam Architecture 2011. *Leisure interest:* photography. *Address:* c/o KIT Publishers, Mauritskade 63, 1092 AD Amsterdam, Netherlands.

BIELECKI, Jan Krzysztof, MSc; Polish politician and economist; b. 3 May 1951, Bydgoszcz; s. of Anastazy Bielecki and Janina Bielecka; m. Barbara Bielecka 1976; one s. one d.; ed Economics Coll., Sopot, Gdańsk Univ.; Asst Lecturer, Gdańsk Univ. 1973–81 (lost his job for his alleged anti-Communist political activities); Head of Research Unit, Centre for Training Managerial Staff, Ministry of Trade and Ministry of Machine Industry 1972–82; trade union and workers' rights activist, expert for econ. affairs, Solidarity Trade Union 1980–81; continued union activity under martial law as assoc. of underground regional and nat. authorities; lorry driver 1982–85; CEO Doradca consulting co-operative, Sopot 1985–90; Deputy to Sejm (Parl.) 1989–93, mem. Civic Parl. Caucus 1989–91, Leader Parl. Liberal-Democratic Congress Caucus; Prime Minister of Poland Jan.–Dec. 1991; Minister for Poland–EU Relations 1992–93; mem. Liberal-Democratic Congress (mem. Provisional Bd Presidium) 1989–94; apptd by Polish Govt to Bd of Dirs EBRD, London 1993–2003; Pres. and CEO Bank Pekao SA 2003–10; Sr Econ. Adviser to Prime Minister Donald Tusk; Chair. Council of the Polish Inst. of Int. Affairs. *Publications include:* Histoire de l'Europe 1997; numerous articles in nat. and int. specialist newspapers and magazines. *Leisure interests:* horse riding, tennis, football. *Address:* Economic Council, Chancellery of the Prime Minister, 1/3 Ujazdowskie Avenue, 00-583 Warsaw, Poland (office). *Telephone:* (22) 6947292 (office). *Fax:* (22) 6946155 (office). *E-mail:* economic.council@kprm.gov.pl (office). *Website:* www.premier.gov.pl (office).

BIELENBERG, David, BS (AgricEng); American business executive; *Chairman, CHS Inc.;* ed Oregon State Univ., Texas A&M Univ. Exec. Program for Agricultural Producers, Nat. Asscn of Corp. Dirs Director Professionalism course (Certificate of Dir Educ.); fmr mem. Bd of Dirs and Pres. Wilco Farmers Cooperative, Mt Angel, Ore., Chair. East Valley Water Dist; mem. Bd of Dirs CHS Inc. 2002–06, 2009– (also Asst Sec.-Treas. 2012), Chair. 2012–, Chair. Exec. Cttee; operates a diverse agricultural business near Silverton, Ore. *Address:* CHS, 5500 Cenex Drive, Inver Grove Heights, MN 55077, USA (office). *Telephone:* (651) 355-6000 (office). *E-mail:* info@chsinc.com (office). *Website:* www.chsinc.com (office).

BIELSA, Rafael; Argentine politician and business executive; *Executive Chairman, Aeropuertos Argentina 2000 SA;* b. 15 Feb. 1953, Rosario, Santa Fe; m. Andrea DArza; two c. from previous m.; ed Univ. de Rosario; Asst Fed. Tribunals of Rosario 1974–78; various positions at Ministry of Justice, Ministry of Educ. and Office of the Presidency; Minister of Foreign Affairs, International Trade and Worship 2003–05; mem. Chamber of Deputies for Buenos Aires 2005–07; Sec., Secretaría de Programación para la Prevención de la Drogadicción y la Lucha Contra el Narcotráfico (SEDRONAR) 2011–13; Exec. Chair. Aeropuertos Argentina 2000 SA 2013–mem. Partido Justicialista. *Address:* Aeropuertos Argentina 2000 SA, Honduras 5663, Buenos Aires C1414BNE, Argentina (office). *Telephone:* (11) 4779-6900 (office). *Website:* www.aa2000.com.ar (office).

BIEMANN, Klaus, PhD; American (b. Austrian) chemist and academic; *Professor Emeritus of Chemistry, Massachusetts Institute of Technology;* b. 1926, Innsbruck, Austria; widowed; ed Univ. of Innsbruck; joined MIT 1955, fmr Prof. of Chem., now Prof. Emer.; mem. NAS 1993–; Fellow, American Acad. of Arts and Sciences 1966; Stas Medal, Belgian Chemical Soc. 1962, Powers Award 1973, NASA Exceptional Scientific Achievement Medal 1977, Fritz Pregl Medal, Austrian Microchemical Soc. 1977, Newcomb-Cleveland Prize 1978, first ACS Frank H. Field and Joe L. Franklin Award in applied Mass Spectrometry 1986, Thomson Medal 1991, Pehr Edman Award 1992, ACS Analytical Chem. Award 2001, Benjamin Franklin Medal in Chem., The Franklin Inst. 2007. *Achievements include:* developed the use of mass spectrometry in organic chem. and biochemistry and its application to alkaloids, peptides, proteins and other natural products; sent miniaturized gas chromatograph/mass spectrometer to Mars as part of Viking Mission to look for organic compounds at surface of Red Planet 1976; has been called "the father of organic mass spectrometry". *Publications:* Mass Spectrometry: Organic Chemical Applications 1962; more than 350 publs on devt of mass spectrometry as chemical analysis tool to determine structure of complex molecules of biological and medical interest. *Address:* 174 Fort Point Road, Alton Bay, NH 03810, USA (home). *Telephone:* (603) 875-3046 (home). *E-mail:* kbiemann@mit.edu (office). *Website:* web.mit.edu/chemistry (office).

BIENEN, Henry S., BA, MA, PhD; American political scientist and university administrator; *President Emeritus, Northwestern University;* b. 5 May 1939; m. Leigh Bienen; three d.; ed Cornell Univ. and Univ. of Chicago; Asst Prof., Princeton Univ. 1966–69, Assoc. Prof. of Politics and Int. Affairs 1969–72, Prof. of Politics and Int. Affairs 1972–81, William Stewart Tod Prof. of Politics and Int. Affairs 1981–85, James S. McDonnell Distinguished Univ. Prof. and Dean of the Woodrow Wilson School of Public and Int. Affairs 1985–94; Pres. Northwestern Univ. 1995–2009, Pres. Emer. 2009–; Visiting Prof., Makerere Coll., Kampala, Uganda 1963–65, Univ. Coll., Nairobi, Kenya 1968–69, Columbia Univ. 1971–72, Univ. of Ibadan, Nigeria 1972–73; Fellow, Center for Advanced Studies in Behavioral Sciences, Stanford Univ. 1976–77; Polsky Fellow, Aspen Inst. 1982–83; mem. Inst. for Advanced Studies, Princeton 1984–85; consultant to US Dept of State 1972–88, Nat. Security Council 1978–79, Agency for Int. Devt 1980–81, CIA 1982–88 (mem. Sr Review Panel in late 1980s), World Bank 1981–89, Hambrecht and Quist Investment Co., Boeing Corpn, Carnegie Corpn, Ford Foundation, Rockefeller Foundation, John D. and Catherine T. MacArthur Foundation; Chair. United Football League; Vice-Chair. Rasmussen Coll. 2009–; mem. Bd of Dirs The Bear Stearns Cos Inc., Deltak Inc., Council on Foreign Relations (Chair. Nominating and Governance Cttee and mem. Exec. Cttee), Chicago Council on Foreign Relations (mem. Exec. Cttee); mem. Bd Govs Argonne Nat. Lab. (mem. Exec. and Nominating Cttees); mem. Exec. Cttee Asscn of American Univs; mem. Cttee on Roles of Academic Health Centers in the 21st Century, Nat. Acads Inst. of Medicine; mem. Bd Univ. Corpn for Advanced Internet Devt (Internet 2) 1998–2002; mem. American Political Science Asscn; Hon. DHumLitt (Northwestern Univ.) 2009; Univ. of Chicago Professional Achievement Alumni Award 2000, Niagara Peace & Dialogue Award, Niagara Foundation 2008, Carnegie Corpn Academic Leadership Award for innovative leadership in higher educ. *Address:* Office of the President Emeritus, Arthur Rubloff Building, 375 East Chicago Avenue, Room 11-410, Chicago, IL 60611, USA (office). *Telephone:* (312) 503-7460 (office). *Fax:* (312) 503-5388 (office). *E-mail:* hsbienen@northwestern.edu (office). *Website:* www.northwestern.edu/Bienen (office).

BIEŃKOWSKA, Elżbieta, MA, MBA; Polish politician; *Deputy Prime Minister and Minister of Infrastructure and Development;* b. 4 Feb. 1964, Katowice, Silesia; ed Jagiellonian Univ., Polish Nat. School of Public Admin, Warsaw School of Econs; began admin. career working in Business Dept of Silesian Voivodeship, involved in local application of EU's Phare programme; mem. Civic Platform; Minister of Regional Devt 2007–13; Deputy Prime Minister and Minister of Infrastructure and Devt 2013–. *Address:* Ministry of Infrastructure and Development, 00-926 Warsaw, Wspólna 2/4, Poland (office). *Telephone:* (22) 2737000 (office). *E-mail:* info@mir.gov.pl (office). *Website:* www.mir.gov.pl (office).

BIESENBACH, Klaus; German gallery curator; *Director MoMA PS1 and Chief Curator at Large, The Museum of Modern Art (MoMA);* b. 1967, Bergisch Gladbach, North Rhine-Westphalia; Founding Dir Kunst-Werke Inst. for Contemporary Art, Berlin 1991–, Berlin Biennale 1996–; joined MoMA PS1 (fmrly P.S.1 Contemporary Art Center), New York as a curator 1996, apptd a curator in MoMA Dept of Film and Media 2004, Chief Curator Dept of Media 2006– (subsequently Dept of Media and Performance Art 2009), presented major retrospective of work of Marina Abramović 2010, currently Dir MoMA PS1 and Chief Curator at Large, MoMA; adviser to Christine Macel and Hans Ulrich Obrist for Based in Berlin (six-week exhbn); co-staged, with Hans Ulrich Obrist, 11

Rooms, an installation of durational performance works by Marina Abramović, Tino Sehgal, Simon Fujiwara, amongst others, at Manchester Int. Festival 2011; restaged Abramovic's The Artist Is Ever-Present at Dasha Zhukova's Garage, Moscow 2011; turned MoMA P.S.1 into a temporary day shelter for displaced residents following Hurricane Sandy 2012. *Address:* MoMA PS1, 2225 Jackson Avenue, Long Island City, NY 11101-4309 (office); The Museum of Modern Art, 11 West 53rd Street, New York, NY 10019, USA (office). *Telephone:* (718) 784-2084 (MoMA PS1) (office); (212) 708-9400 (MoMA) (office). *E-mail:* mail_ps1@moma.org (office); info@moma.org (office). *Website:* momaps1.org (office); www.moma.org (office).

BIÉTRY, Charles-Pierre; French sports reporter and television executive; *Director, Al Jazeera Sport France;* b. 5 Nov. 1943, Rennes; ed Centre de formation des journalistes, Paris; reporter, Agence-France Presse 1966–84; Dir of Sports, Canal+ 1984–98; Dir of Sports and adviser to Chair., France Télévision 1999–2001; Producer and consultant, Onzeo (TV satellite channel of town of AS Saint-Etienne and RC Lens) 2006–; Editorial Dir L'Équipe TV –2011; Dir Al Jazeera Sport France 2011–; Pres. PSG omnisports 1992–98, Paris Saint-Germain July–Dec. 1998; Vice-Pres. Créteil June–July 2001; mem. Admin. Council, FC Lorient 2004–05, 2005–06; Recruiter for Stade Rennes 2007–; Hon. Pres. Brittany Football Asscn 1997–. *Address:* Al Jazeera Sport France, PO Box 23123, Doha, Qatar (office). *Telephone:* 489-7446 (office). *Fax:* 489-7472 (office). *E-mail:* press.int@aljazeera .net (office). *Website:* www.aljazeerasport.net (office); english.aljazeera.net (office).

BIFFI, HE Cardinal Giacomo; Italian ecclesiastic; b. 13 June 1928, Milan; ordained 1950; consecrated Bishop (Titular Church of Fidene) 1975; Archbishop of Bologna 1984–2003, Archbishop Emer. 2003–; cr. Cardinal Priest of SS Giovanni Evangelista e Petronio 1985. *Address:* Villa Edera, Via S. Ruffillo 5, Lazzaro di Savena, 40068 Bologna, Italy (home). *Telephone:* (51) 482027 (home).

BIG BOI; American rap artist; b. (Antoine André Patton), 1 Feb. 1975, Savannah, Ga; ed Tri-City High School, Atlanta; mem., Outkast (with Andre 3000, aka Dré) 1992–, signed to LaFace Records; designed Outkast Clothing line; also solo artist; Source Award for Best New Rap Group of the Year 1995, American Music Awards for Best Hip Hop/R&B Group 2003, 2004, Grammy Award for best urban/ alternative performance 2004, World Music Awards for Best Group, Best Pop Group, Best Rap/Hip-Hop Artist 2004, MTV Europe Best Group Award 2004, Best Song Award, Best Video Award (both for Hey Ya) 2004. *Recordings include:* albums: with Outkast: Southernplayalisticadillacmuzik 1994, ATLiens 1996, Aquemini 1998, Stankonia 2000, Big Boi And Dre Present... 2002, Speakerboxxx/The Love Below (Grammy Awards for Album of the Year, Best Rap Album 2004, American Music Award for Best Rap/Hip-Hop Album 2004) 2003, My Life In Idlewild 2005, Idlewild 2006; solo: Sir Lucious Left Foot: The Son of Chico Dusty 2010. *Address:* William Morris Agency, 1325 Avenue of the Americas, New York, NY 10019, USA (office); c/o LaFace Records, A&R Department, 1 Capital City Plaza, 3350 Peachtree Road, Suite 1500, Atlanta, GA 30326, USA. *Telephone:* (212) 586-5100 (office). *Fax:* (212) 246-3583 (office). *Website:* www.outkast.com; www .bigboi.com.

BIGELOW, Kathryn Ann; American film director, producer and screenwriter; b. 27 Nov. 1951, San Carlos, Calif.; d. and only c. of the late Ronald Elliot Bigelow and Gertude Kathryn Bigelow (née Larson); m. James Cameron (q.v.) 1989 (divorced 1991); ed San Francisco Art Inst. and Columbia Univ., New York; worked with Art and Language performance group, UK; awarded scholarship to Ind. Study Program, Whitney Museum, New York; named to the TIME 100 list of most influential people of the year 2010. *Films include:* The Set Up (short), The Loveless 1982, Near Dark 1987, Blue Steel 1990, Point Break 1991, Strange Days (Saturn Award for Best Dir 1995) 1995, The Weight of Water 2000, K-19: The Widowmaker 2002, Mission Zero 2007, The Hurt Locker (numerous awards, including BAFTA Award for Best Dir 2010, Academy Award for Best Dir (first woman) 2010, Directors Guild of America Award for Outstanding Directing, Critics' Choice Award for Best Dir, Nat. Soc. of Film Critics Award for Best Dir, Hollywood Film Festival Dir of the Year) 2009, Zero Dark Thirty (New York Film Critics' Circle Award for Best Dir, amongst others) 2012. *Television includes:* Wild Palms (miniseries, episode 3) 1993, Homicide: Life on the Street (three episodes) 1998–99, Karen Sisco (one episode) 2004, The Miraculous Year 2011. *Address:* c/o Ken Stovitz, Creative Artists Agency, 2000 Avenue of the Stars, Los Angeles, CA 90067, USA (office). *Telephone:* (424) 288-2000 (office). *Fax:* (424) 288-2900 (office). *Website:* www.caa.com (office).

BIGGAM, Sir Robin Adair, Kt; British business executive and chartered accountant; b. 8 July 1938, Carluke; s. of Thomas Biggam and Eileen Biggam; m. Elizabeth McArthur Biggam (née McDougall) 1962; one s. two d.; ed Lanark Grammar School; CA, Peat Marwick Mitchell 1960–63, ICI 1964–81; ICL Finance Dir 1981–84; Exec. Dir Dunlop 1984–85; Chair. Cadcentre Ltd 1983–86; Man. Dir BICC PLC 1986–87, CEO 1987–91, Deputy Chair. 1991–, Chair. 1992–96; Dir Fairey Group PLC 1995– (Chair. 1996–2001); Chair. Ind. TV Comm. 1997–2003; Chair. Macquarie European Infrastructure 2000–05; Dir (non-exec.) Chloride Group PLC 1985–87, Lloyds Abbey Life PLC (fmrly Abbey Life Group) 1985–90, Redland Group PLC 1991–97, British Aerospace PLC 1994–2003, British Energy 1996–2002 (Deputy Chair. 2001–02); Pres. German-British Chamber of Industry and Commerce 1996–98; Chancellor, Univ. of Luton (now Univ. of Bedfordshire) 2001–09; mem. Inst. of Chartered Accountants of Scotland. *Leisure interests:* golf, gardening, swimming, watching TV, fishing.

BIGGS, Peter Martin, CBE, DSc, FRS, FRCVS, FRCPath, CBiol, FBS, FMedSci; British veterinary scientist and academic (retd); b. 13 Aug. 1926, Petersfield, Hants.; s. of Ronald Biggs and Cecile Biggs (née Player); m. Alison Janet Molteno 1950; two s. one d.; ed Bedales School, Petersfield, Cambridge School, Mass., Royal Veterinary Coll., London, Univ. of Bristol; with RAF 1944–48; with Royal Veterinary Coll., London 1948–53; Research Asst, Dept of Veterinary Anatomy, Univ. of Bristol 1953–55; Lecturer in Veterinary Clinical Pathology, Dept of Veterinary Medicine 1955–59; Prin. Scientific Officer, Houghton Poultry Research Station 1959–66, Sr Prin. Scientific Officer 1966–1971, Deputy Dir 1971–74, Dir 1974–86; Dir Inst. for Animal Health 1986–88; Chief Scientific Officer 1981–88; Visiting Prof. of Veterinary Microbiology, Royal Veterinary Coll. London 1982–2008, Hon. Prof. of Veterinary Microbiology 2009–, Vice-Chair. of Council 2002–08; Andrew D. White Prof.-at-Large, Cornell Univ., USA 1988–94; Vice-Pres.

British Veterinary Asscn 1996–98; Fellow, Inst. of Biology 1973, Pres. 1990–92; Fellow, Royal Coll. of Pathologists 1978, Royal Coll. of Veterinary Surgeons 1979, Royal Veterinary Coll. 1983; Hon. Fellow, Royal Agricultural Soc. of England 1986; Hon. Dr of Veterinary Medicine (Ludwig-Maximilians Univ., Munich); Dr hc (Univ. of Liège) and numerous others; Wolf Foundation Prize in Agric. 1989; Dalrymple-Champneys Cup and Medal of the British Veterinary Asscn 1973, Chiron Award, British Veterinary Asscn 1999. *Publications:* more than 100 scientific papers. *Leisure interests:* music making, natural history. *Address:* 'Willows', London Road, St Ives, PE27 5ES, England (home). *Telephone:* (1480) 463471 (home). *E-mail:* petermartinbiggs@btinternet.com (home).

BIGOT, Charles André Marie; French aviation engineer and business executive; b. 29 July 1932, Angers; s. of Charles Bigot and Marcelle Pousset; m. Marie-Odile Lambert 1959; one s. three d.; ed Ecole Sainte-Geneviève, Versailles, Ecole Nat. Supérieure de l'Aéronautique, Ecole Polytechnique and Cranfield Coll. of Aeronautics, Centre de Perfectionnement Affaires; aeronautical engineer 1957–61; Tech. Dir of Aeronautical Services, Ministry of Aeronautics, CNRS 1961–63; Dir of launch vehicle div., Centre Nat. des Etudes Spatiales (CNES) 1963–70; Deputy Dir Centre Spatial de Brétigny 1970–71; Dir of Devt Air Inter 1971–75; Soc. d'Etudes et de Réalisations Industrielles (Seri-Renault Eng), Dir-Gen. 1975–80; Commercial Dir Soc. Nat. Industrielle Aérospatiale (Snias) 1980–82; Dir-Gen. Arianespace 1982–90, Pres.-Dir-Gen. 1990–98, Hon. Chair. 1998–; mem. Bd of Dirs Ellipso, Inc., Washington, DC 1998–; mem. Int. Acad. of Astronautics, Acad. Nat. de l'Air et de l'Espace; Chevalier, Légion d'honneur, Commdr, Ordre nat. du Mérite; Médaille de Vermeil, CNES. *Address:* c/o Board of Directors, Ellipso, Inc., 4410 Massachusetts Avenue, NW, Suite 385, Washington, DC 20016, USA.

BIGUM, Jens, MSc; Danish business executive and fmr university administrator; b. 28 July 1938, Gislum; ed Royal Veterinary and Agricultural Univ., Copenhagen; Admin. Officer, Oxexport 1965–70; Financial Man. Mejeriselskabet Danmark amba 1970–72, Financial Dir 1972; Dir MD Foods amba 1987–92, Man. Dir 1992–2000 (renamed Arla Foods), Man. Dir Arla Foods amba 2000–04, also Dir and Deputy Chair. Arla Foods UK PLC 2003–; Chair. Chr. Hansen Holding A/S 2005–06; Chair. Aarhus Univ. –2013; Dir Carlsberg Breweries A/S 1997–, Chair. 2002–09, Deputy Chair. Carlsberg A/S 2002–09; Kt of the Dannebrog 1993. *Address:* c/o Office of the Chairman, Aarhus University, 8000 Aarhus, Denmark. *E-mail:* jens.bigum@arlafoods.com.

BÍLÁ, Lucie; Czech singer; b. (Hana Zaňáková), 7 April 1966, Otvovice; d. of Josef Zaňák; fmr pnr Petr Kratochvíl; one s.; m. Vaclav Noid Barta; co-owner Theatre Ta Fantastika, Prague; has toured throughout Western Europe; has performed in charity concerts in Czech Repub.; numerous awards including Czech Grammy Prize 1992–96, Most Popular Singer (Czech Repub.) 1994–2007, Czech Musical Acad. Prize 1997, Czech Nightingale Trophy 1996–2004, 2007–08. *Recordings include:* albums: Missariel 1993, Lucie Bílá 1994, Hvezdy jako hvezdy (Stars as Stars) 1998, Uplne naha (Totally naked) 1999, Jampadampa 2003, Laska je laska (Love is love - Best Of) 2004, Koncert (Concert) 2006, Woman 2007, Bang Bang! 2009, Bíle Vánoce 2010, Modi 2012. *Theatre includes:* Les Misérables 1992, Dracula 1995, Rat-Catcher 1996, Joan of Arc (Thalia Prize) 2000, Love is Love 2004, Elixir Zivota 2006, Carmen 2008. *Films include:* Horká kaše 1988, Divoká srdce 1989, Volná noha 1989, Praáků̇m, těm je hej 1990, Zkoušové období 1990, Fontána pro Zuzanu 2 1993, Princezna ze miejna 1994, King Ubu 1996, Čas dluhů 1998. *Publications include:* Nyní ji to vim (Now I Know It Already) 1999, Jen kratka navsteva potesi (Just short visit delights) 2007. *Leisure interest:* family. *Address:* Agentura 44, s.r.o. Karlova 8, 110 01 Prague 1, Czech Republic. *E-mail:* produkce@luciebila.com (office). *Website:* www.luciebila.com.

BILALI, Mohamed Gharib, MA; Tanzanian nuclear scientist and politician; *Vice-President;* b. 6 Feb. 1945; ed Howard Univ., Univ. of California, Berkeley, USA; joined Univ. of Dar es salaam as Lecturer in Physics 1976, Head of Dept of Physics and in charge of Nuclear Physics Unit 1983, Head of Faculty of Science 1988–1990; Fellow, Univ. of Singapore under IAEA 1984–85; apptd Prin. Sec. to Ministry of Science, Tech. and Higher Educ. 1990; Chief Minister, Supreme Revolutionary Council of Zanzibar 1995–2000; Vice-Pres. of Tanzania 2010–; Chair. Dodoma Univ. Council 2007–; mem. CCM (Party for Democracy and Progress). *Address:* Office of the Vice-President, Luthuri Street, PO Box 5380, Dar es Salaam, Tanzania (office). *Telephone:* (22) 2113857 (office). *Fax:* (22) 2113856 (office). *E-mail:* ps@vpo.go.tz (office). *Website:* vpo.go.tz (office).

BILDT, Carl; Swedish politician and diplomatist; *Minister of Foreign Affairs;* b. 15 July 1949, Halmstad; m. Mia Bohman 1984; one s. one d.; ed Univ. of Stockholm; Chair. Confed. of Liberal and Conservative Students 1973–74, European Democrat Students 1974–76; mem. Stockholm Co. Council 1974–77; Political Advisor on Policy Co-ordination Ministry of Econ. Affairs 1976–78; Under-Sec. of State for Co-ordination and Planning at the Cabinet Office 1979–81; mem. Parl. 1979–2001; mem. Exec. Cttee Moderate Party 1981, Leader 1986–99; mem. Advisory Council on Foreign Affairs 1982–99; mem. Submarine Defence Comm. 1982–83; mem. 1984 Defence Policy Comm. 1984–87; Prime Minister of Sweden 1991–94; EU Peace Envoy in Fmr Yugoslavia 1995; High Rep. of the Int. Community in Bosnia and Herzegovina 1995–97; Vice-Chair. Int. Democrat Union 1992–99, Chair. 1992–99; Special Envoy of Sec.-Gen. of the UN to the Balkans 1999–2001; Chair. At-Large-Membership Study Cttee Internet Corpn for Assigned Names and Numbers (ICANN) 2001–02; currently Chair. Bd of Dirs Kreab Group (public affairs and strategic communication cos), Nordic Venture Network, Teleoptimering AB; Minister of Foreign Affairs 2006–; mem. Bd of Dirs Centre for European Reform, Vostok Nafta, Lundin Petroleum, HiQ, Öhmans; Trustee RAND Corpn; Fellow, Inst. for the Study of Terrorism and Political Violence, Univ. of St Andrews, Scotland; mem. IISS, London. *Publications:* Landet som steg ut i kylan (The Country that Stepped Out into the Cold) 1972, Framtid i frihet (A Future in Freedom) 1991, Hallanning, svensk, europe (A Citizen of Holland, Sweden and Europe) 1991, Peace Journey 1997. *Address:* Ministry for Foreign Affairs, Gustav Adolfs torg 1, 103 39 Stockholm, Sweden (office). *Telephone:* (8) 405-10-00 (office). *Fax:* (8) 723-11-76 (office). *E-mail:* registrator@foreign.ministry.se (office); carl@bildt.net. *Website:* utrikes.regeringen.se (office); www.bildt.net.

BILE, Pastor Micha Ondo, MSc; Equatorial Guinean mining engineer, diplomatist and politician; b. 2 Dec. 1952, Nsinik-Esawong; m.; six c.; ed Inst. of Mining,

Krivoi-Rog Univ.; engineer, Mines and Quarries Section, Dept of Mines and Hydrocarbons, Ministry of Mines and Energy 1982, Chief of Section 1983–84, Dir-Gen. Dept 1984–94, Sec.-Gen. Ministry 1994–95; Perm. Rep. to UN 1995–2001; Minister of External Relations, Int. Co-operation and Francophone Affairs 2003–12; Kt (Second Class), Order of Independence. *Address:* c/o Ministry of External Relations, International Co-operation and Francophone Affairs, Malabo, Equatorial Guinea (office).

BILLAUD, Bernard; French fmr civil servant; b. 3 Sept. 1942, Béziers; s. of Bernard Billaud and Raymonde Mazet; m. Claude Devitry 1967; two s. one d.; ed Inst. d'études politiques de Paris and Ecole nat. d'admin, Faculté de droit de Paris; obtained Diplôme de Inst. d'études politiques de Paris and Diplôme d'études supérieures de droit public; auditor 1968, Public Auditor Cour des Comptes 1976, Conseiller maître 1989, now hon.; Adviser to French Embassy, Holy See 1974–76; Official Rep. to the Prime Minister 1976; Sr Lecturer Inst. d'études politiques de Paris 1977–92; Dir of Staff, Mayor of Paris 1979–83; mem. comm. Vieux Paris 1983–; Pres. comm. on historical works of Ville de Paris 1983–2009; Dir-Gen. Int. Relations, Paris 1983–84; Gen. Commr of the French Language 1987–89; Prime Minister's Rep. of Admin. Council of AFP 1993–98, France 3 1995–98; Vice-Pres. organizing Cttee for 'de la Gaule à la France' 1996; Pres. du conseil d'admin de l'Ecole nationale des chartes 2004–07; Commdr, Légion d'honneur, Officier, Ordre nat. du Mérite, Grand Croix Ordre de Saint-Grégoire-le-Grand, Grand Medaille de Vermeil, Ville de Paris 2010. *Publications include:* L'aide de l'Etat à l'enseignement privé 1966, Georges Bidault – Les éditoriaux de "l'aube" (1938–1940) 2001, D'un Chirac l'autre 2005. *Leisure interest:* history. *Address:* 12 rue des Jardins Saint Paul, 75004 Paris, France (home). *Telephone:* 1-48-87-91-68 (home).

BILLINGTON, James Hadley, PhD; American historian, academic and librarian; *Librarian of Congress;* b. 1 June 1929, Bryn Mawr, Pa; s. of Nelson Billington and Jane Coolbaugh; m. Marjorie A. Brennan 1957; two s. two d.; ed Princeton Univ. and Univ. of Oxford, UK; army service 1953–56; Instructor in History, Harvard Univ. 1957–58, Fellow, Russian Research Center 1958–59, Asst Prof. of History 1958–61; Assoc. Prof. of History, Princeton Univ. 1962–64, Prof. 1964–73; Dir Woodrow Wilson Int. Center for Scholars, Washington, DC 1973–87; Librarian of Congress, Library of Congress, Washington, DC 1987–; Visiting Research Prof., Inst. of History, USSR Acad. of Sciences 1966–67, Univ. of Helsinki 1960–61, Ecole des Hautes Etudes en Sciences Sociales, Paris 1985, 1988; Guggenheim Fellow 1960–61; mem. Bd of Dirs John F. Kennedy Center for the Performing Arts; mem. American Acad. of Arts and Sciences, American Philosophical Soc.; Foreign mem. Russian Acad. Sciences; mem. Bd of Foreign Scholarships, Fulbright Program 1971–76 (Chair. 1973–75); writer/host, The Face of Russia (TV series) 1998; Chevalier des Arts et des Lettres, Légion d'honneur, Kt Commdr's Cross of the Order of Merit (Germany) 1996, Commdr Nat. Order of the Southern Cross (Brazil), Order of Merit (Italy), Order of Friendship (Russia) 2008; 40 hon. degrees; Gwangha Medal (Repub. of Korea), Woodrow Wilson Award 1992, UCLA Medal 1999, Pushkin Medal 2000, Karamzin Prize, Foreign Literature Library, Moscow 2005, Likhachev Prize, Likhachev Foundation, St Petersburg 2006, Lafayette Prize, French-American Cultural Foundation 2007, EastWest Inst. Outstanding Leadership Award 2007, Presidential Citizens Medal 2008. *Publications include:* Mikhailovsky and Russian Populism 1958, The Icon and the Axe: An Interpretive History of Russian Culture 1966, Fire in the Minds of Men: Origins of the Revolutionary Faith 1980, Russia Transformed: Breakthrough to Hope 1992, The Face of Russia 1998, Russia in Search of Itself 2004; contribs to books and journals. *Address:* Library of Congress, 101 Independence Avenue, SE, Washington, DC 20540-0002, USA (office). *Telephone:* (202) 707-5000 (office). *Fax:* (202) 707-1714 (office). *Website:* www.loc.gov (office).

BILLINGTON, Michael Keith, OBE, BA; British drama critic and author; b. 16 Nov. 1939, Leamington Spa, Warwicks., England; s. of Alfred R. Billington and Patricia Bradshaw; m. Jeanine Bradlaugh 1977; one d.; ed Warwick School and St Catherine's Coll., Oxford; Public Liaison Officer, Theatre Royal, Lincoln 1962–64; writer on theatre, film and cinema, The Times 1965–71; Drama Critic, The Guardian 1971–, Country Life 1988–; presenter of various BBC Radio arts programmes including Options, Kaleidoscope, Meridian, etc. 1971–91; writer on London arts scene for The New York Times 1984–94; writer and presenter of TV profiles of Peter Hall, Alan Ayckbourn, Peggy Ashcroft 1988–90; Hon. Fellow, St Catherine's Coll., Oxford 2005; Dr hc (Warwick) 2009; IPC Critic of the Year 1974, Theatre Critic of the Year 1993, 1995, 1997. *Publications:* The Modern Actor 1973, How Tickled I Am: A Celebration of Ken Dodd 1977, Alan Ayckbourn 1984, Stoppard: The Playwright 1987, Peggy Ashcroft 1988, Approaches to Twelfth Night 1990, One Night Stands: A Critic's View of British Theatre 1971–1991 1993, The Life and Work of Harold Pinter 1996, Stage and Screen Lives (ed.) 2001, Harold Pinter 2007, State of the Nation: British Theatre since 1945 (Theatre Book Prize 2007) 2007. *Leisure interests:* cricket, opera, travel. *Address:* 15 Hearne Road, London, W4 3NJ, England (home). *Telephone:* (20) 8995-0455 (home). *Fax:* (20) 8742-3496 (home). *E-mail:* michael.billington@guardian.co.uk (office). *Website:* www.guardian.co.uk/profile/michaelbillington (office).

BIN LADEN, Bakr Mohammed; Saudi Arabian business executive; *Chairman, Saudi Binladin Group;* b. 1947; s. of Mohammad Awad bin Laden; half-brother of the late Osama bin Laden; ed Univ. of Miami, Fla, USA; Chair. Saudi Binladin Group (took over leadership of construction co. from his brother the late Salem M. Bin Laden); ranked by Arabian Business amongst the Power 500: The Worlds's Most Influential Arabs (48th) 2012. *Address:* Saudi Binladin Group Bldg, Prince Mohd Bin Abdul Aziz Street, Al Rawdah District, Jeddah 21492, Saudi Arabia (office). *Telephone:* (2) 664-3033 (office). *Fax:* (2) 664-3261 (office). *E-mail:* info@sbg .com.sa (office). *Website:* www.sbg.com.sa (office).

BINAY, Jejomar (Jojo) C.; Philippine lawyer and politician; *Vice-President;* b. 11 Nov. 1942, Makati; s. of Diego Binay and Lourdes Cabauatan; m. Elenita Sombillo; five c.; ed Philippine Normal Coll., Univ. of the Philippines; taught law, political science and public admin at Philippine Coll. of Commerce, Philippine Women's Univ. and St Scholastica's Coll.; Mayor of Makati 1986–98, 2001–10; Vice-Pres. of the Philippines 2010–; Chair. Metropolitan Manila Devt Authority 1990–92, 1998–2001; fmr Vice-Chair. Pasig River Rehabilitation Comm.; fmr Traffic Czar for Metro Manila; Pres. PDP-Laban Party. *Address:* Office of the Vice-President, PNB Financial Center, 7th Floor, President Diosdado Macapagal Blvd, Pasay City, 1300 Metro Manila, Philippines (office). *Telephone:* (2) 8333311 (office).

Fax: (2) 8316676 (office). *E-mail:* vp@ovp.gov.ph (office). *Website:* www.ovp.gov.ph (office).

BINDING, Günther, DrIng, DPhil; German professor of art and architecture; *Emeritus Professor, University of Cologne;* b. 6 March 1936, Koblenz; s. of Kurt Binding and Margot Binding (née Masur); m. Elisabeth Dietz 1969; one s. two d.; ed gymnasium in Arnsberg and Cologne, Technische Hochschule, Aachen and Univs of Cologne and Bonn; Dir Lower Rhine section, Rheinisches Landesmuseum, Bonn 1964–70; Prof., Univ. of Cologne 1970–2000, Rector 1981–83, Pro-Rector 1983–85, now Prof. Emer.; Vice-Pres. W German Rectors' Conf. 1982–84; mem. Sächsische Akad. der Wissenschaften 1999–, Wissenschaftliche Gesellschaft an der Universität Frankfurt 2002–06; Ruhrpreis für Kunst und Wissenschaft 1966, Josef-Humar-Preis 1986, Rheinland-Taler 1987. *Publications include:* 40 books and 320 articles about European architecture and history of art. *Address:* University of Cologne, Albertus-Magnus-Platz, 50923 Cologne (office); Wingertsheide 65, 51427 Berg.-Gladbach, Germany (home). *Telephone:* (221) 470-4440 (office); (2204) 64956 (home). *E-mail:* guenther.binding@uni-koeln.de. *Website:* www.guentherbinding.de (office).

BINDRA, Abhinav, BBA; Indian air rifle shooter; b. 28 Sept. 1982, Dehradun; s. of Apjit Singh Bindra and Babli Bindra; ed Univ. of Colorado, USA; Nat. Champion 1999–2003, 2005, Jr World Record Holder, Air Rifle, Munich 2001, European Circuit Champion (seven gold, four silver, one bronze) 2002, Commonwealth Games, Manchester (gold and silver medalist) 2002, Asian Shooting Championship (silver medalist) 2003, World Cup, Munich (bronze medalist) 2003, All American Shooting Championship, Colorado Springs (gold medalist) 2004, Commonwealth Games Record Holder 2004, Asian Shooting Championship, Bangkok (gold medalist) 2005, Commonwealth Games, Melbourne (gold, silver, bronze medalist) 2006, World Champion, Air Rifle World Championship, Zagreb 2006, Air Rifle Asian Shooting Championship (gold medalist) 2007, Air Rifle Australian Cup, Sydney (gold medalist) 2007, INTERSHOOT Netherlands (gold, silver medalist) 2010, Beijing Olympic (gold medalist) 2008; Dir Abhinav Futuristics Ltd, Abhinav Hotels and Inns Pvt. Ltd; mem. Cen. Selection Cttee, Nat. Youth Awards 2008–09; Dr hc (SRM Univ., Chennai) 2008; Arjuna Award 2000, Rajiv Gandhi Khel Ratna 2001, Maharaja Ranjit Singh Award 2001, K.K. Birla Award 2002, UT Government Most Elite Sportsman Award 2002, Uttaranchal Praman Patra Award 2003, Punjab Praman Patra Award 2006, NDTV - India Sportsman of the Year 2008, Madhya Pradesh Khel Ratna 2008, Padma Bhushan 2009, Padma Bhushan 2009, Rajiv Gandhi Award 2009, Bharat Shiromani Award 2009, India Youth Sports Icon 2009, The Sportsman of the Year, SAHARA Indian Sports Awards. *Address:* Abhinav Futuristics Limited, SCO 62-63, Sector 34-A, Chandigarh, India (office). *Telephone:* (172) 2645978 (office); (172) 5074620 (office). *Fax:* (172) 2647940. *E-mail:* info@abhinavfuturistics.com (office). *Website:* www.abhinavfuturistics .com (office); www.abhinavbindra.com.

BINGAMAN, Jesse Francis (Jeff), Jr, BA, JD; American politician and lawyer; b. 3 Oct. 1943, El Paso, Tex.; s. of Jesse Francis Bingaman and Frances Bethia (née Ball); m. Anne Kovacovich 1968; one s.; ed Silver High School, Harvard and Stanford Univs; grew up in Silver City, NM; admitted to the NM Bar 1968; served in US Army Reserve 1968–74; Pnr, Campbell, Bingaman & Black, Santa Fe 1972–78; Attorney-Gen. of NM 1979–82; Senator from New Mexico 1983–2013 (retd), Chair. Energy and Natural Resources Cttee 2001–03, 2007–13, Chair. Cttee Outreach for the Senate Democratic Caucus; Democrat; Hon. DHumLitt (New Mexico State Univ.) 2008; Distinguished Eagle Scout Award, Boy Scouts of America. *Address:* c/o 703 Hart Senate Building, Washington, DC 20510, USA.

BINGHAM, H. Raymond, BS, MBA; Singaporean business executive; *Chairman, Flextronics International Ltd;* ed Weber State Univ., Harvard Business School, USA; held sr man. positions at Marriott Corpn, Red Lion Hotels and Inns, Agrico Overseas Investment Co. and N-ReN International; Exec. Vice-Pres. and Chief Financial Officer Cadence Design Systems, Inc. 1993–99, mem. Bd of Dirs 1997–2004, Pres. and CEO 1999–2004, Exec. Chair. 2004–05; Man. Dir General Atlantic LLC (pvt. equity firm) 2006–10, also Co-head of Palo Alto, Calif. office; mem. Bd of Dirs Flextronics International Ltd 2005–, Chair. 2008–; mem. Bd of Dirs Freescale Semiconductor, Inc., KLA Tencor Corpn, Oracle Corpn, STMicroelectronics NV; Co-founder and Dir Silicon Valley Educ. Foundation; mem. Bd of Dirs Nat. Parks Conservation Asscn; named an Outstanding Director by the Outstanding Director Exchange (div. of the Financial Times) 2009. *Address:* General Atlantic LLC, 228 Hamilton Avenue, Palo Alto, CA 94301, USA (office); Flextronics International Ltd, 2 Changi South Lane, 486123, Singapore (office). *Telephone:* (650) 251-7800 (Palo Alto) (office); 6299-8888 (office). *Fax:* (650) 251-9672 (Palo Alto) (office); 6543-1888 (office). *E-mail:* board@flextronics.com (office). *Website:* www.generalatlantic.com (office); www.flextronics.com (office).

BINGHAM, John, CBE, FRS; British scientist, plant breeder and farmer; b. 19 June 1930; s. of Thomas Frederick Bingham and Emma Maud Lusher; m. Jadwiga Anna Siedlecka 1983; one s.; ed Univ. of East Anglia; mem. staff, Plant Breeding Inst. of Cambridge (subsequently Plant Breeding International Cambridge Ltd) 1954–86, Deputy Chief Scientific Officer 1981–91; research in plant breeding, culminating in production of improved winter wheat varieties for British agric.; Pres. Royal Norfolk Agric. Asscn 1991; Hon. Fellow, Royal Agric. Soc. of England 1983, Nat. Inst. of Agric. Botany; Hon. DSc (East Anglia); Mullard Medal, Royal Soc. 1975, Royal Agric. Soc. of England Research Medal 1975, Massey Ferguson Nat. Award for Services to UK Agric. 1984. *Leisure interests:* farming and wildlife conservation (one floral meadow discovered now classified as Site of Special Scientific Interest). *Address:* Hereward Barn, Church Lane, Mattishall Burgh, Dereham, Norfolk, NR20 3QZ, England. *Telephone:* (1362) 858354.

BINMORE, Kenneth George, CBE, PhD, FBA; British economist and academic; *Professor Emeritus of Economics and Research Fellow, University College London;* b. 27 Sept. 1940, London; s. of Ernest Binmore and Maud Binmore (née Holland); m. Josephine Ann Lee 1972; two s. two d.; ed Imperial Coll., London; Prof. of Math., LSE 1974–88; Prof. of Econs, Univ. of Mich. 1988–93; Prof. of Econs, Univ. Coll. London 1991–2003, Prof. Emer. and Research Fellow 2003–; Dir Centre for Econ. Learning and Social Evolution 1994–2003; Fellow, Econometric Soc., American Acad. of Arts and Sciences. *Publications include:* 11 books, including Mathematical Analysis 1977, Economics of Bargaining 1986, Fun and Games 1992, Playing Fair: Game Theory and the Social Contract I 1994, Just Playing: Game Theory and

the Social Contract II 1998, Natural Justice 2004, Rational Decisions 2009; 125 published papers. *Leisure interest:* philosophy, watercolors. *Address:* Department of Economics, University College London, Gower Street, London, WC1E 6BT, England (office); Newmills, Whitebrook, Monmouth, Gwent, NP25 4TY, Wales (home). *Telephone:* (20) 7504-5864 (office); (1600) 860691 (home). *Fax:* (20) 7916-2774 (office); (1600) 860691 (home). *E-mail:* k.binmore@ucl.ac.uk (office). *Website:* else.econ.ucl.ac.uk/newweb/displayProfile.php?key=2 (office).

BINNIG, Gerd; German physicist; b. 20 July 1947, Frankfurt am Main; s. of Karl Franz Binnig and Ruth Bracke Binnig; m. 1st Lore Wagler 1969; one s. one d.; m. 2nd Renate Binnig 2003; ed Johann Wolfgang Goethe Univ., Univ. of Frankfurt; mem. Physics Group, IBM Zürich Research Lab., Rüschlikon 1978–2005, Group Leader 1984–2005; Assignment to IBM Almaden Research Centre, San José, Calif., collaboration with Stanford Univ. 1985–86, 1987; IBM Fellow 1986; Visiting Prof., Stanford Univ. 1986–88; Foreign Assoc. mem. NAS, Washington, DC 1987; mem. IBM Acad. 1989, Bd Mercedes Automobil Holding AG 1989–93, Bd Daimler Benz Holding 1990–; Founder, Head of Research and mem. Advisory Bd Definiens AG 1994–; Hon. Prof., Univ. of Munich 1986–; Hon. Fellow, Royal Microscopical Soc. 1988; OM (FRG) 1987; Physics Prize, German Physical Soc. 1982, Otto-Klung-Weberbank Prize 1983, EPS Europhysics Prize 1984, King Faisal Int. Prize for Physics (jtly) 1984, Hewlett Packard Europhysics Prize (jtly) 1984, Nobel Prize for Physics (with E. Ruska and H. Rohrer) 1986, Eliot Cresson Medal, Franklin Inst., Phila 1987, Distinguished Service Medal, Minnie Rosen Award, Ross Univ. 1988, Bayerischer Verdienstorden 1992, named to Nat. Inventors Hall of Fame 1994. *Publications include:* Aus dem Nichts 1989. *Leisure interests:* music, reading, swimming, golf. *Address:* Definiens AG, Trappentoen str. 1, 80339 Munich, Germany (office). *Telephone:* (89) 2311800 (office). *Fax:* (89) 23118090 (office). *E-mail:* gclark@ricochetpr.com (office). *Website:* www.definiens.com.

BINNING, Paviter (Pavi) Singh; American business executive; *President, George Weston Ltd;* held several Sr Corp. and Operational Finance positions at Diageo PLC from 1986, as Corp. Finance Dir, Group Financial Controller, Chief Financial Officer (CFO) of Europe and CFO of Americas; CFO Telent PLC (fmrly Marconi Corpn PLC) 2003–06; Finance Dir Hanson plc 2006–, Exec. Dir 2007–, Exec. Dir Hanson Ltd 2009–; fmr Prin. Accounting Officer, Nortel Networks Corpn, Exec. Vice-Pres. and CFO Nortel Networks Corpn 2007–10, Chief Restructuring Officer 2009–10; CFO George Weston Ltd 2010–12, Pres. 2011–; fmr Dir, Solex PLC, Electrolux Ltd, Loblaw Cos Ltd; Fellow, Chartered Inst. of Man. Accountants (UK). *Address:* George Weston Ltd, 22 St Clair Avenue East, Suite 1901, Toronto, ON M4T 2S7, Canada (office). *Telephone:* (416) 922-2500 (office). *Fax:* (416) 922-4395 (office). *E-mail:* info@weston.ca (office). *Website:* www .weston.ca (office).

BINNS, Malcolm, ARCM; British pianist; b. 29 Jan. 1936, Nottingham; s. of Douglas Priestley Binns and May Walker; ed Bradford Grammar School, Royal Coll. of Music; soloist with numerous leading orchestras and conductors around the world (including Boulez, Boult, Dorati, Haitink and Rattle) 1960–; toured with Scottish Nat. Orchestra and Limbourg Orchestra 1987–88; regular performer at Wigmore Hall 1958–, the Promenade Concerts 1962–; concerts at Aldeburgh, Leeds, Three Choirs and Canterbury Festivals; solo and concerto performances broadcast regularly on BBC; Chappell Medal 1956, Medal of Worshipful Co. of Musicians 1956. *Recordings:* more than 30 recordings, including piano sonatas by Bax, Ireland and Bridge for the British Music Soc. 2007, Balakirev Piano Concerti 1 and 2, Rimsky-Korsakov Piano Concerto (English Northern Philharmonia) 1992. *Leisure interests:* gardening, collecting antique gramophone records. *Address:* c/o Michael Harrold Artist Management, 13 Clinton Road, Leatherhead, Surrey, KT22 8NU, England (office); 233 Court Road, Orpington, Kent, BR6 9BY, England (home). *Telephone:* (1372) 375728 (office); (1689) 831056 (home). *E-mail:* management@angelus.co.uk (office). *Website:* www.angelus.co.uk (office).

BINNS, Hon. Patrick (Pat) George, MA; Canadian politician and diplomatist; *Consul General to New England;* b. 8 Oct. 1948, Sask.; s. of Stan Binns and Phyllis Binns; m. Carol Binns; three s. one d.; ed Univ. of Alberta; worked with PEI Rural Devt Council 1972–78; mem. Legis. Ass. representing 4th Kings Dist 1978–88, fmr Minister of Industry, Municipal Affairs, Fisheries, Environment, Labour, Housing, responsibilities for Econ. Devt; mem. House of Commons representing Cardigan, Ottawa 1984–88; Pres. Island Bean Ltd and Pat Binns & Assocs 1988–96; Leader, Progressive Conservative Party of PEI 1996–2007, MLA for Dist 5, Murray River-Gaspereaux 1996–2007, Premier, Pres. of Exec. Council, Minister Responsible for Intergovernmental Affairs 1996–2007, Minister of Agric., Fisheries and Aquaculture 2006–07; Amb. to Ireland 2007–10, Consul Gen. to New England, Boston, Mass, USA 2010–. *Address:* Canadian Consulate General, Three Copley Place, Suite 400, Boston, MA 02116, USA (office). *Telephone:* (617) 247-5100 (office). *Fax:* (617) 247-5190 (office). *E-mail:* bostn@international.gc.ca (office).

BINOCHE, Juliette; French actress; b. 9 March 1964, Paris; d. of Jean-Marie Binoche and Monique Stalens; one s. by André Halle, one d. by Benoît Magimel; ed Nat. Conservatory of Drama and private theatrical studies. *Films include:* Les nanas, La vie de famille, Rouge Baiser, Rendez-Vous, Mon beau-frère a tué ma soeur, Mauvais Sang, Un tour de manège, Les amants du Pont-Neuf, The Unbearable Lightness of Being, Wuthering Heights 1992, Damage 1992, Trois Couleurs: Bleu 1993, Le Hussard sur le Toit 1995, The English Patient (Acad. Award for Best Supporting Actress 1996, Berlin Film Festival Award 1996, BAFTA Award 1997) 1996, Alice et Martin 1999, Les Enfants du Siècle (Children of the Century) 1999, La Veuve de Saint-Pierre 2000, Chocolat 2001, Code Unknown 2001, Décalage horaire (Jet Lag) 2002, Caché 2005, Country of My Skull 2004, Bee Season 2005, Mary 2005, Paris, je t'aime 2006, A Few Days in September 2006, Breaking and Entering 2006, Le Voyage du ballon rouge 2007, Désengagement 2007, Dan in Real Life 2007, Paris 2007, Summer Hours 2008, Certified Copy 2009 (Cannes Film Festival Award for Best Actress), The Son of No One 2011, Sponsoring 2011, Elles 2011, Cosmopolis 2012. *Play:* Naked (Almeida, London) 1998. *Address:* c/o UTA, 9560 Wilshire Boulevard, Floor 5, Beverly Hills, CA 90212, USA.

BIO-TCHANÉ, Abdoulaye, MA; Benin international organization official and economist; *President, West African Development Bank;* b. 1952, Parakou; divorced; three c.; ed Univ. of Dijon, France, Centre Ouest-Africain de Formation et d'Etudes, Dakar, Senegal; economist, Cen. Bank for W African Countries (BCEAO), Dakar, Asst to Gov 1992–96, Dir Econ. and Monetary Survey Dept 1996–98; Minister of Finances and Economy 1998–2002; Dir IMF African Dept 2002–08; Pres. West African Devt Bank 2008–. *Address:* West African Development Bank, 68, Avenue de la Libération, BP 1172, Lomé, Togo (office). *Telephone:* 221-59-06 (office). *Fax:* 221-52-67 (office). *E-mail:* boadsiege@boad.org (office). *Website:* (office); www.abiotchane.org.

BIONDI, Frank J., Jr, BA, MBA; American business executive; b. 9 Jan. 1945, New York; s. of Frank Biondi and Virginia Willis; m. Carol Oughton 1974; two d.; ed Princeton and Harvard Univs; Assoc., Corp. Finance, Prudential Securities, New York 1969, Shearson-Lehman Inc. New York 1970–71; Prin. Frank Biondi & Assocs, New York 1972; Dir Business Analysis, Teleprompter Corpn New York 1972–73; Asst Treas., Assoc. Dir Business Affairs, Children's TV Workshop, New York 1974–78; Dir Entertainment Planning, HBO, New York 1978, Vice-Pres. Programming Operations 1979–82, Exec. Vice-Pres. Planning and Admin. 1982–83, Pres. and CEO 1983, Chair. and CEO 1984; Exec. Vice-Pres. Entertainment Business Sector, The Coca-Cola Co. 1985,; Chair. and CEO Coca-Cola TV 1986; Pres., CEO and Dir Viacom Int. Inc. New York 1987–96, Pres., CEO and Dir Viacom Inc. 1987–96; Chair., CEO Universal Studios Inc. 1996–98; mem. Bd of Dirs Amgen 2002–, Hasbro 2002–, Cablevision Systems 2005–, RealD Inc., Seagate Technology 2005–, Yahoo Inc. 2008–; Pres. Biondi Reiss Capital Man., New York 1998; fmr Sr Man. Dir Waterview Advisors LLC (private equity fund); Trustee, Claremont Graduate Univ.; Founding mem. Board of Councilors, School of Cinema-Television, Univ. of Southern California. *Address:* 110 North Rockingham Avenue, Los Angeles, CA 90049, USA.

BIONDI, Matt, MA; American teacher and fmr swimmer; b. 8 Oct. 1965, Moraga, Calif.; m. Kirsten Biondi 1995; two s. one d.; ed Univ. of California, Berkeley, Lewis & Clarke Coll.; mem. USA Water Polo Team, then became freestyle swimmer; career highlights include Olympic Games: 50m freestyle 1st (1988), 2nd (1992) 100m freestyle 1st (1988); 200m freestyle 3rd (1988); 100m butterfly 2nd (1988); 4x100m freestyle 1st (1984, 1988, 1992); 4x200m freestyle 1st (1988); 400m medley 1st (1988, 1992); World Championships: 100m freestyle 1st (1986, 1991); world records: 50m freestyle 22.14 (Seoul 1988), 100m freestyle 48.42 (Austin 1988), 400m medley 3:34.84 (Atlanta 1996), 4x100m freestyle 3:16.53 (Seoul 1988); spokesman Olympic Movt; mem. Int. Hall of Fame Selection Cttee; mem. US Olympic Hall of Fame; math. teacher at Parker School (secondary school), Kamuela, Hawaii 2001–, launched school swim team 2004; Int. Swimming Hall of Fame 1997, World Swimmer of the Year 1998. *Address:* c/o Parker School, 65–1224 Lindsey Road, Kamuela, HI 96743 USA.

BIOT, Jacques; French engineer, academic and university administrator; *President, École Polytechnique;* ed École Polytechnique; engineer from Corps des Mines; dedicated first years of professional career to industrial recovery and innovation funding within Ministry of Industry and Research; then served as adviser, in charge of Industry and Technology, in the Prime Minister's office –1985; subsequently held exec. positions in French biopharmaceutical cos, Roussel Uclaf, then Pasteur Mérieux Serums and Vaccines (both later integrated into the Sanofi Group); Founder and Pres. JNBD (strategic consulting firm) 1992–2012; also served as an Ind. Dir and Deputy Chair. Guerbet Laboratories; investor in French start-ups in the healthcare field; mem. Scientific and Tech. Comm. of the Corps des Mines 2003–; participated, as Chair. École des Mines d'Alès, in working parties in charge of designing strategy of Écoles des Mines and in formation of Mines Telecom Inst.; Chair. Admin. Council and Pres. École Polytechnique 2013–. *Address:* École Polytechnique, 91128 Palaiseau Cedex, France (office). *Telephone:* 1-69-33-33-33 (office). *Website:* www.polytechnique.edu (office).

BIRCH, Bryan John, PhD, FRS; British mathematician and academic; *Professor Emeritus of Mathematics, University of Oxford;* b. 25 Sept. 1931, Burton-on-Trent, Staffs., England; s. of Arthur Jack Birch and Mary Edith Birch; m. Gina Margaret Christ 1961; two s. one d.; ed Shrewsbury School, Trinity Coll., Cambridge; Research Fellow, Trinity Coll. 1956–60; Harkness Fellow, Princeton Univ. 1957–58; Fellow, Churchill Coll., Cambridge 1960–62; Sr Lecturer, later Reader, Univ. of Manchester 1962–65; Reader in Math., Univ. of Oxford 1966–85, Prof. of Arithmetic 1985–98, Prof. Emer. 1998–, Fellow, Brasenose Coll. 1966–98, Emer. Fellow 1998–; Del. of Oxford University Press 1988–98; Ed. Proceedings of the London Mathematical Society 2001–03; Sr Whitehead Prize 1993, De Morgan Medal 2007. *Publications:* scholarly articles, particularly on number theory. *Leisure interests:* theoretical gardening, opera, watching marmots and, of course, mathematics. *Address:* Mathematical Institute, 24–29 St Giles, Oxford, OX1 3LB (office); Green Cottage, Boars Hill, Oxford, OX1 5DQ, England (home). *Telephone:* (1865) 735367 (home). *E-mail:* birch@maths.ox.ac.uk (office). *Website:* www.maths .ox.ac.uk (office).

BIRCH, Peter Gibbs, CBE; British business executive; b. 4 Dec. 1937; m. Gillian Benge 1962; three s. one d.; ed Allhallows School, Devon; served Royal West Kent Regt 1957–58; with Nestlé Co. 1958–65; Sales Man. Gillette 1965–69, Gen. Sales Man. Gillette Australia 1969–71, Man. Dir Gillette NZ 1971–73, Gen. Man. Gillette South East Asia 1973–75, Group Gen. Man. Gillette, Africa, Middle East, Eastern Europe 1975–81, Man. Dir Gillette UK 1981; mem. Bd of Dirs Abbey Nat. (fmrly Abbey Nat. Bldg Soc.) 1984–98, Chief Exec. 1984–88, Chief Exec. Abbey Nat. PLC 1988–98; mem. Bd of Dirs Hoskyns Group 1988–93, Argos 1990–98, Scottish Mutual 1992–98, Dalgety 1993–98, N. M. Rothschild and Sons 1998–2007, Travelex 1999–2001, Sainsbury's Bank PLC 2002–, Dah Sing Bank Ltd 2006–, Banco Finantia SA 2007–08; Sr Dir (non-exec.) Trinity Mirror PLC 1999–2007; mem. Bd of Dirs Land Securities PLC 1997–2007 (Chair. 1998–2007); Chair. Trinity PLC 1998–99; Legal Services Comm. 2000–03; Kensington Group PLC 2000–07, UCTX Ltd 2001; Chair. Council of Mortgage Lenders 1991–92, Clubs for Young People 2010–; Deputy Chair. Lamprell PLC 2007–08 (Chair. Feb.–Dec. 2008); fmr Pres. Middx Asscn of Boys' Clubs. *Leisure interests:* active holidays, swimming, cycling, skiing.

BIRD, Sir Adrian Peter, Kt, CBE, PhD, FRS, FRSE, FMedSci; British geneticist and academic; *Buchanan Professor of Genetics, University of Edinburgh;* b. 3 July 1947; s. of Kenneth George Bird and Aileen Mary Bird; m. 1st 1976; one s. one d.; m. 2nd Catherine Mary Abbott 1993; one s. one d.; ed Univs of Sussex and Edinburgh; Damon Runyon Fellow, Yale Univ., USA 1972–73; Postdoctoral

Fellowship, Univ. of Zurich, Switzerland 1974–87, MRC, Edin.; mem. scientific staff, Mammalian Genome Unit; Sr Scientist, Inst. for Molecular Pathology, Vienna 1988–90; Buchanan Prof. of Genetics, Univ. of Edinburgh 1990–, Dir Wellcome Trust Centre for Cell Biology 1999–2011, Gov. Wellcome Trust 2000–10; fmr Chair. Scientific Advisory Bd Rett Syndrome Research Foundation, Breakthrough Breast Cancer UK, now Trustee and Scientific Advisor; mem. Bd of Eds, Molecular and Cellular Biology, Molecular Cell; Trustee, Cancer Research UK, Kirkhouse Trust; Hon. DrSc (Sussex) 2010; Louis Jeantet Prize for Medical Research 1999, Gabor Medal, Royal Soc. 1999, Gairdner Foundation Prize 2011, GlaxoSmithKline Prize 2012. *Publications include:* numerous papers in scientific journals. *Address:* Wellcome Trust Centre for Cell Biology, University of Edinburgh, Michael Swann Building, King's Buildings, Mayfield Road, Edinburgh, EH9 3JR, Scotland (office). *Telephone:* (131) 650-5668 (office). *Fax:* (131) 650-5379 (office). *E-mail:* a.bird@ed.ac.uk (office). *Website:* www.wcb.ed.ac.uk/ research/bird (office); birdlab.bio.ed.ac.uk (office).

BIRD, Harold Dennis (Dickie), OBE; British fmr international umpire and fmr cricketer; *President, Yorkshire County Cricket Club;* b. 19 April 1933, Barnsley, Yorks., England; s. of James Harold Bird and Ethel Bird (née Smith); ed Raley Secondary Modern School, Barnsley; right-hand batsman and right-arm medium-fast bowler; played for Yorks. Co. Cricket Club 1956–59, Leicestershire Co. Cricket Club 1960–64; played in 93 First-class matches, scored 3,314 runs (average 20.71, highest score 181 not out 1959) with two hundreds; First-class Umpire 1970–98; umpired 68 Test matches (world record 1973–96), 69 limited-overs ints (1973–95), including 1975, 1979, 1983 and 1987–88 World Cups (officiating in the first three finals), 92 one-day int. matches and seven Sharjah (UAE) tournaments; only person to umpire both men's and women's World Cup Finals; served on Int. Umpires Panel 1994–96; MCC Advanced Cricket Coach; f. Dickie Bird Foundation (for less privileged children) 2004; Pres., Yorkshire Co. Cricket Club 2014–; Hon. Life mem. MCC, Yorks. Co. Cricket Club, Leics. Co. Cricket Club, Barnsley Football Club; Freeman Borough of Barnsley 2000; Hon. DUniv (Sheffield Hallam) 1996; Hon. LLD (Leeds) 1997; Hon. DCL (Huddersfield) 2008; Yorks. Personality of the Year 1977, Rose Bowl, Barnsley Council 1988, Variety Club of GB Yorkshire Award 1988, Carlsberg-Tetley Yorkshireman of the Year 1996, People of the Year Award 1996, Radar Abbey Nat. 1996, Special Sporting Award, Variety Club of GB 1997, Lifelong Achievement Award 1998, Professional Cricketers Asscn Special Merit Award 1998, Yorkshire Co. Cricket Club 50 Years Service Award 1998, The Barnsley Millennium Award of Merit for outstanding services to the community and to cricket and in particular for the promotion of the image and civic pride of the Borough 2000, England and Wales Cricket Bd 30 Years of Service Award, Anglo-American Sporting Club Award for services to cricket, BBC TV Sports Awards, Yorkshire Hall of Fame 2006; statue erected in his honour, Barnsley 2008. *Radio:* Down Your Way with Brian Johnston 1975, Harry Carpenter Show (BBC) 1975, Desert Island Discs with Sue Lawley 1996. *Television appearances include:* The Terry Wogan Show (BBC) 1988, This is Your Life (ITV) 1992, BBC Grandstand 1996, Document of the Year (BBC 2) 1996, Newsnight (BBC 2) 1996, A Question of Sport (six times) 1999, The Clive Anderson Show 1998, Through the Keyhole (three times), Breakfast with Frost and Songs of Praise (BBC), The Gloria Hunniford Show (ITV, four times), Ready Steady Cook (BBC 2), They Think It's All Over (BBC 1), The Young Ones (BBC 1) 2010. *Publications:* Not Out 1978, That's Out 1985, From the Pavilion End 1988, Dickie Bird – My Autobiography (best-selling sports autobiog. in history) 1997, White Cap and Bails 1999, Dickie Bird's Britain 2002. *Leisure interest:* watching football. *Address:* White Rose Cottage, 40 Paddock Road, Staincross, Barnsley, Yorks., S75 6LE, England (home). *Telephone:* (1226) 384491 (home).

BIRD, Lester Bryant, BA; Antiguan lawyer and politician; *Leader, Antigua Labour Party;* b. 21 Feb. 1938; m.; one s. four d.; ed Antigua Grammar School, Univ. of Michigan, USA, Gray's Inn, UK; lawyer in pvt. practice 1969–76; Leader, Antigua Labour Party (ALP) 1971–; Senator, Upper House of Parl. and Leader of Opposition in Senate 1971–76; mem. Parl. 1976–; Deputy Premier and Minister of Econ. Devt, Tourism and Energy 1976–81; Deputy Prime Minister and Minister of Foreign Affairs, Econ. Devt, Tourism and Energy 1981–91; Minister of External Affairs, Planning and Trade 1991–94; Prime Minister of Antigua and Barbuda 1994–2004, Minister of External Affairs, Planning, Social Services and Information 1994, of Communications, Civil Aviation and Int. Transport 1996–98, of Foreign Affairs, Social Services, Civil Aviation and Int. Transport and Information 1998–99, of Foreign Affairs, Caribbean Community Affairs, Defence and Security and Merchant Shipping 1999–2001, of Justice and Legal Affairs 2001–04; del. to numerous Caribbean and int. confs. *Address:* Antigua Labour Party (ALP), S46 North Street, POB 948, St John's, Antigua, West Indies (office). *Telephone:* 462-2235 (office). *E-mail:* alp@antigualabourparty.net (office). *Website:* www .antigualabourparty.net (office).

BIRD, Phillip Bradley (Brad); American director, writer, actor and producer; b. 11 Sept. 1957, Kalispell, Mont.; m. Elizabeth Canney 1988; three c.; ed Corvallis High School, Ore.; trained as Disney animator; first person to receive a solo writing credit on feature-length film (The Incredibles) from Pixar Animation Studios; provided voices of Don Carlo in Doctor of Doom 1979, Edna Mode in The Incredibles 2004 and Ambrister Minion in Ratatouille 2007; ranked 23rd on EW's The 50 Smartest People in Hollywood 2007, Lifetime Achievement Award, Venice Film Festival 2009. *Films directed:* Amazing Stories: Book Two (segment 'Family Dog'; also writer) 1992, The Iron Giant 1999, The Incredibles (also writer) 2004, Jack-Jack Attack (also writer) 2005, One-Man Band (producer) 2005, Ratatouille (also screenplay) 2007, Mission: Impossible - Ghost Protocol 2011. *Animator:* Animalympics 1980, The Plague Dogs 1982. *Address:* c/o Jake Bloom, Bloom Hergott Diemer Rosenthal LaViolette & Feldman, LLP, 150 South Rodeo Drive, Third Floor, Beverly Hills, CA 90212, USA.

BIRDSALL, Nancy, BA, MA, PhD; American research institute director; *President, Center for Global Development;* ed Newton Coll. of the Sacred Heart, Paul H. Nitze School of Advanced Int. Studies (SAIS), Johns Hopkins Univ., Yale Univ.; Research Asst, Overseas Liaison Cttee, American Council on Educ. 1969–70; Social Science Analyst, Int. Communications Program, Smithsonian Inst. 1972–76; joined World Bank 1979, Economist, Devt Econs Dept 1979–82, Sr Economist, Country Policy Dept 1982–84, Staff Dir, World Devt Report 1984 1983–84, Chief, Policy and Research Div., Population, Health and Nutrition Dept

1984–87, Chief, Population and Human Resources Operations Div., Brazil Dept 1987–90, Chief, Environment Div., Latin America Region 1990–91, Dir Policy Research Dept 1991–93; Exec. Vice-Pres. IDB 1993–98; Sr Assoc. and Dir, Econ. Reform Project, Carnegie Endowment for Int. Peace 1998–2001; Sr Fellow (non-resident), Brookings Inst. 1998–; Founder and Pres. Center for Global Devt, Washington, DC 2001–; Visiting Prof., School of Advanced Int. Studies, Johns Hopkins Univ. 2006; fmr Adviser to Admin. of UNDP Rockefeller Foundation; fmr Consultant to Asia Soc., AAAS, UN Fund for Population Activities; fmr Chair. Int. Center for Research on Women; mem. Bd of Dirs Population Asscn of America 1987–89, Int. Center for Research on Women 1989–98 (Chair. 1995–97), Overseas Devt Council 1998–2000, Population Council 1995–2004, Social Science Research Council 1996–99, Peterson Inst. for Int. Econs 2001–, Per Jacobssen Foundation 2003–, Center for Interfaith Action 2008–, ACCION 2009–; fmr mem. Bd Social Science Research Council, Overseas Devt Council, cttees and working groups of NAS. *Publications include:* Population Growth and Economic Development 1986, Financing Health in Developing Countries: An Agenda for Reform (co-author) 1987, Unfair Advantage: Labor Market Discrimination in Developing Countries (co-ed.) 1991, The East Asian Miracle: Economic Growth and Public Policy (co-ed.) 1993, Opportunity Forgone: Education in Brazil (co-ed.) 1996, Pathways to Growth: Comparing East Asia and Latin America (co-ed.) 1997, Beyond Tradeoffs: Market Reform and Equitable Growth in Latin America (co-ed.) 1998, Population Matters: Demographic Change, Economic Growth and Poverty in the Developing World (co-author) 1999, Distributive Justice and Economic Development (co-ed.) 2000, New Markets, New Opportunities? Economic and Social Mobility in a Changing World 2000, Washington Contentious: Economic Policies for Social Equity in Latin American (co-author) 2001, Delivering on Debt Relief: From IMF Gold to a New Aid Architecture (co-author) 2002, Financing Development: The Power of Regionalism (co-ed.) 2004, Reality Check: The Distributional Impact of Privatization in Developing Countries (co-ed.) 2005, Rescuing the World Bank (ed.) 2006, The White House and the World: A Global Development Agenda for the Next U.S. President (ed.) 2008, Cash on Delivery Aid: A New Approach to Foreign Aid (co-author) 2010, The Global Financial Crisis: The Beginning of the End of the Development Agenda? (ed.) 2011; more than 75 articles in scholarly journals and chapters in books. *Address:* Center for Global Development, 1800 Massachusetts Avenue, Suite 301, NW Washington, DC 20036 (office); 3225 33rd Place, NW Washington, DC 20008, USA (home). *Telephone:* (202) 416-0700 (office). *Fax:* (202) 416-0750 (office). *E-mail:* nbirdsall@cgdev.org (office); president@cgdev.org (office). *Website:* www.cgdev.org (office).

BIRGENEAU, Robert J., PhD, FRS, FInstP, FAAS, FRSC; Canadian physicist, academic and university administrator; b. 25 March 1942, Toronto; m. Mary Catherine Birgeneau; ed Univ. of Toronto and Yale Univ., USA; instructor, Yale Univ. 1966–67; Nat. Research Council of Canada Postdoctoral Fellow, Univ. of Oxford, UK 1967–68; mem. tech. staff, Bell Labs 1968–74, Research Head, Scattering and Low Energy Physics 1975; Prof. of Physics, MIT 1975–82, Cecil and Ida Green Prof. of Physics 1982–2000, Assoc. Dir, Research Lab. of Electronics 1983–86, Head, Condensed Matter, Atomic and Plasma Physics 1987–88, Head, Dept of Physics 1988–91; Dean of Science, Univ. of Toronto 1991–2000, Pres. Univ. of Toronto 2000–04; Chancellor and Prof. of Physics, also Prof. of Materials Science and Eng, Univ. of California, Berkeley 2004–13 (retd); mem. Advisory Bd World Premier Research Center, Tohoku Univ., Japan 2007; Fellow, American Physical Soc., American Acad. of Arts and Sciences 1987, American Philosophical Soc. 2006, AAAS; Foreign Assoc. NAS 2004; Fellow, Neutron Scattering Soc. of America 2008; Morris Loeb Lecturer, Harvard Univ. 1986, H.L. Welsh Lecturer, Univ. of Toronto 1994, A.W. Scott Lecturer, Cambridge Univ. 2000, Tercentennial Lecturer, Yale Univ. 2001; Dr hc (Tsinghua Univ.) 2007, Hon. DEng (Colo School of Mines) 2007; numerous awards including Yale Science and Eng Alumni Achievement Award 1981, Wilbur Lucius Cross Medal, Yale Univ. 1986, Oliver E. Buckley Prize for Condensed Matter Physics, APS 1987, Bertram Eugene Warren Award, ACA 1988, DOE Materials Science Outstanding Accomplishment Award 1988, IUPAP Magnetism Award 1997, J.E. Lilienfeld Award, APS 2000, American Acad. of Arts and Sciences Founders Award 2006, Level Playing Field Inst. Lux Award 2007, Carnegie Corpn Academic Leadership Award 2008, Karl T. Compton Medal for Leadership in Physics, American Inst. of Physics 2012. *Address:* c/o Office of the Chancellor, 200 California Hall, #1500, Berkeley, CA 94720-1500, USA.

BIRKAVS, Valdis, PhD, DrIur; Latvian politician and lawyer; *Chairman, Strategic Partnership of Construction Development;* b. 28 July 1942, Riga; s. of Voldemars Birkavs and Veronika Birkavs (née Zihelmane); one s.; ed Riga Industrial Polytech. School, Univ. of Latvia; expert, Sr Researcher, Head of Div., Latvian Research Lab. of Forensic Medicine and Criminology 1969–86; Lecturer, Univ. of Latvia 1969–86, Deputy Dean Law Faculty 1986–89; Founder and Pres. Latvian Bar Asscn 1988–; Deputy to Supreme Council of Latvian Repub. from Popular Front of Latvia 1990–93, Deputy Chair. Legis. Cttee, Deputy Chair. Supreme Council of Latvian Repub. 1992–93; Prime Minister of Latvian Repub. 1993–94; Minister of Foreign Affairs 1994–99; Minister of Justice 1999–2000; currently Chair. Latvian Cttee, Business Software Alliance; Chair. Strategic Partnership of Construction Devt; mem. Club of Madrid, Wise Man Group for Nordic-Baltic Co-operation; Royal Order of the Polar Star (Sweden) 1995, Dannebrog Order (Denmark) 1997, Norwegian Royal Order 1998, Légion d'honneur 1997, Grand Master Three Star Order of Latvia 1999, Medal of the Order of Malta 2002, Order of Lithuania 2003, Medal of Baltic Ass. *Publications:* contrib. of more than 200 articles. *Leisure interests:* golf, yachting, reading, downhill skiing. *Address:* Strategic Partnership of Construction Development, Riga 1010, Latvia (office). *Telephone:* (2) 949-8195 (office). *Fax:* (2) 6745-1099 (office). *E-mail:* valdis.birkavs@gmail.com (office). *Website:* www.basp.lv (office).

BIRKE, Adolf Mathias, PhD, FRHistS; German historian and academic; b. 12 Oct. 1939, Wellingholzhausen; s. of Matthias Birke and Maria Birke (née Enewoldsen); m. 1st Linde D. Birn 1968; m. 2nd Sabine Volk 1988; one s. two d.; ed Univ. of Berlin; Prof. of Modern History, Free Univ. of Berlin 1979; Visiting Prof. of German and European Studies, Trinity Coll., Univ. of Toronto, Canada 1980–81; Asst St Antony's Coll., Oxford; Prof. of Modern History, Univ. of Bayreuth 1982–85; Prof. of Modern History, Univ. of Munich 1995–2000, now Prof. Emer.; Dir German Historical Inst., London 1985–94; Chair. Prince Albert Soc. 1983–95; Heisenberg Fellow 1979; mem. Royal Historical Soc.; Corresp. mem. Berliner Wissenschaftlichen Gesellschaft; Fed. Cross of Merit 1996; Cusanuswerk

Grant 1962. *Publications:* Bischof Ketteler und der deutsche Liberalismus 1971, Pluralismus und Gewerkschaftsautonomie 1978, Britain and Germany 1987, Nation ohne Haus. Deutschland 1945–1961 1989, (4th edn) 1998, Prince Albert Studies (ed.) Vols I–XIII 1983–95, Die Herausforderung des europäischen Staatensystems 1989, Princes, Patronage and the Nobility (ed with R. Asch) 1991, The Quest for Stability (ed. with R. Ahmann and M. Howard) 1992, Control Commission for Germany (British Element) (11 vols) Inventory (with H. Booms and O. Merker) 1993, Die Bundesrepublik Deutschland. Verfassung: Parlament und Parteien 1997, Deutschland und Grossbritannien 1999, An Anglo-German Dialogue (co-ed. with Magnus Brechtken and Alaric Searle) 2000; numerous articles on 19th- and 20th-century German and English history. *Leisure interests:* music, walking. *Address:* Friedenstr. 16, 06114 Halle, Germany (home).

BIRKERTS, Gunnar, FAIA; Latvian architect; *President, Gunnar Birkerts and Associates Inc.;* b. 17 Jan. 1925, Riga; s. of the late Peter Birkerts and of Merija Shop Birkerts; m. Sylvia Zvirbulis 1950; two s. one d.; ed Technische Hochschule, Stuttgart, Germany; went to USA 1949; est. own practice 1959, Pres. Gunnar Birkerts and Assocs Inc. 1963–; Prof. of Architecture, Univ. of Mich. 1959–90, Prof. Emer. 1990–; numerous guest lectureships USA, Canada, Mexico and Europe; Architect-in-Residence, American Acad. in Rome 1976; Fellow, Latvian Architects' Asscn; mem. Latvian Acad. of Sciences; Order of Three Stars, Latvia; Dr hc (Riga Tech. Univ., Latvia) 1990; over 50 awards for projects, including American Acad. of Arts and Letters Brunner Memorial Prize in Architecture, Latvian Acad. of Sciences Great Medal. *Leisure interests:* tennis, swimming, music. *Address:* 65 Grove Street, 241, Wellesley, MA 02482, USA (home). *Telephone:* (781) 235-4091 (home). *Fax:* (781) 235-4167 (home). *E-mail:* gunnarbirk@aol.com (office). *Website:* www.gunnarbirkerts.com (office).

BIRKIN, Jane, OBE; French (b. British) actress and singer; b. 14 Dec. 1946, London; d. of David Birkin and Judy Campbell; m. John Barry (divorced); one d.; one d. with the late Serge Gainsbourg (Charlotte Gainsbourg); one s. with Jacques Doillon; Chevalier des Arts et des Lettres; Gold Leaf Award Canada 1968, Triomphe du cinéma 1969, 1973, Victoire de la musique (for best female singer) 1992. *Theatre includes:* Carving a Statue 1964, Passion Flower Hotel 1965, La Fausse suivante 1985, L'Aide-Mémoire 1993, Créatrice et Interprète de Oh! pardon tu dormais 1999, Electra by Sophocles. *Films include:* The Knack 1965, Blow Up 1966, Les Chemins de Katmandou 1969, Je t'aime moi non plus 1976, Mort sur le Nil 1978, Jane B par Agnès V 1988, Oh pardon! Tu dormais 1992, Noir comme le souvenir 1995, La fille d'un soldat ne pleure jamais 1999, The Last September 2000, Ceci est mon corps 2001, Reines d'un jour 2001, Merci Docteur Rey 2002, Mariées mais pas trop 2003, Boxes (actor and dir) 2007. *Recordings include:* albums: Je T'aime (Beautiful Love) 1970, Lolita Go Home 1975, Ex Fan des Sixties 1978, Baby Alone in Babylone 1983, Lost Song 1987, Au Bataclan 1987, Je Suis Venue Te Dire Que Je M'en Vais 1992, Jane B., Vol. 1 1993, Concert Integral a l'Olympia 1997, Je T'aime Moi Non Plus 1998, Quoi Generique TV 1998, Jane Birkin Coffret 1998, Ballade de Johnny 1998, A la Legere 1998, Jane en Concert au Japan 2001, Jane Birkin et Serge Gainsbourg 2001, Arabesque 2003, Rendez-Vous 2004, Fictions 2006, Enfants d'Hiver 2008; singles: (songs by Serge Gainsbourg) C'est la vie qui veut ça, La Baigneuse de Brighton, Je t'aime moi non plus (Le Métier trophy 1970), Di doo dah, Le Canari est sur le balcon, Baby Song, Si ça peut te consoler, Tu n'es pas le premier garçon, Lolita Go Home, Love for Sale, La Ballade, Ex-fan des sixties, Baby Alone in Babylone (Grand Prix du disque, Acad. Charles-Cros). *Publication:* Oh pardon! Tu dormais 1999. *Address:* Les Visiteurs du Soir, 40 rue de la Folie Regnault, Paris 75011, France (office). *Telephone:* 1-44-93-02-02 (office). *Fax:* 1-44-93-04-40 (office). *E-mail:* david@visiteurdusoir.com (office). *Website:* www.janebirkin.com (office).

BIRKIN, Sir (John) Derek, Kt, TD, CBIM; British business executive; b. 30 Sept. 1929; s. of Noah Birkin and Rebecca Birkin (née Stranks); m. Sadie Smith 1952; one s. one d.; ed Hemsworth Grammar School; Man. Dir Velmar Ltd 1966–67, Nairn Williamson Ltd 1967–70; Deputy Chair. and Man. Dir Tunnel Holdings Ltd 1970–75, Chair. and Man. Dir 1975–82; Dir Rio Tinto-Zinc (then RTZ) Corpn 1982–96, Deputy Chief Exec. 1983–85, Chief Exec. and Deputy Chair. 1985–91, Chair. 1991–96; Chair. Watmoughs (Holdings) PLC 1996–98; Dir Smiths Industries Ltd 1977–84, British Gas Corpn 1982–85, George Wimpey PLC 1984–92, CRA Ltd (Australia) 1985–94, Rio Algom Ltd (Canada) 1985–92, The Merchants Trust PLC 1986–99, British Steel PLC (formerly British Steel Corpn) 1986–92, Barclays Bank PLC and Barclays PLC 1990–95, Merck & Co. Inc. (USA) 1992–2000, Carlton Communications PLC 1992–2001, Unilever PLC 1993–2000; mem. Council, Industrial Soc. 1985–97, UK Top Salaries Review Body 1986–89; Trustee, Royal Opera House 1990–93, Dir 1993–97; Hon. LLD (Bath) 1998. *Leisure interests:* opera, rugby, cricket.

BIRLA, Basant Kumar; Indian business executive; *Chairman, Century Textiles and Industries Ltd;* b. 16 Feb. 1921; s. of Ghanshyam Das Birla and Mahadevi; m. Sarala Birla 1942; one s. two d.; Chair. Century Textiles and Industries Ltd, BK Birla Group, Century Enka Ltd, Jay Shree Tea and Industries Ltd, Kesoram Industries and Cotton Mills Ltd, Bharat Commerce and Industries Ltd; Gov. Birla Inst. of Tech., Krishnarpan Charity Trust, BK Birla Inst. of Eng and Tech., Pilani; Order of Menelik II (Ethiopia). *Publications include:* Svantah Sukhaya (autobiography), and numerous others. *Leisure interests:* music, art, literature, photography, sports. *Address:* Century Textiles and Industries Ltd, Century Bhavan, Dr Annie Besant Road, Worli, Mumbai, 400 030, India (office). *Telephone:* (22) 24957000 (office). *Fax:* (22) 24309491 (office). *E-mail:* info@birlacentury.com (office). *Website:* www.birlacentury.com (office).

BIRLA, Kumar Mangalam, BCom, MBA; Indian business executive; *Chairman, Aditya Birla Group;* b. 14 June 1967, Jeddah, Saudi Arabia; s. of Aditya Vikram Birla; m. Neerja Birla; one s. two d.; ed London Business School, UK; Chair. Aditya Birla Group 1997–; Hindalco Industries Ltd (aluminium manufacturing subsidiary); apptd mem. Governing Bd Securities and Exchange Bd of India 1998, also served as Chair. Cttees on Corp. Governance and Insider Trading; mem. Cen. Bd of Dirs Reserve Bank of India; mem. Bd Tata Iron and Steel Co., Larsen & Toubro, Maruti Udyog Ltd; mem. Bd of Dirs G.D. Birla Medical Research and Educ. Foundation; mem. Bd of Govs Birla Inst. of Tech. and Science, Indian Inst. of Man.; mem. London Business School's Asia Pacific Advisory Bd; has served on various professional and regulatory bds including Prime Minister's Advisory Council on Trade and Industry, Nat. Council of Confed. of Indian Industry, Apex Advisory

Council of Associated Chambers of Commerce and Industry of India, Govt of UP's High Powered Investment Task Force; Hon. Fellow, London Business School, All India Man. Asscn; Hon. DLitt (Banaras Hindu Univ.); Dr hc (G. D. Pant Univ. of Agriculture & Technology) 2008, (SRM Univ.) 2008, (Visvesvaraya Technological Univ., Karnataka) 2012; Man. Man of the Year, Bombay Man. Asscn 2000, Golden Peacock Nat. Award for Business Leadership, Inst. of Dirs 2001, Mumbai Pradesh Youth Congress's Rajiv Gandhi Award for Business Excellence and Contribution to the Country 2001, Outstanding Business Man of the Year, Nat. HRD Network, Pune 2001, Qimpro Platinum Standard Award, Qimpro Foundation 2002, Business Leader of the Year, Economic Times Awards 2003, 2013, Lakshya–Business Visionary Award, Nat. Inst. of Industrial Eng 2003, Young Achiever Award, Indo-American Soc. 2003, Ernst & Young Indian Entrepreneur of the Year 2005, Udyog Ratna, PHD Chamber of Commerce and Industry 2005, Global Indian Leader of the Year, NDTV Profit 2007, AIMA–JRD Tata Corp. Leadership Award 2008, Business Leader of the Year, All India Man. Asscn 2010, GQ Business Leader of the Year Award, Condé Nast India Pvt. Ltd 2011, Entrepreneur of the Year, Flagship Award, Forbes India Leadership Awards 2012, NASSCOM's Global Business Leader Award 2012. *Address:* Aditya Birla Centre, 1st Floor, S. K. Ahire Marg, Worli, Mumbai 400 030, India (office). *Telephone:* (22) 66525000 (office). *Fax:* (22) 66525741 (office). *E-mail:* pragnya.ram@adityabirla.com (office). *Website:* www.adityabirla.com (office).

BIRLA, Sudarshan Kumar; Indian fmr business executive; *Chairman Emeritus, S K Birla Group;* fmr Chair. Mysore Cement Ltd, Birla Eastern Ltd, Birla Metals Ltd, Digjam Ltd; fmr Chair. SK Birla Group, currently Chair. Emer.; fmr Dir Century Textiles and Industries Ltd, Birla Brothers Pvt. Ltd.

BIRLE, James Robb, BS; American insurance industry executive (retd); b. 25 Jan. 1936, Philadelphia, Pa; ed Villanova Univ.; numerous positions at General Electric Co. 1958–1988, including Sr Vice-Pres. and Group Exec.; Gen. Pnr, Blackstone Group 1988–94, CEO Collins & Aikman Group 1988–94; Founder and Chair. Resolute Pnrs LLC (pvt. investment firm) 1994–; mem. Bd of Dirs Mass Mutual Life Insurance Co. 1992, Chair. 2005–07, Lead Dir 2007–08; mem. Bd of Dirs IKON Office Solutions, Conn. Health and Educ. Facilities Authority, Transparency Int.; Trustee, Villanova Univ. 1993–; Hon. DEng (Villanova Univ.) 1992; J. Stanley Morehouse Memorial Award, Villanova Univ. 1988. *Address:* 2 Pine Lane East, Village of Golf, FL 33436, USA (office).

BIRNBAUM, Daniel, PhD; Swedish author, art critic, philosopher, teacher and curator; *Rector, Städelschule Art Academy, Frankfurt am Main;* b. 1963, Stockholm; ed Stockholm Univ.; spent childhood and youth in Geneva, Vienna, Boston and Stockholm; art critic at Expressen and Dagens Nyheter daily newspapers, Stockholm 1988; Lecturer in Philosophy, Stockholm Univ. 1990–95; Lecturer in Art Theory, Univ. Coll. of Art, Craft and Design, Stockholm 1995–97; Founding mem. Artnode Stockholm (internet site for art and theory and venue for art and tech.) 1996; Dir IASPIS (Int. Artists Studio Programme in Sweden) 1997–2000; Contributing Ed., Artforum, New York 1999; Rector Städelschule Art Acad., Frankfurt am Main, Germany 2001–; Dir Kunsthalle Portikus, Frankfurt am Main 2001–; Int. Bd mem. Yokohama Triennial of Contemporary Art 2001–; Manifesta Foundation, Amsterdam 2002–. *Publications:* Defining Contemporary Art: 25 Years in 200 Pivotal Artworks 2011. *Address:* Staatliche Hochschule für Bildende Künste, Städelschule, Dürerstrasse 10, 60596 Frankfurt am Main, Germany (office). *Telephone:* (69) 605008-0 (office). *E-mail:* info@staedelschule.com (office). *Website:* www.staedelschule.com (office).

BIRT, Baron (Life Peer) cr. 2000, of Liverpool in the County of Merseyside; **John Birt,** Kt, MA, FRTS; British business executive; *Adviser, Terra Firma;* b. 10 Dec. 1944, Liverpool; s. of Leo Vincent and Ida Birt; m. 1st Jane Frances Lake 1965 (divorced 2006); one s. one d.; m. 2nd Eithne Victoria Wallis CB 2006; ed St Mary's Coll., Liverpool, St Catherine's Coll., Oxford; Television Producer of Nice Time 1968–69, Jt Ed. World in Action 1969–70, Producer The Frost Programme 1971–72, Exec. Producer Weekend World 1972–74, Head of Current Affairs, London Weekend Television (LWT) 1974–77, Co-Producer The Nixon Interviews 1977, Controller of Features and Current Affairs, LWT 1977–81, Dir of Programmes 1982–87; Deputy Dir-Gen. BBC 1987–92, Dir-Gen. 1992–2000; Vice-Pres. Royal TV Soc. 1994–2000 (Fellow 1989); mem. Media Law Group 1983–94, Working Party on New Technologies 1981–83, Broadcasting Research Unit, Exec. Cttee 1983–87, Int. Museum of TV and Radio, New York 1994–2000, Opportunity 2000 Target Team, Business in the Community 1991–98; Adviser to Prime Minister on criminal justice 2000–01, Strategy Adviser 2001–05; Adviser to McKinsey and Co. Inc. 2000–05; Adviser, Terra Firma (pvt. equity firm) 2005–, Capgemini UK plc 2006–10; Chair. Lynx Capital Ventures 2000–04, WRG Holdings 2006, Infinis Ltd 2006–07 (after sale of WRG waste disposal business), Maltby Capital Ltd 2007–10; mem. Bd of Dirs (non-exec.) PayPal (Europe) Ltd 2004– (Chair. 2010–), Eutelsat 2006–; Visiting Fellow, Nuffield Coll., Oxford 1991–99; Hon. Fellow, Univ. of Wales, Cardiff 1997, St Catherine's Coll., Oxford 1992; Hon. DLitt (Liverpool John Moores) 1992, (City) 1998, (Bradford) 1999, (Westminster) 2010; Emmy Award US Nat. Acad. of Television, Arts and Sciences. *Publication:* The Harder Path – The Autobiography. *Leisure interest:* walking, football, cinema. *Address:* House of Lords, London, SW1A 0PW, England.

BIRTWISTLE, Sir Harrison, Kt, CH; British composer; b. 1934, Accrington, Lancs.; m. Sheila Birtwistle 1958; three s.; ed Royal Manchester Coll. of Music and Royal Acad. of Music, London; Dir of Music, Cranborne Chase School 1962–65; Visiting Fellow, Princeton Univ. (Harkness Int. Fellowship) 1966; Cornell Visiting Prof. of Music, Swarthmore Coll., Pa 1973–74; Slee Visiting Prof., State Univ. of New York, Buffalo 1975; Assoc. Dir Nat. Theatre 1975–88; Composer-in-Residence, London Philharmonic Orchestra 1993–98; Henry Purcell Prof. of Composition, King's Coll., London 1994–2001; Visiting Prof., Univ. of Alabama at Tuscaloosa 2001–02; Dir of Contemporary Music, RAM 1996–2001; works have been widely performed at major festivals in Europe including the Venice Biennale, the Int. Soc. of Contemporary Music Festivals in Vienna and Copenhagen, the Warsaw Autumn Festival and at Aldeburgh, Cheltenham and Edinburgh; co-f. (with Sir Peter Maxwell Davies) The Pierrot Players; Hon. FRNCM 1990 Chevalier, Ordre des Arts et des Lettres; Siemens Prize 1995; Grawemeyer Award, Univ. of Louisville 1987, Ivor Novello Award for Classical Music 2006. *Operatic and dramatic works:* The Mask of the Goat (cantata) 1965, Punch and Judy (one-act opera) 1966, The Visions of Francesco Petrarca (sonnets for baritone

and orchestra) 1966, Monodrama for soprano, speaker, ensemble 1967, Down by the Greenwood Side (dramatic pastoral) 1969, The Mask of Orpheus 1973, Ballet, Frames, Pulses and Interruptions 1977, Bow Down 1977, Yan Tan Tethera 1983, Gawain 1988, The Second Mrs Kong 1992, The Last Supper 1999. *Orchestral works:* Chorales for Orchestra 1962, Three Movements with Fanfares 1964, Nomos 1968, An Imaginary Landscape 1971, The Triumph of Time 1970, Grimethorpe Aria for Brass Band 1973, Melencolia I 1976, Silbury Air for small orchestra 1977, Still Movement for 13 solo strings 1984, Earth Dances 1985, Endless Parade for trumpet, vibraphone, strings 1987, Ritual Fragment 1990, Antiphonies for piano and orchestra 1992, The Cry of Anubis for tuba and orchestra 1994, Panic 1995, Night's Black Bird (British Composer Award, British Acad. of Composers and Songwriters 2005), Concerto for Violin and Orchestra (British Composer Award, British Acad. of Composers and Songwriters 2012) 2011. *Choral works and narration:* Monody for Corpus Christi for soprano and ensemble 1959, A Description of the Passing Year for chorus 1963, Entr'actes and Sappho Fragments for soprano and ensemble 1964, Carmen Paschale for chorus and organ 1965, Ring a Dumb Clarion for soprano, clarinet, percussion 1965, Cantata for soprano and ensemble 1969, Nenia on the Death of Orpheus for soprano and ensemble 1970, The Fields of Sorrow for two sopranos, chorus, ensemble 1971, Meridian for mezzo, chorus, ensemble 1970, Epilogue: Full Fathom Five for baritone and ensemble 1972, arrangement for 16 solo voices and three instruments 1979, On the Sheer Threshold of the Night for four solo voices and 12-part chorus 1980, White and Light for soprano and ensemble 1989, Four Poems by Jaan Kaplinski for soprano and ensemble 1991, The Woman and the Hare, for soprano, reciter and ensemble 1999, Ring Dance of the Nazarene (British Composer Award, British Acad. of Composers and Songwriters 2005). *Instrumental works:* Refrains and Choruses for wind quintet 1957, The World is Discovered for ensemble 1960, Tragoedia for ensemble 1965, Three Lessons in a Frame 1967, Chorales from a Toyshop 1967, Verses for Ensembles 1969, Ut heremita solus, arrangement of Ockeghem 1969, Hoquetus David, arr of Machaut 1969, Medusa for ensemble 1970, Chronometer for 8-track tape 1971, For O For O the Hobby Horse is Forgot for six percussion 1976, Carmen Arcadiae Mechanicae Perpetuum for ensemble 1977, Pulse Sampler 1980, Clarinet Quintet 1980, Secret Theatre 1984, Words Overheard 1985, Fanfare for Will 1987, Salford Toccata for brass band and bass drum 1988, Nine Movements for string quartet 1991, An Uninterrupted Endless Melody for oboe and piano 1991, Five Distances for five instruments 1992, Tenebrae for soprano and ensemble 1992, Night for soprano and ensemble 1992, Movement for string quartet 1992, Slow Frieze for piano and 13 instruments 1996, Pulse, Shadows 1997, Harrison's Clocks for piano 1998, The Silk House Tattoo for two trumpets and percussion 1998, Three Niedecker Verses for soprano and cello 1998, Exody 1998, The Axe Manual 2000, The Shadow of Night 2001, Theseus Game 2002, The Io Passion 2004, Night's Black Bird 2004, Orpheus Elegies 2004, The Tree of Strings (Royal Philharmonic Soc. Award for Best Chamber-Scale Composition 2009) 2007, The Minotaur 2008, Tree of Strings 2008, The Corridor 2009, Angel Fighter 2010, Piano Trio 2011, Oboe Quartet 2011. *Theatre:* music for Hamlet, Nat. Theatre 1975, The Oresteia, Nat. Theatre 1986, The Bacchae, Nat. Theatre 2002. *Address:* Allied Artists Agency, 42 Montpelier Square, London, SW7 1JZ, England (office).

BIRULÉS Y BERTRÁN, Ana Maria, PhD; Spanish politician and fmr business executive; b. 28 June 1954, Gerona; ed Univ. of Barcelona, Univ. of California, Berkeley; worked for regional Govt of Catalonia; Banco Sabadell 1990–97, negotiated acquisition of Banco NatWest 1996; Man. Dir Retevisión 1997–2000; Minister of Science and Tech. 2000–04; Bd mem. Circulo de Economia de Barcelona. *Address:* c/o Ministry of Science and Technology, Paseo de la Castellana 160, 28071 Madrid, Spain.

BISCHOFF, Manfred, Dr rer. pol; German business executive; *Chairman of the Supervisory Board, Daimler AG;* b. 22 April 1942, Calw; ed Univs of Tübingen and Heidelberg; Asst Prof. of Econ. Politics and Int. Trade, Alfred-Weber-Inst., Univ. of Heidelberg 1968–76; joined Daimler-Benz AG 1976, Project Co-ordinator for Mercedes Benz Cross Country Cars, Corp. Subsidiaries, M&A Dept 1976–81, Int. Products, M&A, Finance Dept 1981–88 (Vice-Pres. Finance Cos and Corp. Subsidiaries), mem. Bd of Man. and Chief Financial Officer Mercedes do Brazil, São Paulo 1988–89, Deutsche Aerospace AG (later Daimler-Benz Aerospace AG) 1989–95, mem. Bd of Man. Daimler-Benz AG (later DaimlerChrysler AG then Daimler AG) 1995–2003, Chair. Supervisory Bd 2007–, also Chair. Presidential Cttee; mem. Bd of Man., Pres. and CEO DASA (now European Aeronautic Defence and Space Co.—EADS) 1995–2000, Chair. EADS 2000–09; mem. Bd of Man. Mitsubishi Motors Corpn 2000–03; Chair. Supervisory Bd MTU Aero Engines, Munich 2000–03; mem. several supervisory bds, including Royal KPN NV, SMS GmbH (Chair.), Unicredit SpA, Voith AG (Chair.); Pres. European Asscn of Aerospace Industries 1995–96, Fed. of German Aerospace Industries 1996–2000; Verdienstkreuz (First class) der Bundesrepublik Deutschland 2011, Bayerischer Verdienstorden. *Address:* Daimler AG, 70546 Stuttgart, Germany (office). *Telephone:* (711) 170 (office). *Fax:* (711) 1722244 (office). *E-mail:* dialog@daimler.com (office). *Website:* www.daimler.com (office).

BISCHOFF, Sir Winfried Franz Wilhelm (Win), Kt, BCom; British/German investment banker; *Chairman, Financial Reporting Council;* b. 10 May 1941, Aachen, Germany; s. of the late Paul Helmut Bischoff and Hildegard Bischoff (née Kühne); m. Rosemary Elizabeth Leathers 1972; two s.; ed Marist Brothers, Johannesburg and Univ. of the Witwatersrand; with Int. Dept, Chase Manhattan Bank 1962–63; joined Company Finance Div., J. Henry Schroder & Co. Ltd, London 1966, Man. Dir Schroders Asia Ltd, Hong Kong 1971–82, Dir J. Henry Schroder & Co. Ltd 1978–94 (Chair. 1983–94), Dir Schroders PLC 1983 (Group Chief Exec. 1984–95), Chair. Schroders PLC 1995–2000, then Citigroup Europe (after acquisition of Schroders by Citigroup) 2000–07, interim CEO Citigroup Nov.–Dec. 2007, Chair. Citigroup 2007–09; Chair. Lloyds Banking Group 2009–14; Chair. Financial Reporting Council 2014–; mem. Nat. Advisory Bd of UK Career Acad. Foundation (Chair. –2010), Akbank International Advisory Bd; current Chair. of Advisory Council, The CityUK; Dir (non-exec.) Cable and Wireless PLC 1991– (Deputy Chair. 1995–2003), The McGraw Hill Cos 1999–, Land Securities PLC 1999–2008, Eli Lilly and Co., Indianapolis 2000–, IFIL, Finanziaria di Partecipazioni SpA, Italy 2001–04, Siemens Holdings PLC 2001–03, AkBank, Turkey 2007–08; Johnson Hon. Fellow, St Anne's Coll. Oxford 2001; Dr hc (City Univ.) 2000. *Leisure interests:* opera, music, golf. *Address:* Financial Reporting

Council, Fifth Floor, Aldwych House, 71–91 Aldwych, London, WC2B 4HN, England (office). *Telephone:* (20) 7492-2300 (office); (20) 7492-2301 (office). *E-mail:* enquiries@frc.org.uk (office). *Website:* www.frc.org.uk (office).

BISH-JONES, Trevor Charles, BSc (Pharm); British business executive; *Chief Operating Officer, United Electronics Company (eXtra);* b. 23 April 1960; m. Amanda Bish-Jones 1991; two d.; ed Varndean Grammar School, Portsmouth School of Pharmacy; research chemist, The Tosco Corpn, Colo 1980–81; Store Man. Boots PLC 1981, rising to Sr Man. position –1994; various man. positions with Dixons Group 1994–2002, including Commercial Dir PC World 1994–95, Marketing Dir Dixons PLC 1995, Man. Dir The Link, Man. Dir Dixons, Dir Currys 2000–02; CEO Woolworths Group PLC 2002–08; moved to Middle East 2010; COO United Electronics Co. (also known as eXtra) 2010–; part Owner and Creator of Mypeoplebiz.com (online recruitment platform); has held non-exec. roles at Royal London (Financial Services) 2006–10, ConcertLive (Media) 2009–; Gov. Ashridge Business School; Dir (non-exec.), Royal London Mutual Insurance Soc. Ltd 2005–10. *Leisure interests:* horse riding, motorbikes. *Address:* United Electronics Company, PO Box 76688, Khobar 31952, Saudi Arabia (office). *Telephone:* (3) 858-1532 (office). *Fax:* (3) 858-1653 (office). *Website:* www.extrastores.com (office); www .mypeoplebiz.com.

BISHARA, Shukri, BEcons, MEconSc; Palestinian banker and politician; *Minister of Finance;* ed American Univ. of Beirut, Univ. Coll. London, UK; fmr Chair. AIMS (financial advisory co.), Damascus; fmr Vice-Chair. Palestine Electric Co.; fmr CEO Housing Bank for Trade and Finance; numerous high-level positions within the Arab Bank, including Chief Banking Officer, Sr Exec. Vice-Pres. and country head for Palestine and France, also Regional Man., Europe-Arab Bank; fmr Asst Group Head for Middle East and N Africa, Fidelity Bank, USA; fmr Chair. Palestine Investment Fund; Minister of Finance 2013–. *Address:* Ministry of Finance, POB 795, Sateh Marhaba, al-Birah, Ramallah, Palestinian Territories (office). *Telephone:* (2) 2825255 (office). *Fax:* (2) 2848900 (office). *E-mail:* mof@mof .ps (office). *Website:* www.mof.gov.ps (office).

BISHOP, Bronwyn Kathleen; Australian solicitor and politician; *Speaker, House of Representatives;* b. (Bronwyn Kathleen Setright), 19 Oct. 1942, Sydney; d. of Kathleen Congreve; m. Alan Bishop (divorced); two d.; ed Univ. of Sydney; early acting role in TV drama series Divorce Court 1960s; practising solicitor 1967–; writer and producer Law for Mr and Mrs Everyman (radio series) during early 1970s; mem. Senate for New South Wales 1987–94 (resgnd); mem. House of Reps (Parl.) for Mackellar, NSW 1994–, Speaker 2013–; Minister for Defence Industry, Science and Personnel 1996–98, for Aged Care 1998–2001; Patron Opera Australia; mem. Liberal Party of Australia, Pres. Balmoral Br. 1973–79, NSW Br. 1985–87. *Address:* PO Box 6022, Parliament House, Canberra, ACT 2600, Australia (office). *Telephone:* (2) 6277-4382 (office). *E-mail:* Bronwyn.Bishop.MP@ aph.gov.au (office). *Website:* www.aph.gov.au/house (office).

BISHOP, James Drew, BA; British journalist; b. 18 June 1929, London; s. of the late Sir Patrick Bishop and Vera Drew; m. Brenda Pearson 1959; two s.; ed Haileybury Coll., Hertford and Corpus Christi Coll., Cambridge; reporter, Northampton Chronicle 1953; editorial staff of The Times (London) 1954–70, Foreign Corresp. 1957–64, Foreign News Ed. 1964–66, Features Ed. 1966–70; Ed. The Illustrated London News 1971–87, Newsweek Int. Diary 1977–86; Editorial Dir Orient Express, Connections and Natural World Magazines 1981–94; Ed.-in-Chief, Illustrated London News Publs 1987–94; contrib. to The Annual Register 1960–88, mem. Advisory Bd 1970–; Chair. Editorial Bd Natural World 1981–97, Asscn of British Eds 1987–95; Dir Int. Thomson Publishing Co. 1980–85; Chair. Nat. Heritage 1998– (Trustee 1994–). *Publications:* A Social History of Edwardian Britain 1977, Social History of the First World War 1982, The Story of The Times (with O. Woods) 1983, Illustrated Counties of England (ed.) 1985, The Sedgwick Story 1998. *Leisure interests:* reading, walking. *Address:* Black Fen, Stoke by Nayland, Suffolk, CO6 4QD, England (home). *Telephone:* (1206) 262315 (office). *Fax:* (1206) 262876 (office). *E-mail:* jamesbishop3@tiscali.co.uk (home).

BISHOP, John Michael, MD; American scientist, academic and university administrator; b. 22 Feb. 1936; m. 1959; two c.; ed Gettysburg Coll. and Harvard Univ.; intern in internal medicine Mass. Gen. Hosp., Boston 1962–63, Resident 1963–64; Research Assoc. in Virology, NIH, Washington, DC 1964–66, Sr Investigator 1966–68, Asst Prof. to Assoc. Prof. 1968–72; Prof. of Microbiology and Immunology, Univ. of Calif. Medical Center, San Francisco 1972–, Prof. of Biochemistry and Biophysics 1982–, Univ. Prof. 1994–2000, Chancellor 1998–2009 (now Chancellor Emer.), Dir G. W. Hooper Research Foundation 1981–; Gairdner Foundation Int. Award 1984, Medal of Honor, American Cancer Soc. 1984, Nobel Prize for Physiology or Medicine 1989, and many other awards and distinctions. *Address:* UCSF School of Medicine, Department Microbiology and Immunology, 513 Parnassus Avenue, San Francisco, CA 94143-0402, USA (office). *Telephone:* (415) 476-5158 (office). *E-mail:* bishop@cgl.ucsf.edu (office). *Website:* hooper.ucsf .edu/hooper/bishop_lab.html (office).

BISHOP-KOVACEVICH, Stephen (see Kovacevich, Stephen).

BISIGNANI, Giovanni, LLM; Italian airline executive; *Chairman, Council on Aviation, Travel and Tourism, World Economic Forum;* b. 1946, Rome; m.; one d.; ed Univ. of Rome and Harvard Business School; Sr Asst Prof. in Public Law, Univ. of Rome 1969; with First Nat. City Bank, New York 1970; research and econ. planning, EFIM, Rome 1973–76; Asst to Pres. ENI, Rome 1976–79; Chief of Staff, IRI, Rome 1979–89, Corp. Sr Vice-Pres. (Foreign Affairs) 1981–83, Corp. Exec. Vice-Pres. and Head of Foreign Affairs 1983–89, IRI Rep. on Bd of Finsider, Italstat, SME, Fincantieri 1979–89; Man. Dir and CEO Alitalia 1989–94; Pres. Tirrenia di Navigazione SpA 1994–98; Man. Dir and CEO SM Logistics–Gruppo Serra Merzario SpA 1998–2000; CEO Opodo (European airline-owned online travel agency) 2001–02; Founding mem. Exec. Cttee Int. Air Transport Asscn 1989–94, Dir-Gen. and CEO 2002–11; Chair. Asscn of European Airlines 1992, Chair. Galileo International (global computer reservation system group) 1993–94; mem. Advisory Bd United Technologies 1998–2001; mem. Bd Assolombarda, Milan 1998–2000, NATS Ltd 2002–, SaFran, Air Castle, ILVA (IRI steel co.), Italo-German Chamber of Commerce, Inst. for Int. Affairs; Visiting Prof. School of Engineering, Cranfield Univ., UK; Hon. DSc (Cranfield Univ.). *Publications:* articles on law, economic and financial subjects in professional publs. *Leisure*

interests: golf, tennis, riding. *Address:* 12–14 De Vere Gardens, London, W8 5AE, England (office). *E-mail:* bisignanig@gmail.com (home). *Website:* www.iata.org.

BIŠKUPIĆ, Božo, LLB, MA; Croatian lawyer and politician; b. 26 April 1938, Mala Mlaka; m.; one d.; f. Biškupić Collection 1964; worked as lawyer in Zagreb 1974–80; collated and ed monographs in the Graphics Inst. in Zagreb and fine art in the Nat. and Univ. Library; f. Vukovar Museum in Exile and project on contemporary Croatian art for the Museum of Croatian Art, Mostar; mem. Croatian Democratic Union (HDZ) 1990–; Dir Republican Fund for Culture, Ministry of Culture 1990–92; Asst Minister of Culture and Educ. 1993–83; Deputy Mayor of Zagreb 1993–95; Minister of Culture 1995–2000, 2003–10; mem. Parl. 2000–; Vladimir Nazor Award 1993. *Leisure interests:* music, chess. *Address:* c/o Ministry of Culture, 10000 Zagreb, Runjaninova 2, Croatia.

BISSET, Jacqueline; British actress; b. (Winnifred Jacqueline Fraser-Bisset), 13 Sept. 1944, Weybridge, Surrey, England; ed French Lycée, London; Chevalier, Légion d'honneur 2010. *Films include:* The Knack 1965, Two for the Road 1967, Casino Royale 1967, The Sweet Ride 1968, The Detective 1968, Bullitt 1968, The First Time 1969, Airport 1970, The Grasshopper 1970, The Mephisto Waltz 1971, Believe in Me 1971, The Life and Times of Judge Roy Bean 1972, Stand Up and Be Counted 1972, The Thief Who Came to Dinner 1973, Day for Night 1973, Murder on the Orient Express 1974, The Spiral Staircase 1974, End of the Game 1974, St Ives 1975, The Deep 1976, Le Magnifique 1977, Sunday Woman 1977, The Greek Tycoon 1978, Secrets 1978, Too Many Chefs 1978, I Love You, I Love You Not 1979, When Time Ran Out 1980, Rich and Famous 1981, Inchon 1981, Class 1982, Under the Volcano 1983, Forbidden 1986, Choices 1986, High Season 1988, Scenes from the Class Struggle in Beverly Hills 1989, Wild Orchid 1989, La Cérémonie 1995, The Maid, A Judgement in Stone, Once You Meet a Stranger 1996, The Honest Courtesan 1996, Let the Devil Wear Black 1998, Dangerous Beauty 1998, Joan of Arc 1999, In the Beginning 2000, Jesus 2000, Britannic 2000, The Sleepy Time Gal 2001, Sundance Holiday Gift Pack 2003, Latter Days 2003, Swing 2004, Fascination 2004, Domino 2005, Save the Last Dance 2 2006, Death in Love 2008, Two Jacks 2012. *Television includes:* Nip/Tuck (series) 2006, Carolina Moon (film) 2007, An Old Fashioned Thanksgiving (film) 2008, The Eastmans (film) 2009, An Old Fashioned Christmas (film) 2010, Rizzoli & Isles (series) 2011, Dancing on the Edge (series) (Golden Globe Award for Best Supporting Actress in a Series, Mini-series, or TV Movie 2014) 2013. *Address:* c/o Annabel Karouby, Agence Cinéart, 28 rue de Mogador, 75009 Paris, France (office). *E-mail:* a.karouby@cineart.fr (office). *Website:* www.cineart.fr (office).

BISSON, Thomas Noel, PhD; American historian and academic; *Henry Charles Lea Professor Emeritus of Medieval History, Harvard University;* b. 30 March 1931, New York, NY; s. of Thomas A. Bisson and Faith W. Bisson; m. Margaretta C. Webb 1962; two d.; ed Port Washington High School, New York, Haverford Coll., Univ. of California, Berkeley and Princeton Univ.; Instructor in History, Amherst Coll. 1957–60; Asst Prof., Brown Univ. 1960–65; Assoc. Prof., Swarthmore Coll. 1965–67; Assoc. Prof., Univ. of California, Berkeley 1967–69, Prof. 1969–87; Prof., Harvard Univ. 1986–, Henry Charles Lea Prof. of Medieval History 1988–2005, Emer. 2005–, Chair. Dept of History 1991–95; mem. American Philosophical Soc., American Acad. of Arts and Sciences; Fellow, Medieval Acad. of America (Pres. 1994–95), Royal Historical Soc., British Acad., Institut d'Estudis Catalans etc.; Creu de Sant Jordi (Generalitat of Catalonia) 2001; Dr hc (Barcelona) 1991; Guggenheim Fellow 1964–65. *Publications include:* Assemblies and Representation in Languedoc in the Thirteenth Century 1964, Medieval Representative Institutions: Their Origins and Nature 1973, Conservation of Coinage: Monetary Exploitation and its Restraint in France, Catalonia and Aragon (c. AD 1000–c. AD 1225) 1979, Fiscal Accounts of Catalonia under the Early Count-Kings 1151–1213 (two vols) 1985, The Medieval Crown of Aragon: A Short History 1986, Medieval France and Her Pyrenean Neighbors 1989, Tormented Voices: Power, Crisis and Humanity in Rural Catalonia 1140–1200 1998, The Crisis of the Twelfth Century 2009; articles in journals. *Leisure interests:* classical music, English literature. *Address:* 21 Hammond Street, Cambridge, MA 02138, USA (home). *Telephone:* (617) 354-0178 (home). *E-mail:* tnbisson@fas.harvard.edu (office). *Website:* www .fas.harvard.edu/~history (office).

BITI, Tendai Laxton; Zimbabwean lawyer and politician; b. 6 Aug. 1966, Dzivarasekwa, Harare; ed Goromonzi High School, Univ. of Zimbabwe Law School; joined Honey and Blackenberg (law firm), Pnr 1992; co-f. Movt for Democratic Change 1999, Sec.-Gen. 2000–05; MP for Harare E 2000–, mem. Cttee on Budget, Finance and Econ. Devt, fmr mem. Parl. Portfolio Cttee on Lands, Agric., Water Devt, Rural Resources and Resettlement, Cttee on Defence and Home Affairs; Minister of Finance 2009–13. *Address:* c/o Ministry of Finance, Private Bag 7703, Causeway, Harare, Zimbabwe (office).

BITOV, Andrei Georgevich; Russian writer; b. 27 May 1937, Leningrad (St. Petersburg); m. Inga Petkevich; one d.; ed Leningrad Mining Inst.; evacuated 1939–44; worked as stevedore and lathe operator 1958–62; Researcher, Leningrad Mining Inst. 1962; started writing 1960; mem. of 'Young Prose' group in 1960s with Vasiliy Aksyonov and Anatoliy Gladilin (q.v.); contrib. to Metropol 1979; Co-founder Russian PEN Centre, Pres. 1992–, Vice-Pres. International PEN 2003–; Hon. Citizen of Yerevan; Chevalier, nat. Ordre des Arts et des Lettres 1993; Dr hc (Yerevan State Univ.) 1997; Andrey Bely Prize (Russia) 1990, Pushkin Prize (Germany), Bunin Award 2006. *Publications include:* The Big Balloon 1963, Such a Long Childhood 1965, A Summer Place 1967, Apothecary Island 1968, Way of Life 1972, Seven Journeys 1976, Days of Man 1976, Pushkin House (Best Foreign Book Prize, Paris 1990) 1978, Sunday (short stories) 1980, A Man in the Landscape 1987, The Flying Monakhov (Russian State Prize 1992) 1990, We Woke Up in a Strange Country 1991, Awaiting Monkeys 1993, The Possessed (Russian State Prize 1997, Northern Palmira Prize 1997) 1995, Empire in Four Dimensions (collected works), (Vols 1–4) 1996, Inevitability of Non-Written 1998, Life in Windy Weather 2000. *Address:* Krasnoprudnaya str. 30/34, Apt 14, 107140 Moscow, Russia. *Telephone:* (495) 209-45-89 (office); (495) 264-12-93 (home).

BITSCH, Hans-Ullrich; German architect, industrial designer and academic; *Professor, Peter Behrens School of Architecture, University of Düsseldorf;* b. 13 June 1946, Essen; s. of Prof. Heinz W. Bitsch and Lore L. Bitsch (née Falldorf); m. Evelyn R. Koch 1981; two s.; ed Saarbrücken, State Coll. of Art, Saarbrücken and Illinois Inst. of Tech.; architect, Univ. of Saarbrücken 1968; Instructor, Int. Inst. of

Design, Washington, DC, USA 1969; Visiting Lecturer, Harrington Inst., Chicago, Ill. 1970–71; Prof., Dept of Architecture, Univ. of Düsseldorf 1972–; Pres. German Inst. of Interior Architects 1977–82; Visiting Prof., Univ. of Texas 1981; Prof., Univ. of Naples 1997–; Pres. Professor Bitsch & Assocs (design and architectural office), Düsseldorf; Pres. World Congress of Int. Fed. of Internal Designers, Hamburg 1983; several awards for architecture and design. *Publications:* Menschengerechte Gestaltung des Kassenarbeitsplatzes 1978, Farbe und Industrie-Design 1982, Design und Formentwicklung von Stuhlen 1988, Visuelle Wahrnehmung in Architektur und Design 1989, Projekt Hotel 1992, Architectural Visions for Europe 1994, Stilströmungen 1998, Studien aus dem Architekturbüro 1999. *Leisure interests:* skiing, sailing, photography. *Address:* Peter Behrens School of Architecture, Room A1.41, Department of Applied Sciences, University of Düsseldorf, Georg-Glock-Strasse 15, 40474 Düsseldorf (office); Kaiser-Wilhelm-Ring 23, Rive Gauche, 40545 Düsseldorf, Germany. *Telephone:* (211) 4351122 (office); (211) 95449000. *Fax:* (211) 553814 (office). *E-mail:* hans-ulrich.bitsch@fh-duesseldorf.de (office); prof.bitsch@web.de. *Website:* arc.fh-duesseldorf.de (office).

BITTERLICH, Joachim; German/French business executive, consultant and diplomatist (retd) and academic; *Affiliate Professor, Economics, Law and Social Sciences, ESCP Europe, Paris;* b. 10 July 1948, Saarbrücken-Dudweiler; m. 1969; two s. one d.; ed Univ. of Saarbrücken, Ecole Nat. d'Admin; entered Foreign Office 1976; posted to Algiers 1978–81; Perm. Rep. to EC, Brussels 1981–85; Adviser, Pvt. Office of the Minister of Foreign Affairs 1985–87; Head of European Policy Dept, Fed. Chancellor's Office 1987–93; Dir of Foreign Policy, Econ. Co-operation and External Security, Fed. Chancellor's Office and Foreign and Security Policy Adviser to Fed. Chancellor 1993–98; Amb. and Perm. Rep. to N Atlantic Council, Brussels 1998–99; Amb. to Spain 1999–2003; Exec. Vice-Pres. for Int. Affairs, Veolia Environnement, Paris 2003–12, Chair. Veolia Environment Germany 2009–12, mem. Bd of Admin, Veolia Propreté –2012, Veolia Transport –2012, ENA; Affiliate Prof., Econs, Law and Social Sciences, ESCP Europe, Paris 2012–; Pres., Sr Adviser and CEO FDR-Foncière des Régions Paris, EY Paris, Cranemere Frankfurt/New York, HESAM Paris; Vice-Pres. France-China Cttee –2012; mem. Supervisory Bd DEKRA eV, Stuttgart 2014; mem. Bd of Trustees, Friends of Europe; Vice-Pres. Notre Europe; mem. Deutsche Gesellschaft für Auswärtige Politik; Assoc. mem. IISS, London, Euro 50 Group, Atlantik-Brücke, Berlin, Boao-Forum (China), People for Global Transformation (think tank), New Delhi and others; numerous decorations and awards, including Hon. CBE 1992, Grosses Silbernes Ehrenzeichen mit Stern (Austria) 1994, Grande Oficial do Ordem de Rio Branco (Brazil) 1995, Officier, Légion d'honneur 1996, Grande Ufficiale dell Ordine al Merito (Italy) 1997, Orden do Infante Dom Enrique (Portugal) 1998, Gran Cruz de la Orden del Mérito Civil (Spain) 1998, Officier des Palmes académiques 1994. *Publications include:* Commentaire du traité de l'Union Européenne 1999, (new edn 2006), L'Europe du futur 2004, France-Allemagne: mission impossible? Comment relancer la construction européenne 2005, Le Futur de la politique énergétique de l'Union européenne: avons-nous besoin d'une Haute Autorité Européenne pour l'énergie 2006, (new edn 2009), EU-Treaties: A Legal Commentary (co-author) 2012; numerous articles in newspapers and journals. *Address:* 4 rue Charles Dickens, 75016 Paris, France (home); Reinhardtstrasse 23, 10117 Berlin, Germany (office). *Telephone:* 1-42-15-16-80 (home); (30) 30882703 (office). *E-mail:* jbitterlich@escpeurope.eu (office); joachim@bitterlich.fr (office). *Website:* www.escpeurope.eu (office).

BIWOTT, Nicholas Kiprono, BA; Kenyan politician; b. 1934, Keiyo Dist; m.; ed Kapsabet Govt African School and Univ. of Melbourne, Australia; served in Ministry of Information and Broadcasting 1959–60; several positions in Cen. Govt 1965–79, including Dist Officer, Ministry of Home Affairs, Asst Sec., Sr Asst Sec., UnderSec. and Deputy Sec.; mem. Parl. 1979–, Minister of Regional Devt, Science and Tech. 1979–82, Minister of Energy 1982–91, Minister of State in the Office of the Pres. 1997, Minister of E African and Regional Co-operation 1998–99, Minister of Tourism, Commerce, and Industry 1999–2001, Minister of Trade and Industry 2001–02; Chair. Kenya African Nat. Union (KANU) 2006. *Address:* Kenya African National Union (KANU), KICC POB 72394, Nairobi, Kenya (office). *Telephone:* (20) 332383 (office).

BIYA, Paul, LenD; Cameroonian politician and head of state; *President;* b. 13 Feb. 1933, Mvomeka'a; m. 1st Jeanne (née Atyam) Biya (deceased); one c.; m. 2nd Chantal Biya 1994; ed Ndem Mission School, Edea and Akono Seminaries, Lycée Leclerc, Yaoundé, Univ. of Paris, Inst. d'Etudes Politiques, Inst. des Hautes Etudes d'Outre-Mer, Paris; Head of Dept of Foreign Devt Aid 1962–63; Dir of Cabinet in Ministry of Nat. Educ., Youth and Culture 1964–65; on goodwill mission to Ghana and Nigeria 1965; Sec.-Gen. in Ministry of Educ., Youth and Culture 1965–67; Dir of Civil Cabinet of Head of State 1967–68; Minister of State, Sec.-Gen. to Pres. 1968–75; Prime Minister 1975–82; Pres. of Cameroon 1982–; Second Vice-Pres., Central Cttee, mem. Union Nationale Camerounaise (UNC), Pres. 1983–85; Pres. Rassemblement Démocratique du Peuple Camerounais (RDPC) 1985–; mem. Politbureau; Hon. Prof. (Univ. of Beijing); Commdr de l'Ordre de la Valeur Camerounaise, Commdr of Nat. Order of FRG and of Tunisia, Great Commdr of the Medal of St George UK, Great Commdr of Order of Nigeria, Grand Cross of Nat. Order of Merit of Senegal, Grand Officier, Légion d'honneur, Grand Collier of the Ordre of Ouissam Mohammadi, Morocco; Dr hc (Univ. of Maryland); Peace Laureate, Centre European Peace Studies 1988. *Publication:* Communal Liberalism 1987. *Address:* Office of the President, Palais de l'Unité, Yaoundé, Cameroon (office). *Telephone:* 2223-4025 (office). *Website:* www.camnet.cm/celcom/homepr.htm (office).

BIYANI, Kishore, BCom, PGD; Indian business executive; *Founder and Group CEO, The Future Group;* b. 9 Aug. 1961, Mumbai; m. Sangita Biyani; two d.; ed HR Coll. of Commerce; Founder, Pantaloon Retail (India) Ltd 1997, Chair. and Man. Dir 2005–; Founder, Big Bazaar 2001; Founder and Group CEO, The Future Group 2006–; Man. Partner and Chair., Indivision Capital Fund 2006–; Man. Dir and Exec. Dir Future Ventures India Ltd 2007–; Non-Exec. Chair., Future Capital Holdings 2006–; Dir Jagran Prakashan Ltd 2005–, Ambit Investment Advisory Co. Ltd 2005–, Fame India Ltd 2010–, Embassy Property Developments Ltd 2010–, Galaxy Entertainment Corpn Ltd –2011; mem. Bd National Innovation Foundation in India, New York Fashion Bd; Ernst & Young Entrepreneur of the Year Award (Services Sector) 2006, Lakshmipat Singhania – IIM Lucknow Young Business Leader Award 2006, CNBC First Generation Entrepreneur of the Year

Award 2006. *Publication:* It Happened in India: The Story of Pantaloons, Big Bazaar, Central and the Great Indian Consumer 2007. *Address:* The Future Group, Future Media (India) Ltd, Future Retail Home Office, Tower C, 7th Floor, 247 Park, LBS Marg, Vikhroli West, Mumbai, Maharashtra, 400 083 (office); Knowledge House, Shyam Nagar, Mumbai, Maharashtra, 200 060, India (office). *Telephone:* (22) 61190000 (office); (22) 30841300 (office). *Fax:* (22) 66442201 (office). *Website:* www.futuregroup.in (office).

BJARNASON, Björn, cand. jur.; Icelandic journalist and politician; *President, Atlantic Treaty Association;* b. 14 Nov. 1944, Reykjavik; s. of Bjarni Benediktsson and Sigríður Björnsdóttir; m. Rut Ingólfsdóttir; two c.; ed Univ. of Iceland; Ed. Almenna bókafélagið (book publr) 1971–74; Foreign News Ed. Vísir 1974; Div. Chief, Prime Minister's Office 1974, Deputy Sec.-Gen. 1975–79; journalist, Morgunblaðið 1979–84, Asst Ed. 1984–91; mem. Parl. (Independence Party) for Reykjavik 1991–2009; Minister of Educ., Science and Culture 1995–2002, of Justice and Ecclesiastical Affairs 2003–09 (resgnd); currently Pres. Atlantic Treaty Asscn; mem. Reykjavik City Council 2002–06; Ed./Publr Evropuvaktin 2010–. *Publications:* The Security of Iceland, Five Roads to Nordic Security 1973, Strategic Factors in the North Atlantic 1977, No Other Option in Security Affairs: The Resurgence of Liberalism 1979, Iceland and Nuclear Weapons, Nuclear Weapons Policy in the North, Copenhagen 1982, From the Prime Ministry to Morgunbladid 1983, Iceland's Security Policy: Vulnerability and Responsibility 1985, Í hita kalda stríðsins (In the Heat of the Cold War) 2001, Hvað er Íslandi fyrir bestu? (What is Best for Iceland?) 2009, Rosabaugur yfir Íslandi (Threatening Baugur over Iceland) 2011; numerous articles. *Leisure interests:* swimming, hiking, books, films and farming. *Address:* Háahlíð 14, 105 Reykjavík, Iceland. *Telephone:* 5512261. *E-mail:* bjorn@bjorn.is. *Website:* www.bjorn.is; www.evropuvaktin.is.

BJARNASON, Gudmundur; Icelandic administrator and fmr politician; b. 9 Oct. 1944, Húsavík; s. of Bjarni Stéfánsson and Jakobina Jónsdóttir; m. Vigdís Gunnarsdóttir; three d.; ed Húsavík Secondary School and Co-operative Coll.; with Co-operative Soc., Húsavík 1963–67; Húsavík Br. Co-operative Bank of Iceland 1967–77, Br. Dir 1977–80; elected mem. Húsavík Town Council 1970, Chair. 1974; mem. Althing 1979–99; Minister of Health and Social Security 1987–91, of Environment and Agric. 1995–99; mem. Althing Appropriation Cttee 1979–87, 1991–95, Vice-Chair. 1983–87; Chair. Cttee on Housing Affairs; Chair. Icelandic Asscn of Heart Patients 2007–; mem. Jt Cttee on public projects; Gen. Man. Housing Financing Fund (ind. govt inst. that grants house mortgages) 1999–2010; Bd Research Council; mem. Icelandic del. to Parl. Ass. of Council of Europe 1991–95. *Address:* Kirkjusandur 5, 105 Reykjavik, Iceland (home). *Telephone:* 553-9898 (home).

BJERREGAARD, Ritt; Danish fmr politician; b. 19 May 1941, Copenhagen; d. of Gudmund Bjerregaard and Rita Bjerregaard; m. Søren Mørch 1966; mem. Parl. 1971–95, 2001–05; Minister of Educ. 1973, 1975–78, for Social Affairs 1979–81; Chair. Parl. Group, Social Democratic Party (SDP) 1981–92, 1987–92, Deputy Chair. 1982–87; Chair. Parl. Cttee on Public Accounts 1990–95; mem. Parl. Ass. of Council of Europe 1990–95; Pres. Danish European Movt 1992–94; Vice-Pres. Parl. Ass. of CSCE 1992–95; Vice-Pres. Socialist Int. Women 1992–94; EU Commr for Environment 1995–99; Minister of Food, Agric. and Fisheries 2000–01; Lord Mayor of Copenhagen 2006–09; mem. Trilateral Comm., Centre for European Policy Studies. *Publications:* several books on politics in general and the role of women in politics. *Leisure interests:* her apple farm, organic farming, the environment. *Address:* Jens Juels Gade 4, 2100 Copenhagen Ø, Denmark (home). *Telephone:* 35430897 (home). *Website:* www.ritt.dk.

BJØERNDALEN, Ole Einar; Norwegian professional biathlete; b. 27 Jan. 1974, Drammen; m. Nathalie Santer 2006; ed Norwegian Ski Gymnas; gold medals (Individual, Sprint), Junior/Youth World Championships, Ruhpolding 1993; winner of eight Olympic gold medals: gold medal (Sprint) in Nagano, Japan 1998, four gold medals (Sprint, Pursuit, Individual, Relay) in Salt Lake City, USA 2002 (became third Olympian to win four gold medals at a single Winter Games), gold medal (Relay) in Vancouver 2010, two gold medals (Sprint and Mixed Relay) in Sochi, Russia 2014; World Championships: gold medals (Team), Pokljuka 1998, (Sprint, Mass Start), Khanty-Mansiysk 2003, (Sprint, Pursuit, Mass Start, Relay), Hochfilzen 2005, (Sprint, Pursuit), Antholz 2007, (Pursuit), Östersund 2008, (Individual, Sprint, Pursuit, Relay), Pyeongchang 2009, (Relay, Mixed Relay), Khanty-Mansiysk 2011, (Relay, Mixed Relay), Ruhpolding 2012, (Relay), Nové Město 2013; World Cup (Overall) titles 1997–98, 2002–03, 2004–05, 2005–06, 2007–08, 2008–09; winner FIS Cross-Country World Cup, Sweden 2006; winner four gold medals Biathlon World Championships, South Korea 2009; most medalled Olympian in the history of the Winter Games, with 13 medals; Norwegian Sportsperson of the Year 2002, Egebergs Ærespris 2002. *Leisure interests:* motorbikes, climbing, off-road, cycling. *Address:* Skavelandsvei 12E, Trondheim 7022, Norway (office). *Website:* www.oleeinarbjoerndalen.com.

BJÖRCK, Anders; Swedish politician; b. 19 Sept. 1944, Nässjö; m. Py-Lotte Björck; one d.; Nat. Pres. Swedish Young Moderates 1966–71; MP 1968–2009; mem. Parl. Ass. Council of Europe 1976–91, Pres. (Speaker) 1989–91; Minister of Defence 1991–94; First Deputy Speaker of Swedish Parl. 1994–2009; mem. Bd Swedish Broadcasting Co. 1978–91, Swedish TV Co. 1979–91; mem. numerous govt comms dealing with constitutional matters, the mass media, environmental protection. *Publications:* various articles on defence, foreign policy and constitutional issues.

BJÖRK; Icelandic singer, songwriter, musician, record producer and actress; b. (Björk Guðmundsdóttir), 21 Nov. 1965, Reykjavík; m. Thór Eldon (divorced); one s., one d.; first solo release aged 11; fmr singer for various Icelandic groups, including Exodus, Tappi Tikarras; singer, Kukl, later renamed The Sugarcubes 1986–92; solo artist 1992–; BRIT Award for Best Int. Newcomer 1994, MTV European Music Award for Best Int. Female Artist 1994, 1996, 1997, Q Inspiration Award 2005, MOJO Inspiration Award 2007, Polar Music Prize 2010. *Films:* Dancer in the Dark (Cannes Film Festival Best Actress Award 2000) 2000, Drawing Restraint 9 2005, Anna and the Moods (voice) 2007. *Recordings include:* albums: with The Sugarcubes: Life's Too Good 1988, Here Today, Tomorrow Next Week 1989, Stick Around For Joy 1992, It's It 1992; solo: Björk 1977, Debut 1993, Post 1995, Telegram 1996, Homogenic 1997, Selmasongs 2000, Vespertine 2001,

Dancer in the Dark 2001, Greatest Hits 2002, Family Tree 2002, Medúlla 2004, Army of Me: Remixes and Covers (charity album) 2005, Drawing Restraint 9 (OST) 2005, Volta 2007, Voltaic 2009, Biophilia 2011. *Address:* Quest Management, 36 Warple Way, Unit 1D, London, W3 0RG, England (office); c/o Nonesuch Records, Warner Music Group, 75 Rockefeller Plaza, New York, NY 10019, England (office). *Telephone:* (20) 8749-0188 (office); (212) 275-2000 (office). *Fax:* (20) 8749-0080 (office). *E-mail:* info@quest-management.com (office); info@nonesuch.com (office). *Website:* www.quest-management.com (office); www.nonesuch.com (office); www .bjork.com.

BJÖRK, Claes; Swedish business executive; joined Skanska AB 1967, moved to USA 1971, responsible for Skanska's construction operations in USA 1983, Pres. Skanska (USA) Inc. 1987, Sr Vice-Pres. Skanska AB, Head of Skanska USA Operations –1997, mem. Group Man. Skanska AB 1995, Pres. and Group CEO 1997–2002, Chair. Scancem Cement Co. 1998–2000; Chair. Swedish-American Chamber of Commerce 1992–95, currently mem. Bd of Dirs; mem. Bd of Dirs Granite Construction Inc. 2006–, Qliktech Inc. –2009, Consolidated Management Group; mem. Bd Banister Foundation 1990–; mem. Bd of Trustees, American Scandinavian Foundation; Lucia Trade Award, Swedish-American Chamber of Commerce.

BJORKEN, James Daniel, BS, PhD; American physicist and academic; *Professor Emeritus, Stanford Linear Accelerator Center, Stanford University;* b. 1934; ed Massachusetts Inst. of Tech., Stanford Univ.; Research Assoc., then Asst Prof., Stanford Univ. 1959–62, Assoc. Prof., then Prof., Stanford Linear Accelerator Center 1962–79, Theoretical Physicist 1989–98, Prof. Emer. 1998–; Theoretical Physicist and Assoc. Dir for Physics, Fermi Lab. 1979–89; Eastman Prof., Univ. of Oxford, UK 1995–96; mem. NAS, American Acad. of Arts and Sciences; Foreign mem. Swedish Acad. of Sciences; Hon. PhD (Univ. of Turin, Italy); Putnam Fellow 1954, Dannie Heinemann Prize in Math. Physics, American Physical Soc., Ernest Orlando Lawrence Medal, Dept for Energy, Dirac Medal, Abdus Salam Int. Centre for Theoretical Physics 2004. *Publications include:* Relativistic Quantum Mechanics (co-author) 1964, Relativistic Quantum Fields (co-author) 1965. *Address:* Stanford Linear Accelerator Center, 2575 Sand Hill Road, Menlo Park, CA 94025, USA (office). *Telephone:* (650) 926-3300 (office). *E-mail:* bjorken@slac.stanford.edu (office). *Website:* www.slac.stanford.edu (office).

BJÖRKLUND, Leni, BA; Swedish politician; b. 5 July 1944; ed Uppsala Univ.; Research Asst, Dept of Pedagogical Studies, Stockholm Inst. of Educ. 1969–71; Educ. Consultant, Nat. Bd of Educ. 1971–74; Expert, Dept for Cultural Affairs, Ministry of Educ. and Science 1974–76; Municipal Commr Municipality of Järfälla 1977–79; Co. Council Commr Stockholm Co. Council 1980–98; Man. Dir of Planning and Rationalisation, Inst. for Health and Social Services 1989–99; Sec.-Gen. Church of Sweden 1999–2002; Minister of Defence 2002–06; mem. SDP, held numerous party positions including Vice-Chair. Exec. Cttee Stockholm Co. SDP; currently First Vice-Chair. Civilförsvarsförbundet (Civil Defense League); fmr Chair. Expert Group on Public Finance (ESO); mem. Nat. Heritage Bd, Mid-Sweden Univ.; fmr Chair. Swedish Medical Research Council; fmr Vice-Chair. Stockholm Co. Admin Bd; fmr mem. Foundation of Strategic Research; Hon. DrMed (Karolinska Institutet). *Address:* Civilförsvarsförbundet, Box 2034, 169 02 Solna, Sweden. *E-mail:* info@civil.se. *Website:* www.civil.se.

BJÖRKMAN, Olle Erik, PhD, DSc, FAAS; American (b. Swedish) professor of plant biology; *Member of Faculty, Department of Plant Biology, Carnegie Institution of Washington;* b. 29 July 1933, Jönköping, Sweden; s. of Erik Gustaf Björkman and Dagmar Kristina Björkman (née Svensson); m. Monika Birgit Waldinger 1955; two s.; ed Univs of Stockholm and Uppsala; Research Fellow, Swedish Natural Science Research Council, Univ. of Uppsala 1961–63; Postdoctoral Fellow, Carnegie Inst. of Washington Dept of Plant Biology, Stanford, Calif. 1964–65, Faculty mem. 1966–, Prof. of Biology by courtesy, Stanford Univ. 1977–; mem. Cttee on Carbon Dioxide Effects, US Dept of Energy 1977–82, Cttee on Bioscience Research in Agric. 1984–85; Scientific Adviser, Desert Research Inst., Nevada 1980–81; mem. Editorial Bd Planta 1993–96; mem. NAS; Fellow, American Acad. of Arts and Sciences; Corresp. (Foreign) mem. Australian Acad. of Sciences; Foreign mem. Royal Swedish Acad. of Sciences; Linnaeus Prize, Royal Swedish Physiographic Soc. 1977, The Stephen Hale's Award, American Soc. of Plant Physiologists 1986, The Selby Award, Australian Acad. of Sciences 1987, The Barnes Life Membership Award, American Soc. of Plant Biologists 2001. *Publications:* Experimental Studies on the Nature of Species V (co-author) 1971, Physiological Processes in Plant Ecology 1980, more than 170 articles in scientific journals. *Leisure interest:* opera. *Address:* Carnegie Institution of Washington Department of Plant Biology, 260 Panama Street, Stanford, CA 94305 (office); 3040 Greer Road, Palo Alto, CA 94303, USA (home). *Telephone:* (650) 858-0880 (home). *E-mail:* olle_bjorkman@msn.com (home). *Website:* carnegiedpb.stanford.edu (office).

BJORKMAN, Pamela J., BA, PhD; American biologist and academic; *Max Delbrück Professor of Biology and Investigator, Howard Hughes Medical Institute, California Institute of Technology;* b. Portland, Ore.; m. Kai Zinn; two c.; ed Univ. of Oregon and Harvard Univ.; Post-doctoral Researcher, Harvard Univ. 1984–87, Stanford Univ. 1987–88; Asst Prof., California Inst. of Tech. 1988–95, Assoc. Prof. 1995–98, Prof. 1998–2004, Max Delbrück Prof. of Biology 2004–, Asst Investigator, Howard Hughes Medical Inst. Div. of Biology 1989–95, Assoc. Investigator 1995–98, Investigator 1988–99, 2005–, Full Investigator 2000–05, Exec. Officer for Biology 2000–; currently also Adjunct Prof. of Biochemistry, School of Medicine, Univ. of Southern California, Los Angeles; fmr Pew Scholar in the Biomedical Sciences; fmr American Cancer Soc. Post-doctoral Fellow; fmr American Soc. of Histocompatibility and Immunogenetics Young Investigator; mem. NAS 2001–, American Acad. of Arts and Sciences, American Philosophical Soc., American Crystallographic Asscn, American Soc. for Cell Biology, American Asscn of Immunologists; William B. Coley Award for Distinguished Research in Fundamental Immunology 1993, Gairdner Foundation Int. Award (co-author) 1994, AAI-PharMingen Investigator Award 1996, Paul Ehrlich and Ludwig Darmstaedter Award, L'Oréal-UNESCO Women in Science Award 2006, Max Planck Research Award, James R. Klinenberg Science Award, Arthritis Foundation. *Publications:* numerous papers in scientific journals on the structures of proteins mediating the immune response and on protein crystallography. *Address:* Howard Hughes Medical Institute, Division of Biology, Office 361 Broad, MC 114-96, California

Institute of Technology, 1200 E California Blvd, Pasadena, CA 91125, USA (office). *Telephone:* (626) 395-8350 (office). *Fax:* (626) 792-3683 (office). *E-mail:* bjorkman@ caltech.edu (office). *Website:* www.its.caltech.edu/~bjorker (office).

BJØRNEBOE, Gunn-Elin Aasprong, Cand. med. (MD), MA, PhD; Norwegian physician, academic and university administrator; *Director, University of Oslo;* b. 6 April 1956; ed Univ. of Oslo; fmr Adjunct Prof., Dept of Community Medicine, Univ. of Tromsø; has extensive man. experience and completed the Solstrand Leadership Devt Programme; fmr Admin. Man. and fmr Dir Nat. Nutrition Council; Deputy Dir Gen. Directorate of Health and Social Affairs –2007; Prof., Dept of Nutrition, Univ. of Oslo, Dir Univ. of Oslo 2007–. *Publications:* several book chapters as well as scientific papers in professional journals. *Address:* University Director's Office, University of Oslo, Administration Building, 9th Floor, Problemveien 7, 0316 Oslo, Norway (office). *Telephone:* 22-85-63-01 (office). *Fax:* 22-85-44-42 (office). *E-mail:* universitetsdirektor@uio.no (office). *Website:* www.uio.no/english/about/organisation/management/unidir (office).

BJØRNHOLM, Sven, DPhil; Danish physicist; b. 8 Sept. 1927, Tønder; s. of Lt-Col H. L. Bjørnholm and Inger Hillerup; m. Iran Park 1957; two s. one d.; ed Tech. Univ. of Denmark, Sorbonne, Paris and Univ. of Copenhagen; Research Asst, Niels Bohr Inst., Copenhagen 1955–68; Assoc. Prof., Univ. of Copenhagen 1968–96; visiting scientist at research insts in France, USSR, USA, Germany and Brazil 1951–97; mem. Bd Int. Fed. of Insts of Advanced Study 1972–77, Danish Natural Science Research Council 1973–79, Danish Energy Policy Council 1976–86, IUPAP Comm. on Nuclear Physics 1978–84, EC Comm. on Research and Devt 1980–82; Pres. Danish Physical Soc. 1978–80; mem. Royal Danish Acad., Danish Acad. of Tech. Sciences, Royal Physiographical Soc. of Lund, Sweden, Danish Pugwash Cttee; Officier, Ordre des Palmes académiques; Ole Rømer Award 1965, Ulrich Brinch Award 1973. *Publications:* Energy in Denmark 1990–2005 1976; and articles on the structure and reactions of atomic nuclei and metal clusters, including fission, in professional journals. *Address:* The Niels Bohr Institute, Blegdamsvej 17, 2100 Copenhagen Ø (office); Fuglevangsvej 6B, 1962 Frederiksberg C, Denmark (home). *Telephone:* 33-22-48-85 (home).

BJURSTRØM, Hanne Inger; Norwegian lawyer, politician and fmr academic; *Minister of Labour;* b. 1960; m.; two c.; ed Inst. for Foreign Students, Univ. of Florence, Italy, Univ. of Oslo, Univ. of London and London School of Econs, UK; legal consultant (women's rights), Univ. of Oslo 1981–82, Scientific Asst (maritime law) 1984–85, part-time teacher and External Examiner (Admin. Law) 1987–2006; Visiting Researcher, Inst. for Social Research 1992; Sr Exec. Officer/Adviser, Legislation Dept, Ministry of Justice 1987–94; Political Sec. to Commr for Finance and Planning, Rune Bjerke, Oslo City Govt 1994–95; Corp. Counsellor, Aker Oil and Gas Technology PLC 1995–97; barrister training for lawyers (mandatory) 1996; Agent, Attorney Gen. of Civil Affairs 1997–2000; Vice-Pres. and Judge, The Labour Court 2000–03; Sr Adviser with responsibility for devt of Norway's cap and trade system (climate change), Ministry of Environment 2003–07, Norway's Chief Negotiator under UN climate change negotiations 2007–09; Minister of Labour 2009–; mem. Cttee overseeing official policy review (pricing of public information) 1993; Norwegian Adviser to Council of Europe (Civil Law) 1993–96; mem. Nat. Cttee for Research Ethics (Social Sciences, Law, Humanities) 1997–2003, complaints bd relating to decisions made by Data Inspectorate (protection of personal privacy) 2001–08; Deputy Bd mem. European Surveillance Authority Coll. 2001–04; Leader of UN ECE Convention on Access to Information, Public Participation in Decision-making and Access to Justice in Environmental Matters 2005–08; leader of dispute cttee (workplace environment) 2006–08; Deputy mem. Oslo City Govt 1980–83, Oslo School Bd 1980–83, Oslo Price Bd 1980–83, Norwegian Children and Youth Council 1982–83; mem. Oslo Municipal Youth Cttee 1981–83; Bd mem. Norwegian Student Soc. 1982, Chateu Neuf 1982, Ullevål Hosp. 1996–99. *Address:* Ministry of Labour, Akersgt. 64, PO Box 8019 Dep, 0030 Oslo, Norway (office). *Telephone:* 22-24-90-90 (office). *Fax:* 22-24-87-11 (office). *E-mail:* postmottak@ad.dep.no (office). *Website:* www.regjeringen.no/ad (office).

BJURSTRÖM, Per Gunnar, PhD; Swedish academic; b. 28 March 1928, Stockholm; s. of Gunnar Bjurström and Claire Bjurström (née Hellgård); m. 1st Eva Gunnars 1957 (divorced 1983); two d.; m. 2nd Görel Cavalli-Björkman; Asst Curator, Nat. Museum 1950–68, curator of prints and drawings 1968–79; Dir Nat. Swedish Art Museums 1980–89; Guest Prof., Yale Univ. 1968; Prof., Nat. Gallery of Art, Washington, DC 1990–91; mem. Bd Gen. Art Asscn of Sweden 1964–, Prince Eugen's Waldemarsudde 1980–89; Vice-Chair. Soc. of Art History 1965–91; Chair. Int. Cttee of Museums of Fine Art 1983–88; mem. Royal Acad. of Letters, History and Antiquities and Royal Acad. of Fine Art, Ateneo Veneto, Venice. *Publications:* Giacomo Torelli and Baroque Stage Design 1961, Stage Design in Sweden 1964, Feast and Theatre in Queen Christina's Rome 1966, German Drawings in Swedish Public Collections 1972, French Drawings in Swedish Public Collections 1–3 1976, 1982, 1986, Italian Drawings in Swedish Public Collections 1–4 1979, Johan Tobias Sergel 1975, Three Decades of Swedish Graphic Art 1946–1976, Roman Baroque Scenery 1977, Philip von Schantz 1979, Claude Lorrain Sketchbook 1984, Nationalmuseum 1792–1991 1992, Karl Axel Pehrson 1992, I, Alexander Roslin 1993, Nicola Pio as a Collector of Drawings 1994, Art at the Karolinska Hospital 1997, Evert Lundquist Grafiker 2004, Kännare (On Connoisseurship) 2005. *Address:* Folkungagatan 142, 116 30 Stockholm, Sweden (home). *Telephone:* (8) 641-7093 (home). *E-mail:* per.bjurstrom@tele2.se (home).

BLACK, Dame Carol M., DBE, CBE, FRCP, FMedSci, FACP, MD; British physician and academic; *National Director for Health and Work;* m.; ed Dixie Grammar School, Market Bosworth, Univ. of Bristol, Royal Coll. of Physicians; Consultant Rheumatologist, West Middlesex Univ. Hospital 1981–89; Consultant Rheumatologist, Royal Free and Univ. Coll. Medical School, Univ. of London 1989–94, Prof. of Rheumatology 1994–2006, Prof. Emer. 2006–; Medical Dir Royal Free Hospital, London 2000–02; Chair. Nuffield Trust for Research and Policy Studies in Health Services 2006–; Nat. Dir for Health and Work 2006–; Pro-Chancellor, Univ. of Bristol 2007–; Public Appointments Amb., Govt Equalities Office, Cabinet Office 2009–; Chair. of Research Cttee and Vice-Chair. of Bd, Imperial Coll. Healthcare Charity 2008–; Chair. Skills for Health, Widening Participation Strategy Group, Dept of Health 2009–; Chair., Governance Bd, Centre for Workforce Intelligence 2010–; elected to Royal Coll. of Physicians 1996, Clinical Vice-Pres. 1999–2002, Pres. 2002–06; Dir (non-exec.), NHS Inst. for Innovation and Improvement 2006–; mem. Nat. Inst. for Health and Clinical

Excellence (NICE) Appraisal Cttee 1999–2002, Partners Council 2002–06; mem. Nat. Specialist Commissioning Advisory Group 2000–04; mem. Imperial Cancer Research Fund Council 2002–04; mem. Council of Acad. of Medical Sciences 2002–06; mem. Postgraduate Medical Educ. and Training Bd 2003–07; mem., CBRC Scientific Advisory Bd, Guy's and St. Thomas's Medical School 2007–; mem. Advisory Bd, Business in the Community, Nat. Campaign Business Action on Health 2008–; Founding mem. Cttee, Queen's Awards for Voluntary Services 2009–; mem. Wellbeing Through Work Expert Reference Group, NHS Wales 2009–, Advisory Bd, Centre for Organisational Health and Well-Being, Univ. of Lancaster 2009–, Employee Engagement Task Force, Dept of Business Innovation and Skills 2011–, Life Sciences Skills Strategy Bd, Cogent 2011–, Int. Advisory Bd, US Preventive Medicine 2011–; Foreign Assoc., Inst. of Medicine, Washington, DC 2006; Fellowship of Univ. Coll. London 2004; Trustee, Nat. Portrait Gallery 2010–; Master, American Coll. of Physicians 2005; Companion, Chartered Man. Inst. 2004; mem. Bd of Govs. The Health Foundation 2004–07; Hon. Pres. Scleroderma Soc. 2006–, Raynaud's and Scleroderma Asscn 2007–, British Lung Foundation 2007–; Hon. Patron, Treat Trust, Wales 2009–; Hon. Physician, Royal Soc. of Musicians of Great Britain 2008–; Hon. Fellow, Lucy Cavendish Coll., Univ. of Cambridge 2004, Univ. Coll. London 2004; Hon. MD (Nottingham); Hon. DrSc (Bristol, Leicester, Sheffield, Hertfordshire, Exeter, Glasgow, Southampton). *Leisure interests:* hill-walking, running, opera, reading, travel. *Address:* Centre for Rheumatology and Connective Tissue Disease, Centre for Rheumatology, Department of Medicine, Royal Free Hospital, Pond Street, London, NW3 2QG, England (office). *Telephone:* (20) 7794-0432 (office). *Fax:* (20) 7794-0432 (office). *Website:* www.ucl.ac.uk/medicine/rheumatology-RF/index.html (office).

BLACK, Cathleen (Cathie) Prunty; American publishing executive; b. 26 April 1944, Chicago, Ill.; d. of James Hamilton Black and Margaret Black (née Harrington); m. Thomas E. Harvey 1982; two c.; ed Trinity Coll., Washington, DC; sold advertising for magazines such as Holiday and Travel & Leisure; joined New York magazine in 1970, Publr 1979; helped launch Ms. magazine 1972, Assoc. Publr; Pres. and Publr USA Today 1983–91, mem. Bd Dirs and Exec. Vice-Pres. Marketing, Gannett Co. Inc. (parent-co.) 1985–91; Pres. and CEO Newspaper Asscn of America 1991–95; Pres. Hearst Magazines, New York 1996–2010, Chair. 2010, mem. Bd of Dirs Hearst Corpn 1996–; Chancellor, New York City Dept of Educ. Jan.–April 2011; mem. Bd of Dirs Coca-Cola Co. 1990–91, 1993–, International Business Machines Corpn (IBM) 1995–, Women.com Networks Inc. 1999–, Advertising Council; Chair. Magazine Publrs of America 1999–2001; Trustee, Univ. of Notre Dame; mem. Council on Foreign Relations; hon. degrees from St Mary's Coll., South Bend, Ind., Capitol Coll., Laurel, Md, Ithaca Coll., NY, Lehigh Univ., Bethlehem, Pa, Simmons Coll., Boston, Mass, Trinity Washington Univ., Washington, DC, Trinity Coll., Hartford, Conn., Marymount Coll., Tarrytown, NY, Loyola Univ., New Orleans, La, Hamilton Coll., Clinton, NY; Woman of the Year Award Financial Women's Asscn 1986–87, Advertising Age Publishing Executive of the Year 2000, named by Crain's New York Business one of its 100 Most Influential Business Leaders 2002, ranked by Fortune magazine amongst the 50 Most Powerful Women in Business in the US (24th) 2002, (26th) 2003, (30th) 2004, (34th) 2005, (38th) 2006, (43rd) 2007, (49th) 2008, (46th) 2009, ranked by Forbes magazine amongst The World's 100 Most Powerful Women (91st) 2005, (92nd) 2006, (94th) 2007, (67th) 2010; Lifetime Achievement Award, Magazine Publrs of America 2005, named Corp. Publr of the Year, The Delaney Report 2006, Prism Award, New York Univ. 2007. *Publication:* Basic Black: The Essential Guide for Getting Ahead at Work (and in Life) 2007. *Address:* c/o New York City Department of Education, Tweed Courthouse, 52 Chambers Street, New York, NY 10007, USA; c/o Crown Publishing Group Publicity Department, Random House Inc., 1745 Broadway, New York, NY 10019, USA. *E-mail:* crownpublicity@randomhouse.com. *Website:* www.randomhouse.com/author/79886/cathie-black.

BLACK, Robert Lincoln, MD, FAAP; American pediatrician and academic; *Voluntary Clinical Professor of Pediatrics, Stanford University;* b. 25 Aug. 1930, Los Angeles; s. of Harold Black and Kathryn Stone; m. Jean Wilmott McGuire 1953; two s. one d.; ed Stanford Univ., Kings County Hosp., Brooklyn, Stanford Univ. Hosp.; Capt. in USAF Medical Corps 1956–58; Asst Clinical Prof., Stanford Univ., Clinical Prof. 1962–, Assoc. Prof. 1968–79, Prof. of Pediatrics 1980, currently Voluntary Clinical Prof. of Pediatrics; mem. Bd of Dirs Lyceum of Monterey Peninsula 1973–; mem. Bd Mid Coast Health System Agency 1975–81; mem. various cttees of American Acad., of Pediatrics 1962–, Alt. Chapter Chair. 1984–87; Consultant, State of Calif. Dept of Health Service 1962– and of Office of Statewide Health Planning 1975–81; mem. State Maternal, Child, Adolescent Health Care Bd 1984–93; mem. Inst. of Medicine, NAS, Calif. State Maternal, Child, Adolescent Health Bd; Fellow, American Acad. of Pediatrics (FAAP); mem. Bd of Educ. Monterey Peninsula Unified School Dist 1965–73; Martin Gershman Award for Child Advocacy, American Acad. of Pediatrics 1996, Physician of the Year, Monterey County Medical Soc. 2001, Child Advocacy Award, American Acad. of Pediatrics 2003. *Publications:* California Health Plan for Children, California's Use of Health Statistics in Child Health Planning. *Leisure interests:* music, hiking, travel, photography. *Address:* 920 Cass Street, Monterey, CA 93940, USA (office). *Telephone:* (831) 372-5841 (office). *Fax:* (831) 372-4820 (office). *E-mail:* rblack@chomp.org (office).

BLACK OF BRENTWOOD, Baron (Life Peer), cr. 2010, of Brentwood in the County of Essex; **Guy Vaughan Black,** MA, FRSA, MCIPR; British newspaper executive; *Executive Director, Telegraph Media Group;* b. 6 Aug. 1964, Chelmsford, Essex; s. of Monica Black and Thomas Black; Civil Partner, Mark Bolland; ed Brentwood School, Essex, Peterhouse, Cambridge; Grad. Trainee, Corp. Banking Div., BZW 1985–86; Desk Officer, Conservative Party Research Dept 1986–89; Special Adviser to Sec. of State for Energy 1989–92; Account Dir, Westminster Strategy 1992–94; Assoc. Dir, Lowe Bell Good Relations 1994–96; Dir Press Complaints Comm. 1996–2003; Dir of Communications, Conservative Party 2004–05; Exec. Dir, Telegraph Media Group 2005–; Dir Advertising Standards Bd of Finance 2005–, Press Standards Bd of Finance 2007– (Chair. 2009–); Conservative mem. Brentwood Dist Council 1988–92; Trustee, Sir Edward Heath Charitable Foundation 2006–10, Imperial War Museum 2007–, Imperial War Museum Foundation 2010–; Chair. Commonwealth Press Union Media Trust 2009–; mem. Council, Royal Coll. of Music 2009–; Hon. mem. London Press Club; Sir Herbert Butterfield Prize for History, Univ. of Cambridge 1985. *Publication:* The Eclipse of Socialism (with Tim Collins) 1988. *Leisure interests:* reading, music,

playing the piano, cats. *Address:* Telegraph Media Group, 111 Buckingham Palace Road, London SW1A 0DT, England (office). *Telephone:* (20) 7931-3806 (office). *E-mail:* guy.black@telegraph.co.uk (office). *Website:* www.telegraph.co.uk (office).

BLACK OF CROSSHARBOUR, Baron (Life Peer), cr. 2001, of Crossharbour in the London Borough of Tower Hamlets; **Conrad Moffat Black,** Kt, BA, LLL, MA, LittD; British (b. Canadian) publisher, business executive, author, columnist and investor; *Chairman, Conrad Black Capital Corporation;* b. 25 Aug. 1944, Montreal, Quebec; s. of George Montegu and Jean Elizabeth Black (née Riley); m. 1st Joanna Catherine Louise Black 1978 (divorced 1991); two s. one d.; m. 2nd Barbara Amiel 1992; ed Carleton, Laval, McGill Univs; Chair. and CEO Ravelston Corpn Ltd; Chair. Hollinger Int. 1985–2004, acquired Daily Telegraph newspaper group 1985, Chair. Telegraph Group –2004; CEO Chair. Argus Corpn 1978–2005; Chair. Conrad Black Capital Corpn; mem. Advisory Bd, The Nat. Interest, Washington, DC; Patron, The Malcolm Muggeridge Foundation; charged with 17 counts of criminal offences by US Dept of Justice, which sought life imprisonment and fine of $140 million 2005, four counts dropped, nine led to acquittals, remaining four vacated unanimously by US Supreme Court after spending 29 months in a low security fed. prison, two counts revived by a lower court but US Supreme Court refused to grant leave to appeal these May 2011, resentenced to a reduced term of 42 months and a fine of $125,000, returned to prison to serve remaining 13 months of his sentence June 2011, released from prison and deported to Canada May 2012, granted a one-year temporary resident's permit to re-enter Canada as he had renounced his Canadian citizenship in 2001; fined $4.1 million and barred from becoming dir of a US co. 2013; Kt Commdr, Order of St Gregory the Great, OC –2014, PC –2014; Hon. LLD (St Francis Xavier) 1979, (McMaster) 1979, (Windsor) 1979, (Carleton) 1992. *Publications:* Duplessis 1977, A Life in Progress (autobiog.) 1994, Franklin D. Roosevelt: Champion of Freedom 2003, Richard Milhous Nixon: The Invincible Quest 2007. *Address:* 3044 Bloor Street West, Suite 296, Toronto, ON M8X 2Y8, Canada (home). *Telephone:* (416) 241-7758 (home). *Fax:* (416) 241-5026 (home). *E-mail:* jmaida@blackam.net (office).

BLACKADDER, Dame Elizabeth Violet, DBE, MA, RA, RSA; British artist; b. 24 Sept. 1931, Falkirk, Scotland; m. John Houston 1956 (died 2008); ed Falkirk High School, Edinburgh Coll. of Art and Univ. of Edinburgh; teacher of art, St Thomas of Aquinas School, Edin. 1958–59; Librarian, Fine Art Dept, Univ. of Edin. 1959–61; teacher, Edin. Coll. of Art 1962–86; Scottish Arts Council retrospective Exhbn Edin., Sheffield, Aberdeen, Liverpool, Cardiff 1981–82; participant in numerous group shows in UK, USA, Canada etc. British Painting 1952–77; Royal Acad., London 1977; HM Painter and Limner in Scotland 2000–; work includes drawings and watercolours (especially botanical), prints, lithographs, portraits, tapestries and stained glass (window commissioned by Nat. Library of Scotland 1987); Hon. FRSE; Hon. DLitt (Heriot-Watt) 1989, (Strathclyde) 1998; Dr hc (Edin.) 1990, (Stirling, St Andrews, London); Hon. LLD (Aberdeen) 1997, (Glasgow) 2001; Jt Winner, Watercolour Foundation Award, RA Summer Exhbn 1988. *Publication:* Favourite Flowers (with Deborah Kellaway) 1994. *Address:* 57 Fountainhall Road, Edinburgh, EH9 2LH, Scotland. *Telephone:* (131) 667-3687 (home).

BLACKBOURN, David Gordon, BA, PhD, FRHistS; British historian and academic; *Coolidge Professor of History and Director, Minda de Gunzburg Center for European Studies, Harvard University;* b. 1 Nov. 1949, Spilsby, Lincs.; s. of Harry Blackbourn and Pamela Jean Blackbourn; m. Deborah Frances Langton; one s. one d.; ed Leeds Modern Grammar School, Christ's Coll., Cambridge; Research Fellow, Jesus Coll., Cambridge 1973–76; Lecturer in History, Queen Mary Coll., Univ. of London 1976–79, Birkbeck Coll. 1979–85, Reader in Modern History 1985–89, Prof. of Modern European History 1989–92; Coolidge Prof. of History, Harvard Univ., USA 1992–; Dir Minda de Gunzburg Center for European Studies 2007–; lectures and contribs to confs in UK, Ireland, Germany, France, Italy, fmr Yugoslavia, USA and Canada 1973–; Fellow, Inst. for European History, Mainz, FRG 1974–75; Research Fellow, Alexander von Humboldt Foundation, Bonn-Bad Godesberg, FRG 1984–85, 1994–95; Visiting Kratter Prof. of German History, Stanford Univ., Calif., USA 1989–90; Fellow, Guggenheim Foundation, New York 1994–95; Sec. European History Soc. 1978–81, mem. Cttee 1981–86; mem. Academic Advisory Bd, German Historical Inst., London 1983–92; mem. Editorial Bd Past and Present 1988–; mem. European Sub-cttee of Labour Party Nat. Exec. Cttee 1978–80, Academic Advisory Bd, Inst. for European History, Mainz, Germany 1995–2005, Cttee on Hon. Foreign mems, American Historical Asscn 2000–02; Pres. Conf. Group on Cen. European History, American Historical Asscn 2003–04; mem. Advisory Bd, Edmund Spevack Memorial Foundation 2003–06, mem. Bd, Friends of the German Historical Inst., Washington, DC 2004, Chair. Bd 2007–; mem. Academic Advisory Bd Lichtenberg Coll. Univ. of Goettingen 2007–; Ed. Penguin Custom Editions: The Western World Database 2000–; consultant to SMASH/The History Channel, USA; Fellow, American Acad. of Arts and Sciences 2007; gave Annual Lecture of German Historical Inst., London 1998, Malcolm Wynn Lecture, Stetson Univ., Fla. 2002, George C. Windell Memorial Lecture, Univ. of New Orleans 2006, Crayenborgh Lecture, Leiden Univ., Netherlands 2007, Jakob and Wilhelm Grimm Lecture, Univ. of Waterloo, Canada 2010; American Historical Asscn Book Prize 1996, Walter Channing Cabot Fellow, Harvard Univ. 2003–04, George L. Mosse Prize, American Historical Asscn 2007, Charles A. Weyerhaeuser Prize, Forest History Soc. 2007. *Publications:* Class, Religion and Local Politics in Wilhelmine Germany 1980, The Peculiarities of German History (with Geoff Eley) 1984, Populists and Patricians: Essays in Modern German History 1987, Volksfrömmigkeit und Fortschrittsglaube im Kulturkampf 1988, The German Bourgeoisie (co-ed. with Richard J. Evans) 1991, Marpingen: Apparitions of the Virgin Mary in Bismarckian Germany 1993, The Fontana History of Germany: The Long Nineteenth Century, 1780–1918 1997, The Conquest of Nature: Water, Landscape and the Making of Modern Germany 2006; scholarly articles in English, German, French, Serbo-Croat, Japanese and Italian; contribs to several magazines and the BBC. *Leisure interests:* family, reading, music, sport, politics. *Address:* Minda de Gunzburg Center for European Studies, Harvard University, 27 Kirkland Street, Cambridge, MA 02138, USA (office). *Telephone:* (617) 495-4303, ext. 228 (office). *Fax:* (617) 495-8509 (office). *E-mail:* dgblackb@fas.harvard.edu (office). *Website:* www.fas.harvard.edu/~history (office).

BLACKBURN, Elizabeth Helen, AC, BSc, MSc, PhD, FRS; Australian/American biochemist and academic; *Morris Herzstein Professor of Biology, Department of*

Biochemistry and Biophysics, University of California, San Francisco; b. 26 Nov. 1948, Hobart, Australia; d. of Harold Stewart Blackburn and Marcia Constance Jack; m. John Sedat 1975; one s.; ed Univ. of Melbourne, Australia and Univ. of Cambridge, UK; Researcher, Molecular Biology Lab., Univ. of Cambridge 1971–74; Post grad. Researcher, Yale Univ., USA 1975–77; mem. Faculty Univ. of California, Berkeley 1978–90; Prof., Dept of Microbiology and Immunology, Univ. of California, San Francisco 1990, Dept Chair. 1993–99, currently Morris Herzstein Prof. of Biology and Physiology, Dept of Biochemistry and Biophysics; Steven and Michele Kirsch Foundation Investigator Fellowship 2000; Non-Resident Fellow, Salk Inst.; Memorial Sloan-Kettering Cancer Center Katharine Berkan Judd Award Lectureship 2001; Pres. American Soc. for Cell Biology 1998, American Asscn for Cancer Research 2010; mem. Bd Genetics Soc. of America 2000–02; mem. Pres.'s Council on Bioethics 2001–04; mem. American Acad. of Excellence 2000, Inst. of Medicine 2000; Foreign Assoc. NAS 1993; Fellow, American Acad. of Arts and Sciences 1991, American Acad. of Microbiology 1993, AAAS 2000, Royal Soc. of NSW 2010; Hon. DSc (Yale) 1991; Australian Soc. for Microbiology Prize 1967, Travelling Gowrie Research Scholar 1971–73, Anna Fuller Fund Fellowship 1975–77, Eli Lilly Research Award for Microbiology and Immunology 1988, NAS Award in Molecular Biology 1990, Gairdner Foundation Award 1998, Australia Prize 1998, California Scientist of the Year 1999, Novartis-Drew Award for Biomedical Science 1999, Feodor Lynen Award 2000, Dickson Prize in Medicine 2000, American Cancer Soc. Medal of Honor 2000, American Asscn for Cancer Research-Pezcoller Foundation Int. Award for Cancer Research 2001, General Motors Cancer Research Foundation Alfred P. Sloan Award 2001, Bristol-Meyers Squibb Award for Distinguished Achievement in Cancer Research 2003, Dr A. H. Heineken Prize for Medicine 2004, American Soc. for Cell Biology Public Service Award 2004, Benjamin Franklin Medal in Life Science 2005, Albert Lasker Award for Basic Medical Research (with Carol W. Greider and Jack W. Szostak) 2006, Genetics Prize, Peter Gruber Foundation 2006, Vanderbilt Prize in Biomedical Science 2007, named to the TIME 100 2007, L'Oréal-UNESCO Award for Women in Science 2008, Nobel Prize in Physiology or Medicine (with Carol W. Greider and Jack W. Szostak) 2009, inducted into California Hall of Fame 2011. *Publications include:* numerous articles in scientific journals. *Leisure interest:* music. *Address:* Department of Biochemistry and Biophysics, University of California, 600 16th Street, GH-S312F, Box 2200, San Francisco, CA 94158-2517, USA (office). *Telephone:* (415) 476-2824 (office); (415) 476-7284 (Lab.) (office). *Fax:* (415) 514-2913 (office). *E-mail:* telomer@itsa.ucsf.edu (office); elizabeth .blackburn@ucsf.edu (office). *Website:* biochemistry.ucsf.edu/labs/blackburn (office).

BLACKBURN, Jean-Pierre, BBA, MA; Canadian politician and business executive; b. 6 July 1948; ed Université du Québec, Chicoutimi; MP (Jonquière) 1984–93, 2006–11; fmr Parl. Sec. to Minister of Nat. Defence; fmr Pres. Blackburn Communication Inc.; Minister of Labour and Minister of the Econ. Devt Agency of Canada for the Regions of Quebec 2006–08, of Nat. Revenue and Minister of State (Agric.) 2008–10, of Veterans Affairs 2010–11. *Address:* c/o Veterans Affairs Canada, Office of the Minister of Veterans Affairs, 16th Floor, 66 Slater Street, Ottawa, ON K1A 0P4, Canada.

BLACKBURN, Jeffrey Michael, BA, MBA, FCIB, FRSA, CVO; British business executive; *Senior Vice-President, Business Development, Amazon.com Inc.;* b. 16 Dec. 1941, Manchester; s. of Jeffrey Blackburn and Renee Blackburn; m. 2nd Louise Clair Jouny 1987; two s.; one s. one d. from previous m.; ed Northgate Grammar School, Ipswich, Dartmouth Coll., Grad. School of Business, Stanford Univ., USA; Chief Man. Business Advisory Service, Lloyds Bank 1979–83; Dir and CEO Jt Credit Card Co. Ltd (Access) 1983–87, Leeds Permanent Building Society 1987–93; CEO Halifax Building Society (now Halifax PLC) 1993–98; Asst Vice-Pres. Deutsche Morgan Grenfell 1998; joined Amazon.com Inc. 1998, Vice-Pres. Operations Integration 2002–03, Vice-Pres. European Customer Service 2003–04, Vice-Pres. Business Devt 2004–06, Sr Vice-Pres. Business Devt 2006–; Pres. Chartered Inst. of Bankers 1998–99; mem. Bd of Dirs DFS Furniture PLC 1999–, George Wimpey PLC 1999–, Town Centre Securities PLC 1999–2003; mem. court, Univ. of Leeds 1989–2000; Companion, Chartered Man. Inst.; Gov. Nat. Youth Orchestra 1999–; Trustee, Duke of Edin.'s Award 1998–; Hon. DUniv (Leeds Metropolitan) 1998; Hon. DLitt (Huddersfield) 1998. *Leisure interest:* the arts. *Address:* Amazon.com Inc., PO Box 81226, Seattle, WA 98108-1226, USA (office). *Telephone:* (206) 266-2171 (office). *Fax:* (206) 266-1355 (office). *Website:* www .amazon.com (office).

BLACKBURN, Simon W., PhD, DPhil, FBA; British philosopher and academic; *Distinguished Research Professor, University of North Carolina, Chapel Hill;* b. 12 July 1944, Bristol, England; s. of Cuthbert Blackburn and Edna Blackburn; m. Angela Bowles 1968; one s. one d.; ed Clifton Coll., Bristol and Trinity Coll., Cambridge; Research Fellow, Churchill Coll. Cambridge 1967–69; Fellow and Tutor in Philosophy, Pembroke Coll. Oxford 1969–90; Ed. Mind 1984–90; Edna J. Koury Distinguished Prof. of Philosophy, Univ. of North Carolina, Chapel Hill, USA 1990–2000, currently part-time Distinguished Research Prof.; Adjunct Prof., ANU 1993–; Prof. of Philosophy, Univ. of Cambridge 2001–11, Fellow; Prof., New Coll. of the Humanities; Pres. Aristotelian Soc. 2009–10; Vice-Pres. British Humanist Asscn; Foreign Hon. mem. American Acad. of Arts and Sciences 2007; Hon. LLD (Sunderland); Hon. DLitt (Glasgow). *Publications:* Reason and Prediction 1970, Spreading the Word 1984, Essays in Quasi-Realism 1993, The Oxford Dictionary of Philosophy 1994, Ruling Passions 1998, Truth (co-ed.) 1999, Think: A Compelling Introduction to Philosophy 1999, Being Good 2001, Lust 2004, Truth: A Guide for the Perplexed 2005, Plato's Republic: A Biography 2006, How to Read Hume 2008. *Leisure interests:* walking, photography, sailing. *Address:* Trinity College, Cambridge, CB2 1TQ (office); 141 Thornton Road, Cambridge, CB3 0NE, England (home). *Telephone:* (1223) 528278 (office). *E-mail:* swb24@cam.ac.uk (office). *Website:* www.phil.cam.ac.uk/~swb24 (office).

BLACKER, Coit D., A, MS, PhD; American political scientist, academic, research institute director and international relations consultant; *Director and Senior Fellow, Freeman Spogli Institute for International Studies, Stanford University;* ed Occidental Coll., Fletcher School of Law and Diplomacy, Tufts Univ.; Professor Stanford Univ. 1978–, and succession of other positions at Stanford, including Dir of Studies, Center for Int. Security and Arms Control, co-Chair. Int. Relations and Int. Policy Studies Programs, Olivier Nomellini Family Univ. Fellow in Under-

graduate Educ., Deputy Dir, Freeman Spogli Inst. for Int. Studies, now Dir and Sr Fellow; Assoc. Prof. School of Int. Relations, Univ. of Southern Calif., Dir ad interim Peace and Conflict Studies Program; Special Asst for Nat. Security Affairs to US Senator Gary Hart, then to Pres. Clinton during first admin.; Sr Dir Russian, Ukrainian and Eurasian Affairs, Nat. Security Council; co-Dir Aspen Inst. US-Russia Dialogue 1998–2003; mem. study group US Comm. on Nat. Security in the 21st Century; mem. Council on Foreign Relations; mem. Bd of Dirs Int. Research and Exchanges Bd, Washington, DC; Chair. Exec. Cttee of the Int. Initiative 2005–; mem. Stanford Bd of Trustees Cttee on Devt 2004–07; Dr hc (Russian Acad. of Sciences Inst. of Far Eastern Studies) 1993; Laurance and Naomi Carpenter Hoagland Prize for Undergraduate Teaching 2001. *Publications include:* International Arms Control: Issues and Agreements (co-Ed.) 1984, Reluctant Warriors: the United States, The Soviet Union and Arms Control 1987, Hostage to Revolution: Gorbachev and Soviet Security Policy, 1985–91 1993, NATO After Madrid: Looking to the Future (Vol I) (co-Ed.) 1999, Belarus and the Flight from Sovereignty 2001, Arms Control 2002. *Address:* Freeman Spogli Institute for International Studies, Stanford University, Encina Hall, C137, Stanford, CA 94305-6055, USA (office). *Telephone:* (650) 725-5368 (office). *Fax:* (650) 725-3435 (office). *E-mail:* cblacker@stanford.edu (office). *Website:* www.iis-db.stanford.edu (office).

BLACKMAN, Honor; British actress; b. 22 Aug. 1926, London; film début in Fame is the Spur 1947. *Films include:* Green Grow the Rushes 1951, Come Die My Love 1952, The Rainbow Jacket 1953, The Glass Cage 1954, Dead Man's Evidence 1955, A Matter of Who 1961, Goldfinger 1964, Life at the Top 1965, Twist of Sand 1967, The Virgin and the Gipsy 1970, To the Devil a Daughter 1975, Summer Rain 1976, The Cat and the Canary 1977, Talos—The Mummy, To Walk With Lions, Bridget Jones's Diary 2001, Jack Brown and the Curse of the Crown 2001, Colour Me Kubrick: A Trueish Story 2005, Summer Solstice 2005, Reuniting the Rubins 2010, Cockneys vs Zombies 2011, I, Anna 2012. *Plays include:* Mademoiselle Colombe 2000, Cabaret 2007. *TV appearances include:* Four Just Men 1959, Man of Honour 1960, Ghost Squad 1961, Top Secret 1962, The Avengers 1962–64, The Explorer 1968, Visit from a Stranger 1970, Out Damned Spot 1972, Wind of Change 1977, Robin's Nest 1982, Never the Twain 1982, The Secret Adversary 1983, Lace 1985, The First Modern Olympics 1986, Minder on the Orient Express 1986, Dr. Who 1986, William Tell 1986, The Upper Hand (series) 1990–96, Jack and the Beanstalk: The Real Story 2001, Revolver 2001, Midsomer Murders 2003, The Royal 2003, Coronation Street 2004, Revolver (series) 2005, New Tricks (series) 2004, Summer Solstice (film) 2005, Sound (film) 2007, Hotel Babylon (series) 2009. *Website:* www.honorblackman.co.uk.

BLACKMORE, Rayburn, BA; Dominican politician; *Minister of Public Works, Energy and Ports;* b. Mahaut; ed Humber Coll., York Univ., Canada; served as police officer for seventeen years, attaining rank of Sergeant –2000; MP (Dominica Labour Party—DLP) for Mahaut 2005–; fmr Parl. Sec., later Minister of State in Prime Minister's Office with responsibility for Security; Minister of Nat. Security, Immigration and Labour 2007–10, of Public Works, Energy and Ports 2010–; Chair. Nat. Symposium on Crime 2003; Chair. Regional Security System –2008. *Address:* Ministry of Public Works, Energy and Ports, Government Headquarters, Kennedy Avenue, Roseau, Dominica (office). *Telephone:* 4482401 (office). *Fax:* 4488960 (office). *E-mail:* burnray@hotmail.com (office).

BLACKSTONE, Baroness (Life Peer), cr. 1987, of Stoke Newington in Greater London; **Rt Hon. Tessa Ann Vosper Blackstone,** PC, BSc, PhD; British politician and university vice-chancellor; b. 27 Sept. 1942, London, England; d. of the late Geoffrey Vaughan Blackstone, CBE, GM and of Joanna Blackstone; m. Tom Evans 1963 (divorced, died 1985); one s. one d.; ed Ware Grammar School, London School of Econs, Univ. of London; Assoc. Lecturer, Enfield Coll. 1965–66; Asst Lecturer, then Lecturer, Dept of Social Admin., LSE 1966–75; Fellow, Centre for Studies in Social Policy 1972–74; Adviser, Cen. Policy Review Staff, Cabinet Office 1975–78; Prof. of Educational Admin., Univ. of London Inst. of Educ. 1978–83; Deputy Educ. Officer (Resources), then Clerk and Dir of Educ., Inner London Educ. Authority 1983–87; Master, Birkbeck Coll., Univ. of London 1987–97; mem. (Labour), House of Lords 1987–, Opposition Spokesperson on Educ. and Science, House of Lords 1990–92, on Foreign Affairs 1992–97; Minister of State in Dept of Educ. and Employment 1997–2001; Minister of State for the Arts, Dept for Culture, Media and Sport 2001–03; Dir, Royal Opera House 1987–97, Trustee 2010–; Chair. General Advisory Council BBC 1987–91, RIBA Trust 2003–10, Great Ormond Street Hosp. Trust 2009–; Chair. Bd of Trustees, Inst. for Public Policy Research 1988–97; Chair. British Library Bd 2011–, Orbit Group Bd 2013–; Co-Chair. Franco-British Council 2013–; mem. Bd of Dirs Thames TV 1991–92, Rover Learning Business Bd 1991–97, Granada Learning 2003–07, VT Group 2004–, Teachers TV 2004–09, Mott MacDonald 2005–08; Visiting Prof., LSE 2003–05; Vice-Chancellor, Univ. of Greenwich 2004–11; Trustee, British Museum (Natural History) 1992–97; Hon. Fellow, LSE 1995, Birkbeck Coll. 1998, Canterbury Christchurch Univ. 2010; Hon. DLitt (Bradford) 1990, (Bristol Polytechnic) 1991; Hon. DUniv (Middlesex) 1993, (Strathclyde) 1996, (Leeds Metropolitan) 1996; Hon. LLD (Aberdeen) 1994, (St Andrews) 1995; Dr hc (Dauphine, Sorbonne, Paris) 1998, (Univ. of Rome Roma 3) 2005, (Queen's, Belfast) 2007, (Kent) 2011, (Greenwich) 2012. *Publications:* A Fair Start 1971, Education and Day Care for Young Children in Need 1973, Social Policy and Administration in Britain 1975; co-author: Students in Conflict 1970, The Academic Labour Market 1974, Disadvantage and Education 1982, Education Policy and Educational Inequality 1982, Response to Adversity 1983, Testing Children 1983, Inside the Think Tank: Advising the Cabinet 1971–83, 1988, Prisons and Penal Reform 1990, Race Relations in Britain 1997. *Leisure interests:* tennis, walking, ballet, opera, bridge. *Address:* House of Lords, Westminster, London, SW1A 0PW, England (office). *Telephone:* (20) 7219-5409 (office). *E-mail:* blackstonet@parliament.uk (office). *Website:* www.parliament.uk/biographies/lords/baroness-blackstone/3561 (office).

BLACKWELL, Julian Toby; British bookseller; b. 10 Jan. 1929; s. of the late Sir Basil Henry Blackwell and Marion Christine Soans; m. Jennifer Jocelyn Barley Wykeham 1953; two s. one d.; ed Winchester Coll., Trinity Coll., Oxford; served 5th Royal Tank Regt 1947–49; 21st SAS (TA) 1950–59; Dir and Chair. various Blackwell cos 1956–99; Chair. Blackwell Group Ltd 1980–94; Pres. Blackwell Ltd (retd) 1995–99, Chair. 1996–99 (retd); Chair. Council, ASLIB 1966–68; Pres.

Booksellers' Assen 1980–82; Chair. Thames Business Advice Centre 1986–97, Heart of England TEC 1989–94, Fox FM 1989–98, Cottontail Ltd 1990; apptd Chair. Son White Memorial Trust 1991, Milestone Group; DL (Oxfordshire) 1988; Hon. DLitt (Robert Gordon) 1997, DUniv (Sheffield Hallam) 1998. *Leisure interests:* sawing firewood, sailing. *Address:* c/o Blackwell UK, 50 Broad Street, Oxford, OX1 3BQ, England.

BLACKWELL, Kimberly L., MD; American oncologist and academic; *Assistant Professor in Radiation Oncology, School of Medicine, Duke University;* b. 1969; two s.; ed Duke Univ., Mayo Medical School; currently Prof. of Medicine and Asst Prof. of Radiation Oncology, Duke Univ. Medical Center, also Dir Breast Cancer Program, Duke Cancer Inst., Durham, NC; prin. investigator or co-prin. investigator in over 50 clinical trials in breast cancer. *Publications:* author or co-author of over 60 articles or book chapters in journals including Clinical Cancer Research, The Journal of Clinical Oncology, Cancer, Radiation Research, Molecular Cancer Therapeutics. *Address:* Duke University Medical Center 3893, Durham, NC 27710, USA (office). *Telephone:* (919) 668-1748 (office). *Fax:* (919) 681-0874 (office). *Website:* medicine.duke.edu (office).

BLACKWELL, Baron (Life Peer), cr. 1997, of Woodcote in the County of Surrey; **Norman Roy Blackwell,** MA, PhD, MBA; British business executive and fmr civil servant; b. 29 July 1952, London, England; s. of Albert Edward Blackwell and Frances Evelyn Blackwell (née Lutman); m. Brenda Clucas 1974; three s. two d.; ed Latymer Upper School, Trinity Coll., Cambridge, Wharton Business School, Univ. of Pennsylvania (Thouron Scholar); Jr Exhibitioner RAM 1963–69; Chair. Cambridge Univ. Conservative Asscn 1973; with Strategic Planning Unit, Plessey Co. 1976–78, McKinsey & Co. 1978–86, 1988–95 (Partner 1984), Prime Minister's Policy Unit 1986–88, Head 1995–97 Dir of Group Devt NatWest Group 1997–2000; Chair. Smartstream Technologies Group 2001–05, Interserve plc 2006–, Scottish Widows Group 2012–; Dir, Dixons Group 2000–03, Corp. Services Group 2000–06, SEGRO Plc 2001–10, Standard Life 2003–12, Halma Plc 2010–, Lloyds Banking Group Plc 2012–; Special Adviser, KPMG Corp. Finance 2000–09; Chair. Centre for Policy Studies 2000–09; mem. Bd Office of Fair Trading 2003–10, Ofcom 2009–; mem. (Conservative) House of Lords 1997–. *Leisure interests:* classical music, walking. *Address:* House of Lords, Westminster, London, SW1A 0PW, England (office). *Telephone:* (20) 7219-8672 (office). *E-mail:* blackwelln@parliament.uk (office). *Website:* www.parliament.uk/biographies/lords/norman-blackwell/27109 (office).

BLAGA, Vasile; Romanian politician; *President, Democratic Liberal Party;* b. 26 July 1956, Petrileni, Bihor Co.; m.; two c.; ed Nat. Defence Coll., Timişoara Polytechnic Univ.; work team head, SC Hiperion SA, Bihor, then workshop head, plant section deputy head, plant section coordinating head, manager, 1981–90; Deputy of Bihor for Nat. Salvation Front party 1990–91; Prefect of Bihor 1991–93; Gen.-Dir, Oradea Customs Regional Authority 1993–96; Senator of Bihor 1996–2000, of Bucharest 2004–; Minister of Admin and Interior Affairs 2004–07, interim Minister of the Interior Oct. 2009, Minister of Devt and Tourism Nov. 2009, of the Interior and Admin. Reform Dec. 2009–10 (resgnd); cand. for Mayor of Bucharest 2008; Pres. Senate 2011–12; Founding mem. Democrat Party (PD, later renamed Democratic Liberal Party (Partidul Democrat Liberal—PD-L)), Pres. of Bihor Co. PD Org. 1991–97, Sec.-Gen. PD 1997–2001, 2005–08, Sec.-Gen. PD-L 2008–11, Pres. PD Bucharest, party Vice-Pres. 2001–04, Pres. 2012–; mem. Nat. Council of Justice and Truth Alliance 2003–04. *Address:* Partidul Democrat Liberal, 011825 Bucharest, Sector 1, Al. Modrogan 1, Romania (office). *Telephone:* (21) 2303701 (office). *Fax:* (21) 2302262 (office); (21) 2301625 (office). *E-mail:* office@pd.ro (office). *Website:* www.pd-l.ro; www.vasileblaga.ro.

BLAGOJEVICH, Rod R., BA, JD; American fmr politician; b. 10 Dec. 1956, Chicago; s. of Rade Blagojevich and Millie Blagojevich (née Govedarica); m. Patricia Blagojevich; two d.; ed Northwestern Univ., Pepperdine Univ.; est. pvt. law practice, Chicago 1983; Asst State Attorney, Cook Co. 1983–92; mem. Ill. Gen. Ass. 1992–96; mem. US House of Reps, Washington, DC 1997–2003; Gov. of Ill. 2003–09, impeached and removed from office, convicted of 17 public corruption charges, sentenced to 14 years in prison 2011; Democrat; Library Man of the Year, American Library Asscn, Friends of Libraries USA, Whitehouse Conf. on Libraries. *Publication:* The Governor 2009.

BLAHNIK, Manolo, CBE; Spanish couturier; b. 28 Nov. 1942, Santa Cruz, The Canary Islands; ed Univ. of Geneva; studied architecture and literature but left univ. and travelled to Paris 1968; moved to London and worked briefly as photographer for Sunday Times 1970; cr. first shoe collection 1972; Founder and Dir Manolo Blahnik Int. Ltd; opened shop in Chelsea, London 1973, USA 1981, Hong Kong 1991; biannual collections in London and New York; Hon. Royal Designer for Industry, Royal Soc. of Arts (GB) 2001; La Medalla de Oro en Merito en las Bellas Artes 2002, Hon. CBE (GB) 2007; Dr hc (Royal London Coll. of Art) 2001; Council of Fashion Designers of America Awards 1987, 1990, 1998, American Leather New York Award 1991, British Fashion Award 1992, Neiman Marcus Award 1993, 2000, Accessory Designer of the Year, British Fashion Council 1990, 1999, 2003, Footwear News Designer of the Year Award 1998, 2003, Lifetime Achievement Award 2011, Silver Slipper Award, Houston Museum of Fine Art 1999, La Aguja de Oro (Spain) 2001, La Medalla de Oro de Canarias 2003, Accessory Designer of the Year Award, British Style Awards 2003, Pinnacle in Art & Design Award, Pratt Inst., New York (USA) 2005, Lifetime Achievement Award, Telva Magazine 2005, Prix de la Mode: Outstanding Achievement Award, Marie Claire (Spain) 2008, André Leon Talley Lifetime Achievement Award, Savannah Coll. of Art & Design (USA) 2011. *Publications:* Manolo Blahnik Drawings 2003, Manolo's New Shoes 2010, The Tale of the Elves and the Shoemaker (illustrator) 2011; various int. publs on fashion. *Leisure interests:* painting, reading, watching old films. *Address:* 49–51 Old Church Street, London, SW3 5BS, England (office). *Telephone:* (20) 7352-8622 (office). *Website:* www.manoloblahnik.com (office).

BLAINEY, Geoffrey Norman, AC; Australian historian and author; b. 11 March 1930, Melbourne, Vic.; s. of Rev. Samuel C. Blainey and Hilda Blainey; m. Ann Heriot 1957; one d.; ed Ballarat High School, Wesley Coll., Univ. of Melbourne; freelance historian 1951–61; Reader in Econ. History, Univ. of Melbourne 1963–68, Prof. 1968–76, Ernest Scott Prof. of History 1977–88, Dean of Faculty of Arts 1982–87; Prof. of Australian Studies, Harvard Univ., USA 1982–83; columnist in daily newspapers 1974–; Deputy Chair. Nat. Inquiry into Museums

1974–75; Commr, Australian Heritage Comm. 1976–77; Chair. Australia Council 1977–81, Chair. Fed. Govt's Australia-China Council 1979–84, Chair. Commonwealth Literary Fund 1971–73; Pres. Council, Queen's Coll., Univ. of Melbourne 1971–89; Chair. Australian Selection Cttee Commonwealth Fund (Harkness) Fellowships 1983–90; Chancellor Univ. of Ballarat 1994–98; Dir Royal Humane Soc. 1996–2004; Gov. Ian Potter Foundation 1991–; Councillor, Nat. Council for the Centenary of Fed. 1997–2002 (Chair. 2001–02), Australian War Memorial 1997–2004; Del. to Australian Constitutional Convention 1998; Hon. LLD (Melbourne, Ballarat); Gold Medal, Australian Literature Soc. 1963, Capt. Cook Bicentenary Literary Award 1970, Britannica Award for dissemination of learning, New York 1988, Dublin Prize 1986, Australian Authors' Soc. Book of the Year 2000, Centenary Medal 2003. *Television includes:* The Blainey View (10-part series for ABC) 1982–83. *Publications include:* The Peaks of Lyell 1954, Centenary History of the University of Melbourne 1957, Gold and Paper: A History of the National Bank 1958, Mines in the Spinifex 1960, The Rush That Never Ended 1963, A History of Camberwell 1965, If I Remember Rightly: The Memoirs of W. S. Robinson 1966, The Tyranny of Distance 1966, Wesley College: The First Hundred Years (co-author and ed.) 1967, Across a Red World 1968, The Rise of Broken Hill 1968, The Steel Master 1971, The Causes of War 1973, Triumph of the Nomads: A History of Ancient Australia 1975, A Land Half Won 1980, Our Side of the Country 1984, All for Australia 1984, The Great Seesaw 1988, A Game of Our Own 1990, Eye on Australia 1991, Odd Fellows 1992, The Golden Mile 1993, Jumping over the Wheel 1993, A Shorter History of Australia 1994, White Gold 1997, A History of AMP 1999, In Our Time 1999, A Short History of the World 2000, This Land is All Horizons 2001, Black Kettle and Full Moon: Daily Life in a Vanished Australia 2003, A Very Short History of the World 2004, A Short History of the Twentieth Century 2005, A History of Victoria 2006, Sea of Dangers: Captain Cook and His Rivals 2009, A Short History of Christianity 2011. *Leisure interests:* travel, wood chopping, Australian football. *Address:* PO Box 257, East Melbourne, Vic. 8002, Australia (home). *Telephone:* (3) 9417-7782 (home).

BLAIR, Rt Hon. Anthony (Tony) Charles Lynton, BA, PC; British barrister, consultant and fmr politician; *Special Envoy, Quartet on the Middle East;* b. 6 May 1953, Edinburgh, Scotland; s. of Leo Blair and the late Hazel Blair; m. Cherie Booth (q.v.) 1980; three s. one d.; ed Fettes Coll., Edinburgh, St John's Coll., Oxford; barrister, specializing in trade union and employment law; MP for Sedgefield 1983–2007; Shadow Spokesman on the Treasury 1984–87, on Trade and Industry 1987–88, on Energy 1988–89, on Employment 1989–92, on Home Affairs 1992–94; Leader of the Labour Party 1994–2007; Prime Minister, First Lord of the Treasury and Minister for the Civil Service 1997–2007 (re-elected 2001, 2005); Special Envoy to Middle East on behalf of Quartet (USA, Russia, EU and UN) 2007–; mem. Bd of Dirs World Econ. Forum Foundation Bd 2007–; f. Tony Blair Sports Foundation 2007, Tony Blair Faith Foundation; Founder and Patron, Africa Governance Initiative; Sr Adviser, JP Morgan Chase & Co. 2008–; Adviser, Zurich Financial Services working on int. politics and climate change 2008–, Khosla Ventures working on investment in environmentally friendly technologies 2010–, Albanian Govt in joining EU 2013; Howland Distinguished Fellow, Yale Univ. 2008–09; Hon. Bencher, Lincoln's Inn 1994; Hon. LLD (Northumbria) 1995; numerous awards including Charlemagne Prize 1999, Ellis Island Medal of Honor for Int. Leadership 2003, US Congressional Gold Medal of Honor 2003, Polio Eradication Champion, Rotary International 2006, US Presidential Medal of Freedom 2009, Philadelphia Liberty Medal 2010. *Publications:* New Britain: My Vision of a Young Country 1996, The Third Way 1998, A Journey 2010. *Address:* The Office of Tony Blair, PO Box 60519, London, W2 7JU, England (office). *E-mail:* info@tonyblairoffice.org (office). *Website:* www.tonyblairoffice.org (office); www .tonyblairfaithfoundation.org (office); www.africagovernance.org (office).

BLAIR, Cherie (see BOOTH, Cherie).

BLAIR, Dennis Cutler, BA; American naval officer (retd) and government official; b. 4 Feb. 1947, Kittery, Me; s. of Capt. Carvel Hall Blair and Abbie Dora Blair (née Ansel); m. Diane Blair; one s. one d.; ed US Naval Acad., Univ. of Oxford, UK; commissioned as ensign in USN, attained rank of Vice-Adm., Commdr USS Cochrane 1984–86, Naval Staff, Pearl Harbor 1988–89, Kittyhawk Battle-group 1993–95; Assoc. Dir Mil. Support, CIA 1995–96, also mem. Nat. Security Council; Dir Jt Staff 1996–99; C-in-C US Pacific Command, HI 1999–2002 (retd); Sr Fellow, Inst. for Defence Analyses 2002–03, Pres. 2003–07, then consultant; US Dir of Nat. Intelligence, Washington, DC 2009–10 (resgnd); held John M. Shalikashvili Chair in Nat. Security Studies, Nat. Bureau of Asian Research and Gen. of the Army Omar N. Bradley Chair of Strategic Leadership, Dickinson Coll. and US Army War Coll.; served as Deputy Exec. Dir Project on Nat. Security Reform; mem. IISS Council, Energy Security Leadership Council of Securing America's Future Energy, Aspen Homeland Security Council; mem. Bd of Dirs Nat. Bureau of Asian Research, Nat. Cttee on US-China Relations; mem. Bd of Trustees Freedom House; Defense Distinguished Service Medal with three oak leaf clusters, Defense Superior Service Medal, Legion of Merit, Meritorious Service Medal, Navy and Marine Corps Commendation Medal, Navy and Marine Corps Achievement Medal, Nat. Intelligence Distinguished Service Medal with star. *Publication:* Military Engagement: Influencing Armed Forces Worldwide to Support Democratic Transitions 2013.

BLAIR, Gordon Purves, CBE, PhD, DSc, FREng, FIMechE; British engineer and academic; *Professor Emeritus of Mechanical Engineering, Queen's University Belfast;* b. 29 April 1937, Larne, Northern Ireland; s. of Gordon Blair and Mary H. J. Blair; m. Norma Margaret Millar 1964; two d.; ed Larne Grammar School and Queen's Univ. Belfast; Asst Prof., Mechanical Eng, New Mexico State Univ., USA 1962–64; Lecturer in Mechanical Eng, Queen's Univ. Belfast 1964–71, Sr Lecturer 1971–73, Reader 1973–76, Prof. of Mechanical Eng 1976–96, Prof. Emer. 1996–, Prof. and Head of Dept of Mechanical and Industrial Eng 1982–88, Dean of Faculty 1985–88, Pro-Vice-Chancellor 1989–94; f. Prof. Blair and Associates (software co.); Fellow, SAE; Colwell Technical Merit Award (SAE), Crompton Lanchester Medal (IMechE), Trident TV Award (IBA). *Publications:* The Basic Design of Two-Stroke Engines 1990, The Design and Simulation of Two-Stroke Engines 1996, The Design and Simulation of Four Stroke Engines 1999; more than 100 tech. papers in int. journals. *Leisure interests:* golf, fishing, motorcycling. *Address:* 9 Ben Madigan Park South, Newtonabbey, Co. Antrim, BT36 7PX (home); Ashby Building, The Queen's University of Belfast, Belfast, BT9 5AH, Northern Ireland. *Telephone:*

(28) 9037-0368 (home). *Fax:* (28) 9037-0372 (home). *E-mail:* gpb@ profblairandassociates.com (office); g.p.blair@qub.ac.uk (home). *Website:* www .profblairandassociates.com (office).

BLAIS, Marie-Claire, CC; Canadian writer; b. 5 Oct. 1939, Québec City; d. of Fernando Blais and Véronique Nolin; ed studied in Québec, Paris, France and USA; Guggenheim Foundation Fellowship, New York 1963, 1964; mem. Royal Soc. of Canada, Acad. Royale de Belgique, Acad. des Lettres françaises; Hon. mem. Boivin Center of French Language and Culture, Univ. of Massachusetts, USA; Hon. Prof., Univ. of Calgary 1978; Chevalier, Légion d'honneur; Dr hc (York Univ., Toronto) 1975, (Lyon) 2003, (Ottawa) 2004, (Lyon) 2005; Prix de la langue française 1961, Prix France-Québec 1964, Prix Médicis 1966, Prix de l'Acad. Française 1983, Prix Athanase-David (Québec) 1983, Prix Nessim Habif (Acad. Royale de Belgique) 1991, Prix de la Fondation Prince Pierre de Monaco, Prix du Gouverneur Général (Canada) (three times), Prix Gilles Corbeil 2005, Matt Cohen Award 2006, and others. *Publications:* La belle bête 1959, Tête blanche 1960, Le jour est noir 1962, Existences (poems) 1964, Une saison dans la vie d'Emmanuel 1965, L'insoumise 1966, Les voyageurs sacrés 1966, David Sterne 1967, L'océan 1967, L'exécution 1968, Manuscrits de Pauline Archange 1968, Vivre, vivre 1969, Les apparences 1970, Le loup 1972, Un Joualonais sa Joualonie 1973, Théâtre radiophonique 1974, Fièvre 1974, Une liaison parisienne 1976, La nef des sorcières 1976, Les nuits de l'underground 1978, Le sourd dans la ville 1980, Visions d'Anna 1982, Pierre 1984, Sommeil d'hiver 1985, Fière 1985, L'île 1988 (plays), L'ange de la solitude (novel) 1989, Un jardin dans la tempête (play) 1990, Parcours d'un Ecrivain: Notes Américaines (essay) 1993, L'Exile (short stories) 1993, Soifs (novel) 1995, Théâtre (Ed.), Des Rencontres Humaines 2002, Dans la foudre et la lumière (novel) 2002, Noces à midi au-dessus de l'abîme (play) 2004, Augustino et le choeur de la destruction (novel) 2007, Naissance de Rebecca à l'ère des Tourments (Gov. Gen's Award for Fiction) 2008, Mal au Bal des Prédateurs 2010. *Leisure interests:* painting and drawing, cycling, handwriting analysis, travel. *Address:* Agence Goodwin, 839 Sherbrooke Estate, Suite 2, Montréal, H26 1K6, Canada (office); 717 Windsor Lane, Key West, FL 33040, USA (home). *Telephone:* (514) 598-5252 (office); (305) 292-9450 (home). *Fax:* (514) 598-1878 (office). *E-mail:* goodleim@qc.aira.com (office).

BLAIS, Hon. Pierre, PC, BA, LLL; Canadian lawyer, judge, politician and fmr academic; *Chief Justice, Federal Court of Appeal;* b. 30 Dec. 1948, Berthier-sur-Mer, Québec; m. Chantal Fournier; two s. two d.; ed Sainte-Anne-de-la-Pocatière Coll., Laval Univ.; mem. House of Commons 1984–93; Parl. Sec. to Minister of Agric. 1984–86, to Deputy Prime Minister 1986–87; Solicitor-Gen. of Canada 1989–90; Minister of State (Agric.) 1990; Minister of Consumer and Corp. Affairs 1990–93; Minister of Justice, Attorney-Gen. and Pres. Privy Council 1993; Partner, Langlois Gaudreau law practice, Québec 1993–98; Judge, Fed. Court of Canada, Trial Division and ex officio mem. Court of Appeal and Judge, Court Martial Appeal Court of Canada 1998; mem. Competition Tribunal 2002–08; Pres. Public Servants Disclosure Protection Tribunal 2007–08; Judge, Fed. Court of Appeal 2008–, Chief Justice 2009–; Fellow, Inst. of Advanced Legal Studies, Univ. of London, UK 2008. *Leisure interests:* skiing, reading, swimming. *Address:* Federal Court of Appeal, Supreme Court Building, Kent and Wellington Streets, Ottawa, ON K1A 0H9, Canada (office). *Telephone:* (613) 943-9259 (office). *Website:* www.fca-caf.gc.ca (office).

BLAKE, Christopher, BE; New Zealand composer, civil servant and arts administrator; *Chief Executive, New Zealand Symphony Orchestra;* b. 1949, Christchurch; ed Univ. of Canterbury, Univ. of Southampton, UK; fmr Chief Exec., Dept of Internal Affairs; fmr Gen. Man. Nat. Opera of New Zealand, Auckland Philharmonia Orchestra and Canterbury Orchestra; fmr Man. Concert FM, Radio New Zealand Concert; Foundation Chief Exec., Ministry for Culture and Heritage 1991–97; Chief Exec. and Nat. Librarian, Nat. Library of New Zealand 1997–2002; currently Chief Exec. and Sec. for Labour, Dept of Labour; Chief Exec., New Zealand Symphony Orchestra 2012–; numerous comms for a wide range of performers and ensembles. *Publications include:* Music in New Zealand Spring 1989. *Address:* New Zealand Symphony Orchestra, PO Box 6640, Wellington 6141 (office); New Zealand Symphony Orchestra, Level 2, 101 Wakefield Street, Wellington 6011, New Zealand (office). *Telephone:* (4) 801-3890 (office). *Fax:* (4) 801-3891 (office). *E-mail:* info@nzso.co.nz (office). *Website:* www.nzso.co.nz (office).

BLAKE, Francis (Frank) S., BA, JD; American lawyer and business executive; *Chairman and CEO, The Home Depot Inc.;* b. 30 Aug. 1949, Boston, Mass; s. of George Baty Blake and Rosemary Blake (née Shaw); m. Anne McChristian 1977; one s. one d.; ed Harvard Coll., Columbia Univ. School of Law; Legis. Aide, Jt Cttee on Social Welfare, Mass Legislature, Boston 1971–73; law clerk, US Court of Appeals, NY 1976–77, to Justice Stevens, US Supreme Court, Washington, DC 1976–78; Assoc., Leva, Hawes, Symington, Martin & Oppenheimer 1978–81; Deputy Counsel to Vice-Pres. George Bush, The White House 1981–83; Partner, Swidler Berlin & Strelw 1983–85; Gen. Counsel, US Environmental Protection Agency 1985–88; Vice-Pres. and Gen. Counsel, GE Power Systems 1991–95, Vice-Pres. Business Devt & Alliances 1995–98, Pres. Business Devt 1998–2000, Sr Vice-Pres. Corp. Business Devt and Gen. Counsel 2000–01; Deputy Sec. US Dept of Energy 2001–02; Exec. Vice-Pres. Business Devt and Corp. Operations, The Home Depot Inc. 2002–07, Vice-Chair. and Exec. Vice-Pres. 2006–07, Chair. and CEO 2007–; mem. Bd of Dirs Southern Co., Atlanta 2004–, Hudson Inst., Washington, DC, Georgia Aquarium. *Address:* The Home Depot Inc., 2455 Paces Ferry Road, NW, Atlanta, GA 30339-4024, USA (office). *Telephone:* (770) 433-821 (office). *Fax:* (770) 384-2356 (office). *E-mail:* info@homedepot.com (office). *Website:* www .homedepot.com (office).

BLAKE, John Clemens, MA, RCA; American artist; b. 11 Jan. 1945, Providence, RI; s. of John Holland Blake and Elizabeth Clemens (now Romano); ed Carnegie Inst. of Tech. (now Carnegie-Mellon Univ.), Yale Univ., Royal Coll. of Art, London; freelance visual artist in various media including drawing, installations, photographic constructions, film and time-based works, etc.; teaching positions include Hull Polytechnic 1975–76, London Coll. of Printing 1978–82, S Glamorgan Inst. of Higher Educ., S Wales 1983–84, W. de Kooning Academie, Rotterdam 1988–2009; residencies include Hokkaido Fellowship, Japan 1984, Banff Centre for the Arts, Canada 1992, Bemis Center for the Arts, Ômaha, Neb., USA 2000; Fulbright Fellow 1967–69; Nat. Endowment (USA) 1977; has lived and worked in London and Amsterdam/Woerden 1967–; Nat. Endowment for the Arts 1977, Arts Council

Award (UK) 1979, Hokkaido Foundation Award (Japan) 1984. *Works in public collections:* Stedelijk Museum, Amsterdam, Museum Fodor, Amsterdam, Rijksmuseum Kroller-Muller, Otterlo, British Council, London, Eastern Arts Asscn, Cambridge, Musée de Toulon, France, Nat. Gallery of Australia, Melbourne, Stadhuis Middelburg, Netherlands, Tate Gallery, London, Museum Sztucki, Łódź, Arts Council of GB, London, Frans Hals Museum, Haarlem, Victoria & Albert Museum, London, Haagsgemeentemuseum, The Hague, Rijksdienst Collectie, Netherlands, Museum Pavillions, Almere, Netherlands, Muzeum Narodowe, Warsaw, Van Reekum Museum, Apeldoorn, Netherlands, New Museum of Contemporary Art, Warsaw, Museum of Contemporary Art, Krakow, Poland. *Commissioned works and works in public spaces include:* photo-construction installation (outdoor) for Entrepotdok (residential and business complex), Amsterdam 1987, Verpleeghuis 'De Vijf Havens' (jtly), Zevenkamp 1989, Light Trap (jtly) for St Jacobus Ziekenhuis, Zwijndrecht 1990, Veurs Coll., Leidesche-dam, Netherlands 1991, Haags Montessori Lyceum, The Hague 1991, photo-construction for 'De Cascade', Prov. Archive Offices, Groningen 1998, Dukaat/De Aker (residential and business complex, in collaboration with Tangram Archi-tekten), Osdorp, Amsterdam 2000, outdoor installation incorporating two tram shelters and related object for Kunsthalte With de Withstraat – 'De hals', Museum Quarter/Westersingel, Rotterdam 2000. *Films:* Tongue Film, Arrest 1970, Rose, Focus A/B, Untitled (Juggler) 1972, Five Glass Panes Broken/Not Broken 1973, Bridge Film 1974. *Publications:* catalogue of ICA, London 1980, De Vleeshal in De Vleeshal – Their Eves/Hun Ogen (two catalogues) (co-author) 1983, 600 Eyes for Krzysztofory (text and photos) 1987, River – A Work in Almere (text and photos) 1991, Guard 1991, River 1991, John Blake on Aleph 1993, On the Ideal Place 1994, Remember Wtedy i Teraz – Teraz i Wtedy: John Blake's Works in Poland 1980–1994 1995, John Blake: Bunker – München 1996, De Hals: Kunsthalte with de Withstraat 1996, S-P-I-N-E (with Peter Mason) 2002. *Address:* c/o J. P. Blonk, Gedempte Binnengracht 19A, 3441 AE Woerden, Netherlands (office). *Telephone:* (348) 481850 (office). *E-mail:* Jb@studiojohnblake.com. *Website:* www .studiojohnblake.com.

BLAKE, Sir Peter Thomas, Kt, CBE, RA, ARCA, RDI; British artist; b. 25 June 1932, Dartford, Kent; s. of Kenneth William Blake; m. 1st Jann Haworth 1963 (divorced 1982); two d.; m. 2nd Chrissy Wilson 1987; one d.; ed Gravesend Tech. Coll., Gravesend School of Art, Royal Coll. of Art; third assoc. artist of Nat. Gallery, London 1994–96; works exhibited in Inst. of Contemporary Art 1958, 1960, Guggenheim Competition 1958, Cambridge 1959, Royal Acad. 1960, Musée d'Art Moderne, Paris 1963; works in perm. collections, Trinity Coll., Cambridge, Carlisle City Gallery, Tate Gallery, Arts Council of GB, Museum of Modern Art, New York, Victoria and Albert Museum, other maj. galleries; designed cover of Beatles' album Sgt Pepper's Lonely Hearts Club Band 1967, posters for Live Aid 1985, Live 8 2005; Dr hc (RCA), (Brunel) 2010, (Roehampton) 2010, (Leeds) 2011. *Publications:* illustrations for Oxford Illustrated Old Testament 1968, Venice Fantasies, several Arden Shakespeares, Alice Through the Looking Glass, Peter Blake's ABC, Peter Blake Alphabets, Peter Blake Design, Paris Escapades 2011, and in various periodicals and magazines. *Leisure interests:* sculpture, wining and dining, going to rock and roll concerts. *Address:* c/o Waddington Galleries Ltd, 11 Cork Street, London, W1X 2LT, England.

BLAKE, Sir Quentin Saxby, Kt, CBE, OBE, RDI, MA, FCSD; British artist, writer, illustrator and teacher; b. 16 Dec. 1932, Sidcup, Kent, England; s. of William Blake and Evelyn Blake; ed Downing Coll., Cambridge, London Inst. of Educ., Chelsea School of Art; freelance illustrator 1957–; Tutor, RCA 1965–86, Head of Illustration Dept 1978–86, Sr Fellow RCA 1988, Visiting Prof. 1989–; first British Children's Laureate 1999–2001; Hon. Fellow, Univ. of Brighton 1996, Downing Coll. Cambridge 2000, Cardiff Univ. 2006, Hon. RA; Officier, Ordre des Arts et des Lettres 2002; Dr hc (London Inst.) 2000, (Northumbria) 2001, (RCA) 2001, (Open Univ.) 2006, (Loughborough) 2007, (Anglia Ruskin Univ.); Hon. DLitt (Cambridge) 2004. *Publications include:* Patrick 1968, Angelo 1970, Mister Magnolia 1980, Quentin Blake's Nursery Rhyme Book 1983, The Story of the Dancing Frog 1984, Mrs Armitage on Wheels 1987, Mrs Armitage Queen of the Road, Quentin Blake's ABC 1989, All Join In 1992, Cockatoos 1992, Simpkin 1993, La Vie de la Page 1995, The Puffin Book of Nonsense Verse 1996, Mrs Armitage and the Big Wave 1997, The Green Ship 1998, Clown 1998, Drawing for the Artistically Undiscovered (with John Cassidy) 1999, Fantastic Daisy Artichoke 1999, Words and Pictures 2000, The Laureate's Party 2000, Zagazoo 2000, Tell Me a Picture 2001, Loveykins 2002, A Sailing Boat in the Sky 2002, Laureate's Progress 2002, Angel Pavement 2004, The Life of Birds 2005; illustrations for over 250 works for children and adults, including collaborations with Roald Dahl, Russell Hoban, Joan Aiken, Michael Rosen, John Yeoman, Michael Morpurgo. *Address:* c/o AP Watt at United Agents LLP, 12–26 Lexington Street, London, W1F 0LE, England (office); Flat 8, 30 Bramham Gardens, London, SW5 0HF, England (home). *Telephone:* (20) 3214-0800 (office). *Fax:* (20) 3214-0801 (office). *E-mail:* info@unitedagents.co.uk (office). *Website:* www.apwatt.co.uk (office); www .quentinblake.com.

BLAKE, Yohan; Jamaican track and field athlete; b. 26 Dec. 1989, St James; s. of Shirley Blake and Veda Blake; ed St Jago High School; gold medal, 100m, 200m, Caribbean Free Trade Asscn (CARIFTA) Games (Youth), Bacolet 2005, gold medal, 200m, 4×100m relay, CARIFTA Games (Junior), Les Abymes 2006, gold medal, 100m, 200m, 4×100m relay, Central American and Caribbean (CAC) Junior Championships (U20), Port of Spain 2006; gold medal, 4×100m relay, bronze medal, 100m, World Junior Championships, Beijing 2006; gold medal, 100m, 4×100m relay, CARIFTA Games (Junior), Providenciales 2007; silver medal, 100m, bronze medal, 4×400m relay, Pan American Junior Championships, São Paulo 2007; gold medal, 100m, CARIFTA Games (Junior), Basseterre 2008; silver medal, 4×100m relay, World Junior Championships, Bydgoszcz 2008; gold medal, 100m (9.92 seconds, became youngest 100m world champion ever), 4×100m relay, World Championships, Daegu 2011; won 100m, Diamond League, Zurich 2011, 200m, Brussels 2011; gold medal, 100m, Int. Asscn of Athletics Feds (IAAF) World Challenge, Berlin 2011, gold medal, 100m, Kingston 2011, silver medal, 200m, Ostrava 2011, gold medal, 200m, Kingston 2012; gold medal, 4×100m relay, silver medal, 100m, 200m, Olympic Games, London 2012; est. YB Afraid Foundation 2011; holds nat. (junior) record for 100m, is the youngest sprinter to have broken 10-second barrier (at 19 years, 196 days); coached by Glen Mills; Austin Sealy Trophy for Most Outstanding Athlete, CARIFTA Games 2007. *Leisure interest:*

cricket. *Address:* c/o Racers Track Club, 3 Port of Spain Drive, University of the West Indies, Mona, Kingston, Jamaica. *Telephone:* 970-4854. *E-mail:* admin@racersstrackclub.com; contact@ybafraidfoundation.org (office). *Website:* www.racerstrackclub.com; www.ybafraid.com (office).

BLAKELY, Sara, BA; American business executive; *Founder, Spanx Inc.;* b. 21 Feb. 1971, Clearwater, Fla; m. Jesse Itzler 2008; one s.; ed Florida State Univ.; began career as sales rep. with Danka Business Systems (fax and photocopier co.), Tampa; f. Spanx Inc. (based on own prototype design for shapewear lingerie) 2000; f. Sara Blakely Foundation (charitable foundation) 2006; TV appearances include The Rebel Billionaire (Fox TV) 2004, judge on American Inventor (ABC) 2007; named by Forbes Magazine as world's youngest self-made female billionaire 2012, named as one of TIME magazine's 100 Most Influential People 2012, ranked by Forbes magazine amongst The World's 100 Most Powerful Women (90th) 2013. *Address:* Spanx Inc., 3344 Peachtree Road NE, #1700, Atlanta, GA 30305, USA (office). *Telephone:* (404) 321-1608 (office). *Website:* www.spanx.com (office).

BLAKEMORE, Colin (Brian), PhD, ScD, DSc, FRS, FMedSci, CBiol; British neuroscientist and academic; *Professor of Neuroscience, Universities of Oxford and Warwick;* b. 1 June 1944, Stratford-upon-Avon; s. of Cedric Norman and Beryl Ann Blakemore; m. Andrée Elizabeth Washbourne 1965; three d.; ed King Henry VIII School, Coventry, Corpus Christi Coll., Cambridge, Univ. of California, Berkeley, USA; Harkness Fellowship, Univ. of California, Berkeley 1965–67; Univ. Demonstrator, Physiological Lab., Univ. of Cambridge 1968–72, Lecturer in Physiology 1972–79, Fellow and Dir of Medical Studies, Downing Coll. Cambridge 1971–79; Visiting Prof., New York Univ. 1970, MIT 1971, Univ. of Toronto 1984, McMaster Univ. 1992, Univ. of California, Davis 1980, 1995–97; Visiting Scientist, Salk Inst., San Diego 1982–83, 1992; Locke Research Fellow, Royal Soc. 1976–79; Waynflete Prof. of Physiology, Univ. of Oxford 1979–2007; Prof. of Physiology, Univ. of Warwick; Professorial Fellow, Magdalen Coll. Oxford 1979–; Vice-Chair. European Dana Alliance for the Brain 1996–; CEO MRC 2003–07; Vice-Pres. BAAS 1990–97, 1998–2001, Pres. 1997–98, Chair. 2001–03; Pres. Physiological Soc. 1997–2000, Physiological Soc. 2001–03, Biosciences Fed. 2002–04; Dir McDonnell-Pew Centre for Cognitive Neuroscience, Oxford 1990–2003, MRC Interdisciplinary Research Centre for Cognitive Neuroscience, Oxford 1996–2003; Assoc. Dir MRC Research Centre in Brain and Behaviour, Oxford 1990–96; Commr UK Drug Policy Comm. 2006–; mem. Advisory Council Asscn of the British Pharmaceutical Industry 2007–; Chair. Gen. Advisory Cttee on Science, Food Standards Agency 2007–, A*STAR – Duke-NUS Grad. Medical School Partnership in Neuroscience, Singapore 2007–; Dir (non-exec.) Harkness Fellows Asscn and Transatlantic Trust 2001–, Physiological Soc. 2001–, SANE 2001–, Biosciences Fed. 2002–, Coalition for Medical Progress, British Technology Group plc 2007–; Assoc. Ed. NeuroReport 1989–2003; Ed.-in-Chief IBRO News 1986–2000; mem. Editorial Bd Perception 1971, Behavioral and Brain Sciences 1977, Journal of Developmental Physiology 1978–86, Experimental Brain Research 1979–89, Language and Communication 1979, Reviews in the Neurosciences 1984–, News in Physiological Sciences 1985, Clinical Vision Sciences 1986, Chinese Journal of Physiological Sciences 1988, Advances in Neuroscience 1989–, Vision Research 1993–, Int. Review of Neurobiology 1996–, EuroBrain 1998, American Journal of Bioethics 2006–; Leverhulme Fellowship 1974–75; Lethaby Prof., RCA, London 1978; Storer Lecturer, Univ. of California, Davis 1980, Regents' Prof. 1995–96; Macallum Lecturer, Univ. of Toronto 1984; Fellow, World Econ. Forum 1994–98; Founder Fellow, Acad. of Medical Sciences 1998–; Foreign mem. Royal Netherlands Acad. of Arts and Sciences 1993; mem. Experimental Psychology Soc. 1968–, Research Defence Soc. (Chair. of Council 2007–) 1969–, European Brain and Behaviour Soc. 1972–, Int. Brain Research Org. 1973–, Cambridge Philosophical Soc. 1975–, Soc. foe Neuroscience 1981–, Oxford Medical Soc. 1986–, Child Vision Research Soc. 1986–, British Asscn for the Advancement of Science (Pres. 1997–98, Chair. 2001–03) 1989–, Int. Soc. for Myochemistry 1989–, European Biomedical Research Asscn (founder mem.) 1994–, Inst. of Biology 1996–, Worshipful Co. of Spectacle Makers (mem. Livery 1998–) 1997–, Fed. of European Neuroscience Socs 2000–; Patron and mem. Professional Advisory Panel Headway (Nat. Head Injuries Asscn) 1997–; Patron Asscn for Art, Science, Eng and Tech. (ASCENT) 1997–; Freeman of the City of London 1997; Hon. Pres. World Cultural Council 1983–; Hon. Prof., Peking Union Medical Coll. 2005; Hon. Fellow, Corpus Christi Coll. Cambridge 1994, Cardiff, Univ. of Wales 1998, Downing Coll. Cambridge 1999; Hon. FRCP 2004; Hon. Fellow, BAAS 2001, Inst. of Biology 2004, Indian Acad. of Neurosciences 2007, British Pharmacological Soc. 2007; Hon. mem. Chelsea Arts Club 1992, Alpha Omega Alpha Honor Medical Soc. 1996, Physiological Soc. 1998, Maverick Club 1999, Motor Neurone Disease Asscn; Hon. Assoc. Rationalist Press Asscn 1986, Rationalist Int. 2000, Cambridge Union Soc. 2003; Hon. DSc (Aston) 1992, (Salford) 1994, (Manchester) 2005, (Aberdeen) 2005, (King's Coll. London) 2007; Hon. DM (Nottingham) 2008; Robert Bing Prize, Swiss Acad. of Medical Sciences 1975, Man of the Year, Royal Soc. for Disability and Rehabilitation 1978, John Locke Medal, Worshipful Soc. of Apothecaries 1983, Netter Prize, Acad. Nat. de Médecine, Paris 1984, Bertram Louis Abrahams Lecture, Royal Coll. of Physicians 1986, Cairns Memorial Lecture and Medal, Soc. of British Neurological Surgeons 1986, Norman McAllister Gregg Lecture and Medal, Royal Australian Coll. of Ophthalmologists 1988, Royal Soc. Michael Faraday Medal 1989, Robert Doyne Medal, Oxford Ophthalmology Congress 1989, John P. McGovern Science and Soc. Lecture and Medal 1990, Montgomery Medal 1991, Sir Douglas Robb Lectures, Univ. of Auckland 1991, Osler Medal, Royal Coll. of Physicians 1993, Ellison-Cliffe Medal, Royal Soc. of Medicine 1993, Charles F. Prentice Award, American Acad. of Optometry 1994, Annual Review Prize Lecture, Physiological Soc. 1995, Centenary Lecture, Univ. of Salford 1996, Alcon Prize 1996, Newton Lecture 1997, Cockcroft Lecture, UMIST 1997, Memorial Medal, Charles Univ., Prague 1998, Alfred Meyer Award, British Neuropathological Soc. 2001, Inst. of Biology Charter Award and Medal 2001, Baly Medal, Royal Coll. of Physicians (Dyster Trust) 2001, British Neuroscience Asscn Outstanding Contrib. to Neuroscience 2001, Menzies Medal, Menzies Foundation, Melbourne 2001, Bioindustry Asscn Award for Outstanding Personal Contrib. to Bioscience 2004, Lord Crook Gold Medal, Worshipful Co. of Spectacle Makers 2004, Edinburgh Medal, City of Edinburgh 2005, Science Educator Award, Soc. for Neuroscience 2005, Kenneth Myer Medal, Howard Florey Inst., Univ. of Melbourne 2006. *Films:* several educational films on neuroscience (Silver Award, BMA Film Competition 1972, Silver Award, Padua Int. Film Festival 1973, BMA Certificate of Educational

Commendation 1974). *Radio:* The Reith Lectures (BBC Radio 4) 1976, Machines with Minds (five-part series) 1983. *Television:* Royal Inst. Christmas Lectures 1983, The Mind Machine (13-part series) 1988. *Publications:* Handbook of Psychobiology (ed.) 1975, Mechanics of the Mind 1977, Mindwaves (ed.) 1987, The Mind Machine 1988, Images and Understanding (ed.) 1990, Vision: Coding and Efficiency 1990, Sex and Society 1999, Oxford Companion to the Body 2001, The Physiology of Cognitive Processes (co-ed.) 2003, The Roots of Visual Awareness (co-ed.) 2003; contribs to Constraints on Learning 1973, Illusion in Art and Nature 1973, The Neurosciences Third Study Program 1974 and to professional journals and to nat. newspapers and magazines. *Leisure interests:* running and the arts. *Address:* Room 5609, Nuffield Department of Clinical Medicine, University of Oxford, John Radcliffe Hospital, Oxford, OX3 9DU, England (office). *Telephone:* (1865) 228964 (office). *Fax:* (1865) 222901 (office). *E-mail:* colin.blakemore@ndm.ox.ac.uk (office). *Website:* www.dpag.ox.ac.uk (office).

BLAKEMORE, Michael Howell, AO, OBE; Australian theatre and film director; b. 18 June 1928, Sydney; s. of Conrad Blakemore and Una Mary Blakemore (née Litchfield); m. 1st Shirley Bush 1960; one s.; m. 2nd Tanya McCallin 1986; two d.; ed The King's School, NSW, Sydney Univ., Royal Acad. of Dramatic Art, UK; actor with Birmingham Repertory Theatre, Shakespeare Memorial Theatre etc. 1952–66; Co-Dir Glasgow Citizens' Theatre 1966–68 (first production The Investigation); Assoc. Artistic Dir Nat. Theatre, London 1971–76; Dir Players, New York, USA 1978; Resident Dir Lyric Theatre, Hammersmith, London 1980; Scottish Television Theatre Award (Arturo Ui) 1969, Variety Poll of London Critics Award (Forget-Me-Not Lane) 1971, Plays & Players Award (The Front Page) 1972, Evening Standard Award (A Personal History of the Australian Surf) 1982, Drama Desk Awards, New York (Noises Off) 1983, (Copenhagen) 2000, (Kiss Me Kate) 2000, Hollywood Drama League Award (Noises Off) 1984, Evening Standard Awards for Best Musical Theatre (City of Angels) 1993, (Kiss Me Kate) 2001, Film Critics Circle of Australia Award (Country Life) 1994, Molière Award, France (Copenhagen) 1999, Tony Awards (Copenhagen, Kiss Me Kate) 2000, Critics Circle Award (Kiss Me Kate) 2001, Helpmann Award, Australia (Copenhagen) 2003; inducted into American Theater Hall of Fame 2010. *Films include:* A Personal History of the Australian Surf (writer and dir) 1981, Privates on Parade (dir) 1983, Country Life (writer and dir) 1994. *Productions include:* UK: A Day in the Death of Joe Egg 1967, Arturo Ui 1969, Forget-Me-Not Lane 1971, Design for Living 1973, Separate Tables 1976, Privates on Parade 1977, Candida 1977, Make and Break 1980, Travelling North 1980, The Wild Duck 1980, All My Sons 1981, Noises Off 1982, Benefactors 1984, Lettice and Lovage 1987, Uncle Vanya 1988, Tosca (Welsh Nat. Opera) 1992, City of Angels 1993, Kiss Me Kate 2001, The Three Sisters 2003; at National Theatre, London: The National Health 1969, Long Day's Journey into Night 1971, The Front Page 1992, Macbeth 1992, The Cherry Orchard 1973, Plunder 1976, After the Fall 1990, Copenhagen 1998 (also in France 1999, Australia 2003 and USA 1999), Democracy 2004; USA: A Day in the Death of Joe Egg 1968, Noises Off 1983, Benefactors 1986, City of Angels 1989, Lettice & Lovage 1990, Death Defying Acts 1995, The Life 1997, Kiss Me Kate 1999, Copenhagen 1999, Deuce 2007, Is He Dead 2007, Blithe Spirit 2009. *Television productions include:* Long Day's Journey into Night 1972, Hay Fever (Denmark) 1978, Tales from the Hollywood Hills (USA) 1988. *Publications include:* Next Season (novel) 1969, Australia Fair? (anthology) 1985, Arguments with England (autobiography) 2004, Stage Blood (autobiography) 2013. *Leisure interest:* surfing. *Address:* 47 Ridgmount Gardens, London, WC1E 7AT, England (home). *Telephone:* (20) 7209-0608 (home). *Fax:* (20) 7209-0141 (home).

BLAKENHAM, 2nd Viscount (cr. 1963), of Little Blakenham; Michael John Hare, PC, OBE, DL; British business executive; b. 25 Jan. 1938, London; s. of the late 1st Viscount Blakenham and Hon. Beryl Nancy Pearson; m. Marcia P. Hare 1965; one s. two d.; ed Eton Coll. and Harvard Univ., USA; nat. service 1956–57; with English Electric Co. 1958; with Lazard Brothers 1961–63; with Standard Industrial Group 1963–71; with Royal Doulton 1972–77; Chief Exec. Pearson PLC 1978–90, Chair. 1983–97; Chair. Financial Times 1983–93; Pnr, Lazard Partners 1984–97 (Dir Lazard Bros. 1975–97); Dir MEPC PLC 1990–98 (Chair. 1993–98); Chair. Royal Soc. for Protection of Birds 1981–86; Chair. Suffolk Together; fmr Chair. Commission on the Governance of the National Trust, UK; mem. Bd of Dirs Sotheby's Holdings Inc. (now Sotheby's) 1987–, UK–Japan 2000 Group 1990–, Lafarge SA 1997–2008; Pres. Sussex Wildlife Trust 1983–, Bristol Trust for Ornithology 2001–05; mem. Int. Advisory Bd Lafarge 1979–97 (Dir 1997–); mem. Int. Advisory Group Toshiba 1997–; mem. House of Lords Select Cttee on Science and Tech. 1984–88, Nature Conservancy Council 1986–90; Trustee, The Royal Botanic Gardens, Kew 1991–2003 (Chair. 1997–2003); Trustee, Blakenham Trust; Conservative; Order of the Rising Sun (Japan) 2002. *Address:* House of Lords, London, SW1A 0PW; 1 St Leonard's Studio, London, SW3 4EN, England (home).

BLAKERS, Andrew, PhD; Australian scientist and academic; *Foundation Director, Centre for Sustainable Energy Systems, Australian National University;* currently Foundation Dir Centre for Sustainable Energy Systems and Dir Australian Research Council (ARC) Centre for Solar Energy Systems, ANU; fmr Humboldt Fellow; has held ARC QEII and Sr Research Fellowships; Fellow, Acad. of Technological Sciences and Eng., Inst. of Energy, Inst. of Physics; Banksia Award, Environmental Leadership in Infrastructure & Services 2005, Aichi World Expo Global Eco-Tech 100 Award 2005, Australian Inst. of Energy Innovation in Energy Science & Eng Award 2005, Australian Inst. of Physics Alan Walsh Medal for services to industry 2006, ACT Sustainable Cities Environmental Innovation Award 2006, ACT Sustainable Cities Overall Award 2006, Engineers Australia Australian Eng Excellence Award 2007, Int. Solar Energy Soc. Weeks Award 2007, Engineers Australia (ACT Div.) Eng Excellence Award 2007, Chairman's Award, duPont Innovation Awards 2008. *Achievements include:* co-invented, with Dr Klaus Weber, sliver cell photovoltaic tech. which uses one-tenth of the silicon used in conventional solar panels, with similar power, performance and efficiency. *Publications:* more than 200 scientific papers in professional journals on photovoltaic and solar energy systems, particularly advanced thin film silicon solar cell tech. and solar concentrator cells, components and systems; 12 patents. *Address:* Room E224, Department of Engineering (Bldg 32), Australian National University, Canberra, ACT 0200, Australia (office). *Telephone:* (2) 6125-5905 (office). *Fax:* (2) 6125-0506 (office). *E-mail:* andrew.blakers@anu.edu.au (office). *Website:* solar.anu.edu.au (office).

BLANC, Christian; French business executive and politician; b. 17 May 1942, Talence, Gironde; s. of Marcel Blanc and Emcarma Miranda; m. Asa Hagglund 1973; two d.; ed Ecole Montgolfier, Bordeaux, Lycée Montesquieu, Bordeaux and Inst. d'Etudes Politiques, Bordeaux; Asst Dir Sopexa-Scandinavie 1969; Société centrale d'équipement du territoire 1970–74; Chef du bureau, State Secr. for Youth and Sport 1974–76; Asst Del.-Gen. Agence technique interministérielle pour les loisirs et le plein air 1976–80; Dir du Cabinet to Edgard Pisani, mem. of Comm. of EC, Brussels 1981–83; Prefect, Commr, République des Hautes-Pyrénées 1983–84; special Govt assignment, New Caledonia 1985; Prefect for Seine-et-Marne 1985–89; Special Prefect 1989; Chair. and CEO RATP 1989–93; Chair. and CEO Air France (Admin. Council) 1993–97; Dir Middle East Airlines 1998–99, Marceau Investissements 1998–; Chair. Merrill Lynch France SA 2000–02; presidential cand. 2002; Dir Action contre la Faim 1998–, Chancellery Univs of Paris 1991–2001; Pres. Karaval 2001–; f. L'Ami Public; mem. Assemblée Nationale for Yvelines 2002–08, 2010–; Sec. of State of Région Capitale (Great Paris) 2008–10 (resgnd); Founder and Chair. Energies démocrates 2002–; Chevalier, Légion d'honneur, Officier, Ordre nat. du Mérite. *Publication:* Le Lièvre et la Tortue (jtly) 1994, La Croissance ou le chaos 2006. *Address:* Assemblée Nationale, 126 rue de l'Université, 75355 Paris Cedex 07 (office); Constituency Office, 18 avenue de Bellevue, 78150 Le Chesnay, France (office). *Telephone:* 1-39-54-46-00 (office). *Fax:* 1-39-66-02-00 (office). *E-mail:* cblanc@assemblee-nationale.fr (office); cblanc@christian-blanc.net. *Website:* www.assemblee-nationale.fr (office); www.christian-blanc.net.

BLANC, Georges; French chef, author and business executive; *CEO, Georges Blanc Parc & Spa;* b. 2 Jan. 1943, Bourg-en-Bresse; s. of Jean Blanc and Paule Blanc (née Tisserand); m. Jacqueline Masson 1966; two s. one d.; ed Ecole Hôtelière de Thonon-les-Bains; worked at Réserve de Beaulieu and Grand Hôtel de Divonne; mil. service as chef to Adm. Vedel on the Foch and the Clémenceau; returned to work in family business 1965, became head of firm 1968; Man. Dir Georges Blanc SA, CEO Georges Blanc Parc & Spa; Maître Cuisinier de France 1975; finalist in Meilleur Ouvrier de France competition 1976; has organized numerous events abroad to promote French cuisine; Founder mem., Second Vice-Pres. Chambre Syndicale de la Haute Cuisine Française 1986; Muncipal Councillor, Vonnas 1989; Officier, Ordre nat. du Mérite, Commdr, Légion d'honneur, Commdr du Mérite agricole, des Arts et des Lettres, Chevalier des Palmes Académiques. *Publications:* Mes recettes 1981, La cuisine de Bourgogne (co-author), La nature dans l'assiette 1987, Le livre blanc des quatre saisons 1988, Les Blanc (jtly) 1989, Le Grand Livre de la Volaille (jtly) 1991, De la vigne à l'assiette 1995, la Cuisine de nos mères 2000, Cuisine de la vigne à la Carte 2000, Plat du jour 2003, Fêtes des Saveurs 2004, La Vie en Blanc 2008, Le plus simple du Meilleur 2009. *Leisure interests:* skiing, tennis. *Address:* Relais & Châteaux Georges Blanc Parc & Spa, 01540 Vonnas (Ain), France (home). *Telephone:* (4) 74-50-90-90 (home). *Fax:* (4) 74-50-08-80 (home). *E-mail:* gblanc@georgesblanc.com (home). *Website:* www.georgesblanc.com (home).

BLANC, Pierre-Louis, MenD, MèsL; French diplomatist; *President, Council of Francophone Affairs;* b. 18 Jan. 1926; s. of Lucien Blanc and Renée Blanc; m. 1st (wife deceased); one s. two d.; m. 2nd Jutta Freifrau von Cramm 1988; ed Univ. of Paris, Paris Inst. of Political Studies and Ecole Nat. d'Admin; served in French embassies in Rabat 1956, Tokyo 1962, Madrid 1965; served in Office of Pres. of Repub. 1967–69; pvt. staff of Gen. de Gaulle 1969–70; Acting Deputy Dir for Asia/Oceania, Govt of France 1969–71; Cultural Counsellor, London 1971–75; Deputy Dir for Personnel and Gen. Admin., Ministry of Foreign Affairs 1975; Dir Ecole Nat. d'Admin 1975–82; Amb. to Sweden 1982–85, to Greece 1985–87; Perm. Rep. to UN, New York 1987–91; Pres. Council of Francophone Affairs 1992–; Vice-Pres. Soc. des Amis des Archives de France 1994–2000; Commdr, Légion d'honneur 1992. *Publications:* De Gaulle au soir de sa vie 1990, Valise Diplomatique 2004, Retour à Colombey 2012, Arille, Compagnon de Napoléon 2013. *Leisure interest:* writing. *Address:* 549 Chemin de Gergouven, 84560 Ménerbes, France. *Telephone:* 4-90-72-26-52 (home).

BLANC, Raymond René Alfred; French chef; b. 19 Nov. 1949, Besançon; s. of Maurice Blanc and Anne-Marie Blanc; two s.; ed Besançon Tech. Coll.; various positions 1968–76, mil. service 1970–71; Man. and Chef de cuisine, Bleu, Blanc, Rouge, Oxford 1976–77; opening of Les Quat'Saisons, Oxford as Chef Proprietor 1977; opening of Maison Blanc, patisserie and boulangerie 1978, Dir and Chair. 1978–88; opening of Le Manoir aux Quat'Saisons 1984; opening of La Petit Blanc Brasserie in Oxford 1996, in Cheltenham 1998, in Birmingham 1999, in Manchester 2000, in Tunbridge Wells 2004, La Petete Blanc (re-launched as Brasserie Blanc) 2006; Consultant to Maison Blanc 2009; weekly recipe column in the Observer newspaper 1988–90; mem. Acad. Culinaire de France, British Gastronomic Acad., Restaurateurs' Asscn of GB; rep. GB at Grand Final of Wedgwood World Master of Culinary Arts, Paris 2002; Hon. OBE; Hon. DBA (Oxford Brookes Univ.) 1999; European Chef of the Year 1989, Personalité de l'Année 1990, Craft Guild of Chefs Special Award 2002, AA Restaurant Guide Chef of the Year 2004, Lifetime Achievement Award 2009, Chef of the Year Award 2009, many awards for both the restaurant and hotel. *Television:* Blanc Mange (series) 1994, Passion for Perfection (series, Carlton TV) 2002, The Restaurant (series, BBC2) 2007–, Kitchen Secrets 2010, 2011, The Very Hungry Frenchman 2012. *Publications:* Recipes from Le Manoir aux Quat'Saisons 1988, Cooking for Friends 1991, Blanc Mange 1994, A Blanc Christmas 1996; contrib. to Take Six Cooks 1986, Taste of Health 1987, Restaurants of Great Britain 1989, Gourmet Garden 1990, European Chefs 1990, Masterchefs of Europe 1998, Blanc Vite 1998, Foolproof French Cooking 2002, A Taste of My Life 2008. *Leisure interests:* classical music, opera, swimming, tennis, sailing. *Address:* Le Manoir aux Quat'Saisons, Church Road, Great Milton, Oxford, OX44 7PD, England (home). *Telephone:* (1844) 278881 (office). *Fax:* (1844) 278847 (home); (1844) 277212 (office). *E-mail:* raymond.blanc@blanc.co.uk (office). *Website:* www.raymondblanc.com; www.manoir.com.

BLANCHARD, James J., BA, MBA, JD; American lawyer, diplomatist and fmr politician; *Partner, DLA Piper US LLP;* b. 8 Aug. 1942, Detroit, Mich.; m. 2nd Janet Eifert; one s.; ed Michigan State Univ. and Univ. of Minnesota; admitted to Mich. Bar 1968; Legal Aid, elections bureau, Office of the Sec. of State, Mich. 1968–69; Asst Attorney-Gen., State of Mich. 1969–74, Admin. Asst to Attorney-Gen. 1970–71, Asst Deputy Attorney-Gen. 1971–72; mem. House of Reps 1975–83; Gov. of Mich. 1983–91; Pnr, Verner, Liipfert, Bernhard, McPherson and Hand

1991–93; Amb. to Canada 1993–96; Pnr, DLA Piper US LLP, Washington, DC 1996–, Chair. Emer. Government Affairs Practice Group; Chair. Bd of Trustees, Meridian International Center; Co-Chair. Canada-US Law Inst.; Vice-Pres. Foundation for the National Archives; mem. Bd of Dirs Enbridge, Inc; fmr mem. Pres.'s Comm. on Holocaust; several honorary degrees; Foreign Affairs Award for Public Service 1996, numerous other awards. *Publication:* Behind the Embassy Door 1998. *Address:* DLA Piper US LLP, 500 8th Street, NW, Washington, DC 20004, USA (office). *Telephone:* (202) 799-4303 (office). *Fax:* (202) 799-5303 (office). *E-mail:* james.blanchard@dlapiper.com (office). *Website:* www.dlapiper.com (office).

BLANCHARD, Olivier Jean, PhD; French economist and academic; *Economic Counsellor and Director of Research Department, International Monetary Fund;* b. 27 Dec. 1948, Amiens; m. Noelle Golinelli 1973; three d.; ed Univ. of Paris and Massachusetts Inst. of Tech.; Asst Prof., Harvard Univ., USA 1977–81, Assoc. Prof. 1981–83; Assoc. Prof., MIT, Cambridge, Mass, USA 1983–85, Prof. of Econs 1985–, Class of 1941 Prof. 1994–, Chair. Econs Dept 1998–2003; Econ. Counsellor and Dir Dept of Research, IMF 2008–; Vice-Pres. American Econ. Asscn 1995–96; Fellow, Econometric Soc.; mem. American Acad. of Arts and Sciences. *Publications:* Lectures on Macroeconomics (with S. Fischer) 1989, Reform in Eastern Europe 1991, Pour l'Emploi et Cohésion Sociale 1994, Spanish Unemployment: Is There a Solution? 1994, The Economics of Transition 1996, Macroeconomics 1997. *Leisure interest:* tennis. *Address:* International Monetary Fund, 700 19th Street NW, Washington, DC 20431; Department of Economics, E52-357, Massachusetts Institute of Technology, Cambridge, MA 02139, USA (office). *Telephone:* (202) 623-7000 (DC) (office); (617) 253-8891 (office). *Fax:* (202) 623-4661 (DC) (office); (617) 258-8112 (office). *E-mail:* publicaffairs@imf.org (office); blanchar@mit.edu (office). *Website:* www.imf.org (office); econ-www.mit.edu (office).

BLANCHETT, Cate; Australian actress; b. 14 May 1969, Melbourne, Vic.; m. Andrew Upton 1997; three s.; ed Univ. of Melbourne, Nat. Inst. of Dramatic Art; Co-Artistic Dir Sydney Theatre Co. 2008–; BAFTA Award for Best Actress 1999, Best Actress, Nat. Bd of Review 2001, Golden Camera Award 2001, Career Achievement Award, Palm Springs Int. Film Festival 2007. *Plays include:* Top Girls 1992–93, Kafka Dances (1993 Newcomer Award), Oleanna (Rosemont Best Actress Award) 1993, Hamlet 1994, Sweet Phoebe 1995, The Tempest 1995, The Blind Giant is Dancing 1995, Plenty 1999, Hedda Gabler 2004, A Streetcar Named Desire 2009, Uncle Vanya 2010. *Films include:* Police Rescue 1994, Parklands 1996, Paradise Road 1997, Thank God He Met Lizzie 1997, Oscar and Lucinda 1997, Elizabeth 1998 (Golden Globe Award), Dreamtime Alice (also co-producer), Bangers 1999, The Talented Mr Ripley 1999, An Ideal Husband 1999, Pushing Tin 1999, Bandit 2000, The Man Who Cried 2000, The Gift 2000, Bandits 2000, The Lord of the Rings: The Fellowship of the Ring 2001, Charlotte Gray 2001, The Shipping News 2002, The Lord of the Rings: The Two Towers 2002, Heaven 2002, Veronica Guerin 2003, The Lord of the Rings: The Return of the King 2003, Coffee and Cigarettes 2003, The Aviator (Best Supporting Actress, Screen Actors Guild Awards 2005, Best Actress in a Supporting Role, BAFTA Awards 2005, Best Supporting Actress, Acad. Awards 2005) 2004, The Life Aquatic 2004, Stories of Lost Souls 2005, Little Fish 2005, Babel 2006, The Good German 2006, Notes on a Scandal (Best Supporting Actress, Toronto Film Critics Asscn) 2006, I'm Not There (Best Actress, Venice Film Festival 2007, Golden Globe for Best Supporting Actress 2008) 2007, Elizabeth: The Golden Age 2007, Indiana Jones and the Kingdom of the Crystal Skull 2008, Ponyo (English version, voice) 2008, The Curious Case of Benjamin Button 2008, Robin Hood 2010, The Last Time I Saw Michael Gregg 2011, Hanna 2011, The Hobbit: An Unexpected Journey 2012, A Cautionary Tail (short) 2012, Blue Jasmine (Best Actress, Nat. Soc. of Film Critics, Golden Globe Award for Best Actress in a Motion Picture, Drama, Screen Actors Guild Award for Outstanding Performance by a Female Actor in a Leading Role, BAFTA Award for Best Actress in a Leading Role, Academy Award for Best Actress in a Leading Role 2014) 2013, The Turning 2013, The Hobbit: The Desolation of Smaug 2013, The Monuments Men 2014, How to Train Your Dragon 2 (voice) 2014, Knight of Cups 2014, The Hobbit: There and Back Again 2014. *Television includes:* Police Rescue (series) 1994, Heartland (mini-series) 1994, G.P. (series) 1994, Bordertown (mini-series) 1995, Family Guy (series) 2012. *Address:* c/o Hylda Queally, Creative Artists Agency, 2000 Avenue of the Stars, Los Angeles, CA 90067, USA (office); c/o Robyn Gardiner, PO Box 128, Surry Hills, 2010 NSW, Australia. *Telephone:* (424) 288-2000 (office). *Fax:* (424) 288-2900 (office). *Website:* www.caa.com (office).

BLANCHFLOWER, David G., CBE, BA, MSc, PhD; American/British economist and academic; *Bruce V. Rauner 1978 Professor of Economics, Dartmouth College;* b. 2 March 1952; ed Univ. of Leicester, UK, Univ. of Wales, Univ. of London (Queen Mary Coll.); Research Officer, Inst. for Employment Research, Univ. of Warwick 1984–86; Lecturer, Dept of Econs, Univ. of Surrey 1989–89; Assoc. Prof., Dept of Econs, Dartmouth Coll. 1989–93, Prof. 1993–, Bruce V. Rauner 1978 Prof. of Econs 2002–, Dept Chair. 1998–2000, Assoc. Dean of Faculty of Social Sciences 2000–01; Research Assoc., Nat. Bureau of Econ. Research (NBER); Research Fellow, CESifo, Center for Econ. Studies, Univ. of Munich, Germany; Research Fellow, Inst. for the Study of Labor (IZA), Univ. of Bonn; mem. Monetary Policy Cttee, Bank of England 2006–09; mem. Editorial Bd Small Business Econs, Scottish Journal of Political Economy, Industrial and Labor Relations Review; Richard A. Lester Prize, Princeton Univ. 1994. *Publications:* numerous articles in professional journals. *Address:* Department of Economics, Dartmouth College, 6106 Rockefeller Hall, Hanover, NH 03755, USA. *Telephone:* (603) 646-2536. *Fax:* (603) 646-2122. *E-mail:* blanchflower@dartmouth.edu. *Website:* www.dartmouth.edu/~economic; www.dartmouth.edu/~blnchflr.

BLAND, Sir (Francis) Christopher (Buchan), Kt; British business executive; b. 29 May 1938, Japan; s. of James Franklin MacMahon Bland and Jess Buchan Bland (née Brodie); m. Jennifer Mary, Viscountess Enfield 1981; one s. two step-s. two step-d.; ed Sedbergh and Queen's Coll., Oxford; 2nd Lt 5th Royal Inniskilling Dragoon Guards 1956–58; Lt, Northern Irish Horse (TA) 1958–69; Dir NI Finance Corpn 1972–76; Deputy Chair., IBA 1972–80; Chair., Sir Joseph Causton & Sons 1977–85, LWT (Holdings) 1984–94, Century Hutchinson Group 1984–89, Life Sciences Int. (fmrly Philicom) PLC 1987–97, NFC 1994–2000; Chair., British Telecommunications PLC (now BT Group) 2001–07; Dir, Nat. Provident Inst. 1977–88, Storehouse PLC 1988–93; mem. for Lewisham, GLC 1967–70; mem.

Burnham Cttee 1970; Chair. Bow Group 1969–70; Ed., Crossbow 1971–72; mem. Prime Minister's Advisory Panel on Citizen's Charter 1991–94; Chair., NHS Review Group on Nat. Training Council and Nat. Staff Cttees 1982, Hammersmith and Queen Charlotte's Hosps (fmrly Hammersmith) SHA 1982–94, Hammersmith Hosps NHS Trust 1994–96; mem. BBC Bd of Govs 1996–2001; Chair. RSC 2004–; Hon. LLD (South Bank) 1994. *Achievements include:* mem. Irish Olympic Fencing Team 1960. *Leisure interests:* fishing, skiing, reciting poetry. *Address:* Blissamore Hall, Clanville, Andover, Hants., SP11 9HL; 10 Catherine Place, London, SW1E 6HF, England. *Telephone:* (20) 7834-0021; (1264) 772274 (Andover).

BLANK, Sir (Maurice) Victor, Kt, MA; British business executive; b. 9 Nov. 1942; s. of Joseph Blank and Ruth Blank (née Levey); m. Sylvia Helen Richford 1977; two s. one d.; ed Stockport Grammar School, St Catherine's Coll., Oxford; solicitor, Supreme Court; joined Clifford-Turner as articled clerk 1964, Solicitor 1966, Partner 1969; Dir and Head Corp. Finance Charterhouse Bank 1981, Chief Exec. 1985–96, Chair. 1985–97, Chief Exec. Charterhouse PLC 1985–96, Chair. 1991–97, Dir Charterhouse Europe Holding 1993–, Chair. 1993–97; Chair. Wellbeing of Women 1989–; Deputy Chair. Great Universal Stores (renamed GUS PLC) 1996–2000, Chair. 2000–06 (Dir 1993–2006); Founding Chair. Trinity Mirror 1999–2006; Chair. Lloyds TSB Group plc (renamed Lloyds Banking Group plc following acquisition of HBOS plc Jan. 2009) 2006–09; Dir (non-exec.) Coats Ltd (fmrly Coats Viyella PLC), Chubb PLC (fmrly Williams PLC); Chair. Industrial Devt Advisory Bd; mem. Financial Reporting Council 2002–07; mem. Council, adviser to Environmental Change Unit and Chair. Devt Programme Advisory Bd, Univ. of Oxford 2000–07; Sr Adviser, Texas Pacific Group; Chair. UJS Hillel, Council of Univ. Coll. School, Royal Coll. of Obstetricians and Gynaecologists' health research charity; mem. CBI Boardroom Issues Group, Jewish Leadership Council, Orchestra of the Age of Enlightenment; Patron, Royal Coll. of Obstetricians and Gynaecologists; apptd UK Business Amb. 2010; Hon. Fellow, St Catherine's Coll. Oxford; Hon. FRCOG. *Publication:* Weinberg and Blank on Take-overs and Mergers (co-author) 1971. *Leisure interests:* cricket, family, tennis, theatre. *Address:* c/o Wellbeing of Women, 27 Sussex Place, Regent's Park, London, NW1 4SP, England.

BLANK, Rebecca M., BS, PhD; American economist, academic and government official; *Chancellor, University of Wisconsin-Madison;* b. 19 Sept. 1955, Mo.; m. Hanns Kuttner; one d.; ed Univ. of Minnesota, Massachusetts Inst. of Tech.; Consultant and Educational Coordinator, Data Resources, Chicago Office 1976–79; Asst Prof. of Econs and Public Affairs, Dept of Econs and Woodrow Wilson School of Public and Int. Affairs, Princeton Univ. 1983–89; Sr Staff Economist, Council of Econ. Advisers, Washington, DC 1989–90, mem.-nominee 1997–98, mem. 1998–99; Visiting Asst Prof. of Econs, MIT 1988–89; Assoc. Prof. of Econs, Northwestern Univ. 1989–94, Prof. of Econs 1994–99, Research Faculty, Center for Urban Affairs and Policy Research 1989–99, Assoc. Prof., School of Educ. and Social Policy 1989–93, Dir Jt Center for Poverty Research 1996–97; Joan and Sanford Weill Dean of Public Policy, Gerald R. Ford School of Public Policy, Univ. of Michigan 1999–2007, Henry Carter Adams Collegiate Prof. of Public Policy, Gerald R. Ford School of Public Policy Prof. of Econs, Dept of Econs, Co-Dir Nat. Poverty Center 2002–08; Robert S. Kerr Visiting Fellow, Econ. Studies, Brookings Inst. 2007–08, Robert S. Kerr Sr Fellow, Econ. Studies 2008–09; Under-Sec. for Econ. Affairs 2009–12, Acting Deputy Sec. of Commerce 2010–12, Deputy Sec. of Commerce 2012–13, Acting Sec. of Commerce 2012–13; Chancellor Univ. of Wisconsin-Madison 2013–; Faculty Research Fellow, Nat. Bureau of Econ. Research 1985–90, Faculty Research Assoc. 1990–2009; Faculty Assoc. NAS 2004–; Co-Ed. Journal of Human Resources 1995–97; Labour Economics 2004–07 (Assoc. Ed. 2007–); mem. Bd of Eds, American Economic Review, 1993–97, American Economic Journal: Economic Policy 2007–09; mem. Advisory Bd, Journal of Public Economics 1993–97, Journal of Economic Education 1992–97 2002–09, Feminist Economics 1994–97; mem. Bd of Dirs MRDC (fmrly Manpower Demonstration Research Corpn) 1993–97, Center for Budget and Policy Priorities 1994–97, 2000–09, Economic Policy Inst. 2008–09; mem. Bd of Trustees, Urban Inst. 2007–09; mem. Advisory Council, Spotlight on Poverty and Opportunity 2007–09; mem. Scientific Advisory Cttee, DIW (research/policy think tank), Berlin, Germany 2001–04; mem. Hon. Advisory Council, DIW-DC 2008–09; mem. Advisory Cttee, New Hope Project (job training and employment programme), Milwaukee, Wis. 1992–97, Advisory Cttee on Poverty Research, Russell Sage Foundation 1994–97, Research Advisory Cttee, W.E. Upjohn Inst. for Employment Research 1995–96, 2000; mem. Visiting Cttee, Kennedy School of Govt, Harvard Univ. 2004–09; mem. NAS, mem. Div. Cttee for the Behavioral and Social Sciences and Educ. (DBASSE), Nat. Research Council 2003–08, DBASSE Exec. Cttee mem. 2005–08, Chair. Workshop to Reconsider the Fed. Poverty Measure, Cttee on Nat. Statistics 2004–05, Panel on Methods for Assessing Discrimination, Cttee on Nat. Statistics 2001–04; Pres. Asscn for Public Policy Analysis and Man. 2007, Exec. Cttee mem. 2006–08, Policy Council mem. 2001–04; mem. American Econ. Asscn (mem. Exec. Cttee 1995–97, Vice-Pres. American Econ. Asscn 2007), Nat. Acad. of Social Insurance; Lifetime Nat. Assoc., Nat. Acads of Sciences 2004; Fellow, American Acad. of Arts of Sciences 2005, Soc. of Labor Economists 2006; Hon. PhD (Univ. of Maryland) 2012; Outstanding Alumni Achievement Award, Univ. of Minnesota 2008, Winter Commencement Speaker, Coll. of Liberal Arts, Univ. of Minnesota 2008, Eleanor Roosevelt Fellow, American Acad. of Political and Social Science 2010, numerous named lectures. *Publications include:* Do Justice: Linking Christian Faith and Modern Economic Life 1992, Social Protection vs. Economic Flexibility: Is There a Tradeoff? (ed. and author of two articles) 1994, It Takes A Nation: A New Agenda for Fighting Poverty 1997, Finding Jobs: Work and Welfare Reform (co-ed. with David Card and co-author of two articles) 2000, The New World of Welfare (co-ed. with Ron Haskins and co-author of two articles) 2001, Is the Market Moral? A Dialogue on Religion, Economics, and Justice (with William McGurn) 2004, Measuring Racial Discrimination (with Marilyn Dabady and Connie Citro) 2004, Working and Poor: How Economic and Policy Changes are Affecting Low Wage Workers (co-ed. with Sheldon Danziger and Robert Schoeni and co-author of two articles) 2006, Insufficient Funds: Savings, Assets, Credit and Banking Among Low-Income Households (co-ed. with Michael S. Barr and co-author of one article) 2009, Changing Inequality 2011; several book chapters and book reviews and numerous articles in professional journals. *Address:* Office of the Chancellor, 161 Bascom Hall, 500 Lincoln Drive, Madison, WI 53706, USA (office). *Telephone:* (608)

262–9946 (office). *E-mail:* chancellor@news.wisc.edu (office). *Website:* www .chancellor.wisc.edu (office).

BLANKFEIN, Lloyd Craig, BA, JD; American lawyer and business executive; *Chairman and CEO, Goldman Sachs;* b. 1954, The Bronx, New York City; m. Laura Susan Jacobs 1983; three c.; ed Harvard Univ. and Harvard Univ. Law School; corp. tax lawyer, Donovan, Leisure, Newton & Irvine 1978–81; joined J. Aron div. of Goldman Sachs as a gold bar and coin salesman 1981, Head or Co-head Currency and Commodities Div. 1994–97, Co-head Fixed Income, Currency and Commodities Division (FICC) 1997–2002, Vice-Chair. Goldman Sachs, with man. responsibility for FICC and Equities Div. 2002–04, mem. Bd of Dirs Goldman Sachs 2003–, Pres. and COO 2004–06, Chair. and CEO 2006–; mem. Dean's Advisory Bd of Harvard Law School, Dean's Council, Harvard Univ., Advisory Bd of Tsinghua Univ. School of Econs and Man.; mem. Bd of Overseers, Weill Medical Coll. of Cornell Univ.; mem. Bd of Dirs Partnership for New York City; ranked by Forbes magazine amongst The World's Most Powerful People (18th) 2009, (42nd) 2010, (43rd) 2011, (36th) 2012, (27th) 2013. *Address:* The Goldman Sachs Group, 85 Broad Street, 17th Floor, New York, NY 10004, USA (office). *Telephone:* (212) 902-1000 (office). *Fax:* (212) 902-3000 (office). *E-mail:* info@gs.com (office). *Website:* www.goldmansachs.com (office).

BLANNING, Timothy Charles William, LittD, FBA; British academic; *Fellow in History, Sidney Sussex College, Cambridge;* b. 21 April 1942, Wells, Somerset, England; s. of Thomas Walter Blanning and Gwendolen Marchant-Jones; m. Nicky Susan Jones 1988; one s. one d.; ed King's School, Bruton, Somerset, Sidney Sussex Coll., Cambridge; Research Fellow, Sidney Sussex Coll. 1965–68, Fellow 1968–, Asst Lecturer in History, Univ. of Cambridge 1972–76, Lecturer 1976–87, Reader in Modern European History 1987–92, Prof. of Modern European History 1992–2009. *Publications include:* Joseph II and Enlightened Despotism 1970, Reform and Revolution in Mainz 1743–1803 1974, The French Revolution in Germany 1983, The Origins of the French Revolutionary Wars 1986, The French Revolution: Aristocrats versus Bourgeois? 1987, Joseph II 1994, The French Revolutionary Wars 1787–1802 1996, The French Revolution: Class War or Culture Clash? 1998, The Culture of Power and the Power of Culture 2002, The Pursuit of Glory: Europe 1648–1815 2007; Ed.: The Oxford Illustrated History of Modern Europe 1996, The Rise and Fall of the French Revolution 1996, History and Biography: Essays in Honour of Derek Beales (with Peter Wende), Reform in Great Britain and Germany 1750–1850 1999, The Short Oxford History of Europe: The Eighteenth Century 2000, The Short Oxford History of Europe: The Nineteenth Century 2000, Unity and Diversity in European Culture *c.* 1800 2006, The Triumph of Music 2008, The Romantic Revolution 2010. *Leisure interest:* music. *Address:* Sidney Sussex College, Cambridge, CB2 3HU, England (office). *Telephone:* (1223) 338854 (office). *Fax:* (1223) 338884 (office). *E-mail:* tcb1000@cam .ac.uk (office).

BLASHFORD-SNELL, Col John Nicholas, OBE, FRSGS; British explorer, writer and broadcaster; *President, Scientific Exploration Society;* b. 22 Oct. 1936, Hereford, Herefords.; s. of the late Rev. Prebendary Leland John Blashford-Snell and Gwendolen Ives Blashford-Snell (née Sadler); m. Judith Frances Sherman 1960; two d.; ed Victoria Coll., Jersey, Royal Mil. Acad., Sandhurst; commissioned in Royal Engineers 1957; Commdr Operation Aphrodite (Expedition), Cyprus 1959–61; Instructor, Jr Leaders Regt Royal Engineers 1962–63; Instructor, RMA, Sandhurst 1963–66; Adjt, 3rd Div. Engineers 1966–67; Commdr The Great Abbai Expedition (Blue Nile) 1968; attended Staff Coll., Camberley 1969; Chair. Scientific Exploration Soc. 1969–2009, currently Pres.; Commdr Dahlak Quest Expedition 1969–70, British Trans-Americas Expedition (Darien Gap) 1971–72; Officer Commdg 48th Field Squadron, Royal Engineers 1972–74; Commdr, Zaïre River Expedition 1974–75; CO, Jr Leaders Regt, Royal Engineers 1976–78; Dir of Operations, Operation Drake 1978–81; Staff Officer, Ministry of Defence 1978–91, Consultant 1992–; Commdr, Fort George Volunteers 1982; Operations Dir, Operation Raleigh 1982–88, Dir-Gen. 1989–91; Dir SES Tibet Expedition 1987; Leader, Kalahari Quest Expedition 1990, Karnali Quest Expedition 1991, Karnali Gorges Expedition 1992, numerous exploration projects thereafter; Trustee, Operation New World 1995–; Chair. Just a Drop Charity 2001–04, Pres. 2004–, The Liverpool Construction-Crafts Guild 2003–05, Pres. 2005–; Pres. The British Travel Health Asscn 2006–; Freeman of the City of Hereford; Hon. Pres. The Vole Club 1996–; Hon. Life Pres. The Centre for Fortean Zoology 2003–; Hon. Fellow, Liverpool John Moores Univ. 2010; Hon. DSc (Durham); Hon. DEng (Bournemouth) 1997; The Livingstone Medal, The Darien Medal (Colombia) 1972, The Segrave Trophy, Paul Harris Fellow, Rotary International, Royal Geographical Soc. Patrons' Medal 1993, Gold Medal, Inst. of Royal Engineers 1994, La Paz Medal (Bolivia) 2000. *Publications include:* Weapons and Tactics (with T. Wintringham) 1970, The Expedition Organiser's Guide (with Richard Snailham) 1970, Where the Trails Run Out 1974, In the Steps of Stanley 1975, Expeditions the Experts' Way (with A. Ballantine) 1977, A Taste for Adventure 1978, Operation Drake (with M. Cable) 1981, In the Wake of Drake (with M. Cable) 1982, Mysteries: Encounters with the Unexplained 1983, Operation Raleigh, The Start of an Adventure 1987, Operation Raleigh, Adventure Challenge (with Ann Tweedy) 1988, Operation Raleigh, Adventure Unlimited (with Ann Tweedy) 1990, Something Lost Behind the Ranges 1994, Mammoth Hunt (with Rula Lenska) 1996, Kota Mama: Retracing the Lost Trade Routes of Ancient South American Peoples (with Richard Snailham) 2000, East to the Amazon (with Richard Snailham) 2002. *Leisure interests:* shooting, food, photography, cryptozoology. *Address:* Scientific Exploration Society, Expedition Base, Motcombe, nr Shaftesbury, Dorset, SP7 9PB, England (office). *Telephone:* (1747) 854456 (office). *E-mail:* jbs@ses-explore.org (office). *Website:* www.johnblashfordsnell.org.uk.

BLATHERWICK, Sir David (Elliott Spiby), KCMG, OBE, MA; British diplomatist (retd); *Chairman, Egyptian-British Chamber of Commerce;* b. 13 July 1941, Lincoln, Lincs., England; s. of Edward S. Blatherwick; m. (Margaret) Clare Crompton 1964; one s. one d.; ed Lincoln School, Wadham Coll., Oxford; Foreign Office 1964; Second Sec., Embassy in Kuwait 1968–70; First Sec., Embassy in Dublin 1970–73; FCO 1973–77; Head of Chancery, Cairo 1977–80; NI Office, Belfast 1981–83; FCO 1983–85; sabbatical, Stanford Univ., USA 1985–86; Head of Chancery, Perm. Mission to UN, New York 1986–89; Prin. Finance Officer and Chief Insp., FCO 1989–91; Amb. to Ireland 1991–95, to Egypt 1995–99; Chair. Egyptian-British Chamber of Commerce 1999–; Jt Chair. Anglo-

Irish Encounter 2003–08; Trustee, British Univ. in Egypt 2005–. *Publication:* The Politics of International Telecommunications 1987. *Leisure interests:* walking, sailing, music. *Address:* Egyptian-British Chamber of Commerce, PO Box 4EG, 299 Oxford Street, London, W1A 4EG, England (office). *Telephone:* (20) 7499-3100 (office). *Fax:* (20) 7499-1070 (office). *E-mail:* info@theebcc.com (office). *Website:* www.theebcc.com (office).

BLATTER, Johann W. (Gianni), PhD; Swiss physicist and academic; *Professor of Theoretical Physics, Institute of Theoretical Physics, ETH Zürich;* b. 10 Nov. 1955; ed Eidgenössische Technische Hochschule Zürich (ETH Zürich); Researcher, Brown Boveri Co. (later Asea Brown Boveri), Baden, Switzerland 1983, 1987–93; fmr Post-Doctoral Researcher, Cornell Univ., Ithaca, NY, USA; Assoc. Prof., Inst. of Theoretical Physics, ETH Zürich 1993–96, Prof. of Theoretical Physics 1996–, Head of Dept 2007–; Fellow, American Physical Soc. *Address:* Institute of Theoretical Physics, HPZ G 10, Schafmattstr. 32, Hönggerberg, 8093 Zürich, Switzerland (office). *Telephone:* (44) 633-2568 (office). *Fax:* (44) 633-1115 (office). *E-mail:* johann.blatter@itp.phys.ethz.ch (office). *Website:* www.itp.phys.ethz.ch (office).

BLATTER, Joseph Sepp, BBA; Swiss international organization official and sports administrator; *President, Fédération Internationale de Football Association;* b. 10 March 1936, Visp, Viège; one d.; ed Sion and St Maurice Colls, Univ. de Lausanne; footballer (played for Swiss amateur league in top div.) 1948–71; mem. Bd Xamax Neuchâtel Football Club 1970–75; fmr Sec. Tourist Office, Valais; Sec.-Gen. Swiss Fed. of Ice-Hockey 1964; pursued journalistic and public relations activities in the fields of sport and pvt. industry; fmr Dir of Sports Timing and Public Relations, Longines SA; Tech. Dir of Devt Programmes, FIFA 1975–81, Gen. Sec. 1981–90, CEO 1990–98, Pres. 1998–; mem. IOC 1999–; mem. Swiss Asscn of Sportswriters, Panathlon Club; Hon. mem. Swiss Football Asscn; Olympic Order, knighthood (with title of Dato') from Sultanate of Pahang, Order of Good Hope (South Africa), Order of Independence (First Class) (Jordan), Grand Cordon du Wissam Alaouite (Morocco), Medalla al Mérito Deportivo (Bolivia), Grand Cordon de l'Ordre de la République Tunisienne, Rank of Grand Officer of Wissam Al Arch (Morocco), Order of Merit in Diamond, Union of European Football Asscns (UEFA), Award of Merit (Yemen), Chevalier de la Légion d'honneur, Order of the Two Niles (Sudan), Commdr de l'Ordre Nat. du 27 Juin 1977 (Djibouti), Supreme Companion of Tambo (SA), Ordre de la Médaille de la Reconnaissance (Commdr Grade) (Cen. African Repub.), Commdr's Cross with Star of the Order of Merit (Hungary) 2006, Commdr de l'Ordre Nat. du Lion (Senegal) 2006, 1st Grau da Ordem do Dragoeiro (Cape Verde) 2006, Das Grosse Verdienstkreuz (Germany) 2006, Collar Estrella del Centenario de la Asociación de Fútbol (Paraguay) 2006, Danaker (Kyrgyzstan) 2006; Hon. DArts (De Montfort Univ.), Hon. PhD (Nelson Mandela Metropolitan Univ., SA) 2006; 'International Humanitarian of the Year' and 'Golden Charter of Peace and Humanitarianism', Int. Humanitarian League for Peace and Tolerance, American Global Award for Peace, Asian Football Conf. Diamond of Asia Award 2006, ranked by Forbes magazine amongst The World's Most Powerful People (53rd) 2009, (65th) 2010, (63rd) 2011, (69th) 2012–13, numerous awards from clubs, nat. asscns and confeds. *Address:* FIFA, FIFA-Strasse 20, PO Box 8044, Zürich, Switzerland (office). *Telephone:* (43) 222-7777 (office). *Fax:* (43) 222-7878 (office). *Website:* www.fifa.com (office).

BLATTMANN, René, LicIurU; Bolivian judge; b. 28 Jan. 1948, La Paz; m. Marianne Blattmann; one s. two d.; ed Bolivian Univ., La Paz, Univ. of Basle, Switzerland, Acad. of American and Int. Law, USA, Int. Faculty of Comparative Law, France and Italy; Prof. of Criminal Law, San Andrés State Univ., La Paz 1973–80, Bolivian Catholic Univ., La Paz 1990–94; Attorney at Law 1975–93; Minister of Justice and Human Rights 1994–97; Chief of Human Rights and Justice Area, UN Human Rights Verification Mission in Guatemala 1998–2000; Dir Andrean Jurists Comm. (CAJ) 1997–2002; Judge, Trial Div., Int. Criminal Court 2003–09, Second Vice-Pres. 2006–09, assigned to Trial Chamber I for the Courts First Trial (Prosecutor vs. Thomas Lubanga in the situation of the Democratic Republic of Congo) 2007; mem. La Paz Bar Asscn, Bolivian Bar Asscn, Andrean Jurists Comm.; Hon. Life mem. Wilshire Bar Asscn, LA, USA 1977–; Hon. mem. Experts Asscn on Criminal Law of Bogota and Cundinamarca, Colombia 1995; Bundesverdienstkreuz 2005; Dr hc (Univ. of Basle) 1998, (Humboldt Univ., Berlin) 2010; Robert J. Storey Int. Award of Leadership, Southwestern Legal Foundation, Univ. of Texas at Dallas 1995, Diosa Temis Medal, Nat. Foundation Fora and Interdisciplinary Studies of Colombia 1995, Monseñor Leonidas Proaño Latin American Prize of Human Rights, Latin American Asscn of Human Rights (ALDHU) 1995, Carl Bertelsmann Int. Prize 2001; distinctions from Bolivian Nat. Police 1995, Journalists Asscn of La Paz 1996, Superior Court of Justice of Santa Cruz 1997, Superior Court of Justice of Tarija 1997, Nat. Chamber of Commerce 1997, City Council of La Paz 2000. *Address:* c/o International Criminal Court, Maanweg 174, 2516 AB The Hague, Netherlands. *Telephone:* (70) 515-85-15. *E-mail:* pio@icc-cpi.int.

BLATTY, William Peter, MA, DHumLitt; American writer and screenwriter; b. 7 Jan. 1928, New York, NY; s. of Peter Blatty and Mary Blatty (née Mouakad); m. Julie Alicia Witbrodt 1983; three s. three d.; ed Georgetown Univ., George Washington Univ. and Seattle Univ.; served in USAF 1951–54; ed. with US Information Agency 1955–57; Publicity Dir Univ. of Southern Calif. 1957–58; Public Relations Dir Loyola Univ., Los Angeles 1959–60; Acad. Award of Acad. Motion Picture, Arts and Sciences 1973, Acad. of Fantasy, Science Fiction and Horror award 1980, Stoker Award for Lifetime Achievement 1998. *Screenplays:* The Man from the Diner's Club 1961, Promise Her Anything 1962, John Goldfarb, Please Come Home 1963, A Shot in the Dark 1964, The Great Bank Robbery 1967, What Did You Do in the War, Daddy? 1965, Gunn 1967, Darling Lili 1968, Mastermind 1976, The Exorcist (Acad. Award for Best Adapted Screenplay 1973, Golden Globe for Best Picture and Best Writing) 1973, The Ninth Configuration (also known as Twinkle, Twinkle, 'Killer' Kane, also dir and producer) (Golden Globe for Best Writing) 1980, The Exorcist III 1990, Exorcist: The Beginning 2004. *Writing for television:* Watts Made Out of Thread (series episode) (American Film Festival Blue Ribbon and Gabriel Award). *Publications:* Which Way to Mecca, Jack? 1959, John Goldfarb, Please Come Home 1963, I, Billy Shakespeare 1965, Twinkle, Twinkle, 'Killer' Kane 1966, The Exorcist 1970, I'll Tell Them I Remember You (autobiog.) 1973, The Exorcist: From Novel to Film 1974, The Ninth Configuration 1978, Legion 1983, Demons Five, Exorcists Nothing 1996,

Elsewhere 1999, Dimiter 2010, Crazy 2010. *Address:* c/o Tor/Forge, Tom Doherty Associates, LLC, 175 Fifth Avenue, New York, NY 10010, USA (office).

BLAVATNIK, Leonard (Len), MS, MBA, PhD; American (b. Ukrainian) business executive and philanthropist; *Chairman and President, Access Industries, Inc.;* b. (Leonid Valentinovich Blavatnik), 14 June 1957, Odessa, Ukraine; m. Emily Blavatnik; ed Moscow Inst. of Transport Eng, Columbia Univ. and Harvard Business School, USA; emigrated with his family from Russia to USA 1978; served in various man. positions at Arthur Andersen & Co., Macy's Dept Stores and General Atlantic Partners; f. Access Industries industrial group, New York 1986, Chair. and Pres. 1986–; fmr Man. Dir Access Technology Capital; co-f. Russian-American investment group Renova 1990; Partner, Faena Group; Chair. Supervisory Bd LyondellBasell Industries 2007–10; Vice-Chair. Kennan Council of the Woodrow Wilson Center, Washington, DC; Dir of numerous cos in the Access portfolio (including Basell Holdings BV), Wmg Acquisition Corpn 2004–, TNK-BP International Ltd, Svenska Bredbandsbolaget AB and other cos, United Company RUSAL (UC RUSAL) 2009–, Public Jt Stock Co. TNK-BP Holding 2009–10; fmr Dir Tyumen Oil Co., OAO SUAL Holding of Sual Group; fmr mem. Advisory Bd Eurasia Group Ltd; serves on academic boards at Univ. of Cambridge, Harvard Business School and Tel-Aviv Univ.; Dir, The White Nights Foundation of America, 92nd Street Y, The Center for Jewish History, New York; mem. Global Advisory Bd Center for Int. Business and Man., Univ. of Cambridge; mem. Bd of Dean's Advisors, Harvard Business School; Dir, Warner Music Group Corpn 2004–08; mem. Bd Govs New York Acad. of Sciences. *Address:* Access Industries Inc., 730 5th Avenue, 20th Floor, New York, NY 10019-4105, USA (office). *Telephone:* (212) 247-6400 (office). *E-mail:* info@accessindustries.com (office). *Website:* www.accessindustries.com (office).

BLAY-AMIHERE, Kabral; Ghanaian diplomatist and journalist; *Chairman, National Media Commission of Ghana;* fmr Ed. The Independent newspaper, Ghana, arrested for publishing criticism of mil. regime 2000; fmr Pres. West African Journalists' Asscn; High Commr to Sierra Leone 2001–05, Amb. to Côte d'Ivoire 2005–09; currently Chair. National Media Commission of Ghana; fmr Dir Ghana Inst. of Journalism; Dr hc (Univ. of Sierra Leone) 2007. *Publications include:* Tears for a Continent: An American Diary, Fighting for Freedom: The Autobiography of an African Journalist, Between the Lion and the Elephant: Memoirs of an African Diplomat. *Address:* Office of the Chairman, National Media Commission of Ghana, Abdul Nasser Avenue, Ridge, Accra, Ghana (office).

BLAZWICK, Iwona, OBE; British art critic and curator; *Director, Whitechapel Art Gallery, London;* b. 1955, London; ed Exeter Univ.; Dir AIR Gallery, London 1984–86; Curator, Inst. of Contemporary Arts (ICA), becoming Dir of Exhbns 1987–93; Commissioning Ed. Phaidon Press during 1990s; ind. curator for museums and public arts projects in Europe and Japan 1993–97; Head of Exhbns, Tate Modern 1997–2001; Dir Whitechapel Art Gallery, London 2001–; Visiting Tutor at several art colls and acads in Europe and Canada; Series Ed. Documents of Contemporary Art; mem. several cultural juries including Turner Prize 1993, Jerwood Painting Prize 1997, Wexner Prize 2002, Vincent Prize, Max Mara Art Prize for Women, Golden Lion Award, Venice Biennale; mem. London Cultural Strategy Group; Fellow, RCA; hon. degrees from London Metropolitan Univ., Univ. of Plymouth. *Publications include:* numerous exhbn catalogues; An Endless Adventure, An Endless Passion, An Endless Banquet 1989, Alan Charlton: Paintings 1991, Katharina Fritsch 2002, Lawrence Weiner, Ilya Kabakov, Tate Modern: the Handbook (ed.), Century City (ed.), Fresh Cream (ed.) 2000. *Address:* Whitechapel Gallery, 77-82 Whitechapel High Street, London, E1 7QX, England (office). *Telephone:* (20) 7522-7888 (office). *Fax:* (20) 7377-1635 (office). *E-mail:* info@whitechapelgallery.org (office). *Website:* www.whitechapelgallery.org (office).

BLEARS, Rt Hon Hazel Anne, PC, BA; British politician; b. 14 May 1956, Salford, Greater Manchester, England; d. of Arthur Blears and Dorothy Blears; m. Michael Halsall 1989; ed Wardley Grammar School, Trent Polytechnic; trainee solicitor, Salford Council 1978–80; in pvt. practice 1980–81; solicitor, Rossendale Council 1981–83, Wigan Council 1983–85; Councillor, Salford City Council 1984–92; Prin. Solicitor, Manchester City Council 1985–97; contested Tatton 1987 and Bury South 1992 general elections; MP (Labour) for Salford 1997–2010, for Salford and Eccles 2010–; Parl. Pvt. Sec. to Alan Milburn: as Minister of State, Dept of Health 1998, as Chief Sec., HM Treasury 1999; Parl. Under-Sec. of State, Dept of Health 2001–03; Minister of State, Home Office 2003–06; Minister without Portfolio 2006–07; Sec. of State for Communities and Local Govt 2007–09 (resgnd); mem. Intelligence and Security Cttee 2010–; mem. North West Exec., Labour Party 1997–99, Nat. Policy Forum 1997–2001, Leadership Campaign Team 1997–98, Labour Party Devt Co-ordinator and Deputy to Ian McCartney 1998–2001, Leader, Parl. Campaign Team 2003–, Labour Party Nat. Exec. Cttee 2004–, Chair. Labour Party 2006–07; Chair. Social Action Forum 2010–12. *Publications:* Communities in Control 2003, The Politics of Decency 2004. *Leisure interests:* dance, motorcycling. *Address:* House of Commons, Westminster, London, SW1A 0AA (office); Constituency Office, 201 Langworthy Road, Salford, M6 5PW, England (office). *Telephone:* (20) 7219-3000 (office); (161) 925-0705 (constituency) (office). *E-mail:* blearsh@parliament.uk (office). *Website:* www.parliament.uk/biographies/commons/hazel-blears/456 (office); www.hazelblears.co.uk.

BLEASDALE, Alan; British playwright and novelist; b. 23 March 1946; s. of George Bleasdale and Margaret Bleasdale; m. Julia Moses 1970; two s. one d.; ed Wade Deacon Grammar School, Widnes, Padgate Teachers Training Coll.; schoolteacher 1967–75; Hon. DLitt (Liverpool Polytechnic) 1991; BAFTA Writers Award 1982, Royal TV Soc. Writer of the Year 1982. *Publications include:* Scully 1975, Who's Been Sleeping in My Bed? 1977, No More Sitting on the Old School Bench 1979, Boys from the Blackstuff 1982, Are You Lonesome Tonight? (Best Musical, Evening Standard Drama Awards 1985) 1985, No Surrender (film script) 1986, Having a Ball 1986, It's a Madhouse 1986, The Monocled Mutineer (televised 1986) 1986, GBH (TV series) 1991, On the Ledge 1993, Jake's Progress (TV, Best Writer, Monte Carlo Int. TV Festival 1996) 1995, Oliver Twist 1999 (Best Drama Series, TV and Radio Industries Club 2000), The Sinking of the Laconia (TV script) 2010. *Leisure interest:* rowing. *Address:* c/o Stephen Durbridge, The Agency, 24 Pottery Lane, Holland Park, London, W11 4LZ, England (office). *Telephone:* (20) 7727-1346 (office). *E-mail:* sd-office@theagency.co.uk (office); info@theagency.co.uk (office). *Website:* www.theagency.co.uk (office).

BLECHA, Karl; Austrian fmr politician; *President, Society for Austro-Arab Relations;* b. 16 April 1933, Vienna; s. of Karl Matthias Blecha and Rosa Blecha; m. 1st Ilse Steinhauser 1965; m. 2nd Burgunde Teuber 1982; two d.; m. 3rd Rosi Belcheva 1999; one d.; ed Univ. of Vienna; vocational adviser in Vienna Employment Exchange and later reader in publishing firm; Founder and Dir Inst. for Empirical Social Research 1963–75; mem. Lower Austrian SPÖ (Austrian Socialist Party) Exec. 1964–90; mem. Nationalrat 1970–89; Gen. Sec. SPÖ HQ 1976–81, Vice-Chair. SPÖ 1981–89; Federal Minister of the Interior 1983–89; Founder and Man. Dir Mitropa Inst. for Econ. and Social Research, Vienna 1989–; fmr Chair. Socialist Student Movt, Socialist Young Generation, Austrian Asscn for Cultural Affairs; Pres. Austrian Soc. for Promotion of Research 1994–; Pres. Austrian Union of Pensioners 1999–, Council of Sr in Austria 1999–, Society for Austro-Arab Relations, Social Democratic Party Retirees Asscn; mem. Nat. Council 1970–83, Feb.–April 1989; mem. Advisory Bd Mediamixx Group. *Publications include:* numerous essays on sociology and various articles and brochures on political principles. *Address:* Society for Austro-Arab Relations, Anschützgasse 1, 1150 Vienna (office); Mitropa Institute for Economic and Social Research, Stubenring 14, 1010 Vienna, Austria (office). *Telephone:* (1) 31372-0 (office); (664) 340-42-86 (office). *Fax:* (1) 31372-12 (office). *E-mail:* office@mitropa-institut.at (office). *Website:* www.saar.at (office); mitropa-institute.eu (office).

BLENCATHRA, Baron (Life Peer), cr. 2011, of Penrith in the County of Cumbria; **Rt Hon. David John,** PC; British politician; b. 16 May 1953, Cromarty, Ross and Cromarty, Scotland; ed Fortrose Acad., Univ. of Aberdeen; elected to House of Commons in by-election as MP (Conservative) for Penrith and The Border 1983–2010; Asst Govt Whip 1987–88, Govt Whip 1988–89; Parl. Sec. to Ministry of Agric., Fisheries and Food 1989–92; Minister of State at Dept of the Environment 1992–93, at Home Office 1993–97; returned to back benches 1997–2001; Opposition Chief Whip 2001–03, 2003–05; returned to back benches 2005–10; mem. House of Commons Comm. 2006; Chair. Jt Cttee on Statutory Instruments 2006, mem. Liaison 2006. *Address:* House of Lords, Westminster, London, SW1A 0PW, England (office). *Telephone:* (20) 7219-3000 (office).

BLENDON, Robert J., ScD, MPH, MBA; American academic; *Senior Associate Dean for Policy Translation and Leadership Development, Harvard University;* b. 19 Dec. 1942, Philadelphia, Pa; s. of Edward G. Blendon and Theresa M. Blendon; m. Marie C. McCormick 1977; ed Marietta Coll., Univ. of Chicago and Johns Hopkins Univ., Baltimore, Md; Instructor, Johns Hopkins Univ. School of Hygiene and Public Health 1969, Asst to Assoc. Dean (Health Care Programs) 1969–70, Asst Prof. 1970–71, Asst Dir for Planning and Devt, Office of Health Care Programs 1970–71; Special Asst for Health Affairs to Deputy Under-Sec. for Policy Co-ordination, Dept of Health Educ. and Welfare 1971–72, Special Asst for Policy Devt to Asst Sec. for Health and Scientific Affairs 1971–72; Visiting Lecturer, Princeton Univ. 1972–80, Co-ordinator, Medicine in Modern America Course 1980–; Sr Vice-Pres. The Robert Wood Johnson Foundation 1980–87; Prof., Dept of Health Policy and Political Analysis, Harvard Univ. School of Public Health 1987–, Chair. 1987–96, Sr Assoc. Dean for Policy Translation and Leadership Devt 2010–, Richard L. Menschel Prof. of Public Health and Prof. of Health Policy and Political Analysis; Prof., Kennedy School of Govt 1987–; numerous other professional appointments; Distinguished Investigator Award, AHSR 2000, Warren G. Mitofsky Award. *Publications:* numerous articles in professional journals. *Address:* Harvard University School of Public Health, Kresge Building, Room 402, 677 Huntington Avenue, Boston, MA 02115 (office); 478 Quinobequin Road, Waban, MA 02468-2127, USA (home). *Telephone:* (617) 432-4502 (office); (617) 965-8279 (home). *E-mail:* rblendon@hsph.harvard.edu (office). *Website:* www.hsph .harvard.edu/faculty/robert-blendon (office).

BLESSED, Brian; British actor; b. 9 Oct. 1936, Mexborough, S Yorks., England; s. of William Blessed and Hilda Wall; m. Hildegard Zimmermann 1978; one d.; ed Bolton-on-Dearne Secondary Modern School, Bristol Old Vic Theatre School; began acting career in repertory cos, mainly Nottingham and later Birmingham Repertory Co.; appeared with RSC as Claudius in Hamlet, Hastings in Richard III, Exeter in Henry V; one-man show An Evening with Brian Blessed; Pres. Council for Nat. Parks; Hon. DLitt (Bradford), (Sheffield). *Theatre includes:* Cats, Metropolis, Lion In Winter, Chitty Chitty Bang Bang, London Palladium, State of Revolution, The Relapse, Royal Nat. Theatre. *Films include:* The Christmas Tree 1966, Asterix the Gaul (voice) 1967, Till Death Us Do Part 1969, The Same Skin 1970, The Last Valley 1971, The Trojan Women 1971, Henry VIII and His Six Wives 1972, Man of La Mancha 1972, King Arthur, the Young Warlord 1975, Flash Gordon 1980, High Road to China 1983, Asterix and the Big Fight (voice: English version) 1989, Henry V 1989, Waiting for Godot 1991, Robin Hood: Prince of Thieves 1991, Back in the U.S.S.R. 1992, Freddie as F.R.O.7. (voice) 1992, Agincourt 1415: The Triumph of the Longbow (video) (narrator) 1993, Much Ado About Nothing 1993, Chasing the Deer 1994, The Bruce 1996, Hamlet 1996, King Lear: A Critical Guide (video documentary short) 1997, Macbeth 1997, King Lear (also dir) 1999, Star Wars: Episode I – The Phantom Menace 1999, Tarzan 1999, Day Return (short) 2000, The Mumbo Jumbo 2000, Olympiad 448 BC: Olympiad of Ancient Hellas (narrator) 2004, Alexander 2004, Midsummer Dream 2005, Day of Wrath 2006, The Conclave 2006, As You Like It 2006, Back in Business 2007, Agent Crush 2008, Mr. Bojagi (short) 2009, Re-Evolution 2011, The Pirates! In an Adventure with Scientists! 2012. *Television includes:* role of Fancy Smith in Z Cars 1963–78, Ghost Squad (series) 1963, The Three Musketeers (mini-series) 1966–67, The Further Adventures of the Musketeers (series) 1967, The Troubleshooters (series) 1968, Cold Comfort Farm (mini-series) 1968, The Avengers (series) 1967–69, Barrister at Law (film) 1969, Randall and Hopkirk (Deceased) (series) 1969, The Wednesday Play – Son of Man 1969, The Wednesday Play – Wine of India 1970, Whom God Hath Joined (film) 1970, Jackanory (series) (storyteller) 1971, The Expert (series) 1971, Shirley's World (series) 1971, The Venturers (film) 1972, Public Eye (series) 1973, Justice (series) 1973, Love Story (series) 1973, ITV Sunday Night Theatre – Lorna and Ted 1973, Hadleigh (series) 1973, Arthur of the Britons (series) 1972–73, BBC Play of the Month – The Recruiting Officer 1973, Boy Dominic (series) 1974, Notorious Woman (mini-series) 1974, The Great Alfred (film) 1975, The Sweeney (series) 1975, Churchill's People (series) 1975, Thriller (series) 1975, NBC Special Treat (series) 1975, The Story of David (film) 1976, The Day After Tomorrow (film) 1976, Space: 1999 (series) 1975–76, I, Claudius (mini-series) 1976, Survivors (series) 1977, A Christmas Carol (film) 1977, Blakes 7 (series) 1978, ITV Playhouse – Double Agent 1969, The Aphrodite Inheritance

(mini-series) 1979, Tales of the Unexpected (series) 1979, ITV Playhouse – Saint Vitus' Dance 1979, Leap in the Dark (series) 1980, The Little World of Don Camillo (series) 1981, Cosmic Princess (film) 1982, Black Adder (series) 1983, The Hound of the Baskervilles (film) 1983, The Master of Ballantrae (film) 1984, The Last Days of Pompeii (mini-series) 1984, Return to Treasure Island (series) 1986, Doctor Who (series) 1986, The Kenny Everett Television Show (series) 1986, William Tell (series) 1987, My Family and Other Animals (series) 1987, David Macaulay: Pyramid (film) 1988, Once in a Life Time (film) 1988, Boon (series) 1989, Minder (series) 1989, War and Remembrance (mini-series) 1988–89, Blood Royal: William the Conqueror (film) 1990, The Castle of Adventure (series) 1990, Galahad of Everest 1991, Lovejoy (series) 1991, Prisoner of Honor (film) 1991, Blood and Dust (film) 1992, Exam Conditions (film) 1992, Lady Chatterley (series) 1993, MacGyver: Lost Treasure of Atlantis (film) 1994, Johnny and the Dead (series) 1995, Kidnapped (film) 1995, Catherine the Great (film) 1996, The History of Tom Jones, a Foundling (mini-series) 1997, Dennis the Menace (series) 1998, Adam's Family Tree (series) 1999, The Big Knights (series) 1999, The Greatest Store in the World (film) 1999, The Nearly Complete and Utter History of Everything (film) 1999, Devil's Harvest 2003, Winter Solstice (film) 2003, Let's Write a Story (series documentary) 2004, The Legend of the Tamworth Two (film) 2004, Alexander the Great (video documentary) (narrator) 2006, Mist: The Tale of a Sheepdog Puppy (film) 2006, Peppa Pig (series) 2006–10, Doctors (series) 2007–11, Kika & Bob (mini-series) 2008, The Wrong Door (series) 2008, Family Guy (series) 2008, The Royal (series) 2008, Henry 8.0 (series) 2009, Fee Fi Fo Yum (series) 2010, Little Princess (series) 2010, The Legend of Dick and Dom (series) 2010–11. *Publications:* The Turquoise Mountain, The Dynamite Kid, Nothing's Impossible, Blessed Everest, Quest to the Lost World. *Leisure interests:* mountaineering, judo (black belt), Koi Carp and animal welfare. *Address:* c/o Stephen Gittins, 7 Hatton Garden, London, EC1N 8AD, England (office). *Telephone:* (20) 7831-9709 (office). *E-mail:* info@aimagents.com (office); email@aimagents.com (office). *Website:* www .aimagents.com (office).

BLESSING, Martin, MBA; German banker; *Chairman, Board of Managing Directors, Commerzbank AG;* b. 6 July 1963, Bremen; m.; three d.; ed Univ. of Frankfurt, Univ. of St Gallen, Switzerland, Univ. of Chicago, USA; apprenticeship at Dresdner Bank AG, Frankfurt 1983–84, Jt Man. Pvt. Customers 1997–2000; univ. studies 1984–88; Frankfurt and New York consultant, McKinsey 1989–96, Pnr 1994; Chair. Advance Bank AG, Munich 2000–01; mem. Bd of Man. Dirs Commerzbank AG, Frankfurt 2001– (responsible for retail banking div. 2001–04, for Information Tech. and Transaction Banking and for Mittelstand Banking Depts of Corp. Banking and Financial Insts 2004–07), Chair. 2008–; mem. Supervisory Bd AMB Generali, Heidelberger Druckmaschinen, ThyssenKrupp Services. *Leisure interests:* jogging, skiing, running the marathon. *Address:* Commerzbank AG, 60261 Frankfurt am Main, Germany (office). *Telephone:* (69) 13620 (office). *Fax:* (69) 285389 (office). *E-mail:* info@commerzbank.com (office). *Website:* www.commerzbank.com (office).

BLETHYN, Brenda Anne, OBE; British actress; b. 20 Feb. 1946, Ramsgate, Kent, England; d. of William Charles Bottle and Louisa Kathleen Bottle; partner Michael Mayhew 1977; ed St Augustine's RC School, Ramsgate, Thanet Tech. Coll., Guildford School of Acting; with Nat. Theatre (now Royal Nat. Theatre) 1975–90; mem. Poetry Soc. 1976–; Hon. DLitt (Kent) 1999, (Surrey) 2006; numerous awards including Boston Film Critics' Award 1997, LA Film Critics' Award 1997, Golden Globe 1997, London Film Critics' Award 1997, BAFTA 1997. *Theatre appearances include:* for Royal Nat. Theatre: A Midsummer Night's Dream, Troilus and Cressida, Bedroom Farce, Tales From the Vienna Woods, The Guardsman, Fruits of Enlightenment, Madras House, The Provoked Wife, Strife, Force of Habit, Tamburlaine, Plunder (also Old Vic), Camilla Ringbinder Show, Bloody Neighbours (at ICA), The Mysteries 1979, The Double Dealer 1982, Dalliance 1987, The Beaux Stratagem 1989; for Comedy Theatre, London: Steaming (Theatre Critics' Best Supporting Actress Award) 1981; for Vaudeville Theatre, London: Benefactors 1984; for Royal Exchange Theatre, Manchester: A Doll's House 1987, Born Yesterday 1988, An Ideal Husband 1992; for RSC: Wildest Dreams 1993; for Bush Theatre, London: Crimes of the Heart; for Almeida Theatre, London: The Bed Before Yesterday 1994; for Donmar Theatre, London, Habeas Corpus 1996; for Nuffield Theatre, Southampton: The Dramatic Attitudes of Miss Fanny Kemble; for Manhattan Theater Club, New York: Absent Friends (Theatre World Award for Outstanding New Talent 1996) 1996; Mrs Warren's Profession (West End, London) 2002–03. *Films:* Witches, A River Runs Through It 1992, Secrets and Lies (Golden Globe Best Actress 1996, Best Actress Award, Cannes Film Festival 1996, London Film Critics' Circle Best Actress of the Year Award 1996, Boston Critics' Circle Best Actress Award 1996, LA Critics' Circle Best Actress Award 1996, British Acad. Award: Best Actress 1997, Premier Magazine Best Actress Award 1997) 1996, Remember Me 1996, Music From Another Room 1997, Girls' Night 1997, Little Voice (Dallas Fort Worth Critics' Asscn Best Supporting Actress 1999) 1999, Saving Grace (Sundance Film Festival Audience Award 2000, Variety Club of Great Britain Best Screen Actress Award 2001) 1999, On the Nose, In the Winter Dark, Night Train 1999, Daddy and Them 1999, RKO 281 1999, The Sleeping Dictionary 2000, Yellow Bird, Pumpkin 2000, Anne Frank – The Whole Story 2001, Lovely and Amazing 2001, Plots with a View 2002, Sonny 2002, Blizzard 2002, Beyond the Sea 2004, A Way of Life 2004, On a Clear Day 2005, Pride and Prejudice 2006, Atonement 2007, Clubland 2007, Dead Man Running 2009, My Angel 2011. *Television includes:* Mona, All Good Things, Grown Ups, The Imitation Game, That Uncertain Feeling, Floating Off, Claws, Sheppey, Yes Minister, Alas Smith and Jones, The Shawl, Rumpole, Maigret, Bedroom Farce, The Double Dealer, Death of an Expert Witness, The Storyteller, The Richest Woman in the World, The RNT Mysteries, Henry VI (Part I) 1981, King Lear 1983, Chance in a Million 1983–85, The Labours of Erica 1987, The Bullion Boys 1993, The Buddha of Suburbia 1993, Sleeping with Mickey 1993, Outside Edge (Television's Best Comedy Actress Award) 1994–96, First Signs of Madness 1996, Between the Sheets 2003, Belonging 2004, Mysterious Creatures 2006, War and Peace 2007, Law & Order: Special Victims Unit 2008, The New Adventures of Old Christine (series) 2008, Vera (series) 2011–12, King of the Teds (film) 2012. *Publication:* Mixed Fancies (memoir) 2006. *Leisure interests:* reading, swimming, cryptic crosswords, running. *Address:* c/o Independent Talent Group Limited, Oxford House, 76 Oxford Street, London, W1D 1BS, England. *Telephone:*

(20) 7636-6565. *Fax:* (20) 7323-0101. *E-mail:* info@independenttalent.com. *Website:* www.independenttalent.com.

BLEWETT, Neal, AC, MA, DPhil, FRHistS, FASSA; Australian politician; b. 24 Oct. 1933, Sydney; s. of James Blewett and Phyllis Blewett (née Kerrison); m. Jill Myford 1962 (died 1988); one s. one d.; ed Launceston High School, Tasmania, Univ. of Tasmania, Univ. of Oxford, UK; Lecturer, Univ. of Oxford 1959–64; Prof., Dept of Political Theory and Insts, Flinders Univ. 1974–77; MP for Bonython, South Australia 1977–94; Minister for Health 1983–87, for Community Services and Health 1987–90, for Trade and Overseas Devt 1990–91, Minister for Social Security 1991–93; High Commr in UK 1994–98; Pres. Australian Inst. of Int. Affairs 1998–2006; Pres. Alcohol and Other Drugs Council of Australia 2002–; mem. Exec. Bd WHO 1995–98; Visiting Prof., University of Adelaide, Univ. of Sydney 1999–; Hon. Fellow, Jesus Coll. (Oxford); Hon. DLit (Hull), Hon. LLD (Tasmania, ANU) 2003; Dr hc (Univ. of Technology, Sydney) 2010. *Publications:* Playford to Dunstan: The Politics of Transition (with Dean Jaensch) 1971, The Peers, the Parties and the People 1972, A Cabinet Diary 1999. *Leisure interests:* reading, bush walking. *Address:* 32 Fitzroy Street, Leura, New South Wales 2780, Australia. *Telephone:* (2) 4784-3478 (home). *Fax:* (2) 4784-3478 (home).

BLIER, Bertrand; French film director and screenwriter; b. 14 March 1939, Paris; s. of the late Bernard Blier and of Gisèle Brunet; m. Catherine Florin 1973; one d.; also one s. by Anouk Grinberg; ed Lycée Claude Bernard, Paris; Grand Prix Nat. du Cinema 1989. *Films include:* Hitler, connais pas 1963, Si j'étais un espion (Breakdown) 1967, Les valseuses (Making It) 1974, Calmos 1975, Préparez vos mouchoirs (Oscar for Best Foreign Film) 1977, Buffet froid (three Césars) 1979, Beau-père 1981, La femme de mon pote (My Best Friend's Girl) 1983, Notre histoire (Separate Rooms) 1984, Tenue de soirée 1986, Trop belle pour toi (Cannes Special Jury Prize 1989) 1988, Merci la vie 1991, Tango 1992, Un deux trois – soleil 1993, Mon homme 1996, Les acteurs 2000, Les côtelettes 2003, Combien tu m'aimes? 2005, Le Bruit des glaçons 2010. *Publications:* several novels and film scripts. *Address:* c/o Artmédia, 10 avenue Georges V, 75008 Paris (office); 11 rue Margueritte, 75017 Paris, France (home).

BLIGE, Mary J.; American singer and songwriter; b. 11 Jan. 1971, New York; m. Kendu Isaacs 2003; solo artist; numerous tours and live appearances; has collaborated with numerous musicians, including George Michael, Lauryn Hill; American Music Award for Favorite Female Hip-Hop/R&B Artist 2003, for Favorite Female Soul/R&B Artist 2006, Grammy Award for Best Pop Collaboration with Vocals (jtly) 2004, BET Award for Best Female R&B Artist 2006, nine Billboard Awards 2006, Grammy Award for Best Female R&B Vocal Performance (for Be Without You) 2007. *Films:* I Can Do Bad All By Myself 2009. *Recordings include:* albums: What's The 411? 1992, My Life 1994, Mary Jane 1995, Share My World 1997, The Tour 1998, Mary 1999, No More Drama 2001, Ballads 2001, Love & Life 2003, The Breakthrough (American Music Award for Favorite Soul/R&B Album 2006, Grammy Award for Best R&B Album 2007, Best R&B/Soul Album by a Female Artist, Soul Train Awards 2007) 2005, Growing Pains (Grammy Award for Best Contemporary R&B Album 2009) 2007, Stronger with Each Tear 2009, My Life II: The Journey Continues 2011. *Address:* Steve Lucas Associates, 156 West 56th Street, New York, NY 10019, USA (office). *Website:* www.mjblige.com.

BLIKLE, Andrzej, PhD; Polish mathematician and academic; *Professor Emeritus, Institute of Computer Science, Polish Academy of Sciences;* b. 24 Sept. 1939, Warsaw; s. of Jerzy Blikle and Aniela Blikle; m.; one s.; ed Warsaw Univ.; master of confectioner's trade 1975; scientific worker, Inst. of Math., Polish Acad. of Sciences 1963–71, Computational Centre, Polish Acad. of Sciences 1971–77, Prof., Inst. of Computer Science, Polish Acad. of Sciences 1977–2004, Prof. Emer. 2004–; Pres. and CEO A. Blikle Ltd 1991– (Chair. 2008–); Pres. Family Business Initiative 2008–; mem. Polish Math. Soc. 1962–, Polish Information Processing Soc. 1981– (Pres. 1987–93), Asscn for Theoretical Computer Science 1982–, Academia Europaea 1993; mem. European Acad. of Sciences; Hon. mem. Polish Information Processing Soc.; Golden Cross of Merit 1987, Cross of Merit 2005; Young Mathematician Award, Polish Math. Asscn 1967, Golden Award, Polish Tech. and Scientific Publisher 1989, Jan Kilinski Silver Medal of Merit, Bd of Polish Craft Asscn 2001, Warsaw Medal of Merit 2001, Tadeusz Kotarbinski Medal, Polish Acad. of Sciences 2008. *Publication:* MetaSoft Primer – Towards a Metalanguage for Applied Denotational Semantics Series: Lecture Notes in Computer Science (Vol. 288) (co-ed.) 1987. *Leisure interests:* skiing, windsurfing, films, history. *Address:* ul. Czarnieckiego 82, 01-541 Warsaw, Poland (home). *Telephone:* (22) 8396365 (home). *Fax:* (22) 8396365 (office). *E-mail:* andrzej.blikle@ blikle.pl (office). *Website:* www.moznainaczej.com.pl (office).

BLINDER, Alan Stuart, AB, MSc, PhD; American economist and academic; *Gordon S. Rentschler Memorial Professor of Economics and Public Affairs, Princeton University;* b. 14 Oct. 1945, Brooklyn, New York; s. of Morris Blinder and Shirley Blinder; m. Madeline Schwartz 1967; two s.; ed Princeton Univ., London School of Econs, Massachusetts Inst. of Tech.; Deputy Asst Dir US Congressional Budget Office 1975; Gordon S. Rentschler Memorial Prof. of Econs, Princeton Univ., NJ 1982–2007, of Econs and Public Affairs 2007–, Dir Center for Econ. Policy Studies 1989–93, Co.-Dir 1996–2011; mem. Council of Econ. Advisers to Pres. Clinton 1993–94; Vice-Chair. Bd of Govs, Fed. Reserve System 1994–96; Vice-Chair. G7 Group 1997–; Pnr, Promotory Financial Group 2000–; mem. American Philosophical Soc. 1996–; Fellow, American Acad. of Arts and Sciences 1991–. *Publications include:* Growing Together: An Alternative Economic Strategy for the 1990s 1991, Central Banking in Theory and Practice 1998, Asking About Prices: A New Approach to Understanding Price Stickiness (jtly) 1998, Economics, Principles and Policy (jtly) 2000, The Fabulous Decade: Macroeconomic Lessons from the 1990s (jtly) 2001, The Quiet Revolution: Central Banking Goes Modern 2004, Offshoring of American Jobs: What Response from U.S. Economic Policy? (jtly) 2009. *Address:* Department of Economics, Princeton University, 105 Fisher Hall, Princeton, NJ 08544, USA (office). *Telephone:* (609) 258-4023 (office). *Fax:* (609) 258-5398 (office). *E-mail:* blinder@princeton.edu (office). *Website:* www .princeton.edu/blinder (office).

BLISS, (John William) Michael, CM, PhD, FRSC; Canadian historian, academic and writer; *University Professor Emeritus of History, University of Toronto;* b. 18 Jan. 1941, Kingsville, Ont.; s. of Quartus Bliss and Anne L. Crow; m. Elizabeth J. Haslam 1963; one s. two d.; ed Kingsville Dist High School and Univ.

of Toronto; Teaching Asst, Harvard Univ. 1967–68; Dept of History, Univ. of Toronto 1968–72, Prof. 1975–99, Univ. Prof. 1999–2006, Prof. Emer. 2006–, also held cross-appointments to Faculty of Medicine and to Inst. for History and Philosophy of Science and Tech.; Sr Fellow, Massey Coll.; Hon. Fellow, Royal Coll. of Physicians and Surgeons of Canada; Hon. DLitt (McGill) 2001; numerous awards including Tyrrell Medal 1987, RSC 1988, Oswald T. Avery Medal, Dalhousie History of Medicine Soc. 1998. *Publications include:* A Living Profit 1974, A Canadian Millionaire: The Life of Sir Joseph Flavelle (Sir John A. Macdonald Prize, Canadian Historical Asscn, F.-X. Garneau Medal) 1978, The Discovery of Insulin (William A. Welch Medal, American Asscn for the History of Medicine 1984, City of Toronto Book Award 1983) 1982, Banting: A Biography 1984, Northern Enterprise: Five Centuries of Canadian Business (Nat. Business Book Award for the best book about business published in Canada, Award of Merit of Asscn for Canadian Studies) 1987, Plague: A Story of Smallpox in Montreal 1991, Right Honourable Men: The Descent of Canadian Politics from Macdonald to Mulroney 1994, William Osler: A Life in Medicine (Canadian Historical Asscn Ferguson Prize for the best book of the year in a field of history other than Canadian, Jason Hannah Medical Award, RSC) 1999, Harvey Cushing: A Life in Surgery 2005, The Making of Modern Medicine: Turning Points in the Treatment of Disease 2010; essays in various newspapers and magazines. *Address:* Department of History, University of Toronto, Sidney Smith Hall, 100 St. George Street, Toronto, ON M5S 3G3, Canada (office). *Telephone:* (416) 978-3363 (office). *Fax:* (416) 978-6647 (office). *E-mail:* m.bliss@sympatico.ca; history@chass.utoronto.ca (office). *Website:* www.history.utoronto.ca (office).

BLISS, Timothy Vivian Pelham, PhD, FRS, FMedSci; British neuroscientist and academic; *Visiting Worker, Division of Neurophysiology, National Institute for Medical Research;* b. 27 July 1940, Weymouth; s. of Pelham Marryat Bliss and Elizabeth Bliss (née Sproule); m. 1st Virginia Catherine Morton-Evans 1975; one step-s. two step-d.; m. 2nd Isabel Frances Vasseur; two step-s.; one d. by Katherine Clough; ed McGill Univ., Montreal; mem. of scientific staff, MRC at Nat. Inst. for Medical Research 1967–, Head, Div. of Neurophysiology 1988–2006, Visiting Worker 2006–, Head, Neurosciences Group 1996–2006; Visiting Prof., Dept of Physiology, Univ. Coll. London 1993–; Trustee, Sir John Soane's Museum 2003–08, Feldberg Foundation; mem. Scientific Advisory Cttee, Lister Foundation; Bristol Myers Squibb Prize for Neuroscience 1991, Feldberg Prize 1994, British Neuroscience Asscn Award for Outstanding Contribution to British Neuroscience 2003, Royal Society Croonian Lecture 2012, Fondation Ipsen Prize for Neuronal Plasticity (jt winner) 2013. *Publications:* more than 100 papers in scientific journals relating to the neural basis of learning and memory. *Leisure interests:* architecture, food, wine, naval history, travelling. *Address:* 18 Market Place, Aylsham, Norfolk, NR11 6EH, England (home). *Telephone:* (1263) 734216 (home). *E-mail:* tbliss@nimr.mrc.ac.uk (office).

BLIX, Hans Martin, LLD, PhD; Swedish lawyer and international official (retd); b. 28 June 1928, Uppsala; s. of Gunnar Blix and Hertha Blix (née Wiberg); m. Eva Kettis 1962; two s.; ed Uppsala Univ., Univ. of Cambridge, UK, Columbia Univ., New York, USA, Univ. of Stockholm; Asst Prof. of Int. Law, Univ. of Stockholm 1960–63; Legal Consultant on Int. Law, Foreign Ministry 1963–76; Under-Sec. of State for Int. Devt Co-operation, Foreign Ministry 1976–78, 1979–81; Minister for Foreign Affairs 1978–79; Dir-Gen. IAEA, Vienna 1981–97; mem. Swedish del. to UN Gen. Ass. 1961–81; mem. del. to Conf. on Disarmament, Geneva 1962–78; Exec. Chair. UN Monitoring, Verification and Inspection Comm. for Iraq 2000–03; Hon. Chair. World Nuclear Asscn; Commdr, Légion d'honneur 2004; Dr hc (Moscow State Univ.) 1987, (several other univs); Henry de Wolf Smyth Award 1988, Gold Medal, Uranium Inst. (now World Nuclear Asscn) 1997, Olof Palme Prize 2003. *Publications include:* Treaty-Making Power (dissertation), Statsmyndigheternas Internationella Förbindelser (monograph) 1964, Sovereignty, Aggression and Neutrality 1970, The Treaty-Maker's Handbook 1973, Disarming Iraq: The Search for Weapons of Mass Destruction 2004; numerous articles in scientific journals. *Leisure interests:* Oriental rugs, hiking, art.

BLIZNAKOV, Vesselin Vitanov; Bulgarian scientist and politician; b. 18 June 1944, Straldga, Yambol Dist; m.; ed Vassil Kkaragyizov High School, Yambol, Medical Acad., Sofia; began career in general practice, Bourgas Dist 1972–75; Researcher Assoc. and Head of Lab., Nat. Centre for Radio-Biology and Radiation Protection, Sofia 1976–86, Head, Radiation Protection Dept 1986–99; Chair. Bulgarian Nuclear Soc. 1999–2001; fmr mem. Civil Cttee for Protection of Nuclear Power Plant Kozloduy; co-owner Dr. Atanas Shterev's Clinic; mem. Nat. Ass. for Vratsa 2001–05, for Haskovo 2005–, Chair. Energy Cttee 2001–05, mem. Foreign Policy, Defence and Security Cttees 2001–05; Deputy Chair. Parl. Group of Simeon II Nat. Movt 2001–03; mem. Del. to Jt Bulgarian-EU Parl. Cttee 2001; Minister of Defence 2005–08; mem. Governing Council, European Nuclear Soc. 1999–2001.

BLOBEL, Günter, MD, PhD; American (b. German) cell biologist and academic; *Professor, Rockefeller University;* b. 21 May 1936, Waltersdorf, Silesia (now Poland); m. Laura Maioglio-Blobel; ed Univ. of Tübingen, Univ. of Wisconsin; emigrated to USA 1960 (now naturalized citizen); internship in various German hosps 1960–62; joined cell biology lab. of George Palade, Rockefeller Univ., New York, Asst Prof. 1969–73, Assoc. Prof. 1973–76, Prof. 1976–, now Head of Cell Biology Lab.; Investigator, Howard Hughes Medical Inst., Rockefeller Univ. 1986–; Founder Friends of Dresden Inc. 1994; Co-founder and Chair. Scientific Advisory Bd Chromocell Corpn; mem. Bd of Dirs Nestlé, Int. Flavors & Fragrances 2000–; mem. Bd of Scientific Govs Scripps Research Inst.; mem. NAS, American Philosophical Soc., Pontifical Acad. of Sciences; Dr hc (Rockefeller Univ.) 2013; Gairdner Foundation Int. Award 1982, Louisa Gross Horwitz Prize 1989, Albert Lasker Award 1993, King Faisal Int. Prize 1996, Nobel Prize in Physiology or Medicine for work on signal and transport mechanisms of proteins 1999, Ellis Island Medal of Hon. 2000. *Leisure interests:* architecture, classical music, landscapes. *Address:* Rockefeller University Cell Biology Laboratory, 66th and York Avenue, New York, NY 10021 (office); The Howard Hughes Medical Institute, The Rockefeller University, 1230 York Avenue, New York, NY 10021 (office); 1100 Park Avenue, Apt 10D, New York, NY 10128, USA (home). *Telephone:* (212) 327-8096 (office); (212) 369-3552 (home). *Fax:* (212) 327-7880 (office); (212) 534-5556 (home). *E-mail:* Gunter.Blobel@rockefeller.edu (office); blobel@rockvax.rockefeller .edu (office). *Website:* www.rockefeller.edu/labheads/blobel/blobel-lab.html (office).

BLOCHER, Christoph; Swiss politician and business executive; *Vice-President, Swiss People's Party;* b. 11 Oct. 1940; m. Sylvia Blocher; one s. three d.; ed attended univ. in Zürich, Montpellier and Paris; joined legal dept Ems-Chemie AG 1969, acquired co. 1983, Pres. and Rep to the Bd ems–Chemie Holding AG 1984–; mem. Meilen Dist Council 1974–78; mem. Zürich Canton Council 1975–80; Pres. Swiss People's Party (Schweizerische Volkspartei), Zürich Canton 1977–; mem. Nat. Ass. 1979–; Founder and Pres. Aktion für eine unabhängige und neutrale Schweiz (AUNS) 1986–; mem. Swiss Fed. Council 2003–07, Minister of Justice and Police Affairs 2004–07; Vice-Pres., Swiss People's Party 2008–. *Address:* Federal Council, Federal Palace, West Wing, 3003 Bern; Schweizerische Volkspartei, Brückfelderstr. 18, 3000 Bern, Switzerland (office). *Telephone:* (31) 3005858 (office). *Fax:* (31) 3005859 (office). *E-mail:* christoph@blocher.ch (office). *Website:* www.svp.ch (office); www.blocher.ch.

BLOCK, Gene D., AB, MA, PhD; American biologist, academic and university administrator; *Chancellor, University of California, Los Angeles;* b. 1948, Monticello, NY; m. Carol Block; two c.; ed Stanford Univ., Univ. of Oregon; postdoctoral work, Stanford Univ. 1975–78; joined Faculty at Univ. of Virginia 1978, Vice-Provost for Research 1993–98, Vice-Pres. for Research and Public Service 1998–2001, Pres. and Provost 2001–07; Chancellor Univ. of California, Los Angeles (UCLA) 2007–; Fellow, AAAS; Commonwealth of Va Outstanding Public Service Award 1984. *Achievements:* inventor of several devices, holds a patent for a non-contact respiratory monitor for the prevention of Sudden Infant Death Syndrome. *Leisure interest:* avid collector of vacuum-tube radios. *Address:* Office of the Chancellor, University of California, Los Angeles, 405 Hilgard Avenue, 2147 Murphy Hall, Los Angeles, CA 90095-1405, USA (office). *Telephone:* (310) 825-2151 (office). *Fax:* (310) 206-6030 (office). *E-mail:* chancellor@ucla.edu (office). *Website:* www.chancellor.ucla.edu (office).

BLOCK, Ned Joel, PhD; American academic; *Silver Professor, Departments of Philosophy, Psychology and Center for Neural Science, New York University;* b. 21 Aug. 1942, Chicago; s. of Eli Block and Blanche Rabinowitz; m. Susan Carey 1970; one d.; ed Massachusetts Inst. of Tech., St John's Coll., Oxford, UK, Harvard Univ.; Asst Prof., MIT 1971–77, Assoc. Prof. 1977–83, Prof. of Philosophy, Dept of Linguistics and Philosophy 1983–96, Chair. of Philosophy 1989–95; Prof. of Philosophy, New York Univ. 1996–, Silver Prof., Depts of Philosophy, Psychology and Center for Neural Science 2005–; Visiting Prof., Harvard Univ. 2002–03; Distinguished Visiting Prof., Univ. of Hong Kong 2008–09; Townsend Visitor, Univ. of California, Berkeley 2008–09; Pres. Soc. for Philosophy and Psychology 1978–79, Asscn for the Scientific Study of Consciousness; Chair. MIT Press Cognitive Science Bd 1992–95; NSF Fellow 1985–86, 1988–89; Robert A. Muh Alumni Award in the Humanities, Arts and Social Sciences, MIT 2005; Nat. Endowment for the Humanities Fellow 2006–07; Fellow, American Council of Learned Socs, Center for Study of Language and Information, American Acad. of Arts and Sciences 2004–, Cognitive Science Soc.; Guggenheim Fellow, Petrus Hispanus Lecturer, Univ. of Lisbon, Jack Burstyn Memorial Lecturer, Manhattan Marymount, Francis W. Gramlich Lecturer, Dartmouth, Burman Lecturer, Univ. of Umea, Sweden 2004–05, Lone Star Tourist 2004–05, Jack Smart Lecturer, ANU 2008–09, Lansdowne Lecturer, Univ. of Victoria 2009–10, Josiah Royce Lecturer, Brown Univ. 2009–10, Royal Inst. of Philosophy Annual Lecturer 2009–10, Thalheimer Lecturer, Johns Hopkins Univ. 2010–11, William James Lecturer, Harvard Univ. 2011–12, Immanuel Kant Lecturer, Stanford Univ. 2011–12, John Locke Lecturer, Univ. of Oxford 2012–13, Jean Nicod Lecturer and Jean Nicod Prize, Paris Univ. 2014, Marc Jeannerod Lecturer 2014–(15). *Publications:* The IQ Controversy (with G. Dworkin) 1976, Readings in Philosophy of Psychology (Vol. 1) 1980, (Vol. 2) 1981, Imagery 1981, The Nature of Consciousness (with O. Flanagan and G. Güzeldere), Functionalism, Consciousness and Representation – Collected Papers (Vol. 1) 2007; articles chosen for The Philosophers' Annual 1983, 1990, 1995, 2002. *Address:* Department of Philosophy, New York University, Room 405, 5 Washington Place, New York, NY 10003 (office); 37 Washington Square West, New York, NY 10011, USA (home). *Telephone:* (212) 998-8322 (office). *Fax:* (212) 995-4179 (office). *E-mail:* ned.block@nyu.edu (office). *Website:* www.nyu.edu/gsas/dept/philo/faculty/block (office).

BLOEMBERGEN, Nicolaas, DPhil; American (b. Dutch) scientist and academic; *Professor of Optical Sciences, University of Arizona;* b. 11 March 1920, Dordrecht, Netherlands; s. of Auke Bloembergen and Sophia M. Quint; m. Huberta D. Brink 1950; one s. two d.; ed Univs of Utrecht and Leiden; Research Fellow, Leiden Univ. 1947–49; Soc. of Fellows, Harvard Univ. 1949–51, Gordon McKay Assoc. Prof. 1951–57, apptd Prof. of Applied Physics 1957, Rumford Prof. of Physics 1974–80, Gerhard Gade Univ. Prof. 1980–90, Prof. Emer. 1990–; Prof. of Optical Sciences, Univ. of Arizona 2001–; Guggenheim Fellow 1957; Lorentz Guest Prof., Leiden 1973; Raman Visiting Prof., Bangalore Univ. 1979; Visiting Prof., Coll. de France 1980; mem. NAS; Corresp. mem. Royal Dutch Acad. of Sciences; Foreign mem. Indian Acad. of Sciences, Akad. Leopoldina (GDR), Royal Norwegian Inst. of Science; Foreign Assoc. mem. Acad. des Sciences, Inst. de France 1981–; Commdr, Order of Orange 1988; Hon. DSc (Laval Univ., Québec, Univ. of Conn., Hartford Univ., Univ. of Mass., Univ. of Cen. Fla); Hon. DSc (Moscow State Univ.) 1997, (N Carolina State Univ.) 1998, (Harvard Univ.) 2000; Buckley Prize, American Physical Soc., Liebmann Prize, Inst. of Radio Engineers, Ballantine Medal, Franklin Inst., Royal Dutch Acad. of Arts and Sciences, Half Moon Trophy, Netherland Club of New York, Nat. Medal of Science 1974, Lorentz Medal, Royal Dutch Acad. of Sciences 1978, Frederick Ives Medal, Optical Soc. of America 1979, Alexander von Humboldt Sr US Scientist Award, Munich 1980, shared Nobel Prize in Physics 1981 for contrib. to development of laser spectroscopy, Medal of Honor, IEEE 1983, Byvoet Medal, Univ. of Utrecht 2001. *Publications:* Nuclear Magnetic Relaxation 1961, Nonlinear Optics 1965, Encounters in Magnetic Resonance 1996, Encounters in Nonlinear Optics 1996; over 300 papers in professional journals. *Leisure interests:* travel, skiing, tennis. *Address:* Optical Sciences Center, University of Arizona, 1630 East University Boulevard, Tucson, AZ 85747, USA (office). *Telephone:* (520) 626-3479 (office); (520) 647-3772 (home). *Fax:* (520) 621-5300 (office). *E-mail:* nbloembergen@optics.arizona.edu (office). *Website:* www.optics.arizona.edu/faculty/Resumes/Bloembergen.htm (office).

BLOKHIN, Oleg Vladimirovich; Ukrainian football coach, politician and fmr footballer; *Manager, FC Dynamo Kiev;* b. 5 Nov. 1952, Kiev, Ukrainian SSR, Soviet Union; s. of Volodimir Ivanovich Blokhin and Katerina Zakharivna Adamenko

(fmr sprint hurdler); m. Irina Ivomovna Deryugina (divorced early 1990s); one d.; ed Kiev Physical Culture Inst. and Kiev Univ.; forward; played for Dinamo Kiev youth team 1962–69, sr team 1969–88, Vorwärts Steyr 1988–89, Aris Limassol 1989–90; played 432 matches in USSR Championships, 112 matches for USSR team (record) 1972–88; scored over 200 career goals; fmr coach, Greek clubs Olympiacos 1990–93 (won Greek Cup 1990, 1992, Greek Super Cup 1992), PAOK Saloniki 1993–94, 1997–98, Ionikos 1994–97, 1999–2002, AEK Athens 1998–99; coach Ukraine nat. football team 2003–07, 2011–12, FC Moscow 2007–08, Chornomorets Odesa (Sportive Dir) 2009–11; Man. FC Dynamo Kiev 2012–; Chair. Oleg Blokhin Int. Fund 1994–; elected to Verkhovna Rada (Parl.) 1998, 2002, mem. Cttee on Problems of Youth Policy and Sport; mem. Batkishchina faction 1999–, CP faction 2002–; mem. United Social Democratic Party of Ukraine 2002–; Soviet Top League Top Scorer 1972, 1973, 1974, 1975, 1977, Soviet Top League All-Time Goals and Appearances Leader, Ukrainian Footballer of the Year 1972, 1973, 1974, 1975, 1976, 1977, 1978, 1980, 1981, Soviet Footballer of the Year 1973, 1974, 1975, Golden Boot Award 1975, European Footballer of the Year (first Ukrainian player) 1975, Best Footballer of USSR 1973–75, seven times Champion USSR, five times winner USSR Cup, winner Cup Winners' Cup 1975, winner Supercup 1975, UEFA Cup Winners' Cup Top Scorer 1985–86, USSR nat. football team All-Time Goals and Caps Leader, Ukraine's Golden Player Rep., UEFA Jubilee Awards 2004. *Address:* c/o FC Dynamo Kiev, vul. Hrushevskoho 3, 1001 Kiev, Ukraine. *Website:* www.fcdynamo.kiev.ua/en.

BLOM-COOPER, Sir Louis Jacques, Kt, LLB, DrIur, QC, FRSA; British lawyer and writer; *Associate Tenant, Doughty Street Chambers;* b. 27 March 1926; s. of Alfred Blom-Cooper and Ella Flesseman; m. 1st 1952 (dissolved 1970); two s. one d.; m. 2nd Jane E Smither 1970 (died 2006); one s. two d.; ed Seaford Coll., King's Coll., London, Municipal Univ. of Amsterdam and Fitzwilliam Coll., Cambridge; army service 1944–47; called to Bar, Middle Temple 1952, Bencher 1978; mem. Home Sec.'s Advisory Council on the Penal System 1966–78; Chair. Howard League for Penal Reform 1973–84; Chair. Panel of Inquiry into death of Jasmine Beckford 1985; on several comms of inquiry 1986–87; academic appointment, Univ. of London 1962–84; Judge Court of Appeal, Jersey and Guernsey 1989–96; Ind. Commr for the Holding Centres, NI 1993–2000; Chair. Mental Health Act Comm. 1987–94, Press Council 1989–90, Nat. Asscn for Victim Support Schemes (NASS) 1994–97; currently Assoc. Tenant, Doughty Street Chambers, London; Dr hc (Ulster) 1995; Hon. LittD (E Anglia) 1997; Hon. LLD (Loughborough), (Ulster), (Univ. of East Anglia). *Publications:* Bankruptcy in Private International Law 1954, The Law as Literature 1962, The A6 Murder (A Semblance of Truth) 1963, A Calendar of Murder (with T. P. Morris) 1964, Language of the Law 1965, Separated Spouses (with O. R. McGregor and C. Gibson) 1970, Final Appeal: A Study of the House of Lords in its Judicial Capacity (with G. Drewry) 1972; ed. Progress in Penal Reform 1975, Law and Morality (with G. Drewry) 1976, The Falling Shadow (jtly) 1995, The Birmingham Six and Other Cases 1997, With Malice Aforethought (with T. Morris) 2004, The Penalty of Imprisonment: Why 60 Per Cent of the Prison Population Should Not Be There 2008, The Judicial House of Lords 1876–2009 (co-ed.) 2009, Murder, Manslaughter and Other Forms of Unlawful Killing (with Prof. Terence Morris) 2011. *Leisure interests:* watching and reporting on Association football, reading, music, writing, broadcasting. *Address:* 1 Bayes House, Augustas Lane, London, N1 1QT (home); Southminster Hall, Southminster, Essex CM0 7EH, England (home). *Telephone:* (20) 7607-3127 (London) (home). *E-mail:* louisblomcooper@gmail.com (home).

BLOMSTEDT, Herbert Thorsson; Swedish conductor; b. 11 July 1927, Springfield, Mass, USA; s. of Adolphe Blomstedt and Alida Armintha Thorson; m. Waltraud Regina Peterson 1955 (died 2003); four d.; ed Royal Acad. of Music, Stockholm, Uppsala Univ., Mozarteum, Salzburg, Austria, Schola Cantorum, Basel, Switzerland, Juilliard School, New York, USA, Tanglewood, Mass; Music Dir, Norrköping Symphony Orchestra 1954–61; Prof. of Conducting, Swedish Royal Acad. of Music 1961–70; Perm. Conductor, Oslo Philharmonic 1962–68; Music Dir Danish Radio Symphony Orchestra 1967–77, Dresden Staatskapelle Orchestra 1975–85, Swedish Radio Symphony Orchestra 1977–82; Music Dir and Conductor, San Francisco Symphony Orchestra 1985–95, Conductor Laureate 1995–; Music Dir NDR Symphony Orchestra, Hamburg 1996–98, Leipzig Gewandhaus Orchestra 1998–2005; mem. Royal Acad. of Music, Stockholm 1965; Hon. Conductor NHK Symphony, Tokyo 1985, Bamberg Symphony Orchestra 2006, Danish Nat. Symphony Orchestra 2006, Swedish Radio Symphony Orchestra 2006, Gewandhausorchester, Leipzig; Kt Royal Order of the North Star (Sweden); Kt Royal Order of Dannebrog (Denmark); Grosses Verdienstkreuz der Bundesrepublik Deutschland 2003; Hon. DMus (Andrews), Hon. PhD (Gothenburg) 1999, Dr hc (Southwestern-Adventist Univ., Tex.) 1993; Jenny Lind Scholarship, Swedish Royal Acad. of Music, Litteris et Artibus, Gold Medal (Sweden), Deutscher Schallplattenpreis 1978, Golden Reward Prize, Tokyo 1984, Grand Prix du Disque 1989, Gramophone Award, London 1990, Record Acad. of Japan Award 1991, Ditson Award for Distinguished Services to American Music, Columbia Univ., New York 1992, Grammy Awards 1993, 1996, Schallplattenpreis der Deutschen Musikkritik 1994, Ehrenpräsident der Stiftung Musikforschung Zentralschweiz 2001, Anton-Bruckner-Preis der Betil-Östbo-Bruckner-Stiftung, Linz 2001, Haederpris, Carl Nielsen Soc., Denmark 2002, Julio Kilenyi Medal of Honor, Bruckner Soc. of America. *Publications:* Till Kennedomen om Johann Christian Bachs Symfonies 1951, Lars-Erik Larsson och Lars Convertinor (co-author) 1957, Berwald: Sinfonie Singulière 1965. *Leisure interests:* hiking, history, philosophy, literature, art. *Address:* KünstlerSekretariat am Gasteig, Rosenheimer Strasse 52, 81669 Munich, Germany (office). *Telephone:* (89) 444-8879-0 (office). *Fax:* (89) 444-9522 (office).

BLÖNDAL, Halldór; Icelandic politician; b. 24 Aug. 1938, Reykjavík; m. Kristrún Eymundsdóttir; ed Akureyri High School; teacher and journalist, Morgunbladid 1959–80; mem. staff Authorised Public Accountant office, Akureyri 1976–78; Chief Surveyor of the State Account 1976–87; mem. Bd Dirs Regional Devt Inst. 1983–91, Agric. Bank of Iceland 1985–91; mem. Independence Party, Vice-Chair. Parl. Group 1983–91; mem. Parl. for Northeastern Dist 1979–2007, Speaker of the Althingi (Parl.) 1999–2005, Chair. Cttee on Foreign Affairs 2005–07, Chair. Icelandic Del. to West Nordic Council 2005–07; Minister of Transport and Communications 1991–99, of Communications and Agric. 1991–95; Rep. to UN Gen. Ass. 1983; mem. Icelandic Del. to Council of Europe 1984–86. *Address:*

Sjálfstæðisflokkurinn (Independence Party), Háaleitisbraut 1, 105 Reykjavík, Iceland. *Telephone:* 5151700. *Fax:* 5151717. *E-mail:* xd@xd.is. *Website:* www.xd.is.

BLOOM, Barry R., BS, DrSc, MA, PhD; American immunologist, academic and university administrator; *Distinguished Service Professor, Department of Immunology and Infectious Diseases and Joan L. and Julius H. Jacobson Professor of Public Health, School of Public Health, Harvard University;* ed Amherst Coll., Harvard Univ., Rockefeller Univ.; consultant to White House on Int. Health Policy 1977–78; joined faculty Albert Einstein Coll. of Medicine 1964, Prof. 1973–90, Chair. Dept of Microbiology and Immunology, 1978–90; Dean of Faculty, Harvard School of Public Health 1998–, Joan L. and Julius H. Jacobson Prof. of Public Health 1998–, also Distinguished Service Prof., Dept of Immunology and Infectious Diseases; Investigator, Howard Hughes Medical Inst. 1990–98; Chair. Tech. and Research Advisory Cttee to Global Programme on Malaria, WHO; Founding Chair., Bd of Trustees, Int. Vaccine Inst., South Korea; fmr Chair. Advisory Cttee on Health Research, Leprosy Research and Tuberculosis Research Cttees, WHO, Scientific and Tech. Advisory Cttees, UNDP/World Bank/WHO Special Programme for Research and Training, Vaccine Advisory Cttee on UNAIDS; mem. Ellison Medical Foundation Scientific Advisory Bd; mem. Wellcome Trust Pathogens, Immunology and Population Health Strategy Cttee; mem. Nat. Advisory Bd, Howard Hughes Medical Inst. 1990–98; mem. Scientific Advisory Bd Earth Inst., Columbia Univ.; mem. Advisory Council, Paul G. Rogers Soc. for Global Health Research; fmr Pres. Fed. of American Socs for Experimental Biology; fmr mem. US AIDS Research Cttee, Nat. Advisory Council, Nat. Inst. for Allergy and Infectious Diseases; fmr mem. Scientific Advisory Bd Nat. Center for Infectious Diseases for Disease Control and Prevention; fmr mem. Nat. Advisory Bd Fogarty Int. Center, NIH; fmr mem. Governing Bd Inst. of Medicine; Fellow, American Acad. of Arts and Sciences; mem. NAS, Inst. of Medicine, AAAS, American Asscn of Immunologists (Pres. 1984), American Philosophical Soc.; Bristol-Myers Squibb Award for Distinguished Research in Infectious Diseases, Novartis Award in Immunology (jtly) 1998; Robert Koch Gold Medal 1999. *Address:* Department of Immunology and Infectious Diseases, Harvard School of Public Health, Building 1, Room 813, Boston, MA 02115, USA (office). *Telephone:* (617) 432-7684 (office). *E-mail:* bbloom@hsph.harvard.edu (office). *Website:* www.hsph.harvard.edu (office).

BLOOM, Claire, CBE; British actress; b. (Patricia Claire Blume), 15 Feb. 1931, Finchley, London, England; d. of Edward Blume and Elizabeth Grew; m. 1st Rod Steiger 1959 (divorced 1969, died 2002); m. 2nd Philip Roth 1990 (divorced 1995); ed Badminton School, Bristol, Fern Hill Manor, New Milton, Guildhall School of Music and Drama, London under Eileen Thorndike, Central School of Speech and Drama, London and in New York; Oxford Repertory Theatre 1946, Stratford-on-Avon 1948; first major stage appearances in The Lady's Not For Burning 1948, Ring Around the Moon 1950; at Old Vic 1951–53; Fellow, Guildhall School of Music and Drama 1975. *Other stage performances include:* Duel of Angels 1956, 1967, Andromache in The Trojan Women 1964, Sascha in Ivanov, London 1966, Nora in A Doll's House, New York 1971, London 1973, Hedda Gabler in Hedda Gabler, New York 1971, Mary Queen of Scots in Vivat, Vivat Regina!, New York 1972, A Streetcar Named Desire, London (Evening Standard Drama Award for Best Actress) 1974, The Innocents, USA 1976, Rosmersholm, London 1977, The Cherry Orchard, Chichester Festival 1981, When We Dead Awaken 1990, The Cherry Orchard, USA 1994, Long Day's Journey into Night, USA 1996, Electra, New York 1998, Conversations after a Burial, London 2000, A Little Night Music 2003, Whispering Psyche 2004, Six Dance Lessons in Six Weeks 2006–07. *Films include:* The Blind Goddess 1948, The Shepherdess and the Chimneysweep (voice: English version) 1952, Limelight 1952, Innocents in Paris 1953, The Man Between 1953, Richard III 1955, Alexander the Great 1956, The Brothers Karamazov 1958, The Buccaneer 1958, Look Back in Anger 1959, Three Moves to Freedom 1960, The Wonderful World of the Brothers Grimm 1962, The Chapman Report 1962, The Haunting 1963, 80,000 Suspects 1963, The Teacher from Vigevano 1963, Alta infedeltà 1964, The Outrage 1964, The Spy Who Came in from the Cold 1965, Charly 1968, The Illustrated Man 1969, Three into Two Won't Go 1969, A Severed Head 1970, Red Sky at Morning 1971, A Doll's House 1973, Islands in the Stream 1977, Beauty and the Beast (short) 1981, Clash of the Titans 1981, Always 1984, Déjà Vu 1985, Sammy and Rosie Get Laid 1987, Brothers 1988, Crimes and Misdemeanours 1989, Pas de deux (short) 1990, The Princess and the Goblin (voice) 1991, The Age of Innocence (uncredited) 1993, Mad Dogs and Englishmen 1995, Mighty Aphrodite 1995, Daylight 1996, Shakespeare's Women and Claire Bloom, Wrestling with Alligators 1998, The Book of Eve 2002, The Republic of Love 2003, Imagining Argentina 2003, Daniel and the Superdogs 2004, Kalamazoo? 2006, The King's Speech 2010, While We Were Here 2012. *Television appearances:* The Marvellous History of St. Bernard (film) 1952, BBC Sunday-Night Theatre – Martine 1952, Producers' Showcase (series) 1955–57, Robert Montgomery Presents – Victoria Regina 1957, Shirley Temple's Storybook – Beauty and the Beast 1958, Playhouse 90 – Misalliance 1959, Checkmate 1961, Anna Karenina (film) 1961, Wuthering Heights (film) 1962, Camera Three – Claire Bloom Reads Poetry 1964, ITV Play of the Week – Ivanov 1966, Theatre of Stars – A Time to Love 1967, Soldier in Love (film) 1967, The Bell Telephone Hour – The Many Faces of Romeo and Juliet 1967, Late Night Horror – The Triumph of Death 1968, The Going Up of David Lev (film) 1973, Wessex Tales – An Imaginative Woman 1973, Great Mysteries – Ice Storm 1974, Aquarius (series) 1974, A Legacy (series) 1975, Backstairs at the White House (mini-series) 1979, The Oresteia (mini-series) 1979, The Famous History of the Life of King Henry the Eight (film) 1979, Hamlet, Prince of Denmark (film) 1980, CBS Library – Misunderstood Monsters 1981, Brideshead Revisited (mini-series) 1981, Cymbeline (film) 1982, Separate Tables (film) 1983, American Playhouse – The Ghost Writer 1984, Ellis Island (mini-series) 1984, King John (film) 1984, Time and the Conways (film) 1985, Ann and Debbie (film) 1985, Florence Nightingale (film) 1985, Shadowlands (film) (BAFTA Award for Best Actress) 1985, Promises to Keep 1985, Oedipus the King 1985, This Lightning Always Strikes Twice (film) 1985, Liberty (film) 1986, The Theban Plays by Sophocles (series) 1986, Hold the Dream (film) 1986, Anastasia: The Mystery of Anna (film) 1986, Queenie (film) 1987, The Belle of Amherst 1986, Intimate Contact (film) 1987, Beryl Markham: A Shadow on the Sun (film) 1988, The Lady and the Highwayman (film) 1989, The Camomile Lawn (mini-series) 1991, The Mirror Crack'd from Side to Side 1992; The Poetry Hall of Fame (film) 1993, It's Nothing Personal (film) 1993, Remember (film) 1993, As the World Turns (series)

1993–95, American Masters (series documentary) 1994, A Village Affair (film) 1995, Family Money (series) 1997, What the Deaf Man Heard (film) 1997, Imogen's Face (series) 1998, The Lady in Question (film) 1999, Tales from the Madhouse (mini-series) 2000, Love and Murder (film) 2000, Yesterday's Children (film) 2000, Law & Order: Criminal Intent (series) 2004, Jericho (series) 2005, Doc Martin (series) 2005, Marple: By the Pricking of My Thumbs (film) 2006, Trial & Retribution (series) 2006, The Chatterley Affair (film) 2006, The Ten Commandments (film) 2006, New Tricks (series) 2008, Fiona's Story (film) 2008, Doctor Who (series) 2009–10, The Bill (series) 2010; also performs her one-woman shows Enter the Actress and These are Women, A Portrait of Shakespeare's Heroines, throughout the USA. *Publications:* Limelight and After 1982, Leaving a Doll's House 1996. *Leisure interests:* walking, music. *Address:* c/o Jeremy Conway, 18–21 Jermyn Street, London, SW1Y 6HB, England. *Telephone:* (20) 7287-0077. *Fax:* (20) 7287-1940.

BLOOM, Floyd Elliott, AB, DSc, MD, FAAS; American physician, research scientist and academic; b. 8 Oct. 1936, Minneapolis, Minn.; m. 1st D'Nell Bingham 1956 (died 1973); two c.; m. 2nd Jody Patricia Corey 1980; ed Southern Methodist Univ., Washington Univ., Hahnemann Univ., Univ. of Rochester, Mount Sinai Univ. Medical School, Thomas Jefferson Univ.; intern, Barnes Hosp., St Louis 1960–61, resident internal medicine 1961–62; Research Assoc., Nat. Inst. of Mental Health (NIMH), Washington, DC 1962–64; Fellow, Depts of Pharmacology, Psychiatry and Anatomy, Yale Univ. School of Medicine 1964–66, Asst Prof. 1966–67, Assoc. Prof. 1968; Chief of Lab. of Neuropharmacology, NIMH 1968–75, Acting Div. of Special Mental Health 1973–75; Commissioned Officer, Public Health Service 1974–75; Prof., Salk Inst., La Jolla, Calif. 1975–83; Founder and mem. Bd of Dirs Alkermes Inc. 1987–; Dir Div. of Preclinical Neuroscience and Endocrinology, Scripps Research Inst., La Jolla 1983–89, Chair. Dept of Neuropharmacology 1989–2005, Prof. Emer., Dept of Molecular and Integrative Neuroscience 2005–; Ed.-in-Chief Science Magazine 1995–2000; Founding CEO, Chief Scientific Officer and Chair. Neurome, Inc. 2000–06; Chair. Nat. Medical Council 2000–; mem. Nat. Advisory Mental Health Council 1976–80, Comm. on Alcoholism 1980–81; mem. Scientific Advisory Bd Neurocrine Inc. 1993–2000, Neurobiological Tech. Inc. 1994–98, Healthcare Ventures Inc. 1998–2000, Advancis Pharmaceuticals 1999–, SafeMed 2003–, Saegis Pharmaceuticals 2004–; Trustee, Washington Univ., St Louis 1998–; mem. AAAS (Pres. 2002–03), NAS 1977–, Inst. of Medicine, American Philosophical Soc., American Acad. of Arts and Sciences, Swedish Acad. of Sciences; Dr hc (Southern Methodist Univ.) 1983, (Washington Univ.) 1998; A. Cressy Morrison Award, New York Acad. of Sciences 1971, Mathilde Solowey Award 1973, McAlpin Research Achievement Award, Mental Health Asscn 1980, Steven Beering Medal 1985, Janssen Award, World Psychiatry Asscn 1989, Herman von Helmholtz Award 1991, Meritorious Achievement Award, Council of Biology Eds 1999, Distinguished Service Award, American Psychiatric Asscn 2000, Walsh McDermott Award, Inst. of Medicine 2004, Bernard and Rhoda Sarnat Award for Mental Health Research, Inst. of Medicine 2005. *Publications include:* Biochemical Basis of Neuropharmacology (with J. R. Cooper and R. H. Roth) 1971, Brain, Mind and Behavior (with Lazerson and Hofstadter) 1984, Brain Browser (with W. Young and Y. Kim) 1989; Ed. Peptides: Integrators of Cell and Tissue Function 1980, Neuro-Psychopharmacology: The Fourth Generation of Progress 1994, Handbook of Chemical Neuroanatomy 1997, The Primate Nervous System 1997, Funding Health Sciences Research (with M. Randolph) 1990. *Leisure interests:* cruise travel, fine food and wine, abstract art. *Address:* Scripps Research Institute, 10550 North Torrey Pines Road, La Jolla, CA 92037-1000 (office); 628 Pacific View Drive, San Diego, CA 92109, USA (home). *Telephone:* (858) 784-9730 (office). *Fax:* (858) 784-8851 (office). *E-mail:* fbloom@scripps.edu (office). *Website:* www.scripps.edu/np (office).

BLOOM, Harold, PhD; American academic and writer; *Sterling Professor of Humanities and English, Yale University;* b. 11 July 1930, New York; s. of William Bloom and Paula Lev; m. Jeanne Gould 1958; two s.; ed Cornell and Yale Univs, Pembroke Coll., Cambridge, UK; mem. Faculty, Yale Univ. 1955–, Prof. of English 1965–77, DeVane Prof. of Humanities 1974–77, Prof. of Humanities 1977–, Sterling Prof. of Humanities and English 1983–; Visiting Prof., Hebrew Univ. Jerusalem 1959, Breadloaf Summer School 1965–66, Soc. for Humanities, Cornell Univ. 1968–69; Visiting Univ. Prof., New School of Social Research, New York 1982–84; Charles Eliot Norton Prof. of Poetry, Harvard Univ. 1987–88; Berg Visiting Prof. of English, New York Univ. 1988–2004; mem. American Acad. and Inst. of Arts and Letters, American Philosophical Soc.; Fulbright Fellow 1955, Guggenheim Fellow 1962; Dr hc (St Michael's Coll., Univ. of Rome, Univ. of Bologna, Univ. of Coimbra, Boston Coll., Yeshiva Univ., Univ. of Mass. at Dartmouth, Univ. of Buenos Aires); Newton Arvin Award 1967, Melville Cane Award, Poetry Soc. of America 1970, Zabel Prize, American Inst. of Arts and Letters 1982, MacArthur Foundation Fellowship 1985, Christian Gauss Prize 1989, Gold Medal for Criticism, American Acad. of Arts and Letters 1999, Int. Prize of Catalonia 2002, Alfonso Reyes Prize (Mexico) 2003, Hans Christian Anderson Bicentennial Prize (Denmark) 2005. *Publications:* Shelley's Mythmaking 1959, The Visionary Company 1961, Blake's Apocalypse 1963, Commentary to Blake 1965, Yeats 1970, The Ringers in the Tower 1971, The Anxiety of Influence 1973, Wallace Stevens: The Poems of Our Climate 1977, A Map of Misreading 1975, Kabbalah and Criticism 1975, Poetry and Repression 1976, Figures of Capable Imagination 1976, The Flight to Lucifer: A Gnostic Fantasy 1979, Agon: Towards a Theory of Revisionism 1981, The Breaking of the Vessels 1981, The Strong Light of the Canonical 1987, Freud: Transference and Authority 1988, Poetics of Influence: New and Selected Criticism 1988, Ruin the Sacred Truths 1989, The Book of J 1990, The American Religion 1991, The Western Canon 1994, Omens of Millennium 1996, Shakespeare: The Invention of the Human 1998, How to Read and Why 2000, Stories and Poems for Extremely Intelligent Children of All Ages 2000, Genius: A Mosaic of One Hundred Exemplary Creative Minds 2002, Hamlet: Poem Unlimited 2003, Best Poems of the English Language: Chaucer to Hart Crane 2003, Where Shall Wisdom be Found? 2004, The Names Divine: Jesus and Yahweh 2005, Yetziat: Fallen Angels, Demons and Devils 2006, Till I End My Song: A Gathering of Last Poems 2010, The Anatomy of Influence: Literature as a Way of Life 2011, The King James Bible: A Literary Appreciation 2011. *Leisure interest:* reading. *Address:* Department of English, WHC 202, Yale University, 63 High Street, POB 208302, New Haven, CT 06520-8302, USA (office). *Telephone:*

(203) 432-0029 (office). *E-mail:* harold.bloom@yale.edu (office). *Website:* www.yale.edu/english (office).

BLOOM, Myer, PhD, FRSC; Canadian physicist and academic; *Professor Emeritus of Physics, University of British Columbia;* b. 7 Dec. 1928, Montreal; s. of Israel Bloom and Leah Ram; m. Margaret P. Holmes 1954; one s. one d.; ed Baron Byng High School, McGill Univ. and Univ. of Illinois at Urbana; NRC Travelling Postdoctoral Fellow, Univ. of Leiden, Netherlands 1954–56; Research Assoc., Univ. of BC 1956–57, Asst Prof. 1957–60, Assoc. Prof. 1960–63, Prof. of Physics 1963–94; Prof. Emer. 1995–; Visiting Prof., Harvard Univ. 1964–65, Kyoto Univ. 1965, Univ. de Paris Sud 1971–72, 1978–79, Univ. of Rome 1986, Danish Tech. Univ. 1986; mem. Canadian Asscn of Physicists; Alfred P. Sloan Fellow 1961–65; Fellow, American Physical Soc., Canadian Inst. for Advanced Research 1991–2000; Hon. DTech (Tech. Univ. of Denmark) 1994; Hon. DIur (Concordia Univ., Montreal) 1995; Hon. DSc (British Columbia) 2000; Steacie Prize 1967, Biely Prize 1969; Canadian Asscn of Physicists Gold Medal 1973; Science Council of BC Chair.'s Award for Career Achievements 1992, Izaak Walton Killam Memorial Prize for Natural Sciences 1995. *Publications:* numerous research and review articles. *Leisure interests:* hiking, skiing, squash, wine-making. *Address:* c/o David Bloom, 1616 McLean Drive, Vancouver, BC V5L 3P3, Canada (home).

BLOOM, Orlando Jonathan Blanchard; British actor; b. 13 Jan. 1977, Canterbury, Kent; m. Miranda Kerr 2010; ed The King's School Canterbury, St Edmund's School, Canterbury, Guildhall School of Music and Drama, London, Hampstead Fine Arts Coll., London; early acting experience with Nat. Youth Theatre; cinema debut in Wilde 1997; UNICEF Goodwill Amb. 2009–; hon. degree (Kent at Canterbury) 2010. *Films:* The Lord of the Rings: The Fellowship of the Ring (Empire Award for Best Debut 2002) 2001, Black Hawk Down 2001, The Lord of the Rings: The Two Towers 2002, Ned Kelly 2003, Pirates of the Caribbean: The Curse of the Black Pearl 2003, The Lord of the Rings: The Return of the King 2003, The Calcium Kid 2004, Troy 2004, Haven 2004, Kingdom of Heaven 2005, Elizabethtown 2005, Pirates of the Caribbean: Dead Man's Chest 2006, Pirates of the Caribbean: At World's End 2007, New York, I Love You 2009, Sympathy for Delicious 2009, Main Street 2010, The Good Doctor 2011, The Three Muskateers 2011, The Hobbit: An Unexpected Journey 2012. *Television:* Casualty 1994–96, Midsomer Murders 2000, Extras 2006. *Plays:* In Celebration (Duke of York's Theatre, London) 2007. *Address:* Creative Artists Agency, 2000 Avenue of the Stars, Los Angeles, CA 90067, USA (office). *Telephone:* (424) 288-2000 (office). *Fax:* (424) 288-2900 (office). *Website:* www.caa.com (office).

BLOOM, Sir Stephen Robert, Kt, MA, MD, DSc, FRCP, FRCPath, FMedSci, FSB; British physician, academic and biomedical researcher; *Head of Division of Investigative Science, Imperial College London;* b. 24 Oct. 1942, Maidstone, Kent, England; s. of Arnold Bloom and Edith Nancy Bloom (née Fox); m. Margaret Janet Sturrock 1965; two s. two d.; ed Univ. of Cambridge; Medical Unit Registrar, Middx Hosp., London 1970–72; MRC Clinical Research Fellow 1972–74; Sr Lecturer, Royal Postgraduate Medical School, Hammersmith Hosp. 1974–78, Reader in Medicine 1978–82, Prof. of Endocrinology 1982–, Head Dept of Endocrinology and Metabolic Medicine, Dir of Pathology and Therapy Services, Hammersmith Hosps NHS Trust 1996–; Prof. of Medicine, Imperial Coll. School of Medicine (ICSM) (fmrly Royal Postgraduate Medical School) 1982–, Dir of Metabolic Medicine and Chief of Service for Chemical Pathology 1994–; Chair. Div. of Diabetes, Endocrinology and Metabolism, ICSM 1997–; Vice-Pres. (Sr Censor) Royal Coll. of Physicians 1999–2001; Sec. Soc. for Endocrinology 1999–2001, Chair. 2001–; Fellow, Soc. of Biology. *Publications:* Gut Hormones (ed.) 1978, Endocrine Tumours 1985, Surgical Endocrinology 1992. *Leisure interests:* jogging, classical music, computing. *Address:* Department of Metabolic Medicine, Division of Investigative Science, Imperial College London at Hammersmith Hospital, 6th Floor, Commonwealth Building, Du Cane Road, London, W12 0NN, England (office). *Telephone:* (20) 8383-3242 (office). *Fax:* (20) 8383-3142 (office). *E-mail:* s.bloom@imperial.ac.uk (office). *Website:* www1.imperial.ac.uk/medicine/people/s.bloom (office).

BLOOMBERG, Michael Rubens, MBA; American politician and UN official; *Special Envoy of the Secretary-General for Cities and Climate Change, United Nations;* b. 14 Feb. 1942, Medford, Mass; m. (divorced); two c.; ed Johns Hopkins Univ., Harvard Univ.; with Salomon Brothers (investment bank) 1966–81, made Partner 1972; Founder, Chief Exec., Chair. Bloomberg Financial Markets 1981–, Founder-Pres. Bloomberg LP 1982–; Publr Bloomberg Business News, Bloomberg Magazine, Bloomberg Personal Magazine; Gen. Man. Bloomberg Television, Bloomberg Radio WBBR-AM 1130; Mayor of New York 2001–13; Special Envoy of the Sec.-Gen. for Cities and Climate Change, UN 2014–; Chair. Bd of Trustees, Johns Hopkins Univ. –2002; mem. Bd Lincoln Center for Performing Arts, Jewish Museum, New York, Police and Fire Widow's and Children's Fund, Metropolitan Museum of Art and numerous other bodies; Trustee, Big Apple Circus; ranked by Forbes magazine amongst The World's Most Powerful People (20th) 2009, (23rd) 2010, (17th) 2011, (16th) 2012, (29th) 2013. *Publication:* Bloomberg by Bloomberg (autobiog.) 1998. *Address:* Office of the Secretary-General, United Nations, New York, NY 10017, USA (office). *Telephone:* (212) 963-1234 (office). *Fax:* (212) 963-4879 (office). *Website:* www.un.org (office).

BLOOMER, Jonathan, BSc, ARCS, FCA, CIMgt; British insurance industry executive; *Executive Chairman, Jardine Lloyd Thompson Employee Benefit Solutions Ltd;* b. 23 March 1954; m. Judy Bloomer (née May); one s. two d.; ed Imperial Coll., London; joined Arthur Andersen 1974, Man. Pnr of European Insurance Practice –1994; Group Finance Dir Prudential PLC 1995–2000, Group CEO 2000–05, also mem. Bd of Dirs; Pnr, Cerberus European Capital Advisors LLP 2006–12, Exec. Chair. Lucida plc 2006–12; Exec. Chair. Jardine Lloyd Thompson Employee Benefit Solutions Ltd 2013–, Arrow Global Group plc 2013–; fmr Chair. Scottish RE Group Ltd; Deputy Chair. Financial Services Practitioner Panel 2001–03, Chair. 2003–05; mem. Bd of Dirs Railtrack PLC 1999–2002, Asscn of British Insurers 2001–05, Geneva Asscn 2001–05, Hargreaves Lansdown PLC 2006–; Trustee and Treasurer Nat. Soc. for the Prevention of Cruelty to Children; mem. Urgent Issues Task Force of Accounting Standards Bd 1995–99. *Leisure interests:* rugby, boats.

BLOOMFIELD, Sir Kenneth Percy, KCB, MA, MRIA; British public servant; b. 15 April 1931, Belfast, NI; s. of Harry Percy Bloomfield and Doris Bloomfield; m.

Mary E. Ramsey 1960; one s. one d.; ed Royal Belfast Academical Inst. and St Peter's Coll., Oxford; joined NI Civil Service 1952; Private Sec. to Minister of Finance 1956–60; Deputy Dir British Industrial Devt Office, New York 1960–63; Asst later Deputy Sec. to Cabinet, NI 1963–72; Under-Sec. NI Office 1972–74; Perm. Sec., Office of Exec. of NI 1974–75; Perm. Sec., Dept of Environment, NI 1975–81, Dept of Econ. Devt 1981–84; Head of NI Civil Service and Second Perm. Under-Sec. of State, NI Office 1984–91; Nat. Gov., Chair. Broadcasting Council for NI, BBC 1991–99; Chair. Children in Need Trust 1992–98; NI Higher Educ. Council 1993–2001, NI Victims Commr 1997–98, Bangor and Holywood Town Centre Man. Ltd 2001, BBC Audit Cttee, NI Chief Execs Forum, Higher Educ. Council for NI; fmr Chair. NI Legal Services Comm.; Pres. Ulster People's Coll. 1996–; mem. NI Advisory Bd Bank of Ireland 1991–2001, Green Park Trust 1996–2001; Hon. Fellow, St Peter's Coll. Oxford; Hon. LLD (Belfast), Hon. DUniv (Open Univ.) 2000, Hon. DLitt (Univ. of Ulster) 2002; NI Chamber of Commerce Award for Personal or Corp. Excellence 1990. *Publications include:* Stormont in Crisis (a memoir) 1994, We Will Remember Them 1998, A Tragedy of Errors 2007, A New Life 2008. *Leisure interests:* reading history and biographies, writing, swimming. *Address:* 16 Larch Hill, Holywood, Co. Down, BT18 0JN, Northern Ireland (home). *Telephone:* (28) 9042-8340 (home). *Fax:* (28) 9042-8340 (home). *E-mail:* kenbloomfield@tiscali.co.uk (home).

BLUM, Brad, BA, MBA; American business executive; *CEO, Blum Enterprises LLC;* b. 1954; m.; two step-s.; ed Denison Univ., Granville, OH, Northwestern Univ. J. L. Kellogg Business School, Evanston, Ill.; joined General Mills as Asst Product Man. Big G (Cereal) Div. 1978, served 16 years in marketing, Gen. Man., becoming Vice-Pres. of Marketing, Cereal Partners Worldwide, Morges, Switzerland 1990–94; Sr Vice-Pres. of Marketing, Olive Garden Div., Darden Restaurants June–Dec. 1994, Pres. Dec. 1994–1997, Exec. Vice-Pres. and Dir Darden Restaurants 1997–2002, Vice-Chair. March–Dec. 2002; Chief Exec. Burger King Corpn 2003–2004 (resgnd); Founder and CEO Blum Enterprises LLC (restaurant industry consultancy) 2005–; CEO Romano's Macaroni Grill 2008–10; Chair. Econ. Devt Bd, City of Winter Park, Fla; mem. Bd of Trustees Atlantic Center for the Arts; mem. Advisory Bd Sun Trust Bank; Multi-unit Foodservice Operators Operator of the Year 2000. *Leisure interests:* tennis, skiing, motor racing. *Address:* Blum Enterprises LLC, 250 S Park Avenue 510, Winter Park FL 32789-4388, USA (office). *Telephone:* (407) 622-5700 (office).

BLÜM, Norbert, DPhil; German politician; b. 21 July 1935, Rüsselsheim; s. of Christian Blüm and Margarete Blüm (née Beck); m. Marita Binger 1964; one s. two d.; ed Volksschule; apprentice, Opel AG, Rüsselsheim, 1949–53, toolmaker 1953–57; worked in building trade and as lorry driver while studying evenings 1957–61; univ. student in Cologne and Bonn 1961–67; Ed. Soziale Ordnung 1966–68; Chief Man. Social Comm. of Christian Democrat employees' Asscn 1968–75, Regional Chair. Rhineland-Palatinate 1974–77, Fed. Chair. 1977–87; mem. Fed. Exec. CDU 1969–; mem. Bundestag 1969–81, 1983–2002; Deputy Chair. CDU 1981–2000; Senator for Fed. Affairs for Berlin 1981; Minister of Labour and Social Affairs 1982–98; Regional Chair. CDU North Rhine-Westphalia 1987–98; mem. IG Metall; fmr Chair. Kindernothilfe Stiftung (Children in Need Foundation); Karl-Valentin-Orden 1987, Heinrich-Brauns Preis 1990, Leipzig Human Rights Award 2001 and numerous other awards and prizes. *Publications include:* Reform oder Reaktion–Wohin geht die CDU 1972, Gewerkschaften zwischen Allmacht und Ohnmacht 1979, Werkstücke 1980, Die Arbeit geht weiter–zur Krise der Erwerbsgesellschaft 1983, 40 Jahre Socialstaat Bundesrepublik Deutschland 1989, Politikals Balanceakt 1993, Dann Willichs mal probieren–Geschichten vom Lachen und Weinen 1994, Sommerfrische-Regentage inclusive 1995, Die Glücksmargerite–Geschichten zum Vorlesen 1997, Diesseits und Jenseits der Politik 1998. *Leisure interests:* reading, walking. *Address:* c/o Kindernothilfe Stiftung, Düsseldorfer Landstraße 180, 47249 Duisburg, Germany.

BLUM, Tim; American gallery owner and art dealer; *Co-Owner, Blum & Poe;* b. 5 Aug. 1965; m. Maria Blum 1993; moved to Tokyo to work as an art dealer 1990; returned to Los Angeles 1994 and with Jeff Poe opened small exhbn space in art gallery complex in Santa Monica 1994; introduced Japanese artists Takashi Murakami and Yoshito Nara in USA; Co-Owner Blum & Poe gallery, expanded to larger spaces in 2003 and 2009; regularly exhibits local and internationally recognized artists, including Chiho Aoshima, J. B. Blunk, Slater Bradley, Chuck Close, Nigel Cooke, Carroll Dunham, Sam Durant, Kōji Enokura, Anya Gallaccio, Mark Grotjahn, Tim Hawkinson, Drew Heitzler, Julian Hoeber, Zhang Huan, Zhu Jinshi, Matt Johnson, Susumu Koshimizu, Friedrich Kunath, Shio Kusaka, Linder, Sharon Lockhart, Florian Maier-Aichen, Victor Man, Dave Muller, Takashi Murakami, Yoshitomo Nara, Matt Saunders, Hugh Scott–Douglas, Nobuo Sekine, Jim Shaw, Dirk Skreber, Kishio Suga, Henry Taylor, Keith Tyson, Lee Ufan, Chris Vasell and Michael Wilkinson. *Address:* Blum & Poe, 2727 S La Cienega Blvd, Los Angeles, CA 90034, USA (office). *Telephone:* (310) 836-2062 (office). *Fax:* (310) 836-2104 (office). *E-mail:* info@blumandpoe.com (office). *Website:* www.blumandpoe.com (office).

BLUM, Yehuda Z., PhD; Israeli diplomatist, lawyer and academic; *Hersch Lauterpacht Professor of International Law, Hebrew University of Jerusalem;* b. 2 Oct. 1931, Bratislava, Czechoslovakia (now Slovakia); s. of Joseph Blum and Selda Blum (née Dux); m. Moriah Rabinovitz-Teomim; two s. one d.; ed Hebrew Univ., Univ. of London, England; detained in Nazi concentration camp of Bergen-Belsen 1944; Asst to Judge Advocate-Gen. of Israel Defence Forces 1956–59; Sr Asst to Legal Adviser, Ministry for Foreign Affairs 1962–65; UNESCO Fellow, Univ. of Sydney July–Aug. 1968; Office of UN Legal Counsel Sept.–Dec. 1968; Sr Research Scholar, Univ. of Michigan Law School 1969; Visiting Prof., School of Law, Univ. of Texas 1971, New York Univ. 1975–76, Univ. of Michigan Law School 1985, Cardozo School of Law, New York 1991, 2000, Univ. of Southern California 1991–92, Tulane Univ., New Orleans 1994, 2003, Univ. of Miami 1999, Univ. of California, Berkeley 2002; Dir Harry Sacher Inst. for Legis. Research and Comparative Law, Hebrew Univ. of Jerusalem 1977–78, Hersch Lauterpacht Prof. of International Law 1991–; mem. Israeli del., Third UN Conf. on Law of the Sea 1973, 31st Session of UN Gen. Ass. 1976; Perm. Rep. to UN 1978–84; Law Ed. Encyclopedia Hebraica 1973–78; Hon. DrJur (Yeshiva Univ.) 1981; Jabotinsky Prize 1984. *Publications include:* Historic Titles in International Law 1965, Secure Boundaries and Middle East Peace 1971, For Zion's Sake 1987, Eroding the United

Nations Charter 1993; more than 40 articles in Hebrew, English and German, on various int. law topics. *Address:* Faculty of Law, Hebrew University, Mount Scopus, Jerusalem 91905, Israel (office). *Telephone:* (2) 5882562 (office). *Fax:* (2) 5823042 (office). *E-mail:* msblumy@mscc.huji.ac.il (office). *Website:* law.huji.ac.il/eng (office).

BLUME, Judy, BS; American writer; b. 12 Feb. 1938, Elizabeth, NJ; d. of Rudolph and Esther (née Rosenfeld) Sussman; m. 1st John M. Blume 1959 (divorced 1975); one s. one d.; m. 2nd George Cooper 1987; one step-d.; ed New York Univ.; Founder and Trustee The Kids Fund 1981; mem. PEN Club, Authors' Guild, Nat. Coalition Against Censorship, Soc. of Children's Book Writers and Illustrators, Key West Literary Seminar, Nat. Coalition Against Censorship; Hon. LHD (Kean Coll.) 1987; Chicago Public Library Carl Sandburg Freedom to Read Award 1984, Civil Liberties Award, American Civil Liberties Union of Atlanta 1986, American Library Asscn Margaret A. Edwards Award for Lifetime Achievement 1996, Library of Congress Living Legends Award, Medal for distinguished contrib. to American Letters, Nat. Book Foundation 2004; Nat. Book Foundation Medal for Distinguished Contribution to American Letters 2004. *Publications:* juvenile fiction: The One in the Middle Is the Green Kangaroo 1969, Iggie's House 1970, Are You There God? It's Me, Margaret (Outstanding Book of the Year Award 1970, Nene Award 1975, Young Hoosier Award 1976, North Dakota Children's Choice Book Award 1979, Great Stone Face Award 1980) 1970, Then Again, Maybe I Won't 1971, Freckle Juice (Michigan Young Reader's Award 1980) 1971, It's Not the End of the World 1972, Tales of a Fourth Grade Nothing 1972, Otherwise Known as Sheila the Great (South Carolina Children's Book Award 1982) 1972, Deenie 1973, Blubber (Outstanding Book of the Year Award 1974, North Dakota Children's Choice Award 1983) 1974, Forever 1975, Starring Sally J. Freedman as Herself 1977, Superfudge (Golden Sower Award 1983, Iowa Children's Choice Award 1983, Arizona Young Readers' Award, Georgia Children's Book Award, California Young Reader Medal Reader's Choice Award 1984, Great Stone Face Award 1985, 1986) 1980, Tiger Eyes (Buckeye Children's Book Award 1983, Iowa Teen Award 1985, Colorado Blue Spruce Young Adult Book Award 1985) 1981, Fudge-a-mania (California Young Reader Medal, Iowa Children's Choice Award, Nene Award, Nevada Young Reader's Award, Sunshine State Young Reader's Award, Pennsylvania Young Reader's Choice Award, Michigan Readers' Choice Award) 1983, The Pain and the Great One (Young Readers' Choice Award 1989) 1984, Just As Long As We're Together 1987, Here's to You, Rachel Robinson (Parents' Choice Award) 1993, Places I Never Meant To Be (ed) 1999, Double Fudge 2002, The Pain and the Great One: Soupy Saturdays 2008, The Pain and the Great One: Cool Zone 2008, The Pain and the Great One: Going, Going, Gone! 2009, The Pain and the Great One: Friend or Fiend? 2009; adult fiction: Wifey 1978, Smart Women 1983, Summer Sisters 1998; non-fiction: Letters to Judy: What Kids Wish They Could Tell You 1986, The Judy Blume Memory Book 1988. *Address:* c/o Suzanne Gluck, William Morris Agency, 1325 Avenue of the Americas, New York, NY 10022, USA (office); c/o Tashmoo Productions, 1075 Duval Street, Suite C21 #236, Key West, FL 33040, USA. *E-mail:* JudyB@judyblume.com. *Website:* www.judyblume.com.

BLUMENTHAL, Richard M., BA, JD; American lawyer and politician; *Senator from Connecticut;* b. 13 Feb. 1946, Brooklyn, NY; s. of Martin A. Blumenthal and Jane Blumenthal (née Rosenstock); m. Cynthia Allison Markle; three s. one d.; ed Harvard Coll., Univ. of Cambridge, UK (Fiske Fellowship), Yale Univ. Law School; Editorial Chair. The Harvard Crimson; summer intern reporter for Washington Post, London Bureau, UK; Ed.-in-Chief Yale Law Journal; served in US Marine Corps Reserve, honourably discharged with rank of Sergeant; served as aide to Daniel P. Moynihan (later Senator Moynihan) when Asst to Pres. Richard Nixon, and as law clerk to Hon. Jon O. Newman, US Dist Court, Conn. 1973–74, and to Supreme Court Justice Harry A. Blackmun 1974–75; Admin. Asst to Senator Abraham A. Ribicoff 1975–76; US Attorney for the Dist of Conn. 1977–81, and Chief Fed. Prosecutor of Conn.; volunteer counsel for Nat. Asscn for the Advancement of Colored People (NAACP) Legal Defense Fund 1981–86; Partner, Cummings & Lockwood law firm 1981–84, Silver Golub & Teitell LLP, Stamford, Conn. 1984–90; Founder and Chair. Citizens Crime Comm. of Conn. 1982; mem. Conn. House of Reps for 145th Dist 1984–87; won special election to fill vacancy in 27th Dist of Conn. Senate 1987–90; Attorney Gen. of Conn. 1991–2011; Senator from Conn. 2011–, mem. Special Cttee on Aging 2011–, Judiciary Cttee 2011–, Armed Services Cttee 2011–, Health, Educ. Labor and Pensions Cttee 2011–; Democrat; Raymond E. Baldwin Award for Public Service, Quinnipiac Univ. School of Law 2002. *Address:* 702 Hart Senate Office Building, Washington, DC 20510 (office); 30 Lewis Street, Suite 101, Hartford, CT 06103, USA (office). *Telephone:* (202) 224-2823 (DC) (office); (860) 258-6940 (Hartford) (office). *Fax:* (202) 224-9673 (DC) (office); (860) 258-6958 (Hartford) (office). *Website:* blumenthal.senate.gov (office).

BLUMENTHAL, W(erner) Michael, PhD; American business executive; b. 3 Jan. 1926, Oranienburg, Germany; s. of Ewald Blumenthal and Rose Valerie (Markt) Blumenthal; ed Univ. of California, Berkeley and Princeton Univ., USA; went to US 1947, naturalized 1952; Research Assoc., Princeton Univ. 1954–57; Vice-Pres., Dir Crown Cork Int. Corpn 1957–61; Deputy Asst Sec. of State for Econ. Affairs, Dept of State 1961–63; also served as USA Rep. to UN Comm. on Int. Commodity Trade; President's Deputy Special Rep. for Trade Negotiations (with rank of Amb.) 1963–67; Chair. US Del. to Kennedy Round tariff talks in Geneva; Pres. Bendix Int. 1967–70; Dir Bendix Corpn 1967–77, Vice-Chair. June–Dec. 1970, Pres. and Chief Operating Officer 1971–72, Chair. and CEO 1972–77; Sec. of the Treasury 1977–79; Dir Burroughs Corpn (now Unisys) 1979–90, Vice-Chair. 1980, CEO 1981–90, Chair. 1990; Sr Advisor Lazard Frères & Co. 1990–96; Dir, Jewish Museum Berlin 1997–; mem. Council on Foreign Relations; Charter Trustee Emer., Princeton Univ.; Große Verdienstkreuz. *Publications:* The Invisible Wall 1998, From Exile to Washington: A Memoir of Leadership in the Twentieth Century 2013. *Leisure interests:* tennis, skiing. *Address:* 227 Ridgeview Road, Princeton, NJ 08540, USA (office). *Telephone:* (609) 497-7676 (office). *Fax:* (609) 497-1888 (office).

BLUMGART, Leslie Harold, BDS, MD, FACS, FRCS (Glas.), FRCSE, FRCPS; British academic and surgeon; *Enid A. Haupt Professor of Surgery, Memorial Sloan-Kettering Cancer Center;* b. 7 Dec. 1931, South Africa; s. of Harold Herman Blumgart and Hilda Blumgart; m. 1st Pearl Navias 1955 (deceased); m. 2nd Sarah

Raybould Bowen 1968; two s. two d.; ed Jeppe High School, Johannesburg, Univ. of Witwatersrand, Univ. of Sheffield, UK; Sr Lecturer and Deputy Dir, Dept of Surgery, Welsh Nat. School of Medicine, Cardiff 1970–72; St Mungo Prof. of Surgery, Univ. of Glasgow, Hon. Consultant Surgeon, Glasgow Royal Infirmary 1972–79; Prof. of Surgery and Dir Dept of Surgery, Royal Postgraduate Medical School, Univ. of London and Hon. Consultant, Hammersmith Hosp., London 1979–86; Prof. of Visceral and Transplantation Surgery, Univ. of Bern and Inselspital Bern, Switzerland 1986–91; Enid A. Haupt Prof. of Surgery, Memorial Sloan-Kettering Cancer Center, New York 1991–, Chief of Section of Hepato-Biliary Surgery and Dir Hepato-Biliary Program 1995–2007; Prof. of Surgery, Cornell Univ. Medical Coll. 1993, American Surgery Soc.; Moynihan Fellowship, Asscn of Surgeons of GB and Ireland 1972; mem. Hong Kong Surgical Soc., Hellenic Surgical Soc., LA Surgical Soc.; Pres. Int. Biliary Asscn 1986; Hon. Fellow, Royal Coll. of Surgeons in Ireland; Hon. mem. Soc. for Surgery of the Alimentary Tract, USA, Danish Surgical Soc. 1988, Asscn Française de Chirurgie, Yugoslav Soc. of Surgery, Soc. Italiana di Chirurgia 2002, Austrian Soc. of Surgery 2007, French Acad. of Surgery 2008; Order of Prasidda Prabala Gorkha-Dakshin Bahu (Nepal) 1984; Hon. DSc (Sheffield) 1998. *Publications include:* Essentials of Medicine and Surgery for Dental Students (with A. C. Kennedy), 4th Edn 1982, The Biliary Tract, in Clinical Surgery Int., Vol. 5 1982, Liver Surgery, in Clinical Surgery Int., Vol. 12 (with S. Bengmark) 1986, Difficult Problems in General Surgery 1989, Surgery of the Liver and Biliary Tract, Vols 1 and 2 (3rd edn) 2000, Surgery of the Liver, Biliary Tract and Pancreas, Vols 1 and 2 (4th edn); numerous publs concerned with medical educ., gastrointestinal surgery and aspects of oncology with particular interest in surgery of the liver, pancreas and biliary tract. *Leisure interests:* watercolour painting, wood carving. *Address:* Memorial Sloan-Kettering Cancer Center, 1275 York Avenue, New York, NY 10065 (office); 447 East 57th Street, 3E, New York, NY 10022, USA (home). *Telephone:* (212) 639-5526 (office); (212) 755-0836 (home). *Fax:* (212) 794-5852 (office). *E-mail:* blumgarl@mskcc.org (office). *Website:* www.mskcc.org (office).

BLUNDELL, Sir Tom Leon, Kt, DPhil, FRS, FMedSci; British biochemist, academic, entrepreneur and administrator; *Professor Emeritus and Director of Research, Department of Biochemistry, University of Cambridge;* b. 7 July 1942, Brighton, Sussex, England; s. of Horace Leon Blundell and Marjorie Blundell; m. Bancinyane Lynn Sibanda 1987; one s. two d.; ed Steyning Grammar School, Brasenose Coll., Oxford; Jr Research Fellow in Molecular Physics, Linacre Coll., Oxford 1968–70; Lecturer, Hertford Coll., Oxford 1970–72; Lecturer in Biological Sciences, Univ. of Sussex 1973–76; Prof. of Crystallography, Birkbeck Coll., London 1976–90, Fellow 1997; Dir-Gen. Agricultural and Food Research Council (AFRC) 1991–94; Chief Exec. Biotechnology and Biological Sciences Research Council (BBSRC) 1994–96, Chair. 2009–; Sir William Dunn Prof. of Biochemistry, Univ. of Cambridge 1995–2009, Fellow, Sidney Sussex Coll. 1995–, Head, Dept of Biochemistry 1996–2009, Chair. School of Biological Sciences 2003–09, Prof. Emer. 2009–, currently Dir of Research, also Dir Int. School of Crystallography 1982–; Chair. Scientific Advisory Bd Bioprocessing Ltd 1996–99; Dir (non-exec.) Celltech 1997–2004 (Chair. Scientific Advisory Bd 1998–2004); Scientific Adviser, Oxford Molecular Ltd 1996–99; mem. R&D Bd SmithKline Beecham 1997–99, Bd Babraham Inst., Cambridge 1996–2003; Hon. Dir Imperial Cancer Research Fund Unit of Structural Molecular Biology 1989–96; Chair. Biological Sciences, Science and Eng Research Council (SERC) Council 1983–87, SERC Council 1989–90, AFRC Council 1985–90, Advisory Council on Science and Tech. 1988–90, Royal Comm. on Environmental Pollution 1998–2005, Science Advisory Bd 2000–11; Co-founder and Dir (non-exec.) Astex Technology 1999–2011, Chair. Scientific Advisory Bd, Astex Pharmaceuticals 2011–13; consultant, Pfizer 1983–90; Pres. UK Biochemical Soc. 2009–12; Deputy Chair. Inst. of Cancer Research, London 2009–; mem. Bd Parl. Office of Science and Tech. 1998–2005; Trustee, Daphne Jackson Trust 1996–2011, Lawes Trust 1996–2007; mem. Academia Europaea 1993, Council, Royal Soc. 1997–99; Foreign Assoc. Acad. of Sciences for the Developing World 2008–; Corresp. mem. Chilean Acad. of Science 2011, Pres. Science Council 2011–; Fellow, EMBO 1985–; Foreign Fellow, Indian Nat. Science Acad. 1994; Hon. Fellow, Royal Agricultural Soc. of England 1993, Brasenose Coll., Oxford 1989–, Linacre Coll., Oxford 1991–; Dr hc (Stirling) 2000, (Sussex) 2001, (Pavia) 2002; Hon. DSc (London) 2003 and numerous other hon. degrees; Gold Medal, Inst. of Biotechnologies 1987, Sir Hans Krebs Medal 1987, CIBA Medal 1988, Feldberg Prize 1988, Medal of Soc. for Chemical Industry 1995, Nat. Equal Opportunities Award 1996, Pfizer European Prize for Innovation 1998, Biochemical Society Award 2013, Hon. Fellows Prize, Cambridge Philosophical Soc. 2013. *Publications include:* Protein Crystallography 1976, Progress in Biophysics and Molecular Biology (ed.) 1980–; various publs in Nature, Journal of Molecular Biology. *Leisure interests:* opera, playing jazz, foreign travel, walking. *Address:* Department of Biochemistry, 80 Tennis Court Road, University of Cambridge, Cambridge, CB2 1GA, England (office). *Telephone:* (1223) 333628 (office). *E-mail:* tlb20@cam.ac.uk (home). *Website:* www.bioc.cam.ac.uk/people/uto/blundell (office).

BLUNKETT, Rt Hon. David, PC, BA; British politician; b. 6 June 1947; m. 1st (divorced); four s.; m. 2nd Dr Margaret Williams 2009; ed Univ. of Sheffield; worked for E Midlands Gas Bd before entering univ.; subsequently taught industrial relations and politics at Barnsley Coll. of Tech.; joined Labour Party 1963; mem. Sheffield City Council 1970–87, Leader 1980–87; mem. S. Yorks. Co. Council 1973–77; MP for Sheffield Brightside 1987–; elected to Nat. Exec. Cttee (NEC) of Labour Party 1983, Chair. NEC Local Govt Cttee 1984; Local Govt Front Bench Spokesman in Opposition's Environment Team 1988–92; Shadow Sec. of State for Health 1992–94, for Educ. 1994–95, for Educ. and Employment 1995–97; Sec. of State for Educ. and Employment 1997–2001, for the Home Dept 2001–04 (resgnd); Sec. of State for Work and Pensions 2005 (resgnd); Vice-Chair. Labour Party 1992–93, Chair. 1993–94; Academician, Acad. of Social Sciences 2012. *Publications:* On a Clear Day (autobiog.) 1995; co-author: Local Enterprise and Workers' Plans 1981, Building from the Bottom: the Sheffield Experience 1983, Democracy in Crisis: the Town Halls Respond 1987, Politics and Progress 2001, The Blunkett Tapes: My Life In The Bearpit (autobiog.) 2006. *Leisure interests:* walking, sailing, poetry. *Address:* House of Commons, London, SW1A 0AA, England (office). *Telephone:* (20) 7219-4043 (office); (114) 273-5987 (constituency office) (office). *Fax:* (20) 7219-5903 (office).

BLUNT, Charles William, BEcons, CPA; Australian politician and business executive; *CEO, American Chamber of Commerce in Australia;* b. 19 Jan. 1961; s. of R. S. G. Blunt; mem. House of Reps (for Richmond, NSW) 1984–90, Shadow Minister for Community Service 1987; Exec. Dir Nat. Party 1980–84, Leader 1989–90; CEO American Chamber of Commerce in Australia 1990–; Chair. Maxis Ltd, Permo-Drive Technologies Ltd, Pacific Star Resorts Ltd, Capital Policy and Trade Pty Ltd, Palamedia Ltd; Man. Dir American Business Services Pty Ltd. *Leisure interests:* tennis, squash, golf, motor racing, travel, trekking. *Address:* Suite 4, Gloucester Walk, 88 Cumberland Street, Sydney, NSW 2000, Australia.

BLUNT, Matt Roy, BA; American consultant and fmr politician; *Senior Advisor, The Ashcroft Group, LLC;* b. 20 Nov. 1970, Greene Co., Mo.; s. of Roy Blunt; m. Melanie Blunt 1997; two s.; ed Jefferson City's public high school, US Naval Acad., Annapolis, Md; spent five years on active duty with USN as Eng Officer aboard USS Jack Williams (FFG-24) and then as Navigator and Admin. Officer aboard USS Peterson (DD-969), currently Lt-Commdr, USNR; mem. Mo. State House of Reps for 139th Legis. Dist 1998–2000; Sec. of State for Mo. 2001–05; served in support of Operation Enduring Freedom 2001–02; Gov. of Mo. 2005–09; Sr Advisor, Ashcroft Group 2009–, Solamere Capital; mem. Bd of Dirs Copart; Republican; four USN and Marine Corps Achievement Medals and Humanitarian Service Medal. *Address:* The Ashcroft Group, LLC, 950 North Glebe Road, Suite 530 Arlington, VA 22203, USA (office). *Telephone:* (703) 247-5454 (office). *Fax:* (703) 247-5446 (office). *E-mail:* mblunt@ashcroftgroupllc.com (office). *Website:* www.ashcroftgroupllc.com (office).

BLUNT, Roy D., BA, MA; American politician and fmr college administrator; *Senator from Missouri;* b. 10 Jan. 1950, Niangua, Mo.; s. of Leroy O. Blunt and Neva Dora Blunt (née Letterman); m. 1st Roseann Ray 1967 (divorced 2002); two s. one d.; m. 2nd Abigail Perlman 2003; one s. (adopted) ed Southwest Baptist Univ., Missouri State Univ. (then Southwest Missouri State Univ.); teacher, Marshfield High School, Mo. 1970–73; instructor, Drury Coll., Springfield 1973–82; Co. Clerk and Chief Election Official of Greene Co. 1973–85; Republican nominee for Lt Gov. of Mo. 1980; Sec. of State of Mo. (first Republican in 50 years) 1985–93; unsuccessful cand. for Gov. of Mo. 1992; Pres. Southwest Baptist Univ. 1993–96; mem. US House of Reps for 7th Congressional Dist of Mo. 1997–2011, Chief Deputy Majority Whip 1999–2002, Asst Majority Leader (Majority Whip) 2002–07, Interim Majority Leader 2005–06, Asst Minority Leader (Minority Whip) 2007–09; Senator from Mo. 2011–, mem. Appropriations Cttee 2011–, Select Cttee on Intelligence 2011–, Commerce, Science and Transportation Cttee 2011–; del., Atlantic Treaty Assen Conf. 1987; mem. Bd of Dirs Center for Democracy; mem. Missouri Mental Health Advocacy Council 1998–99, Exec. Bd American Council of Young Political Leaders 1998–99; Chair. Missouri Housing Devt Comm., Kansas City 1981, Republican State Convention, Springfield 1980; Chair. Gov.'s Advisory Council on Literacy; Co-Chair. Missouri Opportunity 2000 Comm. 1985–87; active in local American Red Cross, Muscular Dystrophy Assen, and others; mem. Nat. Assen of Secs of State (Chair. Voter Registration and Educ. Cttee, Sec., Vice-Pres. 1990), American Council of Young Political Leaders, Kiwanis, Masons, Smithsonian Council for American Art; Trustee, State Historical Soc. of Missouri; Republican; named one of The 10 Outstanding Young Americans, US Jaycees 1986, Springfield's Outstanding Young Man, Jaycees 1980, Missouri's Outstanding Young Civic Leader 1981, Missouri Republican of the Year 2002, Distinguished Member of Congress Award, American Wire Producers Assen 2002, Health Leadership Award, American Assen of Nurse Anesthetists 2003, Arthur T. Marix Congressional Leadership Award, Mil. Officers Assen of America 2004, Community Health Defender Award, Nat. Assen of Community Health Centers Inc. 2005. *Publications:* Missouri Election Procedures: A Layman's Guide 1977, Jobs Without People: The Coming Crisis for Missouri's Workforce 1989. *Address:* 260 Russell Senate Office Building, Washington, DC 20510, USA (office). *Telephone:* (202) 224-5721 (office). *Fax:* (202) 224-8149 (office). *Website:* blunt.senate.gov (office).

BLY, Robert Elwood, MA; American writer and poet; b. 23 Dec. 1926, Madison, Minn.; s. of Jacob Thomas Bly and Alice Bly (née Aws); m. 1st Carolyn McLean 1955 (divorced 1979); m. 2nd Ruth Counsell 1980; five c.; ed Harvard Univ. and Univ. of Iowa; served in USN 1944–46; Founder and Ed. The Fifties 1958–, later The Sixties and Seventies Press; f. American Writers Against the Vietnam War 1966; Fulbright Award 1956–57, Amy Lowell Fellow 1964–65, Guggenheim Fellow 1965–66, Rockefeller Foundation Fellow 1967, Nat. Book Award in Poetry 1968, Distinguished Artist Award, McKnight Foundation 2002, Maurice English Poetry 2002, Robert Frost Medal, Poetry Soc. of America 2013. *Publications include:* poems: Silence in the Snowy Fields 1962, The Light Around the Body 1967, Chrysanthemums 1967, Ducks 1968, The Morning Glory: Another Thing That Will Never Be My Friend 1969, The Teeth Mother Naked at Last 1971, Poems for Tennessee (with William Stafford and William Matthews) 1971, Christmas Eve Service at Midnight at St Michael's 1972, Water Under the Earth 1972, The Dead Seal Near McClure's Beach 1973, Sleepers Joining Hands 1973, Jumping out of Bed 1973, The Hockey Poem 1974, Point Reyes Poems 1974, Old Man Rubbing his Eyes 1975, The Loon 1977, Visiting Emily Dickinson's Grave and Other Poems 1979, This Tree Will Be Here for a Thousand Years 1979, Finding An Old Ant Mansion 1981, The Man in the Black Coat Turns 1982, Four Ramages 1983, The Whole Moisty Night 1983, Out of the Rollling Ocean 1984, Mirabai Versions 1984, In the Month of May 1985, A Love of Minute Particulars 1985, Loving a Woman in Two Worlds 1985, Selected Poems (ed.) 1986, The Moon on the Fencepost 1988, The Apple Found in the Plowing 1989, What Have I Ever Lost By Dying?: Collected Prose Poems 1993, Gratitude to Old Teachers 1993, Meditations on the Insatiable Soul 1994, Morning Poems 1997, Eating the Honey of Words: New and Selected Poems 1999, The Best American Poetry (ed.) 1999, The Night Abraham Called to the Stars 2001, My Sentence was a Thousand Years of Joy 2005, The Urge to Travel Long Distances 2005, My Sentence Was a Thousand Years of Joy 2006, Talking into the Ear of a Donkey 2011; prose poems: The Morning Glory 1973, This Body is Made of Camphor and Gopherwood 1977, This Body is Made of Eating the Honey of Words: New and Selected Poems 1999, The Best American Poetry (ed.) 1999; prose: Iron John 1990; criticism: A Poetry Reading Against the Vietnam War 1966, The Sea and the Honeycomb 1966, Forty Poems Touching on Recent American History (ed.) 1967, Leaping Poetry 1975, The Soul is Here for its Own Joy 1995; trans. of vols of poetry from Swedish, Norwegian, German, Spanish and Hindi. *Address:* 1904 Girard Avenue South, Minneapolis, MN 55403, USA (home). *Website:* www.robertbly.com (home).

BLYTH OF ROWINGTON, Baron (Life Peer), cr. 1995, of Rowington in the County of Warwickshire; **James Blyth,** MA, FRSA; British business executive; b. 8 May 1940; s. of Daniel Blyth and Jane Power Carlton; m. Pamela Anne Campbell Dixon 1967; one d. (one s. deceased); ed Spiers School, Univ. of Glasgow; with Mobil Oil Co. 1963–69, Gen. Foods Ltd 1969–71, Mars Ltd 1971–74; Dir and Gen. Man. Lucas Batteries Ltd 1974–77, Lucas Aerospace Ltd 1977–81; Dir Joseph Lucas Ltd 1977–81; Head of Defence Sales, Ministry of Defence 1981–85; Man. Dir Plessey Electronic Systems 1985–86; CEO Plessey Co. PLC 1986–87; CEO Boots Co. PLC 1987–98, Deputy Chair. 1994–98, Chair. 1998–2000; Dir (non-exec.) Imperial Group PLC 1984–86, Cadbury-Schweppes PLC 1986–90, British Aerospace 1990–94, Anixter Int. Inc. 1995–, NatWest Group 1999–2000; Dir Diageo PLC 1998–2008 (Chair. 2000–2008); fmr Vice-Chair. Greenhill & Co., now Sr Adviser; mem. Council, Soc. of British Aerospace Cos 1977–81; Gov. London Business School 1987–96 (Hon. Fellow 1997); Pres. ME Assen 1988–93; Chair. Advisory Panel on Citizen's Charter 1991–97; Patron Combined Services Winter Sports Assen 1997–2002; Liveryman, Coachmakers'and Coach Harness Makers' Co.; Hon. LLD (Nottingham) 1992. *Leisure interests:* skiing, tennis, paintings, theatre. *Address:* House of Lords, London, SW1A 0PW, England (office). *Telephone:* (20) 7219-5353 (office).

BO, Xilai, MA; Chinese politician; b. 3 July 1949, Dingxiang, Shanxi Prov.; s. of Bo Yibo (one of the Eight Elders of the CCP); m. 1st Li Danyu; one s.; m. 2nd Gu Kailai 1986; one s.; ed Peking Univ., Graduate School, Chinese Acad. of Social Sciences; worked in hardware factory, No. 2 Light Industry Bureau, Beijing 1968; joined CCP 1980; fmrly cadre, Research Dept of Secr. of CCP Cen. Cttee and Gen. Office of CCP Cen. Cttee; Vice-Sec. then Sec. CCP Cttee of Dalian Econ. and Technological Devt Zone; Sec. CCP Jinzhou Dist Cttee; Deputy Mayor (also Acting Mayor) of Dalian, Liaoning Prov. 1992–93, Mayor 1993–2000; Deputy Sec. CCP Dalian City Cttee 1995–99, Sec. 1999–2000; mem. CCP Prov. Cttee Standing Cttee, Liaoning Prov. 1999, Deputy Sec. CCP Prov. Cttee 2001–04; Vice-Gov. Gov. Liaoning Prov. 2001 (also Acting Gov.), Gov. 2001–04; mem. 16th CCP Cen. Cttee 2002–07; Minister of Commerce 2004–07; Sec., CCP Chongqing Municipal Cttee 2007–12 (removed from office); suspended from the Politburo April 2012; mem. 17th CCP Cen. Cttee 2007–12, mem. Politburo 2007–12; expelled from CCP Nov. 2012; on trial Aug. 2013 accused of accepting bribes and abuse of power, found guilty and sentenced to life imprisonment.

BOADEN, Helen, BA; British broadcasting executive; *Director, BBC Radio;* b. 1 March 1956, Colchester, Essex, England; d. of William John Boaden and Barbara Mary Boaden; m. Stephen Burley 1994; ed Univ. of Sussex; Care Asst, Hackney Social Services, London 1978; Reporter, Radio WBAI, NY, USA 1979, Radio Tees and Radio Aire 1980–83; Producer, BBC Radio Leeds 1983–85; Reporter, File on 4, Radio 4 1985–91, Brass Tacks, BBC 2 1985–91; Presenter, Woman's Hour, Radio 4 1985–91, Verdict, Channel 4 1991–; Ed., File on 4, Radio 4 1991–94; Head of Network Current Affairs, BBC Manchester (first woman in position) 1994–97; Head of Business Programmes, BBC News 1997, Head of Current Affairs and Business Programmes 1998–2000; Controller, BBC Radio 4 2000–04, BBC 7 2002–04; Dir BBC News 2004–11, Dir BBC News Group, with additional responsibility for the Global News div., and mem. Exec. Bd 2011–13, Dir BBC Radio 2013–; Fellow, Radio Acad., Chair. 2003–; Hon. Fellow, Univ. of the Arts, London; Dr hc (East Anglia, Sussex, York, Open Univ.); Sony Gold Award (File on 4 investigation into AIDS in Africa in 1987), Sony Gold Award (File on 4 investigation into bullying in Feltham Young Offenders Inst. 1993), Radio Station of the Year 2003, 2004, ranked by Forbes magazine amongst The World's 100 Most Powerful Women (51st) 2011. *Leisure interests:* walking, food, travel. *Address:* BBC Radio, Broadcasting House, Portland Place, London, W1A 1AA, England (office). *Website:* ww.bbc.co.uk/radio (office).

BOAGIU, Anca-Daniela; Romanian engineer and politician; b. 30 Nov. 1968, Constanta; one adopted s.; ed Ovidius Univ., Constanta; Asst to Dir Gen., S.E.Co.L SpA 1994–95, Construction Site Man. 1995–96; Dir Dept of External Financing Programmes, Nat. Admin of Roads 1996–97; Dir Dept for External Financial Relations, Ministry of Transport 1997–99; Dir Programme for Industrial Restructuring and Professional Conversion (RICOP) 1999–2000; Admin. of External Financing Projects, Programme for the Restructuring the Pvt. Sector 1999–2000; Minister of Transport June–Dec. 2000; Deputy of Romanian Parl. 2000–08, Senator, Senatul 2008– (Vice-Pres. 2010–); Vice-Pres. of Parl. Cttee for European Integration 2004–05; Minister of European Integration 2005–07; Minister of Transport and Infrastructure 2010–12 (resgnd); mem. friendship parl. groups with Italy, Tunisia and Germany; mem. Romania-EU Jt Parl. Cttee; mem. European Parl. Network; Rep. Democratic Liberal Party (PD-L) within the working group of mems of European Parl.; mem. and Exec. Sec., PD-L; Chevalier, Légion d'honneur 2010. *Address:* Calea Moşilor 199, Sector 2, Bucharest, Romania. *E-mail:* anca .boagiu@gmail.com. *Website:* www.ancaboagiu.ro.

BOARDMAN, Christopher (Chris) Miles, MBE, MSc; British fmr professional cyclist; b. 26 Aug. 1968; s. of Keith Boardman and Carole Boardman; m. Sally-Anne Edwards 1988; six c.; ed Hilbre Secondary School and Withens Coll.; competed in nine world championships; holder of various nat. records and 20 nat. titles; bronze medal, Commonwealth Games, Edinburgh 1986; two bronze medals, Commonwealth Games, Auckland 1990; gold medal, 4,000m individual pursuit, Olympic Games, Barcelona 1992, Double World Champion (pursuit and time trial) 1994; winner Tour de France Prologue and holder Yellow Jersey 1994, 1997, 1998; World Record for distance cycled in one hour 1993 and 1996; won World 4,000m cycling championships, broke his own world record Sept. 1996; retd Oct. 2001; Co-founder Boardman Bikes; mem. English Sports Council (now Sport England) 1996; mem. Bd Nat. Cycling Strategy; expert adviser to British cycling team 2004 Olympic Games; equipment and technical manager to TeamGB cyclists during 2008 Olympic Games; writes for various publications, including Diver magazine, Pro Cycling, commentator for ITV and BBC covering major cycling events; Hon. DSc (Brighton) 1997; Hon. MSc (Liverpool); Man of Year Award, Cheshire Life magazine 1997. *Publication:* Chris Boardman's Complete Book of Cycling. *Leisure interests:* carpentry, swimming, scuba diving, writing, archery, family. *E-mail:* media@chrisboardman.com (office). *Website:* www.chrisboardman.com (office).

BOARDMAN, Sir John, Kt, MA, FSA, FBA; British archaeologist and academic; *Professor Emeritus of Classical Archaeology and Art, University of Oxford;* b. 20 Aug. 1927; s. of the late Frederick Boardman and Clare Wells; m. Sheila Stanford

1952; one s. one d.; ed Chigwell School and Magdalene Coll., Cambridge; Asst Dir British School, Athens 1952–55; Asst Keeper, Ashmolean Museum, Oxford 1955–59; Reader in Classical Archaeology, Univ. of Oxford 1959–78, Lincoln Prof. of Classical Archaeology and Art 1978–94, Hon. Fellow 1995, now Prof. Emer.; Fellow, Merton Coll., Oxford 1973–78, Hon. Fellow 1978–, Sub-Warden 1975–78; Prof. of Ancient History, Royal Acad. of Arts 1989–; conducted excavations on Chios 1953–55, Crete 1964–65, in Tocra, Libya 1964–65; Visiting Prof., Columbia Univ. 1965; Geddes-Harrower Prof., Univ. of Aberdeen 1974; Fellow, Inst. of Etruscan Studies, Florence 1983, Austrian and German Archaeological Insts; Foreign mem. Royal Danish Acad.; Assoc. mem. Acad. des Inscriptions et des Belles Lettres, Institut de France; Corresp. mem. Bavarian Acad. of Sciences; Foreign mem. American Philosophical Soc., Accad. dei Lincei, Rome, Russian Acad. of Sciences; Hon. RA; Hon. MRIA; Dr hc (Athens) 1991, (Sorbonne) 1994; Kenyon Medal (British Acad.) 1995, Onassis Prize for Humanities 2009. *Publications include:* Cretan Collection in Oxford 1961, Island Gems 1963, Archaic Greek Gems 1968, Athenian Black Figure Vases 1974, Escarabeos de Piedra de Ibiza 1984, The Oxford History of the Classical World (with others) 1986, Athenian Red Figure Vases: Classical period 1989, Oxford History of Classical Art 1993, The Diffusion of Classical Art in Antiquity 1994, Greek Sculpture, Later Classical 1995, Runciman Prioxe 1995, Early Greek Vase Painting 1997, Persia and the West 2000, The History of Greek Vases 2001, Greek Gems and Finger Rings 2001, The Archaeology of Nostalgia 2002, Classical Phoenician Scarabs 2003, The World of Ancient Art 2006; articles in learned journals. *Address:* 11 Park Street, Woodstock, Oxford, OX20 1SJ (home); Beazley Archive, Classics Centre, Oxford, OX1 3LU, England. *Telephone:* (1993) 811259 (home); (1865) 278084. *Fax:* (1865) 610237 (office). *E-mail:* john.boardman@ashmus.ox.ac.uk (office).

BOARDMAN, Norman Keith, AO, PhD, ScD, FAA, FRS, FTSE; Australian biochemist and academic; b. 16 Aug. 1926, Geelong, Vic.; s. of William R. Boardman and Margaret Boardman; m. Mary C. Shepherd 1952; two s. five d.; ed Melbourne Univ., St John's Coll., Cambridge, UK; Research Officer, Wool Research Section, CSIRO 1949–51; Sr Research Scientist, Div. of Plant Industry, CSIRO 1956–61, Prin. Research Scientist 1961–64; Fulbright Scholar, UCLA, USA 1964–65; Sr Prin. Research Scientist, Div. of Plant Industry, CSIRO 1966–68, Chief Research Scientist 1968–77, mem. of Exec., CSIRO 1977–85, Chair. and Chief Exec. 1985–86, CEO 1986–90, post-retirement Fellow 1990–97; Pres. Australian Biochemical Soc. 1976–78; fmr Chair. Nat. Science and Industry Forum; Treas. Australian Acad. of Science 1978–81; Dir Sirotech Ltd 1986–90, Landcare Australia Ltd 1990–98; Sec. for Science Policy, Australian Acad. of Science 1993–97; mem. Australian Research Grants Cttee 1971–75, ANU Council 1979–89, 1990–91, Australian Centre for Int. Agric. Research 1982–88, CRA Scientific Advisory Bd 1983–98, Prime Minister's Scientific Council 1989–90; Foreign mem. Korean Acad. of Science and Tech.; Hon. DSc (Newcastle Univ.); David Syme Research Prize, Melbourne Univ. 1967, Centenary Medal, Lemberg Medal, Australian Biochemical Soc. 1969. *Publications include:* scientific papers on plant biochemistry, particularly photosynthesis and structure, function and biogenesis of chloroplasts. *Leisure interests:* listening to music, reading, walking. *Address:* 6 Somers Crescent, Forrest, ACT 2603, Australia (home). *Telephone:* (2) 6295-1746 (home). *Fax:* (2) 6260-6889 (home). *E-mail:* keithboardman@bigpond .com.

BOASE, Martin, MA; British advertising executive; b. 14 July 1932, Sheffield; s. of Alan Boase and Elizabeth Grizelle Boase (née Forster); m. 1st Terry Ann Moir 1960 (divorced 1971); one s. one d.; m. 2nd Pauline Valerie Brownrigg 1974; one s. one d.; ed Rendcomb Coll., New Coll., Oxford; with Pritchard Wood and Partners 1961–68; Pnr, The Boase Massimi Pollitt Partnership (subsequently Boase Massimi Pollitt PLC, now part of Omnicom UK PLC), Chair. 1977–89, Chair. Omnicom UK PLC 1989–95; Chair. Predator Three PLC 1990–97; Chair. Advertising Ass>cn 1987–92, Kiss 100 FM 1993–2000, Maiden Outdoor 1993–2006, British TV Advertising Awards Ltd 1993–2000, Herald Investment Trust 1994–2009, Investment Trust of Investment Trusts 1995–2005, Heal's 1997–2002, Jupiter Dividend and Growth Investment Trust PLC, 1999–2008, Global Professional Media PLC 1999–2005, New Star Investment Trust 2000–06, New Media Industries PLC 2001–05; Dir Omnicom Group Inc. 1989–93, EMAP PLC 1991–2000, Taunton Cider PLC 1993–97, Matthew Clark PLC 1995–98; mem. Inst. of Practitioners in Advertising. *Leisure interest:* the Turf.

BOATENG, Ozwald, OBE; British fashion designer; m. Gyunel Boateng; two c.; has designed for Pierce Brosnan, Mick Jagger, Will Smith, Stephen Baldwin, Laurence Fishburne, Billy Zane and others; signed exclusive licensing deal with Marchpole Holdings to produce new formal and casual wear ranges 2002–; Creative Dir of Menswear, Givenchy 2003–07; British Menswear Designer of the Year Award 2001. *Address:* 30 Savile Row, London, W1S 3PT, England (office). *Telephone:* (20) 7440-5237 (office). *Website:* www.ozwaldboateng.co.uk (office).

BOATENG, Baron (Life Peer), cr. 2010, of Akyem in the Republic of Ghana and of Wembley in the London Borough of Brent; **Paul (Yaw) Boateng,** PC, LLB; British diplomatist, politician, lawyer and broadcaster; b. 14 June 1951, Hackney, London, England; s. of Kwaku Boateng and Eleanor Boateng; m. Janet Alleyne 1980; two s. three d.; ed Ghana Int. School, Accra Acad., Apsley Grammar School and Univ. of Bristol; solicitor, Paddington Law Centre 1976–79; solicitor and Pnr, B. M. Birnberg & Co. 1979–87; called to the Bar, Gray's Inn 1989; Legal Adviser, Scrap Sus Campaign 1977–81; mem. GLC (Labour) for Walthamstow 1981–86, Chair. Police Cttee 1981–86, Vice-Chair. Ethnic Minorities Cttee 1981–86; MP (Labour) for Brent S 1987–2005; Home Office mem. House of Commons Environment Cttee 1987–89; Opposition Frontbench Spokesman on Treasury and Econ. Affairs 1989–92, on Legal Affairs, Lord Chancellor's Dept 1992–97; Parl. Under-Sec. of State, Dept of Health 1997–98; Minister of State 1998–2001, Deputy Home Sec. 1999–2001; Minister for Young People 2000–01; Financial Sec. to HM Treasury 2001–02, Chief Sec. 2002–05; High Commr to S Africa 2005–09; Chair. Afro-Caribbean Educ. Resource Project 1978–86, Westminster CRC 1979–81; Gov. Police Staff Coll., Bramshill 1981–84; mem. Home Sec.'s Advisory Council on Race Relations 1981–86, WCC Comm. on Programme to Combat Racism 1984–91, Police Training Council 1981–85; Exec. Nat. Council for Civil Liberties 1980–86; mem. Court of Univ. of Bristol 1994–; Interim Chair. Africa Intellectual Property Trust; Dir, ENO 1984–97; Dir (non-exec.) Aegis Defence Services Ltd 2009–; mem. Bd of Govs, LSE 2011; Gov., English Speaking Union; mem. Unified Bd, Food for the

Hungry; Trustee, Museum of London 2009–; Patron, Barbara Kwateng Lupus Trust, MTN-Ghana Foundation; Hon. LLD (Lincoln Univ., USA, Univ. of Bristol). *Television work includes:* Behind the Hardlines (BBC), Nothing but the Truth (Channel 4). *Publications include:* Reclaiming the Ground (contrib.) 1993, Introduction to Sense and Sensibility, The Complete Jane Austen 1993. *Leisure interests:* opera, swimming, art history. *Address:* House of Lords, Westminster, London, SW1A 0PW, England (office). *Telephone:* (20) 7219-5353 (office). *Website:* www.parliament.uk/biographies/lords/paul-boateng/25159 (office).

BOATSWAIN, Anthony; Grenadian economist and politician; *Minister of Education and Human Resource Development;* ed Long Island Univ., USA, Univ. of Toronto, Canada; early career as teacher at McDonald Coll. St John's Christian Secondary School; held several positions in Public Service including Perm. Sec., Deputy Dir Gen. and Chief Econ. Planner, Ministry of Finance; fmr Gen. Man. Grenada Industrial Devt Corpn; fmr Chair. Marketing and Nat. Importing Bd, Grenada Ports Authority, Land Devt Control Authority; fmr mem. Bd of Dirs Grenada Bd of Tourism, Grenada Banana Cooperative Soc., Grenada Bureau of Standards, Grenada Chamber of Industry and Commerce, Grenada Devt Bank; elected MP for St Patrick W 1999, re-elected 2003; Minister of Finance and Planning 2003–07, of Econ. Devt and Planning 2007; apptd Senator 2010; Minister of Educ. and Human Resource Devt 2013–; mem. New Nat. Party. *Address:* Ministry of Education and Human Resource Development, Ministry of Education Building, Ministerial Complex, Botanical Gardens, Tanteen, St George's, Grenada (office). *Telephone:* 440-2737 (office). *Fax:* 440-6650 (office). *Website:* www .grenadaedu.com (office).

BOBBITT, Philip Chase, AB, JD, PhD; American academic and government official; *Herbert Wechsler Professor of Jurisprudence, Columbia University;* b. 22 July 1948, Temple, Tex.; ed Princeton Univ., Yale Univ., Univ. of Oxford, UK; Asst Prof. of Law, Univ. of Texas School of Law 1976–79, Prof. 1979, A. W. Walker Centennial Chair 1996–2007; Jr Research Fellow, Nuffield Coll., Univ. of Oxford 1982–84, Research Fellow 1984–85, Anderson Sr Research Fellow 1985–91, mem. Modern History Faculty 1984–91; Sr Research Fellow, War Studies Dept, Kings Coll. London, UK 1994–97; Assoc. Counsel to Pres. of USA for Intelligence and Int. Security 1980–81; Legal Counsel to US Senate Intra-Contra Cttee 1987–88; Counsellor on Int. Law, US State Dept 1990–93; Dir for Intelligence, Nat. Security Council 1997–98, Sr Dir of Critical Infrastructure 1998–99, Sr Dir for Strategic Planning 1999; Herbert Wechsler Prof. of Jurisprudence, Columbia Univ. 2007–; Fellow, American Acad. of Arts and Sciences; life mem. American Law Inst.; mem. Council on Foreign Relations, Pacific Council on Int. Policy, Int. Inst. for Strategic Studies; fmr Trustee, Princeton Univ. *Publications include:* Tragic Choices (co-author) 1978, Constitutional Fate 1982, Democracy and Deterrence 1987, US Nuclear Strategy (co-author) 1989, Constitutional Interpretation 1991, The Shield of Achilles: War, Peace and the Course of History 2002, Terror and Consent: The Wars for the Twenty-First Century 2008. *Address:* Oakwell, 1505 Windsor Road, Austin, TX 78703, USA (office). *Telephone:* (512) 472-2779 (office). *Fax:* (512) 471-6460 (office). *E-mail:* bobbitt@law.columbia.edu (office).

BOBINAC, Franjo, BEcons, MSc, MBA; Slovenian business executive; *President and CEO, Gorenje Group;* b. 16 Oct. 1958, Celje; m. Polonca Bobinac; one s. one d.; ed Univ. of Ljubljana, Ecole Supérieure de Commerce, Paris, France; began career with Emo Celje 1983–86; Asst to Dir of Export, Gorenje gospodinjski aparati d.d. (Gorenje Household Appliances) 1986–91, Export Dir 1990, Marketing Dir 1991–93, Gen. Dir Gorenje Sidex France 1993–98, mem. Man. Bd, Gorenje d.d. 1998–, Pres. Man. Bd 2003–, currently also CEO; fmr Pres. BIO 19 Organizing Cttee; Pres. Slovenian Handball Fed.; mem. Supervisory Bd ETI Izlake; mem. Man. Cttee, Chamber of Commerce and Industry of Slovenia, Council, Bled School of Man., Steering Cttee, Int. Asscn Conseil Européen de la Construction d'appareils Domestiques 2010–, Jozef Stefan Inst.; Chevalier, Ordre nat. du Mérite 2009; Award by the Chamber of Commerce and Industry of Slovenia for exceptional results, Janez Vajkard Valvasor Medal, Int. Asscn of Business Communicators Merit Excel Award (Excellence in Communication Leadership), Slovenian Asscn for Public Relations Primus Award for Best Slovenian Manager. *Address:* Gorenje gospodinjski aparati d.d., Partizanska 12, 3503 Velenje, Slovenia (office). *Telephone:* (3) 8991000 (office). *Fax:* (3) 8991460 (office). *E-mail:* franjo .bobinac@gorenje.si (office). *Website:* www.gorenje.com (office).

BOBONAZAROVA, Oinihol; Tajikistani lawyer and politician; b. 10 June 1948, Java dist; m.; one s. one d.; ed Faculty of Law, Tajik State Univ.; has taught at Faculty of Law, Tajik State Univ. since 1976, Dean of Faculty 1989–; human rights lawyer known for advocacy of human rights with non-governmental org. Perspective-Plus, has also worked with Western insts including OSCE and Open Society Foundations, chaired Bd of Open Society Inst. Assistance Foundation – Tajikistan (under auspices of Soros Foundations Network); convicted for being mem. of an opposition party, but later pardoned early 1990s; Adviser on Human Rights to Tajikistan Rep. of OSCE 1996–2004; mem. Islamic Rebirth Party of Tajikistan (IRPT); apptd to represent United Reformist Forces (merger of IRPT, Social Democratic Party and several non-governmental groups and others in opposition) Sept. 2013; opposition cand. in presidential election 6 Nov. 2013. *Address:* Islamic Rebirth Party of Tajikistan, 734000 Dushanbe, pos. Kalinina, Kuchai Tukhagul 55, Tajikistan (office). *Telephone:* (372) 27-25-30 (office). *Fax:* (372) 27-53-93 (office).

BOBROW, Martin, CBE, DScMed, FRS, FRCP, FRCPath, FMedSci; British medical scientist, geneticist and academic; b. 6 Feb. 1938, Johannesburg, South Africa; s. of Joe Bobrow and Bessie Bobrow; m. Lynda Strauss; three d.; ed Univ. of Witwatersrand, S Africa; Prof. of Human Genetics, Univ. of Amsterdam 1981–82; Prince Philip Prof. of Paediatric Research, United Medical and Dental Schools of Guy's and St Thomas' Hosps, London, 1982–95; Prof. and Head, Dept of Medical Genetics, Univ. of Cambridge 1995–2005, Dir (non-exec.) Addenbrooke's Hosp.; mem. Black Advisory Group on possible increased incidence of cancer in W Cumbria 1983–84, Cttee to examine ethical implications of gene therapy 1989–93, NHS Cen. R&D Cttee, Dept of Health 1991–97, Gene Therapy Advisory Cttee 1993–94, Lewisham NHS Trust Bd 1994–95, Nuffield Council on Bioethics 1996–2003 (fmr Deputy Chair.), Human Genetics Advisory Comm. 1997–99; fmr mem. MRC; Gov. Wellcome Trust 1996–2007, Deputy Chair. 2004–07; Chair. Muscular Dystrophy Campaign 1995–2010; fmr Chair. ULTRA (Unrelated Living Transplant Regulating Authority), COMARE (Dept of Health Advisory Cttee on

Radiation in the Environment); Founder Acad. of Medical Sciences 1998. *Publications:* papers in science books and journals 1967–. *Address:* Department of Medical Genetics, Cambridge Institute for Medical Research, Wellcome/MRC Building, Addenbrooke's Hospital, Cambridge, CB2 2XY, England (office). *Telephone:* (1223) 331154 (office). *Fax:* (1223) 331206 (office). *E-mail:* lms28@cam.ac.uk (office). *Website:* www.cimr.cam.ac.uk/medgen (office).

BOBUŢAC, Valeriu; Moldovan politician and diplomatist; b. 13 March 1945, Khankaun; m. Maria Bobutac; two c.; ed Lvov Trade-Econ. Inst., Ukraine, Higher CP School, Kiev, Ukraine; worked in Comsomol, First-Sec. Cen. Cttee then Sec. Cen. Cttee Moldovan CP; Deputy Minister of Econs and Reforms; Amb. to Russia 1997–99, 2001; Prime Minister of Moldova 1999–2000; at Ministry of Foreign Affairs 2002–05; Amb. to Hungary (also accred to Slovenia, Croatia, Bosnia and Herzegovina, Holy See) 2005–09, also Rep. to Danube Comm. 2005–09.

BOC, Emil, DPhil; Romanian politician and academic; *President, Democratic Liberal Party;* b. 6 Sept. 1966, Răchiţele; s. of Ioan Boc and Ana Boc; m. Oana Boc 1994; two d.; Sr Law Lecturer; Deputy, Romanian Parl. 2000–04, Vice-Chair. of Legal, Discipline, and Immunity Cttee 2000–04, Vice-Chair. Cttee for Elaboration of Bills Concerning the Revision of Romania's Constitution 2001–04; mem. parl. friendship groups with UK, South Africa, Repub. of Korea 2000–04; Mayor of Cluj-Napoca 2004–08; fmr Vice-Pres. Democratic Liberal Party (PD-L), Pres. 2008–; Prime Minister 2008–09, 2009–12 (resgnd), Acting Prime Minister Oct.–Dec. 2009; Acting Minister of Educ., Research and Innovation Oct.–Dec. 2009; apptd Acting Minister of Labour, Family and Social Protection 2011. *Publication:* Separation of Powers in the State 2000. *Address:* Democratic Liberal Party (Partidul Democrat Liberal—PD-L), 011825 Bucharest, Sector 1, Al. Modrogan 1, Romania (office). *Telephone:* (21) 2303701 (office). *Fax:* (21) 2301625 (office). *E-mail:* boc@yahoo.com (home); office@pd.ro (office). *Website:* www.pdl.org.ro (office).

BOCCARDO, Archbishop Renato; Italian ecclesiastic; *Archbishop of Spoleto-Norcia;* b. 21 Dec. 1952, Sant'Ambrogio; ordained priest 1977; apptd Titular Bishop of Aquipendium 2004; Sec. Pontifical Council for Social Communications 2003–; Sec. Governorate of the Vatican City State 2005–09; Archbishop of Spoleto-Norcia 2009–; mem. Congregazione per le Cause dei Santi 2012–. *Address:* Arcivescovado, Via Aurelio Saffi 13, 06049 Spoleto, Italy (office). *Telephone:* (07) 4323101 (office). *Website:* www.arcidiocesidispoleto-norcia.it.

BOCELLI, Andrea; Italian singer (tenor); b. 22 Sept. 1958, Lajatico, Pisa; s. of the late Alessandro Bocelli and of Edi Bocelli; m. Enrica Cenzatti 1992; two s.; m. Veronica Berti 2014; one d.; ed Univ. of Pisa; began piano lessons aged six, later learned to play the flute, saxophone, trumpet, trombone, harp, guitar and drums; became blind following a football accident aged 12; won first song competition, Margherita d'Oro in Viareggio with O sole mio aged 14; earned money performing in piano bars; completed law school and spent one year as a court-appointed lawyer; won Newcomers section of Sanremo Music Festival 1994; has recorded 13 solo studio albums, of both pop and classical music, two greatest hits albums and nine complete operas; biggest-selling solo artist in history of classical music; duet with Celine Dion, The Prayer, for animated film The Quest for Camelot, won Golden Globe for Best Original Song 1999; Grande Ufficiale, Ordine al merito della Repubblica Italiana 2006, Grand Officer, Orden al Mérito de Duarte, Sánchez y Mella (Dominican Repub.) 2009; named one of People Magazine's 50 Most Beautiful People 1998, honoured with a star on Hollywood Walk of Fame 2010, World Music Award for World's Best-selling Classical Artist 2010, America Award, Italy-USA Foundation 2012, Classic BRIT Award for Int. Artist of the Year in association with Raymond Weil 2012. *Recordings include:* albums: Bocelli 1995, Viaggio Italiano 1995, Romanza 1997, Aria 1998, Sacred Arias 1999, Sogno 1999, Verdi 2000, La Bohème 2000, Verdi Requiem 2001, Cieli di Toscana 2001, Sentimento (Classical BRIT Award for Best Album 2003) 2002, Tosca 2003, Aria: The Opera Album 2005, MW 2006, Vivere 2007, Incanto 2008, My Christmas 2009, Andrea Chénier 2010, Carmen: Duets & Arias 2010, Concerto: One Night in Central Park 2011, Notte Illuminata 2011, Opera 2012, Roméo et Juliette 2012. *Publications:* The Music of Silence: A Memoir (La musica del silenzio) (autobiog.) 2000 (reworked 2010). *Address:* c/o Michele Torpedine, MT Opera and Blues Production and Management, via Mario Musolesi, 40138 Bologna, Italy (office). *Telephone:* (51) 251117 (office). *Fax:* (51) 251123 (office). *E-mail:* mtorped@tin.it (office). *Website:* www.mt-operaandblues.it (office); www.andreabocelli.org.

BOCEVSKI, Ivica, BJur; Macedonian politician and teacher; *Social Sciences Teacher, Nova International Schools;* b. 15 June 1977, Skopje; m.; one d.; ed Nikola Karev High School, SS Cyril and Methodius Univ., Skopje, Univ. of Pittsburgh, USA; fmr columnist, Utrinski Vesnik; Co-founder and fmr Exec. Dir Inst. for Democracy, Skopje; Chief of Staff, Office of the Deputy Prime Minister for Econ. Affairs 2004–06; Analyst, Ministry of Foreign Affairs 2006–07; Govt Spokesman 2007–08; Deputy Prime Minister, responsible for European Integration 2008–09; Social Sciences Teacher, NOVA Int. Schools 2010–. *Publications:* several expert articles in domestic and foreign journals. *Address:* Nova International Schools, 1000 Skopje, Prashka 27, Former Yugoslav Republic of Macedonia (office). *Telephone:* (2) 3076402 (office). *Fax:* (2) 3076299 (office). *E-mail:* info@nova.edu .mk (office). *Website:* www.nova.edu.mk (office).

BOCHEŃSKI, Jacek; Polish writer and essayist; b. 29 July 1926, Lvov; m.; one d.; ed State Coll. of Theatrical Arts, Warsaw; Co-founder and Ed. Zapis (first Polish underground periodical) 1977–81; Pres. Polish PEN Club 1996–99; currently Pres. Authors & Composers Assocn's Council; Solidarity Prize 1987, Polish PEN Club Parandowski Prize 2006, Gloria Artis Golden Medal 2009. *Radio:* Post-Breakdown, Naso Poet, The Elderly Man's Fantasies 1998–2002. *Television and stage plays:* Taboo, Post-Breakdown. *Publications include:* fiction: Farewell to Miss Syngilu 1960, Roman Trilogy: Divine Julius 1961, Taboo 1965, Naso Poet 1969, Post-Breakdown 1987, The Elderly Man's Fantasies 2004, Tiberius Caesar 2009; non-fiction: Bloody Italian Rarities 1982, Thirteen European Exercises 2005, Antiquity after Antiquity 2010; several essays and contribs to magazines on politics and culture. *Address:* ul. Sonaty 6 m. 801, 02-744 Warsaw, Poland (home). *E-mail:* jacek.bochenski@gazeta.pl. *Website:* www.jacekbochenski.blox.pl.

BOCHNIARZ, Henryka Teodora, PhD; Polish economist and politician; *President, Polish Confederation of Private Employers;* b. 29 Oct. 1947, Świebodzin; m. Zbigniew Bochniarz 1969; one s. one d.; ed Warsaw School of Econs and Foreign Trade Research Inst.; Asst, Deputy Head Agric. Div., Foreign Trade Research

Inst., Warsaw 1976–80, Asst Prof., Lecturer 1980–84, Dir Agric. Div. and Negotiator 1984–90; Research Asst, Int. Inst. of Socialist Econ. Systems, Moscow, USSR (now Russian Fed.) 1978; Visiting Asst Prof., Vienna Inst. for Comparative Econ. Systems 1983–84; Sr Fulbright Scholar and Visiting Prof., Dept of Agric. and Applied Econs, Univ. of Minn., USA 1985–87; Dir Proexim Ltd 1988–90; Pres. Nicom Consulting Ltd, Warsaw 1990–91, 1992–, Asscn of Econ. Consultants in Poland 1991–; Minister of Industry and Trade 1991–92; Pres. Polish Business Roundtable 1996–99, Polish Confed. of Pvt. Employers 1999–; Co-Chair. (with Leszek Balcerowicz q.v.) Cttee on Deregulation of the Polish Economy 1998–; currently Exec. Pres. Polish Business Council; mem. Bd Dirs TVN SA, Computer-land SA, ITI SA; mem. Polish Del. to UN Cttee on Agric., Econ. Comm. for Europe, Geneva, Switzerland 1976–85; Visiting Prof., Dept of Agricultural and Applied Econs, Univ. of Minnesota, USA 1985–87; mem. Negotiating Group on Agric., Uruguay Round GATT talks 1987. *Publications include:* Polish Agricultural Trade (annual reports) 1975–90, Poland: The Impact of Foreign Trade Policy on Self-Sufficiency in Agriculture 1987; numerous papers and contribs to professional journals. *Leisure interests:* skiing, volleyball, theatre. *Address:* Polskej Konfederacji Pracodawców Prywatnych Lewiatan (Polish Confederation of Private Employers), ul. Klonowa 6, 00-591 Warsaw (office); c/o Nicom Consulting Ltd, 10 Inwalidów Square, 01-552 Warsaw, Poland. *Telephone:* (22) 845-95-50 (office). *Fax:* (22) 845-95-51 (office). *E-mail:* pkpp@prywatni.pl (office). *Website:* www .prywatni.pl (office); www.nicom.pl (office); www.bochniarz.pl.

BOCK, Kurt, PhD; German business executive; *Chairman of the Board of Executive Directors, BASF SE;* b. 1958, Rahden, Eastern Westphalia; m.; three c.; ed Univs of Münster and Cologne, Pennsylvania State Univ., USA, Univ. of Bonn; joined Finance Div., BASF AG 1985, mem. of staff to BASF's Chief Financial Officer (CFO) 1987–91, Dir of Tech., Planning and Controlling, Eng Plastics, BASF AG 1991–94, Sr Vice-Pres. Finance 1992–94, Sr Vice-Pres. Finance and Accounting, Robert Bosch GmbH, Stuttgart, Germany 1994–96, Man. Dir Robert Bosch Ltda, Campinas, Brazil 1996, CFO BASF Corpn, NJ, USA 1998–2000, Pres. Logistics & Information Services, BASF AG 2000–03, mem. Bd of Exec. Dirs and CFO BASF AG (renamed BASF SE 2008) 2003–11, Chair. and CEO BASF Corpn, USA 2007–, Chair. Bd of Exec. Dirs BASF SE 2011–, responsible for Legal, Taxes & Insurance, Strategic Planning & Controlling, Communications & Govt Relations, Global Exec. Human Resources, Investor Relations and Compliance. *Address:* BASF SE, Carl-Bosch Strasse 38, 67056 Ludwigshafen, Germany (office). *Telephone:* (621) 60-0 (office); (621) 60-20916 (Corporate Media Relations) (office). *Fax:* (621) 60-92693 (office); (621) 60-42525 (office). *E-mail:* presse.kontakt@basf .com (office); info@basf.de (office). *Website:* www.basf.com (office); www.basf.de (office).

BOCKERIA, Leo Antonovich, DrMedSci; Russian cardio-vascular surgeon and academic; *Chairman and Head, A. Bakulev Scientific Centre for Cardiovascular Surgery, Russian Academy of Medical Sciences;* b. 22 Dec. 1939, s. of F. Anton Bockeria and Olga M. Bockeria; m.; two d.; ed I. M. Sechenov First Moscow Medical Inst. (now Sechenov First State Medical Univ.); with A. Bakulev Scientific Centre for Cardiovascular Surgery (SCCVS) 1968–, Chair. and Head 1994–, Dir, SCCVS Prof. Burakovsky Research Inst. of Cardiosurgery 1993–; mem. Russian Acad. of Medical Sciences 1994–, Russian Acad. of Sciences 2011–; main research in cardiovascular surgery, hyperbaric oxygenation, treatment of cardiopulse violation problems; apptd mem. Public Chamber of the Russian Fed. 2005, Chair. Comm. for the Formation of a Healthy Lifestyle 2006–; Lenin Prize 1976, USSR State Prize 1986, Russian Fed. State Prize 2002, Russian Govt Prize 2003, Russian Acad. Prize 2004, Moscow City Prize 2009. *Publications:* numerous articles on cardiovascular surgery. *Leisure interests:* painting, collecting encyclopaedias and dictionaries. *Address:* Bakulev Scientific Centre for Cardiovascular Surgery, 135 Roublevskoye shosse, 121552 Moscow, Russia (office). *Telephone:* (495) 414-75-71 (office). *Fax:* (495) 414-78-67 (office). *E-mail:* leoan@heart-house.ru (office). *Website:* www.bakulev.ru (office).

BOCLET, Franck; French fashion designer; Collection Man. Kenzo 1984–85; Product Man. Arrow 1985–89; Licensing Man. Courreges 1989–90; Artistic Dir for Francesco Smalto 1990–2007; Chief Men's Designer for Emanuel Ungaro 2007–10; CEO Franck Boclet 2010–; consultant, FBN Consulting 2012–. *Address:* Franck Boclet, 53 Avenue Montaigne, 75008 Paris, France (office). *Telephone:* 9-81-99-30-44 (office). *Website:* www.franckboclet.fr (office).

BOCUSE, Paul; French restaurateur; b. 11 Feb. 1926, Collonges-au-Mont-d'Or, Rhône; s. of Georges Bocuse and Irma Roulier; m. Raymonde Duvert 1946; one s. one d.; ed Ecole primaire, Collonges-au-Mont-d'Or and Pensionnat Saint-Louis, Lyons; restaurateur (in business passing from father to son since 1765), Collonges-Mont-d'Or; restaurateur, French Pavilion, Disneyworld, Orlando, Fla, USA; Pres. Asscn Eurotoques 1989–, L'Ecole des Arts Culinaires et de l'Hôtellerie Ecully 1991–95; Pres. Meilleur Ouvrier de France: Section Cuisine-Restauration 1991–; Founder and Hon. Pres. Inst. Paul Bocuse, Lyon; mem. Asscn des maître-cuisiniers de France; Officier, Légion d'honneur 1975, Ordre nat. du Mérite, Chevalier des Palmes académiques, Officier du Mérite agricole. *Publications:* La Cuisine du marché 1976, Bocuse dans votre cuisine 1982, La cuisine du gibier (in collaboration) 1984, Bon appétit 1989, Cuisine de France 1990, La bonne chère 1995. *Leisure interests:* underwater fishing. *Address:* Institute Paul Bocuse, Château du Vivier, BP 25, 69131 Ecully Cedex (office); Restaurant Paul Bocuse, 40 rue de la Plage, 69660 Collonges-au-Mont d'Or, France (office). *Telephone:* (4) 72-18-02-20 (office). *Fax:* (4) 78-43-33-51 (office). *E-mail:* info@institutpaulbocuse.com (office); paul.bocuse@bocuse.fr (office). *Website:* www.bocuse.fr (office); www .institutpaulbocuse.com (office).

BOD, Péter Ákos, PhD; Hungarian economist, politician and academic; *Professor and Chairman, Economic Policy Department and Director, Institute of Economics, Corvinus University of Budapest;* b. 28 July 1951, Szigetvár; s. of Andor Bod and Rózsa Nagy; m.; two s. one d.; ed high school, Miskolc, Univ. of Economics, Budapest; worked as researcher, Dept Head, Inst. for Econ. Planning 1975–90; UNDP adviser in Ghana 1986–87; mem. of Parl. (Hungarian Democratic Forum) 1990–91; Minister of Industry and Trade 1990–91; Pres. Nat. Bank of Hungary 1991–94; mem. Bd EBRD, London 1995–97; Prof. and Chair. Econ. Policy Dept and Dir Inst. of Econs, Corvinus Univ. of Budapest 2001–; Personal Econ. Adviser to Pres. of the Repub. 2001–05; Vice-Pres. Hungarian Econ. Soc. 2009–; Medal of Merit, Pres. of the Repub. 2005, Commdr's Cross (Hungarian Repub.) 2011;

Popovics Award, Hungarian Nat. Bank 2002. *Publications:* The Entrepreneurial State in the Contemporary Market Economy 1987, Foundations of Economic Theory and Policy 1999, The World of Money – The Money of the World 2001, Economic Policy 2002, Introduction into Finance and Financial Policy 2008, Foundation of Finance 2012 (all in Hungarian). *Leisure interests:* tennis, music, history. *Address:* 1093 Budapest, Fövam tér 8, Corvinus University of Budapest, Hungary (office). *Telephone:* (1) 482-5370 (office). *Fax:* (1) 482-5034 (office). *E-mail:* petera.bod@uni-corvinus.hu (office). *Website:* www.corvinus.hu (office).

BODE, Lucian Nicolae; Romanian politician; b. 27 Oct. 1974, Valcau de Jos, Salaj; m.; one c.; ed Faculty of Electrotechnics and Informatics, Univ. in Oradea, Advance Training Program in Int. Relations, Romanian Diplomatic Inst., Ministry of Foreign Affairs, Nat. Coll. of Defence 'Carol I', Nat. Univ. of Defence, Faculty of History and Philosophy, Babes-Bolyai Univ., Cluj-Napoca; Service Engineer, Br. of Electricity Distribution in Zalau, S.C. Electrica SA 2001–08, also spokesperson, head of service and trade union pres.; Sec. Biroul Permanent Judetean (BPJ), Partidul Democrat (PD), Salaj 2001–02, Vice-Pres. 2002–05, Sec. Gen. 2005–07, Sec. Gen. BPJ Partidul Democrat Liberal (PD-L), Salaj 2007–08, Pres. BPJ PD-L Salaj 2008–; Minister of Economy, Trade and Business Environment 2011–; Pres. Electrica Zalau Trade Union 2003–08; Councillor, Local Council of Valcau de Jos 2000–04, Co. Councillor in Salaj 2004–08; Founding mem. Prodemos Zalau Asscn. *Address:* c/o Ministry of the Economy, Trade and the Business Environment, 010096 Bucharest 1, Calea Victoriei 152, Romania. *E-mail:* dezbateri_publice@minind.ro.

BODE, Ridvan Vait, MSc; Albanian economist and politician; b. 26 May 1959, Korcë; s. of Vait Bode; m.; ed Gen. High School, Gjirokaster, Agricultural Univ., Tirana, Mediterranean Agricultural Inst. (DSPU), Montpellier, France; Head, Finance Div., Perrenjas City Admin, Librazhd Dist 1983–89; Lecturer on Financial Analysis and Accountability, Tirana Agrarian Univ. 1991–95; Dir-Gen. Albanian Customs Gen. Dept 1995–96; elected mem. Parl. (Democratic Party of Albania—DPA) for Devoli Dist 1996–97, 2001–; Minister of Finance 1996–97, 2009–13; mem. DPA Nat. Council and Presidency 1997, Gen. Sec. 1997–; Collaborator and part-time Lecturer, Faculty of Econs, Univ. of Tirana 2002–. *Publications:* numerous papers on financial analysis. *Address:* Democratic Party of Albania (Partia Demokratike e Shqipërisë), Rruga Punëtorët e Rilindjes 1, 1001 Tirana, Albania (office). *Telephone:* (4) 2228091 (office). *Fax:* (4) 2223525 (office). *E-mail:* denonco@pd.al (office). *Website:* www.perpara.al (office).

BODE, Thilo, PhD; German business executive and consultant; *Executive Director, Foodwatch;* b. 1947, nr Munich; ed Univ. of Munich, Univ. of Regensburg; int. consultant, Lahmeyer Int., Frankfurt; Project Man. German Bank for Reconstruction and Devt 1978–81; ind. consultant for int. orgs, govts and businesses 1981; Special Asst to Chief Exec. of int. corpn 1986; Exec. Dir Greenpeace Germany 1989–95, Greenpeace Int. 1995–2001; Founder and Exec. Dir Foodwatch 2002–. *Publications:* Die Demokratic verrät ihre Kinder 2003. *Address:* Foodwatch, Brunnenstrasse 181, 10119 Berlin, Germany (office). *Telephone:* (30) 2404760 (office). *Fax:* (30) 240476-26 (office). *E-mail:* bode@foodwatch.de (office). *Website:* www.foodwatch.de (office).

BODEK, Arie, BS, PhD; American physicist and academic; *George E. Pake Professor of Physics, University of Rochester;* b. 1947, Tel-Aviv, Israel; ed Massachusetts Inst. of Tech.; Research Assoc., Lab. for Nuclear Science, MIT 1972–74; Milkan Fellow, Calif. Inst. of Tech. 1974–76; Asst Prof. of Physics, Univ. of Rochester, NY 1977–80, Assoc. Prof. 1980–87, Prof. 1987–, George E. Pake Prof. of Physics 2005–, Assoc. Chair. Dept of Physics and Astronomy 1995–98, Chair. 1998–2007; mem. Editorial Bd several journals including European Physics Journal 1992–; Fellow, American Physical Soc. 1985, Japan Soc. for the Promotion of Science 1986–87; Alfred P. Sloan Fellow, Univ. of Rochester 1978, Panofsky Prize in Experimental Particle Physics, American Physical Soc. 2004, Grad. Teaching Award, Univ. of Rochester 2004. *Publications:* more than 700 articles in scientific journals. *Address:* Department of Physics and Astronomy, University of Rochester, Bausch & Lomb 354, Rochester, NY 14627, USA (office). *Telephone:* (585) 275-5445 (office). *Fax:* (585) 273-3237 (office). *E-mail:* bodek@pas.rochester.edu (office). *Website:* www.pas.rochester.edu/urpas/faculty_page/bodek_arie (office).

BODEN, Margaret Ann, OBE, ScD, PhD, FBA; British cognitive scientist and professor of cognitive science; *Research Professor of Cognitive Science, Centre for Research in Cognitive Science, University of Sussex;* b. 26 Nov. 1936, London; d. of Leonard F. Boden and Violet Dorothy Boden (née Dawson); m. John R. Spiers 1967 (divorced 1981); one s. one d.; ed Newnham Coll., Cambridge (Major Scholar) and Harvard Grad. School (Harkness Fellow); Lecturer in Philosophy, Univ. of Birmingham 1959–65; Lecturer, then Reader in Philosophy and Psychology, Univ. of Sussex 1965–80, Prof. 1980–, Founding Dean School of Cognitive and Computing Sciences 1987, Research Prof. of Cognitive Science, Centre for Research in Cognitive Science 2002–; Curator Univ. of London Inst. for Advanced Study 1995–; Co-founder, Harvester Press Ltd 1970, Dir 1970–85; Vice-Pres. British Acad. 1989–91, Royal Inst. of GB 1993–95, Chair. of Council 1993–95, mem. of Council 1992–95; mem. Advisory Bd for the Research Councils 1989–90, Academia Europaea 1993–, Animal Procedures Cttee 1995–99; Fellow, American Asscn for Artificial Intelligence 1993–, European Coordinating Cttee for Artificial Intelligence 1999–; Hon. DSc (Sussex) 2001, (Bristol) 2002, Hon. DUniv (Open) 2004. *Publications:* Purposive Explanation in Psychology 1972, Artificial Intelligence and Natural Man 1977, Piaget 1979, Minds and Mechanisms 1981, Computer Models of Mind 1988, Artificial Intelligence in Psychology 1989, The Philosophy of Artificial Intelligence (ed.) 1990, Dimensions of Creativity (ed.) 1994, Artificial Intelligence and the Mind (co-ed.) 1994, The Philosophy of Artificial Life (ed.) 1996, Artificial Intelligence (ed.) 1996, The Creative Mind (2nd edn) 2004, Mind as Machine 2006, Creativity and Art 2010. *Leisure interests:* dressmaking, travelling, passion for India and Polynesia. *Address:* Centre for Research in Cognitive Science, University of Sussex, Falmer, Brighton, BN1 9QJ, England (office). *Telephone:* (1273) 678386 (office). *Fax:* (1273) 671320 (office). *E-mail:* maggieb@cogs.susx.ac.uk (office). *Website:* www.cogs.susx.ac.uk (office).

BODEWIG, Kurt; German politician; b. 26 April 1955, Rheinberg; m.; two s.; ed commercial coll.; joined SPD 1973, mem. Nat. Exec. Cttee 2000–05; held various party posts 1982–98; mem. Bundestag 1998–2009; Minister of Transport, Building

and Housing 2000–02; Maritime Amb. of EU 2006–; Chair. Baltic Sea Forum e.V., Bd Trustees German-Lithuanian-Forum; Deputy Chair. Cttee on the Affairs of the EU; Pres. Deutsche Verkehrswacht e.V.; mem. European Council and Parl. Ass., Baltic Sea Parl. Conf.; Deputy mem. NATO Parl. Ass. *Address:* Deutsche Verkehrswacht e.V., Budapester Straße 31, 10787, Berlin, Germany (office). *Telephone:* (30) 516510544 (office). *Fax:* (30) 516510569 (office). *E-mail:* mail@kurt-bodewig.de. *Website:* www.kurt-bodewig.de.

BODEWITZ, Hendrik Wilhelm, PhD; Dutch professor of Sanskrit (retd); b. 13 Oct. 1939, Gramsbergen; s. of Johan Adriaan Bodewitz and Jennigjen Lenters; m. Janneke van Uchelen 1964; one s. one d.; ed Lyceum Coevorden, Univ. of Utrecht; Lecturer in Sanskrit, Utrecht Univ. 1966–68, Prof. 1976–92, Dean of Faculty 1980–82, 1984–86; Sr Lecturer, Leiden Univ. 1969–76, Prof. 1992–2002; mem. Netherlands Royal Acad.; Founding mem. Academia Europaea. *Publications:* Jaiminīya Brāhmaṇa I, 1-65, with a study of the Agnihotra and the Prāṇāgnihotra 1973, The daily evening and morning offering according to the Brāhmaṇas 1976, The Jyotiṣṭoma Ritual: Jaiminīya Brāhmaṇa I, 66-364 1990, Kauṣitaki Upaniṣad 2002; articles: Vedic agham: evil or sin, distress or death? 2007, The Vedic Concepts āgas and enas 2007, Sins and Vices, their Enumerations and Specifications in the Veda 2008, The Special Meanings of śrama and other derivations of the root śram in the Veda 2008, The refrain kasmai devaya havia vidhema 2009, On the Interpretation of Bhagavad Gita (Vol. I–VI) 2009, The Dialogue of Yama and Yami 2009, The Legend of Urvaśī and Pururavas and Their Dialogue 2011, The Chronology of the Upaniṣads and Their Basic Ideas 2011, Vedic Terms Denoting Virtues and Merits 2013. *Address:* Stolberglaan 29, 3583 XL Utrecht, Netherlands (home). *Telephone:* (30) 2510047 (home).

BODIN, Manfred; German banker; b. 14 Nov. 1939, Münster; m.; ed German Savings Banks Acad.; Stadtsparkasse, Münster 1960–64; Stadtsparkasse, Witten 1964–70; mem. Man. Bd Kreissparkasse Recklinghausen 1970–75, Chair. 1976–83; Chair. Man. Bd Sparkasse Essen 1984–91, Norddeutsche Landesbank Girozentrale NORD/LB 1991–2004; Chair. Lower Saxony Bd of Trustees, German Econ. Research; Vice-Pres. German Savings Banks Asscn, Chamber of Trade and Commerce, Hanover-Hildesheim, Lower Saxony Foundation; mem. Fed. Asscn of Public Sector Banks, Lower Saxony Savings Banks Asscn; mem. Advisory Bd Deutsche Bundesbank; mem. Bd Carolo-Wilhelmina Technical Univ., Braunschweig.; Hon. Registrar Lower Saxon Inst. for Economic Research, Hon. Consul Kingdom of Denmark; Knight's Cross of the Order of Dannebrog (Denmark); Dr hc (Tech. Univ. Braunschweig) 1996; Lower Saxony Land Medal. *Leisure interests:* art, sailing.

BODINE, Barbara K., BA MA; American diplomatist, academic and university administrator; *Diplomat In Residence and Lecturer of Public Affairs, Woodrow Wilson School of Public and International Affairs, Princeton University;* b. 1948, St Louis, Mo.; ed Univ. of California, Santa Barbara, Fletcher School of Law and Diplomacy, Chinese Univ. of Hong Kong; career mem. Foreign Service, initial tours Hong Kong and Bangkok; Country Officer then Political-Mil. Officer, Bureau of Nr East Affairs, Office of Arabian Peninsula Affairs, later Deputy Office Dir; Congressional Fellow, Office of US Senator Robert Dole; Deputy Prin. Officer in Baghdad, US State Dept. 1980s, Deputy Chief of Mission in Kuwait (held captive by Iraqi invading forces for 137 days) 1990, Assoc. Co-ordinator for Operations early 1990s, Acting Co-ordinator for Counterterrorism 1990s; Dean of Professional Studies, Foreign Service Inst., US State Dept, later Dir of East African Affairs, Amb. to Yemen (arranged release of captured Americans) 1999–2001, US Co-ordinator for Cen. Iraq April–May 2003, Sr Advisor Bureau of Political-Mil. Affairs 2003; fmr Sr Research Fellow and Dir of the Governance Initiative in the Middle East, Kennedy School, Harvard Univ., also fmr Fellow at Center for Public Leadership and Inst. of Politics; fmr Robert Wilhelm Fellow, MIT Center for Int. Studies; currently Diplomat In Residence and Lecturer of Public Affairs, Woodrow Wilson School of Public and Int. Affairs, Princeton Univ.; Treasurer, Alumni Asscns, Univ. Calif., Santa Barbara; Diplomat-in-Residence, Global and Int. Studies Program, Univ. Calif., Santa Barbara 2001–02; Regent-desig. Univ. of Calif. 2002–03, ex-officio Regent 2003–04, Vice-Pres. Alumni Asscns of the Univ. of Calif. 2004–; US Sec. of State Award for Valor (for work in occupied Kuwait) 1990, Univ. Calif., Santa Barbara Distinguished Alumni Award 1991, US Dept of State Distinguished Honor Award (for work in Yemen) 2001. *Address:* Woodrow Wilson School of Public and International Affairs, Princeton University, 432 Robertson Hall, Princeton, NJ 08544-1013, USA (office). *Telephone:* (609) 258-7765 (office). *Fax:* (609) 258-2809 (office). *E-mail:* bbodine@princeton.edu (office). *Website:* wws.princeton.edu (office).

BODKIN, Teresina; Montserratian statistician and government official; *Speaker of the Legislative Council;* fmr secondary school teacher; Dir Dept of Statistics, Govt of Montserrat 1995–2010; Speaker Legis. Council (first woman) 2010–. *Address:* Office of the Speaker, Legislative Council, Brades, Montserrat (office).

BODMAN, Samuel Wright, III, ScD; American academic, business executive and fmr government official; b. 26 Nov. 1938, Chicago, Ill.; s. of Samuel W. Bodman Jr and Lina B. Bodman; m. 1st Lynda Schubert 1984; three c.; m. 2nd Diane Barber 1997; ed Cornell Univ. and Massachusetts Inst. of Tech.; Instructor, MIT 1964, Asst Prof. 1964–68, Assoc. Prof. 1968–70, Dir School of Chemical Eng Practice, American Cyanamid Co. 1965–67; Tech. Dir American Research and Devt Corpn 1964–70; Founding Pnr, Fidelity Ventures Ltd 1970–86, Vice-Pres. Commercial Devt 1971–75, Pres. Fidelity Man. and Research Co. 1976–86, Pres. and COO FMR Corpn (parent holding co. of Fidelity Investments) 1982–86, Exec. Vice-Pres. and Dir Fidelity Group of Mutual Funds 1980–86; Pres. and COO Cabot Corpn 1987–88, Chair., CEO 1988–2002; US Deputy Sec. of Commerce 2002–04; US Sec. of Energy, Washington, DC 2004–09; Dir DuPont, Cabot Corpn, Bank of Boston Corpn, Westvaco Inc., Continental Cablevision Inc., Index Tech. Corpn, John Hancock Financial Services, Thermo Electron Corpn, Security Capital Group Inc.; Trustee Mitre Corpn, Babson Coll., Isabella Stewart Gardner Museum, New England Aquarium; mem. Corpn, MIT, Chair. Chemical Eng Visiting Cttee; mem. American Acad. of Arts and Sciences. *Address:* c/o E.I. DuPont de Nemours and Co., 1007 Market Street, Wilmington, DE 19898, USA. *Telephone:* (302) 774-1000. *Website:* www2.dupont.com/DuPont_Home/en_US/index.html.

BODMER, Sir Walter Fred, Kt, PhD, FRS, FRCPath, FMedSci; British research scientist, academic and university administrator; *Head, Cancer and Immunoge-*

netics Laboratory, Weatherall Institute of Molecular Medicine, University of Oxford; b. 10 Jan. 1936, Frankfurt am Main, Germany; s. of Ernest Julius Bodmer and Sylvia Emily Bodmer; m. Julia Gwynaeth Pilkington 1956 (died 2001); two s. one d.; ed Manchester Grammar School, Clare Coll., Cambridge; Research Fellow, Clare Coll., Cambridge 1958–60, Fellow 1961, Hon. Fellow 1989; Demonstrator, Dept of Genetics, Univ. of Cambridge 1960–61; Fellow, Visiting Asst Prof., Dept of Genetics, Stanford Univ. 1961–62, Asst Prof. 1962–66, Assoc. Prof. 1966–68, Prof. 1968–70; Prof. of Genetics, Univ. of Oxford 1970–79, Prin. Hertford Coll., Oxford 1995–2005, currently Head of Cancer and Immunogenetics Lab., Weatherall Inst. of Molecular Medicine; Vice-Pres. Royal Inst. 1981–82; Pres. Royal Statistical Soc. 1984–85; Pres. British Asscn for Advancement of Science 1987–88, Chair. of Council 1996–2003; mem. Advisory Bd for the Research Councils 1983–88; Chair. BBC Science Consultative Group 1981–87; mem. BBC Gen. Advisory Council; Chair. Bd of Trustees, British Museum (Natural History) 1989–93; Pres. Human Genome Org. 1990–92; Dir-Gen. Imperial Cancer Research Fund 1991–96 (Dir of Research 1979–91); Chancellor Univ. of Salford 1995–2005; Chair. Cttee on the Public Understanding of Science (COPUS) 1990–94; Pres. Int. Fed. of Asscns for the Advancement of Science and Tech. 1992–94; Dir (non-exec.) Fisons PLC 1990–96; Chair. UK Nat. Radiological Protection Bd 1998–2003, Leukaemia Research Fund Medical and Scientific Panel 2003–09; Pres. British Assoc. for Cancer Research 1998–2002; Foreign Assoc. NAS; Hon. Vice-Pres. Research Defence Soc. 1990–; Hon. Fellow, Green Coll., Oxford, Keble Coll., Oxford, Hertford Coll., Oxford, Clare Coll., Cambridge, Royal Soc. of Medicine; Hon. FRCP; Hon. FRCS; Hon. FRSE; Foreign Hon. mem. American Acad. of Arts and Sciences, American Asscn of Immunologists, Companion of Trinity Laban 2008; Hon. MD (Bologna, Birmingham); Hon. DSc (Bath, Oxford, Hull, Edin.) 1990, (Aberdeen, Lancaster) 1994, (London, Plymouth, Salford) 1996, (UMIST) 1997; Hon. DUniv (Surrey) 1990; William Allan Memorial Award, American Soc. of Human Genetics 1980, Conway Evans Prize, Royal Coll. of Physicians/Royal Soc. 1982, Rabbi Shai Shacknai Memorial Prize Lectureship in Immunology and Cancer Research 1983, John Alexander Memorial Prize and Lectureship, Univ. of Pennsylvania Medical School 1984, Royal Inst. Christmas Lecturer 1984, Rose Payne Distinguished Scientist Lectureship 1985, Ellison Cliffe Lecture and Medal 1987, Neil Hamilton-Fairley Medal, Royal Coll. of Physicians 1990, Faraday Award, Royal Soc. 1994, Dalton Medal, Manchester Literary and Philosophical Soc. 2002, D.K. Ludwig Award 2002, Seroussi Research Award 2003, Royal Medal, Royal Soc. 2013. *Publications:* co-author: The Genetics of Human Populations 1971, Our Future Inheritance – Choice or Chance? 1974, Genetics, Evolution and Man 1976, The Book of Man 1994; more than 700 papers in scientific and medical journals. *Leisure interests:* playing piano, riding, swimming, scuba diving. *Address:* Weatherall Institute of Molecular Medicine, University of Oxford, John Radcliffe Hospital, Oxford OX3 9DS, England (office). *Telephone:* (1865) 222356 (office). *Fax:* (1865) 222431 (office). *E-mail:* walter.bodmer@hertford.ox.ac.uk (office). *Website:* www .imm.ox.ac.uk (office).

BODROV, Sergey Vladimirovich; Russian screenwriter and film director; b. 28 June 1948, Khabarovsk; m. Carolyn Cavallaro; one s. (died 2002); ed Inst. of Energetics, All-Union Inst. of Cinematography. *Films include:* Golosa voyny 1974, Balamut (writer) 1978, Lyubimaya zhenshchina mekhanika Gavrilova (writer) 1981, Molodye lyudi (writer) 1983, Sladkiy sok vnutri travy (also writer) 1984), Yurka - syn komandira (writer) 1984, Ochen vazhnaya persona (writer) 1984, Neprofessionaly (also writer) 1985, Ne khodite, devki, zamuzh (writer) 1985, Ya tebya nenavizhu (also writer) (TV) 1986, Moy dom na zelyonykh kholmakh (writer) 1986, Na pomoshch, brattsy! (writer) 1988, Frantsuz (writer) 1988, S.E.R. - Svoboda eto rai (also writer) 1989, Krejzi 1989, Katala (also writer) 1989, ...I vsya lyubov (writer) 1989, Nash chelovek v San-Remo (writer) 1990, Ya khotela uvidet angelov (also writer) 1992, Belyy korol, krasnaya koroleva (Russkie) (also writer) 1992, Somebody to Love (writer) 1994, Kavkazskiy plennik (also writer) (Nika Award) 1996, Est - Ouest (writer) 1999, Running Free 1999, Syostry (story) 2001, The Quickie (also writer) 2001, Bear's Kiss (also writer) 2002, Shiza (writer) 2004, Nomad 2004, Mongol: Part One (also writer) (Nika Award) 2007, A Yakuza's Daughter Never Cries (also writer) 2010. *Address:* 117513 Moscow, Leninsky prosp. 129, korp. 3, Apt 20, Russia. *Telephone:* (495) 438-38-04.

BOECKMANN, Alan Lee, BEng; American construction industry executive; ed Univ. of Arizona; joined Fluor Corpn as engineer 1974, various man. positions in Calif., Tex., SC, S Africa and Venezuela, becoming Vice-Pres., DuPont Alliance and Head of Eng Div., also Pres. and CEO Fluor Daniel, mem. Bd of Dirs, Pres. and CEO Fluor Corpn 2001–02, Chair. and CEO 2002–11, Chair. (non-exec.) 2011–12; Chair. Eng and Construction Govs, World Econ. Forum; mem. Bd of Dirs Burlington Northern Santa Fe, LLC 2001–, Burlington Northern Santa Fe, Nat. Petroleum Council 2001–, BHP Billiton 2008–11, Sempra Energy 2011–, Archer Daniels Midland Co. 2004–08, 2012–, American Petroleum Inst., Boys and Girls Clubs of America, Southern Methodist Univ.'s Cox School of Business; mem. Business Roundtable, World Econ. Forum, Univ. of Arizona's Coll. of Eng's Industry Advisory Council; was instrumental in formation of World Econ. Forum's Partnering Against Corruption Initiative 2004. *Address:* c/o Fluor Corpn, 6700 Las Colinas Blvd, Irving, TX 75039, USA. *E-mail:* info@fluor.com.

BOEDHOE, Wonnie; Suriname economist and politician; b. 1962; fmr Lecturer, Anton de Kom Univ., Paramaribo; Adviser, Coopers & Lybrand/Warwick Research Inst. Suriname Structural Adjustment Programme 1992–96; fmr Researcher, Ministry of Transport, Trade and Industry, then Ministry of Planning and Devt; Dir Nationale Ontwikkelings Bank van Suriname NV –2010; Minister of Finance 2010–11; mem. Megacombinatie political alliance (MC). *Address:* c/o Ministry of Finance, Tamarindelaan 3, Paramaribo, Suriname.

BOEDIONO, MEcons, PhD; Indonesian academic, government official and fmr central banker; *Vice-President;* b. 25 Feb. 1943, Blitar, Jawa Timur; ed Univ. of Western Australia, Monash Univ., Melbourne, Australia, Wharton School, Univ. of Penn., USA; fmr Lecturer, Faculty of Econs, Gajah Mada Univ., Togyakarta; Deputy Gov. Bank Indonesia in charge of fiscal monetary policy 1997–98, Gov. Bank Indonesia 2008–09; State Minister for Nat. Planning and Devt 1998–99; Minister of Finance and State Enterprises Devt 2001–04; Coordinating Minister for the Economy 2005–08; Vice-Pres. of Indonesia 2009–. *Address:* Office of the Vice-President, Jalan Merdeka Selatan 6, Jakarta Pusat, Indonesia (office). *Telephone:* (21) 363539 (office).

BOEDORO, Philip; Ni-Vanuatu politician; *Speaker of the Parliament;* b. 21 May 1958, Maewo; ed Voreas High School; fmr police officer; fmrly self-employed in own security business; MP for Maewo Constituency 2002–, Chair. Parl. Institutional Cttee, Speaker of Parl. 2013–; mem. Vanuaaku Pati (VP). *Address:* Parliament of Vanuatu, PMB 9025, Port Vila, Vanuatu (office). *Telephone:* 22229 (office). *Fax:* 24330 (office). *Website:* www.parliament.gov.vu (office).

BOEHM, Gottfried Karl, DPhil; German art historian and academic; *Professor of Art History, University of Basel;* b. 19 Sept. 1942, Braunau, Bohemia; s. of Karl Boehm and Olga Boehm; m. Margaret Hunold 1980; one d.; ed Univs of Cologne, Vienna and Heidelberg; Lecturer in History of Art, Ruhr Univ. Bochum 1975–79, Prof. 1977; Prof. of History of Art, Justus Liebig Univ., Giessen 1979–86, Univ. of Basel 1986–; Dir Nat. Centre of Competence in Research; Perm. Fellow, Inst. für die Wissenschaften vom Menschen, Vienna 1981–; Fellow, Wissenschaftskolleg, Berlin 2001–02; Corresp. mem. Heidelberger Acad. of Sciences 2006–; Ehrenkreuz für Wissenschaft und Kunst (First Class) (Austria). *Publications:* Studien zur Perspektivität, Philosophie und Kunst in der frühen Neuzeit 1969, Zur Dialektik der ästhetischen Grenze 1973, Philosophische Hermeneutik 1976, Die Hermeneutik und die Wissenschaften 1978, Bildnis und Individuum, Über den Ursprung der Porträtmalerei in der italienischen Renaissance 1985, Paul Cézanne, Montagne Sainte-Victoire 1988, Konrad Fiedler, Schriften zur Kunst 1991, Was ist ein Bild? 1994, Beschreibungskunst-Kunstbeschreibung. Ekphrasis von der Antike bis zut Gegenwart 1995, Canto d'amore. Klassizistische Moderne in Musik und bildender Kunst 1996, Paul Cézanne und die Moderne 1999, Der Maler Max Weiler. Das Geistige in der Natur 2001, Homo Pictor 2001, Zwischen-Räume. Malerei, Relief und Skulptur im Werk von Ellsworth Kelly 2002, Der Topos des Lebendigen: Bildgeschichte und ästhetische Erfahrung (in Dimensionen ästhetische Erfahrung) 2003, Mit durchdringendem Blick 2003, Die Härte der Grossen Dinge: Arp und Schwitters in ihren frühen Jahren 2004, Jenseits der Sprache? Anmerkungen zur Logik der Bilder (in Iconic Turn: Die Neue Macht der Bilder) 2004, Ausdruck und Dekoration: Henri Matisse auf dem Weg zu sich selbst 2005, Zeit-Räume. Zum Begriff des plastischen Raumes. Im Schatten von Lessings 'Laokoon' 2006, Das Ende als Anfang – Eine Reflexionsfigur der modernen Kunst, in: End of Art – Endings in Art / La fin de l'art – Les fins dans les arts / Ende der Kunst – Enden in der Kunst 2006, Unbestimmtheit. Zur Logik des Bildes, in: Bild und Einbildungskraft 2006, Wie Bilder Sinn erzeugen 2007. *Address:* Kunstgeschichtliches Seminar, St Alban-Graben-8, 4051 Basel (office); Sevogelplatz 1, 4051 Basel, Switzerland (home). *Telephone:* (61) 2066292 (office); (61) 3116241 (home). *Fax:* (61) 2066297 (office). *E-mail:* gottfried.boehm@unibas.ch (office). *Website:* www .unibas.ch/kunsthist (office); www.eikones.ch (home).

BOEHM, Peter M., BA, MA, PhD; Canadian diplomatist; *Associate Deputy Minister of Foreign Affairs;* b. 26 April 1954, Kitchener, Ont.; ed Wilfrid Laurier Univ., Waterloo, Ont., Norman Paterson School of Int. Affairs, Carleton Univ., Ottawa, Ont., Univ. of Edinburgh, UK; joined Canadian Foreign Service 1981, held several positions at Dept of Foreign Affairs and Int. Trade, including Dir of Econ. Summit Div. in Policy Staff of Dept, and Co-ordinator of Halifax G-7 Econ. Summit 1995, apptd Minister (Political and Public Affairs), Embassy in Washington, DC 1997, Amb. and Perm. Rep. to OAS, Washington, DC 1997–2005; Asst Deputy Minister, N America, Dept of Foreign Affairs and Int. Trade 2005–08; Amb. to Germany 2008–12; Assoc. Deputy Minister of Foreign Affairs 2012–; Commonwealth Scholarship to Univ. of Edinburgh 1978, Canadian Foreign Service Officer Award for contrib. to establishment of peace in Cen. America 1993, Public Service of Canada's Outstanding Achievement Award. *Address:* Foreign Affairs, Trade and Development Canada, 125 Sussex Drive, Ottawa, ON K1A 0G2, Canada (office). *Telephone:* (613) 944-2771 (office). *Fax:* (613) 947-8497 (office). *E-mail:* peter.boehm@international.gc.ca (office). *Website:* www.international.gc.ca (office).

BOEHNER, John, BA; American politician; *Speaker of the House of Representatives;* b. 17 Nov. 1949, Cincinnati, Ohio; s. of Earl Henry Boehner and Mary Anne Boehner; m. Debbie Boehner 1973; two d.; ed Xavier Univ., Cincinnati; early career as Sale Rep. then Pres. Nucite Sales; Trustee, Union Township, Ohio 1982–84; mem. Ohio State Legislature 1984–90; mem. US House of Reps, Washington, DC 1990–, Chair. House Cttee on Educ. and the Workforce 2001–06, fmr mem. House Agric. Cttee, House Majority Leader 2006–07, House Minority Leader 2007–11, Speaker of the House 2011–; ranked by Forbes magazine amongst The World's Most Powerful People (67th) 2011, (65th) 2012, (66th) 2013. *Leisure interests:* golf, wine. *Address:* Office of the Speaker, H-232 The Capitol, Washington, DC 20515 (office); 1011 Longworth H.O.B., Washington, DC 20515, USA (office). *Telephone:* (202) 225-0600 (Office of the Speaker) (office); (202) 225-6205 (office). *Fax:* (202) 225-5117 (Office of the Speaker) (office); (202) 225-0704 (office). *Website:* www .speaker.gov (office); johnboehner.house.gov (office).

BOEL, (Else) Mariann Fischer; Danish politician; b. 15 April 1943, Aasum, Funen; d. of Hans Boel and Valborg Boel; Man. Sec. at export co., Copenhagen 1965–67, Finance Man. 1967–71; mem. Munkebo Municipal Council 1982–91, 1994–97, Second Deputy Mayor 1986–90; Chair. Liberal Party Kerteminde constituency 1987–89; mem. Folketing for Funen Co. 1990–, Chair. Food, Agric. and Fisheries Cttee 1994–98, Trade and Industry Cttee 1998–99, Fiscal Affairs Cttee 1998–99; Minister of Food, Agric. and Fisheries 2001–04; EU Commr for Agric. and Rural Devt 2004–10; mem. Cen. Bd, Liberal Party 1990–, mem. Man. Cttee Parl. Liberal Party 1990–; Chair. High Schools' Secr. 1993–; mem. Nat. Assessment Council 1994–98, Nat. Tax Tribunal 1998–2001; mem. Cttee of Reps Østifterne 1991–; mem. Bd of Govs Boel Fund 1992–. *Address:* c/o Venstre, Søllerødvej 30, 2840 Holte (office); Dr. Tværgade 59, 3. sal, 1302 Copenhagen K, Denmark.

BOER, Dick; Dutch business executive; *Chairman of the Management Board and CEO, Royal Ahold NV;* b. 31 Aug. 1957; spent more than 17 years in various retail positions for SHV Holdings in the Netherlands and abroad, and for Unigro NV; joined Ahold as CEO Ahold Czech Repub. 1998, Pres. and CEO Albert Heijn 2000–03, Pres. and CEO Ahold's Dutch operating cos 2003–06, COO Ahold Europe 2006–11, mem. Corp. Exec. Bd 2007, Chair. Man. Bd and CEO Royal Ahold NV 2011–; Pres. European Retail Round Table; mem. Exec. Bd The Confederation of Netherlands Industry and Employers (VNO-NCW), Advisory Bd G-star, Advisory Bd Red Cross Hosp. Beverwijk, Supervisory Bd AMS Sourcing BV. *Address:* Royal Ahold NV, Piet Heinkade 167–173, 1019 GM Amsterdam, Netherlands (office).

Telephone: (20) 509-51-00 (office). *Fax:* (20) 509-51-10 (office). *E-mail:* info@ahold .com (office). *Website:* www.ahold.com (office).

BOESAK, Rev. Allan; South African clergyman and politician; b. 23 Feb. 1946, Kakamas; s. of Andreas Boesak and Sarah Helena Boesak; m. 1st Dorothy Rose Martin 1969; one s. three d.; m. 2nd Elna Botha 1991; two d.; ed Univ. of Western Cape, Theological Univ., Kampen, Netherlands, Union Theological Seminary; prominent anti-apartheid campaigner; elected Pres. World Alliance of Reformed Churches, Ottawa 1982; co-f. United Democratic Front 1983; Pres. Asscn of Christian Students in SA 1984–90; Vice-Pres. South African Council of Churches 1984–87; fmr mem. Dutch Reformed Mission Church; mem., African Nat. Congress (ANC) 1991–2008, Leader in Western Cape 1991–98; Dir Foundation for Peace and Justice 1991; faced 32 theft and corruption charges 1997; on trial for fraud Aug. 1998; sentenced to six years' imprisonment March 1999, sentence halved on appeal May 2000; conviction for misuse of aid money set aside, conviction for theft upheld 2000; released on parole June 2001; granted presidential pardon 2005; mem. Congress of the People 2008–09; Hon. DD (Victoria) 1983, (Yale) 1984, (Interde-nominational Theological Center, Atlanta) 1985; Hon. DIur (Warwick) 1989; Third World Prize 1989. *Publications:* Farewell to Innocence 1976, Black and Reformed 1984, Walking on Thorns 1984, A Call for an End to Unjust Rule 1986, If This is Treason, I am Guilty (Speeches) 1988, Comfort and Protest 1988, Shadows of the Light 1996, Tot Sterwens Toe (poems) 2001, Running with Horses: Reflections of an Accidental Politician 2009. *Leisure interests:* reading, walking, sports, music. *Address:* 16 Villa Bellini, Constantia Street, Strand 7140, South Africa (home). *Telephone:* (21) 854-4937 (home). *E-mail:* boesak@mweb.co.za (home).

BOFF, Leonardo Genezio Darci, DPhil, DTheol; Brazilian academic, writer and editor; b. 14 Dec. 1938, Concórdia, Santa Catarina; s. of Mansueto Boff and Regina Fontana Boff; ed Inst. Teológico Franciscano, Petrópolis, Univ. of Munich, Germany; Prof. of Systematic Theology and of Franciscan Spirituality, Inst. Teológico Franciscano, Petrópolis, Rio de Janeiro 1971–92, also Prof. of Theology of Liberation; Adviser to Latin American Conf. of Religions (CLAR) 1971–80, to Nat. Conf. of Brazilian Bishops (CNBB) 1971–80; mem. Editorial Bd of Revista Eclesiástica Brasileira 1971–92; mem. Bd of Dirs Vozes publishing house 1971–92; Pres. Bd of Eds, Theology and Liberation collection 1985; mem. Editorial Bd Concilium; ordered by Roman Curia to period of 'obedient silence' 1985–86; Dr hc (Turin, Lund); Paz y Justicia Award, Barcelona, Menschenrechte in der Kirche Award, Herbert Haag Foundation, FRG and Switzerland, Right Livelihood Award, Stockholm 2001. *Publications include:* over 60 books including Jesus Christ Liberator 1971, Die Kirche als Sakrament im Horizont der Welterfahrung 1972, Theology of Captivity and Liberation 1972, Ecclesiogenesis 1977, The Maternal Face of God 1979, Church: Charisma and Power 1980, Theology Listening to People 1981, St Francis: A Model for Human Liberation 1984, Trinity and Society 1988, The Gospel of the Cosmic Christ 1989, The New Evangelization: The Perspective of the Oppressed 1990, Ecology and Spirituality 1991, Mística e Espiritualidade 1994, Nova Era: a Consciência Planetária 1994, Igreja: entre Norte e Sul 1995, Ecology: Cry of the Earth, Cry of the Poor 1995, Casamento entre o céu e a terra 2001, Princípio de compaixão e cuidado 2001, Fundamentalismo. A globalização e o futuro da humanidade 2002, Liberating Grace 2005, Fundamen-talism, Terrorism and the Future of Humanity 2007, Church, Charism and Power 2011. *Leisure interests:* gardening, social work at the 'favelas', child minding. *E-mail:* contato@leonardoboff.com (office). *Website:* leonardoboff.com

BOFFO, Dino; Italian journalist and editor; *Editor-in-Chief, TV2000;* b. 19 Aug. 1952, Asolo; Ed.-in-Chief and Man. Dir Avvenire (daily newspaper) and News Ed. SAT 2000 satellite TV network 1994–2009; Ed.-in-Chief TV2000 (TV network) 2010–; Sec.-Gen. Azione Cattolica Italiana; taught course on communications and citizenship at Catholic Univ. of the Sacred Heart, Milan 2002–03;; Premio Ambrogino d'oro 2010. *Address:* TV2000, Via Aurelia, 796 00165 Rome, Italy (office). *Telephone:* (6) 66508-918 (office). *Fax:* (6) 66508-737 (office). *E-mail:* dir .rete@tv2000.it (office). *Website:* www.tv2000.it (office).

BOFILL, Ricardo; Spanish architect; b. 5 Dec. 1939, Barcelona; s. of Emilio Bofill and Maria Levi; two s.; ed Ecole Française, Barcelona, architectural studies in Geneva; Founder-mem. and leader, Taller de Arquitectura, Paris, Barcelona; Dr hc (Univ. of Hamburg, Germany) 1968, (Metz Univ., France) 1995; Hon. Fellow, FAIA 1985, Bund Deutscher Architekter (BDA) Bonn, Germany 1996; Associació de Disseny Industrial del Foment de les Arts Decoratives (ADI-FAD) Award in Architecture for building on calle Nicaragua 99, Barcelona, Spain 1963, American Soc. of Interior Designers Int. Prize, New York, 1978, Architecte Agrée Degree Ordre National des Architectes, Paris, France 1979, Ciudad de Barcelona Prize of Architecture 1980, Architect in Belgium, Ordre des Architectes Conseil du Brabant, Brussels 1989, Chicago Architecture Award, Ill. Council/American Inst. of Architects/Architectural Record, Chicago 1989, Académie Internationale de Philosophie de lArt, Bern, Switzerland 1989, Lifetime Achievement Award, Israeli Building Center 2009; Officier de l'Ordre des Arts et des Lettres Degree, Ministry of Culture, Paris, France 1984. *Works include:* headquarters for Cartier, Christian Dior, Axa Insurance, BNP Paribas, JP Morgan, Shiseido; also Shangri-la Hotel, Beijing, Corso Karlin and Corso II, Prague, Donnelley Building, Chicago, Metz Theatre, Barcelona Theatre, Rothschild wine cellars, Palacio de Congresos, Madrid, Shepherd School of Music, Houston, Tex., USA. *Publications:* Memory Future 1993, L'Architecture des villes (co-author) 1995, Spazi di una vita (co-author) 1996. *Leisure interests:* traveliing, sea, desert. *Address:* Taller de Arquitectura, 14 Avenida Industria, 08960 Saint Just Desvern, Barcelona, Spain (office). *Telephone:* (3) 4999900 (office). *Fax:* (3) 4999950 (office). *E-mail:* rbofill@ bofill.com (office). *Website:* www.bofill.com (office).

BOFINGER, Helge; German architect and academic; *Professor of Design and Building Theory, Faculty of Architecture, University of Dortmund;* b. 30 March 1940, Stettin/Pommern; s. of Christa Bofinger and Hans Ullrich Bofinger; m. Margret Schreib Schmitz-Mathies 1965; ed Ratsgymnasium Goslar, Tech. Univ. of Brunswick; Scientific Asst, Tech. Univ. of Brunswick 1968–69; est. Bofinger & Partner (with wife), Brunswick 1969–81, Berlin 1974–, Wiesbaden 1978–; Visiting Prof., Univ. of Dortmund 1979–81, Prof. of Design and Building Theory, Faculty of Architecture 1986–; Hon. Prof., Univ. of Buenos Aires, Argentina 1985; Visiting Prof. and Lecturer, Venice, Amsterdam, Rotterdam, Buenos Aires, São Paulo, Brasília, Curitiba, Shanghai 1984–91; Hon. Prof. (Tbilisi) 1995; Deubau Special Prize 1979, German Architectural Prize 1983, Hon. Prize, Transcaucasian

Biennale, Tbilisi 1988, German Civil Engineering Prize 1992, Renault Traffic Award 2002. *Publications:* Architecture in Germany 1979, Young Architects in Europe 1983, Helmut Jacoby – Master of Architectural Drawing (ed.); numerous contribs to German and int. architectural magazines. *Address:* Bofinger & Partner Architekten Architects, Biebricher Allee 49, 65187 Wiesbaden, Germany (office). *Telephone:* (611) 87094 (office). *Fax:* (611) 87095 (office). *E-mail:* bofinger@bofinger -partner.de (office). *Website:* www.bofinger-partner.de (office).

BOGAN, Sir Nagora Y., MBE, KBE, LLB; Papua New Guinea diplomatist and business executive; *Chairman, Nambawan Super Ltd;* b. Sept. 1956, Lae; m. Lady Nohoranie; two c.; ed Univ. of Papua New Guinea; fmr Sr Civil Servant, Internal Revenue Service; Oceania Del. to Commonwealth Asscn of Tax Admin 1988–91; Chair. Policy Working Group on Tax and Customs, Govt of Papua New Guinea 1988–91, Chair. Man. Cttee 1991–95, First Commr Gen. Internal Revenue Comm. 1992–95; Amb. to USA (also accred to Mexico and Canada) 1995–2003; Chair. Bd of Dirs Public Officers Superannuation Fund (public sector pension fund) 2002–; Chair. Nambawan Super Ltd 2009–; Pres. Indigenous Business Council; Chan-cellor, Papua New Guinea Univ. of Technology (Unitech) 2012–; mem. Bd of Dirs Mapai Transport Ltd. *Address:* Nambawan Super Ltd, Level 6, Era Rumana Building, Port Moresby, NCD, Papua New Guinea (office). *Website:* www .nambawansuper.com.pg (office).

BOGATIKOV, Oleg A., PhD; Russian geologist and academic; *Head, Zavaritski Laboratory of General Petrography, Institute of Geology of Ore Deposits, Petrography, Mineralogy and Geochemistry, Russian Academy of Sciences;* b. 15 Dec. 1934; m.; two d.; ed Moscow Inst. of Geological Survey; Jr, then Sr Researcher, Scientific Sec., Lead Researcher, Inst. of Geology of Ore Deposits, Petrography, Mineralogy and Geochemistry 1957–, Head of Zavaritski Lab. of Gen. Petrography 1975–, also currently Chair. Interdisciplinary Petrographic Cttee; mem. Russian Acad. of Sciences (Sec. 2002); Ed.-in-Chief Petrologiya; A. E. Fersman Prize 1985, State Prize of the Russian Fed. 1997, Prize of the Govt of the Russian Fed. 1999. *Publications include:* numerous scientific articles and monographs. *Leisure interest:* travelling. *Address:* Institute of Geology of Ore Deposits, Petrography, Mineralogy and Geochemistry, Russian Academy of Sciences, 119017 Moscow, Staromonetny Per., 35, Russia (office). *Telephone:* (495) 951-72-70 (office). *Fax:* (495) 951-15-87 (office). *E-mail:* oleg@igem.ru (office). *Website:* www.igem.ru (office).

BOGDANCHIKOV, Sergey, DSc; Russian petroleum industry executive; b. 10 Aug. 1957; ed Buguruslansky Oil Tech. School, Ufa Petroleum Inst.; began career in oil and gas industry, Sakhalin Island 1981; joined Sakhalinmornefftegaz 1988, Gen. Dir 1993–97; mem. Bd of Dirs Rosneft Oil Co. 1995–2010, Vice-Pres. 1997–98, Chair. Man. Bd and Pres. 1998–2010, Dir (non-exec.) 2010–, mem. Bd of Dirs OJSC Rosneftegaz; mem. Union of Oil and Gas Producers of Russia; Pres. Union of All-Russian Public Asscns 'All-Russian Asscn of Summer Olympic Sports'. *Address:* c/o Rosneft Oil Co., Moscow 115998, 26/1, Sofiyskaya Embankment, 1, GSP-8, Russia.

BOGDANOR, Vernon, CBE, MA, FRSA, FBA; British academic; *Research Professor, Institute of Contemporary History, King's College London;* b. 16 July 1943, London, England; s. of Harry Bogdanor and Rosa Weinger; m. Judith Beckett 1972 (divorced 2000); two s.; m. 2nd Sonia Robertson 2009; ed Queen's Coll. and Nuffield Coll., Oxford; Fellow, Brasenose Coll., Oxford 1966–2010, Sr Tutor 1979–85, 1996–97; mem. Council of Hansard Soc. for Parl. Govt 1981–97; Special Adviser, House of Lords Select Cttee on European Communities 1982–83; adviser to Govts of Czech Repub., Slovakia, Hungary and Israel on constitutional and electoral matters 1988–; Reader in Govt, Univ. of Oxford 1989–96, Prof. of Govt 1996–2010, Prof. Emer. 2010–; Gresham Prof. of Law, Gresham Coll., London 2004–07; Research Prof., Inst. of Contemporary History, King's Coll., London 2010–; mem. UK del. to CSCE Conf., Oslo 1991; Special Adviser, House of Commons Public Service Cttee 1996; mem. Int. Advisory Council, The Israel Democracy Inst. 2010–; Fellow, Acad. of Social Sciences 2009; Hon. Fellow, Soc. for Advanced Legal Studies 1997, Queen's Coll., Oxford 2009, Hon. Bencher, Middle Temple 2010; Chevalier, Légion d'honneur 2009; Hon. DLitt (Kent) 2010; Mishcon Lecturer 1994, Magna Carta Lecturer 2006, Sir Isaiah Berlin Prize for Lifetime Contribution to Political Studies. *Publications include:* Devolution 1979, The People and the Party System 1981, Multi-party Politics and the Constitution 1983, What is Proportional Representation? 1984, The Blackwell Encyclopaedia of Political Institutions (ed.) 1987, Comparing Constitutions (co-author) 1995, The Monarchy and the Constitution 1995, Politics and the Constitution 1996, Power and the People 1997, Devolution in the United Kingdom 1999, The British Constitution in the Twentieth Century (ed.) 2003, Joined-Up Government (ed.) 2005, The New British Constitution 2009, From New Jerusalem to New Labour: British Prime Ministers from Attlee to Blair (ed.) 2010, The Coalition and the Constitution 2011. *Leisure interests:* music, walking, talking. *Address:* Institute for Contemporary History, Strand Building, King's College, Strand, London, WC2R 2LS (office); 21 Edmunds Walk, East Finchley, London, N2 0HU, England (home).

BOGDANOV, Michael, MA, DLitt, FRWCMD; British theatre, film and televi-sion director and writer; *Artistic Director, Wales Theatre Company;* b. 15 Dec. 1938, London, England; s. of Francis Bogdin and Rhoda Rees; m. 1st Patricia Ann Warwick 1966; two s. one d.; m. 2nd Ulrike Engelbrecht 2000; one s. one d.; ed Trinity Coll., Dublin, Munich Univ., Sorbonne, Paris; trained as Producer/Dir, BBC 1966; Producer/Dir Radio Telefís Eireann 1966–69; Asst Dir RSC 1970–71; Assoc. Dir Tyneside Theatre Co. 1971–73; Assoc. Dir Leicester Haymarket Theatre 1973, also Artistic Dir Phoenix Theatre 1973–77; Dir Young Vic Theatre 1978–80; Assoc. Dir Royal Nat. Theatre 1980–88; f. (with Michael Pennington) English Shakespeare Co. 1986, Artistic Dir 1986–98; Intendant Deutsches Schauspiel-haus, Hamburg 1988–92; Artistic Dir, Wales Theatre Co. 2003–; Sr Fellow, De Montfort Univ. 1992; Assoc. Dir Peter Brook (q.v.)'s production of A Midsummer Night's Dream, RSC 1971; Producer/Dir UK Holocaust Memorial Day Event, Cardiff 2006; Vice-Chair. Dirs Guild of GB; Chair. Welsh Arts Awards; Fellow, Swansea Univ. 2008; mem. Academi, Wales; Hon. Prof., Univ. of Wales 1993, Univ. of Glamorgan 2009, Univ. of Sunderland 1997; Hon. Fellow, Welsh Coll. of Music and Drama 1994; Hon. Fellow, in Drama, Trinity Coll., Dublin 1997; Hon. Fellow, Univ. of Swansea 2009, Shakespeare Birthplace Trust 2010; Dr hc (Trinity Coll., Dublin) 2005. *Plays include:* Two Gentlemen of Verona, Teatro Escobar, São Paulo, Brazil, Rabelais (Jean-Louis Barrault) 1971, Sir Gawain and the Green Knight

1977, Hunchback of Notre Dame, Nat. Theatre 1977, The Taming of the Shrew, RSC, Hamlet, Stuttgart and Düsseldorf (Soc. of West End Theatres Dir of the Year 1979) 1978–79, Knight of the Burning Pestle, RSC, The Seagull, Tokyo 1980, The Romans in Britain, Mayor of Zalamea, The Hypochondriac, Uncle Vanya, all for Nat. Theatre; Hiawatha (Nat. Theatre) 1980, 1981, 1982; Lorenzaccio, You Can't Take it With You, Nat. Theatre 1983; Hamlet, Dublin Abbey Theatre 1983, Romeo and Juliet, Tokyo Imperial Theatre (Japan Critics Circle Dir of the Year 1983) 1983; The Story of a Horse, Ancient Mariner, both for Nat. Theatre 1984; The Mayor of Zalamea, Washington 1984, Measure for Measure, Stratford, Ont. (Toronto Critics Dir of the Year Award 1985) 1985, Donnerstag aus Licht, Covent Garden 1985, Romeo and Juliet, RSC 1986, Julius Caesar, Hamburg 1986, Henry IV (parts I and II), Henry V, UK, Europe, Canada, USA 1986–87, Reineke Fuchs, Hamburg 1987, The Wars of the Roses (seven-play history cycle) (Dir of the Year, Laurence Olivier Award 1989) 1987–89; Montag aus Licht, (Stockhausen) La Scala 1988; Coriolanus, The Winter's Tale, Macbeth, The Tempest, The Venetian Twins, RSC 1993, 1998, 1999, Peer Gynt 1995, 1999, Faust 1996, Macbeth 1997, Timon of Athens 1997, Troilus and Cressida 2000, The Merry Wives of Windsor 2001, Ludlow Festival 2002–04, A Servant of Two Masters, Hamburg 2003, Under Milk Wood (50th Anniversary production for Wales Theatre Co.) 2003–04, Lady Hamilton, Hamburg 2004, Twelfth Night, Cymbeline and The Merchant of Venice, Wales Theatre Co. 2004, Lone Star Love (The Merry Wives of Texas), New York 2004, Amazing Grace and Hamlet, Wales Theatre Co. 2005, Der Garderobier (The Dresser), Hamburg 2006, Fiddler on the Roof, Aberystwyth 2006, A Child's Christmas in Wales 2006, Waiting for Godot, Hamburg (Rolf Mares Prize for Best Dir 2006, Pegasus Prize Best Production 2007), Salto Mortale, Hamburg 2007, Valuing Freedom, Cardiff 2007, Contender, West Side Story, The Servant of Two Masters (all Wales Theatre Co.) 2007, Frost/Nixon and Elling, Hamburg 2008, Ein Bisschen Ruhe vor dem Storm, Hamburg 2009, The Thorn Birds (Wales Theatre Co.) 2009, Sommernachtsdroem, at the opening of the New Ohnsorg Theater, Hamburg 2011, Onkel Vanya, The King's Speech and ROT, Hamburg 2012, Mephisto (world premiere), Hamburg 2013. *Films:* Shakespeare on the Estate (BAFTA Award) 1995, A Light in the Valley (RST Award), The Tempest in Britain (BBC), Macbeth (Granada/Channel 4), The Welsh in Shakespeare (BBC Wales). *Television includes:* Channel 4 series Shakespeare Lives, also for Channel 4, Hiawatha, Macbeth (Channel 4), The Tempest in Bute Town (BBC Wales) 1996, A Light in the Valley (BBC) (Royal TV Soc. Best Regional Film 1999), A Light on the Hill (BBC), A Light in the City (BBC), Killing Time (BBC). *Publications:* Hiawatha 1981, The Magic Drum 1983, Ancient Mariner, Reineke Fuchs 1988, The English Shakespeare Company (jtly) 1992, Shakespeare, the Director's Cut Vol. 1 2004, Vol. 2 2005, Vol. 3 2013, Take As Directed 2013. *Leisure interests:* cricket, reading, music, wine, Celtic history. *Address:* Coach House Productions, 21 Dogo Street, Pontcanna, Cardiff, CF11 9JJ (office); 9 Fairleigh Road, Pobtcanna, Cardiff, CF11 9JT, Wales (home). *Telephone:* (29) 21153726 (office). *E-mail:* mbogdin@hotmail .com. *Website:* www.walestheatrecompany.co.uk (office).

BOGDANOV, Vladimir Leonidovich, DEcon; Russian energy industry execu- tive; *Director-General, OJSC Surgutneftegas;* b. 28 May 1951, Suyerka, Tyumen Oblast; m.; one d.; ed Tiumen Industrial Inst., Acad. of Nat. Economy; worked for Nizhnevartovsk Drilling Admin as Driller Asst, Driller, Sr Engineer, Chief Deputy Technological Dept, Chief of Shift 1973–76; Chief, Sr Technologist, Sr Engineer Surgut Drilling Works Administration No. 2, Industrial Asscn (Surgutneftegas) 1976–78; Chief Deputy Drilling Dept, Deputy CEO, Deputy, Head of Drilling Dept Industrial Asscn (Ugansknegegas) 1978–80; Deputy CEO for Northern regions and Head of Drilling Dept Surgutneftegas 1980–83; Deputy Drilling Chief Glavtyumenneftegas 1983–84; CEO Surgutneftegas (now OJSC Surgutneftegas) 1984–, Chair. and CEO 1990, now Dir-Gen.; Delegate Tyumen Regional Council from Surgut 1985–90; mem. Bd of Dirs Kirishineftteproduct 1994–, Lenneftepro- duct 1994–, Bulk Plant (Ruchi) 1994–, Red Oiler (Krasnyi Neftyanik) 1994–, Onegoneft 1994–, Mosbusinessbank 1996–, ONEXIM Bank 1996–, Nafta Moscow 1997–, AKB Rosbank 2002–; mem. Issuer Council, Fed. Comm. on Securities Market 1999–, Industrial Council 2000–, Steering Cttee, Delovaya Rossiya 2001–; mem. Acad. of Mining Sciences, Acad. of Natural Sciences, Nat. Council on Corp. Governance; Corresp. mem. Acad. of Technological Sciences; Trustee, Global Energy Int. Prize; Fellow of the Technology Academy of the Russian Federation Fellow of the Academy of Mining Sciences of the Russian Federation; Hon. Citizen of Leningradskaya Oblast, Khanty-Mansiysky Autonomous Okrug – Yugra, and two municipal entities of Tyumenskaya Oblast – the city of Surgut and Surgutsky Dist; Order of the Badge of Honour, Order of the Red Banner of Labour, Order of Merit for the Fatherland (IV Degree, III Degree, II Degree), Order of Honour; Entrepreneur of the Year, Russian Union of Industrialists and Entrepreneurs 2000, Medal for Exploitation of Mineral Resources and Devt of the West-Siberian Petroleum Complex, The Honoured Worker of the Russian Oil and Gas Industry; awards granted by the Repub. of Sakha (Yakutia): Badge of Civil Merit, Order of the Polar Star. *Address:* OJSC Surgutneftegas, ul. Kukuyevitskogo 1, Surgut 628415, Tyumen, Russia (office). *Telephone:* (3462) 42-61-33 (office). *Fax:* (3462) 33-32-35 (office). *E-mail:* secret_b@surgutneftegas.ru (office). *Website:* www .surgutneftegas.ru (office).

BOGDANOV, Vsevolod Leonidovich; Russian journalist; *Chairman, Russian Union of Journalists;* b. 6 Feb. 1944, Arkhangelsk Region; m.; three d.; ed Leningrad State Univ.; corresp., ed. in newspapers, radio and TV Magadan 1961–76; Head of Dept of Periodicals, State Cttee of Publs 1976–89; Dir-Gen. TV programmes State Radio and TV Cttee 1989–92; Chair. Russian Union of Journalists 1992–; Prof., Leningrad State Univ.; Pres. Nat. Journalist Trade Union 1999–; Pres. Int. Confed. of Journalists' Unions 1999–. *Leisure interests:* book rarities, fishing, hunting, Russian cuisine, music. *Address:* Russian Union of Journalists, Zubovsky blvd 4, 1199911 Moscow, Russia (office). *Telephone:* (495) 637-51-01 (office). *Fax:* (495) 637-44-55 (office). *E-mail:* inter@ruj.ru (office). *Website:* www.ruj.ru (office).

BOGDANOVICH, Peter; American film director, writer, producer and actor; b. 30 July 1939, Kingston, NY; s. of Borislav Bogdanovich and Herma Bogdanovich (née Robinson); m. 1st Polly Platt 1962 (divorced 1970); two d.; m. 2nd Louise Straten 1988 (divorced 2001); actor, American Shakespeare Festival, Stratford, Conn. 1956, NY Shakespeare Festival 1958; Dir and Producer of off-Broadway plays The Big Knife 1959, Camino Real, Ten Little Indians, Rocket to the Moon 1961, Once in a Lifetime 1964; film feature writer for Esquire, New York Times,

Village Voice, Cahiers du Cinéma, Los Angeles Times, New York Magazine, Vogue, Variety etc. 1961–; Owner The Holly Moon Co. Inc. 1992–; mem. Dirs Guild of America, Writers' Guild of America, Acad. of Motion Picture Arts and Sciences; NY Film Critics' Award 1971 and BAFTA Award for Best Screenplay (The Last Picture Show) 1971, Writers' Guild of America Award for Best Screenplay (What's Up, Doc?) 1972, Pasinetti Award, Critics' Prize, Venice Festival (Saint Jack) 1979 and other awards and prizes. *Films include:* The Wild Angels (2nd unit dir, co-writer, actor) 1966, Targets (dir, co-writer, producer, actor) 1968, The Last Picture Show (dir, co-writer) 1971, Directed by John Ford (dir, writer) 1971, What's Up Doc? (dir, co-writer, producer) 1972, Paper Moon (dir, producer) 1973, Daisy Miller (dir, producer) 1974, At Long Last Love (dir, writer, producer) 1975, Nickelodeon (dir, co-writer) 1976, Saint Jack (dir, co-writer, actor) 1979, They All Laughed (dir, writer) 1981, Mask (dir) 1985, Illegally Yours (dir, producer) 1988, Texasville (dir, producer, writer) 1990, Noises Off (dir, exec. producer) 1992, The Thing Called Love (dir) 1993, Who The Devil Made It (dir) 1997, Mr Jealousy (actor) 1997, Highball (actor) 1997, Coming Soon (actor) 1999, Rated X (actor) 2000, The Independent (actor) 2000, The Cat's Meow (dir) 2003, Scene Stealers (actor) 2003, Infamous (actor) 2006, The Doorman (actor) 2007, Broken English (actor) 2007, Dedication (actor) 2007, The Dukes (actor) 2007, The Fifth Patient (actor) 2007, Humboldt County (actor) 2008, The Doorman (actor) 2008, Queen of the Lot (actor) 2010, Abandoned (actor) 2010. *Television:* The Great Professional; Howard Hawks (co-dir, wrote), BBC 1967, The Sopranos 2000–07; dir: Saintly Switch 1999, The Sopranos 1999, Hustle 2004, The Mystery of Natalie Wood 2004; regular commentator for CBS This Morning 1987–89; actor: Northern Exposure, CBS 1993, Fallen Angels 1995, Painted Word 1995, To Sir With Love II 1996, Naked City: A Killer Christmas 1998. *Publications include:* The Cinema of Orson Welles 1961, The Cinema of Howard Hawks 1962, The Cinema of Alfred Hitchcock 1963, John Ford 1968, Fritz Lang in America 1969, Allan Dwan, the Last Pioneer 1971, Pieces of Time, Peter Bogdanovich on the Movies 1961–85, The Killing of the Unicorn: Dorothy Stratten (1960–80) 1984, A Year and a Day Calendar (ed.) 1991, This is Orson Welles (with Orson Welles) 1992, Who the Devil Made It 1997, Who the Hell's In It? 2004. *Address:* c/o William Pfeiffer, 30 Lane of Acres, Haddonfield, NJ 08033; c/o CAA, 9830 Wilshire Boulevard, Beverly Hills, CA 90212-1804, USA (office).

BOGLE, Ellen Gray; Jamaican diplomatist and government official (retd); b. 9 Oct. 1941, St Andrew; d. of Victor Gray Williams and Eileen Averil (née Rampie); one s. one d.; ed St Andrew High School for Girls, Univ. of the West Indies; Dir Foreign Trade Div., Ministry of Foreign Affairs, with responsibility for formulation of Jamaica's Foreign Trade policy 1978–81; fmr Jamaica Nat. Export Corpn; High Commr in Trinidad & Tobago 1981–89; High Commr in UK 1989–94; fmr Amb., Ministry of Foreign Affairs and Foreign Trade; Amb. and Special Envoy to the Asscn of Caribbean States and CARICOM 1997; fmr Under-Sec. Bilateral and Regional Affairs, Ministry of Foreign Affairs and Foreign Trade; represented Jamaica at numerous int. confs; Int. Trade Consultant, Lascelles DeMercado Co. Ltd 2002–09; Commdr Order of Distinction 1987. *Leisure interests:* gardening, reading, cooking, listening to music. *Address:* c/o Ministry of Foreign Affairs and Foreign Trade, 21 Dominica Drive, Kingston 5, Jamaica (office).

BOGNER, Willy, Jr.; German business executive, film director and fashion designer; *Chairman and Managing Director, Willy Bogner GmbH & Co. KGaA;* b. 23 Jan. 1942, Munich; s. of the late Willy Bogner Sr and Maria Bogner; m. Sonia Ribeiro 1973; ed Altes Realgymnasium, Munich and business and technical studies in Munich and Hohenstein; Chair. and Man. Dir Willy Bogner GmbH & Co. KGaA (sportswear co. f. in 1932 by Willy Bogner Sr); Founder and Man. Willy Bogner Film GmbH, Munich 1968–; mem. German Nat. Olympic Cttee; dir of documen- tary, advertising, sports (especially skiing) films; Bundesverdienstkreuz Medal 1996, Goldene Seidenschleif 1999. *Films include:* Skivision 1974, 1975, 1979, Skifaszination, Ski Fantasie 1981, Crystal Dreams 1982, Feuer und Eis 1986, Feuer, Eis und Dynamit 1990, White Magic 1994, Mountain Magic 1999, Ski to the Max 2001, Skimagination 2009, Magic in Motion 2010; directed ski scene sequences in On Her Majesty's Secret Service 1969, Snow Job 1972, The Spy Who Loved Me 1977, For Your Eyes Only 1981, A View to a Kill 1985. *Achievements include:* several times German ski champion and participated in Winter Olympics, Squaw Valley 1960, Innsbruck 1964 and World Ski Champion- ships, Chamonix 1962, Portillo (Chile) 1966. *Leisure interests:* sport (tennis, skiing, golf), sailing, flying, filming and photography. *Address:* Willy Bogner GmbH & Co. KGaA, Sankt-Veit-Strasse 4, 81673 Munich, Germany (office). *Telephone:* (89) 436060 (office). *Fax:* (89) 43606429 (office). *E-mail:* communication@bogner.com (office). *Website:* www.bogner.com (office).

BOGOLLAGAMA, Rohitha; Sri Lankan lawyer and politician; b. 5 Aug. 1954, Nikaweratiya; m.; two c.; ed Ananda Coll. and Sri Lanka Law Coll.; apptd attorney 1976; fmr Chair. Sri Lanka Cement Corpn, Sathosa Printers; fmr Dir Foreign Employment Bureau; Legal and Political Adviser to Voice of America project in Sri Lanka 1991–99; Chair. and Dir-Gen. Bd of Investment of Sri Lanka 1993–2000; mem. Parl. (United National Party—UNP) 2000–10, served on Parl. Consultative Cttees on Finance, Foreign Affairs, Defence, Industrial Devt and Investment Promotion and Power and Energy 2000–05, Chair. Cttee on Public Enterprises 2005–07, Minister of Industrial Devt 2001–04, of Enterprise Devt and Investment Promotion 2004–07, of Foreign Affairs 2007–10. *Address:* No 40/13, Longdon Place, Colombo 7, Sri Lanka. *Telephone:* (11) 2501944. *Fax:* (11) 2501948. *Website:* www .rohithabogollagama.lk.

BOGOLUBOV, Hennady; Ukrainian business executive and philanthropist; *Co- Owner, Privat Group;* m.; two c.; Co-owner of Privat business group; first made his fortune in 1990 trading in computer parts, then est. one of Ukraine's first privately owned banks, PrivatBank; group now owns stake in oil drilling co. Ukrnafta and has interests in two western Ukrainian oil refineries and ore pits, also controls ferroalloy plants in Ukraine, Romania, Russia, Poland and USA; Pres. Dniprope- trovsk Jewish Philanthropic Fund; f. Bogolyubov Foundation (charity); The Yad Vashem Soc. in Ukraine Award in recognition of his activity on behalf of Yad Vashem 2005. *Leisure interest:* enjoys sports. *Address:* PrivatBank, 50 Naber- ezhnaya Pobedy Street, Dnepropetrovsk, Ukraine (office). *Telephone:* (0562) 390000 (office). *Fax:* (0562) 390271 (office). *E-mail:* hotline@pbank.com.ua (office). *Website:* www.privatbank.ua/info/index3.stm (office). www .bogolyubovfoundation.com.

BOGOMOLOV, Oleg Timofeyevich, DEcon; Russian economist; *Professor and Honorary Director, Institute of International Economic and Political Studies, State University of Management;* b. 20 Aug. 1927, Moscow; s. of T. I. Bogomolov and K. P. Zhelybaeva; m. 1st Larisa Sokolova (died 1962); one s.; m. 2nd Inna Yermakova 1966 (divorced 1977); m. 3rd Tatyana Yarikova 1978; ed Moscow Inst. of Foreign Trade; Ministry of Foreign Trade 1949–50; with CMEA 1954–56; Scientific Inst. for Economical Researches of State Cttee for Planning 1956–62; mem. CPSU 1950–90, Section Chief, Econ. Research Inst., State Planning Cttee 1958–62, Head of Advisors Group (Cen. Cttee of CPSU) 1962–69; Lecturer, then Prof., Moscow Univ. 1967–77; Dir Inst. of Econs of the World Socialist System of Acad. of Sciences (later Inst. of Int. Econ. and Political Studies) 1969–97, Hon. Dir 1997–; mem. Council of Ministers Cttee for Mutual Co-operation with Socialist Countries 1970–86; mem. External Cttee, Int. Econ. Asscn 1992–2011 (Hon. Pres. 2011–); People's Deputy of USSR 1989–91; mem. Advisory Council to the Pres. 1990–92; Deputy, State Duma (Parl.) 1993–95; mem. USSR (now Russian) Acad. of Sciences 1981, Exec. Cttee of Int. Social Science Council, UNESCO 1996–2003; decorations include Order of October Revolution, Order of Red Banner (twice), Orders of Merit to Fatherland (Third and Fourth Degrees). *Publications:* Socialism between Past and Future 1990, Russia and the Commonwealth of Independent States, Trends and Risks of Post-Soviet Development; Market Transformation in Russia: Prospects Still Uncertain 1992, Europe in Global Change 1993, Economics in a Changing World of the Tenth Congress of the IEA 1994, Reformy glazami amerikanskikh i rossiyskikh uchenynykh 1996, Reforms in the Mirror of International Comparison 1998, My Chronicle of Transition Time 2000, Reflections about the Past and the Actualities 2007, World Economy in the Era of Globalization 2007, Nejekonomicheskije grani ekonomiki: nepoznannoje vzaimovlijanije 2008, Non-economic Facets of Economy: Unknown Mutial Influance 2010, Global Economy and Socio-economic Models on the Threshold of a New Epoch 2012. *Leisure interests:* photography, music, tennis. *Address:* Novocheremushrinskaya str. 42-A, 117418 Moscow, Russia (office). *Telephone:* (495) 120-82-00 (office). *Fax:* (495) 120-83-71 (office). *E-mail:* o.t.bogomolov@mail.ru (office). *Website:* bogomolof.com.

BOGOSIAN, Eric, BA; American actor and writer; b. 24 April 1953, Woburn, Mass; s. of Henry Bogosian and Edwina Bogosian; m. Jo Anne Bonney 1990; two c.; ed Univ. of Chicago and Oberlin Coll.; Obie Award 1986, 1990, 1994, Drama Critics' Circle Award, Berlin Film Festival Silver Bear Award 1988. *Films include:* Born in Flames 1983, Special Effects 1984, Chasing the Dragon 1987, Arena Brains 1988, Talk Radio 1988, Suffering Bastards 1989, Dolores Claiborne 1995, Under Siege 2: Dark Territory 1995, The Substance of Fire 1996, Beavis and Butt-Head Do America (voice) 1996, Deconstructing Harry 1997, In the Weeds 2000, Wake Up and Smell the Coffee 2001, Ararat 2002, Igby Goes Down 2002, Charlie's Angels: Full Throttle 2003, Wonderland 2003, King of the Corner 2004, Heights 2004, Blade: Trinity 2004, Heights 2005, Cadillac Records 2008, Don't Go in the Woods 2010. *Television includes:* The Caine Mutiny Court-Martial 1988, Last Flight Out 1990, Witch Hunt 1994, High Incident 1995, A Bright Shining Lie 1998, Blonde 2001, Shot in the Heart 2001, Love Monkey (series) 2006, Law & Order: Criminal Intent (series) 2006–10. *Plays include:* The New World, Men Inside, The Ricky Paul Show, Funhouse, Talk Radio, subUrbia, Griller, Drinking in America, Pounding Nails in the Floor with My Forehead, Sex, Drugs, Rock & Roll, Wake Up and Smell the Coffee, Red Angel, Humpty Dumpty, This is Now!, 100 (Monologues) 2013. *Publications:* Mall 2000, Wasted Beauty 2005, Perforated Heart 2009. *Address:* c/o Emily Gerson-Saines, Brookside Artist Management, 250 West 57th Street, Suite 2303, New York, NY 10107, USA (office).

BOGOV, Dimitar, MSc, MBA; Macedonian economist and central banker; *Governor, National Bank of the Republic of Macedonia;* b. 24 Dec. 1967; ed Univ. of St Cyril and Metodius, Skopje, City Univ. Thessaloniki, Greece, Sheffield Univ., UK; Adviser for Nat. Accounts and Head of Div., State Statistical Office 1993–98, Adviser for Macroeconomics to Gen. Man. 1999–2001; Assoc. Account Man., Macedonian Business Resource Centre 1998–99; Head of Macroeconomics Dept, Ministry of Finance 2001–02; Co-founder and mem. Center for Econ. Analysis, Skopje 2003–07; mem. Supervisory Bd Zito Luks AD Skopje (food mfr) 2005–07; Chief Economist, Stopanska Banka AD 2002–07; Vice-Gov. Nat. Bank of Repub. of Macedonia (central bank) 2007–11, Gov. 2011–; mem. Cttee of Govs, Vienna Econ. Forum. *Address:* Office of the Governor, National Bank of the Republic of Macedonia, 1000 Skopje, bul. Kuzman Josifovski Pitu 1, former Yugoslav republic of Macedonia (office). *Telephone:* (2) 3108108 (office). *Fax:* (2) 3108357 (office). *E-mail:* governorsoffice@nbrm.mk (office). *Website:* www.nbrm.mk (office).

BOHAN, Marc; French couturier; b. 22 Aug. 1926, Paris; s. of Alfred Bohan and Geneviève Baudoux; m. Huguette Rinjonneau (deceased); one d.; ed Lycée Lakanal, Sceaux; Asst with Piguet 1945, later with Molyneux and Patou; Dior org. London 1958, later Paris, Artistic Dir Soc. Christian Dior 1960–89; Artistic Dir Hartnell, London 1990–92; designed costumes for numerous films 1961–89, for Athens Opera 1992–96; Chevalier, Légion d'honneur, Ordre de Saint-Charles (Monaco); Médaille de la Ville de Paris. *Leisure interests:* classical music, theatre, reading, antiques. *Address:* 35 rue du Bourg à Mont, 21400 Châtillon-sur-Seine, France (home).

BOHATYROVA, Raisa Vasylivna, DMedSc; Ukrainian gynaecologist and politician; b. 6 Jan. 1953, Bakal, Chelyabinsk Oblast, Russian SFSR, USSR; m. Ihor Oleksandrovych Bohatyrov; two s.; ed Kharkiv Medical Inst., T. H. Shevchenko Nat. Univ., Kyiv; Machinist, Kramatorg Clothing Factory 1970–71; Intern Physician, Therapy Centre No 2, Horlivka 1977–79; Obstetric Gynaecologist, later Head of Professional Cttee and Deputy Head Physician, Kramatorg Cen. Town Therapy Centre 1979–91; People's Deputy of Ukraine (MP) 1990–94, 2000–08; Deputy, later First Deputy, then Minister of Health 1994–2000; Academic Consultant to Pres. of Ukraine 2000–; mem. Party of Regions –2008, Leader Parl. faction in Verkhovna Rada (Parl.) 2002–08; mem. Parl. Ass., Council of Europe 2006–08; Chair. Nat. Security and Defence Council 2007–12; Deputy Prime Minister 2012–14; Minister of Health 2012–14 (dismissed); Sec., Supervisory Council, 'Ukraina–Dityam' Nat. Social Protection Fund for Mothers and Children 1997–2003; Hon. Pres. Chamber of Tendering of Ukraine 2006–07; Hon. Citizen of Donetsk Oblast 2007; Order of St Stanislaus 1999, Honoured Physician of Ukraine 2001, Order of Princess Olha (Third Degree) 2002; State Prize of Ukraine in Science and Tech. 1999, ranked by Focus magazine amongst the top 10 most influential women in Ukraine 2006–10. *Address:* c/o Ministry of Health, 01021 Kyiv, vul. M. Hrushevskoho 7, Ukraine. *E-mail:* moz@moz.gov.ua.

BOHIGAS GUARDIOLA, Oriol, DArch; Spanish architect; b. 20 Dec. 1925, Barcelona; s. of Pere Bohigas and María Guardiola; m. Isabel Arnau 1957; five c.; ed Escuela Técnica Superior de Arquitectura, Barcelona; partnership with Josep Martorell 1951– and with David Mackay 1962– Oriol Capdevila and Francesc Gual 2000–, forming MBM Arquitectes; Chair. of Composition, Escuela Técnica Superior de Arquitectura, Barcelona (ETSAB) 1971–, Head of ETSAB 1977–80; Head of Urban Planning Dept, Barcelona City Council 1980–84; Councillor of Culture 1991–94; Pres. Joan Miró Foundation 1981–88, Barcelona Athenaeum 2003–11; mem. Accademia Nazionale di San Luca, Rome 1981, Royal Swedish Acad. of Engineering Sciences 1991, Académie d'Architecture de Paris 1991, Real Académia de Bellas Artes de San Fernando 2011; Hon. mem. Sociedad Colombiana de Arquitectos 1982, Asscn of Architects of Bulgaria 1987, Bund Deutscher Architecten 1990, Hon. FAIA 1993, Hon. FRIBA 1996,; Ordem dos Arquitetos Lisboa (Portugal) 2010; Dr hc (Darmstadt) 1992, (Menéndez y Pelayo) 1995, Hon. Chair. Universitat Politécnica de Catalunya 1995; numerous awards including Gold Medal for Artistic Merits, City of Barcelona 1986, Medal of Urbanism, Acad. d'Architecture de Paris 1988, Sikkens Award, Rotterdam 1989, Gold Medal for Architecture, Consejo Superior de Arquitectos de España, Madrid 1990, Creu de Sant Jordi, Generalitat de Catalunya 1991, Volker Stevin Innovatieprijs Award, Rotterdam 1992, RIBA Royal Gold Medal to City of Barcelona (with others) 1999, Gold Medal, Artistic Circle of St Lluc, Barcelona 2004, ArpaFIL Architecture Prize, Mexico 2004, Pres. Macia Medal, Barcelona 2006, Gold Medal, COAC, Barcelona 2007, Nat. Award of Architecture, Madrid 2006, Culture's Nat. Award for his Professional and Artistic Path, Barcelona 2011; firm awarded First Prize in many architectural competitions including Foment de les Arts Decoratives for best bldg in Barcelona 1959, 1962, 1966, 1976, 1979, 1984, 1991, Delta de Plata (industrial design) 1966, 1976, First Prize, Internationale Bauhausstellung Berlin 1981, Un Progetto per Siena, Italy 1990, FAD Award for the Olympic Port 1991, Gold Medal, 'Barcelona 92' 1992, 'Cardiff Bay', Wales 1993, Eric Lyons Housing Award for bldg in Olympic Village, Barcelona 1994, 'Mission Perrache-Confluent', Lyon, France 1997, 'London's Arc of Opportunity', UK 1999, 'Programma di riqualificazione urbana dell'area De-Cecco', Pescara, Italy 2000, Prize of City of Barcelona for the Pompeu Fabra Univ. bldg 2001, Design for HUB Museum competition, Barcelona 2001, Canfranch, Award Década for the Olympic Port, Barcelona 2001,competition Groot Zieken Gasthuis-terrein, 's-Hertogenbosch, The Nederlands 2003, Silver Jubilee Cup for the Vision for Plymouth Plan, UK 2006, Urbanistica Award for new railway station in Parma, Italy 2009, urban planning of Via Trentgo, Parma, Italy 2010, urban planning of Hyères city centre, France 2010, Trophée ARCHIZINC 2012 for La Casa dels Xuklis 2012, Teula de Plata Award, Col.legi d'Arquitectes de Catalunya 2012, Gold Medal, Generalitat de Catalunya 2013. *Publications include:* Barcelona entre el plà Cerdà i el barraquisme 1963, Arquitectura modernista 1968, Contra una arquitectura adjetivada 1969, La arquitectura española de la Segunda República 1970, Polemica d'arquitectura catalana 1970, Reseña y catálogo de la arquitectura modernista 1972, Proceso y erótica del diseño 1972, Once arquitectos 1976, Reconstrucció de Barcelona 1985, Combat d'incerteses. Dietari de records 1989, Dit o fet. Dietari de records II 1992, Gràcies i desgràcies de Barcelona 1993, el Present des del Futur. Epistolari Públic 1994–1995 1996, Del dubte a la Revolució. Epistolari públic 1995–1997 1998, Modernidad en la arquitectura de la España Republicana 1998, Oriol Bohigas. Realismo, urbanidad y fracasos 1999, Tra Strada del Dubbio e Piazza della Revoluzione. Epistolario sulle arti, l'architettura e l'urbanistica 2003, Cartes de la Baralla. Epistolari públic sobre cultura i política 2003, Modernité en l'architecture dans l'espagne républicaine 2004, Contra la incontinencia urbana. Reconsideración moral de la arquitectura y la ciudad 2004, Contra la incontinència urbana. Reconsideració moral de l'arquitectura i la ciutat 2004, Epistolario 1951–1994 2005, Contro l'incontinenza urbana. Riconsiderazione morale sull'architettura e la città 2008, Passar Comptes Dietari de records III 2012. *Address:* MBM Arquitectes, Plaça Reial 18, 08002 Barcelona, Spain (office). *Telephone:* (93) 3170061 (office); (93) 4124771 (home). *Fax:* (93) 3177266 (office). *E-mail:* obohigas@mbmarquitectes.cat (office). *Website:* www.mbmarquitectes.cat (office).

BOHL, Friedrich; German lawyer and politician; b. 5 March 1945, Rosdorf, Göttingen; s. of Heinrich Bohl and Gerda Heyden; m. Elisabeth Bocking; two s. two d.; ed Univ. of Marburg; lawyer 1972–, notary 1976–; mem. CDU and Jungen Union (JU) 1963–; local Chair. JU Marburg-Biedenkopf 1964–70; Dist Chair. JU Mittelhessen 1969–73; mem. Prov. Parl. Hessen 1970–80, Chair. Legal Cttee 1974–78; Acting Chair. CDU Landtagsfraktion 1978–80; Chair. CDU Kreistagsfraktion Marburg-Biedenkopf 1974–90; mem. Fed. Bundestag 1980–, Parl. Man. CDU/CSU Bundestagsfraktion 1984–91; Fed. Minister for Special Tasks and Head of Fed. Chancellery 1991–98; Head of Press and Information, Fed. Govt 1998; mem. Exec. Bd Deutsche Vermögensberatung AG 1991–2009, Chair. Supervisory Bd 2009–; Pres. von Behring-Röntgen Foundation 2011–; Bundesverdienstkreuz (1st Class) 1987. *Address:* c/o Von Behring-Röntgen-Stiftung, Schloss 1, 35037 Marburg; Finkenstrasse 11, 35043 Marburg Cappel, Germany (home). *Telephone:* 41333 (home).

BOHRER, Karl Heinz, PhD, Dr. habil.; German academic; *Professor Emeritus of Modern Literature, University of Bielefeld;* b. 26 Sept. 1932, Cologne; m. Undine Gruenter 1991; one s. one d.; ed Univ. of Göttingen, Univ. of Heidelberg; Prof. of History of Modern Literature, Univ. of Bielefeld 1982–1997, Prof. Emer. 1997–; Visiting Prof. of Comparative Literature, Stanford Univ. 2003–; Ed. Merkur 1984–2011; J.H. Merck Prize 1978, Lessing Prize 2000, Gadamer Prize 2001, Prize of the Bavarian Acad. of Arts 2005, Prize of the Berlin Acad. of Arts 2007. *Publications:* Die gefährdete Phantasie oder Surrealismus und Terror 1970, Der Lauf des Freitag – Die lädierte Utopie und der Dichter 1973, Die Ästhetik des Schreckens 1978, Plötzlichkeit. Der Augenblick des ästhetischen Scheins 1981, Mythos und Moderne 1983, Der romantische Brief, Die Entstehung aesthetischer Subjektivität 1987, Nach der Natur, Über Politik und Ästhetik 1988, Die Kritik der Romantik 1989, Das absolute Präsens. Die Semantik ästhetischer Zeit 1994, Der Abschied. Theorie der Trauer 1996, Die Grenzen des Aesthetischen 1998, Ästhetische Negativität 2002, Ekstasen der Zeit: Augenblick, Gegenwart, Erinnerung 2003, Imaginationen des Bösen 2004, Großer Stil 2007, Das Tragische: Erscheinung, Pathos, Klage 2009, Selbstdenker und Systemdenker 2011, Der

Granatsplitter: Erzählung einer Jugend 2012. *Address:* 110 Lansdowne Way, London, SW8 2EP, England (home); Universtät Bielefeld, Fakultät für Linguistik und Literaturwissenschaft, 33501 Bielefeld (office); Franziskastr. 9, Cologne, Germany. *Telephone:* (20) 7162-2386 (home). *Fax:* (20) 7501-0067 (home).

BOISCLAIR, André, MPA; Canadian fmr politician; b. 14 April 1966, Montréal; s. of Marc-André Boisclair; ed Jean-de-Brébeuf Coll., Univ. of Laval, John F. Kennedy School of Govt, Harvard Univ., USA,; elected to Quebec Nat. Ass. representing Gouin riding 1989 (youngest mem. ever elected); Govt House Leader 2001–04 (resgnd); Minister of Immigration and Citizens 1996–98, Minister of Social Solidarity 1998–2001, Minister of the Environment and Water 2001–03; Leader, Parti Québécois 2005–07 (resgnd); Adjunct Prof., Strategic Communication, Concordia Univ. 2008–12; Pres. Bd Regroupement des événements majeurs internationaux 2010–11; Advisor to t Bd Questerre Energy 2011–12; Del. Gen. of Quebec in New York 2012–13.

BOISSET, Yves; French author and film director; b. 14 March 1939, Paris; s. of Raymond Boisset and Germaine Bonnet; m. Mishline Paintault 1964; two s.; ed Lycée Louis-le-Grand, Faculté des Lettres, Paris and Inst. des Hautes Etudes Cinématographiques; journalist on Cinéma, Paris-Jour etc. 1958–63; Asst Dir to Yves Ciampi 1959, to Jean-Pierre Melville 1962, Claude Sautet and Antoine Bourseiller 1964, Vittorio de Sica and René Clemént 1965, Ricardo Freda 1966; TV and film dir 1967–; Chevalier des Arts et des Lettres. *Films include:* Coplan sauve sa peau 1968, Cran d'arrêt 1969, Un condé 1970, Le Saut de l'ange 1971, L'Attentat (Grand Prix, Moscow Film Festival 1972) 1972, R.A.S. 1973, Dupont Lajoie (Silver Bear, Berlin Film Festival 1974) 1974, Folle à tuer 1975, Le Juge Fayard dit le Sheriff (Prix Louis Delluc 1977) 1976, Un taxi mauve 1977, La Clé sur la porte 1978, La Femme flic (Award for Best Dir, Karlov Vivary Festival 1979) 1979, Allons z'enfants 1981, Espion lève-toi 1982, Le Prix du danger 1983, Canicule 1984, Bleu comme l'Enfer 1986, La Travestie 1988, Radio Corbeau 1989, La Tribu 1991. *Television includes:* La Fée carabine 1987, Le Suspect 1989, Double Identity 1990, Les Carnassiers 1991, Morlock 1993, L'Affaire Seznec (Best Film, Best Screenplay, Best Dir, seven D'Or Awards 1993) 1993, L'Affaire Dreyfus (Silver Prize, Monte Carlo TV Festival 1995) 1995, Morlock: Le tunnel 1996, Les Amants de rivière rouge (mini-series) 1996, La Fine équipe 1997, Une leçon particulière 1997, Le Pantalon (Best Film, Best Dir 1997) 1997, Sam 1999, Dormir avec le diable 2001, Cazas 2001, Jean Moulin 2002, Le Blues des Medias 2003, Ils Veulent Cloner le Christ 2004, Les Mystères Sanglants de l'OTS 2005, La Bataille D'Alger 2006, L'Affaire Salengro 2008, Douze balles dans la tête pour Pierre Laval 2009. *Publications:* 20 ans de cinéma américain 1962, La vie est un choix 2011. *Leisure interests:* athletics, basketball, tennis. *Address:* 61 boulevard Inkerman, 92200 Neuilly-sur-Seine (office); 88 boulevard Victor Hugo, 92200 Neuilly-sur-Seine, France (home). *Telephone:* 1-47-47-52-05 (home). *E-mail:* yves.boisset@yahoo.fr (home).

BOISSIER, Patrick Marie René; French business executive; *Chairman and CEO, DCNS;* b. 18 Feb. 1950, Versailles; s. of Pierre Boissier and Françoise Boissier (née Hennebicque); m. Isabelle Joly 1972; two s. one d.; ed École Polytechnique, Harvard Business School, USA; engineer, Cegedur Rhenalu 1973–75, Forges de Crans 1976–79, Asst Factory Man. Cegedur 1980–83, Man. Pipes Div. 1984–87, Gen. Man. 1987–90; Deputy Chair. and CEO Tréfimétaux 1990–93; Dept Head Péchiney 1994; Gen. Man. Heating and Air-Conditioning Div., Elfi 1994–97; Chair. and CEO Technibel 1994–97; Gen. Man., then Chair. and CEO Chantiers d'Atlantique 1997–2006; CEO GEC Alsthom Leroux Naval (later Alstom Leroux Naval) 1997–2006; Chair. Alstom Marine 1998–2006; mem. Supervisory Bd Vallourec 2000–, Vice-Pres. 2005–; CEO Cegelec electrical engineering group 2007–; Chair. and CEO DCNS (fmrly Direction Technique des Constructions Navales and Direction des Constructions Navales) shipbuilders 2009–; mem. Advisory Bd Steria; mem. Bd of Dirs Sperian; Chair. European Shipbuilders Asscn Cttee 2004–; mem. Acad. des Technologies; Chevalier, Ordre nat. du Mérite, Légion d'honneur. *Leisure interest:* sailing. *Address:* DCNS, 40–42 rue du Docteur Finlay, 75732 Paris, Cedex 15, France (office). *Telephone:* 1-40-59-50-00 (office). *Fax:* 1-40-59-56-48 (office). *E-mail:* patrick.boissier@dcnsgroup.com (office); boissier@academie-technologies.fr (office). *Website:* www.dcnsgroup.com (office).

BOISSON, Jacques-Louis, PhD, LLD; Monegasque diplomatist and government official; *Secretary of State, Principality of Monaco;* b. 8 Jan. 1940, Monaco; s. of Robert Boisson and Léonie-Jeanne Gastaud; m. Carmen Gómez Parejo; one s.; ed Institut d'Etudes Politiques, Institut des Relations Int., Paris, Faculté de Droit et de Sciences Economiques, Aix-en-Provence, Acad. of Int. Law, Netherlands; int. civil servant (responsible for training, research and protection of human rights) UNESCO 1968–83; Amb. to France 1984–93, 2006–08, to Spain 2003–04; Perm. Rep. to UN, New York 1993–2003; Del. to Council of Europe 2004–06; Amb. to Int. Org. of Francophony 2006–08; Perm. Del. to UNESCO 2007–08; Sec. of State (Head of Govt) 2008–; Grand Officier, Ordre de Grimaldi (Monaco), Commdr, Ordre de St Charles (Monaco), Chevalier, Ordre des Palmes académiques, Légion d'onneur. *Publications:* Le Particularisme Institutionnel de la Principalité de Monaco 1966, Le Droit de la Nationalité Monégasque 1968, La Protection Internationale des Minorités, Vers un Enseignement Universel des Droits de l'Homme, L'Autorité internationale des Fonds Marins 2001; numerous articles on the protection and promotion of int. human rights 1971–99. *Leisure interests:* baroque music, opera, philosophy, poetry. *Address:* Palais Princier, 98000 (office); 31 blvd Charles III, 98000, Monaco (home). *Telephone:* 93-25-18-31 (office); 93-25-59-64 (home). *Fax:* 93-30-26-26 (office). *E-mail:* jboisson@palais.mc (office); carfac .boisson@monaco.mc.

BØJER, Jørgen R. H.; Danish diplomatist; *Chairman, Danish Centre for International Studies and Human Rights;* b. 5 March 1940, Hjørring; s. of Svend Rud Hansen Bøjer and Ingeborg Bøjer (née Frederiksen); m. Lone Heilskov 1964; two d.; ed Univ. of Århus, Institut d'Etudes Politiques, Paris; became Foreign Service Officer 1967, Sec., Embassy in Prague 1971; Head of Section, Ministry of Foreign Affairs, Copenhagen 1973, Dir 1982, Deputy Under-Sec. 1992; Visiting Fellow, Stanford Univ. 1978; Counsellor, Embassy in Washington, DC 1979; Amb. to Egypt (also accred to Sudan and Somalia), then to Austria, Slovenia, Bosnia and Herzegovina; Perm. Rep. to Int. Orgs, Vienna 1993; Perm. Rep. to UN, New York 1997–2001, Co-Chair. UN Int. Conf. on Financing for Devt 2001; Amb. to Czech Repub. 2001–07; Chair. Danish Centre for Int. Studies and Human Rights 2006–.

Address: Danish Centre for International Studies and Human Rights, Strandgade 56, 1401 Copenhagen K, Denmark (office). *Telephone:* 32-69-86-86 (office). *Fax:* 32-69-86-00 (office). *E-mail:* dcism@dcism.dk (office). *Website:* www.dcism.dk (office).

BOJINOV, Bojidar; Bulgarian lawyer and legal adviser; b. 30 Jan. 1939, Pleven City; s. of Boris Bojinov and Nina Bojinova; m. Fani Vladimorova; one s. two d.; ed Charles Univ., Prague; lawyer, Pleven 1967–72; Legal Adviser to Bulgarian Chamber of Commerce and Industry (BCCI), Sofia 1972–77, Dir Patent and Trade Marks Div. 1977–85, Vice-Pres. BCCI 1985–93, Pres. 1993–2009; Arbitrator at BCCI Court of Arbitration 1975–2004; currently Pnr, Bojinov & Bojinov Ltd (law firm); mem. Advisory Council to Pres. of Repub. on Foreign Investments, Nat. Council for Tripartite Cooperation, Council of Econ. Growth 2002–; fmr Pres. Asscn of Black Sea Zone Chambers of Commerce and Industry, Asscn of Balkan Chambers, Bulgarian Nat. Group of AIPP. *Leisure interests:* music, art, skiing, tennis. *Address:* Patents and Trademarks Bureau, Bojinov & Bojinov Ltd, 38 Alabin Street, PO Box 728, 1000 Sofia (office). *Telephone:* (2) 9862974 (office). *Fax:* (2) 9873209 (office); (2) 9863508 (office). *E-mail:* office@ptmbojinov.com (office).

BOK, Derek, MA, JD; American lawyer, university administrator and academic; *300th Anniversary University President Emeritus, Professor Emeritus and Faculty Chair, Hauser Center for Non-Profit Organizations, Harvard University;* b. 22 March 1930, Bryn Mawr, Pa; s. of late Curtis Bok and Margaret Plummer (now Mrs. W. S. Kiskadden); m. Sissela Ann Myrdal (d. of Karl Gunnar and Alva Myrdal) 1955; one s. two d.; ed Stanford Univ., Harvard Univ., George Washington Univ. and Inst. of Political Science, Univ. of Paris; served in US Army 1956–58; Asst Prof. of Law, Harvard Univ. 1958–61, Prof. 1961, Dean 1968–71, 300th Anniversary Univ. Prof. 1991, now Prof. Emer.; Pres. Harvard Univ. 1971–91, now Pres. Emer., Interim Pres. 2006–07; Dir, Nat. Chair. Common Cause 1999–; Chair. Spencer Foundation 2002–; Faculty Chair. Hauser Center for Non-Profit Orgs 2002–. *Publications include:* The First Three Years of the Schuman Plan, Cases and Materials on Labor Law (with Archibald Cox), Labor and the American Community (with John Dunlop), The Federal Government and the University, Beyond the Ivory Tower: Social Responsibilities of the Modern University 1982, Higher Learning 1986, Universities and the Future of America 1990, The Cost of Talent 1993, The State of the Nation 1997, The Shape of the River (jtly) 1998, The Trouble with Government 2001, Universities in the Marketplace 2004, The Politics of Happiness: What Government Can Learn from the New Research on Well-Being 2010. *Leisure interests:* gardening, tennis, swimming. *Address:* Hauser Center for Nonprofit Organizations, 5 Bennett Street, Cambridge, MA 02138 (office); John F. Kennedy School of Government, Harvard University, 79 John F. Kennedy Street, Cambridge, MA 02138, USA (office). *Telephone:* (617) 495-1199 (office). *Fax:* (617) 496-6886 (office). *E-mail:* derek_bok@harvard.edu (office). *Website:* www.ksg .harvard.edu/hauser (office).

BOKOVA, Irina Georgieva, MBA; Bulgarian diplomatist, politician and UN official; *Director-General, United Nations Educational, Scientific and Cultural Organization (UNESCO);* b. 12 July 1952; d. of Georgi Bokov; m.; two c.; ed First English Language School, Sofia, Moscow State Inst. of Int. Relations, Russia, Univ. of Maryland, John F. Kennedy School of Govt, Harvard Univ., USA; Attaché and Third Sec., Ministry of Foreign Affairs, Sofia 1977–82, Third Sec., Perm. Mission to UN, New York 1982–84, Third, later Second Sec., UN Dept, Ministry of Foreign Affairs 1984–86, Adviser to Minister of Foreign Affairs (rank of First Sec.) 1986–90, First Sec., European Security Dept 1991–92, State Sec. on European Integration 1995–97, Minister of Foreign Affairs 1996–97, Adviser to Minister of Foreign Affairs (rank of Amb.) Feb.–Sept. 1997, Amb. to France 2005–09; mem. Constituent Nat. Ass. 1990–91; mem. Narodno Sobranie (Parl.) for Bulgarian Socialist Party 2001; Dir-Gen. UNESCO, Paris 2009–; NATO Fellow, Program for Cen. and Eastern Europe on democratic insts focusing on the nat. and legal mechanism for the protection of minorities 1992–94. *Publications:* numerous articles on foreign policy and European integration issues. *Address:* Office of the Director General, UNESCO, 7 place de Fontenoy, 75352 Paris 07 SP, France (office). *Telephone:* 1-45-68-10-00 (office). *Fax:* 1-45-67-16-90 (office). *E-mail:* bpi@ unesco.org (office). *Website:* www.unesco.org (office); www.bokova.eu (home); www .irinabokova.com (office).

BOKROS, Lajos, PhD; Hungarian economist, banker, academic and politician; b. 26 June 1954, Budapest; s. of Lajos Bokros and Irén Szarka; m. Maria Gyetuai; one s. one d.; ed Univ. of Econs, Budapest, Univ. of Panama; Research Fellow, Financial Research Inst., Hungarian Ministry of Finance, Budapest 1980–86, Chief of Public Finance Div. 1986–87; Deputy Gen. Man. Econ. Dept, Nat. Bank of Hungary 1987–89, Man. Dir 1989, Dir Capital Market Dept 1989–91; Chair. Budapest Stock Exchange 1990–95; Chair. and CEO Budapest Bank 1991–95; Chair. Budapest Stock Exchange in early 1990s; Minister of Finance 1995–96; Sr Adviser, Financial Sector Devt, IBRD 1996–97, Dir Pvt. and Financial Sector Devt, ECA 1997–99, Dir Financial Advisory Services, Europe and Cen. Asia 1999–2004; Prof. of Econs and Public Policy, Cen. European Univ. 2004–, also Sr Vice-Pres. for Research and Int. Projects and COO; Chief Econ. Adviser to Prime Minister of Croatia 2002–, to Deputy Prime Minister of Poland 2001–; MEP 2009–, mem. Cttee on Budgets, Del. for relations with Albania, Bosnia and Herzegovina, Serbia, Montenegro and Kosovo; f. Modern Magyarország Mozgalom (Modern Hungary Movement) political party 2013; mem. Bd of Dirs State Property Agency 1990–91. *Publications:* Development Commodity Production, Market Economy 1984, Market and Money in the Modern Economy 1985, Public Finance Reform during Transition – The Experience of Hungary (co-author) 1998, Visegrad Twins' Diverging Path to Relative Prosperity 2000, Financial Transition in Europe and Central Asia – The World Bank (co-author) 2001, Competition and Solidarity – Comparative Economic Studies 2004. *Address:* European Parliament, 60, rue Wiertz, 1047 Brussels, Belgium (office). *Telephone:* (2) 284-57-07 (office). *Fax:* (2) 284-97-07 (office). *E-mail:* lajos.bokros@europarl.europa.eu (office). *Website:* www .europarl.europa.eu (office).

BOKSENBERG, Alexander, CBE, PhD, FRS, FInstP, FRAS; British astronomer and academic; *Honorary Professor of Experimental Astronomy, University of Cambridge;* b. 18 March 1936; s. of Julius Boksenberg and Ernestina Steinberg; m. Adella Coren 1960; one s. one d.; ed Stationers' Co.'s School, Univ. of London, Univ. of Cambridge; SRC Research Asst, Dept of Physics and Astronomy, Univ. Coll. London 1960–65, Lecturer in Physics 1965–75, Head of Optical and Ultraviolet Astronomy Research Group 1969–81, Reader in Physics 1975–78, SRC Sr Fellow

1976–81, Prof. of Physics and Astronomy 1978–81; Sherman Fairchild Distinguished Scholar, Calif. Inst. of Tech. 1981–82; Dir Royal Greenwich Observatory 1981–93, Royal Observatories (Royal Greenwich Observatory, Royal Observatory, Edin., Isaac Newton Group of Optical Telescopes, Canary Islands, Jt Astronomy Centre, Hawaii) 1993–96; Hon. Prof. of Experimental Astronomy, Univ. of Cambridge 1991–; Research Prof. Inst. of Astronomy Univ. of Cambridge and PPARC Sr Research Fellow, Univs of Cambridge and London 1996–99; Extraordinary Fellow, Churchill Coll., Cambridge 1996–, mem. Council 1998–2003; Visiting Prof., Dept of Physics and Astronomy, Univ. Coll. London 1981–, Astronomy Centre, Univ. of Sussex 1981–89; Exec. Ed. Experimental Astronomy 1995–; Hon. Pres. Astronomical Soc. of Glasgow 1995–; Chair. New Industrial Concepts Ltd 1969–81; Pres. West London Astronomical Soc. 1978–; Chair. SRC Astronomy Cttee 1980–81; mem. ESA Hubble Space Telescope Instrument Definition Team 1973–95, S African Astronomical Observatory Advisory Cttee 1978–85, British Council Science Advisory Cttee 1987–91, Anglo-Australian Telescope Bd 1989–91 (Deputy Chair. 1991–92), Max Planck Institut für Astronomie Advisory Cttee 1991–95, European Southern Observatory Vis. Cttee 1993–95, Council and Trustee Royal Soc. 1995–97 (Technical Steering Group 1997–98, Chair. Int. Exchanges Far East Panel 2000–), Int. Astronomical Union Finance Cttee 1997–2000, UK-Japan N+N Bd on Cooperation in Astronomy 1997–, PPARC VISTA Review Bd 1999–2000, Foundation Cttee UK Nat. Comm. for UNESCO (Chair. Science Cttee 2000–03, mem. Council 2000–03, Chair. Steering Cttee UK Nat. Comm. for UNESCO Campaign Group 2003–04; Fellow, Royal Soc. 1978–, Univ. Coll. London 1991–; Asteroid (3205) named Boksenberg 1988; 37th Herstmonceux Conf. The Hubble Space Telescope and the High Redshift Universe in honour of Alec Boksenberg 1996; lecture tours: Royal Soc./Russian Acad. of Sciences 1989, Royal Soc./Chinese Acad. of Sciences 1995, British Council India 1999 and Royal Soc./Japan Acad. 1999; Freeman Clockmakers Co. 1984; Liveryman 1989; Dr hc (l'Observatoire de Paris) 1982; Hon. DSc (Sussex) 1991; Hannah Jackson Medal and Gift 1998, Royal Soc. Hughes Medal 1999, Glazebrook Medal and Prize 2000. *Publications:* Modern Technology and its Influence on Astronomy 1990 (ed.); 220 contribs to learned journals. *Leisure interest:* skiing. *Address:* University of Cambridge, Institute of Astronomy, The Observatories, Madingley Road, Cambridge, CB3 0HA, England (office). *Telephone:* (1223) 339909 (office). *Fax:* (1223) 339910 (office). *E-mail:* boksy@ast.cam.ac.uk (office). *Website:* www.ast .cam.ac.uk/IoA (office).

BOLAÑOS GEYER, Enrique; Nicaraguan business executive and fmr head of state; b. 13 May 1928, Masaya, nr Managua; s. of Nicolás Bolaños Cortés and Amanda Geyer; m. Lila T. Abaunza 1949 (deceased); four s. (three deceased) one d.; ed Colegio Centro-América, Granada, St Louis Univ., USA, Instituto Centroamericano de Administración de Empresas; worked as farmer 1952–59; Gen. Man. Fábrica de Calzados Lorena SA, Masaya 1956–59; Spanish teacher, Berlitz School of Languages, St Louis, Mo., USA 1960–62; Gen. Man. Cía. Leonesa de Productos Lácteos SA, León 1962–64; Chair. Bd Impresora Serigráfica SA, Managua 1967–73; Founder and Chair. numerous cos in Grupo Bolaños-SAIMSA; Head of COSEP (pvt. business asscn) 1979–90; Vice-Pres. of Nicaragua 1997–2000; Pres. of Nicaragua 2002–06; f. Fundación Enrique Bolaños; fmr mem. Partido Liberal Constitucionalista (PLC); mem. Alianza por la República 2004–; Hon. mem. Int. Raoul Wallenberg Foundation; Rubén Darío Medal, Cardinal Mindszenty Foundation Freedom Award, Democracy Service Medal, Nat. Endowment for Democracy 2003. *E-mail:* info@enriquebolanos.org. *Website:* www.enriquebolanos.org.

BOLAÑOS ZAMORA, Rodrigo Alberto, MA, PhD; Costa Rican economist and central banker; *Governor, Banco Central de Costa Rica;* b. 1951; m.; ed Instituto Tecnologico Autonomo de México, Univ. of Chicago, USA; Sec., Ministry of Finance 1984–85, Minister of Finance 1989–90; various man. roles at Banco Central de Costa Rica 1985–86, Gov. 1995–98, 2010–; Pres. Bolsa Nacional de Valores (stock exchange) 1986–89, 1990–95; Exec. Pres. Fondo Latinoamericano de Reservas 2008–10; sr positions with IDB and Inter-American Investment Co. (Corporación Interamericana de Inversiones); Partner, Econálisis (consultancy); fmr consultant for several int. orgs including USAID, World Bank, IDB and UN. *Address:* Office of the Governor, Banco Central de Costa Rica, Avdas Central y Primera, Calles 2 y 4, Apdo 10058, 1000 San José, Costa Rica (office). *Telephone:* 2243-3333 (office). *Fax:* 2243-4566 (office). *Website:* www.bccr.fi.cr (office).

BOLD, Luvsanvandangiin; Mongolian economist and politician; *Minister of External Relations;* b. 1961, Ulan Bator; Vice-Chair. and Sec.-Gen. Mongolian Students' Asscn 1989–91; Chair. Centre of Youth and Students of Mongol Origin 1992–93; mem. Parl. 1996–2000, 2008–; Chair. Bd of Dirs Golomt Bank 2000–04; Minister of Defence 2008–12, of External Relations 2012–; Pres. Asscn of Mongolian Banks 2000–05; mem. Mongolian Social-Democratic Party. *Address:* Ministry of External Relations, Enkh Taivny Örgön Chölöö 7a, Sükhbaatar District, Ulan Bator, Mongolia (office). *Telephone:* (51) 262788 (office). *Fax:* (11) 322127 (office). *E-mail:* info@mfat.gov.mn (office). *Website:* www.mfat.gov.mn (office).

BOLDON, Ato; Trinidad and Tobago athlete; b. 30 Dec. 1973, Port of Spain; ed Univ. of California, Los Angeles; resident in USA since 1988; coached by John Smith; Cen. American and Caribbean record-holder at 60m indoors (6.49 seconds), 100m (9.86 seconds) and 200m (19.77 seconds); gold medal World Jr Championships 100m and 200m 1992; fourth Commonwealth Games 100m 1994; bronze medal World Championships 100m 1995; gold medal NCAA Championships 100m 1996; bronze medals Olympic Games 100m and 200m 1996; 100m World Champion 1997, 1999; gold medal World Championships 200m 1997; gold medal Goodwill Games, New York 200m 1998; gold medal Commonwealth Games 100m 1998; silver medal Olympic Games 100m 2000, bronze medal 200m; youngest sprinter ever to run under 10 seconds in the 100m and under 20 seconds in the 200m; *Website:* www.atoboldon.com (office).

BOLDYREV, Yuri Yuryevich; Russian politician; b. 29 May 1960, Leningrad; m. 1990; one s.; ed Leningrad Electrotech. Inst., Leningrad Inst. of Finance and Econs; worked as engineer at Cen. Research Inst. of Vessel Electronics and Tech. 1983–89; mem. CPSU 1987–90; USSR People's Deputy 1989–91; mem. del. of 28 CPSU Congress; left CPSU 1990; mem. Council of Reps, then of Co-ordination Council of Democratic Russia Movt 1990–91; mem. Higher Advisory Council to Chair. of Russian Supreme Soviet (later to Pres. of Russian Fed.) 1990–92; consultant, Russian Govt Feb.–March 1992; Chief State Inspector of Russian Fed.,

Chief Control Man. of Admin. of Presidency 1992–93; mem. Centre of Econ. and Political Research (Epicentre) 1993–94; mem. Duma (Parl.) 1993–95; Founder-mem. and Deputy Chair. Yabloko Movt 1993–95, left Party Sept. 1995; Deputy Chair. Accountant Chamber of Russian Fed. 1995–2001; Head of St Petersburg electoral cands, Spravedlivaya Rossiya party (Fair Russia) 2007; *Website:* yuriboldyrev.ru.

BOLGER, Dermot; Irish writer, dramatist and poet; b. 6 Feb. 1959, Finglas, Dublin; s. of Roger Bolger and the late Bridie Flanagan; m. Bernadette Clifton 1988 (died 2010); two s.; ed St Canice's BNS, Finglas and Benevin Coll., Finglas; worked as factory hand, library asst and professional author; Founder and Ed. Raven Arts Press 1979–92; Founder and Exec. Ed. New Island Books, Dublin 1992–; mem. Arts Council of Ireland 1989–93; elected mem. Aosdána 1991–; Playwright in Asscn, The Abbey (Nat.) Theatre 1997; Writer Fellow, Trinity Coll., Dublin 2003; Writer in Residence, Farmleigh House, Dublin 2008; A.E. Memorial Prize 1986, Macauley Fellowship 1987, A.Z. Whitehead Prize 1987, Samuel Beckett Award 1991, Edinburgh Fringe First Awards 1991, 1995, Stewart Parker BBC Award 1991, The Hennessy Irish Literature Hall of Fame Award 2003, Irish Times/EBS Prize for Best New Irish Play of 2004, Worldplay Int. Radio Prize for Best Script 2005, Irish Newspapers Commentator of the Year 2012. *Plays:* The Lament for Arthur Cleary 1989, Blinded by the Light 1990, In High Germany 1990, The Holy Ground 1990, One Last White Horse 1991, A Dublin Bloom 1994, April Bright 1995, The Passion of Jerome 1999, Consenting Adults 2000, From These Green Heights 2004, The Townlands of Brazil 2006, Walking the Road 2007, The Consequences of Lightning 2008, The Parting Glass 2010, Tea Chests & Dreams 2012, Ulysses – A Stage Version of Joyce's Novel 2012. *Radio:* The Woman's Daughter 2005, Hunger Again 2006, The Fortunestown Kid 2006, The Night Manager 2007, The Kerlogue 2007, Moving In Day 2008, Accident & Emergency 2010, Outline Permission 2012. *Television screenplay:* Edward No Hands 1996. *Publications:* novels: Night Shift 1985, The Woman's Daughter 1987, The Journey Home 1990, Emily's Shoes 1992, A Second Life 1994, Father's Music 1997, Finbar's Hotel (co-author) 1997, Ladies Night at Finbar's Hotel (co-author) 1999, Temptation 2000, The Valparaiso Voyage 2001, The Family on Paradise Pier 2005, A Second Life: A Renewed Novel 2010, New Town Soul 2010, The Fall of Ireland 2012; poetry: The Habit of Flesh 1979, Finglas Lilies 1980, No Waiting America 1981, Internal Exile 1986, Leinster Street Ghosts 1989, Taking My Letters Back, new and Selected Poems 1998, The Chosen Moment 2004, External Affairs 2008, The Venice Suite – A Voyage through Loss 2012; editor: The Dolmen Book of Irish Christmas Stories 1986, The Bright Wave: Poetry in Irish Now 1986, 16 on 16: Irish Writers on the Easter Rising 1988, Invisible Cities: The New Dubliners: A Journey through Unofficial Dublin 1988, Invisible Dublin: A Journey through its Writers 1992, The Picador Book of Contemporary Irish Fiction 1993, 12 Bar Blues (with Aidan Murphy) 1993, The New Picador Book of Contemporary Irish Fiction 2000, Druids, Dudes and Beauty Queens: The Changing Face of Irish Theatre 2001, The Ledwidge Treasury 2007, Night & Day: 24 Hours in the Life of Dublin 2008. *Leisure interests:* soccer, golf. *Address:* c/o New Island Books, 2 Brookside, Dundrum Road, Dublin 14, Ireland (office). *Telephone:* (1) 2989937 (office). *E-mail:* marketing@newisland.ie (office). *Website:* www.dermotbolger.com (office).

BOLGER, James Brendan, PC, ONZ; New Zealand politician, diplomatist and business executive; b. 31 May 1935, Taranaki; s. of Daniel Bolger and Cecilia Bolger (née Doyle); m. Joan Maureen Riddell 1963; six s. three d.; ed Opunake High School; farmer of sheep and beef cattle, Te Kuiti 1965–72; mem. Parl. 1972–98; Parl. Under-Sec. to Minister of Agric. and Fisheries, Minister of Maori Affairs, Minister in Charge of Rural Banking and Finance Corpn 1975–77, Minister of Fisheries and Assoc. Minister of Agric. 1977–78, Minister of Labour 1978–84, of Immigration 1978–81, Prime Minister of New Zealand and Minister in Charge of Security Intelligence Service 1990–97; Leader Nat. Party 1986–98; Leader of the Opposition 1986–90; Amb. to USA 1998–2002; Pres. ILO 1983, New Zealand/US Council; Chair. Kiwibank 2001–10, New Zealand Post Ltd 2002–10, Ian Axford Foundation 2002–, Gas Industry Company and Trustees Executors Ltd 2004–, Mount Cook Alpine Salmon Ltd; Chair. Advisory Bd World Agricultural Forum 2002–; Chancellor Waikato Univ. 2007–; mem. Bd of Dirs New Zealand Trade Liberalisation Network Inc.; mem. Collegium Int.; Trustee, Rutherford Trust; Patron Inst. of Rural Health 2004–; Founding Patron New Zealand United World Coll. Trust 2007–, NZ Business Excellence; Distinguished Fellow, New Zealand Inst. of Dirs 2011; Hon. DSc (Khon Kaen Univ., Thailand) 1994; Hon. DLitt (Massey Univ.) 2002; Queen's Silver Jubilee Medal 1977, NZ Commemoration Medal 1990, NZ Suffrage Centennial Medal 1993. *Publication:* A View from the Top (political autobiog.). *Leisure interests:* hiking, reading, politics. *Address:* Sommeville Road, PO Box 406, Te Kuiti, New Zealand (home). *Telephone:* (7) 8786-213 (home). *Fax:* (7) 8786-215 (home).

BOLING, Edward J., MS, EdD; American academic and fmr university administrator; *President Emeritus, University of Tennessee;* b. 19 Feb. 1922, Sevier Co., Tenn.; s. of Sam R. Boling and Nerissa Boling (née Clark); m. Carolyn Pierce 1950; three s.; ed Univ. of Tennessee and George Peabody Coll.; with Union Carbide Corpn of Oak Ridge, Tenn. 1951–54; Tenn. State Budget Dir 1954–58; Commr of Finance and Admin. 1958–61; Vice-Pres. for Devt and Admin., Univ. of Tenn. 1961–70, Pres. Univ. of Tenn. 1970–88, Pres. Emer. 1988–, Univ. Prof. 1988–92; mem. Educ. Comm. of States 1970–92, mem. Southern Regional Educ. Bd 1957–61, 1970–81, 1983–90, 1992–96; Chair. Tenn. Resource Valley 1991–92; fmr mem. Bd of Dirs Magnavox, The Signal Co., Philips Electronics, Allied Signal, Home Fed. Bank; Trustee Lifetime Leadership of Univ. of Tennessee Award 2010. *Publications:* Forecasting University Enrolment with D.A. Gardiner) 1952, Methods of Objectifying the Allocation of Tax Funds to Tennessee State Colleges 1961. *Leisure interests:* boating, tennis, skiing, travel. *Address:* 4911 Westover Terrace, Knoxville, TN 37914, USA (home). *Telephone:* (865) 523-6882 (home). *E-mail:* ejb@utk.edu (home).

BOLKESTEIN, Frederik (Frits), MPh, LLM; Dutch fmr politician; *President, TeldersStichting;* b. 1933; m.; three c.; ed Oregon State Univ., Gemeentelijke Univ. Amsterdam, Univ. of London, Univ. of Leiden; with Shell Group 1960–76; Dir Shell Chimie, Paris 1973–76; mem. of Parl. for VVD (Liberals) 1978–82, 1986–88, 1989–99; Minister for Foreign Trade 1982–86; Chair. Atlantic Comm., Netherlands 1986–88; Minister of Defence 1988–89; Chair. VVD Parl. Group 1990–98;

Pres. Liberal Internationale 1996–99; EU Commr for Internal Market, Financial Services, Customs and Taxation 1999–2004; Pres. TeldersStichting (Telders Foundation) (VVD think-tank) 2004–; mem. Supervisory Bd Central Bank of The Netherlands; mem. Bd of Dirs Air France-KLM; mem. Royal Inst. of Int. Affairs. *Play:* Floris Count of Holland. *Leisure interest:* tennis. *Address:* TeldersStichting, Koninginnegracht 55a, 2514 AE The Hague, Netherlands (office). *E-mail:* info@teldersstichting.nl (office). *Website:* www.teldersstichting.nl (office); www.fritsbolkestein.com.

BOLKIAH, HRH Crown Prince, Haji al-Muhtadee Billah; Brunei; b. 17 Feb. 1974, Istana Darul Hana, Bandar Seri Begawan; s. of HM Sultan Haji Hassanal Bolkiah Mu'izzuddin Waddaulah and HM Raja Isteri Pengiran Anak Hajah Saleha; m. HRH Pengiran Anak Isteri Pengiran Anak Sarah binti Pengiran Salleh Ab Rahaman 2004; one s. one d.; ed Univ. of Brunei Darussalam, Oxford Centre for Islamic Studies, England; proclaimed Crown Prince 10 Aug. 1998; attachments to various govt ministries and depts, and to private cos; Sr Minister at the Prime Minister's Office; Gen., Royal Brunei Armed Forces; Deputy Inspector Gen., Royal Brunei Police Force; Chair. Autoriti Monetari Brunei Darussalam (AMBD) (Monetary Authority of Brunei Darussalam); Hon. GCVO 1998. *Address:* c/o Istana Nurul Iman, Bandar Seri Begawan, BA 1000, Brunei (office). *Website:* www .crownprince.bn.

BOLKIAH, HRH Prince Haji Jefri; Brunei politician; b. 6 Nov. 1954; s. of HM Sultan Omar Ali Saifuddin III and HM Raja Isteri Pengiran Anak Damit; brother of Sultan Haji Hassanal Bolkiah Mu'izzuddin Waddaulah of Brunei; m.; 18 c.; fmrly Minister of Culture, Youth and Sports, Deputy Minister of Finance; Minister of Finance 1988–97; fmr Chair. Royal Brunei Airlines, Brunei Investment Agency; fmr Propr Asprey & Garrard.

BOLKIAH, HRH Prince Mohamed; Brunei politician; b. 27 Aug. 1947, brother of Sultan Haji Hassanal Bolkiah Mu'izzuddin Waddaulah of Brunei; ed Royal Mil. Acad., Sandhurst, UK; Minister of Foreign Affairs 1984–. *Address:* Ministry of Foreign Affairs, Jalan Subok, Bandar Seri Begawan (office); Hijau Baiduri, Bukit Kayangan, Jalan Tutong, Bandar Seri Begawan BD 2710, Brunei (home). *Telephone:* (2) 261177 (office); (2) 244101 (office). *Fax:* (2) 261709 (office); (2) 244659 (office).

BOLKIAH MU'IZUDDIN WADDAULAH, HM Sultan and Yang di-Pertuan of Brunei Darussalam, Haji Hassanal, DK, PSPNB, PSLI, SPBM, PANB; *Head of State, Prime Minister, Minister of Defence and Minister of Finance;* b. 15 July 1946, Brunei Town (now called Bandar Seri Begawan); s. of Sultan Haji Omar 'Ali Saifuddien Sa'adul Khairi Waddien, KCMG and PENGIRAN RAJA ISTERI PENGIRAN ANAK DAMIT; m. HM Raja Isteri Pengiran Anak Hajah Saleha 1965; two s. (including HRH Prince Haji al-Muhtadee Billah) four d.; also m. Mariam Abd Aziz 1981 (divorced 2003); two s. two d.; also m. HRH Pengiran Isteri Azrinaz Mazhar Hakim 2005 (divorced 2010); one s. one d.; ed privately and Victoria Inst., Kuala Lumpur, Malaysia and Royal Mil. Acad., Sandhurst, UK; appointed Crown Prince and Heir Apparent 1961; Ruler of State of Brunei Oct. 1967–; Prime Minister of Brunei Jan. 1984–, Minister of Finance and Home Affairs 1984–86, of Defence Oct. 1986–, also of Finance; Sovereign and Chief of Royal Orders instituted by Sultans of Brunei; Head of Dept of Islamic Religious Faith and Royal Custom and Tradition; est. the Sultan Haji Hassanal Bolkiah Foundation; Hon. Gen. of the British Army 1984; Hon. Air Marshal, RAF 1992; Hon. Patron World Org. of the Scout Movt 1993; Hon. Adm. of the RN 2001; Hon. Col, Special Service Group (Pakistan) 2004; Hon. mem. Indonesian Satgas Atbara Special Operations Unit 2008; Royal Family Order of the Crown of Brunei; Order of the Crown of the Realm (Malaysia) 1980; Hon. CMG 1968, Hon. GCMG 1972, Hon. GCB 1992; Collar of the Order of the Nile (Egypt) 1984, Adipurna (or First Class) of the Star of the Repub. of Indonesia 1984, Collar of the Supreme Order of the Chrysanthemum (Japan) 1984, Order of al-Hussein bin Ali (Jordan) 1984, The Civil Order of Oman, First Class (Oman) 1984, Grand Order of Mugunghwa (South Korea) 1984, Order of Khalifa (Bahrain) 1988, Collar of the Order of Muhammad (Morocco) 1988, Raja of the Order of Sikatuna (Philippines) 1988, Order of Rajamitrabhorn (Thailand) 1988, First Class of the Order of Temasek (Singapore) 1990, Mil. Distinguished Service Order (Singapore) 1990, Order of the Netherlands Lion, Nishan-e-Pakistan 1992, Grand Croix, Légion d'honneur 1996, Grand Cross, Special Class of the Order of Merit of the FRG 1998, Punong Komandante (Chief Commdr) of the Philippine Legion of Honour 1998, Collar of the Order of Badr Chain (Saudi Arabia) 1999, Kt, Royal Order of the Seraphim (Sweden) 2004, Phoxay Lane Xang (Laos) 2004, Order of Prince Yaroslav the Wise, 1st Class (Ukraine) 2004 and Cross of Honour 2007; Hon. DLitt (Univ. of Brunei Darussalam) 1989; Hon. LLD (Univ. Malaya) 1992, (Univ. of Aberdeen) 1995, (Univ. of Queensland) 2001, (Univ. of the Philippines) 2003, (Nat. Univ. of Singapore) 2005; Hon. DCL by Diploma (Univ. of Oxford) 1992; Hon. PhD (Nat. Univ. of Malaysia) 1997; Hon. Dr of Political Science (Int. Islamic Univ., Malaysia) 2001, (Chulalongkorn Univ., Thailand) 2002; Hon. Dr of Int. Relations (Beijing Foreign Studies Univ.) 2001; Hon. Dr of Humanities and Culture (Gadjah Mada Univ., Indonesia) 2003; Dr hc (Kyiv Polytechnic Inst.) 2004, (Moscow State Inst. of Int. Relations) 2005; Hon. Dr of Philosophy and Humanities (Universitas Indonesia) 2011; Peace Award, Foundation for Peace Together (Italy) 1989, Pres.'s Gold Medal Award, Royal Coll. of Surgeons of Edinburgh 2000, first Companion of the Coll., Royal Coll. of Gen. Practitioners (UK) (cr. in his honour) 2013. *Leisure interests:* collecting automobiles, playing polo, golf and badminton, race car driving, piloting helicopters and aircraft. *Address:* Istana Nurul Iman, Bandar Seri Begawan, BA 1000, Brunei (office). *Telephone:* (2) 229988 (office). *Fax:* (2) 241717 (office). *E-mail:* info@jpm.gov.bn (office). *Website:* www.pmo.gov.bn.

BOLLAÍN, Icíar; Spanish actress and screenwriter; b. (María Icíar Bollaín Pérez-Míinguez), 12 June 1967, Madrid; two c.; film debut in El Sur (The South) 1983; Pnr, La Iguana (film production co.) 1991–; writer and dir of feature film Hola, ¿estás sola? (Best New Dir Award and Audience Award, Valladolid Int. Film Festival) 1995. *Film appearances include:* El Sur 1983, Al acecho 1987, Malaventura 1988, Sublet 1991, Un Paraguas para tres 1992, Entretiempo 1992, Dime una mentira 1993, Jardines colgantes 1993, Land and Freedom 1995, El techo del mundo 1995, Subjudice 1998, Leo 2000, La balsa de piedra (The Stone Raft) 2002, Nos miran 2002, La Noche del hermano 2005. *Films written include:* Los amigos del muerto 1993, Hola, ¿estás sola? 1995, Flores de otro mundo (co-written with Julio Llamazares, Best Film in Int. Critics' Week, Cannes Film

Festival) 1999, Amores que matan 2000, Poniente 2000, Te doy mis ojos 2003. *Films directed include:* Baja corazón 1992, Los amigos del muerto 1993, Hola, ¿estás sola? 1995, Flores de otro mundo (co-written with Julio Llamazares, Best Film in Int. Critics' Week, Cannes Film Festival) 1999, Amores que matan 2000, Te doy mis ojos 2003, Hay motivo 2004, Mataharis 2007. *Address:* Producciones La Iguana S.L., Jardín de San Federico, 15–1D, 28009 Madrid, Spain (office). *Telephone:* (91) 4010254 (office). *Fax:* (91) 3095008 (office). *E-mail:* iguana@la -iguana.com (office). *Website:* www.la-iguana.com (office).

BOLLAND, Marc; Dutch retail executive; *CEO, Marks and Spencer Group plc;* ed Groningen Univ., London Business School, Institut Européen d'Admin des Affaires (INSEAD); worked at Heineken NV for over 20 years, fmr COO and mem. Bd of Dirs; CEO William Morrison Supermarkets PLC 2006–09; CEO Marks and Spencer Group plc 2009–; Dir (non-exec.) Manpower Inc. 2004–; Chair. Supervisory Bd Hotel de l'Europe, Amsterdam; mem. Dutch Centre for Trade Devt, American Chamber of Commerce, Netherlands. *Address:* Marks and Spencer Group plc, Waterside House, 35 North Wharf Road, London, W2 1NW, England (office). *Telephone:* (20) 7935-4422 (office). *Fax:* (845) 303-0170 (office). *Website:* www.marksandspencer.com (office).

BOLLARD, Alan, PhD; New Zealand central banker and international organization official; *Executive Director, Asia-Pacific Economic Cooperation Secretariat;* b. 1951, Auckland; s. of Edward (Ted) Bollard; m. Jenny Morel; two s.; ed Univ. of Auckland; Dir New Zealand Inst. of Econ. Research 1987–94; Chair. New Zealand Commerce Comm. 1994–2008; Sec. to the Treasury 1998–2002; Gov. Reserve Bank of New Zealand 2002–12; Exec. Dir APEC Secr. 2013–; served as Alternate Gov. to Asian Development Bank, World Bank Group, IMF; Companion, Ordre national du Mérite, 2012; Dr hc (Univ. of Auckland) 2007, (Massey Univ.) 2012. *Publications include:* Crisis: One Central Bank Governor & the Global Financial Collapse (with Sarah Gaitanos) 2010, The Rough Mechanical 2012, Small Business in New Zealand, The Structure and Dynamics of New Zealand Industries. *Address:* APEC Secretariat, 35 Heng Mui Keng Terrace, Singapore 119616, Singapore (office). *Telephone:* 68919600 (office). *Fax:* 68919690 (office). *E-mail:* info@apec.org (office). *Website:* www.apec.org (office).

BOLLIGER, Herbert, Lic. Oec., MBA; Swiss business executive; *CEO, Federation of Migros Cooperatives;* b. 23 Nov. 1953; m. Beatrice Bolliger; two c.; ed Univ. of Zurich; with Bayer AG, Zurich 1980–83; joined Fed. of Migros Cooperatives 1983, Controller 1983–86, Head of Finance/IT Migros, Berne and mem. Bd of Dirs 1987–94, Head of IT Migros Group 1994–97, Man. Dir Migros Aare 1997–2005, CEO Migros 2005–, also Chair. Migrosbank AG; Chair. Hotelplan AG; mem. Bd of Dirs Magazine zum Globus AG, Migros Beteiligungen AG, Denner AG, Interio AG, Gurten–Park im Grüene, 'Im Grüene' Foundation Rüschlikon; Del. to Nat. Climate Forum, Thun Sept. 2007. *Address:* Federation of Migros Cooperatives, Limmatstrasse 152, 8031 Zurich, Switzerland (office). *Telephone:* (44) 277-21-11 (office). *Fax:* (44) 277-25-25 (office). *E-mail:* media@migros.ch (office). *Website:* www .migros.ch (office).

BOLLING, Claude; French jazz pianist, composer and band leader; b. 10 April 1930, Cannes; s. of Harry Bolling and Geneviève Brannens; m. Irène Dervize-Sadyker; two s.; ed Nice Conservatory, studied with pvt. music teachers, including Bob Colin, Earl Hines, Maurice Duruflé, Willie 'The Lion' Smith, André Hodeir; worked with Dizzy Gillespie, Stéphane Grappelli, Rex Stewart, Roy Eldridge, Sidney Bechet, Albert Nicholas, Lionel Hampton, The Ellingtonians, Carmen McRae, Jo Williams; formed groups Les Parisiennes, Claude Bolling Big Band; Hon. Citizen of Los Angeles; Commdr, Ordre des Arts et des Lettres 2006, Chevalier, Ordre nat. du Mérite, Officier Légion d'honneur 2010; Médaille d'or Maurice Ravel, SACEM Gold Medal and Grand Prix 1984. *Compositions include:* piano solos, duos, trios and all instrumental combinations, including jazz, big band and symphony orchestra; written and recorded with Jean-Pierre Rampal (Suite for Flute), Alexandre Lagoya (Guitar Concerto), Maurice André (Toot Suite), Pinchas Zukerman (Suite for Violin), Yo-Yo Ma (Suite for Cello). *Compositions for film:* more than 100 film soundtrack scores, including Le Jour et l'Heure 1963, Borsalino 1970, Le Magnifique 1973, Flic Story 1975, California Suite 1978, L'Homme en Colère 1979, The Awakening 1980, Willie and Phil 1980, La Mandarine, Le Mur de l'Atlantique, On ne meurt que deux fois 1985, Netchaiev est de retour 1991, Hasards ou coïncidences 1998. *Compositions for television include:* Jazz Memories, Les Brigades du Tigre (series) 1974–83, Chantecler 1977, Claudine à l'école 1978, L'étrange monsieur Duvallier (series) 1979, Georges Dandin 1980, Le calvaire d'un jeune homme impeccable 1981, Panurge 1982, Les Dalton en cavale 1983, Lucky Luke (series) 1984, La garçonne 1988, Renseignements généraux (series) 1989–90, L'amant de ma soeur 1991, Ce que savait Maisie 1995, Antoine 1996, Maintenant ou jamais 1997, Letter from an Unknown Woman 2001. *Leisure interests:* ecology, model railroading. *Address:* 20 avenue de Lorraine, 92380 Garches, France (office). *Telephone:* 1-47-41-41-84 (office). *Fax:* 1-47-01-03-63 (office). *E-mail:* bollingclaude@wanadoo.fr. *Website:* www.claude-bolling.com (home).

BOLLINGER, Lee Carroll, DJur; American lawyer, academic and university administrator; *President, Columbia University;* b. 30 April 1946, Santa Rosa, Calif.; s. of Lee Bollinger and Patricia Bollinger; m. Jean Magnano Bollinger; one s. one d.; ed Univ. of Oregon, Columbia Univ. Law School; began career as law clerk, US Court of Appeals 1971–72, then US Supreme Court, Washington, DC 1972–73; Faculty mem. Univ. of Michigan Law School 1973–94, Dean 1987–94; Provost and Prof. of Govt, Dartmouth Coll. 1994–96; Pres. Univ. of Michigan 1996–2002; Pres. Columbia Univ. 2002–; Deputy Chair. Fed. Reserve Bank of New York 2010, Chair. 2011; mem. Bd of Dirs Washington Post Co. 2007–; mem. Bd Gerald R. Ford Foundation, RSC, Pulitzer Prize; Trustee, Kresge Foundation, Inst. of Int. Educ.; Fellow, American Acad. of Arts and Sciences, American Philosophical Soc.; Clark Kerr Award for Distinguished Leadership in Higher Educ. 2005, Nat. Humanitarian Award, Nat. Equal Justice Award. *Publications include:* The Tolerant Society: Freedom of Speech and Extremist Speech in America 1986, Images of a Free Press 1991, Eternally Vigilant: Free Speech in the Modern Era 2002, Uninhibited, Robust, and Wide Open: A Press for a New Century 2010; numerous books, articles and essays in scholarly journals. *Address:* Office of the President, Columbia University, 535 West 116th Street, 202 Low Library, New York, NY 10027, USA (office). *Telephone:* (212) 854-9970 (office). *Fax:* (212) 854-9973 (office). *E-mail:* officeofthepresident@columbia.edu (office). *Website:* www.columbia.edu/content/office-president-1.html (office).

BOLLORÉ, Vincent Marie, LLM; French financial investor and industrialist; *Chairman and CEO, Groupe Bolloré;* b. 1 April 1952, Boulogne-Billancourt (Hauts-de-Seine); s. of Michel Bolloré and Monique Bolloré (née Follot); m. Sophie Fossorier 1977; three s. one d.; ed Lycée Janson-de-Sailly, Université Paris X Nanterre; with EIB 1970–75; Deputy Man. Cie financière Rothschild 1976–81; Chair. and CEO Groupe Bolloré and Bolloré Papermills 1981–, Bolloré, Inc., USA 1981–, Banque Rivaud 1996–; mem. Bd of Dirs Banque de France 1988–; mem. Supervisory Bd Vallourec 2004–07; mem. Bd Dirs then Chair. Havas 2005–; mem. Bd of Dirs Natexis Banques Populaires 2006–, Médiamétrie 2007–, Mediobanca, Financière Moncey, Plantations des Terres Rouges 2008–; mem. Exec. Cttee Conseil nat. du patronat français (CNPF) 1987–96; Chair. Cen. Cttee Armateurs de France 1993–95, Fondation de la deuxième chance 1998; f. Direct8 (TV channel) 2005 (transferred to Groupe Canal+ 2011), DirectSoir (first free evening newspaper in France) 2006; launched Autolib' electric car service in Paris (modelled on Vélib' bike-sharing scheme) 2011; Chevalier, Légion d'honneur, Grand Officier, Ordre du Lion (Senegal), Légion d'honneur (Côte d'Ivoire); Entrepreneur de l'année 1986, Man. de l'année 1987. *Address:* Groupe Bolloré, Tour Bolloré, 31–32 quai Dion Bouton, 92811 Puteaux (office); Havas, 2 alle de Longchamp, 92281 Suresnes Cedex, France (office). *Telephone:* 1-58-47-90-00 (office). *Fax:* 1-58-47-99-99 (office). *Website:* www.bollore.com (office); www.havas .com (office).

BOLLOYEV, Taimuraz Kazbekovich; Russian/Ossetian business executive; b. 23 Feb. 1953, North Ossetia; m.; ed Moscow Inst. of Food Industry; mechanic, then Head of Beer Production, Stepan Razin factory, Leningrad, Chief Technologist 1987–91; Dir Industrial Union, Vsevolzhsk, Leningrad Region 1984–87; Dir-Gen. Baltika (beer manufacturer) 1991–2004, Pres. 1998–2004; acquired St Petersburg Clothing Factory and Trud Factory (uniform manufacturer) 2005; est. Real Estate Investment Trust Baltika 2005; Vice-Pres. Olympstroi Corpn (designer and builder of facilities for 2014 Winter Olympic facilities in Sochi)–2009, Pres. 2009–11 (resgnd); Order of Honour. *Leisure interests:* classical music, football, Russian baths, wrestling, fishing, cooking. *Address:* c/o Olympstroi Corporation, Sochi, Krasnodar Region, Russia.

BOLSHOV, Leonid Aleksandrovich, DS; Russian physicist; *Director, Institute of Nuclear Safety (IBRAE), Russian Academy of Sciences;* b. 23 July 1946, Moscow; m.; three c.; ed Moscow State Univ.; engineer, Jr then Sr Researcher, later Head of Lab., Moscow Kurchatov Inst. of Atomic Energy (Troisk Br.) 1970–91; Dir Inst. of Nuclear Safety (IBRAE), Russian Acad. of Sciences 1991–; participated in mitigation of consequences of Chernobyl nuclear accident 1986; mem. Scientific Council, Ministry of Emergency Affairs; Head of Section, Science and Tech. Council, Rosatom (State Atomic Energy Corpn); mem. nuclear safety group Eurobank; Corresp. mem. Russian Acad. of Sciences 1997; mem. Editorial Bd Atomnaya Energiya journal; Order of Courage 1997, Order of Honour 2006; USSR State Prize 1988. *Publications:* over 300 scientific publs and monographs on physics of solid surfaces, non-linear optics, physics of laser thermonuclear synthesis and problems of nuclear power safety. *Address:* Institute of Nuclear Safety (IBRAE), Russian Academy of Sciences, Bolshaya Tulskaya str. 52, 115191 Moscow, Russia (office). *Telephone:* (495) 952-24-21 (office). *Fax:* (495) 958-00-40 (office). *E-mail:* bolshov@ibrae.ac.ru (office). *Website:* www.ibrae.ac.ru (office).

BOLT, Usain St Leo, OJ, CD; Jamaican athlete; b. 21 Aug. 1986, Sherwood Content, Trelawny; s. of Wellesley Bolt and Jennifer Bolt; ed William Knibb Memorial High School; holds world records for 100m at 9.58 seconds and 200m at 19.19 seconds, both set at World Championships, Berlin 2009; holds Olympic records for 200m at 19.30 seconds (set at Olympic Games, Beijing 2008), 100m at 9.63 seconds, and as men. Jamaican team, 4×100m relay at 36.84 seconds (set at Olympic Games, London 2012); first man to win all three events at a single Olympics since Carl Lewis in 1984, and first man in history to set world records in all three at a single Olympics; made first appearance on world stage at Int. Assocn of Athletics Feds (IAAF) World Youth Championships, Debrecen, Hungary 2001 (set new personal best of 21.73 seconds in 200m); moved to Kingston to train with Jamaica Amateur Athletic Asscn at Univ. of Tech.; gold medal, 200m, World Jr Championships (youngest-ever gold medallist), Kingston 2002, 200m, World Youth Championships, Sherbrooke 2003; silver medal, 4×100m and 4×400m relays, World Jr Championships, Kingston 2002; first jr sprinter to run 200m in under 20 seconds with time of 19.93 seconds at CARIFTA Games 2004; turned professional 2004; missed most of his first two seasons due to injuries; eliminated in first round of 200m heats at Athens Olympics 2004; gold medal, Int. Assocn of Athletics Feds (IAAF) World Cup, Athens 2006; beat Don Quarrie's 200m Jamaican nat. record with time of 19.75 seconds in 2007; set his first 100m world record with time of 9.72 seconds at Reebok Grand Prix, New York City, May 2007; gold medal, 100m, 200m and 4×100m relay, Olympic Games, Beijing 2008, World Championships, Berlin 2009, Olympic Games, London 2012, World Championships, Moscow 2013; gold medal, World Athletics Final, Thessaloniki 2009; gold medal, 200m and 4×100m relay (set world record time of 37.04 seconds), World Championships, Daegu 2011; silver medal, 200m, World Championships, Osaka 2007; won 100m race in Diamond League in 9.79 seconds 2012; by winning three gold medals at 2013 World Championships became the most successful athlete in 30-year history of the athletics world championships; announced intention to retire after 2016 Rio Olympics Sept. 2013; coached by Glen Mills 2004–; Dr hc (Univ. of the West Indies); IAAF Rising Star Award 2002, 2003, IAAF World Athlete of the Year 2008, 2009, 2011, 2012, Track & Field Athlete of the Year 2008, 2009, BBC Overseas Sports Personality of the Year 2008, 2009, 2012, Laureus World Sportsman of the Year 2009, 2010, 2013, UNESCO Champion for Sport 2012, ESPY Award 2013. *Publication:* Usain Bolt. My Story: 9.58 2010. *Leisure interests:* music, dancing, sports, especially cricket and football (fan of Manchester United and Real Madrid), played basketball in the NBA All-Star Weekend Celebrity Game. *Address:* c/o Jamaica Athletics Administrative Association Ltd, PO Box 272, Kingston 5, Jamaica (office). *Telephone:* 978-7102 (office). *Fax:* 946-0003 (office). *E-mail:* athleticsja@cwjamaica.com (office). *Website:* www.usainbolt .com.

BOLTANSKI, Christian; French artist; b. 6 Sept. 1944, Paris; s. of Etienne Boltanski and Marie-Elise Ilari-Guérin; m. Annette Messager; participant in numerous group exhbns in Europe, USA, Canada and Australia; Prof. Ecole Nationale Supérieure des Beaux Arts 1986; Grand Prix nat. de la Sculpture 1990,

Roland-Preis 1997, Kunstpreis 2001, Goslau Kaiserring Prize, Monchhausmuseum Goslar 2001, Laureate of the Praemium Imperiale, Japan Art Asscn 2006, Créateurs sans frontières Award, Cultures France 2007. *Publications:* L'Album de la Famille B. 1971, Les Compositions Photographiques 1976, Murales 1977. *Address:* 146 boulevard Carmélina, 92240 Malakoff, France. *Telephone:* 1-46-57-63-71. *Website:* www.christian-boltanski.com.

BOLTEN, Joshua (Josh) Brewster, BA, JD; American lawyer, business executive and fmr government official; *Managing Director, Rock Creek Global Advisors LLC;* ed Princeton Univ., Stanford Univ. Law School; fmr Ed. Stanford Law Review; law clerk, US Dist Court, San Francisco 1980; Int. Trade Counsel to US Finance Cttee 1985–89, fmr Gen. Counsel to US Trade Rep.; Exec. Dir for Legal and Govt Affairs, Goldman Sachs Int., London 1994–99; Policy Dir Bush-Cheney presidential campaign 1999–2000; Asst to Pres., Deputy Chief of Staff for Policy, The White House 2001–03, Dir Office of Man. and Budget (OMB) 2003–06; White House Chief of Staff 2006–09; Co-founder and Man. Dir Rock Creek Global Advisors LLC 2011–; mem. Bd of Dirs US Holocaust Memorial Museum (Vice-Chair.), ONE Campaign. *Address:* Rock Creek Global Advisors LLC, 1401 I Street, NW, Suite 1120, Washington, DC 20005, USA (office). *Telephone:* (202) 903-0600 (office). *Fax:* (202) 903-0601 (office). *E-mail:* jbolten@rockcreekadvisors.com (office). *Website:* www.rockcreekadvisors.com (office).

BOLTON, John Robert, BA, JD; American lawyer, academic, fmr government official and fmr diplomatist; *Senior Fellow, American Enterprise Institute for Public Policy Research;* b. 20 Nov. 1948, Baltimore, Md; s. of Edward Jackson Bolton and Virginia Bolton (née Godfrey); m. Gretchen Brainerd 1986; one d.; ed Yale Univ.; Assoc., Covington & Burling (law firm), Washington, DC 1974–81, Pnr 1983–85; Gen. Counsel, USAID 1981–82, Asst Admin. for Program and Policy Coordination 1982–83; Asst Attorney-Gen. for Legis. Affairs, US Dept of Justice 1985–88, Asst Attorney-Gen., Civil Div. 1988–89; Asst Sec. for Int. Org. Affairs, US State Dept 1989–93; Pnr, Lerner, Reed, Bolton & McManus LLP (law firm), Washington, DC 1993–99; Of Counsel, Kutak Rock 1999–2001; Sr Vice-Pres. American Enterprise Inst. for Public Policy Research, Washington, DC 1999–2001, Sr Fellow 2007–; Under-Sec. of State for Arms Control and Int. Security, US State Dept 2001–05; Perm. Rep. to UN, New York (recess appointment) 2005–06; Of Counsel, Kirkland & Ellis (law firm) 2008–; Sr Fellow, Manhattan Inst. 1993; Adjunct Prof., George Mason Univ. Law School 1994–2001; Pres. Nat. Policy Forum 1995–96; mem. US Comm. on Int. Religious Freedom 1999–2001. *Publications:* Surrender is Not an Option: Defending America at the United Nations and Abroad 2008, How Barack Obama is Endangering our National Sovereignty 2010. *Address:* American Enterprise Institute, 1150 Seventeenth Street, NW, Washington, DC 20036, USA (office). *Telephone:* (202) 862-5892 (office). *Fax:* (202) 862-7192 (office). *E-mail:* christine.samuelian@aei.org (office). *Website:* www.aei.org (office).

BOLY, Yéro; Burkinabè politician; b. 1954, Komki-Ipala; m.; ed Ecole Nat. d'Admin; subprefect, Dori region 1978–80, l'Oudalan region 1980; civil servant, Ministry of the Interior 1983; Sec.-Gen. Namentenga Prov. and Prefect, Boulsa region 1983–84; High Commr, Gnagna Prov. 1984–86; Amb. to Côte d'Ivoire 1986–88, to Libya 1988–95, to Iran 1990–92; Minister for Regional Affairs and Security 1995–2000; Head of Presidential Staff 2000–04; Minister of Defence and War Veterans 2004–11; Grand Officier, Ordre Nat. de Côte d'Ivoire 1988, Officier, Ordre du Mérite 2004, Commdr, Ordre Nat. du Burkina Faso 2004; Médaille d'Honneur des Sapeurs Pompiers 2000, Médaille d'Honneur de la Police Nationale 2005. *Address:* c/o Ministry of Defence, 01 BP 496, Ouagadougou 01, Burkina Faso (office).

BOMBIERI, Enrico, PhD; American (b. Italian) mathematician and academic; *IBM von Neumann Professor Emeritus of Mathematics, Institute for Advanced Study, Princeton University;* b. 26 Nov. 1940, Milan; ed Univ. of Milan, Trinity Coll., Cambridge, UK; Prof. of Math., Univ. of Pisa 1966–73; Prof. of Math., Scuola Normale Superiore, Pisa 1974–; Visiting mem. Inst. for Advanced Study, Princeton, NJ, USA 1977, IBM von Neumann Prof. of Math. 1984–2011, Prof. Emer. 2011–; mem. Exec. Cttee Int. Math. Union 1979–82; mem. Accad. Nazionale dei Quaranta, Rome, Accad. Nazionale dei Lincei, European Acad. of Sciences, Arts and Humanities; Foreign mem. Acad. des Sciences, Paris 1984, Royal Swedish Acad., Academia Europaea, Accad. Nazionale dei XL, Rome; Fellow, NAS, American Acad. of Arts and Sciences; Cavaliere di Gran Croce al Merito della Repubblica 2002; Fields Medal, Int. Congress of Mathematicians, Vancouver 1974, Balzan Int. Prize 1980, Premio Internazionale Pitagora 2006, Joseph Doob Prize, American Math. Soc. 2008, Feltrinelli Prize, King Faisal Int. Prize for Science (with Terence Tao) 2010. *Publications:* Geometric Measure Theory and Minimal Surfaces 1973, Le Grand Crible dans la théorie analytique des nombres (The Large Sieve in Analytic Number Theory) 1974, Seminar on Minimal Submanifolds 1983, An Introduction to Minimal Currents and Parametric Variational Problems 1985, Number Theory, Trace Formulas, and Discrete Groups 1989. *Address:* Simonyi Hall 213, School of Mathematics, Institute for Advanced Study, Einstein Drive, Princeton, NJ 08540, USA (office). *Telephone:* (609) 734-8397 (office). *Fax:* (609) 924-8399 (office). *E-mail:* eb@math.ias.edu (home); gustafss@ias.edu (home). *Website:* www.ias.edu/people/faculty-and-emeriti/bombieri (office).

BON, Michel; French business executive; *Chairman, Devoteam SA;* b. 5 July 1943, Grenoble; s. of Emmanuel Bon and Mathilde Bon (née Aussedat); m. Catherine Brunet de Sairigné; four c.; ed Ecole Supérieure Sciences Economiques et Commerciales, Paris Inst. of Political Studies, Ecole Nationale d'Admin., Stanford Business School; auditor, Ministry of Finance 1971–75; banker, Crédit Nat. 1975–78; joined Crédit Agricole 1978, Head of Commitments, later Deputy CEO 1981–85; Deputy CEO, later CEO and Chair., Carrefour 1985–92; Head Nat. Job Placement Agency 1993–95; Chair. France Télécom 1995–2002; Chair. (non-exec.) Orange (after merger with France Télécom) 2001–02; Chair. Supervisory Bd Editions du Cerf 1997–, Devoteam SA 2006–; Chair. Supervisory Council Ecole Supérieure Sciences Economiques et Commerciales, Inst. Pasteur 2003–05, Institut de l'Entreprise 2001–04; Sr Adviser Roland Berger Strategy Consultants, Vermeer Capital; fmr mem. Advisory Bd Banque de France; Officier, Légion d'honneur; Chevalier du Mérite agricole; Officier, Ordre nat. du Mérite; Man. of the Year 1991, 1992, 1998. *Address:* Devoteam SA, 73 rue Anatole France, 92300, Levallois-Perret (office); 4 avenue de Camoëns, 75116 Paris, France (home). *Telephone:* 1-41-49-48-23 (office); 1-42-88-84-90 (home). *E-mail:* michel.bon@devoteam.com (office); michel.bon@wanadoo.fr.

BON JOVI, Jon; American singer, songwriter, musician (guitar), record producer and actor; b. (John Francis Bongiovi, Jr) 2 March 1962, Perth Amboy, NJ; m. Dorothea Hurley 1989; three s. one d.; singer in local bands Raze, Atlantic City Expressway; Founder-mem. and lead singer in rock group Bon Jovi 1983–88, 1992–; solo artist 1988–; numerous tours, radio, TV and live appearances world-wide; soundtrack for numerous films; Owner man. co. BJM; Owner record label Jambco; Founder and primary Owner Philadelphia Soul of the Arena Football League 2004–; American Music Awards for Favorite Pop/Rock Band 1988, for Favorite Pop/Rock Single 1991, Nordoff-Robbins Music Therapy Silver Clef 1990, Golden Globe Award for Best Original Song from a Motion Picture (for Blaze of Glory) 1991, BRIT Award for Best Int. Group (with band) 1995, VH-1 Award for Favorite Video (for It's My Life) 2000, Grammy Award for Best Country Collaboration with Vocals (with Jennifer Nettles) 2007. *Films include:* Young Guns II: Blaze of Glory (uncredited) 1990, Moonlight and Valentino (Motion Picture Club Premier Performance Award) 1995, The Leading Man 1996, Little City 1997, Destination Anywhere (video) 1997, No Looking Back 1998, Home-grown 1998, Row Your Boat 1998, U-571 2000, Pay It Forward 2000, Ally McBeal 2001–02, Vampires: Los Muertos 2002, Cry Wolf 2005, Pucked 2006, New Year's Eve 2011. *Television includes:* Unsolved Mysteries 1988, Sex and the City (series) 1999, Ally McBeal (series) 2002. *Recordings include:* albums: with Bon Jovi: Bon Jovi 1984, 7800° Fahrenheit 1985, Slippery When Wet 1986, Bon Jovi Live 1987, New Jersey 1988, Keep The Faith 1991, Cross Road (compilation) 1994, These Days 1995, Crush 2000, One Wild Night 1985–2001 (live) 2001, Tokyo Road: Best of Bon Jovi (compilation) 2001, Bounce 2002, Distance 2003, This Left Feels Right (compilation) 2003, Have a Nice Day 2005, Lost Highway 2007, The Circle 2009, Greatest Hits (compilation) 2010, What About Now 2013; solo: Young Guns II: Blaze of Glory 1990, Destination Anywhere 1997; box set: 100,000,000 Bon Jovi Fans Can't Be Wrong 2004. *Address:* c/o Bon Jovi Management, PO Box 237040, New York, NY 10023, USA (office). *Telephone:* (212) 336-9413 (office). *Fax:* (212) 336-5385 (office). *Website:* www.bonjovi.com.

BOND, Alan, AO; Australian business executive; b. 22 April 1938, London, England; s. of Frank Bond and Kathleen Bond; m. 1st Eileen Hughes 1956 (divorced); two s. two d.; m. 2nd Diana Bliss 1995; ed Perivale School, London and Fremantle Boys' School, WA; Founder and Exec. Chair. Bond Corpn Holdings Ltd 1969–90, now consultant; interests in brewing, property, oil and gas, electronic media, minerals, airships; declared bankrupt April 1992; sentenced to 2¹/²years' imprisonment for dishonesty but found not guilty after retrial Nov. 1992; sentenced to three years' imprisonment for fraud 1996; sentenced to four years' imprisonment for fraud Feb. 1997; sentence extended to seven years Aug. 1997; released March 2000; Syndicate Head, Americas Cup Challenge 1983 Ltd; currently Owner, Strategic Assets Investments Ltd, Capital Asset Enterprises; Australian of the Year 1978, Australia Winners of 1983 Americas Cup Challenge. *Leisure interest:* yachting.

BOND, Alan Maxwell, PhD, DSc, FAA, FRACI, FRSC; Australian chemist and academic; *R.L. Martin Distinguished Professor of Chemistry and Federation Fellow, Monash University;* b. 17 Aug. 1946, Cobden, Vic.; s. of the late Ian T. Bond and Joyce M. Bond; m. Tunde-Maria Bond 1969; two s.; ed Univ. of Melbourne; Sr Demonstrator, Dept of Inorganic Chem., Univ. of Melbourne 1970–73, Research Fellow 1973–78; Foundation Prof. of Chem., Deakin Univ. 1978–90; Prof. of Chem., La Trobe Univ. 1990–95; Prof. of Chem., Monash Univ. 1995–, Deputy Head Dept of Chem. 1996–97, 1999, Head, School of Chem. 2000–02, R.L. Martin Distin-guished Prof. of Chem., Fed. Fellow 2004–; 150th Anniversary Royal Soc. of Chem., Robert Boyle Fellow in Analytical Chem., Univ. of Oxford 1991, Hinshelwood Lecturer 1998, Vallee Visiting Prof. 2004–; mem. numerous editorial bds, including Reviews in Analytical Chemistry 1971–, Bulletin of Electrochemistry 1987–, Inorganica Chimica Acta 1988–, Journal of Electroanalytical Chemistry 1997–, Green Chemistry 1999, Encyclopedia of Analytical Science (second edn) 2001–; mem. Chem. Panel, Australian Research Council 1993–95, Council, Australian Acad. of Science 1993–96 (Vice-Pres. 1995–96), ACS, USA Electro-chemical Soc.; Fulbright Fellow 1972; Fellow, Japan Soc. for Promotion of Science 1990, IUPAC, Royal Australian Chemical Inst.; Erskine Fellowship 1993; Christensen Fellowship, St Catherine's Coll., Oxford 1998; Fed. of Asian Chemical Socs Foundation Lectureship 1993; Rennie Medal 1975, David Syme Prize 1978, Australian Analytical Chem. Medal 1989, Stokes Medal 1992, Liversidge Award, Australian and NZ AAS 1992, Australian Research Council Special Investigator Award 1997–99, Royal Soc. of Chem. (London) Electrochemistry Group Medal 1997, Royal Australian Chemical Inst. H.G. Smith Medal 1998, Royal Soc. of Vic. Medal 1999, Burrows Medal 2000, Faraday Medal, Royal Soc. of Chem. 2000, Gov.-Gen.'s Centenary Medal for Service to Australian Soc. and Science in Electro-chemistry 2003, Craig Medal, Australian Acad. of Science 2004, Reilley Award 2005. *Publications:* Modern Polarographic Methods in Analytical Chemistry 1981, Broadening Electrochemical Horizons 2002; more than 600 publs on different aspects of electrochemistry. *Leisure interest:* cricket. *Address:* School of Chemistry, Monash University, Clayton, Vic. 3800, Australia (office). *Telephone:* (3) 9905-1338 (office). *Fax:* (3) 9905-4597 (office). *E-mail:* alan.bond@sci.monash.edu.au (office). *Website:* www.chem.monash.edu.au/staff/bond.html (office).

BOND, Christopher Samuel (Kit), BA, LLB; American lawyer and fmr politician; *Partner, Public Finance and Public Law Practice Group, Thompson Coburn LLP;* b. 6 March 1939, St Louis, Mo.; s. of Arthur Doerr Bond and Elizabeth Green Bond; m. 1st Carolyn Reid 1967 (divorced 1995); m. 2nd Linda Bond 2002; one s.; ed Deerfield Acad., Mass, Woodrow Wilson School of Public and Int. Affairs, Princeton Univ., Univ. of Virginia; clerk, Fifth Circuit, US Court of Appeals 1963–64; with Covington & Burling (law firm), Washington, DC 1964–67; in pvt. practice 1968; Asst Attorney-Gen., Chief Counsel of Consumer Protection Div. 1969–70; State Auditor, Mo. 1970–72; Gov. of Mo. 1973–77, 1981–84; Chair. Republican Govs Asscn 1974–75, Midwestern Govs Conf. 1976; mem. Exec. Cttee Nat. Govs Conf. 1974–75; Chair. NGA Cttee on Econ. Devt 1981–82; Pres. Great Plains Legal Foundation, Kansas City, Mo. 1977–81; Partner, Gage & Tucker (law firm), Kansas City and St Louis 1981–87, Thompson Coburn LLP, Washington, DC and St Louis 2011–; Senator from Mo. 1987–2011 (retd), Chair. Senate Small Business Cttee 1995–2001; Republican; Hon. LLD (Westminster and William Jewell Colls, Mo.) 1973; Hon. DLitt (Drury Coll., Springfield, Mo.) 1976. *Publications include:* The Next Front: Southeast Asia and the Road to Global Peace with Islam (co-author) 2009. *Address:* Thompson Coburn LLP, 1909 K Street

NW, Suite 600, Washington, DC 20006-1167 (office); Thompson Coburn LLP, One US Bank Plaza, St Louis, MO 63101-1611 (office); 14 South Jefferson Road, Mexico, MO 65265, USA (home). *Telephone:* (202) 585-6946 (Washington, DC) (office); (314) 552-6000 (St Louis) (office). *Fax:* (202) 508-1033 (Washington, DC) (office); (314) 552-7000 (St Louis) (office). *E-mail:* info@thompsoncoburn.com (office). *Website:* www.thompsoncoburn.com (office).

BOND, Edward; British playwright, director and poet; b. 18 July 1934, London; m. Elisabeth Pablé 1971; Northern Arts Literary Fellowship 1977–79; resident theatre writer, Univ. of Essex 1982–83; City of Lyon Medal 2007; Hon. DLitt (Yale) 1977; George Devine Award 1968, John Whiting Award 1968, Obie Award 1976. *Publications:* plays: The Pope's Wedding 1962, Saved 1965, Narrow Road to the Deep North 1968, Early Morning 1968, Passion 1971, Black Mass 1971, Lear 1972, The Sea 1973, Bingo 1974, The Fool 1976, A-A-America! (Grandma Faust and The Swing) 1976, Stone 1976, The Bundle 1978, The Woman 1979, The Worlds 1980, The Activist Papers 1980, Restoration 1981, Summer: A Play for Europe 1982, Derek 1983, Human Cannon 1985, The War Plays (Red Black and Ignorant, The Tin Can People, Great Peace) 1985, Jackets 1989, In the Company of Men 1990, September 1990, Olly's Prison 1993, Tuesday 1993, Coffee: A Tragedy 1994, At the Inland Sea (A Play for Young People) 1996, Eleven Vests (A Play for Young People) 1997, The Crime of the Twenty-first Century 1999, The Children (A Play for Two Adults and Sixteen Children) 2000, Chair 2000, Have I None 2000, Existence 2002, Born 2004, The Balancing Act 2004, The Short Electra 2004, My Day (Song Cycle for Children) 2005, The Under Room 2006, Arcade 2006, Tune 2007, People 2007, A Window 2009, There Will Be More 2010, Collected Plays (nine vols) 1977–2011 2011, Innocence 2011, The Broken Bowl 2011, The Edge 2012, The Chair Trilogy 2012; short stories: Fables 1982; opera librettos of music by Hans Werner Henze: We Come to the River 1977, The English Cat 1983; ballet libretto of music by Henze: Orpheus 1982; translations: Chekhov's The Three Sisters 1967, Wede-kind's Spring Awakening 1974, Wedekind's Lulu: A Monster Tragedy (with Elisabeth Bond-Pablé) 1992; other: Theatre Poems and Songs 1978, Collected Poems 1978–1985 1987, Notes on Post-Modernism 1990, Letters (five vols) 1994–2001, Notes on Imagination 1995, Selected Notebooks Vol. 1 2000, Vol. 2 2001, The Hidden Plot: Notes on Theatre and the State 2000. *Address:* c/o Casarotto Ramsay, Waverley House, 7–12 Noel Street, London, W1F 8GQ, England (office). *Telephone:* (20) 7287-4450 (office). *Fax:* (20) 7287-9128 (office). *E-mail:* tom@casarotto.uk.com (office). *Website:* www.casarotto.uk.com (office).

BOND, (Horace) Julian; American civil rights leader and academic; *Professor Emeritus, Department of History, University of Virginia;* b. 14 Jan. 1940; s. of Horace Mann Bond and Julia Agnes Bond (née Washington); m. 1st Alice Louise Clopton 1961 (divorced 1989); three s. two d.; m. 2nd Pamela Sue Horowitz 1990; ed Morehouse Coll.; Co-founder Cttee on Appeal for Human Rights, Atlanta Univ. 1960; Co-founder Student Non-violent Co-ordinating Cttee 1960, Communications Dir 1961–66; reporter and feature writer, Atlanta Inquirer 1960–61, Man. Ed. 1963; mem. Ga House of Reps 1966–75, excluded 1966 by House for criticizing US involvement in Viet Nam, exclusion overruled in Supreme Court; mem. Ga Senate 1975–87; Prof., Drexel Univ. 1988–89; Pappas Fellow, Univ. of Pennsylvania 1989; Visiting Prof., Harvard Univ. 1989, 1991, Univ. of Virginia 1990; Distinguished Prof. in Residence, American Univ. 1991–; Teacher, Nat Endowment for Human-ities Seminar, Harvard Univ. 1996–2001; Prof., Univ. of Virginia 1998–90, Prof. Emer. 1990–; Chair. Nat. Asscn for the Advancement of Colored People (NAACP) 1998–2010; Pres. Emer. Southern Poverty Law Center; Pres. Inst. of Southern Studies; mem. Bd of Dirs Delta Ministry Project of Nat. Council of Churches, Robert F. Kennedy Memorial Fund, Martin Luther King Jr Center for Social Change, Center for Community Change, Southern Regional Council, New Democratic Coalition and other bodies; mem. Nat. Advisory Council of American Civil Liberties Union, Southern Correspondents Reporting Racial Equality Wars; hon. degrees from 25 colls and univs. *Publications:* A Time to Speak, A Time to Act, Gonna Sit at the Welcome Table; poems and articles in books and periodicals. *Address:* Corcoran Department of History, University of Virginia, 154 Nau Hall, South Lawn, Charlottesville, VA 22904; 4805 Mt Hope Drive, Baltimore, MD 21215 (office); 5435 41st Place, NW, Washington, DC 20015, USA. *Telephone:* (202) 244-1213 (home). *Website:* history.virginia.edu (office).

BOND, J. Richard (Dick), OC, BSc, MS, PhD, FRS, FRSC, FAPS, FInstP, CPhys; Canadian astrophysicist and academic; *University Professor, University of Toronto;* scientist, Gamma Ray Astronomy, Jet Propulsion Lab., Pasadena, Calif. 1975–76; Research Asst, Kellogg Radiation Lab., California Inst. of Tech. (Caltech) 1973–78; Postdoctoral Fellow/Lecturer in Astronomy, Univ. of California, Berkeley 1978–81; Research Fellow, Inst. of Astronomy, Univ. of Cambridge, UK 1982–83, Fellow of Churchill Coll.; mem. Inst. of Theoretical Physics, Univ. of California, Santa Barbara (UCSB) 1984, 1988–2000; Directeur de Recherche Associée, 4ème échelon, Institut d'Astrophysique de Paris 1993–94, 1996; mem. Isaac Newton Inst., Cambridge, UK 1999; Moore Scholar, Caltech 2002; mem. Kavli Inst. for Theoretical Physics (KITP), USCB 2002, KITP China, Beijing 2007; Humboldt Fellow, Max Planck Inst. for Astrophysics 2006–07; Assoc. mem. Perimeter Inst. for Theoretical Physics 2002; Asst Prof. of Physics, Stanford Univ. 1981–85, Assoc. Prof. 1985–87; Assoc. Prof., Canadian Inst. for Theoretical Astrophysics (CITA) 1985–87, Prof. 1987–99, Acting Dir CITA 1990–91, 1994–95, Dir 1996–2001, 2001–06; Cross-appointed Prof., Depts of Astronomy and Physics, Univ. of Toronto 1985–, Univ. Prof. 2000–; Dir Canadian Inst. for Advanced Research (CIFAR) Cosmology and Gravity Program 2002–, CIFAR Sr Fellow; Visiting Scientist, Nuclear Theory, Neils Bohr Inst. 1976–77; Visiting Research Physicist, Inst. for Theoretical Physics, Univ. of California, Santa Barbara Feb.–June 1995; Visiting Prof., 1ère class, Univ. of Paris/IAP/IAS 2003; Visiting Scientist, Inst. for Astronomy, Univ. of Hawaii 2008, Stanford Inst. for Theoretical Physics, Stanford Univ. 2008, KIPAC and SLAC 2008; Visiting Faculty Assoc., Caltech 2008; Sacker Visitor, Inst. of Astronomy, Univ. of Cambridge 2008; mem. American Astronom-ical Soc., American Physical Soc., Canadian Astronomical Soc., Canadian Asscn of Physicists, Inst. of Physics, Int. Astronomical Union, RSC, Royal Soc. of London; Assoc., CIFAR 1985–85, Fellow 1986; Foreign Assoc., NAS 2011; Fellow, American Physical Soc. 1998; Hon. Foreign mem. American Acad. of Arts and Sciences 2003; Order of Ontario; Richard P. Feynman Fellowship, Caltech 1974–75, Alfred P. Sloan Foundation Research Fellow 1985–89, E.W.R. Steacie Fellow, NSERC 1989–91, E.W.R. Steacie Prize, NRC 1989, Beals Prize, Canadian Astronomical Soc. 1995, CAP/CRM Prize in Theoretical and Math. Physics 1998, Exchange

Lecturer, Institut de France, Acad. des Sciences/RSC 1998, Dannie Heineman Prize, AAS and AIP 2002, Moore Scholar, Caltech 2002, Inaugural mem. Etobian Gallery of Distinction, ECI, Toronto 2003, NSERC Award of Excellence 2003, Herzberg Gold Medal 2006, Killam Prize in the Natural Sciences 2007, Alexander von Humboldt Research Award 2007, Cosmology Prize, The Gruber Foundation 2008, RSC Henry Marshall Tory Medal 2009, Medal for Lifetime Achievement in Physics, Canadian Asscn of Physicists (first astrophysicist) 2010, Queen Elizabeth II Diamond Jubilee Medal 2012. *Publications:* book chapters and reviews; more than 300 papers in peer-reviewed journals. *Address:* McLennan Phys Labs, 14th floor, Room 1408, Canadian Institute for Theoretical Astrophysics, 60 St George Street, University of Toronto, Toronto, ON M5S 3H8, Canada (office). *Telephone:* (416) 978-6874 (office). *Fax:* (416) 978-3921 (office). *E-mail:* bond@cita.utoronto.ca (office). *Website:* www.cita.utoronto.ca/~bond (office).

BOND, Sir John Reginald Hartnell, Kt; British business executive; *Chairman, Xstrata plc;* b. 24 July 1941, Oxford, England; s. of the late Capt. R. H. A. Bond and of E. C. A. Bond; m. Elizabeth Caroline Parker 1968; one s. two d.; ed Tonbridge School, Kent, Cate School, Calif., USA; joined The Hongkong and Shanghai Banking Corpn (later became HSBC) 1961; worked in Hong Kong, Thailand, Singapore, Indonesia and USA; Chief Exec. Wardley Ltd (Merchant Banking) 1984–87; Chair. Hongkong Bank of Canada 1987–98; Exec. Dir Hongkong and Shanghai Banking Corpn (responsible for the Americas) 1988–89, Commercial Banking, Hong Kong 1990–91; Pres. and CEO Marine Midland Bank, Inc., Buffalo, USA (subsidiary of HSBC Holdings PLC) 1991–92, Chair. HSBC Americas Inc. 1997; Deputy Chair. HSBC Bank PLC (fmrly Midland Bank) 1996–98 (Dir 1993), Chair. 1998–2006; Chair. HSBC Bank Middle East (fmrly British Bank of the Middle East) 1998–2006; Group CEO HSBC Holdings PLC 1993–98, Group Chair. 1998–2006 (Dir 1990–); Dir (non-exec.) Vodafone Group plc, Chair. 2006–11; Dir (non-exec.) and Chair. Xstrata plc 2011–; Dir Hang Seng Bank Ltd 1990–96, Bank of England 2001–; Sr Adviser Kohlberg Kravis Roberts 2006–; Dir (non-exec.) London Stock Exchange 1994–99, British Steel 1994–98, Orange PLC 1996–99, Ford Motor Co., USA 2000–09 (adviser to Exec. Chair. 2006–09), A.P. Møller-Mærsk A/S (Denmark), Shui On Land Ltd (Hong Kong SAR); Chair. Inst. of Int. Finance, Washington, DC 1998–2003; adviser to Northern Trust, Chicago, KKR Asia; mem. of various advisory bodies in China: China Devt Forum, China Banking Regulatory Comm. Int. Advisory Bd, Tsinghua School of Econs and Man. at Tsinghua Univ.; Gov. The English-Speaking Union 1997–; Hon. Fellow, London Business School 2003; Hon. DEcon (Richmond American Univ., London) 1998; Hon. DLit (Loughborough) 2000, (Sheffield) 2002; Hon. LLD (South Bank) 2001; Foreign Policy Asscn Medal, New York 2003, Magnolia Gold Award, Shanghai Municipal People's Govt 2003. *Leisure interests:* golf, skiing, reading biographies. *Address:* Xstrata plc, Bahnhofstrasse 2, PO Box 102, 6301 Zug, Switzerland (office). *Telephone:* (41) 726-60-70 (office). *Fax:* (41) 726-60-55 (office). *E-mail:* info@xstrata.com (office). *Website:* www.xstrata.com (office).

BONDEVIK, Kjell Magne; Norwegian politician, diplomatist and clergyman; *President, Oslo Centre for Peace and Human Rights;* b. 3 Sept. 1947, Molde, Co. of Møre og Romsdal; s. of Margit Bondevik and Johs Bondevik; m. Bjørg Bondevik 1970; two s. one d.; ed Free Faculty of Theology, Univ. of Oslo; ordained minister in (Lutheran) Church of Norway 1979; Deputy Chair. Christian Democratic Youth Asscn 1968–70, Chair. 1970–73; Deputy mem. Storting 1969–73, mem. 1973–; Political Vice-Chair. Christian Democratic Party 1975–83, Chair. 1983–95; Minister of Church and Educ. 1983–86, Deputy Prime Minister 1985–86, Minister of Foreign Affairs 1989–90; Chair. Christian Democratic Party's Parl. Group 1981–83, 1986–89, 1993–97; Prime Minister of Norway 1997–2000, 2001–05; UN Sec.-Gen.'s Special Humanitarian Envoy for the Horn of Africa 2006–07; Founder and Pres. Oslo Centre for Peace and Human Rights 2006–; mem. Bd Norwegian Atlantic Cttee, Club of Madrid; Hon. mem. The Int. Raoul Wallenberg Foundation; Grand Cross of St Olav 2004; Hon. DTech (Brunel) 1997; Dr hc (Suffolk) 2000, (Wonkurang) 2000; Wittenberg Award, Luther Inst. 2000. *Publication:* Et liv i spenning (A life of excitement/tension) 2006, Fortellingen om Aung San Suu Kyi (The story of Aung San Suu Kyi) (children's book) 2009. *Address:* Oslo Centre for Peace and Human Rights, Ovre Slottsgate 11, 0157 Oslo, Norway (office). *Telephone:* 23-13-66-70 (office). *Fax:* 23-13-66-77 (office). *E-mail:* post@oslocenter .no (office). *Website:* www.oslocenter.no (office).

BONDS, Barry Lamar; American fmr professional baseball player; b. 24 July 1964, Riverside, Calif.; s. of the late Bobby Bonds (fmr San Francisco Giants player); m.; three c.; ed Serra High School, San Mateo, Calif., Arizona State Univ.; outfielder; drafted by Pittsburgh Pirates in first round (6th pick) 1985 amateur draft, played with Pirates 1985–92, signed as free agent San Francisco Giants 1992–2007, filed for free agency status Oct. 2007; hit 73 home runs 2001 (single-season major league baseball home run record); hit 756th home run on 7 Aug. 2007 to set record of most career home runs; National League Most Valuable Player 1990, 1992, 1993, 2001, 2002, 2003, 2004; National League batting champion 2002 (.370 avg.), 2004 (.362 avg.); f. Bonds Family Foundation; Most Valuable Player (National League), Baseball Writers' Asscn of America 1990, 1992, 1993, 2001, 2002, 2003, 2004, Maj. League Player of Year, Sporting News 1990, 2001, 2004, Nat. League Player of Year, Sporting News 1990, 1992, 1993, 2001, 2002, 2003, 2004. Gold Glove Award 1990–98, Silver Slugger Award 1990–94, 1996–97, 2000–04, 13 All-Star appearances. *Website:* www.barrybonds.com.

BONDURANT, Stuart, BS, MD; American physician, academic and university administrator; *Dean Emeritus and Professor Emeritus of Medicine, School of Medicine, University of North Carolina;* b. 9 Sept. 1929, Winston-Salem, NC; m. 1st Margaret Fortescue 1954 (divorced); one s. two d.; m. 2nd Susan Haughton Ehringhaus 1991; ed Univ. of North Carolina, Duke Univ. School of Medicine; Assoc. Dir Indiana Univ. Cardiovascular Research Center, Indiana Univ. Medical Center, Indianapolis, Ind. 1961–67; Chief, Medical Br. Artificial Heart-Myocardial Infarction Program, Nat. Health Inst., NIH 1966–67; Prof. and Chair., Dept of Medicine, Albany Medical Coll., Physician-in-Chief, Albany Medical Center Hosp., New York 1967–74, Pres. and Dean 1974–79; Prof. of Medicine, Univ. of NC 1979, now Prof. Emer., Dean, Univ. of NC School of Medicine 1979–94, now Dean Emer.; Interim Exec. Vice-Pres. and Exec. Dean, Georgetown Univ. Medical Center 2004–07; Dir Center for Urban Epidemiology Studies, NY Acad of Medicine 19954–96; Chair. North Carolina Biotechnology Center 1988–92; fmr Pres. American Coll. of Physicians, Asscn of American Physicians; fmr Interim Pres. Inst. of Medicine, NAS; fmr Vice-Pres. American Heart Asscn, American Soc. for Clinical Investigation; mem. Bd of Dirs Pharmaceutical Product Development, Inc.; Hon. FRCPE; Hon. DSc (Indiana 1980); Thomas Jefferson Award, Univ. of NC 1998.

BONE, Sir Roger, KCMG, BA; British diplomatist and business executive; *President, Boeing UK Ltd;* ed Palmer's School, Grays, Essex, Univ. of Oxford; career diplomat, overseas assignments in Moscow, Washington, DC, and with UK Rep. to EU, Brussels; Pvt. Sec. to Foreign Sec. 1982–84; Visiting Fellow in Int. Relations, Harvard Univ., USA 1984–85; Asst Under-Sec. of State, FCO 1991–95, Amb. to Sweden 1995–99, to Brazil 1999–2004; Pres. Boeing UK Ltd 2005–; mem. Bd of Dirs F & C Investment Trust plc, Continental Data Graphics Ltd, Nat. Centre for Univs and Business; Trustee Royal United Services Inst.; Council mem. Air League, Brazilian Chamber of Commerce; apptd one of Prime Minister's UKTI Ambs for British Businesses. *Address:* Boeing UK Ltd,16 St James Street, London, SW1A 1ER, England (office). *Telephone:* (20) 7930-5000 (office). *Fax:* (20) 7739-9190 (office). *Website:* www.boeing.com (office).

BONELL, Carlos Antonio; British musician, teacher, guitarist and composer; b. 23 July 1949, London; s. of Carlos Bonell and Ana Bravo; m. Pinuccia Rossetti 1975; two s.; ed William Ellis School, Highgate and Royal Coll. of Music, under John Williams; solo début as solo guitarist, Wigmore Hall, London 1971; concerto début with Royal Philharmonic Orchestra 1975; American début, Avery Fisher Hall, New York 1978; concert appearances with all the prin. British orchestras; appearances with John Williams, Teresa Berganza, Pinchas Zukerman 1975–; formed Carlos Bonell Ensemble 1983; Prof. Royal Coll. of Music 1972–, London Coll. of Music 1983–; Hon. ARCM. *Recordings include:* Guitar Music of Spain 1975, Guitar Music of the Baroque 1976, Showpieces 1981, Rodrigo Concerto 1981, Paganini Trios and Quartets 1983, Twentieth Century Music for Guitar 1987, Once Upon a Time, with Xer-Wai (violin) 1992, Walton Bagatelles and Anon in Love 1993, Britten Folksongs (with Philip Langridge) 1994, The Sea in Spring 1997, The Private Collection 1998, Kinkachoo I Love You (Millennium Guitar, The First 1000 Years) 2000, Trinity Coll. Grade pieces 2003, Carlos Bonell plays Gordon Mizzi 2003, Guitar Classics 2004. *Publications:* 20 First Pieces 1982, Tarrega: Fantasia on "La Traviata", 3 Spanish Folk Songs, Purcell: Music from the Fairy Queen, Fantasy for 3 Guitars 1995, Technique Builder 1997, Millennium Guitar, The First 1000 Years 2000. *Leisure interests:* reading, walking, snooker, films. *Address:* Patrick Allen, Connaught Artists Management Ltd, Penhurst House, 352-356 Battersea Park Road, London, SW11 3BY, England (office). *Telephone:* (20) 7978-0144 (office). *E-mail:* classicalmusic@connaughtartists.com (office); carlos@carlosbonell.com. *Website:* www.carlosbonell.com.

BONET, Pep; Spanish architect and designer; b. 19 Nov. 1941, Barcelona; m. Marta Monné 1964; three s.; ed High School of Architecture, Barcelona; f. Studio Per architectural practice, with Cristian Cirici, Lluis Clotet and Oscar Tusquets 1965; began producing furniture and bldg components, co-f. BD Ediciones de Diseño (now BD Barcelona Design) 1972; taught at School of Architecture, Barcelona 1975–78, Washington School of Architecture, St Louis, Mo., USA 1981; Deltas ADI-FAD Award 1967, 1976, 1986, 1990, 1991, Azulejo de Oro Award 1970, Nat. Restoration Award 1980, FAD Award for Architecture 1965, 1970, 1972, 1987, Architecture and Town Planning award 1987 for Triángulo de Oro Sports Centre, Madrid. *Major works include:* (Feria de Barcelona) Plaza Universo 1983–85, Rius i Taulet pavilion 1987, Iberia pavilion 1987, Lleida-Parallel pavilion 1989; Triángulo de Oro Sports Centre 1985, Canillejas civic centre 1985 (Madrid); Granollers Olympic sports centre, COOB-92. *Leisure interest:* playing jazz (tenor saxophone). *Address:* C/Pujades 63, 08005 Barcelona, Spain. *Telephone:* (93) 4855494. *Fax:* (93) 3091472.

BONETTI, Mattia; Swiss designer, decorator and artist; b. 2 May 1952, Lugano; s. of Giorgio Bonetti and Stella Frossard; m. Isabelle Forestier 1990; two d.; ed Centro Scolastico Industrie Artistiche, Lugano; decorated Bernard Picasso's Boisgeloup Castle 1987, Christian Lacroix Showroom and Graphics 1987–88; designs for cafeteria, Schloss Regensburg Thurn und Taxis Museum, Germany 1990; Banque Bruxelles-Lambert, Geneva 1991; packaging for Nina Ricci Cosmetics 1992, 1994; Water Carafe design for Ricard 1995; designed tramway for city of Montpellier 1998, designed second tramway 2006; Venetian Renaissance Glass show installation, Musée des Arts Décoratifs, Paris 2003; Emile Gallé show installation, Musée d'Orsay, Paris 2004; designed choir for Metz Cathedral 2006; Musée d'Orsay: Art Nouveau Revival installation 2009; designed Hôtel Cristal, Champs Elysées, Paris 2009; Hon. Citizen, City of Villeurbanne; Chevalier, Ordre des Arts et des Lettres 1995; 'Créateurs de l'Année 1991' (France). *Publications:* Mattia Bonetti and Elizabeth Garouste 1990, Garouste and Bonetti 1996, 1998, Elizabeth Garouste and Mattia Bonetti 1981–2001, Mattia Bonetti Drawings 2005, Mattia Bonetti 2008, Mattia Bonetti (by Rizzoli-Skira) 2010. *Leisure interests:* swimming, photography. *Address:* 10 rue Rochebrune, 75011 Paris (office); 1 rue Oberkampf, 75011 Paris, France (home). *Telephone:* 1-48-05-61-21 (office); 1-48-05-86-51 (home). *Fax:* 1-48-05-61-29 (office); 1-48-05-86-51 (home). *E-mail:* mattiabonetti@noos.fr (office).

BONFIELD, Sir Peter (Leahy), Kt, CBE, FREng, FIEE, FRSA; British business executive; b. 3 June 1944; s. of George Bonfield and Patricia Bonfield; m. Josephine Houghton 1968; ed Hitchin Boys' Grammar School and Univ. of Loughborough; Div. Dir Texas Instruments Inc. Dallas, Tex., USA 1966–81; Group Exec. Dir Worldwide Operations, ICL 1981–84, Man. Dir 1984, Chair. and CEO ICL PLC 1987–97, Deputy Chair. 1997–2000; Deputy Chief Exec. STC PLC 1987–90; Chair. and CEO British Telecommunications PLC 1996–2002; Chair. NXP Semiconductors N.V.; Chair. of Council and Senior Pro-Chancellor, Univ. of Loughborough; mem. Bd of Dirs L.M. Ericsson 2002–, Mentor Graphics Corpn 2002–, TSMC 2002–, Sony Corpn; Board Mentor, CMi, Belgium; mem. Advisory Bd Longreach Group, Hong Kong, New Venture Partners LLP; Advisor Apax Partners LLP; Sr Advisor Rothschild, London; Chair. East West Inst., UK; Vice-Pres. British Quality Foundation 1993–2012; Amb. for British Business; Liveryman, Information Technologists' Co. 1992; Trustee Cutty Sark Trust 2002–; Fellow, British Computer Soc. 1990, Chartered Inst. of Marketing 1990, Inst. of Eng and Tech.; Freeman, City of London 1990, Hon. Citizen, Dallas, TX; Commdr, Order of the Lion (Finland) 1995; Dr hc (Open Univ.) 1997; Hon. DTech (Loughborough) 1988, (Brunel) 1997, (Nottingham) 1998, (Northumbria) 1999, (Royal Holloway) 2001, (Cranfield) 2001, (Essex) 2001; Nat. Electronics Council Mountbatten Medal 1995,

Inst. of Man. Gold Medal 1996. *Leisure interests:* music, sailing, skiing. *Address:* Truchas Associates Limited, PO Box 129, Shepperton, Middlesex, TW17 9WL, England (office). *Website:* www.sirpeterbonfield.com.

BONGO ONDIMBA, Ali; Gabonese politician and head of state; *President;* b. 9 Feb. 1959, Brazzaville, Repub. of Congo; s. of Omar Bongo (fmr Pres. of Gabon) and Patience Dabany; m. 2nd Sylvia Ajma Valentin; three s. one d.; ed Univ. of Paris Sorbonne I, France; High Personal Rep. of the Pres. of the Repub. 1987–89; Minister of Foreign Affairs and Cooperation 1989–91 (resgnd); Deputy (Parti démocratique gabonais) for Bongoville, Nat. Ass. 1991–99, for Haut-Ogooué Prov. 2001–09; Minister of Nat. Defence 1999–2009 (resgnd); Pres. of Gabon 2009–. *Leisure interests:* sports, music. *Address:* Présidence de la Republique, BP 546, Libreville, Gabon (office). *Telephone:* (1) 72-76-00 (office). *E-mail:* cabinetpr@ presidence.ga (office). *Website:* www.presidentalibongo.com (office).

BONHAM CARTER, Helena, CBE; British actress; b. 26 May 1966, Golders Green, London; d. of the late Hon. Raymond Bonham Carter and of Elena Bonham Carter; (great granddaughter of British Prime Minister Lord Asquith); partner Tim Burton; one s. one d. *Plays include:* The Barber of Seville 1992, Trelawny of the "Wells" 1992. *Films include:* A Room with a View 1985, Lady Jane 1986, Maurice (uncredited) 1987, La maschera 1988, Six Minutes with Ludwig (short) 1988, Francesco 1989, Getting it Right 1989, Hamlet 1990, Where Angels Fear to Tread 1991, Howards End 1992, Mary Shelley's Frankenstein 1994, The Glace Bay Miners' Museum 1994, A Little Loving 1995, Mighty Aphrodite 1995, Margaret's Museum 1995, Jeremy Hardy Gives Good Sex (video) 1995, Twelfth Night 1996, Portraits chinois 1996, The Petticoat Expeditions 1997, The Theory of Flight 1997, The Wings of the Dove (numerous awards including London Film Critics Circle Award for British Actress of the Year, Nat. Bd of Review Award for Best Actress, Toronto Film Critics Asscn Award for Best Actress) 1997, Keep the Aspidistra Flying 1997, The Revengers' Comedies 1998, The Theory of Flight 1998, Fight Club 1999, Women Talking Dirty 1999, Carnivale (voice) 2000, Football (short) 2001, Planet of the Apes 2001, Novocaine 2001, The Heart of Me 2002, Till Human Voices Wake Us 2002, Big Fish 2003, Charlie and the Chocolate Factory 2005, Conversations with Other Women 2005, Wallace & Gromit in the Curse of the Were-Rabbit (voice) 2005, Corpse Bride (voice) 2005, Sixty Six 2006, Harry Potter and the Order of the Phoenix 2007, Sweeney Todd: The Demon Barber of Fleet Street 2007, Terminator Salvation 2009, Harry Potter and the Half-Blood Prince 2009, Alice in Wonderland 2010, The King's Speech (BAFTA Award for Best Supporting Actress 2011) 2010, Harry Potter and the Deathly Hallows: Part 1 2010, Toast 2010, Harry Potter and the Deathly Hallows: Part 2 2011, Dark Shadows 2012, Les Misérables 2012, The Lone Ranger 2013. *Television appearances include:* A Pattern of Roses (film) 1983, Miami Vice (series) 1987, Screen Two (series; The Vision) 1987, A Hazard of Hearts (film) 1987, Theatre Night (series; Arms and the Man) 1989, The Early Life of Beatrix Potter 1990, Jackanory (series) 1991, Brown Bear's Wedding (film) 1991, Dancing Queen (film) 1993, Fatal Deception: Mrs. Lee Harvey Oswald (film) 1993, A Dark Adapted Eye (film) 1994, Butter (short) 1994, Absolutely Fabulous (series) 1994, Humanoids from the Deep (film) 1996, 1914–1918 (series) 1996, Merlin (mini-series) 1998, The Nearly Complete and Utter History of Everything (film) 1999, Live from Baghdad (film) 2002, Henry VIII (film) 2003, Magnificent 7 (film) 2005, Enid (film) 2009, The Gruffalo (voice) 2009, The Gruffalo's Child (short) (voice) 2011. *Address:* c/o Nicola van Gelder, Conway van Gelder Grant Ltd, 8/12 Broadwick Street, London, W1F 8HW, England. *Telephone:* (20) 7287-1070. *E-mail:* nicki@conwayvg.co.uk. *Website:* www.conwayvangeldergrant.com.

BONHOEFFER, Tobias, PhD; German/American neurobiologist; *Director, Max Planck Institute of Neurobiology;* b. 9 Jan. 1960, Berkeley, Calif.; ed Max Planck Inst. for Biological Cybernetics, Tübingen; Rockefeller Univ., New York, USA 1989–90; Max Planck Inst. for Brain Research, Frankfurt 1991–93, Max Planck Inst. of Psychiatry, Martinsried, nr Munich 1993–98, Dir and Scientific Mem., Max Planck Inst. of Neurobiology 1998–; Assoc. Neuroscience Research Program, Neuroscience Inst.; mem. German Neuroscience Soc., Faculty 1000, Academia Europaea, European Molecular Biology Org., Nat. Acad. of Sciences Leopoldina 2010–; Attempto Prize for Young Neuroscientists, Tübingen Univ., Ernst Jung Prize 2004. *Publications:* numerous articles on visual system, cerebral cortex devt, neuronal plasticity and optical imaging. *Address:* Max Planck Institute of Neurobiology, Am Klopferspitz 18, 82152 Munich Martinsried, Germany (office). *Telephone:* (89) 8578-3751 (office). *Fax:* (89) 8578-2481 (office). *E-mail:* office .bonhoeffer@neuro.mpg.de (office). *Website:* www.neuro.mpg.de (office).

BONIFACE, Pascal, PhD; French political scientist and academic; *Founding Director, Institute for International and Strategic Relations;* b. 25 Feb. 1956, Paris; m.; three c.; ed Lycée Saint-Exupery, Mantes-la-Jolie, Univ. of Paris XIII Villetaneuse, Institut d'Etudes Politiques de Paris; Ed., Strategic Yearbook 1985–; worked with Socialist parl. group in Nat. Ass. 1986–88; Lecturer at Insts of Political Studies, Lille and Paris; currently Prof. of Int. Relations, Inst. for European Studies, Univ. of Paris VIII; currently columnist, La Croix (France), La Vanguardia (Spain), Al-Ittihad (UAE); currently Sec.-Gen., Football Foundation; Chair. Cttee for Future of Football, French Fed. of Football; Founding Dir Inst. for Int. and Strategic Relations 1991–; Adviser to Ministers Jean-Pierre Chevenement and Pierre Joxe 1988–92; mem. Advisory Bd Inst. for Nat. Defence Studies 1998–2004; mem. High Council for Int. Cooperation 1999–2003; mem. UN Advisory Bd on Disarmament Matters 2001–05; Chevalier, Légion d'honneur, Ordre nat. du Mérite. *Publications include:* over 40 books as author or ed., dealing with int. relations, nuclear deterrence and disarmament, European security, French int. policy, sport in int. relations. *Address:* Institut de relations internationals et stratégiques (IRIS), 2 bis rue Mercoeur, 75011 Paris, France (office). *Telephone:* 1-53-27-60-62 (office). *Fax:* 1-53-27-60-70 (office). *E-mail:* boniface@iris -france.org (office). *Website:* www.iris-france.org (office).

BONILLA, Manuel Acosta; Honduran diplomatist and lawyer; b. 13 Jan. 1929, El Progreso, Yoro; Dr Isidoro Acosta, Prof. Adela Bonilla de Acosta; m. Dr Anna Lucia Marchetti de Acosta; four c.; ed Universidad Autónoma de Mexico, Universidad Autónoma de Honduras; Head Int. Relations, Civil Aviation Authority 1953–54; Dir Gen. Welfare, Legal Adviser, Ministry Labour and Social Security 1954–56; Chair. Nat. Electoral Council 1964–65; Minister of Econ. Affairs and Finance 1965–71; Minister of Finance and Public Credit 1972–75; Minister and Adviser, Pres. and Nat. Coordinator, State Modernization Programme 1990–94;

mem. Central American Parl. 1991, First Vice-Chair., then Chair. Human Rights Cttee; Perm. Rep. to UN, New York 2002–06; Deputy Chair. Fundación Iras Ulargui (youth scholarship and children's home); mem. Nat. Law Acad. *Publications:* numerous articles, chapters, and co-authored works.

BONINGTON, Sir Christian John Storey (Chris), Kt, CVO, CBE; British mountaineer, writer and photographer; *Chancellor, University of Lancaster;* b. 6 Aug. 1934, Hampstead, London; s. of the late Charles Bonington and Helen Anne Bonington (née Storey); m. Muriel Wendy Marchant 1962; three s. (one s. deceased); ed Univ. Coll. School, Hampstead, Royal Mil. Acad., Sandhurst; commissioned in Royal Tank Regt 1956–59; Instructor, Army Outward Bound School 1959–61; man. trainee, Unilever 1961–62; writer and photographer 1962–; Vice-Pres. Army Mountaineering Assen 1980–; Pres. LEPRA 1985–, British Orienteering Fed. 1986– (now Hon. Pres.), British Mountaineering Council 1988–91 (Vice-Pres. 1976–79, 1985–88, now Patron), Council for Nat. Parks 1992–2000, The Alpine Club 1995–99; Chair. (non-exec.) Berghaus 1998–; Chair. Mountain Heritage Trust 2000–; Chancellor Univ. of Lancaster 2005–; 19 expeditions to the Himalayas, including four to Mount Everest and first ascent of south face of Annapurna 1970, British Everest Expedition 1972, Brammah, Himalayas 1973, Changabang, Himalayas 1974, British Everest Expedition (first ascent, SW Face) 1975, Mount Vinson, Antarctica 1983, Panch chuli II, Himalayas (first ascent, W Ridge) 1992, Maslin, Greenland (first ascent) 1993, Rangrik Rang, India (first ascent) 1994, Drangnag-Ri, Nepal (first ascent) 1995, Danga II 2000; reached Everest summit 1985; motivational/after-dinner speaker; Hon. Fellow, UMIST, Lancashire Polytechnic; Hon. Pres. Hiking Club; Hon. MA (Salford); Hon. DSc (Sheffield) 1976, (Lancaster) 1983; Hon. DCL (Northumbria) 1996; Hon. DUniv (Sheffield Hallam) 1998; Hon. DLitt (Bradford) 2002; Founders Medal, Royal Geographical Soc. 1971, Lawrence of Arabia Medal 1986, Livingstone Medal 1991, David Livingstone Medal, Royal Scottish Geographical Soc. 1991. *Publications include:* I Chose to Climb (autobiog.) 1966, Annapurna South Face 1970, The Next Horizon (autobiog.) 1973, Everest South West Face 1973, Changabang 1974, Everest the Hard Way 1976, Quest for Adventure 1981, Kongur: China's Elusive Summit 1982, Everest: The Unclimbed Ridge (with Dr Charles Clarke) 1983, The Everest Years 1986, Mountaineer 1989, The Climbers 1992, Sea, Ice and Rock (with Robin Knox-Johnston) 1992, Great Climbs (co-ed. with Audrey Salkeld) 1994, Tibet's Secret Mountain – The Triumph of Sepu Kangri (with Dr Charles Clarke) 1999, Boundless Horizons 2000, Chris Bonington's Everest 2002, Mountaineer – Thirty Years of Climbing on the World's Great Peaks 2007. *Leisure interests:* mountaineering, orienteering. *Address:* Badger Hill, Hesket Newmarket, Wigton, Cumbria, CA7 8LA, England. *Telephone:* (16974) 78286. *Fax:* (16974) 78238. *E-mail:* chris@bonington.com. *Website:* www.bonington.com.

BONINO, Emma, PhD; Italian politician; b. 9 March 1948, Bra, Turin; d. of Filippo Bonino and Catterina Barge; ed Bocconi Univ., Milan; mem. Camera dei Deputati (Chamber of Deputies, lower house of parl.) 1976–1983, re-elected 1986, 1992, 1994, 2006; Pres. Parl. Group, Radical Party 1981; mem. European Parl. 1979–2006; Founder, Centro Informazione Sterilizzazione e Aborto 1975, No Peace without Justice; Pres. Transnational Radical Party 1991–93, Sec. 1993–94; EC Commr for Consumer Policy, EC Humanitarian Office and Fisheries 1995–99; Leader, Rosa nel Pungo party; unsuccessful cand. in presidential elections 1999, 2013; presented own list in general elections 2001; mem. Bd of Dirs Int. Crisis Group; Distinguished Visiting Prof., American Univ. of Cairo; Minister for EU Policies 2006–08; mem. Senate (upper house of parl.). 2008–13, Vice-Pres. 2008–13; Minister of Foreign Affairs 2013–14; Gran Cruz de la Orden de Mayo (Argentina) 1995, Order of the Prince Branimir (Croatia) 2002; European Personality of the Year 1996, European Communicator of the Year 1997, Premio Principe de Asturias (Spain) 1998, Gonfalone d'Argento Award 2002, Premio Presidente della Repubblica 2003, Premio Campione 2003, Prix Femmes d'Europe 2004, Open Soc. Prize 2004, Premio Galileo 2005. *Leisure interests:* sailing, diving. *Address:* c/o Ministry of Foreign Affairs, Piazzale della Farnesina 1, 00194 Rome, Italy.

BONNAFÉ, Jean-Laurent; French business executive; *CEO, BNP Paribas SA;* b. 14 July 1961; ed École Polytechnique and École des Mines; CEO Banca Nazionale del Lavoro Spa 2006–11; COO BNP Paribas Securities Services S.C.A. Sept.–Dec. 2008, Chair. BNP Paribas Development, COO BNP Paribas SA 2008–11, mem. Exec. Bd and CEO BNP Paribas Fortis 2009–11, Dir of BNP Paribas SA 2010–, CEO BNP Paribas SA 2011–, French Retail Banking Exec. of BNP Paribas (Canada) Valeurs Mobilières Inc., Head of French Retail Banking, BNP Paribas North America, Inc., BNP Paribas Hungaria Bank Rt., COO BNP Paribas Wealth Management; mem. Bd of Dirs Carrefour SA 2008–, BNP Paribas Personal Finance, Banca Nazionale del Lavoro (Italy), BNP Paribas Fortis (Belgium). *Address:* BNP Paribas SA, 16 boulevard des Italiens, 75009 Paris, France (office). *Telephone:* 1-40-14-45-46 (office). *Fax:* 1-40-14-45-46 (office). *E-mail:* info@bnpparibas.com (office). *Website:* www.bnpparibas.com (office).

BONNAIRE, Sandrine; French film actress; b. 31 May 1967, Gannat, Auvergne; m. Guillaume Laurant 2003; two d.; film debut in La Boum 1980; Chevalier des Art et des Lettres; Venice Film Festival Award 1995, Grand prix nat. du cinéma, Ministry of Culture 1987, Cesar Award 1983, Best Actress Award 1986. *Plays include:* The Good Person of Sechuan 1989. *Films include:* A Nos Amours (César Award 1983) 1983, Le Meilleur de la Vie 1983, Vagabond (Best Actress Award 1986) 1985, La Puritaine 1986, Sous le Soleil de Satan 1987, Jaune Revolver 1987, Monsieur Hire 1989, Dans la Soinée 1990, Joan of Arc 1992, La Cérémonie 1995, Judgment in Stone, Circle of Passion 1996, Secret défense 1998, The Colour of Lies 1999, East–West 2000, Mademoiselle 2001, Femme fatale 2002, C'est la vie 2002, Confidences trop intimes 2003, L'equipier 2003, Le Cou de la Girafe 2003, Quelques jours avec moi, Des innocents a l'Echine, Peaux de vaches, Le ciel de Paris, L'Equipier 2004, Je crois que je l'aime 2007, Demandez la permission aux enfants 2007, Elle s'appelle Sabine 2007 (dir), Un coeur simple 2008, L'empreinte de l'ange 2008, Joueuse 2009. *Television includes:* Une femme en blanc 1996, La maison des enfants 2002, Le Procès de Bobigny 2006, Signature (series) 2011. *Publication:* Elle s'appelle Sabine 2007. *Address:* c/o Intertalent, 5 rue Clément Marot, 75008 Paris, France (office). *Telephone:* 1-47-23-40-00.

BONNEFOY, Yves Jean, LèsL; French writer and poet; b. 24 June 1923, Tours; s. of Elie Bonnefoy and Hélène Maury; m. Lucille Vines 1968; one d.; ed Lycée Descartes, Tours, Faculté des Sciences, Poitiers and Faculté des Lettres, Paris;

Prof., Collège de France 1981; contrib. to Mercure de France, Critique, Encounter, L'Ephémère, La Nouvelle Revue Française etc.; has travelled in Europe, Asia and N America; lectures or seminars at Brandeis, Johns Hopkins, Princeton, Williams Coll., Calif., Geneva, Nice, Yale, CUNY, New York and other univs; Commdr des Arts et des Lettres; Hon. DHumLitt (American Coll., Paris, Univ. of Chicago, Univ. of Neuchâtel, Trinity Coll., Dublin, Rome, Edin., Siena, Oxford, Naples); Prix Montaigne 1980, Grand Prix de poésie (Acad. Française) 1981, Prix Florence Gould 1987, Grand Prix national 1993, Prix de la Fondation Cino-del-Duca 1995, Prix Balzan 1995, Prix Prince Louis de Polignac 1998, American Acad. of Arts and Letters Award, Franz Kafka Prize 2007, Prix Mario Luzi 2010, Prix Viareggio 2011, Griffin Trust for Excellence in Poetry's Lifetime Recognition Award 2011, and numerous other prizes. *Publications:* poems: Du mouvement et de l'immobilité de Douve 1953 (English 1968), Hier régnant désert 1958, Pierre écrite 1964 (English 1976), Selected Poems 1968, Dans le leurre du seuil 1975, Poèmes (1947–1975) 1978, Ce qui fut sans lumière 1987, Entretiens sur la Poésie 1990, Début et fin de la neige 1991, Les planches courbes 2001, Raturer outre 2010; essays: L'Improbable 1959, Arthur Rimbaud 1961 (English trans. 1973), Un rêve fait à Mantoue 1967, Le nuage rouge 1977, Rue traversière 1977; on art: Peintures murales de la France Gothique 1954, Miró 1963, Rome 1630 1969, L'Arrière-Pays 1972, Entretiens sur la poésie 1981, La Présence et l'Image 1983, Récits en rêve 1987, La Vérité de Parole 1988, Alberto Giacometti 1991, La vie errante 1993, Remarques sur le dessin 1993, Dessin, couleur et lumière 1995, Théâtre et poésie: Shakespeare et Yeats, l'Encore aveugle 1998, Zao-Wou-ki (jtly) 1998, Lieux et destins de l'image 1999, La Communauté des traducteurs 2000, Baudelaire: La Tentation de l'oubli 2000, Keats et Léopardi 2000, Sous l'Horizon du Langage 2001, Remarques sur le regard 2001, Breton à l'avant de soi 2001, Poésie et architecture 2001, L'Enseignement de Léopardi 2001, Le poète et le flot mouvant des multitudes 2003, Le sommeil de personne 2004, La stratégie de l'énigme 2006, L'imaginaire métaphysique 2006, Goya: les peintures noires 2006, Dans un débris de miroir 2006, L'alliance de la poésie et de la musique 2007, Ce qui alarma Paul Celan 2007, La Poésie à voix haute 2007, Le Grand Espace 2008, Notre besoin de Rimbaud 2009, Deux Scènes et notes conjointes 2009, La beauté dès le premier jour 2010, La communauté des critiques 2010, Le siècle où la parole a été victime 2010, L'inachevable 2010, L'heure présente 2011, Sous le signe de Baudelaire 2011; co-ed. L'Ephémère, trans. of Shakespeare, W. B. Yeats, Keats, Léopardi, Petrarque. *Address:* Collège de France, 11 place Marcelin Berthelot, 75005 Paris, France (office). *E-mail:* yves.bonnefoy@college-de-france.fr (office).

BONNELAME, (Emile Patrick) Jérémie; Seychelles politician and diplomatist; *Chairman, Constitutional Appointment Authority;* b. 24 Oct. 1938, Mahe; ed Inst. Catholique de Paris, Inst. Ecuménique pour les Développement des Peuples, Paris, France, Sion School of Theology, Lucerne School of Theology, Switzerland, Univ. of Québec in Montréal, Canada; teacher, Modern Secondary School of Seychelles 1967–75; Dir-Gen. of Information 1978–79; Prin.-Sec., Ministry of Educ. 1979–80, of External Relations 1981–83, of Educ. and Information 1983–86; Minister of Manpower 1986–88, of Transport 1988–89, of Agric. and Fisheries 1989–93, of Foreign Affairs 1997; Sec.-Gen. Indian Ocean Comm. 1993–97; Perm. Rep. to UN, New York 1997–2007, Amb. to USA 2005–07; Chair. Constitutional Appointment Authority 2007–; Ed.-in-Chief L'Echo des Iles; Pres. Ministerial Council, Tuna Asscn; Co-ordinator Western Indian Ocean Tuna Org. (WIOTO); Gov. Int. Fund for Agricultural Devt; Head of Del. of Seychelles to numerous int. meetings of UN, OAU, ECA, FAO, UNESCO, EU, UNDP. *Leisure interests:* reading, fishing. *Address:* Office of the Chairman, Constitutional Appointment Authority, PO Box 1087, Ground Floor, La Ciotat Building, Mont Fleuri, Mahé, Seychelles (office).

BONNEMAIN, François; French broadcasting executive and fmr journalist; *CEO, TV5 Monde;* b. 9 Oct. 1942; s. of Georges Bonnemain and Renée Charpentier; ed Centre de formation des journalistes de Paris; with Associated Press (AP), Agence France-Presse (AFP), then France-Soir; joined TF 1 TV channel, in charge of political news 1972; Ed. in Chief TF 1 1977; apptd Ed. FR 3 TV channel 1981; Dir News and Current Affairs, France-Inter 1982; Political Ed. Hebdo (weekly magazine); Tech. Adviser to Prime Minister Jacques Chirac on Audiovisual Information 1986–88, to Mayor of Paris (Chirac) 1988–94; Man. Dir Radio-Télévision française d'outre-mer (RFO) 1994–95; mem. Conseil Supérieur de l'audiovisuel (CSA) 1996–99; Dir Chaîne Parl.-Sénat 2000–; Dir Human Resources, France Télévision 2000–02; Adviser to Prime Minister Jean-Pierre Raffarin 2004–05; CEO TV5 Monde 2006–. *Leisure interest:* fine cuisine. *Address:* TV5 Monde, Avenue de Wagram, 75017 Paris (office); Chaîne Parlementaire-Sénat, 15 rue de Vaugirard, 75291 Paris Cedex 06, France (home). *Website:* www.tv5.org (office).

BONNER, Gerald, MA, FSA; British academic (retd); *Reader Emeritus, Durham University;* b. 18 June 1926, London; s. of Frederick J. Bonner and Constance E. Hatch; m. Priscilla J. Hodgson 1967; one s. one d.; ed The Stationers' Co.'s School, London and Wadham Coll., Oxford; mil. service 1944–48; Asst Keeper, Dept of Manuscripts, British Museum 1953–64; Lecturer in Theology, Durham Univ. 1964, promoted to personal Readership 1969, Reader Emer. 1989–; Convener and Sec., Bedan Conf., Durham 1973; Distinguished Prof. of Early Christian Studies, Catholic Univ. of America 1991–94; delivered Cathedral Lecture, Durham 1970, Augustine Lecture, Villanova Univ. Pa, 1970, Otts Lectures, Davidson Coll., NC 1992; Visiting Prof. in Augustinian Studies, Villanova Univ. 1999; Johannes Quasten Medal 1994. *Publications:* The Warfare of Christ 1962, St Augustine of Hippo: Life and Controversies 1963, Famulus Christi: Essays in Commemoration of the Thirteenth Centenary of the Venerable Bede (ed.) 1976, God's Decree and Man's Destiny 1987, St Cuthbert, His Cult and His Community (co-ed. with D. Rollason and C. Stancliffe), Church and Faith in the Patristic Tradition: Augustine, Pelagianism and Early Christian Northumbria 1996, Augustine of Hippo: The Monastic Rules 2004, Freedom and Necessity: St Augustine's Teaching on Divine Power and Human Freedom 2007, A Last Apology for Pelagianism? 2010; articles in the Augustinus-Lexikon (Basle) 1986– and other learned journals including Journal of Ecclesiastical History, Journal of Theological Studies. *Leisure interests:* reading, antiquarianism, (moderate) wine-drinking and any sort of history. *Address:* 7 Victoria Terrace, Durham, DH1 4RW, England (home). *Telephone:* (191) 386-3407 (home).

BONNER, John Tyler, PhD; American biologist and academic; *George M. Moffett Professor Emeritus, Department of Ecology and Evolutionary Biology, Princeton*

University; b. 12 May 1920, New York, NY; s. of Paul Hyde Bonner and Lilly Marguerite Stehli; m. Ruth Ann Graham 1942 (deceased); three s. one d.; ed Harvard Univ.; US Air Corps 1942–46; Asst Prof., then Prof., Princeton Univ., New Jersey 1947–58, George M. Moffett Prof. 1966–90, George M. Moffett Prof. Emer. 1990–, Chair. Dept of Biology 1965–77, 1983–84, 1987–88; Bernard Visiting Prof., Williams Coll. 1989; Raman Visiting Prof., Indian Acad. of Sciences 1990; Sheldon Travelling Fellow, Panama, Cuba 1941; Rockefeller Travelling Fellow, Paris 1953; Guggenheim Fellow, Edin. 1958, 1971–72; NSF Sr Postdoctoral Fellow, Univ. of Cambridge 1963; Commonwealth Foundation Book Fund Fellow, Edin. 1971, 1984–85; Josiah Macy Jr Foundation Book Fund Fellow, Edin. 1978; fmr mem. Editorial Bd American Naturalist, American Scientist and other publs; mem. American Philosophical Soc., NAS; mem. Oxford Surveys in Evolutionary Biology 1982–93; Fellow, American Acad. of Arts and Sciences; Hon. Fellow, Indian Acad. of Sciences 1992; Hon. DSc (Middlebury Coll.) 1970, (Princeton Univ.) 2006, Hon. LLD (Concordia Univ.) 2003, Hon. DLitt (Univ. Coll. of Cape Breton) 2004. *Achievement:* pioneer in use of cellular slime moulds to understand evolution and devt. *Television:* Professor Bonner and the Slime Moulds (BBC Horizon programme) 1984. *Publications:* Morphogenesis: An Essay on Development 1952, Cells and Societies 1955, The Evolution of Development 1958, The Cellular Slime Molds 1959, The Ideas of Biology (several edns in trans.) 1962, Size and Cycle 1965, The Scale of Nature 1969, On Development: The Biology of Form 1974, The Evolution of Culture in Animals (several edns in trans.) 1980, On Size and Life 1983, The Evolution of Complexity 1988, Life Cycles 1993, Sixty Years of Biology: Essays on Evolution and Development 1996, First Signals: The Evolution of Multicellular Development 2000, Lives of a Biologist: Adventures in a Century of Extraordinary Science (ForeWord Magazine Book of the Year Award 2002) 2002, Why Size Matters 2006, The Social Amoebae: The Biology of the Cellular Slime Molds 2009; ed. abridged edn of Growth and Form (D'Arcy Thompson) 1961; more than 230 articles and book reviews. *Leisure interests:* fishing, walking. *Address:* 1025 NE 33rd Avenue, Portland, OR 92732, USA (home). *Telephone:* (609) 651-6503 (home). *E-mail:* jtbonner@princeton.edu (office). *Website:* www.princeton.edu/eeb (office).

BONNER, Paul Max, OBE, FRTS; British television executive (retd); b. 30 Nov. 1934, Banstead, Surrey; s. of Frank Bonner and Jill Bonner; m. Jenifer Hubbard 1956 (died 2013); two s. one d.; ed Felsted School; with Longmans Green & Co., Publrs 1952; trainee reporter, Southend Standard 1953; Nat. Service 1953–55; Asst Press Officer, E. K. Cole Ltd 1955; freelance work for Evening Standard 1955; Trainee Studio Asst, BBC, Bristol 1955–56, Studio Man. 1956–58, Acting Asst Producer, Talks Dept, West Region 1958–59, Production Asst, Talks Dept, TV 1961–65, Sr Producer, Travel and Features Programmes 1965–74, Ed. BBC Community Programmes 1974–77, Special Asst to Controller BBC2 1977, Chair. Small Integrated Multi-Role Production Unit Study Group 1977, Head of Science and Features Dept, TV 1978–81; Channel Controller, Channel Four TV Co. Ltd 1981–83, Controller of Programmes and Exec. Dir 1983–87; Dir of Programme Planning Secr. ITV Asscn 1987–92, Dir ITV Network Centre Secr. 1993–94; Dir House of Commons Broadcasting Unit Ltd 1989–94; Chair. Edin. TV Festival 1979; a Man., Royal Inst. 1982–85; Gov. of Nat. Film and TV School 1981–88; Bd mem. Broadcasting Support Services 1981–93; Chair. Media Group, Cttee on Public Understanding of Science 1981–93; mem. Classic FM Consumer Panel 2009–11. *Television documentaries include:* Climb up to Hell 1967, The Search for the Real Che Guevara 1971, Who Sank the Lusitania? 1972. *Publications:* The Third Age of Broadcasting 1983, Independent TV in Britain (Vol. 5: ITV and IBA 1981–92 1994, (Vol. 6: C4, TV-am, Cable & Satellite 1981–92) 2002. *Leisure interests:* photography, music. *Address:* 9 Alan Road, London, SW19 7PT, England (home). *Telephone:* (20) 8947-6635 (home).

BONNET, Christian, DenD; French politician and business executive; b. 14 June 1921, Paris; s. of Pierre Bonnet and Suzanne Delebecque; m. Christiane Mertian 1943 (died 1999); five c. (one s. deceased); ed Univ. of Paris and Ecole des sciences politiques; Pres. Les Grandes Marques de la conserve 1952–61, Del. Conseil supérieur de la conserve; MRP Deputy for Morbihan 1956–58; Deputy for the second constituency of Morbihan 1956–83; Gen. Councillor, Belle-Ile 1958–2001; Mayor of Carnac 1964–96; fmr Sec.-Gen. Républicains Indépendants; Chair. Cttee on Merchant Marine budget; Pres. Supervisory Council, Caisse des dépots et consignations; Sec. of State for Supply, Housing and Territorial Devt 1972–74; Minister of Agric. 1974–77, of the Interior 1977–81; Senator for Morbihan 1983–2001. *Address:* 56340 Carnac, France (home).

BONNEY, Barbara; American singer (soprano); b. 14 April 1956, Montclair, NJ; d. of Alfred Bonney III and Janet Gates; m. 1st Håkan Hagegård 1989; m. 2nd Maurice Whittaker; ed Univ. of New Hampshire, Mozarteum, Austria; chorus mem. Darmstadt City Opera 1979–83; with Frankfurt Opera 1983–84; maj. early appearances include Der Rosenkavalier, Covent Garden 1984, Metropolitan Opera, New York 1990, Die Zauberflöte, La Scala 1985, Falstaff, Metropolitan Opera 1990, The Marriage of Figaro, Covent Garden 1995, Zurich Opera, Metropolitan Opera 1998, 1999, Les Boréades, Salzburg Festival 1999, Idomeneo, San Francisco 1999; noted especially for Mozart and Strauss interpretations; appeared regularly as recitalist accompanied by Geoffrey Parsons; Visiting Prof., RAM; mem. Swedish Acad. of Music; Dr hc (New Hampshire), (Bowdoin Coll.), (Royal Acad. of Music). *Recordings include:* Le Nozze di Figaro, Don Giovanni, Die Zauberflöte, Die Fledermaus, Fidelio, Hansel und Gretel, The Merry Widow, Vocalise, Miss Sallie Chisum Remembers Billy The Kid, Emily Dickinson Songs, Samuel Barber's Hermit Songs, Six Elizabethan Songs, Frauenliebe und-leben, Les mamelles de Tirésias, Diamonds in the Snow (Gramophone Award for Best Solo Vocal Recording), While I Dream. *Leisure interests:* textiles, interior decorating, calligraphy. *Address:* Michael Storrs Music Ltd, 11 Maiden Lane, London, WC2E 7NA, England (office). *Telephone:* (20) 7078-1440 (office). *Fax:* (20) 7078-1456 (office). *E-mail:* info@michaelstorrsmusic.co.uk (office). *Website:* www.michaelstorrsmusic.co.uk (office); www.barbarabonney.com (office).

BONNICI, Josef, MA, PhD; Maltese economist, fmr politician and central banker; *Governor, Central Bank of Malta;* b. 15 April 1953, Birzebbuga; m. Rita Oliva; two c.; ed Univ. of Malta, Simon Fraser Univ., Canada; Sr Lecturer in Econs, Deakin Univ., Australia 1980–88; Visiting Prof., Univ. of Malta 1988, Prof. of Econs 1988–2004; Econ. Adviser to Prime Minister 1988–92; appointed adviser to Council of Europe in Co-ordinated Social Research Programme 1992; mem. Parl.

1992–2004; Parl. Sec. Ministry of Finance 1993–95; Minister of Econ. Services 1995–96; Shadow Minister and Opposition Spokesman for Econ. Devt 1996–98; Minister for Econ. Services 1998–2003; Gov. Central Bank of Malta 2011–; mem. European Court of Auditors 2004–10; mem. Del. to OSCE, to Council of Europe, Jt Malta EU Parl. Cttee; mem. Nat. Comm. for Higher Educ. in Malta 2006–; mem. Nationalist Party; Dr hc (Rikkyo) 1996. *Publications:* Macroeconomics 1996; articles on econs in Malta and in professional econ. journals. *Address:* Pjazza Kastilja, Valletta VLT 1060, 1615 Luxembourg Ville, Luxembourg (office). *Telephone:* 25500000 (office). *Fax:* 25502500 (office). *E-mail:* jbonnici@waldonet .net.mt (office); info@centralbankmalta.org (office). *Website:* www .centralbankmalta.org (office); www.josefbonnici.com (office).

BONNICI, Ugo Mifsud (see Mifsud Bonnici, Ugo).

BONNIN, Didier; French business executive; *CEO, Sergio Rossi SpA;* began career at Arthur Andersen; held several sr positions with Louis Vuitton; CEO Céline Production, Florence –2003; Industrial Dir Bottega Veneta, Gucci Group NV 2003–07, CEO Sergio Rossi SpA 2007–. *Address:* Sergio Rossi, Via Pontaccio 13, 20121 Milan, Italy (office). *Telephone:* (02) 7632081 (office). *Fax:* (02) 76320833 (office). *E-mail:* press.office@sergiorossi.it (office). *Website:* www.sergiorossi.com (office).

BONO; Irish rock singer, songwriter and humanitarian; *Lead Singer, U2;* b. (Paul Hewson), 10 May 1960, Dublin; m. Alison Stewart 1982; ed Mount Temple School; Founder-mem. and lead singer, the Feedback 1976, renamed the Hype, finally renamed U2 1978–; numerous concerts, including Live Aid Wembley 1985, Self Aid Dublin, A Conspiracy of Hope (Amnesty International Tour) 1986, Smile Jamaica (hurricane relief fundraiser) 1988, Very Special Arts Festival, White House, Washington, DC 1988; numerous tours world-wide; Foreign Hon. Fellow, American Acad. of Arts and Sciences 2009; Portuguese Order of Liberty 2005; Hon. KBE 2007; 22 Grammy Awards with U2, including Best Rock Performance by a Duo or Group with Vocal (for Desire) 1988, BRIT Awards for Best Int. Act 1988–90, 1992, 1998, 2001, Best Live Act 1993, Outstanding Contribution to the British Music Industry 2001, JUNO Award 1993, World Music Award 1993, Grammy Award for Song of the Year, Record of the Year, Best Rock Performance by a Duo or Group with Vocal (all for Beautiful Day) 2000, Grammy Awards for Best Pop Performance by a Duo or Group with Vocal (for Stuck In A Moment You Can't Get Out Of), for Record of the Year (for Walk On), for Best Rock Performance by a Duo or Group with Vocal (for Elevation) 2001, American Music Award for Favourite Internet Artist of the Year 2002, Ivor Novello Award for Best Song Musically and Lyrically (for Walk On) 2002, Golden Globe for Best Original Song (for The Hands That Built America, from film Gangs of New York) 2003, Grammy Awards for Best Rock Performance by a Duo or Group with Vocal, Best Rock Song, Best Short Form Music Video (all for Vertigo) 2004, TED Prize 2004, Nordoff-Robbins Silver Clef Award for lifetime achievement 2005, Q Award for Best Live Act 2005, Digital Music Award for Favourite Download Single (for Vertigo) 2005, Meteor Ireland Music Award for Best Irish Band, Best Live Performance 2006, Grammy Awards for Song of the Year, for Best Rock Performance by a Duo or Group with Vocal (both for Sometimes You Can't Make it in Your Own), for Best Rock Song (for City of Blinding Lights) 2006, Ambassadors of Conscience Award, Amnesty International 2006, Liberty Medal 2007, Visionary Award, Palm Springs Film Festival 2014, Golden Globe Award for Best Original Song (Ordinary Love in Mandela: Long Walk to Freedom) 2014. *Plays include:* Spider-Man: Turn Off The Dark (music and lyrics by Bono and The Edge), Broadway, New York 2011–14. *Films include:* Rattle and Hum 1988, The Million Dollar Hotel (co-writer) 2000. *Recordings include:* albums: Boy 1980, October 1981, War 1983, Under a Blood Red Sky 1983, The Unforgettable Fire 1984, Wide Awake In America 1985, The Joshua Tree (Grammy Award for Album of the Year, Best Rock Performance by a Duo or Group with Vocal) 1987, Rattle and Hum 1988, Achtung Baby (Grammy Award for Best Rock Performance by a Duo or Group with Vocal 1992) 1991, Zooropa (Grammy Award for Best Alternative Music Album) 1993, Passengers (film soundtrack with Brian Eno) 1995, Pop 1997, The Best Of 1980–90 1998, All That You Can't Leave Behind (Grammy Award for Best Rock Album 2001) 2000, The Best Of 1990–2000 2002, How To Dismantle An Atomic Bomb (Meteor Ireland Music Award for Best Irish Album 2006, Grammy Awards for Album of the Year, for Best Rock Album 2006) 2004, No Line on the Horizon 2009. *Address:* c/o Principle Management, 30–32 Sir John Rogersons Quay, Dublin 2, Ireland (office). *E-mail:* nadine@numb.ie (office). *Website:* www.u2.com.

BONO MARTÍNEZ, José; Spanish politician; b. 14 Dec. 1950, Salobre; m. Ana Maria Rodriguez Mosquera (divorced); four c.; ed Colegio de la Inmaculada, Alicante, Univ. of Deusto; worked as lawyer until 1979; mem. Congreso de los Diputados (Congress of Deputies) for Albacete 1979–83, for Toledo 2008–, Pres. Congreso de los Diputados 2008–11; Pres. Castilla-La Mancha region 1983–2004; Minister of Defence 2004–06; fmr Prof. of Political Law, Universidad Complutense de Madrid; mem. Partido Socialista Obrero Español (Spanish Socialist Workers' Party).

BONSE-GEUKING, Wilhelm; German mining engineer and business executive; *Chairman of the Supervisory Board, Evonik Industries AG;* b. 26 Aug. 1941, Arnsberg, Sauerland; m.; three s.; Chair. Veba Oel AG (following acquisition by BP) 1995–2002, Head of BP Germany –2004, European Head of BP Group, Group Vice-Pres. and mem. Exec. Man. of BP Group 2003–06; Chair. Supervisory Bd Evonik Industries AG 2007–; Chair. Exec. Bd RAG Foundation 2007–; apptd to Energy and Climate Advice Panel of State Govt of North Rhine-Westphalia; Chair. Comm. on Econ. Growth and Innovation, Econ. Council of CDU; Chair. Bd of Trustees, Foundation of the Int. Charlemagne Prize, Aachen, Zollverein Foundation; mem. Zollverein Fed. of Catholic Entrepreneurs (BKU). *Address:* Evonik Industries AG, Rellinghauser Straße 1–11, 45128 Essen, Germany (office). *Telephone:* (201) 177-01 (office). *Fax:* (201) 177-3475 (office). *E-mail:* info@evonik .com (office). *Website:* www.evonik.com (office).

BONYNGE, Richard, AO, CBE; Australian conductor; b. 29 Sept. 1930, Sydney, NSW; s. of C. A. Bonynge; m. Dame Joan Sutherland 1954 (died 2010); one s.; ed NSW Conservatorium of Music, Royal Coll. of Music, London; trained as a pianist; debut as conductor with Santa Cecilia Orchestra, Rome 1962; conducted first opera Faust, Vancouver 1963; Musical Dir Sutherland/Williamson Grand Opera Co., Australia 1965; Artistic Dir Vancouver Opera 1974–77; Musical Dir Australian

Opera 1976–86; has conducted La Sonnambula, La Traviata, Faust, Eugene Onegin, L'Elisir d'amore, Orfeo, Semiramide, Giulio Cesare, Lucia di Lammermoor, Norma, The Tales of Hoffmann and many more; has revived many operas not in the repertoire, including Les Huguenots, La Fille du Régiment, Maria Stuarda, Lucrezia Borgia and Thérèse; Hon. Assoc. Accademia Filarmonica di Bologna 2007; Commdr Ordre Nat. des Arts et des Lettres 1989. *Videos include:* Les Huguenots, La Fille du Régiment, The Merry Widow, Norma, Die Fledermaus and The Magic Flute. *Recordings include:* opera: Alcina, La Sonnambula, Norma, Beatrice di Tenda, I Puritani, Faust, Semiramide, Lakmé, La Fille du Régiment, Messiah, Don Giovanni, Les Huguenots, L'Elisir d'amore, Lucia di Lammermoor, Rigoletto, Les Contes d'Hoffmann, Thérèse, Le Toréador, The Land of Smiles and Giuditta, Lucrezia Borgia, Maria Stuarda, Giulio Cesare, Merry Widow, L'Oracolo, Esclarmonde, Le Roi de Lahore, Suor Angelica, Die Fledermaus, Hamlet, I Masnadieri, La Traviata, Il Trovatore; ballet: Le Diable à Quatre, Giselle, Marco Spada, La Péri, Les Sylphides, Coppélia, Sylvia, Le Carillon, La Cigale, Le Papillon, La Boutique Fantastique, Aschenbrödel, The Nutcracker, Sleeping Beauty, Swan Lake, La Sonnambula; recitals: Tchaikovsky and Grieg Piano Concertos, Kalman's Die Herzogin von Chicago, Die Czardasfurstin. *Recordings include:* recordings with Pavarotti, Tebaldi, Sumi Jo, Jerry Hadley, Deborah Riedel, Rosamund Illing, Yvonne Kenny, Cheryl Barker. *Publications:* The Joan Sutherland Album (with Dame Joan Sutherland) 1986, A Collector's Guide to Theatrical Postcards 1988. *Address:* Ingpen & Williams Ltd, 7 St George's Court, 131 Putney Bridge Road, London, SW15 2PA, England (office).

BOODAI, Marwan Marzouk; Kuwaiti airline industry executive; *Chairman and CEO, Jazeera Airways;* CEO Boodai Corpn 1995–; f. Jazeera Airways 2005, currently Chair. and CEO; mem. Advisory Bd World Econ. Forum's Global Growth Cos. *Address:* Jazeera Airways, POB 29288, 13153 Safat, Kuwait City, Kuwait (office). *Website:* www.jazeeraairways.com (office).

BOOLELL, Arvin, LLM, MB, BCH, BAO, MRCP, MRCS; Mauritian physician and politician; *Minister of Foreign Affairs, Regional Integration and International Trade;* b. 26 May 1953; s. of the late Sir Satcam Boolell; ed Nat. Univ. of Ireland, Royal Coll. of Surgeons, Ireland; fmr medical practitioner; mem. Nat. Ass. 1987–; Minister of Agric. and Nat. Resources 1995–2000, of Agro-Industry and Fisheries 2005–08, of Foreign Affairs, Regional Integration and Int. Trade 2008–. *Address:* Ministry of Foreign Affairs, International Trade and Co-operation, New Government Centre, 5th Floor, Port Louis, Mauritius (office). *Telephone:* 201-1648 (office). *Fax:* 208-8087 (office). *E-mail:* mfa@mail.gov.mu (office). *Website:* foreign.gov.mu (office).

BOOMGAARDEN, Georg; German diplomatist; b. 24 June 1948, Emden; m.; three c.; ed Univ. of Kiel; entered Higher Foreign Service 1974, Desk Officer, Cultural Section, Embassy in Moscow 1976–80, Press Officer, Embassy in Buenos Aires 1980–83, Desk Officer, Cen. America Div., Fed. Foreign Office 1983–86, Head of the Information Processing Div. 1986–89, Amb. to Nicaragua 1989–92, Head of Econ. Service, Embassy in Moscow 1992–95, Head of Div. responsible for Southern Latin America, Fed. Foreign Office 1995–99, Dir for Latin American Affairs 1999–2003, Amb. to Spain 2003–05, State Sec., Fed. Foreign Office 2005–08, Amb. to UK 2008–13. *Address:* Federal Ministry of Foreign Affairs, 11013 Berlin, Germany (office). *Telephone:* (30) 18170 (office). *Fax:* (30) 18173402 (office). *E-mail:* poststelle@auswaertiges-amt.de (office). *Website:* www .auswaertiges-amt.de (office).

BOON, David Clarence, MBE, Dipl. Bus. Man.; Australian fmr professional cricketer; *International Match Referee, International Cricket Council;* b. 29 Dec. 1960, Launceston, Tasmania; s. of Clarence Leonard Boon and Lesley Mary Boon; m. Philippa Louise Wright 1983; one s. two d.; ed Launceston Church Grammar School; right-hand batsman; teams: Tasmania 1978–79 to 1998–99 (Capt. 1992–93 to 1998–99), Durham, England (Capt.) 1997–99, for Australia played 107 Test matches 1984–96, scoring 7,422 runs (average 43.65) including 21 hundreds and holding 99 catches, highest score 200; toured England 1985, 1989 and 1993; scored 23,413 First-class runs (68 hundreds), highest score 227; 181 limited-overs ints; Marketing Man. Trust Bank Australia 1991–; Marketing and Special Events Co-ordinator 1999; Australian selector 2000–11; Gen. Man. Cricket Operations Tasmania 2004–11; Int. Match Referee, ICC (Int. Cricket Council); Patron Road Trauma Support Group, World Vision; Int. Cricketer of the Year 1987–88, Wisden Cricketer of the Year 1994. *Publications:* In the Firing Line (with A. Mark Thomas), Under the Southern Cross (autobiog.) 1996. *Leisure interests:* gardening, golf, music. *Address:* 113 King Street, Sandy Bay, Tasmania 7005, Australia.

BOONSITHI, Chokwatana, PhD; Thai business executive; b. 25 July 1937, Bangkok; ed Wat Suthat Secondary School; Chair. Saha Group (consumer goods conglomerate), Pipat Paniangvait; Pres. Thai President Foods 1995–; Advisory Chair. International Laboratories Corpn Ltd; mem. Advisory Cttee Thai-Japanese Asscn; mem. Bd of Dirs Champ Ace Co. Ltd, I.C.C. International Public Co. Ltd; Chair. Thanulux Public Co. Ltd –2010, now Advisory Dir; Chair. Waseda Education (Thailand) Co. Ltd; Order of the Sacred Treasure, Gold Rays with Neck Ribbon (Govt of Japan) 2002; Dr hc (Burapha Univ.) (Thammasat Univ.), (National Institute of Development Administration), (Univ. of the Thai Chamber of Commerce), (Khon Kaen Univ.), (Waseda Univ., Japan), (Rajamangala Univ. of Technology). *Address:* Saha Group, 2156 New Petchburi Road, Bangkapi, Huay Kwang, Bangkok 10320, Thailand (office). *Website:* www.sahagroup.thailand.com (office).

BOONYARATGLIN, Gen. Sonthi; Thai army officer (retd) and politician; *Leader, Matubhum (Motherland) party;* b. 2 Oct. 1946; m. two wives, Sukanya and Piyada; ed Armed Forces Academies Preparatory School, Chulachomklao, Royal Mil. Acad.; commissioned into Royal Army Infantry Corps, went on to lead several top units, including Special Warfare Command based in Lopburi Prov.; Deputy Army Commdr 2004–05, C-in-C Royal Thai Army (first Muslim) 2005–07 (retd); Pres. Admin. Reform Council (de facto head of govt) following overthrow of elected govt of Thaksin Shinawatra in coup d'état 19 Sept.–1 Oct. 2006; Chair. Council for Nat. Security (mil. junta that ruled the kingdom) 2006–07; Deputy Prime Minister in charge of nat. security 2007–09; Leader, Matubhum (Motherland) party 2009–; US Army Commendation Medal, with Valor device 1970, Victory Medal, Viet Nam War 1972, Freeman Safeguarding Medal (Second Class) 1973, Companion (Fourth Class), Order of the Crown of Thailand 1976, Border Service Medal (Thailand)

1982, Commdr (Third Class) of The Most Noble Order of the Crown of Thailand 1984, Chakra Mala Medal (Thailand) 1989, Kt Commdr (Second Class) of The Most Noble Order of the Crown of Thailand 1989, Kt Commdr (Second Class) of the Most Exalted Order of the White Elephant 1991, Kt Grand Cross (First Class) of the Most Noble Order of the Crown of Thailand 1995, Kt Grand Cross (First Class) of the Most Exalted Order of the White Elephant 1999. *Address: c/o* Office of the Prime Minister, Government House, Thanon Nakhon Pathom, Bangkok 10300, Thailand. *Telephone:* (2) 280-3526. *Fax:* (2) 282-8792. *E-mail:* webmaster@opm.go.th.

BOORMAN, John, CBE; British film director, producer and screenwriter; b. 18 Jan. 1933; s. of George Boorman and Ivy Boorman (née Chapman); m. 1st Christel Kruse 1956; one s. three d.; m. 2nd Isabella Weibrecht 1994; one s. two d.; ed Salesian Coll., Chertsey; Broadcaster and critic, BBC Radio, also contributor to Manchester Guardian and magazines 1950–54; army service 1951–53; Film Editor, ITN London 1955–58; Dir and Producer Southern TV 1958–60; Head of Documentaries, Bristol, BBC TV; left BBC to work as film dir; Chair. Nat. Film Studios of Ireland 1975–85; Gov. British Film Inst. 1983–94, co-f. Merlin Films Group 1989; f. magazine Day by Day; Chevalier de l'Ordre des Arts et des Lettres 1985; Best Dir Prize, Cannes Festival 1970, 1998; BAFTA Fellowship Award 2004, numerous film awards. *Television:* Dir Citizen 1963, The Newcomers 1960–64. *Films:* Catch Us If You Can 1965, Point Blank 1967, Hell in the Pacific 1968, Leo the Last 1969, Deliverance 1970, Zardoz 1973, The Heretic 1976, Excalibur 1981, The Emerald Forest 1985, Hope and Glory (Golden Globe Award 1988) 1987, Where the Heart Is 1989, I Dreamt I Woke Up 1991, Beyond Rangoon 1994, Two Nudes Bathing 1995, The General 1998, The Tailor of Panama 2001, In My Country 2005, The Tiger's Tail 2006, The Wonderful Wizard of Oz 2010. *Publications:* The Legend of Zardoz 1973 (novel), Money into Light 1985, Hope and Glory 1987, Projections 1 1992, Projections 2 1993, Projections 3 1994, Projections 4 1/2 (co-ed.) 1995, Projections 5 1996, Projections 6 1997, Projections 7 1997, Projections 8 1998; co-ed. A Year in Film 1993, Adventures of a Suburban Boy (autobiog.) 2003. *Leisure interests:* hacking the Wicklow Hills, losing gracefully at tennis, planting trees. *Address:* Merlin Films Group, 16 Upper Pembroke Street, Dublin 2, Ireland. *Telephone:* (1) 6764373. *Fax:* (1) 6764368. *E-mail:* info@merlinfilms.com. *Website:* www.merlinfilms.com.

BOOS, Georgy Valentinovich, CandTechSc; Russian engineer, politician and business executive; *President, Boos Lighting Group Managing Company;* b. 22 Jan. 1963, Moscow; m.; six c.; ed Moscow Energy Inst.; Sr Engineer, All-Union Research Inst. of Light Tech., also teacher of math., secondary school 1986–91; Founder, Dir-Gen., then Pres., Svetoservis Co. 1991–96; mem. State Duma 1996–98, 1999–2005, Deputy Speaker 2003–05 (joined Yedinstvo and Otechestvo Union (later Yedibaya Rossiya) 2000); Head of State Taxation Service of Russian Fed. Sept.–Dec. 1998; Minister of Revenue Dec. 1998–May 1999; Gov. of Kaliningrad Oblast 2005–10; currently Pres. Boos Lighting Group Man. Co., Moscow; mem. Bd of Dirs IDGC Holding Jt Stock Co.; Pres. Int. Acad. of Information Technologies 1999–; Prof. and Full Mem. Acad. of Security, Defence and Law-and-Order 2004–; mem. Int. Acad. of Social Sciences 2008–; Order of Honour 2004, Order of Holy Prince Daniel of Moscow (Russian Orthodox Church) 2006, 4th Class Order of Merit for the Fatherland 2008, 2nd Class Order of the Silver Cross of Philanthropist (IASS) 2008; Medal for the Memory of the 850th Anniversary of Moscow 1997, Medal for Merit in the Implementation of the All-Russia Census 2002, Medal for the Memory of the 300th Anniversary of Saint Petersburg 2003, Medal of the 70th Anniversary of the Armed Forces of the USSR, Medal for the 15th Anniversary of the Council of Federation 2008. *Achievements include:* designer of architectural illumination of Moscow 1996. *Address:* Boos Lighting Group Managing Company, 1296266 Moscow, 6, 1st Rizshkiy pereulok, Russia (office). *Telephone:* (495) 785-20-95 (office). *Fax:* (495) 785-20-96 (office). *E-mail:* info@bl-g.ru (office). *Website:* www.bl-g.ru (office).

BOOTH, Cherie, CBE, QC, LLD, FRSA; British barrister; *Queen's Counsel, Matrix Chambers;* b. 23 Sept. 1954, Bury; d. of Anthony Booth and Gale Booth (née Smith); m. Anthony Charles Lynton Blair (Tony Blair (q.v.)) 1980; three s. one d.; ed Seafield Grammar School, Crosby, Liverpool, London School of Econs; called to Bar (Lincoln's Inn) 1976, Asst Recorder 1996–99, Recorder 1999–, Bencher 1999–; pupillage with Alexander Irvine (now Lord Irvine of Lairg q.v.) 1976–77; Tenant New Court Chambers 1977–91, 4/5 Gray's Inn Square, London 1991–2000, Matrix Chambers 2000–; parl. cand. for Thanet 1983; apptd QC 1995; Gov. LSE 1998–; Chancellor John Moores Univ., Liverpool 1998–2008, Chancellor Emer. 2008–, Hon. Fellow; Pres. Comm. of Inquiry into UK Prison and Penal System 2007–; Pres. Barnardo's 2001–07 (currently Hon. Vice-Pres.), Kids Club Network, Family Mediators Asscn; Patron Refuge, The Citizenship Foundation, CLIC-Sargeant (Cancer Care for Children), Breast Cancer Care 1997–, Islington Music Centre 1999–, Victim Support London, SCOPE, Greater London Fund for the Blind, Home Start Islington, Mary Ward Legal Centre, Noah's Ark, NOJOS Awards, Downside Up, Age Exchange, The Merlyn Trust; Fellow, International Soc. of Lawyers for Public Service, Howard League for Penal Reform; Founder Cherie Blair Foundation for Women 2008, Africa Justice Foundation 2011; Patron Asian Univ. for Women, Chittagong, Bangladesh 2009–11, Chancellor 2011–; Hon. Bencher, King's Inn, Dublin 2002, Hon. Fellow, LSE 2003, Open Univ., Inst. of Advanced Legal Studies, Hon. Pres. Plater Coll., Hon. Patron Genesis Appeal; Hon. DUniv (Open) 1999, Hon. LLD (Westminster), (Liverpool) 2003, Hon. DLitt (UMIST) 2003; ranked by Forbes magazine amongst The 100 Most Powerful Women (12th) 2004, (62nd) 2005, Eleanor Roosevelt Val-Kill medal 2007, Justitia Omnibus Award 2012. *Publications include:* The Goldfish Bowl 2004, The Negligence Liabilty of Public Authorities 2005, Speaking for Myself 2008. *Leisure interests:* family, reading, the arts, keeping fit. *Address:* Matrix Chambers, Griffin Building, Gray's Inn, London, WC1R 5LN, England (office). *Telephone:* (20) 7563-5050 (office); (20) 7298-0830 (home). *Fax:* (20) 7723-6525 (office). *E-mail:* boothc@matrixlaw.co.uk (office). *Website:* www.matrixlaw.co.uk (office).

BOOTH, Chris; New Zealand sculptor; b. 30 Dec. 1948, Kerikeri, Bay of Islands; m.; two s. one d.; ed Ilam School of Fine Arts, Univ. of Canterbury, Christchurch; undertook specialist sculpture studies with Barbara Hepworth, Denis Mitchell, John Milne and Quinto Ghermandi 1968–70; numerous solo and collective exhbns; represented in public and pvt. collections including Int. Land Art Collections; Frances Hodgkins Fellowship, Univ. of Otago 1982; int. mem. Royal Soc. of British

Sculptors 1990–2009, Int. Sculpture Centre, USA; elected for Art in Motion Biennale, Bos van Ypeij, Netherlands 2003; public and pvt. commissions in UK, Germany, Netherlands, Italy, France, Denmark, Australia, USA and NZ 1988–; Christchurch/Seattle Sister City Comm. Award 1996, Greenham Common Trust Prize 1998, 10th Millfield Int. Sculpture Comm., Somerset 1998, Artists in Industry Project, Vic., Australia 1998–99, Hanover 2000 Expo, Steinbergen, Germany 2000, Kinetic Art Org. Int. Competition, USA 2002. *Major commissions:* Gateway, Albert Park, Auckland 1990, Rainbow Warrior Memorial, Matauri Bay 1990, Tuuram Cairn, Deakin Univ., Warrnambool, Australia 1996, In Celebration of a Tor, Grizedale, Cumbria, UK 1993, Cave, Takahanga Marae, Kaikoura 1996, Wiyung Tchellungnai-Najil, Evandale Sculpture Walk, Gold Coast, Australia 1997, Tranekaer-Vader, Tickon, Langeland, Denmark 1998, Wairau Strata, Seresin Estate, Marlborough 2000, Bukker Tillibul, Swinburne Univ., Lilydale, Melbourne 2001, Waka and Wave (collaboration with Te Warihi Hetaraka), Whangarei District Council, NZ 2003, Kroller-Muller Museum Sculpture Garden, Netherlands 2003–05, Nga Uri O Hinetuparimaunga, Hamilton Gardens Entrance Sculpture (collaboration with Diggeress Te Kanawa), Hamilton City Council, NZ 2004–05, Echo van de Veluwe, Kröller-Müller Museum (Sculpture Park), Otterlo, Netherlands 2004–05, Subterranean Living Sculpture System, Eden Project, Cornwall, UK 2006–, Ciclo, San Miguel de Allende, Mexico 2007–, Te Whiringa o Manoko, Kerikeri, NZ 2007–09, JET commission for Royal Botanic Gardens, Sydney 2007. *Television documentaries include:* When a Warrior Dies (documentary on bombing of Greenpeace ship Rainbow Warrior and the creation of the memorial to the ship and its crew) 1995, Sculpture in the Park 1996, New in Netherlands (documentary on Kröller-Müller Museum Sculpture), Respecting the Earth (documentary for Maori TV on the making of Nga Uri o Hinetuparimaunga, entranceway sculpture to the Hamilton Gardens). *Publications include:* Chris Booth Sculpture 1993, Balanced Stone 1998, Chris Booth: Sculpture in Europe, Australia and New Zealand 2001, Woven Stone: The Sculpture of Chris Booth 2007. *Address:* PO Box 816, Kerikeri, 0245, New Zealand (office). *Telephone:* (9) 407-1331 (home). *Fax:* (9) 401-7413 (office). *E-mail:* chris@chrisbooth.co.nz (office). *Website:* www.chrisbooth.co.nz (office).

BOOTH, Lewis William Killcross, CBE, BEng; British automotive industry executive; b. 7 Nov. 1948, Liverpool, England; m.; two c.; ed Univ. of Liverpool; chartered man. accountant; joined Ford Motor Co. 1978 as Financial Analysis Co-ordinator, Product Devt Div., later various man. positions with Ford Europe 1980–1992, Finance Dept, Ford USA 1992–96, Group Man. Dir South Africa Motor Corpn (SAMCOR) 1997–2000, Pres. Ford Asia Pacific, Africa and Tech. Staffs 2000–02, Pres. and COO Ford of Europe GmbH 2003–08, Group Vice-Pres. Ford Motor Co. 2003–05, Exec. Vice-Pres. Ford Europe Operations 2005–08, Exec. Vice-Pres. Premier Automotive Group 2005–08, Chief Financial Officer and Exec. Vice-Pres. Ford Motor Co. 2008–12, Group Vice-Pres. Ford Motor Credit Co. LLC, Chair. Volvo Car Corpn, Ford Europe, fmr Chair. Jaguar Brand, Ford of Europe GmbH, Land Rover Brand, Ford Motor Co., Chair. (non-exec.) Cars Div. of Ford Motor Co., Vice-Chair. Ford Otomotiv Sanayi AS, Dir, Ford Motor Credit Co. LLC, Ford Motor Co., Ford of Europe GmbH, Land Volvo Brand, Mahindra & Mahindra Ltd 2000–, Ford Otosan 2003–, Mazda Motor Corpn 2003–08; Sr Advisor for Corp. Strategy, Mazda Motor Corpn 2002, Pres. and CEO 2002–03; Dir (non-exec.) Rolls-Royce 2011–. *Address:* Ford Motor Co., One American Road, Dearborn, MI 48126, USA (office). *Telephone:* (313) 322-3000 (office). *Fax:* (313) 845-7512 (office). *E-mail:* info@ford.com (office). *Website:* www.ford.com (office).

BOOTHROYD, Baroness (Life Peer), cr. 2000, of Sandwell in the County of West Midlands; **Rt Hon. Betty Boothroyd,** OM, PC; British parliamentarian; b. 8 Oct. 1929, Dewsbury, Yorks.; d. of Archibald Boothroyd and Mary Boothroyd; ed Dewsbury Coll. of Commerce and Art; sec., Labour Party HQ 1955–60; legis. asst to US congressman, Washington, DC 1960–62; sec. and personal asst to various sr Labour politicians 1962–73; mem. Hammersmith Borough Council 1965–68; contested various elections and by-elections 1957–70; MP (Labour) for West Bromwich 1973, for West Bromwich West 1974–2000; Asst Govt Whip 1974–76; mem. Labour Party Nat. Exec. 1981–87; Deputy Speaker 1987–92; Speaker of the House of Commons 1992–2000; currently Hon. Cross Bencher, House of Lords; Chancellor, Open Univ. 1994–2006; Hon. Bencher, Middle Temple 2011; several hon. degrees from British univs including Hon. LLD (Cambridge) 1994, Hon. DCL (Oxford) 1995, (St Andrews) 2002; Parliamentarian of the Year 1992, Personality of the Year, Communicator of the Year. *Publication:* Betty Boothroyd – The Autobiography 2001. *Address:* House of Lords, Westminster, London, SW1A 0PW, England. *Telephone:* (20) 7219-8673 (office).

BOOZMAN, John Nichols; American optometrist and politician; *Senator from Arkansas;* b. 10 Dec. 1950, Fort Smith, Ark.; s. of Fay Winford Boozman, Jr and Marie Boozman (née Nichols); m. Cathy Marley; three d.; ed Northside High School, Fort Smith, Univ. of Arkansas, Southern Coll. of Optometry; entered pvt. practice as Co-founder Boozman-Hof Regional Eye Clinic, Rogers, Ark. 1977; served two terms on Rogers Public School Bd; mem. US House of Reps for 3rd Congressional Dist of Ark. 2001–11, served as Asst Whip, as Chair. Veterans Affairs Econ. Opportunity Sub-cttee; Senator from Ark. 2011–, mem. Commerce, Science and Transportation Cttee 2011–, Environment and Public Works Cttee 2011–; mem. NATO Parl. Ass., Rogers (Arkansas) Bd of Educ. 1994–2001; mem. Int. Acad. of Sports Vision, Arkansas Optometric Asscn, American Optometric Asscn, Fellowship of Christian Athletes; Republican; Spirit of Enterprise Award, US Chamber of Commerce 2001, 2002, 2003, Hero of the Taxpayer Award, American for Tax Reform 2001, 2002, 2003, Small Business Advocate Award, Small Business Survival Cttee 2004, Brighter Vision Award, Age-Related Macular Degeneration Alliance International 2006, Award for Manufacturing Legis. Excellence, Nat. Asscn of Mfrs 2010, A in English Award, US English, Inc. 2010, Distinguished Advocate Award, Asscn of Educ. & Rehabilitation of the Blind & Visually Impaired (Arkansas chapter). *Achievements include:* est. low vision programme at Arkansas School for the Blind, Little Rock; worked as volunteer optometrist at area clinic providing medical services to low-income families. *Address:* 320 Hart Senate Office Building, Washington, DC 20510, USA (office). *Telephone:* (202) 224-4843 (office). *Fax:* (202) 228-1371 (office). *Website:* boozman .senate.gov (office).

BOR, Naci; Turkish professor of physiology; *Professor Emeritus, Medical Faculty, Hacettepe University;* b. 20 Feb. 1928, Bor; s. of Cemal Bor and Zekiye Bor; m.

Sema Bor; two d.; ed Istanbul Univ.; researcher in cardiac physiology, Emory Univ., Atlanta 1958–61; est. research in foetal physiology, Philadelphia Presbyterian Hosp.; Lecturer, Univ. of Pa; Founding Dir of Physiology, Hacettepe Univ. Medical School 1963, f. Medical and Surgical Research Centre 1976, Chair. 1976, Prof. of Physiology, Hacettepe Univ. Medical Faculty, Prof. Emer. 1995–; Prof. of Physiology, East Mediterranean Univ. Medical Faculty; Chair. Anadolu Health and Research Foundation; mem. Science Council, Turkish Scientific and Tech. Nat. Research Council; Founder and Ed. Doga (scientific journal), Turkish Journal for Medical Sciences; Founding Fellow, Islamic Acad. of Sciences (IAS), mem. Council 1994, Founding Ed. IAS Journal 1988, Medical Journal of IAS; numerous TV and radio broadcasts on health and health research; American Heart Asscn Research Award 1958, Turkish Scientific and Tech. Research Council Prize for Lifetime Medical Research 1992. *Leisure interest:* essentials of Sufism. *Address:* Mithat Pasa Caddesi, 66/5, 06420 Kizilay, Ankara (office); Cevizli Dere Caddesi, No. 130/7, Yeni Oran, Ankara, Turkey (home). *Telephone:* (312) 4250319 (office); (312) 4762914 (home). *Fax:* (312) 4259487 (office). *E-mail:* nacibor@bir.net.tr (office). *Website:* www.medicaljournal-ias.org (office).

BORAH, Nayan Mani, BE; Indian business executive; ed Indian School of Mines, Dhanbad, Norwegian Inst. of Tech., Trondheim; Reservoir Engineer, Oil India Ltd 1974, later Group Gen. Man., Main Producing Area, Gen. Man. of Geosciences, Dir (Operations) 2004–10, Chair. and Man. Dir 2008–12, also mem. Business Devt Cttee; mem. Bd of Dirs Numaligarh Refinery Ltd 2006–11; mem. Academic Council, Dibrugarh Univ., Soc. of Petroleum Engineers, Soc. of Petroleum Geophysics. *Leisure interests:* reading, playing golf. *Address:* c/o Oil India Limited, Plot No. 19, Near Film City, Sector 16A, Noida 201 301, India.

BORCHERDS, Richard Ewen, PhD, FRS; British mathematician and academic; *Professor, Department of Mathematics, University of California, Berkeley;* b. 29 Nov. 1959, South Africa; s. of Dr Peter Howard Borcherds and Margaret Elizabeth Borcherds (née Greenfield); m. Ursula Gritsch; ed Trinity Coll., Cambridge; Research Fellow, Trinity Coll. 1983–87; Morrey Asst Prof., Univ. of Calif., Berkeley 1987–88, Prof. of Math. 1993–96, 1999–; Royal Soc. Univ. Residential Fellow, Univ. of Cambridge 1988–92, Lecturer 1992–93, Royal Soc. Prof., Dept of Math. 1996–99; Jr Whitehead Prize 1992, Prize of the City of Paris 1992, Fields Medal 1998. *Publications:* numerous papers in mathematical journals. *Leisure interest:* films. *Address:* Department of Mathematics, 927 Evans Hall, University of California, Berkeley, CA 94720-3840, USA (office). *Telephone:* (510) 642-8464 (office). *Fax:* (510) 642-8204 (office). *E-mail:* reb@math.berkeley .edu (office). *Website:* math.berkeley.edu/~reb (office).

BORDA, Dionisio, MA, PhD; Paraguayan politician and economist; b. San Juan, Misiones; ed Univs of Wisconsin and Massachusetts, USA; Prof. of Econs, Universidad Nacional de Asunción; Adviser to Nat. Congress 1994–96; Minister of Finance 2003–05 (resgnd), 2008–12; Founder and Dir Center of Analysis and Dissemination of the Paraguayan Economy (CADEP); fmr Visiting Prof., Univ. of Indiana. *Publications:* Presupuesto, Política Fiscal y Desempeño Económico en la Transición 2001, Globalización y Crisis fiscal (Ed.) 2003, Seguridad Social (Ed.) 2003. *Address:* c/o Ministry of Finance, Chile 128 esq. Palmas, Asunción, Paraguay (office).

BORDABERRY HERRÁN, Pedro; Uruguayan lawyer and politician; b. 28 April 1960, Montevideo; s. of Juan Maria Bordaberry (fmr Pres. of Uruguay); m.; three c.; ed British School of Montevideo, Universidad de la República; Nat. Dir of Industrial Property, Ministry of Industry, Energy and Mining 1993–94, Under-Sec., Ministry of Tourism 2000, Minister of Industry and Energy 2002–03, of Sports and Youth 2003–04, of Tourism 2004–05; unsuccessful cand. for Mayor of Montevideo 2005; f. Vamos Uruguay group within Partido Colorado 2007, Sec.-Gen. Partido Colorado 2009–11, unsuccessful cand. for Pres. of Uruguay 2009; Senator 2010–; fmr Pres. Uruguayan Rugby Union. *Leisure interest:* rugby. *Address:* Partido Colorado, Andrés Martínez Trueba 1271, 11100 Montevideo, Uruguay (office). *Telephone:* (2) 4090180 (office). *Website:* www.parlamento.gub.uy (office); www.vamosuruguay.com.uy (office).

BORDER, Allan Robert, AO; Australian fmr professional cricketer; b. 27 July 1955, Cremorne, Sydney, NSW; s. of John Border and Sheila Border; m. Jane Hiscox 1980; two c.; ed Mosman Primary School, N Sydney Tech. School, N Sydney Boys' High School; fmr clerk; work in motor trade; left-hand middle-order batsman, left-arm slow bowler; teams: NSW 1976–80, Glos., England 1977 (1 match), Queensland 1980–96 (Capt. 1983–89), Essex, England 1986–88; Capt. Australian Nat. Team 1984–94; 156 (record) Tests for Australia 1978–94, including record unbroken sequence of 153 matches, record 93 (unbroken sequence 1984–94) as Capt., scoring 11,174 runs (average 50.56) including 27 hundreds and then holding record 156 catches; scored 27,131 first-class runs (70 hundreds); toured England 1979 (World Cup), 1980, 1981, 1983 (World Cup), 1985, 1989, 1993 (last three as Capt.); then record 273 limited-overs ints, record 178 as Capt.; with Ronald McConnell Holdings 1980–84; mem. Nat. Cricket Selection Panel 1998–2005, 2006, Queensland Cricket Bd 2001–; Int. Cricket Council (ICC) Amb. to developing regions, mem. ICC Cttee; cricket commentator for Fox Sports Australia; Wisden Cricketer of the Year 1982, Australian Sports Medal in 2000, inducted into Sport Australia Hall of Fame 1990, Australian Cricket Hall of Fame 2000, ICC Cricket Hall of Fame. *Publication:* A Peep at the Poms 1986. *Leisure interests:* golf, tennis, reading. *Website:* www.foxsports.com.au/cricket.

BORDIER, Roger; French writer; b. 5 March 1923, Blois; s. of Robert Bordier and Valentine Jeufraux; m. Jacqueline Bouchaud; ed secondary school; journalist in the provinces, later in Paris; contrib. to Nouvelles Littéraires and Aujourd'hui; radio and TV writer; Officier, Ordre des Arts et des Lettres; Prix Renaudot 1961. *Publications:* poems: Les épicentres 1951; novels: La cinquième saison 1959, Les blés 1961, Le mime 1963, L'entracte 1965, Un âge d'or 1967, Le tour de ville 1969, Les éventails 1971, L'océan 1974, Meeting 1976, Demain l'été 1977; plays: Les somnambules 1963, Les visiteurs 1972; essays: L'objet contre l'art 1972, Le progrès: Pour qui? 1973, L'art moderne et l'objet 1978, A la recherche de Paris 2004; novels: La grande vie 1981, Les temps heureux 1983, La longue file 1984, 36 La fête 1985, La belle de mai 1986, Les saltimbanques de la Révolution 1989, Vel d'hib 1989, Les fusils du 1er Mai 1991, Chroniques de la Cité Joyeuse 1995, Le Zouave du Pont de l'Alma 2001; other: L'interrogatoire, dialogue 1998. *Address:*

Editions Albin Michel, 22 rue Huyghens, 75014 Paris (office); 8 rue Geoffroy St Hilaire, 75005 Paris, France (home).

BORDYUZHA, Gen. Nikolai Nikolayevich; Russian fmr army officer, politician and diplomatist; *Secretary General, Collective Security Treaty Organization (CSTO);* b. 22 Oct. 1949, Orel; m.; one s.; ed Perm Military Eng School, Moscow Inst. of Political Science, Military Acad. of the Gen. Staff of Armed Forces of the Russian Fed., Diplomatic Acad. of the Russian Fed.; service in army and state security forces 1972–91; Deputy Head, Personnel Dept, Fed. Agency of Govt Communications and Information of Russian Presidency 1991–92; Deputy Commdr, Frontier Forces 1992–94; Deputy Dir, Fed. Frontier Service 1995–98, Dir 1998; Chief of Staff of Presidential Exec. Office and Sec., Russian Fed. Security Council 1998–99; Head, State Customs Cttee 1999; Amb. to Denmark 2000–03; Sec. Gen. Collective Security Treaty Organization (CSTO) 2003–; Order of Services to the Motherland, Fourth Class (Russia), of Courage (Russia), of Friendship (Russia), of Friendship of Peoples (Belarus), Dostyk (Kazakhstan), Danaker (Kyrgyzstan), numerous medals. *Leisure interest:* fishing. *Address:* Collective Security Treaty Organization (CSTO), 3/2 Sverchkov pereulok, 101000 Moscow, Russia (office). *Telephone:* (495) 621-37-86 (office). *Fax:* (495) 623-43-46 (office). *E-mail:* odkb@gov.ru (office). *Website:* www.odkb.gov.ru (office).

BOREL, Jacques Paul; French restaurant and hotel executive and consultant; b. 9 April 1927, Courbevoie; s. of William Borel and Marie Borel (née Le Monnier); m. Christiane Roubit 1949; two s. one d.; ed Lycées Condorcet and Carnot, Paris, Ecole des Hautes Etudes Commerciales; mem. Sales Force, IBM France 1950–57, Man. Saigon (Viet Nam) Br. Office, IBM; f. restaurant chain Jacques Borel 1957, became Compagnie des Restaurants Jacques Borel (CRJB) 1960, then Jacques Borel Int. (J.B. Int.) 1970, Pres., Dir-Gen.–1977; Pres. J.B. Enterprises Soc. 1977; Dir Sofitel Jacques Borel, Jacques Borel Belgie NV-Belgique SA, Jacques Borel Do Brasil, Jacques Borel Deutschland, Jacques Borel Italia, Jacques Borel Nederland, Jacques Borel Iran, Jacques Borel Misr (Egypt), Jacques Borel Venezuela, Hoteles Jacques Borel (Barcelona), Farah Maghreb (Casablanca); Founder Syndicat Nat. des Restaurants Economiques (now Syndicat Nat. des Chaînes d'Hôtels et de Restaurants de Tourisme et d'Entreprise) 1966; Pres. Groupement HEC Tourisme-Hôtellerie; f. Club VAT 1994, Club TVA (group campaigning for reduction of VAT in hotel and restaurant industry) 2000; Chevalier, Légion d'honneur 2008. *Leisure interests:* music, painting, sailing. *Address:* Jacques Borel VAT CLUB, 29 Champs-Élysées, 75008 Paris, France. *Website:* www.vatclubjacquesborel.co.uk.

BOREN, David Lyle, MA, JD; American lawyer, university administrator and fmr politician; *President, University of Oklahoma;* b. 21 April 1941, Washington, DC; s. of Lyle H. Boren and Christine Boren (née McKown); m. 1st; one s. one d.; m. 2nd Molly Shi 1977; ed Yale Univ., Univ. of Oxford, Univ. of Oklahoma; mem. Okla House of Reps 1966–74; Chair. Govt Dept, Okla Baptist Univ. 1969–74; Gov. of Okla 1975–79; Senator from Okla 1979–94; Pres. Univ. of Okla 1994–; Rhodes Scholar 1965; mem. Bd of Trustees, Yale Univ. 1988–97; Henry Yost Award as Educ. Advocate of the Year, American Asscn of Univ. Profs 1993, Mory's Cup, Mory's Asscn, Yale Univ. 2004. *Leisure interests:* family, reading, rowing, tennis. *Address:* Office of the President, University of Oklahoma, Evans Hall Room 110, 660 Parrington Oval, Norman, OK 73019-3073 (office); 750 West Boyd, Norman, OK 73019, USA (home). *Telephone:* (405) 325-3916 (office). *Fax:* (405) 325-7605 (office). *Website:* www.ou.edu (office).

BORG, Alan Charles Nelson, CBE, PhD, FSA; British museum director; b. 21 Jan. 1942; s. of Charles J. N. Borg and Frances M. O. Hughes; m. 1st Anne Blackmore 1964 (divorced); one s. one d.; m. 2nd Lady Caroline Hill 1976; two d.; ed Westminster School, Brasenose Coll., Oxford, Courtauld Inst. of Art, London; Lecteur d'anglais, Univ. d'Aix-Marseille 1964–65; Lecturer, History of Art, Indiana Univ. 1967–69; Asst Prof. of History of Art, Princeton Univ. 1969–70; Asst Keeper of the Armouries, HM Tower of London 1970–78; Keeper, Sainsbury Centre for Visual Arts, Univ. of East Anglia 1978–82; Dir-Gen. Imperial War Museum 1982–95; Chair. Nat. Inventory of War Memorials 1988–95, Advisory Cttee on Public Records 1993, Vice-Pres. Founding Museum 2010–; Dir Victoria and Albert Museum 1995–2001; Pres. Elizabethan Club 1994–2000; Gov. Westminster School 1997–; Librarian, Order of St John 2007–; Hon. Liveryman, Worshipful Co. of Painters 1997; Hon. FRIBA 2001; Hon. Freeman, Worshipful Co. of Cooks 2011; Dr hc (Sheffield Hallam) 2000. *Publications include:* Architectural Sculpture in Romanesque Provence 1972, European Swords and Daggers in the Tower of London 1974, Torture and Punishment 1975, Heads and Horses 1976, Arms and Armour in Britain 1979, The Vanishing Past 1981, War Memorials 1991, History of the Painter-Stainers Company 2002, History of the Worshipful Company of Cooks 2011, A History of Vauxhall Gardens 2011; articles in learned journals. *Leisure interests:* fencing, music, travel. *Address:* Telegraph House, 36 West Square, London, SE11 4SP, England (home).

BORG, Anders E.; Swedish economist and politician; *Minister of Finance;* b. 11 Jan. 1968, Stockholm; m. Sanna Borg; three c.; ed De Geer School, local authority adult secondary educ., Norrköping, Uppsala and Stockholm Univs; Chair. Uppsala Univ. Student Union 1989, Föreningen Heimdal 1989; leader writer, Svenska Dagbladet 1990–91; Political Adviser, Prime Minister's Office, Coordination Secr., with responsibility for coordination of Ministry of Health and Social Affairs, Ministry of Public Admin, Ministry of Culture and Ministry of Educ. and Science 1991–93; Political Adviser to Carl Bildt at Prime Minister's Office 1993–93; Chief Economist, Transferator Alfred Berg 1995–98; Chief Economist, ABN Amro Bank, Stockholm 1998–99; Head of Econ. Analysis Dept, Skandinaviska Enskilda Banken (SEB) 1999–2001; adviser on monetary policy issues to Exec. Bd Riksbank (Swedish Cen. Bank) 2001–02; Chief Economist and Admin. for Moderate Party 2002–06; Minister of Finance 2006–; mem. Expert Group on Public Finance 1992–96, Bd Swedish Labour Market Admin 2005. *Address:* Ministry of Finance, Drottninggatan 21, 103 33 Stockholm, Sweden (office). *Telephone:* (8) 405-10-00 (office). *Fax:* (8) 21-73-86 (office). *E-mail:* registrator@finance.ministry.se (office). *Website:* www.regeringen.se (office).

BORG, Björn Rune; Swedish business executive and fmr professional tennis player; b. 6 June 1956, Stockholm; s. of Rune Borg; m. 1st Mariana Simionescu 1980 (divorced 1984); one s. by Jannike Bjorling; m. 2nd Loredana Berte 1989 (divorced 1992); ed Blombacka School; professional player since 1972; Italian Champion 1974, 1978; French Champion 1974, 1975, 1978, 1979, 1980, 1981;

Wimbledon Champion 1976, 1977, 1978, 1979, 1980 (runner-up 1981); WCT Champion 1976; four times runner-up in US Open; Grand Prix Masters Champion 1980, 1981; World Champion 1979, 1980; played Davis Cup for Sweden 1972, 1973, 1974, 1975, 1976, 1977, 1978, 1979, 1980; Winner Stockholm Open 1980; announced retirement from tennis Jan. 1983, two brief comebacks 1984, 1992; later played in srs tour; f. Björn Borg Enterprises Ltd; Sweden's Sportsperson of the Century, voted second-best tennis player ever by Sports Illustrated and l'Equipe newspaper. *Publication includes:* Bjorn Borg – My Life and Game (with Eugene Scott) 1980. *Leisure interest:* fishing. *Address:* c/o International Management Group, McCormack House, Hogarth Business Park, Burlington Lane, Chiswick, London W4 2TH, England (office). *Telephone:* (20) 8233-5300 (office). *Fax:* (20) 8233-5301 (office). *E-mail:* www.imgworld.com (office).

BORG, Joseph (Joe), LLD; Maltese politician and lawyer; b. 19 March 1952; m. Isabelle Agius; one s. one d.; ed Lyceum, Univ. of Malta, Univ. of Wales; practising lawyer 1976–; legal adviser to cos and corpns in Malta and abroad; Lecturer, Univ. of Malta 1979–88, Sr Lecturer 1988; adviser on EU matters to Minister of Foreign Affairs 1989–95; mem. Bd of Govs Malta Int. Business Authority 1989–92, Bd of Dirs of Cen. Bank 1992–95; MP 1995–2004; Shadow Minister for Industry and EU Impact on Malta 1996–98; mem. Foreign Affairs Parl. Cttee, EU-Malta Jt Cttee 1996–98; Parl. Sec., Ministry of Foreign Affairs 1998–99; Minister of Foreign Affairs 1999–2004; EU Commr without Portfolio 2004, for Fisheries and Maritime Affairs 2004–10; Hon. LLM (Wales). *Address:* c/o European Commission, Rue de la Loi 200, 1049 Brussels, Belgium (office).

BORG, Tonio, LLD; Maltese politician and lawyer; *Commissioner for Health and Consumer Policy, European Commission;* b. 12 May 1957; s. of Carmelo Borg and Maria Gemma Zarb; m. Adele Galea 1982; one s. two d.; ed St Aloysius Coll. and Univ. of Malta; Lecturer in Public Law, Univ. of Malta; exec. mem. of European Union Young Christian Democrats 1983–85; Dir Mid-Med Bank 1987–92; Pres. of Nationalist Party Gen. Council 1988–95; mem. of European Cttee for Prevention of Torture and Inhuman or Degrading Punishment or Treatment 1990–95; MP 1992–; mem. Planning Authority 1992–95; mem. of Council of Europe Ass. 1992–95; mem. Jt Parl. Cttee of the European Parl. and Maltese House of Reps 1992–95, 1996–98; Minister for Home Affairs 1995–96, 1998–2003, for Justice and Home Affairs 2003–08, for Foreign Affairs and Deputy Prime Minister 2008–12; Commissioner for Health and Consumer Affairs, EC 2012–; mem. Nationalist Party. *Leisure interests:* reading, cycling. *Address:* European Commission, rue de la Loi 200, 1049 Brussels, Belgium (office). *Telephone:* (2) 299-11-11 (office). *Fax:* (2) 295-01-38 (office). *Website:* europa.eu (office).

BORGEAUD, Pierre, DiplEng; Swiss business executive; b. 31 March 1934; m.; three c.; ed Swiss Fed. Inst. of Tech.; with Research Dept, Sulzer Bros Ltd 1959–73, Man. Sulzer Eng Works and Swiss Locomotive and Machine Works, Winterthur 1973–75, Gen. Man., Sulzer Bros Ltd (now Sulzer Man. Ltd) 1975–81, Pres. and CEO 1981–88 (Chair. 1988–2000, Del. 1999), fmr mem. Bd of Dirs; Chair. Presidential Bd of Swiss Fed. of Commerce and Industry 1987–93; Vice-Chair. Clariant Ltd 2000–03; fmr mem. Bd of Dirs Swiss Bank Corpn, Bühler Ltd, Pirelli Int. Ltd, Winterthur Insurance Co.; mem. Advisory Bd Brainforce AG.

BORGES, Jacobo; Venezuelan painter; b. 28 Nov. 1931, Caracas; ed Escuela de Artes Plásticas Cristóbal Rojas, Caracas and Ecole des Beaux Arts, Paris; mem. of Young Painters' Group and illustrator of magazines and record covers while in Paris 1951–56, also exhibited in French nat. exhbns; Prof. of Scenography and Plastic Analysis, Escuela de Artes Plásticas Cristóbal Rojas, Caracas 1958–65; Prof. of Scenography, Theatre School of Valencia and Dir Experimental Art Centre, Univ. Centre de Venezuela 1966–; has taught at Int. Summer Acad., Salzburg, Austria 1995–96, 98–99, 2000–04; int. exhbns at Guggenheim Museum, New York 1964, 1965; Artist-in-Residence, Mexico City 1993; Museo Jacobo Borges created to house his work 1995; Nat. Painting Prize 1963, Armando Reverón Bienal Prize 1965. *Major works:* La Lámpara y la Silla 1951, La Pesca 1957, Sala de Espera 1960, Todos a la Fiesta 1962, Ha Comenzado el Espectáculo 1964, Altas Finanzas 1965; series of Las Jugadoras and Las Comedoras de Helados 1965–66. *Website:* www.museojacoboborges.org.ve.

BORGES, Jorge; Cape Verde economist and politician; *Minister of Foreign Affairs;* worked for several years with EU at HQ in Brussels and in Botswana and Zimbabwe; Adjunct State Sec. to Minister of Economy, Growth and Competitiveness 2007; Sec. of State for Foreign Affairs –2011, Minister of Foreign Affairs 2011–. *Address:* Ministry of Foreign Affairs, Palácio das Comunidades, Achada de Santo António, CP 60, Praia, Santiago, Cape Verde (office). *Telephone:* 2607853 (office). *Fax:* 2619270 (office).

BORGES, Victor Manuel Barbosa; Cape Verde politician; *Independent Consultant, EFG Consulting;* b. 24 May 1955, Assomada; s. of André Borges and Maria Luisa Barbosa Borges; m. Leopoldina Maria Varela Furtado; one s. two d.; fmr Minister of Educ., Culture and Sports with portfolio of Human Resources Devt; Minister of Foreign Affairs, Co-operation and Communities 2004–08; mem. Governing Bd of UNESCO for Lifelong Learning; Ind. Consultant, EFG Consulting. *Address:* Rua Cidade de Funchal, 8 CP 133-A ASA, Praia, Cape Verde (office). *Telephone:* (262) 2368 (office). *E-mail:* victorborges@sapo.cv (office).

BORGO BUSTAMANTE, Enrique, MA, JD; Salvadorean business executive, lawyer, politician and diplomatist; b. 1928; ed Universidad de El Salvador, Rome Univ., Italy; Judge, First Instance Criminal Court, San Vicente 1955–57; attorney, Salvadoran Social Security Inst. 1957–60; attorney, Cen. Bank of El Salvador 1961–63; Dir Banco Cuscatlán 1975–79; Legal Adviser, Taca Int. Airlines 1975–80, CEO 1981–94; Vice-Pres. of El Salvador 1994–99; mem. Cen. American Congress 1999–2000; apptd Amb. to Spain 2004; fmr Partner, Consortium Centro America Abogados, El Salvador; Borgo, Avila & Cordova; Gentleman of the Order of Santiago 2008.

BORIES, Christel; French business executive; *President and CEO, Engineered Products Group, Rio Tinto Alcan Inc.;* b. 1964; ed Hautes Etudes Commerciales School of Management, Paris; worked for Booz Allen & Hamilton; Man. Corporate Value Assocs; joined Pechiney 1993, later Head of Packaging Div., Pres. and CEO Alcan Packaging and Sr Vice-Pres. Alcan Inc. (following takeover of Pechiney by Alcan) 2003–, Pres. and CEO Engineered Products Group (now Rio Tinto Alcan Engineered Products Group) 2006–; Chair. Exec. Cttee European Aluminium Asscn 2007–08; mem. Bd of Dirs Atlas Copco AB 2008–; ranked 24th by the Financial Times amongst Top 25 Businesswomen in Europe 2005. *Address:* Rio Tinto Alcan France S.A.S., 7, place du Chancelier Adenauer, 75218 Paris Cedex 16; 87, avenue Raymond Poincare, 75116 Paris, France. *Telephone:* 1-56-28-20-00 (office). *Website:* www.alcan.com (office).

BORISEVICH, Nikolai Aleksandrovich; Belarusian physicist; b. 21 Sept. 1923, Luchnoy Most, Beresinsky Dist; m. Irina Pavlovna Borisevich 1949; two s.; ed Byelorussian State Univ.; guerilla, then served in Soviet Red Army 1941–45; Deputy Dir Inst. of Physics, Byelorussian Acad. of Sciences 1955–69 (Head of Lab. 1957–); Head of Lab., Lebedev Inst. of Physics, USSR (now Russian) Acad. of Sciences 1987–; Deputy to USSR Supreme Soviet 1969–89; mem. Byelorussian (Belarus) Acad. of Sciences 1969 (Pres. 1969–87, Hon. Pres. 1992–; Corresp. mem. USSR (now Russian) Acad. of Sciences 1972–81, mem. 1981–; Foreign mem. Czechoslovakian Acad. 1977, Slovenian Acad. of Sciences and Arts 1981; titular mem. European Acad. of Arts, Sciences and Humanities 1991; Order of Red Star 1944, 1945; Order of Patriotic War (First Degree) 1945, (Second Degree) 1985; Order of Red Banner of Labour 1967; Order of Lenin 1971, 1975, 1978, 1983; Order of October Revolution 1973; Order of Friendship 2001; Order of F. Skariny 2003; Hon. PhD (Jena) 1985; USSR State Prize 1973, Hero of Socialist Labour 1978, Lenin Prize 1980, Gold Medal, Czechoslovak Acad. 1983, Slovenian Acad. 1983, Belarus State Prize 1998. *Publications:* Exited States of Complex Molecules in Gas Phase 1967, Infrared Filters 1977; over 270 scientific articles. *Address:* 7, Apt 20, Y. Kupala str., 220030 Minsk, Belarus (home). *Telephone:* (17) 227-4559 (home).

BORISOV, Lt-Gen. Boyko Metodiev, DS; Bulgarian politician; *Leader, Citizens for European Development of Bulgaria (GERB—Grazhdani za evropeysko razvitie na Balgariya);* b. 13 June 1959, Bankya; m. Stela Borisova (divorced); one d.; partner Tsvetelina Borislavova; ed Higher Specialized School, Ministry of the Interior; early career as police officer, Sofia 1978, Platoon Commdr 1982, later Co. Commdr; Lecturer, Higher Inst. for Officer Training and Scientific Research, Ministry of the Interior 1985–90; f. WON-1 Ltd (security co.) 1991; mem. Bulgarian Communist Party –1990, Nat. Movt Simeon II 2001–06; Sec.-Gen., Ministry of the Interior 2001–05; Mayor of Sofia 2005–09; Founder and Leader Citizens for European Devt of Bulgaria (GERB) 2006–; Prime Minister 2009–13 (resgnd); mem. World Org. of Security Co.; has actively participated in karate championships since 1978, currently has 7th dan black belt; Chair. Bulgarian Karate Fed., fmr Coach, Bulgarian Nat. Karate Team and int. karate referee; Sign of Honour (Second Degree), Bulgaria 2003, Cross for Police Contrib. with Red Star, Spain 2003, Medal of Honour of the French Police, Medal for Operational Friendship and Co-operation, Russia, Commdr, Order of the Star of Italian Solidarity 2006. *Address:* Citizens for European Development of Bulgaria (GERB—Grazhdani za evropeysko razvitie na Balgariya), 1463 Sofia, pl. Balgariya 1, NDK Administration Building 17, Bulgaria (office). *Telephone:* (2) 490-13-13 (office). *Fax:* (2) 490-09-51 (office). *E-mail:* pr@gerb.bg (office). *Website:* www.gerb.bg (office).

BORITH, Ouch; Cambodian diplomatist; *Secretary of State, Ministry of Foreign Affairs and International Cooperation;* b. 2 Nov. 1957, Phnom-Penh; m.; five c.; ed Medical Faculty, Phnom-Penh, Inst. of Sociology, Moscow; French trans., Ministry of Foreign Affairs 1979–80, Dir Dept of UN Humanitarian Org., Ministry of Foreign Affairs 1980–83, Dir Dept of Asia and Pacific Affairs 1987–90; Counsellor in charge of Political Affairs, Embassy in Moscow 1983–87; Amb. to Viet Nam 1990–92; Chargé d'affaires, Perm. Mission to UN, New York 1992–93, Deputy Perm. Rep. 1993–97, Perm. Rep. 1998; currently Sec. of State, Ministry of Foreign Affairs and Int. Co-operation. *Address:* Ministry of Foreign Affairs and International Co-operation, 3 rue Samdech Hun Sen, Khan Chamkarmon, Phnom-Penh, Cambodia (office). *Telephone:* (23) 214441 (office). *Fax:* (23) 216144 (office). *E-mail:* mfaicasean@online.com.kh (office). *Website:* www.mfaic.gov.kh (office).

BORJA CEVALLOS, Rodrigo, PhD, DJur; Ecuadorean politician and academic; b. 19 June 1937, Quito; s. of Luis Felipe Borja de Alcázar and Aurelia Cevallos; m. Carmen Calisto de Borja; one s. three d.; ed Cen. Univ. of Ecuador; Deputy in Nat. Congress 1962–82; founder and fmr Leader Partido Izquierda Democrática; Prof. of Political Sciences, Cen. Univ. of Ecuador 1963–88; Pres. of Ecuador 1988–92; presidential candidate 2002; Pres. Law School Asscn, Cen. Univ. of Ecuador 1958; mem. Special Comm. of Lawyers on Ecuador's Political Constitution 1966; Hon. Mem. Charles Darwin Foundation; Hon. Prof. Universidad Nacional de Mar del Plata, Argentina, Universidad Autónoma de Santo Domingo, Dominican Repub.; Dr hc (Sorbonne, Paris), (Universidad de Buenos Aires), (Universaidad de San Andrés de Bolivia), (Univ. of N Carolina, Ashville, USA), (Universidad Nacional de Santiago, Dominican Repub.), (Universidad Ricardo Palma, Lima); Cristóbal Gabarrón International Award for Thought and Humanities 2010. *Publications:* Political Constitutional Law (2 vols) 1964, 1971, Socialismo Democrático (Democratic Socialism) 1983, El Asilo Diplomático en América (Diplomatic Asylum in the Americas), La democracia en América Latina (Democracy in Latin America), A Political Dictionary, Historia de una Claudicación, Tratado de Derecho Político y Constitucional, La Etica del Poder, Desarrollo del Derecho Constitucional Ecuatoriano, Derechos Humanos: una nueva perspectiva, Democracia y Populismo, La lucha de América Latina por la Democracia, Recovecos de la Historia, Sociedad, Cultura y Derecho; numerous essays. *Address:* c/o Izquierda Democrática, Polonia 161, entre Vancouver y Eloy Alfaro, Quito, Ecuador.

BORKO, Yuri Antonovich, DEcon; Russian economist; *Head, European Integration Department, Institute of Europe, Russian Academy of Sciences;* b. 6 Feb. 1929, Rostov-on-Don; m. Yelena Borisovna Borko; two s.; ed Moscow State Univ.; researcher, Inst. of World Econ. and Int. Relations USSR (now Russian) Acad. of Sciences 1962–63; Ed. and mem. of Bd journal World Econ. and Int. Relations 1963–69; Head of Div. Inst. of Information on Social Sciences, USSR (now Russian) Acad. of Sciences 1970–90; Head of Div., Deputy Dir, Head of Research Centre of European Integration, Head of Centre of European Documentation, Prof., Inst. of Europe, Russian Acad. of Sciences 1990–; Jean Monnet Chairholder 2001–; Pres. Russian Asscn of European Studies 1992–. *Publications include:* works on problems of European integration, European Community policy and int. relations between Russia and European Community. *Leisure interests:* skiing, books, music. *Address:* Institute of Europe, 125993 Moscow, Mokhovaya str. 11, stroenye 3B (office); 127018 Moscow, Sovetskoy Armii str. 13–43, Russia (home). *Telephone:* (495) 292-10-23 (office); (495) 289-21-66 (home). *Fax:* (495) 200-

42-98 (office). *E-mail:* europe@ieras.ru (office). *Website:* www.ieras.ru (office); www.edc-aes.ru (office).

BORLOO, Jean-Louis, MBA; French lawyer and politician; *President, Union des Démocrates et Indépendants;* b. 7 April 1951, Paris; m. Béatrice Schönberg 2005; ed Ecole des Hautes Etudes Commerciales-Institut Supérieur des Affaires (HEC-ISA), Univ. of Manchester, UK; began career as finance lawyer, Paris; est. own law firm; fmr teacher of Financial Analysis, HEC-ISA; Mayor of Valenciennes 1989–2002, Deputy Mayor 2002–08; mem. European Parl. 1989–92; Regional Counsellor for Nord-Pas-de-Calais 1992–93, 1998; mem. Assemblée Nationale 1993–2002, 2007–; Spokesman, Union pour la Démocratie Française (UDF) 2001–02; joined Union pour la majorité présidentielle (now Union pour un Mouvement Populaire—UMP) 2002; Minister-Del. of Towns and Urban Redevelopment, attached to Minister of Social Affairs, Labour and Solidarity 2002–04; Minister of Employment, Labour and Social Cohesion 2004–05, of Employment, Social Cohesion and Housing 2005–07, of the Economy, Finance and Employment May–June 2007, for Ecology, Energy, Sustainable Devt and Spatial Planning June 2007–10; Pres. Parti Radical de Gauche (assoc. party of UMP) 2007–11; Pres. and Leader, Union des démocrates et indépendants (Union of Democrats and Independents) party 2012–. *Publications:* Un Homme en colère 2002, L'Architecte et l'Horologer 2007. *Address:* Union des Démocrates et Indépendants, 27 boulevard Raspail, 75007 Paris, France (office). *Telephone:* 1-53-71-20-17 (office). *E-mail:* contact@parti-udi.fr (office). *Website:* www.parti-udi.fr (office).

BORMAN, Frank, American business executive and fmr astronaut; b. 14 March 1928, Gary, Ind.; s. of Edwin Borman and late Marjorie Borman; m. Susan Bugbee 1950; two s.; ed US Mil. Acad., California Inst. of Tech., USAF Aerospace Research Pilots' School; pilot training, Williams Air Force Base, Arizona; assigned to various fighter squadrons in US and Philippines; Instructor in Thermodynamics and Fluid Mechanics, US Mil. Acad. 1957; Instructor, USAF Aerospace Research Pilots' School 1960–62; selected by NASA as astronaut Sept. 1962, Command Pilot, Gemini VII 1965, Commdr Apollo VIII spacecraft which made flight round the moon Dec. 1968, Deputy Dir for Flight Operations, NASA, –1969, Field Dir NASA Space Station Task Group 1969–70; Vice-Pres. Eastern Airlines Inc. 1970–74, Vice-Pres. for Eastern Operations 1974–75, Pres. 1975–85, CEO 1975–86, Chair. of Bd 1976–86; Vice-Chair. Texas Air Corp. 1986–92; Chair. and CEO Patlex Corp. 1988–92, Chair. Bd Autofinance Group Inc. (parent of Patlex) 1992–95; NASA Exceptional Service Medal, Harmon Int. Aviation Trophy 1966, Gold Space Medal, Int. Aeronautics 1969, Encyclopedia Britannica Achievement in Life Award 1980. *Publication:* Countdown: An Autobiography 1988. *Leisure interests:* restoring aeroplanes, building model aeroplanes. *Address:* 4530 Blue Lake Drive, Boca Raton, FL 33431, USA (home).

BORN, Adolf, Czech artist; b. 12 June 1930, České Velenice; m. Emilie Košáková; one d.; ed Pedagogical Faculty of Charles Univ., Prague School of Applied Art, Acad. of Graphic and Plastic Arts; illustration, animated cartoons, film co-operation with Jiří Brdečka 1955–; illustrated 250 children's books including Robinson Crusoe 1971, The Isle of Penguins, La Fontaine's Fables; author of 45 cartoon films for children; Chevalier, Ordre des Arts et des Lettres; Gold Medal for Brecht's Mother Courage, Leipzig 1965, Premio preferri di Imperie, Italy 1965, Dattero d'Oro 1966, Albatross Prize for Lifelong Work, Prague 2000. *Films:* co-dir. (with Macourek and Doubrava) of films The Life of Birds, The Life of Children. *Television:* serial Mach and Šebestová. *Leisure interests:* travel, animals. *Address:* Dvorecká 18, Prague 4, 14700 Czech Republic.

BORN, Gustav Victor Rudolf, MB, ChB, DPhil, FRS, FRCP; British professor of pharmacology; *Research Professor, William Harvey Research Institute, St Bartholomew's Hospital Medical College;* b. 29 July 1921, Göttingen, Germany; s. of the late Prof. Max Born (jt winner 1954 Nobel Prize for Physics); m. 1st Wilfrida Ann Plowden-Wardlaw 1950 (divorced 1961); two s. one d.; m. 2nd Dr Faith Elizabeth Maurice-Williams 1962; one s. one d.; ed Oberrealschule, Göttingen, Germany, Perse School, Cambridge, Edinburgh Acad. and Univs of Edinburgh and Oxford; Medical Officer, RAMC 1943–47; Research Asst, Graham Research Lab., Univ. Coll. Hosp. Medical School, London 1947–49; studentship, training in research methods of MRC 1949–52; mem. scientific staff, Toxicology Research Unit, MRC 1952–53; Sr Research Officer Nuffield Inst. for Medical Research and Medical Lecturer, St Peter's Coll., Oxford 1953–60; Vandervell Prof. of Pharmacology, Royal Coll. of Surgeons and Univ. of London 1960–73; Sheild Prof. of Pharmacology, Univ. of Cambridge and Fellow, Gonville and Caius Coll., Cambridge 1973–78; Prof. of Pharmacology, King's Coll., London 1978–86, Prof. Emer. 1986–; Research Prof., William Harvey Research Inst., St Bartholomew's Hospital Medical Coll. 1988–; fmr mem. Council of the Int. Soc. of Thrombosis and Haemostasis (Pres. 1977–79), Cttee of British Pharmacological Soc., Working Party on Antihaemophilic Globulin of MRC, Official Cttee of Enquiry into Relationship of Pharmaceutical Industry with Nat. Health Service, Medical Advisory Bd, British Council and numerous other cttees and bds; mem. Nat. Akad. of Sciences Leopoldina; Hon. Fellow, St Peter's Coll., Oxford, Hon. FRCS, Hon. Life mem. New York Acad. of Sciences, and other hon. memberships; Chevalier, Ordre nat. du Mérite; Hon. DSc (Bordeaux, Paris, Brown Univ.), Hon. MD (Münster, Leuven, Edinburgh, Munich, Loyola Univ., Chicago, Düsseldorf); Royal Soc. Royal Medal, Paul Morawitz Prize, Robert Pfleger Prize, Alexander von Humboldt Award 1995, Gold Medal for Medicine, Jung Foundation, British Pharmacological Soc. Wellcome Gold Medal and Prize 2009. *Publications include:* more than 300 scientific publs. *Leisure interests:* music, history. *Address:* The William Harvey Research Institute, St Bartholomew's and the Royal London School of Medicine and Dentistry, Charterhouse Square, London, EC1M 6BQ (office); 5 Walden Lodge, 48 Wood Lane, London, N6 5UU, England (home). *Telephone:* (20) 7882-6070 (office). *Fax:* (20) 7882-6071 (office). *E-mail:* g.v.born@qmul.ac.uk (office). *Website:* www.whri.qmul.ac.uk (office).

BORNER, Silvio, Swiss economist and academic; b. 24 April 1941; s. of Walter Borner and Meta Borner; m. Verena Barth 1966; two d.; ed St Gall Grad. School and Yale Univ., USA; Prof. of Econs, Univ. of St Gallen 1974–78, of Political Econs, Univ. of Basle 1978–2009, currently Head of Summer School in Law, Econs and Public Policy. *Publications:* Die 'sechste Schweiz'—überleben auf dem Weltmarkt, New Forms of Internationalization: An Assessment, Einführung in die Volks-wirtschaftslehre, International Finance and Trade in a Polycentric World. *Leisure interests:* sports (active) and culture. *Address:* c/o WWZ der Universität Basel,

Abteilung Wirtschaft und Politik, Peter Merian-Weg 6, Postfach, 4002 Basle, Switzerland.

BORODIN, Pavel Pavlovich; Russian politician and economist; *State Secretary, Union of Russia and Belarus;* b. 25 Oct. 1946, Shakhudya, Nizhnii-Novgorod region; m. Valentina Borodina; one d. three adopted s.; ed Higher CPSU School, Moscow Inst. of Chemical Machine Construction, Ulyanovsk Inst. of Agric.; joined Yakutskgeologiya co. as economist 1978, Deputy Dir-Gen. until 1990; Mayor of Yakutsk 1993; Russian Soviet Federated Socialist Repub. People's Deputy, mem. Cttee on Problems of Women, Family Protection and Childhood 1990–93; moved to Moscow 1993; mem., then Man., then Chair. of Presidential Admin. 1993–2000; State Sec. Union of Russia and Belarus 2000–; detained in USA on request of Swiss Govt Prosecutor, extradited to Switzerland for money laundering 2002, case closed 2002; Leader, Great Russia—Eurasian Union electoral bloc, State Duma elections 2003; Order for Service to Motherland; State Prize of Russian Fed. *Leisure interests:* football, pets. *Address:* Executive Committee of Union of Russia and Belarus, 220000 Minsk, Kirova str. 17, Belarus (office). *Telephone:* (17) 229-34-34 (office). *Website:* www.belarus.mid.ru (office).

BORODINA, Olga Vladimirovna; Russian singer (mezzo-soprano); b. Leningrad (now St Petersburg); d. of Vladimir Nikolaevich and Galina Fedorovna Borodin; m. Ildar Abdrazakov; three s.; ed Leningrad Conservatory (student of Irina Bogacheva); soloist of Kirov (now Mariinsky) Theatre of Opera and Ballet 1987–; debut as Delilah in Samson and Delilah at Royal Opera House, Covent Garden with Plácido Domingo 1992; leading roles in operas including Marfa in Khovanshchina, Konchakovna in Prince Igor, Poline in Queen of Spades, Lubava in Sadko, Marina Mnichek in Boris Godunov, Cinderella in La Cenerentola, Carmen, Amneris in Aïda, Eboli in Don Carlos, Isabella in The Italian Girl in Algiers, Laura in La Gioconda, Delilah in Samson and Delilah, La Principessa in Adriana Lecouvreur, Giulietta in Les Contes d'Hoffmann, Marguerite in La Damnation de Faust; regular performances in all major opera houses as well as recitals and concerts world-wide; winner of First Prizes: All-Union Glinka Competition 1987, Int. Rosa Poncell Competition, New York 1987, Int. Francisco Viñas Competition, Barcelona 1989, People's Artist of Russia 2002, State Prize of Russia 2007. *Recordings include:* Verdi Requiem, Chicago Symphony Orchestra, conductor Riccardo Muti (Grammy Award for Best Classical Album, first Russian to win a Grammy Award) 2011. *Leisure interest:* fishing. *Address:* c/o NFBM Ltd, 3rd Floor, 24 Endell Street, London, WC2H 9HQ, England (office). *Telephone:* (20) 7359-4771 (office). *Fax:* (20) 3292-1913 (office). *E-mail:* nicola-fee@nfbm.com (office). *Website:* www.nfbm.com (office).

BOROS, Christian; German art collector and media executive; b. 1964, Zabrze (German: Hindenburg), Upper Silesia, Poland; m. Karen Lohmann; ed studied communication design with Bazon Brock in Wuppertal; f. Boros communication agency 1990; cr. ad campaign for music channel VIVA 1994; began collecting art aged 18; first purchase, Intuition Box, an early multiple of Joseph Beuys; discovered the photographer Wolfgang Tillmans in London 1990; collected the Young British Artists Damien Hirst, Tracey Emin, Steven Gontarski and Sarah Lucas, and the German Zeitgeist artists Michel Majerus, Daniel Pflumm, the American artists Elizabeth Peyton, Anselm Reyle and the Danish artist Olafur Eliasson; owns pvt. museum of contemporary art, Bunker in Berlin. *Address:* Boros Group, Hofaue 63, 42103 Wuppertal (office); Sammlung Boros, Bunker, Reinhardtstr. 20, 10117 Berlin -Mitte, Germany (office). *Telephone:* (202) 24843-0 (Wuppertal) (office); (30) 27594065 (Berlin) (office). *Fax:* (202) 24843-19 (Wuppertal) (office). *E-mail:* info@sammlung-boros.de (office). *Website:* www.sammlung-boros.de (office).

BOROSS, Péter, PhD; Hungarian lawyer and politician; b. 27 Aug. 1928, Nagybajom; m. Ilona Papp (died 2010); two c.; ed Eötvös Loránd Univ. of Budapest; with Budapest Metropolitan Council 1951–56; dismissed for membership of revolutionary cttee and revolutionary council 1956; kept under police surveillance until 1959; employed as unskilled worker 1964; organized catering and tourist coll. training; catering chain dir 1971; mem. Council Coll. of Trade and Catering; mem. Hungarian League of Human Rights, Hungarian Chamber of Economy; Founder, Nation Bldg Foundation 1988; Minister of State for Office of Information and Office of Nat. Security 1990–94; Minister of Interior 1990–93; Prime Minister of Hungary 1993–94; mem. Parl. (Hungarian Democratic Forum—MDF) 1994–98; Chair. Nat. Security Cttee of Parl. 1994–96; Sr Counsellor and Adviser to Prime Minister 1998–2009; mem. Hungarian Democratic Forum –2010.

BOROVKOV, DSc; Russian mathematician and academic; *Professor, Head of Probability and Statistics Chair, Novosibirsk University;* b. 6 March 1931, Moscow; s. of Aleksey and Klaudia Borovkov; m. Svetlana Borovkov 1975; two s.; ed Moscow Univ.; Postgraduate, Research Assoc. Steclev Math. Inst. 1954–60; Head of Probability and Statistics Dept, Sobolev Inst. of Math., Siberian Branch USSR (now Russian) Acad. of Sciences 1960–, Deputy Dir 1981–91; Prof., Head of Probability and Statistics Chair, Novosibirsk Univ. 1965–; Corresp. mem. USSR (now Russian) Acad. of Sciences 1966–90, full mem. 1990–; mem. Int. Statistical Inst., Bernulli Soc.; Friendship of Nations Order 1981, Order Merit to Fatherland, Fourth Degree 2002; Badge of Honours 1975, State Prize 1979, Russian Fed. Govt Prize in Educ. 2003, Russian Acad. of Science Markov Prize 2003. *Publications:* Stochastic Processes in Queuing Theory 1976, Wahrscheinlichkeitstheorie 1976, Asymptotic Methods in Queuing Theory 1980, Statistique Mathématique 1987, Ergodicity and Stability of Stochastic Processes, 1998, Probability Theory 1998, Mathematical Statistics 1998, Asymptotic Analysis of Random Walks: Heavy-Tailed Distributions (jtly with K.A.Borovkov) 2008; more than 200 works on contiguous problems of theory probabilities and mathematical statistics. *Address:* Sobolev Institute of Mathematics, Koptyug prospekt 4, Novosibirsk 630090 (office); 12/1 Trofimuk str., Novosibirsk 630090, Russia (home). *Telephone:* (383) 363-45-89 (office); (383) 330-23-53 (home). *Fax:* (383) 333-25-98 (office). *E-mail:* borovkov@math.nsc.ru (office). *Website:* www.math.nsc.ru (office).

BOROWSKI, Marek Stefan; Polish politician; b. 4 Jan. 1946, Warsaw; m.; one s.; ed Main School of Planning and Statistics (now Warsaw School of Econs), Warsaw; Sr Economist, Centrum Dept stores, Warsaw 1968–82; Ministry of Nat. Economy 1982–91, Deputy Minister 1989; deputy to Sejm (Parl.) 1991–2001, Vice-Marshal of Sejm 1996–2001, Marshal (Speaker) 2001–04; Deputy Prime Minister, Minister of Finance and Head Econ. Cttee of Council of Ministers 1993–94; Minister/Head

Council of Ministers Office 1995–96; mem. Polish United Workers' Party (PZPR) 1967–68, 1975–90; mem. Social Democracy of Polish Repub. 1990–99, Democratic Left Alliance 1999–2004 (Vice-Chair.); Leader, Polish Social Democracy Party (Socjaldemokracja Polska—SDPL) 2004–08; Senator 2011–. *Leisure interests:* brain teasers, bowling, board and card games, classical and light music, science fiction books by Stanislaw Lem. *Address:* Biuro Senatorskie Marka Borowskiego, 03-408 Warsaw, ul. Targowa 81 lok. 107A (office); Senat, 00-902 Warsaw, ul. Wiejska 6, Poland. *Telephone:* (22) 881-77-65 (office). *E-mail:* biurosenatorskie@marekborowski.pl. *Website:* www.marekborowski.pl (home).

BORRA TOLEDO DE JIMÉNEZ, Dora Virginia, MEconSc; Peruvian economist and politician; b. 1943, Lima; ed Universidad Nacional Mayor de San Marcos, Universidad Inca Garcilaso de la Vega, Universidad ESAN, Lima; Adviser to Office of the Presidency of the Council of Ministers 2008; Minister of State, Ministry of Women and Social Devt 2006–07, Head of Decentralized Public Inst. Direct Assistance Programme (DAP) 1988–90, Dir Presidency of the Council of Ministers DAP 1987–88; Exec. Dir Instituto Trabajo y Familia 2002–06, 2008–09; Minister of Women and Social Devt 2010–11; fmr Exec. Dir Sembrando Devt Programme; mem. Alianza Popular Revolucionaria Americana. *Address:* c/o Ministry of Women and Social Development, Jirón Camaná 616, Lima 1, Peru (office).

BORRELL FONTELLES, Josep, MA, DEconSci; Spanish politician and academic; b. 24 April 1947, Pobla Segur, Lérida; divorced; two c.; ed Polytechnic Univ. and Complutense Univ. Madrid, Institut français du Pétrole, France, Stanford Univ., USA; engineer and Dir Dept of Systems, CESPA (Compañía Española de Petróleos) 1972–81, elected as trade-union rep.; mem. Socialist Workers' Party (PSOE) Madrid 1975–, mem. Partit dels Socialistes de Catalunya Nat. Exec. 1992–2004, mem. PSOE Fed. Exec. 1997–2004, won PSOE's primary elections to become party cand. for office of Prime Minister 1998; elected as councillor in Spain's first democratic municipal elections 1979; Deputy, Treasury and Econ. Planning for Prov. Del. Madrid 1979–82; Under-Sec. Budget and Public Spending 1982–84, Sec. of State for the Treasury 1984–91, Deputy for Barcelona in Legis. Ass. 1986–91; Minister of Public Works and Transport 1991–96, of the Environment 1993–96; Chair. Parl. Cttee on European Affairs 1999–2004; mem. European Parl. 2004–09, Pres. 2004–07, Chair. European Parl. Devt Cttee 2007–09, mem. European Convention 2002–03; Dir European Studies Seminar, International Univ. of Santander and of Malaga Univ. at Ronda 2000–08; Pres. European Univ. Inst. 2010–12; currently Research Assoc., Complutense Inst. of International Studies, Universidad Complutense de Madrid; mem. Bd of Dirs Abengoa, Notre Europe (Jacques Delors Inst.); Grand Cross, Order of Charles III. *Address:* Complutense Institute for International Studies, Universidad Complutense de Madrid, Av Séneca, 2, 28040 Madrid, Spain (office).

BORRIE, Baron (Life Peer), cr. 1995, of Abbots Morton in the County of Hereford and Worcester; **Gordon Johnson,** Kt, QC, FRSA; British lawyer; b. 13 March 1931; s. of Stanley Borrie; m. Dorene Toland 1960 (died 2010); ed John Bright Grammar School, Llandudno and Univ. of Manchester; called to Bar, Middle Temple 1952; Bencher 1980; Barrister, London 1954–57; Lecturer, later Sr Lecturer in Law, Coll. of Law 1957–64, Univ. of Birmingham 1965–68, Prof. of English Law and Dir Inst. of Judicial Admin. 1969–76, Dean Faculty of Law 1974–76; Dir-Gen. Office of Fair Trading 1976–92; Dir (non-exec.) Woolwich Building Society 1992–2000, Three Valleys Water Services 1992–2003, Mirror Group Newspapers 1993–99, Telewest Communications 1994–2001, General Utilities 1998–2003; Chair. Accountancy Foundation 2000–03, Advertising Standards Authority 2001–07; mem. Parole Bd for England and Wales 1971–74, Consumer Protection Advisory Cttee 1973–76, Equal Opportunities Comm. 1975–76; Pres. Inst. of Trading Standards Admin 1992–97; Chair. Comm. on Social Justice 1992–94, Money Advice Trust 1993–95; mem. Council of Ombudsman for Corp. Estate Agents 1992–98; Labour cand. Croydon 1955, Ilford 1959; Gov. Birmingham Coll. of Commerce 1966–70; Hon. LLD (City of London Polytechnic) 1989, (Manchester) 1990, (Hull) 1991, (Dundee) 1993, (Nottingham Trent) 1996, (Univ. of the West of England) 1997, (Nottingham) 2005. *Publications:* Commercial Law 1962, The Consumer, Society and the Law (with Prof. A. L. Diamond) 1963, Law of Contempt (with N.V. Lowe) 1973, The Development of Consumer Law and Policy 1984. *Leisure interests:* gastronomy, piano playing, travel. *Address:* 4 Brick Court, Temple, London, EC4Y 9AD (office); Manor Farm, Abbots Morton, Worcestershire, WR7 4NA, England (home). *Telephone:* (20) 7353-4434; (1386) 792330.

BÖRSIG, Clemens, PhD; German banker; *Chairman of the Supervisory Board and Director, Deutsche Bank AG;* b. 1948; ed Univ. of Mannheim; Asst Prof., Univs of Mannheim and Munich 1973–77; held several positions at Mannesmann Group, Dusseldorf 1977–85, including Head of Corp. Planning at Mannesmann-Kienzle GmbH and Chief Financial and Admin. Officer at Mannesmann-Tally; Head of Corp. Planning and Controlling, Robert Bosch GmbH, Stuttgart 1985–97, mem. Man. Bd 1990–97; Chief Financial Officer and mem. Man. Bd RWE AG, Essen 1997–99; Chief Financial Officer Deutsche Bank AG 1999–2006, mem. Man. Bd 2001–06, also Chief Risk Officer responsible for corp. governance, mem. Supervisory Bd 2006–, Chair. 2006–; Deputy Chair. Supervisory Bd Eurohypo AG –2005; mem. Supervisory Bd Bayer AG, Linde AG 2006–, Daimlerchrysler AG (now Daimler AG) 2007–. *Address:* Deutsche Bank AG, Taunusanlage 12, 60262 Frankfurt am Main, Germany (office). *Telephone:* (69) 910-00 (office). *Fax:* (69) 910-34225 (office). *E-mail:* webmaster@db.com (office). *Website:* www.db.com (office).

BORSIK, János, DJur; Hungarian trade union official; *President, Autonomous Trade Union Confederation;* b. 22 June 1946; m.; two s.; ed Janus Pannonius Univ. of Sciences, Pécs; locomotive fitter 1964–88; locomotive driver 1968–86; trade union officer 1986–; consultant on labour law; Pres. Autonomous Trade Union Confed. (Autonóm Szakszervezetek Szövetsége—ASzSz) 2000–; Vice-Pres. Mozdonyvezetok Szakszervezet (MoSZ) 2000. *Leisure interests:* literature, theatre, sports. *Address:* ASZSZ, Benczúr utca 45, 1068 Budapest (office); Oktogon 3, 1066 Budapest, Hungary (home). *Telephone:* 4131934 (office). *Fax:* 4612480 (office). *E-mail:* autonom@t-online.hu (office).

BORST, Piet, MD, PhD; Dutch biochemist; *Staff Member, Netherlands Cancer Institute;* b. 5 July 1934, Amsterdam; s. of Prof. J. Borst and A. Borst-de Geus; m. Jinke C. S. Houwing 1957; two s. one d.; ed Gymnasium, Amsterdam, Univ. of Amsterdam; Research Asst, Lab. of Biochemistry, Univ. of Amsterdam 1958–61; Post-doctoral Research Fellow, Dept of Biochemistry, New York Univ. 1963–64; Prof. of Biochemistry and Molecular Biology, Univ. of Amsterdam 1965–83, Head of Section for Medical Enzymology, Lab. of Biochemistry 1966–83, Dir Inst. of Animal Physiology 1972–80, Extraordinary Prof. of Clinical Biochemistry 1983–; Dir of Research Netherlands Cancer Inst., Amsterdam 1983–99, staff mem. 1999–; mem. Royal Netherlands Acad. of Arts and Sciences 1978, Hollandsche Maatschappij der Wetenschappen 1983, Academia Europaea 1989; Foreign mem. Royal Soc. of GB 1986; Foreign Assoc. NAS 1991; Foreign Hon. mem. American Acad. of Arts and Sciences 1995; Commdr, Order of the Dutch Lion 1999, Hon. CBE; Dr hc (Leiden) 2003; Hon. LLD (Dundee); Royal Dutch/Shell Prize for the Life Sciences 1981, Federatie van Medisch Wetenschappelijke Verenigingen Prize 1984, Paul-Ehrlich and Ludwig-Darmstaedter Prize (jtly) 1984, Ricketts Award, Univ. of Chicago 1989, Dr G. Wander Award of the Wander Foundation, Berne 1990, Gold Medal, Genootschap voor Natuur-, Genees- en Heelkunde, Amsterdam 1990, Dr H. P. Heineken Prize for Biochemistry and Biophysics, Amsterdam 1992, Gold Medal, Koch Foundation, Cologne 1992, Hamilton Fairley Award for Clinical Research, ESMO 2000. *Publications include:* over 300 scientific articles in biochemistry, molecular biology and cell biology. *Leisure interests:* tennis, windsurfing, skiing, cello, bridge. *Address:* Netherlands Cancer Institute, Plesmanlaan 121, 1066 CX Amsterdam (office); Meentweg 87, 1406 KE Bussum, Netherlands (home). *Telephone:* (20) 5122880 (office); (35) 6914453 (home). *Fax:* (20) 6691383 (office). *E-mail:* p.borst@nki.nl (office). *Website:* www.nki.nl (office).

BORTNIKOV, Lt.-Gen. Aleksandr Vasilyevich; Russian government security official; *Head, Federal Security Service (FSB);* b. 15 Nov. 1951, Perm; m.; one s.; ed Leningrad Inst. for Railway Eng; joined Leningrad KGB 1975, Deputy Head, Fed. Security Service (FSB) Directorate for St Petersburg and Leningrad Oblast in charge of counter-intelligence operations –2003, Head of Directorate 2003–04, Deputy Dir FSB and Head of Econ. Security Service 2004–08, Head of FSB 2008–; mem. Bd of Dirs Sovkomflot; Order of Merit for the Fatherland (Third and Fourth Classes), Order of Mil. Merit, Medal of Honour; Diploma of the Govt of the Russian Fed. 2006. *Address:* Federal Security Service (FSB), 103031 Moscow, ul. Bolshaya Lubyanka, Building 1/3, Russia (office). *Telephone:* (495) 914-43-69 (office). *E-mail:* fsb@fsb.ru (office). *Website:* www.fsb.ru (office).

BORUBAYEV, Altai; Kyrgyzstani mathematician and politician; b. 1950, Karaoy, Kyrgyzia; ed Kyrgyz State Univ.; teacher, Frunze Polytechnic Inst. 1975–76; teacher, Sr Teacher, Head of Chair., Dean, Pro-Rector Kyrgyz State Univ. 1976–92, Rector 1998–2000; Rector, Kyrgyz State Pedagogical Inst. 1994–98; First Deputy Minister of Educ. 1992–94; Chair. (Speaker) Ass. of People's Reps Chamber of Zhogorku Kenesh (Parl.) 2000; mem. Nat. Acad. of Sciences 2000, Russian Acad. of Social and Pedagogical Sciences. *Publications:* three monographs, over 100 articles. *Address:* c/o Zhogorku Kenesh, 720003 Bishkek, ul. Abdymomunov 207, Kyrgyzstan (office).

BORYSIEWICZ, Sir Leszek, MA, PhD, FRS, FRCP, FMedSci; British physician, academic and university administrator; *Vice-Chancellor, University of Cambridge;* b. 13 April 1951, Cardiff, Wales; s. of Polish parents who settled in Wales after World War II; m. Gwenllian Borysiewicz; ed Cardiff High School, Welsh Nat. School of Medicine; postdoctoral research in London 1977; Registrar, Dept of Medicine, Hammersmith Hosp. 1979–80; joined Royal Postgraduate Medical School, London initially as MRC Clinical Training Fellow, then Lister Research Fellow and Sr Lecturer 1980–86; Wellcome Trust Sr Lecturer in Infectious Diseases, Addenbrooke's Hosp., Cambridge 1987–88; Lecturer in Medicine, Univ. of Cambridge 1988–91, Vice-Chancellor 2010–, fmr Fellow, Wolfson Coll., now Hon. Fellow; Prof. of Medicine, Univ. of Wales Coll. of Medicine 1991–2001; Prin., Faculty of Medicine, Imperial Coll. London 2001–04, Deputy Rector, Imperial Coll. London 2004–07; mem. Council of MRC 1995–2000 Chief Exec. MRC 2007–10; Chair. UK Clinical Research Collaboration's Integrated Academic Training Awards Panel 2005–07; HEFCE RAE Main Panel A Assessment Panel; Gov. Wellcome Trust 2006–07; Chair. Nat. Health Service (Wales) R&D Grants Cttee; Acting Dir NHS (Wales) Research and Devt 1994–96; mem. Council, Cancer Research UK 2002–05; Dir (non-exec.) North Thames Regional Health Authority 2003–04; Founding Fellow, Acad. of Medical Sciences 1996, mem. Council 1997–2002. *Address:* Vice-Chancellor's Office, University of Cambridge, The Old Schools, Trinity Lane, Cambridge, CB2 1TT, England (office). *Telephone:* (1223) 332290 (office). *E-mail:* v-c@admin.cam.ac.uk (office). *Website:* www.admin.cam.ac.uk/offices/v-c (office).

BORZAKOVSKIY, Yuriy; Russian middle distance runner; b. 12 April 1981, Kratovo; m. Irina; one s.; winner 800m., European Cup Super League, Paris 1999, Annecy 2002; Gold Medal 800m., World Youth Games, Moscow 1998, European Jr Championships, Riga 1999, European Indoor Championships, Gent 2000, World Indoor Championships, Lisbon 2001, Athens Olympics 2004; Gold Medal 400m. European U23 Championships, Amsterdam 2001; Silver Medal 800m., IAAF Grand Prix Final, Melbourne 2001, IAAF World Championships, Paris 2003, Helsinki 2005; Silver Medal 4 x 400m. European Championships, Munich 2002, Bronze Medal IAAF World Indoor Championships Moscow 2006, Bronze Medal IAAF World Championships Osaka 2007, Gold Medal European Indoor Championships 2009, Bronze Medal IAAF World Outdoor Championships 2011, Gold Medal European Championships 2012; retd 2013.

BORZOV, Valeriy Filippovich; Ukrainian sports administrator, politician and fmr athlete; b. 20 Oct. 1949, Sambor, Lvov Region, Ukraine; s. of Philipp Petrovich Borzov and Valentina Georgiyevna Borzova; m. Lyudmila Turishcheva 1978 (divorced); one d.; ed Kiev State Inst. of Physical Culture; competed Olympic Games Munich 1972, winning gold medals at 100m and 200m; bronze medal at 100m, Montreal 1976; European Junior Champion 100m and 200m 1968; European Champion 100m 1969; 100m and 200m 1971, 100m 1974; European Indoor Champion 60m 1970, 1971, 1972, 50m 1974, 1975, 1976; held European record at 100m and 200m and world record at 60m; Minister of Sport and Youth Ukrainian Repub. 1991–97; mem. Int. Olympic Cttee, Jt Asscn of Summer Olympic Sports 1994–; Chair. State Cttee for Physical Culture and Sport 1996–97; Chair. Nat. Olympic Cttee of Ukraine 1990–98; mem. Parl. 1998–2006; f. Nat. Olympic Acad. of Ukraine; Merited Master of Sport. *Leisure interests:* fishing, hunting.

BOS, Caroline Elisabeth, BA, MSc; Dutch art historian and urban planner; *Founder and Director, UNStudio;* b. 17 June 1959, Rotterdam; d. of the late Peter Bos and Ellen Guibal; m. Ben van Berkel; one d.; ed Birkbeck Coll., London, UK, Utrecht Univ.; freelance journalist 1982–88; Co-founder (with Ben van Berkel) and Dir Van Berkel & Bos Architectur Bureau 1988–99; Co-founder and Dir UNStudio (network of specialists in architecture, urban devt and infrastructure), Amsterdam 1998–; has lectured at Princeton Univ., Berlage Inst., Amsterdam, Acad. of Fine Arts, Vienna, Acad. of Architecture, Arnhem; Int. FRIBA 2009; Eileen Gray Award 1983, British Council Fellowship 1986, Charlotte Köhler Prize 1991; winning entry for Police HQ, Berlin 1995, Museum Het Valkof 1995, La Defense Offices Almere (Netherlands) 1999, Agora Theater, Lelystad 2003, Te Papa Museum, Wellington Waterfront, Waitangi, NZ 2005, Charles Jencks Award 2007. *Projects include:* switching substation, Amersfoort 1989–93, Erasmus Bridge, Rotterdam 1990–96, Villa Wilbrink, Amersfoort 1992–94, Möbius House, 't Gooi 1993–98, Rijksmuseum Twente, conversion and extension, Enschede 1992–96, Museum Het Valkhof, Nijmegen 1995–99, Masterplan of station area, Arnhem 1996–2005, Willemstunnel, Arnhem 1996–99, City Hall and Theatre, Ijsselstein 1996–2000, Lab. for NMR facilities, Utrecht 1996–2000, switching station, Innsbruck 1998–2001, Mercedes-Benz Museum, Stuttgart (Hugo Haring Prize 2008) 2006, VillA NM 2007, Galleria Dept Store, Seoul, South Korea 2007, Theatre Agora, Lelystad 2007, Star Place Dept Store, Kaohsiung, Tawian 2008, Music Theater, Graz 2009; current projects include mixed-use devt in Hangzhou, China, Theatre, St Petersburg, restructuring of Harbour Ponte Parodi, Genoa. *Address:* UNStudio, Stadhouderskade 113, 1073 AX Amsterdam, The Netherlands (office). *Telephone:* (20) 5702040 (office). *Fax:* (20) 5702041 (office). *E-mail:* info@unstudio.com (office). *Website:* www.unstudio .com (office).

BOS, Wouter Jacob; Dutch business executive and fmr politician; *Partner, KPMG Advisory NV;* b. 14 July 1963, Vlaardingen; ed Grammar School, Zeist and Free Univ. of Amsterdam; Man. Consultant, Shell Netherlands Refinery BV 1988–90, Policy Adviser, Rotterdam 1990–92, Gen. Affairs Man. Shell Romania Exploration BV, Bucharest 1992–93, Staff Planning and Devt Man., Shell Cos in China, Hong Kong 1993–96, Consultant, New Markets, Shell International Oil Products, London 1996–98; mem. Parl. (Partij van de Arbeid) 1998–2000, 2002–07, Parl. Leader PvdA 2002–07; mem. Partij van de Arbeid (PvdA), Leader 2002–10; Sec. of State for Finance (Taxes) 2002–02; Deputy Prime Minister and Minister of Finance 2007–10; Partner, KPMG Advisory NV 2010–. *Address:* KPMG Advisory NV, Laan van Langerhuize I, 1186 DS Amsterdam, Netherlands (office). *Telephone:* (20) 6567428 (office). *Fax:* (20) 6567000 (office). *E-mail:* bos.wouter@ kpmg.nl (office). *Website:* www.kpmg.nl (office).

BOSKIN, Michael Jay, MA, PhD; American economist, academic, consultant and fmr government official; *T. M. Friedman Professor of Economics and Hoover Institution Senior Fellow, Stanford University;* b. 23 Sept. 1945, New York; s. of Irving Boskin and Jean Boskin; m. Chris Dornin 1981; ed Univ. of California, Berkeley; Asst Prof., Stanford Univ., Calif. 1970–75, Assoc. Prof. 1976–78, Prof. 1978–86, Wohlford Prof. of Econs 1987–92, T. M. Friedman Prof. of Econs and Hoover Inst. Sr Fellow 1993–, Dir, Centre for Econ. Policy Research 1981–88; Chair. Pres.'s Council of Econ. Advisers 1989–93; Pres., Boskin & Co., Calif. 1993–; Research Assoc., Nat. Bureau of Econ. Research 1976–; Chair. Congressional Comm. on the Consumer Price Index 1995–96; Pres. International Atlantic Econ. Soc. 2005–06; mem. Advisory Bd Nat. Income and Product Accounts, US Dept of Commerce, Bureau of Econ. Analysis 2000–; mem. Governor's Council of Econ. Advisors 2003–; Visiting Prof., Harvard Univ. 1977–78; Faculty Research Fellow, Mellon Foundation 1973; Distinguished Faculty Fellow, Yale Univ. 1993; Visiting Scholar, American Enterprise Inst. 1993; mem. Bd of Dirs ExxonMobil Corpn, Oracle Corpn, Shinsei Bank; several prizes and awards including Abramson Award for Outstanding Research, Nat. Asscn of Business Economists 1987, Distinguished Teaching Award, Stanford Univ. 1987, W.S. Johnson Award for Contributions to Free Enterprise, Nat. Fed. of Ind. Business 1990, Medal of the Pres. of the Italian Repub. 1991, Distinguished Public Service Award, Stanford Univ. 1993, Adam Smith Prize, Nat. Asscn of Business Economists 1998. *Publications:* Too Many Promises: The Uncertain Future of Social Security 1986, Reagan and the Economy: Successes, Failures, Unfinished Agenda 1987, Frontiers of Tax Reform 1996, Capital Technology and Growth 1996, Toward a More Accurate Measure of the Cost of Living 1996; contrib. articles in various professional journals. *Leisure interests:* tennis, skiing, reading, theatre. *Address:* Stanford University, 213 HHMB, Stanford, CA 94305, USA (office). *Telephone:* (650) 723-6482 (office). *Fax:* (650) 723-6494 (office). *E-mail:* boskin@hoover .stanford.edu (office). *Website:* www.stanford.edu/~boskin (office).

BOSNICH, Brice, BSc, PhD, FRS; Australian chemist and academic; *Professor, Department of Chemistry, University of Chicago;* b. 1936, Queensland; ed Univ. of Sydney, Australian Nat. Univ.; Dept of Industrial and Scientific Research Postdoctoral Fellow, Univ. Coll., London 1962–63; ICI Fellow, 1963–66; Lecturer, Univ. of Toronto 1966–69, Assoc. Prof. 1970–75, Prof. 1975–87; Prof., Dept of Chemistry, Univ. of Chicago 1987–; Visiting Fellow, Research School of Chem., ANU; Killam Fellow, Univ. of Toronto 1979–91; Noranda Award in Inorganic Chem., Canadian Inst. of Chem. 1978, Organometallic Medal, Royal Soc. of Chem. 1994, Nyholm Award Medal, Royal Soc. of Chem. 1995, ACS Award in Inorganic Chem. 1998. *Address:* University of Chicago, Department of Chemisty, SCL 121, 5735 South Ellis Avenue, Chicago, IL 60637, USA (office). *Telephone:* (773) 702-0287 (office). *Fax:* (773) 702-0805 (office). *E-mail:* bos5@uchicago.edu (office). *Website:* chemistry.uchicago.edu (office).

BOSSANO, Hon. Joseph (Joe) J., BSc (Econ), BA; Gibraltarian politician; *Minister of Enterprise, Training and Employment, and of Health and Safety;* b. 10 June 1939; m. 1st Judith Baker 1967 (divorced 1988); three s. one d.; m. 2nd Rose Torilla 1988; ed Gibraltar Grammar School, Univ. of Birmingham, London School of Econs, UK; factory worker 1958–60; merchant seaman 1960–64; Sec. Integration with Britain Movt 1964; mem. Man. Cttee Tottenham Constituency Labour Party 1965–68; fmr mem. IWBP Exec. Cttee; Leader, Gibraltar Socialist Labour Party 1977–2011; Leader of the Opposition 1988–91; Sec. Gibraltar Br., Commonwealth Parl. Assen 1980–88; Br. Officer TGWU (Gibraltar) 1974–88; Chief Minister of Gibraltar, with responsibility for Information 1988–96; Minister of Enterprise, Training and Employment, and of Health and Safety 2011–. *Leisure interests:* carpentry, fishing, thinking and linguistics. *Address:* Ministry of

Enterprise, Training, Employment, and of Health and Safety, Unit 75, Harbours Walk, Rosia Road (office); 2 Gowland's Ramp, Gibraltar (home). *Telephone:* 2001100 (office). *Fax:* 20073981 (office). *E-mail:* employment.service@gibraltar.gov .gi (office); hqgslp@gibtelecom.net (home).

BOSSE, Christine (Stine), LLM; Danish lawyer and insurance industry executive; *CEO, TrygVesta A/S;* b. 1960; four c.; ed Univ. of Copenhagen, Institut Européen d'Admin des Affaires (INSEAD), France, Wharton School of Univ. of Pennsylvania, USA; served with Tryg Forsikring A/S 1987–2001, joined TrygVesta 1987, Head of Claims Dept 1988–90, Head of Underwriting Dept 1990–91, Deputy Functional Man. responsible for product and concept devt, Claims and Underwriting Dept 1991–93, Personnel Man. 1993–95, Human Resource Dir 1995–99, Sr Vice-Pres. 1999–2002, currently Group CEO TrygVesta A/S, also CEO Tryg i Danmark smba and Tryg Forsikring A/S (subsidiaries), Man. Dir TrygVesta Forsikring A/S; Chair. Danish Insurance Asscn, Hjertebarnsfonden, Ejendomsselskabet af 8. maj 2008 A/S; mem. Bd of Dirs Forsikring og Pension, Grundfos Management A/S, Poul Due Jensens Fond, TDC A/S 2004–06, Nordea Bank AB 2008–, Grundfos DK A/S –2009, Amlin plc; Ind. Dir, Flügger A/S 2002–; mem. Danish Welfare Comm.; mem. Supervisory Bd Forsikring & Pension (F&P), TDC; Chair. Supervisory Bd Vesta Forsikring AS, ApS KBIL 9 NR. 2032, Tryg Ejendomme A/S, TrygVesta IT A/S; ranked by the Financial Times amongst the Top 25 Businesswomen in Europe (15th) 2005, (11th) 2006, (13th) 2007, ranked by Fortune magazine amongst the 50 Most Powerful Women in Business outside the US (40th) 2008, (33rd) 2009–10. *Address:* TrygVesta A/S, Klausdalsbrovej 601, 2750 Ballerup, Denmark (office). *Telephone:* 70-11-20-20 (office). *Fax:* 44-20-67-00 (office). *E-mail:* trygvesta@trygvesta.com (office). *Website:* www.trygvesta.com (office).

BOSSI, Umberto; Italian politician; *Secretary, Federation of Northern League Movements;* b. 19 Sept. 1941, Cassano Magnago, Varese; m.; four c. (two by Manuela Marrone); ed Pavia Univ.; f. Lombard Autonomy League 1982; Leader, Lombard League 1984–; Senator 1987; Sec. Fed. of Northern League Movts 1989–;elected Deputy for Div. III (Lombardy 1), Dist 3, Milan 2001; Minister without Portfolio, responsible for Reforms and Devolution 2001–04 (resgnd); Minister without Portfolio for Federal Reform 2008–11. *Address:* Lega Nord, via C. Bellerio 41, 20161 Milan, Italy (office). *Telephone:* (02) 662341 (office). *Fax:* (02) 66234266 (office). *E-mail:* webmaster@leganord.org (office). *Website:* www .leganord.org (office).

BOSSIDY, Lawrence Arthur, BA; American business executive and writer; b. 5 March 1935, Pittsfield, Mass.; m. Nancy Bossidy 1956; three s. six d.; ed Colgate Univ.; joined General Electric Co. 1957, Chief Operating Officer, General Electric Credit Corpn (now GE Capital Corpn) 1979–81, Exec. Vice-Pres. and Pres. Services and Materials Sector 1981–84, Vice-Chair. and Exec. Officer, General Electric Co. 1984–91, fmr Chair. and Dir Gen. Electric Credit Corpn; Chair. and CEO Allied Signal Inc. 1991–99, Chair. Honeywell International Inc. (after merger of Allied Signal and Honeywell 1999) 1999–2000, 2001–02; mem. Bd of Dirs Merck & Co. 1992–2007, Champion Int. Corpn, J.P. Morgan & Co. Inc., Berkshire Hills Bancorp Inc.; mem. Exec. Bd Aurora Capital Group; CEO of the Year, Financial World magazine 1994, Chief Executive of the Year, CEO Magazine 1998. *Publications:* Execution: The Discipline of Getting Things Done 2002, Confronting Reality: Doing What Matters to Get Things Right (with Ram Charan) 2004. *Address:* c/o Aurora Capital Group, 10877 Wilshire Blvd, 21st Floor, Los Angeles, CA 90024, USA.

BOSSON, Bernard; French lawyer and politician; b. 25 Feb. 1948, Annecy; s. of Charles Bosson and Claire Bosson; m. Danielle Blaise 1976; one d.; ed Coll. Saint-Michel and Faculté de Droit de Lyon; barrister, Annecy 1976–; Mayor of Annecy 1983–2007; Deputy in Nat. Ass. 1986–93, 1995–2007; Sec. of State, Ministry of the Interior 1986, Del. Minister, Ministry of Foreign Affairs 1986–88; Minister of Public Transport and Tourism 1993–95; Deputy Vice-Pres. Del. for EC 1988; Vice-Pres. Mouvement européen 1990–97; Sec.-Gen. Centre des Démocrates sociaux 1991; mem. Union pour la démocratie française, Vice-Pres. 1998.

BOST, Eric M., BA, MA; American diplomatist (retd) and university administrator; *Assistant Director for External Relations and Special Assignments, Vice-President for Global Initiatives, Borlaug Institute of International Agriculture, Texas A&M University;* b. 1952, Concord, NC; ed Univ. of North Carolina, Univ. of South Florida; served in a variety of positions in several state social welfare agencies and pvt. and non-profit orgs; Deputy Dir Ariz. Dept of Econ. Security 1994–97; Chief Exec. and Admin. Officer, Tex. Dept of Human Services 1997–2001; Under-Sec. for Food, Nutrition, and Consumer Services, US Dept of Agric., Washington, DC 2001–06; Amb. to South Africa 2006–09; Vice-Pres. for Global Initiatives, Texas A&M Univ. 2009–11, Asst Dir for External Relations and Special Assignments, Borlaug Inst. for Int. Agric. 2011–. *Leisure interest:* travelling. *Address:* Borlaug Institute of International Agriculture, Texas A&M University, 578 John Kimbrough Blvd, AGSV Building, Room 201, College Station, TX 77843-2477, USA (office). *Telephone:* (979) 458-3406 (office). *Fax:* (979) 845-5663 (office). *E-mail:* Eric.Bost@ag.tamu.edu (office). *Website:* borlaug.tamu.edu (office).

BOSTRIDGE, Ian Charles, CBE, MA, DPhil; British singer (tenor); b. 1965, London; s. of the late Leslie John Bostridge and of Lilian Winifred (née Clark); m. Lucasta Miller 1992; two c.; ed Westminster School, Univs of Oxford and Cambridge; debut recital performance in Wigmore Hall, London 1993; operatic debut in Edin. Festival 1994; has since performed at Carnegie Hall and Lincoln Center, New York, Salzburg Festival, Théâtre du Châtelet, Philharmonie, Berlin etc.; annual lieder recitals Munich Opera Festival; Hon. Fellow Corpus Christi Coll., Oxford; Hon. DMus (St Andrews); awards include Gramophone Solo Vocal Awards 1996, 1998, Time Out Classical Music Award 1999, Edison Award 1999, 2002, Grammy Award (opera) 1999, Critics' Choice Classical Brit Award (for The English Songbook) 2006, Preis der Deutschen Schallplattenkritik 2001, Acad. Charles Cros, Grand Prix du Disque 2001. *Television:* Winterreise (Channel 4) 1997, Britten Serenade (BBC) 1999, The South Bank Show (ITV) 2000, Janacek documentary (BBC 4) 2004. *Opera:* A Midsummer Night's Dream, Edin. Festival 1994, The Magic Flute, ENO 1996, The Turn of the Screw, Royal Opera House 1997, 2002, The Bartered Bride, Sadler's Wells 1998, L'incoronazione di Poppea, Munich Festival 1998, The Diary of One Who Vanished, Munich and New York 1999, The Rake's Progress, Munich Festival 2002, Don Giovanni, Royal Opera

House, Covent Garden 2003, Ades and The Tempest, Covent Garden 2004, The Rape of Lucretia, Munich 2004, Aldeburgh 2011. *Recordings include:* Britten 2005, Wolf: Lieder 2006, Schubert: Lieder and Sonata 2007, Great Handel 2007, Schubert: The Wanderer: Lieder and Fragments 2008, Schubert: Schwanengesang 2009, Three Baroque Tenors 2010. *Publications:* Witchcraft and its Transformations 1650–1750 1997, A Singer's Notebook 2011. *Leisure interests:* reading, cooking, looking at pictures. *Address:* c/o EMI Classics, 27 Wrights Lane, London, W8 5SW, England (office). *Telephone:* (20) 7795-7000 (office). *Website:* www.emiclassics.co.uk (office).

BOSTRÖM, Rolf Gustav, PhD; Swedish physicist and academic; *Professor Emeritus, Swedish Institute of Space Physics;* b. 15 April 1936, Kalmar; s. of Gustav Boström and Greta Boström (née Bergström); m. Barbro Karlsson 1962; one s.; ed Royal Inst. of Tech.; Research Assoc., Dept of Plasma Physics, Royal Inst. of Tech. 1961–71, Sr Physicist 1971–75, Assoc. Prof. 1975–76; Prof., Uppsala Div. of Swedish Inst. of Space Physics (fmrly Uppsala Ionospheric Observatory) 1976–2002, Prof. Emer. 2002–; Head Dept of Space Physics, Uppsala Univ. 1988–96; mem. Royal Swedish Acad. of Sciences. *Publications:* scientific papers on space plasma physics. *Leisure interests:* hiking, angling. *Address:* Klippvägen 22, 756 52 Uppsala, Sweden (home). *Telephone:* (18) 32-02-61 (home). *E-mail:* rolf.g.bostrom@telia.com (office).

BOSWORTH, Stephen Warren; American diplomatist; *Dean, The Fletcher School of Law and Diplomacy, Tufts University;* b. 4 Dec. 1939, Conn.; s. of Warren Charles Bosworth and Mina Bosworth; m. Christine Bosworth; two s. two d.; ed Dartmouth Coll. and George Washington Univ.; joined Foreign Service 1962, assignments in Paris, Madrid and Panama City, later Amb. to Tunisia 1979–81, the Philippines 1984–87, Repub. of Korea 1997–2001; various positions with US Dept of State including Deputy Asst Sec. for Econ. Affairs and for Inter-American Affairs, Dir of Policy Planning and Head of Office of Fuels and Energy; Pres. US-Japan Foundation 1988–96; Exec. Dir Korean Peninsula Energy Devt Corpn 1995–97; Dean, The Fletcher School of Law and Diplomacy, Tufts Univ. 2001–; Special Rep. for N Korea Policy, Dept of State 2009–11; Adjunct Prof., School of Int. and Public Affairs, Columbia Univ. 1990–94; Order of the Rising Sun, Gold and Silver Star (Japan) 2006; Distinguished Service Award, Dept of State 1976, 1986, Distinguished Service Award, Dept of Energy 1979. *Publications:* articles: Why Do They Hate Us? The Reasons are Many, The History Long, Because We Are Big, So Powerful, The Boston Globe 2001, Adjusting to the New Asia (with Morton Abramowitz), Foreign Affairs 2003. *Address:* The Fletcher School of Law and Diplomacy, 160 Packard Avenue, Tufts University, Medford, MA 02155, USA (office). *Telephone:* (617) 627-3050 (office). *Fax:* (617) 627-3508 (office). *E-mail:* stephen.bosworth@tufts.edu (office). *Website:* www.fletcher.tufts.edu (office).

BOT, Bernard Rudolf (Ben), DJur; Dutch diplomatist and politician; *President, Netherlands Institute of International Relations;* b. 21 Nov. 1937, Jakarta, Indonesia; s. of Th. H. Bot and E. W. van Hal; m. Christine Bot-Pathy 1962 (deceased); three c.; ed St Aloysius Coll., The Hague, Univ. of Leiden, Acad. of Int. Law, The Hague and Harvard Law School, USA; Deputy Perm. Rep. of Netherlands to North Atlantic Council, Brussels 1982–86; Amb. to Turkey 1986–89; Sec.-Gen. Ministry of Foreign Affairs 1989–92; apptd Perm. Rep. to EU 1992; Minister of Foreign Affairs 2003–07; currently Pres. Netherlands Inst. of Int. Relations (Clingendael); Kt, Order of Netherlands Lion, Officier, Order of Orange-Nassau and other decorations. *Publications:* Non-recognition and Treaty Relations 1968; numerous articles on the Common Market, European political co-operation, NATO and other political matters. *Leisure interests:* cycling, painting, skiing. *Address:* Clingendael, POB 93080, 2509 AB The Hague (office); Meines & Partners, Lange Voorhout 26, 2514 EE The Hague, The Netherlands (office). *Telephone:* (70) 3622552 (office). *Fax:* (70) 3637875 (office). *E-mail:* info@clingendael.nl (office); bernardbot@meinespartners.nl (office). *Website:* www.clingendael.nl (office).

BOTELHO, João; Portuguese film director; b. 11 May 1949, Lamego; m. Leonor Pinhão; three c.; ed Nat. Conservatory Film School, Lisbon; involved in film socs in Coimbra and Oporto; film critic for newspapers; f. film magazine M. *Films include:* Alexandre e Rosa (short, co-Dir) 1978, Conversa acabada (The Other One) 1980, Um adeus português (A Portuguese Goodbye) 1985, Tempos difíceis (Hard Times) 1987, No dia dos meus anos (On my Birthday) 1992, Aqui na Terra (Here on Earth) 1993, Três Palmeiras (Three Palm Trees) 1994, Tráfico (Traffic) 1998, Se a Memória Existe (If Memories Exist) 1999, Quem és tu? (Who are you?) (Mimmo Rotella Foundation Prize, Venice Film Festival) 2001, O Fatalista 2005, A Luz na Ria Formosa 2005, True and Tender Is the North 2008, Para Que Este Mundo Não Acabe! 2009, Disquiet 2010, Anquanto la Lhéngua fur Cantada 2012. *Address:* c/o Associação Portuguesa de Realizadores, Rua de Palmeira 7, r/c, 1200 Lisbon, Portugal.

BOTELHO, Maurício; Brazilian business executive; *Chairman, Embraer-Empresa Brasileira de Aeronautica SA;* Exec. Vice-Pres. Técnica Nacional de Engenharia Ltda.1992; Exec. Officer, Cia. Bozano 1995; CEO CMW Equipamentos SA 1985–95; CEO Stelar Telecom (fmrly Odebrecht Automação & Telecomunicações Ltda.) 1988–95; Pres. and CEO Empresa Brasileira de Aeronautica SA (Embraer) 1995–, Chair. 2006–; Pres. Mogno Consultoria de Negócios Ltda. (business consultancy); Commdr, Ordem do Rio Branco (Brazil); Chevalier, Legion d'Honneur; BACCF Excellence Award 1999. *Address:* Embraer, Av. Brig. Faria Lima 2170, Putim 12227-901, S. Jose dos Campos, São Paulo, Brazil (office). *Telephone:* (12) 345-1000 (office). *Fax:* (12) 321-8238 (office). *Website:* www.embraer.com (office).

BOTERO, Fernando; Colombian artist; b. 19 April 1932, Medellín; s. of David Botero and Flora Botero; m. 2nd Cecilia Botero 1964; m. 3rd Sophia Vari; four c.; first group exhbn, Medellín 1948; first solo exhbn, Galería Leo Matiz, Bogotá 1951; studied at Acad. San Fernando and El Prado Museum, Madrid 1952; visited Paris and Italy and studied art history with Roberto Longhi, Univ. of Florence 1953–54; lived in Mexico 1956; solo exhbn Pan American Union, Washington, DC 1957, Colombia 1958–59; lived in New York 1960–; first solo exhbn in Europe, Baden-Baden and Munich 1966; visited Italy and Germany 1967, studied work of Dürer; travelling retrospective exhbn of 80 paintings in five German museums 1970; solo exhbn Hannover Gallery, London 1970; moved to Paris 1973; concentrated on Sculpture 1976–77, first solo exhbn of sculpture, Foire Int. d'Art Contemporain,

Paris 1977; retrospective exhbn, Hirshorn Museum and Sculpture Garden, Washington, DC 1979; first solo exhbn in Japan, Tokyo, Osaka 1981; outdoor sculpture exhbn, Chicago 1994; paintings in public collections in Belgium, Finland, Germany, Israel, Italy, S. America, Spain and USA; Guggenheim Nat. Prize for Colombia 1960, Lifetime Achievement in Contemporary Sculpture Award, International Sculpture Center 2012.

BOTHA, Roelof Frederik (Pik), BA, LLB; South African politician; b. 27 April 1932, Rustenburg; m. 1st Helena Bosman 1953; two s. two d.; m. 2nd Ina Joubert 1998; ed Volkskool, Potchefstroom, Univ. of Pretoria; joined Dept of Foreign Affairs 1953, served with diplomatic missions in Europe 1956–66; mem. S African legal team in SW Africa case, Int. Court of Justice, The Hague 1963–66, 1970–71; Agent of S African Govt, Int. Court of Justice 1965–66; Legal Adviser, Dept of Foreign Affairs 1966–68, Under-Sec. and Head SW Africa and UN sections 1968–70; mem. Parl. for Wonderboom 1970–74, for Westdene 1977–94, re-elected 1994–96, served on various select parl. cttees 1970–74; Sec., Foreign Affairs Study Group of Nat. Party's mems of Parl. 1974; Amb. and Perm. Rep. to UN, New York 1974–77; Amb. to USA 1975–77; Minister of Foreign Affairs 1977–94, of Mineral and Energy Affairs 1994–96, for Information 1980–86; mem. S African Del. to UN Gen. Assembly 1967–69, 1971, 1973–74; Leader Nat. Party in Transvaal 1992–96; Grand Cross, Order of Good Hope, Decoration for Meritorious Service (SA), Grand Cordon, Order of the Brilliant Star (Taiwan). *Leisure interests:* hunting and fishing. *Address:* PO Box 16176, Pretoria North 0116, South Africa.

BOTHAM, Sir Ian Terence, Kt; British fmr professional cricketer; *Chairman, Mission Sports Management;* b. 24 Nov. 1955; s. of Leslie Botham and Marie Botham; m. Kathryn Waller 1976; one s. two d.; ed Buckler's Mead Secondary School, Yeovil; right-hand batsman, right-hand, fast-medium bowler; teams: Somerset 1974–86 (Capt. 1984–85), Worcs. 1987–91, Queensland 1987–88, Durham 1992–93; 102 Tests for England 1977–92, 12 as Capt., scoring 5,200 runs (average 33.54, highest score 208) including 14 hundreds, taking 383 wickets (average 28.40) and holding 120 catches; scored 1,673 runs and took 148 wickets v. Australia; became first player to score a century and take 8 wickets in an innings in a Test match, v. Pakistan (Lord's) 1978; took 100th wicket in Test cricket in record time of 2 years 9 days 1979; achieved double of 1,000 runs and 100 wickets in Tests to create world record of fewest Tests (21) and English records of shortest time (2 years 33 days) and at youngest age (23 years 279 days) 1979; became first player to have scored 3,000 runs and taken 250 wickets in Tests (55) Nov. 1982; first player to score a century and take 10 wickets in a Test match, v. India; scored 19,399 runs (38 hundreds) and took 1,172 wickets in first-class cricket; toured Australia 1978–79, 1979–80, 1982–83 and 1986–87; has also played soccer for Scunthorpe United and Yeovil; mem. Sky Sports cricket commentary team 1995–; Tech. Advisor, England Cricket Team 1996; Chair. Mission Sports Man. 2000–; mem. MCC Cricket Cttee 1995, Sports Council 1995–, Laureus World Sports Acad.; Columnist, Daily Mirror; Hon. MSc (UMIST); Wisden Cricketer of the Year 1978, Lifetime Achievement Award, BBC Sports Personality of the Year 2004, inducted into Int. Cricket Council Hall of Fame 2009. *Publications include:* It Sort of Clicks 1986, Cricket My Way 1989, Botham: My Autobiography 1994, The Botham Report (with Peter Hayter) 1997, Head On: The Autobiography 2007. *Leisure interests:* shooting, golf, flying, fishing. *Address:* Mission Sports Management, Park House, Northfields, London, SW18 1DD, England (office). *Telephone:* (20) 8704-4165 (office). *Fax:* (20) 8704-4169 (office). *E-mail:* adam@missionsportsmanagement.com (office). *Website:* www.missionsportsmanagement.com (office).

BOTHWELL, Thomas Hamilton, DSc, MD, FRCP, FRSSA; South African physician and professor of medicine; *Honorary Professorial Research Fellow, University of the Witwatersrand;* b. 27 Feb. 1926; s. of Robert Cooper Bothwell and Jessie Isobel Bothwell (née Hamilton); m. Alexandrine Moorman Butterworth 1957; one s. two d.; ed St John's Coll., Johannesburg, Univ. of Witwatersrand, Univ. of Oxford, UK, Univ. of Washington, USA; physician, later Sr Physician Dept of Medicine, Univ. of the Witwatersrand 1956–67, Prof. of Medicine and Head Dept of Medicine 1967–91; Chief Physician Johannesburg Hosp. 1967–91; Dir MRC Iron and Red Cell Metabolism Research Unit, Univ. of the Witwatersrand 1969–91, Dean of Medicine 1992–93, Hon. Professorial Research Fellow 1993–; Hon. FCP; Hon. FACP; Dr hc (Univs of Cape Town, Natal, Witwatersrand); Gold Medal, SA Medical Research Council 1987; Medal of the SA Asscn for the Advancement of Science 1980, Biennial Award of the Nutrition Soc. of Southern Africa 1988, John F. W. Herschel Medal of the Royal Soc. of SA 1993, William D. Davis Award, Hemochromatosis Research Foundation 1993, Science-for-Society Gold Medal, Acad. of Science of SA 2005. *Publications:* more than 260 articles in the field of iron metabolism, 55 chapters, seven monographs and two books: Iron Metabolism 1962, Iron Metabolism in Man 1979. *Leisure interests:* reading, walking, dogs. *Address:* c/o Department of Medicine, University of the Witwatersrand, Medical School, 7 York Road, Parktown 2193, Johannesburg, South Africa. *Telephone:* (11) 728-2180 (home). *Fax:* (11) 728-2180 (home).

BOTÍN, Ana Patricia; Spanish banking executive; *CEO, Santander UK plc;* b. 4 Oct. 1960, Santander; d. of Emilio Botín-Sanz de Sautuola y García de los Ríos and Paloma O'Shea, 1st Marquise of O'Shea; m. Guillermo Morenés Mariátegui; three s.; ed Bryn Mawr Coll. and Harvard Univ., USA; began career with JP Morgan, New York and Madrid 1981, various positions in Latin American Div. including Vice-Pres. –1988; CEO Banco Santander de Negocios and Exec. Vice-Pres. Banco Santander 1994–99; Founder, Chair. and CEO Suala Capital Advisers 1999–2002; Jt Pres. Banco Santander Central Hispano (BSCH), Chair. of subsidiary Banco Banesto, Madrid 2002–10, CEO Santander UK plc 2010–; Chair. coverlink.com; Exec. Chair. Razona (tech. consulting and systems integrations co.) 1999–; mem. Foro Iberoamerica, Trilateral Comm.; mem. Int. Advisory Bd J.E. Robert Cos (int. real estate investment and asset man. firm) 2002–; mem. Int. Advisory Bd New York Stock Exchange, Council of Georgetown Univ.; ranked by Fortune magazine amongst the 50 Most Powerful Women in Business outside the US (20th) 2003, (sixth) 2004, (eighth) 2005, (ninth) 2006–07, (11th) 2008–09, (15th) 2010, (14th) 2011, (26th) 2012, ranked by Forbes magazine amongst The World's 100 Most Powerful Women (94th) 2004, (99th) 2005, (73rd) 2006, (40th) 2007, (51st) 2008, (45th) 2009, (38th) 2010, (77th) 2011, ranked by the Financial Times amongst Top 25 Businesswomen in Europe (first) 2005, (first) 2006, (fourth) 2007, named by Merco the most reputed woman in Spain 2010. *Leisure interest:* golf. *Address:* Santander UK plc, 2 Triton Square, Regent's Place, London, NW1 3AN, England (office). *Telephone:* (870) 607-6000 (office). *E-mail:* info@santander.co.uk (office). *Website:* www.santander.co.uk (office); www.aboutsantander.co.uk (office).

BOTÍN-SANZ DE SAUTUOLA Y GARCÍA DE LOS RÍOS, Marquis Consort of O'Shea; **Emilio;** Spanish banker; *Executive Director and Chairman, Banco Santander SA;* b. 1 Oct. 1934, Santander, Cantabria; s. of Emilio Botín y Sanz de Sautuola and Ana María García de los Ríos y Caller; m. Paloma O'Shea Artiñano, 1st Marquise of O'Shea; two s. four d.; ed Colegio de la Inmaculada, Gijón, Univ. of Valladolid, Univ. of Duesto, Bilbao; apptd a Dir of the bank 1960, inherited Banco de Santander 1986, Pres. 1986–99 (absorbed Banesto 1993), Co-Pres. Banco Santander Central Hispano SA (following merger of Banco de Santander with Banco Hispano Americano and Banco Central 1999) 1999–2002, Exec. Dir and Chair. 2002–, also Chair. Exec. Cttee, Int. Cttee, Tech., Productivity and Quality Cttee; Dir (non-exec.) Shinsei Bank Ltd. *Leisure interests:* hunting, fishing, golf, the arts. *Address:* Ciudad Grupo Santander, Edificio Pereda, 1st Floor, Avenida de Cantabria s/n, 28660 Boadilla del Monte, Madrid, Spain (office). *Telephone:* (91) 2890000 (office). *E-mail:* info@gruposantander.com (office). *Website:* www.santander.com (office).

BOTNARU, Ion, PhD; Moldovan diplomatist and UN official; *Director, General Assembly and ECOSOC Affairs Division, United Nations;* b. 19 Aug. 1954, Pitusca, Calarasi; s. of Toma Botnaru and Tatiana Sheremet; m. 1979; one s. one d.; ed Inst. of Oriental Studies, Moscow, Moscow State Univ.; fmr translator and interpreter of Turkish and English; Sr Researcher, Inst. of History Studies, Nat. Acad. of Science, Chişinău 1983–84; Prof. of Contemporary History of Asia and Africa, Chişinău State Univ. 1987–89; Deputy Dir-Gen. Dept of Protocol, Ministry of Foreign Affairs 1989–90, Dir-Gen. Dept of Political Affairs 1990–92, Deputy Minister 1992–93, Minister 1993–94; Amb. to Turkey (also accred to Kuwait and Egypt) 1994–98, 2002; Amb. and Perm. Rep. to UN, New York 1998–2002; fmr Chief, UN Gen. Ass. Affairs Br., Dept for Gen. Ass. and Conf. Man., currently Dir Gen. Ass. and ECOSOC Affairs Div.; mem. Moldovan del. to UN Gen. Ass. 1992; Head of Moldovan del. to UN World Conf. on Human Rights 1993; mem. Asscn of Orientalists 1985–. *Publications:* The Army and Politics in Turkey 1986, Islam and Political Parties in Turkey 1989, The Process of Democratisation in Moldova—Political Aspects 1993; numerous papers and articles. *Address:* Room S-3080, General Assembly and ECOSOC Affairs Division, Department for General Assembly and Conference Management, United Nations, New York, NY 10017, USA (office). *Telephone:* (212) 963-0725 (office). *Fax:* (212) 963-5305 (office). *E-mail:* botnaru@un.org (office).

BOTSTEIN, David, BS, PhD; American biologist and academic; *Anthony B. Evnin '62 Professor of Genomics and Director, Lewis-Sigler Institute, Princeton University;* b. 8 Sept. 1942, Switzerland; ed Bronx High School of Science, Harvard Univ., Massachusetts Inst. of Tech., Univ. of Michigan; taught at MIT, later Prof. of Genetics; Vice-Pres. (Science), Genentech, Inc. 1987–90; Chair. Dept of Genetics, Stanford Univ. 1990–2003; Anthony B. Evnin '62 Prof. of Genomics and Dir, Lewis-Sigler Inst., Princeton Univ. 2003–, Dir Integrated Science Program; Eli Lilly & Co. Award in Microbiology 1978, Genetics Soc. of America Medal (co-recipient) 1988, Allan Award, American Soc. of Human Genetics (co-recipient) 1989, Gruber Prize in Genetics 2003, Albany Medical Center Prize in Medicine and Biomedical Research (co-recipient) 2010, Agilent Thought Leader Award (co-recipient), Dan David Prize Laureate 2012, Breakthrough Prize in Life Sciences (co-recipient) 2013. *Publications:* numerous papers in professional journals. *Address:* 120 Carl Icahn Laboratory, Lewis-Sigler Institute for Integrative Genomics, Washington Road, Princeton University, Princeton, NJ 08544, USA (office). *Telephone:* (609) 258-7005 (office); (609) 258-8585 (lab.). *Fax:* (609) 258-7070 (office). *E-mail:* botstein@princeton.edu (office). *Website:* www .princeton.edu/genomics/botstein (office).

BOTT, Martin Harold Phillips, MA, PhD, FRS; British earth scientist and academic; *Professor Emeritus of Geophysics, Durham University;* b. 12 July 1926, Stoke-on-Trent; s. of Harold Bott and Dorothy Bott (née Phillips); m. Joyce Cynthia Hughes 1961; two s. one d.; ed Claysmore School, Dorset, Keble Coll. Oxford (army short course) and Magdalene Coll. Cambridge; Nat. Service in army (Royal Signals) 1945–48, rank of Lt; Turner & Newall Research Fellow, Durham Univ. 1954–56, Lecturer in Geophysics 1956–63, Reader 1963–66, Prof. 1966–88, Research Prof. in Geophysics 1988–91, Prof. Emer. 1991–; Head of Dept of Geological Sciences 1970–73, 1976–82; Chair. British Nat. Cttee for Geodesy and Geophysics 1985–89; Murchison Medal, Geological Soc. of London 1977, Clough Medal, Geological Soc. of Edinburgh 1979, Sorby Medal, Yorks. Geological Soc. 1981, Wollaston Medal, Geological Soc. of London 1992. *Achievements include:* completed climbing the Scottish Munros at age of 76 Sept. 2002. *Publications:* The Interior of the Earth (revised edn) 1982, Structure and Development of the Greenland–Scotland Ridge: new methods and concepts (co-ed.) 1983, Sedimentary Basins of Continental Margins and Cratons (ed.) 1976 and many scientific papers in journals. *Leisure interests:* Reader Emer. (Anglican Church), mountain walking, garden slavery, etc. *Address:* 11 St Mary's Close, Shincliffe, Durham, DH1 2ND, England (home).

BOTTAI, Bruno; Italian diplomatist; *President, Società Dante Alighieri;* b. 10 July 1930, Rome; ed Univ. of Rome; entered Ministry of Foreign Affairs 1954, served abroad in Tunis, Brussels, London and Holy See and Ministry of Foreign Affairs 1955–76; Amb. to the Holy See and the Sovereign Mil. Order of Malta 1979; Dir-Gen. of Political Affairs, Ministry of Foreign Affairs 1981–85; Amb. to UK 1985–87; Sec.-Gen. Ministry of Foreign Affairs 1987–94; Amb. to the Holy See 1994–97; Chair. Int. Balzan Foundation; Pres. Società Dante Alighieri 1995–; Foundation-Milan Pres. Balzan Prize 1999. *Leisure interest:* modern paintings. *Address:* Palazzo Firenze, Piazza Firenze 27, 00186 Rome, Italy. *Telephone:* (06) 6873692/4/5 (office); (06) 6786427 (home). *Fax:* (06) 6873692 (office). *E-mail:* presidente@ladante.it (office). *Website:* www.ladante.it (office).

BOTTOMLEY OF NETTLESTONE, Baroness (Life Peer), cr. 2005, of St Helens in the County of Isle of Wight; **Rt Hon. Virginia (Hilda Brunette Maxwell) Bottomley,** PC, BA, MSc, DL; British politician and business executive; *Chair of the Board Practice, Odgers Berndtson;* b. 12 March 1948, Dunoon, Argyll, Scotland; d. of the late W. John Garnett and of Barbara Garnett (née Rutherford-Smith); m. Sir Peter Bottomley, MP; one s. two d.; ed Putney High School, Univ. of Essex, London School of Econs; Behavioural Scientist 1971–84;

Vice-Chair. Nat. Council of Carers and their Elderly Dependants 1982–88; Dir Mid Southern Water Co. 1987–88; mem. MRC 1987–88; MP for Surrey SW 1984–; Parl. Pvt. Sec. to Minister of State for Educ. and Science 1985–86, to Minister for Overseas Devt 1986–87, to Sec. of State for Foreign and Commonwealth Affairs 1987–88; Parl. Under-Sec. of State, Dept for the Environment 1988–89; Sec., Conservative Backbench Employment Cttee 1985; Fellow, Industry Parl. Trust 1987; Minister of State (Minister for Health) 1989–92; Sec. of State for Health 1992–95; Sec. of State for Nat. Heritage 1995–97; Pnr and Chair of the Bd Practice, Odgers Berndtson 2000–; mem. Supervisory Bd Akzo Nobel 2000–12; Nat. Pres. Abbeyfield Soc. 2003–09; Co-Chair. Women's Nat. Comm. 1991–92; mem. Court of Govs, LSE 1985–, British Council 1997–2001, House of Commons Select Cttee on Foreign Affairs 1997–99; Dir (non-exec.) BUPA 2009–, Smith & Nephew Plc 2012–; Gov. Ditchley Foundation 1991–, London Univ. of the Arts 1999–; JP, Inner London 1975 (Chair. Lambeth Juvenile Court 1981–84); Lay Canon, Guildford Cathedral; Pro-Chancellor Univ. of Surrey 2005–; Chancellor, Univ. of Hull 2006–; Trustee, The Economist; DL (Surrey) 2006; Freeman City of London 1989; Hon. LLD (Portsmouth) 1992; Hon. DSc (Aston) 2012. *Leisure interest:* family. *Address:* Odgers Berndtson, 20 Cannon Street, London, EC4M 6XD (office); House of Lords, Westminster, London, SW1A 0PW, England. *Telephone:* (20) 7529-1066 (office); (20) 7219-5060. *E-mail:* bottomleyv@parliament.uk. *Website:* www.parliament.uk/ biographies/lords/virginia-bottomley/25740.

BOUABRÉ BOHOUN, Paul-Antoine; Côte d'Ivoirian economist and politician; b. 1957; fmr Minister of State, Economy and Finance; Minister of State, Minister of Planning and Devt 2005, 2007–11; mem. Front populaire ivoirien. *Address:* c/o Ministry of Planning and Development, 16éme étage, Immeuble SCIAM, Abidjan Plateau, Côte d'Ivoire (office). *Telephone:* 20-20-08-42 (office). *Fax:* 20-20-08-65 (office). *E-mail:* gvode@plan.gouv.ci (office).

BOUARÉ, Lassine; Malian politician; b. 1959, Massala, Ségou region; ed École nat. d'admin publique, Rabat, Morocco, École nat. d'admin, Paris, France; began career with Admin Reform Comm. 1990–94; Head of Devt Unit, Office for Decentralization and Institutional Reform 1994–2000; Tech. Adviser, Ministry of Territorial Admin and Local Communities 2000–01; Tech. Adviser, Office of the Pres. 2002–03; Dir Nat. Inst. of Social Welfare 2003–09; Minister Delegate at the Ministry of Economy and Finance 2009–11, Minister of the Economy and Finance 2011–12. *Address:* c/o Ministry of the Economy and Finance, Bamako, Mali (office).

BOUASONE, Bouphavanh; Laotian politician; b. 3 June 1954, Salavan Province; ed in USSR; student activist in 1970s; fmr Pres. State Planning Cttee; fmr Third Deputy Prime Minister, First Deputy Prime Minister 2003–06, Prime Minister 2006–10. *Address:* c/o Office of the Prime Minister, Ban Sisavat, Vientiane, Laos.

BOUBLIL, Alain Albert; French writer and dramatist; b. 5 March 1941, Tunis; four s.; wrote libretto and lyrics for: La Révolution Française 1973, Les Misérables 1980, Abbacadabra 1984, Miss Saigon 1989, Martin Guerre 1996, The Pirate Queen 2006, Marguerite 2008; Le Journal d'Adam et Eve (play) 1994; two Tony Awards, Two Grammy Awards, two Victoire de la Musique Awards, Molière Award (all for Les Misérables), Evening Standard Drama Award (for Miss Saigon), Laurence Olivier Award (for Martin Guerre). *Leisure interests:* theatre, opera, cinema, tennis.

BOUCHAIN, Patrick; French architect; b. 31 May 1945, Paris; ed Acad. des Beaux-Arts, internships at Jacques Dumond (decorator), André Hermant (architect), Henry Malvaux (painter); Prof. of Drawing and Architecture, École Camondo, Paris 1972–74, École des Beaux-Arts de Bourges 1974–81, École de Création industrielle, Paris 1981–83; adviser to Jack Lang at Ministry of Culture, then to Pres. Établissement public du Grand Louvre 1992–94; Dir Atelier public d'architecture et d'urbanisme, Blois 1990–93; has a background in theatre, circuses and urban festivals; relies on collaborations to develop an alternative urban planning; projects use several specialists rather than a single contractor;; leader, spectacle of the Grandes Roues on Champs-Elysées in Paris as part of the Millennium celebrations 1999–2000; curated French pavilion at the Venice Architecture Biennale 2006; architect of the Pompidou Centre travelling on tour 2011. *Works include:* Magasin, Grenoble 1985, Zingaro Theatre, Aubervilliers 1988, Dromesko Birdcage, Lausanne 1991, Admin. and Tech. Centre, Valeo à La Verrière 1995, registered office of Thomson Multimédia, Boulogne-Billancourt 1997, transformation of the old LU factories in Nantes for CRDC 1999, Musée int. des Arts modestes, Sète 2000, Capital of the Centaur Theatre, Marseille 2001, Academy Fratellini, St Denis 2002, La Condition Publique, Roubaix 2004, Pool Baths, Begles 2005, French Pavilion at Venice Architecture Biennale 2006, National City of the history of immigration, Paris 2007, transformation of the slaughterhouses Channel, Calais 2007, Burgundy restaurant Michel Troisgros 'La Colline du Colombier' 2008, renovation of the restaurant La Grenouillère 2011; architectural installations 'L'amour de l'art' for first Biennale d'art contemporain de Lyon 1991, 'Tous, ils changent le monde', Lyon Biennale 1993. *Collaborations include:* with numerous contemporary artists, including Daniel Buren ('Les deux plateaux', court of the Palais Royal) 1986, Sarkis, Ange Leccia, Bartabas (Celebration of the battle of Valmy) 1989, Joseph Kosuth (Figeac) 1989, Claes Oldenbourg ('Le vélo enseveli', Parc de la Villette) 1990, Jean-Luc Vilmouth ('Comme deux tours', Châtellerault) 1994. *Publications include:* La condition publique 2004, Construire autrement 2006, Construire ensemble/Le Grand ensemble 2010, Histoire du Palais Royal. Les Deux Plateaux/Daniel Buren (with Daniel Buren, Edith Hallauer, Michel Nuridsany) 2010. *Address:* c/o Institut Français d'Architecture, ZA Les Portes du Vexin, 1 chemin de la Chapelle St Antoine, 95300 Ennery, France. *Telephone:* 1-46-33-90-36. *Fax:* 1-34-43-83-81. *Website:* www.ifa.fr.

BOUCHARD, Benoît, BA, LèsArts; Canadian fmr politician and fmr diplomatist; b. 16 April 1940, Roberval, Québec; m. Jeannine Lavoie; three c.; ed Laval Univ.; teacher, Coll. Classique, Coll. Notre-Dame, then Prin. Coll. Notre-Dame and Villa étudiante, Roberval; Dir-Gen. St Félicien CEGEP 1979; alderman, Roberval 1973–80; MP for Roberval, Québec 1984–93, served as Minister of State (Transport) 1984–85, Minister of Communications 1985–86, of Employment and Immigration 1986–88, of Transport 1988–90, of Industry, Science and Tech. 1990–91, of Nat. Health and Welfare 1991–93; Amb. to France 1993–96; Chair. Transportation Safety Bd of Canada 1996–2001; treaty negotiator for Canadian

Govt with Innus people of Québec 2004–10. *Address:* 1120 Rachelle, Roberval, QC G8H 2B9, Canada (home). *Telephone:* (418) 275-8365 (office). *E-mail:* benbouch@ cgocable.ca (office).

BOUCHARD, Lucien, BA, BSc, LLL; Canadian lawyer, diplomatist and fmr politician; *Partner, Davies Ward Phillips & Vineberg LLP;* b. 22 Dec. 1938, Saint-Coeur-de-Marie, Lac Saint-Jean, Québec; s. of Philippe Bouchard and Alice Simard; m. Audrey Best; two s.; called at Collège de Jonquière, Univ. of Laval; called to Québec Bar 1964; pvt law practice in Chicoutimi until 1985; mem. numerous comms and orgs connected with labour relations, both in public and pvt. sectors; Pres. Saguenay Bar 1978; Amb. to France 1985–88; Sec. of State of Canada 1988; MP 1988–2001; Minister of the Environment 1989–90; resgnd from Conservative Party 1990 to lead Bloc Québécois; Chair. and Leader, Bloc Québécois 1991–96; Leader Parti Québécois 1996–2001; Leader of Opposition, House of Commons 1993–95; Prime Minister of Québec 1996–2001; currently Partner, Davies Ward Phillips & Vineberg LLP (law firm); mem Bd of Dirs Transcontinental Inc., Saputo Inc., Centre d'études et de recherches internationales de l'Université de Montréal, Groupe BMTC, TransForce Inc; Commdr, Légion d'Honneur 2002; Grand officier, Ordre national du Québec 2008. *Publications:* À visage découvert 1992; articles in legal and labour relations journals. *Address:* Davies Ward Phillips & Vineberg LLP, 26th Floor, 1501 McGill College Avenue, Montreal, PQ H3A 3N9, Canada (office). *Telephone:* (514) 841-6515 (office). *E-mail:* lbouchard@dwpv.com (office). *Website:* www.dwpv.com (office).

BOUCHÈNE, Abderrahmane; Algerian publisher; b. 1941, Algiers; m.; four c.; ed Algeria and Lausanne Univs; worked in family clothing shop; admin. posts at Société nat. d'édition et de diffusion, Entreprise nat. du livre and Ministry of Culture; f. Editions Bouchène publishing house, Kouba, in late 1980s; by 1990 owner of two bookshops in Algiers, one in Riad-El-Feth; forced to flee Algeria and close business 1994; exile in Tunisia 1994–96; moved to Paris and set up new co. specializing in Algerian historical texts and historical anthropology of Maghreb socs. *Address:* Editions Bouchène, 113–115 rue Danielle Casanova, 93200 Saint-Denis, Paris, France (office). *Telephone:* 1-48-20-93-75 (office). *Fax:* 1-48-20-20-78 (office). *E-mail:* edbouchene@wanadoo.fr (office). *Website:* www.bouchene.com (office).

BOUCHER, Mark Verdon; South African professional cricketer; b. 3 Dec. 1976, East London, Cape Prov.; ed Selborne Coll.; wicketkeeper batsman; right-handed batsman; right-arm medium pace bowler; plays for Border 1995–2003, S Africa 1997–2012 (Capt. Test side 2001–02), Warriors 2004–, ICC (Int. Cricket Council) World XI, Royal Challengers Bangalore 2009–10, Kolkata Knight Riders 2011, Africa XI, Cape Cobras; First-class debut: 1995/96; Test debut: Pakistan v S Africa, Sheikhupura 17–21 Oct. 1997; One-Day Int. (ODI) debut: NZ v S Africa, Perth 16 Jan. 1998; T20I debut: S Africa v NZ, Johannesburg 21 Oct. 2005); played in 147 Tests, took 1 wicket and scored 5,515 runs (5 centuries, 35 half-centuries), highest score 125, average 30.30; played in 295 ODIs and scored 4,686 runs (1 century, 26 half-centuries), highest score 147 not out, average 28.57; played in 25 T20Is and scored 268 runs, highest score 36 not out, average 17.86; has played in 212 First-class matches, scored 8,803 runs (10 centuries, 53 half-centuries), highest score 134, average 33.34; put on, with Pat Symcox, 195 to set new Test ninth-wicket partnership record 1998; first wicketkeeper in Test cricket history to reach milestone of 400 dismissals 2007; holds Test record of 999 dismissals 2012; retd from int. cricket after sustaining eye injury during tour of England 10 July 2012; South Africa Player of the Year 1998, 2000, 2006, Wisden Cricketer of the Year 2009. *Address:* c/o Cricket South Africa, Wanderers Club, 21 North Street, Illovo, PO Box 55009, Northlands, Johannesburg 2116, South Africa. *Telephone:* (11) 880-2810. *Fax:* (11) 880-6578. *E-mail:* info@cricket.co.za. *Website:* www.cricket.co.za; www.markboucher.co.za.

BOUCHEZ, Élodie; French actress; b. 5 April 1973, Montreuil-sous-Bois, Seine-Saint-Denis, Île-de-France; m. Thomas Bangalter; two c. *Films include:* Stan the Flasher 1990, Tous les garçons (short) 1992, Tango 1993, Le cahier volé 1993, Les mots de l'amour (short) 1994, Le péril jeune 1994, Les roseaux sauvages (Wild Reeds) (César Award for Most Promising Actress) 1994, Le plus bel âge... 1995, Mademoiselle Personne 1996, Clubbed to Death (Lola) 1996, A toute vitesse 1996, The Proprietor 1996, Les fantômes du samedi soir (voice) 1997, C'est Noël déjà (short) 1997, La divine poursuite 1997, Le ciel est à nous 1997, Flammen im Paradies 1997, Je veux descendre (short) 1998, La vie rêvée des anges (Best Actress Award, Cannes Film Festival 1998) 1998, Zonzon 1998, J'aimerais pas crever un dimanche 1998, Louise (Take 2) 1998, Les kidnappeurs 1998, Meurtre d'une petite grue 1999, Lovers 1999, Blame It on Voltaire 2000, Too Much Flesh 2000, CQ 2001, The Beatnicks 2001, Le petit poucet 2001, Being Light 2001, Dreams of Trespass 2002, La merveilleuse odyssée de l'idiot Toboggan (segment 'Les mots de l'amour') 2002, The War in Paris 2002, Le pacte du silence 2003, Stormy Weather 2003, À quoi ça sert de voter écolo? (short) 2004, America Brown 2004, Toi, vieux (short) 2004, Shooting Vegetarians 2005, The Brice Man 2005, Sorry, Haters 2005, Ma place au soleil 2007, Héros 2007, I Hate My Best Friends' Kids 2007, Après lui 2007, Tel père telle fille 2007, Seuls Two 2008, Driving Elodie (short) 2009, The Imperialists Are Still Alive! 2010, Happy Few 2010. *Television includes:* Les compagnons de l'aventure (series) 1990–91, La lettre inachevée (film) 1993, 3000 scénarios contre un virus (series) 1994, Les Cordier, juge et flic (series) 1994, Les brouches (film) 1994, Tous les garçons et les filles de leur âge... (series) 1994, Premières neiges (film) 1999, Alias (series) 2005–06, The L Word (series) 2006–07, Douce France (film) 2009.

BOUCHIER, Ian Arthur Dennis, CBE, MB, ChB, MD, FRCP, FRCPE, FRSA, FRSE, FFPHM, FSB, FMedSci; British professor of medicine (retd); b. 7 Sept. 1932, Cape Town, S Africa; s. of E. A. Bouchier and May Bouchier; m. Patricia N. Henshilwood 1959; two s.; ed Rondebosch Boys' High School and Univ. of Cape Town; jr staff positions, Groote Schuur Hosp., Cape Town 1955–60; Registrar, Lecturer, Royal Free Hosp., London 1961–63; Research Fellow, Boston Univ. 1963–65; Sr Lecturer, Univ. of London 1965–70, Reader in Medicine 1970–73; Prof. of Medicine, Univ. of Dundee 1973–86, Univ. of Edinburgh 1986–97; Sec.-Gen. World Org. of Gastroenterology 1982–90, Pres. 1990–98; Chief Scientist for Scotland 1992–97; mem. Chief Scientist Cttee; Visiting Prof., Univ. of Michigan 1979, Madras Medical Coll. 1981, McGill Univ. 1983, Royal Postgraduate Medical School 1984, Univ. of Hong Kong 1988, China Medical Univ. 1988, Univ. of Dunedin 1989, Keio Univ. 1991; mem. Council, British Soc. of Gastroenterology

1987–90 (Pres. 1994–95); mem. Council, Royal Soc. of Edinburgh1986–89, British Soc. of Gastroenterology 1992–; Corresp. mem. Italian Soc. of Gastroenterology, Royal Catalonian Acad. of Medicine; mem. numerous editorial bds; Hon. FCP(SA); Hon. mem. South African Soc. of Gastroenterology, Japanese Soc. of Gastroenterology; Hon. MD (Iasi). *Publications:* 28 textbooks and 600 articles mainly on gastroenterological topics. *Leisure interests:* music of Berlioz, history of whaling, cooking. *Address:* 8A Merchiston Park, Edinburgh, EH10 4PN, Scotland.

BOUDOU, Amado, DEcon, MEconSc; Argentine economist and politician; *Minister of Economy and Public Finance;* b. 1963, Buenos Aires; ed Nat. Univ. of Mar del Plata, Centro de Estudio Macroeconómicos Argentinos; Asst Prof. of Econs, Univ. Nacional de Tres de Febrero 2000; Asst Prof., Centro de Estudio Macroeconómicos Argentinos 2001–02; Asst Prof., Univ. Argentina de la Empresa 2001–05; with Sales Dept, Venturino ESHIUR SA 1990–95; Project Man. ECOPLATA SA 1995–98; Co-ordinator, Administración Nacional de la Seguridad Social 2000, Gen. Man. Comptroller's Office 2001, later Finance Dir, Sec.-Gen. 2008–09; Sec. of Housing and Finance, Dist of La Costa 2003–05; Minister of Economy and Public Finance 2009–. *Address:* Ministry of Economy and Public Finance, Hipólito Yrigoyen 250, C1086AAB Buenos Aires, Argentina (office). *Telephone:* (11) 4349-5000 (office). *E-mail:* infoprensa@mecon.gov.ar (office). *Website:* www.mecon.gov.ar (office).

BOUDREAUX, Gail Koziara, BA, MBA; American business executive; *CEO, UnitedHealthcare;* m. Terry Boudreaux; two s.; ed Chicopee Comprehensive High School, Mass, Dartmouth Coll., Columbia Univ. Business School; fmr professional basketball player, including for Dartmouth Big Green Women's basketball team 1978–82; joined Aetna Inc. as Regional Man., becoming Gen. Man., Pacific Northwest Market, Vice-Pres., Customer Service, Sr Vice-Pres., later Pres. Group Insurance; Pres. Blue Cross and Blue Shield of Illinois 2002–05; Exec. Vice-Pres., External Operations, Health Care Services Corpn (HCSC) 2005–08; Pres. UnitedHealthcare 2008–11, CEO 2011–, Exec. Vice-Pres. UnitedHealth Group 2008–; mem. Bd of Dirs Dental Network America, Health Care Services Corpn Insurance Services, Fort Dearborn Life Insurance Co., Metropolitan Planning Council; Dir Genzyme Corpn 2004–; named Ivy League Player of the Year for three consecutive seasons, twice an Academic All-American and third team All-American, NCAA Silver Anniversary Award 2007, Minneapolis/St Paul Business Journal Women in Business Industry Leader Award 2009, ranked by Forbes magazine amongst The World's 100 Most Powerful Women (54th) 2009, ranked by Fortune magazine amongst the 50 Most Powerful Women in Business in the US (38th) 2009, (34th) 2010, (30th) 2011, (28th) 2012. *Leisure interest:* tennis. *Address:* UnitedHealth Group Inc., 9900 Bren Road East, Minnetonka, MN 55343, USA (office). *Telephone:* (952) 936-1300 (office). *Fax:* (952) 936-1819 (office). *Website:* www.uhc.com (office).

BOUDRIA, Don, PC, BA; Canadian fmr politician; *Senior Counsellor, Hill+Knowlton Canada;* b. 30 Aug. 1949, Hull, Québec; m. Mary Ann Morris 1971; one s. one d.; ed Eastview High School, Univ. of Waterloo; entered Fed. Govt 1966, held various positions including Chief Purchasing Agent –1981; Councillor, Cumberland Township 1976–80, fmr mem. Cumberland Township Housing Corpn; mem. Ontario Legis. for Prescott-Russell 1981–84, Opposition Critic of Govt Services 1981–82, of Community and Social Services 1982–83, of Consumer and Commercial Relations 1983–84; mem. Parl. for Glengarry-Prescott-Russell 1984–2005 (retd); Opposition Critic on Fed. Supply and Services, mem. Standing Cttee on Agriculture 1984, Opposition Critic on Public Works 1985, Govt Operations 1987, Canada Post and Govt Operations 1988; Deputy Opposition Whip 1989, Asst House Leader for the Official Opposition and Govt Operations Critic 1990–93, Deputy Govt Whip 1994; mem. Int. Liberal Caucus 1984, Chair. 1985–87; Minister of Int. Co-operation and Francophonie 1996–97, Minister of State and Leader of Govt in House of Commons 1997–2002, Minister of Public Works and Govt Services Jan.–May 2002, Minister of State and Leader of the Govt in House of Commons 2002–03; currently Sr Counsellor, Hill+Knowlton Canada; Founding Pres. Ont. Section, Int. Asscn of French-speaking Parliamentarians; mem. Bd of Dirs International Election Monitoring Inst., Canadian Asscn of Former Parliamentarians; Founding mem. Sarsfield Knights of Columbus; currently Chair. Canadian Section FIPA. *Publication:* Busboy: From Kitchen to Cabinet 2005. *Leisure interests:* history, music, downhill skiing. *Address:* Hill+Knowlton Canada, 55 Metcalfe Street, Suite 1100, Ottawa, ON K1P 6L5 (office); 3455 Dessaint Crescent, Sarsfield, ON K0A 3E0, Canada (home). *Telephone:* (613) 238-4371 (office). *Website:* hkstrategies.ca (office).

BOUGIE, Jacques, OC; Canadian business executive and academic; *Adjunct Professor, Department of Management, HEC Montréal;* b. 1947, Montreal; ed Univ. de Montréal; joined Alcan 1979, Man. Beauharnois Works, then various positions in Winnipeg, Toronto and Montreal in major project devt, planning and gen. man., responsible for fabricating operations in N America, Pres., COO Alcan Aluminium Ltd 1989–93, Pres., CEO 1993–2001; Adjunct Prof., HEC Montréal 2002–; fmr Vice-Chair. Business Council on Nat. Issues; mem. Bd Dirs Abitibi-Consolidated Inc., Nova Chemicals Inc. 2001, McCain Foods Ltd, Rona Inc. 2003–05; Chair. Int. Advisory Council, CGI Group Inc. 2004. *Address:* Department of Management, HEC Montréal, Côte-Sainte-Catherine Building, 3000 Côte-Sainte-Catherine Road, Montréal, PQ H3T 2A7, Canada (office). *Telephone:* (514) 340-6000 (office). *Fax:* (514) 340-6411 (office). *E-mail:* jacques.bougie@hec.ca (office). *Website:* www .hec.ca/management (office).

BOUH, Yacin Elmi; Djibouti politician; b. 4 June 1962; ed Univ. of Nantes, France; Minister of the Economy, Finance and Planning, in charge of privatization 1997–2005, Minister of Interior and Decentralization 2005–11; fmr mem. Bd of Govs Islamic Devt Bank. *Address:* c/o Ministry of the Interior and Decentralization, BP 33, Djibouti, Djibouti (office).

BOUHAMED CHAABOUNI, Habiba, DèsSc; Tunisian medical geneticist and academic; ed Faculty of Medicine, Tunis; est. first genetic counselling service and launched epidemiological studies on consanguinity in northern Tunisia 1981, set up medical genetics and consultation service to carry out antenatal diagnostic tests 1993; fmr Prof. of Medical Genetics, Univ. of Tunis, Head of Dept of Congenital and Hereditary Diseases, Charles Nicolle Hosp., Tunisia, Dir Human Genetics Research Lab. and Faculty of Medicine, Tunis; fmr mem. Tech. Comm. of Arab League for Genetic Diseases Prevention and Genetic Counselling, represented

Tunisia in Cttee of Governmental Experts to prepare UNESCO draft declaration on the Human Genome; mem. Soc. Tunisienne des Sciences Médicales, Soc. Tunisienne de Pédiatrie, American Soc. of Human Genetics, European Soc. of Cytogenetics; L'Oréal-UNESCO Women in Science Award 2006. *Publications:* more than 100 scientific papers on the analysis and prevention of hereditary disorders. *Address:* University of Tunis El Mar, BP 94, Tunis 1068, Tunisia (office).

BOUHIA, (Haya) Hynd, SM, MA, PhD; Moroccan economist and business executive; *Director-General, Casablanca Stock Exchange;* b. 21 Oct. 1972, Casablanca; m. Khalid Zerouali; one s.; ed Ecole Centrale, Paris, France, Johns Hopkins School for Advanced Int. Studies and Harvard Univ., USA; joined World Bank Young Professional Program, Washington, DC 1996, worked on Bank's lending operations 1996–2001, worked as Water and Environmental Economist in Middle East and N Africa (MENA) Region, in Latin America Region on water sector strategy for Argentina and water quality control in Brazil and SE Asia Region, Special Asst to Vice-Pres. for MENA Region –2001, Sr Financial Officer in Capital Market Operations unit of Banking, Capital Markets and Financial Eng Dept, World Bank Treasury 2001–04; econ. adviser to Prime Minister of Morocco 2004–08; Dir-Gen. Casablanca Stock Exchange 2008–; mem. Washington Conservatory of Music (performs classical piano); Hon. Prize of Casablanca Conservatory of Music for Piano performances; ranked by Forbes magazine amongst 100 Most Powerful Women (29th) 2008. *Publications:* Water in the Macro Economy: Application of an Integrated Analytical Model 2001; several academic papers and book chapters. *Leisure interest:* athletic and fitness activities. *Address:* 57 Avenue du Phare-Bourgogne, 20 000, Casablanca, Morocco (office). *Telephone:* (22) 364214/364216 (office). *Fax:* (22) 364210 (office). *E-mail:* hbouhia@hotmail.com (office). *Website:* www.casablanca-bourse.com/homeen.html (office).

BOULANGER, Daniel; French writer; b. 24 Jan. 1922, Compiègne, Oise; s. of Michel Boulanger and Hélène Bayart; m. 2nd Clémence Dufour; four s. three d.; ed Petit Séminaire Saint-Charles, Chauny; sub-ed., Affaires économiques 1946–48; writer 1948–; has written scripts or screenplays for over 100 films, including Cartouche 1962, L'Homme de Rio 1963, Les Tribulations d'un Chinois en Chine 1965, La Vie de Château 1966, Le Voleur 1967, Le Diable par la Queue 1968, Le Roi de Coeur (Prix Louis-Delluc) 1969, Les Maries de l'An II 1971, L'Affaire Dominici 1973, Police Python 1975, Une femme fidèle 1976, La Menace 1976, Cheval d'Orgueil 1980, Chouans 1988, La Révolution Française 1989; numerous plays; mem. Acad. Goncourt 1983–2008; Officier, Légion d'honneur, Ordre nat. du Mérite, Commdr, des Arts et des Lettres; Rose d'or des Rosati 1973, Prix Pierre de Monaco for complete body of work 1979, Prix Kléber Haedens 1983. *Publications include:* novellas: Les Noces du Merle (Prix de la Nouvelle) 1963, L'été des Femmes (Fête Ste Beuve 1966) 1964, Le Chemin des Caracoles 1966, Le jardin d'Armide 1969, Mémoire de la Ville 1970, Vessies et Lanternes (Prix de l'Académie française) 1971, Fouette Cocher (Prix Goncourt de la Nouvelle) 1974; novels: Jules Bouc 1987, La Confession d'Omer 1991, Un Eté à la diable 1992, Ursacq 1992, Le Retable Wasserfall 1994, Caporal Supérieur 1994, Le Miroittier 1995, Tombeau d'Héraldine 1997, Talbard 1998, Le Ciel de Bargetal 1999, Clémence et Auguste 2000, Les Mouches et l'âne 2001, Cache-Cache 2002, Du temps qu'on plaisantait 2003, La Poste de Nuit 2004, Le ciel est aux petits porteurs 2006; poems: Tchadiennes 1969, Retouches (Prix Max Jacob 1970) 1969, A la courte paille 1993, Etiquettes 1994, Taciturnes 1995, Images mes catins 1999, Fenêtre mon navire 2008, Vestiaire des anges 2012. *Address:* 22 rue du Heaume, 60300 Senlis, France (home).

BOULEZ, Pierre; French composer and conductor; b. 26 March 1925, Montbrison; s. of Léon Boulez and Marcelle Calabre; ed Paris Conservatoire; studied with Messiaen, Vaurabourg-Honegger and Leibowitz; Dir of Music to Jean-Louis Barrault theatre co. 1948; aided by Barrault and Madeleine Renaud Barrault he founded the Concert Marigny which later became the Domaine Musical, Paris; Prin. Guest Conductor Cleveland Symphony Orchestra 1968; Prin. Conductor BBC Symphony Orchestra 1971–75; Musical Dir New York Philharmonic 1971–77; Dir Inst. de Recherches et de Coordination Acoustique/Musique (IRCAM) 1975–91, Hon. Dir 1992–; Founder and Pres. Ensemble Intercontinental 1977–98; Prof. Collège de France 1976–95; Prin. Guest Conductor Chicago Symphony Orchestra 1995–2006, Conductor Emer. 2006–; conducted the centenary production of Wagner's Ring, Bayreuth 1976–80; Hon. Conductor, Staatskapelle Berlin 2005, Vienna Philharmonic 2005, Fellow British Acad. of Composers and Songwriters 2005, Distinguished Musician Award Inc. Soc. of Musicians 2006–07; Hon. CBE; Dr hc (Cambridge) 1980, (Basel) 1980, (Los Angeles) 1984, (Oxford) 1987, (Brussels) 1988; Prize of the Siemens Foundation 1979, Praemium Imperiale, Japan Art Asscn 1989, Polar Music Prize, Sweden 1996, Wolf Foundation Prize in Arts 2000, Grawemeyer Award 2001, Inc. Soc. of Musicians Distinguished Musician Award 2005, Gramophone Hall of Fame 2012. *Compositions include:* First Piano Sonata 1946, Sonatina for Flute and Piano 1946, Le Visage nuptial (5 poems of René Char for 2 solo voices, female choir and orch.) 1946–50, Second Piano Sonata 1948, Le Soleil des eaux (2 poems by René Char for voice and orchestra) 1948, Livre pour Quatuor (string quartet) 1949, Le Marteau sans maître (cantata for voice and instruments to texts by René Char, also ballet 1965) 1955, Structures (2 pianos) 1964, Third Piano Sonata 1957–58, Improvisations sur Mallarmé (soprano and chamber ensemble) 1958, Doubles (orchestra) 1958, Poésie pour pouvoir (orchestra) 1958, Tombeau (soprano and orchestra) 1959, Pli selon Pli 1958–62, Figures-Doubles-Prismes 1964/74, Eclat and Eclat/Multiples 1965, Domaines 1968–69, cummings ist der dichter 1970, explosante-fixe for 8 solo instruments 1973, Rituel 1974, Messagesquisse 1977, Notations 1979, Répons 1981–86, Dérive 1984, Dialogue de l'ombre double 1984, Mémoriale 1985, le Visage nuptial 1989, . . . explosante-fixe . . . for midi-flute, 2 solo flutes, ensemble and electronics 1993, Anthèmes 2 1997, sur Incises 1998, Notations VII 1999, Dérive 2 2002–05. *Publications:* Penser la musique aujourd'hui 1966, Relevés d'apprenti (essays) 1967, Par volonté et par hasard 1975, Points de repère 1981, Le pays fertile: Paul Klee 1989, Orientations: Collected Writings 1986. *Address:* IRCAM, 1 place Igor Stravinsky, 75004 Paris, France (office). *Telephone:* 1-42-77-95-01 (office). *Fax:* 1-44-78-15-40 (office). *E-mail:* secretariat.pierre .boulez@ircam.fr (office).

BOULLIER, Éric René; French motorsport manager; *Team Principal, Lotus F1 Formula One Team;* b. 9 Nov. 1973, Laval; ed French Institut Polytechnique des Sciences Appliquees; Chief Engineer, Spanish Racing Engineering team 2002; Man.

and Tech. Dir, Driot-Arnoux Motorsport (DAMS) team, France 2003–08, Team Principal 2007–08; CEO Gravity Sport Man. 2008–10; Team Principal, Renault F1 Team 2010–11, Lotus F1 Formula Team 2012–; Vice-Chair. Formula One Teams Asscn 2011–. *Address:* Lotus Renault GP, Whiteways Technical Centre, Enstone, Oxon. OX7 4EE, England (office). *Telephone:* (1608) 678000 (office). *Fax:* (1608) 678609 (office). *E-mail:* pressoffice@lotusrenaultgp.com (office). *Website:* www .lotusrenaultgp.com (office); www.teamsassociation.org (office).

BOULUD, Daniel; French chef and restaurateur; b. 25 March 1955, St Pierre de Chandieu, Rhône; began career as apprentice chef at age 14; spent two years as chef in Copenhagen; chef, European Comm., Washington DC 1981; opened first restaurants, The Polo Lounge, Westbury Hotel, and Le Régence, Hotel Plaza Athenée, New York; Exec. Chef Le Cirque, New York 1986–92; opened Daniel restaurant 1993 (Gourmet Magazine Top Table Award), Café Boulud, New York Sept. 1998, DB Bistro Moderne June 2001, Café Boulud, Florida 2003, numerous other restaurants; Founding Pnr, Payard Patisserie & Bistro –2000; Owner, Feast & Fêtes Catering and Daniel Boulud CONNOISSEUR (direct mail co.); mem. Bd of Dirs Citymeals-on-Wheels 1999–; contrib. Elle Décor; Bon Appétit Magazine Chef of the Year, Outstanding Restaurateur, James Beard Foundation 2006. *Publications include:* Cooking with Daniel Boulud 1993, Daniel Boulud's Café Boulud Cookbook 1999, Chef Daniel Boulud Cooking in New York City 2002, Letters to a Young Chef (jt author) 2003, Daniel's Dish: Entertaining at Home with a Four-Star Chef 2003, Braise: A Journey through International Cuisine 2006; Easy Cooking with Great Chefs (Ed.) monthly newsletter. *Address:* c/o Daniel, 60 East 65th Street, New York NY 10065, USA (office). *Website:* www.danielboulud.com (office).

BOUMA, Johannes, PhD; Dutch soil scientist and academic; b. 29 Oct. 1940, 't Bildt; s. of S. Bouma and J. Bouma (née Werff); m. Marianne Wiebols 1969; one s. one d.; ed Agricultural Univ., Wageningen, Univ. of Wisconsin USA; Asst Prof., Soils Dept, Univ. of Wis., Madison 1969–73, Assoc. Prof. 1973–75; Head of Soil Physics Dept, Netherlands Soil Survey Inst., Wageningen 1975–82, Deputy Dir in charge of research 1982–86; Prof. of Soil Science, Agricultural Univ. of Wageningen 1986–2002, Scientific Dir Environmental Sciences Group Research Centre 2002–04; mem. Netherlands Scientific Council for Govt Policy 1998–2003; mem. Royal Dutch Acad. of Sciences 1989; Corresp. mem. German Soil Science Asscn 1982; Fellow, Soil Science Soc. of America 1985; Officer of the Order of Orange-Nassau 2001. *Publications:* several books and various articles in tech. journals. *Leisure interests:* jogging, cycling. *Address:* Alterra, PO Box 47, 6700 AA Wageningen (office); Spoorbaanweg 35, 3911 CA Rhenen, Netherlands (home). *Telephone:* (317) 613469 (home). *E-mail:* johan.bouma@wur.nl (office); johan .bouma@planet.nl (home).

BOUNGNANG, Volachit; Laotian politician and army officer; *Vice President;* b. 1936; m. Keosaychay Sayasone; fmr army officer; fmr Gov. Savannaket, then Mayor Vientiane Municipality; apptd mem. Politburo 1996; Minister of Finance and Deputy Prime Minister 1999–2001; Prime Minister of Laos 2001–06; Vice Pres. 2006–. *Address:* Office of the Vice President, rue Lane Xang, Vientiane, Laos. *Telephone:* (21) 214200 (office). *Fax:* (21) 214208 (office).

BOUQUET, Carole; French actress; b. 18 Aug. 1957, Neuilly-sur-Seine; m. 1st Jean-Pierre Rassam (deceased), one s.; m. 2nd Jacques Liebowitch (divorced); pnr Francis Giacobetti, one s.; fmr Face of Chanel No. 5. *Films include:* Cet Obscur Objet du Désir 1977, Buffet Froid 1979, Le Manteau d'Astrakan 1979, For Your Eyes Only 1981, Le Jour des Idiots 1981, Bingo Bango 1982, Dream One 1983, Mystère 1983, Dagobert 1984, Rive droite, Rive gauche 1984, Double Messieurs 1985, Special Police 1985, Le Mal d'Aimer 1986, Jenatsch 1986, On se dépêche d'en rire 1987, Bunker Palace Hotel 1988, Trop Belle pour toi (César for Best Actress) 1990, Grosse Fatigue 1994, A Business Affair 1994, Lucie Aubrac 1997, In All Innocence, The Bridge, Tango 1993, En plein cœur 1998, Un pont entre deux rives 1999, Le Pique-nique de Lulu Kreutz 2000, Embrassez qui vous voudrez 2002, Blanche 2002, Bienvenue chez les Rozes 2003, Feux Rouges 2004, Les Fautes d'orthographe 2004, Nordeste 2005, Travaux, on sait quand ça commence 2005, L'Enfer 2005, Aurore 2006, Un ami parfait 2006, Si c'était lui 2007, Les Enfants de Timpelbach 2007, Les Hauts murs 2008, You'll Miss Me 2009, Protéger et servir 2010, Libre échange 2010, Impardonnables 2011, Bad Girl 2012. *Television:* Ruy Blas (film) 2002, L'éloignement (film) 2009, Le grand restaurant II (film) 2011. *Plays include:* Phèdre, Théâtre Dejazet, Paris 2002. *Address:* c/o Intertalent, 5 rue Clément-Marot, 75008 Paris, France (office).

BOURCE, Ludovic; French composer and actor. *Film scores include:* Mes amis 1999, OSS 117: Cairo, Nest of Spies 2006, Here to Stay (documentary) (original music) 2009, OSS 117: Lost in Rio 2009, The Artist (Broadcast Film Critics Asscn Award for Best Composer 2011, Chicago Film Critics Asscn Award for Best Original Score 2011, European Film Award for Best Composer 2011, Washington, DC Area Film Critics Asscn Award for Best Score 2011, Golden Globe Award for Best Original Score 2012) 2011. *Film roles in:* OSS 117: Lost in Rio 2009.

BOURDAIS DE CHARBONNIÈRE, Eric; French business executive; *Chairman of the Supervisory Board, Michelin;* b. 1939; began career with JP Morgan 1965, various positions including commercial banker, Controller and Treas., New York and Paris 1965–81, Chair. and CEO JP Morgan (France) 1981–85, Sr Vice-Pres. JP Morgan Continental Europe 1985–87, Exec. Vice-Pres. JP Morgan Europe 1987–90; Chief Financial Officer, Compagnie Générale des Établissements Michelin 1990–2000, Chair. Supervisory Bd 2000–; mem. Bd of Dirs Thomson 2003–, also Chair. Audit Cttee; mem. Supervisory Bd Oddo & Cie, ING Group 2004–; Compagnie Générale des Établissements Michelin, 12 cours Sablon, 63000 Clermont-Ferrand, France. *Telephone:* (4) 73-98-59-00 (office). *Fax:* (4) 73-98-59-04 (office). *E-mail:* info@michelin.com (office). *Website:* www.michelin.com (office).

BOURDEAU, Philippe François, PhD, FAAS; Belgian academic and fmr European Community official; b. 25 Nov. 1926, Rabat, Morocco; s. of Michel Bourdeau and Lucienne Imbrecht; m. Flora Gorirossi 1954; three d.; ed Gembloux, Belgium and Duke Univ. USA; Asst Prof., State Univ. of North Carolina 1954–56, Yale Univ. 1956–58, 1960–62; Prof., Univ. of Belgian Congo 1958–60; Head, Radiobiology Dept, EURATOM, Jt Research Centre, Ispra, Italy 1962–71; Head of Div. then Dir research programmes in environment and in non-nuclear energy, Comm. of EC, Brussels 1971–91; Prof., Univ. Libre de Bruxelles 1972–96; Head, European Environment Agency Task Force 1991; Chair. Scientific Cttee, European Environmental Agency; mem. Belgian Royal Acad. *Publications:* scientific papers in the fields of environment policy, ecophysiology, ecotoxicology. *Leisure interests:* reading, sport. *Address:* ULB, CP 130/02, 50 avenue F.D. Roosevelt, 1050 Brussels, Belgium (office). *E-mail:* bourdeau@ulb.ac.be (office).

BOURESLI, Amani Khaled; Kuwaiti academic, business executive and government official; ed Southern Illinois Univ., USA; fmr Asst Prof. then Prof., Dept of Finance, Kuwait Univ.; Founder and Chair. Capital Standards (regional credit ratings agency); Minister of Trade and Industry 2011–12; mem. Bd of Dirs Burgan Bank –2011; Economic Policy and Knowledge Devt Achiever Award, Middle East Excellence Awards Inst. 2010. *Address:* c/o Ministry of Trade and Industry, Ministry Complex Block 1/2, PO Box 2944, Safat, Kuwait (office). *E-mail:* bouresli@cba.edu.kw (office). *Website:* www.capstandards.com.

BOURGAIN, Jean, PhD; Belgian mathematician and academic; *Professor, School of Mathematics, Institute for Advanced Study, Princeton;* b. 28 Feb. 1954, Ostend; ed Free Univ. of Brussels; Research Fellowship, NSF (NFWO), Belgium 1975–81; Prof., Free Univ. of Brussels 1981–85; J.L. Doob Prof. of Math., Univ. of Illinois, USA 1985–; Prof., Institut des Hautes Études Scientifiques (IHÉS), France 1985–95; Lady Davis Prof. of Math., Hebrew Univ. of Jerusalem, Israel 198; Fairchild Distinguished Prof., Calif. Inst. of Tech. 1991; Prof., School of Math., Inst. for Advanced Study, Princeton, NJ 1994–; mem. Editorial Bd Annals of Mathematics, Journal de l'Institut de Mathématique de Jussieu, Publications Mathématiques de l'IHES, Duke Math Journal, International Mathematical Research Notices, Geometrical and Functional Analysis, Journal d'Analyse de Jérusalem, Journal of Functional Analysis, Duke Journal of Mathematics, Journal of the European Mathematical Society, Comptes Rendus Académie Sciences, Paris, Monografic Matematyczne, Applied and Computational Harmonic Analysis; Associé Etranger, Acad. des Sciences, 2000; Foreign mem. Polish Acad. 2000, Academia Europaea 2000, Royal Swedish Acad. of Sciences 2009, Royal Flemish Acad. of Arts and Sciences 2013; Foreign Assoc. NAS 2011; Dr hc (Université Marne-la-Vallée, France) 1994, (Hebrew Univ. of Jerusalem) 1991, (Free Univ. of Brussels) 1995; Alumni Prize, Belgium NSF 1979, Empain Prize, Belgium NSF 1983, Salem Prize 1983, Damry-Deleeuw-Bourlart Prize, Belgian NSF 1985, Langevin Prize, Acad. française 1985, E. Cartan Prize, Acad. française 1990, Ostrowski Prize, Ostrowski Foundation (Basel, Switzerland) 1991, Fields Medal, ICM Zurich 1994, Shaw Prize in Math. 2010, Crafoord Prize in Math., Royal Swedish Acad. of Sciences (co-recipient) 2012. *Address:* Simonyi Hall 203, School of Mathematics, Institute for Advanced Study, Princeton, NJ 08540, USA (office). *Telephone:* (609) 734-8397 (office). *Fax:* (609) 951-4459 (office). *E-mail:* bourgain@math.ias.edu (office). *Website:* www.math.ias.edu/people/faculty/bourgain (office).

BOURGES, Hervé; French administrator, diplomatist and journalist; b. 2 May 1933, Rennes, Ile-et-Vilaine; s. of Joseph Bourges and Marie-Magdeleine Desjeux; m. Marie-Thérèse Lapouille 1966; ed Lycée de Biarritz, Coll. Saint-Joseph, Reims, École supérieure de journalisme; Ed. then Ed.-in-Chief Témoignage Chrétien 1956–62; attached to Keeper of the Seals 1959–62, Dir Algerian Ministry of Youth and Popular Education, attached to Ministry of Information; Asst Lecturer Univ. de Paris II 1967–; Founder and Dir École supérieure de journalisme de Yaoundé, Cameroun 1970–76; Dir then Pres. Admin. Council École nat. supérieure de journalisme de Lille 1976–80; Dir Information Service and Dir-Gen.'s Messenger UNESCO 1980–81, Amb. to UNESCO 1994–95; Dir then Dir-Gen. Radio France Int. 1981–83; Chair. and Dir-Gen. TV Française 1 (TF1) 1983–87, Hon. Pres. 1987–93; Hon. Pres. Admin. Council, Ecole Supérieure de Journalisme de Lille 1992–; Dir-Gen. Radio Monte Carlo (RMC) 1988; Pres. and Dir-Gen. Société financière de radiodiffusion (Sofirad) 1989–91; Pres. Canal Horizon 1990–91, Conseil Supérieur de L'Audio-Visuel (CSA) 1995–2001; Pres. L'Union internationale des journalistes de la presse de langue française (UIJPLF) 2001; Comité permanent de la diversité de France Télévisions 2009–; Commdr, Légion d'honneur 2011; Croix de la Valeur Militaire. *Film:* L'Algérie à l'épreuve du pouvoir (documentary). *Publications:* L'Algérie à l'épreuve du pouvoir 1967, La Révolte étudiante 1968, Décoloniser l'information 1978, Les cinquante Afriques (jtly) 1979, Le village planétaire (jtly) 1986, Une Chaîne sur les bras 1987, Un amour de télévision (jtly) 1989, La Télévision du Public 1993, De mémoire d'éléphant (autobiog.) 2000, Le règne de la terreur sacrée (with Liess Boukra) 2001, Entretiens (with Jean-Michel Djian) 2003, Léopold Sédar Senghor, lumière noire 2006, L'Afrique n'attend pas 2010. *Website:* www.ftv-diversite.fr.

BOURGUIGNON, François, DEcon, DEA, PhD; French economist; *Associate Chair Paris School of Economics;* b. 22 May 1945, Paris; m.; ed Ecole Nationale de la Statistique et des Analyses Economique (ENSEA), Univ. of Paris VI, Univ. of Western ON, Canada, Univ. of Orléans; Expert de coopération (VSN), Univ. of Chile 1969–70; Asst Prof., Univ. of Toronto, Canada 1975–78; Consultant, OECD Devt Center 1971–72; Research Fellow, Laboratoire d'économie politique de l'Ecole normale supérieure, CNRS, Paris 1978–85; Research Fellow, Centre d'observation économique, Chambre de Commerce et d'Industrie de Paris 1971–72; Prof. of Econs, Ecole des Hautes Etudes en Sciences Sociales (EHESS), Dir Centre d'Economie Quantitative et Comparative 1986–87, Founder and first Dir of Delta (jt research unit CNRS, EHESS and Ecole Nat. Supérieur) 1988; Advisor to Chief Economist, Banque Mondiale 1999–2000; mem. Conseil d'Analyse Economique (advisory group to Prime Minister), Paris; Visiting Prof., Concordia Univ., Montreal, Canada 1979, Birkbeck Coll., London, UK 1984, Univ. of Geneva, Switzerland 1989–90, Università Commerciale Luigi Bocconi, Milan, Italy 1992–95; Chief Economist and Sr Vice-Pres., Devt Econs, World Bank, Washington, DC 2003–07, Dir Devt Research Group 2003, est. Devt Impact Evaluation Initiative (DIME); fmr Dir and now Assoc. Chair, Paris School of Econs 2007–; Prof. of Econs, Ecole des hautes études en sciences sociales; Ed. World Bank Economic Review, European Economic Review; fmr consultant, UN, EC, ILO; Pres. European Soc. for Population Econs 1995, Comité d'évaluation du RSA (revenu de solidarité active); mem. Scientific Cttee of WIDER (UN, Helsinki), Universidad Torcuato di Tella (Argentina), Centro Luca d'Agliano, Turin, Council of Econ. Advisors of the French Prime Minister, Exec. Cttee of EUDN (European Devt Network), EC Advisory Group on Societal Analysis, Evaluation Cttee of European Research Council, Brussels, Copenhagen Consensus Panel; Fellow, Econometric Soc. 1986; Chevalier, Ordre nat. du Mérite 1991, Ordre de la Légion d'honneur 2010; Dr hc (Université du Québec à Montréal) 2001, (Geneva) 2005, (Western Ontario) 2009, (Liège) 2009 Merrit Brown Prize for the best thesis, Univ.

of Western Ontario 1975, CNRS Bronze Medal 1982, El Fasi Prize for Devt Econs, Asscn des Universités de langue française (Aupelf/Uref), Médaille d'argent, CNRS 1997. *Publications include:* Statistical Analysis of Incomes in Chile (in Spanish) 1970, International Labour Migrations and Economic Choices – The European Case (with G. Gallais-Hamonno) 1977, L'économie française au XIX^esiècle – Analyse macroéconomique (with M. Lévy-Leboyer) 1985 (English trans.: A Macroeconomic Model of France during the 19th Century: An Essay in Econometric Analysis) 1990, Foreign Trade and Income Distribution (with C. Morrisson *et al.*) 1989, Théorie micro-économique: L'équilibre concurrentiel (with P.-A. Chiappori and P. Rey) 1992, Equity and Adjustment in Developing Economies (with C. Morrisson) 1992, Growth and Macro-economic Crisis in Côte d'Ivoire (with J.-C. Berthélémy) 1996, Handbook of Income Distribution (co-ed. with A. Atkinson) 2000, The Impact of Economic Policies on Poverty and Income Distribution: Evaluation Techniques and Tools (co-ed. with L. Pereira da Silva) 2003, The Microeconomics of Income Distribution Dynamics in East Asia and Latin America (co-ed. with F. Ferreira and N. Lustig) 2005, The Impact of Macroeconomic Policies on Poverty and Income Distribution (co-ed. with M. Bussolo and L. Pereira) 2008, Trajectoires et enjeux de l'économie mondiale (with François Boutin-Dufresne) 2010; several book chapters; numerous articles in specialist journals. *Address:* 48 boulevard Jourdan, Building E, Office EEP, Paris School of Economics, 75014 Paris, France (office). *Telephone:* 1-43-13-63-49 (office). *E-mail:* francois.bourguignon@parisschoolofeconomics.eu (office). *Website:* www .parisschoolofeconomics.eu (office).

BOURGUIGNON, Philippe Etienne, MScEcon, MBA; French business executive; *CEO, Exclusive Resorts;* b. 11 Jan. 1948, Salins les Bains; s. of Jacques Bourguignon and Paule Clément; m. Martine Lemardeley 1977; one s. one d.; ed Univ. of Aix; analyst, Synthèse Documentaire, Paris 1971–72; Project Man. Systembau, Munich 1973; Vice-Pres. Devt Accor, Novotel Asia, Middle East 1974–79; Exec. Vice-Pres. Accor North America, New York 1979–84; Pres. and CEO Accor Asia Pacific, Los Angeles 1984–88; Sr Vice-Pres. Real Estate Devt Euro Disney, Paris 1989–92; Pres. Euro Disney SA, Paris 1992, Chair. and CEO 1993–97; Exec. Vice-Pres. for Europe Walt Disney Co. 1996–97; Chair. Bd of Dirs Club Méditerranée 1997–2002; Man. Dir World Econ. Forum Aug.–Oct. 2003, Co-CEO 2003–04; Chair. Aegis Media France 2004–06; Vice-Chair. Revolution Resorts (div. of Revolution LLC) 2006–07, Vice-Chair. Revolution Places Group and CEO Revolution Places Development 2007–; CEO Miraval Resort 2009–; CEO Exclusive Resorts 2011–; Pres. Young Pres. Org. 1990; Pres. Exec. Comm. for Paris' bid for Olympic Games 2008 1998; mem. Bd of Dirs eBay Inc 1999–, American Chamber of Commerce in France; mem. Econ. Council Confed. of French Industries and Services; Chair. YPO French Chapter 1990; Chevalier, Légion d'honneur, Officier, Ordre nat. du Mérite, Wissam Al Alaoui Order (Morocco). *Leisure interests:* sailing, reading, tennis, skiing. *Address:* Exclusive Resorts, 1515 Arapahoe Street, Tower 3, Suite 300, Denver, CO 80202, USA (office). *Telephone:* (866) 863-2688 (office). *Website:* www.exclusiveresorts.com (office).

BOURHANE, Ali; Comoran international civil servant; *Senior Adviser, African Development Bank;* b. 2 April 1946; m. Neila Bourhane; one s. one d.; ed Univ. of Bordeaux, Ecole Nationale d'Administration, Paris and Univ. of Toulouse; Research Fellow, Univ. of Toulouse 1971; Prof. of Math., Comoros 1972–75; civil servant 1980–85; Sr Economist, IMF, Washington, DC 1985–90; Alt. Exec. Dir IBRD 1990–94, Exec. Dir 1994–99; currently Sr Adviser African Devt Bank, Tunis. *Leisure interests:* reading (religion, African history and anthropology, Devt Econs), tennis, running. *Address:* African Development Bank, Angle des Trois Rues: Avenue du Ghana, Rue Pierre de Coubertin, Rue Hedi Nouira, POB 323, 1002 Tunis (office); Apartment A41, Venus, Rue Hedi Novira, Ennassa 2, 2037 Tunis, Tunisia (home). *Telephone:* (71) 102-686 (office); (71) 816-152 (home). *E-mail:* a.bourhane@afdb.org (office); alboucom@hotmail.com (home).

BOURHANE, Nourdine; Comoran politician; *Vice-President, with responsibility for Land Settlement, Infrastructure, Town Planning and Housing;* b. 1958; Prime Minister of Comoros 1997–98; Vice-Pres., with responsibility for Land Settlement, Town Planning and Housing 2011–. *Address:* Ministry of Land Settlement, Town Planning and Housing, BP 12, Moroni, Comoros (office). *Telephone:* 7744500 (office). *Fax:* 7732222 (office).

BOURJINI, Salah Amara, MA (Econs), PhD; Tunisian UN official; b. 17 Jan. 1938, Lekef; m. 1967; one s. two d.; engineer in planning and statistics, Tunis 1963–67; Lecturer in Econs, Univ. of Kansas, USA 1969–72; Prof., Univ. of Tunis 1972–80; Adviser to Minister of Economy 1972–76; Deputy Dir-Gen. Ministry of Foreign Affairs 1976–80; Deputy UN Resident Rep. and UN Co-ordinator, Algeria 1980–82; Chief, Div. for Regional Programme, Arab States, UNDP, New York 1982–87, UN Resident Rep. and UN Co-ordinator, Iraq 1987–92, UN Resident Rep. and UN Co-ordinator, Libya 1992; Chevalier de la République; various UN service awards. *Publications:* Human Capital Investment and Economic Growth 1974, New International Economic Order 1978; articles on devt, educ. and trade. *Leisure interests:* tennis, swimming, music.

BOURNE, Larry Stuart, BA, MA, PhD, FRSC, MCIP, RPP; Canadian geographer and academic; *Professor Emeritus of Geography and Planning, University of Toronto;* b. 24 Dec. 1939, London, Ont.; s. of Stuart H. Bourne and Florence Bourne; m. Paula T. O'Neill 1967; one s. one d.; ed Univs of Western Ontario, Alberta and Chicago; Asst Prof. of Geography, Univ. of Toronto 1967–69, Assoc. Prof. and Assoc. Dir, Centre for Urban and Community Studies (CUCS) 1969–82, Prof. and Dir 1973–78, 1979–84, Prof. of Geography and Planning, Co-ordinator of Grad. Studies 1985–89, 1991–94, Dir Grad. Planning Program 1996–98, 1999–2002, 2004–06, Prof. Emer. 2006–; Research Assoc., Centre for Urban and Community Studies and Global Cities Program; Visiting Scholar, Univ. of Monash, Australia and LSE, UK 1972–73, Centre for Environmental Studies, London, UK 1978–79; Visiting Prof., Univ. of Alberta, Univ. of Texas, USA 1984, Marburg (FRG) 1985, Melbourne 1988, Meiji Univ. Tokyo 1991, Univ. of Tokyo 1996, Ben Gurion Univ. 1998, Seoul Nat. Univ. 1999; Chair. Comm. on Urban Systems and Devt, Int. Geographical Union 1988–92; consultant to local, nat. and int. agencies; Pres. Canadian Asscn of Geographers 1993–94, North American Regional Science Council 1994–95; Hon. DES (Waterloo) 1999; Hon. DLitt (New Brunswick) 2008; Award for Scholarly Distinction, Canadian Asscn of Geographers 1985, Honors Award, Asscn of American Geographers 1985, Elected to Royal Soc. of Canada 1986, Award for Service to Geography (Ont. Div. Canadian Asscn of Geographers)

1990, Teaching Award, Univ. of Toronto 1999, Massey Medal, Royal Canadian Geographical Society, 2004, Laureat d'honneur, Int. Geographical Union 2012. *Publications:* 19 books, including Urban Systems: Strategies for Regulation 1975, The Geography of Housing 1981, Internal Structure of the City 1982, Urbanization and Settlement Systems 1984, Urban Systems in Transition 1986, The Changing Geography of Urban Systems 1989, Urbanization and Urban Growth 1991, Changing Social Geography of Canadian Cities 1993, People and Places 2000, Canadian Urban Regions 2011; over 250 articles in journals and professional reports. *Address:* Department of Geography, University of Toronto, 100 St George Street, Toronto, ON M5S 3G3 (office); 26 Anderson Avenue, Toronto, ON M5P 1H4, Canada (home). *Telephone:* (416) 978-1593 (office); (416) 486-7819 (home). *Fax:* (416) 946-3886 (office); (416) 978-6729 (home). *E-mail:* bourne@geog.utoronto.ca (office); larry.bourne@utoronto.ca (home). *Website:* www.geog.utoronto.ca/people/faculty/bourne/outline-lb (office).

BOURNE, Matthew Christopher, OBE, BA; British dancer and choreographer; b. 13 Jan. 1960, London; s. of Harold Jeffrey (Jim) Bourne and June Lillian Bourne (née Handley); ed Laban Centre for Movt and Dance; Founder and Artistic Dir Adventures in Motion Pictures 1987–2002; Co-founder (with Robert Noble and) Artistic Dir New Adventures 2002–, Resident Artist, Sadler's Wells Theatre 2005–, Resident Co., Sadlers Wells Theatre 2006–; Hon. Fellow, Laban Centre 1997, Companion, Trinity Laban Conservatoire of Music and Dance 2011, Companion, Liverpool Inst. of Performing Arts 2012; Dr hc (Open Univ.) 2007, (De Montford Univ.) 2007, (Univ. of Plymouth) 2010, (Kingston Univ.) 2010, (Roehampton Univ.) 2011; Tony Award 1999, Astaire Award 1999 (for Swan Lake), Hamburg Shakespeare Prize for the Arts 2003, Theatre Mans Asscn Special Award 2007, British Inspiration Award (for Arts) 2010, Dance Film Asscn Dance in Focus Award 2013. *Dance:* Overlap Lovers 1987, Town and Country 1991, Nutcracker 1992, 2002, Highland Fling 1994, Swan Lake 1995, Cinderella 1997, The Car Man 2000–01 (also televised Channel 4), My Fair Lady (Olivier Award for Best Theatre Choreographer 2002) 2001, South Pacific 2002, Play Without Words (Olivier Awards for Best Entertainment and Best Theatre Choreographer 2003) 2002, Mary Poppins (with Stephen Mear) (Olivier Award for Best Theatre Choreographer 2005) 2004, Edward Scissorhands 2006, Dorian Gray 2008. *Publication:* Matthew Bourne and his Adventures in Motion Pictures 1999. *Leisure interests:* theatre, cinema, music. *Website:* www.new-adventures.net.

BOURNE, Stephen, MA, FCA, FRSA; British publisher; *President, Cambridge University Press;* b. 20 March 1952, Kampala, Uganda; s. of Colyn M. Bourne and Kathleen Bourne; m. Stephanie Ann Bickford 1978; one s. one d.; ed Berkhamsted School, Univ. of Edinburgh; with Deloitte Haskins and Sells, London and Hong Kong 1974–80; with Exxon Chemical Asia-Pacific, Hong Kong 1980–86; Financial Dir Asia, Dow Jones Telerate, London and Hong Kong 1986–89, Gen. Man. Northern Europe 1989–94; Man. Dir, Financial Printing Div., St Ives PLC, London 1994–96; Devt Dir, Cambridge Univ. Press 1997–2000, Chair. of Printing Div. 2000–, CEO 2002–12, Pres. 2012–; Pres. Cambridge Connections International, Britten Sinfonia, The Theatre Royal, Bury St Edmunds; Bd mem. The Wine Soc.; mem. Publishing Studies Advisory Bd, Univ. Coll. London, City Univ., London Coll. of Communication; Fellow, Clare Hall, Cambridge, Inst. of Printing; Liveryman, The Stationers' Co.; Prince of Wales' Amb. for East of England, Business in the Community 2009, China Special Book Award 2011. *Leisure interests:* fine wines, performing arts, cricket, skiing, Real Tennis. *Address:* Cambridge University Press, UPH, Shaftesbury Road, Cambridge, CB2 8BS (office); Falmouth Lodge, Snailwell Road, Newmarket, CB8 7DN, England (home). *Telephone:* (1223) 325184 (office). *E-mail:* sbourne@cambridge.org (office). *Website:* www.cambridge.org (office).

BOURRIAUD, Nicolas; French curator and art critic; *Director, École Nationale Supérieure des Beaux-Arts;* b. 1965; Paris Corresp., Flash Art (magazine) 1987–1995; Co-founder, Documents sur l'art 1992–2000, Perpendiculaire 1995–98; Founding Dir Palais de Tokyo, Paris 1999–2005; Adviser to Ukrainian collector Victor Pinchuk 2006; Gulbenkian Curator of Contemporary Art, Tate Britain, London 2008–10; Dir École Nationale Supérieure des Beaux-Arts, Paris 2011–. *Publications:* Postproduction 2000, Relational Aesthetics 2002, Altermodern 2009, The Radicant 2009. *Address:* Ecole nationale supérieure des Beaux-arts, 14, rue Bonaparte, 75006 Paris, France (office). *Telephone:* 1-47-03-50-00 (office). *Website:* www.beauxartsparis.com (office).

BOURSEILLER, Antoine; French theatre director and producer; b. 8 July 1930, Paris; s. of Marcel Edouard Bourseiller and Denise Fisteberg; m. Chantal Darget 1966 (deceased); one s. one d.; Dir of Theatre, Studio des Champs-Elysées 1960–63, Poche 1964–66, Centre Dramatique National de Marseille 1966–75, Recamier 1975–78, Orléans 1980–82; Dir-Gen. Opéra-Théâtre de Nancy et de Lorraine 1982–96; Artistic Adviser, Théâtre de Tarascon 2003–05; Officier, Légion d'honneur; Commdr des Arts et des Lettres. *Operas directed:* La Clémence de Titus (Aix-en-Provence Festival) 1973, Le Barbier de Seville (Théâtre Lyrique du Sud) 1979, Mireille (Geneva) 1981, (London) 1983, Carmen (Nancy) 1981, Woyzeck (Angers) 1982; Boulevard Solitude 1984, Cantate d'Octobre, Erwartung 1986, Donna Abbandonata 1987, King Priam 1988 (all at Nancy); Lulu (Nantes), Lady Macbeth de Mtsensk (Nancy) 1989; La Noche Triste 1989, Lohengrin L'Homme de Mancha (Brussels-Liège) 1994, 1998, Voyage à Reims (Liège) 2000. *Films:* Cleo de 5 à 7, 2 places pour le 26, Masculin Feminin, La Guerre est finie. *Plays directed:* Va donc chez Torpe 1961, Axel 1963, L'Amérique 1964, Metro Fantôme 1965, Striptease 1965, Silence, l'arbre... 1967, Les Brigands 1972, Jean Harlow 1972, Leuco 1974, Kennedy's Children 1975, La Tour 1976, S.T. 1979, The Idiot 2005, Le Bagne 2006, Hamlet/Lorenzo 2006, Lorenzaccio 2007, parution chez Actes Sud. Artes du livre Sans Relâche 2008, Figures de l'enrol amoureux l'Ane d'Or, Festival Avignon 2009, Corrida, theatre du Rond-Point du Champs-Elysees 2009, Notre-Dame des Fleurs 2010. *Publications:* Sans relâche 2008. *Address:* 9 rue Stanislas, 75006 Paris, France (home). *Telephone:* 6-14-32-22-88 (mobile) (office); 1-46-33-05-27 (home).

BOUSNINA, Mongi; Tunisian academic, diplomatist and international organization executive; b. Tunis; ed Univ. of Paris (Sorbonne); fmr Minister of Culture; fmr Amb. to Morocco, to France; apptd Prof., Univ. of Tunis 1970, Prof. Lecturer 1981; Dir-Gen. Arab League Educational, Cultural and Scientific Org. (ALECSO) 2001–09; Gen. Co-ordinator for the Arab Participation Programme at the

Frankfurt Book Fair 2004; Medal of the Republic, Seventh of November Medal, Alaoui Medal (Morocco), Higher Oscar Medal of Culture (Egypt).

BOUSQUET, Jean; French couturier and fmr politician; *CEO, Cacharel;* b. 29 March 1932, Nîmes; s. of Célestin Bousquet and Rosa Pyronnet; m. Dominique Sarrut 1965; one s. one d.; ed Ecole Tech. de Nîmes; dress cutter, Jean Jourdan, Paris 1955–57; Founder and CEO Soc. Jean Cacharel 1964–, of subsidiaries abroad 1972–; Mayor of Nîmes 1983–95; Deputy (UDF) for Gard, Assemblée Nat. 1986–97; mem. Radical Party 1993–96; Acad. Award for export achievement 1969, Man of the Year, Jeune Chambre économique française 1985. *Leisure interests:* travel, football, golf, skiing. *Address:* Cacharel, 36 rue Tronchet, 75009 Paris, France (office). *Telephone:* 1-42-68-38-88 (office). *Fax:* 1-42-68-38-77 (office). *Website:* cacharel.com (office).

BOUSQUET, Rufus; Saint Lucia politician; Man. Dir Luxury Vacation Homes 1997–2006; mem. House of Ass. (Parl.) for Choiseul 2006–11; Minister for External Affairs, Int. Financial Services, Information and Broadcasting 2006–07, for Industry, Trade, Commerce, Investment and Consumer Affairs 2008–09, for External Affairs, Int. Trade and Investment 2009; mem. United Workers Party (UWP), fmr Deputy Leader and Chair. Public Relations Cttee.

BOUTEFLIKA, Abdul Aziz; Algerian head of state; *President and Minister of National Defence;* b. 2 March 1937, Oujda; ed Morocco; Maj., Nat. Liberation Army and Sec. of Gen. Staff; mem. Parl. for Tlemcen 1962; Minister of Youth, Sports and Tourism 1962–63, of Foreign Affairs 1963–79; Counsellor to the Pres. March 1979–80; Pres. of Algeria and Minister of Nat. Defence 1999–; mem. FLN Political Bureau 1964–81, mem. Cen. Cttee 1989; mem. Revolutionary Council 1965–79; led negotiations with France 1963, 1966, for nationalization of hydrocarbons 1971; leader of dels to many confs of Arab League, OAU 1968, Group of 1977 1967, Non-aligned Countries 1973, Pres. Seventh Special Session of UN Gen. Ass. 1975, Int. Conf. on Econ. Co-operation, Paris 1975–76; Pres. 29th UN Gen. Ass. 1974; mem. Nat. Council Moujahidin (Nat. Liberation Army) 1990–. *Address:* Office of the President, el-Mouradia, Algiers (office); 138 Chemin Bachir Brahimi, El Biar, Algiers, Algeria. *Telephone:* (21) 69-15-15 (office); (21) 60-34-59 (home). *Fax:* (21) 69-15-95 (office). *Website:* www.el-mouradia.dz (office).

BOUTERSE, Col Désiré (Desi) Delano; Suriname politician and head of state; *President;* b. 13 Oct. 1945, Paramaribo; led mil. coup 1980, Chair. Nat. Mil. Council (de facto Leader) 1980–88 (resgnd); Pres. 1982; led mil. coup 1990, Chief of Army 1990–92 (resgnd); Pres. Nationale Democratische Partij 1992–99, 2006–; political adviser to Pres. 1996–99; convicted of drug trafficking in absentia, Netherlands 1999; mem. Parl. 2005–; unsuccessful cand. in presidential election 2005; Pres. of Suriname 2010–. *Address:* Office of the President, Kleine Combéweg 2–4, Centrum, Paramaribo, Suriname (office). *Telephone:* 472841 (office). *Fax:* 475266 (office). *E-mail:* kabpressur@sr.net (office). *Website:* www.kabinet.sr.org (office).

BOUTON, Daniel; French business executive; b. 10 April 1950, Paris; ed Ecole nat. d'Admin; Insp. of Finance, Ministry of Finance 1973–76, Budget Dept, Ministry of Finance 1977–86, Chief of Staff to Alain Juppé, Deputy Minister in charge of the Budget 1986–88; Exec. Vice-Pres. Société Générale 1991, CEO 1993–2008, Chair. 1997–2009 (resgnd); Founder and Pres. DMJB Conseil (consultancy) 2009; mem. Bd of Dirs Total SA 1997–, Veolia 2003–; Sr Adviser, Rothschild & Cie Banque, CVC Capital Partners; Chevalier, Légion d'honneur, Ordre nat. du Mérite. *Address:* DMJB Conseil, 26 rue d'Artois, 75008 Paris, France (office).

BOUTROS, Fouad; Lebanese politician and lawyer; b. Nov. 1917, Beirut; m. Tania Shehade 1953; one s. two d.; ed Coll. des Frères, Beirut, St Joseph Univ. Law School; clerk, Mixed Appeal Court, Beirut 1939; Judge, Civil Court of Mount Lebanon 1942; Judge, Mixed Civil and Commercial Tribunal of Beirut 1944–46; Head, State Legal Dept 1946–47; Examining Magistrate, Mil. Court 1944–47; attorney at law 1947–; Minister of Educ. and Planning 1959–60; mem. Chamber of Deputies 1960–68; Deputy Speaker (Vice-Pres.), Chamber of Deputies 1960–61; Minister of Justice 1961–64; Vice-Pres. Council of Ministers, Minister of Educ. and Defence April–Dec. 1966; Vice-Pres. Council of Ministers, Minister of Foreign Affairs and Tourism Feb.–Oct. 1968; Vice-Pres. Council of Ministers, Minister of Foreign Affairs 1976–82, and of Defence 1976–78; numerous decorations, including Grand Cross, Order of Gregory the Great 1997, Grand Officier, Ordre Nat. du Cèdre 2011. *Publications:* Ecrits politiques 1997, Memories of Fouad Boutros 2009; numerous lectures and political articles in the press, in Arabic and French. *Leisure interests:* reading, walking. *Address:* Hazmieh, Gardenia Street, Ghaleb Center, PO Box 45-224, Beirut (office); Sursock Street, Fouad Boutros Building, Beirut, Lebanon (home). *Telephone:* (5) 459411 (office); (1) 201500 (home). *Fax:* (5) 457992 (office); (5) 458933 (office); (1) 217216 (home). *E-mail:* raniahabre@hotmail.com (office); tboutros@dm.net.lb (home).

BOUTROS GHALI, Boutros, LLB, PhD; Egyptian politician and international civil servant; *President, Curatorium Administrative Council, Hague Academy of International Law;* b. 14 Nov. 1922, Cairo; m. Leia Nadler; ed Cairo Univ. and Univ. of Paris, France; fmr Prof. of Int. Law and Int. Relations and Head Dept of Political Sciences, Cairo Univ. 1949–77; fmr mem. Cen. Cttee Arab Socialist Union; Pres. Cen. of Political and Strategic Studies; f. Al Ahram Al Iktisadi, Ed. 1960–75, f. Al-Siyassa Ad-Dawlya; Minister of State for Foreign Affairs 1977–91, Deputy Prime Minister for Foreign Affairs 1991–92; Sec.-Gen. of UN 1992–96; Sec.-Gen. Org. Int. de la Francophonie 1997–2002; Chair. South Centre 2003–06; Pres. Egyptian Nat. Council of Human Rights, Cairo 2003–12; Vice-Pres. Egyptian Soc. of Int. Law 1965; Pres. Curatorium Administrative Council, Hague Acad. of Int. Law; mem. Cttee on Application of Conventions and Recommendations of Int. Labour Org. 1971–79; Pres. Centre of Political and Strategic Studies (Al-Ahram) 1975–; mem. Int. Comm. of Jurists, Geneva and Council and Exec. Cttee of Int. Inst. of Human Rights, Strasbourg; mem. UN Comm. of Int. Law 1979–92, Secretariat Nat. Democratic Party 1980–92, Parl. 1987–92; Onassis Foundation Prize 1995, recipient of honorary titles and awards from 24 countries. *Publications include:* Contribution à l'étude des ententes régionales 1949, Cours de politique et de droit diplomatique et consulaire 1951, Le principe d'égalité des états et les organisations internationales 1961, Foreign Policies in World Change 1963, L'Organisation de l'unité africaine 1969, La ligue des états arabes 1972, Les Conflits des frontières en Afrique 1973; also numerous books in Arabic and contribs to periodicals. *Leisure interests:* the works of Matisse, collecting old pens from the Ottoman Empire. *Address:* Hague Academy of International Law, Peace Palace, Carnegieplein 2, 2517 KJ The Hague, Netherlands (office); 2 avenue Epnipgiza, Cairo, Egypt (home). *Website:* www.hagueacademy.nl/?curatorium-and -administration-of-the-academy (office).

BOUTROS-GHALI, Yousuf, BA, PhD; Egyptian economist and politician; ed Cairo Univ., Massachusetts Inst. of Tech., USA; Sr Economist, IMF 1981–86; Econ. Adviser to Prime Minister and Gov. of Cen. Bank of Egypt 1986–93; Minister of State for Int. Cooperation 1993–95, Minister of State at Council of Ministers 1993–95; Minister of State for Econ. Affairs 1996–97, Minister of Economy 1997–99, Minister of Economy and Foreign Trade 1999–2001, of Foreign Trade 2001–2004, of Finance 2004–11; Chair. International Monetary and Financial Committee, IMF 2008–11; fmr Lecturer of Econs, American Univ. in Cairo and MIT, Assoc. Prof. of Econs, Cairo Univ.; fmr Dir Centre for Econ. Analysis, Council of Ministers; mem. Bd of Dirs Nat. Bank of Egypt 1991–93. *Publications:* 22 papers and books on devt and theoretical issues in field of econs. *Address:* c/o Ministry of Finance, Ministry of Finance Towers Cairo (Nasr City), Egypt.

BOUVET, Jean-Christophe; French actor, director and screenwriter; b. 24 March 1947, Paris. *Film appearances include:* La philosophie dans le boudoir 1969, Change pas de main 1975, Le pendule 1976, Les pornocrates 1976, Le théâtre des matières 1977, Le borgne 1980, C'est la vie 1981, Loin de Manhattan 1982, L'archipel des amours 1983, En haut des marches 1983, Sous le soleil de Satan 1987, Les dents de ma mère 1991, J'embarassa pas 1991, Krapatchouk 1992, Bouvet son texte 1992, Les nuits fauves 1992, Terre sainte 1994, Dadou 1994, La cité de la peur 1994, L'eau froide 1994, J'aime beaucoup ce que vous faites 1995, Dialogue au sommet 1996, Des progrès en amour 1996, Le complexe de Toulon 1996, Le rocher d'Acapulco 1996, L'@mour est à réinventer 1996, Vicious Circles 1997, Un arrangement 1997, Le passager 1997, Le Plaisir (et ses petits tracas) 1998, Pain au chocolat 1998, Le comte de Monte Cristo 1998, L'examen de minuit 1998, Out! 1999, Le domaine 1999, Glória 1999, Les passagers 1999, Recto/Verso 1999, Lovers 1999, Une rue dans sa longueur 2000, Taxi 2 2000, Cosmocrator 2000, Lise et André 2000, La chambre obscure 2000, Effraction 2001, Le chien, le chat et le cibachrome 2001, La boîte 2001, Being Light 2001, Jojo la frite 2002, Le nouveau Jean-Claude 2002, La sirène rouge 2002, Le cou de Clarisse 2003, Taxi 3 2003, Saltimbank 2003, En famille 2003, Notre musique 2004, Mensonges et trahisons 2004, Prisonnier 2004, Comme un frère 2005, Journal IV 2005, Il sera une fois 2005, La comédie du pouvoir 2005, Marie-Antoinette 2006, Les brigades du tigre 2006, La France 2007, Des Indes à la planète Mars 2008, The Wolberg Family 2009, Black Venus 2010, Let My People Go! 2011, Chaos 2012, Gare du Nord 2013, Hasta mañana 2013. *Films directed and written include:* Le troisiéme wagon 1981, En veux-tu, en voilà (TV) 1982, Peinture à l'eau (TV) 1983, En voilà 2 (TV) 1983, Et de trois (TV) 1988, Les dents de ma mère 1991, Bouvet et son texte 1992. *Address:* Agence Artistique Terenga, 32, rue Yves Toudic, Paris 75010, France (office). *Telephone:* 1-53-36-72-91 (office). *Fax:* 1-53-36-71-85 (office). *E-mail:* terenga@noos .fr (office). *Website:* www.terenga.com (office).

BOUYGUES, Martin; French business executive; *Chairman and CEO, Bouygues SA;* b. 3 May 1952; s. of Francis Bouygues; three c.; ed Univ. of Paris Dauphine; joined Bouygues Group 1974, site supervisor for Les Halles shopping complex, Paris 1974–78, f. Maison Bouygues 1978, Chair. and CEO Saur 1986, mem. Bd of Dirs Bouygues SA 1982–, Vice-Chair. 1987–89, Chair. and CEO 1989–; Chair. SCDM; mem. Bd of Dirs TF1, Sodeci, CIE; mem. Supervisory Bd Paris-Orléans; Chevalier, Légion d'honneur, Ordre nat. du Mérite. *Leisure interests:* hunting, boating. *Address:* Bouygues Headquarters, 32 avenue Hoche, 75378 Paris Cedex 08, France (office). *Telephone:* 1-44-20-10-00 (office). *Fax:* 1-44-20-14-99 (office). *E-mail:* presse@bouygues.com (office). *Website:* www.bouygues.com (office).

BOVENDER, Jack O., Jr, BSc; American healthcare industry executive (retd); ed Duke Univ.; served in Navy Service Medical Corps, attained rank of Lt; fmr Asst Admin., Community Gen. Hosp., Thomasville, NC; joined HCA (Hospital Corpn of America) Inc., CEO Medical Center Hosp., Largo, Fla and West Fla Regional Medical Center, Pensacola, later several man. positions 1985–92, including Vice-Pres. HCA Atlanta Div., Pres. HCA Eastern Group Operations, Exec. Vice-Pres. and COO HCA 1992–94, 1997–2001, Pres. and CEO 2001–02, Chair. and CEO 2002–09 (retd); mem. Bd of Dirs Bank of America 2012–; Founding mem. Nashville Health Care Council; fmr Dir Nashville Community Foundation, Frist Foundation, Tennessee Performing Arts Center, Center for Non-Profit Man.; mem. Duke Univ. Health System Bd; mem. Bd of Visitors, Duke Univ. Fuqua School of Business, Bd of Trustees, Duke Univ. 2007–; Hon. mem. Bd of Visitors, Duke Univ. Divinity School; Best CEO in America for healthcare facilities, Institutional Investor magazine 2003, 2004, 2005, Gold Medal Award, American Coll. of Healthcare Execs 2007, Distinguished Alumni Award, Duke Univ. 2012. *Address:* c/o Secretary, Duke University, PO Box 90030, Durham, NC 27708, USA.

BOWAO, Charles Zacharie, Dr.Sci.Hum.; Republic of Congo professor of philosophy and politician; ed Université Cheikh Anta Diop, Dakar, Senegal; Prof., Dept of Philosophy, Université Marien Ngouabi, Brazzaville, also Dir of Philosophical Training; Official, Comm. nat. d'organisation des élections 2002; Minister at the Presidency in charge of Co-operation, Humanitarian Action and Solidarity –2009, Minister at the Presidency responsible for Nat. Defence 2009–12; mem. Parti congolais du travail (PCT), mem. Cen. Cttee; Dir Editorial Bd, Géopolitique Africaine (journal). *Publications:* Autour de la méthode (de Descartes à Feyerabend) 1997, Gaston Berger: Introduction à une philosophie de l'avenir 1997, Bonne gouvernance et développement 1997, La mondialité: entre histoire et avenir 2004, Pour la refondation du PCT: La refondation politique à l'aune de la nouvelle espérance 2006. *Address:* c/o Ministry of Defence, Brazzaville, Republic of Congo (office).

BOWE, Riddick Lamont; American professional boxer; b. 1967, Brooklyn, New York; s. of Dorothy Bowe; m. 1st Judy Bowe 1986 (divorced); one s. two d.; 2nd Terri Bowe; amateur boxer 1982–89, professional boxer 1989–, won World Boxing Asscn, World Boxing Confed., Int. Boxing Fed. titles 1992, World Boxing Asscn, Int. Boxing Fed. titles 1993, World Boxing Org. title 1995, defeating two challengers in that year to retain title; Silver Medal Super Heavyweight Div., Olympic Games, Seoul, 1988; ranked Undisputed Heavyweight Champion 1992–93, 1995; retd from boxing 1996; briefly with US Marine Corps; pleaded guilty to fed. charge of abduction June 1998, served 18 months, released 2004; announced resumption of

boxing career 2004; 43 wins and one loss, with one no-contest, and 33 knockouts. *E-mail:* joemelendez@msn.com.

BOWEN, Gregory, BEng, MEng; Grenadian politician; *Minister of Communications and Works, Physical Development, Public Utilities and Information Communications Technology;* m.; five c.; ed Presentation Brothers Coll., Univ. of the West Indies, Univ. of Saskatchewan, Canada; several diplomas and certificates in Financial Man., Eng Man. and Business; taught at Presentation Brothers Coll. and Anglican High School; Lecturer, Inst. for Further Educ. 1980–81; Planning and Devt Engineer, Grenada Electricity Services Ltd 1983, later Man.; Senator and Minister for Communications, Works, Public Utilities, Energy and Transport 1995–2003; mem. Parl. for St George South East 1999–; apptd Deputy Prime Minister and Minister of Agric., Lands, Forestry and Fisheries, Public Utilities, Energy and The Marketing and Nat. Importing Bd 2003; Minister of Communications and Works, Physical Devt, Public Utilities and Information Communications Tech. 2013–; mem. ASME, Inst. of Diesel and Gas Turbine Engineers, Grenada Inst. of Professional Engineers, American Soc. of Agricultural Engineers. *Leisure interest:* guitar playing. *Address:* Ministry of Works, Physical Development and Public Utilities, Ministerial Complex, 4th Floor, Botanical Gardens, Tanteen, St George's, Grenada (office). *Telephone:* 440-2271 (office). *Fax:* 440-4122 (office). *E-mail:* ministryofworks@gov.gd (office).

BOWEN, Most Rev. Michael George, STL, PhL; British ecclesiastic; *Archbishop Emeritus of Southwark;* b. 23 April 1930, Gibraltar; s. of Maj. C. L. J. Bowen and Mary J. Pedley; ed Downside Abbey School, Trinity Coll., Cambridge and Gregorian Univ., Rome; army service 1948–49; in the wine trade 1951–52; Venerable English Coll., Rome 1952–59; ordained RC priest 1958; curate, Earlsfield and Walworth, Diocese of Southwark 1959–63; teacher of Theology, Pontifical Beda Coll., Rome 1963–66; Chancellor, Diocese of Arundel and Brighton 1966–70, Coadjutor Bishop 1970–71, Bishop of Arundel and Brighton 1971–77; Archbishop and Metropolitan, Diocese of Southwark 1977–2003, Archbishop Emer. 2003–; Vice-Pres. Catholic Bishops' Conf. England and Wales 1996–99; Pres. 1999–2000; Freeman City of London 1984. *Leisure interests:* golf, tennis. *Address:* c/o Archbishop's House, 150 St George's Road, London, SE1 6HX, England. *Telephone:* (20) 7928-2495. *Fax:* (20) 7928-7833.

BOWEN, Ray M., PhD; American engineer, academic and fmr university administrator; *Professor Emeritus, Department of Mechanical Engineering and President Emeritus, Texas A&M University;* b. 30 March 1936, Fort Worth, Tex.; s. of Winfred Herbert Bowen and Elizabeth Williams Bowen; m. Sara Elizabeth Gibbons Bowen 1958; one s. one d.; ed Texas A&M Univ., California Inst. Tech.; Assoc. Prof. of Mechanical Eng, Louisiana State Univ. 1965–67; Prof. of Mechanical Eng, Rice Univ. 1967–83, Chair. Dept of Mechanical Eng 1972–77; Div. Dir, NSF 1982–83, Acting Asst Dir Eng to Deputy Asst Dir 1990–91; Prof. and Dean of Eng, Univ. of Kentucky 1983–89; Vice-Pres. for Academic Affairs, Oklahoma State Univ. 1991–93, Interim Pres. 1993–94; Pres. Texas A&M Univ. 1994–2002, Pres. Emer. 2002–, Prof., Dept of Mechanical Eng and Sara and John H. Lindsey '44 Chair 2002–10, Prof. Emer. 2010–; mem. Nat. Science Bd 2002– (Chair. 2010–12), Soc. of Scholars, Johns Hopkins Univ., Fellow, American Soc. for Eng Educ., American Astronautical Soc. *Publications:* Introduction to Continuum Mechanics for Engineers, Introduction to Vectors and Tensors (co-author), Rational Thermodynamics (contrib.); contrib. of numerous articles to professional journals. *Leisure interests:* travelling, opera. *Telephone:* (979) 845-2217 (office). *E-mail:* rbowen@ tamu.edu (office). *Website:* www.mengr.tamu.edu (office).

BOWEN, Tim; British music industry executive; Head of Business Affairs, Sony Music UK, then Head, Sony Music Publishing Int., New York 1982–86; Man. Dir CBS/Columbia Records UK 1986–91; Sr Vice-Pres. Marketing and Business Affairs, Universal Music Int. 1994–99, Exec. Vice-Pres. 1999–2001; COO BMG Europe 2002–03, Chair. BMG Entertainment, UK and Ireland 2003–04, Chair. Sony BMG UK & Ireland, Canada, Australia, New Zealand, South Africa 2004–06, COO Sony BMG 2006–08; currently Prin., BPM Entertainment, London; *Website:* www.bpm-entertainment.co.uk.

BOWEN, William Gordon, BS, PhD; American academic; *President Emeritus, Princeton University;* b. 6 Oct. 1933, Cincinnati, Ohio; s. of Albert A. Bowen and Bernice Pomert; m. Mary Ellen Maxwell 1956; one s. one d.; ed Denison and Princeton Univs; Asst Prof. of Econs, Princeton Univ. 1958–61, Assoc. Prof. 1961–65, Prof. 1965–87, Dir of Grad. Studies, Woodrow Wilson School of Public and Int. Affairs 1964–66, Provost Princeton Univ. 1967–72, Pres. 1972–88, Pres. Emer. 1988–; Lecturer, Univ. of Oxford, UK 2000; Regent Smithsonian Inst. 1980, now Regent Emer.; Pres. Andrew W. Mellon Foundation, New York 1988–2006; Co-Chair. Research Alliance for New York City Public Schools 2009–12; Dir NCR Corpn 1975–91; mem. Bd of Overseers, Teachers Insurance and Annuity Asscn and College Retirement Equities Fund 1995–2010; Trustee, Denison Univ. 1966–75, 1992–2000, Center for Advanced Study in the Behavioral Sciences 1973–84, 1986–92, Reader's Digest 1985–97, American Express 1988–2006, ISTOR 1995–, Merck and Co. 1986–2009, Ithaka Harbors, Inc.; Woodrow Wilson Fellow, Ford Foundation Fellow, Social Science Research Council Faculty Research Fellow, Ford Foundation Faculty Research Fellow, James Madison Medal, Princeton Univ., Joseph Henry Medal, Smithsonian Inst., Grawemeyer Award in Educ., Rolex Achievement Award, Asscn for the Study of Higher Educ., Phyllis Franklin Award, Modern Language Asscn, Teachers' Coll. Distinguished Service Award, Pierre Boudreau Leadership Award, José Vasconcelos World Award of Educ., Clark Kerr Award for Distinguished Leadership in Higher Educ., Nat. Humanities Medal 2012. *Publications:* The Wage-Price Issue: A Theoretical Analysis 1960, Performing Arts: The Economic Dilemma (with W. J. Baumol) 1966, The Economics of Labor Force Participation (with T. A. Finegan) 1969, Ever the Teacher 1987, Prospects for Faculty in the Arts and Sciences (with J. A. Sosa) 1989, In Pursuit of the PhD (with Neil L. Rudenstine) 1992, Inside the Boardroom: Governance by Directors and Trustees (with T. Nygren, S. Turner and E. Duffy) 1994, The Charitable Nonprofits 1994, Universities and Their Leaderships (ed. Harold Shapiro) 1998, The Shape of the River: Long-Term Consequences of Considering Race in College and University Admissions (with Derek Bok) 1998, The Game of Life: College Sports and Educational Values 2001, At a Slight Angle to the Universe (also Romanes Lecture, Univ. of Oxford) 2001, Reclaiming the Game: College Sports and Educational Values (with Sarah A. Levin) 2003, Equity and Excellence in Higher Education 2005, Crossing the Finish Line: Completing

College at America's Public Universities 2009, The Board Book 2009, Lesson Learned 2010. *Address:* c/o Andrew W. Mellon Foundation, 151 East 61st Street, New York, NY 10065, USA (office). *Telephone:* (212) 826-8114 (office).

BOWER, Gordon H., MS, PhD; American psychologist and academic; *Albert Ray Lang Professor Emeritus of Psychology, Stanford University;* b. 30 Dec. 1932, Scio, Ohio; s. of Clyde W. Bower and Mabelle Bosart Bower; m. Sharon Anthony 1957; one s. two d.; ed Western Reserve (now Case Western Reserve) and Yale Univs; Woodrow Wilson Fellowship for Grad. Study, Univ. of Minnesota 1954–55; NIMH Fellowship for Grad. Study, Yale Univ. 1956–59; Asst Prof., Stanford Univ. 1959–63, Assoc. Prof. 1963–65, Prof. 1965–75, Albert Ray Lang Prof. of Psychology 1975–2008, Prof. Emer. 2008–, Chair. Dept of Psychology 1978–82, Assoc. Dean, Stanford Univ. 1983–86; Ed. The Psychology of Learning and Motivation 1964–92; Pres. Western Psychological Asscn 1990–91, 2004–05, American Psychological Soc. 1991–93; mem. NAS, American Acad. of Arts and Sciences, Soc. of Experimental Psychologists (Pres. 1989), American Philosophical Soc.; Distinguished Fellow and Founding Mem., Cognitive Science Soc. 2008; Dr hc (Univ. of Chicago) 1991, (Indiana State Univ.) 1993, (Univ. of Basel, Switzerland) 2003; Distinguished Scientist Contrib. Award, American Psychology Asscn 1979, Warren Medal, Soc. of Experimental Psychologists, Wilbur Cross Medal, Yale Univ. 1986, Presidential Citation for scientific contributions, American Psychological Asscn 2002, Nat. Medal of Science 2005, Lifetime Contributions Award, Western Psychological Asscn 2006, Outstanding Grad. Student Mentoring Award, Western Psychological Asscn 2011. *Publications:* co-author of five books and more than 250 scientific papers. *Leisure interests:* reading, sport. *Address:* Department of Psychology, Jordan Hall, Building 420, Room 314, Stanford University, Stanford, CA 94305, USA (office). *Telephone:* (650) 725-2417 (office). *Fax:* (650) 725-5699 (office). *E-mail:* gbower@stanford.edu (office). *Website:* www-psych.stanford.edu (office).

BOWERING, George Harry, OC, MA; Canadian writer, poet and academic; *Professor Emeritus, Simon Fraser University;* b. 1 Dec. 1936, Penticton, BC; s. of Ewart Bowering and Pearl Bowering (née Brinson); m. 1st Angela Luoma 1962 (died 1999); one d.; m. 2nd Jean Baird 2006; ed Victoria Coll., Univ. of British Columbia, Univ. of Western Ontario; served as Royal Canadian Air Force photographer 1954–57; Lecturer, Univ. of Calgary 1963–66; Writer-in-Residence, Sir George Williams Univ., Montreal 1967–68, Lecturer 1968–71; Prof., Simon Fraser Univ., Burnaby, BC 1972–2001, Prof. Emer. 2001–; First Parl. Poet Laureate 2002–04; Order of BC 2005; Hon. DLit (British Columbia) 1997, (Western Ontario) 2003; Gov.-Gen.'s Award for poetry 1967, for fiction 1980, bpNichol Chapbook Awards for Poetry 1991, 1992, Canadian Authors' Asscn Award for Poetry 1993, Lt-Gov.'s Award for Literary Excellence 2011, Alumni Award of Distinction, Univ. of British Columbia 2011. *Play:* The Home for Heroes 1962. *Radio plays:* George Vancouver (CBC) 1972, Sitting in Mexico (CBC) 1973, Music in the Park (CBC) 1986, The Great Grandchildren of Bill Bissett's Mice (CBC) 1989. *Television play:* What Does Eddie Williams Want? (CBC) 1966. *Publications include:* poetry collections: Sticks & Stones 1963, Points on the Grid 1964, The Man in Yellow Boots/El hombre de las botas amarillas 1965, Rocky Mountain Foot 1969, The Gangs of Kosmos 1969, Touch: Selected Poems 1960–1969 1971, In the Flesh 1974, The Catch 1976, Poem & Other Baseballs 1976, The Concrete Island 1977, Another Mouth 1979, West Window: Selected Poetry 1982, Smoking Mirrow 1982, Seventy-One Poems for People 1985, Delayed Mercy & Other Poems 1986, George Bowering Selected: Poems 1961–1992 1993; chapbooks: How I Hear Howl 1967, Two Police Poems 1969, The Sensible 1972, Layers 1–13 1973, In Answer 1977, Uncle Louis 1980, Spencer & Groulx 1985, Quarters 1991, Do Sink 1992, A, You're Adorable 1998, 6 Little Poems in Alphabetical Order 2000, Joining the Lost Generation 2002; long poems: Sitting in Mexico 1965, George,Vancouver 1970, Geneve 1971, Autobiology 1972, Curious 1973, At War With the US 1974, Allophanes 1976, Kerrisdale Elegies 1984, His Life: A Poem 2000, Baseball: A poem in the magic number 9 2003, Changing on the Fly 2004, Vermeer's Light 2006, Fulgencio 2008, A Little Black Strap 2009, My Darling Nelly Grey 2010; novels: Mirror on the Floor 1967, A Short Sad Book 1977, Burning Water 1980, En eaux troubles 1982, Caprice 1987, Harry's Fragments 1990, Shoot! 1994, Parents from Space 1994, Piccolo Mondo 1998, Diamondback Dog 1998, Pinboy 2012; short story collections: Flycatcher & Other Stories 1974, Concentric Circles 1977, Protective Footwear 1978, A Place to Die 1983, Standing on Richards 2004, The Box 2009; non-fiction: Al Purdy 1970, Three Vancouver Writers 1979, The Mask in Place 1983, Craft Slices 1985, Imaginary Hand 1988, Bowering's B.C. 1996, Egotists and Autocrats – The Prime Ministers of Canada 1999, A Magpie Life (memoir) 2001, Cars (memoir) 2002, Stone Country (history) 2003, Left Hook (criticism) 2005, Baseball Love (memoirs) 2006, Horizontal Surfaces (chapbook) 2010, The Diamond Alphabet 2011, How I Wrote Certain of My Books (essays) 2011, Words, Words, Words (essays) 2012. *Leisure interests:* motor trips to see baseball games in Canada, USA, Mexico, Cuba, Italy, Australia, etc. *Address:* 4403 West 11th Avenue, Vancouver, BC V6R 2M2, Canada. *Telephone:* (604) 224-4898. *E-mail:* bowering@sfu.ca.

BOWERS-BROADBENT, Christopher Joseph, FRAM; British organist and composer; *Organist and Choirmaster of Gray's Inn and Organist of the West London Synagogue;* b. 13 Jan. 1945, Hemel Hempstead, Herts.; s. of Henry W. Bowers-Broadbent and Doris E. Mizen; m. Deirdre Cape 1970; one s. one d.; ed Berkhamsted School, King's Coll. Cambridge and Royal Acad. of Music; Organist and Choirmaster of St Pancras Parish Church 1965–88; Organist of West London Synagogue 1973–; Organist and Choirmaster of Gray's Inn 1983–; debut organ recital, Camden Festival 1966; Prof. of Organ, RAM, London 1976–92; Three Choirs Festival Composers' Competition Prize 1978. *Recordings include:* Trivium, O Domina Nostra, Méditations sur le Mystère de la Sainte Trinité, Mattins Music, Duets and Canons. *Operas include:* The Pied Piper 1972, The Seacock Bane 1979, The Last Man 1983–2000, The Face 2012. *Leisure interests:* sketching, silence. *Address:* 94 Colney Hatch Lane, Muswell Hill, London, N10 1EA, England. *Telephone:* (20) 8883-1933. *Fax:* (20) 8883-8434; (20) 8888-8434. *E-mail:* kitbb@ btinternet.com. *Website:* www.christopherbowers-broadbent.com.

BOWIE, David; British singer and actor; b. (David Robert Jones), 8 Jan. 1947, Brixton, London, England; s. of Hayward Stenton Jones and of the late Margaret Mary Jones (née Burns); m. 1st Angela Barnett 1970 (divorced 1980); one s.; m. 2nd Iman Abdul Majid 1992; one d.; solo singer and songwriter 1966–; numerous tours,

live and TV appearances; film actor 1967–; mem. and lead singer, Tin Machine 1989–91; f. Bowieart.com (online art dealership); Guest Curator of High Line Festival, New York 2007; Silver Clef Award for Outstanding Achievement 1987, Ivor Novello Award for Outstanding Contribution to British Music 1990, BRIT Award for Outstanding Contribution to Music 1996; Commdr, Ordre des Arts et des Lettres. *Films:* The Image 1967, The Virgin Soldiers 1969, Love You Till Tuesday 1969, The Man Who Fell to Earth 1976, Schöner Gigolo, armer Gigolo (trans. as Just a Gigolo) 1979, Christiane F 1980, Cat People 1982, The Hunger 1983, Merry Christmas Mr Lawrence 1983, Yellowbeard 1983, Ziggy Stardust and the Spiders from Mars 1983, Into the Night 1985, Absolute Beginners 1986, Labyrinth 1986, The Last Temptation of Christ 1988, The Linguini Incident 1990, Twin Peaks: Fire Walk with Me 1992, Basquiat 1996, Trainspotting 1996, Il Mio West 1998, Everybody Loves Sunshine 1999, Mr Rice's Secret 2000, The Prestige 2006, Arthur and the Invisibles (voice) 2006, August 2008. *Television:* The Pistol Shot (film) 1968, Baal (film) 1982, The Hunger (series) 1999–2000, Extras (series) 2006, Imagine (series) 2007, SpongeBob SquarePants (series) 2007. *Play:* The Elephant Man (New York) 1980. *Compositions include:* When the Wind Blows (theme) 1986, The Buddha of Suburbia (music, BBC series) 1993. *Recordings include:* albums: solo: David Bowie 1969, The Man Who Sold The World 1971, Hunky Dory 1971, The Rise And Fall Of Ziggy Stardust And The Spiders From Mars 1972, Aladdin Sane 1973, Pin-Ups 1973, Diamond Dogs 1974, David Live 1974, Young Americans 1975, Station To Station 1976, Low 1977, Heroes 1977, Lodger (with Brian Eno) 1979, Scary Monsters and Super Creeps 1980, Let's Dance 1983, Tonight 1984, Never Let Me Down 1987, Black Tie White Noise 1993, Outside 1995, Earthling 1997, Hours 1999, Bowie At The Beeb (radio sessions and concerts) 2000, Heathen 2002, Reality 2003, Club Bowie 2004, The Next Day 2013; single: Where Are We Now? (video and download) 2013; with Tin Machine: Tin Machine 1989, Tin Machine II 1991. *Leisure interests:* boxing, martial arts instruction, listening to Polish and Chinese Communist music. *Address:* Isolar Enterprises, 641 Fifth Avenue, Suite 22Q, New York, NY 10022, USA (office). *Telephone:* (212) 308-9345 (office). *Website:* www.davidbowie.com.

BOWLES, Erskine, BS, MBA; American investment banker, fmr university administrator and fmr government official; *Senior Advisor, Carousel Capital;* b. 1945, Greensboro, NC; s. of Hargrove 'Skipper' Bowles; m. Crandall Bowles 1971; three c.; ed Univ. of North Carolina, Columbia Univ. Grad. School of Business; with Morgan Stanley & Co. New York; Bowles Hollowell Conner & Co. Charlotte, NC 1975–93; Admin., Small Business Admin., Washington, DC 1993–94; Deputy Chief of Staff to Pres., The White House, Washington, DC 1994–97, Chief of Staff 1997–99; Pnr, Forstmann Little & Co., Charlotte 1999–2001; unsuccessful campaigns for US Senate from NC 2002, 2004; Pres. Univ. of NC 2006–10, Pres. Emer. 2010–; Co-founder and Sr Advisor, Carousel Capital 2006–; Co-Chair. (with Alan K. Simpson) Nat. Comm. on Fiscal Responsibility and Reform 2010; Co-founder (with Alan K. Simpson) The Campaign to Fix the Debt; mem. Bd of Dirs Morgan Stanley, Norfolk Southern Corpn, North Carolina Mutual Life Insurance Co., Cousins Properties, Inc., Belk, Inc., Facebook Inc. 2011–; apptd UN Deputy Special Envoy to tsunami affected countries in SE Asia 2005; fmr Pres. Juvenile Diabetes Foundation; fmr Trustee Duke Endowment, Golden LEAF Foundation; fmr Chair. Rural Prosperity Task Force, NC; Co-founder Dogwood Equity 2002; mem. North Carolina Advisory Bd DonorsChoose; eight hon. degrees from US univs. *Address:* Carousel Capital, 201 North Tryon Street, Suite 2450, Charlotte, NC 28202, USA (office). *Telephone:* (704) 372-2040 (office). *Website:* www .carouselcapital.com (office); www.fixthedebt.org.

BOWMAN, Philip; Australian business executive; *Chairman, Miller Group;* b. Melbourne; ed Univ. of Cambridge, UK; served in accountancy positions in venture devt in Iran, Australia and USA; fmr CEO and Chair. Bass Taverns; Dir of Finance and Admin Coles Myer Ltd, Australia 1995–98; Finance Dir Allied Domecq 1998–99, CEO 1999; fmr non-exec. Chair. (non-exec.) Liberty plc; CEO Scottish Power plc 2006–07; CEO Smiths Group plc 2007–12; Chair. Miller Group 2012–; mem. Bd of Dirs Scottish & Newcastle plc, Burberry plc. *Address:* Office of the Chairman, Miller Group, Miller House, 2 Lochside View, Edinburgh Park, Edinburgh EH12 9DH, Scotland (office). *Telephone:* (870) 336-5000 (office). *Website:* www.miller.co.uk (office).

BOWMAN, William Scott (Scotty); Canadian sports executive and fmr professional ice hockey coach; *Senior Advisor, Chicago Blackhawk Hockey Team, Inc.;* b. 18 Sept. 1933, Verdun, PQ; m. Suella Bowman; three s. two d.; early and short career as player then minor league coach in Montréal Canadiens system; began Nat. Hockey League (NHL) coaching career as Coach St Louis Blues 1967–71, then Montréal Canadiens 1971–79, winning Stanley Cups 1973, 1976–79; Coach and Gen. Man. Buffalo Sabres 1979–87; left NHL and worked as analyst for CBCs 'Hockey Night in Canada' TV programme 1987; returned to NHL as Dir of Player Personnel Pittsburgh Penguins 1987–91, then Coach 1991–93, winning Stanley Cup 1992; Coach Detroit Red Wings 1993–2002, winning Stanley Cup 1997, 1998, 2002; records include winning nine Stanley Cups, coaching 1,244 NHL regular-season wins (next highest total is 781), 223 post-season wins; retd at end of 2002 season, consultant, Detroit Red Wings 2002–08; Sr Advisor, Chicago Black Hawks 2008–; NHL Jack Adams Award for Outstanding Coach 1977, 1996, NHL Lester Patrick Award for outstanding service to hockey in the United States 2001; mem. Hockey Hall of Fame 1991, Mich. Sports Hall of Fame 1999, Greater Buffalo Sports Hall of Fame 2000; Canada Walk of Fame 2003. *Address:* Chicago Blackhawk Hockey Team, Inc., 1901 West Madison Street, Chicago, IL 60612, USA (office). *Telephone:* (312) 455-7000 (office). *Fax:* (312) 455-7041 (office). *Website:* www .chicagoblackhawks.com (office).

BOWNESS, Sir Alan, Kt, CBE, MA; British art historian; b. 11 Jan. 1928; s. of George Bowness and Kathleen Bowness (née Benton); m. Sarah Hepworth-Nicholson 1957; one s. one d.; ed Univ. Coll. School, Downing Coll., Cambridge, Courtauld Inst. of Art, Univ. of London; with Friends' Ambulance Unit and Friends' Service Council 1946–50; Regional Art Officer, Arts Council of GB 1955–57; Courtauld Inst. 1957–79, Deputy Dir 1978–79; Reader, Univ. of London 1967–78, Prof. of History of Art 1978–79; Visiting Prof., Humanities Seminar, Johns Hopkins Univ., Baltimore 1969; Dir Tate Gallery 1980–88, Henry Moore Foundation 1988–94 (Trustee 1984–88, 1994–2003); mem. Arts Council 1973–75, 1978–80, Art Panel 1960–80 (Vice-Chair. 1973–75, Chair. 1978–80), Arts Film Cttee 1968–77 (Chair. 1972–75); mem. Fine Arts Cttee, British Council 1960–69,

1970–93 (Chair. 1981–93); mem. Exec. Cttee, Contemporary Art Soc. 1961–69, 1970–86, Cultural Advisory Cttee, UK Nat. Comm. for UNESCO 1973–82; Gov. Chelsea School of Art and London Inst. 1965–88; Hon. Sec. Asscn of Art Historians 1973–76; Dir Barbara Hepworth Museum, St Ives, Cornwall 1976–88; mem. Council Royal Coll. of Art 1978–99; Trustee, Yorkshire Sculpture Park 1979–, Handel House Museum 1994–2001 (Chair. 1997–2001); mem. int. juries for Premio Di Tella, Buenos Aires 1965, São Paulo Bienal 1967, Lehmbruck Prize, Duisburg 1970, Rembrandt Prize 1982, Venice Biennale 1986, Heiliger Prize 1998; Hon. Fellow, Downing Coll., Cambridge 1980, Univ. of the West of England, Bristol 1980, Courtauld Inst. of Art 1985; Chevalier, Ordre des Arts et des Lettres 1973; Hon. DLitt (Liverpool) 1988, (Leeds) 1995, (Exeter) 1996. Publications: William Scott Paintings 1964, Impressionists and Post Impressionists 1965, Henry Moore: Complete Sculpture 1955–64 1965, Modern Sculpture 1965, Barbara Hepworth Drawings 1966, Alan Davie 1967, Recent British Painting 1968, Gauguin 1971, Barbara Hepworth: complete sculpture 1960–69 1971, Modern European Art 1972, Ivon Hitchens 1973, Picasso 1881–1973 (contrib.) 1973, The Genius of British Painting (contrib.) 1975, Henry Moore: Complete Sculpture 1964–73 1977, Henry Moore: Complete Sculpture 1974–80 1983, Henry Moore: Complete Sculpture 1981–86 1988, The Conditions of Success 1989, British Contemporary Art 1910–1990 (contrib.) 1991, Bernard Meadows 1995. Leisure interests: going to concerts, opera, theatre. Address: 91 Castelnau, London, SW13 9EL; 16 Piazza, St Ives, Cornwall, TR26 1NQ, England. Telephone: (20) 8846-8520 (London); (1736) 795444 (St Ives).

BOWYER, (Arthur) William, RA, RP, RWS; British artist; b. 25 May 1926, Leek, Staffs.; s. of Arthur Bowyer and Emma Bowyer; m. Vera Mary Small 1951; two s. one d.; ed Burslem School of Art, Royal Coll. of Art; Head of Fine Art, Maidstone Coll. of Art 1971–82; Hon. Sec. New English Art Club 1968–98; mem. Royal Soc. of Painters in Watercolour. Leisure interests: cricket, snooker. Address: 12 Cleveland Avenue, Chiswick, London, W4 1SN, England. Telephone: (20) 8994-0346. Website: www.bowyerfineart.co.uk.

BOXER, Barbara, BA; American politician; Senator from California; b. 11 Nov. 1940, Brooklyn, NY; d. of Ira Levy and Sophie Levy (née Silvershein); m. Stewart Boxer 1962; one s. one d.; ed Brooklyn Coll.; stockbroker, New York 1962–65; journalist, then Assoc. Ed. Pacific Sun 1972–74; Congressional Aide, Democratic 5th Congressional Dist, San Francisco 1974–76; mem. Marin Co. Bd of Supervisors, San Rafael, Calif. 1976–82, Pres. 1980–81; mem. US House of Reps from 6th Calif. Dist, Washington, DC 1982–93; Senator from California 1993–, mem. Foreign Relations Cttee, Chair. Environment and Public Works Cttee, Chair. Subcttee on Near Eastern and S Asian Affairs, Chief Deputy Whip in Majority 2007–; mem. Bd of Dirs Golden Gate Bridge Highway and Transport Dist, San Francisco 1978–82; Pres. Democratic New Mems Caucus 1983–; f. Senate Mil. Family Caucus 2010; Democrat; numerous awards. Publications: novels: A Time to Run 2005, Blind Trust 2009. Address: 112 Hart Senate Office Building, Washington, DC 20510-0001, USA (office). Telephone: (202) 224-3553 (office). Website: boxer .senate.gov (office).

BOXSHALL, Geoffrey Allan, BSc, PhD, FRS; British/Canadian zoologist; Merit Researcher (Deputy Chief Scientific Officer), Natural History Museum, London; b. 13 June 1950, Oyen, Alberta; s. of John Edward Boxshall and Sybil Irene Baker; m. Roberta Gabriel Smith 1972; one s. three d.; ed Churcher's Coll., Univ. of Leeds; Higher Scientific Officer, British Museum (Natural History) 1974–76, Sr Scientific Officer 1976–80, Prin. Scientific Officer 1980–91, Sr Prin. Scientific Officer 1991–97, Merit Researcher (Deputy Chief Scientific Officer) 1997–; Visiting Prof., Queen Mary Coll., Univ. of London 1996; Vice-Chair. MarBEF (EU-funded Network of Excellence 2004–09; Vice-Pres. World Asscn of Copepodologists 1990–93, Pres. 1999–2002; Pres. The Ray Soc. 2004–07; mem. Exec. Cttee Marine Biological Asscn 2003–07; Mem. of Council, Soc. for Man. of European Biodiversity Data 2004, Sir Alister Hardy Foundation for Ocean Science 2010–13; Mem. of Council, The Linnean Soc. 2010–13, Vice-Pres. 2012–13; Sec., Zoological Soc. of London 2011–; Hon. Prof., Univ. of St Andrews 2006; Hon. Vice-Pres. Marine Biological Asscn of the UK 2007; Scientific Medal of the Zoological Soc. of London 1986, Excellence in Research Award, Crustacean Soc. 1998, Linnean Soc. Medal for Zoology 2004, Homage Award, Brazilian Crustacean Soc. 2004, Monoculus Award, World Asscn of Copepodologists 2008, Plymouth Marine Science Lecturer 2010. Publications include: co-author: Dictionary of Ecology, Evolution and Systematics, Illustrated Dictionary of Natural History, Copepod Evolution, An Introduction to Copepod Diversity. Leisure interests: travel, tennis, lexicography. Address: Department of Life Sciences, Natural History Museum, Cromwell Road, London, SW7 5BD, England (office). Telephone: (20) 7942-5749 (office). Fax: (20) 7942-5054 (office). E-mail: g.boxshall@nhm.ac.uk (office). Website: www.nhm.ac .uk/research-curation/staff-directory/zoology/g-boxshall/index.html (office).

BOYARCHIKOV, Nikolai Nikolayevich; Russian choreographer; Artistic Director, Mussorgsky Academic Opera and Ballet Theatre; b. 27 Sept. 1935, Leningrad; s. of Maria Boyarchikova; m. Larissa Klimova; ed Leningrad Vaganova School of Choreography, Leningrad State Conservatory; soloist Mussorgsky Academic Opera and Ballet Theatre (fmrly Leningrad Maly State Academic Opera and Ballet Theatre) 1954–71, Artistic Dir 1977–; chief choreographer Perm Opera and Ballet Theatre 1971–77; Glinka Prize 1977, People's Artist of Russia 1985, State Prize of Russian Fed., Order of Friendship 1996. Theatre productions include: Romeo and Juliet 1972, Tsar Boris 1975, Robber 1982, Quiet Don 1988. Address: Mussorgsky Theatre, 1 Arts Square, 191011 St Petersburg, Russia. Telephone: (812) 219-19-78.

BOYARCHUK, Aleksander Alekseyevich; Russian astrophysicist and academic; Chairman, Department of Experimental Astronomy, Lomonosov Moscow State University; b. 21 June 1931, Grozny; s. of Aleksei Boyarchuk and Maria Boyarchuk; m. Margarita Yevgenyevna Boyarchuk (née Kropotova) 1955; one s.; ed Leningrad State Univ.; Researcher, Deputy Dir Crimea Astrophysical Observatory USSR Acad. of Sciences 1953–87; Dir Inst. of Astronomy 1987, now Science Supervisor; also Chair., Department of Experimental Astronomy, Lomonosov Moscow State Univ.; mem. USSR (now Russian) Acad. of Sciences 1987; Acad.-Sec. Dept of Gen. Physics and Astronomy 1996–; Ed.-in-Chief Astronomy Reports; Pres. Int. Astronomical Union 1991–94; mem. Int. Astronomical Acad., Royal Astronomical Soc. of UK, American Astronomical Soc., American Physical Soc.; USSR State Prize. Publications include: more than 200 works on astrospectroscopy,

physics of star atmospheres, construction of astronomic equipment, cosmic studies. Address: Faculty of Physics, Lomonosov Moscow State University, Moscow 119991, GSP-1, 1-2 Leninskiye Gory (office); Institute of Astronomy, 109017 Moscow, Pyatnitskaya str. 48, Russia (office). Telephone: (495) 951-09-24 (Institute) (office). Fax: (495) 951-55-57 (office). E-mail: aboyar@inasan.rssi.ru (office). Website: www.phys.msu.ru/eng (office); www.inasan.rssi.ru (office).

BOYARSKY, Mikhail Sergeyevich; Russian actor and singer; b. 26 Dec. 1949, Leningrad; s. of the late Sergei Boyarsky; m. Larisa Luppian; one s. one d.; ed Leningrad Inst. of Theatre, Music and Cinematography; fmrly with Lensovet Theatre, appeared in musicals Interview in Buenos Aires, Troubadour and His Friends; cinema debut 1974, more than 60 roles; Artistic Dir Benefice Theatre; People's Actor of Russian Fed. 1984, People's Artist of Russia 1995. Films include: Starshiy syn 1975, Sentimentalnyy roman 1976, Ma-ma 1976, Kak Ivanushka-durachok za chudom khodil 1976, Dikiy Gavrila 1976, Poka bezumstvuyet mechta 1978, Komissiya po rassledovaniyu 1978, Nesravnennyy Nakonechnikov 1981, Kuda on denetsya! 1981, Dusha 1981, Tamozhnya 1982, Lishniy bilet 1983, Geroy eyo romana 1984, Gum-gam 1985, Chelovek s bulvara Kaputsinov 1987, Uznik zamka If 1988, Iskusstvo zhit v Odesse 1989, Vivat, gardemariny! 1991, Choknute 1991, Mushketyory 20 let spustya 1992, Tayna korolevy Anny ili mushketyory 30 let spustya 1993, Plachu vperyod! 2001, Klyuchi ot smerti (Keys to Death 2) 2002, Novogodnyye muzhchiny (New Year's Men) 2004, Schastlivyi (Happy) 2005, Vy ne ostavte menya (Don't Leave Me) 2006. Television includes: Don Sezar de Bazan 1989, Tartyuf 1992, Koroleva Margo (series) 1996, Zal ozhidaniya (series) 1998, Idiot (miniseries) 2003. Address: Naberezhnaya Moiki 31, Apt. 2, 191186 St Petersburg; c/o Benefice Theatre, 24 Moyki reki nab, St. Petersburg, Russia. Telephone: (812) 311-37-97. E-mail: info@boyarskiy.su. Website: www.boyarskiy .su.

BOYCE, Baron (Life Peer), cr. 2003, of Pimlico in the City of Westminster; **Adm. Michael (Cecil) Boyce,** Kt, KG, GCB, OBE, DL; British naval officer; Lord Warden and Admiral of the Cinque Ports and Constable of Dover Castle; b. 2 April 1943, Cape Town, S Africa; s. of the late Commdr Hugh Boyce and Madeline Boyce (née Manley); m. 1st Harriette Gail Fletcher 1971 (divorced 2005); one s. one d.; m. 2nd Fleur Margaret Ann Rutherford (née Smith); ed Hurstpierpoint Coll., Royal Naval Coll., Dartmouth Royal Coll. of Defence Studies; joined RN 1961; qualified submariner 1965, TAS 1970, served in HM submarines Anchorite, Valiant and Conqueror 1965–72, commanded HM submarines Oberon 1973–74, Opossum 1974–75, Superb 1979–81, frigate HMS Brilliant 1983–84, Capt. (SM) Submarine Sea Training 1984–86; Royal Coll. Defence Staff 1988; Sr Naval Officer ME 1989; Dir Naval Staff Duties 1989–91; Flag Officer, Sea Training 1991–92, Surface Flotilla 1992–95; Commdr Anti-Submarine Warfare Striking Force 1992–94; Second Sea Lord and C-in-C Naval Home Command 1995–97; Flag ADC to the Queen 1995–97; C-in-C Fleet, C-in-C Eastern Atlantic Area and Commdr Naval Forces NW Europe 1997–98; First Sea Lord 1998–2001; Chief of Defence Staff 2001–03; First and Prin. Naval ADC to the Queen 1998–2001, ADC 2001–03; Lord Warden and Adm. of the Cinque Ports and Constable of Dover Castle 2004–; Col Commdt SBS 2003–; Gov. Alleyn's School 1995–2005; mem. Bd of Dirs W.S. Atkins 2004–, VT Group PLC 2004–10; Chair. HMS Victory Preservation Co. 2012–; Pres. Officers Asscn 2003–12, London Dist St John Ambulance 2003–11, Submarine Museum 2005–; mem. Council White Ensign Asscn 2003–13 (Chair. 2007–10), Royal Nat. Lifeboat Inst. 2004– (Chair. 2008–13); Trustee, Nat. Maritime Museum 2004–13; King of Arms, Order of the Bath 2009–; DL Greater London 2003–; Patron Sail4Cancer 2003–, Submarine Asscn 2003–; Freeman of the City of London 1999, Younger Brother, Trinity House 1999–2006, Elder Brother 2006–; Hon. Freeman Drapers' Co. 2005–08, Liveryman 2008–, Court 2011–; Master 2013–; KStJ, Commdr, Legion of Merit (USA) 1999, Bronze Oak Leaf (USA) 2003; Hon. LLD (Portsmouth) 2005; Dr hc (Canterbury Christ Church Univ.) 2011; Hon. DCL (Kent) 2013. Leisure interests: squash, tennis, real tennis, sailing, windsurfing, opera, ballet. Address: House of Lords, Westminster, London, SW1A 0PW, England (office). E-mail: boycem@parliament.uk (office). Website: www .parliament.uk/biographies/lords/lord-boyce/3630 (office).

BOYCE, Ralph L. (Skip), BA, MPA; American business executive and fmr diplomatist; President, Boeing Southeast Asia, The Boeing Co.; b. 1 Feb. 1952, Washington, DC; m. Kathryn Sligh; two c.; ed George Washington Univ., Princeton Univ.; joined Foreign Service 1976, Staff Asst to Amb., Embassy in Tehran 1977–79, Commercial Attaché, Embassy in Tunis 1979–81, Financial Economist, Embassy in Islamabad 1981–84, Special Asst, then Adviser to Deputy Sec. of State, State Dept 1984–88, Political Counsellor, Embassy in Bangkok 1988–92, Deputy Chief of Mission, Embassy in Singapore 1992–93, Chargé d'affaires a.i. 1993–94, Deputy Chief of Mission, Embassy in Bangkok 1994–98, Deputy Asst Sec. for E Asia and Pacific Affairs 1998–2001, Amb. to Indonesia 2001–04, to Thailand 2004–07; Pres. Boeing Southeast Asia, The Boeing Co. 2008–. Address: Boeing International Corporation, Wheelock Place #13-02, 501 Orchard Road, Singapore 238880 (office). Telephone: 67329435 (office). Website: www.boeing.com (office).

BOYCOTT, Geoffrey, OBE; British sports commentator and fmr professional cricketer; b. 21 Oct. 1940, Fitzwilliam, Yorks.; s. of the late Thomas Wilfred Boycott and Jane Boycott; m. Rachael Swinglehurst 2003; one d.; ed Kinsley Modern School, Hemsworth Grammar School; fmrly in civil service; right-hand opening batsman; teams: Yorkshire 1962–86 (Capt. 1971–78), Northern Transvaal 1971–72; 108 Tests for England 1964–82, 4 as Capt., scoring then record 8,114 runs (average 47.72) including 22 hundreds; scored 48,426 first-class runs (151 hundreds); completed 100 hundreds for Yorkshire 1985, 7th batsman to achieve this for a county; toured Australia 1965–66, 1970–71, 1978–79 and 1979–80; only Englishman to achieve average of 100 in English County season 1971; repeated this achievement in 1979; scored 100th hundred, England v. Australia, Headingley, Leeds Aug. 1977; became 18th batsman in history of game to score 100 hundreds and the first to achieve this in a Test match; mem. Gen. Cttee; served as coach for Pakistan's Nat. Acad. 2001; cricket commentator for BBC and Sky –1998, talkSPORT –2003, Channel 4 2004–05, BBC Test Match Special for England's tour of Pakistan 2005, Cricket on Five 2006–, Ten Sports 2006–, BBC Cricket Team for Ashes series 2006–07; Wisden Cricketer of the Year 1965, Winner of Walter Lawrence Trophy 1970, inducted into Int. Cricket Council Hall of Fame 2009. Publications: Geoff Boycott's Book for Young Cricketers 1976, Put to the Test: Ashes Series in Australia 1978/79 1979, Geoff Boycott's Cricket Quiz 1979,

Boycott on Batting 1980, Opening Up 1980, In the Fast Lane 1981, Master Class 1982, Boycott – The Autobiography 1987, Boycott on Cricket 1990, Geoffrey Boycott on Cricket 1999, The Best XI 2008. *Leisure interest:* golf. *Website:* www .geoffboycott.com.

BOYCOTT, Rosie; British journalist and author; *Chair, London Food Board;* b. 13 May 1951; d. of Charles Boycott and Betty Boycott; m. 1st David Leitch (divorced); one d.; m. 2nd Charles Howard 1999; ed Cheltenham Ladies Coll., Kent Univ.; f. Spare Rib 1972; est. Virago Books 1973; worked on Village Voice (magazine), New York; subsequently edited Arabic women's magazine in Kuwait; Features Ed. Honey; Deputy Ed. Daily Mail's Male and Femail pages; Ed. Discount Traveller; Commissioning Ed. The Sunday Telegraph; Deputy Ed. Harpers & Queen 1989; Deputy Ed. and Features Ed. (British) Esquire 1991, Ed. 1992–96, of Ind. on Sunday 1996–98, of the Ind. 1998, of the Express 1998–2001, of the Express on Sunday 1998–2001; Chair., Panel of Judges, Orange Prize for Fiction 2001; Chair. London Food Bd 2010–; mem. Exec. Cttee English PEN. *Publications include:* A Nice Girl Like Me (autobiog.) 1983, All For Love 1985, Our Farm: A Year in the Life of a Smallholding 2007. *Address:* London Food Board, Greater London Authority, City Hall, The Queen's Walk, London, SE1 2AA, England (office). *Telephone:* (20) 7983-4595 (office). *Website:* www.london.gov.uk/london-food/general/london-food (office).

BOYD, Sir John Dixon Iklé, KCMG, MA; British fmr diplomatist and fmr university administrator; b. 17 Jan. 1936, Cambridge; s. of the late Prof. James Dixon Boyd and of Amélie Lowenthal; m. 1st Gunilla Kristina Ingregerd Rönngren 1968 (divorced 1977); one s. one d.; m. 2nd Julia Daphne Raynsford 1977; three d.; ed Westminster School, Clare Coll., Cambridge, Yale Univ., USA; joined HM Foreign Service 1962, in Hong Kong 1962–64, Third Sec., Embassy in Beijing 1965–67, at FCO 1967–69, Asst Under-Sec. of State 1984, Deputy Under-Sec. of State 1987–89, Chief Clerk 1989–92, at Embassy in Washington, DC 1969–73, First Sec., Embassy in Beijing 1973–75; on secondment to Treasury 1976; Econ. Counsellor, Embassy in Bonn 1977–81, Counsellor (Econ. and Social Affairs), Perm. Mission to UN, New York 1981–84; Political Adviser, Hong Kong 1985–87; Amb. to Japan 1992–96; Master Churchill Coll., Cambridge 1996–2006; Chair. Bd of Govs Bedales School 1966–2001, David Davies Memorial Inst. 1997–2001; Co-Chair. Nuffield Languages Inquiry 1998–2000; Vice-Chair. Yehudi Menuhin Int. Violin Trust Ltd 1996–; Dir UK-Japan 21st Century Group 2006–; Dir (non-exec.) British Nuclear Fuels PLC 1997–2000; Adviser, East Asia Inst., Univ. of Cambridge 1998–2005; mem. ASEM (Asia-Europe Meeting) 'Vision Group' 1998–2000, ANA Advisory Group 2003–; Trustee, British Museum 1996–2006 (Chair. 2002–06), Sir Winston Churchill Archive Trust 1996–2006, Cambridge Union (also Chair.) 1997–2006, Margaret Thatcher Archive Trust 1997–2006, Cambridge Foundation 1997–2005, The Wordsworth Trust 1997–, Great Britain-Sasakawa Foundation 2001–, Council of Senate Cambridge Univ. 2001–04, Huang Hsing Foundation 2001–, RAND (Europe) UK 2001–, Joseph Needham Research Inst. 2005–; Syndic Fitzwilliam Museum 1997–2002; Gov. RSC 1996–2005; Hon. Fellow, Clare Coll., Cambridge 1994, Westminster School 2003, Life Fellow, Churchill Coll., Cambridge 2006. *Publications:* contrib. articles to Asian Affairs and others. *Leisure interests:* music, books, sheep farming, fly-fishing. *Address:* 87 Elizabeth Street, London, SW1W 9PG, England. *Telephone:* (20) 7730-8389. *E-mail:* jul.boyd@gmail.com.

BOYD, Joseph Walker, BA; American music industry executive, film producer and writer; b. 5 Aug. 1942, Boston, Mass; s. of Joseph M. Boyd and Elizabeth Walker Boyd; ed Harvard Univ.; Gen. Man. Elektra Records UK 1965–66; Man. Dir Witchseason Productions Ltd 1966–71; Dir Music Services, Warner Bros Films 1971–73; Man. Dir Osiris Films 1976–79; Vice-Pres. Broadway Pictures, New York 1979–80; Man. Dir Hannibal Records Ltd 1980–91; Vice-Pres. A&R, Rykodisc Inc. 1991–98; A&R Dir Hannibal/Ryko Latino Labels 1999; Grammy Award 1974. *Publication:* White Bicycles: Making Music in the 1960s 2007. *Leisure interests:* history, tennis. *Address:* c/o Serpents Tail Press, 3A Exmouth House, Pine Street, London, EC1R 0JH, England (office). *Telephone:* (20) 7841-6300 (office). *Website:* www.serpentstail.com (office); www.joeboyd.co.uk.

BOYD, Sir Michael, Kt, MA; British theatre director; b. 6 July 1955, Belfast, Northern Ireland; s. of John Truesdale Boyd and Sheila Boyd; partner Caroline Hall; one d.; one s. one d. (twins) by previous partner; ed Latymer Upper School, London, Daniel Stewart's Coll., Edinburgh and Univ. of Edinburgh; Trainee Dir, Malaya Bronnaya Theatre, Moscow; Trainee Asst Dir Belgrade Theatre, Coventry, Asst Dir 1980–82; Assoc. Dir Crucible Theatre, Sheffield 1982–84; Founding Artistic Dir Tron Theatre, Glasgow 1985–96; Assoc. Dir RSC 1996–2003, Artistic Dir 2002–12. *Productions include:* for Tron Theatre: The Trick is to Keep Breathing, Macbeth, Good, The Real World, Crow, Century's End, Salvation, The Baby, Clyde Nouveau, The Guid Sisters; for the RSC: The Broken Heart 1994–95, Measure for Measure 1996–97, The Spanish Tragedy, Much Ado About Nothing 1997–98, Troilus and Cressida 1998–99, A Midsummer Night's Dream 1999–2000, Romeo and Juliet 2000–01, Henry VI, Parts I, II and III and Richard III (Olivier Award for Best Dir 2001, South Bank Award 2001) 2000–01, The Tempest 2002, Hamlet 2004, Twelfth Night 2005, The Histories (eight play cycle) 2006–08, The Grain Store 2009, As You Like It, 2009–11, Antony and Cleopatra 2010–11; other theatre productions include: Miss Julie (Haymarket Theatre, West End) 1999, Commedia (Lyric Hammersmith) 1983, Othello (Lyric Hammersmith) 1984, A Passion in Six Days (Crucible Theatre, Sheffield), Hard to Get (Traverse Theatre, Edinburgh), Hedda Gabler (Leicester Haymarket), The Alchemist (Cambridge Theatre Co.). *Leisure interests:* walking, reading, music, cooking. *Address:* c/o Royal Shakespeare Company, Royal Shakespeare Theatre, Waterside, Stratford-upon-Avon, Warwicks., CV37 6BB, England.

BOYD, Sir Robert, Kt, MA, MB, BChir, FRCP, FFPHM, FRCPCH, FMedSci; British paediatrician; b. 14 May 1938, Cambridge, England; s. of James Dixon Boyd and Amélie Boyd; m. Meriel Cornelia Talbot 1966; one s. two d.; ed Ley's School, Clare Coll., Cambridge, Univ. Coll. Hosp., London; jr posts, Hosp. for Sick Children, Great Ormond Street, Brompton Hosp., Univ. Coll. Hosp. (UCH), London 1962–65; Sir Stuart Halley Research Fellow and Sr Registrar, UCH 1966–71; Goldsmiths MRC Travelling Fellow, Univ. of Colorado Medical Center, USA 1971–72; Sr Lecturer and Hon. Consultant, UCH Medical School 1972–80; Sec., Academic Bd, British Paediatric Asscn 1976–79, Chair. 1987–90; Asst Registrar Royal Coll. of Physicians 1980–81; Prof. of Paediatrics, Univ. of

Manchester 1981–96, Dean 1989–93, Visiting Prof. 2003–; Prin. St George's Hosp. Medical School and Prof. of Paediatrics 1996–2003, Pro-Vice-Chancellor for Medicine, Univ. of London 2000–03, Deputy Vice-Chancellor 2002–03; Chair. Manchester Health Authority 1994–96, Nat. Primary Care R&D Centre, Univs of Manchester, Salford and York 1994–96, Dir Nat. Health Service (NHS) Research and Devt, Greater Manchester 2004–08; Chair. Council of Heads of UK Medical Schools 2001–03, Lloyds TSB Foundation for England and Wales 2003–, Council for Assisting Refugee Academics 2004–; Ed. Placenta 1989–95; mem. Health Cttee Universities UK 1997–2003, Asscn of Medical Research Charities Scientific Advisory Cttee 1996–2002, Task Force 'Supporting Research & Development in the NHS' 1994; mem. Council, Royal Veterinary Coll. 1999–2003; Gov. Kingston Univ. 1998–2003, Univ. of Manchester 2004–; Hon. Consultant, St Mary's Hosp., Manchester and Booth Hall Children's Hosp., Manchester 1981–96, St George's Healthcare Nat. Health Service Trust, London 1996–2003, Hon. Fellow, American Pediatric Soc.; Hon. DSc (Kingston, Keele). *Publications include:* Paediatric Problems in General Practice (co-author) 1982; contribs to Placental and Fetal Physiology and Paediatrics and Health Administration. *Leisure interests:* cooking, reading, holidays. *Address:* The Stone House, Skellorn Green, Adlington, Macclesfield, Cheshire, SK10 4NU, England (home). *Telephone:* (1625) 872400 (home). *E-mail:* rboyd@doctors.org.uk.

BOYD, William Andrew Murray, CBE, MA, FRSL; British writer; b. 7 March 1952, Ghana; s. of Dr Alexander Murray Boyd and Evelyn Boyd; m. Susan Anne Boyd (née Wilson) 1975; ed Gordonstoun School, Glasgow Univ., Jesus Coll., Oxford; lecturer in English, St Hilda's Coll., Oxford 1980–83; TV critic, New Statesman 1981–83; Officier, Ordre des Arts et des Lettres; Hon. DLitt (St Andrews), (Glasgow), (Stirling). *Film appearance:* Rabbit Fever 2006. *Publications include:* A Good Man in Africa (Whitbread Prize 1981, Somerset Maugham Award 1982) 1981 (screenplay 1994), On the Yankee Station 1981, An Ice-Cream War (John Llewellyn Rhys Prize) 1982, Stars and Bars 1984 (screenplay 1988), School Ties 1985, The New Confessions 1987, Scoop (screenplay) 1987, Brazzaville Beach (McVities Prize and James Tait Black Memorial Prize) 1990, Aunt Julia and the Scriptwriter (screenplay) 1990, Mr Johnson (screenplay) 1990, Chaplin (screenplay) 1992, The Blue Afternoon (novel) 1993, A Good Man in Africa (screenplay) 1994, The Destiny of Nathalie 'X' 1995, Armadillo 1998 (screenplay 2001), Nat Tate: An American Artist 1998, The Trench (screenplay, also dir) 1999, Sword of Honour (screenplay) 2001, Any Human Heart 2002, Fascination 2004, Bamboo (collection of literary reviews) 2005, A Waste of Shame (screenplay) 2005, Restless (novel) (Costa Book Award for Novel of the Year, Yorkshire Post Book of the Year 2007) 2006, Granta 100 (Ed.) 2008, The Dream Lover (short stories) 2008, Ordinary Thunderstorms (novel) 2009, Waiting for Sunrise (novel) 2012. *Leisure interests:* tennis, strolling. *Address:* The Agency, 24 Pottery Lane, Holland Park, London, W11 4LZ, England (office).

BOYD OF DUNCANSBY, Baron (Life Peer), cr. 2006, of Duncansby in the County of Caithness; **Colin Boyd,** PC, QC, BA (Econ), LLB, FRSA, LARTPI; British lawyer; b. 7 June 1953, Falkirk; s. of David Hugh Aird Boyd and Betty Meldrum Boyd; two s. one d.; ed Wick High School, George Watson's Coll., Edinburgh, Univ. of Manchester and Univ. of Edinburgh; qualified as solicitor 1978; called to Bar 1983; Legal Assoc. Royal Town Planning Inst. 1990; Advocate Depute (prosecutor) 1993–95; QC 1995; Solicitor-Gen. for Scotland, UK Govt 1997; Solicitor-Gen., Scottish Exec. 1999–2000; Lord Advocate of Scotland 2000–06; Hon. Fellow, Inst. of Advanced Legal Studies 2001. *Leisure interests:* reading, walking, watching rugby. *Address:* House of Lords, London, SW1A 0PW, England (office). *Telephone:* (20) 7219-3000 (office). *E-mail:* boydcd@parliament.uk (office).

BOYD OF MERTON, 2nd Viscount, cr. 1960 of Merton-in-Penninghame, Co. Wigtown; **Simon Donald Rupert Neville Lennox-Boyd,** MA; British business executive (retd); b. 7 Dec. 1939, London; s. of the late Alan Lennox-Boyd (1st Viscount Boyd of Merton) and of Lady Patricia Guinness; m. Alice Mary Clive 1962; two s. two d.; ed Eton Coll., Christ Church, Oxford; Deputy Chair. Arthur Guinness & Sons 1981–86; Vice-Chair. Save the Children Fund 1979–82, Chair. 1987–93; Chair. Stonham Housing Asscn 1992–98, Trustee, Guinness Trust 1974–; Dir The Iveagh Trustees Ltd. *Leisure interest:* forestry. *Address:* Ince Castle, Saltash, Cornwall, PL12 4QZ, England. *Telephone:* (1752) 842672. *Fax:* (1752) 847134 (home). *E-mail:* boydince@aol.com (home).

BOYE, Mame Madior; Senegalese politician and lawyer; b. 1940; ed Faculty of Legal and Econ. Sciences, Dakar, Centre Nat. d'Etudes Judiciaires, Paris; fmr Deputy Procurator of Repub.; Judge, First Vice-Pres. First Class Regional Court, Dakar; fmr Pres. Dakar Court of Appeal; Minister of Justice and Keeper of the Seals 2000–01; Prime Minister of Senegal 2001–02; Special Rep. for the Promotion of the Protection of Civilians in Armed Conflicts, African Union 2004–; mem. Parti Démocratique Sénégalais. *Address:* Siege de L'Union Africaine, PO Box 3243, Addis Ababa, Ethiopia (office). *Telephone:* (1) 517700 (office). *Fax:* (1) 517844 (office). *Website:* www.africa-union.org (office).

BOYER, Yves, PhD; French research institute director and academic; *Deputy Director, Fondation pour la Recherche Stratégique;* b. 9 Oct. 1950, Blois; m. Isabelle Kraft 1978; one s. one d.; ed Inst. d'Etudes Politiques, Paris and Paris-Panthéon Univ.; Deputy Gen. Sec. SOFRESA, Paris 1978–80; Bureau des Etudes Stratégiques et des Négociations Internationales, Secr. Gén. de la Défense Nationale 1980–82; Defence Consultant and Research Assoc., IISS, London 1982–83; Sr Researcher, Inst. Français des Relations Internationales 1983–88; Research Fellow, Woodrow Wilson Center 1986; fmr Deputy Dir CREST, Ecole Polytechnique; Prof., Army Acad. 1986–, Staff Coll. 1992–; currently Prof. of Int. Relations, Ecole polytechnique, Paris; also currently Deputy Dir Fondation pour la Recherche Stratégique; Chair. French Soc. for Mil. Studies (SFEM), Working Groups for the French Ministry of Defence's Scientific Advisers; mem. Editorial Bd, Annuaire Français de Relations Internationales; Chevalier, Ordre des Palmes académiques. *Publications:* Oxford Handbook of War (co-ed with J. Lindley-French) 2012. *Address:* Fondation pour la Recherche Stratégique, 4 bis rue des Pâtures, 75013 Paris (office); 2 rue de Haut Bourg, 41000 Blois, France (home). *Telephone:* (1) 43-13-77-66 (office). *Fax:* (1) 43-13-77-78 (office). *E-mail:* y.boyer@frstrategie.org (office). *Website:* www.frstrategie.org (office).

BOYKO, Yuriy Anatoliyovych; Ukrainian engineer and politician; *Deputy Prime Minister;* b. 9 Oct. 1958, Horlivka, Donetsk region; m. Vera Dimitrievna

Boyka; three s. three d.; ed Mendeleyev Moscow Inst. of Chemical Tech.; began career as Foreman and Gen. Man., Zorva Rubizhanskiy chemical plant; various man. positions with Lisichansknaftoorgsintez JSC (now LiNOS), and Ukrvybuhprom State Corpn; fmr Chair. Bd Ukrtatnafta (oil refining co.) and Chair. Supervisory Bd Ukrtransnafta (oil transportation co.); Head, Naftogaz of Ukraine (nat. oil and gas co.) and Sr Deputy Minister of Fuel and Energy 2002–05, Minister of Fuel and Energy 2006–07, of Energy and Coal Industry 2010–12; Deputy Prime Minister 2012–; mem. Verkhovna Rada (Supreme Council, Parl.) 2007–, Deputy Chair. Cttee on Fuel and Energy Complex, Nuclear Policy and Nuclear Safety; Hero of Ukraine, Order of Merit, 3rd Class, Order of St Seraphim of Sarov, 2nd Class. *Address:* Office of the Cabinet of Ministers, 01008 Kyiv, vul. M. Hrushevskoho 12/2, Ukraine (office). *Telephone:* (44) 254-05-84 (office). *Fax:* (44) 254-05-84 (office). *E-mail:* web@kmu.gov.ua (office). *Website:* www.kmu.gov.ua (office).

BOYLE, Danny; British film director; b. 20 Oct. 1956, Bury, Lancs.; Artistic Dir Royal Court Theatre 1982–87; Artistic Dir of the Opening Ceremony, London Olympic Games 2012; Fellow, British Film Inst. 2010; Golden Ephebe Award 1997. *Films:* Shallow Grave 1994, Trainspotting 1996, A Life Less Ordinary 1996, Twin Town (exec. producer) 1996, The Beach 1999, Alien Love Triangle 1999, 28 Days Later 2002, Alien Love Triangle 2002, Millions 2004, Sunshine 2007, Slumdog Millionaire (Best Film Nat. Bd of Review 2008, Golden Globe Award for Best Dir 2009, BAFTA Award for Best Dir 2009, Acad. Award for Best Picture 2009, Acad. Award for Best Dir 2009) 2008, 127 Hours 2010. *Theatre includes:* Royal Court Theatre: The Grace of Mary Traverse, Genius, Saved; RSC: The Pretenders, The Last Days of Don Juan, The Silent Woman; Nat. Theatre: Frankenstein 2011. *Television:* Elephant (producer) 1989, The Greater Good (dir, series) 1991, Mr Wroe's Virgins (dir) 1993, Not Even God is Wise Enough (dir) 1993, National Theatre Live (series), Frankenstein 2011. *Address:* c/o Robert Newman, The Endeavor Agency, 9601 Wilshire Blvd, 10th Floor, Beverly Hills, CA 90212; c/o D6A, 7920 West Sunset Boulevard, Los Angeles, CA 90046, USA (office).

BOYLE, Thomas Coraghessan (T. C.), BA, MFA, PhD; American academic and writer; *Professor, Department of English, University of Southern California;* b. 2 Dec. 1948, Peekskill, NY; m. Karen Kvashay 1974; two s. one d.; ed SUNY at Potsdam, Univ. of Iowa; Founder-Dir, Creative Writing Program 1978–86, Asst Prof. of English 1978–82, Assoc. Prof. of English 1982–86, Prof. of English 1986–, Univ. of Southern California; mem. Nat. Endowment of the Arts literature panel 1986–87; Nat. Endowment for the Arts grants 1977, 1983; Guggenheim Fellowship 1988, mem. American Acad. of Arts and Letters 2009–; Hon. DHumLitt (SUNY) 1991; PEN/Faulkner Award 1988, Commonwealth Club of California Gold Medal for Literature 1988, O. Henry Short Story Awards 1988, 1989, Prix Passion Publishers' Prize, France 1989, Eds' Choice, New York Times Book Review 1989, Harold D. Vursell Memorial Award, American Acad. of Arts and Letters 1993, Prix Médicis Étranger 1997. *Publications:* Descent of Man 1979, Water Music 1982, Budding Prospects 1984, Greasy Lake 1985, World's End 1987, If the River was Whiskey 1989, East is East 1990, The Road to Wellville 1993, Without a Hero 1994, The Tortilla Curtain 1995, Riven Rock 1998, T.C. Boyle Stories 1998, A Friend of the Earth 2000, After the Plague 2001, Drop City 2003, The Inner Circle 2004, Tooth and Claw 2006, Talk Talk 2006, The Women 2009, Wild Child 2010, When the Killing's Done 2011, San Miguel 2012; contrib. to numerous anthologies and periodicals. *Address:* Department of English, University of Southern California, Los Angeles, CA 90089, USA (office). *Telephone:* (213) 740-3734 (office). *E-mail:* tcb@tcboyle.com (office). *Website:* www.tcboyle.com.

BOZANGA, Georges; Central African Republic politician; Minister of Finance and Budget –June 2013. *Address:* Ministry of Finance and the Budget, BP 696, Bangui, Central African Republic (office). *Telephone:* 21-61-38-05 (office).

BOZANGA, Simon-Narcisse; Central African Republic politician and lawyer; b. 26 Dec. 1942, Bangassou; ed Univs. of Nancy and Paris, France; Dir of Legal Studies, Ministry of Foreign Affairs 1972–74, Sec.-Gen. 1974–78; Amb. to Gabon 1978–79; Sec.-Gen. to Govt 1979–80; Minister of Justice 1980–81; Prime Minister and Head of Govt April–Sept. 1981 (deposed by mil. coup); Dir-Gen. Société Centrafricaine des Hydrocarbures (CentraHydro) 1982; Adviser, Transitional Constitutional Court 2004–. *Address:* Transitional Constitutional Court, Bangui, Central African Republic.

BOZANIĆ, HE Cardinal Josip, MTS, LLM; Croatian ecclesiastic; *Archbishop of Zagreb;* b. 20 March 1949, Rijeka; s. of Ivan Bozanić and Dinka Valković; ed Lower Seminary of Pazin, Faculties of Theology, Rijeka and Zagreb, Pontifical Gregorian Univ. and Pontifical Lateran Univ., Rome; ordained priest by Bishop of Krk, Karmelo Zazinović 1975; Sec. to Bishop of Krk 1975–76; Parish Priest 1976–78; Chancellor of Diocesan Curia in Krk 1986–87; Gen. Priest 1987–89; Prof. of Canon Law and Theology, Seminary of Rijeka 1987; elected Bishop of Krk 1989; consecrated by Cardinal Franjo Kuharić 1989; Admin. of Archdiocese of Rijeka-Senj 1996; Archbishop of Metropolitan See of Zagreb 1997–; Pres. Croatian Conf. of Bishops; Vice-Pres. Council of European Bishops' Confs; cr. Cardinal (Cardinal-Priest of San Girolamo dei Croati) 2003–; participated in Papal Conclave 2005, 2013; del. to Special Ass. for Europe, World Synod of Bishops, The Vatican 1999. *Address:* Archdiocese of Zagreb, Kaptol 31, p.p. 553, 10001 Zagreb, Croatia (office). *Telephone:* 4894802 (office). *Fax:* 4816104 (office). *E-mail:* Josip.Bozanic@hbk.hr (office). *Website:* zagreb.hbk.hr (office).

BOZER, Ali Husrev, Dr in Law; Turkish academic, judge and government official; *Board Member, AxA A.S.;* b. 28 July 1925, Ankara; s. of Mustafa Fevzi Bozer and Zehra Bozer; m.; three s.; ed Ankara and Neuchâtel Univs and Harvard Law School; Asst judge, Ankara 1951; Asst, Faculty of Law, Ankara Univ. 1952–60, Agrégé 1955–60, Head of Dept 1961, apptd Prof. of Commercial Law 1965; Prof. of Law Çankaya Univ. 1992–, also Law Faculty, Ankara Univ., Law Faculty, Gazi Univ.; lawyer at bar, Ankara 1952–; Dir Inst. de Recherche sur le Droit commercial et bancaire 1960–; Judge, European Court of Human Rights 1974–76; mem. Admin. Council, Turkish Radio-TV Corpn 1968–71, Vice-Pres. 1971–73; Minister of Customs and Monopolies 1981–83, of State for Relations with EEC 1986–90; Deputy Prime Minister and Minister of State 1989–90; Minister of Foreign Affairs Feb.–Oct. 1990; fmr Pres., now Hon. Pres. European Assocn of Former Parliamentarians of the Member Countries of the European Council or the EU; mem. Bd AxA A.S.; Officier Légion d'honneur 1993; Merite Européan 1992.

Publications: Les droits d'administration et de jouissance de père et mère sur les biens de l'enfant, Nantissement commercial, Aperçu général sur le droit des assurances sociales en droit turc, Droit commercial pour les employés de banques, Papiers valeurs pour les employés de banques, Droits des Assurances, Droit des Obligations, Insurance Law, Contracts Law, Negotiable Instruments; monographs and articles in several reviews in Turkish and French; articles published on Turkish relations with European Union. *Leisure interests:* theatre, music, sport, tennis, swimming. *Address:* Ahmet Rasim sok. 35/5, Çankaya, Ankara, Turkey (home). *Telephone:* (312) 4424112 (home). *Fax:* (312) 4424113 (home).

BOŽINOVIĆ, Davor, BA, MA, PhD; Croatian diplomatist and government official; b. 27 Dec. 1961, Pula; m.; two c.; ed Univ. of Zagreb, George C. Marshall European Center for Security Studies, Garmisch-Partenkirchen, Germany; Adviser, Secr. for Defence 1987–90; Chair. Draft Bd, Ministry of Defence 1990–94; Sr Adviser, Dept for Consular Affairs, Ministry of Foreign Affairs (MFA) 1994–96, Counsellor, Embassy in Sarajevo 1996, Deputy Head and Head of Dept on Neighbouring Countries, MFA 1997–99, Asst Minister of Foreign Affairs 1999, Coordinator for relations with Yugoslavia, MFA 2000, Chargé d'affaires a.i., Embassy in Belgrade 2001, Amb. to Serbia and Montenegro 2002–04; Chief of Staff, Office of the Pres. 2004; Perm. Rep. to NATO, Brussels 2005–08, State Sec. for European Integration, Ministry of Foreign Affairs and European Integration (MFAEI) 2008–09, State Sec. for Political Affairs 2009, Special Envoy of the Prime Minister for SE Europe March–Dec. 2010; Minister of Defence 2010–11; negotiator during Croatia–EU accession negotiations; fmr Lecturer, Faculty of Political Science, Univ. of Zagreb, MFAEI Diplomatic Acad., Ban Josip Jelacic War Coll.; has lectured at Woodrow Wilson Int. Scientific Center, Washington, DC, German Marshall Fund, Washington, DC, Johns Hopkins Univ., Baltimore, Md, USA, Diplomatic Acad. of Russian Ministry of Foreign Affairs, Moscow. *Publications include:* NATO-Euro-Atlantic Integration 2008, Mutual Transition NATO-EU-Southeast Europe 2010. *Address:* Chief of Cabinet, 10000 Zagreb, Sarajevska cesta 7 (Building No. 15), Croatia (office).

BOZIZÉ, Jean Francis; Central African Republic government official; s. of fmr Pres. François Bozizé Yangovounda; served in several positions in the Ministry of Nat. Defence, War Veterans, War Victims, Disarmament and the Restructuring of the Armed Forces, including Chief of Staff to the Minister, Deputy Minister, Minister–Del. at the Presidency in charge of Nat. Defence, War Veterans, War Victims, Disarmament and the Restructuring of the Armed Forces 2008–13. *Address:* c/o Ministry of National Defence, War Veterans, War Victims, Disarmament and the Restructuring of the Armed Forces, Bangui, Central African Republic (office).

BOZIZÉ YANGOVOUNDA, Gen. François; Central African Republic army officer and fmr head of state; opposition leader 1981–93, led unsuccessful coup 1983; spent many years in exile in Togo; presidential cand. 1993; supported Pres. Ange-Felix Patasse in suppressing coups 1996–97; sacked as Army Chief; participated in unsuccessful coup against Pres. 2001, took control of N Bangui before escaping to Chad with 300 supporters; launched several rebel attacks from base in Chad 2001–02; led successful coup March 2003, suspended constitution and dissolved Parl.; self-proclaimed Pres. of Cen. African Repub. 2003–05, elected 2005, Pres. 2005–13, Minister of Defence 2005–08, also Minister of Nat. Defence, War Veterans, War Victims, Disarmament and the Restructuring of the Armed Forces; fled to Democratic Repub. of Congo following attack by rebel forces March 2013.

BRABECK-LETMATHE, Peter, BA; Austrian business executive; *Chairman, Nestlé SA;* b. 13 Nov. 1944, Villach; ed Univ. of World Trade, Vienna; fmrly with Findus Austria; joined Nestlé Group as salesman 1968, becoming new products specialist 1970, Nat. Sales Man. 1970, later Dir of Marketing, Nestlé Chile, frozen food and ice-cream specialist, Nestlé HQ 1975, Marketing and Sales Div. Man., Chiprodal (Chile) 1976, Asst to Regional Man. for S America, Nestlé HQ 1980, Man. Dir Nestlé Ecuador 1981, Nestlé Venezuela 1983, Sr Vice-Pres. and Head of Culinary Products Div., Nestlé SA, Vevey 1987, Exec. Vice-Pres. and Head of Strategic Business Group 2 1992, Group CEO (desig.) Nestlé SA, Vevey 1995–97, Group CEO 1997–2008, Vice-Chair. 2001–05, Chair. 2005–, also Chair. Chairman's and Corp. Governance Cttee, Nomination Cttee, Chair. Nestlé Health Science SA; Vice-Chair. L'Oréal SA 1997–, Crédit Suisse Group 2000–05, 2008–; mem. Bd of Dirs Exxon Mobil Corpn (USA) 2010–, Delta Topco Ltd (Formula 1), Jersey 2010– (Chair. 2012–); Chair. Int. Business Council of World Econ. Forum; Deputy Chair. The Prince of Wales Int. Business Leaders' Forum; mem. European Round Table of Industrialists, Int. Asscn for the Promotion and Protection of Pvt. Foreign Investments; mem. Foundation Bds World Econ. Forum, Foundation for the Int. Fed. of Red Cross and Red Crescent Socs; La Orden Mexicana del Aguila Azteca, Austrian Cross of Honour; Hon. LLD (Univ. of Alberta, Canada) 2012; Schumpeter Prize for outstanding contrib. in economics. *Address:* Nestlé, Avenue Nestlé 55, 1800 Vevey, Switzerland (office). *Telephone:* (21) 921-18-85 (office). *Fax:* (21) 921-18-85 (office). *E-mail:* info@nestle.com (office). *Website:* www.nestle.com (office).

BRABHAM, Sir John Arthur (Jack), Kt, OBE; Australian fmr racing driver; b. 2 April 1926, Sydney, Australia; s. of C. T. Brabham; m. 1st Betty Evelyn (divorced); three s.; m. 2nd Margaret Brabham; ed Hurstville Tech. Coll.; served in RAAF 1944–46; started engineering business 1946; Midget Speedway racing 1946–53; numerous wins driving a Cooper-Bristol, Australia 1953–54; went to Europe 1955; Australian Grand Prix 1955, 1963; World Champion, Formula II 1958, 1966; Formula II Champion of France 1964; World Champion Driver 1959–60, 1960–61, 1966; came first in Monaco and UK Grandes Epreuves 1959; won Grand Prix of Netherlands, Belgium, France, UK, Portugal, Denmark 1960, Belgium 1961, France 1966, 1967, UK 1966; began building own cars 1961; winner Formula 1 Mfrs Championship 1966, 1967; fmr Chair. Jack Brabham (Ewell) Ltd; fmr Dir Engine Developments Ltd; Ferodo Trophy 1964, 1966; Australian of the Year 1966; BRDC Gold Star 1966, BARC Gold Medal 1959, 1966, 1967. *Publications:* Jack Brabham's Book of Motor Racing 1960, When the Flag Drops 1971, The Jack Brabham Story 2004. *Leisure interests:* flying, scuba diving, water skiing, cruising. *Address:* c/o Lady Brabham, Suite 404, Bag No. 1, Robina Town Centre, Queensland, 4230, Australia. *Telephone:* (7) 5564-7072 (office). *Fax:* (7) 5564-9872 (office).

BRACHER, Karl Dietrich, DPhil; German historian, political scientist and academic; *Professor Emeritus, University of Bonn;* b. 13 March 1922, Stuttgart; s. of Theodor Bracher and Gertrud Zimmermann; m. Dorothee Schleicher (niece of Dietrich Bonhoeffer) 1951; one s. one d.; ed Gymnasium, Stuttgart, Univ. of Tübingen and Harvard Univ., USA; Research Asst and Head of Dept, Inst. of Political Science, Berlin 1950–58; Lecturer, German Hochschule für Politik, Berlin; Privatdozent and Prof., Free Univ., Berlin 1955–58; Prof. of Political Science and Contemporary History, Univ. of Bonn 1959–, now Prof. Emer.; Pres. Comm. for History of Parl. and Political Parties, Bonn 1962–68; Fellow, Center for Advanced Study in the Behavioral Sciences, Stanford, USA 1963–64; Chair. German Asscn of Political Science 1965–67; mem. Inst. for Advanced Study, Princeton, USA 1967–68, 1974–75; mem. Wilson Center, Washington, DC, USA 1980–81; Chair. Bd, Inst. für Zeitgeschichte, Munich 1980–88, German Asscn of Foreign Policy, German PEN Centre; Visiting Prof., Sweden 1962, Univ. of Oxford 1971, Tel-Aviv Univ. 1974, Japan 1975, European Univ. Inst., Florence 1975–76, Seattle 1984; Corresp. Fellow, British Acad., American Philosophical Soc., Austrian Akad. der Wissenschaften; mem. Deutsche Akad. für Sprache und Dichtung, Rhenish-Westfalian Acad. of Sciences; Ed. Vierteljahrshefte für Zeitgeschichte; mem. Editorial Bd, Politische Vierteljahresschrift until 1970, Neue Politische Literatur, Bonner Historische Forschungen, Journal of Contemporary History, Government and Opposition, Societas, Zeitschrift für Politik, Tempo Presente, Risorgimento, European Journal of Int. Affairs, History of the Twentieth Century, Bonner Schriften zur Politik und Zeitgeschichte, Quellen zur Geschichte des Parliamentarismus, Dokumente zur Deutschlandpolitik; Hon. mem. American Acad. of Arts and Sciences; Verdienstorden für Wissenschaft und Kunst (Order of Merit for Science and Art) 1992; Hon. DHumLitt (Florida); Hon. DJur (Graz); Hon. Dr rer. pol (Berlin); Dr hc (Paris); Premio Storia Acqui 1973, Bentinck-Preis 1981, Curtius-Preis 1994. *Publications:* Conscience in Revolt (with others) 1954, Die Auflösung der Weimarer Republik 1955, Staat und Politik (with E. Fraenkel) 1957, Die Nationalsozialistische Machtergreifung (with others) 1960, Propyläen Weltgeschichte (vol. nine) (Dutch trans.) 1960, The Foreign Policy of the Federal Republic of Germany 1963, Problems of Parliamentary Democracy in Europe 1964, Adolf Hitler 1964, Deutschland zwischen Demokratie und Diktatur 1964, Theodor Heuss 1965, Modern Constitutionalism and Democracy (co-ed. two vols) 1966, Internationale Beziehungen (with E. Fraenkel) 1969, The German Dictatorship (English, Italian, Spanish, French, Japanese, Hebrew trans.) 1970, Nach 25 Jahren (ed.) 1970, Das deutsche Dilemma 1971 (English trans. 1974), Western Europe (in Times History of Our Times) 1971, Democracy (in Europe Tomorrow) 1972, Zeitgeschichtliche Kontroversen 1976, Die Krise Europas seit 1917 1976 and 1992 (Italian trans.), Schlüsselwörter in der Geschichte 1978, Geschichte und Gewalt 1981, Bibliographie zur Politik (co-ed.) 1970, 1976, 1982, Zeit der Ideologien 1982 (English, Spanish and Italian trans. 1985), Nationalsozialistische Diktatur 1983, Das Gewissen steht auf 1984, Die totalitäre Erfahrung 1987, Geschichte der BR Deutschland 1981–87, Verfall und Fortschritt im Denken der frühen römischen Kaiserzeit 1987, Die Weimarer Republik 1998, Deutschland zwischen Krieg und Frieden 1991, Staat und Parteien (co-ed.) 1992, Wendezeiten der Geschichte 1992, Deutschland 1933–1945 1993, Hitler et la dictature allemande 1995, Turning Points in Modern Times 1995, Geschichte als Erfahrung 2001, Politik, Geschichte und Kultur 2009. *Leisure interest:* playing piano and chamber music, mountain walking. *Address:* Stationsweg 17, 53127 Bonn, Germany. *Telephone:* 284358.

BRACHES, Ernst; Dutch academic (retd); b. 8 Oct. 1930, Padang, Indonesia; s. of Godfried Daniel Ernst Braches and Zeni Jansz; m. Maartje van Hoorn 1961; three s., one foster s.; ed Univ. of Amsterdam; asst, Univ. of Amsterdam 1957–65; Keeper of Western Printed Books, Univ. Library, Leiden 1965–73; Dir Rijksmuseum Meermanno-Westreenianum, The Hague 1973–77; Dir Univ. of Amsterdam Library 1977–88, Prof. of History of the Printed Book, Univ. of Amsterdam; Hon. mem. Soc. de la Reliure Originale, Paris. *Publications include:* Henry James: Engel en Afgrond 1983, Lord Peter Whimsey as a Book Lover 1989, The Scheffers Type 1990, Gutenberg's Scriptorium 1991, The Steadfast Tin Soldier of Joh Enschede en Zonen 1992, Alle nieuwe kunst wordt eerst niet begrepen 2003, Nieuwe Kunst en het boek 2003, Nieuwe Kunst Documentatie 2006, Dutch Art Nouveau and Book Design 1892–1903 2009, Kommentar zum Tod in Venedig 2014. *Address:* Vrijburglaan 53, 2051 LB Overveen, Netherlands. *Telephone:* (23) 5253246. *Fax:* (23) 5253246.

BRACKEN, Richard M., BSc, MSc; American business executive; *Chairman and CEO, HCA Inc.;* b. 14 Sept. 1952; m. Judith Bracken; four c.; ed San Diego State Univ., Medical Coll. of Virginia; joined HCA (Hospital Corpn of America) Inc. 1981, has held numerous man. positions including CEO Green Hospital, Scripps Clinic and Research Foundation, San Diego, Centennial Medical Center, Nashville, Pres. Pacific Div. 1995–97, Pres. Western Group 1997–2001, COO 2001–09, mem. Bd of Dirs 2002–, Pres. 2002–09, Pres. and CEO Jan.–Dec. 2009, Chair. and CEO 2009–; fmr mem. Bd of Dirs California Hosp. Asscn, Fed. of American Hosp., St Luke's Community Center, United Way of Metropolitan Nashville; mem. American Soc. of Corp. Execs, Business Council, Nashville Healthcare Council, Community Foundation of Middle Tennessee Bd; Fellow, American Coll. of Healthcare Execs. *Address:* HCA Inc., 1 Park Plaza, Nashville, TN 37203, USA (office). *Telephone:* (615) 344-9551 (office). *Fax:* (615) 344-2266 (office). *E-mail:* info@hcahealthcare.com (office). *Website:* www.hcahealthcare.com (office).

BRACKS, Hon. Stephen (Steve) Phillip, AC, DipBusStudies, GradDipEduc; Australian politician; b. 15 Oct. 1954, Ballarat Vic.; m.; two s. one d.; ed Ballarat Univ.; secondary commerce teacher 1976–81; employment project worker and municipal recreation officer 1981–85; Exec. Dir Ballarat Educ. Centre 1985–89; Statewide Man. Victoria's Employment Programmes 1989–1993; Adviser to Premier of Vic. 1990; Prin. Adviser to Fed. Parl. Sec. for Transport and Communications 1993; Exec. Dir Victorian Printing Industry Training Bd 1993–94; mem. Parl. (Labour) 1994–; Deputy Chair. Public Accounts and Estimates Cttee 1996–99; Shadow Minister for Employment, Industrial Relations and Tourism 1994–96; Shadow Treas., Shadow Minister for Finance and Industrial Relations 1996–99; Premier of Vic., Minister for Multicultural Affairs 1999–2007, Treas. of Vic. 1999–2000, Minister for Veterans' Affairs 2004–07; Adviser to Prime Minister of Timor-Leste (East Timor) Xanana Gusmao 2007–; Chair. United Super Pty Ltd (Cbus) 2008–; Ind., Chair. Australian Subscription TV and Radio Asscn (ASTRA) 2008–13; Sr Adviser KPMG 2007–12, Nat. Australia Bank 2008–13; mem. Bd Jardine Lloyd Thompson Pty Ltd 2007–, Bank of Sydney 2010–; Australia Automotive Industry Envoy 2009–13; adviser to several major Australian finance and service sector corpns; Hon. Chair. 2010 Road World Cycling Championship. *Leisure interests:* camping, cycling, distance swimming, tennis. *Address:* Old Treasury Building, 20 Spring Street, Melbourne, Vic. 3000, Australia (office). *Telephone:* (3) 9651-2223 (office). *E-mail:* info@stevebracks.com.au (office). *Website:* www.stevebracks.com.au (office).

BRADBEER, Sir (John) Derek (Richardson), Kt, OBE, MA, TD, DL; British lawyer; b. 29 Oct. 1931; s. of William Bertram Bradbeer and Winifred Bradbeer (née Richardson); m. Margaret Elizabeth Chantler 1962; one s. one d.; ed Canford School, Sidney Sussex Coll., Cambridge; admitted solicitor 1959; Partner, Wilkinson Maughan (fmrly Wilkinson Marshall Clayton & Gibson) 1961–97; mem. Criminal Injuries Compensation Bd 1988–2000, Criminal Injuries Compensation Appeals Panel 1996–2008; mem. Disciplinary Cttee Inst. of Actuaries 1989–96, Insurance Brokers Registration Council 1992–96; mem. Council, Law Soc. 1973–94, Vice-Pres. 1986–87, Pres. 1987–88; Pres. Newcastle-upon-Tyne Inc. Law Soc. 1982–83; Gov. Coll. of Law 1983–2002 (Chair. 1990–99); Dir Newcastle and Gateshead Water PLC 1978–90, Sunderland and South Shields Water PLC 1990–2002; Chair. North East Water 1992–2002; Deputy Chair. Northumbrian Water Group 1996–2002; UK Vice-Pres. Union Int. des Avocats 1988–92; Vice-Chair. N of England Territorial Auxiliary and Volunteer Reserve Asscn 1988–90, Chair. 1990–96; DL Tyne and Wear 1988; Hon. DUniv (Open Univ.) 2000, Hon. DLaws (Coll. of Law) 2007. *Leisure interests:* reading, gardening, sport, fine art. *Address:* Forge Cottage, Shilvington, Newcastle-upon-Tyne, NE20 0AP (home); Criminal Injuries Compensation Appeals Panel, 11th Floor, Cardinal Tower, Farringdon Road, London, EC1M 3HS, England (office). *Telephone:* (1670) 775214 (home). *Fax:* (1670) 775214 (home). *E-mail:* bradbeer4@aol.com (home).

BRADEMAS, John, DPhil; American university administrator and fmr politician; *President Emeritus, New York University;* b. 2 March 1927, Mishawaka, Ind.; s. of Stephen J. Brademas and Beatrice Goble; m. Mary Ellen Briggs 1977; ed Harvard Univ. and Univ. of Oxford, UK; Legis. Asst to Senator Pat McNamara; Admin. Asst to Rep. Thomas L. Ashley 1955; Exec. Asst to presidential nominee Stevenson 1955–56; Asst Prof. of Political Science, St Mary's Coll. Notre Dame, Ind. 1957–58; mem. 86th–96th Congresses from 3rd Ind. Dist, Chief Deputy Majority Whip 93rd–94th Congresses; Majority Whip 95th–96th Congresses; Pres. New York Univ. 1981–92, Pres. Emer. 1992–, currently Pres. King Juan Carlos I of Spain Center, New York Univ. Foundation; Chair. Pres.'s Comm. on the Arts and Humanities 1994; fmr Chair. American Ditchley Foundation, now Gov. Ditchley Foundation; fmr Chair. Fed. Reserve Bank of New York, Nat. Endowment for Democracy 1993–2001; fmr mem. Bd of Dirs RCA/NBC, Scholastic Inc., New York Stock Exchange, Rockefeller Foundation; Founder John Brademas Center for the Study of Congress, New York Univ.; fmr mem. Cen. Comm. WCC, Trilateral Comm., Bd Aspen Inst., Overseers of Harvard, New York Stock Exchange, Rockefeller Foundation; Trustee, New York Univ., World Conf. of Religions for Peace; mem. Nat. Acad. of Educ., Acad. of Athens, Nat. Acad. of Educ. of Argentina, European Acad. of Sciences and Arts; Fellow, American Acad. of Arts and Sciences; Hon. Fellow, Brasenose Coll., Oxford; Gran Cruz de la Orden de Alfonso X el Sabio (Spain) 1997, Grand Cross of the Order of Makarios the III (Cyprus) 2007; hon. degrees from 51 colls and univs; Annual Gold Medal of Spanish Inst. 1984, Public Leadership in the Arts Awards 2004, and many other awards and distinctions. *Publications:* Anarcosindicalismo y revolución en España, 1930–37 1974, Washington, DC to Washington Square 1986, The Politics of Education: Conflict and Consensus on Capitol Hill 1987. *Leisure interests:* reading, travel. *Address:* Office of the President Emeritus, New York University King Juan Carlos I Center, 53 Washington Square South, New York, NY 10012, USA (office).

BRADFORD, Barbara Taylor, OBE; British writer and journalist; b. Leeds, England; d. of Winston Taylor and Freda Walker; m. Robert Bradford 1963; reporter, Yorkshire Evening Post 1949–51, Women's Ed. 1951–53; Fashion Ed. Woman's Own 1953–54; columnist, London Evening News 1955–57; Exec. Ed. London American 1959–62; Ed. Nat. Design Centre Magazine 1965–69; syndicated columnist, Newsday Specials, Long Island 1968–70; nat. syndicated columnist, Chicago Tribune-New York (News Syndicate), New York 1970–75, Los Angeles Times Syndicate 1975–81; Dir Library of Congress; Bd mem. American Heritage Dictionary, Police Athletic League, Author's Guild Foundation 1989–; Girls Inc.; Hon. DLit (Leeds) 1990, (Bradford) 1995, Hon. DHumLitt (Teikyo Post Univ.) 1996; numerous awards and prizes. *Television:* ten novels adapted into TV miniseries. *Publications include:* Complete Encyclopaedia of Homemaking Ideas 1968, A Garland of Children's Verse 1968, How to be the Perfect Wife 1969, Easy Steps to Successful Decorating 1971, How to Solve your Decorating Problems 1976, Decorating Ideas for Casual Living 1977, Making Space Grow 1979, A Woman of Substance (novel) 1979, Luxury Designs for Apartment Living 1981, Voice of the Heart 1983, Hold the Dream 1985, Act of Will (novel) 1986, To Be The Best 1988, The Women in his Life (novel) 1990, Remember (novel) 1991, Angel (novel) 1993, Everything to Gain (novel) 1994, Dangerous to Know (novel) 1995, Love in Another Town (novel) 1995, Her Own Rules 1996, A Secret Affair 1996, Power of a Woman 1997, A Sudden Change of Heart 1998, Where You Belong 2000, The Triumph of Katie Byrne 2001, Three Weeks in Paris 2002, Emma's Secret 2003, Unexpected Blessings 2004, Just Rewards 2006, The Ravenscar Dynasty 2007, Heirs of Ravenscar 2007, Being Elizabeth 2008, Breaking the Rules 2009, Playing the Game 2011. *Leisure interests:* boating, travelling, art collecting. *Address:* Bradford Enterprises, 450 Park Avenue, New York, NY 10022, USA (office). *Telephone:* (212) 308-7390 (office). *Fax:* (212) 935-1636 (office). *E-mail:* btbweb@barbarataylorbradford.com. *Website:* www.barbarataylorbradford.com.

BRADFORD, Max, MCom; New Zealand economist, consultant and fmr politician; b. 1942, Christchurch; s. of Robert Bradford and Ella Bradford; m. 1st Janet Grieve (divorced); m. 2nd Rosemary Bradford; two step-d.; ed Univ. of Canterbury; fmr mem. staff, Treasury; fmr mem. staff IMF, Washington, DC; fmr Chief Exec. NZ Bankers' Asscn; MP (Nat. Party) for Tarawera (now for Rotorua) 1990–2002; Minister of Labour, Energy, Immigration and Business Devt 1996–98, of Labour, Energy, Defence, Enterprise and Commerce 1998–99, of Tertiary Educ. 1999; fmr Chief Exec. Nat. Party; fmr Dir Castalia Strategic Advisors Ltd; f. Bradford and Associates (consultancy). *Leisure interests:* fishing, music, reading, sailing. *Address:* Bradford & Associates, 1/214 Oriental Parade, Wellington 6002

Wellington 6002, New Zealand (office). *E-mail:* max.bradford@paradise.net.nz. *Website:* www.maxbradford.co.nz.

BRADLEE, Benjamin Crowninshield, AB; American newspaper editor; *Vice-President at Large, Washington Post;* b. 26 Aug. 1921, Boston; s. of Frederick Bradlee and Josephine de Gersdorff; m. 1st Jean Saltonstall 1942; one s.; m. 2nd Antoinette Pinchot 1956; one s. one d.; m. 3rd Sally Quinn 1978; one s.; ed Harvard Univ.; reporter, New Hampshire Sunday News, Manchester 1946–48, Washington Post 1948–51; Press Attaché, Embassy in Paris 1951–53; European corresp. Newsweek, Paris 1953–57; reporter, Washington Bureau, Newsweek 1957–61, Sr Ed. and Chief of Bureau 1961–65; Man. Ed. Washington Post 1965–68, Vice-Pres. and Exec. Ed. 1968–91, Vice-Pres. at Large 1991–; Chair. History of St Mary's City Comm. 1992–; Dr hc (Georgetown Univ.) 2006; Burton Benjamin Award 1995. *Publications:* That Special Grace 1964, Conversations with Kennedy 1975, A Good Life: Newspapering and Other Adventures (autobiography) 1995, A Life's Work: Fathers and Sons 2012. *Address:* 1150 15th Street, NW, Washington, DC 20071-0001, USA (home). *Telephone:* (202) 334-7510 (home).

BRADLEY, Clive, CBE, MA (Hons); British publishing and media executive and barrister; *Convenor, Confederation of Information Communication Industries;* b. 25 July 1934, London, England; s. of Alfred Bradley and Annie Kathleen Bradley; ed Felsted School, Essex, Clare Coll., Cambridge, Yale Univ., USA; barrister (Middle Temple); with BBC 1961–63; Broadcasting Officer, Labour Party 1963–65; Political Ed., The Statist 1965–67; Group Labour Adviser, Int. Publishing Corpn and Deputy Gen. Man. Daily Mirror and Sunday Mirror 1967–73; Dir The Observer 1973–75; Chief Exec. The Publishers Asscn 1976–97; Convenor Confed. of Information Communication Industries 1984–; Chair. Central London Valuation Tribunal 1972–2006, Age Concern Richmond upon Thames 1999–2003, Richmond upon Thames Arts Council 2003–09, BookPower 2008–11; Gov. Felsted School 1972–2009. *Publications:* many articles and broadcasts on politics, econs, industrial relations, industry media and current affairs. *Leisure interests:* politics, reading, walking. *Address:* 8 Northumberland Place, Richmond upon Thames, Surrey, TW10 6TS, England. *Telephone:* (20) 8940-7172. *E-mail:* bradley_clive@btopenworld.com.

BRADLEY, David John, MA, DM, FRCP, FRCPath, FFPHM, FIBiol, FMedSci; British medical scientist and academic; *Ross Professor Emeritus, Ross Institute of Tropical Hygiene, London School of Hygiene and Tropical Medicine, University of London;* b. 12 Jan. 1937; s. of the late Harold Robert Bradley and of Mona Bradley; m. Lorne Marie Farquhar 1961 (divorced 1989); two s. two d.; ed Wyggeston Grammar School, Leicester, Selwyn Coll., Cambridge and Univ. Coll. Hosp. Medical School, London; Univ. Coll. Hosp. 1960–61; Medical Research Officer, Ross Inst. Bilharzia Research Unit, Mwanza, Tanzania 1961–64; Lecturer, Makerere Medical School, Univ. of East Africa 1964–66, Sr lecturer in Preventive Medicine 1966–69; Royal Soc. Tropical Research Fellow 1969–73; Sr Research Fellow, Staines Medical Fellow, Exeter Coll., Oxford 1971–74; Clinical Reader in Pathology, Univ. of Oxford Clinical Medical School 1973–74; Prof. of Tropical Hygiene, Univ. of London, Dir and Head of Dept Ross Inst. of Tropical Hygiene, London School of Hygiene and Tropical Medicine 1974–2000, Ross Prof. Emer. 2000–, currently Distinguished Visiting Scientist, School of Geography and the Environment, Univ. of Oxford; Chair. Div. of Communicable and Tropical Diseases 1982–88; fmr Pres. Royal Soc. of Tropical Medicine and Hygiene; Visiting Prof., Univ. of Wales Coll. of Medicine 1995–; corresp. mem. German Tropenmedizingesellschaft; Foreign Corresp. mem. Royal Belgian Acad. of Medicine; Dr hc (Univ. of Leicester); Chalmers Medal, Royal Soc. of Tropical Medicine and Hygiene, Macdonald Medal, Royal Soc. of Tropical Medicine and Hygiene, Harben Gold Medal, Royal Inst. of Public Health. *Publications:* five books and more than 150 papers on tropical medicine and related topics. *Leisure interests:* natural history, landscape gardens, travel. *Address:* School of Geography and the Environment, South Parks Road, Oxford, OX1 3QY; Ross Institute, London School of Hygiene and Tropical Medicine, Keppel Street, London, WC1E 7HT (office); Flat 3, 1 Taviton Street, London, WC1H 0BT, England. *Telephone:* (20) 7927-2216 (office); (20) 7383-0228 (home). *Fax:* (20) 7580-9075 (office). *E-mail:* David.Bradley@lshtm.ac.uk (office); david.bradley@zoo.ox.ac.uk (office). *Website:* www.lshtm.ac.uk (office); www.geog.ox.ac.uk (office).

BRADLEY, Donal Donat Conor, CBE, BSc, PhD, ARCS, FRS, FInstP, FIET, FRSA; British physicist and academic; *Lee-Lucas Professor of Experimental Physics, Director, Centre for Plastic Electronics and Vice-Provost (Research), Imperial College London;* ed Wimbledon Coll., Imperial Coll., London, Royal Coll. of Science, Univ. of Cambridge Cavendish Lab.; served as Royal Coll. of Science Union Departmental Rep. for Physics; BP-funded Research Assoc. 1987; Unilever Research Fellow in Chemical Physics, Corpus Christi Coll., Cambridge 1987–89; Toshiba Fellow within Chemical Lab., Toshiba R&D Center, Kawasaki, Japan 1987–88; Univ. Asst Lecturer in Physics, Cavendish Lab., Cambridge 1989–93, Coll. Lecturer in Physics and Title A Fellow, Churchill Coll. 1989–93, Dir of Studies in Physics 1992–93; Reader in Dept of Physics, Univ. of Sheffield 1993–95, Prof. 1995–2002, f. Molecular Electronic Materials and Devices Group, Warden of Tapton Hall of Residence 1994–99, Co-Dir Centre for Molecular Materials 1994–95, Dir 1995–2000, Royal Soc. Amersham Int. Sr Research Fellowship 1996–97, Leverhulme Research Fellowship 1997–98; Prof. of Experimental Solid State Physics, Imperial Coll. London 2000–, Head of Experimental Solid State Physics Group 2001–04, 2005, Dir of Imperial College London Consultants Ltd 2005–06, Head of Dept 2005, Lee-Lucas Prof. 2006–, Deputy Prin., Faculty of Natural Sciences 2008–09, first Dir Centre for Plastic Electronics 2009–, Pro-Rector (Research) 2011–13, Chair. Coll.'s Research Cttee and mem. Coll. Man. Bd 2011–13, Vice-Provost (Research) and mem. Provost's Bd 2013–; Adjunct Chair Prof., Dept of Physics and Inst. of Advanced Materials, Hong Kong Baptist Univ. 2012; Chief Int. Academic Advisor, Faculty of Science, Harbin Inst. of Tech., China 2012; Trustee, Rank Prize Funds 2013; Fellow, Inst. of Eng and Tech. 2013; Hon. Prof., Nanjing Tech. Univ. 2013; Silver Medal and Fellowship, Royal Soc. of Arts 1983, Daiwa Award 1994, EU Descartes Prize 2003, Jan Rajchman Prize, Soc. for Information Display 2005, European Latsis Prize for Nanoengineering, European Science Foundation 2005, Research Excellence Award, Imperial Coll. London 2006, Brian Mercer Award for Innovation, Royal Soc. 2007, Faraday Medal, Inst. of Physics 2009, Faraday Medal, Inst. of Eng and Tech. 2010, Bakerian Lecturer, Royal Soc. 2010, Founders Prize, combined Inst. of Physics, RSC and Inst. of

Materials, Minerals and Mining, Polymer Physics Group 2013. *Publications include:* numerous papers in professional journals; one patent. *Address:* Room 4.08A, Faculty Building, Imperial College, South Kensington Campus, London, SW7 2AZ, England (office). *Telephone:* (20) 7594-2638 (office). *Fax:* (20) 7594-2077 (office). *E-mail:* d.bradley@imperial.ac.uk (office). *Website:* www.imperial.ac.uk/people/d.bradley (office); www.imperial.ac.uk/plasticelectronics (office).

BRADLEY, Donald Charlton, BSc, PhD, DSc, FRSC, CChem, FRSA, FRS; British inorganic chemist and academic; *Professor Emeritus, Queen Mary College, University of London;* b. 7 Nov. 1924, London; m. 1st Constance Joy Hazeldean 1948 (died 1985); one s.; m. 2nd Ann Levy (née MacDonald) 1990; ed Hove Co. School for Boys, Birkbeck Coll., Univ. of London; Research Asst, British Electrical and Allied Industries Research Asscn 1941–47; Asst Lecturer in Chem., Birkbeck Coll. 1949–52, Lecturer 1952–59; Prof. of Chem., Univ. of Western Ont. 1959–64; Prof. of Inorganic Chem., Queen Mary Coll., Univ. of London 1965–87, Prof. Emer. 1988–, Head of Chem. Dept 1978–82, Fellow 1988; Chair. Bd of Studies in Chem. and Chemical Industries, Univ. of London 1977–79; mem. Senate, London Univ. 1981–87; Pres. Dalton Div. Royal Soc. Chem.; MRI (mem. Council 1987–93, Hon. Sec. 1988–93); Exec. Ed. Polyhedron 1982–97; Fellow, Royal Soc. 1980; Freeman City of London 1996; Ludwig Mond Medal and Lectureship, Royal Soc. Chem. 1987, Royal (Queen's) Medal, Royal Soc. 1998, Bakerian Prize Lecture 2010. *Publications:* Metal Alkoxides (jt author) 1978, Alkoxo and Aryloxo Derivatives of Metals (jt author) 2001; over 260 scientific papers. *Leisure interests:* travelling, gardening, music, archaeology. *Address:* Birkbeck, University of London, Malet Street, Bloomsbury, London WC1E 7HX (office); Department of Chemistry, Queen Mary College, University of London, Mile End Road, London, E1 4NS (office); 171 Shakespeare Tower, Barbican, London, EC2Y 8DR, England (home). *Telephone:* (20) 7882-5025 (office); (20) 7638-2054 (home). *E-mail:* d.c.bradley@qmul.ac.uk (office); don@bradleyhome.net (home). *Website:* www.chem.qmul.ac.uk (office).

BRADLEY, Michael Carl, MBE; British trade union official; *General Secretary, General Federation of Trade Unions;* b. 17 Feb. 1951, Birmingham, England; s. of Ronald William Bradley and Doris Florence Bradley (née Hill); m. Janice Bradley (née Holmes) 1973; ed Aldridge Grammar School, Brooklyn Coll., Birmingham; Exec. Officer, Inland Revenue 1971–74; Payroll Admin. Smedley H.P. Foods 1974–80; Researcher, Transport and Gen. Workers Union (TGWU) 1980–82; Staff Section Organizer, Nat. Union of Lock and Metal Workers 1982–87, Gen. Sec. 1988–92; Gen. Sec. Gen. Fed. of Trade Unions 1993–; mem. Unity Trust Advisory Cttee 1986–, Social Security Appeals Tribunal 1986–98, Governing Council, Ruskin Coll., Oxford 1994–, Trade Union Labour Party Liaison Cttee 1996–; Chair. Trade Union Co-ordinating Cttee 2003–; Gov. The Northern Coll., Barnsley 2000–; Trustee, Trade Union Unit Charitable Trust 2000–; Hon. Fellow, Oxford Brookes Univ. 2006. *Leisure interests:* sport, reading, music. *Address:* General Federation of Trade Unions, 4th Floor, Headland House, 308–312 Gray's Inn Road, London, WC1X 8DP, England (office). *Telephone:* (20) 7520-8340 (office). *Fax:* (20) 7520-8350 (office). *E-mail:* mike@gftu.org.uk (office). *Website:* www.gftu.org.uk (office).

BRADLEY, Stephen Edward; British diplomatist and consultant; b. 4 April 1958; m. Elizabeth Bradley; one s. one d.; ed Balliol Coll., Oxford, Fudan Univ., Shanghai; joined FCO 1981, Afghan/Pakistan Desk, S Asian Dept 1981–83; Second Sec., Econ., later First Sec., Chancery, British Embassy, Tokyo 1983–87; Deputy Political Adviser to Hong Kong Govt 1988–93; FCO French Desk, W European Dept 1995; Deputy Head of Near East and N Africa FCO Dept 1996–97; Head of W Indian Atlantic Dept 1997–98; Dir of Trade and Investment Promotion, British Embassy, Paris 1999–2002; Minister, Deputy Head of Mission and Consul Gen., British Embassy, Beijing 2002; Consul-Gen., Hong Kong Special Admin. Region 2003–08; currently Independent Consultant to Grosvenor five, Hong Kong; Marketing Dir, Guinness Peat Aviation, Hong Kong 1987–88, Assoc. Dir, Lloyd George Investment Man., Hong Kong 1993–95, New Millennium Experience Co. 1998–99; mem. Bd of Dirs Husky Energy Inc. 2010–, Swire Properties Ltd 2010–. *Leisure interests:* books, gardens, travel, hiking. *Address:* Grosvenor Ltd, Suite 3505, Jardine House, One Connaught Place, Hong Kong Special Administrative Region, People's Republic of China. *Website:* www.grosvenor.com.

BRADLEY, William (Bill) W., BA, MA; American business executive, fmr politician and fmr professional basketball player; *Managing Director, Allen & Company LLC;* b. 28 July 1943, Crystal City, Mo.; s. of Warren W. Bradley and Susan Crowe; m. Ernestine Schlant 1974; one d.; ed Princeton Univ., Univ. of Oxford, UK; served in USAF Reserve 1967; after graduating from Princeton Univ., attended Univ. of Oxford as Rhodes Scholar; returned to USA to play professional basketball with New York Knickerbockers of Nat. Basketball Asscn (NBA) 1967–77; Senator from New Jersey 1979–96; Payne Dist Prof., Inst. for Int. Studies, Stanford Univ. 1997–98; Sr Advisor and Vice-Chair. of Int. Council, J.P. Morgan & Co. 1997–99; unsuccessful bid for Democratic Party nomination for President of US 2000; Chief Outside Advisor, McKinsey & Co.'s non-profit practice 2001–04; currently Man. Dir Allen & Company LLC (investment bank); mem. Bd of Dirs Quinstreet Inc. 2004–; mem. Advisory Bd Hakluyt & Co. (UK) 2005–, Eurasia Foundation; fmr Visiting Prof., Stanford Univ., Univ. of Notre Dame, Univ. of Maryland; host, American Voices radio show on Sirius Satellite Radio; Hon. DCL (Univ. of Oxford) 2003; elected mem. Basketball Hall of Fame. *Achievements include:* Olympic gold medalist (basketball) 1964. *Publications:* Life on the Run 1976, The Fair Tax 1984, Time Present, Time Past 1996, Values of the Game 1998, The New American Story 2007. *Address:* c/o Allen & Company LLC, 711 Fifth Avenue, 9th Floor, New York, NY 10022 (office); 1661 Page Mill Road, Palo Alto, CA 94304, USA (office). *Telephone:* (212) 832-8000 (office). *Fax:* (212) 832-8023 (office).

BRADMAN, Godfrey Michael, FCA; British business executive; b. 9 Sept. 1936; s. of William I. Bradman and Anne Bradman (née Goldsweig); m. Susan Bennett 1975; two s. three d.; Sr Pnr, Godfrey Bradman & Co. (chartered accountants) 1961; Chair. Bankers London Mercantile Corpn 1969; Jt Chair. Broadgate Devts 1984–91; Chair. European Land and Property Corpn PLC 1992–2003, Ashpost Finance Ltd 1993–2004, Vic. Quay 1993–2000, Pondbridge Europe Ltd 1994–2000; Founder CLEAR (Campaign for Lead-Free Air) 1981–91; Jt Founder and Pres. Campaign for Freedom of Information 1983–, Founder and Chair. Citizen Action and European Citizen Action 1983–91; Chair. Friends of the Earth Trust 1983–91; Founder and Dir AIDS Policy Unit 1987–90; Pres. Soc. for the Protection of Unborn Children Educational Research Trust 1987–2006; mem. Bd of Dirs Property and

Land Investment Corpn 2001–11, Midatech Ltd 2004–13, Bridgehall Real Estate Ltd 2012–, UK Residential Properties Ltd 2013–; mem. Council UN Int. Year of Shelter for the Homeless 1987; mem. governing body London School of Hygiene and Tropical Medicine 1988–91; Founder and Jt Chair. Parents Against Tobacco Campaign; Founder Opren Victims Campaign; Trustee Right to Life Charitable Trust; Wilkins Fellow, Cambridge 1999; Hon. Fellow, King's Coll. London, Downing Coll., Cambridge; Hon. DSc (Salford). *Leisure interest:* reading. *Address:* 1 Berkeley Street, London, W1J 8DJ, England (home). *Telephone:* (20) 7706-0189 (home). *E-mail:* gb@godfreybradman.com (office).

BRADSHAW, Ben; British jounalist and politician; b. 30 Aug. 1960, London; pnr Neal Dalgleish; ed Univ. of Sussex, Univ. of Freiburg, Germany; reporter, Exeter Express & Echo 1984, Eastern Daily Press, Norwich 1985, BBC Radio Devon 1986, BBC Radio Four (The World at One) 1991–97; MP (Labour) for Exeter 1997–, Parl. Pvt. Sec. to Minister of State at Dept of Health 2000–01, Parl. UnderSec. of State at FCO 2001, Minister in the Foreign Office 2001, Deputy Leader of the Commons 2002, Under-Sec. of State at Dept of Environment, Food and Rural Affairs 2003–06, Sec. of State at Dept for Culture, Media and Sport 2009–10, also Minister for the South West; mem. GMB, NUJ, Usdaw (trade unions); Sony News Reporter Award 1993, Charity Champions Award for Animal Welfare. *Leisure interests:* hiking, theatre. *Address:* House of Commons, London, SW1A 0AA, England (office). *Telephone:* (20) 7219-6597 (office). *Fax:* (20) 7219-0950 (office). *E-mail:* ben .bradshaw.mp@parliament.uk (office). *Website:* www.benbradshaw.co.uk.

BRADSHAW, Peter, BA, FRS; American (b. British) professor of aerodynamics; *Professor Emeritus of Engineering, Stanford University;* b. 26 Dec. 1935, Torquay, Devon, England; s. of J. W. N. Bradshaw and F. W. G. Bradshaw (née Finch); m. Sheila Dorothy Brown 1968; ed Torquay Grammar School, St John's Coll., Cambridge; Scientific Officer, Aerodynamics Div., Nat. Physical Lab., Teddington 1957–69; Sr Lecturer, Dept of Aeronautics, Imperial Coll., London 1969–71, Reader 1971–78, Prof. of Experimental Aerodynamics 1978–88; Thomas V. Jones Prof. of Eng, Dept of Mechanical Eng, Stanford Univ. 1988–95, Prof. Emer. 1996–; Hon. DSc (Exeter) 1990; Royal Aeronautical Soc. Bronze Medal 1971, Royal Aeronautical Soc. Busk Prize 1972, AIAA Fluid Dynamics Award 1994. *Publications include:* Experimental Fluid Mechanics 1964, An Introduction to Turbulence 1971, Momentum Transfer in Boundary Layers (with T. Cebeci) 1977, Engineering Calculation Methods for Turbulent Flow (with T. Cebeci and J. H. Whitelaw) 1981, Convective Heat Transfer (with T. Cebeci) 1984. *Leisure interests:* ancient history, walking. *Address:* Flow Physics and Computational Engineering Group, Department of Mechanical Engineering, Stanford University, Stanford, CA 94305-3035, USA (office). *Telephone:* (650) 725-0704 (office). *Fax:* (650) 725-3525 (office). *E-mail:* bradshaw@stanford.edu (office). *Website:* www.stanford.edu/~bradshaw (office).

BRADY, Conor, BA, MA; Irish journalist and academic; b. 24 April 1949, Dublin; s. of Conor Brady and Amy MacCarthy; m. Ann Byron 1971; two s.; ed Mount St Joseph Cistercian Abbey, Univ. Coll. Dublin; reporter Irish Times 1969–73, Asst Ed. 1977–81, Dir and Deputy Ed. 1984–86, Ed. and Group Editorial Dir 1986–2002, Ed. Emer. 2002–; Ed. Garda Review 1973–74; Tutor, Dept of Politics, Univ. Coll. Dublin 1973–74 Presenter/Reporter RTE News At One and This Week 1974–75; Ed. The Sunday Tribune 1981–82; Chair. Bd of Counsellors, European Journalism Centre, Maastricht 1993–98; Pres. World Eds' Forum, Paris 1995–2000; mem. Bd of Dirs World Press Freedom Cttee, Federation International des Editeurs de Journeaux 1995–2000; Commr, Garda Síochána Ombudsman Comm. 2006–11; fmr Chair. British-Irish Asscn; Visiting Prof., John Jay Coll., CUNY; Sr Teaching Fellow, Michael Smurfit Grad. School of Business, Univ. Coll. Dublin; Cttee Mem. UNESCO Int. Press Freedom; Award for Outstanding Work in Irish Journalism 1979. *Publications:* Guardian of the Peace 1974, Up With The Times 2005, Cead Bliain Faoi Rath: The Story of Cistercian College Roscrea 1905–2005 (co-ed.) 2005, A June of Ordinary Murders 2012. *Leisure interests:* travel, reading, swimming. *Address:* c/o Garda Síochána Ombudsman Commission, 150 Abbey Street Upper, Dublin 1, Ireland.

BRADY, James S., BS; American lawyer and fmr government official; *Trustee, Brady Center to Prevent Gun Violence;* b. 29 Aug. 1940, Centralia, Ill.; m. Sarah Kemp; one s., one d.; ed Univ of Illinois; staff member, Minority Leader US Senate Everett Dirksen 1961–62; Honor Intern, US Dept of Justice 1962 then returned to Ill.; mem. Faculty, Southern Ill. Univ. 1964–65; Asst Nat. Sales Man. and Exec. Man. to Pres., Lear-Seigler 1965–66; Dir Legislation and Public Affairs Ill. State Medical Soc. 1966–68; Chicago Office Man. Whitaker and Baxter 1968–69; Exec. Vice-Pres. James and Thomas Advertising and Public Relations 1969–73; Communications Consultant 1973 then Special Asst, US Sec. Housing and Urban Devt, Washington, DC 1973–75; Special Asst Dir US Office of Man. and Budget 1975–76; Asst US Sec. of Defense 1976–77; joined staff of Senator William V. Roth Jr. 1977–79; Press Sec. presential candidate John Connally 1979; Dir Public Affairs Reagan-Bush Cttee and Spokesperson Office of Pres.-Elect 1980; Asst to Pres. Ronald Reagan and White House Press Sec. 1981–88; suffered gunshot wound to head during attempt to assassinate Pres. Reagan March 1981; f. Brady Campaign to Prevent Gun Violence (fmrly Handgun Control) 1988, Hon. Trustee Brady Center to Prevent Handgun Violence (fmrly Center to Prevent Handgun Violence); Vice-Chair. Nat. Head Injury Foundation, Nat. Org. on Disability; numerous awards including Robert A. Taft Award for Outstanding Service to Republican Party, Significant Sigma Chi Award, Distringuished Eagle Award from Boy Scouts of America, Lincoln Award; with wife awards include Advancement Communications Award, Lenore and George W. Romney Citizen Volunteer Award, John W. Gardner Leadership Award, Margaret Chase Smith Award, Jules Cohen Memorial Award; White House Press Briefing Room officially named James S. Brady Briefing Room 2000. *Address:* Brady Center to Prevent Gun Violence, 1225 Eye Street, NW, Suite 1100, Washington, DC 20005 (office). *Telephone:* (202) 289-7319 (office). *Fax:* (202) 408-1851 (office). *Website:* www.bradycenter.org (office).

BRADY, Nicholas F., BA, MBA; American investment banker, financial executive and fmr government official; *Chairman, Darby Overseas Investment Ltd;* b. 11 April 1930, New York; s. of James C. Brady and Eliot Brady; m. Katherine Douglas 1952; three s. one d.; ed Yale and Harvard Univs; with Dillon, Read and Co. Ltd 1954–82, Chair. and CEO 1982–88; Chair. Purolater Inc. 1971–87; Sec. of the Treasury, Washington, Dc 1988–93; apptd to US Senate from NJ 1982; Chair. Templeton Latin American Investment Trust 1994–; Founder and Chair. Darby

Overseas Investments 1994–; mem. Bd of Dir Amerada Hess Corpn, Holowesko Partners Ltd, Weatherford International; Dir/Trustee US Templeton Funds; served on five Presidential comms including Chair. Presidential Task Force on Market Mechanisms (known as Brady Comm.), mem. Scowcroft Comm. on Strategic Forces, Kissinger Comm. on Cen. America, Packard Comm. on Defense Man.; fmr Chair. Jockey Club, New York. *Address:* Darby Overseas Investments Ltd 1133 Connecticut Avenue, NW, Suite 400, Washington, DC 20036, USA (office). *Telephone:* (202) 872-0500 (office). *Fax:* (202) 872-1816 (office). *E-mail:* contact@doil.com (office). *Website:* www.darbyoverseas.com (office).

BRADY, Roscoe Owen, MD; American medical research scientist and academic; *Scientist Emeritus, National Institutes of Health;* b. 11 Oct. 1923, Philadelphia, Pa; s. of Roscoe O. Brady and Martha Roberts Brady; m. Bennett Carden Manning 1972; two s.; ed Pennsylvania State Univ., Harvard Medical School and Univ. of Pennsylvania; Thyroid Clinic Assoc., Massachusetts Gen. Hosp., Boston; Nat. Research Council Fellow, Dept of Biochemistry, Univ. of Pennsylvania School of Medicine 1948–50, also US Public Health Special Research Fellow and Fellow in Clinical Medicine; Officer-in-Charge, Dept of Chem., US Naval Medical School 1952–54; Section Chief, Nat. Inst. of Neurological Diseases and Blindness (now Nat. Inst. of Neurological Disorders and Stroke), NIH 1954–67, Acting Chief, Lab. of Neurochemistry 1967–68, Asst Chief 1969–71, Chief, Developmental and Metabolic Neurology Br. 1972–2006, now Scientist Emer., NIH; Professorial Lecturer, Dept of Biochemistry, George Washington Univ. School of Medicine 1963–; Adjunct Prof. of Biochemistry, Dept of Biochemistry, Georgetown Univ. School of Medicine 1965–; mem. of medical staff, Children's Hosp., Washington, DC 1992–; mem. NAS, Inst. of Medicine; Dr hc (Uppsala) 2005; Gairdner Foundation Int. Award 1973, Cotzias Award, American Acad. of Neurology 1980, Passano Foundation Award 1982, Lasker Foundation Award 1982, Kovalenko Medal, NAS 1991, Alpert Foundation Prize, Harvard Medical School 1992, US Nat. Medal of Tech. and Innovation 2007. *Publications:* Neurochemistry of Nucleotides and Amino Acids (co-ed. with D. B. Tower) 1960, The Basic Neurosciences (ed.) 1975, The Molecular Basis of Lysosomal Storage Disorders (co-ed. with J. A. Barranger) 1984; more than 470 scientific publs. *Leisure interests:* piano, cycling. *Address:* Building 10, Room 3D03, National Institutes of Health, 9000 Rockville Pike, Bethesda, MD 20892-1260, USA (office). *Telephone:* (301) 496-3286 (office); (301) 881-3474 (home). *Fax:* (301) 496-9480 (home). *E-mail:* bradyr@ninds.nih.gov (office); bradyroscoe@yahoo.com (home). *Website:* www.neuroscience.nih.gov (office).

BRADY, HE Cardinal Seán Baptist, DCL; Irish ecclesiastic; *Archbishop of Armagh and Primate of All Ireland;* b. 16 Aug. 1939, Laragh, Co. Cavan; s. of the late Andrew Brady and Teresa Smith; ed Caulfield Nat. School, St Patrick's Coll. Cavan, St Patrick's Coll., Maynooth, Irish Coll., Rome and Lateran Univ.; ordained priest 1964; language teacher, St Patrick's Coll., Cavan 1967–80; Diocesan Sec., Kilmore 1973–80; mem. Cavan Co. Bd of Gaelic Athletic Asscn; Vice-Rector Irish Coll., Rome 1980, Rector 1987–94; Parish Priest, Ballyhaise, Co. Cavan 1994; Coadjutor Archbishop of Armagh 1995–96, Archbishop of Armagh and Primate of All Ireland 1996–; cr. Cardinal (Cardinal-Priest of SS. Quirico e Giulitta) 2007; participated in Papal Conclave 2013; Chair. Irish Episcopal Conf. *Leisure interest:* Gaelic football. *Address:* Ara Coeli, Cathedral Road, Armagh, BT61 7QY, Northern Ireland (home). *Telephone:* (28) 37522045 (home). *Fax:* (28) 37526182 (home). *E-mail:* admin@aracoeli.com (office). *Website:* www.archdioceseofarmagh.com (home).

BRADY, Thomas Edward Patrick, Jr (Tom); American football player; b. 3 Aug. 1977, San Mateo, Calif.; s. of Tom Brady, Sr and Galynn Johnson-Brady; m. Gisele Bündchen 2009; one s. one d.; one s. with Bridget Moynahan; ed Junipero Serra High School, Univ. of Michigan; picked in 1995 Major League Baseball draft in 18th round as a catcher by the Montreal Expos; played coll. football for Univ. of Michigan and set record for completing 214 of 350 passes and 15 touchdowns 1999; drafted as quarterback by New England Patriots of Nat. Football League (NFL) 2000–, became youngest quarterback to win a Super Bowl 2001 season, won second Super Bowl 2003, third 2005; holds NFL record for most touchdown passes in a single regular season; tied with Kurt Warner for fifth-highest career passer rating of all time (93.3); Pro Bowl 2001, 2004, 2005, 2007, 2009, 2010, 2011, 2012, First-team All-Pro 2007, 2010, Second-team All-Pro 2005, Super Bowl MVP XXXVI, XXXVIII, AFC Champion 2001, 2003, 2004, 2007, 2011, Sports Illustrated Sportsman of the Year 2005, Sporting News Sportsman of the Year 2007, AP Male Athlete of the Year 2007, AP NFL MVP 2007, 2010, AP NFL Offensive Player of the Year 2007, 2010, AFC Offensive Player of the Year 2007, 2010, 2011, NFL Comeback Player of the Year 2009, New England Patriots All-time leader (Passing touchdowns), NFL 2000s All-Decade Team. *Television includes:* guest star host, Saturday Night Live 2005, appeared on The Simpsons 2005, Family Guy 2006. *Leisure interests:* golf, reading. *Address:* New England Patriots, 1 Patriot Place, Foxborough, MA 02035-1388, USA. *Telephone:* (508) 543-8200. *Fax:* (508) 543-0285. *Website:* www.patriots.com; www.facebook.com/TomBrady.

BRAGG, Baron (Life Peer), cr. 1998, of Wigton in the County of Cumbria; **Melvyn Bragg,** BA, MA, FRS, FRSL, FRTS; British author and television presenter; b. 6 Oct. 1939, Wigton, Cumbria, England; s. of Stanley Bragg and Mary E. Park; m. 1st Marie-Elisabeth Roche 1961 (deceased); one d.; m. 2nd Catherine M. Haste 1973; one s. one d.; ed Nelson-Thomlinson Grammar School, Wigton and Wadham Coll., Oxford; BBC Radio and TV Producer 1961–67; TV Presenter and Ed. The South Bank Show for ITV 1978–2010; Head of Arts, London Weekend TV 1982–90, Controller of Arts and Features 1990–2010; Deputy Chair. Border TV 1985–90, Chair. 1990–96; novelist 1965–; writer and broadcaster 1967–, writer and presenter of BBC Radio Four's Start the Week 1988–98, In Our Time 1998–; Routes of English 1999–, The Adventure of English 2001; mem. Arts Council and Chair. Literature Panel of Arts Council 1977–80; Pres. Cumbrians for Peace 1982–, Northern Arts 1983–87, Nat. Campaign for the Arts 1986–; Gov. LSE 1997–; Chancellor Univ. of Leeds 1999–; mem. Bd Really Useful Co. 1989–90; Pres. Nat. Acad. of Writing –2009, MIND; Appeal Chair. Royal Nat. Inst. for the Blind Talking Books Appeal 1998–2005; Hon. Fellow, Lancashire Polytechnic 1987, The Library Asscn 1994, Wadham Coll. Oxford 1995, Univ. of Wales, Cardiff 1996, Domus Fellow, St Catherine's Coll., Oxford 1990; Hon. DLitt (Liverpool) 1986, (CNAA) 1990, (Lancaster) 1990, (South Bank) 1997, (Leeds) 2000, (Bradford) 2000; Hon. DUniv (Open Univ.) 1988; Hon. DCL (Northumbria) 1994; Hon. DSc (UMIST)

1998, (Brunel) 2000; Dr hc (St Andrews) 1993, (Sunderland) 2001; John Llewellyn Rhys Memorial Award 1968, PEN Award for Fiction 1970, Richard Dimbleby Award for Outstanding Contribution to TV 1987, Ivor Novello Award for Best Musical 1985, VLV Award 2000, WHSmith Literary Award 2000, four Prix Italia Awards, various BAFTA Awards including Acad. Fellowship 2010, South Bank Show Life Achievement Award. *Plays:* Mardi Gras 1976, Orion 1977, The Hired Man 1985, King Lear in New York 1992. *Screenplays:* Isadora, The Music Lovers, Jesus Christ Superstar, A Time to Dance. *Publications:* novels: For Want of a Nail 1965, The Second Inheritance 1966, Without a City Wall 1968, The Hired Man 1969, A Place in England 1970, The Nerve 1971, The Hunt 1972, Josh Lawton 1972, The Silken Net 1974, A Christmas Child 1976, Autumn Manoeuvres 1978, Kingdom Come 1980, Love and Glory 1983, The Cumbrian Trilogy 1984, The Maid of Buttermere 1987, A Time to Dance (televised 1992) 1990, Crystal Rooms 1992, Credo 1996, The Sword and the Miracle 1997, The Soldier's Return 1999, A Son of War 2001, Remember Me 2008; non-fiction: Speak for England 1976, Land of the Lakes 1983, Laurence Olivier 1984, Rich, The Life of Richard Burton 1988, The Seventh Seal: A Study on Ingmar Bergman 1993, On Giants' Shoulders 1998, The Adventure of English 2003, Crossing the Lines 2005, Twelve British Books That Changed the World 2006, The South Bank Show: Final Cut 2010, In Our Time (ed.) 2010. *Leisure interests:* walking, watching football. *Address:* 12 Hampstead Hill Gardens, London, NW3 2PL, England. *Telephone:* (20) 7261-3128. *Fax:* (20) 7261-3299.

BRAGHIŞ, Dumitru; Moldovan politician and business executive; *Co-Leader, Moldova Noastra Alliance;* b. 28 Dec. 1957, Grătieşti; ed Institutul Politehnic din Chişinău; First Sec., Komsomol, Moldovan SSR 1989–91; Dir-Gen. Dept of Foreign Econ. Relations, Ministry of the Economy and Reform 1995; First Deputy Minister of Economy and Reform 1997–99; Prime Minister of Moldova 1999–2001; mem. Parl. 2000–; Leader Social-Democratic Alliance 2001–03; Co-Leader Moldova Noastra (AMN–Our Moldova) Alliance, following merger of Social-Democratic Alliance and two other centrist parties 2003–. *Address:* Alianţa Moldova Noastra, str. Puşkin a, Chişinău, Moldova (office). *Telephone:* (2) 54-85-38. *E-mail:* vitalia@ch.moldpac.md. *Website:* www.amn.md.

BRAHIC, André; French astronomer and astrophysicist; *Director, Laboratory Gamma-gravitation, Commissariat a l'Energie Atomique;* b. 1942, Paris; Prof., Université de Paris VII Denis Diderot, Dir Lab. Gamma-gravitation, Commissariat a l'Energie Atomique; worked with Évry Schatzman and Michel Hénon on supernovas, chaos theory, the dynamics of galaxies, planetary rings and the formation of the Solar System; specialist in exploration of Solar System by space probes; developed one of main models for rings of Saturn 1974; mem. Voyager spacecraft Imaging Team 1981; co-discoverer, with Bruno Sicardy and William Hubbard, of the rings of Neptune (five years before photographic confirmation by Voyager) 1984; mem. Cassini spacecraft Imaging Team 2004; Carl Sagan Medal for Excellence in Public Communication in Planetary Science, Div. for Planetary Sciences 2001, Prix Jean-Perrin 2006. *Publications include:* Enfants du Soleil (Children of the Sun) 1999, Planètes et Satellites 2001, Lumières d'étoiles – Les couleurs de l'invisible (with Isabelle Grenier) 2008; chapter: Saturn's Rings Seen by Cassini Spacecraft: Discoveries, Questions and New Problems, in, Traffic and Granular Flow (co-ed. Schadschneider, Poschel, Kuhne and Schreckenberg) 2005; numerous scientific papers in professional journals. *Address:* CEA/Saclay, 91191 Gif-sur-Yvette Cedex, France (office). *Telephone:* 1-69-08-60-00 (office). *E-mail:* brahic@cea.fr (office). *Website:* www.centre-saclay.cea.fr (office).

BRAHIMI, Abdelhamid, DEcon; Algerian politician and academic; b. 2 April 1936, Constantine; m.; one c.; officer, Nat. Liberation Army 1956–62; Wali of Annaba (Govt Rep. in province of Annaba) 1963–65; Dir OCI (Algerian-French Bd for promotion of industrial co-operation) 1968–70; Prof. of Econs, Univ. of Algiers 1970–75; Chair. SONATRACH Inc., USA 1976–78; Minister of Planning and Regional Devt 1979–83; Prime Minister of Algeria 1984–88; fled to UK after assassination attempt 1990s; currently Dir-Gen., Centre for Maghreb Studies, London. *Publications include:* Dimensions et perspectives du monde arabe 1977, Stratégies de développement pour l'Algérie (1962-1991) 1992, Justice sociale et développement en économie islamique 1993, Le Maghreb à la croisée des chemins à l'ombre des transformations mondiales (1956-1995) 1996, Aux origines de la tragédie algérienne (1958-2000) 2000.

BRAHIMI, Lakhdar; Algerian UN official, diplomatist and politician; *Joint Special Representative of the United Nations and the League of Arab States for Syria;* b. 1 Jan. 1934; m.; three c.; ed in Algeria and France; FLN Rep. in SE Asia 1956–61; Perm. Rep. to Arab League, Cairo 1963–70; Amb. to UK 1971–79, to Egypt and Sudan; Diplomatic Adviser to Pres. of Algeria 1982–84; Under-Sec.-Gen., League of Arab States 1984–91, Special Envoy Arab League Tripartite Cttee to Lebanon 1989–91; Minister of Foreign Affairs 1991–93; Rapporteur, UN Conf. on Environment and Devt (Earth Summit) 1992; Special Rep. of UN Sec.-Gen. in South Africa –1994, in Haiti 1994–96; Under-Sec.-Gen. for Special Assignments in Support of Preventive and Peacemaking Efforts of the Sec.-Gen. 1997; Special Envoy of UN Sec.-Gen. in Afghanistan, UN Special Mission to Afghanistan 1997–99, Special Rep. 2001–04; Special Envoy of UN Sec.-Gen. in Angola 1998; Special Adviser to UN Sec.-Gen. 2004–05 (retd); currently Distinguished Sr Fellow, Centre for the Study of Global Governance, LSE; Joint Special Rep. of the UN and the League of Arab States for Syria 2012–; Chair. UN panel for evaluation of peace-keeping operations March–Aug. 2000; other special missions to Zaïre (now Democratic Repub. of the Congo), Yemen, Liberia, and Iraq; Special Rep. of the UN Sec.-Gen. for Afghanistan and Head, UN Assistance Mission in Afghanistan 2001–03; Dir Visitor Inst. for Advanced Study, Princeton 2007; mem. The Elders 2007–, Comm. on Legal Empowerment of the Poor (UNDP), Global Leadership Foundation; Chair. Ind. Panel on Safety and Security of UN Personnel and Premises 2007; Governing Bd mem. Stockholm International Peace Research Inst.; Harvard Law School Great Negotiator Award 2002, Dag Hammarskjöld Hon. Medal, German UN Asscn 2004, Laureate of the Special Jury Prize for Conflict Prevention, Foundation Chirac 2010. *Address:* Department of Political Affairs, United Nations, New York, NY 10017, USA (office). *Telephone:* (212) 963-1234 (office). *Fax:* (212) 963-4879 (office). *Website:* www.un.org (office).

BRAHMS, Hero Heinrich, B. Dipl.-Kfm; German business executive; *Senior Advisor, Société Générale Corporate & Investment Banking;* b. 6 July 1941,

Munster; s. of Johannes Brahms and Ursula Brahams (née Stuhlmann); ed Univ. Munster; fmrly with SKET Schwermaschinenbau Magdeburg and Deutsche Waggonbau AG; joined Hoesch AG, Dortmund 1969, becoming Man. Dir 1982–91; Vice-Chair. Treuhandanstalt (privatization agency), Berlin 1991–94; Chief Financial Officer Kaufhof Holding AG, Cologne 1994–95; Chair. Supervisory Bd Bremer Vulkan (shipyard) 1995; mem. Exec. Cttee and Chief Financial Officer Linde AG 1996–2004; mem. Supervisory Bd Karstadtquelle AG (renamed Arcandor AG 2007) 2003–08, Chair. 2005–08; Second Vice-Chair. Supervisory Bd Zumtobel AG 2008–, Telefunken Holding AG, 2009–; mem. Supervisory Bd and Vice-Chair. Georgsmarienhuette Holding GmbH; mem. or fmr mem. Supervisory Bd Deutsche Post AG –2004, Wincor Nixdorf AG 2004–, Morgan Stanley AG, Madeleine Schickedanz Co. KG; mem. Shareholders' Cttee M.M. Warburg & Co. Holding KGaA; Sr Advisor (non-exec.) SG Corporate & Investment Banking (SG CIB) 2004–. *Address:* SG Corporate & Investment Banking, Tour S.G., 17 cours Valmy, 92987 Paris, Île-de-France, France (office). *Telephone:* 1-42-13-45-45 (office). *Fax:* 1-42-13-46-15 (office). *E-mail:* info@sgcib.com (office). *Website:* www.sgcib.com (office).

BRAITHWAITE, Sir Rodric Quentin, GCMG; British fmr diplomatist; b. 17 May 1932, London; s. of Henry Warwick Braithwaite and Lorna Constance Davies; m. Gillian Mary Robinson 1961; four s. (one deceased) one d.; ed Bedales School, Christ's Coll., Cambridge; mil. service 1950–52; joined Foreign Service 1955, Third Sec., Embassy in Jakarta 1957–58, Second Sec., Embassy in Warsaw 1959–61, Foreign Office 1961–63, First Sec. (Commercial), Embassy in Moscow 1963–66, First Sec., Embassy in Rome 1966–69, Foreign Office 1969–72, Head of European Integration Dept (External) 1973–75, Head of Planning Staff 1979–80, Asst Under-Sec. of State 1981, Deputy Under-Sec. of State 1984–88, Head of Chancery, Office of Perm. Rep. to EEC, Brussels 1975–78, Minister (Commercial), Embassy in Washington, DC 1982–84, Amb. to Soviet Union 1988–92; Foreign Policy Adviser to Prime Minister 1992–93; Chair. Jt Intelligence Cttee 1992–93; currently Sr Consultant in Global Investment Banking, Deutsche Bank AG, London; Chair. Britain Russia Centre 1994–2000, Moscow School of Political Studies 1998–; mem. European Strategy Bd ICL 1994–2000, Supervisory Bd Deutsche Bank Moscow 1998–99, Bd Ural Mash Zavody (Moscow and Ekaterinburg) 1998–99; mem. Advisory Bd Sirocco Aerospace 2000–03; mem. RAM 1993–2002 (Chair. Bd of Govs 1998–2002); Visiting Fellow, All Souls Coll. Oxford 1972–73; Hon. Fellow, Christ's Coll. Cambridge; Hon. FRAM; Hon. Prof. (Birmingham) 2000; Dr hc (Birmingham) 1998. *Publications include:* Engaging Russia (with Blackwill and Tanaka) 1995, Russia in Europe 1999, NATO at Fifty: Perspectives of the Future of the Atlantic Alliance (jtly) 1999, Across the Moscow River 2002, Moscow 1941 2006, Afgantsy 2011. *Leisure interests:* chamber music (viola), sailing, Russia.

BRAKS, Gerrit J. M., MAgr; Dutch politician; b. 23 May 1933, Odiliapeel; s. of Theodorus H. Braks and Helena Johanna Kroef; m. Frens Bardoel 1965 (died 2000); two s. three d.; ed Agricultural Univ., Wageningen; worked on parents' farm –1955; Asst Govt Agricultural Advisory Service, Eindhoven 1955–58; Directorate for Int. Econ. Co-operation, Ministry of Agric. and Fisheries 1965–66; Deputy Agricultural Attaché, Perm. Mission of Netherlands to EEC, Brussels 1966–67; Sec. North Brabant Christian Farmers' Union (NCB), Tilburg 1967–69; Agricultural Counsellor, Perm. Mission of Netherlands to EEC 1969–77; mem. Second Chamber of Parl. 1977–80, 1981–82; Chair. Standing Cttee on Agric., Second Chamber 1979–80 parl. year; Minister of Agric. and Fisheries 1980–81, 1982–90; mem. First Chamber of Parl. (Christian Democratic Appeal—CDA) 1991–; Pres. Catholic Broadcasting Org. 1991–96; Chair. and Pres. Céhavé Farmers Cooperative 1995–; mem. Interpal. Benelux Council 1996–2001; Pres. of Senate 2001–03; Govt Commr 'Floriade 2002'; currently ind. adviser; Commdr, Order of Netherlands Lion and other decorations. *Leisure interests:* gardening and golf. *Address:* Ruwenbergstraat 4, 5271 Sint-Michielsgestel AG, Netherlands (home). *Telephone:* (73) 5514759 (home); (6) 52303360 (home). *E-mail:* g.braks@planet.nl (home).

BRALY, Angela Fick, BA, JD; American lawyer and business executive; b. 1 July 1961, Dallas, Tex.; m.; three c.; ed Texas Tech. Univ., Southern Methodist Univ. School of Law; Partner, Lewis, Rice & Fingersh LC (law firm), St Louis 1987–99; joined RightCHOICE Managed Care Inc. (now Blue Cross Blue Shield of Mo., an operating subsidiary of WellPoint Inc.) as Gen. Counsel 1999, Pres. and CEO 2003–05, Exec. Vice-Pres., Gen. Counsel and Chief Public Affairs Officer WellPoint, Inc. 2005–07, Pres. and CEO 2007–12, Chair. 2010–12 (resgnd); mem. Bd of Dirs The Procter & Gamble Co., Blue Cross Blue Shield Asscn, Council for Affordable Quality Healthcare, Nat. Inst. for Health Care Man., America's Health Insurance Plans, Cen. Indiana Corp. Partnership; mem. United Way Women's Initiative Cttee, ABA, American Health Lawyers Asscn; named one of Modern Healthcare magazine's Top 25 Women in Healthcare 2007, 2011, named by The Wall Street Journal No. 1 on list of Women to Watch 2007, ranked by Fortune magazine amongst the 50 Most Powerful Women in Business in the US (fourth) 2007, (fifth) 2008, (fourth) 2009–10, (fifth) 2011, ranked by Forbes magazine amongst The World's 100 Most Powerful Women (16th) 2007, (fourth) 2008, (eighth) 2009, (12th) 2010, (41st) 2011, (24th) 2012. *Address:* c/o WellPoint, Inc., 120 Monument Circle, Indianapolis, IN 46204, USA. *E-mail:* boardofdirectors@wellpoint.com.

BRAMALL, Baron (Life Peer), cr. 1987, of Bushfield in the County of Hampshire; **Field Marshal The Lord Edwin Noel Westby Bramall,** KG, GCB, OBE, MC, KStJ; British army officer (retd); b. 18 Dec. 1923, Tunbridge Wells, England; s. of the late Maj. Edmund Haselden Bramall and Katherine Bridget Bramall (née Westby); m. Dorothy Avril Wentworth Vernon 1949; one s. one d.; ed Eton Coll.; commissioned in King's Royal Rifle Corps 1943, served in North-west Europe 1944–45, occupation of Japan 1946–47; Instructor, School of Infantry 1949–51; served Middle East 1953–58; Instructor, Army Staff Coll. 1958–61; on staff of Lord Mountbatten with special responsibility for reorg. of Ministry of Defence 1963–64; CO 2nd Green Jackets (King's Royal Rifle Corps) 1965–66; Commdr 5th Airportable Brigade 1967–69; GOC 1st Div. BAOR 1972–73; rank of Lt-Gen. 1973; Commdr British Forces Hong Kong 1973–76; Col Commdt 3rd Royal Green Jackets 1973–84; Col 2nd Gurkhas 1976–86; rank of Gen. 1976; C-in-C UK Land Forces 1976–78; Vice-Chief of Defence Staff (Personnel and Logistics) 1978–79; Chief of Gen. Staff and ADC Gen. to HM The Queen 1979–82; rank of Field

Marshal 1982; Chief of Defence Staff 1982–85; Lord Lt of Greater London 1986–98; Pres. of MCC 1988–89; Trustee Imperial War Museum 1983–, Chair. 1989–98; JP London 1986; KStJ 1986; Golden Medallion for Service to Christian-Jewish Dialogue 2001. *Publication:* The Chiefs: The Story of the United Kingdom Chiefs of Staff (co-author) 1993. *Leisure interests:* cricket, painting, travel, tennis. *Address:* House of Lords, London, SW1A 0PW, England.

BRAMMERTZ, Serge, PhD; Belgian lawyer, UN official and author; *Prosecutor, International Criminal Tribunal for the former Yugoslavia (ICTY);* b. 17 Feb. 1962, Eupen; ed Univ. of Louvain-la-Neuve, Univ. of Liège, Albert Ludwig Univ., Germany; Deputy Prosecutor, then Chief Deputy Prosecutor, Court of First Instance, Eupen 1996–97, before becoming Deputy to the Prosecutor-Gen., Liège Court of Appeal; Fed. Prosecutor of the Kingdom of Belgium 1997–2002; Scientific Asst, then Prof. of Law, Univ. of Liège –2002; Deputy Prosecutor, Int. Criminal Court in charge of Investigations Div. of Office of the Prosecutor 2003–07; Commr UN Int. Ind. Investigation Comm. into the murder of fmr Lebanese Prime Minister Rafiq Hariri 2006–07; Prosecutor, Int. Criminal Tribunal for the fmr Yugoslavia (ICTY) 2008–; assisted Council of Europe as expert on organized crime; also served on Justice and Internal Affairs Cttee of EC and as adviser for Int. Org. for Migration, leading major research studies on cases of cross-border corruption and trafficking in human beings in Cen. Europe and the Balkans. *Publications:* has published extensively in int. academic journals on global terrorism, organized crime, corruption, int. co-operation in criminal matters and corruption and int. criminal law. *Address:* Office of the Prosecutor, International Criminal Tribunal for the former Yugoslavia, Churchillplein 1, 2517 JW The Hague, Netherlands (office). *Telephone:* (70) 512-53-60 (office). *Fax:* (70) 512-53-58 (office). *E-mail:* brammertz@un.org (office). *Website:* www.un.org/icty (office).

BRANAGH, Sir Kenneth Charles, Kt; British actor and director; b. 10 Dec. 1960, Belfast, Northern Ireland; s. of William Branagh and Frances Branagh; m. 1st Emma Thompson 1989 (divorced 1998); m. 2nd Lindsay Brunnock 2003; ed Meadway Comprehensive School, Reading, Royal Acad. of Dramatic Art (RADA); f. Renaissance Theatre Co. 1987 (resgnd 1994), Renaissance Films PLC 1988 (resgnd 1994), Shakespeare Film Co. 1999; mem. Bd BFI 1993–97; Officier des Arts et des Lettres; Hon. DLitt (Queen's, Belfast) 1990, (Univ. of Birmingham) 2001; Bancroft Gold Medal, RADA 1982. *Theatre includes:* Another Country (Soc. of W End Theatres Award for Most Promising Newcomer) 1982, The Madness 1983, Francis, Henry V, Hamlet, Love's Labour's Lost, Golden Girls, Tell Me Honestly (writer and dir) 1986, Romeo and Juliet (producer and dir) 1986, Public Enemy (writer, actor) 1986, Napoleon (dir) 1987, Twelfth Night (dir) 1987, Much Ado About Nothing, As You Like It, Hamlet, Look Back in Anger 1989, Napoleon: The American Story (dir) 1989, King Lear (actor, dir) 1989, Midsummer Night's Dream (actor, dir) 1989, Uncle Vanya (co-dir) 1991, Coriolanus (actor), Hamlet (actor, RSC) 1992, The Play What I Wrote (dir) 2001–03, Richard III (actor) 2002, Edmond (actor, Royal Nat. Theatre) 2003, Ducktastic (Albery Theatre, London, dir) 2005, Ivanov (actor, Wyndham's Theatre) 2008, Macbeth (actor, co-dir) (Manchester Theatre Award for Best Actor 2014) 2013. *Films include:* High Season, A Month in the Country, Henry V (actor, dir, writer) (Evening Standard Best Film, NY Film Critics' Circle Best Dir Award, BAFTA Award for Best Dir, European Film Award for Best Dir 1990, European Actor of the Year, European Film Awards 1990) 1989, Dead Again (actor, dir) 1991, Peter's Friends (actor, dir, producer) 1992, Swing Kids (actor) 1992, Swan Song (dir) 1992, Much Ado about Nothing (actor, dir, producer) (British Producer of the Year, London Film Critics' Circle 1993) 1993, Mary Shelley's Frankenstein (actor, dir) 1994, Othello (actor) 1995, In the Bleak Midwinter (dir, writer) 1995, Hamlet (actor, dir, producer) 1996, The Theory of Flight 1997, The Proposition 1997, The Gingerbread Man 1997, Celebrity 1998, Wild, Wild West 1998, Love's Labour's Lost (actor, dir, producer) 2000, How to Kill Your Neighbor's Dog 2002, Rabbit Proof Fence 2002, Harry Potter and the Chamber of Secrets (British Supporting Actor of the Year, London Film Critics' Circle) 2002, Five Children and It 2004, The Magic Flute (dir) 2006, As You Like It (dir) 2006, Sleuth (dir) 2007, Valkyrie 2008, The Boat That Rocked 2009, My Week with Marilyn (Supporting Actor of the Year, London Film Critics' Circle) 2011, Thor (dir) 2011. *Radio includes:* Hamlet (actor, dir) 1992, Romeo and Juliet (actor, dir) 1993, King Lear (actor) 1994, Bequest to the Nation 2005. *Television includes:* The Boy in the Bush, Billy (Trilogy), To the Lighthouse, Maybury, Derek, Coming Through, Ghosts, Fortunes of War, Strange Interlude, The Lady's Not for Burning, Shadow of a Gunman, Conspiracy (Emmy Award for Best Actor 2001), Shackleton 2002, Warm Springs 2004, 10 Days to War (series) 2008, Wallander (series) (also exec. producer) (BAFTA Award for Best Actor 2009) 2008–12. *Publications include:* Public Enemy (play) 1988, Beginning (memoirs) 1989, The Making of Mary Shelley's Frankenstein 1994, In the Bleak Midwinter 1995, screenplays for Henry V, Much Ado About Nothing, Hamlet. *Address:* Shepperton Studios, Studio Road, Shepperton, Middx, TW17 0QD, England.

BRANCH, Taylor, AB; American writer; b. 14 Jan. 1947, Atlanta, Ga; m. Christina Macy; one s. one d.; ed Univ. of North Carolina, Princeton Univ.; mem. staff, The Washington Monthly magazine, Washington, DC 1971–73, Harper's magazine, New York 1973–75, Esquire magazine, New York 1975–76; John S. Guggenheim Fellowship 1983; John D. and Catherine T. MacArthur Fellowship 1991; Christopher Award 1988, Nat. Humanities Medal 1999, Dayton Literary Peace Prize for Lifetime Achievement 2008. *Publications include:* Blowing the Whistle: Dissent in the Public Interest (with Charles Peters) 1972, Second Wind: The Memoirs of an Opinionated Man (with Bill Russell) 1979, The Empire Blues 1981, Labyrinth (with Eugene M. Propper) 1982, Parting the Waters: America in the King Years 1954–63 (Nat. Book Critics Circle Award for General Non-fiction 1988, Pulitzer Prize in History 1989, Los Angeles Times Book Award 1988, Melcher Book Award 1988, English-Speaking Union Book Award 1989, Anisfield-Wolf Book Award 1989) 1988, Pillar of Fire: America in the King Years 1963–65 (American Bar Association Silver Gavel Award 1999, Sidney Hillman Book Award 1999) 1998, At Canaan's Edge (Chicago Tribune Heartland Prize for Non-Fiction 2006) 2006, The Clinton Tapes: Wrestling History with the President 2009, The Cartel: Inside the Rise and Imminent Fall of the NCAA (e-book) 2011, The King Years: Historic Moments in the Civil Rights Movement 2013; other: Blind Ambition (ghostwriter for John Dean) 1976; contrib. of articles to magazines and journals, including 'The Shame of College Sports' in The Atlantic, 2011. *Address:* 1806 South Road, Baltimore, MD 21209, USA (office). *E-mail:* info@taylorbranch .com (office). *Website:* www.taylorbranch.com.

BRANCO, Joaquim Rafael; São Tome and Príncipe politician; b. 1953; Minister of Foreign Affairs 2000–01, of Public Works 2003; Prime Minister 2008–10; fmr Pres. Movt for the Liberation of São Tomé and Príncipe–Social Democratic Party. *Address:* Movimento de Libertação de São Tomé e Príncipe–Partido Social Democrata (MLSTP—PSD), Estrada Riboque, Edif. Sede do MLSTP, São Tomé, São Tomé and Príncipe (office).

BRAND, Stewart, BS; American editor, writer and publisher; *President, The Long Now Foundation;* b. 14 Dec. 1938, Rockford, Ill.; m. 1st Lois Jennings 1966 (divorced 1972); m. 2nd Ryan Phelan 1983; one s. from a previous relationship; ed Phillips Exeter Acad., Stanford Univ.; served in US Army 1960–62; fmrly with Merry Pranksters; consultant to Gov. of Calif. 1976–78; research scientist Media Lab., MIT 1986; Visiting Scholar Royal Dutch/Shell 1986; f. America Needs Indians, Whole Earth Review 1985, Point Foundation, Hacker's Conf.; co-f. The Well (Whole Earth 'Lectronic Link—internet bulletin bd) 1985–, Global Business Network consultancy 1988–, The Long Now Foundation 1996– (also Pres.), All Species project 2000–; Trustee, Santa Fe Inst. 1989–. *Television:* How Buildings Learn (writer and presenter) 1997. *Publications:* Two Cybernetic Frontiers 1974, The Media Lab: Inventing the Future at MIT 1987, How Buildings Learn 1994, The Clock of the Long Now 2000, Whole Earth Discipline: An Ecopragmatist Manifesto 2009, SALT Summaries, Condensed Ideas About Long-term Thinking (with Brian Eno) 2011; ed. (or co-ed.) and publr: The Last Whole Earth Catalog 1968–72 (Nat. Book Award), Whole Earth Epilog 1974, Whole Earth Epilog: Access to Tools 1974, The Co-Evolution Quarterly 1974–85, The Next Whole Earth Catalog 1980–81, The (Updated) Last Whole Earth Catalog: Access to Tools (16th edn) 1975, Space Colonies, Whole Earth Catalog 1977, Soft-Tech 1978, The Next Whole Earth Catalog: Access to Tools 1980, (revised 2nd edn) 1981, Whole Earth Software Catalog (Ed.-in-Chief) 1983–85, Whole Earth Software Catalog for 1986, '2.0 edition' of above title (Ed.-in-Chief) 1985, News That Stayed News 1974–1984: Ten Years of CoEvolution Quarterly 1986. *Address:* The Long Now Foundation, Fort Mason Center, Landmark Building A, San Francisco, CA 94123 (office); 3E Gate 5 Road, Sausalito, CA 94965, USA (home). *Telephone:* (415) 561-6582 (office). *Fax:* (415) 561-6297 (office). *E-mail:* sb@gbn.org (home). *Website:* www.longnow .org (office); sb.longnow.org.

BRANDAUER, Klaus Maria; Austrian actor; b. 6 Feb. 1944, Bad Aussee; m. Karin Brandauer 1965 (died 1992); m. 2nd Natalie Krenn 2007; ed Acad. of Music and Dramatic Arts, Stuttgart; mem. Burgtheater, Vienna; extensive stage repertoire; Cannes Film Festival Prize for film Mephisto 1981; appeared as Jedermann at Salzburg Festival 1983, as Speer, Almeida Theatre, London 1999;. *Films include:* Mephisto 1980, Colonel Redl 1985, Out of Africa (Golden Globe Award for Best Supporting Actor - Motion Picture 1986) 1985, Burning Secret 1988, Hannussen 1988, Russia House, Angel in Hell 1989, Streets of Gold 1989, The French Revolution 1989, The Artisan (also dir), Becoming Colette 1991, White Fang 1991, The Resurrected, Seven Minutes (also dir), Felidae (voice), Marco and the Magician (also dir), Die Wand (dir), Rembrandt, Introducing Dorothy Dandridge 1999, Druids 2001, Jedermanns Fest 2002, Between Strangers 2002, Poem - Ich setzte den Fuss in die Luft, und sie trug 2003, Tetro 2009, Manipulation 2011, The Strange Case of Wilhelm Reich 2012. *Television includes:* Quo Vadis?, Perlasca, un eroe italiano 2002, Die Entführung aus dem Serail 2003,. *Address:* Bartensteingasse 8/9, 1010 Vienna, Austria.

BRANDIS, George, BA, LLB, QC, RCL (Oxon); Australian lawyer and politician; *Attorney-General and Minister for the Arts;* b. 22 June 1957, Sydney; divorced; ed Univ. of Queensland, Magdalen Coll., Oxford, UK; called to Bar, Queensland 1985; apptd Sr Counsel, Supreme Court of Queensland 2006, QC 2013; mem. Senate for Sydney 2004–, Deputy Leader of Opposition in Senate 2010–13, Deputy Leader of Govt in Senate 2013–; Minister for Arts and Sport Jan.–Dec. 2007; Shadow Attorney-Gen. 2007–13; Shadow Minister for the Arts 2010–13; Attorney-Gen. 2013–, also Minister for the Arts 2013–; Vice-Pres. Exec. Council 2013–; mem. Liberal Party of Australia. *Publications:* Liberals Face the Future: Essays on Australian Liberalism (with T Harley and D Markwell) 1984, Australian Liberalism: The Continuing Vision (with Y Thompson and T Harley) 1986. *Address:* Attorney-General's Department, Central Office, 3–5 National Circuit, Barton, ACT 2600, Australia (office). *Telephone:* (2) 6141-6666 (office). *Fax:* (2) 6141-2553 (office). *Website:* www.ag.gov.au (office).

BRANDMÜLLER, HE Cardinal Walter, PhD; German ecclesiastic, historian and academic; *President Emeritus, Pontifical Committee for Historical Sciences;* b. 5 Jan. 1929, Ansbach, Bavaria; ed Ludwig-Maximilians Univ., Munich; ordained priest, Diocese of Bamberg 1953; carried out pastoral work in Church of St John, Kronach 1953–57, Church of St Martin, Bamberg 1957–60; Prof. of Church History and Patrology, Univ. of Dillingen 1969–70; Prof. of Modern and Medieval Church History, Univ. of Augsburg 1970–97; Parish Priest of the Assumption, Walleshausen, Diocese of Augsburg 1971–98; Canon of the Chapter of St Peter's Basilica 1997–2010; specialist in the history of the Church Councils; Founder and Ed. Annuarium historiae conciliorum (journal) 1969, of series 'Konziliengeschichte' (37 vols) 1979–; mem. Pontifical Cttee for Historical Sciences 1981–98, Pres. 1998–2009, Pres. Emer. 2009–; Pres. Int. Comm. for Comparative Church History 2000–06; Titular Archbishop of Caesarea in Mauretania 2010–; cr. Cardinal (Cardinal-Deacon of S. Giuliano dei Fiamminghi) (non-voting) 20 Nov. 2010; Hon. Prelate 1983, Corresp. mem., Accad. degli Intronati, Siena, Ordinary mem. Pontifical Theological Acad., Rome, Hon. citizenship of Genazzano 2007, of Geltendorf 2011; Kt of Holy Sepulchre of Jerusalem 1981, Cross of the Order of Merit (FRG) 1990, First Class Cross of Honour, Pro litteris et artibus (Austria) 2001, Grand Cross, Order of Holy Sepulchre of Jerusalem 2010; František-Palacký-Medal, Czechoslovakian Acad. of Sciences 2001. *Publications:* The Council of Pavia-Siena 1423-1424 1974, Ignaz von Döllinger on the Eve of the First Vatican Council: A Provocation and the Answer 1977, Handbook of Bavarian Church History (three in four vols) 1991–99, The Council of Constance 1414-1418 (Vol I) 1991, (Vol II) 1997, Galilei and the Church 1994, Holocaust in Slovakia and the Catholic Church 2003, Light and Shadows: Church History Amid Faith, Fact and Legend 2008. *Address:* 00120 Città del Vaticano, Rome, Italy (office). *Website:* www.vatican.va (office).

BRANDTZAEG, Svein Richard, BEcons, PhD; Norwegian business executive; *President and CEO, Norsk Hydro ASA;* b. 23 Dec. 1957, Haugesund; s. of Svein Brandtzaeg and Kari Brandtzaeg (née Bjorlo); m. Turid Anita Merkesvik; three c.;

ed Norwegian Univ. of Science and Tech., Trondheim, Norwegian School of Man., Univ. of Auckland, NZ; started career as Project Man., ASV Group; joined Norsk Hydro, Karmøy 1986, various positions within Hydro's aluminium business including Vice-Pres. Casthouses Norway 1998–2000, Pres. Hydro Magnesium, Brussels 2000–01, Pres. Hydro Aluminium Metal Products 2002–03, Pres. Hydro Aluminium Rolled Products 2003–06, Pres. Aluminium Products Business 2006–09, Pres. and CEO Norsk Hydro ASA 2009–. *Address:* Office of the CEO, Norsk Hydro ASA, Drammensveien 260, 0283 Oslo, Norway (office). *Telephone:* 22-53-81-00 (office). *Fax:* 22-53-27-25 (office). *Website:* www.hydro.com/en (office).

BRANKOVIĆ, Nedžad, MSc, PhD; Bosnia and Herzegovina engineer, politician and professor; b. 28 Dec. 1962, Višegrad; m.; two c.; ed Univ. of Sarajevo; served with Bosnia-Herzegovina Army then apptd to head logistics team attached to Gen. Staff; with IPSA (Inst. for Transport and Communications), Sarajevo 1987–92; Dir-Gen. BiH Railways 1993–98; Dir-Gen. Energoinvest Co. (eng firm) 1998–2002; Sr Teaching Asst, Faculty for Transport and Communications, Univ. of Sarajevo; Minister of Transport and Communications, Fed. of Bosnia and Herzegovina 2003–07, Prime Minister 2007–09 (resgnd); mem. Party of Democratic Action (SDA). *Address:* c/o Party of Democratic Action, (Stranka Demokratske Akcije), 71000 Sarajevo, Mehmeda Spahe 14, Bosnia and Herzegovina (office). *Telephone:* (33) 216906 (office). *Fax:* (33) 650429 (office). *E-mail:* centrala@sda.ba (office). *Website:* www.sda.ba (office).

BRANSCOMB, Lewis McAdory, MS, PhD; American physicist and academic; *AETNA Professor Emeritus of Public Policy and Corporate Management and Director Emeritus, Public Policy Program, John F. Kennedy School of Government, Harvard University;* b. 17 Aug. 1926, Asheville, NC; s. of Bennett Harvie Branscomb and Margaret Vaughn Branscomb; m. 1st Anne Wells 1951 (died 1998); one s. one d.; m. 2nd Constance Hammond Mullin 2005; ed Duke and Harvard Univs; Instructor in Physics, Harvard Univ. 1950; Lecturer in Physics, Univ. of Maryland 1950–51; Chief, Atomic Physics Section, Nat. Bureau of Standards, Washington, DC 1954–60, Chief Atomic Physics Div. 1960–62; Chair. Jt Inst. for Lab. Astrophysics 1962–65, 1968–70; Chief, Lab. Astrophysics Div., Nat. Bureau of Standards, Boulder, Colo 1962–69; Dir Nat. Bureau of Standards 1969–72; Chief Scientist, Vice-Pres. IBM Corpn 1972–86; Prof., Dir Public Policy Program Kennedy School of Govt, Harvard Univ. 1986–96, now Dir Emer., AETNA Prof. of Public Policy and Corp. Man. 1988–96, Prof. Emer. 1996–; Adjunct Prof., Univ. of California, San Diego School of Int. Relations and Pacific Studies, Distinguished Research Fellow, Inst. for Global Conflict and Cooperation, Univ. of California; Visiting Prof., Vanderbilt Univ. 1999–2000; mem. tech. assessment advisory council, Office of Tech. Assessment, US Congress 1990–95; mem. Bd, Mobil Corpn, MITRE Corpn; mem. Nat. Acad. of Sciences (mem. Council 1972–75, 1998–), Inst. of Medicine, Nat. Acad. of Eng; Fellow, American Acad. of Arts and Sciences, American Philosophical Soc.; mem. Nat. Acad. of Public Admin, Harvard Univ. Bd of Overseers, Comm. on Global Information/Infrastructure 1995–; Trustee, Carnegie Inst. of Washington 1973–90, Vanderbilt Univ., Nat. Geographic Soc., Woods Hole Oceanographic Inst., LASPAU 1999–2004; 16 hon. degrees; several awards. *Publications:* Empowering Technology 1993, Confessions of a Technophile 1994, Korea at the Turning Point 1996, Investing in Innovation 1998, Taking Technical Risks 2000; numerous articles in professional journals. *Leisure interests:* skiing, sailing. *Address:* John F. Kennedy School of Government, Harvard University, Mailbox 57, 79 John F. Kennedy Street, Cambridge, MA 02138-5801 (office); 1600 Ludington Lane, La Jolla, CA 92037, USA (home). *Telephone:* (617) 495-1853 (office); (858) 454-6871 (home). *Fax:* (858) 456-1752 (home). *E-mail:* lewis_branscomb@harvard.edu (office); lbranscomb@branscomb .org (home). *Website:* ksgfaculty.harvard.edu/Lewis_Branscomb (office); www .branscomb.org (home).

BRANSON, Sir Richard Charles Nicholas, Kt; British business executive; *Chairman, Virgin Group Ltd;* b. 18 July 1950, Blackheath, London; s. of Edward James Branson; m. 1st Kristen Tomassi 1969 (divorced 1979); m. 2nd Joan Templeman 1989; one s. one d.; ed Stowe School; set up Student Advisory Centre (now Help) 1970; f. Virgin mail-order co. 1969, first Virgin record shop 1971, recording co. 1973, nightclub (The Venue) 1976, Virgin Atlantic Airlines 1984; f. and Chair. Virgin Retail Group, Virgin Communications, Virgin Travel Group, Voyager Group; took Virgin Music Group public 1986, bought back shares 1988 (rotating chairmanship 1991, Chair. 1991–92, now Life Pres. after sale of shares 1992); Group also includes publishing, broadcasting, construction, heating systems, holidays; Chair. UK 2000 1986–88, Pres. 1988–; Dir Intourist Moscow Ltd 1988–90; f. The Healthcare Foundation 1987, Virgin Books 1989 (sold to Random House 2007), Virgin Radio 1993, Virgin Rail Group Ltd 1996, Virgin Express 1996 (merged with SN Brussels Airlines forming Brussels Airlines 2006), V2 Records 1997 (sold to Universal Music Group 2007), Virgin Mobile (sold to NTL/ NTL:Telewest 2006 and re-launched as Virgin Media 2007) 1999, Virgin Blue (Australia) 2000, Virgin Galactic (space tourism co.) 2004, Virgin Comics 2006, Virgin Animation 2006, Virgin Health Bank 2007, Virgin Nigeria 2007, Virgin America 2007, Virgin Fuels 2009; launched Virgin Cola (drink) 1994, Babylon (restaurant) 2001, Virgin Vodka (drink); crossed Pacific in hot air balloon with Per Lindstrand 1991; world record for fastest crossing of the Channel in amphibious vehicle 2004; made unsuccessful attempt with his children at eastbound record crossing of Atlantic Ocean under sail in 99ft (30m) sloop, Virgin Money (also known as Speedboat) 2008; Chair. jury of first Picnic Green Challenge 2007; set up global science and tech. prize, The Virgin Earth Challenge 2007; hosted environmental gathering at his pvt. island, Necker Island (part of British Virgin Islands) in Caribbean with several prominent entrepreneurs, celebrities and world leaders to discuss global warming-related problems March 2008; Patron Int. Rescue Corps, Prisoners Abroad; Commr Broadband Comm. for Digital Devt 2010, Global Comm. on Drug Policy 2011; Hon. DTech (Loughborough) 1993; Dr hc (Kaunas Technology Univ.) 2013; Blue Riband Title for Fastest Atlantic Crossing 1986, Segrave Trophy 1987, ranked No. 85 on list of 100 Greatest Britons (BBC) 2002, ranked No. 86 on list of 100 Worst Britons (Channel 4) 2003, ranked by Time Magazine amongst Top 100 Most Influential People in the World 2007, UN Correspondents Asscn Citizen of the World Award 2007, German Media Prize 2011, Pres.'s Merit Award, Nat. Acad. of Recording Arts and Sciences 2012. *Film and TV appearances:* Friends, Baywatch, Birds of a Feather, Only Fools and Horses, Goodness Gracious Me, Tripping Over, Live & Kicking, The Rebel Billionaire 2004, Around the World in 80 Days 2004, Casino Royale 2006, Superman Returns 2006, Rabbit Fever 2006.

Publications: Losing My Virginity (autobiography) 1998, Screw It, Let's Do It 2006, Business Stripped Bare: Adventures of a Global Entrepreneur 2008. *Leisure interest:* sailing. *Address:* Virgin Group Ltd, 120 Campden Hill Road, London, W8 7AR, England (office). *Telephone:* (20) 7229-1282 (office). *Fax:* (20) 7727-8200 (office). *Website:* www.virgin.com (office).

BRANSTAD, Terry Edward, BA, JD; American university administrator, healthcare administrator, politician and state governor; *Governor of Iowa;* b. 17 Nov. 1946, Leland, Ia; s. of Edward Arnold Branstad and Rita Branstad (née Garland); m. Christine Ann Johnson 1972; two s. one d.; ed Univ. of Iowa, Drake Univ.; served in US Army 1969–71; admitted to Iowa Bar; Sr Partner, Branstad-Schwarm law firm, Lake Mills, Iowa –1982; mem. Iowa House of Reps 1973–78; Lt-Gov. of Iowa 1979–82; Gov. of Iowa 1983–99, 2011–; Chair. Educ. Comm. of the US 1997–98; Founder Branstad & Assocs, West Des Moines 1999; fmr Partner, Kayfman, Patee, Branstad & Miller, Washington, DC; fmr financial adviser, Robert W. Baird & Co.; Chair. Pres.'s Comm. for Excellence in Special Educ. 2001–03; Pres. and CEO Des Moines Univ. Osteopathic Medical Center 2003–09; mem. Bd of Dirs American Legion of Iowa Foundation, Iowa Health Systems, Cementech, Featherlite, Liberty Bank, Living History Farms, Advanced Analytical Technologies, Inc., American Inst. of Certified Public Accountants; Chair. Nat. Govs Asscn 1989–90; Visiting Prof., Univ. Iowa; mem. Farm Bureau, American Inst. of Certified Public Accountants (public mem. 2003), Council of State Govts (Chair. 1991), Midwest Gov. Conf., Midwestern Govs' Asscn 1986–87, Republican Govs Asscn (Task Chair. 1997), Nat. Govs Asscn (Chair. 1989), Univ. of Iowa Alumni Asscn (Distinguished Alumni Award 1999), American Legion, Sons of Norway, Kts of Columbus, Lions; Republican; Hon. mem. Des Moines Rotary; Army Commendation Medal; Hon. LHD (Univ. Osteopathic Medical and Health Service, Buena Vista Coll., Marycrest Coll.); Hon. LLD (Clarke Coll., Dubuque). *Address:* Office of the Governor, State Capitol, 1007 East Grand Avenue, Des Moines, IA 50319-0001 (office); Office of State-Federal Relations, State of Iowa, 400 North Capitol Street, Suite 359, Washington, DC 20001, USA (office). *Telephone:* (515) 281-5211 (Des Moines) (office); (202) 624-5479 (DC) (office). *Fax:* (515) 281-6611 (Des Moines) (office); (202) 624-8189 (DC) (office). *Website:* governor.iowa.gov (office).

BRAR, Davinder S., BE, MBA; Indian business executive; ed Thapar Inst. of Eng and Tech., Univ. of Delhi; Systems and Business Analyst, Associated Cement Co. 1974–77; Pres. Ranbaxy Laboratories Ltd 1996–99, CEO and Man. Dir 1999–2004; Chair. GVK Biosciences Pvt. Ltd 2004–, Davix Man. Services Pvt. Ltd; mem. Bd of Dirs Central Bd Reserve Bank of India –2007, Mphasis-BFL 2004–, moksha8 Pharmaceuticals, Maruti Suzuki India Ltd Inc. 2006–, Barista Coffee Co. Ltd, India Trade Promotion Org., Indian Inst. of Man., Lucknow, Suraj Hotels Pvt. Ltd, Madhubani Investments Pvt. Ltd, Suraj Overseas Pvt. Ltd, Green Valley Land and Devt Pvt. Ltd, Inogent Labs Pvt. Ltd, Confed. of Indian Industry, Nat. Inst. of Pharmaceutical Education and Research; Advisor Bd of Dirs Codexis Inc., USA 2005–; Dean's Medal, Tufts Univ. School of Medicine, Gold Medal, Faculty of Man. Studies, Univ. of Delhi 1974.

BRASH, Donald (Don) Thomas, MA, PhD; New Zealand banker and politician; b. 24 Sept. 1940, Wanganui; s. of Rev. Dr Alan A. Brash; m. 1st Erica Beatty 1964; m. 2nd Je Lan Lee 1989; two s. one d.; ed Christchurch Boys' High School, Canterbury Univ. and Australian Nat. Univ.; Gen. Man. Broadband Corpn Ltd 1971–81; Gen. Man. Finance and Computer Sector, Fletcher Challenge Ltd 1981–82; Man. Dir NZ Kiwifruit Authority 1982–86; Man. Dir Trust Bank Group 1986–88; Gov. Reserve Bank of New Zealand 1988–2002; mem. NZ Monetary and Econ. Council 1974–78, NZ Planning Council 1977–80; mem. Parl. (Nat. Party) 2002–; Nat. Spokesperson (Opposition) on Finance 2002–03; Leader, Nat. Party and Parl. Opposition 2003–06; Distinguished Fellow, New Zealand Asscn of Economists 2007; Dr hc (Canterbury) 1999; NZIER-Qantas Econs Award 1999. *Publications:* New Zealand's Debt Servicing Capacity 1964, American Investment in Australian Industry 1966. *Leisure interest:* kiwifruit growing. *E-mail:* mail@ donbrash.com. *Website:* www.donbrash.com.

BRASSARD, Gilles, PhD, FRSC; Canadian quantum physicist, computer scientist and academic; *Canada Research Chair in Quantum Information Processing, Université de Montréal;* ed Cornell Univ., USA; Faculty mem. Université de Montréal since 1980s, currently Canada Research Chair in Quantum Information Processing 2001–; Foreign mem. Latvian Acad. of Sciences 1998; Fellow, Canadian Inst. for Advanced Research (CIFAR) 2002, Int. Asscn for Cryptologic Research 2006; Dr hc (ETH, Zurich) 2010; E.W.R. Steacie Memorial Fellowship 1992, Prix Urgel-Archambault 1992, 'Grand Débrouillard', Les Débrouillards 1993, Université de Montréal Teaching Prize 1993, Prix Steacie 1994, Scientist of the Year, La Presse 1995, Killam Research Fellow 1997, Prix Marie-Victorin 2000, Rank Prize in Opto-electronics 2006, NSERC Award of Excellence 2006, Personality of the Year in Information Tech. FiQ 2007, IACR Distinguished Lecturer 2008, Gerhard Herzberg Canada Gold Medal for Science and Eng 2009, Killam Prize for Natural Sciences, Canada Council for the Arts 2011. *Achievements include:* with Charles H. Bennett, developed the BB84 protocol, the most secure method of encrypting information for confidential transfer from one party to another 1984, discovery hailed as one of the "10 emerging technologies that will change the world" by MIT 2003. *Publications:* Algorithmique: Conception et analyse (with P. Bratley) 1987, Modern Cryptology, Lecture Notes in Computer Science, Vol. 325 1988, Advances in Cryptology – Proceedings of Crypto '89, Santa Barbara, Calif. Aug. 1989, Lecture Notes in Computer Science, Vol. 435 (ed.) 1990, Fundamentals of Algorithmics (with P. Bratley) 1996; numerous papers in professional journals. *Address:* Département d'informatique et de recherche opérationnelle, Pavillon André-Aisenstadt, 2215 chemin de la Tour, Montréal, PQ H3T 1J4, Canada (office). *Telephone:* (514) 343-6807 (office). *Fax:* (514) 343-5834 (office). *E-mail:* brassard@iro.umontreal.ca (office). *Website:* www.iro.umontreal.ca/~brassard (office).

BRASSEUR, Claude; French actor; b. (Claude Espinasse), 15 June 1936, Paris; s. of the late Pierre Espinasse (known as Pierre Brasseur) and of Odette Joyeux; m. 2nd Michèle Cambon 1970; one s.; ed René Girard and René Simon drama schools, Paris; Beatrix Dussane Trophy 1974, César Awards for Best Supporting Actor in Un éléphant ça trompe énormément 1976, Best Actor in La guerre des polices 1980; Chevalier, Ordre Nat. du Mérite. *Plays include:* Un ange passe, L'enfant du dimanche, Match 1964, La calèche 1966, Britannicus 1966, Du côté de chez l'autre

1971, Les jeux de la nuit 1974, George Dandin 1987, Le Souper 1989, Dîner de cons 1993, La Dernière salve 1995, À torts et à raisons 1999. *Films include:* Rue des prairies, Les yeux sans visage 1959, Le noeud de vipères, La verte moisson, Pierrot la tendresse 1960, Le caporal épinglé, La bride sur le cou 1961, Germinal 1962, Dragées au poivre, Peau de banane 1963, Bande à part, Lucky Joe 1964, L'enfer (unfinished), Le chien fou, Du rififi à Paname 1966, Un homme de trop, Caroline chérie 1967, La chasse royale, Catherine ou il suffit d'un amour 1968, Le viager, Le portrait de Marianne, Un cave 1971, Une belle fille comme moi 1972, Bel ordure 1973, Les seins de glace 1974, Il faut vivre dangereusement, L'agression 1975, Attention les yeux 1976, Barocco, Le grand Escogriffe, Un éléphant ça trompe énormément 1976, Monsieur papa, Nous irons au paradis, L'état sauvage 1977, L'argent des autres, Une histoire simple 1978, La guerre des polices 1979, La boume 1980, Une langouste au petit déjeuner, Une robe noire pour un tueur, L'ombre rouge, Une affaire d'hommes 1981, Josepha, Guy de Maupassant 1982, Légitime violence 1982, T'es heureuse? Moi toujours 1983, la Crime 1983, Signes extérieurs de richesse 1983, Souvenir, Le Léopard 1984, Palace 1985, Les loups entre eux 1985, La gitane 1986, Taxi Boy 1986, Descente aux enfers 1986, George Dandin 1988, Radio Corbeau 1989, l'Union sacrée 1989, l'Orchestre Rouge 1989, Dancing Machine 1990, Sale comme un Ange 1991, Le Bal des Casse-Pieds 1992, Le Souper 1992, le Fil de L'Horizon 1993, Le plus beau pays du monde et fait d'hiver 1999, Fait d'hiver 1999, La Taule 2000, Toreros et les Acteurs 2000, Malabar Princess 2004, L'Amour aux trousses 2005, Les Parrains (voice) 2005, Camping 2006, J'invente rien 2006, Les Petites Vacances 2006, Le Héros de la famille 2006, Fauteuils d'orchestre 2006. *Television appearances include:* Le paysan parvenu, La misère et la gloire, Don Juan, Le mystère de la chambre jaune (as Rouletabille), Les eaux mêlées, Vidocq, Les nouvelles aventures de Vidocq, l'Équipe, L'argent, Véga 1999, Soraya 2003, Franck Keller 2003. *Leisure interests:* boxing, swimming, football, bobsleighing, skiing. *Address:* c/o Artmédia, 20 avenue Rapp, 75007 Paris, France.

BRATHWAITE, Rt Hon. Sir Nicholas, Kt, OBE, PC, BEd; Grenadian educationalist, administrator and politician (retd); b. 8 July 1925, Carriacou; s. of Charles Brathwaite and Sophia Brathwaite; m.; three s. one d.; ed Univ. of West Indies; fmr teacher, Sr Tutor, Prin. Teachers' Coll.; fmrly Chief Educ. Officer; fmr Minister of Social Affairs; fmr Commonwealth official; Chair. Interim Council est. after US invasion of Grenada and deposition of fmr mil. Govt 1983–84; Leader Nat. Democratic Congress (NDC) 1989–94; Prime Minister 1990–95, also fmr Minister of Home Affairs, Nat. Security, Foreign Affairs, Finance, Personnel and Man. and Carriacou and Petit Martinique Affairs. *Address:* Villa 'A', St George's, Grenada (home).

BRATUŠEK, Alenka, BA, MA; Slovenian public official and politician; b. 31 March 1970, Celje; one s. one d.; ed Faculty of Natural Sciences and Tech. and Faculty for Social Sciences, Univ. of Ljubljana; worked for a small textile co. following graduation; with Ministry of the Economy 1995–99, helped set up small business promotion network; moved to Ministry of Finance 1999, Head of Budget Directorate 2004, played active role in preparations for Slovenian EU Council presidency 2007–08; mem. Nat. Ass. (list of Zoran Janković – Positive Slovenia) 2011–, Chair. Comm. for Public Finance Control, mem. Cttee on Finance and Monetary Policy, Cttee on Justice, Public Admin and Local Self-Govt; Pres. Positive Slovenia party Jan. 2013–; Prime Minister 2013–14. *Address:* c/o Office of the Prime Minister, 1000 Ljubljana, Gregorčičeva 20, Slovenia (office). *Website:* pozitivnaslovenija.si (office).

BRAUCHLI, Marcus, BA; American journalist and pubishing executive; b. 19 June 1961, Boulder, Colo; s. of Christopher R. Brauchli and Margot L. Brauchli; m. Maggie Farley; ed Columbia Univ.; began career as copyreader for AP-Dow Jones 1984; foreign correspondent in Hong Kong, Dow Jones Newswires 1984–87, in Scandinavia 1987–88, in Japan 1988–95, Head, China Bureau 1995–99; News Ed. Wall Street Journal 1999–2000, Nat. News Ed. 2000–03, Global News Ed. 2003–05, Deputy Man. Ed. 2005–07, Man. Ed. 2007–08 (resgnd); Exec. Ed., The Washington Post 2008–12. *Address:* c/o The Washington Post, 1150 15 St. NW, Washington, DC 20071, USA.

BRAUER, Arik; Austrian artist; b. 4 Jan. 1929, Vienna; s. of Simon Moses Brauer and Hermine Brauer; m. Naomi Dahabani 1957; three d.; ed Wiener Kunstakademie; underground, Vienna 1942–45; after studies in Vienna travelled in Africa, France, Spain, Austria, Greece and Israel 1950–58, USA, E Africa, Ethiopia, Japan 1965–74; Prof. Acad. of Fine Arts Vienna 1986; one-man exhbns 1956–, in Austria, Germany, Switzerland, France, Denmark, Liechtenstein, Italy, Canada, Sweden, Yugoslavia, Bulgaria, Norway, Japan, Israel and USA; world travelling exhbn 1979–; group exhbns, including travelling exhbns with Wiener Schule des Phantastischen Realismus 1962–, in W Europe, USA, S. America, Poland, Yugoslavia, Israel, Iran, Turkey, Japan; Scenery for The Seven Mortal Sins (Vienna 1972), Bomarzo (Zürich 1970); scenery and costumes for Medea (Vienna 1972), The Magic Flute (Paris 1977); book, design and costumes for Sieben auf einen Streich (Vienna 1978); mural design for Univ. of Haifa, Israel 1982–; designer Brauerhaus, Vienna 1983–95; Guest Lecturer, Int. Summer Acad. for Fine Arts, Salzburg 1982, 83; two gold records for Erich Brauer LP (poetry, music and songs) 1971. *Publications:* Zigeunerziege 1976, Runde Fliegt 1983. *Leisure interests:* alpinism, skiing, windsurfing. *Website:* www.arikbrauer.com.

BRAUER, Stephen Franklin, BEcons; American business executive and diplomatist; *Chairman, President and CEO, Hunter Engineering Company;* b. 3 Sept. 1945, St Louis, Mo.; m. Camilla Thompson Bauer 1971; three c.; ed Westminster Coll.; First Lt, US Army Corps of Engineers 1967–70, tour of duty in Viet Nam; joined Hunter Engineering Co. 1971, Exec. Vice-Pres. and COO 1978–81, Pres. and CEO 1981–2001, Chair., Pres. and CEO 2003–; Amb. to Belgium 2001–03; mem. Bd of Dirs Ameren Corpn 2006–13; pnr and part-owner of St Louis Cardinals professional baseball team; Trustee St Louis Art Museum, Missouri Botanical Garden (Pres. Bd Trustees), Smithsonian Inst., Washington, DC, Washington Univ.; Hon. Consul of Belgium in Missouri state 1987–2001. *Leisure interest:* baseball. *Address:* Hunter Engineering Company, 11250 Hunter Drive, Bridgeton, MO 63044 USA (office). *Telephone:* (314) 731-3020 (office). *Fax:* (314) 731-1776 (office). *Website:* www.hunter.com (office).

BRAUMAN, John I., PhD; American chemist and academic; *J.G. Jackson-C.J. Wood Professor Emeritus of Chemistry, Stanford University;* b. 7 Sept. 1937,

Pittsburgh, Pa; s. of Milton Brauman and Freda S. Brauman; m. Sharon Lea Kruse 1964; one d.; ed Massachusetts Inst. of Tech., Univ. of California, Berkeley, Univ. of California, Los Angeles; Asst Prof., Stanford Univ. 1963–69, Assoc. Prof. 1969–72, Prof. 1972–80, J. G. Jackson-C. J. Wood Prof. 1980, now Prof. Emer., Chair. 1979–83, 1995–96; Deputy Ed. Science 1985–2000, Chair. Sr Editorial Bd 2000–; mem. editorial bds several journals including Nouveau Journal de Chimie 1977–85, Chemical Physics Letters 1982–85, Chemical and Engineering News 1982–84, Journal of Physical Chemistry 1985–87; mem. Nat. Research Council Bd on Chemical Sciences and Tech., advisory panels of NASA, Nat. Science Found., Atomic Energy Comm.; mem. NAS and AAAS; ACS Award in Pure Chemistry 1973, Harrison-Howe Award 1976, ACS, James Flack Norris Award in Physical Organic Chemistry 1986, Arthur C. Cope Scholar Award 1986, R.C. Fuson Award 1986, NAS Award in Chemical Sciences 2001, Linus Pauling Award 2002, National Medal of Science Award 2002, Willard Gibbs Medal 2003. *Publications:* over 270 publs in scientific journals. *Address:* Department of Chemistry, Stanford University, Stanford, CA 94305-5080 (office); 849 Tolman Drive, Palo Alto, CA 94305, USA (home). *Telephone:* (415) 723-3023 (office); (415) 493-1378 (home). *Fax:* (650) 725-0259 (office). *E-mail:* brauman@stanford.edu (office). *Website:* www.stanford.edu/dept/chemistry/faculty/brauman (office).

BRAUN, Ewa, MA; Polish costume designer, production decorator and art director; *Lecturer, Polish National Film, Television and Theatre School;* b. 2 Aug. 1944, Kraków; ed Warsaw Univ.; costume designer, Documentary Film Producers 1967–72; interior decorator, Art Dir, Film Production Agency 1972–99; mem. Polish Film Makers 1994–; Lecturer, Polish Film, Television and Theatre School, Łódź 1999–. *Films:* interior decorations and designs in over 60 films including Illumination 1972, Jealousy and Medicine 1973, Hotel Pacific 1975, Camouflage 1977, Career of Nikodem Dyzma 1979, Queen Bona 1980, C.K. Dezerterzy 1985, Young Magician (Gdańsk Bronze Lions 1987) 1986, Europe, Europe 1990, Eminent Domain 1991, Coupable d'innocence 1992, The Silent Touch 1992, Schindler's List (Acad. Award for Art Direction/Set Decoration 1994) 1993, Les Milles 1995, Holy Week 1995, Bandit 1996, Palais de la Santé 1997, Brother of Our God 1997, Jacob the Liar 1997, Gold Deserts 1998. *Leisure interests:* movies, travels, music, literature. *Address:* Polish National Film, Television and Theatre School, ul. Targowa 61/ 63, 90-323 Łódź, Poland (office). *Telephone:* (42) 6749494 (office); (22) 6428153 (home). *Fax:* (42) 6748153 (office). *E-mail:* braunewa@hotmail.com (home); ebraun@parta.onet.pl (home). *Website:* www.filmschool.lodz.pl.

BRAUN, Volker; German poet and playwright; b. 7 May 1939, Dresden; ed Univ. of Leipzig; Asst Dir Deutsches Theater, Berlin 1972–77, Berlin Ensemble 1979–90; Brother Grimm Prof., Univ. of Kassel 1999–2000; mem. Akad. der Künste, Berlin, Deutsche Akademie für Sprache und Dichtung, Sächsischen Akademie der Künste; Heinrich Mann Prize 1980, Bremen Literature Prize 1986, Nat. Prize, First Class 1988, Berlin Prize 1989, Schiller Commemorative Prize 1992, Deutschen Kritikerpreis 1996, Erwin Schrittmatter Prize 1998, Georg Büchner Prize 2000. *Plays:* Die Kipper 1965, Grosser Frieden 1979, Dmitri 1982, Die Ubergangsgesellschaft 1987, Lenins Tod 1988, Transit Europa: Der Ausflug der Toten 1988, Böhmen am Meer 1992. *Publications:* Provokation für mich 1965, Vorläufiges 1966, KriegsErklärung 1967, Wir und nicht sie 1970, Gedichte 1972, Gegen die symmetrische Welt 1974, Es genügt nicht die einfache Wahrheit 1975, Unvollendete Geschichte 1977, Training des aufrechten Gangs 1979, Hinze-Kunze-Roman 1985, Langsamer knirschender Morgen 1987, Verheerende Folgen magnelnden Anscheins innerbetrieblicher Demokratie (essays) 1988, Der Stoff zum Leben 1990, Bodenloser Satz 1990, Der Wendehals: Eine Enterhaltung 1995, Lustgarten Preussen 1996, Wir befinden uns soweit wohl. Wir sind erst einmal am Ende 1998, Tumulus 1999, Das Wirklichgewollte 2000, Das unbesetzte Gebiet 2004, Auf die schönen Possen 2005, Das Mittagsmahl (Ver.di-Literature Prize) 2007, Machwerk oder Das Schichtbuch des Flick von Lauchhammer 2008, Die hellen Haufen 2011. *Address:* Wolfshagenerstrasse 68, 13187 Berlin, Germany (home).

BRAUNGART, Michael, PhD; German chemist and academic; *Professor of Process Engineering, University of Lüneburg;* ed Univs of Darmstadt, Konstanz and Hannover; fmr Greenpeace activist, led formation of Chem. Section of Greenpeace International, Leader of Greenpeace Chem. 1985; now Prof. of Process Eng, Univ. of Lüneburg 1994–, also Dir interdisciplinary materials flow man. Masters programme; Founder and Scientific Dir Environmental Protection Encouragement Agency International Umweltforschung GmbH, Hamburg 1987–; Co-founder and Prin. McDonough Braungart Design Chemistry, Charlottesville, Va, USA; Co-founder and Scientific Dir HUI Hamburger Umweltinstitut eV 1989; currently holds Cradle-to-Cradle for Innovation and Quality Chair, Rotterdam School of Man., Erasmus University; Visiting Prof., Univ. of Twente 2010–, TU Delft 2011–. *Publications:* Hannover Principles of Design: Design for Sustainability 2000, Cradle to Cradle: Remaking the Way We Make Things 2002. *Address:* Trostbrücke 4, 20457 Hamburg, Germany (office). *Telephone:* (40) 879762-0 (office). *Fax:* (40) 879762-26 (office). *E-mail:* braungart@braungart.com (office). *Website:* www.braungart.com (office).

BRAUNWALD, Eugene, MD; American cardiologist and academic; *Hersey Distinguished Professor of Theory and Practice of Physical Medicine, Harvard Medical School;* b. 15 Aug. 1929, Vienna, Austria; m. 1st Nina Starr 1952 (deceased); three d.; m. 2nd Elaine Smith 1994; ed New York Univ.; successively Chief of Section of Cardiology, Clinic of Surgery, Cardiology Br. and Clinical Dir Nat. Heart, Lung & Blood Inst. 1958–68; Prof. and Chair. Dept of Medicine, Univ. of Calif., San Diego School of Medicine 1968–72; Hersey Prof. of Theory and Practice of Physical Medicine, Harvard Medical School 1972–96, Hersey Distinguished Prof. of Theory and Practice of Physical Medicine 1996–, Faculty Dean for Academic Programs 1996–2003; Sr Consultant in Medicine, Mass. Gen. Hosp. 1994–; Vice-Pres. Academic Programs Partners Healthcare System 1996–2003; Herrmann Blumgart Prof. of Medicine 1980–89; Chair. Dept of Medicine, Peter Bent Brigham Hosp. (now Brigham & Women's Hosp.) 1972–96; Founding Chair. TIMI Study Group, Brigham & Women's Hosp. 1984–; 14 hon. degrees; J. Allyn Taylor Int. Prize in Medicine 1993, Libin/AHFMR Prize for Excellence in Cardiovascular Research 2004, and many other awards. *Publications:* over 1,200 articles, reviews and book chapters. *Address:* TIMI Study Group, 350 Longwood Avenue, Boston, MA 02215, USA (office). *Telephone:* (617) 732-8989 (office). *Fax:*

(617) 975-0955 (office). *E-mail:* ebraunwald@partners.org (office). *Website:* www .timi.org (office).

BRÄUTIGAM, Hans Otto, DJur, LLM; German fmr diplomatist and fmr politician; b. 6 Feb. 1931, Völklingen, Saar; s. of Maximilian Bräutigam and Margarethe Sauerwald; m. Dr Hildegard Becker 1961; two s.; ed Bonn Univ. and Harvard Law School, USA; Research Asst in Int. Law, Heidelberg 1958–62; served in foreign service of FRG 1962–74; Deputy Head, Perm. Representation of FRG to GDR 1974–77, Dir Fed. Chancellor's Office, Bonn 1977–80; Foreign Office, Bonn 1980–82, Perm. Rep. to GDR 1982–89; Perm. Rep. of FRG to UN, New York 1989–90; Brandenburg Minister of Justice 1990–99; mem. Bd of Dirs Foundation for Remembrance, Responsibility and Future, Berlin 2000–02, Chair. 2004–06; Grosses Verdienstkreuz mit Stern der Bundesrepublik Deutschland. *Leisure interests:* arts, literature. *Address:* Eichenallee 37, 14050 Berlin, Germany (home). *Telephone:* (30) 3048037 (home). *Fax:* (30) 3048037 (home). *E-mail:* hobraeutigam@gmx.de (home).

BRAVO, Dwayne James John; Trinidad and Tobago professional cricketer; b. 7 Oct. 1983, Santa Cruz, Trinidad; all-rounder; right-handed batsman; right-arm medium-fast bowler; plays for West Indies, Kent, Trinidad & Tobago, Univ. of West Indies Vice-Chancellor's X, Mumbai Indians 2008–; First-class debut: 2001/02; Test debut: England v West Indies, Lord's 22–26 July 2004; One-Day Int. (ODI) debut: West Indies v England, Georgetown 18 April 2004; T20I debut: NZ v West Indies, Auckland 16 Feb. 2006. *Address:* c/o National Cricket Centre, Clifford Roach Drive, Balmain, Couva, Trinidad.

BRAVO, Rose Marie; American retail executive; *Vice-Chairman, Burberry Ltd;* ed Bronx High School of Science and Fordham Univ., Bronx, New York; began retailing career at Abraham & Strauss 1971–74; joined R. H. Macy and Co., New York as assoc. buyer 1974, various positions 1974–87, Chair. and CEO I. Magnin Specialty Div. 1987–92; Pres. Saks Fifth Avenue, New York 1992–97; CEO Burberry Ltd, London, UK 1997–2006, Vice-Chair. 2006–, mem. Bd Burberry Group PLC 1997–; mem. Bd Tiffany & Co., The Estee Lauder Cos, Inc., Nat. Italian American Foundation; Vice-Chair. Kennedy Center's Corp. Fund Bd; mem Advisory Bd Fashion Group International, The Fashion Inst. of Tech., New York; Trustee Fordham Univ.; honoured for excellence in retailing by Nat. Italian American Foundation, March of Dimes, City of Hope, Eleanor Lambeth Award, Council of Fashion Design Awards, New York 2003, ranked by Fortune magazine amongst 50 Most Powerful Women in Business outside the US (29th) 2003, (13th) 2004, (13th) 2005, ranked by Forbes magazine amongst 100 Most Powerful Women (63rd) 2005, ranked by the Financial Times amongst Top 25 Businesswomen in Europe (ninth) 2005. *Address:* Burberry Ltd, 18–22 Haymarket, London, SW1 4DQ, England (office). *Telephone:* (20) 7968-0412 (office). *Fax:* (20) 7318-2666 (office). *Website:* www.burberry.com (office).

BRAVO DE LA PARRA, María Alejandra, BSc, MSc, PhD; Mexican biochemist and academic; *Researcher, Institute of Biotechnology, National Autonomous University of Mexico (UNAM);* b. 29 April 1961; m. Dr Mario Soberon; ed Nat. Autonomous Univ. of Mexico (UNAM); Research Visitor, Plant Genetic Systems, Ghent, Belgium 1990–91; Researcher, Inst. of Biotechnology, UNAM; included in list of Experts on Biosafety under Cartagena Protocol Security and Convention on Biological Diversity, Univ. of Colombia 2003; mem. Nat. Acad. of Sciences 2002; Gabino Barreda Medal (Licenciatura) 1985, Gabino Barreda Medal (Doctorado) 1989, Award from Nat. Acad. of Sciences in Natural Sciences 1998, National Univ. Distinction for Young Academics, UNAM 2000, Award for Best Research in Agricultural Biotechnology, AgroBIO-Mexico 2003, Laureate for Latin America, L'Oréal-UNESCO Awards for Women in Science 2010. *Publications:* numerous papers in professional journals; six patents. *Address:* Instituto de Biotecnología, UNAM, Cuernavaca, Morelos, Mexico (office). *E-mail:* bravo@ibt.unam.mx (office). *Website:* www.ibt.unam.mx (office).

BRAYBROOKE, David, PhD, FRSC; Canadian/American philosopher, academic and author; *Professor Emeritus of Government, Professor of Philosophy and Centennial Commission Chair in the Liberal Arts, University of Texas at Austin;* b. 18 Oct. 1924, Hackettstown, NJ; s. of Walter Leonard Braybrooke and Netta Rose Braybrooke (née Foyle); m. 1st Alice Boyd Noble 1948 (divorced 1982); two s. one d.; m. 2nd Margaret Eva Odell 1984 (divorced 1994); m. 3rd Gomyo Michiko 1994; ed Hobart Coll., New School for Social Research, Downing Coll., Cambridge, UK, Columbia Univ., Harvard and Cornell Univs, USA, New Coll., Oxford, UK; Instructor, History and Literature, Hobart and William Smith Colls 1948–50; Teaching Fellow, Econ., Cornell Univ. 1950–52; Instructor, Philosophy, Univ. of Mich., USA 1953–54, Bowdoin Coll. 1954–56; Asst Prof. of Philosophy, Yale Univ., USA 1956–63; Assoc. Prof. of Philosophy and Politics, Dalhousie Univ., Halifax 1963–65, Prof. 1965–88, McCulloch Prof. of Philosophy and Politics 1988–90, Prof. Emer. 1990–; Prof. of Govt, Prof. of Philosophy and Centennial Comm. Chair in the Liberal Arts Univ. of Texas at Austin 1990–2005, Prof. Emer. 2005–; Visiting Fellow, Wolfson Coll., Cambridge, UK 1985–86; Fellowships of Canada Council and Social Sciences and Humanities Research Council, Canada; Fellowship, American Council of Learned Socs 1952–53, Rockefeller Foundation Grant 1959–60, Guggenheim Fellow 1962–63. *Publications:* A Strategy of Decision: Policy Evaluation as a Social Process (with C. E. Lindblom) 1963, Philosophical Problems of the Social Sciences 1965, Three Tests for Democracy 1968, Traffic Congestion Goes through the Issue-Machine 1974, Ethics in the World of Business 1983, Philosophy of Social Science 1987, Meeting Needs 1987, Logic on the Track of Social Change (with B. Bryson and P. K. Schotch) 1995, Social Rules (co-author) 1996, Moral Objectives, Rules and the Forms of Social Change 1998, Natural Law Modernized 2001, Utilitarianism: Resorations, Repairs, Renovations 2004, Analytical Political Philosophy 2006. *Leisure interests:* reading (poetry, fiction, history), listening to music, walking. *Address:* Department of Government, University of Texas at Austin, Austin, TX 78712, USA (office); Department of Philosophy, Dalhousie University, Halifax, NS B3H 3J5, Canada (office); 1500 Scenic Drive, 300, Austin, TX 78703, USA (home); 1 Prince Street 510, Dartmouth, NS, B2Y 4L3, Canada (home). *Telephone:* (902) 494-3810 (Canada) (office); (902) 466-3660 (Canada) (home); (512) 479-8963 (USA) (home); (512) 471-5121 (USA) (office). *E-mail:* braybrookedb@yahoo.com (office). *Website:* www.utexas.edu/cola/ depts/government (office).

BRAYFIELD, Celia Frances; British author and journalist; *Reader in Creative Writing, Brunel University, London;* b. 21 Aug. 1945, Wembley Park; d. of the late Felix Brayfield and Ada Ellen Brayfield (née Jakeman); one d.; ed St. Paul's Girls' School, Universitaire de Grenoble; feature writer, Daily Mail 1969–71, TV critic, Evening Standard 1974–82, The Times 1983–88; columnist, Sunday Telegraph 1989–90, The Times 1998–; contrib. to numerous other media; Dir Nat. Acad. of Writing 1999–2003; Sr Lecturer in Creative Writing, Brunel Univ., London 2005–06, Director 2006–10, Reader 2007–; Sr Lecturer in Creative Writing, Bath Spa Univ. 2010–; Trustee, One Parent Families 1988–; mem. Soc. of Authors. *Publications include:* The Body Show Book 1981, Glitter: The Truth About Fame 1985, Pearls 1987, The Prince 1990, White Ice 1993, Harvest 1995, Bestseller 1996, Getting Home 1998, Sunset 1999, Heartswap 2000, Mr Fabulous and Friends 2003, Wild Weekend 2004, Deep France 2004, Arts reviews 2008; contrib. various journals, magazines and newspapers. *Leisure interests:* family life, the arts. *Address:* Curtis Brown Ltd, Haymarket House, 28–29 Haymarket, London, SW1Y 4SP, England (office). *Telephone:* (20) 7393-4400 (office). *Fax:* (20) 7393-4401 (office). *Website:* www.curtisbrown.co.uk (office); www.celiabrayfield.com. *E-mail:* celia.brayfield@brunel.ac.uk (office); celia@celiabrayfield.com (office).

BRÁZ DE AVIZ, HE Cardinal João; Brazilian ecclesiastic and academic; *Prefect, Congregation for Institutes of Consecrated Life and Societies of Apostolic Life;* b. 24 April 1947, Matra; ed Major Seminary 'Rainha dos Apostolos', Curitiba, Faculty of Palmas, Pontifical Gregorian Univ. and Pontifical Lateran Univ., Rome; ordained priest, Diocese of Apucarana, Parana 1972; served as Rector of Major Seminary Apucarana and Londrina; fmr Prof. of Dogmatic Theology, Theological Inst. Paul VI, Londrina; fmr mem. Council of Priests and Coll. of Consultors and Gen. Coordinator of the Diocesan Pastoral Apucarana; apptd Auxiliary Bishop of Vitória, Espirito Santo and Titular Bishop of Flenucleta 1994, Bishop of Ponta Grossa, Parana 1998–2002, Archbishop of Maringá, Parana 2002–04, Archbishop of Brasília, DF 2004–11; Prefect of the Congregation for Institutes of Consecrated Life and Societies of Apostolic Life 2011–13, 2013–; cr. Cardinal (Cardinal-Deacon of Sant'Elena fuori Porta Prenestina) 2012; participated in Papal Conclave 2013. *Address:* Congregation for Institutes of Consecrated Life and Societies of Apostolic Life, Palazzo della Congregazioni, Piazza Pio XII 3, 00193 Rome, Italy (office). *Telephone:* (06) 69884121 (office); (06) 69892511 (office); (06) 69884128 (office). *Fax:* (06) 69884526 (office). *E-mail:* civcsva.pref@ccscrlife.va (office). *Website:* www .vatican.va/roman_curia/congregations/ccscrlife (office).

BREAM, Julian, CBE, FRCM, FRNCM; British classical guitarist and lutenist; b. 15 July 1933, London, England; s. of Henry G. Bream; m. 1st Margaret Williamson; one adopted s.; m. 2nd Isobel Sanchez 1980 (divorced); ed Royal Coll. of Music, London; began professional career Cheltenham 1947, London debut, Wigmore Hall 1950; has made many transcriptions for guitar of Romantic and Baroque works; commissioned new works from Britten, Walton, Henze and Arnold; tours throughout the world, giving recitals as soloist and with the Julian Bream Consort (f. 1960); many recitals with Sir Peter Pears and Robert Tear, and as guitar duo with John Williams; 60th Birthday Concert, Wigmore Hall, London 1993; Hon. DUniv (Surrey) 1968, Hon. DMus (Leeds) 1984; Villa-Lobos Gold Medal 1976, Gramophone Award for Best DVD (for My Life in Music) 2007, Lifetime Achievement Award, Gramophone Classical Music Awards 2013; numerous recording awards. *Leisure interests:* playing the guitar, cricket, table tennis, gardening, backgammon. *Address:* c/o Hazard Chase Ltd, 25 City Road, Cambridge, CB1 1DP, England (office). *Telephone:* (1223) 312400 (office). *Fax:* (1223) 460827 (office). *E-mail:* info@hazardchase.co.uk (office). *Website:* www .hazardchase.co.uk (office).

BREARLEY, John Michael (Mike), OBE; British psychoanalyst, author, journalist and fmr professional cricketer; b. 28 April 1942, Harrow, Middx, England; s. of the late Horace Brearley and Midge Brearley; partner, Mana Sarabhai; two c.; ed City of London School, St John's Coll., Cambridge, Univ. of California, Irvine, USA; right-hand opening batsman, occasional wicket-keeper; played for Univ. of Cambridge 1961–64, captained Univ. of Cambridge 1963, 1964; awarded county cap (Middx) 1964; Capt. of Middx (winning County Championships four times and Gillette Cup twice) 1971–82; Test debut 1976; Capt. of England in 31 Tests 1977–80, 1981; played in 39 Tests, scored 1,442 runs, highest score 91, average 22.88; went on tours of S Africa 1964–65, Pakistan 1967, India, Sri Lanka and Australia 1976–77, Pakistan 1977–78, Australia 1978–79, Australia and India 1979–80; holds record for most runs scored at Univ. of Cambridge (4,310 at an average of 38.48) 1964; scored 312 not out for MCC Under-25 v. North Zone, Peshawar 1967; Pres. MCC 2007–08; Lecturer in Philosophy, Univ. of Newcastle-upon-Tyne 1968–71; Assoc. mem. British Psycho-Analytical Soc. 1985, Full mem. 1990, Pres. 2008–10; part-time cricket journalist for The Times; Hon. Fellow, St John's Coll., Cambridge 1997; Hon. DCL (Newcastle) 1984, (Lancaster) 1999, Dr hc (Oxford Brookes) 2006; Wisden Cricketer of the Year 1977. *Publications:* (with Dudley Doust) The Return of the Ashes 1978, The Ashes Retained (with Dudley Doust) 1979, Phoenix: The Series That Rose from the Ashes 1982, The Art of Captaincy 1985, 2001, Arlott in Conversation with Mike Brearley (with John Arlott) 1986. *Address:* c/o Middlesex County Cricket Club, Lord's Cricket Ground, St John's Wood Road, London, NW8 8QN, England. *Telephone:* (20) 7289-1300. *Website:* www.middlesexccc.com.

BREAUX, John B., JD; American business executive and fmr politician; *Senior Counsel, Patton Boggs LLP;* b. 1 March 1944, Crowley, La; s. of Ezra Breaux and Katie Breaux; m. Lois Gail Daigle 1964; two s. two d.; ed Southwestern Univ., State Univ. of Louisiana; called to La Bar 1967; Partner, Brown, McKernan, Ingram and Breaux 1967–68; Legislative Asst to US Congressman 1968–69; Dist Asst 1969–72; mem. 92nd–99th Congresses from 7th Dist, La 1971–87; Senator from Louisiana 1987–2005 (retd), Chief Deputy Whip 1993–2005; Chair., Democratic Senatorial Campaign Cttee, Nat. Water Alliance 1987–88; Sr Man. Dir Clinton Group, Inc. (investment firm) 2005; f. Breaux-Lott Leadership Group 2008, acquired by Patton Boggs LLP, Sr Counsel, Patton Boggs LLP 2005–; Sr Advisor, Riverstone Holdings LLC 2005; fmr Distinguished Prof., Manship School of Mass Communication, Louisiana State Univ.; mem. Bd of Dirs CSX Transportation; apptd by Pres. Bush as Vice-Chair. nat. comm. to make recommendations or changes to current US tax laws 2005; Co-Chair. Nat. Bipartisan Comm. on Future of Medicare 1998–99; American Legion Award, Neptune Award, American Oceanic Org. 1980. *Address:* Patton Boggs LLP, 2550 M Street, NW, Washington, DC 20037, USA (office).

Telephone: (202) 457-5290 (office). *Fax:* (202) 457-6315 (office). *Website:* www.pattonboggs.com (office).

BRECHER, Michael, PhD, FRSC; Canadian political scientist and academic; *R.B. Angus Professor of Political Science, McGill University;* b. 14 March 1925, Montreal, Quebec; s. of Nathan Brecher and Gisela Hopmeyer; m. Eva Danon 1950; three d.; ed McGill and Yale Univs; mem. Faculty, McGill Univ. 1952–, Prof. 1963–, R.B. Angus Prof. of Political Science 1993–; Pres. Int. Studies Asscn 1999–2000; Visiting Prof., Univ. of Chicago 1963, Hebrew Univ., Jerusalem 1970–75, Univ. of California, Berkeley 1979, Stanford Univ. 1980; Nuffield Fellow 1955–56; Rockefeller Fellow 1964–65; Guggenheim Fellow 1965–66; f. Shastri Indo-Canadian Inst. 1968 (Pres. 1969–71); Watumull Book Prize, American Hist. Asscn 1960, Killam Awards, Canada Council 1970–74, 1976–79, Woodrow Wilson Book Award, American Political Science Asscn 1973, Fieldhouse Award for Distinguished Teaching, McGill Univ. 1986, Distinguished Scholar Award, Int. Studies Asscn 1995, Léon-Gérin Quebec Prize 2000, Award for High Distinction in Research, McGill Univ. 2000, Lifetime Achievement Award, American Political Science Asscn 2009. *Publications include:* The Struggle for Kashmir 1953, Nehru: A Political Biography 1959, The New States of Asia 1963, Succession in India 1966, India and World Politics 1968, Political Leadership in India 1969, The Foreign Policy System of Israel 1972, Israel, the Korean War and China 1974, Decisions in Israel's Foreign Policy 1975, Studies in Crisis Behavior 1979, Decisions in Crisis 1980, Crisis and Change in World Politics 1986, Crises in the 20th Century (Vols I, II) 1988, Crisis, Conflict and Instability 1989, Crises in World Politics 1993, A Study of Crisis 1997, 2000, Millennial Reflections on International Studies (Vols 1–5) 2002, International Political Earthquakes 2008; over 85 articles in journals. *Address:* Department of Political Science, McGill University, 855 Sherbrooke Street West, Montreal, PQ H3A 2T7, Canada (office); 3450 Drummond Street, Apt 1701, Montreal, PQ H3G 1Y3, Canada (home). *Telephone:* (514) 398-4800 (office). *Fax:* (514) 398-1770 (office). *E-mail:* michael.brecher@mcgill.ca (office). *Website:* www.mcgill.ca/politicalscience (office).

BRÉCHIGNAC, Catherine, DSc; French physicist; *Secrétaire perpétuel, French National Academy of Sciences;* b. 12 June 1946, Paris; d. of Jean Teillac and Andrée Teillac (née Kerleguer); m. Philippe Bréchignac 1969; two s. one d.; ed Ecole Normale Supérieure, Fontenay-aux-Roses; Research Asst, CNRS 1971–78, Supervisor 1978–85, Dir of Research 1985–91, Del. to the Scientific Dir, Dept of Physical and Math. Sciences 1985–89, Dir of Aimé Cotton Lab. 1989–95, Scientific Dir Dept of Physical and Math. Sciences 1995–97, Dir-Gen. CNRS 1997–2000, Exec. Pres. 2006–10; Assoc. Researcher Institut d'astrophysique d'Ottawa, Canada 1979–80; Visiting Prof., Ecole Polytechnique de Lausanne 1987–; Adjunct Prof. then Distinguished Visiting Scholar, Georgia Tech. Univ., USA 2001–; Pres. Int. Council for Science (ICSU) 2008–, High Council of Biotechnologies 2009–; Amb.-Del. for Science, Tech. and Innovation to Minister of Foreign Affairs; Corresp. mem. French Acad. des Sciences 1997 (mem. 2005, Secrétaire perpétuel 2011–), American Acad. of Arts and Sciences 2011–; mem. French Acad. of Tech. 2000–; Officier, Légion d'honneur, Ordre nat. du Mérite; Dr hc (Univ. of Berlin, Georgia Tech. Inst., Atlanta, Ecole polytechnique fédérale de Lausanne); Acad. des Sciences Prize 1991, CNRS Silver Medal 1994, Holweck Prize and Medal 2003. *Leisure interests:* opera, painting, literature. *Address:* 23 quai de Conti, 75006 Paris, France (office). *Telephone:* 1-44-41-45-05 (office). *E-mail:* catherine.brechignac@academie-sciences.fr (office). *Website:* www.academie-sciences.fr (office).

BRÉCHOT, Christian, PhD; French medical researcher and professor of cell biology; *Director-General, Institut Pasteur;* b. 23 July 1952, Paris; s. of Claude Bréchot and Marie-Louise Bréchot (née Tisne); m. 1st (divorced); one s. two d.; m. 2nd Patrizia Paterlini; two s.; ed Lycée Montaigne, Paris, Lycée Louis le grand, Paris, Univ. of Paris VII, Inst. Pasteur; Prof. of Cell Biology, Necker-Enfants Malades Faculty of Medicine, Univ. of Paris V 1989–2001; Head, Hybridotest Lab., Inst. Pasteur 1990–98; Head, Institut nat. de la santé et de la recherche médicale (INSERM) Research Unit U.370, Necker Hosp., Paris 1993–2001, Head, Liver Unit, Necker Hosp. 1997–2001, Head, Nat. Reference Centre on the molecular epidemiology of viral hepatitis, Inst. Pasteur and INSERM U.370 1998–2001, Dir-Gen. INSERM 2001–07 (resgnd); Vice-Pres. Institut Mérieux 2008; Dir-Gen. Inst. Pasteur 2013–; WHO study co-ordinator for standardization of PCR in diagnosis of HIV infections 1988–91; mem. Scientific Cttee, Asscn pour la Recherche sur le Cancer 1988–2001, Agence Française du Sang 1993–96; mem. Inst. Universitaire de France 1992–, European Asscn for Virological Diagnosis, American Asscn for the Study of Liver Diseases, French Asscn for the Study of the Liver, European Asscn for the Study of the Liver (Sec. 1993–97); Biotrol Award 1982, Fondation pour la Recherche Médicale Award 1982, Abott Award for research on viral hepatitis 1983, Ligue Française contre le cancer Paris Award for research on liver cancer and hepatitis B virus 1985, APMS Award for research on prevention of transmissible diseases 1987, French Medical Soc., René Fauvert Award 1987, French Acad. of Medicine Award 1996, Fondation de France Jean Valade Award 2000. *Leisure interests:* paintings, tennis, rugby. *Address:* Institut Pasteur, 25-28 rue du Docteur Roux, 75015 Paris, France (office). *Telephone:* 1-45-68-80-00 (office). *Fax:* 1-43-06-98-35 (office). *Website:* www.pasteur.fr (office).

BRECHTEFELD, Natan Teewe, BA, LLB; I-Kiribati lawyer and politician; b. 27 May 1961, Abemama; s. of Teewe and Bwebweniti; m. Tebaraoi Tangimate; five c.; ed Univ. of the South Pacific, Fiji, Univ. of Papua New Guinea, Otago Univ., New Zealand; mem. Maneaba Ni Maungatabu (Parl.) for Abemama –2011; Minister for Communications, Transport and Tourism Devt –2007, of Finance and Econ. Devt 2007–11; mem. Boutokaan Te Koaua Party; State Advocate, Office of Attorney General, Kiribati; Asst Attorney Gen., Marshall Islands; CEO Kiribati Oil Co. (KOIL). *Leisure interest:* cycling. *Address:* Asemama, Kiribati (home). *E-mail:* n_teewe@yahoo.com (home).

BRECKENRIDGE, Sir Alasdair Muir, Kt, CBE, MD, MSc, FRCP, FRCPE, FRSE; British scientist and academic; *Chairman, Emerging Science and Bioethics Advisory Committee;* b. 7 May 1937, Arbroath, Scotland; s. of Thomas Breckenridge and Jane Breckenridge; m. Jean M. Boyle 1967; two s.; ed Bell-Baxter School, Cupar, Fife and Univ. of St Andrews; House Physician and Surgeon, Dundee Royal Infirmary 1961–62; House Physician, Registrar, Lecturer, Sr Lecturer, Hammersmith Hosp. and Royal Postgraduate Medical School 1963–74; Prof. of Clinical Pharmacology, Univ. of Liverpool 1974–2002, Prof. Emer. 2002–;

mem. Cttee on Safety of Medicines 1981, Chair. 1999–2003; Chair. Medicines and Healthcare Products Regulatory Agency (MHRA) 2003–12; Chair. Emerging Science and Bioethics Advisory Cttee 2012–; Councillor Int. Union of Pharmacology 1981–87; Foreign Sec. British Pharmacological Soc. 1983–91, Dir Research and Devt, Mersey Region 1992–96; Vice-Chair. Advisory Cttee on Drugs 1985–98; mem. Council Royal Coll. of Physicians 1983–86, Panel of Tropical Diseases, Wellcome Trust 1984–88, WHO Steering Cttee on Chemotherapy of Malaria 1987–91, MRC Physiological Systems and Disorders Bd 1987–91, Council MRC 1992–96, Cen. Research and Devt Cttee, Nat. Health Service 1991–95, Council, Acad. of Medical Sciences; Chair. NW Regional Office of the Nat. Health Service 1996–99; Chair. Jt Medical Advisory Cttee of Higher Educ. Funding Councils of the UK 1998–2002; mem. Bd of Dirs Univ. Coll. London Hosps 2012–; Goulstonian Lecturer, Royal Coll. of Physicians 1975; Paul Martini Prize for Clinical Pharmacology 1974, Poulson Medal (Norwegian Pharmacological Soc.) 1988, Lilly Prize (British Pharmacological Soc.) 1993. *Publications:* articles in scientific and medical journals. *Leisure interest:* golf. *Address:* Cree Cottage, Feather Lane, Wirral, L69 3BX, England (home). *Telephone:* (151) 342-1096 (home).

BREDESEN, Philip Norman (Phil), Jr, AB; American politician, business executive and state governor; *Co-Chairman, Achieve, Inc.;* b. 21 Nov. 1943, Oceanport, NJ; s. of Phillip Norman Bredesen, Sr and Norma Lucille Bredesen (née Walborn); m. 1st Susan Cleaves 1968 (divorced 1974); m. 2nd Andrea Conte 1974; one s.; ed Red Jacket Cen. School, NY, Harvard Coll.; computer programmer, Itek Corpn, Mass 1967–70; Dir of Systems Devt G.D. Seale & Co. 1971–73, Div. Man. 1973–75; Dir of Special Projects Hosp. Affiliates Int. Nashville 1976–80; f. Healthplans Corpn (later HealthAmerica Corpn) 1980, Chair. and CEO 1980–86 (sold co.); co-f. Coventry Corpn 1986, Chair. 1986–90; co-f. Clinical Pharmaceuticals 1986, Chair. 1986–93; Mayor of Nashville and Davidson Co. 1991–99; Pres. Bredex Corpn 2000–02; Gov. of Tenn. 2003–11; f. Nashville's Table 1989, mem. Bd of Dirs 1989–91; Founder Land Trust for Tenn. 1999, Chair. 1999–2001; Co-Chair. Achieve, Inc. (bipartisan and educ. reform org.) 2009–; mem. Bd of Dirs United Cerebral Palsy 1988–92, United Way of Middle Tennessee 1985–90, Nashville Symphony 1985–91, Univ. School, Nashville 1986–95, Nashville Publrs' Library Foundation 1997–2007, Tennessee State Univ. Foundation; mem. Bd of Trustees, Frist Center for Visual Arts 1998–2003, Chair. Finance Cttee 2000–03; Democrat. *Leisure interests:* oil painting, flying glider planes, jogging, hunting, fishing, skiing, hiking, reading, computers. *Address:* 1724 Chickering Road, Nashville, TN 37215-4908, USA (home); Achieve, Inc., 1400 16th Street NW, Suite 510, Washington, DC 20036; Bipartisan Policy Center, Suite 1000, 1225 I Street NW, Washington, DC 20005, USA. *Telephone:* (202) 419-1540 (Achieve, Inc.); (202) 204-2400 (Bipartisan Policy Center). *Fax:* (202) 828-0911 (Achieve, Inc.); (202) 637-9220 (Bipartisan Policy Center). *E-mail:* info@achieve.org; bipartisaninfo@bipartisanpolicy.org. *Website:* www.achieve.org; www.bipartisanpolicy.org.

BREDIN, Jean-Denis, LèsL; French lawyer; b. 17 May 1929, Paris; m. Danièle Hervier; two c. (including Frédérique Bredin); ed Lycée Charlemagne and Facultés de Droit et des Lettres, Paris; called to the Bar 1950–; Prof. Faculté de Droit, Rennes 1958, Lille 1967; Founding Partner, Bredin Prat (law firm) 1965–; Adviser to Council for Higher Educ. 1968–69; Prof. of Pvt. Law, Univ. of Paris-Dauphine 1969; Prof. Univ. of Paris I 1971–93, Prof. Emer. 1993–; worked with Edgar Faure on higher educ. reform 1968; Vice-Pres. Mouvement des radicaux de gauche 1976–80; Pres. Man. Bd Bibliothèque Nationale 1983–88; Vice-Pres. Comm. Moinot 1981; Pres. Comm. for Reform of Cinema 1982; Adviser on Audiovisual Matters to Prime Minister 1985; mem. Acad. Française 1989–; Prix Gobert 1984. *Publications include:* Traité de droit commercial international 1967, La République de Monsieur Pompidou 1974, Les Français au pouvoir 1977, Eclats 1976, Joseph Cailleux 1980, L'Affaire 1983, Un coupable 1985, L'Absence 1986, La Tâche 1988, Weisbuch 1989, Un enfant sage 1990, Battements de coeur 1991, Bernard Lazare 1992, Comédie des Apparences 1994, Encore un peu de temps 1996, Convaincre, dialogues sur l'éloquence 1997, L'Affaire 1998, Une singulière famille 1999, Rien ne va plus 2000, Lettre à Dieu le fils 2001, Un tribunal au garde-à-vous 2002, Et des amours desquelles nous parlons 2004, Mots et pas perdus: images du Palais 2004, On ne meurt qu'une fois: Charlotte Corday 2006. *Address:* Bredin Prat, 130, rue du Faubourg Saint-Honoré, 75008 Paris, France (office). *Telephone:* 1-44-35-35-51 (office). *Fax:* 1-42-89-10-73 (office). *E-mail:* jdb@bredinprat.com (office). *Website:* www.bredinprat.fr (office)

BREEDLOVE, Gen. Philip M., BCE, MS; American air force officer and international organization official; *Supreme Allied Commander, Europe, NATO;* b. 21 Sept. 1955; m. Cindy Breedlove; one s. one d.; ed Georgia Inst. of Tech., Arizona State Univ., Air Command and Staff Coll., Nat. War Coll.,; commissioned 1977, First Lt 1979, Capt. 1981, F-16 Aircraft Commdr and Instructor Pilot, 614th Tactical Fighter Squadron, Torrejon AB, Spain 1983–85, Air Liaison Officer, 602nd Air Support Operations Group, Kitzingen AB, West Germany 1985–87, F-16 Pilot, 526th Tactical Fighter Squadron, Ramstein AB, West Germany 1987–88, F-16 Flight Commdr, then Asst Operations Officer, 512th Tactical Fighter Squadron, Ramstein AB, Germany 1988–90, Chief of Air Operations, UN Command and Korea/US Combined Forces Command, Yongsan Army Garrison, South Korea 1991–93, Commdr 80th Fighter Squadron, Kunsan AB, South Korea 1993–94, 27th Operations Group, Cannon AFB, New Mexico 1997–99, 8th Fighter Wing, Kunsan AB, South Korea 2000–01, 56th Fighter Wing, Luke AFB, Arizona 2002–04, 31st Fighter Wing, Aviano AB, Italy 2004–05, 3rd Air Force, Ramstein AB, Germany 2008–09, USAF in Europe, Air Forces HQ Allied Air Command, Ramstein 2012–13, Sr Mil. Asst to Sec. of Air Force 2001–02, Vice-Dir for Strategic Plans and Policy on the Jt Staff –2008, Deputy Chief of Staff for Operations, Plans and Requirements, Air Force HQ 2009–11, Vice-Chief of Staff, USAF 2011–12, Dir, Jt Air Power Competence Centre, Kalkar Germany 2012–13, NATO Supreme Allied Commdr, Europe and Commdr of US European Command 2013–; attained rank of Maj. 1988, Lt-Col 1993, Col 1998, Brig.-Gen. 2003, Maj.-Gen. 2006, Lt-Gen. 2008, Gen. 2011; Seminar XXI Fellow, MIT; Legion of Merit (with three oak leaf clusters), Defense Meritorious Service Medal (with two oak leaf clusters), Meritorious Service Medal (with three oak leaf clusters), Air Force Distinguished Service Medal, Defense Superior Service Medal, Aerial Achievement Medal, Joint Service Commendation Medal, Air Force Achievement Medal, Combat Readiness Medal (with bronze oak leaf cluster), Nat. Defense Service Medal (with bronze service star), Global War on Terrorism Service Medal, Korea Defense Service Medal, Air Force Overseas Short Tour Service Ribbon (with two bronze oak leaf clusters), Air Force Overseas Long Tour Service Ribbon (with four bronze oak leaf clusters), Air Force Longevity Service Award (with one silver and three bronze oak leaf clusters), Air Force Training Ribbon, Inter-American Defense Board Medal (with gold award star); Jt Meritorious Unit Award (with bronze oak leaf cluster), Air Force Outstanding Unit Award (with four bronze oak leaf clusters). *Address:* North Atlantic Treaty Organization, Blvd Léopold III, 1110 Brussels, Belgium (office). *Telephone:* (2) 707-41-11 (office). *Fax:* (2) 707-45-79 (office). *E-mail:* natodoc@hq.nato.int (office). *Website:* www.nato.int (office); www.aco.nato.int/shape.aspx (office).

BREEDON, Timothy (Tim) James, CBE, MA, MSc; British insurance industry executive; m.; three c.; ed Calthorpe Comprehensive School, Fleet, Hants., Farnborough Coll., Worcester Coll. Oxford, London Business School; began career with Standard Chartered Bank 1981–85; joined Legal & General Investment Man. Ltd 1987, Man. Quantitative Products and Index Funds 1987, Dir Index Funds 1994, Man.-Dir (Index Funds) 2000–02, mem. Bd of Dirs and Group Dir (Investments) 2002–05, Deputy Group Chief Exec. Legal & General Group Plc 2005–06, Group Chief Exec. 2006–12; mem. Bd of Dirs Asscn of British Insurers, Chair. 2010–12; fmr mem. Bd of Dirs The Investment Man. Asscn, The Financial Reporting Council. *Address:* c/o Legal & General Group Plc, One Coleman Street, London, EC2R 5AA, England. *E-mail:* info@landg.com.

BREEN, Edward D., Jr, BS; American business executive; *Chairman, Tyco International Inc.;* m.; three c.; ed Grove City Coll.; joined General Instrument (GI) Corpn 1978, Sr Vice-Pres. of Sales 1988–94, Pres. GI Broadband Networks Group 1994–97, Chair., Pres. and CEO GI 1997–2000; Vice-Pres. Motorola 2000–02, Pres. Motorola Broadband Communications Sector 2000–01, Pres. Motorola Networks Sector 2001–02, Pres. and COO Motorola Jan.–July 2002; Chair. and CEO Tyco International Inc. July 2002–2012, Chair. (non-exec.) 2012–; Lead Dir Comcast Corpn 2005–11; mem. Advisory Bd New Mountain Capital (pvt. equity firm); Trustee Grove City Coll.; Vanguard Award, Nat. Cable TV Asscn 1998, ranked by CableFAX magazine as one of the top 15 of the 100 most influential people in cable 1999. *Address:* Tyco International Inc., 9 Roszel Road, Princeton, NJ 08540, USA (office). *Telephone:* (609) 720-4200 (office). *Website:* www.tyco.com (office).

BREGGIN, Peter Roger, BA, MD; American psychiatrist; b. 5 Nov. 1936, New York, NY; m. 3rd Ginger Ross 1984; one c. (and three c. from two previous marriages); ed Harvard Coll., Case Western Reserve School of Medicine, State Univ. of New York, Upstate Medical Center, Massachusetts Mental Health Centre; consultant, Nat. Inst. of Mental Health 1966–68; psychiatrist in pvt. practice 1968–; Founder and Dir Int. Center for Study of Psychiatry and Psychology 1972–2002, Dir Emer. 2002–; Adjunct Prof. of Conflict Resolution George Mason Univ. 1990–96; Faculty Assoc. Dept of Counselling Johns Hopkins Univ. 1996–99; Ed. numerous journals, including Journal of Mind and Behaviour, International Journal of Risk and Society in Medicine, The Humanistic Psychologist, Review of Existential Psychology and Psychiatry; Founding Ed. Ethical Human Sciences and Services 1999–; Ludwig von Mises Award of Merit 1987, Minn. Mental Health Asscn Advocacy Award 1990, honours from Harvard Coll. *Publications:* College Students in a Mental Hospital: Contribution to the Social Rehabilitation of the Mentally Ill (co-author) 1962, Electroshock: Its Brain-Disabling Effects 1979, Psychiatric Drugs: Hazards to the Brain 1983, Toxic Psychiatry 1991, Talking Back to Prozac (with Ginger Breggin) 1994, Brain-Disabling Treatments in Psychiatry 1997 (revised edn 2008), The Heart of Being Helpful 1997 (new paperback edn 2006), The War Against Children of Color (with Ginger Breggin) 1998, Talking Back to Ritalin 1998, Your Drug May Be Your Problem (with David Cohen) 1999 (revised edn 2007), Reclaiming Our Children: A Healing Solution for a Nation in Crisis 2000, Talking Back to Ritalin: What Doctors Aren't Telling You About Stimulants and ADHD 2001, The Anti-Depressant Fact Book: What Your Doctor Won't Tell You About Prozac, Zoloft, Paxil, Celexa, and Luvox 2001, The Ritalin Fact Book: What Your Doctor Won't Tell You 2002, Dimensions of Empathic Therapy (co-ed.) 2002, Medication Madness: A Psychiatrist Exposes the Dangers of Mood-Altering Medications 2008, Wow, I'm an American! How to Live Like Our Nation's Heroic Founders 2009, Psychiatric Drug Withdrawal: A Guide for Prescribers, Therapists, Patients and their Families 2012; numerous articles in scientific journals. *Address:* 101 East State Street, #112, Ithaca, NY 14850, USA. *Telephone:* (607) 272-5328; (607) 272-5354. *Fax:* (607) 272-5329. *E-mail:* psychiatricdrugfacts@hotmail.com. *Website:* www.breggin.com.

BRÉGIER, Fabrice; French aeronautics industry executive; *President and CEO, Airbus SAS;* b. 16 July 1961, Dijon; ed École Polytechnique and École des Mines; began career as a test engineer at Creys-Malville nuclear power station 1983–84; Sales Man. for Péchiney (Japan) 1984–86; joined Directions Régionales de l'Industrie de la Recherche et de l'Environnement, Alsace, Ministry of Industry 1986–89; Dir of Econ. and Financial Affairs, Ministry of Agric. 1989–90; Tech. Advisor to Minister of Foreign Trade 1990–91, to Minister of Post and Telecommunications 1991–93; joined Matra Défense (later Matra BAe Dynamics) as Chair. Apache MAW GIE (co-operation with Dasa) and Eurodrone GIE (with STN-Atlas) 1993–96, Dir of Stand-Off activities (Apache, Scalp EG/Storm Shadow), Matra BAe Dynamics 1996–98, CEO Matra BAe Dynamics 1998–2001; CEO MBDA (European missile systems co. cr. by Aerospatiale Matra, British Aerospace and Finmeccanica) 2001–03; Pres. and CEO Eurocopter Group, European Aeronautic Defence and Space Co. (EADS) 2003–06, Head of EADS' Eurocopter Div. 2005–06, COO Airbus SAS 2006–12, Pres. and CEO 2012–, mem. EADS Exec. Cttee, commissioned by Louis Gallois to improve overall operational performance of the Group, tasked with implementing the Power 8 reorganization plan and the A350 XWB programme; Chevalier, Légion d'honneur. *Address:* Airbus SAS, 1 Rond point Maurice Bellonte, 31707 Blagnac Cedex, France (office). *Telephone:* (5) 61-93-33-33 (office). *Fax:* (5) 61-93-49-55 (office). *Website:* www.airbus.com (office).

BREGU, Majlinda Enver, PhD; Albanian politician; b. 19 May 1974, Tirana; m.; two c.; ed Sami Frashëri Gymnasium, Univ. of Tirana, Univ. of Urbino, Italy; worked for Albanian Radio-TV 1992–2002; interships, NOVA Inst. for Research and Social Policy Oslo, Norway, Viadrina Univ., Germany 1997–2004; Lecturer on Social Sciences and Gender Issues, Univ. of Tirana 1996–; Visiting Prof., McGill Univ., Canada 2000; mem. Partia Demokratike e Shqipërisë (Democratic Party of Albania), Co-ordinator of Social Policies at Political Orientation Cttee 2004, mem. Nat. Council 2004, Head of the sub-comm. on Minors and Gender Equality

2005–07; mem. Kuvendi Popullor (Parl.) 2005–, Head, Parl. Del. to European Parl. 2005–07, Chair. Parl. Sub-comm. for Juveniles and Equal Opportunities (in co-operation with Children's Human Rights Centre of Albania) 2006, mem. Health and Social Issues Parl. Comm. 2005–07; Minister of European Integration 2009–13; Spokesperson, Council of Ministers 2009–13. *Publications:* co-author: Qualitative Research for Social Sciences 2003, Media Monitoring on Domestic Violence 2003, Domestic Violence and Judiciary System 2005, Assesment of Health Care Workers 2006, National Strategy for Gender Equality 2006; ed.: Prostitute. Ci passerano davanto nel Regno dei Cieli 2004. *Address:* Kuvendi Popullor, Bulevardi Dëshmorët e Kombit 4, Tirana, Albania. *E-mail:* majlindabregu@yahoo .com. *Website:* www.parlament.al.

BREIEN, Anja; Norwegian film director; b. 1940; ed Inst. des hautes études cinématiques, France; mem. European Film Acad.; Aamot-statuetten Prize 1982, Hon. Amanda 2005. *Short films include:* Vokse opp (Part 1 of Dager fra 100 år) 1967, 17. Mai: en film om ritualer 1969, Ansikter 1971, Murer rundt fengslet 1972, Herbergister 1973, Mine Søsken, goddag 1974, Gamle 1975, Fjellet 1989, Solvorn 1997, A se en båt med seil (To see a boat in sail; UIP/EFA Prize, Berlin Film Festival 2001, Best Short Feature, Toronto 2001) 2000, Uten Tittel (Untitled) 2005, Riss 2009, Fra tyggegummiens historie (From the History of the Chewing Gum) 2012. *Feature films include:* Voldtekt/Tilfellet Anders (Rape/Le viol) (Norsk Kritikerlags Pris) 1971, Hustruer (Wives) (Silver Hugo Award, Chicago 1976) 1975, Den Allvarsamme Leken (Games of Love and Loneliness) (Silver Hugo Award, Chicago 1977) 1977, The Swedish (Guldbogga) 1978, Arven (Next of Kin/The Inheritance) (Norske kinosjefers Sølvklumpen Award) 1979, Forfølgelsen (Witch Hunt) 1981, Papirfuglen (Paper Bird) (Silver Hugo Award, Chicago 1984) 1984, Hustruer: ti år etter (Wives: Ten Years After) (Norwegian Film Prize Amanda for Best Film 1985) 1985, Smykketyven (Twice upon a Time) 1990, Hustruer III (Wives III) 1996, Solvorn 1997, Jezidi (Yezidi) 2009,; has also written script for film Trollsyn (Second Sight) (dir by Ola Solum) 1994. *Publications:* Forfølgelsen (script) 1981, Trollsyn (script) 1995, Kaniaw (novel) 2006. *Leisure interest:* skiing. *Address:* Norwegian Film Institute, Dronningens 6T. 16, 0152 Oslo, Norway (office). *Telephone:* 95-21-49-49. *E-mail:* anja@mfu.no (office).

BREILLAT, Catherine; French film director, screenwriter and novelist; *Professor of Auteur Cinema, European Graduate School;* b. 13 July 1948, Bressuire; currently Prof. of Auteur Cinema, European Grad. School, Switzerland. *Film roles include:* Last Tango in Paris 1972, Dracula Père et Fils 1977. *Films directed include:* Une vraie jeune fille (A Real Young Girl) 1975 (released 2000), Tapage nocturne (Nocturnal Uproar) 1979, 36 Fillette (Virgin) 1988, Sale comme un ange (Dirty Like an Angel) 1990, Parfait Amour (Perfect Love, jtly) 1996, Romance 1999, A ma soeur! (Fat Girl) 2001, Brève traversée (Brief Crossing) 2001, Scènes intimes 2002, Sex is Comedy 2002, Anatomie de l'enfer 2004, Une Vieille Maîtresse (The Last Mistress) 2007, Barbe bleue 2009, La Belle Endormie 2010, Bad Love 2011; screenplays: Catherine et Cie (Catherine & Co., jtly) 1975, Bilitis 1977, La peau (The Skin) 1981, Et la nave va (And the Ship Sails On) 1983, L'araignée de satin (The Satin Spider) 1984, Police 1985, Milan noir (Black Milan, jtly) 1987, Zanzibar (jtly) 1988, La nuit de l'océan (The Night of the Ocean, jtly) 1988, Aventure de Catherine C. (The Adventure of Catherine C., jtly) 1990, Le diable au corps 1990, La Thune (Money, jtly) 1991, Couples et amants (Couples and Lovers, jtly) 1994, Viens jouer dans la cour des grands (TV) 1997, Selon Matthieu 2000. *Publications include:* L'homme facile (novel), Tapage nocturne 1979, Romance 1999, Le livre du plaisir 1999, Une vraie jeune fille 2000, A ma soeur! 2001, Pornocratie 2001, Ein Mädchen 2001, Abus de faiblesse 2009. *Address:* European Graduate School, Alter Kehr 20, Ringacker, 3953 Leuk-Stadt, Switzerland (office). *Telephone:* 274749917 (office). *Fax:* 274749969 (office). *Website:* www.egs.edu (office).

BREIMER, Douwe Durk, PhD; Dutch fmr university rector, pharmacologist and academic; b. 24 Nov. 1943, Gaasterland; m. Joan Breimer; four c.; ed Univs of Groningen and Nijmegen; apptd Prof. of Pharmacology, Leiden Univ. 1975, mem. Bd, Rector Magnificus and Pres. Exec. Bd Leiden Univ. 2001–07; Foreign Assoc. mem. Inst. of Medicine of NAS, Nat. Innovation Platform; Knight of the Order of the Dutch Lion; Dr hc (Ghent Univ., Uppsala Univ., Semmelweis Univ. (Budapest), Univ. of Navarra, Hoshi Univ. (Tokyo), Univ. of London, Université de Montréal). *Publications:* more than 500 scientific papers on pharmacokinetics, pharmacodynamics and drug metabolism. *Address:* c/o Office of the President, Leiden University, LACDR, PO Box 9502, 2300 RA Leiden, Netherlands (office). *Telephone:* (71) 5274707 (office); (71) 5176410 (home). *Fax:* (71) 5176420 (office). *E-mail:* ddbreimer@lacdr.leidenuniv.nl (office).

BREJON DE LAVERGNÉE, Arnauld, DenL; French museum curator; *Director of Collections, Mobilier National;* b. 25 May 1945, Rennes; s. of Jacques Brejon de Lavergnée and Monique Perquis; m. Barbara Mercillon 1977; four c.; ed Univ. of Sorbonne, Paris; trainee curator, Louvre Museum, Museums of Cluny and Dijon 1969–70; Visiting Fellow, Acad. of France in Rome 1971–72; Curator Museum of Cluny 1973–76; Curator Dept of Painting, Louvre Museum 1976–87; Gen. Curator of Heritage 1987; Curator Museum of Fine Arts, Lille 1987–2003 (oversaw 220 million French franc restoration project 1992–97); Dir of Collections, Mobilier National 2003–; Corresp. mem. Acad. of Fine Arts 1993–, Acad. of Bologne; Fotillon Fellow, Yale Univ. 1977; Chevalier, Légion d'honneur, Ordre nat. du Mérite, Ordre des Arts et des Lettres; Getty Center Art History Grant 1984, Prix nat. de Muséographie 1987. *Publications include:* L'art italien dans les collections françaises, La collection du Bailli de Breteuil, Une monographie sur Simon Vouet, La collection des tapissiers de Louis XIV. *Address:* Mobilier National, 42 avenue des Gobelins, 75013 Paris, France (office). *Telephone:* 1-44-08-52-02 (office). *Fax:* 1-40-13-46-74 (office). *E-mail:* arnauld.brejon@culture.gouv.fr (office). *Website:* www .mobiliernational.culture.gouv.fr.

BREMAÏDOU, Christophe; Central African Republic politician; fmr mem. Commission Electorale Indépendant; fmr Minister of Econ. Reform; Minister of Finance and the Budget 2013; Pres. Alliance pour la Solidarité et le Développement 2011. *Address:* c/o Ministry of Finance and the Budget, BP 696, Bangui, Central African Republic (office).

BREMAN, Jan; Dutch professor of comparative sociology; b. 24 July 1936, Amsterdam; Dir Centre of Asian Studies, Univ. of Amsterdam; Prof. Inst. of Social Studies, The Hague, now Emer.; extensive anthropological research in India and Indonesia 1962–; devt consultant on social policies in Asia; mem. Nat. Advisory

Council on Devt Cooperation in the Netherlands; mem. Royal Netherlands Acad. of Sciences and Humanities. *Publications:* Of Patronage and Exploitation 1974, Landless Labour in Colonial Java 1984, Of Peasants, Migrants and Workers 1985, Taming the Coolie Beast 1989, Beyond Patronage and Exploitation 1993, Wage Hunters and Gatherers 1994, Footloose Labour: Working India's Informal Economy (Edgar Graham Prize 1998) 1996, The Labouring Poor in India 2003, The Making and Unmaking of an Industrial Working Class 2006, The Poverty Regime in Village India 2007, The Jan Breman Omnibus 2007, Outcast Labour in Asia 2010. *Address:* 48 Kloveniersburgwal, 1012 CX Amsterdam, Netherlands (office). *Telephone:* (20) 5252262 (office). *E-mail:* j.c.breman@uva.nl (office).

BREMER, Kåre, PhD; Swedish botanist, academic and fmr university administrator; *Professor, Stockholm University;* b. 17 Jan. 1948, Lidingö; m. Birgitta Bremer; one s. one d.; ed Stockholm Univ.; Asst Prof., later Assoc. Prof. of Systematic Botany, Stockholm Univ. 1972–75, 1976–80, Vice-Chancellor (Rector) 2004–13, Prof. 2013–; Head of Curator Dept of Phanerogamic Botany, Swedish Museum of Natural History 1980–89; Research Assoc. and B.A. Krukoff Curator of African Botany, Mo. Botanical Garden, USA 1985–86; Prof. of Systematic Botany, Uppsala Univ. 1989–2004, Dean of Biology 1993–99; Foreign mem. Linnean Soc. of London 1998; Fellow, Royal Swedish Acad. of Sciences; Lund Royal Physiographic Soc. Linnaeus Prize 1999, HM The King's Gold Medal 2006. *Publications:* numerous papers in learned journals. *Address:* Stockholm University, 106 91 Stockholm, Sweden (office). *Telephone:* (8) 167327 (office). *E-mail:* kare.bremer@su .se (office). *Website:* karebremer.wordpress.com.

BREMER, L. Paul, III, BA, MBA; American business executive, fmr diplomatist and fmr government official; *Chairman, Board of Advisors, Global Secure Corporation;* ed Yale Univ., Institut d'études politiques, Paris, Harvard Grad. School of Business Admin; joined US State Dept, Special Asst to six Secs of State, service at US Embassies in Afghanistan and Malawi; fmr Deputy Chief of Mission, US Embassy, Norway; Amb. to Netherlands 1983–86; fmr Exec. Sec., State Dept and Amb. at Large for Counter Terrorism; Presidential Envoy to Iraq and Admin. Coalition Provisional Authority 2003–04; Man. Dir Kissinger Assocs 1989–2000; fmr Chair. and Chief Exec. Marsh Crisis Consulting Co.; Pres. and CEO World T.E.A.M. Sports 2010–12; currently Chair. Bd of Advisors, Global Secure Corpn; Chair. Nat. Comm. on Terrorism 1999; fmr Dir Air Products and Chemicals Inc., Akzo Nobel NV, Harvard Business School Club of New York, Netherland-America Foundation; fmr Trustee Econ. Club of New York; Founder and Pres. Lincoln/ Douglass Scholarship Foundation; mem. Pres.'s Homeland Security Advisory Council 2002; mem. IISS, Council on Foreign Relations; fmr mem. NAS Comm. on Science and Tech.; State Dept Superior Honor Award, two Presidential Meritorious Service Awards, Distinguished Honor Award, Presidential Medal of Freedom 2004. *Publications:* My Year in Iraq 2006. *Address:* Global Secure Corporation, 2600 Virginia Avenue, Suite 600, Washington, DC 20037, USA (office). *Telephone:* (202) 333-8400 (office). *Fax:* (202) 333-0082 (office). *E-mail:* info@globalsecurecorp .com (office). *Website:* www.globalsecurecorp.com (office).

BREMI, Ulrich; Swiss business executive and politician; b. 6 Nov. 1929, Zurich; s. of Heinrich Bremi-Sennhauser and Johanna Bremi-Sennhauser; m. Anja Bremi-Forrer; two d.; ed School of Mechanical Eng, Winterthur and Swiss Fed. Inst. of Tech., Zürich; CEO Kaba Holding Ltd Zürich 1962–90; Chair. Bd Neue Zürcher Zeitung 1988–99, Georg Fischer AG 1989–98, Swiss Reinsurance Co. 1992–2000, Flughafen-Immobilien-Gesellschaft 1992–2000; mem. Swiss Nat. Parl. 1975–91, Chair. 1990–91; Hon. Senator, Univ. of St Gallen 2000; Hon. Counsellor, ETH Zurich. *Address:* Zollikerstrasse 57, 8702 Zürich, Switzerland (office). *Telephone:* (44) 3952010 (office). *Fax:* (44) 3952019 (office). *E-mail:* ulrich.bremi@bremi.ch (office). *Website:* www.bremi.ch (office).

BREMKAMP, Detlev; German business executive; b. 2 March 1944, Hamburg; insurance apprenticeship, Allianz Versicherungs AG 1963–65, skills devt in UK Commercial Union Insurance, Willis Faber and Lloyd's of London 1969–70, posted to Munich HQ as First Clerk and dept dir 1971, apptd Head of Fire Dept and Dir of Insurance sector 1974, advanced to Exec. Bd of Allianz Versicherungs AG (holding co. for damage and casualty business) 1980; Sr Strategic Adviser to European Business, Lehman Brothers Inc. 2005–08, mem. European Advisory Council; mem. Man. Bd and Head of Europe II, Allianz SE 1991–, Allianz AG, Munich 2000–05, responsible for Western, Northern and Southern Europe, reinsurance, alternative risk transfer and assistance/travel insurance and served as Head of Europe II; Deputy mem. Man. Bd Allianz Versicherung 1981–82, Full mem. 1983–87, Man. Dir and Gen. Man. Allianz Europe Ltd, Amsterdam 1987–90; Chair. Supervisory Bd Hochtief AG –2011; Dir, Converium Holding AG 2006–, Allianz Portugal SA, Assurances Gènèrales de France, Lloyd Adriatico, Allianz Nederland Group and vorstand of Allianz; mem. Supervisory Bd ABB AG, HSH Nordbank AG 2009–, ACIF, AGF RAS Holding BV (Chair.), Allianz Financial & Insurance Services GmbH, Allianz General Insurance Co. SA, Allianz Life Insurance Co. SA, Allianz Portugal SA, Allianz Global Risks Rückversicherungs-AG, Allianz Risk Transfer, Reaseguros SA (Spain), Companhia de Seguros (Portugal), Cornhill Insurance PLC (UK), Dresdner ABD Securities Ltd (Hong Kong), Dresdner Kleinwort Wasserstein (Japan) Ltd, Elmonda Assistance (France, Chair.), Lloyd Adriatico (Italy), RAS International II BV, RINV (NewCo) (Chair.), Zwolsche Algemeene NV (Netherlands), Bayerische Hypovereinsbank AG (Germany), Royal Nederland Verzekeringsgroep NV; mem. Econ. Advisory Council Bayerische Landesbank 2005–09; Dir RAS International NV, Assurances Generales de France 1998–2005, SCOR Holding (Switzerland) Ltd 2006–; Dir (non-exec.) Riunione Adriatica Di Sicurtà SpA (RAS) 1997–. *Address:* c/o Hochtief AG, Opernplatz 2, 45128 Essen, Germany.

BREN, Donald L., BA; American real estate investment industry executive and philanthropist; *Chairman, The Irvine Company Inc.;* b. 11 May 1932, Los Angeles, Calif.; s. of Milton H. Bren and Marion Bren (née Newbert); m. 1st Diane Bren; three c.; m. 2nd Mardelle Bren 1977 (divorced); one d.; m. 3rd Brigitte Muller 1998; one s.; three c. by two fmr companions; ed Univ. of Washington; served as officer in US Marine Corps; f. Bren Co. to build homes in Orange Co., Calif. 1958, later renamed California Pacific Homes; Founder and Pres. Mission Viejo Co., Orange Co. 1963, sold interest in co. 1967; joined a group of investors to purchase The Irvine Co. from The Irvine Foundation 1977, later mem. Exec. Cttee and Vice-Chair., bought out partners and elected Chair. 1983–, sole shareholder 1996–; f. Donald Bren Foundation; mem. Bd of Trustees, Chapman Univ., California Inst. of

Tech. (Caltech), LA County Museum of Art, Orange County Museum of Art; Fellow, American Acad. of Arts and Sciences; Semper Fidelis Award, Marine Corps Univ. Foundation 1998, and its Gen. Leonard F. Chapman Medallion 2003, Univ. of California Presidential Medal 2004, ranked by BusinessWeek ninth nationally among philanthropists 2009. *Leisure interests:* skiing, tennis, sailing, windsurfing. *Address:* The Irvine Company Inc., 550 Newport Center Drive, Newport Beach, CA 92660, USA (office). *Telephone:* (949) 720-2000 (office). *Fax:* (949) 720-2218 (office). *E-mail:* webmaster@irvinecompany.com (office). *Website:* www.irvinecompany .com (office); www.donaldbren.com.

BRENCIU, Marius; Romanian singer (tenor); b. 11 Nov. 1973, Braşov; s. of Radu Brenciu and Maria-Elena Brenciu; m.; ed Andrei Saguna High School, Univ. of Music, Bucharest; began singing in choir of local Orthodox church aged 12; teaching asst, Univ. of Music, Bucharest 1997–2000; debut as Don Ottavio in Mozart's Don Giovanni at Bucharest Opera 1997; Perm. Leading Singer, Romanian Nat. Opera, Bucharest; recent opera activities include Rodolfo (La Bohème) in Hamburg and Tel-Aviv, Alfredo (La traviata) in Berlin, Rome and Brussels, Almaviva (Il Barbiere di Siviglia) in Lyon and Lisbon, Adorno (Simon Boccanegra) in Hamburg, Macduff (Macbeth) at Edinburgh Festival and Amsterdam; debut at New York Met in La rondine (Puccini) 2008, also sang in Paris and Toulouse; sang Nemorino (L'elisir d'amore) in Berlin and Tel-Aviv, Edgardo (Lucia di Lammermoor) in Amsterdam and Lensky (Eugen Onegin) in Vienna, Munich, Berlin, Zurich, Toulouse, Lyon, Tokyo, Lisbon, Genf, Israel and Cardiff and title role in Idomeneo (Mozart); sang Prunier (La rondine) at New York Met 2013, Alfredo Germont (La traviata) in Sofia 2013–14, Lenski (Eugene Onegin) in Naples 2014; regular collaborations with conductors including Claudio Abbado, Seiji Ozawa, Lorin Maazel, Zubin Mehta, Simone Young, Ion Marin, Kent Nagano, Valéry Gergiev, Sylvain Cambreling, Marco Armiliato, Ton Koopman, Lothar Zagrosek, Sir Charles Mackerras, Stefan Soltesz, Gianandrea Noseda, Jacques Delacôte, Mstislav Rostropovich, Herbert Blomstedt, Kiril Petrenko, Dan Ettinger; with orchestras including Berlin Philharmonic, Gewandhaus Orchestra, Rotterdam Philharmonic Orchestra, NDR Symphony Orchestra, BBC Philharmonic, Academy of Ancient Music, Orchestre Philharmonique de Radio France and Orquesta Nacional de Espana; other repertoire includes Requiem (Verdi), Mass in C Minor (Mozart), Messa di Gloria (Puccini), Messe Solennelle (Gounod), A Child of our Time (Tippett); winner Julian Gayarre Int. Competition, Georges Enescu Int. Competition, Second Prize and Opera Prize, Queen Elizabeth Competition, Brussels 1999, First Prize, Young Artists Int. Auditions, New York 2001, Winner Cardiff Singer of the World (also Song Prize) 2001. *Recordings include:* George Enescu's Vox Maris with Lawrence Foster. *Leisure interests:* literature, foreign languages, history, surfing the net. *Address:* c/o Luisa Petrov, Glauburgstr. 95, 60318 Frankfurt am Main, Germany (office). *Telephone:* (69) 5970377 (office). *Fax:* (69) 59748–08 (office). *E-mail:* luisapetrov@web.de (office).

BRENDE, Børge, BA; Norwegian politician; *Minister of Foreign Affairs;* b. 25 Sept. 1965, Odda; s. of Knut Brendeseter and Kari Wesche; m.; two s.; ed Norwegian Univ. of Science and Tech.; mem. Trondheim Municipal Exec. Bd (Kommunalråd) 1992–97; mem. Storting (Parl.) 1997–2007; Minister of the Environment 2001–04, of Trade and Industry 2004–05, of Foreign Affairs 2013–; Chair. PD Burma (int. network of political leaders promoting democracy in Burma) 2005–07; Man. Dir World Econ. Forum, Geneva 2008–09, 2011–13; Sec.-Gen. Red Cross Norway 2009–11; mem. Bd Norwegian School of Econs and Business Admin 2009–12; Trustee The Oslo Center for Peace and Human Rights 2009–12; Chair. Mesta (road maintenance co.) 2010–13; mem. Bd of Dirs Statoil 2012–13; mem. China Council for Int. Cooperation on Environment and Devt 2005–; mem. Foundation Bd Global Shapers Community 2012–; mem. Conservative Party (Høyre), Deputy Chair. 1994–98; Grand Cross, Order of Merit (Italy), Order of the Phoenix 2004, Commdr, Order of St Olav 2005. *Address:* Ministry of Foreign Affairs, 7 juni pl./Victoria Terrasse, POB 8114 Dep., 0032 Oslo, Norway (office). *Telephone:* 23-95-00-00 (office). *Fax:* 23-95-00-99 (office). *E-mail:* post@mfa .no (office). *Website:* www.regjeringen.no/ud (office).

BRENDEL, Alfred; Austrian pianist and writer; b. 5 Jan. 1931, Wiesenberg; s. of Ing. Albert and Ida Brendel (née Wieltschnig); m. 1st Iris Heymann-Gonzala 1960 (divorced 1972); one d.; m. 2nd Irene Semler 1975; one s. two d.; studied piano under Sofija Deželić (Zagreb), Ludovika v. Kaan (Graz), Edwin Fischer (Lucerne), Paul Baumgartner (Basel), Edward Steuermann (Salzburg); studied composition under A. Michl (Graz) and harmony under Franjo Dugan (Zagreb); first piano recital Musikverein Graz 1948; concert tours through Europe, Latin America, North America 1963–2008, Australia 1963, 1966, 1969, 1976; has appeared at many music festivals, including Salzburg 1960–2008, Vienna, Edinburgh, Aldeburgh, Athens, Granada, Lucerne, Puerto Rico, London Proms and has performed with most of the major orchestras of Europe and USA, etc.; mem. American Acad. of Arts and Sciences; Hon. RAM; Hon. RCM; Hon. Fellow, Exeter Coll. Oxford 1987; Commdr, Ordre des Arts et des Lettres 1985, Hon. KBE 1989, Ordre pour le Mérite (Germany) 1991; Hon. DMus (London) 1978, (Oxford) 1983, (Warwick) 1991, (Yale) 1992, (Exeter) 1998, (Southampton) 2002, Hon. DLitt (Sussex) 1981, Dr hc (Cologne) 1995; Premio Città de Bolzano, Concorso Busoni 1949, Grand Prix du Disque 1965, Edison Prize (five times 1973–87), Grand Prix des Disquaires de France 1975, Deutscher Schallplattenpreis (four times 1976–84, 1992), Wiener Flötenuhr (six times 1976–87), Gramophone Award (six times 1977–83), Japanese Record Acad. Award (five times 1977–84, with Scottish Symphony Orchestra/Sir Charles Mackerras 2002), Japanese Grand Prix 1978, Franz Liszt Prize (four times 1979–83), Frankfurt Music Prize 1984, Diapason D'Or Award 1992, Heidsieck Award for Writing on Music 1990, Hans von Bülow-Medaille, Kameradschaft der Berliner Philharmoniker eV, 1992, Cannes Classical Award 1998, Ehrenmitgliedschaft der Wiener Philharmoniker 1998, Léonie Sonnings Musikpris, Denmark 2002, Ernst von Siemens Musikpreis 2004, Prix Venezia 2007, Praemium Imperiale 2009, Gramophone Lifetime Achievement Award 2010. *Recordings:* extensive repertoire; Beethoven's Complete Piano Works, Beethoven Sonatas, three sets of Beethoven Concertos (with Vienna Philharmonic Orchestra and Simon Rattle) 1998. *Publications:* essays on music and musicians in Phono, Fono Forum, Österreichische Musikzeitschrift, Music and Musicians, Hi-Fi Stereophonie, New York Review of Books, Die Zeit, Frankfurter Allgemeine Zeitung, Musical Thoughts and Afterthoughts 1976, Nachdenken über Musik 1977, Music Sounded Out (essays) 1990, Musik beim

Wort genommen 1992, Fingerzeig 1996, Störendes Lachen während des Jaworts 1997, One Finger Too Many 1998, Kleine Teufel 1999, Collected Essays on Music 2001, Augerechnet Ich (aka The Veil of Order: In Conversation with Martin Meyer) 2001, Spiegelbild und Schwarzer Spuk (poems) 2003, Cursing Bagels (poems) 2004, Alfred Brendel über Musik 2005. *Leisure interests:* books, theatre, the visual arts, films, baroque and romanesque architecture, unintentional humour, kitsch. *Address:* c/o Ingpen & Williams, 7 St George's Court, 131 Putney Bridge Road, London, SW15 2PA, England (office). *Telephone:* (20) 8874-3222 (office). *Fax:* (20) 8877-3113 (office). *E-mail:* info@ingpen.co.uk (office).

BRENDISH, Clayton (Clay) M., CBE, BSc, MSc, CEng, FBCS, CMgr FCMI; British business executive; *President, Chartered Management Institute;* served as an Adviser to the Govt on the efficiency of the Civil Service, as an Adviser to the Chancellor of the Duchy of Lancaster and the Office of Public Services on their respective Next Steps Agencies 1993–2000; played key role in the privatization of HM's Stationery Office, Civil Service Occupational Health and Safety Agency, Recruitment and Assessment Services and Chessington Computer Centre; co-f. CMG Admiral PLC (acquired Admiral PLC) 1979, Exec. Chair. 1979–2000, Exec. Deputy Chair. CMG Plc (following CMG's merger with Admiral) 2000–01; Chair. (non-exec.) Close Beacon Investment Fund 1995–, Echo Research Ltd 2003–, Anite plc 2005–, SThree Plc 2010–; External Chair. The Meteorological Office; Chair. GlobeOp Financial Services SA 2007–09; Dir (non-exec.), Ordnance Survey 1993–96, BT Group PLC 2002–11, Close Beacon Investment Fund 1995–, Elexon plc, Echo Research Ltd; Dir, Defence Logistics Organisation, Defence Communication Services Agency, Test and Itchen Asscn Ltd, Herald Investment Trust Plc 2001–12, Group NBT plc; fmr Chair. Exec. Bd Inst. of Man. (Chartered Man. Inst. since 2002), Pres. 2001–, Chair. Information Tech. Task Group, mem. Remuneration Cttee, Chartered Fellow; Trustee, Economist Newspapers Ltd 1999–; mem. Admin. Bd, Elster Group SE 2011–12; mem. Ind. TV Comm. 2000–, Council City Univ., London 2000–, Malaysian British Business Council –2001; Trustee, Economist Newspapers Ltd. *Address:* Chartered Management Institute, 2 Savoy Court, Strand, London, WC2R 0EZ, England (office). *Telephone:* (20) 7497-0580 (office). *Fax:* (20) 7497-0463 (office). *E-mail:* enquiries@managers.org.uk (office). *Website:* www.managers.org.uk (office).

BRENNAN, David R., BBA; American pharmaceutical industry executive; m.; four c.; ed Gettysburg Coll.; joined Merck as sales rep. 1975, Gen. Man. Chibret Int. (French subsidiary) 1990–92; joined AstraMerck 1992, was responsible for business planning and devt at Astra Pharmaceuticals, Sr Vice-Pres. of Commercial Operations, AstraZeneca Pharmaceuticals LP (N America) 1999–2001, Pres. and CEO AstraZeneca LP (N America) 2001–06, Exec. Bd Dir AstraZeneca 2005–12, CEO AstraZeneca PLC 2006–12; Pres. Int. Fed. of Pharmaceutical Mfrs and Asscns; Past Chair. Pharmaceutical Research and Mfrs of America (PhRMA), Southeastern Pennsylvania Chapter of the American Heart Asscn; mem. Exec. Bd European Fed. of Pharmaceutical Industries and Asscns, European Roundtable of Industrialists, Nat. Inst. of Health Roundtable on Evidence Based Medicine; Commr UK Comm. for Employment and Skills 2007–; mem. Bd Philadelphia Orchestra; Hon. mem. Bd of Dirs CEO Roundtable on Cancer. *Leisure interests:* scuba diving, cycling, amateur photography. *Address:* c/o AstraZeneca PLC, 15 Stanhope Gate, London, W1K 1LN, England.

BRENNAN, Hon. Sir (Francis) Gerard, Kt, AC, KBE, GBS (Hong Kong), LLB, QC; Australian judge (retd); b. 22 May 1928, Rockhampton, Queensland; s. of Hon. Mr Justice Frank T. Brennan and Gertrude Brennan; m. Patricia O'Hara 1953; three s. four d.; ed Christian Brothers' Coll., Rockhampton, Downlands Coll., Toowoomba and Univ. of Queensland, Brisbane; admitted to Bar 1951, QC 1965; Pres. Bar Asscn of Queensland 1974–76, Australian Bar Asscn 1975–76, Admin. Review Council 1976–79, Admin. Appeals Tribunal 1976–79; mem. Exec. Law Council of Australia 1975–76, Australian Law Reform Comm. 1975–77; Additional Judge, Supreme Court of ACT 1976–81; Judge, Australian Industrial Court 1976–81, Fed. Court of Australia 1977–81; Justice, High Court of Australia 1981–95; Chief Justice of Australia 1995–98; External Judge, Supreme Court of Fiji 1999–2000; Non-perm. Judge, Court of Final Appeal of Hong Kong 2000–12; Foundation Scientia Prof. of Law, Univ. of New South Wales 1998; Chancellor, Univ. of Tech., Sydney 1998–2004; Hon. LLD (Univ. of Dublin Trinity Coll.) 1988, (Univ. of Queensland) 1996, (ANU) 1996, (Melbourne Univ., Univ. of Tech., Sydney) 1998, (Univ. of New South Wales) 2005; Hon. DLitt (Central Queensland Univ.) 1996; Hon. DUniv (Griffiths Univ.) 1996, (Univ. of Tech., Sydney) 2005. *Address:* c/o Suite 3003, Piccadilly Tower, 133 Castlereagh Street, Sydney, NSW 2000, Australia. *Telephone:* (2) 9261-8704 (office). *Fax:* (2) 9261-8113 (office).

BRENNAN, John J. (Jack), AB, MBA; American business executive; *Chairman Emeritus and Senior Advisor, The Vanguard Group Inc.;* b. 1954, Boston, Mass; s. of Frank Brennan; m. Catherine Brennan; two s. one d.; ed Dartmouth Coll., Harvard Business School; Assoc., New York Bank for Savings 1976–78; Planning Assoc., S.C. Johnson & Son 1980–82; joined Vanguard Group Inc. 1982, Asst to Chair. 1982–85, Chief Financial Officer 1985–89, Pres. 1989–96, CEO 1996–2008, Chair. 1998–2009, Chair. Emer. and Sr Advisor 2010–; fmr Chair. Investment Company Inst., Financial Accounting Foundation; Dir, Guardian Life Insurance Co. of America, LPL Financial Holdings Inc.; fmr Dir, The Hanover Insurance Group; Lead Gov., FINRA Bd Govs; Trustee, The Vanguard Charitable Endowment Program, Univ. of Notre Dame. *Address:* The Vanguard Group Inc., PO Box 1110, Valley Forge, PA 19482-1110, USA (office). *Telephone:* (610) 648-6000 (office). *Fax:* (610) 669-6605 (office). *E-mail:* info@vanguard.com (office). *Website:* www.vanguard.com (office).

BRENNAN, John Owen, BA, MA; American government official; *Director, Central Intelligence Agency;* b. 22 Sept. 1955; m. Kathy Pokluda; three c.; ed Fordham Univ., American Univ., Cairo, Univ. of Texas, Austin; career trainee, Operations Directorate, CIA 1980, joined Directorate of Intelligence, CIA 1981, Political Officer, Embassy in Jeddah, Saudi Arabia 1982–84, various positions with Office of Near Eastern and South Asian Analysis, CIA 1984–89, Head of Terrorism Analysis, CIA Counterterrorist Center 1990–92, Daily intelligence briefer to Pres. Bill Clinton 1994–95, Exec. Asst to CIA Deputy Dir 1995–96, Station Chief, CIA, Riyadh, Saudi Arabia 1996–99, Chief of Staff to CIA Deputy Dir 1999–2001, Deputy Exec. Dir, CIA 2001–03, Dir, Terrorist Threat Integration Center 2003–04, Interim Dir, Nat. Counterterrorism Center 2004–05, Dir, CIA 2013–; Asst to Pres., Deputy Nat. Security Adviser for Homeland Security and Counterterrorism, Nat.

Security Council 2009–13; Pres. and CEO, The Analysis Corpn 2005–08; Chair. Intelligence and Nat. Security Alliance 2007–08; Nat. Security Medal, Distinguished Intelligence Medal, Distinguished Career Intelligence Medal. *Address:* CIA Headquarters, Washington, DC 20250, USA (office). *Telephone:* (703) 482-0623 (office). *Fax:* (703) 482-1739 (office). *Website:* www.cia.gov (office).

BRENNECKE, Joan F., BS, MS, PhD; American chemist and academic; *Keating-Crawford Professor of Chemical and Biomolecular Engineering, University of Notre Dame;* ed Univ. of Texas, Univ. of Illinois; mem. Faculty, Univ. of Notre Dame, Ind. 1989–, currently Keating-Crawford Prof. of Chemical and Biomolecular Eng, Dir Notre Dame's Energy Center; Past Chair. Council for Chemical Research; mem. Editorial Bd Green Chemistry; mem. AIChE, ACS, American Soc. for Eng Educ.; numerous awards, including NSF Presidential Young Investigator Award 1991, ACS Ipatieff Prize 2001, AIChE Professional Progress Award 2006, John M. Prausnitz Award, Conf. on Properties and Phase Equilibria for Product and Process Design 2007, Julius Stieglitz Lecturer, Chicago section of ACS and Univ. of Chicago 2008. *Publications:* numerous papers in professional journals on supercritical fluid tech., ionic liquids, thermodynamics, environmentally benign chemical processing and carbon dioxide separation, storage and usage. *Address:* 180 Fitzpatrick Hall, Department of Chemical and Biomolecular Engineering, University of Notre Dame, Notre Dame, Ind. IN 46556, USA (office). *Telephone:* (574) 631-5847 (office); (574) 631-7709 (Lab.) (office). *Fax:* (574) 631-8366 (office). *E-mail:* jfb@nd.edu (office). *Website:* www.nd.edu/~jfb (office).

BRENNEMAN, Ronald Alvin, BSc, MSc; Canadian petroleum industry executive; ed Univ. of Toronto, Univ. of Manchester, Sr Exec. Program, Sloan School of Business, Massachusetts Inst. of Tech.; joined Imperial Oil Ltd 1969, Operations Man. 1977, various man. roles 1978–83, with Exxon Corpn (parent co.), NY 1983–86, becoming Vice-Pres. then Pres. Imperial Oil Ltd 1992–94, CEO Esso Benelux 1994–97, Gen. Man. of Corp. Planning, Exxon, Dallas 1997–99; mem. Bd of Dirs, Pres. and CEO Petro-Canada 2000–09, Exec. Vice-Chair. Suncor Energy Inc. (following merger with Petro-Canada) 2009–10; mem. Bd of Dirs The Bank of Novia Scotia (Scotiabank) 2000–, BCE Inc., WestJet Airlines Ltd, Syncrude Canada Ltd 2004–08; fmr mem. Canadian Petroleum Asscn, Canada Safety Council, United Way of Calgary and of Toronto; Trustee, United Way of Greater Toronto, Hosp. for Sick Children. *Address:* Office of the Chairman, Scotiabank, Scotia Plaza, 44 King Street West, Toronto, ON M5H 1H1, Canada (office). *Telephone:* (416) 866-6161 (office). *Fax:* (416) 866-3750 (office). *E-mail:* email@scotiabank.com (office). *Website:* www.scotiabank.com (office).

BRENNER, David J., BA, MSc, MA, MSc, PhD; British physicist and academic; *Higgins Professor of Radiation Biophysics, College of Physicians and Surgeons, Columbia University;* b. 9 June 1953, Liverpool; ed Univ. of Oxford, St Bartholomew's Hosp., Univ. of London, Univ. of Surrey; Postdoctoral Fellow, Los Alamos Scientific Lab. 1979–81, Staff mem. 1981–83; Assoc Research Scientist, Radiological Research Lab., Coll. of Physicians and Surgeons, Columbia Univ., New York 1983–86, Asst Prof. of Radiation Oncology 1986–92, Assoc. Prof. 1992–93, Prof. and Dir Center for Radiological Research 1994–, Higgins Prof. of Radiation Biophysics 2008–; also Dir Columbia Univ. Radiological Research Accelerator Facility; Miller Prof., Univ. of California, Berkeley 2002; mem. Editorial Bd Radiation and Environmental Biophysics 2002–; mem. Nat. Council on Radiation Protection and Measurements; Hon. DSc (Oxford) 1996; Univ. of Oxford Carter Physics Prize 1974, Radiation Research Soc. Annual Research Award 1991, Robert D. Moseley Award for Radiation Protection in Medicine, Nat. Council on Radiation Protection and Measurements 1992, Jean Roy Memorial Lecturer, Canadian Asscn of Radiation Oncology 2002, G. William Morgan Lecturer, Health Physics Soc. 2008, Selby Lecturer, Memorial Sloan Kettering Cancer Center 2009, Douglas Lea Lecturer, UK Radiation Oncology Congress 2009. *Publications include:* Radon, Risk and Remedy 1989, Making the Radiotherapy Decision 1996; numerous articles in scientific journals. *Address:* Center for Radiological Research, Columbia University, 630 West 168th St, New York, NY 10032, USA (office). *Telephone:* (212) 305-5660 (office). *Fax:* (212) 305-3229 (office). *E-mail:* djb3@columbia.edu (office). *Website:* www.columbia.edu/~djb3 (office).

BRENNER, Sydney, CH, MB, DPhil, FRS, FRCP; British scientist and academic; *Distinguished Research Professor, Salk Institute for Biological Studies;* b. 13 Jan. 1927, Germiston, South Africa; s. of Morris Brenner and Lena Brenner (née Blacher); m. May Woolf Balkind; two s. (one step-s.) two d.; ed Univ. of the Witwatersrand, Johannesburg and Oxford Univ.; Lecturer in Physiology, Univ. of Witwatersrand 1955–57; mem. Scientific Staff, MRC 1957–92, Dir MRC Lab. of Molecular Biology, Cambridge 1979–86, Dir Molecular Genetics Unit, Cambridge 1986–92; mem. Scripps Inst., La Jolla, Calif. 1992–94; Dir Molecular Sciences Inst., Berkeley, Calif. 1996–2001; Distinguished Research Prof. Salk Inst. for Biological Studies, La Jolla, Calif., USA 2001–; mem. MRC 1978–82, 1986–90; Fellow, King's Coll., Cambridge 1959–; Hon. Prof. of Genetic Medicine, Univ. of Cambridge Clinical School 1981–87; Foreign Assoc., NAS 1977; Foreign mem., American Philosophical Soc. 1979; Foreign Assoc., Royal Soc. of S. Africa 1983; Foreign mem. Real Academia de Ciencias 1985; External Scientific mem. Max Planck Soc. 1988; mem. Academia Europaea 1989; Corresp. Scientifique Emérite de l'INSERM, Associé Etranger Académie des Sciences, France, Fellow American Acad. of Microbiology; Foreign Hon. mem. American Acad. of Arts and Sciences 1965, Hon. mem. Deutsche Akademie der Naturforscher Leopoldina 1975, Soc. for Biological Chemists 1975, Hon. Fellow, Exeter Coll. 1985, Hon. Fellow, Indian Acad. of Sciences 1989, Hon. mem. Chinese Soc. of Genetics 1989, Hon. Fellow, Royal Coll. of Pathologists 1990, Hon. Fellow, Acad. Medical Sciences 1999, Hon. mem. Assoc. of Physicians of GB and Ireland 1991; Hon. DSc (Dublin, Witwatersrand, Chicago, London, Leicester, Oxford, La Trobe); Hon. LLD (Glasgow) 1981, (Cambridge) 2001; Hon. DLitt (Singapore); Hon. Dr rer. nat (Jena); Warren Triennial Prize 1968, William Bate Hardy Prize, Cambridge Philosophical Soc. 1969, Gregor Mendel Medal of German Acad. of Science Leopoldina 1970, Albert Lasker Medical Research Award 1971, Gairdner Foundation Annual Award (Canada) 1978; Royal Medal of Royal Soc. 1974, Prix Charles Leopold Mayer, French Acad. 1975, Krebs Medal, Fed. of European Biochemical Socs 1980, Ciba Medal, Biochemical Soc. 1981, Feldberg Foundation Prize 1983, Neil Hamilton Fairley Medal, Royal Coll. of Physicians 1985, Croonian Lecturer Royal Soc. of London 1986, Rosenstiel Award, Brandeis Univ. 1986, Prix Louis Jeantet de Médecine (Switzerland) 1987, Genetics Soc. of America Medal 1987,

Harvey Prize, Israel Inst. of Tech. 1987, Hughlings Jackson Medal, Royal Soc. of Medicine 1987, Waterford Bio-Medical Science Award (The Research Inst. of Scripps Clinic) 1988, Kyoto Prize (Inamori Foundation) 1990, Gairdner Foundation Award (Canada) 1991, Copley Medal (Royal Soc.) 1991, King Faisal Int. Prize for Science (King Faisal Foundation) 1992, Bristol-Myers Squibb Award for Distinguished Achievement in Neuroscience Research 1992, Albert Lasker Award for Special Achievement 2000, Nobel Prize for Physiology or Medicine 2002, Dan David Prize 2002. *Leisure interest:* rumination. *Address:* Brenner Laboratory, Salk Institute for Biological Studies, 10010 North Torrey Pines Road, La Jolla, CA 92186-5800 (office); 22 Black Hill, Ely, Cambs. CB7 2BZ, England (home). *Telephone:* (858) 453-4100 (office). *E-mail:* sbrenner@salk.edu (office). *Website:* www.salk.edu (office).

BRENT, Richard P., MA, PhD, DSc, FAA, FIEEE, FACM, FIMA, FAustMS, FSIAM; Australian computer scientist, mathematician and academic; *Professor Emeritus, Australian National University;* b. 1946, Melbourne, Vic.; s. of Oscar Brent and Nancy Brent; m. Erin O'Connor 1969 (died 2005), two s.; m. Judy-anne Osborn 2007; ed Melbourne Grammar School, Monash Univ., Stanford Univ., USA; Research Scientist, IBM T.J. Watson Research Center, Yorktown Heights, New York, USA 1971–72; Research Fellow, ANU, Canberra 1972–78, Prof. of Computer Sciences 1978–98, Australian Research Council Fed Fellow and Prof., Math. Sciences Inst. 2005–10, Distinguished Prof. of Math. and Computer Science 2010–11, Prof. Emer. 2011–; Prof. of Computing Science, Univ. of Oxford 1998–2005, Fellow, St Hugh's Coll. 1998–2005; Conjoint Prof. of Math., CARMA, Univ. of Newcastle, NSW 2010–; Fellow, Inst. of Math. and its Applications, Asscn for Computing Machinery (USA), Soc. for Industrial and Applied Math. (USA), Australian Math. Soc.; Foreign Fellow, Bangladesh Acad. of Science; Australian Math. Soc. Medal 1984, Forsythe Memorial Lecturer 1990, Hannan Medal 2005. *Publications include:* Algorithms for Minimization without Derivatives 1973, Topics in Computational Complexity and the Analysis of Algorithms 1980, Modern Computer Arithmetic (with Paul Zimmermann) 2010. *Leisure interests:* music, chess, bridge, walking. *Address:* Mathematical Sciences Institute, Australian National University, Canberra, ACT 0200, Australia (office). *E-mail:* europa@rpbrent.com (office). *Website:* maths-people.anu.edu.au/~brent (office).

BRENTON, Howard, BA; British playwright; b. 13 Dec. 1942, Portsmouth, Hants., England; s. of Donald Henry Brenton and Rose Lilian Brenton (née Lewis); m. Jane Fry 1970; two s.; ed Chichester High School for Boys and St Catharine's Coll., Cambridge; resident writer, Royal Court Theatre, London 1972–73; Writer-in-Residence, Univ. of Warwick 1978–79; Granada Artist-in-Residence, Univ. of Calif., Davis 1997; Arts and Humanities Research Bd Fellowship, Univ. of Birmingham 2000; Hon. Dr of Arts (North London) 1996, (Westminster), (Portsmouth); John Whiting Award 1970, Standard Best Play of the Year Award 1976, Standard Best Play of the Year (with David Hare) 1985. *Publications include:* Revenge (play) 1969, Christie in Love 1969, Scott of the Antarctic (or What God Didn't See) 1970, Lay By (co-author) 1972, Plays for Public Places 1972, Hitler Dances 1972, Magnificence 1973, Brassneck (with David Hare) 1973, The Churchill Play 1974, Government Property 1975, The Saliva Milkshake 1975, Weapons of Happiness 1976, The Paradise Run (TV play) 1976, Sore Throats 1979, Plays for the Poor Theatre 1980, The Romans in Britain 1980, Thirteenth Night 1981, The Genius 1983, Desert of Lies (TV play) 1983, Sleeping Policemen (with Tunde Ikoli) 1983, Bloody Poetry 1984, Pravda (with David Hare) 1985, Dead Head 1986, Greenland 1988, Diving for Pearls (novel) 1989, Iranian Nights (with Tariq Ali) 1989, Hess is Dead 1990, Moscow Gold (with Tariq Ali) 1990, Berlin Bertie 1992, Hot Irons (Essays and Diaries) 1995, Playing Away (opera) 1994, Goethe's Faust, Parts I and II (adaptation) 1995, Plays I 1996, Plays II 1996, In Extremis 1997, Ugly Rumours (with Tariq Ali) 1998, Collateral Damage (with Tariq Ali and Andy de la Tour), Nasser's Eden (play for radio) 1999, Snogging Ken (with Tariq Ali and Andy de la Tour) 2000, Kit's Play 2000, Spooks (TV series) 2002–05, Paul (play) 2005, In Extremis (play) 2006, Never So Good (play) 2008, Anne Boleyn (play) 2010, Danton's Death (version) 2010, The Ragged Trousered Philanthropists (adaptation) 2010, 55 Days (play) 2012, The Interrogation of Ai Weiwei (play) 2013, Dances Of Death (adaptation) 2013, The Guffin (play) 2013, Drawing the Line (play) 2013. *Leisure interest:* painting. *Address:* c/o Casarotto Ramsay Ltd, Waverley House, 7–12 Noel Street, London, W1F 8GQ, England (office). *Telephone:* (20) 7287-4406 (office). *Fax:* (20) 7287-9128 (office). *E-mail:* info@casarotto.co.uk (office). *Website:* www.casarotto.co.uk (office).

BRESCH, Heather, BA; American pharmaceutical company executive; *CEO, Mylan;* ed Univ. of West Virginia; joined Mylan (pharmaceutical co.) 1992, has held numerous positions including Head of North America operations, later COO and Chief Integration Officer, led integration of Matrix Laboratories and Merck KGaA's generics business, Pres. Mylan –2012, mem. Bd of Dirs and CEO 2012–; fmr Chair. and Vice-Chair. Generic Pharmaceutical; ranked by Fortune magazine amongst the 50 Most Powerful Women in Business in the US (47th) 2012. *Address:* Mylan, 1500 Corporate Drive, Canonsburg, PA 15317, USA (office). *Telephone:* (724) 514-1800 (office). *E-mail:* iinfo@mylan.com (office). *Website:* www.mylan.com (office).

BRESLOW, Ronald Charles, AB, PhD; American chemist and academic; *University Professor of Chemistry, Columbia University;* b. 14 March 1931, Rahway, NJ; s. of Alexander Breslow and Gladys Fellows; m. Esther Greenberg 1956; two d.; ed Harvard Univ.; Instructor, Columbia Univ. 1956–59, Assoc. Prof. 1959–62, Prof. 1962–67, Mitchill Prof. of Chem. 1966–, Chair. Dept of Chem. 1976–, Univ. Prof. 1992–; A.R. Todd Visiting Prof., Univ. of Cambridge 1982; mem. NAS, Chair. Div. of Chem. 1974, Procurator 1984; mem. Exec. Cttee, Div. of Organic Chem., ACS, Chair. Div. of Organic Chem. 1970–71, Pres. of ACS 1996; Ed. Benjamin Inc. 1962–; mem. Editorial Bd Organic Syntheses 1965–, Bd of Eds Journal of Organic Chemistry 1968, Tetrahedron, Tetrahedron Letters 1977, Chemical Engineering News 1980–83; mem. Advisory Bd Chemical and Engineering News 1980; Chair. Bd of Scientific Advisers, Sloan Foundation 1981–; mem. Bd of Scientific Advisers, General Motors 1982–; Trustee, American-Swiss Foundation for Scientific Exchange Inc. 1969–71, Rockefeller Univ. 1981–; mem. American Acad. of Arts and Sciences, American Philosophical Soc., European Acad. of Science 2004; Foreign mem. Royal Soc.; Fellow, AAAS 1986; Foreign Fellow, Indian Acad. of Science 1992; Hon. mem. Korean Chemical Soc. 1996, Royal Soc. of Chem. (UK) 1996, Japan Chemical Soc. 2002; Foreign Hon. mem.

Royal Soc. 2000; numerous awards, including Sloan Fellowship 1961–63, ACS Award in Pure Chem. 1966, Fresinius Award 1966, Mark van Doren Award 1969, Baekeland Medal 1969, Centenary Lecturer, Chemical Soc., London 1972, Remsen Medal 1977, Roussel Prize 1978, ACS James Flack Norris Award in Physical Organic Chem. 1980, Annual Ciba Foundation Lecturer, London 1982, Richards Medal in Chem. 1984, Arthur Cope Award 1987, Nichols Medal 1989, NAS Chem. Medal 1989, Swiss Chemical Soc. Paracelsus Medal 1990, US Nat. Medal of Science 1991, ACS Priestley Medal 1999, ACS Bader Award in Bioorganic Chem. 2002, Esselen Award for Chem. in the Public Interest 2002, Robert A. Welch Award in Chem. 2003, ACS Willard Gibbs Medal 2004, Auburn Univ. Kosolapoff Award 2005, Chemical Heritage Foundation Othmer Gold Medal 2006, ACS Paul Gassman Medal 2006, Organic Syntheses/Wiley Award 2007, Westheimer Medal 2013. *Publications:* Organic Reaction Mechanisms 1965, Chemistry Today and Tomorrow 1996; more than 400 scientific papers. *Leisure interest:* piano performance. *Address:* Department of Chemistry, Columbia University, 3000 Broadway, Mail Code 3105, New York, NY 10027 (office); 44 West 77th Street, New York, NY 10024, USA (home). *Telephone:* (212) 854-2170 (office). *Fax:* (212) 854-2755 (office). *E-mail:* rb33@columbia.edu (office). *Website:* www.columbia.edu/cu/chemistry/breslow (office).

BRESSANI, Ricardo, PhD; Guatemalan biochemist; *Head, Food Science and Technology Centre, Research Institute, Universidad de Valle;* b. 28 Sept. 1926, Guatemala; s. of César Bressani and Primina Castignoli de Bressani; m. Alicia Herman 1949; five s. two d.; ed Univ. of Dayton, Iowa State Univ. and Purdue Univ., USA; Visiting Prof., MIT, Rutgers Univ.; Ed.-in-Chief, Archivos Latino-americanos de Nutrición; Head and Research Dir, Div. of Agric. and Food Sciences, Inst. of Nutrition of Cen. America and Panama (INCAP) 1988–; Head of Food Science and Tech. Centre, Research Inst., Univ. de Valle; mem. Directive Cttee Agroindustrial Rural Devt (PRODAR), Costa Rica 1991–; Corresp. Academic mem. Acad. of Medical, Physical and Natural Sciences of Guatemala 1990–; Foreign mem. NAS; mem. American Inst. of Food Technologists, Acad. of Science of the Int. Union for Food Science and Tech.; Orden del Quetzal en el Grado de Gran Cruz 1999; Dr hc (Purdue), (Universidad del Valle de Guatemala); Babcock Hart Award 1970, McCollum Award 1976, World Science Award 'Albert Einstein' 1984, Abraham Horowitz Award 1990, Ibero-American Prize in Science and Tech., Mexico 2001, Danone Int. Prize of Nutrition 2003, Distinguished Alumnus Award, Univ. of Dayton 2012. *Publications:* more than 500 scientific publns in related professional fields, including books, monographs and articles in scientific journals. *Leisure interests:* swimming, horseback riding, agricultural conservation. *Address:* Institute of Nutrition of Central America and Panama, Calzada Roosevelt 6-25 zona 11, PO Box 1188, 01011 Guatemala City (office); Centro de Ciencia y Tecnología de Alimentos, Instituto de Investigaciones, Universidad del Valle de Guatemala, 18 avenida 11-95 zona 15, Vista Hermosa III, 01015 Guatemala City (office); 6a calle 'A' 7-74 zona 9, Guatemala City, 01009 Guatemala (home). *Telephone:* (502) 2472-3762 (Inst. of Nutrition); (502) 2364-0336 (Univ.); (502) 2332-6125 (home). *Fax:* (502) 2473-6529 (Inst. of Nutrition) (office); (502) 2364-0212 (Univ.) (office). *E-mail:* bressani@incap.org.gt (office); bressani@incap.ops-oms.org (office); bressani@uvg.edu.gt (office). *Website:* www.incap.org.gt (office); www.uvg.edu.gt (office).

BRETH, Andrea; German theatre director; *Director-in-Residence, Vienna Burgtheater;* b. 31 Oct. 1952, Rieden, Allgau; d. of Prof. Herbert Breth and Maria Breth (née Noether); ed Darmstadt, Heidelberg; Dir Bremen, Hamburg, Berlin 1976, Zürich, Bochum 1980, Freiburg (Bernarda Albas Haus, Lorca) 1984, Schauspielhaus Bochum (Le Sud, Green; The Last, Gorki) 1986–90, Burgtheater, Vienna (Zerbrochener Krug, Kleist) 1990, Schaubuhne Berlin (Einsamer Weg, Schnitzler) 1991 and (Nachtasyl, Gorki) 1992, Burgtheater Vienna (End of the Beginning, O'Casey) 1991, Tschulimsk, Wampilow (Letzten Sommer) 1992, Kaiser (Von morgens bis mitternachts) 1993, (Hedda Gabler) 1993, (Orestes) 1995, (Die Möwe) 1995; Art Dir Berliner Schaubühne am Leniner Platz 1992–97; Dir-in-Residence, Vienna Burgtheater 1997–; mem. der Darstellenden Künste, Frankfurt, Akademie der Künste berlin; Fritz-Kortner-Prize 1987, Nestroy-Award 2003, and other awards. *Leisure interests:* literature, music, paintings, theatre. *Address:* Burgtheater, Dr. Karl-Lueger-Ring 2, 1010 Vienna, Austria (office). *Telephone:* (1) 51444-4140 (office). *Fax:* (1) 51444-4440 (office). *Website:* www.burgtheater.at (office).

BRETON, Guy, BA, MD; Canadian radiologist, academic and university administrator; *Rector, Université de Montréal;* b. 1 April 1950, Saint-Hyacinthe, Quebec; ed Séminaire de Saint-Hyacinthe, Univ. of Sherbrooke; served residency in diagnostic radiology at McGill Univ., while obtaining additional training in neuroradiology at Montreal Neurological Inst. and Hosp.; Assoc. Clinical Prof., Dept of Radiology, Radio-Oncology and Nuclear Medicine, Faculty of Medicine, Université de Montréal 1979–94, Full Prof. 1994–, Head of Dept 1996–2003, Exec. Vice-Dean of Post-Doctoral Medical Studies and Hosp. Affairs, Faculty of Medicine 2003–06, helped establish integrated university health network (RUIS), Exec. Vice-Rector Université de Montréal 2006–10, Rector 2010–; involved in operations and admin of Hôpital Saint-Luc early 1980s, later of Centre hospitalier de l'Université de Montréal (CHUM), Head of hospital's Radiology Dept, Dir of Planning for CHUM and Special Advisor to Chair. and CEO; played role in CHUM project 2000–06, Vice-Pres. SICHUM in planning of care, services, education and research, and Dir of Planning, CHUM 2010–; Pres. and CEO of pvt. radiology clinic in Québec 1983–97; Pres. Asscn des radiologistes du Québec 1987–97, Canadian Heads of Academic Radiology 1998–2000; fmr Chair. Medical Affairs Cttee of Conf. of Rectors and Prins of Quebec Univs; fmr mem. Bd CHUM, Fondation du CHUM, Hôpital Maisonneuve-Rosemont, Hôpital du Sacré-Cœur de Montréal, Canadian Asscn of Univ. Business Officers and Québec-Transplant; Albert Jutras Prize, Asscn des radiologistes du Québec 2009. *Publications:* author or co-author of 100 scientific publs in professional journals. *Address:* Office of the Rector, Université de Montréal, PO Box 6128, Station Centre-ville, Montréal, PQ H3C 3J7, Canada (office). *Telephone:* (514) 343-6991 (office). *Fax:* (514) 343-2354 (office). *E-mail:* recteur@umontreal.ca (office). *Website:* www.umontreal.ca (office).

BRETON, Thierry; French government official and business executive; *CEO and Chairman of the Management Board, Atos Origin;* b. 15 Jan. 1955; m.; three c.; ed Lycée Louis Le Grand, Supelec Electrical Eng . School, Paris and French Inst. for Nat. Defence Studies (IHEDN); nat. mil. service as teacher of information tech.

and math., French Lycée, New York 1979–81; Chair. and CEO Forma Systèmes 1981–86; Chief Adviser of Minister for Information and New Technologies, Ministry of Educ. and Research 1986–88; CEO Futuroscope de Poitiers (science and tech. theme park) and CEO Futuroscope Telecommunications Platform 1986–90; CEO CGI Group 1990–93; CEO and Vice-Chair. Bd Dirs Bull Group 1993–97; Chair. and CEO Thomson SA and Thomson Multimedia 1997–2002; Chair. and CEO France Telecom SA 2002–05; Minister of the Economy, Finance and Industry 2005–07; CEO and Chair. Man. Bd Atos Origin 2008–; mem. Bd of Dirs Carrefour SA 2008–; Chevalier, Légion d'honneur, Commdr, Ordre nat. du Mérite. *Publications:* Softwar 1984, Vatican III 1985, Netwar 1987, La Dimension Invisible 1991, La Fin des Illusions 1992, Le Lievre et la Tortue 1994. *Address:* Atos Origin, Tour les Miroirs–Bat C, 18 avenue d'Alsace, 92926 Paris, La Défense 3 Cedex, France (office). *Telephone:* 1-55-91-20-00 (office). *Fax:* 1-55-91-20-05 (office). *Website:* www.atosorigin.com (office).

BRETSCHER, Mark Steven, MA, PhD, FRS; British/Swiss research scientist (retd); b. 8 Jan. 1940, Cambridge, England; s. of Egon Bretscher and Hanni Bretscher (née Greminger); m. Barbara M.F. Pearse 1978; one s. one d.; ed Abingdon School, Gonville and Caius Coll., Cambridge; research student, Gonville and Caius Coll., Cambridge 1961–64; Post-doctoral Visitor, Stanford Univ., USA 1964–65; Scientific Staff mem. MRC Lab. of Molecular Biology, Cambridge 1965–2012, Head, Div. of Cell Biology 1984–95; Visiting Prof., Harvard Coll., USA 1974–75, Stanford Univ. 1984–85; Friedrich-Miescher Prize 1979. *Television:* Bags of Life (Horizon, BBC) 1974. *Publications:* scientific papers in professional journals. *Leisure interest:* silviculture. *Address:* Ram Cottage, Commercial End, Swaffham Bulbeck, Cambs., CB25 0ND, England (home). *Telephone:* (1223) 811276 (home). *E-mail:* msb@mrc-lmb.cam.ac.uk (office). *Website:* www2.mrc-lmb .cam.ac.uk/personal/bretscher/msb_home.html (office).

BREUER, Michael; German accountant and politician; *Chairman, Rheinische Sparkassen- und Giroverband (Rheinische Savings Bank and Giro Association);* b. 2 Oct. 1965, Brühl, North Rhine-Westphalia; ed Abitur in Lechenich, Univ. of Bonn; grew up in Erftstadt-Ahrem; mil. service in Munster and Lüneburg; mem. CDU 1983–, co. and dist chair. Jungen Union, mem. North Rhine-Westphalia State Parl. and mem. Bd CDU Parl. Group Cttee 1995–, Spokesman for Budgetary Control 1995–2005; Dist Chair. CDU Cen. Rhine (Cologne, Bonn, Leverkusen, Rhine Erft) 1999–, mem. regional-level Party Council of CDU North-Rhine-Westphalia; Minister for Fed., European and Int. Affairs, State of North Rhine-Westphalia 2005–07; worked for KPMG German trust 1993–2004; ind. certified public accountant and tax adviser 2004–05; Chair. Rheinische Sparkassen- und Giroverband (Rheinische Savings Bank and Giro Asscn), Düsseldorf 2008–. *Address:* Rheinischer Sparkassen- und Giroverband, Kirchfeldstraße 60, 40217 Düsseldorf, Germany (office). *Telephone:* (211) 3892-01 (office). *Fax:* (211) 3892-240 (office). *E-mail:* info@rsgv.de (office). *Website:* www.rsgv.de (office).

BREUER, Rolf-Ernst, DJur; German banker; b. 1937; ed Univs of Lausanne, Munich and Bonn; Spokesman, Bd of Man. Dirs and Chair., Group Exec. Cttee, Deutsche Bank AG, Frankfurt 1997–2002, Chair. Supervisory Bd 2002–06 (resgnd); numerous other commercial appointments. *Address:* c/o Deutsche Bank, 60262 Frankfurt am Main, Germany (office).

BREWER, Janice Kay (Jan); American politician and state governor; *Governor of Arizona;* b. 26 Sept. 1944, Hollywood, Calif.; d. of of the late Perry Wilford Drinkwine and Edna C. Drinkwine (née Bakken); m. Dr John Leon Brewer; three s. (one deceased); ed Glendale Community Coll.; qualified as radiological technologist; mem. Ariz. House of Reps from 19th Dist 1983–97; Chair. Bd of Supervisors, Maricopa Co. 2001–03; Sec. of State of Ariz. 2003–09; Gov. of Ariz. 2009–; mem. or fmr mem. Nat. Org. of Women, American Legis. Exchange Council, Nat. Fed. of Republican Women, Luke Fighter Country Partnership, Hope and a Future, Child Help USA, Arizonans for Children, Arrowhead Republican Women's Club, Maricopa Co. SMI Comm., Arizona Rifle and Pistol Asscn, Japanese-American Citizens League; Republican; named Woman of Year, Chiropractic Asscn of Arizona 1983, Legislator of Year, Behaviour Health Asscn of Arizona 1991, Freedom Award, Veterans of Arizona 1994. *Address:* Office of the Governor, Executive Tower, 1700 West Washington Street, Phoenix, AZ 85007, USA (office). *Telephone:* (602) 542-4331 (office). *Fax:* (602) 542-1381 (office). *Website:* www .governor.state.az.us (office); azgovernor.gov (office).

BREWER, Rosalind G., BS; American business executive; *President and CEO, Sam's Club, Walmart;* ed Spelman Coll., Advanced Man. Program at The Wharton School, Director's Coll. at Univ. of Chicago School of Business/Stanford School of Law; worked for Kimberly-Clark Corpn, starting as a scientist in non-woven technology and product devt before becoming Vice-Pres. Global Non-wovens sector 2004–06; joined Wal-Mart Stores, Inc. (now Walmart) as Regional Vice-Pres., responsible for operations in Georgia 2006, promoted to Pres. of SE Operating Div., later Exec. Vice-Pres. and Pres. South business unit of Walmart US, Exec. Vice-Pres. and Pres. Walmart East –2011, Pres. and CEO Sam's Club (first woman and first African American CEO of a Walmart business unit) 2012–; mem. Bd of Dirs Lockheed Martin, Molson Coors Brewing Co. 2006– (mem. Human Resources/Compensation Cttee); mem. Bd of Trustees Spelman Coll., Westminster Schools, Atlanta; named to Black Enterprise's 75 Most Powerful Women In Business list 2010, ranked by Fortune magazine amongst the 50 Most Powerful Women in Business in the US (35th) 2010, (23rd) 2011, (13th) 2012, ranked by Forbes magazine amongst The World's 100 Most Powerful Women (50th) 2012, (44th) 2013. *Address:* Walmart, 702 SW 8th Street, Bentonville, AR 72716-8611, USA (office). *Telephone:* (479) 273-4000 (office). *Fax:* (479) 277-1830 (office). *E-mail:* info@walmartstores.com (office). *Website:* walmartstores.com (office).

BREYER, Stephen, AB, BA, LLB; American lawyer, academic and judge; *Associate Justice, Supreme Court;* b. 15 Aug. 1938, San Francisco, Calif.; s. of Irving Breyer and Anne Breyer; m. Joanna Hare 1967; one s. two d.; ed Stanford Univ., Magdalen Coll. Oxford Univ. and Harvard Univ. Law School; law clerk to Mr Justice Arthur Goldberg, US Supreme Court 1964–65; Special Asst to Asst US Attorney-Gen., Antitrust Div. US Dept of Justice 1965–67; Asst Prof. of Law, Harvard Univ. 1967–70; Prof. of Law, Harvard Law School 1970–80; Prof., Kennedy School of Govt Harvard Univ. 1977–80; Lecturer, Harvard Law School 1981–; Asst Special Prosecutor, Watergate Special Prosecution Force 1973; Special Counsel, Admin. Practices Subcttee, US Senate Judiciary Cttee 1974–75, Chief

Counsel, Senate Judiciary Cttee 1979–80; Circuit Judge, US Court of Appeals for the First Circuit 1980–94, Chief Judge 1990–94; mem. US Sentencing Comm. 1985–89; Judicial Conference of the US 1990–94; Assoc. Justice, US Supreme Court 1994–; Visiting Lecturer, Coll. of Law, Sydney, Australia 1975; Visiting Prof., Univ. of Rome 1993; Fellow, American Acad. of Arts and Sciences. *Publications:* The Federal Power Commission and the Regulation of Energy (with P. MacAvoy) 1974, Administrative Law and Regulatory Policy (with R. Stewart) 1979, Regulation and Its Reform 1982, Breaking the Vicious Circle: Towards Effective Risk Regulation 1993, Making our Democracy Work: A Judge's View 2010; numerous articles and book chapters. *Address:* United States Supreme Court, One First Street, NE, Washington, DC 20543, USA (office). *Telephone:* (202) 479-2977 (office). *Fax:* (202) 479-2963 (office). *Website:* www.supremecourtus.gov (office).

BREYTENBACH, Breyten; South African/French poet and writer; b. 16 Sept. 1939, Bonnievale; m. Yolande Ngo Thi Hoang Lien 1962; ed Univ. of Cape Town; Visiting Prof., Univ. of Cape Town 2000–02, also Univ. of Natal, Princeton Univ.; Dr hc (Univ. of Cape Town), (Univ. of Natal, Durban); Hertzog Prize 1984, 1999, Rapport Prize 1986, Alan Paton Award 1994, CNA Prize, Jan Campert Foundation Special Prize, Van der Hoogt Prize. *Publications:* poetry: The Iron Cow Must Sweat (A.P.B. prize 1965) 1964, The House of the Deaf 1967, Gangrene 1969, Lotus 1970, The Remains 1970, Scrit: Painting Blue a Sinking Ship 1972, In Other Words 1973, Foot Writing 1976, Sinking Ship Blues 1977, And Death White as Words. An Anthology 1978, In Africa Even the Flies Are H 1978, Flower Writing 1979, Eclipse 1983, YK 1983, Buffalo Bill 1984, Living Death 1985, Judas Eye 1989, As Like 1990, Nine Landscapes of our Times Bequeathed to a Beloved 1993, The Handful of Feathers 1995, The Remains. An Elegy 1997, Paper Flower 1998, Lady One 2000, Iron Cow Blues 2001, Lady One: Of Love and other Poems 2002, The Undanced Dance: Prison Poetry 1975–1983 2005, The Windcatcher 2007, Voice Over: A Nomadic Conversation with Mahmoud Darwish (Max Jacob Prize, Mahmoud Darwish Literature Prize 2010) 2009; prose: Catastrophes (A.P.B. Prize 1965) 1964, The Tree Behind the Moon 1974, The Anthill Bloats … 1980, A Season in Paradise 1980, Mouroir: Mirror Notes of a Novel 1983, Mirror Death 1984, End Papers 1985, The True Confessions of an Albino Terrorist 1985, Memory of Snow and of Dust 1987, All One Horse. Fiction and Images 1989, Sweet Heart 1991, Return to Paradise. An African Journal (Alan Paton Award) 1992, The True Confessions of an Albino Terrorist 1994, The Memory of Birds in Times of Revolution 1996, Dog Heart: A Travel Memoir 1998, Word Work 1999, A Veil of Footsteps 2008, All One Horse 2008, Mouroir: Mirror Notes of a Novel 2008, Intimate Stranger 2009, Notes From The Middle World: Essays 2009, Notes from the Middle World 2009.

BREZIGAR, Barbara; Slovenian lawyer and government official; b. 1 Dec. 1953, Ljubljana; m.; two c.; ed Univ. of Ljubljana; Dist State Prosecutor, Ljubljana Public Prosecutor's Office 1980, Vice-Pres. 1994, Head of Office 1995, apptd head of special team of prosecutors dealing with organized crime 1996–99; Supreme State Prosecutor 1998–2000, 2000–05; Minister of Justice in caretaker Govt of Andrej Bajuk 2000; presidential cand. 2002; Nat. mem. for Slovenia at Eurojust 2004–05; State Prosecutor Gen., Repub. of Slovenia 2005–11. *Address:* c/o Office of the State Prosecutor General, Trg OF 13, 1000 Ljubljana, Slovenia (office).

BREZIS, Haim; French academic; *Professor of Mathematics, Institut Universitaire de France;* b. 1 June 1944, Riom-ès-Montagnes; s. of Jacob Brezis and Rebecca Brezis; m. Michal Govrin 1982; two d.; ed Univ. of Paris; Prof. of Math., Pierre et Marie Curie Univ. 1974–, Inst. Universitaire de France 1997–; Visiting Prof. New York Univ., Univ. of Chicago, Princeton Univ., MIT, Hebrew Univ.; Visiting Distinguished Prof. Rutgers Univ., Technion (Haifa); mem. Acad. des Sciences, Academia Europaea; Foreign Hon. mem. NAS USA, American Acad. of Arts and Sciences; Hon. mem. Romanian Acad., Real Academia Madrid, Royal Acad. of Belgium; numerous hon. degrees; Prix. Ampère 1985. *Publications:* Analyse Fonctionnelle 1983, Ginzburg-Landau vortices 1994, Un mathématicien juif 1999. *Leisure interest:* Hebraic studies. *Address:* Analyse Numérique, Université Pierre et Marie Curie, 4 place Jussieu, 75252 Paris Cedex 05 (office); 18 rue de la Glacière, 75013 Paris Cedex 13, France (home). *Telephone:* 1-44-27-42-98 (office); 1-43-36-15-10 (home). *Fax:* 1-44-27-72-00 (office). *E-mail:* brezis@ccr.jussieu.fr (office).

BRIANÇON, Pierre, LLM; French journalist; b. 3 Aug. 1954, Tunis, Tunisia; s. of Claude Briançon and Geneviève Pochard; three c.; ed Université Paris II, Institut d'Etudes Politiques, Paris; journalist, Forum International 1979; Econs and Business Ed. Libération 1981–88, Moscow Corresp. 1988–91, USA Bureau Chief, Washington 1992–95, Ed.-in-Chief 1996–98; contrib. France Inter radio 1982–86; Asst Editorial Dir L'expansion 1998–2000; Chief Dow Jones Newswire Paris Bureau 2003–06; Paris corresp. Breaking-Views.com 2006–; Dir Startup Avenue (econ. information site) 2004–06; fmr CEO and Chair. B to B Avenue.com. *Publications include:* A Droite en sortant de la gauche? 1986, Héritiers du désastre 1992, Messier Story 2002, San Quentin Jazz Band 2008. *Address:* c/o Breaking Views Ltd, 80 rue Taitbout, 75009 Paris, France (office). *Telephone:* 1-53-20-99-27 (office). *Fax:* 1-53-20-99-27 (office). *E-mail:* pierre.briancon@ breakingviews.com (office). *Website:* www.breakingviews.com.

BRICEÑO, Hon. John, BBA; Belizean politician; b. 17 July 1960, Orange Walk Town; m. Rossana Briceño; three s.; ed Muffles High School, St John's Coll., Belize City, Univ. of Texas at Austin, USA; mem. Parl. for Orange Walk Cen. Div. (People's United Party) 1993–; Deputy Prime Minister 1998–2007, also Minister of Natural Resources and the Environment 1998–2007, of Commerce Trade and Industry 1999–2007, of Local Govt 2005–07; Deputy Leader People's United Party –2008, Leader 2008–. *Leisure interests:* reading, music, cinema. *Address:* People's United Party (PUP), 3 Queen Street, Belize City, Belize (office). *Telephone:* 223-2428 (office). *Fax:* 223-3476 (office). *Website:* www.pupbelize.bz (office).

BRICQ, Nicole; French politician; b. 10 June 1947, La Rochefoucauld (Charente); ed Univ. of Bordeaux IV; Regional Councillor for Île-de-France 1983–89; Deputy (Parti socialiste—PS) to Nat. Ass. for the Sixth Dist of Seine-et-Marne 1997–2002; mem. Senate of France, representing Seine-et-Marne département 2004–14, Vice-Pres. Finance Cttee 2008; Minister of Ecology, Sustainable Devt and Energy May–June 2012, of Foreign Trade 2012–14. *Address:* c/o Ministry of Foreign Trade, 92055 La Défense Cedex, France (office). *Telephone:* 1-40-81-21-22 (office).

BRIDGEMAN, John Stuart, CBE, TD, DL, BSc, CIMgt, FRGS, FRSA, FID; British business executive; b. 5 Oct. 1944; s. of the late James Alfred George Bridgeman and Edith Celia Bridgeman (née Watkins); m. Lindy Jane Fillmore 1967; three d.; ed Whitchurch School, Cardiff, Univ. Coll., Swansea, McGill Univ., Montreal; with Alcan Industries 1966–69, Aluminium Co. of Canada 1969–70, Alcan Australia 1970, Commercial Dir Alcan UK 1977–80, Vice-Pres. (Europe), Alcan Basic Raw Materials 1978–82, Man. Dir, Extrusion Div., British Alcan Aluminium PLC 1983–87, British Alcan Enterprises 1987–91, Dir of Corp. Planning, Alcan Aluminium Ltd, Montreal 1992–93, Man. Dir British Alcan Aluminium PLC 1993–95; Chair. Aluminium Extruders' Asscn 1987–88 (mem. Council 1982–91); mem. Monopolies and Mergers Comm. 1990–95; Dir-Gen. Office of Fair Trading 1995–2000; Dir Regulatory Impact Unit, Cardew & Co. Corp. Financial Advisers 2001–03; Chair. Direct Marketing Authority 2000–07 (currently Ind. Appeals Commr), Audit and Standards Cttee Warwicks. Co. Council 2000–, Howtocomplain.com 2000–, Warwickshire Police Authority 2001–08, Regulatory Cttee British Horseracing Authority (BHA) 2007–08 (fmrly Chair. Jockey Club Regulatory Bd, Regulatory Dir BHA 2009–12); ind. complaints adjudicator, Asscn for TV on Demand 2007–10; consultant with law firm Norton Rose 2000–02; Chair. Standards Cttee, Worcs. Co. Council; Visiting Prof. of Man., Keele Univ. 1992–2010, Imperial Coll. London 2001–04, Univ. of Surrey 2004–07; Chair. N Oxon. Business Group 1984–92, Enterprise Cherwell Ltd 1985–91, N Oxon Coll. 1989 (also Gov. 1985–98), Oxfordshire Econ. Partnership 2000–07; Pres. Oxford Gliding Club 1998–2006; Vice-Pres. Aluminium Fed. 1995 (mem. Bauxite Advisory Group 1977–81), UK-Canada Chamber of Commerce 1995–96 (Pres. 1997–98); Deputy Chair. Heart of England Trading and Enterprise Council 1989–2002, Chair. 2000–02; mem. Bd British Waterways 2006– (Chair. Fair Trading Cttee 2007–, Wales Advisory Bd 2008–, Vice-Chair. British Waterways 2009–); Dir, Oxford Orchestra da Camera 1996–2000, Oxford Psychologists Press 2001–06; commissioned, TA and Reserve Forces 1978, Queen's Own Yeomanry 1981–84, Maj. REME (V) 1985–94, Staff Coll. 1986, mem. Territorial Auxiliary and Volunteer Reserve Asscn, Oxon. and E Wessex 1985–2000; Hon. Col 5 (Queen's Own Oxfordshire Hussars) Squadron 31 (City of London) Signal Regt 1996–, mem. South Eastern Reserve Forces and Cadets Assoc (SERFCA) 2001–09, Defence Science Advisory Council 1991–94; mem. British Airways NE Consumer Council 1978–81, Defence Science Advisory Council 1991–94, Nat. Employer Liaison Cttee for Reserve Forces 1992–2002 (Chair. 1997–2002), Council of UK-Canada Colloquia 1993–98, 2003– (Treas. 2005), Cttee Canada Club 1994–2010; Fellow, Univ. of Wales, Swansea 1997; Chair. of Trustees, Banbury Sunshine Centre 2003–; Trustee, Foundation for Canadian Studies 1995–2010 (Vice-Chair. 2005–10), Oxon. Community Foundation 1996–2002, Oxfordshire Yeomanry Trust 1997–, Canal and River Trust 2011–; DL (Oxon.) 1989; High Sheriff, Oxon. 1995–96; Hon. Fellow, Univ. of Wales, Swansea 1997, Inst. of Credit Man. 1998; Hon. mem. Inst. of Consumer Affairs 1999; mem. Court of Assts, Worshipful Co. of Turners 2004– (Master Steward 2011); Dr hc (Sheffield Hallam) 1996; US Aluminum Asscn Prize 1988. *Leisure interests:* horses, Oxfordshire affairs, Territorial Army, gardening, shooting, skiing. *Address:* c/o The Reform Club, 104 Pall Mall, London, SW1Y 5EW, England; c/o Glamorgan County Cricket Club, SWALEC Stadium, Cardiff, CF11 9XR, Wales.

BRIDGEMAN, Rt Hon. The Viscountess Victoria Harriet Lucy, (Harriet Bridgeman), CBE, MA, FRSA; British fine arts specialist, picture library executive, art historian and editor; *Executive Chairman, The Bridgeman Art Library;* b. (Victoria Harriet Lucy Turton), 30 March 1942, Co. Durham; d. of Ralph Meredyth Turton and Mary Blanche Turton (née Chetwynd Stapylton); m. Viscount Bridgeman 1966; four s. (one deceased); ed St Mary's School, Wantage, Trinity Coll., Dublin; worked as editorial trainee with The Lady magazine; Exec. Ed. The Masters 1965–69; Ed. Discovering Antiques 1970–72; est. own co. producing books and articles on fine and decorative arts; Founder and Exec. Chair. The Bridgeman Art Library 1971–; Cttee mem. British Asscn of Picture Libraries and Agencies; Founder Artists Collecting Soc. 2006; European Woman of the Year (Arts Section) Award 1997, Int. Business Woman of the Year 2005. *Publications include:* Encyclopaedia of Victoriana, Needlework: An Illustrated History, The British Eccentric 1975, Society Scandals 1977, Beside the Seaside 1977, Guide to the Gardens of Europe 1980, The Last Word 1982 (all jtly with Elizabeth Drury), eight titles in Connoisseur's Library series. *Leisure interests:* reading, family, travel. *Address:* The Bridgeman Art Library, 17–19 Garway Road, London, W2 4PH (office); 19 Chepstow Road, London, W2 5BP (home); Watley House, Sparsholt, Winchester, Hants., SO21 2LU, England (home). *Telephone:* (20) 7727-4065 (London) (office); (20) 7727-5400 (London) (home); (1962) 776297 (Winchester) (home). *Fax:* (20) 7792-8509 (London) (office); (20) 7792-9178 (London) (home); (1962) 776297 (Winchester) (home). *E-mail:* harriet .bridgeman@bridgemanart.co.uk (office). *Website:* www.bridgemanart.com (office).

BRIDGES, Jeff; American actor; b. 4 Dec. 1949, Los Angeles; s. of the late Lloyd Bridges and of Dorothy Bridges; m. Susan Bridges; three d.; acting debut aged eight; Career Achievement Award, Nat. Bd of Review 2004. *Films include:* Halls of Anger 1970, The Last Picture Show 1971, Fat City 1971, Bad Company 1972, The Last American Hero 1973, The Iceman Cometh 1973, Thunderbolt and Lightfoot 1974, Hearts of the West 1975, Rancho Deluxe 1975, King Kong 1976, Stay Hungry 1976, Somebody Killed her Husband 1978, Winter Kills 1979, The American Success Company 1980, Heaven's Gate 1980, Cutter's Way 1981, Tron 1982, Kiss Me Goodbye 1982, The Last Unicorn 1982, Against All Odds 1984, Jagged Edge 1985, 8 Million Ways to Die 1986, The Morning After 1986, Nadine 1987, See You in the Morning 1990, Texasville 1990, The Fabulous Baker Boys 1990, The Fisher King 1991, American Heart, The Vanishing, Blown Away 1994, Fearless 1994, Wild Bill, White Squall 1995, The Mirror Has Two Faces 1996, The Big Lebowski 1997, Arlington Road 1998, Simpatico 1999, The Muse 1999, The Contender 2000, K-Pax 2002, Lost in La Mancha (voice) 2002, Seabiscuit 2003, The Door in the Floor 2004, The Moguls 2005, Tideland 2005, Stick It 2006, Surf's Up (voice) 2007, How to Lose Friends & Alienate People 2008, Iron Man 2008, The Open Road 2009, A Dog Year 2009, The Men Who Stare at Goats 2009, Crazy Heart (Golden Globe for best performance by an actor in a motion picture—drama 2010, Academy Award for Best Actor in a Leading Role 2010) 2009, True Grit 2010, TRON: Legacy 2010, Pablo 2012. *Television:* Raising the Hammoth (voice) 2000, National Geographic: Lewis and Clark – Great Journey West 2002. *Address:* c/o Rick Nicita, Creative Artists Agency, 2000 Avenue of the Stars, Los Angeles, CA 90067, USA.

BRIERLEY, Sir Ronald (Ron) Alfred, Kt; New Zealand business executive and investor; b. 2 Aug. 1937, Wellington; s. of J. R. Brierley; ed Wellington Coll.; Chair. Brierley Investments Ltd 1961–89 (Founder 1961, Founder Pres. 1990–); Deputy Chair. Bank of NZ 1987–89; Chair. Industrial Equity Pacific Ltd 1966–90, Guinness Peat Group PLC 1990–2010 (Dir (non-exec.) 2010–), Tozer Kemsley & Millbourn Holdings PLC 1986, The Citizens & Graziers Life Assurance Co. Ltd 1990–91; Dir Ariadne Australia Ltd 1989–91, The Australian Gas Light Co. 1987–, Australian Oil & Gas Corpn Ltd, Mid-East Minerals Ltd 1992–, Metals Exploration Ltd 1992–, Tyndall Australia Ltd 1992–, Advance Bank Australia 1990–; mem. NZ Cricket Council, NZ Cricket Foundation; Dir Sydney Cricket & Sports Ground Trust. *Leisure interests:* cricket, ballet, stamp collecting, chess. *Address:* Guinness Peat Group plc, 78 Pall Mall, London, SW1Y 5ES, England. *Telephone:* (20) 7663-3992.

BRIGGS, Baron (Life Peer), cr. 1976, of Lewes in the County of Sussex; **Asa Briggs,** BSc, MA, FBA; British historian; b. 7 May 1921, Keighley, Yorks., England; s. of William Walker Briggs and Jane Briggs; m. Susan Anne Banwell 1955; two s. two d.; ed Keighley Grammar School and Sidney Sussex Coll., Cambridge; Cryptographer, Bletchley Park 1942–45; Fellow, Worcester Coll., Oxford 1945–55, Reader in Recent Social and Econ. History, Univ. of Oxford 1950–55; Prof. of Modern History, Univ. of Leeds 1955–61; Prof. of History, Univ. of Sussex 1961–76, Dean of Social Studies 1961–65, Pro-Vice-Chancellor 1961–67, Vice-Chancellor 1967–76; Provost Worcester Coll., Oxford 1976–91; Chancellor, Open Univ. 1979–94; Pres. Workers Educational Asscn 1958–67; Chair. Appts Comm. Press Council 1972–88; mem. Univ. Grants Cttee 1959–67; Trustee, Int. Broadcast Inst. 1968–86, Hon. Trustee 1990–; Gov. British Film Inst. 1970–76; Chair. European Inst. of Educ. 1974–84; mem. Council of UN Univ. 1974–80; Chair. Cttee on Nursing 1970–72, Heritage Educ. Group 1976–86, Commonwealth of Learning 1988–93; Pres. Social History Soc. 1976–, Ephemera Soc. 1984–, Victorian Soc. 1983–; Vice-Pres. Historical Asscn 1986–; Vice-Chair. of Council, UN Univ. 1974–80; Hon. mem. American Acad. of Arts and Sciences 1970–; Hon. LLD, Hon. DLitt, Hon. DSc; Marconi Medal for Services to Study of Broadcasting 1975, Medal of French Acad. for Architecture 1982, Wolfson History Prize 2001. *Publications:* Patterns of Peacemaking (with D. Thomson and E. Meyer) 1945, History of Birmingham, 1865–1938 1952, Victorian People 1954, Friends of the People 1956, The Age of Improvement 1959 (revised edn 2000), Ed. Chartist Studies 1959, History of Broadcasting in the United Kingdom, Vol. I 1961, Vol. II 1965, Vol. III 1970, Vol. IV 1979, Vol. V 1995, Victorian Cities 1963, The Nineteenth Century (ed.) 1970, Cap and Bell (with Susan Briggs) 1972, Essays in the History of Publishing (ed.) 1974, Essays in Labour History 1918–1939 1977, Governing the BBC 1979, From Coalbrookdale to the Crystal Palace 1980, The Power of Steam 1982, Marx in London 1982, A Social History of England 1983, The BBC—The First Fifty Years 1985, The Collected Essays of Asa Briggs, (Vol. 1, 2, 3), The Franchise Affair (with Joanna Spicer) 1986, Victorian Things 1988, The Longman Encyclopedia (ed.) 1989, Haut-Brion: An Illustrious Lineage 1994, The Channel Islands: Occupation and Liberation 1940–45 1995, Fins de Siècle (co-ed.) 1996; co-author Modern Europe 1789–1989 1996, The History of Bethlem 1997, Chartism 1998, Go to It! War: Working for Victory on the Home Front, 1939–45 2000, Michael Young: Social Entrepreneur 2000, A Social History of the Media (with Peter Burke) 2002, A History of Longmans and Their Books, 1724–1990: Longevity in Publishing 2008, Secret Days: Code-Breaking in Bletchley Park 2011, Special Relationships: People and Places 2012. *Leisure interest:* memories of travel and great lunches and dinners. *Address:* The Caprons, Keere Street, Lewes, Sussex, BN7 1TY, England (home). *Telephone:* (1273) 474704 (home). *Fax:* (1273) 474704 (home). *E-mail:* pat.spencer@ukgateway.net (office).

BRIGGS, Raymond Redvers, NDD, DFA, FSCD, FRSL; British writer, illustrator and cartoonist; b. 18 Jan. 1934, Wimbledon, London, England; s. of Ernest R. Briggs and Ethel Bowyer; m. Jean Taprell Clark 1963 (died 1973); ed Rutlish School, Merton, Wimbledon School of Art and Slade School of Fine Art, London; freelance illustrator 1957–; part-time lecturer in illustration, Brighton School of Art 1961–87; children's author 1961–; mem. Soc. of Authors; Hon. Fellow, Univ. of the Arts London; awards include Kate Greenaway Medal 1966, 1973, BAFTA Award, Francis Williams Illustration Award, Victoria & Albert Museum 1982, Broadcasting Press Guild Radio Award 1983, Children's Author of the Year 1992, Kurt Maschler Award 1992, Illustrated Book of the Year Award 1998, Smarties Silver Award 2001, Lifetime Achievement Award, Cartoon Art Museum. *Radio play:* When the Wind Blows, The Man. *Publications:* The Strange House 1961, Midnight Adventure 1961, Ring-a-Ring o' Roses 1962, Sledges to the Rescue 1963, The White Land 1963, Fee Fi Fo Fum 1964, The Mother Goose Treasury 1966, Jim and the Beanstalk 1970, The Fairy Tale Treasury 1972, Father Christmas 1973 (also film version), Father Christmas Goes on Holiday 1975, Fungus the Bogeyman 1977, The Snowman 1978 (also film version), Gentleman Jim 1980 (also stage version), When the Wind Blows 1982 (stage and radio versions 1983, animated film version 1987), The Tinpot Foreign General and the Old Iron Woman 1984, The Snowman Pop-Up 1986, Unlucky Wally 1987, Unlucky Wally Twenty Years On 1989, The Man 1992, The Bear 1994 (also film version), Ethel and Ernest 1998, UG 2001, Blooming Books (with Nicolette Jones) 2003, The Puddleman 2004. *Leisure interests:* second-hand books, walking, gardening, fishing. *Address:* Weston, Underhill Lane, Westmeston, nr Hassocks, Sussex, BN6 8XG, England.

BRIGGS, Winslow Russell, MA, PhD; American biologist and academic (retd); *Professor Emeritus, Carnegie Institution of Washington;* b. 29 April 1928, St Paul, Minn.; s. of John Briggs and Marjorie Briggs (née Winslow); m. Ann Morrill 1955; three d.; ed Harvard Univ.; Instructor in Biological Sciences, Stanford Univ. 1955–57, Asst Prof. 1957–62, Assoc. Prof. 1962–66, Prof. 1966–67, 1973–93, Dir Dept of Plant Biology, Carnegie Inst. of Washington, Stanford 1973–93, now Prof. Emer.; Prof. of Biology, Harvard Univ. 1967–73; mem. NAS; Dr hc (Univ. of Freiburg, Germany) 2002; Guggenheim Fellow 1973–74, American Soc. of Plant Physiologists Stephen Hales Award 1994, ACS/US Dept of Agric. Sterling Hendricks Award 1995, Philip C. Hamm Award (Minn.) 1999, Anton Lang Memorial Lecturer, Michigan State Univ. 1999, Asscn Int. de Photobiologie Finsen Medal 2000, Int. Prize for Biology, Japan Soc. for the Promotion of Science 2009.

Publications: Life on Earth (with others) 1973; more than 250 articles in professional journals and books. *Leisure interests:* hiking, Chinese cooking, park volunteer. *Address:* Department of Plant Biology, Carnegie Institution for Washington, 260 Panama Street, Stanford, CA 94305 (office); 480 Hale Street, Palo Alto, CA 94301-2207, USA (home). *Telephone:* (650) 325-1521 (ext. 207) (office); (650) 739-4207 (office); (650) 324-1455 (home). *Fax:* (650) 325-6857 (office). *E-mail:* briggs@stanford.edu (office). *Website:* dpb.carnegiescience.edu/labs/briggs -lab (office).

BRIGHT, Roger, CB, MA (Cantab.); British civil servant; *Chief Executive and Second Commissioner, The Crown Estate;* ed Univ. of Cambridge; joined Dept of the Environment 1973, held series of sr positions, including Prin. Pvt. Sec. and Press Sec. to Sec. of State –1991; apptd Deputy CEO Housing Corpn 1991; held sr posts at Personal Investment Authority, including Chief Exec., and subsequently Head of Investment Business (Personal Investment Authority firms) Dept, Financial Services Authority; Dir of Finance and Admin, The Crown Estate 1999–2001, mem. Bd of Dirs 2000–, Chief Exec. 2001–; mem. Governing Council of City Univ.; Dir (non-exec.) London First, Heritage of London Trust. *Address:* The Crown Estate, 16 New Burlington Place, London, W1S 2HX, England (office). *Telephone:* (20) 7851-5000 (office). *E-mail:* enquiries@thecrownestate.co.uk (office). *Website:* www.thecrownestate.co.uk (office).

BRIGHTMAN, Sarah; British actress and singer; d. of Grenville Brightman and Pauline Brightman (née Hall); m. Andrew Lloyd Webber 1984 (divorced 1990); fmr mem. Pan's People and Hot Gossip groups; concerts world-wide. *Performances include:* Cats, Requiem, The Phantom of the Opera, Aspects of Love (music all by Andrew Lloyd Webber), I and Albert, The Nightingale, The Merry Widow, Trelawney of the Wells, Relative Values, Dangerous Obsession, The Innocents. *Recordings:* albums include: As I Came of Age 1990, Sarah Sings the Music of Andrew Lloyd Webber 1992, Dive 1993, Surrender 1995, Fly 1995, Timeless 1997, Eden 1999, La Luna 2000, Classics 2001, Harem 2003, Diva 2006, Symphony 2008, A Winter Symphony 2008. *Address:* c/o Claudia Dorrell, Dorrell Management, 2nd Floor, Lyme Wharf, 191 Royal College Street, London, NW1 0SG, England. *Telephone:* (870) 420-5088. *Fax:* (870) 420-5188. *E-mail:* claudia@ dorrellmanagement.com. *Website:* www.sarah-brightman.com (home).

BRIGHTY, (Anthony) David, CMG, CVO; British diplomatist (retd); *Chairman, Anglo Spanish Cultural Foundation;* b. 7 Feb. 1939; m. 1st Diana Porteous 1963 (divorced 1979); two s. two d.; m. 2nd Jane Docherty 1982 (divorced 1996); m. 3rd Susan Olivier 1997; ed Clare Coll., Cambridge; joined FCO 1961, Third Sec., Embassy in Brussels 1962–64, Third Sec., Embassy in Havana 1964–66, Second Sec. 1966–67, with FCO 1967–69; Asst Man. S.G. Warburg & Co. 1969–71; at FCO 1971–73, Head of Chancery, Saigon 1973–75, First Sec., UK Mission, New York 1975–78; Royal Coll. of Defence Studies 1979; at FCO 1979–83, Counsellor, Embassy in Lisbon 1983–86, Dir of Cabinet of Sec.-Gen. to NATO, FCO 1986–87, Amb. to Cuba 1989–91, to Czech Repub. and Slovakia (non-resident) 1991–94, to Spain and Andorra (non-resident) 1994–98; Dir (non-exec.) EFG Pvt. Bank 1999–2006; Chair. Co-ordinating Cttee on Remuneration (NATO, OECD, etc.) 1999–2006; Dir (non-exec.) Henderson European Microcap Trust 2000–04; Chair. Anglo-Spanish Soc. 2001–07, Friends of the British Library 2004–07, Anglo-Spanish Cultural Foundation 2005–; Robin Humphries Fellow, Inst. of Latin American Studies, Univ. of London 2003. *Address:* 15 Provost Road, London, NW3 4ST, England.

BRIGMANIS, Augusts; Latvian agronomist and politician; *Chairman, Centre Party Latvian Farmers' Union;* b. 19 July 1952, Jelgava; m. Elita Brigmane; three c.; ed Latvian Acad. of Agric.; worked on his farm in Pūre following graduation; First Sec., Latvian Communist Party, Saldus Dist Cttee 1985–87; adviser to Minister for Agric., Aigars Kalvitis 1999; elected Pres. Latvian Farmers' Union 2000; unsuccessful cand. for Rīga City Council 2001; Chair. Centre Party Latvian Farmers' Union (forms part of the Greens' and Farmers' Union—ZZS) 2000–; mem. Saeima (Parl.) for Zemgale constituency 2010–, Chair. ZZS Parl. Group, Sec., Human Rights and Public Affairs Cttee (mem. Children and Youth Affairs Sub-cttee), Chair. Govt Review Cttee. *Address:* Centre Party Latvian Farmers' Union (Centriskā partija Latvijas Zemnieku savienība), Republikas lauk. 2, Rīga 1010, Latvia (office). *Telephone:* 6732-3628 (office). *Fax:* 6702-7467 (office). *E-mail:* augusts.brigmanis@lzs.lv (office); augusts.brigmanis@saeima.lv (office); lzs@ latnet.lv (office). *Website:* www.lzs.lv (office).

BRILLINGER, David Ross, BA, MA, PhD, FRSC; Canadian professor of statistics; *Professor of Statistics, University of California, Berkeley;* b. 27 Oct. 1937, Toronto, Ont.; s. of Austin C. Brillinger and Winnifred E. Simpson; m. Lorie Silber 1961; two s.; ed Univ. of Toronto and Princeton Univ.; Woodrow Wilson Nat. Fellow 1959–60; Bell Telephone Laboratories Grad. Fellowship 1960–61; Social Science Research Council Fellow, LSE, UK 1961–62, Lecturer 1964–66, Reader 1966–69; Lecturer in Math., Princeton Univ., concurrently mem. Tech. Staff, Bell Telephone Labs 1962–64; Visiting Assoc. Prof., Univ. of California, Berkeley 1967–68, Prof. of Statistics 1969–, Miller Research Prof. 1973, Chair. Statistics Dept 1979–81; Instructional Lecturer, 12th Biennial Seminar, Canadian Math. Congress 1969; Visiting Prof. of Math., Univ. of Auckland, NZ 1976; Short Term Visitor, CSIRO, Australia 1977; Visiting Maclaurin Fellow, NZ Inst. of Math. and Its Applications 2010; Ed. International Statistical Review 1987–91; Assoc., Soc. of Actuaries; mem. Int. Statistical Inst. 1974, Royal Statistical Soc.; Foreign mem. Norwegian Acad. of Science and Letters 2004, Brazilian Acad. of Science 2006; Fellow, Inst. of Math. Statistics 1969, American Statistical Assocn 1972, AAAS 1983, American Acad. of Arts and Sciences 1993; Founding Fellow, Fields Inst. for Research in Math. Sciences 2002; Hon. mem. Probability and Statistics Section, Cuban Soc. of Math. and Computation 2001, Statistical Soc. of Canada 2010; Hon. DMath (Waterloo) 2003; Hon. DSc (Western Ontario) 1999, (McMaster) 2008; S.H. Janes Medal, Victoria Univ., Toronto 1959, Canada Council Scholarship 1959, Guggenheim Fellow 1975–76, 1982–83, Wald Lecturer 1983, R.A. Fisher Award 1991, Gold Medal, Statistical Soc. of Canada 1992, Lecturer PIMS Inaugural Meeting 1997, Parzen Prize for Statistical Innovation 2001, Huggins Lecturer, Acadia Univ., NS 2004, Neyman Lecturer, IMS 2005, PIMS 10th Anniversary Distinguished Lecturer 2007. *Publications:* Time Series: Data Analysis and Theory 1975, Directions in Time Series 1980. *Address:* Department of Statistics, University of California, Berkeley, CA 94720-3860, USA (office). *Telephone:* (510)

642-0611 (office). *Fax:* (510) 642-7892 (office). *E-mail:* brill@stat.berkeley.edu (office). *Website:* www.stat.berkeley.edu/~brill (office).

BRIM, Orville Gilbert, Jr., PhD; American fmr foundation administrator and author; b. 7 April 1923, Elmira, New York; s. of Orville Gilbert and Helen Whittier Brim; m. Kathleen J. Vigneron 1944; two s. two d.; ed Yale Univ.; Instructor in Sociology, Univ. of Wisconsin 1952–53, Asst Prof. of Sociology 1953–55; Sociologist, Russell Sage Foundation, New York 1955–60, Asst Sec. 1960–64, Pres. 1964–72; author and consultant 1972–74; Pres. Foundation for Child Devt 1974–85; Chair. Automation Eng Lab. 1959–67, Special Comm. on the Social Sciences, NSF 1968–69; mem. Drug Research Bd, NAS 1964–65; Vice-Chair. Bd of Trustees, American Insts for Research 1971–88, Chair. 1988–90; MacArthur Foundation Research Program on Successful Aging 1986–89; Dir McArthur Foundation Research Network on Successful Midlife Devt 1989–2002; Pres. Life Trends Inc. 1991–2002; Interim Pres. Social Science Research Council 1998–99; Kurt Lewin Memorial Award 1979, Soc. Research in Child Devt Award for Distinguished Scientific Contributions to Child Devt Research 1985. *Publications:* Sociology and the Field of Education 1958, Education for Child Rearing 1959, Personality and Decision Processes 1962, Intelligence: Perspectives 1965, Socialization after Childhood: Two Essays 1966, American Beliefs and Attitudes Toward Intelligence 1969, The Dying Patient 1970; ed.: Lifespan Development and Behavior, Vols II–VI 1979–84, Constancy and Change in Human Development 1980, Ambition: How We Manage Success and Failure throughout Our Lives 1992, How Healthy Are We?: A National Study of Well-being at Midlife 2004, Look At Me! The Fame Motive from Childhood to Death 2009. *Leisure interests:* sports and world ocean beaches. *Address:* 503 River Drive, Vero Beach, FL 32963, USA (home). *Telephone:* (772) 231-3647 (home). *Fax:* (772) 234-8559 (home).

BRIN, Sergey Mihailovich, BS, MS; American (b. Russian) computer scientist, computer software executive and entrepreneur; *Co-founder and Director of Special Projects, Google Inc.;* b. 21 Aug. 1973, Moscow; s. of Michael Brin and Eugenia Brin; m. Anne Wojcicki 2007; one s.; ed Eleanor Roosevelt High School, Univ. of Maryland, College Park, Stanford Univ.; emigrated to USA aged six; interned at Wolfram Research, makers of Mathematica 1993; co-f. Google Inc. with Larry Page (q.v.), Co-Pres. 1998–2001, Pres. of Tech. 2001–11, Dir of Special Projects 2012–; mem. AmBAR (networking org. for Russian-speaking business professionals in USA); mem. Nat. Acad. of Eng 2009; Fellow, NSF; Hon. MBA (IE Business School) 2003; Marconi Award (with Larry Page) 2004, named (with Larry Page) "Persons of the Week" by ABC World News Tonight 2004, Economist Innovation Award (with Larry Page) 2005, named one of the World's Most Influential People by Time Magazine 2005, ranked No. 1 (with Larry Page) by PC World Magazine amongst the 50 Most Important People on the Web 2007, named by Fortune Magazine as one of the 25 Most Powerful People in Business 2007, ranked (with Larry Page) by Forbes magazine amongst The World's Most Powerful People (jt fifth) 2009, (jt 22nd) 2010, (jt 30th) 2011, (jt 20th) 2012, (jt 17th) 2013. *Film:* Broken Arrows (exec. producer) 2009. *Publications:* more than a dozen academic papers including Extracting Patterns and Relations from the World Wide Web, Dynamic Data Mining: A New Architecture for Data with High Dimensionality (with Larry Page), Scalable Techniques for Mining Casual Structures, Dynamic Itemset Counting and Implication Rules for Market Basket Data, Beyond Market Baskets: Generalizing Association Rules to Correlations. *Address:* Google Inc., 1600 Amphitheatre Parkway, Mountain View, CA 94043, USA (office). *Telephone:* (650) 253-0000 (office). *Fax:* (650) 253-0001 (office). *E-mail:* sergey.m.b@ mysergeybrin.com. *Website:* www.google.com (office).

BRINDLE, Ian, FCA, BA; British business executive; *Chairman, Financial Reporting Faculty Group, Institute of Chartered Accountants in England and Wales;* b. 17 Aug. 1943; s. of John Brindle and Mabel Brindle (née Walsh); m. Frances Elisabeth Moseby 1967; two s. one d.; ed Blundells School, Manchester Univ.; articled Price Waterhouse London 1965, Toronto 1975, partner 1976–2001, mem. Supervisory Cttee 1988–98, Dir Auditing and Business Advisory Services 1990–91, Sr Partner 1991–98; Chair. PricewaterhouseCoopers UK (following merger with Coopers and Lybrand) 1998–2001, Sr Partner UK 1991–98; mem. Auditing Practices Cttee Consultancy Cttee of Accounting Bodies 1986–90, Chair. 1990; mem. Accounting Standards Bd 1993–2001; mem. Council Inst. of Chartered Accountants in England and Wales 1994–97 (Chair. Financial Reporting Faculty Group 2008–), mem. Financial Reporting Council 1995–; Deputy Chair. Financial Reporting Review Panel 2001–08. *Leisure interests:* tennis, golf, classical music. *Address:* c/o Institute of Chartered Accountants in England and Wales, Metropolitan House, 321 Avebury Boulevard, Milton Keynes, MK9 2FZ (office); Milestones, Packhorse Road, Bessels Green, Sevenoaks, Kent, TN13 2QP, England (home). *Telephone:* (1908) 248250 (office). *E-mail:* contactus@icaew.com (office). *Website:* www.icaew.com/en (office).

BRINDLEY, Giles Skey, MA, MD, FRCP, FRS; British physiologist and academic; *Professor Emeritus, University of London Institute of Psychiatry;* b. (Giles Skey), 30 April 1926, Woking, Surrey, England; s. of Arthur James Benet Skey and Dr Margaret Beatrice Marion Skey (née Dewhurst), later Brindley; m. 1st Lucy Dunk Bennell 1959 (divorced); m. 2nd Dr Hilary Richards 1964; one s. one d.; ed Leyton Co. High School, Downing Coll., Cambridge, London Hosp. Medical School; clinical and research posts 1950–54; Russian Language Abstractor, British Abstracts of Medical Sciences 1953–56; Demonstrator, then Lecturer and Reader in Physiology, Univ. of Cambridge 1954–68; Prof. of Physiology, Univ. of London Inst. of Psychiatry 1968–91, Prof. Emer. 1991–; Hon. Dir MRC Neurological Prostheses Unit 1968–92; Partner, Brindley Surgical Implants 1991–2001; Hon. Consultant Physician, Maudsley Hosp. 1971–92; Fellow, King's Coll., Cambridge 1959–62, Trinity Coll., Cambridge 1963–68; Chair. Editorial Bd Journal of Physiology 1964–66; Visiting Prof., Univ. of Calif., Berkeley 1968; Hon. FRCS 1988; Hon. FRCSE 2000; Liebrecht-Franceschetti Prize, German Ophthalmological Soc. 1971, Feldberg Prize, Feldberg Foundation 1974, St Peter's Medal, British Assocn of Urological Surgeons 1987. *Compositions:* Tyrolean Suite for wind quintet 1999, The Waterman's Daughter for soprano and woodwind quartet 2001, The Four Temperaments, variations on a theme from Schoenberg's wind quintet 2004, The Standard-bearer, the Wave-reader and the Milker of Goats for woodwind quartet and undilector 2004, Lantern Festival for mezzo-soprano and piano 2005, Lost is My Wallet for baritone and guitar 2006, The Sun on the Sea for soprano and piano 2007, Midnight Dance for fute choir 2008, Suite for Small Orchestra 2010.

Publications: Physiology of the Retina and Visual Pathway 1960, numerous scientific papers. *Leisure interests:* designing and playing musical instruments, composing chamber music. *Address:* 102 Ferndene Road, London, SE24 0AA, England. *Telephone:* (20) 7274-2598. *E-mail:* gsbrindley@btinternet.com.

BRINDLEY, Dame Lynne Janie, DBE, MA, FLA, FRSA, CCMI; British librarian; *Master, Pembroke College Oxford;* b. 2 July 1950, London; d. of Ivan Blowers and Janie Blowers (née Williams); adopted d. of Ronald Williams and Elaine Williams (née Chapman); m. Timothy Stuart Brindley 1972; ed Truro High School, Univ. of Reading, Univ. Coll., London; Head of Marketing and of Chief Exec.'s Office, British Library 1979–85, Chief Exec. British Library 2000–12; Dir of Library and Information Services, also Pro-Vice Chancellor, Univ. of Aston 1985–90; Prin. Consultant, KPMG 1990–92; Librarian and Dir of Information Services, LSE 1992–97; Librarian and Pro-Vice Chancellor, Univ. of Leeds 1997–2000, Visiting Prof. of Knowledge Man. 2000–10; Visiting Prof. of Information Man., Leeds Metropolitan Univ. 2000–03; Master, Pembroke Coll. Oxford 2013–; mem. Int. Cttee on Social Science Information, UNESCO 1992–97, Lord Chancellor's Advisory Cttee on Public Records 1992–98, Stanford Univ. Advisory Council for Libraries and Information Resources 1999–, Resource Bd 2002–05, Eng and Physical Sciences Research Council User Panel 2002–04, Ithaka Bd; non-exec. mem. Arts & Humanities Research Council 2008–, Ofcom (telecoms and media regulator) 2011–, Wolfson Trust Panel 2012–; Trustee, Thackray Medical Museum, Leeds 1999–2001; Freeman, City of London 1989, Liveryman, Goldsmiths' Co. 1993, Court of Assistants Goldsmiths' Co. 2006; Hon. Fellow, Univ. Coll., London 2002, Univ. of Wales 2007; Hon. DLitt (Nottingham Trent) 2001, (Oxford) 2002, (Leicester) 2002, (Sheffield) 2004, (Reading) 2004, (Leeds) 2006, (Aston) 2008; Hon. DPhil (London Guildhall) 2002; Hon. DSc (City) 2005; 12 further hon. degrees, most recently from Trinity Coll., Dublin and Univ. of London. *Publications include:* numerous articles on the digital society, copyright and information man. *Leisure interests:* classical music, theatre, modern art, hill walking. *Address:* Pembroke College, Pembroke Square, St Aldates, Oxford OX11DW, England (office). *E-mail:* lynnebrindley@me.com. *Website:* www.pmb.ox.ac.uk (office).

BRINES, Francisco; Spanish poet; b. 1932, Oliva, Valencia; ed Univ. de Deusto, Univ. of Valencia, Univ. of Salamanca; fmr Reader of Spanish Literature, Univ. of Cambridge, UK; fmr Prof. of Spanish Literature, Univ. of Oxford, UK; mem. Royal Spanish Acad. 2001– (replaced playwright Antonio Buero upon his death); Valencian Literature Award 1967, Nat. Award for Spanish Literature 1999, Creativity Award 'Ricardo Marín' 2004, IV Poetry Prize Federico García Lorca 2007, Queen Sofía Award for Poetry 2010. *Publications:* Las brasas (Premio Adonais 1959) 1960, El santo inocente 1965, Palabras a la oscuridad (Premio de la Crítica 1967) 1966, Aún no 1971, Ensayo de una despedida 1960–71 1974, Insistencias en Luzbel 1977, Poesía. 1960–81 1984, Poemas excluidos 1985, El otoño de las rosas (Premio Nacional de Literatura 1987) 1986, La rosa de las noches 1986, Poemas a DK 1986, Espejo Ciego 1993, La última costa (Fastenrath Prize 1998) 1995, Breve antología personal 1997, Selección de poemas 1997, Poesía completa (1960–97) 1997, Antología poética 1998, Ensayo de una despedida 1998, La Iluminada Rosa Negra 2003, Amada vida mía 2004. *Address:* Royal Spanish Acad., 4 Felipe IV, 28014 Madrid, Spain (office). *Telephone:* (91) 4201478 (office). *Fax:* (91) 4200079 (office). *E-mail:* prorae@rae.es (office). *Website:* www.rae.es (office).

BRINK, André Philippus, MA; South African writer and academic; *Honorary Professor, Department of English Language and Literature, University of Cape Town;* b. 29 May 1935, Vrede; s. of Daniel Brink and Aletta Brink (née Wolmarans); three s. one d.; ed Lydenburg High School, Potchefstroom Univ., Sorbonne, Paris; began writing at an early age; first novel (Afrikaans) published 1958; on return from Paris became mem. and spokesman of young Afrikaans writers' group Sestigers; returned to Paris 1968; went back to South Africa to resist apartheid through writing; novel Kennis van die Aand banned 1973 (first Afrikaans novel to be banned); began to write in English as well; Dir several plays, but abandoned theatre owing to censorship; resumed playwriting 1996; Founder-mem. Afrikaans Writers' Guild; Prof. of Afrikaans and Dutch Literature, Rhodes Univ. (previously lecturer) 1980–89; Prof. of English, Univ. of Cape Town 1991–2000, now Hon. Prof.; Chevalier Légion d'honneur 1983, Commdr Ordre des Arts et des Lettres 1992; Hon. DLitt (Witwatersrand) 1985, (Univ. of Free State) 1997, (Montpellier) 1998, (Rhodes) 2001, (Pretoria) 2003; Reina Prinsen Geerlings Prize 1964, CNA Award for Literature, South Africa 1965, 1978 and 1982, Martin Luther King Memorial Prize 1979, Prix Médicis Etranger, France 1979, Biannual Freedom of Speech Prize by Monismanien Foundation, Univ. of Uppsala 1991, Premio Mondello (Italy) 1997, Commonwealth Prize for Literature (Africa) 2003, Sunday Times Fiction Award 2004. *Publications include:* File on a Diplomat 1966, Looking on Darkness (novel) 1974, An Instant in the Wind (novel) 1976, Rumours of Rain (novel) 1978, A Dry White Season (novel) 1979, A Chain of Voices (novel) 1982, Mapmakers (essays) 1983, The Wall of the Plague (novel) 1984, The Ambassador (novel) 1985, A Land Apart (co-ed with J M Coetzee) 1986, States of Emergency (novel) 1988, An Act of Terror (novel) 1991, The First Life of Adamastor (novel) 1993, On the Contrary (novel) 1993, Imaginings of Sand (novel) 1996, Reinventing a Continent (essays) 1996, Devil's Valley (novel) 1998, The Rights of Desire (novel) 2000, The Other Side of Silence (novel) 2002, Before I Forget (novel) 2004, Praying Mantis 2004, Other Lives: A Novel in Three Parts 2008, A Fork in the Sand (auto-biog.) 2009; several plays 1965–75, The Jogger 1997. *Address:* Department of English Language and Literature, University of Cape Town, Rondebosch 7701, South Africa (office). *Fax:* (21) 685-3945 (home). *Website:* web.uct.ac.za/depts/english.

BRINKHORST, Laurens Jan, LLM, MA; Dutch politician, academic, diplomatist and consultant; b. 18 March 1937, Zwolle; ed Leiden Univ., Columbia Univ., New York, USA; worked for Shearman & Sterling law firm, New York; worked at Europe Inst., Leiden Univ., Dir Europe Inst. and Sr Lecturer in the Law of Int. Orgs 1965; Chair Extraordinary Prof. of Int. Environmental Law; Chair of European Law, Groningen Univ. 1967–73; State Sec. for Foreign Affairs with European Affairs portfolio 1973–77; mem. House of Reps of States Gen. 1977–82; mem. Democraten 66 (D66), Leader Parl. Party 1981–82, now Hon. mem.; Head, Del. of Comm. of European Communities in Japan 1982; Dir-Gen. of Environment, Consumer Protection and Nuclear Safety, EC 1987–89, of Environment, Nuclear

Safety and Civil Protection 1989; mem. European Parl. 1994–99; Minister of Agric., Nature Man. and Fisheries 1999–2002; European Affairs Adviser, NautaDutilh law firm, Brussels 2002; Minister of Econ. Affairs 2003–04; Deputy Prime Minister and Minister of Econ. Affairs 2004–06 (resgnd); mem. Bd of Dirs Salzburg Seminar, Int. Inst. of Sustainable Devt, LJB Europe Consult BV; Prof. of Int. and European Law and Governance, Univ. of Leiden –2011; Coordinator EC for the Project No. 6 Trans-eur. Network; Dr hc (Sofia). *Address:* Lange Houtstraat 23C, 2511 CV The Hague, Netherlands (office). *Telephone:* (70) 30-20-165 (office). *Fax:* (70) 42-77-345 (office). *E-mail:* l.j.brinkhorst@gmail.com (office); office@ljbeurope.eu (office).

BRINKLEY, Alan, BA, PhD; American historian and academic; *Provost and Allan Nevins Professor of History, Columbia University;* b. 2 June 1949, Washington, DC; s. of the late David Brinkley; m. Evangeline Morphos 1989; one d.; ed Princeton and Harvard Univs; Asst Prof. of History, MIT 1978–82; visiting position, Harvard Univ. 1980, Dunwalke Assoc. Prof. of American History 1982–88; Prof. of History, Grad. School and Univ. Center, CUNY 1988–91; visiting positions, Princeton Univ. 1991, Univ. of Turin 1992, New York Univ. 1993, École des Hautes Études en Sciences Sociales, Paris 1996; Prof. of History, Columbia Univ. 1991–98, Allan Nevins Prof. of History 1998–, Provost 2003–08; Harmsworth Prof. of American History, Univ. of Oxford 1998–99; Fellow, Soc. of American Historians 1984– (Exec. Bd mem. 1989–); mem. American Historical Asscn, Org. of American Historians (Exec. Bd mem. 1990–93), Century Foundation (Trustee 1995–, Chair. 1999–), Nat. Humanities Center (Trustee 2004–), American Acad. of Arts and Sciences; Nat. Endowment for the Humanities Fellowship 1972–73, American Council of Learned Socs Fellowship 1981, Robert L. Brown Prize, Louisiana Historical Asscn 1982, Nat. Book Award for History 1983, Guggenheim Fellowship 1984–85, Woodrow Wilson Center for Int. Scholars Fellowship 1985, Joseph R. Levenson Memorial Teaching Prize, Harvard Univ. 1987, Nat. Humanities Center Fellowship 1988–89, Media Studies Center Fellowship 1993–94, Russell Sage Foundation Fellowship 1996–97, Great Teacher Award, Columbia Univ. 2003. *Publications:* Voices of Protest: Huey Long, Father Coughlin, and the Great Depression 1982, American History: A Survey 1983, The Unfinished Nation: A Concise History of the American People 1993, The End of Reform: New Deal Liberalism in Recession and War 1995, Eyes of the Nation: A Visual History of the United States (with others) 1997, New Federalist Papers (with Kathleen Sullivan and Nelson Polsby) 1997, Liberalism and Its Discontents 1998, The Chicago Handbook for Teachers (co-ed.) 1999, The Reader's Companion to the American Presidency (co-ed.) 2000, Franklin Delano Roosevelt 2009, The Publisher: Henry Luce and His American Century 2010, Memories of the Bush Administration 2011; contribs to scholarly books and journals. *Address:* Office of the Provost, 205 Low Library, Columbia University, New York, NY 10027, USA (office). *Telephone:* (212) 854-2403 (office). *E-mail:* ab65@columbia.edu (office). *Website:* www.columbia.edu/cu/history (office).

BRINKLEY, Amy Woods; American banking executive; *Global Risk Executive, Bank of America;* ed Univ. of North Carolina; began her career as man. trainee in Commercial Credit Department Dept, Bank of America 1978, later Corp. Banking Officer, Asia Pacific Area of Int. Div., later Commercial Banker in Greensboro, NC, Exec. Vice-Pres. and Sr Consumer Credit Policy Exec. 1990, Marketing Group Exec. 1993–99, Pres. Consumer Products 1999–2001, Chair. Credit Policy and Deputy Corp. Risk Man. Exec. 2001–02, Global Risk Exec., mem. Risk and Capital Cttee and Man. Operating Cttee 2002–; mem. Bd Carolinas HealthCare System, Private Export Funding Co. (PEFCO); mem. Bd of Advisors, Partners in Out-of-School Time, N Carolina Dance Theatre (fmr Chair. Bd of Trustees); fmr mem. Univ. of N Carolina Bd of Visitors; Trustee, Princeton Theological Seminary; ranked by Fortune magazine amongst 50 Most Powerful Women in Business in the US (22nd) 2003, (19th) 2004, (25th) 2005, (23rd) 2006, (23rd) 2007, (22nd) 2008, named by US Banker magazine amongst Most Powerful Women in Banking (first) 2005, ranked by Forbes magazine amongst 100 Most Powerful Women (48th) 2008. *Address:* Bank of America Corpn, Corporate Center, 100 N Tryon Street, Charlotte, NC 28255, USA (office). *Telephone:* (800) 432-1000 (office). *Fax:* (704) 386-6699 (office). *Website:* www.bankofamerica.com (office).

BRINKLEY, Robert Edward, CMG, MA; British independent consultant and fmr diplomatist; *Chairman, The BEARR Trust;* b. 21 Jan. 1954; m. Mary Brinkley; three s.; ed Stonyhurst Coll., Lancs., Corpus Christi Coll., Oxford; joined FCO, London 1977, mem. staff 1982–88, 1992–96; mem. UK Del. to Comprehensive Test Ban Negotiations, Geneva 1978; assigned to Embassy in Moscow 1979–82, 1996–99, to Embassy in Bonn 1988–92; Head of FCO/Home Office Jt Entry Clearance Unit 2000–02; Amb. to Ukraine 2002–06; High Commr to Pakistan 2006–09; Business Devt Man., Associated British Foods plc (on secondment) 2010–11; int. affairs consultant 2011–; Chair. The BEARR Trust; Visiting Fellow, Ukrainian Catholic Univ. *Leisure interests:* reading, walking, swimming, music (violin).

BRINKMAN, Leonard Cornelis (Elco), Dr rer. pol; Dutch politician and national organization official; b. 5 Feb. 1948, Dirksland; m. J. Salentijn; three c.; ed Gymnasium, Dordrecht, Free Univ., Amsterdam; research post in the Public Admin. Dept, Free Univ. 1969–74; mem. Co-ordination Office for North of West Holland conurbation 1974–75; Head of Office of Sec.-Gen., Ministry of Home Affairs 1976–79, Dir-Gen. 1980–82; Minister for Welfare, Health and Cultural Affairs 1982–89; Pres. Het Nederlandse Rode Kruis (Netherlands Red Cross) 2001–11; Christian Democratic Alliance. *Publications:* articles on public admin. in specialist journals.

BRINSTER, Ralph L., VMD, PhD; American physiologist and academic; *Richard King Mellon Professor of Reproductive Physiology, University of Pennsylvania;* b. Montclair, NJ; ed School of Agric., Rutgers Univ., New Brunswick, NJ, School of Veterinary Medicine and Grad. School of Arts and Sciences, Univ. of Pennsylvania; Postdoctoral Fellow, Jackson Lab., Bar Harbor, ME 1960, Marine Biological Lab., Woods Hole, Mass 1962; Teaching Fellow, Dept of Physiology, School of Medicine, Univ. of Pennsylvania 1960–64, Instructor 1964–65, Asst Prof. of Physiology, School of Veterinary Medicine 1965–66, Assoc. Prof. of Physiology, Dept of Animal Biology 1966–70, Program Dir, Reproductive Physiology Training Program 1968–83, Program Dir, Veterinary Medical Scientist Training Program 1969–84, Prof. of Physiology, School of Veterinary Medicine and Grad. School of Arts and Sciences and Grad. Faculty 1970–, Richard King Mellon Prof. of Reproductive

Physiology, School of Veterinary Medicine and Grad. School 1975–; mem. Inst. of Medicine (NAS) 1986, NAS 1987, American Veterinary Medical Asscn, American Physiological Soc., American Soc. of Cell Biology, Soc. for the Study of Fertility (GB), Soc. for the Study of Reproduction; Fellow, American Acad. of Arts and Science 1986, AAAS 1989, American Acad. of Microbiology 1992; Hon. MD (Univ. of the Basque Country) 1994; Hon. DSc (Rutgers Univ.) 2000; Nat. Medal of Science, USA 2010; Distinguished Service Award, US Dept of Agric. 1989, Pioneer Award, Int. Embryo Transfer 1992, Charles-Leopold Mayer Prize, Acad. des Sciences (France) 1994, Alumni Award of Merit, Univ. of Pennsylvania School of Veterinary Medicine 1995, Prize in Developmental Biology, March of Dimes 1996, John Scott Award for Scientific Achievement, City Trusts of Philadelphia 1997, Bower Award and Prize for Achievement in Science, Franklin Inst. 1997, Carl Hartman Award, Soc. for the Study of Reproduction 1997, honoured by Special Festschrift Issue, International Journal of Developmental Biology 1998, Pioneer in Reproduction Research Award, Nat. Inst. of Child Health and Human Devt (NICHHD) 1998, George Hammel Cook Distinguished Alumni Award, Rutgers Univ. 1999, Charlton Lecturer, Tufts Univ. School of Medicine 2000, Ernst W. Bertner Award, Univ. of Texas M. D. Anderson Cancer Center 2001, selected for Hall of Honor, NICHHD 2003, Wolf Prize in Medicine (Israel) 2003, Gairdner Foundation Int. Award 2006, Int. Soc. for Transgenic Technology Prize 2011, Career Excellence in Theriogenology Award 2012. *Publications:* more than 360 articles in scientific journals. *Address:* School of Veterinary Medicine, University of Pennsylvania, 3850 Baltimore Avenue, Philadelphia, PA 19104, USA (office). *Telephone:* (215) 898-8805 (office). *Fax:* (215) 898-0667 (office). *Website:* www2.vet.upenn.edu (office).

BRINTON, Baroness (Life Peer), cr. 2011, of Kenardington in the County of Kent; **Sarah (Sal) Brinton;** British politician and organization executive; *Executive Director, Association of Universities in the East of England;* b. 1 April 1955, Paddington, London; d. of Tim Brinton, fmr Conservative MP for Gravesend; m.; several c.; ed Benenden School, Kent, Churchill Coll., Cambridge, Cen. School of Speech and Drama, London; began career at BBC TV as a floor man. in mid-1970s, worked on programmes including Playschool, Grandstand and Doctor Who; has worked as a venture capitalist; joined Liberal Party 1975, served as Vice-Chair. Fed. Policy Cttee, fmr mem. Fed. Conf. Cttee; managed New Cambridge Research Co. Ltd 1984–87; Bursar Lucy Cavendish Coll., Cambridge 1992–97, Selwyn Coll., Cambridge 1997–2002; Cambridgeshire Co. Councillor 1993–2004; unsuccessful Parl. cand. (Liberal Democrat) for SE Cambridgeshire at Gen. Elections 1997, 2001, for Watford 2005, 2010; mem. Liberal Democrat Educ. and Higher Educ. Working Group 1993–97, Fed. Conf. Cttee 2004–, Fed. Policy Cttee 2004– (Vice-Chair. 2006–), Schools Working Group 2008–; Founder-mem. Bd East of England Devt Agency 1998–2004 (Deputy Chair. 2001–04); Chair. Cambridgeshire Learning and Skills Council 2000–06; regional skills champion and Chair. regional skills forum and Framework for Employment and Skills Action –2004; self-employed consultant in training and skills; mem. Asscn of Univs in the East of England 2006–, Exec. Dir –2011; Dir (non-exec.) St John's Innovation Centre, Univ. for Industry (Learndirect), Ufi Ltd, East of England International; Dir and Trustee, Christian Blind Mission UK Ltd, Ufi Charitable Trust; Hon. PhD (Anglia Ruskin Univ.) 2003; East Anglian Entrepreneurial Businesswoman of the Year Award 1997. *Address:* Association of Universities in the East of England, Victory House, Vision Park, Chivers Way, Histon, Cambs., CB24 9ZR (office); House of Lords, Westminster, London, SW1A 0PW; 128 Langley Road, Watford, WD17 4AR, England (home). *Telephone:* (1223) 200816 (office); (20) 7219-5353; 7768-821187 (mobile). *Fax:* (1223) 202822 (office); (20) 7219-5979. *E-mail:* sal@watfordlibdems.org.uk (office); salbrinton.org.uk (office); auee2@eeda.org.uk (office). *Website:* www.auee.ac.uk (office); www.uni-east.ac.uk (office); www.salbrinton.org.uk.

BRIQUET MARMOL, Armando; Venezuelan politician; *President, Fundación Justicia y Democracia;* b. 3 June 1970, Caracas. s. of Juan Francisco Briquet and Dorisabel Marmol Briquet; m. Teresa Saavedra de Briquet; two s.; ed Colegio El Peñón, Universidad Central de Venezuela, Universidad Católica Andrés Bello, Advanced Course IV Local Public Man., Zaragoza, Spain; mem. Nat. Swimming Team for ten years; Gen. Man. for Health and Social Issues, Caracas City Council 1996–98; Man. Dir Office of Pres. of Nat. Congress 1999; Man. Dir Municipality of Baruta 2000–03; Dir of Intergovernmental Affairs 2003–05; Gen. Co-ordinator in Caracas, Primero Justicia party 2002–04, Nat. Organizing Sec. 2004–06, Campaign Chief for presidential cand. Julio Borges 2005–06, Nat. Sec.-Gen. 2006–07, mem. Nat. Bd; currently Pres. Fundación Justicia y Democracia; elected mem. Legis. Council of Miranda State 2008; a campaign manager in presidential election 2012. *Address:* Primero Justicia, Planta de Oficianas, Centro Comercial Chacaito, Chacaito, Caracas, Venezuela (office). *Telephone:* (212) 952-9733 (office). *E-mail:* contacto@fjd.com.ve (office). *Website:* www.primerojusticia.org.ve (office); fjd.com.ve (office).

BRISVILLE, Jean-Claude Gabriel; French writer and playwright; b. 28 May 1922, Bois-Colombes/Hauts-de-Seine; s. of Maurice Brisville and Geneviève Gineste; m. 2nd Irène Kalaschnikowa 1963; one s. one d. by first m.; ed Lycée Jacques Decour, Paris; literary journalist 1946–; Reader, Hachette 1951–58; Sec. to Albert Camus 1957–59; Deputy Literary Dir Juilliard 1959–64, Literary Dir 1964–70; Head of Drama Video Section, ORTF 1971–75; Literary Dir Livre de poche 1976–81; Chevalier, Légion d'honneur, Chevalier, Ordre des Arts et des Lettres; Prix du Théâtre de la Société des Auteurs et Compositeurs Dramatiques. *Plays include:* Le Fauteuil à bascule (Prix Ibsen, Prix de la meilleure création dramatique) 1982, Le Bonheur à Romorantin, L'entretien de M. Descartes avec M. Pascal le jeune, La Villa bleue, Les Liaisons dangereuses (adaptation), Le Souper (Prix du Théâtre, Acad. Française) 1990, L'Officier de la Garde 1990, L'Antichambre 1991, Contre-jour 1993, Dernière Salve 1995, Sept comédies en quête d'acteurs 2007. *Publications include:* narrative works: Prologue 1948, D'un amour (Prix Sainte-Beuve) 1954, La Fuite au Danemark 1962, La petite Marie 1972, La Zone d'ombre 1976, La révélation d'une voix et d'un nom 1982, Vive Henri IV 2002; essays; stories for children. *Address:* 85 rue Republique, 59172 Roeulx, France (home). *Telephone:* 3-27-43-27-75 (home).

BRITO, Carlos, MBA; Brazilian business executive; *CEO, Anheuser-Busch InBev;* b. 1960; ed Fed. Univ. of Rio de Janeiro, Stanford Univ., USA; worked for Shell Oil and Daimler Benz –1989; Financial Analyst, Brahma, AmBev (now

InBev) 1989–91, Plant Man. 1991–92, Head Softdrink Div. 1992–96, Head Beer Sales 1997–2001, Head Operations 2002–03, CEO Ambev Jan.–Aug. 2004, Zone Pres. for N America (after merger with Interbrew) 2004–05, CEO InBev 2005–08, CEO Anheuser-Busch InBev (following takeover of Anheuser-Busch) 2008–. *Address:* Anheuser-Busch InBev, Brouwerijplein 1, Leuven 3000, Belgium (office). *Telephone:* (16) 24-71-11 (office). *Fax:* (16) 24-74-07 (office). *E-mail:* info@ab-inbev.com (office). *Website:* www.ab-inbev.com (office).

BRITT, Glenn A.; American media executive; *Chairman, President and CEO, Time Warner Cable Inc.;* ed Dartmouth Coll., Amos Tuck School of Business Admin; joined Time Inc. in Controller's Dept 1972, rose successively to Vice-Pres.-Treas. Manhattan Cable Television, Inc. 1974–77, Finance Dir Time-Life Books Iran Project 1977–80, Vice-Pres. Network and Studio Operations for Home Box Office, Inc. (HBO), Dir of Business Devt, Time Inc.'s video group 1980–81, Sr Vice-Pres., Finance, American Television and Communications Corpn (Time Inc.'s cable TV unit) 1981–84, Sr Vice-Pres., Finance, Time Inc.'s Video Group 1984, Sr Vice-Pres. and Chief Financial Officer (CFO) Home Box Office 1984–86, Vice-Pres. Time Inc. and Treas. 1986–88, Vice-Pres., Finance 1988, Vice-Pres. and CFO 1988–90, Exec. Vice-Pres. 1990 (following merger between Time Inc. and Warner Communications), Sr Vice-Pres. and Treas. Time Warner Inc. –1990, Pres. and CEO Time Warner Cable Ventures, Pres. 1999–2001, Chair. and CEO Time Warner Cable div., Time Warner Entertainment Co., LP (now a subsidiary of co.) 2001–, CEO Time Warner Cable 2001–, Pres. 2006–, Chair. 2009–; mem. Bd of Dirs Nat. Cable & Telecommunications Asscn, Paley Center for Media, Pearl Harbor Memorial Fund, Xerox Corpn; Trustee, Teachers Insurance and Annuity Asscn; numerous awards, including CTPAA Pres.'s Award 2004, Kaitz Foundation Diversity Champion 2005, NAMIC Stanley B. Thomas Jr Lifetime Achievement Award 2006, The Media Inst.'s American Horizon Award 2006, NCTA's Vanguard Award for Distinguished Leadership 2006, Cable Positive's Joel G. Berger Award 2007, Broadcasting & Cable's Hall of Fame 2008. *Address:* Time Warner Cable Inc., 60 Columbus Circle, 17th Floor, New York, NY 10023, USA (office). *Telephone:* (212) 364-8200 (office). *E-mail:* info@timewarnercable.com (office). *Website:* www.timewarnercable.com (office).

BRITTAN, Sir Samuel, Kt, MA; British writer and journalist; *Columnist, Financial Times;* b. 29 Dec. 1933, London; brother of Lord Brittan of Spennithorne; ed Kilburn Grammar School, Jesus Coll., Cambridge; journalist on The Financial Times 1955–61, prin. economic commentator 1966–, Asst Ed. 1978–95; Econs Ed. The Observer 1961–64; Adviser, Dept of Econ. Affairs 1965; Research Fellow, Nuffield Coll., Oxford 1973–74; Visiting Fellow 1974–82; Visiting Prof., Chicago Law School, USA 1978; mem. Peacock Cttee on Finance of the BBC 1985–86; Hon. Prof. of Politics, Univ. of Warwick 1987–92; Hon. Fellow, Jesus Coll., Cambridge 1988; Chevalier, Légion d'honneur 1993; Hon. DLitt (Heriot-Watt) 1985; Hon. DUniv (Essex) 1995; first winner Sr Harold Wincott Award for financial journalists 1971, George Orwell Prize for political journalism 1980, Ludwig Erhard Prize 1987. *Publications:* Steering the Economy (3rd edn 1970), Left or Right: The Bogus Dilemma 1968, The Price of Economic Freedom: A Guide to Flexible Rates 1970, Is There an Economic Consensus? 1973, Capitalism and the Permissive Society 1973 (new edn A Restatement of Economic Liberalism 1988), The Delusion of Incomes Policy (with Peter Lilley) 1977, The Economic Consequences of Democracy 1977, How to End the 'Monetarist' Controversy 1981, Role and Limits of Government: Essays in Political Economy 1983, There Is No Such Thing As Society 1993, Capitalism with a Human Face 1995, Essays, Moral, Political and Economic 1998, Against the Flow 2005, Inside the Department of Economic Affairs: Samuel Brittan, the Diary of an 'Irregular' 2012. *Address:* The Financial Times, Number 1 Southwark Bridge, London, SE1 9HL, England (office). *Telephone:* (20) 7873-3000 (office). *Fax:* (20) 7873-4343 (office). *E-mail:* samuel.brittan@ft.com (office). *Website:* www.samuelbrittan.co.uk.

BRITTAN OF SPENNITHORNE, Baron (Life Peer), cr. 2000, of Spennithorne in the County of North Yorkshire; **Rt Hon. Leon Brittan,** Kt, PC, QC, DL; British politician, barrister and investment banker; *Vice-Chairman, UBS Investment Bank;* b. 25 Sept. 1939, London, England; s. of the late Dr Joseph Brittan and of Rebecca Brittan; brother of Sir Samuel Brittan; m. Diana Peterson 1980; two step-d.; ed Haberdashers' Aske's School, Trinity Coll., Cambridge, Yale Univ., USA; Chair. Cambridge Univ. Conservative Asscn 1960; Pres. Cambridge Union 1960, debating tour of USA 1961; called to Bar, Inner Temple 1962 (Bencher 1983); Chair. Bow Group 1964–65; contested N Kensington seat 1966, 1970; Ed. Crossbow 1966–68; mem. Political Cttee Carlton Club, Cttee of the British Atlantic Group of Young Politicians 1970–78; Vice-Chair. of Govs of Isaac Newton School 1968–71; MP for Cleveland and Whitby 1974–83, for Richmond (N Yorks.) 1983–88; QC 1978; Vice-Chair. Parl. Conservative Party Employment Cttee 1974–76; Opposition Spokesman on Devolution and House of Commons Affairs 1976–78, on Devolution and Employment 1978–79; Minister of State, Home Office 1979–81; Chief Sec. to the Treasury 1981–83, Home Sec. 1983–85; Sec. of State for Trade and Industry 1985–86; Commr with responsibility for Competition Policy and Financial Insts, Comm. of the European Communities (EC) 1989–92, for Econ. Relations 1993–94, for External Trade and Relations with N America and parts of Asia 1995–99, a Vice-Pres. 1989–99; consultant, Herbert Smith 2000–06; Vice-Chair. UBS Investment Bank 2000–; Advisory Dir Unilever 2000–04, Dir (non-exec.) 2004–10; Chair. Lotis group of Int. Financial Services London (IFSL) 2001–06; Trade Adviser to Prime Minister David Cameron 2010–11; Distinguished Visiting Fellow Inst. of Policy Studies 1988; Hersch Lauterpacht Memorial Lecturer, Univ. of Cambridge 1990; Chair. Soc. of Conservative Lawyers 1986–89; Vice-Chair. Nat. Asscn of School Govs and Mans 1970–78; Chancellor Univ. of Teesside 1993–2005; Deputy Lt, Co. of N Yorks. 2001–; Hon. DCL (Newcastle) 1990, (Durham) 1992; Hon. LLD (Hull) 1990, (Bath) 1995; Hon. DL (Bradford) 1992; Hon. DEcon (Korea Univ.); Dr hc (Edin.) 1991. *Publications:* The Conservative Opportunity (contrib.), Millstones for the Sixties (co-author), Rough Justice, Infancy and the Law, How to Save your Schools, A New Deal for Health Care 1988, Defence and Arms Control in a Changing Era 1988, Discussions on Policy 1989, Monetary Union: the Issues and the Impact 1989, Europe: Our Sort of Community (Granada Guildhall Lecture) 1989, Hersch Lauterpacht Memorial Lectures (Univ. of Cambridge) 1990, European Competition Policy 1992, Europe: The Europe We Need 1994, A Diet of Brussels 2000. *Leisure interests:* walking, cricket, opera. *Address:* 1 Finsbury Avenue, London, EC2M 2PP (office); House of Lords, Westminster, London, SW1A 0PW, England (office). *Telephone:* (20) 7568-6305 (office). *Fax:* (20) 7568-6520

(office). *E-mail:* leon.brittan@ubs.com (office). *Website:* www.ubs.com (office); www
.parliament.uk/biographies/lords/leon-brittan/26671 (office).

BRITZ, Robert, BSc; American financial executive; b. 1951; ed Manhattan Coll.,
Harvard Business School; joined New York Stock Exchange (NYSE) 1972, various
man. posts in corp. marketing, then Man. Dir Corp. Business Devt, Vice-Pres. New
Listings and Client Service, Sr Vice-Pres., Exec. Vice-Pres., Group Exec. Vice-Pres.
overseeing operation of NYSE market, tech. and information products, mem.
Office of Chair. 1995–2001, Co-COO, Pres. and Exec. Vice-Chair. 2001–05 (retd);
fmr mem. Bd of Dirs The Stanley Works, Securities Industry Automation Corpn
(SIAC), Sector Inc. *Address:* c/o New York Stock Exchange, 11 Wall Street, 6th
Floor, New York, NY 10005, USA (office).

BRIX, Emil, Mag. phil, Dr phil; Austrian historian and diplomatist; *Ambassador
to UK;* b. 1956, Vienna; ed Univ. of Vienna; joined Austrian Foreign Service 1982;
Sec., Austrian People's Party (ÖVP) 1984–86; worked in office of Fed. Minister for
Science and Research 1986–89; Gen. Consul in Kraków 1990–95, Man. Austrian
Inst. for Culture, London 1995–99, Dir for Cultural Programmes 2000–02, Dir-
Gen. for Foreign Cultural Policies, Fed. Ministry for European and Int. Affairs
2002–09, Amb. to UK 2010–; Deputy Chair. Inst. for the Danube Region and Cen.
Europe 1995–; Sec. Gen. Austrian Research Inst. 2000–10; Pres. EU Nat. Insts of
Culture 2007–08; Head of Civil Society in Austria (research group); mem.
Presidium, Austrian Research Asscn 2009–; mem. Polish Acad. of Arts and
Sciences 2011; Dr hc (Univ. of Drohobych) 2003, (Univ. of Cluj Napoca) 2005;
Anton Gindely Prize, Vienna 1983, European Culture Prize 'New Cultures in the
New Europe', Krynica 2008. *Publications:* numerous books and articles on the
Austrian and European history of the 19th and 20th centuries, including Die
Frauen der Wiener Moderne (with Lisa Fischer) 1994, Schweiz und Österreich.
Eine Nachbarschaft in Mitteleuropa (with Urs Altermatt) 1996, Liberalismus.
Grundlagen und Perspektiven (with Wolfgang Mantl) 1996, Memoria Austriae 1
Menschen – Mythen – Zeiten (with Ernst Bruckmüller and Hannes Stekl) 2004.
Address: Embassy of Austria, 18 Belgrave Mews West, London, SW1X 8HU,
England (office). *Telephone:* (20) 7344-3250 (office). *Fax:* (20) 7344-0292 (office).
E-mail: london-ob@bmeia.gv.at (office). *Website:* www.bmeia.gv.at/london (office).

BRIXNER, Ulrich, Dr rer. pol; German banker; b. 1941, Munich; ed Univ. of
Mannheim; fmrly CEO GZ Bank; Chair. and CEO DZ BANK AG (formed by
merger of GZ Bank and DG Bank Deutsche Genossenschaftsbank) 2001–07; mem.
Supervisory Bd Südzucker AG. *Address:* c/o DZ BANK AG, Deutsche Zentral-
Genossenschaftsbank, Platz der Republik, 60265 Frankfurt am Main, Germany
(office).

BRIZ ABULARACH, Jorge; Guatemalan politician and business executive; b. 27
Sept. 1955, Guatemala City; m.; ed Univ. Rafael Landívar de Guatemala; trained
as lawyer; Dir Chamber of Commerce 1985–86, Vice-Pres. 1987–88, Pres. 1989–91,
1995–99, 2001–03; Leader Partido Movimiento Reformador (MR–Movt. for Reform
Party) 2002–; elected mem. of Parl. 2003–; Minister of Foreign Affairs 2004–06;
Pres. Coordinating Cttee, Asscn of Agric., Commerce, Industry and Finance
(CACIF) 1990–96, Dir 2000–03; Pres. Perm. Secr. of Latin American Chambers of
Commerce and Industry (CAMACOL) 1997–98; fmr Dir Fed. of Chambers of
Commerce of Cen. America (CAMACOL); mem. Financial Bd of Guatemala
1992–2002; del. to IMF, World Bank, Inter-American Devt Bank and EU; Gran
Oficial, Orden al Mérito Bernardo O'Higgins (Chile) 1997, Orden José Cecilio del
Valle (Guatemala) 1999. *Address:* c/o Ministry of Foreign Affairs, 2a Avda La
Reforma 4–47, Zona 10, Guatemala City, Guatemala (office).

BRIZUELA DE AVILA, María Eugenia, MBA; Salvadorean lawyer and
politician; b. 31 Oct. 1949, San Salvador; m. Ricardo Antonio Avila Araujo; three
c.; ed Geneva Univ., Switzerland, Sorbonne Univ., Paris, France, Dr. José Matías
Delgado Univ. of El Salvador, Cen. American Inst. of Business, Nicaragua; Pres.
Admin. Council for Int. Insurance, Salvadorean Asscn for Study of Insurance
Rights 1995–98, Salvador Foundation for the Devt of Women 1995–98; Co-
ordinator 'The New Alliance', Govt of El Salvador 1999–; Minister of Foreign
Affairs 1999–2004; Pres. Banco Salvadoreño 2004, later CEO and mem. Bd of Dirs;
Pres. Gen. Ass., OAS, Inter-American Cttee against Terrorism; Chair. of Bd
International de Seguros 1996–99; apptd Exec. Pres. Hongkong and Shanghai
Banking Corpn (HSBC) 2006, Regional Dir for Corp. Sustainability in Latin
America 2007, Chief Exec. of HSBC 2008, then Sec. of Salvadoran HSBC Bd, SA;
apptd Dir of FEPADE 1997; moderator Aspen Inst.; mem. El Salvador Lawyers'
Asscn 1985–, Chamber of Arbitration and Conciliation, Inst. of Notary Rights
1985–, Juridicial Studies Centre 1989–, Cen. America Leadership Initiative; Exec.
mem. Social Security Inst. 1994, Social Investment Fund 1995; Distinguished
Professional of the Year, Dr. Jose Matias Delgado Univ. 2006, Palme d'Or top
prize, Chamber of Commerce and Industry 2007. *Address:* c/o Ministry of Foreign
Affairs, Calle El Pedregal, Blvd Cancillería, Ciudad Merliot, Antiguo Cuscatlán,
San Salvador, El Salvador.

BROAD, Eli, BA, CPA; American business executive and philanthropist; b. 6 June
1933, New York, NY; s. of Leon Broad and Rebecca Broad (née Jacobson); m.
Edythe Lois Lawson 1954; two s.; ed Michigan State Univ.; Asst Prof., Detroit Inst.
of Tech. 1956; Co-founder, Chair., Pres. and CEO AIG SunAmerica Life Insurance
Co. (fmrly Kaufman & Broad, Inc.), LA 1957–2001; Chair. of numerous cos,
including CalAmerica Life Insurance Co., KB Home (fmrly Kaufman & Broad
Home Corpn) 1989–93, Stanford Ranch Co.; mem. Exec. Cttee Fed. Nat. Mortgage
Asscn 1972–73; mem. California Business Roundtable 1986–2000; Regent
Smithsonian Inst. 2004–09; Co-owner Sacramento Kings and Arco Arena
1992–99; Dir LA World Affairs Council 1988– (Chair. 1994–99), DARE America
1989–95 (Hon. Dir 1995–); Chair. Mayor's Housing Policy Comm. 1974–75; mem.
Advisory Council, Town Hall of California 1985–87; mem. Contemporary Art
Comm., Harvard Univ. Art Museum 1992–; mem. Bd of Overseers, Univ. of
Southern California Keck School of Medicine 1999–, Bd of Dirs EdVoice 2001–;
Trustee, Pitzer Coll., Claremont, Calif. 1970–82 (Chair. Bd of Trustees 1973–79,
Life Trustee 1982–), Haifa Univ., Israel 1972–80, Windward School, Santa Monica,
Calif. 1972–77, California State Univ. 1978–82 (Vice Chair. Bd of Trustees
1979–80, Trustee Emer. 1982–), Museum of Contemporary Art, LA 1980–93,
UCLA Foundation 1986–, Caltech 1993–, Trustee, Comm. for Econ. Devt 1993–95;
Founder and Trustee, The Broad Foundation 1999–; numerous philanthropic
donations, including funds to build the Frank Gehry-designed Walt Disney

Concert Hall 2003; mem. Bd Future Generation Art Prize; Fellow, American Acad.
of Arts and Sciences 2001; Chevalier, Légion d'honneur 1994; Golden Plate Award,
American Acad. of Achievement 1971, Humanitarian Award, NCCJ 1977, Public
Affairs Award, Coro Foundation 1987, KCET-Los Angeles Visionary Award 1999,
Julius Award, Univ. of Southern California 2001, Teach for America Educational
Leadership Award 2001, United Way Alexis de Tocqueville Award 2002, Exem-
plary Leadership in Man. Award, Anderson School, UCLA 2002, Carnegie Medal of
Philanthropy 2007, David Rockefeller Award, Museum of Modern Art 2009,
William E. Simon Prize for Philanthropic Leadership, Philanthropy Roundtable
(co-recipient with his wife) 2013. *Publication:* The Art of Being Unreasonable:
Lessons in Unconventional Thinking 2012. *Address:* The Broad Foundations,
10900 Wilshire Boulevard, 12th Floor, Los Angeles, CA 90024, USA (office).
Telephone: (310) 954-5000 (office). *Fax:* (310) 954-5051 (office). *E-mail:* info@
broadfoundation.org (office). *Website:* www.broadfoundation.org (office); www
.broadeducation.org (office).

BROADBENT, Jim; British actor and writer; b. 24 May 1949, s. of the late Roy
Broadbent and Dee Broadbent; m. Anastasia Lewis 1987; two step-s.; ed Leighton
Park School, Reading, Hammersmith Coll. of Art, London Acad. of Music and
Dramatic Arts (LAMDA); actor 1972–; mem. Nat. Theatre and RSC; wrote and
appeared in short film A Sense of History (Clermont-Ferrand Int. Film Festival
Award). *Theatre:* The Recruiting Officer, A Winter's Tale, The Government
Inspector, A Flea in Her Ear, Goose Pimples, Our Friends in the North, Habeas
Corpus. *Films include:* The Shout, Breaking Glass, The Dogs of War, The Good
Father, Superman IV, Life is Sweet, Enchanted April, The Crying Game, Widow's
Peak, Princess Caraboo, Richard III, The Borrowers, Little Voice, The Avengers,
Topsy Turvy 1999, Moulin Rouge (Acad. Award for Best Supporting Actor 2002,
BAFTA Award for Best Supporting Actor 2002) 2001, Bridget Jones's Diary 2001,
Iris (Golden Globe for Best Supporting Actor) 2001, Gangs of New York 2002,
Nicholas Nickleby 2002, Bright Young Things 2003, Around the World in Eighty
Days 2004, Vanity Fair 2004, Vera Drake 2004, Bridget Jones: The Edge of Reason
2004, The Chronicles of Narnia: The Lion, the Witch and the Wardrobe 2005, Art
School Confidential 2006, Free Jimmy (voice) 2006, Hot Fuzz 2007, And When Did
You Last See Your Father? 2007, Indiana Jones and the Kingdom of the Crystal
Skull 2008, Inkheart 2008, The Young Victoria 2009, The Damned United 2009,
Harry Potter and the Half-Blood Prince 2009, Perrier's Bounty 2009, Another Year
2010, Harry Potter and the Deathly Hallows: Part 2 2011, Arthur Christmas
(voice) 2011, The Iron Lady 2011, Filth 2012, Cloud Atlas 2012. *Television
includes:* Not the Nine O'Clock News, Sense of History (also writer), Murder Most
Horrid, Only Fools and Horses, The Victoria Wood Show, Silas Marner,
Blackadder, Birth of a Nation, Gone to the Dogs, Gone to Seed, The Peter
Principle, The Gathering Storm, The Young Visitors, Spider-Plant Man 2005,
Longford (BAFTA Award for Best Actor 2007) 2006, Einstein and Eddington 2008,
Any Human Heart 2010, Exile 2011. *Address:* c/o Harriet Robinson, ICM, 76
Oxford Street, London, W1D 1BS, England (office). *Telephone:* (20) 7636-6565
(office).

BROADBENT, Hon. John Edward (Ed), OC, CC, PhD; Canadian politician and
academic; b. 21 March 1936, Oshawa, Ont.; s. of Percy E. Broadbent and Mary A.
Welsh; m. 1st Yvonne Yamaoka 1961 (divorced 1967); one s. one d.; m. 2nd Lucille
Munroe 1971 (died 2006); one step-s. and one adopted d.; ed High School in
Oshawa, Trinity Coll., Toronto, London School of Econs, UK; fmr mem. RCAF;
Prof. of Political Science, York Univ., Ont. 1965–68; MP for Oshawa-Whitby
1968–79, for Oshawa 1979–90; Co-Chair. Policy Review Cttee for New Democratic
Party Fed. Convention 1969; Chair. Fed. Caucus 1972–74, Parl. Leader of Fed.
Caucus 1974–75; Nat. Leader of New Democratic Party (NDP) 1975–89; Vice-Pres.
Socialist Int. 1978–90, Hon. Pres. 1991–; Pres. Int. Centre for Human Rights and
Democratic Devt 1990–96; Fellow, All Souls Coll., Oxford 1996–97; J.S. Woods-
worth Chair, Inst. for the Humanities, Simon Fraser Univ. 1997–99; Skelton-Clark
Fellow, Queen's Univ. 1999–2000, Fellow, School of Policy Studies; MP represent-
ing riding of Ottawa Centre 2004–06 (retd); came out of retirement to help
negotiate a formal coalition agreement between the Liberals and New Democratic
Party 2008; announced creation of the Broadbent Inst. 2011; Hon. LLD (Dalhousie
Univ.) 1990, (York Univ.) 1991; Hon. DLitt (Trinity Coll., Oxford) 1990, (Toronto
Univ.) 1990; Nation Builder of the Year, Globe and Mail 2005. *Publication:* The
Liberal Rip-Off 1970. *Leisure interests:* reading contemporary fiction, listening to
music, skiing. *Address:* c/o New Democratic Party of Canada, 279 Laurier Avenue
West, Suite 300, Ottawa, ON K1P 5J9, Canada. *E-mail:* info@ndp.ca.

BROADBENT, Sir Richard, Kt; British business executive; *Non-Executive
Chairman, Tesco plc;* began career at HM Treasury; with Schroders 1986–99;
Exec. Chair. HM Customs and Excise 1999–2003; mem. Man. Bd of UK Civil
Service 1999–2003; mem. Bd of Dirs Barclays plc 2003–11, Sr Ind. Dir 2004–11,
Deputy Chair. 2010–11; mem. Bd of Dirs Arriva plc 2004–10, Chair. 2004–10;
mem. Bd of Dirs Tesco plc July 2011–, Chair. (non-exec.) Nov. 2011–; Trustee,
Relate. *Address:* Tesco plc, New Tesco House, Delamare Road, Cheshunt, Herts.,
EN8 9SL, England (office). *Telephone:* (1992) 632222 (office). *Fax:* (1992) 630794
(office). *E-mail:* info@tesco.com (office). *Website:* www.tesco.com (office).

BROCK, Gunnar, MBA; Swedish business executive; *Chairman, Stora Enso;* b.
1950; ed Stockholm School of Econs; various positions with Tetra Pak including
Man. Dir, Pres. Tetra Pak Europe and Exec. Vice Pres. Tetra Pak Group 1974–92,
Pres. and CEO 1994–2000; Pres. and CEO Alfa Laval Group 1992–94; CEO Thule
International 2001–02; Pres. and CEO Atlas Copco Group July 2002–09; Chair.
Stora Enso 2010–; Dir OM-Gruppen, Lego AS, Denmark; mem. Royal Swedish
Acad. of Eng Sciences (IVA). *Address:* Stora Enso, World Trade Center,
Klarabergsviadukten 70, C4, PO Box 70395, 107 24 Stockholm, Sweden (office).
Telephone: (10) 460-00-00 (office). *Fax:* (8) 10-60-20 (office). *Website:* www
.storaenso.com (office).

BROCK, John F.; American business executive; *Chairman and CEO, Coca-Cola
Enterprises Inc.;* b. 1948; with Procter & Gamble Inc. 1972–83; joined Cadbury
Schweppes North America 1983, various sr positions, becoming mem. Bd and Man.
Dir, Global Beverages Div. 1996, COO 1999–2002; CEO Interbrew (later InBev SA
following merger with AmBev 2004) 2003–05; Dir, Pres. and CEO Coca-Cola
Enterprises Inc. 2006–08, Chair. and CEO 2008–; Dir (non-exec.) Reed Elsevier
PLC; Dir Georgia Inst. of Tech. Presidential Advisory Bd; USA Beverage Industry
Exec. of the Year 2000. *Address:* Coca-Cola Enterprises Inc., 2500 Windy Ridge

Parkway, Atlanta, GA 30339, USA (office). *Telephone:* (770) 989-3000 (office). *Fax:* (770) 989-3788 (office). *E-mail:* info@cokecce.com (office). *Website:* www.cokecce .com (office).

BROCKES, Jeremy Patrick, PhD, FRS; British biologist and academic; *MRC Research Professor, University College, London;* b. 29 Feb. 1948, Haslemere, Surrey, England; s. of Bernard Brockes and Edna Heaney; ed St John's Coll., Cambridge, Univ. of Edinburgh; Asst, then Assoc. Prof. of Biology, California Inst. of Tech. (Caltech), USA 1978–83; mem. MRC Biophysics Unit, King's Coll., London 1983–88; mem. Ludwig Inst. for Cancer Research 1988–97; Prof. of Cell Biology, Univ. Coll., London 1992–97, MRC Research Prof., Dept of Structural and Molecular Biology 1997–; Scientific Medal, Zoological Soc. of London 1986, AAAS Newcomb Cleveland Prize 2008. *Publication:* Amphibian Limb Regeneration: Rebuilding a Complex Structure 1997, Plasticity and Reprogramming of Differentiated Cells in Amphibian Regeneration 2002, Molecular Basis for the Nerve Dependence of Limb Regeneration in an Adult Vertebrate 2007. *Leisure interest:* soprano saxophone. *Address:* Department of Structural and Molecular Biology, Darwin Building, University College London, Gower Street, London, WC1E 6BT, England (office). *Telephone:* (20) 7679-4483 (office). *E-mail:* j.brockes@ucl.ac.uk (office). *Website:* www.ucl.ac.uk/smb/academic-staff/jeremy_Brockes/index (office).

BROCKINGTON, Ian Fraser, MP, MD, FRCP, FRCPsych; British psychiatrist and academic; *Professor Emeritus of Psychiatry, University of Birmingham;* b. 12 Dec. 1935, Chillington, Devon, England; s. of Fraser Brockington and Joyce Brockington; m. Diana Hilary Pink 1969; two s. two d.; ed Winchester Coll., Univ. of Cambridge, Univ. of Manchester Medical School; Wellcome Research Fellow, Royal Postgraduate Medical School and Univ. of Ibadan, Nigeria 1966–69; Visiting Prof., Univ. of Chicago, USA 1980–81, Washington Univ., St Louis, USA 1981; Prof. of Psychiatry, Univ. of Birmingham 1983–2002, Prof. Emer. 2002–; Visiting Prof., Univ. of Chicago 1980–81, Washington Univ. in St Louis 1981, Univ. of Nagoya, Japan 2002, Univ. of Kumamoto, Japan 2003, Inst. of Psychiatry, London 2009; Pres. The Marcé Society 1982–84; Founder and first Pres. Women's Mental Health section, World Psychiatric Asscn; est. Eyry Press 2002; Cottman Fellow, Monash Univ. 1988. *Publications:* monographs: Motherhood and Mental Health 1996, Eileithyia's Mischief: The Organic Psychoses of Pregnancy, Parturition and the Puerperium 2006, Menstrual Psychosis and the Catamenial Process 2008; papers on African heart diseases 1966–80, on schizoaffective psychosis, methods of clinical psychiatric research, pregnancy-related psychiatric disorders. *Leisure interests:* family activities, choral singing, French, Italian and German literature, publishing, distance running. *Address:* Lower Brockington Farm, Bredenbury, Bromyard, Herefords., HR7 4TE, England (home). *Telephone:* (1885) 3245 (home). *E-mail:* i.f.brockington@bham.ac.uk.

BRÖDER, Ernst-Günther, DEcon; German banker, economist and international consultant; b. 6 Jan. 1927, Cologne; ed Univs of Cologne, Mainz, Freiburg and Paris; mem. Corpn staff, Bayer AG, Leverkusen 1956–61; Projects Dept, World Bank (IBRD) 1961–64; joined KfW-Bankengruppe (fmrly Kreditanstalt für Wiederaufbau) 1964, Deputy Man. 1968–69, Man. 1969–75, mem. Man. Bd 1975–84, Man. Bd Spokesman 1980–84; Dir European Investment Bank (EIB) 1980–84, Pres. and Chair. Bd of Dirs 1984–93, Hon. Pres. 1993–; Chair. Inspection Panel, IBRD 1994–96, 1998–99, mem. 1997–98; mem. Supervisory Bd DEG Deutsche Finanzierungsgesellschaft für Beteiligungen in Entwicklungsländern GmbH 1980–84; mem. Panel of Conciliators, Int. Centre for Settlement of Investment Disputes 1976–, Special Advisory Group, Asian Devt Bank 1981–82; high decorations in Germany, Belgium, Italy and Luxembourg.

BRODER, Samuel E., BS, MD; American physician; *Chief Medical Officer, Celera Corporation;* b. 24 Feb. 1945, Łódź, Poland; m. Gail Broder; two d.; moved to USA 1949; ed Univ. of Michigan and Stanford Univ.; Clinical Assoc., Nat. Cancer Inst. (NCI), Bethesda, Md 1972, Investigator, Medicine Br. 1975, Sr Investigator, Metabolism Br. 1976, in charge of lab. overseeing new drug trials 1981–89, Dir NCI 1989–95; Sr Vice-Pres. for Research and Devt IVAX Corpn 1995–98; Chief Medical Officer, Celera Corpn 1998–; mem. Inst. of Medicine; Arthur S. Flemming Award, Leopold Griffuel Award. *Publications:* AIDS: Modern Concepts and Therapeutic Challenges (ed.) 1987; more than 300 papers in scientific journals. *Leisure interests:* long walks, playing cards, cinema, dinner with friends. *Address:* Celera Corpn, 1401 Harbor Bay Parkway, Alameda, CA 94502, USA (office). *Telephone:* (510) 749-4200 (office). *E-mail:* info@celera.com (office). *Website:* www .celera.com (office).

BRODERICK, Matthew; American actor; b. 21 March 1962, New York City; s. of James Broderick and Patricia Broderick; m. Sarah Jessica Parker (q.v.) 1997; one s. two d. *Theatre includes:* Valentine's Day (workshop production), Torch Song Trilogy, Brighton Beach Memoirs (Tony Award), Biloxi Blues,The Widow Claire, How to Succeed in Business Without Really Trying (Tony Award), The Producers, The Odd Couple 2005. *Films include:* War Games, Ladyhawke, 1918, On Valentine's Day, Ferris Bueller's Day Off, Project X, Biloxi Blues, Torch Song Trilogy, Glory, Family Business, The Freshman, Lay This Laurel, Glory, Out on a Limb, The Night We Never Met, The Lion King (voice), Road to Welville, Mrs Parker and the Vicious Circle, Infinity (also dir), The Cable Guy, Addicted to Love, The Lion King II: Simba's Pride (voice), Godzilla, Election, Inspector Gadget 1999, Walking to the Waterline 1999, You Can Count on Me 2000, Suspicious Minds 2001, Good Boy! (voice) 2003, Marie and Bruce 2004, Lion King 1 1/2 (voice) 2004, Stepford Wives 2004, Last Shot 2004, Strangers with Candy 2005, The Producers: The Movie Musical 2005, Deck the Halls 2006, Then She Found Me 2007, Bee Movie (voice) 2007, Diminished Capacity 2008, Finding Amanda 2008, Wonderful World 2009, Margaret 2011, Tower Heist 2011. *Television includes:* Master Harold . . . and the Boys, Cinderella, Jazz 2001, The Music Man 2003, Beach Lane (film) 2010, Louie (series) 2010. *Address:* c/o CAA, 9830 Wilshire Boulevard, Beverly Hills, CA 90212, USA.

BRODEUR, Yves; Canadian diplomatist; *Permanent Representative, North Atlantic Treaty Organization;* ed Université Laval, Québec; completed studies in Architecture at Université Laval, Québec and worked as architect; joined Dept of External Affairs and Int. Trade 1982, served in Media Relations Office, Ottawa 1982–83, Second Sec. and Vice-Consul, Embassy in Ankara 1983–85, Analyst, Political and Strategic Analysis Secr., Ottawa 1985–87, Analyst in South, SE Asia Relations Div. 1987, Chief of Staff to the Deputy Minister of Foreign Affairs

1988–89, First Sec., OECD, Paris 1989–93, Policy Advisor, Foreign Affairs and Defence, Privy Council Office 1993–95, Departmental Spokesperson and Press Secretary to the Minister of Foreign Affairs 1995–96, Counsellor (Political) and Head of Political Affairs Section, Perm. Mission of Canada to EU Brussels 1996–2000, Dir of Communications and Spokesperson, NATO 2001–03, Amb. to Turkey (also accred to Azerbaijan and Georgia) 2005–07, Dir Media Relations Office and Director General of the Communications Bureau 2003–05, Asst Deputy Minister for the Afghanistan Task Force 2007–09, Asst Deputy Minister of Int. Security Br. and Political Dir 2009–11, Amb. and Perm. Rep. to NATO, Brussels 2011–. *Address:* Joint Delegation of Canada to NATO, Blvd Léopold III, 1110 Brussels, Belgium (office). *Telephone:* (2) 707-71-10 (office).

BRODHEAD, Richard H., PhD; American university administrator and writer; *President, Duke University;* b. Dayton, Ohio; m. Cynthia Brodhead; one s.; ed Yale Univ.; mem. Faculty, Yale Univ. 1972–2004, later A. Bartlett Giamatti Prof. of English and American Studies –2004, served as Chair. Dept of English for six years, Dean of Yale Coll. 1993–2004; Prof. of English and Pres. Duke Univ. 2004–; spent eight summers teaching high school teachers at Bread Loaf School, Middlebury, Vt; has lectured widely in univs at home and in Europe and Asia; mem. Business-Higher Educ. Forum; Trustee Carnegie Corpn of New York; fmr Pres. J. William Fulbright Foreign Scholarship Bd; mem. American Acad. of Arts and Sciences; DeVane Medal for Outstanding Teaching, Yale Univ. *Publications:* The Good of This Place: Values and Challenges in College Education; has written or ed more than a dozen books on Nathaniel Hawthorne, Herman Melville, Charles W. Chestnutt, William Faulkner, Harriet Beecher Stowe, Louisa May Alcott, Richard Wright and Eudora Welty, among others. *Address:* Office of the President, Duke University, 207 Allen Building, Box 90001, Durham, NC 27708-0001, USA (office). *Telephone:* 919) 684-2424 (office). *Fax:* (919) 684-3050 (office). *E-mail:* president@duke.edu (office). *Website:* about.duke.edu/leadership/brodhead (office).

BRODIE, H(arlow) Keith H(ammond), MD, FRSM; American psychiatrist and academic; *James B. Duke Professor of Psychiatry and Professor of Law and President Emeritus, Duke University;* b. 24 Aug. 1939, Stamford, Conn.; s. of Lawrence Sheldon and Elizabeth Hammond Brodie; m. Brenda Ann Barrowclough 1967; three s. one d.; ed Princeton Univ. and Columbia Univ. Coll. of Physicians and Surgeons; Internship, Ochsner Foundation Hosp., New Orleans 1965–66; Asst Resident in Psychiatry, Columbia-Presbyterian Medical Center, New York 1966–68; Clinical Assoc., Sec. on Psychiatry, Lab. of Clinical Science, Nat. Inst. of Mental Health 1968–70; Asst Prof., Dept of Psychiatry, Stanford Univ. School of Medicine 1970–74; Program Dir, Gen. Clinical Research Center, Stanford Univ. School of Medicine 1973–74; Prof. and Chair., Dept of Psychiatry, Duke Univ. School of Medicine 1974–82, Chief, Psychiatry Service, Duke Univ. Hosp. 1974–82, Chancellor Duke Univ. 1982–85, Acting Provost 1982–83, Pres. 1985–93, Pres. Emer. 1993–; James B. Duke Prof. of Psychiatry and Behavioral Sciences 1981–, Prof., Dept of Psychology, Prof. Law 1980–; Chair. Cttee on Substance Abuse and Mental Health Issues in AIDS Research 1992–95; mem. Coll. of Physicians and Surgeons of Columbia Univ. Asscn of Alumni Gold Medal 1985, Carnegie Council on Adolescent Devt 1986–97, Nat. Review and Advisory Panel for Improving Campus Race Relations, Ford Foundation 1990–94; Hon. LLD (Richmond) 1987; Strecker Award, Inst. of Pennsylvania Hosp. 1980, Distinguished Alumnus Award, Ochsner Foundation Hosp. 1984, Distinguished Medical Alumni Award, Columbia Univ. 1985, NC Award for Science 1990, William C. Menninger Memorial Award 1994. *Publications:* The Importance of Mental Health Services to General Health Care 1979, co-author Modern Clinical Psychiatry 1982, co-ed. American Handbook of Psychiatry (Vol. 6 1975, Vol. 7 1981, Vol. 8 1986), Co-Critical Problems in Psychiatry 1982, Signs and Symptoms in Psychiatry 1983, Aids and Behavior: An Integrated Approach 1994, Keeping an Open Door: Passages in a University Presidency 1996, The Research University Presidency in the Late Twentieth Century (co-author) 2005; also numerous articles. *Leisure interests:* tennis, reading, hiking. *Address:* 3211 Shannon Road, Suite 603, Durham, NC 27707 (office); 63 Beverly Drive, Durham, NC 27707, USA (home). *Telephone:* (919) 403-8070 (office). *Fax:* (919) 493-3628 (office). *E-mail:* brodie@duke.edu (office). *Website:* medspace.mc.duke.edu/h-keith-h-brodie (office).

BRODY, Adrien; American actor; b. 14 April 1973, Queens, New York; s. of Elliot Brody and Sylvia Plachy; ed American Acad. of Dramatic Arts, High School for the Performing Arts; first worked in off-Broadway productions; television debut in PBS movie Home at Last 1988; other TV appearances include Home at Last 1988, Annie McGuire (series) 1988. *Films include:* New York Stories 1989, King of the Hill 1993, Jailbreakers 1994, Angels in the Outfield 1994, Solo 1996, Bullet 1996, The Undertaker's Wedding 1997, The Last Time I Committed Suicide 1997, The Thin Red Line 1998, Sweet Jersey 1998, Ten Benny 1998, Summer of Sam 1999, Six Ways to Sunday 1999, Oxygen 1999, Liberty Heights 1999, Restaurant 2000, Harrison's Flowers 2000, Bread and Roses 2001, Love the Hard Way 2001, The Affair of the Necklace 2001, Dummy 2002, The Pianist (Acad. Award for Best Actor 2003) 2002, Harrison's Flowers 2002, The Singing Detective 2003, The Village 2004, The Jacket 2005, King Kong 2005, Hollywoodland 2006, The Tehuacan Project 2007, The Darjeeling Limited 2007, Giallo (also producer) 2009, Fantastic Mr Fox (voice) 2009, Predators 2010, Wrecked (also exec. producer) 2011, Detachment 2011, Third Person 2013, The Grand Budapest Hotel 2014. *Address:* c/o Jeff Kwatinetz, The Firm, 9465 Wilshire Blvd., 6th Floor, Beverly Hills, CA 90212; c/o Creative Artists Agency, 2000 Avenue of the Stars, Los Angeles, CA 90067, USA. *Telephone:* (310) 860-8000 (The Firm). *Fax:* (310) 860-8100 (The Firm).

BRODY, Alexander, BA; Hungarian/American advertising executive and writer; b. (Sándor Bródy), 28 Jan. 1933, Budapest, Hungary; s. of János Brody and Lilly Brody (née Pollatschek); ed Princeton Univ.; with Young & Rubicam Inc. 1953–83; Vice-Pres., Man. Young & Rubicam Inc., Frankfurt, Germany 1965–67; Sr Vice-Pres., Head, European Operations, Young & Rubicam Inc. 1967–70; Int. Pres. Young & Rubicam Inc., Brussels and New York 1970–82; Pres. and CEO DYR Worldwide, New York 1984–87; Pres. Int. Ogilvy & Mather Worldwide 1987–93; returned to Hungary to concentrate on writing 1993; organizer of the Sandor Brody Literary Award for journalists in honour of his grandfather 1995–; Order of Merit of the Hungarian Repub. 2004, Order of Merit of the Hungarian Repub., Civil Div. 2005. *Publications;* Gondok és gondolatok (Thoughts and Concerns) 1998, Húszezeregy éjszaka – Almok és mesék a valóságról (Twenty Thousand and

One Nights – Dreams and Tales of Reality) 2001, Alibi hat hónapra 1. Evés-ivás (Alibi for Six Months 1. Eating-drinking) 2001, Alibi hat hónapra 2. Kert (Alibi for Six Months 2. Garden) 2002, Alibi hat hónapra 3. (Alibi for Six Months 3. Horses) 2002, Késóbb, mint soha. . . 2002, Alibi hat hónapra 4. Fürdő (Alibi for Six Months 4. Bath) 2003, Alibi hat hónapra 5. Urak – Dámák (Alibi for Six Months 5. Men – Queens) 2003, Alibi hat hónapra 1–4 (alibi for Six Months 1–4) 2003, Alibi hat hónapra 6. (Alibi for Six Months 6. Luck) 2004, Hunyady Margit (Margaret Hunyady) 2006, Hét évtized íze (Seven Decades of Flavours) 2008.

BRODY, Jane Ellen, MS; American journalist and author; *Personal Health Columnist, New York Times;* b. 19 May 1941, Brooklyn, New York; d. of Sidney Brody and Lillian Kellner; m. Richard Engquist 1966; twin s.; ed New York State Coll. of Agric., Cornell Univ., Univ. of Wisconsin; reporter, Minneapolis Tribune 1963–65; science writer, personal health columnist, New York Times 1965–; mem. Advisory Council, New York State Coll. of Agric. 1971–77; Dr hc (Princeton Univ., Hamline Univ., Univ. of Minnesota School of Public Health, State Univ. of New York School of Public Health); Howard Blakeslee Award, American Heart Asscn 1971, Science Writers' Award, ADA 1978, J.C. Penney Univ. of Missouri Journalism Award 1978, Lifeline Award, American Health Foundation 1978. *Publications:* Secrets of Good Health (with R. Engquist) 1970, You Can Fight Cancer and Win (with A. Holleb) 1977, Jane Brody's Nutrition Book 1981, Jane Brody's New York Times Guide to Personal Health 1982, Jane Brody's Good Food Book 1985, Jane Brody's Good Food Gourmet 1990, Jane Brody's Good Seafood Book (with Richard Flaste) 1994, Jane Brody's Cold and Flu Fighter 1995, Jane Brody's Allergy Fighter 1997, The New York Times Book of Health 1997, The New York Times Book of Women's Health 2000, The New York Times Book of Alternative Medicine 2001, Jane Brody's Guide to the Great Beyond 2009. *Address:* New York Times, 620 Eighth Avenue, New York, NY 10018, USA (office). *E-mail:* engquist@nytimes.com (office). *Website:* www.nytimes.com (office); janebrody.net (home).

BRODY, William R., BS, MS, PhD, MD; American physician, biomedical engineer, research institute director and fmr university administrator; *President, Salk Institute for Biological Studies;* b. 4 Jan. 1944, Stockton, Calif.; m. Wendy Brody; two c.; ed Massachusetts Inst. of Tech. and Stanford Univ., Univ. of California, San Francisco; Fellow, Dept of Cardiovascular Surgery, Stanford Univ. School of Medicine 1970–71, Intern, Dept of Surgery 1971–72, Resident, Dept of Cardiovascular Surgery 1972–73; Clinical Assoc., Surgery Br., Nat. Heart, Lung, and Blood Inst., Bethesda, Md 1973–75; Resident, Dept of Radiology, Univ. of California, San Francisco 1975–77; Assoc. Prof. of Radiology and, by courtesy, Electrical Eng, Stanford Univ. School of Medicine 1977–82, Dir of Research Labs, Div. of Diagnostic Radiology 1977–84, Dir Advanced Imaging Techniques Lab., Dept of Radiology 1978–84, Prof. of Radiology and, by courtesy, Electrical Eng 1982–86, on unpaid leave of absence 1984–86; Martin Donner Prof. and Dir Dept of Radiology, The Johns Hopkins Univ. School of Medicine 1987–94, Prof. of Biomedical Eng 1987–94, Prof. of Electrical and Computer Eng 1987–94, Radiologist-in-Chief, The Johns Hopkins Hosp. 1987–94, Pres. The Johns Hopkins Univ. 1996–2008; Prof. of Radiology, Univ. of Minnesota 1994–96, Provost, Academic Health Center 1994–96; Pres. The Salk Inst., La Jolla, Calif. 2009–; Founder and Consultant, Resonex, Inc. 1983–84, Pres. 1984–86, Pres. and CEO 1986–87, Chair. 1987–89; mem. Bd of Dirs Mercantile Bankshares Corpn 1997–, Medtronic Inc. 1998–, AEGON USA 2000–; mem. Selection Cttee Goldseker Foundation 1996–, Int. Academic Advisory Cttee, Singapore 1997–, Governing Cttee Whitaker Foundation 1997–, Exec. Cttee Council on Competitiveness 1998–, Bd Dirs The Commonwealth Fund 2000–, CareFirst Inc. 2004–, FBI's Nat. Security Higher Educ. Advisory Bd 2005–; mem. Pres.'s Foreign Intelligence Advisory Bd 2003–05; fmr mem. Bd Minnesota Orchestra Asscn, Corpn of Massachusetts Inst. of Tech.; mem. Nat. Acad. of Eng, Inst. of Medicine, NAS, AAAS; Fellow, IEEE, American Coll. of Radiology, American Coll. of Cardiology, American Heart Asscn, Int. Soc. of Magnetic Resonance in Medicine, American Inst. of Biomedical Eng, American Acad. of Arts and Sciences; Founding Fellow, American Inst. of Medical and Biological Eng; Trustee Baltimore Museum of Art 1997–, Baltimore Community Foundation 2004–; Hon. mem. Canadian Asscn of Radiologists; Prize Manuscript Award, Western Thoracic Surgical Soc. 1974, Established Investigator Award, American Heart Asscn 1980–84, Outstanding Alumnus Award, Univ. of California, San Francisco 1994. *Publications:* Digital Radiography: Proceedings of the Stanford Conference on Digital Radiography. Society for Photooptical Instrumentation Engineers (SPIE). Proceedings Vol. 315 (ed.) 1981, Digital Radiography 1984, Computer Applications to Assist Radiology. Proceedings of the 11th S/CAR Symposium (co-ed.) 1992; more than 120 publs and one patent (US Patent No. 4,445,226, 1984) in the field of medical imaging; bimonthly columns for Diagnostic Imaging 1990–94. *Address:* Salk Institute for Biological Studies, P.O. Box 85800, San Diego, CA 92186-5800, USA (office). *Telephone:* (858) 453-4100 (office). *Fax:* (858) 453-8534 (office). *E-mail:* communications@salk.edu (office). *Website:* www.salk.edu (office).

BROECKER, Wallace (Wally) Smith, BA, MA, PhD; American geophysicist and academic; *Newberry Professor, Department of Earth and Environmental Sciences and Scientist, Lamont-Doherty Earth Observatory, Columbia University;* b. 1931; ed Wheaton Coll.; transferred to Columbia Univ., worked at Lamont Geological Observatory, currently Newberry Prof., Dept of Earth and Environmental Sciences and Scientist, Lamont-Doherty Earth Observatory; mem. American Acad. of Arts and Sciences, NAS; Fellow, American Geophysical Union, European Geophysical Union; Crafoord Prize in Geosciences, Royal Swedish Acad. of Sciences 2006, Nat. Medal of Science, Maurice W. Ewing Medal, American Geophysical Union, NAS Alexander Agassiz Medal, Urey Medal, European Asscn for Geochemistry, V. M. Goldschmidt Award, Geochemical Soc., Vetlesen Prize, G. Unger Vetlesen Foundation, Wollaston Medal, Geological Soc. of London, Roger Revelle Medal, American Geophysical Union, Tyler Prize for Environmental Achievement, Univ. of Southern California, Blue Planet Prize, The Asahi Glass Foundation, Benjamin Franklin Medal in Earth and Environmental Science, The Franklin Inst. 2008, Balzan Prize 2008. *Achievements include:* best known for discovery of role played by ocean in triggering abrupt climate changes that punctuated glacial time, in particular, development and popularization of idea of global 'conveyor belt' linking circulation of global ocean; inadvertently coined phrase 'global warming' when he published paper entitled: Climate Change: Are We on the Brink of a Pronounced Global Warming? 1975. *Publications:* Chemical Equilibria in the Earth (co-author) 1971, Chemical Oceanography 1974, Tracers in the Sea 1982, How to Build a Habitable Planet 1988, Greenhouse Puzzles 1993, The Glacial World According to Wally 1995, Greenhouse Puzzles: Keeling's World, Martin's World, Walker's World 1998, Fixing Climate: What Past Climate Changes Reveal About the Current Threat – And How to Counter It (co-author) 2008; more than 400 scientific papers in professional journals on Pleistocene geochronology, radiocarbon dating and chemical oceanography, including oceanic mixing based on stable and radioisotope distribution. *Address:* Lamont-Doherty Earth Observatory, Columbia University, PO Box 1000, 301 Comer 61, Route 9W, Palisades, NY 10964-8000, USA (office). *Telephone:* (845) 365-8413 (office). *E-mail:* broecker@ldeo.columbia.edu (office). *Website:* www.ldeo.columbia.edu (office).

BROERS, Baron (Life Peer), cr. 2004, of Cambridge in the County of Cambridgeshire; **Alec Nigel Broers,** ScD, FRS, FREng; British electrical engineer and academic; b. 17 Sept. 1938, Calcutta, India; s. of Alec W. Broers and of Constance A. Broers (née Cox); m. Mary T. Phelan 1964; two s.; ed Geelong Grammar School, Melbourne Univ. and Gonville & Caius Coll. Cambridge; mem. research staff and man. of photon and electron optics groups, IBM Thomas Watson Research Center 1965–80; Man., Semiconductor Lithography and Process Devt and Advanced Devt, IBM East Fishkill Lab. 1981–84; mem. Corp. Tech. Cttee, IBM Corp. HQ 1984; Prof. of Electrical Eng, Univ. of Cambridge 1984–96, Prof. Emer. 1996–, Head, Electrical Div. 1984–92, of Dept of Eng 1992–96; Dir (non-exec.) Vodafone Group 1998–2000, Vodafone PLC 2000–, Lucas Industries Group 1995–96, R.J. Mears 2003–; Adviser, Warburg Pincus 2003–; Chair. House of Lords Select Cttee on Science and Tech. 2004–; Fellow, Trinity Coll., Cambridge 1984–90; Master, Churchill Coll., Cambridge 1990–96, Fellow 1996–; Vice-Chancellor, Univ. of Cambridge 1996–2003; Pres. Royal Acad. of Eng 2001–06; Foreign Assoc. Nat. Acad. of Eng (USA); IBM Fellow 1977; Hon. Fellow, Gonville and Caius Coll. Cambridge 1996–, Trinity Coll. Cambridge 1999–, Univ. of Wales, Cardiff 2001–, St Edmund's Coll. Cambridge 2004–, Imperial Coll. London 2004–; Hon. DEng (Glasgow) 1996; Hon. DSc (Warwick) 1997; Hon. LLD (Melbourne) 2000; Hon. DUniv (Anglia Polytechnic) 2000; Dr hc (Greenwich) 2000, (UMIST) 2002, (Peking) 2002; Prize for Industrial Applications of Physics, American Inst. of Physics 1982, Cledo Brunetti Award, Inst. of Electrical and Electronic Engineers 1985. *Publications:* patents, papers and book chapters on electron microscopy, electron beam lithography and integrated circuit fabrication. *Leisure interests:* music, sailing, skiing.

BROGGINI, Andrea, Dr iur, LLM; Swiss business executive; *Chairman, Federation of Migros Cooperatives;* mem. Bd of Dirs Migros-Genossenschafts-Bund (Fed. of Migros Co-operatives) 2004–, Chair. 2012–; Dir, Generali Schweiz Holding AG, Fondiaria-SAI SpA, Banca Euromobiliare (Suisse) SpA, Florenz, March Ltd, Hamilton & Knorr-Bremse SfS GmbH, Munich; Ind. Dir Fastweb SpA 2008–. *Address:* Federation of Migros Cooperatives, Limmatstrasse 152, 8031 Zurich, Switzerland (office). *Telephone:* (44) 277-21-11 (office). *Fax:* (44) 277-25-25 (office). *E-mail:* media@migros.ch (office). *Website:* www.migros.ch (office).

BROKAW, Thomas (Tom) John, BA; American broadcast journalist and writer; b. 6 Feb. 1940, Webster, S Dakota; s. of Anthony O. Brokaw and Eugenia Conley; m. Meredith Lynn Auld 1962; three d.; ed Univ. of South Dakota; morning news KMTV, Omaha 1962–65; news ed., anchorman, WSB-TV, Atlanta 1965–66; reporter, corresp., anchorman KNBC-TV, Los Angeles 1966–73; White House corresp. NBC, Washington, DC 1973–76; anchorman, Saturday Night News, New York 1973–76; host, Today Show, New York 1976–82; anchor and Man. Ed., NBC Nightly News 1982–2004 (retd), Special Corresp. NBC News 2005–; mem. Bd of Dirs Council on Foreign Relations, Cttee to Protect Journalists, Int. Rescue Cttee; mem. advisory cttee Reporters Cttee for Freedom of Press, Gannett Journalism Center, Columbia Univ.; Trustee, Norton Simon Museum of Art, Pasadena, Calif.; mem. American Acad. of Arts and Sciences; Dr hc (Univ. of South Dakota), (Washington Univ., St. Louis), (Syracuse Univ.), (Hofstra Univ.), (Boston Coll.), (Emerson Coll.), (Simpson Coll.), (Duke Univ.) 1991, (Notre Dame Univ.) 1993; Hon. DHL (Dartmouth Coll.) 2005; two Dupont Awards, Peabody Award, Alfred I. duPont-Columbia Univ. Award for Excellence in Broadcast Journalism 1997, ten Emmy Awards including Emmy for Outstanding Interview 2003, Records of Achievement Award, Foundation for the Nat. Archives 2005, George Catlett Marshall Medal, Asscn of the US Army 2005, Edward R. Murrow Award for Lifetime Achievement in Broadcasting, Wash. State Univ. 2006, Sylvanus Thayer Award, US Military Acad. at West Point 2006, Walter Cronkite Award for Journalism Excellence, Ariz. State Univ. 2006; elected to TV Hall of Fame 1997. *Publications:* The Greatest Generation 1998, The Greatest Generation Speaks 1999, An Album of Memories 2001, A Long Way from Home 2002, Boom! Voices of the Sixties 2007, The Time of Our Lives: A Conversation about America 2011. *Address:* c/o Board of Directors, Council on Foreign Relations, The Harold Pratt House, 58 East 68th Street, New York, NY 10021, USA (office).

BROLIN, Josh; American actor; b. 12 Feb. 1968, Santa Monica, Calif.; s. of James Brolin and Jane Cameron Agee; m. 1st Alice Adair, two c.; m. 2nd Diane Lane. *Films include:* The Goonies 1985, Thrashin' 1986, Bed of Roses 1996, Flirting with Disaster 1996, Nightwatch 1997, Best Laid Plans 1999, Hollow Man 2000, Slow Burn 2000, Melinda and Melinda 2004, Into the Blue 2005, The Dead Girl 2006, Grindhouse - Planet Terror 2007, In the Valley of Elah 2007, No Country for Old Men 2007, American Gangster 2007, W. 2008, Milk 2008, Wall Street: Money Never Sleeps 2010, True Grit 2010, Men in Black III 2012, Gangster Squad 2012. *Television includes:* Picnic 2000, Mister Sterling 2003, Into the West 2005. *Address:* WME, 9601 Wilshire Blvd, Beverly Hills, CA 90210, USA (office).

BROMBERG, Serge; French film collector, director and producer; *Founder, Lobster Films;* b. 26 April 1961, Saint-Maur-des-Fossés (Val-de-Marne); ed École Supérieure de Commerce, Paris; Founder Lobster Films 1985; Founder Steamboat Films 2006; Artistic Dir Annecy Festival 1999–; Dir silent film DVD collection of Arte 2000–; mem. and Admin. Asscn française de lutte contre les myopathies, Institut de Myologie; Admin. Cinémathèque française 1999–2007, École de la Poudrière 2000–, Fondation GAN pour le cinéma 2004–; Officier, Ordre des Arts et des Lettres 2010; Prix Jean Mitry. *Films directed:* Inferno (documentary) (also writer and producer) 2009, Le voyage extraordinaire (documentary) (also writer) 2011. *Films produced:* The Lost World (producer of alternative version) 2000, Jean Vigo: Le son retrouvé (video documentary short) 2001, 8 mai 1945, la capitulation (documentary) 2005, Coster Bill of Paris (producer of alternative version) 2005,

The Hunchback of Notre Dame (producer of alternative version) 2006, Poil de carotte (restoration producer of alternate version) 2007, The Flying House (short) (assoc. producer) 2011. *Television includes:* La mafia à Hollywood (documentary) (producer) 2002, Discovering Cinema: Learning to Talk (documentary) (writer and producer) 2003, Discovering Cinema: Movies Dream in Color (documentary) (writer and producer) 2004, Arletty, Lady Paname (documentary) (producer) 2007; director: Chaplin Today: City Lights (documentary short) 2003. *Address:* Lobster Films, 13 rue Lacharrière, 75011 Paris, France (office). *Telephone:* 1-43-38-69-69 (office). *Fax:* 1-43-57-26-05 (office). *E-mail:* lobster@lobsterfilms.com (office). *Website:* www.lobsterfilms.com (office).

BRON, Eleanor, BA; British actress and author; b. 14 March 1938, Stanmore; d. of Sydney Bron and Fagah Bron; ed North London Collegiate School and Newnham Coll. Cambridge; started at Establishment Night Club, toured USA 1961; TV satire, Not So Much a Programme, More a Way of Life 1964–65; co-wrote and appeared in TV series Where Was Spring? 1969, Beyond a Joke 1972, After That This 1975; Dir Actors' Centre 1982–93, Soho Theatre Co. 1993–2000. *Stage appearances include:* Private Lives, Hedda Gabler, Antony and Cleopatra, Madwoman of Chaillot, Hamlet; appeared at Royal Exchange in Uncle Vanya, Heartbreak House, Oedipus, The Prime of Miss Jean Brodie, Present Laughter; appeared at Nat. Theatre in The Duchess of Malfi, The Cherry Orchard, The Real Inspector Hound, The Miser, The White Devil, Desdemona – If You Had Only Spoken! (one-woman show), Dona Rosita The Spinster, A Delicate Balance, Be My Baby, Making Noise Quietly, Twopence to Cross the Mersey 2005, The Clean House 2006, In Extremis 2007, All About My Mother 2007, The Late Middle Classes 2010. *Television appearances include:* BBC TV Play for Today: Nina 1978, Rumpole of the Bailey 1979, Dr Who 1979, 1985, A Month in the Country 1985, French & Saunders 1990, The Hour of the Lynx 1991, Absolutely Fabulous 1992, 1994, 2003, The Blue Boy 1994, Vanity Fair 1998, Ted and Alice 2002, Fat Friends 2000–05, Casualty 1909 2009, Foyle's War 2010, Midsomer Murders 2012. *Films:* Help!, Alfie, Two for the Road, Bedazzled, Women in Love, The National Health, Turtle Diary, Little Dorritt, The Attic, Deadly Advice 1994, Black Beauty 1993, A Little Princess 1994, The House of Mirth 2000, Iris 2001, The Heart of Me 2002, Love's Brother 2003, Wimbledon 2004, StreetDance 2010, Hyde Park on Hudson 2012. *Concert appearances (as narrator) include:* Façade, Carnival des Animaux, Peter and the Wolf, Bernstein's Symphony No. 3 with BBC Symphony Orchestra; with Counterpoise: works by Edward Rushton, David Matthews. *Publications include:* Song Cycle (with John Dankworth) 1973; verses for Saint-Saëns Carnival of the Animals 1975; Is Your Marriage Really Necessary? (with John Fortune) 1972, Life and Other Punctures 1978, The Pillow Book of Eleanor Bron 1985, Desdemona – If You Had Only Spoken! (trans. of original by Christine Brückner) 1992, Double Take (novel) 1996, Cedric Price Retriever (co-ed.) 2005. *Address:* c/o Rebecca Blond, 69A King's Road, London, SW3 4NX, England. *Telephone:* (20) 7351-4100. *Fax:* (20) 7351-4600.

BRON, Zakhar; Russian violinist and academic; *Professor of Violin, Hochschule für Musik Köln;* b. 1947, Uralsk; ed Stoliarski School of Music, Odessa, Gnessin Conservatoire, Moscow, Tchaikovsky Conservatoire; studied with Boris Goldstein and Igor Oistrakh; has taught at Musikhochschule, Lübeck, Glinka Conservatoire, Novosibirsk, RAM, London, Rotterdam Conservatoire, Reina Sofia School, Madrid; currently Prof. of Violin, Hochschule für Musik, Cologne; lectures and gives masterclasses in many countries; has performed with many maj. int. orchestras; prizewinner Wieniawski Int. Violin Competition, Poznań, Queen Elizabeth Competition, Brussels; Verdienstkreutz am Bande (Germany). *Address:* Hochschule für Musik Köln, Dagobertstr. 38, 50668 Cologne, Germany. *Telephone:* (221) 9128180. *Fax:* (221) 131204. *E-mail:* zakharbron@web.de (home). *Website:* www.zakharbron.com (home).

BRONFMAN, Charles Rosner, PC, CC; Canadian/American business executive; b. 27 June 1931, Montreal, Québec; s. of the late Samuel Bronfman and Saidye Bronfman (née Rosner); m. 1st Barbara Baerwald; s. one d.; m. 2nd Andrea Morrison 1982 (died 2006); m. 3rd Bonita Rocheone 2008 (divorced 2012); m. 4th Rita Mayo 2012; ed Selwyn House School, Trinity Coll., McGill Univ.; joined The Seagram Co. Ltd 1951, Pres. and Co.-Chair. 1986–2000 9 co. sold to Vivendi); Chair., prin. owner Montreal Expos 1968–90; fmr Chair. Koor Industries Ltd; Chair. The Jerusalem Report, Andrea and Charles Bronfman Philanthropies, Claridge Israel LLC, The CRB Foundation, United Jewish Communities; mem. Int. Advisory Corpn of Canada; Hon. Pres. United Israel Appeal of Canada; mem. of Bd Washington Inst. for Near E Policy, The Kravis Center for Performing Arts, Fla; Co-founder and Co-Chair. Birthright Israel; Chair. (non-exec.) The Nat. Jewish Center for Learning and Leadership; Hon. DPhil (Hebrew Univ. of Jerusalem), Hon. DL (McGill Univ., Montreal), (Concordia Univ., Montreal), (Univ. of Waterloo), (Univ. of Toronto), Hon. DHumLitt (Branders). *Leisure interests:* tennis, golf. *Website:* www.acbp.net.

BRONFMAN, Edgar Miles, Jr; American business executive; b. 16 May 1955, Montreal; s. of the late Edgar Miles Bronfman; m. 1st Sherri Brewer 1979 (divorced 1991); three c.; m. 2nd Clarissa Alcock 1994; three c.; began career working in British and US film industries as producer; joined family firm Seagram as Asst to Pres. 1982, Man. Dir Seagram Europe in London 1982–84, Pres. House of Seagram 1984–88, Exec. Vice-Pres. US Operations 1988–89; Pres. and COO J.E. Seagram Corpn New York 1989–94; Pres. and CEO Seagram Co. Ltd 1994–2000 (after merger with Vivendi to form Vivendi Universal), Vice-Chair. Bd of Dirs Vivendi Universal 2000–03; attempted to buy back Seagram assets in 2003 but failed; Chair. and CEO Lexa Pnrs LLC, then with Thomas H. Lee Pnrs acquired Warner Music Group, Chair. and CEO 2004–11, Chair. 2011–12; fmr Acting Pres. MCA Inc.; mem. Bd of Dirs French & Associates 2001–; Chair. Bd of Dirs Endeavor (non-profit); Gen. Pnr, Accretive Tech. Pnrs LLC (venture capital firm); Chair. Governing Bd, World Jewish Congress 2007–; *Website:* www.endeavor.org.

BRONIAREK, Zygmunt; Polish journalist and broadcaster (retd); b. 27 Aug. 1925, Warsaw; s. of Wacław Broniarek and Marianna Broniarek; m. Elzbieta Sarcewicz 1972; ed Warsaw School of Econs; radiotelegraphic operator and stenographer, Czytelnik publrs, Warsaw 1945–48; Corresp. Trybuna Ludu 1950–90, Perm. Corresp. in USA 1985; in USA 1955, 1958, 1974, Latin America 1956, Paris 1959–60, 1969–73, Washington 1960–67, East Africa 1975, West Africa 1976, Nordic countries 1977–82; mem. Polish United Workers' Party (PZPR) 1956–90; Corresp. Polish Radio and TV, for Finland and Sweden; Chair. Polish

Assc n of Int. Journalists and Writers 1974–77; mem. Bd of Foreign Press Asscn, Stockholm 1979–81; mem. Presidium of Journalists' Asscn, Polish People's Repub. 1983–85; Vice-Pres. Polish Club of Int. Journalism 1984–85, 1991–; Corresp., Trybuna Ludu, LA Olympic Games 1984; Special Corresp. in Australia 1984; Corresp., Trybuna Ludu, USA 1985–90; presenter The Guests of Mr. Broniarek (TV), The Inner History of the Great Policy (TV) 1983, Behind the Scenes of Int. Politics (TV) 1983–85; retd 1990; columnist, Trybuna 1996–, Rynki Zagraniczne 1998–, Swiat Elit 2005–, Biznes Trendy 2006–, Europerspektywy 2009–, Miesięcznk 2009–, Mieszkaniec 2009–, Głoswetarana 2009–; Gold Cross of Merit, Order of Banner of Labour (Second Class) 1984, Commdr's Cross with Star of Infante Dom Henrique the Navigator (Portugal), Commdr's Cross with Star of Polonia Restituta 2002, Gold Medal of Merit for Defence of Poland 2010, Golden Figurine and Diploma of Merit for Hard Work approved by Pres. 2011; Int. Journalists Club of Polish Journalistic Asscn Prize 1978, Golden Screen Award of Weekly Ekran 1984, Victor Prize (TV) 1985, Polish Club of Int. Journalism (First Prize) 1990, Bolesław Prus Award, First Class (SD PRL) 1984, Hon. Silver Ace of Polish Promotion Corpn 1995, City of Warsaw Award of Merit 2000, Gold Medal, Polish Acad. of Success 2000, Leader of Polish Journalism 2005. *Publications:* Od Hustonu do Mississipi 1956, Gorące dni Manhattanu 1961, Walka o Pałac Elizejski 1974, Kto się boi rewolucji (co-author) 1975, Angola zrodzona w walce 1977, Od Kissingera do Brzezińskiego 1980, Szaleństwo zbrojeń (co-author) 1982, Źródła spirali zbrojeń (co-author) 1985, Szczeble do Białego Domu 1986, Tajemnice Nagrody Nobla 1987, Ronald Reagan w Białym Domu 1989, Jak nauczyłem się ośmiu języków 1991, Biały Dom i Jego Prezydenci 1992, Wesoła spowiedź 1993, Książę Karol w Polsce 1994, Sekrety korespondenta zagranicznego 1995, Okiem światowca 1999, Kronika towarzyska Warszawy 2002, 365 dni z angielskim 2002, Kulisy polityki 2003, Papiez Pius X, syn Polaka a Pasja Mela Gibsona 2004, Broniarek o sobie, inni o Broniarku 2005, TVN Series Kulisy Slawy (Hall of Fame) 2008, Książę Karol Praprawnukpolki 2010. *Leisure interests:* good company, good food. *Address:* ul. Gałczyńskiego 12 m. 9, 00-362 Warsaw, Poland (office). *Telephone:* (22) 8263304 (office). *Fax:* (22) 8276202 (home).

BRONSTEIN, Alexander Semenovich, DrMed; Russian therapist (internist); *Director-General, Centre for Endosurgery and Lithotripsy;* b. 19 Sept. 1938, Khmelnitsky, Ukrainian SSR, USSR; s. of Semen Bronstein and Rebecca Yangarber; m. Inna Vladimirovna Kunina 1939; two d.; ed Moscow Sechenov Inst. of Medicine; gen. practitioner of polyclinic, therapist, Moscow hosp.; Intern, Jr, then Sr Researcher, Inst. of Proctology 1964–76; Head, Div. of Gastroenter-ology, Moscow clinic 1976–90; Pres., Dir-Gen. Centre for Endosurgery and Lithotripsy 1993–; Prof., Moscow Sechenov Acad. of Medicine; mem. Editorial Bd, International Medical Journal; Academician, Russian Acad. of Nat. Sciences; Order of St Constantine the Great; Merited Dr of Russian Fed. *Publications:* Clinical Medicine (two vols) and more than 150 scientific works. *Leisure interests:* classical music, tennis, singing. *Address:* Centre for Endosurgery and Lythotripsy, Entusiastov shosse 62, 111125 Moscow (office); Petrovsko-Razumovskaya Allea 20, Apt 18, Moscow, Russia (home). *Telephone:* (495) 305-15-83 (office). *Fax:* (495) 305-22-09 (office). *E-mail:* bronshtein@celt.ru (office). *Website:* www.celt.ru (office).

BROOK, Adrian G., PhD; Canadian chemist and academic; *University Professor Emeritus, Department of Chemistry, University of Toronto;* b. 21 May 1924, Toronto, Ont.; s. of Frank A. Brook and Beatrice M. Wellington; m. Margaret E. Dunn 1954; two s. one d.; ed Lawrence Park Collegiate and Univ. of Toronto; Lecturer in Chem., Univ. of Toronto 1953–56, Asst Prof. 1956–60, Assoc. Prof. 1960–62, Prof. 1962–89, Acting Chair. Dept of Chem. 1969–71, Chair. 1971–74, Chair. Univ. of Toronto Research Bd 1976–81, Univ. Prof. 1987–89, Univ. Prof. Emer. 1989–; Nuffield Fellow 1950–51; ACS Stanley Kipping Award 1973; CIC Medal, Chem. Inst. of Canada 1986, Killam Prize, Canada Council 1994. *Publications:* more than 140 papers on aspects of organic chem. *Leisure interest:* computers. *Address:* Department of Chemistry, University of Toronto, 80 Saint George Street, Toronto, ON M5S 3H6 (office); 7 Thornwood Road, Apt 202, Toronto, ON M4W 2R8, Canada (home). *Telephone:* (416) 978-3573 (office); (416) 920-8383 (home). *Fax:* (416) 978-8775 (office). *E-mail:* abrook@chem.utoronto.ca (office). *Website:* www.chem.utoronto.ca (office).

BROOK, Peter Stephen Paul, CH, CBE, MA; British theatre director, film director and writer; b. 21 March 1925, Chiswick, London, England; s. of Simon Brook; m. Natasha Parry 1951; one s. one d.; ed Westminster and Gresham's Schools and Magdalen Coll., Oxford; joined RSC 1962; Producer, Co-Dir Royal Shakespeare Theatre; f. Centre for Theatre Research, Paris 1970, opened Théâtre des Bouffes du Nord, Paris 1974–2010, Co-Dir with Stéphane Lissner (q.v.) 1998–2005; Dir Int. Centre for Theatre Creations; Officier des Arts et des Lettres, Légion d'honneur, Praemium Imperiale; Hon. DLitt (Birmingham), (Strathclyde) 1990; Freiherr von Stein Foundation, Shakespeare Award 1973, Wexner Prize (Ohio State Univ.) 1991, Onassis Int. Award 1993, Times Award 1994, Dan David Prize, 2005. *Films include:* The Beggar's Opera 1952, Moderato Cantabile 1959, Lord of the Flies 1963, Marat/Sade 1967, Tell Me Lies 1967, King Lear 1969, Meetings With Remarkable Men 1976–77, La Tragédie de Carmen 1983, The Mahabharata 1989 (also producer), The Tragedy of Hamlet 2002. *Productions include:* Dr Faustus 1943, Pygmalion, King John, Lady from the Sea 1945, Romeo and Juliet (at Stratford) 1947, Dir of Productions at Covent Garden Opera 1949–50, Faust (at Metropolitan Opera, New York) 1953, The Dark is Light Enough (London) 1954, House of Flowers (New York) 1954, Cat on a Hot Tin Roof (Paris) 1956, Eugene Onegin (New York) 1958, View from the Bridge (Paris) 1958, The Fighting Cock (New York) 1959, Irma la Douce 1960, King Lear 1963, The Physicists (New York) 1964, The Marat/Sade (New York) 1965, US (London) 1966, Oedipus (Seneca) 1968, A Midsummer Night's Dream 1970, Orghast (Iran) 1971, The Conference of the Birds 1973, Timon of Athens (Paris) 1974, The Ik (Paris) 1975, (London) 1976, (USA) 1976, Ubu (Paris) 1977, Meetings with Remarkable Men (film, also dir screenplay) 1977, Antony and Cleopatra (Stratford and London) 1978, Measure for Measure (Paris) 1978, Conference of the Birds, L'os (Festival Avignon and Paris) 1979, (New York) 1980, The Cherry Orchard (Paris) 1981, (New York) 1988, (Moscow) 1989, La Tragédie de Carmen (opera) (Paris) 1981, (film) 1983, Le Mahabharata (Avignon and Paris) 1985, (world tour) 1988, Woza Albert! (Paris) 1989, La Tempête (Paris) 1990, Impressions de Pelléas (opera) 1992, L'Homme Qui (Paris) 1993, 1997, The Man Who 1994, Oh! Les Beaux Jours (Lausanne) 1995, (Paris) 1996, Don Giovanni (opera) 1998, Je suis un phénomène (Paris) 1998, Le Costume (Paris) 1999, The Tragedy of Hamlet (Paris) 2000, Far

Away (Paris) 2002, La Tragédie d'Hamlet (Paris) 2002, La Mort de Krishna (Paris) 2002, Ta Main Dans La Mienne (Paris) 2003, Tierno Bokar (Paris) 2004, Le Grand Inquisiteur (Paris) 2004, Fragments (Paris, London, New York) 2008, Warum Warum 2008, Love Is My Sin (Paris), Eleven and Twelve (London) 2009, Une Flûte Enchantée (opera) (world tour) 2010–11, The Suit (Paris and world tour) 2012. *Publications:* The Empty Space 1968, The Shifting Point: Forty years of theatrical exploration 1946–87, 1987, There Are No Secrets 1993 (appeared in USA as The Open Door: Thoughts on Acting and the Theatre), Threads of Time (autobiog.) 1998, Evoking Shakespeare 1999, The Quality of Mercy: Reflections on Shakespeare 2013. *Leisure interests:* painting, playing the piano, air travel. *Address:* CIRT, 37 bis boulevard de la Chapelle, 75010 Paris, France (office).

BROOK, Robert Henry, MD, ScD, FACP; American physician and professor of medicine; *Director, Health Program and Vice-President, RAND Corporation;* b. 3 July 1943, New York; s. of Benjamin N. Brook and Elizabeth Berg; m. 1st Susan Weiss 1966; m. 2nd Jacqueline Kosecoff 1981; one s. three d.; ed Univ. of Arizona, Johns Hopkins Medical School, Johns Hopkins School of Hygiene and Public Health; mil. service, US Public Health Services 1972–74; Dir Health Program, RAND Corpn 1990–, Vice-Pres. 1998–; Prof. of Medicine and Public Health, UCLA Center for Health Sciences 1974–; Dir Robert Wood Johnson Clinical Scholars Program 1974–; mem. Inst. of Medicine, NAS, American Soc. of Clinical Investigation, American Asscn of Physicians; Commendation Medal Richard and Hinda Rosenthal Foundation Award Baxter Health Services Research Prize 1988 Sonneborn Distinguished Lecturer, Univ. of Pa, Distinguished Health Services Researcher, Asscn of Health Services Research Robert J. Glaser Award of Soc. of Gen. Internal Medicine, Johns Hopkins Soc. of Scholars Hollister Univ. Lecturer, Northwestern Univ. Nat. Cttee for Quality Assurance Health Quality Award 2001, Research America 2000 Advocacy Award for Sustained Leadership 2001, Inst. of Medicine Gustav O. Lienhard Medal 2005, American Asscn of Medical Colls David Rogers Award 2007. *Publications:* over 300 articles on quality of medical care. *Leisure interests:* tennis, swimming, golf. *Address:* The RAND Corporation, PO Box 2138, 1776 Main Street, Santa Monica, CA 90401-3297 (office); 1474 Bienvenida Avenue, Pacific Palisades, CA 90272-2346, USA (home). *Telephone:* (310) 393-0411 (office); (310) 454-0766 (home). *Fax:* (310) 451-6917 (office); (310) 454-2797 (home). *E-mail:* brook@rand.org (office). *Website:* www.rand.org (office).

BROOKE, Beth A., BS; American business executive; *Global Vice-Chair, Public Policy, Ernst & Young LLP;* ed Purdue Univ.; served as Tax Services Coordinator, later Nat. Dir Tax Consulting Services and Man. Partner, Nat. Tax Dept; joined Ernst & Young 1981, held several leadership roles, including US Nat. Dir of Tax Advisory Services and Global and Americas Vice-Chair for Public Policy, Sustainability and Stakeholder Engagement, currently Global Vice-Chair, Public Policy, Ernst & Young LLP, mem. Ernst & Young's Americas Exec. Bd; worked in Dept of Treasury; mem. Bd of Dirs TechnoServe Inc., Atlantic Council of United States, March of Dimes Public Policy Advisory Council, Nat. Women's Hall of Fame Advisory Council; Bd mem. The White House Project, Women's Leadership Bd, Harvard Kennedy School, Women's Advisory Bd, World Economic Forum; Fellow, Life Management Inst.; Henry Crown Fellow, Aspen Inst., also mem. Bd of Trustees; Pathways Envoy State Dept; mem. Committee of 200; mem. del. to UN Comm. on Status of Women; mem. Audit Advisory Cttee, Dept of Defence; ranked by Forbes magazine amongst The World's 100 Most Powerful Women (41st) 2006, (70th) 2007, (79th) 2008, (100th) 2011, (99th) 2012, (96th) 2013. *Address:* Ernst & Young, 1101 New York Avenue NW, Suite 601, Washington, DC 20005 (office); Ernst & Young, 5 Times Square, New York, NY 10036-6530 (office). *Telephone:* (202) 293-7500 (Washington, DC) (office); (212) 773-3000 (New York) (office). *Fax:* (202) 465-3149 (Washington, DC) (office); (212) 773-6350 (New York) (office). *Website:* www.ey.com (office).

BROOKE, Christopher Nugent Lawrence, CBE, MA, LittD, FBA, FRHistS, FSA; British historian and academic; *Professor Emeritus, University of Cambridge;* b. 23 June 1927, Cambridge, England; s. of Zachary Nugent Brooke and Rosa Grace Brooke (née Stanton); m. Rosalind Beckford Clark 1951; three s. (one deceased); ed Winchester Coll., Gonville and Caius Coll., Cambridge; Fellow, Gonville and Caius Coll., Cambridge 1949–56, 1977–, Asst Lecturer, Univ. of Cambridge 1953–54, Lecturer 1954–56, Dixie Prof. of Ecclesiastical History 1977–94, Prof. Emer. 1994–; Prof. of Medieval History, Univ. of Liverpool 1956–67; Prof. of History, Westfield Coll., London 1967–77; Pres. Soc. of Antiquaries 1981–84; mem. Royal Comm. on Historical Monuments 1977–83, Reviewing Comm. on Export of Works of Art 1979–82; Corresp. mem. Monumenta Germaniae Historica, Bavarian Acad. of Sciences; Corresp. Fellow, Medieval Acad. of America; Fellow, Società Internazionale di Studi Francescani; Hon. DUniv (York) 1984; Lord Mayor's Midsummer Prize City of London 1981. *Publications include:* The Letters of John of Salisbury Vol. I (ed.) 1955, From Alfred to Henry III 1961, The Saxon and Norman Kings 1963, Europe in the Central Middle Ages 1964, Gilbert Foliot and his Letters (with A. Morey) 1965, Time the Archsatirist 1968, The Twelfth Century Renaissance 1969, Structure of Medieval Society 1971, London 800–1216 (with G. Keir) 1975, Marriage in Christian History 1977, The Letters of John of Salisbury vol. II (ed.) 1979, Oxford (fmrly Nelson's) Medieval Texts (gen. ed.) 1979–87, Nelson's History of England (gen. ed.), Councils and Synods Vol. I (co-ed. with D. Whitelock and M. Brett) 1981, Popular Religion in the Middle Ages, 1000–1300 (with Rosalind Brooke) 1984, A History of Gonville and Caius College 1985, Oxford and Cambridge (with Roger Highfield and Wim Swaan) 1988, A History of the University of Cambridge (four vols) 1988–2004, The Medieval Idea of Marriage 1989, Churches and Churchmen in Medieval Europe (with R. B. Brooke) 1999, Jane Austen: Illusion and Reality 1999, The Age of the Cloister 2001; contribs: articles and reviews to professional journals. *Address:* Gonville and Caius College, Cambridge, CB2 1TA, England (home).

BROOKE, Edward William, LLD, LLM; American lawyer and fmr politician; b. 26 Oct. 1919, Washington, DC; s. of Edward Brooke and Helen Brooke; m. 2nd Anne Fleming 1979; ed Howard Univ. and Boston Univ.; Capt., US Army, World War II; admitted to Mass Bar 1948; Chair. Finance Comm., Boston 1961–62; Attorney-Gen. of Mass 1963–67; US Senator from Mass (first African-American to be elected by popular vote to US Senate) 1967–79; Chair. Boston Opera Co.; fmr Pnr, O'Connor & Hannan, Washington, DC; Chair. Nat. Low-Income Housing Coalition 1979–; Counsel, Csaplar & Bok, Boston 1979–; Ltd Pnr, Bear Stearns, New York 1979; Fellow, ABA, American Acad. of Arts and Sciences; Republican; 34

hon. degrees; Presidential Medal of Freedom 2004, Congressional Gold Medal 2009. *Publications:* The Challenge of Change 1966, Bridging the Divide: My Life 2006. *Address:* 60 Edgewater Drive, Unit: Lanai South, Coral Gables, FL 33133, USA (home).

BROOKE OF SUTTON MANDEVILLE, Baron (Life Peer), cr. 2001, of Sutton Mandeville in the County of Wiltshire; **Peter Leonard Brooke,** CH, PC, MA, MBA, FSA; British politician; b. 3 March 1934, London; s. of Lord Brooke of Cumnor, CH, PC and Baroness Brooke of Ystradfellte, DBE; m. 1st Joan Smith 1964 (died 1985); four s. (one deceased); m. 2nd Lindsay Allinson 1991; ed Marlborough Coll., Balliol Coll., Oxford, Harvard Business School, USA; Research Asst, Inst. pour l'Etude des Méthodes de Direction de l'Entreprise (IMEDE), Lausanne and Swiss Corresp. of Financial Times 1960–61; Spencer Stuart Man. Consultants 1961–79, Chair. of parent co. 1974–79; MP for City of London and Westminster S. 1977–97, for Cities of London and Westminster 1997–2001; Govt Whips' Office 1979–83; Dept of Educ. and Science Parl. Under-Sec. 1983–85; Minister of State, HM Treasury 1985–87, Paymaster Gen. 1987–89; Chair. Conservative Party 1987–89; Sec. of State for NI 1989–92, for Nat. Heritage 1992–94; Chair. Commons Select Cttee on NI 1997–2001; mem. House of Lords 2001–; Chair. Asscn of Conservative Peers 2004–06; lay mem. Univ. of London Council 1994–2006, Deputy Chair. 2001–02, Chair. and Pro-Chancellor 2002–06; Pres. British Antique Dealers Asscn 1995–2005, British Art Market Fed. 1996–, Friends of Wiltshire Churches 2008–; Trustee Wordsworth Trust 1974–2001, Cusichaca Project 1978–98; Lay Adviser, St Paul's Cathedral 1980–99; Chair. Churches Conservation Trust 1995–98; Sr Fellow, RCA 1987, Presentation Fellow, King's Coll. London 1989, Hon. Fellow, Queen Mary and Westfield Coll. 1996, Univ. of Wales Lampeter 2009; Hon. DLitt (Westminster) 1999, (London Guildhall Univ.) 2001, Hon. LLB (London) 2006. *Leisure interests:* churches, conservation, cricket, visual arts. *Address:* House of Lords, London, SW1A 0PW, England (office). *Telephone:* (20) 7219-2150 (office). *E-mail:* brookep@parliament.uk (office).

BROOKHART, Maurice S., BA, PhD; American chemist and academic; *William R. Kenan, Jr Professor of Chemistry, University of North Carolina;* b. 1943, North Carolina; ed Johns Hopkins Univ., Univ. of California, Los Angeles; NSF Postdoctoral Fellow, UCLA 1968; NATO Postdoctoral Fellowship, Univ. of Southampton, UK 1968–69; William R. Kenan, Jr Prof. of Chem., Univ. of North Carolina 1969–; Visiting Prof., Univ. of Wisconsin 1974, Univ. of Rennes, France 1981, 1987, Univ. of Oxford 1982–83, Univ. of Bordeaux 1989, CNRS Inst. for Co-ordination Chem., Toulouse 1989, Univ. of California, Berkeley 1996, Instituto de Investigaciones Quimicas, Seville 1997; Sr Humboldt Fellow, Univ. of Marburg 2001, Max Planck Inst., Muelheim 2003; Assoc. Ed., Organometallics 1990–96; Medicinal Chem. Study Section, DRG, NIH 1997–2001; mem. Editorial Advisory Bd, Organic Letters, Journal of Polymer Science, Advanced Synthesis and Catalysis; mem. NAS 2001; Fellow, American Acad. of Arts and Sciences 1996, AAAS 2001; Dr hc (Univ. of Rennes) 2000; ACS Award in Organometallic Chem. 1992, North Carolina Section ACS Distinguished Speaker Award 1992, ACS A.C. Cope Scholar Award 1994, Japan Soc. for the Promotion of Science Fellowship 1995, ACS Co-operative Research Award in Polymer Science and Eng (co-recipient) 1998, Charles H. Stone Award, Piedmont Section, ACS 1998, RSC Centenary Lecturer 2000, ACS Award in Polymer Chem. 2003, North Carolina Award in Science 2008, Willard Gibbs Medal, ACS Chicago Local Section 2010. *Publications:* more than 270 papers in professional journals; 22 US patents. *Address:* Department of Chemistry, University of North Carolina, Chapel Hill, NC 27599-3290, USA (office). *Telephone:* (919) 962-0362 (office). *Fax:* (919) 962-2388 (office). *E-mail:* mbrookhart@unc.edu (office). *Website:* www.chem.unc.edu/people/faculty/brookhart (office).

BROOKNER, Anita, CBE, BA, PhD, FRSL; British academic, writer and art historian; b. 16 July 1928, London; d. of Newson Brookner and Maude Brookner; ed James Allen's Girls' School, King's Coll., London, Courtauld Inst. and Paris; Visiting Lecturer in Art History, Univ. of Reading 1959–64; Lecturer, Courtauld Inst. of Art 1964–77, Reader in Art History 1977–87; Slade Prof., Univ. of Cambridge 1967–68; Fellow, New Hall Cambridge, King's Coll. London; Commdr, Ordre des Arts et Lettres 2002; Hon. DLitt (Loughborough Univ. of Tech.) 1990; Dr hc (Smith Coll., USA). *Publications:* fiction: A Start in Life 1981, Providence 1982, Look at Me 1983, Hôtel du Lac (Booker Prize) 1984, Family and Friends 1985, A Misalliance 1986, A Friend from England 1987, Latecomers 1988, Lewis Percy 1989, Brief Lives 1990, A Closed Eye 1991, Fraud 1992, A Family Romance 1993, A Private View 1994, Incidents in the rue Laugier 1995, Altered States 1996, Soundings 1997, Visitors 1997, Falling Slowly 1998, Undue Influence 1999, The Bay of Angels 2000, The Next Big Thing 2002, The Rules of Engagement 2003, Leaving Home 2005, Strangers 2009; non-fiction: An Iconography of Cecil Rhodes 1956, J. A. Dominique Ingres 1965, Watteau 1968, The Genius of the Future: Studies in French Art Criticism 1971, Greuze: The Rise and Fall of an Eighteenth-Century Phenomenon 1972, Jacques-Louis David, a Personal Interpretation: Lecture on Aspects of Art 1974, Jacques-Louis David 1980; editor: The Stories of Edith Wharton (two vols) 1988; contrib. to books and periodicals, including Burlington Magazine. *Address:* 68 Elm Park Gardens, London, SW10 9PB, England (home). *Telephone:* (20) 7352-6894 (home).

BROOKS, Albert; American actor, writer and director; b. (Albert Einstein), 22 July 1947, Beverly Hills, Calif.; s. of Harry Brooks and Thelma (Leeds) Einstein; began career with several successful comedy albums then directing short comedy films for TV shown on Great American Dream Machine (PBS) and Saturday Night Live (NBC). *Films include:* (actor) Taxi Driver 1976, Private Benjamin 1980, Twilight Zone: The Movie 1983, Unfaithfully Yours 1983, Terms of Endearment 1983, Broadcast News 1987, I'll Do Anything 1994, The Scout 1994, Critical Care 1997, Out of Sight 1998, Dr Dolittle (voice) 1998, The Muse 1999; (dir, writer and actor) Real Life 1979, Modern Romance 1982, Lost in America 1985, Defending Your Life 1991, Mother 1996 (NY Soc. of Film Critics' Award, Nat. Soc. of Film Critics' Award for Best Screenplay), The Muse 1999, My First Mister 2000, Finding Nemo (voice) 2003, The In-Laws 2003, Looking for Comedy in the Muslim World 2006, The Simpsons Movie (voice) 2007. *Television includes:* The Simpsons (voice) 1990–2005; dir, writer short films Saturday Night Live 1975–76. *Recordings include:* Comedy Minus One, A Star is Bought. *Address:* c/o Toni Howard, International Creative Management Inc. (ICM), 8942 Wilshire Blvd., Beverly

Hills, CA 90211; 1880 Century Drive Park East, #900, Los Angeles, CA 90067-1609, USA.

BROOKS, James L.; American screenwriter, director and producer; b. 9 May 1940, North Bergen, NJ; s. of Edward M. Brooks and Dorothy Helen Sheinheit; m. 1st Marianne Catherine Morrissey 1964 (divorced); one d.; m. 2nd Holly Beth Holmbert 1978; one s. one d.; ed New York Univ.; writer CBS News, New York 1964–66; writer-producer documentaries Wolper Productions, LA 1966–67; founder and owner Gracie Films 1984; mem. Guild of America, Writers' Guild of America, TV Acad. of Arts and Sciences, Acad. of Motion Picture Arts and Sciences. *TV series include:* creator Room 222 1968–69 (Emmy Award for Outstanding New Series); co-creator, producer Mary Tyler Moore Show 1970–77 (Emmy Awards for Comedy Writing, Outstanding Comedy Series, Peabody Award, Writers' Guild of America Award, Humanitas Award and others); writer, producer Paul Sand in Friends and Lovers 1974; co-creator, co-exec. producer series Rhoda Show 1974–75 (Emmy and Humanitas Awards); co-creator, exec. producer Taxi 1978–80 (Emmy, Film Critics' Circle, Golden Globe and Humanitas Awards); co-exec. producer, co-writer Cindy 1978; co-creator, exec. producer The Associates 1979; exec. producer, co-exec. producer, co-creator The Tracey Ullman Show 1986–90 (3 Emmy Awards for Outstanding Variety or Comedy Series, 2 Emmy Awards Outstanding Writing Variety or Music Show), The Simpsons 1990– (3 Emmy Awards), The Critic (exec. producer) 2000, What About Joan (exec. producer) 2001. *Films include:* producer, writer, dir Terms of Endearment 1983 (Golden Globe Best Screenplay and Best Picture Awards, Acad. Awards for Best Film, Best Dir, Best Screenplay, Dirs' Guild of America Award for Best Dir), Spanglish 2004, How Do You Know 2010; writer, dir, producer Broadcast News 1987 (New York Film Critics' Awards for Best Picture, Best Dir, Best Screenplay); exec. producer Big 1988, The War of the Roses 1989; producer Jerry Maguire 1996, As Good As It Gets 1997, Riding in Cars With Boys 2001. *Address:* Gracie Films, c/o Sony Film Corporation, 10202 West Washington Boulevard, Culver City, CA 90232, USA (office). *Telephone:* (310) 244-4222 (office). *Fax:* (310) 244-1530 (office). *Website:* www.graciefilms.com (office).

BROOKS, Mel; American actor, writer, producer and director; b. (Melvin Kaminsky Brooks), 28 June 1926, Brooklyn, New York; m. 1st Florence Baum; two s. one d.; m. 2nd Anne Bancroft 1964 (died 2005); one s.; script writer for TV series Your Show of Shows 1950–54, Caesar's Hour 1954–57, Get Smart 1965; set up feature film production co. Brooksfilms; Kennedy Center Honor 2009. *Television include:* Get Smart (writer) 1965–70, The Nutt House (writer) 1989, Mad About You (Emmy Award for Outstanding Guest Actor in a Comedy Series 1997, 1998, 1999) 1996–99, Curb Your Enthusiasm 2004, Inside Comedy 2012. *Films include:* The Critic (writer, cartoon) (Academy Award 1964) 1963, The Producers (writer, dir) (Acad. Award for Best Screenplay) 1968, The Twelve Chairs (writer, dir, actor) 1970, Shinbone Alley (writer) 1971, Blazing Saddles (writer, dir, actor) 1974, Young Frankenstein (writer, dir) 1974, Silent Movie (writer, dir, actor) 1976, High Anxiety (writer, dir, actor, producer) 1977, The Muppet Movie (actor) 1979, The Elephant Man (exec. producer) 1980, History of the World Part I (writer, dir, actor, producer) 1981, My Favourite Year 1982, To Be or Not to Be (actor, producer) 1983, The Doctor and the Devils (exec. producer) 1985, Solarbabies (exec. producer) 1986, Fly I 1986, Spaceballs (writer, dir, actor, producer) 1987, 84 Charing Cross Road (exec. producer) 1987, Fly II 1989, Life Stinks (writer, dir, actor, producer) 1991, The Vagrant (exec. producer) 1992, Robin Hood: Men in Tights (writer, dir, actor, producer) 1993, The Little Rascals (actor) 1994, Dracula: Dead and Loving It (writer, dir, actor, producer) 1995, Svitati (actor) 1999, The Producers: The Movie Musical 2005. *Musicals include:* The Producers (producer, co-writer, composer) (Tony Awards for Best Book, Best Score, Best Musical 2001, Evening Standard Award for Best Musical 2004, Critics Circle Theatre Award for Best Musical 2005) 2001, Young Frankenstein 2007. *Address:* c/o The Culver Studios, 9336 W Washington Boulevard, Culver City, CA 90232, USA (office).

BROOKS, Rebekah; British newspaper editor; b. 27 May 1968; d. of the late Robert Wade and Deborah Wade; m. Charlie Brooks 2009; ed Appleton Hall, Cheshire and Univ. of the Sorbonne, Paris; began career as Features Ed., later Assoc. Ed. and Deputy Ed. News of the World –1998, Ed. 2000–03; Deputy Ed. The Sun 1998–2000, Ed. 2003–09; CEO News International –2011 (resgnd); Founder-mem. and Pres. Women in Journalism. *Address:* c/o News International, 1 Virginia Street, Wapping, London, E98 1XY, England.

BROOKS, (Troyal) Garth, BS; American country singer, songwriter and musician (guitar); b. 7 Feb. 1962, Tulsa, Okla; s. of Troyal Raymond and Colleen Carroll Brooks; m. 1st Sandra Mahl 1986; three c.; m. 2nd Trisha Yearwood 2005; ed Oklahoma State Univ.; mem. American Soc. of Composers, Authors and Publrs (ASCAP), Country Music Asscn, Acad. of Country Music; Acad. of Country Music Entertainer of the Year 1991, 1992, 1993, 1994, Male Vocalist of the Year Award 1991, Horizon Award 1991, Country Music Asscn Entertainer of the Year award 1991, 1992, Grammy Award for Best Male Country Vocalist 1992, Best Male Country Music Performer 1992, 1993, Best Male Musical Performer, People's Choice Awards 1992–95, Country Music Award for Artist of the Decade 1999, American Music Award for Favorite Country Artist 2000, Special Award of Merit 2002, inducted into Country Music Hall of Fame 2012. *Recordings:* albums: Garth Brooks 1989, No Fences (Acad. of Country Music Album of the Year 1991, CMA Award for Best Album 1991) 1990, Ropin' The Wind 1991, Beyond The Season 1992, The Chase 1992, In Pieces 1993, The Hits 1994, Fresh Horses 1995, Sevens 1997, In The Life Of Chris Gaines 1999, Garth Brooks & The Magic Of Christmas 1999, Double Live (American Music Award for Favorite Country Album 2001) 2000, Scarecrow 2001, The Entertainer 2006; singles: If Tomorrow Never Comes 1989, The Dance (Acad. of Country Music Song of Year, CMA Award for Best Single) 1991, Friends in Low Places (Acad. of Country Music Single Record of Year) 1991, If Tomorrow Never Comes (American Music Country Song of Year) 1991, Tour EP 1994, To Make You Feel My Love 1998, One Heart At A Time 1998, Lost In You 1999, Call Me Claus 2001, The Thunder Rolls, We Shall Be Free, Somewhere Other Than The Night, Learning to Live Again. *Television specials:* This is Garth Brooks 1992, This is Garth Brooks Too 1994, Garth Brooks: The Hits 1995, Garth Brooks Live in Cen. Park 1997. *Address:* c/o Scott Stern, G. B. Management Inc., 1111 17th Avenue S, Nashville, TN 37212, USA (office). *Website:* www.garthbrooks.com.

BROOME, David McPherson, CBE; British fmr professional show jumper, sports administrator and farmer; b. 1 March 1940, Cardiff, Wales; s. of Fred Broome and Amelia Broome; brother of veteran show jumper Liz Edgar; m. Elizabeth Fletcher 1976; three s.; ed Monmouth Grammar School for Boys; European show jumping champion, riding Sunsalve, Aachen 1961, riding Mr Softee, Rotterdam 1967 and Hickstead 1969; world champion, riding Beethoven, La Baule (France) 1970; professional world champion, riding Sportsman and Philco, Cardiff 1974; mem. of six British Olympic teams (including Barcelona 1992); Master of Foxhounds. *Publications:* Jump-Off 1970, Horsemanship (with S. Hadley) 1983. *Leisure interests:* hunting, shooting, golf. *Address:* Mount Ballan Manor, Crick, Chepstow, Monmouthshire, NP26 5XP, Wales. *Telephone:* (1291) 420777; (1291) 418125. *E-mail:* charlotte@theshowground.com. *Website:* www.theshowground.com.

BROSNAN, Pierce; Irish actor; b. 16 May 1953, Navan, Co. Meath; s. of Tom Brosnan and May Smith; m. Cassandra Harris (died 1991); one s.; m. Keely Shaye Smith 2001; two s.; ed Drama Center; London stage appearances include Wait Until Dark, The Red Devil Battery Sign (cast in role of McCabe in British premiere by Tennessee Williams), Filumenia; co-f. (with Beau St. Clair) Irish Dreamtime (production co.) 1996; Hon. OBE 2003. *Films include:* The Mirror Crack'd 1980, The Long Good Friday, Nomads, The Fourth Protocol, Taffin, The Deceivers, Mister Johnson, The Lawnmower Man, Mrs Doubtfire 1993, Love Affair 1994, Robinson Crusoe 1995, Mars Attacks! 1996, The Mirror Has Two Faces 1996, Dante's Peak 1997, The Nephew 1998, The Thomas Crown Affair 1999, Grey Owl 2000, The Tailor of Panama 2001, Laws of Attraction 2004, After the Sunset 2004, The Matador 2005, Seraphim Falls 2006,Married Life 2007, Mamma Mia! 2008, The Ghost Writer 2010, Remember Me 2010, Salvation Boulevard 2011, I Don't Know How She Does It 2011, The Bald Hairdresser 2012; role of James Bond in Goldeneye 1994, Tomorrow Never Dies 1997, The World is Not Enough 1999, Die Another Day 2002. *TV appearances include:* role of detective in Remington Steele (series), Noble House (mini-series), Nancy Astor, Around the World in Eighty Days, The Heist, Murder 101, Victim of Love, Live Wire, Death Train, Robinson Crusoe 1994, The James Bond Story 1999, Bag of Bones (mini-series) 2011. *Address:* Irish Dreamtime, 3110 Main Street, Suite 200, Santa Monica, CA 90405; c/o Guttman Associates, 118 South Beverly Drive, Suite 201, Beverly Hills, CA 90212, USA (office). *Telephone:* (310) 449-3411 (Irish Dreamtime). *Fax:* (310) 586-8138 (Irish Dreamtime). *Website:* www.piercebrosnan.com.

BROTMAN, Jeffrey (Jeff) H., BA, MA, JD; American lawyer and retail executive; *Chairman, Costco Wholesale Corporation;* b. 1943; m. Susan Brotman; two c.; ed Univ. of Washington; Co-founder (with Jim Sinegal) and Chair. Costco Wholesale Corpn 1983–93, Vice-Chair. 1993–94, Chair. 1994–; Dir Starbucks Coffee 1988–99, Garden Botanika 1989–98, Seattle-First Nat. Bank 1990–99, The Sweet Factory Inc. 1992–98, Million-Dollar Roundtable at United Way of King County; Regent Univ. of Washington 1998–, Vice-Pres. Bd of Regents 2002–03, Pres. 2004–; Co-Chair. King County United Way Campaign Bd 1997–; Trustee, Seattle Art Museum 1990–, Seattle Foundation 1991–, Univ. of Washington Medical Center Bd 1991–. *Address:* Costco Wholesale Corporation, 999 Lake Drive, Issaquah, WA 98027, USA (office). *Telephone:* (425) 313-8100 (office). *Fax:* (425) 313-8103 (office). *E-mail:* info@costco.com (office). *Website:* www.costco.com (office).

BROTODININGRAT, Soemadi Djoko Moerdjono; Indonesian diplomatist; *Chief Negotiator, Indonesia-EFTA Economic Partnership Agreement;* b. 13 June 1941, Solo, Cen. Javan Prov.; m.; one s. one d.; ed Gadjah Mada Univ., Int. Inst. of Public Admin, France; with Dept of Foreign Affairs 1965–, Head of Section and later of Staff), Directorate of Information 1965–71; Third then Second Sec., Embassy in Brussels 1971–75; Deputy Dir of Social and Cultural Relations, Dept of Foreign Affairs 1975–78; First Sec., Counsellor, Perm. Mission to UN, New York 1978–82, Minister Counsellor 1984–88; Deputy Dept, Directorate of Multilateral Econ. Co-operation, Dept of Foreign Affairs 1982–84, Dept 1988–91; Amb. and Perm. Rep. to UN, Geneva 1991–95; Dir for Foreign Econ. Relations, Dept of Foreign Affairs 1995–98; Amb. to Japan and Federated States of Micronesia 1998–2002, to USA (also accred to Grenada, St Lucia, St Vincent and Dominica) 2002–05; Chief Negotiator for the Econ. Partnership Agreement with Japan 2005–07; Special Envoy for Climate Change 2007; Lecturer, Center of Educ. and Training, Ministry of Foreign Affairs 2005–; mem. Bd of Govs Asia-Europe Foundation/ASEF 2009–; Sr Advisor, Minister of Defence 2009–; Chief Negotiator, Indonesia-EFTA Econ. Partnership Agreement 2010–; Sr Advisor, HD Asia Advisory; mem. Bd of Commrs Astra International, DBS Bank Indonesia. *Address:* Ministry of Foreign Affairs, Jalan Taman Pejambon 6, 10th Floor, Jakarta 10110, Indonesia (office); Ministry of Defence, Jalan Medan Merdeka Barat 13–14, Jakarta 10200 (office). *Telephone:* (21) 3858052 (office). *Fax:* (21) 3848863 (office). *E-mail:* soemadibrotodiningrat@yahoo.com (office). *Website:* www.deplu.go.id (office); www.dephan.go.id (office).

BROUGHTON, Sir Martin Faulkner, Kt, FCA; British business executive and chartered accountant; *Chairman, British Airways PLC;* b. 15 April 1947, London, England; s. of Edward Broughton and Laura Faulkner; m. Jocelyn Mary Rodgers 1974; one s. one d.; ed Westminster City Grammar School; joined British-American Tobacco Co. (BAT) 1971, with group's Brazilian subsidiary Souza Cruz 1980–85, Finance Dir BAT Industries 1988–93, Group Chief Exec. and Deputy Chair. 1993–98, Chair. BAT PLC (following demerger) 1998–2004; Finance Dir Eagle Star 1985–88, Chair. 1992–93, Chair. Wiggins Teape Group 1989–90; Dir (non-exec.) Whitbread 1993–2000; Dir (non-exec.) British Airways PLC 2000–, Deputy Chair. (non-exec.) 2003–04, Chair. (non-exec.) 2004–, Chair. Nominations Cttee; Pres. CBI 2007–09, Deputy Pres. 2009–; Ind. Dir British Horseracing Bd 1999–2004, Chair. 2004–07; Co-Chair. Transatlantic Business Dialogue 2006–08, currently European Chair.; mem. Financial Reporting Council 1998–, European Round Table of Industrialists. *Leisure interests:* golf, football, horse racing, the theatre. *Address:* British Airways PLC, Waterside, PO Box 365, Harmondsworth, West Drayton, UB7 0GB, England (office). *Telephone:* (844) 493-0787 (office); (20) 8759-5511 (office). *Fax:* (20) 8738-9801 (office). *E-mail:* info@britishairways.com (office). *Website:* www.britishairways.com (office).

BROUSSARD, Bruce D.; American business executive; *President and CEO, Humana Incorporated;* CEO McKesson Specialty/US Oncology, Inc. (purchased by McKesson in 2010) –2010, held several sr exec. roles, including Chief Financial Officer, Pres., CEO and Chair.; Pres. Humana Inc. 2011–12, mem. Bd of Dirs, Pres. and CEO 2013–; mem. Bd of Dirs America's Health Insurance Plans and its Exec.

Cttee; mem. Business Roundtable. *Address:* Humana Inc., 500 West Main Street, Louisville, KY 40202, USA (office). *Telephone:* (502) 580-1000 (office). *Fax:* (502) 580-3677 (office). *E-mail:* info@humana.com (office). *Website:* www.humana.com (office).

BROVTSEV, Vadim Vladimirovich; Russian business executive and politician; b. 26 July 1969, Chelyabinsk (now Ozyorsk), Russian SFSR, USSR; m.; two c.; served in Soviet Strategic Rocket Forces; Chair. Vermikulit (construction co.), Chelyabinsk 2005–09; Prime Minister of the 'Repub. of South Ossetia' 2009–12, also Acting Pres. Dec. 2011–12. *Address:* c/o Office of the Prime Minister of the 'Republic of South Ossetia', 100001 Tskhinvali, ul. Khetgurova 1, South Ossetia, Georgia. *E-mail:* ospress@yandex.ru.

BROWDER, Felix Earl, MA, PhD; American mathematician, academic and university administrator; *University Professor, Rutgers University;* b. 31 July 1927, Moscow, Russia; s. of Earl Browder and Raissa Berkmann; m. Eva Tislowitz 1949; two s.; ed Yonkers High School and Princeton Univ.; CLE Moore Instructor in Math., MIT 1948–51; Instructor in Math., Boston Univ. 1951–53; US Army 1953–55; Asst Prof. of Math., Brandeis Univ. 1955–56; Asst Prof., then Prof., Yale Univ. 1956–63; Prof. of Math., Univ. of Chicago 1963–72, Louis Block Prof. of Math. 1972–82, Max Mason Distinguished Service Prof. 1982–87, Chair. Math. Dept 1971–76, 1979–85; Visiting Prof., MIT 1961–62, 1977–78; Vice-Pres. for Research, Rutgers Univ. 1986–91, Univ. Prof. 1986–; Pres. American Math. Soc. 1999–2001; ed. of numerous journals; mem. NAS (mem. Council 1992–95, Governing Bd Nat. Research Council 1994–95); Fellow, American Acad. of Arts and Sciences; Dr hc (Paris) 1990; Nat. Medal of Science 1999. *Publications:* Problèmes non-linéaires 1966, Functional Analysis and Related Fields 1970, Nonlinear Functional Analysis (two vols) 1970, 1976, Mathematical Heritage of Henri Poincaré 1984, Nonlinear functional analysis and its applications (two vols) 1985; numerous papers in mathematical journals. *Leisure interests:* reading, especially in philosophy, history and classics. *Address:* Department of Mathematics, Rutgers University, Hill Center – Busch Campus, 110 Frelinghuysen Road, Piscataway, NJ 08854-8019, USA (office). *Telephone:* (732) 445-2393 (office); (732) 297-6040 (home). *E-mail:* browder@math.rutgers.edu (office). *Website:* math.rutgers.edu/people/index.php?type=faculty&id=35 (office).

BROWN, Adriane M., BSc, MA; American automotive industry executive; *President and CEO, Transportation Systems, Honeywell International Inc.;* ed Old Dominion Univ., Norfolk, Va, Massachusetts Inst. of Tech. (Sloan Fellow); Vice-Pres. and Gen. Man. Environmental Products Div., Corning Inc. 1980–94, Vice-Pres. and Gen. Man. Automotive Products business 1994–99; Vice-Pres. and Gen. Man. Aircraft Landing Systems, Honeywell Aerospace 1999, later Vice-Pres. and Gen. Man. Engine Systems and Accessories, Pres. and CEO Transportation Systems, Honeywell International Inc., Torrance, Calif. 2005–; mem. Bd of Dirs Jobs for America's Graduates; mem. Exec. Leadership Council, Arizona Women's Forum; named one of Top 100 Leading Women in the Automotive Industry 2005. *Address:* Honeywell Transportation Systems, 23326 Hawthorne Blvd, # 200, Torrance, CA 90505, USA (office). *Telephone:* (310) 791-9101 (office). *Website:* www.honeywell.com (office).

BROWN, Cedric Harold, FREng, FICE; British business executive; b. 7 March 1935; s. of William Herbert Brown and Constance Dorothy Brown (née Frances); m. Joan Hendry 1956; one s. three d.; ed Sheffield, Rotherham and Derby Colls of Tech.; East Midlands Gas Bd 1953–59; Eng Asst Tunbridge Wells Borough Council 1959–60; Eng posts, East Midlands Gas Bd 1960–75; Dir of Eng East Midlands Gas 1975–78; joined British Gas Corpn (now British Gas PLC) 1978; Dir Morecambe Bay Project 1980–87; Regional Chair. British Gas West Midlands 1987–89; Dir and Man. Dir Exploration and Production 1989; Man. Regional Services 1989–91; Sr Man. Dir 1991; Chief Exec. British Gas PLC 1992–96; Chair. CB Consultants 1996–, Intellihome PLC 1997–, Atlantic Caspian Resources PLC 1999–, Business Champions-East Midlands Devt Agency 2001–, Lachesis Investment Advisory Cttee 2002–; Pres. Institution of Gas Engineers 1996–97, Fellow; Dir Bow Valley Industries 1988–92, Orb Estates 2000–; mem. Advisory Council on Business and the Environment 1993–95. *Publications include:* tech. papers. *Leisure interests:* sport, countryside, places of historic interest.

BROWN, Christina Hambley (Tina), (Lady Evans), MA, CBE; American (b. British) magazine editor, television presenter and author; b. 21 Nov. 1953, Maidenhead, Berks., England; d. of the late George Hambley Brown and Bettina Iris Mary Brown (née Kohr); m. Sir Harold Matthew Evans 1981; one s. one d.; ed Univ. of Oxford; columnist, Punch magazine 1978; Ed.-in-Chief Tatler Magazine 1979–83, of Vanity Fair Magazine, New York 1984–92, London 1991–92; Ed. The New Yorker 1992–98, Talk magazine 1999–2002; Partner and Chair. Talk Media 1998–2002, Talk Miramax Books 1998–2002; columnist, Washington Post 2003–; Founder and Ed.-in-Chief The Daily Beast (internet news site) 2008–13, Newsweek (after jt venture with Daily Beast to form The Newsweek Daily Beast Co.) 2010–13; Most Promising Female Journalist, Katherine Pakenham Prize Sunday Times 1973, Young Journalist of the Year 1978, Univ. of Southern Calif. Distinguished Achievement in Journalism Award 1994, four George Polk Awards, five Overseas Press Club awards, ten National Magazine Awards, inducted into Magazine Editors' Hall of Fame 2007, ranked by Forbes magazine amongst The World's 100 Most Powerful Women (34th) 2010, (81st) 2011, (77th) 2012. *Publications:* Under the Bamboo Tree (play) (Sunday Times Drama Award) 1973, Happy Yellow (play) 1977, Loose Talk – Adventures on the Street of Shame 1979, Life as a Party 1983, The Icarus Complex 2005, The Diana Chronicles 2007. *Address:* c/o The Daily Beast, IAC Headquarters, 555 West 18th Street, New York, NY 10011, USA.

BROWN, Dan; American writer; b. 1965, Exeter, New Hampshire; m. Blythe Newlon 1997; ed Phillips Exeter Acad., Amherst Coll.; English teacher 1986–1996. *Publications include:* 187 Men to Avoid (as Danielle Brown) 1995, Digital Fortress 1998, Angels and Demons 2001, Deception Point 2002, The Da Vinci Code (British Book Award for Book of the Year 2005) 2003, The Lost Symbol 2009, Inferno 2013. *Address:* c/o Heide Lange, Sandford J. Greenburger Associates Inc., 55 Fifth Avenue, New York, NY 10003, USA (office). *Telephone:* (212) 206-5600 (office). *Fax:* (212) 463-8718 (office). *E-mail:* queryHL@sjga.com (office). *Website:* www.greenburger.com (office). *Website:* www.danbrown.com.

BROWN, Donald David, MS, MD; American biologist and academic; *Member of Staff, Department of Embryology, Carnegie Institution and Adjunct Professor, Department of Biology, Johns Hopkins University;* b. 30 Dec. 1931, Cincinnati, Ohio; s. of Albert L. Brown and Louise R. Brown; m. Linda Weil 1957; one s. two d.; ed Walnut Hills High School, Cinn., Dartmouth Coll and Univ. of Chicago; Intern, Charity Hosp., New Orleans 1956–57, Sr Asst Surgeon, US Public Health Service, Bethesda 1957–59; Postdoctoral Fellow, Pasteur Inst. 1959–60, Dept of Embryology, Carnegie Inst. of Washington, Baltimore 1960–62, staff mem. 1963–, Dir 1976–94; Adjunct Prof., Dept of Biology, Johns Hopkins Univ. 1968–; Pres. Life Sciences Research Foundation 1981–; Pres. American Soc. of Cell Biology 1992; US Steel Award in Molecular Biology 1973, V. D. Mattia Award 1976, New York Acad. of Science Boris Pregel Award 1977, Ross Harrison-ISDB Award 1981, Texas Univ. Cancer Center Ernst W. Bertner Award 1982, Columbia Univ. Louisa Gross Horwitz Award 1985, Rosensteil Award 1985, Miami Winter Symposium Feodor Lynen Medal 1987, E. B. Wilson Award 1996, American Soc. of Developmental Biology Lifetime Achievement Award 2009. *Address:* Carnegie Institution, Department of Embryology, 3520 San Martin Drive, Baltimore, MD 21218 (office); 6511 Abbey View Way, Baltimore, MD 21212, USA (home). *Telephone:* (410) 246-3052 (office); (410) 377-0812 (home). *Fax:* (410) 243-6311 (office). *E-mail:* brown@ciwemb.edu (office). *Website:* www.ciwemb.edu/labs/brown/index.php (office); www.bio.jhu.edu/directory/faculty/brown/default.html (office).

BROWN, Edmund Gerald (Jerry), Jr, AB, JD; American lawyer, politician and state governor; *Governor of California;* b. 7 April 1938, San Francisco, Calif.; s. of Edmund Gerald Brown and Bernice Layne; m. Anne Gust 2005; ed Univ. of Santa Clara, Sacred Heart Novitiate, Univ. of California, Berkeley, Yale Law School; worked as a law clerk to Calif. Supreme Court Justice Mathew Tobriner 1964–65, Attorney, Tuttle & Taylor (law firm) Los Angeles 1966–69; mem. Board of Trustees, Los Angeles Community Coll. 1969–70; Calif. Sec. of State 1971–74; Gov. of Calif. 1975–83, 2011–; Chair. Calif. State Democratic Party 1989–90; unsuccessful Democratic presidential cand. 1992; Mayor of Oakland, Calif. 1999–2007; Attorney Gen. of Calif. 2007–11; fmr Pnr, Reavis & McGarth (law firm); f. Oakland School for the Arts, Oakland Mil. Inst. *Publication:* Dialogues 1988. *Address:* Office of the Governor of California, State Capitol Building, Sacramento, CA 95814 (office); Washington Office of the Governor, State of California, 444 North Capitol Street, Suite 134, Washington, DC 20001, USA (office). *Telephone:* (916) 445-2841 (Sacramento) (office); (202) 624-5270 (DC) (office). *Fax:* (916) 558-3160 (Sacramento) (office); (202) 624-5280 (DC) (office). *Website:* gov.ca.gov (office).

BROWN, Hon. Ewart Frederick, Jr, BSc, MD, MPH, JP; Bermudian physician and politician; b. 1946, Bermuda; s. of Ewart Brown and Helene Brown; m. Wanda Henton Brown; four s. from previous m.; ed Berkeley Inst., Howard Univ., Washington DC, USA, Howard Coll. of Medicine, Univ. of California, Los Angeles; represented Bermuda at Commonwealth Games, Kingston, Jamaica, where he ran the 400m and 1600m relay 1966; spent many years practising medicine in USA, including at Vermont-Century Medical Clinic, Los Angeles –1993; Medical Dir Bermuda HealthCare Services Ltd; MP for Warwick West 1993–98, for Warwick South Cen. 1998–; Minister of Transport 1998–2003, Deputy Premier and Minister of Transport 2003–04, Deputy Premier and Minister of Transport and Tourism 2004–06, Premier and Minister of Transport and Tourism 2006–10 (resgnd); Leader Bermuda Progressive Labour Party 2006–10; certified Diplomat of American Bd of Family Practice; Diplomat of American Bd of Quality Assurance and Utilization Review Physicians; fmr Vice-Pres. Union of American Physicians and Dentists; fmr Asst Prof., Dept of Family Practice, Charles R. Drew Univ. of Medicine and Science; fmr Dir, Marcus Garvey School, Los Angeles; fmr mem. Bd Union of American Physicians and Dentists (California Fed.); fmr mem. Bd Dirs Marina Hills Hosp., Los Angeles; fmr physician consultant to Rev. Jesse Jackson (1988 US presidential cand.); fmr mem. California State Comm. on Maternal, Child and Adolescent Health; founding Commr Bd of Prevention Commrs for South Cen. Los Angeles Regional Centre for Devt Disabilities; Founder and Chair. Western Park Hosp., Calif.; fmr Coordinator Summer Health Task Force, Nat. Urban Coalition, Washington, DC; fmr Sec. Charles R. Drew Medical Soc., Los Angeles; mem. Nat. Medical Asscn, American Coll. of Utilization Review Physicians, Golden State Medical Asscn, American Medical Asscn, American Acad. of Family Physicians, American Public Health Asscn, Charles R. Drew Medical Soc.; fmr Trustee Howard Univ., Charles R. Drew Univ. of Medicine and Science; Howard Univ. Service Awards 1968, 1972, Physician's Recognition Award, American Medical Asscn 1977, Community Leadership Award, DuBois Academic Inst. 1982, Pacesetter Award, Nat. Asscn for the Advancement of Colored People 1984, Humanitarian of the Year Award, Marcus Garvey School, Los Angeles 1991, Scroll Award, Union of American Physicians and Dentists 1993. *Leisure interests:* travel, exercising, golf. *Address:* Progressive Labour Party, Alaska Hall, 16 Court Street, Hamilton, HM 17, Bermuda (office). *Telephone:* 292-2264 (office). *Fax:* 295-7890 (office). *E-mail:* info@plp.bm (office). *Website:* www.plp.bm (office).

BROWN, Gavin; British art gallery owner; b. 1963, Croydon, London, England; m. Lucy Barnes (divorced); three d.; ed Newcastle-upon-Tyne Polytechnic, Whitney Museum of American Art, USA; moved to New York 1988; worked at several art galleries, including Pat Hearn Gallery, Brooke Alexander Editions, Lisa Spellman's 303 Gallery; opened Gavin Brown's Enterprise 1994, represents artists Franz Ackermann, James Angus, Uri Aran, Thomas Bayrle, Dirk Bell, Jennifer Bornstein, Joe Bradley, Kerstin Brätsch, Martin Creed, Verne Dawson, Jeremy Deller, Peter Doig, Urs Fischer, Dara Friedman, Mark Handforth, Jonathan Horowitz, Alex Katz, Christopher Knowles, Udomsak Krisanamis, Ella Kruglyanskaya, Mark Leckey, Bjarne Melgaard, Silke Otto-Knapp, Laura Owens, Oliver Payne, Oliver Payne & Nick Relph, Elizabeth Peyton, Steven Pippin, Rob Pruitt, Nick Relph, Steven Shearer, Frances Stark, Katja Strunz, Sturtevant, Spencer Sweeney and Rirkrit Tiravanija; Owner Passerby (bar) 1999–2008; expanded to the West Coast by opening a large warehouse in Los Angeles with gallery artist Laura Owens 2013; has also been running a project space from his own house, promoted through Instagram. *Address:* Gavin Brown's Enterprise, 620 Greenwich Street, New York, NY 10014, USA (office). *Telephone:* (212) 627-5258 (office). *Fax:* (212) 627-5261 (office). *E-mail:* gallery@gavinbrown.biz (office). *Website:* www.gavinbrown.biz (office).

BROWN, Gregory Q., BA; American business executive; *Chairman and CEO, Motorola Solutions, Inc.;* b. 14 Aug. 1960; ed Rutgers Univ.; held several sales and marketing positions with AT&T 1983–87; joined Ameritech 1987, Pres. Custom Business Services and Ameritech New Media, Inc. 1994–96; Chair. and CEO Micromuse, Inc., San Francisco 1999–2003; joined Motorola 2003, held several exec. positions including Exec. Vice-Pres., CEO Commercial, Govt and Industrial Solutions 2003–05, Exec. Vice-Pres. Networks and Enterprise 2005–07, mem. Bd Dirs 2007–, Pres. and COO Motorola, Inc. March–Dec. 2007, Pres. and Co-CEO 2008–11, Chair. and CEO Motorola Solutions, Inc. (following separation of Motorola into Motorola Mobility and Motorola Solutions) 2011–; apptd by White House to serve on Nat. Security Telecommunications Advisory Cttee 2004–, Pres.'s Man. Advisory Bd 2011–, Skills for America's Future Bd 2011–; mem. Bd Dirs Commercial Club of Chicago, World Business Chicago, Northwestern Memorial Hosp.; mem. Business Council, Business Roundtable, Technology CEO Council, Exec. Cttee of the US-China Business Council; mem. Bd of Trustees and Bd of Overseers, Rutgers Univ. *Address:* Motorola Solutions, Inc., 1303 East Algonquin Road, Schaumburg, IL 60196, USA (office). *Telephone:* (847) 576-5000 (office). *Fax:* (847) 576-5372 (office). *E-mail:* info@motorolasolutions.com (office). *Website:* www.motorolasolutions.com (office).

BROWN, Hank, JD, LLM, CPA; American university administrator, lawyer and fmr politician; b. 12 Feb. 1940, Denver, Colo; s. of Harry W. Brown and Anna M. Hanks; m. Nana Morrison 1967; one s. two d.; ed Univ. of Colo and George Washington Univ.; Lt USN 1962–66; tax accountant, Arthur Andersen 1967–78; admitted Colo Bar 1969; Asst to Pres. Monfort of Colo Inc., Greeley 1969–70, Corp. Counsel 1970–71, Vice-Pres. Monfort Food Distribution 1971–72, Vice-Pres. Corp. Devt 1973–75, Int. Operations 1975–78, Lamb Div. 1978–80; mem. US House of Reps (97th–101st) Congresses from Colo 4th Dist; mem. Colo State Senate 1972–76, Asst Majority Leader 1974–76; US Senator from Colorado (102nd Congress) 1991–97; mem. Senate Judiciary, Budget and Foreign Affairs Cttees 1991–97; Pres. Univ. of N Colo 1998–2002; Pres. and CEO Daniels Fund 2002–05; Pres. Univ. of Colo 2005–08; Republican; Order of Merit, Poland, Grand Cordon of the Order of the Brilliant Star, Repub. of China, Nishan-I-Quaid-I-Azam, Pakistan; Hungarian Presidential Gold Medal, Air Medal, Viet Nam Service Medal, Nat. Western Stock Show Citizen of the West Award 2008. *Leisure interest:* skiing. *Address:* c/o University of Colorado, 35 SYS, 914 Broadway, Boulder, CO 80309-0035, USA (home).

BROWN, Harold, PhD; American physicist, academic and fmr government official; *Counsellor and Trustee, Center for Strategic and International Studies;* b. 19 Sept. 1927, New York City; s. of A. H. Brown and Gertrude Cohen; m. Colene McDowell 1953; two d.; ed New York City public schools and Columbia Univ.; Lecturer in Physics, Columbia Univ. 1947–48, Stevens Inst. of Tech. 1949–50; Univ. of Calif. Radiation Laboratory, Berkeley 1950–52; Livermore Radiation Laboratory, 1952–61, Dir 1960–61; mem. Polaris Steering Cttee, Dept of Defense 1956–58; Consultant to Air Force Scientific Advisory Bd 1956–57; mem. Scientific Advisory Cttee on Ballistic Missiles to Sec. of Defense 1958–61; mem. President's Science Advisory Cttee 1961; Dir, Defense Research and Eng 1961–65; Sec. of Air Force 1965–69; Pres. Calif. Inst. of Tech. 1969–77; US Sec. of Defense 1977–81; Distinguished Visiting Prof. of Nat. Security Affairs, School of Advanced Int. Studies, Johns Hopkins Univ. 1981–84, Chair. Johns Hopkins Univ. Foreign Policy Inst. 1984–92; business consultant 1981–; Dir Philip Morris Int., Evergreen Holdings Inc.; Pnr Warburg, Pincus and Co. 1990–2007; Counsellor and Trustee, Center for Strategic and Int. Studies 1992–; mem. Del. to Strategic Arms Limitation Talks 1969–76; mem. NAS, Nat. Acad. of Eng; Hon. DEng (Stevens Inst. of Tech.); Hon. LLD (Long Island Univ., Gettysburg Coll., Occidental Coll., Univ. of Calif. Los Angeles, Univ. of S Carolina, Franklin and Marshall Coll., Univ. of the Pacific, Brown Univ.); Hon. DSc (Univ. of Rochester); Presidential Medal of Freedom 1981, Fermi Award 1993. *Publications:* Thinking About National Security: Defense and Foreign Policy in a Dangerous World 1983, The Strategic Defense Initiative: Shield or Snare? (ed.) 1987, Star Spangled Security 2012. *Leisure interests:* tennis, swimming, reading. *Address:* Center for Strategic and International Studies, 1800 K Street, Suite 400, NW, Washington, DC 20006, USA (office). *Telephone:* (202) 887-0200 (office). *Fax:* (202) 775-3199 (office). *E-mail:* webmaster@csis.org (office). *Website:* www.csis.org (office).

BROWN, Rt Hon. (James) Gordon, PC, MA, PhD; British politician and UN official; *Special Representative of the Secretary-General for Global Education, United Nations;* b. 20 Feb. 1951, Glasgow, Scotland; s. of the late Rev. J. Brown and J. Elizabeth Brown; m. Sarah Macaulay 2000; two s. one d. (deceased); ed Kirkcaldy High School, Univ. of Edinburgh; Rector, Univ. of Edinburgh 1972–75, Temporary Lecturer 1976; Lecturer, Glasgow Coll. of Tech. 1976–80; journalist and Current Affairs Ed., Scottish TV 1980–83; MP (Labour) for Dunfermline East 1983–2005, for Kirkcaldy and Cowdenbeath 2005–; Chair. Labour Party Scottish Council 1983–84; Opposition Chief Sec. to the Treasury 1987–89; Shadow Sec. of State for Trade and Industry 1989–92; Shadow Chancellor of the Exchequer 1992–97; Chancellor of the Exchequer 1997–2007; Prime Minister 2007–10; Minister for the Civil Service 2007–10; First Lord of the Treasury 2007–10; Leader, Labour Party 2007–10; Jt Hon. Treas. (ex-officio), Commonwealth Parl. Asscn (UK Br.) 1997–99, fmr Jt Hon. Sec., Vice-Pres. 2007–10; Special Rep. of the Sec.-Gen. for Global Educ., UN 2012–; mem. Chair. Interim Cttee IMF 1999–; mem. Transport and Gen. Workers' Union; Hon. DCL (Newcastle) 2007; ranked 29th by Forbes magazine amongst The World's Most Powerful People 2009. *Publications include:* The Red Paper on Scotland (ed.) 1975, A Voter's Guide to the Scottish Assembly (with Christopher Harvie) 1979, The Politics of Nationalism and Devolution (with H. M. Drucker) 1980, Scotland: The Real Divide (co-ed. with Robin Cook) 1983, Maxton: A Biography 1986, Where There is Greed: Margaret Thatcher and the Betrayal of Britain's Future 1989, John Smith: Life and Soul of the Party (with J. Naughtie) 1994, Values, Visions and Voices (with T. Wright) 1995, Speeches 1997–2006 2006, Courage: Eight Portraits 2007, Britain's Everyday Heroes 2007, Wartime Courage 2008. *Leisure interests:* reading, writing, football and tennis. *Address:* Office of the Secretary-General, United Nations, New York, NY 10017, USA (office); House of Commons, Westminster, London, SW1A 0AA, England (office). *Telephone:* (212) 963-1234 (office); (20) 7219-2968 (office). *Fax:* (212) 963-4879 (office); (20) 7219-5734 (office). *E-mail:* browng@parliament.uk (office). *Website:* www.un.org/sg (office); www.parliament.uk/biographies/commons/mr-gordon-brown/591 (office).

BROWN, James (Jim) Nathaniel; American actor and fmr professional football player; b. 17 Feb. 1936, St Simons Island, Ga; s. of Swinton Brown and Theresa Brown; m. Sue Jones; two s. one d.; ed Manhasset High School Long Island, Syracuse Univ.; All-American running back and lacrosse player at Syracuse Univ.; fullback for Cleveland Browns 1957–65; played in nine straight NFL (Nat. Football League) Pro Bowls; NFL's leading rusher in eight of his nine seasons; NFL Most Valuable Player—MVP 1958, 1963, 1965; All-NFL 1957–61, 1963–65; career totals include: 118 games played, 12,312 rushing yards, 262 receptions, 15,459 combined net yards, 756 points scored, 126 touchdowns, 106 rushing touchdowns, average 104 yards per game, 5.2 yards per carry; retd from football to pursue acting career 1966; co-f. Negro Industrial Economic Union (NIEU) 1966; works with Coor Golden Door, Barriers and Vital Issues inmates and ex-convicts training programmes 1980–; Founder and Pres. Amer-I-Can Program Inc. 1988–, Chair. Amer-I-Can Foundation for Social Change 1993–; mem. Bd Rebuild LA Project 1992–; hired as sports analyst for the Ultimate Fighting Championship 1993; currently serves as Exec. Advisor to the Cleveland Browns; Syracuse All-America 1956, NFL Rookie of the Year 1957, Hickok Belt Winner 1964, Jim Thorpe Trophy 1965, inducted into Pro Football Hall of Fame 1971 (second youngest ever, at 35), to Lacrosse Hall of Fame 1984, to Coll. Football Hall of Fame 1995, Walter Camp All-Century Team, named by The Sporting News as greatest professional football player ever 2002. *Films include:* Rio Conchos 1964, Dirty Dozen 1967, Mercenaries 1968, Ice Station Zebra 1968, The Split 1968, Riot 1969, Kenner 1969, 100 Rifles 1969, . . .tick. . .tick. . .tick. . . 1970, Grasshopper 1970, Slaughter 1972, Black Gunn 1972, Slaughter's Big Rip-Off 1973, Slams 1973, I Escaped from Devil's Island 1973, Three the Hard Way 1975, Kid Vengeance 1977, Fingers 1978, Pacific Inferno 1979, One Down, Two to Go 1982, Running Man 1987, I'm Gonna Git You Sucka 1988, Crack House 1989, L.A. Heat 1989, Twisted Justice 1990, Killing American Style 1990, Divine Enforcer 1991, Original Gangstas 1996, Mars Attacks! 1996, He Got Game 1998, Any Given Sunday 1999, New Jersey Turnpikes 1999, Any Given Sunday 1999, On the Edge 2002, She Hate Me 2004, Animal (video) 2005, Dream Street 2010. *Television includes:* I Spy (one episode) 1967, Cops and Robbers (one episode) 1967, Police Story (one episode 1977, End of the Line (one episode) 1977, CHiPs (three episodes, High Times, Roller Disco: Part 1, Roller Disco: Part 2) 1979–83, T.J. Hooker (two episodes, Anatomy of a Killing, Raw Deal 1983–84, Knight Rider (one episode, Knight of the Drones 1984, Cover Up (one episode, Midnight Highway) 1984, Lady Blue (one episode) 1985, The A-Team (one episode, Quarterback Sneak) 1986, Highway to Heaven (one episode, Whose Trash Is It Anyway?) 1988, Hammer, Slammer, & Slade 1990, Soul Food (three episodes, Survival Techniques, The Son Also Rises, Pagan Poetry) 2004, Sucker Free City 2004, Sideliners 2006. *Publication:* Out of Bounds (autobiography, with Steve Delsohn) 1989. *Address:* The Amer–I–Can Program, 269 South Beverly Drive, #1048, Los Angeles, CA 90212, USA. *Telephone:* (310) 652-7884. *Fax:* (310) 652-9353. *E-mail:* info@amer-i-can.org. *Website:* www.amer-i-can.org.

BROWN, John Joseph, AO; Australian politician; *Emeritus Chairman, Tourism Task Force Limited;* b. 19 Dec. 1931, Sydney, NSW; s. of Norman Leslie Brown and Eva May Spencer; m. Jan Murray 1963 (divorced); four s. one d.; ed St Patrick's Coll., Strathfield and Sydney Univ.; worked as distributor and co. dir in wholesale meat business; Alderman, Parramatta City Council 1970–77; MP for Parramatta, NSW 1977–90; Minister for Sport, Recreation and Tourism 1983–87 (also Minister assisting the Minister for Defence), for Admin. Services 1983–84; Chair. NSW Wholesale Meat Traders' Asscn 1974–76, Tourism Task Force Ltd 1989 (now Emer. Chair.), Environmental Choice 1992–94, London/Sydney Air Race; Dir Tourism Assets Ltd 1992–98, Sea World Man. Ltd 1993–98, Duty Free Operators Accreditation Bd 1998–, Sport Industry Australia, Macquarie Tourism and Leisure, Canterbury Bankstown Leagues Club; est. Sport and Tourism Youth Foundation (fmrly the John Brown Foundation); mem. Sydney Olympics 2000 Bid Cttee, Co-founding Dir Sydney Olympic Games Organizing Cttee; mem. Australasian Meat Industry Employees' Union, Sport and Tourism, Advisory Council of the Australian Opera, Advertising Standards Council; Labor Party; Patron Les Clefs d'Or; Olympic Silver Order of Merit 1986, Australian of the Year 1986, Gold Award, Australian Inst. of Marketing, Distinguished Service Award, US Sports Acad., Australian Sport Medal 2000. *Leisure interests:* golf, jogging, horse racing, theatre, opera, gardening. *Address:* c/o Tourism Task Force Ltd, PO Box R 1804, Royal Exchange, Sydney, NSW 1225, Australia. *Telephone:* (2) 9240-2000. *Fax:* (2) 9240-2020. *E-mail:* jj.brown@bigpond.com (home); jbrown@ttf.org.au (office). *Website:* www.ttf.org.au.

BROWN, Joyce F., BA, PhD; American educator and academic administrator; *President, Fashion Institute of Technology;* ed Marymount Coll., Inst. for Educational Man. at Harvard Univ., New York Univ.; held several sr admin. posts at CUNY, including Acting Pres. Bernard Baruch Coll. and Vice-Chancellor CUNY, Prof. of Clinical Psychology, Grad. School and Univ. Center –1998, Prof. Emer. 1998–, directed numerous special initiatives, including the Urban Summit of Big City Mayors, as well as collaborations between the New York City Bd of Educ. and the univ.; served as a New York City Deputy Mayor for Public and Community Affairs; cr. and directed programmes with Govt of South Africa, including the Professional Devt Program; Pres. (first woman) Fashion Inst. of Tech., State Univ. of NY 1998–; Pres. The FIT Foundation; mem. Bd of Dirs Ralph Lauren Corpn; served on state-wide comms and task forces on the black family, child care and domestic violence; Trustee, Marymount Coll. 1994–2000; honoured by numerous educational, cultural and civic orgs, including New York Univ., Marymount Coll., Clark Atlantic Univ., The Town Hall, Thurgood Marshall Coll. Fund, Brooklyn Chamber of Commerce, New York Co. Supreme Court, Staten Island Econ. Devt Corpn. *Address:* President's Office, Fashion Institute of Technology, 227 West 27th Street, New York, NY 10001-5992, USA (office). *Telephone:* (212) 217-4000 (office). *E-mail:* info@fitnyc.edu (office). *Website:* www.fitnyc.edu (office).

BROWN, Lawrence (Larry); American basketball coach and fmr basketball player; b. Brooklyn, NY; m. Shelly Brown; one s. four d.; ed Long Beach High School, NY; Univ. of North Carolina; played college basketball Univ. of North Carolina 1960–63; asst coach 1965–67; played for Akron, OH (AAU) 1964–65, then began professional career in American Basketball Asscn (ABA) with New Orleans Buccaneers 1967–68, Oakland Oaks 1968–69, Washington Capitols 1969–70, Virginia Squires 1970–71, Denver Nuggets 1971–72; mem. gold-medal winning US Olympic basketball team 1964; ABA All-Star team 1968–70, Most Valuable Player

ABA All-Star Game 1968; won ABA Championship with Oakland 1969; began coaching career as Head Coach of Carolina Cougars 1973–74, then Denver Rockets 1975–76, Denver Nuggets 1977–79 (all ABA), three-time ABA Coach of the Year 1973, 1975, 1976; switched to college coaching going to UCLA 1979–81, led team to Nat. Collegiate Athletic Asscn (NCAA) championship game 1980; returned to professional ranks as Head Coach with Nat. Basketball Asscn (NBA) New Jersey Nets 1981–83; returned to college coaching going to Univ. of Kansas 1983–88, won NCAA Championship 1988; returned to professional coaching going to NBA San Antonio Spurs 1988–93, Los Angeles Clippers 1991–93, Indiana Pacers 1993–97, Philadelphia 76ers 1997–2003, Detroit Pistons 2003–05 (won NBA championship 2004), New York Knicks 2005–06; Exec. Vice-Pres. Philadelphia 76ers 2007–08; Head Coach, Charlotte Bobcats 2008–10 (resgnd); returned to college coaching with Southern Methodist Univ. 2012–; won 900th NBA game 2003–04 (seventh coach to win 900 games); in 22 seasons as NBA coach has record of 987 wins and 741 losses (.571), ranking fourth all-time among NBA coaches and first amongst active coaches; only coach in NBA history to take seven different teams to play-offs; Asst Coach of gold-medal winning Team USA, Olympic Games, Sydney 2000, Head Coach of bronze-medal winning Team USA, Olympic Games, Athens 2004; winning Head Coach NBA All-Star Game 2001; NBA coach of the year 2001; elected Naismith Memorial Hall of Fame. *Leisure interests:* golf. *Address:* Moody Coliseum, 6024 Airline Road, University Park, TX 75205, USA. *Website:* www .smumustangs.com/sports/m-baskbl/smu-m-baskbl-body.html.

BROWN, Lawrence Michael, MA, PhD, DSc, FRS; British/Canadian physicist and academic; *Professor Emeritus of Physics, University of Cambridge;* b. 18 March 1936, Windsor, Ont.; s. of B. W. Brown and Edith Brown; m. Susan Drucker 1965; one s. two d.; ed Univ. of Toronto, Univ. of Birmingham, UK; work in Cambridge 1960–, Fellow, Gonville and Caius Coll. 1963–77, Robinson Coll. 1977–, Univ. Demonstrator in Physics 1966, Reader in Structure and Properties of Materials, Dept of Physics 1983–89, Prof. of Physics 1989–2001, Prof. Emer. 2001–; Rosenhain Medal, Inst. of Metals 1980, Robert Franklin Mehl Award, TMS 1991, Van Horn Distinguished Lecturer, Case Western Reserve Univ., USA 1994, Guthrie Medal and Prize, Inst. of Physics 2000, Frontiers of Electron Microscopy and Materials Science (FEMMS) Prize Lecturer 2007. *Publications:* many papers in Philosophical Magazine and Acta Metallurgica (now Acta Materialia). *Leisure interests:* reading, gardening. *Address:* Cavendish Laboratory, J.J. Thomson Avenue, Cambridge, CB3 0HE (office); 74 Alpha Road, Cambridge, CB4 3DG, England (home). *Telephone:* (1223) 337076 (office); (1223) 362987 (home). *E-mail:* lmb12@cam.ac.uk (office).

BROWN, Mark; Cook Islands politician; *Minister of Finance, Telecommunications and Internal Affairs;* m. Daphne Brown; one s. one d.; worked for Cook Islands Party 2000–10, currently Vice-Pres.; MP for Takuvaine-Tutakimoa 2010–; Minister of Finance and Economic Man., Business Trade and Investment Bd, Cook Islands Investment Corpn, Commerce Comm., Financial Intelligence Unit, Telecommunication, Financial Services Devt Authority, Financial Supervisory Comm., Nat. Superannuation, and Public Expenditure and Review Cttee Audit (PERCA) 2010–. *Address:* Ministry of Finance, POB 120, Rarotonga, Cook Islands (office). *Telephone:* 22878 (office). *Fax:* 23877 (office). *E-mail:* etuatina@mfem.gov .ck (office). *Website:* www.mfem.gov.ck (office).

BROWN, Melanie Janice; British singer; b. 29 May 1975, Leeds, England; m. 1st Jimmy Gulzar 1998 (divorced); two d.; m. 2nd Stephen Belafonte 2007; mem. Touch, later renamed The Spice Girls 1993–2001, as Melanie B (later Melanie G) or 'Scary Spice', reunion tour 2007–08; numerous tours, concerts, television and radio appearances; world tours include UK, Europe, India, USA; solo artist 1998–; two Ivor Novello songwriting awards 1997, Smash Hits Award for Best Band 1997, BRIT Awards for Best Single (for Wannabe) and for Best Video (for Say You'll Be There) 1997, for Best Performance of the last 30 years 2010, three American Music Awards 1998, Special BRIT Award for Int. Sales 1998. *Film includes:* Spiceworld: The Movie 1997. *Television includes:* presenter This is My Moment (ITV 1) 2001. *Recordings include:* albums: with The Spice Girls: Spice 1996, Spiceworld 1997, Forever 2000, Greatest Hits 2007; solo: Hot 2003, LA State of Mind 2005. *Website:* www.melaniebrown.com.

BROWN, Michael Stuart, BA, MD; American geneticist and academic; *The W.A. (Monty) Moncrief Distinguished Chair in Cholesterol and Arteriosclerosis Research, Regental Professor and Paul J. Thomas Chair in Medicine, Southwestern Medical Center, University of Texas;* b. 13 April 1941, Brooklyn, NY; s. of Harvey Brown and Evelyn Katz; m. Alice Lapin 1964; two d.; ed Univ. of Pennsylvania; Intern, then Resident, Massachusetts Gen. Hosp., Boston 1966–68; served with US Public Health Service 1968–70; Clinical Assoc., NIH 1968–71; Asst Prof., Univ. of Texas Southwestern Medical School, Dallas 1971–74, Paul J. Thomas, Prof. of Genetics and Dir Center of Genetic Diseases 1977–, now The W.A. (Monty) Moncrief Distinguished Chair in Cholesterol and Arteriosclerosis Research, Regental Prof. and Paul J. Thomas Chair in Medicine, Southwestern Medical Center; mem. NAS, American Soc. for Clinical Investigation, Asscn of American Physicians, Inst. of Medicine, Royal Soc. (London); numerous hon. degrees; Passano Award, Johns Hopkins Univ. 1978, Lita Annenberg Hazen Award 1982; co-recipient with Joseph L. Goldstein: ACS Pfizer Award 1976, NAS Lounsbery Award 1979, Gairdner Foundation Int. Award 1981, Louisa Gross Horwitz Prize 1984, William Allan Award, American Soc. of Human Genetics 1985, Albert Lasker Medical Research Award 1985, Nobel Prize in Medicine or Physiology 1985, Nat. Medal of Science USA 1988, Warren Alpert Foundation Prize, Harvard Medical School 1999, Kober Medal, Asscn of American Physician 2002, Albany Medical Center Prize 2003, Herbert Tabor Award, American Soc. for Biochemistry and Molecular Biology 2005, Woodrow Wilson Award for Public Service 2005, Builders of Science Award, Research!America 2007, Stadtman Distinguished Scientist Award, American Soc. for Biochemistry and Molecular Biology 2011. *Address:* The University of Texas Southwestern Medical Center, 5323 Harry Hines Boulevard, Dallas, TX 75390-9046, USA (office). *Telephone:* (214) 648-2179 (office). *E-mail:* mike.brown@utsouthwestern.edu (office). *Website:* profiles.utsouthwestern.edu/profile/10894/michael-brown.html (office); www4 .utsouthwestern.edu/moleculargenetics/pages/brown/lab.html (office).

BROWN, Rt Hon. Nicholas (Hugh), PC, BA; British politician; *Chief Whip and Parliamentary Secretary to the Treasury;* b. 13 June 1950; s. of the late R. C. Brown and G. K. Brown (née Tester); ed Swatenden Secondary Modern School, Tunbridge

Wells Tech. High School, Univ. of Manchester; trade union officer Gen. and Municipal Workers' Union, Northern Region 1978–83; mem. Newcastle-upon-Tyne City Council 1980–83; MP (Labour) for Newcastle-upon-Tyne E 1983–97, for Newcastle-upon-Tyne E and Wallsend 1997–; Labour spokesman on Legal Affairs 1987–92, on Treasury Affairs 1988–94, on Health 1994–95; Deputy Chief Opposition Whip 1995–97; Chief Whip and Parl. Sec. to the Treasury 1997–98, 2008–, Sec. of State for Agric., Fisheries and Food 1998–2001; Minister of State for Work, Dept for Work and Pensions 2001–03. *Address:* Chief Whip's Office, 9 Downing Street, London, SW1A 2AG, England (office). *Telephone:* (20) 7276-2020 (office). *Fax:* (20) 7276-2015. *E-mail:* ministers@hm-treasury.gov.uk (office). *Website:* www.hm-treasury.gov.uk (office).

BROWN, Pauline; American business executive; *Chairman, LVMH Moët Hennessy Louis Vuitton Inc.;* began career as a man. consultant at Bain & Co.; fmr Vice-Pres. of Strategic Planning and New Business Devt, Estée Lauder Cos Inc.; held roles as Sr Vice-Pres. of Corp. Strategy and Global Business Devt, Avon Products Inc.; Man. Dir, The Carlyle Group, working on firm's global consumer and retail team 2006–10; ind. investor and adviser to emerging luxury brands 2010–12; Chair. LVMH Moët Hennessy Louis Vuitton Inc. 2013–. *Address:* LVMH Inc., 19 East 57th Street, New York, NY 10022, USA (office). *Telephone:* (212) 931-2700 (office). *Fax:* (212) 931-2730 (office). *Website:* www.lvmh.com (office).

BROWN, Richard H. (Dick), BSc; American business executive; *Executive Officer, Joseph E. Seagram & Sons, Inc.;* b. 3 June 1947, New Brunswick, NJ; ed Ohio Univ.; began working in telecommunications industry 1974; fmr Vice-Pres. Sprint Corpn; Pres. CEO Illinois Bell 1990; mem. Bd of Dirs and Vice-Chair. Ameritech Corpn 1993–94; fmr Pres. and CEO H & R Block Inc. 1995–96; mem. Bd of Dirs and CEO Cable & Wireless (C&W) PLC, London 1996–98; Chair. and CEO Electronic Data Systems Co. 1999–2003; Exec. Officer, Joseph E. Seagram & Sons, Inc.; mem. Bd of Dirs Vivendi Universal, Browz Group, LC and Browz, LLC, Pharmacia & Upjohn Co., LLC 1993–, The Seagram Co. Ltd 1997–2000, The Home Depot Inc. 2000–06, DuPont Qualicon, Inc. 2001–; Ind. Dir, EI DuPont de Nemours & Co. 2001–; mem. Business Roundtable, Business Council, Pres.'s Advisory Cttee on Trade and Policy Negotiations, US-Japan Business Council, French-American Business Council, Pres.'s Nat. Security Telecommunications Advisory Cttee, Pres.'s Council of Advisors on Science and Tech., Econ. Club of Chicago; Pres. Boston Univ.; fmr Provost and fmr Prof., MIT; Trustee, Southern Methodist Univ., Rush-Presbyterian-St Luke's Medical Center; Vice-Chair. Bd of Trustees, Ohio Univ. Foundation; mem. NAS, American Acad. of Arts and Sciences, Nat. Acad. of Eng; Hon. DrIur (Ohio Univ.); Hon. PhD (James Madison Univ.). *Address:* Joseph E. Seagram & Sons, Inc., 375 Park Avenue, New York, NY 10152, USA (office). *Telephone:* (212) 572-7000 (office). *Fax:* (212) 572-1022 (office).

BROWN, Robert A., BS, MS, PhD; American engineer, academic and university administrator; *President, Boston University;* b. 1951; m. Beverly Brown; two s.; ed Univ. of Texas at Austin; Instructor, Dept of Chemical Eng and Material Science, Univ. of Minnesota 1978; Asst Prof. of Chemical Eng, Massachusetts Inst. of Tech. (MIT) 1979–82, Assoc. Prof. 1982–84, Prof. 1984–2005, Arthur Dehun Little Prof. of Chemical Eng 1986–92, Warren K. Lewis Prof. 1992–2005, Dean of Eng 1996–98, Provost 1998–2005; Pres. Boston Univ. 2005–; Exec. Ed. Journal of Chemical Engineering Science 1991–2004; mem. Pres.'s Council of Advisors on Science and Tech. 2006–08, Council on Competitiveness 2011–, Exec. Cttee Asscn of Ind. Colls and Univs in Mass 2007– (Chair. 2010–11); mem. and Chair. Academic Research Council, Ministry of Educ., Singapore 2006–; mem. Bd Nat. Research Foundation, Singapore 2006–; Dir, E.I. du Pont de Nemours & Co. 2007–; Trustee, Aalto Univ. Foundation, Finland 2008–10, Universities Research Asscn, Washington, DC 2009–; mem. Nat. Acad. of Eng 1991, American Acad. of Arts and Sciences 1994, NAS 2001; Hon. Citizen of Singapore; numerous honours and awards, including Univ. of Texas at Austin Grad. School Outstanding Alumnus/a Award 2003, named by AIChE to list of 100 Most Influential Chemical Engineers of the Modern Era 2008. *Publications:* over 250 papers in areas related to mathematical modelling of transport phenomena in materials. *Address:* Office of the President, University of Boston, 8th Floor, 1 Silber Way, Boston MA 02215, USA (office). *Telephone:* (617) 353-2200 (office). *Fax:* (617) 353-3278 (office). *E-mail:* president@bu.edu (office). *Website:* www.bu.edu/president (office).

BROWN, Robert James (Bob), MB, BS; Australian physician and politician; *Senator for Tasmania;* b. 27 Dec. 1944, Oberon, NSW; pnr, Paul Thomas 1996; ed Blacktown Boys High School, Univ. of Sydney; elected School Capt. in sr year; medical practice, Canberra, London, Sydney, Perth, Launceston 1969–80; moved to Tasmania to work in Launceston gen. practice 1972; cand. for United Tasmania Group 1975; Dir The Wilderness Soc. 1979–84; emerged as leader of campaign to prevent construction of Franklin Dam late 1970s, spent 19 days in Hobart's Risdon Prison 1983; elected to Tasmanian House of Ass. 1983–93, Leader of five Green inds, formed accord with Labor Party 1989–92; unsuccessful cand. for Fed. House of Reps 1993; extensive tours of Australian cities and towns as Australian Greens Nat. Spokesperson 1994–96; Senator for Tasmania (first Australian Greens Senator) 1996–, re-elected 2001, 2007; hosted first Global Greens Conf., Canberra 2001; Leader, Australian Greens 2005–; elected first Fed. Parl. Leader of The Greens 2005–; Founding Pres. Australian Bush Heritage Fund (now Bush Heritage Australia) 1990–96; Australian of the Year, The Australian newspaper 1983, UNEP Global 500 Award 1987, Goldman Environmental Prize (USA) 1990, World's Most Inspiring Politician, BBC Wildlife magazine 1996, Nat. Trust Australian Nat. Treasure 1998, Rainforest Action Network Environmental Hero 2006, My Favourite Australian 2008. *Publications:* several books, including Wild Rivers 1983, Lake Pedder 1986, Tarkine Trails 1994, The Greens (with Peter Singer) 1996, Memo for a Saner World 2004, Tasmania's Recherche Bay 2005, Earth 2009. *Leisure interests:* photography, bushwalking, poetry, philosophy. *Address:* GPO Box 404, Hobart, TAS 7001 (office); Parliament House, Canberra, ACT, Australia (office). *Telephone:* (3) 6224-3222 (Hobart) (office); (2) 6277-3170 (Canberra) (office). *Fax:* (3) 6224-2999 (Hobart) (office); (2) 6277-3185 (Canberra) (office). *E-mail:* senator.bob.brown@aph.gov.au (office). *Website:* www.bobbrown .org.au (office); www.aph.gov.au/senate/senators/homepages/s-qd4.htm (office).

BROWN, Scott Philip, BA, JD; American lawyer and politician; *Counsel, Nixon Peabody LLP;* b. 12 Sept. 1959, Kittery, Maine; m. Gail Huff; two d.; ed Wakefield High School, Tufts Univ., Boston Coll. Law School; mem. US Army Nat. Guard 1979–, holds rank of Col in Judge Advocate Gen. Corps, head defence attorney for the New England States; began career in public service as mem. Wrentham, Massachusetts Bd of Assessors 1987–90; mem. Wrentham Bd of Selectmen 1995–98; served in Massachusetts House of Reps 1998–2004; elected three times to Massachusetts Senate from Norfolk, Bristol & Middlesex Dist 2004–10; Senator from Massachusetts 2010–13, mem. Cttee on Armed Services, Cttee on Veterans' Affairs, Homeland Security and Governmental Affairs Cttee, Cttee on Small Business and Entrepreneurship; Counsel, Nixon Peabody LLP (law firm), Boston 2013–; commentator, Fox News 2013–; Republican; Army Commendation Medal for meritorious service in homeland security, Meritorious Service Medal. *Address:* Nixon Peabody LLP, 100 Summer Street, Boston, MA 02110, USA (office); . *Telephone:* (617) 345-1381 (office). *Fax:* (855) 297-5465 (office). *E-mail:* sbrown@ nixonpeabody.com (office). *Website:* www.nixonpeabody.com (office).

BROWN, Sherrod, BA, MA; American politician; *Senator from Ohio;* b. 9 Nov. 1952, Mansfield, Ohio; m. Connie Schultz; two d. one step-s. one step-d.; ed Yale Univ. and Ohio State Univ.; taught at Mansfield br. campus, Ohio State Univ. 1979–81; Ohio State Rep. 1975–82; Ohio Sec. of State 1982–91; mem. US House of Reps for the 13th Dist 1993–2006, ranking minority mem. on House Energy and Commerce Cttee's Health Sub-cttee, also served on Sub-cttee on Telecommunications and the Internet and Sub-cttee on Commerce, Trade and Consumer Protection, mem. House Int. Relations Cttee, Sub-cttee on Asia and the Pacific; Senator from Ohio 2007–; mem. Congressional Progressive Caucus; Democrat; American Public Health Asscn Distinguished Public Health Legislator of 2002, Congressional Leadership Award, Nat. Asscn of Public Hosps and Health 2005, Congressional Leadership Award, American Coll. of Emergency Physicians 2002, Paul G. Rogers Award, Asscn of Academic Health Centers 2002, recognized by Acad. of Medicine of Cleveland and Northern Ohio Medical Assen. *Publications:* Congress from the Inside: Observations from the Majority and the Minority, Myths of Free Trade: Why American Trade Policy Has Failed. *Address:* 713 Hart Senate Office Building, Washington, DC 20510, USA (office). *Telephone:* (202) 224-2315 (office). *Fax:* (202) 228-6321 (office). *Website:* brown.senate.gov (office); www .sherrodbrown.com (office).

BROWN, Shona L., PhD; American business executive; *Senior Vice-President of Business Operations, Google Inc.;* ed Carleton Univ., Canada, Univ. of Oxford, UK (Rhodes Scholar), Stanford Univ.; has taught in Dept of Industrial Eng and Grad. School of Business, Stanford Univ. and within McKinsey's mini-MBA programme; Pnr, McKinsey & Co., worked with tech. clients in Toronto and Los Angeles and Leader, Global Strategy Practice 1995–2003; Vice-Pres. Business Operations, Google Inc. 2003–06, Sr Vice-Pres. Business Operations 2006–. *Publications:* Competing on the Edge: Strategy as Structured Chaos (co-author) 1998; numerous articles in both applied and academic journals. *Address:* Google Headquarters, 1600 Amphitheatre Parkway, Mountain View, CA 94043, USA (office). *Telephone:* (650) 253-0000 (office). *Fax:* (650) 253-0001 (office). *Website:* www.google.com (office).

BROWN, Trisha, BA; American choreographer; *Artistic Director, Trisha Brown Dance Company;* b. 25 Nov. 1936, Aberdeen, Wash.; ed Mills Coll., Calif.; with Judson Dance Theater 1960s; Founder and Artistic Dir Trisha Brown Dance Co. 1970–; mem. Nat. Council on the Arts 1994–97; Fellow, American Acad. of Arts and Sciences 2009–; Hon. mem. American Acad. of Arts and des Letters; Officier des Arts et Lettres 2000; numerous hon. doctorates; Nat. Endowment for the Arts Fellowship in Choreography (five times), John Simon Guggenheim Memorial Foundation Fellowship in Choreography (twice), MacArthur Foundation Fellowship Award 1991, Samuel H. Scripps American Dance Festival Award 1994, Prix de la Danse de la Soc. des Auteurs et Compositeurs Dramatiques 1996, New York State Gov.'s Arts Award 1999. *Dance:* has choreographed numerous dances for alternative spaces including rooftops and walls 1961–; Opal Loop/Cloud Installation 1980, Son of Gone Fishin' 1981, Set and Reset 1982, Lateral Pass 1985, Carmen (opera) 1986, Newark 1987, Astral Convertible 1989, Foray Forêt 1990, Astral Converted (50") 1991, For M.G.: The Movie 1991, One Story as in Falling 1992, Another Story as in Falling 1993, Yet Another Story 1994, Long and Dream 1994, If You Couldn't See Me 1994, You Can See Us 1995, M.O. 1995, Twelve Ton Rose 1996, Canto/Pianto 1997, L'Orfeo (opera) 1998, Five Part Weather Invention 1999, Rapture to Leon James 2000. *Address:* Trisha Brown Dance Company, 625 West 55th Street, 2nd Floor, New York, NY 10019, USA (office). *Telephone:* (212) 582-0040 (office); (212) 977-5365 (office). *Website:* www.trishabrowncompany.org (office).

BROWN, William Charles Langdon, CBE; British banker (retd); b. 9 Sept. 1931, London, England; s. of Charles Leonard Brown and Kathleen May Tizzard; m. Nachiko Sagawa 1959; one s. two d.; ed John Ruskin School, Croydon, Ashbourne Grammar School, Derbyshire; with Chartered Bank of India, Australia and China, serving throughout Far East 1954–75, Area Gen. Man., Hong Kong 1975–87, Sr Gen. Man. (London) for Asia Pacific Region 1987; Exec. Dir Standard Chartered Bank PLC (SCB) 1987, Man. Dir 1988, Deputy Group Chief Exec. 1988, Group Deputy Chair. 1989–91, Dir (non-exec.) 1991–94; Dir and Treasurer Royal Commonwealth Soc. 1991–95, Commonwealth Trust 1991–95; Dir HongKong Investment Trust PLC 1991–97; Dir (non-exec.) Kexim Bank UK Ltd 1992–2003, Arbuthnot Latham & Co. Ltd 1993–99; Chair. (non-exec.) Atlantis Japan Growth Fund Ltd 1996–2002; Unofficial mem. Legis. Council of Hong Kong 1980–85; Hon. DScS (Chinese Univ., Hong Kong) 1987. *Leisure interests:* mountain walking, yoga, skiing, philately, photography, classical music. *Address:* Penthouse B, 15 Portman Square, London, W1H 6LJ (home); Appleshaw, 11 Central Avenue, Findon Valley, Worthing, Sussex, BN14 0DS, England (home). *Telephone:* (20) 7487-5741 (home); (1903) 873175 (home). *Fax:* (20) 7486-3005 (home). *E-mail:* wclbrown@yahoo.co.uk (home).

BROWNBACK, Samuel Dale (Sam), BS, JD; American lawyer and politician; *Governor of Kansas;* b. 12 Sept. 1956, Garnett, Kan.; s. of Robert Brownback and Nancy Brownback; m. Mary S. Stauffer; two s. three d. (two c. adopted); ed Kansas State Univ. and Univ. of Kansas; raised in farming family in Parker, Kan.; elected student body pres., Kan. State Univ.; State Pres. Nat. FFA Org., Nat. Vice-Pres. 1976–77; spent a year working as a broadcaster, hosting a weekly half-hour show, KKSU; admitted to Kansas Bar 1982; Partner, law firm in New York; Instructor in Law, Kan. State Univ.; Sec. Agricultural State of Kansas, Topeka 1986–93; City Attorney, Ogden & Leonardville, Kan.; mem. US Congress from 2nd Kansas Dist 1995–96; Senator from Kan. 1996–2011 (retd), mem. Foreign Relations Cttee,

Chair. Sub-cttee on East Asian and Pacific Affairs; unsuccessful campaign for Republican nomination for Pres. of US 2007; Gov. of Kansas 2011–; Vice-Chair. Riley Co. Republican Cttee; Commr, US Helsinki Comm.; Pres. Kansas Prayer Breakfast; mem. ABA, Nat. Future Farmers of America (Vice-Pres. 1977), American Judicature Soc., American Agricultural Law Assen, Riely Co. Bar Assen, Kansas Bar Assen; Republican; named a Kansan of Distinction 1988, Manufacturing Excellence Award, Nat. Assen of Mfrs 2001, Honor Award, Oncology Nursing Soc. 2002, US Oncology Medal of Honor 2002, Pro Deo et Patria Medal, Christendom Coll., Va 2005. *Publication:* From Power to Purpose: A Remarkable Journey of Faith and Compassion (with Jim Nelson Black) 2007. *Address:* Office of the Governor, Capitol, 300 SW 10th Avenue, Suite 241S, Topeka, KS 66612-1590 (office); Washington Office of the Governor, State of Kansas, 500 New Jersey Avenue NW, Suite 400, Washington, DC 20001, USA (office). *Telephone:* (785) 296-3232 (Topeka) (office); (202) 715-2923 (DC) (office). *Fax:* (785) 296-7973 (Topeka) (office); (202) 638-1045 (DC) (office). *Website:* governor.ks .gov (office).

BROWNE, Anthony; British writer, artist and illustrator; b. 1946, Sheffield, m.; two c.; ed Leeds Coll. of Art; fmr medical illustrator, Leeds Royal Infirmary; fmr greetings card illustrator; Illustrator-in-Residence, Tate Britain 2001–02; Children's Laureate 2009–11; Hon. D.Ed (Kingston Univ.) 2005; Boston Globe Book Award, Hans Christian Andersen Award 2000. *Publications:* Through the Magic Mirror 1976, A Walk in the Park 1977, Bear Hunt 1979, Look What I've Got! 1980, Hansel and Gretel 1981, Bear Goes to Town 1982, Gorilla (Kate Greenaway Medal, Kurt Maschler Emil Award) 1983, The Visitors Who Came to Stay 1984, Willy the Wimp 1985, Knock, Knock, Who's There 1985, Willy the Champ 1985, Piggybook 1986, Kirsty Knows Best 1988, Alice's Adventures in Wonderland (Kurt Maschler Emil Award) 1988, Little Bear Book 1988, I Like Books 1988, Things I Like 1989, A Bear-y Tale 1989, The Tunnel 1990, Trail of Stones 1990, Changes 1990, Willy and Hugh 1991, The Night Shimmy 1991, Zoo (Kate Greenaway Medal) 1992, The Big Baby 1993, The Topiary Garden 1993, The Daydreamer 1994, King Kong 1994, Willy the Wizard 1995, Willy the Dreamer 1997, Voices in the Park (Kurt Maschler Emil Award) 1998, My Dad 2000, Willy's Pictures 2000, The Animal Fair 2002, The Shape Game (Honor Book, Boston Globe-Horn Book Awards) 2003, Into the Forest 2004, My Mum 2008, Silly Billy 2006, My Brother 2007, Little Beauty 2008, Me and You 2011, How Do You Feel? 2011. *Address:* c/o Walker Books, 87 Vauxhall Walk, London, SE11 5HJ, England (office). *E-mail:* childrenslaureate@booktrust .org.uk (office). *Website:* www.walker.co.uk (office); www.childrenslaureate.org.uk (office).

BROWNE, Jackson; American singer, songwriter and musician (guitar, piano); b. 9 Oct. 1948, Heidelberg, Germany; m. 1st Phyllis Major 1975 (died 1976); one s.; m. 2nd Lynne Sweeney 1981 (divorced 1983); one s.; fmr mem., Nitty Gritty Dirt Band 1966; solo singer, songwriter, musician 1967–; Co-founder Musicians United for Safe Energy (MUSE), Nukefree.org, Success through the Arts Foundation; numerous tours and concerts, festival appearances and benefit concerts; Hon. DMus (Occidental Coll.) 2004; John Steinbeck Award 2002, inducted into Rock and Roll Hall of Fame 2004, Songwriters Hall of Fame 2007, NARM Harry Chapin Humanitarian Award 2008. *Compositions include:* songs recorded by Tom Rush; Nico; Linda Ronstadt; The Eagles; co-writer with Glenn Frey, Take It Easy. *Recordings include:* albums: Jackson Browne 1972, For Everyman 1973, Late For The Sky 1974, The Pretender 1976, Running On Empty 1978, Hold Out 1980, Lawyers In Love 1983, Lives In The Balance 1987, World In Motion 1989, I'm Alive 1993, Looking East 1996, The Naked Ride Home 2002, Solo Acoustic Vol. 1 2005, Solo Acoustic Vol. 2 2008, Time the Conqueror 2008, Love Is Strange: En Vivo Con Tino (with David Lindley) 2010. *Address:* c/o Michael Jensen, Jensen Communications, 101 East Green Street. Suite 12, Pasadena, CA 91105, USA (office). *Telephone:* (626) 585-9575 (office). *Fax:* 626) 213-3964 (office). *E-mail:* info@ jensencom.com (office). *Website:* www.jensencom.com (office); www.jacksonbrowne .com.

BROWNE, Michael (Mike); Saint Vincent and the Grenadines government official; Minister of Educ., Youth and Sport –2005, of Foreign Affairs and of Commerce and Trade May–Dec. 2005. *Address:* c/o Ministry of Foreign Affairs, Administrative Centre, Kingstown, Saint Vincent and the Grenadines (office).

BROWNE, Air Chief Marshal Norman Anil Kumar; Indian air force officer; b. 15 Dec. 1951; m. Kiran Browne; one s. one d.; ed St Joseph's Coll., Nat. Defence Acad., Air Force Acad., Air Command and Staff Coll., USA; joined Air Force as Operational Fighter Squadron 1972, mem. first two batches of pioneer pilots that went to train with Number 226 Operational Conversion Unit at RAF Lossiemouth on Jaguar Deep Penetration Strike Aircraft, Commdr Number 16 Squadron 'The Cobras' 1990–92, also Fighter Combat Leader, fmr Instructor, Tactics and Air Combat Devt Establishment and Defence Services Staff Coll., USA; has held various operational and staff positions including Jt Dir Air War Strategy Cell, Air HQ, Chief Operations Officer and Air Officer Commanding SU-30 base, Air-I at Western Air Command, Asst Chief of the Air Staff (Intelligence), Deputy Chief of the Air Staff 2007–09, Vice-Chief of the Air Staff Jan.–July 2011, Chief of the Air Staff 2011–14; est. Indian Defence Wing in Tel Aviv, Israel 1997, Defence Attaché 1997–2000; Hon. ADC to Pres. of India; Param Vishist Seva Medal, Ati Vishist Seva Medal, Vayu Sena Medal. *Address:* c/o Indian Air Force, Directorate of Public Relations, Ministry of Defence, Room Number 91, South Block, New Delhi, 110 106, India.

BROWNE OF LADYTON, Baron (Life Peer), cr. 2010, of Ladyton in Ayrshire and Arran; **Des Browne,** PC, LLB; British politician and lawyer; b. 22 March 1952, Ayrshire; m.; two s.; ed St Michael's Acad., Kilwinning, Univ. of Glasgow; admitted as solicitor 1976; joined Ross, Harper and Murphy (law firm), Kilmarnock; Co-founder McCluskey Browne (law firm) –1993; unsuccessful cand. for MP for Argyll and Bute 1992; called to the Bar 1993, served as specialist child law advocate; MP for Kilmarnock and Loudoun 1997–2005, for New Kilmarnock and Loudoun 2005–10; Parl. Pvt. Sec. to Sec. of State for Scotland Donald Dewar 1998–99, for Adam Ingram 2000; Parl. Under-Sec. of State, NI Office 2001–03; Minister of State, Dept for Work and Pensions (Work) 2003–04; Minister of State, Home Office (Citizenship, Immigration and Nationality) 2004–05; Chief Sec. to Treasury 2005–06; Sec. of State for Defence 2006–08, for Scotland 2007–08; Prime Minister's Special Envoy for Sri Lanka 2009–; Sec. Scottish Labour Party Working Party on Prison System 1988–90; mem. Commons Select Cttees on NI Affairs 1997–98,

Public Admin 1999–2000; Jt Cttee on Human rights 2001; mem. Labour Party Departmental Cttees for NI, Treasury, Civil Liberties Group 1997–2001; Hon. Sec. Labour Party Departmental Cttee for Social Security 1997–2001. *Address:* House of Lords, London, SW1A 0PW, England (office).

BROWNE OF MADINGLEY, Baron (Life Peer), cr. 2001, of Madingley in the County of Cambridgeshire; **(Edmund) John (Philip) Browne,** BSc, MS, FRS, FREng, FInstP, FInstPet, CIMgt; British business executive; *Managing Director and Managing Partner, Riverstone Europe;* b. 20 Feb. 1948, Hamburg, Germany; ed Univ. of Cambridge, Stanford Univ., Calif., USA; joined BP 1966, held various exploration and production posts in Anchorage, New York, San Francisco, London and Canada 1969–83, Group Treas. and Chief Exec. BP Finance Int. 1984–86, Exec. Vice-Pres. and Chief Financial Officer The Standard Oil Co., Cleveland, Ohio 1986–87, BP America and CEO Standard Oil Production Co. (following BP/ Standard merger) 1987–89, Man. Dir and CEO BP Exploration, London 1989–91, Man. Dir The British Petroleum Co. PLC 1991–95, Group CEO 1995–98, Group CEO BP Amoco (now BP PLC) 1998–2007 (resgnd); Man. Dir and Man. Pnr, Riverstone Europe 2007–; Lead Non-Executive Dir, Cabinet Office 2010–; mem. Supervisory Bd Daimler Chrysler AG 1998–2001, Chair.'s Council 2001–04; Chair. Cuadrilla Resources, Performance Theatre Advisory Group, International Advisory Bd, Russian Museum, Accenture Global Energy Bd, Stanhope Capital Advisory Bd 2010–, Mubadala Oil and Gas International Advisory Bd; Chair. Emer. Advisory Bd, Stanford Grad. School of Business; Pres. Royal Acad. of Eng 2006–11; Vice-Pres. Prince of Wales Business Leaders Forum; Chair. Bd of Trustees Queen Elizabeth Prize Foundation 2011–, John Browne Charitable Trust; mem. Bd of Dirs (non-exec.) Foster + Pnrs 2007–, Fairfield Energy Ltd, White Rose Energy Ventures LLP, Goldman Sachs 1999–2007, SmithKline Beecham 1996–99, Intel Corpn 1997–2006, Apax Pnrs Worldwide 2006–07; Trustee, British Museum 1995–2005, Tate Gallery 2007– (Chair. 2009–), Blavatnik School of Govt Foundation 2011–, Needham Research Inst., Cambridge China Development Trust, Cambridge Foundation; Chair. Advisory Bd Cambridge Business School; Global Counsellor, Conference Bd, Inc.; mem. Deutsche Bank Advisory Bd for Climate Change, Schlumberger Business Consulting Advisory Group, Deutsche Bank Europe Advisory Bd, British-American Business Council (also fmr Chair.), Cambridge Consultative Cttee and Chem. Appeal (also fmr Chair.), Guild of Cambridge Benefactors, Council of the Foundation for Science and Tech., Bd of Catalyst, School of Econs and Man., Tsinghua Univ. (Chair. Advisory Bd); Fellow, Inst. of Mining and Metallurgy; Sr Mem. St Anthony's Coll. Oxford; apptd by Prime Minister David Cameron to lead Whitehall efficiency initiative 2010; Hon. Fellow, St John's Coll. Cambridge; Hon. FIChemE; Hon. FGS; Hon. FIMechE; Hon. FRSC; Hon. Trustee, Chicago Symphony Orchestra; Hon. DEng (Heriot Watt, Colorado School of Mines, Belfast); Hon. DTech (Robert Gordon); Hon. LLD (Dundee, Thunderbird, Notre Dame); Hon. DUniv (Sheffield Hallam); Hon. DSc (Cranfield, Hull, Leuven, Warwick, Mendeleyev University of Chemical Technology—Moscow, Buckingham); Hon. DLitt (Arizona State Univ.); Prince Philip Medal, Royal Acad. of Eng 1999, Henry Shaw Medal, Missouri Botanical Gardens, Gold Medal, Inst. of Man., Ernest C. Arbuckle Award, Stanford Business School Alumni Asscn 2001, Soc. of Petroleum Engineers Public Service Award 2002. *Address:* House of Lords, London, SW1A 0PW; RiverStone Management, 2nd Floor, Mint House, 77, Mansell Street, London, E1 8AF, England (office). *Telephone:* (20) 7219-5353 (House of Lords); (20) 7977-1600 (office). *E-mail:* spaynter@riverstonellc.com (office). *Website:* www.rsml.co.uk (office).

BROWNE-WILKINSON, Baron (Life Peer), cr. 1991, of Camden, in the London Borough of Camden; **Nicolas Christopher Henry Browne-Wilkinson,** PC, QC, BA; British judge; *Chairman, Financial Markets Law Committee, Bank of England;* b. 30 March 1930, London; s. of the late Canon A.R. Browne-Wilkinson and Molly Browne-Wilkinson; m. 1st Ursula de Lacy Bacon 1955 (died 1987); three s. two d.; m. 2nd Hilary Tuckwell 1990; ed Lancing Coll., Magdalen Coll., Oxford; called to Bar, Lincoln's Inn 1953, Bencher 1977; QC 1972; Jr Counsel to Registrar of Restrictive Trading Agreements 1964–66, to Attorney-Gen. in Charity Matters 1966–72, in bankruptcy, to Dept of Trade and Industry 1966–72; a Judge of the Courts of Appeal of Jersey and Guernsey 1976–77; Judge of the High Court, Chancery Div. 1977–83; a Lord Justice of Appeal 1983–85; Vice-Chancellor of the Supreme Court 1985–91; Lord of Appeal in Ordinary 1991–2000, Sr Law Lord 1998–2000; currently Chair. Financial Markets Law Cttee, Bank of England; Pres. Employment Appeal Tribunal 1981–83, Senate of the Inns of Court and the Bar 1984–86; Fellow, St Edmund Hall, Oxford 1986, Magdalen Coll. 1993, American Coll. of Trial Lawyers, American Law Inst. *Leisure interests:* gardening, music. *Address:* House of Lords, London, SW1A 0PW (office); Financial Markets Law Committee, c/o Bank of England, Threadneedle Street, London, EC2R 8AH, England. *Telephone:* (20) 7219-3202 (office). *Website:* www.bankofengland.co.uk.

BROWNER, Carol Martha, BA, JD; American lawyer and fmr government official; *Senior Counselor, Albright Stonebridge Group;* b. 16 Dec. 1955, Miami, Fla; d. of Michael Browner and Isabella Browner (née Hugues); m. 1st Michael Podhorzer (divorced); one s.; m. 2nd Thomas Joseph Downey 2007; two step-c.; ed Univ. of Florida; gen. counsel of a Cttee of Fla Legis. 1979–83; Assoc. Dir Citizen Action, Washington, DC 1983–86; mem. staff Senator Lawton Chiles 1986–89; mem. staff Senate Cttee on Energy and Natural Resources 1989; Legis. Dir on staff of Senator Al Gore 1989–90; Head of Dept of Environmental Regulation, State of Fla 1990–93; Admin. Environmental Protection Agency 1993–2001, Co-founder and Prin. The Albright Group LLC (consulting firm), Washington, DC 2001–08, also Prin. Albright Capital Management (investment advisory firm), Sr Counselor, Albright Stonebridge Group 2011–; Coordinator for Energy and Climate, The White House, Washington, DC 2009–11; mem. Exec. Cttee, Center for American Progress; fmr mem. Bd of Dirs Audubon Soc., League of Conservation Voters, Alliance for Climate Protection; Outstanding Mother of the Year, Nat. Mother's Day Cttee 1997, Woman of the Year, Glamour magazine 1998, Guy M. Bradley Lifetime Achievement Award, S Florida Chapter of Audubon Soc., Lifetime Environmental Achievement Award, New York State Bar Asscn. *Address:* Albright Stonebridge Group, 110 New York Avenue, NW, Suite 900, Washington, DC 20005, USA (office). *Telephone:* (202) 842-7222 (office). *Fax:* (202) 370-3599 (office). *Website:* www.albrightstonebridge.com (office).

BROWNING, Keith Anthony, BSc, PhD, DIC, FRS, ARCS; British meteorologist and academic; *Professor Emeritus, Department of Meteorology, University of*

Reading; b. 31 July 1938, Sunderland, England; s. of James Anthony Browning and Amy Hilda Greenwood; m. Ann Baish 1962; one s. two d.; ed Imperial Coll. of Science and Tech., Univ. of London; Research Atmospheric Physicist, Air Force Cambridge Research Labs, Mass, USA 1962–66; Prin. then Chief Meteorological Officer, Meteorological Office Radar Research Lab., Royal Signals and Radar Establishment, Malvern, Worcs. 1966–74, 1975–85; Chief Scientist, Nat. Hail Research Experiment, Nat. Center for Atmospheric Research, Boulder, Colo, USA 1974–75; Deputy Dir (Physical Research), Meteorological Office, Bracknell, Berks. 1985–89, Dir of Research 1989–91; Visiting Prof., Dept of Meteorology, Univ. of Reading 1988–94, Visiting Scientist, Jt Centre for Mesoscale Meteorology 1991–92, Dir 1992–2003, Prof. in Dept of Meteorology 1995–2003, Prof. Emer. 2003–; Visiting Prof. of Atmospheric Science, School of Earth and Environment, Univ. of Leeds 2006–12; Dir Univs Weather Research Network 2000–03, Univs Facility for Atmospheric Measurements 2001–03; Chair. Meteorology & Atmospheric Physics Sub-cttee of British Cttee for Geodesy and Geophysics 1985–89, GEWEX Cloud System Study 1992–95; mem. Natural Environment Research Council 1984–87, Scientific Steering Group, Global Energy and Water Cycle Experiment 1988–97, Jt Scientific Cttee, World Climate Research Programme 1990–94, Scientific Steering Cttee, World Weather Research Programme 1996–2005; Pres. Royal Meteorological Soc. 1988–90; mem. Academia Europaea 1989–; Foreign Assoc., Nat. Acad. of Eng (USA) 1992–; Fellow, American Meteorological Soc. 1975–, Hon. mem. 2010–; Chartered Meteorologist and Fellow, Royal Meteorological Soc., Hon. mem. 2006–; Ministry of Defence L. G. Groves Memorial Prize 1969, Inst. of Physics Charles Chree Medal 1981, Symons Gold Medal 2001 and three other awards from Royal Meteorological Soc., Carl Gustaf Rossby Medal 2003 and two other awards from American Meteorological Soc. *Publications:* more than 200 articles on meteorology in learned journals since 1962. *Leisure interests:* home, garden, photography, walking, piano. *Telephone:* (1539) 433615 (home). *E-mail:* kandabrowning@googlemail.com (office).

BROWNLOW, Kevin; British film historian and television director; b. 2 June 1938, Crowborough, Sussex; s. of Robert Thomas Brownlow and Niña Fortnum; m. Virginia Keane 1969; one d.; ed Univ. Coll. School, Hampstead; joined World Wide Pictures 1955; became film ed., then co-dir 1964; with Thames TV 1975–90; Hon. Acad. Award, Acad. of Motion Picture Arts and Sciences 2010. *Films include:* It Happened Here 1964, Winstanley 1975 (both with Andrew Mollo). *Television includes:* 13-part series Hollywood 1980, three-part Unknown Chaplin 1983, three-part British Cinema (producer only) 1986, three-part Buster Keaton: A Hard Act to Follow 1987, two-part Harold Lloyd 1988, three-part D. W. Griffith 1993, six-part Cinema Europe: The Other Hollywood 1995 (all with David Gill), Universal Horror 1998, Lon Chaney: A Thousand Faces 2000, The Tramp and the Dictator (with Michael Kloft) 2002, Cecil B. De Mille: American Epic 2003; with Christopher Bird: Buster Keaton: So Funny It Hurt 2004, Garbo 2005, I'm King Kong: The Exploits of Merion C. Cooper 2005. *Publications:* Parade's Gone By 1968, The War, the West and the Wilderness 1978, Napoleon (Abel Gance's Classic Film) 1983, Behind the Mask of Innocence 1990, David Lean: A Biography 1996, Mary Pickford Rediscovered 1999, Winstanley: Warts and All 2009, The Search for Charlie Chaplin 2010. *Address:* c/o Photoplay Productions, 21 Princess Road, London, NW1 8JR, England (office). *Telephone:* (20) 7722-2500 (office).

BROWSE, Sir Norman Leslie, Kt, MD, FRCP, FRCS; British government official and surgeon (retd); *President, States of Alderney, Channel Islands;* b. 1 Dec. 1931, London; s. of Reginald Browse and Margaret Browse; m. Jeanne Menage 1957; one s. one d.; ed St Bartholomew's Hosp. Medical Coll. and Univ. of Bristol; Capt. RAMC 1957–59; Sr House Officer and Registrar, Bristol 1959–62; Lecturer in Surgery, Westminster Hosp. 1962–65; Harkness Fellow, Research Assoc. Mayo Clinic, Rochester, Minn. 1964–65; Reader in Surgery and Consultant Surgeon, St Thomas' Hosp. 1965–72, Prof. of Vascular Surgery 1972–81, Prof. of Surgery 1981–96, Consulting Surgeon 1996–; Hon. Consultant to Army and RAF 1980–96; Prof. of Surgery, United Medical and Dental Schools 1981–96; Prof. Emer. Univ. of London 1996–; Pres. States of Alderney, CI 2002–; Pres. Royal Coll. of Surgeons of England 1992–95; Chair., Jt Consultants Cttee 1994–98, Lord Brock Memorial Trust 1994–2001; Vice-Chair. British Vascular Foundation 1997–; Visiting Prof. and Lecturer, Cape Town, Johannesburg, Perth, Sydney, Melbourne, Brisbane, Boston, Ann Arbor, San Diego, Los Angeles, Vancouver, Seattle, Singapore, Hong Kong, Madras, Sri Lanka, Delhi, Kuwait, Paris, Marseille, Barcelona, Amsterdam, Copenhagen, Stockholm, Helsinki; mem. Council Marlborough Coll. 1990–2001; Gov. American Coll. of Surgeons 1997–2003; Fellow, King's Coll., London 2000–; Patron HOPE 2002–; Hon. Fellow Royal Coll. of Physicians and Surgeons (Glasgow) 1993; Hon. FRACS 1994; Hon. Fellow in Dental Surgery 1994; Hon. Fellow Royal Coll. of Surgeons in Ireland 1995; Hon. FACS 1995; Hon. Fellow Faculty of Accident and Emergency Medicine 1995; Hon. FRCSE 1996; Hon. Fellow Coll. of Medicine of S Africa 1996; Distinguished Alumnus, Mayo Clinic 1993; Hon. Freeman Worshipful Co. of Barbers 1997; Arris and Gale Medal 1968, Abraham Colles Medal 1990, Kinmouth Medal 1991, Vicary Medal 2000, Ratschow Medal 2007. *Publications:* Physiology and Pathology of Bed Rest 1964, Symptoms and Signs of Surgical Disease 1978, Reducing Operation for Lymphoedema 1986, Diseases of the Veins 1989, Diseases of the Lymphatics (co-author) 2003. *Leisure interests:* marine art, medieval history, sailing. *Address:* Corbet House, Butes Lane, Alderney, GY9 3UW, Channel Islands (home). *E-mail:* norman.browse@ virgin.net (home).

BROYLES, William Dodson, Jr, MA; American journalist; b. 8 Oct. 1944, Houston; s. of William Dodson and Elizabeth (née Bills) Broyles; m. 1st Sybil Ann Newman 1973; one s. one d.; m. 2nd Linda Purl 1988 (divorced 1992); m. 3rd Andrea Bettina Berndt; three c.; ed Rice Univ., Houston, Oxford Univ.; Marine Corps Reserve 1969–71; teacher Philosophy Naval Acad. 1970–71; Asst Supt Houston Public Schools 1971–72; Ed.-in-Chief Texas Monthly 1972–82; Ed.-in-Chief California Magazine 1980–82; Ed.-in-Chief Newsweek Magazine 1982–84; Columnist, US News and World Report 1986; mem. Advisory Council, Harry Ransom Center, Univ. of Texas at Austin; Bronze Star, inducted into Texas Film Hall of Fame 2002. *Television:* China Beach (co-producer, exec. consultant) 1988–91. *Films:* screenwriter: Apollo 13 (with Al Reinert) 1995, Entrapment 1999, Cast Away 2000, Planet of the Apes 2001, Unfaithful 2002, The Polar Express 2004, Jarhead 2005, Flags of Our Fathers 2006. *Publications:* Brothers in Arms: A Journey from War to Peace 1986, Cast Away: The Shooting Script 2001, All Aboard the Polar Express (Ed.) 2004. *Address:* Harry Ransom Center, University of Texas at Austin, PO Drawer 7219, Austin, TX 78713-7219, USA (office). *Fax:* (512) 471-9646 (office). *Website:* www.hrc.utexas.edu (office).

BRUCE, Christopher, CBE; British ballet dancer and choreographer; b. 3 Oct. 1945, Leicester; s. of Alexander Bruce and Ethel Parker; m. Marian Meadowcroft 1967; two s. one d.; ed Rambert School, London; dancer, Ballet Rambert, London 1963–80, Assoc. Dir 1975–79, Assoc. Choreographer 1979–87, Artistic Dir Rambert Dance Co. 1994–2003; Assoc. Choreographer, English Nat. Ballet (fmrly London Festival Ballet), London 1986–91; Assoc. Choreographer, Houston Ballet 1989–; choreographer for Kent Opera, Nederlands Dans Theater, Ballet du Grand Théâtre de Genève, etc; Hon. Life mem. Amnesty Int. 2010; Dr hc (De Montfort) 2000; Hon. DLitt (Exeter) 2001; Evening Standard Inaugural Dance Award 1974, Int. Theatre Inst. Award 1993, Evening Standard Ballet Award 1996, Critic's Circle Award for Outstanding Achievement in Dance 2002, Critic's Circle Award for Best Choreography 2010. *Ballets include:* George Frideric 1969, For Those Who Die as Cattle 1971, There Was a Time 1972, Weekend 1974, Ancient Voices of Children 1975, Black Angels 1976, Cruel Garden 1977, Night with Waning Moon 1979, Dancing Day 1981, Ghost Dances 1981, Berlin Requiem 1982, Concertino 1983, Intimate Pages 1984, Ceremonies 1986, Swansong 1987, Symphony in Three Movements 1989, Rooster 1991, Waiting 1993, Crossing 1994, Meeting Point 1995 (for 'United We Dance' Int. Festival celebrating 50 years of UN), Quicksilver (tribute to Marie Rambert to celebrate Rambert Dance Co.'s 70th anniversary) 1996, Stream 1996, Four Scenes 1998, God's Plenty 1999, Hurricane 2000, Grinning in Your Face 2001, 3 Songs, 2 Voices 2005, A Steel Garden 2005, Hush 2006, Shift 2007, Dance at the Crossroads 2007, Ten Poems 2009, Für Alina 2011. *Address:* c/o Rambert Dance Company, 94 Chiswick High Road, London, W4 1SH, England; c/o Houston Ballet, 1921 West Bell Street, Houston, TX 77019, USA. *Website:* www.rambert.org.uk; www.houstonballet.org.

BRUCKHEIMER, Jerry, BA; American film and television producer; b. 1945, Detroit, Mich.; m. Linda Bruckheimer; ed Univ. of Arizona; fmr producer of TV commercials; formed Don Simpson/Jerry Bruckheimer Productions with the late Don Simpson 1983; formed Jerry Bruckheimer Films 1996; entered into partnership with Paramount 2014; Hon. DFA (Univ. of Arizona Coll. of Fine Arts); ShoWest Producer of the Year 1999, David O. Selznick Lifetime Achievement Award 2000, Emmy Award 2004, 2005, 2006, Nat. Bd of Review Producers Award 2004, Variety Showman of the Year 2006, Salute to Excellence, Museum of TV and Radio 2006, Norman Lear Achievement in TV Award 2007, American Cinematheque Award 2013. *Films include:* (assoc. producer) Culpepper Cattle Company 1972, Rafferty and the Gold Dust Twins 1975, (producer) Farewell My Lovely 1975, March or Die 1977, Defiance 1980, American Gigolo 1980, Thief 1981, Cat People 1982, Young Doctors in Love 1982, Flashdance 1983, Beverly Hills Cop 1984, Thief of Hearts 1984, Top Gun 1986, Beverly Hills Cop II 1987, Days of Thunder 1990, The Ref (exec. producer) 1994, Dangerous Minds 1995, Bad Boys 1995, Crimson Tide 1995, The Rock 1996, Con Air 1997, Enemy of the State 1998, Armageddon 1998, Gone in 60 Seconds 2000, Coyote Ugly 2000, Remember the Titans 2000, Pearl Harbor 2001, Black Hawk Down 2002, Bad Company 2002, Kangaroo Jack 2003, Pirates of the Caribbean 2003, Bad Boys 2003, Veronica Guerin 2003, King Arthur 2004, National Treasure 2004, Pirates of the Caribbean: Dead Man's Chest 2006, Glory Road 2006, Deja Vu 2006, Pirates of the Caribbean: At World's End 2007, National Treasure: Book of Secrets 2007, Confessions of a Shopaholic 2009, G-Force 2009, Prince of Persia: The Sands of Time 2010, The Sorcerer's Apprentice 2010, Pirates of the Caribbean: On Stranger Tides 2011, The Lone Ranger 2013, Beware the Night 2014. *Television includes:* exec. producer CSI: Crime Scene Investigation 2000–13, The Amazing Race 2001–13, CSI: Miami 2002–12, Without a Trace 2002–09, Cold Case 2003–10, The Amazing Race Asia 2006–10, CSI: New York 2004–13, E-Ring 2005–06, Just Legal 2005–06, Close to Home 2005–07, Modern Men 2006, Justice 2006–07, Eleventh Hour 2008–09, The Forgotten 2009–10, Dark Blue 2009–10, Miami Medical 2010, The Amazing Race: China Rush 2010, The Whole Truth 2010, Jerry Bruckheimer's Chase 2010–11, The Amazing Race Australia 2011, Take the Money and Run 2011, Hostages 2013, Marshal Law: Texas 2013. *Leisure interest:* ice hockey. *Address:* c/o Jerry Bruckheimer Films Inc., 1631 10th Street, Santa Monica, CA 90404, USA (office). *Telephone:* (310) 664-6260 (office). *Fax:* (310) 664-6261 (office). *Website:* www.jbfilms.com (office).

BRUCKMANN, Gerhart, PhD; Austrian politician and statistician; b. 9 Jan. 1932, Vienna; s. of Friedrich Bruckmann and Anny Bruckmann (née Pötzl); m. Hilde Bartl 1961; two s.; ed Univ. of Graz, Vienna and Rome, Antioch Coll., USA; with Austrian Fed. Chamber of Commerce 1957–67; Prof. of Statistics, Univ. of Linz 1967–68, Univ. of Vienna 1968–92; Dir Inst. for Advanced Studies 1968–73; Consultant Int. Inst. for Applied Systems Analysis 1973–83; Council mem. 1983–86; mem. Parl. 1986–94, 1999–2002; Bd mem. Austrian Sr Citizens' Union 1998–; Exec. Officer European Sr Citizens' Union 1998–2001; mem. Austrian Acad. of Sciences; Hon. PhD (Linz) 1998. *Publications:* Auswege in die Zukunft 1974, Sonnenkraft statt Atomenergie 1978, Groping in the Dark (with D. Meadows and J. Richardson) 1982, Megatrends für Österreich 1988, Österreicher wer bist du? 1989. *Leisure interest:* collecting anchor building blocks. *Address:* Österr. Seniorenbund, Lichtenfelsgasse 7, 1010 Vienna (office); Zehenthofgasse 11, 1190 Vienna, Austria (home). *Telephone:* (431) 40126-151 (office). *Fax:* (431) 4066-266 (office).

BRUCKNER, Pascal, DèsSc, PhD; French writer and lecturer; b. 15 Dec. 1948, Paris; s. of René Bruckner and Monique Bruckner; m. Violaine Barret 1970 (divorced 1973); one s.; also one d. by Caroline Thompson; ed Lycée Henri IV, Univ. de Paris I (Sorbonne), Univ. Paris VII (Jussieu); annual travels in Asia 1977–90; Lecturer, Inst. d'Etudes Politiques, Paris 1990–94; Visiting Prof., Univ. of San Diego and New York Univ. 1986–95; mem. Bd of Dirs Action contre la faim 1983–88; mem. Cercle de l'Oratoire (French think tank) 2001–; Chevalier des Arts et des Lettres, Légion d'honneur 2002. *Theatre:* many of his books have been played on stage throughout Europe and in India. *Publications include:* Le Nouveau Désordre Amoureux 1977, Lune de Fiel 1982 (adapted for screen by Roman Polanski under the title Bitter Moon 1992), Le sanglot de l'homme blanc 1983, Le palais des claques 1986, Le Divin Enfant 1992, La Tentation de l'Innocence (Prix Médicis) 1995, Les Voleurs de Beauté (Prix Renaudot) 1997, Les ogres anonymes 1998, L' Euphorie perpétuelle, essai sur Le devoir de bonheur 2000, Misère de la prospérité. La religion marchande et ses ennemis (Sénat Prix du Livre d'économie)

2002, Au secours, le Père Noël revient 2003, L'amour du prochain 2006, La Tyrannie de la pénitence: Essai sur le masochisme en Occident 2006; translations in 25 countries. *Leisure interests:* piano, sports, fantasy films. *Address:* 8 rue Marie Stuart, 75002 Paris, (home); c/o Editions Denoel, 9 Rue de Cherche-Midi, 75248 Paris, France (office). *Telephone:* 1-40-26-68-79 (home). *Fax:* 1-40-56-34-37 (home). *E-mail:* bruckner@wanadoo.fr (home); contact@lemeilleurdesmondes.org (office). *Website:* www.lemeilleurdesmondes.org (office).

BRÜDERLE, Rainer, BEcons; German politician; *Chairman, Parliamentary Group, Freie Demokratische Partei;* b. 22 June 1945, Berlin; m.; ed Gutenberg Univ., Mainz; mem. FDP (Freie Demokratische Partei—Free Democratic Party) 1973–, becoming FDP Dist Chair. for Rheinhessen-Vorderpfalz, Deputy Chair. Mainz Dist FDP 1981–83, FDP Chair. in Land of Rhineland-Palatinate 1983–, mem. FDP Fed. Exec. Cttee (Bundesvorstand) 1983–; Dir Office of Econ. Affairs and Transport Devt, city of Mainz 1975–77, Dir Office of Econ. Affairs and Real Estate 1977–81, Full-time City Councillor and Head of Dept of Econ. Affairs 1981; mem. Rhineland-Palatinate Landtag (State Parl.) 1987–98, Rhineland-Palatinate Minister of Economy and Transport 1987–94, of Economy, Transport, Agric. and Viticulture 1994–98, Deputy Minister-Pres. of Rhineland-Palatinate 1988–98; mem. Bundestag (Parl.) 1998–, Deputy Chair. FDP Parl. Group 1998–2011, Chair. 2011–; Fed. Minister of Econs and Tech. 2009–11; Chair. Bd of Supervisory Dirs KfW Bankengruppe 2010–11. *Address:* Freie Demokratische Partei, Thomas-Dehler-Haus, Reinhardtstr. 14, 10117 Berlin, Germany (office). *Telephone:* (30) 28495820 (office). *Fax:* (30) 28495822 (office). *E-mail:* fdp-point@fdp.de (office). *Website:* www.fdp-bundespartei.de (office); www.rainer-bruederle.de.

BRUECKNER, Keith Allan, MA, PhD; American fmr academic; b. 19 March 1924, Minneapolis; s. of Leo John Brueckner and Agnes Holland Brueckner; m. Bonnie Brueckner; two s. one d.; ed Univs of Minnesota and California, Berkeley, Inst. for Advanced Study, Princeton; Asst Prof., Indiana Univ. 1951–54, Assoc. Prof. 1954–55; Physicist, Brookhaven Nat. Lab., New York 1955–56; Prof. of Physics, Univ. of Pennsylvania 1956–59; apptd Prof. of Physics, Univ. of California, San Diego 1959; Vice-Pres. and Dir of Research, Inst. for Defense Analyses, Washington, DC 1961–62; Tech. Dir KMS Tech. Center, San Diego 1968–71; Exec. Vice-Pres. and Tech. Dir KMS Fusion Inc., Ann Arbor 1971–74; Consulting Ed., Pure and Applied Physics Series, Academic Press 1964–; mem. NAS; Hon. DSc (Indiana) 1976; Dannie Heinemann Prize for Mathematical Physics 1963. *Publications:* numerous articles in scientific journals. *Leisure interests:* mountain climbing, skiing, sailing, surfing. *Address:* 3120 Almahurst Row, La Jolla, CA 92037, USA. *Telephone:* (858) 452-6920.

BRUEL, Jean-Marc André; French business executive; *Chairman, Firmenich SA;* b. 18 Feb. 1936, Akbou, Algeria; s. of René Bruel and Jeanine Poirson; m. Anne-Mary Barthod 1962; two s. two d.; ed Ecole Centrale des Arts et Manufactures; Head of Tech. Services, Rhodiaceta, Brazil 1964; Dir nylon polyester factory, Rhône-Poulenc, Brazil 1968; Deputy Dir-Gen. of Textile Poduction Rhône-Poulenc, Brazil 1971; Deputy Dir-Gen. Div. of Plant Hygiene, Groupe Rhône-Poulenc 1975, Dir-Gen. 1976; Asst to Pres. and mem. Exec. Cttee Rhône-Poulenc 1979–80, Deputy Dir-Gen. 1980, Dir-Gen. 1982–84; mem. Exec. Cttee Sandoz, Basle 1985–87; Dir-Gen. Rhône Poulenc 1987–92, Vice-Pres. 1992–99; Pres. Rhône Poulenc Chimie 1987–92; Vice-Pres. European Council of Fed. of Chemical Industry (Cefic) 1988; Pres. Soc. of Chemical Industry 1993–94, Villette Enterprises 1995–2005, Institut Curie 1998–2002; mem. Supervisory Bd Sanofi-Aventis 1999–2004, ind. dir 2004–; Chair. Firmenich SA, Geneva 2000–; mem. Bd of Dirs Rhodia 2002–05; Chevalier Légion d'honneur, Officier Ordre nat. du Mérite. *Leisure interests:* tennis, sailing. *Address:* Firmenich SA, Route de La Plaine 125, 1283 La Plaine, Geneva, Switzerland (office); 105 bis rue de Longchamp, 92200 Neuilly-sur-Seine, France (home). *Telephone:* (22) 780-22-11 (office). *Fax:* (22) 754-14-73 (office). *Website:* www.firmenich.com (office).

BRUFAU NIUBÓ, Antonio, MBA; Spanish business executive; *Chairman and CEO, Repsol YPF SA;* b. 1948, Mollerussa, Lérida; ed Univ. of Barcelona, IESE Business School, Univ. of Navarra; fmr Partner and Head of Audit Div., Arthur Andersen; Asst Gen. Man. La Caixa 1998, Man. Dir La Caixa Group 1999–2004; mem. Bd of Dirs Repsol YPF SA 1996–, Chair. and CEO 2004–; Chair. Man. Cttee, mem. Global E & P Cttee, Global Downstream Cttee, Human Resources Cttee; Chair. Gas Natural SDG 1997–2004, Vice-Chair. 2004–; Chair. Comupet Madrid 2008, S.L., Fundation Repsol YPF; Pres. Círculo de Economía de Barcelona 2002–05; mem. European Round Table of Industrialists, Advisory Bd of CEIM Confederación Empresarial de Madrid – CEOE, Asociación Española de Directivos, Círculo de Economía, Foundation Privada Instituto Ildefons Cerdà, Foundation CEDE (Confederación Española de Directivos y Ejecutivos); Chair. Consorcio Interinstitucional GlobalLleida; fmr mem. Bd of Dirs Enagás, Abertis, Aguas de Barcelona, Colonial, Suez, Caixa Holding, CaixaBank France, CaixaBank Andorra; mem. Exec. Cttee ICC; Global Business Leader Award, American Chamber of Commerce in Spain (AmchamSpain) 2009, Best Businessman of the Year, Spanish Chamber of Commerce of the Repub. of Argentina (CECRA) 2010, Entrepreneur of the Year, Fed. of Spanish Chambers of Commerce in Europe (FEDECOM) 2010. *Address:* Repsol YPF SA, Méndez Álvaro 44, 28045 Madrid, Spain (office). *Telephone:* (91) 7538100 (office). *Fax:* (902) 303145 (office). *E-mail:* info@repsol.com (office). *Website:* www.repsol.com (office).

BRUGUERA, Sergi; Spanish fmr professional tennis player; b. 16 Jan. 1971, Barcelona; s. of Luis Bruguera; coached by his father; turned professional 1988; winner French Open 1993, 1994, finalist 1997; Olympic silver medal, Atlanta, USA 1996; winner of 17 titles (three doubles); retd 2002; currently plays Delta Tour of Champions. *Address:* Delta Tour of Champions, ATP Tennis International Headquarters, 201 ATP Boulevard, Ponte Vedra Beach, FL 32082, USA. *Telephone:* (904) 285-8000. *Fax:* (904) 285-5966. *Website:* www.atptennis.com/championstour/default.asp.

BRUININKS, Robert H., BA, MA, PhD; American university administrator, psychologist and academic; *President, University of Minnesota;* m. Dr Susan Andrea Hagstrum; three s.; ed Western Michigan Univ., George Peabody Coll. (now part of Vanderbilt Univ.; Asst Prof., Dept of Educational Psychology, Univ. of Minnesota 1968, later Prof., Dean, Exec. Vice-Pres. and Provost Univ. of Minnesota, Pres. 2002–; Fellow, American Assen on Mental Retardation, American Psychological Assen, American Psychological Soc.; named by Minnesota

Monthly magazine Minnesotan of the Year 2004. *Publications:* more than 90 journal articles and 70 book chapters, as well as training materials and several nationally standardized tests. *Address:* Office of the President, University of Minnesota, 202 Morrill Hall, 100 Church Street SE, Minneapolis, MN 55455, USA (office). *Telephone:* (612) 626-1616 (office). *Fax:* (612) 625-3875 (office). *E-mail:* UPres@umn.edu (office). *Website:* www1.umn.edu (office).

BRUMMELL, Paul, BA, MA; British diplomatist; *Ambassador to Romania;* b. 28 Aug. 1965, Harpenden, Herts., England; s. of Robert George Brummell and June Brummell; m. Adriana Mitsue Ivama Brummell; ed St Albans School, St Catharine's Coll., Cambridge; joined HM Diplomatic Service 1987; Third Sec., later Second Sec., Islamabad 1989–92; with FCO, London 1993–94; First Sec., Rome 1995–2000; Deputy Head Eastern Dept, FCO 2000–01; Amb. to Turkmenistan 2002–05, to Kazakhstan (also accred to Kyrgyzstan) 2005–09; High Commr to Barbados (also accred to Antigua and Barbuda, Dominica, Grenada, Saint Kitts and Nevis, Saint Lucia, and Saint Vincent and the Grenadines) 2009–13, concurrently UK Rep. to CARICOM and the Org. of Eastern Caribbean States 2010–13 and Consul Gen. to the Dutch Caribbean 2011–13; Amb. to Romania 2014–. *Publications:* Turkmenistan: The Bradt Travel Guide 2005, Kazakhstan: The Bradt Travel Guide 2008. *Address:* British Embassy, 010463 Bucharest, Str. Jules Michelet 24, Sector 1, Romania (office). *Telephone:* (21) 2017200 (office). *Fax:* (21) 2017299 (office). *E-mail:* press.bucharest@fco.gov.uk (office). *Website:* www .gov.uk/government/world/organisations/british-embassy-bucharest (office); www .gov.uk/government/world/romania (office).

BRUNDIN, Clark Lannerdahl, BS, PhD; American/British engineer, academic and university administrator (retd); b. 21 March 1931, Los Angeles, Calif., USA; s. of Ernest Brundin and Elinor Brundin (née Clark); m. Judith Anne Maloney 1959; two s. two d.; ed Whittier High School, California Inst. of Tech., Univ. of California, Berkeley; electronics petty officer, USN 1951–55; Assoc. in Mech. Eng, Univ. of California, Berkeley 1956–57, Research Engineer, Inst. of Eng Research 1959–63; Demonstrator, Dept of Eng Science, Univ. of Oxford 1957–58, Lecturer 1963–85, Vice-Chair. Gen. Bd of Faculties, Univ. of Oxford 1984–85, Fellow and Tutor in Eng, Jesus Coll. Oxford 1964–85, Sr Tutor 1974–77, Estates Bursar 1978–84, Hon. Fellow 1985–; Gov. Oxford Polytechnic 1978–83, Cokethorpe School 1983–96, Magdalen Coll. School 1987–99, Coventry School Foundation; Vice-Chancellor Univ. of Warwick 1985–92; Visiting Prof., Univ. of California, Santa Barbara 1978; Visiting Scholar, Center for Higher Educ. Studies, Univ. of California, Berkeley 1997–2004; Liberal Democrat City Councillor, Oxford 2004–12; Chair. Anchor Housing Asscn 1985–91; Dir Blackwell Science Ltd 1990–98; Dir Heritage Projects (Oxford) 1986–97, Finsbury Growth Trust PLC 1995–2000, Charities Aid Foundation America 1997–2000 (Pres. 1998–2000); Founding Dir Oxford Univ. School of Man. Studies 1992–96; Pres. Templeton Coll., Oxford 1992–96; mem. Eng Bd, CNAA 1976–82; Hon. Fellow, Jesus Coll., Oxford 1985, Green Templeton Coll., Oxford 2011; Freeman, City of Oxford 2013; Hon. LLD (Warwick) 2005. *Publications:* articles on rarefied gas dynamics and education. *Leisure interests:* sailing, mending old machinery, all types of music. *Address:* Jesus College, Oxford, OX1 3DW, England (office).

BRUNDTLAND, Gro Harlem, Cand. med., MPH; Norwegian politician, diplomatist, physician and international organization official; *Secretary-General's Special Envoy on Climate Change, United Nations;* b. 20 April 1939, Oslo; d. of Gudmund Harlem and Inga Harlem; m. Arne Olav Brundtland 1960; three s. (one deceased) one d.; ed Oslo Univ. and Harvard Univ., USA; Consultant, Ministry of Health and Social Affairs 1965–67; Medical Officer, Oslo City Health Dept 1968–69; Deputy Dir School Health Services, Oslo 1969; Minister for Environmental Affairs 1974–79; Deputy Leader Labour Party 1975–81, Leader Labour Parl. Group 1981–92; Prime Minister of Norway Feb.–Oct. 1981, 1986–89, 1990–96; mem. Parl. Standing Cttee on Foreign Affairs, fmr mem. Parl. Standing Cttee on Finance; mem. of Storting (Parl.) 1977–97; Dir-Gen. WHO 1998–2003; Chair. UN World Comm. on Environment and Devt 2003–05; UN Sec.-Gen.'s Special Envoy on Climate Change 2007–; consultant, Pepsi Co.; fmr Vice-Chair. Sr Secondary Schools' Socialist Asscn, Students' Asscn of Labour Party; mem. Council of Women World Leaders, Club of Madrid; Founding mem. The Elders group, Johannesburg, S Africa 2007; Dr hc (Oxford) 2001; Third World Prize for Work on Environmental Issues 1989, Indira Gandhi Prize 1990, Onassis Foundation Award 1992, Scientific American Policy Leader of the Year Award 2003, Thomas Jefferson Foundation Medal in Architecture 2008, Zayed Int. Prize for the Environment (Category 1) 2008. *Publications:* articles on preventive medicine, school health and growth studies. *Leisure interest:* cross-country skiing. *Address:* United Nations, New York, NY 10017, USA (office). *Telephone:* (212) 963-1234 (office). *Fax:* (212) 963-4879 (office). *Website:* www.un.org (office).

BRUNEKREEF, Bert, BSc, MSc, PhD; Dutch environmental scientist and academic; *Professor of Environmental Epidemiology and Director of the Institute for Risk Assessment Sciences, University of Utrecht;* b. 3 March 1953, Utrecht; ed Univ. of Wageningen; worked at US Environmental Protection Agency (EPA) monitoring lab. . Las Vegas, Nev., USA 1978–79; Asst Prof., Dept of Environmental and Tropical Health (later Dept of Environmental Sciences), Univ. of Wageningen 1979–86, Assoc. Prof. 1986–93, Prof. 1993–, Dept of Environmental and Occupational Health moved to Utrecht Univ. and merged with existing Research Inst. of Toxicology Div. to create Inst. for Risk Assessment Sciences (IRAS) 2000, IRAS absorbed Dept of Food Safety and Veterinary Public Health 2005, Dir IRAS 2005–, currently Prof. of Environmental Epidemiology in Faculty of Veterinary Medicine and in Faculty of Medicine; Academy Prof., Royal Netherlands Acad. of Arts and Sciences 2009; Visiting Prof., Harvard School of Public Health, USA 1986–87; Councillor, Int. Soc. for Environmental Epidemiology (ISEE) –1995, Pres. ISEE 2000–01; Co-ordinator European Study of Cohorts for Air Pollution Effects (ESCAPE) 2008–12; adviser on nat. and int. panels in the field of environmental health, including Dutch Nat. Health Council (also mem.), WHO, USA EPA; Kt, Order of the Netherlands Lion 2011; Dr hc (Catholic Univ. of Louvain) 2008; John Goldsmith Award, Int. Soc. for Environmental Epidemiology 2007, European Lung Foundation Award 2007, Dr A.H. Heineken Prize for Environmental Sciences, Royal Netherlands Acad. of Arts and Sciences 2008. *Publications:* co-author of more than 300 peer-reviewed journal articles in the field of environmental epidemiology and exposure assessment. *Address:* Institute for Risk Assessment Sciences, Faculty of Veterinary Medicine, PO Box 80.163, 3508 TD Utrecht, The

Netherlands (office). *Telephone:* (30) 2539490 (office). *Fax:* (30) 2537727 (office). *E-mail:* b.brunekreef@uu.nl (office). *Website:* www.uu.nl (office).

BRUNER, Jerome Seymour, BA, PhD; American psychologist, academic and professor of law; *University Professor, School of Law, New York University;* b. 1 Oct. 1915, New York; s. of Herman Bruner and Rose Bruner; m. 1st Katherine Frost 1940 (divorced 1956); one s. one d.; m. 2nd Blanche Marshall McLane 1960 (divorced 1984); m. 3rd Carol Fleisher Feldman; ed Duke and Harvard Univs; US Intelligence 1941–42; Assoc. Dir Office of Public Opinion Research, Princeton 1942–44; Political Intelligence, France 1943; Research, Harvard Univ. 1945–72, Prof. of Psychology 1952–72, Dir Center for Cognitive Studies 1961–72; Ed. Public Opinion Quarterly 1943–44; Lecturer, Salzburg Seminar 1952; Bacon Prof., Univ. of Aix-en-Provence 1965; Watts Prof. of Psychology, Oxford Univ. 1972–80; Univ. Prof., New School for Social Research, New York 1981–88; Research Prof. of Psychology, New York Univ. 1988–96, Sr Researcher Fellow, Law School 1991–96, Univ. Prof. 1996–; Fellow, New York Inst. for the Humanities; mem. American Acad. of Arts and Sciences; Hon. DSc (Northwestern) 1965, (Sheffield) 1970, (Bristol) 1965, (Columbia) 1991; Hon. MA (Oxford) 1972; Hon. LLD (Temple) 1965, (Cincinnati) 1966, (New Brunswick) 1966, (Yale) 1978; Hon. DLitt (N Mich.) 1969, (Duke) 1969, (York Univ.) 1993; Dr hc (Sorbonne) 1974, (Leuven) 1976, (Ghent) 1977, (Madrid) 1986, (Free Univ. of Berlin) 1988, (Rome) 1992, (Harvard) 1996, (Bologna) 1996, (Salerno) 2001, (Crete) 2002; Int. Balzan Foundation Prize 1987. *Publications:* Mandate from the People 1944, A Study of Thinking 1956, The Process of Education 1960, On Knowing: Essays for the Left Hand 1962, Toward a Theory of Instruction 1966, Processes of Cognitive Growth: Infancy, (Vol. III) 1968, The Relevance of Education 1971, Under Five in Britain 1980, Communication as a Language 1982, In Search of Mind 1983, Child's Talk 1983, Actual Minds, Possible Worlds 1986, Acts of Meaning 1990, The Culture of Education 1996, Minding the Law 2000, Making Stories 2002; also co-author of several books. *Leisure interests:* sailing, drama. *Address:* New York University School of Law, 40 Washington Square South, New York, NY 10012, USA (office). *Telephone:* (212) 998-6463 (office); (212) 674-7816 (home). *Fax:* (212) 995-4881 (office); (212) 673-6118 (home). *E-mail:* brunerj@juris.law.nyu.edu (office); jerome.bruner@nyu.edu (home). *Website:* www.law.nyu.edu/faculty/profiles/affiliated/brunerj.html (office).

BRUNET, Michel, LèsSc, PhD, DSc; French palaeontologist, palaeoanthropologist and academic; *Professor of Human Palaeontology, Collège de France;* b. 1940, Vienne (Poitou); ed Univs of Paris and Poitiers; formed with colleague Emile Heintz a team to search for extinct apes in Afghanistan 1970s, expedition was unsuccessful; Founder and current Head of int. transdisciplinary team MPFT (Mission Paléoanthropologique Franco-Tchadienne), a scientific collaboration between Univs of Poitiers, N'Djamena and Centre Nationale d'Appui à la Recherche; Head, Institut International de Paléoprimatologie, Evolution et Paléoenvironnements, Univ. of Poitiers 2000–07; Prof. of Human Palaeontology, Coll. de France 2007–; Hon. mem. Soc. of Vertebrate Paleontology, USA 2008; Chevalier, Ordre de la Légion d'honneur, Officier, Ordre nat. du Mérite, Officier, des Palmes académiques, Officier, Ordre Nat. du Tchad; Prix Fontanes Prize 1977, Philip Morris Scientific Prize (Paleoanthropology) 1996, Dan David Prize 2003. *Achievements include:* moved to Africa 1980s, described a new Chadian hominid species, *Australopithecus bahrelghazali* (nicknamed Abel), dated around 3.5 Ma 1995, published in Nature an almost complete cranium of claimed oldest human ancestor: *Sahelanthropus tchadensis* (nicknamed Toumai) discovered in Chad in 2001 2002. *Address:* Collège de France, 3 rue d'Ulm, 75231 Paris Cedex 05, France (office). *Telephone:* 1-44-27-16-11 (office); 1-44-27-10-39 (Asst) (office). *Fax:* 1-44-27-10-59 (office). *E-mail:* michel.brunet@college-de-france.fr (office). *Website:* www .college-de-france.fr (office).

BRUNETTA, Renato; Italian politician, labour economist, academic and government official; b. 26 May 1950, Venice; ed Marco Foscarini Liceo Classico, Venice and Univs of Padua, Cambridge, UK and Rotterdam, Netherlands; researcher in political sciences, Univ. of Padua 1975–77, Prof. of Labour Econs 1978–82; Gen. Sec. Fondazione G. Brodolini, Rome 1980–; Chief Consultant, Econ. Adviser to Ministry of Labour 1983–88; Sec., Italian Asscn of Labour Economists 1985–87; Vice-Pres., OECD Manpower and Social Affairs Cttee 1988–89; Prof. of Labour Econs, Rome Univ. II 'Tor Vergata' 1990–; mem. Scientific Cttee on European Integration, Ministry of Foreign Affairs 1990–92, Taskforce for Programming and Econ. Policy, Ministry of the Budget 1990–; mem. European Parl. 1999–; Econ. Adviser to Prime Minister 2004–06; Minister for Public Admin. and Innovation 2008–11; Ed. Economia & Lavoro (quarterly review), Rome 1980–; Founder and Ed. Labour (four-monthly journal) 1987–; Pres. Comm. on Information for CNEL (Nat. Council of Economy and Labour) 1989–94, Councillor 1995; mem. European Asscn of Labour Economists 1989–93, ASPEN-Italy 1989–; fmr Vice-Pres. Cttee on Industry, External Trade, Research and Energy; Premio St Vincent (for Econs) 1988, Premio Tarantelli (for Econs) 1993, Scanno Prize 1994, Rodolfo Valentino Int. Prize 2000. *Publications:* Economia del Lavoro 1981, Multilocalizzazione produttiva come strategia d'impresa 1983, Squilibri, conflitto, piena occupazione 1983, Spesa pubblica e conflitto 1987, Microeconomia del lavoro: Teorie e analisi empiriche 1987, Labour Relations and Economic Performance (ed.) 1990, Il Modello Italia 1991, Economics for the New Europe 1991, Il conflitto e le relazioni di lavoro negli anni '90 1992, Disoccupazione, Isteresi, Irreversibilità 1992, Retribuzione, costo del lavoro. Regolazione e deregolazione; il capital umano; la destrutturazione del mercato (ed.) 1992, La fine della società dei salariati 1994, Sud: Alcune idee perché il Mezzogiorno non resti com'è 1995, Venezia XXI, Cronache di una transizione difficile 2004, Quindici piu Direci: Il difficile camminodell'integrazione europea (jt author) 2004, Il coraggio e la paura, Scritti de economia e politica 1999–2003 2004; articles and essays on labour econs and industrial relations; Columnist, Il Sole 24 ore, Il Giornale. *Leisure interests:* photography, history of Venice, gastronomy. *Address:* Palais de l'Europe Louise Weiss, 67070 Strasbourg, France (office). *Telephone:* (3) 88-17-53-93 (office). *Fax:* (3) 88-17-93-93 (office). *E-mail:* rbrunetta@europarl.eu.int. *Website:* www .renatobrunetta.it.

BRUNETTI, Wayne H., BSc; American energy industry executive (retd); ed Univ. of Florida, Harvard Business School; fmr Exec. Vice-Pres. Florida Power & Light Co.; fmr Pres. and CEO Man. Systems International; Chair., Pres. and CEO New Century Energies –2000; joined Public Service Co. of Colo 1994, Pres. and CEO 1994, later Chair., Pres. and CEO; Chair., Pres. and CEO Southwestern

Public Service Co., Cheyenne Light, Fuel and Power Co.; Chair., Pres. and CEO Xcel Energy Inc. 2001–03, Chair. and CEO 2003–05 (retd); Dir, Cheyenne Light, Fuel and Power Co. 1994–, NRG Energy Inc. 2000–03, Synenco Energy Inc. 2006–, OGE Energy Corpn 2008–; fmr Chair. Denver Asscn of Commerce and Industry, 2000 Mile High United Way Campaign; Dir Capital City Partnership, Minn. Orchestral Asscn, Juran Center for Leadership and Quality, Labour Relations Cttee, Chamber of Commerce of the USA; mem. Nat. Petroleum Council, Minn. Business Partnership, Colo Renewable Energy Task Force; fmr Cttee mem., Electric Power Research Inst., Edison Electrical Inst. (EEI), also EEI First Vice-Chair. *Publications:* Achieving Total Quality in Integrated Business Strategy and Customer Needs. *Address:* c/o Xcel Energy Inc., 414 Nicollet Mall, Minneapolis, MN 55401-1993, USA. *E-mail:* info@xcelenergy.com.

BRUNI, Carla; Italian/French model and singer; b. (Carla Gilberta Bruni Tedeschi), 23 Dec. 1967, Turin; fmr partner of Raphaël Enthoven; one s.; m. Nicolas Sarközy de Nagy Bocsa 2008; one d.; ed Univ. of Paris; began career as model, City Models, Paris 1986; appeared in GUESS? advertising campaigns 1987; catwalk model for Chistian Dior, Paco Rabanne, Chanel, Givenchy, Yves Saint Laurent and John Galliano 1990s; listed as one of world's top 20 highest-paid models, Business Age 1998; retd from catwalk modelling 1998; signed to Versace to model fragrance advertisements 1998; signed to record label Naïve, launched singing career 2002; First Lady of France (as wife of Pres. of French Repub.) 2008–12; f. Carla Bruni-Sarkozy Foundation 2009; ranked by Forbes magazine amongst The World's 100 Most Powerful Women (35th) 2010. *Films include:* Prêt-à-Porter 1994, Unzipped (uncredited) 1995, Catwalk 1996, Paparazzi 1998, Yves Saint Laurent: His Life and Times 2002, La caravane des enfoirés 2007, Starko! 2008, (500) Days of Summer 2009, Midnight in Paris 2011. *Film music:* En la ciudad (song Tout le monde) 2003, Le divorce (song Quelqu'un m'a dit) 2003, In the City (writer and performer Tout le monde) 2003, Conversations with Other Women (music Le Plus Beau du Quartier, J'en connais, L'excessive) 2005, The Lake House (performer La Noyée 1970) 2006, Colors en sèrie: Rosa: Enganxós o diví (song and lyrics and performer Quelqu'un m'a dit) 2007. *Television includes:* Die Schönsten Frauen der Welt – Carla Bruni 1995, Ombre et lumière 2003, Lo + plus 2003, Qui veut gagner des millions? 2004, Vivement dimanche prochain 2005, 2008, 2009, 2010, Le grand journal de Canal+ 2005, 2008, 2009, Campus, le magazine de l'écrit: Nouveau campus en direct! 2006, Turin 2006: XX Olympic Winter Games (mini-series) 2006, Symphonic show spécial Sidaction 2007, Stars of Europe 2007, Tenue de soirée: Cannes 2007, Later with Jools Holland 2008, Wetten, dass...? 2008, Somebody Told Me About... Carla Bruni (documentary) 2008, Late Show with David Letterman 2008, Sidaction 2009 2009, Chuck: Chuck vs First Class 2010, Melody Gardot: The Accidental Musician 2010. *Recordings include:* albums: Quelqu'un m'a dit 2002, No Promises 2007, Comme si de rien n'était 2008. *Leisure interests:* playing guitar, spending time with her cats. *Website:* www .carlabrunisarkozy.org/en; www.carlabruni.com.

BRUNI, Jorge Ricardo; Uruguayan lawyer and politician; b. 1941; ed Univ. de la República, Montevideo; Lecturer, Dept of Law, Univ. de la República 1991–96; with Banco de Previsión Social 1992; fmr Co-ordinator, Legal Dept, Central Unica de Trabajadores del Uruguay (trade union); columnist, La República de Montevideo; UnderSec., Ministry of Labour and Social Security 2005–09; Minister of the Interior 2009–10. *Address:* c/o Ministry of the Interior, Mercedes 953, 11100 Montevideo, Uruguay (office).

BRUNO, Franklin (Frank) Roy, MBE; British fmr professional boxer; b. 16 Nov. 1961, London; s. of the late Robert Bruno and of Lynette Bruno (née Campbell); m. Laura Frances Mooney 1990 (divorced 2001); one s. three d.; ed Oak Hall School, Sussex; began boxing with Wandsworth Boys' Club, London 1970; mem. Sir Philip Game Amateur Boxing Club 1977–80; won 20 out of 21 contests as amateur; professional career 1982–96; won 38 out of 42 contests as professional 1982–89; European heavyweight champion 1985–86 (relinquished title), world heavyweight title challenges against Tim Witherspoon 1986, Mike Tyson 1989; staged comeback, won first contest 1991; lost 4th world title challenge against Lennox Lewis Oct. 1993; WBC heavyweight champion 1995–96, lost title to Mike Tyson 1996; announced retirement Aug. 1996; numerous appearances in pantomimes; fmr presenter, BBC TV; SOS Sports Personality of the Year 1990; TV Times Sports Personality of the Year 1990, Lifetime Achievement Award, BBC Sports Personality of the Year Awards 1996. *Publications:* Personality: From Zero to Hero (with Norman Giller) 1996, Frank (autobiog., with Kevin Mitchell) (Sky Sports Autobiography of the Year 2006) 2005. *Leisure interests:* music, training, swimming. *Address:* Little Billington, Leighton Buzzard, Beds., LU7, England.

BRUNTON, Sir Gordon Charles, Kt; British business executive; *Chairman, Communications and General Consultants Ltd;* b. 27 Dec. 1921, London; s. of Charles A. Brunton and Hylda Pritchard; m. 1st Nadine Sohr 1946 (divorced 1965); one s. (one s. deceased) two d.; m. 2nd Gillian A. Kirk 1966; one s. one d.; ed Cranleigh School and London School of Econs; war service 1942–46; joined Tothill Press 1947, Exec. Dir 1956; Man. Dir Tower Press Group 1958; Exec. Dir Odhams Press 1961; joined Thomson Org. 1961, Dir 1963, Man. Dir and CEO Int. Thomson Org. PLC (fmrly Thomson British Holdings) and Thomson Org. Ltd 1968–84; Man. Dir Thomson Publications 1961; Chair. Thomson Travel 1965–68; Pres. Int. Thomson Org. Ltd 1978–84; Dir Times Newspapers Ltd 1967–81, Bemrose Corpn 1974 (Chair. 1978–91), Sotheby Parke Bernet Group PLC 1978–85, Cable and Wireless PLC 1981–91, Yattendon Investment Trust PLC 1985–2001; fmr non-exec. Dir Cable and Wireless PLC, South Bank Bd (Arts Council); Pres. Periodical Publishers' Asscn 1972–74, 1981–82, Nat. Advertising Benevolent Soc. 1973–75; Chair. Econ. Devt Council for Civil Eng 1978–84, Appeals Cttee, Ind. Adoption Soc., Communications and Gen. Consultants Ltd 1985–, Mercury Communications Ltd 1986–90, Cavendish Shops 1985–93, Community Industry Ltd 1985–92, The Racing Post PLC 1985–97, Ingersoll Publications 1988–91, Verity Group PLC (fmrly Wharfedale PLC) 1991–97, Green Field Leisure Group Ltd 1992–2011, PhoneLink PLC (now GB Group PLC) 1993–2001, Galahad Gold PLC 2003–07, Euram Consulting Ltd, Focus Investments Ltd, Cavendish Retail, Racing Int. Ltd and other limited cos; Gov. and Fellow LSE, Henley Man. Coll. 1983–86; Pres. The History of Advertising Trust 1981–84; mem. Council, Templeton Coll. (fmrly Oxford Cen. for Man. Studies); mem. South Bank Bd, Arts Council 1985–92. *Leisure interests:* books, breeding horses. *Address:* North Munstead Stud Farm,

North Munstead Lane, Godalming, Surrey, GU8 4AX, England. *Telephone:* (1483) 424181 (office); (1483) 416313 (home). *Fax:* (1483) 426043 (office).

BRUS, Louis E., BA, PhD; American chemist and academic; *Samuel Latham Mitchill Professor, Columbia University;* Lt, USN, US Naval Research Lab., Washington, DC 1969–73; Mem. Tech. Staff, AT&T Bell Labs, Murray Hill, NJ 1973–84, Distinguished Mem. Tech. Staff 1984–96; Prof. of Chem., Columbia Univ. 1996–, Prof. of Chemical Eng and Applied Chem. 1997–, Thomas Alva Edison Prof. 2001–04, Samuel Latham Mitchill Prof. 2004–, Scientific Head, Columbia NSF MRSEC IRG on Complex Films 1998–2008 Co-Dir Columbia Dept of Energy EFRC Energy Research Center 2009–14; Visiting Prof., Univ. of Paris VI (Pierre et Marie Curie) 2002; Vice Chair. Gordon Research Confs 1997, Chair. 1998; mem. Editorial Bd of several journals, including Journal of Chemical Physics 1988–91, Journal of Physical Chemistry 1990–93, 2003–06, Journal of the American Chemical Society 1990–96, Nano Letters 2000–04, ACS Nano 20007–, Accounts of Chemical Research 2012–15; mem. numerous review cttees; mem. NAS 2004–; Foreign mem. Norwegian Acad. of Science and Letters 2009; Fellow, American Physical Soc. 1980, American Acad. of Arts and Sciences 1998; NSF Predoctoral Fellow 1966–69, Univ. of Chicago Herman Bloch Award 1995, Irving Langmuir Prize in Chemical Physics, American Physical Soc. 2001, ACS E.I. Pont de Nemours & Co. Award in the Chem. of Materials 2005, R.W. Wood Prize, Optical Soc. of America (co-recipient) 2006, Inaugural Kavli Prize in Nanoscience (with S. Iijima) 2008, J. Willard Gibbs Medal, ACS (Chicago Section) 2009, NAS Prize in the Chemical Sciences 2010, R.T. Major Medal, Merck and Univ. of Connecticut 2010, Distinguished Alumnus Award Rice Univ. 2010, ACS Peter Debye Award in Physical Chem. 2011, Bower Award and Prize for Achievement in Science, Franklin Inst. 2012, Welch Foundation Award in Chem. 2013. *Address:* Department of Chemistry, Columbia University, Havemeyer Hall, MC 3125, 3000 Broadway, New York, NY 10027, USA (office). *Telephone:* (212) 854-4041 (office). *Fax:* (212) 932-1289 (office). *E-mail:* leb26@columbia.edu (office). *Website:* www .columbia.edu/cu/chemistry (office).

BRUSKIN, Grisha (Brouskine Grigori); Russian artist; b. 21 Oct. 1945, Moscow; s. of David Brouskin and Bassia Strunina; m. 1st Ludmila Dmitrieva 1975 (divorced 1978); m. 2nd Alexandra Makarova 1982; one d. one adopted s.; ed Art High School, Moscow, Moscow Textile Inst.; mem. Soviet Artists' Union 1968; work includes paintings, gouaches, drawings, sculptures, performances; work included in first Sotheby's auction in Moscow, designed poster for Chicago Art Exhbn 1988; now lives and works in New York; solo exhbns in Moscow 1976, 1984, Vilnius, Lithuania 1983, Marlborough Gallery, New York 1990; numerous group exhbns including The Painter and Modernism, Moscow 1987, 100 Years of Russian Art, Barbican, London and in Chicago, Berne, Seoul, Cologne, Chicago, New York, Barcelona, Paris, Munich, Düsseldorf, Lisbon, Brussels, Berlin, Copenhagen 1988–; works in Art Inst. of Chicago, Jewish Museum, New York, Museum of Modern Art, New York, Nat. Museum of Israel, Jerusalem etc. *Leisure interests:* literature, music. *Address:* c/o Marlborough Galleries, 40 West 57th Street, New York, NY 10019, USA.

BRUSTEIN, Robert Sanford, MA, PhD; American drama critic, actor and producer; *Founding Director and Creative Consultant, American Repertory Theatre;* b. 21 April 1927, New York, NY; s. of Max Brustein and Blanche Brustein (née Haft); m. 1st Norma Cates 1962 (died 1979); one s. one step-s.; m. 2nd Doreen Beinart 1996; one step-s. one step-d.; ed Amherst Coll., Yale Univ. Drama School, Columbia Univ.; played about 70 roles in theatre groups and TV plays 1950–; Instructor, Cornell Univ. 1955–56, Vassar Coll. 1956–57; Lecturer, Columbia Univ. 1957–58, Asst Prof. 1958–63, Assoc. Prof. 1963–65, Prof. 1965–66; Prof. of English, Yale Univ., Dean of Yale Drama School, Artistic Dir and Founder Yale Repertory Theatre 1966–79; Founder and Artistic Dir, American Repertory Theatre, Loeb Drama Center, Cambridge, Mass 1980–2002, Founding Dir and Creative Consultant 2002–; Prof. of English, Harvard Univ. 1979–2002; Sr Fellow, Nat. Arts Journalism Program, Columbia Univ. 2003, Nat. Endowment for the Arts Arts Journalism Inst. in Theatre and Musical Theatre, Univ. of Southern California 2004–05; Drama Critic, The New Republic 1959–67, 1978–, Contributing Ed. 1959–79; regular contrib. to New York Times 1972–, Huffington Post; Advisory Ed., Theatre Quarterly 1967–; Guest Critic, The Observer, UK 1972–73, 1978–, Contributing Ed. 1959–; Trustee, Sarah Lawrence Coll. 1973–77; panel mem. Nat. Endowment for the Arts 1970–72, 1981–84; mem. American Acad. of Arts and Sciences 1999; Hon. LittD (Lawrence Univ.) 1968, (Amherst Coll.) 1972; Hon. LHD (Beloit Coll.) 1975; Hon. Dr of Arts (Bard Coll.) 1981; Fulbright Fellow 1953–55, Guggenheim Fellow 1961–62, George E. Nathan Prize in Criticism 1962, Ford Fellow 1964–65, George Polk Memorial Award in Criticism 1964, Jersey City Journal Award in Theatre Criticism 1967, Eliot Norton Award for Theatre, New England Theatre Conf. Award for Excellence in Theme, Award, Outstanding Achievement in American Theater, New England Theater Council 1985, Tiffany Award for Excellence in Theater, Soc. for Performing Arts Administrators 1987, American Acad. of Arts and Letters Distinguished Services to Arts Award 1995, ATHE Award for Lifetime Achievement in the Theater 2000, inducted into American Theatre Hall of Fame 2002, Lifetime Achievement Award, US Inst. for Theatre Tech. 2003, Chair.'s Award for Achievement in Theatre, Nat. Corp. Theatre Fund 2003, Gann Academy Award for Excellence in the Performing Arts 2005, Tao House award, Eugene O'Neill Foundation 2008, Nat. Medal of Arts 2010, inducted into Players Club Hall of Fame 2011, Pirandello Medal, Medal from Egyptian Govt for contribs to world theatre. *Plays:* Demons 1995, Nobody Dies on Friday 1996, The Face Lift 1999, Spring Forward, Fall Back, Shakespeare Trilogy: The English Channel, Mortal Terror, The Last Will; short plays: Poker Face 1999, Chekhov on Ice 2000, Divestiture, AnchorBimbo, Noises, Terrorist Skit, Airport Hell, Beachman's Last Poetry Reading, Sex For a Change, Kosher Kop. *Television:* writer and narrator of a WNET series called The Opposition Theatre 1966. *Publications:* Introduction to the Plays of Chekhov 1964; Ed. The Plays of Strindberg 1964; author: The Theatre of Revolt: An Approach to Modern Drama 1964, Seasons of Discontent: Dramatic Opinions 1959–1965 1965, The Third Theatre 1969, Revolution as Theatre: Notes on the New Radical Style 1971, The Culture Watch: Essays on Theatre and Society, 1969–1974 1975, The Plays and Prose of Strindberg (ed.), Critical Moments: Reflection on Theatre & Society, 1973–1979 1980, Making Scenes: A Personal History of the Turbulent Years at Yale, 1966–1979 1981, Who Needs Theatre: Dramatic Opinions 1987, Reimagining American Theatre 1991, Dumbocracy in America: Studies in the Theatre of Guilt,

1987–1994 1994, Culturak Calisthenics: Writings on Race, Politics, and Theatre 1998, Three Farces and a Funeral 2000, Divestiture 2001, The Siege of the Arts: Collected Writings, 1994–2001 2001, Letters to a Young Actor: A Universal Guide to Performance 2005, Millennial Stages: Essays and Reviews 2001–2005 2006, Doctor Hippocrates is Out: Please Leave a Message (anthology of theatrical and cinematic satire on medicine and physicians) 2008, The Tainted Muse: Prejudices and Preconceptions in Shakespeare's Works and Times 2009, Rants and Raves: Opinions, Tributes, and Elegies 2011, Winter Passages: Essays and Criticism 2014. *Address:* American Repertory Theatre, Loeb Drama Center, Harvard University, 64 Brattle Street, Cambridge, MA 02138, USA. *Telephone:* (617) 495-2668. *Fax:* (617) 495-1705. *E-mail:* info@americanrepertorytheater.org. *Website:* americanrepertorytheater.org.

BRUTON, John Gerard, BA, BL; Irish politician, diplomatist, barrister, farmer and company director; *President, International Financial Services Centre Ireland;* b. 18 May 1947, Dublin; s. of Matthew Joseph Bruton and Doris Mary Delany; m. Finola Gill 1981; one s. three d.; ed Clongowes Wood Coll., Univ. Coll., Dublin, King's Inn, Dublin; mem. Dáil Éireann (House of Reps) 1969–2004; Fine Gael Spokesman on Agric. 1972–73; Parl. Sec. to Minister for Educ. 1973–77, to Minister for Industry and Commerce 1975–77; Fine Gael Spokesman on Agric. 1977–81, on Finance Jan.–June 1981; Minister of Finance 1981–82, of Industry, Trade, Commerce and Tourism 1982–86, of Finance 1986–87; Deputy Leader of Fine Gael 1987–90, Leader 1990–2001, Fine Gael Spokesman on Industry and Commerce 1987–89, on Educ. 1989–90, Vice-Pres. 2010–; mem. Parl. Ass., Council of Europe 1989–91, British-Irish Parl. Body 1993–94, Parl. Ass., WEU 1997–; Prime Minister of Ireland 1994–97; Leader of Opposition 1997–2001; Amb. and Head of EU Del. to USA 2004–09; mem. Fine Gael Front Bench 2002; Pres. Int. Financial Services Centre Ireland 2010–, European Sustainable Materials Platform 2012–; Gov. Ditchley Foundation 1999–2012; Hon. Citizen, Sioux City, Iowa, USA; Commdr, Grand Cross of the Royal Order of the Polar Star (Sweden), Kt Grand Cross with Gold Star, Sacred Mil. Constantinian Order of St George; Hon. LLD (Memorial Univ., St John's, Newfoundland), (Nat. Univ. of Ireland), (Univ. of Missouri). *Publications:* Reform of the Dail 1980, A Better Way to Plan the Nation's Finances 1981. *Leisure interests:* history, folk music, tennis. *Address:* Cornelstown, Dunboyne, Co. Meath, Ireland (home). *E-mail:* jgbcor@gmail.com (office). *Website:* www.johnbruton.com.

BRUTUS, Duly; Haitian diplomatist and politician; *Minister of Foreign Affairs and Religion;* elected to Chamber of Deputies (Parl.) 1990, Pres. 1991–92; Perm. Rep. to OAS 2004–14, Chair. OAS Cttee on Hemispheric Security 2013; Minister of Foreign Affairs and Religion 2014–. *Address:* Ministry of Foreign Affairs and Religion, boulevard Harry S Truman, Cité de l'Exposition, Port-au-Prince, Haiti (office). *Telephone:* 2222-8482 (office). *Fax:* 2223-1668 (office). *E-mail:* webmaster@ maehaitiinfo.org (office). *Website:* www.mae.gouv.ht (office).

BRUYNINCKX, Hans, MPS, PhD; Belgian political scientist; *Executive Director, European Environment Agency;* b. 20 March 1964, Schoten; ed Catholic Univ. Leuven, Colorado State Univ., USA; 20 years' research experience in environmental, sustainable devt and climate change policy; fmr Researcher and Lecturer, Colorado State Univ., Canisius Coll., Buffalo, NY and Wageningen Univ., Netherlands; Prof. of Int. and European Environmental Politics, Catholic Univ. Leuven –2013, also Dir HIVA Research Inst. for Work and Soc. 2010–13; Exec. Dir European Environment Agency 2013–; Founding mem. Leuven Centre for Global Governance Studies. *Address:* European Environment Agency, 6 Kongens Nytorv, 1050 Copenhagen K, Denmark (office). *Telephone:* 33-36-71-00 (office). *Fax:* 33-36-71-99 (office). *E-mail:* eea@eea.europa.eu (office). *Website:* www.eea.europa.eu (office).

BRYAN, Elizabeth, BA (Econ), MA (Econ); Australian business executive; *Non-Executive Chairman, Caltex Australia Limited;* ed Australian Nat. Univ., Univ. of Hawaii, USA; experience in financial services industry, in govt policy and admin, and on bds of cos and statutory orgs since late 1970s; served for six years as Man. Dir Deutsche Asset Man. and its predecessor org., NSW State Superannuation Investment and Man. Corpn; Chair. UniSuper Ltd; mem. Bd of Dirs Ridley Corpn Ltd 2001–07, Westpac Banking Corpn 2006–, Australian Inst. of Co. Dirs; mem. Bd of Dirs Caltex Australia Ltd 2002–, Ind. Chair. (non-exec.) 2007–, Chair. Nomination Cttee. *Address:* Caltex Australia Ltd, GPO Box 3916, Sydney, NSW 2001 (office); Caltex Australia Ltd, Level 24, Market Street, Sydney, NSW 2000, Australia (office). *Telephone:* (2) 9250-5000 (office). *Fax:* (2) 9250-5742 (office). *E-mail:* info@caltex.com.au (office). *Website:* www.caltex.com.au (office).

BRYAN, Richard H., LLB; American lawyer and fmr politician; *Partner, Lionel Sawyer & Collins;* b. 16 July 1937, Washington, DC; m. Bonnie Fairchild; three c.; ed Univ. of Nevada, Hastings Coll. of Law, Univ. of California; admitted to Nev. Bar 1963, US Supreme Court Bar 1967; Deputy Dist Attorney, Clark Co., Nev. 1964–66; Public Defender, Clark Co. 1966–68; Counsel, Clark Co. Juvenile Court 1968–69; mem. Nev. Ass. 1969–71; Nev. Senate 1973–77; Attorney-Gen., Nev. 1979–83; Gov. of Nev. 1983–89; Senator from Nev. 1989–2001; Partner and mem. Exec. Cttee, Lionel, Sawyer & Collins (law firm) 2001–; mem. Bd of Trustees, Las Vegas Global Economic Alliance 2001–, Econ. Devt Authority of Western Nev. (EDAWN), Las Vegas Chamber of Commerce; mem. Bd of Dirs Las Vegas Performing Arts Center; mem. City of Las Vegas Centennial Cttee; Chair. Preserve Nevada; mem. Order of the Coif; rated in The Best Lawyers in America 2008–13, named Distinguished Nevadan by Nevada System of Higher Educ. 2011. *Address:* Lionel Sawyer & Collins, 1700 Bank America Plaza, 300 South Fourth Street, Las Vegas, NV 89101, USA (office). *Telephone:* (702) 383-8916 (office). *Fax:* (702) 383-8845 (office). *E-mail:* rbryan@lionelsawyer.com (office). *Website:* www .lionelsawyer.com (office).

BRYAN, Andy D., BEcons, MBA; American business executive; *Chairman, Intel Corporation;* ed Univ. of Missouri, University of Kansas; held positions in finance at Ford Motor Co. and Chrysler Corpn –1981; joined Intel as Controller for the Commercial Memory Systems Operation 1981–83, Systems Group Controller 1983–87, Dir of Finance 1987–90, Vice-Pres. and Dir of Finance, Intel Products Group 1990–94; Chief Financial Officer 1994–99, Sr Vice-Pres. 1999–2007, Chief Financial and Enterprise Services Officer 1999–2007, Chief Admin. Officer 2007–11, Head of Tech. and Manufacturing Group 2009–11, mem. Bd of Dirs and Vice-Chair. Intel Corpn 2011–12, Chair. 2012–. *Address:* Intel Corporation,

2200 Mission College Boulevard, Santa Clara, CA 95054-1537, USA (office). *Telephone:* (408) 765-8080 (office). *Fax:* (408) 765-9904 (office). *E-mail:* info@intel .com (office). *Website:* www.intel.com (office).

BRYANT, (Dewey Phillip) Phil, BA, MA; American politician, state governor and educator; *Governor of Mississippi;* b. 9 Dec. 1954, Moorhead, Miss.; s. of Dewey C. Bryant and Estelle R. Bryant; m. Deborah Hays; one s. one d.; ed Hinds Community Coll., Univ. of Southern Mississippi, Mississippi Coll.; worked as Service Manager at Jackson Mack Sales; later insurance investigator; taught Mississippi political history at Mississippi Coll.; mem. Mississippi House of Reps 1990–95, Vice-Chair. Insurance Cttee; apptd State Auditor 1996–99, elected 1999–2008; Lt Gov. 2008–12; Gov. of Mississippi 2012–; Republican. *Address:* Office of Governor, PO Box 139, Jackson, MS 39205, USA (office). *Telephone:* (601) 359-3150 (office). *Fax:* (601) 359-3741 (office). *Website:* www.governorbryant.com (office).

BRYANT, John; British journalist; *Chairman, Press Association Trust;* trainee journalist, The Scotsman; fmr Exec. Ed. The Daily Mail; fmr Managing Ed. The Times 1986, then Deputy Ed.; fmr Ed. The Sunday Correspondent 1990, The European; Consulting Ed. The Daily Mail –2005; Ed.-in-Chief Telegraph Newspapers 2005–, acting Ed. The Daily Telegraph 2005; Chair. Press Asscn Trust 2008–; Chair. Editorial Bd, London Evening Standard 2009–. *Publications include:* non-fiction: 3:59.4 2005, The London Marathon 2006. *Address:* London Evening Standard, Northcliffe House, 2 Derry Street, London, W8 5TT, England (office). *Website:* www.standard.co.uk (office).

BRYANT, John Martin, MA, CEng, FIM, FREng; British business executive; b. 28 Sept. 1943, Cardiff, Wales; s. of William George Bryant and Doris Bryant; m. Andrea Irene Emmons 1965; two s. one d.; ed West Monmouth School, Pontypool, St Catharine's Coll., Cambridge; grad. trainee, Steel Co. of Wales 1965–68; various tech., production, personnel positions at British Steel 1968–78, Works Man. Hot Rolled Products 1978–87, Dir Coated Products 1987–90, Dir Tinplate 1990–92, Man. Dir Strip Products 1995–99, Exec. Dir 1996–98, Chief Exec. 1999; Chief Exec. Corus PLC 1999–2001; Chair. Actoris Group Ltd 2009–; mem. Bd of Dirs ASW PLC 1993–95, Bank of Wales PLC 1996–2001, Welsh Water PLC 2001–, Glas Cymru Ltd 2001–, Costain Group PLC 2002–13; Fellow, Royal Acad. of Eng; Hon. DSc (Wales) 2000. *Leisure interests:* all sports, particularly squash and rugby, family. *Address:* Broadway Farm, 24 Roger Lane, Laleston, Bridgend, CF32 0LA, Wales. *Telephone:* (1656) 647558. *Fax:* (1656) 664348. *E-mail:* drjmbryant@aol.com.

BRYANT, Kobe; American professional basketball player; b. (Kobe Bean Bryant), 23 Aug. 1978, Philadelphia, Pa; s. of Joe 'Jellybean' Bryant and Pam Bryant; m. Vanessa Laine 2001; two d.; ed Lower Merion High School, Pa; position: guard; moved with family to Italy where he lived until 1992; selected from high school by Charlotte Hornets in first round (13th pick overall) 1996 Nat. Basketball Assen (NBA) draft, draft rights traded to LA Lakers; youngest-ever NBA all-star starter at 19 years of age 1998; five times NBA champion with Lakers (2000, 2001, 2002, 2009, 2010); played in gold medal-winning US Nat. Team at FIBA Americas Championships, Las Vegas 2007; played in gold medal-winning Team USA, Olympic Games, Beijing 2008, London 2012; official Amb. for After-School All-Stars; est. Kobe Bryant China Fund; NBA All-Star 1998, 2000–12, NBA Most Valuable Player in All-Star Game 2002, 2007, 2009 (shared award with Shaquille O'Neal), 2011, NBA Scoring Champion 2005–06, 2006–07, NBA Most Valuable Player 2008, NBA Finals Most Valuable Player 2009, NBA Finals MVP Award 2009, 2010. *Television:* Moesha (series) 1996. *Address:* Los Angeles Lakers, 555 North Nash Street, El Segundo, CA 90245, USA (office). *Telephone:* (310) 426-6031 (office). *Website:* www.nba.com/lakers (office); www.kb24.com.

BRYARS, Gavin, BA; British composer; b. 16 Jan. 1943, Goole, Yorks., England; s. of Walter Joseph Bryars and Miriam Eleanor Bryars; m. 1st Angela Margaret Bigley 1971 (divorced 1993); two d.; m. 2nd Anna Tchernakova 1999; one s. one step d.; ed Goole Grammar School, Univ. of Sheffield, Northern School of Music and pvt composition study with Cyril Ramsey, George Linstead and Benjamin Johnston; freelance double bassist 1963–66; Lecturer in Liberal Studies, Northampton Coll. of Tech. 1966–67; freelance composer/performer 1968–70; Lecturer in Music, Portsmouth Polytechnic 1969–70; Sr Lecturer, School of Fine Art, Leicester Polytechnic 1970–78, Sr Lecturer and Head of Music, School of Performing Arts 1978–85; Prof. of Music, De Montfort Univ. 1985–96; Assoc. Research Fellow, Dartington Coll. of Arts 2004–08; collaborations with artists, including Aphex Twin, John Cage, Brian Eno, Tom Waits; mem. Collège de Pataphysique, France 1974–, Regent 2007–; Ed. Experimental Music Catalogue 1972–81; British Rep. Int. Soc. for Contemporary Music Festival 1977; Visiting Prof., Univ. of Hertfordshire 1999–2003; Arts Council Comms 1970, 1980, 1982, Bursary 1982; Music Juror, Akademie Schloss Solitude, Stuttgart 1990–92; freelance composer 1994–; Hon. Fellow, Bath Spa Univ. 2008; Dr hc (Plymouth) 2006. *Compositions include:* The Sinking of the Titanic 1969, Jesus' Blood Never Failed Me Yet 1971, Out of Zaleski's Gazebo 1977, The Vespertine Park 1980, Medea (opera with Robert Wilson) 1982, My First Homage for two pianos 1978, Effarene 1984, String Quartet No. 1 1985, Pico's Flight 1986, By the Vaar for double bass and ensemble 1987, The Invention of Tradition 1988, Glorious Hill 1988, Cadman Requiem 1989, String Quartet No. 2 1990, Four Elements (dance piece) 1990, The Black River for soprano and organ 1991, The White Lodge 1991, The War in Heaven for chorus and orchestra 1993, Epilogue from 'Wonderlawn' for four players 1994, Three Elegies for Nine Clarinets 1994, The North Shore for solo viola and small orchestra 1994, After Handel's Vesper 1995, Cello Concerto 1995, The Adnan Songbook 1996, Doctor Ox's Experiment (opera) 1997, String Quartet No. 3 1998, The Porazzi Fragment for strings 1998, Biped (ballet) 1999, First Book of Madrigals 2000, Violin Concerto 2000, G (opera) 2001, Second Book of Madrigals 2001, Double Bass Concerto 2002, Book of Laude 2003, Writings on Water (ballet) 2003, Third Book of Madrigals 2003, Eight Irish Madrigals 2004, New York (percussion concerto) 2004, From Egil's Saga 2004, Creamer Etudes 2005, New York 2005, Paper Nautilus 2006, The Stones of the Arch 2006, Nothing Like the Sun 2007, Amjad 2007, Nine Irish Madrigals 2007, To Define Happiness 2007, Sonnets from Scotland 2007–09, Trondúr I Gøtu 2008, Anail Dé 2008–09, St Brendan Arrives at the Happy Land of the Saints 2009, Four Songs from Northern Seas 2009, Four I Tatti Madrigals 2009, At Portage and Main 2009, The First Light (ballet) 2010, The Solway Canal 2010, The Morrison Songbook 2010, Ramble on Cortona 2010, Reverence (ballet) 2011, Dido and Orfeo (after Purcell and Gluck) (ballet) 2011, Lauda 40 and 41

2011, Four Battiferri Madrigals 2011, Children's Songs 2012, The Open Road 2012, Psalm 141 2012, Lauda 42 2012, Three Choral pieces from the Faroe Islands 2012, The Voice of St Columba 2012, After the Underworlds 2012, Through the Halls 2012, The Beckett Songbook 2012–13, Marilyn Forever (opera) 2013. *Films:* Sea and Stars (Nat. Film Bd of Canada) 2003, Season of Mists 2008, Our Chekhov 2010, Proezd Serova 2012–13. *Radio:* I Send You This Cadmium Red (BBC Radio 3, with John Berger and John Christie) 2002, Egil's Last Days (BBC Radio 3) 2004, The Pythagorean Comma (BBC Radio 3) 2012. *Television:* Last Summer (CBC TV, Dir Anna Tchernakova) 2000. *Publications:* contribs to Music and Musicians, Studio International, Art and Artists, Contact, The Guardian, Arcana, Modern Painters, Parkett, Open Space (Moscow). *Leisure interests:* cricket (mem. Yorks. Co. Cricket Club), football, Dalmatians. *Address:* c/o Schott and Co. Ltd, 48 Great Marlborough Street, London, W1F 7BB, England (office). *Telephone:* (20) 7534-0750 (office). *Fax:* (20) 7534-0759 (office). *E-mail:* sally.groves@schott-music.com (office); gbproductions@gavinbryars.com (office). *Website:* www.schott-music.com (office); www.gavinbryars.com.

BRYCE ECHENIQUE, Alfredo; Peruvian writer; b. 19 Feb. 1939, Lima; Premio Nacional de Literatura de Perú 1972, Premio Passion, France 1983, Encomienda de Isabel la Católica, Spain 1993, Premio Nacional de Narrativa, Spain 1998, Encomienda de Alfonso X El Sabio, Spain 2000, Premio Grinzane Cavour, Piemonte, Italy 2002, Premio Planeta, Spain 2002; Commdr, Ordre des Arts et des Lettres 2000. *Publications include:* Huerto cerrado (short stories) 1968, Un mundo para Julius (novel) 1970, La felicidad ja ja (short stories) 1974, Tantas veces Pedro (novel) 1977, A vuelo de buen cubero y otras crónicas (non-fiction) 1977, La vida exagerada de Martín Romaña (novel) 1981, El hombre que hablaba de Octavia de Cádiz 1984, Magdalena peruana y otros cuentos (short stories) 1986, Crónicas personales 1986, La última mudanza de Felipe Carrillo (novel) 1988, Dos señoras conversan (novella) 1990, Permiso para vivir (Antimemorias) (memoir) 1993, No me esperen en abril (novel) 1995, A trancas y barrancas (articles) 1997, Reo de nocturnidad (novel) 1997, Guía triste de París (short stories) 1999, La amigdalitis de Tarzán (novel) 1999, El huerto de mi amada 2002, Doce cartas a dos amigos 2003, Entrevistas escogidas 2004, Entre la soledad y el amor 2005, Las obras infames de Pancho Marambio 2007, Dándole pena a la tristeza 2012. *Website:* www .bryce-echenique.com.

BRYDEN, Alan, Dipl in Nuclear Physics; British/French international organization executive; *Secretary-General, International Organization for Standardization Policy;* b. 1945; m. Laurence Bryden; three c.; ed Ecole Polytechnique, Paris, Ecole des Mines, Paris and Univ. d'Orsay, France; began career in metrology with Nat. Bureau of Standards (now Nat. Inst. of Standards and Tech.), USA; Dir-Gen. Laboratoire Nat. d'Essais 1981–99; f. Eurolab (European Fed. of Measurement, Testing and Analytical Labs), Pres. 1990–96; Dir-Gen. AFNOR (French nat. standardization inst.) 1999–2003; mem. Council Int. Org. for Standardization (ISO) 1999–2003, Sec.-Gen. 2003–; fmr Vice-Pres. European Cttee for Standardization Policy; fmr Vice-Pres. Cttee on Tech. Barriers to Trade in GATT (now WTO); fmr Chair. Labs Cttee of Int. Lab. Accreditation Co-operation; Ordre nat. du Mérite 1988, Chevalier, Légion d'honneur 1995. *Leisure interests:* riding, sailing. *Address:* International Organization for Standardization, Case Postale 56, 1211 Geneva 20, Switzerland (office). *Telephone:* (22) 7490217 (office). *Fax:* (22) 7333440 (office). *E-mail:* bryden@iso.org (office). *Website:* www.iso.org (office).

BRYDON, Donald Hood, CBE; British business executive; *Chairman, Royal Mail Group;* b. 25 May 1945, Stirling, Scotland; s. of James Hood Brydon and Mary Duncanson Brydon (née Young); m. 1st Joan Victoria 1971 (divorced 1995), one s. one d.; m. 2nd Corinne Susan Jane Green 1996; ed George Watson's Coll., Edinburgh, Univ. of Edinburgh; with Econs Dept, Univ. of Edinburgh 1967–70; with British Airways Pensions Fund 1970–77; Barclays Investment Man.'s Office 1977–81, Deputy Man. Dir Barclays Investment Man. Ltd 1981–86; Dir BZW Investment Man. 1986–88, Man. Dir 1988–91, Chair., CEO BZW Asset Man. Ltd 1991–94, Chair. (non-exec.) 1994–95, Deputy Chief Exec. Barclays de Zoete Wedd 1994–96, Acting CEO 1996; Chair. and CEO AXA Investment Managers 1997–; Chair. Smiths Group 2004–13; Chair. Royal Mail Group 2009–; Chair. Sage Group 2012–; Chair. MRC 2012–; mem. Bd of Dirs Stock Exchange 1991–98, Edinburgh Inca Investment Trust 1996–2002, Allied Domecq 1997–2005, AXA UK (fmrly Sun Life and Provincial Holdings) 1997–2002, Amersham 1997–2004, Scottish Power 2003–07; Chair. European Children's Trust 1999–2001, Fund Man. Asscn 1999–2001, Financial Services Practitioner Panel 2001–03, TNS 2005–08, ifs School of Finance 2006–10, EveryChild 2002–08; Pres. European Asset Man. Asscn 1999–2001. *Publications:* Economics of Technical Information Services (co-author) 1972. *Address:* Royal Mail Group, 100 Victoria Embankment, London, EC4Y 0HQ, England (office). *Telephone:* (20) 7449-8099 (office). *E-mail:* donald .brydon@royalmail.com (office).

BRYMER, Charles E. (Chuck), BA; American advertising executive; *President and CEO, DDB Worldwide;* b. 30 July 1959, Louisville, Ky; s. of Robert L. Brymer and Natalie Brymer; m. Tracy Brymer; four c.; ed Coll. of Communications & Information, Univ. of Kentucky; worked at various TV stations and advertising agencies while at coll.; opened and ran BBDO's Houston office 1982–85; joined Interbrand Group (int. consultancy specializing in brands and branding) 1985, served as Founding Pres. of the UK co.'s US div., Interbrand acquired by Omnicom Group 1993, Pres. and CEO Interbrand 1994–2006, Pres. and CEO Omnicom-owned DDB Worldwide 2006–; helped create Businessweek's World's Most Valuable Brands feature; has advised US State Dept on the USA's int. image; mem. Bd Regal Entertainment Group, Ad Council 2007, Chamber of Commerce of the US; named one of Fortune Magazine's People to Watch 1986. *Publications:* Brands and Branding (co-author) 2004, The Nature of Marketing: Marketing to the Swarm as Well as the Herd 2009. *Address:* Roberts+Langer DDB, 437 Madison Avenue, New York, NY 10022, USA. *Telephone:* (646) 289-7300. *Fax:* (212) 759-3120. *E-mail:* info@ddb.com. *Website:* www.ddb.com.

BRYN, Kåre; Norwegian diplomatist; b. 12 March 1944; m.; four c.; ed Norwegian School of Econs and Business Admin; Trainee, Ministry of Foreign Affairs 1969, Attaché/Second Sec., Embassy in London 1971–74, First Sec., Embassy in Belgrade 1974–76, Exec. Officer, Ministry of Foreign Affairs 1976–79, First Sec., later Counsellor, Perm. Mission of Norway, Geneva 1979–84, Head of Div., Ministry of Foreign Affairs 1984, Asst Dir-Gen. 1985–89, Dir-Gen. Dept for Natural Resources and Environmental Affairs 1989–99, Norwegian Rep. to Int.

Whaling Comm. (IWC) 1995–99, Amb. and Perm. Rep. to EFTA and WTO, Geneva 1999–2003 (Chair. WTO Gen. Council 2000–01), Amb. to the Netherlands 2003–06; Sec.-Gen. EFTA 2006–12. *Address:* c/o European Free Trade Association, 9–11 rue de Varembé, 1211 Geneva 20, Switzerland.

BRYNGDAHL, Olof; Swedish scientist and academic; *Professor, University of Essen;* b. 26 Sept. 1933, Stockholm; s. of Carl Olof Bryngdahl and Ingeborg M. Pihlgren; m. Margaretha Schraut 1959; ed Royal Inst. of Tech. Stockholm; Research Assoc. Inst. for Optical Research, Stockholm 1956–64; staff mem. Xerox Research Lab. Rochester, NY 1964–65; Man. IBM Research Lab. San José, Calif. 1966–69; Sr scientist, IBM Research Lab. Yorktown Heights NY 1970; Prin. Scientist, Xerox Research Lab., Palo Alto, Calif. 1970–77; Prof., Inst. d'Optique, Univ. of Paris 1975–76; Prof., Univ. of Essen 1977–; Fellow, Optical Soc. of America. *Publications:* more than 200 scientific articles; 14 patents in optics. *Address:* University of Essen, 45117 Essen, Universitätsstrasse 2, Germany (office). *Telephone:* (201) 1832562 (office). *E-mail:* olof.bryngdahl@uni-due.de (office).

BRYNTSALOV, Vladimir Alekseyevich; Russian business executive; b. 23 Nov. 1946, Cherkessk; m. 1st; one d.; m. 2nd Natalya Bryntsalova; one s. one d.; ed Inst. of Construction and Eng; engineer, then Head Construction Dept in Stavropol 1970–80; expelled from CPSU for 'petty bourgeois inclination'; pvt. enterprise activities started late 1980s; f. co-operative Pchelka (Bee) 1987; bought stock shares of pharmaceutical factories, f. Co. Ferein 1992 (produces over one third of all medicaments in Russia), Hon. Pres. 1996–; mem. State Duma (Parl.) 1995–1999 (joined Our Home–Russia faction 1997); f. Russian Socialist Party 1998; re-elected as ind. cand. 1999; Deputy Chair. Yedinstvo i Otechestvo party; cand. for Presidency of Russia 1996. *Address:* Ferein, 117105 Moscow, Nagatinskaya str. 1, Russia. *Telephone:* (499) 611-13-20 (office); (495) 111-00-79 (office). *E-mail:* info@ferain.ru (office). *Website:* www.ferain.ru (office).

BRYSON, Bill; American writer; b. 1951, Des Moines, Ia; m.; four c.; ed Drake Univ.; travelled to UK and worked as orderly in mental hosp. 1973; worked as journalist for The Times and the Independent; returned with his family to USA 1993; apptd to selection panel, Book of the Month Club 2001; Commr for English Heritage; Chancellor Durham Univ. 2005–11; Pres. Campaign to Protect Rural England 2007–; Hon. DCL (Durham) 2004, Hon. OBE 2006. *Publications:* Penguin Dictionary of Troublesome Words (re-printed as Bryson's Dictionary of Troublesome Words) 1985, The Lost Continent 1987, The Mother Tongue: English and How It Got That Way, Made in America 1994, Neither Here Nor There: Travels in Europe 1995, Notes From a Small Island 1995, A Walk in the Woods 1998, I'm a Stranger Here Myself (essays, aka Notes From a Big Country) 1999, In a Sunburned Country (aka Down Under) 2000, The Best American Travel Writing (ed.), African Diary 2002, A Short History of Nearly Everything (Aventis Prize 2004, Descartes Science Communication Prize 2005) 2003, The Life and Times of the Thunderbolt Kid (memoirs) 2006, Shakespeare: A Short Life (biog.) 2007, Bryson's Dictionary for Writers and Editors 2008, At Home: A Short History of Private Life 2011. *Address:* The Marsh Agency, 50 Ablemarle Street, London, W1S 4BD, England (office); c/o Publicity Department, Transworld Publishers, 61–63 Uxbridge Road, London, W5 5SA, England. *Telephone:* (20) 7493-4361 (office). *Fax:* (20) 7495-8961 (office). *Website:* www.marsh-agency.co.uk (office); www.cpre.org .uk; www.randomhouse.com/features/billbryson.

BRYSON, John E., LLB, JD; American energy industry executive and government official; b. 1944; ed Stanford Univ., Yale Law School; Dir Edison International 1990–, Chair. and CEO 1990–99, Chair., Pres. and CEO 2000–, Dir Southern California Edison (subsidiary) 1990–99, 2003–, Chair. and CEO 1990–99, Chair. 2003–, Chair., Edison Mission Energy (subsidiary) 2000–02; Sec. of Commerce 2011–12; fmr mem. Bd of Dirs The Boeing Co., Pacific American Income Shares Inc., Western Asset Funds Inc., The Walt Disney Co., W. M. Keck Foundation; Trustee, California Inst. of Tech.; fmr Chair. Calif. Business Roundtable; fmr Trustee, Stanford Univ. *Address:* c/o Department of Commerce, 1401 Constitution Avenue, NW, Washington, DC 20230, USA.

BRZEZINSKI, Zbigniew Kazimierz, PhD; American academic and fmr government official; *Counsellor, Center for Strategic and International Studies;* b. 28 March 1928, Warsaw, Poland; s. of Tadeusz Brzezinski and Leonia Roman; m. Emilie Anna (Muska) Benes 1955; two s. one d.; ed McGill and Harvard Univs; settled in N America 1938; Instructor in Govt and Research Fellow, Russian Research Center, Harvard Univ. 1953–56; Asst Prof. of Govt, Research Assoc. of Russian Research Center and of Center for Int. Affairs, Harvard Univ. 1956–60; Assoc. Prof. of Public Law and Govt, Columbia Univ. 1960–62, Prof. 1962–89 (on leave 1966–68, 1977–81) and Dir Research Inst. on Communist Affairs 1961–77 (on leave 1966–68); mem. Policy Planning Council, Dept of State 1966–68; mem. Hon. Steering Cttee, Young Citizens for Johnson 1964; Dir Foreign Policy Task Force for Vice-Pres. Humphrey 1968; Asst to the Pres. for Nat. Security Affairs 1977–81; mem. Nat. Security Council 1977–81; Counsellor, Center for Strategic and Int. Studies, Washington, DC 1981–; Robert E. Osgood Prof. of American Foreign Policy, Paul Nitze School of Advanced Int. Studies, Johns Hopkins Univ. 1989–; mem. Council on Foreign Relations, New York, Bd of Trustees, Freedom House; Fellow, American Acad. of Arts and Sciences 1969; Order of White Eagle (Poland) 1995, Order of Merit (Ukraine) 1996, Masaryk Order 1998, Gedymin Order 1998; Dr hc (Alliance Coll.) 1966, (Coll. of the Holy Cross) 1971, (Fordham Univ.) 1979, (Williams Coll.) 1986, (Georgetown Univ.) 1987, (Catholic Univ. of Lublin) 1990, (Warsaw Univ.) 1991; Guggenheim Fellowship 1960, Ford Fellowship 1970, Presidential Medal of Freedom 1981. *Publications include:* Political Controls in the Soviet Army 1954, The Permanent Purge–Politics in Soviet Totalitarianism 1956, Totalitarian Dictatorship and Autocracy (with Carl Joachim Friedrich) 1957, The Soviet Bloc–Unity and Conflict 1960, Ideology and Power in Soviet Politics 1962, Africa and the Communist World (ed. and contrib.) 1963, Political Power: USA/USSR (with Samuel P. Huntington) 1964, Alternative to Partition: For a Broader Conception of America's Role in Europe 1965, Dilemmas of Change in Soviet Politics (ed. and contrib.) 1969, Between Two Ages: America's Role in the Technetronic Era 1970, The Fragile Blossom: Crisis and Change in Japan 1972, The Relevance of Liberalism 1977, Power and Principle: Memoirs of the National Security Adviser 1977–1981 1983, Game Plan: A Geostrategic Framework for the Conduct of the US-Soviet Contest 1986, In Quest of National Security 1988, The Grand Failure: The Birth and Death of Communism in the 20th

Century 1989, *Out of Control: Global Turmoil on the Eve of the Twenty-First Century* 1993, *The Grand Chessboard: American Primacy and its Geostrategic Imperatives* 1996, *The Geostrategic Triad: Living with China, Europe, and Russia* 2000, *The Choice: Global Domination or Global Leadership* 2004, *Second Chance: Three Presidents and the Crisis of American Superpower* 2007, *America and the World: Conversations on the Future of American Foreign Policy* (with Brent Scowcroft) 2008, *Strategic Vision: America and the Crisis of Global Power* 2012; contrib. to numerous publs, journals and periodicals. *Address:* Center for Strategic and International Studies, 1800 K Street NW, Washington, DC 20006, USA (office). *Telephone:* (202) 833-2408 (office). *Fax:* (202) 833-2409 (office). *E-mail:* zb@ csis.org (office). *Website:* www.csis.org (office).

BU, Changsen, BSc, MSc; Chinese business executive and academic; *Chairman and CEO, Shandong Energy Group Company Ltd;* ed Shandong Coll. of Mining Tech., China Univ. of Mining and Tech.; worked as Section Chief of Geology and Survey Div., Taoyang Mine, Feicheng Mining Group, subsequently Deputy Div. Chief of Geology and Survey Div., Feicheng Mining Group, later Dir Liangbaosi Mine Preparation Office, then Man. of Taoyang Mine, of Guojiazhuang Mine, then Deputy Chief Engineer, Feicheng Mining Group, later Deputy Chief Econ. Man., then Asst to the Gen. Man., Deputy Gen. Man. Feicheng Mining Group; fmr Deputy Dir Coal Industry Bureau of Shandong Prov., mem. Party Cttee of Shandong Prov. Econ. and Information Tech. Comm. and Dir of Coal Industry Bureau of Shandong Prov.; Chair. and CEO Shandong Energy Group Co. Ltd 2011–; Adjunct Prof. and Doctoral Supervisor, China Univ. of Mining and Tech., Shandong Univ. of Science and Tech.; mem. Special Talent Project 2010–11. *Address:* Shandong Energy Group Co. Ltd, 10777 Jingshi Road, Jinan City 250014, Shandong Province, People's Republic of China (office). *Telephone:* (531) 66597812 (office), (531) 66597799 (office). *Fax:* (531) 66597700 (office). *E-mail:* web@snjt.com (office). *Website:* www.snjt.com (office).

BU HE, (Yun Shuguang); Chinese party and government official; b. 24 March 1926, Inner Mongolia; s. of the late Ulanfu and Yun Ting; m. Zhulanqiqige 1947; one s. two d.; ed Yan'an Inst. for Nationalities, Nationalities Coll. of Yan'an Univ.; joined CCP 1942; Lecturer and Deputy Dir Political Dept of Nei Mongol Autonomous Coll. in Chifeng 1946; CCP Br. Sec. and Dir of Nei Mongol Art Troupe 1947–53; Leading Party Group Sec. and Deputy Dir Nei Mongol Cultural Bureau 1954–64; Acting mem. Standing Cttee of CCP Cttee, Nei Mongol and Sec. and Dir of CCP Cttee of Cultural and Educ. Comm., Nei Mongol 1966; Sec. Municipal Party Cttee of Baotou 1974–77; Dir Propaganda Dept of CCP Cttee, Nei Mongol 1978; Deputy Dir State Nationalities Affairs Comm. 1978–81; Sec. CCP Cttee and Mayor of Huhhot City 1978–81; Deputy Sec. CCP Cttee, Nei Mongol 1981–82; mem. of 12th CCP Central Cttee 1982–87; Deputy Sec. CCP Cttee and Chair. Provincial Govt, Nei Mongol 1983; mem. 13th CCP Cen. Cttee 1987–92; Vice-Chair. 8th NPC Standing Cttee 1993–98, 9th NPC 1998–2003; Chair. Regional Fed. of Literary and Art Circles 1954–65; mem. 2nd, 3rd, 4th Council of Chinese Fed. of Literary and Art Circles. *Publications:* The Basic Knowledge of Autonomy in the Nationalities Region, the Nationalities Theory of Marxism and the Party's Nationalities Policies, The Animal Husbandry in Inner Mongolia Today, In the Sea of Poems (poetry collection), Bu He's Collection of Theses in Literature and Art. *Leisure interests:* calligraphy, literature and art-writing. *Address:* c/o Office of the Regional Governor, Hohhot, Nei Mongol, People's Republic of China.

BUAINAIN, Ganem Fadhel al-; Bahraini politician; *Minister of State for Foreign Affairs;* mem. Majlis al-Nuab (Council of Reps) for Muharraq Eighth Constituency –2012; Minister of State for Foreign Affairs 2012–; Pres. Al-Asala Islamic Soc. *Address:* Ministry of Foreign Affairs, POB 547, Government House, Government Rd, Manama, Bahrain (office). *Telephone:* 17227555 (office). *Fax:* 17212603 (office). *E-mail:* info@mofa.gov.bh (office). *Website:* www.mofa.gov.bh (office).

BUARQUE DE HOLLANDA, Anna Maria, (Ana de Hollanda); Brazilian singer, songwriter and politician; *Minister of Culture;* b. 12 Aug. 1948, São Paulo; d. of Sérgio Buarque de Hollanda and Maria Amélia Alvim Buarque de Hollanda; ed Int. School of Theater of Latin America and the Caribbean, Cuba; stage debut aged 16 at Coll. of Rio Branco; Dir Centro Cultural São Paulo 1983–85; Sec. of Culture, City of Osasco 1986–88; musical tours throughout Brazil and Angola, Cuba, Uruguay 1988–2000; Dir Centro de Música da Funarte (Fundação Nacional de Artes) 2003–07; Minister of Culture 2011–; fmr mem. Partido Comunista Brasileiro. *Recordings:* solo albums: Tão Simples 1995, Um Filme 2001, Só na Canção 2009. *Address:* Ministry of Culture, Esplanada dos Ministérios, Bloco B, 4° andar, 70068-900, Brasília DF, Brazil (office). *Telephone:* (61) 2024-2000 (office). *Fax:* (61) 3225-9162 (office). *E-mail:* gm@cultura.gov.br (office). *Website:* www .cultura.gov.br (office).

BUBALO, Predrag, LLM, LLD; Serbian politician; b. 14 Oct. 1954, Vladicin Han; m.; one s. one d.; ed Faculty of Law, University of Novi Sad; joined Livnica Kikinda (foundry co.) as Adviser to Gen. Man. 1977, Eng Man. 1981–90, Financial Man. 1991–94, Head, office in Beijing 1994–2000, Man. AUTO-KUCA (Livnica Kikinda subsidiary) 2000–02, Gen. Man. Livnica Kikinda 2002–04; Minister of International Economic Relations March–Oct. 2004, Coordinator, Ministry of Economy July–Oct. 2004, Minister of the Economy 2004–06, of Trade and Services 2007–08; mem. Democratic Party of Serbia (DPS).

BUBKA, Sergey Nazarovich; Ukrainian politician, sports official and fmr athlete; *Vice-President, Council, International Association of Athletics Federations;* b. 4 Dec. 1963, Voroshilovgrad (now Lugansk); s. of Nazar Bubka and Valentina Bubka; m. Lilya Tioutiounik 1983; two s.; ed Kiev State Inst.; fmr pole vaulter; turned professional, represented USSR 1981–91, Ukraine 1991–2001 (retd); set 17 world records outdoors and 18 indoors; cleared 6m or better in more than 44 competitions; first man to clear 6m feet both indoors and out 1991; holds current world outdoor record of 6.14m (20 feet 1³/₄ inches) set in Sestriere, Italy July 1994 and current world indoor record of 6.15m set in Donetsk, Ukraine Feb. 1993; six-time Int. Asscn of Athletics Feds (IAAF) world champion Helsinki 1983, Rome 1987, Tokyo 1991, Stuttgart 1993, Gothenburg 1995, Athens 1997; gold medal, Olympic Games, Seoul, South Korea 1988; mem. IOC Exec. Bd, IOC Evaluation Comm. for 2008, IOC Athletes' Comm. –2008, IAAF Council 2001– (Vice-Pres. 2011–), Bd Nat. Olympic Cttee of Ukraine (Pres. 2005–); Chair. IOC Athletes' Comm.; Pres. S. Bubka Sports Club; mem. Parl. (For United Ukraine,

Regions of Ukraine faction) 2002–06; unsuccessful cand. for IOC Pres. 2013; mem. Champions for Peace club; Best Sportsman of the Soviet Union 1984, 1985, 1986, Prince of Asturias Award in Sports 1991, L'Equipe Sportsman of the Year 1997, Track and Field Best Pole Vaulter of the Last Half-Century, UNESCO Champion for Sport 2003, Panathlon Int. Flambeau d'Or 2005, Marca Leyenda 2005, inducted into IAAF Hall of Fame 2012. *Publication:* An Attempt is Reserved (in Russian) 1987. *Address:* Ukrainian National Olympic Committee, 39–41 Khoryva Street, Kiev 04071, Ukraine (office). *Telephone:* (44) 379-12-77 (office). *E-mail:* office@noc -ukr.org (office). *Website:* www.noc-ukr.org (office); www.iaaf.org/athletes/ukraine/ sergey-bubka-365; www.sergeybubka.com.

BUCHACHENKO, Anatoly Leonidovich, DrChemSc; Russian chemical physicist; b. 7 Sept. 1935, Arkhangelsk region; s. of L. P. Buchachenko and A. S. Buchachenko; m. M. S. Buchachenko 1960; one s. one d.; ed Gorky Univ.; post grad., Jr then Sr scientific Asst 1958–68; Head of Lab. of USSR (now Russian) Acad. of Sciences Inst. of Chemical Physics 1970–, Vice-Dir 1989–94, Dir 1994–96; Head of Dept 1996; Head of Dept of Chemical Kinetics, Moscow State Univ. 1988–; Prof. 1975–; mem. USSR (now Russian) Acad. of Sciences 1987; State Prize 1977, Lenin Prize 1986. *Publications:* works on the physical chemistry of free radicals, chemical reactions, spin chemistry, molecular ferromagnets. *Leisure interests:* wood architecture modelling. *Address:* N. N. Semenov Institute of Chemical Physics of the Russian Academy of Sciences, 1 Academyya Semenova Prospect, Chernogolovka, Noginskyy Region, Moscow oblast 142432, Russia (office). *Telephone:* (495) 993-57-07 (office); (495) 331-31-70 (home). *Fax:* (496) 515-54-20 (office). *Website:* www.icp.ac.ru (office).

BUCHANAN, Isobel Wilson; British singer (soprano); b. 15 March 1954, Glasgow, Scotland; d. of Stewart Buchanan and Mary Buchanan; m. Jonathan Stephen Geoffrey King (actor Jonathan Hyde) 1980; two d.; ed Cumbernauld Comprehensive High School and Royal Scottish Acad. of Music and Drama; professional debut in Sydney, Australia with Richard Bonynge and Joan Sutherland 1976–78; British debut, Glyndebourne 1978; US and German debuts 1979; Vienna Staatsoper debut 1979; ENO debut 1985, Paris Opera debut 1986; now freelance artist working with all major opera cos and orchestras and giving recitals; teaches and regularly gives master classes and acts as adjudicator in music festivals and competitions. *Recordings:* Beethoven's Ninth Symphony, Werther, Mozart Arias and Duets. *Leisure interests:* cooking, reading, gardening, yoga, knitting. *E-mail:* isobel@totalfiasco.co.uk (office).

BUCHANAN, J. Robert, MD; American medical scientist and academic; *Professor of Medicine, School of Medicine, Harvard University;* b. 8 March 1928, Newark, NJ; m. Susan Carver; one s. one d.; ed Amherst Coll. and Cornell Univ. Medical School; Intern, then Asst Resident Physician, New York Hosp. 1954–58, Research Fellow in Medicine 1956–57; Research Fellow in Endocrinology, Cornell Univ. Medical Coll., New York 1960–61; WHO Travelling Fellow 1963; Instructor in Medicine, Cornell Univ. Medical Coll. 1961–63, Asst Prof. 1963–67, Asst to Chair. Dept of Medicine 1964–65, Assoc. Dean 1965–69, Clinical Assoc. Prof. 1967–69, Assoc. Prof. 1969–71, Prof. 1971–76, Acting Dean, then Dean 1969–76; Prof. of Medicine, Univ. of Chicago, Ill. 1977–82; Assoc. Dean, Pritzker School of Medicine, Chicago 1978–82; Prof. of Medicine, Harvard Medical School, Boston, Mass. 1982–; Gen. Dir. Mass. Gen. Hosp. 1982–94; Gen. Dir Emer. 1994–; physician at hosps in New York, Chicago and Boston 1956–; mem. Admin. Bd, Council of Teaching Hosps 1984–89, mem. Exec. Council 1985–; Dir Mass. Div., American Cancer Soc. 1984–; Bd of Dirs Bank of New England 1986–91, AMI Holdings 1991–, Exec. Cttee Mass. Hosp. Asscn 1987– (Chair. 1990–91), Charles River Labs; Chair. Council of Teaching Hosps, Asscn of American Medical Colls 1988–89; mem. NAS Cttee to review Inst. of Medicine, American Cancer Soc., Mass. Div., Soc. of Medical Admins; Chair. Educ. Comm. for Foreign Medical Grads 1994–; Fellow, American Coll. of Physicians; Founding Trustee, Aga Khan Univ.; Hon. ScD (Amherst Coll.); Hon. LHD (Rush Univ.); Hon. MD (Peking Union Medical Coll., Beijing, China). *Publications:* numerous papers and articles in journals. *Leisure interests:* boating, gardening. *Address:* 5 Chestnut Hill Road, POB 669, Killingworth, CT 06419, USA (office). *Telephone:* (860) 663-2637 (home). *Fax:* (860) 663-3058 (home). *E-mail:* jrobertbuchan@aol.com (home). *Website:* hms .harvard.edu/hms/home.asp (office).

BUCHANAN, Patrick (Pat) Joseph, MS; American journalist and fmr government official; b. 2 Nov. 1938, Washington; s. of William Buchanan and Catherine Crum; m. Shelley A. Scarney 1971; ed Georgetown and Columbia Univs; editorial writer, St Louis Globe Democrat 1962–64, asst editorial writer 1964–66; Exec. Asst to Richard Nixon 1966–69; Special Asst to Pres. Nixon 1969–73; consultant to Pres. Nixon and Pres. Ford 1973–74; Asst to Pres., Dir of Communications, White House, Washington, DC 1985–87; syndicated columnist, political commentator, New York Times special features 1975–78, Chicago Tribune-New York News Syndicate 1978–85, Tribune Media Services 1987–91, 1993–95; commentator, NBC Radio Network 1978–82; co-host Crossfire (TV Show) Cable News Network 1982–85, 1987–91, 1993–95, 1997; appeared as host and panellist in TV shows 1978–; Ed.-in-Chief PJB—From the Right (newsletter) 1990–91; moderator, Capital Gang TV show CNN 1988–92; Chair. The American Cause 1993–95, 1997–, Pat Buchanan & Co., Mutual Broadcasting System 1993–95; unsuccessful cand. for Republican Presidential nomination 1992, 1996; Republican. *Publications:* The New Majority 1973, Conservative Votes, Liberal Victories 1975, Right from the Beginning 1988, Barry Goldwater, The Conscience of A Conservative 1990, The Great Betrayal 1998, A Republic, not an Empire 2000, State of Emergency 2006, Day of Reckoning 2008. *Address:* The American Cause, 501 Church Street, Suite 315, Vienna, VA 22180 (office); 1017 Savile Lane, McLean, VA 22101, USA (home). *Telephone:* (703) 255-2632 (office). *Fax:* (703) 255-2219 (office). *E-mail:* americancause@gmail.com (office). *Website:* www .theamericancause.org (office).

BUCHANAN, Robin William Turnbull, MBA, FCA, FRSA; American/British business executive and academic administrator; *Senior Adviser, Bain & Company;* b. 2 April 1952; s. of Iain Buchanan and Gillian Pamela Buchanan (née Hughes-Hallett); m. Diana Tei Tanaka 1986; one s. one d.; ed Harvard Business School (Baker Scholar); with Mann Judd Landau (now Deloitte & Touche) 1970–77; with American Express Int. Banking Corpn 1979–82; with Bain & Co. Inc. 1982–, Bain Capital 1982–84, Man. Pnr, London 1990–96, Sr Pnr, London 1996–2007, Sr Adviser 2007–; Dean, then Pres. London Business School 2007–09; Dir (non-exec.)

Liberty International plc 1997–2008, Shire plc (fmrly Shire Pharmaceuticals Group plc) 2003–08, Schroders plc 2010–; mem. Trilateral Comm., Northern Meeting, Highland Soc., Professional Standards Advisory Bd, Inst. of Dirs, Editorial Bd European Business Journal; mem. Advisory Council, Prince's Trust, Int. Advisory Council, Recipco; Fellow, Salzburg Seminar, Liveryman Worshipful Co. of Ironmongers. *Address:* Bain & Company, 40 Strand, London, WC2N 5RW, England (office). *Telephone:* (20) 7969-6070 (office). *Fax:* (20) 7960-6072 (office). *E-mail:* rbuchanan@mba1979.hbs.edu (office).

BÜCHNER, Ton, MSc (CivilEng), MBA; Dutch engineer and business executive; *Chairman of the Board of Management and CEO, Akzo Nobel NV;* b. 1965; ed Delft Univ. of Tech., Int. Inst. for Man. Devt, Switzerland, Stanford Univ. Exec. Program, USA; early career spent in oil and gas construction industry involving roles at Allseas Engineering in Europe and AkerKvaerner in SE Asia before joining Sulzer in 1994; worked in a range of Sulzer operations until apptd to Exec. Cttee as Div. Pres. 2001, Pres. and CEO Sulzer Corpn 2007–12; Chair. Bd of Man. and Exec. Cttee and CEO Akzo Nobel NV 2012–. *Address:* Akzo Nobel NV, Strawinskylaan 2555, 1077 ZZ Amsterdam, Netherlands (office). *Telephone:* (20) 502-7833 (office). *Fax:* (20) 502-7604 (office). *E-mail:* media.relations@akzonobel .com (office). *Website:* www.akzonobel.com (office).

BUCHWALD, Christoph; German publishing executive; *Publisher, Uitgeverij Cossee;* b. 30 Nov. 1951, Tübingen; ed Freie Universität, Berlin, Technische Universität, Berlin; fmrly Ed. Hanser, Munich; fmrly Publr Luchterhand Literaturverlag; fmrly with Suhrkamp Verlag KG, Frankfurt; Co-founder and Publr Uitgeverij Cossee, Amsterdam; Kt, Orde van Oranje-Nassau (Netherlands) 2011. *Address:* Uitgeverij Cossee, Kerkstraat 361, 1017 HW Amsterdam, Netherlands (office). *Telephone:* (20) 5289911 (office). *Fax:* (20) 5289912 (office). *E-mail:* buchwald@cossee.com (home). *Website:* www.uitgeverijcossee.nl (office).

BUCHWALD, Stephen L., ScB, PhD; American chemist and academic; *Camille Dreyfus Professor of Chemistry, Massachusetts Institute of Technology;* b. 1955, Bloomington, Ind.; ed Brown, Columbia and Harvard Univs; NSF Predoctoral Fellow, Harvard Univ. 1977–82; Myron A. Bantrell Postdoctoral Fellow, California Inst. of Tech. 1982–84; Asst Prof. of Chem., MIT 1984–89, Assoc. Prof. 1989–93, Prof. 1993–, Camille Dreyfus Prof. 1997–; Assoc. Ed. Advanced Synthesis and Catalysis and Chemical Science; consultant to several cos; mem. NAS 2008; Fellow, American Acad. of Arts and Sciences 2000; Harold Edgerton Faculty Achievement Award, MIT, ACS Arthur C. Cope Scholar Award, ACS Award in Organometallic Chem. 2000, NIH MERIT Award, Bristol-Myers Squibb Distinguished Achievement Award 2005, CAS Science Spotlight Award 2005, ACS Award for Creative Work in Synthetic Organic Chem. 2006, Siegfried Medal Award in Chemical Methods which Impact Process Chem. 2006, Gustavus J. Esselen Award for Chem. in the Public Interest 2010, ACS Arthur C. Cope Award 2013. *Publications:* more than 390 papers in professional journals and 43 issued patents. *Address:* Massachusetts Institute of Technology, Room 18-490, 77 Massachusetts Avenue, Cambridge, MA 02139, USA (office). *Telephone:* (617) 253-1885 (office). *Fax:* (617) 253-3297 (office). *E-mail:* sbuchwal@mit.edu (office). *Website:* web.mit.edu/chemistry/buchwald (office).

BUCK, Linda B., PhD; American physiologist and academic; *Affiliate Professor of Physiology and Biophysics, University of Washington;* ed Univ. of Wash., Univ. of Tex. Southwestern Medical Center, Dallas; Postdoctoral Fellow, Columbia Univ. Coll. of Physicians and Surgeons 1980-84; Assoc., Howard Hughes Medical Inst., Columbia Univ. 1984–91; Asst Prof., Dept of Neurobiology, Harvard Medical School 1991–96, Assoc. Prof. 1996–2001, Prof. 2001–02; Asst Investigator Howard Hughes Medical Inst. (HHMI) 1994–97, Assoc. Investigator, 1997–2000, Full Investigator 2001–; Affiliate Prof. of Physiology and Biophysics, Univ. of Wash. 2003–; Full Mem. Basic Sciences Div., Fred Hutchinson Cancer Research Center 2002–; Fellow, AAAS, American Acad. of Arts and Sciences; mem. NAS; mem. Bd of Dirs International Flavors and Fragrances Inc. 2007–; Lewis S. Rosenstiel Award, Unilever Science Award, Perl/UNC Neuroscience Prize, Gairdner Foundation Int. Award, Nobel Prize in Physiology or Medicine (jtly with Richard Axel) 2004. *Publications:* numerous articles in professional publs; books include The Human Olfactory Receptor Gene Family (co-author) 2004, The Mouse Olfactory Receptor Gene Family (co-author) 2004. *Address:* Fred Hutchinson Cancer Research Center, 1100 Fairview Avenue North, POB 19024, Seattle, WA 98109-1024 (office); Howard Hughes Medical Institute, 4000 Jones Bridge Road, Chevy Chase, MD, 20815-689, USA (office). *Telephone:* (206) 667-6316 (office); (301) 215-8500 (office). *Fax:* (206) 667-1031 (office). *E-mail:* lbuck@fhcrc.org (office); webmaster@ hhmi.org (office). *Website:* www.fhcrc.org (office); www.hhmi.org (office).

BUCKINGHAM, (Amyand) David, CBE, FRS, FRSC, FInstP, FRACI; Australian chemist and academic; *Professor Emeritus of Chemistry, University of Cambridge;* b. 28 Jan. 1930, Sydney, NSW; s. of Reginald Joslin Buckingham and Florence Grace Buckingham; m. Jillian Bowles 1965; one. s. two d.; ed Barker Coll., Hornsby, NSW, Univ. of Sydney, Corpus Christi Coll., Cambridge; Lecturer, then Student and Tutor, Christ Church, Univ. of Oxford 1955–65, Univ. Lecturer in Inorganic Chem. 1958–65; Prof. of Theoretical Chem., Univ. of Bristol 1965–69; Prof. of Chem., Univ. of Cambridge 1969–97, Fellow, Pembroke Coll., Cambridge 1970–97, Hon. Fellow 2008, Prof. Emer. 1997–; Pres. Faraday Div. of RSC 1987–89, Cambridge Univ. Cricket Club 1990–2009; mem. Council Royal Soc. 1999–2001; mem. ACS; Corresp. mem. Australian Acad. of Science; Foreign mem. American Acad. of Arts and Sciences, Royal Swedish Acad. of Sciences; Foreign Assoc., NAS; Fellow, Royal Australian Chemical Inst., American Physical Soc., Optical Soc. of America; Dr hc (Université de Nancy I) 1979; Hon. DSc (Sydney) 1993, (Antwerp) 2004; Harrie Massey Medal, Inst. of Physics 1995, Hughes Medal, Royal Soc. 1996, Faraday Medal, RSC 1998, Townes Medal, Optical Soc. of America 2001, Inaugural Ahmed Zewail Prize 2007. *Achievement:* Cricket Blue, Univ. of Sydney 1953. *Publications:* The Laws and Applications of Thermodynamics 1964, Organic Liquids: Structure, Dynamics and Chemical Properties 1978, The Principles of Molecular Recognition 1993; more than 330 papers in scientific journals. *Leisure interests:* cricket, woodwork, travel, walking. *Address:* Department of Chemistry, University of Cambridge, Cambridge, CB2 1EW (office); Crossways, 23 The Avenue, Newmarket, Cambs., CB8 9AA, England (home). *Telephone:* (1223) 336372 (office); (1638) 663799 (home). *Fax:* (1223) 336362 (office). *E-mail:* adb1000@cam.ac.uk (office). *Website:* www.ch.cam.ac.uk/person/ adb1000 (office).

BUCKLAND, David John; British artist, theatre director and filmmaker; *Director, Cape Farewell;* b. 15 June 1949, London, England; s. of Denis Buckland and Valarie Buckland; partner Siobhan Davies 1978; one s. one d.; ed Dorchester Secondary Modern School, Dorset, Hardye's Grammar School, Dorchester, Deep River High School, Ottawa and London Coll. of Printing; has participated in group exhbns and work appears in public collections in London, New York, Chicago, Los Angeles, Paris etc.; Artistic Dir Siobhan Davies Dance Co.; Lecturer, RCA, London Coll. of Printing, Chicago Art Inst.; 21 set and costume designs for dance, including Rambert Dance Co., Siobhan Davies Dance Co., English Nat. Ballet and work for TV; Northern Arts Fellow 1972–73; Kodak Bursary 1978; Founder and Dir Cape Farewell environmental project 2000–; three commissions from MasterCard, Vanguard Insurance and Royal Caribbean completed; Minn. First Bank Award 1988–90. *Leisure interests:* multi-hull sailor, arts, theatre, travel, hill walking. *Address:* Cape Farewell, The Science Museum's Dana Centre, 165 Queen's Gate, South Kensington, London, SW7 5HD, England (office). *Telephone:* (20) 7620-6235 (office). *Fax:* (20) 7401-8231 (office). *E-mail:* davidbuckland@capefarewell.com (office). *Website:* www.capefarewell.com (office).

BUCKLEY, Sir George William, Kt, BSc, PhD; British business executive; *Chairman, Arle Capital LLP;* b. 23 Feb. 1947; ed Univs of Southampton and Huddersfield; fmr Man. Dir Cen. Services Div., British Railways Bd, UK; fmr Pres. Electric Motors Div. and Automotive and Precision Motors Div., Emerson Electric Co., St Louis, Mo., USA; joined Brunswick Corpn 1997, Chair. and CEO 2000–05; Chair., Pres. and CEO 3M Company 2005–12; Chair. Arle Capital LLP 2012–; Chair. Expro International; Dir (non-exec.) Technogym; mem. Bd of Dirs PepsiCo, Hitachi, Archer Daniels Midland, Stanley Black & Decker; Hon. DSc (Huddersfield). *Address:* Arle Capital Partners Ltd, 12 Charles II Street, London, SW1Y 4QU, England (office). *Telephone:* (20) 7979-0000 (office). *E-mail:* info@arle.com (office). *Website:* www.arle.com (office).

BUCKLEY, James Lane, BA, LLB; American fmr politician and judge (retd); b. 9 March 1923, New York, NY; s. of William F. Buckley and Aloise Steiner Buckley; m. Ann F. Cooley 1953; five s. one d.; ed Yale Univ.; served in USN 1943–46; Senator from New York 1971–77; Under-Sec. of State for Security Assistance 1981–82; Pres. Radio Free Europe–Radio Liberty 1982–85; Circuit Judge, US Court of Appeals, DC Circuit 1985–2001, Sr Judge, retd 2001; Co-Chair. US Del. to UN Conf. on Environment, Nairobi 1982; Chair. US Del. to UN Conf. on Population, Mexico City 1984; Republican. *Publications:* If Men Were Angels 1975, Gleanings from an Unplanned Life 2006, Freedom at Risk 2010. *Leisure interests:* natural history, American History. *Address:* PO Box 597, Sharon, CT 06069 (office); 28 Great Elm Drive, Sharon, CT 06069, USA (home). *Telephone:* (860) 364-2207 (home).

BUCKLEY, Michael; Irish banker; *Chairman, DCC PLC;* b. Cork; m. Anne Buckley; fmr stockbroker and civil servant in Ireland and EU; joined Allied Irish Bank PLC (AIB) 1991, Exec. Dir 1995–2001, Man. Dir Capital Markets Div. 1994–99, Head Polish Div. 1999–2001, Group Chief Exec. 2001–05; Chair. DCC PLC 2008–; Adjunct Prof. and Chair. Advisory Bd, Dept of Econs, Nat. Univ. of Ireland, Univ. Coll. Cork; Chair. Irish Chamber Orchestra; Dir M&T Bank Corpn, UK Asset Resolution Ltd. *Address:* DCC House, Brewery Road, Stillorgan, Blackrock, Co. Dublin, Ireland (office). *Telephone:* (1) 2799 400 (office). *Website:* www.dcc.ie (office).

BUCKLEY, Stephen, MFA; British artist and university professor; *Professor Emeritus, University of Reading;* b. 5 April 1944, Leicester; s. of Nancy Throsby and Leslie Buckley; m. Stephanie James 1973; one s. one d.; ed Univs of Newcastle-upon-Tyne and Reading; taught at Canterbury Coll. of Art 1969, Leeds Coll. of Art 1970, Chelsea School of Art 1971–80; Artist in Residence, King's Coll., Cambridge 1972–74; Prof. of Fine Art, Univ. of Reading 1994–2009, currently Prof. Emer.; worked with Rambert Dance Co., London 1987–88; works in public collections in Chile, Sweden, UK, Venezuela, USA, NZ, Australia; comms include Neal Street Restaurant 1972, mural painting for Penguin Books 1972, Leith's Restaurant 1973; included in over 30 public collections world-wide; prizewinner, John Moores Exhbn 1974, 1985, Chichester Nat. Art Exhbn 1975, Tolly-Cobbold Exhbn 1977. *Address:* c/o Austin/Desmond Fine Art, Pied Bull Yard, 68–69 Great Russell Street, London, WC1B 3BN, England. *Telephone:* (20) 7242-4443 (office). *Fax:* (20) 7404-4480 (office). *E-mail:* contact@stephenbuckley.com (office). *Website:* www .stephenbuckley.com.

BUCKOVSKI, Vlado, PhD; Macedonian politician; *Chairman, Socijaldemok-ratski Sojuz na Makedonije—SDSM (Social Democratic Alliance of Macedonia);* b. 2 Dec. 1962, Skopje; ed Univ. of Skopje; expert legal collaborator for Parl. 1987–88; Jr Teaching Asst of Roman Law, Univ. of Skopje 1988–91, Sr Teaching Asst 1992–99, Docent 1999–, Assoc. Prof., Faculty of Law 2004–; mem. State Election Comm. 1998–2000; Party Spokesman Socijaldemokratski Sojuz na Makedonije— SDSM (Social Democratic Alliance of Macedonia) 1999–2001, Vice-Pres. SDSM 1999–2004, Chair. 2004–; Chair. Council of Skopje 2000–01; Minister of Defence May–Nov. 2001, Oct. 2002–04; Prime Minister of Fmr Yugoslav Repub. of Macedonia 2004–06. *Publications include:* academic papers on public law. *Address:* Socijaldemokratski Sojuz na Makedonije—SDSM (Social Democratic Alliance of Macedonia), 1000 Skopje, Bihačka 8, Macedonia (office). *Telephone:* (2) 3135380 (office). *Fax:* (2) 3120462 (office). *E-mail:* contact@sdsm.org.mk (office). *Website:* www.sdsm.org.mk (office).

BUCKSTEIN, Mark Aaron, BS, JD; American lawyer, mediator and arbitrator; *President, Professional Dispute Resolutions, Inc.;* b. 1 July 1939, New York, NY; s. of Henry Buckstein and Minnie Buckstein; m. Rochelle J. Buchman 1960; one s. one d.; ed New York Univ. Law School and City Coll. of New York; with various New York law firms 1963–69; Sr Partner, Baer, Marks & Upham (law firm), New York 1969–86; Special Prof. of Law, Hofstra Univ. Law School 1980–93; Adjunct Prof. of Law, Rutgers Univ. Law School 1993–96; Florida Adjunct Prof., Florida Atlantic Univ. 2004–07; Sr Vice-Pres., Gen. Counsel and mem. Bd of Dirs Trans World Airlines Inc. 1986–92; Exec. Vice-Pres., Gen. Counsel, GAF Corpn and International Speciality Products, Inc., NJ 1993–96; Counsel, Greenberg, Traurig, Fort Lauderdale, Fla 1996–99; Pres. Professional Dispute Resolutions, Inc., Boca Raton, Fla 1999–; Dir, Bayswater Realty and Capital Corpn, Travel Channel Inc.; mem. American Arbitration Assan 1970– (Exec. Vice-Pres. and Pres.-Designate 1992–93); mem. FINRA Dispute Resolution (fmrly NASD Regulation) 1996–.

Leisure interests: tennis, puzzles, reading, music. *Address:* Professional Dispute Resolutions, Inc., 2424 North Federal Highway, Suite 150, Boca Raton, FL 33432-2803 (office); 5832 Waterford, Boca Raton, FL 33496, USA (home). *Telephone:* (561) 417-6602 (office); (561) 994-6067 (home). *Fax:* (561) 417-6604 (office); mabresolve@aol.com (office). *Website:* www.professionaldisputeresolutions.com (office).

BUCYANAYANDE, Tress, MSc; Ugandan agriculturalist and politician; *Minister of Agriculture, Animal Industry and Fisheries;* b. 1 Jan. 1938; m.; ed Bukalasa Agricultural Coll., Univ. of West Virginia and Univ. of Wisconsin, USA; Dist Agricultural Officer, Kabale and Masaka 1962–69, then Area Extension Adviser and Deputy Regional Agricultural Officer, Buganda; Gen. Man. Kinyara Sugar Works 1972–76; Asst Commr for Agric. 1982–87, Deputy Commr for Agric. 1988–91; Man. Dir Uganda Coffee Devt Authority 1993–2000; Farmer and Consultant on Agric. 2001–05; Dir of Agric., Entebbe HQ 1990–92; mem. Parl. for Bufumbira South; Minister of Agric., Animal Industry and Fisheries 2011–; mem. Nat. Resistance Movt. *Address:* Ministry of Agriculture, Animal Industry and Fisheries, PO Box 102, Entebbe (office); PO Box 77, Kisoro, Uganda (office). *Telephone:* (41) 320841 (office). *E-mail:* tbucyanayandi@parliament.go.ug (office).

BUDAKIAN, Raffi Ohannes, BS, MS, PhD; American physicist and academic; *Professor of Physics, University of Illinois at Urbana-Champaign;* b. 22 Aug. 1969, Istanbul, Turkey; s. of Sirahuys Budakian and Nazar Budak; m. Adrienne Lo; one s. one d.; ed Univ. of California, Los Angeles; fmr Researcher, Physics Dept, UCLA; currently Prof. of Physics, Univ. of Illinois at Urbana-Champaign; Visiting Scientist, IBM Almaden Research Center, San Jose, Calif. 2002–05; Edwin Pauly Merit Fellowship, UCLA 1994–98, E. Lee Kinsey Award in Physics, UCLA 1994, IBM Research Div. Award for Single Spin Detection 2004, World Tech. Award in Materials, The World Tech. Network (co-recipient) 2005. *Achievements* include: part of team that made first demonstrations of magnetic resonance force microscopy (MRFM) 1992, work reached key milestone with manipulation and detection of individual electron spin 2004. *Publications:* numerous scientific papers in professional journals on experimental condensed matter physics, magnetic resonance force microscopy, ultra-sensitive force/displacement detection, design and fabrication of micro- and nanomechanical devices. *Address:* Room 106 MRL, Department of Physics, University of Illinois at Urbana-Champaign, 1110 West Green Street, Urbana, IL 61801-3080, USA (office). *Telephone:* (217) 333-3065 (office). *Fax:* (217) 244-8544 (office). *E-mail:* budakian@illinois.edu (office). *Website:* physics.illinois.edu (office).

BUDD, Sir Alan Peter, Kt, GBE, BSc (Econ), PhD; British economist and academic; *Member of Council, Institute for Fiscal Studies;* b. 16 Nov. 1937, Kent, England; s. of Ernest Budd and Elsie Budd; m. Susan Millott 1964; three s.; ed Oundle School, London School of Econs, Univ. of Cambridge; Lecturer in Econs, Univ. of Southampton 1966–69; Ford Foundation Visiting Prof., Carnegie-Mellon Univ., USA 1969–70; Sr Econ. Adviser, HM Treasury 1970–74, Chief Econ. Adviser to HM Treasury 1991–97; Sr Research Fellow, London Business School 1974–81, Prof. of Econs 1981–88, Fellow 1997; Econ. Adviser, Barclays Bank 1988–91; Provost, The Queen's Coll., Oxford 1999–2008; Chair. Tax Law Review Cttee, Inst. for Fiscal Studies 2002–; Chair. UK Office for Budget Responsibility May–Aug. 2010; mem. Bank of England Monetary Policy Cttee 1997–99; Visiting Prof., Univ. of New South Wales, Australia 1983; Grocers' Co. Scholarship; Leverhulme Undergraduate Scholarship; Chair. Gambling Review Body 2000–01; Gov. Nat. Inst. of Econ. and Social Research 1998–; Chair. (non-exec.) Oxford Biosensors Ltd 2001–02; Hon. Fellow, The Queen's Coll., Oxford; Hon. DSc (Salford). *Publication:* Politics of Economic Planning 1978. *Leisure interests:* music, gardening, reading. *Address:* c/o Queen's College, Oxford, OX1 4AW, England (office). *Website:* www.ifs.org.uk (office).

BUDD, Sir Colin Richard, Kt, KCMG, BA; British diplomatist (retd); b. 31 Aug. 1945, Harpenden, Herts.; s. of B. W. Budd, QC and M. A. Budd (née Burgin); m. Agnes Smit; one s. one d.; ed Univ. of Cambridge; entered Diplomatic Service 1967, overseas assignments in Warsaw, Islamabad, Bonn and Brussels, Head of Political Section, Embassy in The Hague 1980–84, various positions in European Div., FCO, Deputy Sec., Cabinet Office 1996–97, Deputy Under-Sec. of State and Dir of EU and Econ. Affairs 1997–2001, Amb. to the Netherlands 2001–05; Commr, Comm. for Racial Equality 2006–07; Lay mem. QC Selection Panel 2009–13; mem. Prime Minister's Advisory Cttee on Business Appointments 2010–; *Telephone:* (20) 7223-7211 (home). *E-mail:* acbudd@hotmail.com (office).

BUDIMIR, Gen. (retd) Živko; Bosnia and Herzegovina politician and army officer (retd); *President, Federation of Bosnia and Herzegovina;* b. 20 Nov. 1962, Vir, nr Posušje, Herzegovina; m. Darija Kuna; two s. one d.; ed Aeronautical Tech. Mil. Coll., Rajlovac, War Coll. of Armed Forces of Repub. of Croatia 'Ban Josip Jelačić'; mem. League of Communists of Yugoslavia 1979–86; mem. Yugoslav People's Army 1984–86; long career in army, positions included Bn Commdr, Logistics Adviser, Hrvatsko vijeće obrane (HVO, Croatian Defence Council), Deputy Commdr, Jt HQ of Fed. Army following Washington Agreement, Commdr-in-Chief HVO following Dayton Agreement; elected mem. City Council of Mostar 2008; Pres. Fed. of Bosnia and Herzegovina March 2011– (suspended April–May 2013); mem. Croatian Party of Rights (Hrvatska stranka prava) 2006–13; f. Party of Justice and Trust 2013. *Address:* Office of the Federation Presidency, 71000 Sarajevo, Musala 9 (office); 88000 Mostar, Ante Starčevića bb, Bosnia and Herzegovina. *Telephone:* (33) 212986 (Sarajevo) (office); (36) 318905 (Mostar). *Fax:* (33) 220437 (Sarajevo) (office); (36) 313255 (Mostar). *E-mail:* info@fbihvlada.gov .ba (office). *Website:* www.fbihvlada.gov.ba (office).

BUDIŠA, Dražen; Croatian fmr politician and linguist; *Editor, Školska Knjiga;* b. 25 July 1948, Drniš; m. Nada Budiša; three s.; ed Zagreb Univ.; Pres. of Students' League of Zagreb 1971; Pres. Croatian Social-Liberal Party (Hrvatska socijalno-liberalna stranka—HSLS) 1990–96, 2002–04; Minister in Croatian Govt 1991–92; mem. House of Reps (Parl.) of Croatia 1992, 1995–2003; presidential cand. 2000; currently Ed., Školska Knjiga. *Publications:* Beginning of Printing in Europe 1984, Heritage of Croatian Reformers in Custody of the National and University Library 1985, Humanism in Croatia 1988, Croatian Books Published in Venice from 15th to 18th Centuries 1990. *Leisure interest:* gardening. *Address:* Školska Knjiga, 28, 10000 Zagreb, Croatia (office). *Website:* www.skolska.com.hr (office).

BUERGENTHAL, Thomas, LLM, JD, SJD; American judge and academic; *Lobingier Professor of International and Comparative Law, George Washington*

University Law School; b. 11 May 1934, Lubochna, Slovakia; s. of Mundek Buergenthal and Gerda Buergenthal; m. 2nd Marjorie Julia Buergenthal (née Bell); three s. from previous m.; ed Bethany Coll., W Va, New York Univ. Law School (Root Tilden Scholar), Harvard Law School; became US citizen 1957; mem. (Judge, then Pres.) Inter-American Court on Human Rights 1979–91; mem. (Judge, then Pres.) Admin. Tribunal, IDB 1989–94; mem. UN Truth Comm. for El Salvador 1992–93, UN Human Rights Comm. 1995–99; mem. Claims Resolution Tribunal for Dormant Accounts, Switzerland 1998–99, Vice-Chair. 1999; Judge, Int. Court of Justice 2000–10; mem. Faculty, George Washington Univ. Law School, Washington, DC 1989–2000, Lobingier Prof. Emer. of Int. and Comparative Law 2000–10, reappointed Lobingier Prof. 2010–; mem. New York Bar, Dist of Columbia Bar, US Supreme Court Bar; Hon. Pres. American Soc. of Int. Law 2001–09; Dr hc (Bethany Coll.) 1981, (Heidelberg Univ.) 1986, (Free Univ. of Brussels) 1994, (State Univ. of New York) 2000, (American Univ., Washington, DC) 2002, (Univ. of Minnesota) 2003, (George Washington Univ.) 2004, (Univ. of Gottingen) 2007, (New York Univ.) 2008, (Brandeis Univ.) 2011; Manley O. Hudson Medal, American Soc. of Int. Law 2002, Gruber Foundation Int. Justice Prize 2008, Goler Butcher Human Rights Prize, and numerous other awards. *Publications* include: Law-Making in the International Civil Aviation Organization 1969, International Protection of Human Rights (with L. B. Sohn) 1973, Protecting Human Rights in the Americas (with D. Shelton, fourth edn) 1995, International Human Rights (with D. Shelton and D. Stewart, fourth edn) 2007, Public International Law (with S. Murphy, fourth edn) 2007, A Lucky Child 2009. *Address:* George Washington University Law School, 2000 H Street NW, Washington, DC 20052, USA (office). *Telephone:* (202) 994-6120 (office). *Fax:* (202) 994-5654 (office). *E-mail:* tbuergen@law.gwu.edu (office). *Website:* www.law.gwu.edu/Faculty/profile.aspx?id=1758 (office).

BUFE, Uwe-Ernst, PhD; German business executive and chemist; *Deputy Chairman of the Supervisory Board, Akzo Nobel NV;* b. 22 May 1944, Teschen; m.; two c.; ed Technische Universität, Munich; with Spang and Co. 1971–74; Product Man., Degussa Frankfurt 1974, Corp. Devt and Inorganic Chemicals 1981, mem. Bd Degussa AG 1987, Corp. Devt Degussa Corpn 1977, Exec. Vice-Pres. Chemical Group 1985, Chair. and CEO 1996–99, Chair. Degussa-Hüls AG 1999–2003; Deputy Chair. Supervisory Bd, Akzo Nobel NV 2003–; mem. Supervisory Bd Solvay SA, Umicore SA, Kali + Salz AG; Dir (non-exec.) SunPower Inc. *Address:* Akzo Nobel NV, Strawinskylaan 2555, 1077 ZZ Amsterdam, The Netherlands. *Telephone:* (20) 502-7555. *Fax:* (20) 502-7604 (office). *E-mail:* info@akzonobel.com. *Website:* www.akzonobel.com.

BUFFET, Marie-George; French politician; *National Secretary, Parti Communiste Français;* b. 7 May 1949, Sceaux (Hauts-de-Seine); d. of Paul Kossellek and Raymonde Rayer; m. Jean-Pierre Buffet 1972; two c.; joined Parti Communiste Français (PCF) 1969, elected to PCF Cen. Cttee 1987, mem. Nat. Bureau 1994, Head Nat. Women's Cttee 1996, elected to Nat. Secr. 1997, Nat. Sec. 2001–; municipal councillor, then Deputy Mayor Châtenay-Malabry (Hauts-de-Seine) 1977–83; Nat. Ass. Deputy for Seine-Saint-Denis 1997–; Minister for Youth and Sport 1997–2002. *Address:* Parti Communiste Français, 2 place du Colonel Fabien, 75019 Paris, France (office). *Telephone:* 1-40-40-12-12 (office). *Fax:* 1-40-40-13-56 (office). *E-mail:* pcf@pcf.fr (office). *Website:* www.pcf.fr (office).

BUFFETT, Warren Edward; American financier and investor; *Chairman and CEO, Berkshire Hathaway Inc.;* b. 30 Aug. 1930, Omaha, Neb.; s. of Howard Homan Buffett and Leila Stahl; m. 1st Susan Thompson 1952 (died 2004); two s. one d.; m. 2nd Astrid Menks 2006; ed Wharton Business School, Univ. of Pennsylvania, Univ. of Nebraska, Columbia Univ. Business School; worked as investment salesman for father's brokerage firm 1951–54; Graham-Newman Corpn, New York City 1954–56; formed Buffett Partnership, Omaha 1956–69, Chair. and CEO Berkshire Hathaway Inc. (investment co.), Omaha, Neb. 1969–, Nat. Indemnity Co., Buffalo Evening News; mem. Bd of Dirs Salomon Brothers 1987, interim Chair. and CEO 1991–92; mem. Bd of Dirs Coca-Cola Co. (second largest stockholder in co.) 1989–2006; f. Buffet Foundation; Co-Chair. Goldman Sachs 10,000 Small Businesses initiative; ranked by Forbes magazine amongst The World's Most Powerful People (14th) 2009, (33rd) 2010, (20th) 2011, (15th) 2012, (13th) 2013, Presidential Medal of Freedom 2010, named, along with Bill Gates, by Foreign Policy as the most influential global thinker 2010, named by TIME magazine as one of the most influential people in the world 2012. *Address:* Berkshire Hathaway Inc., 3555 Farnam Street, Suite 1440, Omaha, NE 68131, USA (office). *Telephone:* (402) 346-1400 (office). *Fax:* (402) 346-3375 (office). *E-mail:* berkshire@berkshirehathaway.com (office). *Website:* www.berkshirehathaway.com (office).

BUFI, Ylli; Albanian politician; b. 25 May 1948, Tiranë; m. Zana Bufi 1978; two d.; Minister of Foodstuff Industry 1990–91, of Food and Light Industry Feb.–May 1991, of Nutrition May–June 1991; Prime Minister of Albania June–Dec. 1991; Minister of the Public Economy and Privatization –2000; mem. Leading Cttee of Socialist Party; mem. Parl., Chair. Cttee on Industry, Energetics, Transport and Telecommunications, Cttee on Economy, Finance and Privatization 2002–. *Address:* c/o Ministry of the Public Economy and Privatization, c/o Këshilli i Ministrave, Tirana, Albania. *E-mail:* ybufi@hotmail.com.

BUGÁR, Béla; Slovak politician; *Chairman, Bridge (Most-Híd) party;* b. 7 July 1958, Bratislava; ed Slovak Tech. Univ., Bratislava; early career as mechanical engineer in heavy engineering plants 1982–90; mem. Fed. Ass. of Czechoslovakia 1990–92; mem. Nat. Council of the Slovak Repub. (Parl.) 1992–, Deputy Speaker 1998–2006, 2010–, Acting Speaker Feb.–July 2006; mem. Hungarian Christian-Democratic Movt (MKDH) 1990–98, Chair. 1991–98; Leader of Party of the Hungarian Coalition 1998–2007; Co-founder and Chair. Bridge (Most-Híd) party (promoting inter-ethnic co-operation) 2009–. *Address:* Bridge (Most-Híd), Trnavská cesta 37, 831 04 Bratislava, Slovakia (office). *Telephone:* (2) 4911-4555 (office). *Fax:* (2) 4911-4555 (office). *E-mail:* bela_bugar@nrsr.sk (office); office@most-hid.sk (office). *Website:* www.most-hid.sk (office).

BUHARI, Maj.-Gen. Muhammadu; Nigerian government official and army officer (retd); b. 17 Dec. 1942, Daura, Katsina Prov. of Kaduna; m. Safinatu Yusuf 1971; two d.; ed Katsina Prov. Secondary School, Nigerian Mil. Training Coll., Mons Officers' Cadet School, Aldershot, UK; joined Army 1962; commissioned 1963; served in 2nd Bn in Congo (now Zaïre) 1963–64; Army Service Corps

1964–66; staff and command appointments in 1st and 3rd Infantry Divs; Defence Service Staff Coll., Wellington, India 1972–73; Acting Dir of Supply and Transport, Nigerian Army 1974–75; Mil. Gov. of North Eastern State (divided into three States Feb. 1976) 1975–76, of Borno State Feb.–March 1976; Fed. Commr for Petroleum 1976–78; Chair. Nigerian Nat. Petroleum Corpn 1976–80; Mil. Sec. Nigerian Army 1978; mem. Supreme Mil. Council 1976–77; overthrew Govt of Shehu Shagari (q.v.); Head of State, Chair. Supreme Mil. Council and C-in-C of Armed Forces 1983–85; detained 1985–88, released 1988; mem. All Nigeria's People's Party (ANPP), presidential cand. 2003, 2007, 2011; Chair. Special Trust Fund 1994–. *Leisure interests:* tennis, squash, polo. *Address:* c/o All Nigeria People's Party, Plot 274, Central Area, Behind NICON Plaza, Abuja; GRA, Daura, Katsina State, Nigeria.

BUHL RASMUSSEN, Jørgen, BEcons, MBA; Danish business executive; *President and CEO, Carlsberg A/S;* b. 18 Aug. 1955; ed Copenhagen School of Econs and Business Admin; Research Man. and Consultant IFH Research Int. (Unilever), Denmark 1979–82; Product Group Man. A/S Lagerman, Slagelse 1982–85; Marketing Man. Pet Food, MasterFoods Denmark 1985–87; Nordic Marketing Dir Duracell Denmark 1987–88, Gen. Man. Duracell Denmark and Finland 1988–93, Gen. Man. Duracell UK and Ireland 1993–95, Area Dir Duracell N Europe 1995–97; Pres. Gillette Group N Europe 1997–99, Pres. Gillette Group AMEE (Africa, Middle East, E Europe) 2001–06; mem. Exec. Bd Carlsberg A/S 2006–, Exec. Vice-Pres. 2006–07, Pres. and CEO 2007–. *Address:* Carlsberg A/S, 100 Ny Carlsberg Vej, 1799 Copenhagen V, Denmark (office). *Telephone:* 33-27-33-00 (office). *Fax:* 33-27-48-08 (office). *Website:* www.carlsberggroup.com (office).

BUICAN, Denis, DèsScNat, DèsL et ScHum; Romanian/French academic, biologist and philosopher of biology; *Honorary Professor, Université de Paris X Nanterre;* b. 21 Dec. 1934, Bucharest; s. of Dumitru Peligrad and Elena Buican; ed Bucharest Univ., Faculté des Sciences de Paris, Univ. de Paris I-Sorbonne; teaching asst, Bucharest Univ. 1956–57, Prin. Scientific Researcher 1957–60, Course Leader Gen. Biology and Genetics with History of Science course 1960–69, Invited Prof. 1990–; Invited Prof. First Class, History of Sciences, Faculté des Sciences, Univ. de Paris 1969–70, Univ. de Paris-Sorbonne 1970–74, Assoc. Prof., History and Philosophy of Science 1970–74; Assoc. Prof., History and Philosophy of Science, Univ. of Dijon 1974–80; Assoc. Prof., History of Sciences, Univ. of Paris I Panthéon-Sorbonne 1980–83; Assoc. Prof. First Class, History of Sciences, Univ. of Paris X 1983–86; Invited Prof. Collège de France 1984, 1993; Prof. First Class, Univ. of Paris X Nanterre 1986–2003, Hon. Prof. 2003–; Hon. Citizen of Saliste (Romania) 2003; Grand Prix, Acad. Française 1989. *Achievements include:* developed new synergetic theory of evolution and Biognoseology theory of knowledge. *Publications include:* Histoire de la génétique et de l'évolutionnisme en France 1984, La Génétique et l'évolution 1986, Génétique et pensée évolutionniste 1987, Darwin et le darwinisme 1987, Lyssenko et le lyssenkisme 1988, L'Evolution et les évolutionnismes 1989, La Révolution de l'évolution 1989, L'Explosion biologique, du néant au Sur-être 1991, Dracula et ses avatars de Vlad l'Empaleur à Staline et Ceausescu 1991, Charles Darwin 1992, Mendel et la génétique d'hier et d'aujourd'hui 1993, Les Métamorphoses de Dracula 1993, Biognoséologie: Evolution et révolution de la connaissance 1993, Jean Rostand 1994, Histoire de la Biologie 1994, Evolution de la pensée biologique 1995, L'Evolution aujourd'hui 1995, L'Evolution: la grande aventure de la vie 1995, Ethologie comparée 1996, Dictionnaire de Biologie 1997, L'Evolution et les théories évolutionnistes 1997, L'Epopée du vivant, L'Evolution de la biosphère et les avatars de l'Homme 2003, Le Darwinisme et les évolutionnismes 2005, Memorii 2007, L'Odyssée de l'Evolution 2008, Darwin dans l'histoire de la pensée biologique 2008, Mendel dans l'histoire de la génétique 2008, Mosaïque profane 2010, Biologie, Histoire et Philosophie 2010, Darwin et l'épopée de l'évolutionnisme 2012; poetry books: Arbre seul 1974, Lumière aveugle 1976, Mamura 1993, Spice (poèmes anciens et nouveaux) 2006, Margaritare negre (Perles noires) 2008, Roue de torture-Roue de lumière 2009. *Leisure interests:* literature and the arts. *Address:* 15 rue Poliveau, 75005 Paris, France (home). *Telephone:* 1-43-36-33-97 (home).

BUIJNSTERS, Petrus Jacobus Adrianus Maria (Piet J.); Dutch historian and academic; *Professor Emeritus of Dutch Literature, Radboud University Nijmegen;* b. 18 Oct. 1933, Breda; s. of Adriaan Buijnsters and Johanna Wirken; m. Leontine Smet 1961; two s. two d.; ed Univs of Nijmegen and Tübingen; f. Werkgroep 18e Eeuw (with C. M. Geerars) 1968; apptd Prof. of Dutch Literature, Univ. of Nijmegen (now Radboud Univ. Nijmegen) 1971, now Prof. Emer.; mem. Royal Netherlands Acad. of Arts and Sciences; Anne Frank Foundation Prize 1964, Jan Campbert Stiching Prize 1974, Menno Hertzberg Prize 1981, GH 's-Gravesandestraat Prize 2005. *Publications include:* Tussen twee werelden: Rhijnvis Feith als dichter van 'Het Graf' 1963, Hiëronymus van Alphen 1746–1803 1973, Bibliografie der geschriften van en over Betje Wolff en Aagje Deken 1979, Levens van beruchte personen. Over de criminele biografie in Nederland gedurende de 18e eeuw 1980, Nederlandse literatuur van de achttiende eeuw 1984, Wolff en Deken, een biografie 1984, Het verzamelen van boeken. Een handleiding 1985, Briefwisseling van Betje Wolff en Aagje Deken 1987, Spectatoriale geschriften 1991, Justus van Effen (1684–1735). Leven en werk 1992, Bibliofilie in de kinderkamer. Over het verzamelen en bestuderen van oude kinderboeken 1995, Het Nederlandse antiquariaat tijdens de Tweede Wereldoorlog 1997, Bibliografie van Nederlandse school- en kinderboeken 1700–1800 (with Leontine Buijnsters-Smet) 1997, Lust en leering. Geschiedenis van het Nederlandse kinderboek in de negentiende eeuw (with Leontine Buijnsters-Smet) (Menno Hertzbergerprijs 2002) 2001, Papertoys. Speelprenten en papieren speelgoed in Nederland (1640–1920) (with Leontine Buijnsters-Smet) 2005, Geschiedenis van het Nederlandse antiquariaat: 1750–2006 2007, Sluikhandel met juffrouw Duizer 2007, Effectief verplegen 0: handboek voor evidence based verpleegkundig handelen (co-author) 2009, Geschiedenis van de Nederlandse bibliofilie: boeken prentverzamelaars 1750–2010 2010, Geschiedenis van antiquariaat en bibliofilie in België (1830–2012) 2013. *Leisure interest:* book collecting. *Address:* Centre for Language Studies, Radboud University Nijmegen, PO Box 9103, 6500 HD Nijmegen (office); Witsenburgselaan 35, 6524 TE Nijmegen, The Netherlands (home). *Telephone:* (80) 225466 (home).

BUIRA, Ariel, MA; Mexican economist and academic; *Professor of Economics, Universidad Iberoamericana;* b. 20 Sept. 1940, Chihuahua; s. of Antonio Buira and

Enriqueta Seira de Buira; m. Janet Clark 1965; two s.; ed Univ. of Manchester, UK; Lecturer, Centre for Econ. and Demographic Studies, El Colegio de México 1966–68; Prof. of Econs, Grad. School of Business, Instituto Tecnológico de Monterrey 1968–70; Economist, IMF 1970–74; Econ. Adviser to Gov., Man. for Int. Research, Banco de México, SA 1975–78, Deputy Dir then Dir for Int. Orgs and Agreements 1982–94, then Deputy Gov. and mem. Bd of Govs; Del. to Conf. on Int. Econ. Co-operation (CIEC) (Financial Affairs Comm.) 1976–77; Alt. Exec. Dir, IMF 1978–80, Exec. Dir for Mexico, Spain, Venezuela, Cen. America 1980–82; Chair. Bd of Dirs BLADEX 1985–94; mem. Bd of Govs Bank of Mexico 1994–96; Amb. to Greece 1998–2001; Sr mem., St Antony's Coll., Oxford 2001–02; Special Envoy of Pres. of Mexico and Chair. of Panel, UN Int. Conf. on Financing for Devt 2002; Dir Secretariat, Intergovernmental Group of Twenty Four on Int. Monetary Affairs and Devt (G–24) 2002–06; currently Prof. of Econs, Univ. Iberoamericana, Mexico, DF; Order of the Phoenix (Greece) 2001; First Prize, Course on Econ. Integration, Coll. Européen des Sciences Sociales et Economiques 1963, Medal of the City of Athens 2001. *Publications include:* 50 Años de Banca Central (jtly) 1976, LDC External Debt and the World Economy 1978, Directions for Reform – The Future of the International Monetary System (jtly) 1984, México: Crisis Financiera y Programa de Ajuste in América Latina: Deuda, Crisis y Perspectivas 1984; Is There a Need for Reform? 1984; contrib.: Politics and Economics of External Debt Crisis – The Latin American Experience 1985, Incomes Policy (ed. V. L. Urquidi) 1987, Money and Finance Vol. I (R. Tandon) 1987, Adjustment with Growth and the Role of the IMF 1987, La Economía Mundial: Evolución y Perspectivas 1989, Una Evalución de la Estrategia de la Deuda 1989, Los Determinantes del Ahorro en México 1990, Evolución de la Estrategia de la Deuda 1990, International Liquidity and the Needs of the World Economy (Vol. IV) 1994, Reflections on the International Monetary System 1995, Can Currency Crises be Prevented or Better Managed? (co-ed. Jan Joost Teunissen) 1996, The Potential of the SDR for Improving the International Monetary System 1996, Reflections on the Mexican Crisis of 1994 1996; and numerous articles and essays; as ed.: The IMF and the World Bank at Sixty 2005, Introduction (in The IMF and the World at Sixty) 2005, The IMF at Sixty: An Unfulfilled Potential? (in The IMF and the World at Sixty) 2005, Reforming the Governance of the IMF and the World Bank 2005, The Bretton Woods Institutions: Governance Without Legitimacy? (in Reforming the Governance of the IMF and the World Bank) 2005; as contrib. and ed.: The Governance of the IMF in a Global Economy, An Analysis of IMF Conditionality (in Challenges to the World Bank and the IMF: Developing Country Perspectives) 2003; as contrib.: Curbing the Impact of Shocks (in Protecting the Poor; ed. Jan Joost Teunissen and Age Akkerman) 2005, Does the IMF Need More Financial Resources? (in Reform of the IMF for the 21st Century; ed. Edwin M. Truman) 2006. *Leisure interests:* music, literature. *Address:* Ruben Dario 45, piso 9, Col. Ricon del Bosque, México, DF 11560, Mexico (home). *Telephone:* (55) 5250-1711 (home). *Fax:* (202) 623-6000 (office). *E-mail:* abuiras@yahoo.com.mx (home).

BUITER, Willem Hendrik, CBE, BA, PhD, FBA; American/British economist and academic; *Chief Economist, Citigroup Inc.;* b. 26 Sept. 1949, The Hague, Netherlands; s. of Hendrien Buiter van Schooten and Harm Geert Buiter; m. 1st Jean Archer 1988; two c.; m. 2nd Anne C. Sibert 1998; ed Univ. of Cambridge, Yale Univ.; Asst Prof. of Econs and Int. Affairs, Woodrow Wilson School, Princeton Univ. 1975–79; Prof. of Econs, Univ. of Bristol 1980–82; Cassel Prof. of Econs with Special Reference to Money and Banking, LSE 1982–85, Prof. of European Political Economy 2005–11; Prof. of Econs, Yale Univ. 1985–94, Juan T. Trippe Prof. of Int. Econs 1990–94; Prof. of Int. Macroeconomics, Univ. of Cambridge 1994–2000; external mem. Monetary Policy Cttee, Bank of England 1997–2000; Chief Economist and Special Counsellor to the Pres., EBRD 2000–05; Chair. Council of Econ. Advisers, Netherlands Parl. 2005–07; Chief Economist, Citigroup Inc. 2010–; Consultant IMF, IBRD, IDB 1979–; adviser, Goldman Sachs 2005–09; adviser to House of Commons Treasury Select Cttee, UK 1980–82, Netherlands Ministry of Educ. 1985–86, EC, DGII 1982–85; Fellow, British Acad. 1998, European Econ. Asscn 2004; Corresp. mem. Royal Netherlands Acad. of Sciences 1989–; Research Assoc., Nat. Bureau of Econ. Research 1979–2011; Research Fellow, Centre for Econ. Policy Research 1983–; Dr hc (Amsterdam) 2012; Royal Netherlands Acad. of Sciences Dr Hendrik Muller Prize for the behavioural and social sciences 1999, N.G. Pierson Medal (Netherlands) 2000. *Publications:* Temporary and Long-run Equilibrium 1979, Budgetary Policy, International and Intertemporal Trade in the Global Economy 1989, Macroeconomic Theory and Stabilization Policy 1989, Principles of Budgetary and Financial Policy 1990, International Macroeconomics 1990, Financial Markets and European Monetary Cooperation: The Lessons of the 92–93 ERM crisis (with Giancarlo Corsetti and Paolo Pesenti) 1997. *Leisure interests:* tennis, theatre, westerns, science fiction and fantasy novels, poetry. *Address:* Citigroup Centre, Canada Square, Canary Wharf, London, E14 5LB, England (office); Apt 1201, The Aldyn, 60 Riverside Boulevard, New York, NY 10069, USA (home). *Telephone:* (20) 7986-5944 (office). *Fax:* (20) 7986-3221 (office). *E-mail:* willem.buiter@citi.com (office). *Website:* www.citigroup .com (office); www.willembuiter.com.

BUJAK, Zbigniew; Polish politician and trade union official; b. 29 Nov. 1954, Łopuszno; ed Warsaw Univ.; worked in Polfa Pharmaceutical plant, Grodzisk Mazowiecki, then Ursus Mechanical Works 1973–81; nat. service in airborne commando div. 1974–76; organizer of strike in Ursus Works in July 1980; assoc. Workers' Cttee for solidarity with striking coastal workers Aug. 1980; Chair. Founding Cttee Solidarity Trade Union, Mazowsze Region 1980; mem. Nat. Consultative Comm. of Solidarity, took part in negotiations with Govt 1981; under martial law in hiding, continued union activity 1981–86; Chair. Bd Mazowsze Region in Provisional Exec. Comm. of Solidarity 1982–86; arrested May 1986, pardoned Sept. 1986; mem. Nat. Exec. Comm. of Solidarity 1987–90; Chair. Citizens' Cttee of Solidarity 1989–90; took part in Round Table debates in Groups for Political Reform and for Economy and Social Policy Feb.–April 1989; Chair. Council of Warsaw Agreement of Citizens' Cttees 1990–91; one of founders and leaders Citizens' Movt–Democratic Action (ROAD) 1990–91; Deputy to Sejm (Parl.) 1991–97, Chair. Sejm Comm. of Admin. and Internal Affairs 1993–97; Chair. Cen. Bd of Customs 1999–2001; Chair. of Democratic-Social Movt 1991; Co-Founder and Vice-Chair. Union of Labour (UP) 1992–98; mem. Freedom Union (UW) Party 1998–; fmr mem. Socialist Rural Youth Union; Robert F. Kennedy Human Rights Award 1988. *Publication:* Przepraszam za Solidarność 1991. *Address:* Główny Urząd Ceł, ul. Świętokrzyska 12, 00-916 Warsaw, Poland.

Telephone: (22) 6944946 (office). *E-mail:* gabinet_prezesa_guc@guc.gov.pl (office). *Website:* www.guc.gov.pl (office).

BUJOLD, Genevieve; Canadian actress; b. 1 July 1942, Montreal; m. Paul Almond 1967 (divorced); one s.; ed Montréal Conservatory of Drama; fmr cinema usherette in Montreal. *Films include:* La guerre est finie, La fleur de l'age, Entre la mer et l'eau douce, King of Hearts, The Thief of Paris, Isabel, Anne of the Thousand Days, The Act of the Heart, The Trojan Women, The Journey, Earthquake, Alex and the Gypsy, Kamouraska, Obsession, Swashbuckler, Another Man Another Chance, Coma, Murder by Decree, Final Assignment, The Last Flight of Noah's Ark, Monsignor, Tightrope, Choose Me, Trouble in Mind, The Moderns, Dead Ringers, False Identity, Secret Places of the Heart, A Paper Wedding, Star Trek: Generations, An Ambush of Ghosts, Mon Ami Max, Dead Innocent 1996, The House of Yes 1997, Last Night 1998, Eye of the Beholder 1999, Alex in Wonder 2001, La Turbulence des fluides 2002, Jericho Mansions 2003, Finding Home 2003, Downtown: A Street Tale 2004, Mon petit doigt m'a dit 2005, Disappearances 2006, Délivrez-moi 2006, The Trotsky 2009, Pour l'amour de Dieu 2011, Still 2012. *Stage appearances include:* The Barber of Seville, A Midsummer Night's Dream, A House... A Day. *TV appearances include:* St Joan, Antony and Cleopatra, Mistress of Paradise, Red Earth, White Earth, Star Trek. *Address:* c/o WME, 9601 Wilshire Blvd, Beverly Hills, CA 90210, USA (office).

BUJON DE L'ESTANG, François; French diplomatist and business executive; *President, FBE International Consultants;* b. 21 Aug. 1940, Neuilly-sur-Seine, Hauts-de-Seine; s. of Henry Bujon de l'Estang and Vera Markels; m. Anne Jacquin de Margerie 1963; four c.; ed Institut Politique de Paris, Ecole Nat. d'Admin, Harvard Grad. School of Business Admin, USA; Office of Perm. Sec., Ministry of Foreign Affairs 1966; Special Adviser on staff of Pres. of Repub. 1966, Deputy to Pres.'s Diplomatic Adviser –1969; Second, then First Sec., Embassy in Washington, DC 1969–73; First Sec. and Second Counsellor in London 1973–75; Adviser on Int. Affairs to Del. Gen. for Energy, Ministry of Industry 1975–77; Dir for Int. Relations, Atomic Energy Commissariat 1978–79; French Rep. on Bd of Govs of IAEA 1979; Chief of Staff to Minister of Industry 1980–81; f. COGEMA Inc., Washington, DC 1982, Pres. and CEO 1982–86; apptd Amb. to Mexico 1986 (did not take up post); Sr Adviser to Prime Minister Jacques Chirac for Diplomatic Affairs, Defence and Co-operation 1986–88; Amb. to Canada 1989–91, to USA 1995–2002, rank of Amb. of France 1999; mem. Bd of Dirs Sofratome, Technicatome and Eurodif 1979–80, Copperweld Corpn (Imetal Group) 1982–86; Sr Vice-Pres. Compagnie de Navigation Mixte and Via Banque 1991–92; Chair. and CEO SFIM 1991–92, mem. Bd Dirs 1991–93; Pres. Harvard Business School Club of France 1992–95; Founder FBE International Consultants 1992, Pres. 1992–95, 2003–; mem. Bd Dirs Banque Indosuez 1993–95, CNES 2003–10, Institut Pasteur 2003–05, Tembec Inc. 2005–07, Thales 2003–09, IFRI 2003–09; mem. Int. Advisory Bd Total 2004–; Chair. Citigroup France 2003–10, Sr Int. Adviser 2010–12, mem. European Advisory Bd, Citigroup 2003–12; Vice-Chair. French-American Foundation US 2003–, mem. Bd French-American Foundation France 2008–; Chair. Bd of Trustees, MB American Center for Arts & Culture 2013–; Officier, Legion d'honneur, Commdr, Ordre nat. du Mérite. *Address:* FBE International Consultants, 38 rue Marbeuf, 75008 Paris, France (office). *Telephone:* 1-42-25-55-53 (FBE) (office). *Fax:* 1-42-25-55-56 (FBE) (office). *E-mail:* fbe@fbe-international.com (office). *Website:* www.the-international.com (office).

BUKEJLOVIĆ, Pero, MEng; Bosnia and Herzegovina politician and engineer; b. 9 Aug. 1946, Bušletic, Doboj municipality; m.; one s.; ed Univs of Sarajevo and Zagreb; various positions as engineer; Gen. Man. Trudbenik Co.; Minister of Industry and Tech. 2001–03; worked in private sector 2003–05, 2006–; Prime Minister of Republika Srpska 2005–06; represented the Serbian Democratic Party. *Address:* c/o Office of the Prime Minister, 78000 Banja Luka, trg Republike Srpske 1, Bosnia and Herzegovina. *E-mail:* kabinet@vladars.net.

BUKENYA, Gilbert Balibaseka, MSc, MD, PhD; Ugandan professor of public health and politician; b. May 1949, Wakiso Dist; m.; three c.; ed Makerere Univ. Medical School, Royal Inst. of Public Health and Hygiene, London, UK, Ross Inst., London School of Hygiene and Tropical Medicine, Univ. of Queensland, Australia; internship in Uganda; following studies in public health in London returned to Uganda in 1983; Lecturer, Inst. of Public Health, Makerere Univ. 1983–84, Dir 1989, Assoc. Prof. 1993, Dean Faculty of Medicine 1995; Lecturer, Dept of Community Medicine, Univ. of Papua New Guinea 1984–87, Head of Dept 1987–89; Assoc. Prof., Tulane Univ. School of Public Health, New Orleans, La, USA 1995; Adjunct Prof. of Int. Health, Case Western Reserve Univ., Cleveland, OH, USA 2004; MP for Busiro North 1996–, Chair. Movt Caucus; Minister of State for Trade and Minister in charge of the Presidency; Vice-Pres. of Uganda 2003–11; Chair. Nat. Advisory Cttee on Environmental Health and Maternal and Child Health, Papua New Guinea 1985–91, Bd of Examiners, Coll. of Allied Health Sciences Health Inspectors' Programme 1985–91; Vice-Chair. Network of African Postgraduate Public Health Training Schools, WHO-Afro Region 1992–94, Chair. 1994–96. *Address:* c/o Office of the President, Parliament Building, POB 7168, Kampala, Uganda (office). *Telephone:* (41) 258441 (office). *Fax:* (41) 256143 (office). *E-mail:* vp@statehouse.go.ug (office). *Website:* www.statehouse.go.up (office).

BUKHARY, Tan Sri Syed Mokhtar al-; Malaysian business executive; *Executive Chairman, Al-Bukhary Foundation;* b. 1952, Alor Star; m. Puan Sri Sharifah Zarah Al-Bukhary; five c.; began career in meat and later rice trading; f. transport business 1973; owns stakes in numerous cos in Malaysia and abroad, including Malaysian Mining Corpn (MMC), Johor Port Bhd, Malakoff (ind. power producer), Gas Malaysia; investment interests include plantations, property devt, construction, power generation, retailing, information tech., infrastructure and ports; f. Syarikat Impian Teladan Sendirian Bhd; Owner SKS Ventures; Exec. Chair Al-Bukhary Foundation; mem. Bd Syarikat Bina Puri Holdings Berhad; mem. United Malays Nat. Org.; Panglima Setia Mahkota, Dato' Setia Mahkota Kedah, announced and awarded Tokoh Ma'al Hijrah by The Yang Di Pertuan Agong of Malaysia in recognition of his contrib. to nation building 2008. *Address:* Al-Bukhary Foundation, Kuala Lumpur, Malaysia (office).

BUKOVAC, Martin J., PhD; American horticulturist and academic; *Distinguished Professor Emeritus, Department of Horticulture, Michigan State University;* b. 12 Nov. 1929, Johnston City, Ill.; s. of John Bukovac and Sadie Fak; m. Judith A. Kelley 1956; one d.; ed Mich. State Univ.; Asst Prof., Dept of

Horticulture, Mich. State Univ. 1957–61, Assoc. Prof. 1961–63, Prof. 1963–92, Univ. Distinguished Prof. 1992–, now Distinguished Prof. Emer.; Biological Science Collaborator, USDA/Agricultural Research Service 1982–2003; Postdoctoral Fellow, Univs of Oxford and Bristol, UK 1965–66; Dir Mich. State Univ. Press 1983–91; Adviser, Eli Lilly Co. 1971–88; Pres. Martin J. Bukovac Inc. 1996–; Fellow, AAAS, American Soc. of Horticultural Science; mem. NAS, Editorial Advisory Bd Horticultural Abstracts 1990–2003, Editorial Bd Encyclopedia of Agricultural Science 1991–96, Int. Editorial Bd, Horticultural Science, Kertészetic Tudomány, Budapest 1989–2003; mem. Int. Advisory Bd, Life Sciences Div., Center for Nuclear Sciences, Grenoble 1993–2000; Hon. DrAgr (Bonn) 1995; Alexander von Humboldt Award for Sr Scientist 1995, Gold Veitch Memorial Medal, Hall of Fame, American Soc. for Horticultural Science 2001, Royal Horticultural Soc. 2003, Spiridon Brusina Medal, Croatian Soc. of Natural Sciences 2004. *Publications:* over 350 research articles. *Leisure interests:* photography, sports. *Address:* A390B Plant and Soil Sciences, Michigan State University, East Lansing, MI 48824-1325 (office); 4428 Seneca Drive, Okemos, MI 48864-2946, USA (home). *Telephone:* (517) 355-5191 (ext. 393) (office); (517) 349-1952 (home). *Fax:* (517) 353-0890 (office). *E-mail:* bukovacm@msu.edu (office). *Website:* www.hrt.msu.edu/faculty/bukovac.htm (office).

BUKOVSKY, Vladimir Konstantinovich, MA; Russian writer and scientist; b. 30 Dec. 1942, Belebey; s. of Konstantin Bukovsky and Nina Bukovsky; ed Moscow State Univ., Univ. of Cambridge; worked at Moscow Centre of Cybernetics; arrested for possessing banned literature 1963, confined to Leningrad Psychiatric Prison Hosp. for 15 months; arrested for demonstration on behalf of Soviet writers 1965, confined for eight months in psychiatric institutions; arrested for civil rights work 1967, on trial Sept. 1967 and sentenced to three years' corrective labour; arrested for delivering information on psychiatric abuse to the West 1971, on trial 1972 and sentenced to two years in prison, five in a labour camp and five in exile; after world-wide campaign for his release, was exchanged for Chilean Communist Party leader Luis Corvalán in Zürich Dec. 1976; citizenship restored 1992; research work, Stanford Univ., Calif. 1982–90; f. Centre for Democracy in Support of New Russia, New York; co-founder political group 'Committee 2008' 2004 (aimed to promote free and fair 2008 presidential elections; last meeting 2005); nominated candidate 2008 presidential elections 2007; hon. mem. several human rights orgs, several PEN clubs; lives in England; Konrad Adenauer Freedom and Literature Prize 1984. *Publications:* short stories in Russia's Other Writers 1970 and in Grani, Opposition–Eine neue Geisteskrankheit in der USSR (German edn) 1972, A Manual on Psychiatry for Dissenters (with Semyon Gluzman) 1974, To Build a Castle: My Life as a Dissenter (in English; trans. in Swedish, Italian, Spanish, French and German) 1978, Cette lancinante douleur de la liberté 1981, The Peace Movement and the Soviet Union 1982. *Leisure interests:* the arts, architecture. *Website:* bukovsky.org/official/ (office).

BULAI, Igor Borisovich, CandHist; Russian diplomatist; *Consul General, Kirkenes, Norway;* b. 17 May 1947, Moscow; m.; two c.; ed Moscow State Inst. of Int. Relations, Inst. of USA and Canada Acad. of Sciences; Jr Researcher, Inst. of USA and Canada 1973–79; Instructor, Div. of Information Cen. Cttee CPSU 1979–85; Counsellor, Embassy in Washington, DC 1985–91; with Dept of Information, USSR Ministry of Foreign Affairs 1991–92; Head, Dept of Information and Press, Ministry of Foreign Affairs of Russia 1992–98; Consul-Gen. in Edin. 1998–2001; mem. staff, Dept for Information and Press and Head of Press Centre, Ministry of Foreign Affairs 2001–05; currently Consul Gen. in Kirkenes, Norway. *Address:* Consulate of the Russian Federation, Postbox 98, 9900 Kirkenes, Norway (office). *Telephone:* 78-99-37-37 (office). *Fax:* 78-99-37-42 (office). *E-mail:* genkons@online.no (office). *Website:* kirkenes.rusembassy.org (office).

BULATOVIĆ, Momir, CandEconSc; Montenegrin politician; b. 21 Sept. 1956, Belgrade, Yugoslavia; ed Titograd Univ.; fmr mem. League of Communists of Montenegro, then Leader, Republican League of Communists; Chair. Democratic Party of Socialists 1990–98; Chair. Socialist People's Party of Montenegro 1998–2001; Pres. of Montenegro 1990–98; Prime Minister of Yugoslavia 1998–2001. *Address:* c/o Socialist People's Party of Montenegro, Podgorica, Montenegro.

BULATOVIĆ, Predrag; Montenegrin politician; b. 16 July 1956, Kolašin; m.; three d.; ed Faculty of Mechanical Eng, Univ. of Montenegro, Podgorica; various admin., teaching and exec. positions, Univ. of Montenegro 1975–80; Sec. of Montenegro Youth Org. and Socialist Fed. Repub. of Yugoslavia Youth Org. 1982–84; worked for Radoje Dakić Factory, Podgorica 1985–89; began career as professional politician 1989–; elected to Ass. of Repub. 1990–; elected to Fed. Ass. of Fmr Yugoslavia 2001–02, Chair. Foreign Policy Cttee 2000–03; Pres. Parliamentary Group of Democratic Party of Socialists (DPS) 1992–97; Vice-Pres. Socialist People's Party of Montenegro (SSPM–following division of DPS 1997) 1997–2001, Pres. 2001–02; Vice-Pres. Parl. Group of SSPM 1997–2001; mem. Montenegro Ass. 2006–, mem. Cttee for Int. Relation and European Integration; several Awards and Prizes from Univ. of Montenegro. *Address:* 13 Jula No. 49, Podgorica (home); Vaka Djurovica No. 5, Podgorica, Montenegro (office). *Telephone:* (20)-272 421 (office). *Fax:* (20) 272-421 (office). *Website:* www.snp.cg.yu (office).

BÜLBÜLOĞLU, Polad, PhD; Azerbaijani composer, singer, film actor and diplomatist; *Ambassador to Russia;* b. 4 Feb. 1945, Baku; s. of Bul-Bul; ed Azerbaijan State Conservatory; head of pop-music ensembles 1975–87; Head of Azerbaijan State Philharmonic 1987–88; apptd Minister of Culture 1988; elected mem. Milli-Medjlis 1995; Dir-Gen. Int. Org. TURKSOI 1994; Prof., Int. Humanitarian Acad.; currently Amb. to Russia; Hon. Prof., Azerbaijan Univ. of Culture and Arts; Om emerit al (Moldova) 2005, Order of Independence 2005, Order of Friendship (Russia) 2005; Song of the Year Award (for Will Be Delighted by the Sun Again 1977, I am In Love 1978, Beloved Country 1979, Tell Your Eyes 1980), People's Artist of Azerbaijan 1982, Kazakhstan Nat. Award of Peace and Progress 2010. *Music:* symphonic works, chamber and instrumental music, musical, vocal cycles, incidental music, pop-songs. *Address:* Embassy of Azerbaijan, 125009 Moscow, Leontyevskii per. 16, Russia (office); Fioletova street 6/8, Apartment 53, Baku, Azerbaijan (home). *Telephone:* (495) 629-43-3 (office); (12) 4932177 (home). *Fax:* (495) 202-50-72 (office). *E-mail:* embassy@azembassy.msk.ru (office). *Website:* www.azembassy.ru (office).

BULCKE, Paul; Belgian business executive; *CEO, Nestlé SA;* b. 1954, Roeselare; m.; three c.; ed Univs of Louvain and Ghent, Belgium, Program for Exec. Devt, IMD Business School, Switzerland; financial analyst, Scott Graphics International, Bornem, Belgium 1977–79; with Nestlé Group, Vevey, Switzerland 1979–, marketing trainee, Nestlé SA (Switzerland, Spain, Belgium) 1979–80, Marketing, Sales and Div. functions, Nestlé Peru, Nestlé Ecuador and Nestlé Chile 1980–96, Man. Dir Nestlé Portugal 1996–98, Man. Dir Nestlé Czech and Slovak Repubs 1998–2000, Man. Dir Nestlé Germany, Frankfurt am Main 2000–03, Exec. Vice-Pres. responsible for Zone Americas: USA, Canada, Latin America, Caribbean 2004–08, CEO Designate and mem. designate Bd Nestlé SA 2007–08, mem. Bd Dirs and CEO 2008–, Administrateur Délégué, Nestlé Health Science SA; Co-Chair. Supervisory Bd Cereal Partners Worldwide (Switzerland); Bd mem. and Co-Chair. Governance Cttee, Consumer Goods Forum; mem. Bd Roche Holding Ltd (Switzerland). *Address:* Nestlé SA, 1800 Vevey, Switzerland (office). *Telephone:* (21) 924-21-11 (office). *Fax:* (21) 921-18-85 (office). *E-mail:* webmaster@nestle.com (office). *Website:* www.nestle.com (office).

BULDAKOV, Aleksey Ivanovich; Russian actor; b. 26 March 1951, Makarovka, Altai Territory; m.; ed Pavlodar Drama Theatre Studio; worked in theatres in Pavlodar, Ryazan, Karaganda, Moscow. *Films include:* Skvoz ogon 1982, Rodilsya ya v Sibiri... 1982, Semyon Dezhnev 1983, Nebyvalshchina 1983, Vosem dney nadezhdy 1984, Vot moya derevnya... 1985, Radi neskolkikh strochek 1985, Parol znali dvoye 1985, Nauchis tantsevat 1985, Tikhoye sledstviye 1986, Ledyanye tsvety 1986, Ill Omen 1986, Moonzund 1987, V dvukh shagakh ot 'Raya' 1987, Yedinozhdy solgav 1987, Strannik 1987, Khotite – lyubite, khotite – net... 1987, Khleb – imya sushchestvitelnoe 1988, Utomlyonnoye solntse 1988, Ozhog 1988, Komu na Rusi zhit... 1989, Karaul 1990, Dva shaga do tishiny 1991, Khmel – Film vtoroy: Iskhod 1991, Khmel – Film pervyy: Krepost 1991, Belye odezhdy (TV Series) 1991, Tram-tararam, ili bukhty-barakhty 1993, Val'siruyushchiye navernyaka 1994, Molba o proshchenii 1994, Peculiarities of the National Hunt 1995, Ya – Russkiy soldat 1995, Syn za ottsa... 1995, Shirli-Myrli 1995, Love-Service 1995, Pionerka Meri Pikford 1996, Vozvrashchenie 'Bronenostsa' 1996, Privet, duralei! 1996, Peculiarities of the National Fishing 1998, Yubiley prokurora 1998, Na boykom meste 1998, Checkpoint 1999, Zorka venera 2000, Peculiarities of the National Hunt in the Winter 2001, The Hero of Her Romance 2001, Plemyannik ili Russkiy biznes 2 2002, Peculiarities of the National Politics 2003, Antikiller 2: Antiterror 2003, Soviet Park 2006, Vechernyaya skazka 2007, Igra 2008, Gitler kaput! 2008, Utomlyonnye solntsem 2: Predstoyanie 2010, Chelovek s kharu Kaputsinok 2010, Olimpiyskaya derevnya 2011, Rzhevskiy protiv Napoleona 2012, Popugay Club (voice) 2013. *Television includes* Mesto deystviya (film) 1983, V lesakh pod Kovelem (film) 1985, Protivostoyanie (mini-series) 1985, All Costs Paid (film) 1988, Voydi v kazhdyy dom (mini-series) 1990, Keshka i spetsnaz (short) 1991, Dela smeshnye, dela semeynye (series) 1996, Koroleva Margo (series) 1996, Operation Happy New Year (film) 1996, Klubnichka (series) 1997, Dose detektiva Dubrovskogo (series) 1999, Chto skazal pokoynik (series) 2000, Idealnaya para (series) 2001, Uchastok (mini-series) 2003, Parni iz stali (mini-series) 2005, Zakoldovannyy uchastok (series) 2006, Priklyucheniya soldata Ivana Chonkina (film) 2007, Chuzhie tainy (series) 2007, Prodolzhenie sleduet (series) 2008, Utomlennye solntsem 2 (mini-series) 2011, Lesnik (series) 2011–14. *Address:* 121096 Moscow, Kastanayevskaya str. 23, korp 4, Apt 27, Russia. *Telephone:* (495) 144-02-73.

BULGAK, Vladimir Borisovich, CandTechSc, DEconSc; Russian politician and business executive; b. 9 May 1941, Moscow; m.; one d.; ed Moscow Electrotech. Inst. of Communications, Inst. of Man. of Nat. Econ., USSR State Cttee on Science and Tech.; instructor, then sec. Moscow City Komsomol Cttee 1963–68; for 15 years worked in Moscow radio trans. network; head of depts USSR Ministry of Telecommunications 1983–90; Minister 1990–91; Minister of Telecommunications Russian Fed. 1991–97; Deputy Chair. Govt of Russian Fed. 1997–98, 1998–99; Minister of Science and Tech. April–Sept. 1998; Chair. TV-Holding Svyazinvest 1999–2001, Comincom-Combellga group 1999–2003; fmr Chair. Insurance Group Nasta; mem. Council of Dirs Sovintel (operating company of Golden Telecom) 2004–; mem. Int. Acad. of Informatization, Russian Acad. of Tech. Sciences, Russian Acad. of Natural Sciences; USSR State Prize. *Publications:* several textbooks on communication techniques; over 100 articles and papers. *Address:* c/o Golden Telecom, 115114 Moscow, 1 Kozhevnicheskii prospect, Russia.

BULGURLU, Bülent, MS, PhD; Turkish business executive; b. 1947, Ankara; m.; three c.; ed Ankara Eng and Architectural Faculty, Norwegian Tech. Univ., Trondheim; Construction Engineer, Elliot Strömme A/S, Oslo 1972; Asst Lecturer and Researcher, Norveç Tech. Univ. 1972–77; Project Man., Intes San. ve Tic. AŞ 1977–79; Construction Engineer, Garanti Insaat AŞ Oct.–Dec. 1979, Planning and Construction Man. 1979–81, Site Coordination Construction Man. 1981–82, Asst Gen. Man. 1982–84, Asst Gen. Man. (Tech.) 1984–86, Asst Gen. Man. (Production) Tech. Processes (by proxy) 1986–88, Gen. Man. 1988–90, Gen. Man. Garanti Koza Insaat AŞ 1990–96; Vice-Pres. Tourism and Services Group, Koç Holding AŞ 1996–2000, Pres. Tourism and Services Group 2000–01, Pres. Tourism and Construction Group 2001–03, Pres. Durable Goods and Construction Group 2004–07, mem. Bd of Dirs and CEO 2007–13, Dir 2010–; fmr Vice-Chair. Arcelik AŞ; fmr Deputy Chair. Izocam Ticaret ve Sanayi AŞ; mem. Bd of Dirs Grundig Elektronik AS, Aygaz AŞ, Arcelik AŞ, Ford Otomotiv Sanayi AŞ 2007–, Turkiye Petrol Rafinerileri AŞ 2007–, Yapi Kredi Koray 2007–, Otokar Otobus Karoseri Sanayi AŞ 2008–, TOFAS Turk Otomobil Fabrikasi AŞ –2011, Izocam; mem. Turkish Industrialists' and Businessmen's Asscn (TÜSIAD), Altunizade Rotary Club, T.E.D.Club, Anatolian Club, Turkish Marine Environment Protection Asscn, Turkish Tourism Investors Asscn, Chaîne de Rotisseurs. *Address:* Koç Holding AŞ, Nakkaştepe Aziz Bey Sok. 1, Kuzguncuk, 34674 Istanbul, Turkey (office). *Telephone:* (216) 5310000 (office). *Fax:* (216) 5310099 (office). *E-mail:* info@koc.com.tr (office). *Website:* www.koc.com.tr (office); www.rmk-museum.org.tr (office).

BULIN, Gen. René Henri; French aeronautical engineer; b. 8 Aug. 1920, Langres; s. of Louis Bulin and Louise Bulin (née Walter); m. 1st Claudine Prostot 1955 (deceased); m. 2nd Catherine Tambuscio 1982; ed Ecole Polytechnique Paris, Ecole Nationale Supérieure de l'Aéronautique; engineer responsible for setting up Centre d'Essais des Propulseurs (Fort de Villeras) 1946–53; French Air Force pilot 1947; Head of Operations Dept and Instructor, Ecole Nationale de l'Aviation Civile 1953–56; Deputy Dir, then Dir Air Navigation Secrétariat Général de l'Aviation Civile 1956–61; first Dir-Gen. European Org. for the Safety of Air Navigation (EUROCONTROL) 1963–78, responsible for having set up the Air Traffic Services Agency, Brussels and the EUROCONTROL Experimental Centre, Brétigny-sur-Orge and for establishing the Upper Area Control Centres, Maastricht, Netherlands, Karlsruhe, Germany, Shannon, Ireland, the EUROCONTROL Inst. of Air Navigation Services, Luxembourg and the Users Charge Service, Brussels; Adviser Thomson-CSF 1978–83; Special Adviser to EC Aeronautical Comm.; Commdr, Légion d'honneur; Grand Croix du Mérite (Germany); Grand Croix du Mérite Aeronautique (Spain); Commdr (Portugal, Austria, Belgium, Luxembourg); Officier (Ethiopia). *Address:* Altirama, 23 avenue Frédéric Mistral, 06130 Grasse, France. *Telephone:* (4) 93-70-60-58. *E-mail:* renebulin1@libertysurf.fr; infocentre@eurocontrol.int.

BULL, Deborah Clare, CBE; British ballerina, writer, broadcaster, creative director and cultural commentator; *Director, Cultural Partnerships, King's College London;* b. 22 March 1963, Derby; d. of Rev. Michael John Bull and Doreen Audrey Franklin Bull (née Plumb); ed Royal Ballet School; joined Royal Ballet 1981, Prin. Dancer 1992–2001, teacher of Nutrition, Royal Ballet School 1996–99; Dir Clore Studio Upstairs, Royal Opera House 1999–2001, Creative Dir, ROH2, Royal Opera House 2002–08, Creative Dir, Royal Opera House 2008–12; Dir Cultural Partnerships, King's Coll., London 2012–; mem. Dance Panel, Arts Council 1998–96, Arts Council 1998–2005; Gov. South Bank Centre 1997–2003, BBC Bd Govs 2003–06, Foundation, Prix de Lausanne 2012–, ARHC Cultural Value Project Advisory Group 2012–; Commr, Warwick Comm. on Cultural Value 2013–; mem. Council Arts & Humanities Research Council 2013–; columnist, The Telegraph 1999–2002; Patron Nat. Osteoporosis Soc., Foundation for Community Dance, Journalism Foundation; Hon. Pres. Voices of British Ballet; Dr hc (Derby) 1998, (Sheffield) 2001, (Open Univ.) 2005, (Kent) 2010; Prix de Lausanne 1980, Dancer of the Year, Sunday Express and The Independent on Sunday 1996, Overall Prize Dancescreen Monaco 2002. *Dance includes:* appearances with Royal Ballet include leading roles in La Bayadère (Gamzatti), Swan Lake (Odette/Odile), The Sleeping Beauty (Aurora), Don Quixote (Kitri), Steptext (first staging in UK for her by William Forsythe) 1995; appeared in Harrogate Int. Festival 1993, 1995, An Evening of British Ballet, Sintra Festival, Portugal 1994, 1995, Diamonds of World Ballet Gala, Kremlin Palace, Moscow 1996, Rite of Spring, Teatro dell'Opera, Rome 2001–02. *Radio includes:* regular contrib. to BBC Radio 4 including Breaking the Law 2001, Law in Order 2002, A Dance Through Time 2002, Hothouse Kids 2009, After I Was Gorgeous 2011, Steps in Time 2011, Dance for Your Life 2012, Deborah Bull's Dance Nation 2012, Desert Island Discs (BBC Radio 4) 2013, The Essay (BBC Radio 3) 2013. *Television includes:* Dance Ballerina Dance (writer, presenter) 1998, Travels with my Tutu (writer, presenter) 2000, Coppélia, Royal Ballet (live broadcast), Rambert Dance Co., Sadler's Wells (live broadcast), BBC 1 and BBC 2 Proms (live broadcast), The Dancer's Body (writer, presenter) 2002, Saved for the Nation (presenter) 2006, Bolshoi Unseen (presenter) 2013. *Publications include:* The Vitality Plan 1998, Dancing Away 1998, The Faber Guide to Classical Ballets (with Luke Jennings) 2004, The Everyday Dancer 2011; numerous articles and reviews in newspapers and dance magazines. *Leisure interests:* reading, writing, walking, cycling, dancing, talking, theatrical and arts experiences. *Address:* c/o Rosemary Scoular, United Agents, 12–26 Lexington Street, London, W1F 0LE, England (office). *Telephone:* (20) 3214-0893 (office). *E-mail:* rscoular@unitedagents.co.uk (office). *Website:* www.unitedagents.co.uk (office); www.deborahbull.com.

BULL, Sir George, Kt; British business executive; b. 16 July 1936, London; s. of Michael Bull and Hon. Noreen Hennessy; m. Tessa Freeland 1960; four s. one d.; ed Ampleforth Coll.; Coldstream Guards 1954–57; joined Twiss Browning & Hallowes 1958; Gilbey Vintners Ltd 1970; Dir Int. Distillers and Vintners (IDV) 1973; Man. Dir IDV Europe 1977; Deputy Man. Dir IDV Ltd 1982; Dir Grand Metropolitan Ltd 1985; Chief Exec. IDV Ltd 1987; Chair. and CEO IDV Ltd (Drinks Sector of Grand Metropolitan PLC) 1988; Chair. and CEO Grand Met Food Sector 1992; Group Chief Exec. Grand Metropolitan PLC 1993, Chair. Grand Metropolitan PLC 1996–97; Co.-Chair. Diageo (after merger with Guinness PLC) 1997–98; Chair. J Sainsbury PLC 1998–2004; Dir (non-exec.) BNP Paribas UK Holdings 2000–04, The Maersk Co. Ltd 2001–06, Marakon Assocs 2002–06; mem. Advisory Bd Marakon Assocs 2002–; Chevalier, Légion d'honneur 1994. *Leisure interests:* golf, photography. *Address:* The Old Vicarage, Arkesden, Saffron Walden, Essex, CB11 4HB, England (home).

BULL, William V. S., MA; Liberian diplomatist; b. 1946, Monrovia; ed Univ. of Liberia, Univ. of Pittsburgh, USA; joined Bureau of African and Asian Affairs, Ministry of Foreign Affairs 1972; Counsellor and Deputy Chief of Mission, Washington, DC 1976, Chargé d'affaires 1980; Asst Minister for American Affairs, Monrovia 1981, for African and Asian Affairs 1982–86, Prin. Deputy to Minister of Foreign Affairs 1987–90; Amb. and Perm. Rep. to UN, New York 1990–98; Amb. to UK 1998–2000, to USA 2000–03; Acting Foreign Minister –2010; Amb. to USA 2010–12. *Address:* Ministry of Foreign Affairs, Mamba Point, PO Box 10-9002, 1000 Monrovia 10, Liberia (office). *Telephone:* 226763 (office). *Website:* www.mofa.gov.lr (office).

BULLARD, Robert D., PhD; American sociologist and academic; *Edmund Asa Ware Distinguished Professor of Sociology and Director, Environmental Justice Resource Center, Clark Atlanta University;* b. 1946; ed Iowa State Univ.; currently Edmund Asa Ware Distinguished Prof. of Sociology, Clark Atlanta Univ., Founder and Dir Environmental Justice Resource Center 1994–; featured in CNN People You Should Know, Bullard: Green Issue is Black and White July 2007, named by Newsweek magazine as one of 13 Environmental Leaders of the Century 2008. *Publications:* Invisible Houston: The Black Experience in Boom and Bust 1987, In Search of the New South: The Black Urban Experience in the 1970s and 1980s 1989, Houston: Growth and Decline in a Sunbelt Boomtown (co-author) 1989, Dumping in Dixie: Race, Class and Environmental Quality, 1990, Confronting Environmental Racism: Voices From the Grassroots (ed.) 1993, Unequal Protection: Environmental Justice and Communities of Color (ed.) 1994, Residential Apartheid: The American Legacy (co-ed.) 1994, Just Transportation: Dismantling Race and Class Barriers to Mobility (co-ed.) 1997, People of Color Environmental Groups Directory 2000, 2000, Sprawl City: Race, Politics and Planning in Atlanta, Washington, DC (co-ed.) 2000, Just Sustainabilities: Development in an Unequal

World (co-author) 2003, Highway Robbery: Transportation Racism and New Routes to Equity (co-author) 2004, The Quest for Environmental Justice: Human Rights and the Politics of Pollution 2005, In the Wake of the Storm: Environment, Disaster and Race After Katrina (co-author) 2006, Toxic Wastes and Race at Twenty: 1987–2007 2007, Growing Smarter: Achieving Livable Communities, Environmental Justice, and Regional Equity 2007, The Black Metropolis in the Twenty-First Century: Race, Power, and the Politics of Place 2007, Deadly Waiting Game Beyond Hurricane Katrina: Government Response, Unnatural Disasters, and African Americans 2009, Race, Place and Environmental Justice After Hurricane Katrina: Struggles to Reclaim, Rebuild, and Revitalize New Orleans and the Gulf Coast 2009. *Address:* Environmental Justice Resource Center, Clark Atlanta University, 223 James P. Brawley Drive, Atlanta, GA 30314, USA (office). *Telephone:* (404) 880-6911 (office). *Fax:* (404) 880-6909 (office). *E-mail:* ejrc@cau.edu (office). *Website:* www.ejrc.cau.edu (office).

BULLER, Arthur John, BA, MB, BSc, PhD, FRCP, FIBiol, FRSA; British physiologist and academic; *Professor Emeritus, Faculty of Medicine, University of Bristol;* b. 16 Oct. 1923; s. of Thomas Alfred Buller and Edith May Buller (née Wager); m. Helena Joan Pearson 1946; one s. two d. (one deceased); ed Duke of York's Royal Mil. School, Dover, St Thomas' Hosp. Medical School; Kitchener Scholar 1941–45; Lecturer in Physiology St Thomas' Hosp. 1946–49; Maj. RAMC, Specialist in Physiology, Jr Sec., Mil. Personnel Research Cttee 1949–53; Lecturer in Medicine, St Thomas' Hosp. 1953–57; Reader in Physiology, King's Coll., London 1961–65; Gresham Prof. of Physic 1963–65; Prof. of Physiology, Univ. of Bristol 1965–82, Dean Faculty of Medicine 1976–78, Prof. Emer. 1982–; Chief Scientist (on secondment), Dept of Health and Social Security 1978–81; Visiting Prof., Monash Univ., Australia 1972; Royal Soc. Commonwealth Fellow, Canberra, Australia 1958–59; mem. Bd of Govs Bristol Royal Infirmary 1968–74, Avon Health Authority 1974–78, MRC 1975–81; Chair. Neurosciences and Mental Health Bd, MRC 1975–77; External Scientific Adviser, Rayne Inst., St Thomas' Hosp. 1979–85; Research Devt Dir, Muscular Dystrophy Group of GB and NI 1982–90; mem. BBC, IBA Cen. Appeals Advice Cttee 1983–88; Hon. Consultant in Clinical Physiology, Bristol Dist Hospital 1970–85; Emergency Reserve Decoration (Army); Long Fox Memorial Lecturer, Univ. of Bristol 1978, Milroy Lecturer, Royal Coll. of Physicians 1983. *Publications:* articles in books and journals on normal and abnormal physiology. *Leisure interests:* clarets and conversation. *Address:* Flat 13, Turnpike Court, Hett Close, Ardingly, Haywards Heath, RH17 6GQ, England (home). *Telephone:* (1444) 891873 (home). *E-mail:* arthur.buller@btinternet.com.

BULLOCK, Sandra; American actress; b. 26 July 1964, Arlington, Va; d. of John Bullock and Helga Bullock; m. Jesse James 2005 (divorced 2010); ed East Carolina Univ.; grew up in Germany and Washington, DC; frequent appearances on European stage with opera-singer mother; appeared in off-Broadway productions including No Time Flat (WPA Theatre); f. Fortis Films (production co.). *Films include:* Hangmen 1987, A Fool and His Money 1988, Breakin' the Rules 1989,Religion, Inc. 1989, Love Potion No. 9 1992, The Vanishing 1993, When the Party's Over 1993, The Thing Called Love 1993, Fire on the Amazon 1993, Demolition Man 1993, Wrestling Ernest Hemingway 1993, Speed 1994, Who Do I Gotta Kill? 1994, While You Were Sleeping 1995, The Net 1995, Stolen Hearts 1996, Two If By Sea 1996, Moll Flanders, A Time to Kill 1996, In Love and War 1996, Speed 2 1997, Hope Floats (also exec. producer) 1998, Making Sandwiches (short, also writer) 1998, Practical Magic 1998, Prince of Egypt (voice) 1998, Forces of Nature 1999, Gun Shy 1999, 28 Days 2000, Famous 2000, Miss Congeniality 2000, Murder by Numbers 2001, Exactly 3:30 2001, Divine Secrets of the Ya-Ya Sisterhood 2002, Two Weeks' Notice 2002, Crash 2004, Loverboy 2005, Miss Congeniality 2: Armed and Fabulous 2005, The Lake House 2006, Infamous 2006, Premonition 2007, The Proposal 2009, All About Steve 2009, The Blind Side (Golden Globe for Performance by an Actress in a Motion Picture — Drama 2010, Acad. Award for Best Actress in a Leading Role 2010) 2009, Extremely Loud & Incredibly Close 2011, The Heat 2013, Gravity 2013, Aningaaq (short, voice) 2013. *Television includes:* Bionic Showdown: The Six Million Dollar Man and the Bionic Woman (film) 1989, Starting from Scratch (series) 1989, The Preppy Murder (film) 1989, Working Girl (NBC mini-series) 1990, Lucky Chances (mini-series) 1990, George Lopez (series) 2002–04. *Address:* c/o CAA, 2000 Avenue of the Stars, Los Angeles, CA 90067; Fortis Films, 8581 Santa Monica Blvd, Suite 1, West Hollywood, CA 90069, USA. *Telephone:* (310) 659-4533 (Fortis).

BULLOCK, Steve, BA, MA, JD; American lawyer, politician, state governor and academic; *Governor of Montana;* b. 11 April 1966, Missoula, Mont.; m. Lisa Bullock; ed Helena High School, Claremont McKenna Coll., Columbia Univ.; served as Chief Legal Counsel to Mont. Sec. of State Mike Cooney; worked with Montana Dept of Justice for four years, first as Exec. Asst Attorney Gen., later as Acting Chief Deputy 1997–2001, also served as Legis. Dir; unsuccessful cand. for Mont. Attorney Gen. 2000; practised law with Steptoe & Johnson, Washington, DC 2001–04; Adjunct Prof., George Washington Univ. Law School 2001–04; returned to Mont. to work in pvt. practice in Helena 2004–08; Attorney Gen. of Mont. 2009–13; Gov. of Montana 2013–; Democrat. *Address:* Office of the Governor, PO Box 200801 State Capitol, Helena, MT 59620-0801, USA (office). *Telephone:* (406) 444-3111 (office). *Fax:* (406) 444-5529 (office). *E-mail:* governor@mt.gov (office). *Website:* governor.mt.gov (office).

BULMAHN, Edelgard, MA; German politician; *Vice-President of Bundestag;* b. 4 March 1951, Minden; m.; ed Petershagen Aufbaugymnasium and Hanover Univ.; high school teacher for seven years; mem. SPD 1969–; mem. Bundestag (SPD) 1987–, Vice-Pres. 2013–; SPD Parl. Group Deputy Spokesman on Research and Tech. 1990–94, mem. Exec. Cttee SPD Parl. Group 1991–98, Exec. Cttee SPD 1993–, Chair. Parl. Cttee on Educ., Science, Research, Tech. and Tech. Assessment 1995–96, Spokesman on Educ. and Research 1996–98, mem. Cttee for Econ. Affairs and Tech. 2005–09, mem. Cttee on Foreign Affairs 2009–; Fed. Minister of Educ. and Research 1998–2005; Chair. European Space Agency (ESA) at ministerial level 2001–05. *Address:* Bundestag, Platz der Republik 1, 11011 Berlin, Germany (office). *Telephone:* (30) 22773798 (office). *Fax:* (30) 22776868 (office). *E-mail:* edelgard.bulmahn@bundestag.de (office); edelgard.bulmahn@wk.bundestag.de (office). *Website:* www.bundestag.de (office); www.edelgard-bulmahn.de.

BULMER-THOMAS, Victor Gerald, OBE, MA, DPhil; British economist, academic and international consultant; *Visiting Professor, Department of History,*

Florida International University; b. 23 March 1948, London; s. of the late Ivor Bulmer-Thomas and of Joan Bulmer; m. Barbara Swasey 1970; two s. one d.; ed Westminster School, New Coll. and St Antony's Coll., Oxford; Research Fellow, Fraser of Allander Inst. 1975–78; Lecturer in Econs, Queen Mary Coll., Univ. of London 1978–87, Reader 1987–90, Prof. of Latin American Econs 1990–98, Prof. Emer. 1998–, Dir Inst. of Latin American Studies 1992–98, Sr Research Fellow 1998–2001; Dir Chatham House (Royal Inst. of Int. Affairs) 2001–06; Visiting Prof., Fla Int. Univ., Miami 2007–; Dir Schroders Emerging Countries Fund 1996–2003, Deutsche Latin America Companies Trust 2004, New India Investment Trust 2004–; fmr Dir Gartmore Latin America New Growth Fund SA; fmr consultant for EC, IDB; Order of San Carlos (Colombia) 1998, Order of the Southern Cross (Brazil) 1998. *Publications:* Input-Output Analysis for Developing Countries 1982, The Political Economy of Central America since 1920 1987, Studies in the Economics of Central America 1988, Britain and Latin America: A Changing Relationship (ed.) 1989, The Economic History of Latin America Since Independence 1994, The New Economic Model in Latin America and Its Impact on Income Distribution and Poverty (ed.) 1996, Thirty Years of Latin American Studies in the UK 1997, United States and Latin America: The New Agenda (ed.) 1999, Regional Integration in Latin America and the Caribbean: The Political Economy of Open Regionalism (ed.) 2001, The Cambridge Economic History of Latin America, Vol. I: The Colonial Era and the Short Nineteenth Century, Vol. II The Long Twentieth Century (co-ed.) 2005. *Leisure interests:* music (viola), tennis, walking, canoeing, underwater photography. *Address:* Department of History, Florida International University, University Park (DM-397), Miami, FL 33199, USA (office). *Telephone:* (305) 348-3883 (office). *Fax:* (305) 348-3561 (office). *Website:* www.fiu.edu/~history (office).

BUMAYA HABIB, André; Rwandan politician; *Leader, Parti démocratique idéal (PDI);* fmr Minister of Labour and Public Service; Minister of Foreign Affairs and Regional Co-operation 2000–02; Leader, Parti démocratique idéal (PDI) (fmrly Parti démocratique islamique). *Address:* Parti démocratique idéal (PDI), Kigali, Rwanda (office).

BUMÇI, Aldo Tonin, BA, MA; Albanian politician; b. 11 June 1974, Tirana; ed Eastern Mediterranean Univ., Northern Cyprus, Bilkent Univ., Turkey; Researcher, Albanian Inst. for Int. Studies, Tirana 1999, becoming Deputy Exec. Dir –2005; mem. Kuvendi Popullor (Parl.) for Tirana 2005–, mem. Cttee on Legal Affairs, Public Admin and Human Rights, Cttee on European Integration; Minister of Justice 2005–07, of Tourism, Culture, Youth and Sports 2011–12, of Foreign Affairs April–Sept. 2013; mem. Democratic Party of Albania. *Address:* Kuvendi Popullor, Bulevardi Dëshmorët e Kombit 4, Tirana, Albania (office). *E-mail:* info@parlament.al (office). *Website:* www.parlament.al (office).

BUMPERS, Dale Leon, LLD; American lawyer and fmr politician; b. 12 Aug. 1925, Charleston, Ark.; s. of William Rufus Bumpers and Lattie (née Jones) Bumpers; m. Betty Flanagan 1949; two s. one d.; ed Univ. of Arkansas and Northwestern Law School; Propr Charleston Hardware and Furniture Co. 1951–66, Angus Breeding Farm 1966–70; Attorney, Charleston, Ark. 1951–70; Gov. of Arkansas 1971–74; Senator from Arkansas 1975–99; fmr Dir Center for Defense Information; Counsel, Arent Fox Kintner Plotkin & Kahn, Washington, DC 2000–09; Democrat; Univ. of Arkansas-Fayetteville founded the Dale Bumpers Coll. of Agricultural, Food and Life Sciences in his honour 1995. *Leisure interests:* reading, tennis, hunting. *Address:* c/o Arent Fox LLP, 1717 K Street NW, Washington, DC 20036, USA. *E-mail:* bumpers.dale@arentfox.com.

BÜNDCHEN, Gisele Caroline; Brazilian model, actress and fashion designer; b. 20 July 1980, Três de Maio; d. of Valdir Bündchen and Vânia Bündchen (née Nonnenmacher); m. Tom Brady 2009; one s. one d.; grew up in Horizontina, Rio Grande do Sul; has participated in modelling campaigns for Valentino, Tommy Hilfiger, Chloe, Celine, Versace, Christian Dior, Michael Kors, Ralph Lauren, Victoria's Secret, Louis Vuitton and Dolce & Gabbana; introduced own skin care product line, Sejaa Pure Skincare 2010; currently owns a hotel in Brazil; UNEP Goodwill Amb.; VH1/Vogue Model of the Year Award 1999, ranked by Forbes magazine amongst The World's 100 Most Powerful Women (72nd) 2010, (60th) 2011, (83rd) 2012, (95th) 2013, ranked third on The 20 Youngest Power Women of 2011. *Films:* Taxi 2004, The Devil Wears Prada 2006, cameo role in Apple Get a Mac campaign. *Address:* c/o img models NY, 304 Park Avenue South, 12 Floor, New York NY 10010, USA (office). *Website:* www.imgmodels.com (office); www.giselebundchen.com.br.

BUNDU, Abass, PhD; Sierra Leonean lawyer, diplomatist and business consultant; b. 3 June 1948; s. of Isatu Kallay Bundu and Pa Santigie; m. Khadija Allie 1976; two s. three d.; ed Australian Nat. Univ., Canberra, Univ. of Cambridge, UK; Asst Dir, Commonwealth Secr., London 1975–82; mem. of Parl. for Port Loko NE 1982–90; Minister of Agric., Natural Resources and Forestry 1982–85; Exec. Sec., Econ. Community of W African States (ECOWAS) 1989–93; Sec. of State for Foreign Affairs and Int. Co-operation 1993–95; unsuccessful presidential cand. (People's Progressive Party) 1996; Co-founder Afcan International (consultancy) 1997; Yorke Award, Univ. of Cambridge. *Leisure interests:* tennis, swimming. *Address:* Afcan International, 40 UN Drive, Cockerill, South Freetown, Sierra Leone (office). *Telephone:* (22) 230581 (office). *E-mail:* abassbundu@hotmail.com (office). *Website:* www.afcanholdings.com (office).

BUNDY, Colin James, BA, DPhil; British historian, academic and university administrator; *Warden, Green College, Oxford;* m.; two c.; ed Univ. of Natal, Univ. of Witwatersrand, Merton Coll. Oxford; Research Fellow, Queen Elizabeth House, Oxford 1979–80, Dept for External Studies, Oxford 1980–84; fmr Sr Lecturer, Manchester Polytechnic; Dir Inst. for Historical Research, Univ. of the W Cape 1992–94, Vice-Rector 1994–97; Vice-Chancellor and Prin. Univ. of Witwatersrand 1997–2001; Dir and Prin. School of Oriental and African Studies (SOAS), London 2001–06; Deputy Vice-Chancellor Univ. of London 2003–06; Warden, Green Coll., Oxford 2006–; Hon. Fellow, Kellogg Coll., Oxford. *Publications:* History, Revolution and South Africa 1987, Remaking the Past: New Perspectives in South African History 1987, Hidden Struggles in Rural South Africa: Politics & Popular Movements in the Transkei & Eastern Cape 1890–1930 (co-author) 1987, The History of the South African Communist Party 1991. *Leisure interests:* cricket, chess, music and hiking. *Address:* Office of the Warden, Green College, Radcliffe Observatory, Woodstock Road, Oxford, OX2 6HG, England (office). *Telephone:*

(1865) 274770 (office). *Fax:* (1865) 274796 (office). *E-mail:* colin.bundy@green.ox.ac .uk. *Website:* www.green.ox.ac.uk (office).

BUNDY, James Abbott, AB, MFA; American theatre director and academic; *Dean, School of Drama, Yale Univesity;* b. 8 May 1959, Boston; s. of McGeorge Bundy and Mary L. Bundy; m. Anne Tofflemire 1988; two d.; ed Harvard Coll., London Acad. of Music and Dramatic Art, Yale School of Drama; Man. Dir Cornerstone Theater Co., New York 1989–91; Assoc. Producing Dir The Acting Company 1996–98; Artistic Dir Great Lakes Theater Festival, Cleveland 1998–2002; Adjunct Prof. of Theatre, Case Western Reserve Univ., Cleveland –2002; Artistic Dir Yale Repertory Theatre, New Haven, Conn. 2002–, Prof. of Drama, Yale School of Drama 2002–, Dean 2002–; mem. Bd of Dirs Theatre Communications Group 2007–; fmr Dir Calif. Shakespeare Festival, Ala Shakespeare Festival, Lincoln Center Theater Dirs Lab, Juilliard School Drama Div.; Trustee Groton School 2003–; Tom Killen Award, Conn. Critics Circle 2007. *Address:* Yale School of Drama, 222 York Street, New Haven, CT 06520 (office); Yale Repertory Theatre, PO Box 208244, New Haven, CT 06505, USA (office). *Telephone:* (203) 432-1234 (office). *Fax:* (203) 432-1521 (office). *E-mail:* james .bundy@yale.edu (office). *Website:* drama.yale.edu (office); www.yalerep.org (office).

BUNE, Poseci Wagalevu; Fijian politician and diplomatist; ed Queen Victoria School, Royal Coll. of Public Admin., London; joined Public Service Dept 1966, apptd Sr Admin. Officer 1972, attached to Australian Embassy, Bangkok 1973, joined Perm. Mission to UN, New York 1973, apptd First Sec. 1973, Counsellor, Mission to EEC 1976–80; Western Divisional Commr, Ministry of Rural Devt 1981–85; Amb. to EEC (also accred to Belgium, Luxembourg, Netherlands, France and Italy) 1985–87; Perm. Sec. for Public Service 1987–95, Perm. Sec. to Govt and for Public Service 1990–95; Perm. Rep. to UN 1995–2000; mem. Parl. for Macuata 2001–; Leader, Veitokani ni Lewenivanua Vakarisito (Christian Democratic Alliance); Minister for Public Service and Public Sector Reform 2007–08. *Address:* c/o Ministry of Public Enterprises and Public Sector Reform, Government Bldgs, POB 2278, Suva, Fiji.

BUNGEI, Wilfred Kipkemboi; Kenyan athlete; b. 24 July 1980, Kabirirsang, nr Kapsabet; second cousin of Kenyan-born Danish fmr athlete Wilson Kipketer; ed Samoei High School; middle distance runner; ranked World No. 1 over 800m in 2002 and 2003; set personal best of 1:42.34 in Rieti 2002; part of 4×800m relay team that holds world record 2008; Silver Medal, World Jr Championships, Annecy, France 1998, World Championships, Edmonton 2001; Bronze Medal, African Championships, Radès 2002, World Indoor Championships, Birmingham 2003; finished first at Int. Asscn of Athletics Feds (IAAF) World Athletics Final, Monaco 2003, fifth at Olympic Games, Athens 2004, fourth at World Championships, Helsinki 2005, first at IAAF World Athletics Final, Monaco 2005; Gold Medal, World Indoor Championships, Moscow 2006; Bronze Medal, IAAF World Athletics Final, Stuttgart 2006; finished first at World Championships, Osaka 2007; Gold Medal, Olympic Games, Beijing 2008. *Address:* c/o Kenya Athletics Federation, PO Box 46722, Aerodrome Road, Riadha House, 00100 Nairobi West, Kenya. *Telephone:* (2) 605021. *Fax:* (2) 605020. *E-mail:* athleticskenya@gt.co.ke. *Website:* www.athleticskenya.org.

BUNIN, Igor Mikhailovich; Russian political commentator; *Director-General, Political Technologies Centre;* b. 25 Feb. 1946, Moscow; m.; one d.; ed Moscow State Univ.; Sr Researcher, Inst. of World Econs and Int. Relations, USSR Acad. of Sciences 1973–82; Chief Researcher, Inst. of Int. Workers' Movt 1982–92; Chief Scientific Expert, Int. Foundation of Socio-Econ. and Political Studies (Gorbachev Foundation) 1992–93; Dir Centre of Business Initiatives, Ekspertiza 1992–93; Dir-Gen. Political Technologies Centre 1993–; Dir-Gen. Ind. Information Site of Political Comments (www.politcom.ru) 2001–. *Publications include:* Socialists and Political Struggle in France in the 1980s 1989, New Russian Businessmen and Myths of Post-Communist Mentality 1993, Businessmen of Russia: 40 Stories of Success 1994, Experience of Formation 1994, Financial and Industrial Groups and Conglomerates in Economics and Politics of Russia 1997, Political Processes in the Regions of Russia 1998, The '99 Elections: Results and Lessons 2000, Political Prognosis as the Art of the Possible: Contemporary Russian Politics, A Course of Lectures 2003. *Address:* Political Technologies Centre, Bolshoi Zlatoustovsky per. 8/7 office 73–95, 101000 Moscow, Russia (office). *Telephone:* (495) 206-80-30 (office). *Fax:* (495) 20682-58 (office). *E-mail:* info@cpt.ru (office). *Website:* www.cpt .ru (office).

BUNNAG, Marut; Thai politician and lawyer; b. 21 Aug. 1925, Bangkok; s. of Phra Sutthikarnvinijchai and Mrs Phongsri; m. Phantipha Bunnag; two c.; ed Thammasat Univ.; with Ministry of Justice –1952; Marut Bunnag Int. Law Office law practice 1952–; Minister of Justice 1979; mem. Parl. (Democratic Party) 1983–, served as Speaker of the House of Reps and Pres. Nat. Ass.; Minister of Public Health 1983–86, Sept.–Dec. 1990, of Educ. 1988; Deputy Leader, Democrat Party, Sr Adviser; part-time Lecturer, Thai Bar Asscn, Thammasart Univ., Chulalongkorn Univ., Mahidol Univ., Ramkhamhaeng Univ., etc.; mem. World Peace Through Law Centre, Int. Bar Asscn, Law Asscn for Asia and the Pacific (Pres.). *Address:* c/o Marut Bunnag International Law Office, Forum Tower, 22nd Floor, 184/130–136 Ratchadaphisek Road, Huaykwang, Bangkok 10320 (office); 45/1 Pradipat Road, Kwaeng Samsane-nai, Khet Phyathai, Bangkok 10400, Thailand (home). *Telephone:* (2) 645-2556 (office); (2) 271-1081 (home). *Fax:* (2) 645-2568 (office). *E-mail:* marut@loxinfo.co.uk (office). *Website:* www.marut.th.com (office).

BUNROD, Gen. Somtad; Thai government official and army officer (retd); served in special warfare unit of Thai army; fmr Army Jt Chief of Staff; Minister of Defence 2006–11. *Address:* c/o Ministry of Defence, Thanon Sanamchai, Bangkok 10200, Thailand (office).

BUNSUMPUN, Prasert, BEng, MBA; Thai energy executive; *Chairman, IRPC Public Co. Ltd;* b. 20 Feb. 1952; ed Chulalongkorn Univ., Utah State Univ., Harvard Univ. and Nat. Defense Coll., USA, King Prajadhipoks Inst.; Dir Dept of Petroleum Procurements & Contracts, Petroleum Authority of Thailand (PTT) 1986–91, Asst Gov. of Marketing 1991–92, Sr Vice-Pres., Marketing Downstream Oil Business 1992–96, Pres. PTT Oil 1996–99, Pres. PTT Gas Business Group 2000–01, Sr Exec. Vice-Pres. PTT Gas Business Group 2001–03, Pres. and CEO PTT Public Co. Ltd 2003–11, Sec. 2007–11, Chair. PTT Global Chemical Public Co. Ltd Feb.–June 2010, 2011–, Vice-Chair. 2010–11; Chair. Thai Lube Base Public

Co. Ltd 2005–; Chair. of the Bd and Chair. Exec. Cttee IRPC Public Co. Ltd 2011–, Dir 2009–; mem. Bd of Dirs PTT Exploration and Production PLC (Chair. 2007–11), Trans Thai-Malaysia (Thailand) Co. Ltd, PTT Natural Gas Distribution Co. Ltd, PTT Aromatics and Refining Public Co. Ltd 2007–11, PTT Global Chemical Public Co. Ltd 2005–, Thai Olefin Public Co. Ltd, Thai Petroleum Pipeline Co. Ltd, Nat. Petrochemical PLC, Thaioil Co. Ltd –2010, Thaioil Power Co. Ltd, Independent Power (Thailand) Co. Ltd, Siam City Bank Public Co. Ltd –2010, Krungthai Bank Public Co. Ltd 2011–; Ind. Dir Shin Corpn Public Co. Ltd 2011–; mem. Nat. Legis. Ass. 2006–08; Pres. Utah Univ. Alumni, USA; Chair. Thailand Business Council for Sustainable Devt 2011–, Community Enterprise Inst., Churalongkorn Univ. Eng Alumni; mem. Nat. Legis. Ass. 2006–08; Hon. DEng (Chulalongkorn Univ.), Hon. Dr of Man. (Nat. Inst. of Devt Admin), Hon. Dr of Man. Science (Petchaburi Rajabhat Univ.). *Address:* IRPC Public Co. Ltd, 555/2 Energy Complex Building B, 6th Vibhavadi-Rangsit Road, Kwaeng Chatuchak Khet, Chatuchak, Bangkok 10900, Thailand (office). *Telephone:* (2) 649-7000 (office). *Fax:* (2) 649-7001 (office). *E-mail:* info@irpc.co.th (office). *Website:* www .irpc.co.th (office).

BUORA, Carlo Orazio; Italian business executive; b. 26 May 1946, Milan; m.; two s.; ed Bocconi Univ., Milan; began career at Banca Nazionale del Lavoro 1972; Head of Finance and Admin, Merloni Finanziaria 1979–82; Finance Dir SNIA Viscose 1982–89 (co. acquired by Fiat 1984), Deputy Dir Gen. Telettra SpA 1989; Gen. Man. Benetton Group 1989–91; joined Pirelli SpA 1991, Dir and CEO 1999–2006; apptd Jt CEO Olivetti SpA 2001; CEO and Man. Dir Telecom Italia SpA 2001–11; mem. Bd of Dirs Riunione Adriatica Di Sicurta SpA, Olimpia SpA, RCS MediaGroup SpA, FC Internazionale SpA, Pirelli Labs SpA, Tecnost SpA, Mediobanca SpA; mem. Bd of Man. HDP Holding di Partecipazioni SpA, Mediobanca SpA, RAS SpA, Tecnost SpA; mem. Advisory Cttee EuroQube Fund.

BURBIDGE, (Eleanor) Margaret Peachey, PhD, FRS; American (b. British) astronomer and academic; *Professor Emerita of Physics, University of California, San Diego;* b. 12 Aug. 1919, Davenport, England; d. of Stanley John Peachey and Marjorie Peachey (née Stott); m. Geoffrey Burbidge 1948 (died 2010); one d.; ed Frances Holland School, London and Univ. Coll., London; Second Asst, Asst Dir and acting Dir Univ. of London Observatory 1946–51; Research Fellow, Yerkes Observatory, Harvard Coll. Observatory 1951–53, Calif. Inst. of Technology 1955–57; Research Fellow and Assoc. Prof. Univ. of Chicago 1957–62; Assoc. Research Physicist, Univ. of Calif., San Diego 1962–64, Prof. 1964, Univ. Prof. 1984–91, Prof. Emer. 1991–, Research Prof., Dept of Physics 1990–, Dir Center for Astrophysics and Space Sciences 1979–88; Dir Royal Greenwich Observatory 1971–73; Ed. Observatory 1948–51; mem. Editorial Bd Astronomy and Astrophysics 1969–85; Lindsay Memorial Lecture, NASA 1985; mem. Royal Astronomical Soc., American Astronomical Soc. (Pres. 1978), American Acad. of Arts and Science, NAS, AAAS (Fellow 1981, Pres. 1982), American Philosophical Soc., Soc. Royale des Sciences de Liège, Astronomical Soc. of the Pacific, New York Acad. of Sciences; Fellow, Univ. Coll., London, Lucy Cavendish Coll., Cambridge, Girton Coll., Cambridge; Hon. DSc (Smith Coll., Mass, Rensselaer Political Inst. and Univs of Sussex, Leicester, Bristol, Chicago, Mich., Mass, City Univ., London, Notre Dame, London and Williams Coll.); numerous prizes and awards including Helen B. Warner Prize (jtly with Geoffrey Burbidge) 1959, Karl G. Jansky Lectureship, Nat. Radio Astronomy Observatory 1977, Bruce Gold Medal, Astronomical Soc. of the Pacific 1982, Nat. Medal of Science, USA 1983, Einstein Medal 1988, Gold Medal, Royal Astronomical Soc. (jtly with Geoffrey Burbidge) 2005. *Publications:* Quasi-Stellar Objects (with Geoffrey Burbidge) 1967; numerous articles in scientific journals. *Address:* Center for Astrophysics and Space Sciences, University of California, Mail Code #0424, La Jolla, CA 92093, USA (office). *E-mail:* mburbidge@ucsd.edu (office).

BURBULIS, Gennady Eduardovich; Russian politician; b. 4 Aug. 1945, Pervouralsk, Sverdlovsk (now Ekaterinburg); s. of Eduard Kazimirovich Burbulis and Valentina Ivanovna Belonogova; m. Natalia Kirsanova; one s.; ed Ural State Univ.; Lecturer Ural Polytechni Inst. 1974–83; Head of Chair., Deputy Dir Inst. of Non-Ferrous Metals 1983–89; USSR People's Deputy 1989–90; formed Discussion Tribune, Sverdlovsk 1988; elected to Congress of People's Deputies 1989; mem. Inter-Regional Group; Chief of Staff to Boris Yeltsin 1991; State Sec. RSFSR (now Russian Fed.) 1991–92, State Council Sec. 1991–92; First Deputy Chair. Russian Govt 1991–92, Sec. of State May–Nov. 1992, Head of Advisors' Team Nov.–Dec. 1992; Founder and Pres. Int. Humanitarian and Political Cen. Strategy 1993–; mem. State Duma (Parl.) 1993–99, mem. Cttee for Geopolitics; Deputy Gov. Novgorod Region 1999–2001; Chair. Observational Bd Novotrubny factory, Pervouralsk 1997–98; Rep. of Novgorod Region to Council of Fed. 2002–05, Chair. Fed. Council Comm. on Methodology of Exercising the Fed. Council's Constitutional Powers 2002, currently Adviser to Chair. of Federation Council. *Publication:* Profession – Politician 1999. *Leisure interests:* poetry, playing soccer and tennis. *Address:* Council of Federation, 103426 Moscow, B. Dmitrovca 26, Russia (office). *Telephone:* (495) 292-61-23 (office). *Fax:* (495) 926-69-50 (office). *E-mail:* GEBurbulis@council.gov.ru (office). *Website:* council.gov.ru (office).

BURCH, Lt-Col (retd) David, OBE, JP, ED; Bermudian army officer (retd) and politician; ed Royal Mil. Acad., Sandhurst, UK; spent 20 years as Reinsurance Underwriting Man.; Commanding Officer, The Bermuda Regt 1994–97 (retd); Consultant to Ministry of Works and Eng and Housing 2005, Minister of Works and Eng and Housing 2005–06, Minister of Public Safety and Housing 2006–07, of Labour, Home Affairs and Housing 2007–10, of Nat. Security 2010–11; fmr Govt Leader in the Senate; host, weekly radio talk show Bermuda Speaks: Sundays with the Colonel; mem. Progressive Labour Party; mem. Bermuda Sea Cadet Asscn, Royal Artillery Asscn; Efficiency Decoration for outstanding mil. service 1990, First Clasp 1996. *Address:* c/o Ministry of National Security, Government Administration Bldg, 1st Floor, 30 Parliament St, Hamilton HM12, Bermuda (office).

BURCH, Tory; American fashion designer, business executive and philanthropist; *Creative Director and CEO, Tory Burch LLC;* b. 17 June 1966, Valley Forge, Pa; d. of the late Buddy Robinson and of Reva Robinson; m. 1st William Macklowe; m. 2nd Christopher Burch 1997 (divorced 2006); three s. (including twins) three step-d.; ed Agnes Irwin School, Rosemont, Pa, Univ. of Pennsylvania; moved to New York City and began career working with fashion designers, including Zoran, a Yugoslavian designer; worked at Harper's Bazaar magazine; copywriter for Polo

Ralph Lauren and worked for Vera Wang; began fashion label, known as TRB by Tory Burch (later as Tory Burch) 2004, began as business operation in her Upper East Side apartment and then into free-standing boutiques, now numbering 26, opened flagship store in the NoLIta (North of Little Italy) neighbourhood of Manhattan, New York 2004, label endorsed by Oprah Winfrey 2005; has designed outfits for Cameron Diaz, Oprah Winfrey, Jennifer Lopez, Uma Thurman and Hilary Swank; sold minority stake in co. to Mexican pvt. equity firm Tresalia Capital 2009; f. Tory Burch Foundation 2008; mem. Bd Memorial Sloan-Kettering Cancer Center; Chair. Spring Gala for the American Ballet Theatre 2006; Rising Star Award for Best New Retail Concept, Fashion Group International 2005, Accessory Brand Launch of the Year Award, Accessories Council of Excellence 2007, Council of Fashion Designers of America winner (Accessories Designer of the Year) 2008, ranked by Forbes magazine amongst The World's 100 Most Powerful Women (88th) 2010, (69th) 2013. *Television:* appeared as herself in fourth episode of Gossip Girl (teen drama series) 2009, Fashion King (cameo) 2012. *Address:* Tory Burch Corporate Offices & Showroom, 11 West 19th Street, 7th Floor, New York, NY 10011, USA (office). *Telephone:* (212) 683-2323 (office). *Fax:* (212) 683-3876 (office). *E-mail:* press@toryburch.com (office). *Website:* www.toryburch.com (office); www.toryburchfoundation.org; www.toryburchfoundation.org; www.toryburch.com.

BURD, Steven A., BS, MA; American retail executive; b. Valley City, ND; m. Chris Burd; two c.; ed Carroll Coll., Univ. of Wisconsin; worked for Arthur D. Little, New York 1981–87; man., Safeway Stores, Kohlberg Kravis Roberts & Co. 1986–91; consultant Stop and Shop Cos, Boston 1988–89; consultant and interim CEO Fred Meyer Inc., Portland, Ore. 1991–92; Pres. Safeway Inc. 1992–2012, CEO 1993–2013, Chair. 1998–2013; mem. Bd of Dirs Kohl's Corpn; mem. US Dept of Homeland Security's Pvt. Sector Sr Advisory Cttee 2003–. *Address:* c/o Safeway Inc., 5918 Stoneridge Mall Road, Pleasanton, CA 94588-3229, USA. *E-mail:* info@safeway.com.

BURDA, Hubert, DPhil; German publisher and author; *CEO, Hubert Burda Media;* b. 9 Feb. 1940, Heidelberg; s. of Franz Burda and Aenne Lemminger; m. Maria Furtwängler; ed Univ. of Munich; Man. Bild & Funk 1966–74; partner, Burda GmbH 1974, currently CEO and Acting Partner, Hubert Burda Media; Co-Publr Elle-Verlag GmbH, Munich; Founder Hubert Burda Centre for Innovative Communications, Ben-Gurion Univ. in Beer Sheva, Israel; Co-founder Europe Online SA, Luxembourg, European Publishers Council; currently Pres. Asscn of German Magazine Publishers; currently also Chair. of the Council, Munich Ludwig-Maximilians Univ.; est. Felix Burda Foundation 2001; f. Petrarca Prize (for poetry), Bambi (Media-Prize), Corp. Art Prize 1997; Publr Anna, Bunte, Burda Moden, Das Haus, Elle, Elle Bistro, Elle Deco, Elle TopModel, Focus, Focus Online, Focus TV, Freundin, Freizeit Revue, Futurekids, Glücks Revue, Haus + Garten, Lisa, Lisa Kochen & Backen, Lisa Wohnen & Dekorieren, Mein schöner Garten, Meine Familie & ich, Norddeutsche Neueste Nachrichten, Schweriner Volkszeitung, Starwatch Navigation, Super Illu, Super TV, TraXXX, Verena; Bd mem. German School of Journalism, Munich; Great Cross of Merit (Germany); Interfaith Gold Medallion, Council of Christians and Jews 1999, European Print Media Prize, Gold Medal Freedom of Speech, European Asscn of Communications Agencies, Leo Baeck Prize, Cen. Council of Jews in Germany 2006. *Address:* Hubert Burda Media, Arabellastrasse 23, 81925 Munich, Germany (office). *E-mail:* info@hubert-burda-media.com (office). *Website:* www.hubert-burda-media.com (office); www.hubert-burda.de (office).

BURDETT-COUTTS, William Walter, MA; British artistic director and film and television producer; *Artistic Director, Riverside Studios Ltd;* b. 17 Feb. 1955, Harare, Zimbabwe; s. of William A. F. Burdett-Coutts and Nancy C. Burdett-Coutts (née Gervers); one s. two d.; ed Radley Coll., Oxford, Rhodes Univ., South Africa, Univ. of Essex; Artistic Dir Assembly Rooms, Edinburgh 1981–; Festival Dir Mayfest, Glasgow 1987–90; Head of Arts Granada TV 1990–93; Dir Riverside TV Studios Ltd 1998–, Chair. 2002–, currently Artistic Dir Riverside Studios Ltd; Exec. Producer Assembly Film and TV 1994–2004, Dir Assembly Media Group Ltd 2007–11; Chair. Kiss 102 1993–97, Kiss 105 1996–97; Festival Dir Brighton Comedy Festival 2002–. *Address:* Riverside Studios, Crisp Road, London, W6 9RL, England (office). *Telephone:* (20) 8237-1075 (office). *Fax:* (20) 8237-1071 (office). *E-mail:* wbc@riversidestudios.co.uk (office). *Website:* www.riversidestudios.co.uk (office).

BUREAU, Jérôme, DHist; French journalist; *Director of Communications, Métropole Télévision 6 (M6);* b. 19 April 1956, Paris; m. Fabienne Pauly 1999; two c. (and two from previous marriage); journalist with Libération 1978–81; Sr Reporter L'Équipe Magazine 1981–87, Ed.-in-Chief 1989–93; Ed.-in-Chief Le Sport 1987–88; Editorial Dir L'Équipe, L'Équipe-TV 1997–2003, L'Équipe Magazine, Vélo, XL, Tennis de France 1993–2003, lequipe.fr 1999–2003; TV and Radio Producer, Sport FM 2004; Dir of Communications, Métropole Télévision 6 (M6) 2004–. *Publications:* L'Amour-Foot 1986, Les Géants du football 1996, L'année du football 2004, Euro 2004: la grande fête du football 2004, Les champions d'Athènes 2004, Braaasil: Les magiciens du football 2005. *Leisure interests:* cookery, bullfighting. *Address:* Métropole Télévision 6 (M6), 89 avenue Charles de Gaulle, 92575 Neuilly sur Seine cedex (office); 20 avenue Pernety, 75014 Paris, France (home). *E-mail:* jerome.bureau6@wanadoo.fr (home). *Website:* www.m6.fr (office).

BURENGA, Kenneth L.; American publishing executive; b. 30 May 1944, Somerville, NJ; s. of Nicholas Burenga and Louanna Chamberlin; m. Jean Case 1964; one s. one d.; ed Rider Coll.; budget accountant, Dow Jones & Co., S Brunswick, NJ 1966–67, Asst Man. Data Processing Control 1968–69, staff asst for systems devt 1970–71, Man. Systems Devt and Control 1972–76, Circulation Marketing Man. 1977–78, Circulation Sales Dir 1979–80, Vice-Pres. Circulation and Circulation Dir 1980–86; Chief Financial Officer and Admin. Officer, Dow Jones & Co., New York 1986–88, Exec. Vice-Pres. and Gen. Man. 1989–91, Pres. and COO 1991, Pres. and CEO –1998 (retd); fmr Gen. Man. Wall Street Journal 1989; mem. Bd of Dirs Dow Jones Courier. *Leisure interest:* cattle farming. *Address:* 1076 Grona Schandua Road, Fredericksburg, TX 78624-7624, USA (home). *Telephone:* (830) 997-9944 (home).

BURG, Avraham, BA; Israeli politician; b. 1955; s. of Dr. Josef Burg; m. Yael Burg; six c.; ed Hebrew Univ., Jerusalem; army service; mem. Knesset 1988–2004, Speaker 1999–2003; mem. Finance and State Control Cttees 1988–92; Chair.

Educ. Cttee 1992–95; mem. Cttee for the Advancement of the Status of Women 1992–95; Chair. Jewish Agency for Israel 1995–99; fmr Chair. Zionist Movt, Co-Chair. World Jewish Restitution Organisation 1995–1999, Deputy Chair. World Jewish Congress; mem. int. cttee that negotiated settlement with Swiss banks 1995–1999, mem. Board of Claims Conference 1995–1999. *Publication:* The Holocaust is Over: We Must Rise from its Ashes 2007. *Address:* c/o The Knesset, Kiryat Ben-Gurion, Hakirya, Jerusalem 91950, Israel (office).

BURGEN, Sir Arnold (Stanley Vincent), Kt, MD, FRS; British scientist; b. 20 March 1922, London, England; s. of Peter Burgen and Elizabeth Burgen (née Wolfers); m. 1st Judith Browne 1946 (died 1993); two s. one d.; m. 2nd Olga Kennard 1993; ed Christ's Coll., Finchley, London, Middlesex Hosp. Medical School; Demonstrator, later Asst Lecturer, Middlesex Hosp. Medical School 1945–49; Prof. of Physiology, McGill Univ., Montreal 1949–62; Deputy Dir McGill Univ. Clinic, Montreal Gen. Hospital 1957–62; Sheild Prof. of Pharmacology, Univ. of Cambridge 1962–71; Dir Nat. Inst. of Medical Research, London 1971–82; Master Darwin Coll., Cambridge 1982–89, Deputy Vice-Chancellor, Univ. of Cambridge 1983–89; mem. MRC 1969–71, 1973–77, Hon. Dir MRC Molecular Pharmacology Unit 1967–72; Pres. Int. Union of Pharmacology 1972–75; Vice-Pres. Royal Soc. 1980–86, Foreign Sec. 1981–86; Fellow, Downing Coll., Cambridge 1962–71, Hon. Fellow 1972; mem. Bureau, European Science and Tech. Asscn 1994–; Ed. European Review 1993–; mem. Deutsche Akad. der Naturforscher Leopoldina 1984; Corresp. mem. Royal Acad. of Spain 1984; Foreign Assoc. NAS; Pres. Academia Europaea 1988–94; Academician of Finland; Hon. FRCP (Canada); Hon. DSc (McGill, Leeds, Liverpool); Hon. MD (Zurich) 1983, (Utrecht); Hon. DUniv (Surrey) 1983; Wellcome Gold Medal 1999. *Publications:* papers in journals of pharmacology and physiology. *Leisure interests:* sculpture, music. *Address:* 8A Hills Avenue, Cambridge, CB1 7XA, England. *Telephone:* (1223) 415381. *Fax:* (1223) 363852. *E-mail:* asvb@cam.ac.uk (office).

BURGESS, Sir Robert George, Kt, DL, BA, PhD; British academic administrator; *Vice-Chancellor, University of Leicester;* b. 23 April 1947, Sherborne, Dorset; s. of George Burgess and Olive Burgess (née Andrews); m. Hilary Margaret Mary Joyce 1974; ed Durham Univ., Univ. of Warwick; Lecturer, Univ. of Warwick 1974–84, Sr Lecturer 1984–88, Dept Chair. 1985–88, Dir Centre for Educational Devt Appraisal and Research 1987–99, Chair. Faculty of Social Sciences 1988–91, Prof. of Sociology 1988–99, Founding Chair. Grad. School 1991–95, Pro-Vice-Chancellor 1995–99; Vice-Chancellor, Univ. of Leicester 1999–; mem. Research Resources Bd, Econ. and Social Research Council 1991–96, mem. Council 1996–2000, Chair. Postgraduate Training Bd 1997–2000 (mem. 1989–93, Vice-Chair. 1996–97); Founding Chair. UK Council for Grad. Educ. 1993–99; Chair. East Midlands Univs Asscn 2001–04; mem. Higher Educ. Funding Council for England (HEFCE) Review of Postgraduate Educ. 1995–96, HEFCE Quality Assessment, Learning and Teaching Cttee 2003–07; Bd UCAS 2001–11 (Chair. 2005–11), Jt Equality Steering Group 2001–03, Bd British Library 2003–10; Trustee and Chair., Higher Educ. Acad. 2003–; apptd Deputy Lt of Leicestershire 2010; Chair. UUK/Guild HE Managing and Recording Student Achievement (The Burgess Groups) 2004–, Econ. and Social Research Council (ESRC) Teaching and Learning Research Programme 2004–09, Research Information Network 2005–11, Nat. Centre for Social Research 2012–; Academician, Acad. of Learned Socs in the Social Sciences 2000, Acad. of Social Sciences; DL 2010, UCEA Bd 2013–; Kt Bachelor for services to Higher Educ. locally and nationally 2010; Hon. DLitt (Staffordshire) 1998, Hon. DUniv (Northampton) 2007, Hon. EdD (De Montfort) 2013. *Publications include:* Experiencing Comprehensive Education 1983, In the Field 1984, Education, Schools and Schooling 1985, Sociology, Education and Schools 1986, Implementing In-Service Education (co-author) 1993, Research Methods 1993, Reflections of the University of Leicester (with Joanne Wood) 2010; ed. of more than 24 books on social research methodology and the sociology of educ. *Leisure interests:* some gardening, music, walking. *Address:* Vice-Chancellor's Office, University of Leicester, Leicester, LE1 7RH, England (office). *Telephone:* (116) 252-2322 (office). *Fax:* (116) 255-8691 (office). *E-mail:* vc@le.ac.uk (office). *Website:* www.le.ac.uk (office).

BURGHARDT, Günter, PhD, DrJur; German lawyer, academic, international organization official and fmr diplomatist; *Senior Counsel, Mayer Brown Europe-Brussels LLP;* b. 27 April 1941, Krosswitz; m. Rita Byl; three c.; ed Univs of Hamburg, Paris and Strasbourg; mem. of Legal Service, EC 1970, Desk Officer for External Relations (USA, Canada and Australia), for Devt of EC External Relations Network and Asst to Dir-Gen. Sir Roy Denman 1972–80, Deputy Head of Cabinet to Commr Karl-Heinz Narjes 1981–84, to Pres. Jacques Delors 1985–88, Political Dir, Sec. Gen. of the Comm. under Pres. Delors 1988–93, Dir-Gen. of External Relations (Europe and Newly Ind. States), Common Foreign and Security Policy and External Service under Commr Hans van den Broek 1993–99, Dir-Gen. of External Relations for Commr Chris Patten 1999–2000; Amb. and Head Del. of EC to USA 2000–05; Visiting Prof., European Political and Admin. Studies Dept and EU Int. Relations and Diplomacy Studies Dept Coll. of Europe, Bruges 2005–; Sr Counsel, Mayer Brown Europe-Brussels LLP, Brussels 2005–; Bundesverdienstkreuz 1. Klasse. *Address:* Mayer Brown Europe-Brussels LLP, Avenue des Arts 52, 1000 Brussels (office); Vossenlaan 12, 3080 Tervuren (home); c/o Department of EU International Relations and Diplomacy Studies, College of Europe, Dijver 11, 8000 Bruges, Belgium (office). *Telephone:* (2) 502-55-17 (Mayer Brown) (office); (50) 47-72-51 (office). *Fax:* (2) 502-54-21 (Mayer Brown) (office); (50) 47-72-50 (office). *E-mail:* gburghardt@mayerbrown.com (office). *Website:* www.mayerbrown.com (office).

BURGIN, Victor, ARCA, MFA; British artist, writer and academic; *Millard Professor Emeritus of Fine Art, Goldsmiths College, London;* b. 24 July 1941, Sheffield; s. of Samuel Burgin and Gwendolyne A. Crowder; m. 1st Hazel P. Rowbotham 1964 (divorced 1975); m. 2nd Francette Pacteau 1988; two s.; ed Firth Park Grammar School, Sheffield, Sheffield Coll. of Art, Royal Coll. of Art, London and Yale Univ., USA; Sr Lecturer, Trent Polytechnic, Nottingham 1967–73; Prof. of History and Theory of Visual Arts, Faculty of Communication, Polytechnic of Cen. London 1973–88; Prof. of Art History, Univ. of Calif., Santa Cruz 1988–95, Prof. of History of Consciousness 1995–2001, Prof. Emer. of History of Consciousness 2001–; Millard Prof. of Fine Art Goldsmiths Coll., Univ. of London 2001–06, now Millard Prof. Emer.; Prof. of Media Philosophy and History of Consciousness, European Graduate School; Deutscher Akademischer Austauschdienst Fellowship

1978–79; Picker Professorship, Colgate Univ., Hamilton, New York 1980; mem. arts advisory panel, Arts Council of Great Britain 1971–76, 1980–81; numerous mixed and solo exhbns at galleries around the world from 1965; Hon. DUniv (Sheffield Hallam) 2005. *Publications include:* Work and Commentary 1973, Thinking Photography 1982, The End of Art Theory 1986, Between 1986, Passages 1991, In/Different Spaces 1996, Some Cities 1996, Venice 1997, Shadowed 2000, The Remembered Film 2005, Voyage to Italy 2007, Incomplete Components of a Practice 2008, Situational Aesthetics 2009, Parallel Texts: Interviews and Interventions About Art 2011; contrib. to exhbn catalogues. *Address:* c/o Goldsmiths College, New Cross, London, SE14 6NW, England (office). *Telephone:* (20) 7919-7671 (office). *Fax:* (20) 7919-7673 (office). *E-mail:* v.burgin@gold.ac.uk (office). *Website:* www.goldsmiths.ac.uk/departments/visual-arts (office).

BURGMANS, Antony, MA; Dutch business executive; b. 13 Feb. 1947, Rotterdam; one s. one d.; ed Nijenrode Univ., Univ. of Stockholm, Sweden, Univ. of Lancaster, UK; joined Unilever NV 1972, Marketing Asst, Lever Netherlands and Indonesia, Marketing and Sales Dir Lever, Netherlands 1982–85, Lever Germany 1985–88, Chair. PT Unilever Indonesia 1988–91, Dir Unilever (Personal Care Products Div.) 1991–94, (Ice Cream and Frozen Foods—Europe) 1994–98, Chair. Unilever European Cttee 1994–98, Vice-Chair. Unilever NV 1998–99, Chair. 1999–2007 (retd); Chair. WWF Netherlands; mem. Supervisory Bd Akzo Nobel, AEGON, SHV, TNT Express; Dir (non-exec.) BP PLC; Commdr, Order of Orange Nassau 2007, Hon. KBE (UK) 2008; Dr hc (Lancaster) 2005; UN Humanitarian of the Year Award 2007. *Leisure interests:* golf, skiing, Dutch painters, soccer. *Address:* BurGo BV, Lange Vijverberg, 12, 2513 AC The Hague, Netherlands (office). *Telephone:* (70) 3460831 (office). *Fax:* (70) 3469904 (office). *E-mail:* antony.burgmans@burgobv.nl (office).

BURGO, Carlos Augusto Duarte de, BEcons, MSc; Cape Verde politician and central banker; *Governor, Central Bank of Cape Verde;* b. 5 March 1958, Nova Sintra, Ilha da Brava; ed Martin Luther Univ., Halle-Wittenberg, Germany, Catholic Univ. of Louvain, Belgium, Univ. of Iowa, USA; Prof. of Econs, Instituto Amílcar Cabral 1983–90, Dir 1987–90; Deputy, Assembleia Nacional for Brava constituency 1991–2001, Pres. Special Perm. Comm. for Finance 2000; Pres. Municipal Ass. of Brava 2000–04; Minister of Finance, Planning and Regional Devt 2001–03; currently Gov. Banco de Cabo Verde (BCV, Central Bank of Cape Verde Islands); mem. Nat. Council and Political Comm., Partido Africano da Independência de Cabo Verde (PAICV). *Address:* Banco de Cabo Verde, Av.Amílcar Cabral, CP 101, Praia, Cape Verde (office). *Telephone:* 2617192 (office); 2607180 (office). *Fax:* 2614447 (office). *Website:* fevora@bcv.cv (office); www.bcv.cv (office).

BURGOS VARELA, Jorge; Chilean lawyer, fmr diplomatist and politician; *Minister of National Defence;* b. 24 June 1956, Providencia; m. María Patricia Salas; three s.; ed Universidad de Chile; began career as Vice-Pres., Public Safety Coordinating Council; Chief of Staff and Legal Adviser to Minister of Interior 1990–93; Acting Mayor, Metropolitan Region 1992; Sec. of War 1993–96; Amb. to Ecuador 1996–2000; Sec. of the Interior 2000–01; mem. Camera de Diputados (Parl.) for Dist 21 (Nuñoa y Providencia) 2002–, Chair. Standing Cttee on Constitution, Legislation and Justice 2002–03, Special Cttee on Public Safety 2003–04, Leader, Christian Democrat Parl. Group 2005–, First Vice-Pres. Chamber of Deputies 2006–; Minister of Nat. Defence 2014–; mem. Partido Demócrata Cristiano. *Address:* Ministry of National Defence, Edif. Diego Portales, 22°, Villavicencio 364, Santiago, Chile (office). *Telephone:* (2) 2222-1202 (office). *Fax:* (2) 2633-0568 (office). *E-mail:* correo@defensa.cl (office). *Website:* www.defensa.cl (office); www.jorgeburgos.cl.

BURGUBURU, Jean-Marie, LLM; French lawyer and international organization official; *President, Union Internationale des Avocats;* ed Univ. of Paris, French Inst. for Higher Nat. Defence Studies, French Inst. for Higher Nat. Security Studies; lecturer at Univs of Paris and Bordeaux, in several law schools and at Industrial Property Centre, Univ. of Alicante, Spain; mem. Paris Bar 1966–, Chair. 2004–05, mem. Paris Bar Council 1991–; spent more than 40 years at Gide Loyrette Nouel (int. law firm), Partner 1976–2010; currently Int. Counsel, Debevoise & Plimpton LLP, Paris; Chair. French Nat. Cttee of Union Internationale des Avocats (UIA) 2006–08, First Vice-Pres. UIA 2010–12, Pres. 2012–, Pres. Int. Bar Leaders Senate (UIA consultative body and discussion forum) 2008–; mem. Conseil Nat. des Barreaux (French Law Soc.), Vice-Pres. of its int. comm.; fmr mem. French del. to Council of Bars and Law Socs of Europe, Int. Asscn for Protection of Intellectual Property, Conseil Supérieur de la Propriété Industrielle 1996–2010. *Address:* Union Internationale des Avocats, 25 rue du Jour, 75001 Paris, France (office). *Telephone:* 1-44-88-55-66 (office). *Fax:* 1-44-88-55-77 (office). *E-mail:* uiacentre@uianet.org (office). *Website:* www.uianet.org (office).

BURJANADZE, Nino, JD, PhD; Georgian politician, lawyer and professor of international law; *Chairman, Democratic Movement—United Georgia;* b. 16 July 1964, Kutaisi; d. of Anzor Burjanadze and Tina Morchadze; m. Badri Bitsadze 1960; two s.; ed Akaki Tsereteli School, Kutaisi, Tbilisi State Univ., Moscow Lomonosov State Univ.; Prof. of Int. Relations and Int. Law, Tbilisi State Univ. 1991–; consultant to Ministry of Environmental Protection 1991–92, Parl. Cttee on Foreign Relations 1992–95; mem. Parl. 1995–, Deputy Chair. Cttee on Constitutional Legal Affairs and Rule of Law 1995–98, Chair. 1998–99, Chair. Cttee on Foreign Relations 2000–01, Chair. (Speaker) of Parl. of Georgia 2001–04, 2004–08; Rapporteur, Gen. Cttee on Democracy, Human Rights and Humanitarian Issues, OSCE Parl. Ass. 1998–2000, Vice-Pres. OSCE Parl. Ass. 2000–; Pres. Parl. Ass. of Black Sea Econ. Co-operation 2001–02; fmr mem. Citizens' Union of Georgia, initiated efforts to organize opposition alliance of United Democrats, Nat. Movt and New Rights Party 2003; formed Burjanadze Democrats electoral bloc Aug. 2003; Founder and Chair. Democratic Movement—United Georgia 2008–; Interim Pres. of Georgia Nov. 2003–Jan. 2004, Nov. 2007–Jan. 2008; Chair. Perm. Parl. Del. to UK 1995–98; Co-Chair. EU–Georgian Parl. Co-operation Cttee 1999–2000; Pres. Black Sea Econ. Co-operation Parl. Ass. 2001–02; mem. Young Lawyers Asscn, Int. Justice Asscn, Int. Marine Justice Asscn, US Int. Justice Asscn; participant in numerous int. confs; led protest demonstration in Tbilisi demanding resignation of Pres. Mikheil Saakashvili May 2011. *Publications include:* Legal Problems of International Organisations of a New Type; more than 40 articles on issues related to int. law and int. relations. *Address:* Democratic Movement—United Georgia, 0160 Tbilisi, Abuladze 8, Georgia (office). *Telephone:* (32) 255-03-

77 (office). *Fax:* (32) 255-03-77 (office). *E-mail:* nino.burjanadze64@gmail.com (office); mail@democrats.ge (office). *Website:* www.democrats.ge (office).

BURK, Martha; American psychologist and national organization official; *Chairperson, National Council of Women's Organizations;* ed Univ. of Texas; political psychologist and women's equity expert; fmr Univ. Research Dir, Prof. of Man. and adviser to political campaigns and orgs; Co-Founder and Pres. Center for Advancement of Public Policy, Washington, DC; currently Chair. Nat. Council of Women's Orgs; fmr mem. Comm. for Responsive Democracy, Advisory Cttee of Americans for Workplace Fairness, Sex Equity Caucus of Nat. Asscn for the Educ. of Young Children, Bd Dirs Nat. Org. for Women; mem. Bd Wider Opportunities for Women; Chair. Legislative Task Force for Nat. Cttee on Pay Equity; mem. advisory bd to several other nat. orgs including Univ. of Texas, US Bureau of Indian Affairs, US Dept of Educ., US Dept of State, NSF, Kansas House of Reps Smithsonian Inst., Women's Int. News Gathering Service, Nat. Educ. Asscn, Search for Common Ground and US Information Agency; numerous TV and radio broadcasts and frequent contrib. to major newspapers and magazines on public policy; Ed. Washington Feminist Faxnet. *Address:* National Council of Women's Organizations, 1050 17th Street NW, Suite 250, Washington, DC 20036, USA (office). *Telephone:* (202) 293-4505 (office). *Fax:* (202) 293-4507 (office). *E-mail:* ncworg@aol.com (office). *Website:* www.womensorganizations.org (office).

BURKE, Bernard Flood, PhD; American physicist and astrophysicist; *Professor Emeritus of Astrophysics, Massachusetts Institute of Technology;* b. 7 June 1928, Boston, Mass; s. of Vincent Paul Burke and Clare Aloyse Brine; m. 1st Jane Chapin Pann 1953 (died 1993); three s. one d.; m. 2nd Elizabeth King Platt 1998; ed Massachusetts Inst. of Tech.; mem. of staff, Carnegie Inst. of Washington 1953–65; Chair. Radio Astronomy Section, Carnegie Inst. of Washington, Dept of Terrestrial Magnetism 1962–65; Prof. of Physics, MIT 1965–2000, William Burden Prof. of Astrophysics 1981–2001, Prof. Emer. 2001–; Visiting Prof., Leiden Univ. 1971–72, Manchester Univ. 1992–93; Pres. American Astronomical Soc. 1986–88; Ed. Comments on Astrophysics 1984–87; Trustee Associated Univ. Inc. 1972–90; Trustee and Vice-Chair. NE Radio Observatory Corpn 1973–82, Chair. 1982–95; Oort Lecturer, Leiden Univ. 1993, Karl Jansky Lecturer, Nat. Radio Astronomy Observatory 1998; Visiting Scholar, Carnegie Inst. of Washington 1998; mem. Nat. Science Bd 1990–96; mem. Nat. Acad. of Science, American Acad. of Arts and Sciences; Sr Fellow, Carnegie Inst. of Washington 1997; Fellow, AAAS; Sherman Fairchild Scholar, Calif. Inst. of Tech. 1984–85; Smithsonian Regents Fellow 1985; Helen B. Warner Prize, American Astron. Soc. 1963, Rumford Prize, American Acad. of Arts and Sciences 1971, NASA Achievement Award 1989, 1998, Oort Lecturer, Univ. of Leiden 1997, Karl Jansky Lecturer, Nat. Radio Astronomy Observatory 1997. *Publications:* Microwave Spectroscopy 1953–54, Radio Noise from Jupiter 1955–61, Galactic Structure 1959–, Very Long Baseline Interferometry 1968–, Interstellar Masers 1968–, Gravitational Lenses 1980–, Interferometry in Space 1984–, Introduction to Radio Astronomy (2nd edn) (co-author) 2002; miscellaneous publs in radio astronomy 1955–. *Leisure interests:* skiing, sailing, hiking, chamber music. *Address:* Room 37-641, Massachusetts Institute of Technology, Department of Physics, Cambridge, MA 02139 (office); 34 Bradbury Street, Cambridge, MA, 02138 USA (home). *Telephone:* (617) 253-2572 (office); (617) 354-1209 (home). *Fax:* (617) 253-0861 (office). *E-mail:* bfburke@space.mit .edu (office); bfburke@comcast.net (home).

BURKE, Kathy; British actress and director; b. 13 June 1964, London; ed Anna Scher's Theatre School, London. *Play:* Smaller (dir) 2006. *TV includes:* Harry Enfield's Television Programme 1990–92, Absolutely Fabulous 1992–96, Mr Wroe's Virgins (Royal TV Soc. Award) 1993, Harry Enfield and Chums 1994–97, Common as Muck 1994–97, Tom Jones 1997, Gimme Gimme Gimme 1999–2001, The Catherine Tate Show 2007, Walking and Talking 2012. *Films:* Scrubbers 1983, Nil by Mouth (Best Actress, Cannes Film Festival 1997, Best Actress, British Ind. Film Awards 1998) 1997, Elizabeth 1998, This Year's Love 1999, Love, Honour and Obey 2000, The Martins 2001, Once Upon a Time in the Midlands 2002, Anita and Me 2003, Flushed Away (voice) 2006, Tinker, Tailor, Soldier, Spy 2011. *Theatre includes:* Mr Thomas, London, Bond Bang-a-Bang, London (Dir). *Address:* c/o Hatton McEwan, POB 37385, London, N1 7XF, England.

BURKE, Nazim; Grenadian lawyer and politician; *Minister of Finance;* ed Concordia Univ., Univ. of Windsor, York Univ., Queen's Univ., Canada; Perm. Sec., Ministry of Trade 1979–83; lawyer, Burke, Sealy-Burke (law firm), Toronto 1992–2000; Founding Pnr Ciboney Chambers Law Firm 2000; mem. Grenada House of Reps 2003–; Minister of Finance 2008–, now also Minister of Planning, Economy, Energy and Co-operatives; mem. Nat. Democratic Congress Party, fmr Public Relations Officer. *Address:* Ministry of Finance, Financial Complex, The Carenage, St George's, Grenada (office). *Telephone:* 440-2741 (office). *Fax:* 440-4115 (office). *E-mail:* finance@gov.gd (office). *Website:* finance.gov.gd (office).

BURKE, Philip George, CBE, PhD, FRS, FRAS, FInstP, MRIA; British mathematical physicist and academic; *Professor Emeritus, Queen's University, Belfast;* b. 18 Oct. 1932, London, England; s. of Henry Burke and Frances Mary Burke (née Sprague); m. Valerie Mona Martin 1959; four d.; ed Univ. Coll. of the South West of England, Exeter, Univ. Coll., London; Research Fellow, Univ. Coll. London 1956–57, Lecturer, Computer Unit 1957–59, Fellow 1986–; Research Physicist, Alvarez Bubble Chamber Group and Watson's Theory Group, Lawrence Radiation Lab., Berkeley, Calif. 1959–62; Research Fellow, later Prin. Scientific Officer, then Sr Prin. Scientific Officer, Atomic Energy Research Establishment, Harwell 1962–67; Prof. of Math. Physics, Queen's Univ., Belfast 1967–98, Prof. Emer. 1998–, Head Dept of Applied Math. and Theoretical Physics 1974–77, Dir School of Math. and Physics 1988–90; Chair. Inter-Council High Performance Computing Man. Cttee 1996–98; Head Div. Theory and Computational Science, Science and Eng Research Council, Daresbury Lab., Cheshire 1977–82 (jt appointment with Queen's Univ.); Founding and Prin. Ed., Computer Physics Communications 1969–79, Hon. Ed. 1980–; mem. UK Science and Eng Research Council 1989–94, Chair. Supercomputing Man. Cttee 1991–94; mem. Council Royal Soc. 1990–92; mem. American Physical Soc.; Hon. DSc (Exeter) 1981, (Queens Univ., Belfast) 1999; Inst. of Physics' Guthrie Medal and Prize 1994, Sir David Bates Prize 2000, Will Allis Prize 2012. *Publications:* author or co-author of eight books; more than 350 articles in numerous specialist journals. *Leisure interests:* walking, books, music. *Address:* Brook House, Norley Lane, Crowton, Northwich, Cheshire, CW8 2RR, England (home); Department of Applied Mathematics and Theoretical Physics, David Bates Building, Queen's University, Belfast, BT7 1NN, Northern Ireland (office). *Telephone:* (28) 9097-6034 (office); (1928) 788301 (home). *E-mail:* p.burke@qub.ac.uk (office).

BURKE, HE Cardinal Raymond Leo, BA, MA, STB, MA, STL, STD; American ecclesiastic; *Prefect of the Supreme Tribunal of the Apostolic Signatura;* b. 30 June 1948, Richland Center, Wis.; s. of Thomas Burke and Marie Burke; ed Holy Cross Seminary, La Crosse, Wis., Catholic Univ. of America, Washington, DC (Basselin Scholar), Pontifical Gregorian Univ., Rome; ordained priest, Diocese of La Crosse 1975; served as Asst Rector, Cathedral of St Joseph the Workman, La Crosse; also taught religion at Aquinas High School, La Crosse; Moderator of the Curia and Vice-Chancellor of La Crosse Diocese 1984–89; Bishop of La Crosse 1994–2003; Archbishop of Saint Louis, Mo. 2004–08; apptd first American Defender of the Bond of the Supreme Tribunal of the Apostolic Signatura 1989, mem. Supreme Tribunal of the Apostolic Signatura 2006–, Prefect 2008–13, 2013–; Pres. Comm. for Advocates 2008–; mem. Pontifical Council for Legis. Texts 2008–, Congregation for the Clergy 2008–, Congregation for Bishops 2009–, Congregation for Divine Worship and the Discipline of the Sacraments 2010–, Congregation for the Causes of Saints 2010–; ed Cardinal (Cardinal-Deacon of S. Agata de' Goti) 2010; participated in Papal Conclave 2013; mem. Bd of Trustees, Catholic Univ. of America; Kt Commdr with Star, Order of the Holy Sepulchre 1997; Hon. DHumLitt (Ave Maria Univ.) 2005, (Christendom Coll.) 2007. *Address:* Supremo Tribunale della Segnatura Apostolica, Palazzo della Cancelleria 1, 00186 Rome, Italy (office). *Telephone:* (06) 69887520 (office). *Fax:* (06) 69887553 (office). *Website:* www.vatican.va/roman_curia/tribunals/apost_signat (office).

BURKE, Richard T.; American business executive; *Non-Executive Chairman, UnitedHealth Group;* b. 1944, Raleigh, NC; m. Jude Burke; five c.; ed Georgia State Univ., Univ. of Virginia; f. UnitedHealth Inc. (later UnitedHealth Group), Dir 1977–, Chair. and CEO 1974–88, Chair. (non-exec.) 2006–; CEO Physicians Health Plan of Minnesota (now MEDICA) 1977–87; Owner and CEO Phoenix Coyotes (professional sports franchise of Nat. Hockey League) 1995–2001; Dir First Cash Financial Services Inc. 1993–2009, Meritage Homes Corpn (fmrly Meritage Corpn) 2004–. *Address:* UnitedHealth Group, PO Box 1459, Minneapolis, MN 55440-1459, USA (office). *Telephone:* (952) 936-1300 (office). *Website:* www.unitedhealthgroup .com (office).

BURKE, Stephen B., BA, MBA; American media executive; *CEO, NBCUniversal;* m.; five c.; ed Colgate Univ., Harvard Business School; joined The Walt Disney Co. 1986, helped develop and found The Disney Stores, Pres. and COO Euro Disney SA from 1992, later served as Pres. of ABC Broadcasting; joined Comcast as Pres. of Comcast Cable 1998, led integration of AT&T Broadband with Comcast, COO Comcast Corpn –2011, CEO NBCUniversal 2011–; mem. Bd of Dirs NBCUniversal, Berkshire Hathaway Inc., J.P. Morgan Chase & Co., The Children's Hosp. of Philadelphia. *Address:* NBCUniversal Media LLC, 30 Rockefeller Plaza, New York, NY 10112, USA (office). *Telephone:* (212) 664-4444 (office). *Fax:* (212) 664-4085 (office). *E-mail:* info@nbcuni.com (office). *Website:* www .nbcuni.com (office).

BURKE, Sir Thomas Kerry, Kt, BA; New Zealand politician; b. 24 March 1942, Christchurch; m. 1st Jennifer Shiel (divorced 1984); two s.; m. 2nd Helen Paske 1984 (died 1989); one s.; ed Univ. of Canterbury, Christchurch Teachers' Coll.; general labourer in Auckland 1965–66, Factory del., Auckland Labourers' Union; teacher, Rangiora High School 1967, Chair. Rangiora Post-Primary Teachers' Asscn 1969–71; MP for Rangiora 1972–75, for West Coast 1978–90; teacher, Greymouth High School 1975–78; Minister of Regional Devt and of Employment and Immigration 1984–87; Speaker, New Zealand Parl. 1987–91. *Leisure interests:* skiing, swimming.

BURKE, Tom, CBE, BA, FRSA; British/Irish environmental policy adviser; *Founding Director, E3G;* b. (David Thomas Burke), 5 Jan. 1947, Cork, Ireland; s. of J. V. Burke and Mary Bradley; ed St Boniface's Coll., Plymouth, Univ. of Liverpool; Great George's Community Arts Project 1969–70; Lecturer, Carlett Park Coll., Cheshire 1970, Old Swan Tech. Coll. 1971–73; Local Groups Co-ordinator, Friends of the Earth 1973–75, Exec. Dir 1975–79, Dir of Special Projects 1979–80, Vice-Chair. 1980–81; Policy Adviser, European Environment Bureau 1978–88, mem. Exec. Cttee 1988–91; Sec.-Gen. Bergen 1990 NGO Conf. 1988–90; Dir The Green Alliance 1982–91 (mem. Exec. Cttee 1979–82, 1997–), Sustainability Ltd 1987–89; Sec. Ecological Studies Inst. 1987–92; Special Adviser to Sec. of State for Environment 1991–97; Environmental Policy Adviser, Rio Tinto plc 1996–, BP PLC 1997–2001; mem. Council English Nature 1999–2005; Adviser, Cen. Policy Group, Office of the Deputy Prime Minister 2002–, Sr Adviser to Special Rep. on Climate Change 2005–; Founding Dir E3G, London 2003–; Chair. Review of Environmental Governance in NI 2006–07; Chair. Editorial Advisory Bd ENDS 2005–; Visiting Fellow, Cranfield School of Man. 1990–94; Visiting Prof., Imperial Coll. London 1997–, Univ. Coll. London 2003–; mem. Bd of Dirs Earth Resources Research 1975–87, Waste Man. Advisory Council 1976–80, Packaging Council 1978–82, Exec. Cttee Nat. Council for Voluntary Orgs and Chair. Planning and Environment Group 1984–89, UK Nat. Cttee for European Year of the Environment 1986–88, Council, Royal Soc. for Nature Conservation 1993–97; mem. Council Royal Soc. of Arts 1990–92 (mem. Environment Cttee 1989–96), Overseas Cttee, Save the Children Fund 1992–97, Exec. Bd World Energy Council Comm. 1990–93; Dir (non-exec.) Earth Resources Research 1975–88; Fellow Inst. of Energy; mem. Co-operative Insurance Services Environ Trust Advisory Cttee 1990–92, 1997–2001, OECD High Level Advisory Group on the Environment 1996–98; stood as SDP cand., Gen. Elections 1983, 1987; mem. Council London Sustainable Devt Comm. 2002–06, American Chem. Council Leadership Dialogue (USA) 2003–07; Advisory Bd Center for Environmental Leadership in Business (USA), Council Inst. of Environmental Man.; Patron UK Law Asscn 2008–; Hon. Visiting Fellow, Manchester Business School 1984–86; Hon. Prof., Faculty of Laws, Univ. Coll. London; Royal Humane Soc. Testimonials on Vellum 1966, on Parchment 1968, UNEP Global 500 Laureate 1991. *Publications:* Europe: Environment 1981, Pressure Groups in the Global System (co-author) 1982, Ecology 2000 (co-author) 1984, The Green Capitalists (co-author) 1987, Green Pages (co-author) 1988, Ethics, Environment and the Company (with Julie Hill) 1990, Connecting the Dots 2009. *Leisure interests:* photography, birdwatching. *Address:* E3G, 47 Great Guildford Street, London, SE1 0ES, England (office).

Telephone: (20) 7593-2020 (office). *E-mail:* tom.burke@riotinto.com (office); tom@ tomburke.co.uk. *Website:* www.e3g.org (office); www.tomburke.co.uk.

BURKE, (Ulick) Peter, MA, FRHistS, FBA; British historian and academic; *Professor Emeritus of Cultural History, University of Cambridge;* b. 16 Aug. 1937, Stanmore, London, England; s. of John Burke and Jenny Burke (née Colin); m. 1st Susan Patricia Dell 1972 (divorced 1983); m. 2nd Maria Lucía García Pallares 1989; ed St Ignatius' Coll., Stamford Hill, St John's Coll., Oxford, St Antony's Coll., Oxford; Asst Lecturer, then Lecturer, then Reader in History (later Intellectual History), School of European Studies, Univ. of Sussex 1962–78; Lecturer in History, Univ. of Cambridge 1979–88, Reader in Cultural History 1988–96, Prof. of Cultural History 1996–2004, Prof. Emer. 2004–; Fellow, Emmanuel Coll. Cambridge 1979–; Visiting Prof., Univ. of São Paulo, Brazil 1986, 1987, Nijmegen Univ. 1992–93 and Groningen Univ. 1998–99, The Netherlands, Heidelberg Univ., Germany 2002; Fellow, Wissenschaftskolleg, Berlin 1989–90, Netherlands Inst. for Advanced Study 2005; Hon. PhD (Lund), (Copenhagen), (Bucharest), (Zurich); Erasmus Prize, Academia Europaea 1999. *Publications include:* The Renaissance Sense of the Past 1969, Culture and Society in Renaissance Italy 1972, Venice and Amsterdam 1974, Popular Culture in Early Modern Europe 1978, Sociology and History 1980, Montaigne 1981, Vico 1985, Historical Anthropology of Early Modern Italy 1987, The Renaissance 1987, The French Historical Revolution: The Annales School 1929–1989 1990, The Fabrication of Louis XIV 1992, History and Social Theory 1992, Antwerp: A Metropolis in Europe 1993, The Art of Conversation 1993, The Fortunes of the Courtier 1995, Varieties of Cultural History 1997, The European Renaissance 1998, A Social History of Knowledge 2000, Eyewitnessing 2001, (co-author) A Social History of the Media 2002, Languages and Communities in Early Modern Europe 2004, A Social History of Knowledge Vol. 2 2011. *Leisure interest:* travel. *Address:* Emmanuel College, Cambridge, CB2 3AP (office), 14 Warkworth Street, Cambridge, CB1 1EG, England (home). *Telephone:* (1223) 334272 (home). *Fax:* (1223) 334426 (office). *E-mail:* upb1000@cam.ac.uk (office). *Website:* www.hist.cam.ac.uk (office).

BURKHALTER, Didier Eric; Swiss politician; *President and Head, Federal Department of Foreign Affairs;* b. 17 April 1960, Neuchâtel; m.; three s.; ed Univ. of Neuchâtel; staff mem., Univ. of Neuchâtel 1981–82; Econs Ed., Soc. for Swiss Econ. Devt, Geneva 1984–86; mem. FDP-The Liberals 1985–, Ed. in Chief National (Neuchâtel FDP newspaper) 1985–89, FDP Cantonal Sec. for Neuchâtel 1986–89; mem. Hauterive NE Communal Council 1988–90, Neuchâtel Communal Council 1991–2005 (Pres. 1994, 1998, 2001); mem. Neuchâtel Cantonal Parl. 1990–2001; mem. Nat. Council 2003–07, Council of States 2007–09; mem. Swiss del. to Parl. Ass. of OSCE 2005–09; mem. Fed. Council 2009–, Head of Fed. Dept of Home Affairs 2009–11, of Foreign Affairs 2012–, Vice-Pres., Swiss Confed. 2013, Pres. (Head of State) 2014–. *Leisure interests:* cycling, swimming, football, hiking, travel. *Address:* Federal Department of Foreign Affairs, Bundeshaus West, 3003 Bern, Switzerland (office). *Telephone:* 313222111 (office). *Fax:* 313234001 (office). *E-mail:* info@eda.admin.ch (office). *Website:* www.eda.admin.ch (office).

BURLAND, John Boscawen, CBE, DSc, FRS, FREng, FICE, FIStructE; British scientist, academic and civil engineer; *Professor Emeritus of Soil Mechanics, Imperial College London;* b. 4 March 1936, Little Chalfont, Bucks., England; s. of John Whitmore Burland and Margaret Irene Burland (née Boscawen); m. Gillian Margaret Burland (née Miller) 1963; two s. one d.; ed Parktown Boys' High School, Univ. of the Witwatersrand, Johannesburg, S Africa, Univ. of Cambridge; engineer, Ove Arup and Partners, London 1961–63; Sr Scientific Officer then Prin. Scientific Officer, Bldg Research Station (BRS), Watford 1966–72, Head of Geotechnics Div. 1972–79, Asst Dir, BRS 1979–80; apptd Prof. of Soil Mechanics, Imperial Coll., London 1980, now Prof. Emer.; mem. Italian Prime Minister's Cttee for stabilizing the Leaning Tower of Pisa; Hon. Fellow (Imperial Coll., London, Emmanuel Coll., Cambridge, Cardiff Univ.); Kt Commdr, Royal Order of Francis I, Italy, Commendatore Ordine della Stella di Solidarietà Italiana; Hon. DEng (Heriot-Watt, Glasgow), Hon. DSc (Nottingham, Warwick), Hon. DSc (Eng) (Univ. of Witwatersrand); Kelvin Medal, Baker Medal, Kevin Nash Gold Medal, Gold Medal, Inst. of Structural Engineers, Gold Medal, Inst. of Civil Engineers, Public Promotion of Engineering Medal, Royal Acad. of Engineering. *Publications:* numerous papers on soil mechanics and civil eng. *Leisure interests:* golf, painting, sailing. *Address:* Department of Civil and Environmental Engineering, Imperial College, South Kensington Campus, London, SW7 2AZ, England (office). *Telephone:* (20) 7594-6079 (office). *Fax:* (20) 7594-5934 (office). *E-mail:* j.burland@ imperial.ac.uk (office). *Website:* www.cv.imperial.ac.uk (office).

BURLATSKY, Fedor Mikhailovich, DPhil; Russian journalist, writer and politician; b. 4 Jan. 1927, Kiev; s. of Mikhail Burlatsky and Sofia Burlatsky; m. 1st Seraphyma Burlatsky 1952 (divorced 1974); two s.; m. 2nd Kyra Burlatsky 1974; one d.; ed Tashkent Law Inst.; journalist, Tashkent 1948–50; post grad. at Inst. of State Law, USSR Acad. of Sciences 1950–53; journalist with Kommunist 1953–59; head of section in Cen. Cttee Dept for Liaison with Communist and Workers' Parties of Socialist Countries 1959–65; political observer with Pravda 1965–67; Deputy Dir of USSR Inst. of Sociological studies 1968–72; head of section, USSR Inst. of State and Law (later Chief Scientific Researcher 1990–) and Head of Philosophy Dept, Inst. of Social Science, Cen. Cttee of CPSU 1975–88; Vice-Pres. Soviet Assoc. of Political Science 1976, currently Pres.; USSR People's Deputy 1989–91; Chair. Sub cttee on Humanitarian, Scientific and Cultural Co-operation, Cttee on Foreign Affairs 1989–91; political observer Literaturnaya Gazeta 1983–90, Ed.-in-Chief 1990–91; Chair. of Public Comm. for Int. Co-operation on Humanitarian Problems and Human Rights 1987–90; Dir Public Consultative Council to Chair. of State Duma 1993–96; Chief Scientific Researcher Inst. of State and Law 1992–; Visiting Prof. Heidelberg Univ. 1988, Harvard Univ. 1992, Oxford Univ. 1993; Pres. Euro-Asian Fund for Humanitarian Co-operation 1996–, Int. League for Defence of Culture; Chair., Scientific Council on Politology, Pres. Russian Acad. of Sciences 1995–; Pres. Fund 'International Cultural Co-operation' 2003–, Fund 'Euro-Atlantic State Co-operation' 2003–; mem. Acad. of National Sciences 1993, Acad. of Socio-Political Sciences 1996; Italian Senate Prize 1988. *Publications include:* Mao Zedong (biography) 1976, The Modern State and Politics 1978, The Legend of Machiavelli 1987, New Thinking 1988, Leaders and Advisers 1990, Khrushchev and the First Russian Spring 1992, The End of the Red Empire 1993, Russian Sovereigns–Age of the Reformation 1996. *Leisure interest:* tennis.

Address: Novovagankovsky per. 22, Apt 90, 123022 Moscow, Russia (home). *Telephone:* (495) 291-85-06 (home).

BURLEIGH, A. Peter; American diplomatist and government official; b. 7 March 1942, Los Angeles, Calif.; ed Colgate Univ.; Teaching Fellow, Wharton School, Univ. of Pennsylvania; Deputy Asst Sec. of State, Bureau of Near Eastern and South Asian Affairs 1987–89, Prin. Deputy Asst Sec. of State for Intelligence and Research 1989–91; Co-ordinator Office of Counter-Terrorism 1991–92; Prin. Deputy Asst Sec. of State for Personnel 1992–95; Amb. to Sri Lanka (also accred to the Maldives) 1995–97; Deputy Rep. to UN 1997–99, Chargé de Mission 1998–99; Amb. in Residence and Distinguished Visiting Prof., Univ. of Miami 2004–08; Chargé d'affaires a.i., Embassy in New Delhi 2009, 2011–12; Fulbright Scholar; mem. American Foreign Service Asscn, Kathmandu Valley Preservation Trust, American Acad. of Diplomacy; numerous Dept of State Superior Honor Awards, Sr Foreign Service Presidential Award, Meritorious Service Award, Sec. of State's Distinguished Service Medal 2000, Presidential Distinguished Service Award 2000. *Address:* 2300 Riverlane Terrace, Fort Lauderdale, FL 33312-4762, USA. *Telephone:* (954) 327-2912. *Fax:* (954) 585-6022. *E-mail:* apburl@bellsouth .net.

BURNAT, Emad; Palestinian farmer and documentary filmmaker; m.; four c.; first film experience as cameraman for Israeli producer Guy Davidi on documentary Keywords 2010; film Five Broken Cameras nominated for Acad. Award 2013 (first nomination for a Palestinian). *Film:* Five Broken Cameras (documentary, co-produced with Guy Davidi) (Best Documentary, Jerusalem Film Festival, Sundance Film Festival Directing Award 2013, Int. Emmy Award 2013). *Website:* emadburnat.com (office).

BURNETT, Erin Isabelle, BA; American journalist, news broadcaster and television presenter; *Anchor and Chief Business and Economics Correspondent, CNN Worldwide;* b. 1976, Mardela Springs, Md; ed St Andrew's School, Middletown, Del., Williams Coll., Williamstown, Mass; began career as a financial analyst for Goldman Sachs in investment banking div. 1998; was offered a position at CNN as writer and booker for CNN's Moneyline; moved to Citigroup to serve as Vice-Pres. for Citigroup/CitiMedia, responsible for all anchoring of Citigroup online financial news network; accepted position with Bloomberg Television 2003, anchor of Bloomberg on the Markets and In Focus 2003–05; host of CNBC's Street Signs and co-anchor of Squawk on the Street 2005–11, anchored several documentaries, including India Rising: The New Empire, City of Money and Mystery, The Russian Gamble, On Assignment: Iraq, and Dollars & Danger: Africa, The Final Investment Frontier; contributed to NBC's Today 2001–11, Meet the Press 2008–11, MSNBC's Morning Joe; Anchor and Chief Business and Econs Corresp., CNN Worldwide (div. of Turner Broadcasting System, Inc., a Time Warner Co.) 2011–, anchors weekday general news programme and contributes to CNN's coverage of nat. and int. breaking news events, contributing reporter to CNN.com; mem. Council on Foreign Relations; selected as one of Fortune magazine's Top 40 Under 40 2009. *Television includes:* boardroom adviser, The Apprentice USA (series) 2008–10, co-host, Weekend Today (series) 2010, Too Big to Fail (film) 2011. *Address:* c/o Creative Artists Agency, 2000 Avenue of the Stars, Los Angeles, CA 90067, USA (office); CNN, 1 Time Warner Center, New York, NY 10019, USA (office). *Telephone:* (424) 288-2000 (office). *Fax:* (424) 288-2900 (office). *Website:* www.caa.com (office); edition.cnn.com (office).

BURNETT, Sir Keith, Kt, CBE, BA, DPhil, FRS, DFInstP; British physicist, academic and university administrator; *Vice-Chancellor, University of Sheffield;* b. 1953, Llwynypia, Wales; m. Anne Burnett; one s. one d.; ed Univ. of Oxford; began career as Research Assoc., Jt Inst. for Lab. Astrophysics, Colo, USA; fmr Asst Prof. of Physics, Univ. of Colorado; Physics Lecturer, Imperial Coll., London 1984–87; Lecturer in Physics and Fellow of St John's Coll. Oxford 1987, becoming Chair. of Physics, Univ. of Oxford, Head of Div. of Math., Physical and Life Sciences 2005–07; Vice-Chancellor Univ. of Sheffield 2007–; mem. Universities UK, Yorkshire Univs, Russell Group; Dir Worldwide Univs Network, Sheffield Univ. Enterprises Ltd; Fellow, Inst. of Physics; Inst. of Physics Thomas Young Medal and Prize 1997, Royal Soc. Wolfson Merit Award 2003. *Publications:* Spectral Line Shapes 1983, Ultracold Atoms and Bose-Einstein-Condensation 1996; author or co-author of nearly 200 scientific papers in the fields of atomic, molecular and laser physics. *Leisure interests:* Chinese language and culture. *Address:* Office of the Vice-Chancellor, University of Sheffield, Western Bank, Sheffield, S10 2TN, England (office). *Telephone:* (114) 222-1000 (office). *E-mail:* vc@sheffield.ac.uk (office). *Website:* www.shef.ac.uk/vc (office).

BURNETT, Mark; British television producer; *President, Mark Burnett Productions, Inc.;* b. 17 July 1960, London; m. 1st Dianne J. Valentine (divorced 2003); two s.; m. 2nd Roma Downey 2007; one step-d.; ed ; enlisted in British Army aged 17, Section Commdr in Parachute Regiment, served with 3rd Bn, Parachute Regt (3 PARA) 1978–82, saw action during Falklands War; moved to USA 1982; worked as a security guard in Beverly Hills, Calif. for one year then later worked in an insurance office; rented plot at Venice Beach and sold T-shirts at weekends 1985; joined a French adventure competition Raid Gauloises 1991; bought format rights and brought a similar competition, Eco Challenge, to USA which launched career as TV producer; best known as the producer of Survivor and the creator of The Apprentice; four Emmy Awards and four People's Choice Awards. *Address:* Mark Burnett Productions, Inc., 640 North Sepulveda Blvd, Los Angeles, CA 90049, USA (office). *Telephone:* (310) 903-5400 (office).

BURNHAM, Rt Hon. Andrew Murray (Andy), PC, MA; British politician; *Shadow Secretary of State for Health;* b. 7 Jan. 1970, Aintree, Merseyside, England; m. Marie-France Van Heel 2000; one s. two d.; ed St Aelred's Roman Catholic High School (now St Aelred's Catholic Tech. Coll.), Newton-le-Willows, Fitzwilliam Coll., Cambridge; joined Labour Party aged 14 during miners' strike 1984; researcher for Tessa Jowell MP 1994–97; joined Transport and Gen. Workers' Union 1995; researcher, Nat. Health Service Confed. Aug.–Dec. 1997; Admin. with Football Task Force 1998; Special Adviser to Chris Smith MP, Dept for Culture, Media and Sport 1998–2001; MP (Labour) for Leigh 2001–, mem. Health Select Cttee 2001–03; Parl. Pvt. Sec. to Home Sec. David Blunkett 2003–04, Parl. Under-Sec. of State for Immigration, Citizenship and Nationality 2005–06, Minister of State at Dept of Health 2006–07, Chief Sec. to Treasury 2007–08, Sec. of State for Culture, Media and Sport 2008–09, for Health 2009–10; Shadow Sec. of

State for Health May–Oct. 2010, 2011–, for Educ. Oct. 2010–11; unsuccessful cand. in Labour Party leadership election Sept. 2010; Election Co-ordinator Oct. 2010–11; fmr Hon. Chair. Leigh Rugby League Club. *Leisure interest:* Everton Football Club. *Address:* House of Commons, Westminster, London, SW1A 0AA (office); Leigh Parliamentary Office, 10 Market Street, Leigh, WN7 1DS, England (office). *Telephone:* (20) 7219-8250 (London) (office); (1942) 682353 (Leigh) (office). *E-mail:* andy.burnham.mp@parliament.uk (office). *Website:* www.parliament.uk/ biographies/commons/andy-burnham/1427 (office).

BURNHAM, Christopher Bancroft, BA, MPA; American investment banker and fmr UN official; *Managing Director and Vice-Chairman, Deutsche Asset Management;* b. 1956, New York City; ed Washington & Lee Univ., Harvard Univ., Georgetown Univ. Nat. Security Studies Program; served in US Marine Corps Reserve, veteran of first Gulf War, led one of the first infantry units to reach and liberate Kuwait City in 1991; elected to Conn. House of Reps three times, served as Asst Minority Leader; fmr investment banker with Credit Suisse First Boston and Advest Corp. Finance; Treas. of Conn. 1994; fmr CEO PIMCO's Columbus Circle Investors (asset man. and mutual fund co.), fmr Vice-Chair. PIMCO's mutual fund group; Asst Sec. for Resource Man. and Chief Financial Officer, State Dept 2002–05; UN Under-Sec.-Gen. for Man. 2005–06; Man. Dir and Vice-Chair. Deutsche Asset Man. (DeAM), Deutsche Bank, New York 2006–, Global Co-head DeAM's Climate Change Business 2008–; "Legislator of the Year", Connecticut Children's Coalition 1988, Combat Action Ribbon, Navy Unit Citation, Marine Corps Unit Citation 1991, "Friend of Democracy Award", Connecticut Common Cause for authoring legislation to stop 'Pay to Play' 1995, Outstanding Citizen Award, Greenwich Chambers of Commerce 1996, Nat. Govt Finance Officer's Asscn Award for excellence in financial reporting (first ever awarded to any state treasury) 1996, Individual Excellence Award, New England Asscn of Comptrollers 1997, Asscn of Govt Accountants 'CEAR' Award for excellence in financial reporting (first ever awarded to Dept of State) 2002, 2003, 2004, Presidential Award for Man. Excellence for "Innovative and Exemplary Practices in Budget and Performance Integration" 2004, US Sec. of State's Award for Distinguished Service (highest award in Dept) 2005. *Address:* Deutsche Asset Management, Deutsche Bank, 60 Wall Street, New York, NY 10005, USA (office). *Telephone:* (212) 250-2500 (office). *E-mail:* info@db.com (office). *Website:* www.db.com (office).

BURNHAM, James B., AB, PhD; American economist, banker and academic; *Distinguished Service Professor of Finance, Palumbo Donahue School of Business, Duquesne University;* b. 22 Oct. 1939, New York, NY; s. of James Burnham and Marcia Burnham (née Lightner); m. Anne Mullin 1964; two s. two d.; ed Milton Acad., Princeton Univ., Washington Univ., St Louis; Economist and Special Asst, Federal Reserve Bd, Washington, DC 1969–71; Sr Economist, Mellon Bank, Pittsburgh, Pa 1971–74, Vice-Pres. 1974–81, Sr Vice-Pres. 1985, Office of Govt Affairs 1979–81, Chair. Country Review Cttee 1977–81; Staff Dir and Special Asst to Chair., Pres.'s Council of Econ. Advisors 1981–82; US Exec. Dir IBRD, Washington, DC 1982–85; John M. Olin Visiting Prof., Center for the Study of American Business, Washington Univ., St Louis 1989–90; Prof. of Finance, John F. Donahue Grad. School of Business, Duquesne Univ. 1990–, now Distinguished Service Prof. of Finance, Palumbo Donahue School of Business; mem. American Econs Asscn, Nat. Asscn of Business Economists; Fulbright Scholar, Univ. of São Paulo, Brazil 1962, Murrin Prof. in Global Competitiveness, Fulbright Sr Research Grant (Turkey) 2005. *Publications:* articles on contemporary economic subjects. *Leisure interests:* canoeing, bridge. *Address:* Palumbo Donahue School of Business, Duquesne University, 507 Rockwell Hall, Pittsburgh, PA 15282, USA (office). *Telephone:* (412) 396-5118 (office). *Fax:* (412) 396-1797 (office). *E-mail:* burnham@ duq.edu (office). *Website:* www.duq.edu/academics/schools/business/faculty-and -research/faculty-directory/burnham-phd-james-j (office); www.jamesbburnham .typepad.com.

BURNS, Conrad Ray; American lobbyist and fmr politician; *Senior Advisor, GAGE Business Consulting and Government Affairs;* b. 25 Jan. 1935, Gallatin, Mo.; s. of Russell Burns and Mary Frances Burns (née Knight); m. Phyllis Jean Kuhlmann; one s. one d.; ed Univ. of Missouri; Field Rep. Polled Hereford World magazine, Kansas City 1963–69; Public Relations Officer, Billings Livestock Cttee, Mont. 1969–73; Founding Pres. Ag-Network 1975–86; Farm Dir KULR TV 1974; Commr Yellowstone Co. 1987–89; mem. Republican Party; Senator from Montana 1989–2007, Chair. Appropriations Sub-cttee of Mil. Construction, Cttee on Science and Transportation, Sub-cttee of Cttees, Energy and Natural Resources Cttee, mem. Ageing Cttee, Small Business Cttee; Sr Advisor, GAGE Business Consulting and Government Affairs, Washington C 2007–; mem. Nat. Asscn of Farm Broadcasters. *Leisure interest:* football officiating. *Address:* GAGE Business Consulting and Government Affairs, 122 C Street, NW, Suite 380, Washington, DC 20001, USA (office). *Telephone:* (202) 393-4262 (office). *Fax:* (202) 393-1002 (office). *Website:* www.gage.cc (office).

BURNS, Duncan Thorburn, BSc, MA, PhD, DSc, FICI, CChem, FRSC, FRSE, MRIA; British chemist and academic; *Professor Emeritus of Analytical Chemistry, Queen's University, Belfast;* b. 30 May 1934, Wolverhampton, England; s. of James Thorburn Burns and Olive Mary Constance Burns (née Waugh); m. 1st Valerie Mary Vinton 1961 (divorced 1994); one s. two d.; m. 2nd Celia Mary Thorburn Burns 1994; ed Whitcliffe Mount School, Univ. of Leeds; Asst Lecturer in Physical Chem., Medway Coll. of Tech. 1958–59, Lecturer 1959–63; Sr Lecturer in Analytical Chem., Woolwich Polytechnic 1963–66, Loughborough Univ. 1966–71, Reader 1971–75; Prof. of Analytical Chem., Queen's Univ., Belfast 1975–99, Prof. Emer. 1999–, Sr Research Fellow, School of Chem. 2009–; Redwood Lecturer, Royal Soc. of Chem. 1982, Pres. Analytical Div. 1988–90, Visiting Research Prof. 2012; Visiting Prof., Kasetsart Univ., Bangkok; Fellow, Inst. of Chem. in Ireland, European Chemist; Hon. mem. Pharmaceutical Soc. of NI 2001; numerous awards including Boyle/Higgens Gold Medal, Inst. of Chem. of Ireland 1990, Ehren Nadel in Gold, Analytical Inst. Technische Univ. Wien 1990, AnalaR Gold Medal, Royal Soc. of Chem. 1990, SAC Gold Medal, Royal Soc. of Chem. 1993, Fritz Pregl Medal, Austrian Chemical Soc. 1993, Sigillum Magnum, Univ. of Bologna 1996, Div. of Analytical Chem. (DAC) Tribute, European Asscn for Chemical and Molecular Sciences 2005, Award for Service, Royal Soc. of Chem. 2009. *Publications:* nine books and more than 400 papers. *Leisure interest:* history of chemistry. *Address:* The School of Chemistry, The Queen's University of Belfast, Belfast BT9 5AG (office); 318 Stranmillis Road, Belfast, BT9 5EB, Northern Ireland (home).

Telephone: (28) 9097-5442 (office); (28) 9066-8567 (home). *E-mail:* d.t.burns@qub
.ac.uk (office); profburns@chemistry.fsbusiness.co.uk (home).

BURNS, John Fisher; British journalist; *Chief of Bureau for London, New York
Times;* b. 4 Oct. 1944, Nottingham; s. of Air Cdre R. J. B. Burns and Dorothy Burns
(née Fisher); m. 1st Jane Pequegnat 1972 (divorced); m. 2nd Jane Scott-Long 1991;
two s. one d.; ed Stowe School, McGill Univ., Canada and Harvard Univ., USA;
China correspondent, Globe and Mail, Toronto, Canada; Foreign Corresp., New
York Times 1975–80, Soviet Union 1981–84, China 1984–86, Canada 1987–88,
Afghanistan 1989–90, Persian Gulf 1990, Balkans 1991–94, India 1994–98,
Special Corresp. for Islamic Affairs 1999–2002, Chief of Bureau for Baghdad
2002–07, Chief of Bureau for London 2007–; Chief of Bureau for Pakistan and
Afghanistan, Washington Post 2002; Visiting Fellow, King's College, Cambridge
1998–99; Pulitzer Prize for Int. Reporting 1993 (co-winner for reporting from
Bosnia), 1997 (for coverage of the Taliban regime in Afghanistan); George Polk
Prize for Foreign Correspondence 1978, 1997. *Leisure interests:* golf, music, motor
racing. *Address:* The New York Times, London Bureau, 66 Buckingham Gate,
London SW1E 6AU, England (office). *Telephone:* (20) 7799-5050 (office). *Website:*
www.nytimes.com (office).

BURNS, Kenneth (Ken) Lauren, BA; American film director and film producer;
b. 29 July 1953, Brooklyn, New York; s. of Robert Burns and Lyla Burns; m. 1st
Amy Stechler Burns (divorced); two c.; m. 2nd Julie Deborah Brown 2003; ed Ann
Arbor Pioneer High School, Mich., Hampshire Coll.; Co-founder Florentine Films;
Dr hc (Bowdoin Coll.) 1991, (Amherst Coll.) 1991, (Univ. of New Hampshire),
(Franklin Pierce Coll.), Notre Dame Coll.), (Coll. of St Joseph), (Springfield Coll.),
(Pace Univ.), (Univ. of NC, Chapel Hill). *Films include:* Brooklyn Bridge 1981, The
Shakers: Hands to Work, Hearts to God 1984, The Statue of Liberty 1985, Huey
Long 1985, Thomas Hart Benton (TV) 1988, The Congress (TV)) 1988, The Civil
War (TV miniseries, more than 40 major film and TV awards including two Emmy
Awards, two Grammy Awards, Producer of the Year Award from Producer's Guild,
People's Choice Award, Peabody Award, DuPont-Columbia Award, D.W. Griffiths
Award, Lincoln Prize) 1990, Empire of the Air: The Men Who Made Radio 1991,
Baseball (TV miniseries, numerous awards including Emmy, CINE Golden Eagle
Award, Clarion Award, TV Critics Awards for Outstanding Achievement in Sports
and Special Programming) 1994, The West (producer, Erik Barnouw Prize) 1996,
Thomas Jefferson (TV miniseries) 1997, Lewis & Clark: The Journey of the Corps
of Discovery 1997, Frank Lloyd Wright (Peabody Award) 1998, Not for Ourselves
Alone: The Story of Elizabeth Cady Stanton and Susan B. Anthony (TV miniseries,
Peabody Award) 1999, Jazz (TV miniseries) 2001, Mark Twain (TV, Leon Award
for Best Documentary, St Louis Film Festival) 2001, Horatio's Drive: America's
First Road Trip (TV) 2003, Unforgivable Blackness: The Rise and Fall of Jack
Johnson (three Primetime Emmy Awards) 2004, The War 2007. *Publication:* The
Civil War (with Geoffrey C. Ward), Baseball (with Geoffrey C. Ward), Lewis and
Clarke: The Journey of the Corps of Discovery (with Dayton Duncan), The War
(with Geoffrey C. Ward) 2007. *Address:* Florentine Films, PO Box 613, Walpole,
NH 03608, USA (office). *Telephone:* (603) 756-3038 (office). *Fax:* (603) 756-4389
(office). *Website:* www.florentinefilms.com (office).

BURNS, R. Nicholas, MA; American diplomatist and academic; *Professor of the
Practice of Diplomacy and International Politics, John F. Kennedy School of
Government, Harvard University;* b. 28 Jan. 1956, Buffalo, NY; m. Elizabeth
Baylies; three d.; ed Univ. of Paris, Boston Coll., Johns Hopkins School of
Advanced Int. Studies; before entering Foreign Service worked in US Embassy in
Mauritania and as programme officer for AT Int.; Vice-Consul and Staff Asst to
Amb., Cairo 1983–85; political officer, Consulate-Gen., Jerusalem 1985–87; staff
officer, Operations Center and Secr., Dept of State 1987–88, Special Asst to
Counsellor 1989–90; Adviser to Pres. George Bush on Greece, Turkey and Cyprus
and Dir for Soviet (later Russian) Affairs; Special Asst to Pres. Clinton and Sr Dir
for Russia, Ukraine and Eurasia Affairs; Spokesman, Dept of State and Acting
Asst Sec. for Public Affairs 1995–97; Amb. to Greece 1997–2001; Perm. Rep. to
NATO, Brussels 2001–05; Under-Sec. Of State for Political Affairs 2005–08
(resgnd); currently Prof. of the Practice of Diplomacy and International Politics,
John F. Kennedy School of Govt, Harvard Univ., also Dir Future of Diplomacy
Project and Faculty Chair for Programs on the Middle East and on India and South
Asia, mem. Bd of Dirs Belfer Center for Science and International Affairs; mem.
Council on Foreign Relations, Order of St. John, Int. Inst. for Strategic Studies;
Order of the Terra Mariana (Estonia); Dr hc (Worcester Polytechnic Inst.) 1997;
Superior Honor Award (three times), James Clement Dunn Award for Excellence
1994, Charles E. Cobb Award for Trade Devt by an Amb. 2000, Woodrow Wilson
Award for Distinguished Govt Service (Johns Hopkins Univ.) 2002. *Address:*
Littauer 374, John F. Kennedy School of Government, 79 JFK Street, Cambridge,
MA 02138, USA (office). *Telephone:* (617) 495-2495 (office). *E-mail:*
nicholas_burns@hks.harvard.edu (office). *Website:* belfercenter.ksg.harvard.edu
(office).

BURNS, Sir (Robert) Andrew, Kt, KCMG, MA, FRSA; British diplomatist; *UK
Envoy for Post-Holocaust Issues, Foreign and Commonwealth Office;* b. 21 July
1943, London, England; s. of the late Robert Burns CB, CMG and Mary Burns (née
Goodland); m. Sarah Cadogan 1973; two s. one step-d.; ed Highgate School, Trinity
Coll. Cambridge, School of Oriental and African Studies, Univ. of London; joined
Diplomatic Service 1965, served in New Delhi 1967–71, FCO, London and UK Del.
to CSCE 1971–75, First Sec. and Head of Chancery, Bucharest 1976–78, Pvt. Sec.
to Perm. Under-Sec. and Head of Diplomatic Service, FCO 1979–82, Fellow,
Center for Int. Affairs, Harvard Univ., USA 1982–83, Counsellor (Information)
and Head of British Information Services, Washington, DC and New York
1983–86, Head of S Asian Dept, FCO 1986–88, Head of News Dept 1988–90, Asst
Under-Sec. of State (Asia), FCO 1990–92; Amb. to Israel 1992–95; Deputy Under-
Sec. of State (non-Europe, Trade and Investment Promotion) 1995–97; British
Consul-Gen., Hong Kong Special Admin. Region and Macao 1997–2000; High
Commr to Canada 2000–03; UK Envoy for Post-Holocaust Issues 2010–; Int. Gov.
BBC 2005–06; Dir JP Morgan Chinese Investment Trust 2003–, Aberdeen All Asia
Investment Trust 2008–; Chair. Council, Royal Holloway, Univ. of London
2004–11, Anglo-Israel Asscn 2004–05, 2008–11, Hestercombe Gardens Trust
2005–, Advisory Council British Expertise 2006–10; mem. Cttee of Univ. Chairs
2009–11, British North America Cttee 2004–, Bd Govs Guildhall School of Music
and Drama; Fellow, Portland Trust 2004–; Trustee, Canadian Studies Foundation;

Patron, British Friends of the Abraham Fund Initiatives; Hon. Pres. Canada UK
Colloquia 2003–, China Asscn 2009–. *Publication:* Diplomacy, War and Parliamentary Democracy 1989. *Leisure interests:* music, theatre, Exmoor. *Address:*
Human Rights and Democracy Department, Foreign and Commonwealth Office,
King Charles Street, London, SW1A 2AH, England (office). *Telephone:* (20) 7008-
4340 (home). *E-mail:* andrew.burns@fco.gsi.gov.uk (office). *Website:* www.gov.uk/
government/organisations/foreign-commonwealth-office (office).

BURNS, Stephanie A., PhD; American business executive; *Chairman, President
and CEO, Dow Corning Corporation;* ed Iowa State Univ.; postdoctoral research in
organic chemistry, Université Montpellier, Sciences et Techniques du Languedoc,
France; joined Dow Corning Corpn 1983, Researcher 1983–87, Product Devt Man.
for Electronics Industry 1987–94, Dir of Women's Health 1994–97, Science and
Tech. Dir for Europe, Brussels, Belgium 1997–99, Industry Dir for Life Sciences in
Europe 1999, European Electronics Industry Dir 1999–2000, Exec. Vice-Pres.
2000–03, apptd mem. Bd Dirs 2000, Pres. and COO 2003–04, Pres. and CEO
2004–06, Chair., Pres. and CEO 2006–; mem. Bd of Dirs GlaxoSmithKline plc,
Manpower Inc., Michigan Molecular Inst., Chemical Bank Midland Area, Ameri-
can Chem. Council, Dow Corning/Genencor Int. Partnership, The Conference
Board; mem. Advisory Bd Chemical and Engineering News; mem. Exec. Cttee Soc.
of Chemical Industry; mem. ACS; Trustee Midland Community Center; Michigan
Woman Exec. of the Year 2003, ranked by Forbes magazine amongst 100 Most
Powerful Women (81st) 2004, (82nd) 2005, (84th) 2006, (86th) 2007, (91st) 2009,
Vanguard Award, Chemical Educ. Foundation 2006. *Address:* Dow Corning
Corporation, 2200 West Salzburg Road, Midland, MI 48686, USA (office).
Telephone: (989) 496-4000 (office). *Fax:* (989) 496-4393 (office). *Website:* www
.dowcorning.com (office).

BURNS, Baron (Life Peer), cr. 1998, of Pitshanger in the London Borough of
Ealing; **Terence Burns,** GCB, BAEcon; British economist and business executive;
Chairman, Abbey National plc; b. 13 March 1944, Durham; s. of the late Patrick
Owen Burns and Doris Burns; m. Anne Elizabeth Powell 1969; one s. two d.; ed
Houghton-le-Spring Grammar School and Victoria Univ. of Manchester; held
various research positions at London Business School 1965–70, Lecturer in Econs
1970–74, Sr Lecturer in Econs 1974–79, Dir Centre for Econ. Forecasting 1976–79,
Prof. of Econs 1979; Chief Econ. Adviser to HM Treasury and Head, Govt Econ.
Service 1980–91; Perm. Sec. to Treasury 1991–98; Chair. Inquiry into Hunting
1999; Chair. Financial Services and Markets Jt Cttee 1999, Nat. Lottery Comm.
2000–01, Abbey National plc 2002–, Channel 4 Television Corpn 2009–; Deputy
Chair. Marks & Spencer Group 2005–06, Chair. 2006–08; Dir (non-exec.) Legal
and General Group PLC 1999–2001, Pearson 1999–2010, British Land 2001–05,
Banco Santander 2004–; Vice-Pres. Soc. of Business Economists 1985–99, Pres.
1999–; Fellow, London Business School 1989–; mem. Council Royal Econ. Soc.
1986–91, Vice-Pres. 1992–; Visiting Prof., Durham Univ. 1995–; Gov. RAM 1998–;
Hon. DScS (Manchester) 1992. *Leisure interests:* Dir Queen's Park Rangers
Football team 1996–2001, music and golf. *Address:* Abbey plc, Grupo Santander,
The Causeway, Worthing, West Sussex, BN99 6DA (office); House of Lords,
London, SW1A 0PW, England (office). *E-mail:* burnst@parliament.uk (office).
Website: www.abbey.com (office).

BURNS, Ursula M., MSc (MechEng); American business executive; *Chairman
and CEO, Xerox Corporation;* b. 20 Sept. 1958, New York; m. Lloyd Bean; two c.; ed
Brooklyn Polytechnic Inst. of New York, Columbia Univ., New York; mechanical
eng summer intern, Xerox Corpn in 1980, Exec. Asst to Chair. and CEO 1991–92,
held several positions in eng, including product devt and planning, led several
business teams, including office colour and fax business, office network copying
business and departmental business unit 1992–2000, Sr Vice-Pres. Corp. Strategic
Services 2000–01, Pres. Document Systems and Solutions Group 2001–02, Sr Vice-
Pres. and Pres. Business Group Operations 2002–07, mem. Bd of Dirs 2007–, Pres.
Xerox Corpn 2007–09, CEO 2009–, Chair. 2010–; mem. Bd of Dirs American
Express Corpn, Boston Scientific Corpn, FIRST (For Inspiration and Recognition
of Science and Tech.), Nat. Asscn of Manufacturers, PQ Corpn, Univ. of Rochester,
The Rochester Business Alliance, CASA – The Nat. Center on Addiction and
Substance Abuse at Columbia Univ.; named by Pres. Obama to help lead the White
House nat. programme on STEM (science, tech., eng and math.) 2009–; Vice-Chair.
President's Export Council 2010–; ranked 28th by Fortune magazine amongst the
Most Powerful Black Executives 2002, ranked by Fortune magazine amongst the
50 Most Powerful Women in Business in the US (44th) 2003–04, (48th) 2005, (27th)
2006, (11th) 2007, (tenth) 2008, (ninth) 2009–10, (eighth) 2011, (seventh) 2012,
named by Time/CNN Annual on List of Global Business Influentials 2003, named
by US Black Engineering & Information Technology magazine one of 50 Most
Important African-Americans in Tech. 2003, 2004, ranked by Forbes magazine
amongst The World's 100 Most Powerful Women (55th) 2008, (14th) 2009, (20th)
2010, (27th) 2011, (17th) 2012, (14th) 2013. *Address:* Xerox Corporation, 45 Glover
Avenue, Norwalk, CT 06856-4505, USA (office). *Telephone:* (203) 968-3000 (office).
Website: www.xerox.com (office).

BURNS, William Joseph, BA, MPhil, DPhil; American diplomatist; *Deputy
Secretary of State;* b. 11 April 1956, Fort Bragg, NC; m. Lisa Carty; two d.; ed La
Salle Univ., Univ. of Oxford, UK (Marshall Scholar); entered Foreign Service 1982;
Political Officer, US Embassy, Amman; mem. staff, Bureau of Near E Affairs,
Office of Deputy Sec. of State; Special Asst to the Pres., Sr Dir for Near E and S
Asian Affairs, Nat. Security Council; Acting Dir and Prin. Deputy Dir State Dept's
Policy Planning; Minister-Counsellor for Political Affairs, Moscow; Exec. Sec.,
State Dept and Special Asst to Sec. of State; Amb. to Jordan 1998–2001; Asst Sec.
of State for Near Eastern Affairs 2001–05; Amb. to Russia 2005–08; Under-Sec. of
State for Political Affairs 2008–11, Deputy Sec. of State 2011–; three hon. doctorate
degrees; two Distinguished Honor Awards, James Clement Dunn Award, five
Superior Honor Awards, two Presidential Distinguished Service Awards, named to
TIME Magazine's list of the 50 Most Promising American Leaders Under Age 40
1994, and to TIME's list of 100 Young Global Leaders 1994, Robert C. Frasure
Memorial Award 2005, Charles E. Cobb, Jr Ambassadorial Award for Initiative
and Success in Trade Devt 2006. *Publication:* Economic Aid and American Policy
Toward Egypt, 1955–1981 1985. *Address:* Department of State, 2201 C Street NW,
Washington, DC 20520, USA (office). *Telephone:* (202) 647-4000 (office). *Fax:* (202)
647-6738 (office). *Website:* www.state.gov/p (office).

BURNSTOCK, Geoffrey, PhD, DSc, FRS, FAA, FMedSci; Australian/British scientist and academic; *President, Autonomic Neuroscience Centre, Royal Free and University College Medical School;* b. 10 May 1929, London, England; s. of James Burnstock and Nancy Green; m. Nomi Hirschfeld 1957; three d.; ed London and Melbourne Univs; Nat. Inst. for Medical Research, London 1956–57; Post-Doctoral Fellow, King's Coll., London 1957; Dept of Pharmacology, Univ. of Oxford 1957–59; Dept of Physiology, Illinois Univ. 1959; Sr Lecturer, Dept of Zoology, Melbourne Univ. 1959–62, Reader 1962–64, Prof. and Chair. 1964–75, Assoc. Dean (Biological Sciences) 1969–72, Prof. Emer. 1993–; Visiting Prof., Dept of Pharmacology, Univ. of Calif. 1970; Vice-Dean, Faculty of Medical Sciences, Univ. Coll., London (UCL) 1980–83, Prof. of Anatomy 1975–, Head of Dept of Anatomy and Developmental Biology 1975–97, Convenor, Centre for Neuroscience 1979–, Fellow 1996, Dir Autonomic Neuroscience Inst., Royal Free and Univ. Coll. Medical School, UCL 1997–, now Pres. Autonomic Neuroscience Centre; Contract Prof., Univ. of Siena 1985–87, Univ. of Milan 1993–94; Visiting Prof., Royal Soc. of Medicine Foundation, New York 1988; Chair. Scientific Advisory Bd, Eisai London Ltd 1990–96; Chair. Bd of Clinical Studies, Royal Nat. Orthopaedic Hosp. Trust 1996; Pres. Int. Soc. for Autonomic Neuroscience 1995–2000, Int. Neurovegetative Soc. 1995–, British Assen (Medical), Purine Club 2009–; Founder FMedSci 1998; mem. Academia Europaea 1992; mem. Russian Soc. of Neuropathology 1993; Ed.-in-Chief, Journal of Autonomic Neuroscience, Purinergic Signalling, Open Pharmacology, Neuroscience Journals; mem. Bd of over 30 journals; Fellow, Real Academia Nacional de Farmacia, Spain 2003–; Hon. FRCS; Hon. FRCP; Hon. MRCP 1987; Hon. Fellow, British Pharmacological Soc. 2007; Hon. mem. Australian Physical Soc. 2008; Dr hc (Antwerp) 2002, (J.W. Goethe-Universität) 2007, (Leipzig) 2011; Royal Soc. of Vic. Silver Medal 1970, Special Award, NIH Conf., Bethesda 1989, Royal Medal, Royal Soc. 2000, Janssen Award for Lifetime Achievement 2000, Copernicus Gold Medal 2009, Annual Award, British Neuroscience Assen 2009, Gaddum Memorial Award, British Pharmacological Soc. 2010, The Erasmus Medal, Academia Europaea 2012. *Publications include:* books: Adrenergic Neurons: Their Organisation, Function and Development in the Peripheral Nervous System 1975, An Atlas of the Fine Structure of Muscle and its Innervation 1976; Ed. Purinergic Receptors 1981, Somatic and Autonomic Nerve-Muscle Interactions 1983, Peptides: A Target for New Drug Development 1991, Cardiovascular Biology of Purines 1998; series Ed. The Autonomic Nervous System (Vols 1–14) 1992–97, Neural-Endothelial Interactions in the Control of Local Vascular Tone 1993, Nitric Oxide in Health and Disease 1997, Cardiovascular Biology of Purines 1998; also author of over 1,800 publns in scientific and medical journals and books. *Leisure interests:* wood sculpture, tennis. *Address:* Autonomic Neuroscience Centre, University College Medical School, Royal Free Campus, Rowland Hill Street, London, NW3 2PF, England (office). *Telephone:* (20) 7830-2948 (office). *Fax:* (20) 7830-2949 (office). *E-mail:* g.burnstock@ucl.ac.uk (office). *Website:* www.ucl.ac.uk/ani (office).

BURNYEAT, Myles Fredric, CBE, BA, FBA; British academic; *Emeritus Fellow, All Souls College, University of Oxford;* b. 1 Jan. 1939; s. of Peter James Anthony Burnyeat and Cynthia Cherry Warburg; m. 1st Jane Elizabeth Buckley 1971 (divorced 1982); one s. one d.; m. 2nd Ruth Sophia Padel 1984 (divorced 2000); one d.; m. 3rd Heda Segvic 2002 (died 2003); ed Bryanston School and King's Coll., Cambridge; Russian Interpreter, RN 1959; Asst Lecturer in Philosophy, Univ. Coll., London 1964, Lecturer 1965; Lecturer in Classics, Univ. of Cambridge 1978, Lecturer in Philosophy, Robinson Coll. 1978, Fellow 1978–96, Hon. Fellow 2006–; Laurence Prof. of Ancient Philosophy, Univ. of Cambridge 1984–96, Sr Research Fellow in Philosophy, All Souls Coll., Oxford 1996–06, Emer. Fellow 2006–; Foreign Hon. mem. American Acad. of Arts and Sciences 1992–; Hon. DLitt (St Andrews) 2012. *Publications:* Philosophy As It Is (co-ed.) 1979, Doubt and Dogmatism (co-ed.) 1980, Science and Speculation (co-ed.) 1982, The Sceptical Tradition (ed.) 1983, The Theaetetus of Plato 1990, The Original Sceptics (co-ed.) 1997, A Map of Metaphysics Zeta 2001, Aristotle's Divine Intellect 2008, Explorations in Ancient and Modern Philosophy (two vols) 2012. *Leisure interest:* travel. *Address:* All Souls College, Oxford, OX1 4AL, England (office). *Fax:* (1865) 279299 (office).

BURR, Richard; American politician; *Senator from North Carolina;* m. Brooke Burr; two s.; ed R. J. Reynolds High School, Wake Forest Univ.; family moved to Winston-Salem, NC when he was a young child; various positions with Carswell Distributing 1977–94; elected to US Congress from N Carolina 1994–2005, wrote Food and Drug Admin Modernization Act ('Burr Bill') 1997, Vice-Chair. House Energy and Commerce Cttee 2001, mem. House Select Cttee on Intelligence and Task Force on Terrorism 2001; Senator from N Carolina 2005–; Co-Chair. Partnership for a Drug Free N Carolina; mem. Bd Brenner Children's Hosp., Idealliance; mem. Bd of Visitors, West Point. *Address:* 217 Russell Senate Office Building, Washington, DC 20510, USA (office). *Telephone:* (202) 224-3154 (office). *Fax:* (202) 228-2981 (office). *Website:* burr.senate.gov (office).

BURRELL, Leroy; American athletics coach and fmr professional athlete; b. 21 Feb. 1967, Lansdowne, Philadelphia; m. Michelle Finn (fmr Olympic sprinter); two s.; ed Pen Wood High School, Lansdowne and Univ. of Houston, TX; fmr sprinter and long jumper; set world record, 100m in 9.90 seconds at US Championships, New York June 1991; set another world record 100m of 9.85 seconds July 1994; Olympic gold medal 4×100m relay, Barcelona 1992; Head Coach, Track and Field, Univ. of Houston 1998–.

BURRINGTON, Ernest; British newspaper executive; b. 13 Dec. 1926; s. of the late Harold Burrington and of Laura Burrington; m. Nancy Crossley 1950; one s. one d.; reporter, Oldham Chronicle 1941–44, reporter and sub-ed. 1947–49; mil. service 1945–47; sub-ed. Bristol Evening World 1950; sub-ed. Daily Herald, Manchester 1950, night ed. 1955, London night 1957; night ed. IPC Sun 1964, Asst ed. 1965; Asst ed. and night News Int. Sun 1969; deputy night ed. Daily Mirror 1970; Deputy Ed. Sunday People 1971, Assoc. Ed. 1972; Ed. The People 1985–88, 1989–90; Dir Mirror Group Newspapers 1985–92, Deputy Chair. and Asst Publr 1988–91, Man. Dir 1989–91, Chair. 1991–92; Chair. Syndication Int. 1989–92; Deputy Chair. Mirror Publishing Co. 1989–91; Dir Mirror Group Magazine and Newsday Ltd 1989–92, Legionstyle Ltd 1991–92, Mirror Colour Print Ltd 1991–92; Dir (non-exec.) Sunday Correspondent 1990, The European 1990–91, IQ Newsgraphics 1990–92, Sygma Picture Agency, Paris 1990–91; Deputy Publr Globe Communications, Montreal, Canada 1993–95, Exec. Vice-Pres. and Assoc. Publr

1995–96; Pres. Atlantic Media 1996–98; Consultant Head of Marketing Harveys PLC, UK 1998–2000; mem. Council Nat. Press Assen 1988–92, Int. Press Inst. British Exec. 1988–92; Trustee, Int. Centre for Child Studies 1986–90; Life mem. NUJ 1960–; Hon. Life mem. NUJ 1996; Hon. Red Devil (Manchester United Football Club) 1985. *Leisure interests:* travel, bridge, Manchester United FC. *Address:* 17499 Tiffany Trace Drive, Boca Raton, FL 33487, USA (home); South Hall, Dene Park, Shipbourne Road, Tonbridge, TN11 9NS, England (home). *Telephone:* (561) 995-9897 (USA) (home); (1732) 368517 (England) (home). *Fax:* (561) 995-9897 (USA) (home); (1732) 368517 (England) (home). *E-mail:* burrington@aol.com (home).

BURRIS, Roland Wallace, BA, JD; American attorney, politician and fmr banker; b. 3 Aug. 1937, Centralia, Ill.; s. of Earl L. Burris and Emma M. Burris (née Curry); m. Berlean Miller 1961; one s. one d.; ed Centralia High School, Southern Illinois Univ., Carbondale, Univ. of Hamburg, Germany, Howard Univ., Washington, DC; Nat. Bank Examiner, Office of Comptroller, Currency for US Treasury Dept, Washington, DC 1963–64; called to Ill. Bar 1964; worked at Continental Illinois National Bank and Trust Company 1964–73, positions included tax accountant, tax consultant, commercial banking officer, Vice-Pres.; Dir Dept of Central Management Services, State of Ill. 1973–77, Comptroller 1979–91, Attorney-Gen. 1995–98; Nat. Exec. Dir and COO Operation Push Jan.–Oct. 1977; Man. Partner, Jones Ware & Grenard 1995–98; Of counsel, Buford & Peters LLC (law firm) 1999–2002, Burris, Wright, Slaughter & Tom LLC 2002–07; Sr Counsel, Gonzalez Saggio & Harlan LLP 2007–09; Man. and CEO Burris & Lebed Consulting LLC 2002–09; Senator from Ill. 2009–10 (retd); fmr Adjunct Prof., MPA Program, Southern Illinois Univ. 1995–98; Chair. Ill. Comm. of African-American Males 1992–94; Chair. Nat. Assen of Attorneys Gen. Civil Rights Comm. 1993–95; Chair. Ill. State Justice Comm. 1994–96; Pres., Nat. Assen of State Auditors, Comptrollers and Treasurers 1981–82; Founder and Pres. Nat. Forum on State Leaders 1982–; Trustee, Govt Finance Officers Assen of US and Canada 1987–91; Trustee, Financial Accounting Foundation Bd 1991–94; served three years on Exec. Bd as Trustee, Govt Finance Office of US and Canada; fmr Vice-Chair. Cttee on Illinois Govt; fmr mem. of Bd Ill. Criminal Justice Authority, Law Enforcement Foundation of Ill., Ill. Supreme Court Cttee for Civil Jury Instructions, mem. Nat. Center for Responsible Gaming 1996–2005, Auditorium Theater of Chicago 2001–06, Better Business Bureau 2008; mem. ABA, Ill. Bar Assen, Cook Co. Bar Assen (Public Service Award 1975), Chicago Bar Assen, Nat. Assen for Advancement of Colored People (Pres.'s Award 1991), Howard Univ. Law School Alumni Assen, Southern Illinois Univ. Alumni Assen, Southern Illinois Univ. Foundation, Mental Health Assen of Greater Chicago, US Jaycees, Chicago Area Council of Boy Scouts of America; Hon. LLD (Nat. Louis Univ., Evanston, Ill., Tougaloo Coll., Miss.); Distinguished Service Award, Chicago South End Jaycees 1968, named as one of The Ten Outstanding Young Men of Chicago 1970, 1972, 1,000 Successful Black Men of America, Fortune magazine 1973, Blackbook's Outstanding Business Man of Year 1974, Community Service Award, Operation Push 1975, 100 Most Influential Black Americans, Ebony Magazine 1979–95, named Man of the Year, Goodwill Industries 1980, Outstanding Alumnus Award, Howard Univ. Law School Alumni Assen 1980, 1989, Donald L. Scantlebury Memorial Award for State Leadership 1982, Award of Financial Reporting Achievement, Govt Finance Officers Assen (USA and Canada) 1985, Three Outstanding Financial Officers, Crain's Chicago Business 1986, Distinguished Public Service Award, B'nai B'rith 1988, One of the Top Three Govt Financial Officers in the Nation, City and State Magazine 1989, State Auditors, Comptrollers, & Treasurers Service Award, Govt Finance Officers Assen 1990, Outstanding Black Manitoba, 21st Century Comm. of African American Males 1991, Defender of Justice Award, Nat. Center for Juvenile Justice 1991, Peace & Justice Award, Kappa Alpha Psi 1991, Distinguished Accomplishments in the Field of Law, Nat. Bar Assen 1993, Distinguished Service Award for Excellence in Crime Prevention, Chicagoland Chamber of Commerce 1993, Ten Most Distinguished Alumni in the History of the University Wall of Fame, Southern Illinois Univ., Carbondale 1997, Hall of Fame, Centralia, Ill., Centralia High School Alumni Assen Award 2008. *Address:* Burris & Lebed Consulting, LLC, 35 East Wacker Drive, Suite #500, Chicago, IL 60601-2105, USA (office). *Telephone:* (312) 566-0202 (office). *Fax:* (312) 566-0041 (office).

BURROW, Sharan Leslie, BA; Australian international trade union official; *General Secretary, International Trade Union Confederation;* b. (Sharan Leslie Murphy), 27 May 1954, Warren, NSW; ed Univ. of New South Wales, Charles Sturt Univ.; became an organizer for NSW Teachers' Fed., Bathurst; Pres. Bathurst Trades and Labour Council 1980s; fmr Sr Vice-Pres. NSW Teachers' Fed.; fmr mem. Bd Curriculum Corpn; Vice-Pres. Education International 1995–2000; Pres. Australian Educ. Union 1993–2000; Pres. Australian Council of Trade Unions (second woman) 2000–10; Pres. (first woman) Int. Confed. of Free Trade Unions (ICFTU) Asia Pacific Region Org. 2000–04, Pres. ICFTU (first woman) 2004–06, Pres. Int. Trade Union Confed. (ITUC) 2006–10, Gen. Sec. 2010–; mem. Governing Body of ILO (chaired Workers' Group of Sub-cttee on Multinational Enterprises), Stakeholder Council of Global Reporting Initiative. *Address:* International Trade Union Confederation, Blvd du Roi Albert II 5, Bte 1, 1210 Brussels, Belgium (office). *Telephone:* (2) 224-02-11 (office). *Fax:* (2) 201-58-15 (office). *E-mail:* sharan .burrow@ituc-csi.org (office). *Website:* www.ituc-csi.org (office).

BURROWS, (James) Stuart, OBE, DMus; British singer (tenor); b. 7 Feb. 1933, Cilfynydd, Pontypridd, South Wales; s. of Albert Burrows and Gladys Irene Burrows (née Powell); m. Enid Lewis; one s. one d.; ed Trinity Coll., Carmarthen; sang in concerts at first; stage debut with Welsh Nat. Opera as Ismaele in Nabucco 1963; school teacher until debut at Royal Opera House, Covent Garden 1967; sang Don Ottavio in Don Giovanni, Jenek in Bartered Bride, Ernesto in Don Pasquale, Rodolfo in Bohème, Oedipus Rex with Stravinsky in Athens 1965; Covent Garden from 1967 as Beppe in Pagliacci, Tamino in Magic Flute, Ottavio in Don Giovanni, Fenton in Falstaff, Elvino in La Sonnambula, Lensky in Onegin, Ernesto in Don Pasquale, Alfredo in Don Pasquale, Pinkerton in Butterfly, Alfredo in Traviata, Idomeneo, Titus in La Clemenza di Tito, Faust; USA from 1967 as Tamino, Lensky, Pinkerton, Ottavio, Des Grieux; Vienna Staatsoper in 1970 as Tamino and Ottavio, Faust, Pinkerton, Salzburg Festival from 1970 in Mozart roles; Metropolitan Opera from 1971 as Ottavio, Tamino, Pinkerton, Faust, Alfredo and Belmonte; Paris Opéra, 1975 as Ottavio, Belmonte; a leading lyric tenor and has sung in world's major opera houses, including San Francisco, Vienna, Paris, Buenos Aires

(Théâtre Cologne) and Brussels (Théâtre de la Monnaie) as well as Covent Garden and Metropolitan Opera, New York; toured Far East with Royal Opera 1979 and sang with co. at Olympic Festival, Los Angeles 1984; four US tours with Metropolitan Opera; appearances at Aix-en-Provence and Orange Festivals, and at Hamburg, Geneva, Houston (Des Grieux), Santa Fe (Tamino, Alfredo) and Boston; sang Mozart's Titus at Brussels 1982, Covent Garden 1989, Mozart's Basilio at Aix 1991; concert appearances throughout Europe and N America, under Solti, Barenboim, Mehta, Ozawa, Bernstein and Ormandy, including two recitals in Brahmssaal, Vienna; numerous concert appearances in music by Bach and Handel; numerous TV and radio broadcasts; in demand as an adjudicator and singing teacher and for masterclasses; Hon. Freedom of the Borough, Rhondda Cynon Taff, South Wales 2008; Hon. DMus (Wales) 1981; Dr hc (Carmarthen) 1989, (Univ. Coll. of Wales, Aberystwyth) 1992; Blue Riband, National Eisteddfod of Wales 1959, Fellowships from Aberystwyth and Cardiff Univs and Trinity Coll., Camarthen, The Stuart Burrows Int. Voice Competition set up in his honour 2006. *Television:* Stuart Burrows Sings (BBC series) 1978–85, BBC TV films of Faust, La Bohème and Rigoletto. *Recordings include:* Die Zauberflöte, Don Giovanni, Die Entführung aus dem Serail, La Clemenza di Tito, La Damnation de Faust, Les Contes d'Hoffmann, Maria Stuarda, Anna Bolena, Eugene Onegin, The Midsummer Marriage, Messiah, Grande Messe des Morts (Berlioz), Les Nuits d'Eté, Das Klagende Lied, Beethoven's 9th (Choral) Symphony and single discs of Mozart arias, Operetta Favourites, German and French songs, popular ballads and Welsh songs, including The Stuart Burrows Edition 2006. *Leisure interests:* breeding koi carp, gardening, snooker, listening to music. *Address:* 29 Blackwater Grove, Alderholt, Fordingbridge, SP6 3AD, England (office). *E-mail:* stuartburrows@ nicholls.f9.co.uk (office); meryl@nicholls.f9.co.uk (office). *Website:* www .stuartburrows.f9.co.uk (office).

BURROWS, Richard; Irish business executive and banker; *Chairman, British American Tobacco plc;* b. 16 Jan. 1946, Dublin; m.; four c.; began career as chartered accountant; joined Irish Distillers 1971, Man. Dir Old Bushmills Distillery 1972–76, Gen. Man. Irish Distillers 1976–78, CEO 1978–91, Chair. and CEO Irish Distillers (acquired by Pernod Ricard SA 1988) 1978–2000, Dir-Gen. Pernod Ricard SA 2000, Co-CEO 2000–05, mem. Bd of Dirs 2004–; apptd to Court of Bank of Ireland 2000, Deputy Gov. 2002–05, Sr Ind. Dir 2003–09, Gov. 2005–09 (resgnd); Dir (non-exec.) British American Tobacco plc, London Sept. 2009–, Chair. Nov. 2009–; Dir Cityjet Ltd 2007–; Dir (non-exec.) Rentokil Initial, Carlsberg; Chair. Nat. Devt Corpn 1984–88, Scotch Whisky Asscn 2006–07; Pres. Irish Business and Employers Confed. 1998–2000; mem. Trilateral Comm.; Royal Dublin Soc. Gold Medal Award for Excellence in Industry 2005. *Leisure interests:* sailing, watching rugby. *Address:* British American Tobacco plc, Globe House, 4 Temple Place, London, WC2R 2PG, England (office). *Telephone:* (20) 7845-1000 (office). *Fax:* (20) 7845-2118 (office). *Website:* www.bat.com (office).

BURSÍK, Martin, RNDr; Czech politician; *Deputy Prime Minister and Minister for the Environment;* b. 12 Aug. 1959, Prague; ed Faculty of Natural Sciences, Charles Univ., Prague; signatory of civic initiative 'Civil Liberty Movement' 1989; involved in Civic Forum from outset, mem. and subsequently Deputy Chair. following split in party; switched to Free Democrats (Svobodní Demokraté) –2003; Chair. Environmental Protection Cttee, Prague City Ass. 1994–98, specialized in waste man. and transport, mem. Environment Protection Cttee 1998–2002; unsuccessful cand. for Mayor of Prague; later joined Christian and Democratic Union – Czechoslovak People's Party (KDU-ČSL); Minister for the Environment 1998; consultant in field of energy and environmental protection 1998–2005; external energy and environment adviser to Minister for the Environment 2002–05; mem. Strana zelených (Czech Green Party) 2004–, Chair. 2005–; mem. Parl. (Green Party) 2006–; Deputy Prime Minister and Minister for the Environment 2007–; Dir Ecoconsulting s.r.o. *Address:* Ministry of the Environment, Vršovická 65, 100 10 Prague 10, USA (office). *Telephone:* (267) 121111 (office). *Fax:* (267) 310308 (office). *E-mail:* posta@mzp.cz (office). *Website:* www.env.cz (office).

BURSON, Harold, BA; American public relations executive and consultant; *Chairman, Burson-Marsteller;* b. 15 Feb. 1921, Memphis; s. of Maurice Burson and Esther Burson; m. Bette Foster 1947; two s.; ed Univ. of Miss.; Acting Dir Ole Miss News Bureau 1938–40; reporter Memphis Commercial Appeal 1940; Asst to Pres. and Public Relations Dir, H. K. Ferguson Co. 1941–43; operated own public relations firm for six years; Chair. Burson-Marsteller 1953–, CEO 1953–88; Public Relations Adviser to Pres. Reagan 1989–94; Dir World Environmental Center 1998–; Exec. Vice-Pres. Young and Rubicam Inc., mem. Exec. Cttee 1979–85; Garrett Lecturer on Social Responsibility, Columbia Univ., Grad. School of Business 1973; Exec.-in-Residence, Univ. of Ky Coll. Comm. 2000; Visiting Prof., Leeds Univ. 2001; Vice-Pres. and mem. Exec. Cttee, Nat. Safety Council 1964–77; Int. Trustee World Wildlife Fund 1977–81; Trustee and mem. Exec. Cttee Foundation for Public Relations Research and Educ. 1978–84; Founder and Sec. Corporate Fund, John F. Kennedy Centre for the Performing Arts 1977; Dir Kennedy Cen. Productions Inc. 1974–89; presidential appointee to Fine Arts Comm. 1981–85, to Exec. Cttee Young Astronauts Co. 1984–88; mem. Advisory Cttee, Medill School of Journalism, Northwestern Univ. 1985, Grad. School of Business, Emory Univ. 1986; mem. Public Relations Soc. of America, Int. Public Relations Asscn of Business Communicators, Overseas Press Club, NY Soc. of Security Analysts, Exec. Cttee, Catalyst Inc. 1977–88, Public Relations Advisory Cttee, US Information Agency 1981; assoc. mem. NY Acad. of Medicine; Counsellor, Nat. Press Foundation; Trustee The Economic Club of NY, Ray Simon Inst. of Public Relations, Syracuse Univ. 1985; Chair. Jt Council on Econ. Educ., Public Relations Seminar 1983; Hon. Prof. Fudan Univ., Shanghai 1999; Hon. DHumLitt (Boston Univ.) 1988; Public Relations Professional of the Year Award (Public Relations News) 1977, Gold Anvil Award (Public Relations Soc. of America) 1980, Univ. of Miss. Alumni Hall of Fame 1980, Silver Em Award (Miss. Press Asscn) 1982, Arthur Page Award, Univ. of Tex. 1986, Horatio Alger Award 1986, Nat. Public Relations Achievement Award, (Ball State Univ.), Inside PR Life Achievement Award 1993. *Publications include:* The Making of Burson-Marsteller 2004. *Leisure interests:* stamp collection, West Highland White terriers. *Address:* Burson-Marsteller, 230 Park Avenue South, New York, NY 10003-1513, USA. *Telephone:* (212) 614-4444 (office). *Fax:* (212) 598-5679 (office). *E-mail:* harold_burson@nyc.bm.com (office). *Website:* www.bm.com.

BURSTYN, Ellen; American actress; b. (Edna Rae Gillooly), 7 Dec. 1932, Detroit, Mich.; d. of John Austin and Coriene Marie Gillooly (née Hamel); m. 1st William C. Alexander 1950 (divorced 1957); m. 2nd Paul Roberts 1958 (divorced 1962); m. 3rd Neil Burstyn 1964 (divorced 1972); one s. and one adopted s.; ed Cass Tech. High School, Detroit, study acting with Lee Strasberg at The Actor's Studio, New York; had several jobs before becoming an actress; went to Texas to model and then to New York as a showgirl on The Jackie Gleason Show 1952; worked as a nightclub dancer in Montreal; Broadway debut in Fair Game 1957; appeared on TV series The Doctors 1963; gained notice for her role in Goodbye Charlie 1964; cast as female lead in The Last Picture Show 1971; Co-Artistic Dir The Actor's Studio 1982–88; Pres. Actors' Equity Asscn (first woman) 1982–85; Dir Judgement (off Broadway) 1981, Into Thin Air 1985; mem. jury, Berlin Int. Film Festival 1977 (Co-head of jury 1988), Cannes Film Festival 1981; ordained minister; chosen by People Magazine as one of the 50 Most Beautiful People in the World 2001, Lifetime Achievement Award in Acting, Savannah Film Festival 2005, Career Achievement in Acting Award, the Hamptons Film Festival 2006, became the 20th person (and one of only 12 actresses) to have won the Triple Crown of Acting (Academy Award 1975, Tony Award 1975, Emmy Award 2009) 2009. *Stage productions include:* Fair Game 1957, Same Time Next Year 1975, 84 Charing Cross Road, Shirley Valentine 1989–90. *Films:* as Ellen McRae: For Those Who Think Young 1964, Goodbye Charlie 1964, Pit Stop 1969; as Ellen Burstyn: Tropic of Cancer (uncredited) 1970, Alex in Wonderland 1970, The Last Picture Show (Best Supporting Actress, New York Film Critics' Award, Nat. Soc. of Film Critics' Award) 1971, The King of Marvin Gardens 1972, The Exorcist 1973, Harry and Tonto 1974, Alice Doesn't Live Here Anymore (Best Actress, Acad. Awards, British Acad. Awards) 1974, Providence 1977, A Dream of Passion 1978, Same Time, Next Year 1978, Resurrection 1980, Silence of the North 1981, The Ambassador 1984, Twice in a Lifetime 1985, Hanna's War 1988, Dying Young 1991, Grand Isle 1991, The Cemetery Club 1993, The Color of Evening 1994, When a Man Loves a Woman 1994, Roommates 1995, The Baby-Sitters Club 1995, How to Make an American Quilt 1995, Cross the Line 1996, The Spitfire Grill 1996, Liar 1997, Playing by Heart 1998, The Yards 1999, You Can Thank Me Later 1999, Walking Across Egypt 1999, Requiem for a Dream 2000, Distance (short) (voice over) 2001, Divine Secrets of the Ya-Ya Sisterhood 2002, Red Dragon 2002 (voice) (uncredited), Cross the Line 2005, The Wicker Man 2006, The Fountain 2006, 30 Days 2006, Charlotte's Web 2006, The Elephant King 2006, The Stone Angel 2007, Lovely, Still 2008, The Loss of a Teardrop Diamond 2008, W. 2008, The Velveteen Rabbit 2009, Greta 2009, The Mighty Macs 2009, Main Street 2010, Another Happy Day 2011, Some Day This Pain Will Be Useful to You 2011. *Television films:* Thursday's Game 1974, The People vs. Jean Harris 1981, Surviving 1985, Into Thin Air 1985, Act of Vengeance 1986, Something in Common 1986, Pack of Lies 1987, Look Away 1987, When You Remember Me 1990, Mrs. Lambert Remembers Love 1991, Taking Back My Life: The Nancy Ziegenmeyer Story 1992, Shattered Trust: The Shari Karney Story 1993, Getting Out 1994, Getting Gotti 1994, Primal Secrets 1994, My Brother's Keeper 1995, Follow the River 1995, Our Son, the Matchmaker 1996, Timepiece 1996, A Deadly Vision 1997, Flash 1997, The Patron Saint of Liars 1998, Night Ride Home 1999, Mermaid 2000, Dodson's Journey 2001, Within These Walls 2001, Brush with Fate 2003, The Madam's Family: The Truth About the Canal Street Brothel 2004, The Five People You Meet in Heaven 2004, Our Fathers 2005, Mrs. Harris 2005, Mitch Albom's For One More Day 2007, Possible Side Effects 2009. *Television series:* as Ellen McRae: Kraft Television Theatre 1958, The Christmas Tree 1958, Westinghouse Desilu Playhouse 1960, The DuPont Show of the Month 1960, Michael Shayne 1961, Letter to Loretta 1961, Surfside 6 1961, The Dick Powell Show 1961, Dr. Kildare 1961, Cheyenne 1961, Bus Stop 1962, The Detectives 1962, Checkmate 1962, Kraft Mystery Theater 1962, Ben Casey 1962, I'm Dickens, He's Fenster 1962, The Many Loves of Dobie Gillis 1962, Perry Mason 1962, The Real McCoys 1962, Gun Law 1962, Laramie 1963, 77 Sunset Strip 1961–63, The Defenders 1963, Going My Way 1963, Wagon Train 1963, The Big Brain 1963, Kraft Suspense Theatre 1964, Theatre of Stars 1964, The Greatest Show on Earth 1964, The Doctors 1964–65, For the People 1965, The Time Tunnel 1966, The Big Valley 1967, Iron Horse 1967–68, Insight 1968, The Virginian 1969; as Ellen Burstyn: Gun Law 1971, The Bold Ones: The Lawyers 1972, The Ellen Burstyn Show 1986–87, A Will of Their Own (mini-series) 1998, That's Life 2000–02, The Book of Daniel 2006, Law & Order: Special Victims Unit 2008, Big Love 2007–11, Political Animals 2012. *Address:* c/o Creative Artists Agency, 2000 Avenue of the Stars, Los Angeles, CA 90067, USA. *Telephone:* (424) 288-2000. *Fax:* (424) 288-2900. *Website:* www.caa.com.

BURT, Sir Peter Alexander, Kt, MA, MBA, FCIBS, FRSE; British business executive; *Chairman, Promethean Investments plc;* b. 6 March 1944; s. of Robert W. Burt and May H. Rodger; m. Alison Mackintosh Turner 1971; three s.; ed Merchiston Castle School, Edin., Univs of St Andrews and Pennsylvania; joined Hewlett Packard, Calif., USA 1968–70; worked for CSL, Edin. 1970–74, then Edward Bates & Sons Ltd 1974; moved to Bank of Scotland 1975, Int. Div. 1975–88 (Head 1985), Asst Gen. Man. 1979–84, Divisional Gen. Man. 1984–85, Jt Gen. Man. 1985–88, Treas. and Chief Gen. Man. 1988–96, mem. Bd of Dirs 1995–03, Chief Exec. 1996–2001, Gov. 2001–03; Exec. Deputy Chair. HBOS (formed after merger of Halifax PLC with Bank of Scotland) 2001–03; Chair. Gleacher Shacklock LLP (investment bank) 2003–08, Promethean Investments plc 2005–; Chair. (non-exec.) ITV PLC (formed by merger of Carlton Communications and Granada) 2004–07; Dir Shell Transport and Trading 2002–04, Royal Dutch Shell 2004–06, Templeton Emerging Markets Investment Trust plc 2004–; mem. High Constables and Guard of Honour Holyrood House, Edin. *Leisure interests:* golf, skiing, gardening, reading. *Address:* Auldhame House, Auldhame, North Berwick, EH39 5PW, England (home). *Telephone:* (1620) 893375 (home). *Fax:* (1620) 893375 (home). *Website:* www.prometheaninvestments.com.

BURT, Robert Amsterdam, MA, JD; American lawyer and academic; *Alexander M. Bickel Professor of Law, Yale University;* b. 3 Feb. 1939, Philadelphia, Pa; s. of Samuel Mathew Burt and Esther Amsterdam Burt; m. Linda Gordon Rose 1964; two d.; ed Princeton, Oxford and Yale Univs; Law Clerk, US Court of Appeals, Dist of Columbia Circuit 1964–65; Asst Gen. Counsel, Exec. Office of the Pres. of USA 1965–66; Legis. Asst, US Senate 1966–68; Assoc. Prof. of Law, Chicago Univ. 1968–70; Assoc. Prof. of Law, Univ. of Michigan 1970–72, Prof. of Law 1972–73, Prof. of Law and Prof. of Law in Psychiatry 1973–76; Prof. of Law, Yale Univ. 1976–, Southmayd Prof. of Law 1982–93, Alexander M. Bickel Prof. 1993–; Special

Master US Dist Court, Conn. 1987–92; Rockefeller Fellowship in Humanities 1976; mem. Bd of Dirs, Benhaven School for Autistic Persons 1977–, Chair. 1983–96, Mental Health Law Project 1985–, Chair. 1990–2000; Dir Yale Hillel Foundation 1996–; mem. Inst. of Medicine and NAS 1976, Advisory Bd Open Soc. Inst. Project on Death in America 1993–2004; John Simon Guggenheim Fellowship 1997. *Publications:* Taking Care of Strangers: The Rule of Law in Doctor-Patient Relations 1979, Two Jewish Justices: Outcasts in the Promised Land 1987, The Constitution in Conflict 1992, Death is That Man Taking Names 2002. *Leisure interests:* cello, swimming, bicycling. *Address:* Yale Law School, PO Box 208215, 127 Wall Street, New Haven, CT 06520 (office); 66 Dogwood Circle, Woodbridge, CT 06525, USA (home). *Telephone:* (203) 432-4960 (office); (203) 393-3881 (home). *Fax:* (203) 432-4982 (office); (203) 393-1292 (home). *E-mail:* robert.burt@yale.edu (office). *Website:* www.law.yale.edu (office).

BURTON, Ian, (Burtoni), MA, PhD, FRSC; Canadian/British environmental scientist, geographer, scholar and consultant; *Scientist Emeritus, Meteorological Service of Canada;* b. 24 June 1935, Derby, England; s. of Frank Burton and Elsie Victoria Barnes; m. 1st Lydia Demodoff 1962 (divorced 1977); one s. one d.; m. 2nd Anne V. T. Whyte 1977 (divorced 1995); one s. two d.; m. 3rd Elizabeth May; one d.; ed Derby School, Univ. of Birmingham, Univ. of Chicago and Oberlin Coll. Ohio; Lecturer, Indiana Univ. 1960–61, Queen's Univ., Kingston, Ont. 1961; Consultant, Ford Foundation, India 1964–66; Prof., Univ. of Toronto 1968–90, Adjunct Prof. 1990–, Dir Inst. for Environmental Studies 1979–84, now Prof. Emer.; Prof. of Environmental Science, Univ. of East Anglia, UK 1972–73; Sr Adviser, Int. Devt Research Centre, Ottawa 1972–75; Sr Connaught Fellow, École des Hautes Études en Sciences Sociales, Paris 1984–86; Dir Int. Fed. of Insts for Advanced Study 1986–92; Dir Environmental Adaptation Research, Atmospheric Environmental Service, Meteorological Service of Canada 1990–96, Scientist Emer. 1996–; mem. Bd of Dirs Foundation for Int. Training 1994–; mem. Ind. World Comm. on the Oceans 1995–98; mem. Int. Soc. of Biometeorology, Vice-Pres. 1996–2002, Pres. 2002–05; numerous cttee and consultant assignments with UNESCO, WHO, UNEP, Rockefeller Foundation, UNDP, World Bank Global Environment Facility, World Resources Inst., Intergovernmental Panel on Climate Change, European Comm., Ford Foundation, projects in Sudan and Nigeria etc.; mem. Jury, St Francis Environment Prize; Fellow, TWAS—the acad. of sciences for the developing world; Order of Zvonkova (USSR) 1968; Burtoni Award 2003. *Publications:* co-author: The Human Ecology of Coastal Flood Hazard in Megalopolis 1968, The Hazardousness of a Place: A Regional Ecology of Damaging Events 1971, The Environment as Hazard 1978; co-ed.: Readings in Resource Management and Conservation 1986, Environmental Risk Assessment 1980, Living with Risk 1982, Geography, Resources and Environment 1986, Climate Change and Adaptation 2007. *Leisure interests:* swimming, hiking, cricket. *Address:* Meteorological Service of Canada, 4905 Dufferin Street, Downsview, ON M3H 5T4 (office); 26 St Anne's Road, Toronto, ON M6J 2C1, Canada (home). *Telephone:* (416) 739-4314 (office); (416) 538-2034 (home). *Fax:* (416) 739-4297 (office). *E-mail:* ian.burton@ec .gc.ca (office); burtoni.ian@gmail.com (home). *Website:* www.msc-smc.ec.gc.ca (office).

BURTON, Hon. Mark; New Zealand politician; b. 16 Jan. 1956, Northampton, England; m. Carol Burton; two s. one d.; ed Wanganui Boys' Coll., Univ. of Waikato, Massey Univ., NZ Council of Recreation and Sport; began career in community and social work, adult educ. and recreation; fmr employee Red Cross, Dept of Social Welfare, Palmerston North City Council; fmr Community Educ. Organiser, Cen. N Island; MP for Tongariro 1993–96, for Taupo 1996–; Sr Labour Party Whip 1996–99; Minister of Defence, State-Owned Enterprises and Tourism 1999–2005, also Minister of Internal Affairs and Veterans' Affairs 1999–2002; Deputy Leader of the House 1999–2007; Minister Responsible for Fire Service Comm. 2004–05; Minister of Justice and of Local Govt and in Charge of Treaty of Waitanagi Negotiations and Minister Responsible for Law Comm. 2005–07; Pres. Japan Karate NZ; NZ 1990 Medal. *Address:* Parliament Buildings, PO Box 10–041, Wellington, New Zealand (office). *Telephone:* (4) 817-8134 (office). *E-mail:* Helen .Kennelly@parliament.govt.nz (office). *Website:* www.ps.parliament.govt.nz (office).

BURTON, Richard St John Vladimir, CBE, RIBA; British architect and artist; b. 3 Nov. 1933, London; s. of Percy Basil Harmsworth Burton and Vera (née Poliakoff Russell); m. Mireille Dernbach-Mayen 1956; three s. one d.; ed Bryanston, Architectural Asscn School of Architecture; Dir Ahrends Burton and Koralek 1961–2002; currently artist; founder and Trustee, Makepeace School for Craftsmen in Wood 1977–83; Chair. of numerous cttees including Arts Council of England Architecture Advisory Group, Nat. Steering Cttee Per Cent for Art 1990–92, RIBA Steering Group on Architectural Educ. 1991–93, Health Bldgs for the 21st Century; NHS Estates 1991–93, Patient Care Study 1993, Building a 2020 Vision: Future Healthcare Environments; Chair. NHS Design Brief Working Group 2001–04; mem. ACE Visual Arts Panel 1994–98; Patron, Arts for Health, Axis, Healing Arts, Isle of Wight. *Design projects include:* Chichester Theological Coll. 1964, Trinity Coll. Dublin Library 1967, Templeton Coll., Oxford 1965–96, Hooke Park Coll., Dorset 1983–90, St Mary's Hosp., Isle of Wight 1991, Lawson Practice Primary Care Centre, London 1997, Housing Estates, Basildon, Essex 1974–80, New British Embassy, Moscow 1988–2000. *Publications:* Ahrends Burton and Koralek 1991, (jtly) Collaborations: The Architecture of ABK 2002. *Leisure interests:* building and writing. *Address:* Ahrends Burton and Koralek, Unit 1, 7 Chalcot Road, London, NW1 8LH (office). *Telephone:* (20) 7586-3311 (office). *Fax:* (20) 7722-5445 (office). *E-mail:* abk@abklondon.com (office); rsvb@blueyonder.co .uk (home). *Website:* www.abk.co.uk (office).

BURTON, Tim; American film director and screenwriter; b. 25 Aug. 1958, Burbank, Calif.; pnr Helena Bonham Carter; one s. one d.; ed California Arts Inst.; began career as animator, Walt Disney Studios; Chevalier, Ordre des Arts et des Lettres 2010; short-length film awards include two from Chicago Film Festival, Golden Lion Lifetime Achievement Award, Venice Int. Film Festival 2007. *Films as director:* Vincent (also animator) 1982, Luau 1982, Hansel and Gretel (TV) 1982, Frankenweenie (short, for Disney) 1984, Pee-Wee's Big Adventure 1985, Alfred Hitchcock Presents (TV episode, The Jar) 1985, Beetlejuice 1988, Batman 1989, Edward Scissorhands (also prod.) 1991, Batman Returns (also prod.) 1992, Ed Wood (also prod.) 1994, Mars Attacks! (also prod.) 1996, Sleepy Hollow 1999,

Planet of the Apes 2001, Big Fish 2003, Charlie and the Chocolate Factory 2005, Corpse Bride (also prod.) 2005, Sweeney Todd: The Demon Barber of Fleet Street (Best Dir, Nat. Bd of Review 2007, Golden Globe for Best Musical or Comedy 2008) 2007, Alice in Wonderland (also producer) 2010, Dark Shadows 2012, Frankenweenie (also producer) 2012. *Films as producer:* Beetlejuice (TV series) 1993, Family Dog (TV series) 1993, The Nightmare Before Christmas 1993, Cabin Boy 1994, Batman Forever 1996, James and the Giant Peach 1996, Lost in Oz (TV series) 2000, 9 2009, Abraham Lincoln: Vampire Hunter 2012. *Film screenplays:* The Island of Doctor Agor 1971, Stalk of the Celery 1979, Vincent 1982, Luau 1982, Beetlejuice (story) 1988, (TV series creator) 1989, Edward Scissorhands (story) 1990, The Nightmare Before Christmas (story) 1993, Lost in Oz (TV pilot episode story) 2000, Point Blank (TV series) 2002. *Film appearance:* Men in Black III. *Publications:* My Art and Films 1993, The Melancholy Death of Oyster Boy and Other Stories 1997, Burton on Burton 2000; various film tie-in books. *Address:* Chapman, Bird & Grey, 1990 South Bundy Drive, Suite 200, Los Angeles, CA 90025, USA (office). *Website:* www.timburton.com (office).

BURWELL, Sylvia Mathews, AB, BA; American foundation president and government official; *Director, Office of Management and Budget;* b. 1965, Hinton, W Va; d. of Dr William Mathews and Cleo Mathews; m. Stephen Burwell; one c.; ed Harvard Univ., Oxford Univ.; Assoc., McKinsey & Co., New York 1990–92; Staff Dir, Nat. Econ. Council, Washington, DC 1993–94; Chief of Staff to Treasury Sec. Robert Rubin 1995–97; Deputy White House Chief of Staff to Pres. Bill Clinton 1997–98; Deputy Dir, Office of Man. and Budget (OMB) 1998–2001, Dir 2013–; nominated as Sec. of Health and Human Services April 2014; COO, Bill and Melinda Gates Foundation 2001–05, Pres., Gates Foundation Global Devt Program 2006–11; Pres. Walmart Foundation 2012; Dir MetLife and Metropolitan Life Insurance Co. 2004; mem. Univ. of Washington Medicine Bd, Pacific Council on Int. Policy, Aspen Strategy Group, Nike Foundation Advisory Group; mem. Governing Council, Miller Center of Public Affairs, Univ. of Virginia; chosen by Wall Street Journal as one of The 50 Women to Watch 2005. *Address:* Office of Management and Budget, Executive Office of the President, 725 17th Street, NW, Washington, DC 20503, USA (office). *Telephone:* (202) 395-3080 (office). *Fax:* (202) 395-3888 (office). *Website:* www.whitehouse.gov/omb (office).

BURWITZ, Nils, BA (Fine Arts); German freelance artist, sculptor and lecturer; b. 16 Oct. 1940, Swinemünde; s. of Ulrich Burwitz and Johanna Lohse; m. Marina Schwezova 1964; two s. one d.; ed Univ. of Witwatersrand and postgrad. studies in London, Fribourg and Salzburg; emigrated to S Africa 1958; settled in Balearic Islands 1976; 202 solo exhbns, including 36 Exposures 1971 and restrospective exhbn in Sollerich Palace, Palma, Majorca 1985, Pretoria Art Museum, Pretoria 1991, Nat. Gallery 1992, Kunsthalle Munich-Germering 1995; lecturer at Lessinghaus, Herzog Bibliothek, Wolfenbüttel 2002; visual concept for stage works Iconostasis 1967–68, 8 Birds 1969, 8 Beasts 1970, Gentlemen (with R. Kirby) 1972, Mobile (with V. Rodzianko), London 1972, Retalls de l'Ignorancia (with R. Esteras) 1978, Llagrimes del Vienès (with A. Ballester) 1995; stained glass windows in churches of St Philip and St James and Sta Eulalia, Palma de Mallorca, Monastery of Lluch, La Ermita de la Santísima Trinidad, Royal Carthusian Monastery, Valldemossa, Majorca, Cupola for Castillo Hotel Son Vida, Palma de Mallorca, Cathedral, Palma de Mallorca; Founder Libra Press 1984; opened Funda Art Centre, Soweto, SA 1986; works in around 90 public collections including: Albertinum, Vienna, Albertinum, Dresden, Fitzwilliam Museum, Cambridge, Museum Ludwig, Cologne, Nat. Gallery, Warsaw, Nat. Portrait Gallery, Washington, DC, Museum of Modern Art, Tokyo, State Museum of Prints and Drawings, Berlin, British Museum, London, Victoria and Albert Museum, London, Sculpture for Plaza de la Concordia, Sa Pobla; has collaborated in three video documentaries in SA and Namibia; posters for UNHCR 2001, OAU 2001, Max Planck Inst. (Einstein's Legacy) 2005; portfolios: Locust Variations 1967, It's About Time 1973, Tidal Zone 1974, Heads or Tails? 1981, 9 Terraces 1986, The Journey to Dresden 1989, Marinas Terraces 1995, The Invisible Miró 2000, Journey to Berlin 2014; numerous honours and awards, including Gold Medal (Design), Johannesburg 1963, African Arts Centre Award, Durban 1971, Art Critics' Award, XI Graphic Biennale, Ljubljana 1975, Prix de la Ville de Monaco 1981, Primer Premio 'Ciutat de Palma' 1982, Merit Award, II Biennale of Painting, Barcelona 1987, Balearic European Citizen Award 1999, Premio Importantes, Diario de Mallorca 2002, Bishop Teodor Ubeda Memorial Award 2004. *Publications:* On the Razor's Edge 1995, Walking the Tightrope 2002. *Leisure interests:* swimming, diving. *Address:* Calle Rosa 22, 07170 Valldemossa, Majorca, Balearic Isles, Spain. *Telephone:* (971) 612838. *E-mail:* nils@burwitz-art .com. *Website:* www.burwitz-art.com.

BURZAN, Dragiša, MS, PhD; Montenegrin politician and diplomatist; b. 1950, Podgorica; m. Vesna Burzan; one s. two d.; ed Univ. of Montenegro, Univ. of Belgrade, Univ. of Essex, UK; mem. staff, Dept of Natural Sciences, Univ. of Montenegro 1976–98; Founder Democratic Alternative 1989; mem. Reform Forces of Fmr Yugoslavia 1991; Co-founder Montenegro Party 1992, Int. Sec. 1992–; mem. Parl. (Montenegro) 1992–96; Deputy Prime Minister of Montenegro with portfolios of Educ., Labour and Welfare, Health, Culture, Sport, Secr. of Information, Secr. for Int. and Science Cooperation, Commissariat for Refugees, etc. 1998–2001; Minister of Labour and Social Welfare 2001–02, of Foreign Affairs 2003–04; Amb. of Serbia and Montenegro to UK 2004–06, Amb. of Montenegro to UK 2007–11; Chair. Parl. Comm. investigating abduction of group of Muslims in Bosnia; Vice-Pres. SDP 1996–2000; Co-founder Monitor (weekly). *Publications:* numerous articles on physics in scientific journals. *Address:* Ministry of Foreign Affairs and European Integration, 81000 Podgorica, Stanka Dragojevića 2, Montenegro (office). *Telephone:* (20) 201530 (office). *Fax:* (20) 224670 (office). *E-mail:* dragisa .burzan@mfa.gov.me (office). *Website:* www.mip.gov.me (office).

BUSAIDI, Sayyid Badr bin Saud bin Hareb al-; Omani politician; currently Minister Responsible for Defence Affairs. *Address:* Ministry of Defence, POB 113, Muscat 113, Oman (office). *Telephone:* 24312605 (office). *Fax:* 24702521 (office).

BUSCEMI, Steve; American actor and film director; b. 13 Dec. 1957, Brooklyn, NY; m. Jo Andres 1987; one s.; ed Valley Stream Cen. High School, NY; moved to Manhattan following high school graduation to study acting with John Strasberg; worked as bartender, ice-cream truck driver, stand-up comedian; New York City Fireman, Engine Co. No. 55, Little Italy Section 1980–84; began writing and performing theatre pieces with Mark Boone, Jr; film debut in The Way It Is 1984;

first lead role in Parting Glances 1986; directed several episodes of TV series The Sopranos 1999, appeared in series 2004; currently volunteer fireman, NY. *Films include:* The Way It Is 1984, Tommy's 1985, Parting Glances 1986, Heart 1987, Kiss Daddy Goodnight 1988, Vibes 1988, New York Stories 1989, Slaves of New York 1989, Mystery Train 1989, Coffee and Cigarettes II 1989, Borders 1989, King of New York 1990, Miller's Crossing 1990, Barton Fink 1991, Zandalee 1991, Billy Bathgate 1991, In the Soup 1992, CrissCross 1992, Reservoir Dogs 1992, Who Do I Gotta Kill? 1992, Claude 1993, Rising Sun 1993, Twenty Bucks 1993, Ed and His Dead Mother 1993, Floundering 1994, The Hudsucker Proxy 1994, Airheads 1994, Somebody to Love 1994, Pulp Fiction 1994, Living in Oblivion 1995, Dead Man 1995, Things to Do in Denver When You're Dead 1995, Fargo 1996, Trees Lounge 1996, Kansas City 1996, Escape from L.A. 1996, Con Air 1997, The Real Blonde 1997, The Wedding Singer 1998, The Big Lebowski 1998, The Impostors 1998, Armageddon 1998, Louis & Frank 1998, Animal Factory 2000, 28 Days 2000, Ghost World 2000, Final Fantasy: The Spirits Within 2001, The Grey Zone 2001, Monsters Inc. 2001, The Laramie Project 2002, Love in the Time of Money 2002, 13 Moons 2002, Mr Deeds 2002, Spy Kids 2: Island of Lost Dreams 2002, Deadrockstar 2002, Spy Kids 3-D: Game Over 2003, Coffee and Cigarettes 2003, Big Fish 2003, Home on the Range 2004, The Sky is Green 2004, Romance & Cigarettes 2005, Art School Confidential 2004, The Island 2005, A License to Steal 2005, Cordless 2005, Delirious 2005, Paris, je t'aime 2006, Monster House 2006, Charlotte's Web (voice) 2006, Interview 2007, I Think I Love My Wife 2007, I Now Pronounce You Chuck & Larry 2007, I'm Dirty! (video short) 2008, Igor (voice) 2008, The Messenger 2009, City of War: The Story of John Rabe 2009, Rage 2009, Handsome Harry 2009, Saint John of Las Vegas 2009, G-Force (voice) 2009, Youth in Revolt 2009, Fight for Your Right Revisited (short) 2010, Grown Ups 2010, The Chosen One 2010, Pete Smalls Is Dead 2010, Rampart 2011, On the Road 2012, Hotel Transylvania 2012. *Films directed include:* What Happened to Pete? 1992, Trees Lounge 1996, Animal Factory 2000, Lonesome Jim 2005, Interview 2007. *Films produced include:* Animal Factory 2000, Symbiopsychotaxiplasm: Take 2 1/2 (documentary) (exec. producer) 2005, Lonesome Jim 2005, Saint John of Las Vegas (exec. producer) 2009. *Films written include:* What Happened to Pete? 1992, Trees Lounge 1996, Interview 2007. *Television includes:* The Simpsons (series) 2007, 30 Rock (series) 2007–11, ER (series) 2008, Boardwalk Empire (Golden Goble Award for Best Performance by an Actor in a TV Series – Drama 2011) 2010–11, Portlandia (series) 2011. *Address:* c/o WME Entertainment, 9601 Wilshire Boulevard, Beverley Hills, CA 90210, USA (office).

BUSCH, August A., III; American brewery industy executive; *Director, Anheuser-Busch Companies Inc.;* b. 16 June 1937, St Louis, Mo.; s. of the late August A. Busch, Jr; one s.; ed Univ. of Arizona; began career with family-business Anheuser-Busch Cos Inc. (brewery, theme-park operator and mfr of alumnium cans), mem. Bd of Dirs 1963–, Pres. 1974–2002, CEO 1975–2002, Chair. 1977–2006; mem. Bd of Dirs Emerson Electric Co., SBC Communications Inc.; Beverage Forum Lifetime Achievement Award 2003. *Address:* Anheuser-Busch Companies Inc., 1 Busch Place, St Louis, MO 63118, USA (office). *Telephone:* (314) 577-2000 (office). *Fax:* (314) 577-2900 (office). *Website:* www.anheuser-busch.com (office).

BUSCH, August Adolphus, IV, MBA; American brewing industry executive; b. 15 June 1964, St Louis, Mo.; s. of August Busch, III and Susan Busch (née Hornibrook); m. Kathryn (Kate) Thatcher 2006 (divorced 2009); ed Parkway West High School, Ballwin, Mo., St Louis Univ., Int. Brewing Inst., Berlin; joined Anheuser-Busch as apprentice brewer 1985, Vice-Pres. Brand Man. 1994–96, Vice-Pres. Marketing 1996–2000, Group Vice-Pres. Marketing and Wholesale Operations 2000–02, Pres. 2002–08, CEO 2006–08 (co. sold to InBev), mem. Bd of Dirs 2006–08, of Anheuser-Busch InBev 2008–11; mem. Bd of Dirs FedEx Corpn 2003–08; f. Great Rivers Habitat Alliance; Hon. DBA (Webster Univ.) 2006. *Leisure interests:* holds advanced black belt degrees in Judo, Tae-Kwon-Do and Hapkido. *Address:* c/o Anheuser-Busch Companies, LLC, 1 Busch Place, St Louis, MO 63118, USA. *E-mail:* info@anheuser-busch.com.

BUSCH, May Chien, MBA; British/American investment banker; *Chief Operating Officer, Morgan Stanley & Co International Ltd;* ed Harvard Coll., Harvard Business School; joined Morgan Stanley Dean Witter 1985, later Head of Debt Capital Markets in Europe for Corporates, later Man. Dir and Co-Head of European Coverage of Global Capital Markets, Morgan Stanley & Co. Int. Ltd 2002–04, Head of Firm Relationship Man. 2004–06, COO 2006–; mem. Council for Industry and Higher Educ., Advisory Bd SEO London UK Internship Programme. *Address:* Morgan Stanley Investment Management Ltd, 25 Cabot Square, Canary Wharf, London, E14 4QA, England (office). *Telephone:* (20) 7425-8000 (office). *Fax:* (20) 7425-7832 (office). *E-mail:* info@morganstanley.com (office). *Website:* www .morganstanley.com (office).

BUSEK, Erhard, DJur; Austrian politician and international organization official; *President, Instituts für den Donauraum und Mitteleuropa (Institute for the Danube Region and Central Europe);* b. 25 March 1941, Vienna; m. Helga Busek; ed Univ. of Vienna; Second Sec. Parl. Austrian People's Party (ÖVP); joined Fed. Exec. Cttee of Austrian Econ. Fed. 1968, Deputy Sec.-Gen. 1969, Sec.-Gen. 1972–76; Gen. Sec. ÖVP 1975–76; mem. Parl. 1975–78; City Councillor, Vienna City Senate 1976–78, 1987–89; Deputy Mayor of Vienna 1978–87; Deputy Fed. Chair. ÖVP 1983–91, Chair. 1991–95; Pres. Austrian Research Community; Fed. Minister of Science and Research 1989–94, of Educ. and Culture 1994–95, Vice-Chancellor 1992–95; with Instituts für den Donauraum und Mitteleuropa (Inst. for the Danube Region and Central Europe—IDM) 1995–; Co-ordinator for South-eastern European Co-operative Initiative 1996–; Pres. European Forum Alpbach 2000–; Special Co-ordinator Stability Pact for SE Europe 2002–08; Visiting Prof. of the Practice of Public Policy Studies, Duke Univ., USA 1995–; Perm. Sr Fellow, Centre for Research into European Integration, Bonn; Pres. Gustav Mahler Youth Orchestra, Österreichischen Volksliedwerkes, Stipendienwerkes 'pro scientia'; Jt-Pres. Technologieforums Sloweniens; Adviser, Economic Initiative for Kosovo 2008–; Dr hc (Univs of Kraków, Bratislava, Czernowitz and Ruse). *Publications include:* Projekt Mitteleuropa 1986, Aufbruch nach Mitteleuropa (with G. Wilflinger) 1986, Wissenschaft, Ethik und Politik (with M. Peterlik) 1987, Wissenschaft und Freiheit – Ideen zu Universalität und Universalität (with W. Mantl and M. Perterlik) 1989, Heimat – Politik mit sitz im Leben 1994, Mensch im Wort 1994, Mitteleuropa: Eine Spurensicherung 1997, Politik am Gängelband der

Medien 1998, Österreich und der Balkan – Vom Umgang mit dem Pulverfass Europas 1999, Eine Reise ins Innere Europas – Protokoll eines Österreichers 2001, Offenes Tor nach Osten 2003, Die Europäische Union auf dem Weg nach Osten 2003. *Address:* Institut für den Donauraum und Mitteleuropa, Hahngasse 6/1/24, 1090 Vienna, Austria (office). *E-mail:* idm@idm.at (office). *Website:* www.idm.at (office).

BUSER, Walter Emil, DrIur; Swiss government official; b. 14 April 1926, Lausen; s. of Emil Buser and Martha Buser; m. Renée Vuille 1947; ed Humanistic Gymnasium, Basel, Univs of Basel and Berne; Ed. Sozialdemokratische Bundeshauskorrespondenz 1950–61; legal consultant 1962–64; Head, legal and information service, Fed. Dept of Interior 1965–67; Vice-Chancellor of the Swiss Confed. 1968–81, Chancellor 1981–91; Hon. Dozent (Basel). *Publications:* Das Bundesgesetz über die Ordnung des Arbeitsverhaltnisses vom 27.6.19, Die Rolle der Verwaltung und der Interessengruppen im Entscheidungsprozess der Schweiz, Betrachtungen zum schweizerischen Petitionsrecht, Die Organisation der Rechtsetzung, in Hundert Jahre Bundesverfassung 1874–1974, Das Institut der Volksinitiative in rechtlicher und rechtspolitischer Sicht. *Address:* c/o Federal Chancellery, Swiss Confederation, 3003 Berne, Switzerland.

BUSH, Barbara; fmr First Lady; b. 8 June 1925, Rye, NY; d. of Marvin Pierce and Pauline Pierce (née Robinson); m. George Herbert Walker Bush (q.v.) 1945; four s. including George W. Bush and John Ellis (Jeb) Bush, one d.; ed Smith Coll.; mem. Bd of Dirs, Reading is Fundamental (also Hon. Chair. Advisory Bd), Business Council for Effective Literacy; mem. Advisory Council, Soc. of Memorial Sloan-Kettering Cancer Center; Hon. Chair. Advisory Council, Literacy Volunteers of America; Pres. Ladies of the Senate 1981–88; founder and Hon. Chair. Barbara Bush Foundation for Family Literacy 1989–; numerous hon. degrees; Outstanding Mother of the Year Award 1984, Distinguished Leadership Award, United Negro Coll. Fund 1986, Distinguished American Woman Award, Mt St Joseph Coll. 1987, Free Spirit Award, Freedom Forum 1985. *Publications:* C. Fred's Story, Millie's Book, Barbara Bush: A Memoir 1994. *Address:* c/o Barbara Bush Foundation for Family Literacy, 1201 15th Street, NW, Suite 420, Washington, DC 20005, USA. *Website:* www.barbarabushfoundation.com.

BUSH, George Herbert Walker, BA (Econs); American fmr head of state; b. 12 June 1924, Milton, Mass.; s. of the late Prescott Sheldon Bush and of Dorothy Walker; m. Barbara Bush (née Pierce) (q.v.) 1945; four s. (including George Walker Bush, John Ellis (Jeb) Bush) one d.; ed Phillips Acad., Andover, Mass. and Yale Univ.; naval carrier pilot USN 1942–45; Co-founder, Bush-Overbey Oil Devt Co. 1951; Co-founder, Dir Zapata Petroleum Corpn 1953–59; Founder, Pres. Zapata Offshore Co. 1956–64, Chair. 1964–66; mem. House of Reps for 7th Dist of Texas 1967–71; Perm. Rep. to UN 1971–72; Chair. Republican Nat. Cttee 1973–74; Head US Liaison Office, Peking (now Beijing) 1974–75; Dir CIA 1976–77; Vice-Pres. of USA 1981–89, Pres. of USA 1989–93; Republican; Sr Adviser, Asia Advisory Bd, Carlyle Group 1998–2003; apptd UN Special Envoy in Pakistan and Kashmir earthquake zone 2005; Hon. KBE (UK); DFC, three Air Medals; Hon. GCB 1993; numerous hon. degrees; Churchill Award 1991, Presidential Medal of Freedom 2010. *Publications:* Looking Forward: An Autobiography (with Victor Gold) 1988, A World Transformed (with Brent Scowcroft) 1998, All the Best, George Bush 1999. *Leisure interests:* tennis, jogging, boating, fishing, golf. *Address:* Suite 900, 10000 Memorial Drive, Houston, TX 77024-3422, USA (office). *Telephone:* (713) 686-1188 (office).

BUSH, George Walker, BA, MBA; American business executive, politician and fmr head of state; b. 6 July 1946, New Haven, Conn.; s. of George Herbert Walker Bush (q.v.) (fmr Pres. of USA) and Barbara Bush (née Pierce) (q.v.); brother of John Ellis (Jeb) Bush; m. Laura Welch Bush; twin d.; ed Yale Univ. and Harvard Business School; trained as F-102 fighter pilot, Tex. Air Nat. Guard 1968; CEO Bush Exploration, Midland, Tex. 1975–83; Chair. and CEO Spectrum 7 Energy Corpn (merged with Harken Energy Corpn 1986) 1983–87; worked in father's presidential campaign 1988; Man. Gen. Pnr, Texas Rangers professional baseball team 1989–94; Gov. of Tex. 1995–2000; Pres. of USA 2001–09. *Publications:* A Charge To Keep (with Karen Hughes) 2000, Decision Points 2010. *Address:* Office of George W. Bush, PO Box 259000, Dallas, TX 75225-9000, USA (office).

BUSH, John Ellis (Jeb), BA; American business executive, politician and fmr state official; b. 11 Feb. 1953, Midland, Tex.; s. of George Herbert Walker Bush (q.v.), fmr Pres. of USA and Barbara Bush (q.v.); brother of George W. Bush (q.v.), fmr Pres. of USA; m. Columba Bush; two s. one d.; ed Univ. of Texas; co-f. Codina Group (real estate devt co.), Miami, Fla 1981, Pres. and COO; Sec. of Commerce, State of Fla 1987–88; unsuccessful bid for Fla Gov.'s office 1994; f. Foundation for Fla's Future 1995, serving as Chair.; Gov. of Florida 1999–2007; Founder and Chair. Foundation for Excellence in Education; mem. Pvt. Equity Advisory Bd, Lehman Brothers Holdings Inc. 2007–08; Republican. *Address:* c/o Office of the Chairman, Foundation for Excellence in Education, PO Box 10691, Tallahassee, FL 32302, USA. *Website:* www.excelined.org.

BUSH, Kate, CBE; British singer, songwriter, musician and record producer; b. 30 July 1958, Bexleyheath, Kent, England; pnr Danny McIntosh; one s.; numerous live and TV appearances; Dir Novercia Ltd; Founder Fish People label; guest and backing vocalist for numerous artists, including Peter Gabriel, Roy Harper, Prince, Midge Ure; BPI Awards for Best Vocalist 1979, 1987, Ivor Novello Award for Outstanding British Lyrics (for The Man With The Child In His Eyes) 1979, BRIT Award for Best Female Artist 1987, Q Magazine Award for Best Classic Songwriter 2001, Ivor Novello Award for Outstanding Contribution to British Music by a Songwriter 2002. *Film:* The Line, The Cross and The Curve (writer, dir and actor) 1993. *Recordings include:* albums: The Kick Inside 1978, Lionheart 1978, Never for Ever 1980, The Dreaming 1982, Hounds Of Love 1985, The Whole Story 1986, The Sensual World 1989, This Woman's Work 1990, The Red Shoes 1993, Aerial 2005, Director's Cut 2011, 50 Words for Snow 2011. *E-mail:* admin@ katebush.com. *Website:* www.katebush.com.

BUSH, Laura Welch, BA, MLS; American public servant and teacher; b. Midland, Tex.; m. George W. Bush 1977; twin d.; ed Southern Methodist Univ., Univ. of Tex.; worked as teacher at Longfellow Elementary School, Dallas, Tex. 1968–69; teacher, John F. Kennedy Elementary School 1969–72; librarian, Houston Public Library 1973–74, Dawson Elementary School, Austin, Tex. 1974–77; First Lady of Tex. 1995–2000; First Lady of US 2001–09; ranked by

Forbes magazine amongst 100 Most Powerful Women (fourth) 2004, (46th) 2005, (43rd) 2006, (60th) 2007, (44th) 2008. *Publication:* Spoken from the Heart (autobiog.) 2010. *Address:* c/o Office of George W. Bush, PO Box 259000, Dallas, TX 75225-9000, USA (office).

BUSH, McKeeva, OBE, JP; Cayman Islands business executive and politician; b. 20 Jan. 1955, West Bay; m. Kerry Bush; two c.; mem. Legis. Ass. (parl.) for West Bay 1984–; mem. Exec. Council (renamed Cabinet 2003) as Mem. (Minister) for Health and Human Services 1992–94, for Community Devt, Sports, Women's and Youth Affairs and Culture 1994–97, for Tourism, Environment and Transport 2000–01, for Tourism, Environment, Devt and Commerce 2001–05; Founding mem. United Democratic Party 2001; Leader of the Opposition 2005–09; Leader of Govt Business 2001–05, May–Nov. 2009; Premier of the Cayman Islands and Minister responsible for Financial Services, Tourism and Devt Nov. 2009–12; Hon. MSc (Int. Coll. of the Cayman Islands); Cayman Islands Football Asscn Order of Merit. *Address:* United Democratic Party, Godfrey Nixon Road, George Town, Grand Cayman, Cayman Islands. *Telephone:* 943-3338. *E-mail:* info@udp.ky. *Website:* www.udp.ky.

BUSH, Wesley (Wes) G., BSc, MSc; American defence industry executive; *Chairman, President and CEO, Northrop Grumman Corporation;* ed Massachusetts Inst. of Tech., Univ. of California, Los Angeles; worked at Aerospace Corpn and Comsat Labs; joined TRW as systems engineer 1987, served in several man. positions including Vice-Pres. TRW Ventures, Vice-Pres. and Gen. Man. Telecommunications Programs Div., Pres. and CEO Aeronautical Systems UK; Corp. Vice-Pres. and Pres. of Space Tech., Northrop Grumman Corpn 2002–05, Vice-Pres. and Chief Financial Officer (CFO) 2005–06, Pres. 2006–, also CFO 2006, COO 2007–10, mem. Bd of Dirs 2009–, CEO 2010–, Chair. 2011–. *Address:* Northrop Grumman Corpn, 2980 Fairview Park Drive, Falls Church, VA 22042, USA (office). *Telephone:* (703) 280-2900 (office). *Fax:* (office). *E-mail:* onewebmaster@ngc.com (office). *Website:* www.northropgrumman.com (office).

BUSHATI, Ditmir, LLM; Albanian lawyer and politician; *Minister of Foreign Affairs;* b. 24 March 1977, Shkodra; m. Aida Bushati; one s. one d.; ed Faculty of Law, Univ. of Tirana, Univ. of Leiden, the Netherlands; fmr Researcher on European Affairs, European Centre for Public Law, Univ. of Athens, Greece; trained in int. affairs at several univs and research centres, including Harvard Univ., Acad. of Int. Law, Dallas, USA, Abo Univ. Acad., Finland; Founding Dir European Movt in Albania; then Dir of Legal Approximation, Ministry of European Integration, part of team negotiating Stabilization and Asscn Agreement with EU; worked as Advisor on European Affairs to Deputy Prime Minister, as Legal Advisor to Constitutional Court, Office of the Pres. of Albania and Int. Criminal Tribunal for the fmr Yugoslavia; Analyst for Freedom House for the Nations in Transition Report 2007–08; fmr Nat. Reporter for European Soc. of Int. Law; Nat. Co-ordinator, Open Society Foundation's project monitoring Albania's progress in European integration process 2006–08; worked as consultant for various projects of EU, World Bank, USAID, Deutsche Gesellschaft für Internationale Zusammenarbeit, OSI, Friedrich Ebert Stiftung, Int. Org. for Migration, Netherlands Devt Org. (SNV); has lectured on European Law and EU enlargement process at different insts and univs in Albania and Kosovo; mem. Parl. (Socialist Party) in Tirana Dist 2009–, Chair. Parl. Cttee for European Integration 2011–13, mem. Jt EU-Albania Parl. Cttee 2009–13; mem. Steering Cttee, Socialist Party of Albania 2011–; Minister of Foreign Affairs 2013–; various fellowships and research grants, including TEMPUS, NUFFIC, Victor Folsom, Kokkalis, TMC Asser Inst. *Publications:* numerous scientific papers and articles in areas related to EU enlargement process, public int. law and European law. *Address:* Ministry of Foreign Affairs, Bulevardi Gjergj Fishta 6, Tirana, Albania (office). *Telephone:* (4) 2364090 (office). *Fax:* (4) 2362084 (office). *E-mail:* info@mfa.gov.al (office). *Website:* www .mfa.gov.al (office).

BUSQUIN, Philippe; Belgian politician; b. 6 Jan. 1941; m.; ed Université Libre de Bruxelles; fmr Prof. of Biology and Physics; Deputy for Hainaut 1977–78, for Charleroi 1978–; Minister of Nat. Educ. 1980–81, of the Interior and Nat. Educ. Feb.–Dec. 1981, for the Budget and Energy (French region) 1982–85, of the Economy and Employment (French region) Feb.–May 1988, of Social Affairs 1988–92; Chair. Parti Socialiste (PS) 1992–99; Vice-Pres. Socialist Int. 1992–, PES 1995–; EU Commr responsible for Science, Research and Devt and the Jt Research Centre 1999–2004. *Address:* c/o European Commission, 200 rue de la Loi, 1049 Brussels, Belgium (office).

BUSSEL, James Bruce, BS, MD; American paediatrician, haematologist, oncologist and academic; *Professor of Pediatrics, Weill Cornell Medical College;* ed Yale Univ., Coll. of Physicians and Surgeons, Columbia Univ.; completed residency in paediatrics at Cincinnati Children's Hosp., Ohio; returned to New York City to undertake jt fellowship in Pediatric Hematology/Oncology at Memorial Sloan-Kettering Cancer Center and New York-Presbyterian Hosp., Chief Fellow 1980–81; currently Prof. of Pediatrics, Weill Cornell Medical Coll., also Prof. of Pediatrics in Obstetrics and Gynecology and Prof. of Pediatrics in Medicine; Attending Pediatrician, New York-Presbyterian Hosp.; Ratnoff Prof. of Hematology, Case Western Reserve Univ. 2008; Alpha Award, American Blood Resources Asscn for Contribs in Immunohematology 1998, selected as one of 15 reps of American Soc. of Hematology for SPARKII 2003, King Faisal Int. Prize for Medicine (co-recipient) 2012. *Publications:* more than 90 papers in professional journals. *Address:* Weill Cornell Medical College, 1300 York Avenue, New York, NY 10065 (office); 525 East 68th Street, Payson Pavilion 695, New York, NY 10065, USA (office). *Telephone:* (212) 746-3400 (office). *Fax:* (212) 746-5121 (office). *Website:* weillcornell.org/physician/jamesbussel (office).

BUSSELL, Darcey Andrea, CBE; British ballet dancer; b. 27 April 1969, London; d. of Philip M. Bussell and Andrea Williams; m. Angus Forbes 1997; two d.; ed Arts Educational School and Royal Ballet School; joined Sadler's Wells Royal Ballet (later Birmingham Royal Ballet) 1987; debut with leading role in The Prince of The Pagodas (Kenneth MacMillan) 1988; soloist, Royal Ballet 1988, first soloist 1989, prin. ballerina 1989–2006, guest artist 2006–07; appearances with Royal Ballet include leading roles in The Spirit of Fugue (created for her by David Bintley), first Royal Ballet performances of Balanchine's Rubies and Stravinsky Violin Concerto and leading roles in Agon, Symphony in C, Tchaikovsky pas de deux, Apollo (Terpsichore), Prodigal Son (Siren), Duo Concertante, Ballet Imperial

and Serenade, Kenneth Macmillan's The Prince of the Pagodas (role of Princess Rose created for her), Winter Dreams (role of Masha created for her), Manon (title role), Song of the Earth, Elite Syncopations, Raymonda, Romeo and Juliet, Requiem, Mayerling and Anastasia, Frederick Ashton's Cinderella (title role), Monotones II, Les Illuminations (Sacred Love), Birthday Offering, Les Rendezvous, William Forsyth's In the middle, somewhat elevated and Herman Scherman (pas de deux), Glen Tetley's La Ronde (Prostitute), Ninette de Valois' Checkmate (Black Queen), Ashley Page's Bloodlines (creator of leading role) and ...now langourous, now wild..., Twyla Tharp's Push Comes to Shove (co. premiere), Jerome Robbins' The Concert (Ballerina), Antony Tudor's Lilac Garden (Caroline), Roland Petit's Le Jeune Homme et La Mort, Balanchine's The Four Temperaments and Themes and Variations, Alistair Marriot's Kiss; classical repertory includes leading roles in Swan Lake (Odette/Odile), The Sleeping Beauty (Princess Aurora), The Nutcracker (Sugar Plum Fairy), La Bayadère (Nikiya and Gamzatti), Cinderella (title role), Giselle (title role), Raymonda Act III (title role); numerous appearances on TV and abroad as guest with other ballet cos in Paris, St Petersburg, New York, Australian Ballet, La Scala; in Viva La Diva touring production (with Katherine Jenkins) 2007–08; currently lives in Australia; Pres. Royal Acad. of Dance 2010–; mem. Bd of Dirs Sydney Dance Co. 2008–; Hon. DLit (Oxford) 2009; Prix de Lausanne 1989, Dance and Dancers Magazine Dancer of the Year 1990, Variety Club of GB Sir James Garreras Award 1991, Evening Standard Ballet Award 1991, Jt Winner Cosmopolitan Achievement in the Performing Arts Award 1991, Olivier Award 1992. *Television includes:* judge, Strictly Come Dancing (UK) 2012–. *Publications:* Life in Dance (with Judith Mackrell) 1998, Favourite Ballet Stories, The Young Dancer, Pilates for Life 2005, Darcey Bussell's Dance Body Workout 2007, Magic Ballerina children's book series 2008–. *Leisure interests:* sketching/painting, arts. *Address:* c/o Sydney Dance Company, The Wharf, Pier 4, Hickson Road, Walsh Bay, NSW 2000, Australia (office). *Website:* www.rad.org.uk; www.darceybussell.com.

BUSSEREAU, Dominique; French politician; b. 13 July 1952, Tours, Indre-et-Loire; ed Institut d'études politiques, Paris; Conseiller Général, Charente-Maritime 1985–, Pres. Conseil Gen. 2008–; Deputy (4ème circonscription) for Charente-Maritime, Assemblée nationale 1986–88, 1993–2002, 2007–, mem. Comm. des Lois, comité directeur du fonds d'investissement pour le développement économique et social des territoires d'outre-mer (fidestom); Conseiller régional de Poitou-Charentes 1992–93, March–April 2004; Mayor of Saint-Georges-de-Didonne, Charente-Maritime 1989–2002, 1er adjoint au Maire 2002–08, Conseiller municipal 2008–; Sec. of State, Transport and Sea 2002–04, for the Budget and Budgetary Reform, Ministry of the Economy, Finances and Industry March–Nov. 2004; Minister of Agric., Food, Fishing and the Countryside 2004–05, of Agric. and Fishing 2005–07, Sec. of State for Ecology, Energy, Sustainable Devt and Spatial Planning, responsible for Transport 2007–10; mem. Union pour un Mouvement Populaire (UMP); Pres. Asscn Avenir Transports; Commdr, Ordre du Mérite agricole, Ordre du Mérite maritime, Ordre du Mérite Agricole (Senegal), Grand Cordon, Order of the Rising Sun (Japan) 2007. *Address:* 85, bd de la République, 17076 La Rochelle Cedex 9, France (office). *Telephone:* 5-46-31-70-00. *Fax:* 5-46-31-17-17. *E-mail:* info@cg17.fr.

BUSTAMANTE, Jean-Marc; French artist, sculptor and photographer; b. 1952, Toulouse; conceptual and installation artist, has incorporated ornamental design and architectural space in his works, has also worked with film; with Bernard Bazile operated under jt name BazileBustamante 1983–87; teaches at Rijksakademie, Amsterdam. *Address:* 43, rue de la Bruyère, 75009 Paris, France (office).

BUSTAMANTE PONCE, Fernando, MPA; Ecuadorean politician; *Minister of Government, Worship, Police and Municipalities;* ed Catholic Univ. of Chile, Harvard Univ.,; fmr Prof., San Francisco Univ., Quito; Minister of Internal and External Security Policy Co-ordination 2007-08, of Govt, Worship, Police and Municipalities 2008–; columnist diario Hoy. *Address:* Ministry of Government, Worship, Police and Municipalities, Espejo y Benalcázar, Quito, Ecuador (office). *Telephone:* (2) 295-5666 (office). *Fax:* (2) 295-8360 (office). *E-mail:* febusta@hoy .com.ec; informacion@mingobierno.gov.ec (office). *Website:* www.mingobierno.gov .ec (office).

BUSTANI, José Mauricio, LLB; Brazilian diplomatist and government official; *Ambassador to France;* b. 5 June 1945, Porto Velho, Rondônia; m. Janine-Monique Bustani; two s. one d.; ed Pontifício Universidade Católica (Law School), Rio de Janeiro, Rio Branco Inst.; joined Ministry of Foreign Relations 1967, Asst to Assoc. Sec.-Gen. for Int. Orgs 1967–70, 1975–77; posted to Brazilian Embassy in Moscow 1970–73, Vienna 1973–75, Brazilian Mission to the UN 1977–84, Embassy in Montevideo 1984–86 Consulate-Gen. Montreal 1987–92; Head Dept for Tech., Financial and Devt Policy, Ministry of Foreign Relations 1992–93; Dir-Gen. Dept for Int. Orgs 1993–97; Dir-Gen. UN OPCW, The Hague 1997–2002; Amb. to UK 2003–08, to France 2008–; del. to numerous int. confs. including UNIDO, Vienna 1973–75, UN Conf. on the Law of the Sea (13 sessions 1974–93), UN Gen. Ass. 1977–83, UN Special Sessions on Disarmament 1978–82, UN Emergency Sessions on Afghanistan 1980, Namibia 1981. *Address:* Embassy of Brazil, 34 cours Albert 1er, 75008 Paris, France (office). *Telephone:* 1-45-61-63-00 (office). *Fax:* 1-42-89-03-45 (office). *E-mail:* imprensa@bresil.org (office). *Website:* www.bresil.org (office).

BUSUJIMA, Kunio; Japanese business executive; *Founder, Sankyo Co. Ltd;* b. 1925; m.; four c.; began career with Heiwa Corpn (gaming co.); f. Sankyo Co. Ltd (pachinko slot machine co.) 1966, Chair. 1966–2008, currently Hon. Chair., Dir and Sr Adviser. *Address:* Sankyo Co. Ltd, 3-29-14 Shibuya, Shibuya-ku, Tokyo 150 8327, Japan (office). *Telephone:* (3) 5778-7773 (office). *Fax:* (3) 5778-6731 (office). *Website:* www.sankyo-fever.co.jp (office).

BUTAGIRA, Francis K., LLB, LLM; Ugandan diplomatist; *Ambassador to Germany;* b. 22 Nov. 1942, Bugamba; m.; seven c.; ed Dar es Salaam Univ. Coll., Harvard Univ., USA, School of Oriental and African Studies, London, UK; State Attorney, Ministry of Justice 1967; Lecturer in Law, Nsamizi Law School 1968; Head of Law Dept, Law Devt Center 1969–70; Chief Magistrate of Buganda Road Law Courts 1973, of Mbarara 1974; High Court Judge 1974–79; mem. Nat. Consultative Council 1979–80; mem. Parl. 1980–85, also served as Pres. Jt Ass. of the European Econ. Community and the African, Caribbean and Pacific Group of States 1981–83; Chair. Legal and Security Affairs Cttee Nat. Resistance Council (Parl.) 1989–96; Amb. to Ethiopia and Perm. Rep. to Org. of African Unity, Addis

Ababa 1998; led team of Ugandan negotiators in talks leading to establishment of E African Community 1999; fmr High Commr in Kenya and Perm. Rep. to UNEP and UN–HABITAT, Nairobi; served as mediator in Sudanese peace talks sponsored by Intergovernmental Authority on Devt 2000–03; Amb. and Perm. Rep. to UN, New York 2003–09, Chair. UN Gen. Ass. Third Cttee (Social, Humanitarian and Cultural) 2005–09; Amb. to Germany 2009–; Sr Partner, Butagira & Co. (law firm) 1989–; Uganda Investment Authority Golden Award for Attraction of Investment 2002. *Address:* Embassy of Uganda, Axel-Springer-Str. 54A, 10117 Berlin, Germany (office). *Telephone:* (30) 24047556 (office). *Fax:* (30) 24047557 (office). *E-mail:* ugembassy@yahoo.de (office).

BUTCHER, Hon. David John, BA (Hons); New Zealand/British economist, consultant and fmr politician; *Consultant, David Butcher and Associates;* b. 19 Sept. 1948, England; s. of Frank George Butcher and Dorothy May Butcher; m. Mary Georgina Hall 1980; two d.; ed Victoria Univ. of Wellington; Research Economist, Dept of Labour 1972–74; Field Officer, Clerical Workers Union and New Zealand Labourers Union, Hawke's Bay, Wellington 1976–78; MP for Hastings 1978–90; Parl. Under-Sec. to Ministers of Agric., Lands and Forests 1984–87; Minister of Energy, of Regional Devt 1987–90, Assoc. Minister of Finance 1987–88, of Regional Devt 1987–90, of Commerce 1988–90; Consultant, David Butcher and Assocs (econ. consultancy) 1992–; Sr Man., Ernst & Young, Wellington 1995–96; mem. Labour Party; Fellow, New Zealand Inst. of Man.; mem. New Zealand Asscn of Economists, NZ Soc. of Public Admin, Inst. of Man. Consultants New Zealand, New Zealand Asscn of Former MPs; Commemorative Medal 1990. *Achievement:* helped dismantle agricultural subsidies, new taxation regime for livestock, dismantled unnecessary protection for manufacturing, helped put in place deregulation of telecommunications, electricity; helped establish Information Communications Networking Co. Mongolia, first ever nationwide Netco; employed by int. agencies to offer advice in more than 30 different countries. *Publications include:* Agriculture in a More Market Economy 1985, Lessons for the Future from the Free Market Economy, Open the Way to Competition 2007, Parliamentary Committees in Westminster Systems, UNDP Dhaka Bangladesh 2006, Electricity Sectors in CAREC Member Countries (co-author) 2005; contrib. to Privatization Yearbook 1993, 1994, 1995, 1999; numerous speeches and articles. *Leisure interests:* swimming, reading, classical music, family history, photography. *Address:* PO Box 5279, Wellington 6145, New Zealand (home). *Telephone:* (4) 476-9001 (office), 21-438630 (mobile) (office). *E-mail:* david@dba.org.nz (office). *Website:* www.dba.org.nz (office).

BUTCHER, Eugene (Gene) Corning, BS, MD; American immunologist and academic; *Professor of Pathology, Stanford University;* b. 6 Jan. 1950, St Louis, Mo.; ed Massachusetts Inst. of Tech., Washington Univ., St Louis; Residency in Pathology (Anatomic), Dept of Pathology, Stanford Univ., Calif. 1976–77, 1979–80, NIH Postdoctoral Fellowship, Dept of Pathology 1977–79, Sr Fellow, American Cancer Soc., Calif. Div., Dept of Pathology 1980–82, Asst Prof., Dept of Pathology, Stanford Univ. Medical Center 1982–89, Assoc. Prof. 1989–99, Prof. 1999–; Staff Physician, Veterans Admin Palo Alto Health Care System 1982–, Dir Serology and Immunology Section, Veterans Admin Palo Alto Health Care System 1982–; Co-Dir Immunohistologic Diagnosis Service, Surgical Pathology, Stanford 1983–93; Univ. Lecturer, Univ. of Texas Southwest Medical Center 1996; Burroughs-Wellcome Visiting Prof., Univ. of New Mexico 1996; mem. American Asscn of Pathologists, American Asscn of Immunologists, Asscn of American Physicians 2003, Fed. of American Socs for Experimental Biology, American Soc. for Investigative Pathology, Mars Soc., Planetary Soc.; Eloranta Award 1971, PLU (Hon. Chem. Soc.) 1972, Richard S. Brookings Award for Excellence in Medical Student Research 1976, Scholar, Leukemia Soc. of America 1982–87, Established Investigator, American Heart Asscn 1987–92, Warner-Lambert/Parke-Davis Award for meritorious research in experimental pathology, American Soc. for Investigative Pathology 1989, Marjorie J. Williams Lecturer, Asscn of Veterans Admin Pathologists 1989, AAI-Huang Foundation Meritorious Career Award, American Asscn of Immunologists 1999, William S. Middleton Award (Highest Research Award from Dept of Veterans Affairs) 2001, Stanford Univ. Outstanding Inventor Award 2004, Crafoord Prize in Polyarthritis, Royal Swedish Acad. of Sciences (co-recipient) 2004, invited to membership of Scientific Advisory Bd, 'SystemsX' (Swiss nat. initiative in systems biology) 2005. *Publications:* Over33 reviews and 280 scientific papers in professional journals on the trafficking of white blood cells, including their interactions with the endothelial lining of blood vessels at sites of leukocyte extravasation, and their chemotactic responses in tissues; nine US patents. *Address:* Department of Pathology, Stanford University School of Medicine, Lane Building, Mailcode 5324, Stanford, CA 94305-5324, USA (office). *Telephone:* (650) 852-3369 (office). *Fax:* (650) 858-3986 (office). *E-mail:* ebutcher@stanford.edu (office); marthas1@stanford.edu (office). *Website:* med .stanford.edu/profiles/Eugene_Butcher (office); butcherlab.stanford.edu (office).

BUTCHER, John Charles, ONZM, PhD, DSc, FRSNZ; New Zealand mathematician and academic; *Honorary Research Professor and Professor Emeritus of Mathematics, University of Auckland;* b. 31 March 1933, Auckland; s. of Charles Hastings Butcher and Alice Lilac Cornwall Butcher (née Richards); m. 1st Patricia Frances Nicolas 1957 (divorced 1989); two s. one d.; m. 2nd Jennifer Ann Wright (née Bowman) 1990; ed Dargaville, Taumarunui and Hamilton High Schools, Univ. of New Zealand (Auckland Univ. Coll.), Univ. of Sydney, Australia; Lecturer in Applied Math., Univ. of Sydney 1959–61; Sr Lecturer in Math., Univ. of Canterbury 1961–64; computer scientist, Stanford Linear Accelerator Center, USA 1965–66; Prof. of Math., Univ. of Auckland 1966–79 (Head of Math. Dept 1967–73), of Computer Science 1980–88 (f. Dept of Computer Science 1980), Head, Applied and Computational Math. Unit 1989–94, 1997–98, Prof. of Math. 1989–98, Hon. Research Prof. and Prof. Emer. 1999–; various visiting lectureships and professorships in USA, UK, Sweden, Austria, Germany, USSR, Netherlands 1965–; mem. Editorial Bd Acta Numerica, Applied Numerical Mathematics, Numerical Algorithms, Journal of Universal Computer Science; Life mem., Fellow and Past Pres. NZ Math. Soc.; mem. American Math. Soc. 1966, Soc. for Industrial and Applied Math. (USA), Australian and NZ Industrial and Applied Math.; Fellow, Inst. of Math. and its Applications (UK) 1972; Officer, New Zealand Order of Merit 2013; Award for Math. Research, NZ Math. Soc. 1991, Hector Medal, Royal Soc. of NZ 1996, Jones Medal, Royal Soc. of NZ 2010, Van Wijngaarden Award 2011. *Publications:* The Numerical Analysis of Ordinary Differential Equations: Runge-Kutta and General Linear Methods 1987 (second edn as

Numerical Methods for Ordinary Differential Equations 2008); approx. 160 papers on numerical analysis and other topics. *Leisure interests:* classical music, bridge. *Address:* Room 424B, Department of Mathematics, University of Auckland, Private Bag 92019, Auckland (office); 16 Wallace Street, Herne Bay, Auckland, New Zealand (home). *Telephone:* (9) 3737599 (ext. 88747) (office); (9) 3762743 (home). *Fax:* (9) 3737457 (office). *E-mail:* butcher@math.auckland.ac.nz (office). *Website:* www.math.auckland.ac.nz/~butcher (office); jcbutcher.com.

BUTHELEZI, Rt Rev. Bishop Manas, STM, PhD; South African ecclesiastic; b. 10 Feb. 1935, Mahlabathini; s. of Absalom Buthelezi and Keslinah Mkhabase; m. Grace Mhlungu 1963; two s. two d.; ed St Francis Coll. and Yale and Drew Univs, USA; high school teacher 1957; Visiting Prof., Heidelberg Univ., FRG 1974, Wesley Seminary 1975; Bishop, Cen. Diocese, Evangelical Lutheran Church 1977–2000, Bishop Emer. 2000–; Pres. South African Council of Churches 1984–91; mem. Comm. on Studies, Lutheran World Fed. 1970–77, Comm. on World Mission and Evangelism, WCC 1975–83; mem. Standing Cttee Faith and Order Comm., Pvt. Sector Council on Urbanization, Int. Comm. on Lutheran/Catholic Dialogue, Iliff School of Theology; St John's Visiting Prof., Lutheran Theological Seminary at Phila 2001; several hon. degrees. *Leisure interests:* music and photography. *Address:* PO Box 1210, Roodepoort 1725, South Africa.

BUTHELEZI, Chief Mangosuthu Gatsha, BA; South African politician; b. 27 Aug. 1928, Mahlabatini; s. of the late Chief Mathole Buthelezi and Princess Magogo; m. Irene Audrey Thandekile Mzila 1952; three s. four d.; ed Adams Coll., Fort-Hare Univ.; installed as Chief of Buthelezi Tribe 1953; assisted King Cyprian in admin. of Zulu people 1953–68; elected leader of Zululand territorial authority 1970; Chief Minister of KwaZulu 1976–94; Minister of Home Affairs (in Gov. of Nat. Unity) 1994–2004; Pres. Inkatha Freedom Party; Kt Commdr Star of Africa (Liberia), Commdr Ordre Nat. du Mérite 1981; Hon. LLD (Zululand and Cape Town); George Meany Human Rights Award 1982. *Publications include:* South Africa: My Vision of the Future 1990. *Address:* Inkatha Freedom Party, Albany House North, 4th Floor, Albany Grove, PO Box 443, Durban 4000, South Africa. *Website:* www.fp.org.za.

BUTIME, Col Tom; Ugandan government official; joined Nat. Resistance Army guerrillas 1981; mil. training in Libya 1982; Acting Minister of Foreign Affairs 2004–05, also served as Minister of State for Int. Affairs and Second Deputy Prime Minister; Minister of State for Karamoja Affairs 2006 (resgnd). *Address:* c/o Ministry of Foreign Affairs, 2a/b Apollo Kaggwa Road, PO Box 7048, Kampala, Uganda. *E-mail:* info@mofa.go.ug.

BUTKEVIČIUS, Algirdas, MS, DScS; Lithuanian politician and economist; *Prime Minister;* b. 19 Nov. 1958, Paežeriai, Radviliškis dist; m. Janina Butkevičienė; one d.; ed Radviliškis, Šeduva dist high school, Vilnius Eng Construction Inst., Lithuanian Acad. of Man., Kaunas Technological Univ., German Man. Acad., Würzburg, studies in Denmark and USA; construction work supt, Vilkaviškis Region Industrial Union 1982–85, Exec. Cttee 1985–90; Head of Dept of Econs and Finance, Deputy Gov. Vilkaviškis Region 1991–95; Marketing Dir, SC Vilkauta 1995–96; Vilkaviškis Dist Council mem. 1990–97, 2000–02, mem. Vilkaviškis Municipal Bd 1995–97; mem. Lithuanian Social Democratic Party (LSDP) 1992–, Chair. Vilkaviškis Br. 1995–97, Deputy Chair. LSDP 1999–2005, Chair. 2009–, Chair. LSDP Parl. Group 2009; mem. Seimas (Parl.) 1996–, Chair. Treasury Sub-cttee 1996–2001, Budget and Finance Cttee 2001–04, Family Budget and Finance Cttee and Cttee on European Affairs 2005–06; Minister of Finance 2004–05 (resgnd), of Transport and Communications 2006–08; unsuccessful LSDP cand. in presidential election 2009; Prime Minister 2012–. *Leisure interest:* sports. *Address:* Office of the Prime Minister, Gedimino pr. 11, Vilnius 01103 (office); Zircnūnus 38A -31, Vilnius, Lithuania (home). *Telephone:* (8) 706-63711 (office); (6) 984-2492 (home). *Fax:* (8) 706-63895 (office). *E-mail:* mptarnyba@lrv.lt (office). *Website:* www.lrv.lt (office).

BUTLER, Basil Richard Ryland, CBE, MA, FREng; British business executive; b. 1 March 1930, Hexham, Northumberland, England; s. of Hugh Montagu Butler and Annie Isabel Butler (née Wiltshire); m. Lilian Joyce Haswell 1954; one s. two d.; ed Denstone Coll., Staffs., St John's Coll., Cambridge; 2nd Lt, 5th Royal Inniskilling Dragoon Guards; Operations Man. Sinclair and BP Colombian Inc. 1968–70, Operations Man. BP Alaska Inc. 1970–72, Gen. Man. BP Petroleum Devt Ltd 1978–81, Chief Exec. BP Exploration Co. Ltd 1981–86, Dir 1986–89, Man. Dir BP Co. PLC 1986–91; Dir BP Solar International 1991–99, Chair. 1991–95; Chair. European Council of Applied Sciences and Eng 1993–98; Dir Brown and Root Ltd 1991–97, Chair. 1993–97; Dir Murphy Oil Corpn 1991–2002; Gen. Man. Kuwait Oil Co. Ltd 1972–75, Sullom Voe Devt 1975–78; Chair. KS Biomedix Holdings PLC 1995–2001; Pres. Inst. of Petroleum 1990–92; mem. Council Royal Acad. of Eng 1993–2002, Hon. Sec. Int. Activities 1995–98, Sr Vice-Pres. 1996–99; Cdre, Royal Western Yacht Club of England 2004–08; Freeman, City of London. *Leisure interests:* sailing, music. *Address:* c/o Royal Academy of Engineering, London, SW1P 5DG, England.

BUTLER, Sir David Edgeworth, Kt, CBE, MA, DPhil, FBA; British psephologist; b. 1924; s. of Prof. Harold E. Butler and Margaret Pollard; m. Marilyn S. Evans (Marilyn Butler) 1962; three s.; ed St Paul's School, Princeton Univ., USA and New Coll., Oxford; J.E. Procter Visiting Fellow, Princeton Univ. 1947–48; student, Nuffield Coll. Oxford 1949–51, Research Fellow 1951–54, Fellow 1954–92, Emer. Fellow 1992–, Dean and Sr Tutor 1956–64; Personal Asst to British Amb. in Washington, DC 1955–56; Co-Ed. Electoral Studies 1982–92; Hon. DUniv (Paris) 1978, (Essex) 1993; Hon. DSc (Queen's Univ. Belfast) 1985, (Teesside) 1998; Hon. LLD (Plymouth) 1997. *Publications include:* The Study of Political Behaviour 1958, Elections Abroad (ed.) 1959, British Political Facts 1900–1960 (with J. Freeman), Political Change in Britain 1969, The Canberra Model 1973, Coalitions in British Politics (ed.) 1978, Policy and Politics (co-ed. with A. H. Halsey), Referendums (with A. Ranney) 1978, British Political Facts 1900–79 (with A. Sloman), European Elections and British Politics (with D. Marquand) 1981, Democracy at the Polls (with A. Ranney) 1981, Democracy and Elections (with V. Bogdanor) 1983, Governing without a Majority 1983, A Compendium of Indian Elections 1984, Party Strategies in Britain (with P. Jowett) 1985, Sovereigns and Surrogates (with A. Low) 1991, Failure in British Government (with others) 1994, India Decides (with P. Roy) 1995, Referendums Around the World (co-ed.) 1995, British Politics and European Elections (with Martin Westlake) 2000, British

Political Facts 1900–2000 (with G. Butler) 2000, The British General Election of 2001 2001; also numerous books on the British electoral system and British elections since 1945. *Address:* Nuffield College, Oxford, OX1 1NF, England. *Telephone:* (1865) 278500.

BUTLER, Sir James (Jim), Kt, KCB, CBE, FCA; British chartered accountant; b. 15 March 1929, Batheaston; m. Margaret Butler (née Copland); one s. two d.; ed Marlborough Coll., Clare Coll., Cambridge; articled clerk, Peat Marwick (chartered accountants) 1952; negotiated Peat Marwick's merger with Klynveld Main Goerdeler to form KPMG 1986–87; Sr Pnr, Peat Marwick (UK arm of KPMG) 1987–93; Chair. KPMG Int. 1991–93; Dir Camelot PLC 1994–2002 (Deputy Chair. 1995), Royal Opera House 1994–99, Wadworth and Co. Ltd 1994–, Nicholson, Graham & Jones 1994–2005. *Leisure interests:* bridge. *Address:* Littleton House, Crawley, Winchester, Hants., SO21 2QF, England. *Telephone:* (1962) 880206 (home). *Fax:* (1962) 886177 (home). *E-mail:* jbutler603@aol.com (home).

BUTLER, James Walter, MBE, RA, RWA, FRBS; British sculptor; b. 25 July 1931, London, England; s. of Walter Arthur Butler and Rosina Kingman; m. Angela Elizabeth Berry 1975; five d.; ed Maidstone Grammar School, Maidstone School of Art, St Martin's School of Art, City & Guilds of London Art School, Royal Coll. of Art; worked as stone carver; taught sculpture and drawing, City & Guilds Art School; professional sculptor working on public and pvt. comms and exhbns; works in various galleries; mem. Soc. of Portrait Sculptors, Royal West of England Acad. *Leisure interest:* astronomy. *Address:* Valley Farm Studios, Radway, Warwick, CV35 0UJ, England (office). *Telephone:* (1926) 641938 (office); 7831-847129 (mobile). *Fax:* (1926) 640624 (office). *E-mail:* info@jamesbutler-ra .com (office). *Website:* www.jamesbutler-ra.com (office).

BUTLER, Hon. Richard William, AC, DUniv; Australian diplomatist and academic; *Global Diplomat in Residence and Clinical Professor, Center for Global Affairs, New York University;* b. 13 May 1942; s. of H. H. Butler; m. Barbara Evans 1974; three s. one d.; ed Randwick Boys High School, Univ. of Sydney, Australian Nat. Univ.; Second Sec., Embassy and Perm. Mission to UN, Deputy Perm. Rep. IAEA, Vienna 1966–69; First Sec. Mission to UN, New York 1970–73; Deputy High Commr, Singapore, 1975–76; Prin. Pvt. Sec. to Leader of Opposition 1976–77; Counsellor, Bonn Embassy 1978–81; Minister-Del. to OECD, Paris, Amb. and Perm. Rep. to UN (Disarmament Matters), Geneva 1983–88; Amb. to Thailand 1989–92; Amb. and Perm. Rep. to Supreme Nat. Council of Cambodia 1991–92; Amb. and Perm. Rep. to UN, New York 1992–97; Exec. Chair. UN Special Comm. on Iraqi Disarmament 1997–99; Diplomat-in-Residence, Council on Foreign Relations, New York 1999–2002; Gov. of Tasmania 2003–04 (resgnd); Global Diplomat in Residence and Clinical Prof., Center for Global Affairs, School of Continuing and Professional Studies, New York University 2008–. *Publications:* The Greatest Threat 2000, Saddam Defiant 2000. *Leisure interests:* art, music, rugby. *Address:* Center for Global Affairs, School of Continuing and Professional Studies, New York University, 145 4th Avenue, New York, NY 10003, USA (office). *Website:* www.scps.nyu.edu/areas-of-study/global-affairs (office).

BUTLER, William Elliott, BA, MA, JD, LLM, PhD, LLD, FRSA, FSA; American/British legal scholar and academic; *John Edward Fowler Distinguished Professor of Law, Dickinson School of Law, Pennsylvania State University;* b. 20 Oct. 1939, Minneapolis, Minn., USA; s. of the late William E. Butler and Maxine Swan Elmberg; m. 1st Darlene Johnson (died 1989); two s.; m. 2nd Maryann Gashi 1991; ed Hibbing Junior Coll., The American Univ., Harvard Law School, Russian Acad. of Sciences, Johns Hopkins School of Advanced Int. Studies, Univ. of London, UK, Kyiv Univ. of Law, Ukraine; Research Asst, Washington Center for Foreign Policy Research, Johns Hopkins Univ. 1966–68; Research Assoc. in Law and Assoc., Russian Research Center, Harvard Univ. 1968–70; Reader in Comparative Law, Univ. of London 1970–76, Prof. of Comparative Law 1976–2005, Dean, Faculty of Laws 1988–90, Prof. Emer. 2005–, mem. Council, School of Slavonic and East European Studies 1973–93, Dean, Faculty of Laws, Univ. Coll. London 1977–79, Vice-Dean 1979–81, Dir Vinogradoff Inst. 1982–2005, Professorial Research Assoc., SOAS, Univ. of London 2006–; Dean, Faculty of Law and Speranskii Prof. of Int. and Comparative Law, Moscow Higher School of Social and Econ. Sciences 1995–2005; John Edward Fowler Distinguished Prof. of Law, Dickinson School of Law, Penn State Univ. 2005–, mem. Faculty Council, School of Int. Affairs 2007–, mem. Senate, Penn State Univ. 2008–; Professorial Lecturer in Int. Law, Johns Hopkins School of Advanced Int. Studies 2009; Partner, White & Case 1994–96, Price Waterhouse Coopers 1997–2001; Sr Partner, Phoenix Law Assocs, Moscow 2002–12; Special Counsel, Comm. on Econ. Reform, USSR Council of Ministers 1989–91; consultant, IBRD; adviser and consultant to govts of Russian Fed., Belarus, Ukraine, Kyrgyzstan, Kazakhstan, Tajikistan, Uzbekistan; Legal Adviser, UN Office on Drugs and Crime (UNODC) 2006–08; Visiting Scholar, Moscow State Univ. 1972, 1980, Mongolian State Univ. 1979, Inst. of State and Law, USSR Acad. of Sciences 1976, 1981, 1983, 1984, 1988, Harvard Law School 1982; Visiting Prof., New York Univ. Law School 1978, Ritsumeikan Univ. 1985, Harvard Law School 1986–87, Washington and Lee Univ. 2005; mem. Russian Court of Int. Commercial Arbitration 1995–, Expert Council on Reform of Corp. Man., Ministry of Econ. Devt and Trade of Russian Fed. 2004–06, Int. Commercial Arbitration Court of Kazakhstan 2012–, Court of Int. Commercial Arbitration of Ukraine 2013–; Academician, Russian Acad. of Natural Sciences, Nat. Acad. of Sciences of Ukraine, Nat. Acad. of Legal Sciences of Ukraine, Int. Acad. of the Book and Art of the Book, Russian Acad. of Legal Sciences; mem. Sr Common Room, St Antony's Coll. Oxford, UK 2004–; mem. Exec. Council, Russian Asscn of Maritime Law 2008, American Law Inst. 2009–; G.I. Tunkin Medal 2003, Ivan Fedorov Medal 2004, FISAE (Int. Fed. of Ex-libris Socs) Certificates of Honour, Medal 'For Fidelity of Law', Supreme Court of Ukraine 2012. *Publications:* more than 4,000 books, articles, reviews and translations, including Soviet Law 1983, The Non-Use of Force in International Law 1989, Perestroika and International Law 1990, The History of International Law in Russia 1647–1917 1990, Foreign Investment Legislation in the Republics of the Former Soviet Union 1993, Russian Law of Treaties 1997, Russian Legal Texts 1998, Russian Law 1999, 2003, 2009, Constitutional Foundations of the CIS Countries 2000, American Bookplates 2000, Russian Company Law 2000, Russian-English Legal Dictionary 2001, Foreign Investment Laws in the CIS 2002, The Law of Treaties in Russia and the CIS 2002, Civil Code of the Russian Federation 2003, 2008, 2009, Russian Company and Commercial Law 2003, Narcotics and HIV in Russia 2005, Russian

Intellectual Property Law (fourth edn) 2005, Russian Foreign Relations and Investment Law 2006, Russian Legal Biography (with V. A. Tomsinov) 2007, Civil Code of Uzbekistan 2007, Civil Code of Kazakhstan 2008, Russia and the Law of Nations in Historical Perspective 2009, The Nakaz of Catherine the Great (with V. A. Tomsinov) 2010, Russian Criminal Law and Procedure 2011. *Leisure interests:* book collecting, bookplate collecting. *Address:* 155 Mt Rock Road, Newville, PA 17241-8916 (home); Dickinson School of Law, Penn State University, Lewis Katz Hall, 333 West South Street, Carlisle, PA 17013, USA (office). *Telephone:* (717) 776-7359 (home); (717) 240-5227 (office). *Fax:* (717) 240-5126 (office). *E-mail:* webakademik@aol.com (home); web15@psu.edu (office). *Website:* www.dsl.psu .edu/faculty/butler (office).

BUTLER, William T., BA, MD; American immunologist, academic, university administrator and petrochemical industry executive; ed Western Reserve Univ., Oberlin Coll.; served as Chief Clinical Assoc., Lab. of Clinical Medicine, Nat. Inst. of Allergy and Infectious Diseases, Washington, DC; joined faculty Baylor Coll. of Medicine, Houston 1966, served in several positions including Prof. of Internal Medicine and Microbiology and Immunology, Assoc. Dean, Dean of Admissions, Exec. Vice Pres. and Dean 1976–79, Pres. and Pres. 1979–96, Chancellor 1996–2004, Chancellor Emer. 2004–; mem. Bd of Dirs Lyondell Chemical Co., Houston 1989–2007, Chair. 1997–2007 (retd); mem. Bd of Dirs Browing-Ferris Industries, C. R. Bard Inc; mem. Inst. of Medicine. *Publications:* numerous publications in the fields of immunology, infectious disease and medical admin. *Address:* c/o Lyondell Chemical Company, 1221 McKinney Street, Suite 700, Houston, TX 77010, USA (office).

BUTLER OF BROCKWELL, Baron (Life Peer), cr. 1998, of Herne Hill in the London Borough of Lambeth; **Frederick Edward Robin Butler,** KG, GCB, CVO, PC, MA; British public servant; *Non-Executive Member, King's Health Partners;* b. 3 Jan. 1938, Poole, Dorset; s. of the late Bernard Butler and Nora Butler (née Jones); m. Gillian Lois Galley 1962; one s. two d.; ed Harrow School, University Coll., Oxford; with HM Treasury 1961–69, Pvt. Sec. to the Financial Sec. 1964–65, Sec. Budget Cttee 1965–69; seconded to Cabinet Office as mem. Cen. Policy Review Staff 1971–72; Pvt. Sec. to Prime Minister 1972–74, 1974–75, 1982–85; Head of General Expenditure Policy Group 1977–80; Principal Establishment Officer, HM Treasury 1980–82; Second Perm. Sec., Public Services 1985–87; Sec. to Cabinet and Head of Home Civil Service 1988–98; Master Univ. Coll., Oxford 1998–2008; Chair. Cttee to review intelligence on weapons of mass destruction 2004; mem. (non-exec.) King's Health Partners–; Chair. of Govs Dulwich Coll. 1997–2003; Gov. Harrow School 1975–91 (Chair. of Govs 1988–91); mem. Royal Comm. for Lords' Reform 1999; Hon. Fellow, Univ. Coll. Oxford 1989, Kings Coll. London 2011; Hon. DSc (Cranfield) 1994, Hon. LLD (Exeter) 1998, Hon. DCL (London) 1999. *Leisure interests:* competitive games, opera. *Address:* House of Lords, London, SW1A 0PW, England. *E-mail:* lord.butler@univ.ox.ac.uk.

BUTLER-SLOSS, Baroness (Life Peer), cr. 2006, of Marsh Green in the County of Devon; **(Ann) Elizabeth (Oldfield) Butler-Sloss,** DBE, GBE, PC, FRSM; British judge (retd); b. 10 Aug. 1933; d. of the late Sir Cecil Havers and Enid Snelling; m. Joseph William Alexander Butler-Sloss 1958; two s. one d.; ed Wycombe Abbey School; called to Bar, Inner Temple 1955, Bencher 1979; contested Lambeth, Vauxhall as Conservative Cand. 1959; practising barrister 1955–70; Registrar, Prin. Registry of Probate, later Family Div. 1970–79; Judge, High Court of Justice, Family Div. 1979–87; Lord Justice of Appeal 1988–99; Pres. of Family Div. 1999–2005; Chair. Crown Appointments Comm. 2002; Lord of Appeal 2006–09; fmr Vice-Pres. Medico-Legal Soc.; Chair. Cleveland Child Abuse Inquiry 1987–88; Chair. Advisory Council, St Paul's Cathedral 2000–09; currently Chair. Nat. Comm. on Forced Marriage; Pres. Honiton Agricultural Show 1985–86; Treas. Inner Temple 1998; mem. Judicial Studies Bd 1985–89; Hon. Fellow, St Hilda's Coll., Oxford 1988, Visiting Fellow 2001–; Fellow, Kings Coll., London 1991, mem. Council 1992–98; Chancellor Univ. of W of England 1993–2011; Trustee, Human Trafficking Foundation; mem. House of Lords 2006–; Hon. FRCP; Hon. FRCPsych; Hon. FRCPaed; Hon. LLD (Hull) 1989, (Bristol) 1991, (Keele) 1991, (Brunel) 1992, (Exeter) 1992, (Manchester) 1995, (Cambridge) 2000, (Greenwich) 2000, (East Anglia) 2001, (Liverpool) 2001, (Ulster) 2004, (London) 2004; Hon. DLit (Loughborough Univ. of Tech.) 1993; Hon. DUniv (Univ. of Cen. England) 1994, (Open Univ.), (LSE) 2009. *Publications:* Jt Ed. Phipson on Evidence (10th edn), Corpe on Road Haulage (2nd edn), fmr Ed. Supreme Court Practice 1976, 1976. *Address:* House of Lords, London, SW1A 0PW, England. *Telephone:* (20) 7219-4044. *Fax:* (20) 7219-5979. *E-mail:* butlerslosse@parliament.uk.

BUTLER-WHEELHOUSE, Keith Oliver, BComm; British business executive; *Chairman, Chamberlin PLC;* b. 29 March 1946, Walsall; s. of the late Kenneth Butler-Wheelhouse and May Butler-Wheelhouse; m. Pamela Anne Bosworth Smith 1973; two s.; ed Technicon, Port Elizabeth, Univ. of Witwatersrand and Univ. of Cape Town Grad. School of Business; Ford Motor Co. S Africa 1965–85; Dir of Tech. Operations, Gen. Motors S Africa 1985–86; Chair. and CEO Delta Motor Corpn 1987–92; Pres. and CEO Saab Automobile 1992–96; Chief Exec. Smiths Group (fmrly Smiths Industries) PLC 1996–2007; Chair. (non-exec.) Chamberlin PLC 2012–. *Leisure interests:* golf, tennis, shooting, skiing, keeping fit. *Address:* Chamberlin PLC, Chuckery Road, Walsall, WS1 2DU, England (office). *Telephone:* (1922) 707-100 (office). *Fax:* (1922) 638-370 (office). *Website:* www .chamberlin.co.uk (office).

BUTLIN, Martin Richard Fletcher, CBE, MA, DLit, FBA; British museum curator and art historian; b. 7 June 1929, Birmingham; s. of K. R. Butlin and Helen M. Butlin (née Fletcher); m. Frances C. Chodzko 1969; ed Trinity Coll., Cambridge and Courtauld Inst. of Art., Univ. of London; Asst Keeper, Tate Gallery, London 1955–67, Keeper of the Historic British Collection 1967–89; Mitchell Prize (jtly) 1978. *Publications:* A Catalogue of the Works of William Blake in the Tate Gallery 1957, 1971, 1990, Samuel Palmer's Sketchbook of 1824, 1962, 2005, Turner Watercolours 1962, Turner (with Sir John Rothenstein) 1964, Tate Gallery Catalogues: The Modern British Paintings, Drawings and Sculpture (with Mary Chamot and Dennis Farr) 1964, The Later Works of J. M. W. Turner 1965, William Blake 1966, The Blake-Varley Sketchbook of 1819 1969, The Paintings of J. M. W. Turner (with E. Joll) 1977, 1984, The Paintings and Drawings of William Blake 1981, Aspects of British Painting 1550–1800 1988, Turner at Petworth (with Mollie Luther and Ian Warrell) 1989, The Oxford Companion to J. M. W. Turner (co-ed. with Evelyn Joll and Luke Herrmann) 2001, William Blake's Watercolour

Inventions in Illustration of The Grave by Robert Blair 2010; catalogues, articles, reviews etc. *Leisure interests:* music, travel. *Address:* 74C Eccleston Square, London, SW1V 1PJ, England (home). *Telephone:* (20) 7828-8245 (home).

BUTOLA, Ranbir Singh, BA, MBA; Indian oil industry executive; *Chairman, Indian Oil Corporation Ltd;* b. 5 May 1954; ed Faculty of Man. Studies, Univ. of Delhi; worked in a nationalized bank and also in Govt of India dept –1991; joined Oil And Natural Gas Corpn Ltd (ONGC) as Deputy Gen. Man. Finance and Accounts) 1991, Dir (Finance), ONGC Videsh Ltd (subsidiary of ONGC) 2002–04, Man. Dir and CEO ONGC Videsh Ltd 2004–11; Man. Dir Indian Oil Corpn Ltd (IndianOil) 2004–11, mem. Bd of Dirs and Chair. 2011–; apptd mem. Bd of Dirs and Chair. Imperial Energy Corpn plc 2009; Chair. Chennai Petroleum Corpn Ltd 2011–; Chair. Governing Council, Petroleum Fed. of India; Certified Assoc., Indian Inst. of Bankers. *Leisure interests:* travelling, reading. *Address:* Indian Oil Corporation Ltd, Corporate Office, 3079/3, J.B. Tito Marg, Sadiq Nagar, New Delhi 110 049, India (office). *Telephone:* (11) 26260000 (office). *E-mail:* info@iocl .com (office). *Website:* www.iocl.com (office).

BUTOR, Michel; French writer and lecturer; b. 14 Sept. 1926, Mons-en-Baroeul, Nord; s. of Emile Butor and Anne Brajeux; m. Marie-Josephe Mas 1958; four d.; ed Univ. of Paris; teacher at Sens, France 1950, Minieh, Egypt 1950–51, Manchester, UK 1951–53, Salonica, Greece 1954–55, Geneva, Switzerland 1956–57; Visiting Prof., Bryn Mawr and Middlebury, USA 1960, Buffalo, USA 1962, Evanston, USA 1965, Albuquerque, USA 1969–70, 1973–74, Nice and Geneva 1974–75; Assoc. Prof., Vincennes 1969, Nice 1970–73; Prof. of Modern French Literature, Geneva 1975–91; Reader, Éditions Gallimard 1958–; Chevalier, Ordre nat. du Mérite, Ordre des Arts et des Lettres; Hon. PhD (Univ. of Mainz) 1995, (Univ. of Massachusetts) 1999, (Univ. of Thessaloniki) 2001; Prix Felix Fénéon 1957, Prix Renaudot 1957, Grand prix de la critique littéraire 1960. *Publications:* novels: Passage de Milan 1954, L'emploi du temps 1956, La modification 1957, Degrés 1960, Intervalle 1973; essays: Le Génie du lieu 1958, Répertoire 1960, Histoire extraordinaire 1961, Mobile 1962, Réseau aérien 1963, Description de San Marco 1963, Les oeuvres d'art imaginaires chez Proust 1964, Répertoire II 1964, Portrait de l'artiste en jeune singe 1967, Répertoire III 1968, Essais sur les essais 1968, Les mots dans la peinture 1969, La rose des vents 1970, Le génie du lieu II 1971, Dialogue avec 33 variations de L. van Beethoven 1971, Répertoire IV 1974, Matière de rêves 1975, Second sous-sol 1976, Troisième dessous 1977, Boomerang 1978, Quadruple Fond 1981, Répertoire V 1982; poetry: Illustrations 1964, 6,801.000 litres d'eau par second 1965, Illustrations II 1969, Travaux d'approche 1972, Illustrations III 1973, Illustrations IV 1976, Envois 1980, Brassée d'Avril 1982, Exprès 1983, Herbier Lunaire 1984, Mille et un plis 1985, Le Retour du Boomerang 1988, Improvisations sur Flaubert 1991, Patience, Collation 1991, Transit A, Transit B 1993, Improvisations sur Michael Butor 1994, L'Utilité Poétique 1995, Le Japon depuis la France, un rêve à l'ancre 1995, Curriculum Vitae 1996 (jtly), Gyroscope 1996, Ici et là 1997, Improvisations sur Balzac 1998, Entretiens 1999, M. Butor par M. Butor 2003, Anthologie nomade 2004, L'Horticulteur itinérant 2004, Octogénaire 2006, Seize Lustres 2006, Oeuvres complètes I–IV 2006, V–VI 2007, VII–VIII 2008, IX–X 2009, XI–XII 2010. *Leisure interest:* teaching. *Address:* à l'Ecart, 216 Place de l'Eglise, 74380 Lucinges, France (office).

BÚTORA, Martin, PhD; Slovak diplomatist, sociologist, academic and author; *Honorary President, Institute for Public Affairs;* b. 7 Oct. 1944; m.; four c.; Ed.-in-Chief, Bratislava student paper 1966–67, Deputy Ed.-in-Chief 1969; Ed. Kulturny Zivot 1968; Research Asst, Research Inst. of Labour and Social Studies 1971–77; sociologist and psychotherapist at outpatient clinic for alcohol and drug addiction, Bratislava 1978; freelance writer and researcher 1988–; Co-founder and Leader Public Against Violence; Co-founder and first Pres. Inst. for Public Affairs (IVO) 1997–99, Hon. Pres., Programme Dir and Analyst 2003–; Adviser to Pres. Havel on Human Rights Issues and Dir Human Rights Section, Office of Pres. of Fed. Repub. 1990–92; Sr Assoc. mem. St Anthony's Coll. 1993; taught at Faculty of Social Sciences, Charles Univ., Prague 1991–92, Trnava Univ. 1993–97; Amb. to USA 1999–2003; unsuccessful cand. in presidential election 2004; Order of Ľudovít Štúr 2000;German Marshall Fund Fellow 1993, Exec. Educ. Fellow, Woodrow Wilson School of Public and Int. Affairs 1993, Democracy Service Medal, Nat. Endowment for Democracy, Washington, DC 1999, Ján Papánek Medal 2000, Celebration of Freedom Award, American Jewish Cttee 2002, Czech and Slovak Freedom Lecturer, Woodrow Wilson Center, Washington, DC 2012. *Publications include:* Active Citizenship and the Nongovernmental Sector in Slovakia: Trends and Perspectives 2012; numerous journals and magazine articles on post-communist transition, civil society, NGOs, political behaviour, foreign policy issues, ethnicity, nationalism and anti-Semitism. *Address:* Institute for Public Affairs (Inštitút pre verejné otázky), Baštová 5, 811 03 Bratislava, Slovakia (office). *Telephone:* (2) 5443-4030 (office). *Fax:* (2) 5443-4041 (office). *E-mail:* butora@ivo.sk (office). *Website:* www.ivo.sk/166/en/people/martin-butora (office).

BUTROS, Albert Jamil, PhD; Jordanian academic and diplomatist; *Professor Emeritus of English, University of Jordan;* b. 25 March 1934, Jerusalem; s. of Jamil Issa Butros and Virginie Antoine Butros (née Albina); m. Ida Maria Albina 1962; four d.; ed Univs of London and Exeter, UK, Columbia Univ., USA; taught English and math. in two pvt. schools, Amman 1950–55; instructor, Teachers' Coll., Amman 1958–60; Lecturer in English, Hunter Coll., CUNY 1961; Instructor, Miami Univ., Oxford, Ohio 1962–63; Asst Prof. of English, Univ. of Jordan 1963–65, Assoc. Prof. 1965–67, Prof. 1967–79, Acting Chair. Dept of English 1964–67, Chair. 1967–73, 1974–76, Dean of Research and Graduate Studies 1973–76, Prof. of English 1985–2004, Prof. Emer. 2004–; Visiting Prof. of English, Ohio Wesleyan Univ., Delaware, Ohio 1971–72, Jordan Univ. for Women, Amman 1995–96; Dir-Gen. and Pres. Royal Scientific Soc., Amman 1976–84; Sr Research Fellow, Int. Devt Research Centre, Ottawa, Canada 1983–84, Gov. 1986–98; Special Adviser to HRH Crown Prince Hassan of Jordan 1984–85; Amb. to UK 1987–91, (also accred to Ireland 1988–91, to Iceland 1990–91); mem. Bd of Trustees, Philadelphia Univ., Amman 1995–2009; Rapporteur, Cttee on the Jordan Incentive State Prize in Trans. 2001, Cttee on Selection for the Shoman Foundation Prize for Young Arab scholars in the Humanities and Social Sciences 2002, Cttee on Selection of Outstanding Researchers in Jordan 2004; Fellow, World Acad. of Art and Science 1986–; mem., Int. Advisory Bd Jordan Journal of Modern Languages and Literature 2007–; Istiqlal Order, First Class 1987, Order

of Merit (Grande Ufficiale), Italy 1983, KStJ 1991. *Publications:* Leaders of Arab Thought 1969; several articles in learned journals; several translations including parts of Chaucer into Arabic; long paper on the English language and non-native writers of fiction in English, published 2004, Geoffrey Chaucer, Introduction and Selected Translations (in Arabic) 2009. *Leisure interests:* reading, writing, translation, art, world affairs. *Address:* Department of English, University of Jordan, Amman, Jordan (office). *Telephone:* (6) 535-5000 (office); (6) 515-7870 (home). *Fax:* (6) 535-5511 (office); (6) 515-7870 (home). *E-mail:* albertbutros@gmail .com (home). *Website:* www.ju.edu.jo (office).

BUTT, Michael Acton, OBE, MA, MBA; British business executive; *Chairman, Axis Capital Holdings Ltd;* b. 25 May 1942, Thruxton, Hants.; s. of Leslie Acton Kingsford Butt and Mina Gascoigne Butt; m. 1st Diana Lorraine Brook 1964; two s.; m. 2nd Zoe Benson 1986; ed Rugby School, Magdalen Coll., Oxford and Institut Européen d'Admin des Affaires (INSEAD), France; joined Bland Welch Group 1964; Dir Bland Payne Holdings 1970; Chair. Sedgwick Ltd 1983–87; Deputy Chair. Sedgwick Group PLC 1985–87, Eagle Star Holdings PLC 1987–91; Chair. and CEO Eagle Star Insurance Co. 1987–91; Dir BAT Industries PLC 1987–91, Marceau Investissements SA (France) 1987–94, Phoenix International (Bermuda) 1992–97, Bank of N. T. Butterfield & Son Ltd (Bermuda) 1996–2002; Pres. and CEO Mid Ocean Ltd 1993–98, Chair. and CEO Mid Ocean Reinsurance Co. Ltd 1993–98; Dir Exel Capital Ltd 1998–99, XL Capital Ltd 1998–2002; Chair. Axis Capital Holdings Ltd 2002–; Dir Istituto Nazionale delle Assicurazioni 1994–97; Bd mem. and mem. Int. Advisory Council, INSEAD 1982–. *Leisure interests:* travel, tennis, opera, reading, family, the European movt. *Address:* Axis Capital Holdings Ltd, Axis House, 92 Pitts Bay Road, Pembroke, HM 08, Bermuda (office); Leamington House, 50 Harrington Sound Road, Hamilton Parish, CR 04, Bermuda (home). *Telephone:* 496-2600 (office); 293-1378 (home). *Fax:* 405-2720 (office); 293-8511 (home). *E-mail:* michael.butt@axis.bm (office). *Website:* www.axiscapital.com (office).

BUTT, Noor Mohammed, PhD, DSc; Pakistani nuclear solid state physicist (retd); *Professor and Chairman, Preston Institute of Nano Science and Technology;* b. 3 June 1936, Sialkot City; s. of late Ferozuddin Butt and Sardar Begum; m. Gulzar Butt; two s. one d.; ed Punjab Univ., Univ. of Birmingham, UK; fmrly Chief Scientist and Dir Gen., Pakistan Inst. of Nuclear Science and Tech.; currently Prof. and Chair. Preston Inst. of Nano Science and Tech. (PINSAT), Preston Univ., Islamabad; fmr Vice-Pres. Crystallography Soc. of Pakistan; Pres. Pakistan Nuclear Soc. 1995–97; Treas. Pakistan Acad. of Sciences 1994–98; Chair. Pakistan Science Foundation 2005–08, Nat. Comm. on Nano-Science and Tech.; mem., Expert Group, Ministry of Science and Technology; Visiting Scientist, AERE, Harwell, UK, Univ. of Oxford, Int. Centre for Theoretical Physics, Trieste, Reactor Inst., Stockholm, Sweden; IAEA nuclear energy consultant; occasional appearances on Pakistan radio and TV; Fellow, Islamic Acad. of Sciences; Sitara-i-Imtiaz from Pres. of Pakistan 1991; Open Gold Medal in Physical Sciences, Pakistan Acad. of Sciences 1990, 8th Kharazmi Prize (co-recipient) (Iran) 1995, Scientist Emer., PAEC, Life Title 1996. *Publications:* Waves and Oscillations (text book) 1973, International Seminar on Solid State Physics (ed.) 1974, CTBT and its Implications (ed.) 1996; ed. of eight books; more than 140 research papers on nuclear solid state physics; journals and conf. proceedings. *Leisure interest:* photography, playing with grandchildren. *Address:* Preston Institute of Nano Science and Technology (PINSAT), Preston University, Sector H-8/1, Islamabad (office); H: 155, St 15, Sector E-7, Islamabad, Pakistan (home). *Telephone:* (51) 4430597 (ext. 409) (office); (51) 2652242 (home). *Fax:* (51) 4430648 (office). *E-mail:* nmbutt36@yahoo.com (office). *Website:* www.preston.edu.pk (office).

BUTT, Air Chief Marshal Tahir Rafique, MSc; Pakistani air force officer; *Chief of Air Staff;* b. 1955; m.; three c.; ed Staff Coll., Turkey, Nat. Defence Univ., Pakistan Air Force Acad.; joined Pakistan Air Force as Gen. Duty Pilot 1977, served as Deputy Dir Plans, Dir Flight Safety, Asst Chief of the Air Staff (Personnel Branch), Asst Chief of the Air Staff (Training), Dir Gen. Nat. Accountability Bureau, Air Officer, Commdg Southern Air Command, Deputy Chief of the Air Staff (Personnel), Vice-Chief of Air Staff 2010–12, Chief of Air Staff 2012–; fmr Commdt Nat. Security Coll., Nat. Defence Univ.; Hilal-i-Imtiaz, Sitara-i-Imtiaz, Tamgha-i-Basalat. *Address:* Air Force Headquarters, Mushaf Avenue, Islamabad, Pakistan (office). *Website:* www.paf.gov.pk (office).

BUTTENHEIM, Lisa M.; American UN official; *Special Representative of the Secretary-General and Head, United Nations Peacekeeping Force in Cyprus;* b. 1954; d. of Curtis R. Buttenheim; m. Jean-Claude Aimé; ed Stanford Univ., Johns Hopkins Univ. School of Advanced Int. Studies; joined UN 1983, served in various positions including in Exec. Office of Sec.-Gen., in Office of Under-Secs-Gen. for Special Political Affairs, New York and UN Truce Supervision Org., Jerusalem, Sr Political Adviser, Office of Dir-Gen., UN, Geneva 1997–2003, also assignments as Chief of Staff, Office of the Special Rep. of Sec.-Gen. UN Interim Admin Mission in Kosovo and Dir and Sr Adviser, Office of the Special Envoy for Balkans, Geneva, Dir and Head of UN Office, Belgrade 2003–04, Dir Asia and Middle East Div., Dept of Peacekeeping Operations 2004–07, Dir Asia and Pacific Div. 2008, Dir Middle East and West Asia Div., Dept of Political Affairs 2009–10, Special Rep. of UN Sec.-Gen. and Head of Mission, UN Peacekeeping Force in Cyprus (UNFICYP) 2010–. *Address:* UNFICYP Headquarters, PO Box 21642, 1590 Nicosia, Cyprus (office). *E-mail:* unficyp-public-information-office@un.org (office). *Website:* www.unficyp .org (office).

BUTTERWORTH, David, Eur Ing, BSc (Eng), FREng, FIChemE, FRSA; British chemical engineer; b. 24 Oct. 1943; m. Pauline Morgan 1966; one s.; ed Univ. Coll., London; Visiting Engineer, MIT, USA 1976–77; Group Leader, UKAEA 1977–89; Man. Dir Heat Transfer and Fluid Flow Service 1989–95, Sr Consultant in heat transfer 1995–; Visiting Prof., Univ. of Bristol 1993–, Cranfield Univ. 1995–2002, Aston Univ., Birmingham 1996–2001; Pres. UK Heat Transfer Soc. 1988–89; Gen. Sec. Aluminium Plate-Fin Heat Exchanger Mfrs Asscn (ALPEMA) 1995–2008; AIChE Kern Award 1986. *Publications:* Introduction to Heat Transfer 1977, Two-Phase Flow and Heat Transfer 1977 (co-author) (Russian trans. 1980), Condensers, Theory and Practice 1983, Design and Operation of Heat Exchangers (co-ed.) 1992, New Developments in Heat Exchangers (co-ed.), The 8th UK National Conference on Heat Transfer 2004. *Leisure interests:* landscape painting, cooking. *Address:* 29 Clevelands, Abingdon, Oxon., OX14 2EQ, England. *Telephone:* (1235)

525955. *Fax:* (1235) 200906. *E-mail:* davebutterworth@aol.com; davebutterworth@compuserve.com.

BUTTIGLIONE, Rocco; Italian academic and politician; *Vice-President, Camera dei Deputati;* b. 16 June 1948, Gallipoli, Lecce; m.; four d.; fmr Acting Chancellor, Int. Acad. of Philosophy, Liechtenstein; Prof. of Political Science, Saint Pius V Univ., Rome; Minister of European Union Affairs 2001–05, of Cultural Assets and Activities 2005–06; Sec.-Gen. Partito Popolare Italiano 1994–95, Cristiani Democratici Uniti 1995–2002; Pres. Unione dei Democratici Cristiani e di Centro (UDC) 2002–; Vice-Pres. Camera dei Deputati 2008–; Dr hc (Univ. Cattolica di Lublino, Univ. Francisco Marroquín). *Address:* Camera dei Deputati, Palazzo di Montecitorio, Rome (office); Unione dei Democratici Cristiani e di Centro, Via dei Due Macelli 66, 00182 Rome, Italy (office). *Telephone:* (06) 67603316 (office); (06) 69791001 (office). *Fax:* (06) 6791574 (office). *E-mail:* dlwebmast@camera.it (office); info@udc-italia.it (office). *Website:* www.camera.it (office); www.udc-italia.it (office).

BUTTON, Jenson Alexander Lyons, MBE; British racing driver; b. 19 Jan. 1980, Frome, Somerset; s. of the late John Button (fmr Rallycross driver) and of Simone Lyons; ed Selwood Middle School, Frome Community Coll.; began karting aged eight; Formula Ford Festival Winner 1998, British Formula Ford Champion 1998; first drove in Formula One in 2000 season, with Williams team; youngest driver to score points in Formula One aged 20 years, 67 days (Brazilian Grand Prix 2000); switched to Benetton 2001–03 (became Renault F1 2002); moved to BAR 2003 (renamed Honda for 2006 season), won first Grand Prix in Hungary after 113 races 6 Aug. 2006, Honda withdrew from sport Dec. 2008, man. buy-out of team by Ross Brawn Feb. 2009, drove Mercedes-engined car in 2009 Championship; Formula One World Champion 2009; signed for Vodafone McLaren Mercedes Nov. 2009–; runner-up, Formula One World Championship 2011; Australian Grand Prix 2012; won Belgian Grand Prix 2012; resides in Monaco; McLaren Autosport BRDC Award 1998, Lorenzo Bandini Trophy 2001, British Competition Driver of the Year 2003, Hawthorn Memorial Trophy 2004, 2005, 2006, Int. Driver of the Year 2004, British Competition Driver of the Year 2006, Laureus Breakthrough of the Year Award 2010. *Leisure interests:* triathlon, car collection includes a McLaren MP4-12c. *Address:* McLaren Technology Centre, Chertsey Road, Woking, GU21 4YH, England (office). *Telephone:* (1483) 261000 (office). *Fax:* (1483) 261010 (office). *E-mail:* info@mclaren.com (office). *Website:* www.mclaren.com (office); www.jensonbutton.com.

BUXTON, Andrew Robert Fowell, CMG, FIB; British banker; b. 5 April 1939, London; m. Jane Margery Grant 1965; two d.; ed Winchester Coll. and Pembroke Coll., Oxford; joined Barclays Bank Ltd 1963; Gen. Man. Barclays Bank PLC 1980, CEO 1992–93, Chair. 1993–99; Deputy Chair. (non-exec.) Xansa PLC 1999–2007; Chair. Heart of the City; Pres. British Bankers' Assen 1997–2002; mem. Bd of Dirs Capitaland Ltd; mem. Court, Bank of England 1997–2001, Guild of Int. Bankers 2001, Panel on Takeovers and Mergers 2001; Gov. Imperial Coll. of Science and Technology; fmr Visiting Prof., City Univ.; currently Visiting Prof., Cass Business School; Hon. DSc (City). *Address:* Cass Business School, City University London, 106 Bunhill Row, London, EC1Y 8TZ, England (office). *Telephone:* (20) 7040-8600 (office). *Website:* www.cass.city.ac.uk (office).

BUYOYA, Maj. Pierre; Burundian politician and fmr head of state; *President, Foundation for Unity, Peace and Democracy;* b. 24 Nov. 1949, Mutangaro, Rutovu; m. Sophie Buyoya 1978; one s. three d.; ed Royal Mil. Acad., Brussels, staff coll. in France, war coll. in Germany; degree in social science and mil. affairs; mem. Cen. Cttee UPRONA Party 1979–87; fmr COO Ministry of Nat. Defence; led mil. coup against fmr Pres. Bagaza Sept. 1987; Pres. of Third Repub. and Minister of Nat. Defence 1987–92; Chair. Mil. Cttee for Nat. Salvation 1987–93; Pres. Foundation for Unity, Peace and Democracy 1994–; Pres. of Burundi 1987–93, 1996–2003; mem. Senate 2003–. *Publications:* Building Peace in Burundi – Mission Impossible 1998. *Leisure interests:* reading, football, swimming. *Address:* BP 2006, Bujumbura, Burundi (office). *Telephone:* (2) 20796 (office); (2) 13208 (home). *Fax:* (2) 20816 (office). *E-mail:* fupd2003@yahoo.fr (office).

BUYSSE, Baron Paul Henri Maria; Belgian business executive; *Chairman, NV Bekaert SA;* b. 17 March 1945, Antwerp; m.; five c.; various marketing and sales functions, Ford Motor Co. 1966–76; Gen. Man. Car Sales & Marketing, Deputy Man. Dir British Leyland Belgium NV 1976–79, Exec. Dir Tenneco Belgium 1980–84, Man. Dir J.I. Case Benelux 1980–84, Gen. Man. Europe N, J.I. Case, Int. Harvester and Poclain 1984–88; Group Man. Dir Hansen Transmissions Int. 1988; Group Chief Exec. BTR Automotive & Eng Group (London) 1989, Group Chief Exec. BTR Eng and Dunlop Overseas 1991, Exec. Dir BTR PLC 1992–97; CEO Vickers PLC 1998–2000; Chair. NV Bekaert SA 2000–; Dir (non-exec.) Bd of Generale Bank, Censor Nat. Bank of Belgium; Chair., mem. Exec. Cttee and Dir King Baudouin Foundation; Chair. Prince Filip Foundation; Hon. Pres. Antwerp Chamber of Commerce & Industry; Hon. Dean of Labour, Emer. 2003–; Kt, Order of Leopold 1988; Officer, Order of Orange-Nassau 1994; Officier, Order nat. du Mérite 1996; Hon. CBE 1997; Commdr, Order of Leopold II 2001; Grand Officer, Order of Leopold II 2005; Hon. CMG 2005; UNIZO Prize 2003. *Publication:* main author of the Belgian Code for Corporate Governance (Code Buysse). *Leisure interests:* golf, reading. *Address:* NV Bekaert SA, President Kennedypark 18, 8500 Kortrijk, Belgium (office). *E-mail:* paul.buysse@bekaert.com (office). *Website:* www.bekaert.com (office).

BÜYÜKANIT, Gen. (Mehmet) Yaşar; Turkish army officer; b. 1 Sept. 1940, Istanbul; m. Filiz Büyükanıt; one d.; ed Mil. Acad., Infantry School, Army Staff Coll., NATO Defence Coll.; served in different units of Land Forces as Platoon and Commando Co. Commdr 1963–70, then numerous leadership positions including Chief of Operations, 6th Infantry Div., Instructor, Army Staff Coll., Intelligence Div. Basic Intelligence Br. Forces and Systems Section Chief, Supreme HQ Allied Powers Europe (SHAPE), Mons, Belgium, Section then Br. Chief of Gen.-Adm. Br. at Turkish Gen. Staff (TGS) HQ, Commdr of Kuleli Mil. High School and of Presidential Guard Regiment; 2nd Armored Brigade Commdr then Chief of Intelligence Dept, AFSOUTH HQ, Naples, Italy; Sec. Gen. of Turkish Gen. Staff then Supt Turkish Army Acad. 1992–96; 7th Army Corps Commdr 1996–98; Chief of Operations TGS 1998–2000, Deputy Chief 2000–03, Commdr of First Army 2003–04; Commdr Turkish Land Forces 2004–06; Commdr Turkish Armed Forces 2006–08; Turkish Armed Forces (TAF) Medal of Distinguished Service, TAF Medal

of Distinguished Courage and Self-Sacrifice, TAF Medal of Honor, Italian Medal of Honour, USA Legion of Merit, Pakistani Nishan-ı Imtiaz. *Address:* Ministry of National Defence, Milli Savunma Bakanlığı, 06100 Ankara, Turkey (office). *Telephone:* (312) 4254596 (office). *Fax:* (312) 4184737 (office). *E-mail:* meb@meb.gov.tr (office). *Website:* www.msb.gov.tr (office); www.tsk.mil.tr (office).

BUZATU, Gheorghe, DHist; Romanian historian, research institute director and fmr politician; b. 6 June 1939, Sihlea, Vrancea Co., Romania; s. of Ilie Buzatu and Maria Buzatu; m. Constanţa Huiban 1970; one s.; ed Iaşi Univ.; Prof., Ovidius Univ., Constanţa; Prof., Univ. of Craiova, Dir Centre for the Study of International Relations; Scientific Researcher and Dir European History and Civilization Centre of Romanian Acad./Filiala Iaşi; Scientific Researcher, Pvt. Inst. for Romanian Studies Constantin C. Giurescu; Vice-Pres. Senate 2000–04; mem. Parl. Ass. of Council of Europe 2003–04; mem. Acad. of Romanian Scientists; mem. editorial bds several journals including Europa XXI, Dosarele Istoriei, Anuarul Muzeului Marinei Române, Saeculum, Orizont XXI, Istorie şi Civilizaţie; Dr hc (Univ. of Constanţa); Prizes of the Romanian Acad. 1981, 1983, Prize of Flacăra magazine 1992, Prize of Revista de Istorie Militară 1993, 1995, 1996, D. Cantemir Prize, Academia Oamenilor de Stiinţa din Romania 2010. *Publications include:* (in Romanian): Files of the World War 1939–45 1979, Romania and the International Oil Trusts up to 1929 1981, From the Secret History of World War II Vols I and II 1988, 1995, Romania and World War II: A Bibliography (with others) 1981, Titulescu and the Strategy of Peace (ed.) 1982, The Romanians in World History Vols 1–260 (ed.) 1986–2011, Marshal Antonescu versus History, Vols I–V (with others) 1990–2002, Forbidden History 1990, Romania with and without Antonescu 1991, The Romanians in the American Archives (ed.) 1992, Geopolitics (Vol. I) (ed.) 1994, North Iorga, The Man and the Word (Vols I–III) 1971–99, Romania and the World War of 1939–1945 1995, The Romanians in the Kremlin's Archives 1995, The Romanian Right (ed.) 1996, The Secret Archives, Vols I–II (with others) 1998, A History of Romanian Oil 1998, History of the Romanians 1918–1948 (with others) 1999, Stalin (with others) 1999, Romania and the Second World War (with others) 2002, Diplomacy and Romanian Diplomats (Vols 1–2) (with others) 2001–02, Marshal Antonescu at the Judgement of History 2003, Romania and the Great Powers 1939–1947 2003, History of the Romanian Senate (with others) 2004, Parliamentarian Discourses and Debates 1864–2004 (ed.) 2004, Hitler-Stalin-Antonescu I–III 2005–08, Journal of Marshall Antonescu I 1940–1941 2008 (ed.), Journal II 1942–June 1943 2010, Romania Under the Empire of Chaos (1939–1945) 2007, Execution of Marshal Antonescu 2009, The Romanians in Foreign Archives I–II 2009, Romania in War and Peace Equation (1939–1947) (with others) 2009, Opera Omnia (54 vols) 2009–10; (in English): Anglo-Romanian Relations after 1821 (ed.) 1983, North Titulescu and Transylvania 1984, Romania's Options in June 1940 1995, The Oil Policy of Romania until 1918 2004, The Reconstruction of Europe (1944–1947): Romania and the Great Powers 2004; (in Spanish): Breve Historia de Rumania (with others) 1982. *Address:* European History and Civilization Centre of Romanian Academy/Filiala Iaşi, Aleea Mihail Sadoveanu, nr. 3, parter, Iaşi 700490 (office); Splai Bahlui, nr 20A, Bloc I/1, Apartment 5, Iaşi 6600, Romania (home). *Telephone:* (32) 212441 (Iaşi) (office); (24) 1671448 (Constanţa) (office); (72) 2696764 (mobile). *Fax:* (32) 212441 (Iaşi) (office). *E-mail:* ghbuzatu@yahoo.com (office).

BUZEK, Jerzy Karol; Polish politician and chemical engineer; b. 3 July 1940, Śmiłowice; m. Ludgarda Buzek; one d.; ed Silesian Tech. Univ., Gliwice; Scientific Researcher and Prof., Chemical Eng Inst., Polish Acad. of Sciences, Gliwice 1963–97, Prof. of Tech. Science 1997–; mem. Solidarity Trade Union 1980–; organizer of Solidarity underground structures in Silesia; activist of union's regional and nat. leadership; expert and co-author economic program of the Solidarity Election Action (AWS), Chair. Nat. Bd of Social Movt of Solidarity Election Action 1999–2001, Chair. AWS coalition 2001–; Deputy to Sejm (Parl.) 1997–2001; Prime Minister of Poland 1997–2001; Researcher and Pro-Rector Polonia Univ., Częstochowa 2002–; Prof., Mechanical Div., Tech. Univ. of Opole; mem. European Parl. (Silesian Voivodship constituency) (Group of the European People's Party—Christian Democrats and European Democrats) 2004–, Pres. 2009–12, mem. Cttee on Industry, Research and Energy, mem. Temp. Cttee on Climate Change, Substitute mem. Cttee on the Environment, Public Health and Food Safety, mem. Del. to EU-Ukraine Parl. Cooperation Cttee, Substitute mem. Del. for Relations with the Countries of Cen. America; f. Family Foundation together with his wife 1998; est. annual Pro Publico Bono Prize for the best national civic initiatives 1999; Dr hc (Seoul, Dortmund); Laureate, Grzegorz Palka Award 1998. *Publications include:* several dozen articles and monographs on mathematical modelling, desulphurization of exhaust gases and optimization of processes. *Leisure interests:* poetry, theatre, horse riding, tennis, yachting. *Address:* European Parliament, Bâtiment Altiero Spinelli, 05F243, 60 rue Wiertz, 1047 Brussels, Belgium (office). *Telephone:* (2) 284-56-31 (office). *Fax:* (2) 284-97-69 (office). *E-mail:* jbuzek@europarl.eu.int (office). *Website:* www.buzek.pl (office).

BYAM SHAW, Nicholas Glencairn; British publisher; b. 28 March 1934, London; s. of the late David Byam Shaw and Clarita Pamela Clarke; m. 1st Joan Elliott 1956 (divorced 1973); two s. one d.; m. 2nd Suzanne Filer (née Rastello) 1974; m. 3rd Constance Mary Wilson (née Clarke) 1987; ed Royal Naval Coll., Dartmouth; served RN, retiring with rank of Lt 1951–56; on staff of Collins (printers and publrs), Sales Man. 1956–64; joined Macmillan Publrs Ltd as Sales Man. 1964, Deputy Man. Dir 1968, Man. Dir 1970–90, Chair. 1990–97, Deputy Chair. 1998–99; Dir St Martin's Press 1980–99 (Deputy Chair. 1997–99), Pan Books Ltd 1983–99 (Chair. 1986–99), Gruppe Georg von Hotzbrinck, Stuttgart, Germany 1996–99; mem. British Council Publrs' Advisory Cttee, Byam Shaw School Council. *Leisure interests:* travel, gardening, reading, music. *Address:* 9 Kensington Park Gardens, London, W11 3HB, England (home). *Telephone:* (20) 7221-4547 (home).

BYAMBASUREN, Dashiyn; Mongolian politician; b. 20 June 1942, Binder somon Dist, Hentii Prov.; s. of Lombyn Dash and Tsevegeen Perenlee; m. Sanjeen Dulamlkhand 1968; three s. three d.; ed Inst. of Economics and Statistics, Moscow, USSR; apptd Dept Chief, State Statistics Bd; Deputy Chair., then Chair. State Cttee for Prices and Standardization 1970–76; Chair. Construction and Repair Work Trust for Auto Transport 1984, Chief Research Officer, Research Inst. of Project Drafts for Automated Man. Systems 1985, Dir Manager Training Inst., Council of Ministers 1986; Deputy Chair. Council of Ministers 1989–90, First

Deputy Chair. March–Sept. 1990, Prime Minister 1990–92; Pres. Mongolian Devt Foundation, World Mongolian Fed. 1993; fmr mem. Parl.; fmr Chair. Mongolian Democratic Renewal Party; Rector Inst. of Admin. and Man. 1998–2000; Rector Acad. of Man.; Dir Centre for Devt Strategy and System Research 2001; Prof. and Academician, Nat. Acad. of Science. *Publications:* Orchlongiin hurd, Sergen mandakh ireedui, Uuriin javar. *Address:* GPO Box 248, Ulan Bator, Mongolia (home). *Telephone:* 324167 (office). *Fax:* 320090 (office). *E-mail:* byambasuren@cdssr.mn (office). *Website:* www.cdssr.mn (office).

BYATT, Dame Antonia Susan (A.S.), (Dame Antonia Duffy), DBE, BA, FRSL; British writer; b. 24 Aug. 1936, Sheffield, Yorkshire; d. of John F. Drabble, QC and the late Kathleen M. Bloor; sister of Margaret Drabble; m. 1st Ian Charles Rayner Byatt (q.v.) 1959 (divorced 1969); one s. (deceased) one d.; m. 2nd Peter John Duffy 1969; two d.; ed Sheffield High School, The Mount School, York, Newnham Coll., Cambridge, Bryn Mawr Coll., PA, USA and Somerville Coll., Oxford; Extra-Mural Lecturer, Univ. of London 1962–71; Lecturer in Literature, Cen. School of Art and Design 1965–69; Lecturer in English, Univ. Coll., London 1972–81, Sr Lecturer 1981–83; Assoc. Newnham Coll., Cambridge 1977–82; mem. BBC Social Effects of TV Advisory Group 1974–77; mem. Bd of Creative and Performing Arts 1985–87, Bd of British Council 1993–98; Kingman Cttee on English Language 1987–88; Man. Cttee Soc. of Authors 1984–88 (Chair. 1986–88); mem. Literature Advisory Panel of the British Council 1990–98; broadcaster, reviewer and judge of literary prizes; Fellow English Asscn; Hon. Fellow, Newnham Coll. Cambridge 1999, London Inst. 2000, Univ. Coll. London 2004, Somerville Coll. Oxford 2005; Chevalier, Ordre des Arts et Lettres 2003; Hon. DLitt (Bradford) 1987, (Durham, York) 1991, (Nottingham) 1992, (Liverpool) 1993, (Portsmouth) 1994, (London) 1995, (Cambridge) 1999, (Sheffield) 2000, (Kent at Canterbury) 2004, (Oxford) 2007, (Winchester) 2007, (Leiden, Holland) 2010; Premio Malaparte Award, Capri 1995, Toepfer Foundation Shakespeare Prize, Hamburg 2002, Grand Prix littéraire du Metropolis Bleu (Canada) 2009. *Radio:* dramatisation of quartet of novels (BBC Radio) 2002. *Television:* profile on Scribbling (series, BBC 2) 2002, interview with Mark Lawson (BBC 4) 2010. *Films:* Angels and Insects 1996, Possession 2002. *Publications:* fiction: The Shadow of the Sun 1964, The Game 1967, The Virgin in the Garden 1978, Still Life (PEN/Macmillan Silver Pen for Fiction 1986) 1985, Sugar and Other Stories 1987, Possession: A Romance (Booker Prize 1990, Irish Times-Aer Lingus Int. Fiction Prize 1990, Eurasian Regional Award of the Commonwealth Writers' Prize 1991) 1990 filmed 2002, Angels and Insects (novellas) 1992 (filmed 1996), The Matisse Stories 1993, The Djinn in the Nightingale's Eye (Mythopoeic Fantasy Award 1998) 1994, Babel Tower 1996, Elementals, Stories of Fire and Ice 1998, The Biographer's Tale 2000, A Whistling Woman 2002, Little Black Book of Stories 2003, The Children's Book (James Tait Black Memorial Prize 2010) 2009, Ragnarok: the End of the Gods 2012; non-fiction: Degrees of Freedom: The Novels of Iris Murdoch (revised edn as Degrees of Freedom: The Early Novels of Iris Murdoch) 1965, Wordsworth and Coleridge in Their Time (revised edn as Unruly Times: Wordsworth and Coleridge in Their Time) 1970, Iris Murdoch 1976, Passions of the Mind (selected essays) 1991, Imagining Characters: Conversations About Women Writers (with Ignês Sodré) 1995, New Writing 4 (ed. with Alan Hollinghurst) 1995, New Writing 6 (co-ed.) 1997, The Oxford Book of English Short Stories (ed.) 1998, On Histories and Stories (essays) 2000, Portraits in Fiction 2001, Bird Hand Book (with V. Schrager) 2001, Memory (ed., anthology, with Harriet Harvey Wood) 2008; ed. and introduction to numerous works by other writers. *Address:* c/o Rogers, Coleridge & White, 20 Powis Mews, London, W11 1JN, England (office). *Telephone:* (20) 7221-3717 (office). *Fax:* (20) 7229-9084 (office). *Website:* www.asbyatt.com.

BYATT, Sir Ian Charles Rayner, Kt, BA, DPhil; British economist and government official; *Senior Associate, Frontier Economics;* b. 11 March 1932, Preston, Lancs.; s. of Charles Rayner Byatt and Enid Marjorie Annie Byatt (née Howat); m. 1st Antonia Susan Drabble (q.v.) 1959 (divorced 1969); one s. (deceased) one d.; m. 2nd Prof. Deirdre Kelly 1997; two step-s.; ed Kirkham Grammar School, St Edmund Hall and Nuffield Coll., Oxford, Harvard Univ.; Lecturer in Econs, Durham Coll., Univ. of Durham 1958–62, LSE 1964–67; Econ. Consultant, HM Treasury 1962–64; mem. Central Council of Educ. (England) 1965–66; Sr Econ. Adviser, Dept of Educ. and Science 1967–69; Dir of Econs, Ministry of Housing and Local Govt (and subsequently Dept of Environment) 1969–72; Under-Sec., HM Treasury 1972–78, Deputy Chief Econ. Adviser 1978–89, Chair. Advisory Cttee to HM Treasury on Accounting for Econ. Costs and Changing Prices 1986; Dir-Gen. of Water Services 1989–2000; Sr Assoc., Frontier Economics 2001–; Pres. Econs and Business Educ. Asscn 1998–2001; Co-Sec.-Gen. Foundation for Int. Studies in Social Security 2002–02; Adviser to Water Industry Commr for Scotland 2000–04, Chair. 2005–11; mem. Econ. Policy Cttee of EC 1978–89 (Chair. 1982–85), Econ. and Social Research Council 1983–89, Bd of Man., Int. Inst. of Public Finance 1987–90, 2001–06, Council, Royal Econ. Soc. 1983–90 (mem. Exec. Cttee 1987–89), Cttee on Water Services, Econ. and Financial Objectives 1970–73, Public Services Productivity Panel, HM Treasury 2000–02, Chief Sec.'s Advisory Panel on Better Public Services 2002–06, Bd of Public Finance Foundation 1984–89, Bd of Regulatory Policy Inst. 2001–07, Panel of Advisors to NI Govt in reform of water services 2003–06, Council of Man., Nat. Inst. of Econ. and Social Research 1996–2002, Advisory Bd Centre for Management Under Regulation, Warwick Business School 1996–2010, Governing Body of Birkbeck Coll. 1997–2005 (Chair. Finance and Gen. Purposes Cttee 2001–05, Fellow 2005–), Bd of Advisers, St Edmund Hall, Oxford 1998–2003, Int. Advisory Cttee Public Utilities Research Center, Univ. of Florida 2002–; Vice-Pres. Strategic Planning Soc. 1993–, Human City Inst., Birmingham 1999–2002; Treas., Holy Cross Centre Trust, London 1988–2002, Patron 2006–; Chair. Friends of Birmingham Cathedral 1999– (mem. Cathedral Council 2003–), Trustees of David Hume Inst., Edinburgh 2008–11; Trustee, Acad. of Youth, Birmingham 2001–05; Freeman, City of London 1995; Hon. Prof., Univ. of Birmingham; Hon. Fellow, St Edmund Hall, Oxford 2007–; Hon. DUniv (Brunel) 1994, (Univ. of Central England) 2000, (Aston) 2005. *Publications:* The British Electrical Industry 1875–1914 1979, Delivering Better Services to Citizens 2001; articles and book chapters on nationalized industries and public utilities; contrib to govt reports on micro-econ. policy. *Leisure interests:* painting, family life. *Address:* Frontier Economics, MidCity Place, 71 High Holborn, London, WC1V 6DA (office); 34 Frederick Road, Birmingham, B15 1JN, England (home). *Telephone:* (20) 7031-7000 (office); (121) 689-7946 (home). *Fax:* (20) 7031-7001 (office); (121) 454-6438

(home). *E-mail:* ianbyatt@blueyonder.co.uk (home); ian_byatt@yahoo.co.uk (home); ian.byatt@frontier-economics.com (office). *Website:* www.frontier-economics.com (office).

BYATT, Ronald (Robin) Archer Campbell, CMG; British diplomatist (retd); b. 14 Nov. 1930; s. of Sir Horace Byatt and Lady Byatt (née Olga Campbell); m. Ann Brereton Sharpe 1954; one s. one d.; ed Gordonstoun, New Coll., Oxford; joined Diplomatic Service 1959, at Foreign Office 1959, 1963, served in Havana 1961, Kampala 1970, Perm. Mission to UN, New York 1966, Counsellor and Head of Chancery 1977–79, Head of Rhodesia Dept, FCO 1972–75, Asst Under-Sec. of State for Africa 1979–80, High Commr to Zimbabwe 1980–83, Amb. to Morocco 1985–87, High Commr to NZ (also accred to Western Samoa and Gov. of Pitcairn Island) 1987–90; Visiting Fellow, Univ. of Glasgow 1975–76; Civilian Dir Royal Coll. of Defence Studies, London 1983–84; Panel Chair. Civil Service Selection Bd 1992–95; mem. Forestry Comm. Home-Grown Timber Advisory Cttee (Chair. Environment Sub-cttee) 1993–98; Trustee, Beit Trust 1987–2011, UK Antarctic Heritage Trust 1993–2001; Wissem Alaouite (First Class) (Morocco) 1987. *Leisure interests:* birdwatching, sailing, gardening. *Address:* Drim-na-Vullin, Lochgilphead, Argyll, Scotland (home). *E-mail:* byatt.drim@virgin.net (home).

BYCHKOV, Semyon; American conductor; b. 30 Nov. 1952, Leningrad (now St Petersburg), Russia; brother of Yakov Kreizberg; m. Marielle Labèque; ed Leningrad Conservatory (pupil of Musin); invited to conduct Leningrad Philharmonic Orchestra; left USSR 1975; debut with Concertgebouw, Amsterdam and Berlin Philharmonic 1984–85; toured Germany with Berlin Philharmonic 1985; Music Dir Grand Rapid Symphony Orchestra 1980, Buffalo Philharmonic Orchestra 1986–87, Orchestre de Paris 1989–98, Semperoper, Dresden 1999–2003; Prin. Guest Conductor Maggio Musicale Fiorentino 1992–96; Chief Conductor WDR Sinfonieorchester Köln 1997–2010; Günter Wand Conducting Chair BBC Symphony Orchestra 2012–; Otto Klemperer Chair of Conducting, RAM, London; guest conductor with New York Philharmonic, Chicago Symphony, Cleveland Orchestra, Philadelphia Orchestra, Los Angeles Philharmonic, Vienna Philharmonic, Royal Concertgebouw Orchestra, Gewandhausorchester Leipzig, Berlin Philharmonic, Munich Philharmonic, London Symphony, Royal Opera House Covent Garden, Teatro Real Madrid, Metropolitan Opera New York, La Scala Milan, Opéra de Paris, Vienna State Opera; Franco Abbiati Prize 1996. *Recordings:* R. Strauss's Daphne (with Cologne Radio Chorus and Symphony Orchestra) 2005, Elektra (with Chorus and Symphony Orchestra of Westdeutscher Rundfunk, Köln) 2005. *Address:* c/o IMG Artists, The Light Box, 111 Power Road, London, W4 5PY, England (office). *Telephone:* (20) 7957-5800 (office). *Fax:* (20) 7957-5801 (office). *E-mail:* twalton@imgartists.com (office). *Website:* www .imgartists.com (office).

BYCZEWSKI, Iwo, DrIur; Polish lawyer and diplomatist; b. 29 Feb. 1948, Poznań; m. Anna Nehrebecka; two d.; ed Adam Mickiewicz Univ., Poznań and Collège d'Europe, Bruges; mem. staff, Ministry of Justice 1977–82; researcher, Inst. of Econ. Sciences, Polish Acad. of Sciences (PAN) 1982–89; Prin. Expert, Sec. Comm. in Senate Chancellery; Ministerial Adviser, Vice-Dir Council of Minister's Office 1989–90; Dir Personnel Dept, Ministry of Foreign Affairs 1990–91, Under-Sec. of State 1991–95; Perm. Rep. to EU 2001–02; Amb. to Belgium and Luxembourg 2002–03, to Belgium 2005–07; Chair. Supervisory Bd Alcatel Polska SA 1995–; consultant, Hogan and Hartson (American law firm) 1996–; Chair. Centre of Int. Affairs Foundation 1997–. *Address:* c/o Ministry of Foreign Affairs, 00-580 Warsaw, Al. Szucha 23, Poland.

BYDDER, Graeme M., PhD, MD; British radiologist and academic; *Professor of Radiology and Director, Bydder Laboratory, University of California, San Diego;* fmrly with Robert Steiner Magnetic Resonance Unit, MRC Clinical Sciences Centre, Imaging Sciences Dept, Imperial Coll. Faculty of Medicine, Hammersmith Hosp., London, UK, later Prof. and Fellow, Acad. of Medical Sciences; Prof. of Radiology and Dir Bydder Lab., Univ. of California, San Diego 2003–; Taylor Prize, Robarts Research Inst. 1998. *Publications include:* Magnetic Resonance Imaging Atlas of the Brain (co-author) 1989, MRI Atlas of the Brain (co-author) 1990, Advanced MR Imaging Techniques (co-author) 1997. *Address:* Department of Radiology, School of Medicine, University of California, 200 West Arbor Drive, San Diego, CA 92103-8756, USA (office). *Telephone:* (619) 543-3617 (office). *Fax:* (619) 543-3767 (office). *E-mail:* gbydder@ucsd.edu (office). *Website:* www.ucsd.edu (office).

BYERS, Rt Hon. Stephen (John), PC, LLB, FRSA; British politician and business executive; *Chairman, ACWA Services Ltd;* b. 13 April 1953, Wolverhampton; s. of the late Robert Byers; ed Chester City Grammar School, Chester Coll., Liverpool Polytech.; Sr Lecturer of Law Newcastle Polytech. 1977–82; Labour Party MP for Wallsend 1992–97, for Tyneside N 1997–2010; Opposition Whip 1994–95, frontbench spokesman on educ. and employment 1995–97; Minister of State Dept for Educ. and Employment 1997–98; Chief Sec. to the Treasury 1998–99; Sec. of State for Trade and Industry 1999–2001, for Transport, Local Govt and the Regions 2001–02; Chair. (non-exec.) ACWA Services Ltd. *Address:* ACWA Services Ltd, ACWA House, Keighley Road, Skipton, North Yorkshire, BD23 2UE, England (office). *Telephone:* 1756 794-794 (office). *Fax:* 1756 790-898 (office). *Website:* www.acwa.co.uk (office).

BYFORD, Mark, LLB; British broadcasting executive; b. 13 June 1958, Castleford; s. of Sir Lawrence Byford and Lady Muriel Byford (née Massey); m. Hilary Bleiker 1980; two s. three d.; ed Christ's Hospital School, Lincoln; Univ. of Leeds; joined BBC as Holiday Relief Asst 1979, Controller, Regional Broadcasting 1991–94, Deputy Man. Dir 1994–96, Dir 1996–98; Dir BBC World Service and Global News 1998–2004, Deputy Dir Gen. 2003–11; fmr mem. BBC Exec. Cttee; Fellow, Radio Acad. 2000; Royal TV Soc. Journalism Awards 1980, 1982, 1988, Webby Award (World Service) 2001, Sony Radio Special Award (World Service) 2002, One World Special Award (World Service) 2002. *Leisure interests:* family life, soccer, cricket, rock music, being surrounded by children. *Address:* Bolberry House, 1 Clifton Hill, Winchester, Hants., SO22 5BL, England (home). *Telephone:* (1962) 860197 (home).

BYNG, (James Edmund) Jamie, BA; British publishing director; *Managing Director, Canongate Books;* b. 27 June 1969, Winchester; s. of the Earl of Strafford; m. 1st (divorced); one s. one d.; m. 2nd Elizabeth Sheinkman 2005; ed Univ. of Edinburgh; joined Canongate Books as unpaid worker 1992, bought the co. 1994,

Man. Dir 1994–; f. World Book Night; Canongate named Publisher of the Year 2003. *Address:* Canongate Books, 14 High Street, Edinburgh, EH1 1TE, Scotland (office); Canongate Books, Basement, 151 Chesterton Road, London, W10 6ET, England (office). *Telephone:* (131) 557-5111 (office); (20) 8969-6011 (office). *Fax:* (131) 557-5211 (office); (20) 8969-8462 (office). *E-mail:* info@canongate.co.uk (office). *Website:* www.canongate.co.uk (office); www.worldbooknight.org.

BYRNE, David, BA, BL, SC, FRCPI; Irish barrister, politician and university administrator; *Chancellor, Dublin City University;* b. 26 April 1947; m.; three c.; ed Dominican Coll., Newbridge, Univ. Coll. Dublin, King's Inns, Dublin; called to the Bar 1970; mem. Bar Council 1974–87; mem. Exec. Cttee, Irish Maritime Law Asscn 1974–92; called to Inner Bar 1985; mem. Nat. Cttee ICC 1988–97; mem. Govt Review Body on Social Welfare Law 1989, ICC Int. Court of Arbitration, Paris 1990–97, Constitution Review Group 1995–96; External Examiner for Arbitration and Competition Law, King's Inns 1995–97; Attorney-Gen. 1997–99; mem. Council of State, Cabinet Sub-cttees on Social Inclusion, European Affairs, Child Abuse; EU Commr for Health and Consumer Protection (with particular responsibility for Food Safety, Public Health and Consumer Protection) 1999–2004; Chancellor, Dublin City Univ. 2006–; mem. Barristers' Professional Practices and Ethics Cttee 1995–97; participated in negotiation of Good Friday Agreement April 1998; Fellow, Chartered Inst. of Arbitrators of England and Ireland 1998–; f. Free Legal Advice Centre, Dublin; Hon. Treasurer, Bar Council 1982–83. *Publications:* numerous papers on legal affairs. *Address:* Office of the Chancellor, Dublin City University, Dublin 9, Ireland (office). *E-mail:* public.affairs@dcu.ie (office). *Website:* www.dcu .ie (office).

BYRNE, David; American musician, songwriter, composer and director; b. 14 May 1952, Dumbarton, Scotland; s. of Thomas Byrne and Emily Anderson (née Brown) Byrne; m. Adele Lutz 1987; one c.; ed Rhode Island School of Design, Maryland Inst. Coll. of Art; founder mem., Talking Heads 1974–92; solo artist, musician, composer, producer 1980–; producer for artists, including B-52s, Fun Boy 3, Margareth Menezes; producer Index Video 1983–; dir videotapes 1981–; designer stage sets, lighting, album covers and posters 1977–; f. Luaka Bop label 1988; Film Critics' Award for Best Documentary 1985, MTV Video Vanguard Award 1985, Music Video Producers Asscn Award 1992. *Compositions for film, television and theatre:* Stop Making Sense 1984, The Knee Plays 1984, Alive from Off Center 1984, Dead End Kids 1986, True Stories 1986, Tribute 1986, The Kitchen Presents Two Moon July 1986, True Stories 1986, The Forest 1986, Something Wild 1986, The Last Emperor (Acad. Award, Golden Globe, Hollywood Foreign Press Asscn Award for Best Original Score) 1987, Married to the Mob 1988, A Rustling of Leaves: Inside the Philippine Revolution 1988, The Catherine Wheel 1988, Magicians of the Earth: The Giant Woman and The Lightning Man (TV) 1990, Magicians of the Earth: A Young Man's Dream and a Woman's Secret (TV) 1990, Blue in the Face 1995, In Spite of Wishing and Wanting 2002, Young Adam 2003; contrib. songs to numerous other films. *Films:* Stop Making Sense (actor) 1984, True Stories (actor, dir and co-screenwriter) 1986, Checking Out 1988. *Recordings include:* albums: with Talking Heads: Talking Heads '77 1977, More Songs About Buildings And Food 1978, Fear Of Music 1979, Remain In Light 1980, The Name Of This Band Is Talking Heads 1982, Speaking In Tongues 1983, Stop Making Sense 1984, Little Creatures 1985, True Stories 1986, Naked 1988, Popular Favourites: Sand In The Vaseline 1992; solo: My Life In The Bush Of Ghosts (with Brian Eno) 1981, The Knee Plays 1985, The Forest 1988, Rei Momo 1989, Uh-Oh 1992, David Byrne 1994, Feelings 1997, Look Into The Eyeball 2001, Grown Backwards 2004, Big Love: Hymnal 2008, Everything that Happens will Happen Today (with Brian Eno) 2008, Here Lies Love (with Fatboy Slim) 2010, Love This Giant (with St Vincent) 2012. *Publications:* Stay Up Late 1987, What the Songs Look Like 1987, Strange Ritual 1995, Bicycle Diaries 2009, How Music Works 2012. *Address:* Maine Road Management, 195 Chrystie Street, Suite 901F, New York, NY 10002, USA (office). *Telephone:* (212) 979-9004 (office). *Fax:* (212) 979-0985 (office). *E-mail:* mailbox@maineroadmanagement.com (office). *Website:* www.maineroadmanagement.com (office); www.davidbyrne.com.

BYRNE, Edward, AO, MB BS, MD, DSc, MBA, FRCP, FRCPE, FRACP; Australian neuroscientist, academic and university administrator; *Vice-Chancellor and President, Monash University;* b. 1952, UK; m. Melissa Byrne; ed Univs of Tasmania, Melbourne, Adelaide and Queensland; Muscular Dystrophy Research Fellow, Univ. Coll. London (UCL) Inst. of Neurology 1980–82, Exec. Dean of Medicine, Univ. Coll. and Royal Free Medical School and Vice-Provost (Health), UCL 2007–09; Neurology Registrar, Royal Adelaide Hosp. 1978–80; Dir of Neurology, St Vincent's Hosp., Melbourne 1983; Founding Dir Melbourne Neuromuscular Research Unit, Centre for Neuroscience, Univ. of Melbourne, fmr Prof. of Experimental Neurology; Dean, Faculty of Medicine, Nursing and Health Sciences, Monash Univ. 2003–07, Vice-Chancellor and Pres. Monash Univ. 2009–; Dir (non-Exec.) Cochlear Pty Ltd 2002–, BUPA 2008–09, BUPA Australia 2009–; UCL Queen Square Prize for Neurological Research 1982, Bethlehem Griffith Research Medal 2003, Sir Louis Pyke Award for Contribution to Multiple Sclerosis 2004, John Sands Medal 2005, Alumnus of the Year, Univ. of Tasmania 2010. *Publications:* 200 publs on neurology and neuroscience; Poems from the City, a London Interlude. *Leisure interests:* fly fishing, classical music. *Address:* Office of the Vice-Chancellor, Monash University, Melbourne, Vic. 3800, Australia (office). *Telephone:* (3) 9902-9851 (office). *Fax:* (3) 9905-2096 (office). *E-mail:* edward .byrne@monash.edu (office). *Website:* www.monash.edu/about/structure/senior -staff/vice-chancellor (office).

BYRNE, Gabriel; Irish actor; b. 12 May 1950, Dublin; m. Ellen Barkin (q.v.) 1988 (divorced 1999); two c.; ed Univ. Coll. Dublin; archaeologist, then teacher, began acting in amateur productions; joined an experimental repertory co. 1980; first TV appearance in series The Riordans 1982; first cinema role in Excalibur; moved to New York 1987; f. Plurabelle Films (production co.) 1985. *Theatre:* several roles Nat. Theatre, London; A Touch of the Poet (Broadway) 2005. *Films include:* Hanna K, Gothic, Julia and Julia, Siesta, Miller's Crossing, Hakon Hakenson, Dark Obsession, Cool World, A Dangerous Woman, Little Women, Usual Suspects,

Frankie Starlight, Dead Man, Last of the High Kings, Mad Dog Time, Somebody is Waiting 1996, The End of Violence (dir) 1997, This is the Sea 1997, Toby's Story, Polish Wedding 1998, The Man in the Iron Mask 1998, Quest for Camelot (voice) 1998, An Ideal Husband, Enemy of the State 1998, Stigmata 1999, End of Days 1999, Canone inverso – making love 2000, Spider 2002, Virginia's Run 2002, Emmett's Mark 2002, Ghost Ship 2002, Shade 2003, Vanity Fair 2004, P.S. 2004, The Bridge of San Luis Rey 2004, Assault on Precinct 13 2005, Wah-Wah 2005, Played 2006, Jindabyne 2006, Emotional Arithmetic (aka Autumn Hearts: A New Beginning) 2007, Attack on Leningrad 2009, Perrier's Bounty 2009, I, Anna 2012, Capital 2012, All Things to All Men 2013, Just a Sigh 2013; co-producer In the Name of the Father. *Television includes:* Madigan Men 2000, Patrick (voice) 2004, Live from Lincoln Center (episode, Camelot) 2008, In Treatment (Golden Globe Award for Best Actor in a TV Series – Drama 2009) 2008–10, Secret State (series) 2012, Quirke (mini-series) 2013, Vikings (series) 2013. *Address:* c/o ICM, 8942 Wilshire Blvd, Beverly Hills, CA 96211, USA (office); Plurabelle Films, 10125 Washington Blvd, #205, Culver City, CA 90232, USA. *Telephone:* (310) 244-6782 (Plurabelle).

BYRNE, John V., BA, MA, PhD; American oceanographer and academic; *President Emeritus, Oregon State University;* b. 9 May 1928, Hempstead, NY; m. Shirley O'Connor 1954; one s. three d.; ed Hamilton Coll., Clinton, NY, Columbia Univ. and Univ. of Southern Calif.; research geologist, Humble Oil & Refining, Houston, Tex. 1957–60; Assoc. Prof., Oregon State Univ., Corvallis 1960–66, Prof. of Oceanography 1966–, Chair, Oceanography 1968–72, Dean, Oceanography 1972–76, Dean, Research 1976–80, Vice-Pres. Research and Grad. Studies 1980–81, Pres. 1984–95, now Pres. Emer.; Program Dir Oceanography, NSF 1966–67; US Commr to Int. Whaling Comm. 1982–85; Exec. Dir Kellogg Comm. on Future of State and Land Grant Univs 1996–2000; Admin. Nat. Oceanic & Atmospheric Admin., Washington, DC 1981–84; Hon. Assoc. of Arts (Lynn-Benton Community Coll., Ore.); Hon. JD (Hamilton Coll.) 1994; Distinguished Service Award, Oregon State Univ. 1996. *Leisure interests:* music, painting. *Address:* 811 SW Jefferson Avenue, Corvallis, OR 97333, USA (office). *Telephone:* (541) 737-3542. *Fax:* (541) 737-4380. *E-mail:* john.byrne@orst.edu (office).

BYRNE, Rt Hon. Liam Dominic, PC, BA (Hons), MBA; British politician; *Shadow Secretary of State for Work and Pensions and Policy Review Co-ordinator;* b. 2 Oct. 1970, Warrington, Cheshire, England; m.; three c.; ed Burnt Mill School, Harlow, Univ. of Manchester, Harvard Business School, USA (Fulbright Scholar); early positions at Accenture and N.M. Rothschild & Sons; f. e-Government Solutions Ltd computer co. 2000; adviser to Labour Party on re-organisation of Millbank and nat. business campaign 1996–97; MP (Labour) for Birmingham Hodge Hill (by-election) 2004–10, (revised boundary at Gen. Election) 2010–; Under-Sec. of State for Care Services, Dept of Health 2005; Minister of State for Borders and Immigration 2006–08; Minister for the Cabinet Office and Chancellor of the Duchy of Lancaster 2008–09, Chief Sec. to the Treasury 2009–10; Shadow Chief Sec. to the Treasury May–Oct. 2010, Shadow Minister for the Cabinet Office 2010–11, Shadow Sec. of State for Work and Pensions and Policy Review Co-ordinator 2011–; mem. Amicus, Christian Socialist Movt, Fabian Soc.; fmr Assoc. Fellow, Social Market Foundation. *Publications:* Local Government Transformed 1996, Information Age Government 1998, Cities of Enterprise 2002, Britain in 2020 2003, Reinventing Government Again (co-author) 2004, Why Labour Won 2005, A Common Place 2007. *Address:* House of Commons, Westminster, London, SW1A 0AA, England (office). *Telephone:* (20) 7219-6953 (London) (office); (121) 789-7287 (Birmingham) (office). *Fax:* (20) 7219-1431 (London) (office); (121) 789-9824 (Birmingham) (office). *E-mail:* byrnel@parliament.uk (office). *Website:* www .parliament.uk/biographies/commons/liam-byrne/30771 (office); liambyrne.co.uk.

BYRON, Rt Hon. Sir (Charles Michael) Dennis, Kt, PC, LLB, MA; St Christopher and Nevis barrister and judge; *President, Caribbean Court of Justice;* b. 4 July 1943, Basseterre; m. Lady Norma Virgen Byron; ed Fitzwilliam Coll., Univ. of Cambridge, UK; called to the Bar, Hon. Soc. of the Inner Temple, London, Barrister-at-Law, High Court of Justice in England and Wales 1965; pvt. practice as barrister throughout Leeward Islands, with chambers in St Christopher, Nevis and Anguilla 1966–82; apptd High Court Judge 1982; High Court Judge, East Caribbean Supreme Court 1982–90, Acting Chief Justice 1996–99, Chief Justice 1999–2004; Perm. Judge, Int. Criminal Tribunal for Rwanda, Tanzania 2004–07, Pres. 2007–11; Pres. Caribbean Court of Justice, Trinidad and Tobago 2011–; Pres. Commonwealth Judicial Educ. Inst. 2000–; Yogis and Keddy Chair in Human Rights Law, Dalhousie Univ., Nova Scotia, Canada. *Address:* Caribbean Court of Justice, PO Box 1768, 134 Henry Street, Port of Spain, Trinidad and Tobago (office). *Telephone:* 623-2225 (office). *E-mail:* info@caribbeancourtofjustice.org (office). *Website:* www.caribbeancourtofjustice.org (office).

BYZANTINE, Julian Sarkis, ARCM; British classical guitarist and academic; *Senior Lecturer and Head of Classical Guitar Studies, Queensland Conservatorium, Griffith University, Australia;* b. 11 June 1945, London, England; s. of Carl Byzantine and Mavis Harris; ed Royal Coll. of Music (RCM), London and Accad. Chigiana, Siena, Italy; studied with John Williams at RCM, subsequently with Julian Bream and with Andrés Segovia and Alirio Diaz in Siena; taught at RAM, London 1966–68; Sr Lecturer in Guitar, Queensland Conservatorium, Griffith Univ., Australia; London debut, Wigmore Hall 1969; New York debut, Carnegie Hall 1980; has performed in 77 countries; has given concerts with leading British orchestras, including Royal Philharmonic, City of Birmingham Symphony, Scottish Chamber, BBC Symphony; numerous radio and TV appearances; awarded first ARCM for guitar 1966; scholarships to study with Segovia from Vaughan Williams and Gilbert Foyle Trusts. *Recordings include:* five solo albums, two recordings with flautist Gerhard Mallon. *Publications:* Arrangements of Six Albéniz Piano Works for Guitar 1984, Guitar Technique Rationalised 2002. *Leisure interests:* collecting oriental art, archaeology, tennis. *Address:* Flat 1, 42 Ennismore Gardens, London, SW7 1AQ, England. *Telephone:* (20) 7584-7486. *E-mail:* j.byzantine@griffith.edu.au (home). *Website:* www.julianbyzantine.net (home).

C

CAAMAÑO DOMÍNGUEZ, Francisco, DIur; Spanish politician; *Minister of Justice;* b. 8 Jan. 1963, A Coruña; m.; two d.; ed Univ. de Santiago de Compostela; Adjunct Prof., then Prof. of Constitutional Law, Univ. de Santiago de Compostela; counsel to Constitutional Court 1993–2002; Prof. of Constitutional Law, Univ. of Valencia 2002; Dir Democracy and Local Govt Foundation 2001–04; Sec. of State for Constitutional and Parl. Affairs 2004–09; Minister of Justice 2009–. *Address:* Ministry of Justice, San Bernardo 45, 28015 Madrid, Spain (office). *Telephone:* (91) 3904500 (office). *Website:* www.mjusticia.es (office).

CAAN, James; American actor and director; b. 26 March 1940, Bronx, New York; s. of Arthur and Sophie Caan; m. 1st DeeJay Mathis 1961 (divorced 1966); one d.; m. 2nd Sheila Ryan 1976 (divorced 1977); one s.; m. 3rd Linda O'Gara 1995; two c.; ed Michigan State Univ., Hofstra Coll.; made theatre debut in the off-Broadway production of La Ronde 1960; Broadway debut in Blood Sweat and Stanley Poole, 1961; Outstanding Achievement in Acting, Hollywood Film Festival 1999. *Films include:* Irma La Douce 1963, Lady in a Cage 1964, The Glory Guys 1965, Countdown 1967, Games 1967, Eldorado 1967, Journey to Shiloh 1968, Submarine XI 1968, Man Without Mercy 1969, The Rain People 1969, Rabbit Run 1970, T. R. Baskin 1971, The Godfather 1972, Slither 1973, Cinderella Liberty 1975, Freebie and the Bean 1975, The Gambler 1975, Funny Lady 1975, Rollerball 1975, The Killer Elite 1975, Harry and Walter Go to New York 1976, Silent Movie 1976, A Bridge Too Far 1977, Another Man, Another Chance 1977, Comes a Horseman 1978, Chapter Two 1980, Thief 1982, Kiss Me Goodbye 1983, Bolero 1983, Gardens of Stone 1988, Alien Nation 1989, Dad 1989, Dick Tracy 1990, Misery 1991, For the Boys 1991, Dark Backward 1991, Honeymoon in Vegas 1992, Flesh and Bone 1993, The Program 1994, North Star 1995, Boy Called Hate 1995, Eraser 1996, Bulletproof 1996, Bottle Rocket 1996, This Is My Father 1997, Poodle Springs 1997, Blue Eyes 1998, The Yards 1999, The Way of the Gun 1999, In the Boom Boom Room 2000, Luckytown 2000, Viva Las Nowhere 2000, In the Shadows 2001, Night at the Golden Eagle 2002, City of Ghosts 2002, Dogville 2003, This Thing of Ours 2003, Jericho Mansions 2003, Elf 2003, Get Smart 2008, Cloudy with a Chance of Meatballs (voice) 2009, Middle Men 2010, Henry's Crime 2010, Minkow 2011, Detachment 2011, Tower Heist 2011, Small Apartments 2012, That's My Boy 2010, For the Love of Money 2012; dir and actor Hide in Plain Sight 1980, dir Violent Streets 1981; starred in television movie, Brian's Song, 1971, The Warden 2000. *Television includes:* Las Vegas (series) 2003, Hawaii Five-O (series) 2012, and numerous other TV appearances. *Address:* c/o WME, 9601 Wilshire Boulevard, Beverly Hills, CA 90210, USA (office).

CABALLÉ, Montserrat; Spanish singer (soprano); b. 12 April 1933, Barcelona; m. Bernabé Marti (tenor) 1964; one s. one d.; ed Conservatorio del Liceo; studied under Eugenia Kemeny, Conchita Badia and Maestro Annovazi; debut as Mimi (La Bohème), State Opera of Basel; N American début in Manon, Mexico City 1964; US debut in Lucrezia Borgia, Carnegie Hall 1965; appeared at Glyndebourne Festival as the Marschallin in Der Rosenkavalier and as the Countess in The Marriage of Figaro 1965; debut at Metropolitan Opera as Marguerite (Faust) Dec. 1965; frequent appearances at the Metropolitan Opera and numerous other opera houses throughout the USA; has performed in most of the leading opera houses of Europe including Gran Teatro del Liceo, Barcelona, La Scala, Milan, Vienna State Opera, Paris and Rome Operas, Bayerische Staatsoper (Munich), etc. and also at Teatro Colón, Buenos Aires; repertoire of over 40 roles; final performance at the Met in La Bohème 1988; apptd UNESCO Goodwill Amb. 1994; Most Excellent and Illustrious Doña and Cross of Isabella the Catholic 1966, Commdr des Arts et des Lettres 1986; Gold Medal, Gran Teatro del Liceu, Echo Award 2000, Gramophone Lifetime Achievement Award 2007, numerous other awards. *Recordings include:* Lucrezia Borgia, La Traviata, Salomé, Aida, La Canción Romántica Española (Latin Grammy Award for Best Classical Album) 2007. *Address:* Postfach 1462, 26172 Rastede, Germany. *Website:* www.montserratcaballe.com; www.montserrat-caballe.de.

CABALLEROS, Rómulo Alfredo; Guatemalan economist, diplomatist and politician; b. 29 March 1941; m. Nora Wellmann de Caballleros; ed Univ. de San Carlos de Guatemala, Centro Interamericano de Enseñanza Estaística (CIENES), Instituto Latinoamericano de Planificación Economica y Social (ILPES), Univ. de Madrid, Spain; worked at Bank of Guatemala 1962–72; consultant to Dept of Gen. Studies, Secr. Gen. of Econ. Planning 1972–73, Dir 1973–75; consultant to UNDP 1975; Econ. Affairs Exec., Econ. Comm. for Latin America and the Caribbean (CEPAL) 1975–79, Deputy Head of Econ. Devt, Int. Trade and Statistics Section 1976–81, Head of Section 1983–90, Deputy Dir CEPAL Satellite Office, Mexico 1990–92, 1994–96, Dir Planning, Programmes and Operations Div. 1996–97, Dir Sub-regional Office, Mexico 1997–2000; Sec.-Gen. of Econ. Planning 1993; Amb. to Mexico 2000–02; consultant to EC, UN, IDB, World Bank 2002–07; Minister of the Economy 2008–09; currently consultant; Orden del Águila Azteca (Mexico).

CABALLEROS LÓPEZ, Harold Osberto, MA, MBA; Guatemalan lawyer, business executive and politician; *Minister of Foreign Affairs;* b. 20 June 1956, Guatemala City; s. of Osberto Caballeros and Coralia López; m. Cecilia Arimany; two s. two d.; ed Universidad Francisco Marroquin, Univ. of Miami, Harvard Univ., Fletcher School of Law and Diplomacy, Tufts Univ., USA; pvt practice as lawyer 1983–; f. El Shaddai Ministries, 20 years as pastor; f. Visión con Valores political party 2006, Sec.-Gen. 2009–; Minister of Foreign Affairs 2012–; Dean, Universidad San Pablo de Guatemala; Founder and Pres. Radios Vision Corpn. *Publications:* De Victoria en Victoria 1999, Dios te invita a soñar 2002, El poder transformador del evangelio de Jesucristo 2003, El poder transformador del avivamiento 2005. *Address:* Ministry of Foreign Affairs, 2b Avda La Reforma 4-17, Zona 10, Guatemala City, Guatemala (office). *Telephone:* 2410-0010 (office). *Fax:* 2410-0011 (office). *E-mail:* webmaster@minex.gob.gt (office). *Website:* www.minex.gob.gt (office).

CABEZAS MOLINA, Eduardo; Ecuadorean economist, diplomatist and fmr central banker; m. Berta Cabezas; ed Universidad del Ecuador, Queen's Coll., New York, USA; Minister, Embassy in Bonn 1981–84, Amb. to Uruguay 1994, to Guatemala –2003, to UK (also accred to Portugal) 2003–06, 2008–10; Pres. Cen. Bank of Ecuador 2006–08. *Address:* c/o Ministry of Foreign Relations, Trade and Integration, Avenida 10 de Agosto y Carrión E1-76, Quito, Ecuador (office). *Telephone:* (2) 299-3284 (office). *Fax:* (2) 299-3273 (office). *E-mail:* gabminis@mmrree.gov.ec (office). *Website:* www.mmrree.gov.ec (office).

CABEZAS MORALES, Rodrigo Eduardo; Venezuelan politician and economist; *Chairman, Grupo Parlamentario Venezolano;* b. 19 June 1956, Valera, Trujillo state; m.; ed Univ. of Zulia; mem. Faculty, Univ. of Zulia 1982–, currently Prof. and mem. Instituto de Investigaciones; Deputy, Congreso de la República 1990–93, 1994–98, Asamblea Nacional 2000–04, Vice-Chair. Asamblea Nacional Finance Comm. 2000–01, Chair. 2002–06; Minister of Finance 2007–08; Chair. Parlamento Latinoamericano, Grupo Parlamentario Venezolano 2011–; Bd mem. Nat. Council on Culture 2002; mem. Por la Democracia Social (PODEMOS) party. *Address:* Grupo Parlamentario Venezolano, Edificio La Perla, Mezzanina - Piso 1. Caracas Distrito Capital 1010, Correo de Carmelitas Caracas, 5971 Caracas, Venezuela (office). *E-mail:* contacto@podemos.org.ve (office). *Website:* www.parlatino.org.ve (office).

CABI, Martinho N'Dafa; Guinea-Bissau politician; b. 17 Sept. 1957, Nhacra, Oio Prov.; s. of Cabi Imbitna and Tchambu Insol; mem. Balanta ethnic group; joined Partido Africano da Independência da Guiné e Cabo Verde (PAIGC) 1974, various roles including Chair. Cttee for Autonomous Region of Guinea-Bissau, mem. Cen. Cttee 1999, Third Vice-Pres. 2002–07; fmr Minister of Energy; Minister of Nat. Defence 2004–05; Prime Minister 2007–08. *Address:* Partido Africano da Independência da Guiné e Cabo Verde (PAIGC), CP 106, Bissau, Guinea-Bissau (office). *Website:* www.paigc.org (office).

CABLE, Rt Hon. (John) Vincent (Vince), BA, PhD; British politician and economist; *Secretary of State for Business, Innovation and Skills;* b. 9 May 1943, York, N Yorks.; m. 1st Olympia Rebelo 1968 (died 2001); three c.; m. 2nd Rachel Wenban Smith 2004; ed Nunthorpe Grammar School, Fitzwilliam Coll., Cambridge, Univ. of Glasgow; mem. Liberal Party 1963–65, Labour Party 1966–82, Social Democratic Party (SDP) 1982–88; Pres. Cambridge Union 1965; fmr Pres.-elect Cambridge Univ. Liberal Club (resgnd from Liberals before taking up office); Treasury Finance Officer for Govt of Kenya 1966–68; fmr Lecturer in Econs, Univ. of Glasgow, LSE; Councillor (Labour), Glasgow City Council 1971–74; First Sec., FCO 1974–76; Deputy Dir Overseas Devt Inst., including as a Special Adviser to then Sec. of State for Trade and Industry, John Smith MP 1970s; worked as Special Adviser on Econ. Affairs for Commonwealth Sec. Gen., Sir Sonny Ramphal 1983–90; worked for Shell International from 1990, Chief Economist 1995–97; fmr Head of Econs Programme, Chatham House; contested Glasgow Hillhead (Labour) constituency 1970, York (SDP/Liberal Alliance) 1983, 1987, Twickenham (Liberal Democrat) 1992; MP for Twickenham 1997–; Liberal Democrat Spokesperson for the Treasury (EMU and The City) 1997–99, Prin. Spokesperson for Trade and Industry 1999–2003, Shadow Chancellor of the Exchequer 2003–10; Sec. of State for Business, Innovation and Skills and Pres. of the Bd of Trade 2010–; Deputy Leader Liberal Democrat Party 2006–10, Acting Leader 2007; mem. (Select Cttees), Treasury (Treasury Sub-cttee) 1998–99, Treasury 1998–99; mem. Competitiveness Council, Council of the EU 2010–; Fellow, Nuffield Coll., Oxford; Visiting Research Fellow, Centre for the Study of Global Governance, LSE 2001–04; Patron, Polycystic Kidney Disease Charity; Liberal Democrat. *Publications:* Protectionism and Industrial Decline 1983, The New Giants: China and India 1994, The World's New Fissures: The Politics of Identity 1995, Globalisation and Global Governance 1999, Multiple Identities 2005, Public Services: Reform with a Purpose 2005, The Storm: The World Economic Crisis and What It Means 2009, Tackling the Fiscal Crisis: A Recovery Plan for the UK 2009. *Address:* Ministerial Correspondence Unit, Department for Business, Innovation and Skills, 1 Victoria Street, London, SW1H 0ET (office); House of Commons, Westminster, London, SW1A 0AA; Constituency Office, 2A Lion Road, Twickenham, TW1 4JQ, England. *Telephone:* (20) 7215-5621 (Dept) (office); (20) 7219-3000 (Westminster); (20) 8892-0215 (Twickenham). *Fax:* (20) 7215-5468 (Dept) (office). *E-mail:* vince.cable@bis.gsi.gov.uk (office); mpst.cable@bis.gsi.gov.uk (office); cablev@parliament.uk (office); enquiry.enquiry@bis.gsi.gov.uk (office). *Website:* www.bis.gov.uk (office); www.parliament.uk/biographies/commons/vince-cable/25665; vincentcable.org.uk.

CABRAAL, Ajith Nivard; Sri Lankan chartered accountant and central banker; *Governor, Central Bank of Sri Lanka;* est. own man. consultancy before taking up public service 2005; fmr Chair. and/or Dir of several quoted and unquoted public cos; Sec., Ministry of Plan Implementation and Adviser to Pres. on Econ. Affairs –2006, also served as mem. Bd Strategic Enterprises Man. Agency; mem. Govt Team at Geneva Talks with Liberation Tigers of Tamil Eelam Feb. 2006; represented Govt in Millennium Challenge Fund negotiations with US Govt; Gov. Cen. Bank of Sri Lanka 2006–, Chair. Monetary Bd; fmr Eisenhower Fellow; Founder-Chair. Corp. Governance Cttee; fmr Pres. Business Recovery and Insolvency Practitioners Asscn of Sri Lanka; Past Pres. Inst. of Chartered Accountants of Sri Lanka, S Asian Fed. of Accountants, St Peter's Coll. Old Boys Union; fmr mem. Bd Securities and Exchange Comm., Nat. Inst. of Business Man., Postgraduate Inst. of Man., Univ. of Moratuwa. *Publications:* Towards a Sri Lankan Renaissance, Lak Mawata Muthu Potak (A String of Pearls for Mother Lanka, collection of more than 60 short essays submitted to popular nat. newspapers 2003–04). *Address:* Central Bank of Sri Lanka, 30 Janadhipathi Mawatha, POB 590, Colombo 1, Sri Lanka (office). *Telephone:* (11) 2477000 (office). *Fax:* (11) 2477712 (office). *E-mail:* cbslgen@cbsl.lk (office). *Website:* www.cbsl.gov.lk (office).

CABRAL BARRETO, Ireneu; Portuguese judge and government official; *Representative of the Portuguese Republic in the Autonomous Region of Madeira;* b. 5 Feb. 1941, Ponta do Sol, Madeira; ed Coimbra Law Univ.; Asst to Dist Attorney for Ourique, S Vicente, Vila Nova de Famalicão, Vila Verde, Portimão and Lisbon 1964–70; Judge, São Jorge co. 1971–72; Asst to Dist Attorney for Bragança, Évora and Setúbal 1972–75; Deputy Attorney Gen. of Portugal 1975–97; Legal Adviser, Ministry of Trade and Tourism 1975–77; Judge, Supreme Court of Justice 1997–98; mem. European Comm. of Human Rights 1993–99; Judge, European Court of Human Rights, Strasbourg 1998–2011; Rep. of Portuguese Repub. in

Autonomous Region of Madeira 2011–. *Publications:* A Convenção Europeia dos Direitos do Homen (fourth edn) 2010; numerous articles in professional journals. *Address:* Palácio de São Lourenço, Apat n.º 142, Avenida Zarco 9001-902 Funchal, Madeira (office). *Fax:* (291) 234626 (office). *E-mail:* geral@representantedarepublica-madeira.pt (office). *Website:* www .representantedarepublica-madeira.pt (office).

CABREJAS, Santiago Cembrano; Colombian government official and inter-national organization official; *Secretary-General a.i., Andean Community;* ed Jorge Tadeo Lozano Univ.; fmr Dir of Econ. Integration, Ministry of Foreign Trade and Tourism; CEO Gen. Secr., Andean Community (Comunidad Andina) 2008–13, Sec.-Gen. a.i. 2013–. *Address:* Andean Community, Avenue Aramburú Cdra. 4 S/N Esquina con Paseo de la República, San Isidro, Lima 27, Peru (office). *Telephone:* (1) 7106400 (office). *Fax:* (1) 2213329 (office). *E-mail:* contacto@comunidadandina .org (office). *Website:* www.comunidadandina.org (office).

CABRERA, Cesar Benito, BS; American business executive, politician and fmr diplomatist; *Senior Advisor, Husch Blackwell Sanders LLP;* b. San Juan, Puerto Rico; m. Helvetia Barros; one d.; ed Univ. of Puerto Rico, Mayagüez campus; involved in banking, devt and construction industries in Puerto Rico for over 35 years; fmr pres. three devt cos; fmr mem. Bd of Dirs Home Builders Puerto Rico (also Treas.), Fed. Home Loan Mortgage Corpn; Exec. Dir Republican Party of Puerto Rico 1992–2004, Chair. Puerto Rico del. to Republican Nat. Convention 2000; mem. US Presidential Del. at inauguration of Martin Torrijos, Pres. of Panama 2004; Amb. to Mauritius (also accred to Seychelles) 2006–07; currently Sr Advisor, Husch Blackwell Sanders LLP (law firm); Home Builder Multifamily Project of the Year (twice). *Address:* Husch Blackwell Sanders LLP, 750 17th Street, NW, Suite 1000, Washington, DC 20006, USA (office). *Telephone:* (202) 378-2300 (office). *E-mail:* cesar.cabrera@huschblackwell.com (office); cabreracb@ hotmail.com. *Website:* www.huschblackwell.com (office).

CABRERA, Miguel; Venezuelan professional baseball player; b. 18 April 1983, Maracay, Aragua State; s. of Miguel Cabrera and Gregoria Cabrera; m. Rosangel Cabrera; one s. two d.; major league debut at age 20 with Florida Marlins 2003, playing as infielder 2003–07, traded to Detroit Tigers 2008–; mem. Venezuelan nat. team, World Baseball Classic 2009; Major League Baseball Triple Crown 2012. *Achievements include:* led American League in home runs 2008, 2012, RBI (runs batted in) 2010, 2012, batting average 2011, 2012 (won Triple Crown 2012, first player since 1967), American League Most Valuable Player 2012, mem. National League All-Star team 2004–7, American League All-Star team 2010–12. *Address:* c/o Detroit Tigers, Comerica Park, 2100 Woodward Avenue, Detroit, MI 48201-3470, USA (office). *Website:* detroit.tigers.mlb.com (office).

CACCIAVILLAN, HE Cardinal Agostino, DCnL, DCL; Italian ecclesiastic and diplomatist; b. 14 Aug. 1926, Novale; ordained priest of Vicenza 1949; joined Holy See diplomatic service 1959, served in Philippines, Spain, Portugal; Head Documentation and Information Office, Secr. of State, Vatican City 1969–76; Apostolic Pro-Nuncio to Kenya, Apostolic Del. to Seychelles 1976–81; Apostolic Pro-Nuncio to India 1981–90, to Nepal 1985–90, to USA 1990–98; Pres. Admin. Patrimony of the Apostolic See 1998–2002, now Pres. Emer.; mem. Pontifical Comm. for Vatican City State; Perm. Observer to OAS 1990–98; cr. Cardinal 2001, Cardinal-Deacon of Ss Angeli Custodi a Città Giardino; Kt Grand Cross, Order of the Holy Sepulchre. *Address:* c/o Patrimony of the Apostolic See, Palazzo Apostolico, 00120 Vatican City, Italy.

CÁCERES CHÁVEZ, Juan Ramón Carlos Enrique; Salvadorean banker and politician; *Minister of Finance;* ed Univ. of Leuven, Belgium, Universidad Tecnologica de El Salvador; f. Carlos Cáceres Soluciones Financieras (consulting firm); Exec. Dir Asociación Bancaria Salvadoreña (ABANSA) 2006–09; Minister of Finance 2009–. *Address:* Ministry of Finance, Blvd Los Héroes 1231, San Salvador, El Salvador. *Telephone:* 2244-3000 (office). *Fax:* 2244-6408 (office). *E-mail:* webmaster@mh.gob.sv (office). *Website:* www.mh.gob.sv (office); www .carloscaceres.com.sv.

ČAČIĆ, Radimir; Croatian business executive and politician; b. 11 May 1949, Zagreb; m.; ed Univ. of Zagreb; began career with Interpublic, Zagreb 1973–77; Founder, Dir and Prin. Pvt. Shareholder, Coning, Varaždin 1978–2000; Founder Zagal (now Croatia Airlines) 1990; served as Brig. in Croatian Army 1991; mem. Constitutional Comm. for drafting new constitution of Repub. of Croatia 1990; Founding mem. Croatian People's Party—Liberal Democrats (Hrvatska narodna stranka—liberalni demokrati, HNS) 1990–, mem. Presidency 1990, Vice-Pres. 1993, Pres. 1994–2000, 2008–13; mem. Sabor (Parl.) 1995–; Minister for Public Works, Reconstruction and Devt 2000–03, Deputy Prime Minister and Minister of the Economy 2011–12 (resgnd); Pres. Croatian Tennis Fed. 2002–11; Independ-ence War Medal, Order of Prince Domagoj with Neckband. *Leisure interests:* tennis, reading. *Address:* Croatian People's Party—Liberal Democrats, 10000 Zagreb, Kneza Mislava 8, Croatia (office). *Telephone:* (1) 4629111 (office). *Fax:* (1) 4629110 (office). *E-mail:* pr@hns.hr (office). *Website:* www.hns.hr (office).

CADBURY, Sir (Nicholas) Dominic, Kt, MBA; British business executive; *Chairman, Misys PLC;* b. 12 May 1940; s. of the late Laurence John Cadbury and Joyce Cadbury (née Mathews); m. Cecilia Sarah Symes 1972; three d.; ed Eton Coll., Trinity Coll., Cambridge, Stanford Univ., USA; Chief Exec. Cadbury Schweppes PLC 1984–93, Chair. 1993–2000; Dir Economist Group 1990–2003, Chair. 1994–2003; Jt Deputy Chair. Guinness (now Diageo PLC) 1994–97, Deputy Chair. 1996 (Dir 1991–); Jt Deputy Chair EMI Group PLC 1999–; Chair. The Wellcome Trust 2000–06, Transense Techs 2000–03; Pres. Food and Drink Fed. 1999; Dir (non-exec.) Misys PLC 2000–, interim Chair. 2005, Chair. 2006–; mem. Royal Mint Advisory Cttee 1986–94, Pres.'s Cttee CBI 1989–94, Food Asscn 1989–2000, Stanford Advisory Council 1989–95; Chancellor Univ. of Birmingham 2002–13. *Leisure interests:* tennis, golf, shooting. *Address:* Office of the Chairman, Misys PLC, One Kingdom Street, Paddington, London, W2 6BL, England (office). *Telephone:* (20) 3200-5000 (office). *Fax:* (20) 3320-1771 (office). *Website:* misys.com (office).

CADET, Jean, LLM; French fmr diplomatist; b. 15 Oct. 1942; m. Elisabeth Cadet; three c.; ed Inst. d'études politiques de Paris, Ecole Nat. d'Admin, Paris; Attaché Cen. Admin, Ministry of Justice 1968–70, Cen. Admin, Econ. and Financial Affairs 1972–75; apptd Minister Plenipotentiary 1977; Second Sec., Perm. Rep. to EC,

Brussels 1978–82, Minister Counsellor 1986–92; First Sec. in Abidjan 1982–84, in Bonn 1984–86; Amb. to Greece 1992–94, to Austria 1997–2001, to S Africa 2001–03, Amb. (non-resident) to Lesotho 2002–03; to Russian Fed. 2003–06; Sec.-Gen. Inter-ministerial Cttee on European Econ. Cooperation 1995–97; Counsellor for European Affairs, Cabinet of the Prime Minister 1995–97; Conseiller Maitre, Cour des Comptes 2006–11; Officier Légion d'honneur, Officier Ordre nat. du Mérite. *Address:* c/o Cour des comptes, 13 rue Cambon, 75001 Paris, France.

ČAĐO, Stanislav; Bosnia and Herzegovina politician; b. 1961, Bosanska Gradiška; m.; two c.; ed Faculty of Law, Univ. of Banja Luka; worked for Vuk Karadžić publishing co.; Civil Servant, Dept for Social-Political Orgs, Laktaši Municipal Council; fmr Commercial Man., Sim Prom (import and export co.); fmr Gen. Man. Technogas; Minister of Internal Affairs, Republika Srpska 2006–13. *Address:* c/o Ministry of Internal Affairs of Republika Srpska, 78000 Banja Luka, Desanke Maksimović 4, Bosnia and Herzegovina. *E-mail:* kabinet@vladars.net.

CADOGAN, Sir John Ivan George, Kt, CBE, PhD, FRS, FRSE, CChem, FRSC; British chemist, industrialist and academic; *Professorial Fellow, University College of Swansea;* b. 8 Oct. 1930, Pembrey, Carmarthenshire; s. of the late Alfred Cadogan and of Dilys Cadogan; m. 1st Margaret Jeanne Evans 1955 (deceased 1992); one s. one d.; m. 2nd Elizabeth Purnell 1997; ed Grammar School, Swansea and King's Coll., London; research at King's Coll., London 1951–54; Civil Service Research Fellow 1954–56; Lecturer in Chem., King's Coll., London 1956–63; Purdie Prof. of Chem. and Head of Dept, St Salvator's Coll., Univ. of St Andrews 1963–69; Forbes Prof. of Organic Chem., Univ. of Edin. 1969–79; Chief Scientist, BP Research Centre 1979–81; Dir of Research, British Petroleum 1981–92, CEO BP Ventures 1988–92; Dir Gen. Research Council 1994–99; Chair. DNA Research Innovations Ltd 1999–2004; Science Policy Adviser, Science Foundation Ireland 1999-2005; Dir BP Chemicals Int. Ltd, BP Venezuela Ltd; Visiting Prof., Imperial Coll., London 1979–2002; Professorial Fellow, Univ. Coll. of Swansea, Univ. of Wales 1979–; mem. Council, Royal Inst. 1984–87, Royal Comm. on Criminal Justice 1991–93; Past Pres. Royal Soc. of Chem. 1982–84; Gov. Jt Research Centre, EC 1994–; Chair. Fusion Antibodies Ltd 2005–; mem. numerous scientific cttees; Hon. FREng 1992; recipient of 20 fellowships and hon. degrees; several prizes. *Publications:* about 300 papers in professional journals. *Leisure interests:* supporting rugby football, being in France, gardening. *Address:* Department of Chemistry, University of Wales, Singleton Park, Swansea, SA2 8PP, Wales (office). *Telephone:* (1792) 295306 (office). *Website:* www.swan.ac.uk/ chemistry (office).

CADOT, Michel François Jacques; French civil servant and administrator; *Minister of Agriculture;* b. 22 May 1954, Suresnes, Seine; s. of Jean Cadot and Elsa Cadot (née Puiatti); m. Catherine Van Luchene 1981; three s. two d.; ed Lycées Charlemagne and Henri IV, Paris, Univ. of Paris II Panthéon, Ecole Nat. d'Admin.; Civil Admin., Ministry of the Interior 1980; Asst. Prefect, Dir. of Cabinet of Prefect of Oise 1980–82 Sec.-Gen. of Prefecture of Cantal 1982–85; Civil Admin., Embassy in Venezuela 1985–88; Asst. Prefect of Saint-Julien-en-Genevois 1988–89; Civil Admin., Elf Aquitaine 1989–93; Sec.-Gen. Elf Trading S.A. 1989–93; Asst. Prefect of Béziers 1993–95; Prefect of Languedoc-Roussillon 1993–95, of Meuse 1998–2000, of Martinique 2000–04; Dir. Office of Sec. of State for Rural Devt. 1995, of Minister for Agric., Food and Fisheries 2004–06, Advisor to Prime Minister Dominique de Villepin 2006–07, Minister of Agric. 2007–; Dir for Man. of Region of Datar 1995–98. *Address:* Ministry of Agriculture, 78 rue de Varenne, 75349 Paris, France (office). *Telephone:* 1-49-55-60-11 (office). *Fax:* 1-49-55-83-55 (office). *E-mail:* info@agriculture.gouv.fr (office). *Website:* www.agriculture.gouv.fr (office).

CAETANI, Oleg; Italian conductor; b. 1956, Lausanne, Switzerland; s. of Igor Markevitch and Topazia Caetani; m. Susanna Caetani; three d. (two from previous m.); ed studied with Nadia Boulanger, Franco Ferrara in Rome, Kyrill Kondrashin in Moscow and Ilia Mussin in Leningrad; Asst to Otmar Suitner, Staatsoper Berlin 1981–84; Deutsche Nationaltheater Weimar 1984–87; Kapellmeister, Städtische Buhnen Frankfurt am Main; Music Dir Wiesbaden 1992–95, leading the Ring, Tristan und Isolde, La Forza del Destino, Otello, Rimsky's Invisible City of Kitezh and Bluebeard's Castle; guest engagements with Semiramide in Vienna, Les Vêpres Siciliennes in Nice, Lucia di Lammermoor and Tosca at Trieste and Verdi's Falstaff at Stuttgart 1996–97; Zurich Opera with Rigoletto, The Nutcracker, La Bohème and Norma; led Tchaikovsky's Maid of Orleans at Strasbourg 1998, Otello and Turandot at La Scala, Don Pasquale in Florence, The Flying Dutchman in Rome etc.; with ENO Khovanshchina 2003, Sir John in Love 2006, Madam Butterfly 2012; concert repertoire includes all symphonies by Beethoven, Brahms, Schubert, Schumann and Shostakovich, with soloists such as Martha Argerich, Viktoria Mullova, Shlomo Mintz and the late Sviatoslav Richter; Music Dir, Chemnitz 1996–2001; Chief Conductor Designate Melbourne Symphony Orches-tra 2003–04, Chief Conductor and Artistic Dir 2005–09; Winner RAI Competition, Turin 1979, Prizewinner, Herbert von Karajan Competition 1982. *E-mail:* caetanioffice@gmail.com. *Website:* www.olegcaetani.com.

CAFFARELLI, Luis A., MSc, PhD; Argentine/American mathematician and academic; *Sid Richardson Chair, University of Texas, Austin;* b. 8 Dec. 1948, Buenos Aires, Argentina; m. Irene M. Gamba; three s.; ed Univ. of Buenos Aires; expert in free boundary problems for nonlinear partial differential equations; Postdoctoral Researcher, Univ. of Minnesota 1973–74, Asst Prof. 1975–77, Assoc. Prof. 1977–79, Prof. 1979–83; Prof., Courant Inst. of Math. Sciences, New York Univ. 1980–82, 1994–97; Prof., Univ. of Chicago 1983–86; Perm. Faculty mem. Inst. for Advanced Study, Princeton 1986–96; Prof., Univ. of Texas, Austin 1997–, currently holds the Sid Richardson Chair; Pres. of the Jury, Int. Math. Olympiad 1997, 2012; mem. NAS 1991, American Math. Soc., Union Matematica Argentina, Pontifical Acad. of Sciences; Foreign mem. Accad. Nazionale delle Scienze (dei XL, Italy), Accad. Nazionale dei Lincei (Italy), Academia Nacional de Ciencias, Buenos Aires, Academia Nacional de Ciencias, Cordoba, Insituto Lombardo, Accad. di Scienze e Lettere (Italy); Fellow, American Acad. of Arts and Sciences 1986; Hon. Prof., Universidad de Buenos Aires, Universidad de Mar del Plata; Dr hc (Universidad Autónoma de Madrid) 1992, (École Normale Superieure, Paris) 2003, (Universidad de La Plata) 2003, (Universidad de San Luis) 2007), (Univ. of Buenos Aires) 2012; Hon. DSc (Univ. of Notre Dame) 2012, (Univ. of Chicago) 2013; Stampacchia Prize (jtly) 1982, Bocher Prize 1984, Guggenheim Fellowship 1984, Pius XI Gold Medal, Pontifical Acad. of Sciences 1988, Premio Konex, Platino y

Brillantes (Argentina) 2003, Rolf Schock Prize, Royal Swedish Acad. of Sciences 2005, Leroy P. Steele Prize for Lifetime Achievement, American Math. Soc. 2009, Rouse Ball Lecturer, Univ. of Cambridge 2011, Wolf Prize in Math. (jtly with Michael Aschbacher) 2012. *Publications:* Fully Nonlinear Elliptic Equations (co-author) 1995, A Geometric Approach to Free Boundary Problems (co-author) 2005; more than 260 articles on partial differential equations and their applications. *Address:* RLM 10.150, Department of Mathematics, University of Texas at Austin, 1 University Station C1200, Austin, TX 78712-0257, USA (office). *Telephone:* (512) 471-3160 (office). *Fax:* (512) 471-9038 (office). *E-mail:* caffarel@math.utexas.edu (office). *Website:* www.ma.utexas.edu/users/caffarel (office).

CAFFARRA, HE Cardinal Carlo, DCL; Italian ecclesiastic; *Archbishop of Bologna;* b. 1 June 1938, Samboseto di Busseto, prov. of Parma, Emilia Romagna; ed Episcopal Seminary of Fidenza, Studio Teologico Bolognese, Università Cattolica, Milan, Theological Faculty of Northern Italy, Pontifical Gregorian Univ., Rome; ordained priest, Archdiocese of Fidenza 1961; returned to Diocese of Fidenza 1965; taught medical ethics at Faculty of Medicine and Surgery, Università Cattolica campus in Rome; mem. Int. Theological Comm. 1974–84, also held position of Consultor of Congregation for Doctrine of the Faith; Pres. Pontifical John Paul II Inst. for Studies on Marriage and Family 1980, f. sections of the same inst. in USA, Spain and Mexico; Archbishop of Ferrara-Comacchio 1995–2003; Archbishop of Bologna 2003–; cr. Cardinal (Cardinal-Priest of San Giovanni Battista dei Fiorentini) 2006; mem. Exec. Cttee Pontifical Council for the Family 2006–. *Address:* Arcivescovile, Via Altabella 6, 40126 Bologna, Italy (office). *Telephone:* (051) 6480611 (office). *Fax:* (051) 6480734 (office). *E-mail:* canc@bologna.chiesacattolica.it (office). *Website:* www.bologna.chiesacattolica.it/arcivescovi/caffarra/pagine (office).

CAFU; Brazilian fmr professional footballer; b. (Marcos Evangelista de Moraes), 7 June 1970, São Paulo; m. Regina de Morales; defender (right back); played with São Paulo 1989–94 (115 appearances, seven goals, won Campeonato Brasileiro Série A 1991, Copa Conmebol 1994, Supercopa Sudamericana 1993), Juventude 1995, Real Zaragoza 1995, Palmeiras 1996–97 (won Torneio Maria Quitéria 1997), Roma, Italy 1997–2003 (won Serie A 2000–01), AC Milan, Italy 2003–08 (won Serie A 2003–04, Supercoppa Italiana 2004, UEFA Champions League 2007, UEFA Super Cup 2007, FIFA Club World Cup 2007); mem. Brazil nat. team 1990–2006 (retd), 142 int. caps (record), scored five goals; only player to have played in three World Cup final matches, mem. winning team for FIFA World Cup 1994, 2002 (Capt.), FIFA Confederations Cup 1997, Copa América 1997, 1999; Brazilian record of 21 World Cup appearances; Officer, Order of Rio Branco 2008; South American Footballer of the Year 1994, named by Pelé as one of the top 125 greatest living footballers 2004. *Address:* Fundação Cafu, Rua Edward Joseph, 122, cj. 85/86 Morumbi, São Paulo, SP 05709-020, Brazil. *Telephone:* (11) 3772-6630. *E-mail:* cafu@fundacaocafu.org.br (office). *Website:* www.fundacaocafu.org.br.

CAGE, Nicolas; American actor and film company executive; b. (Nicolas Coppola), 7 Jan. 1964, Long Beach, Calif.; s. of Prof. August Coppola and Joy Vogelsang; nephew of Francis Ford Coppola (q.v.); m. 1st Patricia Arquette (q.v.) 1995 (divorced 2001); m. 2nd Lisa Marie Presley 2002 (divorced 2004); m. 3rd Alice Kim 2004, one s.; one s. with Christina Fulton; ed studied theatre at Beverly Hills High; changed his name early in his career to make his own reputation; secured bit part in Fast Times at Ridgemont High 1982; took job selling popcorn at Fairfax Theater; then landed role in his uncle's film Rumble Fish 1983 followed by role as punk-rocker in Valley Girl 1983 (released first) which launched his career; f. Saturn Films (production co.); Dr hc (California State, Fullerton); numerous awards including Acad. Award for Best Actor 1996, Golden Globe Award for Best Actor 1996, Lifetime Achievement Award 1996, P. J. Owens Award 1998, Charles A. Crain Desert Palm Award 2001, UN Global Citizen of the Year Award for humanitarian endeavours 2009. *Films include:* Fast Times at Ridgemont High 1982, Valley Girl 1983, Rumble Fish 1983, Racing with the Moon 1984, The Cotton Club 1984, Birdy 1984, The Boy in Blue 1986, Peggy Sue Got Married 1986, Raising Arizona 1987, Moonstruck 1987, Never on Tuesday (uncredited) 1988, Vampire's Kiss 1989, Tempo di uccidere (aka Le raccourci, aka The Short Cut, aka Time to Kill) 1989, Fire Birds 1990, Wild at Heart 1990, Zandalee 1991, Red Rock West 1992, Honeymoon in Vegas 1992, Amos & Andrew 1993, Deadfall 1993, Guarding Tess 1994, It Could Happen to You 1994, Trapped in Paradise 1994, Kiss of Death 1995, Leaving Las Vegas (Golden Globe Award for Best Actor 1996, Acad. Award for Best Actor 1996) 1995, The Rock 1996, The Funeral 1996, Con Air 1997, Face/Off 1997, City of Angels 1998, Snake Eyes 1998, 8MM 1999, Bringing Out the Dead 1999, Gone in 60 Seconds 2000, The Family Man 2001, Captain Corelli's Mandolin 2001, Christmas Carol: The Movie (voice) 2001, Windtalkers 2002, Sonny 2002, Adaptation 2003, Matchstick Men 2003, National Treasure 2004, Lord of War 2005, The Weather Man 2005, The Ant Bully (voice) 2006, World Trade Center 2006, The Wicker Man 2006, Ghost Rider 2006, Grindhouse 2007, Next 2007, National Treasure: Book of Secrets 2007, Bangkok Dangerous 2007, Knowing 2009, G-Force (voice) 2009, The Bad Lieutenant: Port of Call – New Orleans 2009, Astro Boy (voice) 2009, Kick-Ass 2010, The Sorcerer's Apprentice 2010, Season of the Witch 2011, Angry 2011, Trespass 2011, Ghost Rider: Spirit of Vengeance 2011, Seeking Justice 2011, Stolen 2012, The Frozen Ground 2012, The Croods 2013. *Television includes:* Best of Times 1981, Industrial Symphony No. 1: The Dream of the Brokenhearted 1990. *Address:* c/o Creative Artists Agency, 2000 Avenue of the Stars, Los Angeles, CA 90067, USA (office). Saturn Films, 9000 West Sunset Boulevard, Suite 911, West Hollywood, CA 90069, USA (office). *Website:* www.saturnfilms.com.

CAGIATI, Andrea, LLB; Italian diplomatist; b. 11 July 1922, Rome; s. of Filippo Cagiati and Germaine Dewies; m. Sigrid von Morgen 1968; one s. one d.; ed Univ. of Siena; entered Foreign Service 1948; Sec., Paris 1950–51; Prin. Pvt. Sec. to Minister of State for Foreign Affairs 1951–53; Vice-Consul-Gen., New York 1953–55; Prin. Pvt. Sec. to Minister of State for Foreign Affairs, then with Dept of Political Affairs 1955–57; Counsellor, Athens 1957–60, Mexico 1960–62; Del. Disarmament Cttee, Geneva March–Dec. 1962; mem. Italian del. to UN June 1962; Head NATO Dept 1962–66; Minister-Counsellor, Madrid 1966–68; Amb. to Colombia 1968–71; Inst. for Diplomatic Studies 1971–72; Diplomatic Adviser to Prime Minister 1972–73; Amb. to Austria 1973–80, to UK 1980–86, to the Holy See (Vatican) 1986–88; Vice-Chair. Alitalia 1989–94 (Dir 1987–94); Pres. Fondazione Cagiati-von Morgen 1990–, Fondazione Aristenza Sanitaria Melitense 1997–;

Vice-Pres. Fondazione De Gasperi; Hon. Pres. Circolo Studi Diplomatici, Eurodéfence Italia; Hon. GCVO 1980, Grand Cross of Merit (Italy, Austria, Holy See), Kt, Order of Malta. *Publications:* La Diplomazia 1945, Verso quale avvenire? 1957, I sentieri della vita 1990, Scritti di politica estera (five vols) 1991–2007, Verso l'Europa Unita 2008; and numerous articles on foreign policy and int. affairs. *Leisure interests:* sculpture, golf, shooting. *Address:* 3 Av. degli Astalli, 00186 Rome (office); Largo Olgiata, 15 (49D), 00123 Rome, Italy (home). *Telephone:* (6) 6791052 (office); (6) 30888135 (home). *Fax:* (6) 6781148 (office).

ÇAĞLAYAN, Zafer; Turkish business executive and politician; b. 1957, Muş; m.; two c.; ed Gazi Univ.; fmr Chair. Çağlayanlar Alüminyum Ltd, Akel Alüminyum A.Ş; Chair. Ankara Chamber of Industry (ASO) 1995–2007; Deputy Chair. Turkish Union of Chambers and Commodities Exchanges (TOBB) 2005–07; mem. Parl. (AKP) 2007–; Minister of Industry and Trade 2007–09, Minister of State 2009–11, Minister of Econ. Affairs 2011–13.

CAHILL, Teresa Mary, LRAM, AGSM; British singer (soprano); b. 30 July 1944, Maidenhead, Berks.; d. of Henry D. Cahill and Florence Cahill (née Dallimore); m. 1st John Anthony Kiernander 1971 (divorced 1978); m. 2nd Dr Robert Saxton 2005; ed Notre Dame High School, Southwark, Guildhall School of Music and Drama and London Opera Centre; debut at Glyndebourne 1969, Covent Garden 1970, La Scala, Milan 1976, Philadelphia Opera 1981; Prof., Trinity Coll. of Music, London; specializes in works of Mozart, Strauss, Mahler, Elgar and Tippett; has given concerts with all the London orchestras, Boston Symphony Orchestra, Chicago Symphony Orchestra, at Berlin, Vienna and Bath Festivals and throughout Europe, USA and the Far East; Artistic Adviser, Nat. Mozart Competition 1997–; Adjudicator, Live Music Now 1988– (Musical Adviser 2000–); Gov. Royal Soc. of Music 2000–04; Prof., Vocal Dept, Trinity Laban Conservatoire of Music and Dance, London; masterclasses, Dartington Festival 1984, 1986, 's-Hertogenbosch 1988, 2000, Univ. of Oxford 1995–96, Peabody Inst. 1999, RAM 2002, Bowdoin Coll. 2004; Patron Opera/UK; Worshipful Company of Musicians Silver Medal 1966, John Christie Award 1970. *Recordings include:* works by Elgar, Strauss, Mahler, Mozart, Rachmaninov, Saxton and Lutyens. *Publications:* contrib. to 'Divas in their Own Words', compiled by Andrew Palmer. *Leisure interests:* cinema, theatre, travel, photography, reading and going to sales, from car boots to Sothebys. *Address:* Trinity Laban Conservatoire of Music and Dance, Faculty of Music, King Charles Court, Old Royal Naval College, Greenwich, London, SE10 9JF (office); 65 Leyland Road, London, SE12 8DW, England. *Telephone:* (20) 8852-0847 (home). *Website:* teresacahill.net.

CAHN, John Werner, BS, PhD; American chemist, materials scientist and academic; *Senior NIST Fellow, National Institute of Standards and Technology;* b. 9 Jan. 1928, Cologne, Germany; m. Anne Hessing; three c.; ed Univ. of Michigan, Univ. of California, Berkeley; with Chemical Metallurgy research effort at General Electric Lab., Schenectady, NY 1954–64; Prof., Dept of Metallurgy (now Materials Science), MIT 1964–78; mem. staff, Nat. Inst. of Standards and Tech. (NIST) 1977–, Sr NIST Fellow, Materials Science and Eng Lab. 1984–; Affiliate Prof., Univ. of Washington 1984–; mem. NAS 1973, Nat. Acad. of Eng 1998; Fellow, American Acad. of Arts and Sciences 1974, Japan Soc. for Promotion of Science 1981, World Technology Network, Nat. Museum of Science and Tech., London 1999; Hon. Prof., Jiao Tong Univ., Shanghai 1980; Hon. mem. MRS-India 1992, Japan Inst. of Metals 1994; Hon. Life mem. American Ceramic Soc. 2001; Hon. ScD (Northwestern Univ.) 1990; Dr hc (Université d'Évry, France) 1996; Allied Chemical and Dye Fellowship, Univ. of California, Berkeley 1951, Guggenheim Fellowship, Univ. of Cambridge 1960–61, S.B. Meyer Award, American Ceramic Soc. 1966, Inst. of Metals Lecturer, AIME 1968, MacDonald Lecturer, Canadian Metallurgical Soc. 1969, 1998, Gold Medal, Acta Metallurgica 1977, Dorn Lecturer, Northwestern Univ. 1978, Van Horn Lecturer, Case Western Univ. 1979, Dickson Prize, Carnegie-Mellon Univ. 1981, Golick Lecturer, Univ. of Missouri, Rolla 1982, Distinguished Lecturer, Univ. of Connecticut 1983, Gold Medal, US Dept of Commerce 1984, Von Hippel Award, Materials Research Soc. 1985, Stratton Award, Nat. Bureau of Standards 1986, Distinguished Physics Lecturer, Boston Univ. 1987, Sauveur Award, ASM International 1989, Hilliard Lecturer, Northwestern Univ. 1990, Michelson and Morley Prize, Case Western Univ. 1991, Cyril Stanley Smith Lecturer, Univ. of Chicago 1993, Hume-Rothery Award, TMS 1993, Inland Steel Lecture, Northwestern Univ. 1993, Gold Medal, Japan Inst. of Metals 1994, Rockwell Medal, Hall of Fame for Eng, Science and Tech., and Medal, Int. Tech. Inst. 1994, Harvey Prize, Technion, Israel 1995, Distinguished GE Lecturer in Materials Science, RPI 1998, Nat. Medal of Science 1998, Bakhuys Roozeboon Lecturer and Gold Medal, Royal Netherlands Acad. of Sciences 1999, Emil Heyn Medal, German Metallurgical Soc. 2001, Bower Prize, The Franklin Inst. 2002, Kyoto Prize, Inamori Foundation 2011. *Publications:* about 250 papers in professional journals. *Address:* Materials Science and Engineering Laboratory, Materials Building, National Institute of Standards and Technology, Gaithersburg, MD 20899, USA (office). *Telephone:* (301) 975-5664 (office). *Fax:* (301) 975-4553 (office). *E-mail:* john.cahn@nist.gov (office). *Website:* www.nist.gov (office).

CAHUC, Pierre, DEcon; French economist and academic; *Professor of Economics, Ecole Polytechnique;* b. 18 Jan. 1962; three c.; ed Ecole polytechnique, Agrégation des Universités en Sciences Economiques; Prof. of Econs, Univ. of Paris I-Panthéon-Sorbonne 1992–2003, Research Fellow, CREST-INSEE Laboratoire de Macroéconomie 1998–, Dir Macroeconomic Lab. 2011–; Asst Prof. (Professeur chargé de cours), École Polytechnique, Paris 1998–, Prof. of Econs 2007–; Research Fellow, Inst. for the Study of Labor (IZA), Bonn, Germany 1999–, Program Dir 'Labor Markets and Institutions' 2004–; Research Fellow, Centre for Econ. Policy Research 2001–; mem. Comm. Economique de la Nation 2005–09, Conseil de l'Emploi des Revenus et de la Cohésion Sociale 2005–10, Conseil d'Analyse Economique (Advisory Council of the Prime Minister) 2006–10; Assoc. Ed. American Economic Journals: Macroeconomics, European Economic Review, Labour Economics, Journal of Economics/Zeitschrift für Nationalökonomie; mem. Scientific Cttee Problèmes Economiques, Economie et Statistique; Jr mem. Institut Universitaire de France 1998–2003; Chevalier des Palmes académiques 2004; Prix de thèse, Asscn Française de Science Economique 1989, Prix du 'Meilleur jeune economiste', Le Monde and Le Cercle des Economistes 2001, Prix Risque les Echos 2005, Prix Zerilli-Marimo 2006, Prix du livre d'Economie 2007, Lire magazine Best Essay Prize 2007, Prix du livre des dirigeants, essay section 2007. *Publications include:* Les negociations salariales, des fondements microéconomiques aux implications macroéconomiques 1991, La Nouvelle Microéconomie 1993, La réduction du temps de travail, une solution pour l'emploi? (co-ed.) 1997, Le marché du travail (with Andre Zylberberg) 2001, La microéconomie du marché du travail (with Andre Zylberberg) 2003, Le chômage, fatalité ou nécessité? (with Andre Zylberberg) (Prix Mutation et Travail 2004, Prix Européen du livre d'économie 2004, Prix ManPower 2005 de l'ouvrage de ressources humaines) 2004, Labor Economics (with Andre Zylberberg) 2004; more than 85 articles in professional journals. *Address:* CREST-INSEE, Timbre J 360, 15 Boulevard Gabriel-Peri, 92245 Malakoff, France (office). *Telephone:* 1-41-17-37-17 (office). *E-mail:* pierre.cahuc@gmail.com (office); cahuc@ensae.fr (office).

CAI, Guo-Qiang; Chinese artist; b. 8 Dec. 1957, Quanzhou City, Fujian Prov.; ed Shanghai Theatre Acad.; lived in Japan 1986–95; explored properties of gunpowder in his drawings, experimented with explosives including signature explosion events exemplified in his series Projects for Extraterrestrials; has collaborated with specialists and experts from various disciplines including Issey Miyake, Rafael Vinoly, Zaha Hadid, Tan Dun and Tsai Ming-liang among others; has lived in New York since 1995; core mem. creative team and Dir of Visual and Special Effects for opening and closing ceremonies of Beijing Olympics 2008;; Dir of fireworks festivities for China's 60th Nat. Day, Beijing 2009; Fireworks Artistic Dir, Repub. of China Centennial; core mem. creative team for Taipei Int. Flora Exposition 2010; Japan Cultural Design Prize, Tokyo 1995, Benesse Prize of Transculture Exhbn, 46th Venice Biennale 1995, Oribe Award, Gifu (Japan) 1997, Golden Lion Prize, 48th Venice Biennale Int. 1999, CalArts/Alpert Award in the Arts (USA) 2001, Hiroshima Art Prize, Hiroshima City Culture Foundation (Japan) 2007, Best Monographic Museum Show, Best Installation or Single Work in a Museum, Int. Curators Assccn 20th Fukuoka Prize for Arts and Culture (Japan) 2009, First Place for Best Project in a Public Space (for Cai Guo-Qiang: Fallen Blossoms), AICA 2010, Lifetime Achievement in the Arts (Painting) 24th Praemium Imperiale (Japan) 2012, Medal of Arts, US Dept of State 2012; several awards for Best Exhbn and Best Installation from Int. Curators Assccn; repeatedly listed amongst the UK journal ArtReview's Power 100. *Works in permanent collections include:* Agnes Gund Collection, New York, Annie Wong Art Foundation, Vancouver, BC, Astrup Fernley Museum of Modern Art, Oslo, Centre Pompidou, Paris, City of New York, Cleveland Museum of Art, Contemporary Art Gallery, Art Tower Mito, Japan, Dentsu, Caretta Shiodome, Tokyo, Deste Foundation, Athens, Deutsche Bank Collection, Germany, Fogg Art Museum, Harvard Univ. Art Museums, Fondation Cartier pour l'art contemporain, Paris, Fonds Nat. d'art Contemporain and Musée d'art contemporain Lyon, Fukuoka Asia Art Museum, Fukuoka, Japan, Graphische Sammlung Albertina Wien, Vienna, Guangdong Museum of Art, Guangzhou, China, Hirshhorn Museum and Sculpture Garden, Smithsonian Inst., Washington, DC, Ho-Am Art Museum, Seoul, Issey Miyake Inc., Japan, Iwaki City Art Museum, Japan, The Japan Foundation, Tokyo, Modern Museum, Stockholm, Mori Art Center, Tokyo, Museo Navale di Venezia, Museu de Arte Moderna da Bahia, Bahia, Brazil, Museum of Contemporary Art, Tokyo, Museum of Modern Art, New York, Museum of Modern Art, Saitama, Japan, Queensland Art Gallery, Brisbane, Queens Museum of Art, New York, Riiksmuseum, Kroller-Muller, Netherlands, San Diego Museum of Art, Shiseido Co. Ltd, Tokyo, S.M.A.K.: Museum van Hedendaags Kunst Ghent, Solomon R. Guggenheim Museum, New York, Stadtische Galerie Nordhorn, Germany, Takamatsu City Museum of Art, Japan, Taiwan Museum of Art, Taichung, Tate Collection, London. *Solo projects include:* Primeval Fireball: The Project for Projects, P3 art and environment, Tokyo 1991, Project to Extend the Great Wall of China by 10,000 Meters, Jiayuguan City 1993, The Century with Mushroom Clouds – Projects for the 20th Century, Nevada, Nuclear Test Site, Salt Lake, New York 1996, Cultural Melting Bath: Projects for the 20th Century, Queens Museum of Art, Queens, New York 1997, APEC Cityscape Fireworks Show, Asia Pacific Econ. Cooperation, Shanghai 2001, Explosion Project for Tate Modern, London 2003, Light Cycle Over Central Park, Asia Soc. and Museum, New York 2003, Explosion Project for Central Park, Creative Time, New York 2003, Kite Project for Siwa, Egypt 2003, Explosion Project for the Festival of China, John F. Kennedy Center for the Performing Arts, Washington, DC 2005, Curator DMoCA, Echigo-Tsumari Triennial, Japan 2006. *Address:* Cai Studio, 40 East First Street #1B, New York, NY 10003, USA (office). *Telephone:* (212) 995-0908 (office). *Fax:* (212) 254-0336 (office). *E-mail:* studio@caiguoqiang.com (office). *Website:* www.caiguoqiang.com (office).

CAI, Jin-Yong, BS, PhD; Chinese economist and international organization official; *Executive Vice-President and CEO, International Finance Corporation;* ed Peking Univ., Boston Univ., USA; began career with World Bank Group 1990, worked as Economist in Cen. Europe and S Asia; joined Morgan Stanley 1995, later seconded to China International Capital Corpn; joined Goldman Sachs 2000, apptd Partner 2006, held numerous other sr positions including Participating Man. Dir, Chief Exec. Goldman Sachs Gao Hua Securities Co., Head of China Investment Banking Business; Exec. Vice-Pres. and CEO, IFC 2012–. *Address:* International Finance Corporation, 2121 Pennsylvania Avenue, NW, Washington, DC 20433, USA (office). *Telephone:* (202) 473-3800 (office). *Fax:* (202) 974-4384 (office). *Website:* www1.ifc.org (office).

CAI, Wu, LLD; Chinese government official; *Minister of Culture;* b. Oct. 1949, Wedu Co., Gansu Prov.; ed Beijing Univ.; joined CCP 1973; mem. Communist Youth League of China (CYLC), Cen. Cttee, Standing Cttee 1983–95; fmr lecturer, Beijing Univ.; mem. All-China Youth Fed. and Deputy Sec.-Gen. then Prin. 1983–95; Dir Int. Liaison Dept 1983–95, Research Office, then Deputy Sec.-Gen. 1995–97, Vice-Minister Int. Liaison Dept 1997–2005; Dir Information Office, State Council 2005–08; mem. 17th CCP Cen. Cttee 2007–12, 18th CCP Cen. Cttee 2012–; Minister of Culture 2008–; Prof. of Int. Relations, Beijing Univ. *Address:* Ministry of Culture, 10 Chaoyangmen Bei Jie, Dongcheng Qu, Beijing 100020, People's Republic of China (office). *Telephone:* (10) 65551432 (office). *Fax:* (10) 65551433 (office). *E-mail:* webmaster@whb1.ccnt.com.cn (office). *Website:* www.ccnt.com.cn (office).

CAI, Zhenhua, MA; Chinese fmr table tennis coach and sports official; *Deputy Director, State General Administration of Sport;* b. 3 Sept. 1961, Wuxi, Jiangsu Prov.; ed Hebei Normal Univ.; Head Coach, Chinese men's table tennis team 1991–97, Chief Coach 1997–2004; Chief Coach, Italian table tennis team 1985–89; Deputy Head, Chinese Olympic Del. 2008; Vice-Pres. Chinese Olympic Cttee;

Deputy Dir, State Gen. Admin of Sports 2007–; Chair. All-China Ping-Pong Soc. 2009–, All-China Badminton Soc. 2009–, All-China Soccer Soc. 2014–; fmr Vice-Pres. All-China Youth Fed.; Alt. mem. 17th CCP Cen. Cttee 2007–12, 18th CCP Cen. Cttee 2012–. *Coaching achievements include:* 2000 Olympic Games: 4 gold medals, 3 silver medals, 1 bronze medal; 2001 World Championships: gold medals, 4 silver medals, 5 bronze medals; 2003 World Championships: 4 gold medals; 2004 World Team Championships: 1st men's/women's. *Address:* State General Administration for Physical Culture and Sports, 9 Tiyuguan Road, Chongwen District, Beijing, 100061 People's Republic of China (office). *Telephone:* (10) 87183505 (office). *Fax:* (10) 67110248 (office).

CAIN, James Palmer; American lawyer, business executive and fmr diplomatist; *Of Counsel, Kilpatrick Stockton LLP;* b. High Point, N Carolina; m. Helen Cain; two d.; ed Wake Forest Univ.; with Kilpatrick Stockton (law firm) for twenty years, co-founder Research Triangle office 1985, leave of absence to serve as Pres. and COO Nat. Hockey League Carolina Hurricanes and their parent co., Gale Force Holdings 2000–02, currently Of Counsel; fmr mem. Bd N Carolina Citizens for Business and Industry, Wake Leadership Acad., N Carolina Character Educ. Foundation; fmr regional Chair. American Red Cross, American Diabetes Asscn, Boy Scouts of America annual campaigns; fmr Chair. Food Bank of N Carolina, Communities in Schools of Wake Co., Eastern N Carolina Chamber of Commerce; mem. Republican Nat. Cttee for N Carolina 2003–05; Regional Chair. and State Finance Vice-Chair. for Bush-Cheney '04 campaign; Pres. Bush's Emissary to the Philippines for Inauguration of Pres. Gloria Macapagal-Arroyo 2004; Amb. to Denmark 2005–09; Grand Cross of the Order of the Dannebrog 2009; chosen as Business Leader of the Year by Business Leader Magazine, John Ross Leadership Award, Greater Raleigh Convention and Visitors Bureau, National Outstanding Community Service Award, American Diabetes Asscn 2003. *Publications include:* The American 2008. *Address:* Kilpatrick Stockton LLP, Suite 400, 3737 Glenwood Avenue, Raleigh, NC 27612, USA (office). *Telephone:* (919) 420-1776 (office). *Fax:* (919) 510-6179 (office). *E-mail:* JCain@KilpatrickStockton.com (office); ambcain@gmail.com. *Website:* kilpatrickstockton.com (office).

CAIN, John, LLB; Australian politician; b. 26 April 1931; s. of the late John Cain; m. Nancye Williams 1955; two s. one d.; ed Northcote High School, Scotch Coll. and Melbourne Univ.; mem. Council Law Inst. of Victoria 1967–76, Exec. Law Council of Australia 1973–76; Vice-Chair. Vic. Br. Australian Labor Party 1973–75; Pres. Law Inst., Vic. 1972–73, Chair. Council 1971–72; mem. Legis. Ass. for Bundoora, Vic. 1976–92; Leader of Opposition 1981–82; Premier of Vic. 1982–90; Attorney-Gen. 1982–83; Minister for Fed. Affairs 1982, Minister for Women's Affairs 1982–90, for Ethnic Affairs 1990; Treas. Law Inst., Vic. 1969–70; Professorial Assoc., School of Social & Political Sciences, Melbourne Univ. 1994–; part-time mem. Law Reform Comm. of Australia 1975–77; mem. Commonwealth Secr. Observer Group, South African elections 1994; mem. Trust, Nat. Tennis Centre, Flinders Park 1990–94; Trustee, Melbourne Cricket Ground 1982–98, 1999–2013; Pres. Melbourne Univ. Grad. Union 2005–11; Chair. Hume Global Village Learning Advisory Bd 2004–; mem. Faculty of Business and Law Academic Advisory Bd, Deakin Univ. 2004–, Melbourne and Olympic Parks Trust 2005–2013, Library Bd of Vic. 2005–12 (Pres. 2006–12); Dir and Trustee, LUCRF Community Partnership Trust 2010–. *Publications:* John Cain's Years: Power, Parties and Politics 1994, On With the Show 1998, Off Course (with John Hewitt) 2004. *Leisure interests:* tennis, swimming, jogging. *Address:* 9 Magnolia Road, Ivanhoe, Vic. 3079, Australia.

CAINE, Sir Michael, Kt, CBE; British actor; b. (Maurice Joseph Micklewhite), 14 March 1933, London, England; s. of Maurice Joseph Micklewhite and Ellen Frances Marie Micklewhite (née Burchell); m. 1st Patricia Haines 1954 (divorced); one d.; m. 2nd Shakira Khatoon Baksh 1973; one d.; ed Wilson's Grammar School, Peckham; army service, Berlin and Korea 1951–53; worked at repertory theatres, Horsham and Lowestoft 1953–55; Theatre Workshop, London 1955; mem. IBA 1984–; Hon. Fellow, Univ. of London 1994; Freeman of the City of London 2013; Commdr, Ordre des Arts et des Lettres 2011; BAFTA Award 2000. *Films include:* A Hill in Korea 1956, How to Murder a Rich Uncle 1958, Zulu 1964, The Ipcress File 1965, Alfie 1966, The Wrong Box 1966, Gambit 1966, Funeral in Berlin 1966, Billion Dollar Brain 1967, Woman Times Seven 1967, Deadfall 1967, The Magus 1968, Battle of Britain 1968, Play Dirty 1968, The Italian Job 1969, Too Late the Hero 1970, The Last Valley 1970, Kidnapped 1971, Pulp 1971, Get Carter 1971, Zee and Co. 1972, Sleuth 1973, The Black Windmill 1974, The Wilby Conspiracy 1974, The Destructors (also known as The Marseilles Contract) 1974, Peeper (also known as Fat Chance) 1975, The Romantic Englishwoman 1975, The Man Who Would be King 1975, Harry and Walter Go to New York 1976, The Eagle has Landed 1976, A Bridge Too Far, The Silver Bears 1976, The Swarm, California Suite 1977, Ashanti 1978, Beyond the Poseidon Adventure 1979, The Island 1979, Dressed to Kill 1979, Escape to Victory 1979, Deathtrap 1981, The Hand 1981, Educating Rita 1982, Jigsaw Man 1982, The Honorary Consul 1982, Blame it on Rio 1983, Water 1984, The Holcroft Covenant 1984, Sweet Liberty 1985, Mona Lisa 1985, The Whistle Blower 1985, Half Moon Street 1986, The Fourth Protocol 1986, Hannah and Her Sisters (Academy Award for Best Supporting Actor) 1986) 1986, Surrender 1987, Without a Clue 1988, Dirty Rotten Scoundrels 1988, A Shock to the System 1989, Mr. Destiny 1989, Bullseye 1989, Noises Off 1991, Blue Ice 1992, The Muppet Christmas Carol 1992, On Deadly Ground 1993, Bullet to Beijing 1994, Blood and Wine 1995, 20,000 Leagues under the Sea 1996, Mandela and De Klerk 1996, Curtain Call, Shadowrun, Little Voice 1997, The Debtors 1998, The Cider House Rules (Academy Award for Best Supporting Actor 2000) 1999, Quills 1999, Shiner 2000, Last Orders 2000, Quick Sand 2000, The Quiet American 2001, Austin Powers: Gold Member 2002, The Actors 2002, The Quiet American 2002, Secondhand Lions 2003, The Statement 2003, Around the Bend 2004, The Weather Man 2005, Bewitched 2005, Batman Begins 2005, Children of Men 2006, The Prestige (Best British Actor in a Supporting Role, London Film Critics' Circle Award 2007) 2006, Flawless 2007, Sleuth 2007, The Dark Knight 2008, Harry Brown 2009, Is Anybody There? 2009, Inception 2010, Journey 2: The Mysterious Island 2011, Cars 2 2011, Gnomes and Juliet (voice) 2011, The Dark Knight Rises 2012, Mr. Morgan's Last Love 2013, Now You See Me 2013. *Television includes:* over 100 TV plays 1957–63, Jack the Ripper (mini-series) (Golden Globe Award 1988) 1988, World War 2: When Lions Roared (NBC TV) 1993. *Plays include:* Next Time I'll Sing to You 1963. *Publications:* Michael Caine's File of Facts 1987, Not Many People Know This 1988, What's It All About? 1992, Acting in Film 1993, The

Elephant to Hollywood: The Autobiography 2010, Elephant to Castle 2011. *Leisure interests:* gardening, reading. *Address:* c/o Toni Howard, ICM, 8942 Wilshire Blvd, Beverly Hills, CA 90211, USA; c/o Duncan Heath, Independent Talent Group Ltd, Oxford House, 76 Oxford Street, London, W1D 1BS, England (office). *Telephone:* (20) 7636-6565 (office). *Fax:* (20) 7323-0101 (office). *Website:* www .independenttalent.com (office); www.michaelcaine.com.

CAINE, Uri; American jazz pianist and classical composer; b. Philadelphia; ed Univ. of Pennsylvania; began studying piano with Bernard Pfeiffer; played in bands led by Philly Joe Jones, Johnny Coles, Odean Pope, Hank Mobley, Grover Washington, Mikey Roker and Jymmie Merritt during high school; studied music composition with George Crumb and George Rochenberg at univ. and performed with Joe Henderson, Donald Byrd, J. J. Johnson, Stanley Turrentine, Lester Bowie and Freddie Hubbard; Composer-in-Residence, Los Angeles Chamber Orchestra 2006–09; performed in groups led by Don Byron, Dave Douglas, Terry Gibbs and Buddy DeFranco, Clark Terry, Rashid Ali, Arto Lindsay, Sam Rivers and Barry Altschul, Bobby Watson, Craig Handy, Annie Ross, Arto Lindsay, The Enja Band, Global Theory, The Woody Herman Band, The Master Musicians of Jajouka; performed at What is Jazz? Festival, New York, North Sea Jazz Festival, The Hague, Montréal Jazz Festival, Jazz Across the Borders, Berlin, Texaco Jazz Festival, NY, Umbria Jazz Festival, Gustav Mahler Festival, Toblach, Italy, Vittoria Jazz Festival, San Sebastian Jazz Festival, Newport Jazz Festival, Salzburg Festival, Munich Opera, Holland Festival, Israel Festival, ICRAM and others; Toblacher Komponierhäuschen Award for Best Mahler CD 1997. *Compositions include:* ballet composed for Vienna Volksoper 2000, version of Diabelli Variations for Concerto Köln 2001, Mahler Reimagined, London 2002. *Recordings include:* albums: Sphere Music 1993, Toys 1995, Urlicht/Primal Light 1996, Wagner e Veneza 1997, Blue Wail 1998, Sidewalks of New York 1999, Love Fugue 2000, The Goldberg Variations 2000 (performed by Pennsylvania Ballet 2001), Solitaire 2001, Rio 2001, Bedrock3 2001, Closure (with Mark O'Leary and Ben Perowsky) 2006. *Website:* www.uricaine.com.

CAIO, Francesco, MBA; Italian business executive; *Vice-Chairman, Europe, Investment Banking, Nomura International plc;* b. 23 Aug. 1957; m. Meryl Caio; two c.; ed Politecnico di Milano, INSEAD; consultant with McKinsey, London 1986–1991; CEO Omnitel Pronto Italia (now Vodafone Italy) 1993–96; CEO Merloni (now Indesit) 1997–2000; Founder and CEO Netscalibur (internet service provider) 2000–03; Group CEO Cable & Wireless 2003–06; Vice-Chair., Europe, Lehman Brothers 2006–08, Chair. European Advisory Bd 2008, Vice-Chair., Europe, Investment Banking, Nomura International plc (after acquisition by Nomura of Lehman Brothers' Europe and Middle East investment bank and equities businesses) 2008–; mem. Bd of Dirs Motorola Corpn 2000–03; mem. Int. Advisory Bd, Univ. Bocconi, Milan; head of ind. review on next generation high speed broadband for UK Dept for Business Enterprise and Regulatory Reform 2008; mem. Steering Bd Digital Britain Report 2008–. *Address:* Nomura International plc, 25 Bank Street, London, E14 5LS, England (office). *Telephone:* (20) 7102-1000 (office). *Website:* www.nomura.com (office).

CAIRD, Most Rev. Donald Arthur Richard, BD, MA, DipEd; Irish ecclesiastic; b. 11 Dec. 1925, Dublin; s. of George R. Caird and Emily F. Dreaper; m. Nancy B. Sharpe 1963; one s. two d.; ed Wesley Coll., Dublin and Trinity Coll., Dublin; Curate-Asst, St Mark's, Dundela, Belfast 1950–53, Asst Master and Chaplain The Royal School, Portora 1953–57; Lecturer in Philosophy, Univ. of Wales 1957–60; Rector Rathmichael Parish, Co. Dublin 1960–69; Asst Lecturer in Philosophy, Trinity Coll. Dublin 1962–63; Dean of Ossary, Kilkenny 1969–70; Bishop of Limerick, Ardfert and Aghadoe 1970–76, of Meath and Kildare 1976–85; Archbishop of Dublin, Primate of Ireland and Bishop of Glendalough 1985–96; Chair. Council Alexandra Coll. (Dublin); Chair. Church of Ireland Coll. of Educ.; mem. Bórd na Gaeilge (Govt Bd for Irish Language); Patron Nat. Youth Council of Ireland; Fellow, St Columba's Coll., Dublin; Visiting Prof. of Anglican Studies, Gen. Theological Seminary, New York 1997; Sr Exhibitioner, Foundation Scholar and Sr Moderator, Univ. of Dublin; Life mem. Royal Dublin Soc. 1995–; Hon. DD (Trinity Coll., Dublin) 1988; Hon. LLD (Nat. Univ. of Ireland) 1995; Hon. PhD (Pontifical Univ., Maynooth, Co. Kildare) 2002; Nat. Council for Educational Awards 1993. *Publication:* The Predicament of Natural Theology since the Criticism of Kant, in Directions 1970. *Leisure interests:* walking and swimming. *Address:* 3 Crofton Avenue, Dun Laoghaire, Co. Dublin, Ireland (home). *Telephone:* (1) 2807869 (home). *Fax:* (1) 2301053 (home).

CAIRNCROSS, Frances Anne, CBE, BA, MA; British journalist and academic; *Rector, Exeter College, Oxford;* b. 30 Aug. 1944, Otley, Yorks.; d. of Alexander Kirkland Cairncross and Mary Frances Cairncross; m. Hamish McRae 1971; two d.; ed St Anne's Coll., Oxford, Brown Univ., USA; staff mem. The Times 1967–69, The Banker 1969, The Observer 1969–71; Econs Corresp., The Guardian 1973–81, Women's Ed. 1981–84; Britain Ed., The Economist 1984–89, Public Policy Ed. 1997–2000, Man. Ed. 2000–04; Chair., Econ. and Social Research Council 2001–07; High Sheriff of London 2004–05; Rector, Exeter Coll., Oxford 2004–, also Freedom of Information Officer; Pres. BAAS 2005–06; Sr Fellow, School of Public Policy, UCLA; Visiting Fellow, Nuffield Coll.; mem. Bd of Dirs Stramongate Ltd; regular presenter, Analysis (BBC Radio Four); Hon. Fellow, St Anne's Coll., Oxford, St Peter's Coll., Oxford, RSA; Dr hc (Univs of Glasgow, Birmingham, City, Loughborough, Trinity Coll. Dublin, East Anglia); Inst. of Internal Auditors award for business and management journalism 2003. *Publications:* Capital City (with Hamish McRae) 1971, The Second Great Crash 1973, The Guardian Guide to the Economy 1981, Changing Perceptions of Economic Policy 1981, Second Guardian Guide to the Economy 1983, Guide to the Economy 1987, Costing the Earth 1991, Green, Inc. 1995, The Death of Distance 1997, The Company of the Future 2002. *Leisure interest:* winter swimming. *Address:* Exeter College, Oxford, OX1 3DP, England (office). *Telephone:* (1865) 279605 (office). *E-mail:* rector@ exeter.ox.ac.uk (office). *Website:* www.exeter.ox.ac.uk (office).

CAIRNS, Christopher (Chris) Lance; New Zealand fmr professional cricketer; b. 13 June 1970, Picton, Marlborough; s. of Lance Cairns; right-hand batsman, right-arm fast-medium bowler; teams: Northern Districts 1988–89, Notts. 1988–, Canterbury, New Zealand 1990–2006, Chandigarh Lions 2008 (Capt.); First-class debut: 1988/89; Test debut: Australia v NZ, Perth 24–28 Nov. 1989; ODI debut: NZ v England, Wellington 13 Feb. 1991; in 62 Tests scored 3,320 runs (average 33.53, highest score 158), 218 wickets (average 29.40); T20I debut: NZ v Australia,

Auckland 17 Feb. 2005; in 215 One Day Ints (ODIs) scored 4,950 runs (average 29.46), 201 wickets (average 32.80); 10,702 first-class runs (average 35.32), 647 wickets (average 28.31) in 217 matches; with father Lance Cairns (fmr Test Player), the only father and son to have captured 10 wickets in single Test matches; retd from Test cricket 2004, from ODI cricket 2006; played for Notts. in Twenty20 League; Wisden Cricketer of the Year 2000, PricewaterhouseCoopers No 1 All-rounder in the World 2000, New Zealand Nat. Bank Player of the Year 2001, Redpath Cup for Batting, Windsor Cup for Bowling. *Address:* c/o Nottinghamshire County Cricket Club, Trent Bridge, Nottingham, Notts., NG2 6AG, England. *Telephone:* (115) 982-3000. *Fax:* (115) 982-3037. *E-mail:* administration@nottsccc.co.uk. *Website:* www.nottsccc.co.uk.

CAIRNS, David Adam, CBE, MA, FRSL; British journalist and musicologist; b. 8 June 1926, Loughton, Essex; s. of Sir Hugh William Bell Cairns and Barbara Cairns (née Smith); m. Rosemary Goodwin 1959; three s.; ed Dragon School, Winchester Coll., Oxford, Princeton Univ. Graduate Coll., USA; Library Clerk, House of Commons 1951–53; critic, Record News 1954–56; mem. editorial staff, Times Educational Supplement 1955–58; music critic, Spectator 1958–63, Evening Standard 1958–63; asst music critic, Financial Times 1963–67; music critic, New Statesman 1967–70; mem. staff, Philips Records, London 1968–70, Classic Programme Co-ordinator 1970–73; asst music critic, Sunday Times 1975–84, music critic 1985–92; Leverhulme Research Fellow 1972–74; Distinguished Visiting Prof., Univ. of California, Davis 1985; Distinguished Visiting Scholar, Getty Center for the History of Art and Humanities 1992; Visiting Resident Fellow, Merton Coll., Oxford 1993; Chair. The Berlioz Soc.; Pres. City Music Soc., Putney Music; Founder-Conductor, Thorington Players (amateur orchestra); Officier, Ordre des Arts et des Lettres 1991; Hon. DLitt (Southampton) 2001; British Acad. Derek Allen Memorial Prize 1990, Royal Philharmonic Soc. Award 1990, 1999, Yorkshire Post Prize 1990. *Publications:* The Memoirs of Hector Berlioz (ed. and trans.) 1969, Responses: Musical Essays and Reviews 1973, The Magic Flute (co-author, ENO Opera Guide) 1980, Falstaff (co-author, ENO Opera Guide) 1982, Berlioz: The Making of an Artist 1803–1832 (ASCAP Deems Taylor Award 2001) 1989, Berlioz: Servitude and Greatness 1832–1869 (Whitbread Biog. of the Year 2000, Samuel Johnson Non-Fiction Prize 2000, Prix de l'Académie Charles Croz 2003) 1999, Mozart and his Operas 2006; contrib. of articles on Beethoven and Berlioz, in Viking Opera Guide 1993. *Leisure interests:* conducting, reading, walking, cinema, theatre, cricket, Shakespeare. *Address:* 49 Amerland Road, London, SW18 1QA, England (office). *Telephone:* (20) 8870-4931 (office). *E-mail:* d03.cairns@zen.co.uk (office).

CAIRNS, 6th Earl; Simon Dallas Cairns, BA, CVO, CBE; British business executive; b. 27 May 1939; s. of 5th Earl Cairns and Barbara Jeanne Harrisson; m. Amanda Mary Heathcoat Amory 1964; three s.; ed Eton, Trinity Coll., Cambridge; Chair. VSO 1981–92 (Treas. 1974–81); mem. City Capital Markets Cttee 1989–95; Dir S.G. Warburg Group PLC (fmrly Mercury Int. Group) 1985–95, Vice-Chair. 1987–91; Jt Chair. S. G. Warburg and Co. 1987–95, CEO, Deputy Chair. 1991–95; Chair. Commonwealth Devt Corpn (CDC Group PLC) 1995–2004, BAT Industries 1996–98 (Deputy Chair. June–Dec. 1995); Chair. Allied Zurich 1998–2000, Actis Capital LLP 2004–05; Vice-Chair. Zurich Allied 1998–2000, Zurich Financial Services 1998–2000; Chair. Commonwealth Business Council 1997–2003, Chair. Charities Aid Foundation 2003–10; Overseas Devt Inst. 1994–2002; Receiver Gen. Duchy of Cornwall 1990–2000; Dir Fresnillo PLC 2008–; mem. Bd of Dirs Celtel Int. (now Zain Africa BV 2I) 2005–, Chair. 2007–10; mem. Bd of Dirs Mo Ibrahim Foundation 2006–. *Address:* Bolehyde Manor, Allington, nr Chippenham, Wilts., SN14 6LW, England (home).

CAKTIONG, Tony Tan, BEng; Philippine business executive; *Chairman, President and CEO, Jollibee Foods Corporation;* m. Grace Tan Caktiong; three c.; ed Univ. of Santo Tomas, Manila; opened two ice cream parlours 1975; est. chain of seven hamburger outlets under name Jollibee Foods Corpn 1978 (now nat. and int. fast food chain), currently Chair., Pres. and CEO. *Major acquisitions include* Greenwich Pizza Corpn 1994, Chowking 2000, Hongzhuangyuan 2007, Lao Dong, Taiwan 2008; mem. Bd of Dirs Philippine Long Distance Telephone Co. 2008–, First Gen. Corpn; Philippines Entrepreneur of the Year 2004, Ernst and Young World Entrepreneur of the Year 2004. *Address:* Jollibee Foods Corporation, 10th Floor, Jollibee Plaza Building, F. Ortigas Jr. Road, Ortigas Center, Pasig, Metro Manila 1605, Philippines (office). *Telephone:* (2) 6341111 (office). *Fax:* (2) 6339504 (office). *Website:* www.jollibee.com.ph (office).

CALABRESI, Guido, BS, LLB, MA; American judge and professor of law; b. 18 Oct. 1932, Milan, Italy; s. of Massimo Calabresi and Bianca Maria Finzi-Contini Calabresi; m. Anne Gordon Audubon Tyler 1961; one s. two d.; ed Yale Coll., Magdalen Coll., Oxford, UK and Yale Law School; Asst Instructor, Dept of Econs, Yale Coll. 1955–56; with Thacher & Bartlett (law firm), New York 1957; mem. Conn. Bar 1958; law clerk to Mr Justice Hugo Black, US Supreme Court 1958–59; Asst Prof. of Law, Yale Univ. School of Law 1959–61, Assoc. Prof. 1961–62, Prof. of Law 1962–70; John Thomas Smith Prof. of Law, Yale Univ. 1970–78, Sterling Prof. of Law 1978–95, Sterling Prof. of Law Emer. 1995–, Dean Yale Univ. Law School 1985–94; Judge, US Court of Appeals (Second Circuit) 1994–2009; Corresp. mem. British Acad.; mem. Royal Acad. of Sweden, Accademia delle Scienze di Torino, Accad. Nazionale dei Lincei, American Acad. of Arts and Sciences, American Philosophical Soc.; Commendatore, Repub. of Italy 1994; awarded more than 30 hon. degrees; awards include Laetare Medal, Univ. of Notre Dame 1985, Thomas Jefferson Medal in Law 2000. *Publications:* The Costs of Accidents: A Legal and Economic Analysis 1970, Tragic Choices (with P. Bobbit) 1978, A Common Law for the Age of Statutes 1982, Ideals, Beliefs, Attitudes and the Law: Private Law Perspectives on a Public Law Problem 1985; more than 80 articles on law and related subjects. *Leisure interests:* walking, reading (especially history), gardening, travel, bridge. *Address:* c/o United States Court of Appeals for the Second Circuit, 157 Church Street, New Haven, CT 06510-2100 (office); 639 Amity Road, Woodbridge, CT 06525-1206, USA (home). *Telephone:* (203) 393-0008 (home). *Fax:* (203) 393-1575 (home). *E-mail:* guido.calabresi@yale.edu (home).

CALANTZOPOULOS, André; Swiss business executive; *CEO, Philip Morris International;* ed Swiss Fed. Inst. of Tech., Institut Européen d'Admin des Affaires (INSEAD), France; served as design engineer in automotive industry –1985; joined Philip Morris International Inc. (PMI) as Business Devt Analyst 1985, transferred to Area Operations Dept 1987–90, Gen. Man. Philip Morris Finland 1990–91, Gen.

Man. for PMI in Czechoslovakia 1991–92, Area Dir for Cen. Europe 1992–93, covering the fmr Yugoslavia, Romania and Bulgaria, Area Dir for Hungary and Cen. Europe South 1993–95, Area Dir for Poland and Hungary 1995–96, Man. Dir Poland 1996–99, Pres. Eastern Europe Region 1999–2002, Pres. and CEO Philip Morris International Management SA 2002–08, COO Philip Morris International (following spin-off from Altria Group) 2008–13, mem. Bd of Dirs and CEO 2013–. *Address:* Philip Morris International, Avenue de Cour 107, 1171 Lausanne, Switzerland (office). *Telephone:* (21) 618-61-11 (office). *E-mail:* info@pmi.com (office). *Website:* www.pmi.com (office).

CALATRAVA VALLS, Santiago, PhD; Spanish architect, artist and civil engineer; *Principal, Santiago Calatrava LLC;* b. 28 July 1953, Benimamet, nr Valencia; m. Robertina Marangoni Calatrava; three s. one d.; ed Escuela Tecnica Superior de Arquitectura, Valencia, Fed. Inst. of Tech. (ETH), Zürich, Switzerland; asst. Fed. Inst. of Tech. (ETH), Zürich 1979; undertook small eng comms. 1980s; est. firm Santiago Calatrava LLC, Zürich, 1983, second office Paris 1989, third office Valencia 1991, fourth office New York 2004; won competitions to design and construct Stadelhofen Station, Zürich 1983, Bach de Roda Bridge (commissioned by Olympic Games), Barcelona 1984, Cathedral of St John the Divine, New York 1991; sculptural works include Shadow Machine (large-scale sculpture with undulating concrete fingers) 1993; recently selected to design the expansion of Museo dell'Opera del Duomo, Florence and Symphony Center for the Atlanta Symphony Orchestra, Georgia; mem. Acad. des Arts et Lettres, Paris; Creu Sant Jordi, Barcelona; twelve hon. doctorates; Gold Medal, Inst. of Structural Engineers (UK), City of Toronto Urban Design Award (Canada), Global Leader for Tomorrow, World Econ. Forum, Davos (Switzerland), Algur H. Meadows Award for Excellence in the Arts, Meadows School of the Arts, Gold Medal, Circolo de Bellas Artes, Valencia, Sir Misha Black Medal, Royal Coll. of Art (UK), Leonardo da Vinci Medal, Société pour les Formations des Ingénieurs (France); Príncipe de Asturias Art Prize; Eugene McDermott Award in the Arts, MIT, American Inst. of Architects Gold Medal, Gold Medal for Merit in the Fine Arts, Ministry of Culture (Granada). *Architectural works include:* Alamillo Bridge Viaduct, Seville 1987–92, BCE Place Mall, Toronto 1987–92, Campo Volantin Footbridge, Bilbao 1990–97, Alameda Bridge and Underground Station, Valencia 1991–95, Lyon Airport Station, France 1989–94, City of Arts and Sciences, Valencia 1991–, Oriente Railway Station, Lisbon, Portugal 1993–98, Sondica Airport, Bilbao 2000, The Bridge of Europe, Orléans, France 2000, Bodegas Ysios Winery, Laguardia 2001, Milwaukee Art Museum, USA (Time Magazine 'Best of 2001' designation) 2001, Tenerife Auditorium, Santa Cruz, Canary Islands, 2003, Turtle Bay Bridge, Redding, Calif., USA 2004, Athens Olympic Sports Complex, Greece 2004, World Trade Center Transportation Hub, New York 2004–, Valencia Opera House 2005, Petach Tikvah Bridge, Israel 2005, Quarro Ponte sul Canal Grande, Venice, Italy 2005, Turning Torso Tower, Malmö, Sweden 2005. *Address:* Santiago Calatrava LLC, Parkring 11, 8002 Zürich, Switzerland (office). *Telephone:* (1) 2045000 (office). *Fax:* (1) 2045001 (office). *E-mail:* zurich@scsa-mail.com (office). *Website:* www.calatrava.com (office).

CALCAGNO, HE Cardinal Domenico; Italian ecclesiastic and academic; *President, Administration of the Patrimony of the Apostolic See;* b. 3 Feb. 1943, Tramontana; ed diocesan seminary, Pontifical Gregorian Univ., Rome; ordained priest, Archdiocese of Genoa 1967; several years of parish ministry; fmr Prof. of Theology, Theological Faculty of Northern Italy and, later, at Higher Inst. of Religious Studies of Liguria; served as Pres. of Diocesan Clergy Inst. and was Episcopal Vicar for 'new activities'; held positions as Sec., Italian Priests Comm., Inspector of Italian Episcopal Conf. for Insts of Religious Sciences, Dir of Nat. Missionary Cooperation between Churches, Treas. of the Bishops' Conf., amongst others; Bishop of Savona-Noli 2002–07; apptd Archbishop ad personam 2007; Sec., Admin of the Patrimony of the Apostolic See 2007–11, Pres. 2011–13, 2013–; cr. Cardinal (Cardinal-Deacon of Annunciazione della Beata Vergine Maria a Via Ardeatina) 2012; participated in Papal Conclave 2013. *Address:* Administration of the Patrimony of the Apostolic See, Palazzo Apostolico, 00120 Città del Vaticano, Rome, Italy (office). *Telephone:* (06) 69893403 (office); (06) 69883247 (office). *Fax:* (06) 69883141 (office); (06) 69883591 (office). *E-mail:* segreteria.presidenza@aosa.va (office). *Website:* www.vatican.va (office).

CALDER, Elisabeth (Liz) Nicole, BA; British publisher; b. 20 Jan. 1938, New Zealand; d. of Ivor George Baber and Florence Mary Baber; m. 1st Richard Henry Calder 1958 (divorced 1972); one s. one d.; m. 2nd Louis Baum 2000; ed Palmerston North Girls' High School, NZ and Univ. of Canterbury, NZ; catwalk model in Brazil 1965–68; reader, Metro-Goldwyn-Mayer Story Dept 1969–70; Publicity Man. Victor Gollancz 1971–74, Editorial Dir 1975–78; Editorial Dir (fiction), Jonathan Cape 1979–86; Founding Publishing Dir Book Div., Bloomsbury Publishing 1986–2008, Ed. 2008–09; co-f. Full Circle Editions 2009–; co-f. Women in Publishing 1979; co-f. Groucho Club, London 1984; f. Parati Int. Literary Festival, Brazil 2003; Chair. Royal Court Theatre 2001–05, Vice-Chair. 2005–; Order of Merit for services to culture (Brazil) 2004. *Address:* Full Circle Editions, Parham House, Barn Brick Lane, Framlingham, Woodbridge, Suffolk, IP13 9LQ, England (office). *Website:* www.fullcircle-editions.co.uk (office).

CALDER, John Mackenzie; British publisher, critic, playwright and theatre administrator; *Managing Director, Calder Publishers Ltd;* b. 25 Jan. 1927; m. 1st Mary A. Simmonds 1949; one d.; m. 2nd Bettina Jonic 1960 (divorced 1975); one d.; ed Gilling Castle, Yorks., Bishops Coll. School, Canada, McGill Univ., Montreal, Sir George Williams Coll. and Univ. of Zürich, Switzerland; Founder and Man. Dir John Calder (Publishers) Ltd 1950–91, Calder Publishers Ltd 1991–, Calder and Boyars Ltd 1964–75, f. Calder Bookshop; expanded to Edin. 1971; organized literature confs, Edin. Festival 1962, 1963, Harrogate Festival 1969; f. Ledlanet Nights (music and opera festival) Kinross-shire 1963–74; Pres. Riverrun Press Inc., New York 1978–; Prof. of Literature and Philosophy, Ecole Active Bilingue, Paris 1994–96; Lecturer in History, Univ. of Paris-Nanterre 1995; acquired book-selling business of Better Books, London 1969; Chair. North American Book Clubs 1982–89, Fed. of Scottish Theatres 1972–74; Co-founder Defence of Literature and the Arts Soc.; Dir of other cos associated with opera, publishing etc.; f. Godot Company, Waterloo, London; Theatre Admin. Godot Co.; Chevalier des Arts et des Lettres; Officier, Ordre nat. du Mérite; Dr hc (Edinburgh, Zurich, Napier) 2008. *Plays include:* Lorca, The Voice, The Trust. *Publications:* A Samuel Beckett Reader, The Burroughs Reader 1981, New Beckett Reader 1983, Henry Miller

Reader 1985, Nouveau Roman Reader 1986, The Defence of Literature 1991, The Garden of Eros 1992, The Philosophy of Samuel Beckett 1998, What's Wrong, What's Right (poetry) 1999, Pursuit (autobiography) 2001, Solo (poems); contribs to anthologies. *Leisure interests:* writing, reading, music, theatre, opera, chess, conversation, travelling, promoting good causes, good food and wine. *Address:* Calder Publications Ltd, 51 The Cut, London, SE1 8LF, England (office); 9 rue de Romainville, 93100 Montreuil, France (home). *Telephone:* (20) 7633-0599 (UK) (home); 1-49-88-75-12 (France). *E-mail:* info@calderpublications.com (office). *Website:* www.calderpublications.com (office).

CALDERA, Louis Edward, BS, MBA, JD; American lawyer, university administrator and government official; b. 1 April 1956, El Paso, Tex.; s. of Benjamin Luis Caldera and Soledad Siqueiros; m. Eva Orlebeke Caldera; ed US Mil. Acad., West Point and Harvard Univ.; called to Bar, Calif. 1987; Commdr 2nd Lt US Army 1978, advanced through ranks to Capt. 1982, resigned comm. 1983; Assoc. O'Melveny & Myers (law firm), LA 1987–89, Buchalter, Nemer, Fields & Younger, LA 1990–91; Deputy Co. Counsel, Co. of LA 1991–92; mem. Calif. State Ass., 46th Dist, LA 1992–97, Chair. Banking and Finance Cttee; Man. Dir and COO Corpn for Nat. Service, Washington, DC 1997–98; Sec. of US Army 1998–2001; Vice-Chancellor for Univ. Advancement, Calif. State Univ. System 2002–03; Pres. Univ. of New Mexico 2003–06, mem. faculty School of Law 2006–08; Dir White House Mil. Office, Washington, DC Jan.–May 2009; Sr Fellow, Center for American Progress 2009–10; Vice-Pres. of Programs, Jack Kent Cooke Foundation 2010–12; Pres. Caldera Associates LLC, Washington, DC (consultancy) 2012–; mem. Bd of Dirs IndyMac Bank 2002–08; mem. Bd of Trustees Claremont McKenna Coll., Nat. World War II Museum; mem. Council on Foreign Relations; Democrat; Dr hc (Norwich Univ.) 2000.

CALDERA CARDINAL, Norman José, DPhil; Nicaraguan politician, economist and consultant; b. 21 Oct. 1946, Managua; m. Nora Maria Mayorga Arg Uello; one s. two d.; ed Wentworth Mil. Acad., Lexington, Mo., Univ. of Texas, Columbia Univ., USA; fmr Marketing Supervisor, then Product Man. Kimberley Clark Co.; Finance Gen. Empresas Universales SA 1972, Exports Man. 1975, Gen. Man. 1976; consultant to Agricultural Devt of Latin America Investment Co. 1979, to OAS 1979, to UNCTAD/GATT 1980–96, to GUATEXPRO 1980–84 (apptd Chief Adviser 1984); Adjunct Sec.-Gen. SIECA and COMIECO (Cabinet of Integration and Commerce of Cen. America) 1992–95; consultant to IDB 1995–96, UNCTAD 1996; Econ. Adviser to Pres. of Nicaragua 1996–97; Exec. Sec., Cttee to Reform the Public Admin 1997; Minister of Trade, Industry and Commerce 1999–2001, of Foreign Affairs 2002–06. *Address:* c/o Ministry of Foreign Affairs, Del Cine González al Sur sobre Avda Bolivar, Managua, Nicaragua (office).

CALDERÓN HINOJOSA, Felipe, MEcon, MPA; Mexican lawyer, politician and fmr head of state; b. 18 Aug. 1962, Morelia, Michoacan; s. of Luis Calderón Vega and María del Carmen Hinojosa González; m. Margarita Zavala; two s. one d.; ed Escuela Libre de Derecho, Mexico City, Instituto Tecnológico Autónomo de México (ITAM), Kennedy School of Govt, Harvard Univ., USA; Pres. Partido Acción Nacional (PAN) youth group 1986, Sec.-Gen. 1993, Nat. Pres. 1996–99, Leader Parl. Group 2000–03; Rep. to Mexico City Legis. Ass. 1988; mem. Cámara Federal de Diputados Mexico (Fed. Chamber of Deputies) 1991–94, 2000–03; Dir Banobras 2001–03; Sec. of Energy 2003–04 (resgnd); Pres. of Mexico 2006–12; unsuccessful cand. for Gov. of Michoacan 1995; named as a Global Leader of Tomorrow, World Econ. Forum 1997. *Publication:* El Hijo Desobediente 2006. *Address:* c/o Office of the President, Los Pinos, Col. San Miguel Chapultepec, 11850 México, DF, Mexico (office).

CALDERÓN MARTÍNEZ, Rafael P.; Dominican Republic politician and sociologist; m.; ed Univ. Autónoma de Santo Domingo; lecturer on sociology at various insts in Dominican Repub. and Cen. America 1975–94; Dir-Gen. Planning and Programs, Dist. Council of Santo Domingo 1994–95, mem. Comm. on Modernisation 1998–2000; Tech. Sec. of the Presidency 2000–03; Sec. of State for Finance 2003–04; Dir Dept of Studies and Programs, Caritas Dominicanas 1970–81; Dir-Gen. Centre of Scientific Investigation and Consultation (CENICC) 1973–2000; Gen. Coordinator for Area of Latin America, Mexico, Panama and the Caribbean, Carita Int. 1978–93; Pres. Dominican Asscn of Sociologists 1979–81, Recursos del Futuro Foundation (FUNDARE) 1990–99; Vice-Pres. Amigos de los Niños Foundation 1994–98; currently mem. Chamber of Deputies for Azua; mem. artido Revolucionario Dominicano (PRD). *Publications:* numerous articles in periodicals and nat. journals. *Address:* c/o Partido Revolucionario Dominicano, Espaillat 118, Santo Domingo, DN, Dominican Republic. *Telephone:* 687-2193. *E-mail:* julio.estevez@prd.partidos.com. *Website:* www.prd.partidos.com.

CALDERÓN SOL, Armando; Salvadorean fmr head of state; b. 24 June 1948, San Salvador; m. Elisabeth Aguirre; three c.; ed Univ. of El Salvador; f. Alianza Republicana Nacionalista (ARENA) 1981, elected leader 1988; deputy 1985–88; Mayor of San Salvador 1988–94; Pres. of El Salvador 1994–99. *Address:* c/o Alianza Republicana Nacionalista, Prolongación Calle Arce 2423, entre 45 y 47 Avda Norte, San Salvador, El Salvador.

CALDICOTT, Dame Fiona, DBE, BM, BChir, MA, FRCP, FRCPsych, FRCPI; British psychiatrist and psychotherapist; *Principal, Somerville College, University of Oxford;* b. 12 Jan. 1941; d. of Joseph Maurice Soesan and Elizabeth Jane Soesan (née Ransley); m. Robert Gordon Woodruff Caldicott 1965; one d. (one s. deceased); ed City of London School for Girls, St Hilda's Coll., Oxford Univ.; House Surgeon and Physician, Coventry Hosps 1966–67; GP, Family Planning and Child Welfare 1968–70; training in psychiatry 1970–76; Sr Registrar in Psychiatry, W Midlands Regional Training Scheme 1977–79; Consultant Psychiatrist, Univ. of Warwick 1979–85; Consultant Psychotherapist, Uffculme Clinic, Birmingham 1979–96; Sr Clinical Lecturer in Psychotherapy, Univ. of Birmingham 1982–96; Unit Gen. Man., Mental Health, Cen. Birmingham 1989–91; Clinical Dir Adult Psychiatric and Psychotherapy Service, Mental Health Unit, S Birmingham 1991–94; Medical Dir S Birmingham Mental Health Nat. Health Service (NHS) Trust 1994–96; mem. Sec. of State's Standing Advisory Cttee on Medical Manpower (now Workforce) Planning 1991–2001, on Postgrad. Medical Educ. 1993–99, Council Univ. of Oxford 1998–; Chair. Monospecialist Cttee for Psychiatry 1995– (Sec. 1991–95); Sec. European Bd of Psychiatry 1992–96; Sub-Dean Royal Coll. of Psychiatrists 1987–90, Dean 1990–93, Pres. 1993–96; Chair. Conf. of Medical Royal Colls. 1995–96; Prin. Somerville Coll., Oxford Univ. 1996–; Pro-Vice-

Chancellor Oxford Univ. 2001–02; mem. Union of European Medical Specialists, Broadcasting Standards Council 1996–, Czech Psychiatric Soc. 1994; Fellow Acad. of Medicine, Singapore 1994; Chevalier du Tastevin 1991; Hon. DSc (Warwick) 1997; Hon. MD (Birmingham) 1997. *Publications:* contrib. to Discussing Doctors' Careers (ed. Isobel Allen) 1988; papers in learned journals on psychiatry. *Leisure interests:* family, friends, reading, theatre, wine. *Address:* Somerville College, Oxford, OX2 6HD (office); The Old Rectory, Manor Farm Lane, Balscote, Banbury, OX15 6JJ, England (home). *Telephone:* (1865) 270630 (office); (1295) 730293 (home). *Fax:* (1865) 280623 (office); (1295) 730549 (home). *E-mail:* principals .office@some.ox.ac.uk (office); fiona.caldicott@some.ox.ac.uk (office). *Website:* www .some.ox.ac.uk (office).

CALDWELL, John Bernard, OBE, PhD, DSc; British academic; *Professor Emeritus, Newcastle University;* b. 26 Sept. 1926, Northampton, Northants., England; s. of John R. Caldwell and Doris Caldwell (née Bolland); m. Jean M. F. Duddridge 1955; two s.; ed Bootham School, York, Univs of Liverpool and Bristol; Prin. Scientific Officer, RN Scientific Service 1957–60; Asst Prof., Royal Naval Coll., Greenwich 1960–66; Visiting Prof., MIT 1962–63; Prof. of Naval Architecture, Newcastle Univ. 1966–91, Prof. Emer. 1991–, Head, Dept of Naval Architecture 1966–83, Head, School of Marine Tech. 1975–80, 1986–88, Dean, Faculty of Eng 1983–86; Fellow, Royal Inst. of Naval Architects (RINA), Pres. 1984–87; Dir Nat. Maritime Inst. Ltd 1983–85, Marine Design Consultants Ltd 1985–89, Marine Tech. Directorate 1986–90; mem. Eng Council 1988–94; Fellow, Royal Acad. of Eng; Hon. DSc (Tech. Univ. of Gdansk); NECIS Gold Medal 1973, RINA Froude Medal 1984, Soc. of Naval Architects and Marine Engineers David Taylor Medal (USA) 1987, Eng Council Pres.'s Award of 1995. *Publications include:* more than 70 papers in various eng and scientific publs. *Leisure interests:* music, walking, reading. *Address:* Barkbooth, Winster, Windermere, Cumbria, LA23 3NZ, England. *Telephone:* (15395) 68222. *E-mail:* caldwell892@btinternet .com.

ČALFA, Marián, DrIur; Czech politician and lawyer; b. 7 May 1946, Trebišov, Slovakia; m. Jiřina Čalfová; two d.; ed Charles Univ.; studied law in Prague, subsequently worked in legal and admin. depts of official press agency CTK; Minister without portfolio 1988–89; resgnd from CP of Czechoslovakia; Prime Minister of Czechoslovakia 1989–92; Chair. State Defence Council 1990–92; Deputy to House of Nations of Fed. Ass. CSFR 1990–92; official, Fed. Govt of CSFR July–Oct. 1992; Deputy Chair. Civic Democratic Union—Public Against Violence 1991–92; Co-founder CTL Consulting, Prague 1992–95, Čalfa, Bartošík a partneři, Prague 1995–; Chair. Supervisory Bd I. Silas, Deputy Chair. Alia Chem. 1995; Ed.-in-Chief Legal Adviser 1993–95, Chair. Editorial Bd 1995–99; mem. M. R. Štefánik Foundation 2000–; Grand Cross of the Order of the Crown (Belgium) 1990. *Address:* Calfa, Bartošík a Partneři, Karlovo náměstí 24, 110 00 Prague 1, Czech Republic (office). *Telephone:* 222232380 (office). *Fax:* 222232388 (office). *E-mail:* kancelar@calfabartosik.cz (office). *Website:* www.calfabartosik.cz (office).

CALHEIROS, Renan; Brazilian politician; b. (José Renan Vasconcelos Calheiros), 16 Sept. 1955, Murici; s. of Olavo Calheiros Novais and Ivanilda Vasconcelos Calheiros; m. Verônica Calheiros; three c.; ed Universidade Federal da Alagoas; student Pres., Universidade Federal da Alagoas 1974; State Deputy for Alagoas, Movimento Democrático Brasileiro 1978–80; Leader, Alagoas Legis. Ass. 1980–82; Fed. Deputy, Partido do Movimento Democrático Brasileiro (PMDB) 1982–92, Leader of the House of Deputies 1990–92; Vice Pres. PMDB 1984–85; Senator for Alagoas state 1994–, Minister of State for Justice 1998–99, Leader of PMBD in Fed. Senate 2001–02, 2009–, Pres. of Fed. Senate 2005–07 (resgnd); Exec. Vice Pres. Petrobras Química 1992–94. *Address:* Senado Federal, Praça dos Três Poderes, Anexo 1, Edifício Principal, 15° andar, 70165-920 Brasília, DF, Brazil (office). *Telephone:* (61) 3303-2261 (office). *Fax:* (61) 3311-1695 (office). *E-mail:* renan.calheiros@senador.gov.br (office). *Website:* www.senado.gov.br/ renan (office); www.renancalheiros.com.br.

CALIFANO, Joseph Anthony, Jr, AB, LLB; American lawyer, writer, academic and fmr government official; *Chairman, National Center on Addiction and Substance Abuse, Columbia University;* b. 15 May 1931, Brooklyn, New York; s. of Joseph A. Califano and Katherine Gill Califano; m. 2nd Hilary Paley Byers 1983; two s. one d. from previous marriage; one step-s. one step-d.; ed Holy Cross Coll. and Harvard Univ.; admitted to New York Bar 1955; served in USNR 1955–58; attorney, Dewey Ballantine, Bushby, Palmer Wood, New York 1958–61; Special Asst to Gen. Counsel, US Dept of Defense, Washington, DC 1961–62; Special Asst to US Sec. of Army 1962–63, Gen. Counsel, US Dept of Army 1963–64; Special Asst to Sec. and Deputy Sec. of Defense 1964–65; Special Asst to Pres. 1965–69; US Sec. of Health, Educ. and Welfare 1977–79; Special Counsel to US House of Reps Cttee on Standards of Official Conduct 1982–83; admitted to US District Court; US Court of Appeals for 2nd Circuit; US Supreme Court Bar 1966; mem. ABA, Fed. Bar Asscn, American Judicature Soc.; attorney, Arnold & Porter 1969–71, Williams, Connolly & Califano 1971–77, Califano, Ross & Heineman 1980–82, Dewey, Ballantine, Bushby, Palmer & Wood 1983–92; General Counsel, Democratic Nat. Cttee 1971–72; Prof. of Public Health Policy, Schools of Medicine and Public Health, Columbia Univ. 1992–; Founder and Chair. Nat. Center on Addiction and Substance Abuse, Columbia Univ. 1992–; mem. Democratic Party's Nat. Charter Comm. 1972–74; Chair. Inst. for Social Policy in the Middle East, Kennedy School of Govt, Harvard Univ.; mem. Bd of Dirs Midway Games Inc. 2004–, Willis Group Holdings 2004–, CBS Corpn 2006–; fmr mem. Bd of Dirs Viacom Inc. 2003–05, Primerica Corpn, Automatic Data Processing Inc., K-Mart Corpn, True North Communications, Inc., Warnaco; Trustee Urban Inst.; hon. degrees from Coll. of Holy Cross, Coll. of New Rochelle, Univ. of Michigan, Davis and Elkins Coll., Howard Univ., Univ. of Notre Dame, City Coll., New York; Distinguished Civilian Service Medal, Dept of Army 1964, Dept of Defense 1968; Man of Year Award, Justinian Soc. Lawyers 1966. *Publications:* The Student Revolution, A Global Confrontation 1969, A Presidential Nation 1975, The Media and the Law (with Howard Simons) 1976, The Media and Business (with Howard Simons) 1978, Governing America: An Insider's Report from the White House and the Cabinet 1981, Report on Drug Abuse and Alcoholism 1982, America's Health Care Revolution: Who Lives? Who Dies? Who Pays? 1985, High Society: How Substance Abuse Ravages America and What to Do About It 2007; numerous articles for various newspapers and other publications. *Leisure interest:* jogging. *Address:* Center on Addiction and Substance Abuse, Columbia University, 633 Third

Avenue, 19th Floor, New York, NY 10017-6706, USA. *Telephone:* (212) 841-5200. *Website:* www.casacolumbia.org.

CALIFF, Robert McKinnon, MD; American cardiologist and academic; *Donald F. Fortin, MD, Professor of Cardiology, Vice-Chancellor for Clinical Research and Director of the Duke Translational Medicine Institute, Duke University;* b. 29 Sept. 1951, Columbia, SC; m. Lydia Carpenter 1974; two s. one d.; ed Duke Univ. and Duke Univ. Medical School, Durham, NC; internship in cardiology, Univ. of Calif., San Francisco 1978–79, Resident 1979–80; fellowship in cardiology, Duke Univ. 1978, 1980–83, Attending Physician 1983–, Donald F. Fortin Prof. of Cardiology and Prof. of Internal Medicine 1995–, Dir Duke Clinical Research Inst. 1995–2006, Dir Translational Medicine Inst. 2006–, Assoc. Vice-Chancellor for Clinical Research 1995–2005, Vice-Chancellor for Clinical Research 2005–; mem. Health Sector Advisory Council The Fuqua School of Business; fmr mem. Cardiorenal Advisory Panel US Food and Drug Admin., Pharmaceutical Roundtable of Inst. of Medicine (IOM), IOM Cttee; Dir Co-ordinating Center for Centers for Educ. and Research in Therapeutics; Ed.-in Chief Mosby's American Heart Journal; Contributing Ed. theheart.org; Fellow, American Coll. of Cardiology 1988. *Publications:* Acute Coronary Care (ed.), Textbook of Cardiovascular Medicine (section ed.); more than 600 articles in medical journals. *Leisure interests:* golf, basketball, listening to music. *Address:* Department of Medicine (Cardiology), Duke Clinical Research Institute, 2400 Pratt Street, Suite 7028, Campus PO Box 3850, Durham, NC 27705, USA (office). *Telephone:* (919) 668-8820 (office). *Fax:* (919) 668-7103 (office). *E-mail:* calif001@mc.duke.edu (office). *Website:* www.mc .duke.edu (office).

CALLADINE, Christopher Reuben, ScD, FRS, FREng; British engineer and academic; *Professor Emeritus of Structural Mechanics, University of Cambridge;* b. 19 Jan. 1935, Derby; s. of Reuben Calladine and Mabel Calladine (née Boam); m. Mary Ruth Howard Webb 1964; two s. one d.; ed Nottingham High School, Peterhouse, Cambridge, Massachusetts Inst. of Tech., USA; Lecturer, Dept of Eng, Univ. of Cambridge 1963–79, Reader 1979–86, Prof. of Structural Mechanics 1986–2002, Prof. Emer. 2002–, Fellow, Peterhouse 1960–92, Sr Fellow 1992–2002, Emer. Fellow 2002–; Trustee, EMF Biological Research Trust 2005–, Chair. 2007–; mem. Gen. Bd Univ. of Cambridge 1984–88; mem. Council The Royal Soc. 2000–02; Hon. DEng (Malaysian Univ. of Tech.) 2002; IMechE Ludwig Mond Prize 1966, ICE James Alfred Ewing Medal 1998, ICE Frederick Palmer Prize 2007. *Publications:* Engineering Plasticity 1969, Theory of Shell Structures 1983, Understanding DNA (with H. R. Drew, B. F. Luisi and A. A. Travers) (3rd edn) 2004; many articles in eng and biological journals. *Leisure interest:* mending toys. *Address:* CRC, Department of Engineering, University of Cambridge, Cambridge, CB2 1PZ (office); 25 Almoners Avenue, Cambridge, CB1 8NZ, England (home). *Telephone:* (1223) 764099 (office). *Fax:* (1223) 332662 (office). *E-mail:* crc@eng.cam .ac.uk (office). *Website:* www-civ.eng.cam.ac.uk/crc/crc_web.htm (office).

CALLEJAS ROMERO, Rafael Leonardo; Honduran politician, economist and fmr head of state; b. (Rafael Leonardo Callejas Romero), 14 Nov. 1943, Tegucigalpa; s. of Rafael Callejas Valentine and Emma Romero; m. 1st Nan López (divorced); m. 2nd Norma Regina Gaborit; ed Mississippi State Univ., USA; Under-Sec. for Natural Resources 1972–75; Minister for Agric. and Natural Resources 1978–81; Pres. Cen. Cttee Partido Nacional de Honduras 1982; unsuccessful cand. for Pres. of Honduras 1985, Pres. of Honduras 1990–94; Pres. Honduran Football Asscn 2002–11; mem. FIFA Asscns Cttee; decorations from several countries; Hon. PhD (Mississippi State) 1989, (Georgetown) 1990, (Vermont) 1990, (Pepperdine) 1991, (Guadalajara) 1998, (Vermont, Escuela Agricola El Zamorano). *Leisure interest:* football. *Address:* El Hatillo, Calle Principal, Kilometro 9, Tegucigalpa (home); Edificio Palmira, 5 piso, Frente Hotel Honduras Maya, Tegucigalpa (office); c/o Partido Nacional, Tegucigalpa, Honduras. *Telephone:* 2239-1875 (office); 2211-9359 (home). *Fax:* 2239-2059 (office); 2211-9173 (home). *E-mail:* rcallejas2001@yahoo.com (home).

CALLESEN, Per, MSc; Danish economist and central banker; *Governor, Danmarks Nationalbank;* b. 9 Nov. 1958; m.; two c.; ed Univ. of Copenhagen; Head of Section, Fed. of Danish Industries 1979–86; Special Consultant and Head of Section, Ministry of Finance 1986–91, Head of Div. 1991–93, Deputy Perm. Sec. 1993–2010, responsible for Macroeconomic Policies 1993–2003, Int. Econ. Policies 2003–09; Exec. Dir IMF 2010–11; Gov. Danmarks Nationalbank 2011–; Asst Lecturer, Univ. of Copenhagen 1984–88, External Assoc. Prof. 1988–93; Visiting Fellow, ESRC Modelling Bureau, Univ. of Warwick 1991. *Address:* Office of the Governor, Danmarks Nationalbank, Havnegade 5, 1093 Copenhagen K, Denmark (office). *Telephone:* 33-63-63-63 (office). *Fax:* 33-63-71-03 (office). *E-mail:* nationalbanken@nationalbanken.dk (office). *Website:* www.nationalbanken.dk (office).

CALLIL, Carmen Thérèse, BA, FRSA, FRSL; Australian/British publisher and writer; b. 15 July 1938, Melbourne, Vic.; d. of Frederick Alfred Louis Callil and Lorraine Claire Allen Callil; ed Star of the Sea Convent, Loreto Convent, Melbourne and Melbourne Univ.; settled in UK 1960; Buyer's Asst, Marks and Spencer 1963–65; Editorial Asst, Hutchinson Publishing Co. 1965–66, B.T. Batsford 1966–67, Publicity Man., Granada Publishing 1967–70, André Deutsch 1971–72; f. Carmen Callil Ltd, Book Publicity Co. and Virago Press 1972, Chair. and Man. Dir Virago 1972–83, Chair. 1982–95, Man. Dir Chatto and Windus, The Hogarth Press 1983–93; Co-founder-Dir The Groucho Club, London 1984–94; Publr-at-Large, Random House, UK 1993–94; Ed.-at-Large, Knopf, New York 1993–94; mem. Bd Channel 4 1985–91, Random Century 1989–94; mem. Cttee for The Booker Prize 1979–84, Chair. of Judges, Booker Prize for Fiction 1996; fmr judge, Int. IMPAC Dublin Literary Award, The Orwell Prize; Hon. DLitt (Sheffield) 1994, (Oxford Brookes Univ.) 1995; Hon. DUniv (York) 1995, (Open) 1997; Distinguished Service Award, Int. Women's Writing Guild 1989. *Publications include:* British Council's New Writing 7 (co-ed.) 1998, The Modern Library: The 200 Best Novels in England since 1950 (with Colm Toíbín) 1999, Bad Faith: A Forgotten History of Family and Fatherland 2004. *Leisure interests:* friends, reading, animals, films, gardening, politics, France, Europe. *Address:* c/o Rogers, Coleridge & White Literary Agency, 20 Powis Mews, London, W11 1JN, England (office). *Telephone:* (20) 7221-3717 (office). *Fax:* (20) 7229-9084 (office). *E-mail:* info@rcwlitagency.co.uk (office). *Website:* www.rcwlitagency.co.uk (office).

CALLOW, Simon Philip Hugh, CBE; British actor, director and writer; b. 15 June 1949, London, England; s. of Neil Callow and Yvonne Mary Callow; ed London Oratory Grammar School, Queen's Univ., Belfast, Drama Centre; debut Edinburgh Festival 1973; repertory seasons, Lincoln and Traverse Theatre, Edin.; work at the fringe theatre, the Bush, London; joined Joint Stock Theatre Group 1977, Nat. Theatre 1979; regular book reviewer The Guardian; Freedom of the City of London 2013; Hon. Fellow, Univ. of the Arts, London; Hon. DLitt (Queen's Univ., Belfast) 1999, (Birmingham) 2000, (Open Univ.) 2010; Evening Standard Patricia Rothermere Award 1999. *Stage appearances include:* Passing By 1975, Plumbers Progress 1975, Arturo Ui 1978, Titus Andronicus 1978, Mary Barnes 1978, As You Like It 1979, Amadeus 1979, Sisterly Feeling 1979, Total Eclipse 1982, Restoration 1982, The Beastly Beatitudes of Balthazar B 1982, The Relapse 1983, On The Spot 1984, Melancholy Jacques 1984, Kiss of the Spider Woman 1985, Faust 1988, Single Spies 1988, 1989, The Destiny of Me 1993, The Alchemist 1996, The Importance of Being Oscar 1997, Chimes at Midnight 1997, The Mystery of Charles Dickens 2000–02, Through the Leaves 2003, The Holy Terror 2004 (tour, Duke of York's Theatre, London 2004), The Woman in White (Palace Theatre, London) 2005, Aladdin (Richmond Theatre, London) 2005, Present Laughter (tour) 2006, Equus (tour) 2008, Dr Marigold and Mr Chops (Edinburgh Assembly Rooms and Riverside Studios) 2008–09, Peter Pan (Richmond) 2008, There Reigns Love (Stratford, Ontario) 2008, Waiting for Godot (tour, Theatre Royal, Haymarket) 2009, The Man from Stratford (tour) 2010, Twelfth Night (Nat. Theatre) 2011, Being Shakespeare (Trafalgar Studios) 2011, Tuesday at Tesco's (Assembly Hall, Edinburgh) 2011, Dr Marigold and Mr Chops (tour) 2011, A Christmas Carol (Arts Theatre, London) 2011, Being Shakespeare (Trafalgar Studios) 2012, The Mystery of Charles Dickens (Playhouse Theatre) 2012, A Christmas Carol (Arts Theatre, London) 2012, The Man Jesus (Lyric Theatre, Belfast) 2013, Inside Wagner's Head (Linbury Studios, Royal Opera House) 2013, Chin-Chin (tour) 2013. *Directed:* Loving Reno 1983, Passport 1985, Nicolson Fights Croydon 1986, Amadeus 1986, The Infernal Machine 1986, Così Fan Tutte 1987, Jacques and His Master 1987, Shirley Valentine (theatre production) 1988/89, Die Fledermaus 1989/90, Facades 1988, Single Spies 1988/89, Stevie Wants to Play the Blues 1990, The Ballad of the Sad Café (film) 1991, Carmen Jones (Evening Standard Olivier Award) 1991, My Fair Lady 1992, Shades 1992, The Destiny of Me 1993, Carmen Jones 1994, Il Trittico 1995, Les Enfants du Paradis (RSC) 1996, Stephen Oliver Trilogy 1996, La Calisto 1996, Il Turco in Italia 1997, HRH 1997, The Pajama Game 1999, The Consul 1999, Tomorrow Week (play for radio) 1999, Le Roi Malgré Lui 2003, Everyman 2003, Jus' Like That 2004, The Magic Flute 2008. *Films include:* Amadeus 1983, A Room with a View 1984, The Good Father 1985, Maurice 1986, Manifesto 1987, Mr and Mrs Bridge 1991, Postcards from the Edge 1991, Soft Top Hard Shoulder 1992, Four Weddings and A Funeral 1994, Jefferson in Paris 1994, Victory 1994, Le Passager Clandestin 1995, England, My England 1995, Ace Ventura: When Nature Calls 1995, James and the Giant Peach (voice) 1996, The Scarlet Tunic 1996, Woman In White 1997, Bedrooms and Hallways 1997, Shakespeare in Love 1997, No Man's Land 2000, Thunderpants 2001, A Christmas Carol 2001, George and the Dragon 2004, The Phantom of the Opera 2004, Rag Tale 2005, The Civilization of Maxwell Bright 2005, Bob The Butler 2005, Ripley Under Ground 2005, The Best Man 2005, Some Break (short) 2006, Surveillance 2007, Arn: The Knight Templar 2007, Chemical Wedding 2008, Natural Selection (short) 2010, The Mr. Men Movie (voice, UK version) 2010, Late Bloomers 2011, Save Our Bacon (short) 2011, No Ordinary Trifle 2011, Love's Kitchen 2011, Acts of Godfrey 2012, Miss in Her Teens 2014. *Television includes:* Wings of Song 1977, Instant Enlightenment inc. VAT 1979, La Ronde 1980, Man of Destiny 1982, Chance in a Million 1982–86, Deadhead 1984, Handel 1985, David Copperfield 1986, Cariani and the Courtesan 1987, Old Flames 1989, Patriot Witness 1989, Trial of Oz 1991, Bye Bye Columbus 1992, Femme Fatale 1993, Little Napoleons 1994, An Audience with Charles Dickens 1996, A Christmas Dickens 1997, The Woman in White 1998, Trial-Retribution 1999, 2000, Galileo's Daughter, The Mystery of Charles Dickens 2002, Angels in America (mini-series) 2003, Hans Christian Andersen: My Life as a Fairy Tale (film) 2003, Shoebox Zoo (series) 2004, Agatha Christie's Marple (film) 2004, Doctor Who (series) 2005, 2011, Rome (series) 2005, Midsomer Murders 2006, The Curse of King Tut's Tomb (film) 2007, The Roman Mysteries (series) 2007, The Company (mini-series) 2007, What's on Theatre (series) 2008, Anatomy of Hope (film) 2009, Lewis (series) 2009, The Sarah Jane Adventures (series) 2009, Ice (series) 2011, Comic Relief: Uptown Downstairs Abbey (film) 2011, This is Jinsy (series) 2011, Them from That Thing (mini-series) 2012, Best Possible Taste: The Kenny Everett Story (film) 2012, Agatha Christie: Poirot (series) 2013. *Publications:* Being An Actor 1984 (expanded edn 2004), A Difficult Actor: Charles Laughton 1987, Shooting the Actor, or the Choreography of Confusion (with Dusan Makeyejev) 1990 (expanded edn 2004), Acting in Restoration Comedy 1991, Orson Welles: The Road to Xanadu 1995, Les Enfants du Paradis 1996, Snowdon – On Stage 1996, The National 1997, Love is Where it Falls 1999, Shakespeare on Love 2000, Charles Laughton's the Night of the Hunter 2000, Oscar Wilde and His Circle 2000, The Nights of the Hunter 2001, Henry IV Part 1 2002, Henry IV Part 2 2003, Dicken's Christmas 2003, Orson Welles: Hello Americans 2006, My Life in Pieces: An Alternative Autobiography 2010, Charles Dickens and the Great Theatre of the World 2012; translations of works of Cocteau, Kundera, Prévert, Chabrier; weekly column in Sunday Express, Independent, Country Life; contrib. to The Times, The Sunday Times, The Guardian, The Observer, Evening Standard etc. *Address:* c/o Brebners, The Quadrangle, 130 Wardour Street, London, W1D 5AR, England. *Telephone:* (20) 7413-0869. *Fax:* (20) 7413-0870. *E-mail:* simon.callow@yahoo.co.uk. *Website:* www .simoncallow.com.

CALMAN, Sir Kenneth (Charles), DL, MD, PhD, KCB, FRCP, FMedSci, FRCPE, FRCS, FFPHM, FRSE; British chief medical officer and university administrator; *Chancellor, University of Glasgow;* b. 25 Dec. 1941; s. of Arthur McIntosh Calman and Grace Douglas Don; m. Ann Wilkie 1967; one s. two d.; ed Allan Glen's School, Glasgow, Univ. of Glasgow; Hall Fellow in Surgery, Western Infirmary, Glasgow 1968; Lecturer in Surgery, Univ. of Glasgow 1969, Prof. of Clinical Oncology 1974, Dean of Postgraduate Medicine and Prof. of Postgraduate Medical Educ. 1984–88, Chancellor 2006–; MRC Clinical Research Fellow, Inst. of Cancer Research, London 1972; Chief Medical Officer, Scottish Office Home and Health Dept 1989–91, (at Dept of Health and Social Security) Dept of Educ. and Science (later Dept for Employment, then Dept for Educ. and Employment) 1991–98; Vice-Chancellor and Warden, Durham Univ. 1998–2007 (retd); Deputy Chair. British Library 2008–; Chair. Nat. Trust for Scotland 2010–; mem. Statistics Comm. 2000–; Fellow, Royal Coll. of Surgeons (Glasgow) 1971, Royal Coll. of Gen. Practitioners 1989; Hon. Fellow, Inst. of Cancer Research; Hon. MD (Nottingham) 1994, (Newcastle) 1995, (Birmingham) 1996; Hon. DSc (Strathclyde) 1993, (Westminster) 1995, (Glasgow Caledonian) 1995, (Glasgow) 1996, (Birmingham) 1996, (Brighton) 2000; Hon. DUniv (Stirling) 1992, (Open Univ.) 1996, (Paisley) 1997; Sir Thomas and Lady Dixon Medal, Belfast 1994, Francis Bissett Hawkins Medal, RCP 1995, Crookshanks Medal, RCR 1995, Alexander Hutchinson Medal, Royal Soc. of Medicine (RCS) 1995, Gold Medal, Macmillan Cancer Relief 1996, Heberden (also Orator), British Soc. of Rheumatology 1996, Silver Medal, Royal Coll. of Surgeons in Ireland 1997, Allwyn Smith Medal, Faculty of Public Health Medicine 1998, Bradlaw Medal, RCS Dental Faculty 1999, Thomas Graham Medal, Royal Philosophical Soc., Glasgow 1999. *Publications:* Basic Skills for Clinical Housemen 1971, Basic Principles of Cancer Chemotherapy 1982, Invasion 1984, Healthy Respect 1987, The Potential for Health 1998, Storytelling, Humour & Learning in Medicine 2000; contrib. to Handing on Learning, Health and Healing. *Leisure interests:* gardening, golf, collecting cartoons, Scottish literature, sundials. *Address:* University of Glasgow, Glasgow, G12 8QQ, Scotland (office). *Telephone:* (141) 330-2000 (office). *Website:* www.gla.ac.uk/about/facts/whoswho/chancellor (office).

CALMELS, Virginie; French business executive; *Chairman, Supervisory Board, Euro Disney S.C.A.;* b. 11 Feb. 1971, Talence (Gironde); ed Lycée Marceau, Chartres, Lycée Claude Bernard, Paris, Groupe ESC Toulouse, Institut Européen d'Admin des Affaires (INSEAD); began career as financial auditor, then as Dir, Salustro Reydel 1993–98; Chief Financial Officer (CFO), NC Numericable (Canal+) 1998–99; Admin. and Financial Dir Sky Gate BV, Amsterdam, the Netherlands 1999–2000; Financial Dir, Int. and Devt, Canal+ SA, CFO Canal+ SA 2000–02, Deputy CEO and Co-Deputy Gen. Man. Canal+ SA 2002–03; Gen. Man. Endemol France 2003–07, CEO 2007–13, Exec. Dir and COO Endemol Group Worldwide 2012–13; mem. Supervisory Bd Euro Disney S.C.A. and Euro Disney Associés 2011–, Chair. 2013–; mem. Bd of Dirs Iliad SA 2009–; Vice-Pres. Syndicat des Producteurs et Créateurs d'Emissions de Télévision (ind. TV producers' union) 2004–; mem. Centre d'Etude et de Prospective Stratégique 2004–, Dir 2009–, Vice-Pres. 2010–; mem. Cercle de l'Union Interalliée, Le Siècle; Chevalier, Ordre nat. du Mérite 2008. *Address:* Euro Disney S.C.A., BP 100, 77777 Marne-la-Vallée Cedex 4, France (office). *Telephone:* 1-64-74-59-50 (office). *E-mail:* virginie.calmels@disney.com (office); dlp.corporate.com@disney.com (office). *Website:* corporate.disneylandparis.com (office).

CALMY-REY, Micheline; Swiss politician; b. 8 July 1945, Sion, Valais canton; m. André Calmy; two c.; ed Ecole de commerce, St Maurice, Valais, Grad. Inst. of Int. Studies, Geneva; ran family books business 1977–97; joined Social Democratic Party 1979, Pres. 1986–90; elected Deputy Geneva Grand Council 1981–97, fmr Pres. Finance Comm., fmr Pres. Grand Council; elected to Geneva Conseil d'Etat (Head Dept of Finances) 1997–, Vice-Pres. 2000–01, Pres. 2001–02; mem. Fed. Council 2002–11, Head, Fed. Dept of Foreign Affairs 2002–11; Vice-Pres. of the Swiss Confed. 2006, 2010; Pres. 2007, 2011; mem. Bd of Dirs Caisse d'épargne, Geneva 1986–93, Geneva Int. Airport 1994–97; Vice-Pres., later Pres. Caisse de la pension des employées de la fonction publique 1998–2002; mem. Bd of Dirs Fonds d'équipement communal 1998–2002, Banque Nat. Suisse 2002–.

CALNE, Sir Roy Yorke, Kt, MA, MS, FRCP, FRS; British surgeon, academic and artist; *Professor Emeritus, University of Cambridge;* b. 30 Dec. 1930; s. of Joseph R. Calne and Eileen Calne; m. Patricia D. Whelan 1956; two s. four d.; ed Lancing Coll. and Guy's Hosp. Medical School, London; with RAMC 1954–56; Departmental Anatomy Demonstrator, Univ. of Oxford 1957–58; Sr House Officer, Nuffield Orthopaedic Centre, Oxford 1958; Surgical Registrar, Royal Free Hosp. 1958–60; Harkness Fellow in Surgery, Peter Bent Brigham Hosp., Harvard Medical School 1960–61; Lecturer in Surgery, St Mary's Hosp. London 1961–62; Sr Lecturer and Consulting Surgeon, Westminster Hosp. 1962–65; Prof. of Surgery, Univ. of Cambridge 1965–98, Prof. Emer. 1998–, Fellow, Trinity Hall, Cambridge 1965–98, Emer. 1998–; Ghim Seng Prof. of Surgery, Nat. Univ. of Singapore 1998–2003, Visiting Prof., Dept of Surgery and Medicine 2004–; Pres. Int. Transplantation Soc. 1992–94; mem. Group 90 art group, Singapore; Hon. Consulting Surgeon, Addenbrooke's Hosp., Cambridge 1965–98; Hon. FRCS (Edinburgh) 1992; Grand Officer of the Repub. of Italy 2000, Encomienda con Placa de la Order Civil de Sanidad (Spain) 2008; Hon. MD (Oslo) 1986, (Athens) 1990, (Hanover) 1991, (Thailand) 1993, (Belfast) 1994, (Edinburgh) 2001; Royal Coll. of Surgeons: Hallet Prize, Jacksonian Prize, Hunterian Prof. 1962, Cecil Joll Prize 1966; numerous other honours and awards, including Lister Medal 1984, Hunterian Oration 1989, Cameron Prize 1990, Ellison-Cliffe Medal 1990, Ernst-Jung Prize, Gold Medal of Catalan Transplantation Soc. 1996, King Faisal Int. Prize for Medicine 2001, Prince Mahidol Prize for Medicine 2002, Thomas E. Starzl Prize in Surgery & Immunology 2002, Felix T. Rapaport Memorial Award 2005, Hamdan Award for Medical Research Excellence 2008, Marharshi Sushruta Ginyaanpeeth Prize for advancement of transplantation biology 2009, ASTS-Roche Pioneer Award 2009, Lasker-DeBakey Clinical Medical Research Award (co-recipient) 2012. *Achievements include:* first surgeon to perform a pancreas transplant in UK 1979 and first to perform an intestinal transplant in UK 1992. *Television:* talk on immunosuppression. *Publications include:* Renal Transplantation 1963, Too Many People 1994, Art, Surgery and Transplantation 1996, The Ultimate Gift 1998; books and scientific papers on renal and liver transplantation and gen. surgery. *Leisure interests:* painting, tennis, squash, sculpture. *Address:* 22 Barrow Road, Cambridge, CB2 8AS (home); Department of Surgery, Strangeways Laboratory, 2 Worts Causeway, Cambridge, CB1 8RN, England (office). *Telephone:* (1223) 248777 (office); (1223) 359831 (home). *Fax:* (1223) 740147 (office). *E-mail:* ryc1000@cam.ac.uk (office).

CALOW, Peter, OBE, DSc, PhD, FRSA, FSB; British zoologist and academic; *Research Professor, University of Nebraska-Lincoln;* b. 23 May 1947; two c.; ed Univ. of Leeds; Lecturer, Reader, Univ. of Glasgow 1972–84, Warden Wolfson Hall 1975–84; Prof. of Zoology, Univ. of Sheffield 1984–2004, Prof. Emer. 2004–; Dir Inst. of Environmental Sciences and Tech. 1991–96; Dir Environmental Businesses Network 1998–2000; Founding Ed. Functional Ecology 1986–1999; Pres. SETAC (Europe) 1990–91; Chair. UK Govt Advisory Cttee on Hazardous Substances 1991–2000; Trustee Health and Environmental Sciences Inst.

1996–2002, Int. Life Sciences Inst. 1999–2001; Dir Danish Nat. Environmental Assessment Inst. 2004–06; Prof. of Zoology, Roskilde Univ., Denmark, 2004–12; Research Prof., Univ. of Nebraska-Lincoln 2012–; mem. Council Freshwater Biology Asscn 1995–99, Univ. of Buckingham 1997–2002. *Publications:* author, jt author of 20 books; more than 300 articles in tech. journals. *Leisure interests:* running, reading, writing. *Address:* Office of Research and Economic Development, 230 Whittier Research Center, 2200 Vine Street, PO Box 830857, Lincoln, NE 68583-0857, USA (office). *Telephone:* (402) 472-6035 (office); (402) 405-2892 (cell). *Fax:* (402) 472-9277 (office). *E-mail:* pcalow2@unl.edu (office). *Website:* www .unl.edu (office).

CALTAGIRONE, Francesco Gaetano; Italian business executive; *Chairman, Caltagirone SpA;* b. 1943, Rome; m.; three c.; developed family construction firm into large holding co. with interests in cement manufacturing, real estate, media and construction, currently Chair. Caltagirone SpA, also Chair. of subsidiaries Caltagirone Editore SpA, Il Messaggero SpA, Il Gazzettino SpA, Eurostazioni SpA; Vice-Chair. Assicurazioni Generali 2010–; mem. Bd of Dirs Grandi Stazioni SpA, Ical SpA; Cavaliere del Lavoro 2006. *Address:* Caltagirone SpA, Via Barberini 28, 00187 Rome, Italy (office). *Telephone:* (6) 4541-2293 (office). *Fax:* (6) 4541-2299 (office). *Website:* www.caltagironespa.it (office).

CALVANI, Sandro; Italian academic, diplomatist, international organization official and UN official; *Director, ASEAN Center of Excellence on Millennium Development Goals, Asian Institute of Technology;* b. 16 Aug. 1952, Genoa; m.; four c.; ed Univ. of Genoa, Colorado State Univ., USA; fmr Asst Prof., Univ. of Genoa; Chief of Devt Aid Dept of Caritas, Italy 1980, went on to lead the Caritas Int. del. at FAO, WFP and IFAD and was a mem. of del. of Italian non-governmental orgs to the EC 1985–87, Coordinator for Caritas Foreign Aid Programme 1987, mem. Governing Bd, Devt Cooperation Directorate, Ministry of Foreign Affairs; Founder and first Exec. Dir WHO Pan-African Centre for Disaster Reduction, Addis Ababa, Ethiopia 1988–90, Asst Dir WHO African regional office, Brazzaville, Repub. of the Congo 1990; joined UN System 1992, Country Dir of UN Office on Drugs and Crime (UNODC) Office in Bolivia 1992–95, Dir Barbados-based UNODC Regional Office for the Caribbean 1995–98, Rep. of UNODC to Insts of EU 1998–99, with UNODC Regional Centre in Bangkok, Thailand 1999–2002, Chair. UN Regional working group with remit to contain AIDS epidemic for 30 countries of SE Asia and Pacific 2002, Head of UNODC Office in Colombia 2002–07, Dir UN Interregional Crime and Justice Research Inst., Turin, Italy 2007–10; Dir ASEAN Center of Excellence on Millennium Devt Goals, Asian Inst. of Tech., Bangkok 2010–; fmr Visiting Scientist, Colorado State and Harvard Univs, USA, Louvain Univ., Belgium; mem. Global Agenda Council on Illicit Trade, World Econ. Forum 2008; mem. Scientific Council, Istituto di diritto internazionale della pace Giuseppe Toniolo of Italian Catholic Action, Rome; mem. American Asscn for the Advancement of Science, Asscn of Change Man. Professionals. *Publications:* 20 books and more than 600 articles on sustainable development, human security and human rights. *Address:* ASEAN Regional Center of Excellence on MDGs, Asian Institute of Technology, 19th Floor, One Pacific Place, 142 Sukhumvit Road, Bangkok 10112, Thailand (office). *Telephone:* 8-11715391 (mobile) (office). *Fax:* (2) 516-2126 (office). *E-mail:* arcmdg@ait.asia (office); calvani@ait.asia (office). *Website:* www.arcmdg.ait.asia (office); www.sandrocalvani.it.

CALVERT, Rev. Lorne Albert, BA; Canadian politician; *Leader of the Opposition, Saskatchewan Legislative Assembly;* b. Moose Jaw; m. Betty Sluzalo; two c.; ed St Andrew's Coll. Seminary, Saskatoon, Univ. of Regina, Univ. of Saskatchewan; ordained in United Church of Canada 1976 and served congregations in Perdue, Gravelbourg, Bateman, Shamrock, Coderre, Palmer; Minister Zion United Church, Moose Jaw 1979–86; MLA Sask. 1986–; apptd to Cabinet as Assoc. Minister of Health and Minister Responsible for Wakamow Valley Authority 1992; fmr Minister Responsible for SaskPower and SaskEnergy, Minister of Health, Minister of Social Services, Minister Responsible for Public Service Comm., Minister Responsible for Srs, Minister Responsible for Office of Disabilities; Leader New Democratic Party of Sask. 2001–; Premier of Sask. and Pres. Exec. Council 2001–07; Leader of the Opposition, Saskatchewan Legis. Ass. 2007–. *Address:* Saskatchewan New Democratic Party, 1122 Saskatchewan Drive, Regina, Sask. S4P 0C4, Canada (office). *Telephone:* (306) 525-1322 (office). *Fax:* (306) 569-1363 (office). *E-mail:* info@saskndp.com (office). *Website:* www.saskndp .com (office).

CALVERT, Peter Anthony Richard, BA, MA, PhD, FRHistS; British political scientist, writer and academic; *Professor Emeritus of Comparative and International Politics, School of Social Sciences, University of Southampton;* b. 19 Nov. 1936, Islandmagee, Co. Antrim, Northern Ireland; s. of the late Raymond Calvert and Irene Calvert; m. 1st Diana Elizabeth Farrow 1962; two c.; m. 2nd Susan Ann Milbank 1987; two s.; ed Campbell Coll., Belfast, Queens' Coll., Cambridge, Univ. of Michigan, Ann Arbor, USA; Lecturer, Univ. of Southampton 1964–71, Sr Lecturer 1971–74, Reader 1974–83, Prof. of Comparative and Int. Politics 1984–2002, Prof. Emer. 2002–; Research Fellow, Charles Warren Center, Harvard Univ. 1969–70; Visiting Lecturer/Prof., Birkbeck Coll., London, 1983–84; Co-Ed. Democratization (journal) 1996–2007; Fulbright Scholar 1960, 1969, Ford Foundation grantee 1984–88. *Publications include:* The Mexican Revolution 1910–1914 1968, 2008, A Study of Revolution 1970, The Falklands Crisis 1982, The Concept of Class 1982, The Foreign Policy of New States 1986, Argentina: Political Culture and Instability (with Susan Calvert) 1989, Revolution and Counter Revolution 1990, Latin America in the 20th Century (with Susan Calvert) 1990, 1993, International Politics of Latin America 1994, Politics and Society in the Third World (with Susan Calvert) 1995, The South, the North and the Environment (with Susan Calvert) 1999, Comparative Politics: An Introduction 2002, A Political and Economic Dictionary of Latin America 2004, Politics and Society in the Developing World (with Susan Calvert) 2007, Terrorism, Civil War, and Revolution 2010, Mexico – A Hundred Years of Revolution 2012; editor: The Process of Political Succession 1987, The Central American Security System 1988, 2008, Political and Economic Encyclopedia of South America and the Caribbean 1991, The Resilience of Democracy (with Peter Burnell) 1999, Civil Society in Democratization (with Peter Burnell) 2004, Border and Territorial Disputes of the World (fourth edn) 2004; fiction: The King of the Land of Flopdoodle 2012. *Leisure interest:* non-jarring exercise. *E-mail:* peter@pcalvert24.fsnet.co.uk.

CALVET, Jacques, LenD; French business executive and banker (retd); b. 19 Sept. 1931, Boulogne-sur-Seine; s. of Prof. Louis Calvet and Yvonne Olmières; m. Françoise Rondot 1956; two s. one d.; ed Paris Univ. and Nat. School of Admin., Diplôme d'études supérieures d'économie politique et de sciences économiques, Diplômé de l'Institut Politique de Paris; at Cour des Comptes 1957–63; Chargé de mission to office of Valéry Giscard d'Estaing (Sec. of State for Finance) 1959–62, Dir 1962–66; Dir Financial Affairs, Paris Dist 1966–68; Prin. Pvt. Sec. to Minister of Finance 1968–74; Deputy Gen. Man. Banque Nat. de Paris (BNP) 1974–75, Gen. Man. 1975–79, Chair. 1979–82, Hon. Chair. 1997–; Vice-Chair. Peugeot SA 1982–84, Pres. 1984–97; Chair. Automobiles Peugeot 1982–84, Bd Pres. 1984–, Vice-Pres., Dir-Gen. 1984–89, Pres. 1990–97; Pres. Citroën 1983–97; Pres. Conseil d'Admin. de la Publicité Française 1991–97; Dir Profofina; Chair. European Automobiles Mfrs Asscn 1996; Chair. and Pres. Supervisory Bd Bazar de l'Hôtel de Ville (BHV) 2000–; Vice-Chair. Galeries Lafayette, also Chair. Audit CTTEE; mem. Bd of Dirs Icade (Chair. Audit Cttee), Censor, Société Foncière Lyonnaise, Cottin Frères, Soc. Européenne de Participations Industrielles, Enjoy; mem. Advisory Council Banque de France; Commdr, Légion d'honneur, Officier, Ordre nat. du Mérite, du Mérite agricole,Italian Order of Merit, Chevalier des Palmes académiques. *Publication:* La Grande faillite: Comment l'éviter 1998. *Leisure interest:* tennis, gardening. *Address:* 31 avenue Victor Hugo, 75116 Paris, France (home). *Telephone:* 1-40-67-16-25 (home). *E-mail:* jaccalvet@wanadoo.fr (office).

CALVO, Eddie Baza, BBA; Guamanian lawyer, business executive, politician and state governor; *Governor of Guam;* b. 29 Aug. 1961, Tamuning, Guam; s. of fmr Gov. Paul McDonald Calvo and fmr Guamanian First Lady Rosa Herrero Baza; m. Christine Lujan Sonido; three s. three d.; ed Father Duenas Memorial School, Saint Francis High School, Mountain View, Calif. and Notre Dame de Namur Univ., Belmont, Calif., USA; worked as Gen. Man. Pacific Construction Co. and as Vice-Pres. and Gen. Man. Pepsi Bottling Co. of Guam before entering politics late 1990s; Senator in Guam Legis. 1999–2002, Maite Dist 2004–10, served as Vice-Speaker and Acting Speaker of Legis., Minority Leader in 30th Guam Legislature 2009–11; ran for Lt Gov. of Guam as running mate of Republican gubernatorial cand., Tony Unpingco 2002; Gov. of Guam 2011–; Republican. *Address:* Executive Chamber, PO Box 2950, Hagåtña, GU 96932 (office); Washington Office of the Governor, State of Guam 444 North Capitol Street, Suite 619 Washington, DC 20001, USA (office). *Telephone:* (671) 472-8931 (Hagåtña) (office); (671) 472-8936 (Hagåtña) (office); (202) 434-4855 (DC) (office). *Fax:* (671) 477-4826 (Hagåtña) (office); (202) 434-4856 (DC) (office). *E-mail:* info@mail.gov.gu (office). *Website:* governor.guam.gov (office).

CALZAGHE, Joe, CBE; British professional super-middleweight boxer (retd); b. Hammersmith, London; s. of Enzo Calzaghe and Jackie Calzaghe; joined Newbridge Boxing Club aged nine; won British Amateur Boxing Asscn (ABA) titles 1991 (welterweight), 1992 (light-middleweight), 1993 (middleweight); 2nd to win three ABA titles in consecutive years; professional debut Oct. 1993; won British Super-Middleweight Championship Oct. 1995; won World Boxing Organization World Super-Middleweight Championship Oct. 1997, Int. Boxing Fed. Championship March 2006; 18 defences; won 41 fights including 30 knock-outs, undefeated since turning professional; retd 2009; Professional Boxing Asscn and the Boxing Writers' Club Young Boxer of the Year 1995, BBC Sports Personality of the Year Award 2007. *Publication:* No Ordinary Joe (auto-biog.) 2007. *E-mail:* joe@joecalzaghe.com. *Website:* www.joecalzaghe.com.

CAMACHO, Felix Perez, BBA; American politician, computer software executive and fmr state governor; b. 30 Oct. 1957, Camp Zama, Japan; s. of fmr Gov. of Guam, the late Carlos Garcia Camacho and Lourdes Perez Camacho; m. Joann Gumataotao Garcia Camacho; one s. two d.; ed Father Duenas Memorial School, Marquette Univ., Wis., USA; fmr Insurance Man., Property Casualty Div., Pacific Financial Corpn; Account Admin. IBM Corpn; Deputy Dir Public Utility Agency, Guam 1988–92; Senator, Legislature of Guam 1992–2002, Chair. Cttee on Tourism, Transportation and Econ. Devt 2000–02; Gov. Commonwealth of Guam 2003–11; fmr mem. and Exec. Dir Civil Service Comm.; mem. Nat. Council of State Legislators, Asian Pacific Parliamentarian Union, Kts of Columbus; Republican. *Address:* c/o Office of the Governor, PO Box 2950, Hagåtña, GU 96932, Guam.

CAMAÑO, Eduardo Oscar; Argentine politician; fmr Pres. Partido Justicialista de Quilmes; Pres. of Bloc in Consejal 1983–85; Prov. Deputy 1985–87; Municipal Council, Quilmes 1987–91; Deputy to Nat. Ass. 1991–2007, Vice-Pres. Bloc Justicialista 1994–98, Second Vice-Pres. Chamber of Deputies 1999–2001, Pres. 2001–07, Acting Head of Exec. Br. Dec. 2001–Jan. 2002. *Address:* c/o Partido Justicialista, Domingo Matheu 130, C1082ABD Buenos Aires, Argentina.

CAMARA, Almamy Kabèlè; Guinean economist and government official; ed Univ. of Conakry; intern, Ministry of State Supervision 1979; Deputy Dir-Gen. Alimag (supply co.) 1980–85; Dir Commercial Operations SNG (govt maritime transport co.) 1986–97; Deputy Gen. Man. 1997–2000; Dir-Gen. 2000–01; fmr Dir Gen. Port Autonome De Conakry; Minister of Nat. Defence 2008–09; mem. Exec. Cttee Confed. of African Football, now Vice-Pres. *Address:* c/o Confederation of African Football, 3 Abdel Khalek Sarwat Street, El Hay El Motamayez, PO Box 23, 6th October City, Egypt (office).

CAMARA, Amedi; Mauritanian economist and politician; *Minister of Finance;* b. 31 Dec. 1966, Dafort; m.; four c.; ed Univ. Sidi Mohamed Ben Abdallah, Fez, Morocco, Ecole Nat. de l'Aviation Civile, Toulouse, France; Adviser to Dir-Gen. Société des Aéroports de Mauritanie (SAM), later Financial Dir, SAM 2007–08; Sec.-Gen. Ministry of Industry and Mines 2008–10; Minister of Finance 2010–. *Address:* Ministry of Finance, BP 181, Nouakchott, Mauritania (office). *Telephone:* 525-20-20 (office). *Website:* www.finances.gov.mr (office).

CAMARA, Commdr Abdoul Kabèlè; Guinean lawyer and politician; *Minister-delegate for National Defence;* fmr lawyer, Court of Appeal, Conakry; Overseer of Senegal elections for Parl. Ass. of Francophone Countries 2000; Pres. Bar Asscn of Guinea 2000–06; Minister of Foreign Affairs, Int. Co-operation, African Integration and Guineans Abroad 2007–08, currently Minister-delegate for Nat. Defence. *Address:* Ministry of National Defence, Camp Samory-Touré, Conakry, Guinea (office). *Telephone:* 41-11-54 (office).

CAMARA, Mady Kaba; Guinean politician; fmr Minister of Trade, Minister of Finance 2004, Minister of the Economy and Finance 2004–07, Gov. for Guinea,

IMF Bd of Govs 2006. *Address:* c/o Ministry of the Economy and Finance, face au collège Boulbinet, BP 221, Conakry, Guinea (office).

CAMARA, Gen. Ousmane Arafan; Guinean politician; b. Faranah; fmr personal aide to Pres. Lansana Conté; fmr Deputy Chief-of-Staff of the Armed Forces; Minister of National Defence March–May 2007. *Address:* c/o Ministry of Defence, c/o Office of the President, BP 1000, Boulbinet, Conakry, Guinea (office).

CAMARA, Col-Maj. Yamoussa; Malian army officer and politician; b. 1953, Bancoumana; ed Ecole normale supérieure, Bamako, Ecole supérieure de guerre de Tunis; joined Malian army 1981, Dist Commdr 1991–93, Instructor, Jt Mil. School 1982–83, Deputy Commdr, 133rd Div. 1983–84, Dir Nat. Youth Service Training Centre 1986–88, Head of Operations Div., Army Gen. Staff 1994–96, Adviser to Minister of Armed Forces and War Veterans 2001–03, Commdr, Third Mil. Region 2003, First Mil. Region 2003–05, Operational Controller, Army Gen. Staff 2005, Deputy Chief of Staff Operations 2008, later Chief of Staff of Nat. Guard; rank of Sub-Lt 1981, Lt 1983, Capt. 1988, Commdr 1992, Lt-Col 1997, Col 2002, Col-Maj. 2011; mem. of mil. command group which led coup d'état March 2012; Minister of Defence and War Veterans 2012–13; Silver Star of Nat. Merit with Bee, Chevalier, ordre nat. du Mali; Assalam-2 Campaign Commemorative Medal, Medal of Mil. Merit. *Leisure interests:* running, walking, badminton. *Address:* c/o Ministry of Defence and Veterans, route de Koulouba, BP 2083, Bamako, Mali (office).

CAMARENA BADÍA, Vicente, PhD; Spanish mathematician and academic; *Professor of Applied Mathematics, University of Zaragoza;* b. 26 Aug. 1941, Xátiva, Valencia; s. of Vicente Camarena and Victoria Badía; m. Carmen Grau; one s. four d.; ed Universidad de Zaragoza; Asst Prof. of Math., Universidad de Zaragoza 1966–81, Prof. 1981–84, Rector 1984–92, Prof. of Applied Math. 1992–; mem. Spanish Asscn of Math., Spanish Soc. of Gen. Systems, American Math. Soc., Soc. for Industries and Applied Math., Int. Astronomical Union. *Publications:* Curso de Mecánica 1977–78, Optimización de Trayectorias y efecto de Trampolín Lunar 1972, Formulación Sistemática de la Teoría de Perturbaciones en el Movimiento Orbital 1976, Determinación del Vector Primer de Lawden en Forma Universal y su Aplicación a Problemas de Optimización 1979–83, Elementos Orbitales y Osculadores en Teoría de Perturbaciones, Uniformización de Métodos Canónicos de Perturbaciones 1984, Números y Cálculo con Números: Del 1 al 0, hasta el ∞ 1999. *Leisure interests:* cycling and swimming. *Address:* Universidad de Zaragoza, Centro Politécnico Superior, MªLuna 3, Zaragoza 50018 (office); Latassa 17, Zaragoza, Spain (home). *E-mail:* camarena@unizar.es (office). *Website:* www.cps.unizar.es (office).

CAMBRELING, Sylvain; French conductor; *Principal Conductor, Yomiuri Nippon Symphony Orchestra;* b. 2 July 1948, Amiens; conducting debut with Orchestre de Lyon 1975; Prin. Guest Conductor, Ensemble Intercontemporain, Paris 1976; subsequent appearances in Paris with Orchestre de Paris, Nat. Orchestra of France and Ensemble Intercontemporain; has worked regularly at Paris Opéra since conducting Chéreau's production of Les Contes d'Hoffmann; Glyndebourne Opera debut (The Barber of Seville) 1981; Musical Dir Nat. Opera, Théâtre Royal de la Monnaie, Brussels 1981–91; Music Dir Frankfurt Opera 1990s; Chief Conductor SWR Sinfonieorchester Baden-Baden und Freiburg 1999– (2012); Prin. Conductor, Yomiuri Nippon Symphony Orchestra 2010–; Music Dir Stuttgart Opera (2012–); debut at La Scala (Lucio Silla) 1984, Metropolitan Opera, New York (Romeo et Juliette) 1986; has also appeared at Salzburg, Aix-en-Provence and Bregenz festivals; has worked in UK with Halle and Royal Liverpool Philharmonic orchestras, in Germany with Berlin Philharmonic, Berlin Radio Symphony and other orchestras and in USA. *Address:* c/o International Classical Artists, The Tower Building, 11 York Road, London SE1 7NX, England (office). *Telephone:* (20) 7902-0520 (office). *Fax:* (20) 7902-0530 (office). *E-mail:* info@icartists.co.uk (office). *Website:* www.icartists.co.uk (office); www.sylvaincambreling.com.

CAMBRIDGE, HRH The Duchess of, MA; British royal; b. (Catherine Elizabeth Middleton), 9 Jan. 1982, Reading, Berks.; d. of Michael Francis Middleton and Carole Elizabeth Middleton (née Goldsmith); m. HRH The Duke of Cambridge 2011; one s.; ed St Andrew's School, Pangbourne, Berks., Downe House, Marlborough Coll., Univ. of St Andrews, Scotland; worked for Party Pieces (co. owned by her parents); buyer with Jigsaw Junior (clothing chain) 2006–08; Patron, Action on Addiction, East Anglia's Children's Hospices, The Art Room, Nat. Portrait Gallery 2012–; volunteer in Scout Assen. *Address:* Clarence House, London, SW1A 1BA, England. *Website:* www.royal.gov.uk.

CAMBRIDGE, HRH The Duke of (Earl of Strathearn and Baron Carrickfergus), KG, FRS; British royal; b. (Prince William Arthur Philip Louis), 21 June 1982, London; s. of HRH The Prince of Wales and of the late Diana, Princess of Wales; m. Catherine (Kate) Middleton 2011; one s.; ed Mrs Mynors' Nursery School, Wetherby School, Ludgrove School, Eton Coll., St Andrews Univ., Royal Mil. Acad., Sandhurst, Royal Air Force Coll., Cranwell, Univ. of Cambridge; commissioned as Lt, Blues and Royals Regt, Household Cavalry 2006–09; promoted to Flight Lt with RAF 2009–13, helicopter pilot with Search and Rescue Force, RAF Valley, Anglesey, Wales; Patron of youth homelessness charity, Centrepoint 2005–; Pres. Football Assen 2006–; Patron Tusk Trust 2005–. *Address:* Clarence House, London, SW1A 1BA, England. *Website:* www.royal.gov.uk.

CAMDESSUS, Michel Jean; French international civil servant; *Honorary Governor, Banque de France;* b. 1 May 1933, Bayonne; s. of Alfred Camdessus and Madeleine Cassembon; m. Brigitte d'Arcy 1957; two s. four d.; ed Notre Dame Coll., Betharram, Inst. of Political Studies, Paris, Nat. School of Admin.; civil servant, Treasury, Ministry of Finance 1960–66; Chief, Bureau of Industrial Affairs, Treasury, Ministry of Econ. and Finance 1969–70; Chair. 'Investissements' Sub-cttee of Treasury 1971; Deputy Dir of Treasury 1974–82, Dir 1982–84; Financial Attaché, Perm. Representation, EEC, Brussels 1966–69; mem. Monetary Cttee, EEC 1978, Pres. 1982; Sec. Conseil de Direction du Fonds de Développement Economique et Social 1971; Asst Dir 'Épargne et Crédit' Sub-cttee 1972; Deputy Gov. Banque de France 1984, Gov. 1984–87, Hon. Gov. 1987–; Man. Dir IMF 1987–2000; Pres. Club de Paris 1978–84; Chair. Centre d'études prospectives et d'informations internationales 2000–04, Semaines Sociales de France 2001–07; UN Sec.-Gen. Special Envoy to the Monterrey Conf. 2002; Dir Banque Européenne d'Investissements, Banque Cen. des États de l'Afrique de l'Ouest, Air France, Soc. Nat. des Chemins de fer Français, Crédit Lyonnais (all 1978); Personal Rep. to Africa for French Govt and G8 Heads of State 2002; Grand Officier, Légion d'honneur; Chevalier, Ordre nat. du Mérite; Croix de la Valeur militaire. *Publications:* Notre foi dans ce siècle (with M. Albert, J. Boissonnat), Eau (with Bertrand Badré, Ivan Chéret, Pierre-Frédéric Tenière-Buchot) 2004, Le Sursaut: Vers une nouvelle croissance pour la France 2004, Lettre ouverte aux candidats à l'élection présidentielle 2006, Rapport de la mission sur la modernisation de la distribution du livret A et des circuits de financement du logement social 2007, Réaliser l'objectif constitutionnel d'équilibre des finances publiques 2010, Contrôle des Rémunérations des professionnels de marché 2011, Reform of the International Monetary System (Palais-Royal Initiative) 2011. *Address:* Banque de France, 09–1060, 75049 Paris Cedex 01 (office); 27 rue de Valois, 75001 Paris, France (home). *Telephone:* 1-42-97-73-38 (office). *Fax:* 1-42-97-76-42 (office). *E-mail:* lyliane.huot@banque-france.fr.

CAMERON, Dame Averil Millicent, DBE, MA, PhD, DLitt, FBA, FSA; British historian of late antiquity and Byzantine studies and writer; b. 8 Feb. 1940, Leek, Staffs.; d. of Tom Roy Sutton and Millicent Drew; m. Alan Douglas Edward Cameron 1962 (divorced 1980); one s. one d.; ed Somerville Coll., Oxford, Univ. Coll., London; Asst Lecturer in Classics, King's Coll., London 1965, Lecturer 1968, Reader in Ancient History 1970, Prof. 1978–88, Prof. of Late Antique and Byzantine Studies 1988–94, Dir Centre for Hellenic Studies 1989–94, Fellow 1987–; Warden of Keble Coll., Oxford 1994–2010, Prof. of Late Antique and Byzantine History, Univ. of Oxford 1997–; Pro-Vice-Chancellor, Univ. of Oxford 2001–; Visiting Prof., Columbia Univ., New York 1967–68; Visiting mem. Inst. for Advanced Study, Princeton, NJ 1977–78, Distinguished Visitor 1992; Summer Fellow, Dumbarton Oaks 1980; Sather Prof. of Classical Literature, Univ. of California, Berkeley 1985–86; Visiting Prof., Coll. de France 1987, Lansdowne Lecturer, Victoria, BC 1992; Ed. Journal of Roman Studies 1985–90; Pres. Soc. for the Promotion of Roman Studies 1995–98, Ecclesiastical History Soc. 2005–06, Council for British Research in the Levant 2005–, Fédération internationale des asscns d'études classiques (FIEC) 2009–; Chair. Cathedrals Fabric Comm. for England 1999–2005, Review Group on the Royal Peculiars 1999–2000; Corresp. mem. Akad. der Wissenschaften zu Göttingen 2006; Hon. Fellow, Somerville Coll., Oxford; Hon. DLitt (Warwick, St Andrews, Queen's, Belfast, Aberdeen, London); Hon. DTheol (Lund). *Publications:* Procopius 1967, Agathias 1970, Corippus, In laudem Iustini minoris 1976, Images of Women in Antiquity (ed.) 1983, Continuity and Change in Sixth-Century Byzantium 1981, Constantinople in the Eighth Century (ed.) 1984, Procopius and the Sixth Century 1985, 1996, History as Text (ed.) 1989, The Greek Renaissance in the Roman Empire (ed.) 1990, Christianity and the Rhetoric of Empire 1991, The Byzantine and Early Islamic Near East I (ed.) 1992, II (ed.) 1994, III (ed.) 1995, The Later Roman Empire 1993, The Mediterranean World in Late Antiquity A.D. 395–600 1993 (second edn 2011), Changing Cultures in Early Byzantium (ed.) 1996, Cambridge Ancient History Vol. XIII. The Late Empire (ed.) 1998, Eusebius, Life of Constantine (ed. and trans.) 1999, Cambridge Ancient History Vol. XIV. Late Antiquity: Empire and Successors (ed.) 2000, Fifty Years of Prosopography (ed.) 2003, Cambridge Ancient History Vol. XII. The Crisis of Empire (ed.) 2005, The Byzantines 2006, Doctrine and Debate in the East Christian World (ed.) 2011. *Address:* Keble College, Oxford, OX1 3PG, England (office). *E-mail:* averil.cameron@keble.ox.ac.uk (office).

CÁMERON, Daniel Omar; Argentine government official; *Minister of Energy;* b. 28 March 1954, Río Gallegos, Santa Cruz Prov.; m.; three c.; ed Colegio Nuestra Señora de Luján, Universidad Nacional del Sur, Bahía Blanca, Buenos Aires Technological Inst.; fmr Gen. Man. then Dir state-owned SPSE; fmr adviser to state energy bd of Santa Cruz, then chief adviser to state economy minister and public works ministry; Minister of Economy and Public Works, State of Santa Cruz 1991; Rep. for Santa Cruz to Ofephi (fed. org. of hydrocarbon-producing states) 1991–99 (later Exec. Sec.), also Rep. of Ofephi to fed. govt ministries of economy and public works during privatization of state-owned oil co. YPF (mem. Bd 1998–200); mem. govt comm. that drafted basic energy law 1993, fed. electricity comm. 1998–2002, Man. Cttee, Fed. Trust for Electricity 2002; Minister of Energy 2003–. *Address:* Ministry of Energy, av. Paseo Colón 171, Capital Federal – CP (C1063ACB), Argentina (office). *Telephone:* (11) 4349-8069 (office). *E-mail:* energia@minplan.gov.ar (office). *Website:* energia.mecon.gov.ar (office).

CAMERON, Rt Hon. David William Donald, PC, BA (Hons); British politician; *Prime Minister;* b. 9 Oct. 1966, London, England; s. of the late Ian Donald Cameron and Mary Fleur Cameron (née Mount); m. Samantha Gwendoline Sheffield 1996; two s. (one deceased) two d.; ed Eton Coll., Brasenose Coll., Oxford; raised at Peasemore, Berks.; Head of Political Section, Conservative Research Dept 1988–92; Special Adviser to Chancellor of the Exchequer 1992–93, to Home Sec. 1993–94; Dir of Corp. Affairs, mem. Exec. Bd Carlton Communication plc 1994–2001; unsuccessful parl. cand. for Stafford 1997; MP (Conservative) for Witney 2001–, fmr mem. Home Affairs Select Cttee, Modernisation Cttee, All Party Cttee on Drugs, All Party Media Cttee; Shadow Deputy Leader of the House of Commons 2003; Deputy Chair. Conservative Party 2003; Front Bench Spokesman on Local Govt Finance 2004; Head of Policy Co-ordination –2005; Shadow Sec. of State for Educ. and Skills 2005; Leader, Conservative Party 2005–; Leader of the Opposition 2005–10; Prime Minister 2010–; Minister for the Civil Service 2010–; First Lord of the Treasury 2010–; mem. Exec. British-American Parl. Group; Patron St Mary's Church, Witney, Carterton Educational Trust, Oxon., Victoria County History Trust, Mulberry Bush School, Standlake; ranked by Forbes magazine amongst The World's Most Powerful People (seventh) 2010, (tenth) 2011–12, (11th) 2013. *Leisure interests:* tennis, growing vegetables, cooking, supports Aston Villa Football Club. *Address:* Office of the Prime Minister, 10 Downing Street, London, SW1A 2AA (office); House of Commons, Westminster, London, SW1A 0AA, England. *Telephone:* (20) 7930-4433 (office); (20) 7219-3475. *Fax:* (20) 7925-0918 (office). *Website:* www.number10.gov.uk (office); www.parliament.uk/biographies/commons/david-cameron/25752; www.witneyconservatives.com; www.davidcameronmp.com; www.conservatives.com.

CAMERON, Ian Rennell, CBE, MA, DM, FRCP, FMedSci; British professor of medicine (retd); b. 20 May 1936, London, England; s. of James Cameron and Frances Cameron; m. 1st Jayne Bustard 1964 (divorced); one s. one d.; m. 2nd Jennifer Payne 1980; ed Westminster School, Corpus Christi Coll. Oxford and St Thomas's Hosp. Medical School; jr appointments at St Thomas' Hosp. 1961–64;

Lecturer, St Thomas' Hosp. Medical School 1967, Sr Lecturer 1969, Reader 1975, Prof. of Medicine 1979–94, Dean 1986–89; Research Asst, Dept of Physiology, Univ. Coll., London 1966–68; NIH Postdoctoral Fellowship, Cedars-Sinai Medical Center, Los Angeles and Asst Prof., Dept of Physiology, UCLA 1968–69; Prin. United Medical and Dental Schools of Guys and St Thomas' Hosps 1989–92; Dir Research and Devt South-East Thames Health Authority 1993–94, Bro Taf Health Authority (non-exec.) 1996–99; Provost and Vice-Chancellor, Univ. of Wales Coll. of Medicine 1994–2001; mem. and Treas. GMC 1995–2001; mem. Comm. for Health Improvement 1999–2004; Founder Acad. of Medical Sciences 1998; Hon. Fellow, King's Coll. London 1998, Corpus Christi Coll., Oxford 2000; Hon. LLD (Univ. of Wales) 2001, Hon. DSc (Univ. of Glamorgan) 2001, Hon. PhD (Tokyo Women's Medical Univ., Kobe Gakuin Univ., Japan) 2001. *Publications:* Respiratory Disorders (with N. T. Bateman) 1983; papers in medical and physiological journals. *Leisure interests:* collecting paintings, books and ceramics. *Address:* The Old Mill House, 10 Mill Lane, Middle Barton, Oxon., OX7 7BT, England.

CAMERON, James Francis; Canadian film director, producer, screenwriter, editor and inventor; *Chairman and CEO, Lightstorm Entertainment;* b. 16 Aug. 1954, Kapuskasing, Ont.; s. of Phillip Cameron and Shirley Cameron; m. 1st Sharon Williams 1978 (divorced 1984); m. 2nd Gale Anne Hurd 1985 (divorced 1989); m. 3rd Kathryn Bigelow 1989 (divorced 1991); m. 4th Linda Hamilton 1997 (divorced 1999); one d.; m. 5th Suzy Amis 2000; two d.; ed Stamford Collegiate, Niagara Falls, Fullerton Jr Coll., Calif., California State Univ., Fullerton; f. Lightstorm Entertainment 1990, Head 1992–; CEO Digital Domain 1993–; mem. Advisory Bd Science Fiction Museum and Hall of Fame; Hon. DFA (Carleton Univ.) 1998, Hon. LLD (Ryerson Univ., Toronto) 1998, Hon. DUniv (Univ. of Southampton) 2004; Bradbury Award, Science Fiction and Fantasy Writers of America 1991, inducted into Canada's Walk of Fame 2008, received the 2,396th star on Hollywood Walk of Fame 2009. *Achievements include:* co-developed the digital 3-D Fusion Camera System; completed only the second manned (solo) expedition to the deepest place in the ocean, the Mariana Trench in the western Pacific March 2012. *Films include:* Xenogenesis 1978, Piranha II – The Spawning (dir), The Terminator (dir and screenplay) 1984, Rambo – First Blood Part II (co-screenwriter), Aliens (dir and screenplay), The Abyss (dir and screenplay), Terminator 2 – Judgment Day (co-screenwriter, dir and producer) 1991, Point Break (exec. producer) 1994, True Lies 1994, Strange Days (writer) 1995, Titanic (Acad. Award for Best Dir, film won 11 Acad. Awards equalling record) 1997, Solaris 2002, Ghosts of the Abyss (documentary short; dir and producer) 2003, Volcanoes of the Deep Sea (exec. producer) 2003, Aliens of the Deep (dir and producer) 2005, Avatar (writer, dir and producer) (Golden Globe for Best Motion Picture—Drama 2010, Golden Globe for Best Dir—Motion Picture 2010) 2009, Sanctum (producer) 2010, Cirque du Soleil: Worlds Away (producer) 2012. *Television includes:* Dark Angel (series, exec. producer) 2000, Expedition: Bismarck (producer) 2002, The Lost Tomb of Jesus 2007, Terminator: The Sarah Connor Chronicles (series, writer) 2008–09, Titanic: The Final Word with James Cameron (documentary, exec. producer) 2012. *Publication:* Strange Days 1995. *Address:* Lightstorm Entertainment, 919 Santa Monica Boulevard, Santa Monica, CA 90401, USA (office). *Telephone:* (310) 656-6100 (office). *Fax:* (310) 656-6102 (office).

CAMERON, Peter Duncanson, LLB, PhD, FCIArb; British academic and barrister; *Professor of International Energy Law and Policy and Director, Centre for Energy, Petroleum & Mineral Law, University of Dundee;* b. 21 June 1952, Glasgow, Scotland; s. of Stewart Cameron and Margaret Cameron; m. Qiumin Li 2004; one s. one d.; ed Bishop Vesey Grammar School, High School of Stirling and Univ. of Edinburgh; Lecturer in Law, Univ. of Dundee 1977–86, Prof. of Int. Energy Law and Policy 1997–, also Dir, Centre for Energy, Petroleum & Mineral Law; Visiting Research Assoc., Oxford Univ. Centre for Socio-Legal Studies 1980; Visiting Scholar, Stanford Law School 1985; Adviser, UN Centre on Transnational Corpns 1985–86; Dir Int. Inst. of Energy Law, Univ. of Leiden 1986–97; Chair. Academic Advisory Group and mem. Council, Int. Bar Asscn Section on Energy and Natural Resources Law 1996–2001; Jean Monnet Fellow, European Univ. Inst., Florence, Italy 2001–02, Prof. 2002–05; adviser, UN ESCAP 1988–89; consultant, World Bank 1990–; Visiting Prof., Univ. Autónoma de Madrid 1997–2000; Professorial Fellow, Univ. of Edinburgh Law School 2008–; Visiting Prof., Nat. Univ. of Singapore 2012; mem. Editorial Bd Journal of World Energy Law & Business 2012–; barrister, Middle Temple; door tenant, Tanfield Chambers, London; Fellow, Chartered Inst. of Arbitrators; Research Awards from Asscn of Int. Petroleum Negotiators 1996, 2005. *Publications:* Property Rights and Sovereign Rights: The Case of North Sea Oil 1983, Petroleum Licensing 1984, The Oil Supplies Industry: A Comparative Study of Legislative Restrictions and Their Impact 1986, Nuclear Energy Law After Chernobyl (ed.) 1988, The Regulation of Gas in Europe 1995, Gas Regulation in Western and Central Europe 1998, Kyoto: From Principles to Practice (ed.) 2001, Competition in Energy Markets 2002, 2007, Legal Aspects of EU Energy Regulation (ed.) 2005, International Energy Investment Law: The Pursuit of Stability 2010. *Leisure interests:* long-distance running (marathons: New York, Stockholm, Amsterdam), travel, film. *Address:* Centre for Energy, Petroleum and Mineral Law, University of Dundee, Park Place, Dundee, DD1 4HN (office); 23 Ainslie Place, Edinburgh, EH3 6AJ, Scotland (home). *Telephone:* (1382) 344388 (office). *E-mail:* p.d.cameron@dundee.ac.uk (office). *Website:* www.cepmlp.org (office); www .eisourcebook.org (office).

CAMERON OF LOCHBROOM, Baron (Life Peer), cr. 1984, of Lochbroom in the District of Ross and Cromarty; **Kenneth John Cameron,** LLB, MA, QC, FRSE, FRSA; British lawyer; b. 11 June 1931, Edinburgh, Scotland; s. of Lord Cameron and Eileen Dorothea Burrell; m. Jean Pamela Murray 1964; two d.; ed The Edinburgh Acad., Corpus Christi Coll., Oxford and Univ. of Edinburgh; called to Bar 1958; QC 1972; Chair. Industrial Tribunals (Scotland) 1966–81; Pres. Pensions Appeal Tribunal (Scotland) 1976–84; Chair. Cttee for Investigation in Scotland of Agricultural Marketing Schemes 1980–84; Advocate Depute 1981–84; Lord Advocate 1984–89; Senator of Coll. of Justice in Scotland 1989–2003; Chair. Royal Fine Art Comm. for Scotland 1994–2005; Pres. Scottish Council for Voluntary Orgs 1989–2001; Chancellor's Assessor, Univ. of Edinburgh 1997–2010; Hon. Bencher, Lincoln's Inn, London; Hon. Fellow, Corpus Christi Coll. Oxford, Royal Incorporation of Architects in Scotland, Royal Scottish Acad.

Leisure interest: fishing. *Address:* Stoneyhill House, Musselburgh, Edinburgh, EH21 6RP, Scotland. *Telephone:* (131) 665-1081.

CAMERON WATT, Donald, MA, DLitt, FBA, FRHistS; British historian and academic; *Professor Emeritus of International History, London School of Economics;* b. 17 May 1928, Rugby; s. of Robert Cameron Watt and Barbara Bidwell; m. 1st Marianne R. Grau 1951 (died 1962); m. 2nd Felicia Cobb Stanley 1962 (died 1997); one s., one step-d.; ed Rugby School and Oriel Coll., Oxford; Asst Ed. (Foreign Office Research Dept), Documents on German Foreign Policy 1918–1945, 1951–54, 1951–59; Asst Lecturer in Political History, LSE 1954–56, Lecturer in International History 1957–63, Sr Lecturer 1964–65; Reader in International History, Univ. of London 1966–72, Prof. in International History 1972–82, Stevenson Prof. of International History 1982–93, Prof. Emer. 1993–; Ed. Survey of Int. Affairs, Royal Inst. of International Affairs 1962–71; Historian, Cabinet Office Historical Section 1977–94; Rockefeller Fellow in Social Sciences 1960–61; Fellow, Polish Acad. of Arts and Sciences, Kraków; fmr FRSA; Sec. Comm. for History of International Relations 1982–95, Vice Pres. 1995–; Hon. Fellow, Oriel Coll., Oxford 1998; Wolfson Prize for History 1990. *Publications:* Oxford Poetry 1950 (ed.) 1951, Britain and the Suez Canal 1956, Documents on the Suez Crisis 1957, Britain Looks to Germany 1965, Personalities and Policies 1965, A History of the World in the 20th Century 1967, Contemporary History in Europe 1969, Hitler's Mein Kampf (ed.) 1969, 1992, Current British Foreign Policy 1970–72, Too Serious a Business 1975, 1992, Succeeding John Bull, America in Britain's Place 1900–1975 1983, Documents on British Foreign Affairs 1867–1939 1985–97, How War Came 1989, Argentina Between the Great Powers 1990, Defence Organisation Since the War 2008. *Leisure interests:* cats.

CAMILLERI, Louis C., BA; British business executive; *Chairman, Philip Morris International;* b. 1955, Alexandria, Egypt; comes from a Maltese family that lived in Cairo, Egypt; m. (divorced); three c.; ed Univ. of Lausanne, Switzerland; business analyst with W.R. Grace & Co., Lausanne –1978; joined Philip Morris Europe as a Business Devt Analyst 1978–82, Dir, Business Devt and Planning 1982–86, Vice-Pres., Eastern Europe, Middle East and Africa (EEMA) Region 1986–90, Vice-Pres., Cen. and Eastern Europe 1990–93, Sr Vice-Pres., EU Region 1993–95, Vice-Pres., Corp. Business Strategy Feb.–Aug. 1995, Sr Vice-Pres., Corp. Planning, Philip Morris Cos Inc. (later Altria Group, Inc.), New York Aug.–Dec. 1995, Sr Vice-Pres. and Chief Financial Officer 1996–2002, Pres. and CEO April–Aug. 2002, Chair. and CEO 2002–08, Chair. and CEO Philip Morris International (following spin-off from Altria Group, Inc. March 2008) 2008–13, Chair. 2013–; Pres. and CEO Kraft Foods Int. 1995–2002, mem. Bd of Dirs 2001–07, Chair. 2002–07; Dir (non-exec.) SABMiller 2002–; mem. Bd of Dirs Telmex International SAB 2009–11, América Móvil, SAB de CV 2011–. *Leisure interests:* motorsports, scuba diving. *Address:* Philip Morris International, Avenue de Cour 107, 1171 Lausanne, Switzerland (office). *Telephone:* (21) 618-61-11 (office). *E-mail:* info@pmi.com (office). *Website:* www.pmi.com (office).

CAMILO, Michel; Dominican Republic jazz musician (piano) and composer; b. 4 April 1954, Santo Domingo; m. Sandra Camilo 1975; ed Nat. Conservatory, Santo Domingo, Mannes and Juilliard School of Music, New York; mem. Nat. Symphony Orchestra, Santo Domingo 1970, conductor 1987; moved to New York 1979; debut at Carnegie Hall with trio 1985; Musical Dir Heineken Jazz Festival, Dominican Rep. 1987–92; guest soloist with numerous orchestras 1994–; Co-Artistic Dir Latin-Caribbean Music Festival, Washington, DC 1998; toured internationally with Paquito D'Rivera; Prof. Emer., Univ. Autónoma de Santo Domingo 1992; mem. AfofM, RMA, American Music Center; Dr hc (Univ. Tecnológica de Santiago) 1994, (Berklee Coll. of Music) 2000; Clearwater Jazz Holiday Int. Jazz Award 1993, Emmy Award 1986; Kt Heraldic Order of Christopher Columbus, Silver Cross of the Order of Duarte, Sanchez y Mella 2001. *Recordings include:* albums: The Goodwill Games (theme) (Grammy Award), Calle 54 (OST), Amo mi cama rica (OST) 1970, Why Not! (Grammy Award) 1986, Suntan/Michel Camilo in Trio 1987, Michel Camilo 1988, On Fire 1991, On The Other Hand 1991, Amo tu cama rica (OST) 1992, Rhapsody for two pianos 1992, Suntan 1992, Rendezvous 1993, Los Peores años de nuestra vida (OST) 1994, One More Once 1994, Two Much (OST) 1996, Hands of Rhythm (with Giovanni Hidalgo) 1997, Thru My Eyes 1997, Piano Concerto and Suite 1998, Spain (with Tomatito) 2000, Calle 54 2001, Triangulo 2002, Concerto for piano and orchestra 2002, Solo 2005, Live at the Blue Note 2005, Rhapsody in Blue 2006, Spain Again (with Tomatito) 2006, Spirit of the Moment 2007, Mano a Mano 2011, What's Up? (Latin Grammy Award for Best Latin Jazz Album 2013) 2013. *Address:* c/o Sandra Camilo, Redondo Music & Management Co., PO Box 216, Katonah, NY 10536, USA (office). *Telephone:* (914) 234-6030 (office). *Fax:* (914) 205-3082 (office). *E-mail:* Mijazz@ix.netcom.com (office). *Website:* www.michelcamilo.com.

CAMMARATA, Bernard (Ben); American retail executive; *Chairman, The TJX Companies Inc.;* b. 1941; f. The TJX Cos Inc. (owns TJ Maxx, Marshalls, Home Goods and A.J. Wright dept stores) 1976, Pres. –1999, Chair. and CEO –2000, Acting CEO 2005–06, Chair. 2000–; Co-Chair. Inner-City Scholarship Fund, The Catholic Schools Foundation Inc. 2003–04; mem. Bd of Trustees, Bentley Coll. (Trustee Emer. 2004–), Lahey Clinic, Burlington, Mass; Dir, Heritage Property Investment Trust Inc. (gen. partner of Bradley Operating LP) 1999–. *Leisure interest:* golf. *Address:* The TJX Companies Inc., 770 Cochituate Road, Framingham, MA 01701, USA (office). *Telephone:* (508) 390-1000 (office). *Fax:* (508) 390-2828 (office). *E-mail:* info@tjx.com (office). *Website:* www.tjx.com (office).

CAMOYS, 7th Baron (cr. 1264, called out of abeyance 1839); **(Ralph) Thomas Campion George Sherman Stonor,** GCVO, PC, MA; British banker; b. 16 April 1940; s. of 6th Baron Camoys and Mary Jeanne Stourton; m. Elisabeth Mary Hyde Parker 1966; one s. three d.; ed Eton Coll., Balliol Coll., Oxford; Man. Dir Rothschild Intercontinental Bank Ltd 1969–75; with Amex Bank Ltd 1975–78; Man. Dir Barclays Merchant Bank 1978–84, Exec. Vice.-Chair. 1984–86; Dir Barclays Bank PLC 1984–94; Chief Exec. Barclays de Zoete Wedd Holdings Ltd 1986–87, Deputy Chair. 1987–98; Deputy Chair. Sotheby's Holdings Inc. 1994–97; Dir 3i Group 1991–2002, Perpetual PLC 1994–2000, British Grolux Ltd 1994–; Lord Chamberlain of HM Household 1998–2000; Lord-in-Waiting to HM the Queen 1992–98, Perm. Lord in Waiting 2000–; Pres. River and Rowing Museum, Henley-on-Thames 1998–; mem. Court of Assistants, Fishmongers' Co. 1980–; Consultor Extraordinary Section of Admin. of the Patrimony of the Holy See 1991–2006; Chair. The Tablet Trust 2009–; DL Oxon. 1994–; Order of Gorkha

Dakshina Bahu, 1st Class (Nepal), Kt Grand Cross of the Order of St Gregory the Great 2006; Hon. DLitt (Sheffield) 2001. *Leisure interests:* the arts, family. *Address:* Stonor Park, Henley-on-Thames, Oxon., RG9 6HF, England. *Telephone:* (1491) 638644. *Fax:* (1491) 639348.

CAMP, Jeffery Bruce, RA; British artist; b. 1923, Oulton Broad, Suffolk; s. of George Camp and Caroline Denny; m. Laetitia Yhap 1963; ed Lowestoft and Ipswich Art Schools and Edin. Coll. of Art (under William Gillies); Andrew Grant Scholarship for travelling and study 1944, 1945, David Murray Bursary for landscape painting 1946; painted altarpiece for St Alban's Church, Norwich 1955; Lecturer, Slade School of Fine Art, London 1963–88; mem. London Group 1961; numerous solo and mixed exhbns 1958–; works in numerous public collections in UK; Athena Art Award 1987. *Publications include:* Draw 1981, Paint 1996. *Address:* 27 Stirling Road, London, SW9 9EF, England.

CAMPBELL, Alastair John, MA; British civil servant and journalist; b. 25 May 1957; s. of Donald Campbell and Elizabeth Campbell (née Caldwell); pnr Fiona Millar; two s. one d.; ed City of Leicester Boys School, Gonville and Caius Coll., Cambridge; trainee reporter Tavistock Times and Sunday Independent 1980–82; freelance reporter 1982–83; reporter, Daily Mirror 1982–86, Political Ed. 1989–93; News Ed. Sunday Today 1985–86; Political Corresp. Sunday Mirror 1986–87, Political Ed. 1987–89, columnist 1989–91; Asst Ed. and columnist, Today 1993–95; Press Sec. to Leader of the Opposition 1994–97; Press Sec. to Prime Minister 1997–2001, Dir of Communications and Strategy 2001–03, mem. election campaign team 2005; Pres. Keighley Br., Burnley Football Supporters' Club; Visiting Fellow, Inst. of Politics, Harvard Univ. 2004. *Publications:* The Blair Years 2007, All in the Mind (novel) 2008, Maya (novel) 2010, The Alastair Campbell Diaries Volume One: Prelude to Power 2010. *Leisure interests:* bagpipes, Burnley Football Club. *Address:* c/o Random House, 20 Vauxhall Bridge Road, London, SW1V 2SA, England (office). *Website:* www.alastaircampbell.org.

CAMPBELL, Hon. Alexander Bradshaw, OC, PC, QC, LLD; Canadian lawyer and politician; b. 1 Dec. 1933, Summerside, PEI; s. of the late Thane A. Campbell and Cecilia Bradshaw; m. Marilyn Gilmour 1961; two s. one d.; practised law in Summerside, PEI 1959–66; mem. PEI Legislature 1965–78, Leader of Liberal Party for PEI Dec. 1965–78; Premier of PEI 1966–78; Minister of Devt 1969–72, of Agric. and Forestry 1972–74, Pres. Exec. Council, Minister of Justice, Attorney and Advocate-Gen. 1974–78; Justice, Supreme Court of PEI 1978–94; mem. Privy Council for Canada 1967; mem. and fmr Sec. Summerside Bd of Trade; Past Pres. Y's Men's Club; fmr Vice-Pres. and Exec. mem. PEI Young Liberal Asscn; Pres. Summerside YMCA 1981–91; Elder, United Church, Summerside; Founding Pres. Summerside Area Historical Soc. 1983–88; Founding Chair. Duke of Edinburgh's Awards Cttee (PEI) 1984; Trustee Wyatt Foundation 1990; mem. Heedless Hoarsemen Men's Chorus, Largo, Fla; Co-founder Prince Edward Island Day, Fla; Hon. LLD (McGill, PEI). *Leisure interests:* golf, swimming, gardening. *Address:* Stanley Bridge, Kensington, R.R. #6, Prince Edward Island, C0B 1M0, Canada; 7100 Ulmerton Road, Lot 314, Largo, FL 33771, USA (Winter). *Telephone:* (902) 886-2081 (Summer); (727) 530-9499 (Winter). *E-mail:* alexbcampbell@auracom.com (home).

CAMPBELL, Allan McCulloch, MS, PhD; American biologist and academic; *Professor of Biological Sciences, Stanford University;* b. 27 April 1929, Berkeley, Calif.; s. of Lindsay Campbell and Virginia Campbell; m. Alice Del Campillo 1958; one s. one d.; ed Univ. of Calif. (Berkeley) and Univ. of Ill.; Instructor in Bacteriology, Univ. of Michigan Medical School, Ann Arbor 1953–57; Research Assoc., Carnegie Inst. of Washington, Dept of Genetics 1957–58; Asst Prof. to Prof. of Biology, Univ. of Rochester, 1958–68; Prof. of Biological Sciences, Stanford Univ. 1968–, Barbara Kimball Browning Prof. of Humanities and Sciences 1992–; Fellow, American Acad. of Arts and Sciences; mem. NAS; Hon. DSc (Univ. of Chicago) 1978, (Univ. of Rochester) 1981; Abbott/ASM Lifetime Achievement Award (Microbiology) 2004. *Publications:* Episomes 1969, General Virology 1978. *Address:* Department of Biological Sciences, Stanford University, Stanford, CA 94305 (office); 947 Mears Court, Stanford, CA 94305-1041, USA (home). *Telephone:* (650) 723-1170 (office); (650) 493-6155 (home). *Fax:* (650) 725-1848 (home). *E-mail:* AMC@stanford.edu (office). *Website:* www.stanford.edu/dept/biology (office).

CAMPBELL, Ben Nighthorse, BA; American lawyer and fmr politician; *Senior Policy Advisor, Holland & Knight LLP;* b. 13 April 1933, Auburn, Calif.; m. Linda Price; two c.; ed Univ. of California, San José; educator, Sacramento Law Enforcement Agency; mem. (Democrat) Colo Gen. Ass. 1983–86; mem. US House of Reps 1987–93; Senator from Colo 1993–2005; Sr Policy Advisor Holland & Knight LLP (law firm), Washington, DC 2005–; rancher, jewellery designer; one of 44 chiefs Northern Cheyenne Tribe; mem. American Quarter Horse Assocn, American Indian Educ. Assocn, Aircraft Owners and Pilots Assocn; Ellis Island Medal of Honor 2008. *Address:* Holland & Knight LLP, 2099 Pennsylvania Avenue, NW, Suite 100, Washington, DC 20006, USA (office). *Telephone:* (202) 457-7035 (office). *Fax:* (202) 955-5564 (office). *E-mail:* ben.campbell@hklaw.com (office). *Website:* www.hklaw.com (office).

CAMPBELL, Sir Colin Murray, Kt, LLB; British academic and fmr university administrator; b. 26 Dec. 1944, Aberdeen, Scotland; s. of the late Donald Campbell and Isobel Campbell; m. 1st Elaine Carlisle 1974 (divorced 1999); one s. one d.; m. 2nd Maria Day 2002 (divorced 2004); ed Robert Gordon's Coll., Aberdeen and Univ. of Aberdeen; Lecturer, Faculty of Law, Univ. of Dundee 1967–69, Univ. of Edinburgh 1969–73; Prof. of Jurisprudence, Queen's Univ., Belfast 1974–88, now Prof. Emer.; Vice-Chancellor, Univ. of Nottingham 1988–2008; mem. Council, Soc. for Computers and Law 1973–88, Standing Advisory Comm. on Human Rights 1977–80, Legal Aid Advisory Cttee, NI 1978–82, Mental Health Legislation Review Cttee, NI 1978–82, Nottingham Devt Enterprise 1988–91, Inquiry into Police Responsibilities and Rewards 1992–93; Chair. Ind. Advisory Group on Consumers' Protection in NI 1984, NI Econ. Council 1987–94 (mem. 1985–94), Lace Market Devt Co. 1989–97, Human Fertilisation and Embryology Authority 1990–94, Medical Workforce Standing Advisory Cttee 1991–2001, Food Advisory Cttee 1994–2001, Human Genetics Advisory Comm. 1996–99; Chair. QUBIS Ltd 1983–88, Zeton Ltd 1990; Dir (non-exec.) Swiss Re GB 1999–2005; HM's First Commr for Judicial Appointments 2001–06; Hon. Freeman, City of Nottingham; Hon. LLD (Aberdeen) 2001, (Shanghai Jia-Tong), (Lincoln), (Nottingham). *Publications:* Law and Society (co-author) 1979, Do We Need a Bill of Rights? (ed.)

1980, Data Processing and the Law (ed.) 1984; numerous articles in books and journals. *Leisure interests:* walking, sport, music, reading. *Address:* c/o University of Nottingham, University Park, Nottingham, NG7 2RD, England (office).

CAMPBELL, Finley Alexander, PhD, FRSC; Canadian geologist and academic; *Professor Emeritus, Department of Geology and Geophysics, University of Calgary;* b. 5 Jan. 1927, Kenora, Ont.; s. of Finley McLeod Campbell and Vivian Delve; m. Barbara E. Cromarty 1953; two s. one d.; ed Kenora High School, Portland Univ., Brandon Coll., Univ. of Manitoba, Queen's Univ. Kingston, Ont. and Princeton Univ.; exploration and mine geologist 1950–58; Asst, Assoc. Prof., Univ. of Alberta 1958–65; Prof. and Head, Dept of Geology, Univ. of Calgary 1965–69; Vice-Pres. Capital Resources, Univ. of Calgary 1969–71, Vice-Pres. (Academic) 1971–76, Prof. of Geology 1976–84, Vice-Pres. Priorities and Planning 1984–88, Prof. Emer., Dept of Geology and Geophysics 1988–; Vice-Chair. Canadian Energy Research Inst.; Pres. Emer. Asscn, Univ. of Calgary; Queen's Jubilee Medal 1977, Commemorative Medal for 125th Anniversary of Canada, Distinguished Service Award (Brandon Univ.) 1993 and other awards and distinctions. *Publications:* over 50 publs on geological topics. *Leisure interests:* sailing, golf, music, skiing, ballet. *Address:* Department of Geology and Geophysics, University of Calgary, 2500 University Drive NW, Calgary, AB T2N 1N4 (office); 3408 Benton Drive NW, Calgary AB T2L 1W8, Canada (home). *Telephone:* (403) 220-3258 (office). *E-mail:* campbelf@ucalgary.ca (office). *Website:* www.geo.ucalgary.ca (office).

CAMPBELL, Gordon Arden, CBE, MA, FIChemE, FREng, CBIM; British chemical engineer and business executive; *Chairman, British Nuclear Fuels PLC;* b. 16 Oct. 1946; s. of the late Hugh Eric Campbell and Jessie Campbell; m. Jennifer Vaughan 1970; two d.; ed Oldershaw Grammar School, Churchill Coll., Cambridge; joined Courtaulds Research 1968; Man. Dir British Celanese Ltd 1980–85, Saicor (Pty) Ltd, S Africa 1985–87; Dir Courtaulds PLC 1987–98, Chief Exec. 1996–98; Chair. Acordis Group 1999–2000, Babcock Int. Group PLC 2000–; Pres. Inst. of Chemical Engineers 1998; Pres. Comité Int. de Rayonne et Fibres Synthétiques 1995–98; mem. (non-exec.) UKAEA 1993–96; Dir (non-exec.) A.E.A. Tech. 1996–97, Argos PLC 1997–98, British Nuclear Fuels PLC 2000–, (Chair. 2004–), Accysis Technologies PLC 2005–, HSS Holdings PLC 2005–; Chair. Wade-Allied Holdings 1999–2003, Jupiter Split Trust PLC 2001–04, Jupiter Second Split Trust 2004–, ITI Scotland 2003–05; Vice-Pres. Royal Acad. of Eng 2001–04; Visiting Prof., Strathclyde Univ.; mem. British Heart Foundation Council. *Leisure interests:* golf, skiing, rugby. *Address:* British Nuclear Fuels PLC, 65 Buckingham Gate, London, SW1E 6AP, England (office). *Telephone:* (20) 7202-0865 (office). *Fax:* (20) 799-3224 (office). *Website:* www.bnfl.com (office).

CAMPBELL, Hon. Gordon Muir, BA, MBA; Canadian politician and diplomatist; *High Commissioner to UK;* b. 12 Jan. 1948, Vancouver, BC; s. of Dr Charles Gordon (Chargo) Campbell and Peg Campbell; m. Nancy Campbell; two s.; ed University Hill Secondary School, Dartmouth Coll., Simon Fraser Univ.; taught secondary school in Yola, Nigeria 1970s; Asst to Vancouver Mayor Art Phillips; Gen. Man. of Devt, Marathon Realty 1976–81; f. Citycore Devt Corpn 1981; mem. Vancouver City Council 1984–86; Mayor of Vancouver 1986–93; Leader BC Liberal Party 1993; mem. BC Legislature for Vancouver-Quilchena 1994–2011, for Vancouver-Point Grey 2001; Premier of BC 2001–11; High Commr to UK 2011–; Queen's Golden Jubilee Medal 2002, Order of British Columbia 2011, Queen's Diamond Jubilee Medal 2012; Canadian Olympic Order, Canadian Olympic Cttee 2010, Interfaith Brotherhood Man of the Year, Harald Merilees Tourism Award. *Address:* Canadian High Commission, Macdonald House, 1 Grosvenor Square, London, W1K 4AB, England (office). *Telephone:* (20) 7258-6600 (office); (20) 7258-6328 (office). *Fax:* (20) 7258-6303 (office). *E-mail:* ldn@international.gc.ca (office); collette.lanteigne@international.gc.ca (office). *Website:* www.unitedkingdom.gc.ca (office); www.canada.org.uk (office).

CAMPBELL, Juliet Jeanne d'Auvergne, CMG, MA; British fmr diplomatist and university administrator (retd); *Life Fellow, Girton College, Cambridge;* b. 23 May 1935, London; d. of Wilfred d'Auvergne Collings and Harriet Nancy Draper Bishop; m. Alexander Elmslie Campbell 1983 (died 2002); ed schools in S Africa, Palestine, Lebanon and UK, Lady Margaret Hall, Oxford; joined Foreign Office, London 1957, Del. to Conf. negotiating Britain's proposed entry to EC 1961–63, Second Sec., Bangkok 1964–67, First Sec. Paris (NATO) 1966, First Sec., FCO News Dept 1967–70, Head of Chancery, The Hague 1970–74, First Sec. then Counsellor FCO 1974–77, Counsellor, Paris 1977–80, Royal Coll. Defence Studies 1981, Counsellor, Jakarta 1982–83, Head, Training Dept 1983–87; Amb. to Luxembourg 1987–91; mem. Wilton Park Acad. Council 1992–2000; Mistress Girton Coll., Cambridge 1992–98, Life Fellow 1998–; Deputy Vice-Chancellor, Cambridge Univ. 1993–98; mem. Council Queen's Coll., Harley St 1992–2002; Gov. Marlborough Coll. 1999–2007; Trustee Cambridge European Trust 1994–98, Kurt Hahn Trust 1995–98, Changing Faces (Charity) 1994–2006, Council Royal Soc. for Asian Affairs 2008–; Hon. Fellow, Lady Margaret Hall, Oxford 1992. *Address:* 3 Belbroughton Road, Oxford, OX2 6UZ, England (home). *Telephone:* (1865) 558685 (home). *E-mail:* jencampbell@aol.com (home).

CAMPBELL, Rt Hon Kim Avril Phaedra, BA, LLB, PC QC; Canadian politician and lawyer; b. 10 March 1947, Port Alberni, BC; m. Hershey Felder; ed Univ. of British Columbia, London School of Econs, UK; Lecturer in Science and History, Vancouver Community Coll., in Political Science, Univ. of British Columbia; mem. BC Legis.; elected (Progressive Conservative) House of Commons 1988, Progressive Conservative leader June–Nov. 1993; Minister of State Affairs and Northern Devt 1989–90, Minister of Justice and Attorney-Gen. of Canada 1990–93; Minister of Defence 1993; Prime Minister (first female) June–Nov. 1993; mem. Visiting Cttee Center for Int. Affairs, Harvard Univ. 1995; Consul Gen. of Canada in Los Angeles serving states of California, Utah, Nevada, Arizona, Hawaii and territory of Guam 1996–2000; Visiting Prof. of Practice, John F. Kennedy School of Govt, Harvard Univ. 2001–04; Chair. Council of Women World Leaders 1999–2003, Chair. Emer. 2003–; Pres. Int. Women's Forum 2003–; Sec.-Gen. Club of Madrid 2004–06; Sr Fellow, Gorbachev Foundation of North America; Fellow, John F. Kennedy School of Govt, Harvard Univ.; mem. Int. Council of Asia Soc.; Hon. Fellow, LSE 1994; Dr hc (Brock Univ.) 1998, (Univ. of British Columbia) 2000, (Mt Holyoke Coll., South Hadley, Mass) 2004, (DPS Northeastern Univ., Boston) 1999. *Publication:* Sayings of Chairman Kim 1995, Time and Chance: A Political Memoir of Canada's First Woman Prime Minister (autobiog.) 1996. *Address:* c/o American Program Bureau, 313 Washington Street, Suite 225,

Newton, MA 02458, USA. *Telephone:* (800) 225-4575 (office). *Fax:* (617) 965-6610 (office). *E-mail:* kim_campbell@ksg.harvard.edu. *Website:* www.apbspeakers.com (office).

CAMPBELL, Lewis B., BEng; American transport industry executive; *Chairman, President and CEO, Textron Incorporated;* ed Duke Univ.; 24 years at Gen. Motors, including Gen. Mfg Man., Rochester Products Div., Mfg Man., Chevrolet-Pontiac, Exec. Dir GM/UAW Quality Network, Vice-Pres. Gen. Motors and Gen. Man. Flint Automotive Group 1988–91, Gen. Man. GMC Truck 1991–92; joined Textron Inc. 1992 as Exec. Vice-Pres. and COO, Pres. and COO 1994–98, CEO 1998–, also Chair. 1999– and Pres. 2001–; Dir Bristol-Myers Squibb, Allegheny Energy Inc.; mem. Business Roundtable, Business Council; mem. Bd of Visitors, Fuqua School of Business, Duke Univ. *Address:* 40 Westminster Street, Providence, RI 02903-2596, USA. *Telephone:* (401) 421-2800 (office). *Fax:* (401) 421-2878 (office). *Website:* www.textron.com (office).

CAMPBELL, Naomi; British model; b. 22 May 1970, London; d. of Valerie Morris; ed Barbara Speake Stage School, Italia Conti; fashion model 1985–. *Film appearances include:* Ready To Wear 1994, Miami Rhapsody 1995, Catwalk 1995, Invasion of Privacy 1996, Beautopia 1996, Prisoner of Love 1999, Destinazione Verna 2000, Ali G Indahouse 2002, Fastlane 2003, Fat Slags 2004, The Call 2006, Ugly Betty 2008, Karma, Confessions and Holi 2009, Rose, c'est Paris 2010, Por el Camino 2010. *Albums:* Baby Woman 1994, Love and Tears 1994. *Publications include:* That Wild Lie 1992, Swan 1994, Naomi 2001. *Address:* Women Model Agency, 2nd Floor, 107 Greene Street, New York, 10012, USA. *Telephone:* (20) 7333-0891. *Fax:* (20) 7323-1221.

CAMPBELL, Neve Adrienne; Canadian actress; b. 3 Oct. 1973, Guelph, Ont.; m. 1st Jeff Colt 1995 (divorced 1997); m. 2nd John Light 2007; ed Nat. Ballet School, Canada. *Dance includes:* The Phantom of the Opera, The Nutcracker, Sleeping Beauty. *Films include:* Paint Cans 1994, The Dark 1994, Love Child 1995, The Craft 1996, Scream (Saturn Award for Best Actress 1996, MTV Movie Award for Best Female Performance 1996) 1996, A Time to Kill 1996, Simba's Pride 1997, Scream 2 (MTV Movie Award for Best Female Performance 1996, Blockbuster Entertainment Award for Favourite Actress – Horror 1997) 1997, Wild Things 1998, Hairshirt 1998, 54 1998, Three to Tango 1999, Scream 3 2000, Panic 2000, A Lust for Life 2000, Drowning Mona 2000, Last Call 2003, Blind Horizon 2003, Lost Junction 2003, The Company 2003, When Will I Be Loved 2004, Churchill: The Hollywood Years 2004, Partition 2006, Relative Strangers 2006, Closing the Ring 2006, Love Bites 2007, I Really Hate My Job 2007, Owl Song 2009, Vivaldi 2009, Scream 4 2011, The Glass Man 2011, Singularity 2012. *Television includes:* Catwalk 1992–93, Web of Deceit 1993, Baree 1994, The Forget-Me-Not Murders 1994, Party of Five 1994–98, The Canterville Ghost 1996, Reefer Madness: The Movie Musical 2005, Medium 2007, Burn Up 2008, Sea Wolf (mini-series) 2009, The Philanthropist 2009, Titanic: Blood and Steel (series) 2012, Sworn to Silence (film) 2012. *Address:* Creative Artists Agency, 2000 Avenue of the Stars, Los Angeles, CA 90067, USA. *Telephone:* (424) 288-2000. *Fax:* (424) 288-2900. *Website:* www.caa.com.

CAMPBELL, Philip Henry Montgomery, PhD, FInstP, FRAS; British journalist and academic; *Editor-in-Chief, Nature;* b. 19 April 1951; s. of Hugh Campbell and Mary Montgomery Campbell; m. Judie Yelton 1980 (died 1992); two s.; ed Shrewsbury School, Univ. of Bristol, Queen Mary Coll., London, Univ. of Leicester; postdoctoral research asst, Dept of Physics, Univ. of Leicester 1977–79; Asst Ed. Nature journal 1979–82, Physical Sciences Ed. 1982–88, Ed., Nature journal and Ed.-in-Chief Nature journal and Nature publications 1995–; Dir Nature Publishing Group 1997–; Founding Ed. Physics World magazine 1988–95; Trustee Cancer Research UK; Hon. DSc (Leicester) 1999. *Radio:* broadcasts on BBC World Service. *Publications:* numerous papers and articles in journals, magazines and newspapers. *Leisure interest:* music. *Address:* Nature Publishing Group, The Macmillan Building, 4 Crinan Street, London, N1 9XW, England (office). *Telephone:* (20) 7833-4000 (office). *Fax:* (20) 7843-4640 (office). *E-mail:* exec@nature.com (office). *Website:* www.nature.com (office).

CAMPBELL, Roderick Samuel Fisher, AM, PhD, DSc, MRCVS, FRSE, FRCPath; Australian veterinary scientist and academic; *Professor Emeritus, James Cook University;* b. 5 June 1924, Glasgow, Scotland; s. of Robert Campbell and Harriet Hodson; m. Barbara M. Morris 1956; three s.; ed Allan Glens School, Glasgow, McLaren High School, Callander and Glasgow Veterinary Coll.; Lecturer in Veterinary Pathology, Univ. of Glasgow 1948, Sr Lecturer 1956–69; Prof. and Head, Grad. School of Tropical Veterinary Science, James Cook Univ., Townsville 1969–87, Prof. Emer. 1987–, Chair. Convocation 1992–94, Dir Anton Breinl Centre for Tropical Health and Medicine, Townsville 1990–91; Visiting Prof., Khartoum Univ., Sudan 1964–65, Purdue Univ., USA 1967–68; Deputy Chair. Australian Veterinary Schools Accreditation Cttee 1988–92; Project Man. Balitvet Inst. Project, Bogor, Indonesia 1981–; Consultant, FAO, World Bank, Australian Centre for International Agric. Research, International Devt Program of Australian Univs, Australian Devt Asst Bureau, Ove Arup; Trustee, Indonesia International Animal Science Research and Devt Foundation 1990–93; Fellow, Australian Coll. of Veterinary Science, Australian Coll. of Tropical Medicine, Royal Coll. of Pathology; Hon. DSc (James Cook); Dr hc (Veterinary Medicine and Surgery, Glasgow) 2000; Kesteven Medal for contrib. to Int. Veterinary Science, Pegasus Medal. *Publications include:* numerous scientific papers on infectious diseases, veterinary educ., devt assistance etc. *Leisure interests:* history, music. *Address:* 3/ 27 Epala Street, Carina, Qld 4152 (home); School of Veterinary and Biomedical Sciences, James Cook University, Townsville, Qld 4811, Australia (office). *Telephone:* (7) 3395-0207 (home). *E-mail:* rsfc@ozemail.com.au (home).

CAMPBELL, Sydney, MA (Econ); Belizean fmr central banker; ed Florida Int. Univ.; joined Cen. Bank of Belize 1981, served in various posts including Deputy Gov. –2003, Gov. and Vice-Chair. 2003–08. *Address:* c/o Central Bank of Belize, Gabourel Lane, PO Box 852, Belize City, Belize (office).

CAMPBELL, Sir Walter Menzies (Ming), Kt, CH, CBE, QC, MA, LLB, LLD; British politician and university administrator; b. 22 May 1941; m.; ed Hillhead High School, Univ. of Glasgow, Stanford Univ., USA; ran 200m at 1964 Tokyo Olympic Games and 1966 Commonwealth Games, Capt. UK Athletics Team 1965–66; called to Scottish Bar as Advocate 1968; Chair. Scottish Liberal Party 1975; MP for Fife North East 1987–, Spokesman on Sport and Defence 1988–94,

Shadow Foreign Sec. 1997–2006; Deputy Leader, Liberal Democrat party 2003–06, Leader 2006–07; Chancellor St Andrews Univ. 2006–; Dr hc (Glasgow), (Strathclyde). *Achievements include:* held British 100m record 1967–74. *Publication:* Menzies Campbell: My Autobiography 2008. *Address:* Liberal Democrats, 4 Cowley Street, London, SW1P 3NB, England (office); North East Fife Liberal Democrats, 16 Millgate, Cupar, Fife, KY15 5EG, Scotland (office). *Telephone:* (20) 7222-7999 (office); (1334) 656361 (office). *Fax:* (20) 7799-2170 (office); (1334) 654045 (office). *E-mail:* westminster_office@mingcampbell.org.uk (office); fife_office@mingcampbell.org.uk (office); menzies.campbell.mp@parliament.uk (office). *Website:* www.mingcampbell.org.uk (office).

CAMPBELL-BROWN, Veronica; Jamaican athlete; b. 15 May 1982, Trelawny; d. of Cecil Campbell and Pamella Bailey; m. Omar Brown 2007; ed Vere Tech. High School, Clarendon, Barton Co. Community Coll., Great Bend, Kan. and Univ. of Arkansas, USA; track and field sprint athlete; six-time Olympic medallist, Olympic 200m and World 100m Champion; Gold Medals, 100m and 4×100m, inaugural Int. Asscn of Athletics Feds (IAAF) World Youth Championships 1999; first female to win sprint double at IAAF World Jr Championships 2000; Silver Medal, 4×100m relay, Olympic Games, Sydney 2000; only female athlete to win both 100m and 200m sprints at same World Youth Championships; Silver Medal, 100m, Commonwealth Games, Manchester 2002; Bronze Medal, 100m, Olympic Games, Athens 2004, Gold Medals, 200m and 4×100m; Silver Medals, 100m and 4×100m relay, World Championships, Helsinki 2005; Silver Medal, 200m, Commonwealth Games, Melbourne 2006; Gold Medal, 100m, World Championships, Osaka 2007, Silver Medals, 200m and 4×100m relay; Gold Medal, 200m, Olympic Games, Beijing 2008 (set new personal best time of 21.74 seconds; only second woman in history to win Olympic 200m twice and successfully defend her title); Jamaica Nat. Champion 200m 2009; World Championships 200m (silver medal) 2009; Bronze Medal, 100m London Olympics 2012; World Indoor Champion, 60m 2010; World Leader 100m & 200m 2010; Founder-Chair. Veronica Campbell-Brown Foundation 2011; apptd UNESCO Champion for Sport Amb. 2009. *Publication:* A Better You, Inspirations for Life's Journey. *Address:* On Track Management, PO Box 43023, Atlanta, GA 30336, USA. *Telephone:* (770) 420-1075. *Fax:* (770) 420-1076. *E-mail:* veronica@veronicacampbellbrown.com. *Website:* www.veronicacampbellbrown.com.

CAMPBELL OF SURBITON, Baroness (Life Peer), cr. 2007, of Surbiton in the Royal Borough of Kingston upon Thames; **Jane Susan Campbell,** DBE; British politician; b. 19 April 1959; d. of the late Ronald James Campbell and Jessie Mary Campbell (née Ball); m. Roger Symes; progressed through several local govt equal opportunities roles, principally focusing on disability human rights issues before becoming an Ind. Consultant on Direct Payments 1994–96; co-directed Nat. Centre for Ind. Living 1996–2001; Founding Chair. Social Care Inst. for Excellence 2001–05; Commr, Disability Rights Comm. 2000–07, Equalities and Human Rights Comm. 2007–09; Consultant to Office of Disability Issues in role of Chair. of Right to Control Working Group, Dept of Work and Pensions 2007–12, also in role of Chair. of Ind. Living Scrutiny Group; Chair. All-Party Parl. Disability Group, Ind. mem. House of Lords Appointments Comm. 2008–; Pres. Nat. Disability Archive 2013–. *Address:* House of Lords, Westminster, London, SW1A 0PW, England (office). *Telephone:* (20) 7219-5124 (office). *Fax:* (20) 7219-1303 (office). *E-mail:* campbelljs@parliament.uk (office). *Website:* www.parliament.uk/ biographies/lords/jane-campbell/30865 (office).

CAMPBELL-WHITE, Martin Andrew, FRSA; British business executive; *Joint Chief Executive Officer, Askonas Holt Limited;* b. 11 July 1943; s. of late John Vernon Campbell-White and Hilda Doris Ash; m. Margaret Mary Miles 1969; three s.; ed Dean Close School, Cheltenham, St John's Coll., Oxford, Univ. of Strasbourg, France; with Thomas Skinner & Co. Ltd (Publrs) 1964–66, Ibbs & Tillett Ltd (Concert Agents) 1966–72, Dir 1969–72, Harold Holt Ltd (Concert Agents), subsequently Askonas Holt Ltd 1972–, Dir 1973–, Deputy Chair. 1989–92, Chief Exec. 1992–98, Jt Chief Exec. 1998–; Chair. British Asscn of Concert Agents 1978–81; Council mem. London Sinfonietta 1973–86; Dir Chamber Orchestras of Europe 1983–93; Asst Dir Festival of German Arts 1987; Founding Dir Japan Festival 1991; mem. Bd Première Ensemble 1991–, Riverside Studios 1998–2000; Trustee Abbado Trust for Young Musicians 1987–2006, Salzburg Festival Trust 1996–2000; Exec. Trustee Musicians Benevolent Fund 2006–; Sebetia Ter prize for Culture, Naples, Italy 1999. *Leisure interests:* golf, watching cricket, classical music, travel. *Address:* Askonas Holt Ltd, Lincoln House, 300 High Holborn, London, WC1V 7JH, England (office). *Telephone:* (20) 7400-1700 (office). *Fax:* (20) 7400-1799 (office). *E-mail:* martin.campbell-white@askonasholt.co.uk (office). *Website:* www.askonasholt.co.uk (office).

CAMPESE, David Ian, AM; Australian fmr professional rugby union player; *Managing Director, Goosestep Pty Ltd;* b. 21 Oct. 1962, Queanbeyan, NSW; s. of Tony Campese and Joan Campese; m. Lara Berkenstein 2003; partner Campo's Sports Store; int. debut Australia versus NZ 1982; Capt. Australia team; winner World Cup 1991; world's leading int. try scorer with 64; scored 310 points for Australia; fmrly Australia's most capped player (represented Australia 101 times); Dir David Campese Man. Group 1997–; Man. Dir Goosestep (Co.); Australian Writers Player of the Year 1991, English Rugby Writers Player of the Year 1991, Int. Rugby Hall of Fame 2001, Order of Australia Medal (for services to rugby union) 2002. *Publication:* On a Wing and a Prayer (biog.), My Game, Your Game 1994, Still Entertaining 2003. *Leisure interests:* golf, cooking, music, reading. *Address:* 13 Nicholas Avenue, Concord, Sydney, NSW 2137, Australia. *E-mail:* dcampese@bigpond.net.au (office). *Website:* www.goosestep.com.au (office).

CAMPION, Jane, BA; New Zealand film director and writer; b. 30 April 1954, Wellington; d. of Richard Campion and Edith Campion; ed Victoria Univ., Chelsea School of Arts, London, Australian Film, TV and Radio School, Sydney Coll. of the Arts; Adjunct Prof., Sydney Coll. of the Arts, Univ. of Sydney 2000; Pres. Int. Jury of 54th Mostra Internazionale d'Arte Cinematografica Festival, Venice Film Festival; Hon. DLitt (Victoria Univ. of Wellington) 1999; Women in Hollywood Icon Award, Taormina Arte Diamond Award (Italy), Taormina Arte Award for Cinematic Excellence (Italy) 2004, Vanguard Dir Award 2005, Winner Byron Kennedy Award for Excellence and contrib. to Australian Cinema, Special Career Award 2010. *Films directed include:* Peel (Palme d'Or for Best Short Film, Cannes Film Festival) 1981–82, Girl's Own Story (Best Dir, Best Telemovie, Best

Screenplay at Australian Film Inst. (AFI) Awards, Rouben Mamoulian Award for Best Overall Short Film, Sydney Film Festival, Best Direction, Best Screenplay, Best Cinematography, AFI Awards, First Prize, Cinestud (Press Prize), Amsterdam Film Festival, voted Best Film by critics at Cinestud 1985) 1984, Two Friends (Best Dir, Best Telemovie, Best Screenplay, AFI Awards 1987) 1985, Sweetie (also co-writer) 1988, The Piano (more than 30 int. international awards, including the Palme d'Or (only female winner), Cannes Film Festival, three Acad. Awards, including Best Screenplay, winner Best Dir, New York Film Critics' Circle, Los Angeles Film Critics' Asscn, Australian Film Critics, winner Best Picture, Australian Film Inst.) 1993, The Portrait of a Lady (Best Film, Venice Film Festival 1996) 1996, Holy Smoke 1999, In the Cut 2003, The Water Diary (short film for UNDP) 2005, The Lady Bug (short) 2006, Bright Star (NSW Premier's Literary Award 2010) 2009. *Television includes:* Top of the Lake (series) 2012. *Address:* c/o HLA Management Theatrical Agency Australia, PO Box 1536, Strawberry Hills, Sydney, NSW 2012, Australia (office). *Telephone:* (2) 9549-3000 (office). *Fax:* (2) 9310-4113 (office). *E-mail:* hla@hlamgt.com.au (office).

CAMPORINI, Gen. Vincenzo, FRAeS; Italian military officer; *Chief of Defence General Staff;* b. 1946; ed Air Force Acad., NATO Defence Coll., ITAF Air War Coll.; Staff Officer Personnel Div., Air Staff 1982–83, Aide-de Camp to Chief of Staff 1983–85; Commdr Air Force Flight Test Centre and Rep. to Aerospace Application Study Cttee, Advisory Group for Aerospace Research and Devt, NATO 1988; Head of Plans, Operations and Training Div., Air Force Staff 1993–96; Aviation Insp., The Navy 1996–97; Dir Inspectorate for Flight Safety 1997–98; Head of Mil. Policy and Planning Div., Defence Gen. Staff 1998–2001; Deputy Chief of Defence, Gen. Staff 2001–04; Pres. Italian Centre for High Defence Studies 2004–06; Chief of Staff of Air Force 2006–08; Chief of Defence Gen. Staff 2008–; Grand Kt Cross, Order of Merit, Commdr, Ordre Nat. du Mérite (France); Gold Medal for Flying Merit, Command Gold Medal, Gold Cross for Mil. Service, Italian Defence Gen. Staff Medal of Honour, Santos Dumont Medal. *Address:* Ministry of Defence, Palazzo Baracchini, Via XX Settembre 8, 00187 Rome, Italy (office). *Telephone:* (06) 46911 (office). *E-mail:* pi@smd.difesa.it (office). *Website:* www.difesa.it (office).

CAMPOS E CUNHA, Luis; Portuguese economist and fmr government official; b. 1954; m.; three c.; ed Univ. Católica Portuguesa, Columbia Univ., USA; Asst Prof. of Econs, School of Econs, Universidade Nova de Lisboa 1985–91, Assoc. Prof. 1991–95, Prof. 1995–, Dean, School of Econs 2002–04; Vice-Gov. Banco de Portugal 1996–2002; Minister of Finance and Public Admin, Minister of State March–July 2005; mem. Int. Relations Cttee, European Cen. Bank, Frankfurt 1998–2002; mem. Econ. and Finance Cttee, Brussels 1998–2001; mem. Bd of Dirs (non-exec.) Fundação Serralves 2006–. *Address:* School of Business and Economics, Universidade Nova de Lisboa, Campus de Campolide, 1099-032 Lisbon, Portugal.

CAMUS, Philippe; French business executive; *Co-Managing Partner, Lagardère SCA;* b. 28 June 1948, Paris; ed Ecole Normale Supérieure, Paris, Institut des Etudes Politiques de Paris; Special Project Man. Caisse des Dépôts et Consignations 1972–82; Dir, Sr Man. Lagardère Groupe, Co-Pres. Chair. Financial Cttee 1993–98, Co-Man. Partner Lagardère SCA 1998–, Chair. and CEO Arjil Commanditée – ARCO (Gen. Partner, Group) 1992, now Vice-Chair. and Deputy CEO, Chair. and CEO Lagardère North America, Inc.; Chair. Financial Cttee Matra Group 1982–92; CEO and Chair. Man. Bd Aérospatiale Matra 1999–2000; Co-CEO European Aeronautic Defence and Space Co. (EADS) 2000–05; Chair. Supervisory Bd Banque Arjil 1987–93; Pres. Groupement des Industries Françaises Aéreonautiques et Spatiales (GIFAS) 2001–05, Hon. Chair. 2005–; Sr Man. Dir Evercore Partners Inc. (investment man. co.) 2006–; Chair. Alcatel-Lucent 2008–; mem. Bd of Dirs Crédit Agricole SA, Accor SA, Institut d'Expertise et de Prospective of Ecole Normale Supérieure, Paris Ueroplace Asscn; Perm. Rep. of Lagardère SCA to Bd of Dirs Hachette SA, of Hachette SA to Bd of Dirs Lagardère Services; mem. Supervisory Bd Lagardère Active; Dir, Editions P. Amaury, Schlumberger, Cellfish Media LLC; Chevalier, Légion d'honneur 2000, Officier 2005, Bundesverdienstkreuz 2004; Aviation Week Aerospace Laureate 1989, Prix de la meilleure opération financière 2000. *Address:* Lagardère SCA, 4 rue de Presbourg, 75016 Paris Cedex 16, France (office); Evercore Partners, 10 Hill Street, London, W1J 5NQ, England (office). *Telephone:* 1-40-69-16-00 (Paris) (office); (20) 7268-2700 (London) (office). *Fax:* 1-40-69-21-31 (Paris) (office); (20) 7268-2710 (London) (office). *E-mail:* info@lagardere.fr (office); info@evercore.com (office); execoffice@alcatel-lucent.com (office). *Website:* www.lagardere.fr (office); www.evercore.com (office); www.alcatel-lucent.com (office).

CANAHUATI, Mario Miguel, BE; Honduran diplomatist and politician; b. 12 Sept. 1955, San Pedro Sula; m.; four c.; ed Georgia Inst. of Tech., USA; Gen. Man. for cos Creations Vantage, Industries Pacer, Genesis Apparel; Pres. Distribuidora la Bobina; Pres. Chamber of Commerce and Industries of Cortes, Directorate of the Commerce Econ. System; Vice-Pres. Fed. of Chambers of Commerce and Industry; Dir Honduran Council for Pvt. Enterprise, Council for Sustainable Devt, Nat. Asscn for Industry; pvt. sector rep. Negotiation Cttee of Bilateral Treaties; mem. Bd of Dirs San Pedro Sula Int. Airport, Sula Valley Nat. Comm.; Founder and Pres. Mhotivo Foundation; Vice-Pres. Nueva Vida Foundation; mem. Inter-American Devt Bank's Comm. for Dialogue and Social Politics; Amb. to USA 2002–05; Minister of Foreign Affairs 2010–11.

CANALES CLARIOND, Fernando, MBA; Mexican lawyer, business executive and politician; b. 21 July 1946, Monterrey, Nuevo León; m. Angela Stelzer; two s. two d.; ed Escuela Libre de Derecho, Instituto Tecnológico y de Estudios Superiores de Monterrey, Univ. of the Sorbonne, Paris, France, Instituto de Altos Estudios en La Haya, Holanda; fmr Pres. Grupo IMSA SA de CV, also fmr Man. Dir Corporativo Grupo IMSA, SA de CV; mem. Partido Accion Nacional 1978–; mem. Congress for First Dist of Nuevo León 1979–81; Gov. of Nuevo León 1997–2003; Minister for the Economy 2003–05; Sec. of Energy 2005–06 (by law also Pres. of Bd of PEMEX, CFE and Luz y Fuerza del Centro); currently Pres. Corporación Finestra SA de CV, Monterrey; Pres. Chamber of Commerce of Nuevo León, Monterrey Chamber of Commerce; Vice-Pres. Nat. Confed. of Chambers of Commerce in Mexico; mem. Nuevo León Business Council, IMSS Ass., Movimiento de Promocion Rural, AC, Consejo Coordinador Empresarial; mem. Mexico–USA Comm. of the Ford Foundation. *Address:* c/o Partido Acción Nacional, Avda Coyoacán 1546, Col. del Valle, Del. Benito Juárez, 03100 México, DF, Mexico (office).

CANÇADO TRINDADE, Antônio A., LLB, LLM, PhD; Brazilian professor of international law and judge; *Judge, International Court of Justice;* b. 17 Sept. 1947, Belo Horizonte, Brazil; ed Fed. Univ. of Minas Gerais, Univ. of Cambridge, UK; Prof. of Public Int. Law, Univ. of Brasilia 1978–, Diplomatic Acad. Rio Branco of Brazil 1979–; Lecturer, Hague Acad. of Int. Law 1987, 2005, Lecturer, annual courses of Int. Law organized by OAS Inter-American Juridical Cttee, Rio de Janeiro 1981–82, 1985, 1990–92, 1995–97, 2000–07; Lecturer, annual study sessions of Int. Inst. of Human Rights, Strasbourg, France 1988, 1991, 1993–2007; Lecturer, Interdisciplinary Courses of Inter-American Inst. of Human Rights 1986, 1989, 1991–2001, 2004, 2007; Visiting Prof. ('Cátedra Simón Bolivar'), Univ. of Los Andes, Mérida, Venezuela 1981, 1982, Institut des Hautes Etudes Internationales, Univ. of Paris-II (Panthéon-Sorbonne), France 1988–89, Univ. of Ferrara, Italy 1983, 1986, Univ. of Lisbon, Portugal 1993, Columbia Univ., New York, USA 1998, Tulane Law School, Tulane Univ., New Orleans, USA 1999, Univs of Seville and Deusto, Bilbao, Spain 2002, Washington Coll. of Law, American Univ. May–June 2003, 2004, 2006, Autonomous Univ. of Madrid/ Foundation Ortega y Gasset; External Legal Adviser to Inter-American Inst. of Human Rights 1991–94; Head of Del. of Inter-American Inst. of Human Rights to Cen. American Conf. on Peace and Devt, Tegucigalpa 1994, mem. Bd of Dirs Inter-American Inst. of Human Rights 1988–91, 1991–94, 1996–), *ad hoc* Judge, Inter-American Court of Human Rights 1990–94, Exec. Dir Inter-American Inst. of Human Rights 1994–96, Judge, Inter-American Court of Human Rights 1995–, Vice-Pres. Inter-American Court of Human Rights 1997–99, Pres. 1999–; Judge, Int. Court of Justice, The Hague 2009–; Legal Adviser to Ministry of External Relations 1985–90; Deputy Head of Del. of Brazil to UN Conf. on the Law of Treaties between States and Int. Orgs, Vienna 1986; del. of Brazil to Second UN World Conf. on Human Rights, Vienna 1993; Special Envoy of Minister of External Relations for Questions Pertaining to Human Rights, Santiago, Chile 1993–94; mem. Group of Sr Legal Advisers to UNEP, Nairobi 1990–92; mem. Advisory Cttee of Experts in Int. Environmental Law, UNU 1984–87; mem. Comm. of Jurists of OAS for Nicaragua 1993–94, Comm. of Sr Legal Advisers to Office of UNHCR for final evaluation of process of Int. Conf. on Cen. American Refugees, Mexico City 1994, Comm. of Advisers to UNESCO on Right to Peace as a Human Right; Arbitrator, Int. Centre for Settlement of Investment Disputes 2006–08; Dir Brazilian Journal of International Law 1985–; Co-Dir Brazilian Journal of Human Rights 2001–; Brazilian Ed. International Legal Materials, American Soc. of Int. Law 1981–; mem. Editorial Council, Review "Arquivos" of Ministry of Justice of Brazil 1987–2002; mem. Editorial Bd Brazilian Journal of International Politics 1993–, International Newsletter of University of São Paulo, Brazil 1997–; mem. Int. Council on Human Rights Policy, London 1997, Advisory Bd Council on Human Rights Studies, New Delhi 1998, Steering Cttee of the Project on Int. Courts and Tribunals, New York/The Hague 1998–2001, Curatorium of Hague Acad. of Int. Law 2004, Cttee on the Enforcement of Human Rights Law of Int. Law Asscn, London, Int. Council of Environmental Law, Bonn; mem. Bd of Dirs Inter-American Inst. of Human Rights, San José, Int. Inst. of Human Rights, Strasbourg; Perm. mem. Brazilian Soc. of Int. Law, Instituto Hispano-Luso-Americano de Derecho Internacional 1994 (fmr rapporteur 1996), Academia Mineira de Letras Jurídicas, Academia Brasileira de Letras Jurídicas; mem. Brazilian Bar Asscn, Inst. of Int. Law 1997, Int. Inst. of Humanitarian Law, San Remo, Soc. Française pour le Droit Int., American Soc. of Int. Law, British Inst. of Int. and Comparative Law, Indian Soc. of Int. Law, Asscn des Anciens Auditeurs of Hague Acad. of Int. Law; Assoc. mem. Asociación Argentina de Derecho Internacional; Hon. Pres. Brazilian Inst. of Human Rights; 'Professor Home-nageado' (elected by the students), Univ. of Brasilia, Catholic Univ. of Minas Gerais, Brazil 2002, Tuiuti Univ. of Curitiba, Brazil 2002, Diplomatic Acad. Rio Branco 1999, 2006; holder of many academic and other distinctions; several prizes. *Publications:* numerous books and other publs on int. law. *Address:* International Court of Justice, Peace Palace, Carnegieplein 2, 2517 KJ, The Hague, The Netherlands (office). *Telephone:* (70) 302-2323 (office). *Fax:* (70) 364-9928 (office). *E-mail:* info@icj-cij.org (office). *Website:* www.icj-cij.org (office).

CANCELA, Walter; Uruguayan economist, diplomatist and fmr central banker; *Permanent Representative, European Union;* b. 1950, Montevideo; four c.; ed Universidad de la República; worked at Cen. Bank of Uruguay 1970–78, Centro Cooperativo Uruguayo 1978–85; researcher, Centro Latinoamericano de Economía Humana (CLAEH) 1975–90; Prof., Universidad de la República 1987–2002, Dir Econ. Inst. 2003–; adviser on Uruguay to UN and EC 1990–2000; Pres. Cen. Bank of Uruguay 2005–08; Perm. Rep. to EU, Brussels 2010–. *Address:* Permanent Mission of Uruguay, 22 ave F. D. Roosevelt, 1050 Brussels, Belgium (office).

CANCELLIERI, Anna Maria; Italian government official; b. 22 Oct. 1943, Rome; ed La Sapienza Univ., Rome; joined Ministry of Interior 1972, extensive career in local govt, becoming Prefect of several cities including Vicenza, Bergamo and Brescia 1993–2003, Catania 2003, Head of Genoa Prefecture 2008, Special Commr of Bologna 2010–11, of Parma 2011; Minister of the Interior 2011–13; Minister of Justice 2013–14; Ufficiale dell'Ordine al merito della Repubblica Italiana 1992, Commdr 1993, Grande Ufficiale 2001. *Address:* c/o Ministry of Justice, Via Arenula 71, 00186 Rome, Italy.

CANE, Louis Paul Joseph; French artist; b. 13 Dec. 1943, Beaulieu-sur-Mer; s. of Albert Cane and Andrée Cane (née Pasquier); m. Nicole Rondinella 1970; two d.; ed Collège des Frères Dominicains de Sorèze, Lycée Gassendi de Digne, Ecole Nationale des Arts Décoratifs, Nice, Ecole Nationale Supérieure des Arts Décoratifs, Paris; first exhbn 1970; exhbns at Galerie Yvon, Lambert, Paris 1972, Galerie Templon, Paris, Milan 1973–75, Castelli Gallery, New York 1982, Galerie Beaubourg, Paris (sculptures) 1985–90, Musée de l'Orangerie des Tuileries 1994; regular exhbns in Germany, Sweden, Spain, Belgium, Italy, Australia, Japan, fmr USSR, UK; perm. exhbn at La Galerie 14, Paris; Officier des Arts et Lettres. *Publications:* Louis Cane, artiste-peintre 1967, Toiles découpées 1971, Toiles sol/mur 1972, Annonciations 1982, Déluges 1983, Accouchements 1983, Déjeuners sur l'herbe 1985, Trois graces 1987, 1988, Fleurs et tampons 1989, Nymphéas 1992. *Leisure interests:* 18th-century France, studying 18th-century French bronzes. *Address:* 184 rue Saint Maur, 75010 Paris (office); 37 rue d'Enghien, 75010 Paris, France (home). *Telephone:* 1-42-03-73-31. *Fax:* 1-42-03-01-19.

CANELLA, Guido; Italian architect and academic; *Partner, Canella & Achilli architetti;* b. 19 Jan. 1931, Bucharest, Romania; m. Laura Testori 1960; two s. two d.; ed Polytechnic of Milan; Founding Pnr, Canella & Achilli architetti, Milan 1959–; Prof. of Architectural Composition, Polytechnic of Milan 1970–, Dir Inst. of Architectural Composition 1970–79, Dir Dept of Architectural Design 1979–81; Dir Architecture Section, Triennale of Milan 1978–82; Ed.-in-Chief Hinterland 1977–85, Zodiac 1989–; S. Luca Nat. Acad.; mem. Scientific Cttee Nat. Group of Architecture of Nat. Research Council; Inst. of Architects Prize 1968, Int. Cttee of Architecture Critics Prize 1995. *Major Works:* Segrate Town Hall, Milan 1963, social services and Piazza, Villaggio Incis, Milan 1968; civic centres in Pieve Emanuele, Milan 1971 and Pioltello, Milan 1976; school centres in Opera, Milan 1974, Cesano Boscone, Milan 1975 and Parma 1985; residential complexes in Bollate, Milan 1974, Peschiera Borromeo, Milan 1983, Milan 2002; Law Courts redevelopment in Ancona 1975; town offices and law courts in Legnano, Milan 1982; social services, housing and Piazza in Monte d'Ago, Ancona 1984; theatre projects in Taranto 1988, Aosta 1989, Varese 1990; Church projects at Casamassima, Bari 1991, Modena 2001; auditorium, church and health complex in Peschiera Borromeo, Milan 1983–91; Italian Embassies' projects in Washington and Berlin 1992; Pescara Airport 1992; city planning projects for Milan 1991, Berlin 1992, Como 1993, Beirut 1994, Bucharest 1996, Pordenone 2001; Cinema multiplex, Milan 1997; Motel Inter-Continental, Asmara, Eritrea 1999; museum, Meina, Novara 1997; New City Hall, offices and car park building, Bari 1998; opera house and theatre, Taranto 1998; City Hall extension, Gorgonzola, Milan 2001; New Theatre of Porta Romana and residential complex, Milan 2002; private residence, Woodland, Houston, Texas 2003; restaurant and bookstore complex, Milan 2003. *Publications:* Il sistema teatrale a Milano 1966, Università: ragione, contesto, tipo 1975; articles in various specialist journals. *Address:* Canella & Achilli architetti, Via Revere 9, 20123 Milan, Italy (office). *Telephone:* (02) 4695222 (office). *Fax:* (02) 4813704 (office). *E-mail:* info@canella-achilli.com (office). *Website:* www.canella-achilli.com (office).

CANET, Guillaume; French actor and film director; b. 10 April 1973, Boulogne-Billancourt; m. Diane Kruger 2001 (divorced 2006); ed Saint-Louis-Notre-Dame-Du-Bel-Air school, briefly studied at the Cours Florent; was engaged in a circus aged 10; parents were horses breeders, briefly followed a professional career in horse riding until an accident aged 18 forced him to take up acting. *Films:* Fils unique 1995, Barracuda 1997, Sentimental Education 1998, Ceux qui m'aiment prendront le train (Those Who Love Me Can Take the Train) 1998, En plein cœur (In All Innocence) 1998, Trait d'union (short) 1999, Je règle mon pas sur le pas de mon père (Walking in My Father's Footsteps) 1999, J'peux pas dormir… (short) (also dir) 2000, The Beach (La Plage) 2000, La Fidélité 2000, The Day the Ponies Come Back 2000, Les Morsures de l'aube (Love Bites) 2001, Vidocq (aka Dark Portals) 2001, Le Frère du guerrier (The Warrior's Brother) 2002, Mille millièmes (aka The Landlords) 2002, Mon idole (My Idol) (also dir and assoc. producer) 2002, Jeux d'enfants (Love Me if You Dare) 2003, Les Clefs de bagnole (cameo, as himself) 2003, Narco (aka The Secret Adventures of Gustave Klopp) 2004, Joyeux Noël (Merry Christmas) 2005, L'Enfer (Hell) 2005, Un ticket pour l'espace (A Ticket to Space) 2005, Ne le dis à personne (Tell No One) 2006, Cars (French voice of Flash McQueen) 2006, Ensemble, c'est tout (aka Hunting and Gathering) 2007, Darling 2007, La Clef (The Key) 2007, Les Liens du sang (Rivals) 2008; as dir: Sans regrets 1996, Je taim 1998, Ne le dis à personne (Tell No One) (César Award for Best Dir) 2007, La nouvelle guerre des boutons (War of the Buttons) 2011. *Television:* La colline aux mille enfants 1994, Jeanne 1994, Ils n'ont pas 20 ans 1995, Le juge est une femme (episode Le secret de Marion) 1995, 17 ans et des poussières 1996, Le voyage de Pénélope (The Voyage of Penelope) 1996, Je m'appelle Régine 1996, Le cheval de coeur 1996, Pardaillan 1997, La vacation d'Adrienne (episode Pilot) 1997, Le porteur de destins 1999, Electrochoc 2004; as dir: Scénarios sur la drogue (episode Avalanche) 2000. *Address:* c/o Bertrand de Labbey, VMA, 20 avenue Rapp, 75007 Paris, France. *Telephone:* 1-43-17-37-00. *Fax:* 1-47-20-15-86. *E-mail:* d.leprestre@vma.fr. *Website:* www.vma.fr.

CANGEMI, Joseph P., BS, MS, EdD; American psychologist, academic, consultant and editor; *Professor Emeritus of Psychology/Scholar-in-Residence, Western Kentucky University;* b. 26 June 1936, Syracuse, NY; s. of Samuel Cangemi and Marion Cangemi; m. Amelia Elena Santalo' 1962; two d.; ed State Univ. of NY (SUNY), Oswego, Syracuse and Indiana Univs; taught in Syracuse public schools and in Dominican Repub. 1960–64; Chair. and Lecturer in Psychology, SUNY and Community Coll., Syracuse 1962–65; Supervisor of Educ. and of Training and Devt, US Steel Corpn, Venezuela 1965–68; Teaching Assoc., Indiana Univ., Bloomington 1972, 1973; Asst Prof. to Assoc. Prof., Western Kentucky Univ., Bowling Green 1968–79, Prof. of Psychology and Full mem. Grad. Faculty 1979, now Scholar-in-Residence and Prof. Emer.; Chair. Nat. Bd of Visitors/Advisors, School of Educ., Syracuse Univ.; mem. Bd of Visitors, School of Educ., Indiana Univ.; currently Dir Creative Leadership and Change Inc.; consultant to Firestone, General Motors and numerous cos; Ed. Journal of Human Behavior and Learning 1983–90, Psychology: A Journal of Human Behavior 1977–, Organization Development Journal 1983–88, International Journal of Leadership and Change; mem. Editorial Bd Education and several other publs; mem. American Psychological Assn, Inter-American Soc. of Psychology, Int. Registry of Org. Devt Professionals, Psychologists in Man.; mem. Bd of Trustees, William Woods Univ. 1988–; Diplomate in Professional Counselling, Int. Acad. of Behavioural Medicine, Counselling and Psychotherapy 1994; Hon. LLD (William Woods Univ.) 1996; Dr hc (State Univ. of Humanities, Moscow) 2001; Distinguished Public Service Award, Western Kentucky Univ. 1983, Distinguished Alumnus Award, SUNY 1983, Diplomate American Coll. of Counsellors, American Coll. of Forensic Examiners 1996, Excellence in Productive Teaching Award, Coll. of Educ. and Behavioral Sciences, Western Kentucky Univ. 1977, 1991, 1999, Excellence in Research/Creativity Award, Western Kentucky Univ. Coll. of Ed. and Behavioral Sciences 1987. *Publications:* author, ed. or co-ed. of 20 books and monographs in French, Spanish, Italian, Portuguese, Romanian, Polish, Russian and Chinese and more than 300 papers and articles published in over 80 periodicals, including 31 foreign journals. *Leisure interests:* Latin American music, foreign travel, international exchanges. *Address:* Gary Ransdell Hall 3051, Western Kentucky University, 1906 College Heights Blvd, #21030, Bowling Green, KY 42101-1030 (office); Effective Leadership and Change Inc., 1409 Mount Ayr Circle, Bowling Green, KY 42103-4708, USA (home). *Telephone:* (270) 745-2343 (office); (270) 842-3436 (home). *Fax:* (270) 842-0432 (office); (270) 842-0432 (home). *E-mail:* joseph.cangemi@wku.edu (office). *Website:* www.wku.edu/psychology/staff/joseph_cangemi (office); edtech.wku.edu/~jcangemi (office).

CANI, Shkëlqim, DEcon, PhD; Albanian central banker, economist, politician and academic; *Minister of Finance;* b. 6 May 1956, Tirana; m. Merita Cani; ed Univ. of Tirana; Credit Officer, State Bank of Albania (SBA), Tirana br. 1979–81, Export-Import Officer, SBA Head Office 1981–83, Chief Economist, Research Div. 1984–85, Dir Overseas Dept, mem. Bd of Dirs Cen. Bank 1985–90; Exec. Gen. Man. Commercial Bank of Albania 1990–91, Deputy Gen. Man. 1991–92; ind. financial adviser 1996–97; Gov. Bank of Albania 1997–2004, also Gov. IMF for Albania; currently Prof., Inst. for Econ. and Juridical Consultations, Univ. of Tirana; Project Man. jt Italian-Albanian project L'aqua e il falcone volano insieme 2008; Chair. Tirana Stock Exchange 1997–2002; mem. People's Ass. 1991–96, July–Aug. 1997, 2013–; Vice-Pres. Council of Ministers 1991; Deputy Prime Minister of Albania 1991; Minister of Finance 2013–; mem. Econ. Policies Comm.; mem. Socialist Party of Albania. *Address:* Ministry of Finance, Bulevardi Dëshmorët e Kombit 4, Tirana (office); Faculty of Economics, University of Tirana, Bulevardi Dëshmorët e Kombit, Sheshi Nen Tereza, Tirana, Albania. *Telephone:* (4) 2228405 (office). *Fax:* (4) 2226111 (office). *E-mail:* secretary.minister@minfin.gov.al (office). *Website:* www.minfin.gov.al (office); www.unitir.edu.al.

CANIVET, Guy, JD, FBA; French judge and academic; *Member, Constitutional Council;* b. 23 Sept. 1943, Lons-le-Saunier, Jura; s. of Pierre Canivet and Henriette Barthélémy; m. Françoise Beuzit 1981; two s. two d.; ed Univ. of Dijon; judge, Trial Court of Chartres 1972–75; Public Prosecutor, Paris 1975–77; Sec.-Gen., Trial Court of Paris 1977–83, judge 1983–86; Justice, Court of Appeal, Paris 1986–94, Chief Justice 1996–99; Justice, Cour de Cassation 1994–96, Chief Justice 1999–2007; mem. Constitutional Council (Conseil constitutionnel) 2007–; Assoc. Prof., Institut d'études politiques, Paris 2004–; Founder and Pres. Network of the Pres of the Supreme Judicial Courts of the EU 2004–07; Hon. Bencher, Gray's Inn, London, King's Inn, Dublin; Officier, Ordre nat. du Mérite des Palmes académiques, Commdr, Légion d'honneur, Commdr, Ordre des Arts et des Lettres; Hon. LLD (London, Laval, Manilla, St Kliment Ohridski, Sofia, Tulane, New Orleans, Leicestser). *Publication:* Droit français de la concurrence 1995. *Leisure interests:* music, outdoor recreational activities. *Address:* Conseil constitutionnel, 2 rue de Montpensier, 75001 Paris (office); 8 rue Nicolas Charlet, 75015 Paris, France (home). *Telephone:* 1-40-15-30-03 (office). *Fax:* 1-40-20-93-27 (office). *E-mail:* guy.canivet@conseil-constitutionnel.fr (office). *Website:* www.conseil-constitutionnel.fr (office).

CAÑIZARES LLOVERA, HE Cardinal Antonio, DTheol; Spanish ecclesiastic; *Prefect of the Congregation for Divine Worship and the Discipline of the Sacraments;* b. 15 Oct. 1945, Utiel; ed minor and major seminaries in Valencia, Pontifical Univ. of Salamanca; ordained priest 1970; served as asst pastor and del. for catechesis in Archdiocese of Valencia; taught Catechetical Theology at Univ. of Salamanca and Fundamental Theology at Conciliar Seminary of Madrid; later became Dir and a Prof. of the Inst. of Religious Science and Catechesis, Madrid; sat on several comms and secrs of Spanish Episcopal Conf.; Dir Secr. of Episcopal Comm. for Doctrine of the Faith 1985–92; Founder and first Pres. Asociación Española de Catequistas; fmr Dir Teología y Catequesis (review); Bishop of Avila 1992–96; mem. Congregation for Doctrine of the Faith, Roman Curia 1996; Archbishop of Granada 1996–2002, also Apostolic Admin. of Cartagena Jan.–Oct. 1998, elected Pres. Episcopal Comm. of Educ. and Catechesis 1999; Archbishop of Toledo and Primate of Spain 2002–08; Vice-Pres. Spanish Episcopal Conf. 2008; cr. Cardinal (Cardinal-Priest of San Pancrazio) 2006; Prefect of the Congregation for Divine Worship and the Discipline of the Sacraments 2008–13, 2013–; mem. Pontifical Cttee for Int. Eucharistic Congresses 2010–, Congregation for Doctrine of the Faith, Congregation for Bishops, Pontifical Comm. Ecclesia Dei, Congregation for the Evangelization of Peoples 2013–; mem. Real Academia de la Historia de España 2007–; Dr hc (Universidad CEU Cardenal Herrera) 2006. *Address:* Palazzo delle Congregazioni, Piazza Pio XII 10, 00193 Rome, Italy (office). *Telephone:* (06) 69884005 (office); (06) 69884416 (office). *Fax:* (06) 69883499 (office). *Website:* www.vatican.va/roman_curia/congregations/ccdds/index.htm (office).

CANNADINE, Sir David Nicholas, Kt, DPhil, LittD, FRHistS, FBA, FRSA, FRSL; British historian and academic; *Whitney J. Oates Senior Research Scholar, Princeton University;* b. 7 Sept. 1950; s. of Sydney Douglas Cannadine and Dorothy Mary Hughes; m. Linda Jane Colley (q.v.) 1982; one d. (deceased); ed King Edward's Five Ways School, Birmingham, Clare Coll., Cambridge, St John's Coll., Oxford, Princeton Univ., USA; Resident Fellow, St John's Coll. Cambridge 1975–77, Asst Lecturer in History 1976–80, Lecturer 1980–88; Fellow, Christ's Coll. Cambridge 1977–88, Dir of Studies in History 1977–83, Tutor 1979–81; Prof. of History, Columbia Univ., New York 1988–92, Moore Collegiate Prof. 1992–98; Dir Inst. of Historical Research Univ. of London 1998–2003, Prof. 1998–2003, Queen Elizabeth the Queen Mother Prof. of British History 2003–08, Hon. Fellow 2005–, Consultant, History in Educ. 2008–; Visiting mem., Inst. for Advanced Study, Princeton, NJ 1980–81; Visiting Fellow, Council of the Humanities 2003–05, Whitney J. Oates Sr Research Scholar 2008–; Visiting Prof., Birkbeck Coll., London 1995–97; Visiting Fellow, Whitney Humanities Center, Yale Univ. 1995–96; Visiting Scholar, Pembroke Coll., Cambridge 1997; Pres. Worcs. Historical Soc. 1999–; Vice-Pres. British Records Soc. 1998–, Royal Historical Soc. 1998–2002; Chair. IHR Trust 1999–2003; mem. Advisory Bd Centre for Study of Soc. and Politics, Kingston Univ. 1998–2003, ICBH 1998–2003, Advisory Council Warburg Inst. 1998–2003, Inst. of US Studies 1999–2004, Public Record Office 1999–2004, Inst. of English Studies 2000–03, Inst. of Latin American Studies 2000–04, Kennedy Memorial Trust 2000–, Nat. Trust Eastern Regional Cttee 2000–, Royal Mint Advisory Cttee 2004–, Editorial Bd History of Parliament 2004–, Advisory Council Inst. for the Study of the Americas 2004–; Gov. Ipswich School 1982–88; Fellow, Berkeley Coll., Yale Univ. 1985, J. P. Morgan Library, New York 1992–98; American Council of Learned Socs Fellowship 1990–91; regular radio and TV broadcaster; Gen. Ed. Studies in Modern History 1979–2002, Penguin History of Britain 1989–, Penguin History of Europe 1991–, Historical Research 2000–2003; Trustee Kennedy Memorial Scholarship Fund 1999–, Nat. Portrait Gallery 2000– (Chair. of Trustees 2005–), British Empire and Commonwealth Museum 2003–, Commr English Heritage 2001–; Visiting Fellow, ANU, Canberra 2005 (Adjunct Prof.

2006), Nat. Humanities Center, North Carolina 2006; Chair. Blue Plaques Panel, English Heritage; Hon. Fellow, Christ's Coll. Cambridge 2005; Hon. Prof., Univ. of London 2008; Hon. DLitt (East Anglia, South Bank) 2001, (Birmingham) 2002; T. S. Ashton Prize, Econ. History Soc. 1977, Silver Jubilee Prize, Agric. History Soc. 1977, Lionel Trilling Prize 1991, Governors' Award 1991, Dean's Distinguished Award in the Humanities, Columbia Univ. 1996. *Radio:* A Point of View (BBC Radio 4) 2005–06. *Publications include:* Lords and Landlords: The Aristocracy and the Towns 1774–1967 1980, Patricians, Power and Politics in Nineteenth-Century Towns (ed. and contrib.) 1982, H. J. Dyos, Exploring the Urban Past (co-ed. and contrib.) 1982, Rituals of Royalty: Power and Ceremonial in Traditional Societies (co-ed. and contrib.) 1987, The Pleasures of the Past 1989, The Decline and Fall of the British Aristocracy (Lionel Trilling Prize) 1990, G. M. Trevelyan: A Life in History 1992, Aspects of Aristocracy: Grandeur and Decline in Modern Britain 1994, Class in Britain 1998, History in Our Time 1998, Making History Now 1999, Ornamentalism: How the British Saw Their Empire 2001, In Churchill's Shadow: Confronting the Past in Modern Britain 2002, What is History Now? (ed.) 2002, History and the Media (ed.) 2004, Winston Churchill in the 21st Century (co-ed. and contrib.) 2004, Admiral Lord Nelson, his context and legacy (ed.) 2005, Trafalgar: A Battle and its Afterlife (ed.) 2006, National Portrait Gallery: A Brief History 2007, Empire, the Sea and Global History: Britain's Maritime World c. 1763–1840 (ed.) 2007, History and Philanthropy: Past Present Future (co-ed. and contrib.) 2008, Making History Now and Then: Discoveries, Controversies and Explanations 2008; numerous contribs to other books and learned journals. *Leisure interests:* life, laughter. *Address:* Institute of Historical Research, Senate House, Malet Street, London, WC1E 7HU, England (office). *Fax:* (20) 7862-8754 (office). *E-mail:* jennifer.wallis@sas.ac.uk (office). *Website:* www .history.ac.uk (office).

CANNAVARO, Fabio Mamerto; Italian professional footballer; b. 13 Sept. 1973, Naples. s. of Pasquale Cannavaro and Gelsomina Cannavaro; m. Daniela Cannavaro; two s. one d.; centre-back; played for S.S.C. Napoli 1992–95, Parma FC 1995–2002, FC Internazionale Milano 2002–04, Juventus FC 2004–06, 2009–. Real Madrid (in Spanish Primera División, wearing No. 5 jersey) 2006–09; Serie A debut at Turin's Stadio Delle Alpi against Juventus 1993; mem. two European championship-winning Italy Under-21 teams 1992–94, 1994–96; debut for full nat. team 1997, played in World Cup, France 1998; helped Juventus win Serie A titles 2004/05, 2005/06 (club was stripped of titles and demoted to Serie B by a sports tribunal investigating claims of match fixing); Capt. FIFA World Cup-winning team, Germany 2006; 131 caps for Italy (all-time most capped player); nicknames: Il muro di Berlino (The Berlin Wall), Il umano bus (The Human Bus); has helped establish charity foundation FCF (Fondazione Cannavaro Ferrara), specialising in the procurement of cancer research equipment and surgery for special cases of cancer for a hosp. in Naples; Euro 2000 Team of the Tournament 2000, Oscar del calcio: Serie A Defender of the Year 2005, 2006, Serie A Footballer of the Year 2006, Italian Footballer of the Year 2006; selected in FIFPro World XI 2005–06, 2006–07, European Footballer of the Year 2006, Ballon d'Or, France Football magazine 2006, UEFA Team of the Year 2006, FIFA World Player of the Year (second ever defender) 2006, FIFA World Cup Silver Ball Award 2006, FIFA World Cup Team of the Tournament 2006. *Address:* Juventus FC SpA, Corso Galileo Ferraris, 32, 10128 Turin, Italy. *Telephone:* (011) 65631. *Fax:* (011) 5119214. *E-mail:* fabio@fabiocannavaro.it. *Website:* www.juventus.it; www.fabiocannavaro .it.

CANNELL, Melvin Gilbert Richard, BSc, PhD, DSc, FRSE; British research scientist; b. 12 Aug. 1944, Bungay; s. of Charles Cannell and Joyce Cannell; m. Maria Rietdijk 1966; two d.; ed Bungay Grammar School and Univ. of Reading; research officer, coffee research station, Kenya 1966–71; NERC Inst. of Tree Biology Edin. 1971–74, NERC Inst. of Terrestrial Ecology (now Centre for Ecology and Hydrology) 1974–87, Dir 1987, Prof. (retd), now consultant; Fellow, Inst. of Chartered Foresters; Founder Bd mem. European Forest Inst. *Publications:* Jt Tree Physiology and Yield Improvement 1976, Trees as Crop Plants 1985; over 100 other scientific publs. *Address:* Centre for Ecology and Hydrology, Bush Estate, Penicuik, Midlothian, EH26 0QB (office); Easter Greyfield, Eddleston Road, Peebles, Tweeddale, EH45 9JB, Scotland (home). *Telephone:* (131) 445-4343 (office); (1721) 720144 (home). *Fax:* (131) 445-3943 (office). *E-mail:* mgrc@ceh.ac.uk (office). *Website:* www.ceh.ac.uk (office).

CANNON, John; American business executive; *Executive Vice-President, General Counsel and Chief Public Affairs Officer, WellPoint, Inc.;* ed Denison Univ., Ohio, The Dickinson School of Law at Pennsylvania State Univ.; attorney with Rawle & Henderson, Philadelphia, specialized in litigation and securities law; joined CIGNA Corpn 1988, roles included Sr Vice-Pres. and Deputy Gen. Counsel, Pres. CIGNA Foundation and Chief Counsel for CIGNA Healthcare and CIGNA International –2007; joined WellPoint, Inc. 2007, Exec. Vice-Pres., Gen. Counsel, Corp. Sec. and Chief Public Affairs Officer –2012, Interim Pres. and CEO 2012–13; mem. Bd of Dirs US Chamber of Commerce, Indianapolis Symphony Orchestra. *Address:* WellPoint, Inc., 120 Monument Circle, Indianapolis, IN 46204, USA (office). *Telephone:* (317) 532-6000 (office). *Fax:* (317) 488-6028 (office). *E-mail:* boardofdirectors@wellpoint.com (office). *Website:* www.wellpoint.com (office).

CANNON, Lawrence, BA, MBA; Canadian politician and diplomatist; *Ambassador to France;* b. 6 Dec. 1947; s. of Louis Cannon and Rosemary Power; ed Université de Montréal, Université Laval; Councillor Cap-Rouge 1979–85; mem. Quebec Nat. Ass. 1985–94, Deputy Speaker 1989–94; Minister of Communications 1991–94; fmr Parl. Sec. to Minister of External Trade; fmr consultant; City Councillor, Gastineau 2001; Chair. Outaouais Urban Transit Corpn 2001, Strategic Choices Comm., City of Gatineau; apptd Pres. Asscn du transport urbain du Québec 2004; MP for Pontiac 2006–11; Minister of Transport, Infrastructure and Communities 2006–08, of Foreign Affairs 2008–11; Amb. to France 2012–; fmr Gen. Man., Bd mem. Hull Bicentennial Corpn. *Address:* Embassy of Canada, 35 avenue Montaigne, 75008 Paris, France (office). *Telephone:* 1-44-43-29-00 (office). *Fax:* 1-44-43-29-99 (office). *E-mail:* paris_webmaster@ international.gc.ca (office). *Website:* www.canadainternational.gc.ca/france (office).

CANNON, Michael R., BEng; American computer industry executive; *President of Global Operations, Dell Inc.;* b. 1952; ed Michigan State Univ., Harvard Business School; began career with Boeing Corpn, various man. positions in Mfg

Research and Devt Group; fmr Man. Imprimis Tech., Singapore; fmr Vice Pres., IBM Personal Storage Systems Div., also becoming Vice Pres. of IBM Product Design and Worldwide Mfg; Pres., Dir and CEO Maxtor Corpn 1997–2003; Pres. and CEO Solectron Corpn 2003–07; Pres. of Global Operations, Dell Inc. 2007–; mem. Bd of Dirs Adobe Systems 2003–, US-China Business Council, Silicon Valley Mfg Group. *Address:* Dell Inc., 1 Dell Way, Round Rock, TX 78682-2222, USA (office). *Telephone:* (512) 338-4400 (office). *Fax:* (512) 283-6161 (office). *Website:* www.dell.com (office).

CANNONIER, Craig, BSc, JP; Bermudian business executive and politician; *Premier;* b. 1963, St David's; m. Antoinette Cannonier; four c.; ed Towson State Univ., Baltimore, USA; began career working in retail man.; fmrly with human resources, training and purchasing depts, MarketPlace Group (grocery chain); 10 years as Gen. Man. People's Pharmacy; fmr Relationship Man. Cable & Wireless Bermuda; propr three petrol stations (Esso City Tigermarket, Collector's Hill Esso, Warwick Esso); entered politics 2009, joined Bermuda Democratic Alliance, becoming Leader –2011 (merged into One Bermuda Alliance—OBA 2011), Leader OBA 2011–; mem. House of Ass. (Parl.) for Devonshire S constituency 2011–; Premier of Bermuda 2012–. *Leisure interests:* sports, travelling, boating. *Address:* Office of the Premier, Cabinet Office, Cabinet Bldg, 105 Front Street, Hamilton HM 12, Bermuda (office). *Telephone:* 292-5501 (office). *Fax:* 292-0304 (office). *E-mail:* premier@gov.bm (office). *Website:* www.gov.bm (office).

CANNY, Nicholas Patrick, PhD, FRHistS, FBA, MRIA; Irish historian and academic; *Professor Emeritus, National University of Ireland, Galway;* b. 4 Jan. 1944, Clifden, Co. Galway; s. of Cecil Canny and Helen Joyce; m. Morwena Denis 1974; one s. one d.; ed St Flannan's Coll., Ennis, Co. Clare, Univ. Coll., Galway, Univ. of London, UK, Univs of Pennsylvania, Harvard and Yale, USA; Lecturer in History, Univ. Coll., Galway (now Nat. Univ. of Ireland, Galway) 1972–79, Prof. of History 1980, now Prof. Emer., Dir Moore Inst. for Research in the Humanities 2000–11; mem. Inst. for Advanced Study, Princeton 1979–80; Fellow, Nat. Humanities Center, NC 1985–86; mem. Irish Manuscripts Comm. 1980–, Nat. Archives Advisory Council 1986–96; Chair. Irish Comm. on Historical Sciences 1991–97; Distinguished Visiting Prof., New York Univ. 1995; Fellow-in-Residence, Netherlands Inst. for Advanced Study 2000–01; Prof. invité, École des Hautes Études en Sciences Sociales, Paris 2005; Sr Parnell Research Fellow, Magdalene Coll., Cambridge 2005–06; Pres. Royal Irish Acad. 2008–11; Corresponding Fellow, British Acad. 2005; mem. Academia Europaea 1995–; Foreign mem. American Philosophical Soc. 2007–; mem. Scientific Council, European Research Council 2011; Irish Historical Research Prize 1976, 2003. *Publications include:* The Elizabethan Conquest of Ireland 1976, The Upstart Earl: The Social and Mental World of Richard Boyle 1982, From Reformation to Restoration: Ireland 1534–1660 1987, Colonial Identity in the Atlantic World 1500–1800 1987, Kingdom and Colony: Ireland in the Atlantic World 1560–1800 1988, Europeans on the Move: Studies on European Migration 1500–1800 1994, The Oxford History of the British Empire (Vol. I): The Origins of Empire 1998, Making Ireland British 1580–1650 2000, Oxford Handbook of the History of the Atlantic World 1450–1840 2011. *Leisure interests:* reading, walking, music. *Address:* Furramelia West, Barna, Co. Galway, Ireland (home).

CANO FERNÁNEZ, Ángel; Spanish business executive; *President and Chief Operating Officer, Banco Bilbao Vizcaya Argentaria SA;* b. 1961, Santander; m.; ed graduate in Econ. and Business Sciences; began career at Arthur Andersen, specializing in finance 1984–91; joined Argentaria as Controller 1991, mem. Exec. Cttee 1998, held various man. positions in Banco Bilbao Vizcaya Argentaria (BBVA) Group SA (following merger between BBV and Argentaria), mem. Exec. Cttee 2000, Group Financial Dir 2001–03, Head of Human Resources and Services Dept 2003–05, Head of Resources 2005–09, Pres. and COO 2009–. *Address:* Banco Bilbao Vizcaya Argentaria SA, Paseo de la Castellana 81, 28046 Madrid, Spain (office). *Telephone:* (915) 377690 (office). *Fax:* (913) 747610 (office). *Website:* www .bbva.com (office); www.bbva.es (office).

CANOGAR, Rafael, BA; Spanish painter; b. 17 May 1935, Toledo; s. of Genaro Rafael Canogar and Alfonsa Canogar; m. 1st Ann Jane McKenzie 1960; m. 2nd Purificación Chaves 1992; six c.; studied under Daniel Vázquez Díaz 1949–54; Founder-mem. El Paso group 1957–60; Visiting Prof., Milles Coll., Oakland, Calif. 1965–66; Artist-in-Residence, DAAD, Berlin 1972, 1974; mem. Exec. Cttee Círculo de Bellas Artes, Madrid 1983–86, Advisory Bd Dept of Fine Arts, Ministry of Culture 1981–82, 1983–84, Bd of Trustees, Museo Nacional de Arte Contemporáneo, Madrid 1983, Admin. Bd Nat. Art Collections 1984–90, Exec. Cttee Fundación de Gremios, Madrid 1984–87; more than 120 solo shows and numerous group exhbns; works held in many public art collections world-wide; mem. Real Academia de Bellas Artes de San Fernando, Madrid 1996; nominated 'Hijo predilecto' (Favourite Son) of City of Toledo 2002; Chevalier, Ordre des Arts et des Lettres 1985, Special Commendation, Orden de Isabel la Católica 1991; Dr hc (Universidad Nacional de Educación a Distancia, Madrid) 2001; Third Prize, Primer Concurso para estampados sobre tejidos de tapicería Gastón y Daniela, Bilbao/Madrid 1955, Premio de Instalación de trabajos concedido por la Revista Nacional de Arquitectura 1955, Second Prize, XVII Exposición Manchega de Artes Plásticas, Valdepeñas, Ciudad Real 1956, Prix de la Critique, Brussels 1960, Palette d'Or, XI Festival Int. de la Peinture, Cagnes-sur-Mer, France 1969, Gran Premio Itamaraty, XI Bienal de São Paulo, Brazil 1971, Premio Sol de Oro, Iberian Daily Sun, Palma de Mallorca 1972, Grand Prix, Int. Triennial of Painting, Sofia, Bulgaria 1982, Premio Nacional de Artes Plásticas, Ministry of Culture 1982, Premio Vídeo Castilla-La Mancha, Consejería de Educación y Cultura 1991, IX Premio de Plástica Cultura Viva de la Asociación Cultura Viva, Madrid 1998, Tomislav Krizman Prize of Honour, Second Hrvatski Trijenale Grafike, Zagreb 2000, XIII Premio Tomás Francisco Prieto, Fundación Casa de la Moneda, Madrid 2002, Placa de Pintor Ilustre, Asociación de Escritores y Artistas Españoles, Madrid 2002, Medalla de Oro al Merito en las Bellas Artes, Ministry of Culture 2003, Premio de Cultura de la Comunidad de Madrid 2005, Medalla de Oro, Feria de Arte Contemporáneo Artesevilla 06 2006, Premio Extraordinario del Jurado, III edición de los Premios Castellano-manchegos del Mundo 2008, XVII Premio Ignazio Silone per La Cultura, Rome 2009, Premio AECA al mejor artista vivo español representado en ARCO Madrid 2010 2010, Premio Nacional de Arte Gráfico, otorgado por la Calcografía Nacional, Real Academia de Bellas Artes de San Fernando XV Premio Real Fundación Toledo 2011, VI Premio 'Juanelo

Turriano', Toledo 2011. *Address:* c/o Bernardino Obregón, 6 Local, 28012 Madrid, Spain (office). *Telephone:* (91) 5287729 (office). *Fax:* (91) 5287729 (office). *E-mail:* info@rafaelcanogar.com (office). *Website:* www.rafaelcanogar.com; catalogo .rafaelcanogar.com/home.aspx.

CANTACUZÈNE, Jean Michel, DS; French director of research (retd); b. 15 Dec. 1933, Bucharest, Romania; s. of Dr Alexandre Cantacuzène and Marianne Cantacuzène (née Labeyrie); m. 1st Anne-Marie Szekely 1956 (divorced); one s. one d.; m. 2nd Danièle Ricard 1971; one s.; ed Ecole Supérieure Chem. Industry, Lyon, Ecole Normale Supérieure, Paris; Asst Prof., Ecole Normale Supérieure, Paris 1960–62, Deputy Dir, Lab. Chimie 1964–67; Scientific attaché, French Embassy, Moscow 1962–64, Counsellor for Science and Tech., Washington, DC 1977–80; Prof. of Organic Chem., Univ. of Paris 1967–73, Titular Prof. 1972–; Counsellor for Scientific Affairs, Ministry of Foreign Affairs, Paris 1971–77; Dir Chem. Scientific Dept, CNRS Paris 1973–77, Sr Counsellor for Industrial Affairs 1988; Scientific Dir Total Co. Française des Pétroles, Paris 1980–90; Chair. Bd SOLEMS 1983–86, AVRIST 1982; mem. Conseil pour l'innovation industrielle 1989–91, Applications Cttee, Acad. of Science (Cadas) 1989–2000, Exec. Cttee groupe Climents français 1990–92; mem. Advisory Comm. for Science and Tech. 1971–75, Chair. Industrial R&D Advisory Cttee, EEC, Brussels 1983–86; mem. Council Nuclear Safety Cttee, 1981–90; Pres. Adit 1992–95; mem. Acad. des Technologies (Paris) 2001–; Officier, Légion d'honneur, Ordre nat. du Mérite, Grand Cross, Merit Nat. Order (Romania) 2000; Le Bel Award of the Chemical Soc. of France 1968. *Publications:* Chimie Organique (three vols) (co-author) 1971–75, America, Science and Technology in the 80s (two vols) 1981, Mille Ans dans les Balkans, Chronique des Cantacuzène dans la Tourmente des Siècles 1992; historical papers in Archiva Genealogica and Biblos and over 100 papers in scientific journals. *Leisure interests:* book collecting, history. *Address:* 52 bis route de Damiette, 91190 Gif-sur-Yvette (home); Académie des Technologies, 28 rue Saint Dominique, 75007 Paris, France (office). *E-mail:* jcantacuzene@wanadoo.fr.

CANTARELLA, Paolo; Italian business executive; b. 4 Dec. 1944, Varallo Sesia/ Vercelli; m. Clara Cantarella; ed Turin Polytechnic; began working in car components industry 1977; Commercial Dir Ages (Fiat Group) 1978; Intersectoral Coordinator and Asst to Man. Dir, Fiat Group 1980; Man. Dir Comau (machine tools) 1983; Man. of Supplies and Distribution, Fiat Auto SpA 1989; Vice-Chair. Maserati SpA (luxury sports cars), Modena 1989, Chair. 1993–96; Man. Dir and Gen. Man. Fiat Auto SpA 1990–96, Chair. 1996–2002; Pres. and CEO Fiat SpA 1996–2002; Pres. European Automobile Mfrs Asscn (ACEA) 2000–02; Co-Chair. EU–Russia Industrialists' Round Table (IRT) 2001; Chair. IVECO NV, Business Solutions (Fiat Group) 2001–02; Dir Polaroid Holding 2003–08; Operating Partner, Advent International 2008–; mem. Bd of Dirs Iride, Inpartner (Investitori & Partner Immobiliari); fmr mem. Bd of Dirs Organizing Cttee of the Olympic 2006 Winter Games, Turin; Knight, Order of Labour Merit 1997.

CANTERBURY, Archbishop of (see Welby, Most Rev. and Rt Hon. Justin Portal).

CANTLEY, Lewis C., BS, MA, PhD; American cell biologist, biochemist and academic; *Margaret and Herman Sokol Professor in Oncology Research, Professor of Cancer Biology in Medicine and Director, Cancer Center, Weill Cornell Medical College and New York-Presbyterian Hospital;* b. 20 Feb. 1949, West Virginia; m. Vicki Sato; ed West Virginia Wesleyan Coll., Cornell Univ., Harvard Coll.; Postdoctoral Researcher, Harvard Univ. 1975–78, Asst Prof. of Biochemistry and Molecular Biology, Faculty of Arts and Sciences 1978–85, Prof. of Cell Biology, Harvard Medical School 1992–2003, William Bosworth Castle Chair in Medicine and Prof. of Systems Biology 2003–12, Dir Cancer Center and Chief of Div. of Signal Transduction, Beth Israel Deaconess Medical Center, Boston, Mass 2007–12; Prof. of Physiology, Tufts Univ. 1985–92; Margaret and Herman Sokol Prof. in Oncology Research, Prof. of Cancer Biology in Medicine and Dir Cancer Center, Weill Cornell Medical Coll. and New York-Presbyterian Hosp. 2012–; Co-founder Agios Pharmaceuticals; mem. Advisory Bd AVEO Pharmaceuticals, TransMolecular, Inc.; mem. NAS 2001; Fellow, American Acad. of Arts and Sciences 1999; ASBMB Avanti Award for Lipid Research 1998, Heinrich Wieland Prize for Lipid Research 2000, Caledonian Prize, Royal Soc. of Edinburgh 2002, Pezcoller-AACR Int. Award for Cancer Research 2005, Rolf Luft Award, Karolinska Inst. 2009, Breakthrough Prize in Life Sciences (co-recipient) 2013. *Publications:* numerous papers in professional journals. *Address:* New York Weill Cornell Medical Center, 525 East 68th Street, Box 123, New York, NY 10065, USA (office). *Telephone:* (646) 317-7418 (office). *Fax:* (212) 832-0172 (office). *E-mail:* lcantley@hms.harvard.edu (office). *Website:* weill.cornell.edu (office); cantley.hms .harvard.edu (office).

CANTO-SPERBER, Monique, PhD; French philosopher, academic and academic administrator; *President, Paris Sciences et Lettres;* b. 14 May 1954, Algeria; m. Dan Sperber (divorced); ed École normale supérieure Paris, Univ. Paris I; Asst, Dept of Philosophy, Univ. de Haute-Normandie 1980–84; Prof., Univ. de Picardie 1984–91; Visiting Researcher, King's Coll. London 1988, Princeton Univ., USA 1989, 1990; Visiting Fellow, Inst. for Advanced Study, Princeton, NJ 1993; Dir of Research, CNRS 1993–95; Visiting Prof., Univ. de Caen 1993–96; Visiting Prof., Institut franco-argentin, Buenos Aires 2000, Stanford Univ. 2001, 2002, 2003; fmr Prof., École des Hautes Études en Sciences Sociales; Head of Dir's Office, École normale supérieure Paris 2003–05, Dir 2005–12; Pres. Paris Sciences et Lettres and PSL Foundation 2012–; mem. Centre Nat. des Lettres Philosophy Comm. 1988–91; mem. Editorial Bd European Journal of Philosophy 1993–96; mem. Comité Consultatif Nat. d'Ethique 2001– (Vice-Pres. 2005–); mem. Commissions 'Violence et télévision' 2002, 'Ethique et justice' 2003, du Grand Emprunt nat. 2009; mem. Acad. royale de Belgique 2008; Chevalier, Ordre des Arts et des Lettres 1997, Légion d'honneur 2000, Officier 2009; Officier, Ordre nat. du Mérite 2005; Prix Marcelle Blum, Acad. française 1991, Prix Philippe Habert des professeurs de sciences politiques 2005. *Radio:* host, Questions d'éthique (France Culture) 2006–. *Publications:* Platon, Menon 1991, Les paradoxes de la connaissance 1991, La Philosophie morale britannique 1994, Dictionnaire d'éthique et philosophie morales (ed.) 1996 (revised 2004), La Philosophie grecque 1997, Les Ethiques grecques 2001, L'Inquiétude morale et la vie humaine 2001 (trans. as Moral Disquiet and Human Life 2008), Le style de la pensée 2002, Les règles de la liberté 2003, Le socialisme libéral 2003, La Bien, la guerre et le terreur 2005, La philosophie morale 2006, Faut-il sauver le libéralisme? (co-author) 2006, Platon

Gorgias 2007, Le libéralisme et la gauche 2008, Essai sur la vie humaine 2008, Naissance et liberté 2008, Que devons-nous faire face aux nouvelles questions d'éthique? 2008, Vies et destins 2009, L'idée de guerre juste 2010, La Morale du monde 2010. *Leisure interests:* sport, music. *Address:* Office of the President, Paris Sciences et Lettres, 62 bis rue Gay Lussac, 75005 Paris, France (office). *Telephone:* 1-75-00-02-89 (office). *E-mail:* contact@univ-psl.fr (office). *Website:* www .parissciencesetlettres.org (office).

CANTONA, Eric Daniel Pierre; French actor and fmr professional footballer; b. 24 May 1966, Marseille; s. of Albert Cantona and Léonor Raurich; m. 1st Isabelle Ferrer 1987 (divorced 2003); one s. one d.; m. 2nd Rachida Brakni 2007; player, Auxerre 1983–88, Martigues 1985–86, Marseille 1988–91 (won Coupe de France 1988, Ligue 1 1989, 1991), Bordeaux (loan) 1989, Montpellier (loan) 1989–90 (won Coupe de France 1990), Nîmes 1991, Leeds United 1992 (League Champions 1992, won Charity Shield 1992), Manchester United 1992–97 (League Champions 1993, 1994, 1996, 1997, Football Asscn Cup 1994, 1996, Charity Shield 1993, 1994, 1996), Capt. 1996–97 (scoring 80 goals in 182 appearances); played for French nat. team 1987–95 (45 appearances, 20 goals), Capt. 1993–96; retd 1997; apptd Capt. French Nat. Beach Football team 1997, Man. 2005–11; Dir of Soccer, New York Cosmos 2011–; Professional Footballers' Asscn Player of the Year 1994, Football Writers' Asscn Footballer of the Year 1996, Premier League 10 Seasons Awards (1992/ 93–2001/02): Overseas Player of the Decade and Overall Team of the Decade. *Play:* Face au Paradis, Théâtre Marigny, Paris 2010. *Films include:* Le Bonheur est dans le Pré 1995, Elizabeth 1998, Mookie 1998, Les Enfants du Marais 1999, La Grande Vie 2001, L'Outremangeur 2003, Les Clefs de bagnole 2003, Une belle histoire 2005, La Vie est à nous! 2005, Le Deuxième souffle 2007, Jack Says 2007, French Film 2008, Looking for Eric 2009, Together Is Too Much 2010, Switch 2011, De force 2011, Porn in the Hood 2012, Les mouvements du bassin 2012. *Television includes:* Le grand journal de Canal+ 2006–12, Papillon noir 2008, La liste 2009. *Leisure interest:* painting. *Address:* c/o Mikado, 36 rue Montorgueil, 75001 Paris, France. *Website:* www.fff.fr; www.nycosmos.com.

CANTOR, Anthony John James; British diplomatist (retd); b. 1 Feb. 1946, London; m. Patricia Cantor; one s. two d.; joined Diplomatic Service 1965, Desk Officer, Finance Dept 1966–68, Third Sec., Rangoon, Burma 1968–71, Third Sec., later Second Sec. (Commercial), Tokyo, Japan 1972–76, Second Sec. (Consular) Accra, Ghana, Lomé, Togo 1977–80, Desk Officer, Aid Policy Dept, FCO 1980–82, Desk Officer, West Indian Atlantic Dept 1982–83, Consul (Commercial), Osaka, Japan 1983–89, Deputy Head of Mission, Hanoi, Vietnam 1990–92, on loan to Dept of Trade and Industry 1992–94, First Sec. (Commercial), Tokyo 1994–95, Deputy Consul Gen., Osaka 1995–98, Desk Officer, EU Dept (Bilateral), FCO 1999–2000, Deputy Commr Gen., Expo 2000, Hanover, Germany 2000, Head of Expo Section, Public Diplomacy Dept, FCO 2000–01; Amb. to Paraguay 2001–05, to Armenia 2006–08; mem. Britain-Burma Soc., Kobe Club (Japan). *Leisure interests:* travel, languages, World War II in Asia.

CANTOR, Charles Robert, PhD, FAAS; American molecular biologist and academic; *Chief Scientific Officer, Sequenom Inc.;* b. 26 Aug. 1942, New York; s. of Ida Diane Banks and Louis Cantor; ed Columbia Coll. and Univ. of California, Berkeley; Asst Prof. of Chem., Columbia Univ. 1966–69, Assoc. Prof. of Chem. and Biological Sciences 1969–72, Prof. 1972–81, Prof. of Genetics and Devt; Sherman Fairchild Scholar, Calif. Inst. of Tech. 1975–76; Deputy Dir Comprehensive Cancer Center, Coll. of Physicians and Surgeons 1981–89; Dir Human Genome Center, Lawrence Berkeley Lab. 1989–90; Prof. of Molecular Biology, Univ. of Calif., Berkeley 1989–92; Prof. of Biomedical Eng, Boston Univ. 1992–, Chair. 1994–98, Dir Center for Advanced Biotech. 1992–; Prof. of Pharmacology 1995–; Prin. Scientist, Human Genome Project, US Dept of Energy 1990–92; Chief Scientific Officer, Sequenon Inc. 1998–; mem. Bd of Dirs 2000–; Assoc. Ed. Annual Review of Biophysics and Biophysical Chemistry 1983–93; Pres. Americas Human Genome Org. 1991–98; mem. Biophysics and Biophysical Chem. Study Section, NIH 1971–75, Proposal Review Panel, Stanford Sychrotron Radiation Lab. 1976–88, Ozone Update Comm., NRC 1983, Research Opportunities in Biology Comm. 1985–89, Comm. on Human Genome 1986–89, Scientific Advisory Bd, Hereditary Disease Foundation 1987–89; mem. Council, Human Genome Org. 1989–92, Vice-Pres. 1990–92, Pres. 1991–98; mem. US Nat. Cttee of Int. Union of Pure and Applied Biophysics 1986–94, Vice-Chair. 1988–91, Chair. 1991–94; Chair. US Dept of Energy Human Genome Coordinating Comm. 1989–92; mem. Advisory Cttee Searle Scholars Program 1987–93, Chair. 1993–94; mem. Advisory Cttee Program in Parasite Biology, MacArthur Foundation 1990–93, Scientific Advisory Council Rosewell Park Cancer Inst. 1992–98, Scientific Advisory Cttee European Molecular Biology Lab. 1989–94, Bd of Scientific Counsellors, Nat. Centre for Biotechnology Information, Nat. Library of Medicine 1990–95; consultant, Incyte Pharmaceuticals Inc. 1992–98, Genelabs Inc. 1988–, Samsung Advanced Inst. of Tech. 2000–; mem. Bd of Dirs Applied Biophysics 1993–99, Visiting Cttee for Biology, Brookhaven Nat. Lab. 1986–89; mem. Bd of Dirs and Chair. Scientific Advisory Cttee Avitech Diagnostics Inc. (fmrly ATGC Inc.) 1992–97, Nomenclature Cttee IUBMB 1989–; Chair. Advisory Cttee European Bioinformatics Inst. 1993–94; mem. USDA Genome Advisory Cttee 1992–98; Co-Chair. Biotechnology Advisory Cttee Fisher Scientific 1994–, Biology Advisory Cttee Lawrence Livermore Nat. Lab. 1995–, Chair. 2000–04; mem. Scientific Advisory Cttee Aclara Inc. 1996–2003, Caliper Inc. 1996–; mem. Bd of Dirs ExSar Inc. (fmrly Carta Inc.) 1999–2004, SIGA Inc. (fmrly Plexus Inc.), The Molecular Sciences Inst. SelectX Pharmaceuticals 2003–04 (Chair. Scientific Advisory Bd 2003–), Keystone Conferences 1999–2006; mem. Scientific Advisory Cttee Odyssey Inc. 2002–; Pres. Biochemist Inc. 2001–2002; Quest Scholar, Quest Diagnostics Inc. 1997–99; mem. Biotech Council, Dept of Energy 1996–99; mem. Unconventional Pathogen Countermeasures Advisory Cttee 1996–2000; mem. Advisory Cttee Uppsala Bio-X 2004–06; Adjunct Prof. of Biomedical Eng, Univ. of Calif., San Diego 2002–; mem. NAS, American Acad. of Arts and Sciences, Biophysics Soc., American Soc. of Biological Chemists, ACS, Analytical Cytology Soc., Harvey Soc., American Soc. of Human Genetics, Biomedical Eng Soc., Biophysical Soc.; Fellow, Alfred P. Sloan Foundation 1969–71; Hon. mem. Japanese Biochemical Soc.; Fresenius Award 1972, Guggenheim Fellow 1973–74, Eli Lilly Award in Biological Chem., ACS 1978, Nat. Cancer Inst. Outstanding Investigator Grantee 1985, Analytica Prize 1988, ISCO Prize 1989, Sober Prize 1990, Emily Gray Prize 2005. *Publications:* Biophysical Chemistry (three vols, with Paul Schimmel), Genomics: The Science and Technology behind the Human Genome Project. *Leisure interests:* gastronomy, *running, skiing. Address:* Sequenom Inc., 3595 John Hopkins Court, San Diego, CA 92121 (office); 526 Stratford Court, Apt E, Del Mar, CA 92014-2767, USA (home). *Telephone:* (858) 202-9012 (office). *Fax:* (858) 858-9020 (office). *E-mail:* ccantor@sequenom.com (office). *Website:* www.sequenom.com (office).

CANTWELL, Maria E., BA; American politician; *Senator from Washington;* b. 13 Oct. 1958, Indianapolis, Ind.; d. of Paul Cantwell and Rose Cantwell; ed Univ. of Miami, Ohio; with Cantwell and Assocs (public relations firm) 1981–87; mem. Washington State House of Reps 1987–92; mem. US House of Reps from 1st Congressional Dist 1993–95; Vice-Pres. of Marketing Progressive Networks (now RealNetworks) 1994–97, Sr Vice-Pres. 1997–2000; Senator from Wash. 2001–. *Address:* 311 Hart Senate Office Building, Washington, DC 20510, USA (office). *Telephone:* (202) 224-3441 (office). *Fax:* (202) 228-0514 (office). *Website:* cantwell .senate.gov (office).

CAO, Bochun; Chinese politician; *Deputy Director, NPC Environment and Resources Protection Committee;* b. Nov. 1941, Zhuzhou City, Hunan Prov.; ed Zhuzhou School of Aeronautical Industry; teacher, Zhuzhou School of Aeronautical Industry 1963; joined CCP 1966; Deputy Chief No. 331 Factory, Aircraft Engine Factory, Political Div., Jiangnan, Zhejiang Prov. 1970–83, Dir No. 331 Factory, Political Dept 1970–83, Deputy Dir No. 331 Factory 1980–83; Deputy Sec. and Head CCP Publicity Dept, Zhuzhou City Cttee 1983, Sec. Zhuzhou City Cttee 1984; Sec. CCP Xiangtan City Cttee 1990; Vice-Gov. Hunan Prov. 1991; Deputy Sec. CCP Liaoning Prov. Cttee 1992–95, Sec. Dalian City Cttee 1992–95; Alt. mem. 14th CCP Cen. Cttee 1992; mem. 15th CCP Cen. Cttee 1997–2002, 16th CCP Cen. Cttee 2002–07, Sec. CCP Guangxi Zhuang Autonomous Regional Cttee 1997–2002; Chair. Standing Cttee Guangxi Zhuang Autonomous Regional People's Congress 2002–06; Deputy Dir 10th NPC Environment and Resources Protection Cttee 2006–. *Address:* Environment and Resources Protection Committee, National People's Congress, Beijing, People's Republic of China.

CAO, Dewang; Chinese business executive and philanthropist; *Chairman, Fuyao Glass Industry Group;* b. 1948, Fuqing, Fujian Prov.; s. of He Ren; left school early and worked as herdsman, chef and fruit seller; started own business as tobacco seller at age 16; joined Fuqing Gao Shan Special Glass Factory as merchandiser 1976, f. Fuyao Group 1987, currently Chair. Fuyao Glass Industry Group; mem. Fujian Prov. CPPCC Cttee; Chair. China Automobile Glass Asscn; Pres. Fujian Golf Asscn; Ernst & Young World Entrepreneur of the Year 2009, listed among Top 10 Economic Figures in China's Economy 2009, named by Ministry of Civil Affairs among China's Top 10 Charitable Persons. *Leisure interest:* golf. *Address:* Office of the Chairman, Fuyao Glass Industry Group, Fuyao Industrial Park, Fuqing 350301, Fujian Province, People's Republic of China (office). *Telephone:* (591) 8538-3777 (office). *Fax:* (591) 8538-2719 (office). *Website:* www.fuyaogroup.com (office).

CAO, Gen. Gangchuan; Chinese politician and army officer; b. Dec. 1935, Wuyang Co., Henan Prov.; ed Third Artillery Tech. School, Zhengzhou City, PLA Russian Tech. School, Dalian, Artillery Mil. Eng Acad. Moscow and PLA Univ. of Nat. Defence; joined PLA 1954; teacher, No. 1 Ordnance Tech. School 1956; mem. CCP 1956–; Asst, PLA Gen. Logistics Dept, Ordinance Dept, Ammunition Div. 1963–69, Gen. Logistics Dept, Mil. Equipment Dept, Munitions Div. 1969–75; Staff Officer and Deputy Dir Gen. Planning Div., Mil. Equipment Dept Gen. Staff HQ 1975–82; Deputy Commdr artillery troops during Sino-Vietnamese border conflict 1979; Deputy Dir Mil. Equipment Dept Gen. Staff HQ 1982–89; Dir Mil. Affairs Dept Gen. Staff HQ 1989–90; Dir Mil. Products Trade Office of Mil. Cttee of Cen. Cttee of CCP 1990–92; Deputy Dir Leading Group for Placement of Demobilized Army Officers; Deputy Sec. Comm. for Disciplinary Inspection; Deputy Chief of Gen. Staff, PLA 1992–96; Minister, State Comm. of Science, Tech. and Industry for Nat. Defence 1996–98; rank of Gen. 1996; Dir PLA Gen. Armaments Dept 1998–; mem. 15th Cen. Cttee CCP 1997–2002, 15th Cen. Cttee CCP Cen. Mil. Comm. 1997–2002, 16th Cen. Cttee CCP 2002–07, 16th Cen. Cttee CCP Politburo 2002–07; Vice-Chair. 16th Cen. Cttee CCP Cen. Mil. Comm. 2002–07; State Councillor 2003–08; Minister of Nat. Defence 2003–08. *Address:* c/o Ministry of National Defence, 20 Jingshanqian Jie, Beijing 100009, People's Republic of China.

CAO, Peixi, MEcon MEng; Chinese engineer and business executive; *Chairman and President, China Huaneng Group;* b. Aug. 1955; ed Party School of CCP Cen. Cttee, Shandong Univ.; has worked in power generation, operation and man. and capital operations since mid-1970s; joined Qingdao Plant, China Huadian Corpn 1972, held positions of technician, Deputy Chief Engineer, Deputy Head and Head of the plant, Asst to Gen. Man., Deputy Gen. Man., Chair. and Party Sec. and Gen. Man. of Shandong Electric Power (Group) Corpn 1995–2002, Deputy Gen. Man. and Party mem. China Huadian Corpn 2002–06; Chair. China Huaneng Group 2008–, Pres. 2009–, also Chair. Huaneng Int. Power Devt Corpn, Huaneng Power Int., Inc., Huaneng Renewables Corpn, Vice-Sec. CCP Huaneng Cttee. *Address:* China Huaneng Group, 40 Xueyuan Nanlu, Beijing 100088, People's Republic of China. *Telephone:* (10) 62291888 (office). *Fax:* (10) 62291899 (office). *E-mail:* info@chng.com.cn (office). *Website:* www.chng.com.cn (office).

CAO, Qingze; Chinese government and party official; b. 1932, Lixian Co., Hunan Prov.; ed No. 3 Br., PLA Mil. and Political Coll., 2nd Field Army; clerical staff, People's Govt Gen. Office, Liangping Co., Sichuan Prov. 1950, CCP Co. Cttee Organization Dept, Liangping Co. 1950; joined CCP 1952; staff mem., CCP Prov. Cttee Agricultural Dept, Sichuan Prov. 1955, CCP Revolutionary Cttee, Sichuan Prov. 1966–76 (Deputy Head Agricultural Group 1978); Deputy Dir Prov. Agricultural Office, Sichuan Prov. 1978; trainee, CCP Cen. Cttee Cen. Party School 1980; Deputy Sec.-Gen. People's Govt, Sichuan Prov. 1981–85; Deputy Sec. later Sec. Comm. for Discipline Inspection of CCP Sichuan Prov. Cttee 1985–93; mem. Standing Cttee, 14th CCP Cen. Cttee 1992–97; mem. Cen. Comm. for Discipline Inspection 1989–97; Deputy Sec. CCP Cen. Comm. for Inspecting Discipline 1992–2002; Minister of Supervision 1993–98; Hon. Pres. Soc. of Supervision. *Address:* c/o Ministry of Supervision, 35 Huayuanbei Lu, Haidan Qu, Beijing 100083, People's Republic of China.

CAO, Lt-Gen. Shuangming; Chinese army officer (retired) and party official; b. 1929, Linxian Co., Henan Prov.; joined CCP 1946; Deputy Commdr PLA Shengyang Mil. Area Command 1987–92, Commdr PLA Air Force 1992–94; rank of Lt-Gen. 1988; mem. 14th CCP Cen. Cttee 1992–97. *Address:* Shengyang Military

Area Command, People's Liberation Army, Shengyang City, Liaoning Province, People's Republic of China.

CAO, Zhi; Chinese politician; b. 1928, Anqiu, Shandong Prov.; joined CCP 1947; Dir Acheng News Report, Acheng Co., Heilongjiang Prov. 1947–48; Sec. CCP Co. Cttee, Acheng Co. 1948–49, Deputy Head CCP Co. Cttee Publicity Dept 1949–51, Head 1951–52; Deputy Section Chief CCP Prov. Cttee Publicity Dept, Heilongjiang Prov. 1952–53, Div. Chief 1953–60, Deputy Dir CCP Prov. Cttee Gen. Office 1960–66; Deputy Sec. CCP Prefectural Cttee, Hejiang Prefecture, Heilongjiang Prov. 1966–70; Vice-Chair. CCP Revolutionary Cttee, Heilongjiang Prov. 1970–77; Leading mem. State Devt and Reform Comm. 1977–78; Head CCP Cen. Cttee Research Office 1978–83; Deputy Head CCP Cen. Cttee Org. Dept 1983–87; Deputy Dir Research Office, Secr. CCP Cen. Cttee 1987–88; Sec.-Gen. 7th Standing Cttee NPC 1988–93, 8th Standing Cttee NPC 1993–98; Vice-Chair. Standing Cttee 9th NPC 1998–2003; Del. 14th CCP Nat. Congress 1992–97, 15th CCP Nat. Congress 1997–2002; Vice-Pres. Cen. Cttee for Comprehensive Man. of Public Security 1993; mem. Hong Kong Special Admin. Region Preparatory Cttee Govt Del. for Hong Kong Hand-Over Ceremony 1997. *Address:* c/o Standing Committee, National People's Congress, Tian'anmen Square, Beijing, People's Republic of China.

CAPASSO, Federico, PhD, FInstP; Italian/American mathematician, physicist, computer scientist and academic; *Robert L. Wallace Professor of Applied Physics and Vinton Hayes Senior Research Fellow in Electrical Engineering, Harvard University;* b. 1949, Rome, Italy; m.; two c.; ed Univ. of Rome; Postdoctoral Fellow Fondazione Bordoni, Rome 1973–74, Research Physicist 1974–76; Visiting Scientist, Bell Labs, Holmdel, NJ 1976–77, mem. Tech. Staff, Bell Labs, Murray Hill, NJ 1977–84, Distinguished Mem. of Tech. Staff 1984–87, Dept Head, Quantum Phenomena and Device Research, Bell Labs Lucent Technologies (fmrly AT&T Bell Labs –1996) 1987–97, Dept Head, Semiconductor Physics Research 1997–2000, Vice-Pres. of Physical Research 2000–02; Robert L. Wallace Prof. of Applied Physics, Harvard Univ. 2003–, Vinton Hayes Sr Research Fellow in Electrical Eng, School of Eng and Applied Sciences (fmrly, Div.); Adjunct Researcher, Inst. for Quantum Studies, Texas A&M Univ. 2009–; mem. NAS 1995, Nat. Acad. of Eng 1995; Fellow, American Physical Soc. 1986, IEEE 1987, Optical Soc. of America 1989, Int. Soc. for Optical Eng (SPIE) 1991, AAAS 1992, American Acad. of Arts and Sciences 1998; US citizenship 1992; Hon. mem. Franklin Inst. 1997; Commendatore of Italian Repub. 2004; Hon. Dr of Electrical Eng (Bologna) 2003; Distinguished Mem. of Technical Staff Award, Bell Labs 1984, IEEE David Sarnoff Award in Electronics 1991, New York Acad. of Sciences Award 1993, Heinrich Welker Memorial Medal (Germany) and Int. Compound Semiconductors Symposium Award 1994, Electronics Letters Prize, IEE (UK) 1995, Newcomb Cleveland Prize, AAAS 1995, Moët Hennessy-Louis Vuitton 'Leonardo da Vinci' Award of Excellence (France) 1995, Medal of Materials Research Soc. 1995, Fellow Award, Bell Labs 1997, Wetherill Medal, Franklin Inst. 1997, Capitolium Prize, Mayor of Rome 1998, Rank Prize in Optoelectronics (UK) 1998, W. Streifer Award for Scientific Achievement, IEEE/Laser & Electro-Optics Soc. 1998, Alessandro Volta Memorial Medal, Univ. of Pavia 1999, NASA Group Achievement Award 2000, Willis E. Lamb Medal for Laser Physics and Quantum Optics 2000, Robert Wood Prize, Optical Soc. of America 2001, Silver Seal, Univ. of Bari 2001, Duddell Medal and Prize, Inst. of Physics (UK) 2002, Goff Smith Prize and Lecture, Univ. of Michigan 2003, Tommasoni & Chisesi Prize for Outstanding Achievements in Physics 2004, Arhur Schawlow Prize in Laser Science, American Physical Soc. 2004, IEEE Edison Medal 2004, Gold Medal, Pres. of Italy 2005, King Faisal Int. Prize for Science 2005, Berthold Leibinger Zukunft Prize (Future Prize) 2010, Julius Springer Prize for Applied Physics 2010. *Publications:* Problems of General Physics (co-ed.) 1976, Picosecond Electronics and Optoelectronics (co-ed.) 1987, Heterojunction Band Discontinuities: Physics and Device Applications (co-ed.) 1987, Quantum Well and Superlattice Physics II. Proceedings SPIE (co-ed.) 1988, Physics of Quantum Electron Devices; Springer Series in Electronics and Photonics, Vol. 28 (co-ed.) 1990, Intersubband Transitions in Quantum Wells: Physics and Applications, Part I (co-ed.) 2000, Intersubband Transitions in Quantum Wells: Physics and Applications, Part II (co-ed.) 2000; numerous book chapters and more than 450 papers in peer-reviewed journals. *Address:* School of Engineering and Applied Sciences, Harvard University, 205A Pierce Hall, 29 Oxford Street, Cambridge, MA 02138, USA (office). *Telephone:* (617) 384-7611 (office); (617) 495-5909 (lab.) (office). *Fax:* (617) 495-2875 (office). *E-mail:* capasso@seas.harvard.edu (office). *Website:* www.seas.harvard.edu/directory/capasso (office).

CAPECCHI, Mario Renato, PhD; American (b. Italian) geneticist and academic; *Distinguished Professor of Human Genetics and Biology and Investigator, Howard Hughes Medical Institute, University of Utah School of Medicine;* b. 6 Oct. 1937, Verona, Italy; m. 2nd Laurie Fraser 1985; one d.; ed Antioch Coll., Harvard Univ.; Jr Fellow in Biophysics, Harvard Univ. 1966–69, Asst Prof. to Assoc. Prof. of Biochemistry, Medical School 1969–73; Prof. of Biology, Univ. of Utah 1973–88, Prof. of Human Genetics, School of Medicine 1989–, Distinguished Prof. 1993–, Investigator, Howard Hughes Medical Inst., Univ. of Utah 1988–; mem. Bd Scientific Counselors, Nat. Cancer Inst.; mem. NAS, American Biochemial Soc., American Soc. of Microbiology, New York Acad. of Science, Int. Genome Soc., Genetics Soc. of America, AAAS, Soc. for Developmental Biology, European Acad. of Sciences, American Acad. of Arts and Sciences 2009–; ACS Biochemistry Award 1969, Bristol-Myers Squibb Award for Distinguished Achievement in Neuroscience Research 1992, Gairdner Foundation Int. 1993, Gen. Motors Corpn Alfred P. Sloan Jr Prize 1994, Kyoto Prize in Basic Sciences 1996, Franklin Medal 1997, Baxter Award 1998, Lasker Award 2001, Nat. Medal of Science 2001, John Scott Medal Award 2002, Pezcoller Foundation-AACR Int. Award 2003, Wolf Prize in Medicine 2002–03, March of Dimes Prize in Developmental Biology 2005, Nobel Prize in Physiology or Medicine (with Sir Martin Evans and Oliver Smithies) 2007 for the discovery of principles for introducing specific gene modifications in mice by the use of embryonic stem cells; American Heart Asscn Distinguished Scientist Award 2008. *Publications:* Targeted Gene Replacement 1994, The Making of a Scientist (Howard Hughes Medical Inst. Bulletin) 1997, Generating Mice with Targeted Mutations 2001, and a total of 141 peer-reviewed manuscripts, books and book chapters. *Address:* Howard Hughes Medical Institute, University of Utah, 15 N 2030 E, Room 5100, Salt Lake City, UT 84112-5331 (office); 778 East 13800 South, Draper, UT 84020, USA (home). *Telephone:* (801) 581-7096 (office). *Fax:*

(801) 585-3425 (office). *E-mail:* mario.capecchi@genetics.utah.edu (office). *Website:* capecchi.genetics.utah.edu (office).

CAPELLAS, Michael D., BBA; American business executive; *Principal, Capellas Strategic Partners;* b. 19 Aug. 1954; m. Marie Capellas; two c.; ed Kent State Univ.; systems analyst, Republic Steel Corpn 1976–81; joined Schlumberger Ltd 1981, holding successive posts as First Corp. Dir for Information Systems, Controller and Treas. of Asia Pacific Operations, Chief Financial Officer Dowell Schlumberger, Operations Man. Schlumberger's Fairchild Semiconductor unit 1981–96; Founder and Man. Pnr, Benchmarking Partners, Cambridge, Mass 1996; Dir of Supply-Chain Man., SAP America 1996–97; Sr Vice-Pres. and Gen. Man. Global Energy Business, Oracle Corpn 1997–98; Chief Information Officer Compaq Computer Corpn 1998–99, Pres. and CEO 1999–2000, Chair. and CEO 2000–02; Pres. Hewlett-Packard Co. (following acquisition of Compaq by Hewlett-Packard) 2002; Chair. and CEO WorldCom (now MCI Group) 2002–04, Pres. and CEO 2004–06; Acting Pres. and CEO Serena Software Inc. 2006–07; Sr Advisor, Silver Lake Partners (investment firm) 2007–; Chair. and CEO First Data Corpn 2007–10; Chair. and CEO VCE 2010–11; Prin., Capellas Strategic Partners 2012–; mem. Bd of Dirs Cisco Systems Inc. 2006–; Trustee American Univ., Washington, DC. *Leisure interests:* community leadership and charity work, golf. *Website:* www .capellaspartners.com.

CAPELLE, Alfred, MA; Marshall Islands civil servant and diplomatist; b. 20 March 1940; m. Mwejo term; five s. three d.; ed Univ. of Hawaii at Manoa; Admin. Aide, Global Assocs, Inc., Kwajalein 1964–66; Mayor, Likiep Atoll 1966–68; elementary school teacher 1968–77; Educ. Specialist, Dept of Educ. 1977–79; Continuing Educ. Programme Co-ordinator, Coll. of Micronesia 1979–82; Chief of Post-Secondary Educ., Ministry of Educ. 1982–83, Language Consultant and Researcher 1996; Dir of Assumption Schools, Assumption Parish, Majuro 1983–86; Resource Protection Officer and CEO, Alele Museum 1986–96; Pres., Coll. of Marshall Islands 1996–2002; Perm. Rep. to UN 2002–08; currently Adviser, Pacific Aquaculture Cooperatives International. *Publications include:* Marshallese-English Dictionary (co-author). *Address:* c/o Pacific Aquaculture Cooperatives International, 6 South Lakeview Drive, Jackson, NJ 08527, USA.

CAPELLINO, Ally, BA; British fashion designer; b. (Alison Lloyd), 1956; ed Middlesex Univ.; worked in Courtaulds Cen. Design Studio 1978–79; est. Ally Capellino Little Hat, initially selling hats and accessories 1979; developed clothing line with accessories for Moscow Olympics collection 1979–80; began selling Ally Capellino label to int. markets 1980; launched menswear collection 1986; first London fashion show 1986; opened shop in Soho, London 1988; launched Hearts of Oak sportswear collection 1990, Mini Capellino children's wear 1991; signed promotional and licensing agreement with Coats Viyella PLC 1992; launched 'ao' collection 1996; opened Ally Capellino shop, London 1997; opened flagship store Tokyo, Japan 1998. *Address:* c/o Goodley PR, 41 Dover Street, Mayfair, London, W1S 4NS, England. *Telephone:* (20) 7493-9600 (office). *E-mail:* info@allycapellino .co.uk (office). *Website:* www.allycapellino.co.uk (office).

CAPELLO, Fabio; Italian professional football manager and fmr professional footballer; b. 18 June 1946, San Canzian d'Isonzo; s. of Guerrino Capello and Evelina Capello; m. Laura Capello; two c.; played for SPAL 1964–67, A.S. Roma 1967–69 (won Coppa Italia 1969), Juventus 1969–76 (won Serie A 1972, 1973, 1975), Associazione Calcio (A.C.) Milan 1976–80 (won Coppa Italia 1977, Serie A 1979), Italian nat. team 1972–76 (32 caps, eight goals); Man. AC Milan 1991–96, 1997–98 (won Serie A 1992, 1993, 1994, 1996, Supercoppa Italiana 1992, 1993, 1994, UEFA Champions League 1994, European Super Cup 1994), Real Madrid 1996–97, 2006–07 (winner La Liga 1997, 2007), A.S. Roma 1999–2004 (won Serie A 2001, Supercoppa Italiana 2001), Juventus 2004–06 (won Serie A 2005, 2006 (Trophy revoked due to Calciopoli scandal), England Nat. Football Team 2008–12 (qualified for 2010 World Cup 2009), Russia Nat. Football Team 2012–; apptd Pres. League Managers Asscn 2008; Serie A Coach of the Year 2005, BBC Sports Personality Coach of the Year 2009-10. *Leisure interests:* fine art enthusiast and collector, opera and classical music. *Address:* Russian Football Union, 115172 Moscow, Ulitsa Narodnaya, 7, Russia. *Telephone:* (495) 926-13-00. *E-mail:* info@rfs .ru. *Website:* www.russiateam.com.

CAPITANICH, Jorge Milton, MEconSc; Argentine accountant and politician; *Chief, Cabinet of Ministers;* b. 28 Nov. 1964, Roque Saenz Peña, Chaco Prov.; ed Universidad Nacional del Nordeste, Instituto Universitario Escuela Superior de Economía y Administración de Empresas (ESEADE); Head of Private Employment Generation Program, Secr. of Assistance in Provincial Econ. Reforms 1994; Under-Sec. of Admin. Co-ordination, Nat. Secr. for Social Devt 1995, Under-Sec. of Social Planning 1998; Acting Minister of Infrastructure and Housing, of Social Devt and Environment, of Public Health, of Work, Employment and Human Resources, and of Social Security 2001; Cabinet Chief, Govt of Argentina 2002; Nat. Senator for Chaco Prov. 2002–07; Gov. of Chaco Prov. 2007–13; Chief, Cabinet of Ministers 2013–. *Publications:* Investigación Sobre El Orígen de las Crisis Provinciales, Federalismo Fiscal y Coparticipación, La Sumergida. Chaco, Propuestas para la Integración. *Address:* Office of the Cabinet Chief, Avda Julio Argentino Roca 782, C1067ABP Buenos Aires, Argentina (office). *Telephone:* (11) 4331-1951 (office). *E-mail:* prensa@jgm.gov.ar (office). *Website:* www.jgm.gov.ar (office).

CAPLIN, Mortimer Maxwell, BS, LLB, JSD; American lawyer, government official and academic; *Senior Partner, Caplin & Drysdale Attorneys;* b. 11 July 1916, New York; s. of Daniel Caplin and Lillian Epstein; m. Ruth Sacks 1942; three s. one d.; ed Univ. of Virginia and New York Univ. Law School; law Clerk to US Circuit Judge 1940–41; legal practice with Paul, Weiss, Rifkind, Wharton & Garrison, New York 1941–50; with USNR, Beachmaster in Normandy landings 1942–45; Prof. of Law, Univ. of Virginia 1950–61, Lecturer and Visiting Prof. 1965–87, Prof. Emer. 1988–; Counsel, Perkins, Battle & Minor 1952–61; US Commr of Internal Revenue 1961–64; Founder and Sr Pnr, Caplin & Drysdale, Washington, DC 1964–; Chair. Nat. Civil Service League 1965–80, American Council on Int. Sports 1975–80, Nat. Citizens' Advisory Cttee 1975–80, Asscn of American Medical Colls., Univ. of Virginia Council of the Arts; Dir Fairchild Corpn, Presidential Reality Corpn, Danaher Corpn 1990–2013; mem. Public Review Bd, Arthur Andersen & Co. 1980–88; mem. House of Dels 1980–92, DC and Fed. Bar Assocns, Va and NY State Bars, American Law Inst.; Ed.-in-Chief Virginia Law Review 1939–40; mem. Bd of Trustees, George Washington Univ. 1964, Bd of

Visitors, Univ. of Virginia Law School Foundation 1982–; Emer. Trustee Shakespeare Theatre, Wolf Trap Foundation and Arena Stage; Hon. LLD (St Michael Coll.) 1964; Raven Award, Alexander Hamilton Award, Univ. of Virgina/ Thomas Jefferson Memorial Foundation Medal in Law 2001 and other awards; Order of the Coif. *Publications:* Doing Business in Other States, Proxies, Annual Meetings and Corporate Democracy; numerous articles on tax and corporate matters. *Leisure interests:* swimming, horseback riding, gardening. *Address:* Caplin and Drysdale, One Thomas Circle, NW, Washington, DC 20005-5802 (office). Apartment 18E, 5610 Wisconsin Avenue, Chevy Chase, MD 20815-4415, USA (home). *Telephone:* (202) 862-5050 (office). *E-mail:* mcaplin@capdale.com (office). *Website:* www.capdale.com (office).

ČAPLOVIČ, Dušan, DrSci; Slovak politician and fmr archaeologist; b. 18 Sept. 1946, Bratislava; ed Comenius Univ.; Sr Researcher and Scientist, Slovak Acad. of Sciences 1980–2002, mem. Presidium 1992–2001, Deputy Pres. 1995–2001, Deputy Dir Archaeological Inst., Nitra 1990–92; mem. Nat. Council 2002–06; Deputy Prime Minister for Knowledge-Based Soc., European Affairs, Human Rights and Minorities 2006–10; mem. Council for Science and Tech. 1992–95; mem. Advisory Bd Ministry of Culture 1995–98. *Address:* c/o Office of the Government, nám. Slobody 1, 813 70 Bratislava, Slovakia (office).

CAPPE, Mel, OC, MA; Canadian diplomatist and economist; *Professor, School of Public Policy and Governance, University of Toronto;* b. 3 Dec. 1948, Toronto; m. Marline (Marni) Cappe (née Pliskin); one s. one d.; ed Univs of Toronto and Western Ontario; joined Canadian public service as a policy analyst 1975; with Treasury Bd 1975–78, Deputy Sec. 1990–94; with Dept of Finance 1978–82; Deputy Dir Investigation and Research, Dept of Consumer and Corp. Affairs 1982–90; Deputy Asst Sec. Dept of Finance 1990, Deputy Sec. Program Br. 1990; fmr Asst Deputy Minister Competition Policy; fmr Asst Deputy Minister Policy Co-ordination; fmr Asst Deputy Minister Corp. Affairs and Legis. Policy; Deputy Minister of the Environment 1994–96, of Human Resources Devt 1996–99; Chair. Employment Insurance Comm. 1996–99; Deputy Minister of Labour 1996–99; Clerk of the Privy Council, Sec. to Cabinet and Head of the Public Service 1999–2002; Special Adviser to Prime Minister 2002; High Commr to UK 2002–06; Pres. and CEO Inst. for Research on Public Policy, Montreal 2006–12; Prof., School of Public Policy and Governance, Univ of Toronto 2012–; Queen's Golden Jubilee Medal 2002, Queen's Diamond Jubilee Medal 2012; Hon. PhD (Univ. of Western Ontario, Univ. of Toronto); Hon. LLD. *Address:* School of Public Policy and Governance, University of Toronto, 14 Queen's Park Crescent, West Toronto, ON M5S 3K9, Canada (office). *Telephone:* (416) 978-2875 (office). *Fax:* (416) 978-5079 (office). *E-mail:* mel.cappe@utoronto.ca (office). *Website:* www.publicpolicy .utoronto.ca (office).

CAPPELLAZZO, Amy, BA, MA; American art dealer; *Deputy Chairman, Christie's Americas and Co-Head of Post-War and Contemporary Art, Christie's International;* ed New York Univ. (Presidential Trustee Scholar), Pratt Inst.; Sr Vice-Pres. and Int. Co-Head of Postwar and Contemporary Art, Christie's auction house 2001–, played key role in historic sale which was the first ever Post-War and Contemporary auction to break the $100 million mark May 2004, Deputy Chair. Christie's Americas 2008–; taught and lectured at New York Univ., Museum of Modern Art, New York, Univ. of Miami, Museum of Fine Arts Boston and at UCLA; Trustee, Pratt Inst.; featured in Crain's Business New York 40 under 40 2006. *Address:* Christie's International, 20 Rockefeller Plaza, New York, NY 10020, USA (office). *Telephone:* (212) 636-2000 (office). *Fax:* (212) 636-2399 (office). *E-mail:* info@christies.com (office). *Website:* www.christies.com (office).

CAPPICHIONI, Gian Carlo; San Marino accountant and politician; b. 19 Feb. 1956, Borgo Maggiore; m.; one s.; served for several years in office of Sec. of State for Finance and Budget; Capitano di Castello (Mayor) of Serravalle 2003–06; mem. Consiglio Grande e Generale (Great and Gen. Council, Parl.) 2006–, mem. Finance, Budget and Planning Comm.; Co-Captain Regent (jt head of state) 2013–14; fmr mem. Consiglio dei XII (parl. advisory council); mem. Partito dei Socialisti e dei Democratici 2005–. *Address:* c/o Office of the Captains-Regent, Contrada Omerelli, 47890 San Marino, San Marino (office).

CAPPON, Claudio; Italian broadcasting executive; *Director-General, Radio-televisione Italiana SpA (RAI);* b. 9 July 1952, Rome; m.; three c.; ed Univ. of Rome; worked for Istituto per la Ricostruzione Industriale for 20 years, specializing in control and man.; Dir of Industrial Activities, Fintecna 1994–96, Dir-Gen. and CEO 1996–98; Deputy Dir-Gen. Radiotelevisione Italiana SpA (RAI) 1998–2001, Dir-Gen. 2001–02, 2006–; CEO Consap (Concessionaria dei servizi assicurativi pubblici) 2002–; Pres. APT (Asscn of TV Producers) 2002–. *Address:* Radio-televisione Italiana SpA, Viale Mazzini 14, 00195 Rome, Italy (office). *Telephone:* (06) 38781 (office). *E-mail:* info@rai.it (office). *Website:* www.rai.it (office).

CAPPS, Thomas E., BA, JD; American business executive; b. 31 Oct. 1935, Wilmington, North Carolina; s. of Edward S. Capps Jr and Agnes Rhodes; m. 1st Jane Paden 1963; two c.; m. 2nd Sandra Lee Hurley; four c.; ed Univ. of North Carolina; in pvt. legal practice, N Carolina and Fla 1966–70; held positions in legal depts of two electric utilities; joined Dominion Resources Inc. 1984, apptd Pres. 1990, Vice-Chair., Pres. and CEO 2000, Chair., Pres. and CEO 2000–03, Chair. and CEO 2003–06, Chair. 2006–07 (retd); Chair. and Dir Virginia Electric and Power Co., Consolidated Natural Gas Co.; mem. Bd of Dirs Amerigroup Corpn 2004–, Associated Electric and Gas Insurance Services Ltd, Shaw Group Inc. 2007–; mem. Bd of Visitors Coll. of William and Mary; Trustee Univ. of Richmond, Virginia Foundation of Ind. Colls.

CAPRA, Carlo; Italian historian and academic (retd); b. 14 Nov. 1938, Quartu S. Elena, Cagliari; s. of Agostino Capra and Maria Maxia; m. Maria Grazia Bosi 1964; one s.; ed Università degli Studi, Milan; teacher of English in state secondary schools –1970; Asst Lecturer in History, Università degli Studi, Milan 1970–72, Reader 1972–81, Assoc. Prof. 1981–86, Prof. 1986–2008, Head, Dept of History 1989–92; mem. Scientific Council, Società Italiana di Studi sul XVIII Secolo; Gen. Ed. Edizione Nazionale delle Opere di Pietro Verri; Co-ed. Società e storia (journal), Storia (series), Settecento italiano (series). *Publications:* Giovanni Ristori da illuminista a funzionario (1755–1830) 1968, Il giornalismo nell'età rivoluzionaria e napoleonica 1976, La Lombardia austriaca nell'età delle riforme 1984, 1987, Cesare Beccaria, Carleggio Vols IV–V di Edizione Nazionale delle Opere (ed.) 1995, I progressi della ragione: Vita di Pietro Verri 2002, Storia moderna 2004, Pietro Verri, Scritti politici della maturità (ed.) 2010. *Leisure interests:* music, cinema. *Address:* Corso Garibaldi 71, Milan 20121, Italy (home). *Telephone:* (02) 86461509 (home). *E-mail:* carlo.capra1@unimi.it (home).

CAPRIATI, Jennifer Maria; American professional tennis player; b. 29 March 1976, New York; d. of Stefano Capriati and Denise Capriati; ed Pasco High School, Fla; coached by her father; winner, French Open Jr 1989, US Open Jr 1989, Wimbledon and US Open Jr Doubles 1989; youngest player in Whiteman Cup 1989; youngest player to reach a professional final (aged 13 years and 11 months at Boca Raton 1990); gold medal (Olympic Games of 1992); Wimbledon debut 1990; semi-finalist French Open 1990, 2002, US Open 1991, 2001, 2003, Wimbledon 1991 (youngest Grand Slam semi-finalist in tennis history); 2001; won Australian Open 2001, 2002, French Open 2001; 15 career professional titles in total (one doubles title); Int. Tennis Fed. World Champion 2001. *Leisure interests:* dancing, golf, music, reading, writing. *Address:* International Management Group, c/o Barbara Perry, 22 East 71st Street, New York, NY 10021, USA.

CAPRILES RADONSKI, Henrique; Venezuelan lawyer and politician; b. 11 July 1972, Caracas; ed Universidad Católica Andrés Bello, Cen. Univ. of Venezuela, IBFD Int. Tax Acad., Amsterdam, Centro Interamericano de Administradores Tributarios, Viterbo, Italy, Columbia Univ., USA; worked for several law firms in private sector, including Nevett & Mezquita Abogados and Hoet, Pelaez, Castillo & Duque; Vice-Pres. Chamber of Deputies (COPEI Party) 1998–99; Mayor, Baruta Municipality of Caracas 2000–08; Gov. of Miranda 2008–June 2012, Dec. 2012–; unsuccessful cand. in presidential elections 2012, 2013; mem. Int. Fiscal Asscn, World Asscn of Young Jurors, Cttee of Taxes, Venezuelan American Chamber of Industry and Commerce;*Website:* www .miranda.gob.ve; www.hayuncamino.com.

CAPRON, Alexander Morgan, LLB; American academic and lawyer; *University Professor and Scott H. Bice Chair in Healthcare Law, Policy and Ethics, University of Southern California;* b. 16 Aug. 1944, Hartford, Conn.; s. of William M. Capron and Margaret Capron (née Morgan); m. 1st Barbara A. Brown 1969 (divorced 1985); m. 2nd Kathleen M. West 1989; four c.; ed Palo Alto High School, Swarthmore Coll. and Yale Law School; law clerk to Chief Judge, US Court of Appeals, DC Circuit 1969–70; Lecturer and Research Assoc., Yale Law School 1970–72; Asst Prof. to Prof. of Law and Prof. of Human Genetics, Univ. of Pennsylvania 1972–82; Exec. Dir Pres.'s Comm. for Study of Ethical Problems in Medicine and Biomedical and Behavioural Research 1979–83; Prof. of Law, Ethics and Public Policy, Georgetown Univ. 1983–84; Topping Prof. of Law, Medicine and Public Policy, Univ. of Southern California 1985–89, Univ. Prof. 1989–, Co-Dir Pacific Center for Health Policy and Ethics 1990–, Henry W. Bruce Prof. of Law 1991–2006, Scott H. Bice Chair in Healthcare Law, Policy and Ethics 2006–, Pres. Univ. Faculty 2009–10, Vice-Dean Law School 2011–13; Dir Ethics, Trade, Human Rights and Health Law, WHO 2002–06; Pres. American Soc. of Law and Medicine 1988–89; Pres. Int. Asscn of Bioethics 2005–07; Chair. Biomedical Ethics Advisory Cttee, US Congress 1988–91, Public Responsibility in Medicine and Research (PRIM&R) 2013–; mem. Nat. Bioethics Advisory Comm. 1996–2001; Hon. Fellow, American Coll. of Legal Medicine; Hon. MA (Univ. of Pennsylvania); several honours and awards. *Publications:* books including Catastrophic Diseases: Who Decides What? (with J. Katz) 1975, Law, Science and Medicine (with others) 1984, Treatise on Health Care Law (with others) 1991; 230 articles in journals and books. *Leisure interests:* gardening, films, travel. *Address:* Gould School of Law, University of Southern California, 699 Exposition Blvd, Los Angeles, CA 90089-0071, USA (office). *Telephone:* (213) 740-2557 (office). *Fax:* (213) 740-5502 (office). *E-mail:* acapron@law.usc.edu (office). *Website:* lawweb.usc.edu/who/faculty/ directory/contactInfo.cfm?detailID=205 (office).

CAPUÑAY, Juan Carlos, BEcons; Peruvian diplomatist and international organization official; *Ambassador to Japan;* b. 1948; ed Nat. Univ. of San Marcos; joined Ministry of Foreign Affairs 1972, Third Sec., Embassy in Tokyo 1973–76, Second Sec. 1976, Second Sec., Perm. Mission to UN, New York 1976–79, First Sec. 1979–82, First Sec., Perm. Mission to OAS 1982–83, Counsellor 1983–86, Minister Counsellor and Alt. Rep. 1986–91, Minister, Embassy in Tokyo and Alt. Rep. to Int. Org. for Tropical Woods 1991–94, Minister, Embassy in Beijing 1994–97, Minister, Chargé d'Affaires to Singapore 1997–98, Amb. to Singapore and Brunei 1998–2003, Amb. and Dir-Gen. Asia-Pacific Econ. Co-operation (APEC) Div., also Sr Official of Peru in APEC Under-Secr. for Asia and Pacific Basin Affairs 2003–07, Amb. and Deputy Exec. Dir APEC Secr. 2007, Exec. Dir 2008; Amb. to Japan 2009–; official decorations from Japan, Repub. of Korea and Chile. *Address:* Embassy of Peru, 4-100-1, Higashi, Shibuya-ku, Tokyo 150-0011, Japan (office). *Telephone:* (3) 3406-4243 (office). *Fax:* (3) 3409-7589 (office). *E-mail:* embperutokyo@embperujapan.org (office).

CAPUS, Steve, BA; American media executive; b. 1963; m. Sophia Faskianos; two s. one d.; ed Temple Univ.; with WCAU-TV, Philadelphia 1986; joined KYW-TV, Philadelphia 1987, Exec. Producer 1990–93; joined NBC as Sr Producer NBC Nightside, 1993, Broadcast Producer NBC News Sunrise 1994, Supervising Producer Today Show 1995, Sr Producer MSNBC daytime news 1996–97, Exec. Producer The News with Brian Williams (MSNBC) 1997–2001, Exec. Producer, Nightly News show 2001–05, Sr Vice-Pres., News Division June–Nov. 2005, Pres. NBC News Nov. 2005–13; Alfred I. DuPont-Columbia Award, four Emmys, six Edward R. Murrow Awards, six Nat. Headliner Awards. *Address:* c/o NBC News, 30 Rockefeller Plaza, New York, NY 10112, USA.

CAPUTO, Dante; Argentine politician, diplomatist and academic; *Secretary for Political Affairs, Organization of American States;* b. 25 Nov. 1943, Buenos Aires; m. Anne Morel; three s.; ed Salvador Univ. of Buenos Aires, Univ. of Paris, Tufts Univ. and Harvard Univ., USA; secondary school teacher 1962–64; Adjunct Prof. of Political Sociology, Salvador Univ., Buenos Aires 1973–74; Assoc. Prof. of Public Admin, Univ. of Buenos Aires 1973–74, Assoc. Prof. of Admin. Systems 1973–74, Prof. of Int. Relations 2000; Prof. of Int. Relations, Nat. Univ. of Quilmes 1996–97, Universidad Nacional de la Plata 1998–99; Nat. Deputy 1989–92, 1997–99; Sec. of State for Tech., Science and Useful Innovations 1999–2001; Dir Center for Social Investigations on State and Admin. 1976; Adjunct Investigator, Nat. Center for Scientific Investigation, France; Minister of Foreign Affairs and of Worship 1983–89; Pres. UN Gen. Ass. 1988–89; Special Rep. of UN Sec.-Gen. in Haiti 1993–94; Vice-Pres. ASO FREP 1996–2000; Dir UNDP Regional Project on

Democratic Devt in Latin America 2001–04; Sec. for Political Affairs, OAS, Washington, DC 2006–; Founder and Dir Bimestre Político y económico, Buenos Aires 1981–92. *Address:* Organization of American States, 17th St and Constitution Ave, NW, Washington, DC 20006, USA (office). *Telephone:* (202) 458-3000 (office). *Fax:* (202) 458-6319 (office). *E-mail:* pi@oas.org (office). *Website:* www.oas .org (office).

CARACCIOLO DI VIETRI, Giovanni; Italian diplomatist; *Ambassador to France;* b. 5 Dec. 1947, Rome; ed Lycée Châteaubriand, Rome, Univ. of Rome; entered Foreign Service 1971, held several positions, including assignment to Directorate Gen. for Personnel and Admin and Minister's Pvt. Office, First Sec., Embassy in Addis Ababa 1977–80, in Washington, DC 1980–86, assigned to Secr. Gen. of Presidency of the Repub., Office of Diplomatic Affairs 1986–87, Adjunct Diplomatic Advisor to Pres. of the Repub. 1987–92, Consul Gen. in Paris 1992–96, Deputy Dir Gen. for Emigration and Social Affairs, Rome 1996–2000, Minister Plenipotentiary and Amb. to Serbia and Montenegro 2000–04, Dir Gen. for the Countries of Europe 2004–6, Amb. and Head of Perm. Mission to Int. Orgs, Geneva 2006–09, Amb. to France 2009–. *Address:* Embassy of Italy, 51 rue de Varenne, 75343 Paris Cedex 07, France (office). *Telephone:* 1-49-54-03-00 (office). *Fax:* 1-45-54-04-10 (office). *E-mail:* ambasciata.parigi@esteri.it (office). *Website:* www .ambparigi.esteri.it (office).

CARAMITRU, Ion; Romanian actor, theatre director and politician; *General Director, National Theatre of Bucharest;* b. 9 March 1942, Bucharest; s. of Aristide Caramitru and Maria Caramitru; m. Michaela Caracas 1975; three s.; ed Theatre and Cinema Art Inst., Bucharest; actor and dir Lucia Sturdza Bulandra Theatre, Bucharest 1965–90, Artistic Dir 1990–93, 1996–2000; Acting Prof., I.L.Caragiale Acad. of Drama and Film, Bucharest 1976–81; mem. Exec. Bureau, Council of Nat. Salvation Front 1989, Pres. of Cultural Cttee 1990; Vice-Pres. of Prov. Council for Nat. Unity (responsibility for cultural and youth problems) Feb.–May 1990; Founder and Pres. ITI Romanian Centre, Romanian Theatre Union (UNITER) 1990–; Minister of Culture 1996–2000; currently Gen. Dir Nat. Theatre of Bucharest; Vice-Pres. PNTCD 2001–06 (resgnd); Hon. OBE 1995, Chevalier des Arts et Lettres 1997; Best Actor of the Year 1975, 1979, 1981, 1985, Cinema magazine FIlm Award 1976, "Special Award of the Jury" for leading part in Luchian, Nat. Film Festival, Costinesti 1984. *Principal roles include:* Romeo, Hamlet, Julius Caesar, Feste, Brutus, Leonce (Büchner), Eugene Marchbanks (Bernard Shaw), Cotrone (Pirandello), Perdican (Musset), Riccardo Fontana (Rolf Hochhuth) etc. *Directed:* Remembrances (Aleksei Arbuzov), Insignificance (Terry Johnson), Dialogues (author's performance), The Third Stake (Marin Sorescu), The Shape of the Table (David Edgar), Home (David Storey); musical theatre: Eminescu (Paul Urmuzescu), My Fair Lady; opera: The Little Sweep (Benjamin Britten), Carmen (Bizet) for Belfast Opera 1993, Eugene Onegin (Tchaikovsky) for Belfast Opera 1994, Bastien and Bastienne (Mozart) for Tăndărică puppet theatre, Bucharest. *Films include:* The Treasure from Old River Bed, The City Blue Gates, Luchian, Oak – Extreme Urgency, The Purse with Dragonflies, High-School Pupils, Civic Education Test-Write, Darkness, Citizen X, Mission Impossible. *Television appearances:* Jude City (BBC serial) 1992, An Exchange of Fire 1993, A Question of Guilt 1993, Two Deaths (BBC TV) 1994. *Leisure interests:* collecting icons, tennis, writing, painted popular eggs. *Address:* National Theatre of Bucharest, 2, Nicolae Bălcescu boulevard, 010051, Sector 1, Bucharest (office); UNITER, 2–4, George Enescu Str., Bucharest; 16, Caderea Bastiliei, Sector 1, Bucharest, Romania (home). *Telephone:* (21) 313 9437 (office); (21) 3113214 (UNITER); (21) 2106337 (home). *Fax:* (21) 3123169 (office); (21) 3120913 (UNITER); (21) 2105783 (home). *E-mail:* contact@tncaragiale.ro (office). *Website:* www.tnb.ro (office).

CARBONEZ, Luc, LLD; Belgian diplomatist; b. 1946; m. Marie-Claire Carbonez-deJager; four d.; ed Univ. of Louvain; joined Diplomatic Corps 1978, has served in numerous positions including Attaché, Embassy in Dublin 1979–80, Embassy Sec., Abidjan 1980–84, Consul, Lille 1984–88, Deputy Head of Mission, Vienna 1988–92; Counsellor for Foreign Affairs, Brussels 1992–94, Minister-Counsellor and Perm. Deputy Rep. of Belgium to EU 1994–97, Amb. to Canada 1997–2002; Dir European Security, Ministry of Foreign Affairs 2002–06; Amb. to the Netherlands 2006–11. *Address:* Federal Public Service of Foreign Affairs, Foreign Trade and Development Co-operation, 15 rue des Petits Carmes, 1000 Brussels, Belgium (office). *Telephone:* (2) 501-81-11 (office). *Fax:* (2) 501-81-70 (office). *E-mail:* contact@ diplobel.fed.be (office). *Website:* www.diplomatie.be (office).

CARCASSES, Moana Jacques Raymond Kalosil; Ni-Vanuatu politician; *Prime Minister;* b. 27 Jan. 1963, Tahiti; m. Marie Louise Milne; Leader, Green Confederation Party 2001–; mem. (Green Confederation Party) Parl.; Minister of Foreign Affairs 2003–04, for Finance and Econ. Devt 2004–05; Deputy Leader of the Opposition 2006–08; Minister of Internal Affairs 2009–10, of Finance and Econ. Man. 2010–11, 2011–12; Prime Minister 2013–. *Leisure interests:* rock and roll, dance (especially Bolero), Elvis Presley, golf, rugby. *Address:* Prime Minister's Office, PMB 9053, Port Vila, Vanuatu (office). *Telephone:* 22413 (office). *Fax:* 26301 (office). *E-mail:* mkcarcasses@vanuatu.gov.vu (office). *Website:* www .governmentofvanuatu.gov.vu (office).

CARCIERI, Donald L. (Don), BA; American business executive, politician, fmr state governor and fmr teacher; b. 16 Dec. 1942, East Greenwich, RI; s. of Nicola J. Carcieri and Marguerite E. Carcieri (née Anderson); m. Suzanne Owren; one s. three d.; ed East Greenwich High School, Brown Univ.; fmr math. teacher, Rogers High School, Newport, RI, Concord Carlisle Regional High School, Concord, Mass; various positions rising to Exec. Vice-Pres., Old Stone Bank 1971–81; Head of Catholic Relief Service's West Indies operation, Kingston, Jamaica 1981–83; joined Cookson America 1983, rising to CEO and Jt Man. Dir Cookson Group Worldwide; Gov. of RI 2003–11; co-f. (with his wife) Academy Children's Science Center, East Greenwich; fmr Chair. Rhode Island Math./Science Educ. Coalition; Dir Providence Center, RI; mem. Catholic Relief Services Leadership Council; Republican. *Address:* c/o Office of the Governor, State House, Room 115, Providence, RI 02903-1196, USA.

CARD, Andrew (Andy) H., Jr, BS; American government official and business executive; b. 10 May 1947, Brockton, Mass.; m. Kathleene Card; three c.; ed USA Merchant Marine Acad., Univ. of South Carolina; served in USN 1965–67; Engineer, Maurice Reidy Engineers, Inc. 1971–72, David M. Berg Inc. 1972–75;

mem. Mass. House of Reps 1975–83; Special Asst for Inter-governmental Affairs, The White House, Washington, DC 1983–87; Dir Office of Intergovernmental Affairs 1988, Asst to Pres. George H. W. Bush and Deputy Chief of Staff 1989–92; New Hampshire Campaign Man. for George H. W. Bush 1987–88; Sec. of Transportation 1992–93; Pres. and CEO American Automobile Mfrs Asscn 1993–98; Vice-Pres. for Governmental Relations, Gen. Motors Corpn 1999–2000; Chief of Staff to President George W. Bush 2000–06 (resgnd); mem. Bd of Dirs Union Pacific Corpn 2006–; Dr hc (Univ. of Massachusetts) 2007; named Legislator of the Year by Nat. Republican Legislators Asscn 1982, Mass. Municipal Asscn Distinguished Legislator Award 1982. *Address:* 1207 Buchanan Street, McLean, VA 22101, USA.

CARDEN, Joan Maralyn, AO, OBE; Australian opera singer (soprano); b. 9 Oct. 1937, Richmond, Vic.; d. of the late Frank Carden and of Margaret Carden (née Cooke); m. William Coyne 1962 (divorced 1980); two d.; ed Trinity Coll. of Music, London, Stuyvesant Scholar at London Opera Centre, voice studies with Thea Phillips and Henry Portnoj, Melbourne, Vida Harford, London, and David Harper, UK/Australia; nat. debut: Grisette in Merry Widow with June Bronhill, Melbourne 1960; int. debut, world premiere of Malcolm Williamson's Our Man in Havana, Sadler's Wells 1963; joined Australian Opera (Opera Australia) 1971: Royal Opera, Covent Garden as Gilda in Rigoletto 1974, Glyndebourne as Anna in Don Giovanni 1977, Scottish Opera as Constanze 1977; soloist, Sydney Opera House from opening 1974–2003; US debut at Houston as Amenaide in Tancredi 1977; Metropolitan Opera tour as Anna in Don Giovanni 1978, Kennedy Center 1980, Miami Opera 1981; Singapore Festival 1983; Adelaide Festival 1984; other appearances include Victoria State Opera, Lyric Opera of Queensland, State Opera of South Australia; over 50 major roles including most Mozart heroines, Liu in Turandot, Marguerite in Faust, Gilda in Rigoletto, four heroines in Contes d'Hoffmann, Natasha in War and Peace, Tatyana in Onegin (in English and Russian), Lakmé, Leonora in Forza del Destino/Il Trovatore, Violetta in La Traviata, Alice in Falstaff, Mimi, Musetta in La Bohème, Madama Butterfly, Eva in Die Meistersinger, Feldmarschallin in Der Rosenkavalier, Elisabetta in Maria Stuarda, Médée, Tosca, Public Opinion in Orpheus in the Underworld, Mother Abbess in Sound of Music, Ida Straus in Titanic 2006, Mother Superior in Harp on the Willow 2007; concerts with Australian, Sydney, Melbourne, and Queensland Symphony Orchestras and for Australian Broadcasting Corpn, Sydney Univ. Graduates Choir (sponsors of Joan Carden Award, Sydney Conservatorium 2004–); repertoire includes Mozart Masses, concert arias, choral works, Vier Letzte Lieder (R. Strauss), Britten, works by Australian composers including Moya Henderson, Peter Sculthorpe, Nigel Butterley; soloist at numerous state and fed. occasions, including 1988 bicentenary, royal and presidential state visits; est. Joan Carden Award, Sydney Conservatorium of Music 2004; Hon. DUniv (Swinburne Univ. of Tech., Melbourne) 2000, (Australian Catholic Univ., Sydney); Dame Joan Hammond Award for Outstanding Service to Opera in Australia 1987, Australian Govt Creative Fellowship 1993, Australian Govt Fed. Centenary Medal 2001. *Recordings include:* Joan Carden Sings Mozart, Great Opera Heroines: Joan Carden, The Australian Opera, Mozart: A Bicentennial Celebration, Stars of The Australian Opera Sing Verdi; Verdi aria in Priscilla, Queen of the Desert, film score. *Leisure interests:* dogs, walking, writing, gardening, reading, history. *Address:* Opera Australia, PO Box 291, Strawberry Hills, NSW 2012, Australia (office). *Telephone:* (2) 9699-1099 (office). *Website:* www.opera-australia.org.au (office).

CARDENAL, Ernesto; Nicaraguan poet, priest and fmr government official; b. 20 Jan. 1925, Granada; s. of Rodolfo Cardenal and Esmerelda Cardenal (née Martínez); ed Univ. of Mexico, Columbia Univ., New York, USA; ordained RC priest 1965–; Minister of Culture 1979–90; Co-founder and Hon. Pres. Casa de los Tres Mundos (literary org.); Premio de la Paz 1980, Queen Sofia Ibero-American Poetry Award 2012. *Publications:* Proclama del conquistador 1947, Gethsemani Ky 1960, Hora 0 1960, Epigramas 1961, Poemas 1961, Salmos 1964, Oración por Marilyn Monroe y otros poemas 1965, La voz de un monje en la era nuclear 1965, El estrecho dudoso 1966, Homenaje a los Indios Americanos 1969, Mayapán 1970, Vida en el amor 1971, La hora cero y otros poemas 1971, Canto nacional al F.S.L.N. 1972, Oráculo sobre Managua 1973, El evangelio en solentiname 1975, La santidad de la revolución 1976, Cátulo marcial 1978, Nueva antología poética 1978, Viaje a New York 1980, Nostalgia del futuro 1982, Crónica de un reencuentro 1982, Waslala 1983, Vuelos de victoria 1984, With Walker in Nicaragua and other early poems 1949–54 1984, Quetzalcoatl 1985, Nuevo cielo y tierra nueva 1985, From Nicaragua with Love: Poems 1976–1986 1986, Cántico cósmico 1989, La noche iluminada de palabras 1991, Los ovnis de oro 1991, El telescopio en la noche oscura 1993, Del monasterio al mundo: correspondencia entre Ernesto Cardenal y Thomas Merton 1998, Vida perdida 1999, Los años de Granada 2002, Las ínsulas extrañas 2002, La revolución perdida 2003, Thomas Merton—Ernesto Cardenal: Correspondencia (1959–1968) 2004, Versos del pluriverso 2005. *E-mail:* escritor@ibw.com.ni (office).

CARDENAS CONDE, Victor Hugo, BA; Bolivian politician and academic; *Leader, Tupac Katari Revolutionary Liberation Movement Party;* b. 4 June 1951, Achica Abajo Aymara Indian community, Omasuyos Prov., Dept of La Paz; m. Lidia Katari 1980; one s. two d.; ed Ayacucho High School, Universidad Mayor de San Andrés; Lecturer, then Prof. in Educ. Sciences, Linguistics and Languages, Faculty of Humanities and Educ., Universidad Mayor de San Andrés 1975–92; Chair. First Nat. Congress for Peasant Unity 1979; consultant on educational issues UNESCO and UNICEF 1990, various other orgs 1992; Prof., Latin American Coll. of Social Sciences 1992–93; Nat. Rep. Tupac Katari Revolutionary Liberation Movt party (MRTKL), Exec. Sec. (Nat. Exec. Cttee) 1993, currently Leader; Pres. Nat. Congress 1993–94, Andean Parl. 1993–94, Science and Tech. Nat. Council 1993–94; Vice-Pres. of Bolivia 1993–97; mem. Culture and Educ. Comm., Bolivian Workers Union 1979, Educ. and Culture Comm., House of Reps 1985–86, political forum of Latin American Inst. for Social Research 1992–93, Exec. Council UNESCO 1995–2000; Fray Bartolomé de las Casas Award (Spain) 1994. *Publications include:* articles on culture, educ. and history in local and foreign books, journals and newspapers. *Address:* Movimiento Revolucionario Túpac Katarí de Liberación, Avda Baptista 939, Casilla 9133, La Paz, Bolivia. *Telephone:* (2) 235-4784.

CÁRDENAS SOLÓRZANO, Cuauhtémoc; Mexican politician; *President, Fundación para la democracia;* b. 1 May 1934, Mexico City; s. of Lázaro Cárdenas and Amalia Solórzano; m. Celeste Batel; two s. one d.; ed Escuela Nacional de Ingenieros, Universidad Nacional Autónoma de México; Senator from Michoacán 1976–82; Under-Sec. for Forestry and Wildlife 1976–80; Gov. of Michoacán 1980–86; cand. for presidency (Frente Democrático Nacional) 1988, (Partido de la Revolución Democrática—PRD) 1994, (Allianza por México) 2000; Pres. PRD 1988–93; Pres. Fundación para la democracia—alternativa y debate 1995–; Mayor of Mexico City 1997–99; Vice-Pres. Socialist International 2003–; Grand officier, Ordre nat. du Mérite (France) 1999; Cardenal Cisneros Medal, Universidad Complutense, Madrid (Spain) 1991. *Publications include:* Nuestra lucha a penas comienza 1988, Nace—una esperanza 1990, El proyecto nacional de la Revolució mexicana, un camino a retomar 1990, La esperanza en marcha. Ideario politico 1998, Palabras de Cárdenas 1999. *Leisure interests:* reading, travel. *Address:* Fundación para la democracia, Guadalajara No. 88 Col. Roma, 06700 México, DF (office); Edgar Allan Poe No. 28-1102, 11560 México, DF, Mexico (home). *Telephone:* (55) 5286-1114 (office). *Fax:* (55) 5286-1114 (office). *E-mail:* c_cardenas@mexico.com (office).

CARDIN, Benjamin L., BA, LLB, JD; American politician; *Senator from Maryland;* b. 5 Oct. 1943, Baltimore, Md; s. of Meyer M. Cardin and Dora Cardin (née Green); m. Myrna Edelman; one s. (died 1998) one d.; ed Baltimore public schools, Univ. of Pittsburgh and Univ. of Maryland School of Law; admitted to Maryland Bar 1967; mem. US House of Reps, 3rd Congressional Dist of Md 1987–2007, House Speaker 1979–86, Chair. Ways and Means Cttee 1974–79, Savings and Loan Oversight Cttee 1986, State Fed. Ass., Nat. Conf. of State Legislatures 1980–81, mem. several other cttees, Chair. Democratic Transition Team 1994; mem. House of Dels, representing Dist 5 and Dist 42 (Baltimore City) 1967–86, Asst Democratic Whip 1987–2003, Sr Democratic Whip 2003–07; Senator from Maryland 2007–, mem. numerous cttees, Chair. Int. Devt and Foreign Assistance, Econ. Affairs and Int. Environmental Protection Sub-cttee 2011–12, Chair. East Asian and Pacific Affairs Sub-cttee 2013–), Co-Chair. CSCE (Helsinki Comm.) 2007–; mem. Gov.'s Comm. on Domestic Relations Laws 1976–86 and numerous other comms; mem. Bd of Trustees, St Mary's Coll. of Maryland 1988–99, mem. Advisory Bd, Center for the Study of Democracy 2002–; mem. Bd of Visitors, Univ. of Maryland School of Law 1989–, Univ. of Maryland, Baltimore Co. 1998–, US Naval Acad. 2007–; Democrat; hon. degrees (Univ. of Baltimore School of Law) 1990, (Univ. of Maryland at Baltimore) 1993, (Baltimore Hebrew Univ.) 1994, (Goucher Coll.) 1996; numerous awards including Israel Freedom Award 1992, Congressional Award, Small Business Council of America 1993, 1999, H. Vernon Eney Award, Maryland Bar Foundation 1996, Representative of the Year Award, Nat. Asscn of Police Organizations 1998, Arthur W. Machen, Jr., Award, Maryland Legal Services Corpn 1998, Dr. Nathan Davis Award for Outstanding Government Service, American Medical Asscn 1999, Jacob K. Javits Award, American Psychiatric Asscn 1999, Congressional Advocate of the Year Award, Child Welfare League of America 2000, 2005, named by Worth Magazine amongst top "100 people who have influenced the way Americans think about money" 2001, Congressional Leadership Award, American Coll. of Emergency Physicians 2001, Public Sector Distinguished Service Award, Tax Foundation 2003, named by Treasury and Risk Management Magazine amongst the 100 Most Influential People in Finance 2004, Congressional Award, Small Business Council of America 2005, Friend of Farm Bureau Award, Maryland Farm Bureau 2009, Lifetime Achievement Award, Law and Health Care Program, Univ. of Maryland School of Law 2009, Anti-Poverty Award, Frederick Co. Community Action Agency 2009, Whitney M. Young, Jr Award, Greater Baltimore Urban League 2011, Conservation Champion, Audubon Soc. 2011, Bird Conservation Leader of the Year Award, American Bird Conservancy 2011, Friend of the Nat. Parks Award, Nat. Parks Conservation Asscn 2011, Congressional Champion Award, Nat. Asscn for Equal Opportunity in Higher Educ. 2012, Chesapeake Conservation Hero Award, Chesapeake Conservancy 2012, Congressional Award, Devt Dist Asscn of Appalachia 2012. *Address:* 509 Hart Senate Office Building, Washington, DC 20510, USA (office). *Telephone:* (202) 224-4524 (office). *Fax:* (202) 224-1651 (office). *Website:* cardin.senate.gov (office); www.bencardin.com.

CARDIN, Pierre; French couturier; b. 2 July 1922, San Biagio di Callatla, Italy; fmrly worked with Christian Dior; f. fashion house 1949; f. Espace Pierre Cardin (theatre group); Dir Ambassadeurs-Pierre Cardin Theatre (now Espace Pierre Cardin Theatre) 1970–; Man. Société Pierre Cardin 1973; Chair. Maxims 1982–; Exhbn at Victoria and Albert Museum 1990; mem. Acad. des Beaux-Arts; Hon. UNESCO Amb. 1991–; Grand Officer, Order of Merit (Italy) 1988; Order of the Sacred Treasure (Gold and Silver Star) 1991; Officier, Légion d'honneur 1997; Fashion Oscar 1985; Council of Fashion Designers of America International Award 2007. *Publications:* Fernand Léger, Sa vie, Son oeuvre, Son rêve 1971, Le Conte du Ver à Soie 1992 (Prix Saint-Exupéry valeurs-jeunesse 1992). *Address:* Haute Couture 14, place Francois-1er, 8e, 75008 Paris (office); 27 avenue Marigny, 75008 Paris, France (office); Pierre Cardin, 7 rue Royale, 75008 Paris (office); Institut de France, 23 quai Conti, 75006 Paris (office). *Website:* www.pierrecardin.com; www.maxims-de-paris.com.

CARDINAL, Douglas Joseph, OC, BArch, FRAIC, RCA; Canadian architect; b. 7 March 1934, Calgary, Alberta; s. of Joseph Treffle Cardinal and Frances Margarete Rach; m. 1st Marilyn Zahar 1973; three s. three d.; m. 2nd Idoia Arana-Beobide 1996; ed Univ. of British Columbia, Univ. of Texas; design architect, Bissell & Halman, Red Deer 1963–64; Prin. Douglas Cardinal Architect, Red Deer 1964–67, Edmonton 1967–76, Douglas J. Cardinal Architect Ltd, Edmonton 1976–1985, Ottawa 1985–; Honour Award, Alberta Asscn of Architects, for St Mary's Church 1969 and Award of Excellence, Canadian Architect Magazine, for Grande Prairie Regional Coll. 1972, Governor General's Award in Visual and Media Arts in March 2001. *Major works include:* St Mary's Church, Red Deer, Alberta, Grande Prairie Regional Coll., Grande Prairie, Alberta, Ponoka Provincial Bldg, Ponoka, Alberta, St Albert Place, St Albert, Alberta, Canadian Museum of Civilization, Hull, Québec, Nat. Museum of the American Indian, Washington, DC. *Publications include:* contribs to Of the Spirit 1977 and Human Values: A Primary Motive in Planning 1981. *Address:* Douglas J. Cardinal Architect Ltd., 14 Lodge Road, Suite 200, Ottawa, ON K2C 3H1, Canada (office). *Telephone:* (613) 440-2262 (office). *Fax:* (613) 440-2187 (office). *E-mail:* info@djcarchitect.com (office). *Website:* www.djcarchitect.com (office).

CARDINALE, Claudia; Italian actress; b. 15 April 1939, Tunis, Tunisia; d. of Franco Cardinale and Yolanda Cardinale; m. Franco Cristaldi 1966; one s.; ed Lycée Carnot and Collège Paul Cambon, Tunis; made first film 1958; awards include Nastro d'Argento, David di Donatello, Grolla d'Oro; UNESCO Goodwill Amb.; Golden Apple for Contrib. to European Cinema, European Actors' Awards 2003. *Films include:* 8½, The Pink Panther, The Leopard, The Professionals, Once Upon a Time in the West, Fury, The Magnificent Showman, La Scoumoune, Fitzcarraldo 1982, Le Ruffian 1982, History (TV), A Man in Love 1988, The French Revolution 1989, Hiver '54, L'abbé Pierre, Mother, 588 Rue Paradis, Son of the Pink Panther 1993, Women Only Have One Thing On Their Minds, Un café... l'addition 1999, Li chiamarono... briganti! 1999, And Now... Ladies and Gentlemen 2002, Le Démon de midi 2005. *Address:* c/o Carole Levi, Via Pisanelli 2, 00196 Rome, Italy.

CARDONA, Manuel, PhD, DrSc, FRSC, FInstP, FAPS; Spanish/German physicist and academic; *Director Emeritus, Max-Planck-Institut für Festkörperforschung;* b. (Manuel Cardona Castro), 7 Sept. 1934, Barcelona, Spain; s. of Juan Cardona and Angela Castro; m. Inge Hecht 1959; two s. one d.; ed Univs of Barcelona and Madrid and Harvard Univ., USA; Research Asst, Harvard Univ. 1956–59; mem. tech. staff, RCA Labs Ltd, Zürich 1959–61, Princeton, NJ 1961–64; Assoc. Prof. of Physics, Brown Univ., Providence, RI 1964–66, Prof. 1966–71; Scientific mem. and Founding Dir Max Planck Institut für Festkörperforschung (Inst. for Solid State Research), Stuttgart 1971–, now Emer. Dir, Business Man. Dir 1973–74; mem. various advisory bds, professional bodies, etc.; mem. Comité Nat. d'Evaluation de la Recherche (France) 1999–2002; Lecturer, Air NZ 2001; mem. NAS, Academia Europaea, Mexican Acad. of Science 2002–, Accad. Nazionale dei Lincei 2008, Inst. of Physics; Fellow, American Physical Soc.; Grand Cross of Alfonso X el Sabio; Dr hc (Madrid, Barcelona) 1985, (Sherbrook Univ., Canada) 1993, (Regensburg) 1994, (Rome) 1995, (Toulouse) 1998, (Thessaloniki) 2001, (Brno) 2002, (Valencia) 2004, (La Laguna, Canary Islands) 2006, (Cinvestav, Mexico) 2010; A.D. Sloan Fellowship 1965–68, Guggenheim Fellowship 1969–70, Prince of Asturias Prize 1988, F. Isakson Prize, American Physical Soc. 1988, Italgas Prize 1993, Mateucci Medal, Italian Physical Soc. 1994, J. Wheatley Prize, American Physical Soc. 1997, E. Mach Medal (Czech Repub.) 1999, Mott Medal and Award (UK) 2001, Blaise Pascal Medal, European Acad. of Science 2004, Leloir Prize (Argentina), Bernadski Medal, Phonon Conf. Prize 2012, Luis Leloir Prize (Argentina) 2012 and numerous other awards and distinctions. *Publications:* Modulation Spectroscopy 1969, Light Scattering in Solids, Vols I–IX 1975–2007, Photoemission in Solids, Vols I–II 1978–81, Fundamentals of Semiconductors 1996 (fourth edn 2010). *Leisure interests:* reading, travel, listening to music. *Address:* Max-Planck-Institut für Festkörperforschung, Heisenbergstrasse 1, 70569 Stuttgart, Germany (office). *Telephone:* (711) 6891710 (office). *Fax:* (711) 6891712 (office). *E-mail:* m.cardona@fkf.mpg.de (office).

CARDOSO, Fernando Henrique, BA, MA, PhD; Brazilian sociologist, academic and fmr head of state; b. 18 June 1931, Rio de Janeiro; m. Ruth Corrêa Leite Cardoso 1953 (died 2008); three c.; ed Univs of São Paulo and Paris, France; Prof., Latin American Inst. for Econ. and Social Planning (ILPES/CEPAL), Santiago 1964–67; Prof. of Sociological Theory, Univ. of Paris-Nanterre 1967–68; Prof. of Political Science, Univ. of São Paulo 1968–69; Visiting Prof., Stanford Univ., USA 1972, Inst. for Econ. and Social Devt Univ. of Paris 1977, Univ. of California 1981; Simon Bolivar Prof., Univ. of Cambridge, UK 1976; Assoc. Dir of Studies, Inst. for Higher Studies in Social Sciences, Univ. of Paris 1980–81; Prof., Collège de France 1981; Prof. at Large, Watson Inst. for Int. Studies, Brown Univ., USA 2003–; Fed. Senator for State of São Paulo 1983–94; fmr Leader, Brazilian Social Democratic Party (PSDB) in Fed. Senate; Govt Leader in Congress 1985–86; Minister of Foreign Affairs 1992–93, of Economy and Finance 1993–94; Pres. of Brazil 1995–2002; founder, Pres. Fundação Instituto Fernando Henrique Cardoso (think tank) 2004, currently Lifetime mem. Bd of Trustees; Co-Pres. Inter-American Dialogue; mem. of Consultative Comm., Inst. for Advanced Study, Princeton Univ. and Rockefeller Foundation, New York; Pres. of Fundação Osesp; mem. Academia Brasileira de Letras 2013; Foreign Hon. mem. American Acad. of Arts and Sciences;; Grand Cross, Order of Rio Branc, Chevalier, Légion d'honneur, Grand Cross, Order of Merit of Portugal, Order of the Bath (UK), Order of Infante D. Henrique (Portugal), Order of Liberty (Portugal), Order of the Elephant (Denmark), Order of the Star of Romania, Grand Cross (or 1st Class), Order of the White Double Cross (Slovakia) 2001, Order of the White Eagle (Poland) 2002; Dr hc (Rutgers) 1978, (Notre Dame, Ill.) 1991, (Santiago) 1993, (Central of Caracas), (Porto and Coimbra), (Sofia, Japan), (Free Univ. of Berlin), (Lumière Lyon 2), (Bologna), (Cambridge), (London), (Hebrew Univ. of Jerusalem) 2001; Hon. Dr of Sociology (ISCTE-IUL, Portugal) 2012; Fulbright Award for Int. Understanding, Prince of Asturias Award for Int. Co-operation 2000, John W. Kluge Prize for Lifetime Achievement in the Study of Humanity, Library of Congress 2012. *Publications:* São Paulo Growth and Poverty 1978, Dependency and Development in Latin America (co-author) 1979, Fernando Henrique Cardoso: Reinventing Democracy in Brazil 1999, The New Global Economy in the Information Age 1993, Charting a New Course: The Politics of Globalization and Social Transformation (co-ed.) 2001, A Arte da Política 2006, Carta a jovem político 2006, The Accidental President of Brazil 2006. *E-mail:* info@ifhc.org.br. *Website:* www.ifhc.org.br.

CARELL, Steve; American comedian and actor; b. 16 Aug. 1963, Acton, Mass; s. of Edwin A. Carell and Harriet T. Koch; m. Nancy Walls; one s. one d.; ed Denison Univ., Granville, Ohio; fmr mem. Second City, Chicago. *Films include:* Bruce Almighty 2003, Anchorman: The Legend of Ron Burgundy 2004, The 40 Year-Old Virgin 2005 (also co-writer) (MTV Movie Award for Best Comedic Performance 2006), Bewitched 2005, Little Miss Sunshine 2006, Evan Almighty 2007, Dan in Real Life 2007, Horton Hears a Who! (voice) 2008, Get Smart 2008, Dinner for Schmucks 2010, Despicable Me 2010, Date Night 2010, Seeking a Friend for the End of the World 2012, Hope Springs 2012, The Way, Way Back 2013, The Incredible Burt Wonderstone 2013. *Television includes:* The Daily Show 1999–2004, The Office 2005–11 (also co-writer) (2006 Golden Globe Award for Best Actor in Television Comedy).

CARENCO, Jean-François Claude, LL.L.; French administrator; *Prefect of of région Haute-Normandie and Seine-Maritime;* b. 7 July 1952, Talence, Gironde; s. of Guy Carenco and Roselyne Carenco (née Dalmas); m. Magali Serre 1977; two d.; ed Lycée Thiers, Marseilles, Stanislas Coll., Paris and Sorbonne Univ., Ecole Nat.

d'Admin.; Councillor of Administrative Tribunal, Marseille 1979–83; Dir.-Gen. of Dist. of Montpellier 1983–88, Sec.-Gen. 1988–90; Sec.-Gen. of New Caledonia 1990–91; Sec.-Gen. of Prefecture of Yvelines 1991–96; Prefect of Saint-Pierre et Miquelon 1996–97, of Tarn-et-Garonne 1997–99, of Guadeloupe 1999–2002, of Haute-Savoie 2002–04, of région Haute-Normandie and Seine-Maritime 2006–; Chief of Staff Minister of Employment, Labour and Social Cohesion, then Employment, Social Cohesion and Housing 2004–06; Chevalier Légion d'honneur, Ordre nat. du Mérite, des Palmes academiques, Chevalier du Mérite de l'Ordre souverain de Malte. *Publications include:* L'Espérance occitane (jtly) 1979. *Address:* Préfecture de la région Haute-Normandie, 7 place de la Madeleine, 76000 Rouen, France (office).

CAREW, David Omashola, BSc (Econ); Sierra Leonean chartered accountant and politician; m.; two c.; ed Univ. of Sierra Leone; joined KPMG accounting and man. consultancy firm as grad. accountant in 1979, seconded to KPMG Nigeria 1979–86, Audit Supervisor in charge of KPMG's clients in banking and financial institutions industry, Kanu, Asst Man., KPMG, Freetown 1986, Asst Man., then Deputy Man., then Man. and later Sr Man. 1986–88, Pnr, KPMG-Sierra Leone 1989, Pnr, KPMG-Gambia 1991, Man. Pnr for KPMG-Sierra Leone and for delivering KPMG services to clients in The Gambia and Liberia –2007, fmr Dir KPMG Peat Marwick, Freetown; Minister of Finance and Devt 2007–09, of Trade and Industry 2009–10; CEO Freetown Nominees Ltd 2010–; Man Dir Omagbemi Holdings; Fellow, Inst. of Chartered Accountants (Nigeria); Fellow and Past Pres. Inst. of Chartered Accountants (Sierra Leone). *Leisure interests:* golf, philanthropy. *Address:* Freetown Nominees Ltd, 1st Floor, Aureol House, 22 Wallace Johnson Street, Freetown, Sierra Leone (office).

CAREY, Chase; American business executive; *President and Chief Operating Officer, 21st Century Fox;* fmr mem. Bd of Dirs, Pres. and CEO Sky Global Networks, Inc.; worked at Columbia Pictures 1981–87; Co-COO Fox Entertainment Group 1998–2002, Inc., also Chair. and CEO Fox TV, mem. Bd of Dirs 1992–2002; Exec. Dir and Co-COO News Corporation 1996–2002, Deputy Chair., Pres. and COO 2009–13 (co. restructured with News Corporation's publishing assets spun off into similarly named News Corp while existing News Corporation renamed 21st Century Fox as its legal successor 2013), mem. Bd of Dirs 2004–07, 2009–, Pres. and COO 21st Century Fox 2013–; mem. Bd of Dirs The DIRECTV Group, Inc. 2003–, Pres. and CEO 2003–09; Trustee Emer., Colgate Univ. *Address:* 21st Century Fox, 1211 Avenue of the Americas, New York, NY 10036, USA (office). *Telephone:* (212) 852-7000 (office). *Fax:* (212) 852-7145 (office). *Website:* www.21cf.com (office).

CAREY, John, MA, DPhil, FRSL, FBA; British literary critic and academic; *Merton Professor Emeritus of English Literature, University of Oxford;* b. 5 April 1934, London, England; s. of Charles William and Winifred Ethel Carey (née Cook); m. Gillian Mary Florence Booth 1960; two s.; ed Richmond and East Sheen County Grammar School, St John's Coll., Oxford; served in East Surrey Regt 1953–54; Harmsworth Sr Scholar, Merton Coll., Oxford 1957–58; Lecturer, Christ Church, Oxford 1958–59; Andrew Bradley Jr Research Fellow, Balliol Coll., Oxford 1959–60; Tutorial Fellow, Keble Coll., Oxford 1960–64, St John's Coll. 1964–75; Merton Prof. of English Literature, Univ. of Oxford 1976–2001, Prof. Emer. 2001–; Chief Book Reviewer, Sunday Times (London) 1976–; T.S. Eliot Memorial Lecturer, Univ. of Kent 1989; Northcliffe Lecturer, Univ. Coll., London 2004; Chair. Booker Prize Judges 1982, 2003, Int. Booker Prize Judges 2005; Judge, WH Smith Prize 1989–95; Hon. Fellow, St John's Coll. Oxford 1991, Balliol Coll. Oxford 1992; Hon. Prof. Univ. of Liverpool 2004–. *Publications:* The Poems of John Milton (co-ed. with Alastair Fowler) 1968, Milton 1969, The Violent Effigy: A Study of Dickens' Imagination 1973, Thackeray: Prodigal Genius 1977, John Donne: Life, Mind and Art 1981, The Private Memoirs and Confessions of a Justified Sinner, by James Hogg (ed.), William Golding: The Man and His Books (ed.) 1986, Original Copy: Selected Reviews and Journalism 1987, The Faber Book of Reportage (ed.) 1987, John Donne (Oxford Authors) (ed.) 1990, The Intellectuals and the Masses 1992, The Faber Book of Science (ed.) 1995, The Faber Book of Utopias (ed.) 1999, Pure Pleasure 2000, What Good are the Arts? 2005, William Golding: The Man Who Wrote Lord of the Flies (James Tait Black Memorial Prize 2010) 2009; articles in Review of English Studies, Modern Language Review etc. *Leisure interests:* beekeeping, swimming, gardening, etching. *Address:* Brasenose Cottage, Lyneham, Oxon., OX7 6QL (home); 57 Stapleton Road, Headington, Oxford, England (home). *Telephone:* (1865) 764304 (home). *E-mail:* john.carey123@btinternet.com (home).

CAREY, Mariah; American singer and songwriter; b. 22 March 1970, Long Island, NY; m. 1st Tommy Mottola 1993 (divorced 1998); m. 2nd Nick Cannon 2008; fmr backing singer, Brenda K. Starr, New York 1988; solo artist 1988–; f. Crave record label 1997; f. Camp Mariah holiday project for inner-city children; Grammy Awards for Best New Artist, Best New Pop Vocal by a Female Artist 1990, Soul Train Awards for Best New Artist, Best Single by a Female Artist 1990, Rolling Stone Award for Best Female Singer 1991, eight World Music Awards 1991–95, seven Billboard Awards 1991–96, four American Music Awards 1992–96, Int. Dance Music Award for Best Solo Artist 1996, American Music Awards Special Award of Achievement 2000, Lady of Soul Award for Best Solo R&B/Soul Single (for We Belong Together) 2005, Vibe Awards for Artist of the Year, for R&B Voice of the Year, for Best R&B Song (for We Belong Together) 2005, American Music Award for Favorite Female Soul/R&B Artist 2005, Female Billboard 200 Album Artist of the Year 2005, Billboard Music Awards for Hot 100 Song of the Year, Hot 100 Airplay of the Year, Rhythmic Top 40 Title of the Year (all for We Belong Together) 2005, Billboard Music Award for Female R&B/Hip-Hop Artist of the Year 2005, Grammy Award for Best Female R&B Vocal Performance (for We Belong Together) 2006. *Recordings include:* albums: Mariah Carey (Soul Train Award for Best Album by a Female Artist) 1990, Emotions 1991, MTV Unplugged (EP) 1992, Music Box 1993, Merry Christmas 1994, Daydream 1995, Butterfly 1997, #1s 1998, Rainbow 1999, Glitter 2001, Charmbracelet 2002, The Remixes 2003, The Emancipation of Mimi (Lady of Soul Award for Best Solo R&B/Soul Album, Vibe Award for Album of the Year, Grammy Award for Best Contemporary R&B Album 2006, Image Award for Best Album 2006) 2005, E=MC2 2008, Memoirs of an Imperfect Angel 2009, Merry Christmas II You 2010. *Television includes:* judge, American Idol 2013. *Films include:* The Bachelor 1999, Glitter (also soundtrack) 2001, WiseGirls 2002, State Property 2 2005, Tennessee 2008, Precious 2009, The Butler 2013. *Website:* www.mariahcarey.com.

CAREY, Peter Philip, FRSL; Australian/American writer and academic; *Executive Director, Creative Writing Program, Hunter College, City University of New York;* b. 7 May 1943, Bacchus Marsh, Vic., Australia; s. of Percival Stanley Carey and Helen Jean Warriner; m. 2nd Alison Summers 1985 (divorced); two s.; m. 3rd Frances Rachel Coady 2007; ed Geelong Grammar School and Monash Univ.; fmr Teacher of Creative Writing, New York Univ., New School, New York, Columbia Univ., Princeton Univ., Barnard Univ.; currently Exec. Dir Creative Writing Program, Hunter Coll., CUNY; Hon. LittD (Queensland); Hon. DLit (Monash), (New School, NY, USA). *Screenplay:* Bliss (co-author), Until the End of the World (co-author). *Publications:* The Fat Man in History (short stories, aka Exotic Pleasures 1981) 1974, War Crimes (short stories) (NSW Premier's Award) 1979, Bliss (novel) (Miles Franklin Award, Nat. Book Council Award, NSW Premier's Award) 1981, Illywhacker (novel) (Age Book of the Year Award, Nat. Book Council Award, Victorian Premier's Award) 1985, Oscar and Lucinda (Booker Prize for Fiction 1988, Miles Franklin Award, Nat. Book Council Award, Adelaide Festival Award, Foundation for Australian Literary Studies Award) 1988, Until the End of the World 1990, The Tax Inspector (novel) 1991, The Unusual Life of Tristan Smith (novel) (Age Book of the Year Award) 1994, Collected Stories 1995, The Big Bazoohley (children's novel) 1995, Jack Maggs 1997, The True History of the Kelly Gang (Booker Prize 2001) 2000, 30 Days in Sydney: A Wildly Distorted Account 2001, My Life as a Fake 2003, Wrong About Japan 2005, Theft: A Love Story 2006, His Illegal Self 2008, Parrot and Olivier in America 2009, The Chemistry of Tears 2012. *Address:* c/o Amanda Urban, ICM, 825 Eighth Avenue, New York, NY 10019, USA (office). *Telephone:* (212) 556-5764 (office). *E-mail:* aurban@icmtalent.com (office). *Website:* www.hunter.cuny.edu/creativewriting (office); petercareybooks.com.

CAREY OF CLIFTON, Baron (Life Peer), cr. 2002, of Clifton in the City and County of Bristol; **Most Rev. and Rt Hon. George Leonard Carey,** RVO, PC, MTh, PhD; British ecclesiastic and university chancellor; *Chancellor, University of Gloucestershire;* b. 13 Nov. 1935, London; s. of George Thomas Carey and Ruby Catherine Carey; m. Eileen Harmsworth Hood 1960; two s. two d.; ed Bifrons Secondary Modern School, Barking, Essex, King's Coll., London Univ.; Nat. Service, RAF 1954–56; univ. studies and theological training 1957–62; Curate St Mary's, Islington 1962–66; lecturer, Oak Hill Theological Coll. 1966–70, St John's Coll., Nottingham 1970–75; Vicar St Nicholas' Church, Durham 1975–82; Prin. Trinity Theological Coll., Bristol 1982–87; Bishop of Bath and Wells 1987–91; Archbishop of Canterbury 1991–2002; Chancellor, Univ. of Gloucestershire 2003–; Patron or Pres. of 300 orgs; Fellow King's Coll., London; Hon. Bencher Inner Temple; Freeman Cities of London and of Wells 1990; Hon. DLitt (Polytechnic of East London) 1991; Hon. DD (Kent) 1991, (Nottingham) 1992, (Bristol) 1992, (Durham) 1994; Hon. LLD (Bath) 1992; several hon. degrees from American univs; Greek, Hebrew and theological prizes. *Publications:* I Believe in Man 1978, The Great Acquittal 1981, The Church in the Market Place 1983, The Meeting of the Waters 1985, The Gate of Glory 1986, The Great God Robbery 1988, I Believe 1991, Spiritual Journey 1994, My Journey Your Journey 1996, Canterbury – Letters to the Future 1998, Jesus 2000, Know The Truth 2004. *Leisure interests:* walking, football, poetry, music. *Address:* House of Lords, Westminster, London, SW1A 0PW, England. *E-mail:* george@glcarey.co.uk (office).

CARL XVI GUSTAF, HM The King of Sweden (Carl Gustaf Folke Hubertus); b. 30 April 1946; s. of Prince Gustaf Adolf and Sibylla, Princess of Saxe-Coburg-Gotha; m. Silvia Sommerlath (HM Queen Silvia) 1976; two d., Crown Princess Victoria Ingrid Alice Désirée b. 14 July 1977, Princess Madeleine Thérèse Amelie Josephine b. 10 June 1982; one s., Prince Carl Philip Edmund Bertil b. 13 May 1979; ed studied in Sigtuna and Univs of Uppsala and Stockholm; cr. Duke of Jämtland; became Crown Prince 1950; succeeded to the throne on death of his grandfather, King Gustaf VI Adolf 15 Sept. 1973; Chair. Swedish Branch, World Wide Fund for Nature; Hon. Pres. World Scout Foundation; Dr hc (Swedish Univ. of Agricultural Sciences, Stockholm Inst. of Tech., Abo Acad., Finland); US Environmental Protection Agency Award. *Leisure interests:* hunting, sailing and water sports, motor sport, cross-country and downhill skiing, art, music and food. *Address:* The Royal Palace, 111 30 Stockholm, Sweden (office). *Telephone:* (8) 402-60-00 (office). *Fax:* (8) 402-60-05 (office). *E-mail:* info@royalcourt.se (office). *Website:* www.royalcourt.se (office).

CARLESON, Lennart Axel Edvard, PhD; Swedish mathematician and academic; *Professor Emeritus, Mathematics Department, Uppsala University;* b. 18 March 1928, Stockholm; m. Sylvia Elmstedt 1978 (died 2009); one s.; ed Uppsala Univ.; Dir Mittag-Leffler Inst., Djursholm, Stockholm 1968–84; currently Prof. Emer., Math. Dept, Uppsala Univ.; frmly at Royal Inst. of Tech., Stockholm, UCLA, USA; Pres. Int. Math. Union 1978–82; Wolf Prize 1992, Lomonosov Gold Medal 2002, Sylvester Medal 2003, Abel Prize for outstanding work in the field of maths, particularly for his proof of the convergence of the Fourier series 2006. *Publications:* Selected Problems on Exceptional Sets 1967, Complex Dynamics (with T. W. Gamelin) 1993, Matematik för vår tid (Mathematics for Our Time); numerous articles in professional journals on harmonic analysis. *Address:* Vendev 9E, 18269 Djursholm, Sweden (home). *Telephone:* (8) 51241588 (home). *Fax:* (8) 7231788 (office). *E-mail:* carleson@math.kth.se (office); lennar.carleson@gmail.com (home).

CARLIN, John William, BS; American business executive, archivist, academic and fmr state governor; *Visiting Professor/Executive in Residence, School of Leadership Studies, Kansas State University;* b. 3 Aug. 1940, Salina, Kan.; s. of Jack W. Carlin and Hazel L. Carlin (née Johnson); m. 1st Ramona Hawkinson 1962 (divorced 1980); one s. one d.; m. 2nd Lynn Carlin 1997; ed Lindsborg High School, Kansas State Univ.; farmer and dairyman, Smolan, Kan. 1962–80; mem. Kan. House of Reps for 93rd Dist 1970–73, 73rd Dist 1973–79, Minority Leader 1975–77, Speaker 1977–79; Gov. of Kan. 1979–87; Visiting Prof. of Public Admin. and Int. Trade, Wichita State Univ. 1987–88; Visiting Fellow, Univ. of Kansas 1987–88; Pres. Econ. Devt Assocs Inc. 1987–92; Pnr, Carlin and Assocs, Topeka 1989–95; Vice-Chair. and CEO Midwest Superconductivity Inc., Lawrence 1990–94; Pnr, Clark Publishing Inc., Topeka 1991–95; Archivist of the US, Nat. Archives and Records Admin., Washington, DC 1995–2005; Visiting Prof./Exec. in Residence, School of Leadership Studies, Kansas State Univ., also Co-Chair. Advancement

Council for School of Leadership Studies; Pres. Econ. Devt Asscn 1987–92, Vice-Chair. Midwest Superconductivity Inc. 1990–94; mem. Kan. Bioscience Authority 2006–; Chair. Nat. Historical Publications and Records Comm. 1995–2005, Nat. Comm. for Industrialized Farm Animal Production 2006–08; fmr Chair. Nat. Govs Asscn, mem. Nat. Govs Asscn (NGA) Exec. Cttee; fmr Chair. Midwestern Govs Conf.; Democrat; Hon. DIur (Kan.). *Leisure interests:* golf, swimming. *Address:* School of Leadership Studies, Kansas State University, 107 Leadership Studies Building, Manhattan, KS 66506, USA (office). *Telephone:* (785) 532-6346 (office). *E-mail:* jwcarlin@k-state.edu (office). *Website:* www.k-state.edu/leadership (office).

CARLING, William (Will) David Charles, OBE; British sports commentator and fmr rugby union player; b. 12 Dec. 1965, Bradford-on-Avon, Wilts.; m. 1st Julia Carling 1994 (divorced 1996); m. 2nd Lisa Cooke 1999; one s. one step-s. one step-d.; ed Durham Univ.; centre; fmr mem. Durham Univ. Club; mem. Harlequins club; int. debut England versus France 1988; Capt. England team 1988–96; announced retirement from int. rugby 1997 (brief return to the game with Harlequins 1999); played 72 times for England, Capt. 59 times (world record); rugby football commentator 1997–; owner Inspirational Horizons Co., Insights Ltd. *Publications:* Captain's Diary 1991, Will Carling (autobiog.) 1994, The Way to Win (with Robert Heller) 1995, My Autobiography 1998. *Leisure interests:* painting and sketching. *Address:* c/o Mike Burton Management, Bastian House, Brunswick House, Brunswick Road, Gloucester, GL1 1JJ, England (office). *Telephone:* (1542) 419666 (office). *Fax:* (1306) 713605 (office). *E-mail:* will@willcarling.com (office). *Website:* www.willcarling.com.

CARLISLE, Sir James (Beethoven), Kt, GCMG, BDS; Antiguan/British dental surgeon and fmr administrator; b. 5 Aug. 1937; s. of the late James Carlisle and of Jestina Jones; m. 1st Umilta Mercer 1963 (divorced 1973); one s. one d.; m. 2nd Anne Jenkins 1973 (divorced 1984); one d.; m. 3rd Nalda Amelia Meade 1984; one s. one d.; ed Univ. of Dundee; dentist 1972–93; Gov.-Gen. Antigua and Barbuda 1993–2007; Chair. Nat. Parks Authority 1986–90; Chief Scout Antigua and Barbuda 1986–90; mem. American Acad. of Laser Dentistry, Int. Asscn of Laser Dentistry; Hon. Fellow, Dental Surgery Royal Coll. of Surgeons of Edin. 1995; Hon. mem. British Dental Asscn; Kt Grand Cross, Order of Queen of Sheba (Ethiopia) 1995, Kt Grand Collar, Most Distinguished Order of the Nation (Antigua and Barbuda) 2000, Kt of Grace, Kt of Justice, Order of St John; Hon. LLD (Andrews Univ., USA) 1996. *Leisure interests:* gardening, reading, music. *Address:* POB W1644, St John's, Antigua. *Telephone:* (305) 396-3542 (home). *E-mail:* govg@hotmail.com (home).

CARLOS, Roberto; Brazilian singer and songwriter; b. 19 April 1941, Cachoeiro de Itapemirim; s. of Robertino Braga and Laura Moreira Braga; m. 1st Cleonice Rossi 1968 (divorced 1978); one d.; m. 2nd Myrian Rios 1980 (divorced 1989); m. 3rd Maria Rita Simões Braga 1996 (died 1999); two s. one d.; ed Conservatório Musical de Cachoeiro; started performing professionally in 1958; has presented numerous radio and TV programmes; pioneered Jovem Guarda movt in 1970s, influenced by American rock and roll; numerous tours in South America; has performed with Maria Bethânia, Tom Jobim, Chico Buarque, Caetano Veloso, Dorival Caymmi; First Prize, San Remo Festival 1968, Latin Grammy Awards for Best Singer 1989, for Best Brazilian Romantic Album 2005, for Best Brazilian Song 2013. *Recordings include:* Louco por Você 1961, O Inimitável 1968, A Janela, A Distância e Por Amor 1971, Honestly 1981, Se Diverte e já não Pensa em Mim 1988, Amor sem limite 2000, Pra sempre 2003; over 45 albums including Para Sempre Ao Vivo No Pacaembu (Latin Grammy Award for Best Brazilian Romantic Album), Roberto Carlos 2006 (Latin Grammy Award for Best Brazilian Romantic Album), Roberto Carlos-En Vivo 2008, Elas Cantam Roberto Carlos 2009, Esse Cara Sou Eu 2012. *Address:* c/o Sony BMG Brasil, Rua Lauro Muller 116, 40º Andar, Conjunto 4001 a 4003, Botafogo, 22290-160 Rio de Janeiro, Brazil. *Telephone:* (21) 2128-0600 (office). *Website:* www.robertocarlos.com.

CARLOS, Roberto (see ROBERTO CARLOS).

CARLOS MOCO, Marcolino José, PhD; Angolan lawyer and politician; b. 19 July 1953, Huamba Prov.; fmr Gov. Bié and Huambo Provs; mem. Assembléia Nacional 1992–; Prime Minister of Angola 1992–96; fmr Minister of Youth and Sports; mem. Movimento Popular de Libertação de Angola (MPLA), fmr Sec.-Gen. *Address:* Assembléia Nacional, CP 1204, Luanda, Angola (office). *Telephone:* 222334021 (office). *Fax:* 222331118 (office). *E-mail:* assembleianacional@parlamento.ebonet.net (office). *Website:* www.parlamento.ao (office).

CARLOT, Alfred, BA; Ni-Vanuatu diplomatist and politician; b. 11 June 1959; ed Univ. of the South Pacific, Australian Nat. Univ.; early career as secondary school teacher and salesman, Asco Motors Co.; fmr Perm. Sec., Ministry of Foreign Affairs and Perm. Rep. to UN, New York; mem. Parl. for Efate rural 2008–12; fmr Minister of Lands and Natural Resources, of Justice 2010–11, of Foreign Affairs and External Trade 2011–13; mem. Vanuatu Republikan Pati. *Address:* c/o Ministry of Foreign Affairs and External Trade, PMB 9051, Port Vila, Vanuatu (office).

CARLOT KORMAN, Maxime; Ni-Vanuatu politician; *Leader, Vanuatu Republikan Pati;* b. 1942; Prime Minister of Vanuatu 1991–95, Feb.–Sept. 1996, Minister of Foreign Affairs, of Public Service, Planning and Statistics, of Media and Language Services 1993–95; Minister of Infrastructure and Public Utilities –2005, then Minister of Lands; Speaker of Parl. 2009–10, Acting Pres. Aug.–Sept. 2009; fmr Leader, Union of Moderate Parties; Founder and Leader Vanuatu Republikan Pati 1995–. *Address:* Vanuatu Republikan Pati, Port Vila, Vanuatu (office).

CARLSON, Arne Helge, BA; American politician and business executive; b. 24 Sept. 1934, New York; s. of Helge William and Kerstin Carlson (née Magnusson); m. 1st Barbara Carlson (divorced); one s. two d.; m. 2nd Joanne (divorced); m. 3rd Susan Shepard 1985; one d.; ed Williams Coll., Univ. of Minnesota; with Control Data, Bloomington, Minn. 1962–64; Councilman Minneapolis City Council 1965–67; in pvt. business, Minneapolis 1968–69; Legislator, Minn. House of Reps, St Paul 1970–78; State Auditor, State of Minn. 1978–90; Sec. Minn. Housing Finance Agency 1979–91; Gov. of Minn. 1991–98; Chair. IDS Mutual Fund Group, Minneapolis 1999; Ind. Chair. American Express Funds (now RiverSource Funds) 1999–2006, mem. Bd 2006–; mem. Bd of Dirs Minn. Land Exchange Bd, Exec. Council St Paul; Trustee, Minn. State Bd Investment; several awards including Small Business Guardian Award, Nat. Fed. of Ind. Businesses 1994. *Leisure interests:* reading, squash, Univ. of Minnesota basketball and football games.

CARLSON, Lawrence Evan, (Bear), BS, MS, DEng; American engineer and academic; *Professor Emeritus of Mechanical Engineering, University of Colorado;* b. 22 Dec. 1944, Milwaukee, Wis.; s. of John W. Carlson and Louise M. Altseimer; m. Poppy C. Copeland; one s. two d.; ed Univ. of Wisconsin, Univ. of California, Berkeley; Asst Prof., Dept of Materials Eng, Univ. of Illinois at Chicago 1971–74; Asst Prof., Dept of Eng Design and Econ. Evaluation, Univ. of Colorado, Boulder 1974–78, Dept of Mechanical Eng 1978–, currently Prof. Emer. of Mechanical Eng, Founding Co-Dir Integrated Teaching and Learning Lab. 1995–2007 (retd 2010); numerous awards, including Charles Hutchinson Outstanding Teaching Award, Coll. of Eng and Applied Science 2001, John and Mercedes Peebles Innovation in Educ. Award 2004, Bernard M. Gordon Prize (with Jacquelyn Sullivan), Nat. Acad. of Eng 2008, Excellence in Teaching Award, Boulder Faculty Assembly 2009. *Publications:* numerous papers in academic journals. *Address:* University of Colorado, College of Engineering and Applied Science, 1111 Engineering Drive 422, Boulder, CO 80309-0422, USA (office). *Telephone:* (303) 304-9308 (home). *Fax:* (303) 492-2498 (office). *E-mail:* lawrence.carlson@colorado.edu (office). *Website:* www.me.colorado.edu/#!emeritus-faculty-/c24y5 (office); spot.colorado.edu/~carlsole (office).

CARLSSON, Arvid, MD, PhD; Swedish pharmacologist and academic; *Professor Emeritus of Pharmacology, University of Göteborg;* b. 25 Jan. 1923, Uppsala; physician, Univ. of Lund 1951, Asst Prof. 1951–56, Assoc. Prof. 1956–59; Prof. of Pharmacology, Univ. of Göteborg 1959–89, Prof. Emer. 1989–; co-f. Carlsson Research AB 1998; mem. Scientific Advisory Bd, ACADIA Pharmaceuticals 1999–; mem. Swedish Acad. of Sciences; Foreign mem. NAS; numerous awards and prizes include: Magnus Blix Prize, Univ. of Lund 1947, Wolf Prize in Medicine, Jerusalem (jt recipient) 1979, Paul Hoch Prize, American Psychopathological Asscn 1990, Japan Prize in Psychology and Psychiatry 1994, Gold Medal and Hon. Diploma, Swedish Parkinson Asscn 1996, Gold Medal, Soc. of Biological Psychiatry, Toronto 1998, Antonio Feltrinelli Int. Award, Accad. dei Lincei, Rome 1999, Nobel Prize for Medicine (jt recipient) 2000. *Publications:* several hundred specialist articles in journals. *Address:* Carlsson Research AB, Thorild Wulffsgatan 50, 413 19 Göteborg, Sweden (office). *Telephone:* (31) 82-90-45 (office). *Fax:* (31) 82-14-34 (office). *E-mail:* arvid.carlsson@pharm.gu.se (office).

CARLSSON, Gunilla; Swedish politician; b. 11 May 1963, Vadstena, Östergötland; ed Linköping Univ.; accountant 1984–90, accounting man. 1990–94; mem. Vadstena Municipal Council 1989; mem. European Parl. (Group of the European People's Party (Christian Democrats) and European Democrats—EPP-ED) 1995–2002, Leader Moderate Party Del., mem. Cttee on Foreign Affairs, Human Rights, Common Security and Defence Policy 1999–2002, Vice-Chair. EPP 2004–06; mem. Parl. (Riksdag) 2002–, mem. War Del. 2002–, mem. Cttee on Educ. 2002–03, Cttee on EU Affairs 2002–04, Cttee on Foreign Affairs 2003–04, Deputy Chair. Cttee on Foreign Affairs 2004–, Deputy mem. Cttee on EU Affairs 2004–; Minister for Int. Devt Cooperation 2006–13; mem. UN High-Level Panel on Global Sustainability 2010–; Vice-Chair. Moderate Party Youth League 1992–95, apptd mem. Bd of Moderate Party 1999, Second Vice-Chair. Moderate Party 1999–2003, First Vice-Chair. 2003–; Vice-Chair. Nordic Young Conservative Union 1993–94; Vice-Chair. Int. Young Democratic Union 1994–98; Alt. mem. Swedish Del. to Nordic Council 2004. *Address:* c/o Moderata Samlingspartiet, (Moderate Party), Stora Nygt. 30, POB 2080, 103 12, Stockholm, Sweden (office).

CARLSSON, Ingvar Gösta, MA; Swedish politician; b. 9 Nov. 1934, Borås; m. Ingrid Melander 1957; two d.; ed Lund Univ. and Northwestern Univ. USA; Sec. in Statsradsberedningen (Prime Minister's Office) 1958–60; Pres. Social Democratic Youth League 1961–67; mem. Parl. 1964–; Under-Sec. of State, Statsradsberedningen 1967–69; Minister of Educ. 1969–73, of Housing and Physical Planning 1973–76, Deputy Prime Minister 1982–86, Minister of the Environment 1985–86, Prime Minister 1986–91, 1994–96; Co-Chair. Comm. on Global Governance 1995–2001, Inter Action Council 2005–; Chair. Anna Lindh Memorial Fund 2003–; mem. Exec. Cttee Social Democratic Party, Chair. 1972–96. *Publications:* Ur skuggan av Olof Palme 1999, Så tänkte jag 2003. *Address:* c/o Anna Lindhs Minnesfond (Anna Lindh Memorial Fund), Kulturhuset Box 16414, 10327 Stockholm, Sweden. *Telephone:* (8) 411-90-91. *E-mail:* annalindhsminnesfond.se. *Website:* www.annalindhsminnesfond.se.

CARLUCCI, Frank Charles; American fmr politician and business executive; *Chairman Emeritus, Carlyle Group;* b. 18 Oct. 1930, Scranton, Pa; s. of Frank Carlucci and Roxann Carlucci; m. 1st Jean Anthony 1954 (divorced 1974); one s. one d.; m. 2nd Marcia Myers Carlucci 1976; one d.; ed Princeton Univ. and Harvard Grad. School of Business Admin.; with Jantzen Co., Portland, Ore. 1955–56; Foreign Service Officer, Dept of State 1956; Vice-Consul, Econ. Officer, Johannesburg 1957–59; Second Sec., Political Officer, Kinshasa 1960–62; Officer in charge of Congolese Political Affairs, Zanzibar 1962–64, Consul-Gen. 1964–65; Counsellor for Political Affairs, Rio de Janeiro 1965–69; Asst Dir for Operations, Office of Econ. Opportunity 1969–70, Dir 1970; Assoc. Dir Office of Man. and Budget 1971–72, Deputy Dir 1972; Under-Sec. Dept of Health, Educ. and Welfare 1972–74; Amb. to Portugal 1974–77; Deputy Dir CIA 1977–81, Deputy Sec. of Defense 1981–82, Sec. 1987–89; Pres. and COO Sears World Trade Inc. 1983–84, Chair. and CEO 1984–86; Nat. Security Adviser to Pres. of USA 1986–87; Vice-Chair. Carlyle Group, Washington 1989–93, Chair. 1993–2003, Chair. Emer. 2003–; Hon. DHumLitt; Superior Service Award and Superior Honor Award, US Dept of State, Presidential Citizens Award, Distinguished Intelligence Medal and other awards. *Leisure interests:* tennis, swimming. *Address:* The Carlyle Group, 1001 Pennsylvania Avenue, NW, Suite 220 South, Washington, DC 20004-2505, USA (office). *Telephone:* (202) 729-5224 (office). *Fax:* (202) 347–1597 (office). *E-mail:* frank.carlucci@carlyle.com (office). *Website:* www.thecarlylegroup.com (office).

CARLYLE, Joan Hildred; British singer (soprano) and teacher; b. 6 April 1931; d. of Edgar J. Carlyle and Margaret M. Carlyle; m.; two d.; ed Howell's School, Denbigh, N Wales; studied singing with Madame Bertha Nichlass Kempner; Prin. Lyric Soprano, Covent Garden 1955–79; has sung at La Scala Milan, Staatsoper Vienna, Munich, Berlin, Teatro Colón Buenos Aires, San Carlo Naples, Monet Monte Carlo, Nico Milan, Cape Town, Brussels, Geneva, Zurich, Amsterdam, Boston, New York; teaches privately and also in London; gives master classes, promotes young singers and judges prestigious competitions. *Major roles sung in UK include:* Oscar, Un Ballo in Maschera 1957–58, Sophie, Der Rosenkavalier 1958–59, Nedda, Pagliacci (Zeffirelli production) 1959, Mimi, La Bohème 1960, Titania, Midsummer Night's Dream, Britten (Gielgud production) 1960, Pamina, Magic Flute 1962, 1966, Countess, Marriage of Figaro 1963, Zdenka, Arabella (Hartman Production) 1964, Suor Angelica 1965, Desdemona, Othello 1965, Arabella 1967, Marschallin, Der Rosenkavalier 1968, Jenifer, Midsummer Marriage 1969, Donna Anna, Don Giovanni 1970, Reiza, Oberon 1970, Adriana Lecouvreur 1970, Rusalka, Elisabetta, Don Carlos 1975. *Major roles sung abroad include:* Oscar, Nedda, Mimi, Pamina, Zdenka, Micaela, Donna Anna, Arabella, Elisabetta and Desdemona. *Recordings include:* Von Karajan's production of Pagliacci as Nedda, Midsummer Marriage as Jenifer, Medea, Pagliacci from Buenos Aires, Mavra, Purcell Anthology, Voice from the Old House (1/11) 2002, (12/29), (30/42) 2003, Complete versions of Otello, Arabella, Suor Angelica, Highlights from La Bohème 2003, complete versions of Arabella and Adriana Lecouvreur, Rusalka, Oberon, Complete Ballo 1962, 1971, Benevuto Cellini 2004, Die Zauberflote, Samson. *Leisure interests:* gardening, travel, preservation of the countryside, interior design, cooking. *Address:* Laundry Cottage, Hanmer, SY13 3DQ, Clwyd, Wales. *Telephone:* (1948) 830265. *E-mail:* joan@joancarlyle.co.uk (home). *Website:* www.joancarlyle.co.uk (home).

CARLYLE, Robert, OBE; British actor; b. 14 April 1961, Glasgow; s. of Joseph Carlyle and Elizabeth Carlyle; m. Anastasia Shirley 1997; ed N Kelvinside Secondary School, Royal Scottish Acad. of Music and Drama; f. Rain Dog Theatre Co. 1990, productions include: Wasted, One Flew Over the Cuckoo's Nest (Paper Boat Award), Conquest of the South Pole, Macbeth (Paper Boat Award 1992); Scottish BAFTA Award 1995, Royal TV Award 1996, Salerno Film Festival Award 1997, Evening Standard Outstanding British Actor Award 1998, Film Critics' Circle Award for Best Actor 1998, Variety Club Actor of the Year 1998, Bowmore Whisky/Scottish Screen Award for Best Actor 2001, Michael Elliot Award for Best Actor 2001, David Puttnam Patrons Award. *Stage appearances include:* Twelfth Night, Dead Dad Dog, Nae Problem, City, No Mean City, Cuttin' a Rug, Othello. *Films include:* Marooned, Riff Raff 1990, Silent Scream 1990, Safe 1993, Being Human 1993, Priest 1994, Go Now 1995, Trainspotting 1996, Carla's Song 1996, Face 1997, The Full Monty (BAFTA Award for Best Actor 1998) 1997, Ravenous 1999, Apprentices, Plunkett and Macleane 1999, The World is Not Enough 1999, Angela's Ashes 2000, The Beach 2000, There's Only One Jimmy Grimble 2000, To End All Wars 2000, 51st State 2001, Once Upon a Time in the Midlands 2002, Black and White 2002, Dead Fish 2004, Marilyn Hotchkiss' Ballroom Dancing and Charm School 2005, The Mighty Celt 2005, Eragon 2006, 28 Weeks Later 2007, Stone of Destiny 2008, Summer 2008, The Tournament 2009, California Solo 2012. *Television includes:* The Part of Valour 1981, Safe 1993, Cracker 1994, Hamish Macbeth 1995, The Advocates, Arena, Byrne on Byrne, Taggart, The Bill, Looking After Jo Jo 1998, Hitler: The Rise of Evil 2003, Gunpowder, Treason and Plot 2004, Class of '76 2005, Human Trafficking 2005, Born Equal 2006, The Last Enemy (series) 2008, 24: Redemption 2008, Zig Zag Love 2009, The Unloved (Scottish BAFTA for Best TV Actor) 2009, SGU Stargate Universe (series) 2009–11, Once Upon a Time (series) 2011–12. *Address:* c/o ICM, Oxford House, 76 Oxford Street, London, W1D 1BS, England (office).

CARMACK, John; American software industry executive; *Technical Director, id Software;* worked for Softdisk Publishing; co-f. and Technical Dir id Software 1991–, creating influential computer games, including Wolfenstein 3-D, Doom and Quake, notable for enhanced graphic detail and three-dimensional illusion; numerous awards from gaming publs. *Address:* id Software, Town East Tower, Suite 615, 18601 LBJ Freeway, Mesquite, TX 75150, USA (office). *Website:* www.idsoftware.com.

CARMI, Rivka, MD; Israeli paediatrician, geneticist and university administrator; *President, Ben-Gurion University;* ed Hebrew Univ. Medical School, Jerusalem, Harvard Univ., USA; Sr Faculty mem. Faculty of Health Sciences and Soroka Medical Center, Be'ersheva, Dir Clinical Genetics Unit, Soroka Hosp., Prof. and Dean, Faculty of Health Sciences (first woman dean of a faculty of health sciences in Israel) 2000– (fmr Assoc. Dean of Student Affairs), Acting Pres. Ben-Gurion Univ. of the Negev (first woman pres. of Israeli univ.) Feb.–May 2006, Pres. May 2006–; fmr Chair. Selection Cttee Joyce and Irving Goldman Medical School, Instructional Cttee Recanati School for Community Health Professions, Ben-Gurion Univ.; fmr Acting Dir Nat. Inst. for Biotechnology in the Negev; mem. Editorial Bd American Journal for Medical Genetics; mem. and adviser in local and nat. cttees and in int. insts. *Publications:* more than 100 scientific papers on molecular genetics of rare recessive diseases and on community genetics. *Address:* Office of the President, Ben-Gurion University of the Negev, PO Box 653, Be'ersheva 84105, Israel (office). *Telephone:* (8) 6461111 (office). *Fax:* (8) 6479434 (office). *E-mail:* rcarmi@bgumail.bgu.ac.il (office). *Website:* www.bgu.ac.il (office).

CARMICHAEL, Rt Hon. Alexander Morrison (Alistair), PC, LLB; British lawyer and politician; *Secretary of State for Scotland;* b. 15 July 1965, Islay, Scotland; m. Kathryn Jane Eastham 1987; two s.; ed Islay High School, Univs of Glasgow and Aberdeen; Pres. Liberal Club, Univ. of Glasgow; hotel manager 1984–89; contested Paisley South in Gen. Election 1987; qualified as solicitor 1993; Procurator Fiscal Depute for Edinburgh and Aberdeen 1993–96; solicitor, Aberdeen & Macduff 1996–2001; MP for Orkney and Shetland 2001–, mem. Commons Scottish Affairs Cttee 2001–05, 2008–10, Int. Devt Cttee 2001–02, Public Accounts Cttee 2005–06, Consolidation etc. Bills (Jt Cttee) 2008–10, Draft Constitutional Renewal Bill (Jt Cttee) 2008–10, Members' Allowances 2009–10; Liberal Democrat Spokesperson on Energy and Climate Change 2001–05, on Home Affairs 2005–06, on Transport 2006–07, on NI 2007–10, on Scotland 2008–10; Comptroller, HM Household and Deputy Chief Whip, House of Commons 2010–13; Sec. of State for Scotland 2013–; Deputy Leader of Scottish Liberal Democrats; Elder, Church of Scotland; Liberal Democrat; Hon. Pres. Liberal Youth Scotland 2011–. *Leisure interests:* listening to music, theatre, cooking. *Address:* Scotland Office, Dover House, 66 Whitehall, London, SW1A 2AU, (office); House of Commons, Westminster, London, SW1A 0AA, England; Constituency Office, 171 Commercial Street, Lerwick, ZE1 0HX, Shetland, Scotland. *Telephone:* (20) 7270-6741 (Scotland Office) (office); (20) 7219-8181 (Westminster); (1595) 690044 (Lerwick). *Fax:* (20) 7270-6812 (Scotland Office) (office); (1595) 690055 (Lerwick). *E-mail:* alistair.carmichael@scotlandoffice.gsi.gov.uk (office); carmichaela@parliament.uk. *Website:* www.gov.uk/government/organisations/scotland-office (office); www.alistaircarmichael.co.uk.

CARMONA, Anthony Thomas Aquinas, SC, BA, LLB; Trinidad and Tobago fmr judge and head of state; *President*; b. 7 March 1953, Fyzabad; s. of Dennis Stephen Carmona and Barbara Carmona; m. Reema Carmona; one s. one d.; ed Presentation Coll., San Fernando, Univ. of the West Indies; began career as teacher at primary and secondary school levels 1972–75, first at St Hugh's High School and Merle Grove High School, Kingston, Jamaica, later at Palo Seco Govt Secondary and Fyzabad Anglican Secondary Schools; Lecturer in Business Law, San Fernando Technical Inst. 1983–85, also Lecturer, Dept of Language and Linguistics and Sr Tutor, Dept of Govt, Univ. of the West Indies, St Augustine, Trinidad and Tobago; called to the Bar of Trinidad and Tobago 1983, Sr State Attorney 1989, Asst, then Deputy Dir of Public Prosecutions 1994–99; Judge, Supreme Court of Trinidad and Tobago 2004–12; Appeals Counsel at Office of the Prosecutor, Int. Criminal Tribunal for fmr Yugoslavia, The Hague and Int. Criminal Tribunal for Rwanda, Arusha 2001–04; Judge, Int. Criminal Court 2011–13; Pres. of Trinidad and Tobago 2013–. *Address:* Office of the President, President's House, Circular Road, St Ann's, Port of Spain, Trinidad and Tobago (office). *Telephone:* 624-1261 (office). *Fax:* 625-7950 (office). *E-mail:* presoftt@carib-link.net (office). *Website:* www.thepresident.tt (office).

CARMONA ESTANGA, Pedro; Venezuelan politician, economist and oil executive; b. 6 June 1941, Barquisimeto; ed Universidad Católica Andrés Bello, Université Libre de Bruxelles, Belgium; with Aditivos Orinoco 1989–93, Química Venoco 1989–2000, Industrias Venoco 1990–2000, Promotora Venoco 2001; First Vice-Pres. Fedecamaras 1999–2001, Pres. 2001–02; Pres. Andean Enterprise Consultative Council 2000–01; also worked for Venezuelan Confed. of Industry–Conindustria, Venezuelan Asscn of the Chemical and Petrochemical Industries, Venezuelan Asscn of Exporters (AVEX), Chamber of Commerce, Venezuelan–Columbian Integration (CAVECOL); fmr mem. Directive Council Instituto de Estudios Superiores de la Administración de Empresas; fmr mem. Junta del Acuerdo de Cartagena, fmr Pres. Venezuelan Del. to Comisión del Acuerdo de Cartagena; fmr mem. Corporación Andina de Fomento; fmr Dir Instituto de Comercio Exterior, Sistema Económico Latinoamericano; fmr adviser to Directorate of Econ. Policy, Ministry of Foreign Affairs; installed by army as interim Pres. of Venezuela 12 April 2002 following anti-govt protests against Pres. Chavez; placed under house arrest 14 April 2002, accused of rebellion and usurping the presidency, later granted asylum by Colombian Govt; Order of the Sun (Peru), Nat. Order of Merit (Colombia), Bernardo O'Higgins Order (Chile).

CARNEGIE, Sir Roderick Howard, Kt, AC, BSc, BA, MA, MBA, DipAgrEcon, FTSE; Australian business executive; *Chairman, Pacific Edge Group*; b. 27 Nov. 1932, Melbourne, Vic.; s. of D. H. Carnegie and Margaret F. Carnegie; m. Carmen Clarke 1959 (died 2008); three s.; ed Geeelong GS, Trinity Coll., Melbourne, New Coll., Oxford, Harvard Business School; Assoc., McKinsey and Co., Melbourne and New York 1959–64, Prin. 1964–68, Dir 1968–70; Dir CRA 1970, Jt Man. Dir 1971–72, Man. Dir and Chief Exec. 1972–74, Chair. and Man Dir 1974–83, Chair. and Chief Exec. 1983–86; Dir Comalco Ltd, CRA Ltd, Rio Tinto-Zinc Corpn Ltd; Chair. Consultative Cttee on Relations with Japan 1984–87; Pres. German-Australian Chamber of Industry and Commerce 1985; Pres. Business Council of Australia 1987–88; Chair. Hudson Conway Ltd 1987–2000; currently Chair. Pacific Edge Holdings; Vice-Pres. Australian Mining Industry Council 1985; Chair. Salvation Army Council 1992–96, G10 Australia Holdings Ltd 1992–94, Valiant Consolidated Ltd 1993–98, Adacel Techs Ltd 1998–2003, Newcrest Mining Ltd 1994–98; Dir John Fairfax Holdings Pty Ltd 1992–94, Lexmark Holdings Inc. (USA) 1994–98; Patron Australian Centre for Blood Diseases; Commdr's Cross, Order of Merit (Germany) 1991, Centenary Medal 2003; Hon. DSc (Newcastle); Hon. LLD (Monash). *Address:* Pacific Edge Group, PO Box 7458, St Kilda Road, Melbourne, Vic. 8004, Australia (office). *Telephone:* (3) 9863-7242 (office). *Fax:* (3) 9863-7241 (office). *E-mail:* rod@carboniron.com.au (office).

CARNEY, Mark, BA, MA, PhD; Canadian/British central banker; *Governor, Bank of England;* b. 16 March 1965, Fort Smith, NWT; m.; four c.; ed Harvard Univ., Univ. of Oxford, UK; worked at Goldman Sachs 1988–2001, as analyst in London, later working in Tokyo and New York before becoming Man. Dir Goldman's investment banking div., based in Toronto; Deputy Gov. Bank of Canada, responsible for int. issues 2003–04, Adviser to the Gov. 2007–08, Gov. Bank of Canada (youngest cen. banker among the Group of Seven nations) 2008–12; Sr Assoc. Deputy Minister, Dept of Finance 2004–07; served as Canada's Finance Deputy at the G7, G20 and Financial Stability Forum, Chair. G20 Financial Stability Forum 2011–; Gov.-Elect Bank of England Nov. 2012–June 2013, Gov. July 2013–. *Address:* Bank of England, Threadneedle Street, London, EC2R 8AH, England (office). *Telephone:* (20) 7601-4444 (office). *Fax:* (20) 7601-5460 (office). *E-mail:* enquiries@bankofengland.co.uk (office). *Website:* www.bankofengland.co.uk (office).

CARNEY, Rt Hon. Patricia (Pat), CM, BA, PC, MA; Canadian politician and economist; b. 26 May 1935, Shanghai, China; d. of James Carney and Dora Sanders; m. 2nd Paul S. White 1998; one s. one d. from previous marriage; ed Univ. of British Columbia; Adjunct Prof., Univ. of British Columbia; fmrly econ. journalist; f. Gemini North Ltd (consulting firm for socio-econ. impact studies) 1970; first elected MP 1980; Minister of State for Finance, Minister of Finance, Energy, Mines and Resources; Minister of Energy, Mines and Resources 1984–86, of Int. Trade 1986–88; Pres. Treasury Bd April–Oct. 1988; Chair. Cabinet Cttee on Trade; mem. Senate 1990–2008; fmr Chair. Standing Senate Cttee on Energy, the Environment and Natural Resources; mem. Standing Senate Cttee on Foreign Affairs, Aboriginal Peoples, Fisheries; Adjunct Prof., School of Community and Regional Planning, Univ. of British Columbia; mem. Canadian Inst. of Planners, Asscn of Professional Economists of BC; fmr mem. Econ. Council of Canada; Hon. Fellow, Royal Architectural Inst. of Canada 1989; Hon. LLD (Univ. of British Columbia) 1990, (British Columbia Open Univ.) 1991. *Publication:* Trade Secrets: A Memoir 2000. *Website:* www.patcarney.ca.

CARNLEY, Most Rev. Peter Frederick, AC, DD, PhD; Australian archbishop and theologian (retd); b. 17 Oct. 1937, New Lambton, NSW; s. of F. Carnley; m. Carol Ann Dunstan, 1966; one s. one d.; ed St John's Theological Coll., NSW, Trinity Coll., Melbourne Univ., St John's Coll., Univ. of Cambridge; Deacon 1962; Priest 1964; Chaplain, Mitchell Coll. of Advanced Educ., NSW 1970–72; Research Fellow, St John's Coll., Cambridge 1971–72; Warden St John's Coll., Univ. of Queensland 1973–81; Anglican Archbishop of Perth and Metropolitan of the Province of Western Australia 1981–2005, Primate of the Anglican Church of Australia 2000–05; mem. Archbishop of Canterbury's Comm. on Communion and Women in the Episcopate 1988, Int. Anglican Theological and Doctrinal Comm. 1994; Visiting Prof. of Anglican Studies, Gen. Theological Seminary, New York 1993, 1996, 1999; Anglican Co-Chair. Anglican-Roman Catholic Int. Comm. 2003–; Adjunct Prof. of Theology, Murdoch Univ. 2004–; Patron, Australian Council of Christians and Jews 2004–; Lady Margaret Preacher, Univ. of Cambridge 2010; Hon. Fellow, Trinity Coll., Univ. of Melbourne 2000, St John's Coll., Cambridge 2000, Emmanuel Coll., Cambridge 2006; Dr hc (Newcastle) 2000, (Western Australia) 2000, (Charles Sturt) 2001, (Queensland) 2002; Hon. Dr of Sacred Theology (Melbourne Coll. of Divinity) 2004. *Publications:* The Structure of Resurrection Belief 1987, The Yellow Wallpaper and Other Sermons 2001, Faithfulness in Fellowship: Reflections on Homosexuality and the Church 2001, Reflections in Glass: Trends and Tensions in the Contemporary Anglican Church 2004. *Leisure interests:* gardening, music. *Address:* GPO Box 221, Nannup, WA 6275, Australia. *Telephone:* (4) 1188-8203. *E-mail:* pluspeter@westnet.com.au.

ČARNOGURSKÝ, Ján, LLD, JUDr; Slovak politician and lawyer; b. 1 Jan. 1944, Bratislava; s. of Pavol Čarnogurský and Kristína Čarnogurská (née Fašungová); m. Marta Stachová 1970; two s. two d.; ed Charles Univ., Prague; lawyer, Bratislava 1970–81; mem. of Slovak Lawyers' Cen. Office and Czech Lawyers' Cen. Office; banned from legal profession after defence in a political trial 1981; driver, lawyer for a co. Bratislava 1982–86; unemployed, after expulsion from legal profession, continued giving legal advice to members of the political opposition and religious activists 1987–89; held in custody, released and pardoned Aug.–Nov. 1989; First Deputy Premier, Govt of Czechoslovakia 1989–90, Deputy Premier June 1990; Chair. Legis. Council Feb.–Aug. 1990; Chair. Christian Democratic Movt 1990–2000; First Deputy Premier, Govt of Slovak Repub. 1990–91, Prime Minister of Slovak Govt 1991–92; mem. State Defence Council 1991–92; Deputy to Slovak Nat. Council (Slovak Parl.) for KDH (Christian Democratic Movt) 1992–98; Deputy Chair. Parl. Ass. of CSCE 1993–95; Minister of Justice 1998–2002; advocate in pvt sector 2002–; Trustee, Order of the German Kts 1994–; Grand Cross, Order of Merit (Poland) 2008, Mechitar Gosh Medal (Armenia) 2008, Medal of Friendship (Russia) 2010; Slovak Literary Fund Prize (Journalists' Section) 1992. *Publications:* The Bratislava Letters (samizdat), Suffered for the Faith 1987, Seen from Danube 1997, By the Roads of KDH 2007. *Leisure interests:* history, jogging. *Address:* Law Office, Dostojevského rad 1, 81109 Bratislava, Slovakia (office). *Telephone:* (2) 5263-6954 (office). *Fax:* (2) 5263-6955 (office). *E-mail:* jancarnogursky@slovanet.sk (office). *Website:* www.jancarnogursky.sk.

CAROLUS, Cheryl, BA; South African organization executive and diplomatist; b. 27 May 1958, Silvertown; m. Graeme Bloch 1989; ed Univ. of the Western Cape; Gen. Sec. Nat. Exec. Cttee, United Democratic Front (UDF) 1983–87, Fed. of S African Women (FedSAW) 1987, UDF Western Cape Region 1983; UDF Del. Int. Centre for Swedish Labour Movt 1986; mem. Interim Leadership Group, S African Communist Party 1990; mem. Interim Leadership Cttee, African Nat. Congress (ANC) 1990, ANC Rep. at talks with Govt at Groote Schur, Cape Town 1990, Deputy Sec.-Gen. ANC 1994; High Commr to UK 1998–2001; CEO South African Tourism Bd (SATOUR) 2001–04; Chair. South African National Parks (SAN-PARKS) 2004–10; Exec. Chair. Peotona Holdings Ltd; Chair. of the Bd, South African Airways 2009–; mem. Congress of S African Trade Unions, Nat. Educ. Crisis Cttee 1989, OAU, Harare, Bd of Dirs Int. Inst. for Democracy and Electoral Assistance; detained under emergency regulations 1986, 1989; mem. Bd of Dirs Gold Fields Ltd 2009–, De Beers Consolidated Mines Ltd, Fenner Conveyor Belting SA Ltd, Macsteel Service Centres SA, IQ Business Group, Investec Ltd, Investec PLC, Constitution Hill Trust (Proprietary) Ltd; Bd mem. International Marketing Council of South Africa, International Crisis Group, World Wildlife Fund International 2005–, Nat. Parks Trust, Soul City Health Inst.; Dr hc (Univ. of Cape Town) 2004. *Address:* International Crisis Group, 149 Avenue Louise, Level 24, 1050 Brussels, Belgium (office). *Telephone:* (2) 502-90-38 (office). *Fax:* (2) 502-50-38 (office). *E-mail:* brussels@crisisgroup.org (office). *Website:* www.crisisgroup.org/en (office).

CARON, Leslie Claire Margaret; French actress and ballet dancer; b. 1 July 1931, Boulogne-Billancourt; m. 1st George Hormel; m. 2nd Peter Reginald Frederick Hall (q.v.) 1956 (divorced 1965); one s. one d.; m. 3rd Michael Laughlin 1969 (divorced) ed Convent of the Assumption, Paris and Conservatoire de Danse; with Ballet des Champs Elysées 1947–50, Ballet de Paris 1954; Chevalier Légion d'honneur; Officier Ordre nat. du Mérite. *Films include:* An American in Paris 1951, Man with a Cloak 1951, Glory Alley 1952, Story of Three Loves 1953, Lili 1953, Glass Slipper 1955, Daddy Long Legs 1955, Gaby 1956, Gigi 1958, The Doctor's Dilemma 1958, The Man Who Understood Women 1959, The Subterranean 1960, Austerlitz 1960, Fanny 1961, Guns of Darkness 1962, The L-Shaped Room 1962, Father Goose 1964, A Very Special Favor 1965, Promise Her Anything 1965, Is Paris Burning? 1966, Head of the Family 1969, Madron 1970, Chandler 1971, Purple Night 1972, Surreal Estate 1976, The Man Who Loved Women 1977, Valentino 1977, Nicole 1978, Golden Girl 1979, The Contract 1980, All Stars 1980, Chanel Solitaire 1981, Imperative 1982, Deathly Moves 1983, The Train 1987, Courage Mountain 1990, Guns 1990, Damage 1992, The Genius 1993, Guerriers et Captives 1994, Funny Bones 1995, Let It Be Me 1995, The Reef 1996, Chocolat 2000, Le Divorce 2003. *Television includes:* The Wild Bird 1959, Les Fables de La Fontaine 1964, Carola 1973, QB VII 1974, Docteur Erika Werner 1978, Run, Rabbit, Run 1982, Tales of the Unexpected 1982, The Unapproachable 1982, Le Château faible 1983, Master of the Game 1984, La Génie du Faux 1984, L'oiseau bleu 1985, Mon meilleur Noël 1985, Falcon Crest 1987, The Man Who Lived at the Ritz 1988, Lenin: The Train 1990, The Ring 1996, The Last of the Blonde Bombshells 2000, Murder on the Orient Express 2001, Law and Order 2006. *Plays include:* Orvet (Jean Renoir), La Sauvage (Anouilh), Gigi (Anita Loos), 13 rue de l'Amour (Feydan), Ondine (Giraudoux), Carola (Renoir), La Répétition (Anouilh), On Your Toes (Rogers and Hart), Apprends-moi Céline (Maria Pacôme) (played in English in USA as One for the Tango 1985), Grand Hotel (Vicky Baum), George Sand (Bruno Villien), Le Martyre de Saint Sébastien (Debussy), Nocturne for Lovers (Villien), Babar the Elephant (Poulenc); toured France in Apprends-moi Céline 1998–99, Little Night Music, Châtelet, Paris 2010; stage appearances in Paris, London, USA, Germany and Australia; readings of Colette, USA and Australia. *Publication:* Vengeance 1983, Thank Heaven: A Memoir 2009. *Address:* c/o Clifford Stevens, Paradigm Agency, 360 Park Avenue South, New York, NY

10010, USA (office). *Telephone:* (212) 897-6408 (office). *E-mail:* cstevens@ paradigmagency.com (office). *Website:* www.paradigmagency.com (office).

CARP, Daniel A., MS, MBA; American business executive; *Chairman, Delta Air Lines, Inc.;* b. Wytheville, Va; ed Ohio Univ., Rochester Inst. of Tech., Sloan School of Man., Massachusetts Inst. of Tech.; with Kodak 1970–, Asst Gen. Man. Latin American Region 1986–88, Vice-Pres., Gen. Man. 1988–90, Gen. Man. European Marketing Cos 1991, Gen. Man. European, African and Middle Eastern Region 1991, Exec. Vice-Pres. and Asst COO Eastman Kodak Co. 1995–97, Dir, Pres. and COO 1997–2000, Chair., Pres. and CEO 2000–01, Chair. and CEO 2001–05; Chair. (non-exec.) Delta Air Lines, Inc. 2007–; mem. Bd Dirs Liz Claiborne Inc., Norfolk Southern Corpn, Texas Instruments Inc.; mem. Business Roundtable, Business Council; Trustee, Nat. Urban League, George Eastman House; Human Relations Award from American Jewish Cttee Photographic Imaging Div. 1997, Photographic and Imaging Manufacturers Asscn Leadership Award 2001, Diversity Best Practices CEO Leadership Award 2003, PhotoImaging Manufacturers and Distributors Asscn Person of the Year Award 2004. *Address:* Delta Air Lines Inc., PO Box 20706, 1030 Delta Blvd, Atlanta, GA 30320-6001, USA (office). *Telephone:* (404) 715-2600 (office). *Fax:* (404) 715-5042 (office). *E-mail:* info@delta.com (office). *Website:* www.delta.com (office).

CARPENTER, John Howard; American film director and screenwriter; b. 16 Jan. 1948, Carthage, NY; s. of Howard Ralph Carpenter and Milton Jean Carpenter (née Carter); m. 1st Adrienne Barbeau 1979; m. 2nd Sandy King 1990; ed Univ. of Southern California; mem. American Soc. of Composers, Authors and Publrs, Acad. of Motion Picture Arts and Sciences, Dirs Guild of America, West, Writers Guild of America. *Films directed:* The Resurrection of Bronco Billy 1970, Dark Star 1974, Assault on Precinct 13 1976, Halloween 1978, Elvis 1978, The Fog 1979, Escape from New York 1980, The Thing 1982, Christine 1983, Starman 1984, Big Trouble in Little China 1986, Prince of Darkness 1987, They Live 1987, Memoirs of an Invisible Man 1992, In the Mouth of Madness 1995, Village of the Damned 1995, Escape from LA 1996, Vampires 1998, Ghosts of Mars 2001, The Ward 2010. *Television includes:* Someone's Watching Me! 1978, Elvis 1979, Body Bags 1993, Masters of Horror 2005–06. *Leisure interests:* music, helicopter piloting. *Address:* c/o International Creative Management, 8942 Wilshire Boulevard, Beverly Hills, CA 90211, USA.

CARPENTER, Michael A., BSc, MBA; British business executive; *CEO, Ally Financial Inc.;* ed Univ. of Nottingham, Harvard Business School (Baker Scholar), USA; spent nine years as Vice-Pres. and Dir Boston Consulting Group and three years with ICI, UK; Vice-Pres. Corp. Business Devt and Planning, General Electric (GE) Co. 1983–86, Exec. Vice-Pres. GE Capital Corpn 1986–89, Chair., Pres. and CEO Kidder Peabody Group Inc. (subsidiary of GE) 1989–94; Chair. and CEO Travelers Life & Annuity and Vice-Chair. Travelers Group Inc. 1994–98; Chair. and CEO Salomon Smith Barney (following merger that created Citigroup) 1998–2002, Chair. and CEO Citigroup's Global Corp. & Investment Bank, with responsibility for Salomon Smith Barney Inc. and Citibank's corp. banking activities globally 1998–2002, Chair. and CEO Citigroup Alternative Investments 2002–06; f. Southgate Alternative Investments 2007; mem. Bd of Dirs GMAC Financial Services (renamed Ally Financial Inc. 2009) May 2009–, CEO Nov. 2009–; mem. Bd US Retirement Partners, New York City Investment Fund; fmr mem. Bd New York Stock Exchange, General Signal, Loews Cineplex and various other pvt. and public cos; Hon. LLD (Nottingham). *Address:* Ally Financial Inc., 200 Renaissance Center, Detroit, MI 48265-2000, USA (office). *Telephone:* (313) 556-5000 (office). *Fax:* (815) 282-6156 (office). *E-mail:* info@ally.com (office). *Website:* www.ally.com (office).

CARPENTIER, Alain F., DenM, DèsSc; French cardiac surgeon; *Head, Department of Cardiovascular Surgery and Organ Transplantation, Hôpital Européen Georges Pompidou;* b. 11 Aug. 1933, Toulouse; Lab. Researcher, CNRS 1963–66; Founder and Dir, Lab. for the Study of Cardiac Grafts and Prostheses 1967–; apptd Lab. Dir, Univ. of Paris VI 1978, now Prof. Emer.; Head of Dept of Cardiovascular Surgery, l'Hôpital Broussais 1982, of Cardiovascular Surgery and Organ Transplantation, Hôpital Européen Georges Pompidou 1999–; Visiting Prof., New York Univ. 1983, 2001–05; Adjunct Prof., Mount Sinai School of Medicine, New York Univ. 2002–; Visiting Prof., Univ. of Oregon 1986, 1989, Univ. of London 1989, 1996–2002, Cleveland Clinic Foundation 1990, Harvard Univ. 1991, 1996, 1999, 2002, 2005, Univ. of Montreal 1991, 2004–6, Baylor Univ. 1992, Univ. of Washington 1994, 2000, Florida Heart Inst. 1996, 1999, Univ. of Padua 1996, Hôtel Dieu de France de Beyrouth 1996, Univ. of Virginia 1997, Univ. of North Carolina 1998, Univ. of Tokyo 1998, 2000, 2003, Univ. of Bangkok 2000, Univ. of Pavia 2000, Univ. of Mexico 2004, Univ. of Delhi 2006; Scientific Adviser, Edwards LifeSciences Research Centre, Calif. 1975–; Founder and Pres. Heart Inst., Ho Chi Minh City 1991–; Pres. Cttee Télémédecine et technologies pour la santé, Ministry of Nat. Educ., Research and Tech. 1999; mem. Conseil Nat. de la Science, 1998–, l'Acad. des Sciences 2000–, Haut Conseil de la Science et de la Tech. 2006–; Cardiothoracic Surgery Network, European Asscn for Cardio-Thoracic Surgery, French Soc. for Thoracic and Cardiovascular Surgery, Soc. for Heart Valve Disease, American Asscn for Thoracic Surgery, Western Thoracic Surgical Asscn; mem. Bd of Dirs World Heart Foundation; Hon. mem. Mexican Cardiology Soc. 1978–, American Surgical Asscn 1985–, Soc. of Cardiothoracic Surgeons of GB and Ireland 1986–, American Coll. of Surgeons 1988–, American Coll. of Cardiology 1990, Royal Coll. of Doctors and Surgeons of Canada 1991–, Royal Coll. of Surgeons of England 1992–; Officier, Légion d'Honneur, Commdr, Ordre Nat. du Mérite, du Mérite de l'Ordre de Malte, Ordre du Cèdre (Lebanon), Grand Croix, Ordre de Léopold (Belgium); Dr. hc (Bucharest, Romania) 2001, (Pavia, Italy) 2001; Prix de l'Internat, Médaille d'argent 1965, Bronze Medal, CNRS 1967, Prix de l'Asscn française de chirurgie 1967, Grand Prix, Acad. des Sciences 1986, Prix Médecine-Sciences du Rayonnement français 1990, Grand prix mondial Cino del Duca 1996, Grand Prize, The Foundation for Medical Research 1998, Fifth Scientific Achievement Award, American Asscn for Thoracic Surgery 2005, Prix Lasker 2007. *Publications:* Le Mal Universitaire 1988, La Transplantation d'Organes 1994, Philosophie du Progrès en de Cardiologie (jtly) 2002. *Address:* Hôpital Européen Georges Pompidou, 20 rue Leblanc, Paris 75908 Cedex 15, France (office). *Telephone:* 1-56-09-36-01 (office). *Fax:* 1-56-09-36-04 (office). *E-mail:* alain .carpentier@hop.egp.ap-hop-paris.fr (office); prcarpentier@europost.org (office).

CARPENTIER, Jean Claude Gabriel; French aeronautical engineer; *Scientific Adviser, Office Nationale d'études et de recherches aérospatiales (ONERA);* b. 13 April 1926, Haspres; m. Micheline Robinet 1950; ed Ecole Polytechnique, Ecole Nationale Supérieure Aéronautique et Espace; Service technique de l'aéronautique 1950; Direction des recherches et moyens d'essais 1961; Dir Direction des recherches, études et techniques, Ministry of Defence 1977; Pres. Office Nat. d'études et de recherches aérospatiales (ONERA) 1984–91, Sr Consultant 1991–; Scientific Adviser 1991–; Pres. Man. Cttee Nat. Meteorological Bureau 1989–94; Pres. Comité Avion-Ozone 1992–96; Ed. Aerospace Research 1994–; Co-Ed.-in-Chief Aerospace Science and Technology 1997–, Revue Scientifique et Technique de la Défense; mem. Acad. Nat. de l'Air et de l'Espace; Commdr Légion d'honneur, Ordre Nat. du Mérite; Médaille de l'Aéronautique. *Publications:* Flight Mechanics 1952, Autopilots 1953, Inertial Navigation 1962, Recherche Aéronautique et Progrès de l'Aviation 1999. *Leisure interest:* history. *Address:* Office National d'études et de recherches aérospatiales, 29 avenue de la Division Leclerc, PO Box 72, 92322 Chatillon Cedex, France (office). *Telephone:* 1-46-73-40-01 (office). *Fax:* 1-46-73-41-65 (office). *Website:* www.onera.fr (office).

CARPENTIER, Michel André Georges, LenD, LenSc (Econ); French international organization official and international science consultant; b. 23 Oct. 1930, Billy Montigny, Pas de Calais; m. Annick Puget 1956; four s.; ed Ecole des Hautes Etudes Commerciales, Ecole des Sciences Politiques and Univ. of Paris; Commissariat à l'Energie Atomique (CEA) 1958; EURATOM 1959; Head of Dept Industrial, Technological and Scientific Affairs, EC Comm. 1967, Dir-Gen. Environment 1977, Dir-Gen. Energy 1981; Dir-Gen. Task Force for Information Technologies and Telecommunications, EC Comm. 1984; Dir-Gen. Information Technologies and Telecommunications, EC Comm. 1986; Dir-Gen. DG XIII, Telecommunications, Information Markets and Exploitation of Research, EC Comm. 1993–95; Hon. Dir-Gen. and Special Adviser EU Comm. 1996–; industrial adviser 1996–97; Pres. Scientific Cttee Aquitaine Europe Communication 1997; mem. Econ. and Social Cttee, EC Comm., Paris 1995–96; Pres. Centre Informatique Documentaire (CID) 1997–98, Paris, Orientation Cttee, AEC 1998–2004; Vice-Pres. AIACE, Paris; Municipal Councillor for Montcaret 2002–; Hon. mem. IEEE (USA), Royal Swedish Acad. of Eng Science; Chevalier, Légion d'honneur, Ehrenkreuz für Wissenschaft und Forschung (Austria), Commdr, Ordre du Mérite (Luxembourg), Order of the Rising Sun (Japan); Dr hc (Loughborough, Madrid). *Publications:* Telecommunications in Transition (with others) 1992, The French Space Policy 1998. *Leisure interests:* fishing, classical music, opera, reading. *Address:* Domaine de Lespinassat, 24230 Montcaret, France (home). *Telephone:* (5) 53-58-66-05 (home). *Fax:* (5) 53-58-66-05 (home). *E-mail:* m.carpentier@wanadoo.fr.

CARPER, Thomas Richard, BA, MBA; American politician; *Senator from Delaware;* b. 23 Jan. 1947, Beckley, W Va; s. of Wallace Richard Carper and Mary Jean Carper (née Patton); m. Martha Stacy 1986; two s.; ed Ohio State Univ. (Navy ROTC scholarship), Univ. of Delaware; raised in Va; Commdr in USN 1968–73, Capt., USN Reserve 1973–91; industrial devt specialist, then State Treasurer, State of Del., Dover 1976–83; mem. US House of Reps from Del. 1983–93; Gov. of Delaware 1993–2001; Senator from Delaware 2001–, Deputy Whip 2004–11, Co-Chair. Senate Nuclear Caucus, Senate Recycling Caucus, Congressional Fire Services Caucus, Co-Chair. Senate Moderate Democrats Working Group; fmr mem. Nat. Govs Assoc (Vice-Chair. 1997–98, Chair. 1998–99); Hon. Chair. Delaware Special Olympics 1987–; Hon. Co-Chair. Third Way. *Leisure interests:* physical fitness, running, weightlifting, tennis, reading, raising two sons. *Address:* 513 Hart Senate Office Building, Washington, DC 20510 (office); 600 West Matson Run Parkway, Wilmington, DE 19802, USA (home). *Telephone:* (202) 224-2441 (office). *Fax:* (202) 228-2190 (office). *E-mail:* carper@senate.gov (office). *Website:* carper.senate.gov (office).

CARR, Sir (Albert) Raymond Maillard, Kt, MA, DLitt, FRSL, FRHistS, FBA; British historian; b. 11 April 1919, Bath, England; s. of Reginald Henry Maillard Carr and Ethel Gertrude Marion Carr; m. Sara Ann Mary Strickland 1950; three s. one d.; ed Brockenhurst School and Christ Church, Oxford; Gladstone Research Exhibitioner, Christ Church 1941; Fellow, All Souls Coll., Oxford 1946–53, New Coll. 1953–64, St Antony's Coll. 1964–; Dir Latin American Centre 1964–68, Chair. Soc. for Latin American Studies 1966–68; Prof. of History of Latin America, Univ. of Oxford 1967–68, Warden St Antony's Coll. 1968–87; mem. Nat. Theatre Bd 1980; Corresp. mem. Royal Acad. of History, Madrid 1968; Hon. Fellow, Christ Church Coll., St Antony's Coll., Oxford; Grand Cross of the Order of Alfonso El Sabio (for services to Spanish history) 1983; Hon. DLitt (Madrid); Prince of Asturias Award in Social Sciences 1999. *Publications:* Spain 1808–1939 1966, Latin American Affairs (ed.) 1969, The Republic and the Civil War in Spain (ed.) 1971, English Fox Hunting 1976, The Spanish Tragedy: The Civil War in Perspective 1977, Spain: Dictatorship to Democracy (co-author) 1979, Modern Spain 1980, Fox-Hunting (with Sara Carr) 1982, Puerto Rico: A Colonial Experiment 1984, The Spanish Civil War (ed.) 1986, The Chances of Death: A Diary of the Spanish Civil War (ed.) 1995, Visiones de fin de siglo 1999, Spain: A History (ed.) 2001; contrib. to scholarly books and journals. *Leisure interest:* foxhunting. *Address:* 58 Fitzgerace Avenue, London, W14 0SW, England (home). *Telephone:* (20) 7603-6975 (home).

CARR, Jack, DPhil, FRSE; British mathematician and academic; *Professor, Department of Mathematics, Heriot-Watt University;* b. 29 Aug. 1948, Newcastle-upon-Tyne; s. of John George Carr and Elizabeth Eleanor Carr; m. Teresa Nancy Thorpe 1976; one s. two d.; ed Walbottle Secondary School, Univ. of Bath, St Catherine's Coll., Oxford; Lecturer, Heriot-Watt Univ., Edin. 1974–83, Prof. of Math. 1983–; Visiting Prof., Brown Univ., USA 1978–79, Michigan State Univ., USA 1982, Ecole Polytechnique, Lausanne, Switzerland 1983. *Publication:* Applications of Centre Manifolds 1981. *Leisure interest:* cricket. *Address:* Department of Mathematics, School of Mathematical and Computer Sciences, Room CM.G03, Scott Russell Building, Heriot-Watt University, Riccarton, Edinburgh, EH14 4AS (office); 42 Balgreen Avenue, Edinburgh, EH12 5SU, Scotland. *Telephone:* (131) 451-3229 (office). *Fax:* (131) 451-3249 (office). *E-mail:* J.Carr@ ma.hw.ac.uk (office). *Website:* www.ma.hw.ac.uk/maths/People/Frontpages/jack .html (office).

CARR, Robert (Bob) John, BA; Australian politician; b. 28 Sept. 1947; s. of Edward Carr and Phyllis Carr; m. Helena Carr; ed Univ. of New South Wales;

journalist, ABC Radio 1969–71; Educ. Officer, NSW Council 1972–78; mem. NSW Parl. for Maroubra 1983–2005, Leader of the Opposition of NSW 1988–95, Premier of NSW 1995–2005 (resgnd); Senator for NSW 2012–; Minister of Foreign Affairs 2012–13; mem. Int. Task Force on Climate Change 2004; mem. Labor Party; Life mem. Wilderness Soc. 2003–; Kt Grand Cross, Order of Merit of the Italian Repub. 2008; World Conservation Union Int. Parks Merit Award. *Publications include:* Thoughtlines 2002, What Australia Means to Me 2003, My Reading Life 2008. *Address:* Australian Labor Party (ALP), POB 6222, Kingston, ACT 2604, Australia (office). *Telephone:* (2) 6120-0800 (office). *Fax:* (2) 6120-0801 (office). *E-mail:* info@cbr.alp.org.au (office). *Website:* www.alp.org.au (office).

CARR, Roderick (Rod) M., LLB, BCom, MA, MBA, PhD; New Zealand central banker, business executive and university administrator; *Vice-Chancellor, University of Canterbury;* b. 26 Nov. 1958; m.; four c.; ed Wharton Business School, Univ. of Pennsylvania, Columbia Univ., New York, USA, Otago Univ.; fmr Head of Global Payments, Nat. Australian Bank, Melbourne; Deputy CEO and Deputy Gov. Reserve Bank of New Zealand –2003, fmr Acting Gov., re-apptd to Reserve Bank Board of Dirs 2012, Chair. 2013–; Man. Dir Jade Software Corpn Ltd 2003–09; Vice-Chancellor, Univ. of Canterbury 2009–; Chair. National Infrastructure Advisory Bd; mem. Bd of Dirs Lyttelton Port Company Ltd, Taranaki Investment Management Ltd, Canterbury Employers' Chamber of Commerce, New Zealand International Business Forum; mem. Otago Business School Bd of Advisers, Univ. of Canterbury Coll. of Business and Econs; Dir Canterbury Employers' Chamber of Commerce 2006–; Fellow, NZ Inst. of Man.; NZ Hi-Tech Co. Leader of the Year 2006. *Publication:* Productivity and Efficiency in the US Life Insurance Industry. *Leisure interests:* running, swimming, hiking. *Address:* Vice-Chancellor's Office, Private Bag 4800, University of Canterbury, Christchurch 8140, New Zealand (office). *Website:* www.canterbury.ac.nz/vco.

CARR, Sir Roger Martyn, Kt, FRSA; British business executive; *Chairman, BAE Systems plc;* b. 22 Dec. 1946; various sr positions, including CEO Williams PLC and Chair. Thames Water PLC 1984–2000; Chair. Chubb PLC 2000–02; mem. Bd of Dirs Centrica plc 2001–14, Chair. 2004–14, also Chair. Nominations Cttee; mem. Bd of Dirs Cadbury-Schweppes plc 2001–, Deputy Chair. 2003–08, Chair. 2008–; Chair. Mitchells & Butlers plc –2008; Dir (non-exec.) and Chair. BAE Systems plc 2014–; Dir (non-exec.) Six Continents PLC 2002; Pres. CBI 2011–13; Deputy Chair. and Sr Ind. Dir Court of the Bank of England; Sr Adviser, Kohlberg Kravis Roberts Co. Ltd; mem. or fmr mem. Industrial Devt Advisory Bd, Manufacture Council of the CBI, Higgs Cttee on Corp. Governance, Business for New Europe; Trustee, Landau Forte Charitable Trust; Visiting Fellow, Said Business School, Oxford, Companion of the Inst. of Man. *Address:* BAE Systems plc, Stirling Square, 6 Carlton Gardens, London SW1Y 5AD, England (office). *Telephone:* (1252) 373232 (office). *Website:* www.baesystems.com (office).

CARRANZA UGARTE, Luis, DEcon; Peruvian economist, banker and government official; b. 1967; ed Pontifical Catholic Univ. of Peru, Lima, Univ. of Minnesota, USA; worked as official at IMF for several years 1990s; worked in Dept of Econ. Investigation, US Fed. Reserve Bank of Minneapolis 1990s; apptd Deputy Finance Minister and Dir Cen. Bank by Pres. Alejandro Toledo 2004–05 (resgnd); Chief Economist for Latin America and Emerging Markets, Banco Bilbao Vizcaya Argentaria 2005–06; consultant, IDB; Minister of Economy and Finance 2006–08, Jan.–Dec. 2009 (resgnd); Visiting Prof., Univ. of Navarra, Spain. *Address:* c/o Ministry of Economy and Finance, Jirón Junín 339, 4°, Circado de Lima, Lima 1, Peru (office).

CARRARD, François Denis Etienne, Dr. iur.; Swiss lawyer and fmr international organization official; *Senior Partner, Carrard & Associés;* b. 19 Jan. 1938, Lausanne; ed Lausanne, John Muir High School, Pasadena, Calif., USA, Univ. of Lausanne; with audit co., Lausanne 1962; with law firm, Stockholm, Sweden 1963–64; Attorney, Lausanne 1965–, admitted to Bar of Vaud (Swiss Bar) 1967, Sr Pnr, Etude Carrard, Paschoud, Heim et Associés (now Carrard & Associés); Dir-Gen. IOC 1989–2003, currently Sr Adviser in charge of legal affairs; Chair. Montreux Jazz Festival Foundation; fmr Pres. Automobile-Club de Suisse; fmr Vice-Pres. Bd of Vintage Brands of Vaud; fmr mem. Swiss Fed. Comm. of Foreign Indemnities; mem. Ordre des Avocats Vaudois, Fédération Suisse des Avocats, Int. Bar Asscn, Asscn Suisse de l'Arbitrage, Union Internationale des Avocats; Chair. and Dir of various cos; Commdr, Orden del Mérito Civil (Spain) 1992, Officier, Ordre de Saint-Charles (Monaco) 1993. *Address:* Carrard & Associés, PO Box 7191, Place Saint-François 1, 1002 Lausanne, Switzerland (office). *Telephone:* (21) 3491919 (office). *Fax:* (21) 3491920 (office). *E-mail:* fcarrard@carrard-associes.ch (office). *Website:* www.carrard-associes.ch (office).

CARRARO, Franco; Italian sports administrator and business executive; *President, MCC—Mediocredito Centrale SpA;* b. 6 Dec. 1939, Padua; m.; two c.; Pres. Italian Water-skiing Fed. 1962–76, Chair. Tech. Comm. 1963–67; Chair. World Water-skiing Union 1967–73; Chair. football team Milan Calcio 1967–71; fmr Chair. Comm. for Amateur and Professional Football; fmr Chair. Sub-comm. for Professional Football, UEFA, now mem. UEFA Exec. Cttee; Vice-Pres. Italian Nat. Olympic Cttee 1976–78, Pres. 1978–; Vice-Pres. Alitalia 1981–87; Minister of Tourism and Performing Arts 1987–90; Mayor of Rome 1989–93; Chair. Impregilio 1994–99; Pres. MCC—Mediocredito Centrale SpA (bank) 2000–; mem. Int. Olympic Cttee 1982–, Vice-Chair. Comm. for the Olympic Programme 1983–94, Chair. Olympic Programme Working Group 1998–2001, mem. Exec. Bd 2000–04, Chair. Olympic Programme Comm. 2002–; Pres. Italian Football Fed. (Federazione Italiana Gioco Calcio) 1976–78, 2001–06; Chair. Asscn of European Olympic Cttees 1980–87; Chair. Organizing Cttee World Cup Football Championship 1990;. *Achievements include:* fmr champion water skier, Italian jr champion 1953–54, Italian Open champion 1955–60, European champion, slalom and combined 1956 and 1961, European team champion 1958, 1959, 1960; bronze medallist World Championships 1957. *Address:* MCC SpA, Via Piemonte 51, 00187 Rome, Italy (office). *Telephone:* (06) 47911 (office). *Fax:* (06) 47913130 (office). *Website:* www.mcc.it (office).

CARRASQUILLA BARRERA, Alberto, BS, MS, PhD; Colombian politician and economist; b. Bogotá; ed Univ. of Los Andes, Univ. of Illinois, USA; Tech. Man., Banco de la República 1993–97; Prin. Economist, Investigation Div., IDB, Washington, DC 1997–99; Econ. Adviser, Gen. Repub. Controllership 1999–2000; fmr Assoc. Teacher, Univ. of Los Andes, Dean Faculty of Econs

2000–02; Deputy Minister of Finance 2002–03, Minister of Finance 2003–07; fmr Assoc. Investigator, Fedesarrollo. *Address:* c/o Ministry of Finance and Public Credit, Carrera 8a, No 6–64, Of. 305, Bogotá, DC, Colombia (office).

CARRELL, Robin Wayne, MA, PhD, DSc, FRS, FRCP, FRSNZ; New Zealand haematologist and academic; *Professor of Haematology, University of Cambridge;* b. 5 April 1936, Christchurch; s. of Ruane George Carrell and Constance Gwendoline Carrell (née Rowe); m. Susan Wyatt Rogers 1962; two s. two d.; ed Christchurch Boys' High School, Univs of Otago and Canterbury, Univ. of Cambridge, UK; mem. MRC Haemoglobin Unit, Cambridge 1965–68; Dir Clinical Biochemistry, Christchurch Hosp., NZ 1968–75; Lecturer in Clinical Biochemistry, Univ. of Cambridge 1976–78, Prof. of Haematology 1986–; Prof. of Clinical Biochemistry and Dir Molecular Research Lab., Christchurch Clinical School of Medicine, Otago Univ. 1978–86; Commonwealth Fellow, St John's Coll., Cambridge and Visiting Scientist, MRC Lab. of Molecular Biology 1985; Gov. Imperial Coll. London 1997–98, mem. Court 1999–2003; Pres. British Soc. of Thrombosis and Haemostasis 1999; Fellow, Trinity Coll., Cambridge 1987–; Royal Soc. of NZ Hector Medal 1986. *Publications:* articles in scientific journals on genetic abnormalities of human proteins and new protein family, serpins. *Leisure interests:* gardening, walking. *Address:* 19 Madingley Road, Cambridge, CB3 0EG (home); Haematology Department, University of Cambridge, Cambridge Institute for Medical Research, Hills Road, Cambridge, CB2 2XY, England (office). *Telephone:* (1223) 312970 (office). *E-mail:* rwc1000@cam.ac.uk (office).

CARREÑO, Jose Manuel; Cuban ballet dancer; *Principal Dancer, American Ballet Theatre;* b. 25 May 1968, Havana; ed Prov. School of Ballet and Nat. Ballet School, Cuba; with Nat. Ballet of Cuba 1986–90; joined English Nat. Ballet 1990; Prin. Dancer, The Royal Ballet 1993–95; Prin. Dancer, American Ballet Theatre 1995–(2011); numerous appearances in Europe, Latin America, USA and Japan; Gold Medal, NY Int. Ballet Competition 1987, Grand Prix, Int. Ballet Competition, Jackson, MS 1990, Dance Magazine Award 2004. *Repertoire includes:* (with English Nat. Ballet): Solor in La Bayadère, the Prince in Cinderella, Franz in Coppélia, Albrecht in Giselle, the Prince and the Gopak in The Nutcracker, Romeo in Romeo and Juliet, Petruchio in The Taming of the Shrew, pas de deux in A Stranger I Came, Graduation Ball and Prince Igor; (with The Royal Ballet): Bluebird in The Sleeping Beauty, Basilio in Don Quixiote, Oberon and Puck in The Dream, leading role in Caught Dance and Herman Schmerman; (with American Ballet Theatre): title role in Apollo, leading role in Ballet Imperial, Conrad, Ali, the Slave and Lanckendem in Le Corsaire, third sailor in Fancy Free, Danilo in The Merry Widow, pas de deux in The Nutcracker, leading role in Push Comes to Shove, the Son in Prodigal Son, Romeo and Mercutio in Romeo and Juliet, Prince Desire in The Sleeping Beauty, Misgir in The Snow Maiden, Prince Siegfield in Swan Lake, leading role Études, Themes and Variations, Stepping Stones, Raymonda, Petit Mort. *Films:* Born to be Wild, PBS. *Address:* American Ballet Theatre, 890 Broadway, New York, NY 10003, USA (office). *Telephone:* (212) 477-3030 (office); (646) 912-9380 (home). *Fax:* (646) 912-9380 (home). *E-mail:* jcarreno@aol.com (home). *Website:* www.abt.org (office).

CARRERAS, José; Spanish singer (tenor); b. 5 Dec. 1947, Barcelona; s. of José Carreras and Antonia Carreras; m. Ana Elisa Carreras; one s. one d.; opera debut as Gennaro in Lucrezia Borgia, Liceo Opera House, Barcelona 1970–71 season; appeared in La Bohème, Un Ballo in Maschera and I Lombardi alla Prima Crociata at Teatro Regio, Parma, Italy 1972; US debut as Pinkerton in Madame Butterfly with New York City Opera 1972; debut at Metropolitan Opera as Cavaradossi 1974; debut at La Scala as Riccardo in Un Ballo in Maschera 1975; has appeared at major opera houses and festivals including Teatro Colón, Buenos Aires, Covent Garden, London, Vienna Staatsoper, Easter Festival and Summer Festival, Salzburg, Lyric Opera of Chicago; Pres. José Carreras Int. Leukaemia Foundation 1988–; Hon. mem. RAM 1990; Commdr des Arts et des Lettres, Chevalier, Légion d'honneur; Grammy Award 1991, Sir Lawrence Olivier Award 1993, Gold Medal of City of Barcelona, Albert Schweizer Music Award 1996, ECHO Klassik Lifetime Achievement Award 2008, Classical BRIT Lifetime Achievement Award 2009; numerous other awards and prizes. *Recordings include:* Un Ballo in Maschera, La Battaglia di Legnano, Il Corsaro, Un Giorno di Regno, I Due Foscari, Simone Boccanegra, Macbeth, Don Carlos, Tosca, Thais, Aida, Cavalleria Rusticana, Pagliacci, Lucia di Lammermoor, Turandot, Elisabetta, regina d'Inghilterra, Otello (Rossini). *Films include:* La Bohème, I Lombardi, Andrea Chenier, Turandot, Carmen, Don Carlos, La Forza del Destino, Fedora, Jerusalem, My Life. *Publication:* Singing from the Soul 1991. *Address:* c/o José Carreras International Leukaemia Foundation, Muntaner 383, 2n, 08021 Barcelona (office). *Telephone:* (90) 2240480 (office). *Fax:* (93) 2010588 (office). *E-mail:* info@fcarreras .es (office); info@josepcarreras.com (office). *Website:* www.fcarreras.es (office); www.josepcarreras.com

CARRÈRE D'ENCAUSSE, Hélène, DèsSc; French political scientist; *Secretary for Life, Académie française;* b. 6 July 1929, Paris; d. of Georges Zourabichvili and Nathalie von Pelken; m. Louis Carrère 1952; one s. two d.; ed Univ. of Paris, Sorbonne; fmr Prof., Univ. of Paris (Sorbonne); currently Prof., Inst. d'Etudes Politiques, Paris and Dir of Research, Fondation Nationale des Sciences Politiques; Pres. Radio Sorbonne-Radio France 1984–87; Advisor on Reconstruction and Devt, European Bank 1992; fmr mem. Bd of Dirs East-West Inst. for Security Studies; Visiting Prof. at numerous univs in USA; mem. Acad. française, Sec. for Life 2000–; Foreign mem. Russian Acad. of Sciences 2003–, Acad. of Georgia; Assoc. mem. Acad. Royale de Belgique; mem. European Parl. 1994–99; fmr Vice-Pres. Comm. on Foreign Affairs and Defence, on French Diplomatic Archives; mem. Nat. Council for New Devts in Human and Social Sciences 1998; Pres. Statistical Observatory on Immigration and Integration 2004; Hon. mem. Acad. of Georgia; Commdr, Order of Cultural Merit (Monaco) 1999; Grand-Croix de la Légion d'honneur 2011; Officier, Ordre nat. du Mérite; Commdr des Palmes académiques, des Arts et des Lettres, Ordre de Léopold de Belgique; Dr hc (Montréal, Louvain); Prix de la Fondation Louis-Weiss 1986, Prix Comenius 1992, Lomonosov Gold Medal, Russian Acad. of Sciences 2008. *Publications include:* Le marxisme et l'Asie 1965, Réforme et révolution chez les musulmans de l'Empire russe 1966, L'URSS et la Chine devant les révolutions dans les sociétés pré-industrielles 1970, L'Empire éclaté (Prix Aujourd'hui) 1978, Lénine: la révolution et le pouvoir 1979, Staline: l'ordre par la terreur 1979, Le pouvoir confisqué 1982, Le Grand Frère 1983, La déstalinisation commence 1984, Ni paix ni guerre 1986, Le Grand Défi:

bolcheviks et nations 1917–30 1987, Le Malheur russe 1988, La Gloire des nations ou la fin de l'Empire soviétique 1991, Victorieuse Russie 1992, Nicholas II: la transition interrompue (Prix des Ambassadeurs) 1996, Lénine 1998, La Russie inachevée 2000, Catherine II 2002, L'Impératrice et l'abbé un duel littéraire ivédit 2003, L'Empire d'Eurasie 2005, La Deuxième Mort de Staline 2006, Alexandre II. Le printemps de la Russie 2008, La Russie entre deux mondes 2010, Des siècles d'immortalité. L'Académie française 1635–... 2011, Les Romanov – Une dynastie sous le règne du sang 2013. *Address:* Académie française, 23 quai Conti, 75270 Paris Cedex 06 – CS 90618, France (office). *Telephone:* 1-44-41-43-00 (office). *Fax:* 1-43-29-47-45 (office). *E-mail:* contact@academie-francaise.fr (office). *Website:* www.academie-francaise.fr (office).

CARREY, Jim; Canadian/American film actor; b. 17 Jan. 1962, Newmarket, Ont., Canada; s. of Percy Carrey and Kathleen Carrey; m. 1st Melissa Worner 1986 (divorced); one d.; m. 2nd Lauren Holly 2001; began performing in comedy clubs in Toronto aged 17, before moving to Los Angeles 1979; Star on Hollywood Walk of Fame 2000, American Film Inst. Star Award 2005. *Films include:* All in Good Taste 1983, The Sex and Violence Family Hour 1983, Introducing... Janet 1983, Copper Mountain 1983, Finders Keepers 1984, Once Bitten 1985, Peggy Sue Got Married 1986, The Dead Pool 1988, Earth Girls Are Easy 1988, Pink Cadillac 1989, The Itsy Bitsy Spider (voice) 1992, Ace Ventura: Pet Detective (also screenplay) 1994, The Mask 1994, High Strung 1994, Dumb & Dumber 1994, Batman Forever 1995, Ace Ventura: When Nature Calls 1995, The Cable Guy (MTV Movie Award) 1996, Liar Liar (Blockbuster Entertainment Award) 1997, The Truman Show (Golden Globe for Best Performance 1999) 1998, Simon Birch 1998, Man on the Moon (Golden Globe for Best Performance 2000) 1999, Me, Myself & Irene 2000, How the Grinch Stole Christmas 2000, The Majestic 2001, Bruce Almighty 2003, Pecan Pie 2003, Eternal Sunshine of the Spotless Mind 2004, Lemony Snicket's A Series of Unfortunate Events 2004, Fun with Dick and Jane 2005, The Number 23 2007, Horton Hears a Who! (voice) 2008, Yes Man 2008, I Love You Phillip Morris 2009, A Christmas Carol 2009, Mr Pepper's Penguins 2011. *Television includes:* The Duck Factory (series) 1984, Mike Hammer: Murder Takes All 1989, In Living Color (series, also writer) 1990–94, Doing Time on Maple Drive 1992, The Office (series) 2011, 30 Rock (series) 2012. *Address:* c/o Jimmy Miller, 10th Floor, 9200 Sunset Blvd, Los Angeles, CA 90069, USA (office).

CARRICK, Hon. Sir John Leslie, KCMG, AC, BEcons; Australian politician (retd) and educationalist; b. 4 Sept. 1918, Sydney; s. of Arthur James Carrick and Emily Ellen Carrick (née Terry); m. Diana Margaret Hunter 1951; three d.; ed Sydney Tech. High School, Univ. of Sydney; commissioned Univ. of Sydney Regt 1939, served in Australian Imperial Force, Sparrow Force; POW 1942–45; mem. Citizen Mil. Force 1948–51; Gen. Sec. NSW Div. of Liberal Party of Australia 1948–71; mem. Senate 1971–87; mem. Library Cttee 1971–73, Senate Standing Cttee on Educ., Science and the Arts 1971–75, Senate Standing Cttee on Foreign Affairs and Defence 1971–74, Jt Cttee on Foreign Affairs 1971–72, on Foreign Affairs and Defence 1973–75, Senate Standing Cttee on Standing Orders 1978–83, Senate Select Cttee on Human Embryo Experimentation Bill 1985 1985–, Standing Cttee on Regulations and Ordinances 1983–86, Jt Select Cttee on Electoral Reform 1983–87; Opposition Spokesman for Federalism and Intergovernment Relations 1975; Minister for Housing and Construction, for Urban and Regional Devt Nov.–Dec. 1975, for Educ. 1975–79, Minister assisting the Prime Minister in Fed. Affairs 1975–78; Leader of Govt in the Senate 1978–83, Vice-Pres. of Exec. Council 1978–82; Minister for Nat. Devt and Energy 1979–83; Chair. NSW State Govt Cttee Review of Schools 1988–89, Advisory Cttee GERRIC, Univ. of NSW 1997–2006; Pres. Univ. of Sydney Dermatology Research Foundation 1989–2003; Chair. Gas Council of NSW 1990–95; mem. NSW Exec. Cttee, Foundation for Aged Care 1989–2000, Ministerial Advisory Council on Teacher Educ. and Quality of Teaching 1992–95, Advisory Bd Inst. of Early Childhood, Macquarie Univ. 1992–2000; Chair. Inst. of Early Childhood Foundation 2001–; Commonwealth Gov. Roundtable on Indigenous Capacity 2000; Hon. FACE 1994; Hon. DLitt (Sydney) 1988, (Macquarie) 2000, (Univ. of Western Sydney) 2006; Hon. D Educ. (NSW) 2006; Centenary Medal 2000. *Leisure interests:* walking, reading. *Address:* Apt 21, 162E Burwood Road, Concord, NSW 2137, Australia (home). *Telephone:* (2) 9747-8320 (home). *Fax:* (2) 747-8340 (home).

CARRICK, Sir Roger John, Kt, KCMG, LVO; British international consultant and fmr diplomatist; *Chairman, Lime Finance;* b. 13 Oct. 1937, Middx; s. of John Carrick and Florence Carrick; m. Hilary E. Blinman 1962; two s.; ed Isleworth Grammar School, Jt Services School for Linguists and School of Slavonic and E European Studies, Univ. of London; RN 1956–58; joined HM Diplomatic Service 1956; served in Sofia 1962, FCO 1965, Paris 1967, Singapore 1971, FCO 1973–77; Visiting Fellow, Inst. of Int. Affairs, Univ. of Calif., Berkeley 1977–78; Counsellor, Washington, DC 1978; Head, Overseas Estate Dept FCO 1982; Consul-Gen., Chicago 1985–88; Asst Under-Sec. of State (Econ.), FCO 1988–90; Amb. to Indonesia 1990–94; High Commr to Australia 1994–97; currently Chair. Lime Capital; Deputy Chair. Britain-Australia Soc. 1998–99, Chair. 1999–2002, Vice-Pres. 2003–, Pres. West Country Br. 2003–; Dir (non-exec.) cmb technologies 2000–02; Chair. (non-exec.) Charteris Mackie & Baillie Ltd 2001–03; Deputy Chair. The D Group 1999–2007; Dir Strategy International Ltd 2001–07, Chair. 2007–09; Trustee, Chevening Estate 1998–2003, Britain-Australia Bicentennial Trust; Churchill Fellow, Westminster Coll., Mo. 1986; Freeman of the City of London 2002. *Publications:* East-West Technology Transfer in Perspective 1978, RolleroundOz: Reflections on a Journey Around Australia 1998. *Leisure interests:* sailing, reading, music, theatre, travel, public speaking, avoiding gardening. *Address:* Lime Finance, 31 Ironmarket, Newcastle-under-Lyme, Staffs., ST5 1RP, England (office). *Website:* lime-finance.com (office).

CARRIER, Jean-Guy; Canadian business executive and international organization official; *Secretary-General, International Chamber of Commerce;* various positions with Int. Inst. for Systems Analysis, Vienna, Austria, Econ. Council of Canada, CBC and with several global communications consulting firms; several sr positions with WTO 1996–2008, including Publr and Chief Ed.; Acting Sec.-Gen., ICC 2010–11, Sec.-Gen. 2011–, also Dir of Programmes, ICC Research Foundation; mem. UN Global Compact Bd. *Publications include:* My Father's House 1974, Family 1977, A Cage of Bone 1978, The Trudeau Decade (co-author) 1979, Patriots and Traitors 1992, The End of War 1992; numerous articles in nat. and int. media. *Address:* International Chamber of Commerce, 38 cours Albert 1er, 75008 Paris,

France (office). *Telephone:* 1-49-53-28-28 (office). *Fax:* 1-49-53-28-59 (office). *Website:* www.iccwbo.org (office).

CARRIERE, Berthold, MMus; Canadian composer and music director; *Director of Music, Stratford Festival;* b. 27 Feb. 1940, Ottawa; s. of Rolland and Berthe Carriere (Paradis); m. Nancy Carpenter 1969; ed Univs of Montréal and Western Ontario; Musical Dir, Banff School of Fine Arts 1968–72; Resident Musical Dir, Theatre London 1972–74, Dir of Music 1976–77, Assoc. Dir 1976; Dir of Music, Stratford Festival 1976–83, 1985–; Musical Dir, Talk of Toronto 1980–82; Conductor/Arranger, Dominion Day Celebrations 1967; Man of the Year, City of Ottawa 1967, Guthrie Award, Stratford Shakespearean Festival 1976, Dora Mavor Moore Musical Dir Award 1981, 1982, 1987. *Address:* Stratford Festival, POB 1013, Stratford, Ont., N5A 6V4 (office); Box 1273, St Mary's, Ont., N0M 2V0, Canada (home). *Website:* www.stratford-festival.on.ca (office).

CARRILLO ZÜRCHER, Federico, LLB; Costa Rican lawyer, banker and fmr government official; *CEO, Banco Internacional de Costa Rica SA;* b. 29 Sept. 1964, San José; m.; four c.; ed Austin Community Coll. and Univ. of Texas, USA, Univ. of Costa Rica; Fulbright-Hats Scholarship, Northwestern Univ., Evanston, Ill., USA 1990; worked in investment banks in New York 1990–2000, later Exec. Vice-Pres. Lehman Brothers, Inc. and Salomon Brothers; Man. Costa Rican Stock Exchange 2000–04; Dir Tech. Advisory Cttee on Civil Aviation 2004; Minister of Finance 2004–05; Vice-Pres. Cen. American Bank for Econ. Integration 2005–06; CEO Banco Internacional de Costa Rica SA, Panama City 2007–. *Address:* Banco Internacional de Costa Rica SA, Casa Matriz, Calle Manuel Maria Icaza No. 25, Apartado 0816-07810, Panamá, Panama (office). *Website:* www.bicsapan.com (office).

CARRINGTON, Edwin Wilberforce, MSc; Trinidad and Tobago economist and international organization official; *Ambassador, Caribbean Community and Common Market (CARICOM);* b. 23 June 1938; m.; two s. one d.; ed Univ. of the West Indies, McGill Univ., Montreal, Canada; Admin. Cadet, Cen. Planning Unit, Prime Minister's Office 1964; Chief of Econs and Statistics, Caribbean Community and Common Market (CARICOM) 1973–76, Dir Trade and Integration Div. 1973–76, Sec.-Gen. CARICOM 1992–2010 (retd), Amb. to CARICOM 2011–; Deputy Sec.-Gen. African, Caribbean and Pacific (ACP) states 1976–85, Sec.-Gen. 1985; High Commr to Guyana 1991; Sec.-Gen. Caribbean Forum ACP states; Duarte Sanchez y Mella, Gran Cruz de Plata (Dominican Repub.) 1993, Trinity Cross (Trinidad and Tobago 2005, Chaconia Medal Gold (Trinidad and Tobago) 1987, Order of Distinction (Belize) 2001, Companion of Honour (Barbados) 2002, Order of Jamaica (Jamaica) 2003, Cacique Crown of Honour (Guyana) 2003, Cacique's Crown of Honour (Guyana) 2004, Kt Commdr of Most Distinguished Order of Nation (Antigua and Barbuda) 2010, Order of Caribbean Community 2011; Dr hc (Univ. of the West Indies) 2005, (Medgar Evers Coll., CUNY) 1995; Pinnacle Award Nat. Coalition of Caribbean Affairs. *Publications include:* Industrialization by Invitation: The Case of Trinidad and Tobago 1968, The Solution of Economic Problems through Regional Groupings (jtly), Tourism as a Vehicle for Economic Development 1975. *Address:* Caribbean Community and Common Market (CARICOM), POB 10827, Georgetown (office); Colgrain House, 205 Camp Street, Georgetown, Guyana (home). *Telephone:* (2) 222-0001 (office). *Fax:* (2) 222-0171 (office). *E-mail:* info@caricom.org (office). *Website:* www.caricom .org (office).

CARRINGTON, 6th Baron; Peter Alexander Rupert Carrington, KG, GCMG, CH, MC, PC, JP, DL; British politician and international administrator; b. 6 June 1919, London; s. of 5th Baron Carrington and the Hon. Sybil Marion Colville; m. Iona McClean 1942; one s. two d.; ed Eton Coll. and Royal Mil. Coll., Sandhurst; Grenadier Guards 1939, served in NW Europe; Parl. Sec., Ministry of Agric. 1951–54, Ministry of Defence 1954–56; High Commr in Australia 1956–59; First Lord of the Admiralty 1959–63; Minister without Portfolio (at the Foreign Office), Leader of the House of Lords 1963–64; Leader of the Opposition in the House of Lords 1964–70, 1974–79; Sec. of State for Defence 1970–74, also Minister of Aviation Supply 1971–74; Chair. Conservative Party 1972–74; Sec. of State for Energy Jan.–March 1974, for Foreign and Commonwealth Affairs 1979–82, Minister of Overseas Devt 1979–82; Chair. GEC 1983–84; Sec.-Gen. NATO 1984–88; Chair. Christie's Int. PLC 1988–93 (Dir 1988–); sits in the House of Lords as Lord Carrington of Upton 1999–; Dir The Daily Telegraph 1990–2003; EC Negotiating Cttee on Yugoslavia 1991 (resgnd Aug. 1992); Chancellor Univ. of Reading 1992–2007; Sec. for Foreign Correspondence and Hon. mem. Royal Acad. of Arts 1982–; Chair. Bd Trustees, Victoria and Albert Museum 1983–88; Pres. The Pilgrims 1983–2002, VSO 1993–98; mem. Kissinger Associates 1982–84, 1988–; Pres. Chiltern Open Air Museum 1983–; Hon. Bencher of the Middle Temple 1983; Hon. Fellow, St Antony's Coll., Oxford 1982–; Chancellor, Order of St Michael and St George 1984–94; Order of the Garter 1994–; Grand Officier, Légion d'honneur; Hon. LLD (Cambridge) 1981, (Leeds) 1981, (Univ. of Philippines) 1982, (Univ. of Aberdeen) 1985, (Sussex) 1989, (Nottingham) 1993, (Birmingham) 1993; Hon. DUniv (Essex) 1983; Hon. Dr Laws (Univ. of SC) 1983, (Harvard Univ.) 1986; Hon. DLit (Reading) 1989; Hon. DSc (Cranfield) 1983; Hon. DCL (Oxford) 2003; Dr hc (Buckingham) 1989; Presidential Medal of Freedom 1988, Four Freedoms Award 1992, Freedom from Fear Award (Franklin Delano Inst.) 1992. *Publication:* Reflect on Things Past: The Memoirs of Lord Carrington 1988. *Address:* House of Lords, Westminster, London, SW1A 0PW (office); Manor House, Bledlow, Princes Risborough, Bucks., HP27 9PB, England.

CARRIÓN MENA, Francisco, PhD; Ecuadorean diplomatist and academic; b. 8 April 1953, Quito; m.; two c.; ed Univ. Cen. del Ecuador, Quito; joined Foreign Service 1974; Counsellor and Chargé d'affaires a.i., Embassy in Paris 1982–88; Diplomatic Adviser and Co-ordinator to Pres. of Repub. 1988–91; Minister and Chargé d'affaires a.i., Embassy in London 1991–96; Under-Sec. for Nat. Sovereignty, Ministry of Foreign Affairs 1996–98; mem. Ecuador-Peru Peace Negotiation Comms 1996–98; Deputy Minister of Foreign Affairs 1998–2000; Amb. to Spain 2000–05; Minister of Foreign Affairs 2005–07; Researcher, Facultad Latinoamericana de Ciencias Sociales (FLACSO) 2007–; Perm. Rep. to UN, New York 2009–11; apptd Personal Rep. of Pres. of Ecuador to the Yasuni ITT Initiative 2008; Dir-Gen. Andean Observatory of External Politics (OBANPEX) 2009–; Prof. of Int. Relations and Politics, Univ. Cen. del Ecuador and Diplomatic Acad. of Quito 1988–92; apptd Guest Lecturer, Univ. de Salamanca, Spain 2001, Univ. de Alcalá de Henares 2002; mem. Cttee on Protection of Rights of all Migrant Workers and Mems of their Families, Int. Service for Human Rights 2004–07; columnist, El Comercio newspaper, Quito; decorations from govts of Brazil, Chile, Peru, France, Spain and Portugal. *Publications:* several books and numerous articles in scholarly and popular journals on int. affairs. *Address:* Ministry of Foreign Relations, Trade and Integration, Avenida 10 de Agosto y Carrión E1-76, Quito, Ecuador (office). *Telephone:* (2) 299-3200 (office). *Fax:* (2) 299-3273 (office). *E-mail:* gabminis@mmrree.gob.ec (office). *Website:* www.mmrree.gob.ec (office).

CARRIZALES RENGIFO, Col Rámon Alonso; Venezuelan army officer (retd) and politician; b. 8 Nov. 1952, Zaraza, Guarico; m. Yuvirí del Carmen Ortega Lovera; ed Venezuelan Acad. of Mil. Sciences; fmr Col of Venezuelan Armed Forces, retd 1994; Chair. Fondo Nacional de Transporte Urbano (Fontur) 2000–04; Minister of Infrastructure 2004–07, of Housing 2007–08, of Nat. Defence 2009–10 and Vice-Pres. of Venezuela 2008–10 (resgnd). *Address:* c/o Central Information Office of the Presidency, Torre Oeste 18°, Parque Central, Caracas 1010, Venezuela (office). *Telephone:* (2) 572-7110 (office). *Fax:* (2) 572-2675 (office).

CARROLL, Cynthia, MSc, MBA; American business executive; m.; four c.; ed Skidmore Coll., Univ. of Kansas, Harvard Univ.; fmr Sr Petroleum Geologist, Amoco, USA; joined Rolled Products Group, Alcan 1988, apptd Gen. Man. Foil Products, USA 1991, Man. Dir Aughinish Alumina, Ireland, Pres. Bauxite, Alumina and Speciality Chemicals Group 1998–2002, Pres. and CEO Alcan Primary Metal Group 2002–06, also Officer, Alcan Inc., Montreal; Chief Exec. Anglo American plc, London 2007–13, Chair. Exec. Cttee, Chief Exec.'s Cttee, mem. Safety Cttee, Sustainable Devt Cttee; fmr mem. Bd of Dirs AngloGold Ashanti Ltd, Sara Lee Corpn; Chair. Anglo Platinum Ltd; Dir (non-exec.) BP plc, De Beers; Hon. DSc; ranked by Forbes magazine amongst The World's 100 Most Powerful Women (seventh) 2007, (fifth) 2008, (fourth) 2009, (14th) 2010, (35th) 2011, (55th) 2012, ranked by Fortune magazine amongst the 50 Most Powerful Women in Business outside the US (first) 2007–11, (third) 2012, ranked by the Financial Times amongst Top 25 Businesswomen in Europe (second) 2007.

CARROLL, Philip J., BS, MS; American oil industry executive (retd); b. 1937, New Orleans, La; m. Charlene Carroll; three c.; ed Loyola Univ., New Orleans, Tulane Univ. of Louisiana; began career with Shell Oil Co. as petroleum engineer 1961, held positions in exploration and production business 1970s, Man. Dir Shell Int. Gas and Int. Petroleum, London, UK –1986, Head of Admin, Shell Oil Co., Houston, Tex. 1986–93, Pres. and CEO US Operations, Shell Group 1993–98; Chair. and CEO, Fluor Corpn (eng and construction firm), Calif. 1998–2002; apptd Chair. and CEO, advisory bd for Iraqi Oil Ministry 2003; Dir Energy Conservation Div., US Dept of Commerce 1971–74; fmr Exec. Dir Nat. Industrial Energy Council; dir numerous petroleum industry asscns, professional eng orgs, educ. insts and philanthropic and civic groups. *Address:* 2001 Kirby, #1004, Houston, TX 77019, USA. *Telephone:* (713) 522-6099. *Fax:* (713) 522-6062.

CARRON, René Joseph; French banking executive; b. 13 June 1942, Yenne, Savoie; s. of Albert Carron and Claudine Philippe Carron (née Genoud); m. Françoise Dupasquier 1963; three s. one d.; fmr dairy farmer in Yenne; Pres. Yenne br. Crédit Agricole 1981–, Pres. regional br. in Savoie 1992, all Savoie 1994, mem. Bureau 1995–2010, Pres. Fédération nationale du crédit agricole 2000–03, Vice-Pres. 2003–10 Dir 1999–2010, Vice-Pres. Caisse nationale de crédit agricole (CNCA, renamed Crédit Agricole SA 2000) 2000–10, mem. Supervisory Council, Crédit Agricole Indosuez 2000–, Chair. Crédit Agricole SA 2002–10; Chair. SAS Rue La Boétie 2001–03; Deputy Chair. Confédération Nationale de la Mutualité, de la Coopération et du Crédit Agricole; fmr Co-Deputy Chair. Intesa Sanpaolo SpA (fmrly Banca Intesa SpA); mem. Bd of Dirs GDF Suez, Crédit Agricole Indosuez SA, Soc. de banque de financement pour le commerce (Sofinco), Rue Impériale, Crédit Agricole Solidarité et Développement, Fondation du Crédit Agricole Pays de France, Sacam (SAS), Sapacam (SAS), Suez SA, Fiat SpA 2007–, Caisse Locale de Crédit Agricole de Yenne, Gecam (GIE); mem. Supervisory Bd Lagardere SCA 2004–, Lagardere Active Broadcast 2008–; Pres. Savoie Chamber of Agric. 1983–92, Savoie 92 (asscn to promote Winter Olympics in Albertville 1992) 1988–92, Mission prospective du département de la Savoie 1988–98, Groupe d'étude et de mobilisation Espaces ruraux 1991, Steering Cttee for Savoie Strategic Plan Year 2000 1991–98; Counsellor Banque de France de la Savoie 1991– (mem. 1992–, mem. Perm. Comm. 1992–), Conseil d'admin de l'org. du dialogue et de l'intelligence sociale dans la société et l'entreprise (Odisée) 2006–; Vice-Pres. Conseil général de Savoie 1995–98; Mayor of Yenne 1995–2001; mem. Econ. and Social Council 2000–03, Man. Bd. Groupement Européen des Banques Coopératives; Chevalier, Légion d'honneur, Ordre nat. du Mérite, des Arts et des Lettres, Commdr du Mérite agricole. *Address:* Crédit Agricole SA, 91–93 boulevard Pasteur, 75015 Paris, France (office). *Telephone:* 1-43-23-52-02 (office). *Fax:* 1-43-23-34-48 (office). *E-mail:* info@credit-agricole-sa.fr (office). *Website:* www.credit-agricole-sa.fr (office).

CARSBERG, Sir Bryan (Victor), Kt, MSc(Econ); British public servant, academic and chartered accountant; b. 3 Jan. 1939, London, England; s. of Alfred Victor Carsberg and Maryllia Ciceley Carsberg (née Collins); m. Margaret Linda Graham 1960; two d.; ed London School of Econs; accounting practice 1962–64; Lecturer in Accounting, LSE 1964–68, Arthur Andersen Prof. of Accounting 1981–87, Visiting Prof. 1987–89; Visiting Lecturer, Grad. School of Business, Univ. of Chicago 1968–69; Prof. of Accounting, Univ. of Manchester 1969–78; Visiting Prof. of Business Admin., Univ. of California, Berkeley 1974; Asst Dir Research and Tech. Activities, US Financial Accounting Standards Bd 1978–81; Dir of Research, Inst. of Chartered Accountants in England and Wales 1981–87; Dir-Gen. of Telecommunications, Oftel 1984–92; mem. Accounting Standards Bd 1990–94 (Vice-Chair. 1990–92); Dir-Gen. of Fair Trading 1992–95; Sec. Gen. Int. Accounting Standards Cttee 1995–2001; Chair. Pensions Compensation Bd 2001–04; Dir Nynex Cable Communications 1996–97, Cable & Wireless Communications 1997–2000, RM plc 2002–12, Philip Allan (publrs), Novae Group plc 2003–, Inmarsat plc 2005–; Chair. MLL Telecoms Ltd 1999–2002; Pres. Locus 2005–12, e-Homebuying Forum 2010–12; mem. Bd Radio Communications Agency 1990–92, Council of Univ. of Surrey 1990–92, Council of Loughborough Univ. 1999–2011 (Chair. 2001–11), Equality of Access Bd at BT plc 2005–13, Governing Council, Royal Inst. of Chartered Surveyors 2010–13; Hon. Fellow, LSE; Hon. FIA; Hon. RICS; Hon. DSc (East Anglia) 1992; Hon. DLitt (Loughborough) 1994; Hon. D Univ. (Essex) 1995; Hon. LLD (Bath) 1990; Dr hc (Nottingham Trent) 2008; Inst. Medal, W.B. Peat Medal and Prize, Inst. of Chartered Accountants, England,

Chartered Accountants Founding Socs Centenary Award 1988, Blaew Prize for Telecommunications 1992, Sempier Award, Int. Fed. of Accountants 2002. *Publications:* An Introduction to Mathematical Programming for Accountants 1969, Analysis for Investment Decisions 1974, Economics of Business Decisions 1975 and others. *Leisure interests:* theatre, music, opera, physics. *E-mail:* bryan .carsberg@ntlworld.com.

CARSON, Anne, BA, MA, PhD; Canadian academic, poet and writer; *Professor, Department of English, University of Michigan;* b. 21 June 1950, Toronto, Ont.; ed St Michael's Coll., Univ. of Toronto, Univ. of St Andrews, Scotland; Prof. of Classics, Univ. of Calgary 1979–80, Princeton Univ. 1980–87, Emory Univ. 1987–88; fmr John MacNaughton Prof. of Classics, McGill Univ. and Dir of Grad. Studies, Classics; currently Prof., Dept of English, Univ. of Michigan; Guggenheim Fellowship 1999; John D. and Catherine T. MacArthur Foundation Fellowship 2001; Anna-Maria Kellen Fellow, American Acad., Berlin, Germany 2007; Lannan Literary Award 1996, Pushcart Prize for Poetry 1997. *Publications include:* Eros the Bittersweet: An Essay 1986, Short Talks 1992, Plainwater 1995, Glass, Irony and God 1995, Autobiography of Red 1998, Economy of the Unlost 1999, Men in the Off Hours (Griffin Poetry Prize 2001) 2000, The Beauty of the Husband (Poetry Book Soc. T. S. Eliot Prize 2001) 2001, Sophocles' Electra 2001, If Not, Winter: Fragments of Sappho (trans.) 2002, Decreation 2005, Grief Lessons: Four Plays by Euripides (trans.) 2006, An Oresteia (trans.) (PEN Award for Poetry in Translation 2010) 2009, Nox 2010, Antigonick 2012; contribs to anthologies and journals. *Address:* Department of English, University of Michigan, 435 South State Street, 3143 Angell Hall, Ann Arbor, MI 48109, USA (office); 5900 Esplanade Avenue, Montréal, PQ H2T 3A3, Canada (home). *Telephone:* (734) 763-2265 (office). *E-mail:* carsona@umich.edu (office); decreation@hotmail.com (home). *Website:* www.lsa .umich.edu/english (office).

CARSON, William (Willy) Hunter, OBE; British thoroughbred horse breeder and fmr professional jockey; b. 16 Nov. 1942, Stirling, Scotland; s. of Thomas Whelan and Mary Hay Carson (née Hunter); m. 1st Carole Jane Sutton 1962 (divorced 1979); three s.; m. 2nd Elaine Williams 1982; ed Riverside School, Stirling, Scotland; apprentice with Capt. Gerald Armstrong 1957–62; rode first winner Pinker's Pond at Catterick 1962; first jockey to Lord Derby 1968, to Bernard van Cutsem 1971–75, to Maj. Dick Hern 1977–89, to HM The Queen 1977; champion jockey 1972, 1973, 1978, 1980, 1983; rode the winners of 18 English Classics, eight Irish Classics and 68 English Group One races; rode six winners at one meeting July 1990; best horses ridden Nashwan and Dayjur; bred and rode St Leger winner Minster Son 1988; 3,828 career winners in UK (1997); retd 1997 as fourth-most successful ever UK jockey; racing pundit, BBC 1997–; Owner Minster Stud; Dir Swindon Town Football Club 1997–98, Head of Public Relations 1997–, Chair. 2001–; Dr hc (Stirling 1998), Hon. DSc (Chester) 2010. *Publication:* Willie Carson Up Front: A Racing Autobiography 1993. *Leisure interests:* golf, football. *Address:* Minster House, Barnsley, Cirencester, Glos., GL7 5DZ, England. *Telephone:* (1285) 658919. *E-mail:* carson_w@sky.com. *Website:* williecarson.com.

CARSTENS CARSTENS, Agustín Guillermo, BA, MA, PhD; Mexican economist, government official and central banker; *Governor, Banco de México;* b. 1958, Mexico City; m. Catherine Mansell; ed Instituto Tecnológico Autónomo de México, Univ. of Chicago, USA; Intern, Banco de México 1983; left for studies in USA; rejoined Banco de México 1986, Treas. 1987, Dir-Gen. Econ. Research and Chief of Staff in Gov.'s office 1991–94, Chief Economist and Research Dir 1994–98, Gov. 2010–; Alt. Gov. for Mexico at IDB and World Bank 1998–2000; Deputy Sec. of Finance 2000–03, organized UN Conf. on Financing for Devt, Monterrey, meetings of Group of 20 2002; Second Deputy Man. Dir IMF 2003–06; Sec. of Finance and Public Credit 2006–09. *Publications:* has published articles in collections edited by Fed. Reserve Bank of Boston, Univ. of London, OECD, IMF and World Bank and in journals including Columbia Journal of World Business, American Economic Review, Journal of Asian Economics, Journal of International Finance, Cuadernos Económicos del ICE (Spain) and Gaceta de Economía del ITAM (Mexico). *Address:* Banco de México, Avda 5 de Mayo 2, Col. Centro, Del. Cuauhtémoc, 06059 México, DF, Mexico (office). *Telephone:* (55) 5237-2000 (office). *Fax:* (55) 5237-2070 (office). *E-mail:* comsoc@banxico.org.mx (office). *Website:* www.banxico.org.mx (office).

CARSWELL, Baron (Life Peer), cr. 2004, of Killeen in the County of Down; **Robert Douglas Carswell,** PC; British judge (retd); b. 28 June 1934, Belfast, Northern Ireland; s. of Alan E. Carswell and Nance E. Carswell; m. Romayne Winifred Ferris 1961; two d.; ed Royal Belfast Academical Inst., Pembroke Coll., Oxford, Univ. of Chicago Law School, USA; called to the Bar, NI 1957, to English Bar, Gray's Inn 1972; Counsel to Attorney-Gen. for NI 1970–71; QC 1971; Sr Crown Counsel for NI 1979–84; Judge High Court of Justice in NI 1984–93; Lord Justice of Appeal, Supreme Court of Judicature 1993–97; Lord Chief Justice of NI 1997–2004; Lord of Appeal in Ordinary 2004–09; Chancellor, Dioceses of Armagh and of Down and Dromore 1990–97; Chair. Council of Law Reporting for NI 1987–97, Law Reform Advisory Cttee for NI 1989–97, Distinction and Meritorious Service Awards Cttee, DHSS 1995–97; Pres. NI Scout Council 1993–; Pro-Chancellor, Chair. Council, Univ. of Ulster 1984–94; Hon. DLitt (Ulster) 1994. *Publications:* Trustee Acts (NI) 1964; articles in legal periodicals. *Leisure interests:* golf, hillwalking, music, architecture, antiques and conservation, wildlife. *Address:* House of Lords, Westminster, London, SW1A 0PW, England (office).

CARTELLIERI, Ulrich; German lawyer and banker; b. 21 Sept. 1937; ed Univs of Munich and Cologne; joined Deutsche Bank AG, Frankfurt 1970, Man. Dir 1975–77, CEO 1977 82, Chair. Supervisory Bd European Asian Bank 1982, then Chair. Deutsche Bank (Asia Credit) Ltd, Singapore, DB Finance (Hong Kong) Ltd, Hong Kong; AG 1990–98, mem. Deutsche Bank Man. Bd 1981–97, also served as Deputy Chair. Deutsche Bank North America; mem. Supervisory Bd 1997; mem. Supervisory Bd Robert Bosch GmbH; fmr mem. Supervisory Bd Deutsche Solvay-Werke GmbH, Solingen, Deutsche Telephonwerke und Kabelindustrie AG, Berlin, Euro-Pacific Finance Corpn Ltd, Melbourne, Girmes-Werke AG, Grefrath-Oedt, Th. Goldschmidt AG, Essen, Wilhelm Karmann GmbH, Osnabrück, Thyssen Edelstahlwerke AG, Düsseldorf, G. M. Pfaff AG, Kaiserslautern; mem. Bd of Dirs (non-exec.) BAE Systems; fmr Pres. German Soc. on Foreign Affairs; fmr German Co-Chair. German-Japanese Forum. *Address:* c/o Board of Directors, BAE Systems, Stirling Square, Carlton Gardens, London, SW1Y 5AD, England (office). *Telephone:* (1252) 373232 (office). *Fax:* (1252) 383121 (office). *Website:* www .baesystems.com (office).

CARTER, Ashton B., BA, PhD; American academic and government official; *Deputy Secretary of Defense;* b. 24 Sept. 1954, Philadelphia; m. Ava Clayton Spencer 1983; one s. one d.; ed Yale Univ., Univ. of Oxford, UK; early career positions at MIT, US Congressional Office of Tech. Assessment, Rockefeller Univ.; served as Asst Sec. of Defense for Int. Security Policy, US Dept of Defense, Washington, DC 1993–96; Co-Dir Preventive Defense Project and Ford Foundation Prof. of Science and Int. Affairs, Harvard Univ. –2011; Deputy Sec. of Defense 2011–; fmr Sr Pnr, Global Technology Partners; fmr Chair. Advisory Bd MIT Lincoln Labs; fmr Chair. Editorial Bd International Security (journal); fmr mem. Bd of Dirs Mitretek Systems; fmr mem. Defense Science Bd, Defense Policy Bd, Draper Lab. Corpn, Aspen Strategy Group, Council on Foreign Relations, American Physical Soc., IISS, Nat. Cttee on US-China Relations; Fellow, American Acad. of Arts and Sciences; mem. American Acad. of Diplomacy 2009–; Ten Outstanding Young Americans 1987, US Dept of Defense Distinguished Service Medal (twice), Defense Intelligence Medal. *Publications:* Directed Energy Missile Defense in Space 1984, Ballistic Missile Defense 1984, Managing Nuclear Operations 1987, Soviet Nuclear Fusion: Control of the Nuclear Arsenal in a Disintegrating Soviet Union 1991, Beyond Spinoff: Military and Commercial Technologies in a Changing World 1992, A New Concept of Cooperative Security 1992, Cooperative Denuclearization: From Pledges to Deeds 1993, Preventive Defense (jtly) 1997, Keeping the Edge: Managing Defense for the Future (co-ed.) 2001. *Address:* Department of State, 2201 C Street, NW, Washington, DC 20520, USA (office). *Telephone:* (202) 647-4000 (office). *Fax:* (202) 647-6738 (office). *Website:* www.state.gov (office).

CARTER, Brandon, DSc, FRS; British theoretical physicist and academic; *Director of Research, Laboratoire de l'Univers Théorique, Centre National de la Recherche Scientifique (CNRS);* b. 26 May 1942, Sydney, NSW, Australia; s. of Harold B. Carter and Mary Brandon-Jones; m. Lucette Defrise 1969; three d.; ed George Watson's Coll., Edinburgh, Univ. of St Andrews, Pembroke Coll., Cambridge; Research Fellow, Pembroke Coll., Cambridge 1967–72; staff mem., Inst. of Astronomy, Cambridge 1968–72; Asst Lecturer, Dept of Applied Math. and Theoretical Physics, Univ. of Cambridge 1973, Lecturer 1974; Maître de Recherche, CNRS, Paris 1975–85, Dir-Adjoint, Group d'Astrophysique Relativiste, Observatoire de Paris-Meudon 1975–82, Dir 1987–2001, Dir of Research, Laboratoire de l'Univers Théorique 2002–08. *Publications:* Global Structure of the Kerr Family of Gravitational Fields 1968, Black Hole Equilibrium States 1973, Large Number Coincidences and the Anthropic Principle in Cosmology 1974, The General Theory of the Mechanical Electromagnetic and Thermodynamic Properties of Black Holes 1979, The Anthropic Principle and its Implications for Biological Evolution 1983, Covariant Mechanics of Simple and Conducting Strings and Membranes 1990. *Address:* L.U.T.H., Observatoire de Paris-Meudon, 92195 Meudon (office); 19 rue de la Borne au Diable, 92310 Sèvres, France (home). *Telephone:* 1-45-07-74-34 (office). *Fax:* 1-45-07-79-71 (office). *E-mail:* brandon .carter@obspm.fr (office). *Website:* www.luth.obspm.fr (office).

CARTER, Daniel William (Dan); New Zealand professional rugby union player; b. 5 March 1982, Southbridge, Canterbury, South Island; s. of Neville Carter and Bev Carter; engaged to Honor Dillon 2010; ed Ellesmere Coll., Christchurch Boys' High School; plays as fly-half; played for Southbridge Rugby Club as a scrum half from age five; prov. debut for Canterbury against Marlborough 2002; selected to play in the Super 12 (now Super Rugby) franchise for the Crusaders against the Hurricanes 2003; reached final of competition with the Crusaders 2003, 2004, 2005, 2006; scored the most individual points (221) for a player in one season; signed six-month contract with French club side Perpignan 2008, ruptured Achilles tendon playing against Stade Francais Jan. 2009; played for Canterbury in opening game of Air New Zealand Cup 2009; is now the top scorer in Super 12/14 rugby history; Test debut for New Zealand Nat. Rugby Union Team (All Blacks) in Hamilton scoring 20 points against Wales 2003; capped against France in Christchurch, winning 31–23; included in New Zealand's 2003 Rugby World Cup squad, only secured a permanent position as the first five-eighth in the team during tour to UK and France 2004; mem. of winning All Blacks side against British and Irish Lions 2005, in first Test scored two tries, five penalties and four conversions and ended the match with 33 points, passing the previous All Blacks record of 18 points in a Lions Test; became the highest points scorer of all time after scoring a halfway penalty against Wales 27 Nov. 2010, overtook England's Jonny Wilkinson's previous record of 1,178 points although Wilkinson took the record back on 26 Feb. 2011 against France, reclaimed record on 30 July 2011 when he moved to 1,204 points in first Tri Nations match against South Africa; Vice-Capt. for more than 50 tests under Richie McCaw, announced as captain of All Blacks for the first time against Canada Oct. 2011; voted sexiest New Zealand male in a survey 2004, 2005, Int. Rugby Bd (IRB) Int. Player of the Year 2005, judged by US Cable Channel E! Entertainment to be 11th on their list of Sexiest Men in the World 2008, voted by E! as third Sexiest Male Athlete in the World 2010. *Publication:* Dan Carter: Skills & Performance 2006. *Address:* Crusaders, Level 1, PO Box 755, 5 Durham Street, Christchurch (office); c/o New Zealand Rugby Union, PO Box 2172, Wellington 6140, New Zealand. *Telephone:* (3) 379-8300 (office); (4) 499-4995. *Fax:* (3) 365-3565 (office); (4) 499-4224. *E-mail:* info@crfu.co .nz (office); info@nzrugby.co.nz. *Website:* www.crusaders.co.nz (office); www.nzru .co.nz; www.allblacks.com.

CARTER, (Edward) Graydon; Canadian magazine editor; *Editor-in-Chief, Vanity Fair;* b. 14 July 1949; s. of E.P. Carter and Margaret Ellen Carter; m. 2nd Cynthia Williamson 1982 (divorced 2000); four c.; m. Anna Scott 2005; one d.; ed Carleton Univ., Univ. of Ottawa; Ed. Canadian Review 1973–77; writer, Time 1978–83, Life 1983–86; Founder, Ed. Spy 1986–91; Ed. New York Observer 1991–92; Ed.-in-Chief, Vanity Fair 1992–; Co-owner Waverly Inn, Monkey Bar; Hon. Ed. Harvard Lampoon 1989; Advertising Age Editor of the Year 1996, Nat. Magazine Award for Gen. Excellence 1997, 1999, Nat. Magazine Award for Photography 2000, 2002, Nat. Magazine Award for Reviews and Criticism 2003. *Television* as executive producer: 9/11 (CBS) (Emmy Award, Peabody Award) 2002. *Film* as producer: The Kid Stays in the Picture 2002. *Publications:* Vanity Fair's Hollywood (ed.) 2000, Tom Ford: Ten Years (co-author) 2004, What We've Lost 2004, Oscar Night: 75 Years of Hollywood Parties (ed.) 2004, Spy - The Funny Years (co-author, ed.) 2006, Vanity Fair Portraits (ed.) 2008, Vintage Postcards from Vanity Fair: One Hundred Classic Covers, 1913-1936 2011. *Leisure interest:* fly fishing. *Address:* Vanity Fair, Condé Nast Building, 4 Times Square, New York,

NY 10036-6522, USA (office). *E-mail:* letters@vf.com (office). *Website:* www .vanityfair.com (office).

CARTER, James (Jimmy) Earl, Jr, BSc; American politician, international political consultant, farmer and fmr head of state; *Chairman, Carter Center;* b. 1 Oct. 1924, Plains, Ga; s. of the late James Earl Carter, Sr and Lillian Gordy; m. Eleanor Rosalynn Smith 1946; three s. one d.; ed Plains High School, Georgia Southwestern Coll., Georgia Inst. of Tech., US Naval Acad., Annapolis, Md, Union Coll., New York State; served in USN 1946-53, attained rank of Lt (submarine service); peanut farmer, warehouseman 1953–77, businesses include Carter Farms, Carter Warehouses, Plains, Ga; mem. Sumter Co., Ga, School Bd 1955–62 (Chair. 1960–62); State Senator, Ga 1962–66; Gov. of Georgia 1971–74; Pres. of USA 1977–81; Distinguished Prof., Emory Univ., Atlanta 1982–; leader of int. observer teams in Panama 1989, Nicaragua 1990, Dominican Repub. 1990, Haiti 1990; hosted peace negotiations in Ethiopia 1989; visited Democratic People's Repub. of Korea (in pvt. capacity) June 1994; negotiator in Haitian crisis Sept. 1994; visit to Bosnia Dec. 1994; f. Carter Presidential Center 1982; est. Jimmy and Rosalynn Carter Work Project for Habitat for Humanity International 1984; Chair. Bd of Trustees, Carter Center Inc. 1986–, Carter-Menil Human Rights Foundation 1986–, Global 2000 Inc. 1986–, Council of Freely Elected Heads of Govt 1986–, Council of Int. Negotiation Network 1991–; joined The Elders 2007; mem. Americus and Sumter Co. Hosp. Authority 1956–70, Sumter Co. Library Bd 1961; Pres. Plains Devt Corpn 1963; Georgia Planning Asscn 1968; Dir Ga Crop Improvement Asscn 1957–63 (Pres. 1961); Chair. West Cen. Ga Area Planning and Devt Comm. 1964; State Chair. March of Dimes 1968–70; Dist Gov. Lions Club 1968–69; Chair. Congressional Campaign Cttee, Democratic Nat. Cttee 1974; Democrat; several hon. degrees; Ansel Adams Conservation Award, Wilderness Society 1982, World Methodist Peace Award 1984, Albert Schweitzer Prize for Humanitarianism 1987, Onassis Foundation Award 1991, Notre Dame Univ. Award 1992, Matsunaga Medal of Peace 1993, J. William Fulbright Prize for Int. Understanding 1994, Houphouët Boigny Peace Prize, UNESCO (jtly) 1995, UNICEF Int. Child Survival Award (jtly with Rosalynn Carter) 1999, Presidential Medal of Freedom 1999, Eisenhower Medallion 2000, Nobel Peace Prize 2002, American Peace Award (jtly with Rosalynn Carter) 2009, among numerous others. *Publications:* Why Not the Best? 1975, A Government as Good as Its People 1977, Keeping Faith: Memoirs of a President 1982, The Blood of Abraham: Insights into the Middle East 1985, Everything to Gain: Making the Most of the Rest of Your Life 1987, An Outdoor Journal 1988, Turning Point: A Candidate, a State and a Nation Come of Age 1992, Always a Reckoning (poems) 1995, Sources of Strength 1997, The Virtues of Ageing 1998, An Hour Before Daylight 2001, The Hornet's Nest (novel) 2003, Our Endangered Values 2005, Palestine: Peace Not Apartheid 2006, We Can Have Peace in the Holy Land: A Plan that Will Work 2009, White House Diary 2010, Call to Action: Women, Religion, Violence, and Power 2014. *Leisure interests:* reading, tennis. *Address:* The Carter Center, 453 Freedom Parkway, 1 Copenhill Avenue NE, Atlanta, GA 30307, USA (office). *Telephone:* (404) 420-5100 (office). *Fax:* (404) 420-5196 (office). *E-mail:* carterweb@emory.edu (office). *Website:* www.cartercenter.org (office).

CARTER, Marshall, BS, MS, MA; American business executive; *Chairman of the Board of Directors, NYSE Group Inc.;* b. 23 April 1940, Newport News, Va; m. Mary Meehan 1964; one s. one d.; ed US Mil. Acad. at West Point, US Naval Postgraduate School, Monterey, George Washington Univ.; fmr Marine Corps officer; White House Fellow, State Dept and Agency for Int. Devt 1975–76; with Chase Manhattan Bank –1992; Chair. and CEO State Street Bank and Trust Co., State Street Corp. 1992–2001; Fellow, Center for Public Leadership, Kennedy School of Govt, Harvard Univ. 2001–05; Lecturer in leadership and man., Sloan School of Man., MIT; mem. Bd of Dirs New York Stock Exchange 2003–, Chair. 2005–06, Chair. NYSE Group Inc. 2006–; Chair. Bd of Trustees, Boston Medical Center; Fellow, American Acad. of Arts and Sciences 2006; Navy Cross, Bronze Star, Purple Heart. *Address:* NYSE Group Inc., 11 Wall Street, New York, NY 10005, USA (office). *Telephone:* (212) 656-3000 (office). *Website:* www.nyse.com (office).

CARTER, Stephen Lisle, BA, JD; American academic and lawyer; *William Nelson Cromwell Professor of Law, Yale University;* b. 1954, Washington, DC; m.; c.; ed Stanford and Yale Univs; fmr Note Ed. Yale Law Journal; admitted to Bar, Washington, DC 1981; law clerk, Judge Spottswood W. Robinson III, US Court of Appeal, Washington, DC 1979–80; law clerk, Justice Thurgood Marshall, US Supreme Court 1980–81; Assoc. Shea & Gardner, Washington, DC 1981–82; Asst Prof. of Law, Yale Univ. 1982–84, Assoc. Prof. 1984–85, Prof. 1986–91, William Nelson Cromwell Prof. of Law 1991–; Official Adviser to US Pres. Bill Clinton 1993; Hon. LLD (Univ. of Notre Dame) 1996. *Publications include:* non-fiction: Reflections of an Affirmative Action Baby 1991, The Culture of Disbelief 1991, The Confirmation Mess 1994, Integrity 1997, The Dissent of the Governed 1998, Civility 1998, God's Name in Vain 2001, The Violence of Peace: America's Wars in the Age of Obama 2011; novels: The Emperor of Ocean Park 2002, New England White 2007, Palace Council 2008, Jericho's Fall 2009, The Impeachment of Abraham Lincoln 2012. *Address:* c/o Gabrielle Brooks, Knopf Publishing (Author Mail), 1745 Broadway, New York, NY 10019 (office); Yale Law School, POB 208215, New Haven, CT 06520, USA (office). *E-mail:* stephen.carter@yale.edu (office). *Website:* www.law.yale.edu/outside/html/home/index.htm (office); www .stephencarterbooks.com.

CARTER OF BARNES, Baron (Life Peer), cr. 2008, of Barnes in the London Borough of Richmond upon Thames; **Stephen Carter,** LLB; British business executive; *Chief Marketing, Strategy and Communications Officer, Alcatel-Lucent;* b. 12 Feb. 1964, Scotland; m. Anna Carter; two c.; ed Currie High School, Edinburgh, Univ. of Aberdeen; began career as trainee, J. Walter Thompson UK (advertising agency), Man.-Dir 1995–97, CEO 1997–2000; Man.-Dir of UK Operations, NTL (cable TV co.) 2000–02; CEO Ofcom 2003–06; CEO Brunswick Group LLP 2006–08 (resgnd); Dir (non-exec.) Royal Mail 2007–08 (resgnd); Chief of Strategy and Prin. Adviser to Prime Minister 2008–09; Chief Marketing, Strategy and Communications Officer, Alcatel-Lucent 2010–; Chair. Ashridge Business School; Gov. Royal Shakespeare Co.; mem. Bd of Dirs Informa plc 2010–. *Leisure interest:* running. *Address:* House of Lords, London, SW1A 0PW; Informa plc, Informa House, 30-32 Mortimer Street, London, W1W 7RE, England (office).

Telephone: (20) 7219-4776 (House of Lords); (20) 7017-5771 (office). *E-mail:* carterst@parliament.uk.

CARTES JARA, Horacio Manuel; Paraguayan business executive, politician and head of state; *President;* b. 5 July 1956, Asunción; s. of Ramón Telmo Cartes Lind; ed Colegio Goethe, Colegio Internacional, Colegio Cristo Rey, Asunción; began career with internship at Cessna (aircraft co.), Kansas, USA; returned to Paraguay, f. Cambios Amambay (currency exchange co.) 1989 (renamed Banco Amambay 1992); joined Tabacalera del Este SA (tobacco co.) as Partner 1994, f. Tobacco del Paraguay SA 1996, f. Compañía Agrotabacalera del Paraguay SA 2002; now Owner, Grupo Cartes conglomerate (active in fields of tobacco, soft drinks, meat production, transport and banking); imprisoned 1989 for currency dealings, later acquitted; mem. Colorado Party 2009–, selected as Colorado Party cand. for presidential elections 2012; Pres. of Paraguay 2013–; Pres. Club Libertad (football club) 2001–; fmr Selection Dir Paraguayan Football Asscn. *Address:* Office of the President, Palacio de los López, Asunción (office); Partido Colorado, Casa de los Colorados, 25 de Mayo 842, Asunción, Paraguay (office). *Telephone:* (21) 414-0200 (office). *Website:* www.presidencia.gov.py (office).

CARTIER, Jean-Albert; French theatre director; b. 15 May 1930, Marseille; s. of Albert Cartier and Myriem Bordes; m. Solange Ottavy 1959; two d.; ed Lycée Perier, Marseille and Ecole du Louvre; art critic, Combat and numerous reviews; artistic collaborator, France-Inter; arranged several exhbns for Marseille Museum; participated Paris Biennale 1959, 1961, 1963, 1965; Founder and Dir Asscn technique pour l'action culturelle 1966–72; Creator Ballet-Théâtre contemporain, Centre chorégraphique nat. 1968–72; Dir Centre chorégraphique et lyrique nat. 1972; Dir Angers Municipal Theatre 1972–78; Founder and Dir Anjou Arts Festival 1975–77; Creator and Dir Ballet-Théâtre français de Nancy 1978–87; Dir-Gen. Grand Théâtre de Nancy 1979–81, Dir Théâtre Musical, Paris-Châtelet 1980–88; Dir Festival of Paris 1988, 1989, 1991; Dir Théâtre Nat. de l'Opéra de Paris 1988, Gen. Man. 1989–91; Dir of Music, Radio France 1991–94; Dir-Gen. L'Opéra de Nice 1994–97; Creator and Dir Europa Danse 1999–; Chevalier, Légion d'honneur, des Arts et Lettres; Officier, Ordre nat. du Mérite. *Publication:* L'oeuvre du peintre POUGNY (two vols). *Address:* Europa Danse, 18 rue de l'Hôtel de Ville, 75004 Paris (office); 8 rue Vernier, 06000 Nice; 24 rue Saint-Paul, 75004 Paris, France. *Telephone:* 1-42-77-31-34 (office); 1-44-54-06-48 (home). *Fax:* 1-42-77-32-34 (office).

CARTWRIGHT, Gen. James E., MA; American military officer; *Vice-Chairman, Joint Chiefs of Staff;* ed Maxwell Air Command and Staff Coll., Naval War Coll., Newport, RI, MIT; commissioned Second Lt in US Marine Corps 1971, Naval Flight Officer, graduated 1973, Naval Aviator, graduated 1977, operational assignments as an NFO in the F-4 and as a pilot in the F-4, OA-4 and F/A-18, has served in numerous leadership positions including Commdr Marine Aviation Logistics Squadron 12 1989–90, Marine Fighter Attack Squadron 232 1992, Marine Aircraft Group 31 1994–96, Deputy Commanding Gen., Marine Forces Atlantic 1999–2000, Commanding Gen., First Marine Aircraft Wing 2000–02; Commdr US Strategic Command, Offutt Air Force Base, Neb. 2004–07, command areas include full-spectrum global strike, space operations, computer network operations, Dept of Defense information operations, strategic warning, integrated missile defense, combating weapons of mass destruction; staff assignments have included Asst Program Man. for Eng, F/A-18 Naval Air Systems Command 1986–89, Deputy Aviation Plans, Policy and Budgets HQ, US Marine Corps 1993–94, Directorate for Force Structure, Resources and Assessment, J-8 the Jt Chiefs of Staff 1996–99, Dir for Force Structure, Resources and Assessment, J-8 the Jt Chiefs of Staff 2002–04; Vice-Chair. Jt Chiefs of Staff 2007–, Chair. Jt Requirements Oversight Council, Co-Chair Defense Acquisition Bd, mem. Nat. Security Council Deputies Cttee, Nuclear Weapons Council, Missile Defense Exec. Bd; Co-Chair. Deputies Advisory Working Group; Outstanding Carrier Aviator, Asscn of Naval Aviation 1983. *Address:* Office of the Vice-Chairman of the Joint Chiefs of Staff, 400 Joint Staff, Pentagon, Washington, DC 20318-0400, USA (office). *Website:* www.jcs.mil (office).

CARTWRIGHT, Nancy Delaney, PhD, FBA; American/British academic; *Professor, Department of Philosophy, Durham University;* b. 24 June 1944, Pennsylvania; d. of Claudis Delaney and Eva Delaney; m. 1st Bliss Cartwright 1966 (divorced); m. 2nd Ian Hacking 1974 (divorced); m. 3rd Sir Stuart Hampshire 1985 (died 2004); two d.; ed Univs of Pittsburgh and Illinois; Prof. of Philosophy, Stanford Univ. 1983–91; Prof. of Philosophy, Logic and Scientific Method, LSE 1991–2012, Dir Centre for the Philosophy of the Natural and Social Sciences 1993–2001; Prof. of Philosophy, Univ. of California, San Diego 1997–; also currently Prof. of Philosophy, Durham Univ.; Macarthur Foundation Award 1993, Leopoldina 1999. *Publications include:* How the Laws of Physics Lie 1983, Nature's Capacities and Their Measurement 1989, Otto Neurath: Between Science and Politics (with others) 1995, The Dappled World: A Study of the Boundaries of Science 2000. *Address:* Department of Philosophy, University of Durham, 50 Old Elvet, Durham, DH1 3HN, England (office); Department of Philosophy, University of California, San Diego, 9500 Gilman Drive, La Jolla, CA 92093-0302, USA (office). *E-mail:* nancy.cartwright@durham.ac.uk (office). *Website:* www.dur.ac.uk/philosophy (office).

CARTWRIGHT, The Hon. Dame Silvia Rose, PCNZM, DBE, QSO, LLB; New Zealand judge; b. 7 Nov. 1943, Dunedin; d. of Monteith Poulter and Eileen Jane Poulter; m. Peter John Cartwright 1969; ed Univ. of Otago; Pnr, Harkness Henry & Co. barristers and solicitors, Hamilton 1971–81; Dist Court and Family Court Judge 1981–89, Chief Dist Court Judge 1989–93; Judge High Court of NZ 1993–2001; Gov.-Gen. of NZ 2001–06; Judge in Trial Chamber, Extraordinary Chambers in the Courts of Cambodia for the Prosecution of Crimes Committed during the Period of Democratic Kampuchea 2007–; mem. Comm. for the Future 1975–80, Cttee UN Human Rights Convention to eliminate discrimination against women 1992–2000; Chair. Comm. of Inquiry into the Treatment of Cervical Cancer and Other Related Matters, Nat. Women's Hosp. 1987–88; Int. Hon. Mem., Zonta International 2001; Hon. LLD (Otago) 1993, (Waikato) 1994, (Canterbury) 2002; NZ Medal 1990, NZ Suffrage Centennial Medal 1993. *Address:* Extraordinary Chambers in the Courts of Cambodia, National Road 4, Chaom Chau Commune, Dangkao District, Phnom Penh, Cambodia (office). *Telephone:* (23) 219814 (office). *Fax:* (23) 219841 (office). *E-mail:* info@eccc.gov.kh (office). *Website:* www.eccc.gov.kh (office).

CARTY, Donald J., OC; Canadian business executive; *Chairman, Virgin America;* m. Ana Carty; ed Queen's Univ., Kingston, Ont., Harvard Grad. School of Business Admin., USA; various man. positions at Celanese Canada Ltd, Air Canada, Canadian Pacific Railway, American Airlines Inc.; Pres. and CEO CP Air 1985–87; Sr Vice-Pres. (Airline Planning) AMR Corpn 1987–89, Exec. Vice-Pres. (Finance and Planning) AMR Corpn and American Airlines Inc. 1989–95, Pres. AMR Airline Group and American Airlines Inc. 1995–98, Chair., Pres. and CEO AMR Corpn and American Airlines Inc. 1998–2003 (resgnd); Chair. Virgin America Airlines 2006–; Chair. Porter Airlines, Toronto 2006–; mem. Bd of Dirs Dell Computer Inc. 1992–, Vice-Chair. and Chief Financial Officer 2007, Vice-Chair. 2008–; mem. Bd of Dirs CHC Helicopter Corpn, Barrick Gold Corpn, Brinker Int., Canada-US Foundation for Educational Exchange, Hawaiian Holdings Inc.; mem. Nat. Infrastructure Advisory Council 2002–05. *Address:* Virgin America, 555 Airport Blvd., Fl. 2, Burlingame, CA 94010, USA (office). *Telephone:* (650) 762-7000 (office). *Fax:* (650) 762-7001 (office). *Website:* www.virginamerica.com (office).

CARUANA, Sir Peter Richard, Kt, KCMG, QC; Gibraltarian politician, lawyer and fmr government official; b. 15 Oct. 1956; m.; six c.; ed Christian Brothers School, Grace Dieu Manor, Leicester, Ratcliffe Coll. Leicester, Queen Mary Coll., Univ. of London, Council of Legal Educ., London; joined Triay & Triay (law firm), Gibraltar 1979, Pnr specializing in commercial and shipping law 1990–95; joined Gibraltar Social Democrats 1990, Leader Feb. 1991–; elected in Gibraltar's first-ever by-election to House of Ass. May 1991; Leader of Opposition 1992–96; QC for Gibraltar 1998; Chief Minister of Gibraltar 1996–2011 (re-elected 2000, 2003, 2007); Hon. Fellow, Queen Mary Coll., Univ. of London. *Leisure interests:* golf, political and current affairs. *Address:* 10/3 Irish Town (home); c/o Office of the Chief Minister, 6 Convent Place, Gibraltar (office).

CARUANA LACORTE, Jaime; Spanish central bank governor; *General Manager, Bank for International Settlements;* b. 14 March 1952, Valencia; ed Univ. Complutense Madrid; fmr telecommunications engineer; various posts with Ministry of Trade 1979–84; Commercial attaché to the Spanish Commercial Office, New York 1984–87; Man. Dir and CEO Renta 4, SA, SVB 1987–91, Pres. 1991–96; Gen. Dir of the Treasury and Financial Policy 1996–99; mem. Bd SEPP (State Holding Co.) 1996–99; mem. EU Monetary Cttee 1996–99; Pres. SETE (Euro State Co.) 1997–99; Gen. Dir for Supervision, Banco de España 1999–2000, Gov. 2000–06; Counsellor and Dir Monetary and Capital Markets Dept, IMF 2006–09, Gen. Man. BIS 2009–; Chair. Basel Cttee for Banking Supervision 2003–06, Int. Org. of Securities Comms (IOSCO) 2004–06, Int. Asscn of Insurance Supervisors 2004–06, Jt Forum 2004–06; mem. Governing Council, European Cen. Bank 2000–, Financial Stability Forum 2003–, Group of Thirty Consultative Group on Int. Econ. and Monetary Affairs, Inc. (G-30), Washington, DC 2003–. *Publications:* numerous articles on the Spanish financial system, the financing of public admins and the man. of public debt. *Address:* Bank for International Settlements, Centralbahnplatz 2, 4002 Basel, Switzerland (office). *Telephone:* (61) 280-8080 (office). *Fax:* (61) 280-9100 (office). *E-mail:* email@bis.org (office). *Website:* www.bis.org (office).

CARVALHO, Mário Costa Martins de; Portuguese writer, lawyer and academic; *Director of Creative Writing, Instituto Português do Livro e das Bibliotecas (Portuguese Institute for Book and Libraries) (IPLB);* b. 25 Sept. 1944, Lisbon; s. of Domingos Martins Carvalho and Maria Luísa Costa Carvalho; m. Maria Helena Taborda Duarte 1969; two d.; ed Univ. of Lisbon Law School; involved in student resistance to dictatorship; received conviction for political activities; served with Army; in exile in Paris and Lund, Sweden 1973–74; returned to Portugal after revolution of 1974; involved in politics 1974–77; f. law practice 1981; Prof. of Scriptwriting, Cinema School 1999–2001; mem. Bd Portuguese Asscn of Writers; Prof. of Playwriting, Univ. of Lisbon 2000–02; Dir of Creative Writing, Instituto Português do Livro e das Bibliotecas (Portuguese Institute for Book and Libraries) (IPLB) and Portuguese Society of Authors (SPA) 2003–; City of Lisbon Prize, Theatre Prize 1999, several other awards and prizes. *Plays include:* 'Se perguntarem Por Mim, Não Estou', a Rapariga de Varsóvia. *Film:* F.F. Preto e Branco. *Publications:* Contos da Sétima Esfera 1981, O Livro Grande de Terras, Navio e Mariana 1982, A Paixão do Conde de Fróis 1986, Os Alferes 1989, Um Deus Passeando Pela Brisa da Tarde 1995, Era Bom que Trocassemos umas Ideias sobre o Assunto 1995, Fantasia para dois coronéis e uma Piscina 2003. *Address:* R. António Pereira Carrilho 27 R/C, 1000-046 Lisbon (home); Instituto Português do Livro e das Bibliotecas (Portuguese Institute for Book and Libraries) (IPLB), Campo Grande, 83-1°, 1700-088 Lisbon, Portugal (office). *Telephone:* (21) 8460576 (home). *Fax:* (21) 8464227 (home). *E-mail:* advogados.1@netc.pt (office). *Website:* www.iplb.pt (office).

CARVALHO DE ANDRADE, Marcelo, PhD; Brazilian banker and international organization official; *President, Earth Council Alliance;* s. of Atabalipa de Andrade and the late Maria Carvalho de Andrade; m. Lisa Bjornson 1995; ed Univ. Gama Filho, Rio de Janeiro; PNR, T. W. P. Ltd (investment firm), Rio de Janeiro, Earth Capital Partners LLP (responsible for external relations); Co-founder Terra Capital; Founder and Chair. Pro-Natura International (first int. NGO based in Southern Hemisphere to specialize in sustainable devt), Rio de Janeiro 1980s; Advisor (non-exec.), BHP Billiton, DuPont, Shell; mem. Biotechnology Advisory Panel, E. I. du Pont de Nemours & Co. 2004–; Pres. Earth Council Alliance; mem. CONCEC (pvt.-sector advisory panel for Brazilian Govt), Counterpart International, Earth Restoration Corps; George and Cynthia Mitchell Int. Prize for Sustainable Devt 1997. *Address:* Earth Council Alliance, 101 West Broadway, Suite 1800, San Diego, CA 92101, USA (office). *Telephone:* (619) 595-0760 (office). *Fax:* (619) 595-0764 (office). *E-mail:* info@earthcouncilalliance.org (office). *Website:* www.earthcouncilalliance.org (office).

CARVALHO DE AZEVÊDO, Roberto; Brazilian diplomatist and international organization official; *Director-General, World Trade Organization;* b. 3 Oct. 1957, Salvador; m. Maria Nazareth Farani Azevêdo; two d.; ed Univ. of Brasília; joined Foreign Service 1984, served at Embassies in Washington, DC 1988–91 and Montevideo 1992–94, Perm. Mission in Geneva 1997–2001, Deputy Chief of Staff for Econ. Affairs to the Foreign Minister 1995–96, Head, Dispute Settlement Unit 2001–05, Dir Dept of Econ. Affairs 2005–06, Vice-Minister for Econ. and Technological Affairs, Ministry of Foreign Relations 2006–08, Perm. Rep. to WTO, WIPO, UNCTAD, ITU 2008–13; Dir-Gen. WTO 2013–; fmr Rep. to FAO

Codex Alimentarius Comm., Int. Cotton Council, Int. Cotton Advisory Cttee, OECD Trade Cttee. *Address:* World Trade Organization, Centre William Rappard, Rue de Lausanne 154, 1211 Geneva 21, Switzerland (office). *Telephone:* 227395111 (office). *Fax:* 227314206 (office). *E-mail:* enquiries@wto.org (office). *Website:* www .wto.org (office).

CARVILLE, James; American political consultant; b. 25 Oct. 1944, Fort Benning, Ga; s. of Lucille Carville; m. Mary Matalin 1993; two d.; ed Louisiana State Univ.; litigator Baton Rouge 1973–79; managed first campaign 1982, then managed campaign for Gov. of Texas 1983; subsequent successful campaigns included Robert Casey for Penn. Gov. 1986, Wallace Wilkinson for Ky Gov. 1987, Frank Lautenberg for NJ Sen. 1988, Zell Miller for Ga Lt.-Gov. 1990, Harris Wofford for Penn. Sen. 1991; co-f. Carville and Begala (political consulting co.) 1989; co-managed Clinton Presidential Campaign 1992, later sr political adviser to Pres.; numerous int. political clients 1993–, including successful campaign for Ehud Barak for PM Israel 1999; Co-f. Democracy Corps (consultancy and polling co.); Campaign Man. of the Year 1993. *Films include:* The People vs. Larry Flynt 1996, All the King's Men (exec. producer) 2006. *Publications:* All's Fair: Love, War and Running for President (with Mary Matalin) 1995, We're Right, They're Wrong (with Mary Matalin) 1996, And The Horse He Rode In On: The People v. Ken Starr 1998, Stickin': The Case for Loyalty 2000, Take It Back: Our Party, Our Country, Our Future (with Paul Begala) 2006, 40 More Years: How the Democrats Will Rule the Next Generation (with Rebecca Buckwalter-Poza) 2009. *Address:* Democracy Corps, 10 G Street, NE, Suite 400, Washington, DC 20002 (office); Gaslight Inc., 424 South Washington Street, Lower Level, Alexandria, VA 22314, USA (office). *Telephone:* (202) 478-8330 (DC) (office); (703) 739-7777 (office). *Fax:* (202) 289-8648 (DC) (office); (703) 739-7766 (office). *E-mail:* james@carville.info (office). *Website:* www.democracycorps.com (office); www.carville.info (office).

CARY, Anthony Joyce, CMG, MA, MBA; British fmr diplomatist and administrator; *Executive Director, Queen's-Blyth Worldwide;* b. 1 July 1951; m. Clare Cary; three s. one d.; ed Univ. of Oxford, Stanford Business School, USA; entered British Diplomatic Service 1973; with British Mil. Govt in Berlin 1975–78; mem. Policy Planning Staff, FCO 1978–80, EC Dept 1982–84; Pvt. Sec. to Ministers of State Malcolm Rifkind, then Lynda Chalker 1984–86; Head of Chancery, Kuala Lumpur 1986–89; Deputy Chef de Cabinet to Leon Brittan, EC, Brussels 1989–93; Head of EU Dept, FCO 1993–97; Counsellor, Political and Public Affairs, Embassy in Washington, DC 1997–99; Chef de Cabinet to Chris Patten, European Commr for External Relations 1999–2003; Amb. to Sweden 2003–07; High Commr to Canada 2007–10; Int. Juror, Cundill History Prize, McGill Univ. 2011; Exec. Dir Queen's-Blyth Worldwide (partnership between Queen's Univ., Ont. and Blyth Education) 2011–; Commr, Commonwealth Scholarship Comm. 2012–; Harkness Fellow, Stanford Univ. 1980; Hon. Pres. British Cttee of the Canada UK Colloquia 2011–. *Address:* Queen's-Blyth Worldwide (office). *Telephone:* (866) 960-3552 (office). *E-mail:* info@queensblythworldwide.ca (office); qb.worldwide@queensu.ca (office). *Website:* queensblyth.wordpress.com (office).

CASADESUS, Jean Claude; French conductor; *Director, Lille National Orchestra;* b. (Jean Claude Probst), 7 Dec. 1935, Paris; s. of Lucien Probst and Gisèle Casadesus; two s. one d.; ed Paris Nat. Conservatoire and Ecole Normale, Paris; solo timpanist, Concert Colonne 1959–68; percussion soloist, Domaine Musical (with Boulez); Conductor, Paris Opéra 1969–71; Co-Dir Orchestre Pays de Loire 1971–76; Founder and Dir Lille Nat. Orchestra 1976–; appears as guest conductor with leading orchestras in UK, USA, France, Germany, Norway, Russia, Czech Repub., int. music festivals etc.; Pres. Musique Nouvelle en Liberté; Musical Dir, Lille Piano Festival; Commdr, Légion d'honneur, Ordre nat. du Mérite, Grand-Officier des Arts et des Lettres; Chevalier, Ordre des Palmes académiques; Commdr, Order of Orange Nassau (Netherlands); Officer, Order of Léopold (Belgium); Grand Prix de la SACEM and several other prizes and awards for recordings. *Recordings include:* works by Dutilleux (1st Symphony), Berlioz, Mahler, Bizet, Stravinsky, Mozart, Beethoven, Ravel, Debussy, Poulenc, Groupe des Six, Prokofiev, Dukas, Massenet, Milhaud, Honneger, Mussorgsky, Franck, Canteloube – Songs of the Auvergne. *Publications:* Le plus court chemin d'un coeur à un autre (ed.) 1998, La partition d'une vie 2012. *Leisure interests:* yachting, sailing, skiing, tennis. *Address:* Orchestre National de Lille, 30 place Mendès-France, BP 119, 59027 Lille Cedex (office); 2 rue de Steinkerque, 75018 Paris, France (home). *Telephone:* 3-20-12-82-68 (office). *Fax:* 3-20-78-29-10 (office). *Website:* www.onlille.com.

CASAJUANA I PALET, Carles; Spanish diplomatist; b. 24 Oct. 1954, Sant Cugat del Vallès, Barcelona; m. Margarita Massanet; two d.; ed Univ. of Barcelona; entered Spanish Diplomatic Service 1980, posted to Embassies in Bogotá 1980–82, the Philippines 1982–84, with Ministry of Foreign Affairs 1984–87, Perm. Mission to UN, New York 1987–91, Chief of Staff to Sec. Gen. for Foreign Policy, Ministry of Foreign Affairs 1991–96, Amb. to Malaysia 1996–2001 (also accred to Brunei Darussalam 1996–2001, to Viet Nam 1997–98), Amb. Rep. to Political and Security Cttee of EU 2001–04, Sr Diplomatic Adviser to the Prime Minister 2004–08, Amb. to UK 2008–12. *Publications include:* novels: Tap d'escopeta 1987, Bondad 1989, La puresa del porc 1990, Punt de fuga 1992, Esperit d'evasió 1998, Diumenge de temptació 2001, Kuala Lumpur 2005, L'últim home que parlava català (XXIX Premi de les Lletres Catalanes Ramon Llull 2009) 2009; essays: Pla i Nietzsche: afinitats i coincidències 1996. *Address:* Ministry of Foreign Affairs and Co-operation, Plaza de la Provincia 1, 28012 Madrid, Spain (office). *Telephone:* (91) 3799700 (office); (91) 3798300 (office). *E-mail:* informae@maec.es (office). *Website:* www.maec.es (office).

CASALE, Carl M., BS, MBA; American business executive; *President and CEO, CHS Inc.;* b. Willamette Valley, Ore.; m. Kim Casale; ed Oregon State Univ., Washington Univ., St Louis, Mo.; joined Monsanto as a sales rep. in eastern Wash. 1984, held numerous sales, strategy, marketing and tech.-related positions, later Exec. Vice-Pres., North American Commercial Operations, Exec. Vice-Pres., Strategy and Operations –2009, Chief Financial Officer 2009–10; Pres. and CEO CHS Inc. (agricultural cooperative) 2011–; fmr mem. Bd National 4-H Council; Alumni Fellow, Oregon State Univ. Coll. of Agric. 2009. *Address:* CHS, PO Box 64089, St Paul, MN 55164-0089 (office); CHS, 5500 Cenex Drive, Inver Grove Heights, MN 55077, USA (office). *Telephone:* (651) 355-6000 (office). *E-mail:* info@ chsinc.com (office). *Website:* www.chsinc.com (office).

CASANOVA, Corina, Lic. iur.; Swiss lawyer and politician; *Federal Chancellor;* b. 4 Jan. 1956, Ilanz, Graubünden; ed Univ. of Fribourg; admitted to the Bar, Graubünden 1984, pvt. practice as lawyer 1984–86; Red Cross Del. in S Africa, Angola, Nicaragua and El Salvador 1986–90; Del. for Information, Parl. Service of Fed. Ass. 1992–96; joined staff of Fed. Councillor Flavio Cotti, Fed. Dept of Foreign Affairs (DFA) 1996, Adviser to Fed. Councillor Joseph Deiss 1999, Deputy Sec.-Gen., DFA 2002–05; Vice-Chancellor of Switzerland 2005–07, Fed. Chancellor 2008–; mem. Christian Democratic People's Party. *Address:* Federal Chancellery, Bundeshaus West, 3003 Bern, Switzerland (office). *Telephone:* (31) 3223791 (office). *Fax:* (31) 3223706 (office). *E-mail:* webmaster@admin.ch (office). *Website:* www.bk.admin.ch (office).

CASANOVA, Jean-Claude, DEcon; French economist and journalist; *Editor, Commentaire;* b. 11 June 1934, Ajaccio, Corsica; s. of Jean Casanova and Marie-Antoinette Luciani; m. Marie-Thérèse Demargne 1962; two s.; ed Lycée Carnot, Inst. des Hautes Etudes, Tunis, Univ. of Paris, Harvard Univ.; Asst Fondation nat. des sciences politiques 1958; Chief of Staff to Minister of Industry 1958–61; Asst in Law Faculty, Univ. of Dijon 1963; Sr Lecturer then Prof., Faculty of Law and Econ. Sciences, Univ. of Nancy 1964–68; with Univ. of Paris-Nanterre 1968; with Inst. d'Etudes politiques, Paris 1969–; Dir of Studies and Research, Fondation nationale des sciences politiques 1965–90, Pres. 2007–; Tech. Adviser to Minister of Educ. 1972–74; Adviser to Prime Minister Raymond Barre 1976–81; Ed. Commentaire 1978–; leader writer, L'Express 1985–95; regular contrib. to Le Figaro 1996–2001; mem. Comm. on Renovation and Ethics of Public Life 2012–; mem. Econ. and Social Council 1994–2004, Acad. des Sciences morales et politiques 1996–; columnist, Le Monde 2002–; Pres. Fondation nationale des sciences politiques 2007–; Officier, Ordre nat. du Mérite 1996, Commdr, Légion d'honneur 2008. *Address:* Commentaire, 116 rue du Bac, 75007 Paris (office); Fondation nationale des sciences politiques, 27 rue St Guillaume, 75007 Paris; 11–13 rue de l'Aude, 75014 Paris, France (home). *Telephone:* 1-45-49-37-82 (office); 1-43-26-51-95 (home). *Fax:* 1-45-44-32-18 (office). *E-mail:* jcc@commentaire.fr (office); jcc-1@ numericable.fr (home). *Website:* www.commentaire.fr (office).

CASAS-GONZALEZ, Antonio, BA, MA, PhD; Venezuelan economist, business executive and fmr government official; *Economic Adviser and Board Member, Tecnoconsult SA;* b. 24 July 1933, Mérida; m. Carmen Elena Granadino de Casas; five s. one d.; ed George Washington Univ., Georgetown Univ., USA; fmrly Prof. of Econs at various insts; Adviser, Venezuelan Petrochemical Inst. and Asst to Minister of Mines and Hydrocarbons 1957–59; Petroleum and Econ. Counsellor, Embassy in Washington, DC 1959–61; with Inter-American Devt Bank 1961–69; Vice-Minister of Devt 1969; Minister for Nat. Planning Office (CORDIPLAN) 1972; Man. Dir Petróleos de Venezuela (UK) SA 1990–94; Gov. Banco Cen. de Venezuela 1994–99; Vice-Pres. Intergovernmental Group of Twenty-Four on Int. Monetary Affairs 1996–; mem. Bd of Dirs Venezolana de Aviación (VIASA) 1970–73, Corp. Andina de Fomento 1970–73, Banco Cen. de Venezuela 1972–75, Corp. Venezolana de Guyana 1979–82, Petróleos de Venezuela SA 1979–90; currently Econ. Adviser and Bd mem., Tecnoconsult SA; mem. Int. Council Elliot School of Int. Affairs, George Washington Univ.; 16 decorations from nine countries. *Publications include:* América Latina y los problemas de Desarrollo (co-author) 1974, Venezuela y el CIAP (co-author) 1974, La planificación en América Latina (co-author) 1975, World Development (co-author) 1977; articles for various publs. *Leisure interest:* golf. *Address:* Tecnoconsult SA, Av. Sur 11, Monroy a Puente Victoria, No. 33, Caracas 1050-A, Venezuela (office). *Telephone:* (212) 508-2189 (office). *Fax:* (212) 508-2363 (office). *E-mail:* TCcaracas@tecnoconsult.com (office). *Website:* www .tecnoconsult.com (office).

CASE, Stephen M., MA; American business executive; b. 21 Aug. 1958, Honolulu, Hawaii; m. 1st Joanne Case 1985 (divorced 1996); three d.; m. 2nd Jean Case 1998; ed Williams Coll.; worked in marketing dept, Procter & Gamble 1980–82; Man. of New Pizza Devt, Pizza Hut Div., PepsiCo 1982–83; Marketing Asst, Control Video Corpn, Va 1983–85, Marketing Dir Quantum Computer Services (fmrly Control Video then renamed America Online (AOL)) 1985–92, CEO AOL 1992–2001, Chair. 1995–2001; Chair. AOL Time Warner (cr. after merger of Time Warner and AOL) 2001–03, Dir with jt responsibility for corp. strategy 2003, mem. Bd of Dirs –2005 (resgnd); f. Revolution LLC 2005; prin. investor and Chair. Exclusive Resorts LLC, Denver, Colo 2004; prin. investor, Maui Land and Pineapple, HI; f. Case Foundation 1997; f. ABC2, Accelerate Brain Cancer Cure 2001; Entrepreneur of the Year, Incorporated Magazine 1994. *Leisure interests:* reading political science and history. *Address:* c/o The Case Foundation, 1717 Rhode Island Avenue, NW, Seventh Floor, Washington, DC 20036, USA. *Website:* casefoundation.org; www.abc2.org.

CASEY, Robert (Bob) Patrick, Jr, JD; American lawyer and politician; *Senator from Pennsylvania;* b. 13 April 1960, Scranton, Pa; eldest s. of the late Pa Gov. Robert P. Casey and Ellen Casey; m. Terese Foppiano Casey 1985; four d.; ed The Coll. of the Holy Cross, Catholic Univ. of America; taught fifth grade and coached eighth grade basketball team for Jesuit Volunteer Corps, Gesu School, Philadelphia 1983; began practising law in Scranton 1988; Pa State Auditor Gen. 1997–2005; cand. for State Gov. 2002; State Treas. 2005–06; Senator from Pa 2007–, mem. Foreign Relations Cttee, Agric., Nutrition and Forestry Cttee, Health, Educ., Labor and Pensions Cttee, Special Cttee on Aging, Jt Econ. Cttee; Democrat. *Address:* 393 Russell Senate Office Building, Washington, DC 20510, USA (office). *Telephone:* (202) 224-6324 (office). *Fax:* (202) 228-0604 (office). *Website:* casey.senate.gov (office); bobcasey.com (office).

CASH, Pat; Australian sports commentator, tennis coach and fmr professional tennis player; b. 27 May 1965, Melbourne; s. of Patrick Cussen and Dorothy Hart Cash; m. Emily Cash; four c.; ed Whitefriars Coll.; winner, US Open Jr Championship 1982; mem. winning Australian Davis Cup team 1983; in quarter-finals at Wimbledon 1985; finalist Australian Open 1987, 1988; Wimbledon Champion 1987; retd 1997; plays on Masters Tennis circuit; co-f. Pat Cash Tennis Acad.; currently BBC Wimbledon analyst; Australian Tennis Hall of Fame 2003. *Leisure interests:* music, football. *Address:* c/o Duncan Marsh, Red Baron Enterprises, Day and Co, 88 College Road, Harrow, Middx, HA1 1BQ, England; c/o Pat Cash and Associates, PO Box 2238, Footscray, Vic. 3011, Australia (office). *Telephone:* (7956) 447811. *E-mail:* duncan@patcash.co.uk (office). *Website:* www.patcash .net; www.patcash.co.uk.

CASHMORE, Roger John, CMG, MA, DPhil, FRS, FInstP; British physicist and academic; *Chairman, UK Atomic Energy Authority;* b. 22 Aug. 1944, Birmingham, England; s. of C. J. C. Cashmore and E. M. Cashmore; m. Elizabeth Ann Lindsay 1971; one s.; ed Dudley Grammar School, St John's Coll., Cambridge, Balliol Coll., Oxford; Weir Jr Research Fellow, Univ. Coll., Oxford 1967–69; 1851 Research Fellow 1968; Research Assoc. Stanford Linear Accelerator, Calif. 1969–74; Research Officer, Univ. of Oxford 1974–79, Lecturer 1979–90, Reader in Experimental Physics 1990–91, Prof. 1991–98; Research Dir, CERN 1999–2003, Deputy Dir Gen. 2002–03; Prin. Brasenose Coll. Oxford 2002–; Chair. UKAEA 2010–; Boys Prize, Inst. of Physics 1983, Humboldt Research Award 1995. *Publications:* contribs to Physics Review. *Leisure interests:* sports, wine. *Address:* Culham Science Centre, Abingdon, Oxon., OX14 3DB, England (office). *Telephone:* (1235) 466608 (office). *Fax:* (1235) 466209 (office). *E-mail:* r.cashmore1@physics.ox.ac.uk (office).

CASIDA, John Edward, MS, PhD, FRS; American entomologist, toxicologist and academic; *Professor of the Graduate School, University of California, Berkeley;* b. 22 Dec. 1929, Phoenix, Ariz.; s. of Lester Earl Casida and Ruth Casida (née Barnes); m. Katherine Faustine Monson 1956; two s.; ed Univ. of Wisconsin-Madison; served with USAF 1953; Research Asst, Univ. of Wisconsin 1951–53, Asst Prof. then Assoc. Prof. 1954–63, Prof. of Entomology 1959–63; Prof. of Entomology, Univ. of California, Berkeley 1964–2007, William Muriece Hoskins Chair in Chemical and Molecular Entomology 1996–2008, Faculty Research Lecturer 1998, Prof. of the Grad. School 2008–, Dir Environmental Chem. and Toxicology Lab. 1964–2008; Scholar-in-Residence, Bellagio Study and Conf. Centre, Rockefeller Foundation, Lake Como, Italy 1978; Messenger Lecturer, Cornell Univ. 1985; Sterling B. Hendicks Lecturer, US DE of Agric. and ACS 1992–; Lecturer in Science, Third World Acad. of Sciences, Univ. of Buenos Aires 1997; mem. NAS, ACS, Entomological Soc. of America, Soc. of Environmental Toxicology and Chem., European Acad. of Sciences 2004–; Haight Travelling Fellow 1958–59; Guggenheim Fellow 1970–71; Fellow, Entomological Soc. of America 1989; Foreign mem. Royal Soc. 1998; Hon. mem. Soc. of Toxicology, Pesticide Science Soc. of Japan; Hon. DUniv (Buenos Aires) 1997; ACS Int. Award for Research in Pesticide Chem. 1970, ACS Spencer Award in Agric. and Food Chem. 1978, Bussart Memorial Award, Entomological Soc. of America 1989, Wolf Prize in Agric. 1993, Founder's Award, Soc. of Environmental Toxicology and Chem. 1994, Kôrô-sho Prize Pesticide Science Soc. (Japan) 1995, Career Achievement Award, Univ. of California, Berkeley 2009, Distinguished Service Award, American Coll. of Toxicology 2009. *Publications:* numerous papers in scientific journals on pesticide chem. and toxicology, metabolism and mode of action of organic toxicants, and insect biochemistry. *Address:* Department of Environmental Science, Policy and Management, University of California, Berkeley, 114 Wellman Hall, Berkeley, CA 94720 (office); 1570 La Vereda Road, Berkeley, CA 94708, USA (home). *Telephone:* (510) 642-5424 (office). *Fax:* (510) 642-6497 (office). *E-mail:* ectl@berkeley.edu (office). *Website:* ourenvironment.berkeley.edu (office).

CASIMIR, Pierre-Richard, LLB; Haitian lawyer, diplomatist and politician; b. 19 Feb. 1970, Port-au-Prince; ed Haiti State Univ., Univ. of Montreal, Canada; admitted to the Bar 1999; Instructor in Civic Educ., Amicale des Juristes 1994; Dir Legal Assistance Dept, Staff Training and Improvement Acad. 1995–; Program Dir USAID Poor Detainees Legal Assistance Program 1995–99; fmr Legal Asst and Interpreter, US Embassy Ministerial Advisory Team on Justice; fmr Assoc., Cabinet Lissade (law firm), Port-au-Prince; Legal Counsel to Pres. of Haiti 1999; Deputy Dir Pvt. Office of Minister of Justice 2001; mem. Pvt. Office of Pres. of Haiti 2004–05; Consul-Gen. in Montreal 2005–11; Sec. of State for Foreign Affairs 2011–12, Minister of Foreign Affairs and Religion 2012–14; mem. Bar Assocn of Port-au-Prince. *Address:* c/o Ministry of Foreign Affairs and Religion, boulevard Harry S. Truman, Cité de l'Exposition, Port-au-Prince, Haiti (office).

CASINI, Pier Ferdinando; Italian politician; *President, Inter-Parliamentary Union;* b. 3 Dec. 1955, Bologna; m. Roberta Lubich (divorced); two d.; partner, Azzurra Caltagirone; one d.; joined Unione dei Democratici Cristiani e di Centro (UDC) 1980; elected Town Councillor, Bologna 1980; mem. Chamber of Deputies 1983–94, Pres. 2001–06; Mem. European Parl. 1994–2001 (PPE-DE Group); Pres. Inter-Parl. Union 2005–; Pres. Centrist Democrat Int. (CDI) (fmrly Christian Democrat Int.) 2006–; fmr Pres. Christian Democratic Centre; Order of Merit from Austria, Brazil, Chile, France, Germany, Hungary, Lithuania, Luxembourg, Malaysia, Malta, Norway, Peru, Poland, San Marino, Spain. *Address:* Unione dei Democratici Cristiani e di Centro (UDC) (Union of Christian and Centre Democrats), Via dei Due Macelli 66, 00182 Roma, Italy (office); Inter-Parliamentary Union 5, chemin du Pommier, Case postale 330, 1218 Le Grand-Saconnex, Geneva, Switzerland (office). *Telephone:* (06) 69791001 (UDC) (office); 229194150 (IPU) (office). *Fax:* (06) 6791574 (UDC) (office); 229194160 (IPU) (office). *E-mail:* info@udc-italia.it (office); postbox@mail.ipu.org (office); pier@pierferdinandocasini.it (office). *Website:* www.udc-italia.it (office); www.ipu.org (office); www.pierferdinandocasini.it (office).

CASORATI, Francesco; Italian artist; b. 2 July 1934, Turin; s. of Felice Casorati and Daphne Maugham; m. Paola Zanetti 1959; three s.; ed Liceo Artistico dell' Accad. di Torino; held first solo show in Milan 1954; has since exhibited at numerous int. exhbns including Pittori Italiani, Moscow, Budapest, Prague, Sofia 1957–58, Expo, Brussels 1958, Venice Biennale, etc.; numerous solo and group shows in various European cities; taught at Liceo Artistico di Torino 1959–75, Accad. Albertina di Torino 1970–75; holder, Chair. of Decorative Art, Accad. Albertina di Torino 1975–84. *Address:* Via Mazzini 52, Turin; C.so Kossuth 19, Turin, Italy (home). *Telephone:* (011) 831491; (011) 894950 (home).

CASPER, William Earl (Billy); American professional golfer; b. 24 June 1931, San Diego, Calif.; m. Shirley Casper (née Franklin); six c., five adopted c.; ed Univ. of Notre Dame; fmr fruit farmer; professional golfer since 1954; winner, US Open 1959, 1966, Masters 1970; played eight times in Ryder Cup 1961–75; winner of 51 tournaments on pro circuit and several more on seniors tour; won Brazilian Open twice, the Lancôme 1974, Italian Open 1975, Mexican Open 1977; Sr Advisor and Consultant Billy Casper Golf LLC; US PGA Player of the Year 1966, 1970, PGA Hall of Fame 1982, Vardon Trophy (lowest scoring average) 1960, 1963, 1965, 1966, 1968. *Address:* Billy Casper Golf LLC, 8300 Boone Boulevard, Suite 350, Vienna, VA 22182, USA (office). *Telephone:* (703) 761-1444 (office). *Fax:* (703) 893-

3504 (office). *E-mail:* info@billycaspergolf.com (office). *Website:* www.billycaspergolf.com.

CASPERSEN, Sven Lars, MEcon; Danish academic; b. 30 June 1935, Åabenraa; s. of Jes P. Caspersen and Carla Caspersen; m. Eva Caspersen 1962; three s.; Asst Sec., Danish Cen. Bureau of Statistics 1962–64; Deputy Chief, Cen. Statistical Centre of Danish Insurance Cos at Danish Insurance Asscn 1964–68; Assoc. Prof. of Statistics, Copenhagen School of Econs and Business Admin. 1968–73, Head of Dept of Statistics 1970–73; Dean of Social Sciences, Aalborg Univ. 2004, Rector 1976–2004, Chair. Bd 2004–06; Chair. Bd Copenhagen Stock Exchange 1989–96; Chair. Liaison Cttee of Rectors' Conferences of mem. states of the EC 1992–94; Chair. Govt Advisory Council on EU Matters 1993–2001; Chair. European Capital Markets Inst. 1993–95; Vice-Pres. Fed. of Stock Exchanges of the EC 1993–95, Pres. 1995–96; Pres. Int. Asscn of Univ. Pres.'s 1999–2002; Chair. Bd Aalborg Theatre 1986; Dr hc (Vilnius Tech. Univ.) 1993; recipient, Tribute of Appreciation, US Dept of State 1981. *Leisure interests:* chess, bridge, tennis. *Address:* Duebrødrevej 6, 9000 Aalborg, Denmark (home).

CASS, Sir Geoffrey Arthur, Kt, MA (Oxon.), MA (Cantab.), CCMI; British publishing executive and arts and lawn tennis administrator; b. 11 Aug. 1932, Bishop Auckland; s. of the late Arthur Cass and Jessie Cass (née Simpson); m. Olwen Mary Richards, MBE, JP, DL 1957; four d.; ed Queen Elizabeth Grammar School, Darlington and Jesus Coll., Oxford; Nuffield Coll., Oxford 1957–58; RAF 1958–60; ed. Automation 1960–61; Consultant, PA Man. Consultants Ltd 1960–65; Pvt. Man. Consultant, British Communications Corpn and Controls and Communications Ltd 1965; Dir Controls and Communications Ltd 1966–69; Dir George Allen & Unwin 1965–67, Man. Dir 1967–71; Dir Weidenfeld Publrs. 1972–74, Univ. of Chicago Press, UK 1971–86; Chief Exec. Cambridge Univ. Press 1972–92, Consultant 1992–; Sec. Press Syndicate, Univ. of Cambridge 1974–92; Univ. Printer 1982–83, 1991–92; Fellow, Clare Hall, Cambridge 1979–; Trustee Shakespeare Birthplace Trust 1982–94 (Life Trustee 1994–); Chair. Royal Shakespeare Co. 1985–2000 (Deputy Pres. 2000–11), Royal Theatrical Support Trust (fmrly Royal Shakespeare Theatre Trust) 1983–, British Int. Tennis and Nat. Training 1985–90, Nat. Ranking Cttee; mem. Bd of Man., Lawn Tennis Asscn of GB 1985–90, 1993–2000, Deputy Pres. 1994–96, Pres. 1997–99; Chair. Tennis Foundation 2003–07, Pres. 2007–; mem. Cttee of Man., Wimbledon Championships 1990–2002; Pres., Chair. or mem. numerous other trusts, bds, cttees, charitable appeals and advisory bodies particularly in connection with theatre, sport and medicine; Oxford tennis Blue and badminton; Hon. Fellow, Jesus Coll., Oxford 1998; Chevalier, Ordre des Arts et Lettres. *Achievements include:* played in Wimbledon Tennis Championships 1954, 1955, 1956, 1959; British Veterans Singles Champion, Wimbledon 1978. *Publications:* articles in professional journals. *Leisure interests:* tennis, theatre. *Address:* Middlefield, Huntingdon Road, Cambridge, CB3 0LH, England (home). *Website:* www.tennisfoundation.org.uk.

CASSEL, Vincent; French actor; b. 23 Nov. 1966, Paris; s. of Jean-Pierre Cassel; m. Monica Bellucci 1999. *Films include* Les Clés du paradis 1991, Hot Chocolate 1992, Café au Lait 1993, Jefferson in Paris 1995, La Haine 1995, Blood of the Hunter 1995, Adultery: A User's Guide 1995, L'Appartement 1996, L'Elève 1996, Come mi vuoi 1996, Dobermann 1997, Compromis 1998, Mediterranée 1998, Le Plaisir (et ses petits tracas) 1998, Elizabeth 1998, Guest House Paradiso 1999, Messenger: The Story of Joan of Arc 1999, Les Rivières pourpres (Crimson Rivers) 2000, Birthday Girl 2000, The Reckoning 2001, Le Pacte des loups (Brotherhood of the Wolf) 2001, Sur mes lèvres 2001, Shrek 2001, Irréversible (also co-producer) 2002, Ice Age 2002, Blueberry 2004, Spy Bound 2004, Ocean's Twelve 2004, Robots (voice) 2005, Derailed 2005, Sheitan 2006, Ocean's Thirteen 2007, Eastern Promises 2007, Sa majesté Minor 2007, L'instinct de mort 2008, L'ennemi public no. 1 2008, Lascars (voice) 2009, À deriva 2009, Black Swan 2010, Our Day Will Come 2010, The Monk 2011, A Dangerous Method 2011, Trance 2013. *Address:* c/o Adéquat, 80 rue d'Amsterdam, 75009 Paris, France (office); c/o Creative Artists Agency, 2000 Avenue of the Stars, Los Angeles, CA 90067, USA (office). *Telephone:* 1-44-62-69-69 (Paris) (office); (424) 288-2000 (Los Angeles) (office). *Fax:* 1-44-62-69-68 (Paris) (office); (424) 288-2900 (Los Angeles) (office). *E-mail:* agence@agence-adequat.com (office); contact@120films.com. *Website:* www.agence-adequat.com (office); www.caa.com (office).

CASSEL-CROCHON, Jean-Pierre; French actor; b. 27 Oct. 1932, Paris; m. 2nd Anne Célérier 1981; two s. one d.; film debut in 1959; frequent TV appearances, regular theatre activity, music hall; Chevalier, Légion d'honneur 2004. *Theatre includes:* Roméo et Juliette, Chorus Line, Little Black Book, Who's Afraid of Virginia Woolf?, The Collection, Elvire, Festen. *Films include:* Les Jeux de l'Amour, Le Caporal Epinglé, Paris brûle-t-il? Those Magnificent Men in Their Flying Machines, Oh What A Lovely War!, Baxter, The Discreet Charm of the Bourgeoisie, The Three Musketeers, Le Mouton Enragé, Murder on the Orient Express, That Lucky Touch, The Twist, Who is Killing the Great Chefs of Europe?, Les Rendezvous d'Anna, From Hell to Victory, The Return of the Musketeers, Mangeclous, La Truite, Chouans, Mr. Frost, Phantom of the Opera, Theo and Vincent, The Favour, The Watch and the Very Big Fish, Amour et Petit Doigt de Pied, Pétain, Thé Noir au Citron, Casque Bleu, Prêt à Porter 1994, La Cérémonie 1995, Sade, La Patinoire, Les Rivières Pourpres 2000, Michel Vaillant 2002, Narco 2003, The Wooden Camera 2003, Virgil 2004, King Kong Paradise 2005. *Television includes:* Love in a Cold Climate, Shillingbury Tales, Liberty, Casanova, Secret of Sahara, Matter of Convenience, Warburg, The Maid, The French Kill, Notorious, Dust and Blood, Young Indy, La 13e Voiture, Printemps de Chien, Le Fils de Paul, Le Président et la Garde Barrière 1996, Un printemps de chien, Les Tiers mondains 1996, Le Coeur et l'epée, Les Montagnes bleues 1998, Le Coup du Lapin, Histoire d'Amour (Crimes en Série) 1999, Rastignac 2000, Pique-Nique chez Osiris 2000, La Chanson du Maison 2001, La maison du canal 2002, La faux 2002, La Mémoire et le Pardon. *Music:* album: Et maintenant 2000; DVD: Je ne veux pas vivre sans amour 2003. *Publications:* A mes amours 2004. *Address:* Art-Ciné, 36 rue de Ponthieu, 75008 Paris, France. *Telephone:* 1-42-56-04-20 (office). *Fax:* 1-42-56-04-19 (home). *E-mail:* cecilpro@noos.fr (home).

CASSELLS, Peter; Irish civil servant and trade union official; *Executive Chairman, National Centre for Partnership and Performance;* b. 20 Oct. 1949, Co. Meath; m. Paula Carey; legislation officer, Irish Congress of Trade Unions 1973–80, Econ. and Social Affairs Officer 1980–85, Asst Gen. Sec. 1985–87, Gen. Sec. 1987–2000; Chair. Nat. Centre for Partnership and Performance 2001–;

currently Exec. Dir Peter Cassells Consultants Ltd, also Chair. DHR Communications; Dr hc (Nat. Univ. of Ireland) 2002. *Address:* National Centre for Partnership and Performance, 16 Parnell Square, Dublin 1 (office); Peter Cassells Consultants Ltd., Molyneux House, Bride Street, Dublin 8, Ireland. *Telephone:* (1) 8146391 (office). *Fax:* (1) 8146301 (office). *E-mail:* info@ncpp.ie (office). *Website:* www.ncpp.ie (office).

CASSELS, John William Scott, MA, PhD, FRS, FRSE; British mathematician and academic; *Fellow, Trinity College, University of Cambridge;* b. 11 July 1922, Durham City; s. of the late John William Cassels and Muriel Speakman Cassels (née Lobjoit); m. Constance Mabel Merritt (née Senior) 1949 (died 2000); one s. one d.; ed Neville's Cross Council School, Durham, George Heriot's School, Edinburgh and Univs of Edinburgh and Cambridge; Lecturer, Univ. of Manchester 1949–50; Lecturer, Univ. of Cambridge 1950–65, Reader in Arithmetic 1965–67, Sadleirian Prof. of Pure Mathematics 1967–84, Fellow, Trinity Coll., Cambridge 1949–. *Publications:* An Introduction to Diophantine Approximations 1957, An Introduction to the Geometry of Numbers 1959, Rational Quadratic Forms 1979, Economics for Mathematicians 1981, Local Fields 1986, Lectures on Elliptic Curves 1991, Prolegomena to a middlebrow arithmetic of curves of genus 2 (with E.V. Flynn) 1996. *Leisure interests:* The Higher Arithmetic, gardening. *Address:* c/o Trinity College, Trinity Street, Cambridge, CB2 1TQ (office); 3 Luard Close, Cambridge, CB2 8PL, England (home). *Telephone:* (1223) 338400; (1223) 246108 (home).

CASSESE, Sabino; Italian lawyer, judge and academic; *Judge, Corte costituzionale;* b. 20 Oct. 1935, Atripalda; Prof., Faculté Int. de droit comparé, Luxembourg 1966; Prof. of Public Admin. and Prof. of Govt, Dept of Econs, Univs of Ancona and Naples, Political Science Dept, Univ. of Rome, School for Higher Civil Servants, Rome; Dir Inst. of Public Law, Law Dept, Univ. of Rome 1991–93, Prof. of Admin. Law 1993–; Judge, Corte costituzionale (Constitutional Court) 2005–; Fellow, European Inst. of Public Admin., Maastricht 1985–86; Prof., Univ. de Paris I 1986, 1994; Assoc. Prof., Univ. of Nantes 1987; Visiting Prof., Inst. d'Etudes Politiques, Paris 1991, 2005–07; Visiting Scholar, Law School, Univ. of California, Berkeley 1965, LSE 1969, Law School, Stanford Univ., USA 1970, 1975, 1981, 1986; Guest Scholar, Wilson Int. Center for Scholars, Washington, DC 1983; Visiting Scholar and Jemolo Fellow, Nuffield Coll., Oxford 1987–89, 1995; mem. editorial bds of several journals including Rivista di Diritto Pubblico, International Review of Administrative Sciences, Revue européenne de droit administratif, Western European Politics, Revue française d'administration publique; mem. Prime Minister's policy unit 1988–89; fmr consultant to several Govt ministries and Bank of Italy; Minister for the Public Service 1993–94; Grande Ufficiale della Repubblica Italiana, Cavaliere di Gran Croce, Ordino al Merito della Repubblica Italiana; Campano d'Oro, Associazione Laureati Ateneo Pisano 1994, Premio Tarantelli 1993, Prix Alexis de Tocqueville, Inst. européen d'admin. publique 1997. *Publications:* Lo Stato introvabile 1998, Maggioranza e Minoranza. Il problema della democrazia in Italia 1995, La nuova Costituzione economica 2000, Le basi del diritto amministrativo 2000 and many other books. *Address:* Corte costituzionale, Piazza del Quirinale, 41, 00187 Rome (office); Department of Law, University of Rome, Via Orazio Raimondo 00173 Rome, Italy (office). *Telephone:* (06) 46981 (Corte costituzionale) (office); (06) 72591 (office). *Fax:* (06) 4698916 (Corte costituzionale) (office); (06) 7234368 (office). *E-mail:* ccost@cortecostituzionale.it (office). *Website:* www.cortecostituzionale.it (office).

CASSIDY, (Charles) Michael Ardagh, BD, MA; South African evangelist and author; b. 24 Sept. 1936, Johannesburg; s. of Charles Stewart Cassidy and Mary Craufurd Cassidy; m. Carol Bam 1969; one s. two d.; ed Parktown School, Johannesburg, Michaelhouse, Natal, Cambridge Univ., UK, Fuller Theological Seminary, Calif., USA; Founder and Int. Team Leader, interdenominational evangelistic mission team African Enterprise 1962–2002; conducted missions in cities including Cape Town, Johannesburg, Nairobi, Cairo, Lusaka, Gaborone, Monrovia (Liberia), Mbabane (Swaziland); initiated SA Congress on Mission and Evangelism 1973, Pan African Christian Leadership Ass. 1976, SA Christian Leadership Ass. 1979, 2003, Nat. Initiative for Reconciliation 1985, Nat. Initiative for Reformation of S Africa 2003; speaker at events including Lausanne II conf., Manila, Philippines 1989, Missionsfest 1990, N American Renewal Conf. 1990, UN 50th Anniversary, Dublin Castle, Repub. of Ireland 1995; admitted to Anglican Order of Simon of Cyrene 1983; Patron Transformation Africa Prayer Initiative, Christians for Peace in Africa; Hon. Co-Chair. of Lausanne Movement 2012; Hon. HLD (Azusa Pacific Univ., USA) 1993; Paul Harris Fellow, Rotary Award 1997, Michaelhouse St Michael's Award 1997, Fuller Seminary Distinguished Alumnus 2012. *Publications:* Decade of Decisions 1970, Where Are You Taking the World Anyway? 1971, Prisoners of Hope 1974, Relationship Tangle 1974, Bursting the Wineskins 1983, Chasing the Wind 1985, The Passing Summer 1989, The Politics of Love 1991, A Witness For Ever 1995, Window on the Word 1997, Getting to the Heart of Things 2005, What on Earth Are You Thinking for Heaven's Sake? 2006, So You Want to Get Married? 2010, The Church Jesus Prayed For 2012. *Leisure interests:* music, photography, scrapbooks, sport, jogging. *Address:* African Enterprise, PO Box 13140, Cascades 3202, South Africa (office). *Telephone:* (33) 347-7037 (office). *Fax:* (33) 347-1915 (office). *E-mail:* mcassidy@pobox.com (office). *Website:* www.africanenterprise.org.za (office).

CASSIDY, HE Cardinal Edward Idris, AC, DCnL; Australian fmr ecclesiastic; b. 5 July 1924, Sydney, NSW; s. of Harold Cassidy and Dorothy Phillips; ed Parramatta High School, Sydney, St Columba's Seminary, Springwood, St Patrick's Coll. Manly, Lateran Univ. and Pontifical Ecclesiastical Acad., Rome, Vatican City; ordained priest 1949; Asst Priest, Yenda 1950–52; diplomatic service in India 1955–62, Ireland 1962–67, El Salvador 1967–69, Argentina 1969–70; consecrated Archbishop 1970; Titular Archbishop of Amantia 1970; Apostolic Pro-Nuncio in Taiwan 1970–79 (also accred to Bangladesh and Burma 1973–79); Apostolic Del. to Southern Africa and Apostolic Pro-Nuncio to Lesotho 1979–84; Apostolic Pro-Nuncio to the Netherlands 1984–88; Substitute of the Secr. of State 1988–89; Pres. Pontifical Council for Promoting Christian Unity and Comm. for Religious Relations with the Jews 1989–2001; cr. Cardinal-Deacon of S. Maria in Via Lata 1991, Cardinal Priest 2001; Cavaliere, Gran Croce dell'Ordine al Merito della Repubblica Italiana; decorations from El Salvador, Taiwan, Netherlands, Australia, France, Sweden and Germany. *Publications include:* Vatican II – Ecumenism and Interreligious Dialogue 2005, My Years in Vatican Service 2009. *Leisure interests:* tennis, golf, music. *Address:* 16 Coachwood Drive, Warabrook,

NSW 2304, Australia (home). *Telephone:* (2) 4968-9025 (home). *Fax:* (2) 4968-9064 (home). *E-mail:* icassidy4@bigpond.com.

CASSIDY, Kathryn A., BA, MBA; American business executive; *Vice-President, Corporate Treasury, General Electric Company;* m.; three c.; ed Univ. of Connecticut, Fordham Univ.; joined General Electric (GE) 1980, serving in several positions including Man. Dir GE Capital Real Estate, led Real Estate Capital Markets 1996–2000, Vice-Pres. and Treas. General Electric Co. 2001–; mem. Bd of Dirs UCONN Foundation, Building with Books; mem. Treasury Leadership Roundtable, Washington, DC; ranked by Fortune magazine amongst 50 Most Powerful Women in Business in the US (50th) 2005. *Address:* 152 Canyon Road, Wilton, CT 06897-2639; General Electric Company, 3135 Easton Turnpike, Fairfield, CT 06828-0001, USA (office). *Telephone:* (203) 373-2211 (office). *Fax:* (203) 373-3131 (office). *Website:* www.ge.com (office).

CASSON, Mark Christopher, BA, FRSA; British economist and academic; *Professor of Economics, University of Reading;* b. 17 Dec. 1945, Grappenhall, Cheshire, England; s. of Stanley Christopher Casson and Dorothy Nowell Barlow; m. Janet Penelope Close 1975; one d.; ed Manchester Grammar School, Univ. of Bristol, Churchill Coll., Cambridge; Lecturer in Econs, Univ. of Reading 1969–77, Reader 1977–81, Prof. 1981–, Head Dept of Econs 1987–94, Dir Centre for Institutional Performance 2003–; Fellow, Acad. of Int. Business, Univ. of Leeds 1993, Visiting Prof. of Int. Business 1995–; Visiting Fellow, Univ. of London 2004–, Univ. of York 2010–; Visiting Fellow, Lancaster Univ. 2009–; Leverhulme Major Research Fellow 2006–09; mem. Council Royal Econ. Soc. 1985–90; Chair. Business Enterprise Heritage Trust 2000–. *Publications include:* The Future of the Multinational Enterprise 1976, The Entrepreneur: An Economic Theory 1982, Economics of Unemployment: An Historical Perspective 1983, The Firm and the Market: Studies in Multinational Enterprise and the Scope of the Firm 1987, The Economics of Business Culture: Game Theory, Transaction Costs and Economic Welfare 1981, Entrepreneurship and Business Culture 1995, Information and Organization: A New Perspective on the Theory of the Firm 1997, Economics of International Business 2000, Enterprise and Leadership 2000, Oxford Handbook of Entrepreneurship 2006, Economics of Networks 2008, The World's First Railway System 2009, The Multinational Enterprise Revisited 2009, Entrepreneurship: Theory, Networks, History 2010, Markets and Market Institutions 2011, History of Entrepreneurship 2013, The Entrepreneur in History 2013, Large Databases in Economic History 2013. *Leisure interests:* railway history, Church of England activities, book collecting, drawing in pastel. *Address:* School of Economics, University of Reading, PO Box 218, Reading, Berks., RG6 6AA (office); 6 Wayside Green, Woodcote, Reading, Berks., RG8 0QJ, England (home). *Telephone:* (118) 931-8227 (office); (1491) 681483 (home). *Fax:* (118) 975-0236 (office). *E-mail:* m.c.casson@reading.ac.uk (office); mark@casson14.freeserve.co.uk (home). *Website:* www.reading.ac.uk/economics/about/staff/m-c-casson.aspx (office).

CASTA, Laetitia; French model and actress; b. 11 May 1978, Pont-Audemer; d. of Dominique Casta and Line Casta; one d. (with pnr Stephane Sednaoui); launched by Yves Saint Laurent; first maj. advertising campaign for Guess jeans 1993; model, Victoria's Secret 1996–; appeared in Sports Illustrated 1997, 1998, 1999, on covers of Vogue, Elle, Cosmopolitan, Rolling Stone; contracts with L'Oréal, Galeries Lafayette; chosen to represent Marianne (nat. emblem of France) 2000. *Films include:* Astérix et Obélix contre César 1999, La bicyclette bleue, Les ames fortes (TV miniseries) 2000, Gitano 2000, Rue des plaisirs 2002, Errance 2003, Luisa Sanfelice (TV miniseries) 2004, La déraison du Louvre 2002, Le grand appartement 2006, La jeune fille et les loups 2008, Nés en 68 2008, Visage 2009, La nouvelle guerre des boutons (War of the Buttons) 2011. *Address:* c/o Artmedia, 10 ave Georges V, 75008 Paris, France (office).

CASTANEDA, Jorge G., BA, MA, PhD; Mexican politician, academic and writer; *Global Distinguished Professor of Politics and Latin American and Carribbean Studies, New York University;* b. 24 May 1953, Mexico City; s. of the late Jorge Castañeda y Álvarez de la Rosa; ed Princeton Univ., USA, Universite de Paris-I (Pantheon-Sorbonne), Ecole Pratique de Hautes Etudes, Paris I, Univ. of Paris, France; has taught at Nat. Autonomous Univ. of Mexico,Princeton Univ., Univ. of California, Berkeley; Sr Assoc. Carnegie Endowment for Int. Peace 1985–87; Global Distinguished Prof. of Politics and Latin American and Caribben Studies, New York Univ. 1997–; Sec. of State for Foreign Affairs 2000–03; announced campaign for candidacy in 2006 presidential election in 2004, Supreme Court ruled he could not run without support of a registered political party; mem. Bd of Dirs Human Rights Watch; f. San Angel Group 1994; regular columnist for Reforma (Mexican daily newspaper), Los Angeles Times and Newsweek International; John D. and Catherine T. MacArthur Foundation Research and Writing Grant Recipient 1989–91. *Publications include:* 12 books and numerous articles. *Address:* Center for Latin American and Caribbean Studies, King Juan Carlos I of Spain Center, New York University, 53 Washington Square South, Floor 4W, New York, NY 10012, USA (office). *Telephone:* (212) 998-8682 (office). *Fax:* (212) 995-4163 (office). *E-mail:* jorge.castaneda@nyu.edu (office). *Website:* www.nyu.edu/gsas/program/latin (office).

CASTAÑEDA LOSSIO, Oscar Luis; Peruvian lawyer and politician; b. 21 June 1945, Chiclayo, Lambayeque; s. of Carlos Castañeda Iparraguire; ed Colegio Manuel Pardo, Chiclayo, Pontificia Universidad Católica del Perú; began career with Empresa Municipal Administradora del Peaje de Lima (Metropolitan Inst. for Public Transportation); fmr Man. Dir Banco Industrial del Perú; Exec. Pres. Instituto Peruano de Seguridad Social (Nat. Inst. of Public Health) 1990–96; fmr Dir several private and public cos including COFIDE, EMMSA, ENATA, ESMIL, ENACO; mem. Solidaridad Nacional (SN) party, SN presidential cand. 2000; Mayor of Lima 2003–10. *Address:* c/o Office of the Mayor, Municipalidad Metropolitana de Lima, Jr. de la Unión 300 / Jr. Conde de Superunda 177, Lima, Peru (office).

CASTEEN, John Thomas, III, BA, MA, PhD, FACLS; American writer, academic and fmr university administrator; *University Professor and President Emeritus, University of Virginia;* b. 11 Dec. 1943, Portsmouth, Va; s. of John T. Casteen, Jr and Naomi Irene Casteen; m. Elizabeth F. Casteen; two s. three d.; ed Univ. of Virginia; Asst Prof. of English, Univ. of California, Berkeley 1970–75; Assoc. Prof. and Dean, Univ. of Virginia 1975–81, Pres. Univ. of Virginia

1990–2010, also George M. Kaufman Presidential Prof. and Prof. of English, Pres. Emer. 2010–; Sec. of Educ., Commonwealth of Va 1982–85; Pres. and Prof., Univ. of Connecticut 1985–90; Chair. Jefferson Science Assocs LLC, Universitas 21; mem. Bd of Dirs, Wachovia Corpn, Altria Group, Strayer, Inc., Echo360, U21 Global Pte Ltd, SAGE Publs Inc.; Trustee, Chesapeake Bay Foundation, Mariner's Museum, Jamestown-Yorktown Foundation, Woodrow Wilson Int. Center for Scholars; Fellow, American Acad. of Arts and Sciences 2009, American Council of Learned Socs; Hon. LLD (Shenandoah Coll.), (Bentley Coll.) 1992, (Piedmont Community Coll.) 1992, (Bridgewater Coll.) 1993, Transylvania Univ.) 1999; Hon. PhD (Univ. of Edinburgh) 2011; Dr hc (Athens) 1996; Mishima Award 1987, Raven Award, Univ. of Virginia, Outstanding Virginian of 1993, American Asscn of Univ. Profs Jackson Davis Award 1993, Gold Medal, Nat. Inst. of Social Sciences 1998, Higher Educ. Center for Alcohol and Other Drug Prevention's Presidents Leadership Group Award 2002, Architecture Medal for Virginia Service, Virginia Soc. of the AIA 2004, Virginian of the Year 2010, John Hope Franklin Award 2013. *Publications:* 16 stories 1982; numerous essays and articles 1970–. *Leisure interest:* sailing, walking. *Address:* Office of the President Emeritus, University of Virginia, Alderman Library, PO Box 400283, Charlottesville, VA 22904, USA (office). *Telephone:* (434) 924-6243 (office). *Fax:* (434) 243-6688 (office). *E-mail:* jtc@virginia.edu (office). *Website:* www.virginia.edu/presidentemeritus (office).

CASTEL, Charles, MA, LLM; Haitian lawyer, economist and central banker; *Governor, Banque de la République d'Haïti;* ed Haiti State Univ., Port-au-Prince, Columbia Univ., New York, USA, State Univ. of New York, Albany; Head of Commercial and Industrial Law, Ministry of Commerce and Industry 1987–89; fmr Economist, Govt Dept of Central Planning and Demand; Economist, Managerial Support Unit, Electricité d'Haïti 1991–92; Prof. of Finance and Econs, Inst. of Nat. Admin, Man. and Higher Int. Studies, Faculty of Law and Econ. Sciences, Haiti State Univ. 1991–95; Consultant, Nat. Econ. Mission under coordination of UNDP April–June 1993; with Sogebank SA (Société Générale Haïtienne de Banque), Port-au-Prince 1994–95; joined Banque de la République d'Haïti (central bank) 1995, Adviser to Gov. 1995–96, mem. Monetary Policy Cttee 1996, Dir of Legal Affairs 1996–2004, Dir of Banking Supervision 1998–99, Dir-Gen. and mem. Bd of Dirs 2004–07, currently Gov.; mem. Bar Asscn of Port-au-Prince; mem. World Jurist Asscn, Asscn des Economistes Haïtiens, Fondation Haïtienne de l'Environnement. *Address:* Office of the Governor, Banque de la République d'Haïti, angle rues du Pavée et du Quai, BP 1570, Port-au-Prince, Haiti (office). *Telephone:* 2299-1200 (office). *Fax:* 2299-1045 (office). *E-mail:* brh@brh.net (office). *Website:* www.brh.net (office).

CASTELLANETA, Giovanni; Italian diplomatist and business executive; *Chairman, SACE SpA;* b. 11 Sept. 1942, Puglia; ed Faculty of Law, Univ. of Rome 'La Sapienza'; joined Foreign Service 1967, assigned to Embassy in Mogadishu, Somalia 1969–72, Consul, Chambery, France 1972–74, Head of Econ. and Trade Office, Embassy in Lisbon 1974–76, European Affairs Desk, Ministry of Foreign Affairs 1976–78, Chief of Staff to Sec.-Gen., Ministry of Foreign Affairs 1978–81, Head of Press, Information and Cultural Office, Embassy in Paris 1981–84, on special assignment to Prime Minister's Office 1984–85, Deputy Perm. Rep., Mission to UN and Int. Orgs, Geneva 1985–89, Diplomatic Adviser to Treasury Minister, then Spokesman, Ministry of Foreign Affairs 1989–92, Amb. to Iran 1992–95, Head, Office for Coordination of Int. Activity of Italian Regions 1995–97, Special Coordinator, Italian Reconstruction Program for Albania 1997–98, Amb. to Australia (also accred to various insular States in Pacific Ocean) 1998–2001, Foreign Policy Adviser to Prime Minister 2001–05, rank of Amb. of Italy 2002, Personal Rep. of Prime Minister for G8 Summits, Amb. to USA and Perm. Observer to OAS, Washington, DC 2005–09; Deputy Chair. Finmeccanica Group 2005–; Chair. SACE SpA 2009–, Italfondiario SpA 2013–; Pres. Torre SGR SpA 2013–; Great Cross, Order of Merit of the Italian Repub. *Address:* SACE SpA, Piazza Poli 37/42, 00187 Rome, Italy (office). *Telephone:* (06) 67361 (office). *Fax:* (06) 6736225 (office). *E-mail:* info@sace.it (office). *Website:* www.sace.it (office).

CASTELLANOS ESCALONA, Diego Luis, PhD; Venezuelan banker and academic; b. 1 Sept. 1930, Caracas; ed Cen. Univ. of Venezuela; Prof., Cen. Univ. of Venezuela 1959–; Dir Advisory Council to SELA (Foundation for the Co-ordination of Latin American Economies) 1980–82; Sec. of Nat. Econ. Council 1991–98; financial consultant, Industrial Investment Fund (FONCREI) 1984–86; Pres. Banco de Comercia Exterior –2000; Exec. Dir Fundafuturo 1999–2000; Pres. Banco Central de Venezuela 2000–05; Exec. Sec. Venezuelan Council of Industry 1982–83; fmr Perm. Rep. to UN, Geneva. *Publications:* Export: Market Studies Manual 1951, Markets and Commercialization 1963, Principles and Objectives 1972. *Address:* c/o Banco Central de Venezuela, Avda Urdaneta, esq. de Carmelitas, Caracas 1010, Venezuela (office).

CASTELLI, Roberto; Italian engineer and politician; b. 12 July 1946, Lecco, Lombardy; m.; one s.; ed Alessandro Manzoni School, Lecco, Politecnico di Milano; worked as researcher developing technological system of electronic noise reduction; adviser to EC on environmental affairs; joined Lega Nord 1986, elected Deputy for Lecco 1992, 1994, fmr Vice-Pres. of Lega Nord in Chamber of Deputies; elected Senator for Lecco e Bergamo 1996–, Pres. Lega Nord Parl. Group 1999–2001; Minister of Justice 2001–06; Group Leader, Transport Cttee; mem. Budget Cttee of Senate, Parl. Cttee for Impeachments; mem. Jt Cttee on Regional Affairs, Supervision over RAI TV and Radio, Investigations over Terrorism and Massacres; fmr mem. Comm. for Regional Affairs, Comm. on Terrorism; voluntary mem. Nat. Alpine and Speleological Rescue Corps; Hon. Pres. Alpe (Asscn of Free Padan Hikers). *Leisure interests:* ski-alpinism, hiking, sailing, reading. *Address:* Senate (Senato), Piazza Madama, 00186 Rome (office); c/o Lega Nord, Via C. Bellerio 41, 20161 Milan, Italy. *Telephone:* (06) 67061 (office). *E-mail:* castelli_r@posta.senato.it (office); sen.robertocastelli@tin.it. *Website:* www.senato.it (office); www.leganord.org.

CASTELLINA, Luciana, LLB; Italian journalist, politician and writer; *President, Cineuropa.org;* b. 9 Aug. 1929, Rome; m. (divorced); one s. one d.; ed Univ. of Rome; Ed Nuova Generazione (weekly) 1958–62, Il Manifesto (daily) 1972–78, Pace e Guerra (weekly) then Liberazione (weekly) 1992–94; elected mem. Parl. 1976, 1979, 1983; elected mem. European Parl. 1979, 1984, 1989, 1994, Chair. Culture and Media Cttee 1994–96, later Chair. External Econ. Relations Cttee; fmr mem. Presidence Italian Women's Union, directorate Italian CP; Pres.

Cineuropa.org, Italia Cinema Srl, UCCA (ARCI cine clubs); Vice-Pres. Eurovisioni Bd, Eursolar International; Lecturer, Pisa State Univ.; mem. Bd of Dirs Lelio Basso Foundation; Commdr des Arts et des Lettres, Kt Commdr of the Argentine Repub.; European Personality of the Year, San Sebastian Film Festival 2006. *Publications:* Che c'è in America (reports from America) 1972, Family and Society in Marxist Analysis 1974, Il Commino Dei Movimenti 2003, 50 Anni d'Europa 2007, Eurollywood 2009, La scoperta del mondo 2011, Siberiana 2012. *Leisure interest:* films. *Address:* Via di San Valentino 32, 00197 Rome (home); c/o Board of Directors, ARCI, Via dei Monti di Pietralata 16, 00182 Rome, Italy (office). *Telephone:* (06) 41609220 (office). *E-mail:* lcastellina@gmail.com (home).

CASTIGLIONI SORIA, Luis Alberto; Paraguayan politician; b. 31 July 1962, Itacurubí del Rosario; joined Partido Colorado 1979; Perm. Mem. Partido Colorado Nat. Constituent Convention 1991–92; Perm. Mem. Partido Colorado Govt Bd 1992–95; Pres. Capital Sectional Cttee No. 4 1996–2000; Vice-Pres. of Paraguay 2003–07 (resgnd); unsuccessful cand. (Partido Colorado) for Pres. of Paraguay 2008; Gen. Sec. Supreme Council of Int. Parl. for Safety and Peace. *Address:* c/o Asociación Nacional Republicana—Partido Colorado, Casa de los Colorados, 25 de Mayo 842, Asunción, Paraguay (office); International Parliament for Safety and Peace, Via Marchese di Roccaforte, 10, 90143 Palermo, Sicily, Italy. *Telephone:* (21) 44-4137 (office). *Fax:* (21) 49-7857 (office). *Website:* www.anr.org.py (office); www.international-parliament.net.

CASTILLA RUBIO, Luis Miguel, BA, PhD; Peruvian economist, academic and government official; *Minister of Economy and Finance;* ed McGill Univ., Canada, Johns Hopkins Univ., USA; Head of Practice, Macroeconomics and Econ. Devt, Johns Hopkins Univ. 1992–93; several positions with World Bank, Washington, DC including Vice-Pres., Latin America and the Caribbean, Country Operations Analyst 1994, Vice-Pres. North Africa and the Middle East, Chief Economist, Consultant 1996; Economist, Corporación Andina de Fomento, Caracas 1996–2000, Lima 2000–02, Dir of Econ. Studies 2003–05, Chief Economist and Head of Public Policy and Competitiveness 2006–09; Adviser to Exec. Presidency 2009–; Prof. of Intermediate Macroeconomics, Universidad del Pacifico, Lima 2001–02; Deputy Minister of Finance 2010–11, Minister of Economy and Finance July 2011–. *Address:* Ministry of Economy and Finance, Jirón Junín 319, 4°, Circado de Lima, Lima 1, Peru (office). *Telephone:* (1) 3115930 (office). *E-mail:* postmaster@mef.gob.pe (office). *Website:* www.mef.gob.pe (office).

CASTILLO, Eva; Spanish investment banker and business executive; *Chair and CEO, Telefónica Europe;* b. 1962, Madrid; ed Universidad Pontificia de Comillas of Madrid; equity researcher, Beta Capital Sociedad de Valores, SA 1987–92; with Goldman Sachs Int., London, UK in Int. Equities Dept 1992–97; Head of Equity Markets for Spain and Portugal, Merrill Lynch Spain, Madrid 1997–99, Gen. Man. for Spain and Portugal 1999–2000, CEO Merrill Lynch Capital Markets Spain 2000, then COO Europe, Middle East and Africa (EMEA) Equity Markets, then Head of Global Markets and Investment Banking in Spain and Portugal 2003, also Pres. Merrill Lynch Spain, Head of Global Wealth Man. EMEA 2009, including Merrill Lynch Bank and Int. Trust and Wealth Structuring; Chair. and CEO Telefónica Europe 2012–; mem. Bd of Dirs Telefónica SA. *Address:* Telefónica Europe, Distrito Telefónica Edificio Central, 2ª planta Ronda de la Comunicación s/n, 28050 Madrid, Spain (office). *Telephone:* (91) 4823800 (office). *Website:* pressoffice.telefonica.com (office).

CASTILLO BARRANTES, José Enrique, BA, MA, JD; Costa Rican lawyer, diplomatist and politician; b. 27 Aug. 1945, San José; ed Univ. of Costa Rica, Univ. of Bordeaux, France; Lecturer in Criminology and Criminal Law, Univ. of Costa Rica 1971–, Prof. 1986–2000, Founder and first Dir of Graduate Studies in Law, 1981–86, 1995–2004; Dir Gen. UN Latin American Inst. for the Prevention of Crime 1975–94; Partner, Facio y Cañas (law firm) 1980–, Chair. 2006–07; Amb. to France 1986–2000; Minister of Justice 1994–95; Perm. Rep. of Costa Rica to OAS 2007–11; Minister of Foreign Relations 2011–14; mem. Bar Asscn of Costa Rica, Sec. of the Bd 1986; mem. Int. Asscn of Penal Law, Int. Asscn of French Language Criminologists, Int. Asscn of Criminal Law; mem. Scientific Cttee, Int. Soc. of Criminology, Paris 1978–2005, Deputy Sec.-Gen. 1995–2000; Chevalier, Ordre des Palmes académiques 1999. *Publications:* five books including Ensayos sobre la nueva legislación procesal penal (essays) (Bar Asscn of Costa Rica Alberto Brenes Córdoba Award) 1977, Pesadillas de un hombre urbano (Nightmares of an Urban Man, short stories) (Aquileo J.Echeverría Prize) 2003. *Address:* c/o Ministry of Foreign Relations, Avda 7 y 9, Calle 11 y 13, Apdo 10027, 1000 San José, Costa Rica (office).

CASTLE, Michael (Mike) N., BA, LLB; American politician and lawyer; b. 2 July 1939, Wilmington, Del.; s. of J. Manderson and Louisa C. Castle; m. Jane Castle; ed Hamilton Coll. and Georgetown Univ.; called to Del. Bar 1964, DC Bar 1964; Assoc. Connolly, Bove and Lodge (law firm), Wilmington 1964–73, Pnr 1973–75; Deputy Attorney-Gen. State of Del. 1965–66; mem. Del. House of Reps 1966–67; mem. Del. Senate 1968–77; Pnr, Schnee & Castle PA 1975–80; Lt-Gov. State of Del. 1981–85; Gov. of Delaware 1985–93; mem. US House of Reps 1993–; Prin. Michael N. Castle 1981–; Co-founder and mem. Republican Main Street Partnership (fmr Pres.); Republican. *Address:* 1233 Longworth HOB, Washington, DC 20515-0801, USA (office). *Telephone:* (202) 225-4165 (office). *Website:* www.house.gov/castle (office).

CASTON, Geoffrey Kemp, CBE, MA, MPA; British university administrator; b. 17 May 1926, Beckenham, Kent, England; s. of Reginald Caston and Lilian Caston; m. 1st Sonya Chassell 1956; two s. one d.; m. 2nd Judy Roizen 1983; ed St Dunstan's Coll., Peterhouse, Cambridge, Harvard Univ., USA; Sub-Lt RNVR 1945–47; Colonial Office 1951–58; First-Sec. UK Mission to UN 1958–61; Dept of Tech. Co-operation 1961–64; Asst Sec., Dept of Educ. and Science 1964–66; Sec. Schools Council for Curriculum and Examinations 1966–70; Under-Sec., Univ. Grants Cttee 1970–72; Registrar Univ. of Oxford and Fellow, Merton Coll. Oxford 1972–79; Sec. Gen. Cttee of Vice-Chancellors 1979–83; Vice-Chancellor, Univ. of South Pacific, Fiji 1983–92; Visiting Assoc., Center for Studies in Higher Educ., Univ. of California, Berkeley 1978–2003; Distinguished Lecturer in Pacific Studies, Univ. of Hawaii 1992; GAP Project Man., S. Pacific 1994–99; Chair. Commonwealth Scholarship Comm. in the UK 1996–2001; mem. or chair. numerous bds and cttees, nat. and int., including UN Tech. Assistance Cttee 1962–64, UN Visiting Mission to Trust Territory of Pacific Islands 1961, OECD Workshops on Educational Innovation 1969, 1970, 1971, Nat. Inst. for Careers

Educ. and Counselling 1975–83, Exec. Cttee Inter-Univ. Council for Higher Educ. Overseas 1977–83, Libraries Advisory Council (England) 1973–78, Council, Univ. of Papua New Guinea; Trustee, Just World Partners 1993–2000; Hon. LLD (Dundee) 1982; Hon. DLitt (Deakin) 1991; George Long Prize for Jurisprudence, Univ. of Cambridge 1950, Frank Knox Memorial Fellow, Harvard Univ., Symons Medal for Outstanding Service to Commonwealth Univs 2001. *Publication:* The Management of International Cooperation in Universities 1996. *Leisure interest:* cricket. *Address:* 3A Pennsylvania Park, Exeter, Devon, EX4 6HB, England (home). *Telephone:* (1392) 272986 (home). *E-mail:* geoffcaston@yahoo.co.uk (office).

CASTRESANA FERNÁNDEZ, Carlos; Spanish jurist and international organization official; ed Universidad Complutense de Madrid, Institut Int. de Droits de l'Homme, Strasbourg, France; taught criminal law at Univ. of San Francisco and Universidad Carlos III, Madrid; served as prosecutor in circuit courts of Madrid and Catalunya, temporarily dist and investigating judge and magistrate of territorial court of Madrid before being assigned to Special Prosecutor's Office against drug smuggling and money laundering 1993–95; Special Anti-Corruption Prosecutor for Spain's nat. court 1995–2005; Public Prosecutor for Spanish Supreme Court 2005–06; work for Mexico and Cen. America regional office of UN Office on Drugs and Crime (UNODC) 2006–07; Commr Comisión Internacional contra la Impunidad en Guatemala (Int. Comm. against Impunity in Guatemala—CICIG, body established under agreement between UN and Guatemalan Govt) 2007–10 (resgnd); Dr hc (Universidad Central, Chile, Universidad de Guadalajara, Mexico); Human Rights Nat. Prize (Spain) 1997. *Address:* c/o Comisión Internacional contra la Impunidad en Guatemala (CICIG), 5 Avenida 5-55 Zone 14, Torre IV, Nivel 10, Guatemala City, Guatemala.

CASTRILLÓN HOYOS, HE Cardinal Dario; Colombian ecclesiastic; *President Emeritus, Pontifica Commissione Ecclesia Dei;* b. 4 July 1929, Medellín; s. of Manuel Castrillón Castrillón and Maria Hoyos Salas; ed Pontifical Gregorian Univ., Univ. of Louvain; ordained priest 1952; consecrated Bishop 1971, Bishop of Pereira 1976, Archbishop of Bucaramanga 1992–96; Pro-Prefect Congregation for the Clergy 1996–98; elevated to Cardinal-Deacon of SS. Nome di Maria al Foro Traiano 1998–; Prefect of Clergy, Roman Curia 1998–, Pres. Pontifica Commissione Ecclesia Dei, Roman Curia 2000–09, currently Pres. Emer.; Pres. Emer. Congregazione per Il Clero 2006–; Bali Cavaliere di Gran Croce di Giustizia, Gran Priore del Sacro Militaire Ordine Costantiniano di San Giorgio (Spagna) 2003, Gran Oficial Orden del Congreso. *Address:* c/o Piazza della Citta' Leonina, 1, 00193 Rome, Italy.

CASTRO, Fidel (see CASTRO RUZ, Fidel Alejandro).

CASTRO, Gen. Raúl (see CASTRO RUZ, Gen. Raúl Modesto).

CASTRO CALDAS, Júlio de Lemos de; Portuguese politician and lawyer; *Partner, Almeida Sampaio & Associados;* b. 19 Nov. 1943, Lisbon; s. of Eugénio Queiroz de Castro Caldas and Maria Lusitana Mascarenhas de Lemos de Castro Caldas; m. Ana Cristina Ribeiro Sobral Cid; one s. two d.; ed Classic Univ. of Lisbon; Leader, Students' Asscn, Classic Univ. of Lisbon 1963; mil. service in Portuguese Army 1967–70; f. Associação para o Desenvolvimento Económico e Social (SEDES) 1970, Partido Popular Democrático 1974; Legal Adviser to Pres. of Portugal 1976–78; Democratic Alliance mem. Parl. for Viana do Castelo 1979; Leader Parl. Group of Democratic Alliance 1979–82; Minister of Defence, Socialist Party 1999–2001; currently Pnr, Almeida Sampaio & Associados (law firm), Lisbon, mem. Supreme Council of Public Prosecutor's Dept 1980–92; Chair. Bilbao Vizcaya Bank (Portugal) 1995–99; fmr chair. several cos; mem. Portuguese Bar Asscn, Treas. 1988–91, Pres. 1993–99; Pres. European Bar Fed. 1997–99; fmr Dir (non-exec.) Companhia le Seguros Global SA, Carrefour SA. *Address:* Almeida Sampaio & Associados, Av. Duque D'Avila, 66, 1069-075 Lisbon, Portugal (office). *Telephone:* (21) 3536926 (office). *Fax:* (21) 3536927 (office). *E-mail:* castro.caldas@jsc.pt (office). *Website:* www.almeidasampaio-law.com (office).

CASTRO GONZÁLEZ, Sonia; Nicaraguan physician and politician; *Minister of Health;* trained as obstetrician-gynaecologist; Minister of Health 2010–. *Address:* Ministry of Health, Complejo Nacional de Salud 'Dra Concepción Palacios', costado oeste Colonia Primero de Mayo, Apdo 107, Managua, Nicaragua (office). *Telephone:* 2289-7164 (office). *E-mail:* webmaster@minsa.gob.ni (office). *Website:* www .minsa.gob.ni (office).

CASTRO RUZ, Fidel Alejandro, DIur; Cuban fmr head of state; b. 13 Aug. 1926, brother of Raúl Castro Ruz; m. 1st Mirta Diaz-Bilart 1948 (divorced 1955); one s.; m. 2nd Dalia Soto del Valle; five s.; one d. with Natalia 'Naty' Revuelta Clews; one s. one d. with unnamed women; ed Jesuit schools in Santiago and Havana, Univ. de la Habana; law practice in Havana; began active opposition to Batista regime by attack on Moncada barracks at Santiago 26th July 1953; sentenced to 15 years' imprisonment 1953; amnestied 1956; went into exile in Mexico and began to organize armed rebellion; landed in Oriente Province with small force Dec. 1956; carried on armed struggle against Batista regime until flight of Batista Jan. 1959; C-in-C of the Revolutionary Armed Forces 1959–2008; Prime Minister of Cuba 1959–76; Head of State and Pres. of Council of State 1976–2008 (incapacitated 2006, resgnd 2008), Pres. of Council of Ministers 1976–2008; Chair. Agrarian Reform Inst. 1965; First Sec. Partido Unido de la Revolución Socialista (PURS) 1963–65, Partido Comunista de Cuba 1965–2011 (incapacitated 2006, mem. Political Bureau 1976–2011), Head of Nat. Defence Council 1992–2008; Sec.-Gen. Non-Aligned Movt 1979–1983, 2005–08 (incapacitated 2006); Order of Lenin 1972, 1986, Order of the October Revolution 1976, Somali Order (First Class) 1977, Order of Jamaica 1977, Gold Star (Vietnam) 1982; Lenin Peace Prize 1961, Hero of the Soviet Union 1963, Dimitrov Prize (Bulgaria) 1980, Muammar Gaddafi Human Rights Prize 1998. *Publications include:* author or co-author: Ten Years of Revolution 1964, History Will Absolve Me 1968, Fidel (with Frei Betto) 1987, How Far We Slaves Have Come! – South Africa and Cuba in Today's World (with Nelson Mandela) 1991, Cuba at the Crossroads 1997, Capitalism in Crisis: Globalization and World Politics Today 2000, Playa Giron: Bay of Pigs: Washington's First Military Defeat in the Americas 2001, War, Racism and Economic Justice: The Global Ravages of Capitalism 2002, Fidel My Early Years 2004, Che: A Memoir 2005, Fidel & Religion: Conversations with Frei Betto on Marxism & Liberation Theology 2006, Fidel Castro Reader (autobiog.) 2007, The Prison Letters of Fidel Castro 2007, Fidel Castro: My Life: A Spoken Autobiography 2008, Political

Portraits: Fidel Castro Reflects on Famous Figures in History 2008, The Declarations of Havana 2008, Obama and the Empire 2010. *Address:* c/o Palacio del Gobierno, Havana, Cuba.

CASTRO RUZ, Gen. Raúl Modesto; Cuban politician and head of state; *President, Council of State and Council of Ministers;* b. 3 June 1931, Birán; brother of Fidel Alejandro Castro Ruz; m. Vilma Espín 1959 (died 2007); one s. three d.; ed Jesuit School of Colegio Dolores, Santiago, Colegio de Belén, Havana; sentenced to 15 years' imprisonment for insurrection 1953; amnestied 1954; assisted his brother's movement in Mexico and in Cuba after Dec. 1956, made Commdt 1957; Maximum Gen. of the Revolutionary Armed Forces 1959–2008; led Cuban mil. in repulsing force of Cuban exiles in Bay of Pigs invasion April 1961; Second Sec. CP of Cuba Cen. Cttee 1965–2011, First Sec. 2011–; Deputy, Asamblea Nacional del Poder Popular 1976; First Vice-Pres. of the Councils of State and Ministers 1976–2008, Acting Pres. Council of State 2006–08, Pres. Council of State and Council of Ministers 2008–; Acting C-in-C of the Revolutionary Armed Forces 2006–08, C-in-C 2008–; Acting Sec.-Gen. Non-Aligned Movt 2006–08, Sec.-Gen. 2008–09; Order of Lenin 1979, Order of the October Revolution 1981, Orden Máximo Gómez 1998; Medal for Strengthening of Brotherhood in Arms 1977. *Address:* Palacio del Gobierno, Havana, Cuba (office).

CASTRO SALAZAR, René, BE MA PhD; Costa Rican government official and politician; *Minister of the Environment, Energy and Telecommunications;* b. 25 Aug. 1957, St Louis, Mo., USA; ed Univ. of Costa Rica, Harvard Univ., USA; fmr Vice-Minister of the Interior; Minister of Environment and Energy 1994–98, of the Environment, Energy and Telecommunications 2011–; consultant with UNDP 1998–2010; Minister of Foreign Affairs 2010–11; fmr Prof., INCAE Business School; mem. Bd of Dirs Inter Press Service 2001–; fmr Pres. San José City Council; fmr Nat. Dir of Transport; fmr Sec. Gen. Partido Liberacion Nacional. *Publications include:* Evaluación de Proyectos Ambientales, Evaluación de Impacto Ambiental y Sostenibilidad del Desarrollo, Valoración de los servicios ambientales del Bosque: El Caso de Cambio Climático. *Address:* Ministry of the Environment, Energy and Telecommunications, Avdas 8 y 10, Calle 25, Apdo 10104, 1000 San José, Costa Rica (office). *Telephone:* 2233-4533 (office). *Fax:* 2257-0697 (office). *E-mail:* prensa@minae.go.cr (office). *Website:* www.minae.go.cr (office).

CASULE, Slobodan; Macedonian politician and journalist; b. 27 Sept. 1945, Skopje; ed Pontifical Catholic Univ., Lima, Peru; journalist and interpreter, Skopje TV 1965–67, Ed., Foreign Corresp. 1967–74; Latin America Corresp. Tanjung News Agency 1974–80, Chief Ed. 1980–90; Dir and Chief Ed. Macedonian Radio 1990–94, Ed., Commentator 1994–99; Dir-Gen. Nova Makedonija 1999; govt adviser 2000–; Minister of Foreign Affairs 2001–02; mem. Parl. (VMRO-DPMNE) 2002–06; Founder and mem. Human Rights Forum of Macedonia, Int. Relations Forum; mem. European Inst. of Media, Inst. of East–West Dialogue, Int. Fund for Media, US Democratic Inst., Helsinki Watch, Peace in the Country–Peace in the World Org., Journalists' Asscn of Macedonia, Int. Journalists' Asscn; f. TV Skopje. *Address:* c/o Vnatrešno-Makedonska Revolucionerna Organizacija—Demokratska Partija za Makedonsko Nacionalno Edinstvo, 1000 Skopje, Petar Drapshin br. 36, Macedonia (office).

CATERIANO BELLIDO, Pedro Alvaro; Peruvian lawyer, academic and politician; *Minister of Defence;* b. 26 June 1958; ed Pontifical Catholic Univ. of Peru, Univ. Complutense, Madrid, Spain; fmr Dir of External Cooperation and Prof. of Constitutional Law, Univ. of Lima; mem. Congreso (Parl.) for Lima (Movimiento Libertad) 1990–92, mem. Parl. Constitution Cttee, External Relations Cttee; fmr Deputy Minister of Justice and mem. Ministry of Justice Advisory Cttee; Rep. of Peruvian Govt to Inter-American Court of Human Rights, San José, Costa Rica 2012; Minister of Defence 2012–. *Address:* Ministry of Defence, Edif. Quiñones, Avda de la Peruanidad s/n, Jesús María, Lima 1, Peru (office). *Telephone:* (1) 6255959 (office). *E-mail:* webmaster@mindef.gob.pe (office). *Website:* www.mindef.gob.pe (office).

CATHCART, Kevin James, MA, PhD, MRIA; Irish academic; *Professor Emeritus of Near Eastern Languages, University College, Dublin;* b. 9 Oct. 1939, Derrylin, Co. Fermanagh, Northern Ireland; s. of Andrew Cathcart and Elizabeth Cathcart (née Flannery); m. Ann McDermott 1968; two s.; ed Salesian Coll., Cheshire, UK, Mellifont Abbey, Co. Louth, Trinity Coll., Dublin, Pontifical Biblical Inst., Rome, Italy; Lecturer in Hebrew, Pontifical Biblical Inst., Rome 1968; Lecturer in Near Eastern Studies, Univ. of Ottawa, Canada 1968–71, Asst Prof. 1971–73, Assoc. Prof. 1973–74; Sr Lecturer in Semitic Languages and Dept Head, Univ. Coll. Dublin 1974–79, Prof. of Near Eastern Languages and Dept Head 1979–2001, Prof. Emer. of Near Eastern Languages 2001–; Fellow, Campion Hall, Oxford 2001–13, Sr Research Fellow 2013–; Visiting Fellow, St Edmund's Coll., Cambridge 1987–88, 1993–94; Visiting Academic, St Benet's Hall, Oxford 1994; Visiting Prof., Heidelberg 1981, 1986, 1992, Ottawa 1983, Arhus 1986, Toronto 1989, Mainz 1992; mem. Bd Electors (Regius Professorship of Hebrew), Univ. of Cambridge 1989–2009; editorial consultant, Journal of Semitic Studies 1991–; mem. Royal Danish Acad.; Trustee, Chester Beatty Library, Dublin 1974–89, Chair. Bd of Trustees 1984–86. *Publications include:* Nahum in the Light of Northwest Semitic 1973, Back to the Sources: Biblical and Near Eastern Studies (with J. F. Healey) 1989, The Targum of the Minor Prophets (with R.P. Gordon) 1989, The Aramaic Bible (20 vols, co-ed.), The Edward Hincks Bicentenary Lectures 1994, Targumic and Cognate Studies (with M. Maher) 1996, The Letters of Peter le Page Renouf (1822–97) (four vols) 2002–04, The Correspondence of Edward Hincks (three vols) 2007–09. *Leisure interests:* birdwatching, medieval architecture. *Address:* 8 Friarsland Road, Clonskeagh, Dublin 14, Ireland. *Telephone:* (1) 2981589. *E-mail:* kevincathcart@yahoo.co.uk.

CATHCART, (William) Alun; British business executive; *Chairman, Avis Europe;* b. 9 Dec. 1943; mem. Bd of Dirs (non-exec.) Avis Rent A Car Inc. 1980–98, CEO and Deputy Chair. Avis Europe PLC 1999–2003, Chair. (non-exec.) 2004–; Deputy Chair. (non-exec.) Nat. Express Group PLC 1992; Deputy Chair. Belron Int.; Chair. (non-exec.) Selfridges 1998–2003; Chair. (non-exec.) The Rank Group 2001–07; mem. Bd of Dirs Emap plc 2005, Exec. Chair. 2006–08, Chair. (non-exec.) 2008–; Dir Tikkun UK Ltd (charity). *Address:* Avis Europe plc, Avis House, Park Road, Bracknell, Berks., RG12 2EW, England (office). *Telephone:* (1344) 426-644 (office). *Website:* www.avis-europe.com (office).

CATHERWOOD, Sir (Henry) Frederick (Ross), Kt, MA (Cantab.); British fmr politician, industrialist and church leader; b. 30 Jan. 1925, Castledawson, Co. Londonderry, Northern Ireland; s. of Stuart Catherwood and Jean Catherwood; m. Elizabeth Lloyd-Jones 1954; two s. one d.; ed Shrewsbury School and Clare Coll., Cambridge; Chartered Accountant 1951; Sec., Laws Stores Ltd, Gateshead 1952–54; Sec. and Controller, Richard Costain Ltd 1954–55, Chief Exec. 1955–60; Asst Man. Dir British Aluminium Co. Ltd 1960–62, Man. Dir 1962–64; Chief Industrial Adviser, Dept of Econ. Affairs 1964–66; mem. Nat. Econ. Devt Council (NEDC) 1964–71, Dir Gen. 1966–71; mem. British Nat. Export Council 1965–70; Vice-Chair. British Inst. of Man. 1972–74, Chair. 1974–76, Vice-Pres. 1976–; Chair. British Overseas Trade Bd 1975–79; Chair. Mallinson-Denny Ltd 1976–79 (Dir 1974); mem. Bd of Dirs John Laing Ltd 1971–80 (Group Man. Dir and Chief Exec. 1972–74), Goodyear Tyre and Rubber Co. (GB) Ltd 1975–89; Pres. Fellowship of Ind. Evangelical Churches 1977–78; MEP for Cambridgeshire and Wellingborough 1979–84, for Cambridgeshire and N Bedfordshire 1984–94, Vice-Pres. European Parl. 1989–92 (mem. Del. to US Congress 1983–89, to Hungary 1989, to Canada 1991–94), Chair. Cttee for External Econ. Relations 1979–84, Vice-Pres. European Democratic Group 1983–87, Chair. Land Use and Food Policy Inter-group 1987–92, Vice-Chair. Foreign Affairs Comm. 1992–94); mem. Council Royal Inst. of Int. Affairs 1964–77; Treas., Int. Fellowship Evangelical Students 1979–93, Vice-Pres. 1995–2003; Pres. Evangelical Alliance 1992–2001; Hon. Fellow, Clare Coll., Cambridge 1992; Hon. DSc (Aston) 1972; Hon. DScEcon (Queen's Univ., Belfast) 1973; Hon. DUniv (Surrey) 1979. *Publications:* The Christian in Industrial Society 1964, Britain with the Brakes Off 1966, The Christian Citizen 1969, A Better Way 1975, First Things First 1979, God's Time God's Money 1987, Pro-Europe? 1991, David: Poet, Warrior, King 1993, At the Cutting Edge (memoirs) 1995, Jobs and Justice, Homes and Hope 1997, It Can Be Done 2000, The Creation of Wealth 2002. *Leisure interests:* reading, writing, walking. *Address:* Flat 14, Meadowcroft, 16 Trumpington Road, Cambridge, Cambs., CB2 8EX, England (home). *Telephone:* (1223) 309733 (home). *E-mail:* fredandelizabeth@btinternet.com (home).

CATLOW, (Charles) Richard Arthur, MA, DPhil, FRS, FRSC, FInstP; British chemist and academic; *Dean of Faculty of Mathematical and Physical Sciences, University College London;* b. 24 April 1947, Simonstone, Lancs., England; s. of Rolf M. Catlow and Constance Catlow (née Aldred); m. 1st Carey Anne Chapman 1978; one s.; m. 2nd Nora de Leeuw 2000; ed Clitheroe Royal Grammar School and St John's Coll., Oxford; Grad. Scholar, Jesus Coll. Oxford 1970–73; Research Fellow, St John's Coll., Oxford 1970–76; Lecturer, Univ. Coll. London 1976–85, Head, Dept of Chem. 2002–07, Dean of Faculty of Math. and Physical Sciences 2007–; Prof. of Chem., Univ. of Keele 1985–89; Wolfson Prof. of Natural Philosophy, Royal Inst. of GB 1989–, Dir Davy Faraday Research Lab. 1998–2002; Fellow, Acad. of Science 2006; RSC Medal (Solid State Chem.) 1992, RSC Award (Interdisciplinary Science) 1992, 1998, RSC Liversidge Medal 2009. *Publications:* co-author: Computer Simulation of Solids 1982, Mass Transport in Solids 1983, Computer Simulation of Fluids, Polymers and Solids 1989, Applications of Synchrotron Radiation 1990, New Frontiers in Materials Chemistry 1997, Microscopic Properties or Processes in Minerals 1999, Computational Materials Science 2003; more than 800 research papers and several monographs. *Leisure interests:* reading, walking, music. *Address:* MAPS Faculty Office, University College London, Gower Street, London, WC1E 6BT, England (office). *Telephone:* (20) 7679-2818 (office). *Fax:* (20) 7679-7463 (office). *E-mail:* c.r.a.catlow@ucl.ac.uk (office). *Website:* www.chem.ucl.ac.uk/people/catlow (office).

CATMULL, Ed, BS, PhD; American studio executive and computer graphics designer; *President, Pixar Animation Studios;* b. 31 March 1945, Parkersburg, WV; m. Susan Catmull; five c.; ed Univ. of Utah; Vice-Pres. Computer Div., Lucasfilm Ltd 1979–86, managed devt in areas of computer graphics, video editing, video games and digital audio, key developer of RenderMan programme; Co-Founder Pixar Animation Studios 1986, Chief Tech. Officer and exec. mem. 1986–2001, Pres. 2001–, Pres. Pixar and Disney animation studios after acquisition by Walt Disney Co. 2006–; animated films include Toy Story, Toy Story 2, A Bug's Life, Monsters Inc., Finding Nemo, The Incredibles; mem. Acad. of Motion Picture Arts and Sciences, Science and Tech. Awards Cttee; Scientific and Tech. Eng Awards (three), Acad. of Motion Picture Arts and Sciences Award, Coons Award for Lifetime Contrib. to Computer Graphics Industry, Gordon E. Sawyer Award, Acad. of Motion Picture Arts and Sciences 2009. *Address:* Pixar Animation Studios, 1200 Park Avenue, Emeryville, CA 94608, USA (office). *Telephone:* (510) 752-3000 (office). *Fax:* (510) 752-3151 (office). *Website:* www.pixar.com (office).

CATON-JONES, Michael; British film director; b. 15 Oct. 1957, Broxburn, West Lothian, Scotland; m. 1st Beverly Caton (divorced); one d.; m. 2nd Laura Viederman 2000; ed Nat. Film School; worked as stagehand in London West End theatres, wrote and directed first film The Sanatorium and several other short films before being accepted by Nat. Film School; films made while a student include: Liebe Mutter (first prize European film school competition), The Making of Absolute Beginners (for Palace Productions), The Riveter; left School to make serial Brond for Channel 4 TV, then Lucky Sunil (BBC TV). *Films include:* Scandal 1989, Memphis Belle 1990, Doc Hollywood 1991, This Boy's Life 1993, Rob Roy 1995, The Jackal 1997, City By The Sea 2002, Shooting Dogs 2005, Basic Instinct 2 2006. *Address:* c/o William Morris Endeavor, Centre Point, 103 New Oxford Street, London, WC1A 1DD, England (office).

CATTANACH, Bruce Macintosh, BSc, PhD, DSc, FRS; British geneticist (retd); b. 5 Nov. 1932, Glasgow, Scotland; s. of James Cattanach and Margaretta May Cattanach (née Fyfe); m. 1st Margaret Bouchier Crewe 1966 (died 1996); two d.; m. 2nd Josephine Peters 1999; ed Heaton Grammar School, Newcastle-upon-Tyne, King's Coll., Durham and Univ. of Edinburgh; mem. scientific staff, MRC Industrial Mutagenesis Unit, Edinburgh 1959–62, 1964–66; NIH Post-Doctoral Research Fellow, Biology Div., Oak Ridge, Tenn., USA 1962–64; Sr Scientist, City of Hope Medical Centre, Duarte, Calif. 1966–69; Sr Scientist, MRC Radiobiology Unit, Chilton, Oxon. 1969–86, Head of Genetics Div. 1987–96; Acting Dir MRC Mammalian Genetics Unit, Harwell, Oxon. 1996–97. *Publications:* numerous papers in scientific journals. *Leisure interests:* control of inherited disease in pedigree dogs, Boxer dog breeding, exhibiting and judging. *Address:* Downs Edge, Reading Road, Harwell, Oxon., OX11 0JJ, England (home). *Telephone:* (1235) 835410 (home). *E-mail:* bcattanach@steynmere.freeserve.co.uk (home).

CATTANEO, Elena, DrSc; Italian professor of pharmaceutical biotechnology; *Professor of Pharmaceutical Biotechnology, University of Milan;* b. 1962, Milan; m.; one s. one d.; ed Univ. of Milan, Massachusetts Inst. of Tech., USA; researcher of neutral stem cells, MIT, USA; joined Dept of Pharmacological Science, Univ. of Milan 1994, currently Prof. of Pharmaceutical Biotechnology, Dir Lab. of Stem Cell Biology and Pharmacology of Neurodegenerative Diseases, Co-founder and Dir UniStem, the Centre for Stem Cell Research; Coalition Investigator, Huntington's Disease Soc. of America 1997–; Coordinator FIRB (Fondo Investimento per la Ricerca di Base) research programme 2002–05; mem. Italian Del., Genomics and Biotechnology Work Programme, EU, Brussels 2002; mem. Bd of Dirs Euro-StemCell, NeuroNE; mem. Scientific Advisory Bd Hereditary Disease Foundation, Euro-HD Network; Cavaliere Ufficiale (Knight) of the Italian Repub. 2006, Senator for Life (highest Italian honour) 2013; Cure Huntington's Disease Initiative Award, Hereditary Disease Foundation 1997, Le Scienze Prize for Medicine 2001, Presidential Medal, Italy 2001, Marisa Bellisario and Chiara D'Onofrio prizes 2005. *Leisure interest:* cooking. *Address:* Department of Pharmacological Sciences and Centre of Stem Cell Research (UniStem), University of Milan, via Balzaretti 9, 20133 Milan, Italy (office). *Telephone:* 0250318333 (office). *Fax:* 0250318284 (office). *E-mail:* elena.cattaneo@unimi.it (office); cattaneolab@unimi.it. *Website:* users.unimi.it/~spharm/cattaneo.

CATTAUI, Maria Livanos, BA; Swiss international organization official; b. 25 June 1941, New York, USA; m. Stéphane Cattaui (deceased); two s.; ed Harvard Univ., USA; writer/researcher, Encyclopedia Britannica 1965–67; Ed. Time Life Books 1967–69; Dir, then Man. Dir World Econ. Forum 1977–96; Sec.-Gen. ICC 1996–2005; Dir Petroplus Holdings; mem. Bd or Advisory Bd, Int. Crisis Group, EastWest Inst., Inst. of Int. Educ., Nat. Bureau of Asian Research (NBR), The Resolution Project, Schulich School of Business, York Univ., Elliott School of Int. Affairs, ICT4Peace, Inst. for Integrated Transitions, Shift Project; Hon. LLD (York Univ., Toronto).

CATTELAN, Maurizio; Italian artist; b. 1960, Padua; self-taught artist, works include sculpture, multimedia and installations. *Address:* c/o Galerie Emmanuel Perrotin, 5 & 20, rue Louise Weiss, 75001 Paris, France. *Telephone:* 1-42-16-79-79. *Fax:* 1-42-16-79-74. *Website:* www.galerieperrotin.com.

CATTO, Sir Graeme Robertson Dawson, Kt, DSc, MD, FRCP, FRSE, FMedSci; British professor of medicine; *President, College of Medicine;* b. 24 April 1945, Aberdeen, Scotland; s. of William D. Catto and Dora E. Catto (née Spiby); m. Joan Sievewright 1967; one s. one d.; ed Robert Gordon's Coll., Univ. of Aberdeen, Harvard Univ.; House Officer, Aberdeen Royal Infirmary 1969–70, Hon. Consultant Physician and Nephrologist 1977–2000; Research Fellow, then Lecturer, Univ. of Aberdeen 1970–75, Sr Lecturer, then Reader in Medicine 1977–88, Prof. of Medicine and Therapeutics 1988–2000, Dean, Faculty of Medicine and Medical Sciences 1992–98, Vice-Prin. 1995–2000, Prof. of Medicine 2005–09; Chief Scientist, Scottish Exec. (fmrly Scottish Office) Health Dept 1997–2000; Vice-Prin. King's Coll. London 2000–05; Dean, Guy's, King's Coll. and St Thomas' Hosps Medical and Dental School 2000–05, Hon. Nephrologist, Guy's and St Thomas' Hosps NHS Trust 2000–; Pro-Vice-Chancellor Univ. of London 2003–05; Vice-Chair. Aberdeen Royal Hosps NHS Trust 1992–99; mem. Gen. Medical Council (GMC) 1994–2009, Chair. GMC Educ. Cttee 1999–2002, Pres. GMC 2002–09; Chair. Robert Gordon's Coll. Aberdeen 1995–2005, Scottish Stem Cell Network 2008–11; Pres. Asscn for the Study of Medicine 2009–13, Coll. of Medicine 2010–; Chair. Dignity in Dying 2012–, Lathallan School 2012–; mem. Scottish Higher Educ. Funding Council 1996–2002, Specialist Training Authority 1999–2002, Lambeth, Southwark and Lewisham Health Authority 2000–02, South East London Strategic Health Authority 2002–05, Council for the Regulation of Healthcare Professionals 2003–08; Founder-mem. Acad. of Medical Sciences 1998, Treas. 1998–2001; Harkness Fellow, Commonwealth Fund of New York; Fellow in Medicine, Harvard Univ. and Peter Bent Brigham Hosp., Boston 1975–77; Fellow, King's Coll. London 2005; Hon. Fellow, Royal Coll. of Gen. Practitioners 2001, Royal Coll. of Surgeons of Edinburgh 2002, Faculty of Pharmaceutical Medicine 2008, Acad. of Medical Educators 2012; Hon. LLD (Aberdeen) 2002; Hon. DSc (St Andrews) 2003, (Robert Gordon) 2004, (Kent) 2007, (London South Bank) 2008, (London) 2009; Hon. MD (Southampton) 2004, (Brighton) 2010. *Leisure interest:* hills and glens. *Address:* 4 Woodend Avenue, Aberdeen, AB15 6YL; Maryfield, Glenbuchat, Strathdon, Aberdeenshire, AB36 8TS, Scotland. *Telephone:* (1224) 310509 (Aberdeen); (1975) 641317 (Strathdon). *E-mail:* gcatto@btinternet.com.

CATTORETTI, Marco; Italian fashion designer and business executive; *CEO, Tuleh LLC;* pnr, Bryan Bradley; moved to New York and co-f. and co-designed, with Luca Mosca, own fashion collection 'Luca+Marco' 1994; Vice-Pres. Malo, Milan –2007; CEO Tuleh LLC fashion co., New York 2007–. *Films:* costume designer: Hostage 1999, Girlfight 2000, Hamlet 2000, Happy Here and Now 2002, When Will I Be Loved 2004. *Television:* costume designer: The Education of Max Bickford (series) 2001. *Address:* Tuleh LLC, 181 Chrystie Street, Apt 2, New York, NY 10002-1280, USA (office). *Telephone:* (212) 979-7888 (office).

CATZ, Safra Ada, BA, JD; Israeli/American business executive; *President and Chief Financial Officer, Oracle Corporation;* b. 1 Dec. 1961, Holon, Israel; m.; two c.; ed Brookline High School, Wharton School of Univ. of Pennsylvania and Univ. of Pennsylvania Law School; held various investment banking positions 1986–94; Sr Vice-Pres. Donaldson, Lufkin & Jenrette (global investment bank) 1994–97, Man. Dir 1997–99; Sr Vice-Pres. Oracle Corpn April–Oct. 1999, Exec. Vice-Pres. 1999–2004, mem. Bd of Dirs 2001–, Pres. Oracle Corpn with responsibility for global operations 2004–, Chief Financial Officer 2005–08, 2011–, mem. Exec. Man. Cttee; Dir (non-exec.) HSBC Holdings plc 2008–; ranked by Fortune magazine amongst the 50 Most Powerful Women in Business in the US (49th) 2005, (16th) 2008, (12th) 2009, (11th) 2010–11, (tenth) 2012, ranked by Forbes magazine amongst The World's 100 Most Powerful Women (22nd) 2005, (21st) 2006, (28th) 2007, (15th) 2008, (16th) 2009, (40th) 2011, (48th) 2012, (23rd) 2013. *Address:* Oracle Corpn, 500 Oracle Parkway, Redwood City, CA 94065-1675, USA (office). *Telephone:* (650) 506-7000 (office). *Fax:* (650) 506-7200 (office). *E-mail:* info@oracle.com (office). *Website:* www.oracle.com (office).

CAUBET, Marie-Christine; French automotive industry executive; b. (Marie-Christine Bourguignon), 4 Dec. 1950, Salins Les Bains; m.; three c.; ed Institut d'Etudes Politiques, Aix-en-Provence, Centre Européen d'Educ. Permanente (CEDEP), Fontainebleau, Institut Européen d'Admin des Affaires (INSEAD); joined Renault SA as financial analyst in 1973–85, Dir Mantes sales br. 1985–88, Regional Br. Dir 1988–90, Regional Dir Île de France region 1990–93, Marketing Dir for France 1993–97, Regional Dir Renault France Automobiles 1997–2000, Sr Vice-Pres. Market Area France and mem. Renault Man. Cttee 2000–05, Sr Vice-Pres. Market Area Europe 2005–08; Chair. Groupe Volkswagen France 2009–12, Advisor Volkswagen Group 2013–; Chevalier, Ordre nat. du Mérite; ranked by Fortune magazine amongst the 50 Most Powerful Women in Business outside the US (40th) 2005, (50th) 2006, (47th) 2009. *Leisure interests:* sailing, family life. *Address:* Groupe Volkswagen France, 11 avenue de la Boursonne, 02601 Villers-Cotterêt Cedex, France (office). *Telephone:* (3) 23-73-58-00 (office). *E-mail:* marie-christine.caubet@gr-vw.fr (office).

CAUCHON, Hon. Martin, DCL, LLM; Canadian politician and lawyer; *Partner, Gowling Lafleur Henderson LLP;* b. 23 Aug. 1962, La Malbaie, Québec; ed Univ. of Ottawa, Bar School of Québec, Univ. of Exeter, UK, Inst. of Corporate Dirs; practised as civil and commercial lawyer 1985–93; MP for Outremont 1993–2004 (resgnd); apptd Sec. of State responsible for the Econ. Devt Agency of Canada for the Regions of Québec 1996–2002, Minister of Nat. Revenue (responsible for Canada Customs) 1999–2002, Minister of Justice, Attorney-Gen. 2002–03; Pres. Canada-France Inter-parl. Asscn 1994–95; Pres. Liberal Party of Canada (Québec) 1993–95; Vice-Chair. Standing Cttee on Public Accounts 1994; mem. Standing Cttee on Human Resources Devt 1994–96; currently Pnr, Gowling Lafleur Henderson LLP (law firm), Montréal. *Publications:* articles in Revue du Barreau and Bulletin de la Société de droit int. économique. *Address:* Gowling Lafleur Henderson LLP, 1 Place Ville Marie, 37th Floor, Montréal, PQ H3B 3PA, Canada (office). *Telephone:* (514) 392-9529 (office). *Fax:* (514) 878-1450 (office). *E-mail:* martin.cauchon@gowlings.com (office). *Website:* www.gowlings.com (office).

CAUTE, (John) David, (John Salisbury), MA, DPhil, JP, FRSL, FRHistS; British writer; b. 16 Dec. 1936, Alexandria, Egypt; s. of Edward H. C. Caute and Rebecca Perlzweig; m. 1st Catherine Shuckburgh 1961 (divorced 1970); two s.; m. 2nd Martha Bates 1973; two d.; ed Edinburgh Acad., Wellington, Wadham Coll., Oxford; St Antony's Coll., Oxford 1959; army service in Gold Coast 1955–56; Henry Fellow, Harvard Univ. 1960–61; Fellow, All Souls Coll., Oxford 1959–65; Visiting Prof., New York Univ. and Columbia Univ. 1966–67; Reader in Social and Political Theory, Brunel Univ. 1967–70; Regents' Lecturer, Univ. of California 1974, Visiting Prof. Univ. of Bristol 1985; Literary Ed. New Statesman 1979–80; Co-Chair. Writers' Guild 1982. *Plays:* Songs for an Autumn Rifle 1961, The Demonstration 1969, The Fourth World 1973, Brecht and Company (BBC TV) 1979. *Radio plays:* The Demonstration 1971, Fallout 1972, The Zimbabwe Tapes (BBC Radio) 1983, Henry and the Dogs (BBC Radio) 1986, Sanctions (BBC Radio) 1988, Animal Fun Park (BBC Radio) 1995. *Publications include:* At Fever Pitch (novel) (Authors' Club Award 1960, John Llewellyn Rhys Award 1960) 1959, Comrade Jacob (novel) 1961, Communism and the French Intellectuals 1914–1960 1964, The Left in Europe Since 1789 1966, The Decline of the West (novel) 1966, Essential Writings of Karl Marx (ed.) 1967, The Confrontation: A Trilogy, The Demonstration (play), The Occupation (novel), The Illusion 1971, The Fellow-Travellers 1973, Collisions: Essays and Reviews 1974, The Great Fear: The Anti-Communist Purge Under Truman and Eisenhower 1978, Under the Skin: The Death of White Rhodesia 1983, The Baby-Sitters (novel, as John Salisbury) 1978, Moscow Gold (novel, as John Salisbury) 1980, The K-Factor (novel) 1983, The Espionage of the Saints 1986, Sixty Eight: The Year of the Barricades 1988, Veronica or the Two Nations (novel) 1989, The Women's Hour (novel) 1991, Joseph Losey: A Revenge on Life 1994, Dr Orwell and Mr Blair (novel) 1994, Fatima's Scarf (novel) 1998, The Dancer Defects: The Struggle for Cultural Supremacy During the Cold War 2003, Marechera and the Colonel 2009, Politics and the Novel During the Cold War 2010, Isaac and Isaiah: the Covert Punishment of a Cold War Heretic 2013. *Address:* 41 Westcroft Square, London, W6 0TA, England (home).

CAUTHEN, Stephen Mark (Steve); American fmr professional jockey; b. 1 May 1960, Walton, Ky; s. of Ronald Cauthen and Myra Cauthen; m. Amy Rothfuss 1992; two d.; rode first race 1976, first winner 1976, top jockey, USA with 487 winners 1977; at 18, youngest person to win US racing's Triple Crown; moved to UK 1979; champion jockey 1984, 1985, 1987; won Derby on Slip Anchor 1985, on Reference Point 1987; rode 1,704 winners including 10 classics 1979–93 (retd); only jockey to have won Kentucky, Epsom, Irish, French and Italian Derbys; now works on family farm, Ky and as racing commentator on TV; Vice-Pres. Turfway Racing Asscn, Ky; Seagram Prize 1977, Eclipse Award 1977; youngest person to be elected to Racing Hall of Fame. *Address:* 167 South Main Street, Walton KY 41094, USA.

CAVACO SILVA, Anibal, PhD; Portuguese politician, economist, academic and head of state; *President;* b. 15 July 1939, Loulé; s. of Teodoro Silva and Maria do Nascimento Cavaco; m. Maria Cavaco Silva 1963; one s. one d.; ed Univ. of York, UK and Inst. of Econ. and Financial Studies; taught Public Econs and Political Economy, Inst. of Econ. and Financial Studies 1965–67, then at Catholic Univ. 1975–2006 and New Univ. of Lisbon 1977–2002; Research Fellow, Calouste Gulbenkian Foundation 1967–77; Dir of Research and Statistical Dept, Bank of Portugal 1977–85; Minister of Finance and Planning 1980–81; Pres. Council for Nat. Planning 1981–84; Leader, PSD 1985–95; Prime Minister of Portugal 1985–95; mem. Real Academia de Ciencias Morales y Políticas, Spain; Econ. Adviser to Bank of Portugal (Cen. Bank) 1995–2004; Pres. of Portugal 2006–; Social Democrat (PSD) mem. Exec. Cttee Club of Madrid in Democratic Transition and Consolidation; Dr hc (Univ. of York, UK, Universidade da Coruña, Spain); Joseph Bech Prize 1991, Max Schmidleinz Foundation Prize, Carl Bertelsmann Prize. *Publications:* Budgetary Policy and Economic Stabilization 1976, Economic Effects of Public Debt 1977, The Economic Policy of Sá Carneiro's Government 1982, Public Finance and Macroeconomic Policy 1992, A Decade of Reforms 1995, Portugal and the Single Currency 1997, European Monetary Union 1999, Political Autobiography 2002; over 20 articles on financial markets, public economics and Portuguese economic policy. *Leisure interests:* golf, gardening. *Address:* Office of the President, Presidência da República, Palácio de Belém, Calçada da Ajuda, 1349-022 Lisbon, Portugal (office). *Telephone:* (21) 3614600 (office). *Fax:* (21) 3614611 (office). *E-mail:* presidente@presidenciarepublica.pt (office). *Website:* www.presidenciarepublica.pt (office).

CAVALIER-SMITH, Thomas (Tom), PhD, FRS, FRSC, FLS, FIBiol; British/Canadian biologist and academic; *Professor of Evolutionary Biology, University of Oxford;* b. 21 Oct. 1942, London; s. of Alan Hailes Spencer Cavalier-Smith and Mary Maude Cavalier-Smith (née Bratt); m. 1st Gillian Glaysher 1967 (divorced); one s. one d.; m. 2nd Ema E-Yung Chao 1991; one d.; ed Norwich School, Gonville and Caius Coll., Cambridge, King's Coll., London; Guest Investigator and Damon Runyon Memorial Fellow, Rockefeller Univ., New York 1967–69; Lecturer in Biophysics, King's Coll., Univ. of London 1969–82, Reader 1982–89; Prof. of Botany, Univ. of British Columbia 1989–99; Natural Environment Research Council Research Prof., Dept of Zoology, Univ. of Oxford 1999–2007, Prof. of Evolutionary Biology 2000–; Pres. British Soc. for Protist Biology; mem. Council of Int. Congress of Systematic and Evolutionary Biology, Advisory Cttee of Canadian Inst. for Advanced Research's Programme on Integrated Microbial Biodiversity; Fellow, Canadian Inst. for Advanced Research Evolutionary Biology Programme 1988–2007; Int. Prize for Biology 2004, Linnean Medal for Zoology 2007, Frink Medal, Zoological Soc. of London 2008. *Publications:* Biology, Society and Choice (ed.) 1982, The Evolution of Genome Size (ed.) 1985; more than 180 scientific papers on cell and genome evolution, large scale phylogeny and the tree of life, understanding major evolutionary transitions, molecular evolution, cell biology, ultrastructure, ecology, and classification of Protozoa. *Leisure interests:* reading, natural history. *Address:* Department of Zoology, University of Oxford, The Tinbergen Building, South Parks Road, Oxford, OX1 3PS (office); 54 Warwick Street, Oxford, Oxon., OX14 1SX, England (home). *Telephone:* (1865) 281065 (office). *Fax:* (1865) 281310 (office). *E-mail:* tom.cavalier-smith@zoo.ox.ac.uk (office). *Website:* evolve.zoo.ox.ac.uk (office).

CAVALLI, Roberto; Italian fashion designer; b. 15 Nov. 1940, Florence; grandson of Giuseppe Rossi; m. (divorced); two c.; m. 2nd Eva Duringer; three c.; ed Accad. di Belle Arti, Florence; first collection, Palazzo Pitti, Florence 1972. *Fashion lines include:* Just Cavalli, Class, Freedom, Timewear, Angels. *Address:* Press Office, Via Gesu 19, Milan, Italy (office). *Telephone:* (02) 784416 (office). *Fax:* (02) 782361 (office). *E-mail:* press@robertocavalli.it (office). *Website:* www.robertocavalli.it (office).

CAVALLI-SFORZA, Luigi Luca, MA, MD; Italian/American geneticist and academic; *Professor of Genetics and Anthropology, Faculty of Philosophy, Università Vita-Salute San Raffaele, Milan;* b. 25 Jan. 1922, Genoa; m. Albanaria Ramazzotti; three s. one d.; ed Univ of Pavia, Univ of Cambridge, UK; Dir of Research in Microbiology, Istituto Sieroterapico Milanese, Milan 1950–57; Prof. of Genetics, Univ. of Parma 1960–62; Prof. of Genetics, Univ. of Pavia 1962–70, Dir Inst. of Genetics 1962–70; Prof. of Genetics, Stanford Univ. 1970–92, Chair. Dept of Genetics 1986–90, Prof. Emer., School of Medicine 1992–; Prof. of Genetics and Anthropology, Faculty of Philosophy, Universitá Vita-Salute San Raffaele, Milan 2007–; numerous awards. *Publications:* The History and Geography of Human Genes, Genes 1994, Peoples and Languages 2000, Consanguinity Inbreeding and Drift in Italy 2004. *Address:* Population Genetics Laboratory, CNR Institute of Molecular Genetics, 27100 Pavia (office); Via Fatebene Sorelle 18, 20121 Milan, Italy (home). *Telephone:* (02) 36567973 (office). *E-mail:* cavallisforza@gmail.com (home).

CAVALLO, Domingo Felipe (Mingo), DEcon, PhD; Argentine politician, economist, academic and business executive; *Chairman and CEO, DFC Associates LLC;* b. 21 July 1946, San Francisco, Córdoba; s. of Felipe Cavallo and Florencia Cavallo; m. Sonia Abrazián; three s.; ed Nat. Univ. of Córdoba, Harvard Univ., USA; Under-Sec. for Devt . Govt of Prov. of Córdoba 1969–70; Prof. of Econs and Statistics, Nat. Univ. of Córdoba 1969–84; Prof. of Econs, Catholic Univ. of Córdoba 1970–74; Vice-Pres. Bd of Dirs Banco de la Provincia de Córdoba 1971–72; Founding Dir Instituto de Estudios Económicos sobre la Realidad Argentina y Latinoamericana (IEERAL), Fundación Mediterránea 1977–87, Academic Adviser, IEERAL 1987–; fmr Pres., then Gov. Argentine Cen. Bank; mem. World Bank Research Observer Editorial Bd 1987–88, Advisory Cttee Inst. for Econ. Devt of World Bank 1988; Nat. Deputy for Córdoba 1987–91; Minister of Foreign Affairs and Worship 1989–91, of the Economy 1991–92, of the Economy and Public Works 1992–96, 2001; Visiting Prof., Stern School of Business, New York Univ. 1996–97, 2002–03; Founder and Pres. Acción por la República party 1997–2001; Nat. Deputy for Buenos Aires 1997–2001; Publr Forbes Global 1998–99; Founder Fundación Novum Millenium; arrested for alleged involvement in arms smuggling April 2002, released June 2002; Robert Kennedy Visiting Prof. in Latin American Studies, Harvard Univ. 2003–05; currently Chair. and CEO DFC Associates LLC; mem. Group of Thirty Consultative Group on Int. Econ. and Monetary Affairs, Inc., Washington, DC; Corresp. mem. Royal Acad. of Moral and Political Sciences of Spain 1993; Hon. Pres. Fundación Mediterránea (Argentina) 1996; Dr hc in Jurisprudence (Univ. of Genoa, Italy) 1994; Honour Diploma as Academic mem. Econ., Legal and Social Research Inst. of Argentina) 1995; Dr hc in Philosophy (Ben Gurion Univ., Negev, Israel) 1995, Dr hc in Econs (Univ. of Turin, Italy) 1995, Dr hc (Univ. of Paris 1, Pantheon-Sorbonne, France) 1999, Dr hc in Political Sciencies (Univ. of Bologne, Italy) 2000; Premio Universidad Gold Medal and Honor Diploma for Best Student in Univ. of Córdoba 1968, scholarships from OAS and the Ford Foundation for grad. studies at Harvard Univ. 1975–76, Ten Outstanding Young People of the Year Award, Jr Chamber of Buenos Aires 1981, Quality of Research Discovery Award for the research entitled Agriculture and Economic Growth in an Open Economy: The Case of Argentina 1940–73 (jtly with Yair Mundlak), American Agricultural Econs Asscn 1983, Man of the Year Award, Latin Finance Magazine, Santo Domingo 1992, Minister of Finance of the Year Award, Euromoney magazine 1992, Economist of the Year Award, Inst. of Contemporary Studies, Buenos Aires, Argentina 1992, Eagle of the Americas Award, Asscn of American Chambers of Commerce in Latin America (declaring Dr Cavallo Promoter of Int. Trade) 1995, Americas Award, The Americas Foundation, New York 1999. *Publications:* Volver a Crecer 1984, El Desafío Federal 1986, Economía en Tiempos de Crisis 1989, La Argentina Que Pudo Ser (los costos de la represión económica; jtly with Roberto Domenech and Yair Mundlack) 1989, El Peso de la Verdad 1997, Pasion por Crear (with Juan Carlos De Pablo) 2001, Estanflacion (Stagflation) 2008; numerous tech. publs and articles in Argentine and foreign newspapers. *Address:* Hipólito Yrigoyen 250, 1310 Buenos Aires; DFC Associates LLC, Buenos Aires, C1425EEH, Argentina (office); DFC Associates LLC, 8200 Greenboro Drive, Suite 900, McLean, VA 22102, USA (office). *Telephone:* (11) 4804-0862 (Buenos Aires) (office); (703) 462-5437 (McLean) (office).

Fax: (11) 4804-0865 (Buenos Aires) (office). *E-mail:* info@dfcassociates.com (office). *Website:* www.dfcassociates.com (office); www.cavallo.com.ar (office).

ČAVIĆ, Dragan; Bosnia and Herzegovina politician and fmr head of state; b. 10 March 1958, Zenica; m.; one s. one d.; ed Banja Luka Univ.; worked as man. at several state and pvt. enterprises; mem. Parl. 1998–2000; Vice-Pres. Republika Srpska 2000–02, Pres. 2002–06; mem. Serbian Democratic Party of Bosnia and Herzegovina (SDP) (Srpska Demokratska Stranka Bosne i Hercegovine) (SDS BiH), Deputy Pres. 2002–04, Pres. 2004–06. *Address:* c/o Serbian Democratic Party of Bosnia and Herzegovina (SDP) (Srpska Demokratska Stranka Bosne i Hercegovine) (SDS BiH), 78000 Banja Luka, Nikole Tesle 1B, Bosnia and Herzegovina.

CAVIEZEL, James (Jim) Patrick; American actor; b. 26 Sept. 1968, Mount Vernon, Wash.; s. of Jim Caviezel and Maggie Caviezel; m. Kerri Browitt 1997; one s. (adopted); ed Mount Vernon High School, O'Dea High School, Burien Kennedy High School, Seattle, Bellevue Community Coll., Univ. of Wash.; moved to LA and worked as waiter between auditions 1992; modelled for The Gap; Spokesperson for Redeem the Vote (Catholic-Conservative counterpart to Rock the Vote); Dr hc (King's Coll., Wilkes-Barre, Pa) 2003. *Films include:* My Own Private Idaho 1991, Diggstown 1992, Wyatt Earp 1994, Ed 1996, The Rock 1996, G.I. Jane 1997, The Thin Red Line 1998, Ride with the Devil 1999, Resurrection 2000, Frequency 2000, Pay It Forward 2000, Madison 2001, Angel Eyes 2001, The Count of Monte Cristo 2002, High Crimes 2002, Highwaymen 2003, I Am David 2003, The Final Cut 2004, The Passion of the Christ 2004, Bobby Jones: Stroke of Genius 2004, Unknown 2006, Deja Vu 2006, Outlander 2008, The Stoning of Soraya M. 2008, Long Weekend 2008. *Television includes:* Murder, She Wrote 1984, The Wonder Years 1988, The Prisoner 2009. *Leisure interests:* basketball, Indy car racing. *Address:* c/o United Talent Agency, 9560 Wilshire Boulevard, Suite 500, Beverly Hills, CA 90212, USA (office). *Telephone:* (310) 273-6700 (office). *Fax:* (310) 247-1111 (office).

CAVINESS, Madeline Harrison, BA, MA, PhD, FSA; American medieval art historian and academic; *Mary Richardson Professor Emerita, Department of Art History, Tufts University;* b. 1938, London, UK; d. of Eric Vernon Harrison and Gwendoline Fownes Rigden; m. Verne Strudwick Caviness, Jr 1962; two d.; ed Newnham Coll., Cambridge, Harvard Univ.; Prof. of Medieval Art, Tufts Univ. 1981–2007, Mary Richardson Prof. 1987–2007, Prof. Emer. 2007–; Pres., Int. Acad. Union 1998–2001, Int. Center for Medieval Art 1984–87, Medieval Acad. of America 1993–94, Int. Council for Philosophy and Humanistic Studies 2001–04; Vice-Pres. Corpus Vitrearum Int. Bd 1983–87, Pres. 1987–95, Hon. Pres. 2000–; Vice-Pres. New England Medieval Conference 1985, Pres. 1986; Fellow, Soc. of Antiquaries, London 1980; mem. American Acad. of Arts and Sciences 2007–; Fellow, Medieval Acad. of America 1992–; Hon. Phi Beta Kappa, Radcliffe Coll. 1977; Hon. DLitt (Bristol, UK) 2000; John Nicholas Brown Prize, Medieval Acad. 1981, Haskins Medal, Medieval Acad. 1993, Distinguished Sr Scholar Award, American Asscn of Univ. Women Educational Foundation 2005, Tufts Univ. Award for Distinguished Research and Seymour Simches Award for Teaching and Advising 2005. *Publications include:* Early Stained Glass of Canterbury Cathedral (John Nicholas Brown Prize, Medieval Acad. 1981) 1977, Sumptuous Arts at the Royal Abbeys in Reims and Braine (Charles Homer Haskins Medal, Medieval Acad. of America 1993) 1980, Visualizing Women in the Middle Ages: Sight, Spectacle and Scopic Economy 2001, Medieval Art in the West and its Audience 2001, Reframing Medieval Art: Difference, Margins, Boundaries (e-book) 2001. *Leisure interests:* travel, archaeology, gardens. *Address:* 8 Whittier Place, 24H, Boston MA 02114-1497, USA (home); Department of Art and Art History, Tufts University, 11 Talbot Avenue, Medford, MA 02155, USA (office). *Telephone:* (617) 627-3567 (office); (617) 670-4008 (home). *Fax:* (617) 627-3890 (office). *E-mail:* mhcaviness@comcast.net (office); madeline.caviness@tufts.edu (home). *Website:* ase.tufts.edu/art (office); nils.lib.tufts.edu/Caviness (office).

CAWLEY, Charles M.; American financial services executive (retd); ed George-town Univ.; began career in financial services in 1963; joined Maryland Nat. Bank 1972; sr mem. of man. team that est. MBNA America 1982, Pres. 1985–2002, CEO MBNA American Bank 1990–2002, Pres. MBNA Corpn 1991–2003, Chair. and CEO 2002–03 (retd); mem. Bd of Dirs MasterCard Int.; mem. Bd Grand Opera House, Wilmington, Delaware, St Benedict's Preparatory School, George Bush Presidential Library Foundation, Metropolitan Wilmington Urban League; mem. Bd of Trustees Univ. of Delaware; mem. Bd of Regents Georgetown Univ., American Architectural Foundation.

CAWLEY, Evonne Fay Goolagong, AO, MBE; Australian fmr professional tennis player; b. 31 July 1951, Griffith, NSW; d. of the late Kenneth Goolagong and Linda Hamilton; m. Roger Anson Cawley 1975; one s. one d.; ed Willoughby High School, Sydney; professional tennis player 1970–83; Wimbledon Champion 1971, 1980 (singles), 1974 (doubles); Australian Champion 1974, 1975, 1976, 1977; French Champion 1971; Italian Champion 1973; S African Champion 1972; Virginia Slims Circuit Champion 1975, 1976; played Fed. Cup for Australia 1971, 1972, 1973, 1974, 1975, 1976; Capt. Australian Fed. Cup Team 2001–04; consultant to Indigenous Sports Programme; Sports Amb. to Aboriginal and Torres Strait Island Communities 1997–; Amb. and Exec. Dir Evonne Goolagong Sports Trust; f. Evonne Goolagong Getting Started Programme for young girls; Hon. DUniv (Charles Sturt) 2000; Australian of the Year 1982, Int. Tennis Hall of Fame 1988. *Publications:* Evonne Goolagong (with Bud Collins) 1975, Home: The Evonne Goolagong Story (with Phil Jarratt) 1993. *Leisure interests:* fishing, reading, researching Aboriginal heritage, movies, soccer. *Address:* c/o IMG, 281 Clarence Street, Sydney, NSW 2000; PO Box 1347, Noosa Heads, Queensland 4567, Australia. *Telephone:* (7) 5474-0112. *Fax:* (7) 5474-0113.

CAYETANO, Benjamin Jerome, BA, JD; American politician and lawyer; b. 14 Nov. 1939, Honolulu; m. 1st Lorraine Gueco 1958; m. 2nd Vicky Tiu 1997; two s. three d.; ed Farrington High School, Honolulu, Univ. of Calif., Los Angeles and Loyola Law School, Los Angeles; practising lawyer 1971–86; Pnr, Schutter Cayetano Playdon (law firm) 1983–86; mem. Hawaii State Legis. 1975–78, 1979–86; Lt-Gov. of Hawaii 1986–94, Gov. 1994–2002; Chair. W Gov.'s Asscn 1999; Democrat; Hon. LLD (Univ. of the Philippines) 1995, Hon. Dr of Public Service (Loyola Marymount Univ.) 1998; numerous awards for public service including Medal of UCLA 1995, The Aloha Council Boy Scouts of America Harvard

Foundation Leadership Award 1996, Distinguished Citizens Award 1997, Edward A. Dickson Alumnus of the Year Award, UCLA 1998, Distinguished Alumnus of the Year, Loyola Law School 2002. *Publication:* Ben: A Memoir, From Street Kid to Governor 2007. *Address:* 1926 Okoa Place, Honolulu, HI 96821-2651, USA (office).

CAYGILL, Hon. David Francis, LLB; New Zealand politician and lawyer; *Chairman, Electricity Commission;* b. 15 Nov. 1948, Christchurch; s. of Bruce Allott Caygill and Gwyneth Mary Caygill; m. Eileen E Boyd 1974; one s. three d.; ed Univ. of Canterbury; practised law in Christchurch legal firm 1974–78; mem. Christchurch City Council 1971–80; mem. House of Reps (Labour) 1978–90; Minister of Trade and Industry, Minister of Nat. Devt, Assoc. Minister of Finance 1984–87, of Health, Trade and Industry 1987–88, Deputy Minister of Finance 1988, Minister of Finance 1988–90, of Revenue 1988–89, Deputy Leader of the Opposition 1994–96; Pnr, Buddle Findlay, Barristers and Solicitors 1996–; Chair. Accident Compensation Corpn 1998–; Chair. Ministerial Inquiry into the Electri-city Ind. 2000; Deputy Chair. Commerce Comm. 2004–; Chair. Electricity Comm. 2007–; Chair. Educ. NZ Trust, Advisory Cttee on Official Statistics; mem. Canterbury Regional Planning Authority 1977–80; fmr mem. Bd of Dirs Infratil Ltd. *Leisure interests:* collecting classical music records, science fiction, following American politics. *Address:* Electricity Commission, Level 7, ASB Bank Tower, 2 Hunter Street, PO Box 10041, Wellington, New Zealand (office). *Telephone:* (4) 460-8860 (office). *Fax:* (4) 460-8879 (office). *E-mail:* info@electricitycommission .govt.nz (office). *Website:* www.electricitycommission.govt.nz (office).

CAYLA, Véronique; French civil servant and television executive; *President of Arte GEIE and President and CEO, Arte France;* b. 5 July 1950, Saint-Cloud, Paris; m. Philippe Cayla; ed Institut d'Études Politiques, Paris; joined Ministry of Culture 1973, began as Special Asst to Cultural Intervention Fund, joined Office of Sec. of State for Culture 1974, worked at Legal and Tech. Information Service 1976–78, returned to Ministry as a tech. adviser in charge of cinema 1978–85, apptd Deputy Dir Video Library, Paris 1982, Dir 1983–89, Gen. Man. 1989–92; Deputy Head of MK2 and CEO Images LMK SA 1992–99; apptd to Higher Audiovisual Council 1999–2000; joined trio at head of Cannes Film Festival, as CEO, in tandem with Thierry Fremaux, chaired by Gilles Jacob 2000–05; Head of Centre nat. de la cinématographie 2005–11; Pres. Man. Bd Arte EEIG (Arte—Asscn Relative à la Télévision Européenne, f. 1991 and composed of ARTE Deutschland TV GmbH and ARTE France) Jan. 2011–, Pres. and CEO Arte France (new name of La Sept—French TV) March 2011–; Officier, Légion d'honneur, des Arts et des Lettres. *Address:* Arte GEIE, 4 Quai du Chanoine Winterer, BP 20035, 67080 Strasbourg Cedex (office); Arte France, 8 rue Marceau, 92785 Issy-les-Moulineaux Cedex 9, France (office). *Telephone:* (3) 88-14-22-22 (Strasbourg) (office); 1-55-00-77-77 (Issy-les-Moulineaux) (office). *Fax:* (3) 88-14-22-00 (Stras-bourg) (office); 1-55-00-77-00 (Issy-les-Moulineaux) (office). *E-mail:* info@arte.tv (office). *Website:* www.arte.tv (office).

CAYLEY, Andrew T., QC, LLM; British barrister; *Chief International Co-Prosecutor, Extraordinary Chambers in the Courts of Cambodia;* b. 24 March 1964, Rustington, West Sussex, England; s. of Granville Cayley and Elizabeth Cayley; m. Andrea von Matacic; two s. two d.; ed Brighton Coll., Univ. Coll., London, Coll. of Law, Guildford, Royal Mil. Acad., Sandhurst; Asst Solicitor and Articled Clerk with Thomas Eggar, London 1987–91; Legal Officer, British Army 1991–98; Prosecuting Counsel, Office of the Prosecutor, Int. Criminal Tribunal for the Former Yugoslavia (ICTY), The Hague 1994–2001, Sr Prosecuting Counsel 2001–05, Sr Prosecuting Counsel, Int. Criminal Court, The Hague 2005–07; called to the Bar of England & Wales by the Inner Temple 2007; counsel on the defence team for Charles Ghankay Taylor before Special Court for Sierra Leone and also for Ivan Cermak before ICTY 2007–09; Chief Int. Co-Prosecutor, Extraordinary Chambers in the Courts of Cambodia (Khmer Rouge Tribunal) 2009–; Assoc. Tenant, Doughty Street Chambers, London 2011–; mem. Hon. Soc. of the Inner Temple. *Address:* Doughty Street Chambers, 54 Doughty Street, London, WC1N 2LS, England (office); Office of the Co-Prosecutors, Extraordinary Chambers in the Courts of Cambodia, National Road 4, Chaom Chau Commune, Dangkao District, PO Box 71, Phnom Penh, Cambodia (office). *E-mail:* a.cayley@doughtystreet.co.uk (office); cayley@un.org (office). *Website:* www.eccc.gov.kh (office).

CAYROL, Roland; French researcher, opinion pollster and producer; b. 11 Aug. 1941, Rabat, Morocco; m. Annabelle Gomez 1989; two s. two d.; Prof. and Researcher, Nat. Foundation of Political Sciences, Centre de Recherches Politiques de Sciences Po 1968, Research Dir 1978–; Scientific Adviser, Louis Harris France 1977–86; Dir CSA (Opinion polling and market research co.) 1986–98, Dir Gen. CSA Group 1998–2006, Special Adviser 2006–; Special Adviser, Bolloré Group 2006–; Chevalier du Mérite agricole. *Television productions include:* Portrait d'un Président: François Mitterrand (with A. Gaillard) 1985. *Publications:* François Mitterrand 1967, Le Député Français (with J. L. Parodi and C. Ysmal) 1970, La Presse écrite et audiovisuelle 1973, La télévision fait-elle l'élection? (with G. Blumler and G. Thoveron) 1974, La nouvelle communication politique 1986, Les médias 1991, Le grand malentendu, Les Français et la politique 1994, Médias et démocratie: la dérive 1997, Sondages mode d'emploi 2000, La nuit des politiques 2006, La revanche de l'opinion : Médias, sondages, Internet (with Pascal Delannoy) 2007. *Address:* CSA 2 rue de Choiseul, 75002 Paris, France (office). *Telephone:* 1-44-94-59-57 (office). *E-mail:* roland.cayrol@csa.eu (office); roland.cayrol@wanadoo .fr (home). *Website:* www.cevipof.msh-paris.fr (home).

CAZALET, Sir Peter Grenville, Kt, MA; British business executive (retd); b. 26 Feb. 1929, Weymouth; s. of Vice-Adm. Sir Peter Cazalet, KBE, CB, DSO, DSC and Lady (Elise) Cazalet (née Winterbotham); m. Jane Jennifer Rew 1957; three s.; ed Uppingham School and Univ. of Cambridge; Gen. Man. BP Tanker Co. Ltd 1968–70, Regional Co-ordinator, Australasia and Far East, BP Trading Ltd 1970–72, Pres. BP North America Inc. 1972–75, Dir BP Trading Ltd 1975–81, Chair. BP Oil Int. Ltd 1981–89, Man. Dir BP 1981–89, Deputy Chair. 1986–89; Chair. APV PLC 1989–96, Hakluyt & Co. 1998–99, Breamar Seascope Group PLC 2001–02; Chair. Armed Forces Pay Review Body 1989–93; Deputy Chair. (non-exec.) GKN PLC 1989–96; Dir Standard Oil Co., Cleveland, Ohio 1973–76, Peninsular & Oriental Steam Navigation Co. Ltd 1980–99, De La Rue Co. PLC 1983–95, Energy Capital Investment Co. 1995–98, Seascope Shipping Holdings PLC 1997–2001 (Chair. 2000–01); Dir Gen. Maritime Corpn (US) 2000–02; mem. Top Salaries Review Body 1989–94, Lloyds Register of Shipping Bd 1981–86 and Gen. Cttee 1981–99; Vice-Pres. ME Asscn 1982–, China–Britain Trade Group

1993–96 (Pres. 1996–98); Trustee Uppingham School 1976–95; Trustee The Wellcome Trust 1989–92, Gov. The Wellcome Trust Ltd 1992–96; Hon. Sec. King George's Fund for Sailors 1989–2000; Liveryman, Tallow Chandlers' Co. (Master 1991–92), Shipwrights' Co. *Leisure interests:* golf, theatre, fishing.

CAZALOT, Clarence P., Jr, BS; American oil industry executive; *Chairman, President and CEO, Marathon Oil Corporation;* b. 1 Feb. 1951; ed Louisiana State Univ.; joined Texaco Inc. as Geophysicist 1972, becoming Vice-Pres. 1992, also Pres. of Texaco Latin America/W Africa 1992, Pres. Texaco Exploration and Production Inc. 1994–97, Pres. Texaco Int. Marketing and Mfg 1997, Pres. Int. Production 1998, Chair. Texaco Ltd, London 1998–99, Chair. Texaco Worldwide Production 1999–2000; Vice-Chair. USX Corpn 2000, mem. Bd Dirs Marathon Oil Co. (later Corpn) 2000–, Pres. 2000–, CEO 2002–, Chair. 2011–; Chair. Marathon Ashland Petroleum LLC; mem. Bd Dirs Baker Hughes Inc., American Petroleum Inst., Greater Houston Partnership; mem. The Business Council, Advisory Bd of the World Affairs Council of Houston, James A. Baker III Inst. for Public Policy, Bd of Visitors of Univ. of Texas M.D. Anderson Cancer Center, Exec. Advisory Bd of the Houston Minority Supplier Devt Council, Bd of the Bipartisan Policy Cttee Energy Project; mem. American Asscn of Petroleum Geologists, Nat. Petroleum Council, All-American Wildcatters org.; Hon. DHumLitt (Louisiana State Univ.) 2007. *Address:* Marathon Oil Corporation, 5555 San Felipe Road, Houston, TX 77056-2723, USA (office). *Telephone:* (713) 629-6600 (office). *Fax:* (713) 296-2952 (office). *E-mail:* info@marathon.com (office). *Website:* www.marathon.com (office).

CAZENEUVE, Bernard, BA, MA; French lawyer and politician; *Minister of the Interior;* b. 2 June 1963, Senlis (Oise); Gen. Councillor, La Manche 1994–98; Mayor of Octeville 1995–2000; Second Deputy Mayor of Cherbourg, responsible for port affairs and for fmr territory of Octeville 2000–01, Mayor of Cherbourg 2001–12; First Vice-Pres. Regional Council of Lower Normandy for Econ. Devt, Maritime Policy and Tourism 2004–07; First Vice-Pres. Urban Community of Cherbourg 2004–08, Pres. 2008–12; Councillor of Cherbourg-Octeville 2012–; mem. (Parti socialiste) Nat. Ass. for 5th constituency of La Manche 1997–2002, 2007–12, for 4th constituency of La Manche June–July 2012; Jr Minister for European Affairs 2012–14, Minister of the Interior 2014–. *Publications:* Première manche 1993, La Politique retrouvée 1994, La Responsabilité du fait des produits en France et en Europe 2005, Karachi – L'enquête impossible 2011. *Address:* Ministry of the Interior, place Beauvau, 75008 Paris, France (office). *Telephone:* 1-49-27-49-27 (office). *Fax:* 1-43-59-89-50 (office). *Website:* sirp@interieur.gouv.fr (office); www .interieur.gouv.fr (office).

CEBRIÁN ECHARRI, Juan Luis, BS; Spanish writer and journalist; *CEO, El País;* b. 30 Oct. 1944, Madrid; s. of Vicente Cebrián and Carmen Echarri; m. 1st María Gema Torallas 1966 (divorced); two s. two d.; m. 2nd Teresa Aranda 1988; one s. one d.; ed Univ. of Madrid; Sr Ed. newspapers Pueblo, Madrid 1962–67, Informaciones, Madrid 1967–69; Founder-mem. of magazine Cuadernos para el Diálogo, Madrid 1963; Deputy Ed.-in-Chief, Informaciones 1969–74, 1974–76; apptd Dir News Programming, Spanish TV 1974; Founding Ed.-in-Chief newspaper El País, Madrid 1976–88, CEO El País 1988–; Vice-Pres. International Press Inst. 1982–86, Chair. 1986–88, later mem.; CEO Grupo PRISA 1988–, Canal Plus 1989–, Estructura 1989–; Non-Exec. and Proprietary Dir Sogecable SA 1989–; Vice-Pres. SER 1990–; Pres., Asscn of Spanish Newspaper Eds 2003–04; Dir (non-exec.) Media Capital S.G.P.S 2005–; Pres. and CEO Liberty Acquisition Holdings Virginia Inc. 2010–; mem. Royal Acad. of the Spanish Language 1996; Hon. Prof., (Universidad Iberoamericana de Santo Domingo) Dominican Republic; Chevalier, Ordre des Arts et des Lettres; Dr hc (Iberoamericana Univ., Santo Domingo) 1988, (La Plata Univ.) Argentina 2003; Control Prize for Outstanding Newspaper Ed. 1976, 1977, 1978, 1979, Víctor de la Serna Prize for Journalism, Press Asscn Fed. 1977, Outstanding Ed. of the Year (World Press Review, New York) 1980, Spanish Nat. Journalism Prize 1983, Freedom of Expression Medal, F. D. Roosevelt Four Freedoms Foundation 1986, Medal of Honor, Univ. of Miss. 1986, Trento Int. Prize for Journalism and Communication 1987, Gold Medal, Spanish Inst. New York 1988, Medal for Merit, Univ. of Veracruz, Mexico. *Publications:* La Prensa y la Calle 1980, La España que bosteza 1980, ¿Qué pasa en el mundo? 1981, Crónicas de mi país 1985, La rusa Alfaguara 1986, El Tamaño del elefante 1987, Red Doll 1987, La isla del viento 1990, El tamaño del elefante 1993, El siglo de las sombras 1994, Cartas a un joven periodista 1997, Exaltación del vino, y de la alegria 1998, La red 1998, La agonía del dragón 2000, El futuro no es lo que era 2001, Francomoribundia 2003, El Fundamentalismo Democrático 2004. *Leisure interests:* music, literature. *Address:* El País, Miguel Yuste 40, 28037 Madrid, Spain (office). *Telephone:* (91) 3378200 (office). *Fax:* (91) 3048766 (office). *Website:* www.elpais.com (office).

CEBUC, Alexandru, PhD; Romanian art historian and critic; b. 5 April 1932, Păușești-Măglabi; s. of Ion and Ana Cebuc; m. Florica Turcu 1958; one d.; ed Univ. of Bucharest; Head of Dept, Museum of History of City of Bucharest 1957–69; Vice-Pres. Culture Cttee of City of Bucharest 1969–77; Dir Art Museum of Romania 1977–90; Gen. Man. 2000 ARC (publishing and printing firm) 1990–; Order of Cultural Merit, Kt of Italian Repub. *Publications:* The History of the City of Bucharest 1966, The History of Passenger Transportation 1967, Historical and Art Monuments of the City of Bucharest 1968, The Nat. Gallery 1983, Ion Irimescu (monograph) 1983, Etienne Hadju (monograph) 1984, Nicolae Grigorescu (monograph) 1985, H. H. Catargi (monograph) 1987, I. Ianchelevici (monograph) 1989, I. Irimescu – Album Drawings 1994, Encyclopaedia of Plastic Artists in Romania (Vol. I) 1994, Encyclopaedia of Plastic Artists in Romania, (Vol. II) 1999, (Vol. III) 2000. *Leisure interests:* art, music, travelling. *Address:* B. Dul. Carol I, HR 23, Ap. 10, Bucharest (office); Str. Spatarului No. 36, ET. II Ap. 5, Bucharest, Romania. *Telephone:* (1) 3124018 (office). *Fax:* (1) 3124018 (office); (1) 2118617 (home).

CECCATO, Aldo; Italian conductor and music director; b. 18 Feb. 1934, Milan; m. Eliana de Sabata; two s.; ed Milan Conservatory, Hochschule für Musik Berlin; Musical Dir Detroit Symphony Orchestra 1973–77, Hamburg Philharmonic 1974–82; Chief Conductor Hannover Radio Orchestra 1985–, Bergen Symphony 1985–90, Orquesta Nacional de España 1991–94, Brno Philharmonic Orchestra 1995–2002; Musical Dir I Pomeriggi Musicali orchestra 1999–2004, now Dir Emer.; Hon. DMus (Eastern Michigan Univ.). *Leisure interests:* tennis, stamps, books. *Address:* c/o Orchestra I Pomeriggi Musicali, Teatro Dal Verme, via San Giovanni sul Muro 2, 20121 Milan, Italy (office).

CECCHI GORI, Vittorio; Italian film producer and politician; *Head of Gruppo Cecchi Gori;* b. 27 April 1943, Florence, Tuscany; s. of Mario Cecchi Gori; ed Univ. of Rome; began cinematographic career in father's co. Gruppo Cecchi Gori (previously Casa di Produzione Cinematografica); apptd Head of Group 1993, purchased Telemontecarlo and Videomusic (now TMC2) 1995; has produced more than 150 films; fmr Senator (Partido Populare Italiano), mem. Perm. Comm. for Labour and Social Welfare. *Films produced include:* Il bisbetico domato 1980, Asso 1981, Innamorato pazzo 1981, Grand Hotel Excelsior 1982, Attila 1982, La casa stregata 1982, Acqua e Sapone 1983, Softly Softly 1984, Pizza Connection 1985, Joan Lui 1986, Sono un fenomeno paranormale 1985, Scuola di Ladri 1986, Me and My Sister 1987, Il Burbero 1987, Il volpone 1988, La leggenda del santo bevitore (Best Film, Venice Film Festival) 1988, La chiesa 1989, Russicum 1989, La voce della luna 1990, Il segreto 1990, La Femme Nikita 1990, Che ora è? 1990, Il sole buio 1990, La setta 1991, Atlantis 1991, Volere volare 1991, Mediterraneo 1991, Piedipiatti 1991, Miliardi 1991, Johnny Stecchino 1991, Maledetto il giorno che t'ho incontrato 1992, Folks! 1992, Puerto escondido 1992, Man Trouble 1992, Al lupo, al lupo 1992, L'angelo con la pistola 1992, House of Cards 1993, Io speriamo che me la cavo 1993, Caino e Caino 1993, Una pura formalità 1994, Il postino 1994, Occhio Pinocchio 1994, Pisolini, un delitto italiano 1994, Al di là delle nuvole 1995, La scuola 1995, L'uomo delle stelle 1995, Viaggi di nozze 1995, I laureati 1995, Vite strozzate 1996, Tre 1996, Il ciclone 1996, Sono pazzo di Iris Blond 1996, Nirvana 1997, Ovosodo 1997, Le bossu 1997, Naja 1997, I piccoli maestri 1998, La seconda moglie 1998, Viola bacia tittu 1998, La fame e la sete 1999, Canone inverso — Making love 2000, Denti 2000, Faccia di Ricasso 2000, Almost Blue 2000, Commedia sexy 2001, E adesso sesso 2001, Figli 2001, Momo 2001, Imperial Treasures 2001, My Name is Tanino 2002, L'anima gemella 2002, La vita come viene 2003, Opopomoz 2003, L'Amore è eterno finché dura 2004, In questo mondo di ladri 2004, Cose da pazzi 2005, Il Ritorno del Monnezza 2005, Towards the Moon with Fellini 2006, Scusa ma ti chiamo amore 2008. *Address:* c/o Gruppo Cecchi Gori, Via Valadier, 00193 Rome, Italy (office). *Telephone:* (06) 324721 (office). *E-mail:* webmaster@cecchigori.com (office). *Website:* www.cecchigori.com (office).

CECH, Thomas Robert, PhD; American professor of chemistry and biochemistry; *Distinguished Professor, Department of Chemistry and Biochemistry, University of Colorado;* b. 8 Dec. 1947, Chicago; s. of Robert Franklin Cech and Annette Marie Cech (née Cerveny); m. Carol Lynn Martinson 1970; two d.; ed Grinnell Coll., Univ. of California, Berkeley; Postdoctoral Fellow, Dept of Biology, MIT, Cambridge, Mass. 1975–77; Asst Prof., then Assoc. Prof. of Chem., Univ. of Colorado, Boulder 1978–83, Prof. of Chem. and Biochem. and of Molecular, Cellular and Devt Biology 1983–, Distinguished Prof. 1990–; Research Prof., American Cancer Soc. 1987–; Investigator, Howard Hughes Medical Inst. 1988–99, Pres. 2000–09; Deputy Ed. Science; mem. Editorial Bd Genes and Devt; Nat. Science Foundation Fellow 1970–75; Public Health Service Research Fellow, Nat. Cancer Inst. 1975–77; Guggenheim Fellow 1985–86; mem. American Acad. of Arts and Sciences, NAS 1987–; Hon. DSc (Grinnell Coll.) 1987, (Univ. of Chicago) 1991, (Drury Coll.) 1994, (Colorado Coll.) 1999, (Univ. of Maryland) 2000, (Williams Coll.) 2000, (Charles Univ., Prague) 2002; Medal of American Inst. of Chemists 1970, Research Career Devt Award, Nat. Cancer Inst. 1980–85, Young Scientist Award, Passano Foundation 1984, Harrison Howe Award 1984, Pfizer Award 1985, US Steel Award 1987, V.D. Mattia Award 1987, Heineken Prize 1988, Gairdner Foundation Award 1988, Lasker Award 1988, Warren Triennial Prize 1989, Nobel Prize for Chem. 1989, Rosenstiel Award 1989, Nat. Medal of Science 1995, Gregor Mendel Medal 2002. *Leisure interest:* skiing. *Address:* Cristol Chemistry 334B, Department of Chemistry and Biochemistry, University of Colorado, Boulder, CO 80309-0215, USA (office). *Telephone:* (303) 492-8606 (office). *E-mail:* Thomas.Cech@colorado.edu (office). *Website:* www.colorado.edu/chem (office); cechlab.colorado.edu (office).

CEDAIN, Zhoima; Chinese singer; b. 1 Aug. 1937, Xigaze, Xizang (Tibet); ed Shanghai Music Coll.; joined CCP 1961; performed in USSR 1963; in political disgrace during Proletarian Cultural Revolution 1966–76; rehabilitated 1977; mem. Standing Cttee 5th NPC 1978–83; Vice-Chair. 6th CPPCC Tibet Regional Cttee 1987; Vice-Chair. Chinese Musicians' Asscn 1979–; mem. Standing Cttee 6th NPC 1983–88, 7th CPPCC 1988–92; Exec. Vice-Chair. China Fed. of Literary and Art Circles 1988–. *Address:* Chinese Musicians' Association, Beijing, People's Republic of China.

CEDAR, Howard, BS, MD, PhD; Israeli/American biochemist and academic; *Edmond J. Safra Distinguished Professor Emeritus, The Hebrew University of Jerusalem;* b. (Haim Cedar), 12 Jan. 1943, New York; m. Zipporah Cedar; six c.; ed Massachusetts Inst. of Tech., New York Univ.; worked for US Army's Public Health Service and NIH, Bethesda, Md 1970–73; emigrated to Israel with his family 1973; joined Dept of Biochemistry, Hebrew Univ. of Jeruslaem-Hadassah Medical School, first Edmond J. Safra Distinguished Prof. 2008–11, Prof. Emer. 2011–; Prof., Dept for Biochemistry and Genetics of Human Cell and Chair. Dept for Developmental Biology and Cancer Research, The Inst. for Medical Research, Israel-Canada; mem. Israel Acad. of Sciences and Humanities 2003; Israel Prize 1999, Wolf Prize in Medicine (with Aharon Razin) 2008, EMET Prize 2009, Canada Gairdner Award (with Aharon Razin), Gairdner Int. Award 2011, Rothschild Prize 2012. *Publications:* numerous papers in professional journals. *Address:* Department of Developmental Biology and Cancer Research, Faculty of Medicine, The Hebrew University of Jerusalem, Ein Kerem, PO Box 12272, 91120 Jerusalem, Israel (office). *Telephone:* 2-6758167 (office). *Fax:* 2-6415848 (office). *E-mail:* haimc@ekmd.huji.ac.il (office); cedar@cc.huji.ac.il (office). *Website:* medicine.ekmd .huji.ac.il/En/Publications/ResearchersPages/pages/haimc.aspx (office).

CEDAR, Joseph (Yossef); Israeli film director and screenwriter; b. 31 Aug. 1968, New York; s. of Howard (Haim) Cedar and Zipporah Cedar; m. Rose Kellner; three c.; ed Hebrew Univ. of Jerusalem, New York Univ., USA; moved to Israel with family aged six; began career as lighting designer and stage manager with Telad studios, Jerusalem; gained recognition with debut film Time of Favor. *Films:* Time of Favor (six Ophir Acad. Awards including Best Picture) 2000, Campfire (five Ophir Acad. Awards including Best Picture, Best Dir and Best Screenplay) 2004, Beaufort (Silver Bear Award for Best Dir, 2007 Berlin Int. Film Festival, four Ophir Acad. Awards) 2007, Footnote (Best Screenplay Award, 2011 Cannes Film Festival) 2011. *Address:* c/o International Creative Management, 730 Fifth Avenue, New York, NY 10019, USA (office). *Website:* www.icmtalent.com (office).

CEJAS, Paul L., BBA, CPA; American diplomatist and business executive; *Chairman, PLC Investments, Inc.;* b. 4 Jan. 1943, Havana, Cuba; ed Univ. of Miami; Founder, fmr Chair. and CEO CareFlorida Health Systems Inc. –1987; Amb. to Belgium 1998–2001; currently Chair. PLC Investments, Inc., Miami, Fla; Chair. Dade Co. School Bd; mem. Nat. Bd Smithsonian Inst.; mem. Latin American Advisory Bd, Tate Museum, London, UK; mem. Bd of Regents, Fla Univ. System 1994; Chair. Post-Summit Cttee, Hemispheric Summit of the Americas 1994, Fla Partnership of the Americas 1994–97; Rep. US Del. to Gen. Ass., OAS 1996; fmr Dir Miami Art Museum of Dade County; fmr mem. Bd of Dirs Mellon Financial Corpn, Ivax Corpn; fmr Trustee, Univ. of Miami, Florida International Univ.; Hon. PhD (Florida International Univ.) 1988. *Address:* PO Box 191679, Miami, FL 33119, USA.

ČEKANAUSKAS, Vytautas Edmundas; Lithuanian architect; b. 13 May 1930, Šiauliai; m. Teresa Chekanauskienė; one d.; ed Lithuanian Art Inst., Vilnius; architect, then Sr Architect, Group Man., Sr Projects Architect, Inst. of Urban Planning 1985–90; Prof., Lithuania Acad. of Arts (fmrly Inst. of Arts), Vilnius 1974–93, now mem. of the Acad. Senate; mem. USSR (now Russian) Acad. of Arts 1988, Int. Architects Asscn, Lithuanian Union of Architects, Int. Acad. of Architecture; Order of the Lithuanian Grand Duke Gediminas 2000; Lenin Prize 1974, People's Architect of USSR 1975. *Major projects:* has designed exhbn pavilion in Vilnius 1967, produced gen. plan of Lazdynai, residential dist in Vilnius 1968–73, and other projects, including Contemporary Art Centre. *Address:* Senate, Lithuania Academy of Arts, Maironio 6, 2600 Vilnius; U. Paco 13-9, 2000 Vilnius, Lithuania (home).

ÇEKU, Agim; Kosovo politician and military officer; *Minister of the Kosovo Security Force;* b. 29 Oct. 1960, Qyshk, Peja; s. of Hasan Çeku; m. Dragica Çeku; two s. one d.; ed Mil. High School, Belgrade, Zadar Mil. Acad., Croatia, Sr Exec. Course, George Marshall Centre, Germany; began career as Platoon Commdr, Yugoslav People's Army 1984, graduated as an Artillery Officer 1984; Platoon Commdr and Lecturer, School of Reserve Officers of the Artillery Centre, Mil. Acad., Zadar 1986–87, Lecturer and Commdr of Cadets' Co. 1989–91; joined newly formed Croatian Army as Capt. 1991, served as Commdr of an Infantry Bn and rose to rank of Maj. 1992, rank of Col 1993, rank of Brig. Gen. 1995; Chief of Staff of Mil. Dist of Gospiq 1995–99; released from Croatian Army to join Kosovo Liberation Army (KLA) and apptd Chief of Gen. Staff 1999, oversaw KLA demilitarization and formation of Kosovo Protection Corps, Commdr 1999–2006, rank of Lt-Gen. 2006; Prime Minister 2006–08; Pres. Social Democratic Party 2008–; Minister of the Kosovo Security Force 2011–; Order 'Adem Jashari', Medal of Mil. Service (Kosovo); Croatian decorations: Order 'Bana Jelacica', Nikole Subica Zrinskog, Hrvatskog Križa, Hrvatskog Trolista, Hrvatskog Pletera, Medal Iznimni Podhvat, Award for Operation 'Oluja' and 'Domovinske Zahvalnosti'; Award of Excellence from Supreme Allied Commdr Europe Gen. Wesley Clark. *Address:* Ministry of the Kosovo Security Force, 10000 Prishtina (office); Social Democratic Party (Partia Social Demokrate), 10000 Prishtina, Rruga Rexhep Mala 5, Kosovo (office). *Telephone:* (38) 551437 (Ministry) (office); (38) 225645 (SDP) (office). *E-mail:* violeta.reka@ks-gov.net (office). *Website:* mksf-ks.org (office).

CELANT, Germano, PhD; Italian art critic and curator; *Senior Curator of Contemporary Art, Solomon R. Guggenheim Museum;* b. 1940, Genoa; coined term Arte Povera (poor art) 1967; Jt Artistic Dir First Florence Biennale 1996; Curator, 47th Int. Art Exhbn, Venice Biennale 1997; Contributing Ed. Artforum, Interview (art reviews). *Publications include:* Arte povera: Appunti per una guerriglia 1967, The European Iceberg: Creativity in Germany and Italy Today 1985, The Italian Metamorphosis 1943-1968 1994, Mariko Mori: Dream Temple 1999, Carla Accardi 2001, Paolini Giulio 1960-1972 2004, Anselm Kiefer 2007, Vertigo: A Century of Multimedia Art from Futurism to the Web (co-author) 2008, American Twister: Art in Power 1949-2008 2008, Luigi Ghirri: It's Beautiful Here, Isn't It... 2008. *Address:* Solomon R. Guggenheim Museum, 1071 Fifth Avenue, New York, NY 100128-0173, USA (office). *Telephone:* (212) 423-3500 (office). *Website:* www .guggenheim.org (office).

CELESTE, Richard (Dick) F., PhB; American diplomatist, university administrator and fmr state governor; b. 11 Nov. 1937, Cleveland, Ohio; s. of Frank Celeste; m. 1st Dagmar Braun 1962; three s. three d.; m. 2nd Jacqueline Lundquist; one s.; ed Yale Univ. and Univ. of Oxford, UK; Staff Liaison Officer, US Peace Corps 1963; Special Asst to US Amb. to India 1963–67; Officer with Nat. Housing Consultants, Cleveland 1967–74; mem. Ohio House of Reps 1970–74, Majority Whip 1972–74; Lt-Gov. of Ohio 1975–79, Gov. 1983–91; Dir US Peace Corps, Washington, DC 1979–81; Man. Pnr, Celeste and Sabety Ltd (econ. devt consultancy), Cleveland 1991–97; Amb. to India 1997–2001; Pres. Colorado Coll. 2002–11; Chair. Midwestern Govs' Conf. 1987–88; Great Lakes Govs' Asscn 1987–89; Chair. Bd of Trustees Health Effects Inst., Boston; Lifetime Nat. Assoc., The Nat. Acads; Visiting Fellow in Public Policy, Case Western Reserve Univ. 1995–97; mem. Bd of Dirs Nat. Asscn of Ind. Colls and Univs 2006–08, Garden City Co. 2007–; Pres. Colorado Springs Downtown Partnership; Trustee Glimcher Realty Trust 2007–, the CHF International 2012–; mem. Advisory Bd Inst. of Int. Educ. 2003–; Leadership Council of ServiceNation 2008–; mem. Council on Foreign Relations; Hatch Prize, Yale Univ. 1959, Delta Sigma Rho-Tau Kappa Alpha Speaker of the Year Award 2006.

CELIŃSKI, Andrzej, MA; Polish politician; b. 26 Feb. 1950, Warsaw; three s.; ed Warsaw Univ.; co-f. Underground Soc. for Scholarly Courses; mem. Workers' Defence Cttee (KOR) and Solidarity Ind. Self-governing Trade Union; mem. Civic Cttee attached to Solidarity leader Lech Wałęsa (q.v.) 1988–90; participant Round Table plenary debates 1989; Senator 1989–93 (mem. Civic Parl. Caucus, then Democratic Union Caucus); Deputy to Sejm (Parl.) 1993–97; Vice-Chair. Democratic Union (UD) 1993–94; mem. Freedom Union (UW) 1994–99; Chair. Programme Comm., then Vice-Chair. Democratic Left Alliance (SLD) 1999–2004; Minister of Culture and Nat. Heritage 2001–02; mem. Mazowieckie Voivodship regional parl. 2006–07; co-founder Polish Social Democracy (SDPL) 2004 (left party 2008); returned to Sejm as ind. deputy 2008. *Address:* Sejm, Wiejska 4/6/8, 00-902 Warsaw (office); Polish Deputies' Office, Wojewódzka 23/3, 40-026 Katowice, Poland (office). *Telephone:* (32) 2090819 (office). *E-mail:* biuro_celinski@wp.pl (office).

CENNETOĞLU, Banu, BA; Turkish artist; b. 1970, Ankara; ed Bogazici Univ., Istanbul; lived in New York 1996–2002 and Amsterdam 2002–04; guest artist, Rijksakademie, Amsterdam; moved to Istanbul 2006; works with photography, installation and printed media; f. BAS (innovative project space), Istanbul 2006; chosen to represent Turkey at 53rd Int. Venice Biennial 2009. *Address:* BAS, Necati Bey Caddesi no 32/2, Karakoy, Istanbul, Turkey (office). *E-mail:* bcennetoglu@hotmail.com (office). *Website:* www.b-a-s.info (office).

CENTENO, Pavel; Guatemalan economist, academic and government official; *Minister of Public Finance;* ed Univ. of Guadalajara, Mexico; Founding mem. Partido Patriota; economist, Universidad de San Carlos de Guatemala (USAC); econ. and financial adviser to numerous pvt. cos and banking insts; fmr adviser to Vice-Pres., Faculty of Social Sciences, Latin American School of Social Sciences (FLACSO), Guatemala; has taught in Guatemala, Mexico, the Netherlands and Norway at various academic insts including Centro Universitario de Ciencias Económico Administrativas, Univ. of Guadalajara, Univ. of San Carlos, Inst. of European–Latin American Relations, Univ. of Central Netherlands (HMN); fmr adviser to various govt bodies including Planning Secr., Presidency of the Repub.; Minister of Public Finance 2011–. *Address:* Ministry of Public Finance, Centro Cívico, 8A Avenida y 21 Calle, Zona 1, Guatemala City, Guatemala (office). *Telephone:* 2322-8888 (ext. 11810, 11805, 11800) (office). *Fax:* 2322-8907 (office). *Website:* www.minfin.gob.gt (office).

CENTENO NAJARRO, Humberto; Salvadorean politician and fmr trade unionist; *Minister of Internal Affairs;* b. 14 Dec. 1941, Concepcion Ataco Ahuachapán; m.; fmr mem. Partido Comunista; co-f. Salvadorean Asscn of Telecommunications Workers (trade union); mem. Asamblea Legislativa for Ahuachapán (Frente Farabundo Martí para la Liberación Nacional, FMLN) 1994–; Minister of Internal Affairs 2009–. *Address:* Ministry of Internal Affairs, Centro de Gobierno, Edif. B-1, Alameda Juan Pablo II y Avda Norte 17, San Salvador, El Salvador (office). *Telephone:* 2233-7000 (office). *Fax:* 2233-7018 (office). *E-mail:* DT@gobernacion.gob.sv (office); hcenteno@asamblea.gob.sv. *Website:* www.gobernacion.gob.sv (office).

CENTERMAN, Jörgen, MSc; Swedish business executive; *Chairman, Gunnebo Industrier AB;* b. 1951; ed Univ. of Tech. of Lund; joined ABB 1976, worked in Singapore, Sweden, Germany, USA, Switzerland, Head of Automation –2000, Pres. and CEO 2001–02 (resgnd); Chair. HMS Industrial Networks AB 2004–09; Chair. Gunnebo Industrier AB 2008–, also Chair. Dacke PMC, Kemetyl Holding AB; mem. Bd of Dirs Micronic Laser Systems AB 2004–, Telelogic, XPonCard, Segulah Advisor AB; mem. Int. Advisory Group, Blekinge Inst. of Technology. *Address:* Gunnebo Industrier AB, Bruksvägen 3, 590 93 Gunnebo, Sweden (office). *Telephone:* (490) 89-000 (office). *Fax:* (490) 89-198 (office). *E-mail:* info@ gunneboindustries.com (office). *Website:* www.gunneboindustries.com (office).

ČEPĀNIS, Alfreds; Latvian banker and fmr politician; *Deputy Chairman, Trasta komercbanka—TKB (Trust Commercial Bank);* b. 3 Aug. 1943, Kalsnava, Madona Region; m. Ilma Čepane; one d.; ed Jaungolbene School of Agric., Higher CP School in Moscow by correspondence; Comsomol functionary 1968–74; Deputy Chair., Chair. Ventspils District Exec. Cttee 1975–79; Sec. Preili Regional Cttee Latvian CP 1979–84; First Sec. Liepaja Regional CP Cttee 1983–88; Deputy Chair. Council of Ministers 1989–90; mem. Supreme Soviet of Latvia 1990–93; mem. Saeima (Parl.), Deputy Speaker 1993–95; mem. faction Demikratiska Partija Samnieks 1995, Speaker 1996–98; Gen. Man. Euroconsultant (consultancy) 1998–2006; currently Deputy Chair. Trasta komercbanka—TKB (Trust Commercial Bank), Rīga; currently Head Soc. for the Promotion of Latvian–Belarusian Econ. Relations. *Leisure interests:* hunting, literature, theatre. *Address:* Trasta komercbanka, Miesnieku iela 9, Rīga 1050, Latvia (office). *Telephone:* 6702-7777 (office). *Fax:* 6702-7700 (office). *E-mail:* info@tkb.lv (office). *Website:* www.tkb.lv (office).

CERF, Vinton (Vint) Gray, MSc, PhD; American computer scientist; *Chief Internet Evangelist, Google Inc.;* b. 23 June 1943, New Haven, Conn.; m. Sigrid Cerf; two s.; ed Van Nuys High School, Stanford Univ., Univ. of California, Los Angeles; began career working for N American Aviation, Rocketdyne, then IBM; Prof. of Computer Science, Stanford Univ. 1972–76, worked on ARPANET (earliest packet switched computer network); Head of Internet, Packet Radio, Packet Satellite and Network Security Research and Devt Program, Advanced Research Projects Agency (DARPA), US Dept of Defense 1976–82; played key role in devt of the Internet and TCP/IP protocols; Vice-Pres. MCI Digital Information Services 1982–86, led eng of MCI Mail (first commercial email service on internet), Sr Vice-Pres. of Internet Architecture and Tech. 1994–2005; headed several research projects including digital libraries, Corpn for Nat. Research Initiatives 1986–94; f. Internet Soc. (ISOC) 1992, Pres. 1992–95, Chair. 1999; Chief Internet Evangelist, Google Inc. 2005–; currently consultant on Interplanetary Protocol, Jet Propulsion Lab., NASA; mem. US Presidential Information Tech. Advisory Cttee (PITAC) 1997–2001; mem. Bd Internet Corpn for Assigned Names and Numbers (ICANN) 1999–2007, Chair. –2007; Commr, Broadband Comm. for Digital Devt 2010–; serves on several nat., state and industry cttees focused on cyber-security; mem. Bd of Dirs Endowment for Excellence in Educ.; mem. Asscn for Computing Machinery (ACM) 1967, Fellow 1993, Pres. 2012–14; mem. Nat. Science Bd, mem. Bulgarian Pres. Georgi Parvanov's IT Advisory Council 2002–12, Advisory Bd of Eurasia Group, Bd of Advisors of The Liquid Information Co. Ltd (UK); Chair. StopBadware; Co-Chair. Campus Party Silicon Valley; Foreign mem. Royal Swedish Acad. of Eng; Fellow, IEEE, AAAS, American Acad. of Arts and Sciences, Int. Eng Consortium, Computer History Museum, Nat. Acad. of Eng, American Philosophical Soc.; Hon. Chair. IPv6 Forum; Freeman of the City of London; Distinguished Fellow, British Computer Soc. 2011; Presidential Medal of Freedom 2005, Medal of Science (Tunisia); Dr hc from 20 univs; numerous awards including Marconi Fellowship, NEC Computer and Communications Prize, ITU Silver Medal, IEEE Alexander Graham Bell Medal, IEEE Kobi Kobayahsi Award, ACM Software and Systems Award, Yuri Rubinsky Memorial Award 1995, ACM SIGCOMM Award 1996, US Nat. Medal of Tech. 1997, Kilby Award, Lifetime Achievement Award, Yankee Group/Network World/Interop, IEEE Third Millennium Medal, Computerworld/Smithsonian Leadership Award, J.D. Edwards Leadership Award, Charles Stark Draper Prize, Nat. Acad. of Eng 2001, Premio Principe de Asturias de Investigacion Cientifica (Spain) 2002, Alexander Graham Bell Asscn for the Deaf and Hard of Hearing Award, World Inst. on Disability

Annual Award, Library of Congress Bicentennial Living Legend Medal, ACM Turing Award 2005, US Presidential Medal of Freedom 2005, Medal of Science (Tunisia), St Cyril and St Methodius Medal (Bulgaria), Dickinson Coll. Joseph Priestley Award, Japan Prize 2008, HPI Fellowship 2011, inducted into Internet Hall of Fame 2012, Queen Elizabeth Prize for Eng (co-recipient) 2013. *Publications include*: A Protocol for Packet Network Intercommunication (co-author with Bob Kahn) 1974, Networks, Scientific American Special Issue on Communications, Computers, and Networks 1991, Guidelines for Internet Measurement Activities 1991; numerous articles in professional journals. *Leisure interests*: fine wine, gourmet cooking, science fiction. *Address*: Google Inc., 1818 Library Street, Reston, VA 20190, USA (office). *Telephone*: (202) 370-5637 (office). *Fax*: (703) 935-0228 (office). *E-mail*: vint@google.com (office). *Website*: www.google.com (office).

CERIC, Mustafa, PhD; Bosnia and Herzegovina ecclesiastic; *Grand Mufti of Bosnia-Herzegovina and President, Council of Ulema*; b. 5 Feb. 1952, Veliko Cajno; m.; one s. two d.; ed Medressa, Sarajevo, Al-Azhar Univ., Cairo, Egypt, Univ. of Chicago, USA; returned to Bosnia from Egypt and became an imam; Imam of US Islamic Cultural Center of Greater Chicago 1981–87; Grand Imam of Zagreb, Croatia 1987–, of Sanjak, Croatia and Slovenia; Grand Mufti of Bosnia-Herzegovina 1993–; currently Reis-ul-Ulema (Pres. Council of Ulema); Prof., Int. Inst. of Islamic Thought and Civilization, Kuala Lumpur 1991–92; has delivered numerous lectures and led several workshops on inter-religious and inter-faith issues at local and int. confs; mem. Interreligious Council of Bosnia-Herzegovina, Council of 100 Leaders of the World Econ. Forum, European Council for Fatwas and Research, World Conf. on Religion and Peace, European Council of Religious Leaders; mem. Exec. Bd Foundation for Srebrenica/Potocari Memorial and Cemetery, Sarajevo; mem. Sharia'h Bd Bosnia Bank Int., Fiqh Acad., Mecca, Aal Albayt Foundation for Islamic Thought, Jordan, Int. Comm. for Peace Research; mem. Advisory Council Tony Blair Faith Foundation; Trustee, Int. Islamic Univ., Islamabad; co-recipient UNESCO Félix Houphouët-Boigny Peace Prize for Contrib. to World Peace 2003, Int. Council of Christians and Jews Sir Sigmund Sternberg Award for Exceptional Contrib. to Inter-faith Understanding, 2003, Theodor-Heuss-Stiftung Award 2007, Association of Muslim Social Scientists UK Lifetime Achievement 2007, 2008. *Publications*: several books in Bosnian, including Roots of Synthetic Theology in Islam, A Choice Between War and Peace, European Muslim Declaration. *Address*: c/o European Council of Religious Leaders, PO Box 6820, 0130 Oslo, Norway.

ČERNÁK, Ľudovít, Ing., PhDr; Slovak politician and business executive; *President, Sitno Holding a.s.*; b. 12 Oct. 1951, Hliník nad Hronom; s. of Ludovít Černák and Gabriela Černákova (née Chmelova); m. (divorced); three c.; ed Univ. of Tech., Bratislava, Technical Univ., Kosicee, Univ. of Birmingham, UK; man. training in UK 1990; fmr Chair. Slovak Nat. Party (SNP); Minister of Economy 1992–93, 1998–2000; Vice-Chair. Nat. Council 1993–94; fmr mem. Parl. of Slovakia; fmr Vice-Chair. Democratic Union; mem. Int. Cttee for Econ. Reform and Co-operation 2000; in pvt business (investment, finance, offsets) 2000–, Pres. Sitno Holdings a.s.; Pres. Slovak Defence Industry Asscn 2005–07, 2010–; Owner and Pres. Sk Slovan Bratislava Football Club 2005–08; Pres., Slovak-Russian Business Council 2006–12; Hon. Chancellor of Uzbekistan in Slovakia 2009–. *Leisure interests*: family, detective novels, tourism, football. *Address*: Sitno Holding a.s., Zechenterova 328/5, 67 01 Kremnica (office); Sitno Holding a.s., Lakeside Park 1, Tomasikova 64, Bratislava (office); Buková 8, 811 01 Bratislava, Slovakia (home). *Telephone*: (2) 39900007 (office). *Fax*: (2) 39900008 (office). *E-mail*: lcernak@sitno.sk (office). *Website*: www.sitnobusiness.com (office).

CERNAN, Capt. (retd) Eugene (Gene) Andrew, BS, MS; American business executive, fmr navy officer and fmr astronaut; *President and CEO, Cernan Corporation*; b. 14 March 1934, Chicago; s. of Andrew G. Cernan; m. 1st Barbara Cernan 1961 (divorced 1980); m. 2nd Jan Nanna Cernan 1987; three d.; ed Purdue Univ., US Naval Post Grad. School; joined USN 1956, mem. attack squadrons 126, 113, Miramar naval air station, retd as Capt. 1976; joined NASA 1963, originally selected as back-up pilot for Gemini IX-A (manned space flight), later became prime crew 1966, Lunar Module Pilot of Apollo X (fourth manned mission of US space program) 1969, Commdr Apollo XVII (last manned mission to the Moon) 1972, apptd Special Asst to Program Man., Apollo Spacecraft Program, Johnson Space Center 1973, assisted in planning, devt, evaluation of joint US-USSR Apollo-Soyuz mission, served as Sr US negotiator with USSR on Apollo-Soyuz Test Project 1973–75, retd from NASA 1976; Exec. Vice-Pres. International Coral Petroleum Inc. 1976–81; Founder-Pres. and CEO Cernan Corpn 1981–; Exec. Consultant for Aerospace and Govt, Digital Equipment Corp. 1986–92; Chair. Johnson Eng Corpn 1994–2000; mem. Bd of Dirs Smithsonian Nat. Air and Space Museum, Young Astronaut Council, US Space Foundation; mem. Pres.'s Engineering Council, Purdue Univ.; mem. Soc. of Experimental Test Pilots, Asscn of Naval Aviation, Tail Hook Asscn, American Inst. of Aeronautics and Astronautics, American Astronautical Soc., Early and Pioneer Naval Aviators Asscn, Explorers Club; Fellow, American Astronautical Soc.; mem. Bd of Trustees, US Naval Aviation Museum Foundation, NFL Alumni and Major League Baseball Players Alumni, Hope for a Drug-Free America Foundation; Navy Distinguished Flying Cross, Distinguished Service Medal with Star, NASA Distinguished Service Medal, Grand Officer, Order of the White Double Cross (Slovakia); Dr hc (Western State Univ. Coll. of Law) 1969, (Purdue Univ.) 1970, (Drexel Univ.) 1977, (Gonzaga Univ., Slovakia), (Comenius Univ., Slovakia), (Northwestern Univ.) 1978; VFW Nat. Space Medal 1973, Nat. Eng Washington Award 2003, NASA Amb. of Exploration Award 2005, Wright Brothers Master Pilot Award 2006, Lindbergh Spirit Award 2007, Wright Brothers Memorial Trophy 2008, Rotary Nat. Award for Space Achievement 2008, Fed. Aeronautique Internationale Gold Medal for Space 2008, World Recognition Award, Slovakia, Slovakia Presidential Medal of Honor, Daughters of the American Revolution Medal for Space, Sons of the American Revolution George Washington Award, inducted into Nat. Aviation Hall of Fame 2006, US Space Hall of Fame, Naval Aviation Hall of Honor, Int. Aerospace Hall of Fame, and numerous others. *Achievements include*: second American to walk in space and the last man to have walked on the moon. *Film*: In the Shadow of the Moon. *Television*: contrib.: ABC News and Good Morning America. *Publication*: The Last Man on the Moon: Astronaut Eugene Cernan and America's Race in Space (with Donald A. Davis) 1999. *Leisure interests*: hunting, fishing, flying. *Address*: Cernan Corporation, 900 Town and Country Lane 300, Houston, TX 77024-2233, USA (office). *Telephone*: (713) 827-9922 (office). *Website*: www.genecernan.com.

CEROVSKÝ, Gen. Milan, DipEng; Slovak army officer; b. 10 Oct. 1949, Kalinovo; m.; two c.; ed Mil. Acad., Vyškov; Mil. Acad., Brno, Royal Coll. of Defence, London, UK; began career with Hungarian armed forces 1971, positions include platoon and co. Commdr 1971–74; Deputy Chief of Staff 60th Tank Regt, 14th Tank Div., E Mil. Dist, Commdr Tank Battalion; Chief of Staff 63rd Mechanized Regt, 14th Tank Div., Commdr; Chief of Staff 13th Tank Div., Deputy Commdr of Operations, Commdr 1993–94; Commdr 1st Army Corps 1994–98; Chief of Integration and Standardization Admin. of Army Gen. Staff 1998, Chief of Gen. Staff of Army 1998–2002, of Armed Forces 2002–04; rank of Lt-Gen. 1999–2003, Gen. 2003–. *Leisure interest*: sport. *Address*: c/o Ministry of Defence, Kutuzovova 7, 832 28 Bratislava, Slovakia (office). *Telephone*: (2) 4425-0329 (office). *Fax*: (2) 4425-3242 (office). *Website*: www.mod.gov.sk (office).

CERRATO RODRIGUEZ, Wilfredo Rafael; Honduran economist and politician; *Minister of Finance*; b. 1971; s. of Wilfredo Cerrato; ed Universidad Tecnológica Centroamericana, Central American Inst. of Business Admin (INCAE); held positions in pvt. banking and agribusiness cos and public admin, including as Pres. Coalianza—Comisionado para la Promoción de las Alianzas Público Privadas (Comm. for the Promotion of Public-Private Partnerships) –2012; Minister of Finance 2012–. *Address*: Ministry of Finance, Edif. SEFIN, Avda Cervantes, Barrio El Jazmín, Tegucigalpa, Honduras (office). *Telephone*: 2222-0112 (office). *Fax*: 2238-2309 (office). *E-mail*: sgeneral@sefin.gob.hn (office). *Website*: www.sefin.gob.hn (office).

CERUTTI, Dominique; French business executive; *Deputy CEO and President, NYSE Euronext, Inc.*; b. 1961; with Bouygues (civil eng co.), Saudi Arabia 1994–96; joined IBM 1986, served in various man. roles in sales eng and sales man., becoming Dir Personal Systems Group, W Region 1996–98, Exec. Asst to IBM Chair. and CEO, New York 1998–99, Gen. Man. IBM Global Services, W Region 2000, later Gen. Man., IBM Global Services in Europe, Middle East and Africa, Paris, mem. IBM Sr Leadership Team and Gen. Man. IBM SW Europe 2005–09; Deputy CEO NYSE Euronext Paris SA 2009–, Global Head of Tech. 2009–10, also Pres. Euronext Paris and Chair. Managing Bd, Euronext NV, Pres. NYSE Euronext, Inc. at NYSE Technologies, Inc. 2010–. *Address*: NYSE Euronext, Société des bourses françaises, 39 rue Cambon, 75001 Paris, France (office). *Telephone*: 1-49-27-10-00 (office). *Fax*: 1-49-27-14-33 (office). *Website*: www .euronext.fr (office); www.nyse.com (office).

CERUTTI, Guillaume; French business executive and fmr civil servant; *Deputy Chairman Europe and CEO, Sotheby's France*; ed École Nationale d'Admin, Strasbourg, Institut d'Études Politiques de Paris; began career in French Treasury's Dept for Auditing Public Bodies 1991; served as Financial Advisor to the Secrétariat Général pour les Affaires Européennes (Office for European Affairs); Man. Dir Centre Pompidou, Paris 1996–2001; Chief of Staff to the Minister for Culture and Communication, Jean-Jacques Aillagon 2002–04; Head of Dept of Competition Policy, Consumer Affairs and Fraud Control, Ministry for the Economy and Finance 2004–07; CEO Sotheby's France 2007–, Deputy Chair. Sotheby's Europe 2011–; mem. Bd of Dirs Ingenico SA 2010–, Flamel Technologies SA 2011–; Chair. Accentus vocal ensemble; Pres. Inst. for Financing Film and Cultural Industries; mem. Cttee of Honour of the Friends of the French Cinémathèque. *Publication*: Création et Internet (report, with Patrick Zelnik and Jacques Toubon) 2010. *Address*: Sotheby's France, Galerie Charpentier, 76 rue du Faubourg Saint-Honoré, 75008 Paris, France (office). *Telephone*: 1-53-05-53-12 (office). *Fax*: 1-47-42-22-32 (office). *E-mail*: guillaume.cerutti@sothebys.com (office). *Website*: www.sothebys.com (office).

CÉSAR, Carlos Manuel Martins do Vale; Portuguese politician; *President, Regional Government of the Azores*; b. 30 Oct. 1956, Ponta Delgada; s. of Aurélio Augusto César and Maria Natália Martins do Vale César; m. Luísa Maria Assís Vital Gomes; one s.; ed Antero de Quental High School, Faculty of Law, Lisbon; f. Socialist Youth and Socialist Party 1974, mem. Nat. Exec. Socialist Party 1975–; Asst to State Sec. for Public Admin 1977–78; Deputy, Regional Ass. 1980–96, Vice-Pres. –1996; Pres. Regional Govt of the Azores 1996–; mem. State Council, Higher Nat. Defence Council, Higher Internal Security Council, Cttee of the Regions, Ass. of European Regions, Conf. of Presidents of Ultra-peripheral Regions, Conf. of Peripheral Maritime Regions of Europe, Congress of Local Regional Authorities of Europe. *Address*: Residência do Presidente, Governo Regional, Palácio de Santana, 9500-077 Ponta Delgada, The Azores (office). *Telephone*: (296) 301000 (office). *Fax*: (296) 628890 (office). *E-mail*: presidencia@azores.gov.pt (office). *Website*: www .azores.gov.pt (office).

CESCAU, Patrick Jean-Pierre, MBA; French business executive; b. 27 Sept. 1948, Paris; s. of Pierre Cescau and Louise Cescau; m. Ursula Kadanski; one s. one d.; ed Institut Européen d'Admin des Affaires (INSEAD); joined Unilever France as org. officer 1973, sr consultant –1977, held post at Astra-Calvé and served as Chief Accountant, UDL Germany 1980–84, Commercial mem. Edible Fats and Dairy Co-ordination, Rotterdam, Netherlands 1984–86, Financial Dir Unilever Indonesia 1986–89, Nat. Man., Unilever Portugal 1989–91, Chair. PT Unilever Indonesia 1991–95, Pres. and CEO Van den Bergh Foods, USA 1995–96, Pres. and CEO Lipton, USA (following merger of Van den Bergh and Lipton) 1997–98, Controller and Deputy Financial Dir Unilever 1998–99, Financial Dir 1999–2000, Head, Bestfoods integration team 2000–01, Dir Unilever Global Foods Div. 2001, Chair. Unilever PLC and mem. Exec. Cttee, Unilever NV 2004–05, Group CEO 2005–08; Chair., Nat. Asscn of Margarine Mfrs 1996–98; mem. Bd of Dirs Pearson PLC 2002–, INSEAD 2009–; mem. Exec. Cttee, Tea Council 1997–98; Chevalier, Légion d'honneur 2004. *Leisure interests*: arts, reading, photography, theatre. *Address*: c/o Board of Directors, INSEAD, Boulevard de Constance, 77305 Fontainebleau, Paris, France. *Website*: www.insead.edu.

ÇETİN, Hikmet; Turkish politician; b. 1937, Diyarbakir; m.; two c.; ed Ankara Univ. Political Sciences Faculty, Williams Coll., USA; Sec.-Gen. Social Democratic Populist Party (SHP) (merged to form Republican People's Party), Chair. 1995; Deputy from Gaziantep; Minister of Foreign Affairs 1991–94; Deputy Prime Minister and Minister of State 1995–96; Speaker, Turkish Parl. 1997–99; Sr Civilian Rep. for Afghanistan, NATO 2003–06. *Address*: Rafet Canitez Cad. No. 3/47, Oran, Ankara, Turkey (home). *Telephone*: (312) 4903696 (home). *E-mail*: hikmetcetin@superonline.com.

CEYER, Sylvia T., AB, PhD; American physical chemist and academic; *John C. Sheehan Professor of Chemistry, Massachusetts Institute of Technology;* b. Chicago, Ill.; ed Hope Coll., Univ. of California, Berkeley; Post-doctoral Fellow, Nat. Bureau of Standards (now Nat. Inst. of Standards and Tech.) 1979–81; joined MIT Faculty 1981, Class of 1943 Career Devt Chair 1985–88, tenure 1987, W.M. Keck Foundation Professorship in Energy 1991–96, John C. Sheehan Prof. of Chem. 1996–, Assoc. Head of Dept of Chem. 2005–10, Head 2010–; held Chem. Chair of NAS 2002–05; Class I Chair of NAS 2009–12; Fellow, NAS, American Physical Soc., American Acad. of Arts and Sciences; Harold E. Edgerton Award 1988, Baker Memorial Award for Excellence in Undergraduate Teaching 1988, Young Scholar Award, American Assn of Univ. Women 1988, ACS Nobel Laureate Signature Award 1993, MIT School of Science Teaching Prize 1993, MacVicar Faculty Fellow 1998, ACS Willard Gibbs Award 2007, Arthur Smith Award 2008, ACS Langmuir Lectureship, Welch Foundation Lectureship. *Publications:* numerous scientific papers in professional journals on dynamics of interactions of molecules with surfaces of materials. *Address:* Room 6-217, Department of Chemistry, Massachusetts Institute of Technology, 77 Massachusetts Avenue, Cambridge, MA 02139-4307, USA (office). *Telephone:* (617) 253-4537 (office). *Fax:* (617) 253-7030 (office). *E-mail:* stceyer@mit.edu (office). *Website:* ceyer.mit.edu (office).

CEYLAN, Nuri Bilge; Turkish photographer and film director; b. 26 Jan. 1959, Bakırköy, Istanbul; s. of Emin Ceylan and Fatma Ceylan; m. Ebru Ceylan; one s.; ed Istanbul Technical Univ., Boğaziçi Univ., Mimar Sinan Univ.; began career as commercial photographer; juror, Cannes Int. Film Competition 2009. *Films directed include:* Koza (Cocoon) (short film) 1995, Kasaba (The Small Town) 1997, Mayis Sikintisi (Clouds of May) 1999, Uzak (Distant) (Cannes Film Festival Grand Jury Prize and Best Actor Prize 2003) 2002, Iklimler (Climates) (Cannes Film Festival FIPRESCI Movie Critics' Award 2006, five awards at 2006 Antalya Golden Orange Film Festival including Best Dir) 2006, Üç Maymun (Three Monkeys) (Cannes Film Festival Best Dir Award 2008) 2008, Bir Zamanlar Anadolu'da (Once Upon a Time in Anatolia) (Cannes Film Festival Grand Jury Prize) 2011. *Publication:* Turkey Cinemascope (photography). *Address:* NBC Film, Başkurt sok. 19/4, Ürgüp Palas apt., Cihangir, 34422 Istanbul, Turkey (office). *E-mail:* info@nbcfilm.com (office). *Website:* www.nuribilgeceylan.com/bio-english .php (office).

CHA, Laura M., BA, JD, JP; Chinese politician, lawyer and business executive; *Member, Executive Council, Government of the Hong Kong Special Administrative Region;* b. 1949; m.; ed Univ. of Wisconsin, Santa Clara Univ., USA; began career as attorney with Pillsbury, Madison & Sutro, San Francisco, Calif. and Coudert Brothers, Hong Kong 1982–90; joined Securities and Futures Comm. (SFC), Hong Kong 1991, Asst Dir then Sr Dir 1991–94, Exec. Dir 1994–2001, Deputy Chair. 1998–2001; Vice-Chair. China Securities Regulatory Comm. 2001–04, Vice-Chair. Int. Advisory Cttee 2004–; apptd to Exec. Council of Govt of Hong Kong Special Admin. Region (HKSAR) 2004–; mem. Shanghai Int. Financial Advisory Council, Shanghai Municipal Govt 2007–; HKSAR Deputy for 11th NPC, People's Repub. of China 2008–13; Standing mem. CPPCC Shanghai Cttee 2008–; Dir (non-exec.) The Hong Kong and Shanghai Banking Corpn Ltd 2004–, Hong Kong Exchanges and Clearing Ltd 2006–12, Tata Consultancy Services Ltd 2006–12, China Telecom Corpn Ltd 2008–, HSBC Holdings Plc 2011–; Sr Int. Adviser, Foundation Asset Man. AB, Sweden; Chair. Univ. Grants Cttee, Hong Kong 2007–11, Advisory Cttee on Corruption, Ind. Comm. Against Corruption in Hong Kong 2007–; mem. Advisory Bd, Yale Center for Corp. Governance, Yale Univ., USA 2006–13, Yale School of Man. 2010–13; mem. ABA, State Bar of Calif., Int. Council of Asian Soc., New York; JP 1995–2001, 2006; Silver Bauhinia Star Medal 2001, Gold Bauhinia Star Medal 2009. *Address:* 23/F China Merchants Tower, Shun Tak Centre, 168 Connaught Road Central, Hong Kong Special Administrative Region, People's Republic of China (office). *Telephone:* 22381217 (office). *Fax:* 29873538 (office). *E-mail:* anita.yiu@hkri.com (office).

CHA, Louis, (Jin Yong), GBM, OBE, BLaw, MA, PhD; Chinese/Hong Kong novelist and essayist; b. 6 Feb. 1924, Haining, Zhejiang, China; m. three times; two s. (one deceased) two d. from 2nd m.; ed Hangzhou High School, Jiaxing High School, Zhejiang Prov., Faculty of Foreign Languages, Central Univ., Chongqing, Faculty of Law, Dongwu Univ., Soochow Univ., St John's Coll., Cambridge, UK; joined newspaper agency Ta Kung Pao in Shanghai as a journalist 1947, posted to Hong Kong div. as a copy editor 1948, transferred to Hsin Wan Pao as Deputy Ed.; began writing first serialized martial arts novel, The Book and the Sword following his meeting with Chen Wentong 1955; worked as a scenarist-dir and scriptwriter at Great Wall Movie Enterprises Ltd and Phoenix Film Co. 1957–59; co-f., with Shen Baoxin, Ming Pao (Hong Kong daily) 1959, first Ed.-in-Chief; writes fiction in wuxia genre (martial arts and chivalry), widespread following in Chinese-speaking regions, including mainland China, Hong Kong, Taiwan, SE Asia and USA; numerous adaptations of his works into films, TV series, manhua (comics) and video games; mem. Hong Kong Basic Law drafting cttee (resgnd following Tiananmen Square massacre 1989); mem. Preparatory Cttee set up by Chinese Govt to supervise Hong Kong's transition 1996; Hon. Prof., Peking Univ., Zhejiang Univ., Nankai Univ., Soochow Univ., Huaqiao Univ., Nat. Tsing Hua Univ., Hong Kong Univ. (Dept of Chinese Studies), Univ. of British Columbia, Sichuan Univ.; Hon. Fellow, St Antony's Coll., Oxford, Robinson Coll., Cambridge; Wynflete Fellow, Magdalen Coll., Oxford; Grand Bauhinia Medal; Chevalier, Légion d'honneur 1992, Commdr, Ordre des Arts et des Lettres 2004; Dr hc (Hong Kong Univ.), (Hong Kong Polytechnic Univ.), (Open Univ. of Hong Kong), Univ. of British Columbia, (Soka Univ.), (Univ. of Cambridge) 2004; Asteroid 10930 Jinyong (1998 CR2) named after him. *Publications include:* The Book and the Sword 1955–56, Sword Stained with Royal Blood 1956, The Legend of the Condor Heroes 1957–59, Fox Volant of the Snowy Mountain 1959, The Return of the Condor Heroes 1959–61, Other Tales of the Flying Fox 1960–61, Swordswoman Riding West on White Horse 1961, Blade-dance of the Two Lovers 1961, Heaven Sword and Dragon Sabre 1961, A Deadly Secret 1963, Demi-Gods and Semi-Devils 1963–66, Ode to Gallantry 1966–67, The Smiling Proud Wanderer 1967–69, The Deer and the Cauldron 1969–72, Sword of the Yue Maiden 1970. *E-mail:* info@ jinyong.com. *Website:* www.jinyong.com.

CHAABANE, Sadok, PhD; Tunisian professor of law and government official; b. 23 Feb. 1950, Sfax; s. of Jilani Chaabane; m. Dalenda Nouri 1974; one s. two d.; ed Univ. of Tunis; Prof. of Law, Univ. of Tunis 1973, now Assoc. Prof. of Public Law and Political Science; Dir of Studies, Research and Publ. Centre 1975–82; Perm. Sec. of RCD 1988; Sec. of State for Higher Educ. and Scientific Research 1989; Adviser to the Pres. on Political Affairs 1990; Sec. of State for Scientific Research 1991; Prin. Adviser to the Pres. on Human Rights 1991; Minister of Justice 1992–97, of Higher Educ., Scientific Research and Tech. 1999–2004; Minister Counselor to the Pres., responsible for Political Affairs and Human Rights; Pres. Econ. and Social Council (Conseil Economique et social) 2007–11; currently mem. Arbitration Cabinet; fmr Dir Tunisian Inst. of Strategic Studies; Founder-mem. Int. Acad. of Constitutional Law, Int. Law Asscn; Commdr, Order of Nov. 7; Great Cordon of Order of the Repub. *Publications:* Hannibal Redux: The Renewal of Modern Tunisia 1977, The Law of International Institutions 1985, The Way to Pluralism in Tunisia 1997, The Future Challenges of Tunisia, La tunisie politique. *Leisure interests:* law, political affairs. *Address:* 30 Rue Mannoubia Ben Nasr, Manar 3, 2092 Tunis, Tunisia. *Telephone:* (71) 889690; 98-848485 (mobile).

CHAABI, Miloud; Moroccan business executive and politician; *President, Ynna Holding;* b. 1929; m.; six c.; began working as farmer and goat herder in early teens; est. small construction co. at age of 18 years with two employees 1948; est. ceramic co. 1964; Founder-Pres. Ynna Holding; launched Electra 1994, Aswak Assalam (group of supermarkets) 1998, Riad Mogador hotel chain 1999; mem. Majlis al-Nuab (Chamber of Reps) 2002, elected Rep. for city of Essaouira 2007; Founder-Pres. Miloud Chaabi Foundation 1965–. *Address:* Ynna Holding, 233 Boulevard Mohamed V, Casablanca, Morocco (office). *Telephone:* (53) 7219400 (office). *Website:* www.ynna.ma (office).

CHABON, Michael, MFA; American writer; b. 1964, Columbia, Md; m. Ayelet Waldman; two s. two d.; ed Univ. of Pittsburgh, Univ. of California, Irvine; Fellow, American Acad. of Arts and Sciences 2009–; Publishers Weekly Best Book 1995, New York Times Notable Book 1995, O. Henry Award 1999. *Publications:* The Mysteries of Pittsburgh 1988, A Model World (short stories) 1991, The Wonder Boys 1995, Werewolves in Their Youth (short stories) 1995, The Amazing Adventures of Kavalier & Clay (Pulitzer Prize for fiction 2001) 2000, The Final Solution 2005, The Yiddish Policemen's Union (novel) (Nebula Award for Best Novel 2008, Hugo Award for Best Novel 2008) 2007, Gentlemen of the Road 2007, Maps and Legends: Reading and Writing along the Borderlands 2008, Manhood for Amateurs: The Pleasures and Regrets of a Husband, Father, and Son 2009, Telegraph Avenue 2012; contrib. short stories to several magazines. *Address:* Steven Barclay Agency, 12 Western Avenue, Petaluma, CA 94952, USA (office). *Telephone:* (707) 773-0654 (office). *Fax:* (707) 778-1868 (office). *Website:* michaelchabon.com (office).

CHABRAJA, Nicholas D., BA, JD; American lawyer and defence industry executive; *Chairman, General Dynamics Corporation;* b. 6 Nov. 1942, Gary, Ind.; ed Northwestern Univ.; lawyer, Jenner and Block (law firm) 1968–1997, Partner 1984–93; 1986, Special Counsel to US House of Reps 1986; Sr Vice-Pres. and Gen. Counsel, Gen. Dynamics Corpn 1993–94, Exec. Vice-Pres. 1994–96, Vice-Chair. 1996–97, Chair. and CEO 1997–2009, Chair. 2009–; mem. Bd of Dirs Ceridian Corpn, Northern Trust Co. 2007–; mem. Kennedy Center Corp. Fund Bd. *Address:* General Dynamics Corpn, 2941 Fairview Park Drive, Suite 100, Falls Church, VA 22042-4513, USA (office). *Telephone:* (703) 876-3000 (office). *Fax:* (703) 876-3125 (office). *E-mail:* info@gendyn.com (office). *Website:* www.gendyn.com (office).

CHACÓN PIQUERAS, Carme, LLD; Spanish politician; b. 13 March 1971, Esplugues de Llobregat, Barcelona; m.; one s.; ed Univ. of Barcelona, Osgoode Hall Law School, Toronto, Univ. of Kingston, Univ. of Montréal, Canada; Prof. of Constitutional Law, Univ. of Girona 1994–2004; Sec. of Educ., Culture and Research, Exec. Comm., Spanish Socialist Workers' Party (PSOE) 2000–04, mem. Fed. Exec. Comm. 2000–; mem. Parl. (PSOE) for Barcelona 2000–, Vice-Pres. Congress of Deputies (Lower House) 2004–07; Minister of Housing 2007–08, of Defence 2008–11. *Address:* c/o Ministry of Defence, Paseo de la Castellana 109, 28071 Madrid, Spain.

CHACÓN RENDÓN, María Cecilia; Bolivian lawyer and politician; *Minister of National Defence;* ed Universidad Mayor de San Simón, Cochabamba, Universidad Andina; early career with Legal Office for Women, Cochabamba and Solon Foundation; fmr mem. Water Task Force, becoming Chief of Staff, Ministry of Water 2006; served in Ministry of Foreign Affairs, first as Chief of Staff and later Dir-Gen. of Multilateral Relations 2008–11; Minister of Nat. Defence 2011–; fmr Bolivian Nat. Coordinator for various int. orgs including Rio Group, OAS Inter-American Comm. Against Drug Abuse, Int. Cttee for Combating Terrorism. *Address:* Ministry of National Defence, Calle 20 de Octubre 2502, esq. Pedro Salazar, La Paz, Bolivia (office). *Telephone:* (2) 243-2525 (office). *Fax:* (2) 243-3153 (office). *E-mail:* utransparencia@mindef.gob.bo (office). *Website:* www.mindef.gob .bo (office).

CHADERTON MATOS, Roy; Venezuelan politician and diplomatist; b. 17 Aug. 1942; ed Cen. Univ. of Venezuela, Instituto de Altos Estudios de Defensa Nacional; Second Sec., Embassy in Poland 1969–72, First Sec., Embassy in FRG 1973, Embassy in Canada 1975, Counsellor Embassy in Belgium 1977–78, Counsellor, Perm. Mission to UN, New York 1978–79, Counsellor, Embassy in Ottawa 1979, Minister-Counsellor 1979–82, Deputy Perm. Rep. 1982–83, Amb. to Canada 1983–85, Amb. to Gabon 1985–87, to Norway and Iceland 1987–90, Gen. Dir of Int. Political Affairs 1990–93, to Canada 1993–94, Gen. Dir (Vice-Pres.) 1994–95, Amb. to UK and Ireland 1996–2000, to Colombia 2000–02, to USA 2002, Minister of Foreign Affairs 2002–04, Amb. to France 2004–07, to Mexico 2007–08, to OAS 2008–09; mem. Social Christian Party of Venezuela 1958–; Official Rep. 1994; Caballero de Madara Order (Bulgaria), Francisco de Miranda Order, First Class (Venezuela), Bernardo O'Higgins Order (Chile), Great Cross, May Order (Argentina), Great Cross, San Olav Order (Norway), Great Cross, Cruceiro do Sul National Order (Brazil), Great Cord Libertador Order (Venezuela). *Address:* Ministry of Foreign Affairs, Torre MRE, al lado del Correo de Carmelitas, Avda Urdaneta, Caracas 1010, Venezuela (office). *Telephone:* (212) 806-4400 (office). *Fax:* (212) 861-2505 (office). *E-mail:* web.master@mre.gov.ve (office). *Website:* www .mre.gov.ve (office).

CHADIRJI, Rifat Kamil, DipArch, FRIBA; Iraqi architect; b. 6 Dec. 1926, Baghdad; s. of Kamil Chadirji; m. Balkis Sharara 1954; ed Hammersmith School of Arts and Crafts, London; Founder and Sr Partner and Dir Iraq Consult 1952–;

Section Head, Baghdad Bldg Dept Waqaf Org. 1954–57; Dir-Gen. of Housing, Ministry of Planning, Baghdad 1958–59, Head of Planning Cttee Ministry of Housing 1959–63; returned to full-time pvt. practice with Iraq Consult 1963–78; apptd Counsellor to Mayoralty of Baghdad 1980–82; mem. Iraqi Tourist Bd 1970–75; Loeb Fellow, Harvard Univ. 1983; Hon. Fellow, RIBA, AIA; numerous awards including First Prize for Council of Ministers Bldg, Baghdad 1975, First Prize New Theatre, Abu Dhabi, UAE 1977, First Prize, Council of Ministers, Abu Dhabi, UAE 1978. *Works include:* Council of Ministers Bldg, Baghdad 1975, Cabinet Ministers' Bldg, UAE 1976, Nat. Theatre, Abu Dhabi, UAE 1977, Al-Ain Public Library, UAE 1978. *Leisure interests:* photography, travel.

CHADLINGTON, Baron (Life Peer), cr. 1996, of Dean in the County of Oxfordshire; **Peter Selwyn Gummer,** MA, FRSA; British business executive; *CEO, Huntsworth plc;* b. 24 Aug. 1942, Bexley; s. of the late Rev. Canon Selwyn Gummer and (Margaret) Sybille Gummer (née Mason); brother of The Rt Hon Lord Deben (John Selwyn Gummer (q.v.)); m. Lucy Rachel Dudley-Hill 1982; one s. three d.; ed King's School, Rochester, Selwyn Coll., Cambridge; with Portsmouth & Sunderland Newspaper Group 1964–65, Viyella Int. 1965–66, Hodgkinson & Partners 1966–67, Industrial & Commercial Finance Corpn (3i Group) 1967–74; Founder, Chair. and Chief Exec. Shandwick PLC 1974–94, Chair. 1994–2000; Dir (non-exec.) CIA Group PLC 1990–94, non-exec. mem. Halifax Building Society London Bd 1990–94, Dir (non-exec.) Halifax PLC 1994–2001, Black Box Music Ltd 1999–2001, Oxford Resources 1999–2002, Chair. Hotcourses Ltd 2000–04, Britax Childcare Holdings Ltd 2005–; CEO Huntsworth PLC 2000–; mem. EU Select Sub-cttee B (Energy, Industry and Transport), House of Lords 2000–03; Chair. Action on Addiction 2000–07; mem. Nat. Health Service Policy Bd 1991–95, Chair. Royal Opera House 1996–97, Understanding Industry Trust 1991–96, Arts Council of England (fmrly GB) 1991–96, Marketing Group of GB 1993–95, Nat. Lottery Advisory Bd for the Arts and Film 1994–96; Int. Public Relations 1998–2000, Guideforlife.com 2000–02; Dir Walbrook Club 1999–2004; Chair. Chadlington Consultancy 1999–, LAPADA 2011–; mem. Council, Cheltenham Ladies Coll. 1998–2003, Bd of Trustees, American Univ. 1999–2001, British Heart Foundation Mending Broken Hearts Appeal Cttee 2010–; Hon. Fellow, Bournemouth Univ. 1999–; Trustee, Atlantic Partnership 1999–; Governor, The Ditchley Foundation 2008–; Inst. of Public Relations Pres.'s Medal 1988, PR Week Award for Outstanding Individual Contrib. to Public Relations 1994, Ernst & Young Entrepreneur of the Year 2008. *Publications:* articles and booklets on public relations and marketing. *Leisure interests:* opera, cricket, rugby. *Address:* Huntsworth PLC, 15–17 Huntsworth Mews, London, NW1 6DD (office). *Telephone:* (20) 7298-6583 (office). *Fax:* (20) 7493-3048 (office). *E-mail:* lordchadlington@huntsworth.com (office). *Website:* www.huntsworth.co.uk (office).

CHADWICK, Michael J. (Mike), MA, PhD; British environmental scientist and academic; b. 13 Sept. 1934, Leicester, England; s. of John Chadwick and Hilda Corman; m. Josephine Worrall 1958; one s. two d.; ed Godalming Co. Grammar School and Univ. Coll. of North Wales, Bangor; Lecturer, Dept of Botany, Univ. of Khartoum, Sudan 1959–62; Univ. Demonstrator, School of Agric., Univ. of Cambridge 1962–66; Lecturer and Prof., Dept of Biology, Univ. of York 1966–91; Dir Stockholm Environment Inst., Stockholm, Sweden 1991–96; Dir LEAD-Europe, Geneva, Switzerland 1996–; Sr Research Assoc., Stockholm Environment Inst.'s York Centre; now works as pvt. consultant on environmental matters, most recently with MISTRA in Sweden, Intergovernmental Panel on Climate Change, EU projects and Rockefeller Foundation on poverty alleviation and sustainable livelihoods; fmr Sec., British Ecological Soc.; Hon. Visiting Prof., Depts of Environment and Biology, Univ. of York; Award for Contributing to Nobel Peace Prize 2007 given to Intergovernmental Panel on Climate Change. *Publications:* Restoration of Land (with A. D. Bradshaw) 1980, The Relative Sensitivity of Ecosystems in Europe to Acidic Depositions (with J. C. I. Kuylenstierna) 1990, A Perspective on Global Air Pollution Problems (with J. C. I. Kuylenstierna and W. K. Hicks) 2002. *Leisure interests:* music, gardening, travel. *Address:* Stockholm Environment Institute, Grimston House, University of York, Heslington, York, YO10 5DD (office); 3 Skipwith Road, Escrick, York, YO19 6JT, England (home). *Telephone:* (1904) 728025 (office); (1904) 728234 (home). *Fax:* (1904) 728025 (office). *E-mail:* cmjchadwick@aol.com (office).

CHADWICK, Peter, BSc, PhD, ScD, FRS; British mathematician and academic; *Professor Emeritus, School of Mathematics, University of East Anglia;* b. 23 March 1931, Huddersfield, Yorks., England; s. of Jack Chadwick and Marjorie Chadwick (née Castle); m. Sheila G. Salter 1956 (deceased); two d.; ed Huddersfield Coll., Univ. of Manchester, Pembroke Coll., Cambridge; Scientific Officer, then Sr Scientific Officer, Atomic Weapons Research Establishment, Aldermaston 1955–59; Lecturer, then Sr Lecturer in Applied Math., Univ. of Sheffield 1959–65; Prof. of Math., Univ. of East Anglia 1965–91, Prof. Emer. 1991–, Dean, School of Math. and Physics 1979–82, Leverhulme Emer. Fellow 1991–93; Visiting Prof., Univ. of Queensland, Australia 1972; Hon. DSc (Glasgow) 1991. *Publications:* Continuum Mechanics: Concise Theory and Problems 1976, 1999; articles in books and learned journals. *Leisure interests:* walking, music, family and local history. *Address:* 8 Stratford Crescent, Cringleford, Norwich, Norfolk, NR4 7SF, England (home).

CHADWICK, Sir (William) Owen, Kt, OM, KBE, FBA, FRSE; British historian and academic; b. 20 May 1916, Bromley, Kent, England; s. of John Chadwick and Edith Chadwick (née Horrocks); m. Ruth Hallward 1949; two s. two d.; ed St John's Coll., Cambridge; Fellow, Trinity Hall, Cambridge 1947–56, Master of Selwyn Coll., Cambridge 1956–83, Fellow 1983–, Dixie Prof. of Ecclesiastical History, Univ. of Cambridge 1958–68, Regius Prof. of Modern History 1968–83; Vice-Chancellor Univ. of Cambridge 1969–71; Pres. British Acad. 1981–85; Chancellor Univ. of East Anglia 1985–94; Chair. of Trustees Nat. Portrait Gallery 1988–94; Hon. mem. American Acad. of Arts and Sciences; Hon. DD (St Andrews) 1960, (Oxford) 1973, (Wales) 1993; Hon. DLitt (Kent) 1970, (Columbia Univ.) 1977, (East Anglia) 1977, (Bristol) 1977, (London) 1983, (Leeds) 1986, (Cambridge) 1987; Hon. LLD (Aberdeen) 1986; Wolfson Literary Award 1981. *Publications:* From Bossuet to Newman 1957, The Victorian Church (two vols) 1966–70, John Cassian (2nd edn) 1968, The Reformation (20th edn) 1986, The Secularization of the European Mind 1976, The Popes and European Revolution 1981, Britain and the Vatican during the Second World War 1987, Michael Ramsey: A Life 1990, The Christian Church in the Cold War 1992, A History of Christianity 1995, A History of the Popes 1830–1914 1998, The Early Reformation on the Continent 2001; numerous articles and reviews in learned journals. *Leisure interests:* music and gardening. *Address:* 67 Grantchester Street, Cambridge, CB3 9HZ, England (home). *Telephone:* (1223) 314000 (home). *E-mail:* oc207@cam.ac.uk (office).

CHAFEE, Lincoln (Linc) Davenport, BA; American academic, politician and state governor; *Governor of Rhode Island;* b. 26 March 1953, Providence, RI; s. of the late John Lester Hubbard Chafee and of Virginia Chafee (née Coates); m. Stephanie Danforth; one s. two d.; ed Brown Univ., Montana State Univ. Horseshoeing School, Bozeman; farrier, various harness racktracks 1977–83; planner, General Dynamics, Quonset Point 1983; Exec. Dir Northeast Corridor Initiative 1980s; began political career as del. to RI Constitutional Convention 1985–86; with Warwick City Council 1986–92, Mayor of Warwick 1993–99; apptd by Gov. of RI to fill the unexpired term of his father, the late Senator John H. Chafee Nov. 1999, elected Senator from RI 2000–07, mem. Cttee on the Environment and Public Works, Cttee on Foreign Relations, Chair. Sub-cttee on Near Eastern and South Asian Affairs, Jt Econ. Cttee, Sub-cttee on Superfund, Waste Control and Risk Assessment, Sub-cttee on Western Hemisphere, Peace Corps, Narcotics and Terrorism; Gov. of Rhode Island 2011–; Distinguished Visiting Fellow, Thomas J. Watson, Jr Inst. for Int. Studies, Brown Univ. 2007–; mem. Republican Party –2007 (resgnd), Ind. 2007–; Francis M. Driscoll Award for Leadership, Scholarship and Athletics, Brown Univ., Fiscal Responsibility Award, Concord Coalition 2003, Congressional Award, Nat. Breast Cancer Coalition 2004. *Publication:* Against the Tide: How a Compliant Congress Empowered a Reckless President 2008. *Leisure interests:* skiing, horseback trail riding. *Address:* Office of the Governor, 82 Smith Street, Providence, RI 02903, USA (office). *Telephone:* (401) 222-2080 (office). *Fax:* (401) 222-8096 (office). *E-mail:* governor@governor.ri.gov (office). *Website:* www.governor.state.ri.us (office); www.governor.ri.gov (office).

CHAGOURY, Gilbert; Nigerian/Lebanese business executive and diplomatist; *Co-Founder, Chagoury Group;* b. 8 Jan. 1946, Lagos; s. of Ramez Chagoury and Alice Chagoury; m. Rose Marie Chamchoum; four c.; ed Coll. des Frères Chrétiens, Lebanon; f. Grands Moulins du Bénin Flour Mills, Cotonou 1971 (later part of Chagoury Group); co-f. Chagoury Group (large diversified conglomerate with interests in manufacturing, construction, real estate, hospitality and healthcare), Lagos 1971; Amb. of St Lucia to UNESCO and to Holy See 2004–; fmr econ. adviser to Pres. of Benin; Commdr, Order of St Gregory The Great, Ordre des Arts et des Lettres 2000, Ordre Nat. du Benin. *Address:* Chagoury Group, Plot 1684, Sanusi Fafunwa Street, Victoria Island, Lagos, Nigeria (office). *Website:* www .chagourygroup.com (office); www.gilbertchagoury.com (office).

CHAI, Songyue; Chinese politician; b. Nov. 1941, Putuo Co., Zhejiang Prov.; joined CCP 1961; Deputy Sec. CCP Party Cttee, Changguang Coal Mine Co. 1961, later Sec.; Vice-Gov. Zhejiang Prov. 1988–97, Acting Gov. 1997–98, Gov. 1998–2002; mem. CCP Zhejiang Provincial Cttee Standing Cttee 1993–; Deputy Sec. CCP Zhejiang Provincial Cttee 1993–; Alt. mem. 14th CCP Cen. Cttee 1992–97; mem. 15th CCP Cen. Cttee 1997–2002, 16th CCP Cen. Cttee 2002–07; Chair. State Electricity Regulatory Comm. 2002–07; Vice-Chair. 11th CPPCC Nat. Cttee, Econs Cttee 2008–13. *Address:* c/o State Electricity Regulatory Commission, Chang'an Street 86, Xicheng District, West Beijing 100031 People's Republic of China (office). *Telephone:* (10) 58681803 (office). *E-mail:* manager@serc.gov.cn (office). *Website:* www.serc.gov.cn (office).

CHAI, Zhifang; Chinese nuclear physicist; ed Fudan Univ.; Alexander von Humboldt Foundation Fellow, Cologne Univ., Germany 1980–82; fmr Visiting Prof., Purdue Univ., USA, Strasbourg Nuclear Research Centre, France, Delft Univ. and ECN, Netherlands, Tokyo Metropolitan Univ., Japan; currently Prof. and Dir Lab. of Nuclear Analytical Techniques, Inst. of High Energy Physics, Chinese Acad. of Sciences; mem. Hevesy Medal Selection Panel 2006; George Hevesy Medal 2005. *Publications:* author or co-author of around 450 papers in peer-reviewed journals, including Nature, Nature Nanotechnology, Chemical Society Review, JACS, PNAS, Nano Letter, Analytical Chemistry, Environmental Science and Technology, etc and 10 books. *Address:* Laboratory of Nuclear Analytical Techniques, Institute of High Energy Physics, Chinese Academy of Sciences, 19B YuquanLu, Shijingshan District, PO Box 918, Beijing 100049, People's Republic of China (office). *Telephone:* (10) 88233197 (office). *Fax:* (10) 88233374 (office). *E-mail:* chaizf@ihep.ac.cn (office). *Website:* www.ihep.ac.cn (office).

CHAIGNEAU, Pascal Gérard Joël, DèsSc, DenScPol, DenScEcon, DenD; French academic; *Dean, Centre d'Etudes Diplomatiques et Stratégiques;* b. 8 Feb. 1956, Paris; s. of André Chaigneau and Hélène Alexandre; m. Marie-Claude Ratsarazaka-Ratsimandresy 1983; three s.; ed Coll. St Michel de Picpus and Facultés de Droit et des Lettres, Paris; practical work 1974–75; Asst, Ecole des Hautes Etudes Internationales and Ecole Supérieure de Journalisme 1976–78, Prof. 1978–, Dir of Studies 1984–85, Dir-Gen. 1985–90, Admin.-Gen. 1990–; Research, Fondation pour les Etudes de Défense Nationale 1980–82; in charge of course, Univ. de Paris II 1982–90; Maître de conférences, Univ. de Paris V 1990–2000, Professeur des universités 2000–; Professeur des Universités, Directeur du Département de Science Politique, Université Paris Descartes; Sec.-Gen. Centre de Recherches Droit et Défense, Univ. de Paris V 1985–; Founder and Dir Centre d'Études Diplomatiques et Stratégiques 1986–, now Dean; Advocate, Court of Appeal, Paris 1990–; Prof., Centre des Hautes Etudes sur l'Afrique et l'Asie Modernes; Lecturer, Inst. des Hautes Etudes de Défense Nationale; in charge of course, Ecole des Hautes Etudes Commerciales 1990–92, Prof. 1992–; Prof., Collège Interarmes de Défense 1994–; with Bolivian Consulate in France 1994–97; Foreign Trade Counsellor 1995–; many other public appointments; mem. Acad. des Sciences d'Outre-mer, Soc. d'Economie Politique, Royal Soc. of Arts (London); Chevalier, Légion d'honneur; Officier, Ordre nat. du mérite, Commdr, Ordre des Palmes Académiques; Commdr des Arts et des Lettres; decorations from Bolivia, Burkina Faso, Belgium, Honduras, Chad, Madagascar, Niger, etc.; Hon. LLD (Richmond, USA); Dr hc (Nat. Univ. of Bolivia, Université Nationale Mayor de San Andres); Grand Prix de l'Asscn des Ecrivains de Langue Française 1987, Prix de l'Acad. des Sciences Morales et Politiques 1993, Lauréat de l'Institut de France 2012, and other prizes, awards and distinctions. *Publications:* La Stratégie soviétique 1978, La Politique militaire de la France en Afrique 1984,

Rivalités politiques et socialisme à Madagascar 1985, Les Pays de l'Est et l'Afrique 1985, France-océan indien-mer rouge (with others) 1986, Pour une analyse du commerce international 1987, La Guerre du Golfe 1991, Europe: la nouvelle donne stratégique 1993, Les grands Enjeux du monde contemporain 1997, Dictionnaire des Relations Internationales 1998, Gestion des Risques internationaux 2001, Enjeux diplomatiques et stratégiques 2008, Enjeux diplomatiques et stratégiques 2010; chapters in books. *Address:* Centre d'Études Diplomatiques et Stratégiques, 54 avenue Marceau, 75008 Paris (office); 68 avenue de Gravelle, 94220 Charenton-le-Pont, France (home). *Telephone:* 1-47-20-57-47 (office). *Fax:* 1-47-20-57-30 (office). *E-mail:* contact@ceds.fr (office). *Website:* www.ceds.fr (office).

CHAIKA, Yurii Yakovlevich; Russian lawyer and government official; *Prosecutor-General;* b. 1951, Nikolayevsk-on-Amur, Khabarovsk Krai; m.; two c.; ed Sverdlovsk (now Yekaterinburg) Inst. of Law; electrician at shipbuilding factory, Nikolayevsk-on-Amur 1970; joined Prosecutor's Office, Irkutsk Region 1976, held several positions including investigator, Deputy Regional Public Prosecutor, Taishetsk Transport Public Prosecutor, Head, Investigative Div. of East Siberian Transport Public Prosecutor's Office 1983–92, Public Prosecutor of Irkutsk Oblast 1992–95; instructor, Admin. Div., Irkutsk Oblast CPSU Cttee 1984–92; First Deputy Prosecutor-Gen. of Russian Fed. 1995–99, Prosecutor-Gen. April–July 1999, 2006–; Minister of Justice 1999–2006; Hon. Lawyer of the Russian Fed., Hon. Officer, Prosecution Service of the Russian Fed.; Order of Merit for Country, IV Degree, Order of Honour. *Address:* Office of the Prosecutor-General, 125993 Moscow, ul. B. Dmitrovka 15A, Russia (office). *Telephone:* (495) 987-56-56 (office). *Fax:* (495) 292-88-48 (office). *Website:* www.genproc.gov.ru (office).

CHAILLY, Riccardo; Italian conductor; *Chief Conductor, Gewandhausorchester Leipzig;* b. 20 Feb. 1953, Milan; s. of the late Luciano Chailly and of Anna Marie Motta; m. Gabriella Terragni 1987; two s.; ed Giuseppe Verdi and Perugia Conservatories and with Franco Caracciolo and Franco Ferrara; Asst to Claudio Abbado, La Scala, Milan 1972–74; debut as Conductor with Chicago Opera 1974; debut, La Scala 1978, Covent Garden (operatic debut) 1979; concert debut with London Symphony Orchestra and Edin. Festival 1979; American concert debut, Los Angeles Philharmonic, CA 1980; Metropolitan Opera debut 1982; Prin. Guest Conductor, London Philharmonic Orchestra 1982–85; Chief Conductor Radio Symphony Orchestra, Berlin 1982–89; Vienna State Opera debut 1983; appearances Salzburg Festival 1984, 1985, 1986; Japan debut with Royal Philharmonic Orchestra 1984; New York Philharmonic Orchestra debut 1984; Music Dir Bologna Orchestra, Teatro Comunale 1986–93; Chief Conductor Royal Concertgebouw Orchestra, Amsterdam 1988–2004, Conductor Emer. 2004–; Prin. Conductor and Music Dir Giuseppe Verdi Symphony Orchestra, Milan 1999–2005, Conductor Laureate 2005–; Chief Conductor Gewandhausorchester Leipzig 2005–; Hon. mem. RAM, London; Kt Order of Netherlands Lion 1998, Cavaliere di Gran Croce 1998, Abrogino d'Oro, Comune Milano; Gramophone Award Artist of the Year 1998, Diapason d'Or Artist of the Year 1999; Grand' Ufficiale della Repubblica Italiana. *Recordings include:* Beethoven: The Symphonies (ECHO Klassik Award for Conductor of the Year 2012) 2011. *Leisure interests:* music, paintings, the arts in general. *Address:* Gewandhausorchester, Augustusplatz 8, 04109 Leipzig, Germany (office). *Telephone:* (341) 1270331 (office). *E-mail:* pless@gewandhaus.de (office). *Website:* www.gewandhaus.de (office).

CHAISANG, Chaturon, MA; Thai politician; b. 1 Jan. 1956, Chachoengsao; ed State Univ. of New York at Buffalo, American Univ., Washington DC; Asst Sec. to Minister of Finance 1986–87; Sec. Econ. Cttee, House of Reps 1986–88; mem. Parl. Chachoengsao 1986–92, 1995–; Sec. Cttee on Finance, Banking and Financial Insts, House of Reps 1988–91 (mem. 1992); Sec. to Minister of Commerce and adviser to Minister of Agric. 1991; adviser Minister of Science, Tech. and Environment 1992, Ministry of Labour and Social Welfare 1995; Spokesman for New Aspiration Party 1992–95, fmr Sec.-Gen.; Deputy Minister of Finance 1996–2001, Minister attached to Prime Minister's Office 2001, Minister of Justice 2002, Deputy Prime Minister 2002–06; fmr Acting Leader Thai Rak Thai party (now banned); fmr Chair. Cttee of Science and Tech., House of Reps; Kt Grand Cross (First Class) of Crown of Thailand. *Address:* 441/12 Supakij Road, Maung, Chachoengsao 24000, Thailand.

CHAIYAWAN, Vanich; Thai business executive; *Founder and Chairman, Thai Life Insurance Co. Ltd;* b. 1932; m.; eight c.; Founder and Chair. Thai Life Insurance Co. Ltd; Chair. Thai Credit Retail Bank Public Co. Ltd; Dir Thai Asia Pacific Brewery Co. Ltd, fmr Vice-Chair.; Dr hc (Srinakarinvirot Univ.), (Sripatum Univ.). *Address:* Thai Life Insurance Co. Ltd, 121/89 RS Tower, 31st Floor, Ratchadaphisek Road, Dindaeng, Bangkok 10400, Thailand (office). *Website:* www .thailife.com (office).

CHAKARI, Mohammad Sediq; Afghan politician; studied in Saudi Arabia, returned to join fight against invasion by Soviets; served as Minister of Information in early 1990s; currently Deputy, Wolasi Jirga (Lower House of Parl.) (Jamiat-i Islami); Acting Minister of Hajj and Islamic Affairs 2009. *Address:* c/o Ministry of Hajj and Islamic Affairs, nr District 10, Shir Pur, Shar-i-Nau, Kabul, Afghanistan. *Telephone:* (20) 2201338.

CHAKMA, Amit, MASc, PhD; Canadian (b. Bangladeshi) chemical engineer and university administrator; *President and Vice-Chancellor, University of Western Ontario;* b. 1959, Bangladesh; ed Institut Algerien du Petrole, Boumerdès, Algeria, Univ. of British Columbia; Asst Prof. of Chemical and Petroleum Eng, Univ. of Calgary 1988–90, Assoc. Prof. 1990–94, Prof. 1994–96; Prof. of Environmental Eng, Univ. of Regina 1996–2001, Dean of Eng 1996–99, Vice-Pres. (Research) 1999–2001; Prof. of Chemical Eng, Univ. of Waterloo 2001–09, also Vice-Pres. (Academic) and Provost 2001–09; Pres. and Vice-Chancellor, Univ. of Western Ontario 2009–; Chair. World Univ. Service of Canada; mem. Bd of Dirs Ont. Centres of Excellence; mem. Science, Tech. & Innovation Council of Canada; fmr Chair. Advisory Panel on Canada's Int. Educ. Strategy; Visiting Prof., Petroleum and Petrochemical Coll., Chulalongkorn Univ., Thailand 1997–; Adjunct Prof., Hunan Univ., Changsha, People's Repub. of China 1998, Consulting Prof., Huazhong Univ. of Science & Tech. 1998, Wuhan Univ. of Hydraulic and Electrical Eng 2000; Guest Prof., Peking Univ. 2001; Assoc. Ed. Journal of Environmental Informatics 2003–; Fellow, Canadian Acad. of Eng; Canada's Top 40 Under 40 Award 1998, Queen's Diamond Jubilee Medal 2012. *Publications:* more than 100 articles especially in the field of natural gas eng and petroleum waste manage-

ment. *Address:* Office of the President, University of Western Ontario, Stevenson Hall, Suite 2107, London, ON N6A 5B8, Canada (office). *Telephone:* (519) 661-3104 (office). *Website:* president.uwo.ca (office).

CHAKRABARTI, Sir Suma, Kt, KCB, BA, MA; British (b. Indian) economist, banking executive and international organization official; *President, European Bank for Reconstruction and Development;* b. 1969, West Bengal, India; m.; one d.; ed City of London School, New Coll., Oxford, Univ. of Sussex; started career with IMF and World Bank in 1980s; Sr Econ. Asst, British Overseas Devt Admin 1984; fmr Private Sec. to the then Minister of State for Overseas Devt Lynda Chalker; fmr Head of Aid Policy and Resources; worked with HM Treasury 1996; fmr Head of Econ. and Domestic Affairs Secr., Cabinet Office; Dir-Gen. for Regional Devt Programmes, Dept for International Development 2001–02, Perm. Sec. 2002–07; Perm. Sec., Ministry of Justice 2007–12; Pres. EBRD 2012–; mem. Advisory Council, Oxford Dept of International Development; Fellow, Overseas Development Inst.; Hon. Master of the Bench 2009; Dr hc (Univ. of East Anglia) 2010. *Address:* Office of the President, European Bank for Reconstruction and Development, 175 Bishopsgate, One Exchange Square, London, EC2A 2JN, England (office). *Telephone:* (20) 7338-6000 (office). *Fax:* (20) 7338-6100 (office). *E-mail:* generalenquiries@ebrd.com (office). *Website:* www.ebrd.com (office).

CHALABI, Ahmad, PhD; Iraqi politician; *Leader, Iraqi National Congress;* b. 1945, Baghdad; m.; four c.; ed in UK, MIT and Univ. of Chicago, USA; family moved to England following coup d'état and assassination of King of Iraq 1958; fmr Prof. of Math., American Univ. of Beirut; f. Bank of Petra, Jordan 1980, taken over by mil. decree 1989, charged with embezzlement, fraud and misuse of depositor funds by Jordanian court 1991, sentenced in absentia to 22 years' imprisonment 1992; organized conf. of 400 opposition leaders in Northern Iraq 1992; Chair. Exec. Council and Leader, Iraqi Nat. Congress 1992–; survived failed coup 1995; lived in exile in London 1996–2003; returned to Iraq to help establish an interim govt following overthrow of Saddam Hussein's regime April 2003; Deputy Prime Minister 2005–06, Acting Minister of Oil 2005. *Address:* Iraqi National Congress, Baghdad, Iraq (office). *E-mail:* info@inciraq.com (office). *Website:* inciraq.com (office).

CHALANDON, Sorj; French writer and journalist; b. 16 May 1952, Tunis, Tunisia; ed ; writer and journalist for Libération 1973–2007, covered events in Lebanon, Iran, Iraq, Somalia and Afghanistan; has worked for the satirical-investigative newspaper Le Canard enchaîné 1988–; Albert Londres Prize for his articles on Northern Ireland and the Klaus Barbie trial 1988. *Publications:* Le petit Bonzi (Prix du premier roman de l'Université d'Artois, Prix de l'Ecole Normale Supérieure de Cachan, Prix du premier roman du Touquet) 2005, Une promesse (Prix Médicis 2006) 2006, Mon traître (My Traitor) (Prix Jean Freustié, Prix Joseph Kessel, Prix Marguerite Puhl-Demange, Prix Simenon, Prix littéraire de la ville des Sables d'Olonne, Prix Gabrielle d'Estrées, Prix Lettres Frontière 2008) 2008, La légende de nos pères (Prix Ouest du Printemps du Livre 2010) 2009, Retour à Killybegs (Return to Killybegs) (Grand Prix du roman de l'Acad. française 2011) 2011. *Address:* c/o Éditions Grasset, 61 rue des Saint-Pères, 75006 Paris, France. *Telephone:* 1-44-39-22-00. *Fax:* 1-42-22-64-18. *E-mail:* info@grasset.fr. *Website:* www.grasset.fr.

CHALAYAN, Hussein, MBE, BA; British fashion designer; ed Cyprus and Cen. St Martin's School of Art, London; student final year collection featured in Brown's window; set up own label; exhbn of first solo collection, West Soho Galleries, London 1994; second collection shown during London Fashion Week and in Kobe and Tokyo; fourth collection received Absolut Vodka's Absolut Creation Sponsorship Award (first recipient) 1996; solo exhbn (key pieces from past collections), The Window Gallery, Prague 1996; exhibited Buried and Path dresses, Jam (style, music and media) exhbn, Barbican Art Gallery 1996; designs selected for Cutting Edge exhbn, Victoria and Albert Museum 1997; invited to exhibit in Challenge of Materials exhbn, Science Museum 1997; talk at Tate Gallery (with Zaha Hadid, Michael Bracewell and Georgina Starr) on parallels between fashion, art and architecture 1997; Creative Dir, Puma 2008–; Designer of the Year, London Fashion Awards 1998, 2000. *Address:* 71 Endell Road, London, WC2 9AJ, England. *E-mail:* enquiries@husseinchalayan.com. *Website:* www.husseinchalayan.com.

CHALFIE, Martin Lee, PhD; American biochemist and academic; *William R. Kenan, Jr Professor of Biological Sciences, Columbia University;* b. 15 Jan. 1947; s. of the late Eli Chalfie and Vivian Chalfie (née Friedlen); ed Harvard Univ.; teacher, Hamden Hall Country Day School, Conn. 1970–71; postdoctoral research at Lab. of Molecular Biology, Univ. of Cambridge, UK 1977–82; William R. Kenan, Jr Prof. of Biological Sciences, Columbia Univ. 1982–, also Chair. of Biological Sciences; mem. NAS 2004; Nobel Prize in Chem. (jtly) 2008. *Publications:* numerous articles in academic journals. *Address:* Columbia University, Biological Sciences, 1018 Fairchild Center, MC 2446, New York, NY 10027, USA (office). *Telephone:* (212) 854-8870 (office). *Fax:* (212) 865-8246 (office). *E-mail:* mc21@columbia.edu (office). *Website:* www.columbia.edu/cu/biology/faculty/chalfie (office).

CHALFONT, Baron (Life Peer), cr. 1964, of Llantarnam in the County of Monmouthshire; **(Arthur) Alun Gwynne Jones,** PC, OBE, MC, FRSA; British politician and writer; b. 5 Dec. 1919, Llantarnam, Wales; s. of Arthur Gwynne Jones and Eliza Alice Hardman; m. Dr Mona Mitchell 1948; one d. (deceased); ed West Monmouth School; commissioned into S. Wales Borderers (24th Foot) 1940; served in Burma 1941–44, Malaya 1955–57, Cyprus 1958–59; resgnd comm. 1961; Defence Corresp. The Times, London 1961–64; consultant on foreign affairs to BBC TV, London 1961–64; Minister of State for Foreign Affairs 1964–70, Minister for Disarmament 1964–67, 1969–70, in charge of day-to-day negotiations for Britain's entry into Common Market 1967–69; Perm. Rep. to WEU 1969–70; Foreign Ed. New Statesman 1970–71; Chair. All-Party Defence Group House of Lords 1980–96, Pres. 1996–; Chair. Industrial Cleaning Papers 1979–86, Peter Hamilton Security Consultants Ltd 1984–86, UK Cttee for Free World 1981–89, European Atlantic Group 1983–, VSEL Consortium PLC 1987–93, Marlborough Stirling Group 1994–99; Deputy Chair. IBA 1989–90; Chair. Radio Authority 1991–94; Pres. Hispanic and Luso Brazilian Council 1975–80, Royal Nat. Inst. for Deaf 1980–87, Llangollen Int. Music Festival 1979–90; Chair. Abington Corpn (Consultants) Ltd 1981–, Nottingham Building Soc. 1983–90, Southern Mining Corpn 1997–99; Dir W. S. Atkins Int. 1979–83, IBM UK Ltd 1973–90 (mem. IBM Europe Advisory Council 1973–90), Lazard Brothers and Co. Ltd 1983–90,

Shandwick PLC 1985–95, Triangle Holdings 1986–90, TV Corpn PLC 1996–2001; Pres. Freedom in Sport Int.; mem. IISS, Royal Inst.; Hon. Fellow, Univ. Coll. Wales, Aberystwyth 1974. *Publications:* The Sword and the Spirit 1963, The Great Commanders (ed.) 1973, Montgomery of Alamein 1976, Waterloo: Battle of Three Armies (ed.) 1979, Star Wars: Suicide or Survival 1985, Defence of the Realm 1987, By God's Will: A Portrait of the Sultan of Brunei 1989, The Shadow of My Hand (autobiog.) 2000; contrib. to The Times and nat. and professional journals. *Leisure interests:* music, theatre. *Address:* House of Lords, London, SW1A 0PW, England (office).

CHALGHOUM, Mohamed Ridha; Tunisian politician; b. 1962, Gafsa; m.; three c.; ed Institut de Défense Nationale; various positions within Ministry of Finance including fmr Bureau Chief, Dir Gen. of Tax Benefits, Dir of Savings and Financial Markets, Pres. Conseil du marché financier (financial services regulatory authority) –2010, Minister of Finance 2010–11; mem. Nat. Econ. and Social Council 2006–11; Chevalier, Ordre de la République. *Address:* c/o Ministry of Finance, place du Gouvernement, La Kasbah, 1008 Tunis, Tunisia.

CHALHOUB, Patrick, BEcons; French (b. Syrian) business executive; *CEO, Chalhoub Group;* b. 1957; s. of Michel Chalhoub and Widad Chalhoub; m.; two c.; ed Institut d'Etudes Politiques (Sciences Po), Paris; joined Chalhoub Group (family retail business) 1979, currently CEO; distributor of luxury brands throughout Middle East, including LVMH, L'Oréal, Chanel, Ralph Lauren; fmr Chair. French Business Council in Dubai; Founding mem. Rotary Club Dubai, Capital Club; mem. Young Presidents' Org.; Chevalier, Ordre nat. du Mérite; ranked by Arabian Business amongst the Power 500: The World's Most Influential Arabs (98th) 2012. *Address:* Chalhoub Group, PO Box 261075, Jebel Ali, Dubai, United Arab Emirates (office). *Telephone:* (4) 8045500 (office). *Website:* www.chalhoub-group.com (office).

CHALIAND, Gérard, PhD; French academic and writer; ed Institut National des Langues et Civilisations Orientales, Univ. of Paris V; f. magazine Partisans during Algerian war; Prof., Ecole nat. d'admin (ENA), Collège interarmes de défense 1980–89; taught at l'École Supérieure de Guerre 1993–99; Visiting Prof., Harvard Univ., Univ. of Calif., Berkeley, Military Acad., Bogota, Colombia, Univ. of Capetown, SA, Univ. of Salamanca, Spain, Univ. of Manchester, UK; Visiting Fellow, Centre for Conflict and Peace studies; advisor to Centre for Analysis and Planning, Ministry of Foreign Affairs 1984–94; Dir Centre européen d'étude des conflits 1997–2000. *Publications include:* Armed Struggle in Africa 1969, Mythes révolutionnaires du tiers-monde 1977, Atlas stratégique (with J.-P. Rageau) 1987, Anthologie mondiale de la stratégie 1996, Voyage dans le demi-siècle (with Jean Lacouture) 2001, Atlas du nouvel ordre mondial 2003, Histoire du terrorisme: de l'Antiquité à Al-Qaïda 2004, Guerres et civilisations: de l'Assyrie à l'époque contemporaine 2005, L'Amérique en guerre: Irak-Afghanistan 2007. *Address:* 63 Rue Pascal, 75013 Paris, France (home). *Telephone:* 1-43-31-09-12 (home). *E-mail:* gchaliand@aol.com (home).

CHALKER OF WALLASEY, Baroness (Life Peer), cr. 1992, of Leigh-on-Sea in the County of Essex; **Lynda Chalker,** PC; British politician and consultant on business and development in Africa; *Chairman, Africa Matters Ltd;* b. (Lynda Bates), 29 April 1942, Hitchin, Herts.; d. of the late Sidney Henry James Bates and Marjorie Kathleen Randell; m. 1st Eric Robert Chalker 1967 (divorced 1973); m. 2nd Clive Landa 1981 (divorced 2003); ed Heidelberg Univ., Germany, London Univ., Cen. London Polytechnic; statistician with Research Bureau Ltd (Unilever) 1963–69; Deputy Market Research Man., Shell Mex & BP Ltd 1969–72; Chief Exec. Int. Div. of Louis Harris Int. 1972–74; MP for Wallasey 1974–92; Parl. Under-Sec. of State, Dept of Health and Social Security 1979–82, Dept of Transport 1982–83; Minister of State, Dept of Transport 1983–86, FCO 1986–97, Minister for Overseas Devt 1989–97; ind. consultant on Africa and Devt 1997–; Chair. Africa Matters Ltd 1998–; Dir (non-exec.) Capital Shopping Centres 1997–2000, Unilever PLC and NV 1998–2007, Landell Mills Ltd 1999–2001, Ashanti Goldfields Co. 2000–04, Group 5 (Pty) Ltd 2001–, Devt Consultants Int. 2001–05, Equator Exploration Ltd 2005–07; Chair. Greater London Young Conservatives (GLYC) 1969–70; Nat. Vice-Chair. Young Conservatives 1970–71; Chair. London School of Hygiene and Tropical Medicine 1998–2006; Chair. Bd of Medicines for Malaria Venture 2006–; mem. Advisory Bds Lafarge et Cie 2003–, MerchantBridge Int. 2005–, Renaissance Africa 2008–; mem. BBC Gen. Advisory Cttee 1975–79; Hon. Fellow, Queen Mary and Westfield Coll., Inst. of Transportation; Dr hc (Bradford) 1995, (Liverpool), (John Moores), (Cranfield), (Warwick), (Westminster), (East London). *Publications:* We Are Richer Than We Think 1978 (co-author), Africa: Turning the Tide 1989. *Leisure interests:* music, cooking, theatre, driving. *Address:* House of Lords, London, SW1A 0PW; Africa Matters Ltd, 51 Causton Street, London, SW1P 4AT, England (office). *Telephone:* (20) 7976-6850 (office). *Fax:* (20) 7976-4999 (office). *E-mail:* bstendall@africamatters.com (office). *Website:* www.africamatters.com (office).

CHALMERS, Sir Neil Robert, Kt, MA, PhD; British biologist and museum director; b. 19 June 1942, Surrey; s. of William King Chalmers and Irene Margaret Chalmers (née Pemberton); m. Monica Elizabeth Byanjeru Rusoke 1970; two d.; ed King's Coll. School, Wimbledon, Magdalen Coll., Oxford, St John's Coll., Cambridge; Lecturer in Zoology, Makerere Univ. Coll., Kampala, Uganda 1966–69; Scientific Dir Natural Primate Research Centre, Nairobi, Kenya 1969–70; Lecturer, subsequently Sr Lecturer then Reader in Biology, Open Univ. 1970–85, Dean of Science 1985–88; Dir Natural History Museum, London 1988–2004; Warden, Wadham Coll., Oxford 2004–12; Hon. Fellow, Wadham Coll., Oxford 2012–. *Publications:* Social Behaviour in Primates 1979, and other books on animal behaviour; numerous papers in Animal Behaviour and other learned journals. *Leisure interests:* music, golf, swimming.

CHALONER, William Gilbert, PhD, FRS; British botanist and academic; *Professor Emeritus, Royal Holloway, University of London;* b. 22 Nov. 1928; s. of Ernest J. Chaloner and L. Chaloner; m. Judith Carroll 1955; one s. two d.; ed Kingston Grammar School, Univ. of Reading; Lecturer and Reader, Univ. Coll. London 1956–72; Visiting Prof. 1995–2010; Visiting Prof., Pennsylvania State Univ., USA 1961–62; Prof., Univ. of Nigeria 1965–66; Prof. of Botany, Birkbeck Coll. London 1972–79; Hildred Carlile Prof. of Botany and Head of School of Life Sciences, Royal Holloway and Bedford New Coll. 1985–94 (Bedford Coll. 1979–85), Prof. Emer., Geology Dept, Royal Holloway, Univ. of London 1994–; Wilmer D. Barrett (Visiting) Prof. of Botany, Univ. of Massachusetts, USA 1987–91; mem. Bd

of Trustees, Royal Botanic Gardens, Kew 1983–96; Pres. Linnean Soc. 1985–88; fmr mem. of Senate, Univ. of London; fmr mem. Nat. Environment Research Council; Corresp. mem. Botanical Soc. of America 1987–, Associé Etranger de l'Acad. des Sciences; Hon. Fellow, Royal Holloway 2002. *Publications:* papers in scientific journals. *Leisure interests:* swimming, watercolour painting. *Address:* Department of Earth Sciences, Royal Holloway College, Egham, Surrey, TW20 0EX (office); 26 Warren Avenue, Richmond, Surrey, TW10 5DZ, England (home). *E-mail:* w.chaloner@rhul.ac.uk (office).

CHALUPEC, Igor Adam, BEcons; Polish economist and business executive; b. 1966; ed Warsaw School of Econs, Warsaw Univ.; consultant, Polexpert Sp. zo.o 1989–90; consultant, Proexim Sp. zo.o 1990; licensed stockbroker 1991–; Dir Cen. Brokerage House, Bank Pekao SA 1991–95, mem. Man. Bd 1995–2000, Vice-Pres. 2000–03; Under-Sec. of State and Gen. Insp. of Financial Information, Ministry of Finance 2003–04; Pres. and CEO PKN Orlen SA 2004–07; Chair. Supervisory Bd, Unipetrol as, Prague –2007; Chair. Brokerage Houses Asscn 1994–95; mem. Supervisory Bd, Warsaw Stock Exchange 1994–2003; Deputy Chair., Insurance and Pensions Funds Supervisory Comm. 2003–04, Comm. for Banking Supervision 2003–04; mem. European Corp. Governance Forum 2004–, Capital Market Council 2005–. *Leisure interests:* literature, cinema, politics, tennis, bridge. *Address:* c/o PKN Orlen, ul. Chemików 7, 09–411 Płock, Poland (office).

CHALYI, Aleksei Mikhailovich, DTechSci; Russian politician; *de facto Mayor of Sevastopol;* b. 13 June 1961, Sevastopol; ed Sevastopol Tech. Inst.; Founder, Chief Tech. Officer and CEO Tauris Electric group 1990–; Chief of Exec. Cttee, Sevastopol City Council (de facto Mayor) Feb. 2014–; built and operates the 35th Coastal Battery museum in Sevastopol; involved with restoration of World War II memorials; produced documentary series Sevastopol Tales; mem. Russian Acad. of Electrotechnology; 'For Faith and Fidelity' Award 2011. *Address:* Division of Media Relations, Legislative Assembly of Sevastopol, 99011 Sevastopol, Lenina 3, Crimea, Ukraine (office). *Telephone:* (692) 54-05-38 (office). *Fax:* (692) 54-03-53 (office). *E-mail:* press@sevsovet.com.ua (office). *Website:* sevsovet.com.ua (office).

CHAM, Prasidh; Cambodian politician; *Senior Minister and Minister of Commerce;* b. 15 May 1951, Phnom Penh; m. Tep Bopha Prasidh; one s. two d.; ed Lycée Descartes, Phnom Penh; mem. Cambodian People's Party (CPP); currently Sr Minister and Minister of Commerce; Sr Adviser to His Holiness Samdech Preah Sometheatheppadey Tep Vong, Supreme Patriarch of the Mohanjkhay Buddhist Clergy 2004–; Order of the Sowathara, Moha Sereywadaan class, Order of the Kingdom of Cambodia Assarith Class 1998, Thipadin Class 2001, Oknha 2002. *Leisure interests:* golf, tennis, volleyball. *Address:* Ministry of Commerce, 20a–b Norodom blvd, Phnom-Penh, Cambodia (office). *Telephone:* (23) 991708 (office). *Fax:* (23) 213288 (office). *E-mail:* moccabdir@yahoo.com (office). *Website:* www.moc.gov.kh (office).

CHAMBAS, Mohamed Ibn, BA, MA, PhD; Ghanaian lawyer, politician and international organization official; *Joint Special Representative of UN Secretary-General and African Union Commission Chairperson for Darfur;* b. 7 Dec. 1950; m.; three c.; ed Univ. of Ghana, Legon, Cornell Univ., Ithaca, USA, Case Western Reserve Univ., Cleveland, USA; fmr Lecturer, Oberlin Coll., Ohio; admitted to practise law in Ghana and State of Ohio, USA; legal practice with Forbes, Forbes & Teamor, Cleveland, Ohio; also practised law with The Greater Cleveland Legal Aid Soc.; Deputy Foreign Sec. of Ghana 1987; MP for Bimbilla (Nat. Democratic Congress) 1993–96, 2000–02, First Deputy Speaker of Parl. 1993–94, mem. Select Cttee on Educ., Cttee on Subsidiary Legislation, Chair. Foreign Affairs Cttee 1993–94; Deputy Foreign Minister 1994; Deputy Minister of Educ. 1997–2000; Exec. Sec. Econ. Community of West African States (ECOWAS) 2002–06, Pres. 2007–10; Sec.-Gen., Secr. of the African, Caribbean and Pacific Group of States, Brussels, Belgium 2010–12; Jt Special Rep. of UN Sec.-Gen. and African Union Comm. Chair. for Darfur 2013–, also Head African Union-UN Hybrid Mission in Darfur (UNAMID) and Jt Chief Mediator 2013–; mem. Cornell Univ. Council 1997–2001, 2003–07, 2009–; Commdr of the Nat. Order of Cote d'Ivoire 2002, Highest Nat. Award (for the restoration of Democracy and putting Nation on Path of Sustainable Econ. Devt) 2005, Order of Volta, 2nd Category (For Distinguished Diplomatic and Public Service to the Country) 2006, Kt Grand Band in the Humane Order of African Redemption (Liberia) 2009, Commdr, Ordre Nat. du Bénin 2010, Grand Officer of the Nat. Order of Merit of the Repub. of Guinea 2010; Hon. LLD (Univ. of Ghana, Legon) 2008; Nat. Legis. Ass. Certificate of Appreciation (for role in signing of Accra Comprehensive Peace Agreement that ended civil war in Liberia) 2006. *Leisure interests:* soccer, horse riding. *Address:* African Union-UN Hybrid Mission in Darfur, PO Box 5041, Grand Central Station, New York, NY 10163-5041, USA (office). *Website:* www.unamid.unmissions.org (office).

CHAMBERLAIN, (George) Richard; American actor; b. 31 March 1935, Los Angeles; s. of Charles Chamberlain and Elsa Chamberlain; ed Los Angeles Conservatory of Music and drama studies with Jeff Corey. *Films include:* Secret of Purple Reef 1960, Thunder of Drums 1961, Twilight of Honor 1963, Joy in the Morning 1965, Petulia 1968, The Madwoman of Chaillot 1969, The Music Lovers 1971, Julius Caesar 1971, Lady Caroline Lamb 1971, The Three Musketeers 1974, Towering Inferno 1974, The Four Musketeers 1975, The Slipper and the Rose 1977, The Swarm 1978, Murder by Phone 1982, King Solomon's Mines 1985, Alan Quartermain and The Lost City of Gold 1987, The Return of the Musketeers 1989, Bird of Prey 1996, River To Drown In 1997, All the Winters That Have Been 1997, The Pavilion 1999, Strength and Honour 2007, I Now Pronounce You Chuck and Larry 2007, Endless Bummer 2008, The Perfect Family 2011. *Stage appearances include:* King Lear, Hamlet, Richard II, The Lady's Not for Burning, Night of the Iguana, Cyrano de Bergerac, My Fair Lady. *Television includes:* Dr. Kildare (series) 1961–65, Portrait of a Lady 1968, The Woman I Love 1973, The Count of Monte Cristo 1975, Centennial (miniseries) 1978, The Good Doctor 1978, The Man in the Iron Mask 1978, Shogun 1980 (Golden Globe Award), The Thorn Birds (miniseries) 1983, Cook & Peary: The Race to the Pole 1983, The Miracle 1985, Wallenberg: A Hero's Story 1985, Dream West (miniseries) 1986, Casanova 1987, The Bourne Identity 1988, Ordeal in the Arctic 1993, The Thorn Birds, The Missing Year 1996, The Lost Daughter 1997, All the Winters That Have Been 1997, Too Rich: The Secret Life of Doris Duke 1999, Blackbeard (miniseries) 2006. *Address:* c/o Eric Gardner, Panacea Entertainment Management and Communications, Ltd, 13587 Andalusia Drive, Camarillo, Calif. 93012, USA. *Telephone:* (805) 491-9400.

CHAMBERLIN, Wendy J., MS; American diplomatist, international organization official and fmr UN official; *President, Middle East Institute;* b. 12 Oct. 1948, Bethesda, Md; two d.; ed Northwestern, Boston and Harvard Univs; joined Foreign Service, Dept of State, Washington, DC 1975, Consular and Econ. Officer, Vientiane 1976–78, Staff Aide, E Asia Bureau, Dept of State 1978–79, Special Asst to Deputy Sec. of State 1979, Political Officer, Kinshasa 1980–82; Pearson Fellow, US Senate, Washington, DC 1982–83; Political-Mil. Officer, Office of Israel Affairs, Dept of State 1983–85, Dir (acting) Office of Regional Affairs, Bureau of Near East-S Asian Affairs 1985–87, Asst Gen. Service Officer, Rabat 1988–89, Special Asst to Under-Sec. for Political Affairs, Dept of State 1989–90; Dir of Counter-Terrorism, Nat. Security Council, Washington, DC 1990–91; Dir Office of Press–Public Affairs, Bureau of Near East-S Asian Affairs 1991–93, Deputy Chief of Mission, Kuala Lumpur 1993–96, Amb. to Laos 1996–99; Prin. Deputy Asst Bureau of Int. Narcotics and Law Enforcement Programs, Washington, DC 1999–2001; Amb. to Pakistan 2001–02; Asst Admin. for Asia and Near East, USAID 2002–04; Deputy UN High Commr for Refugees 2004–Feb. 2005, June 2005–06, Acting High Commr Feb.–June 2005; Pres. Middle East Inst. 2007–; Nat. Security Fellow 1984; mem. Bd of Dirs American Acad. of Diplomacy, The Hollings Center, Sultan Qaboos Cultural Center; Hon. PhD (Northwestern Univ.); numerous meritorious awards from US State Dept. *Address:* Middle East Institute, 1761 N Street, NW, Washington, DC 20036-2882, USA (office). *Telephone:* (202) 785-1141 (office). *Fax:* (202) 331-8861 (office). *E-mail:* executiveassist@mei.edu (office). *Website:* www.mei.edu (office).

CHAMBERS, Anne Cox; American media proprietor and fmr diplomatist; *Co-Director, Cox Enterprises Inc.;* b. 1 Dec. 1919, Ga; d. of the late James M. Cox; sister of Barbara Cox Anthony; m. (divorced); three c.; fmr Dir Fulton Nat. Bank 1973; Amb. to Belgium 1977–81; currently Co-Dir (with sister) Cox Enterprises Inc., parent co. of Cox Radio Inc., Cox Communications Inc., AutoTrader.com LLC, Mannheim Auctions Inc., The Atlanta-Journal Constitution, Atlanta Beat, other enterprises; Chair. Atlanta Newspapers Inc.; Vice-Chair. American Advisory Bd Pasteur Foundation; mem. Bd of Dirs Bank of the South 1977–82, Coca-Cola Co. 1981–91, American Soc. French Legion of Honor, MacDowell Gallery, Cities in Schools, High Museum of Art, Atlanta, Friends of Art and Preservation in Embassies, French American Foundation; Pres. American Friends Int. Lyric Art Festival, Aix-en-Provence; Trustee Int. Council Museum of Modern Art, Nat. Cttee Whitney Museum, Council of American Ambs, Council on Foreign Relations; Ordre de la Couronne, Officier, Légion d'honneur; YMCA Women of Achievement Award 1985. *Address:* Cox Enterprises Inc., 6205 Dunwoody Road, Atlanta, GA 30328, USA (office). *Website:* www.coxenterprises.com (office).

CHAMBERS, John T., BL, BA, BSc, MBA; American computer industry executive; *Chairman and CEO, Cisco Systems, Inc.;* m. Elaine Chambers; two c.; ed West Virginia Univ., Indiana Univ.; with IBM 1976–82; with Wang Labs 1982–90; Sr Vice-Pres., Worldwide Sales and Operations, Cisco Systems, Inc., San Jose, Calif. 1991–94, Exec. Vice-Pres. 1994–95, Pres. 1995, CEO 1995–, Chair. 2006–; Chair. NetAid 1999–; mem. Bd of Dirs Clarify Inc., Arbor Software; co-sponsored Jordan Educ. Initiative in partnership with HM King Abdullah II of Jordan and World Econ. Forum; spearheaded 21st Century Schools initiative in Gulf Coast Region affected by Hurricane Katrina 2005; co-led del. of US business leaders, in partnership with US State Dept, to form the Partnership for Lebanon 2006; formed public-pvt. partnership to help rebuild health care and education models in Sichuan, China following earthquake of May 2008; fmr Vice-Chair. Infrastructure Advisory Council; also served on Pres. George W. Bush's Transition Team and Educ. Cttee and on Pres. Clinton's Trade Policy Cttee; Award for Lifetime Achievement, PricewaterhouseCoopers 1999, Mr Internet, Top 25 Executives Worldwide, Business Week 1999, Internet Industry Leader Award, US Internet Council 2000, CEO of the Year, Chief Executive Magazine 2000, Top 10 Most Influential Leaders Shaping Technology, Time Digital 2000, Best Boss in America, 20/20 2000, #2 CEO in America, Worth Magazine 2000, Top 100 Best Corp. Citizens, Business Ethics Magazine 2001–06, three-time winner, Best Investor Relations by a CEO, Investor Relations Magazine 2002, 2004, 2007, six-time winner, Best CEO, Telecommunications, Data Networking, Institutional Investor Magazine 2003–08, Scholars of the Smithsonian Inst. 2004, Presidential Award: Ron Brown Award for Corp. Leadership, The Business Council 2004, Award for Corp. Excellence, US State Dept 2005, 2010, Excellence in Corp. Philanthropy Award, Cttee to Encourage Corp. Philanthropy 2005, Woodrow Wilson Award for Corp. Citizenship, Woodrow Wilson Center for Excellence in Workplace Volunteer Programs, Points of Light Foundation 2005, Int. Community Service Award, US Chamber of Commerce, Business Civic Leadership Center 2007, Gala Award Honoree, American India Foundation 2007, Clinton Global Citizen Award (pvt. sector), Clinton Global Initiative 2007, Business Leadership Award, NASSCOM (India) 2007–08, 20th Anniversary Leadership Award, City Year 2008, World's 100 Most Influential People, Time Magazine 2008, World's Best CEOs, Barron's top 30 list 2008, 25 Most Powerful People In Business, Fortune 2008, Top 10 CEO Vision Award, InternetNews.com 2008, The World's Most Respected CEOs, Barron's top 30 list 2009, CEO Diversity Leadership Award, Diversity Best Practices 2009, Bower Award for Business Leadership, Franklin Inst. 2012. *Address:* Cisco Systems, Inc., Building 10, 170 West Tasman Drive, San Jose, CA 95134-1706, USA (office). *Telephone:* (408) 526-4000 (office). *Fax:* (408) 526-4100 (office). *E-mail:* jochambe@cisco.com (office). *Website:* www.cisco.com (office).

CHAMBERS, M. Susan; American retail executive; *Executive Vice-President, Global People Division, Walmart;* ed William Jewell Coll., Liberty, Mo.; began career with Amoco Oil Corpn; Dir of Applications Devt, Hallmark Cards Inc. 1985–99; joined Wal-Mart Stores Inc. (now known as Walmart) 1999, Store Club Man. 1999, becoming Vice-Pres., Applications Devt Merchandising, Information Systems Div., Sr Vice-Pres. CMI Benefits and Insurance Admin 2002–03, Exec. Vice-Pres., Risk Man. Benefits Admin 2004–06, Exec. Vice-Pres., Global People Div. 2006–, Dir of Wal-Mart de Mexico SAB De CV 2006–; mem. Business Advisory Bd, Kansas State Univ.; mem. Advisory Council, Women Impacting Public Policy; mem. Philanthropy Roundtable; ranked by Forbes magazine amongst The World's 100 Most Powerful Women (39th) 2009, ranked by Fortune magazine amongst the 50 Most Powerful Women in Business in the US (24th) 2009, (23rd) 2010, (22nd) 2011, (36th) 2012. *Address:* Wal-Mart Stores, Inc., 702 SW 8th Street, Bentonville,

AR 72716-8611, USA (office). *Telephone:* (479) 273-4000 (office). *Fax:* (479) 277-1830 (office). *Website:* walmartstores.com (office).

CHAMBERS, Raymond G (Ray), MBA; American business executive and UN official; *Special Envoy for Malaria and for the Financing of Health-Related Millennium Development Goals, United Nations;* b. 1942, Newark, New Jersey; m. Patti Chambers; one s. two d.; ed Rutgers Univ., Seton Hall Univ.; Co-f. Wesray Capital Corpn 1981; after successful career in field of leveraged buyouts, left Wall Street to concentrate on philanthropic projects 1989; Founding Chair. Points of Light Foundation 1990; Co-f. (with Colin Powell) America's Promise–The Alliance for Youth; Co-f. The Millennium Promise Alliance 2005, Malaria No More (with Peter Chernin) 2006, Nat. Mentoring Partnership, New Jersey Performing Arts Center; UN Sec.-Gen.'s Special Envoy for Malaria 2008–, also for Financing of Health-Related Millennium Devt Goals 2013–; f. Millennium Devt Goals Health Alliance 2012; Co-Chair. GBCHealth 2013–; Dir Population Services Int., Communities in Schools, Univ. of Notre Dame, American Museum of Natural History; f. (with William E. Simoand) Wesray Capital Corpn (also fmr Chair.); mem. Pres.'s Council on Service and Civic Participation; mem. Synergos Inst. Global Philanthropists Circle; William E. Simon Prize for Philanthropic Leadership 2002, UN Correspondents' Asscn Citizen of the Year 2011. *Address:* Office of the Secretary-General, United Nations, New York, NY 10017, USA (office). *Telephone:* (212) 963-1234 (office). *Fax:* (212) 963-4879 (office). *E-mail:* info@malariaenvoy.com (office). *Website:* www.un.org (office); www.malariaenvoy.com (office).

CHAMBERS, Richard Dickinson, PhD, DSc, FRS; British chemist and academic; *Professor Emeritus of Chemistry, Durham University;* b. 16 March 1935, West Stanley, Co. Durham; s. of Alfred Chambers and Elizabeth Chambers (née Allsop); m. Anne Boyd 1959; one s. one d. (deceased); ed Stanley Grammar School, Durham Univ.; postdoctoral research at Univ. of British Columbia, Vancouver 1959–60; Lecturer, Durham Univ. 1960–69, Reader 1969–76, Prof. of Chem. 1976–2003, Chair. and Head of Dept of Chem. 1983–86, Sir Derman Christopherson Research Fellow 1988–89, Research Prof. 2000–03, Prof. Emer. 2003–; Tarrant Visiting Prof., Univ. of Florida, Gainesville 1999; Fulbright Scholar, Case Western Reserve Univ., Ohio 1966–67; Dir (non-exec.) BNFL Fluorochemicals Ltd 1995–2000; ACS Award for Creative Work in Fluorine Chemistry 1991, Moissan Int. Prize 2003. *Publications:* Fluorine in Organic Chemistry 1973, 2004; also numerous articles in scientific journals. *Leisure interests:* opera, golf, watching soccer. *Address:* 5 Aykley Green, Durham, DH1 4LN, England (home). *Telephone:* (191) 386-5791 (home). *E-mail:* r.d.chambers@durham.ac.uk (office). *Website:* www.dur.ac.uk/directory/profile/?id=3271 (office).

CHAMBLISS, Saxby, BA, JD; American lawyer and politician; *Senator from Georgia;* b. 10 Nov. 1943, Warrenton, NC; m. Julianne Chambliss (née Frohbert) 1966; two c.; ed Univ. of Georgia, Univ. of Tennessee; fmr small businessman and attorney, Moultrie; mem. US House of Reps from 8th Dist of Georgia 1994–2003, mem. House Perm. Select Cttee on Intelligence 2001, Chair. Intelligence Sub-Cttee on Terrorism and Homeland Security, Chair. Agric. Gen. Farm Commodities and Risk-Man. Cttee 2001, mem. Armed Services Cttee (f. Congressional Air Power Cttee); Senator from Ga 2003–, Vice-Chair. Select Cttee on Intelligence, mem. Armed Services Cttee, Cttee on Agric., Nutrition and Forestry, Rules Cttee, Special Cttee on Aging; fmr Chair. Congressional Sportsmen's Caucus; Republican; Friend of the Farmer Award, Georgia Farm Bureau 1995, Distinguished Service Award, Georgia Peanut Comm. 1997, W. Stuart Symington Award, Air Force Asscn, named Fed. Legislator of the Year, Safari Club Int. 1999, Minuteman of the Year Award, Reserve Officers Asscn 2005, Harry S. Truman Award, Nat. Guard Asscn 2008, Nat. Legis. Advocacy Award, Naval Reserve Asscn 2008. *Leisure interests:* Little League baseball volunteer, YMCA basketball coach. *Address:* 416 Russell Senate Office Building, Washington, DC 20510, USA (office). *Telephone:* (202) 224-3521 (office). *Fax:* (202) 224-0103 (office). *Website:* chambliss .senate.gov (office).

CHAMBON, Pierre, LèsSc, MD; French biochemist and academic; *Director, Institut Clinique de la Souris;* b. 7 Feb. 1931, Mulhouse; s. of Henri Chambon and Yvonne Weill; m. Brigitte Andersson 1957; two s. one d.; ed Univ. of Strasbourg; Research Asst, Strasbourg Medical School 1956–61, Assoc. Prof. 1962–66; Sabbatical, Dept of Biochemistry, Stanford Univ. Medical School 1966–67; Prof. of Biochemistry, Inst. de Chimie Biologique, Faculté de Médecine, Strasbourg 1967–91; Prof., Universitaire de France, Faculté de Médecine, Louis Pasteur Univ., Strasbourg 1991–93; Prof., Collège de France 1993–2002, Hon. Prof. 2002–; Dir Lab. de Génétique Moléculaire des Eucaryotes (LGME), CNRS 1977–2002; Dir Unité 184 de Biologie Moléculaire et de Génie Génétique, Inst. Nat. de la Santé et de la Recherche Médicale (INSERM) 1978–2002; Dir Inst. of Genetics and Molecular and Cellular Biology (IGBMC), CNRS 1994–2002, Emer. Dir 2002–; Dir Génopôle de Strasbourg Alsace-Lorraine 1999–; Pres. Scientific Bd, Genome Programme, Ministry of Research 1999–2002; Founder and Dir Inst. Clinique de la Souris (ICS) 2002–; mem. numerous scientific and editorial bds etc.; mem. Acad. des Sciences; Foreign mem. NAS, Royal Swedish Acad.; Corresp. mem. Liège Acad.; hon. mem. Chinese Soc. of Genetics; Foreign Hon. mem. American Acad. of Arts and Science, Acad. Royale de Médecine, Belgium; Officier, Ordre Nat. du Mérite 1987, Commdr 1995, Officier, Ordre Nat. de la Légion d'Honneur 1991; Dr hc (Univ. de Liège, Belgium, Univ. of Sapporo, Japan); Prix Rosen 1976, CNRS Gold Medal 1979, Freeman Foundation Prize of New York Acad. 1981, Lounsbery Prize (NAS and Acad. des Sciences) 1982, Oberling Prize 1986, Prix Griffuel 1987, Prix Harvey, Israeli Inst. of Tech. 1987, Prix Henry et MaryJane Mitjavile, Acad. Nat. de Médecine, Paris 1987, King Faisal Int. Prize 1988, Krebs Medal 1990, Prix Roussel 1990, Prix Louis Jeantet 1991, Grand Prix, Fondation for Medical Research 1996, Robert A. Welch Award in Chem. 1998, Louisa Gross Horwitz Prize 1999, Prix AFRT 1999, Albert Lasker Award for Basic Medical Research (jtly) 2004. *Publications:* 400 articles in scientific reviews. *Address:* Institut Clinique de la Souris, 1 Rue Laurent Fries BP 10142, Parc d'Innovation, 67404 Illkirch Cedex (office); IGBMC, 1 rue Laurent Fries, B.P. 163, 67404 Illkirch Cedex, C.U. Strasbourg, France (office). *Telephone:* 3-88-65-32-15 (office). *Fax:* 3-88-65-32-99 (office). *E-mail:* ics@titus.u-strasbg.fr (office); chambon@igbmc.u-strasbg.fr (office). *Website:* www-mci.u-strasbg.fr (office).

CHAMEAU, Jean-Lou, PhD; French civil engineer, academic and university administrator; *President, King Abdullah University of Science and Technology;* b. 1953; m. Dr Carol Carmichael; ed École Nat. Supérieure d'Arts et Métiers

(ENSAM), France, Stanford Univ.; Prof. of Civil Eng, Purdue Univ. 1980; Dir School of Civil and Environmental Eng, Georgia Inst. of Tech. 1991–94, 1995–2001, Provost 2001–06; Pres. Golder Associates Inc. 1994–95; Pres. California Inst. of Tech. 2006–13, Pres. Emer. 2013–; Pres. King Abdullah Univ. of Science and Tech. 2013–; mem. Bd Council on Competitiveness, John Wiley & Sons, MTS Systems, Safran, Academic Research Council of Singapore, Advisory Cttee of InterWest Partners; mem. Acad. des Technologies, Nat. Acad. of Eng; Chevalier, Légion d'honneur 2010; ENSAM Prix Nessim Habif, Nat. Science Foundation Presidential Young Investigator Award, American Soc. of Civil Engineers Arthur Casagrande Award, Soc. of Women Engineers Rodney Chipp Memorial Award. *Address:* King Abdullah University of Science & Technology, Thuwal 23955-6900, Saudi Arabia (office). *Website:* www.kaust.edu.sa/about/admin/president/presidentoffice.html?submenuheader=0 (office).

CHAMLING, Pawan Kumar; Indian politician, poet and writer; *Chief Minister of Sikkim;* b. 22 Sept. 1950, Yangang Busty, South Sikkim; s. of Shri Ash Bahadur Chamling and Smt. Asharani Chamling; m. Tika Maya Chamling; four s. four d.; early career as ind. farmer; entered politics in 1973; Vice-Pres. Dist Youth Congress 1975; Pres. Sikkim Handicapped Persons Welfare Mission 1976–77; Ed. Nava Jyoti 1976–77, Founder Nirman Prakashan 1977, Ed. Nirman (quarterly literary magazine) 1977–; Gen. Sec. and Vice-Pres. Sikkim Prajatantra Congress 1978–84; Pres., Yangang Gram Panchayat 1982; mem. Sikkim Legis. Ass. 1985–; Minister for Industries, Printing and Information and Public Relations 1989–92; f. Sikkim Democratic Front party 1993, Leader 1993–; Chief Minister of Sikkim 1994–; Chair. Sikkim Distilleries Ltd 1985–; Hon. PhD (Manipal Univ.) 2003; numerous awards including Chinton Puraskar 1987, Bharat Shiromani 1996, Man of the Year 1998, The Greenest Chief Minister of India 1998, Man of Dedication 1999, Secular India Harmony Award 1998, Manav Sewa Puraskar 1999, Pride of India Gold Award 1999, Best Citizen of India 1999, Poets' Foundation Award 2001, Nat. Citizens of India Award 2002, Bhanu Puraskar 2010. *Publications* include: Veer koh Parichaya (poem) 1967, Antahin Sapana Meroh Bipana 1985, Perennial Dreams and My Reality, Parambhek Kabitaharu 1991, Pratiwad 1992, Damthang Heejah ra Aajah 1992, Ma koh Hun 1992, Sikkim ra Narikon Maryadha 1994, Crucified Prashna Aur Anya Kabitaye 1996, Sikkim ra Prajatantra 1996, Democracy Redeemed 1997, Prajatantra koh Mirmireymah 1997, Meroh Sapana Ko Sikkim 2002, Perspectives and Vision 2002. *Leisure interests:* reading, writing. *Address:* CM Secretariat, Tashiling, Gangtok, Sikkim 737 101 (office); Ghurpisay, Namchi, South Sikkim 737 126, India (home). *Telephone:* (3592) 222263 (office); (3592) 222536 (home). *Fax:* (3592) 222245 (office); (3592) 224710 (home). *E-mail:* cm-skm@nic.in (office). *Website:* sikkim.nic .in (office); sikkim.nic.in/cmonline/homepage.htm.

CHAMORRO, Violeta Barrios de (see BARRIOS de CHAMORRO, Violeta).

CHAMORRO BARRIOS, Cristiana, BA; Nicaraguan foundation director and editor; *Director, Fundación Violeta Barrios de Chamorro;* d. of Pedro Joaquin Chamorro Cardenal and Violeta Barrios de Chamorro; Dir Diario La Prensa 1986–90, Chair. 1991–93, currently mem. Bd of Dirs and mem. Editorial Advisory Bd; Vice-Pres. Comm. for the Freedom of Expression 1987–93; Adviser to Pres. of Nicaragua Violeta Barrios de Chamorro 1990–97; Ed. Servicio Especial de Mujeres (SEM), Costa Rica; Founder-Dir Fundación Violeta Barrios de Chamorro (non-profit org. for peace, democracy and freedom of expression) 1990–; Excellence in Journalism Award, Inter-American Press Soc., Int. Press Asscn. *Publications:* Anchorman: Editorial on Freedom of Expression and the Republic Of Paper In Nicaragua 1948–1977. *Address:* Fundación Violeta Barrios de Chamorro, CC. Plaza España, Edificio Málaga Módulo B-17, Managua, Nicaragua (office). *Telephone:* (505) 2268-6500 (office). *Fax:* (505) 2268-6502 (office). *E-mail:* cristiana@cablenet.com.ni (office); cristiana.chamorro@ibw.com.ni (office). *Website:* www.violetachamorro.org.ni (office).

CHAN, Agnes, PhD; Japanese singer, academic and international organization official; *Ambassador of the Japan Committee, UNICEF;* b. 20 Aug. 1955, Hong Kong; m. Tsutomu Kaneko 1985; three c.; ed Sophia Univ., Univ. of Toronto, Canada, Stanford Univ., USA; debut single Circle Game released in Hong Kong 1969; Japan debut single Hinagesi no Hana released 1972; performed charity concerts for Cambodia in Hong Kong and Japan 1980, Beijing 1985; Lecturer, Shinshui and Reitaku Univs 1986; Lecturer on Cross-Cultural Communication, Nagoya Women's Cultural Coll. 1993–97, Prof. 1997–; Asst Prof., Mejiro Univ. 1994–97, Prof. 1997–; Prof., Kyouei Univ. 2001; Amb. of Japan Cttee, UNICEF 1998–, travelled to Vietnam, Cambodia, Thailand, Sudan and Philippines on issues of child prostitution and child soldiers; lobbied the law against child prostitution and won its passage in the diet 1999; named Amb. of Hong Kong and Japan 2001; cr. new clothing line called Dear Agnes 1990; opened Chan's Boutique, Odaiba, Tokyo 2001; mem. Bd of Dirs, Wild Bird Asscn of Japan, Children's Dream Foundation, Children's Earth Club, Blue Sky Foundation, Kaijo Hoan Tomo no Kai; mem. Bd of Trustees, Day of Peace of Tokyo, Yokohama Museum, Sung Kei Ling Foundation, Japan and China Goodwill Asscn; TV talk show personality; regular contribs to newspapers and magazines; makes over 100 concert performances and speech tours throughout Japan each year; Hong Kong Top Ten Singers Award 1971, Japan Records Grand Prize 1973, New Artist Award 1973, Shinjuku Music Award 1973, Best New Artist Award 1974, Golden Arrow Award 1974, Japan Cable Music Award 1974, Int. Year of Youth Award (for essay on world peace) 1984, S. J. Grand Prize Winner, Ass
cn of Women Working in Broadcasting 1986, Asscn of Japanese Journalists Special Award 1986, Galaxy Award 1986, Most Popular Name of the Year Award 1988, Best Eye Wear Award 1997; numerous gold and platinum discs. *Television:* Agnes' Music Salon 2006, Kitajima Wink Heart 2007. *Radio:* Agnes' Sunny Side Up, City Snapshot. *Albums include:* more than 100 albums in several different languages. *Publications include:* My Chinese Dishes 1983, Be Peaceful With Songs 1984, We All Are the People Who Live on the Earth 1984, Neo Woman 1993, Mama You Don't Need To Be a Doctor 1994, Hong Kong Guide 1997, The Road Winds Uphill All The Way (co-author) 1999, Positive Child Care 2001, Perfection Couple, Ring of Cullet 2002, This Road Leads to the Hill 2003, Cheers to the World! 2004, The Right Track – To People Who Live For the Future 2005, What the Marriage Life Is? (co-author), Agnes' Style Aging 2006. *Address:* Japan Committee for UNICEF, UNICEF House, 4-6-12 Takanawa, Minato-ku, Tokyo 108-8607, Japan (office). *Telephone:* (3) 5789-2032

(office); (3) 5789-2011 (office). *E-mail:* unicefjc@unicef.or.jp (office). *Website:* www .unicef.or.jp (office); www.agneschan.gr.jp (office).

CHAN, Chuen-po, BA, MA; Taiwanese politician; *Vice-Chairman, Kuomintang;* b. 30 Oct. 1941; ed Tunghai Univ., Harvard Univ., USA; fmr Gen. Man. Taiwan TV; fmr Vice-Chair. Kuanghwa Investment Holdings Co.; mem. Nationalist Party of China (Kuomintang, KMT), numerous positions including Vice-Chair., Sec.-Gen. Cen. Cttee, Deputy Exec. Dir and Chief Exec. Policy Cttee, Vice-Chair., Chair. and Sec.-Gen. Taipei Municipal Cttee, Deputy Dir Secr., Cen. Cttee, Deputy Dir Dept of Policy Research, Dept of Organizational Affairs, Vice-Chair. Taiwan Prov. Cttee, Sec.-Gen. 2005–07, 2009, currently Vice-Chair.; Sec.-Gen. of Presidential Office 2008–09. *Address:* Office of the Vice-Chairman, Kuomintang, 232, Sec. 2, Bade Road, Taipei 10492, Taiwan (office). *Telephone:* (2) 87711234 (office). *Fax:* (2) 23434561 (office). *Website:* www.kmt.org.tw (office).

CHAN, Florinda da Rosa Silva, MBA; Chinese politician; *Secretary for Administration and Justice, Macao Special Administrative Region;* b. June 1954, Macao; ed Int. Open Univ. of Asia (Macao), Univ. of Languages and Culture, Beijing, Nat. Inst. of Public Admin., Beijing; joined Macao Govt 1974, Deputy Dir Macao Economic Services Bureau 1995–98, Dir 1998–99, Sec. for Admin. and Justice, Macao Special Admin. Region 1999–; Commr Exec. Council Macao Special Admin. Region 1999–; Medal of Professional Merit 1987, Medal of Dedication 1988. *Address:* Office of the Secretary for Administration and Justice, Headquarters of the Government, Avenida da Praia Grande, Macao Special Administrative Region, People's Republic of China (office). *Telephone:* 89895179 (office). *Fax:* 28726880 (office). *E-mail:* florindachan.saj@raem.gov.mo (office). *Website:* www.gov.mo (office).

CHAN, Heng Chee, BSocSc (Hons), MA, PhD; Singaporean diplomatist, political scientist and academic; *Ambassador-at-Large;* b. 19 April 1942, Singapore; ed Nat. Univ. of Singapore, Cornell Univ., USA; Asst Lecturer, Nat. Univ. of Singapore 1967–70, Lecturer 1970–75, Sr Lecturer 1976–80, Assoc. Prof. of Political Science 1981–, Head, Dept of Political Science 1985–88, Prof. 1990; Dir Inst. of Policy Studies, Singapore Jan.–Dec. 1988; Amb. and Perm. Rep. to UN, New York 1989–91 (also accred as Amb. to Mexico 1989–91 and High Commr to Canada 1989–91); Exec. Dir Singapore Int. Foundation 1991–96; Amb. to USA 1996–2012, Amb.-at-Large 2012–, Rep. to ASEAN Intergovernmental Comm. on Human Rights 2012–; Dir Inst. of SE Asian Studies 1993; Chair. Nat. Arts Council, Lee Kuan Yew Centre for Innovative Cities at Singapore Univ. of Tech. and Design; mem. Int. Council of Asia Soc. 1991–, Singapore Nat. Cttee of Council for Security Co-operation in the Asia-Pacific 1993–, IISS Council, Hong Kong 1995–, Int. Advisory Bd of Council on Foreign Relations, New York 1995–, Presidential Council for Minority Rights 2012–, Bd of Trustees Nat. Univ. of Singapore 2012–, Bd Govs S. Rajaratnam School of Int. Studies at Nanyang Technological Univ. 2013–, Bd of Lowy Inst. for Int. Policy; Trustee, Asia Soc.; Hon. DLit (Newcastle, Australia) 1994, (Buckingham, UK) 1998; Distinguished Service Order 2011; Woman of the Year (Singapore) 1991, Public Admin Medal (Gold) 1999, Meritorious Service Medal 2005, Inaugural Asia Soc. Outstanding Diplomatic Achievement Award 2012, Inaugural Foreign Policy Outstanding Diplomatic Achievement Award 2012, USN Distinguished Public Service Award 2012. *Publications:* The Dynamics of One Party Dominance: The PAP at the Grassroots (Nat. Book Award (non-fiction) 1978) 1976, A Sensation of Independence: A Political Biography of David Marshall (Nat. Book Award (non-fiction) 1986) 1984, Government and Politics of Singapore (co-ed.), The Prophetic and the Political 1987. *Address:* Ministry of Foreign Affairs, MFA Bldg, Tanglin, off Napier Road, Singapore 248163, Singapore (office). *Telephone:* 63798000 (office). *Fax:* 64747885 (office). *E-mail:* mfa@mfa.gov.sg (office). *Website:* www.mfa.gov.sg (office).

CHAN, Jackie, MBE; Chinese actor, martial artist, film director and film producer; b. (Chan Kong-Sang), 7 April 1954, Hong Kong; s. of Chi-Ping Chan and Lee-Lee Chan; m. Lin Feng-Jiao 1982; one s.; ed Chinese Opera Research Inst.; attached to Beijing opera troupe at age of six; began film career as stuntman; worked in Australia; returned to Hong Kong, roles as stuntman or extra, Shaw Brothers Studios; signed with Golden Harvest 1980; est. The Jackie Chan Charitable Foundation 1988, The Jackie Chan Civil Aviation Foundation 2006; Amb., Hong Kong Tourism Board 2003–, Asia Pacific Tourism 2006–; UN Goodwill Amb. 2004–; Cultural Amb. People's Repub. of China 2006–; Fellow, Hong Kong Acad. of Performing Arts 1998–; Appeal Patron Save China's Tigers Campaign 2006–; took part in Beijing Olympics closing ceremony 2008; Hon. Prin. Qiannan Normal Coll. for Nationalities, People's Repub. of China; Silver Bauhinia Star (Hong Kong) 1999; Hon. DScS (Baptist Univ. Hong Kong) 1996; numerous awards, including Best Picture Award, Hong Kong Film 1989, Best Actor, Golden Horse Awards (Taiwan) 1992, 1993, MTV Lifetime Achievement Award 1995, Best Action Choreography, Hong Kong Film 1996, 1999, Maverick Tribute Award Cinequest San Jose Film Festival 1998, Third Hollywood Film Festival Actor of the Year 1999, Indian Film Awards Int. Achievement Award 2000, Montreal World Film Festival Grand Prix of the Americas 2001, MTV Movie Awards Best Fight Scene 2002, Golden Horse Best Action Choreography (Taiwan) 2004, Hong Kong Film Award for Professional Achievement 2005, mem. American Red Cross Nat. Celebrity Cabinet 2006, Laureus Friends and Ambs Certificate, Laureus Sport for Good 2006, Goodwill Amb., Beijing Olympics 2008. *Films include:* child roles: Big and Little Wong Tin-Bar 1962, The Lover Eternal 1963, The Story of Qui Xiang Lin 1964, Come Drink with Me 1966, A Touch of Zen 1968; adult roles: Fist of Fury (stuntman) 1971, The Little Tiger of Canton 1971, The Heroine 1971, Not Scared to Die 1973, Enter the Dragon (stuntman) 1973, All in the Family 1975, The Himalayan (stuntman) 1975, Hand of Death 1976, New Fist of Fury 1976, Shaolin Wooden Men 1976, Killer Meteors 1977, To Kill with Intrigue 1977, Snake and Crane Arts of Shaolin 1978, Magnificent Bodyguards 1978, Spiritual Kung Fu 1978, Dragon Fist 1978, Snake in Eagle's Shadow 1978, Drunken Master 1978, Fearless Hyena 1979, Fearless Hyena II 1980, The Young Master (also dir) 1980, Battle Creek Brawl 1980, The Cannonball Run 1980, Dragon Lord (dir and actor) 1982, Fantasy Mission Force (stuntman) 1982, Winners and Sinners 1983, Cannonball Run II 1983, Project A (also dir) 1983, Wheels on Meals 1984, My Lucky Stars 1985, Twinkle, Twinkle, Lucky Stars 1985, The Protector 1985, Heart of Dragon 1985, Police Story (Hong Kong Best Film Award) 1985, Armour of God (also co-dir) 1986, Project A II (also dir and writer) 1987, Dragons Forever 1987, Police Story II (also dir, writer and stunt coordinator) 1988, Miracles: Mr. Canton and Lady Rose (also dir, writer and stunt coordinator) 1989, Armour of God II: Operation Condor (also dir, producer, writer and stunt coordinator) 1990, Island of Fire 1991, Twin Dragons 1991 (also stunt choreographer), Police Story III: Supercop (also exec. producer and stunt coordinator) 1992, City Hunter (also producer and stunt coordinator) 1993, Crime Story (also producer and stunt coordinator) 1993, Rumble in the Bronx (also producer, writer, jt stunt coordinator and martial arts dir) 1994, Thunderbolt (also producer and stunt coordinator) 1995, Police Story IV: First Strike (also producer and jt stunt coordinator) 1996, Mr Nice Guy (also producer) 1997, An Alan Smithee Film: Burn Hollywood Burn (special appearance) 1997, Who Am I? (also dir, co-producer, co-writer and stunt coordinator) 1998, Rush Hour (also stunt coordinator) 1999, Gorgeous (also co-producer, co-writer and action choreographer) 1999, Shanghai Noon (also co-producer and exec. producer) 2000, Accidental Spy (also co-producer and stunt choreographer) 2001, Rush Hour II (also stunt choreographer) 2001, The Tuxedo 2002, Shanghai Knights (also stunt choreographer) 2003, The Medallion (also exec. producer) 2003, The Twins Effect 2003, Enter the Phoenix (also exec. producer) 2004, Around the World in 80 Days (exec. producer, actor, stunt coordinator) 2004, New Police Story (also exec. producer, stunt choreographer and action dir) 2004, The Huadu Chronicles: Blade of the Rose 2004, Rice Rhapsody (exec. producer) 2005, The Myth (also exec. producer and stunt dir) 2005, Everlasting Regret (co-producer) 2005, Rob-B-Hood (also exec. producer, writer, stunt choreographer and action dir) 2006, Rush Hour 3 2007, Kung Fu Panda (voice) 2008, The Forbidden Kingdom 2008, Shinjuku Incident 2008, The Spy Next Door 2010, The Karate Kid 2010, Kung Fu Panda 2 (voice) 2011, 1911 2011, Chinese Zodiac 2012. *Publications:* I'm Jackie Chan (autobiog.). *Address:* The Jackie Chan Group, 145 Waterloo Road, Kowloon-Tong, Kowloon, Hong Kong Special Administrative Region, People's Republic of China. *Telephone:* 27940388 (office). *Fax:* 23387742 (office). *E-mail:* jcgroup@jackiechan.com (office). *Website:* www.jackiechan.com (office).

CHAN, Rt Hon. Sir Julius, PC, GCMG, KBE, CBE, GCL; Papua New Guinea politician; *Governor, New Ireland Province;* b. 29 Aug. 1939, Tanga, New Ireland; s. of Chin Pak and Tingoris Chan; m. Stella Ahmat 1966; one d. three s.; ed Marist Brothers Coll., Ashgrove, Queensland and Univ. of Queensland, Australia; Co-operative Officer, Papua New Guinea Admin. 1960–62; Man. Dir Coastal Shipping Co. Pty Ltd; mem. House of Ass. 1968–75, 1982–97, Deputy Speaker, Vice-Chair. Public Accounts Cttee 1968–72; Founder and Parl. Leader of People's Progress Party 1970–97; Minister of Finance and Parl. Leader of Govt Business 1972–77; Deputy Prime Minister and Minister for Primary Industry 1977–78, Prime Minister 1980–82, Deputy Prime Minister 1986–88, Minister of Trade and Industry 1986–88, Deputy Prime Minister 1992–94, Minister for Finance and Planning 1992–94, for Foreign Affairs and Trade 1994–96; Prime Minister 1994–97; mem. Parl. 2007–; Gov. New Ireland Prov. 2007–; Gov. for Papua New Guinea and Vice-Chair. Asian Devt Bank 1975–77; Chair. Eminent Person Group 2003–04; Chancellor Univ. of Vudal 2004–07; Fellowship mem. Int. Bankers' Asscn Inc., USA 1976; Hon. DEcon (Dankook Univ., Seoul) 1978; Hon. DTech (Univ. of Tech., Papua New Guinea) 1983. *Leisure interests:* boating, swimming, travel. *Address:* Office of the Governor, PO Box 130, Kavieng, New Ireland Province, Papua New Guinea.

CHAN, Kwok-Bun, PhD; Canadian sociologist and academic; *Chair Professor, Department of Sociology, Hong Kong Baptist University;* b. 9 April 1950, China; m. Wong Suk-yee; two c.; ed York Univ., Canada; currently Prof. and Head of Dept of Sociology, Hong Kong Baptist Univ.; fmr Dir David C. Lam Inst. for East-West Studies; Sr Lecturer in Sociology, Nat. Univ. of Singapore; mem. Hong Kong Central Policy Unit; Ed. Social Transformation of Chinese Society. *Publications:* Stepping Out: The Making of Chinese Entrepreneurs (co-author) 1995, Chinese Business Networks: State, Economy and Culture (ed.) 2000, Alternate Identities: the Chinese of Contemporary Thailand (co-ed.) 2001, Past Times: A Social History of Singapore (co-ed.) 2003, Chinese Identities, Ethnicity and Cosmopolitanism 2005, Migration, Ethnic Relations and Chinese Business 2005, Conflict and Innovation: Joint Ventures in China (co-ed.) 2006, Work Stress and Coping Among Professionals (ed.) 2007, East-West Identities: Globalization, Localization, and Hybridization (co-ed.) 2007, Circuit Entrepreneurs: A Study of Mobile Chinese Immigrant Entrepreneurs (in Chinese) (co-author) 2007, Our Families, Our Homes: Sociological Studies of Families in Hong Kong and China (in Chinese) (ed.) 2008; several articles in journals, contribs to books. *Address:* Department of Sociology, Hong Kong Baptist University, Kowloon Tong, Hong Kong Special Administrative Region, People's Republic of China (office). *Telephone:* 3411-7130 (office). *Fax:* 3411-7893 (office). *E-mail:* ckb@hkbu.edu.hk (office). *Website:* socweb .hkbu.edu.hk (office).

CHAN, Laiwa, (Chen Lihua); Chinese real estate executive; *President, Fu Wah International Group;* b. 1941, Beijing; started furniture maintenance business 1976; moved to Hong Kong 1982, f. Fu Wah International HK Group (real estate developer) 1988, becoming Pres.; returned to mainland late 1980s; property devts include Changan Club, Beijing, Jinbao Street (luxury shopping district); f. China Red Sandalwood Museum 1999, now curator; mem. CPPCC; ranked by Forbes magazine amongst The World's 100 Most Powerful Women (33rd) 2011, (79th) 2012. *Address:* Fu Wah International Group, 89 Jin Bao Street, Beijing, People's Republic of China (office). *Telephone:* (10) 85229988 (office). *Fax:* (10) 85221386 (office). *E-mail:* gmoffice@fuwahgroup.com (office). *Website:* www.fuwahgroup.com (office).

CHAN, Laurie; Solomon Islands politician and diplomatist; *Ambassador to Taiwan;* b. 6 April 1965; s. of Sir Thomas Chan; mem. Nat. Parl. for W Guadalcanal Constituency 2001–, mem. Bills and Legislation Cttee 2006, Chair. Foreign Relations Cttee 2008; Minister of Finance and Treasury 2002, of Foreign Affairs, Commerce and Tourism 2002–06, of Justice and Legal Affairs 2009; Amb to Taiwan 2012–. *Address:* Embassy of the Solomon Islands, 7/F, 9-1 Lane 62, Tien Mou West Road, Taipei 11156, Taiwan (office). *Telephone:* (2) 28731168 (office). *Fax:* (2) 28735224 (office). *E-mail:* embassy@solomons.org.tw (office). *Website:* www.solomons.org.tw (office).

CHAN, Margaret Fung Fu-chun, OBE, MSc, MScPH, MD, DSc, FFPHM; Chinese physician and international organization executive; *Director-General, World Health Organization;* b. 1947, Hong Kong; m.; one s.; ed Northcote Coll. of Educ., Hong Kong, Univ. of Western Ontario, Canada, Nat. Univ. of Singapore,

Harvard Business School, USA, Tsinghua Univ., Beijing, Nat. School of Admin, Beijing; Rotating Internship, Victoria Hosp., London, Ont. 1977–78; Medical Officer (Maternal and Child Health Services), Dept of Health, Hong Kong 1978–85, Sr Medical Officer (Family Health Services) 1985–87, Prin. Medical Officer (Health Admin) 1987–89, Asst Dir (Personal Health Services) 1989–92, Deputy Dir 1992–94, Dir Dept of Health, Hong Kong Special Admin. Region 1994–2003; Dir Dept of Protection of the Human Environment, WHO 2003–05, Asst Dir-Gen. of Communicable Diseases and Rep. of Dir-Gen. for Pandemic Influenza 2005–06, Dir-Gen. WHO 2006–, Organizer 43rd Session WHO Regional Cttee for the Western Pacific 1992, Chair. 49th Session WHO Regional Cttee for the Western Pacific 1998, WHO Guidelines on Methodologies for Research and Evaluation of Traditional Medicine 2000, WHO Int. Conf. for Drug Regulatory Authorities 2001 Planning Cttee 2000–02, Vice-Chair. WHO Working Group on Framework Convention on Tobacco Control 1999–2000, Moderator WHO Western Pacific Region Ministerial Roundtable on Social Safety Net 1999; Prince Mahidol Award in Public Health (Thailand) 1999, ranked by Forbes magazine amongst The World's 100 Most Powerful Women (37th) 2007, (84th) 2008, (38th) 2009, (68th) 2011, (37th) 2012, (33rd) 2013, and amongst The World's Most Powerful People (58th) 2012, (59th) 2013. *Address:* World Health Organization, Ave Appia 20, 1211 Geneva 27, Switzerland (office). *Telephone:* 227912111 (office). *Fax:* 227913111 (office). *E-mail:* info@who.int (office). *Website:* www.who.int (office).

CHAN, Patrick Lewis, (Chan Wai-Kuan); Canadian figure skater; b. 31 Dec. 1990, Ottawa, Ont.; s. of Lewis Chan and Karen Chan; ed École secondaire Étienne-Brûlé, Toronto, Colorado Coll., USA; began figure skating aged five; invited and/or participated in skating tours, shows and competitions in Canada, USA, China, Taiwan, S Korea, Japan, Europe and elsewhere; Pre-novice Men's Champion, Canadian nat. championships 2003, Men's Novice Champion 2004, Men's Jr Champion 2005; silver medal, World Jr Championships 2007; Men's Champion, Grand Prix of France (Trophée Eric-Bompard) 2007 (youngest in history aged 16), 2008; Four Continents Men's Champion, Vancouver 2009, 2012; six-time Canadian Men's Champion (youngest in history aged 17) 2008–13; Men's Champion, Skate Canada Int. Grand Prix 2008, 2010, 2011; silver medal, World Championships, Los Angeles 2009, Turin 2010, gold medal, Moscow 2011, gold medal Nice 2012, gold medal, London, Ont. 2013; winner, Grand Prix Final, Beijing 2011, Quebec City 2012, third, Sochi 2013; finished fifth in Men's Event at Winter Olympics, Vancouver 2010; Japan Open Champion 2011; set world record of 93.02 points for the highest score in a short programme, at World Championships in Moscow, eclipsing record of 91.30 set by Olympic champion, Evgeni Plushenko 2006, also set world records for highest score in long programme (187.96) and highest overall score (280.98) 27 April 2011; set new world record of 98.37 points in the short programme under the ISU Judging System at World Championships, London, Ont. 2013; mem. Canadian Olympic Cttee Adopt-an-Athlete programme 2008–; Amb. and supporter, Ronald McDonald House Charities of Canada 2008–; Athlete Amb., Right to Play Canada 2010–; featured guest speaker for various figure skating asscns and clubs, nat. tennis youth squad, synchronized swimming asscns, etc.; TD Canada Trust Chinese Canadian Youth of the Year, Chinese Cultural Centre of Greater Toronto 2007, named by Asia Network magazine as Asian of the Year in arts and sports 2008, Ontario Male Athlete of the Year 2009, named by The Globe and Mail as one of the most prominent sports personalities in their annual Power List in Canadian sports 2009, Guinness World Records – for short programme, long programme and combined score 2011, Distinguished Canadian Leadership Award, Univ. of Ottawa 2011, Sportsnet's Canadian Athlete of the Year 2011, QMI Agency Canadian Male Athlete of the Year 2011, Lionel Conacher Award (The Canadian Press' Canadian male athlete of the year) 2011, Lou Marsh Trophy as Canada's top athlete 2011. *Leisure interests:* golf, tennis, skiing, music, video games, cars. *Address:* c/o Insight Sports Ltd, 184 Pearl Street, Suite 302, Toronto, ON M5H 1L5, Canada. *Telephone:* (416) 593-0915. *E-mail:* info@insightsports.com. *Website:* www .insightsports.com; www.patrickchan.ca.

CHAN, Tony F., BS, MS, PhD; American mathematician, computer scientist, academic and university administrator; *President, Hong Kong University of Science and Technology;* ed California Inst. of Tech., Stanford Univ.; fmr Research Fellow, California Inst. of Tech.; taught Computer Science at Yale Univ.; Prof. of Math., UCLA 1986, Chair. Dept of Math. 1997–2001, Dean of Physical Science 2001–06, held hon. jt appointments with Univ.'s BioEngineering Dept and Computer Science Dept, one of the principal investigators who made successful proposal to NSF to form Inst. for Pure and Applied Math. (IPAM) at UCLA, Dir IPAM 2000–01; Asst Dir Math. and Physical Sciences Directorate, NSF 2006–09; Pres. Hong Kong Univ. of Science and Tech. 2009–; fmr mem. NSF Math. and Physical Sciences Advisory Cttee, US Nat. Cttee for Math.; one of five US reps to Gen. Ass. of the Int. Union of Mathematicians 2006; mem. Bd of Trustees King Abdullah Univ. of Science and Tech. (KAUST), Saudi Arabia, Pres.'s Advisory Council of Korea Advanced Inst. of Science and Tech. (KAIST), US Cttee of 100, Selection Cttee for Shaw Prize in Math. Sciences, Steering Cttee of Innovation and Tech. Comm. of Hong Kong Govt; mem. Editorial Bd SIAM Review, SIAM Journal of Scientific Computing, SIAM Journal of Imaging Sciences –2012, Asian Journal of Mathematics; an Ed.-in-Chief of Numerische Mathematik; mem. American Math. Soc., IEEE; Fellow, Soc. of Industrial and Applied Math. (SIAM), AAAS. *Publications:* more than 200 papers in peer-reviewed journals on mathematical image processing and computer vision, Very Large-Scale Integration (VLSI) physical design and computational brain mapping. *Address:* Office of the President, Hong Kong University of Science and Technology, Clear Water Bay, Kowloon, Hong Kong Special Administrative Region, People's Repub. of China (office). *Telephone:* 2358-6113 (office). *Fax:* 2358-0029 (office). *E-mail:* ophkust@ust .hk (office). *Website:* president.ust.hk (office).

CHAN FANG ON SANG, Hon. Anson, GCMG, CBE, JP, BA; Chinese fmr government official; b. 17 Jan. 1940, Shanghai; d. of Fang Zhaoling; m. Archibald Chan Tai-wing 1963; two c.; ed Hong Kong Univ.; held numerous positions at Govt Secr. including Asst Sec., 1963, 1966, Sec. 1988, Asst Financial Sec. 1970, Prin. Financial Sec. 1972, Deputy Sec. for NT 1975, for Social Services 1976–79, Dir Social Welfare Dept 1980, 1982–84, Sec. for Econ. Services 1987–93, Chief Sec. of Hong Kong 1993–2001 (retd); MP in Hong Kong Parl. for Hong Kong Island 2007–08; Founding mem. UNICEF Hong Kong Cttee; Patron and Hon. Adviser, Children's Cancer Foundation; Patron, Enlighten Hong Kong Ltd, SoulTalk

Foundation; Dir Reuters Founders Share Co. Ltd; mem. Salvation Army Advisory Bd; Patron Hong Kong Br. and mem. Bd of Dirs Royal Over-Seas League; Hon. Prof., Jiao Tong Univ. Shanghai, Hon. Fellow, SOAS, London; Grand Bauhinia Medal, Chevalier, Nat. Order of the Legion d'Honneur; Hon. LLD (Hong Kong, Liverpool, Open Univ. of Hong Kong, Hong Kong Chinese Univ., Sheffield); Hon. DHumLitt (Tufts). *Leisure interests:* music, reading, cooking. *Address:* 13C Queen's Centre, 58-64 Queen's Road East, Wanchai, Hong Kong Special Administrative Region, People's Republic of China (office). *Telephone:* 2520-2383 (home). *Fax:* 2520-2380 (home). *E-mail:* afangchan@biznetvigator.com (office).

CHAN-OCHA, Gen. Prayuth; Thai army officer; *Chief of Staff, Royal Thai Army;* b. 1954, Bangkok; m. Naraporn Chan-ocha; two d.; ed Armed Forces Acads Preparatory School, Bangkok, Chulachomklao Royal Mil. Acad., Nakhon Nayok Prov.; fmr commdr of several army divs including Commdr, 2nd Bn, 21st Infantry Regt (Queen's Guard), Chief of Staff, 21st Infantry Regt (Queen's Guard), Deputy Commdr, later Commdr, 21st Infantry Regt (Queen's Guard), Deputy Commdr-Gen., later Commdr-Gen., 2nd Infantry Div. (Queen's Guard), Deputy Army Area Commdr, Region 1, Army Area Commdr, Region 1 2006–08, Chief of Staff, Royal Thai Army 2008–. *Address:* Ministry of Defence, Thanon Sanamchai, Bangkok 10200, Thailand (office). *Telephone:* (2) 222-1121 (office). *Fax:* (2) 226-3117 (office).

CHAN SUK-CHONG, Tanya, LLB, LLM; Hong Kong barrister, actress and politician; b. 14 Sept. 1971; ed Univ. of Hong Kong; mem. Legis. Council for Hong Kong Island constituency 2008–12; mem. Central and Western Dist Council of Hong Kong for Peak constituency, Vice Chair. Culture, Leisure & Social Affairs Cttee; Founding mem. Civic Party, Vice-Chair. 2012–; Dir Hong Kong Mortgage Corpn Ltd, Urban Renewal Authority. *Play:* East Wing, West Wing (political satire). *Address:* Civic Party, Unit 202, 2/F, Blk B, Sea View Bldg, 4–6 Watson Road, North Point, Hong Kong Special Administrative Region, People's Republic of China (office). *Telephone:* 28657111 (office). *Fax:* 28652771 (office). *E-mail:* chantanya@civicparty.hk (office). *Website:* www.civicparty.hk (office).

CHANCELLOR, Alexander Surtees, CBE, BA; British journalist; b. 4 Jan. 1940, Ware, Herts., England; s. of Sir Christopher Chancellor, CMG and Sylvia Mary Chancellor (née Paget); m. Susanna Elizabeth Debenham 1964; two d.; ed Eton Coll., Trinity Hall, Cambridge; with Reuters News Agency 1964–74, Chief Corresp. in Italy 1968–73; with ITV News 1974–75; Ed. The Spectator 1975–84; Ed. Time and Tide 1984–86; Deputy Ed. Sunday Telegraph 1986; Washington Ed. The Independent 1986–88; Ed. The Independent Magazine 1988–92; The New Yorker (Ed. The Talk of the Town) 1992–93; columnist, The Times 1992–93, The Guardian 1996–2012, Slate 1997, The Daily Telegraph 1998–2004, Saga Magazine 2002–. *Publication:* Some Times in America 1999. *Address:* The Court House, Stoke Park, Stoke Bruerne, Towcester, Northants., NN12 7RZ, England. *Telephone:* (1604) 862329. *E-mail:* chancellor@dial.pipex.com.

CHAND, Lokendra Bahadur, BA, LLB; Nepalese politician; b. 15 Feb. 1940, Kurkuriya Village, Bashulinga Village Devt Cttee, Baitadi; s. of Mahavir Chand and Laxmi Chand; m.; seven c.; ed Pithauragarh, India, Tri-Chandra Coll., Kathmandu, DSB Degree Coll., Nainital, India and DAV Post-Grad. Coll., Dehradun, India; Founding mem. Shree Basudev High School, Liskita, served voluntarily as teacher 1961–64; practising advocate 1964–68; Vice-Chair. Lisakita Village Panchayat, Baitadi Dist 1968, Chair. Baitadi Dist Panchayat 1970, Pres. Mahakali Zonal Panchayat 1973, Vice-Chair. and Chair. Rastriya Panchayat (Nat. Ass.) 1974; Founder Rastriya Prajatantra Party (RPP), Chair. 1991, Leader and Pres. Parl. Bd after unification of Thapa and Chand Group 1994; elected mem. Parl. (RPP) for both constituencies of Baitadi Dist 1995, 2008–; Prime Minister of Nepal 1983–85, 1990, 1997, 2002–03; Founding Chair. Mahakali Sewa Samaj 1967; mem. Nepal Red Cross Soc. Cen. Exec. Cttee 1970. *Publications include:* Bahraun Kheladi (Twelfth Player), Visarjan (short stories) (Madan Puruskar Prize), Hiunko Tanna, Indra Dhanush, Aparichit Netako Saathi; also satirical essays, humorous plays and collections of short stories. *Leisure interest:* reading books on contemporary literature. *Address:* Rashtriya Prajatantra Party (RPP), Charumati Bahal, Chabahil, Kathmandu, Nepal. *Telephone:* (1) 4471071. *Fax:* (1) 4423384. *E-mail:* info@rppnepal.com. *Website:* www.rppnepal.org.

CHANDERPAUL, Shivnarine, BA, LLB; Guyanese professional cricketer; b. 16 Aug. 1974, Unity Village, East Coast, Demerara; left-handed batsman; leg-break bowler; plays for Guyana 1991–, West Indies (Capt. 2004–06) 1994–, Durham 2007–09, Royal Challengers Bangalore 2008, Lancashire 2010, Warwickshire 2011–, Khulna Royal Bengal 2012–; First-class debut: 1991/92; Test debut: West Indies v England, Georgetown 17–22 March 1994; One-Day Int. (ODI) debut: India v West Indies, Faridabad 17 Oct. 1994; T20I debut: NZ v West Indies, Auckland 16 Feb. 2006; Sir Garfield Sobers Trophy 2008, Wisden Cricketer of the Year 2008, ICC Player of the Year 2008. *Achievements include:* first Indo-Caribbean in West Indies team to play 100 Tests for the West Indies and has captained them in 14 Tests and 16 ODIs; featured with Ramnaresh Sarwan, making 104 in chasing a world record 418 to win in fourth innings of final Test match versus Australia 2002–03; made fourth fastest century in Test cricket, scoring three figures in 67 balls at Bourda, Guyana in series against Australia 2002–03; only second player to make a double century on debut as Test Capt., scoring an unbeaten 200 March 2005; ranked 5th in Test batting rankings 2008; became fourth West Indian batsman to accomplish 8,000 runs in Test cricket (second highest run scorer after Brian Lara) as well as rising in ranks to second of ICC test rankings 2008; ranked World No. 1 Test Batsman 2012; became the tenth batsman and the second West Indian batsman to pass 10,000 runs in Test cricket April 2012; one of only six players to have gone 1,000 minutes in Test cricket without conceding his wicket, has done this four times and is the only player to have done so more than once; only batsman in history of Test cricket to have faced 1,000 consecutive balls without getting out; one of only four batsmen to have averaged more than 100 in two different calendar years (qualification 400 runs) and the only one other than Sir Donald Bradman to do so in consecutive years; one of only three players to score half-centuries in seven consecutive Test innings. *Address:* c/o West Indies Cricket Board Inc., PO Box 616 W, St John's, Antigua. *Telephone:* 481-2450. *Fax:* 481-2498. *E-mail:* wicb@windiescricket.com.

CHANDLER, Kenneth A.; British journalist and consultant; b. 2 Aug. 1947, Westcliff-on-Sea, Essex; s. of Leonard Gordon Chandler and Beatrix Marie Chandler (née McKenzie); m. Erika Schwartz; five c.; Man. Ed. The New York Post

1978–86, 1993–99, Ed.-in-Chief, then Publr 1999–2002; Ed. Boston Herald 1986–93, Editorial Dir 2004–06; f. ChandlerMedia (media consulting firm), New York 2006, now Chandler Regan Strategies; Exec. Producer Fox TV's A Current Affair 1993; CEO Natural Energy Solutions Corpn 2002–03; mem. Bd of Dirs The Bridge Fund; *Telephone:* (914) 310-0876 (office). *E-mail:* ken@kchandler.com (office). *Website:* chandlermedia.com (office).

CHANDRA, Subhash; Indian media executive; *Chairman, Essel Group;* b. 30 Nov. 1950, Hissar, Haryana; m.; three c.; fmr rice packer in Hissar, Haryana; Founder-Chair. Essel Group 1976, comprising media, packaging, entertainment, tech.-enabled services, infrastructure devt and educ. assets, Group cos include Zee Entertainment Enterprise Ltd, Zee News Ltd, Zee Telefilms Ltd, Zee Turner Ltd, Zee Educ. Learning Systems, Dish TV, Wire & Wireless India Ltd, Essel Propack Ltd, ETC Networks Ltd, E-City Property Man. Services, Essel Infraprojects Ltd, Agrani Satellite Services Ltd, fmr jt owner (with Rupert Murdoch q.v.) of Zee Cinema, Zee TV and Zee India TV; Chair. Ekal Vidyalaya Foundation of India; est. Transnational Alternate Learning for Emancipation and Empowerment through Multimedia (TALEEM) 1996; Founder and Chair. Global Foundation for Civilizational Harmony; fmr Chair. Confed. of Indian Industry; f. Brain Trust of India; Trustee Global Vipassana Foundation; est. Indian Cricket League 2007; Ernst & Young Entrepreneur of the Year Award 1999, Business Standard's Businessman of the Year 1999, Global Indian Entertainment Personality of the Year, Fed. of Indian Chambers of Commerce and Industry 2004, Lifetime Achievement Award, Cable and Satellite Broadcasting Asscn of Asia 2009, The Hall of Fame – Entrepreneur 2010, Int. Emmy Directorate Award (first Indian) 2011, ranked 33rd by Economic Times Corporate Dossier on Corporate India's Definitive Power Listing 2012. *Address:* Essel Group, 135 Continental Building, Dr Annie Besant Road, Worli, Mumbai 400 018, India (office). *Telephone:* (22) 24903926 (office). *Fax:* (22) 24988728 (office). *E-mail:* feedback@esselgroup.com (office). *Website:* www.esselgroup.com (office).

CHANDRASEKARAN, Natarajan, BSc; Indian business executive; *CEO and Managing Director, Tata Consultancy Services;* b. 1963, Mohanur, Tamil Nadu; m. Lalitha Chandrasekaran; one s.; ed Coimbatore Inst. of Tech., Tamil Nadu, Regional Eng Coll., Trichy; joined Tata Consultancy Services 1987, Head of Global Sales 2002, COO –2009, CEO and Man. Dir 2009–, also Chair. Tata Consulting Services Luxembourg SA; Chair. TCS e-Serve Ltd (fmrly Citigroup Global Services Ltd), Dir 2008–; Dir (non-exec.) Diligenta Ltd, Business Support Services; Vice-Chair. Exec. Council, Nat. Asscn of Software and Service Companies 2011–; mem. IEEE, Computer Soc. of India, British Computer Soc.; All India Man. Asscn Business Leader Award 2011. *Address:* Tata Consultancy Services House, Raveline Street, Mumbai 400 001, India (office). *Telephone:* (22) 67789999 (office). *Fax:* (22) 67789000 (office). *E-mail:* investor.relations@tcs.com (office). *Website:* www.tcs.com (office).

CHANDRASEKHARAN, Komaravolu S, MA, MSc, PhD; Indian mathematician and academic; *Professor Emeritus, Eidgenössische Technische Hochschule (ETH), Zürich;* b. 21 Nov. 1920, Masulipatam, India; m. A. Sarada 1944; two s.; ed Presidency Coll., Madras Univ., Inst. for Advanced Study, Princeton, USA; Head, School of Math., Tata Inst. of Fundamental Research, Bombay 1949–65; Prof., ETH, Zürich 1965–88, Prof. Emer. 1988–; Sec., Int. Math. Union 1961–66, Pres. 1971–74; Vice-Pres. Int. Council of Scientific Unions 1963–66, Sec.-Gen. 1966–70; mem. Scientific Advisory Cttee to Cabinet, Govt of India 1961–66; Fellow, Nat. Inst. of Sciences of India, Indian Acad. of Sciences; Foreign mem. Finnish Acad. of Science and Letters 1975; lectured at more than 50 univs in the USA, USSR, Europe and Asia; Hon. Fellow, Tata Inst. of Fundamental Research 1970; Hon. mem. Austrian Acad. of Sciences 1996, American Math. Soc. 1998; Padma Shri 1959, Shanti Swarup Bhatnagar Memorial Award for Scientific Research 1959, Ramanujan Medal 1966. *Publications include:* Fourier Transforms (with S. Bochner) 1949, Typical Means (with S. Minakshisundaram) 1952, Lectures on the Riemann Zeta-function 1953, Notebooks of Srinivasa Ramanujan (two vols) (ed.) 1957, Collected Papers of Hermann Weyl (four vols) (ed.) 1968, Analytic Number Theory 1968, Arithmetical Functions 1970, Elliptic Functions 1985, Hermann Weyl, 1885–1985 (ed) 1986, Classical Fourier Transforms 1989, Siegel's Lectures on the Geometry of Numbers (ed.) 1989, Lectures on Topological Groups 1996, Integration Theory 1996; more than 70 research papers. *Leisure interests:* painting, English literature, music. *Address:* Rämistrasse 101, Hut D15, Eidgenössische Technische Hochschule, 8092 Zürich (office); Hedwigstrasse 29, 8032 Zürich, Switzerland (home). *Telephone:* (44) 6324199 (office); (44) 3819686 (home). *Website:* www.math.ethz.ch (office).

CHANDRASIRI, Maj.-Gen. G. A.; Sri Lankan army officer (retd) and government official; *Governor of Northern Province;* b. 1954; m.; three d.; ed St Mary's Coll., Chilaw, mil. training at Sri Lanka Mil. Acad., Diyatalawa; nat. class soccer player at time of enlistment into Sri Lanka Army; joined Sri Lanka Army Regular Force as Officer Cadet 1974; commissioned as Second Lt to 1st Recce Regt, Sri Lanka Armoured Corps 1976; first cavalry officer to deploy in Jaffna peninsula with a Troop of Armour (wheeled armoured cars) to assist infantry in counter-insurgency operations 1977–81, held appointments of Troop Leader, Regimental Signals Officer and Assistant Adjutant of 1st Recce Regt, Adjutant of 1st Recce Regt, Sri Lanka Armoured Corps 1981–83; apptd Squadron Commdr in own regt 1983–89; went to USA to follow Advance Armour Officers course at Armoured Warfare School, Fort Knox 1989; apptd Instructor at Sir John Kotelawala Defence Univ.; Gen. Staff Officer (Grade I), Operational HQ, Ministry of Defence 1991–92; followed Army Command and Staff Course at Tri Services Command and Staff Coll., Bangladesh 1993; assumed command of 4th Armoured Regt, Sri Lanka Armoured Corps 1994; Sr Command Course, Coll. of Combat Mhow, India; apptd Col of Gen. Staff of 51 Infantry Div., Jaffna 1995, took over command of 511 Infantry Brigade, Jaffna 1996, given command of only Armoured Brigade in Sri Lanka Army 1997–2000, participated in Operation Jayasikuru to link Vavuniya with Jaffna along main supply route (A9) and succeeded in capturing Omanthei Township; apptd Deputy GOC 21 Div. and Area Commdr, Mannar 2002, assigned command of 52 Infantry Div., Jaffna 2002–04, Dir Gen. Gen. Staff of Jt Operations HQ 2004–05, assisted Chief of Defence Staff on decision-making process at jt operational level in counter-terrorist operations; went to India to follow Nat. Defence Coll. course in New Delhi 2005; Commdr Security Forces HQ, Jaffna 2005–09, Chief of Staff of Sri Lanka Army March–July 2009; Gov. Northern Prov.

July 2009–; several decorations and gallantry awards; recipient of Sri Lanka schools soccer colours 1972, awarded trophy for most outstanding officer cadet for mil. tactics at commissioning parade 1976. *Address:* Governor's Secretariat, Kanniya Rd, Varothayanagar, Trincomalee, Sri Lanka (office). *Telephone:* (26) 2226970 (office); (11) 2883371 (Sub-Office) (office). *Fax:* (11) 2885436 (Sub-Office) (office). *E-mail:* governornp@sltnet.lk (office). *Website:* www.np.gov.lk (office).

CHANDY, Oommen, BA, BL; Indian politician; *Chief Minister of Kerala;* b. 31 Oct. 1943, Kumarakom, Kottayam Dist; s. of Puthupally Karottu Vallakkalil K.O Chandy and Baby Chandy; m. Mariamma Oommen; one s. two d.; ed St George High School, Puthupally, CMS Kottayam, SB Coll. Changanassery, Law Coll., Ernakulam; Pres. All Kerala Balajana Sakhyam 1961–62; State Pres. Kerala Students Union 1967–69; Pres. Youth Congress 1970–71; mem. Kerala Legis. Ass. 1970–, Leader of the Opposition 2006–; Minister for Labour 1977–78, for Home Affairs 1981–82, for Finance 1991–94; Convenor United Democratic Front 1991, 2001; Chief Minister of Kerala 2004–05, 2011–; Leader of the Opposition, Kerala 2005–11. *Address:* Cantonment House, Vikas Bhavan, Thiruvananthapuram 695 033 (office); Karottu-Vallakkalil, Puthuppally, Kottayam 686 011, India (home). *Telephone:* (471) 2318330 (office); (481) 2351135. *Fax:* (471) 2315625 (office). *E-mail:* oc@oommenchandy.net (office); office@oommenchandy.net (office). *Website:* www.oommenchandy.net (office).

CHANEY, Frederick Michael, AO, LLB; Australian lawyer and politician; *Chairman, Desert Knowledge Australia;* b. 28 Oct. 1941, Perth, Western Australia; s. of the late Frederick Charles Chaney and of Mavis Mary Bond; m. Angela Margaret Clifton 1964; three s.; ed Univ. of Western Australia; in public service, Papua New Guinea 1964–66; pvt. law practice 1966–74; Senator from WA 1974–90, Senate Opposition Whip 1975, Govt Whip 1976–78; Minister for Admin. Services 1978, Assisting the Minister for Educ. 1978–79, for Aboriginal Affairs 1978–80, Assisting the Minister for Nat. Devt and Energy 1979–80, for Social Security 1980–83; Leader of Opposition in Senate 1983–90; Shadow Minister for Industrial Relations 1987–88, 1989–90, for the Environment 1990–92; Deputy Leader of the Opposition 1989–90; mem. House of Reps for Pearce 1990–93; Chair. Fightback! (Co-ordination and Marketing Group) 1992–93; Researcher and Lecturer, Grad. School of Man., Univ. of Western Australia 1993–95; Chancellor Murdoch Univ., WA 1995–2003; Chair. Desert Knowledge Australia 2005–; mem. Nat. Native Title Tribunal 1995–2000, Deputy Pres. 2000–07; Co-Chair. Reconciliation Australia 2000–05, mem. Bd of Dirs 2000–; Hon. LLD (Murdoch, WA); Hon. DUniv (Australian Catholic Univ.) 2007; Hon. DLitt (Univ. of Western Australia); Sr Australian of the Year 2014. *Leisure interests:* swimming, reading. *Address:* 23B Brown Street, Claremont, WA 6010, Australia. *E-mail:* fredchaney@iinet.net.au.

CHANEY, Michael A., AO, BSc, MBA, FAIM, FAICD; Australian business executive; *Chairman, National Australia Bank Ltd;* ed Univ. of Western Australia and Harvard Business School, USA; fmr adviser on corp. lending and finance, Australian Industry Devt Corpn; worked in finance and petroleum industries in Australia and USA –1983; joined Wesfarmers Ltd 1983, Chief Financial Officer 1984–92, mem. Bd 1988, Man. Dir and CEO 1992–2004, Man. Dir 1992–2005, Dir (non-exec.) 2004–; mem. Bd of Dirs Gresham Partners Holdings Ltd 1985–, Chair. 2005–; Dir (non-exec.) National Australia Bank (Chair. 2005–, also Chair. Nomination Cttee), Woodside Petroleum Ltd 2005– (Chair. 2007–); mem. Bd of Dirs BHP Billiton Ltd 1995–2005, BHP Billiton PLC 2001–05; Chancellor Univ. of Western Australia 2006–; Dir Centre for Ind. Studies 2000–; Chair. Australian Research Alliance for Children and Youth Ltd 2002–07; Pres. Business Council of Australia 2005–07; mem. Council of Nat. Gallery of Australia 2000–06, JP Morgan Int. Advisory Council 2003–, Fellow, Australian Inst. of Co. Dirs; Hon. Pres. Business Council of Australia; Hon. LLD (Univ. of Western Australia). *Address:* National Australia Bank, 500 Bourke Street, 24th Floor, Melbourne, Vic. 3000, Australia (office). *Telephone:* (8) 9322-7913 (Perth) (office); (3) 8641-3500 (Melbourne) (office). *Fax:* (8) 9322-7913 (Perth) (office); (3) 8641-4912 (Melbourne) (office); (3) 9208-5695 (Melbourne) (office). *E-mail:* info@national.com.au (office). *Website:* www.nab.com.au (office).

CHANFIOU, Mzé Aboudou Mohamed; Comoran central banker; *Governor, Banque Centrale des Comores;* Deputy Gov., Banque Centrale des Comores –2011, Gov. 2011–. *Address:* Office of the Governor, Banque Centrale des Comores, pl. de France, BP 405, Moroni, Comoros (office). *Telephone:* 7731814 (office). *Fax:* 7730349 (office). *E-mail:* bancecom@comorestelecom.com (office). *Website:* www .bancecom.com (office).

CHANG, Datuk Brian; Singaporean shipping industry executive; *Executive Chairman, Yantai Raffles Shipyard Pte Ltd;* b. South Africa; m. Annie Chang; three c.; ed London School of Engineering; started career with Vosper Thorneycroft, Singapore, then with Far East Levingston Shipbuilding Pte Ltd (now Kepfels) 1967–70; f. Promet Group (civil and marine eng. contractor) 1970, Exec. Chair. –1994; Founder and Exec. Chair. Yantai Raffles Shipyard Pte Ltd 1994– (shipyard located in Yantai, Shandong, People's Repub. of China). *Address:* Yantai Raffles Shipyard Pte Ltd, No. 1 Claymore Drive #08-04, Orchard Towers, Singapore 229594 (office). *Telephone:* 6735-8690 (office). *Fax:* 6734-5449 (office). *E-mail:* enquire@yantai-raffles.com (office). *Website:* www.yantai-raffles.com (office).

CHANG, Chin-chen, PhD, FIEE; Taiwanese computer scientist and academic; *Professor and Dean of Academic Affairs, National Chung Cheng University;* b. 12 Nov. 1954, Taiwan; m. Ling-Hui Hwang 1981; one s. two d.; ed Nat. Tsing Hua Univ., Hsinchu and Nat. Chiao Tung Univ., Hsinchu; Assoc. Prof., Dept of Computer Eng, Nat. Chiao Tung Univ. 1982–83; Assoc. Prof., Dept of Applied Math., Nat. Chung Hsin Univ. 1983–85, Prof. 1985–89; Prof. and Chair. Dept of Computer Eng, Nat. Chung Cheng Univ. 1989–92, Prof. and Dean Coll. of Eng 1992–95, Prof. and Dean of Academic Affairs 1995–, Acting Pres. 1996–99; Ed. Journal of Information Science and Engineering 1988–93, Journal of the Chinese Institute of Engineers 1990–93, Information Science Applications 1994–; Ed.-in-Chief Information and Education 1987–; reviewer for numerous int. journals of information science; Outstanding Talent in Information Science Award of Repub. of China 1984, several Distinguished Research Awards of Nat. Science Council 1986–. *Publications:* more than 300 tech. papers on database design and information security in leading scientific journals and conf. proceedings; 12 books in Chinese on database design, data structures, computer viruses, information security, cryptography etc.; Ed. Advanced Database Research and Development Series (vols 1, 2, 3) 1992. *Address:* Department of Computer Science and Information Engineering, National Chung Cheng University, Chiayi, Taiwan (office). *Telephone:* (5) 272-0411 (office); (4) 325-9100 (home); (5) 272-0405. *Fax:* (5) 272-0839; (4) 327-7423 (home); (5) 272-0404. *E-mail:* ccc@cs.ccu.edu.tw (office). *Website:* www.cs.ccu.edu.tw/-ccc (office).

CHANG, Chun-hsiung, LLB; Taiwanese politician; b. 23 March 1938; m.; three s. one d.; ed Nat. Taiwan Univ.; defence lawyer in mil. trial following Kaohsiung Incident 1980; mem. Legis. Yuan 1983–2000; Founder-mem. Democratic Progressive Party (DPP) 1986, mem. Cen. Standing Cttee and Cen. Exec. Cttee DPP 1986–2000, Exec. Dir DPP Caucus in Legis. Yuan 1987–88, Gen. Convenor 1990, 1998–99, Sec.-Gen. DPP 2002–05; Sec.-Gen. Office of Pres. 2000; Vice-Premier 2000; Premier 2000–02, 2007–08; currently volunteer with Christian Born Anew Fellowship. *Address:* c/o Democratic Progressive Party, 10/F, 30 Beiping East Road, Taipei, 10051, Taiwan.

CHANG, Dae-whan, MA, PhD; South Korean politician and business executive; *Chairman, Maeil Business Newspaper and TV;* b. 21 March 1952; m.; two c.; ed Univ. of Rochester, USA, Coll. of Europe, Belgium, George Washington Univ., New York Univ., USA; Instructor and Capt., Korea Air Force Acad. 1977–83; mem. Acad. of Int. Business, USA 1984; Dir Planning Office, Maeil Business Newspaper 1986, mem. Bd of Dirs and Dir of Business Devt HQ 1986, Man. Dir 1987, Exec. Dir 1988, Pres. and Publr 1988–2002, Pres. Maeil Business News TV Co. 1993–2002, currently Chair. Maeil Business Newspaper and TV; Acting Prime Minister of Repub. of Korea Aug. 9–28 2002; Lecturer in Int. Business Man., Grad. School of Seoul Nat. Univ. 1988–97; Auditor IPI Korean Nat. Cttee 1988–2002, PFA Korean Nat. Cttee 1991–2002; Dir Korea Newspapers Asscn 1986–2002, Auditor 1996–2002; Founder Vision Korea Campaign 1997–2002, World Knowledge Forum 1998–2002; Chair. Press Foundation of Asia March–Aug. 2002, New York Univ. Korean Alumni Asscn; mem. Advisory Bd Sungkyunkwan Univ. Grad. School of Business, World Asscn of Newspapers 1986–2002; Order of Civil Merit 1992, Dongbag Medal 1992. *Publications include:* (in Korean): International Business Negotiation 1989, New Product Millennium (jtly.) 1997. *Address:* Maeil Business Newspaper Building, 51-9, 1-ga, Bil-dong, Jung-gu, Seoul 100-728, Republic of Korea (office). *Telephone:* (2) 2000-2114 (office). *E-mail:* mkmaster@mk.co.kr (office). *Website:* www.mk.co.kr (office).

CHANG, Fa-Te, BA; Taiwanese business executive; *President and Co-CEO, Cathay Life Insurance;* ed Nat. Chung Hsing Univ.; Pres. and Co-CEO Cathay Life Insurance Co. Ltd 2008–, mem. Bd of Dirs Cathay Financial Holdings. *Address:* Cathay Life Insurance Co. Ltd, 296 Jen Ai Road, Section 4, Taipei 10639, Taiwan (office). *Telephone:* (2) 2755-1399 (office). *Fax:* (2) 2704-1485 (office). *E-mail:* info@cathlife.com.tw (office); service@cathayholdings.com.tw (office). *Website:* www .cathlife.com.tw (office).

CHANG, Hsin-kang (H. K.), BS, MS, PhD; Chinese university administrator and academic; *Yeh-Lu Xun Chair Professor in Social Sciences, Peking University;* ed Nat. Taiwan Univ., Stanford and Northwestern Univs, USA; Asst Prof. of Civil Eng, Coll. of Eng and Applied Sciences, State Univ. of New York, Buffalo, USA 1969–75, Assoc. Prof. 1975–76; Assoc. Prof. of Biomedical Eng and Physiology, Faculty of Medicine, McGill Univ., Montreal, Canada 1976–80, Prof. 1980–84, Adjunct Prof. of Chemical Eng 1980–84; Visiting Prof., Faculté de Médecine, Université Paris-Val de Marne, Créteil, France 1981–82; Prof. of Biomedical Eng, School of Eng and Prof. of Physiology and Biophysics, School of Medicine, Univ. of Southern California, Los Angeles, USA 1984–90, Chair. Dept of Biomedical Eng 1985–90; Prof. of Chemical Eng and Founding Dean, School of Eng, Hong Kong Univ. of Science and Tech. 1990–94; Prof. of Chemical Eng and Dean, School of Eng and Prof. of Medicine, School of Medicine, Univ. of Pittsburgh 1994–96; Univ. Prof. and Pres. City Univ. of Hong Kong 1996–2007; Hon. Prof. and Wei Lun Sr Visiting Scholar, Tsinghua Univ. 2007–; Yeh-Lu Xun Chair Prof. in Social Sciences, Peking Univ. 2007–; Chair. Culture and Heritage Comm., Govt of Hong Kong Special Admin. Region (SAR) 2000–03; Dir (Non-Exec.) Hon Kwok Land Investment Co. Ltd 2007–, PCCW Ltd; mem. Judicial Officers Recommendation Comm., Govt of Hong Kong SAR 1999–2005, Council of Advisors on Innovation and Tech., Govt of Hong Kong SAR 2000–04, CPPCC 2003–; Foreign mem. Royal Acad. of Eng (UK); Gold Bauhinia Star (Hong Kong SAR) 2002; Justice of Peace (Hong Kong SAR) 1999; Chevalier de la Légion d'honneur, Commdr,Ordre des Palmes Académiques (France). *Publications:* five books and many articles in Chinese; more than 100 scientific articles, two research monographs and one Canadian patent. *Address:* Department of Sociology, Peking University, Haidian District, Beijing, People's Republic of China (office). *Website:* www.pku.edu.cn (office).

CHANG, Jin Sook; American/South Korean business executive; *Co-founder and Chief Merchandising Officer, Forever 21;* b. Pusan, S Korea; m. Do Won Chang; two c.; emigrated with her husband from S Korea 1981; co-f. (with her husband) Forever 21 retail chain and opened first store 1984, currently Chief Merchandising Officer; operates more than 480 stores world-wide with more than 34,000 employees; ranked by Forbes magazine amongst The World's 100 Most Powerful Women (39th) 2011. *Address:* Forever 21, Inc., 2001 South Alameda Street, Los Angeles, LA 90058, USA (office). *Telephone:* (213) 741-5100 (office). *Fax:* (213) 741-5161 (office). *E-mail:* info@forever21.com (office). *Website:* www.forever21.com (office).

CHANG, John H., BA, MS; Taiwanese politician; b. 2 May 1941, Kiangsi; m. Helen Chang Huang; three c.; ed Soochow Univ., Georgetown Univ.; Third then Second Sec., Embassy in Washington, DC 1974–78; Section Chief Dept of N American Affairs, Ministry of Foreign Affairs 1978, Deputy Dir 1980–81; Sec.-Gen. Coordination Council of N American Affairs (now TECO/TECRO) 1981–82, Dir of Dept 1982–86; Admin. Vice-Minister of Foreign Affairs 1986–90; Dir-Gen. Dept of Overseas Affairs, Kuomintang Cen. Cttee 1990; Political Vice-Minister of Foreign Affairs 1990–93; Minister of Overseas Chinese Affairs Comm. and Minister of State 1993–96; Minister of Foreign Affairs 1996–97, Deputy Prime Minister 1997; Sec.-Gen. Presidential Office 1999–2000; mem. Li-Fa Yuan (Legislative Yuan) 2002–; mem. Kuomintang Cen. Cttee and Cen. Standing Cttee 1993–, fmr Sec.-Gen. *Publication:* Damansky Island Incident. *Address:* c/o Kuomintang (KMT)

(Nationalist Party of China), 11 Jongshan South Road, Taipei, Taiwan. *Website:* www.kmt.org.tw.

CHANG, Jung, PhD; British writer; b. 25 March 1952, Yibin, Sichuan Prov., China; d. of Chang Shou-Yu and Xia De-Hong; m. Jon Halliday 1991; ed Sichuan Univ., Univ. of York; fmrly worked as a peasant, a 'barefoot doctor', a steelworker and an electrician; Asst Lecturer, Sichuan Univ.; moved to UK to study linguistics 1978; now full-time writer; Dr hc (Buckingham) 1996, (Warwick, York) 1997, (Open Univ.) 1998, (Bowdoin Coll., USA) 2005; Bjørnsonordenen, Den Norske Orden for Literature, Norway 1995. *Publications:* Madame Sun Yat-sen (with Jon Halliday) 1986, Wild Swans: Three Daughters of China (NCR Book Award 1992, UK Writers' Guild Best Non-Fiction Book 1992, Fawcett Soc. Book Award 1992, Book of the Year 1993, Golden Bookmark Award, Belgium 1993, 1994, Best Book Award, Humo, Belgium 1993) 1991, Mao: the Unknown Story (with Jon Halliday) 2005. *Address:* Aitken Alexander Associates Ltd, 18–21 Cavaye Place, London, SW10 9PT, England (office). *Telephone:* (20) 7373-8672 (office). *Fax:* (20) 7373-6002 (office). *E-mail:* reception@aitkenalexander.co.uk (office). *Website:* www .aitkenalexander.co.uk (office).

CHANG, King-yuh, LLM, PhD; Taiwanese government official and academic; *Chairman, Foundation on International and Cross-Strait Studies;* b. 27 April 1937, Hsiangtan County, Hunan; s. of Shao Chu Chang and Hsi-chen Huang; m. Grace Yu 1964; two s.; ed Nat. Taiwan Univ., Nat. Chengchi Univ. and Columbia Univ.; Lecturer, Hofstra Univ., USA 1968–69; Asst Prof., Western Illinois Univ. 1972; Assoc. Prof., Nat. Chengchi Univ. 1972–75, Chair. Dept of Diplomacy 1974–77, Dir Grad. School of Int. Law and Diplomacy 1975–77, Prof. 1975–, Deputy Dir Inst. of Int. Relations 1977–81, Dir 1981–84, Pres. Nat. Chengchi Univ. 1989–94; currently Prof. of Int. Affairs and Strategic Studies, Tamkang Univ.; fmr Chair. Mainland Affairs Council, Exec. Yuan; currently Chair. Foundation on Int. and Cross-Strait Studies; Visiting Fellow, Johns Hopkins Univ. 1976–77; Distinguished Visiting Scholar, Inst. of E Asian Studies, Univ. of California, Berkeley 1983; Dir-Gen. Govt Information Office 1984–87; Dir Inst. of Int. Relations 1987–90; Minister of State, Exec. Yuan 1994–96. *Leisure interests:* reading, mountain climbing and sports. *Address:* Foundation on International and Cross-Strait Studies, 10050 Taipei (office); 1 Chung Hsiao East Road, Sec. 1, Taipei, Taiwan. *Telephone:* (2) 3968760 (office). *Fax:* (2) 3917850 (office). *E-mail:* webfics@ gmail.com (office). *Website:* www.fics.org.tw (office).

CHANG, Manuel, MPhil; Mozambican government official; *Minister of Finance;* b. 22 Aug. 1955, Gaza; s. of the late Chang Dai Fão and Angelina Mugabe; m. Lizete Izilda Adriano Simões Maia; three c.; ed Escola Industrial Mouzinho de Albuquerque, Universidade Eduardo Mondlane, Univ. of London, UK; joined Ministry of Finance 1974, Section Head 1977, Section Head, Service Comm. 1979, Acting Head, Dept of the Treasury 1987, Head, Dept of the Treasury 1988–89, Adjunct Nat. Dir of the Treasury 1989–93, Dir of Nat. Budget 1993–96, Vice-Minister of Planning and Finance –2005, Minister of Finance 2005–; mem. Frente de Libertação de Moçambique (Frelimo) party; Vice-Pres. Fund for the Promotion of Fishing; Pres. of audit council Banco de Moçambique; mem. Bd of Dirs Pipeline Mocambique-Zimbabwe; mem. Admin. Council Correios de Moçambique 1994–96, Silos Granoleiros de Matola. *Leisure interests:* playing football, reading and watching television. *Address:* Ministério do Plano e Finanças, Praça da Marinha Popular, CP 272, Maputo, Mozambique. *Telephone:* 21306808. *Fax:* 21306261. *E-mail:* dnpo@dnpo.uem.mz. *Website:* www.mozambique.mz/governo/mpf/dnpo.

CHANG, Michael, American fmr professional tennis player; b. 22 Feb. 1972, Hoboken, NJ; s. of Joe Chang and Betty Chang; m. Amber Liu; ed Biola Univ.; coached by his brother Carl and others; aged 15 was youngest player since 1918 to compete in men's singles at US Open 1987; turned professional 1988; first played at Wimbledon 1988; winner, French Open 1989, becoming youngest player of a Grand Slam tournament; Davis Cup debut 1989; winner Canadian Open 1990; semi-finalist, US Open 1992, finalist 1996; finalist French Open 1995, semi-finalist Australian Open 1995, finalist 1996; won 34 singles titles; retd Aug. 2003; highest singles ranking: 2nd (1996); apptd USA Tennis High Performance Cttee, US Tennis Asscn 2005–06; Trustee Biola Univ.; est. Chang Family Foundation 1999; inducted into Int. Tennis Hall of Fame 2008. *Publication:* Holding Serve: Persevering On and Off the Court 2001. *Address:* c/o Chang Family Foundation, 28562 Oso Pkwy, D343, Rancho Santa Margarita, CA 92688; Advantage International, 1751 Pinnacle Drive, Suite 1500, McLean, VA 22102, USA (office). *E-mail:* cffoundation@mchang.com. *Website:* mchang.com (office).

CHANG, Richard, BS; Chinese-American business executive and art collector; *Director, Tira Holdings;* ed Stern School of Business, New York Univ.; Dir Tira Holdings (investment firm with interests in media, real estate, hospitality, and fashion); Founder Domus Collection, Beijing (foundation to advance global contemporary art in China) 2008; has sponsored numerous exhbns, including Anish Kapoor at Royal Acad. of Arts, London; Roundtrip: Beijing–New York Now, a selection of works (among them commissioned pieces by Terence Koh and Matthew Day Jackson) from his Domus Collection, presented at Ullens Centre for Contemporary Art, Beijing May 2010; mem. Int. Council, Asia Pacific Acquisitions Cttee at the Tate; Trustee, MoMA for PS1. *Address:* Tira Holdings (Pty) Ltd, 7th Floor Prop Net Building, Cape Town, Western Cape 7530, South Africa (office). *Telephone:* (21) 9497181 (office).

CHANG, Shana; Chinese artist; b. 26 March 1931, Lyon, France; d. of Chang Shuhong; one s.; ed Dunhuang, Boston Museum of Fine Art School and New York; returned to China 1950; asst to architect Liang Sicheng, Qinghua Univ. 1951–56; Prof., Cen. Acad. of Arts and Design 1957–85, Deputy Dean 1982–83, Dean 1983–98; Del. 12th CCP Cen. Cttee 1982, 13th CCP Cen. Cttee; mem. New York Students League 1953; mem. Educ., Science, Culture and Public Health Cttee 8th NPC;; mem. Standing Cttee 9th NPC; fmr Vice-Pres. China Artists Asscn. *Address:* c/o Central Academy of Arts and Design, 34 North Dong Huan Road, Beijing 100020, People's Republic of China (office).

CHANG, Steve, MSc; Taiwanese software industry executive; *Chairman, Trend Micro Inc.;* ed Fu-Jen Catholic Univ., Taiwan, Lehigh Univ., Pa, USA; fmr engineer, Hewlett-Packard; f. AsiaTek Inc. (UNIX software design co.), Taiwan; Co-founder, Chair. and CEO Trend Micro Inc. (software co. specialising in network virus protection and internet security), Calif., USA (now based in Japan) 1988–2005, Chair. 2005–; mem. Bd of Dirs AsiaInfo Holdings, Inc. 2001–; Business

Week Star of Asia Award, Asia Business Leader Award 2004. *Address:* Trend Micro Inc., Shinjuku MAYNDS Tower, 1-1, Yoyogi 2-Chome, Shibuya-ku, Tokyo 151-0053, Japan (office). *Telephone:* (3) 5334-3650 (office). *Fax:* (3) 5334-3651 (office). *Website:* www.trendmicro.com (office).

CHANG, Gen. Wanquan; Chinese military commander and government official; *Minister of National Defence and Member, State Council;* b. 1949, Nanyang City, Henan Prov.; ed Univ. of Nat. Defence; joined PLA 1968, Platoon Leader, Services and Arms, Army 1969–70, Chief of Staff, Army Combat Training Section 1970–74, Chief of Staff, Operations Dept, Lanzhou Mil. Region, Gansu Prov. 1978, Deputy Dir Combat Training Section, Services and Arms, Army 1980–81, Chief of Staff, Div. Command, Services and Arms, Army 1983–85, Deputy Commdr 1985–90, Commdr 1992–94, Dir, Operations Dept, Lanzhou Mil. Region 1990–92, Chief-of-Staff, PLA Services and Arms, Group Army 1994–98, Commdr 2000–02; Dir Campaign Research Dept, Univ. of Nat. Defence 1998–2000; Chief of Staff, Lanzhou Mil. Region 2002–03, Beijing Mil. Region 2003–04, Commdr, Shenyang Mil. Region, Liaoning Prov. 2004–07; attained rank of Maj.-Gen. 1997, Lt-Gen. 2003, Gen. 2007; Dir PLA Gen. Armaments Dept 2007–; Minister of Nat. Defence 2013–; mem. State Council 2013–; mem. State Cen. Mil. Comm. 2008–; mem. 16th CCP Cen. Cttee 2002–07, 17th CCP Cen. Cttee 2007–12, also 17th CCP Cen. . Comm. 2007–12, mem. 18th CCP Cen. Cttee 2012–, also 18th CCP Cen. Mil. Comm. 2012–. *Address:* Ministry of National Defence, 20 Jingshanqian Jie, Beijing 100009, People's Republic of China (office). *Telephone:* (10) 66730000 (office). *Fax:* (10) 65962146 (office). *E-mail:* mod@chinamil.com.cn (office). *Website:* www.mod .gov.cn (office).

CHANG, Xiaobing, BEng, MBA, DBA; Chinese engineer and telecommunications executive; *Executive Director, Chairman and CEO, China United Network Communications Group Company Limited (China Unicom);* b. 1958; ed Nanjing Inst. of Posts and Telecommunications, Tsinghua Univ., Hong Kong Polytechnic Univ.; Deputy Dir Nanjing Municipal Posts and Telecommunications (MPT) Bureau, Jiangsu Prov. 1993–96; Deputy Dir-Gen. Dept of Telecommunications Admin, Ministry of Information Industry 1996–2000, Dir 2000–04; Vice-Pres. China Telecom Group –2004, Pres. 2004–; Exec. Dir, Chair. and CEO China United Network Communications Group Co. Ltd (China Unicom) 2004–, Sec. of Party Leadership Group, CEO and Chair. China Unicom Ltd, Chair. China United Telecommunications Corpn Ltd. *Address:* China Unicom Ltd, 75th Floor, The Center, 99 Queen's Road Central, Hong Kong Special Administrative Region (office); China United Telecommunications Corpn Ltd, No. 133A, Xidan North Street, Xicheng District, Beijing 100032, People's Republic of China (office). *Telephone:* 2126-2018 (Hong Kong) (office); (10) 66505588 (Beijing) (office); (21) 52732228 (Shanghai) (office). *Fax:* 2126-2016 (Hong Kong) (office); (21) 52732220 (Shanghai) (office). *E-mail:* info@chinaunicom.com.hk (office). *Website:* eng .chinaunicom.com (office); www.chinaunicom.com.hk (office); www.chinaunicom .com.cn (office).

CHANG, Yung Ho, BS, MArch; Chinese architect and academic; *Professor, Department of Architecture, Massachusetts Institute of Technology;* b. 1956, Beijing; m. Lijia Lu; ed Najing Inst. of Tech., Beijing, Ball State Univ., USA, Univ. of California, Berkeley; taught at Ball State Univ., Muncie, Ind. 1985–88, Univ. of Michigan (Walter B. Sanders Fellow) 1988–90, Univ. of California, Berkeley 1990–92, Rice Univ. 1993–96; co-f. Atelier Feichang Jianzhu Architects, Beijing 1993; f. Grad. Centre of Architecture, Peking Univ. 1999, Head and Prof. 2004–05; Kenzo Tange Chair, Harvard Univ. Grad. School of Design 2002–03; Prof., MIT 2005–, also Head, Dept of Architecture, 2005–10; Walter B. Sanders Fellow, Univ. of Michigan 1989–90, Steedman Travelling Fellowship, Washington Univ., St Louis 1992; First Place, Shinkenchiku Residential Design Competition, Japan Architect 1986, First Place, From Table to Tablescape Design Competition, Formica Corpn 1988, Winner, Young Architects Forum, Architectural League of New York 1992, UNESCO Prize for Promotion of the Arts 2000, China Architectural Arts Award 2004, American Acad. of Arts and Letters Acad. Award in Architecture 2006. *Publications:* Yung Ho Chang/Atelier Feichang Jianzhu: A Chinese Practice (contrib.) 2002. *Address:* Room 7-337D, Department of Architecture, Massachusetts Institute of Technology, 77 Massachusetts Avenue, Cambridge, MA 02139-4307, USA (office); Atelier Feichang Jianzhu Architects, Yuan Ming Yuan East Gate Nei, Yard No. 1 on northside, Yuan Ming Yuan Dong Lu, Beijing 100084, People's Republic of China (office). *Telephone:* (617) 253-4411 (office). *E-mail:* yungho@mit.edu (office); fcjz@fcjz.com (office). *Website:* architecture.mit.edu (office); www.fcjz.com (office).

CHANG, Zhenming, MBA; Chinese economist and banking executive; *Chairman, CITIC Group;* b. Oct. 1956; ed New York Insurance Inst., USA; joined China International Trust & Investment Corpn (CITIC) Group 1983, Deputy Dir, Capital Dept 1992, seconded to USA as Trader 1992–93, Deputy Man. 1993–94, Deputy Chief Man. in charge of Financial Business 1994–95, apptd Chair. and Pres. CITIC Securities 1995, Dir CITIC Pacific (Hong Kong) Ltd 2000–05, apptd Pres., CEO and Dir CITIC Ka Wah Bank Ltd (CKWB) 2001, Exec. Vice-Chair. 2002–04, Dir and CEO CITIC Int. Financial Holdings Ltd 2002–04, Vice-Chair. 2006–, Dir Capital Market Holdings Ltd, Dir and Exec. Vice-Pres. CITIC Group –2004, Vice-Chair. and Pres. 2006–10, Chair. 2010–; Pres. China Construction Bank 2004–06. *Address:* CITIC Group, Capital Mansion, 6 Xinuan Nanlu, Beijing 10004, People's Republic of China (office). *Telephone:* (10) 64660088 (office). *Fax:* (10) 64661186 (office). *Website:* www.citic.com (office); www.citic.com.cn (office).

CHANG-BRITT, Irene, BA, MBA; Canadian business executive; *President, Pepperidge Farm and Senior Vice-President of Global Baking and Snacking, Campbell Soup Company;* ed Univ. of Toronto, Richard Ivey School of Business at Univ. of Western Ontario; with Kimberly-Clark 1986–99, held progressive marketing positions and assignments in Sales and Research and Devt leadership, later Dir Washroom Systems business; Vice-Pres., Nabisco Biscuits and Snacks, Nabisco Ltd 1999–2000; with Kraft Foods 1999–2005, positions including Sr Vice-Pres. and Gen. Man. Salted Snacks Div. and Post Cereal Div.; Vice-Pres. and Gen. Man., Sauces and Beverages, Campbell Soup Co. 2005–08, Pres., North America Food Service 2008–10, Sr Vice-Pres. and Chief Strategy Officer 2010–12, Sr Vice-Pres. of Global Baking and Snacking April 2012–, Pres. Pepperidge Farm Aug. 2012–; fmr mem. Bd of Dirs Sunoco, Inc.; mem. Bd of Advisors, Catalyst; mem. US Exec. Advisory Bd, Enactus (fmrly Students In Free Enterprise); fmr Chair. NJ Kraft Employee Fund (twice); led two United Way campaigns as Co-Chair. and

Exec. sponsor; Corp. Achievement Award, Org. of Chinese Americans 2002, recognized by NJBiz as one of the Best 50 Women in Business 2008, by Pink magazine as a Top 15 Innovator 2008, by Progressive Grocer as a Top Women in Grocery 2008, Laureate, New Jersey Business Hall of Fame 2011, named by The Philadelphia Business Journal amongst its Women of Distinction 2011. *Address:* Campbell Soup Co., 1 Campbell Place, Camden, NJ 08103-1701, USA (office). *Telephone:* (856) 342-4800 (office). *Fax:* (856) 342-3878 (office). *E-mail:* info@campbellsoupcompany.com (office). *Website:* www.campbellsoupcompany.com (office).

CHANG ESCOBEDO, José Antonio; Peruvian politician and fmr university administrator; b. 19 May 1958; ed Univ. Nacional Federico Villarreal, Hartford Univ., Conn., USA; Gen. Co-ordinator, Dept of Computer Eng and Systems, Univ. de San Martín de Porres, Lima 1984, Dir of Academic Programme, Dept of Computer Eng and Systems 1984–85, Dir School of Computer Eng and Systems 1985–86, Dean, Faculty of Computer Eng and Systems 1986–96, Univ. Rector 1996–2006; Cen. Devt Man., Banco de la Nación 1988–89, Cen. Information Man. 1989; Minister of Educ. 2006–10, Pres., Council of Ministers (Prime Minister) and Minister of Educ. 2010–11; mem. Alianza Popular Revolucionaria Americana; Dr hc (Univ. Nacional de Huacho) 2000, (Univ. Nacional Federico Villarreal) 2006; Gran Oficial, Policia Nacional del Perú 2005. *Address:* c/o Office of the President of the Council of Ministers, Jirón Carabaya, cuadra 1 s/n, Anexo 1105-1107, Lima, Peru (office).

CHANG-HIM, Most Rev. French Kitchener, MPhil, LTh; Seychelles ecclesiastic; *Archbishop Emeritus, Province of the Indian Ocean;* b. 10 May 1938, Seychelles; s. of Francis Chang-Him and Amelia Zoé; m. Susan Talma 1975 (died 1996); twin d.; ed Seychelles Coll., Lichfield Theological Coll. and St Augustine's Coll., Canterbury, UK, Univ. of Trinity Coll. Toronto, Canada, Oxford Centre for Mission Studies, UK; primary school teacher 1958; man. of schools 1973–77; Chair. Teacher Training Coll. Bd of Govs 1976–77; Vicar-Gen. Diocese of Seychelles 1973–79; Archdeacon of Seychelles 1973–79; Bishop of Seychelles 1979–2004; Dean, Prov. of the Indian Ocean 1983–84, Archbishop 1984–95, Archbishop Emer. 2013–; Hon. DD (Univ. of Trinity Coll., Toronto) 1991; Rajiv Ghandi Foundation Lifetime Achievement Award 2003. *Publication:* The Seychellois: In Search of an Identity 1975. *Leisure interests:* international affairs, cooking, gardening, reading. *Address:* PO Box 44, Victoria, Seychelles. *Telephone:* 4248151. *Fax:* 4248151. *E-mail:* bishop@seychelles.net.

CHANG TSONG-ZUNG, Johnson; Chinese art critic and gallery curator; *Founding Director, Hanart T Z Gallery;* has curated Chinese exhbns since 1980s; pioneered participation of Chinese art at int. exhbns; adviser to numerous art collectors, including David Tang; Founding Dir Hanart T Z Gallery 1983–; Curator, Co-founder and mem. Bd Asia Art Archive, Hong Kong 2000; Co-founder Hong Kong chapter of AICA (Int. Asscn of Art Critics); Guest Prof., China Art Acad. *Address:* Hanart T Z Gallery, 202 Henley Building, 5 Queen's Road Central, Hong Kong Special Administrative Region, People's Republic of China (office). *Telephone:* 2526-9019 (office). *Fax:* 2521-2001 (office). *E-mail:* tzchang@hanart .com (office). *Website:* www.hanart.com (office).

CHANGEUX, Jean-Pierre, DèsSc; French medical scientist and academic; *Professor, Laboratoire de Neurobiologie Moléculaire, Institut Pasteur;* b. 6 April 1936, Domont; s. of Marcel Changeux and Jeanne Benoît; m. Annie Dupont 1962; one s.; ed Lycées Montaigne, Louis le Grand and St Louis, Paris and Ecole Normale Supérieure, Ulm; research asst 1958–60; Asst Lecturer, Science Faculty, Univ. of Paris 1960–66; post-doctoral Fellow, Univ. of Calif. 1966, Columbia Univ., New York 1967; Vice-Dir Coll. de France (Chair. of Molecular Biology) 1967; Prof., Laboratoire de Neurobiologie Moléculaire, Institut Pasteur 1974–; Prof., Coll. de France 1975–; Pres. Interministerial Comm. for Preservation of Nat. Artistic Heritage 1989–; Consultative Cttee on Ethics for Life and Medical Sciences 1993–99 (Hon. Pres. 1999–); mem. Soc. Des Amis du Louvre 2004–, Vice-Pres. 2006–; mem. Scientific Bd World Knowledge Dialogue 2007–; Corresp. mem. numerous comms, Turin Acad. of Medicine, Acad. des Sciences, Akad. Leopoldina, Halle, NAS, Swedish and Belgian acads; Commdr, Légion d'honneur, Ordre des Arts et Lettres, Grand Croix, Ordre nat. du Mérite; Alexandre Joannidès prize (Acad. des Sciences), Gairdner Foundation Award 1978, Lounsbery Prize (NAS) 1982, Co-recipient Wolf Foundation Prize 1982, Céline Prize 1985, F.O. Schmitt Prize (Neurosciences Research Inst., New York) 1985, Fidia Neuroscience Award 1989, Bristol-Myers-Squibb Award in Neuroscience 1990; Carl-Gustav Bernhard Medal (Swedish Acad. of Sciences) 1991, Médaille d'Or (CNRS) 1992, Prix Jeantet (Geneva) 1993, Goodman and Gilman Award 1994, Camillo Golgi medal (Accad. Nazionale dei Lincei, Rome) 1994, Sir Hans Krebs medal (Helsinki) 1994, Grand Prix (Fondation de la Recherche Médicale) 1997, Eli Lilly Award 1999, Langley Award, Washington 2000, Prix Balzan 2001, Biotechnology Study Center Award, NY Univ. 2006. *Publications include:* L'homme neuronal 1983, Matière à pensée 1989 (with Alain Connes), Raison et Plaisir 1994, Conversations on Mind, Matter and Mathematics (with Alain Connes) 1995, La Nature et la Règle (with Paul Ricoeur) 1998, L'Homme de vérité 2002, Les passions de l'âme 2006; author and co-author of several research papers on allosteric proteins, on the acetylcholine receptor and on the devt of the nervous system. *Leisure interests:* baroque paintings, organ music. *Address:* Laboratoire de Neurobiologie Moléculaire, Institut Pasteur, 25 rue du Docteur Roux, 75015 Paris (office); 47 rue du Four, 75006 Paris, France (home). *Telephone:* 1-45-68-88-05 (office); 1-45-48-44-64 (home). *Fax:* 1-45-68-88-36 (office). *E-mail:* changeux@pasteur.fr (office). *Website:* www.pasteur.fr (office).

CHANNING, Carol; American actress; b. 31 Jan. 1923, Seattle, Wash.; d. of George Channing and Carol Glaser; m. 3rd Charles Lowe 1956; one s.; m. 4th Harry Kullijian 2003; Special Tony Award 1968, Lifetime Achievement Tony Award 1995. *Plays include:* No for an Answer, Let's Face It, So Proudly We Hail, Lend an Ear (Critics' Circle Award), Gentlemen Prefer Blondes, Wonderful Town, The Vamp, Hello Dolly (Tony Award, Best Actress, Musical 1964) 1963. *Films include:* Paid in Full (1950, The First Traveling Saleslady 1956, All About People (1967, Thoroughly Modern Millie (Golden Globe Award for Best Supporting Actress 1967) 1967, Skidoo 1968, Sgt. Pepper's Lonely Hearts Club Band 1978, Alice in Wonderland (TV) (1985), Where's Waldo? (voice) (TV) 1991, Hans Christian Andersen's Thumbelina (voice) 1994, The Brave Little Toaster Goes to

Mars (voice) 1998. *Address:* c/o WME, 9601 Wilshire Blvd, Beverly Hills, CA 90210, USA.

CHANNING, Stockard, BA; American actress; b. (Susan Stockard), 13 Feb. 1944, New York; m. four times; ed Harvard Univ.; performed in experimental drama with Theatre Co. of Boston 1967. *Films include:* Comforts of the Home 1970, The Fortune 1975, Sweet Revenge 1975, The Big Bus 1976, Grease 1978, The Cheap Detective 1978, Boys Life 1978, Without A Trace 1983, Heartburn 1986, Men's Club 1986, Staying Together 1987, Meet the Applegates 1987, Married to It 1993, Six Degrees of Separation 1993, Bitter Moon 1994, Smoke 1995, Up Close and Personal 1996, Moll Flanders, Edie and Pen, The First Wives Club 1996, Practical Magic 1998, Twilight 1998, Lulu on the Bridge (voice) 1998, The Red Door 1999, Other Voices 1999, Isn't She Great 1999, The Venice Project 1999, Where the Heart Is 2000, The Business of Strangers 2001, Life or Something Like It 2002, Behind the Red Door 2002, Bright Young Things 2003, Le Divorce 2003, Anything Else 2003, Red Mercury 2005, Must Love Dogs 2005, 3 Needles 2005, Sparkle 2007, Multiple Sarcasms 2010. *Stage appearances include:* Two Gentlemen of Verona, New York, San Francisco, LA 1972–73, No Hard Feelings, New York 1973, Vanities, LA 1976, As You Like It 1978, They're Playing Our Song, Lady and the Clarinet 1983, The Golden Age 1983, A Day in the Death of Joe Egg 1985 (Tony Award for Best Actress), House of Blue Leaves 1986, Woman in Mind 1988, Love Letters 1989, Six Degrees of Separation, New York 1990 (also London stage début, Royal Court Theatre 1992), Four Baboons Adoring the Sun 1992. *Television appearances include:* The Stockard Channing Show 1979–80, The West Wing 1999–2006, Batman Beyond 1999–2000, Out of Practice 2005–06 and various television movies including The Truth About Jane 2000, The Piano Man's Daughter 2000, Confessions of an Ugly Stepsister 2002, Hitler: The Rise of Evil 2003, Jack 2004, Sundays at Tiffiny's 2010. *Address:* ICM, c/o Andrea Eastman, 40 West 57th Street, New York, NY 10019, USA.

CHANTLER, Sir Cyril, Kt; British paediatric nephrologist and healthcare administrator; *Chairman, UCL Partners;* b. 1939; m. Shireen Chantler; Gen. Man. Guy's Hosp. 1985–88, Prin. United Medical and Dental School, Guy's and St Thomas's Hosps 1992–98, also Prof. of Paediatric Nephrology –2000 (retd); Pro-Vice Chancellor, Univ. of London 1997–2000; Chair. Great Ormond Street Hosp. for Children NHS Trust 2001–09; Chair. UCL Partners 2009–; Chair. King's Fund; Chair. Strategic Devt Group for Dulwich Community Hosp.; Chair. Council of Heads of UK Medical Schools and Faculties 1998–99; Chair. Beit Memorial Fellowships Bd; Pres. British Asscn of Medical Mans 1991–97; Medical Dir, Well Child Medical Research Fund; mem. Bd of Govs South Bank Univ.; Trustee, Dunhill Medical Trust; mem. Advisory Panel, Assoc. Parl. Health Group; mem. NHS Policy Bd 1989–96; mem. Gen. Medical Council 1994–2003. *Address:* UCL Partners, University College London, Gower Street, London, WC1E 6BT, England (office). *Telephone:* (20) 7679-2000 (office). *Website:* www.ucl.ac.uk (office).

CHANTURIA, Lado; Georgian lawyer, judge and academic; *Professor, Faculty of Law, University of Bremen;* b. 14 April 1963, Jvari; ed Iv. Javakhishvili Tbilisi State Univ., Moscow Legislation Inst., Göttingen Univ., Germany; Asst Prof., Assoc. Prof., then Prof. Faculty of Law, Tbilisi State Univ. 1995–; co-ordinator Civil and Econ. Law Reform Project 1993–96; Research Fellow, Max Planck Inst. for Foreign and Int. Pvt. Law 1996; mem. Council of Justice 1997; Minister of Justice 1998–99; Chief Justice of the Supreme Court of Georgia 1999–2004; Humbolt Fellow and Prof., Faculty of Law, Univ. of Bremen, Germany 2004–; legal advisor to Pres. Michail Saakaschvili 2004–; mem. Int. Advisory Bd, ABA/CEELI Inst., Prague. *Publications:* over 60 published works. *Leisure interests:* soccer, travel. *Address:* GW1, C 1020, University of Bremen, Faculty of Law, 28353 Bremen, Germany (office); Phanaskerteli st. 9/97, 0110 Tbilisi, Georgia (home). *Telephone:* (421) 2187462 (office), (32) 36-02-08 (home). *E-mail:* lado.chanturia@uni-bremen .de (office); chanturialado@yahoo.com (home). *Website:* www.jura.uni-bremen.de (office).

CHANTURIYA, Valentin Alekseyevich; Russian metallurgist; *Director, Research Institute of Complex Exploitation of Mineral Resources, Russian Academy of Sciences;* b. 15 Oct. 1938; m. 2nd Yelena Leonidovna Chanturiya; two s. two d.; ed Moscow Inst. of Steel and Alloys; Jr, Sr Researcher, Head of Lab. Moscow Inst. of Earth Sciences 1969–74; Sr Researcher, Head of Lab., Inst. for Problems of Complex Exploitation of Mineral Resources, Russian Acad. of Sciences 1974–, Deputy Dir 1993–2003, Dir 2003–; Corresp. mem. Russian (fmrly USSR) Acad. of Sciences 1990, mem. 1994–; research in physical and chemical aspects of processing mineral raw materials; Prize of USSR Council of Ministers, Govt Prize, Russian Fed. 1983, 1990, 1998, Melnikov Gold Medal, Presidium Russian Acad. of Sciences 1992, Prize of Pres. of Russian Fed. in Educ. 2001. *Publications include:* Chemistry of Surfacial Phenomena at Flotation 1983, Electrochemistry of Sulphides 1993, Mining Sciences 1997, Modern Problems of Primary Processing of Minerals in Russia 2004, Nanoparticles in Geological Materials Destruction and Extraction Processes 2006. *Leisure interest:* fishing. *Address:* Research Institute of Complex Exploitation of Mineral Resources (IPKON), Russian Academy of Sciences, 111020 Moscow, Kryukovsky tupic 4, Russia (office). *Telephone:* (495) 360-06-06 (office); (495) 348-93-94 (home). *E-mail:* info@ipkonran.ru (office). *Website:* www.ipkonran.ru (office).

CHAO, Charles, BA, MA, MAcc; Chinese business executive; *President and CEO, SINA Corporation;* b. 1965, Shanghai; ed Univ. of Texas, Univ. of Oklahoma, USA, Fudan Univ., Shanghai; fmr news correspondent, Shanghai Media Group; fmr Audit Man., PricewaterhouseCoopers LLP 1993–99; Vice-Pres. of Finance, SINA Corpn 1999–2001, Chief Financial Officer 2001–06, Exec. Vice-Pres. 2002–03, Co-COO 2004–06, Pres., CEO 2006–, also currently Dir; current Co-Chair. China Real Estate Information Corpn; Dir Focus Media; Dir NetDragon Websoft Inc. *Address:* SINA Corporation, 20F Beijing Ideal International Plaza, No. 58 Northwest 4th Ring Road, Haidian District, Beijing 100080, People's Republic of China (office). *Telephone:* (10) 82628888 (office). *Fax:* (10) 82607166 (office). *Website:* corp.sina.com.cn/eng/sina_mng_eng.htm (office).

CHAO, Elaine L., BEcons, MBA; American fmr government official; b. 26 March 1953, Taiwan; d. of James S. C. Chao and Ruth Mulan Chu Chao; m. Mitch McConnell 1993; ed Mount Holyoke, Harvard Business School, Dartmouth Coll., Columbia Univ.; banker, Citicorp 1979–83; White House Fellow 1983–84; Vice-Pres. Syndications Bank America Capital Markets Group, San Francisco 1984–86;

Deputy Admin. US Maritime Admin. 1986–88, Chair. Fed. Maritime Comm. 1988–89; Deputy Sec., US Dept of Transportation 1989–91; Dir Peace Corps 1991–92, est. first Peace Corps in Baltic nations and newly ind. states of fmr USSR; Pres. and CEO United Way America 1992–96; US Sec. of Labor 2001–09; Fellow, Heritage Foundation, Washington, DC 1996–2001, Distinguished Fellow 2009–; mem. Bd of Dirs Wells Fargo & Co. 2011–, Protective Life Corpn 2011–; contrib. to Fox News 2009–; 34 hon. degrees including Hon. LLD (Villanova Univ.) 1989, (Sacred Heart Univ., St John's Univ.) 1991, (Notre Dame) 1998, (St Mary's Coll.) 2002, (N Alabama, Fu-Jen Catholic Univ. 2003); Hon. LHD (Drexel Univ., Niagara Univ.) 1992, (Thomas More Coll.) 1994, (Bellarmine Coll., Univ. of Toledo) 1995, (Univ. of Louisville, Goucher Coll.) 1996, (Centre Coll.) 2003; Outstanding Young Achiever Award, Nat. Council of Women 1986, Harvard Univ. Grad. School of Business Alumni Achievement Award 1994, Woodrow Wilson Award for Public Service 2011. *Address:* Heritage Foundation, 214 Massachusetts Avenue, NE, Washington, DC 20002, USA (office). *Telephone:* (202) 608-6240 (office). *Fax:* (202) 675-1173 (office). *Website:* www.elainelchao.com.

CHAO, Manu; French singer and songwriter; b. 26 June 1961, Paris; one s.; as teenager played in various bands, including Les Hot Pants; formed Mano Negra 1987, band split 1993; first single earned group contract with Virgin; toured Latin America; moved to Spain 1995; formed 10-mem. Radio Bemba Sound System; spent next few years recording in South and Central America; King of Bongo recording featured on soundtrack to Madonna's The Next Big Thing film; British tour 2002; producer for Amadou and Mariam, Akli D; BBC Radio 3 World Music Innovator award 2002, Latin Grammy Award for Best Alternative Song (for Me Llaman Calle) 2007. *Recordings include:* with Mano Negra: Patchanka 1988, Puta's Fever 1989, King Of The Bongo 1991, Hell Of Patchinko 1992, Casa Babylon 1994; solo: Clandestino 1998, Próxima Estación: Esperanza 2001, Sibérie m'aétait contéee 2004, La Radiolina 2007, Estación México 2008, Baionarena 2009. *Website:* www.manuchao.net.

CHAOVARAT, Chanweerakul, BSc; Thai business executive and politician; b. 7 June 1936, Bangkok; m. Tassanee Chanrvirakul; three c.; ed Thammasat Univ.; Man. Dir Sino-Thai Eng & Construction PLC 1962–94, Dir and Chair. Advisory Bd 1998–2007; Chair. Bd of Dirs Stp&I PLC 1975–94, 1998–2007; Deputy Minister of Finance 1994–95, 1996–97; Minister of Public Health Feb.–Sept. 2008; Deputy Prime Minister of Thailand Sept.–Nov. 2008, Acting Prime Minister Nov.–Dec. 2008; Minister of the Interior 2008–11; Leader Bhum Jai Thai (Thai Pride Party) 2009–; mem. (Fifth Class) of the Most Exalted Order of the White Elephant 1982, Commdr (Third Class) 1992, Kt Grand Cross (First Class) 1996, (Special Class) 2004; Commdr (Third Class) of the Most Noble Order of the Crown of Thailand 1991, Kt Grand Cross (First Class) 1995, Kt Grand Cordon (Special Class) 1997; Hon. PhD (Ramkhamhaeng Univ.) 2006. *Address:* Bhum Jai Thai, Suite 2159, 11 Thanon Phaholyothin, Chatuchak, Bangkok 10900, Thailand (office). *Telephone:* (2) 940-6999 (office). *Website:* www.bhumjaithai.com (office).

CHAPLIN, Edward Graham Mellish, CMG, OBE, BA, MA; British diplomatist; *Senior Adviser, Good Governance Group (G3);* b. 21 Feb. 1951; m. Nicola Chaplin; one s. two d.; ed Univ. of Cambridge, Ecole Nationale d'Admin, Paris; entered FCO 1973; served with Middle East Dept 1973–74, Third Sec., Chancery, Oman 1975–77, Second Sec., Chancery, Brussels 1977–78; on secondment as Pvt. Sec. to Lord Pres. of the Council and Leader of the House of Lords 1979–81; Near East and N Africa Dept, FCO 1981–85, Head of Chancery, Tehran, Iran 1985–87, Personnel Operations Dept 1987–89; on secondment with Price Waterhouse as man. consultant 1990–92; Deputy Head of Perm. Mission to UN and Int. Orgs, Geneva 1992–96; Head of Middle East Dept, FCO 1996–99; Amb. to Jordan 2000–02; Dir Middle East and N Africa, FCO 2002–04; Amb. to Iraq 2004–05, to Italy (also accred to San Marino) 2006–11; Sr Adviser, Good Governance Group (G3) 2011–; Visiting Fellow, Centre for Int. Studies, Univ. of Cambridge 2005–06. *E-mail:* egmc51@gmail.com (office).

CHAPLIN, Geraldine; American actress; b. 31 July 1944, Santa Monica, Calif.; d. of Charles Chaplin and Oona (O'Neill) Chaplin; m. Patricio Castilla; two c.; ed pvt. schools, Royal Ballet School, London, UK. *Films include:* Doctor Zhivago 1965, Stranger in the House 1967, I Killed Rasputin 1968, The Hawaiians 1970, Innocent Bystanders 1973, Buffalo Bill and the Indians or Sitting Bull's History Lesson, The Three Musketeers 1974, The Four Musketeers, Nashville 1975, Raise Ravens 1975, Welcome to La Cria, Roseland 1977, Remember My Name, A Wedding 1978, The Mirror Crack'd 1980, Voyage en Douce 1981, Bolero 1982, Corsican Brothers, The Word, L'Amour Par Terre, White Mischief 1988, The Moderns 1988, The Return of the Musketeers, I Want To Go Home, The Children, Chaplin 1992, Jane Eyre, In the Name of God's Poor 1997, Cousin Bette 1998, In the Beginning 2000, Las Caras de la Luna 2001, En la Ciudad sin Límites 2002, Talk to Her 2002, El Puente de San Luis Rey 2004, Without Love 2004, Disappearances 2004, Oculto 2005, Heidi 2005, BloodRayne 2005, Melissa P. 2005, The Orphanage 2006, Miguel and William 2007, Teresa, el cuerpo de Cristo 2007, Miguel and William 2007, Los Totenwackers 2007, Diario de una Ninfómana 2008, Imago Mortis 2008, The Wolfman 2010, There Be Dragons 2011, ¿Para qué sirve un oso? 2011, The Monk 2011, Et si on vivait tous ensemble? 2011, Americano 2011, Memoria de mis putas tristes 2011, O Apóstolo (voice) 2012, Hostias 2012, The Impossible 2012. *Television appearances include:* My Cousin Rachel, A Foreign Field 1994, Gulliver's Travels 1996, The Odyssey 1997, To Walk With Lions 1999, Dinotopia (series) 2002, Winter Solstice 2003, A Christmas Carol 2004, The Bridge of San Luis Rey 2004, Les Aventuriers des mers du Sud 2006.

CHAPMAN, Dinos, MA; British artist; b. 1962, London; brother of Jake Chapman (q.v.); two d.; ed Ravensbourne Coll. of Art, RCA; studied painting at RCA; teacher of textiles in boys' school; worked as asst to artists Gilbert and George; now works jtly with brother Jake; Charles Wollaston Award (for The Marriage of Reason and Squalor), RA Summer Exhbn 2003. *Leisure interests:* cooking, pilates, rowing. *Address:* Chapman Fine Arts, 39 Fashion Street, London, E1 6PX, England. *Fax:* (20) 7247-6914. *Website:* www.whitecube.com/artists/chapman/texts/10.

CHAPMAN, (Francis) Ian, CBE, CBIM, FRSA, FFCS; British publisher; b. 26 Oct. 1925, St Fergus, Aberdeenshire, Scotland; s. of Rev. Peter Chapman and Frances Burdett; m. Marjory Stewart Swinton 1953; one s. one d.; ed Shawlands Acad., Ommer School of Music, Glasgow; served in RAF 1943–44; miner (nat.

service) 1945–47; with William Collins Sons & Co. Ltd (fmrly W.M. Collins Holdings PLC, now Harper Collins) 1947, man. trainee, New York br. 1950–51, Sales Man., London br. 1955; mem. main operating Bd, Group Sales Dir 1959, Jt Man. Dir 1967–76, Deputy Chair. 1976–81, Chair. CEO 1981–89; Deputy Chair. Orion Publishing Group 1993–94, Dir William Collins overseas cos 1968–89: Canada 1968–89, USA 1974–89, South Africa 1978–89, NZ 1978–89, William Collins Int. Ltd 1975–89; Chair. Scottish Radio Holdings PLC (fmrly Radio Clyde) 1972–96 (Hon. Pres. 1996–2000), Harvill Press 1976–89, Hatchards Ltd 1976–89, William Collins Publrs Ltd 1979–81, The Listener Publs PLC 1988–93, RadioTrust PLC 1997–2001, Guinness Publrs Ltd 1991–98; Dir Pan Books Ltd 1962–84 (Chair. 1973–76), Book Tokens Ltd 1981–84, Ind. Radio News 1984–85, Stanley Botes Ltd 1986–89, Guinness PLC (non-exec.) 1986–91; Pres.-Dir Gen. Guinness Media SAS, Paris 1996–99; f. Chapmans Publrs, Chair. and Man. Dir 1989–94; Trustee, Book Trade Benevolent Soc. 1982–2003, The Publishers Asscn 1989–97; mem. Gov. Council SCOTBIC; mem. Council Publishers Asscn 1962–77, Vice-Pres. 1978, Pres. 1979–81; Chair. Nat. Acad. of Writing 2000–03, Vice-Pres. 2003; mem. Bd Book Devt Council 1967, Ancient House Bookshop 1972–89, Scottish Opera, Theatre Royal Ltd 1974–79, IRN Ltd 1983–85; Chair. Advisory Bd Strathclyde Univ. Business School 1985–88; Hon. DLitt (Strathclyde) 1990; Scottish Free Enterprise Award 1985. *Leisure interests:* grandchildren, music, golf, reading. *Address:* Kenmore, 46 The Avenue, Cheam, Surrey, SM2 7QE, England (home). *Telephone:* (20) 8642-1820 (home). *E-mail:* fichapman@25googlemail.com (home).

CHAPMAN, Sir Frank Joseph, Kt, BSc; British engineer and business executive; *Chief Executive, BG Group plc;* b. 17 June 1953, West Ham, London, England; m. 1st Evelyn Hill 1975 (divorced 1995); two d.; m. 2nd Kari Theodorsen 1996; one s. one d.; ed East Ham Tech. Coll. (now Newham Coll. of Further Educ.), Queen Mary Coll., London; worked for BP 1974–78, initially at research centre, Sunbury-on-Thames; with Shell 1978–96; joined British Gas plc as Man. Dir, Exploration and Production 1996, mem. Bd of Dirs BG International 1997–, Chief Exec. BG Group plc (following de-merger of Transco from BG International) 2000–, mem. Group Exec. Cttee, Chair.'s Cttee, Finance Cttee, Sustainability Cttee. *Achievements include:* won Global Challenge from Boston to Portsmouth via La Rochelle in BG Spirit in 2004–05. *Leisure interest:* sailing yachts. *Address:* BG Group plc, 100 Thames Valley Park Drive, Reading, Berks., RG6 1PT, England (office). *Telephone:* (20) 7707-4878 (office). *Fax:* (20) 7707-4858 (office). *E-mail:* info@bg-group.com (office). *Website:* www.bg-group.com (office).

CHAPMAN, Jake, MA; British artist; b. 1966, Cheltenham; brother of Dinos Chapman (q.v.); ed North East London Polytechnic, RCA; studied sculpture at RCA; now works jtly with brother Dinos; Charles Wollaston Award (for The Marriage of Reason and Squalor), RA Summer Exhbn 2003. *Publications:* articles in Frieze art magazine. *Address:* c/o White Cube, 48 Hoxton Street, London, N1 6PB, England (office). *Telephone:* (20) 7930-5373. *E-mail:* enquiries@whitecube .com. *Website:* www.whitecube.com/artists/chapman/texts/10.

CHAPONDA, George Thapatula; Malawi lawyer and politician; *Minister of Education, Science and Technology;* b. 1 Nov. 1942, Mulanje; m.; ed Univ. of Delhi, India, Univ. of Zambia, Yale Univ., USA; lawyer, UNHCR, positions included Deputy Regional Dir for East and Horn of Africa, Addis Ababa, Ethiopia, also worked in Tanzania, Switzerland, Bangladesh, Thailand, Kenya, Somalia 1984–2002; Chair. Univ. Council, Univ. of Malawi 2003–04; mem. Parl. (United Democratic Front) for Mulanje South West constituency 2004–; Minister of Foreign Affairs 2004–05, of Local Govt and Rural Devt 2005, of Educ. 2009, Minister for Justice and Constitutional Affairs 2010–11, Minister of Educ., Science and Tech. 2011–. *Leisure interests:* jogging, reading and football. *Address:* Ministry of Education, Science and Technology, Private Bag 328, Lilongwe 3, Malawi (office). *Telephone:* 1789422 (office). *Fax:* 1788064 (office). *E-mail:* education@ malawi.gov.mw (office). *Website:* www.malawi.gov.mw/Education (office).

CHAPOUTHIER, Georges, PhD (Science), PhD (Arts); French neuroscientist and philosopher; *Emeritus Research Director, Centre National de la Recherche Scientifique (CNRS);* b. 27 March 1945, Libourne; s. of the late Fernand Chapouthier and of Odette Mazaubert; m. Wan Hua Goh; four c.; ed Lycée Montaigne, Lycée Louis-le-Grand and Lycée Saint-Louis, Paris, École normale supérieure, Univs of Paris, Strasbourg and Lyon; long career at CNRS, now Emer. Research Dir. *Publications include:* Psychophysiologie – Le système nerveux et le Comportement (with M. Kreutzer and C. Menini) 1980, L'inné et l'acquis des structures biologiques (co-ed.) 1981, Introduction au fonctionnement du système nerveux (codage et traitement de l'information) (with J. J. Matras) 1982, Mémoire et Cerveau – Biologie de l'apprentissage 1988, Au bon vouloir de l'homme, l'animal 1990, Les droits de l'animal 1992, La biologie de la mémoire, 1994, Les droits de l'animal aujourd'hui (co-ed.) 1997, The Universal Declaration of Animal Rights – Comments and Intentions (co-ed.) 1998, L'homme, ce singe en mosaïque 2001, Qu'est-ce que l'animal? 2004, Biologie de la mémoire 2006, L'être humain, l'animal et la technique (co-ed.) 2007, Plasticity and Anxiety (co-ed.) 2007, La cognition réparée? Perturbations et récupérations des fonctions cognitives (co-ed.) 2008, Kant et le chimpanzé – Essai sur l'être humain, la morale et l'art 2009, La création – définitions et défis contemporains (co-ed.) 2009, O faut bin rigoler in p'tit! (in Saintongeais) 2010, L'homme, l'animal et la machine – Perpétuelles redéfinitions (with F. Kaplan) 2011, La question animale – Entre science, littérature et philosophie (co-ed.) 2011; numerous papers in professional journals. *Address:* Pharmacologie, Institut des sciences biologiques, 47 Blvd de l'Hôpital, Centre National de la Recherche Scientifique, 75013 Paris, France (office). *Telephone:* 1-42-16-16-51 (office). *E-mail:* georges.chapouthier@upmc.fr (office). *Website:* www .cnrs.fr (office).

CHAPPELL, Gregory (Greg) Stephen; Australian business executive, cricket coach and fmr professional cricketer; *Managing Director, Holdfast Consulting Services PLC;* b. 7 Aug. 1948, Unley, Adelaide, S Australia; s. of Arthur Martin Chappell and Jeanne Ellen Chappell (née Richardson); grandson of V. Y. Richardson (Australian Cricket Capt. 1935–36); brother of I. M. Chappell (Australian Cricket Capt. 1971–75); m. Judith Elizabeth Donaldson 1971; two s. one d.; ed St Leonard's Primary School and Plympton High School, Adelaide and Prince Alfred Coll., Adelaide; teams: South Australia 1966–73, Somerset 1968–69, Australia 1970–84 (Capt. Test side 1975–77, 1978–81, 1981/82, 1982/83, ODI side 1975–83), Queensland 1973–84 (Capt. 1970–77, 1979–80); played in 87 Tests, 48 as Capt., scoring 7,110 runs (average 53.86, highest score 247 not out), including 24 hundreds, taking 47 wickets and holding 122 catches, best bowling 5/61; scored 108 on Test debut v England, Perth 1970; only player to have scored a century in each innings of 1st Test as Capt. (v West Indies, Brisbane 1975); holds record for most catches in a Test match (seven, versus England, Perth 1975); scored 24,535 First-class runs (74 hundreds); toured England 1972, 1975, 1977, 1980; joined breakaway World Series Cricket org. 1977–79; Man. Dir AD Sports Technologies (fmrly Fundamental Golf and Leisure Ltd) 1993–95 (Dir 1992–95), Greg Chappell Sports Marketing 1995–98; mem. Australian Cricket Bd 1984–88; State Man. of Cricket, South Australian Cricket Asscn 1998–2003; coach, South Australian Redbacks 1998–2003; Man. Dir Greg Chappell Promotions PLC 2003–07; Man. Dir Holdfast Consulting Services PLC; contracted coaching tours in Pakistan 2005–05; coach India nat. team 2005–07; Head Coach Cricket Australia Centre of Excellence 2008–10; Chair. Cricket Australia Nat. Youth Selection Panel 2009–, currently Nat. Talent Man.; Patron Leukaemia Foundation of SA 1998–2003, Happi Foundation 2001–03; Hon. Life mem. MCC 1985; Hon. MBE 1979; Wisden Cricketer of the Year 1973, Australian Sportsman of the Year 1976, chosen for Australian Team of the Century 2000, elected to Australian Cricket Hall of Fame 2002, to ICC Cricket Hall of Fame 2009. *Publications:* Greg Chappell's Health and Fitness Repair Manual 1998, Greg Chappell's Family Health and Fitness Manual 1999, Greg Chappell, Cricket, The Making of Champions 2004, Fierce Focus (autobiog.) 2011. *Leisure interests:* golf, reading, listening to music. *Address:* Cricket Australia, 60 Jolimont Street, Jolimont, Vic. 3002, Australia (office). *Telephone:* (3) 9653-9975 (office). *E-mail:* greg.chappell@cricket.com.au (office).

CHAPPELLAZ, Jérôme, MSc, PhD Habil.; French geoscientist and research institute director; *Senior Scientist and Director of Research, Laboratoire de Glaciologie et Géophysique de l'Environnement, Centre National de la Recherche Scientifique;* b. 22 Dec. 1964; m.; three c.; ed Joseph Fourier Univ., Grenoble; Researcher (Second Class), CNRS 1990–94, CNRS Researcher (First Class) 1994–2002, CNRS Research Dir (equivalent to Full Prof.) (Second Class) 2002–09, CNRS Research Dir (First Class) 2009, currently Sr Scientist and Dir of Research, Laboratoire de Glaciologie et Géophysique de l'Environnement; Nat. Research Council Resident Research Assoc., NASA/Goddard Inst. for Space Studies, New York, USA 1990–91; mem. American Geophysical Union, European Geosciences Union, Int. Union for Quaternary Research, Comité Nat. français pour la Recherche Arctique et Antarctique; Chevalier, Ordre nat. du Mérite 2010; US Nat. Research Council Postdoctoral Fellowship 1990, Nat. Bronze Medal, CNRS 1993, Grand Prix Jaffé, French Acad. of Sciences (with Jean-Marc Barnola) 2001, EU Descartes Prize for collaborative research (European Project for Ice Coring in Antarctica) 2008, Paul Gast Award, Geochemical Soc. and European Asscn of Geochemistry 2010, European Research Council Advanced Grant 2011. *Publications:* numerous articles in professional journals. *Address:* LGGE, 54 rue Molière, BP96, 38402 Saint Martin d'Hères Cedex, France (office). *Telephone:* (4) 76-82-42-64 (office). *Fax:* (4) 76-82-42-01 (office). *E-mail:* chappellaz@lgge.obs.ujf -grenoble.fr (office). *Website:* www-lgge.obs.ujf-grenoble.fr (office).

CHAPPLE, Field Marshal Sir John (Lyon), GCB, CBE, MA, FZS, FLS, FRGS; British army officer (retd); b. 27 May 1931; s. of C. H. Chapple; m. Annabel Hill 1959; one s. three d.; ed Haileybury and Trinity Coll., Cambridge; joined 2nd King Edward's Own Gurkhas 1954, served Malaya, Hong Kong, Borneo; Staff Coll. 1962, Jt Services Staff Coll. 1969; Commdr 1st Bn 2nd Gurkhas 1970–72; Directing Staff, Staff Coll. 1972–73; Commdr 48 Gurkha Infantry Brigade 1976; Gurkha Field Force 1977; Prin. Staff Officer to Chief of Defence Staff 1978–79; Commdr British Forces, Hong Kong and Maj.-Gen. Brigade of Gurkhas 1980–82; Dir of Mil. Operations 1982–84; Deputy Chief of Defence Staff (Programmes and Personnel) 1985–87; Col 2nd Gurkhas 1986–94; C-in-C UK Land Forces 1987–88; Aide-de-Camp Gen. to the Queen 1987–92; Chief of Gen. Staff 1988–92; Gov. and C-in-C Gibraltar 1993–95; Pres. Zoological Soc. of London 1991–94; Vice-Lord Lt of Greater London 1997–; Services Fellow, Fitzwilliam Coll., Cambridge 1973; mem. Council Nat. Army Museum 1980–93; Pres. Combined Services Polo Assen 1991–, Indian Mil. History Soc. 1991–, Mil. History Soc. 1992–, Soc. for Army Historical Research 1993–, Trekforce 1998–, Sir Oswald Stoll Foundation 1998–, British Schools Exploring Soc. Expeditions 1999–; Trustee World Wide Fund for Nature (UK) 1985–93; mem. Council, Conservation Foundation; mem. Bd of Trustees, King Mahendra Trust for Nature Conservation 1993, currently Chair. King Mahendra United Kingdom Trust for Nature Conservation; Patron, Gap Activity Projects. *Address:* c/o Gap Activity Projects, 44 Queen's Road, Reading, Berks. RG1 4BB, England.

CHARA; Japanese singer; b. (Miwa Watabiki), 13 Jan. 1968, Kawaguchi-shi, Saitama Co.; m. Tadanobu Asano (q.v.) 1994; one d. one s.; began taking piano lessons aged four; signed contract with Epic/Sony Records 1990; first performance debut at Quattro Club, Tokyo 1991; released debut single Heaven and debut album Sweet 1991; TV commercials for Suntory, Shiseido and Marui 1990s; appeared in film Swallowtail Butterfly (Best Actress Award, Japanese Acad. Awards) 1996. *Albums include:* Sweet 1991, Soul Kiss 1992, Violet Blue 1993, Happy Toy 1994, Baby, Baby, Baby XXX 1995, Yen Town Band (soundtrack album for film Swallowtail Butterfly) 1996, Junior Sweet 1997, Strange Fruits 1999, Mood 2000, Caramel Milk 2000, Madrigal 2001, Yokae Mae 2003, Sweet 2004, A Scenery Like Me 2004, Something Blue 2005, Union 2007, Sugar Hunter 2007, Honey 2008, Kiss 2008, Carol 2009, Very Special 2011, Dark Candy 2011. *Address:* Universal Music Japan, 30 Minato-ku, Akasaka, Tokyo 107-8583, Japan. *Website:* www.charaweb .net.

CHARASSE, Michel Joseph; French politician; *Member, Conseil Constitutionnel;* b. 8 July 1941, Chamalières; s. of Martial Henri Charasse and Lucie Castellani; m. Danièle Bas 1978; ed Lycée Blaise Pascal, Clermont-Ferrand, Institut d'Etudes Politiques and Faculté de Droit de Paris; mem. staff, Ministry of Finance 1965–92; Asst Sec.-Gen. Socialist group in Nat. Ass. 1962–67, 1968–81 and FGDS group 1967–68; Principal Executive Officer, Ministry of Economy and Finance 1976; Mayor Puy-Guillaume, Puy-de-Dôme 1977–; Sec.-Gen., Puy-de-Dôme Mayors' Association 1978–2001, Pres. 2001–; Regional Councillor, Auvergne 1979–87; Adviser to Pres. of the Repub. 1982–95; Senator for Puy-de-Dôme 1981–88, 1992–2010; Sec. of Senate 1995–98; Minister-Del. for Budget 1988–92, Minister for Budget April–Oct. 1992; Substitute Judge, High Court of Justice 2004–08; Vice-Pres., Puy-de-Dôme Departmental Council 1988–92, 1998–2001; Treas. Asscn of Mayors of France 1998–2008; full mem. Local Finance Cttee 1995–;

mem. High Council for Int. Co-operation 2000–03; mem. Conseil Constitutionnel, Paris 2010–; Founder, François Mitterrand Inst. 1996– (Pres. 2003–); Chevalier de la légion d'honneur 2011. *Publications:* 55 Faubourg St Honoré 1996, Pensées, Répliques et Anecdotes de François Mitterrand 1998. *Leisure interests:* hunting, fishing, reading. *Address:* c/o Conseil Constitutionnel, 2 rue de Montpensier, 75001 Paris (office); Terre Dieu, 63290 Puy-Guillaume, France (home). *Telephone:* 1-40-15-30-06 (office). 1-40-15-30-31 (office). *Fax:* 1-40-20-93-27 (office); 4-73-94-77-54 (home). *Website:* www.conseil-constitutionnel.fr.

CHARBONNEAU, Hubert, MA, PhD; Canadian demographer and academic; *Professor Emeritus, Department of Demography, University of Montréal;* b. 2 Sept. 1936, Montréal, Québec; s. of Léonel Charbonneau and Jeanne Durand; m. Marie-Christiane Hellot 1961; one d.; ed Univ. of Montréal, Univ. of Paris, France; Sr Lecturer, Dept of Demography, Univ. of Montréal 1962–68, Asst Prof. 1968–70, Assoc. Prof. 1970–76, Prof. 1976–97, Prof. Emer. 1997–; Visiting Prof., Univ. do Paraná, Brazil 1978, 1980, 1983, Univ. de Buenos Aires, Argentina 1994, 1997; Killam Sr Research Scholarship 1974, 1975, 1976; J.B. Tyrrell Historical Medal, Royal Soc. of Canada 1990. *Publications:* author and co-author of several books on demographic topics. *Leisure interests:* genealogy, billiards, cross-country skiing. *Address:* Département de démographie, Université de Montréal, CP 6128, succ. 'Centre-Ville', Montréal, PQ H3C 3J7 (office); 19 avenue Robert, Outremont, PQ H3S 2P1, Canada (home). *Telephone:* (514) 731-5503 (home). *E-mail:* hubert .charbonneau@umontreal.ca (office); hubert.charbonneau@videotron.ca (home). *Website:* www.125.umontreal.ca/Pionniers/Charbonneau.html (office).

CHAREST, The Hon. Jean, PC, LLB; Canadian lawyer and fmr politician; *Partner, McCarthy Tétrault LLP;* b. 24 June 1958, Sherbrooke, Québec; m. Michèle Dionne 1980; one s. two d.; ed Université de Sherbrooke; mem. Sherbrooke Legal Aid Office 1981; Assoc. Beauchemin, Dussault et Charest 1981–84; Progressive Conservative MP for Sherbrooke 1984–12; Asst Deputy Speaker, House of Commons 1984; Minister of State for Youth 1986–90, for Fitness and Amateur Sport 1988–90; Deputy Govt Leader in House of Commons 1989–90; Minister for the Environment 1991–93; Deputy Prime Minister of Canada and Minister of Industry; Leader Progressive Conservative Party 1993–98; Leader Liberal Party in Québec 1998–, Leader of the Opposition 1998–2002; Premier of Québec 2003–12; Partner, McCarthy Tétrault LLP (law firm) 2013–; mem. numerous Cabinet cttees; mem. Queen's Privy Council for Canada 1986; mem. Québec Bar Asscn, Canadian Bar Asscn; Grand Croix of Ordre de la Pléiade 2007, Bavarian Order of Merit 2007, Commdr, Légion d'honneur 2009; Medal of the Acad. of Distinguished Canadians and Americans of the Maple Leaf Foundation 2009, South Australian International Climate Change Leadership Award 2010, Statesman Award, Foreign Policy Asscn 2011, Woodrow Wilson Award for Public Service 2011. *Leisure interests:* skiing, sailing. *Address:* McCarthy Tétrault LLP, Suite 2500, 1000 De La Gauchetière Street West, Montréal, PQ H3B 0A2, Canada (office). *Telephone:* (514) 397-4100 (office). *E-mail:* jcharest@mccarthy.ca (office). *Website:* www.mccarthy .ca (office).

CHARETTE DE LA CONTRIE, Hervé Marie Joseph de; French politician; *President, Chambre du Commerce Franco-Arabe;* b. 30 July 1938, Paris; s. of Hélion de Charette de la Contrie and Jeanne de Nolhac; m. 2nd Michèle Delor; one c. and three c. by previous m.; ed Ecole des Hautes Etudes Commerciales, Inst. d'Etudes Politiques, Paris and Ecole Nat. d'Admin.; Deputy Sec.-Gen. Council of State 1969–72, Maître des requêtes 1973; Ministry of Labour 1973–78; Pres. Admin. Council, Nat. Immigration Office 1977; Dir Office of Minister of Educ. 1978; Pres. Sonacotra 1980–81; Deputy Sec.-Gen. Parti Républicain 1979; returned to Council of State 1981; Deputy to Nat. Ass. 1986, 1988–93, 1997–; Asst Minister, Office of Prime Minister 1986–88; Mayor of St-Florent-le-Vieil 1989–; Vice-Pres. Union pour la Démocratie Française (UDF) 1991; Vice-Pres. Conseil Régional, Pays de la Loire 1992–; Minister of Housing 1993–95, of Foreign Affairs 1995–97; Pres. Parti populaire pour la démocratie française 1995, convention démocratie 2002; Pres. Chambre du Commerce Franco-Arabe 2008–. *Publications:* Ouragon sur la République 1995, Lyautey 1997. *Address:* Mairie, 49410 St-Florent-le-Vieil; Assemblée Nationale, 75355 Paris, France.

CHARKIN, Richard Denis Paul, MA; British publishing executive; *Executive Director, Bloomsbury PLC;* b. 17 June 1949, London, England; s. of Frank Charkin and Mabel Doreen Charkin (née Rosen); m. Susan Mary Poole 1972; one s. two d.; ed Haileybury, Imperial Service Coll., Univ. of Cambridge, Harvard Business School, USA; Science Ed. Harrap & Co. 1972; Sr Publishing Man. Pergamon Press 1973; Medical Ed. Oxford University Press 1974, Head of Science and Medicine 1976, Head of Reference 1980; Man. Dir Academic and Gen. 1984; joined Octopus Publishing Group (Reed Books Int.) 1988, Chief Exec. Reed Consumer Books 1989–94, Exec. Dir Reed Books International 1988–96, Chief Exec. 1994–96; CEO Current Science Group 1996–97; CEO Macmillan Ltd 1998–2007; Exec. Dir Bloomsbury PLC 2007–; Non-Exec. Dir, Inst. of Physics Publishing 2009–; Visiting Prof., Univ. of Arts, London 2004–; Visiting Fellow, Green Coll., Oxford 1987; Chair. Common Purpose 1998–2008; mem. man. cttee John Wisden; mem. Publishers Asscn (Vice-Pres. 2004–05, Pres. 2005–06); Vice-Pres. Int. Publrs Asscn 2012–; Dir, Fed. of European Publrs 2011–. *Publication:* Charkin Blog: The Archive 2008. *Leisure interests:* music, cricket. *Address:* Bloomsbury Publishing PLC, 36 Soho Square, London, W1D 3QY, England (office). *Telephone:* (20) 7631-5628 (office). *Website:* www.bloomsbury.com (office).

CHARKVIANI, Gela; Georgian politician and diplomatist; *Permanent Representative, International Maritime Organization;* b. 1 March 1939, Tbilisi, Georgia; s. of Candide Charkviani and Tamar Djaoshvili; m. Nana Toidze-Charkviani; one s. one d.; ed Tbilisi Inst. of Foreign Languages, Univ. of Michigan, USA; teacher, Tbilisi Inst. of Foreign Languages; author and narrator, TV monthly programme Globe, Georgian TV 1976–94; Vice-Pres. Georgian Soc. for Cultural Relations with Foreign Countries 1984–92; apptd Chief Adviser to Pres. Shevardnadze on Foreign Affairs, Head of Int. Relations, Georgian State Chancellery 1992; teacher of sociology at Tbilisi State Univ. 1982–; Asst to Pres. Saakashvili of Georgia and Presidential Spokesperson 2005–06; Amb. to UK (also accred to Ireland) 2006–09; Perm. Rep., IMO, London 2009–; Chair. Presidential Comm. on Peaceful Caucasus; has lectured in Austria, Germany, Sweden, UK and USA; Order of Honour 1998. *Music:* CD of piano miniatures released 2001. *Television:* author and dir of five-part documentary The Georgians in the Kremlin (Rustavi-II TV) 2004. *Publications include:* trans. of King Lear; G. Charkviani – Lectures, Speeches and a Toast 2008; articles in numerous journals. *Leisure interests:* piano music, exotic cuisines. *Address:* Embassy of Georgia, 4 Russell Gardens, London, W14 8EZ, England (office); Gamsakhurdia str. 14, Tbilisi, Georgia (home). *Telephone:* (20) 7603-7799 (office); (32) 380776 (home). *Fax:* (20) 7603-6682 (office). *E-mail:* imo@mfa.gov.ge (office).

CHARLES, Caroline, OBE; British fashion designer; b. 18 May 1942, Cairo, Egypt; d. of Noel St John Fairhurst and Helen T. Williams; m. Malcolm Valentine 1966; one s. one d.; ed Sacred Heart Convent, Woldingham, Surrey, Swindon Art School; f. Caroline Charles 1963; established retail outlet in London selling Caroline Charles Collection 1979; wholesale business suppliers to leading British shops and stores and exports to USA, Japan, Australia and Europe; Evening Standard Design Award 1983 and other design awards. *Publication:* Weekend Wardrobe. *Leisure interests:* travel, theatre, gardening, tennis, reading. *Address:* 56–57 Beauchamp Place, London, SW3 1NY, England (office). *Telephone:* (20) 7225-3197. *Website:* www.carolinecharles.co.uk.

CHARLES-ROUX, Edmonde; French writer; b. 17 April 1920, Neuilly-sur-Seine; d. of François Charles-Roux and Sabine Gounelle; m. Gaston Defferre 1973 (deceased); ed Italy; served as nurse, then in Resistance Movt, during Second World War, in which she was twice wounded; reporter, magazine Elle 1947–49; Features Ed., French edn of Vogue 1949–54, Ed.-in-Chief 1954–66; mem. Acad. Goncourt 1983–, Chair. 2002–14; Croix de guerre 1940–45, Commdr, Légion d'honneur 2010, Caporal d'honneur, Légion Etrangère 2007; Prix Goncourt 1966, Grand Prix Littéraire de Provence 1977. *Dance:* collaboration with La Compagnie nationale des Ballets de Roland Petit, Marseille. *Publications:* Oublier Palerme 1966, Elle, Adrienne 1971, L'irrégulière ou mon itinéraire Chanel 1974, Le temps Chanel 1979, Stèle pour un bâtard, Don Juan d'Autriche 1980, Une enfance sicilienne 1981, Un désir d'Orient: La jeunesse d'Isabelle Eberhardt 1988, Nomade j'étais: Les années africaines d'Isabelle Eberhardt 1995, L'homme de Marseille 2001, Isabelle du désert 2003 (vol combining Un désir d'Orient et Nomade j'étais). *Leisure interests:* music, sea and sailing. *Address:* c/o Editions Grasset, 61 rue des Saints-Pères, Paris 75006, France. *Website:* www.academie-goncourt.fr/?bibliographie=1016642741.

CHARLESWORTH, Brian, BA, PhD, FRS, FRSE; British biologist and academic; *Senior Honorary Professorial Fellow, Institute of Evolutionary Biology, University of Edinburgh;* b. 29 April 1945, Brighton, Sussex, England; s. of Gustave Charlesworth and Mary Ryan Francis; m. Deborah Charlesworth; one d.; ed Queens' Coll., Cambridge; Post-doctoral Fellow in Population Biology, Univ. of Chicago 1969–71, Prof. of Ecology and Evolution 1985–92, George Wells Beadle Distinguished Service Prof. of Ecology and Evolution 1992–97; Lecturer in Genetics, Univ. of Liverpool 1971–74; Lecturer in Biology, Univ. of Sussex, Brighton 1974–82, Reader in Biology 1982–84; Royal Soc. Research Professorship, Univ. of Edinburgh 1997–2007, Professorial Fellow and Head of Inst. of Evolutionary Biology 2007–10, Sr Hon. Professorial Fellow 2010–; Pres. Genetics Soc. (UK) 2006–09, European Soc. for Evolutionary Biology 2011–13; mem. Genetics Soc. of GB 1966– (mem. Cttee 1981–84), Soc. for the Study of Evolution 1985–2005, 2013– (Pres. 1999), Genetics Soc. of America 1986–99, Soc. for Molecular Biology and Evolution 1995–97, 2001–, European Soc. for Evolutionary Biology 1997–99, 2010–, Research Fellowships Cttee, Royal Soc. 1999– (mem. Awards Cttee 2001–04), Functional Genomics Cttee Wellcome Trust 2000–03, Sectional Cttee A3, Royal Soc. of Edinburgh 2000–03, ERA Initiative Cttee Biotechnology and Biological Sciences Research Council 2001; Assoc. Ed. Current Biology 1992–; mem. Editorial Bd Genetical Research 1996–2000, Philosophical Transactions of the Royal Society 1999–2004; Ed. Biology Letters 2004–; mem. Advisory Bd Journal of Theoretical Biology 1996–2005; Reviewer, Nature, Science, Evolution, Genetics, Genetical Research, Journal of Theoretical Biology, American Naturalist, Molecular Biology and Evolution; Hon. Fellow, American Acad. of Arts and Sciences 1996, Foreign Associate, Nat. Acad. of Sciences USA 2013; Darwin Prize, Univ. of Edinburgh 1994, Darwin Medal, Royal Soc. 2000, Sewall Wright Award, American Soc. of Naturalists 2006, Frink Award, Zoological Soc. of London 2007, Weldon Memorial Award, Univ. of Oxford 2007, Fisher Memorial Lecturer 2009, Darwin-Wallace Medal, Linnaean Soc. 2010. *Publications:* Evolution: A Very Short Introduction (with Deborah Charlesworth) 2003, Elements of Evolutionary Genetics (with Deborah Charlesworth) 2010; more than 300 publs in scientific journals on population genetics and evolutionary biology. *Leisure interests:* reading, classical music, hill-walking. *Address:* Institute of Evolutionary Biology, University of Edinburgh, Ashworth Laboratories, West Mains Road, Edinburgh, Midlothian, EH9 3JT, Scotland (office). *Telephone:* (131) 650-5751 (office). *Fax:* (131) 650-6564 (office). *E-mail:* brian.charlesworth@ed.ac.uk (office). *Website:* www.ed.ac.uk/schools-departments/biology/evolutionary-biology (office).

CHARLTON, John (Jack), OBE, DL; British fmr professional football manager and fmr professional football player; b. 8 May 1935, Ashington, Northumberland; s. of the late Robert Charlton and of Elizabeth Charlton; brother of Sir Robert Charlton (q.v.); m. Patricia Charlton 1958; two s. one d.; ed Hirst Park School, Ashington; player for Leeds United youth team 1950–52, sr team 1952–73 (made 629 appearances, scored 70 goals); 35 full England caps 1965–70, scored six goals; played with winning teams League Championship 1969, Football Assen Cup 1972, League Cup 1968, Fairs Cup 1968, 1971, Charity Shield 1969, World Cup (England v. Germany) 1966; Man. Middlesbrough (Div. 2 Champions 1974) 1973–77, Sheffield Wednesday 1977–83, Newcastle United 1984–85, Repub. of Ireland (qualified for European Championships, West Germany 1988, World Cup, Italy 1990, USA 1994) 1986–95; Football Writers' Assen Footballer of the Year 1967. *Publications:* Jack Charlton's American World Cup Diary 1994, Jack Charlton: The Autobiography 1996. *Leisure interests:* shooting, fishing. *Address:* Cairn Lodge, Dalton, Ponteland, Northumbria, England.

CHARLTON, Sir Robert (Bobby), Kt, CBE; British sports official, fmr professional football player and fmr professional football manager; b. 11 Oct. 1937, Ashington, Northumberland; s. of Robert Charlton and Elizabeth Charlton; brother of Jack Charlton (q.v.); m. Norma Charlton 1961; two d.; ed Bedlington Grammar School, Northumberland; professional footballer with Manchester United 1954–73, played 751 games, scored 245 goals; F.A. Cup winners' medal 1963; First Div. championship medals 1956–57, 1964–65, 1966–67; World Cup winners' medal (with England) 1966; European Cup winners' medal 1968; 106 appearances for England 1957–73, scored record 49 goals; Man. Preston North End

1973–75; Chair. NW Council for Sport and Recreation 1982–; Dir Manchester United Football Club 1984–; mem. Laureus World Sports Acad.; Hon. Fellow, Manchester Polytechnic 1979; Hon. MA (Univ. of Manchester); BBC Sports Personality of the Year Lifetime Achievement Award 2008. *Publications include:* My Soccer Life 1965, Forward for England 1967, This Game of Soccer 1967, Book of European Football, Books 1–4 1969–72, My Manchester United Years: The Autobiography 2007, My Life in Football 2009. *Leisure interest:* golf.

CHARNLEY, Irene; South African business executive; b. 6 May 1960; m. Clement Charnley; two s. one d.; ed Univ. of the Witwatersrand, Harvard Univ., USA; negotiator and strategist, Nat. Union of Mineworkers 1996; Commercial Dir MTN Group (fmrly M-Cell Ltd) 2001–05, Group Exec. Vice-Pres. 2005–07, mem. Bd of Dirs (non-exec.) 2008–, fmr Exec. Dir Johnnic Holdings, fmr Chair. M-Cell (subsidiary); Chair. Orbicom; mem. Bd of Dirs FirstRand Bank 2004–, Pontso Investment Holdings, Time Media Ltd, Metropolitan Life Ltd, Int. Marketing Council of South Africa, Black Econ. Empowerment Task Team; mem. King Committee on Corp. Governance; Trustee Eskom Pension Fund, Johnnic Ikageng Share Trust, Vaal Reefs Trust; World Econ. Forum Global Leader for Tomorrow, Businesswoman of the Year 2000, ranked 48th by Fortune magazine amongst 50 Most Powerful Women in Business outside the US 2002. *Address:* MTN Group Limited, Innovation Centre, 216 14th Avenue, Fairlands (office); Private Bag X9955, Sandton, Johannesburg 2146, South Africa. *Website:* www.mtn.com (office).

CHARPENTIER, Georg, MEcons; Finnish economist and UN official; *Deputy Special Representative of the Secretary-General, Resident and Humanitarian Coordinator, United Nations Support Mission in Libya (UNSMIL);* b. 11 Aug. 1956, El Salvador; m.; three c.; ed Univ. of Helsinki; fmr Secr., Programme de Restructuration du Marché Céréalier, Mali; joined UN in 1984 as Programme Officer, Viet Nam, has held numerous posts including Sr Deputy Resident Rep. in Ethiopia, Deputy Resident Rep. in Lesotho and São Tomé, Asst Resident Rep. in Mauritania, UNDP Rep., ad interim and Humanitarian Coordinator, ad interim, in Congo, UNDP Deputy Dir Bureau for Crisis Prevention and Recovery, Geneva 2002–04, UN Resident Coordinator and UNDP Resident Rep. in Burkina Faso 2004–06, UN Resident and Humanitarian Coordinator and UNDP Resident Rep. in Burundi 2006, Deputy Special Rep. in Côte d'Ivoire 2007–11, Deputy Special Rep. and UN Resident Coordinator and Humanitarian Coordinator for the Sudan 2010–11, Deputy Special Rep. of Sec.-Gen., Resident and Humanitarian Coordinator, UN Support Mission in Libya (UNSMIL) 2011–. *Address:* c/o Radhia Achouri, Director, United Nations Support Mission in Libya (UNSMIL), Tripoli, Libya (office); c/o Office of the Secretary-General, United Nations, New York, NY 10017, USA. *Telephone:* (92) 307-0209 (Tripoli) (office); (212) 963-1234 (New York) (office). *Fax:* (212) 963-4879 (New York) (office). *E-mail:* achouri@un.org (office). *Website:* unsmil.unmissions.org (office).

CHARPY, Christian; French government official; *Director-General, Agence Nationale Pour l'Emploi;* mem. Conseil d'Orientation pour l'Emploi (Employment Policy Council); currently Dir-Gen. Agence Nationale Pour l'Emploi; Pres. World Asscn of Public Employment Service 2006–. *Address:* Agence Nationale Pour l'Emploi, c/o Ministère du Travail, des Relations Sociales et de la Solidarité, 127 rue de Grenelle, 75007 Paris 07 SP, France (office). *E-mail:* info@anpe.fr (office). *Website:* www.anpe.fr (office).

CHARTIER, Roger; French academic; *Director of Studies, Ecole des Hautes Etudes en Sciences Sociales;* b. 9 Dec. 1945, Lyons; s. of Georges Chartier and Laurence Fonvielle; m. Anne-Marie Trépier 1967; one s. one d.; ed Ecole Normale Supérieure, St Cloud; Prof., Lycée Louis-Le-Grand, Paris 1969–70; Asst Prof., Univ. Paris I, Panthéon-Sorbonne 1970–75; Assoc. Prof., Ecole des Hautes Etudes en Sciences Sociales 1975–83, Dir of Studies 1984–; Prof., Collège de France 2007–; Visiting Prof., Univ. of California, Berkeley 1987, Cornell Univ. 1988, Johns Hopkins Univ. 1992; Annual Award, American Printing History Assen 1990; Grand Prix d'Histoire, Acad. Française 1992. *Publications include:* L'Education en France du XVIe au XVIIIe siècle (jtly) 1976, La Nouvelle Histoire (co-ed.) 1978, Histoire de l'Edition Française (ed.) 1982–86, Figures de la gueuserie 1982, Représentation et vouloir politique: Autour des Etats Généraux de 1614 (jtly) 1982, Figure della furfantaria, Marginalità e cultura popolare in Francia tra Cinque e Seicento 1984, Pratiques de la lecture (ed.) 1985, The Cultural Uses of Print in Early Modern France 1987, The Culture of Print (ed.) 1987, Cultural History: Between Practices and Representations 1988, The Cultural Origins of the French Revolution 1991, Correspondence: Models of Letter Writing from the Middle Ages to the Nineteenth Century 1991, The Order of Books 1994, Forms and Meanings: Texts, Performances, and Audiences from Codex to Computer 1995, A History of Reading in the West 1995, Culture écrite et société. L'ordre des livres 1996, On the Edge of the Cliff: History, Language, and Practices 1998, Publishing Drama in Early Modern Europe: The Panizzi Lectures 1998, Le Jeu de la règles 2000, Identités d'auteur dans l'Antiquité et la tradition européenne (co-ed.) 2004, Inscrire et effacer: Culture écrite et littérature 2005. *Address:* Ecole des Hautes Etudes en Sciences Sociales, 54 boulevard Raspail, 75006 Paris (office); Collège de France, 11, Place Marcelin Berthelot, 75231 Paris, France (office). *Telephone:* 1-44-27-12-11 (office); 1-49-54-25-25 (office). *E-mail:* webmestre@ehess.fr (office). *Website:* www.ehess.fr.

CHARTRES, Rt Rev. and Rt Hon. Richard John Carew, Kt, KCVO, PC, DD, DLitt, FSA; British ecclesiastic; *Bishop of London;* b. 11 July 1947, Ware, Herts., England; s. of Richard Chartres and Charlotte Chartres; m. Caroline Mary McLintock 1982; two s. two d.; ed Hertford Grammar School, Trinity Coll. Cambridge, Cuddesdon Theological Coll. Oxford and Lincoln Theological Coll.; ordained deacon 1973, priest 1974; Asst Curate, St Andrew's, Bedford 1973–75; Domestic Chaplain to Bishop of St Albans 1975–80; Chaplain to Archbishop of Canterbury 1980–84; Vicar, St Stephen with St John, Westminster 1984–92; Dir of Ordinands for London Area 1985–92; Gresham Prof. of Divinity 1986–92; Bishop of Stepney 1992–95, of London 1996–; Dean of the Chapels Royal 1995–; Ecclesiastical Patron Prayer Book Soc.; Prelate of Imperial Soc. of Kts Bachelor; Prelate of OBE 1995–; Chair. Churches Main Cttee 1998–2001, Church Bldgs Div.; Hon. Bencher, Middle Temple; Liveryman, Merchant Taylors' Co.; Hon. Freeman, Weavers' Co. 1998, Leathersellers' Co. 1999, Woolmen's Co. 2000, Vintners' Co. 2001, Drapers' Co.; Commdr of the Order of St John; Hon. DLitt (London Guildhall) 1998, Hon. DD (London) 1999, (City) 1999, (Brunel) 1999, (Surrey)

1999, (King's Coll. London) 2010. *Publications:* The History of Gresham College 1597–1997 1998, Tree of Knowledge Tree of Life 2005. *Address:* London Diocesan House, 36 Causton Street, London, SW1P 4AU (office); The Old Deanery, Dean's Court, London, EC4V 5AA, England (home). *Telephone:* (20) 7932-1100 (office); (20) 7248-6233 (home). *Fax:* (20) 7932-1110 (office); (20) 7248-9721 (home). *E-mail:* communications@london.anglican.org (office); bishop@londin.clara.co.uk (office). *Website:* www.london.anglican.org (office).

CHASE, Chevy (Cornelius Crane), MA; American comedian, actor and writer; b. 8 Oct. 1943, New York, NY; s. of Edward Tinsley Chase and Cathalene Crane Chase (née Widdoes); m. 1st Jacqueline Carlin 1976 (divorced 1980); m. 2nd Jayni Chase; three d.; ed Bard Coll., Inst. of Audio Research, Massachusetts Inst. of Tech.; writer and actor, Channel One (satirical revue), The Great American Dream Machine, co-writer and actor, Lemmings (Nat. Lampoon satirical musical), writer and performer Nat. Lampoon Radio Hour, Saturday Night Live (TV series); writer Mad magazine 1969; mem. American Fed. of Musicians, Stage Actors Guild, Actors Equity, American Fed. of TV and Radio Artists; three Emmy Awards, Writers' Guild of America Award, Man of the Year, Harvard Univ. Theatrical Group 1992. *Films:* Walk. . . Don't Walk (short) 196, The Groove Tube 1974, Tunnelvision 1976, Foul Play 1978, Oh Heavenly Dog 1980, Caddyshack 1980, Seems Like Old Times 1980, Under the Rainbow 1981, Modern Problems 1981, Vacation 1983, Deal of the Century 1983, Fletch 1985, European Vacation 1985, Sesame Street Presents: Follow that Bird 1985, Spies Like Us 1985, ¡Three Amigos! 1986, The Couch Trip 1988, Funny Farm 1988, Caddyshack II 1988, Christmas Vacation 1989, Fletch Lives 1989, National Lampoon's Winter Holiday 1989, L.A. Story (uncredited) 1991, Nothing But Trouble 1991, Memoirs of an Invisible Man 1992, Accidental Hero (uncredited) 1992, Last Action Hero (cameo) 1993, Cops and Robbersons 1994, Man of the House 1995, National Lampoon's Vegas Vacation 1997, Dirty Work 1998, Pete's a Pizza (voice) 2000, The One Arm Bandit (short) 2000, Snow Day 2000, Ellie Parker (short) 2001, Orange County 2002, Vacuums 2003, Mariti in affitto 2004, Bad Meat 2004, Ellie Parker 2005, Goose on the Loose 2006, Doogal (voice) 2006, Funny Money 2006, Zoom 2006, Cutlass (short) 2007, Stay Cool 2009, Jack and the Beanstalk 2010, Hotel Hell Vacation (video short) 2010, Presidential Reunion (video short) 2010, Hot Tub Time Machine 2010, Not Another Not Another Movie 2011. *Television includes:* The Great American Dream Machine (series) 1971, Energy Crisis (film) (uncredited) 1974, Saturday Night Live (series) 1975–2007, It's Garry Shandling's Show (series) 1989, The Larry Sanders Show (series) 1995, The Nanny (series) 1997, America's Most Terrible Things (film) 2002, Freedom: A History of Us (series documentary) 2003, The Karate Dog (film) (voice) 2004, The Secret Policeman's Ball (film) 2006, Law & Order (series) 2006, Brothers & Sisters (series) 2007, Family Guy (series) 2007–09, Hjälp! (series) 2009, Chuck (series) 2009, Community (series) 2009–13, CollegeHumor Originals (series) 2011. *Address:* Cornelius Productions, Box 257, Bedford, NY 10506, USA (office).

CHASE, David, MA; American scriptwriter, television director and producer; b. (David DeCesare), 22 Aug. 1945, Mount Vernon, NY; s. of Henry DeCesare and Norma DeCesare; m. Denise Kelly; one d.; ed Wake Forest Univ., NC, School of Visual Arts, New York, New York Univ., Stanford Univ., Calif.; produced episodes of Northern Exposure and The Rockford Files, among other series; cr. TV series The Sopranos, Mystery Writers of America Special Edgar Award for his entire body of work. *Television includes:* Kolchak: The Night Stalker (series) (writer) 1974–75, The Rockford Files (series) (writer, producer) (Emmy Award 1977) 1976–80, Off the Minnesota Strip (film) (writer, producer) (Emmy Award 1979, Writers Guild of America Award 1980) 1980, Moonlight 1982, Alfred Hitchcock Presents (series) (dir) 1985, Almost Grown (series) (writer, dir) 1988–89, Grave of the Vampire (film) 1972, I'll Fly Away (writer, exec. producer) (Norman Felton Award, Producers Guild of America 1993) 1992–93, Northern Exposure (series) (exec. producer) 1993–95, The Rockford Files: A Blessing in Disguise (film) (producer) 1995, The Rockford Files: The Punishment and Crime (writer, producer, dir) 1996, The Sopranos (series) (writer, exec. producer, dir) (Emmy Award for College episode 1998, Golden Globe Award 1999, Norman Felton Award, Producers Guild of America 2000, Outstanding Directorial Achievement Award, Directors Guild of America 1999, Peabody Award 2000, Drama Series of the Year Award, American Film Inst. 2001, Primetime Emmy for Outstanding Writing for a Drama Series & Outstanding Drama Series, Acad. of TV Arts and Sciences 2007) 1999–2007, Treme (series) 2010. *Address:* c/o David Harbert, United Talent Agency, 9560 Wilshire Blvd, Suite 500, Beverly Hills, CA 90212-2401, USA (office). *Telephone:* (310) 273-6700 (office). *Fax:* (310) 247-1111 (office). *E-mail:* webmaster@unitedtalent.com (office). *Website:* www.unitedtalent.com (office).

CHASTAIN, Jessica Michelle, BFA; American theatre, film and television actress, model and singer; b. 24 March 1977, Sacramento, Calif.; ed El Camino High School, Sacramento City Coll., Juilliard School; appeared as Juliet in a production of Romeo and Juliet staged by TheatreWorks, San Francisco 1998; Broadway debut playing Catherine Sloper in The Heiress at the Walter Kerr Theatre 2012; featured by TIME magazine as one of the 100 Most Influential People in the World 2012. *Films include:* Jolene (Best Actress, Seattle Int. Film Festival) 2008, Stolen Lives 2009, The Westerner (short) (also producer) 2010, The Debt 2010, Take Shelter (Best Supporting Actress, Austin Film Critics Assn) 2011, Coriolanus 2011, The Tree of Life (Best Supporting Actress, Satellite Awards, amongst others) 2011, The Help (Breakthrough Actress and Ensemble of the Year Award, Hollywood Film Festival, Spotlight Award, Palm Springs Int. Film Festival, Best Ensemble – Motion Picture, Satellite Awards, Outstanding Cast, Screen Actors Guild Awards, amongst others) 2011, Wilde Salome 2011, Texas Killing Fields 2011, Madagascar 3: Europe's Most Wanted (voice) 2012, Lawless 2012, Tar 2012, Zero Dark Thirty (Best Actress – Motion Picture, Drama, Golden Globe Awards, Best Actress in a Movie, Critics' Choice Movie Awards, Best Actress, Boston Online Film Critics Assn, Best Actress, Broadcast Film Critics Assn (Critics Choice Awards), Best Actress, Chicago Film Critics Assn, Best Actress, Nat. Bd of Review, Best Actress, Washington DC Area Film Critics Assn, amongst many others) 2012, Mama (Best Actress, Fantasporto) 2013, The Disappearance of Eleanor Rigby: His 2013, The Disappearance of Eleanor Rigby: Hers 2013, Miss Julie 2014. *Television includes:* Dark Shadows (movie) 2005, Law & Order: Trial by Jury (series) 2005–06, Close to Home (series) 2006, The Evidence (series) 2006, Pirates: The True Story of Blackbeard (movie) 2006, Journeyman (series) 2007, Agatha Christie: Poirot (series) – Murder on the Orient Express

2010. *Address:* c/o Mosaic Media Group, 9200 West Sunset Blvd, 10th Floor, Los Angeles, CA 90069, USA (office).

CHATEL, Luc Marie; French politician; *Mayor of Chaumont;* b. 15 Aug. 1964, Bethesda, Md, USA; m. Astrid Herrenschmidt (died 2012); Municipal Councillor, Bayard-sur-Marne (Haute-Marne) 1993–95, Chaumont (Haute-Marne) 1996–2001; mem. Regional Council, Champagne-Ardenne 1998–2008, Vice-Pres. 1998–2004; mem. Assemblée nationale (Parl.) for Haute-Marne 2002–10; Mayor of Chaumont 2008–; Sec. of State for Consumer Affairs and Tourism 2007–08, for Industry and Consumer Affairs 2008–09, also Govt Spokesman 2009–10, Minister of Nat. Educ. 2009–10, of Nat. Educ., Youth and Voluntary Orgs 2010–12; mem. Union pour un Mouvement Populaire, Spokesman 2002–07. *Address:* Mairie de Chaumont, Hôtel de Ville, BP 564, 52012 Chaumont Cedex, France (office). *Telephone:* (3) 25-30-60-00 (office). *E-mail:* info@ville-chaumont.fr (office). *Website:* www.ville-chaumont.fr (office).

CHATER, Keith Frederick, PhD, FRS; British geneticist and academic; *Emeritus Fellow, Department of Molecular Microbiology, The John Innes Centre;* b. 23 April 1944, Croydon, Surrey, England; s. of Frederick Ernest Chater and Marjorie Inez Chater (née Palmer); m. Jean Wallbridge 1966; three s. one d.; ed Trinity School of John Whitgift, Croydon, Univ. of Birmingham; scientist, The John Innes Centre, Norwich 1969–, Deputy Head, Dept of Genetics 1989–98, Head 1998–2001, Head, Dept of Molecular Microbiology 2001–04, Emer. Fellow 2004–; Hon. Prof., Univ. of East Anglia 1988–, Chinese Acad. of Sciences Inst. of Microbiology, Beijing 1998–, Huazhong Agricultural Univ., Wuhan 2000–, New-castle Univ. 2006–09, Fred Griffith Review Lecturer, Soc. for Gen. Microbiology 1997, Leeuwenhoek Lecturer, Royal Soc. 2005. *Publications:* Genetic Manipula-tion of Streptomyces (co-ed) 1985, Genetics of Bacterial Diversity (co-ed) 1989, Practical Streptomyces Genetics (co-author) 2000. *Leisure interests:* art, bird-watching, gardening, cooking. *Address:* Department of Molecular Microbiology, John Innes Centre, Norwich Research Park, Colney, Norwich, NR4 7UH (office); 6 Coach House Court, Norwich, NR4 7QR, England (home). *Telephone:* (1603) 450297 (office); (1603) 506145 (home). *Fax:* (1603) 450045 (home). *E-mail:* keith.chater@jic.ac.uk (office); keithchater@yahoo.com (home). *Website:* www.jic.ac.uk/staff/keith-chater.

CHATIKAVANIJ, Korn, BA (Hons), MA; Thai politician; *Deputy Leader, Democrat Party;* b. 19 Feb. 1964; m. Vorakorn Chatikavanij; ed Satit Srinakar-inwirot Demonstration School, Old Malthouse School, Winchester Coll. and St John's Coll., Oxford, UK; worked for S.G. Warburg & Co., London 1985–88; Co-founder and Pres. JF Thanakom Securities Ltd 1988–99; Pres. JPMorgan (Thailand) Ltd (following takeover of JF Thanakom Securities Ltd) 2000–04; mem. Sapha Poothaen Rassadorn (House of Reps) for Bangkok 2005–06, 2007–10; Minister of Finance 2008–11; mem. Democrat Party, currently Deputy Leader and Shadow Deputy Prime Minister; Kt Grand Cordon (Special Class), Most Exalted Order of the White Elephant; The Banker Global Finance Minister of the Year 2010, Asia-Pacific Finance Minister of the Year 2010. *Address:* Democrat Party, 67 Thanon Setsiri, Samsen Nai, Phaya Thai, Bangkok 10400, Thailand (office). *Telephone:* 678-9777 (office). *Fax:* 678-9757 (office). *E-mail:* korn@democrat.or.th (office). *Website:* www.facebook.com/KornChatikavanijDP.

CHATT, Amares, BSc, MSc, PhD; Canadian (b. Indian) nuclear chemist and academic; *Adjunct Professor, Department of Chemistry, Dalhousie University;* b. (Amares Chattopadhyay), S India; ed Univ. of Calcutta, Indian Inst. of Tech., Roorkee, Univ. of Waterloo, Univ. of Toronto; joined Dept of Chem., Univ. of Dalhousie, Halifax, Nova Scotia c. 1975, becoming Prof., also Dir Dalhousie Slowpoke-2 Nuclear Research Reactor, Faculty of Science Killam Prof. in Chem. 2001–06, now Adjunct Prof.; fmr Adviser, IAEA, Vienna; Fellow, Chemical Inst. of Canada 1985–, American Nuclear Soc. 1993–; Pres. Int. Cttee for Activation Analysis 1999–; Francis W. Karasek Award 1993, Radiation Science and Tech. Award 1996, William D. Ehmann Award 1999, American Nuclear Soc., George Hevesy Medal 2001. *Publications include:* Hair Analysis: Applications in the Biomedical and Environmental Sciences (with S.A. Katz) 1988. *Address:* Depart-ment of Chemistry, Dalhousie University, Halifax, NS B3H 4J3, Canada (office). *Telephone:* (902) 494-2474 (office). *Fax:* (902) 494-1310 (office). *E-mail:* a.chatt@dal.ca (office). *Website:* chemistry.dal.ca (office); myweb.dal.ca/chatt (office).

CHATTERJEE, Somnath, BA, MA; Indian lawyer, politician and trade union official; b. 25 July 1929, Tezpur, Assam; s. of Nirmal Chandra Chatterjee and Binapani Debi; m. Renu Chatterjee; one s. two d.; ed Mitra Inst. School, Presidency Coll., Univ. of Calcutta, Jesus Coll., Cambridge and Middle Temple, London, UK; called to Bar from Middle Temple, London; Sr Advocate, Supreme Court, Calcutta High Court; Sr Govt Advocate, Calcutta High Court 1969–70; mem. Communist Party of India—Marxist (CPI-M) 1968–2008 (expelled for violation of party discipline), fmr Leader; mem. Lok Sabha 1971–, Chair. Cttee on Subordinate Legislation 1977–79, 1991–93, Cttee on Privileges 1990–91, Cttee on Railways 1993–96, Cttee on Communications 1996–97, 1998–99, Leader, CPI-M in Lok Sabha 1989–2004, Speaker, Lok Sabha 2004–09; Chair. Bengal Table Tennis Asscn, Life Saving Soc., Kolkata, West Bengal Industrial Devt Corpn, mem. several Parl. Cttees, Cricket Asscn of Bengal, India Int. Centre, India Habitat Centre; Hon. Fellow, Jesus Coll. Cambridge 2007; Outstanding Parliamentarian Award 1996, Baby John Award 2009, Sri Chandrasekharendra Saraswati Nat. Eminence Awards, South Indian Educ. Soc. 2009. *Leisure interests:* gardening, reading, sports. *Address:* Lok Sabha, 17 Parliament House, New Delhi 110 001; P-514, Raja Basanta Roy Road, Calcutta 700 029 (home); 21, Ashoka Road, New Delhi 110 001, India (home). *Telephone:* (33) 4644321 (Calcutta) (home); (11) 3365036 (New Delhi) (home). *Fax:* (33) 4662900 (Calcutta) (home); (11) 3345305 (New Delhi) (home).

CHATTERJEE, Soumitra, (Soumitra Chattopadhyay), MA; Indian actor; b. 19 Jan. 1935, Krishnanagar Dist, West Bengal; s. of Mohitkumar Chatterjee; m. Dipa Chatterjee; one s. one d.; ed Univ. of Calcutta; worked at AIR before pursuing film career; Chair. Kolkata Film Festival Cttee 2007; Padma Bhushan 2004, Banglalive Legendary Award, Dadasaheb Phalke Award 2012. *Films include:* Apur Sansar (The World of Apu) 1959, Kshudista Pashan (Hungry Stones) 1960, Devi (The Goddess) 1960, Teen Kanya 1961, Punasha (Over Again) 1961, Atal Jaler Ahwan (1962), Abhijaan (The Expedition) 1962, Saat Pake Bandha 1963, Charulata (The Lonely Wife) 1964, Kapurush (The Coward) 1965, Kanch Kata Hirey 1965, Ek

Tuku Basa 1965, Akash Kusum (Up in the Clouds) 1965, Prastar Swakshar 1967, Mahashweta 1967, Baghini 1968, Teen Bhuboner Porey 1969, Parineeta (The Fiancee) 1969, Aparachita 1969, Aranyer Din Ratri (Days and Nights in the Forest, USA) 1970, Malyadaan 1971, KhunjeyBerai 1971, Stree 1972, Ashani Sanket (Distant Thunder, USA) 1973, Basanata Bilap 1973, Jadi Jantem 1974, Sonar Kella (The Golden Fortress, USA) 1974, Sangini 1974, Asati 1974, Sansar Seemantey 1975, Datta 1976, Joi Baba Felunath (The Elephant God) 1978, Ganadevata 1979, Naukadubi 1979, Debdas 1979, Heerak Rajar Deshe (The Kingdom of Diamonds) (TV) 1980, Khelar Putul 1981, Amar Geeti 1983, Ghare-Baire (The Home and the World) 1984, Kony 1984, Shyam Saheb 1986, Ekti Jiban (Portrait of a Life) 1987, La Nuit Bengali (Bengali Night) 1988, Ganashatru (An Enemy of the People, UK) 1989, Shakha Proshakha (Tyhe Branches of the Tree) 1990, Mahaprithivi (World Within, World Without) 1992, Wheel Chair 1994, Uttoran (The Broken Journey) 1994, Sopan 1994, Vrindavan Film Studios 1996, Gaach (The Tree) (as himself) 1998, Asukh (Malaise) 1999, Paromitar Ek Din 2000, Dekha 2001, Saanjhbatir Roopkathara (Strokes and Silhouettes) 2002, Abar Aranye (In the Forest Again) 2003, Patalghar 2003, Nil Sanket (Tryst of Blue) 2004, Schatten der Zeit 2004, Faltu 2005, Nishijapon 2005, 15 Park Avenue 2005, The Bong Connection 2006, Podokkhep (Rajat Kamal Nat. Film Award (Silver Lotus Award) for Best Actor 2007) 2007, Minister Fatakesto 2007, Krishnakanter Will 2007, Jara Brishtite Bhijechhilo 2007, Chaader Baari 2007, Ballygunge Court 2007, 10:10 2008. Publications: fmrly co-ed. Ekshan (monthly journal); wrote several poems and plays. Leisure interest: reciting poetry. Website: www.soumitrachatterjee.com.

CHAU, Solina, BA; Hong Kong business executive; Director, Li Ka Shing Foundation; b. (Solina Chau Hoi Shuen), 1961, Hong Kong; ed Diocesan Girls' School, Hong Kong, Univ. of New South Wales, Australia; co-f., with Li Ka-shing, Tom Group (Beijing digital media co.) 1997; business partner in Cheung Kong Group; Dir Li Ka Shing Foundation, makes investments through its business unit, provides grants for medical research and disaster relief in countries world-wide; launched own foundation to focus on educ. and women's initiatives 1996; ranked by Forbes magazine amongst The World's 100 Most Powerful Women (87th) 2012, (80th) 2013. Address: Li Ka Shing Foundation, 7/F Cheung Kong Centre, 2 Queen's Road Central, Hong Kong Special Administrative Region, People's Republic of China (office). E-mail: general@lksf.org (office). Website: www.lksf.org (office).

CHAUDHRY, Amir Husain; Pakistani lawyer and politician; b. 1942, Jammu, India; mem. Nat. Ass. 1985–2008, Speaker 2002–08; mem. Council, Azad Jammu and Kashmir Council 1985–90; Vice-Pres. Muslim Conf., Azad Jammu 1985–90; mem. Pakistan Muslim League. Address: c/o Pakistan Muslim League, PML House, F-7/3, Islamabad, Pakistan (office).

CHAUDHRY, Iftikhar Mohammad, BA, LLB; Pakistani judge; b. 12 Dec. 1948, Quetta; s. of Jan Muhammad Chaudhry; called to Bar 1974; enrolled as Advocate of the High Court 1976, Advocate of the Supreme Court 1985; Advocate Gen., Balochistan 1989–90; Additional Judge, Balochistan High Court 1990–99, also served as Banking Judge, Judge of Special Court for Speedy Trials, Judge of Customs Appellate Courts and Company Judge; Chief Justice, High Court of Balochistan 1999–2000; elevated to Supreme Court 2000, Chief Justice of Pakistan 2005–07, reinstated July–Nov. 2007 (suspended for refusing to ratify Pres. Musharraf's emergency rule), reinstated March 2009–13; Pres. High Court Bar Asscn, Quetta; Chair. Balochistan Local Council Election Authority 1992–, Prov. Review Bd for Balochistan, Enrolment Cttee of Pakistan Bar Council, Supreme Court Bldg Cttee; fmr Chair. Pakistan Red Crescent Soc., Balochistan; mem. Bar Council; Hon. mem. Asscn New York City Bar 2008; Hon. LLD (Nova Southeastern Univ.) 2009; Lawyer of the Year, National Law Journal, USA 2007, Medal of Freedom, Harvard Law School 2008, Lifetime Achievement Award, Karachi Tax Bar Asscn 2012, Hero to Animal Award, PETA, India, Int. Jurists Award, Int. Jurists Council 2012, Lifetime Achievement Award, Sindh High Court Bar Asscn 2012. Address: 54-B Zarghon Road, Quetta, Pakistan (home).

CHAUDHRY, Mahendra Pal; Fijian politician and trade unionist; Secretary General (Leader), Fiji Labour Party; b. 2 Sept. 1942, Ba; s. of the late Ram Gopal Chaudhry and Devi Chaudhry (née Nair); two s. one d.; Sr Auditor, Office of the Auditor Gen. 1960–75; Gen. Sec. Fiji Public Service Asscn 1970–99; Gen. Sec. Nat. Farmers' Union 1978–; Nat. Sec. Fiji Trades Union Congress 1988–92; Minister of Finance April–May 1987 (ousted in May 1987 coup), Founding mem. Fiji Labour Party 1985, Parl. Leader 1992, Sec.-Gen. (Leader) 1994–; Prime Minister and Minister of Finance, Public Enterprise, Sugar Industry and Information 1999–2000; ousted in coup May 2000; re-assumed post of Prime Minister 1 March 2001, dismissed 14 March 2001 by Pres. of Fiji; Leader of the Opposition 2004–; Minister of Finance, Nat. Planning, Public Enterprise and Sugar Reform (in Cdre Josaia Bainimarama's interim govt) Jan. 2007–08 (resgnd); Bharatiya Samman Award, Govt of India 2004. Leisure interests: reading, music, gardening, social work. Address: Fiji Labour Party, PO Box 2162, Suva (office); 30 Varani Street, Suva (office); 3 Hutson Street, Suva, Fiji (home). Telephone: 3373317 (office); 3301865 (home). Fax: 3373173 (office). E-mail: flp@connect.com.fj (office); mahendrachaudhry42@hotmail.com (home). Website: www.flp.org.fj (office).

CHAUDHRY, Muhammad Ejaz, MA; Pakistani civil servant and business executive; b. 8 Oct. 1955; ed Govt Coll., Admin. Staff Coll., Lahore, George Washington Univ., Harvard Univ., USA, Univ. of Dundee, UK, Civil Service Coll., Singapore, Nat. Defence Univ., Islamabad; joined civil service in Dist Man. Group 1980; served in Public Admin in Sindh and Punjab Provinces and Fed. Govt; Asst Commr Larkana, Jakobabad and Liaquatabad 1981–86; Deputy Commr Thatta 1988–89, Karachi Cen. 1989–90, Nawabshah 1990–93; Additional Sec., Home 1994–96; Labour 1996–98, Registrar Cooperatives Punjab 1998–2002; Dist Coordination Officer, Multan 2003–05; Jt Sec., Ministry of Educ. 2005–06; Dir-Gen. Nat. Inst. of Public Admin, Lahore 2007–08; Additional Sec., Ministry of Petroleum and Natural Resources 2008–10, fmr Fed. Sec.; Fed. Sec., Ministry of Privatisation 2010–11; Chair. Oil and Gas Devt Co. Ltd 2011–13; Chair. Bd Inter State Gas System, Govt Holding Pvt. Ltd, Saindak Metals Ltd; mem. Bd of Dirs Hydrocarbon Devt Inst. of Pakistan, Pakistan Gems and Jewellery Devt Corpn, Mari Gas Co. Ltd; mem. Pvt. Power Infrastructure Bd, Alternate Energy Devt Bd. Address: Ministry of Petroleum and Natural Resources, 3rd Floor, Block A, Pakistan Secretariat, Islamabad, Pakistan (office). Telephone: (51) 99210220

(office). Fax: (51) 99213180 (office). E-mail: minister@mpnr.gov.pk (office). Website: www.mpnr.gov.pk (office).

CHAUDHRY, Air Vice-Marshal Shahzad Aslam, MSc; Pakistani air force officer (retd) and diplomatist; m.; five c.; ed Air Command and Staff Coll., USA, Nat. Defence Coll., Islamabad; served in various command/staff and instructional roles during air force career including Officer Commanding F-16 Squadron 1987–89, Officer Commanding F-16 Wing 1996–97, Base Commdr, Pakistan Air Force Base, Rafiqui 2000–02, Air Officer Commanding Southern Air Command 2003, Deputy Chief of Air Staff (Operations), Pakistan Air Force 2003–06; Air Attaché, Pakistan High Comm., London 1992–96; High Commr to Sri Lanka 2006–10; mem. UN Asscn of Sri Lanka; Hilal-e-Imtiaz (Mil.), Sitara-e-Imtiaz (Mil.), Tamgha-e-Basalat, Professional Efficiency Badge. Address: Ministry of Foreign Affairs, Constitution Avenue, Islamabad, Pakistan (office). Telephone: (51) 9210335 (office). Fax: (51) 9207600 (office). E-mail: sadiq@mofa.gov.pk (office). Website: www.mofa.gov.pk (office).

CHAUDHURI, Pratip, MSc; Indian banking executive; b. 1954; m.; one s. one d.; ed Univ. of Rajasthan; joined State Bank of India as Probationary Officer 1974, has served in several positions, credited with merger of State Bank of Saurashtra 2008, fmr Group Exec. of Int. Banking and Deputy Man. Dir, later Man. Dir Int. Banking, State Bank of India –2011, Chief Gen. Man. Chennai, State Bank of India –2011, Chair. State Bank of India (and subsidiaries) 2011–13; apptd Man. Dir State Bank of Saurashtra 2007; Hon. Sec., Indian Banks Asscn. Address: c/o Indian Banks Association, World Trade Centre, 6th Floor, Centre 1 Building, World Trade Centre Complex, Cuff Parade, Mumbai 400 005, India.

CHAUDHURY, Shirin Sharmin, LLB (Hons), LLM, PhD; Bangladeshi lawyer and politician; Speaker, Jatiyo Sangshad (Parliament); b. 6 Oct. 1966, Dhaka; d. of Rafiqullah Chaudhury and Naiyar Sultana; m. Syed Ishtiaque Hossain; one s. one d.; ed Univ. of Dhaka, Univ. of Essex, UK; advocate, Bangladesh Bar Council 1992–94; advocate, High Court Div., Bangladesh Supreme Court 1994–2008, Appellate Div., Bangladesh Supreme Court 2008–09; mem. of lawyers' panel that conducted cases filed against Sheikh Hasina during the army-backed caretaker govt 2007–08; mem. Bangladesh Awami League, fmr Int. Affairs Sec.; MP 2009–; State Minister, Ministry of Women and Children Affairs 2009–13; Speaker (first woman) of Jatiyo Sangshad (Parl.) 2013–; mem. Dhaka Bar Asscn, Supreme Court Bar Asscn; Ed. Bangladesh Legal Decisions; Best Student of the Year Award, Holy Cross Girl Award 1982, Humanitarian Service Award for Leadership role in Prevention of Violence against Women, Asia Soc. Leisure interest: listening to music. Address: Speaker's Chamber, Level 5, West Block, Sangsad Bhaban, Bangladesh Parliament, Shere-Bangla-Nagar, Dhaka, Bangladesh (office). Telephone: (2) 9111999 (office). Fax: (2) 9122254 (office). E-mail: speaker@parliament.gov.bd (office). sschau12@gmail.com (office). Website: www.parliament.gov.bd (office).

CHAUSSADE, Jean-Louis; French business executive; CEO, Suez Environnement; b. 2 Dec. 1951; ed Ecole Spéciale des Travaux Publics, Univ. of the Sorbonne, Paris, Institut d'Etudes Politiques de Paris, Advanced Man. Program at Harvard Business School, USA; joined Degrémont 1978, apptd COO Degrémont Spain, Bilbao 1989, Dir Aguas de Barcelona, apptd CEO Dumez Copisa Spain 1992, COO Lyonnaise des Eaux in S America and COO Suez for S America 1997–2000, Chair. and CEO Degrémont 2000–04, Exec. Vice-Pres. Suez and CEO Suez Environnement 2004–; Chair. Lyonnaise des Eaux (France), SITA France; mem. Bd of Dirs Aguas de Barcelona (Spain), mem. Exec. Cttee GDF Suez. Address: Suez Environnement, 1 rue d'Astorg, 75383 Paris Cedex 08, France (office). Telephone: 1-58-18-50-00 (office). Fax: 1-58-18-50-50 (office). E-mail: suez_env.pressoffice@suez-env.com (office). Website: www.suez-environnement.com (office).

CHAUTALA, Om Prakash; Indian politician; Leader, Indian National Lok Dal; b. 1 Jan. 1935, Sirsa Dist, Haryana; s. of Chaudhari Devi Lal; m. Sneh Lata; two s. three d.; Chief Minister of Haryana 1989, 1990, 1999, 2000–05; Pres. Haryana Unit, Indian Nat. Lok Dal 1999; Pres. Haryana State Janata Dal; Nat. Gen. Sec. Samajwadi Janata Party; currently Leader, Indian Nat. Lok Dal party (later United Nat. Progressive Alliance, after merger with other regional parties), Leader of Opposition, Haryana Vidhan Sabha; Hon. Citizen of Texas, USA. Address: Indian National Lok Dal, 18 Janpath, New Delhi 110 001 (office); Teja Khera Farm House, Teh-Dabwali, Sirsa, India (home). Telephone: (11) 23793409 (office). Website: www.inld.in (office).

CHAUVIN, Yves; French chemist; Honorary Director of Research, Institut Francais du Petrole; b. 10 Oct. 1930; ed École supérieure de chimie-physique-électronique (CPE), Lyon; Research Engineer, Institut Francais du Petrole 1960, later Head of Research, apptd Dir of Research 1991, currently Hon. Dir of Research; Emer. Dir of Research, École supérieure de chimie-physique-électronique, Lyon; mem. French Acad. of Sciences; Académie des sciences Prix Clavel-Lespiau 1990, German Scientific Soc. for Coal and Petroleum Research Karl Engler Medal 1994, Nobel Prize in Chem. (jtly) 2005. Publications include: Progress in Polymer Science 1977. Address: Institut Francais du Petrole, 1 & 4 avenue de Bois-Préau, 92852 Rueil-Malmaison (office); Laboratoire de Chimie Organométallique de Surface, CPE Lyon, 43 Bd du 11 Novembre 1918, 69622 Villeurbanne cedex, France (office). Telephone: 1-47-52-60-00 (office); 4-72-43-17-94 (office). Fax: 1-47-52-70-00 (office); 4-72-43-17-95 (office). Website: www.cpe.fr/lcoms (office).

CHAVALIT, Gen. Yongchaiyudh; Thai politician and army officer (retd); b. 15 May 1932, Bangkok; m. Khunying Phankrua Yongchaiyudh; ed Chulachomklao Royal Mil. Acad., Army Command and Gen. Staff Coll., Fort Leavenworth, Kan., USA; Dir of Operations 1981, Chief of Staff 1985, C-in-C 1986–90, Acting Supreme Commdr 1987–90; Deputy Prime Minister and Minister of Defence 30 March–21 June 1990; Opposition Leader May–Sept. 1992; Minister of Interior 1992–94, of Labour and Social Welfare 1993–94; Deputy Prime Minister July–Oct 1994, Deputy Prime Minister and Minister of Defence 1995–96, 2001–02, 2008 (resgnd); Prime Minister and Minister of Defence 1996–97 (resgnd); Deputy Prime Minister 2008 (resgnd); fmr Leader New Aspiration Party (now Muan Chon party). Address: c/o Muan Chon, 630/182 Thanon Prapinklao, Bangkok 10700, Thailand (office).

CHAVAN, Ashok Shankarrao, MBA; Indian politician; b. 28 Oct. 1958, Mumbai; s. of Shankarrao B. Chavan and Kusumtai Chavan; m. Ameeta Ashok

Chavan; two d.; MP (Indian Nat. Congress) for Nanded constituency 1987–; MLC from Maharashtra Legis. Ass. Constituency 1992–, Minister of State for Public Works, Urban Devt and Home 1993, Minister for Transport, Ports, Cultural Affairs and Protocol 2003; Minister of Revenue, Maharashtra Region 1999–2004, also Minister of Cultural Affairs 2004–10, of Industries 2004–10, of Mines 2004–10, of Protocol 2004–10, Chief Minister 2008–10 (resgnd); Gen. Sec. Maharashtra Pradesh Youth Congress Cttee 1986–89, Maharashtra Pradesh Congress Cttee 1995–99; mem. Consultative Cttee, Ministry of Environment and Forests, Ministry of Personnel, Public Grievances and Pensions; Chair. Sanjay Gandhi Niradhar Yojna 1985; mem. Divisional Rail Users Advisory Cttee S-Cen. Railways 1987–89; mem. Advisory Panel, Cen. Film Censor Bd 1991–92; Pres. Sai Sevabhavi Trust, Nanded. *Leisure interests:* table tennis, reading, travelling. *Address:* Shivaji Nagar, Nanded 431 602, India. *Telephone:* (24) 62234081. *Fax:* (24) 62237732.

CHAVAN, Prithviraj, BE, MS; Indian politician; *Chief Minister of Maharashtra;* b. 17 March 1946, Indore, Madhya Pradesh; s. of D. R. Chavan; m. Satvasheela Chavan; one s. one d.; ed Birla Inst. of Tech. and Science, Pilani, Univ. of California, Berkeley, USA; began career in the field of aircraft instrumentation and anti-submarine warfare in USA; returned to India 1974; elected to 10th Lok Sabha (lower house of Parl.) for Karad Dist 1991, becoming Sec., Congress Party in Parl.; entered Rajya Sabha (upper house of Parl.) 2002; Minister of State in Prime Minister's Office 2004; Minister of State (Additional charge), Ministry of Personnel, Public Grievances and Pensions 2008–09, Minister of State 2009; Minister of State (Ind. Charge), Ministry of Science and Tech. 2009; Minister of State (Ind. Charge), Ministry of Earth Sciences 2009; Minister of State, Ministry of Parl. Affairs 2009; Chief Minister of Maharashtra 2010–; Visiting Prof., Birla Inst. of Tech. and Science, Pilani; Founding mem. Indo-US Parl. Forum; mem. Indian Nat. Congress party; Jt Sec., Constitution Club, New Delhi; mem. Atomic Energy Comm., Space Comm., Council of Indian Inst. of Tech.; mem. Consultative Cttee, Ministry of Finance 1996–97, Prime Minister's Cttee on Infrastructure, Energy Coordination Cttee, Trade and Econ. Relations Cttee, Cttee on Trade and Industry; mem. Prime Ministerial delegation to USA 2005. *Leisure interests:* cricket, reading, photography. *Address:* Office of the Chief Minister, Government of Maharashtra, 6th Floor, Mantralaya, Mumbai 400 032 (office); Patan Colony, Shaniwar Peth, Karad 415 410, India (home). *Telephone:* (22) 22025151 (office); (2164) 220222 (home). *Fax:* (22) 22029214 (office). *E-mail:* chiefminister@maharashtra.gov.in (office). *Website:* www.maharashtra.gov.in (office).

CHAVANAVIRAJ, Saroj, BA, MA; Thai government official and fmr diplomatist; b. 11 May 1942; ed UCLA, Nat. Defence Coll. of Thailand; joined Ministry of Foreign Affairs 1967, Third Sec., Protocol Div. 1967–69, Asst Sec. to Minister, Office of Sec. to the Minister 1969–72; Second Sec., Perm. Mission to UN, New York 1972–76; Chief of East Asian Div., Political Dept, Ministry of Foreign Affairs 1976–77, Asst Sec. to the Minister, Office of the Sec. to the Minister 1977–79, Deputy Dir-Gen. Dept of Political Affairs 1979–80, Dir-Gen. Dept of Int. Orgs 1980–83; Chair. Social Cttee 38th Session of UN Gen Ass., New York 1983; Amb. to Singapore 1983–86; Dir-Gen. Dept of Information, Ministry of Foreign Affairs 1986–88, Dir-Gen. Dept of ASEAN Affairs 1988–90, Dir-Gen. Dept of Political Affairs 1990–92, Deputy Perm. Sec., Office of Perm. Sec. 1992–96, Perm. Sec., Ministry of Foreign Affairs 1996–2000; Amb. to France 2000–02; Adviser to Foreign Minister 2002–08; Minister for Foreign Affairs Sept. 2008; Hon. MBE (UK) 1972, Knight Grand Cordon (Special Class) of the Most Noble Order of the Crown of Thailand 1988, Order of the Sacred Treasure, Gold and Silver Star (Japan) 1991, Knight Grand Cordon (Special Class) of the Most Exalted Order of the White Elephant 1993, Hon. KCMG (UK) 1997, Knight Commander (Second Class, lower grade) of the Most Illustrious Order of Chula Chom Klao 2002. *Address:* c/o Ministry of Foreign Affairs, Thanon Sri Ayudhya, Bangkok 10400, Thailand (office).

CHÁVEZ, Anna Maria, BA, JD; American lawyer and national organization official; *CEO, Girl Scouts of the USA;* b. 1968, Eloy, Ariz.; m. Robert Chávez; one s.; ed Yale Univ., James E. Rogers College of Law at Univ. of Arizona; following graduation, clerked for an Ariz. attorney and then attended Univ. of Arizona Law School; admitted to Bar of US Dist Court for Dist of Ariz., Ariz. Supreme Court, US Supreme Court; Chief of Staff to Deputy Admin., US Small Business Admin (SBA), Washington, DC, Chief of Staff for SBA's Office of Govt Contracting and Minority Enterprise Devt, served as adviser to sr SBA and White House officials on a variety of policy issues; legal counsel for Fed. Highway Admin, Washington, DC 1996–98; also served as an attorney adviser in Office of the Counsel to the Pres., Washington, DC; Sr Policy Advisor to fmr US Sec. of Transportation Rodney E. Slater; returned to Arizona as in-house Counsel and Asst Dir for Div. of Aging and Community Services, Arizona Dept of Econ. Security; Dir of Intergovernmental Affairs under Gov. Janet Napolitano 2003–07, later Deputy Chief of Staff for Urban Relations and Community Devt 2007–09; Head of Girl Scouts of SW Texas 2009–11, CEO Girl Scouts of the USA 2011–; named amongst The NonProfit Times' Power & Influence Top 50, recognized by STEMconnector as one of the 100 Women Leaders in STEM (science, tech., eng and maths), Chair.'s Award, US Hispanic Chamber of Commerce 2012, Women of Excellence Award, Women of the Asscn of Latino Professionals in Finance and Accounting 2012, Adjutant Gen.'s Medal and Diversity Champion Leadership Award, Ariz. Nat. Guard. *Address:* Girl Scouts of the USA, 420 Fifth Avenue, New York, NY 10018-2798, USA (office). *Telephone:* (212) 852-8000 (office). *E-mail:* info@girlscouts.org (office). *Website:* www.girlscouts.org (office).

CHÁVEZ CHÁVEZ, Arturo, LicenDer; Mexican lawyer and government official; b. 1960, Chihuahua; ed Inst. Tecnológico de Estudios Superiores de Monterrey; fmr Under-Sec. of Legal Affairs and Human Rights, Secr. of the Interior; fmr Chief Adviser to Senator Diego Fernández de Cevallos; Procurador Gen. (Attorney Gen.), Chihuahua State 1996–98; subsequently worked in Interior Secr. where positions included Dir of Internal Control, Under-Sec. of Legal Affairs and Human Rights, Under-Sec. of the Interior; Pnr, law firm of Diego Fernández de Cevallos; Procurator Gen. of Mexico 2009–11 (resgnd); mem. Partido Acción Nacional. *Address:* c/o Office of the Procurator-General, Avda Paseo de la Reforma 211–213, Col. Cuauhtémoc, Del. Cuauhtémoc, 06500 México DF, Mexico.

CHÁVEZ FRIAS, Adán, BSc, MA; Venezuelan government official; *Governor of Barinas;* b. 1953, Estado de Mérida; brother of Pres. Hugo Chávez Frias; fmr mem.

Ruptura political movt; Founding mem. Movimiento Bolivariano Revolucionario 2000, Movimiento Quinta República 2000 (MVR); Nat. Dir MVR 2001–, also responsible for electoral policy; elected to Nat. Constituent Ass. for Meridá 2001, served as Vice-Pres. Comisión de Disposiciones Transitorias, Pres. Sub-Comm. for Domestic Policy in Comisión Legislativa Nacional, Pvt. Sec. to Pres. Hugo Chávez; Amb. to Cuba –2006; Presidential Chief of Staff 2006–07; Minister of Educ. 2007–08; Gov. of Barinas 2008–; Pres. Inst. Nacional de Tierras 2001. *Address:* Office of the Governor, Barinas, Estado Barinas, Venezuela (office). *Website:* www.barinas.net.ve (office).

CHAWLA, Navin B., BA, MA; Indian civil servant; b. 30 July 1945, New Delhi; m. Rupika Chawla; two d.; ed St Stephen's Coll., New Delhi, Univ. of London, London School of Econs; entered Admin. Service 1969; Sub-Div. Magistrate, Delhi 1971–73, Additional Dist Magistrate, Delhi 1973–75; Dir, Delhi Financial Corp. 1975–77, Delhi Tourism Devt Corp., Delhi State Industrial Devt Corp. 1975–77; Sec. to Lt Gov., Delhi 1975–77; Collector, Lakshadweep 1977–79; Finance Sec., Pondicherry 1979–80; Additional Sec., later Sec., Town Planning 1979–80; Deputy Sec., Ministry of Labour 1980–81; Dir, Ministry of Labour 1981–84, mem. del. to ILO Conf., Geneva 1982–84; on assignment to ILO, Bangkok 1984–86; on study leave for nine months to study leprosy situation in India 1986–87; Gen. Man. Super Bazar, Delhi 1987–89; Sec., Medical and Public Health, New Delhi Admin 1989–90; Resident Rep. of Govt of Goa in New Delhi 1991–92; Jt Sec., Ministry of Home Affairs, New Delhi Nov. 1992; Jt Sec. (Broadcasting), Ministry of Information and Broadcasting, with special responsibility for Doordarshan and AIR 1992–96; Chair. Delhi Vidyut (Electricity) Bd 1997–98; Prin. Sec., Govt of New Delhi with responsibilities for Services, Gen. Admin Dept, and Information and Publicity 1998–2000; Div. Commr, New Delhi 2000; Prin. Sec., Govt of Pondicherry with responsibilities for Power, Ports, Tourism and Art and Culture Depts and Chair. Pondicherry Tourism Devt Corp. Ltd 2000–01; Special Sec. (with rank of Sec. to Union Govt), Ministry of Environment and Forests July–Sept. 2003; Sec., Union Public Service Comm., New Delhi 2001–03; Sec. (Food and Public Distribution), Dept of Consumer Affairs, Ministry of Consumer Affairs 2003–04; Election Commr 2005–09, Chief Election Commr 2009–10; Fellow, Queen Elizabeth House, Univ. of Oxford 1995–96; Award from Inst. of Dirs, New Delhi 2004, Mazzini Award, Govt of Italy 2005. *Publications include:* The Vocational Rehabilitation and Social Re-integration of the Leprosy Affected in India (report) 1988, Mother Teresa (official biog.) 1992, Faith and Compassion–The Life and Work of Mother Teresa (with photographer Raghu Rai) 1996. *Leisure interests:* social service, reading. *Address:* c/o Office of the Chief Election Commissioner, Nirvachan Sadan, Ashoka Road, New Delhi 110 001, India. *Website:* www.navinchawla.com.

CHAZAL, Gilles; French museum director and curator; *Director, Petit Palais, Paris;* b. 4 Sept. 1946, Paris; s. of Robert Chazal and Raymonde Teulon; m. Martine Flevet 1981; two d.; ed Ecole du Louvre, Univ. of Paris-Sorbonne; Asst to Gallery Dir, Galerie Haut Pavé, Paris 1970–78; Asst, Engravings Collections, Bibliothèque Nationale 1972, Chief Curator, Petit Palais, Musée des Beaux-Arts de la Ville de Paris 1979–98, Museum Dir 1998–; Tutor, Ecole du Louvre 1982–, Institut français de restauration des oeuvres d'art 1987–97, Institut Catholique de Paris 1995–2008; Chevalier, Légion d'honneur, Ordre des Palmes académiques; Officier, Ordre des Arts et des Lettres. *Leisure interest:* running races. *Address:* Petit Palais, Musée des Beaux-Arts de la Ville de Paris, Avenue Dutuit, 75008 Paris, France (office). *Telephone:* 1-53-43-40-35 (office). *Fax:* 1-53-43-40-52 (office). *E-mail:* gilles.chazal@paris.fr (office). *Website:* www.petitpalais.paris.fr (office).

CHAZEN, Stephen I., BA, MA, PhD; American business executive; *President and CEO, Occidental Petroleum Corporation;* ed Rutgers Coll., Univ. of Houston, Michigan State Univ.; Man. Dir and Head of Corp. Finance, Merrill Lynch –1994; Exec. Vice-Pres., Corp. Devt, Occidental Petroleum Corpn 1994–99, Exec. Vice-Pres., Corp. Devt and Chief Financial Officer (CFO) 1999–2004, Sr Exec. Vice-Pres. and CFO Occidental Petroleum Corpn 2004–07, Pres. and CFO 2007–10, Dir, Pres. and COO 2010–11, Pres. and CEO 2011–; mem. Bd of Dirs Lyondell Chemical Co., Premcor Inc., Washington Mutual, Inc., American Petroleum Inst. *Address:* Occidental Petroleum Corporation, 10889 Wilshire Blvd, Los Angeles, CA 90024-4201, USA (office). *Telephone:* (310) 208-8800 (office). *Fax:* (310) 443-6690 (office). *E-mail:* info@oxy.com (office). *Website:* www.oxy.com (office).

CHAZOT, Georges-Christian; French business executive; *Chairman, Prosegur France;* b. 19 March 1939, Algiers; s. of Raymond Chazot and Suzanne Monnet; m. Marie-Dominique Tremois 1962; one s. two d.; ed Lycée Bugeaud, Algiers, Ecole Polytechnique, Paris, Harvard Int. Marketing Inst. and MSEE Univ. of Florida; electronic engineer EMR Sarasota, Florida 1962; Man., Space Electronics, Schlumberger 1965–68, Tech. Dir for Industrial Control 1968–70, Commercial Dir for Instruments and Systems 1970–74, Audio-professional Dir-Gen. 1974–76; Dir-Gen. for Alkaline Accumulators, SAFT 1976–80, Dir-Gen. 1981–83, Pres., Dir-Gen. 1983–88, Hon. Pres. and Admin. 1989; Pres., Dir-Gen. Centre d'Etudes et de Services pour le Développement Industriel (CEI) 1983–86; Vice-Pres., Dir-Gen. Télic Alcatel and Opus Alcatel 1989–90; Pres., Dir-Gen. Alcatel Business Systems 1990–91; Pres. Business Systems Group, Vice-Pres. Alcatel NV 1990–92; Pres., Dir-Gen. Adia France 1992–94; Group Man. Dir Eurotunnel 1994–2000, Chair. Eurotunnel Developments Ltd 2002–04; Chair. GCC Consultants 2001–, Prosegur France 2003–; Vice-Pres. French Chamber of Commerce in GB –2000; Chair. Paris Notre-Dame magazine 2001–; Vice-Chair. Radio Notre Dame 2001–; Dir X-PM Transition Partners 2001–, Giat Industries 2002–; Fellow, Chartered Inst. of Transport; Chevalier, Légion d'honneur 1990; Officier, Ordre nat. du Mérite 1994. *Leisure interests:* opera, sailing, skiing. *Address:* 24 rue de Réservoirs, 78000 Versailles (home); Prosegur France, 21 rue Calmette, 78 Jouy en Josas, France (office). *Telephone:* 1-30-67-75-10 (office); 1-30-21-83-14 (home). *Fax:* 1-30-67-74-91 (office); 1-30-21-83-14 (home). *E-mail:* georges.chazot@fr.prosegur.com (office); georges-christian.chazot@wanadoo.fr (home). *Website:* www.prosegur.fr (office).

CHAZOV, Yevgeny Ivanovich, MD, PhD; Russian politician and cardiologist; *General Director, Russian Cardiology Research Complex, Federal Health and Social Development Agency;* b. 10 June 1929, Gorky; ed Kiev Medical Inst.; mem. CPSU 1962–91, mem. Cen. Cttee 1982–90; Sr Scientific Worker, Inst. of Therapy 1959; Deputy Dir Inst. of Therapy, USSR Acad. of Medical Science 1963–65, Dir Inst. of Cardiology 1965–67; Deputy Minister of Public Health 1967–87, Minister 1987–91; mem. Supreme Soviet 1974–89; Gen. Dir, Russian Cardiology Research

Complex, Fed. Health and Social Devt Agency 1975–; personal physician to Presidents Brezhnev, Andropov, Chernenko and Gorbachev; mem. USSR (now Russian) Acad. of Medical Sciences 1971, USSR (now Russian) Acad. of Sciences 1979; Pres. USSR (now Russian) Soc. of Cardiology 1975; Co-Pres. International Physicians for Prevention of Nuclear War 1980–87; mem. acads of USA, Germany, Hungary, Serbia, Mexico, Poland, Romania; Hon. mem. World Albert Schweitzer Medical Acad., European Acad. of Arts and Science; State Prize 1969, 1976, Hero of Socialist Labour 1978, Lenin Prize 1982, UNESCO Peace Prize 1984, State Prize 2004. *Publications include:* Myocardial Infarction (with others) 1971, Cardiac Rhythm Disorders 1972, Anti-coagulants and Fibrinolytics 1977, Health and Power (memoirs) and other monographs; over 500 articles on cardiology. *Leisure interests:* hunting, photography. *Address:* Russian Cardiology Research Complex, 121552 Moscow, 3D Cherepkovskaya Street 15A, Russia (office). *Telephone:* (495) 415-00-25 (office). *Fax:* (495) 414-61-13 (office). *E-mail:* rcardio-chazov@list.ru (office).

CHE, Yingxin, BA; Chinese banking executive; *Chairman of the Board of Supervisors, Agricultural Bank of China;* b. 1954, Henan Prov.; ed Henan Banking School, Henan CCP Party School; held posts at various local brs of People's Bank of China (PBC), Henan Prov., including Lushi Co. Br. and Luoyang, Sanmenxia and Xinyang Municipal Brs 1980–92, Vice-Pres. Prov. Br., PBC, Henan Prov. 1992–97, Deputy Dir-Gen. Auditing Dept, PBC 1997–98, Dir-Gen. Staff Compliance Dept, PBC 1998–2003, Deputy Disciplinary Officer, Staff Compliance Department 1998–2003; Deputy Dir State Adm. of Foreign Exchange, Prov. Office, Henan Prov. 1992–97; Dir-Gen. Banking Supervision Dept, China Banking Regulatory Comm. 2003–05, Vice-Chair. China Banking Regulatory Comm. 2005–; Chair. Bd of Supervisors, Agricultural Bank of China 2008–. *Address:* Agricultural Bank of China, 69 Jianguomen Nei Avenue, Dongcheng District, Beijing 100005, People's Republic of China (office). *Telephone:* (10) 85109619 (office). *Fax:* (10) 85108557 (office). *E-mail:* webmaster@intl.abocn.com (office); ir@abchina.com (office). *Website:* www.abchina.com (office).

CHEA, Chanto, PhD; Cambodian central banker and politician; *Governor, National Bank of Cambodia;* b. 9 Oct. 1951, Kompon Thom Prov.; m.; ed secondary school, Kampong Thom, Univ. of Commerce, Phnom Penh, Hanoi Univ., Viet Nam; Dir Phnom Penh Municipality Brs 1979–81; Deputy Gov. Nat. Bank of Cambodia 1981–86, Gov. 1998–, Gov. for IMF 1998–; First Vice-Minister, Ministry of Planning 1986, Minister of Planning 1986–98; mem. Parl. (Kampong Thom Constituency) 1993–98; Resident Adjunct Prof., Univ. of Southern California, USA 1995; Hon. PhD (Univ. of Southern California) 1995. *Publications:* Socio-Economic Rehabilitation Plan, 1994–1995 1994, Socio-Economic Survey of Cambodia, 1993–1994 1995, Survey of Industrial Establishment, 1993 1996, First Five Year Socio-Economic Development Plan, 1996–2000 1997, Cambodian Human Resource Development Report 1997, Law on Banking and Financial Institutions 1999, Financial Sector Blueprint for 2001–2010 2001, Law on Negotiable Instruments and Payment Transactions 2005, Draft Law on Financial Leasing 2006, Draft Law on Anti-Money Laundering and Financial Terrorism 2006. *Address:* National Bank of Cambodia, 22–24 boulevard Preah Norodom, BP 25, Phnom Penh, Cambodia (office). *Telephone:* (23) 722563 (office). *Fax:* (23) 426117 (office). *E-mail:* nbc2@online.com.kh (office).

CHEA, Leang, MA; Cambodian lawyer and international organization official; *National Co-Prosecutor, Extraordinary Chambers in the Courts of Cambodia (ECCC);* ed Martin Luther Univ., Halle-Wittenberg, Germany; with Ministry of Justice 1996–2002, posts include Deputy, Training Office and mem. Cambodian Cttee for the Penal Code; Prosecutor, Cambodian Court of Appeals 2002–09; Prosecutor-Gen. Supreme Court 2009–; Nat. Co-Prosecutor, Extraordinary Chambers in the Courts of Cambodia 2006–. *Address:* Office of the Co-Prosecutors, Extraordinary Chambers in the Courts of Cambodia, National Road 4, Chaom Chau Commune, Dangkao District, PO Box 71, Phnom Penh, Cambodia (office). *Telephone:* (23) 219814 (office). *Fax:* (23) 219841 (office). *E-mail:* info@eccc.gov.kh (office). *Website:* www.eccc.gov.kh/en (office).

CHEADLE, Don, BFA; American actor; b. 29 Nov. 1964, Kansas City, Mo.; two c.; ed California Inst. of the Arts. *Films include:* Moving Violations 1985, Punk 1986, Hamburger Hill 1987, Colors 1988, Roadside Prophets 1992, The Meteor Man 1993, Things to Do in Denver When You're Dead 1995, Devil in a Blue Dress 1995, Rosewood 1997, Volcano 1997, Boogie Nights 1997, Bulworth 1998, Out of Sight 1998, Mission to Mars, 2000, The Family Man 2000, Traffic 2000, Things Behind the Sun 2001, Manic, 2001, Swordfish 2001, Rush Hour 2 (uncredited) 2001, Ocean's Eleven (uncredited) 2001, The Hire: Ticker 2002, The United States of Leland 2003, The Assassination of Richard Nixon 2004, Crash 2004 (also producer), Hotel Rwanda 2004, After the Sunset 2004, Ocean's Twelve 2004, Other Side of Simple 2006, The Dog Problem 2006, Reign over Me 2007, Talk to Me 2007, Ocean's Thirteen 2007, Traitor 2008, Hotel for Dogs 2009, Brooklyn's Finest 2009, Iron Man 2 2010, The Guard 2011, Sacks West (short) 2011, Don Cheadle Is Captain Planet (short) 2011, Flight 2012, Captain Planet 3 (short) 2012, Iron Man 3 2013. *Television includes:* The Golden Palace (series) 1992, Picket Fences (series) 1993–95, Lush Life 1993, Rebound: The Legend of Earl 'The Goat' Manigault (film) 1996, The Rat Pack (film) 1998, A Lesson Before Dying (film) 1999, Animated Tales of the World (series) 2000, The Simpsons (series) (voice) 2000, Fail Safe (film) 2000, The Bernie Mac Show (series) 2002, ER (series) 2002, Biography (series documentary) 2003, Independent Lens (series documentary) 2003, Make Your Own Superbowl Ad (film) 2006, Drunk History (series) 2010, House of Lies (series) (Golden Globe Award for Best Performance by an Actor in a Television Series – Comedy or Musical 2013) 2012–13. *Publications:* Not On Our Watch (with John Prendergast) 2007, The Enough Moment: Fighting to End Africa's Worst Human Rights Crimes (with John Prendergast) 2010. *Address:* c/o Creative Artists Agency, 2000 Avenue of the Stars, Los Angeles, CA 90067, USA (office). *Telephone:* (424) 288-2000 (office). *Fax:* (424) 288-2900 (office). *Website:* www.caa.com (office).

CHEARAVANONT, Dhanin; Thai business executive; *Chairman and CEO, Charoen Pokphand (CP) Group;* b. April 1939, Bangkok; m. Vatanalikit Tawee (Khunying); five c.; ed secondary school, Shantou, China and commercial school, Hong Kong; Chair. Charoen Pokphand (CP) Group (conglomerate of 250 cos involved in agribusiness and food, telecommunications, retail and distribution and other industries) and Chia Tai Group, China 1989–; Chair. True Corpn 1993–;

major shareholder in BD Bank, Shanghai (first foreign-owned bank with head office in China); adviser to Chinese Govt during Hong Kong negotiations with UK; Pres. China Asscn of Overseas Chinese Entrepreneurs Asscn 2008–; Businessman of The Year, Forbes Asia Magazine 2011. *Address:* 18 True Tower, Ratchadapisek Road, Huai Kwang, Bangkok 10320, Thailand (office). *Telephone:* (2) 643-1111 (office). *Fax:* (2) 643-1651 (office). *E-mail:* cp@cpthailand.com (office). *Website:* www.cpthailand.com (office).

CHECA CREMADES, Fernando, DenFil y Letras, LicEnD; Spanish professor of art history, arts administrator and writer; *Professor of Art History, Universidad Complutense de Madrid;* b. 14 May 1952, Madrid; s. of Francisco Checa and Concepción Cremades; Lecturer in Art History, Univ. Complutense de Madrid 1976–, Prof. of Art History –1996, 2002–; Dir Prado Museum 1996–2002; Summer Visiting Prof., Inst. of Advanced Studies, Princeton, NJ 1988; Paul Mellon Sr Fellow, Center of Advanced Studies in Visual Arts, Nat. Gallery of Art, Washington, DC 1989; Fae Norton Prof., Oklahoma State Univ. 1995; fmr mem. Ministerial Comm. for Classification of State Collections; organizer of four major exhbns; Premio Extraordinario de Doctorado 1981, Nat. Prize for History 1993. *Publications include:* Pintura y escultura del Renacimiento en España 1983, La imagen impresa en el Renacimiento y el Manierismo 1987, Carlos V y la imagen del héroe en el Renacimiento 1987, Felipe II: mecenas de las artes 1992 (Nat. History Prize, Spain), Tiziano y la Monarquía Hispánica 1994, El coleccionismo en España (jtly) 1984, Las casas del Rey: Casas reales, cazaderos, jardines. Siglos XVI y XVII (jtly) 1986, Carlos V. La imagen del poder en el Renacimiento 1999. *Address:* Department of Art History, Universidad Complutense de Madrid, Ciudad Universitaria, Avda. Seneca 2, 28040 Madrid, Spain (office). *Website:* www.ucm .es (office).

CHECHELASHVILI, Valeri, PhD; Georgian diplomatist and international organization official; *Secretary General, Organization for Democracy and Economic Development (GUAM);* b. 17 March 1961, Tbilisi; s. of Karlo Chechelashvili and Tina Chechelashvili; m. Marine Neparidze; two s. one d.; ed Kiev State Univ., Ukraine; mem. staff, Foreign Econ. Relations Dept, Ministry of Light Industry 1987–88; Deputy Head of Foreign Econ. Relations section, Jt Stock Co. Gruzkurort 1988–89; First Sec. Dept of Int. Econ. Relations, Ministry of Foreign Affairs 1989–90, Deputy Dir 1990–91, First Deputy Dir 1991–92, Dir 1992–94, Deputy Minister of Foreign Affairs 1998–2000; Amb. to Ukraine 1994–98, to Moldova 1996–98; Sec.-Gen. Black Sea Econ. Co-operation 2000–04; Amb. to Russian Fed. 2004–05; Minister of Finance Feb.–June 2005; Amb. to Switzerland and Perm. Rep. to UN and Other Int. Orgs, Geneva July–Nov. 2005; First Deputy Foreign Minister of Georgia 2005–07; Sec. Gen. Org. for Democracy and Econ. Devt 2007–; Second Degree Order for Service, Ukraine 1998, Order for Merit (1st Degree), Ukraine 2002. *Publications:* several articles on econ. co-operation in learned journals. *Leisure interests:* classical music, fiction, tennis. *Address:* GUAM Secretariat, 01001 Kyiv, Sofiyska 2-A, Ukraine (office). *Telephone:* (44) 206-37-37 (office). *Fax:* (44) 206-30-06 (office). *E-mail:* secretariat@guam-organization.org (office). *Website:* guam-organization.org (office).

CHECKLAND, Sir Michael, Kt, BA, CCMI, FCMA; British broadcasting executive; b. 13 March 1936, Birmingham; s. of Leslie Checkland and Ivy Florence Checkland; m. 1st Shirley Checkland 1960 (divorced 1983) (deceased); two s. one d.; m. 2nd Sue Zetter 1987; ed King Edward's Grammar School, Five Ways, Birmingham and Wadham Coll., Oxford; accountant, Parkinson Cowan Ltd 1959–62, Thorn Electronics Ltd 1962–64; Sr Cost Accountant, BBC 1964–67, Head, Cen. Finance Unit 1967, Chief Accountant, Cen. Finance Services 1969, Chief Accountant, BBC TV 1971, Controller, Finance 1976, Controller, Planning and Resource Man., BBC TV 1977, Dir of Resources, BBC TV 1982, Deputy Dir-Gen. BBC 1985–87, Dir-Gen. 1987–92, Dir BBC Enterprises 1979–92 (Chair. 1986–87); Dir Visnews 1980–85; Vice-Pres. RTS 1985–94, Fellow 1987–; Trustee Reuters 1994–2009; Pres. Commonwealth Broadcasting Asscn 1987–88; Vice-Pres. EBU 1991–92; Chair. NCH (fmrly Nat. Children's Home) 1991–2001; Gov. Westminster Coll. Oxford 1992–97, Birkbeck Coll. London 1993–97, Brighton Univ. 1996–97; Dir Nat. Youth Music Theatre 1991–2002, Nynex Cablecomms 1995–97, Wales Millennium Centre 2003–09; Chair. City of Birmingham Symphony Orchestra 1993–2001, Brighton Int. Festival 1993–2002, Higher Educ. Funding Council for England 1997–2001, Brighton Univ. 2002–07; Vice-Pres. Methodist Conf. 1997; mem. Ind. TV Comm. 1997–2003; numerous other appointments; Hon. Fellow Wadham Coll. Oxford 1989; Dr hc (Open Univ.) 1993, (Birmingham) 1999, (Brighton) 2008. *Leisure interests:* sport, music, travel. *Address:* Orchard Cottage, Park Lane, Maplehurst, West Sussex, RH13 6LL, England (home).

CHEE, Soon Juan, PhD; Singaporean neuropsychologist and politician; *Secretary-General, Singapore Democratic Party;* b. 1962; ed Univ. of Georgia, USA; Lecturer in Psychology, Nat. Univ. of Singapore –1993; joined Singapore Democratic Party 1992, currently Sec.-Gen.; Chair. Alliance for Reform and Democracy in Asia; Reagan Fellow, Nat. Endowment for Democracy, Washington, DC; participated in numerous int. orgs, including World Movt for Democracy, Forum of Democratic Leaders in Asia Pacific; participated in Reagan-Fascell Democracy Program at Nat. Endowment for Democracy, Washington, DC 2004; declared a bankrupt by High Court after failing to pay S$500,000 in damages awarded to Prime Minister Goh Chok Tong and Sr Minister Lee Kuan Yew, not allowed to stand for elections until Feb. 2011; fined S$6,000 and sentenced to Queenstown Remand Prison for eight days for contempt of court after he criticized independence of Singapore judiciary; Hon. Research Assoc., Monash Asia Inst. 1997, Human Rights Fellow, Univ. of Chicago 2001, Reagan-Fascell Fellow, Nat. Endowment for Democracy, Washington, DC 2004; Parliamentarians for Global Action Defender of Democracy Award 2003, Liberal Int. Prize for Freedom 2011. *Publications include:* Dare to Change: An Alternative Vision for Singapore 1994, Singapore, My Home Too 1995, The Power of Courage: Effecting Political Change in Singapore Through Nonviolence 2005, A Nation Cheated 2008. *Address:* Singapore Democratic Party, 12A Jalan Gelenggang, Serangoon Road, Singapore, 578192, Singapore (office). *Telephone:* 63981675 (office). *Fax:* 63981675 (office). *E-mail:* speakup@yoursdp.org (office). *Website:* www.yoursdp.org (office); cheesoonjuan.blogspot.com.

CHEETHAM, Anthony John Valerian, BA; British publisher; *Founder and CEO, Head of Zeus;* b. 12 April 1943; s. of Sir Nicolas John Alexander Cheetham;

m. 1st Julia Rollason 1969 (divorced); two s. one d.; m. 2nd Rosemary de Courcy 1979 (divorced); two d.; m. 3rd Georgina Capel 1997; ed Eton Coll., Balliol Coll., Oxford; Editorial Dir Sphere Books 1968; Man. Dir Futura Publs 1973, Macdonald Futura 1979; Chair. Century Publishing 1982–85; Man. Dir Century Hutchinson 1985; Chair. and CEO Random Century Group 1989–91; Founder and CEO Orion Publishing Group (fmrly Orion Books) 1991–2003; Exec. Chair. Quercus Publishing plc 2005–08, Chair. (non-exec.) 2008–09; Assoc. Publr. Atlantic Books 2009–11, Founder and CEO Head of Zeus 2012–. *Publication:* Richard III 1972. *Leisure interests:* tennis, gardening, trees, medieval history. *Address:* Head of Zeus, Clerkenwell House, 45–47 Clerkenwell Green, London, EC1R 0HT, England (office). *Telephone:* (20) 7253-5557 (office). *Website:* www.headofzeus.com (office).

CHEETHAM, Anthony Kevin, BA, DPhil, FRS; British materials scientist and academic; *Goldsmiths' Professor of Materials Science and Fellow of Trinity College, University of Cambridge;* ed St Catherine's Coll. and Wadham Coll., Oxford; Lecturer, Lincoln Coll., Oxford 1971–74, Lecturer in Chemical Crystallography 1974–90, Reader in Organic Materials 1990–91; Prof. of Materials and Chem., Univ. of California, Santa Barbara, USA 1991–2007; Goldsmiths' Prof. of Materials Science, Univ. of Cambridge 2007–, Fellow of Trinity Coll.; RSC Corday-Morgan Medal and Prize 1982, Solid State Chem. Award, Royal Soc. 1988, Leverhulme Medal, Royal Soc. 2008. *Publications:* numerous papers in professional journals. *Address:* Department of Materials Science and Metallurgy, University of Cambridge, 27 Charles Babbage Road, Cambridge, CB3 0FS, England (office). *Telephone:* (1223) 767061 (office). *Fax:* (1223) 334567 (office). *E-mail:* akc30@cam.ac.uk (office). *Website:* www.msm.cam.ac.uk (office).

CHEF, Genia, MA; Russian artist; b. 28 Jan. 1954, Aktyubinsk, Kazakhstan; s. of Vladimir Scheffer and Sinaida Scheffer; m. Elke Schwab 1983; ed Polygraphic Inst., Moscow, Acad. of Fine Arts, Vienna; painter, graphic and computer artist; has provided illustrations for publs including Edgar Allan Poe, Prose and Poetry 1983, American Romantic Tales 1984, Finger World 1993, American Alphabet 1998; numerous appearances on radio and TV in New York, Berlin and Moscow; Kt Commdr, Order of St John, Russian Grand Priory, Imperial Order of St Anna, Third Degree; Fueger Gold Prize, Acad. of Fine Arts, Vienna 1993, Delfina Studio Trust Award, New York 1994, First Prize for Painting at Xth Int. Biennial of Miniature Art, Gornij Milanovac, Serbia 2010. *Publications:* Manifesto of Degeneration 1988, Manifesto of Post-Historicism 1989, Viva Canova! 1995, New Computer Renaissance 2002, Glory of a New Century 2011. *Leisure interests:* music, books, collecting insects and coins. *Address:* 'Künstlerhof', Alt Lietzow 12, 10587 Berlin (office); Schustehrusstr. 1, 10585 Berlin, Germany (home). *Telephone:* (30) 3246479 (home); 173-6162940 (mobile). *E-mail:* geniachef@gmx.de. *Website:* www.artnews.org/geniachef; www.artslant.com/global/artists/show/223967-genia-chef.

CHEHADE MOYA, Omar Karim; Peruvian lawyer and politician; b. 8 Nov. 1970, Lima; m. Ursula Galdos; ed Univ. Inca Garcilaso de la Vega, Lima; Legal Adviser, Nat. Univ. of San Marcos, Lima 2003–05; Consultant lawyer, Ad-hoc Anti-corruption Prosecution 2005–08; Partner, Omar Chehade & Torres la Torre (law firm), Lima 2008–; mem. Congreso (Parl.) for Lima (Gana Perú list) 2011–; Second Vice-Pres. of Peru 2011–12. *Address:* c/o Office of the President, Jirón Carabaya, cuadra 1 s/n, Anexo 1105-1107, Lima, Peru (office).

CHEIFFOU, Amadou; Niger politician and civil servant; *President, Rassemblement social-démocratique–Gaskiya;* fmr regional official of Int. Civil Aviation Org., then Regional Dir Western and Cen. African Office, Dakar; Prime Minister and Minister of Defence 1991–93; fmr Vice-Pres. Convention démocratique et social–Rahama; Founder and Pres. Rassemblement social-démocratique–Gaskiya (RSD) 2004; mem. Assemblée nationale 2004–; unsuccessful cand. for Pres. Niger 2004. *Address:* Rassemblement social-démocratique–Gaskiya, Quartier Poudrière, Niamey, Niger (office). *Telephone:* 20-74-00-90 (office).

CHEMETOV, Paul; French architect and academic; b. 6 Sept. 1928, Paris; s. of Alexandre Chemetoff and Tamara Blumine; m. Christine Soupault 1958; one s. two d.; ed Ecole Nationale Supérieure des Beaux Arts; participated in founding of Atelier d'urbanisme et l'architecture 1961; Prof., Ecole d'architecture, Strasbourg 1968–72; Visiting Prof., UP8 1973; exhibited in the Venice Biennial 1976; Prof. of Architecture, Ecole Nationale des Ponts et Chaussées 1978–89; mem. Directorial Cttee, then Vice-Pres. Plan Construction 1979–87; Visiting Prof., Ecole Polytechnique Fédérale, Lausanne 1993–98; mem. Acad. d'Architecture 1996; Officier, Légion d'honneur, Ordre nat. du Mérite, Ordre des Arts et des Lettres; Prix d'architecture, Cercle d'études architecturales 1965, Grand Prix Nat. d'architecture 1980, Médaille d'honneur d'Architecture 1991. *Publications include:* Architectures – Paris 1848–1914 (jtly) 1980, Cinq projets 1979–82 (jtly) 1983, Paris – Banlieue 1919–1939 (with B. Marrey and M. J. Dumont) 1989, La Fabrique des villes 1992; mem. Territoire de L'Architecte 1995, Vingt Mille Mots pour la Ville 1996, Un architecte dans le siècle 2002, Mecano-factures (jtly) 2006; numerous articles in professional journals. *Address:* Chemetov, 4 square Masséna, 75013 Paris, France. *Telephone:* 1-45-82-85-48. *Fax:* 1-45-86-89-14. *E-mail:* cplush@compuserve.com.

CHEMEZOV, Sergei, PhD; Russian business executive; *CEO, Rostec Corporation;* b. 20 Aug. 1952, Cheremkhovo, Irkutsk; m. Yekaterina Ignatova; four c.; ed Irkutsk Inst. of Nat. Economy, Mil. Acad. of the Gen. Staff of Russian Fed.; worked in Irkutsk Scientific Research Inst. of Rare and Nonferrous Metals; worked with Experimental-Industrial Asscn Beam, represented Beam in GDR 1983–88; Asst to Gen. Dir Sovintersport 1989–96; Head, Dept of Foreign Econ. Relations, Admin of the Pres. of Russian Fed. 1996–99; First Deputy CEO Rosoboronexport (Russian Defence Export) State Corpn 2000–04, CEO 2004–07; CEO Russian Technologies Corpn (now Rostec Corpn) 2007–; Deputy Chair. Rosneft JSC 2013–; mem. Bd of Dirs MMC Norilsk Nickel, OJSC Aeroflot, National Information and Settlement Systems LLC, RUSNANO. *Address:* Rostec Corporation, 119048, Moscow, 24 Usacheva Ul., Russia (office). *Telephone:* (495) 287-25-25 (office). *E-mail:* info@rostec.ru (office). *Website:* rostec.ru (office).

CHEN, Ailian; Chinese dancer, academic and choreographer; b. 24 Dec. 1939, Shanghai; d. of Chen Xi Kang and Yu Xiu Ying; m. Wei Dao Ning; two d.; ed First Coll. of Chinese Dancing; teacher, Beijing Coll. of Dancing 1959–63; Chief Actress, China Opera and Dancing House 1963–; fmr Prof., Arts Dept, Nan Kai Univ., Hainan Univ., Wang Kan Arts Coll.; demonstrations and lectures in Shangdong Prov., Shaanxi Prov., Beijing Univ., Foreign Languages Inst., Post and Telegraph

Inst., Light Industry Inst. and Municipal Dancers' Unions; Chief Dancer, Chinese Art Del. to USSR, USA, France, Spain, Belgium, Denmark, Finland, Sweden, Italy, Norway, Hong Kong, Germany, etc.; f. Chen Ailian Artistic Troupe 1989 (first non-governmental performing org. in China); est. Chen Ailian Dancing School, Beijing 1995; mem. CPPCC Nat. Cttee; mem. Exec. Cttee Chinese Dancers' Asscn; won four gold medals as a traditional dancer at 8th World Youth Festival in Helsinki 1962; Excellent Performance Award, First Nat. Dance Concert, First Prize, Ministry of Culture for Dance Soirée and Princess Wenzhen. *Performances include:* The Peony Pavilion, In the Dusk of Evening, The Oriental Melody, The Lantern Dance, Water, The Sword Dance, Ball Dance, The Song of the Serfs, Women Militia in the Grassland, The Red Silk Dance, A Dream of Red Mansions 2007. *Publications:* I Came From An Orphanage; articles and commentaries on dance. *Leisure interests:* literature, music, traditional opera, travel, mountain climbing. *Address:* Chinese Dancers Association, No.10, Nanli, Nong Zhanguan (Agricultural Exhibition Hall), Beijing 100026, People's Republic of China; Room 101/7, 2 Nanhuadong Street, Hufang Road, Beijing 100050.

CHEN, B. L.; Taiwanese oil industry executive; fmr Dir and Pres. CPC Corpn, Taiwan (fmrly Chinese Petroleum Corpn). *Address:* c/o CPC Corpn, No. 3, Songren Road, Sinyi District, Taipei City 110, Taiwan. *E-mail:* ir@cpc.com.tw.

CHEN, Bangzhu; Chinese politician; b. Sept. 1934, Jiujiang City, Jiangxi Prov.; ed Chonqing Civil Eng Coll.; engineer, Jilin Chemical Industrial Dist Construction Co. 1954–65; engineer, Chief Engineer, Deputy Man., Man. Ministry of Chemical Industry No. 9 Chemical Industrial Construction Co. 1966–80; joined CCP 1975; Chief Engineer, Man. Jiuhua Bldg Co. 1980–84; Mayor of Yueyang and Deputy Sec. CCP Yueyang City Cttee 1983–84; Vice-Gov. Hunan Prov. 1984–89, Acting Gov. 1989–93, Gov. 1993–95; Minister of Internal Trade 1995–98; Vice-Minister State Econ. and Trade Comm. 1998–2000; Alt. mem. 13th CCP Cen. Cttee 1987–92; Deputy Sec. CCP 6th Hunan Provincial Cttee 1989–93; mem. 14th CCP Cen. Cttee 1992–97, 15th CCP Cen. Cttee 1997–2002; Vice-Minister State Econ. and Trade Comm. 1998–2000; mem. Macao Special Admin. Region Preparatory Cttee 1998–99, 9th CPPCC Nat. Cttee Standing Cttee 1998–2003 (Chair. CPPCC Sub-cttee on Human Resources and Environment 2003–08); Hon. Pres. Chinese Asscn for Materials Circulation 1995–. *Address:* c/o Chinese People's Political Consultative Conference, Beijing, People's Republic of China.

CHEN, Bao-lang; Taiwanese business executive; *Chairman, Formosa Petrochemical Corporation;* fmr Pres. CPC Corpn, Taiwan; fmr Chair. Kuokuang Petrochemical Technology Co.; Chair. Formosa Petrochemical Corpn (FPC) 2011–; mem. Special Govt Cttee formed under Industrial Devt Bureau of Ministry of Econ. Affairs assigned to oversee safety at FPC petrochemical complex in Mailiao, Yunlin Co. –2011; Nat. Cheng Kung Univ. Outstanding Alumni Award 2008. *Address:* Formosa Petrochemical Corporation, 1-1, Formosa Plastics Group Industrial Zone, Mailiao, Yunlin, Taiwan (office). *Telephone:* (2) 27122211 (office). *Fax:* (2) 87128050 (office). *E-mail:* fpccpre@fpcc.com.tw (office). *Website:* www.fpcc.com.tw (office); www.fpg.com.tw (office).

CHEN, Gen. Bingde; Chinese army officer and politician; *Chief of General Staff, People's Liberation Army;* b. July 1941, Nantong City, Jiangsu Prov.; ed Mil. Acad. of the Chinese PLA; joined PLA 1961, then Squadron Leader, Platoon Leader, Staff mem. PLA Services and Arms, Army (or Ground Force), Combat Training Section, Regt Chief of Staff, Div. Deputy Chief of Staff, Div. Chief of Staff 1979–81, Div. Commdr 1981–83, Deputy Commdr PLA Services and Arms, Army (or Ground Force) 1983, Maj.-Gen. 1988–95, Lt-Gen. 1995–2002, Chief of Staff, PLA, Nanjing Mil. Region 1985, C-in-C 1996–99, C-in-C Jinan Mil. Region 1999–2004, rank of Gen. 2002–; Dir-Gen. PLA Gen. Armaments Dept 2004–07, Chief of Gen. Staff, PLA 2007–; joined CCP 1962, Deputy Sec. CCP Party Cttee PLA, Nanjing Mil. Region 1996–99; mem. 15th CCP Cen. Cttee 1997–2002, 16th CCP Cen. Cttee 2002–07, 17th CCP Cen. Cttee 2007–12; mem. Cen. Mil. Comm. 2005–. *Address:* PLA General Staff Headquarters, 21, North Andeli Street, Beijing, People's Republic of China.

CHEN, Chao-min; Taiwanese air force officer and government official; b. 10 July 1940; ed Armed Forces Univ. (now Nat. Defence Univ.), Repub. of China Air Force Acad.; Dir of Operations, Office of the Deputy Chief of Gen. Staff for Operations, Ministry of Nat. Defence 1986–88, Commdr 443rd Tactical Fighter Wing 1988–89, Dir 4th Dept 1990–91, Dir Operations Div., Air Force Gen. HQ 1991–92, Insp.-Gen. Inspection Office 1992–93, Gen. Commdr Eastern Command 1993–94, Commdr Air Force Operations Command 1995–97, Deputy Commdr Air Force Gen. HQ 1997–98, C-in-C 1998–2002; strategic adviser to Pres. of Taiwan 2002, Deputy Minister for Armaments 2002–04, Minister of Nat. Defence 2008–09; Exec. Dir Repub. of China Air Force Acad. 1989–90, Supt 1994–95. *Address:* c/o Ministry of National Defence, 2/F, 164 Po Ai Road, Taipei 10048, Taiwan (office).

CHEN, Char-Nie, OBE, JP, MB, MSc, FHKAM(Psychiatry), FHKCPsych, FRCPsych, FRANZCP, DPM; British physician, academic and college principal; *Chairman, Hong Kong Advisory Council on AIDS;* b. 19 July 1938, Fujian Prov., China; s. of the late Kam-Heng Chen and of Mei-Ai Chen-Hsu; m. Chou-May Chien 1970; one s. two d.; ed Nat. Taiwan Univ. and Univ. Coll., London; Rotating Intern, Nat. Taiwan Univ. Hosp. 1964–65, Resident Physician, Dept of Neurology and Psychiatry 1965–68; Sr House Officer, Morgannwg Hosp., Wales 1968–69; Registrar, St George's Hosp. Medical School, London 1969–71, Lecturer and Hon. Sr Registrar 1971–72, 1973–78, Sr Lecturer and Hon. Consultant Psychiatrist 1978–80; Prof., Dept of Psychiatry, Chinese Univ. of Hong Kong 1981–98, Chair. of Dept 1981–93, mem. Univ. Senate 1981, Head of Shaw Coll. 1987–94, mem. Univ. Council 1987–94; mem. Coll. Council, Hong Kong Baptist Coll. 1984–95; Pres. Hong Kong Psychiatric Asscn 1982–84, Hong Kong Soc. of Neurosciences 1983–84, 1988–89; Exec. Chair. Hong Kong Mental Health Asscn 1983–98; Pres. Pacific Rim Coll. of Psychiatrists 1988–99, Dir 1990–; Chair. Action Comm. Against Narcotics 1992–98, Hong Kong Advisory Council on AIDS; Pres. Hong Kong Coll. of Psychiatrists 1993–98; Fellow, Royal Coll. of Psychiatrists 1985–, Royal Australian and NZ Coll. of Psychiatrists 1983–, Royal Soc. of Medicine 1975–, Hong Kong Acad. of Medicine 1993–, Hong Kong Soc. of Sleep Medicine (Pres. 1993–), Hong Kong Coll. of Psychiatrists (Pres. 1994–98, Chief Examiner 1998–); mem. British Asscn for Psychopharmacology 1974–, European Sleep Research Soc. 1976–, British Medical Asscn 1979–, Collegium Internationale Neuro-psycho-pharmacologium 1981–, Hong Kong Medical Asscn 1981–, Int.

Brain Research Org. 1985–, Mental Health Asscn, Hong Kong (Chair. 1983–98, Vice-Pres. 1998–); Corresp. Fellow, American Psychiatric Asscn 1991; Visiting Prof., St George's Hosp. Medical School, London 1984; JP, Hong Kong 1993–; Hon. Fellow, Hong Kong Psychological Soc. 1986–. *Publications:* over 90 scientific papers. *Leisure interests:* reading, travelling, good food. *Address:* Hong Kong Advisory Council on AIDS, 5/F Yaumatei Jockey Club Clinic, 145 Battery Street, Yaumatei, Kowloon, Hong Kong (office); Flat 16B, Block 3, Villa Athena, 600 Sai Sha Road, Ma On Shan, Hong Kong Special Administrative Region, People's Republic of China. *Telephone:* (852) 2633-4192. *Fax:* (852) 2633-3067. *E-mail:* aca@dh.gov.hk (office).

CHEN, Deming, BA, PhD; Chinese government official; b. March 1949, Shanghai; ed Jiangxi Communist Labor Univ. (now Jiangxi Agricultural Univ.); began career in 1969 in Jiangxi, working five years for production team; joined CCP 1974; worked for three years for Jiangxi Agricultural Machinery Bureau, then worked for Jiangsu Food Products Corpn; Asst Dir, Gen. Office, Jiangsu Bureau of Commerce 1984, Deputy Dir 1985; fmr Sec.-Gen., Gen. Office, Jiangsu Prov. Govt; Mayor of Suzhou City 1998–2003; Vice-Gov. Shaanxi Prov. 2004–05, Gov. 2005–06; Vice-Chair. State Devt and Reform Comm. 2006–07; Vice-Minister of Commerce 2007, Minister of Commerce 2007–13; Deputy to 9th NPC 1998–2003, Del. to 16th CCP Cen. Cttee 2002–07, Alt. mem. 17th CCP Cen. Cttee 2007–12. *Address:* c/o Ministry of Commerce, 2 Dongchangan Jie, Dongcheng Qu, Beijing 100731, People's Republic of China (office).

CHEN, Ding-Shinn, MD; Taiwanese physician and academic; *Dean, College of Medicine, National Taiwan University;* b. 6 July 1943, Yin-Ge; ed Coll. of Medicine, Nat. Taiwan Univ.; Researcher, Nat. Cancer Center Research Inst., Tokyo, Japan 1975; Lecturer, Dept of Internal Medicine, Coll. of Medicine, Nat. Taiwan Univ. 1975, Assoc. Prof. 1978, Prof. 1983, Dean, Coll. of Medicine 2001–; Chair. Taiwanese Govt's Hepatitis Control Cttee; Pres. Taiwan Asscn for the Study of the Liver 1996–98, Gastroenterological Soc. of Taiwan 1997–2003, Formosan Medical Asscn 2001–; Vice-Pres. Int. Asscn for the Study of the Liver 2000; Assoc. Ed. Hepatology, Journal of Biomedical Science; mem. Editorial Bd Journal of Hepatology and other int. journals; mem. NIH 1979–80, Academia Sinica 1992; Foreign Assoc. NAS 2005; Trieste Science Prize (jtly), Acad. of Sciences for the Developing World (Third World Acad. of Sciences) 2006. *Achievements include:* famous for his leading role in uncovering the factors responsible for the transmission of the Hepatitis B virus from mothers to infants and for proving that this viral disease is associated not only with liver cirrhosis but also with liver cancer; leading to a programme of mass vaccination against Hepatitis B. *Publications:* more than 550 articles in scientific journals on internal medicine, gastroenterology, viral hepatitis and liver disease. *Address:* Department of Internal Medicine, National Taiwan University Hospital and National Taiwan University College of Medicine, No. 7 Chung-Shan South Road, Taipei, Taiwan (office). *Telephone:* (2) 23562185 (office). *Fax:* (2) 23224793 (office). *E-mail:* dean@ha.mc.ntu.edu.tw (office). *Website:* ntuh.mc.ntu.edu.tw (office).

CHEN, Dun; Chinese business executive; b. Dec. 1928, Tianjin City; Vice-Minister for Coal 1985–90; Gen. Man. China Nat. Coal Corpn 1993; Pres. China Electric Green Technology Group; mem. 7th CPPCC 1987–92, 8th 1993–97. *Address:* China Electric Green Technology Group, Pudong New Area, Shanghai 201204, People's Republic of China. *Telephone:* (21) 5042-8899 (office). *Website:* www.cegt.com.cn (office).

CHEN, Enxiang; Chinese business executive; currently Pres. Henan Coal and Chemical Industry Group Co. Ltd. *Address:* Henan Coal and Chemical Industry Group Co. Ltd, Guo Long Mansion, Zhengzhou 450046, Hebei Province, People's Republic of China (office). *E-mail:* info@hnccgc.com (office). *Website:* www.hnccgc.com (office).

CHEN, Feihu, BA; Chinese accountant and business executive; *President, China Guodian Corporation;* ed Renmin Univ.; fmr Deputy Chief of Dept of Economy Adjustment and State-owned Assets Supervision, Ministry of Electric Power; fmr Deputy Head of Dept of Finance and Asset Operation, Deputy Head and Head of Working Dept of Pres., Head, Office for Structural Reform and Chief Economist of State Power Corpn; Chair. (non-exec.) Guodian Technology & Environment Group Corpn Ltd 2013–, Chair. Strategic Cttee, mem. Remuneration and Appraisal Cttee; Dir, Pres. and mem. Party Cttee, China Guodian Corpn 2013–; Vice-Chair. and Dir (non-exec.), Huadian Power International Corpn Ltd; Vice-Pres. and mem. Party Cttee, China Huadian Corpn; Chair. China Huadian Capital Holdings Co. Ltd, China Huadian Finance Corpn Ltd, Huadian Energy Co. Ltd. *Address:* China Guodian Corporation, 6–8 Fuchengmen Bei Street, Beijing 100034, People's Republic of China (office). *Telephone:* (10) 58682000 (office). *Fax:* (10) 58553900 (office). *E-mail:* cgdcb@cgdc.com.cn (office). *Website:* www.cgdc.com.cn (office).

CHEN, Gang; Chinese composer; b. 10 March 1935, Shanghai; s. of Chen Ge-Xin and Jin Jiao-Li; m. (divorced); two d.; ed Shanghai Conservatory of Music; now Prof. of Composition, Shanghai Conservatory of Music; mem. Council of Chinese Musicians' Asscn; Art Dir Shanghai Chamber Orchestra; Guest Prof., USA, France, Canada and Hong Kong; Sec. Chinese Dramatist Asscn 1987–; Golden Record Prize (five times). *Compositions include:* The Butterfly Lovers (with He Zhan Hao), Violin Concerto 1959, The Sun Shines on Tashikuergan, Violin Solo 1973, Morning on the Miao Mountains, Violin Solo 1975; A Moonlight Spring Night on the Flower-surrounded River, Symphonic Picture 1976, Concerto for Oboe 1985, Wang Zhaojun, Violin Concerto 1986, Chamber Music Ensemble 1989, Dragon Symphony 1991. *Leisure interests:* literature, writing. *Address:* Shanghai Conservatory of Music, 20 Fen Yang Road, Shanghai, People's Republic of China (office). *Telephone:* 4370689 (office).

CHEN, Geng; Chinese petroleum industry executive; b. May 1946; ed Beijing Econs Inst.; Deputy Dir Changqing Petroleum Exploration Bureau 1983–85; Deputy Dir Labour Dept, Ministry of Petroleum Industry 1985–88; Dir Labour Bureau, China Nat. Petroleum Corpn 1988–93, Asst to Gen. Man. 1993–97, Deputy Gen. Man. 1997–98, Gen. Man. 2004–06, also Pres.; Dir PetroChina 2001–06, Pres. 2002–04, Chair. 2004–06; currently External Dir China Ocean Shipping (Group) Co. (COSCO). *Address:* China Ocean Shipping (Group) Company, Ocean Plaza, 158 Fuxingmennei Street, Beijing 100031, People's Republic of China (office). *Telephone:* (10) 6649-3388 (office). *Fax:* (10) 6649-2288 (office). *E-mail:* internet@cosco.com (office). *Website:* www.cosco.com (office).

CHEN, Guangyi; Chinese government official; *Chairman, Overseas Chinese Affairs Committee of the National People's Congress;* b. 7 Aug. 1933, Putian City, Fujian Prov.; s. of Chen Zhaohe and Li Muxin; m. Chen Xiuyun 1961; two s. one d.; ed Northeast China Engineering Coll.; joined CCP 1959; Deputy Div. Chief Prov. Heavy Industry Dept, Gansu Prov. 1960–64; Dir Production Office, Northwest China Nonferrous Metallurgical Design Acad. 1964–75; Div. Chief Prov. Metallurgical Bureau, Gansu Prov. 1977–80; Deputy Dir Prov. Planning Cttee, Gansu Prov. 1980–83; Deputy Sec. CCP Prov. Cttee, Gansu Prov. 1983; Gov. of Gansu Prov. 1983–86; Sec. 5th CCP Cttee, Fujian 1986; Chair. CPPCC 6th Fujian Provincial Cttee 1988; Chair. Fujian Prov. People's Congress Standing Committee 1993–94; mem. 12th CCP Cen. Cttee 1982–87, 13th CCP Cen. Cttee 1987–92, 14th CCP Cen. Cttee 1992–97, 15th CCP Cen. Cttee 1997–2002; Party Cttee Sec. and Head Civil Aviation Gen. Admin. of China 1993–98; Chair. Financial and Econ. Cttee of 9th NPC 1998–2003, Overseas Chinese Affairs Cttee of 9th NPC 2003–; Hon. Pres. Nanjing Aerospace Inst. *Address:* c/o Standing Committee of National People's Congress, Beijing, People's Republic of China.

CHEN, Hong, BSc; Chinese automotive executive; *Vice-Chairman and President, SAIC Motor Corporation Limited;* b. March 1961, Jiashan, Zhejiang Prov.; ed Tongji Univ., Shanghai; joined Shanghai Tractor and Automobile Co. (later Shanghai Automotive Industry Group Corpn—SAIC) 1984, with Shanghai-Volkswagen Automobile Co. Ltd (S-VW) project, Asst to Exec. Vice-Pres. of Human Resources, S-VW 1985–92, also Dir of Policy Research and Pres. S-VW Engine Factory, with Shanghai General Motors Co. Ltd (Shanghai-GM) Sedan Project 1995–97, Vice-Pres. Shanghai-GM 1997–99, later Pres., currently Vice-Chair. and Vice-Sec. Party Cttee of SAIC (Group), Pres. SAIC Motor Corpn Ltd 2004–, Vice-Chair. and Vice-Sec. Party Cttee 2006–; Chair. SsangYong Motor Co. 2005–; mem. CCP 1984–. *Address:* SAIC Motor Corporation Ltd, 5/F Building A, 563 Songtao Road, Zhangjiang, High Technology Park, Pu Dong, Shanghai 201203 (office); SAIC Motor Corporation Ltd, No. 489, Weihai Road, Shanghai 200041, People's Republic of China (office). *Telephone:* (21) 50803757 (office); (21) 22011688 (office). *Fax:* (21) 50803780 (office); (21) 22011188 (office). *E-mail:* info@saicgroup.com (office). *Website:* www.saicgroup.com (office); www.saicmotor.com (office).

CHEN, Houqun; Chinese geologist; *Research Professor and Chairman of the Academic Committee, Institute of Water Resources and Hydropower Research;* b. 3 May 1932, Wuxi, Jiangsu Prov.; ed Tsinghua Univ., Moscow Power Mechanics Inst., USSR; made original contrib. to the theoretical study of seismic hardening of concrete dams and to solving key problems of seismic resistance in maj. civil eng projects such as Xinfengjiang, Ertan and Xiaolangdi dams; presided over the compiling, editing and revising of many nat. standards, including Standard for the Anti-Seismic Design of Hydraulic Structures; built China's first large-scale three-dimensional and six-free-degree earthquake simulation platform; Chair. Standing Cttee, Dept of Civil Eng, Hydraulic and Constructional Eng, Chinese Acad. of Eng; Sr Engineer and Dir Eng Anti-Seismic Research Centre, China Water Conservancy and Hydroelectric Science Research Inst.; currently Research Prof. and Chair. Acad. Cttee, Institute of Water Resources and Hydropower Research; Fellow Chinese Acad. of Eng; Hon. mem. Int. Comm on Large Dams 2011; 20 nat., ministerial and provincial awards for science and tech., including Prize of Progress in Science and Technology, Ho Leung Ho Lee Prize 2001. *Publications:* over 150 research papers. *Address:* Institute of Water Resources and Hydropower Research, A–1 Fuxing Road, Beijing 100038, People's Republic of China (office). *Telephone:* (10) 68415522 (office). *Fax:* (10) 68478065 (home). *E-mail:* engach@mail.cae.ac.cn (office). *Website:* www.iwhr.com (office).

CHEN, Huanyou; Chinese administrator; *Chairman, Standing Committee of Jiangsu Provincial People's Congress;* b. 1934, Nantong City, Jiangsu Prov.; ed East China Military and Political Acad., People's Univ. of China; joined PLA, CCP 1954; Lecturer, Jilin Industrial Univ. 1959–65 (also Sec., Teaching Office 1959–65 and Deputy Sec. CCP Gen. Br. 1959–65); Dir Wuxi Diesel Engine Plant, Jiangsu Prov. 1975–81 (also Deputy Sec. and Sec. CCP Party Cttee 1975–81); Deputy Dir Prov. Econ. Cttee and Nat. Defence Industry Cttee, Jiangsu Prov. 1981–83; mem. Standing Cttee of Jiangsu CCP Prov. Cttee 1984, later Chair. People's Armament Cttee; Deputy to 8th NPC Jiangsu Prov.; Vice-Gov. Jiangsu Prov. 1983–84, Exec. Vice-Gov. 1984–89, Gov. 1989–94; Deputy Sec. CCP Jiangsu Prov. Cttee 1986–93, Sec. CCP Jiangsu Prov. Cttee 1993–2000; Del., 13th CCP Nat. Congress 1987–92, 14th CCP Nat. Congress 1992–97, 15th CCP Nat. Congress 1997–2002; Deputy, 7th NPC 1988–92, 8th NPC 1993–98; Chair. Standing Cttee, Jiangsu Prov. People's Congress 1998–; Hon. Pres. Red Cross Soc. of China, Jiangsu Prov. 1994–. *Address:* 70 W Beijing Road, Nanjing 210000, Jiangsu Province, People's Republic of China. *Telephone:* 025-663 5164.

CHEN, Huiguang; Chinese politician; b. 1938, Yulin City, Guangxi Zhuang Autonomous Region; ed Guangxi Inst. of Coal Mining; successively, Engineer, Mining Technician, Head of Production Section, Deputy Head and Head Dongluo Mining Admin, Guangxi Zhuang Autonomous Region 1961–1980 (also Deputy Sec. CCP Party Cttee 1961–80); joined CCP 1965; Deputy Dir Coal Industry Bureau, Guangxi Zhuang Autonomous Region 1980–83; Sec. CCP Municipal Cttee, Nanning 1983–85; Deputy Sec. CCP Cttee, Guangxi Zhuang 1983–85, (Leading) Sec. 1985–88; mem. 12th CCP Cen. Cttee 1982–87, 13th CCP Cen. Cttee 1987–92; Chair. CPPCC Guangxi Zhuang Autonomous Regional Cttee 1983–; Del. 14th CCP Nat. Congress 1992–97, 15th CCP Nat. Congress 1997–2002; mem. 8th CPPCC Nat. Cttee 1993–98, 9th CPPCC Nat. Cttee 1998–2003. *Address:* 1 Minlelu Road, Nanning City, Guangxi, People's Republic of China.

CHEN, Jiaer; Chinese professor of physics; b. 1 Oct. 1934, Shanghai; ed Jilin Univ.; joined CCP 1952; Lecturer in Physics, Peking Univ. 1955 (also Dir Teaching Staff Office and Deputy Dean), later Assoc. Prof., Prof. of Physics and Doctorate Dir 1984–, Vice-Pres. and Pres. Postgraduate School 1984–96, Pres. Beijing Univ. 1996–99, Vice-Pres. Council of Capital Devt Inst. 1999–; Visiting Scholar, Univ. of Oxford, UK 1963–66; fmr Dir Teaching Staff Office, Hanzhong School, Shaanxi Prov.; Visiting Scientist, South Africa 1982–84; Dir Heavy Ion Physics Research Inst. 1986–2001; Deputy Dir Nat. Natural Sciences Foundation of China 1991–99, Dir 1999–2003; Pres. Beijing Asscn of Science and Tech. 1997–, Asscn of Asia Pacific Physical Socs 1998–2001; Bd Dir China Physics Soc. 1996–99; Academician, Chinese Acad. of Sciences 1993– (mem. 4th Presidium of Depts, Chinese Acad. of Sciences 2000–02); Alt. mem. 15th CCP Cen. Cttee 1997–2002; mem. Third World Academy of Sciences 2002; Fellow Inst. of Physics 2001; Hon. SSc

(Menlo Coll., Calif.) 1999, (Waseda Univ., Japan) 2000, (Chinese Univ. of Hong Kong) 2000, (Loughborough) 2002; numerous awards including First Grade Prize, State Educ. Comm. for Progress in Science and Tech. 1992, 1995, Zhou Pei-yuan Physics Award 1997, Ho Leung Ho Lee Foundation Award 2001. *Address:* National Natural Science Foundation of China, 83 Shuangqing Road, Haidian District, 100085 Beijing (office); Room 4–501, Bldg 12, Lanqiying, Peking University, Beijing, People's Republic of China (home). *Telephone:* (10) 62326876 (office); (10) 62758868 (home). *Fax:* (10) 62327082 (office); (10) 62758868 (home). *E-mail:* chenjer@rose.nsfc.gov.cn (office); chenje@pku.edu.cn (home). *Website:* www.nsfc.gov.cn (office).

CHEN, Jian; Chinese diplomatist and UN official; b. 2 Feb. 1942; m.; one d.; ed Fudan Univ., Beijing Foreign Studies Univ.; attaché, Perm. Mission of China to the UN 1972–77, Third, Second then First Sec. 1980–84, Amb. and Deputy Perm. Rep. to UN 1992–94; attaché, Dept of Int. Orgs and Confs, Ministry of Foreign Affairs 1977–80, Dir, Counsellor then Deputy Dir-Gen. 1985–92; Asst, Office of Exec. Dir representing China at IMF 1984–85; Dir-Gen. Dept of Information and Spokesperson Ministry of Foreign Affairs 1994–96; Asst Minister of Foreign Affairs 1996–98; Amb. to Japan 1998–2001; Under-Sec.-Gen. for Gen. Ass. and Conf Man., UN, New York 2001–07; Pres. UN Asscn of China 2007–12; fmr Rep. to UN Sec. Ass., Security Council, ECOSOC, UNEP, ESCAP and numerous confs and meetings. *Address:* c/o United Nations Association of China, 71 Nanchizi Street, Beijing, 100006, People's Republic of China.

CHEN, Jiangong; Chinese writer; b. Nov. 1949, Beihai, Guangxi Prov.; ed Peking Univ.; started career as coal miner in Jingxi Mine; joined Beijing Writers' Asscn 1981; Sec. of Secr., Chinese Writers' Asscn 1995–2001, 2003–, Vice-Chair. 2001–; currently Curator Nat. Museum of Modern Chinese Literature, Beijing; mem. exec. council, China Overseas Friendship Asscn. *Television:* dramas: Haung Cheng Gen Er, Song of Youth, When We Were Still Young. *Publications:* The Meandering Stream 1980, the Fluttering Flowered Scarf 1981, A Girl with the Eyes of a Red Phoenix 1981, Selected Novels by Chen Jiangong, No. 9 Huluba Alley, Letting Go, Curly Hair, Previous Offence, Phoenix Eyes, Manic Starry Sky, At the Foot of Imperial City, The Selection of Chen Jiangong, Imperial City Wall (co-author) (Excellence Saga Novel Award), Sun Stone (Best Novella Award), Confusion Star Sky, Frizzle (Literature Award), Criminal Record, Slim Eyes (Nat. Award for Best Short Story), Colorful Turban Along with Wind (Nat. Award for Best Short Story), Free Captive Animals (Excellence Novella Award); essays: Be honest to Me, The Flavor of Beijing, Essay Selection of Chen Jiangong, Fess Up. *Address:* c/o Beijing Writers' Association, Beijing, People's Republic of China.

CHEN, Jinhang; Chinese engineer and business executive; *Chairman, China Datang Corporation;* ed Shandong Univ.; Deputy Chief of Shandong Heze Electric Power Bureau 1985–91; Deputy Chief and Chief of Tai'an Electric Power Bureau 1991–96; successively worked as Chief of Accounting Dept, Asst to the Chief, Chair. of Trade Union and Vice-Pres. Shandong Electric Power Corpn 1996–2000; Vice-Pres., later Pres. Shanxi Electric Power Corpn, 2000–01, Chair. Shanxi Zhangze Electric Power Corpn Ltd and Shanxi Yangcheng International Electric Power Co. Ltd 2001–02; Exec. Vice-Pres. State Grid Corpn of China 2002–10; Chair. China Datang Corpn 2010–, Chair. China Datang Corpn Renewable Power Co. Ltd 2010–. *Address:* China Datang Corporation, 1 Guangningbo Street, Xicheng District, Beijing 100032, People's Republic of China (office). *E-mail:* webmaster@china-cdt.com (office). *Website:* www.china-cdt.com (office).

CHEN, Jinhua; Chinese government official and business executive; b. 1929, Qingyang, Anhui Prov.; ed People's Univ. of China, Beijing, Beijing Television Univ.; worker, Ministry of Textile Industry, Ministry of Light Industry 1949; fmr Head, Liaoyang Petrochemical Fiber Corpn, Liaoning Prov., Tianjin Petrochemical Corpn; Vice-Mayor of Shanghai Municipality 1977–83; Gen. Man. China Petrochemical Corpn (Sinopec) 1983–90; Minister in charge of State Econ. Restructuring Comm. 1990–93, State Devt and Reform Comm. 1993–98; Head Co-ordination Group for Tertiary Industries 1993–98; mem. 14th Cen. Cttee CPC 1992–97; Vice-Chair. 9th Nat. Cttee of CPPCC 1998–2003. *Address:* c/o National Committee of Chinese People's Political Consultative Conference, 23 Taipingqiao Street, Beijing, People's Republic of China.

CHEN, Jining, BSc, PhD; Chinese professor of environmental system analysis and university administrator; *President, Tsinghua University;* b. 1964, Lishu Co., Jilin Prov.; ed Tsinghua Univ., Imperial Coll. London, UK; joined CCP 1984; Asst Researcher, Imperial Coll. London 1994–98; Vice-Dean Dept of Environmental Eng, Tsinghua Univ. 1998–99, Dean 1999–2006, Vice-Pres. Tsinghua Univ. 2006–07, Deputy Pres. 2007, Exec. Vice-Pres. 2007–12, Pres. 2012–; mem. Nat. Environmental Advisory Comm.; Deputy Chair. Science and Tech. Cttee of MEP; Vice-Pres. Chinese Soc. for Environmental Sciences; mem. Bd Chinese Environmental Foundation, and other scientific cttees, professional asscns and advisory councils related to water and environment; mem. or fmr mem. editorial bds of several environmental journals; several scientific prizes. *Publications:* author or co-editor of several books; more than 200 papers in professional journals; owner of more than a dozen registered environmental and software patents. *Address:* Office of the President, Tsinghua University, 1 Qinghuayuan, Beijing 100084, People's Republic of China (office). *Telephone:* (10) 62782015 (office). *Fax:* (10) 62770349 (office). *E-mail:* webmaster@tsinghua.edu.cn (office). *Website:* www.tsinghua.edu.cn (office).

CHEN, Jui-Tsung (Ray); Taiwanese business executive; *President and CEO, Compal Electronics, Inc.;* ed Nat. Cheng Kung Univ.; Pres. and CEO Compal Electronics, Inc. 1992–, Chair. and CEO Compal Communications Inc. 2000–, also Gen. Man. in four other cos; fmr Exec. Vice-Pres. Kinpo Electronics Inc.; Chair. TPO Displays Corpn, Arcadyan Technology Corpn; fmr Chair. Royal Philips Electronics NV, Mobile Display Systems Unit; Dir Compal Digital Technology (Kunshan) Co. Ltd, Chunghwa Picture Tubes Ltd 2009–, Compal Electronics Inc. 2009–; Man. Dir Taipei Computer Asscn; named The Best CEO in Taiwan by Institutional Investors 2004, Outstanding Alumni with Exceptional Accomplishment Award, Nat. Cheng Kung Univ. 2006, International Entrepreneur, Entrepreneur of The Year 2010 Award, Ernst & Young Taiwan 2010. *Address:* Compal Electronics, Inc., 581 Ruiguang Road, Neihu District, Taipei 11492, Taiwan (office). *Telephone:* (2) 87978588 (office). *Fax:* (2) 26585001 (office). *E-mail:* info@compal.com (office). *Website:* www.compal.com (office).

CHEN, Jun, PhD; Chinese geochemist, academic and university administrator; *President, Nanjing University;* b. 1954, Yangzhou, Jiangsu Prov.; ed Nanjing Univ.; Prof. of Geochemistry, Dept of Earth Sciences, Nanjing Univ. 1992–, becoming Dean, Dept of Earth Sciences, Vice-Pres. and Exec. Vice-Pres. Nanjing Univ., Pres. 2006–; Standing Dir Chinese Geological Soc., Chinese Soc. for Quaternary Research; Vice-Pres. Chinese Soc. for Mineralogy, Petrology and Geochemistry; mem. Fifth Cttee of Science and Tech., Ministry of Educ.; mem. 11th NPC Standing Cttee 2008–13; several Ministry of Educ. prizes for science and tech. *Address:* Office of the President, University of Nanjing, No. 22 Hankou Road, Nanjing, Jiangsu 210093, People's Republic of China (office). *Telephone:* (025) 3593186 (office). *E-mail:* chenjun@nju.edu.cn (office). *Website:* www.nju.edu.cn/cps/site/NJU/njue/profile/profile/president.htm (office).

CHEN, Kaige; Chinese film director; b. 1954, Beijing; m. Chen Hong; ed Beijing Cinema Coll.; worker, rubber plantation, Yunnan; soldier for four years; Golden Palm Award 1993, New York Film Critics' Best Foreign Film 1993, 28th Moscow Int. Film Festival Lifetime Achievement Award 2006. *Films include:* The Yellow Earth (Best Film, Berlin Film Festival), Life on a String, King of the Children 1988, Farewell My Concubine 1993, The Assassin 1998, The Emperor and the Assassin 1999, Killing Me Softly 2002, He ni zai yi qi (Together with You) 2002, Ten Minutes Older: The Trumpet (segment) 2002, Mo gik (The Promise) 2004, Zhanxiou Village 2007, Mei Lanfang 2008, Sacrifice 2010, Caught in the Web 2012. *Publications:* King of the Children, The New Chinese Cinema (with Tony Raynes) 1989, Bawang bieji 1992. *Address:* William Morris Agency, 151 South El Camino Drive, Beverly Hills, CA 90212 (office); Beijing Cinema College, Beijing, People's Republic of China.

CHEN, Kuiyuan; Chinese party official; *Vice-Chairman, 11th Chinese People's Political Consultative Conference National Committee;* b. 1941; ed Inner Mongolia Teachers' Univ.; joined CCP 1965; fmr mem., Deputy Sec.-Gen., Sec.-Gen. CCP League Cttee Standing Cttee, Hulun Buir League, Inner Mongolia Autonomous Region, Deputy Sec. and Sec. 1983–89; mem. CCP Autonomous Regional Cttee Standing Cttee, Inner Mongolia Autonomous Region 1989–92; Vice-Chair. Inner Mongolia Autonomous Regional People's Congress 1989–92; Deputy Sec. CCP Tibet Autonomous Region Cttee 1992, Sec. 1992–2000; mem. 14th CCP Cen. Cttee 1992–97, 15th CCP Cen. Cttee 1997–2002, 16th CCP Cen. Cttee 2002–07, 17th CCP Cen. Cttee 2007–; apptd First Sec. CCP Party Cttee PLA, Tibet Mil. Region 1996; Sec. CCP Henan Prov. Cttee 2000–02; Pres. Chinese Acad. of Social Sciences 2002–; Vice-Chair. 10th CPPCC Nat. Cttee 2003–08, 11th CPPCC Nat. Cttee 2008–. *Address:* Chinese Academy of Social Sciences, 5 Jianguomennei Dajie, Beijing 100732, People's Republic of China.

CHEN, Lei; Chinese politician; *Minister of Water Resources;* b. 1954, Beijing; ed North China Inst. of Water Conservancy and Hydroelectric Power; joined CCP 1980; Teacher, N China Inst. of Water Resources and Hydroelectric Power 1980–82; Clerk, Tech. Dept, China Irrigation and Drainage Co., Ministry of Water Resources 1985–89, Assoc. Man., Project Planning Dept 1989–92, Man. 1992–93, Deputy Gen. Man. 1993–95, Gen. Man. 1995, Dir, Rural Water Conservancy Dept, Ministry of Water Resources 1996–2000, Dir, Planning Dept 2000–01, Vice-Minister of Water Resources 2001–04, Minister 2007–; mem. Three Gorges Project Construction Cttee 2004–05; Vice-Chair., Autonomous Region People's Govt, Xinjiang Uygur Autonomous Region 2005, Exec. Vice-Chair. 2005–07; mem. 17th CCP Cen. Cttee 2007–12, 18th CCP Cen. Cttee 2012–. *Address:* Ministry of Water Resources, 2 Baiguang Lu, Xiang 2, Xuanwu Qu, Beijing 100053, People's Republic of China (office). *Telephone:* (10) 63202114 (office). *E-mail:* webmaster@mwr.gov.cn (office). *Website:* www.mwr.gov.cn (office).

CHEN, Liangyu; Chinese politician; b. Oct. 1946, Ningbo, Zhejiang Prov.; ed PLA Logistics Engineering Inst., Tongji Univ., Shanghai, Party School, First Bureau of Electrical Machinery, Univ. of Birmingham, UK; joined PLA 1963, soldier, Services and Arms Group Army Unit No. 6716 1968–70; worker, designer, Deputy Section Chief of Infrastructure, Shanghai Pengpu Machinery Factory 1970–83; joined CCP 1980; designer, Shanghai Pengpu Machine Bldg Factory; Sec. CCP Shanghai Electric Appliances Corpn Cttee; Vice-Dir, then Dir Veteran Cadre Dept, Shanghai Municipal Cttee –1985, Vice-Sec.-Gen., then Vice-Sec. Shanghai Municipal Cttee 1992–96; Vice-Sec., then Dist Magistrate Huangpu Dist Cttee 1985–92; Exec. Vice-Mayor of Shanghai 1996–2001, Acting Mayor 2001–02, Mayor 2002–03; Alt. mem. 15th CCP Cen. Cttee 1997–2002, 16th CCP Cen. Cttee 2002–07, Politburo 2002–07, Sec. CCP Municipal Cttee, Shanghai 2002–06 (sacked for misuse of Shanghai pension fund), expelled from CCP and sentenced to 18 years imprisonment on corruption charges 2008.

CHEN, Lu Yu; Chinese television presenter; b. 12 June 1970, Beijing; known as "Oriental Oprah"; host of daily chat show A Date with Lu Yu on Hong Kong-based Phoenix Satellite TV station; working with Sina.com to develop new, daily, Oprah Winfrey-style of talk show; China TV Programme Award for the Best Female Presenter of the Year 2000, named as Most Successful Woman 2007 by Jessica magazine. *Television includes:* Good Morning China, Phoenix Afternoon Express. *Address:* A Date with Lu Yu, Phoenix Satellite TV, Room 306, No. 165 Haidian Road, Haidian District, Beijing, 100080, People's Republic of China (office). *Telephone:* (10) 62510868 (office); (10) 62510511 (office). *Fax:* (10) 62510484 (office). *Website:* www.phoenixtv.com (office).

CHEN, Mingyi; Chinese administrator; *Chairman, Fujian Provincial Committee, Chinese People's Political Consultative Conference;* b. 1940, Fuzhou City, Fujian Prov.; ed Jiaotong Univ., Shanghai; joined CCP 1960; teacher, Jiaotong Univ.; Vice-Gov. Fujian Prov. 1993–94, Gov. 1994–96; Deputy Sec. CCP Fujian Prov. Cttee 1993–95, Sec. 1996–2000; Chair. CPPCC Fujian Prov. Cttee 2001–; Alt. mem. 12th CCP Cen. Cttee 1982–87, 13th CCP Cen. Cttee 1987–92, 14th CCP Cen. Cttee 1992–97, mem. 15th CCP Cen. Cttee 1997–2002; Deputy to 8th NPC 1996. *Address:* Fujian Provincial People's Political Consultative Conference, Fuzhou City, People's Republic of China.

CHEN, Nengkuan, DEng; Chinese physicist; b. 1923, Cili, Hu'nan Prov.; ed Tangshan Eng College, Jiaotong Univ., Yale Univ., USA; fmrly Research Fellow Inst. of Physics and Inst. of Atomic Energy, Chinese Acad. of Sciences; Research Fellow, Chinese Atomic Energy Science Research Inst.; Vice-Dir Science and Tech. Cttee of Ministry of Nuclear Industry; mem. Technological Science Dept, Chinese Acad. of Sciences; Exec. Council mem. Chinese Nuclear Soc.; Meritorious Service

Medal for work on the devt of China's atomic and hydrogen bombs and satellites by the CCP Cen. Cttee, the State Council and the Cen. Mil. Comm. 1999. *Address:* Chinese Academy of Sciences, 52 Sanlihe Road, Beijing 100864, People's Republic of China (office).

CHEN, Ningning, (Diana Chen Ningning), MBA; Chinese business executive; *Chairman, Pioneer Metals Holdings;* b. 1971, Beijing; d. of Lu Hui; ed New York Inst. of Tech.; fmr Fund Man. Prudential Securities, New York; fmr Vice-Pres. Winease Investment, Hong Kong; fmr Exec. Dir and Vice-Chair. China Oriental Group Co. Ltd; Founder and Chair. Pioneer Metals Holdings 1996. *Address:* Pioneer Metals Holdings, 5F China Textile Building, No. 19 Jianguomennei Street, Beijing 100005, People's Republic of China (office). *Telephone:* (10) 65129966 (office). *Fax:* (10) 65285085 (office). *E-mail:* webmaster@pioneer-metals .com (office). *Website:* www.pioneer-metals.com (office).

CHEN, Peisi; Chinese comedian and actor; b. 1953, Ningjin, Hebei; s. of Chen Qiang; worked in Nei Monggo Production and Construction Corps 1969–73; with PLA Bayi Film Studio 1973–; comic sketches in collaboration with Zhu Shimao, at successive Chinese New Year Gala Nights on Chinese Cen. TV; took part in Olympic Torch Relay, Nanjing May 2008. *Films:* Look at This Family, Inside and Outside the Law Court, Sunset Boulevard, Erzi Running a Shop, A Stupid Manager, A Chivalrous Ball-Game Star in the Capital, A Young Master's Misfortune, A Millionaire from the South China Sea, Make a Bomb 1993, Sub-Husband 1993, Her Majesty is Fine 1995, Bao lian deng (voice) 2000, The Secret of the Magic Gourd (voice) 2007. *Plays:* A Dou (producer and lead actor) 2008. *Address:* People's Liberation Army Bayi Film Studio, Beijing, People's Republic of China (office).

CHEN, Qingtai, BSc; Chinese politician and business executive; b. 1937, Fengrun, Hebei Prov.; ed Tsinghua Univ., Beijing; joined CCP 1956; Dir Design Dept, Vice-Chief Engineer, Chief Engineer, Gen. Man., then Chair. Aeolus United Automotive Industry Corpn 1962–88, Chair. Aeolus-Citroen Automobile Co. Ltd; Chair. and CEO Dongfeng Peugeot Citroen Automobile Ltd 1985–92; Deputy Dir State Econ. and Trade Comm. 1992–93, Vice-Minister 1993–98; mem. Chinese Monetary Policy Cttee 1997–; Dir Devt Research Centre of the State Council 1993–98, Deputy Dir 1998–2001; mem. 9th CPPCC Nat. Cttee 1998–2003; Dir Sinopec Corpn 2000–06; Dir Bank of Communications Co. Ltd 2005–, Mindray Medical Int. Ltd 2006–; Dir China Europe Int. Business School 2011–; Nat. Excellent Entrepreneur 1988. *Address:* Development Research Centre of the State Council, Beijing, People's Republic of China (office).

CHEN, Qiqi; Chinese administrator; b. 26 April 1941, Guangdong Prov.; m. Prof. Zheng Sheu Xen; one s.; ed Guangdong Medical School, Medical Coll. of Italy; doctor, Guangdong Leprosy Hosp. 1965–75; teacher, Guangzhou Medical School 1975–81; Vice-Mayor of Guangzhou Municipality 1985; Pres. Guangdong Red Cross; Dir China Red Cross; Vice-Pres. Guangzhou People's Asscn for Friendship with Foreign Countries. *Address:* 1 Fuqian Road, Guangzhou, Guangdong (office); 86 Yue Hwa Road, Guangzhou, Guangdong, People's Republic of China (home). *Telephone:* (20) 330360 (office); (20) 3333100 (home). *Fax:* (20) 340347.

CHEN, Quanxun; Chinese business executive; fmr Chair. Supervisory Bd Shanghai Baosteel Group Corpn; Dir Sichuan Chuantou Energy Co. Ltd 2008; Chair. State-Owned Enterprise Supervisory Panel –2008; currently Chair. China Nonferrous Metals Industry Asscn. *Address:* China Nonferrous Metals Industry Association, Fuxing Road, Haidian District, Beijing 100814, People's Republic of China (office). *Telephone:* (10) 63971861 (office). *E-mail:* public@chinania.org.cn (office). *Website:* www.chinania.org.cn/ (office).

CHEN, Rongzhen; Chinese business executive (retired); b. Aug. 1938, Feidong, Anhui Prov.; Dir Hefei Washing Machine Gen. Factory (later renamed Rongshida Group) 1986–2002, Chair. and Pres. Rongshida Group –2002 (retd). *Address:* c/o Rongshida Group, 669 Changjian Road, Hefei 230088, Anhui Province, People's Republic of China.

CHEN, Sean, (Chen Chun), LLB, LLM; Taiwanese banking executive and politician; b. 13 Oct. 1949; ed Nat. Taiwan Univ., Frankfurt Univ., Germany; man. positions with TaipeiBank and Farmers Bank of China 1975–84, Vice-Pres. and Head of Loan Cttee, Farmers Bank of China 1985–88, Sr Vice-Pres. and Gen. Man. of Strategic Planning 1988–89; Exec. Sec., Legal Affairs Cttee, Ministry of Finance (MOF) 1989, Deputy Dir-Gen., MOF Bureau of Monetary Affairs 1989–94, Dir-Gen., MOF Dept of Insurance 1994–95, Dir-Gen., Bureau of Monetary Affairs 1995–98, Deputy Minister of Finance 1998–2002, Minister of Financial Supervisory Comm. 2008–10, Vice-Premier and concurrently Minister of Consumer Protection Comm. 2010–12, Premier 2012–13; Chair. Taiwan Stock Exchange Corpn 2002–04, Taiwan Cooperative Bank 2004–07, KGI Securities Co. Ltd 2007–08, SinoPac Holdings 2008; mem. Kuomingtang. *Address:* c/o Kuomintang, 232–234 Bade Road, Sec. 2, Taipei 10492, Taiwan.

CHEN, Shineng; Chinese administrator; b. 1938, Jiaxing Co., Zhejiang Prov.; ed Qinghua Univ.; joined CCP 1962; Vice-Minister of Light Industry 1984–93; Gov., Guizhou Prov. 1993–96; Deputy Sec., CCP 7th Guizhou Prov. Cttee 1993–96, Dir Cttee for Comprehensive Man.; Vice-Minister of Chemical Industry 1996; Vice-Chair. NPC Ethnic Affairs Cttee 2003–; Pres. China National Light Industry Council. *Address:* Ethnic Affairs Committee, National People's Congress, Beijing 100723, People's Republic of China.

CHEN, Shui-bian, LLB; Taiwanese politician, civil servant and fmr head of state; b. 18 Feb. 1951, Taiwan; s. of the late Chen Sung-ken and of Chen Li Shen; m. Wu Shu-jen 1975; one s. one d.; ed Nat. Taiwan Univ.; attorney-at-law 1974, Chief Attorney-at-Law, Formosa Int. Marine and Commercial Law Office 1976–80; mem. Taipei City Council 1981–85; Publr Free Time serial magazines 1984; Exec. mem. Taiwan Asscn for Human Rights 1984; in jail 1986–87; mem. Democratic Progressive Party (DPP) 1987–2008, Cen. Standing Cttee 1987–89, 1996–2000, Cen. Exec. 1987–89, 1991–96, Chair. 2002–04 (resgnd), 2007–08 (resgnd); mem. Legis. Yuan (Parl.) 1989–94, Exec. Dir DPP Caucus 1990–93, Convener Nat. Defence Cttee 1992–94, Convener Rules Cttee 1993, mem. Judiciary Cttee 1994; Chair. Formosa Foundation 1990–94, 1999–2000; Mayor of Taipei City 1994–98; Pres. of Taiwan 2000–May 2008; arrested and charged with graft Nov. 2008, sentenced to life imprisonment on charges of embezzlement, accepting bribes and money laundering Sept. 2009; Hon. DEcons (Plekhanov Russian Acad. of Econs)

1995; Hon. LLD (Kyungnam Univ., Repub. of Korea) 1995; Hon. DPolSc (Yong-In Univ., Repub. of Korea) 2000; Dr hc (Nat. Asuncion Univ., Paraguay 2001, (Nat. Autonomous Univ., Honduras) 2001; Man of the Taiwan Parl. 1993, Newsweek magazine Global Young Leaders for the New Millennium 1994, Asiaweek magazine Asia's 20 Young Political Stars 1999, Prize for Freedom, Liberal International 2001, Int. League for Human Rights Award 2003. *Publications:* National Defense Black Box and White Paper (co-author), Series on Justice (four vols), Conflict, Compromise and Progress, Through the Line Between Life and Death, The Son of Taiwan, The First Voyage of the Century: Reflections on Taiwan's First Alternation of Political Power, Believe in Taiwan: Chen Shui-bian's Report to the People, President A-bian: Up Close and Personal, Taiwan, Young and Vibrant: Journeying Down the Road of Progress, The New Middle Road for Taiwan: A New Political Perspective (speech). *Address:* c/o Democratic Progressive Party, 10/F, 30 Beiping East Road, Taipei 10051, Taiwan (office).

CHEN, Suzhi; Chinese politician; b. 1931, Shenyang City, Liaoning Prov.; ed Liaoning Univ.; joined the CCP 1949; factory dir 1978; Vice-Gov. Liaoning in charge of industrial work 1982; Alt. mem. 12th CCP Cen. Cttee 1982–87, 13th Cen. Cttee 1987–92; mem. Standing Cttee CCP Prov. Cttee Liaoning 1982; Dir Liaoning Prov. Trade Union Council 1986; Alt. mem. CCP 12th and 13th Cen. Cttee; mem. Standing Cttee 7th CCP Liaoning Prov. Cttee 1985–; Rep. to CCP 13th Nat. Congress; Vice-Gov. Liaoning Prov. 1988–; Deputy to 8th NPC Liaoning Prov.; Vice-Chair. Liaoning Prov. 8th People's Congress Standing Cttee 1992–, Cttee for Comprehensive Man. of Social Security; mem. NPC Internal and Judicial Affairs Cttee. *Address:* Liaoning Trade Union Offices, Shenyang, People's Republic of China (office).

CHEN, Tan-Sun (Mark), MS, PhD; Taiwanese politician; b. 1935, Tainan County; m. June Chen; three s.; ed Nat. Taiwan Univ., Purdue Univ. and Univ. of Oklahoma, USA; with US Dept of Commerce, Washington, DC 1973–92; mem. Legis. Yuan 1992, 2001–04; Magistrate of Tainan Co. 1993–2001; Minister of Foreign Affairs 2004–06; Sec.-Gen. Office of the Pres. 2006–07; Sec.-Gen. Nat. Security Council 2007; indicted on corruption and forgery charges Sept. 2007; Chair. Taiwanese Asscn of America 1979, World Fed. of Taiwanese Asscns 1979, Formosan Asscn for Public Affairs 1982, Int. Cooperation and Devt Fund 2004; fmr Vice-Chair. Taiwan Foundation for Democracy; mem. Democratic Progressive Party; Dr hc Purdue Univ. 2006. *Leisure interests:* hiking, tennis, swimming, reading, music. *Address:* c/o Democratic Progressive Party, 10/F, 30 Beiping East Rd, Taipei 10051, Taiwan. *Telephone:* (2) 23929989. *Fax:* (2) 23929989. *E-mail:* foreign@dpp.org.tw. *Website:* www.dpp.org.tw.

CHEN, Tian-jy, BSc, PhD; Taiwanese economist, academic and government official; ed Nat. Taiwan Univ., Pennsylvania State Univ., USA; Asst Prof., Dept of Econs, Univ. of Mississippi, USA 1983–85, Drexel Univ. 1986–87; Prof., Dept of Econs, Nat. Taiwan Univ. 1995–; Assoc. Research Fellow, Int. Div., Chung-Hua Inst. for Econ. Research 1985–88, Research Fellow 1988–95, Dir 1991–95, Acting Pres. 2002–03, Pres. 2003–05; Minister of the Council for Econ. Planning and Devt, Exec. Yuan 2008–09. *Address:* c/o Council for Economic Planning and Development, 3 Baocing Road, Taipei 10020, Taiwan (office). *Website:* www.cepd.gov.tw (office).

CHEN, Tsu-Pei, BA; Taiwanese business executive; *President, Cathay Financial Holding Co.;* ed Nat. Chengchi Univ.; Pres. Cathay United Bank, Pres. Cathay Financial Holding Co.; mem. Turnaround Man. Asscn. *Address:* Cathay Financial Group (Cathay Financial Holding Co.), 16th Floor, 296, Sec. 4, Ren Ai Road, Taipei 106, Taiwan (office). *Telephone:* (2) 2708-7698 (office). *Fax:* (2) 2325-2488 (office). *E-mail:* service@cathayholdings.com.tw (office). *Website:* www.cathayholdings .com.tw (office).

CHEN, Wei-jao, MD, MPH, DMSc; Taiwanese surgeon; *Professor Emeritus of Surgery and Public Health, National Taiwan University;* b. 15 Nov. 1939, Taichung; s. of the late Chen Wen-Chiang and of Chen Wu-Ping; m. Shiang Yang Tang 1970; one s. one d.; ed Coll. of Medicine, Nat. Taiwan Univ., Postgraduate Medical School, Tohoku Univ., Japan and School of Hygiene and Public Health, Johns Hopkins Univ., USA; Resident, Dept of Surgery, Nat. Taiwan Univ. Hosp. 1966–70, Visiting Surgeon (Pediatric Surgery) 1975–, Deputy Dir 1989–91; mem. Faculty, Coll. of Medicine, Nat. Taiwan Univ. 1975–, Dean 1991–93, Pres. Nat. Taiwan Univ. 1993–2005, also Prof. of Surgery and Public Health, now Emer.; Fellow in Pediatric Surgery, Tohoku Univ., Japan 1972–75; Visiting Research Assoc. Prof., Univ. of Cincinnati 1981–82; recipient of numerous awards. *Publications include:* Story of Separation of Conjoined Twins 1980, Unilateral Occlusion of Duplicated Mullerian Ducts with Renal Anomaly (jtly) 2000, New Advances in Clinical Nutrition 2004, Taiwan Higher Education: Its Problems and Treatment 2008, National Taiwan University: Prospective for the New Century 2008, I See and I Think 2008, Memoir of Wei Jao Chen 2009; more than 230 scientific papers on surgery, nutrition and public health. *Leisure interest:* hiking. *Address:* 7 Chung-shan South Road, Taipei 100 (office); No. 15, Sec. II, Hsin-Yi Road, Taipei, Taiwan (home). *Telephone:* (2) 2356-2122 (office); (2) 2351-6380 (home). *Fax:* (2) 2341-2969 (office). *E-mail:* chenwjh@ntu.edu.tw (office).

CHEN, Wenchi, MS; Taiwanese business executive; *President and CEO, VIA Technologies, Inc.;* m. Cher Wang; two c.; ed Nat. Taiwan Univ., California Inst. of Tech., USA; held positions of Vice-Pres. Sales and Marketing, ULSI Systems Technology and Sr Architect, Intel; Co-founder, Pres. and CEO Symphony Laboratories, Santa Clara, Calif. –1992; Pres. and CEO VIA Technologies, Inc. 1992–; named Top Star in Asia by Business Week 1999, ranked No. 1 Entrepreneur in Asia by Business Week 2001. *Address:* VIA Technologies, Inc., 1F, 531, Chung-Cheng Road, Hsin-Tien, Taipei 231, Taiwan (office). *Telephone:* (2) 22185452 (office). *Fax:* (2) 22185453 (office). *E-mail:* mkt@via.com.tw (office). *Website:* www.via.com.tw (office).

CHEN, Xianglin; Chinese automobile executive; Pres. Shanghai Automotive Industry Corpn (SAIC) 1983–86, 1995–2006; Dir Shanghai Planning Comm. 1986–93; Vice-Party Sec., Shanghai CP Cttee 1993–94. *Address:* SAIC Motor Corporation Ltd, 489 Weihai Road, Shanghai 200041, People's Republic of China (office).

CHEN, Xieyang; Chinese conductor; *Honorary Music Director, Shanghai Symphony Orchestra;* b. 4 May 1939, Shanghai; s. of Chen Dieyi and Liang Peiqiong; m.

Wang Jianying 1973; ed Music High School, Shanghai Conservatory; Conductor, Shanghai Ballet 1965–84; studied with Prof. Otto Mueller, Yale Univ., USA 1981–82; Conductor, Aspen Music Festival, Group for Contemporary Music, New York, Brooklyn Philharmonia, Honolulu Symphony, Philippines State Orchestra, Hong Kong Philharmonic, Shanghai Symphony Orchestra, Cen. Philharmonic, Beijing 1981–83, Symphony Orchestra of Vilnius, Kaunas, Novosibirsk, USSR 1985, Tokyo Symphony Orchestra 1986, Orchestre Regional de Cannes 2003; Music Dir and Prin. Conductor Shanghai Symphony Orchestra 1984–2009, Hon. Music Dir 2009–; made recording for Kuklos CBE, France 1983; Dir China Musicians' Assen.; Pres. Shanghai Symphonic Music Lovers' Soc.; Excellent Conducting Prize, Shanghai Music Festival 1986. *Address:* Shanghai Symphony Orchestra, 105 Hunan Road, Shanghai 200031, People's Republic of China. *Telephone:* 64335608 (office); 64672915 (home). *Fax:* 64333752 (office). *E-mail:* shso105@sh163.net (office). *Website:* www.sh-symphony.com.

CHEN, Yaobang; Chinese politician; b. 1935, Panyu City, Guangdong Prov.; ed Cen. China Agricultural Coll.; Asst, Cen. China Agricultural Coll. 1957–62; Deputy Chief Div. of Cash Crops Bureau, Ministry of Agriculture 1979–82; joined CCP 1982; Deputy Dir Animal Husbandry and Fisheries, Agricultural Bureau, Ministry of Agric. 1982–84, Vice-Minister 1986–88, Vice-Minister of Agric. 1988–93, Minister of Forestry 1997–98, Minister of Agric. 1998–2003; Deputy Sec. CCP Wuxi City Cttee 1984–86; Del., 13th CCP Nat. Congress 1987–92, 14th CCP Nat. Congress 1992–97; Vice-Minister State Devt and Reform Comm. 1993–97; mem. Science and Tech. Sub-cttee, CPPCC Nat. Cttee 1993–98; Deputy Chief State Flood Control and Drought Relief HQ 1993–98; Deputy Dir Nat. Afforestation Cttee 1993–98, Nat. Cttee on Mineral Reserves 1995–97; Vice-Pres. China Mining Industry Assen 1997; Deputy Dir Beijing Afforestation Cttee 1997;; mem. 15th CCP Cen. Cttee 1997–2002. *Address:* c/o Ministry of Agriculture, Nongzhanguan Nan Li, Chaoyang Qu, Beijing 100026, People's Republic of China (office).

CHEN, Yong; Chinese seismologist; b. Dec. 1942, Chongqing; ed Chinese Univ. of Science and Tech.; Assoc. Research Fellow, Research Fellow, Dir Geophysics Research Inst. of Nat. Bureau of Seismology 1965–85, Vice-Dir Nat. Bureau of Seismology 1985–96; Dean, School of Earth and Space Science, Chinese Univ. of Science and Tech. 2005–; mem. Chinese Acad. of Sciences 1993–, also Deputy Dir-Gen., Seismology Div.; fmr Chair. Comm. on Earthquake Prediction and Hazard, Int. Assen of Seismology and Physics of the Earth's Interior; Exec. Dir Int. Seismological Center –2005; Vice Pres. Chinese Geophysical Soc., Chinese Seismological Soc.; Fellow Third World Acad. of Sciences 2000–; award for Progress in Science and Technology (several times); Holeung Ho Lee Foundation Earth Sciences Prize 2006. *Publications:* seven monographs and over 100 essays; The Great Tangshan Earthquake of 1976. *Address:* National Bureau of Seismology, 61 Fuxing Lu, Beijing 100036, People's Republic of China (office).

CHEN, Yuan, BS, MA; Chinese banker; b. 13 Jan. 1945, Shanghai; s. of Chen Yun; ed China Acad. of Social Sciences, Tsinghua Univ., Beijing; Sec. CCP Cttee of Xicheng Dist, Beijing 1982–84; Dir-Gen. Dept of Commerce and Trade, Beijing Municipal Govt 1984–88; Vice-Gov. People's Bank of China 1988–98; Gov. China Devt Bank 1998–2013; mem. Preparatory Cttee of Hong Kong Special Admin. Region, Vice-Pres. Financial Soc.; mem. Securities Comm. of the State Council; Sec. CCP Xicheng Dist Cttee, Beijing; Alt. Mem. 16th CCP Cen. Cttee 2002–07, 17th CCP Cen. Cttee 2007–12; Vice-Chair. 12th CPPCC Nat. Cttee 2013–; involved with planning proposed BRICS Devt Bank 2013; Dir Inst. for Int. Econs, USA (mem. Advisory Cttee and the Financial Stability Inst.); Deputy Gov., Dir Business and Trade Sanxiang Dept, and Adviser to Postgraduates, People's Bank of China (also Deputy Sec. CCP Party Cttee). *Publications:* The Underlying Problems and Options in China's Economy, Macroeconomic Management: The Need for Deepening Reform, Collected Works. *Address:* c/o China Development Bank, 29 Fuchengmenwai Lu, Xicheng Qu, Beijing 100037, People's Republic of China (office).

CHEN, Yunlin; Chinese politician; b. Dec. 1941, Heishan Co., Liaoling Prov.; ed Beijing Agricultural Univ.; joined CCP 1966; technician, Deputy Dir, Dir Yucuntun Chemical Works, Qiqihar City, Heilongjiang Prov. 1960s–70s (also Deputy Sec. CCP Party Cttee); Deputy Sec. CCP Qiqihar City Cttee 1983; Mayor Qiqihar City 1983; Deputy Sec. CCP Heilongjiang Prov. Cttee 1984 (also mem. Standing Cttee, CCP Prov. Cttee); Dir Comm. for Restructuring the Economy, Heilongjiang Prov. 1984; Vice-Gov. Heilongjiang Prov. 1987–94; Del., 13th CCP Nat. Congress 1987–92; Deputy Dir Cen. Office for Taiwan Affairs of State Council 1999–2003, Dir 2003–08; Pres. Assen for Relations Across the Taiwan Straits 2008–13; Alt. mem. 14th CCP Cen. Cttee 1992–97, mem. 15th CCP Cen. Cttee 1997–2002, 16th CCP Cen. Cttee 2002–07; mem. CCP Qiqihar City Standing Cttee. *Address:* c/o Association for Relations Across the Taiwan Straits, No. 6-1, Guang'anmen Nanjie, Xuanwu District, Beijing, People's Republic of China (office).

CHEN, Zhangliang, PhD; Chinese professor of biology and government official; *Executive Secretary, China Association for Science and Technology;* b. 3 Feb. 1961; ed Huanan Tropical Crops Coll., Washington Univ., USA; Prof., Head of Plant Gene Eng Lab., Biology Dept, Beijing Univ. 1987–92 (youngest full Prof. in China at age of 27), Vice-Pres. Beijing Univ. 1995–2002; Pres. China Agricultural Univ., Beijing 2002–07; Vice-Chair. Guangxi Zhuang Autonomous Region People's Govt 2008–13; Exec. Sec. China Assen for Science and Technology 2013–; mem. Council of Advisors, World Food Prize 2007–; mem. Advisory Bd, Belfer Center for Science and Int. Affairs, Harvard Univ.; UNESCO Javed Husain Prize for Young Scientists 1991. *Publications:* several books and more than 150 research papers; holder of seven patents. *Address:* China Association for Science and Technology, 3 Fuxing Road, Beijing 100863, People's Republic of China (office). *Telephone:* (10) 68571898 (office). *E-mail:* english@cast.org.cn (office). *Website:* english.cast.org.cn (office).

CHEN, Zhili; Chinese politician, academic and fmr physicist; *Vice-Chairman, 11th National People's Congress Standing Committee;* b. 21 Nov. 1942, Xianyou Co., Fujian Prov.; ed Fudan Univ., Shanghai Inst. of Ceramics, Chinese Acad. of Sciences; joined CCP 1961; served in People's Liberation Army, No. 6409 Army Unit, Danyang Lake Farm 1968–70; Assoc. Research Fellow, Chinese Acad. of Sciences 1970–80, 1982–84, Deputy Sec., CP Cttee of the Inst. 1982–84; Visiting

Scholar, Materials Research Lab., Pa State Univ., USA 1980–82; Deputy Sec. CCP Party Cttee, Shanghai Inst. of Ceramics 1983–84; Deputy Sec. and Sec. Science and Tech. Work Cttee, Shanghai CCP Municipal Cttee 1984–86; Alt. mem. 13th CCP Cen. Cttee 1987–92, 14th CCP Cen. Cttee 1992–97; mem. Standing Cttee, Shanghai CCP Municipal Cttee 1988–89, Head Publicity Dept 1988–91, Deputy Sec. Publicity Dept 1989–91; Deputy Sec. CCP Shanghai Municipal Cttee 1991–97; Vice-Minister and Sec. CCP Leading Party Group, State Educ. Comm. 1997–98; Minister of Educ. 1998–2003; apptd mem. State Steering Group of Science, Tech. and Educ. 1998; apptd Vice-Chair. State Academic Degree Cttee 1999; State Councillor 2003–08; mem. 15th CCP Cen. Cttee 1997–2002, 16th CCP Cen. Cttee 2002–07, 17th CCP Cen. Cttee 2007–; Vice-Chair. 11th NPC Standing Cttee 2008–; Pres. All-China Women's Fed. 2008–; Hon. Pres. Shanghai Inst. of Int. Friendship. *Address:* c/o Zhongguo Gongchan Dang (Chinese Communist Party), Beijing; All-China Women's Federation, Beijing, People's Republic of China (office). *Telephone:* (10) 65103556 (office). *Fax:* (10) 85112107 (office). *E-mail:* womenofchina@163.com (office). *Website:* www.womenofchina.cn (office).

CHEN, Zhongshi; Chinese novelist; *Chairman, Shaanxi Provincial Writers' Association;* b. 1942, Xian, Shanxi Prov.; Chair. Shaanxi Prov. Writers' Assen 1993–; Vice-Chair. Chinese Writers' Assen 2001; Hon. Dean, Dept of Humanities, Shiyou Univ. 2004; took part as torchbearer in Olympic Flame Relay, Xian 2008. *Publications include:* Bai Lu Yuan (White Deer Plain) (Mao Dun Prize for Literature 1997) 1993, Early Summer, Mr. Blue Gown, The Cellar 1994, numerous novellas and short stories. *Address:* Shanxi Provincial Writers' Association, Xian, People's Republic of China (office).

CHEN, Zhu, PhD; Chinese haematologist and government official; *Minister of Health;* b. Aug. 1953, Zhenjiang, Jiangsu Prov.; m. Chen Saijuan; one s.; ed Shanghai No. 2 Medical Sciences Univ., St Louis Hosp., Univ. de Paris 7, France; apptd Foreign Resident Doctor, St Louis Hosp., Paris 1984; Research Fellow, Chinese Acad. of Sciences (Div. of Biological Sciences) 1990–; Dir Shanghai Haematology Research Inst. 1995; Deputy Dir Shanghai Research Centre of Life Sciences 1996; Deputy Dir Jt Genetics and Medical Sciences Centre, Shanghai No. 2 Medical Sciences Univ.; undertook over 20 nat. key scientific research projects and int. research projects and achieved results on the treatment of leukaemia with diarsenic trioxide and its molecular mechanism, providing a representative model for cancer research; academician, Chinese Acad. of Sciences 1995–, Vice-Pres. 2000–07; Minister of Health 2007–; Chair. Cen. Cttee 15th Chinese Peasants and Workers Democratic Party 2012–; Hon. DrSc (Univ. of Hong Kong) 2002, Hon. DUniv (York) 2010; Légion d'honneur 2002; Laureate, First Shanghai Honour Award of Medical Science 1994, China Youth Scientists' Prize 1994, Ho Lee and Ho Leung Foundation Prize for Medicine 1996, Shanghai Science Elite Nat. Model Worker 1996, Nat. Outstanding Science and Technology Worker 1996, Yangtze Scholar Awarding Program Top Grade Prize 1999, Outstanding Technician Medal, Ministry of Personnel 1999, US Nat. Foundation for Cancer Research Szent-Györgyi Prize for Progress in Cancer Research 2012. *Address:* Ministry of Health, 1 Xizhinenwai Bei Lu, Xicheng Qu, Beijing 100044, People's Republic of China (office). *Telephone:* (10) 68792114 (office). *Fax:* (10) 64012369 (office). *Website:* www .moh.gov.cn (office).

CHEN, Zhuo Lin; Chinese business executive; *Chairman, Agile Property Holdings Ltd;* b. Guangdong Prov.; m. Luk Sin Fong; Pres. Zhongshan Agile Co. 1992–96, Zhongshan Group Co. 1997–; Gen. Man. Zhongshan Dynasty Furniture Factory 1989–92; Co-founder Agile Property brand name, Chair. Agile Property Holdings Ltd 2005–; Vice-Chair. Zhongshan Qiaozi Enterprise Assen; Hon. Chair. Hong Kong Zhongshan Sanxiang Friendship Assen. *Address:* Agile Property Holdings Ltd, 20/F, 238 Nathan Road, Kowloon, Hong Kong Special Administrative Region, People's Republic of China (office). *Telephone:* (760) 6686868 (office). *Fax:* (760) 6683913 (office). *Website:* www.agile.com.cn (office).

CHEN, Ziming; Chinese writer and dissident; b. 1952; m. Wang Zhihong; imprisoned for 13 years for role in Tiananmen Square pro-democracy demonstrations 1989, released on medical parole 1994, rearrested for staging hunger strike 1995, released on medical grounds 1996; Cttee to Protect Journalists' Int. Press Freedom Award 1991.

CHEN, Zuohuang, MM, DMA; Chinese/American conductor; *Music Director, China National Centre for the Performing Arts;* b. 2 April 1947, Shanghai, Repub. of China; s. of Chen Ru Hui and Li He Zhen; m. Zaiyi Wang 1969; one c.; ed Cen. Conservatory of Music, Beijing, Univ. of Michigan, USA; Musical Dir China Film Philharmonic 1974–76; Assoc. Prof., Univ. of Kansas, USA 1985–87; Prin. Conductor Cen. Philharmonic Orchestra of China 1987–96; Music Dir/Conductor Wichita Symphony Orchestra 1990–2000; Music Dir/Conductor Rhode Island Philharmonic Orchestra 1992–96; Artistic Dir/Conductor China Nat. Symphony Orchestra 1996–2000; Music Dir OFUNAM of Mexico 2002–06, Shanghai Philharmonic Orchestra 2004–08, Incheon Philharmonic Orchestra, Repub. of Korea 2006–10, Guiyang Symphony Orchestra 2010–; Artistic Dir China Nat. Centre for the Performing Arts, Beijing 2007–; guest conductor in more than 20 countries with Zürich Tonhalle Orchestra, Vancouver Symphony Orchestra, Budapest Philharmonic Orchestra and State Symphony, Symphony Orchestra of Hungary, Gulbenkian Orchestra, Iceland Symphony Orchestra, Tanglewood Music Festival Orchestra, Colorado Symphony Orchestra, Pacific Symphony Orchestra, Virginia Symphony Orchestra, Alabama Symphony Orchestra, Russian Philharmonic Orchestra, Haifa Symphony Orchestra, Slovak Radio Symphony Orchestra, Hong Kong Philharmonic Orchestra, Singapore Symphony Orchestra, Pusan Philharmonic Orchestra, Mexico Nat. Symphony Orchestra, Mexico City Philharmonic Orchestra, Taipei City Symphony Orchestra, Macao Symphony Orchestra, amongst others.

CHEN, Zuolin; Chinese politician; b. 1923, Wuwei Co., Anhui Prov.; Vice-Chair. Revolutionary Cttee, Zhejiang Prov. 1975–79; Deputy Sec. CCP Cttee, Zhejiang 1976, Sec. 1977–83; Alt. mem. 11th CCP Cen. Cttee 1977, 12th Cen. Cttee 1982–87; Vice-Gov., Zhejiang 1979–83; Sec.-Gen. Cen. Comm. for Discipline Inspection 1985–87, Deputy Sec. 1987; Deputy Sec. CCP Cen. Discipline Inspection Comm. 1992–; mem. Presidium of 14th CCP Nat. Congress 1992, CCP Standing Cttee, Cen. Leading Group for Party Building Work, Internal and Judicial Affairs Cttee; Deputy to 8th NPC Jiangxi Prov. *Address:* Zhejiang Government Office, 28 Reuminlu Road, Hangzhou, People's Republic of China. *Telephone:* 24911.

CHEN, Zutao; Chinese automobile executive (retired); b. 20 Jan. 1928; s. of Chen Changhao; ed Moscow Baumann Highest Tech. Inst.; joined CCP 1960; First Chief Engineer and Vice Dir for Techniques, Dongfeng Motor Corpn 1965–80; First Chief Engineer, Deputy Man. and Gen. Man., China Nat. Automotive Industry Corpn (CNAIC) 1981–88 (retd); Commr, Ministry of Science and Tech. 1989. *Address:* c/o China National Automotive Industry Corporation, 46 Fucheng Lu, Haidian Qu, Beijing 100036, People's Republic of China.

CHEN TIANQIAO, Timothy, BEcons; Chinese business executive; *Chairman and CEO, Shanda Entertainment;* b. 1973, Xinchang County, Zhejiang; ed Fudan Univ.; various man. positions with Shanghai Lujiazui Group 1994–98; Deputy Dir Office of the Pres. Kinghing Trust & Investment Co. Ltd 1998–99; Co-founder, Chair. and CEO Shanghai Shanda Networking Co. Ltd (now Shanda Entertainment) 1999–, Chair. and CEO Shanda Interactive Entertainment Ltd 1999–; Independent Non-Executive Dir SinoMedia Holding Ltd 2008–11; mem. 11th CPPCC Nat. Cttee 2008–13, 12th CPPCC Nat. Cttee 2013–; Alt. mem. 15th Chinese Communist Youth League Cen. Cttee; youngest mem. China Top 50, Rising Business Star Award, China Central TV 2003. *Address:* Shanda Entertainment, No. 1 Intelligent Office, Building No. 690, Bibo Road, Shanghai 201203, People's Republic of China (office). *Telephone:* (21) 50504740 (office). *Fax:* (21) 50508088 (office). *E-mail:* info@shanda.com.cn (office). *Website:* www.snda.com (office).

CHENAULT, Kenneth Irvine, BA, JD; American financial services company executive; *Chairman and CEO, American Express Company;* b. 2 June 1951, Long Island, NY; s. of Hortensius Chenault and Anne N. Chenault (née Quick); m. Kathryn Cassell 1977; two s.; ed Waldorf School of Garden City, Bowdoin Coll., Harvard Univ. Law School; called to Bar, Mass 1981; Assoc., Rogers & Wells, New York 1977–79; consultant, Bain & Co., Boston 1979–81; Dir Strategic Planning, American Express Co., New York 1981–83, Vice-Pres. American Express Travel Related Services Co. Inc., New York 1983–84, Sr Vice-Pres. 1984–86, Exec. Vice-Pres. Platinum Card/Gold 1986–88, Personal Card Div. 1988–89, Pres. Consumer Card and Financial Services Group 1990–93, Pres. (USA) 1993–95, Vice-Chair. American Express Co., New York 1995–97, Pres. and COO 1997–2000, Chair. and CEO 2001–; mem. Bd of Dirs IBM, Brooklyn Union Gas, Quaker Oats Co., New York Univ. Medical Center; mem. Council of Foreign Relations, New York 1988, ABA; several hon. degrees; listed by Ebony magazine as one of 50 "living pioneers" in the African-American community 1995. *Address:* American Express Company, American Express Tower, World Financial Center, 200 Vesey Street, New York, NY 10285-5104, USA (office). *Telephone:* (212) 640-2000 (office). *E-mail:* info@americanexpress.com (office). *Website:* www.americanexpress.com (home).

CHÊNEVERT, Louis R., BCom; Canadian business executive; *Chairman and CEO, United Technologies Corporation;* b. 25 June 1957; ed Univ. of Montreal, École des Hautes Études Commerciales (HEC), Montreal; worked at General Motors 1979–93, served as Production Gen. Man., St Therese; Vice-Pres. for Operations, Pratt & Whitney Canada 1993–97, Exec. Vice-Pres. 1998–99, Pres. 1999–2006; mem. Bd of Dirs Pres. and COO United Technologies Corpn 2006–08, Pres. and CEO 2008–10, Chair. and CEO 2010–; mem. The US-India CEO Forum, Business Council, Business Roundtable; Founding and current mem. Bd of Dirs Friends of HEC Montréal and Pres. HEC Advisory Bd; mem. Bd of Dirs Congressional Medal of Honor Foundation, Yale Cancer Center's Advisory Bd; Fellow, AIAA 2005; Nouveaux Performant, Quebec 1995, Quebec Quality Movement Harrington Medal 1997. *Address:* United Technologies Corpn, 1 Financial Plaza, Suite 22, Hartford, CT 06103-2608, USA (office). *Telephone:* (860) 728-7000 (office). *Fax:* (860) 728-7979 (office). *E-mail:* invrelations@corphq.utc.com (office). *Website:* www.utc.com (office).

CHENEY, Lynne Vincent, BA, MA, PhD; American academic and writer; *Senior Fellow, American Enterprise Institute for Public Policy Research (AEI);* b. 14 Aug. 1941, Casper, Wyo.; d. of Wayne Vincent and Edna Vincent (née Lybyer); m. Richard B. Cheney (q.v.) 1964; two d.; ed Colorado Coll., Univ. of Colorado, Univ. of Wisconsin; freelance writer 1970–83; Lecturer, George Washington Univ. 1972–77, Univ. of Wyoming 1977–78; researcher and writer Md Public Broadcasting 1982–83; Sr Ed. Washingtonian magazine 1983–86; Chair. Nat. Endowment for Humanities 1986–93; W. H. Brady Fellow, American Enterprise Inst. for Public Policy Research, Washington, DC 1993–95, Sr Fellow 1996–; Commr US Constitution Bicentennial Comm. 1985–87; cr. James Madison Book Award Fund 2003; ranked by Forbes magazine amongst 100 Most Powerful Women (23rd) 2004. *Publications:* Executive Privilege 1978, Sisters 1981, Kings of the Hill (jtly) 1983, The Body Politic 1988, Telling the Truth 1995, America: A Patriotic Primer 2002, A is for Abigail: An Almanac of Amazing American Women 2003, We the People: The Story of Our Constitution 2008. *Address:* American Enterprise Institute, 1150 17th Street, NW, Washington, DC 20036, USA (office). *Telephone:* (202) 862-5800 (office). *Fax:* (202) 862-7177 (office). *E-mail:* lcheney@aei.org (office). *Website:* www.aei.org (office).

CHENEY, Richard (Dick) B., BA, MA; American politician and fmr business executive; b. 30 Jan. 1941, Lincoln, Neb.; s. of Richard H. Cheney and Marjorie Dickey Cheney; m. Lynne Vincent Cheney (q.v.); two d.; ed Univ. of Wyoming, Univ. of Wisconsin; engaged on staff of Gov. of Wis.; Special Asst to Dir White House Office of Econ. Opportunity 1969–70; Deputy to White House Presidential Counselor 1970–71; Asst Dir of Operations, White House Cost of Living Council 1971–73; partner, Bradley, Woods & Co. 1973–74; Deputy Asst to the Pres. 1974–75, White House Chief of Staff 1975–77; Congressman, At-large District, Wyoming, 1978–89; Chair. Republican Policy Cttee 1981–87; Chair. House Republican Conf. 1987; House Minority Whip 1988; Sec. of Defense 1989–93; Sr Fellow American Enterprise Inst. 1993–95; Chair. Bd and CEO Halliburton Co., Dallas, Tex. 1995–2000 (Pres. 1997); Vice-Pres. of USA 2001–09; Presidential Medal of Freedom 1991. *Publication:* In My Time: A Personal and Political Memoir 2011.

CHENG, Andong; Chinese politician; b. Oct. 1936, Huainan City, Anhui Prov.; ed Hefei Polytechnical Univ.; engineer, Mining Admin, Pingxiang City, Jiangxi Prov. 1965–67, Chief Engineer and Deputy Dir 1977–83; Chief Engineer and Deputy Dir Gaokeng Coal Mine, Jiangxi Prov. 1967–1977; mem. CCP 1980–; Mayor of Pingxiang City and Deputy Sec. CCP City Cttee 1983–84; Mayor of Nanchang City, Jiangxi Prov. 1984–90; Asst to Gov. Jiangxi Prov. 1990; Sec. CCP Xian Municipal

Cttee 1990; mem. Standing Cttee CCP Shaanxi Prov. Cttee 1990–94, 1998–, Deputy Sec. Provincial Cttee 1994–2003; Chair. City People's Congress Standing Cttee, Xi'an City, Shaanxi Prov. 1992; Alt. mem. 14th CCP Cen. Cttee 1992–97, mem. 15th CCP Cen. Cttee 1997–2002; Vice-Gov. Shaanxi Prov. 1994, Gov. 1995–2003; Hon. Pres. Bd Hefei Polytechnical Univ. 1995. *Address:* c/o Office of the Governor, Xi'an City, Shaanxi Province, People's Republic of China.

CHENG, Eva, BA, MBA; Chinese business executive; ed Univ. of Hong Kong; govt official in Hong Kong –1977; joined Amway Hong Kong as an Exec. Asst 1977, apptd Pres. Amway Hong Kong 1980, Exec. Vice-Pres. Amway, responsible for markets in Greater China (Amway (China) Co. Ltd) and SE Asia 2005–11, Chair. Amway China and Exec. Vice-Pres. Amway Corpn (global parent firm) –2011, currently Chair. Amway Charity Foundation in China; mem. Bd of Dirs Nestlé, Trinity Ltd, Amway (Malaysia) Holdings Berhad, Haier Electronics Group Co. Ltd, Esprit International 2012–; mem. Exec. Cttee All-China Women's Fed.; mem. CPPCC–Guangdong Comm.; mem. Council on Human Reproductive Tech.; Hon. Pres. All-China Women's Fed. Hong Kong Delegates Asscn, Hong Kong Fed. of Women; Perm. Hon. Cttee Mem. Chinese General Chamber of Commerce; ranked by Forbes magazine amongst 100 Most Powerful Women (88th) 2008, (93rd) 2009. *Leisure interest:* Cantonese opera. *Address:* c/o Amway (China) Co. Ltd, 40 & 41F CITIC Plaza, 233 Tianhe North Road, Guangzhou 510613, Guangdong, People's Republic of China.

CHENG, Eva, (Eva Cheng Yu-wah), JP; Hong Kong politician and civil servant; *Secretary for Transport and Housing;* b. 1960, Hong Kong; ed Diocesan Girls' School, Univ. of Hong Kong; joined Admin. Service 1983, served in various bureaux and depts, including Financial Sec.'s Office, Transport Br., Educ. and Manpower Br., Standing Comm. on Civil Service Salaries and Conditions of Service, as Deputy Head of Cen. Policy Unit 1996–98, Deputy Dir of Admin 1997, Deputy Sec. for Information Tech. and Broadcasting (later renamed Deputy Sec. for Commerce, Industry and Tech.) 1998–2003, Commr for Tourism 2003–06, Perm. Sec. for Econ. Devt and Labour (Econ. Devt) 2006–07, Sec. for Transport and Housing 2007–; Chair. Hong Kong Housing Authority; Gold Bauhinia Star 2011. *Address:* Hong Kong Housing Authority Headquarters, 33 Fat Kwong Street, Ho Man Tin, Kowloon, Hong Kong Special Administrative Region, People's Repub. of China (office). *Telephone:* 2712-2712 (office). *Fax:* 2711-4111 (office). *E-mail:* hkha@housingauthority.gov.hk (office). *Website:* www.housingauthority.gov.hk (office).

CHENG, Jason, MEng; Taiwanese business executive; *President and CEO, Pegatron;* ed Univ. of Southern California, USA; fmr Vice-Pres. Asustek; currently mem. Bd of Dirs, Pres. and CEO Pegatron; mem. Bd of Dirs Unihan, AzureWave. *Address:* Pegatron, 96 Ligong Street, Beitou, Taipei 112, Taiwan (office). *Telephone:* (2) 8143-9001 (office). *Fax:* (2) 8143-7984 (office). *E-mail:* pegatronhr@pegatroncorp.com (office). *Website:* www.pegatroncorp.com (office).

CHENG, Lianchang; Chinese government official; b. 14 May 1931, Jilin; m. Huang Shulan; one s. one d.; ed Jilin Industrial School, People's Univ. of China; joined CCP 1950; Vice-Minister of 7th Ministry of Machine Building 1975–82; Vice-Minister, Exec. Vice-Minister of Astronautical Ind. 1982–88; Sr Engineer and Researcher 1988–; Exec. Vice-Minister of Personnel 1988–94; mem. State Educational Comm. 1988–94; Vice-Pres. Nat. School of Admin. 1994–96; Vice-Chair. Steering Cttee for Enterprise; Standing mem. 8th Nat. Cttee CPPCC 1993–97, 9th Nat. Cttee CPPCC 1998–2003; Prof., China People's Univ.; Fellow World Acad. of Productivity Science 2001; First-class Award, Ministry of Astronautical Ind. 1984, State Council Award for Outstanding Contribution in High-energy Physics 1991. *Publications:* Selected Works (two vols), Textbook for State Public Servant Examination (20 vols). *Leisure interest:* swimming. *Address:* Room 1501, No. 13 Building, Cuiwei Xili, Haidian District, Beijing 100036, People's Republic of China (home); c/o Ministry of Personnel, Hepingli Zhongjie, Beijing 100013 (office). *Telephone:* (10) 68462628 (office); (10) 68258072 (home). *Fax:* (10) 84233851 (office). *E-mail:* chenglch@izb.com (home).

CHENG, Siwei, MBA; Chinese politician; *Director of Science Management Division, National Natural Science Foundation of China;* b. June 1935, Xiang City, Hunan Prov.; ed East China Chemical Eng Inst., Univ. of California at Los Angeles, USA; worker, Shenyang Chemical Eng Research Inst., Liaoning Prov. 1956–58; engineer, Tianjin Chemical Eng Research Inst. 1958–73, Petrochemical Eng Research Inst. (Petroleum Chem. Div.) 1973–81; Chief Engineer, Ministry of Chemical Industry, Science and Tech. Bureau 1984–93, Vice-Chair. Science and Tech. Research Inst. 1988–93; Deputy Dir Ministry of Chemical Industry 1994–96; Vice-Chair. Cen. Cttee China Democratic Nat. Construction Asscn 1994–96, Chair. 1996–; mem. Standing Cttee 8th CPPCC 1993–98; Vice-Chair. Standing Cttee of 9th NPC 1998–2003, Standing Cttee of 10th NPC 2003–; Dir Science Man. Div., Nat. Natural Science Foundation of China 2003–; Chair. China Soft-Science Research Soc.; Hon. DBA (Hong Kong Polytechnic Univ.) 2000; Globalist of the Year 2008. *Address:* National Natural Science Foundation of China, Beijing, People's Republic of China. *Website:* www.nsfc.gov.cn (office).

CHENG, Weigao; Chinese fmr government official; b. 1933, Suzhou City, Jiangsu Prov.; Dir CCP City Cttee, Student Dept and Juvenile Dept, Changzhou City, Jiangsu Prov. 1949–54, Head of CCP Propaganda Dept 1949–54; joined CCP 1950; worker, People's Govt Gen. Office, Changzhou City 1955–62, Deputy Dir 1962–63, Dir 1963–65; Dir Changzhou Tractor Plant 1965–72 (also Sec. CCP Party Cttee 1965–72); Sec. CCP Party Cttee, Shanghuang Coal Mine, Jiangsu Prov. 1972–77; Vice-Chair. Planning Cttee and Chair. Capital Construction Cttee, Changzhou City 1977–80; Sec. CCP City Cttee, Changzhou 1980–84; Deputy, 6th NPC 1983–88; Sec. CCP City Cttee, Nanjing, Jiangsu Prov. 1984–87; mem. Standing Committee, CCP Prov. Cttee, Jiangsu Prov. 1984–87; Deputy Sec. CCP Prov. Cttee, Henan Prov. 1987–90; Vice-Gov. Henan Prov. 1987–88, Gov. 1988–90; Acting Gov. Hebei Prov. 1990–91, Gov. 1991–93; Deputy Sec. CCP Hebei Prov. Cttee 1990–93, Sec. 1993–98; Chair. Standing Cttee of NPC, Hebei Prov. 1998–99; mem. 13th CCP Cen. Cttee 1987–92, 14th CCP Cen. Cttee 1987–92, 15th CCP Cen. Cttee 1997–2002; Deputy, 9th NPC 1998–2003; expelled from CCP for alleged involvement in corruption scandals 2003.

CHENG, Yanan; Chinese sculptor; b. 15 Jan. 1936, Tianjin; d. of Cheng Goliang and Liuo Shijing; m. Zhang Zuoming 1962 (died 1989); one s. one d.; ed Cen. Acad. of Fine Arts, Beijing; sculptor Beijing Architectural Artistic Sculpture Factory 1961–84, Sculpture Studio, Cen. Acad. of Fine Arts 1984–; mem. China Artists'

Asscn. *Address:* 452 New Building of Central Institute of Fine Arts, No 5 Shuaifuyan Lane, East District, Beijing, People's Republic of China.

CHENG, Yu-Tung; Chinese business executive (retd); b. 27 Aug. 1925, Shunde, Guangdong; m.; two c.; Dir New World Development Co. Ltd 1970–2012, Chair. 1982–2012; Chair. New World Hotels (Holdings) Ltd, Chow Tai Fook Enterprises Ltd; Chair. (non-exec.) Lifestyle International Holdings Ltd; Dir Cheng Yu-Tung Family (Holdings) Ltd, Centennial Success Ltd; Dir (non-exec.) Shun Tak Holdings Ltd 1982, Hang Seng Bank Ltd; Hon. Consul for Bhutan; Trustee United Coll., Chinese Univ. of Hong Kong; Hon. LLD (Toronto 1987), Hon. DBA, Hon. DSc (Chinese Univ. of Hong Kong 1993); Grand Bauhinia Medal 2008. *Address:* c/o New World Development Company Limited, 30th Floor, New World Tower 18, Queen's Road, Central Hong Kong Special Administrative Region, People's Republic of China (office).

CHEONG, Yip Seng; Singaporean journalist and editor; *Editorial Advisor, Singapore Press Holdings;* b. June 1943; trainee journalist The Straits Times Press 1963, then Ed. The New Nation, then Ed. The Straits Times, Deputy Ed.-in-Chief English/Malay Newspapers Div., Singapore Press Holdings (including The Straits Times, Business Times, Berita Harian and The New Paper) late 1970s–87, Ed.-in-Chief English/Malay Newspapers Div. 1987–2007, Editorial Advisor Singapore Press Holdings 2007–; mem. Bd of Dirs SBS Transit Ltd; mem. Nat. Univ. of Singapore Council 2004–; Founding mem. Singapore Press Club 1971–; ASEAN Award for Information 1997. *Address:* The Straits Times, SPH News Centre, P2, 1000 Toa Payoh North, Singapore City, 318994, Singapore (office). *Telephone:* 6319-5106 (office). *Fax:* 6737-5576 (office). *E-mail:* cheong@sph.com.sg (office). *Website:* www.straitstimes.com (office); www.sph.com.sg (office).

CHER; American singer and actress; b. (Cherilyn Lapierre Sarkisian), 20 May 1946, El Centro, Calif.; d. of John Sarkisian and Georgina Holt; m. 1st Sonny Bono 1964 (divorced 1975, died 1998); one d.; m. 2nd Gregg Allman 1975 (divorced); one s.; formed singing duo Sonny & Cher with Sonny Bono 1964–74, with TV series; solo artist 1964–, with own TV variety series and night club act; VH1 First Music Award for achievements within the music industry 2005, Lifetime Achievement Award, Glamour Women of the Year Awards 2010. *Theatre:* Come Back to the Five and Dime, Jimmy Dean, Jimmy Dean. *Television:* Sonny & Cher Comedy Hour (CBS) 1971–74, Cher (CBS) 1975–76, Sonny & Cher Show (CBS) 1976–77. *Films:* Chastity 1969, Come Back To The Five and Dime, Jimmy Dean Jimmy Dean 1982, Silkwood 1983, Mask (Cannes Film Festival Best Actress Award) 1985, The Witches of Eastwick 1987, Suspect 1987, Moonstruck (Acad. Award for Best Actress 1988) 1987, Mermaids 1989, Club Rhino 1990, Faithful 1996, If These Walls Could Talk 1996, Nine 1996, Tea with Mussolini 1999, Stuck on You 2003. *Recordings include:* albums: as Sonny & Cher: Baby Don't Go 1965, Look At Us 1965, The Wondrous World Of Sonny & Cher 1966, Good Times 1967, In Case You're In Love 1967, Sonny & Cher Live 1971, All I Ever Need Is You 1972, Live In Las Vegas 1974, Mama Was A Rock 'N' Roll Singer 1974; solo: All I Really Want To Do 1965, Cher 1966, The Sonny Side Of Cher 1966, With Love 1967, Backstage 1968, 3614 Jackson Highway 1969, Cher 1971, Gypsies Tramps and Thieves 1971, Foxy Lady 1972, Half Breed 1973, Bittersweet White Light 1974, Dark Lady 1974, Stars 1975, I'd Rather Believe In You 1976, Cherished 1977, Two The Hard Way 1977, This Is Cher 1978, Take Me Home 1979, Prisoner 1982, I Paralyze 1984, Cher 1987, Heart Of Stone 1989, Outrageous 1989, Love Hurts 1991, It's A Man's World 1995, Believe 1998, Black Rose 1999, Not.Com.mercial 2000, Holdin' Out For Love 2001, Believe 2001, Living Proof 2001, Live: The Farewell Tour 2003. Closer to the Truth 2013; singles: as Sonny & Cher: I Got You Babe 1975, Baby Don't Go 1965, Just You 1965, But You're Mine 1965, What Now My Love 1966, Little Man 1966, The Beat Goes On 1967, All I Ever Need Is You 1971, A Cowboy's Work Is Never Done 1972; solo: All I Really Want To Do 1965, Bang Bang 1966, Gypsies Tramps And Thieves 1971, The Way Of Love 1972, Half Breed 1973, Dark Lady 1974, Take Me Home 1979, Dead Ringer For Love (duet with Meatloaf) 1982, I Found Someone 1987, We All Sleep Alone 1988, After All (duet with Peter Cetera, for film Chances Are) 1989, If I Could Turn Back Time 1989, Jesse James 1989, Heart of Stone 1990, The Shoop Shoop Song (for film Mermaids) 1990, Love And Understanding 1991, Save Up All Your Tears 1991, Oh No Not My Baby 1992, Love Can Build A Bridge (with Neneh Cherry and Chrissie Hynde) 1995, Walking In Memphis 1995, One By One 1996, Paradise Is Here 1996, Believe (Grammy Award for Best Dance Recording 2000) 1998, Strong Enough 1999, All Or Nothing 1999, Dov'e l'Amore 1999, The Music's No Good Without You 2001, Alive Again 2002, A Different Kind Of Love 2002, When The Money's Gone 2003. *Address:* ICM, 10250 Constellation Boulevard, Beverly Hills, CA 90067, USA (office). *Website:* www.cher.com.

CHERESHNEV, Valery Aleksandrovich, DMed; Russian immunologist and academic; *Director, Institute of Ecology and Microorganism Genetics, Russian Academy of Sciences;* b. 24 Oct. 1944, Khabarovsk; m.; two c.; ed Medical Inst., Perm, Russian Acad. of Sciences; researcher, Medical Inst., Perm State Univ. –1988; Dir Inst. of Ecology and Microorganism Genetics, Russian Acad. of Sciences, Ural, Perm State Univ. 1988–; Corresp. mem. Russian Acad. of Sciences 1990–97, mem. 1997–, elected Vice-Pres. Russian Acad. of Sciences, Ural Br. 1999, now Pres.; Chair. The Urals Program; Fellow, World Acad. of Art and Science 2005; Medal for Merits in Labour; Order of Friendship. *Leisure interest:* khatkha yoga. *Address:* Presidium, Ural Branch, Russian Academy of Sciences, Permovmayskaya str., 91, 620219 Yekaterinburg (office); Institute of Ecology and Microorganism Genetics, Golev str. 13, 614081 Perm, Russia (office). *Telephone:* (3432) 74-02-23 (office); (3432) 33-54-54 (home). *E-mail:* chereshnev@prm.uran.ru (office). *Website:* prm.uran.ru (office).

CHÉRIF, Taïeb, MSc, PhD; Algerian aviation official; b. 29 Dec. 1941, Kasr El Boukhari; m.; three c.; ed Univ. of Algiers, Ecole Nationale de l'aviation civile, France, Cranfield Inst. of Tech., UK; Eng Officer, Civil Aviation Directorate, Ministry of Transport, Algiers 1970–71, Deputy Dir of Transport and Aerial Activities 1971–74, Deputy Dir of Air Navigation 1974–75, Dir of Air Transport 1985–87, Dir aeronautical construction project 1987–92; State Sec. for Higher Educ. 1992–94; Algerian Rep., ICAO Council 1998–2003, Sec.-Gen. ICAO 2003–09; Dir Algiers Int. Airport 1975–76; Civil Aviation Consultant 1982–85, 1995–97; Visiting Lecturer, Inst. for Civil Aviation and Meteorology, Algiers 1970–71, Ecole Nationale des Techniciens de l'Aéronautique, Blida 1973–74, Econ. Science Inst., Algiers 1984–85. *Address:* c/o International Civil Aviation Organization, External Relations and Public Information Office, 999 University Street, Montreal, H3C 5H7, Canada.

CHERITON, David R., MMath, PhD; Canadian computer scientist and academic; *Professor of Computer Science, Stanford University;* ed Univ. of Waterloo; began career as Asst Prof., Univ. of BC; currently Prof. of Computer Science, Stanford Univ., Leader, Distributed Systems Group; Co-founder Granite Systems and Kealia Inc. (computer networking equipment cos); early investor in Google, Inc.; SIGCOMM Lifetime Achievement Award 2003. *Address:* Computer Science Department, Stanford University, 353 Serra Mall, Stanford, CA 94305-9025, USA (office). *Telephone:* (650) 723-1131 (office). *E-mail:* cheriton@cs.stanford.edu (office). *Website:* www-dsg.stanford.edu (office); www.stanford.edu (office).

CHERKASKY, Michael G., BA, JD; American lawyer and business executive; *CEO, US Investigations Services Inc.;* b. 2 March 1950, Bronx, NY; m. Betsy Cherkasky; four c.; ed Fieldston School, Case Western Reserve Univ.; began career as law clerk in US Dist Court, Northern Dist of Ohio; Asst Dist Attorney, NY Co. Dist Attorney's Office 1978–85, 1985–93, Deputy Chief of Trial Bureau 40 1983–84, Chief of Trial Bureau 1984–85, Head of Rackets Bureau 1986–90, Chief of Investigations Div. 1990–94; Head of Re-election Campaign of Robert Morgenthau 1985; joined Kroll Assocs 1994, Head of New York Office 1994–96, Head of N America Region 1996–97, COO and Exec. Man.-Dir 1997, Pres. and COO The Kroll-O'Gara Co. (following merger with O'Gara-Hess & Eisenstadt 1997, renamed Kroll Inc. 2001) 1997–2001, Pres. and CEO Kroll Inc. 2001–04, Chair. and CEO Marsh Kroll Inc. (after acqustion of Kroll by March & McLennan Cos) 2004; Pres. and CEO March & McLennan Inc. 2004–08; CEO US Investigations Services Inc., Falls Church, Va 2008–. *Publication:* Forewarned: Why the Government is Failing to Protect Us and What We Must Do to Protect Ourselves 2002. *Address:* US Investigations Services Inc., 7799 Leesburg Pike, Suite 1100 North, Falls Church, VA 22043-2413, USA (office). *Telephone:* (703) 448-0178 (office). *Website:* www.usis.com (office).

CHERKESOV, Col.-Gen. Victor Vasilejvich; Russian security officer and lawyer; *Director, Federal Agency for the Procurement of Military and Special Equipment;* b. 13 July 1950, Leningrad; m. Natalya Sergejvna Cherkesova (née Chaplina); two d.; ed Leningrad State Univ.; investigator Leningrad KGB Dept 1975–; Head Dept of Fed. Security Service St Petersburg and Leningrad Region 1992–98; First Deputy Dir Russian Fed. Security Service 1998–2000; Rep. of Russian Pres. to NW Fed. Dist 2000–2003; mem. Russian Federation Security Council; Dir Fed. Service for Control over Drugs and Psychotropic Substances 2003–08; Dir Fed. Agency for the Procurement of Mil. and Special Equipment 2008–; Order of the Red Star 1985, Order of Honour 2000; 14 medals including Honoured Lawyer of the Russian Fed., Honourable Domestic Intelligence Officer of the Russian Fed., Honourable External Intelligence Officer of the Russian Fed. *Address:* Federal Agency for the Procurement of Military and Special Equipment, c/o Office of the President, 1031324 Moscow, Staraya pl. 4, Russia (office). *Telephone:* (495) 925-35-81 (office). *Fax:* (495) 206-07-66 (office). *E-mail:* president@gov.ru (office). *Website:* www.kremlin.ru (office).

CHERMAYEFF, Peter, AB, MArch, FAIA; American architect; *President, Peter Chermayeff LLC;* b. 4 May 1936, London, England; s. of Serge Ivan Chermayeff and Barbara Chermayeff; m. 1st Clare Brandt (née Scott) 1960; m. 2nd Jane Borden (née Batchelder) 1966; one s. two step-s.; m. 3rd Andrea Petersen 1983; one d.; ed Phillips Acad., Andover, Harvard Coll., Harvard Graduate School of Design; Co-founder Cambridge Seven Assocs Inc. 1962, resigned 1996; Co-founder (with Peter Sollogub and Bobby Poole) Chermayeff, Sollogub & Poole, Inc. 1998–2005, continuing as Chermayeff & Poole, Inc. 2005–09; Founder Peter Chermayeff LLC 2009–; Co-founder, Pres. and CEO of affiliated firm International Design for the Environment Assocs Inc. 1990–2009; mem. Mass Council on Arts and Humanities 1969–72, Bd of Advisers, School of Visual Arts, Boston Univ. 1976–80, Visiting Cttee, Rhode Island School of Design, Providence 1969–75, Bd of Design Consultants, Univ. of Pennsylvania 1976–80; Claude M. Fuess Award "For Distinguished Contribution to the Public Service", Phillips Acad., Andover 1979, AIA Firm of the Year Award (with others at Cambridge Seven Assocs) 1992. *Films include:* producer: Orange and Blue 1962, Cheetah, Zebra, Lion, Elephant & Giraffe (with Jane Borden) 1971, Wildebeest, Rhino, Impala, Gazelle, Baboon & Ostrich (with Andrea Petersen) 1984; exec. producer: Where's Boston? 1975. *Major complete works include:* design: Guidelines and Standards, Mass Bay Transportation Authority 1967, US Exhibition Expo '67 Montreal 1967, New England Aquarium, Boston 1969, 'Where's Boston?' exhbn and show, Boston 1975, San Antonio Museum of Art, San Antonio, Tex. 1981, Nat. Aquarium, Baltimore, Md 1981, 2005, Ring of Fire Aquarium, Osaka, Japan 1990, Tennessee Aquarium, Chattanooga 1992, Genoa Aquarium, Italy 1992, Nivola Museum, Orani, Sardinia 1996, Lisbon Oceanarium 1998, Expansion Nat. Aquarium, Baltimore, Md 2005, Expansion Tennessee Aquarium, Chattanooga 2005; start-up operations: Genoa Aquarium 1992, Lisbon Oceanarium 1998, Scientific Centre of Kuwait 2000. *Work in progress includes:* New Bedford Aquarium, LA, Child (Rainforest) Cedar Rapids, Mammal Partition, Virginia Marine Science Museum, Oberhausen Aquarium, Germany, Cala Gonone Aquarium, Sardinia, Mindelo Aquarium, São Vicente, Cape Verde. *Address:* 111 Highland Road, Andover, MA 01810, USA (office). *Telephone:* (617) 226-1827 (office). *Fax:* (978) 289-5801 (office). *E-mail:* pchermayeff@peterchermayeff.com (office); peter@chermayeff.com (home). *Website:* www.peterchermayeff.com (office); www.idea-aquariums.com (office).

CHERNIN, Peter F.; American media executive; b. 29 May 1951, Harrison, New York; early career as Assoc. Publicity Dir St Martin's Press and Ed. Warner Books; fmr Vice-Pres. of Devt and Production, David Gerber Co.; fmr Exec. Vice-Pres. of Programming and Marketing, Showtime/The Movie Channel Inc.; Pres. and COO Lorimar Film Entertainment 1989–92; joined Fox Broadcasting Co. 1989, Pres. of Entertainment Group 1989–92, Chair. Twentieth Century Fox Film Corpn (now Fox Filmed Entertainment) 1992–2009, Pres. and COO News Corpn 1996–2009, Chair. and CEO Fox Entertainment Group 1998–2009; Chair. Malaria No More; mem. Bd of Dirs Gemstar-TV Guide 2002–, DirecTV 2003–, American Express Co. 2006–. *Address:* c/o News Corporation Limited, 1211 Avenue of the Americas, New York, NY 10036, USA (office).

CHERNOBROVKINA, Tatyana Anatolyevna; Russian ballerina; b. 14 Aug. 1965; m. Dmitry Zababurin; one s.; ed Saratov Ballet School; soloist, Saratov

Theatre of Opera and Ballet 1983–86; soloist, Stanislavsky and Nemirovich-Danchenko Moscow Academic Music Theatre 1987–; prizewinner, 5th Moscow Int. Competition of Ballet Dancers 1985, Merited Artist of Russia 1994, People's Artist of Russia 1999. *Main ballet roles:* Odette/Odile (Swan Lake), Macha (The Nutcracker), Aurora (Sleeping Beauty), Juliet (Romeo and Juliet), Kitry (Don Quixote), Giselle (Giselle). *Address:* Moscow Academic Music Theatre, 103009 Moscow, B. Dmitrovka str. 17, Russia (office). *Telephone:* (495) 229-19-57 (office); (495) 954-14-26 (home). *Fax:* (495) 954-14-26 (home). *Website:* www.stanislavskymusic.ru (office).

CHERNOFF, Herman, PhD; American mathematician and academic; *Professor Emeritus of Statistics, Harvard University;* b. 1 July 1923, New York, NY; s. of Max Chernoff and Pauline Markowitz; m. Judith Ullman 1947; two d.; ed Townsend Harris High School, City Coll. of New York, Brown and Columbia Univs; Research Assoc., Cowles Comm. for Research in Econs, Univ. of Chicago 1947–49; Asst Prof. of Math., Univ. of Illinois 1949–51, Assoc. Prof. 1951–52; Assoc. Prof. of Statistics, Stanford Univ. 1952–56, Prof. 1956–74; Prof. of Applied Math., MIT 1974–85, now Prof. Emer.; Prof. of Statistics, Harvard Univ. 1985–97, Prof. Emer. 1997–; mem. NAS, American Acad. of Arts and Sciences; Dr hc (Ohio State) 1983, (Technion) 1984, (Univ. of Rome, La Sapienza) 1995, (Athens) 1999; Townsend Harris Prize 1982, Wilks Medal 1987. *Publications:* Elementary Decision Theory (with L. E. Moses) 1959, Sequential Analysis and Optimal Design 1972; numerous articles in scientific journals. *Address:* Department of Statistics, SC711, Harvard University, Cambridge, MA 02138 (office); 75 Crowninshield Road, Brookline, MA 02446, USA (home). *Telephone:* (617) 495-5462 (office); (617) 232-8256 (home). *Fax:* (617) 496-8057 (office). *E-mail:* chernoff@stat.harvard.edu (office). *Website:* www.fas.harvard.edu/~stats (office).

CHERNOV, Hon. Alex, AC, AO, QC, BCom, LLB; Australian (b. Lithuanian) lawyer and government official; *Governor of Victoria;* m. Elizabeth Chernov; three c.; ed Melbourne High School, Univ. of Melbourne; emigrated with family to Australia as a young boy; fmr part-time tutor, Ormond and Newman Colls and at Monash Univ.; signed Roll of Counsel at Victoria Bar 1968; QC 1980; practised almost exclusively in commercial and co. law and equity, appearing in Supreme Courts in most states and in Supreme Court of Fiji, at trial and appellate levels, and before High Court of Australia and Privy Council; Ind. Lecturer in Equity for Council of Legal Educ. 1971–75; Hon. Consultant to Australian Law Reform Comm. 1985–87; Chair. Victorian Bar 1985–86; Vice-Pres. Australian Bar Assen 1985–86; Pres. Australian Law Council 1990–91; Vice-Pres. LawAsia 1995–97; mem. Council of Presbyterian Ladies Coll. 1981–90; Chair. Australian Motor Sport Court of Appeal 1985–97; apptd a Judge of Trial Div. of Supreme Court of Victoria 1997, apptd to its Court of Appeal 1998; mem. Council of Univ. of Melbourne 1992–2011, chaired several of its major cttees, Deputy Chancellor 2004–10, Chancellor 2010–11; Gov. of Victoria 2011–; Dr hc (Univ. of Melbourne) 2012. *Publication:* Brooking and Chernov, Tenancy Law and Practice in Victoria (co-author, and ed. of second edn). *Leisure interests:* music, theatre, reading, golf, walking, farming. *Address:* Government House, Government House Drive, Melbourne, VIC 3004, Australia (office). *Telephone:* (3) 9655-4211 (office). *Fax:* (3) 9650-9050 (office). *Website:* www.governor.vic.gov.au (office).

CHERNOV, Vladimir Kirillovich; Russian singer (baritone) and academic; *Professor of Vocal Studies, University of California, Los Angeles;* b. 1956, Belorechensk; m. Olga Chernova; one s.; ed Moscow Conservatory with Georgy Seleznev and Hugo Titz; winner of All-Union Glinka Competition, int. competitions: Tchaikovsky (Moscow), Voci Virdiagni (Vercelli), M. Helin (Helsinki); soloist of Kirov (now Mariinsky) Theatre 1990–; debut in USA 1988 (La Bohème, Boston), in UK 1990 (Forza del Destino, Glasgow); perm. soloist of Metropolitan Opera 1990–, Wiener Staatsoper 1991–; guest singer at La Scala, Chicago Lyric Opera, Mariinsky Opera, La Monnaie (Brussels) and other theatres of Europe and USA; leading parts in operas Queen of Spades, Boris Godunov, Barber of Seville, La Traviata, Eugene Onegin, Don Carlos, War and Peace, The Masked Ball, Faust, Rigoletto, Falstaff, Hérodiade (Hérod), La Cenerentola (Dandini), Nabucco (title role); in concerts and recitals performs opera arias, song cycles of Mahler, Tchaikovsky, romances; Regents' Lecturer, Voice and Opera, UCLA 2005, Prof. of Vocal Studies 2007–; Faculty mem. Opera Scola. *Address:* Robert Lombardo and Associates, 61 West 62nd Street, Suite 6f, New York, NY 10023, USA (office); UCLA Department of Music, 2539 Schoenberg Music Building, Box 951616, Los Angeles 90095-1616, USA (office). *Telephone:* (212) 586-4453 (office); (310) 794-9501 (office). *Fax:* (212) 581-5771 (office); (310) 206-4738 (office). *E-mail:* robert@robertlombardo.com (office); musicwebmaster@arts.ucla.edu (office). *Website:* www.rlombardo.com (office); www.music.ucla.edu/People/Faculty%20bios/VChernov.html; www.vchernov.com.

CHERNOW, Ron, BA, MA; American writer; b. 3 March 1949, New York, NY; m. Valerie Stearn 1979 (died 2006); ed Yale Coll., Pembroke Coll., Cambridge; fmr freelance journalist; Dir of Financial Policy Studies Twentieth Century Fund (think tank) 1982; book reviewer, essayist, TV and radio commentator; mem. PEN American Center (fmr Sec., Pres. 2006–07), Authors' Guild; contrib. to New York Times, Wall Street Journal; United Steelworkers of America Jack London Award 1980, English-Speaking Union of the USA Amb. Book Award 1990. *Publications:* The House of Morgan: An American Banking Dynasty and the Rise of Modern Finance (Nat. Book Award for Nonfiction 1990) 1990, The Warburgs: The Twentieth-Century Odyssey of a Remarkable Jewish Family (George S. Eccles Prize for the best business book 1993) 1993, The Death of the Banker: The Decline and Fall of the Great Financial Dynasties and the Triumph of the Small Investor (essays) 1997, Titan: The Life of John D. Rockefeller Sr 1998, Alexander Hamilton (George Washington Book Prize 2005) 2004, Washington: A Life (Pulitzer Prize for Biography 2011) 2010. *Address:* c/o Penguin Group (USA) Inc., c/o The Penguin Press Publicity, 375 Hudson Street, New York, NY 10014, USA (office).

CHERNUKHIN, Vladimir Anatolyevich; Russian business executive and fmr government official; b. 31 Dec. 1968, Moscow; ed Acad. of Int. Business, Acad. of Finance, Russian Fed. Govt; with Techmashexport Co., Ministry of Foreign Trade 1986–87; with Chimmashexport Co., Ministry of Chemical Machine Construction 1986–87; army service 1987–89; Sr Expert, Technomashimport Ministry of External Econ. Relations 1989–96; Vice-Pres. Dept of Credits, Vnesheconombank 1996, mem. Bd of Dirs Vnesheconombank (Foreign Economic Bank) 1998–2004, Deputy Finance Minister and Vice-Chair. 2000–2002, Chair. 2002–04; acquired

27/35 Poultry, London EC2 for devt 2006; Badge of Honour 2004. *Address:* c/o Vnesheconombank, Adademika Sakharova prosp. 9, 103810 Moscow, Russia.

CHERPITEL, Didier J.; French international organization official and investment banker; b. 24 Dec. 1944, Paris; s. of Bernard Cherpitel and Denise Cherpitel (née Lange); m. Nicole Estrangin 1973; one s. two d.; ed Inst. d'Etudes Politiques, Paris, Univ. of Paris; joined JP Morgan/Morgan Guaranty Trust 1972, various posts in Paris 1972–80, Man. Dir of Investment Banking Operations, Morgan Guaranty Pacific, Singapore 1980–83, Head of Commercial Banking Activities, Brussels 1983–84, Exec. Dir and Head of Capital Markets Activities, London 1984–88, Man. Dir Soc. de Bourse JP Morgan SA, Paris 1988–96, mem. Bd JP Morgan Europe 1994–97, Man. Dir of Pvt. Banking Activities Europe, JP Morgan, London 1977–98; mem. Bd French Stock Exchange (CBV) 1991–96; Admin. and Treas. American Chamber of Commerce in France 1991–96; Man. Dir Security Capital Markets Group Ltd, London 1998–99; Admin. Cie générale d'industrie et de participations (CGIP) 1999–; mem. Bd Wendel Investissements 2002–05, mem. Supervisory Bd 2005–; Chair. Atos Origin 2004–, Managers sans Frontières; Treas. François Xavier Bagnoud Int.; Sec.-Gen. Int. Fed. of Red Cross and Red Crescent Socs, Geneva 2000–03. *Leisure interests:* travel, photography, opera, golf. *Address:* c/o Atos Origin, Tour les Miroirs, Bat. C, 18 avenue d'Alsace, 92926 Paris 3 Cedex, France (office).

CHERTOFF, Michael, BA, JD; American judge and fmr government official; b. 28 Nov. 1953, Elizabeth, NJ; ed Harvard Univ.; Summer Assoc., Miller, Cassidy, Larroca & Lewin (law firm) 1978; Law Clerk, Court of Appeals Second Circuit 1978–79, Supreme Court 1979–80; Assoc., Latham & Watkins 1980–83, Pnr 1994–2001; Asst US Attorney, Attorney's Office, Southern Dist of NY 1983–87, First Asst US Attorney, Dist of NJ 1987–90, US Attorney 1990–94; Special Counsel, US Senate Whitewater Cttee 1994–96; Asst Attorney-Gen., Criminal Div., US Dept of Justice 2001–03; Judge, Court of Appeals Third Circuit 2003–05; US Sec. of Homeland Security, Washington, DC 2005–09. *Address:* c/o Department of Homeland Security, Washington, DC 20528, USA.

CHERUIYOT, Vivian Jepkemoi; Kenyan athlete; b. 11 Sept. 1983, Keiyo Dist, Rift Valley Prov.; specializes in long-distance running; represented Kenya at the Summer Olympic Games, Sydney 2000, Beijing 2008, London 2012; World Champion 2009, 2011, African Champion 2010, Commonwealth Games Champion 2010, Int. Asscn of Athletics Feds (IAAF) Continental Cup Champion 2010; also won IAAF Diamond League title 2010; Bronze Medal, 3,000m, World Youth Championships, Bydgoszcz 1999, 5,000m, All-Africa Games, Johannesburg 1999, 5,000m, World Junior Championships, Kingston 2002; World Championships: Gold Medal, 5,000m, Berlin 2009, Gold Medal, 10,000m, Daegu 2011, Gold Medal, 5,000m, Daegu 2011, Silver Medal, 5,000m, Osaka 2007; Commonwealth Games: Gold Medal, 5,000m, Delhi 2010; Olympic Games: Silver Medal, 5,000m, London 2012, Bronze Medal, 10,000m, London 2012; World Athletics Final: Gold Medal, 5,000m, Stuttgart 2007, Silver Medal, 3,000m, Stuttgart 2007, Silver Medal, 5,000m, Stuttgart 2008, Silver Medal, 3,000m, Stuttgart 2008, Silver Medal, 3,000m, Thessaloniki 2009, Bronze Medal, 3,000m, Stuttgart 2006, Bronze medal, 5,000m, Thessaloniki 2009; World Indoor Championships: Silver Medal, 3,000m, Doha 2010; World Cross Country Championships: Gold Medal, Sr Race, Punta Umbría 2011, Gold Medal, Jr Race, Vilamoura 2000, Silver Medal, Jr Race, Belfast 1999, Bronze Medal, Jr Race, Dublin 2002; competed for Africa and won Gold Medal, 5,000m, Continental Cup Gold, Split 2010; with a time of 14:20.89, set at DN Galan 2011; coached by Ricky Simms; Kenyan Sportswoman of the Year 2011, Women's Track & Field Athlete of the Year 2011, Laureus World Sportswoman of the Year 2011. *Website:* www.viviancheruiyot.com.

CHESHIRE, Sir Ian Michael, Kt; British retail executive; *Group Chief Executive, Kingfisher plc;* m.; three c.; ed Univ. of Cambridge; worked at Guinness and the Piper Trust; more than 20 years' retail experience, including Group Commercial Dir Sears plc; joined Kingfisher as Group Strategy Dir in 1998, subsequently joined main Bd as Chief Exec. of Kingfisher's e-Commerce Div. 2000–02, CEO Int. and Devt, with responsibility for all retail operations outside the UK and France 2002–05, CEO B&Q UK 2005–08, Group Chief Exec. Kingfisher plc 2008–; mem. Bd of Dirs Whitbread plc; mem. Prince of Wales Corp. Leaders Group on Climate Change; mem. Employers' Forum on Disability Pres.'s Group. *Address:* Kingfisher plc, 3 Sheldon Square, Paddington, London, W2 6PX, England (office). *Telephone:* (20) 7372-8008 (office). *Fax:* (20) 7644-1001 (office). *Website:* www.kingfisher.com (office).

CHESHIRE, Air Chief Marshal Sir John (Anthony), KBE, CB, FRAeS; British air force commander and government official; *Chairman, Royal Air Force Charitable Trust;* b. 4 Sept. 1943; m. Shirley Ann Stevens 1964; one s. one d.; ed Ipswich School, Worksop Coll., RAF Coll., Cranwell; specialist in air support, Special Forces until 1980; Commdr Air Wing, Brunei 1980–82, RAF Lyneham 1983–85, Plans Br. HQ Strike Command 1986–87; Defence and Air Attaché, Moscow 1988–90; Deputy Commdt RAF Staff Coll. 1991–92; Asst Chief of Staff for Policy Supreme HQ, Allied Powers, Europe 1992–94; Mil. Rep. to NATO HQ 1995–97; C-in-C Allied Forces NW Europe 1997–2000; Lt-Gov. and C-in-C of Jersey (Channel Islands) 2001–06; Chair. Royal Air Force Charitable Trust 2008–, also Pres. Royal Int. Air Tattoo. *Leisure interests:* int. and defence affairs, creative writing, collecting (affordable) antiques, golf, squash, tennis. *Address:* c/o Royal Air Force Charitable Trust Enterprises, Douglas Bader House, Horcott Hill, Fairford, Glos., GL7 4RB, England (office). *Website:* www.rafcte.com (office).

CHESNAKOV, Aleksei Aleksandrovich, PhD; Russian political scientist; b. 1 Sept. 1970, Baku, Azerbaijan; m.; one d.; ed Moscow State Univ.; Jr, then Sr Researcher, Inst. of Mass Political Movts, Russian-American Univ. 1991–93; Researcher, then Head of Collective of Political Lectures, Centre of Political Conjunction of Russia 1993–97, Dir 1997–; Dir Centre of Social-Political Information, Inst. of Social-Political Studies, Russian Acad. of Sciences 1997; currently Deputy Presidential Domestic Policy Directorate; mem. Presidium Ind. Assoc. Civil Soc. *Publications:* numerous scientific publs on social and political problems; monographs: One Hundred Political Leaders of Russia 1993, Azerbaijan: Political Parties and Organizations 1993, Russia: Power and Elections 1996, Social and Political Situation in Russia in 1996 1997, Russia: New Stage of Neo-liberal Reforms 1998. *Address:* Directorate of Domestic Policy, c/o Office of the President,

103132 Moscow, Staraya pl. 4, Russia. *Telephone:* (495) 925-35-81. *Fax:* (495) 206-07-66. *E-mail:* president@gov.ru. *Website:* www.kremlin.ru.

CHET, Ilan, PhD; Israeli microbiologist, academic and university administrator; *Francis Ariowitsch Chair of Agricultural Biotechnology, Hebrew University of Jerusalem;* b. 12 April 1939, Haifa; m. Ruth Geffen; two s. three d.; ed Hebrew Univ. of Jerusalem; teacher of microbiology (specializing in soil microbiology, fungal physiology and biological control of plant diseases), Faculty of Agric., Hebrew Univ. of Jerusalem 1965–2001, Assoc. Prof. of Microbiology 1975–78, Prof. 1978–2001, Head Dept of Plant Pathology and Microbiology 1981–83, Dean Faculty of Agric. 1986–89, currently Francis Ariowitsch Chair of Agricultural Biotechnology; mem. Senate, Hebrew Univ. of Jerusalem 1978, mem. Exec. Cttee of Hebrew Univ. 1990–92, Bd of Man. 1990–2001, Vice-Pres. for Research and Devt 1992–2001, Chair. Univ. Authority for Research and Devt 1992–2001; Prof., Dept of Biological Chem., Weizmann Inst., Rehovot 2001–, Pres. Weizmann Inst. 2001–06; Dir Otto Warburg Center of Biotechnology in Agric., Rehovot 1983–86, 1990–92; mem. Bd Scientific Incubators Co. 1992–94, Yissum R&D Co. 1992–2001; Chair. Nat. Cttee for Strategic Infrastructure 1998–2001; Chair. Cttee for Agric. and Biotechnology, Nat. Council of Research and Devt 1984–86, Special Projects Cttee, Int. Soc. for Plant Pathology 1989–93; Deputy Sec.-Gen. Union for the Mediterranean 2010–; mem. Nat. Cttee for Biotechnology 1985–92, 1996–97, IUPAC Comm. on Biotechnology 1986–92, Editorial Bd, European Journal of Plant Pathology 1995–; mem. External Adviser to EU Group 1998–2002; panel mem. NATO 2000–03; numerous visiting professorships and lectureships; mem. Israeli Nat. Acad. of Sciences and Humanities 1998; Fellow, American Phytopathological Soc. 1991; Officer's Cross, Order of Merit (Germany) 2001, Ordre national de la Légion d'honneur 2014; Dr hc (Lund) 1991, (Naples), (Haifa Univ.); Max-Planck Research Award 1994, Israel Prize for Agricultural Research 1996, Wolf Prize 1998, E.M.T Prize, European Acad. of Science & Art 2003, Invited Speaker, World Econ. Forum, Davos, Switzerland 2003 and numerous other prizes. *Publications include:* Soil-Plant Interaction (co-ed.) 1986, Innovative Approaches to Plant Disease Control (ed.) 1987, Biotechnology in Plant Disease Control (ed.) 1993; 350 chapters, reviews and articles; 32 patents. *Leisure interest:* antique microscopes and scales. *Address:* Faculty of Agriculture, Hebrew University of Jerusalem, Rehovot 76100, Israel (office). *Telephone:* (8) 9489236 (office); (8) 934219077 (home); (8) 3453032 (home). *Fax:* (8) 9468785 (office). *E-mail:* chet@huji.ac.il (office). *Website:* ufmsecretariat.org (office).

CHEUNG, Barry, BSc, MBA, JP; Hong Kong business executive; *Chairman, UC RUSAL;* ed Univ. of Sussex, UK, Harvard Business School, USA; consultant with McKinsey & Co., Los Angeles and Hong Kong 1987–94; mem. Hong Kong Govt Central Policy Unit (on secondment from McKinsey & Co.) 1993–94; CEO Titan Petrochemicals Group Ltd 2004–08, later becoming Deputy Chair.; Chair. Hong Kong Mercantile Exchange (HKMEx) 2008–; Dir (non-exec.) UC RUSAL 2010–, Chair. 2012–; fmr CEO Camelot Oil Co. Ltd; Chair. Hong Kong Urban Renewal Authority 2007, Chair. Standing Cttee on Disciplined Services Salaries and Conditions of Service 2009, Alt. Chair. Pay Trend Survey Cttee, mem. Standing Comm. on Civil Service Salaries and Conditions of Service 2008, Comm. on Strategic Devt 2009–12; fmr Chair. Corruption Prevention Advisory Cttee, Hong Kong Independent Comm. against Corruption; Gold Bauhinia Star 2010. *Address:* UC RUSAL, Moscow 109240, 13/1, Nikoloyamskaya str., Russia (office). *Telephone:* (495) 720-51-70 (office). *Fax:* (495) 745-70-46 (office). *Website:* www.rusal.ru/en (office).

CHEUNG, Maggie; Hong Kong actress; b. 20 Sept. 1964, Hong Kong; m. Olivier Assayas 1998 (divorced 2001); grew up in Bromley, Kent, UK; fmr fashion model; jury mem., Berlin International Film Festival 1997, Venice Film Festival 1999, Cannes Film Festival 2007, Marrakech International Film Festival 2010; apptd UNICEF Amb. to China 2010; Dr hc (Univ. of Edinburgh) 2011. *Films include:* Yuen fan (Behind the Yellow Line) 1984, Ching wa wong ji (Prince Charming) 1984, Ging chaat goo si (Jackie Chan's Police Force) 1985, Xin tiao yi bai (Heartbeat) 1987, Yue liang, xing xing, tai yang (Moon, Stars & Sun) 1988, Wong gok ka moon (As Tears Go By) 1988, Nan bei ma da (Mother vs Mother) 1988, Liu jin sui yue (Golden Years) 1988, Qiu ai ye jing hun (In Between Love) 1989, Xiao xiao xiao jing cha (Little Cop) 1989, Ketu qiuhen (Song of Exile) 1990, Hong chang fei long (Crying Freeman: Dragon from Russia) 1990, Hei xue (Will of Iron) 1990, Gungun hongchen (Red Dust) 1990, A Fei jing juen (Days of Being Wild) 1991, Yuen Ling-yuk (Centre Stage) (Best Actress Award, Berlin Int. Film Festival) 1992, Shuan long hui (Brother vs Brother) 1992, Jia you xi shi 1992, Dung fong saam hap 1993, Wu xia qi gong zhu (Holy Weapon) 1993, Shen Jing Dao yu Fei Tian Mao (Flying Dagger) 1993, Fei yue mi qing (Enigma of Love) 1993, Chai gong 1993, Bai mei gui (Blue Valentine) 1993, Tian mi mi (Comrades: Almost a Love Story) 1996, Irma Vep 1996, Song jia huang chao (The Soong Sisters) 1997, Augustin, roi du Kung-fu 1999, Fa yeung nin wa (In the Mood for Love) 2000, Ying xiong (Hero) 2002, 2046 2004, Clean (Best Actress Award, Cannes Film Festival) 2004, Ashes of Time Redux 2008, Hot Summer Days 2010, Ten Thousand Waves 2010. *Address:* c/o Golden Harvest, 16/F Peninsula Office Tower, 18 Middle Road, Tsumshatsui/Rowlon, Hong Kong Special Administrative Region, People's Republic of China.

CHEUNG, Yan, (Zhang Nin); Chinese business executive; *Founder and Chairperson, Nine Dragons Paper (Holdings) Ltd;* b. Heilongjiang Prov.; m. Liu Ming Chung; two s.; worked in paper products co. in Shenzhen in early 1980s; moved to Hong Kong 1985, est. waste-paper trading business; moved to Los Angeles 1990, est. paper recycling plant; returned to China 1995, est. Nine Dragons Paper (Holdings) Ltd (packaging manufacturer), Chair. 2006–; mem. Nat. Cttee CPPCC; Exec. Vice-Chair. Overseas Chinese Entrepreneurs Asscn, Guangdong Federation of Industry and Commerce; Vice-Chair. Women's Fed. of Commerce; Pres. Guangdong Overseas Chinese Enterprises Asscn; Exec. Vice-Pres. Hong Kong China Chamber of Commerce; Vice-Pres. China Paper Asscn, China Paper Industry Chamber of Commerce; Hon. Pres. World Dongguan Entrepreneurs, Hon. Citizen, City of Dongguan; Entrepreneur of the Year in China, Ernst & Young 2007, Leader Figure, China Cailun Awards, China Paper Industry Chamber of Commerce 2008, China Charity Award, Ministry of Civil Affairs 2008, Outstanding Entrepreneur in Pulp and Paper Manufacturing Industry in China, China Paper Asscn 2009, Chinese Chamber of Commerce Contributions Award 2010, Outstanding Person on Energy Saving and Emission Reduction in

China 2009, All-China Environment Federation 2010, Outstanding Contribution Award on Poverty Alleviation and Benefiting the Community by a Businessman in the Private Sector in Guangdong Province 2010, ranked by Fortune magazine amongst 50 Most Powerful Women in Business outside the US (24th) 2007, (31st) 2008. *Address:* Nine Dragons Paper (Holdings) Ltd, 31st Floor, Sun Hung Kai Centre, 30 Harbour Road, Wanchai, Hong Kong Special Administrative Region, People's Republic of China (office). *Telephone:* 25116338 (office). *E-mail:* info@ndpaper.com (office). *Website:* www.ndpaper.com (office).

CHEUNG WING LAM, Linus, JP, BSocSc; Chinese business executive; ed Univ. of Hong Kong; Deputy Man. Dir Cathay Pacific Airways Ltd 1971–94; apptd Exec. Dir Cable & Wireless PLC 1995; Chief Exec. and Exec. Dir Hongkong Telecom (HKT) Ltd 1995–2000; Deputy Chair. and Exec. Dir PCCW Ltd (fmrly Pacific Century CyberWorks Ltd) (merged with Cable & Wireless HKT Ltd 2000) 2000–04; Chair. Companhia de Telecomunicações de Macao 1996; Dir China Unicom Ltd 2004–; Chair. Man. Bd, School of Business, Univ. of Hong Kong; Univ. apptd adviser to Chinese Soc. of Macroeconomics of the State Planning Comm., People's Repub. of China 1995; Adjunct Prof., Chinese Univ. of Hong Kong; mem. Council Univ. of Hong Kong. *Address:* China Unicom Limited, 75th Floor, The Center, 99 Queen's Road, Central, Hong Kong Special Administrative Region, People's Republic of China (office).

CHEVALIER, Tracy, MA, FRSL; American writer; b. 19 Oct. 1962, Washington, DC; m.; one s.; ed Oberlin Coll., Univ. of East Anglia, UK; moved to London, England 1984; fmr reference book ed. –1993; mem. Council, Soc. of Authors; Dr hc (Oberlin Coll.) 2013, (Univ. of East Anglia) 2013; Barnes & Noble Discover Award 2000, Ohioana Award 2013. *Publications include:* novels: The Virgin Blue 1997, Girl with a Pearl Earring 1999, Falling Angels 2001, The Lady and the Unicorn 2003, Burning Bright 2007, Remarkable Creatures 2009, The Last Runaway 2013. *Address:* c/o Jonny Geller, Curtis Brown, Haymarket House, 28–29 Haymarket, London, SW1Y 4SP, England (office). *Telephone:* (20) 7393-4400 (office). *E-mail:* hello@tchevalier.com. *Website:* www.tchevalier.com.

CHEVÈNEMENT, Jean-Pierre; French politician; *President, Citizen and Republican Movement;* b. 9 March 1939, Belfort; s. of Pierre Chevènement and Juliette Garessus; m. Nisa Grünberg 1970; two s.; ed Lycée Victor-Hugo, Besançon, Univ. de Paris, Ecole Nationale d'Admin.; joined Section française de l'Int. ouvrière (SFIO) 1964; Commercial Attaché, Ministry of Econ. and Finance 1965–68; Sec.-Gen. Centre d'études, de recherches et d'éducation socialistes (CERES) 1965–71; Commercial Adviser, Jakarta, Indonesia 1969; Political Sec. Fédération socialiste de Paris 1969–70; Dir of Studies, Soc. Eres 1969–71; Co-founder Parti Socialiste (PS) 1971, Nat. Sec. PS 1971–75, 1979–80, mem. Exec. Bureau 1971–81, 1986–93, Steering Cttee 1971–92; Deputy (Belfort) to Nat. Ass. 1973–81, 1986–2002; regional councillor Franche-Comté 1974–88; mem. Bd Dirs Repères magazine; Minister of State, Minister of Research and Tech. 1981–82, of Industry 1982–83, of Nat. Educ. 1984–86, of Defence 1988–91, of the Interior 1997–2000; cand. presidential elections 2002, 2007; First Asst to Mayor of Belfort 1977–83, 1997–2001, Mayor 1983–97, 2001–07; Pres. République Moderne 1983–; Pres. Conseil Régional de Franche-Comté 1981–82, mem. 1986–88, fmr Vice-Pres.; Founder and Pres. Citizens Movt (MDC), 1992–2003, became Citizen and Republican Movement (MRC) 2003, Hon. Pres. MRC 2003–08, Pres. MRC 2008–; mem. Foreign Affairs Comm. Nat. Ass. 1986–88, 1991–93, Finance Comm. 1993–97, 2001–02; Founder Asscn Fondation Res Publica (research foundation) 2004, Pres. 2005–;; Croix de la valeur militaire. *Publications:* (as Jacques Mandrin): L'énarchie ou les mandarins de la société bourgeoise 1967, Socialisme ou socialmédiocratie 1969, Clefs pour le socialisme 1973, Le vieux, la crise, le neuf 1975, Les socialistes, les communistes et les autres, Le service militaire 1977, Etre socialiste aujourd'hui 1979, Apprendre pour entreprendre 1985, Le pari sur l'intelligence 1985, Une certaine idée de la République m'amène à 1992, le Temps des citoyens 1993, Le Vert et Le Noir. Intégrisme, Pétrole, Dollar 1995, France–Allemagne: parlons franc 1996, La République contre les bien-pensants 1999, Défis républicains 2004, Pour l'Europe votez non 2005, La Faute de M. Monnet. La République et l'Europe 2006. *Leisure interest:* chess. *Address:* Citizen and Republican Movement, 9 rue du Faubourg Poissonnière, 75009 Paris (office); Fondation Res Publica, 52 rue de Bourgogne, 75007 Paris, France (office). *Telephone:* 1-44-83-83-00 (MRC) (office); 1-45-50-39-50 (office). *Fax:* 1-45-55-68-73 (office). *E-mail:* contact@mrc-france.org (office); info@fondation-res-publica.org (office). *Website:* www.mrc-france.org (office); www.fondation-res-publica.org (office).

CHEVRIER, Francis, PhD; French economist, academic and institute director; *Director, Institut Européen d'Histoire et des Cultures de l'Alimentation;* b. Belfort; ed Univ. of Strasbourg, Univ. of the Sorbonne, Paris, Sciences Po, Paris, Univ. of Oxford, UK; est. Int. Festival of Geography of St-Dié-of-Vosges 1990; Creator and Dir Rendez-vous de l'Histoire (annual int. meeting in Blois bringing together researchers, educators, journalists, artists and publrs); Founder and Dir Institut Européen d'Histoire et des Cultures de l'Alimentation 2002–. *Publications include:* Les cahiers de la Gastronomie, N° 5, Hiver 2010/2011 2010, Notre gastronomie est une culture: Le repas gastronomique des Français au patrimoine de l'humanité 2011. *Address:* Institut Européen d'Histoire et des Cultures de l'Alimentation, 16 rue Briçonnet, 37000 Tours, France (office). *Telephone:* (2) 47-05-90-30 (office). *Fax:* (2) 47-60-90-75 (office). *E-mail:* contact@iehca.eu (office). *Website:* www.iehca.eu (office).

CHEW, Choon Seng, BMechEng, MSc; Singaporean business executive; *CEO, Singapore Airlines Ltd;* ed Univ. of Singapore and Imperial Coll. of Science and Tech., Univ. of London, UK; joined Singapore Airlines 1972, man. assignments in Japan and Italy, regional apppointments as Sr Vice-Pres. SW Pacific, the Americas and Europe, headed of Planning, Marketing and Finance Divs, Sr Exec. Vice-Pres. (Admin) for Corp. Affairs, Auditing and Finance 2001–03, CEO 2003–; Chair. SMRT Corpn Ltd, Singapore Aircraft Leasing Enterprise; mem. Bd of Dirs Singapore Airport Terminal Services Ltd, SIA Engineering Co., Virgin Atlantic Airways. *Address:* Singapore Airlines Ltd, Airline House, 25 Airline Road, 819829, Singapore (office). *Telephone:* 65415880 (office). *Fax:* 65456083 (office). *Website:* www.singaporeair.com (office).

CHEW, Geoffrey Foucar, PhD; American physicist and academic; *Professor Emeritus of Physics, University of California, Berkeley;* b. 5 June 1924,

Washington, DC; s. of Arthur Percy Chew and Pauline Lisette Foucar; m. 1st Ruth Elva Wright 1945 (died 1971); one s. one d.; m. 2nd Denyse Mettel 1972; two s. one d.; ed George Washington Univ. and Univ. of Chicago; Research Physicist, Los Alamos Scientific Lab. 1944–46; Research Physicist, Lawrence Radiation Lab. 1948–49, Head of Theoretical Group 1967; Asst Prof. of Physics, Univ. of California, Berkeley 1949–50, Prof. of Physics 1957–91, Prof. Emer. 1991–, Chair. Dept of Physics 1974–78, Dean of Physical Sciences 1986–92; Asst Prof., then Assoc. Prof. of Physics, Univ. of Illinois 1950–55, Prof. 1955–56; Fellow, Inst. for Advanced Study 1956; Overseas Fellow, Churchill Coll., Cambridge 1962–63; Scientific Assoc., CERN 1978–79; Prof., Miller Inst. 1981–82; Visiting Prof., Univ. of Paris 1983–84; mem. NAS, American Acad. of Arts and Sciences; Hughes Prize, American Physical Soc. 1962, Lawrence Award, US Atomic Energy Comm. 1969, Berkeley Citation, Univ. of Calif. 1991, Majorana Prize 2008. *Publications include:* The S-Matrix Theory of Strong Interactions 1961, The Analytic S-Matrix 1966; over 100 scientific articles. *Leisure interests:* gardening, hiking. *Address:* 10 Maybeck Twin Drive, Berkeley, CA 94708, USA (home). *Telephone:* (510) 734-2014 (home). *Fax:* (510) 848-4117 (home). *E-mail:* gfchew@sbcglobal.net.

CHEY, Jae-won, BSc, MSc, MA; South Korean business executive; ed Brown, Stanford and Harvard Univs, USA; began career working in research position with Raychem Corpn; held positions in SK-USA, Vice-Pres. at Yamaichi International (America) Inc.; later Sr Man. Dir at SK C&C and Man. Dir at SKC Ltd, Exec. Vice-Pres., SK Telecom 2001–05, Vice-Chair. and Co-CEO SK Holdings Co. Ltd 2005–13. *Address:* c/o SK Holdings Co. Ltd, 99 Seorin-Dong, Jongru-Gu, Seoul 110-110, South Korea.

CHEY, Tae-won, BS, MA, PhD; South Korean energy industry executive; *Chairman and Co-CEO, SK Holdings Co. Ltd;* b. 1961; m.; three c.; ed Korea Univ., Univ. of Chicago, USA; Man. Business Devt, METRA Co., Calif., USA –1991; Gen. Man. SK Networks (fmrly SK Global) Co. Ltd 1991–93, with SK Global America Inc. 1993–96, Man. Dir SK Corpn 1996–97, Exec. Vice-Pres. 1997–98, Chair. 1998–2007, mem. Bd of Dirs, Chair. and CEO SK Holdings Co. Ltd 2007–08, Chair. and Co-CEO 2008–, Chair. and CEO SK Energy Co. Ltd 2007–; Exec. Dir Okedongmu; mem. Int. Business Leaders' Advisory Council; Co-Chair. East Asia Econ. Summit in Malaysia, Asian regional forum of WEF; Invited Prof., Seoul Nat. Univ. 2002, PhD programme in Econs, Univ. of Chicago; arrested on charges of fraud 2003, jailed for seven months in connection with accounting fraud at affiliate SK Networks; selected as one of The Next 100 Leaders, World Econ. Forum 1998, WEF Global Leader for Tomorrow. *Address:* SK Holdings Co. Ltd, 99 Seorin-Dong, Jongru-Gu, Seoul 110-110, South Korea (office). *Telephone:* (2) 2121-5114 (office). *Fax:* (2) 2121-7001 (office). *E-mail:* Byc778@sk.com (office). *Website:* www.sk.com (office); www.skenergy.com (office).

CHHABRIA, Vidya M.; Indian business executive; *Chairperson, Jumbo Group;* b. Bangalore; m. Manohar (Manu) Rajaram Chhabria (deceased); three d.; Chair. Jumbo Group 2002–, cos in group include Shaw Wallace & Co., Maharashtra Distilleries, SKOL Breweries, Shaw Wallace Distilleries, Shaw Wallace Breweries, Hindustan Dorr-Oliver, Mather & Platt, Falcon Tyres, Gordon Woodroffe and Shaw Wallace Hedges; Patron-in-Chief Confed. of Indian Alcoholic Beverage Cos 2003; ranked by Fortune magazine amongst 50 Most Powerful Women in Business outside the US (44th) 2002, (38th) 2003, (38th) 2004, (49th) 2005, ranked by Forbes magazine amongst 100 Most Powerful Women (95th) 2006, (97th) 2007. *Leisure interests:* reading, travelling, Indian music. *Address:* Jumbo Group, PO Box 3426, Union Towers, Sheikh Zayed Road, Dubai, United Arab Emirates (office). *Fax:* (4) 343-7397 (office). *E-mail:* chairman@jumbocorp.com (office). *Website:* www.jumbocorp.com (office).

CHI, Gen. Haotian; Chinese politician and army officer; b. 1929, Zhaoyuan Co., Shandong Prov.; m. Jiang Qingping; ed Anti-Japanese Mil. and Political Coll., Nanjing Mil. Acad., Political Acad. of the Chinese PLA, PLA High Infantry School, Mil. Acad. of the Chinese PLA; joined PLA 1945, CCP 1946; Company Instructor, Field Army, PLA Services and Arms 1946–49; joined Chinese People's Volunteers during Korean War 1951, bn instructor and Deputy Dir PLA Regimental Political Dept; Maj., unit, Nanjing Mil. Region 1958; Deputy Political Commissar, Beijing Mil. Region 1975–77; Deputy Ed.-in-Chief, People's Daily 1977–82; Deputy Chief of Staff PLA 1977–82; Political Commissar, Jinan Mil. Region 1985–87; PLA Chief of Staff 1987–92; Minister of Nat. Defence 1993–1998, 1998–2003, State Councillor 2000–03; Chair. Drafting Cttee for Nat. Defence Law of People's Repub. of China; mem. PRC Cen. Cttee 1992–95, Vice-Chair 1995–2003; rank of Gen. 1988; mem. 14th CCP Cen. Cttee 1992–97, 15th CCP Cen. Cttee 1997–2002; mem. 8th NPC 1993–98, Politburo; State Councillor 1992–95; mem. Macao Special Admin. Region Preparatory Cttee, Govt Del., Macao Hand-Over Ceremony 1999; Hon. Pres. Wrestling Asscn of China; Third-Class People's Hero of East China; World Harmony Award 2010. *Address:* c/o Ministry of National Defence, Jingshanqian Jie, Beijing 100009, People's Republic of China (office).

CHIABRA LEÓN, Gen. Roberto; Peruvian army officer (retd) and politician; b. 1950, Callao; ed Escuela Militar de Chorrillos, Inst. Int. de Derechos Humanos, Costa Rica, Univ. of Piura; fmr instructor, Escuela Militar de Chorrillos, Escuela Superior de Guerra, Centro de Altos Estudios Militares (CAEM); Commdr-in-Chief, Cenepa conflict 1995 (rank of Col, later Brig.-Gen., Gen. Commdr Second Mil. Region 2002, Commdr Gen. of Armed Forces 2002–03; Minister of Defence 2003–07; numerous mil. awards including Medalla Académica del Ejército (Merit, Honour and Distinction), Peruvian Cross of Merit, Marshal Andrés Avelino Cáceres Medal, Grand Cross of Mil. Order Francisco Bolognesi. *Address:* c/o Ministry of Defence, Avda Arequopa 291, Lima 1, Peru (office).

CHIANG, Antonio; Taiwanese journalist and editor; *Publisher and Editor-in-Chief, Taipei Times;* fmr Ed. and Publr The Eighties magazine; fmr Publr The Journalist (weekly political magazine) 1980s; Co-founder and sr journalist, Taipei Times 1998, later Ed.-in-Chief, currently Publr and Ed.-in-Chief; Deputy Sec.-Gen. Nat. Security Council 2000–04. *Address:* Taipei Times, 14/F, 399 Ruiguang Road, Neihu District, Taipei City 11492, Taiwan (office). *Telephone:* (2) 2656-1000 (office). *Fax:* (2) 2656-1099 (office). *E-mail:* letters@taipeitimes.com (office). *Website:* www.taipeitimes.com (office).

CHIASSON, Herménégilde, BA, BFA, MA, MFA; Canadian writer, artist, academic and fmr politician; b. 7 April 1946, Saint-Simon, New Brunswick; m. Marcia Chiasson; one d.; ed Université de Moncton, Mount Allison Univ.,

Université de Paris 1, France, State Univ. of New York, USA Univ. of Paris (Sorbonne); Dir Galerie d'art de l'Université de Moncton 1974; Pres. Galerie Sans Nom 1980; Founding Pres. Éditions Perce-Neige (publishing house) 1984; Pres. Asscn acadienne des artistes professionnels du Nouveau Brunswick 1993–95; Founding Pres. Productions du Phare-Est 1998; invited curator, Anecdotes and Enigmas: The Marion McCain Atlantic Art Exhbn, Beaverbrook Art Gallery 1994; Lt-Gov. of New Brunswick 2003–09; Artist-in-Residence, Univ. of Ottawa 2003, Université de Moncton and Mount Allison Univ. 2009–10; mem. RSC; Chevalier, Ordre des Arts et des Lettres 1990, Ordre des francophones d'Amérique 1993, Kt of the Order of la Pléiade; Dr hc (Université de Moncton) 1999; Prix France-Acadie 1986, 1992, Grand Prix de la francophonie canadienne 1999, Prix quinquennal Antonine-Maillet-Acadie Vie 2003, Prix Montfort 2004, Molson Prize 2011. *Films:* has directed 17 films, including Toutes les photos finissent par se ressembler 1985, Le Grand Jack 1987, Robichaud 1989, Taxi Cormier 1990, Épopée 1996. *Publications include:* numerous books, including Mourir à Scoudouc 1974, Claude Roussel/Sculpteur/Sculptor 1985 (in collaboration with Patrick Condon Laurette), Vous (France-Acadie Prize 1992) 1991, Climats 1996, Conversations (Gov.-Gen.'s Literary Award) 1999; and 15 poetry collections; has written 25 plays, including Pierre, Hélène et Michael 1990, L'exil d'Alexa 1993, Aliénor 1997. *Address:* c/o Éditions Prise de parole, 109 Elm Street, Suite 205, Sudbury, ON P3C 1T4, Canada.

CHIBA, Keiko; Japanese lawyer and politician; b. 11 May 1948; ed Chuo Univ., Tokyo; pvt. practice as lawyer; mem. Japan Socialist Party –1997; mem. Democratic Party of Japan (DPJ) 1997–, fmr Vice-Pres., also Chair. DPJ Admin Cttee; mem. House of Councillors for Kanagawa constituency 1986–2010, Dir Parl. Judicial Cttee; Minister of Justice 2009–10; Sec.-Gen. Japanese Parl. Group for Amnesty International. *Address:* c/o Democratic Party of Japan, 1-11-1, Nagatacho, Chiyoda-ku, Tokyo 100-0014, Japan (office).

CHIBESAKUNDA, Hon. Justice Lombe Phyllis, BL; Zambian lawyer, judge and diplomatist; *Acting Chief Justice;* b. 5 May 1944; ed Chipembi Girls' School, Nat. Inst. of Public Admin, Lusaka, Australian Nat. Univ.; called to the Bar, Gray's Inn, UK 1969; State Advocate Ministry of Legal Affairs 1969–77; pvt legal practice with Jacques and Partners 1972–73; mem. Nat. Ass. (Parl.) for Matero 1973–75; Solicitor Gen. and Deputy Minister of Legal Affairs 1973–75; Amb. to Japan 1975–77; High Commr to UK (also accred Amb. to FRG, the Netherlands and the Holy See) 1977–82; Chair. Industrial Relations Court 1981–86; Judge, High Court, Lusaka 1986–94; Judge in charge of Copperbelt, Luapula, Northern and North-western Provs 1994–97; Judge, Supreme Court 1997–, Acting Chief Justice 2012–; Chair. Perm. Human Rights Comm. 1997–2003; Judge Admin. Tribunal of African Devt Bank 1997–, Vice-Pres. 2005–; Assessor of external examinations, Zambia Inst. of Advanced Legal Educ., Lusaka 2005–; Pres. Zambia Asscn of Women Judges 2005–; Chief Zambian Del., UN Law of the Sea Conf. 1974–79; Rep. UN Comm. on the Status of Women, Vienna, Austria 1984–88; Chair. Equality Cttee Sub-Cttee UN Independence Party's Women's League; f. Social Action Charity, Lusaka; Founder-mem. Link Voluntary Org. 1979, Rotary Club 1994–97, Int. Asscn of Women Judges 1994–97; Life mem. Commonwealth Parl. Asscn; Kt Grand Cross, Order of Pope Pius IX 1979. *Achievements include:* first woman lawyer in Zambia; first woman Solicitor Gen. in Zambia and Africa. *Address:* Supreme Court, Independence Avenue, PO Box 50067, Ridgeway, Lusaka, Zambia (office). *Telephone:* (21) 1256781 (office); (21) 1251330 (office). *Fax:* (21) 1251743 (office). *Website:* www.judiciary.gov.zm (office).

CHICAGO, Judy, MFA; American artist, author and academic; b. (Judy Cohen), 20 July 1939, Chicago, Ill.; m. 1st Jerry Gerowitz 1961 (died 1962); m. 2nd Lloyd Hamrol 1969; m. 3rd Donald Woodman 1985; ed Univ. of California, Los Angeles; taught art at Univ. of California Extension, Los Angeles 1963–69, Univ. of Calif. Inst. Extension, Irvine 1966–69, California State Univ., Fresno (f. art programme for women) 1969–71, Calif. Inst. of the Arts, Valencia (f. first Feminist Art Programme) 1971–73; co-f. Feminist Studio Workshop and Woman's Bldg, Through the Flower Corpn, Los Angeles 1977; Presidential Appt. in Art and Gender Studies, Indiana Univ. 1999; Robb Lecturer, Univ. of Auckland, NZ 1999; Visiting Prof., Artist-in-Residence, Duke Univ. and Univ. of North Carolina, Chapel Hill 2000; Prof. in Residence, Western Kentucky Univ., Bowling Green 2001; "Envisioning the Future" (interdisciplinary and multi-exhbn site project), Pomona Arts Colony/Cal Poly Pomona/Pitzer Coll., Pomona and Claremont, Calif. 2003; First Chancellor's Artists in Residence (with photographer Donald Woodman), Vanderbilt Univ. 2006; Hon. DFA (Smith Coll., Northampton, Mass.) 2000, (Duke Univ., Durham, NC) 2003; Hon. DHumLitt (Lehigh Univ., Bethlehem, Pa) 2000; Int. Lion of Judah Conference Award For Pioneering American Women Jewish Artists 2004, Visionary Woman Award Moore Coll. of Art, Philadelphia 2004; numerous other awards. *Publications:* Through the Flower: My Struggle as a Woman Artist 1975, The Dinner Party: A Symbol of Our Heritage 1979, Embroidering Our Heritage: The Dinner Party Needlework 1980, The Birth Project 1985, Holocaust Project: From Darkness into Light 1993, The Dinner Party/Judy Chicago 1996, Beyond the Flower: The Autobiography of a Feminist Artist 1996, Women and Art: Contested Territory 1999, Fragments from the Delta of Venus 2004, Kitty City: A Feline Book of Hours 2005, The Dinner Party: From Creation to Preservation 2007, Face to Face: Frida Kahlo (with Frances Borzello) 2010. *Leisure interests:* cats and exercise. *Address:* PO Box 1327, Belen, NM 87002, USA (office). *Telephone:* (505) 861-1499 (office). *E-mail:* info@judychicago.com (office). *Website:* www.judychicago.com (office).

CHICO PARDO, Jaime, BEng, MBA; Mexican telecommunications executive; *Vice-Chairman and CEO, Teléfonos de México SA de CV (Telmex);* m.; several c.; ed Universidad Iberoamericana, Univ. of Chicago, USA; spent six years doing M&A work at Banamex Int. Div., later managed operations of cos acquired by bank; then Deputy Man. Dir International Mexican Bank (INTERMEX), London, UK; f. International Financial Engineering (investment bank); Sr Exec. Euzkadi, Gen. Tire de México –1993, Fimbursa –1993; Pres. and CEO Grupo Condumex SA de CV 1993–95; joined Teléfonos de México SA (Telmex) 1995, Vice-Chair. and CEO 1995–; Chair. and CEO Carso Global Telecom 2004–; Co-Chair. IDEAL (Impulsora del Desarrollo y el Empleo en America Latina); Dir America Movil SAB de CV, AT&T, Inc., Grupo Carso, Grupo Financiero Inbursa, Honeywell International, Inc., Prodigy Communications Corpn, Mexican Business Advisory Council, Papalote Children's Museum; Distinguished Corp. Alumni Award 2005. *Address:*

Teléfonos de México SA de CV, Parque Vía 190, Col Cuahtémoc, 06599 Mexico City (office); Carso Global Telecom SAB de CV, Avenida Insurgentes Sur 3500, Piso 5, Edificio Telmex, Colonia Peña Pobre, 14060 Mexico City, DF, Mexico (office). *Telephone:* (55) 5222-1212 (Telmex) (office); (55) 5244-0802 (Carso) (office). *Fax:* (55) 5545-5550 (Telmex) (office); (55) 5244-0808 (Carso) (office). *E-mail:* info@telmex.com.mx (office); info@cgtelecom.com.mx (office). *Website:* www.telmex.com.mx (office); www.cgtelecom.com.mx (office).

CHIDAMBARAM, Palaniappan, BSc, LLB, MBA; Indian lawyer and politician; *Minister of Finance; b.* 16 Sept. 1945, Kanadukathan, Tamil Nadu; s. of the late Shri Palaniappan and of Lakshmi Achi; m. Nalini Chidambaram; one s.; ed Presidency Coll., Madras Univ., Harvard Business School, USA; elected to Lok Sabha (Parl.) 1984; Deputy Minister, Dept of Commerce and Dept of Personnel 1985; Minister of State, Depts of Personnel and Home Affairs 1986–89; Minister of State, Dept of Commerce 1991–92, 1995–96; Minister of Finance 1996–98, 2004–08, 2012–, of Home Affairs 2008–12; Trustee, Rajiv Gandhi Foundation, Indian Literary Asscn. *Publication:* A View from the Outside: Why Good Economics Works for Everyone. *Address:* Ministry of Finance, North Block, 1st Floor, New Delhi 110 001, India (office). *Telephone:* (11) 23092611 (office). *Fax:* (11) 23094075 (office). *E-mail:* secy-dea@nic.in (office). *Website:* www.finmin.nic.in (office).

CHIDYAUSIKU, Godfrey Guwa, LLB; Zimbabwean judge; *Chief Justice, Supreme Court of Zimbabwe; b.* 1 March 1947, Goromonzi; s. of Nyamayaro Chidyausiku and Helen Chidyausiku (née Chogugudza); m. Sheila Chidyausiku; seven s. three d.; ed London Univ., Univ. of Zimbabwe; MP (Ind.) 1974–77, elected Zimbabwe African Nat. Union-Patriotic Front (ZANU-PF) MP 1980; Deputy Minister of Local Govt 1980, of Justice 1981; Attorney-Gen. 1983, apptd High Court Judge 1987, Judge Pres. High Court 1998, Chief Justice of Zimbabwe 2001–; Chair. Constitutional Comm. 1999. *Address:* Chambers of the Chief Justice, Supreme Court of Zimbabwe, CY 870, Causeway, Zimbabwe (office). *Telephone:* (4) 798634-5 (office). *Fax:* (4) 731867 (office).

CHIEN, Eugene Y. H., BS, MS, PhD; Taiwanese politician and professor of engineering; *President and Chairman, Taiwan Institute for Sustainable Energy; b.* 4 Feb. 1946, Taoyuan Co.; m. Wang Kuei-Jung (Gwendolyn Chien); two s. one d.; ed Nat. Taiwan Univ., New York Univ., USA; Assoc. Prof., Tamkang Univ. 1973–76, Prof. and Chair. Dept of Aeronautical Eng 1976–78, Prof. and Dean Coll. of Eng 1978–84; Prof. Emer., Catholic Univ. of Honduras 2002; mem. Legis. Yuan (parl.) 1984–87, Chair. Nat. Defense Cttee 1984–85, Educ. Cttee 1986; Minister of State, Environmental Protection Admin. 1987–91; Minister of Transportation and Communications 1991–93; Nat. Policy Adviser to Pres. 1993–96; Rep., Taipei Rep. Office, UK 1993–97; project consultant, EBRD 1997; Sr Adviser, Nat. Security Council 1997–2000; Deputy Sec.-Gen., Office of the Pres. 2000–02; Minister of Foreign Affairs 2002–04; Chair. Int. Co-operation and Devt Fund 2002–; consultant to various hi-tech cos 2004–; Pres. and Chair. Taiwan Inst. for Sustainable Energy 2007–; Pres. Chinese Inst. of Environmental Eng 1988–91, Chinese Inst. of Engineers 1991–92, Sino-British Cultural and Econ. Asscn 1998–; Hon. Fellow, Cardiff Univ., UK 1998; Ten Outstanding Young Persons of the World Award, Jaycees Int. and Osaka Jaycees, Japan 1985, Chinese Inst. of Environmental Eng Award 1991, Environment Protection Admin Medal 1998, Global Views Environmental Heroes Award 2010. *Publication:* The Asian Regional Economy (co-ed.) 1993. *Leisure interests:* horse riding, reading, swimming, jogging, chess, go chess. *Address:* Taiwan Institute for Sustainable Energy, 5F, No. 35 Kwang Fu N. Road, Taipei, Taiwan (office). *Telephone:* (2) 2768-2655 (office). *Fax:* (2) 2768-7522 (office). *E-mail:* eugenechien@gmail.com (office). *Website:* www.tise.org.tw (office).

CH'IEN, Kuo Fung Raymond, CBE, PhD, JP; Chinese business executive; *Non-Executive Chairman, MTR Corporation Ltd; b.* 26 Jan. 1952, Tokyo, Japan; s. of James Ch'ien and Ellen Ma; m. Whang Hwee Leng; one s. two d.; ed schools in Hong Kong, Rockford Coll., Ill., Univ. of Pennsylvania, USA; Second Vice-Pres. and Economist, Chase Manhattan Bank, New York 1978–81; Vice-Pres. and Dir Spencer Stuart & Assocs, Hong Kong 1981–84; Group Man. Dir Lam Soon Hong Kong Group 1984–97; currently Chair. China.com Inc.; Chair. (non-exec.) MTR Corpn Ltd, Hang Seng Bank Ltd, Ascendas China Commercial Fund Management Ltd; Dir Hongkong and Shanghai Banking Corpn Ltd, Convenience Retail Asia Ltd, The Wharf (Holdings) Ltd, China Resources Power Holdings Co. Ltd, Swiss Reinsurance Co. Ltd; mem. Standing Cttee, CPPCC Tianjin Municipal Cttee; fmr Chair. Fed. of Hong Kong Industries, now Hon. Pres.; mem. Exec. Council 1992–97, Exec. Council Hong Kong Special Admin. Region 1997–2002; Hon. Adviser, China Aerospace Corpn; Hon. Prof., Nanjing Univ.; Gold Bauhinia Star (Hong Kong), Chevalier, Ordre du Mérite agricole 2008; Young Industrialist Award, Fed. of Hong Kong Industrialists 1988, Global Leader for Tomorrow, World Econ. Forum 1993. *Leisure interests:* hiking, tennis, scuba diving, Chinese paintings and ceramics. *Address:* 11/F, ING Tower, 308 Des Voeux Road Central, Hong Kong Special Administrative Region, People's Republic of China (office). *Telephone:* (852) 25430887 (office). *Fax:* (852) 25960245 (office). *E-mail:* anitafok@hk.china.com (office); venus.wong@hk.china.com (office).

CHIEN FU, Fredrick, BA, MA, PhD; Taiwanese fmr politician; *Chairman, Cathay Charity Foundation; b.* 17 Feb. 1935, Beijing; m. Julie Tien; one s. one d.; ed Nat. Taiwan Univ., Yale Univ., USA; Sec. to Premier, Exec. Yuan 1962–63; Visiting Assoc. Prof., Nat. Chengchi Univ. 1962–64; Section Chief, Dept of N American Affairs, Ministry of Foreign Affairs 1964–67, Deputy Dir 1967–69, Dir 1969–72, Dir-Gen. Govt Information Office 1972–75; Visiting Prof., Nat. Taiwan Univ. 1970–72; Admin. Vice-Minister of Foreign Affairs 1975–79, Political Vice-Minister 1979–82; Rep., CCNAA Office in USA 1983–88; Minister of State and Chair. Council for Econ. Planning and Devt, Exec. Yuan 1988–90; Minister of Foreign Affairs 1990–96; apptd mem. Kuomintang (KMT) Cen. Standing Cttee 1988–98; Speaker, Nat. Ass. 1996–98; Visiting Prof., Law School, Soochow Univ. 1997–98, Nat. Taiwan Univ. 1997–99; Pres. Control Yuan 1999–2005; currently Chair. Cathay Charity Foundation and Sr Adviser Cathay Financial Holdings; numerous decorations from more than 25 countries, including Order of Brilliant Star with Grand Cordon 1975, Order of Good Hope, Grand Cross Class (SA) 1979, Order of Propitious Cloud with Special Grand Cordon (Taiwan) 2000, Order of Chung Cheng 2005; Hon. DLit (Wilson Coll.), Hon. LLD (Boston Univ., Idaho State Univ., Sun Kyun Kwan Univ., Caribbean American Univ.), Dr hc (Florida International). *Publications include:* The Opening of Korea: A Study of Chinese

Diplomacy 1876–1885, Speaking as a Friend, More Views of a Friend, Faith and Resilience: The ROC Forges Ahead, Opportunity and Challenge, Memoir of Fredrick F. Chien. *Leisure interests:* reading, golf. *Address:* Cathay Financial Centre, 19th Floor, No. 7, Sung Ren Road, Hsin-yi District, Taipei 11073, Taiwan (office). *Telephone:* (2) 8722-6701 (office). *Fax:* (2) 8789-4242 (office). *E-mail:* fredrickchien@cathaybk.com.tw (office). *Website:* www.cathaybk.com.tw (office).

CHIFFLET, Jean-Paul; French banking executive; *CEO, Crédit Agricole SA; b.* 1949, Tournon-sur-Rhône; ed Institut des Hautes Finances de Paris; joined Crédit Agricole du Sud-Est as Head of Sales Man. 1973, Corp. Sec. Crédit Agricole de la Drôme 1980–86, Corp. Sec. Crédit Agricole du Sud-Est 1986–90, Head of Devt and Lending 1990–92, Deputy CEO Crédit Agricole Ain Saône-et-Loire 1992–95, Deputy CEO Crédit Agricole Centre-Est 1995–97, Head of Relations with Regional Banks, Caisse Nationale de Crédit Agricole 1997–2000, CEO Crédit Agricole Centre-Est 2000–10, CEO Crédit Agricole SA 2010–, also Chair. LCL (Le Crédit Lyonnais) and Chair. Crédit Agricole Corp. and Investment Bank; Chair. Fédération Bancaire Française 2012–13; mem. Conseil Economique et Social, Paris 2007–; mem. and Officer of the Bd of Confédération Nationale de la Mutualité, de la Coopération et du Crédit Agricole; Chevalier, Ordre nat. du Mérite; Officier du Mérite agricole. *Address:* Crédit Agricole SA, 91–93 boulevard Pasteur, 75015 Paris, France (office). *Telephone:* 1-43-23-52-02 (office). *Fax:* 1-43-23-34-48 (office). *E-mail:* info@credit-agricole-sa.fr (office). *Website:* www.credit-agricole-sa.fr (office).

CHIHARA, Charles Seiyo, PhD; American academic; *Professor Emeritus of Philosophy, University of California, Berkeley; b.* 19 July 1932, Seattle, Wash.; s. of George Chihara and Mary Chihara; m. Carol Rosen 1964; one d.; ed Seattle and Purdue Univs, Univ. of Washington, Univ. of Oxford, UK; Faculty mem. Univs of Washington 1961–62, Illinois 1962–63; Faculty mem., Univ. of California, Berkeley 1963–, Prof. 1975–, Prof. Emer. 2000–; Mellon Postdoctoral Fellowship 1964–65, Humanities Research Fellowship 1967–68, Nat. Endowment for the Humanities Fellowship 1985–86, 1994–95, Univ. of California President's Research Fellowship in the Humanities 1996–97. *Publications:* Ontology and the Vicious-Circle Principle 1973, Constructibility and Mathematical Existence 1990, The Worlds of Possibility: Modal Realism and the Semantics of Modal Logic 1998, A Structural Account of Mathematics 2004. *Leisure interests:* tennis, travel. *Address:* Department of Philosophy, University of California, Berkeley, CA 94720 (office); 567 Cragmont Avenue, Berkeley, CA 94708, USA (home). *Telephone:* (510) 525-4023 (home). *Fax:* (510) 525-4103 (home). *E-mail:* charles1@berkeley.edu (office). *Website:* philosophy.berkeley.edu/people/detail/25 (office).

CHIK, Tan Sri Sabbaruddin, BA, MPA; Malaysian business executive and fmr politician; *Chairman, Priceworth Wood Products Bhd; b.* 11 Dec. 1941, Temerloh, Penang; ed Abu Bakar Secondary School, Temerloh, Malay Coll., Kuala Kangsar, Perak, Univ. of Malaya and Inst. of Social Studies, The Hague; Asst State Sec. Negri Sembilan, Prin. Asst Sec. JPM, Dir Planning, GPU/SERU, Dir Int. Trade, Ministry of Trade and Industry, Deputy State Sec. Selangor 1966–81; Gen. Man. Pernes Trading Sdn. Bhd 1981–82; mem. Parl. for Temerloh 1982–99; Deputy Minister of Finance 1982; Minister of Culture, Arts and Tourism 1987–99; mem. UMNO Supreme Council 1984; mem. Bd of Dirs Priceworth Wood Products Bhd (Chair. 2001–), EDEN Inc. Bhd 2002–. *Address:* Priceworth Wood Products Berhad, Suite 04-01A and 04-01B, 4th Floor, Menara Keck Seng, 203 Jalan Bukit Bintang, 55100 Kuala Lumpur, Malaysia (office). *Telephone:* (3) 21443299 (office). *Website:* www.pwpmalaysia.com.my (office).

CHIKÁN, Attila, PhD; Hungarian economist, academic and politician; *Professor, Corvinus University of Budapest; b.* 4 April 1944, Budapest; m. Márta Nagy; one s. one d.; ed Karl Marx Univ. of Econ. Sciences, Budapest, Grad. School of Business, Stanford Univ., USA; Prof., Budapest Univ. of Econ. Sciences and Public Admin (Corvinus Univ. of Budapest since 2004) 1968–, Rector 2000–03, Founder Rajk Laszlo Coll. for Advanced Studies (Dir 1970–2010, Pres. 2010–), Dir Competitiveness Research Centre 2003–; Minister of Econ. Affairs 1998–99; Chair. Council of Econ. Advisers of the Prime Minister 2000–02; First Vice-Pres. Int. Soc. for Inventory Research 1982–; Pres. Fed. of European Production and Industrial Man. Socs 1996, Int. Fed. of Purchasing and Supply Man. 2000–01; Chair. Supervisory Bd, Gedeon Richter Pharmaceutical Plc; Vice-Chair. Supervisory Bd, MOL Plc (oil co.); Pres. and/or CEO of several nat. asscn; mem. editorial bds of several int. journals; mem. Royal Swedish Acad. of Eng; Corresp. mem. Hungarian Acad. of Sciences; Middle Cross, Order of Merit of the Repub. of Hungary; Dr hc (Lappeenranta Univ. of Tech., Finland, Cluj Univ., Romania); Garner Themoin Award, Int. Fed. of Purchasing and Supply Man. *Publications:* author or ed. of several books, including Current Trends in Inventory Research: A Selection of Papers Presented at the Sixth International Symposium on Inventories, Budapest, August 1990, Inventory Models (co-ed.) 1991, Erzsebet Czako Zoltay-Paprika 2002. *Leisure interest:* sports. *Address:* Corvinus University of Budapest, 1093 Budapest IX, Fővám tér 8, Hungary (office). *Telephone:* (1) 482-5569 (office). *Fax:* (1) 482-5290 (office). *E-mail:* chikan@uni-corvinus.hu (office). *Website:* www.uni-corvinus.hu (office).

CHIKANE, Rev. Frank, MA; South African ecclesiastic and government official; *Director-General in the Presidency; b.* 3 Jan. 1951, Soweto; s. of James Mashi and Erenia Chikane; m. Kagiso Oglobry; three s.; ed Turfloop Univ. and Univs of S Africa, Durban and Pietermaritzburg; worked with Christ for All Nations 1975–76; ordained Minister 1980; part-time Research Officer, Inst. of Contextual Theology 1981, Gen. Sec. 1983; Gen. Sec. S African Council of Churches 1987–94; Dir-Gen. in Deputy Pres. Office 1994–99, Dir-Gen. in the Office of Presidency 1999–, also Chancellor of Nat. Orders, also Chair. Forum of S Africa's Dirs-Gen.; mem. Nat. Exec. Cttee, African Nat. Congress 1997–; Sr Research Fellow, Univ. of Cape Town 1995–; Hon. DTheol (Groningen); Diakonia Peace Prize 1986; Star Crystal Award 1987, Third World Prize 1989. *Publications:* Doing Theology in a Situation of Conflict 1983, The Incarnation in the Life of People in South Africa 1985, Children in Turmoil: Effect of the Unrest on Township Children 1986, Kairos Document – A Challenge to Churches, No Life of my Own (autobiog.). *Leisure interests:* reading, keeping fit (mentally, spiritually, physically). *Address:* The Presidency, Union Buildings, West Wing, Government Avenue, Private Bag X1000, Pretoria 0001 (office); University of Cape Town, Private Bag, Rondebosch 7700; 310 Zone 7, Pimville 1808, Soweto, South Africa (home); PO Box 4291, Johannesburg 2000.

Telephone: (12) 3005200 (office). *Fax:* (12) 3238246 (office). *E-mail:* president@po .gov.za (office). *Website:* www.gov.za (office).

CHIKIN, Valentin Vasilevich; Russian journalist; b. 25 Jan. 1932; ed Moscow Univ.; literary corresp. for Moscow Komsomol newspaper 1951–58; mem. CPSU 1956–91, CP of Russian Fed. 1992–; literary corresp., Deputy Ed., Ed. of Komsomolskaya Pravda 1958–71; Deputy then First Deputy Ed.-in-Chief of Sovietskaya Rossiya 1971–84, Ed.-in-Chief 1986–91; First Deputy Pres. of State Cttee on Publishing, Printing and the Book Trade 1984–86; Sec. of USSR Union of Journalists 1986–90; cand. mem. of CPSU Cen. Cttee 1986–91; mem. State Duma (CP faction) 1993–, re-elected 1995, 1999, 2003, 2007. *Address:* Gosudarstvennaya Duma, 103265 Moscow, Okhotnyi ryad 1 (office); Communist Party of the Russian Federation (Kommunisticheskaya partiya Rossiiskoi Federatsii), 103051 Moscow, per. M. Sukharevskii 3/1, Russia. *Telephone:* (495) 692-80-00 (office); (495) 628-04-90. *Fax:* (495) 203-42-58 (office); (495) 292-90-50. *E-mail:* stateduma@duma.ru (office); kprf2005@yandex.ru. *Website:* www.duma.ru (office); www.kprf.ru.

CHIKWANDA, Alexander Bwalya; Zambian business executive and politician; *Minister of Finance;* b. 1938; ed Lund Univ., Sweden; fmr Minister of Health, Planning and Finance, and of Agric.; Minister of Finance 2011–; Dir Sigma Enterprises Ltd; fmr mem. United Nat. Independence Party. *Address:* Ministry of Finance, Finance Bldg, POB 50062, Lusaka, Zambia (office). *Telephone:* (21) 1252121 (office). *Fax:* (21) 1251078 (office). *E-mail:* info@mofnp.gov.zm (office). *Website:* www.mofnp.gov.zm (office).

CHILADZE, Tamaz; Georgian writer; b. 5 March 1931, Signakhi; s. of Ivane Chiladze and Tamar Chiladze; brother of Otar Chiladze; ed Univ. of Tbilisi; first published works in 1951; mem. CPSU 1967–89; Chief Ed. Sabchota Khelovneba 1973–89, Mratobi 1997–; Shota Rustaveli Prize 1992, State Prize of Georgia 1997. *Publications include:* Sun Dial (poems) 1961, A Network of Stars 1961, Pony-trek 1963, The First Day 1965, Who Lives on the Stars 1970, White Smoke 1973, Memory (poems) 1978, Martyrdom of St Shushanik (essay) 1978, Herald of Spring (essay) 1985, The Ray of the Setting Sun (novel) 1993, The Cactus Garden (novel) 1993; plays: Shelter on the Ninth Floor, Murder, Role for a Beginner Actress, Bird Fair, The Day of Appointment. *Address:* 22 Simon Chickovani Street, Flat 7, Tbilisi 0171, Georgia. *Telephone:* (32) 33-49-87. *Fax:* (32) 33-40-75. *E-mail:* shalva@sultanishvili.ge.

CHILDS, David M., BA, MArch, FAIA; American architect; *Consulting Partner, Skidmore, Owings and Merrill LLP;* b. 1 April 1941, Princeton, NJ; two c.; ed Yale Univ., Yale School of Art and Architecture; Design Dir Pennsylvania Avenue Comm., Washington, DC 1968–71; joined Skidmore, Owings and Merrill LLP, Washington, DC 1971, moved to New York City office 1984, currently Consulting Design Pnr; Chair. Nat. Capital Planning Comm. 1975–81; Chair. US Comm. of Fine Arts 2003–08; mem. Bd of Dirs Municipal Arts Soc. of New York; Trustee American Acad. in Rome, Museum of Modern Art, Smithsonian Nat. Portrait Gallery, Nat. Bldg Museum; Fellow, AIA. *Completed projects include:* in Washington, DC: Washington Mall master plan and Constitution Gardens, Nat. Geographic HQ, 1300 New York Avenue, Metro Center, US News and World Report HQ, Dulles Airport Extension, Four Seasons, Park Hyatt and Regent hotels; in New York: Worldwide Plaza on 8th Avenue, 450 Lexington Avenue, Bertelsmann Tower, NY Mercantile Exchange, JFK Airport Arrivals Bldg, Bear Stearns HQ, Stuyvesant School Bridge; other projects include Swiss Bank Center, Stamford, Conn., Deerfield Acad. Natatorium, US Courthouse, Charleston, WV, Lester B. Pearson Int. Airport, Toronto, Canada, Ben Gurion Int. Airport, Tel-Aviv, Israel, West Ferry Circus at Canary Wharf, London, England, US Embassy in Ottawa, Canada. *Address:* Skidmore, Owings and Merrill, 14 Wall Street, 24th Floor, New York, NY 10005, USA (office). *Telephone:* (212) 298-9300 (office). *Fax:* (212) 298-9500 (office). *E-mail:* somnewyork@som.com (office). *Website:* www.som .com (office).

CHILINGAROV, Artur Nikolayevich, CandGeoSc; Russian polar explorer and politician; b. 25 Sept. 1939, Leningrad; m.; one s. one d.; ed Adm. Makarov Higher Marine School of Eng; worked as metalworker in Baltic vessel repair plant; First Sec. Regional Comsomol Cttee in Yakutya; headed drifting station N Pole 19, organized station N Pole 22, head Bellingshausen station in Antarctica, head expedition to free scientific vessel Mikhail Somol in Antarctic, expedition on board atomic ice-breaker Sibir; Deputy Chair. USSR State Cttee on Meteorology 1986–92; counsellor, Chair. Russian Supreme Soviet on problems of Arctic and Antarctic 1991–93; Pres. Asscn of Polar Explorers of the Russian Fed. 1991–, mem. Coordinating Council Polus Expeditionary Centre (organizes expeditions for the Asscn) 2002–; mem. State Duma (Parl.) 1993–, Deputy Speaker 1994–; mem. Org. Cttee Otechestvo Movt 1999; joined Yedinstvo and Otechestvo Union (later Yedinaya Rossiya party); Corresp. mem. Russian Acad. of Natural Sciences; Co-Chair. Russian Foundation of int. humanitarian aid and co-operation; Order of Lenin, Labour Red Banner, Sign of Honour; Hero of the Soviet Union, USSR State Prizes. *Leisure interest:* football. *Address:* c/o Coordinating Council, Polus Expeditionary Centre, 119027 Moscow, 2 Reysovaya Street, 2A, PGK airport Vnukovo; State Duma, 103009 Moscow, Okhotny ryad 1, Russia (office). *Telephone:* (495) 436-28-47 (Polus) (office); (495) 292-80-44 (office). *Fax:* (495) 292-76-50 (office). *E-mail:* mail@polus.org (office). *Website:* www.polus.ru (office).

CHILINGIRIAN, Levon, OBE, FRCM, ARCM; British violinist and academic; *Professor, Royal College of Music;* b. 28 May 1948, Nicosia, Cyprus; nephew of Manoug Parikian; m. Susan Paul Pattie 1983; one s.; ed Royal Coll. of Music (RCM), London; f. Chilingirian String Quartet 1971; has performed in N and S America, Africa, Australasia, Europe and Far East; Prof., RCM 1980–; Musical Dir Camerata Nordica of Sweden; BBC Beethoven Competition 1969, Munich Duo Competition (with Clifford Benson) 1971; Hon. DMus (Sussex) 1992; Cobbett Medal 1995, Royal Philharmonic Soc. Chamber Music Award 1995. *Recordings include:* 10 Mozart quartets, last three Schubert quartets, Debussy and Ravel quartets, Schubert octet and quintet, six Bartok quartets and piano quintet, late and middle Dvořák quartets, Tippett Triple Concerto; music by Panufnik, Tavener, Pärt, Chausson, Grieg, Vierne, Hahn, Komitas, McEwan, Michael & Lennox Berkeley, Mozart and Eliasson (with Chilingirian Quartet and Camerata Nordica). *Publications:* Edvard Grieg's F Major Quartet 1999. *Leisure interests:* reading, backgammon, football. *Address:* c/o Grant Rogers Musical Artists' Management, 8 Wren Crescent, Bushey Heath, Hertfordshire, WD23 1AN,

England (office); 7 Hollingbourne Road, London, SE24 9NB, England. *Telephone:* (20) 8950-2220 (office); (20) 7978-9104. *Fax:* (20) 8950-3570 (office); (20) 7274-5764. *E-mail:* info@ngrartists.com (office); spplchil@aol.com (home). *Website:* www .ngrartists.com (office).

CHILOSI, Alberto, PhD; Italian economist and academic; *Professor of Economic Policy, University of Pisa;* b. 14 Jan. 1942, Modena; s. of Giuseppe Chilosi and Clara Trabucchi; m. Lucia Ponzini; one s.; ed La Spezia Liceo Classico, Univ. of Pisa, Warsaw Cen. School of Planning and Statistics, Poland; Asst, Univ. of Pisa 1966–69, Lecturer in Theory and Policy of Econ. Devt 1972–81, Prof. of Econ. Policy 1981–; Lecturer, then Assoc. Prof. of Econs, Univ. Officielle du Congo, Lubumbashi 1969–72; Pres. Asscn Italiana per lo Studio dei Sistemi Economici Comparati 1988–89. *Publications:* Growth Maximization, Equality and Wage Differentials in the Socialist Economy 1976, Kalecki 1979, Self-Managed Market Socialism with Free Mobility of Labour 1986, L'Economia del Periodo di Transizione 1992, Entrepreneurship and Transition 2002, Stakeholders vs Shareholders in Corporate Governance 2007, The European Union and Its Neighbours 2007, The Long March of Italian Communists from Revolution to Neoliberalism 2010. *Leisure interests:* cycling, swimming. *Address:* Dipartimento di Scienze Economiche, Sede di Scienze Politiche, Via Serafini 3, 56126 Pisa (office); Via S. Andrea 48, 56127 Pisa, Italy (home). *Telephone:* (050) 2212439 (home); (050) 544184 (home). *E-mail:* chilosi@specon.unipi.it (office). *Website:* www .dse.ec.unipi.it/persone/docenti/chilosi/index.htm (office).

CHILTON, Mary-Dell, PhD; American plant biotechnologist and business executive; *Vice-President of Agricultural Biotechnology, Distinguished Science Fellow and Principal Scientist, Syngenta Biotechnology Inc.;* b. 2 Feb. 1939, Indianapolis, Ind.; ed Univ. of Illinois; Postdoctoral Researcher in Microbiology, Univ. of Washington, Seattle; mem. Faculty, Washington Univ. in St Louis 1979–83; hired by Syngenta Biotechnology Inc. (fmrly Ciba-Geigy) 1983, f. biotech research centre at Research Triangle Park 1984, later Vice-Pres. of Agricultural Biotechnology, Distinguished Science Fellow and Prin. Scientist; mem. North Carolina Bd of Science and Tech. 1986; mem. NAS 1985; Fellow, American Acad. of Arts and Sciences 1993, American Acad. of Microbiology 1994; Rank Prize in Nutrition (UK) 1986, David Gottlieb Medal, Univ. of Illinois 1986, ACS Hendricks Medal 1987, John Scott Award, City of Philadelphia 2000, Benjamin Franklin Medal in Life Sciences, Franklin Inst. 2002, CSSA Presidential Award, Crop Science Soc. of America 2011, World Food Prize (co-recipient) 2013. *Publications:* more than 100 scientific publs. *Address:* Syngenta Biotechnology Inc., PO Box 12257, 3054 East Cornwallis Road, Research Triangle Park, NC 27709-2257, USA (office). *Telephone:* (919) 541-8500 (office). *E-mail:* info@syngentabiotech.com (office). *Website:* www.syngentabiotech.com (office).

CHILUMPHA, Cassim, PhD; Malawi politician; ed Univ. of Hull, UK; Minister of Finance 1998–2000; Vice-Pres. and Minister responsible for Statutory Corpns 2004–09; Minister of Energy and Mining April–Dec. 2012; mem. People's Party 2012–. *Address:* c/o People's Party, Lilongwe, Malawi (office).

CHIMPHAMBA, Brown B., BSc, MSc, PhD; Malawi diplomatist, academic and university administrator; *Chairman of the Council, Mzuzu University;* b. 1939, Ntcheu; m.; four c.; ed Fourah Bay Coll., Univ. of Sierra Leone, Univ. Coll. London; various positions at Bunda Coll. of Agric., Univ. of Malawi 1961–81, including Research Assoc., Sr Lecturer, Prof. of Biology, Dean of Faculty of Science, Prin. 1981–90; Prin., Malawi Polytechnic 1991–92; Acting Vice-Chancellor, Univ. of Malawi 1991–92, Vice-Chancellor 1992–2000; Presidential Advisor on Educ. 2000–04; Chair. Nat. AIDS Comm. 2000–04; Perm. Rep. to UN, New York 2004–06; currently Chair. Mzuzu Univ. Council; Fulbright Hayes Fellow; Hon. DLitt (Univ. of Malawi); Certificate of Merit for Devt Work. *Publications include:* numerous scientific publs. *Address:* Mzuzu University, Private Bag 201, Luwinga, Mzuzu 2, Malawi.

CHIMUTENGWENDE, Chenhamo (Chen), MA; Zimbabwean writer, activist and politician; b. 28 Aug. 1943, Mazowe Dist; m. Edith Matore; three s. two d.; ed Univ. of Bradford, UK; Exec. Dir Europe–Third World Research Centre, London 1969–74; Pres. Kwame Nkrumah Inst. of Writers and Journalists, London 1969–77; Deputy Dir and Sr Lecturer in Mass Communications and Int. Affairs, City Univ., London 1978–79; UNESCO Consultant on Mass Communications (Broadcasting) 1979–80; Corresp. for East and Southern Africa, Inter Press Service, Rome 1980–83; Sr Lecturer and Head, School of Journalism, Univ. of Nairobi 1980–82; MP 1985–2008; fmr Minister of Environment and Tourism, of Information, Posts and Telecommunications, of Public and Interactive Affairs; fmr Zanu PF Prov. Chair. for Mashonaland Central; fmr Pres. United New Africa Global Network; Corresp. UNESCO's Int. Social Science Journal 1980–2003; Chair. Africa Star Holdings Ltd 1986; Pres. UN Convention on Climate Change 1996–98; Chair. UN High Level Cttee of Ministers and Sr Officials 1997–98. *Publication:* South Africa: The Press and the Politics of Liberation 1978. *Leisure interests:* music, travelling, reading, public speaking. *Address:* 6 Duthie Road, Belgravia, Harare, Zimbabwe (home). *Telephone:* (4) 704586 (home). *E-mail:* chenchim@yahoo.com (home).

CHIN, Lt-Col Elias Camsek, AA, BA; Palauan army officer and politician; b. 10 Oct. 1949, Peleliu; s. of Taktai Chin and Teiske Kuratomi Chin; m. Miriam Rudimch 1977; one s. one d.; ed Farrington High School, Honolulu, Hawaii, Univ. of Hawaii, Electronic Inst. of Hawaii, Univ. of Hawaii at Manoa, Armor Officer Basic and Advanced Course, US Army Flight School, Air Ground Operations School, US Army Command and Gen. Staff Coll., US Army War Coll., US Army Airborne School, US Army Ranger School, US Army Motor Officer School, US Army Computer School; served for 23 years in army, achieving rank of Lt-Col in US Army before retiring in 1977, commissioned in Armor Corps of US Army 1975, later transferred to Aviation Corps, spent more than 20 years as US Army combat aviator; Minister of Justice 1997–2000, designed and built three-story BRT Building to house Ministry of Justice Office and Bureau of Public Safety Admin; participated in design, building and fund-raising for construction of Father Felix Yaoch Gymnasium 2000; Senator to Sixth Olbiil Era Kelulau (Palau Nat. Congress) 2000–04; Vice-Pres. of Palau 2005–09; Legion of Merit, Meritorious Service Medal with Second Oak Leaf Cluster, Army Commendation Medal with Second Oak Leaf Cluster, Army Achievement Medal with Oak Leaf Cluster, Nat. Defense Service Medal, Army Service Ribbon, Overseas Ribbon, Parachutist

Badge, Army Master Aviator Badge, Ranger Tab. *Leisure interests:* baseball, spear fishing. *Address:* c/o Office of the Vice-President, PO Box 10284, Koror 96940, Palau (office).

CHINAMASA, Patrick Anthony, LLB; Zimbabwean politician; *Minister of Finance;* b. 25 Jan. 1947, Nyanga; s. of Anthony Chinamasa and Regina Maunga; m. Monica Chinamasa; two s. two d.; mem. Zimbabwe African Nat. Union—Patriotic Front (ZANU—PF); fmr Attorney Gen.; Minister of Justice, Legal and Parl. Affairs 2000–13, Acting Minister of Finance Feb. 2009, Minister of Finance 2013–. *Leisure interests:* watching sport, jogging, reading. *Address:* Ministry of Finance, Private Bag 7703, Causeway, Harare, Zimbabwe (office). *Telephone:* (263) 738603 (office). *Fax:* (263) 792750 (office). *Website:* www.mofed.gov.zw (office).

CHINCHILLA MIRANDA, Laura, BA, MA; Costa Rican politician and fmr head of state; b. 28 March 1959, Carmen Central, San José; d. of Rafael Angel Chinchilla Fallas and Emilce Miranda Castillo; m. 1st Mario Alberto Madrigal Díaz 1982 (divorced 1985); one s. with José María Rico Cueto 1996, m. 2000; ed Univ. of Costa Rica, Georgetown Univ., USA; adviser, Ministry of Planning and Political Economy 1989–90; consultant on state reform and structural adjustment programmes 1994–96, including with UNDP, IDB, USAID; Vice-Minister for Public Security and Governance 1994–96, Minister of Public Security 1996–98; Deputy, Asamblea Legislativa (Parl.) 2002–06; Vice-Pres. and Minister for Justice 2006–08, Interim Minister of Public Security April 2008 (resgnd); Pres. of Costa Rica (first woman) 2010–14; mem. Bd Nat. Drugs Council; Pres. Nat. Council on Migration 1996–98; mem. Comm. on Judicial Affairs, mem. Comm. on Int. Affairs 2006–; ranked by Forbes magazine amongst The World's 100 Most Powerful Women (83rd) 2010, (86th) 2011. *Publications:* various publs on admin of justice, public security and police reform. *Address:* Partido Liberación Nacional, Mata Redonda, 125 m oeste del Ministerio de Agricultura y Ganadería, Casa Liberacionista José Figueres Ferrer, Apdo 10051, 1000 San José, Costa Rica.

CHINOFOTIS, Adm. Panagiotis, MA; Greek politician, fmr naval officer and fmr chief of defence; b. 12 Aug. 1949, Athens; m. Maria Chinofotis; ed Hellenic Naval Acad., Hellenic Naval War Coll., Naval War Coll., USA, Salve Regina Univ., Newport, Rhode Island, USA; commissioned as Ensign, Hellenic Navy 1971; fmr Head, Hellenic Navy Gen. Staff (HNGS), NATO and Nat. Exercises and Operational Training; fmr Dir of Studies, Hellenic Naval War Coll.; Commdr, HS Lemnos (warship) 1991–93; worked for Mil. Rep. to NATO 1993–95; Asst Dir Strategic Plans and Policy Directorate, Hellenic Nat. Defence Gen. Staff (HNDGS) 1995–96; Commdr, First Div. of Destroyers and Frigates 1996–97; *Deputy Mil. Rep.* to WEU, Brussels 1997–98, concurrently Chair. Mil. Reps Working Group during Greek presidency of WEU; promoted to Commodore 1998; Deputy Chief of Staff, Hellenic Fleet Command 1998–99; Commdr and Flag Officer, Destroyers and Frigates 1999–2001; Dir A Div. HNGS 2001–02; promoted to Rear-Adm. 2002; Dir D Div. HNDGS 2002–04; C-in-C of Hellenic Fleet 2004–05; promoted to Adm. 2005; Chief of Defence 2005–07; Deputy Minister of Interior 2007–09; mem. New Democracy Party; Hon. Freeman of Newport, Rhode Island, USA, Hon. Freeman of Gavdos Island; Navy Force Formation Command Medal A' and C' Class, Navy Force Meritorious Command Medal A', B' and C' Class, Staff Officer Service Commendation Medal A' and B' Class, Chief of Defence Command Medal, Grand Cross of the Order of Phoenix, Grand Commdr of the Order of Honour. *Address:* 17 Aphrodites Street, Palaio Faliro, Athens 155 61, Greece (home). *Telephone:* (210) 9838797 (home). *E-mail:* chinofotis@yahoo.gr.

CHIOU, I-Jen, MA; Taiwanese politician; b. 9 May 1950; ed Nat. Taiwan Univ. and Univ. of Chicago, USA; Deputy Chief of Staff, Nat. Security Council 2000–02, Sec.-Gen. 2002–03, 2004–07; Sec.-Gen. Exec. Yuan 2000–02, Vice-Pres. 2007–08 (resgnd); Minister without portfolio 2002; Chief of Staff, Office of the Pres. 2003–04, 2007; Minister responsible for Consumer Protection Comm. 2007–08 (resgnd). *Address:* c/o Executive Yuan, 1 Jhongsiao E. Rd, Sec. 1, Taipei 10058, Taiwan (office).

CHIPMAN, John Miguel Warwick, CMG, BA, MA, DPhil; British administrator and academic; *Director-General and Chief Executive, International Institute for Strategic Studies (IISS);* b. 10 Feb. 1957, Montreal, Canada; s. of Lawrence Carroll Chipman and Maria Isabel Prados; m. Lady Theresa Manners 1997; two s.; ed Westmount High School, Montreal, El Estudio, Madrid, Harvard Univ., USA, London School of Econs and Balliol Coll., Oxford; Research Assoc. IISS, London 1983–84; Asst Dir for Regional Security, IISS 1987–91, Dir of Studies 1991–93, Dir IISS 1993, now Dir-Gen. and Chief Exec., Founder IISS Publ Strategic Comments; Research Assoc. Atlantic Inst. for Int. Affairs, Paris 1985–87; Dir Arundel House Enterprises, US Office IISS, Washington, DC, Asia Office IISS, Singapore; mem. Int. Advisory Bd Reliance Industries Ltd, Mumbai; NATO Fellowship 1983. *Achievements include:* was Capt. of Harvard Fencing Team and earned Full Blue while fencing at Oxford. *Publications:* Cinquième République et Défense de l'Afrique 1986, French Power in Africa 1989; ed. and prin. contrib. to NATO's Southern Allies: Internal and External Challenges 1988; articles in journals and book chapters. *Leisure interests:* tennis, skiing, scuba diving, collecting travel books, music. *Address:* International Institute for Strategic Studies, Arundel House, 13–15 Arundel Street, London, WC2R 3DX, England (office). *Telephone:* (20) 7379-7676 (office). *Fax:* (20) 7836-3108 (office). *E-mail:* iiss@iiss.org (office). *Website:* www.iiss.org (office).

CHIPPERFIELD, Sir David Alan, Kt, CBE, DipArch, RA, RIBA; British architect; *Principal, David Chipperfield Architects;* b. 18 Dec. 1953, London, England; s. of Alan John Chipperfield and Peggy Chipperfield (née Singleton); m. Dr Evelyn Stern; two s. one d. and one s. from previous m.; ed Architectural Asscn; Prin. David Chipperfield Architects 1984–; Visiting Prof., Harvard Univ., USA 1987–88, Univ. of Naples, Italy 1992, Univ. of Graz, Austria 1992, Ecole Polytechnique Fédérale de Lausanne, Switzerland 1993–94, London Inst. 1997, Università degli Studi Federico II, Naples 2003, Art Inst., Chicago, USA 2003, Università degli Studi di Sassari, Alghero, Italy 2003, Illinois Inst. of Tech., Chicago 2006; Design Tutor, RCA 1988–89; Prof. of Architecture, Staatliche Akad. der Bildenden Künste, Stuttgart, Germany 1995–2001; Mies van der Rohe Chair, Barcelona School of Architecture, Spain 2001; Hon. Prof., Univ. of the Arts, London 2004–; Royal Designer for Industry 2006; Hon. FAIA 2007; Hon. mem. Bund Deutscher Architekten 2007; Order of Merit (Germany) 2009; Andrea Palladio Prize 1993, RIBA Regional Award 1996, 1998, RIBA Award 1998, 1999, 2002, 2003,

2004, Heinrich Tessenow Gold Medal 1999, Royal Fine Art Comm. Trust/BSkyB Best Building Award 1999, RIBA European and Int. Awards 2007, RIBA Nat. and European Awards 2008, Royal Gold Medal for Architecture 2010, Wolf Foundation Prize in the Arts (Architecture) (jtly) 2010. *Completed projects include:* TAK Design Centre, Kyoto 1990, pvt. museum, Japan 1991, Matsumoto Corp. HQ, Okayama 1992, River and Rowing Museum, Henley-on-Thames, UK 1997, Joseph Menswear, Sloane Avenue, London 1997, Kaistrasse Studios, Düsseldorf 1997, Joseph Store, Sloane Avenue, London 1997, Landeszentralbank HQ, Gera, Germany 2001, Shore Club Hotel, Miami, Ernsting Service Centre, Coesfeld-Lette, Germany 2001, Bryant Park Hotel, New York 2001, Gormley Studio, London 2003, Friedrichstrasse 126, Berlin 2004, Dolce & Gabbana Stores, world-wide 2004, housing, Villaverde, Madrid, Pantaenius House, Hamburg 2005, Hotel Beaumont, Maastricht 2005, Figge Art Museum, Davenport, Ia 2005, Hotel Puerta America, Madrid 2005, Museum of Modern Literature, Marbach am Neckar (RIBA Stirling Prize 2007) 2006, Des Moines Public Library, Ia 2006, America's Cup Bldg 'Veles e Vents', Valencia 2006, BBC Scotland Pacific Quay, Glasgow 2006, Freshfields Bruckhaus Deringer office bldg, Amsterdam 2006, Liangzhu Culture Museum, China 2007, Empire Riverside Hotel, Hamburg 2007, Gallery 'Hinter dem Giesshaus 1', Berlin 2007, Penn Museum Masterplan, Philadelphia 2007, Am Kupfergraben 10, Berlin 2007, Ninetree Village, China, Campus Audiovisual, Barcelona 2008, Kivik Pavilion, Sweden 2008, MW Orthopaedic Centre, Munich 2008, Neues Museum, Berlin 2009, Anchorage Museum, Rasmuson Center, Alaska 2009, City of Justice, Barcelona 2009, Museum Folkwang, Essen 2010, Laboratory bldg, Basel 2010, Kaufhaus Tyrol Dept Store, Innsbruck 2010, Ansaldo City of Cultures, Milan 2011, Salerno Palace of Justice, Italy 2011, The Hepworth Wakefield, W Yorks., UK 2011, Turner Contempary, Margate, UK 2011, Gesellschaftshaus Palmengarten, Frankfurt am Main 2011, Peek & Cloppenburg Flagship Store, Vienna 2011, Aust-Agder Cultural Historic Centre, Arendal, Norway 2012, St Louis Art Museum, St Louis, Mo. 2012, Seal House, London 2012, James Simon Gallery, Berlin 2013. *Publications:* El Croquis (monograph) 1998, 2001, 2004, 2006, David Chipperfield, Idea e Realta 2005, David Chipperfield Architectural Works 1990–2002 2003, David Chipperfield Architects – Form Matters 2009, Neues Museum Berlin 2009. *Address:* David Chipperfield Architects Ltd, 11 York Road, London, SE1 7NX, England (office). *Telephone:* (20) 7620-4800 (office). *Fax:* (20) 7620-4801 (office). *E-mail:* info@davidchipperfield.co.uk (office). *Website:* www.davidchipperfield.co.uk (office).

CHIQUET, Maureen, BA; American business executive; *Global CEO, Chanel SA;* b. 9 March 1963, St Louis, Mo.; m. Antoine Chiquet; two d.; ed Yale Univ.; early career as intern then brand man., L'Oreal, Paris; Merchandise Trainee, Gap Inc., San Francisco 1988, then exec. positions including building Old Navy brand 1994–2002, Pres. Banana Repub. div. 2002–03; Pres. and COO Chanel SA, France 2004–, Global CEO 2007–; mem. Supervisory Bd Vivendi 2009–; mem. Bd of Dirs Peek… Aren't You Curious 2008–; selected by Glamour Magazine as one of the Women of the Year 2008, ranked by Forbes magazine amongst The World's 100 Most Powerful Women (80th) 2007, ranked by Fortune magazine amongst the 50 Most Powerful Women in Business outside the US (13th) 2007, (23rd) 2008, (27th) 2009–12. *Address:* Chanel SA, 135 avenue Charles de Gaulle, 92521 Neuilly-sur-Seine, France (office). *Telephone:* 1-46-43-40-00 (office). *Fax:* 1-47-47-60-34 (office). *Website:* www.chanel.com (office).

CHIRAC, Jacques René; French politician and fmr head of state; b. 29 Nov. 1932, Paris; s. of François Chirac and Marie-Louise Valette; m. Bernadette Chodron de Courcel 1956; two d.; ed Lycée Carnot, Lycée Louis-le-Grand, Ecole Nationale d'Admin and Inst. d'Etudes Politiques, Paris; mil. service in Algeria; auditor, Cour des Comptes 1959–62; Special Asst, Secr.-Gen. of Govt 1962; Special Asst, Pvt. Office of M. Pompidou 1962–65; Counsellor, Cour des Comptes 1965–94; Sec. of State for Employment Problems 1967–68; Sec. of State for Economy and Finance 1968–71; Minister for Parl. Relations 1971–72, of Agriculture and Rural Devt 1972–73, 1973–74, of the Interior March–May 1974; Prime Minister of France 1974–1976, 1986–88; Sec.-Gen. UDR 1974–75, Hon. Sec.-Gen. 1975–76; Pres. RPR (fmrly UDR) 1976–94, Hon. Sec.-Gen. 1977–80; mem. European Parl. 1979; Pres. Regional Council, La Corrèze 1970–79; Municipal Counsellor, Sainte-Féréole 1965–77; Mayor of Paris 1977–95; Pres. of France May 1995–2007; HE The Sovereign Co-Prince of Andorra 1995–2007; Deputy for Corrèze March–May 1967, June–Aug. 1968, March–May 1973, 1976–79, 1981–86, 1988–95; mem. Comm. on Nat. Defence, Nat. Assembly 1980–86; mem. (ex officio) Conseil Constitutionnel 2007–; f. Fondation Jacques Chirac (for sustainable devt and cultural dialogue) 2008; on trial for corruption (first fmr French head of state to stand trial since Philippe Petain) involving the misuse of public money during his time as Mayor of Paris 2011; Grand-Croix, Légion d'honneur, Ordre nat. du Mérite, Croix de la Valeur Militaire, Chevalier du Mérite agricole, des Arts et des Lettres, de l'Étoile noire, du Mérite sportif, du Mérite touristique, Grand Cross of Merit, Sovereign Order of Malta; Prix Louise Michel 1986, Médaille de l'Aéronautique, State Prize of the Russian Federation 2008. *Publications:* Discours pour la France à l'heure du choix, La lueur de l'espérance: réflexion du soir pour le matin 1978, Une Nouvelle France, Réflexions 1 1994, La France pour Tous 1995. *Address:* c/o Conseil Constitutionnel, 2 rue de Montpensier, 75001 Paris, France. *Telephone:* 1-40-15-30-00. *Fax:* 1-40-20-93-27. *E-mail:* relations-exterieures@conseil-constitutionnel.fr. *Website:* www.conseil-constitutionnel.fr.

CHIRICĂ, Andrei; Romanian engineer and organization official; *Chairman, Romanian Association of Telecommunications Engineers;* b. 14 June 1939, Ploieşti; ed Electronics and Telecommunications Coll. of Bucharest; engineer in Radio and TV Dept 1961–68; Chief Engineer, Gen. Direction of Post and Telecommunications 1968–84, then Asst Gen. Dir for matters of research and information in telecommunications, Minister of Communications 1990–94; Pres. Romtelecom SA 1994–95; Pres. C. A. Mobil Rom 1996–; Chair. Romanian Asscn of Telecommunications Engineers (AITR) 2003–. *Publications:* numerous specialized works. *Address:* Asociatia Inginerilor de Telecomunicatii din România, Str. Spatiului nr. 3, 051116, Bucharest 5, Romania (office). *Telephone:* (21) 4005141 (office). *Fax:* (21) 4005721 (office). *E-mail:* andrei.chirica@orange.ro (office); adminstrator@aitr.ro (office). *Website:* www.aitr.ro (office).

CHIRTOACĂ, Dorin; Moldovan politician and government official; *Mayor of Chişinău;* b. 9 Aug. 1978, Chişinău, Moldovan SSR, USSR; s. of Valentina Ghimpu; ed Liceul 'Gheorghe Asachi', Chişinău, Liceul 'C. Negruzzi', Iaşi and Univ. of

Bucharest, Romania, Univ. of Paris I Panthéon-Sorbonne, France; worked for Surprize, Surprize (show broadcast on TVR1) 2001–03; worked for Helsinki Cttee for Human Rights in Moldova 2003–05; Vice-Pres. Liberal Party of Moldova 2005–; Mayor of Chişinău 2007–. *Address:* Office of the Mayor, bd Ştefan cel Mare şi Sfânt 83, Chişinău 2012, Moldova (office). *Telephone:* (22) 221002 (office). *Fax:* (22) 221289 (office). *E-mail:* dorin.chirtoaca@pmc.md (office). *Website:* www.chisinau.md (office).

CHISHOLM, Sir John, Kt, KBE, MSc, FREng, CEng, FIEE; British business executive and international organization official; *Chairman, Nesta;* b. 1946; m. Kitty Chisholm; two c.; ed Univ. of Cambridge; began career with General Motors; fmr Man. Scicon Ltd (part of BP); f. CAP Scientific 1979, fmr Dir CAP Group PLC; Man. Dir Sema Group PLC 1988–91; Chief Exec. DERA 1991–2001; Chief Exec. QinetiQ 2001–05, Exec. Chair. 2005–10; Chair. Medical Research Council 2009–12; Chair. Nesta (charity) 2009–; Pres. Inst. of Eng and Tech. 2005–06; Dir (non-exec.) Expro International PLC 1994–2003, Bespack PLC 1999–2005; Fellow, IEE (Pres. 2005–06), Royal Acad. of Eng, Royal Aeronautical Soc., Inst. of Physics. *Leisure interest:* historic motor racing. *Address:* Nesta, 1 Plough Place, London, EC4A 1DE, England (office). *Website:* www.nesta.org.uk (office).

CHISHOLM, Malcolm H., BS, DrSci, PhD, FRS; British chemist and academic; *Distinguished University Professor, Department of Chemistry, Ohio State University;* b. 15 Oct. 1945, Bombay (now Mumbai), India; s. of Maj. Angus Chisholm and Gweneth Chisholm; m. Cynthia Chisholm; three s.; ed Queen Mary Coll., London Univ.; Postdoctoral Fellow and Lecturer, Univ. of Western Ontario, Canada 1969–72; Lecturer, Princeton Univ., NJ, USA 1972–78; Lecturer, Indiana Univ., Bloomington 1978–2000; Distinguished Prof. of Math. and Physical Sciences, Ohio State Univ. 2000–, Distinguished Univ. Prof., Dept of Chem. 2006–; mem. Advisory Bd several journals including Organometallics 1987–89, Chemical Communications 1989–96, Inorganic Synthesis 1990–, Dalton Transactions 1998–; Guggenheim Fellow 1985–86; Fellow, AAAS 1987–, Royal Soc. 1990, American Acad. of Arts and Sciences 2004, Deutsche Akademie der Naturforscher Leopoldina 2004; Corresp. Fellow, Royal Soc. of Edinburgh 2005; mem. NAS 2005–; various awards from the American Chemical Soc. and the Royal Soc. of Chemistry. *Publications:* over 600 articles in research journals. *Leisure interests:* reading, gardening, squash. *Address:* Department of Chemistry, Ohio State University, 100 West 18th Avenue, Columbus, OH 43210, USA (office). *Telephone:* (614) 292-7216 (office). *Fax:* (614) 292-0368 (office). *E-mail:* chisholm@chemistry.ohio-state.edu (office). *Website:* www.chemistry.ohio-state.edu (office); (office).

CHISHOLM, Sam; New Zealand broadcasting executive; b. 8 Oct. 1939; s. of R. and N. Chisholm; m. Susan Chisholm; one d.; ed King's Coll., South Auckland; CEO and Man. Dir Nine Network, Australia 1976–90, Dir 1980–83; CEO and Man. Dir British Sky Broadcasting (BSkyB) 1990–97, Dir BSkyB 1990–99; Exec. Dir The News Corporation 1993–97; Dir Star TV and Foxtel 1993–97, Telstra 2000–04 Chair. Foxtel 2000–04; Dir Tottenham Hotspur Football Club 1998–2000; Exec. Dir Publishing and Broadcasting Ltd 2004–06; Dir Prime TV New Zealand 2004–06; Chair. Macquarie Radio Network 2002–04; Dir and Life Gov. Victor Chang Cardiac Research Inst. 2000–08; Chair. Chris O'Brien Lifehouse at RPA, Sydney 2010–12, Australian Organ and Tissue Donation Authority 2009–12; Dr hc (Queensland Univ. of Tech.) 2004; Hon. AO 2013; inducted into Australian Television Hall of Fame 2004. *Address:* Bundarbo Station, Jugiong, NSW 2726, Australia (home).

CHISSANO, Joaquim Alberto; Mozambican politician and fmr head of state; *Chairman, Joaquim Chissano Foundation;* b. 22 Oct. 1939, Malehice, Chibuto Dist, Gaza Prov., Portuguese colony of Mozambique (then Portuguese East Africa); m. Marcelina Rafael Chissano; four c.; faculty of medicine in Lisbon, Portugal and Poitiers, France; Founding mem. Frente de Libertação de Mozambique (FRELIMO), Asst Sec. to Pres., FRELIMO in charge of Educ. 1963–66, Sec. to Pres., FRELIMO 1966–69; Chief Rep. FRELIMO in Dar es Salaam 1969–74; Prime Minister, Transitional Govt of Mozambique 1974–75; Minister of Foreign Affairs 1975–86; Pres. of Mozambique and C-in-C of Armed Forces 1986–2005; Pres. FRELIMO 1991–2004; Chair. African Union 2002–04; Special Envoy of the UN Sec.-Gen. for the Lord's Resistance Army-affected areas (Northern Uganda, Democratic Repub. of Congo and Southern Sudan) 2006–09; Chair. Joaquim Chissano Foundation, Forum of Fmr African Heads of State and Govt; mem. Club of Madrid; Order, Augusto César Sandino (Nicaragua) 1988; numerous awards including Chatham House Prize 2006, inaugural $5 million Prize for Achievement in African Leadership, Mo Ibrahim Foundation (given to a fmr African leader who has shown good governance) 2007. *Address:* Fundação Joaquim Chissano, Av. do Zimbabwe 954, Caixa Postal nº 63, Maputo, Mozambique (office); Africa Forum, 351 Schoeman Street, PO Box 6541, Pretoria 0001, South Africa. *Telephone:* (21) 484000 (office); (12) 354-8073. *Fax:* (21) 484001 (office); (12) 354-0857. *E-mail:* info@fjchissano.org.mz (office); info@africaforum.org.za. *Website:* www.fjchissano.org.mz (office).

CHITANAVA, Nodari Amrosievich, PhD; Georgian politician, agricultural specialist and economist; *Director, Economic and Social Problems Research Institute;* b. 10 March 1936, Zugdidi Region, Georgia; s. of Ambrose Chitanava and Tina Chitanava; m. Keto Dimitrovna 1964; two d.; ed Georgian Polytechnic Inst., Moscow High Political School; mem. CPSU 1958–91; Komsomol and party work 1959–; Second Sec. Adzhar obkom 1973–74; Minister of Agric. for Georgian SSR 1974–79; First Deputy Chair., Georgian Council of Ministers 1979–85; Party Sec. for Agric. 1985–89; Chair. Council of Ministers, Georgian SSR 1989–90; Minister of Agric. 1991–93; Dir Econ. and Social Problems Research Inst. 1993–; Chair. Georgian Economists' Soc. *Publications:* 70 scientific works of which there are seven monographs including Social-Economic Problems During Transition Perios (three vols). *Leisure interest:* spending time in the country. *Address:* Institute for Macroeconomics, 16 Zandukeli Str., 380008 Tbilisi; Atheni Str. 16, Tbilisi, Georgia (home). *Telephone:* (32) 93-12-55; (32) 99-75-15 (office); (32) 23-37-53 (home).

CHITOIU, Daniel, PhD; Romanian accountant and politician; b. 11 July 1967; ed Academy of Economic Studies, Bucharest, Inst. of Chartered Accountants of Scotland, UK, Nat. Defence Coll.; Special Insp., Gen. Directorate of State Financial Control, Ministry of Economy and Finance 1990–94; Financial Controller, Court of Accounts of Romania (NAFA) 1994–98, 2001–05; Deputy Gen. Dir, Gen. Directorate of Public Finance and State Financial Control, Ministry of Economy and

Finance 1998–2001, Deputy Chair. (with rank of Sec. of State), Nat. Agency for Fiscal Admin, Co-ordinator of Dept for Admin of State Income, Ministry of Economy and Finance 2005–07, Interim Chair. Nat. Agency for Fiscal Admin Jan.–April 2007, Chair. 2007–08; mem. Nat. Liberal Party (Partidul Naţional Liberal—PNL); mem. Parl. 2008–, Deputy Chair. Comm. for Budget, Finance and Banks 2008–12, mem. 2012–; Minister of the Economy, Trade and the Business Environment May–Dec. 2012; Deputy Prime Minister and Minister of Public Finance 2012–14; Pres. Romanian Chamber of Fiscal Consultants. *Address:* National Liberal Party (PNL) (Partidul Naţional Liberal), 011866 Bucharest 1, Board Aviatorilor 86, Romania (office). *Telephone:* (21) 2310795 (office). *Fax:* (21) 2310796 (office). *E-mail:* dre@pnl.ro (office); daniel_chitoiu@minind.ro. *Website:* www.pnl.ro (office).

CHITTISTER, Joan D., MA, PhD; American social psychologist, writer and lecturer; *Executive Director, Benetvision;* b. 26 April 1936, Dubois, Pa; d. of Harold C. Chittister and Loretta Cuneo Chittister; ed St Benedict Acad. Erie, Mercyhurst Coll. Erie, Pa, Univ. of Notre Dame and Penn State Univ.; elementary teacher, 1955–59, secondary teacher 1959–74; teacher, Penn State Univ. 1969–71; Pres. Fed. of St Scholastica 1971–78; Prioress, Benedictine Sisters of Erie 1978–90; Pres. Conf. of American Benedictine Prioresses 1974–90; Invited Visiting Fellow, St Edmund's Coll., Cambridge, UK 1995–96; mem. Exec. Bd Ecumenical and Cultural Inst. St John's Univ., Collegeville 1976–98; Exec. Dir Benetvision 1990–; mem. Bd of Dirs Nat. Catholic Reporter 1983–2000; Co-Chair. Global Initiative of Women Religious and Spiritual Leaders 2002–, Network of Spiritual Progressives/Tikkun Community 2005–10; mem. Niwano Peace Foundation, Tokyo 2003–06; 12 hon. degrees; numerous awards, including Notre Dame Alumni Asscn Women's Award of Achievement 1997, Distinguished Alumni Award, Penn State Univ. 2000, Catholic Press Asscn Book Award 1996, 1997, 2001, 2004, 2005, 2006, 2008, 2009, 2011, 2012 (three). *Publications include:* Climb along the Cutting Edge: An Analysis of Change in Religious Life 1977, Women, Church and Ministry 1983, Winds of Change: Women Challenge the Church 1986, The Fire in These Ashes: A Spirituality of Contemporary Religious Life 1995, The Psalms: Meditations for Every Day of the Year 1996, Beyond Beijing: The Next Step for Women 1996, Songs of Joy: New Meditations on the Psalms 1997, Light in the Darkness: New Reflections on the Psalms 1998, Heart of Flesh: A Feminist Spirituality for Women and Men 1998, Gospel Days: Reflections for Every Day of the Year 1999, The Story of Ruth: Twelve Moments in Every Woman's Life 2000, The Illuminated Life: Monastic Wisdom for Seekers of Light 2000, Living Well: Scriptural Reflections for Every Day 2000, The Friendship of Women: A Spiritual Tradition 2000, Scarred by Struggle, Transformed by Hope (Asscn of Theological Booksellers Award) 2003, Twelve Steps to Inner Freedom 2003, In the Heart of the Temple 2004, The Way We Were: A Story of Conversion and Renewal 2005, The Tent of Abraham (co-author) 2006, How Shall We Live? 2006, The Ten Commandments 2006, 25 Windows into the Soul 2007, Welcome to the Wisdom of the World 2007, The Gift of Years 2008, The Breath of the Soul 2009, The Liturgical Year 2009, Uncommon Gratitude (with Rowan Williams) 2010, God's Tender Mercy 2010, The Rule of Benedict: A Spirituality for the 21st Century (second edn) 2010, The Monastery of the Heart 2011, Songs of the Heart 2011, The Radical Christian Life 2011, Happiness 2011, Following the Path 2012, Aspects of the Heart 2012, The Art of Life 2012, The Way of the Cross 2013, The Sacred In Between 2013; more than 700 articles and lectures on religious life, peace and justice and on women in church and society. *Leisure interests:* computers, music, reading. *Address:* St Scholastica Priory, 355 East 9th Street, Erie, PA 16503, USA. *Telephone:* (814) 454-4052. *Fax:* (814) 459-8066. *E-mail:* office@benetvision.org. *Website:* www.joanchittister.org; www.eriebenedictines.org.

CHITTOLINI, Giorgio; Italian historian and academic; b. 9 Dec. 1940, Parma; s. of Gino Chittolini and Diva Scotti; m. Franca Leverotti 1977; one d.; Assoc. Prof. of History, Univ. of Pisa 1974–76, Univ. of Pavia 1976–79; Fellow at Villa I Tatti, Florence 1980; Prof. of Medieval History, Univ. of Parma 1981–84; apptd Prof. Univ. of Milan 1985; mem. Bd of Eds, Società e Storia 1979–; mem. Scientific Cttee, Istituto Storico Italo-Germanico, Trento 1989–; Pres. Centro Studi Civiltà del tardo Medioevo 1990–; mem. Int. Comm. for the History of Towns 1995; mem. Giunta storica nazionale. *Publications include:* La formazione dello stato regionale e le istituzioni del contado 1979, Gli Sforza, la chiesa lombarda e la corte di Roma (1450–1535) 1990, Comunità, Governi e Feudi nell'Italia Centrosettentrionale 1995, Materiali di storia ecclesiastica lombarda (series ed.) 1995, Piccole città, grandi città, territori urbani. *Address:* Via Madre Cabrini 7, 20122 Milan, Italy (home).

CHIU, Cheng-hsiung, BA, MA, PhD; Taiwanese banker and politician; b. 19 Feb. 1942; ed Nat. Taiwan Univ., Ohio State Univ., USA; Deputy Dir-Gen., Dept of Banking, Cen Bank of the Repub. of China, Exec. Yuan 1975–76, Deputy Dir-Gen., Dept of Foreign Exchange 1976–81, Dir-Gen., Dept of Banking 1981–88, Deputy Gov. 1988–96; Pres. Hua Nan Commercial Bank 1988; Minister of Finance 1996–2000; Bd Chair. Grand Cathay Securities Corpn 2000–04, EnTie Commercial Bank 2004–07, Hon. Bd Chair. 2007–08; Vice Premier and Minister of the Consumer Protection Comm. 2008–09. *Address:* c/o Consumer Protection Commission, 1 Jihe Road, Taipei 11166, Taiwan.

CHIUARIU, Tudor, LLB; Romanian lawyer, academic and politician; *Senior Partner, Chiuariu & Associates – Attorneys at Law;* b. 13 July 1976, Botoşani; ed Al. I. Cuza Univ., Iaşi, Police Acad., Bucharest, Cen. European Univ., Budapest, Acad. of European Law, Trier, Germany, Leiden Univ., The Netherlands; attorney at law, Iaşi 2000–; mem. Partidul Naţional Liberal (Nat. Liberal Party) 1997–, Vice-Pres. of Youth Org., Iaşi br. 1997–2002, mem. Political Cttee, Iaşi br. 2001–02; Vice-Pres. Court of Honour and Arbitration 2005–09; Lecturer in Law, Petre Andrei Univ., Iaşi 2000–07, George Bacovia Univ., Bacău 2008–; Sec. of State, Office of the Prime Minister 2005–07; Minister of Justice 2007; mem. Parlamentul României 2008–; Pres. Inter-Ministerial Comm. on Civil Servants' Pay System 2005–06; Vice-Pres. Justice and Human Rights Comm. 2002–05; mem. Implementation of Nat. Anticorruption Strategy Cttee 2005–07; currently Sr Pnr, Chiuariu & Assocs; mem. Romanian Bar Asscn 2000–. *Publications include:* numerous articles on Romanian law in professional journals. *Address:* Bd Aviatorilor 52, Etaj 3, Sector 1, 011864 Bucharest, Romania (office). *Telephone:* (21) 3161074 (office). *Fax:* (21) 3161075 (office). *E-mail:* tudor@chiuariulawyers.ro (office). *Website:* www.chiuariulawyers.ro (office); www.cdep.ro (office).

CHIZEN, Bruce R., BS; American business executive; *Venture Partner, Voyager Capital Ltd;* b. 5 Sept. 1955; m.; one s. one d.; ed Brooklyn Coll., City Univ. of New York; Retail Merchandising Man. (Eastern Region) Mattel Electronics 1980–83; Sales Dir (Eastern Region) Microsoft Corpn 1983–87; Founding Sr Man. Claris Corpn 1987, later Vice-Pres. Sales, Worldwide Marketing, Vice-Pres. and Gen. Man. Claris Clear Choice; joined Adobe Systems Inc. 1994, Vice-Pres. and Gen. Man. Graphics Professional Div. and Consumer Div., later Exec. Vice-Pres. Worldwide Products and Marketing, Pres. Adobe Systems Inc. 1999–2005, CEO 2000–07, Strategic Advisor 2007; Sr Advisor, Permira Advisers Ltd 2009–; Venture Partner, Voyager Capital 2009–; Dir Synopsys, Inc. 2001–, PBS Foundation 2005–, Oracle Corpn 2008–, Corpn 2008–, Children's Discovery Museum of San Jose. *Address:* Voyager Silicon Valley, 3000 Sand Hill Road, 3-100, Menlo Park, CA 94025, USA (office). *Telephone:* (650) 854-4300 (office). *Fax:* (650) 854-4399 (office). *Website:* www.voyagercapital.com (office).

CHIZHOV, Ludvig Aleksandrovich; Russian diplomatist; b. 25 April 1936, Radornishl, Zhitomir Region; m.; one s. one d.; ed Moscow Inst. of Int. Relations; fmr mem. CPSU; attaché, Embassy in Tokyo 1960–65, First Sec., Counsellor, 1971–77; Third Sec., Second Sec., Second Far Eastern Dept, Ministry of Foreign Affairs 1966–70, Counsellor, Second Far Eastern Dept 1978–80; Minister Counsellor, Embassy in Tokyo 1980–86; Head of Pacific Ocean Countries Dept, Ministry of Foreign Affairs 1986–89; Russian Amb. to Japan 1990–96; Amb.-at-Large 1996–98; Dir 3rd European Dept, Ministry of Foreign Affairs 1998–2001, on staff of Ministry 2001–2003, Deputy Minister 2003–. *Leisure interests:* music, reading. *Address:* c/o Ministry of Foreign Affairs, 119200 Moscow, Smolenskaya-Sennaya pl. 32/34, Russia (office). *Telephone:* (495) 244-16-06 (office). *Fax:* (495) 230-21-30 (office). *E-mail:* ministry@mid.ru (office). *Website:* www.mid.ru (office).

CHKHEIDZE, Prince; Peter, Dr of Law; Georgian lawyer and diplomatist; *Vice-President, Assembly of Georgian Peoples;* b. 22 Oct. 1941, Tbilisi; s. of the late Peter Chkheidze and Julia Chkheidze; m. Manana Chkheidze 1963; two s.; ed Tbilisi Nat. Univ., Diplomatic Acad. of USSR Ministry of Foreign Affairs and Inst. of State and Law, USSR Acad. of Sciences; various positions with Attorney Service of Repub. of Georgia 1963–75; First Sec., Dept of Int. Orgs, Ministry of Foreign Affairs of USSR 1978; First Sec., Counsellor, then Chief of Dept, Perm. Mission of USSR to the UN 1978–84; leading posts in nat. state and public insts 1984–89; Chair. Ind. Trade Unions Confed. of Repub. of Georgia 1989–91; Deputy Prime Minister of Repub. of Georgia and Perm. Rep. of Govt of Georgia to USSR, later to Russian Fed. 1991–92; Chargé d'affaires a.i., Moscow 1992–93; Amb. to USA 1993–94; Amb. and Perm. Rep. to UN 1993–2002; Amb. to Turkmenistan (also accred to Afghanistan) 2002–04; Vice-Pres. and Exec. Dir Int. Public Org. 'Ass. of Georgian Peoples'; mem. Int. Informatization Acad. 1994–. *Publications:* various publs in fields of law and int. relations 1975–95. *Leisure interests:* literature, art, horse riding. *Address:* Picasso 50, Tbilisi 0183, Georgia (home). *Telephone:* (32) 2537595 (home); 59-9405375 (mobile); 7903-1047033 (mobile). *Fax:* (32) 2537593 (home). *E-mail:* chkheidze7@hotmail.com (office). *Website:* www.georgianpeoples.com (office).

CHKHEIDZE, Revaz (Rezo) Davidovich; Georgian film director; *President, Georgian Film;* b. 8 Dec. 1926, Tbilisi; s. of David Chkheidze and Serapime Gogodze; m. Tinatin Gambashidze 1950 (died 2004); one s. two d.; ed Tbilisi State Theatrical Inst., VGIK Moscow (Film School); Pres. Georgian Film 1972–; Deputy USSR Supreme Soviet 1974–84; Chair. of Cinema 1995–; Prof. of Theatre and Cinema, Univ. of Tbilisi 1997–; USSR People's Artist 1980; All-Union Festival Prize 1973; Lenin Prize 1986, Prize for Prominent Contrib. in the World Cinematography 2005–06. *Films include:* Magdana's Donkey (Golden Palm, Int. Cinema Festival Cannes, Diploma, Edinburgh Int. Festival 1956) 1956 (with T. Abuladze), Our Yard (Golden Medal and First Prize, World Festival of Youth Moscow) 1957, Treasure (Jury Prize, Delhi Int. Film Festival 1961) 1961, A Soldier's Father (Cork Int. Film Festival Prize 1965, Best Foreign Film, Salonik Int. Film Festival, Diploma of San Francisco Festival, Capitol of Rome Prize 1965) 1965, Our Youth 1970, The Seedlings (Special Prizes and Diplomas, Moscow Int. Film Festival) 1973, Your Sun, Earth (Prize and Diploma, All-Union Festival of Vilnius 1981) 1981, Life of Don Quixote and Sancho 1989. *Publications:* Cinema and Life. *Leisure interests:* reading, football. *Address:* Larsi Street 5, Apt 3, 010079 Tbilisi, Georgia (home). *Telephone:* (32) 520627 (office). (32) 525674 (home). *E-mail:* tamarchkheidze2000@yahoo.com (home).

CHKHEIDZE, Temur Georgyevich; Georgian theatre director; *Artistic Director, Tovstonogov Bolshoi Drama Theater;* b. 18 Nov. 1943, Tbilisi; ed Tbilisi Rustaveli State Theatre Inst.; Dir Municipal Zugdidi Drama Theatre 1965–67; Dir Georgia Young Spectators Theatre, Tbilisi 1967–70; Dir Tbilisi Academic Rustaveli Theatre 1970–80; Artistic Dir Academic Mardzhanishvili Theatre, Tbilisi 1980–91; Dir Tovstonogov Bolshoi Drama Theatre 1991–2004, Prin. Dir 2004–07, Artistic Dir 2007–; has appeared as producer at St Peterburg Maryinsky Theatre and Milan La Scala;; Peoples Artist of Russia and Georgia, Lenin Prize 1986. *Address:* Tovstonogov Bolshoi Drama Theater, 190023 St Petersburg, ul. Fontanka 65, Russia (office). *Telephone:* (812) 310-20-05 (office). *E-mail:* bdt@bdt.spb.ru (office). *Website:* www.bdt.spb.ru/theatre.html (office).

CHO, Dae-sik, BA, MBA; South Korean business executive; *Co-CEO and President, SK Holdings Co. Ltd;* ed Korea Univ., Clark Univ., USA; Sr Vice-Pres. of Finance Man. and Strategy Office, SK Holdings Co. Ltd 2007–08, Head of Business Man. Office 2010–11, Chief Financial Officer, Head of Finance Team, Risk Man. and Corp. Auditing Office 2012–13, Co-CEO and Pres. 2013–, Chair. and Sr Man. Dir SK Securities Co. Ltd, Inside Dir, SK Telecom Co. Ltd 2013–. *Address:* SK Holdings Co. Ltd, 99 Seorin-Dong, Jongru-Gu, Seoul 110-110, South Korea (office). *Telephone:* (2) 2121-5114 (office). *Fax:* (2) 2121-7001 (office). *E-mail:* Byc778@sk.com (office). *Website:* www.sk.com (office); www.skenergy.com (office).

CHO, Fujio; Japanese automobile industry executive; *Honorary Chairman, Toyota Motor Corporation;* b. 2 Feb. 1937, Tokyo; m. Emiko Cho; two s.; ed Tokyo Univ.; joined Toyota Motor Corpn 1960, apprentice 1960–66, Production Control Div. 1966–74 (Man. 1974–84), Man. Logistics Admin and Project Man., Production Control Div. 1984–86, Admin Man. 1986–87, Man. Toyota N America Project and Exec. Vice-Pres., Toyota Motor Manufacturing USA 1987–88, Pres. Toyota Motor Manufacturing USA 1988–94, Man. Dir Toyota Motor Corpn 1994–96, Sr Man. Dir 1996–98, Exec. Vice-Pres. 1998–99, CEO and Pres. 1999–2005, Vice-Chair. then

Chair. and Rep. Dir 2006–13, Hon. Chair. 2013–; Ind. Dir, Sony Corpn 2006–12; Vice-Chair. Japan Business Fed. (Nippon Keidanren) 2005–; Chair. Japan Automobile Mfrs Asscn 2006–08, Aioi Insurance Co. Ltd; mem. Advisory Bd Development Bank of Japan Inc.; Hon. British Consul Gen. for Prefectures of Gifu, Mie and Aichi 2007; Officier, Légion d'honneur 2004, Kt Commdr, Most Excellent Order of the British Empire 2006, Grand Cordon, Order of the Rising Sun 2009; included by Time magazine in list of 100 Most Influential People of 2004. *Leisure interests:* golf, fishing, listening to classical music. *Address:* Toyota Motor Corpn, 1 Toyota-Cho, Toyota City, Aichi Prefecture 471-8571, Japan (office). *Telephone:* (5) 6528-2121 (office). *Fax:* (5) 6523-5800 (office). *Website:* www.toyota-global.com (office); www.toyota.co.jp (office).

CHO, Hwan-eik, BA, MBA, PhD; South Korean politician, academic and business executive; *President and CEO, Korea Electric Power Corporation;* ed Choongang High School, Seoul Nat. Univ., New York Univ., USA, Hanyang Univ.; fmr Pres. Korea Trade-Investment Promotion Agency; fmr Vice-Minister of Commerce, Industry and Energy; fmr CEO Korea Export Insurance Corpn; mem. Bd of Dirs, Pres. and CEO Korea Electric Power Corpn 2012–; Dir, Samsung Electro-Mechanics Co. Ltd; Chair-Prof., Hanyang Univ., Ansan Campus. *Address:* Korea Electric Power Corporation, 411 Yeongdong-daero, Gangnam-gu, Seoul 135-791, South Korea (office). *Telephone:* (2) 3456-3114 (office). *Fax:* (2) 556-3694 (office). *E-mail:* info@kepco.co.kr (office). *Website:* www.kepco.co.kr (office).

CHO, Ramaswamy, BSc, BL; Indian journalist, playwright, actor, lawyer and political commentator; b. 5 Oct. 1934, Madras (now Chennai); s. of R. Srinivasan and Rajammal Srinivasan; m. 1966; one s. one d.; ed P.S. High School, Loyola Coll., Vivekananda Coll., Madras and Madras Law Coll., Madras Univ.; practiced as lawyer, Madras High Court 1957; Legal Adviser to T.T.K. Group of Cos 1961–; film scriptwriter and actor 1966–; theatre dir, actor and playwright 1958–; Ed. Thuglak (Tamil political fortnightly) 1970–; Pres. People's Union of Civil Liberties, Tamilnadu 1980–82; nominated mem. of Rajya Sabha (Parl.) 1999–2005; Haldi Gati Award, Maharana of Mewar, for nat. service through journalism 1985, Veerakesari Award for investigative journalism 1986, B. D. Goenka Award for Excellence in Journalism, Panchajanya Award for promotion of nationalism 1998. *Publications:* 23 plays and 10 novels in Tamil; numerous articles on politics, in English and Tamil. *Leisure interest:* photography. *Address:* 46 Greenways Road, Chennai 600 028; 35 Meena Bagh, New Delhi 110 011, India. *Telephone:* (44) 4936913 (Chennai); (11) 3792520 (New Delhi). *Fax:* (44) 24936915. *Website:* www.thuglak.com.

CHO, Yang-ho, MBA; South Korean business executive; *Chairman and CEO, Korean Air;* b. 1949, Incheon; m.; one s. two d.; ed Inha Univ.; joined Korean Air as Man., Americas Regional HQ 1974, becoming Pres. and CEO Korean Air 1992–99, Chair. and CEO 1999–; fmr CEO Korea Airport Service Co. Ltd (currently a Dir); Hanjin Information Systems & Transportation (HIST) Co. (currently a Dir); Chair. S-Oil Corpn 2008–; mem. Bd of Dirs Hanjin Information Systems & Telecommunication Co. Ltd; Commdr, Legion d'onneur; Moran Medal (Korea). *Address:* Korean Air Operations Centre, 1370, Gonghang-dong, Gangseo-gu, Seoul 157-712, South Korea (office). *Website:* www.koreanair.com (office).

CHO, Yung-kil; South Korean politician and army officer (retd); b. 9 May 1940, Yongkwangkun, Chollanamdo Prov.; m. Kang Suk; one s. two d.; ed Kwangju Soongil High School, Army Coll., Nat. Defence Coll., Grad. School of Public Admin, Dongkuk Univ.; commissioned Second Lt 1962; Co. Commdr Tiger Unit, Vietnam War 1962–70; Commdr 26th Brigade, Capital Mechanized Div. 1983–84; Chief of Strategic Planning, Policy Planning Office, Army HQ 1984–87, Dir Special Inspection Group 1987–88, Dir of Strategic Planning 1989–91; Dean of Faculty, Nat. Defence Univ. 1988–89; Commdg Gen. 2nd Corps 1995–97, 2nd Repub. of Korea Army 1998–99; Chair. of Jt Chiefs of Staff 1999–2001; Minister of Nat. Defence 2003–04 (resgnd); United States Legion of Merit 2000, 2001 Order of Mil. Merit Hwarang Medal 1970, Vietnam Hero Medal (Silver) and Bronze Star 1970, United States Bronze Star 1970, Order of Nat. Security Medal (Cheonsu) 1987, (Gukson) 1996, (Tongil) 1999. *Address:* c/o Ministry of National Defence, 1, 3-ga, Yonsan-dong, Yeongsan-gu, Seoul, Republic of Korea (office).

CHOBANOV, Petar, MA, PhD; Bulgarian politician; *Minister of Finance;* b. 20 July 1976, Yambol; ed Univ. of Nat. and World Economy, Sofia; fmr Assoc. Prof. of Int. Finance, Univ. of Nat. and World Economy; Sr Expert at Analyses Unit, Treasury Directorate, Bulgarian Nat. Bank –2005; Exec. Dir Agency for Econ. Analysis and Forecasting 2005–09, participated in the drafting of strategic programme documents, including Convergence Programme and Nat. Strategic Reference Framework; Chair. Financial Supervision Comm. 2009–10; Minister of Finance 2013–, Gov. for Bulgaria, EIB, London, UK. *Address:* Ministry of Finance, 1040 Sofia, ul. G.S. Rakovski 102, Bulgaria (office). *Telephone:* (2) 639-26-34 (office). *Fax:* (2) 987-05-81 (office). *E-mail:* press-office@minfin.bg (office). *Website:* www.minfin.bg (office).

CHOE, Jin Su; North Korean diplomatist; b. 1941, S Hwanghae Prov.; ed Univ. of Int. Affairs, Pyongyang; began career in Ministry of Foreign Affairs, posted to Embassy in Brunei 1969, in Burkina Faso 1974, to Trade Rep. Office, Paris 1978, later Head of W European Affairs, Ministry of Foreign Affairs, Amb. to Switzerland 1986–89, to China 2000–10; Deputy Chief, Workers' Party Cen. Cttee Int. Dept 1995–2000. *Address:* Ministry of Foreign Affairs, Pyongyang, North Korea.

CHOE, Tae-bok; North Korean engineer, academic and government official; *Chairman of Supreme People's Assembly;* b. 1929, N Hamgyong Prov.; ed Mangyongdae Revolutionary School and studies in GDR; Prof. of Chemical Eng, Hamhung Tech. Eng Coll. 1961; Dean of Kimcakeh Eng Coll. 1978, Chair. Educ. Comm. 1981; Minister of Higher Educ. 1985; Sec., Worker's Party Cen. Cttee 1986–; Assoc. mem. Politburo 1990–; Chair. Choe Ko In Min Hoe Ui (Supreme People's Ass.) 1998–. *Address:* Choe Ko In Min Hoe Ui, Pyongyang, Democratic People's Republic of Korea (office).

CHOE, Yong-rim; North Korean politician; b. 20 Nov. 1930; ed Mangyongdae Revolutionary School, Kim Il-sung Univ., Lomonosov Moscow State Univ., USSR; fmr Chief Public Prosecutor; Sec.-Gen., Presidium of Supreme People's Ass. 2005–09; mem. Korean Workers' Party (KWP), Alt. mem. KWP Political Bureau, Chief Sec., Pyongyang City Cttee 2009–10; Premier, Democratic People's Repub. of

Korea 2010–13. *Address:* c/o Korean Workers' Party, Pyongyang, Democratic People's Republic of Korea (office).

CHOEDRA, His Holiness the 70th Je Khenpo Trulku Jigme; Bhutanese ecclesiastic; *Chairman, Council for Ecclesiastical Affairs;* followers believe him to be reincarnation of Maitreya, as well as the Mahasiddha Saraha, Hungchen Kara, Kheuchung Lotsawa, and His Holiness Pema Tsering; elected 70th Je Khenpo of Bhutan 1996, title given to highest religious official of Bhutan, Leader of Cen. Monk Body, also formally the leader of Drukpa sect of Kagyupa School of Tibetan Buddhism; adviser to the King; Chair. Council for Ecclesiastical Affairs (Dratshang Lhentshog). *Address:* Council for Ecclesiastical Affairs (Dratshang Lhentshog), POB 254, Thimphu, Bhutan (office). *Telephone:* (2) 322754 (office). *Fax:* 2) 323867 (office). *E-mail:* dratsang@druknet.bt (office).

CHOI, Gee-sung; South Korean business executive; *Vice-Chairman, Corporate Strategy Office, Samsung Electronics;* b. 2 Feb. 1951; ed Seoul Nat. Univ.; began career at Samsung C&T's Int. Trade Div. 1977, Chief Design Officer and est. co.'s chip business in Europe 1980s, Head, Memory Sales and Marketing, Semiconductor Business, Samsung Electronics 1994–98, Head, Visual Display Div. 1998–2003, Head, Digital Media Business 2003–07, Head, Corp. Design Centre 2007–09, Head, Mobile Communications Div., Head, Telecommunications Networks Business, Pres. and Head, Digital Media and Communications Business 2009, Pres. and CEO Samsung Electronics 2010, Vice-Chair. and CEO 2010–12, Vice-Chair., Corp. Strategy Office 2012–. *Address:* Samsung Electronics Bldg, 1320-10 Seocho-2-dong, Seocho-gu, Seoul 137-857, Republic of Korea (office). *Telephone:* (2) 2255-0114 (office). *Fax:* (2) 2255-0117 (office). *E-mail:* j-npr@ samsung.co.kr (office). *Website:* www.samsung.com (office).

CHOI, Kil-seon; South Korean business executive; s. of Choi Ma-am and Yu Ok-soon; m. Yang Yang-ja 1971; two c.; ed Seoul Nat. Univ.; Lt in Korean Army 1969–71; Exec. Vice-Pres. Hyundai Heavy Industries Co. Ltd (HHI) 1972–92, Pres. Halla Engineering and Heavy Industries (subsidiary co.) 1993–99, Pres. Hyundai Mipo Dockyard, Ulsan 2004–05, Pres. and Co-CEO HHI 2005–11, mem. Bd Dirs 2008–11; Chair. Korea Shipbuilders' Asscn 2003–05; Korean Govt Order of Industrial Merit 1977, Korea CEO Forum Grand Prix Award 2006. *Address:* c/o Hyundai Heavy Industries Co. Ltd, 1, 1, Jeonha-dong, Dong-gu, Gyeonsang nam-do, Ulsan, 682-792, Republic of Korea. *E-mail:* ir@hhi.co.kr.

CHOI, Man-Duen, PhD, FRSC; Canadian mathematician and academic; *Professor of Mathematics, University of Toronto;* b. 13 June 1945, Nanking, China; m. Pui-Wah Ip 1972; two s. one d.; ed Chinese Univ. of Hong Kong, Univ. of Toronto; Lecturer, Dept of Math., Univ. of California, Berkeley 1973–76; Asst Prof., Dept of Math., Univ. of Toronto 1976–79, Assoc. Prof. 1979–82, Prof. of Math. 1982–; mem. American Math. Soc., Canadian Math. Soc., Math. Asscn of America; Israel Halperin Prize 1980, Coxeter-James Prize, Canadian Math. Soc. 1983. *Publications:* numerous articles in mathematical journals. *Leisure interests:* yoga, stamps. *Address:* Department of Mathematics, BA6234, University of Toronto, Toronto, ON M5S 2E4, Canada (office). *Telephone:* (416) 978-3318 (office). *Fax:* (416) 978-4107 (office). *E-mail:* choi@math.toronto.edu (office). *Website:* www.math.toronto .edu (office).

CHOI, Seok-young, BA, MBA; South Korean diplomatist and international organization official; *Deputy Minister for Trade;* b. 1955, Kangleung; m. Kim Young In; one s. one d.; ed Seoul Nat. Univ., Univ. of Heidelberg, Germany, Korea Devt Inst. School of Public Policy and Man.; joined Ministry of Foreign Affairs (MFA) 1979, Consul in Hamburg, Germany 1986–88, First Sec., Embassy in Nairobi 1988–91, Asst Dir Environmental Cooperation Div., MFA 1991–94, Counsellor for Econ. and Trade Affairs, Perm. Mission to UN, Geneva 1994–97, Dir for Environment and Science and Chief Negotiator for 1997 UNGA Special Session, MFA 1997–99, Counsellor and Chief of Econ. Section, Perm. Mission to UN, New York 1999–2002, Adviser to Pres. of UN Gen. Ass. 2001, Deputy Dir-Gen. Multilateral Trade Bureau, MFA 2002–03, Deputy Sr Official to APEC 2002–03, Deputy Exec.-Dir APEC Secr. 2004, Exec.-Dir 2005, Minister of Econ. Affairs, Embassy in Washington, DC 2006, also Deputy Chief of Mission, currently Deputy Minister for Trade; del. to numerous int. and multilateral forums including UN, WTO and APEC. *Publications:* numerous articles on trade, environmental issues and climate change negotiations. *Address:* Ministry of Foreign Affairs and Trade, 37, Sejong-no, Seoul 110-787, South Korea (office). *Telephone:* (2) 2100-2114 (office). *Fax:* (2) 2100-7999 (office). *E-mail:* web@mofat.go.kr (office). *Website:* www .mofat.go.kr (office).

CHOI, Maj.-Gen. Young-bum; South Korean army officer and UN official; *Chief Military Observer and Head, Military Observer Group in India and Pakistan (UNMOGIP), United Nations;* b. 1959; m.; two c.; ed Army Infantry School, Army War Coll., Jt Staff Coll., US Defense System Man. Coll., USA; commissioned into South Korean Army 1982, Commdr Medical Support Group, UN Mission for Referendum in Western Sahara (MINURSO) 2000, Chief, Civil Mil. Cooperation, Centre of Repub. of Korea contingent in Iraq 2006, has also served as Chief Dir, Wartime Operational Control Transition Group, Chief, Ground Forces Br., Korea-US Combined Forces Command, Commdr 111th Regt, 37th Infantry Div.; Chief Mil. Observer and Head, UN Mil. Observer Group in India and Pakistan (UNMOGIP) 2012–; Visiting Scholar, Univ. of Maryland, George Washington Univ. *Address:* United Nations Military Observer Group in India and Pakistan (UNMOGIP), Department of Peacekeeping Operations, United Nations, New York, NY 10017, USA (office). *Telephone:* (212) 963-1234 (office). *Fax:* (212) 963-4879 (office). *Website:* www.un.org/en/peacekeeping/missions/unmogip (office).

CHOI, Young-jin; South Korean diplomatist and UN official; b. 29 March 1948, Seoul; m.; two s.; ed Dept of International Relations, Yonsei Univ., Univ. of Paris I (Panthéon-Sorbonne), Fletcher School of Law, Tufts Univ., Boston; Political Officer, Embassy in Dakar 1977–78, in Paris 1979–81; Dir Cultural Exchanges Div., Ministry of Foreign Affairs, Seoul 1981; Political Counsellor, Embassy in Tunis 1983–85; Dir Int. Orgs Div., Ministry of Foreign Affairs, Seoul 1986, Sr Asst to Minister for Foreign Affairs 1987; Econ. Counsellor, Embassy in Washington, DC 1988–90; First Sr Coordinator, Office of Policy Planning, Ministry of Foreign Affairs, Seoul 1991–93, Dir-Gen. Int. Econ. Affairs Bureau 1994–95; Deputy Exec. Dir, Korean Peninsula Energy Devt Org., New York 1995–97; UN Asst Sec.-Gen. for Peacekeeping Operations 1998–99; Deputy Minister for Policy Planning and Int. Orgs, Seoul 2000–01; Amb. to Austria and Solvenia 2002, also Perm. Rep. to all

int. orgs in Vienna 2002; Chancellor, Inst. of Foreign Affairs and Nat. Security (IFANS), Ministry of Foreign Affairs and Trade 2003; Vice-Minister for Foreign Affairs and Trade 2004–05; Perm. Rep. to UN, New York 2005–07; Special Rep. of the UN Sec.-Gen. in Côte d'Ivoire 2007–12; Amb. to USA 2012–13. *Address:* Ministry of Foreign Affairs, 37, Sejong-no, Seoul 110-787, Republic of Korea (office). *Telephone:* (2) 2100-2114 (office). *Fax:* (2) 2100-7999 (office). *E-mail:* web@ mofa.go.kr (office). *Website:* www.mofa.go.kr (office).

CHOJNACKA, Elisabeth, MA; French harpsichordist; *Professor of Contemporary Harpsichord, Mozarteum Academy of Music;* b. 10 Sept. 1939, Warsaw, Poland; d. of Tadeusz Chojnacki and Edwarda Chojnacka; m. Georges Lesèvre 1966; ed Warsaw Acad. of Music, Ecole Supérieure de Musique and with Aimée van de Wiele, Paris; first recital of contemporary harpsichord, L'Arc, Paris 1971; a performer of contemporary music, she has inspired many composers (including Xenakis, Ligeti, Halffter, Donatoni, Ferrari, Bussotti, Górecki, Takemitsu, etc.) to write works for and dedicate works to her; has created completely new repertoire for solo modern harpsichord, initiated repertoire combining harpsichord with organ, percussion, bandéon, orchestra; soloist with Orchestre de Paris, Cleveland and Minneapolis Orchestras 1974, Suisse Romande Orchestra 1979, Orchestre National de France 1981; Prof. of Contemporary Harpsichord, Mozarteum Acad. of Music, Salzburg 1995–; numerous tours in Europe, USA, Japan and Mexico; appearances at prin. festivals of contemporary music; masterclasses; collaborations with choreographer Lucinda Child 1991–; numerous recordings of classical and contemporary music; Chevalier, Légion d'honneur, Officier des Arts et des Lettres, Croix d'Officier, Ordre de Mérite pour la Pologne; First Prize, Int. Harpsichord Competition, Vercelli, Italy 1968, Orphée Prize 1981, 2000, Grand Prix de la SACEM 1983, Polish Union of Composers' Gloria Artis Medal for Culture 2009. *Publications:* articles in La Revue Musicale. *Leisure interests:* cinema, literature, dancing, genetics, astrophysics, theatre, ballet, paintings. *Address:* 17 rue Emile Dubois, 75014 Paris, France (home). *Telephone:* 1-45-89-52-82 (office); 1-45-65-17-20 (home). *Fax:* 1-45-65-31-90 (office). *E-mail:* e.chojnacka@free.fr (office).

CHOLING, Padma, (Baima Chilin); Chinese (Tibetan) government official; *Governor of Tibet;* b. Oct. 1951, Dengqen, Qamdo Pref.; ed Graduate School, CCP Central Party School; served in People's Liberation Army 1969–86; joined CCP 1970; joined regional govt, Tibet (Xizang) Autonomous Region 1986, Vice-Chair. (Deputy Gov.), Autonomous Region People's Govt 2003–10, Gov. of Tibet 2010–, also Deputy Sec. CCP Tibet Autonomous Regional Cttee 2010–. *Address:* c/o People's Government of Tibetan Autonomous Region, 85000 Lhasa, Tibet, People's Republic of China (office).

CHOMSKY, (Avram) Noam, MA, PhD; American theoretical linguist and writer; *Professor Emeritus, Department of Linguistics, Massachusetts Institute of Technology;* b. 7 Dec. 1928, Philadelphia; s. of William Chomsky and Elsie Simonofsky; m. Carol Schatz 1949 (died 2008); one s. two d.; ed Univ. of Pennsylvania; Asst Prof., MIT 1955–58, Assoc. Prof. 1958–61, Prof. of Modern Languages 1961–66, Ferrari P. Ward Prof. of Modern Languages and Linguistics 1966–76, Inst. Prof. 1976–, currently Prof. Emer.; Visiting Prof., Columbia Univ. 1957–58; NSF Fellow, Inst. for Advanced Study, Princeton, NJ 1958–59; American Council of Learned Socs Fellow, Center for Cognitive Studies, Harvard Univ. 1964–65; Linguistics Soc. of America Prof., UCLA 1966; Beckman Prof., Univ. of California, Berkeley 1966–67; John Locke Lecturer, Univ. of Oxford 1969; Shearman Lecturer, Univ. Coll., London 1969; Bertrand Russell Memorial Lecturer, Univ. of Cambridge 1971; Nehru Memorial Lecturer, Univ. of Delhi 1972; Whidden Lecturer, McMaster Univ. 1975; Huizinga Memorial Lecturer, Univ. of Leiden 1977; Woodbridge Lecturer, Columbia Univ. 1978; Kant Lecturer, Stanford Univ. 1979; Jeanette K. Watson Distinguished Visiting Prof., Syracuse Univ. 1982; Pauling Memorial Lecturer, Oregon State Univ. 1995; mem. American Acad. of Arts and Sciences, Linguistic Soc. of America, American Philosophical Assen, American Acad. of Political and Social Science, NAS, Bertrand Russell Peace Foundation, Deutsche Akademie der Naturforscher Leopoldina, Nat. Acad. of Sciences, Royal Anthropological Inst., Utrecht Soc. of Arts and Sciences; Fellow, AAAS; Corresp. Fellow, British Acad.; Hon. Fellow, British Psychological Soc. 1985, Royal Anthropological Inst.; Hon. DHL (Chicago) 1967, (Loyola Univ., Swarthmore Coll.) 1970, (Bard Coll.) 1971, (Massachusetts) 1973, (Maine, Gettysburg Coll.) 1992, (Amherst Coll.) 1995, (Buenos Aires) 1996; Hon. DLitt (London) 1967, (Delhi) 1972, Visva-Bharati (West Bengal) 1980, (Pennsylvania) 1984, (Cambridge) 1995; Dr hc (Tarragona) 1998, (Guelph) 1999, (Columbia) 1999, (Connecticut) 1999, (Pisa) 1999, (Harvard) 2000, (Toronto) 2000, (Western Ontario) 2000, (Kolkata) 2001; George Orwell Award, Nat. Council of Teachers of English 1987, Kyoto Prize in Basic Sciences 1988, James Killian Award, MIT 1992, Helmholtz Medal, Berlin Brandenburgische Akad. Wissenschaften 1996, Benjamin Franklin Medal, Franklin Inst., Philadelphia 1999, Rabindranath Tagore Centenary Award, Asiatic Soc. 2000, Peace Award, Turkish Publrs Assen 2002, UCD Ulysses Medal, University Coll. Dublin 2013. *Film appearance:* Four Horsemen (documentary) 2012. *Publications include:* Syntactic Structures 1957, Current Issues in Linguistic Theory 1964, Aspects of the Theory of Syntax 1965, Cartesian Linguistics 1966, Topics in the Theory of Generative Grammar 1966, Language and Mind 1968, The Sound Pattern of English (with Morris Halle) 1968, American Power and the New Mandarins 1969, At War with Asia 1970, Problems of Knowledge and Freedom 1971, Studies on Semantics in Generative Grammar 1972, For Reasons of State 1973, The Backroom Boys 1973, Counter-revolutionary Violence (with Edward Herman) 1973, Peace in the Middle East? 1974, Reflections on Language 1975, The Logical Structure of Linguistic Theory 1975, Essays on Form and Interpretation 1977, Human Rights and American Foreign Policy 1978, Language and Responsibility 1979, The Political Economy of Human Rights (two vols, with Edward Herman) 1979, Rules and Representations 1980, Lectures on Government and Binding 1981, Radical Priorities 1981, Towards a New Cold War 1982, Concepts and Consequences of the Theory of Government and Binding 1982, Fateful Triangle: The United States, Israel and the Palestinians 1983, Modular Approaches to the Study of the Mind 1984, Turning the Tide 1985, Knowledge of Language: Its Nature, Origins and Use 1986, Barriers 1986, Pirates and Emperors 1986, Generative Grammar: Its Basis, Development and Prospects 1987, On Power and Ideology 1987, Language and Problems of Knowledge 1987, Language in a Psychological Setting 1987, The Chomsky Reader 1987, The Culture of Terrorism 1988, Manufacturing Consent (with Edward Herman) 1988, Language and Politics

1988, Necessary Illusions 1989, Deterring Democracy 1991, What Uncle Sam Really Wants 1992, Chronicles of Dissent 1992, Year 501: The Conquest Continues 1993, Rethinking Camelot: JFK, the Vietnam War and US Political Culture 1993, Letters from Lexington: Reflections on Propaganda 1993, The Prosperous Few and the Restless Many 1993, Language and Thought 1994, World Orders, Old and New 1994, The Minimalist Program 1995, Powers and Prospects 1996, Class Warfare 1996, The Common Good 1998, Profit over People 1998, The New Military Humanism 1999, New Horizons in the Study of Language and Mind 2000, Rogue States: The Rule of Force in World Affairs 2000, A New Generation Draws the Line 2000, Architecture of Language 2000, Propaganda and the Public Mind 2001, 9-11 2001, Understanding Power 2002, On Nature and Language 2002, Middle East Illusions 2003, Hegemony or Survival: America's Quest for Global Dominance 2003, Failed States: America 2006, Interventions 2007, What We Say Goes 2008, Perilous Power (with Gilbert Achcar) 2008, Hopes and Prospects 2010, Gaza in Crisis: Reflections on Israel's War Against the Palestinians (with Ilan Pappé) 2010; numerous lectures, contribs to scholarly journals. *Address:* Department of Linguistics and Philosophy, Massachusetts Institute of Technology, 77 Massachusetts Avenue, Building 32-D808, Cambridge, MA 02139 (office); 15 Suzanne Road, Lexington, MA 02420, USA (home). *Telephone:* (617) 253-7819 (office); (781) 862-6160 (home). *Fax:* (617) 253-9425 (office). *E-mail:* chomsky@mit.edu (office). *Website:* web.mit.edu/linguistics/www (office).

CHONG, Michael; Canadian politician; b. 22 Nov. 1971, Windsor; m. Carrie Davidson 2002; three s.; ed Centre Wellington Dist High School, Fergus, Univ. of Toronto; fmrly with Barclays Bank, Research Capital Corpn; fmr Chief Information Officer Nat. Hockey League Players' Asscn; fmr sr tech. consultant for redevelopment of Pearson Int. Airport, Greater Toronto Airports Authority; co-f. Dominion Inst. 1997, mem. Bd Govs; MP 2004–, mem. House of Commons Standing Cttee on Industry, Natural Resources, Science and Tech. 2004; Pres. Queen's Privy Council for Canada, Minister of Intergovernmental Affairs and of Sport 2006 (resgnd); mem. Corpn Trinity Coll., Univ. of Toronto; mem. Bd Elora Festival. *Address:* House of Commons, Ottawa, ON K1A 0A6, Canada (office). *Telephone:* (613) 992-4179 (office). *E-mail:* Chong.M@parl.gc.ca (office). *Website:* www.michaelchong.ca (home).

CHONG WONG, William, DrLic; Honduran politician; b. Puerto Cortés; ed Univ. of Southern Mississippi, USA; fmr Prof. and Vice-Pres. La Universidad Tecnologica Centroamericana (UNITEC); Dir Internal Revenue Service 1990–92; Deputy Minister of Finance 2002–04, Minister of Finance 2004–06, 2010–12 (resgnd); mem. Partido Nacional. *Address:* c/o Ministry of Finance, 5a Avda, 3a Calle, Tegucigalpa, Honduras.

CHONGWE, Rodger Masauso Alivas, LLB, SC; Zambian lawyer and politician; *President, Liberal Progressive Front (LPF);* b. 2 Oct. 1940, Chipata; m. Gwenda Fay Eaton 1967; one s. one d.; ed St Mark's Coll., Mapanza, Choma, Munali Secondary School, Lusaka, Univ. of Western Australia School of Law, Perth; Native Courts Asst and Dist Asst, Govt of Northern Rhodesia 1962–63; admitted to practise as barrister, solicitor and Proctor of the Supreme Court of Western Australia and the High Court of the Commonwealth of Australia 1968; admitted as solicitor and barrister before all courts, Zambia 1969; Asst Solicitor, Martin & Co., Lusaka 1969–70, Pnr 1979; Pnr, Mwisiya Chongwe & Co., Lusaka 1970–77; owner, RMA Chongwe & Co., Lusaka 1987; apptd State Counsel 1985; mem. Industrial Relations Court of Zambia 1976–87; Lecturer, Law Practice Inst. 1974–83, Examiner 1975; Dir Tazama Pipelines Ltd 1974–89; Local Dir Jos Hansen & Soehne Zambia Ltd 1983; Dir Standard Chartered Bank of Zambia Ltd 1985; Pres. Liberal Progress Front (LPF) party 1993–, Minister of Local Govt and Housing and Legal Affairs 1997, shot by police 1997, fled Zambia and lived in exile in Australia, returned to Zambia 2003; mem. Int. Bar Asscn 1978, mem. Council 1984–86; Councillor Law Asscn of Zambia 1979, Vice-Chair. 1980, Chair. 1981–86, Councillor 1986, Chair. Human Rights Cttee 1986; Chair. African Bar Asscn 1985; mem. Council of Legal Educ. of Zambia 1982; Commr Law Devt Comm. of Zambia 1981; Exec. mem. Commonwealth Lawyers' Asscn 1983, Sec.-Gen. 1986, Pres. 1990; Gov. Art Centre Foundation 1977; Treasurer Int. Asscn of Artists 1983. *Publications:* numerous papers on legal topics, particularly concerning human rights, the legal profession and legal education. *Address:* Liberal Progressive Front (LPF), POB 31190, Lusaka; Subdivision 36, Farm Number 34A, Great East Road, Lusaka, Zambia (home).

CHOO, Kangsoo, BSc, MSc, PhD; South Korean business executive; *Chairman, Korea Gas Corporation (KOGAS);* b. 9 Feb. 1945; ed Seoul Nat. Univ., Dalhousie Univ., NS, Canada, Korea Univ., Seoul; Man., Hyundai Heavy Industries Co. Ltd 1978; Dir and Sr Vice-Pres., Hyundai Corpn 1980–89, Exec. Vice-Pres., Hyundai Resources Devt Inc. 1990–92, Vice-Pres. and CEO 1993–94, Vice-Pres., Hyundai Corpn 1993–98; Korean Pnr, McKnight & Asscs 1999–2006; Advisor, Korea Resources Corpn Jan.–Dec. 2007; Sr Advisor, STX Energy Inc. 2007–08; Pres. and CEO Korea Gas Corpn (KOGAS) 2008–13, Chair. 2013–; Hon. LLD (Dalhousie) 2013; Tin Tower Order of Industrial Service Merit 1987. *Address:* Korea Gas Corpn, 93 Dolmaro, 215 Jeongja-dong, Bundang-gu, Seongnam, Gyeonggi-do, 463-754, South Korea (office). *Telephone:* (31) 710-0114 (office). *Fax:* (31) 710-0117 (office). *E-mail:* kogasmaster@kogas.or.kr (office). *Website:* www.kogas.or.kr (office).

CHOONG, Yong-ahn, MA, PhD; South Korean economist and academic; *Foreign Investment Ombudsman, Korea Trade-Investment Promotion Agency;* ed Kyung-Pook Nat. Univ., Univ. of Hawaii, Ohio State Univ., USA; Prof. of Econs, Chung-Ang Univ. 1974–2006, Chair Prof., Grad. School of Int. Studies 2006–; consultant to World Bank 1978–88, also adviser to Fed. of Korean Industries 1980 and Bank of Korea 1984–87; UNIDO Chief Tech. Adviser to Govt of Malaysia 1990–93; Chair. Chohung Bank 1999–2002; mem. Presidential Econ. Advisory Council 2002–05; Chair. APEC Econ. Cttee 2002–05; Chair. Korean Nat. Cttee for Pacific Econ. Cooperation (KOPEC) 2001; Pres. Korean Inst. for Int. Econ. Policy 2002–05; Foreign Investment Ombudsman, Korea Trade-Investment Promotion Agency (KOTRA) 2006–; mem. Editorial Bd Global Asia (journal); Pres. Korea Econometric Soc. 1991–93, Korea Int. Econs Asscn 1994–95, Devt Econs Asscn 1997–98, Asscn of Trade and Industry Studies 2000–01; mem. Presidential Council on Nat. Competitiveness 2008–; Economist of the Year, Maeil Business Newspaper 1994, Okita Saburo Policy Research Award, Nat. Inst. of Research Investment of Japan 2000, Free Economy Publication Award, Fed. of Korean Industries 2002. *Publi-*

cations: numerous articles and newspapers in journals. *Address:* Office of the Foreign Investment Ombudsman, Korea Trade-Investment Promotion Agency, 6th Floor, KOTRA Bldg, 13, Heolleungno, Seocho-gu, Seoul 137-749, Republic of Korea (office). *Telephone:* (2) 3460-7635 (office). *Fax:* (2) 3460-7949 (office). *Website:* www.investkorea.org (office).

CHOPLIN, Jean-Luc; French arts management executive; *Director, Théâtre du Châtelet;* b. 1951; m.; three d.; Gen. Dir Roland Petit Ballet 1980–84; Man. Dir Paris Opéra Ballet 1984–89; Vice Pres. of Entertainment, Disneyland Paris 1989–95, Vice-Pres. Creative Devt, Walt Disney Co., LA 1995–2001; Artistic Consultant 2001–02; Programme and Devt Advisor, Robert Wilson's Watermill Center, New York 2001–02; CEO Sadler's Wells, London 2002–04; Dir Théâtre du Châtelet, Paris 2006–. *Address:* Théâtre du Châtelet, 1 place du Châtelet, 75001 Paris, France (office). *Telephone:* 1-40-28-28-40 (office). *Website:* www.chatelet-theatre.com (office).

CHOPPIN, Gregory R., PhD; American chemist and academic; *Senior Scientist and Project Director, Radiochemistry, Institute for International Cooperative Environmental Research, Florida State University;* joined Faculty of Florida State Univ. 1956, Chair. Dept of Chem. 1968–76, Robert O. Lawton Distinguished Prof. of Chem., now Prof. Emer., currently Sr Scientist and Project Dir: Radiochemistry, Inst. for Int. Cooperative Environmental Research; consultant, Lawrence Livermore Nat. Lab., Argonne Nat. Lab., Los Alamos Nat. Lab., Sandia Nat. Labs, as well as several pvt. labs; mem. Editorial Bd Chemistry Central Journal; Hon. DSc (Loyola Univ.); Hon. DTC (Chalmers Univ., Sweden); George Hevesy Medal Award 2005. *Publications:* Introductory Chemistry (co-author) 1972, Nuclear Chemistry (co-author) 1980, Nuclear Chemistry: Theory and Applications 1980, Chemistry (co-author) 1982, Lanthanide Probes in Life, Chemical and Earth Sciences: Theory and Practice (co-author) 1990, Principles and Practices of Solvent Extraction (co-author) 1992, Radio Chemistry and Nuclear Chemistry (co-author) 1995, Separations of F Elements: Proceedings of an ACS Symposium of F Elements Separations Held in San Diego, California, March 13–17, 1994 (co-ed.) 1995, Chemical Separation Technologies and Related Methods of Nuclear Waste Management: Applications, Problems, and Research Needs (co-author) 1999, Radiochemistry and Nuclear Chemistry (co-author) 2001, Chemical Separations in Nuclear Waste Management: The State of the Art and a Look to the Future (co-author) 2002; numerous scientific papers in professional journals on inorganic and nuclear chemistry, especially the lanthanide and actinide elements. *Address:* Institute for International Cooperative Environmental Research, Florida State University, 2035 East Paul Dirac Drive (226 HMB), Tallahassee, FL 32310-3700, USA (office). *Telephone:* (850) 644-5524 (office); (850) 644-3875 (office). *Fax:* (850) 574-6704 (office). *E-mail:* choppin@chem.fsu.edu (home); IICER@mailer.fsu.edu (office). *Website:* www.chem.fsu.edu/faculty/choppin.htm (office); iicer.fsu.edu (office).

CHOPPIN, Purnell Whittington, MD; American scientist and academic; *President Emeritus, Howard Hughes Medical Institute;* b. 4 July 1929, Baton Rouge, La.; s. of Arthur Richard Choppin and Eunice Dolores Choppin (née Bolin); m. Joan H. Macdonald 1959; one d.; ed La State Univ.; Intern, Barnes Hosp., St Louis 1953–54, Asst Resident 1956–57; Postdoctoral Fellow, Research Assoc., Rockefeller Univ., New York 1957–60, Asst Prof. 1960–64, Assoc. Prof. 1964–70, Prof., Sr Physician 1970–85, Leon Hess Prof. of Virology 1980–85, Vice-Pres. Acad. Programs 1983–85, Dean of Grad. Studies 1985; Vice-Pres., and Chief Scientific Officer, Howard Hughes Medical Inst. 1985–87, Pres. 1987–99, Pres. Emer. 2000–, Virology 1973–82; Chair. Virology Study Section, NIH 1975–78; mem. Bd of Dirs Royal Soc. of Medicine Foundation Inc., New York 1978–93, Advisory Cttee on Fundamental Research, Nat. Multiple Sclerosis Soc. 1979–84 (Chair. 1983–84), Advisory Council Nat. Inst. of Allergy and Infectious Diseases 1980–83, Sloan-Kettering Cancer Cttee, New York 1983–84, Comm. on Life Sciences, Nat. Research Council 1982–87, Council for Research and Clinical Investigation, American Cancer Soc. 1983–85; Pres. American Soc. of Virology 1985–86; Fellow, AAAS; mem. NAS (Chair. Class IV medical sciences 1983–86, Section 43 microbiology and immunology 1989–93), mem. council 2000–02, mem. Governing Bd NAS Nat. Research Council 1990–92; mem. Council Inst. of Medicine 1986–92, Exec. Cttee 1988–91; mem. American Philosophical Soc. (mem. Council 1999–2001, Vice-Pres. 2000–06); mem. Asscn of American Physicians, American Soc. of Microbiology, American Asscn of Immunologists and other professional orgs; numerous hon. degrees; Howard Taylor Ricketts Award, Univ. of Chicago 1978, Waksman Award for Excellence in Microbiology, NAS 1984. *Publications:* numerous articles and chapters on virology, cell biology, infectious diseases. *Leisure interests:* fly fishing, stamp collecting. *Address:* Howard Hughes Medical Institute, 4000 Jones Bridge Road, Chevy Chase, MD 20815 (office); 2700 Calvert Street, NW, Washington, DC 20008, USA (home). *Telephone:* (301) 215-8554 (office). *Website:* www.hhmi.org (office).

CHOPRA, Deepak; American writer; b. India; founder and Dir of Educational Programs, Chopra Center 1955–; Fellow, American Coll. of Physicians; mem. American Asscn of Clinical Endocrinologists. *Publications include:* Return of the Rishi 1989, Quantum Healing 1990, Perfect Health 1990, Unconditional Life 1991, Creating Health 1991, Creating Affluence 1993, Ageless Body, Timeless Mind 1993, Restful Sleep 1994, Perfect Weight 1994, The Seven Spiritual Laws of Success 1995, The Path of Love 1996, How to Create Wealth 1999, Everyday Immortality: A Concise Course in Spiritual Transformation 1999, How to Know God: The Soul's Journey into the Mystery of Mysteries 2000, How to Know God 2001, Grow Younger, Live Longer 2002, Golf for Enlightenment 2003, Book of Secrets 2004, Peace is the Way 2005, Buddha 2007, The Third Jesus: the Christ we cannot Ignore 2008, Muhammad 2010. *Address:* Chopra Centre at La Costa Resort and Spa, 2013 Costa del Mar Road, Carlsbad, CA 92009, USA (office). *Telephone:* (760) 494-1600 (office). *Fax:* (760) 494-1608 (office). *E-mail:* felicia@chopra.com (office). *Website:* www.chopra.com (office); deepakchopra.com.

CHOQUEHUANCA CÉSPEDES, David; Bolivian government official; *Minister of Foreign Affairs and Worship;* b. 7 May 1961, Cota Cota Baja; ed Colegio General José Miguel Lanza, Escuela Nacional de Formación de Cuadros Niceto Pérez, Cuba, Universidad Cordillera; Nat. Co-ordinator NINA 1998; Minister of Foreign Affairs and Worship 2006–. *Address:* Ministry of Foreign Affairs and Worship, Calle Ingavi, esq. Junín, La Paz, Bolivia (office). *Telephone:* (2) 237-1150 (office).

Fax: (2) 237-1155 (office). *E-mail:* mreuno@rree.gov.bo (office). *Website:* www.rree .gov.bo (office).

CHORLEY, 2nd Baron, cr. 1945, of Kendal; **Roger Richard Edward Chorley,** FCA; British accountant; b. 14 Aug. 1930; s. of 1st Baron Chorley and Katharine Campbell Hopkinson; m. Ann Debenham 1964; two s.; ed Stowe School, Gonville and Caius Coll., Cambridge; joined Cooper Brothers & Co. (later Coopers & Lybrand) 1955, New York office 1959–60, Pakistan (Indus Basin Project) 1961, Partner 1967–89; Accounting Adviser to Nat. Bd for Prices and Incomes 1965–68; Visiting Prof., Dept of Man. Sciences, Imperial Coll. of Science and Tech., London Univ. 1979–82; mem. Royal Comm. on the Press 1975–77, Finance Act 1960 Tribunal 1974–79, Ordnance Survey Review Cttee 1978–79, British Council Review Cttee 1979–80, Bd British Council 1981–99 (Deputy Chair. 1990–99), Top Salaries Review Body 1981–90, Ordnance Survey Advisory Bd 1983–85, House of Lords Select Cttee on Science and Tech. 1983, 1987, 1990, 2006, Select Cttee on Sustainable Devt 1994–95; elected mem. House of Lords 2001–; Chair. The National Trust 1991–96; fmr Pres. Cambridge Univ. Mountaineering Club, mem. expeditions to Himalayas (Rakaposhi) 1954, Nepal 1957; Vice-Pres. Council for Nat. Parks 1996–; Hon. Sec. Climbers' Club 1963–67; mem. Man. Cttee Mount Everest Foundation 1968–70; Pres. Alpine Club 1983–85; mem. Council Royal Geographical Soc. 1984–, Vice-Pres. 1986–87, Pres. 1987–90; mem. Finance Cttee Nat. Trust 1972–90, Exec. Cttee 1989–96; mem. Council, Royal Soc. of Arts 1987–89, City and Guilds of London Inst.; mem. Nat. Theatre Bd 1980–91; Patron British Mountaineering Council 1996–; Hon. FRICS; Hon. Fellow Central Lancashire Univ. 1993, Hon. Pres. Asscn for Geographic Information 1995–; Hon. DSc (Reading, Kingston); Hon. LLD (Lancaster). *Leisure interest:* mountains. *Address:* House of Lords, Westminster, London, SW1A 0PW, England (office). *Telephone:* (20) 7219-5353 (office).

CHORY, Joanne, AB, PhD; American biologist and academic; *Professor and Director, Plant Molecular and Cellular Biology Laboratory, Salk Institute for Biological Studies;* ed Oberlin Coll., Ohio and Univ. of Illinois at Urbana-Champaign; Postdoctoral Research, Harvard Medical School, Boston, Mass 1984–88; Asst Prof., Plant Biology Lab., Salk Inst., La Jolla, Calif. 1988–94, Assoc. Prof. 1994–98, Dir Plant Molecular and Cellular Biology Lab. 1998–, Prof. 1998– (mem. Academic Council Salk Inst. 1992–94, 1995–97, 2000–03); Adjunct Asst Prof., Biology Dept, Univ. of California, San Diego, La Jolla 1992–94, Adjunct Assoc. Prof. 1994–99, Adjunct Prof. 1999–; Assoc. Investigator, Howard Hughes Medical Inst., La Jolla 1997–; mem. Bd of Dirs Int. Soc. for Plant Molecular Biology 1995–98, Boyce Thompson Inst. for Plant Research 2001–03; mem. Bd on Life Sciences, Nat. Research Council 2001–04, Int. Advisory Cttee 7th Int. Congress of Plant Molecular Biology 2003; mem. Editorial Review Bd Plant Journal 1991–99, Plant Physiology 1992–95, 1998–, Genetics 1993–98, Developmental Genetics 1993–99, Cell 1994–97, 2001–, Genes to Cells 1995–, Current Opinion in Plant Biology 1998–, Science 1998–, BioProtocol 2000–01, Faculty of 1000 Section Head 2001–; Fellow, American Acad. of Arts and Sciences 1998–, AAAS; mem. NAS 1999–, German Nat. Acad. of Sciences (Leopoldina); Assoc. mem. European Molecular Biology Org.; Foreign mem. Royal Soc., UK 2011–; Foreign Assoc. French Acad. of Sciences; Trustees' Scholarship, Oberlin Coll. 1975–77, Anna Fuller Fund Jr Research Fellow, Harvard School of Public Health 1977, Award for Initiatives in Research, NAS 1994, Charles Albert Schull Award, American Soc. of Plant Physiologists 1995, Edna Roe Lecturer, Int. Congress of Photobiology 1996, Gatsby Foundation Flying Fellow 1997, L'Oreal-Helena Rubenstein Award for Women in Science 2000, Kumho Award in Plant Molecular Biology. *Publications:* more than 130 publs in scientific journals. *Address:* Plant Biology Laboratory, Salk Institute for Biological Studies, 10010 N Torrey Pines Road, San Diego, CA 92037, USA (office). *Telephone:* (858) 552-1148 (office). *Fax:* (858) 558-6379 (office). *E-mail:* chory@salk.edu (office). *Website:* www.salk.edu/faculty/chory.html (office).

CHOU, Chang-Hung, BS, MS, PhD; Taiwanese researcher and academic; *Chair Professor and Director, Research Center for Biodiversity, China Medical University;* b. 5 Sept. 1942, Tainan, Taiwan; s. of F. K. Chou and C. Y. Shih Chou; m. Ruth L. H. Yang Chou 1970; one s. one d.; ed Nat. Taiwan Univ., Taipei, Univ. of Calif., Santa Barbara, USA, Univ. of Toronto, Canada; Assoc. Research Fellow, Inst. of Botany, Academia Sinica, Taipei 1972–76, Research Fellow 1976–2002, Dir 1989–96; Prof., Dept of Botany, Nat. Taiwan Univ. 1976–99; Vice-Pres. Nat. Sun Yat-sen Univ. 1999–2002; Pres. Nat. Pingtung Univ. of Science and Tech. 2002–06; Nat. Chair Prof., Ministry of Educ. 2001–04; Chair Prof. and Dir Research Center for Biodiversity, China Medical Univ. 2006–; mem. various nat. cttees for Int. Council of Scientific Unions (ICSU) 1974–; Sec. for Int. Affairs, Academia Sinica 1988–, mem. Council Academia Sinica 1989–, Pacific Science Asscn 1989; mem. Cttee for Science Educ., Ministry of Educ. 1986–, Cttee for Environmental Educ. 1991–, Cttee for Cultural and Natural Preservation Council of Agric. 1990; mem. Council Taiwan Livestock Research Inst. 1976–, Taiwan Forestry Research Inst. 1989–, Council Nat. Sustainable Devt 1997–; Dir Life Science Research Promotion Centre Nat. Science Council 1989–; Visiting Scholar, Oklahoma Univ., Univ. of Texas, Washington State Univ. 1979–80; Pres. Botanical Soc. of Repub. of China (Taiwan) 1983–84, Biological Soc. of Repub. of China (Taiwan) 1987–88; Chair. Nat. Cttee Int. Union of Biological Sciences (IUBS) 1990–, Vice-Pres. IUBS 1997, mem. Exec. Cttee 2007–; Chair. SCOPE Nat. Cttee; Exec. Mem. Pacific Science Asscn; Ed. Botanical Bulletin of Academia Sinica 1989–; Fellow, Third World Acad. of Sciences; mem. Academia Sinica, Taipei; Highest Honor, Soka Univ., Japan 2003; awards from Ministry of Educ. and Science Council of Taiwan. *Publications:* over 200 scientific papers, one univ. textbook; 10 monographs. *Leisure interest:* listening to classical music. *Address:* 91, Hseuh-Shih Road, Taichung 404, Taiwan (office). *Telephone:* (4) 2205-3366 (office). *Fax:* (4) 2207-1500 (office). *E-mail:* choumasa@mail.cmu.edu.tw (office). *Website:* www.cmu.edu.tw (office).

CHOUDHURY, Subir Roy; Indian engineer and business executive; *Chairman and Managing Director, Hindustan Petroleum Corporation Ltd;* ed Univ. of Assam; began career in petroleum industry with Assam Oil Co., Digboi (subsidiary of Burma Oil Co.); joined Hindustan Petroleum Corpn Ltd as a construction engineer 1982, held various positions in co., including Gen. Man. (Supply, Operations and Distribution), Gen. Man. (Pipelines), Gen. Man. Sales (West Zone), Exec. Dir Direct Sales, Dir, Marketing 2004–10, Chair. and Man. Dir Hindustan Petroleum Corpn Ltd 2010–. *Address:* Hindustan Petroleum Corporation Ltd, Petroleum House, 17 Jamshedji Tata Road, Mumbai 400 020, India (office).

Telephone: (22) 22863900 (office). *Fax:* (22) 22872992 (office). *E-mail:* corphq@hpcl .co.in (office). *Website:* www.hindustanpetroleum.com (office).

CHOUHAN, Shivraj Singh, MA; Indian politician; *Chief Minister of Madhya Pradesh;* b. 5 March 1959, Jait village, Sehore Dist; s. of Prem Singh Chouhan and Sundar Bai Chouhan; m. Smt. Sadhana Singh 1992; two s.; ed Barkatullah Univ., Bhopal; Pres. Model Higher Secondary School Students Union 1975; participated in underground movt against Emergency 1976–77, imprisoned in Bhopal Jail; joined Rashtriya Swayamsevak Sangh (Nat. Volunteers' Union—Hindu nationalist org.) 1977; Organizing Sec. Akhil Bhartiya Vidyarthi Parishad (ABVP) 1977–78, Jt Sec. ABVP 1978–80, Gen. Sec. 1980–83, mem. Nat. Exec. of ABVP 1982–83; Jt Sec. Bhartiya Janta Yuva Morcha (BJYM) 1984–85, Gen. Sec. BJYM, Madhya Pradesh (MP) 1985–88, Pres. BJYM, MP 1988–91, Gen. Sec. All India BJYM 1992–, Nat. Pres. 2000–03; mem. Bharatiya Janata Party (BJP), fmr Pres. MP state party unit, Gen. Sec. BJP, MP 1992–94, 1997–98, later Nat. Sec. BJP, Pres. BJP, MP 2005–; elected to State Ass. from Budhni Constituency 1990–91; a convener of Akhil Bhartiya Keshariya Vahini 1991–92; five-time MP (Lok Sabha—Lower House of Parl.) 1991–, first representing Vidisha, currently represents Budhni, Sehore Dist, MP in State Ass., mem. Cttee, Ministry of Human Resources Devt 1992–96, mem. Cttee on Labour and Welfare 1993–96, mem. Hindi Salahkar Samiti 1994–1996, mem. Cttee on Urban and Rural Devt, mem. Consultative Cttee, Ministry of Human Resources Devt 1996–97, mem. Cttee on Urban and Rural Devt and its Sub-Cttee on Ministry of Rural Areas and Employment 1998–99, mem. Cttee on Agric. 1999–2000, mem. Cttee on Public Undertakings 1999–2001, Chair. House Cttee (Lok Sabha), mem. Consultative Cttee, Ministry of Communications 2000–04, mem. Cttee on Agric. 2004, mem. Jt Cttee on Offices of Profit 2004, Sec. Parl. Bd 2004, Sec. (Cen. Election Cttee), Chair. Housing Cttee 2004, mem. Cttee on Ethics 2004; Chief Minister of MP 2005–; Gold Medal in Philosophy, Barkatullah Univ. *Leisure interests:* music, spiritual literature, debates and discussions with friends, sight-seeing, watching movies, Kabaddi, cricket, volleyball. *Address:* Office of the Chief Minister, Bhopal, Madhya Pradesh (office); 1 Shyamla Hills, Bhopal, Madhya Pradesh, India (home). *Telephone:* (755) 2441581 (office), (755) 2442231 (home). *E-mail:* cm@mp.gov.in (office). *Website:* www.mp.gov.in (office); www.shivrajsinghchouhan.in (home).

CHOUINARD, Yvon; American mountaineer, surfer, sportsman, business executive and writer; *Chairman, Patagonia, Inc.;* b. 9 Nov. 1938, Lewiston, Me; m. Malinda Pennoyer 1970; two c.; served in US Army 1962–64; f. Chouinard Equipment for Alpinists (CEA), Inc. 1960; f. Lost Arrow Corpn 1974; f. Patagonia Inc. 1976–; also a kayaker, falconer and fisherman; writer on climbing issues and ethics and also on mixing environmentalism and sound business practice; mem. American Alpine Club. *Achievements include:* participated in second ascent of The Nose on El Capitán 1960, ascent of North American Wall using no fixed ropes 1964; visited Canadian Rockies with Fred Beckey 1961, made several important first ascents, including North Face of Mount Edith Cavell, Beckey-Chouinard Route on South Howser Tower in the Bugaboos, and North Face of Mount Sir Donald; freeclimbed first pitch of Matinee in the Gunks 1961; climbed Cerro Fitzroy in Patagonia by a new route (The Californian Route) 1968. *Publications:* Climbing Ice 1982, Let My People Go Surfing 2005. *Address:* 259 W Santa Clara Street, Ventura, CA 93001, USA (office). *Telephone:* (805) 643-8616 (office). *Fax:* (800) 543-5522 (office). *E-mail:* info@patagonia.com (office). *Website:* www.patagonia.com (office).

CHOUMMALI, Lt-Gen. Saignason; Laotian army officer, politician and head of state; *President;* b. 6 March 1936, Attapu; mem. Nat. Ass.; Deputy Prime Minister and Minister of Nat. Defence –2001; Vice-Pres. of Laos 2001–06, Pres. 2006–; elected Gen. Sec. Phak Pasason Pativat Lao (Lao People's Revolutionary Party) 2006–. *Address:* Office of the President, Vientiane, Laos (office). *Telephone:* (21) 214200 (office). *Fax:* (21) 214208 (office).

CHOVANEC, Milan; Czech business executive and politician; *Minister of the Interior;* b. 31 Jan. 1970, Plzeň; m.; two c.; ed Central School of Econs, Plzeň, Univ. of West Bohemia, Plzeň; worked in Czechoslovak bank –1989; owned business in retail, wholesale and services 1989–99; Partner, Miller-Sü sro 1999–2000; Dir and sole shareholder in Plzeň Furniture Ltd 2001–07; sold share in co. 2007; mem. Czech Social Democratic Party (ČSSD) (Česká strana sociálně demokratická), Chair. Regional Exec. Cttee 2011–13, Vice-Chair. ČSSD 2013–; mem. Ass., City of Plzeň 2002–10, Chair. Audit Cttee 2006–08, First Deputy for region's economy and property 2008–10, Pres. Plzeň Region 2010–14; mem. Chamber of Deputies 2013–; Minister of the Interior 2014–. *Address:* Ministry of the Interior, Nad Stolou 3, PO Box 21, 170 34 Prague 7, Czech Republic (office). *Telephone:* (974) 811111 (office). *Fax:* (974) 833582 (office). *E-mail:* posta@mvcr.cz (office). *Website:* www.mvcr.cz (office).

CHOW, Alan Y., BA, MD; American paediatric ophthalmologist and academic; *Paediatric Ophthalmology Specialist, Hauser Ross Eye Institute and Surgicenter;* b. Glen Ellyn, Ill.; ed Univ. of Chicago, Loyola Univ.; completed internships in Paediatrics at Cincinnati Children's/GSH and in Gen. Surgery at Loyola Univ. where he also completed his ophthalmology residency; fmr Knapp Fellow in Ophthalmic Genetics, Wilmer Eye Inst., Johns Hopkins Univ.; fmr Heed Fellow in Paediatric Ophthalmology, Children's Hosp. Nat. Medical Center; Asst Prof., Rush Univ. Medical Center, Chicago; Visiting Assoc. Prof., Univ. of Illinois Eye Center, Chicago; Adjunct Asst Prof., Tulane Univ. Eye Center; Co-founder and COO Optobionics Corpn, led devt of Artificial Silicon Retina 1990; Paediatric Ophthalmology Specialist, Hauser-Ross Eye Inst. and Surgicenter, Sycamore 2007–; frequent nat. and int. lecturer; reviewer for several peer-reviewed journals; spokesperson for American Acad. of Ophthalmology; grants and awards from NASA, Westinghouse Foundation, NSF, NIH and SBA, Chicago Inventor of the Year (together with his brother Vincent) for work in developing Artificial Silicon Retinal Prosthesis 1996, Tibbetts Award, Small Business Innovation Research Program 2000, RP International's Vision Award (with his brother) 2002, Ernst & Young Entrepreneur of the Year Award in the Chicago area 2003, World Tech. Award in Health and Medicine, The World Tech. Network (with his brother) 2004. *Publications:* numerous articles, book chapters and patents. *Address:* Hauser-Ross Eye Institute and Surgicenter, 2240 Gateway Drive, Sycamore, IL 60178, USA (office). *Telephone:* (815) 756-8571 (office); (888) 286-9221 (office). *E-mail:* info@ hauserross.org (office). *Website:* www.hauserross.org (office).

CHOW, Sir C. K. (Chung Kong), Kt., CEng, BSc, MSc, DEng, FREng, FCGI, FIChemE, FHKEng; British (b. Hong Kong) business executive; *CEO, MTR Corporation Ltd;* b. 9 Sept. 1950; ed Univs of Wisconsin and California, USA, Chinese Univ. of Hong Kong, Harvard Univ., USA; Research Engineer, Climax Chemical Co., New Mexico 1974–76; Process Engineer, Sybron Asia Ltd, Hong Kong 1976–77; joined BOC Group 1977, with Hong Kong Oxygen, Hong Kong and BOC Australia 1977–84, Man. Dir Hong Kong Oxygen 1984–86, Pres. BOC Japan 1986–89, Group Man. Gases Business Devt, BOC Group PLC, UK and USA 1989–91, Regional Dir N Pacific, Tokyo and Hong Kong 1991–93, CEO Gases 1993–96, apptd to Main Bd 1994, Man. Dir 1994–97; CEO GKN PLC 1997–2001, CEO Brambles Industries Ltd 2001–03, CEO MTR Corpn 2003–; Dir (non-exec.) Standard Chartered PLC 1997–2008; Chair. Standard Chartered Bank (Hong Kong) Ltd 2004–10; fmr Pres. Soc. of British Aerospace Cos; mem. Governing Body London Business School; Fellow, Inst. of Chemical Engineers, Chartered Inst. of Logistics and Transport; Hon. Fellow, Inst. of Eng and Tech.; Int. Exec., Acad. of Int. Man. 2001, Exec. of the Year, DHL/South China Morning Post Business Award 2006, Dir of the Year, Hong Kong Inst. of Dirs 2006, Best CEO in Hong Kong Award, FinanceAsia Magazine 2009, 2011. *Address:* MTR Corporation Ltd, GPO Box 9916, Hong Kong Special Administrative Region, People's Republic of China (office). *Telephone:* 29932111 (office). *Fax:* 27988822 (office). *Website:* www .mtr.com.hk (office).

CHOW, Vincent Y., BS; American electrical engineer and business executive; *President, Vega Technology and Systems, Inc.;* ed Illinois Inst. of Tech.; fmr Dir of Operations, Telco Systems; fmr Man. of Reliability Devt, AT&T Bell Labs/ Teletype; Dir of Tech. Operations, Autotech Corpn 1985–89; Dir of Research and Devt, MDA Scientific 1989–94; Co-founder and Vice-Pres., Research and Devt, Optobionics Corpn 1990–94; Pres. Vega Technology and Systems, Inc. (eng consulting firm for optical sensing products and ASIC applications) 1994–; Chicago Inventor of the Year Award (with his brother Alan) for work in developing Artificial Silicon Retina Microchip 1996, Vision Award, RP International (with his brother) 2002, Ernst & Young Entrepreneur of the Year Award in the Chicago area (with his brother) 2003, World Tech. Award in Health and Medicine, The World Tech. Network (with his brother) 2004. *Publications:* more than 220 papers in scientific journals and named inventor on 11 patents. *Address:* Vega Technology and Systems, Inc., 7980 Kingsbury Drive, Bartlett, IL 60133-2348, USA (office). *Telephone:* (630) 855-5068 (office).

CHOW, Yun-Fat; Chinese film actor; b. 18 May 1955, Lamma Island; m. Jasmine Chow 1986; began acting career at TV station TVB, Hong Kong 1973, appearing in over 1,000 TV series; Dr hc (City Univ. of Hong Kong) 2001. *Films include:* The Story of Woo Viet, A Better Tomorrow 1986, God of Gamblers 1989, The Killer 1989, Eighth Happiness, Once a Thief 1991, Full Contact 1992, Hard Boiled 1992, Peace Hotel 1995, Broken Arrow, Anna and the King 1999, Crouching Tiger, Hidden Dragon 2000, King's Ransom 2001, Bulletproof Monk 2003, Yi ma de hou xian dai sheng huo 2006, Man cheng jin dai huang jin jia (Curse of the Golden Flower) 2006, Pirates of the Caribbean: At World's End 2007, The Children of Huang Shi 2008, Dragonball Evolution 2009, Confucius 2010, Shanghai 2010, Let the Bullets Fly 2010. *Address:* Chow Yun Fat International, PO Box 71288, Kowloon Central, Hong Kong Special Administrative Region, People's Republic of China (office); c/o WME, 9601 Wilshire Blvd, Beverly Hills, CA 90210, USA.

CHOW MAN YIU, Paul, JP; Chinese business executive; fmr Exec. Dir Sun Hung Kai Securities Ltd; CEO Hong Kong Securities Clearing Corpn 1990–91; CEO Hong Kong Stock Exchange 1991–97; CEO HSBC Asset Management (Hong Kong) Ltd 1997–2003; Chair. Hong Kong Investment Funds Asscn 2000–01; Exec. Dir and CEO Hong Kong Exchanges and Clearing Ltd 2003–10; Dir Hong Kong Cyberport Management Co. Ltd 2003–07; mem. Advisory Cttee Securities and Futures Comm. 2001–07; Independent non-Exec. Dir China Mobile Ltd 2013–; Hon. Fellow, Univ. of Hong Kong; Silver Bauhinia Star 2005, Gold Bauhinia Star 2010. *Address:* c/o The Stock Exchange of Hong Kong Ltd, 1/F One and Two Exchange Square, Central, Hong Kong Special Administrative Region, People's Republic of China.

CHOWDHURY, A. Q. M. Badruddoza, FRCPE, FRCP (CLAS), TDD; Bangladeshi surgeon, politician and fmr head of state; b. 1 Nov. 1932; s. of Kafil Uddin Chowdhury; m. Hasina Chowdhury; one s. two d.; ed St Gregory High School, Dhaka Coll., Dhaka Medical Coll., Univ. of Wales, UK; practised as physician specializing in treatment of tuberculosis; Founding Sec.-Gen. Bangladesh Nationalist Party 1978–90, fmr Deputy Leader, mem. until 2002; fmr Sr Deputy Prime Minister, Minister of Health and Family Planning, of Foreign Affairs 2001; Pres. of Bangladesh 2001–02; Co-founder and Pres. Liberal Democratic Party 2006–13; fmr Pres. Nat. Anti-Tuberculosis Asscn of Bangladesh, Int. Union Against Tuberculosis; led Bangladesh del. to World Health Conf., Geneva 1978, 1979 and many dels to int. confs on tuberculosis and chest diseases; Hon. Fellow, Coll. of Physicians and Surgeons (Bangladesh); Nat. TV Award 1976. *Publications:* many research papers in nat. and int. journals; essays and plays. *Address:* Liberal Democratic Party, Dhaka (office); Residence Bari Dhar, near Gulshan, Dhaka, Bangladesh (home).

CHOWDHURY, Anwarul Karim, MA; Bangladeshi diplomatist and UN official; b. 5 Feb. 1943, Dhaka; m.; three c.; ed Univ. of Dhaka; Dir-Gen. for S and SE Asia, Foreign Ministry 1979–80, for Multilateral Econ. Co-operation 1986–90; Deputy Perm. Rep. to UN 1980–86, Perm. Rep. 1996–2001, Chair. Fifth Cttee (Admin. and Budgetary) of UN 1997–98); UNICEF Dir for Japan, Australia and NZ 1990–93, Sec. Exec. Bd UNICEF, New York 1993–96 (Chair. Bd 1985–86), UN Under-Sec.- Gen. for Least Developed Countries, Landlocked Developing Countries and Small Island Developing States 2002–07 (retd), currently emisssary for UN Culture of Peace Initiative; Dr hc (Soka Univ., Tokyo); U Thant Peace Award, UNESCO Gandhi Gold Medal for Culture and Peace, Chancellor's Medal for Global Leadership for Peace, Univ. of Massachusetts Boston 2012. *Publications:* contribs to journals on devt and human rights issues. *Address:* Culture of Peace Initiative, United Nations Headquarters, New York, NY 10017, USA. *Website:* cultureofpeace .org.

CHOWDHURY, M. Nurunnabi; Bangladeshi business executive; fmr Chair. Bangladesh Textile Mills Corpn. *Address:* c/o Bangladesh Textile Mills Corpn, Bastra Bhaban, 7–9 Kawran Bazar, Dhaka 1215, Bangladesh.

CHOWDHURY, Shamsher Mobin, BA; Bangladeshi diplomatist and politician; *Vice-Chairman, Bangladesh Jatiyatabadi Dal (Bangladesh Nationalist Party);* ed Pakistan Mil. Acad.; joined Pakistan army 1969, promoted to rank of Maj. 1973; joined Bangladesh Civil Service 1975; Deputy Chief of Protocol and Dir West Europe, Ministry of Foreign Affairs 1975–77, with Embassy in Rome 1977–81, Counsellor, Embassy in Washington, DC 1981–83, Counsellor and Minister, High Comm. in Ottawa 1983–86, Deputy Chief of Mission, Embassy in Beijing 1986–88, Dir-Gen. SAARC Div., Ministry of Foreign Affairs 1988–91, High Commr to Sri Lanka 1991–95, Amb. to Germany 1995–98, to Viet Nam 1998–2001, Foreign Sec. 2001–05, Amb. to USA 2005–07; currently Vice-Chair. Bangladesh Jatiyatabadi Dal (Bangladesh Nationalist Party), also head of Int. Dept; Gallantry Award Bir Bikram (BB). *Address:* Bangladesh Jatiyatabadi Dal (Bangladesh Nationalist Party), 28/1 Naya Paltan, VIP Road, Dhaka 1000, Bangladesh. *Telephone:* (2) 8351929 (office). *Fax:* (2) 8318678 (office). *E-mail:* bnpbd@e-fsbd.net (office). *Website:* www.bnp-bd.com (office).

CHRAPLYVY, Andrew R., BA, MS, PhD; American physicist and business executive; *Optical Technologies Research Vice-President, Bell Labs, Alcatel-Lucent;* ed Washington Univ. in St Louis, Cornell Univ.; with Bell Laboratories 1980–, currently Optical Technologies Research Vice-Pres., Bell Labs, Alcatel-Lucent, Bell Labs Fellow; mem. Nat. Acad. of Eng; Marconi Fellow; Fellow, Optical Soc. of America (OSA), IEEE; Bell Laboratories Pres.'s Gold Award (four times), Lucent Technologies Patent Award 1998, New Jersey Inventor of the Year Award 1999, Thomas Alva Edison Patent Award 1999, IEEE John Tyndall Award 2003, OSA John Tyndall Award 2008, Marconi Prize and Fellowship (co-recipient) 2009, inducted into New Jersey Inventors Hall of Fame 2010, IEEE Alexander Graham Bell Medal (co-recipient) 2013. *Publications:* numerous papers in professional journals. *Address:* Bell Labs, Alcatel-Lucent, 600 Mountain Avenue, Murray Hill, NJ 07974-0636, USA (office). *Telephone:* (908) 582-8500 (office). *Website:* www .alcatel-lucent.com/bell-labs (office).

CHRÉTIEN, Rt Hon. Joseph Jacques Jean, PC, QC, BA, LLD; Canadian lawyer and fmr politician; *Of Counsel, Heenan Blaikie LLP;* b. 11 Jan. 1934, Shawinigan; s. of Wellie Chrétien and Marie Boisvert; m. Aline Chaîné 1957; two s. one d.; ed Laval Univ., Québec; Dir Bar of Trois-Rivières 1962; mem. House of Commons (Liberal) 1963–86; Parl. Sec. to Prime Minister 1965, to Minister of Finance 1966; Minister without Portfolio 1967–68, of Nat. Revenue Jan.–July 1968, of Indian Affairs and Northern Devt 1968–74; Pres. Treas. Bd 1974–76; Minister of Industry, Trade and Commerce 1976–77, of Finance 1977–79, of Justice, Attorney-Gen. of Canada and Minister of State for Social Devt 1980–82, of Energy, Mines and Resources 1982–84, Sec. of State for External Affairs, Deputy Prime Minister June–Sept. 1984; MP for Beauséjour 1990–93, for St Maurice 1993–2003, Prime Minister of Canada 1993–2003, Leader Nat. Liberal Party 1990–2003; Legal Counsel, Lang, Michener, Laurence & Shaw, Ottawa, Toronto and Vancouver 1984–90; special adviser on int. energy and power, Bennett Jones LLP 2004; Of Counsel, Heenan Blaikie LLP, Ottawa 2004–; mem. Barreau du Québec, Ont. Bar Asscn; Hon. LLD (Wilfred Laurier Univ.) 1981, (Laurentian Univ.) 1982, (W Ont.) 1982, (York Univ.) 1986, (Alberta) 1987, (Lakehead) 1988, (Ottawa) 1994, (Meiji) 1996, (Queen's Univ.) 2004, (McMaster Univ.) 2005; Dr hc (Ottawa Univ.) 1994, (Meiji Univ., Japan) 1996, (Warsaw School of Econs, Poland) 1999, (Michigan State Univ.) 1999, (Hebrew Univ., Jerusalem) 2000 (Memorial Univ.) 2000, (Université Catholique Pontificate Madre y Maestra in Santiago de los Caballeros, Dominican Repub.) 2003, (Nat. Univ. of Kyiv-Mohyla Acad., Ukraine) 2007, (Univ. of Western Ontario) 2008; Int. Role Model Award, Equality Forum 2005. *Publications:* Straight from the Heart 1985, Finding a Common Ground 1992. *Leisure interests:* skiing, fishing, golf. *Address:* Heenan Blaikie LLP, 55 Metcalfe Street, Suite 300, Ottawa, ON K1P 6L5, Canada (office). *Telephone:* (613) 236-1668 (office). *E-mail:* jchretien@heenan.ca (office). *Website:* www .heenanblaikie.com (office).

CHRÉTIEN, Raymond A.J., BA, LLL; Canadian lawyer, government official and diplomatist (retd); *Partner and Strategic Advisor, Fasken Martineau;* b. 20 May 1942, Shawinigan, Québec; s. of Maurice Chrétien and Cécille Chrétien (née Marcotte); m. Kay Rousseau; one s. one d.; ed Séminaire de Joliette and Laval Univ.; Quebec Bar Exams 1966; mem. Legal Affairs Div., Div. of External Affairs, Govt of Canada 1966–67, Policy Dir Industry, Investments and Competition 1981–82, Asst Under-Sec. for Manufacturing, Tech. and Transportation 1982–83; Insp.-Gen. 1983–85, Assoc. Under-Sec. of State for External Affairs 1988–91; Third Sec., Perm. Mission to UN, New York 1967–68; Asst Sec., Fed. and Provincial Relations Comm., Privy Council Office 1968–70, Exec. Asst to Sec., mem. Treasury Bd 1970–71; Exec. Asst to Pres., Canadian Int. Devt Agency 1971–72; First Sec., Embassy in Beirut 1972–75; First Sec. and Counsellor, Embassy in Paris 1975–78; Amb. to Zaïre 1978–81, to Mexico 1985–88, to Belgium and Luxembourg 1991–94, to USA 1994–2000, to France 2000–03; Pnr and Strategic Advisor, Fasken Martineau (law firm), Montréal 2004–; UN Sec.-Gen.'s Special Envoy to Cen. Africa 1996; Chair. Centre d'études et de recherches internationales de l'Université de Montréal (CÉRIUM); Pres. Comité des gouverneurs des corridors de commerce Québec-Canada-États-Unis of the Fédération des chambres de commerce du Québec; mem. Bd of Dirs Institut de recherches cliniques de Montréal; mem. Trilateral Comm.; Hon. mem. Bar of US Court of Appeal for the Armed Forces 1988; Order of Aztec Eagle, Mexico 1989, Commdr de la Légion d'Honneur 2003; Hon. DLitt (Brock) 1999; Hon. DJur (Laval) 2001, (State Univ. of New York) 2002. *Address:* Fasken Martineau Dumoulin, Stock Exchange Tower, Suite 3400, POB 242, 800 Place Victoria, Montréal, PQ H4Z 1E9, Canada (office). *Telephone:* (514) 397-5230 (office). *Fax:* (514) 397-7600 (office). *E-mail:* rchretien@ fasken.com (office). *Website:* www.fasken.com (office).

CHRIQUI, Vincent; French government official; *Director General, Centre d'analyse stratégique;* b. 1971; ed École Polytechnique, École Nationale d'Admin; responsible for environmental and agricultural budgets as part of overall Budget 1997–99; responsible for econ. and monetary union to Ministry for the Economy and Finances and, for this reason, mem. EU Econ. Policy Cttee 1999–2001; Finance Man. CDC-Ixis (groupe Caisse des dépôts et consignations—CDC) 2001–02; Budgetary Advisor, Office of François Fillon, Minister of Social Affairs, Labour and Solidarity 2002–04, then to Minister for State Educ., Higher Educ. and Research 2004–05; Parl. Pvt. Sec. to Gérard Larcher, Deputy Sec. for Employment, Labour and Youth Training, Asst Dir, Office of Jean-Louis Borloo, Minister of

Employment, Social Cohesion and Housing 2005–07; Advisor in charge of analysis, then Parl. Advisor to Cabinet of François Fillon (Prime Minister) 2007–10; Dir Gen. Centre d'analyse stratégique (Strategic Analysis Centre) 2010–; Lecturer in Econs, Institut d'études politiques de Paris 1998–2000, Univ. of Paris II Panthéon-Assas 2005. *Address:* Centre d'analyse stratégique, 18 rue de Martignac, 75700 Paris Cedex 07, France (office). *Telephone:* 1-42-75-60-00 (office). *Fax:* 1-45-55-53-37 (office). *E-mail:* strategie@strategie.gouv.fr (office). *Website:* www.strategie .gouv.fr (office).

CHRISTENSEN, Helena; Danish model and photographer; b. 25 Dec. 1968, Copenhagen; d. of Flemming Christensen and Elsa Christensen; one s.; grad. in arithmetic and sociology course; fmr child model; began adult modelling career in Paris 1988; has since worked as one of world's leading models in promotions for Versace, Rykiel, Chanel, Lagerfeld, Revlon, Dior, Prada etc.; has appeared on all major magazine covers working for photographers including Herb Ritts, Bruce Weber, Patrick DeMarchelier, Penn, Steven Meisel, Helmut Newton, and others; Co-founder and fmr Creative Dir Nylon Magazine. *Films include:* Inferno (TV) 1992, March of the Anal Sadistic Warrior 1998, Allegro 2005. *Leisure interests:* photography (black and white), oil/watercolour painting. *Address:* One Management, 42 Bond Street, #2, New York, NY 10012, USA (office). *Telephone:* (212) 431-0054 (office).

CHRISTENSEN, Lars Saabye; Norwegian poet, writer and playwright; b. 21 Sept. 1953, Oslo; Ed., Signaler 1986–90; Commdr, Order of St Olaf 2006, Chevalier, Ordre des Arts et des Lettres 2008; Tarjei Vesaas debutantpris 1976, Cappelenprisen 1984, Rivertonprisen 1987, Kritikerprisen 1988, Sarpsborgprisen 1988, Bokhandlerprisen 1990, Amandaprisen 1991, Doblougprisen 1993, Riks-målsforbundets litteraturpris 1997, Sarpsborgprisen 1999, Aamot-statuetten 2001, Bokhandlerprisen 2001, Brageprisen 2001, Den norske leserprisen 2001, Natt & Dags bokpris 2001, Nordisk Råds Litteraturpris 2002. *Plays:* Columbus' ankomst 1981, Kvitt eller dobbelt 1984, Jokeren 1987, Til pengene tar slutt, Al 1988, Lyset på yttersida 2001, Mekka 1994, Chet baker spiller inkke her 2010. *Publications:* Historien om Gly 1976, Amatøren 1977, Kamelen i mitt hjerte 1978, Jaktmarker 1979, Billettene 1980, Jokeren 1981, Paraply 1982, Beatles 1984, Blodets bånd 1985, Asteder 1986, Sneglene 1987, Herman 1988, Stempler 1989, Versterålen 1989, Bly 1990, Gutten som ville være en av gutta 1992, Ingens 1992, Den akustiske skyggen 1993, Jubel 1995, Den andre siden av blått 1996, Den misunnelige frisøren 1997, Noen som elsker hverandre 1999, Falleferdig himmel 1999, Pasninger 1999, Kongen som ville ha mer enn en krone 1999, Under en sort paraply 1999, Pinnsvinsol 2000, Mann for sin katt 2000, Halvbroren 2001, Maskeblomstfamilien 2003, Sanger og steiner 2003, SATS 2003, Oscar Wildes heis 2004, Modellen 2005, Norske omveier i blues og bilder 2005, Saabyes sirkus 2006, Den arktiske drømmen 2007, Ordiord 2007, Bisettelsen 2008, Visning 2009, Men buicken står der fremdeles 2009, Bernhard Hvals forsnakkelser 2010, Mitt danske album 2010. *Address:* c/o Cappelen Damm AS, 0055 Oslo, Norway (office). *Telephone:* 22-61-65-00 (office). *E-mail:* rights@cappelendamm.no (office). *Website:* www.cappelendamm.no (office).

CHRISTIANSEN, Michael, Cand. jur. (LLM); Danish judge, academic, university administrator and fmr civil servant; *Chairman, Aarhus University;* b. 5 June 1945; ed Univ. of Copenhagen; Sec., Ministry of Justice 1970–73, Acting Deputy Judge, Silkeborg 1973–74, Head of Section, Ministry of Justice 1974–77, consultant 1978–96, Head of Dept 1986–88, Perm. Sec. 1988–92; coach in constitutional law and criminal law and Assoc. Prof. of Criminal Law, Univ. of Copenhagen 1977–83, External Examiner 1999–; Chair. Aarhus Univ. 2013–; Man. Dir Royal Danish Theatre 1992–2008; Chair. Sund og Bælt Holding A/S 1991–2000, Øresundskonsortiet 1993–96, Dan Composer Management 1994–2000, J. Lauritzen Holding A/S 1996–2001, A/S Øresundsforbindelsen 1998–2000, A/S Storebæltsforbindelsen 1998–2000, Schmidt Hammer Lassen Architects 2005–, Roshield A/S 2005–, Danmarks Radio 2008–; Chair. Laval Cttee, European Spallation Source Cttee; mem. Bd of Dirs A/S Politiken 1993–96, Lead Agency A/S 2007–, Have A/S 2008–, Danske Retursystem A/S 2008–, Boxer AB (Denmark) 2008–; Chair. Naturama, Svendborg, Copenhagen Film Festivals Foundation, Nørre Vosborg Manor Inst.; Vice-Chair. Holstebro Concert Hall; Commdr, First Class, Order of the Dannebrog. *Address:* Office of the Chairman, Aarhus University, 8000 Aarhus, Denmark (office). *Telephone:* 40-42-32-48 (office). *E-mail:* mch@adm.au.dk (office). *Website:* www.au.dk (office).

CHRISTIANSON, Wei Sun, BA, JD; American/Chinese lawyer and business executive; *Co-CEO of Asia Pacific and CEO of China, Morgan Stanley;* b. 21 Aug. 1956; m. Jon Christianson; three s.; ed Amherst Coll. and Columbia Univ. Law School, USA; fmr attorney, Orrick Herrington & Sutcliffe, New York, USA; Assoc. Dir of Corp. Finance, Securities and Futures Comm. of Hong Kong 1993–98; Exec. Dir and Beijing Chief Rep., Morgan Stanley 1998–2002; Man. Dir and CEO Morgan Stanley China 2006–; Country Man., China, Credit Suisse First Boston 2002–04, Chair. China 2004–06; mem. Bd of Dirs Estee Lauder Co. 2011–; Co-Chair. Int. Advisory Bd, Columbia Law School; Trustee, Amherst Coll. 2010–; Columbia Law School Medal of Excellence 2006, named by The Wall Street Journal as one of 50 Women to Watch 2006, ranked by Fortune magazine amongst the 50 Most Powerful Women in Business outside the US (41st) 2008, (44th) 2009, (46th) 2010, (42nd) 2011, (41st) 2012, named by US Banker magazine amongst the Top 25 Nonbank Women in Finance (eighth) 2008. *Address:* Morgan Stanley China, 2905 First Avenue, Trade Building 2, Jian'guo Gate, Beijing 100004, People's Republic of China (office). *Telephone:* (10) 65058383 (office). *Fax:* (10) 65058220 (office). *E-mail:* infochina@morganstanley.com (office). *Website:* www.morganstanleychina .com (office).

CHRISTIE, Christopher (Chris) James, BA, JD; American lawyer, politician and state governor; *Governor of New Jersey;* b. 6 Sept. 1962, Mendham, NJ; s. of Bill Christie and Sandra Christie; m. Mary Pat Foster 1986; two s. two d.; ed Livingston High School, Univ. of Delaware, Seton Hall Univ. School of Law; admitted to State Bar of NJ and Bar of US Dist Court, Dist of NJ 1987; Assoc., Dughi, Hewit & Palatucci (law firm), Cranford, NJ 1987–93, Pnr 1993–2002, registered as lobbyist 1998–2001; mem. Morris Co., NJ Bd of Chosen Freeholders 1995–97; unsuccessful bid for a seat in NJ Gen. Ass. 1995; US Attorney for Dist of NJ, US Dept Justice 2002–08; Gov. of New Jersey 2010–; mem. Bd of Trustees, Daytop Village-NJ, Mendham 1998–2002; Officer, Christie Family Foundation 2001–; Chair. Morris Co. Insurance Comm.; mem. Bd of Dirs United Way of Morris

Co., Family Services, Morris Co., Morris Bd Social Services; mem. ABA, NJ State Bar Asscn (fmr mem. Election Law Cttee); Republican. *Address:* Office of the Governor, The State House, PO Box 001, Trenton, NJ 08625, USA (office); Washington Office of the Governor, State of New Jersey, 444 North Capitol Street, Suite 201, Washington, DC 20001, USA (office). *Telephone:* (609) 292-6000 (Trenton) (office); (202) 638-0631 (DC) (office). *Fax:* (609) 777-2922 (Trenton) (office); (202) 638-2296 (DC) (office). *E-mail:* info@state.nj.us (office). *Website:* www .nj.gov/governor (office); www.state.nj.us/governor (office).

CHRISTIE, Julie (Frances); British actress; b. 14 April 1940, Assam, India; d. of Frank St John Christie and Rosemary Christie (née Ramsden); ed Brighton Technical Coll. and Central School of Speech and Drama; Dr hc (Warwick) 1994; Motion Picture Laurel Award, Best Dramatic Actress 1967, Motion Picture Herald Award 1967; Fellow BAFTA 1997. *Films include:* Crooks Anonymous 1962, The Fast Lady 1962, Billy Liar 1963, Young Cassidy 1964, Darling 1964 (Acad. Award 1966), Doctor Zhivago (Donatello Award) 1965, Fahrenheit 451 1966, Far From the Madding Crowd 1966, Petulia 1967, In Search of Gregory 1969, The Go-Between 1971, McCabe & Mrs. Miller 1972, Don't Look Now 1973, Shampoo 1974, Demon Seed, Heaven Can Wait 1978, Memoirs of a Survivor 1980, Gold 1980, The Return of the Soldier 1981, Les Quarantièmes rugissants 1981, The Animals Film (voiceover) 1981, Heat and Dust 1982, The Gold Diggers 1984, Miss Mary 1986, The Tattooed Memory 1986, Power 1987, Fathers and Sons 1988, Dadah is Death (TV) 1988, Fools of Fortune 1989, McCabe and Mrs Miller 1990, The Railway Station 1992, Hamlet 1995, Afterglow 1998, The Miracle Maker (voice) 2000, No Such Thing 2001, Snapshots 2001, I'm With Lucy 2002, A Letter to True 2003, Harry Potter and the Prisoner of Azkaban 2004, Finding Neverland 2004, Troy 2004, Away From Her (Best Actress, Nat. Bd of Review 2007, Golden Globe for Best Actress in a Drama 2008, Outstanding Performance by a Female Actor in a Leading Role, Screen Actors Guild 2008) 2007, New York, I Love You 2009, Glorious 39 2009, The Company You Keep 2010. *Plays:* Old Times 1995, Suzanna Andler 1997, Afterglow 1998. *Address:* c/o MF Management, Drury House, 34–43 Russell Street, London, WC2B 5HA, England (office). *Website:* mfmanagement .com (office).

CHRISTIE, Linford, OBE; British athletics coach, business executive and fmr athlete; b. 2 April 1960, St Andrew's, Jamaica; s. of James Christie and of the late Mabel Christie; one d.; fmr cashier Wandsworth Co-op; mem. Thames Valley Harriers; winner, UK 100m 1985, 1987, 200m 1985 (tie), 1988; winner Amateur Athletics Asscn 100m 1986, 1988, 200m 1988; winner, European 100m record; silver medallist, 100m, Seoul Olympic Games 1988, Winner 100m gold medal, Commonwealth Games 1990, Olympic Games 1992, World Athletic Championships 1993, Weltklasse Grand Prix Games 1994, European Games 1994; winner 100m Zurich 1995; Capt. of British Athletics Team 1995–97; officially retd 1997; Co-Founder (with Colin Jackson q.v.) and Man. Dir Nuff Respect sports man. co. 1992–; successful coach to prominent UK athletes including Katharine Merry and Darren Campbell; Hon. MSc (Portsmouth Univ.) 1993; Male Athlete of the Year 1988, 1992, BBC Sports Personality of the Year 1993. *Publications:* Linford Christie (autobiog.) 1989, To be Honest With You 1995, A Year in the Life of Linford Christie 1996. *Leisure interests:* cooking, gardening. *Address:* c/o Susan Barrett, Nuff Respect, The Coach House, 107 Sherland Road, Twickenham, Middx, TW9 4HB, England. *Telephone:* (20) 8891-4145 (office). *Fax:* (20) 8891-4140 (office). *E-mail:* nuff_respect@msm.com (office). *Website:* www.nuff-respect.co.uk (office).

CHRISTIE, Rt Hon. Perry Gladstone, LLB; Bahamian politician; *Prime Minister;* b. 21 Aug. 1943, Nassau; s. of Gladstone L. Christie and Naomi Christie; m. Bernadette Hanna; two s. one d.; ed Eastern Senior School, New Providence, Univ. of London and Univ. of Birmingham, UK; attorney with McKinney Bancroft and Hughes; f. own law practice Christie Ingraham & Co. (now Christie Davis & Co.); mem. Bd of Dirs Broadcasting Corpn of The Bahamas 1973; mem. Progressive Liberal Party (PLP), Co-Deputy Leader 1993–97, Leader 1997–; Senator 1974; mem. House of Ass. (PLP) for Centerville and Farm Road, New Providence 1977–; Minister of Health and Nat. Insurance 1977–82, of Tourism 1977–82, of Agric., Trade and Industry 1990–93; Prime Minister and Minister of Finance 2002–07, 2012–. *Address:* Office of the Prime Minister, Sir Cecil Wallace Whitfield Centre, West Bay St, PO Box N-3217, Nassau (office); Progressive Liberal Party, Sir Lynden Pindling Centre, PLP House, Farrington Rd, POB N-547, Nassau, Bahamas (office). *Telephone:* 327-5826 (Office of the Prime Minister) (office); 325-5492 (Progressive Liberal Party) (office). *Fax:* 328-0808 (Progressive Liberal Party) (office). *Website:* www.myplp.com (office).

CHRISTIE, William Lincoln, BA; French/American harpsichordist, conductor and musicologist; *Director, Les Arts Florissants;* b. 19 Dec. 1944, Buffalo, NY; s. of William Christie and Ida Jones; ed Harvard Univ., Yale School of Music; studied harpsichord with Ralph Kirkpatrick, Kenneth Gilbert and David Fuller; moved to France 1970; mem. Five Centuries Ensemble 1971–75, René Jacobs' Concerto vocale 1976–80; f. Les Arts Florissants vocal and instrumental ensemble 1979; Prof., Conservatoire Nat. Supérieur de Musique, Paris 1982–95; conducts his own orchestra as well as many leading int. orchestras (Orchestra of the Age of Enlightenment, Glyndebourne 1996, 2005, Berlin Philharmonic, Zurich Opera, Opéra Nat. de Lyon); career highlights include Handel's Theodora, Glyndebourne 1996, Handel's Semele, Aix-en-Provence Festival 1996, Rameau's Hippolyte et Aricie, Paris 1996–97, Lully's Thésée, Barbican, London 1998, Monteverdi's Il ritorno d'Ulisse in patria, Aix-en-Provence 2002, Hercules, Aix-en-Provence 2004, Rameau's Les Paladins, Théâtre du Châtelet 2004, 2006, Brooklyn Acad. of Music 2006, Il Sant'Alessio 2007, The Fairy Queen 2010, Così fan tutte at the Met, etc., Lully's Atys at the Opéra Comique and worldwide tour 2011, La Didone (Théâtre de Caen, Théâtre des Champs Elysées) 2011–12, Charpentier's David et Jonathas (Aix, Edinburgh, Opéra Comique, Théâtre de Caen, Brooklyn Acad. of Music) 2012–13, Rameau's Hippolyte et Aricie, Glyndebourne 2013; Pres. Jury, Concours de Chant Baroque de Chimay, Belgium 2000–; cr. Le Jardin des Voix acad. for young singers in Caen, int. tours 2002, 2005, 2007, 2009, 2011, 2013; Artist-in-Residence (with Les Arts Florissants), Juilliard School, New York 2007–; mem. Royal Acad. of Music, Acad. des Beaux-Arts 2008, Institut de France 2010; Commdr, Légion d'honneur 2010; Officier des Arts et des Lettres; Hon. DMus (Univ. of New York, Buffalo) 1999, (Juilliard School); Prix Edison, Netherlands 1981, Grand prix du disque, Prix mondial de Montreux, Switzerland 1982, Gramophone Record of the Year, UK 1984, 1995, 1997, Deutscher Schallplattenpreis 1987, Grand prix de la Critique (best opera performance) 1987, Prix Opus, USA 1987, Prix int. de musique classique 1992, Prix Grand Siècle Laurent Perrier 1997, Grammy Award for Handel's Acis and Galatea 2000, Grammy and Cannes Classical Awards for Alcina 2001, Harvard Univ. Arts Medal 2002, Royal Philarmonic Award 2003, Liliane Bettencourt Choral Singing Prize, Acad. des Beaux Arts 2004, Prix Georges Pompidou 2005. *Recordings:* numerous recordings including all works for harpsichord by Rameau, works by Monteverdi, Purcell, Handel, Couperin, Charpentier, Desmarest, Mozart, etc. *Leisure interests:* gardening, old houses, cooking. *Address:* Les Arts Florissants, 46 rue Fortuny, 75017 Paris (office); Secrétariat de William Christie, 11 rue de la Cerisaie, 75004 Paris (office); 32 rue du Bâtiment, Thiré, 85210 Sainte-Hermine, France (home). *Telephone:* 1-43-87-98-88 (Arts Florissants) (office). *Fax:* 1-40-67-17-43 (Secrétariat) (office). *E-mail:* w.christie@orange.fr (home). *Website:* www.arts-florissants.com (office); ww.jardindewilliamchristie.fr.

CHRISTO; American (naturalized) artist; b. (Christo Javacheff), 13 June 1935, Gabrovo, Bulgaria; m. Jeanne-Claude Denat de Guillebon (Jeanne-Claude) (died 2009); one s.; ed Acad. of Fine Arts, Sofia and Vienna; went to Paris 1958; solo works include: Wrapped Objects 1958; project for Packaging of Public Building 1960; works with Jeanne-Claude 1961–: Stacked Oil Barrels and Dockside Packages, Cologne 1961–, Iron Curtain Wall of Oil Barrels blocking rue Visconti, Paris, Wrapping a Girl, London 1962, Showcases 1963, Store Front 1964, Air Package and Wrapped Tree, Eindhoven, Netherlands 1966, 42,390 cubic foot Package, Walker Art Center, Minneapolis School of Art 1966, Wrapped Kunsthalle, Bern 1968, 5,600 cubic m. Package for Kassel Documenta 4 1968, Wrapped Museum of Contemporary Art, Chicago 1969, Wrapped Coast, Little Bay, Sydney, Australia, 1969, Valley Curtain, Grand Hogback, Rifle, Colo, suspended fabric curtain 1970–72, Running Fence, Calif. 1972–76, Wrapped Roman Wall, Rome 1974, Ocean Front, Newport 1974, Wrapped Walk-Ways, Kansas City 1977–78, Surrounded Islands, Biscayne Bay, Miami, Fla 1980–83, The Pont Neuf Wrapped, Paris 1975–85, The Umbrellas, Japan-USA 1984–91, Wrapped Reichstag, Berlin 1971–95, Wrapped Trees, Fondation Beyeler and Berower Park, Riehen, Switzerland 1997–98, The Wall, 13,000 oil barrels, Gasometer, Oberhausen, Germany, indoor installation 1999, The Gates, Central Park, New York City 1979–2005, Over the River, Colo, The Mastaba, UAE (in progress); Praemium Imperiale 1995. *Website:* www.christojeanneclaude.net.

CHRISTODOULAKIS, Nikos M., EngDipl, MPhil, PhD; Greek politician and academic; *Professor of Economic Analysis, Athens University of Economics;* b. 27 Oct. 1952, Chania, Crete; ed Nat. Tech. Univ. of Athens and Univ. of Cambridge, UK; fmr mem. Euro-Communist party, linked with student uprising at Athens polytechnic 1973; Sr Research Officer, Dept of Applied Econs, Univ. of Cambridge 1984–86; Fellow, European Univ. of Florence 1989–90; apptd Prof. of Econ. Analysis, Athens Univ. of Econs 1990, Vice-Rector 1992–94, Prof. of Econ. Analysis 2007–; fmr Visiting Research Fellow, London Business School, Tinbergen Inst.; Prof. of Econs, Grad. School, Charles Univ., Prague 1992–93, Univ. of Cyprus 1996; Sec.-Gen. Research and Tech. 1993–96; Econ. Adviser to Prime Minister 1996; Deputy Minister of Finance 1996–2000; Minister of Devt with portfolios of Energy, Industry, Tech., Tourism and Commerce 2000–01; Minister of Economy and Finance 2001–04; mem. Parl. (Socialist Party) for Chania, Crete 2004–07; First Prize, Greek Math. Soc. 1970, Winbolt Prize 1985. *Publications include:* The New Terrain for Growth (in Greek) 1998, Growth, Employment and the Environment 2002, The Pendulum of Convergence (in Greek) 2006, several books and articles on econ. policy, business cycles, growth, forecasting and econ. models. *Leisure interest:* art, swimming, trekking. *Address:* 9 Kolokotroni Street, 10562 Athens, Greece (office). *Telephone:* (21) 03313488 (office). *Fax:* (21) 03313428 (office). *E-mail:* christodoulakis@parliament.gr (office). *Website:* www.christodoulakis.gr (office).

CHRISTODOULOU, Christodoulos, BA, BL, PhD; Cypriot business consultant, fmr government official and fmr central banker; b. 13 April 1939, Avgorou; m.; one d.; ed Pedagogical Acad. of Cyprus, Nicosia, Pantios High School of Political Sciences, Athens and Aristotelian Univ. of Salonica, Greece, Univ. of Wales, UK; Dir Govt Printing Office 1972–85; Perm. Sec., Ministry of Labour and Social Insurance 1985–89; Perm. Sec., Ministry of Agric. and Natural Resources 1989–94; Minister of Finance 1994–99, of the Interior 1999–2002; Gov. of Cen. Bank of Cyprus 2002–07; business consultant 2007–; several awards. *Publications:* several books and articles on legal, social, econ. and political matters. *Leisure interests:* reading, gardening. *Address:* 20 Ionos Street, Office 501, 2406 Nicosia (office); 12 Pritagora Street, 2406 Nicosia, Cyprus (home). *Telephone:* 22673400 (office). *Fax:* 22670400 (office). *E-mail:* a.c.consultants@cytanet.com.cy (office).

CHRISTODOULOU, Demetrios, MA, PhD; Greek/American mathematician, physicist and academic; *Professor of Mathematics and Physics, Eidgenössische Technische Hochschule Zürich;* b. 19 Oct. 1951, Athens; ed Princeton Univ.; Research Fellow, California Inst. of Tech. 1971–72; Prof. of Physics, Univ. of Athens 1972–73; Visiting Scientist, CERN, Geneva, Switzerland 1973–74; at Int. Centre for Theoretical Physics, Trieste 1974–76; Humboldt Fellow, Max Planck Inst., Munich, Germany 1976–81; Visiting mem., Courant Inst. 1981–83, Prof. of Math. 1988–92; Assoc. Prof. of Physics, Syracuse Univ. 1983–85, Prof. of Math. 1985–87; Prof. of Math., Princeton Univ. 1992–2001; Prof. of Math. and Physics, ETH Zürich 2001–; mem. American Acad. of Arts and Sciences 2001, European Acad. of Sciences 2003, NAS 2012; Hon. Prof. of Physics, Univ. of Crete 2011; Taxiarchis of the Order of Phoenix 2000; Dr hc (Athens) 1996, (Nat. Tech. Univ., Athens) 2000, (Brown Univ.) 2001, (Univ. of Cyprus) 2003, (Aristotle Univ. of Thessaloniki) 2010; Otto Hahn Medal, Max Planck Soc. 1981, Invited Address, Int. Congress of Mathematicians, Kyoto 1990, Basilis Xanthopoulos Award, GRG Soc. 1991, MacArthur Fellows Award, MacArthur Foundation 1993, Excellence in the Sciences Award, Acad. of Athens 1996, Guggenheim Fellow 1998, Bôcher Memorial Prize, American Soc. 1999, Zenon Prize, Math. Soc. of Cyprus 2000, Leonardo da Vinci Lecturer, Univ. of Milan 2003, Aristeio Bodossaki, Bodossaki Foundation 2006, Mordell Lecturer, Univ. of Cambridge 2007, Tomalla Prize 2008, Chaire d'État, Collège de France 2009, Plenary Lecturer, Int. Congress of Math. Physics, Prague 2009, Shaw Prize in Math. Sciences (co-recipient) 2012, Calderon-Zygmund Lecturer, Univ. of Chicago 2012, Hon. Plaque, Hellenic Soc. of Relativity, Gravitation and Cosmology 2012, Prize in Science, Letters and Arts, Tech. Univ. of Crete 2012, Inaugural Class of Fellows, American Math. Soc. 2012, Honorary Plaque, Hellenic Math. Soc. 2013. *Publications:* numerous papers in professional journals. *Address:* HG G 48.2, ETH-Zentrum, 8092 Zurich, Switzerland (office). *Telephone:* (44) 6325824 (office). *Fax:* (44) 6321085 (office). *E-mail:* demetri@math .ethz.ch (office). *Website:* www.math.ethz.ch/~demetri (office).

CHRISTOFIAS, Demetris, PhD; Cypriot politician and fmr head of state; b. 29 Aug. 1946, Kyrenia; ed Nicosia Commercial Lyceum, Inst. of Social Sciences and Acad. of Social Sciences, Moscow; joined United Democratic Youth Org. (EDON) 1964, elected mem. Central Council 1969, Cen. Organisational Sec. 1974–77, Sec.-Gen. 1977–87; mem. Anorthotiko Komma Ergazomenou Laou (AKEL) 1964–, Sec.-Gen. 1988–; mem. House of Reps representing Kyrenia 1991–, Pres. House of Reps 2001–08; Pres. of Cyprus 2008–13; Dr hc (Univ. of Macedonia) 2004. *Address:* Anorthotiko Komma Ergazomenou Laou, PO Box 21827, 4 East Papaioannou Street, 1075 Nicosia, Cyprus (office). *Telephone:* 22761121 (office). *Fax:* 22761574 (office). *E-mail:* k.e.akel@cytanet.com.cy (office). *Website:* www.akel.org.cy (office).

CHRISTOPHER, Ann, BA, RA, FRBS; British sculptor; b. 4 Dec. 1947, Watford, Herts., England; d. of the late William Christopher and Phyllis Christopher; m. Kenneth Cook 1969; ed Watford Girls' Grammar School, Harrow School of Art, West of England Coll. of Art; works include bronze sculpture, Castle Park, Bristol 1993, Corten sculpture, Marsh Mills, Plymouth 1996, Bronze Sculpture for offices of Linklaters and Paines solicitors, London 1997, Bronze Sculpture, Great Barrington, USA 1998, Corten Sculpture, Port Marine, UK 2001; represented by Gallery Pangolin and Pangolin London; RBS Silver Medal for Sculpture of Outstanding Merit 1994, Frampton Award 1996, Otto Beit Medal for Sculpture of Outstanding Merit 1997. *Publications:* Sculpture and Drawings 1969–89, Sculpture 1989–94, Selected Works 1995–2007, Marks on the Edge of Space 2010. *Leisure interests:* cinema, travel, architecture.

CHRISTOPHER, Sir (Duncan) Robin Carmichael, Kt, KBE, CMG, MA, MALD; British international organization executive and diplomatist (retd); *Projects Director, GLF Global Leadership Foundation;* b. 13 Oct. 1944, Sussex; m. Merril Stevenson 1980; two d.; ed Keble Coll., Oxford and Fletcher School, Tufts Univ., USA; VSO volunteer in Bolivia; philosophy teacher, Univ. of Sussex 1969; joined FCO 1970, served in Embassy in New Delhi 1972–76, FCO 1976, Deputy High Commr, Lusaka 1980–83, FCO and Cabinet Office 1983–87, Counsellor (Econ. and Commercial), Embassy in Madrid 1987–91, Head, Southern African Dept, FCO 1991–94, Amb. to Ethiopia 1994–97, to Indonesia 1997–2000, to Argentina 2000–04; Sec.-Gen. GLF Global Leadership Foundation 2007–10, Projects Dir 2010–; Trustee, Prospect Burma, Partners for Change (Ethiopia), Redress. *Publications include:* Indonesia in Transition: Democracy or Disintegration? 2000, Justice and Peace 2000 (Czech edn 2007), Remembrance Day 2007. *Leisure interests:* motorcycling, skiing, music. *Address:* GLF Global Leadership Foundation, 25 Knightsbridge, London, SW1X 7LY, England (office). *Telephone:* (20) 7838-7054 (office). *Fax:* (20) 7681-2263 (office). *E-mail:* robin.christopher@g-l-f .org (office); rchristopher2@yahoo.co.uk. *Website:* www.g-l-f.org (office).

CHRISTOPHERSEN, Henning, MEcon; Danish politician; *Chairman, European Institute of Public Administration;* b. 8 Nov. 1939, Copenhagen; s. of Richard Christophersen and Gretha Christophersen; m. Jytte Risbjerg Nielsen 1961; one s. two d.; ed Univ. of Copenhagen; Head of the Economic Section of the Handicrafts Council 1965–70; mem. Folketing 1971–84, mem. of Parl. Finance Cttee 1972–76, Vice-Chair. 1976–78, Minister of Foreign Affairs 1978–79; Deputy Leader, Danish Liberal Party 1972, Acting Party Leader 1977–78, Party Leader 1978–84; Deputy Prime Minister and Minister of Finance 1982–84; Vice-Pres. Comm. responsible for Budget, Financial Control, Personnel and Admin., Comm. of EC (now European Comm.) 1985–89, Econ. and Financial Affairs 1989–95, Co-ordination of Structural Funds 1989–92; a Vice Pres. of EC (now EU) 1993–95; Swedish Prime Minister's Adviser, Council for Baltic Sea Cooperation 1996–2000; Danish Prime Minister's Personal Rep. to European Convention and mem. Presidium 2002–03; Chair. European Inst. of Public Admin., Netherlands 1996–; Pres. The Energy Charter Treaty Conf., Brussels 1998–2007; Chair. Supervisory Bd of Dirs Örestad Devt Cooperation, Copenhagen 1999–; Vice-Chair. Supervisory Bd of Dirs Scania Danmark A/S, Herlev, Denmark 2000–; Sr Partner, Kreab A/B, Brussels 2002–; mem. Bd of Dirs Den Danske Bank 1996–, Int. Advisory Bd Creditanstalt-Bankverein, Austria, European Advisory Cttee on the Opening-up of Public Procurement, Danish Council for European Policy and the Baltic Sea Council, Sweden; Nat. Order of Merit. *Publications:* En udfordring for de Liberale, Taenker om Danmark i Det Nye Europa 1989 and numerous articles on econs. *Leisure interests:* genealogy, history and languages. *Address:* Kreab A/B, Av. de Tervueren 2, 1040 Brussels, Belgium.

CHRISTOV-BAKARGIEV, Carolyn; American/Italian writer, art historian and curator; b. 2 Dec. 1957, Ridgewood, NJ; m. Cesare Pietroiusti; two d.; ed Univ. of Pisa, Italy; began career as art critic and ind. curator; Sr Curator of Exhbns, P.S.1 Contemporary Art Center, New York 1999–2001; Chief Curator, Castello di Rivoli Museum of Contemporary Art, Turin, Italy 2002–08, Dir 2009; Artistic Dir Sydney Biennale 2008; Artistic Dir dOCUMENTA (13), Kassel, Germany 2012; mem. jury, 49th Venice Biennale 2001. *Publications:* Arte Povera (Themes and Movements) 1999, The Moderns 2003, Pierre Huyghe 2004.

CHROMY, Bronisław; Polish sculptor; b. 3 June 1925, Leńcze nr Lanckorona; m.; two d.; ed Acad. of Fine Arts, Kraków 1956; one-man exhbns in Poland and abroad; int. exhbns and competitions; creator of many monuments commemorating victims of World War II; f. Bronislaw Chromy ART Foundation, Kraców; mem. Polish Acad. of Arts and Sciences, Kraków; mem. Union of Polish Artists and Designers 1970–; Commdr Cross with Star Order of Polonia Restituta 1999; Meritorious Medal for Nat. Culture 1986. *Achievements:* some works permanently in museums and pvt collections; sculptures include: Pieta Oświęcimska (Monument) 1963, Smok wawelski, Kraców 1970, Pomnik Żolniercy Polskich (Monument to Polish Soldiers), Katowice 1978, Pomnik jana Pawła II (Monument to John Paul II), Tarnów 1981, Zielonki nr Kraków 1998, Statue of John Paul II, Leńczach 2002, Chopin Monument, Wrocław 2010. *Leisure interests:* music, literature, nature. *Address:* Bronislaw Chromy ART Foundation, ul. Cystersow 11, 31-553 Kracóv, Poland. *Telephone:* (12) 4122260 (home). *Fax:* (12) 4122466 (home). *E-mail:* office@ chromy.art.pl. *Website:* www.chromy.art.pl.

CHRONOWSKI, Andrzej; Polish politician; b. 9 April 1961, Grybów, Nowy Sącz Dist; m. Barbara Chronowski; two s.; ed Acad. of Mining and Metallurgy, Kraków;

helped organize student strikes in univ. cities including Kraków 1980–81; railway repair factory, Nowy Sącz 1987, later Head of Production, Chair. Employees' Council 1991–93; mem. Solidarity Trade Union; Senator 1993–2005; Sec. Solidarity Senate Club Presidium 1993–97; Vice-Marshal of Senate 1997–; Chair. Nowy Sącz Region of Social Movt of Solidarity Electoral Action (RS AWS) 1997, Chair. Małopolski Region, Chair. Senators' Club 2001; Chair. Council of Sądecki Club; Minister of State Treasury 2000–01; Senator to 3rd and 4th term Senate, Deputy Speaker of 4th term Senate 2001–; mem. European Parl. (Group of the European People's Party—Christian Democrats and European Democrats) 2004, mem. Cttee on Budgets; mem. Solidarity Trade Union, Nat. Econ. Cttee, Cttee for Human Rights and Lawfulness, Cttee of Initiatives and Legislative Work. *Leisure interests:* skiing, climbing, time with family. *Address:* ul. Pijarska 17A, 33-300 Nowy Sącz S5C2, Poland (office).

CHRYSOHOIDIS, Michalis; Greek politician; *Minister of Civic Protection;* b. 31 Oct. 1955, Imathia; s. of Vasilis Chrisochoidhis and Anna Chrisochoidhis; m. Aggeliu Hondromelidois; one s. one d.; ed Faculty of Law, Aristotle Univ. of Thessaloníki; Founding mem. Panhellenic Socialist Movement (PASOK) 1974–, held numerous elected posts at local level, elected mem. Cen. Cttee 1990, Sec.-Gen. 2003–; elected to Nat. Parl. 1989; Deputy Minister of Commerce 1994–96, of Devt 1996–99; Minister for Public Order 1999–2003, of Civic Protection 2009–. *Address:* Ministry of Civic Protection, P. Khanellopoulou 4, 101 77 Athens, Greece (office). *Telephone:* (210) 6977000 (office). *Fax:* (210) 6921675 (office). *E-mail:* ydt@otenet .gr (office). *Website:* www.ydt.gr (office).

CHSHMARITIAN, Karen, PhD; Armenian economist and politician; b. 12 Sept. 1959, Yerevan; m.; two c.; ed Yerevan Inst. of Nat. Economy; trained as economist, Georgetown Univ. and Int. Law Inst., Washington, DC 1995; economist, Armenian Br., Research Inst. of Standards and State Planning, USSR 1980; mil. service in Soviet Army 1981–82; Sr Economist, Chief Specialist and Head of Financial Sub-Div., State Supply Cttee, Armenia 1985–90; Deputy Dir-Gen., Haielectramekena-metzar (state co.), Armenia 1990–91; Head of Dept, Ministry of Material Resources, Repub. of Armenia 1991–93, Deputy Minister 1993–96; Head of Foreign Trade Dept, Ministry of Trade, Services and Tourism 1996–97; First Deputy Minister, Ministry of Industry and Trade 1997–98; advisor to Azgayin Zhoghov (Nat. Ass.) 1998–99; Minister of Industry and Trade 1999–2000; Minister of Trade and Econ. Devt 2002–07; mem. Azgayin Zhoghov (Nat. Ass.) (Republican Party of Armenia) 2007–. *Address:* Azgayin Zhoghov (National Assembly), 0095 Yerevan, Marshal Baghramian St 19, Armenia (office). *Telephone:* (10) 58-82-25 (office). *Fax:* (10) 52-98-26 (office). *E-mail:* karen.chshmaritian@parliament.am (office). *Website:* www.parliament.am (office).

CHU, Bo; Chinese politician; *Secretary, Committee of Inner Mongolian Autonomous Region, Chinese Communist Party;* b. Oct. 1944, Tongcheng, Anhui Prov.; ed Tianjin Univ.; joined CCP 1969; Deputy Dir and Deputy Sec. CCP Party Cttee, Yueyang Chemical Works 1975–84; fmr Mayor Yueyang City; Del., 13th CCP Nat. Congress 1987–92; mem. Standing Cttee, CCP Hunan Prov. Cttee 1990, Deputy Sec. CCP Hunan Prov. Cttee 1994–99; Exec. Vice-Gov. Hunan Prov. 1993–94, Vice-Gov. (also Acting Gov.) 1998–99, Gov. 1999–2001; Deputy, 9th NPC 1998–2003; Sec. CCP Cttee of Inner Mongolian Autonomous Region 2001–; Alt. mem. 15th CCP Cen. Cttee 1997–2002, mem. 16th CCP Cen. Cttee 2002–07, mem. 17th CCP Cen. Cttee 2007–; Hon. Pres. Hunan Prov. Merchants' Assscn. *Address:* Chinese Communist Party Committee of Inner Mongolian Autonomous Region, Huhot, Inner Mongolia, People's Republic of China.

CHU, Ivan (Kwok-leung), BSc, MCom; Hong Kong airline industry executive; *CEO, Cathay Pacific Airways Ltd;* b. 1962; ed Univ. of Hong Kong, Univ. of New South Wales, Australia; joined Cathay Pacific Airways Ltd as man. trainee 1984, has served in Hong Kong, China, Taiwan, Thailand and Australia, Gen. Man., Southwest Pacific Div. –2008, Dir of Service Delivery 2008–11, Dir 2011–, Chief Operating Officer 2011–14, CEO, Cathay Pacific Airways Ltd 2014–, also Chair. Hong Kong Dragon Airlines Ltd, AHK Air Hong Kong; Dir John Swire & Sons (HK) Ltd, Swire Pacific 2014–. *Address:* Cathay Pacific, One Pacific Place, 88 Queensway, Hong Kong Special Administrative Region, People's Republic of China (office). *Website:* www.cathaypacific.com (office).

CHU, Lam Yiu; Chinese business executive; *Chairman and President, Huabao International Holdings Ltd;* b. 1971, Sichuan; m. Lam Kwok Man; f. Huabao Food and Flavours and Fragrances Co. Ltd, Shanghai 1996, made public 2006, now called Huabao International Holdings Ltd, Chair. and Pres. 2004–; Deputy Dir China Asscn of Fragrance, Flavour and Cosmetic Industry, China Food Additive Production and Application Industry Asscn; mem. 4th CPPCC Cttee; ranked by Forbes magazine amongst 100 Most Powerful Women (90th) 2007. *Address:* Huabao International Holdings Ltd, Suite 1103, Central Plaza, 18 Harbour Road, Wanchai, Hong Kong Special Administrative Region, People's Republic of China (office). *Telephone:* 28276677 (office). *Fax:* 28278866 (office). *Website:* www.huabao .com.hk (office).

CHU, Li-luan (Eric), BBA, MA, PhD; Taiwanese politician; *Mayor of New Taipei City;* b. 7 June 1961; ed Nat. Taiwan Univ., New York Univ., USA; Asst Prof., CUNY, USA 1990–92; Assoc. Prof., later Prof., Nat. Taiwan Univ. 1992–2001; mem., Legis. Yuan (Parl.) 1999–2001, Convener, Budget Cttee 2000, Convener, Finance Cttee 2001; Magistrate, Taoyuan Co. 2001–09; Vice-Premier 2009; Mayor of New Taipei City 2010–. *Address:* No. 161, Sec. 1, Zhongshan Road, Banqiao District, New Taipei City 22001, Taiwan (office). *Telephone:* (2) 29603456 (office). *Website:* www.ntpc.gov.tw (office).

CHU, Paul Ching-Wu, BS, MS, PhD, JP; American (b. Chinese) physicist and academic; *T.L.L. Temple Chair of Science, Professor of Physics and Founding Director and Chief Scientist, Texas Center for Superconductivity, University of Houston;* b. 12 Feb. 1941, Hunan, People's Repub. of China; ed Cheng-Kung Univ., Taiwan, Fordham Univ., Univ. of California, San Diego; Teaching Asst, Fordham Univ. 1963–65; Research Asst, Univ. of Calif., San Diego 1965–68; mem. Tech. Staff, Bell Labs, Murray Hill, NJ 1968–70; Asst Prof. of Physics, Cleveland State Univ. 1970–73, Assoc. Prof. 1973–75, Prof. 1975–79; Resident Research Assoc., Argonne Nat. Lab., Argonne, Ill. 1972; Visiting Scientist, Stanford Univ., Hansens Physics Lab. 1973; Visiting Staff mem., Los Alamos Scientific Lab., NM 1975–80; Prof. of Physics, Univ. of Houston, Tex. 1979–, also Dir Magnetic Information Research Lab. 1984–88, Dir Space Vacuum Epitaxy Center 1986–88, M.D.

Anderson Chair. of Physics 1987–89, Dir Tex. Center for Superconductivity 1987–2001 (Exec. Dir 2005–11, Founding Dir and Chief Scientist 2011–), T.L.L. Temple Chair. of Science 1987–; Pres. and Prof. of Physics, Hong Kong Univ. of Science and Tech. 2001–09, Pres. Emer. and Univ. Prof. Emer. 2009–; Visiting Miller Research Prof., Univ. of Calif., Berkeley 1991; Prin. Investigator, Lawrence Berkeley Nat. Lab., Berkeley 1999–2005 (Guest Scientist 2005–); mem. Editorial Bd numerous journals, including Indian Journal of Pure and Applied Physics 1992–, Brazilian Journal of Physics 1995–, Science in China 1997–, Chinese Science Bulletin 1997–; mem. numerous advisory bds and cttees, including Coalition for the Commercial Application of Superconductors 1989–, Int. Advisory Cttee, Innovative Center for Frontier Sciences, Ministry of Educ., China 2012–; mem. AAAS 1987, Academia Sinia 1988, NAS 1989, American Acad. of Arts and Sciences 1989, Acad. of Medicine, Eng and Science of Texas 2004; Foreign mem. Chinese Acad. of Sciences 1996; Fellow, American Physical Soc. 1978, Tex. Acad. of Sciences 1992, Hong Kong Inst. of Science 2011; Charter Fellow, Nat. Acad. of Inventors 2013; Hon. Pres. Jiaxing Univ. 2006; Hon. Prof., Physics Inst., Chinese Acad. of Sciences 1979, Zhongshan Univ. 1988, Nankai Univ. 1991, Chinese Univ. of Science and Tech. 1991, Nanjing Univ. 1996, Dongnan Univ. 2003, Nat. Tsinghua Univ. 2009; Hon. Citizen, State of Texas 1987, City of Houston 1987; Hon. Chancellor Taiwan Comprehensive Univ. System 2012–; Dr hc (Chinese Univ. of Hong Kong) 1988, (Northwestern Univ.) 1988, (Fordham) 1988, (Florida Int. Univ.) 1989, (State Univ. of New York at Farmingdale) 1989, (Whittier Coll.) 1991, (Hong Kong Baptist Univ.) 1999, (Providence Univ.) 2005, (Univ. of Macau) 2006, (Loughborough) 2007; numerous awards including Grumman Corpn Leroy Randle Grumman Medal for Outstanding Scientific Achievement 1987, NASA Achievement Award 1987, Univ. of Houston Faculty Research Award 1987, New York Acad. of Sciences Physical and Math. Science Award 1987, APS Int. Prize for New Materials 1988, Nat. Medal of Science 1988, NAS Comstock Award 1988, World Cultural Council Medal of Scientific Merit 1989, St Martin de Porres Award 1990, Texas Instruments Founders' Prize 1990, Int. Conf. on Materials and Mechanisms of Superconductivity, High Temperature Superconductors Bernd Matthias Prize 1994, Sharif Univ. Award 1999, Asscn of American-Chinese Professionals (AACP) Distinguished Achievement Award 2001, American Asscn of Eng Socs John Fritz Medal 2001, Univ. of Houston Esther Farfel Award 2000, Prize Ettore Majorana – Erice/Science for Peace 2007, Chinese Inst. of Engineers Lifetime Achievement Award 2008, Hong Kong Inst. of Engineers Hall of Fame Award 2010. *Publications:* more than 590 scientific papers in professional journals. *Address:* Texas Center for Superconductivity, University of Houston, 202 Houston Science Center, Houston, TX 77204-5002, USA (office). *Telephone:* (713) 743-8222 (home). *Fax:* (713) 743-8201 (office). *E-mail:* cwchu@uh.edu (office). *Website:* www .tcsuh.com (office).

CHU, Steven, BA, PhD; American physicist, academic and government official; b. 28 Feb. 1948, St Louis; s. of Ju Chin Chu and Ching Chen Li; m. 1st Lisa Chu-Thielbar; two s.; m. 2nd Jean Fetter 1997; ed Garden City High School, Univ. of Rochester, Univ. of California, Berkeley; Post-doctoral Fellow, Univ. of California, Berkeley 1976–78; with Bell Labs, Murray Hill, New Jersey 1978–83, Head of Quantum Electronics Research Dept, Bell Labs, Holmdell, New Jersey 1983–87; Prof. of Physics and Applied Physics, Stanford Univ. 1987–2004, Frances and Theodore Geballe Prof. of Physics and Applied Physics 1990–2004, Chair. Physics Dept 1990–93, 1999–2001; apptd Prof. of Physics and Prof. of Molecular and Cell Biology, Univ. of California, Berkeley 2004, Dir Lawrence Berkeley Nat. Lab. 2004–08; US Sec. of Energy, Washington, DC 2009–13; Visiting Prof., Collège de France 1990; Fellow, American Physics Soc. (Chair. Laser Science Topical Group 1989), Optical Soc. of America, American Acad. of Arts and Sciences; Woodrow Wilson Fellow 1970, NSF Doctoral Fellow 1970–74; mem. NAS, American Philosophical Soc., Academia Sinica; Foreign mem. Chinese Acad. of Sciences, Korean Acad. of Science and Eng; Herbert P. Broida Prize for laser spectroscopy 1987, King Faisal Prize for Science 1993, Schawlow Prize 1994, Meggars Award 1994, Humboldt Sr Scientist Award 1995, Science for Art Prize 1995, shared Nobel Prize for Physics 1997 for developing methods of cooling matter to very low temperatures using lasers. *Publications include:* numerous papers on atomic physics and laser spectroscopy. *Leisure interests:* baseball, swimming, cycling, tennis. *Address:* c/o Department of Energy, Forrestal Building, 1000 Independence Avenue, SW, Washington, DC 20585, USA.

CHUA, Nam-Hai, PhD, FRS; Singaporean biologist and academic; *Andrew W. Mellon Professor and Head, Laboratory of Plant Molecular Biology, The Rockefeller University;* b. 8 April 1944; m. Suat-Choo Pearl Chua 1970; two d.; ed Univ. of Singapore and Harvard Univ.; lecturer, Dept of Biochemistry, Univ. of Singapore 1969–71; Research Assoc. Dept of Cell Biology, Rockefeller Univ. 1971–73, Asst Prof. Dept of Cell Biology 1973–77, Prof. and Head, Lab. of Plant Molecular Biology 1988–, Andrew W. Mellon Prof. 1988–; consultant Shanghai Research Centre for Life Sciences, Chinese Acad. of Science 1996–, Global Tech. Centre and Nutrition, Monsanto Co. 1997–; numerous consultancies and bd memberships; Int. Prize for Biology, Japan Soc. for the Promotion of Science 2005. *Publications:* over 260 scientific publs. *Leisure interests:* squash, skiing. *Address:* Laboratory of Plant Molecular Biology, Rockefeller University, 1230 York Avenue, New York, NY 10021, USA (office). *Telephone:* (212) 327-8126 (office). *E-mail:* chua@rockefeller.edu (office). *Website:* www.rockefeller.edu/labheads/chua (office).

CHUA, Sock Koong, CPA; Singaporean accountant and telecommunications industry executive; *Group CEO, Singapore Telecommunications Limited (SingTel);* m.; two d.; ed Univ. of Singapore; Certified Public Accountant and Chartered Financial Analyst; joined Singapore Telecommunications Ltd (SingTel) as Treas. in 1989, Chief Financial Officer 1999–2006, Group Chief Financial Officer and CEO Int. Feb.–Oct. 2006, Deputy Group CEO 2006–07, Group CEO 2007–; mem. Bd of Dirs JTC Corpn, Bharti Tele-Ventures Ltd; Trustee, Singapore Man. Univ.; Best Chief Financial Officer, FinanceAsia magazine's 2004, Best Managed Companies poll 2002, 2003, 2004, ranked by Fortune magazine amongst the 50 Most Powerful Women in Business outside the US (25th) 2002, (41st) 2003, (43rd) 2004, (50th) 2005, (17th) 2006, (15th) 2007, (14th) 2008–10, (eighth) 2011–12, ranked by Forbes magazine amongst The World's 100 Most Powerful Women (71st) 2010, (74th) 2012, (91st) 2013. *Leisure interest:* keeping fit. *Address:* SingTel, 31 Exeter Road, Comcentre #19-00, Singapore 239732 (office). *Telephone:* 68383388 (office). *Fax:* 67328248 (office). *E-mail:* contact@singtel.com (office). *Website:* info .singtel.com (office).

CHUAN, Leekpai, LLB; Thai lawyer and politician; b. 28 July 1938, Muang Dist, Trang Prov.; ed Trang Wittaya School, Silapakorn Pre-Univ. and Thammasat Univ.; studied for two years with Bar Asscn of Thailand; mem. Parl. for Trang Prov. 1969–; Deputy Minister of Justice 1975; Deputy Minister of Justice and Minister, Prime Minister's Office 1976; Minister of Justice 1980, of Commerce 1981, of Agric. and co-operatives 1982–83, of Educ. 1983–86; Speaker, House of Reps 1986–88; Minister of Public Health 1988–89, of Agric. and co-operatives 1990–91; Deputy Prime Minister 1990, Prime Minister of Thailand 1992–95, 1997–2001; Leader Prachatipat (Democrat Party—DP) 1992–2003; Leader of Opposition 1995–96, 1996–97, 2001–; Minister of Defence 1997–2001; Vice-Pres. Prince of Songkhla Univ. Council; Kt Grand Cordon of the Most Noble Order of the Crown of Thailand 1981, Kt Grand Cordon (Special Class) of the Most Exalted Order of the White Elephant 1982, Order of Sukatuna (Special Class), Raja, Philippines 1993, Kt Grand Commdr (Second Class, Higher Grade) of the Most Illustrious Order of Chula Chom Klao 1998, Order of the Sun (Grand Cross), Peru 1999; six hon. degrees. *Leisure interest:* drawing. *Address:* Prachatipat (Democrat Party), 67 Thanon Setsiri, Samsen Nai, Phyathai, 10400, Bangkok 10300 (office); 471/2 Rajaprasop Road, Magasasam, Rajatheri District, Metropolitan 10400, Bangkok, Thailand (home). *Telephone:* (2) 278-4042 (office); (2) 245-4415 (home). *Fax:* (2) 279-6086; (2) 278-4218 (office). *E-mail:* admin@democrat.or.th (office). *Website:* www.democrat.or.th (office); www.chuan.org (office).

CHUBACHI, Ryoji, BA, MA, PhD; Japanese business executive; *Vice-Chairman, Sony Corporation;* b. 4 Sept. 1947; ed Tohoku Univ.; joined Sony Corpn 1977, with Sony Magnetic Products Inc., Ala, USA 1989–92, Gen. Man. Video Tape Div., Recording Media Products Group, Tokyo 1992–94, Gen. Man. Video Tape Dept, Recording Media Div. 1994–98, Pres. Recording Media Co. 1999–2002, Pres. Core Tech. & Network Co. 2002–03, Pres. Micro Systems Network Co. 2003–04, COO in charge of Micro Systems Network Co. June 2004, Pres. Production Strategy Group 2004–05, mem. Bd of Dirs Sony Corpn 2005–, also Rep. Corp. Exec. Officer 2005–, Pres. 2005–09, CEO Global Electronics Business 2005–09, Vice-Chair. and Rep. Corp. Exec. Officer 2009–; mem. Asscn of Radio Industries and Businesses (Dir 2005–), Japan Electronics and Information Tech. Industries Asscn (Vice-Chair. Exec. Bd, Trade Affairs). *Address:* Sony Corporation, 1-7-1 Konan, Minato-ku, Tokyo 108-0075, Japan (office). *Telephone:* (3) 6748-2111 (office). *Fax:* (3) 6748-2244 (office). *E-mail:* info@sony.net (office). *Website:* www.sony.net (office).

CHUBAIS, Anatolii Borisovich, CEconSc, PhD; Russian economist, business executive and politician; *CEO, Russian State Nanotechnology Corporation (Rosnanotech);* b. 16 June 1955, Borisov, Belarusian SSR; m.; one s. one d.; ed Leningrad Inst. of Eng and Econs; engineer and Asst to Chair. Leningrad (now St Petersburg) Inst. of Econs and Eng 1977–82, Asst Prof. 1982–90; Leader, The Young Economists 1984–87; Deputy, then First Deputy Chair. of Leningrad Municipal Council Jan.–Nov. 1991; Minister of State Property 1991–98; Deputy Prime Minister and Chair. State Cttee for Man. of State Property 1991–98; Deputy Prime Minister and Chair. Co-ordination Council for Privatization 1992–94; First Deputy Prime Minister responsible for economy 1994–96; mem. State Duma (Parl.) 1993–95; Chief of Staff of Presidential Exec. Office 1996–97; First Deputy Prime Minister 1997–98, Minister of Finance March–Nov. 1997; Russian Dir EBRD 1997–98; mem. Russian Security Council 1997–98; Head of Russian Fed. Interdepartmental Comm. on Co-operation with Int. Financial and Econ. Orgs and Group of Seven 1998; CEO Unified Energy Systems of Russia 1998–2001, CEO and Chair. Bd of Man. 2001–08; CEO Russian State Nanotechnology Corpn (Rosnanotech) 2008–; Co-Chair. Round Table of Russian and EU Producers 2000–; Pres. Electric Power Council of CIS 2000–07; mem. Int. Advisory Bd JP Morgan Chase 2008–; mem. Man. Bd Russian Union of Mfrs and Entrepreneurs 2000–; mem. Govt Comm. on Co-operation with EU 2000–; joined Union of Rightist Forces 1999, Co-Chair. 2001–04 (resgnd); Hon. PhD (St Petersburg State Eng, Econ. Univ.); Best Minister of Finance Award, Euromoney magazine 1997, three commendations from Pres. of Russian Fed. 1995, 1997, 1998, Int. Union of Economists Int. Award 2001. *Leisure interests:* music, literature. *Address:* Russian State Nanotechnology Corpn (Rosnanotech), 117420 Moscow, ul. Nametkina 12A, Russia (office). *Telephone:* (495) 542-44-44 (office). *Fax:* (495) 542-44-34 (office). *E-mail:* info@rusnano.com (office). *Website:* www .rusnano.com (office); www.chubais.ru (home).

CHUBB, Ian William, AC, MSc, DPhil (Oxon.), FACE; Australian neuroscientist, fmr university administrator and government official; *Chief Scientist of Australia;* b. 17 Oct. 1943, Melbourne, Vic.; JF & C Heymans Research Fellow, Univ. of Ghent, Belgium 1969–71; Wellcome Foundation Scholar, then Jr Research Fellow of St John's Coll., later Royal Soc. Research Fellow, Univ. of Oxford, UK 1971–77; Lecturer, then Sr Lecturer, later Assoc. Prof., School of Medicine, Flinders Univ. 1978–85, Vice-Chancellor Flinders Univ. 1995–2000; Deputy Vice-Chancellor Univ. of Wollongong 1986–90, Hon. Prof. of Biology; Chair. Higher Educ. Council 1990–94, part-time Chair. 1994–97; Deputy Chair. Nat. Bd of Employment, Educ. and Training 1990–94; Sr Deputy Vice-Chancellor and Foundation Dean Faculty of Business and Econs, Monash Univ. 1993–95; Interim Chair., then Deputy Chair. Nat. Cttee for Quality in Higher Educ. 1993–94; Vice-Chancellor ANU 2001–11; Chief Scientist of Australia 2011–; mem. Ministerial Task Force 1989, Prime Minister's Science, Eng and Innovation Council 2000–02, Foreign Affairs Council; mem. Bd of Dirs Australia-New Zealand School of Govt, Australian Vice-Chancellors' Cttee 1996–2006 (later Deputy Pres., Pres. 2000–01); Chair. Group of Eight Univs 2003–05; also served in various capacities on Nat. Health and Medical Research Council and Australian Research Cttee; Fellow, Australian Coll. of Educators; Hon. DSc (Flinders) 2000; Hon. DUniv (ANU) 2011; Hon. DLitt (Charles Darwin Univ.) 2011; Hon. LLD (Monash) 2012; several academic awards, grants from Nat. Health and MRC, Australian Research Grants Scheme and from various foundations, Centenary Medal 2003, ACT's Australian of the Year 2011. *Publications:* numerous articles in scientific journals. *Address:* Office of the Chief Scientist, GPO Box 9839, Canberra, ACT 2601, Australia (office). *Telephone:* (2) 6276-1232 (office). *Fax:* (2) 6213-6558 (office). *E-mail:* chief.scientist@chiefscientist .gov.au (office). *Website:* www.chiefscientist.gov.au (office).

CHUBUK, Ion, DrEcon; Moldovan politician; b. 20 May 1943; ed Odessa Inst. of Agric.; First Deputy Chair. Moldova State Planning Cttee 1984–86; Head of Div. Research Inst. of Agric. 1986–89; Deputy Chair. Moldovan Agricultural-Industrial Council 1989–90; First Deputy Minister of Econs 1990–91; Deputy Prime Minister, Perm. Rep. of Moldovan Govt in USSR Council of Ministers 1991–92; First Deputy Minister of Foreign Affairs 1992–94; First Deputy Minister of Econs April–Dec. 1994; Chair. Moldovan Accountant Chamber 1994–97, Deputy Chair. Accountant Chamber 1999–; Prime Minister of Moldova 1997–99; Deputy Chair. Centrist Union 2000–. *Address:* c/o Centrist Union of Moldova, (Uniunea Centristă din Moldova), Chişinău, str. Tricolorului 35, Moldova (office).

CHUCHOTTAWORN, Pailin, BEng, MEng, DEng; Thai business executive; *President and CEO, PTT Public Co. Ltd;* ed Chulalongkorn Univ., Tokyo Inst. of Tech., Japan.; Exec. Vice-Pres., Petrochemicals and Refining Business Unit, PTT Public Co. Ltd, working as Pres. PTT Asahi Chemical Co. Ltd 2006–08, Sr Exec. Vice-Pres., working as Pres. PTT Polymer Marketing Co. Ltd, PTT Asahi Chemical Co. Ltd 2008–09, Sr Exec. Vice-Pres., PTT, working as CEO IRPC Public Co. Ltd 2009–11, Chief Operations Officer, Upstream Petroleum and Gas Business Group, Acting CEO IRPC Public Co. Ltd June–Sept. 2011, Pres. and CEO PTT Public Co. Ltd 2011–, also Dir and Sec. to the Bd, mem. Nominating Cttee; Dr hc in Sustainable Energy and Environment Tech. and Man. (Rajamangala Univ. of Tech. Rattanakosin, Thailand); Asia Talent Management Award, CNBC Asia Business Leaders Award, Leadership Achievement Award, Asia-Pacific region 2012, Asian Banker Magazine, Best CEO 2012, Finance Asia Magazine. *Address:* PTT Public Co. Ltd, 555 Vibhavadi Rangsit Road, Chatuchak, Bangkok 10900, Thailand (office). *Telephone:* 537-2000 (office). *Fax:* 537-3499 (office). *E-mail:* info@pttplc.com (office). *Website:* www.pttplc.com (office).

CHUCK D; American rap artist; b. (Carlton Ridenhour), 1 Aug. 1960, Long Island, NY; m. Gaye Theresa Johnson; ed Adelphi Univ.; Super Special Mix Show, radio WBAU 1982; own mobile DJ and concert promotion co., Spectrum City; Founder mem. rap group, Public Enemy 1982–; Man. and Promoter, The Entourage (hip hop venue), Long Island, New York 1986; Founder, Offda Books, Under the Radar Publishing 2003; MOBO Award for Outstanding Contrib. to Black Music 2005. *Recordings include:* albums: with Public Enemy: Yo! Bum Rush The Show 1987, It Takes A Nation of Millions To Hold Us Back 1988, Fear of a Black Planet 1990, Apocalypse 91... The Enemy Strikes Black (Soul Train Music Award for Best Rap Album 1992) 1991, Greatest Misses 1992, Muse Sick-n-Hour Mess Age 1994, He Got Game (film soundtrack) 1998, There's a Poison Goin' On... 1999, Revolverlution 2002, Rebirth of a Nation 2005, New Whirl Odor 2005, How you Sell a Soul to a Soulless People who Sold their Soul??? 2007, Most of My Heroes Still Don't Appear on No Stamp 2012, The Evil Empire of Everything 2012; solo: No 1996, The Autobiography of Mistachuck 1996. *Publications include:* Public Enemy (autobiography) 1994, Fight the Power: Rap, Race and Reality (non-fiction, with Yusuf Jah) 1997. *E-mail:* Mistachuck@rapstation.com (office). *Website:* www.rapstation .com; www.publicenemy.com.

CHUDAKOVA, Marietta Omarovna, DLit, PhD; Russian academic; *Professor of Literature, Moscow Literary Institute;* b. (Marietta Khan-Magomedova), 2 Jan. 1937, Moscow; m. Alexander Pavlovich Chudakov (died 2005); one d.; ed Moscow State Univ.; school teacher in Moscow 1959–61; Sr Researcher, Div. of Manuscripts, Div. of Rare Books, Div. of Library Research All-Union Lenin's Public Library 1965–84; Ed.-in-Chief Tynyanovski sborniki 1984–; teacher, Moscow Literary Inst. 1986–, Prof. 1992–; Visiting Prof., Stanford Univ. 1989, Univ. of Southern Calif. 1990, Ecole Normale Supérieure, Paris 1991, Geneva Univ. and European Inst. in Geneva 1994, Ottawa Univ. 1995, Cologne Univ. 1999; Chair. All-Russian Mikhail Bulgakov Fund; mem. Academia Europaea; Prize of Moscow Komsomol for research on Yuri Olesha 1970. *Publications:* Effendi Kapiev (biog.) 1970, Craftsmanship of Yuri Olesha 1972, Talks about Archives 1975, Poetics of Mikhail Zoshchenko 1979, Life of Mikhail Bulgakov 1988, Literature of the Soviet Past 2001, Yeltsin and the Cult 2000, Results and Perspectives of the Contemporary Russian Revolution 2002; more than 350 publs in magazines on literary subjects and political essays. *Leisure interests:* rowing, skiing. *Address:* Moscow Literary Institute, Miklukho-Maklaia str. 39, korp. 2, Apt. 380, 117485 Moscow, Russia (home). *Telephone:* (495) 202-84-44 (office); (495) 335-92-57 (home). *Fax:* (495) 375-78-03 (office). *E-mail:* marietta@online.ru (home).

CHUDINOV, Igor Vitalyevich; Kyrgyzstani politician; b. 21 Aug. 1961; ed Kyrgyz State Univ., Int. Business School, Moscow, Russia; held high-ranking positions in Komsomol; early career as computer programmer; worked in a variety of positions as business exec. 1991–2005; Dir-Gen. Kyrgyzgaz (state co. that procures gas supplies for Kyrgyzstan) 2005–07; Minister of Industry, Energy and Fuel Resources Feb.–Dec. 2007; Prime Minister 2007–09 (resgnd); mem. Ak Zhol party (Bright Road People's Party). *Address:* c/o Ak Zhol, 720000 Bishkek, Toktogul 175/15, Kyrgyzstan (office). *Telephone:* (312) 62-82-45 (office). *Website:* www.akjolnarod.kg (office).

CHUI, Benjamin W., PhD; American electrical engineer; *Consulting Associate, Alissa M. Fitzgerald & Associates;* ed Stanford Univ.; has extensive experience in micro-device design and prototyping; has worked for Lightconnect, Inc. (optical Microelectromechanical systems (MEMS) startup co.); fmr Researcher, IBM Almaden Research Center, San Jose, Calif.; fmr Researcher, Inst. of Microtechnology, Neuchatel, Switzerland; Consulting Assoc., Alissa M. Fitzgerald & Assocs tech. consulting 2005–; World Tech. Award in Materials, The World Tech. Network (co-recipient) 2005. *Achievements include:* part of team that made first demonstrations of magnetic resonance force microscopy (MRFM) 1992, work reached key milestone with manipulation and detection of individual electron spin 2004, designed and fabricated micro-cantilevers used to measure single electron spins. *Publications:* one book and numerous papers on MEMS-related subjects. *Address:* A.M. Fitzgerald & Assocs, LLC, 655 Skyway Road, Suite 118, San Carlos, CA 94070, USA (office). *Telephone:* (650) 592-6100 (office). *Fax:* (650) 592-6111 (office). *E-mail:* info@amfitzgerald.com (office). *Website:* www.amfitzgerald.com (office).

CHUI, Sai On (Fernando Chui), BS, MS, PhD; Chinese government official and fmr public health official; *Chief Executive, Macao Special Administrative Region;* b. 1957, Macao; ed Ling Nam School, Macao, California State Univ., Sacramento and School of Public Health, Univ. of Oklahoma, USA; mem. 5th Legis. Ass., Macao Govt 1992–96; played active role in various local community orgs, including as Exec. Dir Macao Kiang Wu Hosp. Charitable Asscn, as Hon. Pres. Macao Nursing Asscn, and as Chair. Supervisory Bd Macao Asscn for the Mentally Handicapped –1999; apptd by Cen. People's Govt as Sec. for Social Affairs and Culture of Macao Special Admin. Region (SAR) Govt 1999–2009; Chief Exec. Macao SAR 2009–; Guest Prof., Huanan Teachers' Training Univ.; tutor in Chamber of Commerce for

Int. Youth; mem. Youth Cttee of Macao Govt; Headmaster of Kiang Ping School; Pres. Youth Asscn of Kiang Wu Hosp.; mem. and Standing Cttee mem. All-China Youth Fed.; Exec. Man. and Dir of Medical and Health Dept of Tung Sin Tong Charitable Inst.; Pres. Macau Jaycee; Exec. Dir Macao Kiang Wu Hosp. Charitable Asscn; mem. Bd Macau Eye-Bank Foundation; Vice-Pres. Asscn of the Man. Professionals; mem. American Asscn of Public Hygiene, American Asscn for the Man. of Medical Affairs; Hon. Pres. Asscn of Nursing Staff of Macao. *Address:* Office of the Chief Executive, Headquarters of the Government of the Macao SAR, Av. da Praia Grande, Macao Special Administrative Region, People's Republic of China (office). *Telephone:* 28726886 (office). *Fax:* 28725468 (office). 28726168 (office). *E-mail:* info@gov.mo (office). *Website:* www.gov.mo (office).

CHUKA, Charles, BSc, MPhil; Malawi economist and central banker; *Governor, Reserve Bank of Malawi;* ed Chancellor Coll., Univ. of Malawi, Univ. of Glasgow, Scotland; joined Reserve Bank of Malawi 1979, served in various capacities and depts, becoming Gen. Man. for Econ. Services 1997–2003, Gov. 2012–; Sr Adviser to Exec. Dir World Bank, Washington, DC 2003–11; CEO Malawi Telecommunications Ltd 2010–12; Chair. Asscn of African Central Banks 2012–. *Leisure interest:* long-distance running. *Address:* Office of the Governor, Reserve Bank of Malawi, Convention Drive, POB 30063, Capital City, Lilongwe 3, Malawi (office). *Telephone:* 1770600 (office). *Fax:* 1772752 (office). *E-mail:* webmaster@rbm.mw (office). *Website:* www.rbm.mw (office).

CHUKHRAI, Pavel Grigoryevich; Russian film director and screenwriter; b. 14 Oct. 1946, Bykovo, Moscow; s. of the late Grigoriy Chukhrai; m. Maria Zvereva; two d.; ed All-Union State Inst. of Cinematography; actor, cameraman, scriptwriter; mem. Union of Cinematographers, European Acad. of Cinema and TV; Lenin's Komsomol Prize 1981, All-Union Film Festival Prize 1981, four Kinoshock Festival prizes, six Russian Acad. prizes, four Golden Oven Festival prizes, Grand Prix Prague Film Festival, Jury Prize, Int. Film Festival, Japan. *Films include:* Lyudi v okeane (also writer) 1980, Kto zaplatit za udachu? (writer) 1980, Kletka dlya kanareek (also writer) 1983, Zina-Zinulya 1986, Vor (also writer) 1997, Klassik (writer) 1998, Voditel dlya Very (also writer) 2004. *Address:* Bolshaya Pirogovskaya str. 53/55, apt. 177, Moscow, Russia (home). *Telephone:* (495) 246-98-61 (home). *Fax:* (495) 246-98-61 (home). *E-mail:* pavel@girmet.ru (home).

CHULANONT, Gen. Surayud; Thai army officer and politician; *Privy Councillor to His Majesty the King;* b. 28 Aug. 1943, Prachinburi; s. of Lt Col Payom Chulanont and Ampoch Tharab; m. 1st Duang Chulanont; one s.; m. 2nd Thanpuying Chitravadee Chulanont; two s.; ed Chulachomklao Royal Mil. Acad., Jt Staff Coll., USA, Jt Staff Coll. and Nat. Defence Coll., Thailand; started career as Jr Lt, Royal Thai Army 1965, served in infantry, artillery and counterinsurgency units; Instructor, Special Warfare School 1974–76; Aide to C-in-C 1976; Commdr Gen., Special Warfare Command 1992–94, Second Army Area 1994–97, C-in-C 1998–2002, Supreme Commdr 2002–03; PC 2003–; Interim Prime Minister 2006–08, also Minister of the Interior 2007–08; mem. Exec. Cttee Anandamahidol Foundation 2003–; Kt, Order of the Crown of Thailand 1992, Kt, Order of the White Elephant 1995, Kt Grand Commdr, Order of Chula Chom Klao 2001; Freeman Safeguarding Medal 1974, Rama Medal of the Hon. Order of Rama 1990. *Leisure interests:* reading, playing golf, jet skiing, trekking. *Address:* Privy Council Chambers, Sanamchai Road, Pranakorn District, Bangkok 10200, Thailand (office). *Telephone:* (2) 220-7400 (office).

CHUMA, Kouki; Japanese politician; b. 8 Oct. 1936; ed Univ. of Tokyo; with Sumitomo Heavy Industries Ltd 1961; with Research Bureau, Econ. Planning Agency –1969; mem. House of Reps (Osaka 1st Dist) 1976–, Chair. House of Reps Standing Cttee on Science and Tech. 1991, on Local Admin Div. 1993, Special Cttee on Election Laws 1996, Standing Cttee on Foreign Affairs 1997, Special Cttee on Political Ethics and Election Laws 2001, Dir Special Cttee on Decentralization of Govt 1993; Chair. Policy Bd, New Liberal Club 1981; State Sec. for Environment 1984; Parl. Vice-Minister for Home Affairs 1990; Dir Local Admin Div., Liberal Democratic Party (LDP) 1991, Acting Head, Nat. Campaign HQ, LDP 1993, Deputy Chair. Policy Research Council, LDP (Local Admin and Transport) 1995, Chief Deputy Sec.-Gen. LDP 2000, Chair. Research Comm. on Local Govt Admin, LDP 2001, 2003, mem. Gen. Council LDP 2002, Deputy Chair. Gen. Council 2004; Chair. Special Cttee to Promote the Devt of Osaka Bay Area 1996; Sr State Sec. for Transport 1999–02; Sr Vice-Minister of Land, Infrastructure and Transport 2002–05; mem. Research Comm. on Local Admin Systems 2004; Minister of State for Admin. Reform, Regulatory Reform, Special Zones for Structural Reform, and Regional Revitalization 2005–06. *Address:* c/o Liberal-Democratic Party—LDP (Jiyu-Minshuto), 1-11-23, Nagata-cho, Chiyoda-ku, Tokyo 100-8910, Japan. *Telephone:* (3) 3581-6211. *E-mail:* koho@ldp.jimin.or.jp. *Website:* www.jimin.jp; www.chuma-koki.jp.

CHUN, Jung-bae, LLM; South Korean lawyer and politician; b. 12 Dec. 1954; ed Seoul Nat. Univ.; founding-mem. Minbyun (Lawyers for a Democratic Soc.) 1988, Co-ordinator, Chair. Int. Human Rights Cttee; elected mem. Nat. Ass. 1996, 2000, 2004, Chair. House Steering Cttee 2004, mem. Commerce, Industry and Energy Cttee 2005; Chief Sec. to Pres. Nat. Congress for New Politics (NCNP) 1998; Vice-Chair. Policy Cttee, Vice Floor Leader, Millennium Democratic Party 2000, Special Advisor on State Affairs to Presidential Cand. 2002, Chief Sec. Advisory Cttee on Political Reform for Presidential Cand. 2002; Chair. Nat. Security and Int. Relations Cttee, Korea-Japan Parliamentarians' Union 2003, Adviser 2005; Chair. Special Cttee on Political Reform, Uri Party 2003, Chair. Gen. Election Planning Cttee, Clean Election Campaign Cttee 2004, Floor Leader 2004; Minister of Justice 2005–06 (resgnd); mem. UNDP (renamed Democratic Party) 2007–; Pres. Korea–UK Parliamentarians' Friendship Asscn 2005; Baek-Bong Memorial Foundation Clean & Gentle Politician Award 1999, Asscn of Korean Journalists Politician of the Year Award 2001. *Address:* c/o Democratic Party, 15–16 Yeouido-dong, Yeongdeungpo-gu, Seoul 150-701, Republic of Korea. *E-mail:* help@undp.kr. *Website:* minjoo.kr.

CHUNG, Dong-soo, BA, MA; South Korean academic and banking executive; b. 24 Sept. 1945; ed Seoul Nat. Univ., Univ. of Wisconsin, USA; fmr Asst Minister, Planning and Man. Office, Ministry of Planning and Budget; Deputy Minister, Ministry of Environment 2001–02; mem. Bd of Dirs Kookmin Bank 2002–, fmr Chair.; Prof., Sangmyung Univ.; Dir Daewoo Shipbuilding and Marine Eng Co. Ltd. *Address:* c/o Board of Directors, Kookmin Bank, 9-1, 2-ga, Namdaemoon-ro,

Jung-gu, Seoul 100-703, Republic of Korea (office). *Telephone:* (2) 2073-7114 (office). *Fax:* (2) 2073-8360 (office). *Website:* www.kookmin-bank.com (office).

CHUNG, Dong-young, MA; South Korean politician; b. 17 June 1953, Sunchang Co., N Jeolla Prov.; m.; two s.; ed Jeonju High School, Seoul Nat. Univ. and Cardiff Grad. School, Univ. of Wales, UK; imprisoned for involvement in Mincheong Hakryeon Case 1973; reporter, Moonhwa Broadcasting Corpn (MBC) 1978–88, Anchor, MBC Midnight News 1988–89, MBC Los Angeles Corresp., USA 1989–93, Main Anchor, 9 O'Clock News Desk, MBC 1994–96; mem. 15th Nat. Ass. 1996–2000, Cen. Party Affairs Cttee, Nat. Congress for New Politics (NCNP) 16th Nat. Ass. 2000–04; mem. Science, Tech., Information and Telecommunications Cttee; Special Asst to NCNP Pres. Kim Dae-jung and Campaign Planner; Seoul Mayor Electoral Campaign 1998; Spokesman, NCNP 1998–99; mem. and Spokesman, Millennium Democratic Party 2000; mem. Cen. Cttee Uri Party (subsequently renamed United Nat. Democratic Party—UNDP, now Democratic Party) 2003–, Chair. Uri Party 2004–06 (resgnd), UNDP cand. for Pres. of South Korea 2007; Minister of Unification 2005–06. *Address:* c/o Democratic Party, 15–16 Yeouido-dong, Yeongdeungpo-gu, Seoul 150-701, Republic of Korea. *Telephone:* (2) 784-0114. *E-mail:* help@undp.kr. *Website:* minjoo.kr.

CHUNG, Eui-sun, MBA; South Korean business executive; *Vice-Chairman, Hyundai Motors Co.;* b. 18 Oct. 1970; s. of Chung Mong-koo; m.; two c.; ed Korea Univ., Univ. of San Francisco, USA; CEO and Pres. Kia Motors Corpn 2005–09, also Dir Hyundai Mobis and Deputy Head, Hyundai-Kia Planning Div., Vice-Chair. Hyundai Motors Co., Dir 2009–, Vice-Chair. Hyundai Steel 2012–, Vice-Chair. of Hyundai Mobis; Pres. Asian Archery Fed. *Address:* Hyundai Motors Co., 231 Yangjae-dong, Seocho-gu, Seoul 137-938, South Korea (office). *Telephone:* (2) 3464-1114 (office). *Fax:* (2) 965-3148 (office). *Website:* worldwide.hyundai.com (office).

CHUNG, Hong-won, LLB; South Korean lawyer and politician; b. 9 Oct. 1944, Hadong, South Gyeongsang Prov.; ed Sungkyunkwan Univ.; began career as teacher, Inwang elementary school 1963–70; 30-year career as state prosecutor, roles include Prosecutor, Seoul-Busan Public Prosecutor's Office 1974–83, Prosecutor, Legal Affairs Div., Ministry of Justice 1983–86, Chief Prosecutor, Geochang Br., Masan Dist 1986–87, Sr Prosecutor, E Secr., Busan Dist Public Prosecutor's Office 1988–89, Dir for Violent Crime, Supreme Public Prosecutor's Office 1990–93, Sr Prosecutor, Seoul Dist Public Prosecutor's Office 1993–95, Supt Prosecutor, Gwangju Dist Public Prosecutor's Office 2000–02, Busan Dist Public Prosecutor's Office 2002–03; Dir of Planning, Judicial Research and Training Inst. 1987–88, Supt 2003–04; Standing mem. Nat. Election Comm. 2004–06; Pres. Korea Legal Aid Corpn 2008–11; Prime Minister 2013–14 (resgnd following criticism of Govt's handling of the sinking of a passenger ferry); mem. Saenuri Party (New Frontier Party). *Address:* c/o Office of the Prime Minister, 55, Sejongno, Jongno-gu, Seoul 110–760, South Korea.

CHUNG, Joon-yang; South Korean business executive; *CEO, POSCO;* b. 3 Feb. 1948; ed Seoul Nat. Univ.; joined POSCO (Pohang Iron and Steel Co.) 1975, Gen. Man. Steelmaking Dept 1991–98, Deputy Gen. Supt POSCO Tech. Research Lab. 1998–99, Man. Dir POSCO EU Office 1999–2004, Gen. Supt Gwangyang Works 2004–06, Sr Exec. Vice-Pres., COO and Chief Tech. Officer 2006–07, Pres., COO and Chief Tech. Officer 2007–08, Pres. POSCO Eng & Construction Co. Ltd 2008–09, CEO, Exec. Dir and Chair. Exec. Man. Cttee POSCO 2009–, Chair. Posco-China Co. Ltd; Chair. Fed. of Korean Industries, Korea-Australia Econ. Co-operation 2007–, 7th Korea Iron & Steel Asscn 2009–; Pres. Korean Inst. of Metal and Materials 2008–, Nat. Acad. of Eng of Korea 2011–; mem. Exec. Cttee Int. Iron and Steel Inst. 2009–; Rep. of Multi-cultural Families Forum 2011–; Presidential Citation 1992, Technological Prize, Korean Inst. of Metal and Materials 1994, Gold Tower Order of Industrial Service Merit 2007, 8th Prize of Honoured Citizen 2008, CEO of the Year, Maegyeong Economy 2009, 9th Most Honoured Entrepreneur 2011, Grand Prized CEO of Korea in Manufacturing Industry 2011. *Address:* POSCO Head Office, 1 Goedong-dong, Nam-gu, Pohang, Kyungsangbuk-do, 790-600 (office); POSCO, POSCO Centre, 892 Daechi-4-dong, Kangnam-ku, Seoul 135-777, Republic of Korea (office). *Telephone:* (54) 220-0114 (Head Office) (office); (2) 3457-0114 (POSCO Centre) (office). *Fax:* (54) 220-6000 (Head Office) (office); (2) 3457-6000 (POSCO Centre) (office). *E-mail:* info@posco.com (office). *Website:* www .posco.com (office); www.posco.co.kr (office).

CHUNG, Kyung-wha; South Korean violinist; b. 26 March 1948, Seoul; sister of Chung Myung-whun and Chung Myung-wha; m. Geoffrey Leggett 1984; two s.; ed Juilliard School, New York with Ivan Galamian; started career in USA; European debut 1970; has played with major orchestras, including all London orchestras, Chicago, Boston and Pittsburgh Symphony Orchestra, New York, Cleveland, Philadelphia, Berlin, Israel and Vienna Philharmonics, Orchestre de Paris, Royal Concertgebouw Orchestra, Deutsche Oper, San Francisco Symphony, Orchestre National de Lyon, Pittsburgh Symphony Orchestra, Orchestre Philharmonique de Radio-France, Tonhalle-Orchester Zurich; has toured world; played at Salzburg Festival with London Symphony Orchestra 1973, Vienna Festival 1981, 1984, Edinburgh Festival 1981 and at 80th birthday concert of Sir William Walton March 1982; with Hallé Orchestra, BBC Proms, London 1999; Faculty of Music, Juilliard School, New York 2007–, Pre-College 2008–; winner, Leventritt Competition 1968, Medal of Civil Merit 1972, Ho-am Prize 2011. *Recordings:* Concertos by Bartók, Beethoven, Bruch, Mendelssohn, Stravinsky, Tchaikovsky, Vieuxtemps, Walton, Vivaldi's The Four Seasons 2001. *Leisure interests:* arts, family. *Address:* Opus 3 Artists, 470 Park Avenue South, 9th Floor North, New York, NY 10016, USA (office); The Juilliard School, 60 Lincoln Center Plaza, New York, NY 10023-6588, USA (office). *Telephone:* (212) 584-7500 (office); (212) 799-5000. *Fax:* (646) 300-8200 (office). *E-mail:* info@opus3artists.com (office). *Website:* www .opus3artists.com (office); www.juilliard.edu (office).

CHUNG, Mong-joon, MA, PhD; South Korean politician, sports administrator and business executive; b. 17 Oct. 1951, Busan; s. of the late Chung Ju-Yung; brother of Chung Mong-koo; m.; two s. two d.; ed Joongang High School, Coll. of Commerce, Seoul Nat. Univ., Massachusetts Inst. of Tech. and Johns Hopkins Univ., USA; First Lt Reserve Officers Training Corps; joined Hyundai Heavy Industries 1978, Man. Dir 1980, CEO 1982, Adviser 1990–2002; Pres. Hyundai Heavy Industries Co. Ltd (HHI) 1982–87, Chair. 1987; Chair. Ulsan Inst. of Tech. Foundation 1999–; elected mem. (Ind.) Nat. Ass. 1988–; f. Nat. Unity 21 party Nov.

2002; Pres. Korea Football Asscn 1993–2009, Hon. Pres. 2009–; Vice-Pres. FIFA 1994–2011, Hon. Vice-Pres. 2011–, Co-Chair. Korean Organizing Cttee for 2002 FIFA World Cup, Korea-Japan 2002; Chair. Bd of Trustees, Ulsan Univ. 1983– Asan Foundation 2001– (Hon. Chair. The Asan Inst. for Policy Studies 2010–, Hon. Chair. The Asan Nanum Foundation 2011–); Chair. Grand Nat. Party, mem. Supreme Council, Grand Nat. Party; cand. in nat. presidential election 2002; mem. Bd of Trustees, Johns Hopkins Univ., USA 1995–2000, Korea Univ.; mem. Bd of Dirs Salzburg Global Seminar; Hon. PhD (Myongji Univ.) 1998; Hon. LLD (Univ. of Maryland) 1999. *Publications include: Corporate Management Ideology 1982, Relations Between the Government and the Corporate in Japan 1995, This I Say to Japan 2001. *Leisure interests:* football, tennis, golf, equestrianism, hiking. *Address:* The Asan Institute for Policy Studies, 1-176, Sinmunno 2-Ga, Hongno-gu, Seoul 110-062 (office); 345-1, Pyeongchang-dong, Jongno-gu, Seoul, Republic of Korea. *Telephone:* (2) 741-1122 (office). *Fax:* (2) 741-1154 (office). *Website:* www.mjchung.com (office).

CHUNG, Mong-koo, BA, PhD; South Korean automotive industry executive; *Chairman and CEO, Hyundai-Kia Automotive Group;* b. 19 March 1938, Seoul; s. of the late Chung Ju-yung, Founder of Hyundai; brother of Chung Mong-joon and the late Chung Mong-hun; m.; four c.; ed Hanyang Univ.; began career in family-owned business Hyundai Automotive Group 1970, various positions include Man. Hyundai Motor Co. 1983, Head of Hyundai Motor Service, Chair. Hyundai Group 1996–99 (Hyundai-Kia Automotive Group following purchase of Kia Motors 1998), Chair. and Co-CEO Hyundai Motor Co. and Kia Motor Co. 1999–2009, Chair. and CEO Hyundai-Kia Automotive Group 2009–; CEO Hyundai Automotive Group (holding co. of Hyundai Mobis Ameron International Corpn); received three-year suspended jail sentence for embezzling co. funds and breach of duty 2007, pardoned by Pres. of Repub. of Korea; Prof. Emer. of Business Admin, Qinghua Univ., China; Vice-Chair. Fed. of Korean Industries; Hon. PhD (Cen. Connecticut State Univ., Mongol Nat. Univ.); Automotive Hall of Fame Distinguished Service Citation, Nat. Automobile Dealers Asscn 2001, named by BusinessWeek magazine as one of the top managers of 2004, named by Automotive News as one of its three Auto Executives of the Year (Asian award) 2010. *Address:* Hyundai-Kia Automotive Group, 231 Yangjae-dong, Seocho-gu, Seoul 137-1115, Republic of Korea (office). *Telephone:* (2) 3464-1114 (office). *E-mail:* dmkim@hyundai-motor.com (office). *Website:* worldwide.hyundai.com (office).

CHUNG, Moon Soul, BA; South Korean business executive; b. 7 March 1938, Chonbuk Imsil; ed Iksan Men's High School, Won Kwang Univ.; Sr Man. Planning and Coordinating Div., Korea Cen. Intelligence Agency 1962–80; Founder, Chair. and CEO Mirae Corpn 1983–2001, Consultant 2001–, Founder and CEO Lycos Korea 1999–2001; apptd Dir (non-exec.) Kookmin Bank 2001, Chair. 2004; Dir (non-exec.) Dongwon Securities; Dr hc (Korea Advanced Inst. of Science and Tech.) 2009. *Address:* c/o Mirae Corporation, 9-2 Cha-Am-dong, Chonan, Chungcheong-nam 330-200, Republic of Korea.

CHUNG, Myung-whun; South Korean conductor and pianist; *Music Director, Seoul Philharmonic Orchestra;* b. 22 Jan. 1953, Seoul; brother of Chung Kyung-wha and Chung Myung-wha; ed Mannes Coll. of Music and Juilliard School, New York, USA; asst to Carlo Maria Giulini as Assoc. Conductor, Los Angeles Philharmonic 1978–81; moved to Europe 1981, conducting Berlin Philharmonic, Munich Philharmonic, Amsterdam Concertgebouw, Orchestre de Paris, major London orchestras; Music Dir and Prin. Conductor, Radio Orchestra of Saarbrücken 1984–89; in USA has conducted the New York Philharmonic, Nat. Symphony, Washington, DC, Boston Symphony, Cleveland and Chicago Orchestras, Metropolitan Opera, San Francisco Opera 1986–; Guest Conductor, Teatro Comunale, Florence 1987; Musical Dir Opéra de la Bastille, Paris 1989–94; Covent Garden debut, conducting Otello 1997; Music Dir and Prin. Conductor, Orchestra of the Nat. Acad. of Santa Cecilia, Rome 1997–2005; conducted Swedish Radio Symphony Orchestra at London Proms, playing Beethoven's Fourth Piano Concerto and Nielsen's Fifth 1999; Music Dir Asia Philharmonic Orchestra 1997–; Music Dir Radio France Philharmonic Orchestra 2000–; Special Artistic Adviser, Tokyo Philharmonic Orchestra 2001–; Music Dir Seoul Philharmonic Orchestra 2005–; Légion d'honneur 1992; Second Prize, Tchaikovsky Competition, Moscow 1974, Abbiati Prize (Italian critics) 1988, Arturo Toscanini Prize 1989, Victoires de la Musique Best Conductor, Best Lyrical Production, Best French Classical Recording 1995, Record Acad. Prize (Japan), Kumkwan (South Korea). *Address:* c/o Seoul Philharmonic Orchestra, Sejong-ro, Jongno-gu, Seoul 110-821, Korea (office). *Telephone:* (2) 37006300 (office). *Fax:* (2) 37006365 (office). *Website:* www.seoulphil.co.kr/english/main.jsp (office).

CHUNG, Shui-ming (Timpson), BSc, MBA; Chinese business executive and fmr government official; *CEO, Shimao Property Holdings Ltd;* b. 23 Nov. 1951, Hong Kong; two c.; ed Univ. of Hong Kong, Chinese Univ. of Hong Kong; fmr Hong Kong Affairs Adviser to Chinese Govt; fmr mem. Exec. Council, Hong Kong Special Admin. Region, Hong Kong Housing Soc. Exec. Cttee, now Chair., fmr mem. Housing Authority Finance Cttee; fmr Chief Exec. Hong Kong Special Admin. Region Land Fund; Exec. Dir and CEO Shimao Property Holdings Ltd 2004–; mem. Bd of Dirs Hantec Investment Holdings Ltd 2004–06, Man. Dir, Exec. Dir and Deputy Chair. 2006–; Dir (non-exec.) China Everbright Ltd 2012–; External Dir COSCO; Dir China Construction Bank Corpn 2013–; mem. Nat. Cttee, 10th, 11th and 12th CPPCC; Deputy Chair. Council of City Univ. of Hong Kong; mem. Hong Kong Housing Authority; Court mem. Univ. of Hong Kong; Fellow, Hong Kong Inst. of CPAs, Asscn of Chartered Certified Accountants, Hong Kong Soc. of Accountants; fmr Chinese mem. Sino-British Land Comm. *Address:* Shimao Property Holdings Ltd, 36-28F One Lujiazui, 68 Yin Cheng Road Central, Shanghai 200120, People's Republic of China (office). *Telephone:* (21) 86213861 (office). *Website:* www.shimaogroup.com (office).

CHUNG, Hon. Sir Sze-yuen, Kt, GBE, OBE, CBE, GBM, DEng, PhD, DSc, FREng, FIET, CBIM, JP; Chinese/British fmr business executive; b. 3 Nov. 1917, Hong Kong; m. Nancy Cheung 1942 (died 1977); one s. two d.; ed Hong Kong Univ. and Univ. of Sheffield, UK; consulting engineer 1952–56; Gen. Man. Sonca Industries 1956–60, Man. Dir 1960–77, Chair. 1977–88; mem. Hong Kong Legis. Council 1965–74, Sr Unofficial Mem. 1974–78; mem. Hong Kong Exec. Council 1972–80, Sr Unofficial Mem. 1980–88; Chair. Fed. of Hong Kong Industries 1966–70; Chair. Hong Kong Productivity Council 1974–76; Founding Chair. Hong Kong Polytechnic 1972–86, City Polytechnic of Hong Kong 1984–85, Hong Kong

Univ. of Science and Tech. 1987–99, Hong Kong Hosp. Authority 1990–95; Adviser to the Govt of People's Repub. of China on Hong Kong Affairs 1992–97; Founder and Pres. Hong Kong Acad. of Eng Sciences 1994–97; mem. Chinese Govt's Preparatory Cttee for establishment of Hong Kong Special Admin. Region (HKSAR) 1996–97; Convenor HKSAR Exec. Council 1997–99; Chair. Kowloon Motor Bus 1933 Ltd 1999–2014; Chair. Transport International Holdings Ltd 2006–; Hon. FIMechE 1983; Order of the Sacred Treasure (Japan) 1984; Hon. DSc (Hong Kong) 1976; Whitworth Prize, IMechE (London) 1952, Silver Jubilee Medal 1977, Gold Medal, Asian Productivity Org. 1980, and other awards and distinctions. *Publications:* Hong Kong's Journey to Reunification – Memoirs of Sze-yuen Chung; articles in professional journals. *Leisure interest:* swimming. *Address:* 128 Argyle Street, 10/F, Kowloon, Hong Kong Special Administrative Region (office); House 25, Bella Vista, Silver Terrace Road, Clear Water Bay, Kowloon, Hong Kong Special Administrative Region, People's Republic of China (home). *Telephone:* 27610281 (office). *Fax:* 27607493 (office).

CHUNG, Un-chan, BA, MA, PhD; South Korean economist and politician; b. 29 Feb. 1946, Gongju City, S Chungcheong Prov.; m. Choi Sun-Ju; one s. one d.; ed Seoul Nat. Univ., Miami Univ., Princeton Univ., USA; Clerk, Bank of Korea 1970–71; Business Assoc. and Asst Prof. of Money and Financial Markets, Columbia Univ., USA 1976–78; Asst, later Assoc. and Full Prof. of Econs, Seoul Nat. Univ. 1978–2009, Dean, Coll. of Social Sciences 2002, Pres. Seoul Nat. Univ. 2002–06, Dir Seoul Nat. Univ. Inst. for Research in Finance and Econs 2008–09; Prime Minister 2009–10; Visiting Assoc. Prof. of Econs, Univ. of Hawaii, USA 1983; Visiting Scholar, LSE, UK 1986; Visiting Prof., Ruhr-Universität Bochum, Germany 1999; Chair., Financial Devt Cttee, Ministry of Finance and Economy 2000–01; Chair. Cttee on Nat. Pension Devt, Ministry of Health and Welfare 2002; Pres. Korean Money and Finance Asscn 1998–99, Korean Econ. Asscn 2006–07, Korean Social Science Research Council 2008–09; Dir Korea Council of Econ. and Social Research Insts 1999–2001; mem., Pres.'s Council, Univ. of Tokyo 2006–09; Hon. DUniv (Far Eastern Nat. Univ., Russia) 2004. *Publications:* numerous publs on econs. *Leisure interest:* baseball. *Address:* c/o Office of the Prime Minister, 77, Sejong-no, Jongno-gu, Seoul, South Korea (office).

CHUNG, Won-shik; South Korean fmr politician; *President, Paradise Welfare Foundation;* fmr Minister of Educ.; Prime Minister of South Korea 1991–92; Pres. Paradise Welfare Foundation (charity associated with Paradise Group); Adviser, Korea Support Cttee for Int. Vaccine Inst.; mem. Democratic Liberal Party. *Address:* Paradise Welfare Foundation, 186-39, Jangchoong Bldg., Jangchoong-dong 2ga, Joong-gu, Seoul 100-855, Republic of Korea (office). *Telephone:* (2) 2277-3296 (office). *Fax:* (2) 2277-3124 (office). *Website:* www.paradise.or.kr (office).

CHURCHILL, Caryl, BA; British playwright; b. 3 Sept. 1938, London; d. of Robert Churchill and Jan Churchill (née Brown); m. David Harter 1961; three s.; ed Trafalgar School, Montréal, Canada, Lady Margaret Hall, Oxford; first play, Downstairs, performed at Nat. Union of Students Drama Festival 1958; writes mainly for theatre but has also written numerous radio plays and several TV plays. *Stage plays include:* Having a Wonderful Time (Oxford Players, 1960), Owners (Royal Court, London) 1972, Objections to Sex and Violence (Royal Court) 1975, Vinegar Tom (Monstrous Regiment toured 1976), Light Shining in Buckingham-shire (performed by Joint Stock Co., Edinburgh Festival 1976, then Royal Court), Traps (Royal Court) 1977, Cloud Nine (Joint Stock Co., Royal Court) 1979, 1980, Lucille Lortel Theater, New York 1981–83, Top Girls (Royal Court) 1982, 1983, Public Theater, New York 1983, Fen (Joint Stock Co., Almeida Theatre, London 1983, Royal Court 1983, Public Theater, New York 1983), Softcops (RSC 1984), A Mouthful of Birds (Joint Stock, Royal Court and tour 1986), Serious Money (Royal Court 1987, Wyndham Theatre 1987, Public Theater New York 1988), Icecream (Royal Court 1989, Public Theater New York 1990), Mad Forest (Cen. School of Drama, Nat. Theatre Bucharest, Royal Court 1990), Lives of the Great Poisoners (Second Stride Co. Riverside Studios, London and tour 1991), The Skriker (Nat. Theatre 1994), Thyestes (by Seneca, translation; Royal Court Theatre Upstairs 1994); Hotel (Second Stride Co., The Place) 1997, This Is A Chair (Royal Court) 1997, Blue Heart (Out of Joint, Royal Court) 1997, Far Away (Royal Court) 2000, (Albery) 2001, A Number (Royal Court) 2002, Drunk Enough to Say I Love You? (Royal Court) 2006, Seven Jewish Children (Royal Court) 2009, Love and Information (Royal Court) 2012. *Radio includes:* The Ants, Not . . Not . . not . . not enough Oxygen, Abortive, Schreiber's Nervous Illness, Identical Twins, Perfect Happiness, Henry's Past. *Television:* The Judge's Wife, The After Dinner Joke, The Legion Hall Bombing, Fugue (jtly). *Publications include:* Owners 1973, Light Shining 1976, Traps 1977, Vinegar Tom 1978, Cloud Nine 1979, Top Girls 1982, Fen 1983, Fen and Softcops 1984, A Mouthful of Birds 1986, Serious Money 1987, Plays I 1985, Plays II 1988, Objections to Sex and Violence in Plays by Women Vol. 4 1985, Ice Cream 1989, Mad Forest 1990, Lives of the Great Poisoners 1992, The Striker 1994, Thyestes 1994, Blue Heart 1997, This is a Chair 1999, Far Away 2000, A Number 2002, Drunk Enough to Say I Love You? 2006, Bliss/Olivier Choinire 2008; anthologies. *Address:* c/o Mel Kenyon, Casarotto Ramsay & Associates, Waverley House, 7-12 Noel Street, London, W1F 8GQ, England (office). *Telephone:* (20) 7287-4450 (office). *Fax:* (20) 7734-9128 (office). *E-mail:* mel@casarotto.co.uk (office). *Website:* www.casarotto.co.uk (office).

CHURKIN, Vitaly Ivanovich, PhD; Russian diplomatist; *Permanent Representative, United Nations;* b. 21 Feb. 1952; m.; one s. one d.; ed Moscow State Inst. of Int. Relations; Attaché, Translations Dept, Ministry of Foreign Affairs, interpreter for USSR del. to SALT II negotiations 1974–79, Third Sec., USA Dept of Ministry of Foreign Affairs 1979–82, Second Sec. then First Sec., USSR Embassy in Washington, DC 1982–87; expert, Int. Dept of Cen. Cttee CPSU 1987–89; Counsellor, Ministry of Foreign Affairs 1989–90, Dir Information and Press Dept 1990–92, attained rank of Amb. 1990, Deputy Minister of Foreign Affairs of Russia 1992–94, Amb. to Belgium 1994–97, to Canada 1998–2003, Chair. Sr Arctic Officials Cttee 2004–06, Amb. and Perm. Rep. to UN, New York 2006–. *Leisure interest:* tennis. *Address:* Permanent Mission of the Russian Federation to the United Nations, 136 East 67th Street, New York, NY 10065, USA (office). *Telephone:* (212) 861-4900 (office). *Fax:* (212) 628-0252 (office). *E-mail:* rusun@un.int (office). *Website:* www.un.int/russia (office).

CHUROV, Vladimir Yevgenyevich; Russian politician and engineer; *Chairman, Central Electoral Commission;* b. 17 March 1953, St Petersburg; s. of Yevgeny Petrovich Churov and Irina Vladimirovna Churova; m. Larisa Nikolayeva Churova; one s.; ed Leningrad State Univ.; began career working in aerospace design 1977–91; worked for Cttee of Int. Relations of City of St Petersburg 1992–2003, Vice Chair. 1995–2003; Deputy in State Duma 2003–07, Deputy Chair. of the Cttee on CIS and Russian Diaspora; Chair. Cen. Electoral Comm. 2007–; Prof. of Econs, Humanitarian Univ. of Trade Unions, St Petersburg; mem. Liberal Democratic Party of Russia (Liberalno-demokraticheskaya partiya Rossii); Order of Merit for Service to the Fatherland, Order of Friendship 2004. *Publications include:* several books on mil., including the history of the imperial army and White Movement, also popular maritime novels for children. *Leisure interests:* photography, military history, history of architecture. *Address:* Central Election Commission, 109012 Moscow, Bolshoi Cherkassky per. 9, Russia (office). *Telephone:* (495) 606-99-66 (office). *Fax:* (495) 606-97-69 (office). *E-mail:* info@cikrf.ru (office). *Website:* www.cikrf.ru (office).

CHUTE, Robert Maurice, ScD; American poet, biologist and academic (retd); *Professor Emeritus of Biology, Bates College;* b. 13 Feb. 1926, Bridgton, Me; s. of James Cleveland and Elizabeth Davis Chute; m. Virginia Hinds 1946; one s. one d.; ed Fryeburg Acad., Univ. of Maine, Johns Hopkins Univ. School of Hygiene and Public Health; Instructor and Asst Prof., Middlebury Coll. 1953–59; Asst Prof. Northridge State Coll. 1959–61; Assoc. Prof. and Chair. of Biology, Lincoln Univ. 1961; Prof. and Chair. of Biology, then Dana Prof. of Biology, Bates Coll. 1962–93, Prof. Emer. 1993–; Fellow, AAAS; Maine Arts and Humanities Award 1978, Chad Walsh Award (Beloit Poetry Journal) 1997, Maine Writers and Publrs Alliance Poetry Competition 2001, Maine Writers and Publrs Lifetime Distinguished Achievement Award 2011. *Publications:* Environmental Insight 1971, Introduction to Biology 1976, Sweeping the Sky: Soviet Women Flyers in Combat 1999; poetry: Quiet Thunder 1975, Uncle George 1977, Voices Great and Small 1977, Thirteen Moons/Treize Lunes 1982, Samuel Sewell Sails for Home 1986, When Grandmother Decides to Die 1989, Woodshed on the Moon: Thoreau Poems, Barely Time to Study Jesus 1996, Androscoggin Too 1997, Bent Offerings 2003, Reading Nature 2006, Cat Tales, Constellations: Collected Story Poems; novel: Coming Home, Return to Sender; trans.: Thirteen Moons into Micmac Maliseet (native American) 2002; contribs to Kansas Quarterly, Beloit Poetry Review, Bitterroot, South Florida Poetry Review, North Dakota Review, Cape Rock, Fiddlehead, Greenfield Review, Literary Review, Poet Pore, Sow's Ear Poetry Review. *Leisure interests:* walking, reading, films, Thoreau studies. *Address:* 68 Schellinger Road, Poland Spring, ME 04274, USA (home). *Telephone:* (207) 998-1073 (home). *E-mail:* vrchute@gmail.com.

CHYLEK, Petr, PhD; American(b. Czech) atmospheric scientist and academic; *Technical Staff Member, Space and Remote Sensing Sciences, Los Alamos National Laboratory;* ed Charles Univ., Prague, Czech Repub., Univ. of California, Riverside; Research Assoc., Dept of Physics, Indiana Univ., Bloomington 1970–72; Post-doctoral Fellow, Advanced Study Program, Nat. Center for Atmospheric Research, Boulder, Colo 1972–73; Asst Prof., Dept of Atmospheric Science, State Univ. of NY, Albany 1973–75, Research Prof. 1978–86; Assoc. Prof., Dept of Geosciences, Purdue Univ., West Lafayette, Ind. 1975–78; Prof., School of Meteorology, Univ. of Oklahoma, Norman 1986–90; Founder and Co-ordinator Atmospheric Science Program, Dalhousie Univ., Halifax, NS, Canada, Prof. of Physics and Atmospheric Science –2001, Sr Chair in Climate Research 1990–2001, Adjunct Prof. of Physics and Atmospheric Science 2001–; Adjunct Prof. of Physics, New Mexico State Univ., Las Cruces 1990–; Tech. Staff Mem. Space and Remote Sensing Sciences, Los Alamos Nat. Lab., Santa Fe, NM 2001–; Visiting Scientist, Instituto di Fisica de la Atmosfera, Frascati, Italy March–May 1966; Visiting Scientist, Air Resources Laboratory, Nat. Oceanic and Atmospheric Admin, Boulder, Colo 2000–01; Chair. Scientific Program Cttee, Second Int. Conf. on Global Warming and the Next Ice Age, Los Alamos Nat. Lab. 2006; mem. American Meteorological Soc., American Geophysical Union 2006; Fellow, Optical Soc. of America 1991, Los Alamos Nat. Lab. 2006; Hon. Fellow, Center for Earth and Planetary Physics, Harvard Univ. 1976–78; Univ. of California Grad. Fellowship 1968–70, Advanced Study Program Post-doctoral Fellowship, Nat. Center for Atmospheric Research 1972–73, Nat. Research Council Sr Fellowship, White Sands Missile Range 1984–85, paper by Chylek, Kiehl & Ko (1978) reprinted in SPIE Milestone Series as one of milestone papers in field of Light Scattering 1988, Sr Research Chair in Climate Research, Natural Sciences and Eng Research Council of Canada 1990–2000, Distinguished Faculty Summer Fellowship, Naval Research Lab. April–June 1992, paper by Chylek and Srivastava (1983) reprinted in SPIE Milestone Series as one of milestone papers in field of linear optical composite materials 1996, paper by Chylek and Borel (2004) selected by American Geophysical Union Eds as a Journal Highlight 2004, Los Alamos Nat. Lab. Award for Scientific and Tech. Leadership 2004. *Publications:* more than 100 scientific papers in professional journals on remote sensing, atmospheric radiation, climate change, cloud and aerosol physics, applied laser physics and ice-core analysis. *Address:* Space and Remote Sensing Sciences (ISR-2), PO Box 1664, MS B241, Los Alamos, NM 87545, USA (office). *Telephone:* (505) 667-2965 (office). *Fax:* (505) 665-3169 (office). *E-mail:* krodriguez@lanl.gov (office). *Website:* www.lanl.gov/orgs/isr/isr2 (office).

CHYNOWETH, Alan Gerald, BSc, PhD, FIEEE, FInstP; British physicist (retd); b. 18 Nov. 1927, Harrow, Middx; s. of James Charles Chynoweth and Marjorie Fairhurst; m. Betty Freda Edith Boyce 1950; two s.; ed King's Coll., London; Postdoctoral Fellow, Nat. Research Council of Canada, Chem. Div., Ottawa 1950–52; mem. Tech. Staff, Bell Telephone Labs 1953–60, Head of Crystal Electronics Dept 1960–65, Asst Dir Metallurgical Research Lab. 1965–73, Dir Materials Research Lab. 1973–76, Exec. Dir Electronic and Photonic Devices Div. 1976–83, Vice-Pres. Applied Research, Bell Communications Research 1983–92; Survey Dir of NAS Cttee on Survey of Materials Science and Eng 1971–73, Comm. on Mineral Resources and the Environment 1973–75; mem. Nat. Materials Advisory Bd 1975–79, NATO Special Programme Panel on Materials 1977–82, consultant to NATO Advanced Study Inst. Panel 1982–89; mem. Materials Research Soc., Metallurgical Soc.; Alt. Dir Microelectronics and Computer Tech. Corpn 1985–92; Dir Industrial Research Inst. 1990–92; Chair. Tech. Transfer Merit Program, NJ Comm. on Science and Tech. 1992–98; consultant to EC Telecommunications Directorate 1995; Lecturer, Electrochemical Soc. 1983; Co-Ed. Optical Fiber Telecommunications 1979; Assoc. Ed. Solid State Comm. 1975–83; mem. Visiting Cttee, Cornell Univ. Materials Science Centre 1973–76, Natural Sciences Advisory Bd, Univ. of Pennsylvania 1988–92, Advisory Bd Dept

of Electrical Eng and Computer Science, Univ. of California, Berkeley 1987–90, Advisory Bd, Dept of Electrical Eng, Univ. of Southern California 1988–90, Advisory Council Electrical Eng Dept, Pennsylvania State Univ. 1993–98; mem. Office of Science and Tech. Policy Panel on High Performance Computing and Communications 1991–92; mem. IEEE Frederik Philips Award Cttee 1997–2000, Corp. Recognitions Cttee 1999–; Chair. IEEE Recognitions Council IEEE 2003–06; Chair. IEEE Awards Review Cttee 2007–12; Fellow, IEEE, American Physical Soc., Int. Eng Consortium, Inst. of Physics, London; IEEE W. R. G. Baker Prize 1967, IEEE Frederik Philips Award 1992, American Physical Soc. George E. Pake Prize 1992, IEEE Eng Leadership Recognition 1996. *Publications include:* Optical Fiber Telecommunications (with Stewart E. Miller) 1979; over 60 papers in professional journals on solid state physics, 11 patents on solid state devices, NAS reports: Materials and Man's Needs, Materials Conservation through Technology, Resource Recovery from Municipal Solid Wastes. *Leisure interests:* travel, boating. *Address:* 6 Londonderry Way, Summit, NJ 07901, USA (home); 17 Mill Close, Fishbourne, Chichester, PO19 3JW, England (home). *Telephone:* (908) 273-3956 (USA) (home); (1243) 775928 (UK) (home). *E-mail:* algchy@aol.com.

CIAMPI, Carlo Azeglio, LLB; Italian economist, politician, fmr central banker and fmr head of state; b. 9 Dec. 1920, Livorno; s. of Pietro Ciampi and Marie Masino; m. Franca Pilla 1946; one s. one d.; ed Scuola Normale Superiore di Pisa, Pisa Univ.; served in Italian Army 1941–44; with Banca d'Italia 1946, economist, Research Dept 1960–70, Head of Research Dept 1970–73, Sec.-Gen. 1973–76, Deputy Dir-Gen. 1976–78, Dir-Gen. 1978–79, Gov. 1979–93; Chair. Ufficio Italiano dei Cambi, 1979–83 (Hon. Gov. 1994–); Prime Minister 1993–94; Minister of the Treasury and the Budget 1996–98; Pres. of Italy 1999–2006 (retd), Pres. Emer. 2006–; Senator for Life 2006–; Chair. IMF Interim Cttee 1998–99; fmr mem. Bd of Govs for Italy IBRD, IDA, IFC; fmr mem. Cttee of Govs EEC; fmr mem. Bd of Dirs Consiglio Nazionale delle Ricerche, BIS; mem. Istituto Adriano Olivetti di Studi per la Gestione dell'Economia e delle Aziende; Mil. Cross, Grand Officer, Order of Merit of the Italian Repub. Dr hc (École Normale Supérieure) 2005; Charlemagne Award, Aachen 2005; Senator for Life ex officio (highest Italian honour). *Publications:* Un metodo per Governare 1996. *Address:* Senate (Senato), Piazza Madama, 00186 Rome, Italy (office). *Telephone:* (06) 67061 (office). *E-mail:* ciampi_ca@posta.senato.it (office). *Website:* www.senato.it (office).

CIANCHETTE, Peter, BS; American business executive, politician and fmr diplomatist; *Vice-President, Business Development, Cianbro Companies;* b. 1961, Waterville, Me; m. Carolyn Cianchette; one s. one d.; ed Univ. of Maine; more than 20 years of business experience, from serving as sr exec. in Dragon Products Co., to running his own business, Cianchette Enterprises, Inc.; joined consulting firm Pierce Atwood Consulting 1998, served as COO and Exec. Vice-Pres.; Pres. The Cianchette Group (public affairs man. and business consulting firm); Partner, CHK Capital Partners, Portland; served in Maine's State Legislature representing South Portland and Cape Elizabeth in Maine's House of Reps 1996–2000, mem. Jt Standing Cttee on Taxation; Republican nominee for Gov. of Maine 2002; currently Maine's Nat. Republican Committeeman, served as Maine Gen. Chair. of Bush-Cheney 2004 campaign; Amb. to Costa Rica 2008–09; Vice-Pres., Business Devt, Cianbro Companies 2009–; mem. Bd of Dirs Make-A-Wish Foundation of Maine and YES! to Youth; mem. George and Barbara Bush Maine Cultural Center Cttee, Finance Cttee of American Lighthouse Foundation, MaineHealth Corporator; fmr mem. Bd of Dirs Greater Portland Big Brothers/Big Sisters, Boy Scouts of America/Pine Tree Council, Portland Chamber of Commerce, Southern Maine Community Coll. Foundation; fmr Pres. Maine Better Transportation Asscn; fmr Chair. Maine Advancement Program. *Address:* Cianbro Companies, 101 Cianbro Square, PO Box 1000, Pittsfield, ME 04967, USA (office). *Telephone:* (207) 487-3311 (office). *Website:* www.cianbro.com (office).

CIAVATTA, Valeria; San Marino government official; *Co-Captain Regent;* b. 16 Jan. 1959; m. Giovanni Pacelli; two c.; ed Univ. of Urbino; mem. Consiglio Grande e Generale (Parl.) 1993–; Co-Capt.-Regent of San Marino 2003–04, 2014–; Sec. of State for Internal Affairs and Civil Protection 2006–12; mem. Popular Alliance of Democrats (Alleanza Popolare dei Democratici Sammarinese). *Address:* Secretariat of State, Parva Domus, Piazza della Libertà, 47890 (office); Alleanza Popolare dei Democratici Sammarinese (APDS), Via Luigi Cibrario 25, 47893 Cailungo, San Marino (office). *Telephone:* (0549) 907080 (office). *Fax:* (0549) 907082 (office). *Website:* www.consigliograndeegenerale.sml (office).

ÇİÇEK, Cemil; Turkish lawyer and politician; *Speaker, Grand National Assembly;* b. 15 Nov. 1946, Yozgat; m.; three c.; ed Faculty of Law, Istanbul Univ.; Mayor of Yozgat 1984–88; co-f. Motherland Party (now ANAVATAN); mem. Grand Nat. Ass. (Parl.) (Justice and Devt Party), Speaker 2011–; fmr State Minister; Minister of Justice 2003–07; Deputy Prime Minister 2007–11. *Address:* Büyük Millet Meclisi (Grand National Assembly), TBMM 06543, Bakanlıklar, Ankara, Turkey (office). *Telephone:* (312) 4205151 (office). *Fax:* (312) 4206756 (office). *E-mail:* gensek@tbmm.gov.tr (office). *Website:* www.tbmm.gov.tr (office).

CICERONE, Ralph J., MS, PhD; American academic, university administrator and chemist; *President, National Academy of Sciences;* b. Pennsylvania; m. Prof. Carol Cicerone; one d.; ed Massachusetts Inst. of Tech. and Univ. of Illinois; Research Scientist and Lecturer, Dept of Electrical Eng, later Asst Prof., Dept of Electrical and Computer Eng, Univ. of Michigan 1971–78; Research Chemist, Scripps Inst. of Oceanography, Univ. of California, San Diego 1978–80; Sr Scientist and Dir Atmospheric Chem. Div., Nat. Center for Atmospheric Research, Boulder, Colo 1980–89; Daniel G. Aldrich, Jr Chair in Earth System Science, Univ. of California, Irvine 1989–2005, Chair. Dept of Earth System Science 1989–94, Prof. of Chem. 1990–2005, Dean of Physical Sciences 1994–98, Chancellor Univ. of California, Irvine 1998–2005; mem. NAS 1990– (served on Council 1996–99 and on Bd on Sustainable Devt), Chair. Climate Change Science: An Analysis of Some Key Questions study 2001, mem. Cttee on Women in Science and Eng, Advisory Bd Koshland Science Museum, Advisory Cttee Div. of Earth and Life Sciences, Pres. NAS 2005–; fmr Pres. American Geophysical Union; mem. ACS 1974, American Acad. of Arts and Sciences, American Philosophical Soc.; expert on chem. of ozone layer and radiative forcing of climate change; James B. Macelwane Award, American Geophysical Union 1979, UNEP Ozone Award 1997, Bower Award and Prize for Achievement in Science, Franklin Inst. 1999, Roger Revelle Medal, American Geophysical Union 2002, Albert Einstein World Award of Science 2004. *Publications:* more than 100 articles in scientific journals and 200 conf. papers.

Address: Office of the President, National Academy of Sciences, 500 Fifth Street, NW, Washington, DC 20001, USA (office). *Website:* www.nationalacademies.org/president (office).

CICHOCKI, Jacek; Polish sociologist, political scientist and politician; *Head of the Chancellery of the Prime Minister;* b. 17 Dec. 1971, Warsaw; m.; one s. three d.; ed XLII Grad. High School, Faculty of Philosophy and Sociology, Warsaw Univ.; worked at Centre for Eastern Studies in Warsaw 1992–2008, first as an expert in armed conflicts and ethnic problems in the post-Soviet states and subsequently as the Head of the Unit for Dept for the Caucasus and Cen. Asia and Head of Dept for Ukraine, Belarus and the Baltic States, Deputy Dir of the Centre 2001–04, Dir 2007–08; worked as programme asst at the programme of Cen. and Eastern Europe Forum, Stefan Batory Foundation 1995–97; Sec., Office of the Cttee for Special and Intelligence Services, Chancellery of the Prime Minister 2008–11; Minister of the Interior 2011–13; mem. Council of Ministers and Head of the Chancellery of the Prime Minister 2013–; Gold Cross of Merit 2006. *Address:* Chancellery of the Prime Minister, 00-583 Warsaw, Al. Ujazdowskie 1/3, Poland (office). *Telephone:* (22) 6946000 (office). *Fax:* (22) 6252637 (office). *E-mail:* kontakt@kprm.gov.pl (office). *Website:* www.kprm.gov.pl (office); www.premier.gov.pl (office).

CICHY, Leszek; Polish bank executive and mountaineer; b. 14 Nov. 1951, Pruszków; m. Maria Gierałtowska; two s.; ed Warsaw Univ. of Tech.; researcher, Geodesic Dept, Warsaw Univ. of Tech. 1977–90; engineer in Syria 1990–92; mem. of staff, Housing Investments, Warsaw 1992–93, Polski Bank Rozwoju 1993–98; Vice-Chair. Dom Inwestycyjny BRE Banku, Warsaw 1998–99, Bank Współpracy Europejskiej, Warsaw 1999–2000; Dir Kredyt Bank, Warsaw 2000–01; Vice-Chair. and Finance Dir, Capital Group ERGIS 2001–; mem. Polish Alpine Club, Pres. 1995–2000; mountaineering expeditions include Tatra, Alps, Andes, Caucasus, Karakoram and Himalayas; first person to climb Mount Everest in the winter (with partner Krzysztof Wielicki q.v.) 1980; first Pole to climb the Crown of the Earth (highest peaks on every continent) 1980–99. *Publication:* Discussing Everest (co-author) 1982. *Leisure interests:* tennis, skiing, astronomy. *Address:* ul. Na Uboczu 16/49, 02-791 Warsaw, Poland (home).

CICUTTO, Frank J., BCom, MPA, FAIBF, FAICD, FCIOSB; Australian business executive; ed Univ. of New South Wales, Harvard Univ., USA; joined Nat. Bank of Australia (later Nat. Australia Bank) as grad. trainee 1968, served in various man. positions including accountant, Gen. Man., State Man., NSW, Exec. Gen. Man., Products and Services 1994–96, Chief Gen. Man., Australian Financial Services 1996–98, also CEO, Clydesdale Bank, Scotland (subsidiary of Nat. Australia Bank), Man. Dir and CEO Nat. Australia Bank 1999–2004; Chair. ORIX Australia Corpn Ltd 2004–08, also Chair. ORIX New Zealand Ltd; Chair. RUN Corpn Ltd 2005–07; currently Chair. Chord Capital Management Pty Ltd; mem. Bd of Dirs St Vincent's Health 2004–, Melbourne Business School. *Leisure interests:* theatre, rugby, squash, golf. *Address:* c/o Board of Directors, St Vincent's Healthy, PO Box 2900, Fitzroy, VIC 3065, Australia (office).

CIECHANOVER, Aaron, MD, PhD; Israeli physician, molecular biologist and academic; *Professor of Biochemistry, Technion–Israel Institute of Technology;* b. 1 Oct. 1947, Haifa; ed Hebrew Univ. of Jerusalem; mil. service as a doctor in Israeli army; studied protein degradation at biochemical level with Avram Hershko (q.v.) 1976–81; collaborated with Alexander Varshavsky (q.v.) at MIT; currently Dir Rappaport Family Inst. for research in Medical Sciences and Prof. of Biochemistry, Technion–Israel Inst. of Tech.; Albert Lasker Basic Medical Research Award 2000, Nobel Prize in Chem. (jtly) 2004. *Address:* Faculty of Medicine, Technion–Israel Institute of Technology, 1 Efron Street, PO Box 9697, Bat Galim, Haifa, 31096, Israel (office). 4-8514722 (office). *Fax:* 4-8517008 (office). *E-mail:* c_tzachy@netvision.net.il (office); rafael@biomed.technion.ac.il (office). *Website:* www.technion.ac.il/medicine (office).

CIELO FILHO, César Augusto; Brazilian swimmer; b. 10 Jan. 1987, Santa Bárbara d'Oeste, São Paulo; s. of César Cielo and Flaria Cielo; ed Colegio Avanco de Ensino Programado, Auburn Univ., USA; began career at small swimming clubs in his native state; trained at Esporte Clube Barbarense under coach Mario Francisco Sobrinho; later trained at Clube de Campo de Piracicaba under Reinaldo Rosa 2000; transferred to Esporte Clube Pinheiros, São Paulo under Alberto Silva and Gustavo Borges 2003; trained under Australian coach Brett Hawke at Auburn Univ.; competed for eight-time NCAA Nat. Champion Auburn Tigers' Swimming and Diving team; also tutored by short-distance specialist Fernando Scherer 2008; World Championships (short course), Indianapolis 2004: silver medal, 4×100m freestyle; Pan American Games, Rio de Janeiro 2007: gold medal, 50m freestyle, 100m freestyle, 4×100m freestyle, silver medal, 4×100m medley; Olympic Games, Beijing 2008: gold medal, 50m freestyle, bronze medal, 100m freestyle; World Championships (long course), Rome 2009: gold medal, 50m freestyle, 100m freestyle; World Championships, Dubai 2010: gold medal, 50m freestyle, 100m freestyle, bronze medal, 4×100m freestyle, 4×100m medley; World Championships (short course), Guadalajara 2011: gold medal, 50m freestyle, 100m freestyle, 4×100m freestyle, 4×100m medley; World Championships (long course), Shanghai 2011: gold medal, 50m freestyle, 50m butterfly; Pan Pacific Championships, Irvine 2010: gold medal, 50m butterfly, silver medal, 50m freestyle, bronze medal, 100m freestyle; Olympic Games, London 2012: gold medal, 50m freestyle; World Championships (long course), Barcelona 2013: gold medal, 50m freestyle, 50m butterfly; world long course record holder in 50m (20.91s) and 100m freestyle (46.91s) 2009; coll. team: Auburn Tigers 2005–08; swims for Clube de Regatas do Flamengo/Auburn Aquatics; coach Alberto Pinto; Brazilian Swimmer of the Year, TV Globo 2006, NCAA Swimmer of the Year 2007, Athlete of the Year in 2008, 2009. *Leisure interests:* resting, playing video games. *Address:* Auburn Athletics Department, PO Box 351, Auburn, AL 36831-0351, USA. *Telephone:* (334) 844-9750. *E-mail:* athletics@auburn.edu; fcielo@terra.com.br. *Website:* www.auburntigers.com/sports/c-swim/mtt/cielo_cesar00.html; www.cesarcielo.com.br.

CIEMNIEWSKI, Jerzy, JuD; Polish lawyer and politician; b. 2 Aug. 1939, Warsaw; m.; one s.; ed Faculty of Law, Warsaw Univ.; Lecturer, Warsaw Univ. 1962–68; scientific worker, Inst. of Law Studies, Polish Acad. of Sciences, Warsaw 1969–, Lecturer 1972–; mem. Solidarity Independent Self-governing Trade Union 1980–89; Assoc. Understanding Cttee of Creative and Scientific Asscns and Teachers' Solidarity, also scientific worker Social and Labour Study Centre

attached to Nat. Comm. of Solidarity 1980–81; mem. Helsinki Cttee in Poland 1983; participant, Round Table debates, mem. group for law and judicature reform, expert group for political reforms Feb.–April 1989; mem. State Election Comm. during election to the Sejm (Parl.) and Senate 1989; Under-Sec. of State in Office of the Council of Ministers, Sec. of Council of Ministers 1989–91; Deputy to Sejm 1991–98; judge, Constitutional Tribunal 1998–2007; mem. Democratic Freedom Union 1990–94, Freedom Union 1994–, Helsinki Foundation for Human Rights, Centre for Human Rights in Eastern Europe; Awards of Gen. Sec. of Polish Acad. of Sciences 1974, 1976. *Publications:* numerous scientific works, mainly on constitutional law, including Ustawa o systemie konstytucyjnym SFR Jugosławii 1976, Sejm Ustawodawczy RP (1947–1952) 1978 (co-author), Studia nad rządem 1985 (co-author), System delegacki na tle ewolucji ustroju politycznego SFR Jugosławii 1988, Draft of the Constitution of the Republic of Poland (co-author) 1990. *Leisure interests:* family life, walking with dog, general history, painting. *Address:* c/o Tribunał Konstytucyjny, al. J. Ch. Szucha 12A, 00-198 Warsaw, Poland.

CIENFUEGOS ZEPEDA, Gen. Salvador; Mexican army officer and government official; *Secretary of National Defence;* b. 14 June 1948, México City; ed Heroico Colegio Militar; entered Mexican military Jan. 1964, positions include Military and Air Attaché, Embassies in Tokyo and Seoul; fmr Commdr of several Mil. Dists including 7th (Chiapas), 1st (México City), 9th (Guerrero), 5th (Jalisco) 2005; fmr Inspector and Comptroller-Gen. of Army and Air Force; fmr Deputy Dir-Gen., Fed. Register of Firearms and Explosives Control; fmr Dir Center for the Study of the Army and Air Force; Sec. (Minister) of Nat. Defence 2012–; several decorations including mem. Legion of Mil. Honour. *Address:* Secretariat of State for National Defence, Blvd Manuel Avila Camacho, esq. Avda Industria Militar, 3°, Col. Lomas de Sotelo, Del. Miguel Hidalgo, 11640 México DF, Mexico (office). *Telephone:* (55) 2122-8800 (office). *Fax:* (55) 5395-2935 (office). *E-mail:* ggalvang@mail.sedena.gob.mx (office). *Website:* www.sedena.gob.mx (office).

CIKOTIĆ, Selmo, PhD; Bosnia and Herzegovina government official and army officer (retd); b. 25 Jan. 1964, Berane-Ivangrad, Montenegro; m. Tanja Cikotić; one s. one d.; ed Bratstvo i Jedinstvo Mil. High School, Belgrade, Zadar Mil. Acad., Sarajevo Univ.; Duty Officer, Air Defence Educ. Centre, Zadar 1986–92; mem. Bosnia and Herzegovina Army 1992–94; Defence Attaché in Washington, DC 1994–97; Head of Training and Educ. Centre, Joint Command of Fed. of Bosnia and Herzegovina Army 1997–99; Head of Cabinet, Deputy Minister of Defence of Fed. of Bosnia and Herzegovina 1999–2000; Deputy Commdr of 1st Corps, Fed. of Bosnia and Herzegovina Army 2000–01, Commdr 2001–04; retd from active mil. duty 2004 (rank of Brig.-Gen.); CEO OKI Ltd, Sarajevo 2004–07; Minister of Defence 2007–12; mem. Party of Democratic Action (SDA). *Publications:* numerous articles and two books on defence and security. *Leisure interests:* sharpshooting, skiing, mountain biking, swimming, reading. *Address:* c/o Ministry of Defence, 71000 Sarajevo, H. Kreševljakovića 98, Bosnia and Herzegovina.

ÇILLER, Tansu, PhD; Turkish politician and academic; b. 1945, Istanbul; m.; two c.; ed Robert Coll., Boğaziçi Univ., Univ. of Connecticut and Yale Univ., USA; Assoc. Prof. 1978, Prof. 1983; served on academic bds of various univs, mainly in Dept of Econs Boğaziçi Univ.; joined True Path Party (DYP) 1990, Leader 1993–96; mem. Parl. 1991–2002; Minister of State for the Economy 1991; Prime Minister 1993–96; Deputy Prime Minister and Minister of Foreign Affairs 1996–97. *Publications:* nine publs on econs. *Address:* c/o True Path Party, Çetýn Emeç Bul. 117, Balgat, Ankara, Turkey. *Website:* www.dyp.org.tr.

CIMINO, Michael, BFA, MFA; American director and screenwriter; b. 1943, New York; ed Yale Univ.; Chevalier des Arts et des Lettres 2001. *Films include:* Silent Running (writer) 1972, Magnum Force (writer) 1973, Thunderbolt and Lightfoot (also writer) 1974, The Deer Hunter (also producer, Academy Award for Best Dir 1979) 1978, Heaven's Gate (also writer) 1980, Year of the Dragon (also writer) 1985, The Sicilian (also producer) 1987, Desperate Hours (also producer) 1990, The Sunchaser (also producer) 1996, To Each His Cinema (segment) 2007. *Publication:* Big Jane (novel) 2001. *Address:* c/o Jeff Berg, ICM, 8942 Wilshire Blvd., Beverly Hills, CA 90211, USA.

CIMOLI, Giancarlo; Italian administrator and airline industry executive; with SNIA Viscosa 1968–74; Chair. and Man. Dir Ferrovie dello Stato (state railways) 1996–2004; Chair. and CEO Alitalia 2004–07; mem. Bd of Dirs Air France-KLM –2007; mem. Aspen Inst.

CIMOSZEWICZ, Włodzimierz, MA, PhD, DJur; Polish lawyer, politician and farmer; b. 13 Sept. 1950, Warsaw; m.; one s. one d.; ed Faculty of Law, Warsaw Univ.; Research Assoc. and then Asst Prof., Warsaw Univ. 1972–85; Fullbright Scholar, Columbia Univ., New York, USA 1980–81; farm owner and operator 1985–89; mem. Union of Socialist Youth 1968–73 (Chair. Bd, Warsaw Univ. 1972–73), Union of Polish Students/Socialist Union of Polish Students 1968–75 (Chair. Univ. Council 1973), PZPR 1971–90; Deputy to Sejm (Parl.) 1989–2005, (mem. PZPR caucus 1989–90, Chair. SLD Parl. Group 1990–93, Vice-Chair. Nat. and Ethnic Minorities Comm. 1989–91, mem. Parl. Foreign Affairs Comm. 1989, Special Comm. on Territorial Self-Government 1990, Chair. Constitutional Cttee 1995–96), Deputy Speaker 1995–96; mem. Bd Interparliamentary Union 1989–91; presidential cand. for Democratic Left Alliance (SLD) 1990; mem. Parl. Ass. Council of Europe 1992–96; Deputy Chair. Council of Ministers and Minister of Justice and Attorney-Gen. 1993–95; Prime Minister of Poland 1996–97; Chair. European Integration Cttee 1996–97; mem. Podlaskie Prov. Council 1998–2000; Minister of Foreign Affairs 2001–04; elected Marshal (Speaker) Sejm Jan.–Oct. 2005; teacher, Univ. of Białystok 2006–; mem. Senate for Białystok 2007–; Fullbright Scholar, Columbia Univ., New York, USA 1980–81; Chevalier Ordre nat. du Mérite 1997; Kt Order of the Greek Repub. 1997; Dr hc (Univ. of South Carolina) 1997, (Appalachian Univ.) 1998, (Odessa Univ., Ukraine). *Leisure interests:* family, reading, handiwork, hunting, angling, crafts, ecology. *Address:* Senat (Senate), 00-902 Warsaw, ul. Wiejska 6, Poland (office). *Telephone:* (22) 6949265 (office). *Fax:* (22) 6949428 (office). *Website:* www.senat.gov.pl (office).

CINCA MATEOS, Jordi; Andorran banker and politician; *Minister of Finance and Public Service;* b. 1965, Andorra la Vella; m.; one s. two d.; worked for 14 years in Andorran financial sector, including various responsibilities within Dept of Banking; Dir of Marketing and Commercial Banking and mem. Exec. Bd Credit Andorra 2009–11; Govt Gen. Sec. and Spokesman 1990–93; mem. Gen. Council

(Consell Gen.) 1993–96; Minister of Finance and Public Service 2011–; mem. Bd of dirs of several cos in Andorra in the areas of entertainment, insurance, health services and textiles. *Leisure interests:* basketball, running marathons, travel. *Address:* Ministry of Finance and Public Service, Carrer Prat de la Creu 62–64, Edif. Administratiu, Andorra la Vella AD500, Andorra (office). *Telephone:* 875700 (office). *Fax:* 860962 (office). *E-mail:* finances.gov@andorra.ad (office). *Website:* www.finances.ad (office).

CINTRA FRÍAS, Gen. Leopoldo; Cuban army officer and government official; *Minister of the Revolutionary Armed Forces;* b. 17 July 1941, Yara, Granma Prov.; joined Rebel Army 1957, took part alongside Fidel Castro in guerrilla advance and overthrow of Batista regime; ended war with rank of Lt; subsequent army roles include Brigade Chief of Land Artillery, Chief of Army Motorized Div., Chief of Artillery Div., Revolutionary Army Forces Div. 3234, Tank Div. UM-1011, Head of W Army Region 1990–2011; roles abroad include Chief of Tanks Third Brigade, Int. Cuban Troops, Ethiopia, Head of Cuban Mil. Mission, Angola; mem. Asamblea Nacional del Poder Popular (Parl.) 1976–; Minister of the Revolutionary Armed Forces 2011–; mem. Partido Comunista de Cuba, mem. Cen. Cttee and Political Bureau; Repub. of Cuba Nat. Hero Award. *Address:* Ministry of the Revolutionary Armed Forces, Plaza de la Revolución, Havana, Cuba (office). *Website:* www .cubagob.cu/otras_info/minfar/far/minfar.htm (office).

CIOCCA, Pierluigi, DIur; Italian economist, fmr central banker and academic; *Professor, Department of Economics, Università degli Studi di Roma 'la Sapienza';* b. 17 Oct. 1941, Pescara; ed Univ. of Rome, Fondazione Einaudi (Univ. of Turin) and Balliol Coll., Oxford, UK; economist, Research Dept Banca d'Italia (Bank of Italy) 1969–82, Cen. Man. for Cen. Bank Operations 1982–88, Cen. Man. for Econ. Research 1988–95, Deputy Dir-Gen. Bank of Italy 1995–2006; mem. Working Party 3 OECD Econ. Policy Cttee 1997; substitute for Gov. Bank of Italy, Governing Council, European Cen. Bank 1998; mem. Financial Stability Forum 1999, EU Econ. and Financial Cttee 2003; currently Prof., Dept of Econs, Università degli Studi di Roma 'la Sapienza'. *Publications:* La nuova finanza in Italia, Una difficile metamorfosi (1980–2000) 2000. *Address:* Via Cesalpino 12, 00161, Rome, Italy. *Telephone:* (06) 4991-7065. *E-mail:* pierluigi.ciocca@uniroma1 .it. *Website:* dipartimento.dse.uniroma1.it.

CIOFFI, John M., BS, MS, PhD; American electrical engineer and academic; *Hitachi America Professor Emeritus of Engineering, Stanford University;* b. 7 Nov. 1956, Chicago, Ill.; s. of John M. Cioffi Jr and Lorraine M. Cioffi; m. Assia Cioffi; one s. five d.; ed Univ. of Illinois, Urbana-Champaign, Stanford Univ., Calif.; Bell Laboratories 1978–84; IBM Research 1984–86; EE Prof., Stanford Univ. 1986–2008, Hitachi America Prof. of Eng 2002–09, Prof. Emer. 2009–; Co-founder and Chief Tech. Officer, Amati Communications Inc. 1991–97 (acquired by Texas Instruments 1997); Chair. and CEO ASSIA Inc., Redwood City, Calif. (dynamic broadband-connection management software); mem. Bd of Dirs Alto Beam, Marconi Foundation; fmr Dir Marvell Semiconductor, Teknovus, ITEX, and others; mem. Nat. Acad. of Eng 2001; Fellow, IEEE 1996; Int. Fellow, Royal Soc. of Eng (UK) 2009; Dr hc (Edinburgh) 2010; NSF Presidential Investigator 1987–92, Faculty Devt Award, IBM Research 1986–88, Best Paper Award, IEEE Communications Soc. 1990, Outstanding Achievment Award, American Nat. Standards Inst. for contribs to ADSL 1995, Outstanding Alumnus, Univ. of Illinois 1999, IEE J.J. Thomson Medal 2000, IEEE Third Millennium Medal 2000, IEEE Kobayashi Medal 2001, ISSLS Best Paper Prize, IEE 2004, Marconi Prize and Int. Fellowship, Marconi Foundation 2006, Best Paper Award, IEEE ICC (co-recipient) 2006, Best Paper Award, IEEE ICC (co-recipient) 2007, Best Paper Award, IEEE Communications Magazine (co-recipient) 2007, Best Paper Award, IEEE ICC (co-recipient) 2008, IEEE Alexander Graham Bell Medal 2010, Innovation Award, Economist Magazine 2010, Distinguished Alumnus, Univ. of Illinois 2010, Edwin H. Armstrong Award 2013, Kirchmayer Award 2014. *Achievement:* designed world's first ADSL and VDSL modems (design accounts for 98% of world's more than 400 million DSL connections). *Publications:* more than 200 journal papers and 400 conf. papers and more than 100 licensed patents. *Address:* Room 363, David Packard Electrical Engineering Building, Stanford University, 350 Serra Mall, MC 9515, Stanford, CA 94305-9515, USA (office). *Telephone:* (650) 723-2150 (office). *Fax:* (650) 724-3652 (office). *E-mail:* cioffi@stanford.edu (office). *Website:* www.stanford.edu/group/cioffi (office).

CIOLOŞ, Dacian; Romanian agricultural engineer, politician and international organization official; *Commissioner for Agriculture and Rural Development, European Commission;* b. 27 July 1969, Zalău; m.; ed Univ. of Agricultural Sciences and Veterinary Medicine, Cluj-Napoca, Ecole nationale supérieure agronomique de Rennes, Univ. of Montpellier 1, France; agro-economist intern, EC Directorate-Gen. for Agriculture and Rural Devt, Brussels 1997, 1999, mem. EC del. to Romania (worked on EU SAPARD agricultural devt programme) 2002–03; Dir, local rural devt programme, Argeş Co. 1998–99; adviser to Minister of Agric. 2005–07, Under-Sec. of State for European Affairs, Ministry of Agric. May–Oct. 2007, Minister for Agric. and Rural Devt 2007–08; Head of Presidential Comm. on Agricultural Devt Public Policy of Romania 2009–10; Commr for Agric. and Rural Devt, EC, Brussels 2010–; mem. Groupe de Bruges (agricultural think-tank) 2000–. *Address:* Commissioner for Agriculture and Rural Development, European Commission, Rue de la Loi 200, 1049 Brussels, Belgium (office). *Telephone:* (2) 296-10-82 (office); (2) 299-11-11 (switchboard) (office). *Fax:* (2) 299-53-87 (office); (2) 295-01-38 (office). *E-mail:* dacian.ciolos@ec.europa.eu (office). *Website:* ec.europa.eu/commission_2010-2014/ciolos (office).

CIORBEA, Victor; Romanian lawyer and fmr politician; b. 26 Oct. 1954, Ponor Village; s. of Vasile Ciorbea and Eugenia Ciorbea; m. 1977; one d.; ed Law School, Cluj-Napoca, Case Western Reserve Univ., Cleveland, Ohio, USA; judge, Court of Bucharest 1979–84; Prosecutor, Dept Civil Cases, Gen. Prosecutor's Office 1984–87; Asst to Lecturer Law School, Bucharest 1987–90; Pres. Free Trade Unions Fed. in Educ. 1990–96, CNSLR 1990–93, CNSLR-FRĂTIA 1993–94, Democratic Union Confed., Romania 1994–96; Mayor of Bucharest 1996; Prime Minister of Romania 1996–98; mem. Exec. Bd ICFTU, ETUC, CES 1993–94, Congress of Local and Regional Powers, Council of Europe, Strasbourg 1996, European Hon. Senate 1999; rep. of Romania at OIM confs; Vice-Pres. PNTCD 1997–99, Pres. 2001; fmr Vice-Pres. and Chair. Christian Democratic Nat. Peasants' Party (now Popular Christian-Democratic Party of Romania); mem. Bd Alianta Civica 1996; Founding mem. Int. Christian Coalition 1999. *Address:* 3

Rosetti Square, sector 1, Bucharest 70 000, Romania (office). *Telephone:* (21) 3153862 (office).

CIOROIANU, Adrian Mihai, PhD; Romanian politician and academic; b. 5 Jan. 1967, Craiova; ed Univ. of Bucharest and Laval Univ., Canada; Lecturer, History Dept, Univ. of Bucharest 2002–; Adviser to Pres. of Nat. Liberal Party (PNL) 2002; elected to Romanian Senate (PNL) 2004–; Observer, European Parl. 2005–07; mem. European Parl. 2007–; Minister of Foreign Affairs 2007–08 (resgnd); mem. editorial team, Dilema Veche 1998–, Gazeta Sporturilor, Interpres, Scrisul Romanesc (newspapers); TV presenter on TVR1, Realitatea TV, Pax TV 2000–04. *Publications include:* The Ashes of a Century: A Hundred and One Superimposed Stories 2001, The Fire Hidden in Stone: On History, Memory and Other Contemporary Vanities 2002, This Ceauşescu Who Is Haunting the Romanians: The Myth, the Images and the Cult of the Leader in Communist Romania 2005, On the Shoulders of Marx: An Incursion into the History of Romanian Communism 2005, Sic Transit Gloria: The Subjective Chronicle of a Five-Year Plan Completed over Three and a Half Years 2006. *Address:* National Liberal Party, 011866, Bucharest, Boulevard Aviatorilor 86, Romania (office). *Telephone:* (21) 2310795 (office). *Fax:* (21) 2310796 (office). *E-mail:* dre@pnl.ro (office). *Website:* www.pnl.ro (office); cioroianu.ro (home).

CIOSEK, Stanisław, MA; Polish politician and diplomatist; b. 2 May 1939, Pawłowice, Radom Prov.; s. of Józef Ciosek and Janina Ciosek; m. Anna Ciosek 1969; two d.; ed Higher School of Econs, Sopot; spent time as activist in youth orgs 1957–75; Chair. Regional Council of Polish Students' Asscn (ZSP), Gdańsk, Deputy Chair. and Chair. Chief Council, ZSP 1957–73; Chair. Chief Council of Fed. of Socialist Unions of Polish Youth (FSZMP) 1974–75; mem. Polish United Workers' Party (PZPR) 1959–90, Deputy mem. PZPR Cen. Cttee 1971–80, First Sec., Voivodship Cttee PZPR and Chair. Presidium of Voivodship Nat. Council, Jelenia Góra 1975–80, mem. PZPR Cen. Cttee 1980–81, 1986–90, Sec., PZPR Cen. Cttee 1986–88, Alt. mem. Political Bureau of PZPR Cen. Cttee 1988, mem. Political Bureau 1988–89; Deputy to Sejm (Parl.) 1972–85; Minister for Co-operation with Trade Unions 1980–85, for Labour, for Wages and Social Affairs 1983–84, Vice-Chair. Cttee of Council of Ministers for Co-operation with Trade Unions 1983–85; Sec., Socio-Political Cttee of Council of Ministers 1981–85; Sec.-Gen. Nat. Council of Patriotic Movt for Rebirth (PRON) 1988–89; Co-organizer and participant, Round Table debates 1989; Amb. to USSR 1989–91, to Russia 1991–96; Foreign Policy Adviser to Pres. of Poland 1997–2005; Sec.-Gen. Eastern Club; Chair. Council, Polish-Russian Chamber of Commerce and Industry; Commdr's Cross, Order of Polonia Restituta. *Address:* 02-604 Warsaw, ul. Olkuska 7, Poland (office). *Telephone:* (22) 542-8240 (office). *Fax:* (22) 542-8244 (office). *E-mail:* ciosek@ ipgroup.pl (office). *Website:* prihp.pl (office).

CIPRIANI THORNE, HE Cardinal Juan Luis; Peruvian ecclesiastic; *Archbishop of Lima;* b. 28 Dec. 1943, Lima; ed St Mary's Catholic High School, Nat. Univ. of Eng, Univ. of Navarra, Spain; mem. Peruvian nat. basketball team in his youth; ordained priest 1977; apptd Coadjutor Bishop of Ayacucho 1988, Bishop of Turuzi 1988–95, Archbishop of Ayacucho 1995–99, Archbishop of Lima 1999–; cr. Cardinal (Cardinal-Priest of S. Camillo de Lellis) 2001; participated in Papal Conclave 2013; Great Chancellor Pontificia Universidad Católica del Perú; mem. Opus Dei; Class of Grand Cross, Order of the Sun 2009. *Address:* Arzobispado, Plaza de Armas s/n, Apdo. 1512, Lima 100 (office); Calle Los Nogales 249, San Isidro, Lima 27, Peru. *Telephone:* (14) 427-5980 (office); (14) 441-1977. *Fax:* (14) 427-1967 (office); (14) 440-9134. *E-mail:* arzolimas@amauta.rcpnet.pe (office).

CIPUTRA, BEng; Indonesian real estate executive; *President Commissioner, Ciputra Group;* b. 1931; m.; four c.; ed Bandung Inst. of Tech.; co-f. PT Pembangunan Jaya 1961, now Commr; Pres. Commr Ciputra Group 1984–90, 2002–, Pres. Dir 1990–2002; f. PT Metropolitan Devt 1971, now Pres. Commr; Ernst and Young Indonesian Entrepreneur of the Year Award 2007. *Address:* Ciputra Head Office, Prof. Dr. Satrio Kav 6, Jakarta 12940, Indonesia (office). *Telephone:* (21) 5225858 (office). *Fax:* (21) 5274125 (office). *Website:* www.ciputra .com (office).

CIRAC SASTURAIN, Juan Ignacio, LicTheorPhys, PhD; Spanish physicist and academic; *Director of the Theory Division, Max Planck Institute for Quantum Optics;* b. 11 Oct. 1965, Manresa, Catalonia; ed Universidad Complutense de Madrid; Fellow, Formación del Personal Investigador (Prog. Gen.), Dept of Optics, Universidad Complutense de Madrid 1989–91; Titular Univ. Prof., Dept of Applied Physics, Universidad de Castilla-La Mancha 1991–96; Research Assoc., Jt Inst. for Lab. Astrophysics, Univ. of Colorado, USA 1993–94; Prof., Institut für Theoretische Physik, Leopold Franzens Universität Innsbruck 1996–2001; Dir Theory Div., Max Planck Inst. for Quantum Optics and mem. Max Planck Soc. 2001–; Assoc. Ed., Physical Review A 2000–03, Revista Española de Física 2002–05, Review of Modern Physics 2005–; Founding Man. Ed., Quantum Information and Computation 2001–; Corresp. Spanish Acad. of Sciences 2002, Austrian Acad. of Sciences 2003; Fellow, American Physical Soc. 2002; Hon. Prof. of Physics, Tech. Univ. of Munich 2002–; Distinguished Guest Prof., Institut de Ciències Fotòniques (Barcelona) 2003; Distinguished Research Chair, Perimeter Inst., Waterloo, Canada 2009; Dr hc (Universidad Castilla-La Mancha) 2005, (Universidad Politecnica de Catalunya, Barcelona) 2007; Premio Nacional a Investigadores Noveles, Royal Physical Soc. of Spain 1992, Felix Kuschenitz Prize, Austrian Acad. of Sciences 2001, Medal of the Royal Physical Soc. of Spain 2002, Quantum Electronics Prize, European Science Foundation 2005, Prince of Asturias Award for Tech. and Scientific Research 2006, 6th Int. Quantum Communication Award 2006, Nat. 'Blas Cabrera' Prize for Physical, Material and Earth Sciences 2007, 'Académico de Honor', Academia de Ciencias de la Región de Murcia 2007, 'Premios de las artes y de la ciencia' – Castellano-Manchegos del Mundo, Junta Castilla-La Mancha 2009, Carl Zeiss Research Award 2009, BBVA Foundation Frontiers of Knowledge Award 2009, Benjamin Franklin Medal, Franklin Inst. (co-recipient) 2010, Premi Nacional de Pensament i Cultura Científica 2010, Wolf Prize in Physics (co-recipient) 2013. *Publications:* more than 350 papers in professional journals. *Address:* Room B1.41, Max-Planck-Institut für Quantenoptik, Hans-Kopfermann-Str. 1, 85748 Garching, Germany (office). *Telephone:* (89) 32905-736 (office). *Fax:* (89) 32905-336 (office). *E-mail:* ignacio.cirac@mpq.mpg.de (office). *Website:* www.mpq.mpg.de (office).

CIRELLI, Jean-François; French energy industry executive; *Vice-Chairman and President, in charge of the Energy Europe Business line, GDF Suez SA;* b. 9 July 1958, Chambéry; ed Institut d'Etudes Politiques, Ecole Nationale d'Admin, Paris; with Treasury Dept, Ministry of Economy and Finance 1985–95; Tech. Adviser to Pres. of France 1995–97, Econ. Adviser 1997–2002; Deputy Dir Office of the Prime Minister 2002–04; Chair. and CEO Gaz de France Group 2004–08, Vice-Chair. and Pres., in charge of the Energy Europe Business line, GDF Suez SA 2008–, Chair. GDF Suez Trading (France), Eurogas (Belgium), Vice-Chair. GDF Suez Corp. Foundation, Electrabel (Belgium), Dir of GDF Suez Energy Services, Suez Environnement Co. (France), GDF Suez Belgium, International Power (UK); mem. Supervisory Bd Vallourec; mem. Bd of Dirs Neuf Cegetel, Atos. *Address:* GDF Suez SA, 1 place Samuel de Champlain, 92400 Courbevoie, France (office). *Telephone:* 1-44-22-00-00 (office). *E-mail:* info@gdfsuez.com (office). *Website:* www.gdfsuez.com (office); www.suez-environnement.com (office).

CIRIANI, Henri Edouard; French architect and academic; b. 30 Dec. 1936, Lima, Peru; s. of Enrique Ciriani and Caridad Suito; m. Marcelle Espejo 1962; two d.; ed Santa Maria School, Nat. Univ. of Eng and Town Planning Inst., Lima; Asst Architect, Dept of Architecture, Ministry of Devt and Public Works, Lima, Project Architect 1961–64; pvt. practice with Crousse and Paez 1961–63; Asst Prof. of Design, Nat. Univ. of Eng, Lima 1962–64; emigrated to France 1964; f. pvt. practice 1968; Prof. Ecole des Beaux-Arts de Paris 1969–83; Prof. of Architecture, Ecole d'Architecture de Paris-Belleville 1984–2002; Dist Prof., Univ. Nacional de Ingeniería, Lima 1985–; Visiting Prof., Tulane Univ., New Orleans 1984, Univ. Coll., Dublin 1985, Ecole d'Architecture de Grenoble 1988, Univ. of Pennsylvania 1989 and many others; Sir Banister Fletcher Visiting Lecturer, Univ. Coll., London 1986; Prof., Univ. of Navarra 2006–07; Dir Acad. de France, Rome 1987–91; Fondation Le Corbusier 1989–; mem. Int. Acad. of Architecture; Hon. Fellow, RIBA; Chevalier, Légion d'honneur 1997; Nat. Grand Prix of Architecture 1983, Equerre d'Argent 1983, Palme d'Or de l'Habitat 1988, Brunner Memorial Prize 1997. *Public works include:* public housing at Ventanilla Matute 1963, San Felipe 1964, Rimac Mirones 1965, Marne-la-vallée Noisy II 1980, Noisy III 1981, St Denis 1982, Evry 1985, Lognes 1986, Charcot 1991, Bercy 1994, Colombes 1995, urban landscape at Grenoble 1968–74, public facilities at St Denis Child-care Centre 1983, Cen. kitchen for St Antoine Hosp., Paris 1985, Torcy Child-care Centre 1989, Museum of the First World War, Péronne 1992, extension to Ministry of Finance Bldg, Paris 1993, Arles Archaeological Museum 1995, pvt. bldgs at The Hague Apartment Tower 1995, Stadspoort College 2000, Conf. Centre, French Nat. Inst. for Research in Computer Science and Control 2001, Palais de Justice 2006, retrospective exhbns at Institut Français d'Architecture, Paris 1984, Figueira da Foz, Oporto and Lisbon 1985, New York 1985, Tokyo 1987, Lima 1996, New York 1997, Montreal 1997, Venice 1999, Sao Paulo 2005. *Publications:* Pratique de la pièce urbaine 1996, Paroles d'architecte (ed. by Jean Petit Lugano) 1997. *Leisure interests:* drawing, collecting postcards. *Address:* Atelier Ciriani, 61 rue Pascal, 75013 Paris, France (office). *Telephone:* 1-43-37-41-00 (office).

ĆIRIĆ, Nebojša, MBA; Serbian economist and politician; b. 12 Jan. 1974, Bor; ed Davies Laing & Dick Coll., England, London School of Econs, England, London Inst. of Chartered Accountants, England, HEC School of Man., Paris, France, Univ. of Belgrade; Jr Account Man., Ogilvy & Mather, Belgrade 1996–97; expert assoc., Consulting Dept, Econ. Inst., Belgrade 1997–2001; Special Foreign Investment Adviser, Ministry of Int. Econ. Relations 2001–02; Dir for Financial Consulting, Deloitte, Belgrade 2002–07; Asst Minister of the Economy, responsible for Industry and Privatization 2007–08; State Sec., Ministry of the Economy 2008–11, Minister of the Economy and Regional Devt 2011–12. *Address:* c/o Ministry of the Economy and Regional Development, 11000 Belgrade, bul. Kralja Aleksandra 15, Serbia.

CIRY, Michel; French composer, painter, etcher and graphic artist; b. 31 Aug. 1919, La Baule; s. of Georges Ciry and Simone Ciry (née Breune); ed Ecole des Arts Appliqués, Paris; studied music with Nadia Boulanger; religious and secular paintings and etchings; apptd Sec. of Peintres Graveurs Français 1941, painter 1951–; Prof., School of Fine Arts Fontainebleau 1957–58, Académie Julian 1960; fmr mem. Conseil Supérieur de l'Enseignement des Beaux-Arts; Vice-Pres. Comité Nat. de la Gravure 1957–; numerous exhbns in Europe and America including Paris, London, New York, Boston, Amsterdam, Rome and Berlin; works in Museums of Europe and America; has illustrated numerous books including books by Montherlant, Green, Claudel and Mauriac; mem. Acad. des Beaux-Arts, Florence 1964–, Belgian Acad. 1988; Officier, Légion d'honneur, Chevalier des Arts et Lettres, Commdr, Ordre Nat. du Mérite; Prix Nat. des Arts 1945, Grande médaille de vermeil de la Ville de Paris 1962, Grand Prix du Conseil Général de la Seine 1962, Prix de l'Ile de France 1964, Prix Eugène Carrière 1964, Grand Prix de Montrouge 1965, Lauréate Acad. des Beaux-Arts 1968, Prix Wildenstein 1968, Biennale Médaille d'Or, Florence 1972, Prix international de la Biennale du Gemmail d'Art Sacré 1973, Lauréat du Grand Prix Georges Baudry 1984. *Major works:* Chemin de croix 1960–64, Stabat Mater 1960, 1961, 1963, 1965, Fièvres 1965, Christ's Passion 1955, 1957, 1960, 1964, Marie-Madeleine 1961, 1963, 1965, Saint François 1950, 1954, 1959, 1960, 1964, 1965, Saint Dominic 1962. *Compositions include:* five sacred symphonies for choir and orchestra 1951–54, Stèle pour un héros 1949, Pietà 1950, Mystère de Jésus 1953, several chamber works. *Publications:* 24 vols of autobiog., Brisons nos fers 1992. *Address:* La Bergerie, 76119 Varengeville-sur-Mer, Seine-Maritime, France. *Website:* www.michel-ciry.fr.

CISNEROS, Gustavo A.; Venezuelan media executive; *Chairman and CEO, Cisneros Group;* b. 16 Aug. 1947; s. of Diego Cisneros; m. Patricia Phelps; three c.; ed Babson Coll., Wellesley, Mass., USA; Chair. and CEO Cisneros Group (family-owned co. holding stakes in over 70 cos. in 39 countries including Venevisión, Univisión, Chilevisión, Caracol Televisión de Colombia, Playboy TV Latin America, Caribbean Communications Network, Direct TV Latin America and American Online Latin America (AOLA); Dir Panamco Bottling Co., AOL Latin America, Pueblo Int., Inc., Ibero-American Media Partners 1997–; Owner, Los Leones del Caracas baseball team 2001–; Co-founder (with wife Patricia and brother Ricardo) Fundación Cisneros; mem. Bd of Dirs Barrick Gold Corpn, RRE Ventures LLC; Commr Global Information Infrastructure Comm.; charter mem. UN Information and Communications Technologies Task Force; mem. World Business Council, World Econ. Forum; mem. Int. Advisory Councils, Columbia Univ., Babson Coll.; mem. Int. Advisory Bd Barrick Gold Corpn, Council on Foreign Relations; mem. Advisory Cttee, David Rockefeller Center for Latin American Studies, Harvard Univ.; mem. Bd of Advisers for Panama Canal; mem. Chair.'s Int. Advisory Council, Americas Soc.; mem. Bd of Overseers, Int. Center for Econ. Growth; mem. Bd Govs. Joseph H. Lauder Inst. of Man., Wharton School at Univ. of Pennsylvania; mem. Chair.'s Council, Museum of Modern Art; mem. Bd Trustees, Museum of TV and Radio; Americas Soc. Distinguished Service Award 2003, Woodrow Wilson Award for Public Service 2004. *Address:* Cisneros Group, 36 East 61st Street, New York, NY 10021, USA (office); Edeficio Venevisión, Final Avenida La Salle, Colina de los Caobos, Caracas 1050 (office); Fundación Cisneros, Centro Mozarteum, Final Avenida La Salle, Colina de los Caobos, Caracas 1050, Venezuela (office). *Telephone:* (212) 708-9444 (USA) (office); (582) 708-9697 (Venezuela) (office). *E-mail:* info@cisneros.com (office); info@fundacion.cisneros.org (office). *Website:* www.cisneros.com (office); www.venevision.net (office).

CISNEROS, Henry G., BA, Master of Urban & Regional Planning, MPA, DPA; American real estate industry executive and fmr politician; *Executive Chairman, CityView;* b. 11 June 1947, San Antonio, Tex.; s. of J. George Cisneros and Elvira Munguia; m. Mary-Alice Perez; one s. two d.; ed Texam A&M Univ., Harvard Univ., George Washington Univ.; Admin. Asst, Office of the City Man., San Antonio, Tex. May–Sept. 1968, Office of the City Man., Bryan, Tex. 1968–69; Asst Dir, Dept of Model Cities, San Antonio, Tex. 1969–70; Asst to the Exec. Vice-Pres., Nat. League of Cities, Washington, DC 1970–71; Teaching Asst, Dept of Urban Studies and Planning, MIT 1972–74; Faculty mem., Dept of Urban Studies, Trinity Univ. 1974–87, Public Admin program, Univ. of Texas, San Antonio 1974–87; mem. City Council, City of San Antonio 1975–81, Mayor of San Antonio 1981–89; Chair. Cisneros Asset Management Co. 1989–93, Chair. Cisneros Benefit Group, Cisneros Communications; Sec., US Dept of Housing and Urban Devt 1993–97; Pres. and COO Univision Communications, Inc. 1997–2000; Chair. American Sunrise Non-Profit Corpn 2000–; Exec. Chair. CityView, LLC 2000–; Earthquake Assistance Hon. mem. AIA 1986; 23 hon. degrees; numerous awards including White House Fellow, Office of the Sec. of Health, Educ., and Welfare, Washington, DC 1971–72, Ford Foundation Grant recipient, John F. Kennedy School of Govt, Harvard Univ. 1972–74, Jefferson Award, American Inst. of Public Service 1982, Distinguished Leadership Award, American Inst. of Planners 1985, Nat. Recognition Award, Mexican Govt 1985, Pres.'s Award, Nat. League of Cities 1989, First Annual John A. Wilson Public Service Award 1993, Humanitarian Award, Los Angeles Inner City Law Center 2001, Lifetime Achievement Award, Para Los Niños 2001, Congressional Hispanic Caucus Medallion of Excellence for Leadership 2002, Aguila Azteca, Govt of Mexico 2003, Catherine Powell Distinguished Service Award, Texas City Planners Asscn 2004, James W. Rouse Civic Medal of Honor, Enterprise Foundation 2004, Martin Luther King Distinguished Leadership Award, San Antonio 2005, Excellence in Affordable Housing Initiatives, City of San Antonio 2005, Business Man of the Year, Texas Asscn of Mexican-American Chambers of Commerce (TAMACC) 2006, Lifetime Achievement Award, San Antonio Hispanic Chamber of Commerce 2006, listed in the Top 50 Most Influential People in Home Building, Builder Magazine 2006, listed in the Top 101 Top Leaders of the Hispanic Community, Latino Leaders Magazine 2006, Cesar Chavez Award, American Asscn for Affirmative Action 2007, Housing Person of the Year, Nat. Housing Conf. 2007, Builders Hall of Fame Inductee, Nat. Asscn of Home Builders 2007, Nat. Leadership Honoree, Hispanic Elected Local Officials 2008, Hubert H. Humphrey Award, American Political Science Asscn 2008, Habitat for Humanity, Visionary Award 2008, Walter F. Mondale and Edward W. Brooke Fair Housing Award, Nat. Alliance for Fair Housing 2009, Urban Leadership Award, Penn Inst. for Urban Research 2011, Jack Kemp Award, Terwilliger Center, Urban Land Inst. 2011, Leadership Award, Council of Large Public Housing Authorities 2011 Outstanding Corp. Citizen, Hispanic Chamber 2012. *Publications include:* San Antonio's Place in the Technology Economy: A Review of Opportunities and a Blueprint for Action 1982, Target 1990, US Dept of Housing and Urban Devt 1994–97, Opportunity and Progress: A Bipartisan Platform for National Housing Policy (with Jack Kemp, Nick Retsinas and Kent Colton) 2004,Casa y Comunidad: Latino Home and Neighborhood Design (co-ed. with John Rosales) 2006, BuilderBooks (Silver Award, Benjamin Franklin Awards, Publrs Marketing Asscn 2007) 2007, Our Communities, Our Homes: Pathways to Housing and Homeownership in America's Cities and States (with Jack Kemp, Nick Retsinas and Kent Colton) 2007, Latinos and the Nations Future (ed.) 2008, From Despair to Hope: HOPE VI and the Transformation of America's Public Housing (ed.) 2009, in, The Handbook of Infrastructure Investing (ed. Michael Underhill) 2012, Independent for Life (co-ed. with Jane Hickie) 2012. *Leisure interests:* reading, going to the cinema, spending time with his family. *Address:* CityView, 454 Soledad Street, Suite 300, San Antonio, TX 78205 (office); 2002 West Houston Street, San Antonio, TX 78207, USA (home). *Telephone:* (210) 228-9574 (office). *Fax:* (210) 224-7888 (home). *E-mail:* info@cityview.com (office). *Website:* www.cityview.com (office).

CISSÉ, Alioune Badara; Senegalese lawyer and politician; b. 1953; ed legal studies in USA; fmr English teacher; mem. Nat. Ass. (Parl.) for Saint-Louis Nord; Chef de Cabinet for Prime Minister Macky Sall 2005; Local Councillor, Saint-Louis 2009–12, First Deputy Mayor 2009; Minister of Foreign Affairs April–Oct. 2012; fmr mem. Parti démocratique sénégalais (PDS); Founding mem. Alliance pour la république (APR), currently Nat. Co-ordinator. *Address:* c/o Ministry of Foreign Affairs, pl. de l'Indépendance, BP 4044, Dakar, Senegal.

CISSÉ, Amadou Boubacar, BA, MEcon, PhD; Niger civil engineer, politician and banker; *Vice-President (Operations), Islamic Development Bank;* b. 29 June 1948; m.; five c.; ed Ecole Nationale des Ponts et Chaussées and Institut des Sciences Politiques, Paris; fmr sr staff mem. in various capacities with World Bank, including Infrastructure Specialist, Prin. Operations Officer, IFC for Privatization and Financial Adviser to Vice-Pres. Africa Region, Resident Rep. of World Bank in several African countries; fmr Prime Minister of Niger; fmr Minister of Finance and Econ. Reforms; fmr Minister of State in charge of Economy, Finance and Planning; fmr Managing Dir Public Works Dept; fmr Exec. Sec. Railway Authority of Benin-Niger; Vice-Pres. (Operations), Islamic Devt Bank, Jeddah, Saudi Arabia 2002–. *Address:* Islamic Development Bank, PO Box 5925, Jeddah 21432, Saudi Arabia (office). *Telephone:* (2) 6361400 (office). *Fax:* (2) 6366871 (office). *E-mail:* idbarchives@isdb.org (office). *Website:* www.isdb.org (office).

CISSÉ, Soumaïla; Malian software engineer and politician; *President, Union pour la République et la Démocratie;* b. 20 Dec. 1949, Tombouctou; m. Astan Traoré 1972; four s.; ed Univ. of Dakar, Senegal, Univ. of Montpellier, France; software engineer with IBM-France, Groupe Pechiney-France and Groupe Thomson-France 1980–84; Analyst and Project Man. Air Inter, France 1984; Project Co-ordinator, Compagnie Malienne pour le Développement de Textile 1984, becoming Dir of Programs and Man. Control, Acting Gen. Man. 1991; fmr Gen. Man. Agence de Cessions Immobilières, Mali; Co-founder Alliance pour la démocratie au Mali 1991; Sec.-Gen. of the Presidency 1992–93; Minister of Finance 1993–2000, also of Trade 1994–97, of Equipment, Physical Planning, Environment and Urban Devt 2000–02; unsuccessful cand. in presidential elections 2002, 2012, 2013; Commr for Mali, Union Economique et Monétaire Ouest Africain (UEMOA) 2001, Pres. UEMOA Comm. 2004–12; f. Union pour la République et la Démocratie 2003, currently Pres.; Chevalier, Officer and Commdr, Nat. Order of Mali. *Address:* Union pour la République et la Démocratie, Niaréla, rue 268, porte 41, Bamako, Mali (office). *Telephone:* 2021-8642 (office). *E-mail:* contact@urd-mali.net (office). *Website:* www.urd-mali.net (office).

CISSOKO, Diango, LLD; Malian government official; b. 1948; ed Ecole Nat. d'Admin du Mali, Univ. of Caen, France, Inst. Int. d'Admin Publique, Paris, Univ. of Rouen; fmr Lecturer, Ecole des Hautes Etudes, Bamako, Ecole Nat. d'Ingénieurs, Inst. Int. d'Admin, Centre de Formation et d'Appui pour le Développement Local 1985–; Civil Admin., Nat. Directorate of Interior and Correctional Services 1971–72, Deputy Dir of Correctional Services April–Oct. 1972, Dir of Correctional Services, also Dir Bamako Central Prison 1972–79, Nat. Dir of Public Service and Personnel 1982–83; Dir of Cabinet of Minister of Labour and Public Service 1983–84; Minister of Justice and Keeper of the Seals 1984–88; Sec.-Gen., Presidency of the Repub. (with rank of Minister) 1988–89, 2008–11, Minister Sec.-Gen. of the Presidency 1989–91; Deputy Gov. Islamic Devt Bank in Mali 1989–90; Gov. World Bank in Mali 1990–91; consultant 1994–2002; Dir, Office of the Prime Minister (with rank of Minister) 2002–08; Ombudsman 2011–12; Prime Minister 2012–13; mem. Nat. Comm. for Admin. Reform 1983–84; Officer, Ordre Nat. du Mali. *Address:* c/o Office of the Prime Minister, Quartier du Fleuve, BP 790, Bamako, Mali (office).

ÇITAKU, Vlora, MA; Kosovo politician; *Minister of European Integration;* b. 10 Oct. 1980, Prishtina; as a teenager, became an interpreter and a stringer for major Western news outlets at onset of Kosovo war; later a refugee during the war; has been involved with politics since 1999; initially became spokesperson for the Kosovo Liberation Army and joined Democratic Party of Kosovo after its formation; mem. Kosovo Ass. in two mandates –2011; served as an Acting Minister of Foreign Affairs and Deputy Minister of Foreign Affairs 2009; Minister of European Integration 2011–; bd mem. Kosovo charity involved in protecting women against domestic violence. *Address:* Ministry of European Integration, 10000 Prishtina, Rruga Nënë Terezë, Ndërtesa e re e Qeverisë, Kati 9, Kosovo (office). *Telephone:* (38) 20027001 (office). *E-mail:* bardha.ajvazi@rks-gov.net (office). *Website:* www.mei-ks.net (office).

CITERNE, Philippe, BEcons, PhD; French banker; *Co-CEO, Société Générale;* b. 1949; ed Ecole Centrale de Paris; Project Man., Business Dept, INSEE 1972–74; Project Man., Forecasting Dept, Ministry of Finance, becoming Bureau Chief, Energy, Transport and Equipment Div. 1974–79; joined Econ. Research Dept, Société Générale 1979, Dir Econ. Research Dept 1984–86, Dir Financial Man. 1986–90, Dir of Human Resources 1990–95, Deputy CEO in charge of Resources and Services Div. 1995–97, CEO Société Générale 1997–2006, Dir and Co-CEO 2006–. *Address:* Société Générale, 75886 Paris Cedex 18, France (office). *Telephone:* 1-42-14-20-00 (office). *E-mail:* info@socgen.com (office). *Website:* www.socgen.com (office).

ČIUPAILA, Regimantas, PhD; Lithuanian mathematician, engineer, academic and politician; b. 20 Aug. 1956; m. Dalia Čiupaila; two d.; ed Vilnius Univ.; engineer-programmer, Computation Centre, Vilnius Univ. 1991–92; Dir of Foreign Relations, Vilnius Gediminas Tech. Univ. 1992–96, Docent 1992–; Docent, Mykolas Riomeris Univ. 2001–; mem. Liberal and Centre Union (LCU—Liberalų Centro Sąjunga), mem. LCU Bd 2003–; mem. Council of Vilnius City Municipality 1990–96, Vice-Pres. Vilnius City Council 1990–91; mem. Seimas (Parl.), Vice-Pres. European Affairs Cttee, mem. Foreign Affairs Cttee 1996–2000; mem. Parl. Ass. of Council of Europe 1996–2000; mem. European Parl. Jt Cttee 1997–2000; Vice-Pres. Lithuanian Cen. Union 2001–03; Vice-Minister of the Interior 2006–07, Minister of the Interior 2007–08. *Address:* Ministry of the Interior, Šventaragio 2, 01510 Vilnius, Lithuania (office). *Telephone:* (5) 271-7130 (office). *Fax:* (5) 271-8551 (office). *E-mail:* korespondencija@vrm.lt (office). *Website:* www.vrm.lt (office).

CIVILETTI, Benjamin R., AB, LLB; American lawyer and fmr government official; *Chairman, Venable, Baetjer, Howard & Civiletti LLP;* b. 17 July 1935, Peekskill, NY; s. of Benjamin C. Civiletti and Virginia I. Civiletti; m. Gaile Lundgren 1958; two s. one d.; ed Johns Hopkins Univ., Baltimore, Md, Columbia Univ., New York, Univ. of Maryland School of Law; admitted Md Bar 1961; law clerk to Hon. W. Calvin Chesnut, US District Court for Md 1961–62; Asst US Attorney, Md 1962–64; Pnr Venable, Baetjer & Howard (now Venable, Baetjer, Howard & Civiletti LLP) 1964–77, 1981–, Chair. 1996–; Asst Attorney-Gen., Criminal Div., US Dept of Justice, Washington, DC 1977–79, US Attorney-Gen. 1979–81; Chair. and Dir Healthcorp Inc.; Dir Bethlehem Steel Corpn, Wackenhut Corrections Corpn, MBNA America, MBNA International; Trustee Johns Hopkins Univ. 1980–98; mem. Legal Advisory Bd Martindale-Lexus; mem. Bd of Eds Federal Litigation Guide Reporter; mem. ABA, Federal Bar Asscn, Md State Bar, DC Bar Asscn, Bar Asscn of Baltimore City; Fellow, American Bar Foundation, American Law Inst., American Coll. of Trial Lawyers; Kt-Commdr, Order of Merit of the Italian Repub.; Hon. LLD (Univ. of Baltimore), (New York Law School), (St John's Coll.), (Tulane Univ.) (Univ. of Notre Dame), (Univ. of Maryland); Hon. DHumLitt (Towson State Univ.); Equal Justice Award, Baltimore Urban League 1997, Justice Award, American Judicature Soc. 2005. *Leisure interests:* golf, gardening, antiques. *Address:* Venable, Baetjer, Howard & Civiletti LLP, 1800 Mercantile Bank and Trust Building, 2 Hopkins Plaza, Baltimore, MD 21201, USA (office). *Telephone:* (410) 244-7600 (home). *Fax:* (410) 244-7742 (office). *E-mail:* brciviletti@venable.com (office). *Website:* www.venable.com (office).

CIXOUS, Hélène, DèsSc; French academic and author; b. 5 June 1937, Oran, Algeria; d. of Georges Cixous and Eve Klein; one s. one d.; ed Lycée d'Alger, Lycée de Sceaux, Sorbonne; mem. staff. Univ. of Bordeaux 1962–65; Asst Lecturer, Sorbonne 1965–67; Lecturer, Univ. of Paris X (Nanterre) 1967–68; helped found Univ. of Paris VIII (Vincennes) 1968, Chair. and Prof. of Literature 1968–; Founder and Dir Centre d'Etudes Féminines 1974–; Co-Founder of journal *Poétique* 1969; Southern Cross of Brazil 1989; Chevalier de la Légion d'honneur 1994; Officier Ordre nat. du Mérite 1998; Dr hc (Queen's Univ., Kingston, Canada) 1991, (Edmonton, Canada) 1992, (York, UK) 1993, (Georgetown, Washington, DC, USA) 1995, (Northwestern, Chicago, USA) 1996; Prix Médicis 1969, Prix des critiques for best theatrical work of the year 1994, 2000, Amb. of Star Awards, Pakistan 1997. *Theatre:* Portrait de Dora 1976, Le nom d'Oedipe 1978, La prise de l'école de Madhubaï 1984, L'Histoire terrible mais inachevée de Norodom Sihanouk, roi du Cambodge 1985, L'Indiade ou l'Inde de leurs rêves 1987, On ne part pas on ne revient pas 1991, Voile noire voile blanche 1994, L'Histoire qu'on ne connaîtra jamais 1994, La Ville Parjure ou le Réveil des Erinyes 1994, Tambours sur la digue 1999 (Molière Award 2000), Rouen la trentième nuit de mai 31 2001. *Publications include:* Le Prénom de Dieu 1967, Dedans 1969, Le Troisième corps, Les Commencements 1970, Un vrai jardin 1971, Neutre 1972, Tombe, Portrait du Soleil 1973, Révolutions pour plus d'un Faust 1975, Souffles 1975, La 1976, Partie 1976, Angst 1977, Préparatifs de noces au-delà de l'abîme 1978, Vivre l'orange 1979, Anankè 1979, Illa 1980, With ou l'art de l'innocence 1981, Limonade tout était si infini 1982, Le Livre de Promethea 1983, Manne 1988, Jours de l'An 1990, L'Ange au secret 1991, Déluge 1992, Beethoven à jamais 1993, La fiancée juive 1995, Messie 1996, Or, les lettres de mon père 1997, Osnabrück 1999, Les Rêveries de la femme sauvage 2000, Le Jour où je n'étais pas là 2000, Portrait de Jacques Derrida en jeune saint juif 2001, Benjamin à Montaigne, il ne faut pas le dire 2001, Manhattan. Lettres de la Préhistoire 2002; essays: L'exil de James Joyce 1969, Prénoms de personne 1974, La Jeune née 1975, La venue à l'écriture 1977, Entre l'écriture 1986, L'heure de Clarice Lispector 1989, Reading with Clarice Lispector 1990, Readings, the Poetics of Blanchot, Joyce, Kafka, Lispector, Tsvetaeva 1992, Three Steps on the Ladder of Writing 1993, Photos de racines 1994, Stigmata 1998, Escaping Texts 1998. *Address:* Éditions Galilée, 9 rue Linné, 75005 Paris (office); Centre d'études féminines, Université Paris VIII, 2 rue de la Liberté, 93526 Saint-Denis cedex 2, France.

CIZA, Jean; Burundian economist and central banker; *Governor, Banque de la République du Burundi;* b. 8 Dec. 1966, Rubanga, Muhanga Dist, Kayanza Prov.; m.; two c.; ed Univ. du Burundi; worked with USAID on BEST project 1995–96; with Africare Burundi (US non-govt org.) 1996–98; joined Interbank Burundi 1999, becoming Dir Central Market Agency; Dir and CEO Banque Commerciale du Burundi (BANCOBU) –2012; Gov. Banque de la République du Burundi (central bank) 2012–. *Address:* Office of the Governor, Banque de la République du Burundi, ave du Gouvernement, BP 705, Bujumbura, Burundi (office). *Telephone:* 22225142 (office). *Fax:* 22223128 (office). *E-mail:* brb@brb.bi (office). *Website:* www.brb-bi.net (office).

CLAES, Willy; Belgian politician and pianist; b. 24 Nov. 1938, Hasselt; m. Suzanne Meynen 1965; one s. one d.; ed Univ. Libre de Bruxelles; mem. Exec. Cttee Belgian Socialist Party, Jt Pres. 1975–77; mem. Limbourg Council 1964; mem. Chamber of Deputies 1968–94; Minister of Educ. (Flemish) 1972–73, of Econ. Affairs 1973–74, 1977–81, Deputy Prime Minister 1979–81, 1988–94, Minister of Econ. Affairs, Planning and Educ. (Flemish Sector) 1988–91, of Foreign Affairs 1991–94; Sec.-Gen. NATO 1994–95 (resgnd), given suspended three-year prison sentence for corruption Dec. 1998; Pres. European Socialist Party 1992–94; f. Willy Claes Quartet. *Publications include:* Tussen droom en werkelijkheid 1979, La Chine et l'Europe 1980, Livre Blanc de l'Energie 1980, Elementen voor een nieuw energiebeleid 1980, De Derde Weg: beschouwingen over de Wereldcrisis 1987. *Address:* c/o Thienpont: Artiestenbureau, Leernsesteenweg 243A, 9800 Bachte-Maria-Leerne, Deinze; Berkenlaan 62, 3500 Hasselt, Belgium.

CLAIR, Louis Serge; Mauritian politician; *Chief Commissioner, Rodrigues Regional Assembly;* b. 1 April 1940, Rodrigues; s. of Emmanuel Clair and Willida Clair; m. Danielle Limock 1984; two c.; studied philosophy, theology and social sciences in France and TV production in Australia; Dir and Ed. L'Organisation (first local newspaper on island of Rodrigues) 1976–86; Leader Org. du Peuple Rodriguais; mem. Legis. Ass. 1982–2002, Minister for Rodrigues 1982–89, 1989–95, Chief Commr, Rodrigues Regional Ass. 2003–06, 2012–; Grand Commdr of the Star and Key of the Indian Ocean. *Leisure interests:* sight-seeing, gardening. *Address:* Organisation du Peuple Rodriguais, Mont Lubin, Rodrigues, Mauritius (office). *Telephone:* (230) 8310882 (office). *Fax:* (230) 8312404 (office). *E-mail:* chiefcom@mtnet.mn (office).

CLANCY, James, BA; Canadian trade union official; *President, National Union of Public and General Employees;* b. 10 March 1950, Kingston, Ont.; m.; three c.; ed Carleton Univ., Ottawa; social worker in Toronto 1976–84; Pres. Ont. Public Services Employees Union 1984–90; Pres. Nat. Union of Public and Gen. Employees 1990–; Gen. Vice-Pres. Canadian Labour Congress 1990–. *Address:* National Union of Public and General Employees, 15 Auriga Drive, Nepean, ON K2E 1B7, Canada (office). *Telephone:* (613) 228-9800 (office). *Fax:* (613) 228-9801 (office). *E-mail:* mail@nupge.ca (office). *Website:* www.nupge.ca (office).

CLAPPER, James R., Jr, BS, MA; American air force officer (retd) and government official; *Director of National Intelligence;* ed Univ. of Maryland, St Mary's Univ., Tex., Air Command and Staff Coll., Maxwell Air Force Base, Montgomery, Ala, Armed Forces Staff Coll., Norfolk, Va, Air War Coll., Maxwell Air Force Base, Montgomery, Ala, Nat. War Coll., Fort Lesley J. McNair, Washington, DC, Program for Sr Execs in Nat. and Int. Security, Harvard Univ., Harvard Defense Policy Seminar, Harvard Univ.; brief enlistment in US Marine Corps Reserve, transferred to Air Force Reserve Officer Training Corps Program; commissioned as a distinguished mil. grad. from Univ. of Maryland 1963; student, Signal Intelligence Officers Course, Goodfellow Air Force Base, Tex. 1963–64; Analytic Br. Chief, Air Force Special Communications Center, Kelly Air Force Base, Tex. 1964–65; Watch Officer and Air Defense Analyst, 2nd Air Div. (later, 7th Air Force), Tan Son Nhut Air Base, S Viet Nam 1965–66; aide to Commdr and command Briefer, Air Force Security Service, Kelly Air Force Base, Tex. 1966–70; Commdr Detachment 3, 6994th Security Squadron, Nakhon Phanom Royal Thai Air Force Base, Thailand 1970–71; Mil. Asst to the Dir Nat.

Security Agency, Fort George G. Meade, Md 1971–73; aide to Commdr and Intelligence Staff Officer, HQ Air Force Systems Command, Andrews Air Force Base, Md 1973–74; Distinguished Grad., Armed Forces Staff Coll., Norfolk, Va 1974–75; Chief, Signal Intelligence Br., HQ US Pacific Command, Camp H.M. Smith, HI 1975–76, Chief, Signal Intelligence Br., J-23 1976–78; student, Nat. War Coll., Nat. Defense Univ., Fort Lesley J. McNair, Washington, DC 1978–79; Washington, DC area rep. for electronic security command, Deputy Commdr Fort George G. Meade, Md 1979–80, Commdr 6940th Electronic Security Wing 1980–81; Dir for Intelligence Plans and Systems, Office of the Asst Chief of Staff for Intelligence, HQ USAF, Washington, DC 1981–84; Commdr Air Force Tech. Applications Center, Patrick Air Force Base, Fla 1984–85; Asst Chief of Staff for Intelligence, US Forces Korea, and Deputy Asst Chief of Staff for Intelligence, Repub. of Korea and US Combined Forces Command 1985–87; Dir for Intelligence, HQ US Pacific Command, Camp H.M. Smith, HI 1987–89; Deputy Chief of Staff for Intelligence, HQ Strategic Air Command, Offutt Air Force Base, Neb. 1989–90; Asst Chief of Staff for Intelligence, HQ USAF, Washington, DC 1990–91; Dir Defense Intelligence Agency and Gen. Defense Intelligence Program, Washington, DC 1991–95 (retd); promoted Second Lt 1963, First Lt 1965, Capt. 1967, Maj. 1973, Lt Col 1976, Col 1980, Brig. Gen. 1985, Maj. Gen. 1988, Lt-Gen. 1991; briefly served as exec. in several pvt. cos, including Booz Allen Hamilton and SRA International; Dir Nat. Geospatial-Intelligence Agency 2001–06; briefly served as COO Detica DFI (now a US-based subsidiary of BAe Systems) 2006; Intelligence and Nat. Security Alliance Distinguished Prof. in the Practice of Intelligence, Georgetown Univ. 2006–07; Under-Sec. of Defense for Intelligence 2007–10; Dir of Nat. Intelligence 2010–; Defense Distinguished Service Medal, Air Force Distinguished Service Medal, Defense Superior Service Medal, Legion of Merit with two oak leaf clusters, Bronze Star with oak leaf cluster, Defense Meritorious Service Medal, Meritorious Service Medal with oak leaf cluster, Air Medal with oak leaf cluster, Jt Service Commendation Medal, Air Force Commendation Medal, Commdr, Ordre nat. du Mérite, Repub. of Korea Order of Nat. Security of Merit, Nat. Intelligence Distinguished Service Medal. *Address:* Office of the Director of National Intelligence, Washington, DC 20511, USA (office). *Telephone:* (703) 733-8600 (office). *E-mail:* info@dni.gov (office). *Website:* www.dni.gov (office).

CLAPTON, Eric Patrick, CBE; British musician (guitar), singer and songwriter; b. (Eric Patrick Clapp), 30 March 1945, Ripley, Surrey; m. 1st Patti Harrison (née Boyd) 1979 (divorced 1988); one s. (deceased) by Lori Delsanto; one d.; m. 2nd Melia McEnery 2002; three c.; guitarist with Roosters 1963, Yardbirds 1963–65, John Mayall's Bluesbreakers 1965–66, Cream 1966–68, Blind Faith 1969, Derek and the Dominoes 1970, Delaney and Bonnie 1970–72; solo artist 1972–; Dir Clouds House 1993; mem. Bd of Dirs Chemical Dependency Centre 1994–99; f. Crossroads Center 1998; Silver Clef Award for Outstanding Contribution to British Music 1983, six Grammy Awards 1993, Grammy Award for Best Rock Performance by Duo or Group (for The Calling, with Santana) 2000, Grammy Award for Best Male Pop Vocalist 1996, Grammy Lifetime Achievement Award 2006; inducted into Rock and Roll Hall of Fame 2000. *Film appearances:* Tommy 1974, Blues Brothers 2000 1998. *Recordings include:* albums: Disraeli Gears 1967, Wheels of Fire 1968, Goodbye Cream 1969, Blind Faith 1969, Layla 1970, Eric Clapton 1970, Concert For Bangladesh 1971, Eric Clapton's Rainbow Concert 1973, 461 Ocean Boulevard 1974, There's One In Every Crowd 1975, E. C. Was Here 1975, No Reason To Cry 1976, Slowhand 1977, Backless 1978, Just One Night 1980, Another Ticket 1981, Money and Cigarettes 1983, Too Much Monkey Business 1984, Behind The Sun 1985, August 1986, Homeboy 1989, Journeyman 1989, 24 Nights 1991, Rush 1992, Unplugged 1992, Stages 1993, From The Cradle 1994, Crossroads 2 1996, Live In Montreux 1997, Pilgrim 1998, Rock Report: Deserted Cities Of The Heart 1998, Riding With The King (with B. B. King) (Grammy Award for Best Traditional Blues Album 2001) 2000, Reptile (Grammy Award for Best Pop Instrumental Performance 2002) 2001, One More Car One More Rider 2002, Me And Mr Johnson 2004, She's So Respectable 2004, Sessions For Robert J. 2004, Back Home 2005, The Road to Escondido (with J. J. Cale; Grammy Award for Best Contemporary Blues Album 2008) 2006, Clapton 2010, Old Sock 2013. *Publication:* Eric Clapton: The Autobiography 2007. *Address:* c/o Michael Eaton, Bushbranch Ltd, 36 Old Church Street, London, SW3 5BY, England. *Website:* www.ericclapton.com.

CLARDY, Jon Christel, BS, PhD; American chemist and academic; *Co-Director, Institute of Chemistry and Cell Biology, Harvard Medical School;* b. 16 May 1943, Washington, DC; m. Andrea Clardy 1966; two s.; ed Yale Univ., Harvard Univ.; Asst Prof., Iowa State Univ. 1969–72, Assoc. Prof. 1972–75, Prof. 1975–77; Prof., Cornell Univ. 1978–90, Chair. Dept of Chem. 1988–93, Horace White Prof. of Chem. and Chemical Biology 1990–2002, Sr Assoc. Dean, Cornell Coll. of Arts and Sciences 2000–02; Prof., Dept of Biological Chem. and Molecular Pharmacology, Harvard Medical School 2003–, Co-Dir Inst. of Chem. and Cell Biology 2003–; mem. Editorial Advisory Bd Chemistry and Biology 1994–; mem. US Nat. Cttee on Crystallography 1994–98, Vice-Chair. 2000–02, Chair. 2003–; mem. Exec. Cttee American Soc. of Pharmacognosy 1999–2002, Pres. 2003–04, mem. Research Achievement Cttee 1997–2000; mem. Review Cttee Novartis Core Technologies 1997, NIH Nat. Cancer Inst. Developmental Therapeutics 1997–98, mem. Bd of Scientific Counselors 1999–2004; Fellow, Camille and Henry Dreyfus Foundation 1972–77, Alfred P. Sloan Foundation 1973–75, John Simon Guggenheim Memorial Foundation 1984–85, AAAS 1985–, American Acad. of Arts and Sciences 1995–; Hon. Fellow, Woodrow Wilson Nat. Fellowship Foundation 1964–; ACS Akron Section Award 1987, Cornell Univ. Clark Distinguished Teaching Award 1990, ACS Arthur C. Cope Scholar Award 1997, Paul J Scheuer Award 1998, American Soc. of Pharmacognosy Research Achievement Award 2004. *Publications:* over 600 papers in scientific journals. *Address:* Department of Biological Chemistry and Molecular Pharmacology, Harvard Medical School, 240 Longwood Avenue, Boston, MA 02115, USA (office). *Telephone:* (617) 432-2845 (office). *Fax:* (617) 432-3702 (office). *E-mail:* jon_clardy@hms.harvard.edu (office). *Website:* www.iccb.med .harvard.edu (office).

CLARK, Rt Hon. (Charles) Joseph (Joe), CC, PC; Canadian politician, business executive and academic; *President, Joe Clark & Associates Limited;* b. 5 June 1939, High River, Alberta; s. of Charles A. Clark and Grace R. Welch; m. Maureen Anne (née McTeer) 1973; one d.; ed Univ. of Alberta, Dalhousie Univ.; began career as a journalist; Nat. Pres. Progressive Conservative Party of Canada (PCP) Student Fed. 1963–65; First Vice-Pres. PCP Asscn of Alberta 1966–67; Lecturer, Univ. of Alberta 1965–67; Special Asst to Davie Fulton 1967; Exec. Asst

to PCP Leader Robert Stanfield 1967–70; MP for Rocky Mountain 1972–79, for Yellowhead 1979–93, for Kings Hants 2000, for Calgary Centre 2000–04; Leader of PCP 1976–83, 1998–2003; Prime Minister of Canada 1979–80; Sec. of State for External Affairs 1984–91, Minister responsible for Constitutional Affairs, Pres. of Queen's Privy Council 1991–93; UN Sec.-Gen.'s Special Rep. for Cyprus 1993–96; Founder-Pres. Joe Clark & Assocs Ltd, Calgary (consulting firm) 1993–; mem. Bd of Dirs Triton Inc., Globespan Inc., Traugott Construction Management Inc., Biotechnologie pour le developpement durable en Afrique (BDA) 2006–09; mem. Advisory Bd Save the Children Canada; Trustee, Lester B. Pearson Coll. of the Pacific; Visiting Fellow, Univ. of California, Berkeley 1993–94; Distinguished Statesman-in-Residence, School of Int. Service and Sr Fellow, Center for North American Studies, American Univ., Washington, DC 2004–05; Public Policy Scholar, Woodrow Wilson Int. Center for Scholars 2004; Prof. of Practice for Public-Private Sector Partnerships, Inst. for the Study of Int. Devt, McGill Univ. 2006–; mem. Founding Bd Pacific Council on Int. Policy; Vice-Chair. Global Leadership Foundation 2006–, Stratus Royalty Corpn; mem. Inter-American Dialogue 2006–; Hon. Chief, Samson Cree Nation 1992; Hon. LLD (New Brunswick) 1976, (Calgary) 1984, (Alberta) 1985, (Univ. of King's Coll., Concordia Univ.) 1994, (St Thomas, Minn.) 1995, (York) 2000, (Carleton) 2010, (Univ. of British Columbia) 2011; mem. Alberta Order of Excellence 1983, Commdr, Ordre de la Pléiade; Vimy Award 1992. *Publications include:* A Nation Too Good To Lose 1994, How We Lead: Canada in A Century of Change 2014. *Address:* Joe Clark & Associates Ltd, 489 Sussex Drive, Suite Three, Ottawa, ON K1N 6Z5, Canada (office). *Telephone:* (613) 244-0202 (office). *E-mail:* joeclark@cchambers.com (office). *Website:* www.joeclarkandassociates.ca (office).

CLARK, Christina (Christy) Joan; Canadian politician; *Premier of British Columbia;* b. 29 Oct. 1965, Burnaby; d. of Jim Clark and Mavis Clark; m. Mark Marissen (divorced); one s.; ed Simon Fraser Univ., Univ. of Paris (Sorbonne), France, Univ. of Edinburgh, UK; mem. BC Legis. Ass. for Port Moody-Burnaby Mountain 1996–2001, for Port Moody-Westwood 2001–05; Deputy Premier of BC and Minister of Educ. 2001–04, Minister of Children and Family Devt Jan.–Sept. 2004, also Vice-Chair. of Treasury Bd, Premier of BC and Pres. of Exec. Council 2011–; host of Christy Clark Show, CKNW 2007–10; mem. BC Liberal Party, Leader 2011–; YWCA Woman of Distinction Award, Consumer Choice Awards Woman of the Year in BC 2009. *Address:* Office of the Premier, Parliament Bldgs, West Annex, Suite 156, POB 9041, Victoria, BC V8W 9E1, Canada (office). *Telephone:* (250) 387-1715 (office). *Fax:* (250) 387-0087 (office). *E-mail:* premier@ gov.bc.ca (office). *Website:* www.gov.bc.ca/premier (office); www.christyclark.ca/ premier (office).

CLARK, Christopher Richard Nigel, CBE, MIM; British business executive; *Chairman, Severstal' OAO;* b. 29 Jan. 1942, St Austell, Cornwall, England; m. Catherine Ann Mather 1964; two s., one d.; ed Trinity Coll., Cambridge, Brunel Univ., London; career spans 40 years at Johnson Matthey plc (speciality chemicals and precious metals group), Chief Exec. 1998–2004, led Group into FTSE 100 in 2002; several non-exec. positions since 2004; Chair. Associated British Ports 2004–11, Urenco Ltd (int. supplier of enriched uranium to power generating industry) 2005–12, Wagon Plc; Ind. Chair. (non-exec.) Severstal' OAO 2006–, Ruspetro PLC 2011–; mem. Nomination and Remuneration Cttee. *Address:* Severstal' OAO, Moscow 127299, 2–3 Klara Tsetkin Street, Russia (office); Ruspetro PLC, Brunswick Group, 57 St James Street, London SW1A 1LD, England (office). *Telephone:* (20) 7404-5959 (office). *E-mail:* ruspetro@ brunswickgroup.com (office); christopher.clark64@gmail.com. *Website:* www .severstal.com (office); www.ruspetro.com (office).

CLARK, Colin Whitcomb, PhD, FRS, FRSC; Canadian mathematician and academic; *Professor Emeritus of Mathematics, University of British Columbia;* b. 18 June 1931, Vancouver, BC; s. of George Savage Clark and Irene Clark (née Stewart); m. Janet Arlene Davidson 1955; one s. two d.; ed Univs of British Columbia and Washington; instructor, Univ. of California, Berkeley 1958–60; Asst Prof., then Assoc. Prof., Prof. of Math., Univ. of British Columbia 1960–94, Prof. Emer. 1994–; Regents' Prof., Univ. of California, Davis 1986; Visiting Prof., Cornell Univ. 1987, Princeton Univ. 1997; Hon. DSc (Univ. of Victoria) 2001. *Publications include:* Dynamic Modelling in Behavioral Ecology (with M. Mangel) 1988, Mathematical Bioeconomics 1990, 2010, Dynamic State Variable Models in Ecology (with M. Mangel) 2000, Worldwide Crisis in Fisheries 2006. *Leisure interests:* natural history, hiking, gardening. *Address:* 10995 Springmont Gate, Richmond, BC V7E 1Y5 (home); Mathematics Department, University of British Columbia, Vancouver, BC V6T 1Z2, Canada (office). *Telephone:* (604) 274-5379 (office). *Fax:* (604) 822-6074 (office). *E-mail:* colin_clark@shaw.ca (home).

CLARK, Graeme M., AC, MB BS, MSurgery, PhD, MD, FRCSE, FRACS, FAA; Australian surgeon, medical scientist and academic; *Distinguished Researcher at ICT for Life Sciences, Electrical and Electronic Engineering, University of Melbourne;* b. Camden, NSW; ed Scots Coll., Sydney, Univ. of Sydney, Univ. of Keele, UK; Resident Medical Officer, Royal Prince Alfred Hosp., Sydney 1958–61, Lecturer in Anatomy, Faculty of Medicine 1960–61, Registrar in Neurosurgery and Otolaryngology 1961; apptd Sr House Surgeon, Royal Nat. Ear, Nose and Throat Hospital, Hosp. London, UK 1962; worked at Bristol Gen. Hosp. and Royal Victorian Eye and Ear Hosp.; Asst Ear, Nose and Throat (ENT) Surgeon, Alfred Hosp., Melbourne 1966–67, later Sr Hon. ENT Surgeon; Lecturer in Physiology, Univ. of Sydney 1967–69; Sr Research Officer, Nat. Health and MRC of Australia 1969–70; Foundation Prof. of Otolaryngology, Univ. of Melbourne 1970–2004, Hon. Laureate Professorial Fellow, Dir Bionic Ear Inst. 2004–; currently Distinguished Researcher at ICT for Life Sciences, Electrical and Electronic Eng; Fellow, Australian Acad. of Technological Sciences and Eng; Hon. mem. American Otological Soc. 2002; Hon. FRCS, FAudSA, FRSM 2003; Hon. LLD (Monash); Hon. DSc (Wollongong) 2002; Hon. DEng (Chung Yuan Christian Univ., Taiwan) 2003; Hon. MD (Sydney), (Medizinische Hochschule, Hanover); Dr hc (Univ. of Zaragoza, Spain) 2010; Prime Minister's Prize for Science 1985, Australian Achiever's Award, Nat. Australia Day Council 2005, Sr Australian of the Year 2006, Australian Father of the Year Award 2007, Lister Medal 2010, Florey Medal 2011, Lasker–DeBakey Clinical Medical Research Award (co-recipient) 2013. *Achievements include:* pioneered the multiple-channel cochlear implant. *Publications:* Sounds from Silence (autobiog.) 2000, Cochlear Implants: Fundamentals and Applications 2003; numerous papers in professional journals and several patents. *Address:* The Graeme Clark Foundation, PO Box 2031, East Ivanhoe, Vic. 3079, Australia (office). *Telephone:* (3) 8677-2513 (office). *Fax:* (3) 8677-2513 (office). *E-mail:* enquiries@graemeclarkfoundation.org (office). *Website:* graemeclarkfoundation.org (office).

CLARK, Rt Hon. Helen Elizabeth, ONZ, PC, MA; New Zealand politician and international organization official; *Administrator, United Nations Development Programme (UNDP);* b. 26 Feb. 1950, Hamilton; d. of George Clark and Margaret Clark; m. Peter Davis; ed Epsom Girls' Grammar School, Auckland, Auckland Univ.; Jr Lecturer, Dept of Political Studies, Auckland Univ. 1973–75, Lecturer 1977–81; MP for Mount Albert 1981–96, 1999–, for Owairaka 1996–99, mem. Foreign Affairs, Defence and Trade Cttee; Minister of Housing and Minister of Conservation 1987–89, of Health 1989–90, of Labour 1989–90; Deputy Prime Minister 1989–90, Prime Minister of New Zealand Nov. 1999–2008, also Minister for Arts, Culture and Heritage; Deputy Leader of the Opposition 1990–93, Spokesperson on Health and Labour 1990–93, Leader of the Opposition 1993–99; Leader NZ Labour Party 1993–2008; mem. Labour Party 1971–, Spokesperson on Foreign Affairs, on Arts, Culture and Heritage 2008–; Admin. UNDP 2009–, also Chair. UN Devt Group; Peace Prize, Danish Peace Foundation 1986, ranked by Forbes magazine amongst 100 Most Powerful Women (43rd) 2004, (24th) 2005, (20th) 2006, (38th) 2007, (56th) 2008, (65th) 2009, (50th) 2011, (34th) 2012, (21st) 2013. *Leisure interests:* film, theatre, classical music, opera, cross-country skiing, trekking, reading. *Address:* Office of the Administrator, United Nations Development Programme, One United Nations Plaza, New York, NY 10017, USA (office). *Telephone:* (212) 906-5295 (office). *Fax:* (212) 906-5364 (office). *E-mail:* hq@undp .org (office). *Website:* www.undp.org (office).

CLARK, Ian D., CM, BSc, DPhil, MPP; Canadian government official, international civil servant and academic; *Professor, School of Public Policy and Governance, University of Toronto;* b. 15 April 1946, Co. Antrim, Northern Ireland, UK; s. of Sidney Clark and Zella I. Stade; m. Marjorie Sweet 1968; ed Univ. of British Columbia, Univ. of Oxford, UK, Harvard Univ., USA; Exec. Asst to Minister of Urban Affairs 1972–74; Dir then Dir-Gen. Analysis and Liaison Br. Dept of Regional Econ. Expansion 1974–79; Dir then Deputy Sec. Ministry of State for Econ. Devt 1979–82; Deputy Sec. Privy Council Office 1982–87; Deputy Minister, Dept of Consumer and Corp. Affairs 1987–89; Sec. Treas. Bd 1989–94, also Comptroller-Gen. of Canada 1993–94; Exec. Dir IMF 1994–96; Pnr, KPMG, Toronto 1996–98; Pres. and CEO Council of Ont. Univs 1998–2007; Prof., School of Public Policy and Governance, Univ. of Toronto 2007–; Order of Canada; Hon. LLD (Univ. of Victoria) 2008; Harvard Kennedy School Alumni Achievement Award 1997. *Publication:* Academic Transformation: The Forces Reshaping Higher Education in Ontario (with Greg Moran, Michael Skolnik and David Trick) 2009. *Address:* School of Public Policy and Governance, University of Toronto, Canadiana Building, Room 316, 14 Queen's Park Crescent West, Toronto, ON M5S 3K9 (office); 44 Glenview Avenue, Toronto, ON, M4R 1P6, Canada (home). *Telephone:* (416) 978-2841 (office). *Fax:* (416) 978-5079 (office). *E-mail:* id.clark@ utoronto.ca (office). *Website:* www.ian-clark.ca (office).

CLARK, Janet F., BEcons, MBA; American business executive; *Executive Vice-President and Chief Financial Officer, Marathon Oil Corporation;* b. New Orleans, La; d. of Bud Clark; ed Harvard Univ., Wharton School, Univ. of Pennsylvania; began career as investment banker, First Boston Corpn –1990; Chief Financial Officer, Santa Fe Energy Resources/Snyder Oil 1997–99, Exec. Vice Pres. of Corp. Devt and Admin 1999–2001; Sr Vice-Pres. and Chief Financial Officer, Nuevo Energy Co. 2001–04; Chief Financial Officer, Marathon Oil 2004–, also Exec. Vice-Pres. 2005–; mem. Bd of Dirs Dell, Inc, Houston Symphony, YES Prep Public Schools, Teach for America–Houston Regional, Greater Houston Community Foundation; mem. Council of Overseers, Rice Univ.- Jones Graduate School of Man.; mem. Business and Community Advisory Council, Federal Reserve Bank of Dallas; ranked by Forbes magazine amongst 100 Most Powerful Women (65th) 2009. *Leisure interest:* tennis. *Address:* Marathon Oil Corporation, 5555 San Felipe Road, Houston, TX 77056-2723, USA (office). *Telephone:* (713) 629-6600 (office). *Fax:* (713) 296-2952 (office). *Website:* www.marathon.com (office).

CLARK, Johnson (John) Pepper, BA; Nigerian poet, dramatist and academic; b. 3 April 1935, Kiagbodo; s. of Fuludu Bekederemo Clark; m. Ebunoluwa Bolajoko Odutola; one s. three d.; ed Govt Coll. Ughelli, Univ. Coll. Ibadan, Princeton Univ., USA; Ed. The Horn (Ibadan) 1958; Head of Features and editorial writer, Express Group of Newspapers, Lagos 1961–62; Research Fellow, Inst. of African Studies, Univ. of Lagos 1963–64, Lecturer, Dept of English 1965–69, Sr Lecturer 1969–72, Prof. of English 1972–80; consultant to UNESCO 1965–67; Ed. Black Orpheus (journal) 1965–78; Visiting Distinguished Fellow, Center for Humanities, Wesleyan Univ., Conn., USA 1975–76; Visiting Research Prof., Inst. of African Studies, Univ. of Ibadan 1979–80; Distinguished Visiting Prof. of English and Writer-in-Residence, Lincoln Univ., Pa 1989; Visiting Prof. of English, Yale Univ. 1990; Trustee and mem. Petroleum (Special) Trust Fund and Man. Bd, Abuja 1995–; mem. Nat. Council of Laureates (Nigeria) 1992; Foundation Fellow, Nigerian Acad. of Letters 1996; Nigerian Nat. Order of Merit; Nigerian Nat. Merit Award. *Drama includes:* Song of a Goat 1961, Three Plays 1964, Ozidi 1968, The Bikoroa Plays 1985, The Wives' Revolt. *Poetry published includes:* Poems 1962, A Reed in the Tide 1965, Casualties 1970, A Decade of Tongues 1981, State of the Union 1985, Mandela and Other Poems 1988, A Lot From Paradise 1997. *Other publications:* America, Their America 1964, The Example of Shakespeare 1970, Transcription and Translation from the Oral Tradition of the Izon of the Niger Delta; The Ozidi Saga (trans.) 1977, The Hero as a Villain 1978. *Leisure interests:* walking, swimming, collecting classical European and traditional African music. *Address:* 23 Oduduwa Crescent, GRA, Ikeja, Lagos; Okemeji Place, Funama, Kiagbodo, Burutu Local Government Area, Delta State, Nigeria. *Telephone:* (1) 497-8436 (Lagos). *Fax:* (1) 497-8463 (Lagos).

CLARK, Jonathan Charles Douglas, PhD, FRHistS; British historian and academic; *Joyce and Elizabeth Hall Distinguished Professor of British History, University of Kansas;* b. 28 Feb. 1951, London, England; s. of Ronald James Clark and Dorothy Margaret Clark; m. Katherine Redwood Penovich 1996; ed Univ. of Cambridge; Research Fellow, Peterhouse, Cambridge 1977–81; Research Fellow, The Leverhulme Trust; Fellow, All Souls Coll., Oxford 1986–95, Sr Research Fellow 1995; Joyce and Elizabeth Hall Distinguished Prof. of British History, Univ. of Kansas, USA 1995–; Visiting Prof., Cttee on Social Thought, Univ. of

Chicago 1993; Visiting Prof., Forschungszentrum Europäische Aufklärung, Potsdam 2000, Univ. of Northumbria 2001–03, Oxford Brookes Univ. 2009–; Visiting Distinguished Lecturer, Univ. of Manitoba 1999; mem. Ecclesiastical History Soc., Church of England Record Soc., N American Conf. on British Studies, British Soc. for Eighteenth Century Studies. *Publications:* The Dynamics of Change 1982, English Society 1688–1832 1985, Revolution and Rebellion 1986, The Memoirs and Speeches of James, 2nd Earl Waldegrave (ed.) 1988, Ideas and Politics in Modern Britain (ed.) 1990, The Language of Liberty 1660–1832 1993, Samuel Johnson 1994, Edmund Burke's Reflections on the Revolution in France (ed.) 2001, English Society 1660–1832 (revised edn) 2000, Samuel Johnson in Historical Context (co-ed.) 2002, Our Shadowed Present 2003, A World by Itself: A History of the British Isles (ed.) 2010, The Politics of Samuel Johnson (co-ed.) 2012, The Interpretation of Samuel Johnson (co-ed.) 2012; articles on British and American history. *Leisure interest:* history. *Address:* Department of History, University of Kansas, 1445 Jayhawk Boulevard, Lawrence, KS 66045-7590, USA (office). *Telephone:* (785) 864-3569 (office). *Fax:* (785) 864-5046 (office). *E-mail:* jcdclark@ku.edu (office). *Website:* www.history.ku.edu (office).

CLARK, Rt Hon. Joseph (see CLARK, Rt Hon. (Charles) Joseph (Joe)).

CLARK, Mary Higgins, BA; American writer and business executive; b. 24 Dec. 1931, New York; d. of Luke Higgins and Nora Durkin; m. Warren Clark 1949 (died 1964); two s. three d.; ed Fordham Univ.; advertising asst Remington Rand 1946; stewardess, Pan Am 1949–50; radio scriptwriter, producer Robert G. Jennings 1965–70; Vice-Pres., Pnr, Creative Dir, Producer Radio Programming, Aerial Communications, New York 1970–80; Chair. and Creative Dir D.J. Clark Enterprises, New York 1980–; mem. American Acad. of Arts and Sciences, Mystery Writers of America, Authors League; several hon. degrees; Grand Prix de Littérature Policière, France 1980. *Publications:* Aspire to the Heavens, A Biography of George Washington 1969, Where Are the Children? 1976, A Stranger is Watching 1978, The Cradle Will Fall 1980, A Cry in the Night 1982, Stillwatch 1984, Weep No More, My Lady 1987, While My Pretty One Sleeps 1989, The Anastasia Syndrome 1989, Loves Music, Loves to Dance 1991, All Around the Town 1992, I'll Be Seeing You 1993, Remember Me 1994, The Lottery Winner 1994, Bad Behavior 1995, Let Me Call You Sweetheart 1995, Silent Night 1996, Moonlight Becomes You 1996, My Gal Sunday 1996, Pretend You Don't See Her 1997, The Plot Thickens 1997, You Belong to Me 1998, All Through the Night 1998, We'll Meet Again 1999, Before I Say Good-Bye 2000, Deck the Halls (with Carol Higgins Clark) 2000, Daddy's Little Girl 2002, On the Street Where You Live 2002, Mount Vernon Love Story: A Novel of George and Martha Washington 2002, The Second Time Around 2003, Nighttime is My Time 2004, No Place Like Home 2005, Little Girls in Blue 2006, Santa Cruise 2006, Ghost Ship: A Cape Cod Story 2007, I Heard that Song Before 2007, Where Are You Now? 2008, Just Take my Heart 2009, The Shadow of Your Smile 2010, The Lost Years 2012. *Address:* c/o Simon and Schuster, Inc., 1230 Avenue of the Americas, New York, NY 10020, USA (office). *Website:* www.simonsays.com (office).

CLARK, The Hon. Maureen Harding, BCL; Irish criminal lawyer and judge; *Judge, High Court of Ireland;* b. 3 Jan. 1946; ed Bukit Nanas School, Kuala Lumpur, Malaysia, Muckross Park School, Dublin, Trinity Coll. Dublin, Univ. Coll. Dublin, Univ. of Lyons, France; called to Irish Bar 1975, Irish Inner Bar 1991; criminal defence practice 1976–2001; Regional State Prosecutor 1985–91; Lead Counsel, Court of Criminal Appeal, Dublin 1991–2001; elected Judge Int. Criminal Tribunal for the Fmr Yugoslavia (ICTY) 2001; Judge, Int. Criminal Court, The Hague 2003–06; Judge, High Court of Ireland 2006–; governmental adviser on issues relating to victims' rights in sexual offence cases; Sec. and elected mem. Bar Council of Ireland; mem. Int. Asscn of Prosecutors, Irish Women Lawyers Asscn, Irish Human Rights Comm. 2004–; Assoc. mem. ABA; Rep. of Irish Bar to numerous int. legal confs. *Address:* Central Office of the High Court, Four Courts, Ground Floor (East Wing), Inns Quay, Dublin 7, Ireland (office). *Telephone:* (1) 8886000 (office). *Fax:* (1) 8886125 (office). *E-mail:* HighCourtCentralOffice@courts .ie (office). *Website:* www.courts.ie (office).

CLARK, Petula, CBE; British singer and actress; b. (Sally Olwen), 15 Nov. 1932, Epsom, Surrey; d. of Leslie Norman Clarke and Doris Olwen; m. Claude Wolff 1961; one s. two d.; started career as child singer entertaining troops during Second World War; early appearances in films under contract to Rank Organization; made numerous recordings and television appearances in both England and France; success of single Downtown started career in USA; currently Patron Art-Therapie Foundation; two Grammy Awards, Francis Carco Prize 1962, Grand Prix de la Chanson 1964, Radio Caroline Bell Award 1965, Radio Luxembourg Golden Lion Award 1965, Fry's Shooting Star Award 1965, Cash Box Award 1966, Hon. Citizen Award, Greater Reno Chamber of Commerce 1965, Int. Award 1966, Midem Int. Award 1967, Medaille de Vermel de Paris 1970, Waldorf Astoria Award 1975, Achievement in Arts Award 1994, Grammy Hall of Fame Award 2003, Gold Badge Award 2003, Heritage Foundation Pres.'s Award 2004. *Compositions include:* Petula Clark Sings 1956, A Date with Pet 1956, You Are My Lucky Star 1957, Tete à Tete avec Petula Clark 1961, In Other Words 1962, Le Soleil dans le Yeux 1963, Hello Paris 1964, Le James Dean 1964, Downtown 1965, The International Hits 1965, My Love 1966, Just Say Goodbye 1966, I Couldn't Live Without Your Love 1966, The Many Faces of Petula Clark 1967, These Are My Songs 1967, The Other Man's Grass Is Always Greener 1967, Just Pet 1969, Memphis 1970, Today 1971, La Chanson de Marie Madeleine 1972, Come on Home 1974, Live in London 1974, Just Petula 1975, Destiny 1978, Portrait of a Song Stylist 1991, Treasures 1992, Where the Heart Is 1998, Sign of the Times 2001, The Ultimate Collection 2002, In Her Own Write 2007, Then & Now: The Very Best of Petula Clark 2008. *Films include:* Medal for the General 1944, Murder in Reverse 1945, London Town 1946, Strawberry Roan 1947, Here Come the Huggets, Vice Versa, Easy Money 1948, Don't Ever Leave Me 1949, Vote for Huggett 1949, The Huggetts Abroad, Dance Hall, The Romantic Age 1950, White Corridors, Madame Louise 1951, Made in Heaven 1952, The Card 1952, The Runaway Bus 1954, My Gay Dog 1954, The Happiness of Three Women 1955, Track the Man Down 1956, That Woman Opposite 1957, Calling All Cats 1958, Daggers Drawn 1964, Finian's Rainbow 1968, Goodbye Mr Chips 1969, Dame dans l'auto avec des lunettes et un fusil 1970, Drole De Zebres 1977, Second Star to the Right 1980, Twin Town 1997, Billy's Hollywood Screen Kiss 1998, Girl Interrupted 1999, The Yards 2000, How To Kill Your Neighbour's Dog 2003. *Stage* *appearances:* Sound of Music 1981, Someone Like You (also wrote) 1989, Blood Brothers (Broadway) 1993, Sunset Boulevard 1995–96; nat. tour 1994–95, Sunset Boulevard 1995, 1996, New York 1998, US tour 1998–2000, London 2000. *Address:* John Ashby, John Ashby Associates, PO Box 288, Woking, Surrey, GU22 0YN, England (office); Art-Therapie Foundation, 11 Rue de Beaumont, 1206 Geneva, (office). *Telephone:* (14) 8379-9686 (office); 227890540 (office). *Fax:* (14) 8379-9687 (office); 227890551 (office). *E-mail:* info@arttherapie.org (office). *Website:* www.arttherapie.org (office); www.petulaclark.net.

CLARK, R. Kerry, BCom; Canadian healthcare industry executive; b. 29 April 1952, Ottawa, Ont.; ed Queen's Univ.; joined Procter & Gamble Co. 1974, held various man. positions including Group Vice-Pres. Laundry and Cleaning Products, Pres. Procter & Gamble Asia, Pres. of Global Market Devt and Business Operations, Vice-Chair. and Pres. Global Health, Baby and Family Care 2004–06; Pres. and CEO Cardinal Health Inc. 2006–07, Chair. and CEO 2007–09; mem. Bd of Dirs Textron Inc., CompeteColumbus, Hauser Capital Partners LLC, General Mills 2009–; mem. The Business Council, Healthcare Leadership Council, Ohio Business Roundtable, The Columbus Partnership, Dean's Advisory Council for Ohio State Univ.'s Fisher Coll. of Business; Hon. Doctor of Commercial Science (St Bonaventure Univ.). *Address:* General Mills Inc., 1 General Mills Blvd, Minneapolis, MN 55426, USA (office). *Telephone:* (763) 764-7600 (office). *Fax:* (763) 764-7384 (office). *E-mail:* info@generalmills.com (office). *Website:* www.generalmills.com (office).

CLARK, Richard T., BA, MBA; American pharmaceutical industry executive; ed Washington and Jefferson Coll., American Univ.; Lt in US Army 1970–72; Quality Control Inspector, Industrial Engineer, Quality Control Analyst, Lead Supervisor (Pharmaceutical Production), MSD Pharmaceutical 1972–78, Sr New Products Planner 1978–81, Production Man., Elkton Pharmaceutical Labs 1981–83, Man. Industrial Eng, West Point 1983–84, Sr Man. Industrial Eng, MPMD 1984–85, Dir Operations Improvement, MPMD 1985–86, Sr Dir, Man. Eng, MSD/MPMD 1986–89, Exec. Dir, Man. Eng, Merck Pharmaceutical Mfg Div. 1989–91, Vice-Pres., Materials Man. and Man. Eng, Merck Mfg Div. (MMD) 1991–93, Vice-Pres., Procurement and Materials Man., MMD 1993–94, Vice-Pres., N American Operations, MMD 1994–96, Sr Vice-Pres. 1996–97, Sr Vice-Pres., Quality Commercial Affairs, MMD 1997, Exec. Vice-Pres. and COO, Merck-Medco Managed Care 1997–2000, Pres. Medco Health Solutions Inc. 2000–02, Chair. and CEO 2002–03, Pres. MMD 2003–05, mem. Bd of Dirs, Pres. and CEO Merck & Co., Inc. 2005–07, Chair., Pres. and CEO 2007–09, Chair. and CEO 2009–10, Chair. 2010–11 (retd). *Address:* c/o Merck & Co. Inc., 1 Merck Drive, PO Box 100, Whitehouse Station, NJ 08889-0100, USA. *E-mail:* info@merck.com.

CLARK, Robin Jon Hawes, CNZM, DSc, PhD, FRS, FRSA, FRSC; British chemist and academic; *Sir William Ramsay Professor Emeritus of Chemistry, University College, London;* b. 16 Feb. 1935, Rangiora, NZ; s. of Reginald Hawes Clark, JP and Marjorie Alice Clark (née Thomas); m. Beatrice Rawdin Brown, JP 1964; one s. one d.; ed Marlborough Coll., Blenheim, NZ, Christ's Coll., Christchurch, NZ, Canterbury Univ. Coll., Univ. of New Zealand, Univ. of Otago, NZ, Univ. Coll., London; Asst Lecturer in Chem., Univ. Coll. London 1962, Lecturer 1963–71, Reader 1972–81, Prof. 1982–88, Head of Dept of Chem. 1989–99, Dean, Faculty of Science 1987–89, Sir William Ramsay Prof. 1989–2009, now Prof. Emer., mem. Council 1991–94, Fellow, Univ. Coll. London 1992–; mem. Senate and Acad. Council, Univ. of London 1988–93; Visiting Prof., Columbia Univ. 1965, Padua 1967, Western Ontario 1968, Texas A&M 1978, Bern and Fribourg 1979, Auckland 1981, Odense 1983, Sydney 1985, Bordeaux 1988, Pretoria 1991, Würzburg 1997, Indiana 1998, Thessaloniki 1999; mem. Dalton Council Royal Soc. of Chem. 1985–88, Vice-Pres. 1988–90; mem. SRC Inorganic Chem. Panel 1977–80, Science and Eng Research Council (SERC) Post-Doctoral Fellowships Panel 1983, SERC Inorganic Chem. Panel 1993–94; Chair. Steering Cttee Int. Confs on Raman Spectroscopy 1990–92, 11th Int. Conf. on Raman Spectroscopy, London 1988, Advisory Council, Ramsay Memorial Fellowships Trust 1989– (Trustee 1994–); mem. Council, Royal Soc. 1993–94, Royal Inst. 1996– (Vice-Pres. 1997–, Sec. 1998–2004), Tilden 1983, Nyholm 1989, Thomas Graham 1991, Harry Hallam 1993, 2000, Liversidge 2003 and Sir George Stokes 2009 Lecturer and Medallist, Royal Soc. of Chem.; Chair. Univ. of Canterbury, NZ Trust (UK Br.) 2004–; mem. Academia Europaea 1990; Foreign Fellow, Nat. Acad. of Sciences (India) 2007; Int. Fellow, American Philosophical Soc. 2010; numerous radio and TV interviews on arts/science subjects in UK, Italy, France and NZ; invited lectures in over 360 insts in 36 countries; Hon. Fellow, Royal Soc. of NZ 1989, Royal Inst. of GB 2004; Companion of the NZ Order of Merit 2004; Hon. DSc (Canterbury, NZ) 2001; Joannes Marcus Marci Medal, Czech Spectroscopy Soc. 1998, UK-Canada Rutherford Lecturer 2000, T.J. Sidey Medal, Royal Soc. of NZ 2001, Ralph Anderson Lecturer Horners' Co. 2003, Lifetime Achievement Award, New Zealand Soc. 2004, Royal Soc. of London Bakerian Lecturer 2008, Inaugural Franklin-Lavoisier Prize, Maison de la Chimie/Chemical Heritage Foundation 2009, Ralph Anderson Lecturer, Horners' Co. 2003, Barber-Surgeons' Co. Denny Lecturer 2009, Rutherford Lecturer, Univ. of Canterbury 2010, Scientific Instruments Co. Minerva Lecturer 2011, Distinguished Lecturer, Royal Soc. of NZ 2011. *Publications:* The Chemistry of Titanium and Vanadium 1968, The Chemistry of Titanium, Zirconium and Hafnium (co-author) 1973, The Chemistry of Vanadium, Niobium and Tantalum (co-author) 1973, Advances in Spectroscopy Vols 1–26 (co-ed.) 1975–98, Raman Spectroscopy (co-ed.) 1988; more than 500 scientific papers in learned journals on topics in transition metal chemistry, spectroscopy and scientific investigation of artwork and archaeological artefacts. *Leisure interests:* golf, long distance walking, travel, bridge, music, theatre, wine. *Address:* Christopher Ingold Laboratories, University College London, 20 Gordon Street, London, WC1H 0AJ, England (office). *Telephone:* (1923) 857899 (home); (20) 7679-7457 (office). *Fax:* (20) 7679-7463 (office). *E-mail:* r.j.h.clark@ucl.ac.uk (office). *Website:* www.chem.ucl.ac.uk (office).

CLARK, T(imothy) J(ames), BA, PhD; British art historian, academic and author; *Professor Emeritus of Art History, University of California, Berkeley;* b. 12 April 1943, Bristol; m. Anne Wagner; ed Bristol Grammar School, St John's Coll., Cambridge, Courtauld Inst. of Art, Univ. of London; Lecturer, Univ. of Essex 1967–69; Sr Lecturer, Camberwell Coll. of Arts 1970–74; mem. British Section of Situationist International (expelled); was also involved in the group King Mob; taught at UCLA 1974–76; Founding mem. Caucus for Marxism and Art, College

Art Asscn 1976; returned to UK 1976; apptd Prof. and Head of Dept of Fine Art, Univ. of Leeds 1976–80; joined Dept of Fine Arts, Harvard Univ. 1980–88; mem. Faculty, Univ. of California, Berkeley 1988–, George C. and Helen N. Pardee Chair and Prof. of Art History 1988–2010, Prof. Emer. 2010–; Visiting Prof., Dept of History of Art, Univ. of York 2013; Co-curator, Lowry and the Painting of Modern Life, Tate Britain 2013; hon. degree from Courtauld Inst. of Art 2006; Distinguished Teaching of Art History Award, College Art Asscn 1991, Mellon Foundation Distinguished Achievement Award 2005. *Publications include:* The Absolute Bourgeois: Artists and Politics in France, 1848–51 1973, Image of the People: Gustave Courbet and the 1848 Revolution 1973, The Painting of Modern Life: Paris in the Art of Manet and his Followers 1985, Farewell to an Idea: Episodes from a History of Modernism 1999, Afflicted Powers: Capital and Spectacle in a New Age of War (with Iain Boal, Joseph Matthews and Michael Watts: under the name 'Retort') 2005, The Sight of Death: An Experiment in Art Writing 2006, The Painting of Postmodern Life? 2009, Picasso and Truth: From Cubism to Guernica 2013; numerous essays, and articles in London Review of Books and New Left Review. *Address:* Department of Art History, 416 Doe Library #6020, Berkeley, CA 94720, USA (office); Department of History of Art, University of York, Heslington, York, YO10 5DD, England. *Telephone:* (510) 643-7290 (Berkeley) (office); (1904) 322978 (York). *Fax:* (510) 643-2185 (Berkeley) (office); (1904) 323427 (York). *E-mail:* travesty@berkeley.edu (office); history-of-art@york.ac.uk. *Website:* arthistory.berkeley.edu (office); www.york.ac.uk/history-of-art.

CLARK, W. Edmund (Ed), OC, MA, DEcon; Canadian banker; *President and CEO, TD Bank Financial Group;* b. 1947; m. Frances Clark; four c.; ed Univ. of Toronto, Harvard Univ., USA; various sr positions in Fed. Govt of Canada, Ottawa 1974–84, including heading Nat. Energy Program 1980; Head of Corp. and Govt Finance, Merrill Lynch, Toronto 1985–88, Chair. and CEO Morgan Financial Corpn 1988–91; Vice-Chair. and COO CT Financial Services Inc. 1991–94, Pres. and CEO 1994–2000; Chair. and CEO Toronto-Dominion (TD) Canada Trust (following acquisition of CT Financial Services Inc. by TD Bank 2000) 2000, Pres. and COO TD Bank Financial Group 2000–02, Pres. and CEO 2002–, Chair. TD Bank US Holding Co. (and its subsidiary banks), Vice-Chair. TD Ameritrade Holding Corpn; Chair. United Way for the Greater Toronto Area 2010; mem. Bd of Dirs C.D. Howe Inst.; mem. Chair.'s Advisory Council for Habitat for Humanity Toronto. *Address:* TD Bank Financial Group, Toronto-Dominion Centre, King Street West and Bay Street, Toronto, ON M5K 1A2, Canada (office). *Telephone:* (416) 982-8222 (office). *Fax:* (416) 982-5671 (office). *E-mail:* td.capa@td.com (office). *Website:* www.td.com (office).

CLARK, Gen. (retd) Wesley Kanne, BA, MA; American politician and fmr army officer (retd); *Chairman and CEO, Wesley Clark & Associates LLC;* b. 23 Dec. 1944, Little Rock, Ark.; m. Gertrude Clark; one s.; ed US Mil. Acad., West Point, Univ. of Oxford (Rhodes Scholar), UK, Nat. War Coll., Command and Gen. Staff Coll., Armor Officer Advanced and Basic Courses, Ranger and Airborne School; served in US Army 1966–2000, held numerous staff and command positions and rose to rank of 4-star Gen., served in Viet Nam; fmr Sr mil. Asst to Gen. Alexander Haig; fmr Head Nat. Army Training Center; fmr Dir of Strategy Dept of Defense; Sr mem. American negotiating team at Bosnian peace negotiations, Dayton, OH 1995; fmr Head of US Southern Command, Panama; NATO Supreme Allied Commdr in Europe (SACEUR) 1997–2000; Head of US Forces in Europe (USEUCOM) 1997–2000 (retd); consultant, Stephens Inc., Little Rock, Ark. 2000–01, Man. Dir Stephens Group 2001–03; Distinguished Advisor, Center for Strategic and Int. Studies, Washington, DC 2000; Chair. and CEO Wesley Clark & Assocs LLC (consulting firm), Little Rock, Ark. 2003–; Vice-Chair. and Sr Advisor, James Lee Witt Assocs LLC, Washington, DC 2004–; Chair. Rodman & Renshaw LLC, New York 2006–; unsuccessful cand. for Democratic presidential nomination 2003; mil. analyst for CNN 2001–03; Sr Fellow and Lecturer, Ronald W. Burkle Center for Int. Relations, UCLA 2006–; Hon. OBE; Dr hc Drake Univ. 2002; Hon. DHumLitt, Seton Hall Univ. 2002; Hon. LLD, Univ. of Arkansas 2002, Ripon Coll. 2005, Lyon Coll. 2005; Commdr, Légion d'honneur, Kt Grand Cross, Order of Orange-Nassau, Netherlands; Decorated Defense Distinguished Service Medal (three), Distinguished Service Medal, Silver Star, Legion of Merit (four), Bronze Star Medal (two), Purple Heart, Meritorious Service Medal (two), Army Commendation Medal (two), Presidential Medal of Freedom 2000. *Publication:* Waging Modern War: Bosnia, Kosovo and the Future of Combat 2001, Winning Modern Wars 2003, Time to Lead: For Duty, Honor and Country (co-author) 2007. *Address:* 1 Crestmont Drive, Little Rock, AR 72227; Rodman & Renshaw LLC, Wall Street Plaza, 88 Pine Street, 32nd Floor, New York, NY 10005, USA (office). *Telephone:* (212) 850-5600 (office). *E-mail:* rodman@fd.com. *Website:* www.rodmanandrenshaw.com (office).

CLARK OF CALTON, Baroness (Life Peer), cr. 2005; **Lynda Margaret Clark,** QC, LLB, PhD; British lawyer, former law officer and judge; *Senator of the College of Justice;* b. 26 Feb. 1949, Dundee; ed Univ. of St Andrews and Univ. of Edinburgh; Lecturer Univ. of Dundee 1973–76; admitted as Advocate of the Scots Bar 1977; called to the English Bar, Inner Temple 1988, Bencher 2000; contested constituency of Fife NE (Labour Party) 1992; MP (Labour) for Edinburgh Pentlands 1997–2005; Advocate Gen. for Scotland 1999–2006; Senator, Coll. of Justice 2006–; Chancellor's Assessor, Edinburgh Napier Univ. 2008–; mem. Court Univ. of Edinburgh 1995–97; Hon. LLD (Napier) 2007, (Dundee) 2007. *Leisure interests:* reading, arts, swimming. *Address:* Parliament House, Edinburgh, EH7 5BL, Scotland (office).

CLARK OF WINDERMERE, Baron (Life Peer), cr. 2001, of Windermere in the County of Cumbria; **David George Clark,** DL, PC, BA, MSc, PhD; British politician; b. 19 Oct. 1939, Castle Douglas; s. of George Clark and Janet Clark; m. Christine Kirkby 1970; one d.; ed Univs of Manchester, Sheffield; fmr forester, lab. asst and student teacher; Pres. Univ. of Manchester Union 1963–64; trainee man., USA 1964; univ. lecturer 1965–70; MP for Colne Valley 1970–74, for S. Shields 1979–2001; Labour spokesman on Agric. and Food 1973–74, on Defence 1980–81, on Environment 1981–86, on Environmental Protection and Devt 1986–87, on Food, Agric. and Rural Affairs 1987–92, on Defence, Disarmament and Arms Control 1992–97; Pres. Open Spaces Soc. 1979–88; mem. Parl. Ass., NATO 1981–2005; Chancellor of Duchy of Lancaster 1997–98; Chair. Atlantic Council of UK 1998–2001, Forestry Comm. 2001–10; Leader UK Del. to NATO-PA 2001–05; mem. House of Lords 2001–; Visiting Prof. in History and Politics, Univ. of Huddersfield; Freeman of South Tyneside 1999; Hon. Fellow, Univ. of Cumbria.

Publications include: The Industrial Manager 1966, Colne Valley: Radicalisation to Socialism 1981, Victor Grayson: Labour's Lost Leader 1985, We Do Not Want the Earth 1992, The Labour Movement in Westmorland 2012. *Leisure interests:* walking, gardening, watching football. *Address:* House of Lords, Westminster, London, SW1A 0PW, England (office). *Telephone:* (20) 7219-2558 (office). *Fax:* (20) 7219-4885 (office). *E-mail:* clarkd@parliament.uk (office).

CLARKE, Aidan, PhD; Irish historian and academic; *Fellow Emeritus, Trinity College, Dublin;* b. 2 May 1933, Watford, Herts., England; s. of the late Austin Clarke and of Nora Walker; m. Mary Hughes 1962; two s. two d.; ed The High School, Dublin and Trinity Coll., Dublin; Lecturer in Modern History and Politics, Magee Univ. Coll., Derry 1959–65; Lecturer in Modern History, Trinity Coll., Dublin 1965–78, Assoc. Prof. 1978–86, Erasmus Smith's Prof. 1986–2001, Sr Tutor 1971–73, Registrar 1974–76, Bursar 1980–81, Vice-Provost 1981–87, 1989–91, Fellow 1970, now Fellow Emer.; Research Fellow, The 1641 Project 2007–10; Prin. Ed. 1641 depositions on-line; Chair. Irish Historical Soc. 1978–80; mem. Royal Irish Acad. 1982–, Sr Vice-Pres. 1988–89, Sec. Cttee of Polite Literature and Antiquities 1989–90, Pres. 1990–93; Hon. LittD (Dublin) 1992. *Publications include:* The Old English in Ireland 1625–42 1966; contribs to The New History of Ireland, 111: Early Modern Ireland 1976 Prelude to Restoration in Ireland: The End of the Commonwealth, 1659–1660 1999; numerous articles and essays on early modern Irish history. *Address:* 160 Rathfarnham Road, Dublin 14, Ireland (home). *Telephone:* (1) 490-3223 (home). *E-mail:* aclarke@tcd.ie (office).

CLARKE, Brian, FRSA; British artist; b. 2 July 1953, Oldham, Lancs., England; s. of the late Edward Ord Clarke and of Lilian Clarke (née Whitehead); m. Elizabeth Cecilia Finch 1972; one s.; ed Oldham School of Arts and Crafts, Burnley School of Art, The North Devon Coll. of Art and Design; Visiting Prof. of Architectural Art, Univ. Coll. London 1993; mem. Council Winston Churchill Memorial Trust 1985–; Trustee and mem. Cttee Robert Fraser Foundation 1990–; Judge, Royal Fine Art Comm. and Sunday Times Architecture Award 1991, BBC Design Awards 1990; mem. Comm. for Architecture and the Built Environment 1999–2005; Chair. The Architecture Foundation 2007; Sole Executor, Estate of Francis Bacon 1998–; Gov. for Capital City Acad. 2001; Trustee, The Stained Glass Museum 1995, The Lowe Educational Charitable Foundation 2001, Architecture Foundation 2002, Winston Churchill Memorial Trust 2007; Hon. FRIBA 1993; Hon. Liveryman, Worshipful Co. of Glaziers and Master Glass Painters 2012; Hon. DLitt (Huddersfield) 2007; Churchill Fellowship in Architectural Art 1974, Art and Work Award Special Commendation 1989, Europa Nostra Award 1990, The Leeds Award for Architecture Special Award for Stained Glass 1990, European Shopping Centre Award 1995, BDA Auszeichnung guter Bauten, Heildelberg 1996, Cttee of Honour: Foundation Vincent Van Gogh, Arles, France 2001. *Major works include:* St Gabriel's Church, Blackburn 1976, All Saints Church, Habergham 1976, Laver's & Barraud Bldg, London 1981, Olympus Optical Europa GmbH HQ Bldg, Hamburg 1981, King Khaled Int. Airport, Riyadh, Saudi Arabia 1982, Lake Sagami Country Club, Yamanishi, Japan (in asscn with Arata Isozaki) 1988, New Synagogue, Darmstadt, Germany 1988, Victoria Quarter, Leeds 1989, Glaxo Pharmaceuticals, Stockley Park, Uxbridge 1990, Stansted Airport, Essex (in asscn with Sir Norman Foster) 1991, España Telefónica, Barcelona 1991, Number One America Square, London 1991, 35–38 Chancery Lane, London 1991, The Carmelite, London 1992, 100 New Bridge Street, London 1992, façade of Hôtel de Ville des Bouches-du-Rhône, Marseille (with Will Alsop) 1992–94, Glass Dune, Hamburg (with Future Systems) 1992, EAM Bldg, Kassel, Germany 1992–93, New Synagogue, Heidelberg, Germany 1993, SMS Lowe The Grace Bldg, New York 1994, Cliveden Hotel 1994, Schadow Arkaden, Düsseldorf 1994, Norte Shopping, Rio de Janeiro 1995, Rye Hosp., Sussex (with Linda McCartney) 1995, Valentino Village, Noci Italy 1996, Kinderhaus Regensburg Germany 1996, Pfizer Pharmaceuticals, New York 1997, 2001, Willis Corroon Bldg, Ipswich 1997, Offenbach Synagogue 1997, New Catholic Church Obersalbach 1997, Praça Norte Clock Tower 1997, Warburg Dillon Read Stamford CT (stained glass cone) 1998, Al Faisaliah Centre, Riyadh (in asscn with Lord Norman Foster) 2000, Olympus Optical Europa GmbH New HQ Building, Hamburg 2000, Hotel and Thalassotherapy Centre, Nova Yardinia, Italy 2002, Pfizer Security Lobby, New York 2003, Pyramid of Peace, Astana, Kazakhstan (with Norman Foster) 2006, Mosaic Path From Life to Life, a Garden for George Harrison, Chelsea Flower Show, London 2008, stained glass for the Papal Chapel, Apostolic Nunciature, London 2010, stained glass, mosaic, painting, carpet and door furniture for a private house, London 2010, Love Him More (stained glass, paintings and works on paper), Kristy Stubbs Gallery, Texas 2011, The Quick and the Dead – New Paintings, Gemeentesmuseum Den Haag, Netherlands 2011, Works on Paper, Phillips de Pury & Co., space at the Saatchi Gallery, London 2011. *Design:* Hammersmith Hosp., London 1993, Crossrail, Paddington, London (with Will Alsop) 1994, Q206 Berlin 1994, Frankfurter Allee Plaza, Berlin 1994, New Synagogue, Aachen 1994, Hungerford Bridge, London (with Alsop and Störmer) 1996, Center Villa-Lobos, São Paulo 1997, Future Systems Tower NEC 1997, Heidelberg Cathedral 1997, Chep Lap Kok Airport, Hong Kong 1997, West Winter Garden, Heron Quays, London 2001, Design for Stained Glass and Rooflight, Ascot Racecourse 2003, Apax Partners, London 2007, The Watchtower, Point Village, Dublin, Eire (design) 2008. *Leisure interests:* reading, hoarding. *Address:* Brian Clarke Studio, 6A Trading Estate Road, London, NW10 7LU, England (office). *Telephone:* (20) 8961-9636 (office). *E-mail:* mail@brianclarke.co.uk (office). *Website:* www.brianclarke.co.uk (office).

CLARKE, Rt Hon. Charles Rodway, PC, BA, FRSS; British politician; b. 21 Sept. 1950, London, England; s. of Sir Richard Clarke and Brenda Clarke (née Skinner); m. Carol Marika Pearson 1984; two s.; ed Highgate School and King's Coll., Cambridge; Pres. Nat. Union of Students 1975–77; various admin. posts 1977–80; Head, Office of Rt Hon Neil Kinnock, MP 1981–92; Chief Exec. Quality Public Affairs 1992–97; mem. Hackney London Borough Council 1980–86; MP (Labour) for Norwich S 1997–2010; Parl. Under-Sec. of State, Dept for Educ. and Employment 1998–99; Minister of State, Home Office 1999–2001; Chair. Labour Party and Minister without Portfolio 2001–02; Sec. of State for Educ. and Skills 2002–04, Home Sec. 2004–06; mem. Treasury Select Cttee 1997–98, mem. Parl. Cttee 2001–, Labour Party Nat. Policy Forum 2001–; Chair. Labour Party Donations Cttee 2002–. *Leisure interests:* chess, reading, walking. *Address:* The Labour Party, Eldon House, Regent Centre, Newcastle upon Tyne, NE3 3PW, England (office). *Telephone:* (1603) 219902 (office); (870) 5900200 (office). *Fax:*

(1603) 764475 (office). *E-mail:* willcoxs@parliament.uk (office). *Website:* www.charlesclarke.org.uk (office).

CLARKE, (Christopher) Michael, CBE, FRSE; British art gallery director; *Director, Scottish National Gallery;* m. Deborah Clarke; two s. one d.; ed Univ. of Manchester; worked at British Museum, London and Univ. of Manchester –1987; Keeper, then Dir Nat. Gallery of Scotland (now the Scottish Nat. Gallery), Edinburgh 1987–, Dir Playfair Project 1999–2004; Trustee, Lakeland Arts Trust, Cumbria 2010–; Chevalier, Ordre des Arts et des Lettres 2004. *Publications:* The Tempting Prospect: A Social History of English Watercolours 1981, Corot and the Art of Landscape 1991, Oxford Concise Dictionary of Art Terms 2001 (second edn 2010). *Leisure interests:* golf, cycling. *Address:* Curatorial Department, Scottish National Gallery, The Mound, Edinburgh, EH2 2EL, Scotland (office). *Telephone:* (131) 624-6200 (office). *Fax:* (131) 220-0917 (office). *E-mail:* nginfo@nationalgalleries.org (office). *Website:* www.nationalgalleries.org (office).

CLARKE, Sir Christopher Simon Courtenay Stephenson, Kt, QC, FRSA; British judge; *High Court Judge, Queen's Bench Division, Commercial Court;* b. 14 March 1947, Plymouth, Devon, England; s. of the late Rev. John Stephenson Clarke and of Enid Courtenay Clarke; m. Caroline Anne Fletcher 1974; one s. two d.; ed Marlborough Coll. and Gonville and Caius Coll., Cambridge; called to the Bar, Middle Temple 1969; apptd QC 1984; Recorder of the Crown Court 1990–, Deputy High Court Judge 1993–2005, High Court Judge, Queen's Bench Div., Commercial Court 2005–; mem. Courts of Appeal of Jersey and Guernsey 1998; Attorney of the Supreme Court of Turks and Caicos Islands 1975–; Bencher of the Middle Temple 1991; Counsel for the Bloody Sunday Inquiry 1998–2004; Councillor Int. Bar Asscn 1988–90; Chair. Commercial Bar Asscn 1993–95; mem. Bar Council 1993–99; Harmsworth Memorial Scholar, Middle Temple 1969, Lloyd Stott Memorial Prizeman (Middle Temple) 1969, J.J. Powell Prizeman (Middle Temple) 1969. *Leisure interest:* opera. *Address:* Royal Courts of Justice, Strand, London, WC2A 2LL, England (office).

CLARKE, Darren Christopher, OBE; British professional golfer; b. 14 Aug. 1968, Dungannon, Co. Tyrone, NI; m. 1st Heather Clarke 1996 (died 2006); two s.; m. 2nd Alison Campbell 2012; ed Wake Forest Univ., USA; fmr jr mem. Dungannon Golf Club; won East of Ireland Championship 1989, Spanish Amateur Open Championship 1990, Irish Amateur Championship 1990, South of Ireland Championship 1990; turned professional 1990; won Ulster Professional Championship 1992, Irish PGA Championship 1994; won Alfred Dunhill Open 1993, Linde German Masters 1996, Benson & Hedges International Open 1998, Volvo Masters 1998, Compass Group English Open 1999, 2000, 2002, Andersen Consulting Match Play Championship 2000, Smurfit European Open 2001, The Crowns 2001, Dimension Data Pro-Am 2001, NEC Invitational 2003, Benmore Developments Northern Ireland Masters 2003, Mitsui Sumitomo VISA Taiheiyo Masters 2004, 2005, BMW Asian Open 2008, KLM Open 2008, JP McManus Invitational Pro-Am 2010, Iberdrola Open 2011; won Open Championship at Royal St George's 2011; currently plays on European Tour and has previously played on PGA Tour; highest finish of second on European Tour money list 1998, 2000, 2003; represented Ireland as both an amateur and as a professional, at World Cup and Alfred Dunhill Cup; mem. European Ryder Cup teams 1997, 1999, 2002, 2004, 2006, winning on four occasions, apptd a non-playing vice-capt. 2010; Texaco Ireland Sportstar Golf Award 1993, 1997, 1998, 2000, 2003, 2004 (shared), Laureus World Comeback of the Year 2012. *Television:* appeared as himself in Kelly (series) 2000. *Leisure interest:* fishing, cigars, fine wines, cars, Liverpool Football Club. *Address:* c/o Andrew Chandler, International Sports Management Ltd, Cherry Tree Farm, Cherry Tree Lane, Rostherne, Cheshire, WA14 3RZ, England (office). *Telephone:* (1565) 832100 (office). *Fax:* (1565) 832222 (office). *E-mail:* ism@golfism.net (office). *Website:* sportism.net (office); www.darrenclarke.com.

CLARKE, Edmund M., BA, MA, PhD; American computer scientist and academic; *FORE Systems University Professor of Computer Science and Professor of Electrical and Computer Engineering, Carnegie-Mellon University;* ed Univ. of Virginia, Charlottesville, Duke Univ., Durham, NC, Cornell Univ., Ithaca, NY; taught in Dept of Computer Science, Duke Univ. –1978; Asst Prof. of Computer Science, Div. of Applied Sciences, Harvard Univ., Cambridge, Mass 1978–82; joined faculty in Computer Science Dept, Carnegie-Mellon Univ., Pittsburgh, Pa 1982, Full Prof. 1989–, first recipient of FORE Systems Professorship, School of Computer Science 1995–, Univ. Prof. 2008–; fmr Ed.-in-Chief Formal Methods in Systems Design; fmr mem. Editorial Bd Distributed Computing, Logic and Computation, IEEE Transactions in Software Engineering; mem. Organizing Cttee Logic in Computer Science, Steering Cttee Computer-Aided Verification; mem. Nat. Acad. of Eng 2005; Fellow, Asscn for Computing Machinery (ACM), IEEE; Tech. Excellence Award, Semiconductor Research Corpn 1995, ACM Kanellakis Award (co-recipient) 1998, Allen Newell Award for Excellence in Research, Carnegie Mellon Computer Science Dept 1999, IEEE Harry H. Goode Memorial Award 2004, ACM A.M. Turing Award (co-recipient) 2007, CADE Herbrand Award for Distinguished Contribs to Automated Reasoning 2008. *Publications:* numerous scientific papers in professional journals on software and hardware verification and automatic theorem proving. *Address:* Wean Hall 7117, School of Computer Science, Carnegie Mellon University, 5000 Forbes Avenue, Pittsburgh, PA 15213-3891, USA (office). *Telephone:* (412) 268-2628 (office). *Fax:* (412) 268-5576 (office). *E-mail:* edmund.clarke@cs.cmu.edu (office). *Website:* www.cs.cmu.edu/~emc (office).

CLARKE, Geoffrey, RA, ARCA; British artist and sculptor; b. 28 Nov. 1924; s. of John Moulding Clarke and Janet Petts; m.; two s.; ed RCA; exhbns at Gimpel Fils Gallery 1952, 1955, Redfern Gallery 1965, Taranman Gallery 1975, 1976, 1982, Yorkshire Sculpture Park 1994, Chappel Gallery 1994; touring exhbns at Christchurch Mansions, Ipswich 1994, Herbert Art Gallery, Coventry and Pallant House, Chichester 1995; retrospective Exhbn Fine Art Soc. 2000; commissioned work includes: iron sculpture, Time Life Building, New Bond Street; mosaics, Liverpool Univ. Physics Block; stained glass windows for Treasury, Lincoln Cathedral; bronze sculpture, Thorn Electric Building, Upper St Martin's Lane; three stained glass windows, high altar cross and candle-sticks, the flying cross and crown of thorns, all for Coventry Cathedral; screens in Royal Mil. Chapel, Birdcage Walk; other works at Newcastle Civic Centre, Churchill Coll., Aldershot, Suffolk Police HQ, All Souls, W London, The Majlis, Abu Dhabi, York House, N

London, St Paul, Minn. *Address:* Stowe Hill, Hartest, Bury St Edmunds, Suffolk, IP29 4EQ, England. *Telephone:* (1284) 830319.

CLARKE, Graeme Wilber, AO, MA, LittD, FAHA, FSA; Australian professor of classics; *Professor Emeritus, Australian National University;* b. 31 Oct. 1934, Nelson, New Zealand; s. of Wilber P. Clarke and Marjorie E. Clarke (née Le May); m. Nancy J. Jordan 1963; three s. one d.; ed Sacred Heart Coll., Auckland, NZ, Univ. of Auckland, Balliol Coll., Oxford, UK; Lecturer, Dept of Classics, ANU 1957, 1961–63, Deputy Dir Humanities Research Centre 1982–90, Dir 1991–99, Prof. Emer. 2000–, Visiting Fellow, Dept of History 2000–; Sr Lecturer, Dept of Classics and Ancient History, Univ. of Western Australia 1964–66, Assoc. Prof., Dept of Classical Studies, Monash Univ. 1967–68; Prof., Dept of Classical Studies, Univ. of Melbourne 1969–81, Prof. Emer. 1981–; Dir archaeological excavation in N Syria at Jebel Khalid 1984–. *Publications:* The Octavius of Marcus Minucius Felix 1974, The Letters of St Cyprian (four vols) 1984–88, Rediscovering Hellenism (ed.) 1988, Reading the Past in Late Antiquity (ed.) 1990, Identities in the Eastern Mediterranean in Antiquity (ed.) 1998, Jebel Khalid on the Euphrates. Report on Excavations 1986–1996 (Vol. I) 2002, The Terracotta Figurines (ed.) (Vol. 2) 2006, The Pottery (ed.) (Vol. 3) 2011. *Leisure interest:* gardening. *Address:* Department of History, Australian National University, Canberra, ACT 0200 (office); 62 Wybalena Grove, Cook, ACT 2614, Australia (home). *Telephone:* (2) 6125-4789 (office); (2) 6251-4576 (home). *Fax:* (2) 6125-3969 (office). *E-mail:* graeme.clarke@anu.edu.au (office).

CLARKE, John, BA, MA, PhD, ScD, FRS; British physicist and academic; *Professor of Physics, University of California, Berkeley;* b. 10 Feb. 1942, Cambridge, England; s. of Victor P. Clarke and Ethel M. Clarke; m. Grethe Fog Pedersen 1979; one d.; ed Perse School, Cambridge and Univ. of Cambridge; Postdoctoral Scholar, Dept of Physics, Univ. of California, Berkeley 1968–69, Asst Prof. 1969–71, Assoc. Prof. 1971–73, Prof. 1973–, Faculty Research Lecturer 2005; Luis W. Alvarez Memorial Chair in Experimental Physics 1994–99; Faculty Sr Scientist, Lawrence Berkeley Nat. Lab., Berkeley 1969–; Visiting Fellow, Clare Hall, Cambridge 1989; Fellow, AAAS, American Physical Soc., Inst. of Physics; Alfred P. Sloan Foundation Fellowship 1970–72; Adolph C. and Mary Sprague Miller Research Professorship 1975–76, 1994–95;; Foreign Assoc., NAS 2012; Hon. Fellow, Christ's Coll., Cambridge; Guggenheim Fellowship 1977–78, Calif. Scientist of the Year 1987, Fritz London Memorial Award 1987, Joseph F. Keithley Award, American Physical Soc. 1998, Comstock Prize in Physics, NAS 1999, Hughes Medal, Royal Soc. 2004, Lounasmaa Prize, Finnish Acad. of Arts and Sciences 2004. *Publications:* approx. 450 publns in learned journals. *Address:* Department of Physics, 366 LeConte Hall, University of California, Berkeley, CA 94720-7300, USA (office). *Telephone:* (510) 642-3069 (office). *E-mail:* jclarke@berkeley.edu (office). *Website:* www.physics.berkeley.edu/research/faculty/clarke.html (office); physics.berkeley.edu/research/clarke (office).

CLARKE, Rt Hon. Kenneth (Ken) Harry, PC, QC, BA, LLB; British politician; *Minister without Portfolio, Cabinet Office;* b. 2 July 1940; s. of Kenneth Clarke and Doris Clarke (née Smith); m. Gillian Mary Edwards 1964; one s. one d.; ed Nottingham High School and Gonville and Caius Coll., Cambridge; called to the Bar, Gray's Inn 1963; practising mem. Midland circuit 1963–79; Research Sec. Birmingham Bow Group 1965–66; contested Mansfield, Notts. in General Elections 1964, 1966, MP for Rushcliffe Div. of Notts. 1970–; Parl. Pvt. Sec. to Solicitor Gen. 1971–72; an Asst Govt Whip 1972–74, Govt Whip for Europe 1973–74; Lord Commr, HM Treasury 1974; Opposition Spokesman on Social Services 1974–76, on Industry 1976–79; Parl. Sec., Dept of Transport, later Parl. Under-Sec. of State for Transport 1979–82; Minister of State (Minister for Health), Dept of Health and Social Security 1982–85; Paymaster-Gen. and Minister for Employment 1985–87; Chancellor of Duchy of Lancaster and Minister for Trade and Industry 1987–88, Minister for the Inner Cities 1987–88; Sec. of State for Health 1988–90, for Educ. and Science 1990–92, for the Home Dept 1992–93; Chancellor of the Exchequer 1993–97; Shadow Sec. of State for Business, Enterprise and Regulatory Reform 2009–10; Lord Chancellor and Sec. of State for Justice 2010–12; Govt Anti-Corruption Champion 2010–; Minister without Portfolio, Cabinet Office 2012–; mem. Parl. Del. to Council of Europe and WEU 1973–74; Dir Alliance UniChem PLC 1997–2001, Deputy Chair. (non-exec.) 2001–08; Dir Foreign and Colonial Investment Trust 1997–2008, Deputy Chair. British American Tobacco 1998–2009; Dir Ind. News and Media (VIC) 1999–2009; Chair. Savoy Asset Man. PLC 2000–08; Master of Bench, Gray's Inn; Liveryman, Clockmakers' Co. 2001–; Hon. LLD (Nottingham) 1989, (Huddersfield) 1993, Hon. DUniv (Nottingham Trent) 1996. *Publication:* New Hope for the Regions 1969. *Leisure interests:* bird-watching, jazz, cricket, football. *Address:* House of Commons, Westminster, London, SW1A 0AA (office); Constituency Office, Rushcliffe House, 17–19 Rectory Road, West Bridgford, Nottingham, NG2 6BE, England. *Telephone:* (20) 7219-4528 (office); (115) 981-7224. *Fax:* (20) 7219-4841 (office); (115) 981-7273. *E-mail:* clarkek@parliament.uk (office). *Website:* www.parliament.uk/biographies/commons/kenneth-clarke/25686 (office); www.rushcliffeconservatives.com.

CLARKE, Michael John; Australian professional cricketer; *Captain, Australian National Cricket Team;* b. 2 April 1981, Liverpool, NSW; m. Kyly Boldy 2012; lower middle order batsman; right-handed batsman; slow left-arm orthodox bowler; plays for NSW 2000–, Hants. 2004, Australia 2004– (Vice-Capt. Test and ODI sides –2011, Capt. 2011–, Capt. Twenty20 side 2009–), Sydney Thunder 2011–, Pune Warriors India 2012–13; First-class debut: for NSW 1999/2000; Test debut: India v Australia, Bangalore 6–10 Oct. 2004; One-Day Int. (ODI) debut: Australia v England, Adelaide 19 Jan. 2003; T20I debut: NZ v Australia, Auckland 17 Feb. 2005; has played in 102 Tests, taken 30 wickets and scored 8,019 runs (26 centuries, 27 fifties), highest score 329 not out, average 51.40, best bowling 6/9; ODIs: 236 matches, scored 7,683 runs, average 44.66, highest score 130, took 56 wickets, average 38.03, best bowling 5/35; First-class: 171 matches, 12,947 runs, average 48.30, highest score 329 not out, took 41 wickets, average 44.65, best bowling 6/9; only Australian to score a century on both home and away debuts 2004; Capt. Ashes-winning team against England 2013–14; Allan Border Medal 2005, 2009, 2012, Australian Man of the Series in Ashes Series (nominated by England team Dir Andy Flower for his "excellent batting") 2009, Test Cricketer of the Year 2009, 2012, named by Wisden as Leading Cricketer in the World for his performances in 2012, 2013, Sir Garfield Sobers Trophy (as world cricketer of the

year) 2013. *Address:* c/o Level 3, 243 Liverpool Street, East Sydney, NSW 2010, Australia (office); c/o Cricket NSW, PO Box 333, Paddington, NSW 2021; c/o Cricket NSW, Driver Avenue, Moore Park, NSW 2021 Australia. *Telephone:* (2) 8353-7777 (office); (2) 8302-6000. *Fax:* (2) 8353-7788 (office); (2) 8302-6080. *E-mail:* we@sel.com.au (office); info@cricketnsw.com. *Website:* www.sel.com.au (office); www.cricketnsw.com.

CLARKE, Philip; British retail executive; *Group Chief Executive, Tesco plc;* b. Liverpool, England; m. Linda Clarke; two c.; ed Univ. of Liverpool; worked shelf-stacking shift for Tesco supermarket as a schoolboy; joined Tesco plc as grad. trainee 1981, held several roles in store operations, commercial and marketing, Regional Man. in Scotland and North of England 1995, mem. Bd of Dirs 1998–, Int. & IT Dir of Supermarket Group 2004–11, Group Chief Exec. March 2011–; mem. Bd of Dirs Whitbread plc 2006–11. *Leisure interests:* horse riding, sailing, Liverpool Football Club. *Address:* Tesco plc, New Tesco House, PO Box 18, Delamare Road, Cheshunt, Herts., EN8 9SL, England (office). *Telephone:* (1992) 632222 (office). *Fax:* (1992) 644962 (office). *E-mail:* philip.clarke@tesco.com (office). *Website:* www.tesco.com (office).

CLARKSON, Rt Hon. Adrienne, OC, PC, CC, CMM, COM, CD, FRSC, FRAIC, FRCPSC; Canadian broadcaster and fmr government official; *Co-Chair, Institute for Canadian Citizenship;* b. 1939, Hong Kong; d. of William Poy; m. John Ralston Saul; ed Univ. of Toronto, Univ. of Paris (Sorbonne), France; broadcaster with CBC TV 1965–82, 1988–98; Ont.'s Agent-Gen. in Paris 1982–87; Pres. McClelland & Stewart Publishing 1987–88; fmr Chair. Canadian Museum of Civilization, Hull, Quebec; fmr Pres. Exec. Bd IMZ, Vienna (int. audio-visual asscn of music, dance and cultural programmers); Gov.-Gen. of Canada 1999–2005; Co-founder and Co-Chair. Inst. for Canadian Citizenship; Chair. of jury, Man Asian Literary Prize 2007; fmr Bencher of Law Soc. of Upper Canada; Colonel-in-Chief of Princess Patricia's Canadian Light Infantry on February 7, 2007; Order of Friendship of the Russian Fed. 2003; numerous Canadian decorations; 21 hon. doctorates. *TV includes:* Take Thirty, Adrienne at Large, The Fifth Estate, Adrienne Clarkson's Summer Festival, Adrienne Clarkson Presents, Something Special. *Publications include:* A Lover More Condoling 1968, True to You in My Fashion 1971, Heart Matters (memoirs) 2006, Dying to be Sick 2007, Norman Bethune 2009, Room for All of Us 2011; numerous magazine and newspaper articles. *Address:* Institute for Canadian Citizenship, 260 Spadina Avenue, Suite 500, Toronto, ON M5T 2E4, Canada (office). *Telephone:* (416) 593-6998 (office). *Fax:* (416) 593-9028 (office). *E-mail:* icc@icc-icc.ca (office). *Website:* www.icc-icc.ca (office); adrienneclarkson.com.

CLARKSON, Thomas William, BS, PhD; British toxicologist and academic; *J. Lowell Orbison Distinguished Alumni Professor Emeritus, Department of Environmental Medicine and Professor of Biochemistry and Biophysics, and Pharmacology and Physiology, University of Rochester;* b. 1 Aug. 1932, Blackburn, Lancs.; s. of William Clarkson and Olive Jackson; m. Winifred Browne 1957; one s. two d.; ed Univ. of Manchester; Instructor, Univ. of Rochester School of Medicine, USA 1958–61, Asst Prof. 1961–62, Assoc. Prof. 1965–71, Prof. of Biochemistry and Biophysics, and Pharmacology and Physiology 1971–, Head of Div. of Toxicology 1980–86, J. Lowell Orbison Distinguished Alumni Prof. 1983–2008, now Emer., Dir Environmental Health Sciences Center 1986–98, Chair. Dept of Environmental Medicine 1992–98; Scientific Officer, MRC, UK 1962–64; Sterling Drug Visiting Prof., Albany Medical Coll. 1989; Sr Fellowship, Weizmann Inst. of Science, Israel 1964–65; Post-Doctoral Fellow, Nuffield Foundation 1956–57 and US Atomic Energy Comm., Univ. of Rochester, NY 1957–58; mem. Inst. of Medicine of NAS; Dir NASA Center in Space Environmental Health 1991–95; mem. La Academia Nacional de Medicina de Buenos Aires 1984; mem. Collegium Ramazzini 1983; Hon. Dr Med. (Umeå Univ., Sweden) 1986; Merit Award, SOT 1999, Arthur Kornberg Award, Univ. of Rochester 1999. *Publications:* Reproductive and Developmental Toxicology (co-ed.), The Cytoskeleton as a Target for Toxic Agents (co-ed.), Biological Monitoring of Toxic Metals (co-ed.), Advances in Mercury Toxicology (co-ed.); more than 200 published papers. *Address:* Department of Environmental Medicine, University of Rochester School of Medicine, Box EHSC, Rochester, NY 14642, USA (office). *Telephone:* (716) 275-3911 (office). *Fax:* (716) 256-2591 (office). *E-mail:* tom_clarkson@urmc.rochester.edu (office). *Website:* www2.envmed.rochester.edu/envmed (office).

CLARY, David Charles, PhD, ScD, FRS, FRSC, FInstP, FRSA; British chemist and academic; *President, Magdalen College, Oxford;* b. 14 Jan. 1953, Halesworth, Suffolk; s. of Cecil Raymond Clary and Mary Mildred Clary (née Hill); m. Heather Ann Vinson 1975; three s.; ed Colchester Royal Grammar School, Univ. of Sussex, Corpus Christi Coll., Cambridge; researcher, IBM Research Lab., San Jose, Calif. 1977–78; post-doctoral research at Univ. of Manchester 1978–80; Research Lecturer in Chem., UMIST 1980–83; Lecturer, then Reader in Theoretical Chem., Dept of Chem., Univ. of Cambridge 1983–96; Fellow, Magdalene Coll., Cambridge 1983–96, Sr Tutor 1989–93, Fellow Commoner 1996–2002, Hon. Fellow 2002; Prof. of Chem., Dir of Centre for Theoretical and Computational Chem., Univ. Coll. London 1996–2002; Head of Math. and Physical Sciences, Univ. of Oxford 2002–05, Professorial Fellow, St John's Coll., Oxford 2002–05; Pres. Magdalen Coll., Oxford 2005–; Miller Fellow, Univ. of California, Berkeley 2001; Pres. Faraday Div. Royal Soc. of Chem. 2006; mem. Int. Acad. of Quantum Molecular Science 1998; Ed. Chemical Physics Letters 2000–; Fellow, AAAS 2003, American Physical Soc. 2003; mem. Council Royal Soc. 2004–05; Foreign Hon. Mem. American Acad. of Arts and Sciences 2003; Kistiakowsky Lecture, Harvard 2002, Pitzer Lecture, Berkeley 2003, Polanyi Lecture 2004; Annual Medal of Int. Acad. of Quantum Molecular Science 1989; medals of the Royal Soc. of Chem.: Meldola 1981, Marlow 1986 Corday-Morgan 1989, Tilden 1998, Chemical Dynamics 1998. *Achievements include:* developed quantum theory for chemical reactions of polyatomic molecules. *Publications:* more than 300 research papers on chemical physics and theoretical chem. in learned journals. *Leisure interests:* family, football. *Address:* Magdalen College, Oxford, OX1 4AU, England (office). *Telephone:* (1865) 276100 (office). *Fax:* (1865) 286730 (office). *Website:* www.chem.ox.ac.uk (office); www.mag.ox.ac.uk (office).

CLASPER, Michael (Mike), CBE, BEng; British airport executive and music industry executive; *Chairman, HM Revenue and Customs;* b. 21 April 1953, Sunderland; s. of Douglas Clasper and Hilda Clasper; m. Susan Rosemary Shore 1975; two s. one d.; ed Bede School, Sunderland, St John's Coll., Cambridge; with

British Rail 1974–78; joined Proctor & Gamble 1978, Advertising Dir 1985–88, Gen. Man. Proctor & Gamble Holland 1988–91, Man. Dir and Vice-Pres. Proctor & Gamble UK 1991–95, Regional Vice-Pres. Laundry Products, Proctor & Gamble Europe 1995–99, Pres. Global Home Care and New Business Devt, Proctor & Gamble, Brussels 1999–2001; Deputy CEO and Chair. Airports Bd BAA PLC 2001–03, CEO 2003–06; Head of EVP Marketing Sales and Operations, EMI Group 2008; Chair., HM Revenue and Customs 2008–; Dir (non-exec.) ITV plc 2006–; mem. Advisory Council on Business and the Environment 1993–99; mem. Man. Cttee Business and Environment Programme, Univ. of Cambridge Programme for Industry 2000–, Prince of Wales Business and Environment Programme; mem. Investor Bd EMI Group 2007; Fellow, Inst. of Grocery Distribution; Hon. PhD (Sunderland). *Leisure interests:* swimming, cycling, skiing, tennis, golf. *Address:* c/o EMI Group Ltd, 27 Wrights Lane, London, W8 5SW, England (office).

CLATWORTHY, Robert, RA; British sculptor; b. 31 Jan. 1928; s. of E. W. and G. Clatworthy; m. 1st Pamela Gordon 1954 (divorced); two s. one d.; m. 2nd Jane Clatworthy (née Illingworth Stubbs) 1989; ed Dr Morgan's Grammar School, Bridgwater, West of England Coll. of Art, Chelsea School of Art, The Slade; teacher, West of England Coll. of Art 1967–71; Visiting Tutor, RCA 1960–72; mem. Fine Art Panel of Nat. Council for Diplomas in Art and Design 1961–72; Governor, St Martin's School of Art 1970–71; Head of Dept of Fine Art, Central School of Art and Design 1971–75; work in collections of Arts Council, Contemporary Art Soc., Tate Gallery, Victoria and Albert Museum, GLC, Nat. Portrait Gallery (portrait of Dame Elisabeth Frink 1985). *Works include:* public sculptures: Large Bull, Alton Housing Estate, London SW15; Monumental Horse and Rider in grounds of Charing Cross Hosp., London W6. *Address:* Moelfre, Cynghordy, Llandovery, Carmarthenshire, SA20 0UW, Wales (home). *Telephone:* (1550) 720201. *E-mail:* robertclatworthy@hotmail.com (office). *Website:* www.robertclatworthy .homestead.com (office).

CLAUSEN, Christian, MSc (Econs); Danish banking executive; *President and Group CEO, Nordea Bank AB;* b. 6 March 1955, Copenhagen; Man. Dir Privatbørsen, Privatbanken 1988–90, Man. Dir and CEO Unibørs Securities (later Nordea) 1990–96, Man. Dir and CEO Unibank Markets 1996–98, mem. Exec. Bd Unibank 1998–2000, mem. Group Exec. Man. Nordea Bank AB (parent co.) 2001–, also Exec. Vice-Pres., Head of Asset Man. & Life 2000–07, Pres. and Group CEO Nordea Bank AB 2007–; Dir OMX Nordic Exchange Group Oy 2005–. *Address:* Nordea Bank AB, Smålandsgatan 17, 105 71 Stockholm, Sweden (office). *Telephone:* (8) 614-7000 (office). *Fax:* (8) 105-069 (office). *E-mail:* info@nordea .com (office). *Website:* www.nordea.com (office).

CLAUSER, John Francis, BS, MA, PhD; American physicist and consultant; b. 1 Dec. 1942, Pasadena, Calif.; s. of Francis H. Clauser and Catharine M. Clauser; m. Barbara A. Tosse 1996; ed California Inst. of Tech., Columbia Univ., New York; Postdoctoral Research Assoc., Lawrence Berkeley Nat. Lab., Berkeley, Calif. 1969–75; Research Physicist, Lawrence Livermore Nat. Lab. 1975–86; Sr Scientist, Science Applications International Corpn 1986–87; Research Physicist, Consultant and Inventor, J.F. Clauser & Assocs 1988–89, 1997; Research Physicist, Berkeley Fundamental Fysiks Group, Univ. of California 1990–97; mem. Berkeley Fundamental Fysiks Group (informal group of physicists who met weekly to discuss philosophy and quantum physics) 1975–; working with Stuart Freedman, carried out first experimental test of the CHSH-Bell's theorem predictions 1972, first ever observation of quantum entanglement and the first experimental observation of a violation of a Bell inequality; carried out the world's second experimental test of CHSH-Bell' Theorem predictions 1976; Reality Foundation Prize (jtly) 1982, Wolf Prize in Physics (jtly) 2010, named a Thomson Reuters Citation Laureate in Physics with Alain Aspect and Anton Zeilinger 2011. *Achievement:* known for contribs to the foundations of quantum mechanics, in particular the Clauser-Horne-Shimony-Holt (CHSH) inequality. *Publications:* numerous papers in professional journals. *Leisure interest:* sailboat racing. *Address:* 817 Hawthorne Drive, Walnut Creek, CA 94596-6112, USA.

CLAVIER, Christian Jean-Marie; French actor and film producer; b. 6 May 1952, Paris; s. of Jean-Claude Clavier and Phanette Rousset-Rouard; one d. by Marie-Anne Chazel; f. Ouille Productions; Chevalier Ordre nat. du Mérite, Officier Ordre nat. des Arts et des lettres. *Stage appearances include:* Ginette Lacaze, La Dame de chez Maxim's, Non Georges pas ici 1972, Ma tête est malade 1976, Le Pot de terre contre le pot de vin 1977, Amours, coquillages et crustacés 1978, Le Père Noël est une ordure 1979–80, Papy fait de la résistance 1981, Double Mixte 1986–88, Un fil à la patte 1989, Panique au plaza 1995. *Films include:* Que la fête commence 1974, F. comme Fairbanks 1976, Le Diable dans la boîte 1976, L'Amour en herbe 1977, Des enfants gâtés 1977, Dîtes-lui que je t'aime 1977, Les Bronzés font du ski (also co-writer) 1979, Cocktail Molotov 1980, Je vais craquer 1980, Clara et les chics types 1980, Quand tu seras débloqué, fais-moi signe 1981, Elle voit des nains partout 1981, Le Père Noël est une ordure (also co-writer) 1982, Rock and Torah 1982, La Vengeance d'une blonde 1993, les Anges gardiens (also co-writer) 1994, Les Couloirs du temps (also co-writer) 1998, Astérix et Obélix contre César 1999, The Visitors 2000, Astérix et Obélix: Mission Cleopatra 2002, Lovely Rita, sainte patronne des cas désespérés 2003, Albert est méchant 2004, L'Enquête corse 2004, L'Antidote 2005, Les Bronzés 3: amis pour la vie 2006, L'Entente cordiale 2006, Le Prix à payer 2006, L'Auberge rouge 2007. *Television includes:* l'Été 1986, Sueurs froides 1988, Palace 1988, Si Guitry m'était conté 1989, Bougez pas j'arrive 1989, Mieux vaut courir 1989, Fantôme sur l'oreiller (co-writer 1989), Charmante soirée (co-writer 1990), Les Misérables (miniseries) 2000, Napoléon 2002, Kronprinz Rudolf 2006, Kaamelott 2007. *Leisure interests:* skiing, cycling, swimming. *Address:* Ouille Productions, 7 rue des Dames Augustines, 92200 Neuilly, France (office). *Telephone:* 1-41-34-13-34 (office). *Fax:* 1-41-34-13-10 (office). *E-mail:* ouille2@wanadoo.fr (office).

CLAYTON, Adam Charles; British musician (bass guitar); b. 13 March 1960, Chinnor, Oxon., England; s. of Brian Clayton and Jo Clayton; ed Castle Park School, Dalkey, St Columba's, Rathfarnham, Mount Temple Comprehensive School, Dublin; family moved to Malahide, Co. Dublin 1965; Founder-mem. Feedback 1976, renamed The Hype, finally renamed U2 1978–; numerous concerts, including Live Aid Wembley 1985, Self Aid Dublin, A Conspiracy of Hope (Amnesty International Tour) 1986, Smile Jamaica (hurricane relief fundraiser) 1988, Very Special Arts Festival, White House, Washington, DC

1988; numerous tours world-wide; 22 Grammy Awards with U2, including Album of the Year and Best Rock Performance by a Duo or Group with Vocal (for The Joshua Tree) 1987, Grammy Awards for Best Rock Performance by a Duo or Group with Vocal (for Desire) and Best Performance Video, short form (for Where the Streets Have No Name) 1988, BRIT Awards for Best Int. Act 1988–90, 1992, 1998, 2001, Best Live Act 1993, Outstanding Contribution to the British Music Industry 2001, JUNO Award 1992, World Music Award 1992, Grammy Award for Best Rock Vocal by a Duo or Group (for Achtung Baby) 1992, Grammy Award for Best Alternative Music Album (for Zooropa) 1993, Grammy Award for Best Music Video, long form (for Zoo TV Live from Sydney) 1994, Grammy Award for Song of the Year, Record of the Year, Best Rock Performance by a Duo or Group with Vocal (all for Beautiful Day) 2000, Grammy Awards for Best Pop Performance by a Duo or Group with Vocal (for Stuck In A Moment You Can't Get Out Of), for Record of the Year (for Walk On), for Best Rock Performance by a Duo or Group with Vocal (for Elevation), for Rock Album of the Year (All That You Can't Leave Behind) 2001, American Music Award for Favorite Internet Artist of the Year 2002, Ivor Novello Award for Best Song Musically and Lyrically (for Walk On) 2002, Golden Globe for Best Original Song (for The Hands That Built America, from film Gangs of New York) 2003, Grammy Awards for Best Rock Performance by a Duo or Group with Vocal, Best Rock Song, Best Short Form Music Video (all for Vertigo) 2004, TED Prize 2004, Nordoff-Robbins Silver Clef Award for lifetime achievement 2005, Q Award for Best Live Act 2005, Digital Music Award for Favourite Download Single (for Vertigo) 2005, Meteor Ireland Music Award for Best Irish Band, Best Live Performance 2006, Grammy Awards for Song of the Year, for Best Rock Performance by a Duo or Group with Vocal (both for Sometimes You Can't Make it on Your Own), for Best Rock Song (for City of Blinding Lights), for Album of the Year and Best Rock Album of the Year (both for How to Dismantle an Atomic Bomb) 2006, Golden Globe Award for Best Original Song, Motion Picture (Ordinary Love in Mandela: Long Walk to Freedom) 2014; Portuguese Order of Liberty 2005; Ambassadors of Conscience Award, Amnesty International 2006. *Film:* Rattle and Hum 1988. *Recordings include:* albums: Boy 1980, October 1981, War 1983, Under a Blood Red Sky 1983, The Unforgettable Fire 1984, Wide Awake In America 1985, The Joshua Tree (Grammy Award for Album of the Year, Best Rock Performance by a Duo or Group with Vocal) 1987, Rattle and Hum 1988, Achtung Baby (Grammy Award for Best Rock Performance by a Duo or Group with Vocal 1992) 1991, Zooropa (Grammy Award for Best Alternative Music Album) 1993, Passengers (film soundtrack with Brian Eno) 1995, Pop 1997, The Best Of 1980–90 1998, All That You Can't Leave Behind (Grammy Award for Best Rock Album 2001) 2000, The Best Of 1990–2000 2002, How To Dismantle An Atomic Bomb (Meteor Ireland Music Award for Best Irish Album 2006, Grammy Awards for Album of the Year, for Best Rock Album 2006) 2004, No Line on the Horizon 2009. *Address:* c/o Principle Management, 30–32 Sir John Rogersons Quay, Dublin 2, Ireland (office). *E-mail:* candida@numb.ie (office). *Website:* www.u2.com.

CLAYTON, Robert Norman, MSc, PhD, FRS; Canadian/American geochemist and academic; *Enrico Fermi Distinguished Service Professor Emeritus, Department of Chemistry, University of Chicago;* b. 20 March 1930, Hamilton, Ont., Canada; s. of Norman Clayton and Gwenda Clayton; m. Cathleen Shelbourne Clayton 1971; one d.; ed Queen's Univ., Kingston and California Inst. of Tech.; Research Fellow, California Inst. of Tech. 1955–56; Asst Prof., Pennsylvania State Univ. 1956–58; Asst Prof., Univ. of Chicago 1958–62, Assoc. Prof. 1962–66, Prof., Depts of Chem. and of the Geophysical Sciences 1966–80, Enrico Fermi Distinguished Service Prof. 1980–, now Prof. Emer.; mem. NAS; Fellow, AAAS, RSC, Royal Soc., London, American Acad. of Arts and Sciences, Meteoritical Soc., American Geophysical Union; NASA Exceptional Scientific Achievement Medal 1976, George P. Merrill Award, NAS 1980, Goldschmidt Medal, Geochemical Soc. 1981, Leonard Medal, Meteoritical Society 1982, Elliot Cresson Medal, Franklin Inst. 1985, William Bowie Medal, American Geophysical Union 1987, Award in Nuclear Chemistry, ACS 1992, Urey Medal, European Asscn of Geochemistry 1995, US Nat. Medal of Science 2004. *Publications:* over 200 papers in geochemical journals. *Address:* Department of the Geophysical Sciences, University of Chicago, RI 440, 5734 South Ellis Avenue, Chicago, IL 60637 (office); 5201 South Cornell, Chicago, IL 60615, USA (home). *Telephone:* (773) 702-7777 (office). *Fax:* (773) 702-9505 (office). *E-mail:* r-clayton@uchicago.edu (office). *Website:* chemistry.uchicago .edu/faculty/faculty/person/member/robert-n-clayton.html (office).

CLEAVER, Sir Anthony Brian, Kt, MA; British business executive; *Chairman of the Executive Board, Caithness and North Sutherland Regeneration Partnership;* b. 10 April 1938, London; s. of the late William Brian Cleaver and Dorothea Early Cleaver (née Peeks); m. Mary Teresa Cotter 1962 (died 1999); one s. one d.; m. 2nd Jennifer Lloyd Graham 2000; ed Berkhamsted School and Trinity Coll. Oxford; nat. service in Intelligence Corps 1956–58; joined IBM 1962, UK Sales Dir 1976–77, DP Dir, mem. Bd, IBM UK (Holdings) 1977–80, Vice-Pres. of Marketing IBM Europe 1981–82, Asst Gen. Man. IBM UK 1982–84, Gen. Man. 1984–85, Chief Exec. 1986–91, Chair. 1990–94 (retd); Chair. UK Atomic Energy Authority (UKAEA) 1993–96, Chair. Atomic Energy Authority Tech. PLC (after privatisation and flotation of UKAEA) 1996–2001; Chair. Industrial Devt Advisory Bd Dept of Trade and Industry 1993–99, UKAEA 1993–96, The Strategic Partnership 1996–2000, Medical Research Council 1998, IX Holdings Ltd 1999, Baxi Partnership 1999–2000, SThree 2000, UK eUniversities Worldwide Ltd 2000, Working Links (Employment) Ltd 2002, Royal Coll. of Music; Deputy Chair. ENO –2000; Pres. Involvement and Participation Asscn 1997–2002, Inst. of Man. 1998–2000; mem. Bd of Dirs Nat. Computing Centre 1977–80, Gen. Accident PLC (fmrly Gen. Accident) Fire and Life Assurance Corpn 1988–98, Gen. Cable PLC 1994–98 (Chair. 1995–98), Smith and Nephew PLC 1993; mem. Council, Templeton Coll. Oxford 1982–93, Asscn for Business Sponsorship of the Arts 1985–97; mem. Bd Centre for Economic and Environmental Development 1985–98 (Deputy Chair. 1992–98); apptd mem. Cttee on Standards in Public Life, British Govt Panel on Sustainable Devt 1998–2000; Chair. Nuclear Decommissioning Authority 2004–07; Chair. Exec. Bd Caithness and North Sutherland Regeneration Partnership 2008–; Chair. Bd of Govs, Birkbeck Coll. 1989–98; Fellow, British Computer Soc.; Hon. Fellow, Birkbeck Coll. 1999; Hon. LLD (Nottingham) 1991, (Portsmouth) 1996; Hon. DSc (Cranfield) 1995, (City) 2001, (Hull) 2001; Global 500 Roll of Honour (UN Environment Program) 1989. *Leisure interests:* sports, especially cricket, music, especially opera and reading. *Address:* c/o Caithness and North Sutherland Regeneration Partnership, 7A Traill House, Olrig Street, Thurso, KW14 7BJ, Scotland (office).

CLEESE, John Marwood, MA; British actor and writer; b. 27 Oct. 1939, Weston-super-Mare, Somerset, England; s. of Reginald Cleese and Muriel Cleese; m. 1st Connie Booth 1968 (divorced 1978); one d.; m. 2nd Barbara Trentham 1981 (divorced 1990); one d.; m. 3rd Alyce Faye Eichelberger 1992 (divorced 2009); ed Clifton Sports Acad. and Downing Coll., Cambridge; started writing and making jokes professionally 1963; first appearance on British TV 1966; appeared in and co-wrote TV series: The Frost Report, At Last the 1948 Show, Monty Python's Flying Circus, Fawlty Towers, The Human Face; Founder and Dir Video Arts Ltd 1972–89; appeared as Petruchio in The Taming of the Shrew, BBC TV Shakespeare cycle 1981; appeared in Cheers, for which he received an Emmy Award; guest appearances in Third Rock From the Sun, Will and Grace; toured Scandinavia and USA with his Alimony Tour Year One and Year Two 2009, 2010, extended to UK (first tour), visiting Cambridge, Birmingham, Salford, Liverpool, Oxford, Leeds, Edinburgh and finishing in Palmerston North, NZ May–July 2011; Hon. A.D. White Prof.-at-Large, Cornell Univ. 1999–; Hon. LLD (St Andrews). *Films include:* Interlude, The Magic Christian, And Now For Something Completely Different, Monty Python and the Holy Grail, Romance with a Double Bass, Life of Brian, Time Bandits, Privates on Parade, Yellowbeard 1982, The Meaning of Life 1983, Silverado 1985, Clockwise 1986, A Fish Called Wanda (BAFTA Award for Best Film Actor) 1988, Erik the Viking 1988, Splitting Heirs 1992, Mary Shelley's Frankenstein 1993, The Jungle Book 1994, Fierce Creatures 1996, The Out of Towners 1998, Isn't She Great 1998, The World Is Not Enough 1999, The Quantum Project 2000, Rat Race 2000, Pluto Nash 2000, Harry Potter and the Philosopher's Stone 2001, Scorched 2002, Die Another Day 2002, Harry Potter and the Chamber of Secrets 2002, Charlie's Angels: Full Throttle 2003, George of the Jungle 2 (voice) 2003, Shrek 2 (voice) 2004, Around the World in 80 Days 2004, Valiant (voice) 2005, Man About Town 2006, Complete Guide to Guys 2006, L'Entente cordiale 2006, Charlotte's Web (voice) 2006, Shrek the Third (voice) 2007, Igor (voice) 2008, The Day the Earth Stood Still 2008, The Pink Panther 2 2009, The Princess and the Frog (voice) 2009, Shrek Forever After (voice) 2010, Spud 2010, Winnie the Pooh (narrator) 2011. *Publications:* Families and How to Survive Them 1983, Life and How to Survive It (both with Robin Skynner) 1993, The Human Face (with Brian Bates) 2001, The Pythons Autobiography (co-author) 2003. *Leisure interests:* gluttony, sloth. *Address:* c/o David Wilkinson, 115 Hazlebury Road, London, SW6 2LX, England. *Telephone:* (20) 7371-5188. *Fax:* (20) 7371-5161.

CLEGG, Rt Hon. Nicholas William Peter (Nick), PC, MA; British politician; *Deputy Prime Minister;* b. 7 Jan. 1967, Amersham, Bucks.; s. of Nicholas Clegg CBE and Hermance van den Wall Bake; m. Miriam González Durántez; three s.; ed Westminster School, Robinson Coll., Cambridge, Univ. of Minnesota, USA, Coll. d'Europe, Belgium; began career as trainee journalist at The Nation magazine, Washington, DC; Aid and Trade Adviser, EC, Brussels, Belgium 1994–96; Adviser to Sir Leon Brittan 1996–99; Liberal Democrat MEP for E Midlands 1999–2004; joined political lobbying firm GPlus as a fifth partner 2004; part-time Lecturer, Univ. of Sheffield 2004; gave series of seminar lectures in Int. Relations Dept, Univ. of Cambridge 2004; MP (Liberal Democrats) for Sheffield Hallam 2005–; Shadow Spokesperson on Foreign Affairs 2005–06, Shadow Home Sec. 2006–07; Leader, Liberal Democratic Party 2007–; Deputy Prime Minister (in coalition with the Conservative Party under Prime Minister David Cameron) and Lord Pres. Privy Council 2010–; Founding mem. Campaign for Parliamentary Reform; columnist, Guardian Politics Unlimited; first David Thomas Prize, Financial Times 1993. *Publications:* Doing Less to Do More: A New Focus for the EU 2000, Trading for the Future: Reforming the WTO (with Duncan Brack) 2001, Learning from Europe: Lessons in Education (with Richard Grayson) 2002, The Liberal Moment 2009, Change That Works for You: Liberal Democrat General Election Manifesto: Building a Fairer Britain (ed.) 2010; numerous articles in nat. newspapers. *Leisure interests:* skiing, mountaineering. *Address:* Office of the Deputy Prime Minister, 70 Whitehall, London, SW1A 2AS (office); Office of the Leader of the Liberal Democrats, 8-10 Great George Street, London SW1P 3AE (office); Constituency Office, 85 Nethergreen Road, Sheffield, S11 7EH, England (office). *Telephone:* (114) 230-9002 (Sheffield) (office). *Fax:* (114) 230-9614 (Sheffield) (office). *E-mail:* nick.clegg.mp@parliament.uk (office); nickclegg@ sheffieldhallam.org.uk (office). *Website:* www.gov.uk/government/organisations/ deputy-prime-ministers-office (office); www.nickclegg.org.uk (office); www .nickclegg.com (office).

CLEGHORN, John E., OC, FCA, BComm, CA; Canadian banker and business executive; *Chairman, Canadian Pacific Railway Ltd;* b. 7 July 1941, Montreal, PQ; s. of H. W. Edward Cleghorn and Hazel Miriam Dunham; m. Pattie E. Hart 1963; two s. one d.; ed McGill Univ.; Clarkson Gordon & Co. (chartered accountants) 1962–64; sugar buyer and futures trader, St Lawrence Sugar Ltd, Montréal 1964–66; Mercantile Bank of Canada 1966–74; joined Royal Bank of Canada 1974, various sr exec. positions 1975–83, including Pres. 1983, Pres., COO 1986, Pres. CEO 1994–95, Chair. CEO 1995–2001; Chair. SNC-Lavalin Group 2002–07 (retd); mem. Bd of Dirs Canadian Pacific Railway Ltd 2001–, Chair. 2006–; mem. Bd of Dirs Molson Coors Brewing Co.) 2003–; fmr mem. McGill Univ. Bd of Govs, now Govs Emer. and mem. McGill Desautels Faculty of Man.'s Int. Advisory Bd; Chancellor Wilfrid Laurier Univ. 1996–2003; mem. Canadian and BC Insts. of Chartered Accountants; Fellow, Ordre des Comptables Agréés du Québec, Inst. of Chartered Accountants of Ont.; Hon. DCL (Bishop's Univ.) 1989, (Acadia Univ.) 1996; Hon. LLD (Wilfrid Laurier Univ.) 1991. *Leisure interests:* skiing, jogging, tennis, fishing. *Address:* Canadian Pacific Railway Ltd, Gulf Canada Square, 401 9th Ave. SW, Calgary, Alberta T2P 4Z4, Canada (office). *Telephone:* (403) 319-7000 (office). *Website:* www8.cpr.ca (office).

CLELAND, Joseph Maxwell (Max), MA; American fmr politician; b. 24 Aug. 1942, Atlanta, Ga; s. of Joseph Cleland and Juanita Kesler; ed Stetson Univ. Deland, Fla, Emory Univ.; served in US Army during Vietnam War, lost both legs and part of one arm 1968; mem. Ga Senate, Atlanta 1971–75; consultant, Comm. on Veterans Affairs, US Senate 1975–77; Admin. Veterans Affairs, Washington, DC 1977–81; Sec. of State, State of Ga 1982–95; Senator from Georgia 1997–2003; mem. Senate Armed Services Cttee 1997–2002, Cttee on Governmental Affairs 1997–2002, Cttee on Small Businesses 1997–2002, Commerce Cttee 1999–2002;

mem. Nat. Comm. on Terrorist Attacks Upon the US 2002–03 (resgnd); Distinguished Adjunct Prof., American Univ. Washington Semester Program and Fellow, Center for Congressional and Presidential Studies 2003; mem. Bd of Dirs Export-Import Bank of the United States 2003–07; worked for presidential campaign of John Kerry 2004; Democrat; Silver Star and Bronze Star for valorous action in combat. *Publications:* Strong at the Broken Places 2000, Going for the Max!: 12 Principles for Living Life to the Fullest 2000, Heart of a Patriot: How I Found the Courage to Survive Vietnam, Walter Reed and Karl Rove 2009. *Address:* 340 Mockingbird Lane, SE, Smyrna, GA 30082, USA (office).

CLÉMENT, Jérôme; French broadcasting and media executive and writer; *President, ARTE France;* b. 18 May 1945; m.; four c.; ed Institut d'Études Politiques de Paris, École Nat. d'Admin; began career at Ministry of Culture; Cultural and Scientific Councillor, Embassy in Cairo 1980–81; Advisor to the Prime Minister, Pierre Mauroy, in charge of Culture and Communication 1981–84; Gen. Man. Nat. Cinematography Centre 1984–89; Pres. La Sept (today ARTE France) 1989–, took part in negotiations with German reps that resulted in creation of ARTE 1991, Pres. ARTE France 1992–, Vice-Pres. ARTE GEIE and Chair. ARTE 1992–99, 2003–; Pres. and Gen. Man. la Cinquième 1997–2000 (before it became France 5); Admin. for several cultural ventures, including Orchestre de Paris and Théâtre du Châtelet; mem. Senate of Deutsche Nationalstiftung 2007–, Council of Admin of Musée d'Orsay 2010–; Municipal Councillor, town of Clamart, in charge of Culture and Architecture 2000–; fmr Lecturer, Univ. of Paris I, École Nat. Supérieure, Sciences Politiques; Officier, Légion d'honneur; Chevalier, Ordre nat. du Mérite; Commdr des Arts de Letters; Officer, Order of Merit of FRG. *Publications:* Socialisme et Multinationales 1978, Un Homme en Quête de Vertu 1992, Lettres à Pierre Bérégovoy 1993, La culture expliquée à ma fille 2000, Les Femmes et l'Amour 2002, Plus tard, tu comprendras 2005, Dictionnaire Des Papous dans la Tête 2007, Maintenant, Je Sais 2008. *Address:* ARTE G.E.I.E., Service Téléspectateurs, 4 Quai du Chanoine Winterer, CS 20035, 67080 Strasbourg Cedex, France (office); ARTE G.E.I.E., Service Téléspectateurs, Postfach 1980, 77679 Kehl am Rhein, Germany (office). *Telephone:* (3) 88-14-22-55 (Strasbourg) (office); (180) 500-24-88 (Kehl am Rhein) (office). *Fax:* (3) 88-14-21-60 (office). *E-mail:* info@arte.tv (office). *Website:* www .arte.tv (office); www.jeromeclement-presidentartefrance.com.

CLEMENT, Pascal; French government official and barrister; b. 12 May 1945, Boulogne-Billancourt (Hauts-de-Seine); fmr Marketing Dir Rank-Xerox; Mayor of Saint-Marcel-de-Félines (Loire) 1977–2001, mem. Municipal Council; Deputy Nat. Ass. 1978–93, 1995–2005, fmr Chair. Cttee on Constitutional Laws and Legislation; Vice-Chair. Loire Gen. Council 1982–94, Chair. 1994–2008; Minister Del. attached to the Prime Minister, responsible for relations with the Nat. Ass. 1993–95; Keeper of the Seals and Minister of Justice 2005–07. *Address:* c/o Ministry of Justice, 13 place Vendôme, 75042 Paris Cédex 01, France (office).

CLEMENT, The Hon. Tony, PC, BA, LLB; Canadian politician; *President of the Treasury Board;* b. 1961, Manchester, UK; m. Lynne Golding; three c.; ed Univ. of Toronto; fmr Pres. Progressive Conservative Party of Ont.; Prov. Minister of Transportation 1997–99, of the Environment 1999–2000, of Municipal Affairs and Housing 1999–2001, of Health and Long-Term Care 2001–03; defeated in 2003 election; Counsel, Bennett Jones LLP 2003–06; MP for Parry Sound—Muskoka 2006–; Minister of Health and Minister for the Fed. Econ. Devt Initiative for Northern Ont. 2006–08, of Industry 2008–11, Pres. of the Treasury Bd 2011–, Minister for the Federal Econ. Initiative for Northern Ont. 2011–13; Founding Pres. Canadian Alliance 2000. *Address:* Treasury Board of Canada Secretariat, Strategic Communications and Ministerial Affairs, L'Esplanade Laurier, 9th Floor, East Tower 140 O'Connor Street, Ottawa, ON K1A 0R5, Canada (office). *Telephone:* (613) 957-2400 (office). *Fax:* (613) 941-4000 (office). *Website:* www.tbs -sct.gc.ca (office).

CLEMENT, Wolfgang; German politician; b. 7 July 1940, Bochum; five d.; ed Univ. of Münster; journalist, Westfälische Rundschau newspaper –1967, various positions including Deputy Ed.-in-Chief 1968–81; Research Asst. Inst. for Procedural Law, Univ. of Marburg 1967–68; Press Spokesman, SPD Nat. Exec., Bonn 1981–86, resgnd over campaign controversy 1986; Ed.-in-Chief Hamburger Morgenpost newspaper 1986–88; Chief-of-Staff N Rhine-Westphalia State Chancellery 1989–90, Minister without Portfolio 1990–95, Head of Ministry of Industry, Small Business, Tech. and Transport 1995–96; mem. N Rhine-Westphalia State Ass. 1993–2001; elected Deputy Chair. SPD Exec. for State of N Rhine-Westphalia 1996; Premier of State of N Rhine-Westphalia 1998–2002; Deputy Chair. SPD Nat. Exec. 1999–2008 (resgnd); Fed. Minister of Econs and Labour 2002–05. *Address:* c/o Federal Ministry of Economics and Labour, Scharnhorststrasse 34–37, 10115 Berlin, Germany (office).

CLEMENTE, Carmine Domenic, AB, MA, PhD; American professor of anatomy and neurobiology; *Professor Emeritus, University of California, Los Angeles;* b. 29 April 1928, Penns Grove, NJ; s. of Ermanno Clemente and Caroline Clemente (née Friozzi); m. Juliette G. Clemente 1968; ed Univ. of Pennsylvania and Univ. Coll. London; US Public Health Service Fellow and Asst Instructor in Anatomy, Univ. of Pennsylvania 1950–52; Instructor in Anatomy, UCLA 1952–53, Asst Prof. 1954–59, Assoc. Prof. 1959–63, Prof. and Chair. Dept of Anatomy 1963–73, Prof. of Anatomy 1973–94, Prof. Emer. 1994–; Prof. of Surgery (Anatomy), Charles R. Drew Postgrad. Medical School 1974– (mem. Bd 1985–), Dir Brain Research Inst. 1976–87; John Simon Guggenheim Memorial Scholar, Nat. Inst. for Medical Research, Mill Hill, London 1988–89, 1991; Consultant in Surgical Anatomy, Martin Luther King Hosp., Los Angeles 1971; Consultant in Research Neurophysiology, Sepulveda Veterans Admin. Hosp.; mem. Inst. of Medicine of NAS; consultant, Robert Wood Johnson Foundation, Princeton, NJ 1990–; numerous awards and distinctions. *Publications:* Gray's Anatomy 1973–; numerous books, films and some 200 scientific publs including: Anatomy, An Atlas of the Human Body 1975 (5th edition 2007). *Leisure interest:* philately. *Address:* Dept of Neurobiology, UCLA School of Medicine, Los Angeles, CA 90095 (office); 11737 Bellagio Road, Los Angeles, CA 90049, USA (home). *Telephone:* (310) 825-9566 (office); (310) 472-1149 (home). *E-mail:* cdclem@ucla.edu (office).

CLEMENTE, Francesco; Italian painter; b. 23 March 1952, Naples; s. of Marquess Lorenzo Clemente; m. Alba Primiceri 1974; four c.; ed Univ. degli Studi di Roma, La Sapienza; collaborated with Andy Warhol and Jean-Michel Basquiat

1984; mem. American Acad. of Arts and Letters. *Address:* c/o Gagosian Gallery, 980 Madison Avenue, New York, NY 10021, USA.

CLEMENTI, Sir David Cecil, Kt, MA, MBA; British financial executive; *Chairman, King's Cross Central;* b. 25 Feb. 1949, Hunts., England; s. of Air Vice-Marshal Creswell Montagu Clementi and Susan Clementi (née Pelham); m. Sarah Louise (Sally) Cowley 1972; one s. one d.; ed Winchester Coll., Lincoln Coll., Oxford, Harvard Business School, USA; with Corp. Finance Div. Kleinwort Benson Ltd 1975–87, Head 1989–94; Head Kleinwort Benson Securities 1987–89; Chief Exec. Kleinwort Benson Ltd 1994–97; Vice-Chair. Kleinwort Benson Group PLC 1997; Deputy Gov. Bank of England 1997–2002; Chair. Prudential plc 2002–08; Chair. King's Cross Central (partnership to develop 67-acre Central London scheme) 2008–; Chair. Virgin Money Holdings 2011–; Chair. Property Industry Alliance; mem. Monetary Policy Cttee; Dir (non-exec.) Financial Services Authority, mem. Financial Capability Steering Group 2003–, apptd by Sec. of State for Constitutional Affairs to carry out review of regulation of legal services in England and Wales (completed 2004); Dir (non-exec.) Rio Tinto plc 2003–10, Foreign & Colonial Investment Trust PLC 2008–; Pres. Investment Property Forum 2005–; Trustee, Royal Opera House. *Leisure interest:* sailing. *Address:* King's Cross Central, c/o Emma Crowe, London Communications Agency, Middlesex House, 34–42 Cleveland Street, London, W1T 4JE, England. *Telephone:* (20) 7612-8480. *Website:* www.kingscross.co.uk (office).

CLEMENTS, John Allen, MD, FRCP; American paediatrician, physiologist and academic; *Professor of Pulmonary Biology and Professor of Pediatrics Emeritus, University of California, San Francisco;* Research Asst. Cornell Univ. Medical Coll. 1947–49; with US Army studying defences against war gasses 1949–61; with Cardiovascular Research Inst., Univ. of California 1961–; Julius H. Comroe, Jr Prof. of Pulmonary Biology, Univ. of California, San Francisco 1987, currently Prof. of Pulmonary Biology and Prof. of Pediatrics Emer.; Distinguished Lecturer in Medical Science, Mayo Clinic 1993; mem. Nat. Heart, Lung and Blood Inst. Advisory Council 1990–93; mem. NAS 1974; Fellow, American Acad. of Arts and Sciences 2002; Hon. Fellow, American Coll. of Chest Physicians 1978; Hon. Dir La Sociedad Chilena de Enfermedades del Thorax y Tuberculosis 1982; Hon. Life Mem. American Lung Asscn 1983; Hon. MD (Universität Bern) 1990, (Philipps Universität Marburg) 1992; Hon. ScD (Univ. of Manitoba) 1993; Bowditch Lecturer, American Physiological Soc. 1961, Modern Medicine Distinguished Achievement Award 1973, Howard Taylor Ricketts Medal and Award, Univ. of Chicago 1975, 57th Mellon Award, Univ. of Pittsburgh 1976, Edward Livingston Trudeau Medal, American Lung Asscn 1982, Gairdner Foundation Int. Award 1983, Research Achievement Award, American Heart Asscn 1991, Harold and Marilyn Menkes Memorial Lecturer, Johns Hopkins Univ. 1991, Christopher Columbus Discovery Award in Biomedical Research, NIH Christopher Columbus Quincentenary Jubilee Comm. of US Congress 1992, Nat. Medical Research Award, Nat. Health Council 1992, American Acad. of Pediatrics Virginia Apgar Award for Distinguished Contribs to Neonatology 1994, Albert Lasker Award for Clinical Research 1994, Warren Alpert Foundation Prize, Harvard Medical School 1996, Ulf von Euler Memorial Lecturer, Karolinska Inst., Nobel Foundation 1996, Pollin Prize for Pediatric Research, Pharmaceutical Manufacturers Asscn 1997. *Achievements include:* independent discoverer of lung surfactant and elucidator of its composition and functions 1955–; inventor of synthetic surfactant replacements 1980. *Publications:* numerous scholarly articles in journals and books. *Leisure interests:* piano, musical concerts, tennis, swimming, biography, history of science. *Address:* Box 1245, University of California, San Francisco, 3333 California Street, Laurel Heights 150, San Francisco, CA 94143-1245, USA (office). *Telephone:* (415) 476-2864 (office). *E-mail:* john.clements@ucsf.edu (office).

CLEOBURY, Nicholas Randall, MA, FRCO; British conductor; *Associate Director, Orchestra of the Swan;* b. 23 June 1950, Bromley, Kent; s. of John Frank Cleobury and Brenda Julie Cleobury (née Randall); brother of Stephen Cleobury; m. Heather Kay 1978; one s. one d.; ed King's School, Worcester and Worcester Coll., Oxford; Asst Organist, Chichester Cathedral 1971–72, Christ Church, Oxford 1972–76; Conductor, Schola Cantorum of Oxford 1973–76; Chorus Master, Glyndebourne Festival Opera 1977–79; Asst Dir, BBC Singers 1977–79; Prin. Opera Conductor, RAM 1980–87; Guest Conductor, Zurich Opera House 1992–; Music Dir, Oxford Bach Choir 1997–; Artistic Dir, Aquarius 1983–92, Cambridge Symphony Soloists 1990–92, Britten Sinfonia 1992–2005, Sounds New 1996–; Music Dir, Broomhill 1990–94, Artistic Dir, Cambridge Festival 1992, Roxanda Ways Canterbury 2003–; Artistic Adviser, Berkshire Choral Festival 2002–; Assoc. Dir, Orchestra of the Swan 2004–; Artistic Dir, Mid Wales Opera 2009–; has conducted world-wide from Australia to USA 1979–; Fellow, Christ Church Univ. Coll., Canterbury 2005; numerous recordings; Hon. RAM 1985. *Leisure interests:* cricket, food, wine, reading, theatre. *Address:* Robert Gilder and Co., 91 Great Russell Street, London WC1B 3PS, England (office); 20 Denbigh Street, London, SW1V 2ER (office); Barcheston House, Northside Steeple, Aston, Oxfordshire, OX25 4SE, England (home). *Telephone:* (20) 7580-7758 (office); (7831) 148637 (office); (1869) 340363 (home). *E-mail:* cathy@robert-gilder.com (office); nicholascleobury@btinternet.com (home). *Website:* www.robert-gilder.com (office); www.nicholascleobury.net.

CLEOBURY, Stephen John, CBE, MusB, MA, FRCM, FRCO, FRSCM; British conductor and organist; *Director of Music, King's College, Cambridge;* b. 31 Dec. 1948, Bromley, Kent, England; s. of John Frank Cleobury and Brenda Julie Cleobury (née Randall); brother of Nicholas Cleobury; m. 2nd Emma Sian Disley; four d. (two from previous m.); ed King's School, Worcester and St John's Coll., Cambridge; Organist, St Matthew's, Northampton 1971–74; sub-organist, Westminster Abbey 1974–78; Master of Music, Westminster Cathedral 1979–82; Dir of Music, King's Coll. Cambridge 1982–, Organist to the Univ. of Cambridge 1991–; Conductor, Cambridge Univ. Music Soc. 1983–2009, Chorus Dir 2009–; frequent appearances on BBC 2, BBC Radio 3 and Classic FM; freelance conducting and organ playing; mem. Council, Royal School of Church Music 1982–2005; Pres. Inc. Asscn of Organists 1985–87, Cathedral Organists' Asscn 1988–90; mem. Royal Coll. of Organists 1967–2008, Hon. Sec. 1981–90, Pres. 1990–92; Chief Conductor BBC Singers 1995–2007, Conductor Laureate 2007–; Fellow, Royal School of Church Music 2008; Hon. DMus (Anglia Polytechnic) 2001. *Radio:* A Festival of Nine Lessons and Carols (BBC Radio 3). *Television:* Carols from King's (BBC 2), Easter from King's (BBC 2). *Recordings:* directing Choir of King's Coll. Cambridge

and BBC Singers (Decca, EMI, Priory, King's Coll. Cambridge own label). *Publications:* various musical arrangements and writings. *Leisure interests:* reading, opera. *Address:* c/o Robin Tyson, Edition Peters Artist Management Ltd, Edition Peters UK, 2–6 Baches Street, London, N1 6DN, England (office); King's College, Cambridge, CB2 1ST, England (office). *E-mail:* robin.tyson@editionpeters.com (office); choir@kings.cam.ac.uk (office). *Website:* www.editionpeters.com/london/epamstephencleobury.php (office); www.stephencleobury.com. *Telephone:* (1223) 331224 (office). *Fax:* (1223) 331890 (office).

CLÉRISMÉ, Jean-Rénald, BA, MA, MPhil, PhD; Haitian anthropologist, politician and diplomatist; b. 7 Nov. 1937, Arniquet; m. Dr Linda Geralde; three s.; ed Université d'Haiti, New York Univ. and Yale Univ., USA; numerous govt and int. org. positions including Pres. and Co-Pres. of Task Forces, WTO on Budget, Finances and Admin Cttee, Minister Counsellor, Perm. Mission to UN, Geneva, Rep. to UNIDO, Vienna; Amb. to WTO, Int. Trade Center, UNCTAD, ITU, Geneva, Switzerland 2001–03; Del. Plenipotentiary to IAEA, Vienna 2001–03; Del. to Gen. Ass., Complete Test Ban Treaty Org. (CTBTO), Vienna 2003; Minister of Foreign Affairs 2006–08; Sr Adviser to Pres. Rene Preval 2008–11; Fulbright/LASPAU Scholarship, Mellon Fondation Grant. *Publication:* Main-d'oeuvre haïtienne and capital dominicain (Haitian Labor and Dominican Capital) 2003.

CLEVERS, Johannes Carolus (Hans), MD, PhD; Dutch geneticist and academic; *President, Royal Netherlands Academy of Arts and Sciences;* b. 27 March 1957, Eindhoven; ed Univ. of Utrecht; postdoctoral work, Dana-Farber Cancer Inst., Harvard Univ., USA 1986–89; Prof. of Immunology, Univ. of Utrecht 1991–2002, Prof. of Molecular Genetics 2002–; Prof. of Molecular Genetics and Dir Hubrecht Inst. for Developmental Biology and Stem Cell Research, Royal Netherlands Acad. of Arts and Sciences (KNAW), Utrecht 2002–12, Pres. KNAW 2012–; mem. KNAW 2000, American Acad. of Arts and Sciences 2012; Chevalier, Légion d'honneur 2005; Kt, Order of the Netherlands Lion 2012; Spinoza Award (Netherlands) 2001, Louis Jeantet Prize (Switzerland) 2004, Memorial Sloan-Kettering Katharine Berkan Judd Award 2005, Rabbi Shai Shacknai Memorial Prize (Israel) 2006, Josephine Nefkens Prize for Cancer Research (Netherlands) 2008, Meyenburg Cancer Research Award (Germany) 2008, Cancer Soc. Award (Netherlands) 2009, Research Prize, United European Gastroenterology Fed. 2010, Ernst Jung Prize for Medicine (Germany) 2011, Léopold Griffuel Prize, Asscn pour la Recherche sur le Cancer (France) 2012, Dr A.H. Heineken Prize for Medicine 2012, Breakthrough Prize in Life Sciences (co-recipient) 2013. *Publications:* numerous papers in professional journals. *Address:* Hubrecht Institute, Uppsalalaan 8, 3584 CT Utrecht, The Netherlands (office). *Telephone:* (30) 2121831 (office). *Fax:* (30) 2121801 (office). *E-mail:* h.clevers@hubrecht.eu (office). *Website:* www.hubrecht.eu/research/clevers (office).

CLEWLOW, Warren (Alexander Morten); South African business executive and chartered accountant; b. 13 July 1936, Durban; s. of Percy Edward Clewlow; m. Margaret Brokensha 1964; two s. three d.; ed Glenwood High School, Univ. of Natal; joined Barlow Group as Co. Sec. Barlow's (OFS) Ltd 1963; Alt. Dir Barlow Rand Ltd 1974, Dir 1975; mem. Exec. Cttee with various responsibilities Barlow Group 1978–83; CEO Barlow Rand Ltd (now Barloworld) 1983–86, Deputy Chair. and Chief Exec. 1985, Chair. 1991–2007 (resgnd); Chair. Nedbank Ltd and Nedcor Ltd 2004–06; Chair. Pretoria Portland Cement 1993–2004; fmr Dir SA Mutual Life Assurance Soc., Sasol Ltd; Regional Gov. Univ. of Cape Town Foundation; Council mem. South Africa Foundation; Chair. State Pres. Econ. Advisory Council 1985; mem. Bd Asscn of Marketers; Trustee Project South African Trust, Nelson Mandela Children's Fund; Chair. Duke of Edinburgh's South African Foundation, The President's Award for Youth Empowerment Trust; Chair. Bd of Trustees Carl & Emily Fuchs Foundation; Hon. Treas. African Children's Feeding Scheme; Hon. Prof. Univ. of Stellenbosch 1986; Order for Meritorious Service (Gold Class) 1988; Hon. DEcon (Natal) 1988; Businessman of the Year, Sunday Times 1984, Marketing Man of the Year, SA Inst. of Marketing 1984, Dr G. Malherbe Award, Univ. of Natal 1986. *Leisure interests:* tennis, horticulture, historical reading, sugar plantation farmering. *Address:* c/o Carl & Emily Fuchs Foundation, 1st Floor, Block 2, Waterfall Terraces, Waterfall Park, Bekker Road, Midrand, South Africa (office).

CLIFF, Ian Cameron, OBE, MA; British diplomatist; *Ambassador to Kosovo;* b. 11 Sept. 1952, Twickenham, Greater London, England; s. of Gerald Shaw Cliff and Dorothy Cliff; m. Caroline Redman 1988; one s. two d.; ed Hampton Grammar School, Univ. of Oxford; history teacher, Dr Challoner's Grammar School, Amersham 1975–79; joined FCO 1979; First Sec., Khartoum 1982–85, FCO 1985–89, UK Mission to UN, New York 1989–93; Dir Exports to Middle East, Near East and N Africa, Dept of Trade and Industry 1993–96; Deputy Head of Mission, Embassy in Vienna 1995–2001; Amb. to Bosnia and Herzegovina 2001–05, to Sudan 2005–07, Amb. and Head of Del. to OSCE, Vienna 2007–11, Amb. to Kosovo 2011–. *Leisure interests:* music, railways, philately. *Address:* British Embassy, Ismail Qemajli 6, Arberi, Dragodan, Pristina, Kosovo (office). *Telephone:* (38) 254700 (office). *Fax:* (38) 249799 (office); (38) 243062 (office). *E-mail:* ian.cliff@fco.gov.uk (office); britishembassy.pristina@fco.gov.uk (office). *Website:* www.gov.uk/government/world/organisations/british-embassy-pristina (office); www.gov.uk/government/world/kosovo (office).

CLIFF, Jimmy; Jamaican reggae singer and composer; b. (James Chambers), 1 April 1948, St Catherine; one s.; ed Kingston Tech. School; singer, songwriter 1960s–; backing vocalist, London 1963; tours world-wide; concerts include Montreux Jazz Festival 1980, World Music Festival, Jamaica 1982, Rock In Rio II, Brazil 1991, Worlds Beat Reggae Festival, Portand, USA 1992; formed own record label, Cliff Records 1989, own production co. Cliff Sounds and Films 1990; Grammy Award, Best Reggae Recording 1985, MOBO Award for contrib. to Urban Music 2002, inducted into Rock and Roll Hall of Fame 2010. *Films include:* The Harder They Come 1972, Bongo Man 1980, Club Paradise 1986. *Compositions include:* You Can Get It If You Really Want (recorded by Desmond Dekker), Let Your Yeah Be Yeah (recorded by The Pioneers), Trapped (recorded by Bruce Springsteen). *Recordings include:* albums: Hard Road 1967, Jimmy Cliff 1969, Can't Get Enough 1969, Wonderful World 1970, Another Cycle 1971, The Harder They Come 1972, Struggling Man 1974, Follow My Mind 1975, Give Thanx 1978, I Am The Living 1980, Give The People What They Want 1981, Special 1982, The Power and The Glory 1983, Cliff Hanger 1985, Hanging Fire 1988, Images 1990,

Breakout 1992, 100% Pure Reggae 1997, Shout for Freedom 1999, Humanitarian 1999, Live And In The Studio 2000, Wanted (compilation) 2000, Best of Jimmy Cliff 2001, Fantastic Plastic People 2002, Sunshine in the Music 2003, Black Magic 2005, Rebirth (Grammy Award for Best Reggae Album 2013) 2012. *E-mail:* sunpowerproductions3@yahoo.fr (office). *Website:* www.jimmycliff.com.

CLIFFORD, Maxwell (Max); British public relations executive; b. April 1943, Kingston-upon-Thames; s. of Frank Clifford and Lilian Clifford; m. Elizabeth Clifford; one d.; ed secondary modern school, South Wimbledon; worked in dept store (sacked); fmr jr reporter, Merton and Morden News; fmr jr press officer, EMI Records (promoted the Beatles); worked in public relations; Founder Max Clifford Assocs Ltd (press and public relations consultancy) 1968–, clients have included Muhammad Ali, Geoffrey Boycott, Marlon Brando, David Copperfield, Diana Ross, O.J. Simpson, Frank Sinatra, SEAT, Laing Homes, Simon Cowell, Kerry Katona; convicted of indecent assault and sentenced to eight years' imprisonment April 2014. *Publication:* Max Clifford, Read All About It (autobiog. with Angela Levin) 2005. *Address:* Max Clifford Associates Ltd, Moss House, 15-16 Brooks Mews, London, W1K 4DS, England (office). *Telephone:* (20) 7408-2350 (office). *Fax:* (20) 7409-2294 (office). *E-mail:* max@maxclifford.com (office). *Website:* www .maxclifford.com (office).

CLIFFORD, R. Leigh, BEng, MEng Sci; Australian business executive; *Chairman, Qantas Airways Ltd;* ed Univ. of Melbourne; joined Rio Tinto Group 1970, has held posts including Man. Dir Rio Tinto Ltd, Chief Exec. Energy Div., CEO Rio Tinto Group 2000–07 (retd), mem. Bd of Dirs 1994–2007; mem. Bd of Dirs Qantas Airways Aug. 2007–, Chair. Nov. 2007–; mem. Bd of Dirs Bechtel Group Inc. (Chair. Bechtel Australia Pty Ltd), Murdoch Childrens Research Inst., Nat. Gallery of Victoria Foundation; fmr mem. Bd of Dirs Barclays PLC; Sr Advisor to Kohlberg Kravis Roberts & Co.; mem. Council of Trustees of the Nat. Gallery of Victoria; Chair. IEA Coal Industry Advisory Bd 1998–2000. *Address:* Qantas Airways Ltd, Level 12, Exhibition Street, Melbourne, VIC 3000, Australia (office). *Telephone:* (3) 8656-6006 (office). *Fax:* (3) 8656-6011 (office). *Website:* www.qantas .com.au (office).

CLIFFORD, Sir Timothy Peter Plint, Kt, BA, FRSA, FRSE, FSA; British art historian, consultant and fmr museum director; b. 26 Jan. 1946; s. of the late Derek Plint Clifford and Anne Clifford (née Pierson); m. Jane Olivia Paterson 1968; one d.; ed Sherborne, Dorset, Perugia Univ., Courtauld Inst., Univ. of London; Asst Keeper, Dept of Paintings, Manchester City Art Galleries 1968–72, Acting Keeper 1972; Asst Keeper, Dept of Ceramics, Victoria and Albert Museum, London 1972–76; Dir Manchester City Art Galleries 1978–84; Dir Nat. Galleries of Scotland 1984–2001, Dir Gen. 2001–05; mem. Cttee ICOM (UK) 1980–82, Chair. Int. Cttee for Museums of Fine Art 1980–83, mem. Exec. Cttee 1983–88; mem. Bd Museums and Galleries Comm. 1983–88, British Council 1987–92, Exec. Cttee Scottish Museums Council 1984; Vice-Pres. Turner Soc. 1984–86, 1989–; mem. Advisory Council, Friends of the Courtauld Inst.; Pres. Nat. Asscn of Decorative and Fine Arts Socs 1996–2006; Consultant, Simon C. Dickinson Ltd, London 2007–; Comitatio Scientifico, Foundation of Civic Museums of Venice 2009–; Opificio delle Pietre Dure, Florence; Trustee, Royal Yacht Britannia 1998–2011, Hermitage Devt Trust 1999–2003, Wallace Collection 2003–11, Attingham Summer School, The American Friends of the Nat. Galleries of Scotland; Patron, Friends of Sherborne House 1997–, Olympia Art and Antiques Fair 2008–10; Freeman, Goldsmiths Co. 1989, City of London 1989, Liveryman 2007; Cavaliere al Ordine della Repubblica Italiana 1988, Commendatore 1999, Grand Ufficiale della Solidarietà Italiana 2004; Hon. LLD (St Andrews) 1996, (Aberdeen) 2005; Hon. DLitt (Glasgow) 2001; Special Award, BIM 1991, Ateneo Veneto, Italy 1997, Gulbenkian Prize for Charles Jenck's Landform 2004, Garrett Lifetime Award for Business Sponsorship for the Arts 2005. *Publications include:* John Crome (with Derek Clifford) 1968, The Man at Hyde Park Corner: Sculpture by John Cheere (with T. Friedmann) 1974, Vues pittoresques de Luxembourg ... par J.M.W. Turner 1977, Ceramics of Derbyshire 1750–1975 1978, J.M.W. Turner, Acquerelli e incisioni 1980, The Nat. Gallery of Scotland: an Architectural and Decorative History (with Ian Gow) 1988, Raphael: the Pursuit of Perfection (co-author) 1994, Effigies and Ecstasies: Roman Baroque Sculpture and Design in the Age of Bernini (with A. Weston-Lewis) 1998, Designs of Desire: Architectural and Ornament Prints and Drawings 1500–1850 2000, (co-author) A Poet in Paradise: Lord Lindsay and Christian Art 2000, The Age of Titian (co-author) 2004, Choice: Twenty-One Years of Collecting in Scotland 2005, Croatia: Aspects of Art and Architecture 2009. *Leisure interests:* bird watching, entomology.

CLIFTON, James Albert, BA, MD; American gastroenterologist, academic and university administrator; *Roy J. Carver Professor Emeritus, College of Medicine, University of Iowa;* b. 18 Sept. 1923, Fayetteville, NC; s. of James A. Clifton, Sr and Flora McNair Clifton; m. Katherine Rathe 1949; two d. (and one d. deceased); ed Vanderbilt Univ.; Asst Prof. of Medicine, Univ. of Iowa Coll. of Medicine 1954–58, Assoc. Prof. 1958–63, Prof. 1963–76, Roy J. Carver Prof. of Medicine 1976–90, Dir Center for Digestive Diseases 1985–90, Prof. Emer. 1991–, Interim Dean 1991–93, Chief, Div. of Gastroenterology 1953–71, Chair. Dept of Medicine 1970–76, Pres. Univ. of Iowa Retirees Asscn 1999–2000, Emer. Faculty Asscn 2000; Pres. American Coll. of Physicians 1977–78, American Gastroenterological Asscn 1970–71; Chair. Subspecialty Bd in Gastroenterology, American Bd of Internal Medicine 1972–75, American Bd of Internal Medicine 1980–81; mem. Ludwig Inst. for Cancer Research, Zurich, Switzerland 1984–95, Central Soc. for Clinical Research, American Physiological Soc., Asscn of American Physicians, Inst. of Medicine (NAS), Royal Soc. of Medicine, London, Scientific Advisory Cttee, Health Task Force Cttee (NIH), Nat. Advisory Council, Nat. Insts of Arthritis, Metabolism and Digestive Diseases (NIH); consultant to numerous US medical schools; Visiting Scientist, Mount Desert Island Biological Research Lab., Bar Harbor, Maine 1964; Visiting Prof. of Medicine, St Mark's Hosp., Univ. of London, UK 1984–85; Distinguished Medical Alumnus Award, Vanderbilt Univ., Alfred Stengel Award, American Coll. of Physicians, Distinguished Medical Alumnus Award, Univ. of Iowa 2000, Distinguished Mentoring Award 2002. *Publications include:* numerous scientific papers on intestinal absorption of nutrients, gastrointestinal motility and numerous publs regarding philosophy and current affairs in internal medicine. *Leisure interests:* music, photography, travel. *Address:* University of Iowa Hospital and Clinics, 4 J.C.P., Hawkins Drive, Iowa City, IA 52242 (office); 39 Audubon Place, Iowa City, IA 52245, USA (home).

Telephone: (319) 356-1771 (office); (319) 351-1561 (home). *Fax:* (319) 353-6399 (office); (319) 351-1561 (home). *E-mail:* james-clifton@uiowa.edu (office); zybumjim@home.com (home).

CLINTON, George; American singer and bandleader; b. 22 July 1941, Kannapolis, NC; one s.; Founder and leader, The Parliaments in 1950's, changed name to Funkadelic 1969, also performed and recorded as Parliament; solo artist 1982–; Owner, Bridgeport Music; regular worldwide concerts and tours; formed record label, The Ckunspyruhzy 2005–; Hon. DMus (Berklee Coll. of Music) 2012, Lifetime Achievement Award, Nat. Asscn for Advancement of Colored People, Vanguard Award, Oxfam America 2013. *Recordings include:* albums: with The Parliaments: I Wanna Testify 1967, Osmium 1970, Up for the Down Stroke 1974, Chocolate City 1975, Clones of Dr Funkenstein 1976, Mothership Connection 1976, Funkentelechy Vs The Placebo Syndrome 1977, Get Down & Boogie 1977, Live Earth Tour 1977, Motor Booty Affair 1978, Gloryhallastoopid (Pin The Tale On The Funky) 1979, Trombipulation 1980; with Funkadelic: Funkadelic 1970, Free Your Mind... And Your Ass Will Follow 1970, Maggot Brain 1971, America Eats Its Young 1972, Cosmic Slop 1973, Standing On The Verge of Getting It On 1974, Let's Take It to the Stage 1975, Hardcore Jollies 1976, Tales of Kidd Funkadelic 1976, One Nation Under A Groove 1978, Uncle Jam Wants You 1979, The Electric Spanking of War Babies 1981; solo: Computer Games 1982, You Shouldn't Nuf Bit, Fish! 1983, Some of My Best Jokes Are Friends 1985, R&B Skeletons In The Closet 1986, Mothership Connection 1986, The Cinderella Theory 1989, Hey Man... Smell My Finger 1993, Go Fer Yer Funk 1995, P is the Funk 1995, Plush Funk 1995, Testing Positive 4 The Funk 1995, A Fifth of Funk 1995, The Awesome Power of a Fully Operation Mothership 1996, Live & Kickin' 1997, Dope Dogs 1998, Six Degrees of P-Funk 2003, How Late Do You Have 2BB4UR Absent 2006, George Clinton and His Gangsters of Love 2008. *E-mail:* unclejam@georgeclinton.com (office). *Website:* www.georgeclinton.com.

CLINTON, Hillary Rodham, MA, DJur; American lawyer, politician and government official; b. 26 Oct. 1947, Chicago, Ill.; d. of the late Hugh Ellsworth and Dorothy Howell Rodham; m. William (Bill) Jefferson Clinton (q.v.) (fmr Pres. of USA), 1975; one d.; ed Wellesley Coll. and Yale Univ.; joined Rose Law Firm 1977, fmr Sr Partner; Legal Counsel, Nixon impeachment staff, US House Judiciary Cttee, Washington, DC 1974; Asst Prof. of Law, Univ. of Arkansas, Fayetteville and Dir Legal Aid Clinic 1974–77; Lecturer in Law, Univ. of Arkansas, Little Rock 1979–80; Chair. Comm. on Women in the Profession, ABA 1987–91; First Lady of USA 1993–2001; Head of Pres.'s Task Force on Nat. Health Reform 1993–94; newspaper columnist 1995; Senator from New York 2001–09, mem. Armed Services Cttee, Environment and Public Works Cttee, Health, Educ., Labor and Pensions Cttee, Special Cttee on Aging; Co-Chair. Children's Defense Fund 1973–74; unsuccessful cand. for Democratic party nomination for US Pres. 2008; US Sec. of State, Washington, DC 2009–13; mem. Bd of Dirs Southern Devt Bancorp 1986, Nat. Center on Educ. and the Economy 1987, Franklin and Eleanor Roosevelt Inst. 1988, Children's TV Workshop 1989, Public/Pvt. Ventures 1990, Arkansas Single Parent Scholarship Fund Program 1990, Clinton Presidential Center 2004; Hon. LLD (Arkansas, Little Rock) 1985, (Arkansas Coll.) 1988, (Hendrix Coll.) 1992; Hon. DHL (Drew) 1996; numerous awards and distinctions including One of Most Influential Lawyers in America, Nat. Law Journal 1988, 1991, Outstanding Lawyer-Citizen Award, Ark. Bar Asscn 1992, Lewis Hine Award, Nat. Child Labor Law Comm. 1993, Friend of Family Award, American Home Econs Foundation 1993, Humanitarian Award, Alzheimer's Asscn 1994, Elie Wiesel Foundation 1994, AIDS Awareness Award 1994, Grammy Award 1996, Alice Award 2009, Founders Award, Elton John AIDS Foundation 2013, ABA Medal 2013, American Patriot Award, National Defense Univ. Foundation 2013; ranked by Forbes magazine amongst The World's 100 Most Powerful Women (fifth) 2004, (26th) 2005, (18th) 2006, (25th) 2007, (28th) 2008, (36th) 2009, (fifth) 2010, (second) 2011–12, (fifth) 2013, ranked by Forbes magazine amongst The World's Most Powerful People (17th) 2009, (20th) 2010, (16th) 2011. *Publications:* It Takes a Village 1996, Dear Socks, Dear Buddy 1998, An Invitation to the White House 2000, Living History (memoirs) 2003; numerous contribs to magazines and journals. *Leisure interests:* reading, walking, tennis. *Website:* hillaryclintonoffice .com.

CLINTON, William (Bill) Jefferson, JD; American lawyer, fmr politician and fmr head of state; b. 19 Aug. 1946, Hope, Ark.; s. of the late William Jefferson Blythe, III and Virginia Dwire Kelley; m. Hillary Rodham Clinton (q.v.) 1975; one d.; ed Hot Springs High School, Ark., Georgetown Univ., Univ. Coll., Oxford, UK, Yale Law School; Prof., Univ. of Arkansas Law School 1974–76; Democratic nominee for US House of Reps from Third Ark. Dist 1974; Attorney-Gen. of Ark. 1977–79, Gov. of Ark. 1979–81, 1983–93; mem. counsel, Wright, Lindsey & Jennings (law firm) 1981–83; Pres. of USA, The White House, Washington, DC 1993–2001; impeached by US House of Reps for perjury and obstruction of justice Dec. 1998, acquitted in US Senate on both counts Jan. 1999; suspended from practising law in US Supreme Court 2001–06; UN Special Envoy for Tsunami Recovery 2005–07, to Haiti 2009–; Chair. Nat. Constitution Center, Philadelphia 2009–; headed mission to N Korea to free US journalists 2009; Chair. Southern Growth Policies Bd 1985–86; Chair. Nat. Govs Asscn 1987, Co-Chair. Task Force on Educ. 1990–91; Vice-Chair. Democratic Govs Asscn 1987–88, Chair. (elect) 1988–89, Chair. 1989–90; Chair. Educ. Comm. of the States 1987; Chair. Democratic Party Affirmative Action 1975, Southern Growth Policies Bd 1980; Chair. Democratic Leadership Council 1990–91; mem. US Supreme Court Bar, Bd of Trustees, Southern Center for Int. Studies of Atlanta, Ga; Chair. Bd of Dirs Global Fairness Initiative; Founder William J. Clinton Foundation, New York and Clinton Presidential Center, Ark.; Hon. Co-Chair. Club of Madrid; Hon. Fellow, Univ. Coll., Oxford 1992; Hon. DCL (Oxford) 1994; Hon. DLitt (Ulster) 1995; Dr hc (Northeastern Univ.) 1993, (Pace Univ.) 2006, (Univ. of New Hampshire) 2007; co-recipient TED (Tech. Entertainment Design) Prize 2007, ranked by Forbes magazine amongst The World's Most Powerful People (31st) 2009, (50th) 2011–12, (43rd) 2013. *Recordings include:* Peter and the Wolf: Wolf Tracks (Grammy Award, Best Spoken Word Album for Children (jtly) 2004) 2003, My Life (Grammy Award, Best Spoken Word Album) 2005. *Publications include:* Between Hope and History 1996, My Life (memoir) (British Book Award for Biography of the Year 2005) 2004, Giving: How Each of Us Can Change the World 2008, Back to Work: Why We Need Smart Government for a Strong Economy 2011. *Leisure interests:* jogging, swimming, golf, reading. *Address:* William J. Clinton Foundation, 55 West 125th

Street, New York, NY 10027; Clinton Presidential Center, 1200 President Clinton Avenue, Little Rock, AR 72201, USA. *Website:* www.clintonpresidentialcenter.org; www.clintonfoundation.org.

CLINTON-DAVIS, Baron (Life Peer), cr. 1990, of Hackney in the London Borough of Hackney; **Stanley Clinton-Davis,** PC, LLB; British politician, solicitor and international organization official; b. 6 Dec. 1928, London; s. of the late Sidney Davis and of Lily Davis; m. Frances Jane Lucas 1954; one s. three d.; ed Hackney Downs School, Bournemouth School, Mercers' School and King's Coll., London; fmr Councillor and Mayor, London Borough of Hackney; MP for Hackney Cen. 1970–83; Parl. Under-Sec. of State for Trade 1974–79; Opposition Spokesman for Trade 1979–81, for Transport, House of Lords 1990–97; Minister of State, Dept of Trade and Industry 1997–98; Deputy Opposition Spokesman for Foreign Affairs 1981–83; Commr EC for the Environment, Consumer Protection, Nuclear Safety, Forests and Transport 1985–86, for Environment, Transport and Nuclear Safety 1986–88; Chair. Refugee Council 1989–97, Advisory Cttee on Protection of the Sea 1989–97, 1998–2001 (Pres. 2001–03); consultant on European affairs and law, S. J. Berwin & Co. 1989–97, 1998–2003, European Cockpit Asscn 1995–97; Pres. Asscn of Metropolitan Authorities 1992–97, 1998–2003, Airfields Environment Fed. 1994–97, British Airline Pilots Asscn 1994–; Deputy Chair. Labour Finance and Industry Group 1993–; Fellow, King's Coll. and Queen Mary and Westfield Coll., London Metropolitan Univ.; Labour; Grand Cross, Order of Leopold II, for services to EC (Belgium) 1990; Dr hc (Polytechnical Inst., Bucharest) 1993; First Medal for Outstanding Services to Animal Welfare in Europe (Eurogroup for Animal Welfare) 1988. *Publication:* Good Neighbours? Nicaragua, Central America and the United States (co-author) 1982. *Leisure interests:* reading political biographies, golf. *Address:* House of Lords, Westminster, London, SW1A 0PW (office); 22 Bracknell Gate, Frognal Lane, Hampstead, London, NW3 7EP, England (home). *Telephone:* (20) 7435-0541 (home).

CLODUMAR, Kinza (Godfrey); Nauruan politician; b. 1944; entered parl. 1977; prin. financial adviser to Pres. 1992–95; Pres. of Nauru 1997–98, Jan.–May 2003; Minister of Finance several times between 1977–92, also 2003–04; Minister of the Environment 2004; fmr Chair. Nauru Insurance Corpn.

CLONINGER, Kriss, III, BBA, MBA; American insurance industry executive; *President and Chief Financial Officer, Aflac Inc.;* b. 21 Oct. 1947, Houston, Tex.; m. Lisa Cloninger (neé Welch); two c. two step-c.; ed Univ. of Texas, Austin; served as First Lt, USAF 1971–73; Consulting Actuary and Partner, Rudd & Wisdom, Austin, Tex. 1974–77; Prin., KPMG, Atlanta, Ga 1977–92; joined Aflac Inc. as Sr Vice-Pres. and Chief Financial Officer 1992, Sr Vice-Pres. 1992–93, Exec. Vice-Pres. 1993–2001, Pres. and Chief Financial Officer, Treas. and Dir 2001–; mem. Bd of Dirs Total System Services Inc., Tupperware Brands Corpn, RiverCenter for the Performing Arts, Historic Columbus Foundation, Little Blessings Nurturing Center, Columbus, Ga; Fellow, Soc. of Actuaries; named Best CFO in America (insurance/life category) by Institutional Investor magazine (three times). *Address:* Aflac Inc., 1932 Wynnton Road, Columbus, GA 31999, USA (office). *Telephone:* (706) 323-3431 (office). *Fax:* (706) 324-6330 (office). *E-mail:* info@aflac .com (office). *Website:* www.aflac.com (office).

CLOONEY, George Timothy; American actor and film director; b. 6 May 1961, Georgetown, Ky; s. of Nick Clooney and Nina Bruce (née Warren); m. Talia Blasam 1989 (divorced 1993); ed Northern Kentucky Univ.; acting debut on TV 1978; gained recognition by portraying Dr Douglas 'Doug' Ross on long-running medical drama ER 1994–99; Founder Section Eight (production co.) –2006; Co-founder Smoke House (production co.) 2006–; Chevalier des Arts et des Lettres 2007; Spirit of Independence Award 2005, Modern Master Award, Santa Barbara Film Festival 2006, American Cinémathèque Award 2006, Humanitarian Laureate, Robert F. Kennedy for Justice and Human Rights 2010. *Films include:* And They are Off 1982, Grizzly II: The Predator 1987, Return to Horror High 1987, Return of the Killer Tomatoes 1988, Red Surf 1990, Unbecoming Age 1992, The Harvest 1993, From Dusk Till Dawn 1996, Curdled 1996, One Fine Day 1996, Batman & Robin 1997, The Peacemaker 1997, Out of Sight 1998, The Thin Red Line 1998, South Park: Bigger Longer & Uncut (voice) 1999, Three Kings 1999, O Brother, Where Art Thou? (Golden Globe Award for Best Actor – Musical or Comedy 2000) 2000, The Perfect Storm 2000, Rock Star (exec. producer) 2001, Spy Kids 2001, Ocean's Eleven 2001, Insomnia (exec. producer) 2002, Far From Heaven (exec. producer) 2002, Welcome to Collinwood (also producer) 2002, Solaris 2002, Confessions of a Dangerous Mind (also dir) 2002, Spy Kids 3-D: Game Over 2003, Intolerable Cruelty 2003, Criminal (producer) 2004, Ocean's Twelve (also exec. producer) 2004, The Big Empty (exec. producer) 2005, The Jacket (producer) 2005, Good Night, and Good Luck (also dir, co-writer, Satellite Award for Best Original Screenplay 2005, Freedom Award, Critics' Choice Awards 2006, Best Director, Bratislava Film Festival 2005, several awards at Venice Film Festival 2005) 2005, Syriana (also producer, Golden Globe Award for Best Supporting Actor 2006, Acad. Award for Best Supporting Actor 2006) 2006, The Good German 2006, Ocean's Thirteen 2007, Michael Clayton (also exec. producer) (Best Actor, Nat. Bd of Review 2007) 2007, Leatherheads 2008, Burn After Reading 2008, Fantastic Mr Fox (voice) 2009, The Men Who Stare At Goats (also producer) 2009, Up in the Air (New York Film Critics Circle Award for Best Actor, Nat. Bd of Review Award for Best Actor) 2009, The American (also producer) 2010, Touch of Evil (short) 2011, The Ides of March 2011, The Descendants (Golden Globe Award for Best Performance by an Actor in a Motion Picture – Drama 2012) 2011, Gravity (also producer) 2012. *Television includes:* The Nick Clooney Show (series) 1968, Centennial (mini-series) 1978, Riptide (series) 1984, Street Hawk (series) 1984, E/R (series) 1984–85, The Facts of Life (series) 1985–86, Combat High (film) 1986, Roseanne (series) 1988–89, Knights of the Kitchen Table (film) 1990, Sunset Beat (series) 1990, Rewrite for Murder (film) 1991, Baby Talk (series) 1991, Bodies of Evidence (series) 1992–93, Sisters (series) 1993–94, ER (series) 1994–2009, Kilroy (film, writer and producer) 1999, Fail Safe (film, also exec. producer) 2000, K Street (series, exec. producer) 2003, Unscripted (series, dir and exec. producer) 2005, Hope for Haiti Now: A Global Benefit for Earthquake Relief (film, exec. producer) 2010, Memphis Beat (series, exec. producer) 2010–11. *Address:* c/o Bryan Lourd, Creative Artists Agency, 2000 Avenue of the Stars, Los Angeles, CA 90067, USA (office); Stan Rosenfield & Associates Ltd, 2029 Century Park East, Suite 1190, Los Angeles, CA 90067-2931, USA (office); Smoke House, Warner Bros, 4000 Warner Blvd, Bldg 15, Burbank, CA 91522. *Telephone:* (424) 288-2900 (office); (310) 286-

7474 (office); (818) 954-4840. *Fax:* (424) 288-2900 (office); (310) 286-2255 (office); (818) 954-4860. *Website:* www.caa.com (office).

CLOS, Joan; Spanish physician, politician, diplomatist and UN official; *Executive Director, United Nations Human Settlements Programme;* b. 29 June 1949, Parets del Vallés, Barcelona; m.; two c.; ed Universidad Autónoma de Barcelona, Univ. of Edinburgh, UK; worked as anaesthetist; apptd Dir of Public Health 1979; Chair. Spanish Soc. of Epidemiology and Healthcare Admin 1981–91; City Councillor, Barcelona 1983–87, Deputy Mayor in charge of Finance and Budgeting 1990–94; elected Councillor, Barcelona Council for Socialists' Party of Catalonia 1993; Mayor of Barcelona and Chair. Metropolitan Greater Area of Barcelona 1997–2006; apptd Pres. Metropolis 1998, World Asscn of Cities and Local Authorities 2000; Chair. UN Advisory Cttee of Local Authorities 2000–07; Minister of Industry, Tourism and Trade 2006–08; Amb. to Turkey and Azerbaijan 2008–10; Exec. Dir UN Human Settlements Programme 2010–; mem. Council of European Municipalities and Regions 1997–2003; Gold Medal, RIBA 1999, Scroll of Honour Award, UN Human Settlements Programme 2002. *Address:* United Nations Human Settlements Programme (UN-Habitat), POB 30030, Nairobi, Kenya (office). *Telephone:* (20) 621234 (office). *Fax:* (20) 624266 (office). *E-mail:* infohabitat@unhabitat.org (office). *Website:* www.unhabitat.org (office).

CLOSE, Chuck, BA, MFA; American artist; b. (Charles Thomas Close), 1940, Monroe, Wash.; ed Univ. of Washington, Seattle, Yale Univ., Akad. der Bildenen Kunste, Vienna, Austria; works in perm. collections of Museum of Modern Art, New York, Louisiana Museum of Modern Art, Denmark, Centres George Pompidou, Paris, France, Tate Modern, London, UK; works include Big Self-Portrait 1967–68, Self-Portrait/White Ink 1977, Phil/Fingerprint 1978, John/Color Fingerprint 1983, Georgia/Fingerpainting 1984, Leslie 1986, Self-Portrait (spitbite aquatint) 1988, Lucas (seven-step reduction block/linoleum cut print) 1988, Alex/ Reduction Block (silk screen print) 1993, Lucas/Rug 1993, Self-Portrait I 1999, Self-Portrait II 1999, Lyle (etching) 2000, Self-Portrait/Scribble/Etching Portfolio (etching) 2000, Emma (woodblock print) 2002; mem. American Acad. and Inst. of Arts and Letters 1992; Hon. DFA (Colby Coll., Me) 1994, (Univ. of Massachusetts) 1995, (Yale Univ.) 1996; Dr hc (Rhode Island School of Design) 1997; Acad.-Inst. Award in Art, American Acad. and Inst. of Arts and Letters 1991, Univ. of Washington Alumnus Summa Laude Dignatus 1997, Dieu Donné Art Award (jtly) 2000. *Address:* c/o PaceWildenstein, 32 East 57th Street, New York, NY 10022, USA (office). *Telephone:* (212) 421-3292. *Fax:* (212) 421-0835.

CLOSE, Glenn; American actress; b. 19 March 1947, Greenwich, Conn.; d. of William Close and Bettine Close; m. 1st Cabot Wade (divorced); m. 2nd James Marlas 1984 (divorced); one d. by John Starke; m. 3rd David Shaw 2006; ed William and Mary Coll.; joined New Phoenix Repertory Co. 1974; Co-owner The Leaf and Bean Coffee House, Bozeman, Mont. 1991–. *Stage appearances include:* Love for Love, The Rules of the Game, The Singular Life of Albert Nobbs, Childhood, Real Thing (Tony Award), King Lear, The Rose Tattoo, Benefactors, Death and the Maiden, Sunset Boulevard, A Streetcar Named Desire (Royal Nat. Theatre) 2002. *Films include:* The World According to Garp 1982, The Big Chill 1983, The Natural 1984, The Stone Boy 1984, Maxie 1985, Jagged Edge 1985, Fatal Attraction 1987, Dangerous Liaisons 1989, Hamlet 1989, Reversal of Fortune 1989, The House of Spirits 1990, Meeting Venus 1990, Immediate Family 1991, The Paper 1994, Mary Reilly 1994, Serving in Silence: The Margaret Cammermeyer Story 1995, 101 Dalmatians 1996, Mars Attacks! 1996, Air Force One 1997, Paradise Road 1997, Tarzan 1999, Cookie's Fortune 1999, 102 Dalmatians 2000, The Safety of Objects 2001, Pinocchio (voice) 2002, Le Divorce 2003, The Stepford Wives 2004, Heights 2004, Nine Lives 2005, The Chum-scrubber 2005, Tarzan II (voice) 2005, Hoodwinked (voice) 2006, Evening 2007, Hoodwinked Too!: Hood vs Evil (voice) 2011, Albert Nobbs 2011. *Television includes:* The Lion in Winter (Best Actress in a Miniseries or TV Movie, Golden Globe Awards 2005, Screen Actors Guild Awards 2005) 2004, The Shield (series) 2005, Damages (series) (Golden Globe for Best Actress in a TV series 2008, Emmy Award for Outstanding Lead Actress in a Drama Series 2009) 2007–, Pokémon 2010. *Address:* c/o Creative Artists Agency, 2000 Avenue of the Stars, Los Angeles, CA 90067, USA.

CLOSETS, François de; French writer, journalist and producer; b. 25 Dec. 1933, Enghien-les-Bains; s. of Louis-Xavier de Closets and Marie-Antoinette Masson; m. 1st Danièle Lebrun; one s.; m. 2nd Janick Jossin 1970; one s. one d.; ed Lycée d'Enghien, Faculté de Droit de Paris and Inst. d'Etudes Politiques, Paris; Ed. then special envoy of Agence France-Presse in Algeria 1961–65; scientific journalist, Sciences et Avenir 1964–, Acualités Télévisées 1965–68; contrib. L'Express 1968–69; Head of Scientific Service, TV Channel 1 1969–72; Head of Scientific and Tech. Service of TV Channel 2 1972; contrib. to Channel 1 1974; Asst Ed.-in-Chief TF1; Co-producer l'Enjeu (econ. magazine) 1978–88; Dir of Econ. Affairs, TF1 1987; Co-producer, Médiations magazine 1987–93; producer, illustrator Savoir Plus for France 2 1992–2000, Les Grandes Enigmes de la Science for France 2 1992–2003; Grand Prix du reportage du Syndicat des journalistes et écrivains 1966, Prix Cazes 1974, 7 d'or du meilleur journaliste 1985, Prix Aujourd'hui 1985, Roland Dorgelès Prize 1997. *Publications:* L'Espace, terre des hommes, La lune est à vendre 1969, En danger de progrès 1970, Le Bonheur en plus 1974, La France et ses mensonges 1977, Scénarios du futur (Vol. I) 1978, Le monde de l'an 2000 (Vol. II) 1979, Le Système EPM 1980, Toujours plus 1982, Tous ensemble pour en finir avec la syndicatrie 1985, La Grande Manip 1990, Tant et Plus 1992, Le Bonheur d'apprendre, et comment on l'assassine 1996, Le compte à Rebours 1998, L'Imposture informatique 2000, La dernière liberté 2001, Ne dites pas à Dieu ce qu'il doit faire 2004, Plus encore 2006, Le divorce français 2008, Zéro Faute: L'orthographe, une passion française 2009, L'échéance : Français, vous n'avez encore rien vu (with Irène Inchauspé) 2011, Le Monde était à nous (autobiog.) 2012. *Address:* c/o Editions Fayard, 13 rue de la Montparnasse, 75006 Paris, France (office). *E-mail:* fclosets@noos.fr (home).

CLOTET, Lluis; Spanish architect and designer; *Principal, Clotet, Paricio i Associats sl;* b. 31 July 1941, Barcelona; s. of Jaime Clotet and Concepción Clotet; ed Barcelona Escuela Técnica Superior de Arquitectura; worked for Federico Correa and Alfonso Milás's Studio 1961–64; co-f. (with Pep Bonet, Cristian Cirici and Oscar Tusquets) Studio PER 1964; co-f. B.D. Ediciones de Diseño; collaborator, XV Triennale de Milano 1973, Festival of Fine Architecture, Paris 1978, Transformations in Modern Architecture, Museum of Modern Art, New York

1979, Forum Design, Linz 1980, Biennale de Venezia 1980, The House as Image, Louisiana Museum of Modern Art 1981, The Presence of the Past, San Francisco 1982, Ten New Buildings, Inst. of Contemporary Art, London 1983, Contemporary Spanish Architecture, New York 1986; associated with with Ignacio Paricio 1983–; Prof. in Drawing, Barcelona Higher Tech. School in Architecture 1977–84; numerous prizes. *Major works include:* Banco España 1981–89, Water Cistern Ciutadella Park, Barcelona 1985–88, SIMON SA Bldg, Canovelles 1987–88, Museum of Art, Convent dels Angels, Barcelona (Restoration and extension plan) 1984–89, Teleport, Castellbisbal, Barcelona (plan) 1988, Sport Pavilion in Granada, 100 dwellings at the Olympic Village. *Address:* Clotet, Paricio i Associats sl, Pujades 63, 3.pl, 08005 Barcelona, Spain (office). *Telephone:* (93) 4853625 (office). *Fax:* (93) 3090567 (office). *E-mail:* cpa@coac.es (office).

CLOUGH, Ray William, Jr, ScD; American structural engineer and academic; *Byron and Elvira Nishkian Professor of Structural Engineering Emeritus, University of California, Berkeley;* b. 23 July 1920, Seattle; s. of Ray W Clough, Sr and Mildred Eva Nelson; m. Shirley Claire Potter 1942; one s. two d.; ed Univ. of Washington, Seattle, California Inst. of Tech., Pasadena, Calif. and Massachusetts Inst. of Tech., Cambridge, Mass.; served in USAF 1942–46; joined Civil Eng Faculty, Univ. of California, Berkeley as Asst Prof. of Civil Eng 1949, Assoc. Prof. 1954–59, Prof. 1959–83, Chair. Div. of Structural Eng and Structural Mechanics 1967–70, Byron and Elvira Nishkian Prof. of Structural Eng 1983–87, Prof. Emer. 1987–; consultant in structural eng specializing in structural dynamics, computer methods of structural analysis and earthquake eng 1953–; mem. US Army Corps of Engineers Structural Design Advisory Bd 1967–; mem. NAS, Nat. Acad. of Eng; Hon. mem. American Soc. of Civil Eng 1988; Research Prize, Howard Medal, Newmark Medal, Moisieff Medal, Th. von Karman Medal (American Soc. of Civil Engineers), George W. Housner Medal 1996, Prince Philip Medal, Royal Acad. of Eng 1997, Benjamin Franklin Medal in Civil Eng 2006. *Publication:* Dynamics of Structures (with J. Penzien) 1975, 1993. *Leisure interests:* skiing (cross-country) and hiking. *Address:* PO Box 4625, Sunriver, OR 97707-1625, USA (home). *Telephone:* (541) 593-5064 (home). *Fax:* (541) 593-2823 (home). *Website:* semm.berkeley.edu/index.htm (office).

CLUFF, Hon. Col John Gordon (Algy); British business executive; *Executive Chairman and CEO, Cluff Natural Resources Plc;* b. 19 April 1940, Bucklow, Cheshire, England; s. of the late Harold Cluff and of Freda Cluff; m. Blondel Hodge 1993; three s.; ed Stowe School; army officer, served W Africa, Cyprus, Malaysia 1959–64; Chief Exec. Cluff Resources (fmrly Cluff Oil) 1971, Chair. (and Chair. Zimbabwe) 1979, Chair. and CEO Cluff Mining 1996–2003 (acquired by Ashanti Goldfields), Exec. Chair. and CEO Cluff Gold plc 2004–10, Exec. Chair. 2010–11, Chair. (non-exec.) 2011–12, Chair. Cluff Geothermal Plc 2010–, Cluff Natural Resources Plc 2012–; Propr, The Spectator 1981–85, Chair. 1985–2004; Chair. Apollo Magazine Ltd 1985; Trustee Anglo-Hong Kong Trust 1989–, Stowe House Preservation Trust 1999–; Dir Centre for Policy Studies 1998–; Gov. Commonwealth Inst. 1995–, Chair. Conservative Comm. on the Commonwealth 2001; mem. Bd of Govs Stowe School 1998–; Chair. Trustees, War Memorial Trust 2003–. *Leisure interests:* collecting books and paintings, golf, shooting. *Address:* Cluff Natural Resources Plc, Third Floor, 5/8 The Sanctuary, Westminster, London, SW1P 3JS, England (office). *Telephone:* (20) 7887-2630 (office). *Fax:* (20) 7887-2639 (office). *E-mail:* admin@cluffnaturalresources.com (office). *Website:* www.cluffnaturalresources.com (office).

CLUTTON-BROCK, Timothy (Tim) Hugh, MA, PhD, ScD, FRS; British zoologist and academic; *Director of Research, Department of Zoology, University of Cambridge;* b. 13 Aug. 1946; fmrly Prince Philip Prof. of Ecology and Evolutionary Biology and Head of the Large Animal Research Group, Dept of Zoology, Univ. of Cambridge, currently Dir of Research; Fellow of Magdalene Coll.; also holds extraordinary professorships in Dept of Zoology and Entomology and Mammal Research Inst. of Univ. of Pretoria, South Africa; Co-founder Kalahari Meerkat Project; Frink Medal, Zoological Soc. of London 1997, Darwin Medal, Royal Soc. 2012. *Publications:* Readings in Sociobiology (co-ed.) 1978, Red Deer: Behavior and Ecology of Two Sexes (co-author) 1982, Rhum: The Natural History of an Island (Edinburgh Island Biology) (co-ed.) 1987, Reproductive Success: Studies of Individual Variation in Contrasting Breeding Systems (ed.) 1990, The Evolution of Parental Care 1991, Changes and Disturbance in Tropical Rainforest in SouthEast Asia (co-ed.) 2000, Wildlife Population Growth Rates (co-ed.) 2003, Soay Sheep: Dynamics and Selection in an Island Population (co-ed.) 2004, Meerkat Manor – The Story of Flower of the Kalahari 2007; numerous papers in professional journals. *Address:* Room T14, Department of Zoology, University of Cambridge, Downing Street, Cambridge, CB2 3EJ, England (office). *Telephone:* (1223) 336618 (office). *Fax:* (1223) 336676 (office). *E-mail:* thcb@cam.ac.uk (office). *Website:* www.zoo.cam.ac.uk (office).

CLUZEL, Jean, LenD; French politician and business executive; *President, Canal Académie;* b. 18 Nov. 1923, Moulins; s. of Pierre Cluzel and Jeanne Cluzel (née Dumont); m. Madeleine Bonnaud 1947; three s. one d.; ed Lycée de Vichy and Univ. of Paris; Pres. and Dir-Gen. Cluzel-Dumont 1947–71; Municipal Councillor St Pourcain/Sioule 1959–65; Admin., later Senator, Allier 1971, 1980, 1989; Conseiller Général, Moulins-Ouest 1967, 1973, 1979, 1985; Pres. Conseil Général, Allier 1970–76, 1985–92; Senator, Allier 1971, 1980, 1989; mem. l'Union Centriste, Spokesman and Vice-Pres. Comm. des Finances du Senat; Pres. Cttee for Econ. Expansion of Allier 1959–67; Pres. 'Positions' and 'L'Allier Demain', Fed. des Elus Bourbonnais 1972, Univ. Populaire de Bransat 1981, Comité Français pour l'Audiovisuel 1993; Dir Cahiers de l'audiovisuel 1994; Admin. France 2 1998, Singer Polignac Foundation 1999; Perm. Sec. Académie des Sciences Morales et Politiques 1999–2004, now mem. Morale et sociologie, Section II; Founder and Pres. Canal Académie, Institut de France (internet radio service) 2004–; Council mem. Admin. du conseil mondial pour la Radio et la Télévision; mem. Supervisory Cttee European Business School; Officier Légion d'honneur. *Publications:* Horizons Bourbonnais 1973, Les boutiques en colère 1975, Elu de peuple 1977, Télé Violence 1978, L'argent de la télévision 1979, Finances publiques et pouvoir local 1980, Les pouvoirs publics et la transmission de la culture 1983, Les pouvoirs publics et les caisses d'épargne 1984, Les anti-monarque de la Vème 1985, Un projet pour la presse 1986, La loi de 1987 sur l'épargne 1987, La télévision après six réformes 1988, Les finances locales decentralisées 1989, Le Sénat dans la société française 1990, Une ambition pour l'Allier 1992, Une autre bataille de France

1993, Mots pour Mots 1993, Pour qui sont ces tuyaux qui sifflent sur nos têtes? 1993, Feu d'artifices pour fin de législature 1993, L'age de la télévision 1993, Lettre à mes collègues représentants du peuple 1993, Education, culture et télévision 1994, Du modèle canadien à l'appel sud-africain 1996, L'audiovisuel en Europe centrale et orientale 1996, La télévision 1996, Presse et démocratie 1997, L'indispensable Sénat 1998, A propos du Sénat et de ceux qui voudraient en finir avec lui 1999, Anne de France 2002, Propos impertinents sur le cinéma français 2003. *Address:* Canal Académie, 23, quai Conti, 75006 Paris; 12 villa Dupont, 75116 Paris (home); c/o L'Académie des Sciences Morales et Politiques, 23, quai Conti, 75006 Paris, France. *Website:* www.canalacademie.com.

CLUZEL, Jean-Paul, MA; French government official; *President, Etablissement public de la Réunion des musées nationaux et du Grand Palais des Champs-Elysées;* b. 29 Jan. 1947, Paris; ed Ecole Nationale d'Admin, Institut d'Études Politiques de Paris, Pantheon-Assas Paris II Univ., Univ. of Chicago, USA; lived in Paris suburb of Le Kremlin-Bicêtre until 1961; Insp. of Finance 1972–76, 1981–82; adviser to Minister of Foreign Affairs 1979–81, adviser for Africa at Treasury Dept 1982–84; with insurance group GAN 1985–92, responsible for research and devt and int. affairs; Gen. Man. and Dir of the Paris Opera 1992–95; CEO Radio France Internationale 1995–2004; CEO Radio France 2004–09; Pres. Radios francophones publiques 2009–; Pres. Etablissement public de la Réunion des musées nationaux et du Grand Palais des Champs-Elysées (administers 34 nat. museums under authority of Ministry of Culture) 2009–; mem. Bd of Dirs Agence France-Presse, Arte France, Médiamétrie (polling org.), Théâtre du Châtelet; Officier, Légion d'honneur, Ordre nat. du Mérite; Commdr des Arts et des Lettres; Offizierkreuz, Verdienstkreuz 1. Klasse (Germany); Kt, Order of Infante Dom Enrique (Portugal). *Address:* Réunion des Musées Nationaux, 254/256 rue de Bercy, 75577 Paris Cedex 12, France (office). *Telephone:* 1-40-13-48-00 (office). *Fax:* 1-40-13-44-00 (office). *E-mail:* info@rmn.fr (office). *Website:* www.rmn.fr (office); www.grandpalais.fr (office).

CLUZET, François; French actor; b. 21 Sept. 1955, Paris; four c. and one s. with actress Marie Trintignant; ed acting lessons at Cours Simon and Cours de Périmony et Cochet; Prix Jean Gabin 1984. *Films include:* Un enfant sans histoire 1979, Cocktail Molotov 1980, Le cheval d'orgueil (The Horse of Pride) 1980, Les fantômes du chapelier (The Hatter's Ghost) 1982, Coup de foudre (Between Us) 1983, L'Été meurtrier (One Deadly Summer) 1983, Les enragés 1985, Elsa, Elsa 1985, États d'âme 1986, 'Round Midnight (Autour de minuit) 1986, Rue du Départ 1986, Association de malfaiteurs 1987, Chocolat 1988, Une affaire de femmes (Story of Women) 1988, Deux (Two) 1989, Un tour de manège (Roundabout) 1989, Force majeure (Uncontrollable Circumstances) 1989, Trop belle pour toi (Too Beautiful for You) 1989, La Révolution française (The French Revolution) 1989, Olivier, Olivier 1992, A demain (See You Tomorrow) 1992, L'Instinct de l'ange 1993, L'Enfer (Hell) 1994, Le vent du Wyoming (Wind from Wyoming) 1994, Prêt-à-Porter (Ready to Wear) 1994, French Kiss (Paris Match) 1995, Le hussard sur le toit (The Horseman on the Roof) 1995, Enfants de salaud (Bastard Brood) 1996, Le silence de Rak (Best Actor Award, Paris Film Festival 1996) 1997, Rien ne va plus (The Swindle) 1997, La Voie est libre 1998, Fin août, début septembre (Late August, Early September) 1998, Dolce far niente (Sweet Idleness) 1998, L'Examen de minuit (Midnight Exam) 1998, L'Adversaire (The Adversary) 2002, Quand je vois le soleil 2003, Janis et John (Janis and John) 2003, Je suis un assassin (The Hook) 2004, Le domaine perdu (The Lost Domain) 2005, La cloche a sonné 2005, Ne le dis à personne (Tell No One) (César Award for Best Actor 2007, Étoile d'Or for Best Actor 2007) 2006, Ma place au soleil (My Place in the Sun) 2007, La vérité ou presque 2007, Détrompez-vous 2007, Les liens du sang (Rivals) 2008, Paris 2008, Les liens du sang 2008, À l'origine 2009, The Intouchables 2011. *Television includes:* Au théâtre ce soir (episode Madame Jonas dans la baleine) 1977, Histoires de voyous: l'élégant 1979, Chère Olga 1980, Le gros oiseau 1981, Le boulanger de Suresnes 1981, Paris-Saint-Lazare (mini-series) 1982, Julien Fontanes, magistrat (episode Perpète) 1983, Un manteau de chinchilla 1983, Le bout du lac 1984, Série noire (episode Aveugle, que veux-tu?) 1984, La mèche en bataille 1984, Manipulations 1984, Sueurs froides (episode À la mémoire d'un ange) 1988, Lucas 1993, Sweet home 1995, L'huile sur le feu 1996, Le goût des fraises 1998, La cape et l'épée (episode La mise à mort) 1999, Les enfants du printemps (mini-series) 2000, L'Algérie des chimères (mini-series) 2001, Un mois à nous 2002, La famille Guérin (series) 2002, Vénus & Apollon (Venus and Apollo (episode Soin ultime) 2005, Quatre étoiles (Four Stars) 2006. *Address:* c/o Isabelle de la Patellière, VMA, 20 avenue Rapp, 75007 Paris, France (home). *Telephone:* 1-43-17-37-00. *Fax:* 1-47-20-15-86. *E-mail:* d.leprestre@vma.fr. *Website:* www.vma.fr.

CLWYD, Rt Hon. Ann, PC; British politician, journalist and broadcaster; b. 21 March 1937; d. of Gwilym Henri Lewis and Elizabeth Ann Lewis; m. Owen Dryhurst Roberts 1963; ed Holywell Grammar School, The Queen's School, Chester and Univ. Coll., Bangor; fmr BBC studio man., freelance reporter and producer; Welsh corresp. The Guardian and The Observer 1964–79; Vice-Chair. Welsh Arts Council 1975–79; mem. Royal Comm. on NHS 1976–79, Arts Council of GB 1975–80; various public and political appointments; MEP for Mid- and West Wales 1979–84; MP (Labour) for Cynon Valley 1984–; Opposition Front Bench Spokesperson on Women 1987–88, on Educ. 1987–88; Shadow Sec. of State on Overseas Devt and Co-operation 1989–92, on Wales 1992, for Nat. Heritage 1992–93; Opposition Front Bench Spokesperson on Employment 1993–94, on Foreign Affairs 1994–95; mem. Select Cttee on Int. Devt 1997–, on Foreign Affairs 2010–; Chair. All-Party Group on Human Rights 1997–; Chair. INDICT 1997–2003; Prime Minister's Special Envoy on Human Rights in Iraq 2003–10; apptd by Prime Minister to lead review into Nat. Health Service Complaints Procedure 2013–; Hon. Fellow, North East Wales Inst. of Educ. 1996, Univ. of Wales, Bangor 2004; White Robed Bard of the Nat. Eisteddfod 1991; Hon. LLD (Univ. of Wales) 2007. *Address:* House of Commons, Westminster, London, SW1A 0AA, England (office); 6 Dean Court, Dean Street, Aberdare, Mid Glamorgan, CF44 7BN, Wales (office). *Telephone:* (1685) 871394 (Aberdare) (office); (20) 7219-6609 (London) (office). *Fax:* (20) 7219-5943 (London) (office); (1685) 883006 (Aberdare) (office). *E-mail:* clwyda@parliament.uk (office). *Website:* www.parliament.uk (office).

CLYNE, Cameron; Australian banking executive; *Executive Director, Managing Director and Group CEO, National Australia Bank;* Man. Partner, PricewaterhouseCoopers financial services consulting practice across Asia-Pacific 1993–2005, also worked in their financial services practices in New York; Exec. Gen., Group Devt, National Australia Bank Group 2005–07, Man. Dir and CEO Bank of New Zealand 2007–09, Exec. Dir, Man. Dir and Group CEO National Australia Bank 2009–, Chair. National Australia Group Europe Ltd 2012–; selected as a Young Global Leader by the World Econ. Forum 2008. *Address:* National Australia Bank Ltd, 500 Bourke Street, Melbourne, Victoria 3000, Australia (office). *Telephone:* (3) 8641-3500 (office). *Fax:* (3) 9208-5695 (office). *E-mail:* info@nabgroup.com (office). *Website:* www.nabgroup.com (office).

COAKLEY, Rev. Sarah Anne, MA, ThM, PhD; British academic; *Norris-Hulse Professor of Divinity, University of Cambridge;* b. 10 Sept. 1951, London; d. of F. Robert Furber and Anne McArthur; m. James F. Coakley 1975; two d.; ed Blackheath High School for Girls, New Hall, Cambridge and Harvard Divinity School, USA; Lecturer in Religious Studies, Univ. of Lancaster 1976–90, Sr Lecturer 1990–91; Tutorial Fellow in Theology and Univ. Lecturer, Oriel Coll., Oxford 1991–93; Prof. of Christian Theology, The Divinity School, Harvard Univ., USA 1993–95, Edward Mallinckrodt, Jr, Prof. of Divinity 1995–2007; Norris-Hulse Professor of Divinity, Univ. of Cambridge 2007–; Harkness Fellowship 1973–75; Select Preacher, Univ. of Oxford 1991; Visiting Professorial Fellow, Princeton Univ., USA 2003–04; Hon. DTheol (Lund); Hulsean Prize, Univ. of Cambridge 1977, Hulsean Lecturer, Univ. of Cambridge 1991–92, Hulsean Preacher 1996, Samuel Ferguson Lecturer, Univ. of Manchester 1997, Riddell Lecturer, Univ. of Newcastle 1999, Tate-Wilson Lecturer, Southern Methodist Univ. 1999, Prideaux Lecturer, Univ. of Exeter 2000, Jellema Lecturer, Calvin Coll. 2001, Stone Lecturer, Princeton Theological Seminary 2002, Cheney Lecturer, Berkeley Divinity School at Yale 2002, Reynolds Lecturer, Princeton Univ. 2005, Hensley Henson Lecturer, Univ. of Oxford 2005. *Publications:* Christ Without Absolutes: A Study of the Christology of Ernst Troeltsch 1988, The Making and Remaking of Christian Doctrine (co-ed. with David Pailin) 1993, Religion and the Body (ed.) 1997, Powers and Submissions: Spirituality, Philosophy and Gender 2002, Re-thinking Gregory of Nyssa (ed) 2003, Pain and its Transformations: The Interface of Biology and Culture (co-ed.) 2007, Praying for England: Priestly Presence in Contemporary Culture (co-ed with Sam Wells) 2008, Re-thinking Dionysis the Areopagite (co-ed with Charles M. Stang) 2009; contribs to Church of England Doctrine Comm. Reports 1987, 1991; articles in theological journals. *Leisure interests:* musical activities, thinking about the garden. *Address:* Faculty of Divinity, West Road, Cambridge, CB3 9BS, England (office). *Telephone:* (1223) 763002 (office). *Fax:* (1223) 763003 (office). *E-mail:* faculty-office@divinity.cam.ac .uk (office). *Website:* www.divinity.cam.ac.uk (office).

COATES, Anne Voase, OBE; British film editor and producer; b. 12 Dec. 1925, Reigate, Surrey; m. Douglas Hickox (deceased); two s. one d.; ed Bartrum Gables Coll.; worked as nurse, East Grinstead Plastic Surgery Hosp.; Gov., American Acad. of Motion Pictures; Woman in Film Crystal Awards Int. Award 1997, Lifetime Achievement Award, American Cinema Eds 1998, Woman in Film and TV Awards Channel Four Lifetime Achievement Award 2000, BAFTA Fellowship 2007. *Films edited include:* Pickwick Papers 1952, Grand National Night 1953, Forbidden Cargo 1954, To Paris With Love 1955, The Truth About Women 1957, The Horse's Mouth 1958, Tunes of Glory 1960, Don't Bother to Knock 1961, Lawrence of Arabia (Academy Award 1962) 1962, Becket 1964, Young Cassidy 1965, Those Magnificent Men in their Flying Machines (co-ed.) 1965, Hotel Paradiso 1966, Great Catherine 1968, The Adventurers 1970, Friends 1971, The Public Eye 1972, The Nelson Affair 1973, 11 Harrowhouse 1974, Murder on the Orient Express 1974, Man Friday 1975, Aces High 1976, The Eagle Has Landed 1976, The Legacy 1978, The Elephant Man 1980, The Pirates of Penzance 1983, Greystoke: The Legend of Tarzan, Lord of the Apes 1984, Lady Jane 1986, Raw Deal 1986, Masters of the Universe 1987, Farewell to the King (co-ed.) 1989, Listen to Me 1989, I Love You to Death 1990, What About Bob? 1991, Chaplin 1992, In the Line of Fire (Guild of British Film Eds Award) 1993, Pontiac Moon 1994, Congo 1995, Striptease 1996, Out to Sea 1997, Out of Sight 1998, Passion of Mind 2000, Erin Brockovich 2000, Sweet November 2001, Unfaithful 2002, Taking Lives 2004, Catch and Release 2006, The Golden Compass 2007, Extraordinary Measures 2009; producer The Medusa Touch 1978; The Aviator (cameo role) 2005. *Leisure interests:* cinema, theatre, travelling, horseback riding, swimming, skiing. *Address:* 8455 Fountain Avenue, Apartment 621, Los Angeles, CA 90069 (office); c/o United Talent Agency, 9560 Wilshire Blvd, Beverly Hills, CA 90210, USA (office). *Telephone:* (323) 654-7282 (home). *Fax:* (323) 654-4574 (home).

COATES, John Dowling, AC; Australian lawyer and business executive; *President, Court of Arbitration for Sport;* b. 7 May 1950, Sydney, NSW; Special Counsel, Kemp Strang Lawyers. Sydney; Pres. Australian Olympic Cttee 1990–; Council mem. Int. Rowing Fed. 1992–; mem. Int. Council of Arbitration for Sport 1994–, Vice-Pres. 1995–2010, Pres. 2011–, Pres. Court of Arbitration for Sport 2011–; mem. IOC 2001–, Exec. Bd 2009–, Juridical, TV Rights and New Media, 2012 London and 2016 Rio Olympic Games Coordination Comms. *Address:* Court of Arbitration for Sport, Château de Béthusy, Avenue de Beaumont 2, 1012 Lausanne, Switzerland (office). *Telephone:* (21) 613-50-00 (office). *Fax:* (21) 613-50-01 (office). *E-mail:* info@tas-cas.org (office). *Website:* www.tas-cas.org (office).

COATES, John Henry, BA, PhD, FRS; Australian mathematician and academic; *Sadleirian Professor Emeritus of Pure Mathematics, University of Cambridge;* b. 26 Jan. 1945, New South Wales; s. of J. H. Coates and B. L. Lee; m. Julie Turner 1966; three s.; ed Australian Nat. Univ., Ecole Normale Supérieure, Paris, France, Univ. of Cambridge, UK; Asst Prof., Harvard Univ., USA 1969–72; Assoc. Prof. (with tenure), Stanford Univ., USA 1972–75; Lecturer, Univ. of Cambridge, UK 1975–77, Sadleirian Prof. of Pure Math. 1986–2012, Prof. Emer. 2012–, Head of Dept of Pure Math. and Math. Statistics 1991–97; Prof., ANU 1977–78, Université de Paris XI (Orsay) 1978–85; Prof. and Dir of Math., Ecole Normale Supérieure, Paris 1985–86; Professorial Fellow, Emmanuel Coll., Cambridge 1975–77, 1986–; Vice-Pres. Int. Math. Union 1991–95; Fellow, Academia Europa 2008; Dr hc (Ecole Normale Supérieure) 1997, (Heidelberg) 2012; Senior Whitehead Prize 1997. *Leisure interest:* reading, early Japanese porcelain, Oriental art. *Address:* Emmanuel College, Cambridge, CB2 3AP (office); Department of Pure Mathematics and Mathematical Statistics, University of Cambridge, Wilberforce Road, Cambridge, CB3 0WB, England (office). *Telephone:* (1223) 337989 (office). *E-mail:* j.h.coates@dpmms.cam.ac.uk (office). *Website:* www.dpmms.cam.ac.uk (office).

COATS, Daniel Ray (Dan), BA, JD; American lawyer, politician and diplomatist; *Senator from Indiana;* b. 16 May 1943, Jackson, Mich.; s. of Edward R. Coats and Vera E. Coats; m. Marsha Ann Crawford 1965; one s. two d.; ed Wheaton Coll., Ill., Univ. of Indiana; served in US Army 1966–68; Asst Vice-Pres. and Counsel, Mutual Security Life Insurance Co., Fort Wayne, Ind. 1969–75; called to Bar of Ind. 1972; mem. US House of Reps from 4th Dist of Ind. 1981–89; Dist Rep. for Congressman Dan Quayle (q.v.) 1976–80; apptd to fill seat vacated by Senator Quayle following Quayle's election as Vic-Pres. of USA 1988, won 1990 special election to serve remainder of Quayle's unexpired term, as well as 1992 election for full six-year term, Senator from Indiana 1989–99, 2011–, mem. Appropriations Cttee, Energy and Natural Resources Cttee, Select Cttee on Intelligence, Jt Econ. Cttee; Special Counsel, Verner, Liipfert, Bernhard, McPherson & Hand 1999–2001; Amb. to Germany 2001–05; Sr Policy Advisor, Govt Advocacy and Public Policy Practice Group, King & Spalding LLP, Washington, DC 2005–10; fmr lobbyist, Pharmaceutical Research and Mfrs of America; mem. Bd of Trustees American Inst. For Contemporary German Studies 2005–; mem. Bd of Dirs IPALCO, Lear Siegler Services Inc., Int. Republic Inst., The Empowerment Network; Pres. Big Brothers/Big Sisters of America, Ind.; Republican. *Publication:* Mending Fences: Renewing Justice Between Government and Civil Society 1998. *Address:* 493 Russell Senate Office Building, Washington, DC 20510 (office); Indianapolis Office, 1650 Market Tower, 10 West Market Street, Indianapolis, IN 46204, USA (office). *Telephone:* (202) 224-5623 (DC) (office); (317) 554-0750 (Indianapolis) (office). *Fax:* (202) 228-1820 (DC) (office). *Website:* coats.senate.gov (office).

COBBOLD, Rear Adm. Richard, CB, FRAeS; British fmr research institute director and military analyst; served in RN 1961–94, first as seaman officer and helicopter observer, commanded frigates HMS Mohawk and HMS Brazen, then Capt. of 2nd Frigate Squadron in HMS Brilliant; promoted Rear Adm. 1991; Asst Chief Defence Staff Operational Requirements for Sea Systems –1994, ACDS (Jt Systems) 1992–94; mem. Royal Coll. of Defence Studies 1984; Dir of Defence Concepts, Ministry of Defence 1987; Dir Royal United Services Inst. for Defence Studies 1994–2007 (retd); apptd specialist adviser to House of Commons Defence Cttee 1997; Gov., London Nautical School. *Publications:* numerous articles on defence and security issues. *Address:* c/o Royal United Services Institute for Defence Studies, Whitehall, London, SW1 2ET, England.

COBEN, Harlan, BA; American writer; b. 4 Jan. 1962, Newark, NJ; m. Anne Armstrong 1988; two s. two d.; ed Amherst Coll.; mem. MWA (pres. 2008–09), Sisters in Crime. *Publications:* novels: Play Dead 1990, Miracle Cure 1991, Deal Breaker (World Mystery Conference Anthony Award for Best Paperback Original Novel 1996) 1995, Drop Shot 1996, Fade Away (MWA Edgar Award for Best Paperback Original Mystery Novel, Shamus Award for Best Paperback Original Novel, Private Eye Writers of America 1997) 1996, Back Spin 1997, One False Move (WH Smith Fresh Talent Award) 1997, The Final Detail 1999, Darkest Fear 2000, Tell No One 2001, Gone For Good (WH Smith Thumping Good Read Award) 2002, No Second Chance 2003, Just One Look 2004, The Innocent 2005, Promise Me 2006, The Woods 2007, Hold Tight 2008, Long Lost 2009, Caught 2010, Shelter 2011, Live Wire 2011, Seconds Away 2012, Stay Close 2012, Six Years 2013; short stories: A Simple Philosophy 1999, The Key to My Father 2003. *Address:* Aaron Priest Literary Agency, 708 Third Avenue, New York, NY 10017, USA (office). *E-mail:* me@harlancoben.com (office). *Website:* www.harlancoben.com.

COBOS, Julio César Cleto; Argentine engineer and politician; *Vice-President;* b. 30 April 1955, Mendoza; m María Cristina Cerutti; one s two d; ed Universidad Tecnológica Nacional; taught at Universidad Tecnológica Nacional and at Universidad Nacional de Cuyo, Universidad de Mendoza, Dean of Prov. Faculty of Universidad Tecnológica Nacional 1997–2003; joined Unión Cívica Radical 1991, has been involved in Mendoza local politics since early 1990s; Minister of Environment and Public Works, Mendoza Prov. 1999–2000; Gov. of Mendoza Prov. (in a coalition with Recrear Liberals and Federalists) 2003–07; Vice-Pres. of Argentina 2007–. *Publications include:* Principios fundamentales de la hidráulica, Materias integradoras en ingeniería civil. *Address:* c/o Office of the President, Balcarce 50, C1064AAB, Buenos Aires, Argentina (office). *E-mail:* dgi@presidencia .gov.ar (office). *Website:* www.presidencia.gov.ar (office).

COBURN, Thomas (Tom) Allen, BS, MD; American physician, obstetrician and politician; *Senator from Oklahoma;* b. 14 March 1948, Muskogee, Okla; m. Carolyn Coburn 1968; three c.; ed Oklahoma State Univ.; fmr Pres. Coll. of Business Student Council, Oklahoma State Univ.; Mfg Man., Ophthalmic Div., Coburn Optical Industries (family-owned co.), Colonial Heights, Va 1970–78; trained as physician 1978–83; internship in gen. surgery, St Anthony's Hosp., Oklahoma City 1983–84; family practice residency, Univ. of Arkansas, Fort Smith 1984–86; family practice physician, specialising in obstetrics and allergy, Muskogee 1986–94; mem. US House of Reps from Okla 2nd Dist, Washington, DC 1995–2001, mem. House Commerce Cttee; Co-Chair. Pres.'s Advisory Council on HIV/AIDS 2001–; f. Family Caucus; Senator from Okla 2005–; mem. Ark. Medical Soc., Okla Medical Asscn, American Medical Asscn, American Acad. of Otolaryngic Allergy, American Acad. of Family Practice; Republican. *Publication:* Breach of Trust: How Washington Turns Outsiders Into Insiders (with John Hart) 2003. *Address:* 172 Russell Senate Office Building, Washington, DC 20510, USA (office). *Telephone:* (202) 224-5754 (office). *Fax:* (202) 224-6008 (office). *Website:* coburn.senate.gov (office).

COCCOPALMERIO, HE Cardinal Francesco, LTh, DCL; Italian ecclesiastic and academic; *President, Pontifical Council for Legislative Texts;* b. 6 March 1938, San Giuliano Milanese; ed Pontifical Gregorian Univ., Università Cattolica del Sacro Cuore, Milan; ordained priest, Archdiocese of Milan 1962; Prof. of Canon Law, Faculty of Theology, northern Italy 1966–99; Prof., Faculty of Canon Law, Pontifical Gregorian Univ. 1981–; apptd Auxiliary Bishop of Milan and Titular Bishop of Coeliana 1993; Titular Archbishop of Coeliana 2007; mem. Supreme Tribunal of the Apostolic Signatura 2000–, Congregation for the Doctrine of the Faith 2010–; Pres. Pontifical Council for Legis. Texts 2007–13, 2013–; cr. Cardinal (Cardinal-Deacon of San Giuseppe dei Falegnami) 2012; participated in Papal Conclave 2013. *Address:* Pontifical Council for Legislative Texts, Palazzo delle Congregazioni, Piazza Pio XII 10, 00193 Rome, Italy (office). *Telephone:* (06) 69884008 (office). *Fax:* (06) 69884710 (office). *E-mail:* info@vatican.va (office). *Website:* www.vatican.va (office).

COCHRAN, (William) Thad, BA, JD; American politician; *Senator from Mississippi*; b. 7 Dec. 1937, Pontotoc, Miss.; s. of William Holmes Cochran and Emma Grace Cochran (née Berry); m. Rose Clayton 1964; two c.; ed Univ. of Mississippi and School of Law, Univ. of Dublin, Ireland; served as Lt in USNR 1959–61; called to the Bar 1995, pvt. law practice in Jackson, Miss. 1965–72; mem. US House of Reps, Washington, DC 1973–78; Senator from Miss. 1979–, Sec. Republican Conf. 1985–90, Chair. Republican Conf. 1990–96, mem. Agric., Nutrition and Forestry Cttee, Appropriations Cttee, Govt Affairs Cttee, Rules and Admin. Cttee and Select Cttee on Indian Affairs; mem. Bd of Dirs US Naval Acad.; mem. Bd of Regents, Smithsonian Inst.; fmr Pres. Young Lawyers' section of Miss. State Bar; fmr Chair. Miss. Law Inst.; mem. ABA; Trustee, Kennedy Center, Washington, DC; Republican; Dr hc (Kentucky Wesleyan Coll., Mississippi Coll., Blue Mountain Coll., Univ. of Richmond, Tougaloo Coll.). *Address:* 113 Dirksen Senate Office Building, Washington, DC 20510-2402, USA (office). *Telephone:* (202) 224-5054 (office). *Website:* cochran.senate.gov (office).

COCHRANE, John H., SB, PhD; American economist; *AQR Capital Management Professor of Finance, Booth School of Business, University of Chicago*; m. Elizabeth Fama; two s. two d.; ed Massachusetts Inst. of Tech., Univ. of California, Berkeley; Jr Economist, Council of Econ. Advisors 1982–83; Asst Prof., Dept of Econs, Univ. of Chicago 1985–90, Assoc. Prof. 1990–94, Prof. of Finance and Econs, Booth School of Business 1994–, currently AQR Capital Man. Prof. of Finance; Visiting Prof., UCLA Anderson School of Man. 2000–01; Consultant, Research Dept, Fed. Reserve Bank of Chicago 1995–; Research Assoc., Nat. Bureau of Econ. Research; Adjunct Scholar, Cato Inst., Washington, DC; Ed. Journal of Political Economy 1998–2003; Assoc. Ed. of several journals including Journal of Monetary Economics, Journal of Business, Journal of Economic Dynamics and Control; Fellow, Econometric Soc. 2001–; mem. American Finance Asscn (Pres. 2010); Chookaszian Endowed Risk Man. Prize. *Publications:* Asset Pricing (TIAA-CREF Inst. Paul A. Samuelson Award). *Leisure interests:* windsurfing. *Address:* Graduate School of Business, University of Chicago, 1101 E. 58th St, Chicago, IL 60637-1610, USA (office). *Telephone:* (773) 7020-3059 (office). *E-mail:* john.cochrane@gsb .uchicago.edu (office). *Website:* www.chicagobooth.edu/faculty (office).

COCKBURN, William, CBE, TD, FRSA; British business executive; b. 28 Feb. 1943, Edinburgh, Scotland; joined Post Office 1961, Personal Asst to Chair. 1971–73, Asst Dir of Planning and Finance 1973–77, Dir Cen. Finance Planning 1977–78, Dir Postal Finance 1978–79, Dir London Postal Region 1979–82, mem. Bd 1981–95, Man. Dir Royal Mail 1986–92, Chief Exec. The Post Office 1992–95; Chair. Int. Post Corpn 1994–95; Group Chief Exec., WH Smith Group PLC 1995–97; Group Man. Dir British Telecommunications PLC 1997–2001; Chair. Parity Group PLC 2001–04; Deputy Chair. UK Mail Group PLC 2002–; Deputy Chair. AWG PLC 2003–06, now Dir (non-exec.); Dir (non-exec.) Watkins Holdings Ltd 1985–93, Lex Service PLC 1993–2002, Centrica PLC 1997–99; Dir Business in the Community 1990–; Chair. Schoolteachers' Review Body 2002–08; Chair. Senior Salaries Review Body 2008–; Pres. Inst. of Direct Marketing 2001–05; Dir non-Exec. Army Bd; Fellow, Chartered Inst. of Transport; Freeman, City of London. *Address:* c/o Board of Directors, UK Mail Group plc, Express House, Wolseley Drive, Heartlands, Birmingham, B8 2SQ (office); 9 Avenue Road, Farnborough, Hants., GU14 7BW, England (home). *Telephone:* (1753) 706070 (office). *E-mail:* ws.cockburn@btinternet.com (office).

COCKER, James Cecil; Tongan economist, politician and diplomatist; m. Malia Cocker; eight c.; fmr Minister of Finance 1982–91, of Works and Disasters Relief Activities, of Marines, of Police, of Labour and Commerce, fmr Deputy Prime Minister and Minister of Internal Affairs; Consul-Gen. in San Francisco 2006–10. *Address:* c/o Consulate-General of Tonga, 360 Post St, Suite 604, San Francisco, CA 94108, USA (office).

CODRON, Sir Michael Victor, Kt, CBE, MA; British theatre producer; b. 8 June 1930, London, England; s. of Isaac A. Codron and Lily Codron (née Morgenstern); ed St Paul's School, Worcester Coll., Oxford; Dir Aldwych Theatre (also Owner), Hampstead Theatre, Royal Nat. Theatre; known for his productions of the early work of Harold Pinter, Christopher Hampton, David Hare, Simon Gray and Tom Stoppard; Cameron Mackintosh Prof., Univ. of Oxford 1993; mem. Bd of Trustees, Oxford School of Drama; Laurence Olivier Award for Lifetime Achievement. *Plays:* has produced over 300 shows in West End, London including: The Birthday Party 1958, The Caretaker 1960, The Killing of Sister George, Little Malcolm and his Struggle against the Eunuchs, Big Bad Mouse 1966, The Boyfriend (revival) 1967, A Voyage Round My Father, The Homecoming (revival), Dr. Faustus, The Dresser, Three Sisters, Uncle Vanya, The Cherry Orchard 1989, Man of the Moment, Private Lives 1990, The Rise and Fall of Little Voice 1992, Time of My Life, Jamais Vu 1993, Kit and the Widow, Dead Funny, Arcadia, The Sisters Rosensweig 1994, Indian Ink, Dealer's Choice 1995, The Shakespeare Revue 1996, A Talent to Amuse 1996, Tom and Clem 1997, Silhouette 1997, Heritage 1997, Things We Do For Love, The Invention of Love, Alarms and Excursions 1998, Copenhagen 1999, Quartet, Comic Potential 1999, Peggy for You 2000, Blue/Orange 2001, Life After George 2002, Bedroom Farce 2002. *Film:* Clockwise 1986. *Leisure interest:* collecting Caroline of Brunswick memorabilia. *Address:* Aldwych Theatre Offices, Aldwych, London, WC2B 4DF (office); 12 Tower Bridge Wharf, London, E1 9UR, England (home). *Telephone:* (20) 7240-8291 (office); (20) 7925-6243. *Fax:* (20) 7240-8467 (office); (20) 7240-8467.

COE, Jonathan, BA, MA, PhD; British writer; b. 19 Aug. 1961, Birmingham, England; m. Janine McKeown 1989; two d.; ed Trinity Coll., Cambridge, Univ. of Warwick; fmr legal proofreader; Chevalier, Ordre des Arts et des Lettres 2004. *Publications:* The Accidental Woman 1987, A Touch of Love 1989, The Dwarves of Death 1990, Humphrey Bogart: Take It and Like It 1991, James Stewart: Leading Man 1994, What A Carve Up! (John Llewellyn Rhys Prize 1995, Prix du Meilleur Livre Étranger 1996) 1994, The House of Sleep (Writers' Guild Best Fiction Award 1997, Prix Médicis Étranger 1998) 1997, The Rotters' Club (Bollinger Everyman Wodehouse Prize 2001, Premio Arcebispo Juan de San Clemente 2004) 2001, The Closed Circle 2004, Like a Fiery Elephant: The Story of B. S. Johnson (BBC Four Samuel Johnson Prize for non-fiction 2005) 2004, The Rain Before It Falls (Prix de l'Europe de la médiathèque de Bussy Saint-Georges 2010) 2007, The Terrible Privacy of Maxwell Sim 2010, Expo 58 2013; contrib. to periodicals. *Address:* c/o Peake Associates, 14 Grafton Crescent, London, NW1 8SL, England (office).

COE, Baron (Life Peer), cr. 2000, of Ranmore in the County of Surrey; **Sebastian Newbold Coe**, CH, KBE, OBE, BSc; British fmr politician and fmr athlete; *Chairman, British Olympic Association*; b. 29 Sept. 1956, London, England; s. of Peter Coe and Angela Coe; m. Nicola Susan Elliott 1990; two s. two d.; ed Univ. of Loughborough; competed in Olympic Games, Moscow 1980, won Gold Medal at 1500m and Silver Medal at 800m and repeated this in Los Angeles 1984; European Jr Bronze Medallist at 1500m 1975; European Bronze Medallist at 800m 1978; European Silver Medallist at 800m 1982; European 800m Champion 1986; held world records at 800m, 1000m, 1500m and mile; est. new records at 800m, 1000m and mile 1981; mem. 4×400m world record relay squad 1982; only athlete to hold world records at 800m, 1000m, 1500m and mile simultaneously; Pres. first athletes' del. to IOC, Baden-Baden 1981 and mem. first athletes' comm. set up after Congress by IOC 1981–; Conservative MP for Falmouth and Camborne 1992–97; mem. Employment Select Cttee 1992–94, Nat. Heritage Select Cttee 1995–97; Parl. Pvt. Sec. to Chancellor of Duchy of Lancaster 1994–95, to Michael Heseltine 1995–96; Jr Govt Whip 1996–97; Deputy Chief of Staff then Pvt. Sec. to William Hague, Leader of the Opposition 1997–2001; Chair. Diadora UK 1987–94, ADT Health Quest Charitable Trust 1991–; Vice-Chair. Sports Council 1986–89, Sports Aid Trust 1987; Vice-Chair. London 2012 Olympic Games Bid 2003–04, Chair. and Pres. London 2012 Olympic and Paralympic Bid 2004–05, London Organizing Cttee of the Olympic Games and Paralympic Games (in 2012) 2005–12; Chair. British Olympic Asscn 2012–; Chair. FIFA Ethics Cttee 2006–; Vice-Pres. Int. Asscn of Athletics Feds; mem. Health Educ. Authority 1987–92, Health Educ. Council (now Authority) 1986–, Council IAAF 2003–; Vice-Patron Sharon Allen Leukemia Trust 1987–, Olympic Cttee Medical Comm. 1987–95, Sport for All Comm. 1997–; Admin. Steward, British Boxing Bd of Control 1995–; Global Adviser NIKE 2000–; Founding mem. World Sports Acad. 2000–; sports columnist, Daily Telegraph 2000–; Trustee, Youth Sports Trust, British Univ. in Egypt, Sebastian Coe Foundation; Hon. D. Tech. (Loughborough) 1985; Hon. DSc (Hull) 1988; Hon. LLB (Sheffield) 1991; BBC Sports Personality of 1979, Sir John Cohen Memorial Award 1981, Príncipe de Asturias Award (Spain) 1987, BBC Sports Personality of the Year Special Award 2005, BBC Sports Personality of the Year Lifetime Achievement Award 2012. *Publications:* Running Free (with David Miller) 1981, Running for Fitness 1983, The Olympians 1984, More Than a Game 1992, Born to Run (autobiog.) 1992. *Leisure interests:* jazz, theatre, reading, some writing. *Address:* British Olympic Association, 60 Charlotte Street, London, W1T 2NU (office); House of Lords, Westminster, London, SW1A 0PW; Head Office, London 2012, One Churchill Place, Canary Wharf, London, E14 5LN, England. *Telephone:* (20) 7842-5700 (BOA) (office); (20) 7219-5353 (House of Lords); (20) 3201-2000 (London 2012). *E-mail:* boa@boa.org.uk (office). *Website:* www.teamgb .com (office); www.parliament.uk/biographies/lords/sebastian-coe/26649; www .london2012.com.

COELHO, Paulo; Brazilian writer; b. 24 Aug. 1947, Rio de Janeiro; m. Christina Oiticica; ed law school; worked as a dir, theatre actor, songwriter and journalist; collaborated with Brazilian composer and singer Raúl Seixas; imprisoned for alleged subversive activities against Brazilian Govt 1974; made pilgrimage to Santiago de Compostela, Spain 1986; regular columnist for O Globo (newspaper) 2007– and other newspapers world-wide; elected mem. Brazilian Acad. of Arts 2002–, UN Messenger of Peace 2007–; Chevalier, Ordre des Arts et des Lettres 1996, Comendador de Ordem do Rio Branco 1998, Chevalier, Légion d'honneur 2000, Order of St Sophia (Ukraine) 2004, Cruz do Mérito do Empreendedor Juscelino Kubitschek 2006; numerous awards, including Prix Lectrices d'Elle, France 1995, Golden Book Awards, Yugoslavia 1995, 1996, 1997, 1998, 1999, 2000, Flaiano Int. Award, Italy 1996, Super Grinzane Cavour Book Award, Italy 1996, Golden Medal of Galicia, Spain 1999, Crystal Mirror Award, Poland 2000, XXIII Premio Internazionale Fregene, Italy 2001, Bambi Award, Germany 2001, Budapest Prize, Hungary 2005, Goldene Feder Award, Germany 2005, Religion Communicators Council Wilbur Award, USA 2006, Premio Alava en el Corazón, Spain 2006, Asscn of Mexican Booksellers Pergolas Prize 2006, Distinction of Honour from the City of Odense (Hans Christian Andersen Award), Denmark 2007, best selling foreign book in Poland 2007, Best Int. Writer Award, ELLE Awards (Spain) 2008, Guinness World Record for the Most Translated Author for the same book (The Alchemist) 2009. *Publications:* Arquivos do inferno 1982, O Diário de um mago (trans. as The Pilgrimage, aka The Diary of a Magus: The Road to Santiago) 1987, O Alquimista (trans. as The Alchemist) 1988, Brida 1990, O Dom Supremo (trans. as The Gift) 1991, As Valkírias (trans. as The Valkyries) 1992, Maktub 1994, Na margem do rio Piedra eu sentei e chorei (trans. as By the River Piedra I Sat Down and Wept) 1994, Frases 1995, O Monte Cinco (trans. as The Fifth Mountain) 1996, Cartas de Amor do Profeta (trans. as Love Letters from a Prophet) 1997, Manual do guerreiro da luz (trans. as Manual of the Warrior of Light) 1997, Veronika decide morrer (trans. as Veronika Decides to Die) 1998, Palavras essenciais (trans. as The Confessions of a Pilgrim) 1999, O demônio e a Srta Prym (trans. as The Devil and Miss Prym) 2000, Histórias para pais, filhos e netos (trans. as Fathers, Sons and Grandsons) 2001, Onze minutos (trans. as Eleven Minutes) 2003, O Gênio e as Rosas (trans. as The Genie and the Roses, juvenile) 2004, O Zahir (trans. as The Zahir) (Kiklop Literary Award, Croatia 2006, Austrian Booksellers' Platin Book Award 2006) 2005, Like the Flowing River (thoughts and short stories) 2006, A Bruxa do Portobello (trans. as The Witch of Portobello) (EMPiK's Ace Award) 2006, O Vencedor está Só (trans. as The Winner Stands Alone) 2008, O Aleph (trans. as The Aleph) 2010, Manuscrito encontrado em Accra (trans. as Manuscript Found in Accra) 2012. *Address:* c/o Sant Jordi Asociados Agencia Literaria SL, Paseo García Faria, 73–75, 08019 Barcelona, Spain (office). *Telephone:* (93) 2240107 (office). *Fax:* (93) 3562696 (office). *E-mail:* readers@santjordi-asociados.com (office); paulo@paulocoelho.com (office). *Website:* www.santjordi-asociados.com (office); www.paulocoelho.com (home).

COËME, Guy; Belgian politician; *Mayor of Waremme*; b. 21 Aug. 1946, Waremme; m.; two c.; ed Univ. of Liège; mem. Nat. Office, Parti Socialiste (PS) 1970–74, Vice-Pres. PS 1983–; Deputy Mayor, Waremme 1971–74, 1982–87; Prov. Councillor, Liège 1971–74; Deputy, Liège 1974–81, Huy-Waremme 1982–; Burgomaster, Waremme 1987–; Sec. of State for the Wallonne Region, with responsibility for the Environment and Planning 1981–82; Minister-Pres. Wallonne Regional Exec., with responsibility for Water, Rural Devt, Conservation and Admin. Feb.–May 1988; Minister of Nat. Defence 1988–92; Deputy Prime Minister and Minister of Communications and Public Services 1992–94 (resgnd); convicted in government bribery case and received suspended sentenced 1998; cand. in regional elections Huy-Waremme 2004; Pres. Soc. for the Regional Devt of Wallonne 1978; Vice-Pres. Socialist Party 1983; Admin. Soc. for Regional Investment in Wallonne 1979. *Address:* Office of the Mayor, Rue Joseph Wauters, 2, Waremme, Belgium (office). *E-mail:* guy.coeme@waremme.be (office). *Website:* www.waremme.be (office).

COEN, Enrico Sandro, CBE, PhD, FRS, FLS; British geneticist; *Project Leader, Department of Cell and Developmental Biology, John Innes Centre;* b. 29 Sept. 1957, Southport, Lancs.; s. of Ernesto Coen and Dorothea Coen (née Cattani); m. Lucinda Poliakoff 1984; two s. one d.; ed King's Coll., Cambridge; joined John Innes Centre, Norwich 1984, Project Leader 1995–98, Deputy Head Dept of Genetics 1998–2000, Project Leader, Dept of Cell and Developmental Biology 2000–; Foreign Assoc. mem. NAS 2001; Corresp. mem. Botanical Soc. of America 2003; Hon. Lecturer Univ. of E Anglia 1989, Hon. Reader 1994, Hon. Prof. 1998; EMBO Medal, Rome 1996, Science for Art Prize, Paris 1996, Linnean Gold Medal, London 1997, Darwin Medal (jtly), Royal Soc. 2004. *Publications include:* The Art of Genes 1999, Cells to Civilizations 2012; 80 articles in int. scientific research journals. *Leisure interests:* painting, children. *Address:* John Innes Centre, Norwich Research Park, Norwich, NR4 7UH, England (office). *Telephone:* (1603) 450000 (office). *Fax:* (1603) 450045 (office). *E-mail:* enrico.coen@jic.ac.uk (office). *Website:* www.jic.ac.uk (office).

COEN, Ethan; American film producer and screenwriter; b. 21 Sept. 1957, St Louis Park, Minn.; s. of Ed Coen and Rena Coen; brother of Joel Coen (q.v.); m.; ed Princeton Univ.; screenwriter (with Joel Coen) Crime Wave (fmrly XYZ Murders); producer, screenplay; ed. Blood Simple 1984; Dan David Prize (with Joel Coen), Tel-Aviv Univ. 2011. *Films include:* Raising Arizona 1987, Miller's Crossing 1990, Barton Fink (Palme d'Or, Cannes Festival) 1991, The Hudsucker Proxy 1994, Fargo 1996, The Naked Man, The Big Lebowski 1998, O Brother, Where Art Thou? 2000, The Man Who Wasn't There 2001, A Fever in the Blood 2002, Intolerable Cruelty 2003, The Ladykillers 2004, Paris, je t'aime (segment) 2006, No Country for Old Men (Best Film, Nat. Bd of Review 2007, Academy Awards for Best Film, Best Direction, Best Adapted Screenplay 2008) 2007, Burn After Reading 2008, A Serious Man 2009, True Grit 2010, Inside Llewyn Davis (Best Dir (with Joel Coen), Best Film, Nat. Soc. of Film Critics) 2013. *Publication:* Gates of Eden 1998. *Address:* c/o United Talent Agency, 9336 Civic Center Drive, Beverly Hills, CA 90210, USA (office). *Telephone:* (310) 273-6700 (office). *Fax:* (310) 247-1111 (office). *Website:* www.unitedtalent.com (office).

COEN, Joel Daniel; American film director and screenwriter; b. 29 Nov. 1954, St Louis Park, Minn.; s. of Ed Coen and Rena Coen; brother of Ethan Coen (q.v.); m. (divorced); ed Simon's Rock Coll. and New York Univ.; Asst Ed. Fear No Evil, Evil Dead; worked with rock video crews; screenwriter (with Ethan Coen) Crime Wave (fmrly XYZ Murders); Dan David Prize (with Ethan Coen), Tel-Aviv Univ. 2011. *Films include:* (with Ethan Coen): Blood Simple 1984, Raising Arizona 1987, Miller's Crossing 1990, Barton Fink (Palme d'Or, Cannes Festival) 1991, The Hudsucker Proxy 1994, Fargo (Best Dir Award, Cannes Int. Film Festival 1996) 1996, The Big Lebowski 1998, O Brother, Where Art Thou? 2000, The Man Who Wasn't There 2001, Intolerable Cruelty 2003, The Ladykillers 2004, Paris, je t'aime (segment) 2006, No Country for Old Men (Best Film, Nat. Bd of Review 2007, Academy Awards for Best Film, Best Direction, Best Adapted Screenplay 2008) 2007, Burn After Reading 2008, A Serious Man 2009, True Grit 2010, Inside Llewyn Davis (Best Dir (with Ethan Coen), Best Film, Nat. Soc. of Film Critics) 2013. *Address:* c/o United Talent Agency, 9336 Civic Center Drive, Beverly Hills, CA 90210, USA (office). *Telephone:* (310) 273-6700 (office). *Fax:* (310) 247-1111 (office). *Website:* www.unitedtalent.com (office).

COENE, Luc; Belgian government official and central banker; *Governor, National Bank of Belgium;* b. 11 March 1947, Ghent; ed Ghent Univ., Coll. of Europe, Bruges; with Research Dept and Foreign Dept, Nat. Bank of Belgium 1973–79, Adviser to Head of Foreign Dept 1992–95, Vice-Gov. 2003–11, Gov. 2011–; Asst Belgian Admin., IMF 1979–85; Deputy Chef de Cabinet to Minister of Finance 1985; Chef de Cabinet to Vice-Premier and Minister for the Budget 1988; Visiting Scholar, IMF 1988; Econ. Adviser, DG II, EC 1989–92; Senator 1995–99; Chef de Cabinet to the Prime Minister and Sec. to the Council of Ministers 1999–2001, Chair. Chancellery of the Prime Minister and Sec. of the Council of Ministers 2001–03; Minister of State 2003–; mem. Bd of Dirs Nat. Accounts Inst. 2011–; mem. Governing Council and Gen. Council, European Central Bank 2011–; Dir, BIS 2011–; mem. Bd Govs and High Council of Finance, G-10 2006–; Chair. Public Sector Borrowing Requirements Dept 2006–; mem. Bureau of the High Council of Finance 2006–; mem. Exec. Cttee King Baudouin Foundation, Madariaga European Foundation; Chair. Fulbright Fund Man. Cttee; Deputy Chair. Exec. Bd, Théâtre Royal de la Monnaie/Koninklijke Muntschouwburg. *Address:* Banque Nationale de Belgique/Nationale Bank van België, 14 boulevard de Berlaimont, 1000 Brussels, Belgium (office). *Telephone:* (2) 221-20-96 (office). *Fax:* (2) 221-32-10 (office). *E-mail:* pressoffice@nbb.be (office). *Website:* www.nbb .be (office).

COETZEE, J(ohn) M(axwell), MA, PhD; South African/Australian writer and academic; b. 9 Feb. 1940, Cape Town; one s. one d.; ed Univ. of Cape Town, Univ. of Texas, USA; Asst Prof. of English, State Univ. of NY (SUNY), Buffalo 1968–71; Lecturer, Univ. of Cape Town 1972–76, Sr Lecturer 1977–80, Assoc. Prof. 1981–83, Prof. of Gen. Literature 1984–2001; Visiting Prof. of Humanities, Univ. of Adelaide, Australia 2002–; Prof. of Social Thought, Univ. of Chicago, USA 1995–2000, Distinguished Service Prof. 2001–03; Chevalier, Ordre des Arts et des Lettres, Ridder van de Orde van de Leeuw (Netherlands), Order of Mapungubwe (South Africa); Dr hc (Oxford) 2002; Nobel Prize for Literature 2003. *Publications:* Dusklands 1974, In the Heart of the Country 1977, Waiting for the Barbarians 1980, Life and Times of Michael K (Booker-McConnell Prize 1983, Prix Femina Etranger 1985) 1983, Foe 1986, White Writing 1988, Age of Iron (Sunday Express Book of the Year Prize 1990) 1990, Doubling the Point: Essays and Interviews (ed. by David Atwell) 1992, The Master of Petersburg (Premio Mondello 1994, Irish Times Int. Fiction Prize 1995) 1994, Giving Offence: Essays on Censorship 1996, Boyhood 1997, The Lives of Animals (lecture) 1999, Disgrace (Booker Prize 1999, Commonwealth Writers Prize 2000) 1999, The Humanities in Africa 2001, Stranger Shores: Essays 1986–1999 2001, Youth 2002, Elizabeth Costello: Eight Lessons 2003, Slow Man (novel) 2005, Inner Workings (essays) 2007, Diary of a Bad Year (novel) 2007, Summertime (fiction) 2009, Scenes from Provincial Life

2011, The Childhood of Jesus (novel) 2013. *Address:* PO Box 3045, Newton, SA 5074, Australia (office). *E-mail:* john.coetzee@adelaide.edu.au (home).

COEY, John Michael David, DSc, FRS; Irish physicist and academic; *Erasmus Smith's Professor of Natural and Experimental Philosophy, Trinity College Dublin;* b. 24 Feb. 1945, Belfast, Northern Ireland; s. of David S. Coey and Joan E. Newsam; m. Wong May 1973; two s.; ed Tonbridge School, Jesus Coll. Cambridge, UK and Univ. of Manitoba, Canada; Chargé de Recherches, CNRS, Grenoble 1974–78; Lecturer/Prof., Trinity Coll. Dublin 1978–, Prof. of Experimental Physics 1987–2007, Erasmus Smith's Prof. of Natural and Experimental Philosophy 2007–, Head, Dept of Physics 1989–92; Visiting Scientist, IBM Research Center, Yorktown Heights, NY 1976–77, 1988, Univ. of Bordeaux 1984, Centre d'Etudes Nucléaires de Grenoble 1985–86, Johns Hopkins Univ. Applied Physics Lab. 1986, Univ. de Paris 7 1992, Univ. of California, San Diego 1997, Florida State Univ. 1998; Co-inventor, thermopiezic analyser 1986, nitromag 1990; Chief Coordinator, Concerted European Action on Magnets 1987–94; Dir Magnetic Solutions Ltd 1994–; mem. Academic Cttee Magnetism Lab. Inst. of Physics, Beijing 1988–; mem. Royal Irish Acad., Vice-Pres. 1989; mem. Fulbright Fellow 1997–98; Fellow, American Physical Soc. 2000; Foreign Assoc. NAS 2005; Hon. DSc (Inst. Nat. Polytechnique de Grenoble) 1994; Charles Chree Prize and Medal, Inst. of Physics, London, Gold Medal, Royal Irish Acad. 2005, Humboldt Prize 2013. *Publications:* Magnetic Glasses (with K. Moorjani) 1984, Structural and Magnetic Phase Transitions in Minerals (with S. Ghose and E. Salje) 1988, Rare-Earth Iron Permanent Magnets 1996, Permanent Magnetism (with R. Skomski) 1999, Magnetism and Magnetic Materials 2010; numerous papers on magnetic and electronic properties of solids. *Leisure interest:* gardening. *Address:* Department of Physics, University of Dublin Trinity College, Dublin 2 (office); Hillbrook House, Castleknock, Dublin 15, Ireland (home). *Telephone:* (1) 8961470 (office). *Fax:* (1) 6711759 (office). *E-mail:* jcoey@tcd.ie (office). *Website:* www.tcd.ie/Physics (office).

COFFEY, Rev. David Roy, OBE, BA; British Baptist leader and minister of religion; *Global Ambassador, BMS World Mission;* b. 13 Nov. 1941, Purley, Surrey, England; s. of Arthur Coffey and Elsie Maud Willis; m. Janet Anne Dunbar 1966; one s. one d.; ed Spurgeon's Coll., London; ordained to Baptist ministry 1967; Minister, Whetstone Baptist Church, Leicester 1967–72, N Cheam Baptist Church, London 1972–80; Sr Minister, Upton Vale Baptist Church, Torquay 1980–88; Sec. for Evangelism, Baptist Union of GB 1988–91, Gen. Sec. 1991–2005; Pres. Baptist Union 1986–87; Vice-Pres. European Baptist Fed. 1995–97, Pres. 1997–99; Vice-Pres. Baptist World Alliance 2000–05, Pres. 2005–10; Free Churches Moderator and Co-Pres. Churches Together in England 2003–07; Vice-Pres. Council for Christians and Jews 2009–; Chair. Spurgeon's Coll. Council 2012–; Global Amb. for BMS World Mission 2009–; Patron Embrace 2008–; Hon. DD (Dallas Baptist Univ.) 2008, (Palmer Seminary) 2009. *Publications:* Build That Bridge: A Study in Conflict and Reconciliation 1986, Discovering Romans: A Crossway Bible Guide 2000, Joy to the World 2008, All One in Christ Jesus 2009. *Leisure interests:* grandchildren, music, soccer, bookshops, Elgar Soc. *Address:* BMS World Mission, Baptist House, 129 Broadway, Didcot, Oxon., OX11 8XA, England (office). *Telephone:* (1235) 517604 (office).

COFFEY, Shelby, III; American journalist; *Vice-Chairman, Newseum;* m. Mary Lee Coffey; ed Univ. of Virginia; with Washington Post 1968–85, later Asst Man. Ed. for nat. news and Deputy Man. Ed. for features; Ed. US News and World Report 1985–86; fmr Sr Vice-Pres. and Ed. Dallas Times Herald; Deputy Assoc. Ed. Los Angeles Times 1986–88, Exec. Ed. 1988–89, Ed. and Exec. Vice-Pres. 1989–97; Pres. CNN Business News and CNNfn 1999–2001; fmr Exec. Vice-Pres. ABC News; apptd Sr Fellow, Freedom Forum Foundation 2001, currently Vice-Chair. Newseum; Bd mem. Pacific Council on International Policy; mem. Council on Foreign Relations, International Press Inst.; Nat. Press Foundation Ed. of the Year 1994, Ida B. Wells Award 1995. *Publications:* The Art of Leadership in News Organizations. *Address:* Newseum, 555 Pennsylvania Avenue, NW, Washington, DC 20001, USA (office). *Telephone:* (888) 639-7386 (office). *E-mail:* info@newseum .org (office). *Website:* www.newseum.org (office).

COFFMAN, Robert L., AB, PhD; American medical scientist and business executive; *Vice-President and Chief Scientific Officer, Dynavax Technologies;* ed Indiana Univ., Univ. of California, San Diego; fmr Postdoctoral Fellow, Stanford Univ. Medical School; joined DNAX Research Inst. 1981, later Distinguished Research Fellow; Vice-Pres. and Chief Scientific Officer, Dynavax Technologies 2000–; mem. NAS 2006; William S. Coley Award for Research in Immunology (jtly with Dr Tim Mosmann of Univ. of Rochester). *Achievements include:* made fundamental discoveries about the regulation of immune responses in allergic and infectious diseases including discovery of the TH1 and TH2 subsets of T-lymphocytes, the two major types of T-cells that control immune responses. *Address:* Dynavax Technologies, 2929 Seventh Street, Suite 100, Berkeley, CA 94710, USA (office). *Telephone:* (510) 848-5100 (office). *Fax:* (510) 848-1327 (office). *E-mail:* contact@dynavax.com (office). *Website:* www.dvax.com (office).

COFFMAN, Vance D., BS, MS, PhD; American aerospace company executive (retd); b. 3 April 1944; m. Arlene Coffman; two d.; ed Iowa State Univ., Stanford Univ.; joined Lockheed Corpn as guidance and control systems analyst, Space Systems Div. (led devt of several major space programmes) 1967, apptd Div. Vice-Pres. 1985, Div. Vice-Pres. and Asst Gen. Man. 1987, Div. Pres. (responsible for Hubble Space Telescope and MILSTAR satellite communications programme) 1988, Pres. Space Systems Div. Lockheed Missiles & Space Co. and Vice-Pres. Corpn, Exec. Vice-Pres. Corpn –1995; Pres. and COO Space & Strategic Missiles Sector, Lockheed Martin Corpn (following merger of Lockheed and Martin Marietta Corpns) 1995, Pres., COO and Exec. Vice-Pres. –1997, Vice-Chair. 1997–98, CEO 1997–2004, Chair. 1998–2005 (retd); mem. Bd of Dirs Bristol-Myers Squibb 1998, United Negro Coll. Fund 2001, 3M Co. 2002; mem. Nat. Acad. of Eng, Security Affairs Support Asscn; Fellow, American Astronomical Soc. 1991, AIAA 1996; Hon. Dr Aerospace Eng (Embry-Riddle Univ.) 1998; Hon. DEng (Stevens Inst. of Tech.) 1998; Hon. LLD (Pepperdine Univ.) 2000; Professional Progress in Engineering Award, Iowa State Univ. 1989, Distinguished Achievement Citation, Iowa State 1999, Rear Admiral John J. Bergen Industry Award, New York Council of the Navy League 2000, Fleet Admiral Chester W. Nimitz Award, Navy League of USA 2001, Executive of the Year, Washington Techway 2001, Bob Hope

Distinguished Citizen Award, Nat. Defense Industrial Asscn (Los Angeles Chapter) 2002. *Address:* POB 1785, Pebble Beach, CA 93953, USA.

COHAN, Robert Paul, CBE; British choreographer; b. 27 March 1925; s. of Walter Cohan and Billie Cohan; ed Martha Graham School, New York; Partner, Martha Graham School 1950, Co-Dir Martha Graham Co. 1966; Artistic Dir Contemporary Dance Trust Ltd, London 1967–; Artistic Dir and Prin. Choreographer, London Contemporary Dance Theatre 1969–87, Founder-Artistic Dir 1987–89; Artistic Adviser, Batsheva Co., Israel 1980–89; Dir York Univ., Toronto Choreographic Summer School 1977, Gulbenkian Choreographic Summer School, Univ. of Surrey 1978, 1979, 1982 and other int. courses; Gov. Contemporary Dance Trust; Ed., Choreography and Dance (journal) 1988–; Chair. Robin Howard Foundation; with London Contemporary Dance Theatre has toured Europe, S. America, N Africa, USA; maj. works created: Cell 1969, Stages 1971, Waterless Method of Swimming Instruction 1974, Class 1975, Stabat Mater 1975, Masque of Separation 1975, Khamsin 1976, Nympheas 1976, Forest 1977, Eos 1978, Songs, Lamentations and Praises 1979, Dances of Love and Death 1981, Agora 1984, A Mass for Man 1985, Ceremony 1986, Interrogations 1986, Video Life 1986, Phantasmagoria 1987, A Midsummer Night's Dream 1993, The Four Seasons 1996, Aladdin 2000; Hon. Fellow, York Univ., Toronto; Hon. DLitt (Exeter Univ.) 1993, (Univ. of Kent) 1996; Dr. hc (Middx) 1994, (Winchester) 2006; Evening Standard Award for outstanding achievement in ballet 1975, Soc. of West End Theatres Award for outstanding achievement in ballet 1978, UK Dance Critics Circle Award for Lifetime Achievement 2005. *Publication includes:* The Dance Workshop 1986. *Leisure interest:* dancing. *Address:* Saussine, Bouquet, Lussan 30580, France.

COHEN, Abby Joseph, BA, MS, CFA; American economist and investment bank executive; *Senior Investment Strategist and President, Global Markets Institute, Goldman Sachs Group, Inc.;* b. 29 Feb. 1952, Queens, New York; d. of Raymond Joseph Cohen and the late Shirley Joseph (née Silverstein); m. David M. Cohen 1973; two d.; ed Martin Van Buren High School, Cornell Univ., George Washington Univ.; Jr Economist, Fed. Reserve Bd, Washington, DC 1973–76; Economist/ Analyst, T. Rowe Price Assocs, Baltimore, Md 1976–83; Investment Strategist, Drexel Burnham Lambert, New York 1983–90, BZW, New York 1990; Investment Strategist, Goldman, Sachs & Co. 1990–, Man. Dir 1996–, Man. Pnr 1998–, Chair. Investment Policy Cttee, also Chief US Portfolio Strategist, currently Sr Investment Strategist and Pres. Global Markets Inst.; Chair. Inst. of Chartered Financial Analysts; mem. Bd Govs Nat. Economists Club, New York Soc. of Security Analysts; Vice-Chair. Asscn for Investment Man. Research; mem. Nat. Asscn of Business Economists; Trustee/Fellow, Cornell Univ.; Trustee Jewish Theological Seminary of America; Woman Achiever (Woman of the Year) Award, YWCA, New York 1989, ranked 19th by Forbes magazine amongst 100 Most Powerful Women 2005. *Address:* Goldman Sachs Group, Inc., 85 Broad Street, New York, NY 10004, USA (office). *Telephone:* (212) 902-1000 (office). *Fax:* (212) 902-3000 (office). *Website:* www.goldmansachs.com (office).

COHEN, Ben; American business executive; *President, TrueMajority.org;* b. 1951, Brooklyn, NY; ed Calhoun High School, Merrick, LI, Colgate Univ., Skidmore Coll., New School, NY, NY Univ.; various jobs whilst studying pottery and jewellery, including pottery wheel delivery person, paediatric emergency room clerk, taxi cab driver; fmr craft therapist intern, Jacobi Hosp., Bronx, New York and Grand Street Settlement House, Manhattan; craft teacher, Highland Community School, Paradox, NY 1974–77; Co-founder Ben & Jerry's Homemade Inc. (with Jerry Greenfield) 1977, opened first Ice Cream Parlour in Burlington, Vt 1978, held various positions including Marketing Dir, Salesperson, Pres., CEO and Chair., est. Ben & Jerry's Foundation (to oversee donation of 7.5% of profits to non-profit orgs), co. sold to Unilever; f. TrueMajority.org (non-profit educ. and advocacy group); Founding mem. Businesses for Social Responsibility (org. that promotes socially responsible business practices); mem. numerous non-profit orgs; Corp. Giving Award, Council on Econ. Priorities 1988, US Small Business Persons of the Year, US Small Business Admin 1988. *Publications include:* Ben & Jerry's Homemade Ice Cream and Dessert Book (co-author with Jerry Greenfield) 1987. *Address:* TrueMajority.org, 1825 K St., NW, Suite 210, Washington, DC 20006, USA (office). *Telephone:* (802) 735-9110 (office). *Website:* www.truemajority.org (office).

COHEN, Bernard Woolf, DFA; British artist and academic; *Slade Professor Emeritus, University College London;* b. 28 July 1933, London; m. Jean Britton 1959; one s. one d.; ed South West Essex School of Art, St Martin's School of Art, London and Slade School of Fine Art, London; held teaching appointments at several art schools 1957–67; teacher of painting and drawing, Slade School of Fine Art 1967–73, 1977; Visiting Prof., Univ. of New Mexico 1969–70, faculty alumni 1974; Guest Lecturer, Royal Coll. of Art 1974–75; Visiting Artist, Minneapolis School of Art 1964, 1969, 1971, 1975, Ont. Coll. of Art 1971, San Francisco Art Inst., Univ. of Victoria, BC 1975; has lectured at several Canadian univs since 1969; fmrly Principal Lecturer (Painting), Wimbledon School of Art 1980–84; Slade Prof., Chair. of Fine Art, Univ. Coll. London 1988–2000, Prof. Emer. 2000–, Fellow, Univ. Coll. London 1992; Hon. DFA (Univ. of London, Slade School). *Publications:* articles and statements in journals and catalogues. *Leisure interests:* music, cinema, travel, museums. *Address:* 80 Camberwell Grove, London, SE5 8RF, England (home). *Telephone:* (20) 7708-4480 (home). *Fax:* (20) 7708-4480 (home). *E-mail:* bwc44@hotmail.com (home). *Website:* wwwflowerseast.com (office).

COHEN, Jared, BA, MPhil; American author and fmr government official; *Director, Google Ideas;* b. 24 Nov. 1981, Weston, Conn.; m. Rebecca Zubaty; ed Stanford Univ., Univ. of Oxford, UK; mem. Policy Planning Staff, Office of the Sec. of State, US Dept of State, Washington, DC (fmr adviser to Condoleezza Rice and Hillary Clinton) 2006–10; Dir Google Ideas, Google, Inc. 2010–; Adjunct Sr Fellow, Council on Foreign Relations; mem. jury, Tribeca Film Festival; Sec. of State's Meritorious Honor Award 2008, 2010, Tribeca Film Festival Innovation Award 2010, Washington Post and John F. Kennedy School Center for Public Leadership Top American Leaders Award 2011. *Publications include:* One Hundred Days of Silence: America and the Rwanda Genocide 2006, Children of Jihad: A Young American's Travels Among the Youth of the Middle East 2007, The New Digital Age: Re-shaping the Future of People, Nations and Business (co-author) 2013. *Address:* Google, Inc, 76 Ninth Avenue, 4th Floor, New York, NY 10011, USA

(office). *Telephone:* (212) 565-0000 (office). *Fax:* (212) 565-0001 (office). *E-mail:* jacohen@cfr.org (office). *Website:* www.google.com (office).

COHEN, Joel E., BA, MA, PhD, MPh, DrPH; American mathematical biologist and academic; *Abby Rockefeller Mauzé Professor of Populations, The Rockefeller University andProfessor of Populations, Columbia University;* b. 10 Feb. 1944; ed Harvard Univ.; taught at Harvard Univ. 1971–75; Prof., The Rockefeller Univ. 1975–, currently Abby Rockefeller Mauzé Prof. of Populations; also Prof. of Populations, Earth Inst., Columbia Univ., New York 1995–; fmr mem. Bd of Dirs The Nature Conservancy; fmr mem. Bd of Trustees Population Reference Bureau; mem. NAS, American Acad. of Arts and Sciences, American Philosophical Soc.; MacArthur Foundation Fellow; Olivia Schieffelin Nordberg Award for excellence in writing in the population sciences 1997, Fred L. Soper Prize, Pan American Health Org., Washington, DC 1998 for work on Chagas disease, Tyler Prize for Environmental Achievement 1999, City of New York Mayor's Award for Excellence in Science and Tech. 2002. *Publications:* author or ed. of 14 books; numerous scientific papers in professional journals on demography, epidemiology, ecology, pure and applied math., and ecology. *Address:* Laboratory of Populations, The Rockefeller University, 1230 York Avenue, Box 20, New York, NY 10065, USA (office). *Telephone:* (212) 327-8884 (office). *E-mail:* cohen@rockefeller.edu (office). *Website:* lab.rockefeller.edu/cohenje (office).

COHEN, Leonard, CC, BA; Canadian singer, songwriter and poet; b. 21 Sept. 1934, Montreal; s. of Nathan B. Cohen and Masha Klinitsky; two c.; ed McGill Univ.; f. country-and-western band, The Buckskin Boys 1951; initially wrote poetry; moved to New York early 1960s; as a songwriter, over 2,000 renditions of his songs have been recorded; limited edition artwork first displayed to public 2005, lithograph prints have achieved widespread critical acclaim and nearly 600 limited edition prints had been sold by 2010; Dr hc (Dalhousie Univ.) 1970, (McGill Univ.) 1992; Grand Officer, Nat. Order of Quebec 2008; numerous awards including William Harold Moon Award (Recording Rights Org. of Canada) 1984, Juno Hall of Fame 1991, Gov. Gen.'s Performing Arts Award 1993, Canadian Songwriters' Hall of Fame 2006, Rock and Roll Hall of Fame 2008, Grammy Award for Album of the Year on Herbie Hancock's River: the Joni Letters 2008, Grammy Lifetime Achievement Award 2010, Prince of Asturias Award 2011, Glenn Gould Prize 2011, PEN New England Excellence in Lyrics Award 2012. *Recordings include:* albums: The Songs of Leonard Cohen 1968, Songs From A Room 1969, Songs of Love and Hate 1971, Live Songs 1973, New Skin for the Old Ceremony 1974, Greatest Hits 1975, The Best of Leonard Cohen 1976, Death of a Ladies' Man 1977, Recent Songs 1979, Various Positions 1985, I'm Your Man 1988, The Future 1992, Cohen Live 1994, More Best Of 1997, Live Songs 1998, Ten New Songs 2001, Field Commander Cohen 2001, The Essential Leonard Cohen 2002, Dear Heather 2004, Old Ideas 2012. *Film:* Leonard Cohen I'm Your Man 2006. *Publications include:* poetry: Let Us Compare Mythologies (McGill Literary Award) 1956, The Spice-Box of Earth 1961, Flowers for Hitler 1964, Beautiful Losers 1966, Parasites of Heaven 1966, Selected Poems 1956–1968 1968, The Energy of Slaves 1972, Death of a Ladies' Man 1978, Book of Mercy (Canadian Authors' Asscn Literary Award) 1984, Stranger Music: Selected Poems and Songs 1993, Book of Longing 2006; other: The Favourite Game (novel) (Quebec Literary Prize) 1963. *Address:* 9300 Wilshire Boulevard, Suite 200, Beverly Hills, CA 90212, USA (office).

COHEN, Lyor; American music company executive; b. New York; ed Univ. of Miami; financial officer, Bank Leumi; Hip-Hop Performance Promoter, Mix Club, Los Angeles; joined Rush Entertainment 1985, later Partner; Pres. and CEO Island Def Jam Records 1988–2004; Vice-Chair. and CEO US and UK Recorded Music, Warner Music Group 2004–12. *Address:* c/o Warner Music Group, 75 Rockefeller Plaza, New York, NY 10019, USA.

COHEN, Marius (Job), PhD; Dutch politician and academic; *Mayor of Amsterdam;* b. 18 Oct. 1947, Haarlem; s. of Adolf Emiel Cohen and Hetty Koster; m. 1972; one s. one d.; ed Stedelijk Gymnasium Haarlem and Univ. of Groningen; joined PvDA (Netherlands Labour Party) 1967; held a scientific position at Bureau Research of Educ., Leiden Univ. 1971–81; Lecturer, Maastricht Univ. 1981–83, Chair. Comm. that prepared establishment of faculty of law, Prof. of Methods and Techniques, Faculty of Law 1983, Rector Magnificus 1991–93; State Sec. (Deputy Minister) of Educ. 1993–94; mem. Eerste Kamer (Upper House) 1995–98; Interim Dir VRPO TV station Feb.–Aug. 1998; State Sec., Ministry of Justice, with responsibility for Immigration 1998–2000; Mayor of Amsterdam 2001–; Labour Party cand. for Prime Minister in gen. elections 2003; Dr hc (Univ. of Windsor) 2007, (Radboud Univ. Nijmegen) 2008; Cleveringa Lecturer, Univ. of Leiden 2002, named a Time magazine 'European Hero' 2005. *Address:* Office of the Mayor, Postbus 202, 1000 AE Amsterdam, Netherlands (office). *Telephone:* (20) 5522000. *E-mail:* j.cohen@amsterdam.nl (office). *Website:* www.amsterdam.nl (office).

COHEN, Marvin Lou, PhD; American (b. Canadian) physicist and academic; *University Professor of Physics, University of California, Berkeley;* b. 3 March 1935, Montreal, Canada; s. of Elmo Cohen and Molly Zaritsky; m. 1st Merrill Leigh Gardner 1958 (died 1994); one s. one d.; m. 2nd Suzy R. Locke 1996; ed Univs of California, Berkeley and Chicago; mem. Tech. Staff, Bell Labs, Murray Hill, NJ 1963–64; Asst Prof. of Physics, Univ. of California, Berkeley 1964–66, Assoc. Prof. 1966–68, Prof. 1969–95, Univ. Prof. 1995–; Prof., Miller Inst. Basic Research in Science, Univ. of California1969–70, 1976–77, 1988, Chair. 1977–81, Univ. Prof. 1995–, Faculty Research Lecturer 1996–97, Faculty Research Prof., Lecturer 1997–; Distinguished Lecturer in Physics and Electrical Eng, Columbia Univ. 1996; US Rep., Semiconductor Comm., IUPAP 1975–81; Visiting Prof., Univ. of Cambridge, UK 1966, Univ. of Paris 1972–73, Univ. of Hawaii 1978–79, Technion, Haifa, Israel 1987–88; Alfred P. Sloan Fellow, Univ. of Cambridge 1965–67; Guggenheim Fellow 1978–79, 1990–91; Fellow, American Physics Soc. Exec. Council 1975–79, Chair. 1977–78; mem. NAS 1980, American Acad. of Arts and Sciences, Oliver E. Buckley Prize Comm. 1980–81 (Chair. 1981); mem. Govt-Univ.-Industry Research Round Table 1984–, Vice-Chair. Working Group on Science and Eng Talent 1984–, Advisory Bd Tex. Center for Superconductivity 1991– (mem. 1988–90), mem. Research Briefing Panels NAS on Funding and on High Temperature Superconductivity 1987, US-Japan Workshop on Univ. Research 1988–89, Science Policy Bd Stanford Synchrotron Radiation Lab. 1990–92, Visiting Cttee, The Ginzton Lab., Stanford Univ. 1991, American Acad. of Arts and Sciences 1993, Scientific Policy Cttee, Stanford Linear Accelerator Center 1993–95; Assoc. Ed. Materials Science and Engineering 1987, Chair. Exec. Bd

Council, Panel on Public Affairs, Investment Cttee, American Physical Soc. Fellowship Cttee, Congressional Fellowship Cttee, 2003; mem. Advisory Bd International Journal of Modern Physics B 1987–, Editorial Bd Perspectives in Condensed Matter Physics 1987–, AAAS 1993–, mem. Bd of Advisors, Discover Magazine 1998–2000, Prize Cttee for Nanoscience Prize, ACSIN 1999, 2001, Int. Advisory Bd, Nanonetwork Materials, Kamakura, Japan 2000, Advisory Cttee, Inst. of Nano Science and Tech., Hong Kong Univ. of Science and Tech. 2001–; mem. Bd of Govs Weizmann Inst. of Science 2002–; mem. Governing Bd American Inst. of Physics 2003–07; Loeb Lecturer, Harvard Univ. 2004; Chief Scientific Officer, Nanomix Inc. 2006–; Inst. Advisor, Daegu Gyeongbuk Inst. of Science and Tech., Daegu, South Korea 2006–; Organizer of Nobel Symposium, Int. Conf. on the Physics of Semiconductors, Rio de Janeiro, Brazil 2008; mem. Advisory Cttee to the Simons Foundation (Physics, Math. and Computer Science) 2009–10; mem. numerous advisory bds including Korean Inst. for Advanced Study 2011–14, School of Science Advisory Cttee, Hong Kong Univ. of Science and Tech. 2012–14, Cttee and Academic Advisory Cttee to review Atomic, Molecular and Optical Physics, Weizmann Inst. of Science 2012, Advisory Bd, Texas Center for Superconductivity, Univ. of Houston 2012–, Advisory Panel, Samsung Science and Tech. Foundation 2013–; Visiting mem. Inst. for Advanced Study, Hong Kong Univ. of Science and Tech. 2010–15; mem. American Physical Soc. 2002 (Pres. 2005), American Philosophical Soc. 2003, The Berkeley Fellows, Univ. of California 2009; Fellow, AAAS 1997; Hon. Chair. Int. Conf. on the Physics of Semiconductors 2014; Dr hc (Montreal) 2005, (Weizmann Inst., Israel) 2014; Hon. DSc (Hong Kong Univ. of Science and Tech.) 2013; numerous awards including Oliver E. Buckley Prize for Solid State Physics 1979, US Dept of Energy Award 1981, 1990, Julius Edgar Lilienfeld Prize, American Physical Soc. 1994, Outstanding Performance Award, Lawrence Berkeley Nat. Lab. 1995, Invited Speaker, Nobel Symposium 1996, Inauguration Speaker, Korea Inst. for Advanced Study 1996, Nat. Medal of Science 2001, Presidential Award 2002, Technology Pioneer Award, World Econ. Forum 2007, Basic Energy Sciences (DOE) Distinguished Lecturer, Brookhaven Nat. Lab. 2008, Berkeley Citation, Univ. of California 2011, Public Lecture, Fudan Univ., Shanghai, People's Repub. of China 2012, Dickson Prize in Science 2012, Oppenheimer Lecturer, Univ. of California, Berkeley 2013. *Publications:* over 800 articles on research topics. *Leisure interests:* music (clarinet), running. *Address:* Department of Physics, 366 Le Conte Hall, #7300, Berkeley, CA 94720-7300 (office); 201 Estates Drive, Piedmont, CA 94611, USA (home). *Telephone:* (510) 642-4753 (office). *Fax:* (510) 643-9473 (office). *E-mail:* mlcohen@berkeley.edu (office). *Website:* civet.berkeley.edu/cohen/index .html.

COHEN, Sir Philip, PhD, FRS, FRSE; British research biochemist and academic; *Professor of Enzymology and Co-Director, Division of Signal Transduction Therapy, University of Dundee;* b. 22 July 1945, Edgware, Middx, England; s. of Jacob Davis Cohen and Fanny Bragman; m. Patricia T. Wade 1969; one s. one d.; ed Hendon County Grammar School, Univ. Coll., London; SRC/NATO Postdoctoral Fellow, Univ. of Washington, Seattle, USA 1969–71; Lecturer in Biochemistry, Univ. of Dundee 1971–77, Reader 1977–81, Prof. of Enzymology 1981–84, Royal Soc. Research Prof. 1984–2010, Dir MRC Protein Phosphorylation Unit 1990–2012, Dir Scottish Inst. for Cell Signalling 2008–12, currently Prof. of Enzymology and Co-Dir, Div. of Signal Transduction Therapy; Dir Wellcome Trust Biocentre 1997–2007; Fellow, Univ. Coll. London 1993, Acad. of Medical Sciences 1998; mem. Discovery Advisory Bd SmithKline Beecham Pharmaceutical Co. 1993–97; mem. European Molecular Biology Org. 1982, Academia Europaea 1990; Croonian Lecturer, Royal Soc. 1998; Foreign Assoc., NAS 2008; Fellow, American Acad. of Microbiology; Hon. Fellow, Royal Coll. of Pathologists 1998; Hon. mem. British Biochemical Soc. 2003 (Pres. 2006–08), American Soc. of Toxicology 2010; Hon. DSc (Abertay) 1998, (Strathclyde) 1999, (Debrecen, Hungary) 2004, Hon. MD (Linkoping, Sweden) 2004, (St Andrews) 2005, (Dundee) 2007; Anniversary Prize, Fed. of European Biochemical Socs 1977, Colworth Medal 1977, CIBA Medal and Prize 1991, British Biochemical Soc., Prix Van Gysel, Belgian Royal Acads of Medicine 1992, Bruce Preller Prize, Royal Soc. of Edin. 1993, Louis Jeantet Prize for Medicine 1997, Pfizer Award for Innovative Science in Europe 1999, Sir Hans Krebs Medal, Fed. of European Biochemical Socs 2001, Bristol-Myers Squibb Distinguished Achievement Award for Metabolic Research 2002, Royal Medal, Royal Soc. of Edin. 2004, Debrecen Award for Molecular Medicine 2004, Rolf Luft Prize, Karolinska Inst., Sweden 2006, Royal Medal, Royal Soc. 2008, Scottish Enterprise Leading Individual Achievement in the Life Sciences in Scotland 2009, MRC Millennium Medal 2013. *Publications:* Control of Enzyme Activity 1976; more than 500 articles in scientific journals. *Leisure interests:* bridge, chess, golf, ornithology, picking wild mushrooms, cooking. *Address:* Division of Signal Transduction Therapy, MRC Protein Phosphorylation Unit, College of Life Sciences, MSI/WTB Complex, University of Dundee, Dow Street, Dundee, DD1 5EH (office); Inverbay Bramblings, Waterside, Invergowrie, Dundee, DD2 5DQ, Scotland (home). *Telephone:* (1382) 384238 (office); (1382) 562328 (home). *Fax:* (1382) 223778 (office). *E-mail:* p.cohen@dundee.ac.uk (office). *Website:* www.lifesci .dundee.ac.uk/people/philip-cohen (office); www.ppu.mrc.ac.uk/research/?pid=1 (office).

COHEN, Preston Scott, MArch; American architect and academic; *Gerald M. McCue Prof. of Architecture and Chair, Department of Architecture, Graduate School of Design, Harvard University;* b. 1961, Asheville, North Carolina; ed Rhode Island School of Design, Harvard Univ. Grad. School of Design; Adjunct Asst Prof. of Architecture, Ohio State Univ. 1989; f. Preston Scott Cohen (architectural firm), Cambridge, Mass 1989; Design Critic in Architecture, Harvard Univ. Grad. School of Design 1989–92, Asst Prof. of Architecture 1992–95, Assoc. Prof. of Architecture 1995–2001, Prof. of Architecture 2002–03, Dir Master of Architecture Degree Programs 2003–08, Gerald M. McCue Prof. of Architecture 2003–, Chair Dept of Architecture 2008–; Visiting Faculty Mem., Rhode Island School of Design 1993–98; Visiting Assoc. Prof. of Architecture, Princeton Univ. 1997; Perloff Visiting Prof., UCLA 2002; Frank Gehry Int. Visiting Chair, Univ. of Toronto 2004; Young Architects Award, Architectural League of New York 1992, Progressive Architecture Award 1998, 2000, First Prize, Herta and Paul Amir Int. Competition 2003, PA Award, Architecture, Tel Aviv Museum of Art 2004, Acad. Award in Architecture, American Acad. of Arts and Letters 2004. *Publications:* Contested Symmetries and Other Predicaments in Architecture 2001, Permutations of Descriptive Geometry 2002. *Address:* Preston Scott Cohen Inc., 675 Massachusetts

Avenue, Cambridge, MA 02139 (office); Harvard University Graduate School of Design, 48 Quincy Street, Gund Hall, Cambridge, MA 02138, USA (office). *Telephone:* (617) 441-2110 (office); (617) 495-2591 (office). *Fax:* (617) 441-2113 (office); (617) 495-8916 (office). *E-mail:* scott@pscohen (office). *Website:* www .pscohen.com (office); www.gsd.harvard.edu (office).

COHEN, Robert; British cellist, conductor and teacher; *Professor, Royal Academy of Music;* b. 15 June 1959, London, England; s. of Raymond Cohen and Anthya Rael; m. Rachel Smith 1987; four s.; ed Purcell School and Guildhall School of Music (Diploma of Advanced Solo Studies), cello studies with William Pleeth, André Navarra, Jacqueline du Pré and Mstislav Rostropovich; started playing cello aged five; Royal Festival Hall debut (Boccherini Concerto) aged 12; London recital debut, Wigmore Hall, aged 17; Tanglewood Festival, USA 1978; recording debut (Elgar concerto) 1979; concerts USA, Europe and Eastern Europe 1979; since 1980, concerts world-wide with major orchestras and with conductors including Muti, Abbado, Dorati, Sinopoli, Otaka, Mazur, Davis, Tilson-Thomas, Marriner and Rattle; Dir Charleston Manor Festival, E Sussex 1989–; regular int. radio broadcasts and numerous int. TV appearances; plays on the 'Ex-Roser' David Tecchler of Rome cello dated 1723; conductor, various chamber orchestras 1990–, symphony orchestras 1997–; Visiting Prof., RAM 1998–, Prof. 2009–; Prof. of Advanced Cello Studies, Conservatorio della Svizzera Italiana di Lugano 2000–; launched Cello Clinic 2009; performance/choreographic projects in collaboration with Royal Ballet School 2010–11; Fellow, Purcell School for Young Musicians 1992; Hon. RAM 2009; Winner, Suggia Award 1968–72, Winner, Young Concert Artists Int. Competition, New York 1978, English Speaking Union Fellowship 1978, Piatigorsky Prize, Tanglewood Festival 1978, Winner, UNESCO Int. Competition, Czechoslovakia 1981, Robert Helpmann Award (Australia) 2005. *Recordings include:* Elgar Concerto (new Elgar concerto 1993), Dvořák Concerto, Tchaikovsky Rococo Variations, Rodrigo Concierto en modo Galante, Beethoven Triple Concerto, Grieg Sonata, Franck Sonata, Virtuoso Cello Music record, Dvořák Complete Piano trios with Cohen Trio, Schubert String Quintet with Amadeus Quartet, Complete Bach Solo Cello Suites, Howard Blake Diversions, Bliss Concerto 1992, Walton Concerto 1995, Britten Cello Suites 1997, Morton Feldman Concerto 1998, Britten Cello Symphony 1998, Sally Beamish Cello Concerto River 1999, HK Gruber Cello Concerto 2003. *Television:* Bach Sarabandes (BBC), Elgar Cello Concerto (BBC), Beamish Cello Concerto (BBC). *Leisure interests:* photography, alternative therapy, philosophy. *Telephone:* (20) 8444-1065 (office). *E-mail:* office@robertcohen.info (office). *Website:* www .robertcohen.info; www.celloclinic.com; www.thecohenpodtalks.com.

COHEN, Sir Ronald, Kt, MA, MBA; British venture capital executive; *Founder and Chairman, The Portland Trust;* b. 1 Aug. 1945, Egypt; s. of the late Michael Mourad Cohen and Sonia Sophie Cohen (née Douek); m. 1st Carol Marylene Belmont 1972 (divorced 1975); m. 2nd Claire Whitmore Enders 1983 (divorced 1986); m. 3rd Sharon Ruth Harel; one s. one d.; ed Orange Hill Grammar School, Exeter Coll., Oxford (Exhibitioner and Pres. Oxford Union Soc.), Harvard Business School, USA; consultant, McKinsey & Co. (UK and Italy) 1969–71; Chargé de mission, Institut de Developpement Industriel, France 1971–72; Founder, Apax Partners Worldwide LLP (fmrly Apax Partners Holdings Ltd) 1972, Chair. 1972–2005; contested (Labour) Kensington North constituency, Gen. Election 1974, London West, European Parl. election 1979; Founder-Dir British Venture Capital Asscn 1983 (Chair. 1985–86), European Venture Capital Asscn 1985, City Group for Smaller Cos 1992; a Founder and Vice-Chair. European Asscn of Securities Dealers Automated Quotation 1995–2001; Chair. The Portland Trust 2003–; Founder and Dir, Social Finance Ltd 2009–11, Social Finance US 2011–; Chair. Big Society Capital 2012–; Dir, NASDAQ Europe 2001–03; Chair. Tech. Stars Steering Cttee, Dept of Trade and Industry (DTI) 1997–2000, Social Investment Task Force 2000–10, Bridges Ventures Ltd 2002–, Comm. on Unclaimed Assets 2005–07; mem. Advisory Bd, InterAction 1986–, Finance and Industry Cttee, NEDC 1988–90, Wider Share Ownership Cttee 1988–90, City Advisory Group 1993–99, CBI Working Party on Smaller Cos, London Stock Exchange 1993, UK Competitiveness Cttee, DTI 1998–2000, Exec. Cttee Centre for Econ. Policy Research 1996–99, Finance Cttee Inst. for Social and Econ. Policy in ME, Kennedy School of Govt, Harvard Univ. 1997–98, Advisory Bd Fullbright Comm., Harvard Univ. 2007–, Investment Cttee Univ. of Oxford 2007–, Int. Council, Tate Gallery 2004–; Vice-Chair. Ben-Gurion Univ.; Trustee and mem. Exec. Cttee, IISS 2005–10; Trustee, BM 2005–; Hon. Fellow, Exeter Coll., Oxford 2000; Hon. Pres. Community Devt Finance Asscn 2005–07; Henry Fellowship, Harvard Business School, Jubilee Award for services to Israeli business, Alumni Achievement Award 2006. *Publication:* The Second Bounce of the Ball: Turning Risk into Opportunity 2007. *Leisure interests:* music, art, theatre, cinema, tennis. *Address:* The Portland Trust, 42 Portland Place, London, W1B 1NB, England (office). *Telephone:* (20) 7182-7780 (office). *Fax:* (20) 7182-7895 (office). *Website:* www.portlandtrust.org (office).

COHEN, Stanley, BA, PhD; American biochemist and academic; *Distinguished Professor Emeritus, School of Medicine, Vanderbilt University;* b. 17 Nov. 1922, Brooklyn, New York; s. of Louis Cohen and Fruma Feitel; m. 1st Olivia Larson 1951; m. 2nd Jan Elizabeth Jordan 1981; three s.; ed Brooklyn and Oberlin Colls., Univ. of Michigan; Teaching Fellow, Dept of Biochemistry, Univ. of Michigan 1946–48; Instructor, Depts of Biochemistry and Pediatrics, Univ. of Colorado School of Medicine, Denver 1948–52; Postdoctoral Fellow, American Cancer Soc., Dept of Radiology, Washington Univ., St Louis 1952–53; Research Prof. of Biochemistry, American Cancer Soc., Nashville 1976–; Asst Prof. of Biochemistry, Vanderbilt Univ. School of Medicine, Nashville 1959–62, Assoc. Prof. 1962–67, Prof. 1967–86, Distinguished Prof. 1986–2000, Distinguished Prof. Emer. 2000–; mem. Editorial Bds Excerpta Medica, Abstracts of Human Developmental Biology, Journal of Cellular Physiology; mem. NAS, American Soc. of Biological Chemists, Int. Inst. of Embryology, American Acad. of Arts and Sciences; Hon. DSc (Chicago) 1985; Nobel Prize for Physiology and Medicine 1986, and many other prizes and awards. *Leisure interests:* camping, tennis. *Address:* 11306 East Limberlost Road, Tucson, AZ 85749 (home); Department of Biochemistry, Vanderbilt University School of Medicine, 607 Light Hall, Nashville, TN 37232, USA (office). *Telephone:* (615) 322-3318 (office). *Fax:* (615) 322-4349 (office). *Website:* medschool.mc .vanderbilt.edu/biochemistry (office).

COHEN, Stanley, MD; American pathologist; b. 4 June 1937, New York; s. of Herman Joseph Cohen and Eva Lapidus; m. Marion Doris Cantor 1959; two s. one d.; ed Stuyvesant High School, Columbia Coll. and Columbia Univ. Coll. of Physicians and Surgeons; Internship and Residency, Albert Einstein Medical Center and Harvard-Mass. Gen. 1962–64; Instructor, Dept of Pathology, New York Univ. Medical Center 1965–66; Captain, MC, USA, Walter Reed Inst. of Research 1966–68; Assoc. Prof., State Univ. of New York at Buffalo 1968–72, Assoc. Dir, Center for Immunology 1972–74, Prof. of Pathology 1972–74; Assoc. Chair. Dept of Pathology, Univ. of Conn. Health Center 1976–80, Prof. of Pathology 1974–87; Prof., Chair. Bd Hahnemann Univ., Philadelphia 1987–94; Chair. Dept of Pathology, Hahnemann Medical Center 1986–94; Prof., Chair. Univ. Medicine and Dentistry, NJ Medical School 1994; Vice-Pres. American Soc. for Investigative Pathology; Treasurer, Fed. of Socs of Experimental Biology; Kinne Award 1954; Borden Award 1961; Parke-Davis Award in Experimental Pathology 1977; Outstanding Investigator Award, Nat. Cancer Inst. 1986; Co-Chair. Int. Lymphokine Workshop 1979, 1982 and 1984. *Publications:* 200 scientific articles on cellular immunity; ed. 7 books including Mechanisms of Cell-Mediated Immunity 1977, Mechanisms of Immunopathology 1979, The Biology of the Lymphokines 1979, Interleukins, Lymphokines and Cytokines 1983, Molecular Basis of Lymphatic Action 1986, The Role of Lymphatics in the Immune Response 1989. *Leisure interests:* music, photography, karate. *Address:* c/o Department of Pathology and Laborator Medicine, UMDNJ-New Jersey Medical School, 185 South Orange Avenue, Newark, NJ 07103 (office); 79 Ettl Circle, Princeton, NJ 08540-2334, USA (home). *Telephone:* (973) 972-4520 (office). *Fax:* (973) 972-5909 (office). *E-mail:* cohenst@umdnj.com (office).

COHEN, Stanley Norman, BS, MD; American physician, geneticist and academic; *Kwoh-Ting Li Professor, School of Medicine, Stanford University;* b. 17 Feb. 1935, Perth Amboy, New Jersey; s. of Bernard Cohen and Ida Cohen (née Stolz); m. Joanna Lucy Wolter 1961; one s. one d.; ed Rutgers Univ. and Univ. of Pennsylvania School of Medicine; intern, Mount Sinai Hosp., New York 1960–61; Asst Resident in Medicine, Univ. Hosp., Ann Arbor, Mich. 1961–62; Clinical Assoc., Arthritis and Rheumatism Br., Nat. Inst. of Arthritis and Metabolic Diseases 1962–64; Sr Resident in Medicine, Duke Univ. Hosp., Durham, North Carolina 1964–65; American Cancer Soc. Postdoctoral Research Fellow, Dept of Molecular Biology and Dept of Developmental Biology and Cancer, Albert Einstein Coll. of Medicine, Bronx, New York 1965–67, Asst Prof. 1967–68; Asst Prof. of Medicine, Stanford Univ. School of Medicine 1968–71, Head, Div. of Clinical Pharmacology 1969–78, Assoc. Prof. of Medicine 1971–75, Prof. of Genetics 1977 and Prof. of Medicine 1975–, Chair. Dept of Genetics 1978–86, Kwoh-Ting Li Prof. of Genetics 1993–, Prof. and Prin. Investigator, Stanley N. Cohen Lab. –2011; mem. Editorial Bd Proceedings of the National Academy of Sciences, Current Opinion in Microbiology; Trustee, Univ. of Pa 1997–2002; mem. of various scientific orgs, including NAS, Inst. of Medicine, American Philosophical Soc. 2006; Fellow, American Acad. of Arts and Sciences (Chair. Genetics Section 1988–91), American Acad. of Microbiology, AAAS; Einstein Prof., Chinese Acad. of Sciences 2006; Hon. ScD (Rutgers) 1994, (Pennsylvania) 1995; numerous awards including Baldouin Lucke Research Award, Univ. of Pennsylvania School of Medicine 1960, Research Career Devt Award, US Public Health Service 1969, Burroughs Wellcome Scholar Award 1970, Mattia Award, Roche Inst. for Molecular Biology 1977, Albert Lasker Basic Medical Research Award 1980, Wolf Prize in Medicine 1981, Marvin J. Johnson Award, Nat. Biotechnology Award 1989, Nat. Medal of Tech. 1989, ACS Special Award 1992, Lemelson-MIT Prize 1996, Nat. Inventors Hall of Fame 2001, Albany Medical Center Prize in Medicine and Biomedical Research (co-recipient) 2004, Shaw Prize in Life Science and Medicine 2004, New York Acad. of Medicine John Stearns Award for Lifetime Achievement in Medicine 2007, Cold Spring Harbor Lab. Double Helix Medal for Scientific Research 2009, Dean's Medal, Stanford Univ. School of Medicine 2011, Fellow of the Inaugural Class of Acad. of American Asscn for Cancer Research 2013, BayBio DINA Lifetime Achievement Award 2013. *Address:* Department of Genetics, School of Medicine, Stanford University, Stanford, CA 94305-5120, USA (office). *Telephone:* (650) 723-5315 (office). *Fax:* (650) 725-1536 (office). *E-mail:* sncohen@stanford.edu (office). *Website:* sncohenlab.stanford.edu (office).

COHEN, Steven A., BS; American investment manager and art collector; b. 11 June 1956, Great Neck, NY; m. 1st Patricia Cohen; two c.; m. 2nd Alexandra Cohen; five c.; ed Wharton School at Univ. of Pennsylvania; early career on Wall Street as jr trader in options arbitrage dept at Gruntal & Co. 1978, later ran own trading group 1984–92; f. SAC Capital Partners, Stamford, Conn. 1992; owns 7% of search engine Baidu; began collecting art in 2000; mem. Bd of Trustees Brown Univ., Robin Hood Foundation, New York; has appeared on Art News magazine's Top 10 list of biggest-spending art collectors around the world each year since 2002, named by Forbes magazine amongst its Top Billionaire Art Collectors 2005, dubbed by The Wall Street Journal "the hedge fund king" 2006, ranked 94th by TIME magazine on its annual TIME 100 list of the Most Influential People 2007. *Address:* S.A.C. Capital Advisors, LP, 72 Cummings Point Road, Stamford, CT 06902, USA (office). *E-mail:* info@sac.com (office). *Website:* www.careers.sac.com (office).

COHEN, William Sebastian, BA, LLB; American consultant, fmr politician and fmr government official; *Chairman and CEO, Cohen Group;* b. 28 Aug. 1940, Bangor, Me.; s. of Reuben Cohen and Clara Cohen (née Hartley); two s.; ed Bangor High School, Bowdoin Coll., Boston Univ. Law School; admitted to Maine Bar, Mass. Bar, DC Bar; Pnr, Prairie, Cohen, Lynch, Weatherbee and Kobritz, Bangor 1966–72; Asst Co. Attorney, Penobscot Co., Me 1968–70, instructor, Univ. of Maine at Orono 1968–72; mem. Bd of Overseers, Bowdoin Coll. 1973–85; City Councillor, Bangor 1969–72, Mayor of Bangor 1971–72; mem. US House of Reps, Washington, DC 1972–78; Senator from Maine 1979–96; US Sec. of Defense 1997–2001; Founder and CEO The Cohen Group (consulting firm), Washington, DC 2001–; Trustee and Counselor, Center Strategic and Int. Studies 2001–; Fellow of John F. Kennedy Inst. of Politics, Harvard Univ. 1972; mem. Bd of Dirs AIG –2006; Distinguished Public Service, Boston Univ. Alumni Assen 1976, L. Mendel Rivers Award, Non-Commissioned Officers' Asscn 1983, Pres.'s Award, New England Asscn of School Superintendents 1984, Silver Anniversary Award, Nat. Collegiate Athletic Asscn 1987, Nat. Asscn Basketball Coaches, US 1987, numerous other awards. *Publications:* Of Sons and Seasons 1978, Roll Call 1981, Getting the Most Out of Washington 1982 (with Prof. Kenneth Lasson), The Double Man 1985 (with

Senator Gary Hart), A Baker's Nickel 1986, Men of Zeal (with Senator George Mitchell) 1988, One-Eyed Kings 1991, Murder in the Senate (with Thomas B. Allen) 1993. *Leisure interests:* poetry, sport. *Address:* The Cohen Group, 1200 19th Street, NW, Suite 400, Washington, DC 20036, USA (office). *Telephone:* (202) 689-7900 (office). *Fax:* (202) 689-7910 (office). *E-mail:* wsc@cohengroup.net (office). *Website:* www.cohengroup.net (office).

COHEN, Yitzhak; Israeli politician; *Deputy Minister of Finance;* b. 2 Dec. 1951; m.; ten c.; army service; fmr Deputy Mayor of Ashkelon and Sec.-Gen. of El Hama'ayan (Shas-affiliated educational inst.); mem. Knesset (Parl.) 1996–, mem. Labour and Social Affairs and Finance Cttees; Minister of Religious Affairs 1999–2000; Deputy Minister of Finance 2001–03, 2009–; Minister without Portfolio (responsible for religious councils) 2006–09; mem. Shas party. *Address:* The Knesset, HaKiryah, Jerusalem, 91950, Israel (office). *Telephone:* (2) 5311170 (office). *Fax:* (2) 6535469 (office).

COHEN STUART, Martien A., BSc, PhD; Dutch physical chemist and academic; *Professor and Head of Laboratory of Physical Chemistry and Colloid Science, Department of Agrotechnology and Food Sciences, Wageningen University;* b. 25 April 1948, Haarlem; ed Groningen State Univ., Wageningen Univ.; apptd Asst Prof., Physical Chem. and Colloid Science Group, Wageningen Univ. 1980, later Assoc. Prof., Prof. of Physical Chem. and Colloid Science 1996–, currently Head of Lab. of Physical Chem. and Colloid Science, Dept of Agrotechnology and Food Sciences; sabbatical/postdoctoral year in group of Pierre Gilles de Gennes, Paris, worked on wetting and spreading experiments; Scientific Dir, Dutch Polymer Inst., Univ. of Twente; adviser to AkzoNobel in area of colloid and physical chem.; Ed. European Physical Journal E (Soft Matter); mem. Royal Dutch Acad. of Sciences, Royal Netherlands Acad. of Arts and Science; Wolfgang Ostwald Medal, German Kolloid Gesellschaft 2007, AkzoNobel Science Award, Royal Holland Soc. of Sciences and Humanities 2008. *Publications:* numerous papers in scientific journals on statics and dynamics of macromolecules, interfaces, wetting, phase behaviour, self-assembly, networks and gels, emulsions and coalescence, and the physics of macromolecules in living cells. *Address:* Laboratory of Physical Chemistry and Colloid Science, Department of Agrotechnology and Food Sciences, Postbus 8038, 6700 EK Wageningen, The Netherlands (office). *Telephone:* (317) 483369 (office); (317) 482178 (office). *Fax:* (317) 483777 (office). *E-mail:* martien .cohenstuart@wur.nl (office). *Website:* www.pcc.wur.nl (office).

COHEN-TANNOUDJI, Claude Nessim, PhD; French academic; *Honorary Professor, Collège de France;* b. 1 April 1933, Constantine; s. of Abraham Cohen-Tannoudji and Sarah Sebbah; m. Jacqueline Veyrat 1958; two s. one d.; ed Ecole Normale Supérieure; Research Assoc., CNRS 1962–64; Maître de Conférences, then Prof., Faculté des Sciences, Paris 1964–73; Prof., Collège de France 1973–2004, Hon. Prof. 2004–; mem. Acad. des Sciences; Foreign Assoc. NAS; Fellow, American Physical Soc.; Foreign Hon. mem. American Acad. of Arts and Sciences, Accademia dei Lincei, Russian Acad. of Sciences, Nat. Acad. of Sciences, Pontifical Acad. of Sciences, Indian Nat. Acad. of Sciences, Brazilian Acad. of Sciences; Commdr, Ordre nat. du Mérite, Grand Officier, Légion d'honneur; Dr hc (Uppsala, Jerusalem, Brussels, Liege, Tel-Aviv, Sussex); Ampère Prize, Acad. des Sciences 1980, Lilienfeld Prize, American Physical Soc., Charles Townes Award, Optical Soc. of America 1993, Harvey Prize, Technion, Haifa, CNRS Gold Medal 1996, Nobel Prize in Physics 1997. *Publications:* in collaboration: Quantum Optics and Electronic 1965, Quantum Mechanics (two vols) 1973, Photons and Atoms, Introduction to Quantum Electrodynamics 1987, Atom-Photon Interactions: Basic Processes and Applications 1988, Atoms in Electromagnetic Fields 1994, Lévy Statistics and Laser Cooling: How Rare Events Bring Atoms to Rest 2001, Advances in Atomic Physics: An Overview 2011. *Leisure interest:* music. *Address:* Laboratoire Kastler-Brossel, 24 rue Lhomond, 75231 Paris Cedex 05 (office); 38 rue des Cordelières, 75013 Paris, France (home). *Telephone:* 1-47-07-77-83 (office); 1-45-35-02-18 (home). *Fax:* 1-44-32-34-34 (office). *E-mail:* cct@lkb.ens.fr (office). *Website:* www.lkb.ens.fr/Claude-Cohen-Tannoudji?lang=en (office).

COHN, Gary D.; American financial services industry executive; *President and Chief Operating Officer, Goldman Sachs Group;* b. 27 Aug. 1960, Cleveland, Ohio; m. Lisa Pevaroff Cohn; ed American Univ.; has served in various sr man. positions with Goldman Sachs Group including Head of Commodities Div. 1996–99, managed Fixed Income, Currency and Commodities (FICC) macro businesses 1999–2002, Co-COO FICC 2002, Co-Head FICC 2002–, Co-Head Equities 2003–, Co-Head Global Securities 2004–06, mem. Bd of Dirs, Pres. and COO 2006–; mem. Bd of Dirs New York Mercantile Exchange 1998–2000; mem. Treasury Borrowing Advisory Cttee, Bond Market Asscn; Chair. Advisory Bd New York Univ. (NYU) Hosp. for Joint Diseases; Trustee, NYU Hosp., NYU School of Medicine, Harlem Children's Zone, American Univ.; est. Gary D. Cohn Endowed Research Professorship in Finance, American Univ.; Effecting Change Award, 100 Women in Hedge Funds 2005. *Address:* Goldman Sachs Group, 85 Broad Street, New York, NY 10004, USA (office). *Telephone:* (212) 902-1000 (office). *Fax:* (212) 902-3000 (office). *E-mail:* info@goldmansachs.com (office). *Website:* www.goldmansachs.com (office).

COHN-BENDIT, (Marc) Daniel; French/German politician; *Co-President, European Greens–European Free Alliance, European Parliament;* b. 4 April 1945, Montauban, Tarn-et-Garonne, France; s. of Erich Cohn-Bendit and Herta Cohn-Bendit (née David); m. Ingrid Voigt 1997; one c.; ed Odenwaldschule, Heppenheim, Germany, Univ. de Paris X–Nanterre; moved to Germany 1958; student movt's spokesman, Paris 1968; deported from France May 1968; nursery school teacher, Frankfurt 1968–73; co-f. German students' group Revolutionärer Kampf, Bockenheim 1970; co-f. cultural magazine Pflasterstrand 1970, Ed.-in-Chief 1978–84; Deputy Mayor of Frankfurt 1989–97; mem. European Parl. (Greens) 1994–99, (Ecology Greens) 1999–2004, (Alliance 90/Greens) 2004–, Vice-Pres. Parl. Comm. on Culture, Youth, Media and Sport 1994–95, mem. Foreign Affairs Comm, Public Freedoms Comm., N Africa Comm., Deputy mem. Budget Comm., Rapporteur for regional co-operation between states of Fmr Yugoslavia 1996, Rapporteur on foreign affairs Parl. Comm. on Jt EU-Mediterranean Accord, mem. Steering Cttee SOS Europe 1997, Chair. Del. to Jt EU-Turkey Parl. Comm. 1999–2002, Pres. Green Parl. Group 2001–04, Co-Pres. European Greens–European Free Alliance 2004–; Adviser to Joschka Fischer, Vice-Chancellor and Minister of Foreign Affairs 1998; mem. German Green Party 1984, French Green Party 1998–; co-f. Forum Européen de Prévention Active des Conflits (Fepac)

1994; presenter monthly literary programme Literaturclub, Swiss German TV 1995; f. monthly Eurospeed 1997; Dr hc (Catholic Univ. of Tilburg, Netherlands) 1997; Trombinoscope 'Political Discovery' Award 1998. *Documentary films:* (writer) A chacun son allemagne 1976, Nous l'avons tant aimée, la révolution (four films) 1983, C'est la vie (full-length film) 1990, Angst im Rüchen hat jeder von uns 1992. *Publications include:* Obsolete Communism: The Left-Wing Alternative (co-author) 1968, La Révolte étudiante 1968, Le Gauchisme, remède à la maladie sénile du communisme (co-author) 1972, Le Grand bazar 1976, De l'écologie à l'autonomie (co-author) 1981, Nous l'avons tant aimée, la révolution 1987, 1968: die letzte Revolution, die noch nichts vom Ozonloch wusste (co-author) 1988, Rechtsstaat und ziviler Ungehorsam, ein Streitgespräch (co-author) 1988, Einwanderbares Deutschland oder Vertreibung aus dem Wohlstandsparadies? (co-author) 1991, Heimat Babylon, das Wagnis der multikulturellen Demokratie (co-author) 1993, Une envie de politique : entretiens avec Lucas Delattre et Guy Herzlich 1998, Petit dictionnaire de l'euro (co-author) 1998, Xénophobies: histoires d'Europe (co-author) 1998, Sois jeune et tais-toi !, Un pavé dans la mare et la France est-elle soluble dans l'Europe? (co-author) 1999. *Leisure interest:* football. *Address:* European Parliament, Bâtiment Altiero Spinelli 08G201, 60 rue Wiertz/Wiertzstraat 60, 1047 Brussels, Belgium (office). *Telephone:* (2) 284-54-98 (office). *Fax:* (2) 284-94-98 (office). *Website:* www.europarl.europa.eu (office); www.cohn-bendit.de.

COHN-SHERBOK, Daniel (Dan) Mark, MLitt, PhD, DD, MAHL, FRSA; American/British rabbi and academic; *Professor Emeritus of Judaism, University of Wales;* b. 1 Feb. 1945, Denver, Colo, USA; s. of Bernard Sherbok and Ruth Sherbok; m. Lavinia C. Heath 1976; ed Williams Coll., Hebrew Union Coll. and Univ. of Cambridge, UK; rabbi in USA, UK, Australia and South Africa 1968–74; Chaplain, Colorado State House of Reps 1971; Univ. Lecturer in Theology, Univ. of Kent, UK 1975–97; Dir Centre for Study of Religion and Society 1982–90; Visiting Prof. of Judaism, Univ. of Wales, Lampeter 1995–97, Prof. 1997–2009, Prof. Emer. 2010–, Dir Centre for the Study of the World's Religions 2003–09; Visiting Prof., Univ. of Essex, UK 1993–94, Middlesex Univ., UK 1994–, Univ. of St Andrews, UK 1995–96, St Andrew's Biblical Theological Coll., Moscow, Russia 1996, Univ. of Wales, Bangor, Univ. of Vilnius, Lithuania 1999, Durham Univ., UK 2002; Visiting Scholar, Sarum Coll. 2006–; Visiting Prof., St Mary's Univ. Coll. 2008–, York St John Univ. 2012–; Visiting Fellow, Heythrop Coll., Univ. of London 2010–; Visiting Fellow, Centre for Religions for Peace and Reconciliation, Univ. of Winchester 2013–; Fellow, Hebrew Union Coll., Acad. of Jewish Philosophy; Hon. Prof., Aberystwyth Univ. 2010–; Hon. DD (Hebrew Union Coll., Jewish Inst. of Religion) 1995. *Drawings:* The Athenaeum: Sketches (book) 2014. *Publications include:* The Jewish Heritage 1988, Jewish Petitionary Prayer 1989, God and the Holocaust 1989, Rabbinic Perspectives on the New Testament 1990, Issues in Contemporary Judaism 1991, Dictionary of Judaism and Christianity (with Lavinia Cohn-Sherbok) 1991, The Crucified Jew 1992, The Blackwell Dictionary of Judaica 1992, Exodus: An Agenda for Jewish-Christian Dialogue 1992, Not a Nice Job for a Nice Jewish Boy 1993, The Future of Judaism 1994, The American Jew (with Lavinia Cohn-Sherbok) 1994, Jewish and Christian Mysticism (with Lavinia Cohn-Sherbok) 1994, Jewish Mysticism 1995, Atlas of Jewish History 1996, Medieval Jewish Philosophy 1996, Fifty Key Jewish Thinkers 1996, The Jewish Messiah 1997, After Noah: Animals and the Liberation of Theology (with Andrew Linzey) 1997, A Concise Encyclopaedia of Judaism 1998, Understanding the Holocaust 1999, Jews, Christians and Religious Pluralism 2000, Messianic Judaism 2000, Holocaust Theology: A Reader 2001, The Palestinian-Israeli Conflict (with Dawoud El-Alami) 2001, Anti-Semitism 2002, Judaism: History, Belief, Practice 2003, The Dictionary of Jewish Biography 2005, Pursuing the Dream: Jewish Christian Dialogue (with Mary Grey) 2005, The Paradox of Antisemitism 2006, Politics of Apocalypse 2006, Kabbalah and Jewish Mysticism 2006, Dictionary of Kabbalah and Kabbalists 2009, Judaism Today 2011, Introduction to Zionism and Israel 2012, The Palestinian State: A Jewish Justification 2012, Love, Sex and Marriage 2013, Why Can't They Get Along 2014, Illustrated Guide to Judaism 2014, Debating Israel and Palestine 2014. *Leisure interests:* keeping cats, walking, drawing cartoons. *Address:* The Old Coach House, Bwlchllan, SA48 7ED, Wales. *Telephone:* (1570) 470409. *E-mail:* cohnsherbok@googlemail.com.

COHON, Jared L., BS, PhD; American university administrator and academic; *President, Carnegie Mellon University;* ed Univ. of Pennsylvania, Massachusetts Inst. of Tech.; Faculty mem. in Dept of Geography and Environmental Eng, Johns Hopkins Univ. 1973–92, later Asst and Assoc. Dean of Eng and Vice-Provost for Research; Prof. of Environmental Systems Analysis and Dean of School of Forestry and Environmental Studies, Yale Univ. 1992–97; Pres. Carnegie Mellon Univ. 1997–; Legis. Asst for Energy and the Environment to the late Daniel Patrick Moynihan, US Senator from NY 1977–78; mem. Nuclear Waste Tech. Review Bd 1995– (Chair. 1997–2002), Homeland Security Advisory Council 2002– (Chair. Sr Advisory Cttee on Academia and Policy Research); mem. Bd of Dirs Mellon Financial Corpn, American Standard, Inc.; serves on bds of several nat. and local non-profit orgs, including Health Effects Inst., Heinz Center for Science, Econs and the Environment, Council on Competitiveness, Carnegie Museums of Pittsburgh, Pittsburgh Cultural Trust, Urban League of Pittsburgh, Allegheny Conf. on Community Devt; shared Pittsburgh Magazine's 'Pittsburgher of the Year'. *Publications:* Multiobjective Programming and Planning 1978 (re-issued as a Classic of Operations Research 2004); author, co-author or editor of more than 80 professional pubns on environmental and water resource systems analysis. *Address:* Office of the President, Carnegie Mellon University, 5000 Forbes Avenue, Pittsburgh, PA 15213, USA (office). *Telephone:* (412) 268-2201 (office). *E-mail:* jaredcohon@cmu.edu (office). *Website:* www.cmu.edu (office).

ČOLAK, Bariša; Bosnia and Herzegovina politician and lawyer; *Minister of Justice;* b. 1 Jan. 1956, Široki Brijeg; m. Anela Čolak; one s. two d.; ed Univ. of Mostar; Judge, Magistrates Court, Široki Brijeg 1988–93; Deputy Minister of Justice 1993–96; Prime Minister of West Herzegovina Canton 1996–99; Minister of Justice 1999–2001, 2007–; mem. Parl., Fed. of Bosnia and Herzegovina 2001–02; Vice-Pres. and Minister of Security, Bosnia and Herzegovina 2003–07; mem. Croatian Democratic Union of Bosnia and Herzegovina (HDZ BiH). *Address:* Ministry of Justice, 71000 Sarajevo, trg Bosne i Hercegovine 1, Bosnia and Herzegovina (office). *Telephone:* (33) 223501 (office). *Fax:* (33) 223504 (office). *E-mail:* info@mpr.gov.ba (office). *Website:* www.mpr.gov.ba (office).

COLANINNO, Roberto; Italian business executive; *Chairman and CEO, Piaggio & Co SpA;* b. 16 Aug. 1943, Mantua; began career with Fiamm SpA, fmr Chief Exec.; f. jtly Sogefi SpA (finance co.) 1981; mem. Bd several regional and nat. banks in Italy including Mediobanco, Efibanca SpA, Gruppo Bancario Capitalia; CEO Olivetti & Co. 1996–2001; Chair. and CEO Telecom Italia 1999–2001, also Chair. Telecom Italia Mobile SpA 1999–2001; f. Omniaholding SpA 1998; Chair. IMMSI 2002–; Chair. and CEO Piaggio & Co. SpA 2006–; mem. Man. Cttee and Nat. Advisory Cttee Confindustria 1997–2002; Hon. DEcon (Lecce) 2001; Cavaliere del Lavoro. *Address:* Piaggio Group, Viale Rinaldo Piaggio, 25, 56025 Pontedera, Italy (office). *Telephone:* (05) 87272111 (office). *Website:* www.piaggiogroup.com (office).

COLAO, Vittorio, MBA; Italian business executive; *Chief Executive, Vodafone Group Plc;* b. 3 Oct. 1961, Brescia; m. 1992; two c.; ed Bocconi Univ., Milan, Harvard Business School, USA; spent time at Morgan Stanley investment bankers, London, UK; Pnr, McKinsey & Co., Milan 1986–96; joined Omnitel Pronto Italia (now Vodafone Italy) 1996, later COO, CEO 1999–2001, Regional CEO, Southern Europe, Middle East and Africa, Vodafone Group Plc 2001–04, Exec. Dir on main Bd 2002–04, 2006–, Chief Exec., Europe, and Deputy Group Chief Exec. 2006–, Chief Exec. 2008–; CEO RCS MediaGroup, Milan 2004–06; mem. Int. Advisory Bd Bocconi Univ.; reserve officer in the Carabinieri. *Address:* Vodafone Group Plc, Vodafone House, The Connection, Newbury, Berks., RG14 2FN, England (office). *Telephone:* (1635) 33251 (office). *Fax:* (1635) 686111 (office). *E-mail:* info@vodafone.com (office). *Website:* www.vodafone.com (office).

COLARIČ, Jože, BEcons; Slovenian business executive; *President of the Management Board and CEO, KrKa d.d.;* b. 27 Aug. 1955, Brežice; ed Faculty of Econs, Univ. of Ljubljana; joined KrKa d.d (pharmaceutical co.) 1982, Head of Foreign Exchange Trade Dept and later Asst Dir 1982–89, Head of Export Service, Export-Import Div. 1989–91, Deputy Dir 1991–93, Deputy to CEO for Marketing and Finance 1993–97, mem. Man. Bd 1997–, Deputy Pres. 1998–2004, Pres. of Man. Bd and CEO 2005–. *Address:* KrKa d.d., Smarješka cesto 6, 8501 Novo Mesto, Slovenia (office). *Telephone:* (7) 3312111 (office). *Fax:* (7) 3321537 (office). *E-mail:* info@krka.biz (office). *Website:* www.krka.si (office).

COLBORN, Theodora Emily Decker (Theo), BS, MA, PhD; American zoologist, academic and environmental health analyst; *Professor Emeritus of Zoology, University of Florida;* ed Western State Coll. of Colorado, Rutgers Univ., Univ. of Wisconsin; Congressional Fellow 1985–86, Science Analyst, Office of Tech. Assessment, US Congress, Washington, DC 1986–87; Assoc., Conservation Foundation, Washington, DC 1987–88, Consultant, Environmental Health Analysis 1987–90; Sr Fellow, World Wildlife Fund 1988–93 (on sabbatical 1990–93); Sr Fellow, W. Alton Jones Foundation 1990–93; Sr Scientist and Dir Wildlife and Contaminants Program, World Wildlife Fund 1993–2003; Prof. of Zoology, Univ. of Florida, Gainesville 2004–07, Prof. Emer. 2008–; Founder and Pres. The Endocrine Disruption Exchange, Paonia, Colo 2003–08; has served on numerous advisory panels, including US Environmental Protection Agency (EPA) Science Advisory Bd, Ecosystem Health Cttee of Int. Jt Comm. of US and Canada, Science Man. Cttee of Toxic Substances Research Initiative of Canada, EPA Endocrine Disruptor Screening and Testing Advisory Cttee, EPA Endocrine Disruption Methods and Validation Sub-cttee; mem. Bd of Dirs Rachel Carson Council 2006–; mem. Bd of Scientific Advisors, Children's Health Environmental Coalition 2006–; est. and directed Wildlife and Contaminants Program at World Wildlife Fund US; Nat. Water Alliance Award for Excellence in Protecting the Nation's Aquatic Resources 1991, Pew Fellows Award 1993–96, Nat. Conservation Achievement Award in Science, Nat. Wildlife Fed. 1994, Rachel Carson Award, Chatham Coll. 1997, Norwegian Int. Rachel Carson Prize 1999, UNEP Women Leadership for the Environment Award 1997, State of the World Forum, Mikhail Gorbachev, Change Makers Award 1997, Audubon Magazine: A Century of Conservation, 100 Champions of Conservation 1998, Int. Blue Planet Prize, Asahi Glass Foundation, Japan 2000, Rachel Carson Award, Soc. of Toxicology and Environmental Chem. 2003, Rachel Carson Award, Center for Science in the Public Interest 2004, Beyond Pesticides Dragonfly Award 2006, Woman on the Forefront: Leadership and Integrity in Science 2007, Lifetime Achievement Award, Nat. Council for Science and the Environment 2007, Time magazine Global Environmental Heroes Award 2007. *Publications:* Chemically Induced Alterations in Sexual and Functional Development: The Wildlife/Human Connection (ed.) 1992, Our Stolen Future: How We Are Threatening Our Fertility, Intelligence and Survival (co-author) 1996; numerous scientific papers in professional journals on the consequences of prenatal exposure to synthetic chemicals by the developing embryo and foetus in wildlife, lab. animals and humans. *Address:* PO Box 1253, 121 Main Avenue Paonia, CO 81428; University of Florida, PO Box 118525, Gainesville, FL 32611-8525 (office); The Endocrine Disruption Exchange, PO Box 1407, Paonia, CO 81428, USA (office). *Telephone:* (352) 392-1107 (Gainesville) (office); (970) 527-4082 (TEDX) (office); (970) 527-6548. *Fax:* (970) 527-6548. *E-mail:* colborn@tds.net (office). *Website:* www.endocrinedisruption.org (office) www.ourstolenfuture.org (office).

COLCLEUGH, D. W. (Dave), PhD; Canadian business executive (retd) and academic; *Leadership Development Professor, Faculty of Applied Science and Engineering, University of Toronto;* b. Fort Erie, Ont.; m.; two c.; ed Univ. of Toronto and Univ. of Cambridge, UK; research engineer, DuPont Canada, Kingston 1963–68, polymer tech. supervisor, Fibres Div. 1968–73, tech. supt, Explosives Div., North Bay 1973–75, Tech. and Planning Man., Explosives Div., Montréal 1975–79, Rubber Industry Man., Tyre and Industrial Div. 1979–82, Man. of Gen. Products, Mississauga 1982–85, Prin. Consultant, Corp. Planning Div., Wilmington April–Dec. 1985, Gen. Man. of Finishes, Toronto 1985–89, Dir of Corp. Planning and Devt April–Nov. 1989, Vice-Pres. of Mfg and Eng 1989–92, Sr Vice-Pres. with responsibility for Fibres and Intermediates, Eng Polymers Units and Mfg and Eng 1992–94; Vice-Pres., Gen. Man. of Nylon, DuPont Asia-Pacific 1994–95, Pres. 1995–97; Pres. and CEO DuPont Canada Inc. 1997–2003, Chair of Bd 1998–2003 (retd); Leadership Development Professor, Faculty of Applied Science and Eng, Univ. of Toronto 2006–; mem. Bd of Dirs Let's Talk Science (LTS) 2003–, Chair. 2005–; mem. Bd of Dirs ZENON Environmental Inc. 2000–, Hudson's Bay Co., Canadian Chemicals Producers Asscn, Textiles Human Resources Council, Art Gallery of Mississauga; mem. Dean's Advisory Bd Univ. of Toronto; . *Address:* Faculty of Applied Science and Engineering, University of Toronto, 35 St. George Street, Toronto, ON M5S 1A4, Canada (office). *Telephone:*

(416) 978-8605 (office). *E-mail:* colcleugh333@rogers.com (office). *Website:* www .undergrad.engineering.utoronto.ca/home.htm (office).

COLDITZ, Graham A., BSc (Med.), MBBS, MPH, DrPH, MD; Australian epidemiologist and academic; *Niess-Gain Professor, Department of Surgery, School of Medicine, Washington University in St Louis;* b. 1 Nov. 1954, Sydney; ed Univ. of Queensland and Harvard School of Public Health, Boston, Mass, USA; Instructor in Medicine, Harvard Medical School 1986–88, Asst Prof. of Medicine 1988–91, Assoc. Prof. 1991–98, Prof. 1998–2006, Prof. of Epidemiology, Grad. School of Public Health 1998–2006, Program Leader, Cancer Epidemiology, Dana-Farber/ Harvard Cancer Center, Dir of Educ., Harvard Center for Cancer Prevention; Niess-Gain Prof., Dept of Surgery, Washington Univ. School of Medicine, St Louis 2006–, also Assoc. Dir for Prevention and Control, Alvin J. Siteman Cancer Center; Raine Visiting Prof., Univ. of Western Australia 1997; Adjunct Prof., Univ. of Queensland School of Population Health 2001–; fmr Dir, American Cancer Soc. New England Div., Inc., Dir, American Cancer Soc. 2010–13; mem. Inst. of Medicine 2006–; mem. Advisory Cttee on Research, Alberta Cancer Bd 2000–03; Fellow, Australian Faculty of Public Health Medicine, Royal Australian Coll. of Physicians 1990; Frank Knox Memorial Fellowship, Harvard Univ. 1981–83, Faculty Research Award, American Cancer Soc. 1991–96, ACS Clinical Research Professorship Award 2003–, DeWitt S. Goodman Lectureship, American Asscn for Cancer Research 2003, American Cancer Soc. Medal of Honor for Cancer Prevention and Control 2011, Award for Excellence in Cancer Epidemiology and Prevention, American Asscn for Cancer Research-American Cancer Soc. 2012. *Publications:* more than 990 publs in medical journals. *Leisure interests:* vegetable gardening, forest conservation. *Address:* Washington University School of Medicine, 660 South Euclid Avenue, Campus Box 8100, St Louis, MO 63108, USA (office). *Telephone:* (314) 454-7940 (office). *E-mail:* colditzg@wustl.edu (office). *Website:* www.publichealthsciences.wustl.edu (office).

COLDWELL, Pedro Joaquín; Mexican lawyer, politician and company chairman; *Secretary (Minister) of Energy, Chairman, Petróleos Mexicanos (PEMEX);* b. 5 Aug. 1950, Cozumel, Quintana Roo; s. of Nassin Joaquín Ibarra; ed Universidad Iberoamericana; mem. Institutional Revolutionary Party (PRI), has occupied different positions, including Pres. 2011–12; fmr Dir Gen. Fondo Nacional para el Desarrollo Turístico (FONATUR); held seat in Chamber of Deputies, representing First Dist of Quintana Roo 1979–80; Gov. of Quintana Roo fmr Peace and Reconciliation Commr in Chiapas; apptd Amb. to Cuba 1998; Senator (PRI) for Quintana Roo 2006–12; Sec. of Energy 2012–; Chair. Petróleos Mexicanos (PEMEX) 2012–. *Address:* Petróleos Mexicanos (PEMEX), Avenida Marina Nacional 329, Col. Huasteca, 11311 México DF (office); Secretariat of State for Energy, Insurgentes Sur 890, 17°, Col. del Valle, Del. Benito Juárez, 03100 México DF, Mexico (office). *Telephone:* (55) 1944-2500 (PEMEX) (office); (55) 5000-6000 (Secretariat) (office). *Fax:* (55) 5531-6354 (PEMEX) (office); (55) 5000-6222 (Secretariat) (office). *E-mail:* calidad@energia.gob.mx (office). *Website:* www .pemex.com (office); www.energia.gob.mx (office).

COLE, Natalie Maria, BA; American singer; b. 6 Feb. 1950, Los Angeles; d. of Nathaniel Adam Cole (Nat 'King' Cole) and Maria Hawkins; m. 1st Marvin J. Yancy 1976 (divorced); m. 2nd Andre Fisher (divorced); ed Univ. of Massachusetts; recordings of albums and singles 1975–; recipient of eight Grammys and other music awards. *Albums include:* Inseparable 1975, Natalie 1976, Unpredictable 1977, Thankful 1977, Live 1978, I Love You So 1979, We're The Best Of Friends 1979, Don't Look Back 1980, Happy Love 1981, I'm Ready 1983, Unforgettable – A Tribute to Nat 'King' Cole (with Johnny Mathis) 1983, Dangerous 1985, Everlasting 1987, Good To Be Back 1989, Unforgettable 1991, Too Much Weekend 1992, Take A Look 1993, Holly and Ivy 1994, Stardust (two Grammy Awards) 1996, This Will Be 1997, Magic of Christmas 1999, Snowfall on the Sahara 1999, Love Songs (compilation) 2000, Ask a Woman Who Knows 2002, Leavin' 2006, Still Unforgettable (Grammy Award for Best Traditional Pop Vocal Album 2009) 2008, The Most Wonderful Time of the Year 2010. *Publications include:* Angel On My Shoulder 2000, Love Brought Me Back 2010. *E-mail:* babswest@aol.com (office). *Website:* www.nataliecole.com (home).

COLE-HAMILTON, David John, PhD, CChem, FRSC, FRSE; British chemist and academic; *Professor of Chemistry, University of St Andrews;* b. 22 May 1948, Bovey Tracey, Devon, England; s. of A. M. Cole-Hamilton and the late M. M Cartwright; m. 1st Elizabeth A. Brown 1973 (divorced); two s. two d.; m. 2nd Rosemary E. Macrae (née Semple) 2008; ed Haileybury & Imperial Service Coll. and Univ. of Edinburgh; Research Asst and temporary Lecturer, Imperial Coll. London 1974–78; Lecturer, Univ. of Liverpool 1978–83, Sr Lecturer 1983–85; Irvine Prof. of Chem., St Andrews Univ. 1985–, Chair. of Chem. 1985–90; Sir Edward Frankland Fellowship 1985, Corday Morgan Medal and Prize 1983, Industrial Award for Organo-metallic Chem. 1998, Sir Geoffrey Wilkinson Prize, Tilden Lecturer, Royal Soc. of Chem. 2000–01, Eminent Visitor, Catalysis Soc. of S Africa 2004, Sir Geoffrey Wilkinson Prize Lecturer, Royal Soc. of Chem. 2005–06. *Publications:* more than 360 articles on homogeneous catalysis and organometallic chem. *Address:* School of Chemistry, Purdie 340, University of St Andrews, St Andrews, Fife, KY16 9ST (office); 22 Buchanan Gardens, St Andrews, Fife, KY16 9LU, Scotland (home). *Telephone:* (1334) 463805 (office). *Fax:* (1334) 463808 (office). *E-mail:* djc@st-and.ac.uk (office). *Website:* ch-www.st-andrews.ac.uk (office).

COLEGATE, Isabel, FRSL; British writer; b. 10 Sept. 1931, Lincs.; d. of Arthur Colegate and Winifred Colegate; m. Michael Briggs 1953; two s. one d.; ed Runton Hill School, Norfolk; literary agent, Anthony Blond Ltd, London 1952–57; Hon. MA (Univ. of Bath) 1988. *Publications include:* The Blackmailer 1958, A Man of Power 1960, The Great Occasion 1962, Statues in a Garden 1964, The Orlando Trilogy 1968–72, News From the City of the Sun 1979, The Shooting Party (WH Smith Literary Award 1981, filmed 1985) 1980, Three Novels 1984, A Glimpse of Sion's Glory 1985, Deceits of Time 1988, The Summer of the Royal Visit 1991, Winter Journey 1995, A Pelican in the Wilderness – Hermits Solitaries and Recluses 2002. *Address:* c/o Penguin Books, 80 Strand, London, WC2R 0RL, England.

COLEIRO PRECA, Marie-Louise, BA; Maltese politician and head of state; *President;* b. 7 Dec. 1958, Qormi; m. Edgar Preca; one d.; ed Univ. of Malta; mem. House of Reps 1998–, mem. Parl. Perm. Cttee for Social Affairs 1998–; fmr Shadow Minister for Social Policy, for Tourism, for Health; Minister of the Family and Social Solidarity 2013–14; Pres. of Malta 2014–; mem. Nat. Comm. for Fiscal Morality; mem. Del. to Council of Europe; fmr Dir Maltacom PLC; mem. Labour Party, fmr Asst Sec., mem. Nat. Exec., Gen. Sec. 1981–92; Collar of Compañeros de Honor, Orden del Mérito de Malta. *Address:* Office of the President, The Palace, Valletta VLT 1190, Malta (office). *Telephone:* 21221221 (office). *Fax:* 21241241 (office). *Website:* www.president.gov.mt (office).

COLEMAN, David, BA; American business executive and educator; *President and CEO, College Board, New York City;* b. 1970; s. of Aaron Coleman and Elizabeth Coleman; ed Yale Univ., Univ. of Oxford, UK; began career as Consultant with McKinsey & Co. for five years; with McGraw-Hill 2005–07; Cofounder Student Achievement Partners 2007–12; Pres. and CEO, College Board, New York City 2012–; Co-founder, Grow Network; Founding mem. StudentsFirst. *Address:* The College Board, 45 Columbus Avenue, New York, NY 10023, USA (office). *Telephone:* (212) 713-8000 (office). *Website:* www.collegeboard.org (office).

COLEMAN, Lewis W., BA; American business executive; *Lead Independent Director, Northrop Grumman Corporation;* ed Stanford Univ.; with Wells Fargo & Co. in a variety of wholesale and retail positions, including as Head of Int. Banking, Chief Personnel Officer and Chair. Credit Policy Cttee 1973–86; joined Bank of America as Chief Credit Officer 1986, roles included Head of Capital Markets, Head of World Banking Group and Vice-Chair. Bd and Chief Financial Officer, Sr Man. Dir Banc of America Securities LLC (fmr known as Montgomery Securities, and a subsidiary of Bank of America Corpn), San Francisco 1995–98, Chair. 1998–2000; mem. Bd of Dirs Northrop Grumman 2001–, Chair. (non-exec.) 2010–11, Lead Ind. Dir 2011–; mem. Bd of Dirs DreamWorks Animation SKG 2004–, Pres. 2005–, Chief Financial Officer 2007– (currently Acting Chief Financial Officer); Pres. Gordon E. and Betty I. Moore Foundation, San Francisco, Calif. 2000–04; mem. Nat. Acads Bd on Science, Tech. and Econ. Policy, Bd of Global Crop Diversity Trust; Fellow, Nat. Acad. of Arts and Sciences. *Address:* Northrop Grumman Corpn, 1840 Century Park East, Los Angeles, CA 90067-2199 (office); Corporate Secretary, Dreamworks Animation, 1000 Flower Street, Glendale, CA 91201, USA (office). *Telephone:* (310) 553-6262 (Los Angeles) (office). *Fax:* (310) 553-2076 (Los Angeles) (office). *E-mail:* onewebmaster@ngc.com (office). *Website:* www.northropgrumman.com (office); www.dreamworksanimation.com (office).

COLEMAN, Mary Sue, BA, PhD; American fmr university administrator and academic; b. 2 Oct. 1943, Ky; m. Dr Kenneth Coleman; one s.; ed Grinnell Coll., Univ. of North Carolina, Univ. of Texas; mem. Biochemistry Faculty, Univ. of Kentucky 1971–90, Cancer Care Admin 1982–90; Assoc. Provost and Dean of Research, Univ. of North Carolina 1990–92, Vice-Chancellor Grad. Studies and Research 1992–93; Provost and Vice-Pres. of Academic Affairs Univ. of New Mexico 1993–95; Pres. Univ. of Iowa 1995–2002; Pres. Univ. of Michigan 2002–14, also Prof. of Biological Chem. and Medical School Prof.; elected to NAS Inst. of Medicine 1997, Co-Chair. Cttee on Consequences of Uninsurance; Chair. Hitchings-Elion Postdoctoral Fellowship Program, Burroughs-Wellcome Fund 1997; Co-Chair. Nat. Advisory Council on Innovation and Entrepreneurship 2010–; mem. Bd of Dirs Johnson & Johnson 2003–, Meredith Corpn, American Council of Educ. (ACE), Nat. Collegiate Athletic Asscn (NCAA); mem. Knight Comm. on Intercollegiate Athletics 2000–01, Michigan Strategic Econ. Investment and Commercialization Bd; mem. Bd of Trustees Univs Research Asscn, ACE Task Force on Teacher Educ. and Comm. Minorities in Higher Educ., Business-Higher Educ. Forum, Imagining America Pres.'s Council, Asscn of American Univs (AAU) Task Force Research Accountability, NCAA Standards for Success Advisory Bd, Pres.'s Leadership Group for Higher Educ., Center for Alcohol and Other Drug Prevention; fmr mem. Exec. Cttee Asscn AAU; Trustee, Knight Foundation 2005–, Gerald R. Ford Foundation; Fellow, American Acad. Arts and Sciences, AAAS; Dr hc (Grinnell Coll., Luther Coll., Univ. of Kentucky, Albion Coll., Dartmouth Coll., Shanghai Jiao Tong Univ., Northeastern Univ., Univ. of Toledo, Univ. of Notre Dame, Grand Valley State Univ., Univ. of North Carolina, Eastern Kentucky Univ., California Univ. of Tech.); Distinguished Alumnus Award, Univ. of North Carolina, Alumni Award, Grinnell Coll., Humanitarian of the Year, The Michigan Roundtable for Diversity and Inclusion, Trillium Lifetime Achievement Award, Michigan Women's Foundation, named by TIME magazine one of the nation's "10 best college presidents" 2009. *Address:* c/o Office of the President, University of Michigan, 2074 Fleming Administration Building, 503 Thompson Street, Ann Arbor, MI 41809-1340, USA. *E-mail:* presoff@umich.edu.

COLEMAN, Norm, BA, JD; American lawyer and politician; b. Brooklyn; m. Laurie Coleman; one s. one d.; ed Hofstra Univ., Univ. of Iowa; served in Office of Attorney-Gen. of Minn. in various positions including Chief Prosecutor and Solicitor-Gen. of State of Minn. 1976–93; elected Mayor of St Paul (Conservative Democrat) 1993, re-elected 1997 (Republican); unsuccessful Republican cand. for Gov. of Minn. 1998; Senator from Minn. 2003–09, mem. Foreign Relations Cttee, Chair. Sub-Cttee on Western Hemisphere, Peace Corps and Narcotics Affairs; advisor, Republican Jewish Coalition, Washington, DC 2009–. *Leisure interests:* playing basketball with his daughter, juggling, Bob Dylan's music. *Address:* Republican Jewish Coalition, 50 F Street, NW, Suite 100, Washington, DC 20001, USA. *Telephone:* (202) 638-6688. *Fax:* (202) 638-6694. *Website:* www.rjchq.org.

COLEMAN, Ornette; American jazz musician; b. 9 March 1930, Fort Worth, Tex.; s. of Randolph Coleman and Rosa Coleman; m. Jayne Cortez (divorced 1964); one s.; ed Lennox School of Jazz; player of alto and tenor saxophone, trumpet, violin, bassoon; developed Harmoldic music theory; mem. various bands including own Coleman Quartet and Prime Time mid-1970s–, currently with Sound Grammer quartet; has appeared in numerous major festivals world-wide; has toured in Japan, Europe, Africa; Guggenheim Foundation Fellow 1967, 1974; mem. American Acad. of Arts and Letters; Dr hc (Univ. of Pennsylvania), (Bard Coll.), (New School for Social Research), (Berklee School of Music); Praemium Imperiale, Japan Art Asscn 2001, MacArthur Genius Award, American Music Center Letter of Distinction, Lillian Gisch Prize, NY State Gov. Arts Award, Grammy Lifetime Achievement Award 2007. *Film:* Ornette: Made in America 1986. *Compositions include:* Music of Ornette Coleman (works for string quartet and woodwind quintet), Skies of America and over 100 compositions for small jazz group and larger ensembles. *Recordings include:* albums: Something Else 1958, Tomorrow is the Question 1959, The Shape of Jazz to Come 1959, Change of the Century 1960, This is Our Music 1960, Free Jazz 1961, Ornette! 1961, Ornette on

Tenor 1961, The Town Hall Concert 1962, 1963, Chappaqua Suite 1965, Live at the Tivoli 1965, The Great London Concert 1966, The Empty Foxhole 1966, Music of Ornette Coleman 1967, Live in Milano 1968, New York is Now 1968, Love Call 1968, Ornette At 12 1969, Crisis 1969, Friends and Neighbours 1970, The Art of Improvisation 1970, Science Fiction 1972, Skies of America 1972, Twins 1972, Dancing in Your Head 1976, Body Meta 1976, Soapsuds (with Charlie Haden) 1977, Broken Shadows 1982, Opening the Caravan of Dreams 1985, Prime Time/ Time Design 1985, Song X 1986, In All Languages 1987, Virgin Beauty 1988, At the Golden Circle, Stockholm 1987, Naked Lunch 1992, Tone Dialling 1995, Colours: Live from Leipzig 1996, Complete Science Fiction Sessions 2000, Song X (with Pat Metheny) 2005, Sound Grammar (Pulitzer Prize for Music 2007) 2006. *Address:* Sound Grammar, c/o Phrase Text, Inc., POB 20071, London Terrace Station, New York, NY 10011, USA. *Telephone:* (646) 238-9942. *Fax:* (212) 431-1753. *E-mail:* phrasetext@gmail.com. *Website:* www.ornettecoleman.com.

COLEMAN, Sir Robert John, Kt, KCMG, MA, JD; British lawyer, academic and international organization official; *Visiting Professor, School of Law and Social Science, University of Plymouth;* b. 8 Sept. 1943; m. Malinda Tigay Cutler 1966; two d.; ed Devonport High School for Boys, Plymouth, Jesus Coll. Oxford and Univ. of Chicago Law School, USA; Lecturer in Law, Univ. of Birmingham 1967–70; called to the Bar 1969; in practice as barrister-at-law, London 1970–73; Admin., subsequently Prin. Admin., EC 1974–82, Deputy Head of Div. 1983, Head of Div. 1984–87, Dir Public Procurement 1987–90, Dir Approximation of Laws, Freedom of Establishment and Freedom to Provide Services, the Professions 1990–91, Dir-Gen. Transport, EC 1991–99; Dir-Gen. Health and Consumer Protection 1999–2003; Sr Practitioner Fellow, Inst. of Governance, Queen's Univ., Belfast 2003–04, Visiting Research Fellow 2004–07; Visiting Prof., School of Law and Social Science, Univ. of Plymouth 2005–; taught at World Maritime Univ., Malmo, Sweden and Inst. of Int. Maritime Law, Malta 2005–11; EU Liaison Officer, Baltic and Int. Maritime Council 2005–; mem. Admin. Bd European Maritime Safety Agency, Lisbon 2008–12. *Publications include:* numerous articles in professional journals. *Leisure interest:* singing. *Address:* Flete House 3, Ivybridge, PL219NX, England (home). *Telephone:* (1752) 830147 (home). *E-mail:* robert.coleman18@btinternet.com.

COLEMAN, Terence (Terry) Francis Frank, LLB, FRSA; British journalist and writer; b. 13 Feb. 1931; s. of Jack Coleman and D. I. B. Coleman; m. 1st Lesley Fox-Strangeways Vane 1954 (divorced); two d.; m. 2nd Vivien Rosemary Lumsdaine Wallace 1981; one s. one d.; ed 14 schools, latterly Poole Grammar School, Univ. of London; fmr reporter, Poole Herald; fmr Ed. Savoir Faire; fmr Sub-Ed. Sunday Mercury, Birmingham Post; Reporter then Arts Corresp. The Guardian 1961–70, Chief Feature Writer 1970–74, 1976–79, New York Corresp. 1981, Special Corresp. 1982–89; Special Writer with Daily Mail 1974–76; Assoc. Ed. The Independent 1989–91; columnist, The Guardian 1992–; Feature Writer of the Year, British Press Awards 1982, Journalist of the Year (What the Papers Say Award) 1988. *Publications include:* The Railway Navvies (Yorkshire Post Prize for Best First Book of the Year) 1965, A Girl for the Afternoons 1965, Providence and Mr Hardy (with Lois Deacon) 1966, The Only True History: Collected Journalism 1969, Passage to America 1972, An Indiscretion in the Life of an Heiress (Hardy's first novel) (ed.) 1976, The Liners 1976, The Scented Brawl: Collected Journalism 1978, Southern Cross 1979, Thanksgiving 1981, Movers and Shakers: Collected Interviews 1987, Thatcher's Britain 1987, Empire 1994, W. G. Grace: A Biography 1997, Nelson: The Man and the Legend (biog.) 2001, Olivier: The Authorised Biography 2005, Great Interviews of the 20th Century 2008, The Old Vic: The Story of a Great Theatre 2014. *Leisure interests:* cricket, opera and circumnavigation. *Address:* c/o PFD, Drury House, 34–43 Russell Street, London, WC2B 5HA, England (office). *Telephone:* (20) 7344-1000 (office); (20) 7720-2651 (home). *Fax:* (20) 7836-9543 (office). *Website:* www.pfd.co.uk (office).

COLERIDGE, David Ean; British fmr insurance executive; b. 7 June 1932; s. of Guy Cecil Richard Coleridge and Katherine Cicely Stewart Smith; m. Susan Senior 1955; three s.; ed Eton Coll.; with Glanvill Enthoven 1950–57; joined R. W. Sturge & Co. 1957, Dir 1966–95; Chair. A. L. Sturge (Holdings) Ltd (now Sturge Holdings PLC) 1978–95; mem. Cttee of Lloyd's Underwriting Agents Asscn 1974–82, Chair. 1981–82; mem. Council and Cttee of Lloyd's 1983–86, 1988–92; Deputy Chair. Lloyd's 1985, 1988, 1989, Chair. 1991–92; Dir Wise Speke Holdings Ltd 1987–94, Ockham Holdings PLC (now Highway Insurance PLC) 1996– (Chair. 1995). *Leisure interests:* golf, racing, gardening, family. *Address:* 37 Egerton Terrace, London, SW3 2BU, England (home). *Telephone:* (1730) 813277 (home).

COLERIDGE, Nicholas David, CBE; British publisher, journalist and author; *President, Condé Nast International;* b. 4 March 1957, London; s. of David Ean Coleridge (q.v.) and Susan Coleridge (née Senior); m. Georgia Metcalfe 1989; three s. one d.; ed Eton, Trinity Coll., Cambridge; Assoc. Ed. Tatler 1979–81; columnist Evening Standard 1981–84; Features Ed. Harpers and Queen 1985–86, Ed. 1986–89; Editorial Dir Condé Nast Publs 1989–91, Man. Dir Condé Nast UK 1992–, Vice-Pres. Condé Nast International 1999–2012, Pres. 2012–, Dir Condé Nast France, Condé Nast India; Chair. British Fashion Council 2000–03, Fashion Rocks for The Prince's Trust 2003, Periodical Publrs Asscn 2004–07; Vice-Chair. The Campaign for Wool 2009–13, Chair. 2013–; mem. Council RCA 1995–2000; Young Journalist of the Year, British Press Awards 1983, Mark Boxer Award for Editorial Excellence 2001, Professional Publishers Asscn Marcus Morris Lifetime Achievement Award 2013. *Publications include:* Tunnel Vision 1982, Around the World in 78 Days 1984, Shooting Stars 1984, The Fashion Conspiracy 1988, How I Met My Wife and Other Stories 1991, Paper Tigers 1993, With Friends Like These 1997, Streetsmart 1999, Godchildren 2002, A Much Married Man 2006, Deadly Sins 2009, The Adventuress 2012. *Address:* Condé Nast, Vogue House, Hanover Square, London, W1S 1JU (office); 29 Royal Avenue, London, SW3 4QE (home); Wolverton Hall, nr Pershore, Worcs., WR10 2AU, England (home). *Telephone:* (20) 7499-9080 (office). *Website:* www.condenast.co.uk (office).

COLES, Sir (Arthur) John, MA, GCMG; British diplomatist (retd); b. 13 Nov. 1937; s. of Arthur S. Coles and Doris G. Coles; m. Anne M. S. Graham 1965; two s. one d.; ed Magdalen Coll. School, Brackley and Magdalen Coll., Oxford; joined HM Diplomatic Service 1960; Middle Eastern Centre for Arabic Studies, Lebanon 1960–62; Third Sec., Embassy in Khartoum 1962–64; Asst Political Agent, Trucial States (Dubai) 1968–71; Head of Chancery, Cairo 1975–77; Counsellor, Perm. Mission to EEC 1977–80, Head of S Asian Dept, FCO 1980–81, Pvt. Sec. to Prime

Minister 1981–84, Amb. to Jordan 1984–88, High Commr to Australia 1988–91, Deputy Under-Sec. of State, FCO 1991–94, Perm. Under-Sec. of State and Head of HM Diplomatic Service 1994–97; Dir B.G. PLC 1998–2009; Visiting Fellow, All Souls Coll. Oxford 1998–99; Trustee, Imperial War Museum 1999–2004; Chair. Sight Savers International 2001–07. *Publications:* British Influence and the Euro 1999, Making Foreign Policy: A Certain Idea of Britain 2000, Blindness and the Visionary: The Life and Work of John Wilson 2006. *Leisure interests:* walking, cricket, bird-watching, reading, music. *Address:* Kelham, Dock Lane, Beaulieu, Hants., SO42 7YH, England.

COLES, John Morton, MA, PhD, ScD, FBA, FSA, FRSA; British/Canadian archaeologist and academic; b. 25 March 1930, Canada; s. of John L. Coles and Alice M. Brown; m. 1st Mona Shiach 1958 (divorced 1985); two s. two d.; m. 2nd Bryony Orme 1985; ed Univ. of Toronto, Canada, Univs of Edinburgh and Cambridge, UK; Carnegie Scholar 1959–60; Research Fellow, Univ. of Edinburgh 1959–60; Univ. Lecturer and Reader, Univ. of Cambridge 1960–80, Prof. of European Prehistory 1980–86; Visiting Prof., Centre for Maritime Archaeology, Nat. Museum of Denmark 1994; Pres. The Prehistoric Soc. 1978–82; mem. Academia Europaea 1989–, Royal Comm. on Ancient and Historical Monuments of Scotland 1992–2002, Discovery Programme Ireland 2001–05; Corresp. mem. Deutsches Archaeologisches Institut 1979; Fellow, Fitzwilliam Coll. Cambridge 1963–; British Acad. Fellow, Royal Swedish Acad. of Letters, History and Antiquities 1990, 1998, 2002; Visiting Fellow, Japan Asscn for the Promotion of Science 1994–95; Hon. Prof., Univ. of Exeter 1993–2003, Univ. of Hull 1996–99; Hon. FSA (Scotland) 2000; Hon. mem. Inst. of Field Archaeologists 1991; Dr hc (Uppsala) 1997; Chalmers-Jervise Prize 1960, Rhind Lecturer (with B. Coles), Soc. of Antiquaries of Scotland 1994–95, Grahame Clark Medal, British Acad. 1995, ICI Medal (jtly), British Archaeological Awards 1998, Europa Prize for Prehistory 2000, Gold Medal, Soc. of Antiquaries of London 2002, European Archaeological Heritage Prize 2006, Gold Medal, Royal Swedish Acad. of Letters, History and Antiquities 2009. *Publications include:* The Archaeology of Early Man (with E. Higgs) 1969, Field Archaeology in Britain 1972, The Bronze Age in Europe (with A. Harding) 1979, Experimental Archaeology 1979, Prehistory of the Somerset Levels (with B. Orme) 1980, The Archaeology of Wetlands 1984, Sweet Track to Glastonbury (with B. Coles) 1986, People of the Wetlands (with B. Coles) 1989, From the Waters of Oblivion 1991, Arthur Bulleid and the Glastonbury Lake Village 1892–1992 (with A. Goodall and S. Minnitt) 1992, Fenland Survey (with D. Hall) 1994, Rock Carvings of Uppland 1995, Industrious and Fairly Civilised: The Glastonbury Lake Village (with S. Minnitt) 1995, Enlarging the Past (with B. Coles) 1996, Lake Villages of Somerset (with S. Minnitt) 1996, Changing Landscapes: The Ancient Fenland (with D. Hall) 1998, Patterns in a Rocky Land: Rock Carvings in South-West Uppland, Sweden 2000, Shadows of a Northern Past: Rock Carvings of Bohuslän and Østfold 2005; numerous papers on European prehistory, field archaeology, experimental archaeology, wetland archaeology. *Leisure interests:* music, travel, wetlands. *Address:* Fursdon Mill Cottage, Cadbury, Devon, EX5 5JS, England (home). *Telephone:* (1392) 860125 (home). *E-mail:* jmcoles@btinternet.com.

COLES, Robert Martin, AB, LHD, MD; American child psychiatrist, writer and academic; *Professor Emeritus of Psychiatry and Medical Humanities, Department of Psychiatry, Harvard Medical School;* b. 12 Oct. 1929, Boston, Mass.; s. of Philip W. Coles and Sandra Coles (née Young); m. Jane Hallowell 1960; three s.; ed Harvard Coll. and Columbia Univ.; Intern, Univ. of Chicago clinics 1954–55; Resident in Psychiatry, Mass. Gen. Hosp., Boston 1955–56, McLean Hosp., Belmont 1956–57; Resident in Child Psychiatry, Judge Baker Guidance Center, Children's Hosp., Roxbury, Mass. 1957–58, Fellow 1960–61; mem. psychiatric staff, Mass. Gen. Hosp. 1960–62, Clinical Asst in Psychiatry, Harvard Univ. Medical School 1960–62, Research Psychiatrist in Health Services, Harvard Univ. 1963–, Lecturer in Gen. Educ. 1966–, Prof. of Psychiatry and Medical Humanities, Harvard Univ. Medical School 1977, now Prof. Emer.; mem. American Psychiatric Asscn; Fellow, American Acad. of Arts and Sciences; Hon. DrSci (North Carolina) 1979; awards include Pulitzer Prize for vols II and III of Children of Crisis series 1973, Sara Josepha Hale Award 1986. *Publications include:* William Carlos Williams: The Knack of Survival in America 1975, Walker Percy: An American Search 1979, Harvard Diary 1988, Times of Surrender: Selected Essays 1989, The Spiritual Life of Children, Bruce Springsteen's America: The People Listening, a Poet Singing 2004, Handing One Another Along: Literature and Social Reflection 2010; Children of Crisis series; numerous articles in professional journals. *Leisure interests:* tennis, bicycle riding, skiing. *Address:* 81 Carr Road, Concord, MA 01742, USA (home). *Telephone:* (617) 591-9389 (office); (617) 369-6498 (home). *E-mail:* Robert_Coles@hms.harvard.edu.

COLES, Sadie; British gallery owner; first worked as gallery dir for Anthony d'Offay; opened own gallery, Sadie Coles HQ, with paintings by John Currin and an installation by Sarah Lucas (one of the original Young British Artists) 1997, artists represented include Carl Andre, Darren Bader, Matthew Barney, Dirk Bell, Avner Ben Gal, Frank Benson, John Bock, Don Brown, Spartacus Chetwynd, Steven Claydon, William N. Copley, John Currin, Sam Durant, Shannon Ebner, Angus Fairhurst, Urs Fischer, Florian Hecker, Georg Herold, Jonathan Horowitz, David Korty, Gabriel Kuri, Jim Lambie, Hilary Lloyd, Sarah Lucas, Helen Marten, Victoria Morton, J. P. Munro, Laura Owens, Simon Periton, Raymond Pettibon, Elizabeth Peyton, Richard Prince, Ugo Rondinone, Wilhelm Sasnal, Gregor Schneider, Daniel Sinsel, Andreas Slominski, Christiana Soulou, Rudolf Stingel, Nicola Tyson, Paloma Varga Weisz, T. J. Wilcox and Andrea Zittel. *Address:* Sadie Coles HQ, 69 South Audley Street, London, W1K 2QZ, England (office). *Telephone:* (20) 7493-8611 (office). *Fax:* (20) 7499-4878 (office). *E-mail:* info@sadiecoles.com (office). *Website:* www.sadiecoles.com (office).

COLFER, Eoin; Irish children's writer; b. 14 May 1965, Wexford; m. Jackie Colfer; two s.; fmr teacher; invited to write new novel in Hitchhiker's Guide to the Galaxy series 2008; British Book Awards WH Smith Children's Book of the Year 2001, WH Smith Book Award 2002, German Children's Book Award 2004. *Publications:* juvenile: Benny and Omar 1998, Benny and Babe 1999, The Wish List 2000, Artemis Fowl 2001, Artemis Fowl: The Arctic Incident 2002, Artemis Fowl: The Eternity Code 2003, The Seventh Dwarf (novella) 2004, The Legend of Spud Murphy 2004, The Supernaturalist 2004, The Artemis Fowl Files 2004, Artemis Fowl: The Opal Deception 2005, Artemis Fowl and the Lost Colony 2006,

Half Moon Investigations 2006, Airman 2008, Artemis Fowl and the Atlantis Complex 2010, Artemis Fowl: The Last Guardian 2012; for younger children: Going Potty 1999, Ed's Funny Feet 2000, Ed's Bed 2001; has also written plays; other: And Another Thing … Douglas Adams' Hitchhiker's Guide to the Galaxy: Part Six of Three 2009, Plugged 2011. *Address:* 1 Priory Hall, Spawell Road, Wexford, Ireland (office); Brookes Batchellor LLP, 102–108 Clerkenwell Road, London, EC1M 5SA, England. *Website:* www.eoincolfer.com.

COLGAN, Michael Anthony, OBE, BA; Irish theatre, film and television producer; *Artistic Director, The Gate Theatre, Dublin;* b. 17 July 1950, Dublin; s. of James Joseph Colgan and Josephine Patricia Colgan (née Geoghegan); ed Trinity Coll., Dublin; Dir Abbey Theatre, Dublin 1974–78; Co-Man. Irish Theatre Co. 1977–78; Man. Dublin Theatre Festival 1978–80, Artistic Dir 1981–83, mem. Bd of Dirs 1983–; Artistic Dir Gate Theatre, Dublin 1983– (also mem. Bd of Dirs); Exec. Dir Little Bird Films 1986–; Co-founder Blue Angel Film Co. 1999 (producers of The Beckett Film Project with RTE and Channel 4 2000 and Celebration by Harold Pinter with Channel 4 2006); Artistic Dir Parma Festival, Italy 1982; Chair. St Patrick's Festival 1996–99; mem. Bd Millennium Festivals Ltd, Laura Pels Foundation, New York 2000–04, Irish Arts Council 1989–94, Governing Authority, Dublin City Univ. 1998–2001; Chevalier, Ordre des Arts et des Lettres 2007; Hon. LLD (Trinity Coll. Dublin) 2000; Sunday Independent Arts Award 1985, 1987, Nat. Entertainment Award 1996, People of the Year Award 1999, Irish Times Theatre Lifetime Achievement Award 2006. *Plays produced:* Faith Healer (Dublin, New York, Edinburgh), No Man's Land (Dublin, London), I'll Go On (Samuel Beckett), Dublin, Paris, London, New York; Salomé (Oscar Wilde), Dublin, Edin., Charleston, SC; Three Sisters (Anton Chekhov), Dublin and Royal Court Theatre, London; six Beckett Festivals, Dublin, London, New York (all 19 Samuel Beckett stage plays); four Pinter Festivals, Dublin and New York; director: First Love, Faith Healer, 's Last Tape. *World premieres include:* The Birds, Molly Sweeney (Brian Friel), Dublin, London and New York; Port Authority (Conor McPherson); Afterplay (Brian Friel); See You Next Tuesday (Francis Veber); Shining City (Conor McPherson); The Home Place (Brian Friel). *Film:* Beckett on Film (co-producer) 2000: all 19 of Beckett's plays filmed using internationally known dirs and actors (Best Drama Award, South Bank Show 2002, US Peabody Award 2002). *Television:* Two Lives (exec. producer) for RTÉ 1986, Troubles (two hour-two-hour films) for LWT 1996. *Leisure interests:* Schubert, Beckett, New York City, middle distance running, chamber music. *Address:* The Gate Theatre, 1 Cavendish Row, Dublin 1, Ireland (office). *Telephone:* (1) 874-4369 (office). *Fax:* (1) 874-5373 (office). *E-mail:* info@gate-theatre.ie (office). *Website:* www.gate-theatre.ie (office).

COLLARD, Jean Philippe; French pianist; b. 27 Jan. 1948, Mareuil-sur-Aÿ (Marne); s. of Michel Collard and Monique (Philipponnat) Collard; m. 2nd Ariane de Brion; three s. (two from previous m.) one d.; ed Conservatoire Nat. de Musique de Paris; Chevalier, Ordre des Arts et des Lettres, Chevalier, Ordre nat. du Mérite, Chevalier Légion d'honneur 2003. *Recordings include:* music by Bach, Brahms, Debussy, Fauré, Franck, Rachmaninov, Ravel, Saint-Saëns, Schubert, Chopin, Mozart. *Leisure interests:* windsurfing, tennis. *Address:* Angela Sulivan, Sulivan Sweetland, 1 Hillgate Place, Balham Hill, London SW12 9ER, England (office). *Telephone:* (20) 8772-3470 (office). *E-mail:* info@sulivansweetland.co.uk (office); pianojpc@aol.com (home). *Website:* www.sulivansweetland.co.uk (office).

COLLENETTE, David Michael, PC, BA (Hons), MA; Canadian academic, business adviser and fmr politician; *Senior Counsel, Hill & Knowlton;* b. 24 June 1946, London, UK; s. of David H. Collenette and Sarah M. Collenette; m. Penny Collenette 1975; one s.; ed Glendon Coll., York Univ.; fmrly worked in life insurance, plastics and exec. recruitment; fmr Exec. Vice-Pres. Mandrake Man. Consultants; elected to House of Commons 1974, 1980, 1993, 1997, 2000, retd 2004; Parl. Sec. to Postmaster-Gen. 1978–79, to Pres. of Privy Council 1980–81; Minister of State (Multiculturalism) 1983–84; Minister of Nat. Defence and Minister of Veterans Affairs 1993–96, of Transport 1997–2003; mem. Liberal Party; Minister responsible for Crown Corpns 2002–03; Chancellor Royal Mil. Coll. of Canada 1993–96; mem. Int. Advisory Council, Inst. of Int. Studies, Stanford Univ. 1999–2005; Distinguished Fellow, Dept of Political Science, Glendon Coll., York Univ. 2004–; currently Sr Counsel, Hill & Knowlton (consultancy), Canada; Head of Ottawa Transportation Task Force 2007; Fellow and Vice-Chair. (North America), Chartered Inst. of Logistics and Transport, also Int. Vice-Pres.; mem. Bd of Dirs Harbourfront Corpn; Queen's Silver Jubilee Medal 1977, Canada 125 Medal 1992, Queen's Golden Jubilee Medal 2003. *Leisure interests:* swimming, weight lifting, classical music, theatre. *Address:* Hill & Knowlton Canada, Suite 1100, 55 Metcalfe Street, Ottawa, ON K1P 6L5, Canada (office). *Telephone:* (613) 238-4371 (office). *Fax:* (613) 238-8642 (office). *E-mail:* david.collenette@hillandknowlton.ca (office); dcollenette@glendon.yorku.ca (office). *Website:* www.glendon.yorku.ca/publicaffairs; www.davidcollenette.com (office).

COLLETTE, Toni; Australian actress; b. 1 Dec. 1972, Sydney; m. Dave Galafassi 2003; one d.; ed Nat. Inst. for Dramatic Art, Sydney; jury mem. Cannes Film Festival 2007. *Films include:* Spotswood 1991, Muriel's Wedding 1994, This Marching Girl Thing 1994, Arabian Knight (voice) 1995, Lilian's Story 1995, Cosí 1996, The Pallbearer 1996, Emma 1996, Clockwatchers 1997, The James Gang 1997, Diana & Me 1997, The Boys 1997, Velvet Goldmine 1998, 8½ Women 1999, The Sixth Sense 1999, Shaft 2000, Hotel Splendide 2000, Changing Lanes 2002, Dirty Deeds 2002, About a Boy 2002, The Hours 2003, Japanese Story 2003, Connie and Carla 2004, The Last Shot 2004, In Her Shoes 2005, The Night Listener 2006, Little Miss Sunshine (Screen Actors' Guild Award for Outstanding Performance by a Cast 2007) 2006, Like Minds 2006, The Dead Girl 2006, Evening 2007, Nothing is Private 2007, The Black Balloon 2008, Hey Hey It's Esther Blueburger 2008, Mary and Max (voice) 2009, Foster 2011, Friday Night 2011, Jesus Henry Christ 2012. *Television includes:* Tsunami: The Aftermath 2006, United States of Tara (Emmy Award for Outstanding Lead Actress in a Comedy Series 2009, Golden Globe for best performance by an actress in a television series—comedy or musical 2010) 2009–. *Leisure interests:* yoga, mental and spiritual retreats in India, climbing Tibetan Himalayas. *Address:* c/o Shanahan Management, Level 3, Berman House, 91 Campbell Street, Surry Hills, NSW 2010, Australia; United Talent Agency Inc. (UTA), 9560 Wilshire Blvd, Suite 500, Beverly Hills, CA 90212, USA. *Telephone:* (2) 8202-1800; (310) 273-6700 (UTA). *Fax:* (2) 8202-1801; (310) 247-1111 (UTA).

COLLEY, Amadou, BSc, MBA; Gambian central banker; *Governor and Chairman, Central Bank of The Gambia;* b. 10 Oct. 1962, Sanchaba Sulay Jobe, Kombo North Dist, West Coast Region; ed Fourah Bay Coll., Univ. of Sierra Leone, Birmingham Business School, UK; Dir, Banking Dept, Central Bank of The Gambia –2010, Gov. and Chair. 2010–. *Address:* Office of the Governor, Central Bank of The Gambia, 1–2 ECOWAS Avenue, Banjul, The Gambia (office). *Telephone:* 4228103 (office). *Fax:* 4226969 (office). *E-mail:* info@cbg.gm (office). *Website:* www.cbg.gm (office).

COLLEY, Linda Jane, CBE, PhD, FRSL, FBA; British academic and writer; *Shelby M.C. Davis 1958 Professor of History, Princeton University;* b. 13 Sept. 1949, Chester, England; d. of Roy Colley and the late Marjorie Colley (née Hughes); m. David Nicholas Cannadine (q.v.) 1982; one d. (deceased); ed Univs of Bristol and Cambridge; Eugenie Strong Research Fellow, Girton Coll., Cambridge 1975–78, Fellow, Newnham Coll., Cambridge 1978–79, Christ's Coll., Cambridge 1979–81; Asst Prof. of History, Yale Univ., USA 1982–85, Assoc. Prof. 1985–90, Prof. of History 1990–92, Richard M. Colgate Prof. of History 1992–98, Dir Lewis Walpole Library 1982–96; Prof., School of History, LSE 1998–2003, Leverhulme Personal Research Prof., European Inst. 1998–2003; Shelby M.C. Davis 1958 Prof. of History, Princeton Univ., USA 2003–; mem. Bd British Library 1999–2003, Princeton University Press 2007–; mem. Advisory Bd Tate Britain 1999–2003, Paul Mellon Centre for British Art 1999–2003, Research Cttee, British Museum 2012–; Visiting Fellowship, Humanities Research Centre, ANU, Canberra 2005; Glaxo-Smith-Kline Sr Fellowship Nat. Humanities Center, NC 2006; Fletcher Jones Distinguished Fellowship, Huntington Library, Calif. 2010; Birkelund Fellowship, Cullman Center for Scholars and Writers, New York Public Library 2013–14; Hon. Fellow, Christ's Coll., Cambridge 2005; Dr hc (South Bank, London) 1999, (Essex) 2004, (East Anglia) 2005, (Bristol) 2006, (Hull) 2012; Wolfson Prize 1993, Anstey Lecturer, Univ. of Kent 1994, William Church Memorial Lecturer, Brown Univ. 1994, Distinguished Lecturer in British History, Univ. of Texas 1995, Trevelyan Lecturer, Univ. of Cambridge 1997, Wiles Lecturer, Queen's Univ. Belfast 1997, Prime Minister's Millennium Lecture 2000, Raleigh Lecturer, British Acad. 2002, Nehru Lecturer 2002, Bateson Lecturer, Oxford 2003, Chancellor Dunning Trust Lecturer, Queen's Univ., Ont. 2004, Byrn Lecturer, Vanderbilt Univ. 2005, Annual Lecture in Int. History, LSE 2006, C.P. Snow Lecture, Cambridge 2007, Pres's Lecture, Princeton Univ. 2007, Political Science Quarterly Lecture 2007, Gordon B. Hinkley Lecturer 2010, Univ. of Utah, Bosley-Warnock Lecturer, Univ. of Delaware 2010, Annual ISEHR Lecturer, Delhi 2011, Keyser Lecturer, George Washington Univ. 2011, Margaret Macmillan Memorial Lecturer, Univ. of Toronto 2013. *Radio:* Acts of Union, Acts of Disunion (BBC Radio 4) 15 talks 2014. *Publications:* In Defiance of Oligarchy: The Tory Party 1714–60 1982, Namier 1989, Crown Pictorial: Art and the British Monarchy 1990, Britons: Forging the Nation 1707–1837 (Wolfson Prize 1993) 1992, Captives: Britain, Empire and the World 1600–1850 2002, The Ordeal of Elizabeth Marsh: A Woman in World History 2007, Taking Stock of Taking Liberties (catalogue of British Library exhbn) 2008, Acts of Union and Disunion 2013; numerous articles and reviews in UK and American learned journals. *Leisure interests:* travel, looking at art, politics. *Address:* c/o Gill Coleridge, Rogers, Coleridge & White Ltd, 20 Powis Mews, London, W11 1JN, England (office); Department of History, Princeton University, 129 Dickinson Hall, Princeton, NJ 08544-1017, USA (office). *Telephone:* (609) 258-8076 (office). *E-mail:* lcolley@princeton.edu (office). *Website:* his.princeton.edu (office).

COLLIGNON, Stefan Colin, PhD; German economist and academic; *Professor of Political Economy, Sant'Anna School of Advanced Studies;* b. 11 Dec. 1951, Munich; s. of Klaus Collignon and Rosemarie Collignon; m. Judith Zahler 1984; ed Institut d'Etudes Politiques, Paris, Free Univ. of Berlin, Univ. of Dar es Salaam, Tanzania, Queen Elizabeth House, Oxford, UK, London School of Econs; financial analyst, First Nat. Bank in Dallas, Paris 1975–76; teacher, Lindi Secondary School, Deutscher Entwicklungsdienst (German Volunteer Service), Tanzania 1977–79; Man. Dir and Chair. Dorcas Ltd, London 1981–88; Dir Research and Communication, Asscn for the Monetary Union of Europe, Paris 1989–98; Lecturer, Institut d'Etudes Politiques, Paris 1990–95, Free Univ. of Berlin 1997–2000; Prof., Collège d'Europe, Bruges 1998–2005; Centennial Prof. of European Political Economy, LSE 2001–08; Visiting Prof., Harvard Univ. 2005–07, also Assoc., Minda de Gunzburg Centre for European Studies; Prof. of Political Economy, Sant'Anna School of Advanced Studies, Pisa 2007–; Chair. Scientific Cttee Centro Europa Ricerche, Rome 2007–; Visiting Prof., Institut d'Etudes Politiques, Lille 2005–, Univ. of Hamburg 2007–08; Pres. Asscn France-Birmanie 1990–; mem. Bd of Dirs Glunz AG 1998–, Sonae Industria SGPS, Portugal 2003–05. *Publications:* Europe's Monetary Future (Vol. I) 1994, The Monetary Economics of Europe: Causes of the EMS Crisis (Vol. II) 1994, European Monetary Policy (ed.) 1997, Exchange Rate Policies in Emerging Asian Countries 1999, Monetary Stability in Europe 2002, Private Sector Involvement in the Euro 2003, Vive la république europeenne (The European Republic) (Prix du meilleur livre politique 2004) 2003, Rebalancing the Global Economy. Four Perspectives on the Future of the International Monetary System, Europe in Dialogue 2010/01 2010; numerous articles and book chapters on monetary union. *Address:* 11 rue d'Ormesson, 75004 Paris, France (home); Scuola Superiore Sant'Anna, Piazza Martiri della Libertà, 33, 56127 Pisa, Italy (office). *Telephone:* 1-40-27-95-63 (home); (050) 883241 (office). *Fax:* 1-40-27-90-45 (home); (050) 883241 (office). *E-mail:* stefan.collignon@sssup.it (office). *Website:* www.stefancollignon.de (home).

COLLIN, Jean-Philippe, MEng; French business executive; *Executive Vice-President, Automobiles Peugeot;* b. 28 May 1956; ed Ecole Supérieure d'Electricité (Supelec); began career with IBM in 1982, served as man. of components procurement centre in USA and Chair. of one of co.'s Global Purchasing Councils, was also in charge of Tech. and Quality Lab.; joined Valeo 1995, Vice-Pres., Purchasing, for Electronics Div., later promoted to Vice-Pres. Purchasing Valeo Group; Sr Vice-Pres., Sourcing, Thomson 1999–2002, put in charge of spring cost reduction programme 2002, later served as Sr Vice-Pres., Integrated Circuits, Thomson Optical Systems, mem. Thomson Exec. Cttee; Vice-Pres., Purchasing, for PSA Peugeot Citroën, as part of Group's Platforms, Eng and Purchasing Dept 2004–07, reported directly to Chair. and Pres. PSA Peugeot Citroën Group as mem. Extended Exec. Cttee 2007, mem. PSA Peugeot Citroën Man. Bd and Exec. Vice-Pres. Automobiles Peugeot 2008–. *Address:* PSA Peugeot Citroën SA, 75 avenue de la Grande-Armée, 75116 Paris, France (office). *Telephone:* 1-40-66-55-11 (office). *Fax:* 1-40-66-54-14 (office). *E-mail:* info@psa-peugeot-citroen.com (office). *Website:* www.psa-peugeot-citroen.com (office); www.peugeot.com (office).

COLLINGWOOD, Paul David, MBE; British professional cricketer; b. 26 May 1976, Shotley Bridge, Co. Durham, England; s. of David Collingwood and Janet Collingwood; m. Vicki Collingwood; two d.; ed Blackfyne Comprehensive School (now Consett Community Sports Coll.); all-rounder; right-handed batsman; right-arm medium pace bowler; plays for Durham 1995–, England 2001–11 (ODI (One-Day Int.) Capt. 2007–08, T20I Capt. 2007–11), Delhi Daredevils 2009–10, Rajasthan Royals 2011–; First-class debut: against Northants., Riverside, Durham 1996; Test debut: Sri Lanka v England, Galle 2–6 Dec. 2003; ODI debut: England v Pakistan, Birmingham 7 June 2001; T20I debut: England v Australia, Southampton 13 June 2005; has played in 68 Tests, scored 4,259 runs (ten centuries), average 40.56, highest score 206, took 17 wickets, best bowling (innings) 3/23, (match) 3/35; ODIs: 197 matches, scored 5,092 runs, average 35.36, highest score 120 not out, took 111 wickets, average 38.68, best bowling 6/31; First-class: 206 matches, 11,819 runs, average 36.368, highest score 206, took 132 wickets, average 39.38, best bowling 5/52; played for Richmond Cricket Club in Melbourne Premier League 2000–01; only third English batsman to score a double century in Australia 2007; first Durham player to score a Test century for England and first to hit one at Riverside Ground 2007; played in three winning Ashes Test series 2005, 2009, 2010–11; most capped ODI cricketer for England; captained England Twenty20 team to World Twenty20 championship 2010; announced retirement from Test cricket Jan. 2011; writes a fortnightly column for BBC; voted Player of the Year by the Durham mems 2000, Jack Ryder Medal for Best Player in Melbourne Premier League (jt recipient) 2001, Wisden Cricketer of the Year (jt recipient) 2007. *Leisure interests:* playing golf, going to the gym, Sunderland Asscn Football Club. *Address:* c/o Durham County Cricket Club, County Ground, Riverside, Chester-le-Street, DH3 3QR, County Durham, England. *Telephone:* (191) 387-1717. *Fax:* (191) 387-1616. *E-mail:* reception@durhamccc.co.uk. *Website:* www.durhamccc.org.uk.

COLLINS, Billy, AB, PhD; American poet and academic; *Distinguished Professor, Lehman College, City University of New York;* b. 22 March 1941, New York; m. Diane Collins 1979; ed Holy Cross Coll., Univ. of California, Riverside; Prof. of English, Lehman Coll., CUNY 1969–2001, Distinguished Prof. 2001–; Sr Distinguished Fellow, Winter Park Inst., Rollins Coll.; Visiting Writer, Poets House, NI 1993–96, Lenoir-Rhyne Coll. 1994, Ohio State Univ. 1998; Resident Poet, Burren Coll. of Art, Ireland 1996, Sarah Lawrence Coll. 1998–2000; Adjunct Prof., Columbia Univ. 2000–01; conducts summer poetry workshops at Univ. Coll. Galway, Ireland; Library of Congress's Poet Laureate Consultant in Poetry 2001, US Poet Laureate 2001–03; Poet Laureate of New York State 2004–06; Fellow, New York Foundation for the Arts, Nat. Endowment for the Arts, Guggenheim Foundation; NEA Fellowship 1993; Guggenheim Fellowship 1995; New York Foundation for the Arts Poetry Fellowship 1986, Nat. Endowment for the Arts Creative Writing Fellowship 1988, Nat. Poetry Series Competition Winner 1990, Bess Hokin Prize 1991, Literary Lion, New York Public Library 1992, Frederick Bock Prize 1992, Guggenheim Fellowship 1993, Levinson Prize 1995, Paterson Poetry Prize 1999, J. Howard and Barbara M. J. Wood Prize 1999, Pushcart Prize 2002, Mark Twain Prize for Humor in Poetry, Poetry Foundation 2004. *Recording:* The Best Cigarette 1997. *Publications include:* Pokerface 1977, Video Poems 1980, The Apple that Astonished Paris 1988, Questions About Angels 1991, The Art of Drowning 1995, Picnic, Lightning 1998, Taking Off Emily Dickinson's Clothes 2000, Sailing Alone Around the Room: New and Selected Poems 2001, Nine Horses 2002, The Trouble with Poetry 2005, She Was Just Seventeen 2006, Ballistics 2008, Horoscopes for the Dead 2012, Aimless Love 2013; editor: Poetry 180: A Turning Back to Poetry, 180 More: Extraordinary Poems for Everyday Life; poems in many anthologies, including The Best American Poetry 1992, 1993, 1997 and periodicals, including Poetry, American Poetry, Review, American Scholar, Harper's, Paris Review and The New Yorker. *Address:* Steven Barclay Agency, 12 Western Avenue, Petaluma, CA 94952, USA (office); Lehman College, Carman Hall, Room 392, 250 Bedford Park Boulevard West, Bronx, New York, NY 10468 (office); 185 Route 202, Somers, NY 10589, USA (home). *Website:* www.lehman .edu/academics/arts-humanities/english (office); www.bigsnap.com.

COLLINS, Christopher Douglas, FCA; British business executive; b. 19 Jan. 1940, Welwyn; s. of Douglas Collins and Patricia Collins; m. Susan Lumb 1976; one s. one d.; ed Eton Coll.; articled clerk, Peat Marwick Mitchell 1958–64; Man. Dir Goya Ltd 1968–75, Dir 1975–80; amateur steeplechase jockey 1965–75; rep. of GB in three-day equestrian events 1974–80; Steward, Jockey Club 1980–81; mem. Horse Race Betting Levy Board 1982–84; Chair. Aintree Racecourse Ltd 1983–88, Nat. Stud 1986–88; joined Hanson PLC 1989, Dir 1991, Vice-Chair. 1995, Deputy Chair. 1997, Chair. 1998–2005; Chair. Forth Ports PLC 2000–, Racecourse Holdings Trust 2005–; Dir Old Mutual PLC 1999–2005, Chair. 2005–09; Dir The Go-Ahead Group PLC 1999–, Alfred McAlpine PLC 2000–. *Leisure interests:* riding, skiing. *Address:* c/o Old Mutual plc, 5th Floor, Old Mutual Place, 2 Lambeth Hill, London, EC4V 4GG, England. *Telephone:* (20) 7002-7204. *E-mail:* matthew.gregorowski@we.co.uk. *Website:* www.oldmutual.com.

COLLINS, Col (retd) Eileen Marie; American pilot and astronaut (retd) and air force officer (retd); b. 19 Nov. 1956, Elmira, NY; m. Pat Youngs 1987; one s. one d.; ed Elmira Free Acad., Corning Community Coll., Syracuse Univ., Stanford Univ., Webster Univ., Air Force Inst. of Tech.; trained as USAF pilot, Vance Air Force Base, Okla 1979–82; C-141 Aircraft Commdr and Instructor Pilot, Travis Air Force Base, Calif. 1983–85; Asst Prof. of Math. and T-41 Instructor Pilot, USAF Acad., Colo 1986–89; attended Air Force Test Pilot School, Edwards Air Force Base, Calif. 1990; selected by NASA to become astronaut 1991, served in various roles including assignment to Orbiter eng support, mem. support team responsible for Orbiter prelaunch checkout, final launch configuration, crew ingress/egress, landing/recovery, worked in NASA Mission Control as spacecraft communicator (CAPCOM), Astronaut Office Spacecraft Systems Br. Chief, Chief Information Officer, Shuttle Br. Chief, Astronaut Safety Br. Chief, pilot on STS-63 mission 1995 (first woman to pilot space shuttle), STS-84 mission 1997, Commdr STS-93 mission 1999 (first woman to command space shuttle mission), Commdr STS-114 2005; retd from USAF 2005; mem. NASA Advisory Council 2006–; mem. Air Force Asscn, Order of Dedalians, Women Mil. Aviators, US Space Foundation, American Inst. of Aeronautics and Astronautics, Ninety-Nines; Hon. DSc (Univ. Coll. Dublin)

2006; Jackie Robinson Empire State Freedom Medal 1999, Soc. of Women Engineers (SWE) Resnik Challenger Medal 2003; Defense Superior Service Medal, Distinguished Flying Cross, Defense Meritorious Service Medal, Air Force Meritorious Service Medal with one oak leaf cluster, Air Force Commendation Medal with one oak leaf cluster, Armed Forces Expeditionary Medal for Service in Grenada (Operation Urgent Fury) 1983, NASA Outstanding Leadership Medal, NASA Space Flight Medals, Women in Space Science Award, Adler Planetarium 2006; Howard Hughes Memorial Award 2006; elected mem. Aviation Hall of Fame 2009; French Legion of Honor. *Address:* c/o NASA Advisory Council, Washington, DC 20546, USA.

COLLINS, Francis S., BS, MD, PhD; American physician, research scientist and institute director; *Director, National Institutes of Health;* b. Staunton, Va; ed Univ. of Virginia, Yale Univ., Univ. of N Carolina at Chapel Hill; residency in internal medicine, Univ. of N Carolina; Fellowship in Human Genetics, Yale Univ., developed technique called 'positional cloning'; fmr staff mem. Howard Hughes Medical Inst., Univ. of Michigan Medical Center, Ann Arbor, Mich. 1984–93, with research team identified gene for cystic fibrosis 1989, for neurofibromatosis 1990, for Huntington disease 1993, for a familial endocrine cancer syndrome, for type 2 diabetes and gene that causes Hutchinson-Gilford progeria syndrome; Dir Nat. Human Genome Research Inst., NIH, Bethesda, Md 1993–2008, also Sr Investigator, Genome Tech. Br., Dir NIH 2009–; mem. Inst. of Medicine, NAS; co-recipient Gairdner Foundation Int. Award for work on Cystic Fibrosis 1990, Presidential Medal of Freedom 2007. *Publications:* The Language of God: A Scientist Presents Evidence for Belief 2006, The Language of Life: DNA and the Revolution in Personalized Medicine 2010. *Leisure interests:* guitarist and vocalist for The Directors (rock band comprised of NIH scientists and execs). *Address:* National Institutes of Health, 9000 Rockville Pike, Bethesda, MD 20892, USA (office). *Telephone:* (301) 496-4000 (office). *E-mail:* NIHinfo@od.nih.gov (office). *Website:* www.nih.gov (office).

COLLINS, Gerard; Irish fmr politician; b. 16 Oct. 1938, Abbeyfeale, Co. Limerick; s. of the late James J. Collins and Margaret Collins; m. Hilary Tattan; ed Univ. Coll. Dublin; fmr vocational teacher; mem. Dáil 1967–97; Acting Gen. Sec. Fianna Fáil Party 1964–67; Parl. Sec. to Minister for Industry and Commerce and to Minister for the Gaeltacht 1969–70; Minister for Posts and Telegraphs 1970–73; mem. Consultative Ass. of Council of Europe 1973–75; Limerick Co. Council 1974–77; Minister for Justice 1977–81, 1987–89, for Foreign Affairs March–Dec. 1982, 1989–93; Chair. Parl. Cttee on EEC Affairs 1983–87; mem. European Parl. 1994–2004 (Vice-Pres. 1998–99), Leader Fianna Fáil Group, Vice-Pres. Union for Europe Group, Pres. European Parl. Del. to S. Asia and South Asian Asscn for Regional Co-operation (SAARC); Chair. of the EU-South Africa Interparliamentary Del. *Address:* The Hill, Abbeyfeale, Co. Limerick, Ireland (home).

COLLINS, Jackie, OBE; British novelist; b. 4 Oct. 1937, sister of Joan Collins (q.v.); Galaxy Nat. Book Award for Outstanding Achievement 2011. *Screenplays include:* Yesterday's Hero, The World is Full of Married Men, The Stud. *TV mini-series include:* Hollywood Wives (ABC TV), Lucky Chances (NBC TV), Lady Boss (NBC TV). *Publications include:* The World is Full of Married Men 1968, The Stud 1969, Sunday Simmons and Charlie Brick 1971, Lovehead 1974, The World is Full of Divorced Women 1975, Lovers and Gamblers 1977, The Bitch 1979, Chances 1981, Hollywood Wives 1983, Lucky 1985, Hollywood Husbands 1986, Rock Star 1988, Lady Boss 1990, American Star 1993, Hollywood Kids 1994, Vendetta – Lucky's Revenge 1996, Thrill 1998, LA Connections (four-part serial novel) 1998, Dangerous Kiss 1999, Hollywood Wives: The New Generation 2001, Lethal Seduction 2001, Deadly Embrace 2002, Hollywood Divorces 2003, Lovers and Players 2006, Drop Dead Beautiful 2007, Married Lovers 2008, Poor Little Bitch Girl 2010, Goddess of Vengeance 2011. *Address:* Steve Troha, St Martin's Press, 175 Fifth Avenue, New York, NY 10010, USA. *Telephone:* (646) 307-5569. *E-mail:* steve.troha@stmartins.com. *Website:* www.jackiecollins.com.

COLLINS, James J., AB, DPhil; American biomedical engineer and academic; *Professor of Biomedical Engineering, William F. Warren Distinguished Professor, University Professor and Co-Director Center for BioDynamics, Boston University;* b. 26 June 1965, New York, NY; ed Coll. of the Holy Cross, Univ. of Oxford, UK (Rhodes Scholar); Prof. of Biomedical Eng, Boston Univ., also William F. Warren Distinguished Prof., Univ. Prof. and Co-Dir Center for BioDynamics; Founding Faculty mem., Wyss Inst. for Biologically Inspired Eng, Harvard Univ., Visiting Prof., Dept of Systems Biology, Harvard Medical School; Howard Hughes Medical Inst. Investigator; MacArthur Fellow, Metcalf Cup and Prize, Boston Univ. 2000, NIH Dir's Pioneer Award 2007, Anthony J. Drexel Exceptional Achievement Award, Drexel Univ. 2009, Lagrange-CRT Foundation Prize 2010, World Technology Award in Biotechnology 2011. *Publications:* numerous papers in professional journals on synthetic biology, systems biology and antibiotics. *Address:* Biomedical Engineering, Boston University, ERB 307, 44 Cummington Street, Boston, MA 02215, USA (office). *Telephone:* (617) 353-0390 (office); (617) 353-5463 (lab.) (office). *Fax:* (617) 353-5462 (office). *E-mail:* jcollins@bu.edu (office). *Website:* www.bu.edu/bme/people/primary/collins (office); www.bu.edu/abl (office); wyss .harvard.edu (office).

COLLINS, Joan Henrietta, OBE; British actress and author; b. 23 May 1933, London, England; d. of Joseph William Collins and Elsa Collins (née Bessant); sister of Jackie Collins (q.v.); m. 1st Maxwell Reed 1954 (divorced 1957); m. 2nd George Anthony Newley 1963 (divorced 1970); one s. one d.; m. 3rd Ronald S. Kass 1972 (divorced 1983); one d.; m. 4th Peter Holm 1985 (divorced 1987); m. 5th Percy Gibson 2002; ed RADA; actress in numerous stage, film, and TV productions, producer and author; Best TV Actress, Golden Globe, 1982; Favourite TV Performer, People's Choice 1985. *Plays include:* The Last of Mrs Cheyne, London 1979–80, Private Lives London 1990, Broadway 1991, Love Letters (US tour) 2000, Over the Moon, London 2001, Full Circle (UK tour) 2004, Legends (US tour) 2006–07, An Evening with Joan Collins (UK tours, London, New York) 2006–. *Films include:* I Believe in You 1952, Our Girl Friday 1953, The Good Die Young 1954, Land of the Pharaohs 1955, The Virgin Queen 1955, The Girl in the Red Velvet Swing 1955, The Opposite Sex 1956, Island in the Sun 1957, Sea Wife 1957, The Bravados 1958, Seven Thieves 1960, Road to Hong Kong 1962, Warning Shot 1966, The Executioner 1969, Quest for Love 1971, Revenge 1971, Alfie Darling 1974, The Stud 1979, The Bitch 1980, The Big Sleep, Tales of the Unexpected, Neck 1983, Georgy Porgy 1983, Nutcracker 1984, Decadence 1994, In the Bleak

Midwinter 1995, Hart to Hart 1995, Annie: A Royal Adventure 1995, The Clandestine Marriage 1998, Joseph and the Amazing Technicolor Dreamcoat 1999, The Flintstones – Viva Rock Vegas 2000, These Old Broads 2000, Clandestine Marriage 2001, Ozzie 2001, Ellis in Glamourland 2004, Valentino: The Last Emperor 2009, Fetish 2010, Saving Santa 2012, Molly Moon: The Incredible Hypnotist 2013. *Television includes:* Dynasty (series) 1981–89, Cartier Affair 1985, Sins 1986, Monte Carlo 1986, Tonight at 8.30 1991, Pacific Palisades (series) 1997, Will and Grace 2000, Guiding Light 2002, Hotel Babylon 2006, Footballers Wives 2006, Joan Does Glamour 2008, Miss Marple 2009, Verboten Liebe 2010, Rules of Engagement 2011, Happily Divorced 2012. *Publications include:* Past Imperfect 1978, The Joan Collins Beauty Book 1980, Katy, A Fight for Life 1982, Prime Time 1988, Love and Desire and Hate 1990, My Secrets 1994, Too Damn Famous 1995, Second Act 1996, My Friends' Secrets 1999, Star Quality 2002, Joan's Way 2002, Misfortune's Daughters 2004, The Art of Living Well 2007, The World According to Joan 2011, A Passion For Life 2013. *Address:* c/o Peter Charlesworth & Associates, 67 Holland Park Mews, London, W11 3SS, England (office). *Telephone:* (20) 7792-4600 (office). *Fax:* (20) 7792-1893 (office). *E-mail:* info@petercharlesworth.co.uk (office). *Website:* www.joancollins.net (office).

COLLINS, Joseph Jameson, AB, MBA; American communications industry executive; b. 27 July 1944, Troy, New York; s. of Mark Francis Collins and Olive Elizabeth Collins (née Jameson); m. Maura McManmon 1972; one s. three d.; ed Brown Univ., Harvard Business School; several exec. positions with American TV and Communications Corpn (ATC) 1964–84, Chair. and CEO 1988–90; Pres. Home Box Office, Time Inc. 1984–88; Chair. and CEO Time Warner Cable (after merger with ATC) 1990–2001, CEO Time Warner Interactive Video div. 2001–03 (retd); currently Chair. Aegis LLC; mem. Bd of Dirs Comcast Corpn 2004–; Dir Emer. Cable TV Labs Inc.; Distinguished Vanguard Award for Leadership, Nat. Cable and Telecommunications Assocn, President's Award and Grand TAM Award, Cable and Telecommunications Assocn for Marketing. *Address:* c/o Board of Directors, Comcast Corporation, 1500 Market Street, Philadelphia, PA 19102-2148, USA.

COLLINS, Kim; Saint Christopher and Nevis professional athlete; b. 5 April 1976, Saint Kitts; ed Texas Christian Univ.; sprinter; 60m personal best 6.53 seconds (Fayetteville, AR, USA, March 2000); 100m personal best 9.98 seconds (Paris, France, Sept. 2002); 200m 20.20 seconds (Edmonton, Alberta, Canada, Aug. 2001); winner: World Championships 100m 2003, Commonwealth Games 100m 2002; runner-up: World Cup 100m 2002, Indoor World Championships 60m 2003; 3rd: World Championships 200m 2001, 4th: International Amateur Athletics Federation Grand Final 100m 2002; finalist: Olympic Games 100m 2000, World Championships 100m 2001; ranked 1st in 2003; coach Monte Stratton. *Address:* c/o Saint Kitts and Nevis Olympic Association, Olympic House, 18 Taylor's Range, Bosseterre, Saint Kitts. *Telephone:* 465-6601. *Fax:* 465-8321. *Website:* sknoc@caribsurf.com.

COLLINS, Michael; American fmr astronaut and fmr museum director; b. 31 Oct. 1930, Rome, Italy; m. Patricia M. Finnegan 1957; one s. two d.; ed US Mil. Acad., West Point and Harvard Univ.; commissioned by USAF, served as experimental flight test officer, AF Flight Test Center, Edwards AF Base, Calif.; selected by NASA as astronaut Oct. 1963; backup pilot for Gemini VII mission 1965; pilot of Gemini X 1966; command pilot, Apollo XI mission for first moon landing July 1969; Asst Sec. for Public Affairs, Dept of State 1970–71; Dir Nat. Air and Space Museum 1971–78, Under-Sec. Smithsonian Inst. 1978–80; Maj.-Gen. USAF Reserve; Vice-Pres. LTV Aerospace and Defense Co. 1980–85; Pres. Michael Collins Assocs (aerospace consulting firm), Washington, DC 1985–; Fellow, Royal Aeronautical Soc., American Inst. of Aeronautics and Astronautics; mem. Int. Acad. of Astronautics, Int. Astronautical Fed.; Exceptional Service Medal (NASA), DSM (NASA), Presidential Medal of Freedom, DCM (USAF), DFC, F.A.I. Gold Space Medal. *Publications:* Carrying the Fire 1974, Flying to the Moon and Other Strange Places 1976, Liftoff 1988, Mission to Mars 1990.

COLLINS, Pauline, OBE; British actress; b. 3 Sept. 1940, Exmouth, Devon; d. of William Henry Collins and Mary Honora Callanan; m. John Alderton; two s. one d.; ed Convent of the Sacred Heart, Hammersmith, Cen. School of Speech and Drama; Dr hc (Liverpool Polytechnic) 1991. *Stage appearances include:* A Gazelle in Park Lane (stage debut, Windsor 1962), Passion Flower Hotel 1965, The Erpingham Camp 1967, The Happy Apple 1967, 1970, The Importance of Being Earnest 1968, The Night I Chased the Women with an Eel 1969, Come as You Are 1970, Judies 1974, Engaged 1975, Confusions 1976, Rattle of a Simple Man 1980, Romantic Comedy 1983, Woman in Mind, Shirley Valentine (Olivier Award for best actress, London, Tony, Drama Desk and Outer Critics' Circle awards, New York) 1988, 1989, Shades 1992. *Films include:* Shirley Valentine (Evening Standard Film Actress of the Year 1989, BAFTA Best Actress Award 1990) 1989, City of Joy 1992, My Mother's Courage 1997, Paradise Road 1997, One Life Stand 2000, Mrs Caldicott's Cabbage War 2002, From Time to Time 2009, You Will Meet a Tall Dark Stranger 2010, Albert Nobbs 2011, Quartet 2012. *Television includes:* Emergency-Ward 10 (series) 1957, Amerika 1966, The Making of Jericho 1966, Happy 1969, The Liver Birds 1969, Upstairs Downstairs (series) 1974, Kings Cross 1972, No, Honestly (series) 1974, Wodehouse Playhouse (series) 1975, Thomas and Sarah (series) 1979, Long Distance Information 1979, Little Miss Trouble and Friends (series, voice) 1983, Knockback 1984, Tropical Moon Over Dorking 1985, The Black Tower (mini-series) 1985, Forever Green (series) 1989, The Ambassador (series) 1998, Little Grey Rabbit (series) 2000, Man and Boy 2002, Sparkling Cyanide 2003, Bleak House (series) 2005, Doctor Who (series) 2006, What We Did on Our Holiday 2006, Marple: The Pale Horse (film) 2010, Merlin (series) 2010, Mount Pleasant (series) 2011. *Publications include:* Letter to Louise 1992. *Address:* c/o ICM, Oxford House, 76 Oxford Street, London, W1D 1BS, England.

COLLINS, Philip (Phil), LVO; British singer, songwriter, musician (drums) and producer; b. 30 Jan. 1951, Hounslow, London; s. of Greville Collins and June Collins; m. 1st 1976 (divorced); one s. one d.; m. 2nd Jill Tavelman 1984 (divorced 1995); one d.; m. 3rd Orianne Cevey 1999 (divorced); two s.; ed Barbara Speake Stage School; fmr child actor, appearing as Artful Dodger in London production of Oliver Twist; fmr mem. various music groups, including The Real Thing, The Freehold, Hickory, Flaming Youth 1967–70; mem. rock group, Genesis, as drummer 1970–96, as lead singer 1975–96, 2006–; mem. Brand X 1975–; solo artist 1981–; record producer for various artists; Trustee Prince of Wales Trust 1983–; f. Little Dreams Foundation 2000; Hon. DFA (Fairleigh Dickinson Univ.)

1987; Hon. DMus (Berklee Coll. of Music) 1991; Hon. DHist (McMurry Univ.) 2012, Grammy Awards (seven), Ivor Novello Awards (six), BRIT Awards (four), Variety Club of Great Britain Awards (two), Silver Clef Awards (two), Elvis Awards, Golden Globe Award for Best Original Song (two, for Two Hearts, from film Buster and You'll Be in My Heart, from film Tarzan), Acad. Award (for You'll be in My Heart, from film Tarzan) 1999, American Music Award for Favorite Adult Contemporary Artist 2000. *Films include:* as actor: Calamity the Cow 1967, Buster 1988, Frauds 1993. *Recordings include:* albums: with Genesis: From Genesis To Revelation 1969, Trespass 1970, Nursery Cryme 1971, Foxtrot 1972, Genesis Live 1973, Selling England By The Pound 1973, The Lamb Lies Down On Broadway 1974, A Trick Of The Tail 1976, Seconds Out 1977, Wind And Wuthering 1977, And Then There Were Three 1978, Duke 1980, Abacab 1981, Three Sides Live 1982, Genesis 1983, Invisible Touch 1986, We Can't Dance 1991, The Way We Walk: The Shorts 1992, The Way We Walk: The Longs 1993, Calling All Stations 1997, Turn It On Again 1999, Archive 1967–75 1999, Archive 1976–92 2001; with Brand X: Unorthodox Behaviour, Moroccan Roll 1977, Livestock 1977, Product 1979, Do They Hurt? 1980, Is There Anything About? 1982, Xtrax 1986, The Plot Thins 1992, Brand X Featuring Phil Collins 1996, Live At The Roxy 1996, Missing Period 1997, A History 1976–80 1997, The X-Files 1999; solo: Face Value 1981, Hello, I Must Be Going! 1982, No Jacket Required 1985, 12"ers 1987, ...But Seriously 1989, Serious Hits... Live! 1990, Both Sides 1993, Dance Into The Light 1996, ...Hits! 1998, A Hot Night In Paris 1999, Tarzan 1999, Testify 2002, Love Songs: A Complication Old And New 2004, The Platinum Collection 2004, Going Back 2010. *Publications include:* Genesis: Chapter and Verse (with other band mems) 2007, The Alamo and Beyond: A Collector's Journey 2012. *Address:* Hit and Run Music, 30 Ives Street, London, SW3 2ND, England (office). *E-mail:* info@genesis-music.com. *Website:* www.philcollins.co.uk; www.genesis-music.com.

COLLINS, Sir Rory Edwards, Kt, PhD, FRCP, FMedSci, FFPM; British epidemiologist and academic; *BHF Professor of Medicine and Epidemiology and Co-Director, Clinical Trial Service Unit, University of Oxford;* Co-Dir Clinical Trial Service Unit (CTSU), Nuffield Dept of Clinical Medicine, Univ. of Oxford 1985–, BHF Prof. of Medicine and Epidemiology 1996–; Prin. Investigator and Chief Exec. UK Biobank prospective study of 500,000 British men and women aged 40–69 2005–; CTSU awarded a Queen's Anniversary Prize for Higher and Further Educ. 2006, J. Allyn Taylor Int. Prize in Medicine, Robarts Research Inst. 2007. *Publications:* numerous scientific papers in professional journals on the establishment of large-scale epidemiological studies of the causes, prevention and treatment of heart attacks, other vascular disease, and cancer. *Address:* Clinical Trial Service Unit, Richard Doll Building, Old Road Campus, Roosevelt Drive, Oxford, OX3 7LF, England (office). *Telephone:* (1865) 743834 (office). *Fax:* (1865) 743985 (office). *E-mail:* secretary@ctsu.ox.ac.uk (office). *Website:* www.ctsu.ox.ac.uk (office).

COLLINS, Susan Margaret, BA; American politician; *Senator from Maine;* b. 7 Dec. 1952, Caribou, Me; d. of Donald Collins and Patricia Collins; ed St Lawrence Univ., Canton, NY; Prin. Adviser on Business Affairs to Senator Bill Cohen 1975–78; Staff Dir Senate Sub-cttee on Oversight Govt Man. 1981–87; Commr Maine Dept of Professional and Financial Regulation 1987–92; Dir New England Operations, US Small Business Admin 1992–93; Exec. Dir Center Family Business, Husson Coll., Bangor 1993–96; Senator from Maine 1997–, mem. Cttee on Health, Educ., Labor and Pensions 1997–2003, Cttee on Govt Affairs 1997–2003, Armed Services mem., Special Cttee on Ageing; Chair. Maine Cabinet Council on Health Care Policy; cand. for Gov. of Maine 1994; Republican; Outstanding Alumni Award, St Lawrence Univ. 1992, named by American Assocn of Port Authorities as Ports Person of the Year, named by Nat. Fed. of Ind. Businesses as Guardian of Small Business, named by American Diabetes Assocn as Legislator of the Year, honours from other groups, including Veterans of Foreign Wars Assocn and Nat. School Bds Assocn. *Address:* 413 Dirksen Senate Office Building, Washington, DC 20510, USA (office). *Telephone:* (202) 224-2523 (office). *Fax:* (202) 224-2693 (office). *Website:* collins.senate.gov (office).

COLLINS, HE Cardinal Thomas Christopher, BA, MA, BTheol, DST; Canadian ecclesiastic and academic; *Archbishop of Toronto;* b. 16 Jan. 1947, Guelph, Ont.; ed Bishop Macdonell High School, St Jerome Coll., Waterloo, Univ. of Western Ontario, St Peter's Seminary, London, Ont., Pontifical Biblical Inst. and Pontifical Gregorian Univ., Rome; ordained deacon, Diocese of Hamilton, Ont. 1972, ordained priest 1973; served as Assoc. Pastor at Holy Rosary Parish, Burlington and at Christ the King Cathedral, as well as teacher and chaplain at Cathedral Boys' High School; Lecturer in English, King's Coll. from 1978; Lecturer in Scripture, St Peter's Seminary 1978–81, Spiritual Dir 1981–85, Assoc. Prof. of Scripture 1985–86, Dean of Theology and Vice-Rector St Peter's Seminary 1992–95, Rector 1995–97; Assoc. Ed. Discover the Bible 1989–92; Coadjutor Bishop of Saint Paul in Alberta May–June 1997, Bishop of Saint Paul in Alberta 1997–99; Coadjutor Archbishop of Edmonton, Alberta Feb.–June 1999, Archbishop of Edmonton 1999–2006, Apostolic Admin. of Saint Paul in Alberta March–Sept. 2001; Archbishop of Toronto, Ont. 2006–; cr. Cardinal (Cardinal-Priest of San Patrizio) 2012; participated in Papal Conclave 2013; mem. Nat. Comm. of Theology, Canadian Conf. of Catholic Bishops 1997, Chair. Nat. Comm. of Theology 1999–2001, mem. Perm. Council 1999–2003, Chair. Nat. Comm. on Christian Unity 2001–03; mem. Organizing Cttee for World Youth Day, Toronto 2002; Pres. Alberta Conf. of Catholic Bishops 1999–2007; mem. Pontifical Council for Social Communications 2010–. *Address:* Office of the Archbishop, Catholic Pastoral Centre, 1155 Yonge Street, Toronto, ON M4T 1W2, Canada (office). *Telephone:* (416) 934-0606 (ext. 609) (office). *Fax:* (416) 934-3452 (office). *E-mail:* archbishop@archtoronto.org (office). *Website:* www.archtoronto.org (office).

COLLINS OF HIGHBURY, Baron (Life Peer), cr. 2011, of Highbury in the London Borough of Islington; **Ray Edward Harry Collins;** British trade unionist; *General Secretary, Labour Party;* b. 1955; mem. Labour Party 1970s–, campaigned for party in every Gen. Election since 1970; apptd Cen. Office Man., Transport & Gen. Workers' Union (T&GWU) 1984, redesignated Head of Admin 1990–99, Asst Gen. Sec. T&GWU section of Unite 1999–2008, helped steer T&GWU into merger with Amicus, creating Unite; T&GWU Rep. on Labour Party Nat. Policy Forum; mem. Nat. Constitutional Cttee of Labour Party, Gen. Sec. Labour Party 2008–; named by Pink News as the 27th most influential LGBT person in British politics 2007. *Leisure interests:* swimming, reading, cinema, supporter of Arsenal Football Club. *Address:* The Labour Party, 39 Victoria Street, London, SW1H 0HA (office); House of Lords, Westminster, London, SW1A 0PW, England. *Telephone:* (870) 590-0200 (office); (20) 7219-5353. *Fax:* (20) 7219-5979. *E-mail:* info@labour.org.uk (office). *Website:* www.labour.org.uk (office).

COLLIS, Steven H., BCom, BCom (Hons); South African/American chartered accountant and business executive; *President and CEO, AmerisourceBergen Corporation;* ed Univ. of the Witwatersrand, Johannesburg; completed articles of clerkship with Price Waterhouse and received Charter Accountancy licence 1986; fmr mem. Johannesburg Stock Exchange; emigrated to USA; Prin. and Gen. Man. Sterling Medical, Irvine, Calif. –1994; joined AmerisourceBergen Corpn as Gen. Man. of newly formed ASD Specialty Healthcare unit 1994, Exec. Vice-Pres., AmerisourceBergen Corpn and Pres. ABDC (largest subsidiary) –2010, Pres. and COO AmerisourceBergen Corpn 2010–11, mem. Bd of Dirs, Pres. and CEO 2011–. *Address:* AmerisourceBergen Corporation, 1300 Morris Drive, Suite 100, Chesterbrook, PA 19087-5594, USA (office). *Telephone:* (610) 727-7000 (office). *Fax:* (610) 727-3600 (office). *E-mail:* info@amerisourcebergen.com (office). *Website:* www.amerisourcebergen.com (office).

COLLMAN, James Paddock, PhD; American chemist and academic; *George A. and Hilda M. Daubert Professor of Chemistry, Stanford University;* b. 31 Oct. 1932, Beatrice, Neb.; s. of Perry G. Collman and Frances Dorothy Palmer; m. Patricia Tincher 1955; four d.; ed Univs. of Nebraska and Illinois; Instructor, Univ. of NC 1958–59, Asst Prof. 1959–62, Assoc. Prof. 1962–66, Prof. of Organic and Inorganic Chem. 1966–67; Prof., Stanford Univ. 1967–, George A. and Hilda M. Daubert Prof. of Chem. 1980–; mem. NAS, American Acad. of Arts and Sciences; Alfred P. Sloan Foundation Fellow 1963–66; Nat. Science Foundation Sr Postdoctoral Fellow 1965–66; Guggenheim Fellow 1977–78, 1985–86; Churchill Fellow (Cambridge) 1977–; Dr. hc (Univ. of Nebraska) 1988, (Univ. de Bourgogne) 1988; American Chemical Soc. (ACS) Award in Inorganic Chem. 1975, Calif. Scientist of the Year Award 1983, Arthur C. Cope Scholar Award (ACS) 1986, Pauling Award 1990, ACS Award for Distinguished Service in the Advancement of Inorganic Chem. 1991, LAS Alumni Achievement Award, Coll. of Liberal Arts and Sciences Univ. of Ill. 1994, Marker Lecturer Medal 1999, Japanese Coordination Chemistry Award 2008, Ronald Breslow Award for Biomimetic Chemistry 2009. *Publications:* Principles and Applications of Organo-transition Metal Chemistry (with Louis S. Hegedus) 1980, 1987, Naturally Dangerous 2001; and 300 scientific papers. *Leisure interest:* fishing. *Address:* Department of Chemistry, Stauffer II, Room 201, Stanford University, Stanford, CA 94305-5080, USA; 794 Tolman Drive, Stanford, CA 94305-5080, USA (home). *Telephone:* (650) 725-0283 (office); (650) 493-0934 (home). *Fax:* (650) 725-0259 (office). *E-mail:* jpc@stanford.edu (office). *Website:* stanford.edu/group/collman (office).

COLLOMB, Bertrand Pierre Charles, PhD; French business executive; *Honorary Chairman, Lafarge;* b. 14 Aug. 1942, Lyon; s. of Charles Collomb and Hélène Traon; m. Marie-Caroline Collomb 1967; two s. one d.; ed Ecole Polytechnique, Paris, Ecole des Mines, Paris and Univ. of Texas, Austin, USA; worked with French Govt, Founder and Man. Centre for Man. Research, Ecole Polytechnique 1972–75; joined Lafarge as Regional Man. 1975, later Pres. and CEO Ciments Lafarge France, CEO Orsan (Biotechnology Co. of the Lafarge Group) 1983, CEO Lafarge Corp. 1987–88, Vice-Chair. and COO Lafarge 1989, Chair. and CEO 1989–2003, Chair. 2003–07, currently Hon. Chair.; mem. Institut de France (Acad. des Sciences, Morales et Politiques); Commdr, Légion d'honneur, Ordre nat. du Mérite. *Publications:* Plaidoyer pour l'entreprise 2010, Pour une entreprise humainement responsable 2011. *Leisure interests:* horse riding, hunting. *Address:* Lafarge, 61 rue des Belles Feuilles, BP 40, 75782 Paris Cedex 16 (office); 7433 Oakwood Drive, Warrenton, VA 20186, USA (home). *Telephone:* 1-44-34-12-02 (office); (540) 347-0032 (home). *Fax:* 1-44-34-12-07 (office); (540) 347-1134 (home). *E-mail:* bertrand.collomb@lafarge.com or bertrand.collomb@lafarge.com (office).

COLMAN, Sir Michael Jeremiah, 3rd Bt, cr. 1907; British business executive; b. 7 July 1928, London; s. of Sir Jeremiah Colman, 2nd Bt and Edith Gwendolyn Tritton; m. Judith Jean Wallop (née William-Powlett) 1955; two s. three d.; ed Eton Coll.; Capt. Yorks Yeomanry 1967; Dir Reckitt and Colman PLC 1970–95, Chair. 1986–95; First Church Estates Commr 1993–99; Dir Foreign and Colonial Ventures Advisors Ltd 1988–99; Trade Affairs Bd Chemical Industries Asscn 1978–84, Council 1983–84; Council Mem. Royal Warrant Holders Asscn 1977–, Pres. 1984; mem. Gen. Council and Investment Cttee, King Edward's Hosp. Fund for London 1978–2004; Assoc. of Trinity House, mem. Lighthouse Bd 1985–94, Younger Brother 1994; mem. Bd UK Centre for Econ. and Environmental Devt 1985–99, Chair. 1996–99; mem. of the Court of Skinners' Co. 1985– (Master 1991–92); mem. Council of Scouts Asscn 1985–2000; Assoc. Trustee St Mary's Hosp., London 1988–2000; Archbishop's Cross of St Augustine 1999; Hon. LLD (Hull) 1993. *Leisure interests:* farming, shooting, forestry, golf. *Address:* Malshanger, Basingstoke, Hants., RG23 7EY (home); 40 Chester Square, London, SW1W 9HT, England. *Telephone:* (1256) 781750 (home). *E-mail:* malshanger.farm@farmline.com (office).

COLMAN, Peter Malcolm, PhD, FAA, FTSE; Australian medical research scientist; *Head, Structural Biology Division, Walter and Eliza Hall Institute of Medical Research;* b. 3 April 1944, Adelaide, South Australia; s. of Clement Colman and Kathleen Colman; m. Anne Elizabeth Smith 1967; two s.; ed Univ. of Adelaide; Post-Doctoral Fellow, Univ. of Oregon, USA 1969–72, Max Planck Inst., Munich, Germany 1972–75; Queen Elizabeth II Fellow, Univ. of Sydney 1975–77; consultant, Univ. of Utah, USA 1977; Prin. Investigator, Nat. Health and Medical Research Council, Univ. of Sydney 1977–78, Officer, CSIRO 1978–89, Chief Div. of Biomolecular Eng 1989–97, Dir Biomolecular Research Inst. 1991–2000; Professorial Assoc., Univ. of Melbourne 1988–98, Professorial Fellow 1998–2003; Adjunct Prof., La Trobe Univ. 1998–2001; Sr Prin. Research Fellow (NHMRC), Walter and Eliza Hall Inst. of Medical Research, Head, Structural Biology Div. 2001–; Dir Biota Holdings Ltd 1985–91; Fellow, Australian Acad. of Technological Sciences and Eng; Hon. DSc (Sydney), Hon. DUniv (Adelaide); Royal Soc. Victorian Medal 1986, Lemberg Medallist and Lecturer, Australian Biochemical Soc. 1988, Burnet Medal, Australian Acad. of Sciences 1995, Australia Prize 1996, Mayne-Florey Medal 2004, Victoria Prize 2008. *Achievements include:* co-discoverer of neuraminidase inhibitors as medicines for influenza virus infection. *Publications include:* over 100 scientific articles in professional journals, mainly on structural

biology, influenza viruses and apoptosis. *Leisure interest:* music. *Address:* PO Box 321, East Melbourne, Vic. 3002 (home); Walter and Eliza Hall Institute of Medical Research, 1G Royal Parade, Parkville, Vic. 3050, Australia (office). *Website:* www.wehi.edu.au (office).

COLOM CABALLEROS, Álvaro, BEng; Guatemalan industrial engineer, business executive, politician and fmr head of state; b. 15 June 1951, Guatemala City; m. Sandra Torres de Colom (divorced); ed Univ. de San Carlos; Deputy Minister for the Economy 1991; Founder and Pres., Unidad Nacional de la Esperanza (UNE) 2001–; runner up in primary elections for Pres. 2003; Pres. of Guatemala 2008–12; Founder and Pres. Grupo Mega; Exec. Dir Dependencia Presidencial de Asistencia Legal y Resolución de Conflictos sobre la Tierra (CONTIERRA); Founder, Pnr and Production Man. Roprisma, Intraexsa; Man. Dept Industrial de DINAH SA; Dir Clothing Comm., Chamber of Industry and Commerce 1977–82; Vice Pres. Asscn of Guatemalan Exporters 1990–; Dir Fundación para el Análisis y Desarollo de Centroamérica (FADES) 1999–; Adviser, Consejo Nacional de Ancianos Mayas (Mayan Council) 1996–; mem. Consultative Bd, AGEXPRONT 1977–82, Dir 1982–90; Founder and Pres. Nat. Comm. for the Clothing Industry 1984; Adviser, Secretaría de la Paz (SEPAZ) 1997; serves as an ordained Mayan minister. *Address:* Unidad Nacional de la Esperanza (UNE), 2a Avenida 5-11, Zona 9, Guatemala City, Guatemala (office). *Telephone:* 232-4685 (office). *E-mail:* ideas@une.org.gt (office). *Website:* www.une.org.gt (office).

COLOMBANI, Jean-Marie; French journalist; b. 7 July 1948, Dakar, Senegal; m. Catherine Sénès 1976; five c.; ed Lycée Hoche, Versailles, Lycée La Pérouse, Nouméa, New Caledonia, Univ. of Paris II-Assas, Univ. of Paris I Panthéon-Sorbonne, Inst. d'Etudes Politiques, Paris and Inst. d'Etudes Supérieures de Droit Public; journalist, ORTF, later Office of FR3, Nouméa 1973; Ed. Political Service, Le Monde 1977, Head of Political Service 1983, Ed.-in-Chief 1990, Deputy Editorial Dir 1991; Man. Dir S.A.–Le Monde March–Dec. 1994, Chair. of Bd and Dir of Publs 1994–2007, mem. Bd of Dirs 2007–08; Co-founder online magazine in France based on Slate.com 2009; Chair. Advisory Council, Midi-Libre Group 2000–. *Publications:* Contradictions: entretiens avec Anicet Le Pors 1984, L'utopie calédonienne 1985, Portrait du président ou le monarque imaginaire 1985, Le mariage blanc (co-author) 1986, Questions de confiance: entretiens avec Raymond Barre 1987, Les héritiers (co-author), La France sans Mitterrand 1992, La gauche survivra-t-elle aux socialistes? 1994, Le Double Septennat de François Mitterrand, Dernier Inventaire (jtly) 1995, De la France en général et de ses dirigeants en particulier 1996, Le Résident de la République 1998, La Cinquième ou la République des phratries (co-author) 1999, Les infortunes de la Republique 2000, Tous Américains? 2002, France-Amérique: Déliaisons Dangereuses (with Walter Wells) 2004, Au fil du Monde 2007, Un Américain à Paris 2008. *Leisure interest:* cinema. *Address:* 12, rue d' Athènes, 75009, Paris (office); 5 rue Joseph Bara, 75006 Paris, France (office). *Telephone:* 1-79-85-81-14 (office). *E-mail:* infos@slate.fr (office). *Website:* www.slate.fr (office).

COLOMBO, John Robert, CM, BA, DLitt; Canadian editor, author and consultant; b. 24 March 1936, Kitchener, Ont.; m. Ruth F. Brown 1959; two s. one d.; ed Kitchener-Waterloo Collegiate Inst., Waterloo Coll. and Univ. Coll., Univ. of Toronto; editorial asst, University of Toronto Press 1957–59; Asst Ed., The Ryerson Press 1960–63; Instructor, York Univ., Downsview, Ont. 1963–65; Consulting Ed., McClelland & Stewart 1963–70, Ed.-at-Large 1963–; Gen. Ed. The Canadian Global Almanac 1992–2000; Writer-in-Residence, Mohawk Coll., Hamilton, Ont. 1979–80; Consultant, American Man. Asscn/Canadian Man. Centre; Assoc. Northrop Frye Centre, Victoria Coll., Univ. of Toronto; Dir, Colombo & Co.; Order of Cyril and Methodius 1979; Esteemed Kt of Mark Twain 1979; Hon. DLitt (York Univ., Toronto) 1998; Centennial Medal 1967, Harbour Front Literary Prize 1985, Citation, Univ. of Toronto's '300 Graduates of Achievement' 2002, Citation, Univ. Coll.'s '100 Graduates of Influence' 2012. *Television:* presenter: Colombo Quotes (series) (CBC-TV 1978), Unexplained Canada (series), Space Network 2006. *Publications include:* more than 200 books of poetry, prose, reference, science fiction anthologies and translations, including Colombo's Canadian Quotations 1974, Colombo's Canadian References 1976, Colombo's Book of Canada 1978, Canadian Literary Landmarks 1984, 1,001 Questions about Canada 1986, Colombo's New Canadian Quotations 1987, Mysterious Canada 1988, Songs of the Great Land 1989, Mysterious Encounters 1990, The Dictionary of Canadian Quotations 1991, UFOs over Canada 1991, Worlds in Small 1992, The Mystery of the Shaking Tent 1993, Walt Whitman's Canada 1993, Voices of Rama 1994, 1995, Close Encounters of the Canadian Kind 1995, Ghost Stories of Ontario 1995, Haunted Toronto 1996, The New Consciousness 1997, Weird Stories 1999, Ghosts in our Past 2000, 1000 Questions about Canada 2001, The Penguin Book of Canadian Jokes 2002, The Penguin Treasury of Popular Canadian Poems and Songs 2002, The Penguin Book of More Canadian Jokes 2003, O Rare Denis Saurat 2003, True Canadian Ghost Stories 2003, The Midnight Hour 2004, The Denis Saurat Reader 2004, The Monster Book of Canadian Monsters 2004, Early Earth 2006, All the Poems 2006, All the Aphorisms 2006, Autumn in August 2006, Miniatures 2006, The Penguin Dictionary of Popular Canadian Quotations 2006, Terrors of the Night 2007, The Big Book of Canadian Ghost Stories 2008, Whistle While You Work 2008, A Far Cry 2009, The Big Book of Canadian Hauntings 2009, Indifferences 2009, Poems of Space and Time 2010, Tesseracts 14 (co-ed.) 2010, Entresol 2011, Imponderables 2011, Fascinating Canada 2011, Jeepers Creepers 2011, A Quaint and Curious Volume of Forgotten Lore 2012, Less of Light 2011, The Crime Magnet (ed.) 2012, Pipe Dreams 2012. *Leisure interest:* reading. *Address:* 42 Dell Park Avenue, Toronto, ON M6B 2T6, Canada. *Telephone:* (416) 782-6853. *Fax:* (416) 782-0285 (home). *E-mail:* jrc@colombo.ca. *Website:* www.colombo.ca.

COLOMBO, Paolo Andrea, BA (Econ); Italian academic and business executive; *Chairman, Enel SpA;* b. 12 April 1960, Milan; ed Bocconi Univ., Milan, New York Univ., USA; certified chartered accountant and public accountant 1985–; Prof. of Accounting and Financial Reporting, Bocconi Univ. 1989–2010, currently Lecturer, Dept of Accounting; Founding Partner and CEO Borghesi Colombo & Associati financial advisory firm 2006–12; Chair. Enel SpA 2011–; Founding Partner and CEO Colombo & Associati (financial advisory firm) 2012–; Chair. Bd of Statutory Auditors, GE Capital Interbanca; fmr Chair. Bd of Statutory Auditors, Saipem, Aviva Vita, Stream and Ansaldo STS; mem. Bd of Statutory Auditors, A.

Moratti S.a.p.a., Humanitas Mirasole; fmr mem. Bd of Statutory Auditors, Winterthur, Credit Suisse Italy, Banca Intesa, Lottomatica, Montedison, Techint Finanziaria, HDPNet, Internazionale FC; mem. Bd of Dirs Mediaset, Versace; fmr mem. Bd of Dirs Saipem, Telecom Italia Mobile, Pirelli Pneumatici, Publitalia '80 (Mediaset group), RCS Quotidiani, RCS Libri, RCS Broadcast and Fila Holding (RCS Mediagroup), Sias, Interbanca and Aurora (Unipol group). *Address:* Enel SpA, Viale Regina Margherita 137, 00198 Rome (office); Colombo & Associati, Piazza Mercanti 11, 20121 Milan, Italy (office). *Telephone:* (06) 83057610 (Rome) (office); (02) 778787201 (Milan) (office). *Fax:* (06) 83057954 (Rome) (office); (02) 778787225 (Milan) (office). *E-mail:* paoloandrea.colombo@enel.com (office); pcolombo@colombo-associati.it (office). *Website:* www.enel.com (office); www .colombo-associati.it (office).

COLOMBO SIERRA, Agustín, DJur; Argentine diplomatist, government official and international organization official; *Director Relaciones Internacionales e Institucionales, Universidad de Tres de Febrero;* b. 1952, Buenos Aires; ed Univ. of Buenos Aires, Univ. of the Sorbonne-Paris II, France, Univ. of San Andrés; held various positions within several multinational telecommunications cos 1992–2003; Chief of Staff, Secr. of Foreign Relations, Ministry of Foreign Affairs 2003–05, Advisory Group Coordinator and Tech. Policy Del. to World Summit of Information Society Phase I, Geneva 2003, Phase II, Tunis 2005, Chief of Staff, Chancery 2005–06, Under-Sec. for Latin American Policy 2007–10; Exec. Dir Mercosur (Spanish: Mercado Común del Sur, Portuguese: Mercado Comum do Sul, English: Southern Common Market) 2010–11; Dir Relaciones Internacionales e Institucionales, Universidad de Tres de Febrero 2012–; mem. Bd of Educ.ar 2005–, Internet Governance Forum 2006–, Advisory Group of UN Sec.-Gen. 2006–. *Address:* Universidad de Tres de Febrero, Avenue San Martín, 2024 Planta Alta, B1678GPW Caseros, Argentina (office). *Telephone:* (11) 4734-4258 (office). *Website:* www.untrefvirtual.edu.ar (office).

COLOMINA, Beatriz, MA, PhD; Spanish architect and academic; *Professor of History and Architecture, Princeton University;* ed Escuela Tecnica Superior de Arquitectura Universidad de Barcelona; trained as architect, Valencia and Barcelona –1976; Asst Prof., Columbia Univ., New York, USA 1984–88; Asst Prof., Princeton Univ. 1988, later Assoc. Prof. of the History and Theory of Architecture, currently Prof. of History and Architecture; has lectured extensively throughout world including Museum of Modern Art, New York, Architectural Inst. of Japan, Tokyo, Centre for Contemporary Art and Architecture, Stockholm, DIA Art Foundation, New York, Museum of Contemporary Art, Barcelona, Museo de Bellas Artes, Buenos Aires, Harvard and Yale Univs, Architectural Asscn, London, Helsinki Univ., Auckland Univ., Wissenschaftskolleg, Berlin; Titulo de Architecto; recipient of grants and fellowships from Chicago Inst. for Architecture, SOM Foundation, Graham Foundation, Fondation Le Corbusier, Center for Advanced Studies in the Visual Arts, Washington, DC, Canadian Centre for Architecture, Montreal. *Publications include:* Architectureproduction (ed.) 1988, Sexuality and Space (ed.) (AIA Int. Book Award 1993) 1992, Privacy and Publicity: Modern Architecture as Mass Media (AIA Int. Book Award 1995) 1994, The Work of Charles and Ray Eames (co-author) 1997, Frank Gehry Architect (co-author) 2001, Cold War Hothouses (co-ed.) 2004, Doble Exposicion: La Arquitectura a través del Arte 2006, Domesticity at War 2006, Clip/Stamp/Fold: The Radical Architecture of Little Magazines 2010; numerous articles. *Address:* School of Architecture, Princeton University, Princeton, NJ 08544-5264, USA (office). *Telephone:* (609) 258-3741 (office). *Fax:* (609) 258-4740 (office). *E-mail:* colomina@princeton.edu (office). *Website:* www.princeton.edu/~soa (office).

COLTRANE, Robbie, OBE; British actor; b. 31 March 1950, Glasgow, Scotland; m. Rhona Irene Gemmel 2000; one s. one d.; ed Glasgow School of Art; Co-Producer, Young Mental Health (documentary) 1973; Co-writer and Dir Jealousy (BBC) 1992, Brothers Bloom 2007; Peter Sellers Comedy Award, Evening Standard 1990, Best Actor, Royal TV Soc. 1993, Best Actor, Broadcasting Press Guild 1993, Best Actor TV Series, BAFTA 1993, 1994, 1995, Best Actor, Monte Carlo TV Festival 1994, Fipa d'Or for Best Actor, Nice Film and TV Festival 1995, Best Actor in Film or Mini-series, Nat. Cable Ace Awards (USA) 1996, Best Actor in TV Series, Royal TV Soc. 1996, Goldener Gong for Best Actor, German TV 1996. *Stage appearances include:* Waiting for Godot, Endgame, The Bug, Mr Joyce is Leaving, The Slab Boys, The Transfiguration of Benno Blimpie, The Loveliest Night of the Year, Snobs and Yobs, Your Obedient Servant (one-man show) 1987, Mistero Buffo 1990, The Brother's Suit 2005. *Films include:* Mona Lisa, Subway Riders, Britannia Hospital, Defence of the Realm, Caravaggio, Eat The Rich, Absolute Beginners, The Fruit Machine, Slipstream, Nuns On The Run, Huckleberry Finn, Bert Rigby, You're A Fool, Danny, Champion of the World, Henry V, Let It Ride, The Adventures of Huckleberry Finn, Goldeneye, Buddy, Montana, Frogs for Snakes, Message in a Bottle, The World is Not Enough 1999, On the Nose 2000, From Hell 2000, Harry Potter and the Philosopher's Stone 2001, Harry Potter and the Chamber of Secrets 2002, Harry Potter and the Prisoner of Azkaban 2004, Ocean's 12 2004, Harry Potter and the Goblet of Fire 2005, Stormbreaker 2006, Provoked 2006, Harry Potter and the Order of the Phoenix 2007, The Brothers Bloom 2008, Tales of Despereaux 2008, Harry Potter and the Half-Blood Prince 2009, Harry Potter and the Deathly Hallows: Part 1 2010, Part 2 2011, Arthur Christmas (voice) 2011, Brave (voice) 2012, Great Expectations 2012, Effie 2013. *Television includes:* Yes, Prime Minister, The Comic Strip Presents… 1982–2012, Five Go To Rehab, Five Go Mad In Dorset, The Beat Generation, War, Summer School, Five Go Mad on Mescalin, Susie, Gino, Dirty Movie, The Miner's Strike, The Supergrass (feature film), The Ebb-tide, Alice in Wonderland, The Young Ones, Kick Up the Eighties, The Tube, Saturday Night Live, Lenny Henry Show, Blackadder, Tutti Frutti, Coltrane in a Cadillac, Cracker, Boswell and Johnson's Tour of the Western Isles 1990, The Plan Man 2003, Cracker 9/11 2005, Coltrane's B-Road Britain 2007, Murderland (mini-series) 2009, The Gruffalo (voice) 2009, Lead Balloon (series) 2011, The Gruffalo's Child (voice) 2011. *Publications include:* Coltrane in a Cadillac 1992, Coltrane's Planes and Automobiles 1999, B-Road Britain 2008. *Leisure interests:* sailing, film, vintage cars, music, art. *Address:* 125 Gloucester Road, London, SW7 4TE, England (home). *Telephone:* (20) 7373-3323 (home). *E-mail:* cda@cdalondon.com (office).

COLUMBUS, Chris; American film director and screenwriter; b. 10 Sept. 1958, Spangler, Pa; s. of Alex Michael Columbus and Mary Irene Puskar; m. Monica Devereux 1983; two d.; ed New York Univ. Film School; wrote and developed TV

cartoon series Galaxy High School; f. 1942 Productions (production co.). *Screenplays include:* Reckless 1983, Gremlins 1984, The Goonies 1985, The Young Sherlock Holmes 1985, Only the Lonely 1991, Little Nemo: Adventures in Slumberland (jtly) 1992, Nine Months 1995, Christmas with the Kranks 2004. *Films include:* Gremlins 1984, Young Sherlock Holmes 1985, Adventures in Babysitting 1987, Heartbreak Hotel 1988, Home Alone 1990, Only the Lonely 1991, Home Alone 2: Lost in New York 1992, Mrs Doubtfire 1993, Nine Months (also producer) 1995, Jingle All the Way (also producer) 1996, Stepmom (also producer) 1998, Monkey Bone 1999, Bicentennial Man (also producer) 1999, Harry Potter and the Philosopher's Stone (also producer) 2001, Harry Potter and the Chamber of Secrets (also producer) 2002, Rent (also producer) 2005, Night at the Museum (producer) 2006, 4: Rise of the Silver Surfer (producer) 2007, Night at the Museum 2 (producer) 2009, I Love You, Beth Cooper 2009, Perry Jackson and the Lightning Thief (also producer) 2010, The Help (producer) 2011. *TV directed includes:* Amazing Stories, Twilight Zone, Alfred Hitchcock Presents (series). *Address:* c/o Beth Swofford, CAA, 2000 Avenue of the Stars, Los Angeles, CA 90067, USA.

COLWELL, Rita Rossi, BS, MS, PhD; American marine microbiologist, epidemiologist and academic; *Adjunct Professor, Bloomberg School of Public Health, Johns Hopkins University;* b. 23 Nov. 1934, Mass.; d. of Louis Rossi and Louise DiPalma; m. Jack H. Colwell 1956; two d.; ed Purdue Univ. and Univ. of Wash.; Research Asst, Drosophila Genetics Lab. Purdue Univ. 1956–57; Research Asst, Dept of Microbiology, Univ. of Washington 1957–58, Predoctoral Assoc. 1959–60, Asst Research Prof. 1961–64; Asst Prof. of Biology, Georgetown Univ. 1964–66, Assoc. Prof. 1966–72; Prof. of Microbiology, Univ. of Maryland 1972–98, Vice-Pres. for Academic Affairs 1983–87, Founding Dir Center of Marine Biotechnology 1987–91, Founder and Pres. Biotechnology Inst. 1991–98, Distinguished Univ. Prof. 2004–; Distinguished Univ. Prof., Bloomberg School of Public Health, Johns Hopkins Univ. 2004, now Adjunct Prof.; Dir NSF 1998–2004; Chair., Canon US Life Sciences, Inc. 2004–06, Sr Advisor and Hon. Chair. 2006–; fmr Chair. Bd of Govs American Acad. of Microbiology; fmr Pres. AAAS, American Society for Microbiology, Int Union of Microbiological Societies, Sigma Xi Nat Science Hon. Society; mem. NAS, Royal Swedish Acad. of Sciences, Stockholm, American Acad. of Arts and Sciences, American Philosophical Society; numerous hon. doctorates; Gold Medal, Canterbury, UK 1990, Purkinje Gold Award, Prague 1991, Maryland Pate Civic Award 1991, Barnard Medal, Colorado Univ. 1996, Gold Medal, UCLA 2000, Achievement Award, American Asscn of Univ. Women 2001, Carey Award, AAAS 2001, Nat. Medal of Science 2007, Stockholm Water Prize 2010. *Publications:* 16 books, over 600 articles in journals, book chapters, abstracts. *Leisure interests:* gardening, sailing, jogging. *Address:* Bloomberg School of Public Health, 615 North Wolfe Street, Baltimore, MD 21205 (office); 5010 River Hill Road, Bethesda, MD 20816, USA (home). *Telephone:* (410) 955-3720 (office). *Fax:* (410) 955-0617 (office). *E-mail:* rcolwell@jhsph.edu (office). *Website:* www.jhsph.edu (office).

COMANECI, Nadia; American (b. Romanian) fmr gymnast; b. 12 Nov. 1961, Oneşti, Bacău Co.; d. of Gheorghe Comaneci and Stefania-Alexandria Comaneci; m. Bart Connor 1996; one s.; ed Coll. of Physical Educ. and Sports, Bucharest; overall European champion Skien 1975, Prague 1977, Copenhagen 1979; overall Olympic champion, Montreal 1976, first gymnast to be awarded a 10; overall World Univ. Games Champion, Bucharest 1981; gold medals European Championships, Skien 1975 (vault, asymmetric bars, beam), Prague 1977 (bars), Copenhagen 1979 (vault, floor exercises), World Championships, Strasbourg 1978 (beam), Fort Worth 1979 (team title), Olympic Games, Montreal 1976 (bars, beam), Moscow (beam, floor), World Cup, Tokyo 1979 (vault, floor); World Univ. Games, Bucharest 1981 (vault, bars, floor and team title); silver medals European Championships, Skien 1975 (floor), Prague 1977 (vault), World Championships, Strasbourg 1978 (vault), Olympic Games, Montreal 1976 (team title), Moscow 1980 (individual all-round, team title), World Cup, Tokyo 1979 (beam); bronze medal Olympic Games, Montreal 1976 (floor); retd May 1984, jr team coach 1984–89; granted refugee status in USA 1989; currently with Bart Connor Gymnastics Acad., Okla, USA; Contributing Ed. International Gymnast magazine; Prin. (with husband) Perfect 10 Productions, Inc. (TV production co.), Grips, Etc.(gymnastics supply co.); UN Spokesperson for Int. Year of Volunteers 2001; f. Nadia Comaneci Children's Clinic, Bucharest 2004; Vice-Chair. Special Olympics Int.; Vice-Pres. Muscular Dystrophy Asscn; mem. Bd of Dirs Laureus Sports For Good Foundation; Sportswomen of the Century Prize, Athletic Sports Category 1999, Govt Excellence Diploma 2001. *Publication:* Letters to a Young Gymnast 2004. *Address:* c/o Bart Conner Gymnastics Academy, 3206 Bart Conner Drive, POB 720217, Norman, OK 73070-4166, USA (office). *Telephone:* (405) 447-7500 (office). *Fax:* (405) 447-7600 (office). *Website:* www.bartconnergymnastics.com (office); www.bartandnadia .com.

COMĂNESCU, Lazăr, PhD; Romanian diplomatist and politician; b. 4 June 1949, Horezu (Ursani), Vâlcea; m. Mihaela Comănescu; one d.; ed Acad. of Econ. Studies, Bucharest, Sorbonne, Paris; Jr Diplomat, Ministry of Foreign Affairs 1972–82, Counsellor, later Minister-Counsellor, Mission to EU, Brussels 1990–94, Dir EU Directorate, Ministry of Foreign Affairs 1994–95, Dir-Gen. and Adviser to Minister of Foreign Affairs, also Head of Minister's office 1995, State Sec., Ministry of Foreign Affairs 1995–98, Amb. and Head, Mission to NATO and WEU 1998–2001, Amb. and Head of Mission to EU 2001–07, Perm. Rep., EU, Brussels 2007–08; Minister of Foreign Affairs 2008; Amb. to Germany 2009–; Prof. of Int. Econs, Acad. of Econ. Studies, Bucharest 1982–90; mem. Scientific Consultative Bd European Inst. in Romania; mem. Scientific Bd Romanian Inst. for Int. Studies; Founding mem. Warsaw Cen. European Forum; Grand Officer, Romanian Nat. Order of Loyal Service 2000, Romanian Nat. Order of Loyal Service with Great Cross 2007. *Publications:* author of several univ. courses and books; numerous articles in journals. *Address:* Embassy of Romania, Romania Dorotheenstr. 62–66, 10117 Berlin, Germany (office). *Telephone:* (30) 21239202 (office). *Fax:* (30) 21239399 (office). *E-mail:* office@rumaenische-botschaft.de (office). *Website:* berlin .mae.ro (office).

COMASTRI, HE Cardinal Angelo; Italian ecclesiastic; *President of the Fabric of St Peter;* b. 17 Sept. 1943, Sorano; ordained priest 1967; Bishop of Massa Marittima-Piombino 1990–94; Archbishop (Personal Title) of Loreto 1996–2005 (retd); Pres. Fabric of St Peter 2005–13, 2013–; Coadjutor Archpriest of the

Basilica di San Pietro in Vaticano and Coadjutor Papal Vicar for the Vatican City 2005–06, Archpriest of the Basilica di San Pietro in Vaticano and Papal Vicar for the Vatican City 2006–; cr. Cardinal (Cardinal-Deacon of San Salvatore in Lauro) 2007; Dir Italian Bishops' Nat. Vocations Centre 1994; Pres. Nat. Cttee for the Great Jubilee of the Year 2000 1994. *Address:* Fabbrica di San Pietro, 00120 Vatican City, Rome, Italy (office). *Telephone:* (06) 6988-5318 (office). *Fax:* (06) 6988-5518 (office). *E-mail:* info@fsp.va (office). *Website:* www.vatican.va/roman_curia/institutions_connected/uffscavi/index.htm (office).

COMBS, Sean John, (Diddy); American rap artist, record producer, fashion designer and business executive; *Chairman and CEO, Bad Boy Worldwide Entertainment Group;* b. 4 Nov. 1969, Harlem, New York; s. of Melvin Combs and Janice Combs; fmr pnr Misa Hylton-Brim; one s.; fmr pnr Kim Porter; two s. twin d.; ed Mount Saint Michael High School, Bronx, Howard Univ.; early positions at Uptown Records (R&B label) 1990–93; talent spotter for artists such as Jodeci and Mary J. Blige; producer for Ma$e, Sting, MC Lyte, Faith Evans, The Lox, Mariah Carey, Aretha Franklin, 112, Notorious BIG; f. Bad Boy Entertainment record label 1994 (now a part of Bad Boy Worldwide Entertainment Group); remixed and reworked songs by artists including Jackson 5, Sting, Goldie, Trent Reznor and The Police; co-producer (with Jimmy Page) of soundtrack to film Godzilla; soundtrack to approx. 50 films; launched fashion collection under name Sean John 1998, opened flagship store in Manhattan 2002; known as Puff Daddy until 2001, when he changed his pseudonym to P Diddy, then Diddy 2005–; producer of MTV's Making the Band; launched fragrances Unforgiveable 2006, I Am King 2009; Grammy Award for Best Rap Performance by a Duo or Group for I'll Be Missing You, with Faith Evans 1998, for Shake Ya Tailfeather 2004, Council of Fashion Designers of America menswear designer of the year award 2004. *Play:* A Raisin in the Sun (actor) 2004. *Films:* Bad Boy's 10th Anniversary…, The Hits (video) 2004, The Notorious B.I.G.: Ready to Die – The Remaster (video short) 2004, Notorious 2009, Undefeated (documentary) (Academy Award for Best Documentary Feature 2012) 2011. *Television includes:* Making the Band 2 (series) 2002, Borrow My Crew (documentary) 2005, Making the Band 3 (series) 2005, P. Diddy Presents the Bad Boys of Comedy (series documentary) 2005, Celebrity Cooking Showdown (mini-series) 2006, The Making of 'Press Play' (film) 2006, Diddy Makes an Album (film) 2006, Making the Band 4 (series) 2007, Taquita & Kaui (series) 2007, A Raisin in the Sun (film) 2008, If I Were King: Sean John Internship by Design (documentary) 2008, Daddy's Girls (series) 2009, Run's House (series documentary) 2005–09, Making His Band (series) 2009, StarMaker (series) (exec. producer) 2009, (co-exec. producer) 2009, I Want to Work for Diddy (series) 2008–10, Nicki Minaj: My Time Now (documentary) 2010. *Recordings include:* albums: No Way Out (Grammy Award for Best Rap Album 1998) 1997, Forever 1999, The Saga Continues… 2001, We Invented the Remix 2002, Maximum Puff Daddy 2003, Press Play 2006, Last Train to Paris (with Dirty Money) 2010. *Address:* Bad Boy Worldwide Entertainment Group, 1710 Broadway, New York, NY 10019, USA (office). *Telephone:* (212) 381-1540 (office). *Fax:* (212) 381-1599 (office). *Website:* www.diddy.com; www.seanjohn.com; www.badboyonline.com.

COMEY, James Brien, Jr, JD; American lawyer and government official; *Director, Federal Bureau of Investigation;* b. 14 Dec. 1960, Yonkers, NY; m. Patrice Comey; five c.; ed Northern Highlands Regional High School, Coll. of William and Mary, Univ. of Chicago Law School; grew up in Allendale, NY; served as law clerk for then-US Dist Judge John M. Walker, Jr in Manhattan; Assoc., Gibson, Dunn & Crutcher, New York; with US Attorney's Office for Southern Dist of New York 1987–93, served as Deputy Chief of the Criminal Div.; Man. Asst, US Attorney in charge of Richmond Div. of US Attorney for Eastern Dist of Va 1996–2001; Adjunct Prof. of Law, Univ. of Richmond School of Law 1996–2001; US Attorney for Southern Dist of New York 2002–03; US Deputy Attorney Gen. 2003–05; Gen. Counsel and Sr Vice-Pres., Lockheed Martin 2005–10; mem. Sr Man. Cttee, Bridgewater Assocs 2010–13; Sr Research Scholar and Hertog Fellow on Nat. Security Law, Columbia Univ. Law School 2013–; Dir FBI 2013–; mem. Bd of Dirs HSBC Holdings, London 2013; mem. Defense Legal Policy Bd 2012–. *Address:* Department of Justice, Federal Bureau of Investigation, J. Edgar Hoover Building, 950 Pennsylvania Avenue, NW, Washington, DC 20530, USA (office). *Telephone:* (202) 324-3000 (office). *Website:* www.fbi.gov (office).

COMMENDA, Gen. Othmar; Austrian army officer; *Chief of the Defence Staff;* b. 29 May 1956; m. Sabine Commenda; two c. from previous m.; ed Theresian Mil. Acad., Nat. Defence Acad., Vienna, US Army War Coll., Führungsakademie der Bundeswehr, Germany; joined Austrian army 1975, has held numerous positions including Co. Commdr, 14th Tank Bn, Wels 1979, Co. Commdr with UN Disengagement Observer Force Zone (UNDOF), Golan Heights 1983–84, Tactical Training Officer, Nat. Defence Acad., Vienna 1988–91, Commdr, Army Reconnaissance Bn, Mistelbach, Lower Austria 1992–94, Commdr, 3rd Mechanized Brigade, Senftenberg, Chief of Staff and Deputy Brigade Commdr, 3rd Tank Brigade, Mautern an der Donau 1994, with foreign exercise Cooperative Guard 99 under Partnership for Peace operation, Czech Repub., Commdr, 15th Gen. Staff Training Course 1996–2000, Deputy Head of Mil. Policy, Gen. Troop Inspectorate, Ministry of Defence 2000, Chief of Staff, Dept of Defence in the cabinet 2001–03, Chef de Cabinet of Minister of Defence 2003, Head of Project Man., Armed Forces Reform Comm. 2003–04, Head of Dept responsible for restructuring of Austrian Armed Forces under Minister of Defence 2004–08, Deputy Chief of Defence Staff 2008–11, Acting Chief of Defence Staff 2011–13, Chief of Defence Staff 2013–; Großes Ehrenzeichen für Verdienste um die Republik Österreich 2004, Große Goldene Ehrenzeichen für Verdienste um die Republik Österreich 2013; Mil. Service Award 1st, 2nd and 3rd Class, Mil. Service Medal in bronze. *Address:* Federal Ministry of Defence and Sports, Rossauer Lände 1, 1090 Vienna, Austria (office). *Telephone:* (1) 502-01-0 (office). *Fax:* (1) 502-01-10-17-041 (office). *E-mail:* presse@bmlvs.gv.at (office). *Website:* www.bmlv.gv.at (office).

COMOLLI, Jean-Dominique, MEconSc; French business executive and fmr public servant; *Deputy Chairman, Imperial Tobacco Group PLC;* b. 25 April 1948, Bougie, Algeria; s. of Yvan Comolli and Jacqueline Courtin; m. Catherine Delmas 1968; two s. one d.; ed Institut d'Etudes Politiques, Paris, Ecole Nat. d'Admin; civil servant, Budget Dept, Ministry of Economy, Finance and Budget 1977–81, Minister of the Budget's Tech. Adviser to Cabinet, then Prime Minister's Tech. Adviser to Cabinet 1981–86, Asst Dir Budget Dept 1986–88, Prin. Pvt. Sec. to

Minister of the Budget 1988–89, Dir-Gen. Customs and Indirect Duties, Ministry of the Budget 1989–95; Chair. and CEO Soc. Nat. d'Exploitation Industrielle des Tabacs et Allumettes (Seita) 1993–99; Co-Chair. Bd of Dirs Altadis SA (tobacco co. cr. out of merger of Seita and Tabacalera) 1999–2005, Chair. 2005–08, Deputy Chair. Imperial Tobacco Group PLC (following acquisition of Altadis) 2008–; Officier, Légion d'honneur, Chevalier, Ordre nat. du Mérite. *Address:* 43/45 Avenue de Clichy, 75017 Paris (office); 23 avenue de l'Observatoire, 75006 Paris, France (home). *Telephone:* 1-44-97-65-65 (office). *Fax:* 1-44-97-62-43 (office). *E-mail:* jean-dominique.comolli@fr.imptob.com (office). *Website:* www.imperial-tobacco.com (office).

COMPAGNON, Antoine Marcel Thomas; French academic and writer; *Blanche W. Knopf Professor of French and Comparative Literature, Columbia University;* b. 20 July 1950, Brussels, Belgium; s. of Gen. Jean Compagnon and Jacqueline Terlinden; ed Lycée Condorcet, Paris, The Maret School, Washington, DC, USA, Prytanée Militaire, La Flèche, Ecole Polytechnique, Paris, Ecole Nat. des Ponts et Chaussées, Paris, Univ. of Paris VII; with Fondation Thiers and Research Attaché, CNRS 1975–78; Asst Lecturer, Univ. of Paris VII 1975–80; Asst Lecturer, Ecole des Hautes Etudes en Sciences Sociales, Paris 1977–79; Lecturer, Ecole Polytechnique, Paris 1978–85; teacher at French Inst., London 1980–81; Lecturer, Univ. of Rouen 1981–85; Prof. of French, Columbia Univ., New York 1985–91, Blanche W. Knopf Prof. of French and Comparative Literature 1991–; Visiting Prof., Univ. of Pennsylvania 1986, 1990; Prof., Univ. of Le Mans 1989–90; Prof., Univ. of Paris IV-Sorbonne 1994–2006, Collège de France 2006–; Sec. Gen. Int. Asscn of French Studies 1998–2008; Guggenheim Fellow 1988; Visiting Fellow, All Souls Coll., Oxford 1994; Fellow, American Acad. of Arts and Sciences 1997, Academia Europaea 2006; Corresp. Fellow, British Acad. 2009; Commdr des Palmes académiques, Officier de l'ordre du Mérite, Chevalier, Légion d'honneur; Dr hc (King's Coll., London) 2010, (Univ. de Liège) 2013; Prix Claude Lévi-Strauss 2011. *Publications include:* La Seconde Main ou le travail de la citation 1979, Le Deuil antérieur 1979, Nous, Michel de Montaigne 1980, La Troisième République des lettres, de Flaubert à Proust 1983, Ferragosto 1985, critical edn of Marcel Proust, Sodome et Gomorrhe 1988, Proust entre deux siècles 1989, Les Cinq Paradoxes de la modernité 1990, Chat en poche: Montaigne et l'allégorie 1993, Connaissez-vous Brunetière? 1997, Le Démon de la théorie 1998, Baudelaire devant l'innombrable 2003, Les Antimodernes 2005, Le Cas Bernard Faÿ 2009, La Classe de rhéto 2012, Un été avec Montaigne 2013, Une question de discipline 2013; numerous articles on French literature and culture. *Address:* Columbia University, Department of French and Romance Philology, 513 Philosophy Hall, 1150 Amsterdam Avenue, New York, NY 10027, USA (office); Collège de France, 11 place Marcelin-Berthelot, 75005 Paris, France (office). *Telephone:* (212) 854-2500 (New York) (office); 1-44-27-10-79 (Paris) (office). *Fax:* (212) 854-5863 (New York) (office). *E-mail:* amc6@columbia.edu (office); antoine.compagnon@college-de-france.fr (office). *Website:* www.columbia.edu/cu/french (office).

COMPAORÉ, Blaise; Burkinabè head of state and former army officer; *President;* b. 3 Feb. 1951, Ouagadougou; m. Chantal K. Terrasson; one d.; trained as soldier in Cameroon and Morocco; fmr second in command to Capt. Thomas Sankara whom he overthrew in a coup in Oct. 1987; Minister of State to the Pres., then Minister for Justice 1983–87; Chair. Popular Front of Burkina Faso and Head of Govt Oct. 1987–, Interim Head of State June–Dec. 1991, Pres. of Burkina Faso Dec. 1991–, Minister of Nat. Defence and War Veterans 2011–; Assoc. mem. Overseas Acad. of Sciences, France 1995–; Commdr, Ordre Int. des Palmes académiques 2005; Dr hc (Ecole des Hautes Etudes Ints de Paris) 1992, (Soka Univ., Japan) 1995, (Jean-Moulin de Lyon 3 Univ., France) 2004, (Ramkhamaeng Univ., Thailand) 2005. *Address:* Office of the President, 03 BP 7030, Ouagadougou 03, Burkina Faso (office). *Telephone:* 50-30-66-30 (office). *Fax:* 50-31-49-26 (office). *E-mail:* info@presidence.bf (office). *Website:* www.primature.gov.bf (office).

COMPAORE, Jean-Baptiste Marie Pascal, MEconSc, DES; Burkinabè politician, banker and economist; *Vice-Governor, Banque Centrale des Etats de l'Afrique de l'ouest (BCEAO);* b. 12 April 1954, Ouagadougou; m.; four c.; ed Phillipe Zinda Kabore Coll., Ouagadougou, Univ. of Benin, Lome, Togo, Centre Ouest Africain de Formation aux Études Bancaires (COFEB); joined Banque Centrale des États de l'Afrique de l'ouest (BCEAO), Dakar 1981, served in Credit and Inspection Divs, Inspector of Banks, Banking Comm. of W Africa Monetary Union 1990–95, Vice-Gov. BCEAO –2011, Interim Gov. Jan. 2011, currently Vice-Gov.; Counsellor, Dir of Econ. and Social Affairs, Office of the Pres. 1995–96, Sec.-Gen. of Ministry 1996–2000; Minister to the Prime Minister, responsible for Finance and the Budget 2000–02, Minister of Finance and the Budget 2002–07, of the Economy and Finances 2007–08; Gov. IMF, World Bank Group, African Devt Bank, Econ. Community of West African States (ECOWAS); fmr Lecturer (part-time), Lomé Tech. School, Togo; Co-ordinator Program of Admin. Support 1997–; fmr Chair. Inter-Departmental Cttee to Follow-up Recommendations of Arbitrator of Faso; Officier, Commdr, Ordre Nat. Burkina; Commdr, Ordre Nat. (Côte d'Ivoire). *Address:* BCEAO, siège BP 3108, Dakar, Senegal (office). *Telephone:* 33-839-0500 (office). *Website:* www.bceao.int (office).

COMPER, Francis Anthony (Tony), BA; Canadian banker; b. 24 April 1945, Toronto, Ont.; m. Elizabeth Comper 1971; ed Univ. of Toronto; began career with BMO Financial Group 1967, Sr Vice-Pres., Personal Banking 1982, Sr Vice-Pres. and Sr Operations Officer, Treasury Group 1982–84, Man., London, UK Br. 1984–86, Sr Marketing Officer, Corp. and Govt Banking 1986–87, Exec. Vice-Pres., Operation 1987–89, Chief Gen. Man. and COO 1989–90, Pres., COO and Dir 1990–99, Pres. CEO and Dir 1999, Chair., CEO and Dir 1999–2007; Chair. Capital Campaign for the Univ. of Toronto 1997–2002; mem. Bd of Dirs Spectra Energy Corpn, Canadian Inst. of Advanced Research, Harris Bancorp, Inc., Harris Trust and Savings Bank, Toronto, C. D. Howe Inst., C. D. Howe Memorial Foundation, Canadian Club, BMO Nesbitt Burns Inc., Catalyst, NY; Trustee Canadian Centre for Architecture; mem. Int. Advisory Cttee, Li Ka Shing Knowledge Inst. of St Michael's Hosp.; Hon. Chair. Bd of Govs The Yee Hong Centre for Geriatric Care; Hon. DHumLitt (Mount Saint Vincent), Hon. LLD (Univ. of Toronto), Hon. DLitt (Univ. of New Brunswick); Human Relations Award, Canadian Council of Christians and Jews 1998, B'nai Brith Order of Merit 2003, Scopus Award (with his wife), Hebrew Univ. of Jerusalem. *Leisure interests:* golf, tennis, theatre, arts, reading. *Address:* c/o BMO Financial Group, First Bank Tower, First Canadian Place, Toronto, ON M5X 1A1, Canada (office).

COMSTOCK, Beth; American business executive; *Chief Marketing Officer and Senior Vice-President, General Electric Company;* b. Va; m.; two d.; ed Coll. of William and Mary; began career working for a TV news service and in local cable programming in Va; held a succession of communications and publicity positions at NBC, Turner Broadcasting and CBS Entertainment from 1986; Vice-Pres. NBC News Communications 1993–96, Sr Vice-Pres. Communications, NBC 1996–98, Vice-Pres. Corp. Communications, General Electric Co. (GE) 1998–2003, Corp. Vice-Pres. and Chief Marketing Officer, GE 2003–05, Pres. NBC Universal Digital Media and Market Devt (now Integrated Media) 2005–08, Chief Marketing Officer and Sr Vice-Pres. GE 2008–; named by Business Week an innovation "transformer" 2005, named by BtoB Magazine Marketing Exec. of the Year, named by PR Week PR Professional of the Year, Matrix Award, New York Women in Communications 2006. *Address:* General Electric Company, 3135 Easton Turnpike, Fairfield, CT 06828, USA (office). *Telephone:* (203) 373-2211 (office). *Website:* www.ge.com (office).

CONANT, Douglas R.; American food industry executive; *President and CEO, Campbell Soup Company;* began career in marketing dept, General Mills Inc. 1976; joined Kraft Foods 1986; Pres. Nabisco Foods Co. 1995–2000; Pres. and CEO Campbell Soup Co. 2001–; mem. Bd of Dirs Applebee's Int. Inc.; Chair. Bd of Dirs Students In Free Enterprise; Chair. and Trustee The Conference Bd; Chair. Grocery Mfrs Asscn/Food Processors of America; Trustee Int. Tennis Hall of Fame. *Address:* Campbell Soup Company, 1 Campbell Place, Camden, NJ 08103-1701, USA (office). *Telephone:* (856) 342-4800 (office). *Fax:* (856) 342-3878 (office). *Website:* www.campbellsoup.com (office).

CONDÉ, Alpha, DenD; Guinean professor of law, politician and head of state; *President;* b. 4 March 1938, Boké; ed Univ. Paris IV (Sorbonne), France; fmr Prof., Faculty of Law and Econ. Sciences, Univ. Paris I (Panthéon-Sorbonne); co-f. Mouvement Nat. Démocratique (MND) 1977; unsuccessful cand. in presidential elections 1993, 1998; sentenced to five years' imprisonment 2000, pardoned and released 2001; exiled in France 2001–05; Pres. Repub. of Guinea 2010–; Leader, Rassemblement du peuple de Guinée. *Publications:* several books including Guinée, Albanie d'Afrique ou néo-colonie américaine 1972, Quel avenir pour la Guinée 1984, Pour que l'espoir ne meure 1985, Un africain engagé: ce que je veux pour la Guinée 2010. *Address:* Office of the President, BP 1000, Boulbinet, Conakry, Guinea (office). *Telephone:* 30-41-10-16 (office). *Fax:* 30-41-16-73 (office).

CONDÉ, Mamadi; Guinean fmr government official; fmr Minister of Information; Minister of Foreign Affairs and Co-operation 2004–05, 2006–07. *Address:* c/o Ministry of Foreign Affairs, face au Port, ex-Primature, BP 2519, Conakry, Guinea (office).

CONDE DE SARO, Francisco Javier, M.L.; Spanish lawyer, business executive and fmr diplomatist; *President, Sociedad Estatal para Exposiciones Internacionales;* b. 13 March 1946, Madrid; s. of Francisco Javier Conde and María Jesús de Saro; m. Ana Martínez de Irujo; one s. two d.; ed Univ. of Madrid, Diplomatic School, Madrid; Dir-Gen. for Int. Econ. Relations, Ministry of Foreign Affairs 1971; Asst Dir-Gen. for Int. Relations, Directorate of Maritime Fisheries 1976; Dir of Political Affairs for Africa and Asia, Ministry of Foreign Affairs 1978; counsellor Ministry of Transport, Tourism and Communications 1978; Econ. and Commercial Counsellor, Embassy in Rabat 1979–83, in Buenos Aires 1983–86; Dir-Gen. Juridical and Institutional Co-ordination, Sec. of State for EU, Ministry of Foreign Affairs 1986–90, Sec.-Gen. 1994; Amb. to Algeria 1990–94; Perm. Rep. to NATO, Brussels 1996–2000; Perm. Rep. to EU, Brussels 2000–04; Amb. to Japan 2004–06; currently Pres. Sociedad Estatal para Exposiciones Internacionales (State Co. for Int. Exhibitions); Vice-Pres. Foundation Bd Fundación Arquitectura y Sociedad; Kt Commdr of Civil Merit (Spain), of Isabel la Católica (Spain), of Mayo Order (Argentina), of Order of the Lion (Senegal); Kt of Order of El Ouissam El Mohammadi (Morocco); Grand Cross for Naval Merit (Spain), Grand Cross of Merit (Austria). *Address:* Sociedad Estatal para Exposiciones Internacionales, C/ José Abascal, 4–4° B, 28003 Madrid, Spain (office). *Telephone:* (91) 7004000 (office). *E-mail:* info@expo-int.com (office). *Website:* www.expo-int.com (office).

CONDON, Baron (Life Peer), cr. 2001, of Langton Green in the County of Kent; **Paul Leslie Condon,** QPM, DL, CCMI (CIMgt), FRSA; British international organization official and fmr police commissioner; b. 1 Jan. 1946, Dorset; m.; two s. one d.; ed St Peter's Coll. Oxford; joined Metropolitan Police 1967, Insp. 1975–78, Chief Insp. 1978–81; Superintendent, Bethnal Green 1981–82; Staff Officer to Commr as Superintendent, then as Chief Superintendent 1982–84; Asst Chief Constable of Kent 1984–87; Deputy Asst Commr Metropolitan Police 1987–88, Asst Commr 1988–89; Chief Constable of Kent 1989–92; Commr, Metropolitan Police 1993–2000; Dir Anti-Corruption Unit, Int. Cricket Council 2001–; mem. Bd of Dirs (non-exec.) Securicor PLC 2000–, G4S 2004– (Deputy Chair. 2006–), Tenix (Holdings) Ltd, Vidient Systems Inc; Vice-Chair. Private Security Group, House of Lords 2006–; Pres. British Security Industry Assen. *Address:* House of Lords, London, SW1A 0PW, England. *Telephone:* (20) 7219-3617.

CONDOR, Sam Terrence, BA; Saint Christopher and Nevis politician and business executive; b. 4 Nov. 1949; m.; one s. two d.; ed Ruskin Coll., Oxford, Univ. of Sussex, UK; printer, Saint Christopher and Nevis Govt Printery 1967–82; Sr Clerk, Inland Revenue Dept 1980–82; Man. Dir Quality Foods Ltd 1986–95; MP 1989–; Deputy Prime Minister, Minister of Trade, Industry, Caricom Affairs, Youth, Sports and Community Devt 1995–99, Deputy Prime Minister, Minister of Foreign Affairs, Int. Trade and Caricom Affairs, Community and Social Devt and Gender Affairs 2000–01; apptd Deputy Prime Minister and Minister of CARICOM Affairs, Int. Trade, Labour, Social Security, Telecommunications and Tech. 2001; currently Deputy Prime Minister and Minister of Foreign Affairs and National Security, Labour, Immigration and Social Security –2013; Vice-Chair. Young Labour 1980–82, Deputy Leader Saint Christopher and Nevis Labour Party 1990–; mem. Saint Christopher and Nevis Tourist Bd 1975–78; Nat. Football Player 1969–72, Man. and Coach Nat. Football Team 1986–88; Margaret Marsh Prize for Most Outstanding Overseas Student, Ruskin Coll. 1979–80. *Leisure interests:* playing football, jogging, fast walking, drama. *Address:* North Pelican Drive, Bird Rock, Saint Christopher, Saint Christopher and Nevis, West Indies (home). *Telephone:* 465-1545 (home). *E-mail:* dpmin@caribsurf.com (office).

CONEWAY, Peter Richard, MBA; American business executive and fmr diplomatist; *Managing Director, Riverstone Holdings LLC;* b. 13 April 1944,

Cleveland, Ohio; m. Lynn M. Coneway; two d.; ed Coll. of Business Admin, Univ. of Texas, Stanford Univ.; joined Goldman, Sachs & Co. 1969, later fmr Advisory Dir, f. Houston office for Goldman Sachs 1975, named Gen. Pnr 1978, est. firm's equities sales, trading and research div., Tokyo 1987–88, returned to manage Houston office; Amb. to Switzerland (also accred to Liechtenstein) 2006–08; currently Man. Dir Riverstone Holdings LLC, New York; immediate past Chair. and mem. Bd of Visitors for Univ. of Texas M. D. Anderson Cancer Center; apptd to Univ. of Texas System Bd of Regents 1993; fmr mem. Nat. Bd Smithsonian Inst.; mem. Bd of Dirs Cobalt Int. Energy; fmr Chair. Stanford Business School Trust, Houston/Harris County Sports Facility Public Advisory Cttee; fmr Dir Greater Houston Partnership; Trustee, Texas Heart Inst., Houston Museum of Fine Arts; Outstanding Young Texas Ex Award 1983, named a Distinguished Alumnus 2003, McCombs Business School Hall of Fame Award 2004. *Address:* Riverstone Holdings LLC, 1000 Louisiana Street, Suite 1000, Houston, TX 77002, USA (office). *Telephone:* (713) 357-1400 (office). *Fax:* (713) 357-1399 (office). *E-mail:* pconeway@riverstonellc.com (office). *Website:* www.riverstonellc.com (office).

CONFALONIERI-RICCA, Fedele; Italian media executive; *Chairman, Mediaset SpA;* b. 6 Aug. 1937, Milan; ed State Univ. of Milan; Chair. Mediaset SpA (commercial TV broadcaster); mem. Bd of Dirs Il Giornale (nat. daily newspaper); mem. Bd of Dirs and Vice-Pres. Gestevision Telecinco SA 2000–; mem. Bd Italian Confed. of Industry (Confindustria); mem. Exec. Cttee and Bd Lombardy Industrialists Confed. (Assolombarda); Chair. Nat. Television Broadcasters Assen (part of Nat. Broadcasting Fed.); mem. Man. Council of Assonime (Assen for Italian limited liability cos); Founding mem. ACT (European Assen of Commercial Television Broadcasters). *Address:* Mediaset SpA, Viale Europa 46, 6th Floor, 20093 Cologno Monzese, Milan, Italy (office). *Telephone:* (2) 25141 (office). *E-mail:* simone.sole@mediaset.it (office). *Website:* www.mediaset.it (office).

CONILLE, Garry, MA, PhD; Haitian gynaecologist, UN official and politician; b. 26 Feb. 1966; s. of Serge Conille and Marie Antoinette Darbouze; m. Betty Rousseau; two d.; ed Univ. of Haiti, Univ. of North Carolina, USA; with Haitian Assen for Nat. Devt 1994–98; Project Officer, UN Population Fund (UNPF), Haiti 1999–2001, Programme Officer 2001–02, Tech. Adviser, Int. Population Services, Haiti 2002–04, Sub-regional Tech. Adviser, Africa/Ethiopia Div., UNPF 2004–06, Chief Tech. Adviser for Africa region 2007, Team Leader, UNDP Millennium Devt Goals Unit 2008–10, Chief Aide, Office Man. for Special Envoy of UN Sec.-Gen. for Haiti (Bill Clinton) 2010, UNDP Resident Rep. and Humanitarian Coordinator in Niger June–Oct. 2011; Prime Minister 2011–12 (resgnd). *Address:* c/o Office of the Prime Minister, Villa d'Accueil, 1 rue Prosper, Musseau, Port-au-Prince, Haiti. *Website:* garryconille.com.

CONLON, James Joseph, BMus; American conductor; *Music Director, Los Angeles Opera;* b. 18 March 1950, New York; s. of Joseph Conlon and Angeline Conlon; m. Jennifer Ringo; two d.; ed High School of Music and Art, New York and Juilliard School; fmr faculty mem. Juilliard School of Music; since making debut with New York Philharmonic has conducted every major US orchestra and many leading European orchestras; Conductor, New York Philharmonic Orchestra 1974–, Metropolitan Opera, New York 1976–; debut at Metropolitan Opera 1976, Covent Garden 1979, Paris Opera 1982, Lyric Opera of Chicago 1988, La Scala, Milan 1993, Kirov Opera 1994; Music Dir Cincinnati May Festival 1979–, Berlin Philharmonic Orchestra 1979, Rotterdam Philharmonic Orchestra 1983–91, Ravinia Festival 2005–; Musical Adviser to Dir, Paris Opera 1995– (Prin. Conductor 1996–2004); conducted opening of Maggio Musicale, Florence 1985; Gen. Music Dir and Chief Conductor, Cologne Opera 1989–2002; Music Dir Los Angeles Opera 2006–(18); residency at Juilliard School, New York 2007–; has conducted at major int. music festivals and with numerous leading orchestras; Officier, Ordre des Arts et Lettres 1996; Grand Prix du Disque for recording of Poulenc Piano Concertos, Opera News Award 2005, Galileo 2000 Music Prize, Florence 2008. *Recordings:* numerous works by Mozart, Liszt, Poulenc etc.; Rise and Fall of the City of Mahagonny (Grammy Awards for Best Classical Album and Best Opera Recording). *Address:* Opus 3 Artists, 470 Park Avenue South, 9th Floor North, New York, New York, NY 10016, USA (office). *Telephone:* (212) 584-7500 (office). *Fax:* (646) 300-8200 (office). *E-mail:* info@opus3artists.com (office). *Website:* www.opus3artists.com (office).

CONNEH, Sekou Damate, Jr; Liberian politician; *Leader, Progressive Democratic Party;* b. 1960, Gbarnga; s. of Sekou Damate Conneh Sr and Margaret Makay; m. Aisha Keita Conneh; ed William V. C. Tubman Methodist High School; joined Progressive People's Party 1980, served as Sr Coordinator Kokoyah Dist; exiled in Uganda 1980–1985; apptd revenue agent, Ministry of Finance 1986; f. and served as Man. Dir Damate Corpn (import/export co.); Pres. Nat. Exec. Cttee Liberians United for Reconciliation and Democracy (now Progressive Democratic Party) 2003–, currently Leader; f. Damate Peace Foundation. *Address:* Progressive Democratic Party, McDonald Street, Monrovia, Liberia. *Telephone:* (6) 521091.

CONNELL, HE Cardinal Desmond, BA, MA, BD, PhD; Irish ecclesiastic; *Archbishop Emeritus of Dublin;* b. 24 March 1926, Dublin; ed Univ. Coll. Dublin, Maynooth, Univ. of Louvain, Belgium; ordained priest 1951; worked in Dept of Metaphysics, Univ. Coll. Dublin 1953–72, apptd Prof. of Gen. Metaphysics 1972, elected Dean Faculty of Philosophy and Sociology 1983; Archbishop of Dublin 1988–2004, now Archbishop Emer.; cr. Cardinal 2001, apptd Cardinal-Priest of S. Silvestro in Capite; fmr mem. Pontifical Council for the Pastoral Care of Migrants and Itinerant People, Irish Hierarchy's Theological Comm., Diocesan Cttee on Ecumenism. *Address:* c/o Archbishop's House, Drumcondra, Dublin 9, Ireland. *Telephone:* (1) 8373732. *Fax:* (1) 8369796. *E-mail:* communications@dublindiocese .ie. *Website:* www.dublindiocese.ie.

CONNELLY, Deirdre P., BA; American business executive; *President, North American Pharmaceuticals, GlaxoSmithKline plc;* b. San Juan, Puerto Rico; ed Lycoming Coll., Pa, Harvard Univ.'s Advanced Man. Program; joined Lilly as Sales Rep. 1983, Marketing Assoc. in San Juan 1984–89, joined Int. Man. Devt Program at Lilly Corp. Center 1989, Sales Supervisor in Phila, Pa 1989–90, Diabetes Product Man., San Juan 1990–91, Nat. Sales Man. for Puerto Rico affiliate 1991–92, Marketing and Sales Dir for Puerto Rico 1992–93, Dir of Sales and Marketing for Caribbean Basin Region, including Cen. America, Puerto Rico and Caribbean Island countries 1993–95, Gen. Man. Eli Lilly Puerto Rico, SA 1995–97, returned to Indianapolis 1997, held positions of Regional Sales Dir, Exec. Dir

Global Marketing for Evista, and Team Leader for Evista Product Team 1997–2001, Leader, Woman's Health Business Unit in US affiliate 2001–03, Exec. Dir Human Resources for US affiliate 2003–04, Vice-Pres. Human Resources for Pharmaceutical Operations 2004–05, Sr Vice-Pres. Human Resources for Lilly and mem. Operations Cttee and Sr Man. Council 2005, Pres. Lilly USA, Eli Lilly & Co. 2005–09 (resgnd); Pres. North American Pharmaceuticals, GlaxoSmithKline (GSK) plc 2009–, CEO and Pres. Human Genome Sciences Inc. (co. acquired by GSK 2012) 2012–; mem. Bd of Dirs Macy's Inc. 2007–; ranked by Fortune magazine amongst the 50 Most Powerful Women in Business in the US (43rd) 2006, (47th) 2007, (42nd) 2008, (37th) 2009, (27th) 2010, (25th) 2011, (26th) 2012, ranked by Forbes magazine amongst The World's 100 Most Powerful Women (74th) 2009, Outstanding Achievement Award, Lycoming Coll. Alumni Asscn 2007. *Address:* GlaxoSmithKline, 5 Moore Drive, PO Box 13398, Research Triangle Park, NC 27709, USA (office). *Telephone:* (919) 483-2100 (office). *Fax:* (919) 549-7459 (office). *Website:* us.gsk.com (office).

CONNELLY, Jennifer; American actress; b. 12 Dec. 1970; d. of Gerard Connelly and Eileen Connelly; one s. with David Dugan; m. Paul Bettany 2002; one s. one d.; ed Saint Ann's School, Brooklyn, Yale Univ. and Stanford Univ.; fmr model. *Films include:* Once Upon A Time in America 1984, Il mondo dell'orrore di Dario Argento 1985, Seven Minutes in Heaven 1985, The Valley 1985, Phenomena 1985, Labyrinth 1986, Inside the Labyrinth 1986, Some Girls 1988, Etoile 1988, The Hot Spot 1990, Career Opportunities 1991, The Rocketeer 1991, Of Love and Shadows 1994, Higher Learning 1995, Far Harbor 1996, Mulholland Falls 1996, Inventing the Abbotts 1997, Dark City 1998, Requiem for a Dream 2000, Waking the Dead 2000, A Beautiful Mind (Acad. Award, BAFTA Award and Golden Globe Award for Best Supporting Actress 2002) 2001, Pollock 2001, House of Sand and Fog 2003, Hulk 2003, Dark Water 2005, Little Children 2006, Blood Diamond 2006, Reservation Road 2007, The Day the Earth Stood Still 2008, Inheart 2008, He's Just Not That Into You 2009, 9 (voice) 2009, Creation 2009, What's Wrong with Virginia 2010, The Dilemma 2011, Salvation Boulevard 2011. *TV appearances include:* Tales of the Unexpected 1984, The $treet 2001. *Recording:* Monologue of Love (single, in Japanese). *Leisure interests:* hiking, camping, swimming, bike riding, quantum physics, philosophy. *Address:* c/o CAA, 2000 Avenue of the Stars, Los Angeles, CA 90067, USA (office).

CONNERY, Sir Sean, Kt; British actor; b. 25 Aug. 1930, Edinburgh, Scotland; s. of Joseph Connery and Euphamia Connery; m. 1st Diane Cilento 1962 (divorced 1974); one s. one step-d.; m. 2nd Micheline Boglio Roquebrun 1975; served in RN; Dir Tantallon Films Ltd 1972–; Fellow, Royal Scottish Acad. of Music and Drama 1984; mem. Scottish Nat. Party 1992–; Dir Fountainbridge Films (production co.) –2002; Freeman City of Edinburgh 1991; Commdr des Arts et Lettres 1987, Chevalier, Légion d'honneur; Hon. DLitt (Heriot-Watt) 1981, (St Andrew's) 1988; American Cinematique Award 1991, Rudolph Valentino Award 1992, Nat. Board of Review Award, BAFTA Lifetime Achievement Award 1990, BAFTA Fellowship 1998. *Films include:* No Road Back 1955, Time Lock 1956, Action of the Tiger 1957, Another Time, Another Place, Hell Drivers, 1958, Darby O'Gill and the Little People 1959, Tarzan's Greatest Adventure 1959, On the Fiddle 1961, The Longest Day 1962, The Frightened City 1962, Woman of Straw 1964, Marnie 1964, The Hill 1965, A Fine Madness 1966, Shalako 1968, The Molly Maguires 1968, The Red Tent 1969, The Anderson Tapes 1970, The Offence 1973, Zardoz 1974, Murder on the Orient Express 1974, Ransom 1974, The Wind and the Lion 1975, The Man Who Would Be King 1975, Robin and Marian 1976, A Bridge Too Far 1977, The Great Train Robbery 1978, Meteor 1978, Cuba 1979, Outland 1981, The Man with the Deadly Lens 1982, The Untouchables (Acad. Award, Best Supporting Actor 1987) 1986, The Name of the Rose 1987, The Presidio 1988, Rosencrantz and Guildenstern are Dead, A Small Family Business, Indiana Jones and the Last Crusade 1989, Hunt for Red October 1989, The Russia House (BAFTA Award 1990) 1989, Mutant Ninja Turtles 1990, Highlander 2 1990, Medicine Man 1992, Rising Sun 1993, A Good Man in Africa 1994, First Knight 1994, Just Cause 1994, The Rock 1996, Dragonheart 1996, The Avengers 1998, Entrapment 1999, Playing By Heart 1999, Finding Forrester 2000, The League of Extraordinary Gentlemen 2003, Sir Billi the Vet (short) (voice) 2006, Sir Billi (voice) 2012; as James Bond in Dr. No 1962, From Russia with Love 1963, Goldfinger 1964, Thunderball 1965, You Only Live Twice 1967, Diamonds are Forever 1971, Never Say Never Again 1983. *Publication:* Neither Shaken Nor Stirred 1994, Being a Scot (memoirs) (with Murray Grigor) 2008. *Leisure interests:* golf, tennis, reading. *Address:* c/o Creative Artists Agency Inc., 2000 Avenue of the Stars, Los Angeles, CA 90067 (office); Fountainbridge Films, 8428 Melrose Place, Unit C, Los Angeles, CA 90069, USA. *Telephone:* (323) 782-1177 (Fountainbridge). *Website:* www.seanconnery.com.

CONNES, Alain, PhD; French mathematician and academic; *Professor, Collège de France;* b. 1 April 1947, Draguignan (Var); ed Ecole Normale Supérieur, Paris; Research Fellow, CNRS 1970–74, Dir of Research 1981–84; Visiting Research Fellow, Queen's Univ., Kingston, Canada 1975; Assoc. Prof. and Prof., Univ. of Paris VI 1976–80; Long Term Prof. and Léon Motchane Prof., Institut des Hautes Etudes Scientifiques 1979–; Prof., Collège de France (chaire d'Analyse et Géométrie) 1984–; Distinguished Prof., Vanderbilt Univ., Nashville, Tenn., USA 2003–; Ed. Journal of Functional Analysis, Inventiones Mathematicae 1978–98, Communications in Mathematical Physic, Journal of Operator Theor, Ergodic Theory and Dynamical Systems 1981–93, Comptes rendus de l'Académie des sciences, Letters in Mathematical Physics, K-theory, Selecta Mathematica, Publications Mathématiques de l'I.H.E.S., Advances in Mathematics; Corresp. mem. Acad. des Sciences 1980, mem. 1983–; Foreign Assoc. mem. Royal Danish Acad. of Sciences 1980, Norwegian Acad. of Science 1993, NAS 1997, Russian Acad. of Sciences 2003; Foreign Fellow, Royal Soc. of Canada 1996; Hon. Foreign mem. American Acad. of Arts and Sciences 1990; Dr hc (Queen's Univ., Kingston) 1979, (Univ. of Rome Tor Vergata) 1997, (Univ. of Oslo) 1999; Prix aimé Berthé, Acad. des Sciences 1975, Prix Peccot-Vimont, Collège de France 1976, Médaille d'argent, CNRS 1977, Prix Ampère, Acad. des Sciences 1980, Fields Medal 1982, Clay Research Award 2000, Crafoord Prize 2001, CNRS Gold Medal 2004. *Publications:* Matière à pensée (co-author) 1989, Géométrie non commutative 1990, Noncommutative geometry 1994, Conversations on Mind, Matter, and Mathematics (co-author) 1995, Triangle de pensées (co-author) 2000, Triangle of Thought (co-author) 2001; more than 150 publs in scientific journals. *Address:* Collège de France, 3 rue d'Ulm, 75231 Paris Cedex 05, France (office). *Telephone:* 1-44-27-17-05 (office). *Fax:* 1-44-27-17-04 (office). *E-mail:* alain@connes.org (office). *Website:*

www.college-de-france.fr (office); www.ihes.fr (office); www.alainconnes.org; www.vanderbilt.edu (office).

CONNICK, Harry, Jr; American jazz musician (piano), singer and actor; b. 11 Sept. 1967, New Orleans, La; m. Jill Goodacre 1994; ed New Orleans Center for the Creative Arts, Hunter Coll. and Manhattan School of Music; studied with Ellis Marsalis. *Films include:* Memphis Belle 1990, Little Man Tate 1991, Copycat 1995, Independence Day 1996, Excess Baggage 1997, Action League Now!! (voice) 1997, Hope Floats 1998, The Iron Giant (voice) 1999, Wayward Son 1999, My Dog Skip (voice) 2000, The Simian Line 2000, Life Without Dick 2001, Basic 2003, Mickey 2004, The Happy Elf (voice) 2005, Bug 2006, P.S. I Love You 2007, New in Town 2009, Dolphin Tale 2009, When Angels Sing 2011. *Television includes:* South Pacific 2001, Will & Grace (series) 2002–06, Law & Order 2012. *Theatre:* Thou Shalt Not (composer, Broadway) 2001, The Pajama Game (actor, Broadway) 2005. *Recordings include:* albums: 11 1978, Harry Connick Jr 1987, 20 1988, When Harry Met Sally (Grammy Award for Male Jazz Vocal Performance 1990) 1989, Lofty's Roach Soufflé 1990, We Are In Love 1990, Blue Light, Red Light 1991, 25 1992, When My Heart Finds Christmas 1993, Imagination 1994, She 1994, Whisper Your Name 1995, Star Turtle 1995, All Of Me 1996, To See You 1997, Come By Me 1999, 30 2001, Songs I Heard 2001, Other Hours: Connick On Piano, Vol. I 2003, Harry For The Holidays 2003, Only You 2004, Occasion 2005, Harry on Broadway, Act 1 2006, Oh, My Nola 2007, Chanson de Vieux Carré 2007, What a Night! A Christmas Album 2008, Your Songs 2009, In Concert on Broadway 2011, Music from the Happy Elf 2011, Smokey Mary 2013; contrib. music for films Memphis Belle 1990, Little Man Tate 1991. *Address:* Wilkins Management Inc., 323 Broadway, Cambridge, MA 02139, USA (office). *Telephone:* (617) 354-2736 (office). *E-mail:* info@wilkinsmanagement.com (office); info@harryconnickjr.com (office). *Website:* www.hconnickjr.com.

CONNOLLY, Billy, CBE; British actor, comedian, playwright and presenter; b. 24 Nov. 1942, Anderston, Glasgow, Scotland; m. 1st Iris Connolly (divorced 1985); one s. one d.; m. 2nd Pamela Stephenson 1990; three d.; worked as apprentice welder; performed originally with Gerry Rafferty and The Humblebums; first play, The Red Runner, staged at Edinburgh Fringe 1979; Hon. DLitt (Glasgow) 2001, (Nottingham) 2010, Dr hc (Royal Scottish Acad. of Music and Drama, Glasgow) 2006; Freedom of the City of Glasgow 2010. *Theatre:* The Great Northern Welly Boot Show, The Beastly Beatitudes of Balthazar B 1982, What About Dick? 2012. *Films include:* Absolution 1978, Worzel Gummidge: A Cup o' Tea an' a Slice o' Cake 1980, Bullshot 1983, To the North of Katmandu 1986, The Hunting of the Snark 1987, The Return of the Musketeers 1989, The Big Man 1990, Indecent Proposal 1993, Pocahontas (voice) 1995, Treasure Island (Muppet Movie) 1996, Deacon Brodie (BBC Film) 1996, Beverly Hills Ninja 1997, Mrs Brown 1997, Ship of Fools 1997, Middleton's Changeling 1998, The Impostors 1998, Still Crazy 1998, The Debt Collector 1999, The Boondock Saints 1999, Beautiful Joe 2000, An Everlasting Piece 2000, The Man Who Sued God 2001, The Last Samurai 2003, Timeline 2003, Lemony Snicket's A Series of Unfortunate Events 2004, Garfield 2 2006, Open Season (voice) 2006, Fido 2006, The X Files: I Want to Believe 2008, Boondock Saints II 2009, Gulliver's Travels 2010, Open Season 2 2008, Good Sharma 2010, The Ballad of Nessie (voice) 2011, Brave (voice) 2012, Quartet 2012, The Hobbit: The Desolation of Smaug 2013, The Hobbit: There and Back Again 2014, What We Did on Our Holiday 2014; numerous video releases of live performances including Bite Your Bum (Music Week and Record Business Award 1982) 1981, An Audience with Billy Connolly 1985, Billy Connolly – Live in New York 2005, Billy Connolly Live – Was It Something I Said?. *Television includes:* Just Another Saturday (play) 1975, The Elephants' Graveyard (play) 1976, Blue Money 1982, Androcles and the Lion 1984, Return to Nose and Beak (Comic Relief), Head of the Class (series) 1990–91, South Bank Show Special (25th Anniversary Commemoration) 1992, Billy (series) 1992, Billy Connolly's World Tour of Scotland (six-part documentary) 1994, The Big Picture 1995, Billy Connolly's World Tour of Australia 1996, Deacon Brodie 1997, Erect for 30 Years 1998, Columbo: Murder with Too Many Notes 2000, Gentlemen's Relish 2001, Prince Charming 2001, Billy Connolly's World Tour of England, Ireland and Wales 2002, Gentleman's Relish, Billy Connolly's World Tour of New Zealand, Journey to the Edge of the World, Billy Connolly's Route 66 2011, House MD 2012. *Albums include:* The Great Northern Welly Boot Show (contains No. 1 hit D.I.V.O.R.C.E.), Pick of Billy Connolly (Gold Disc) 1982. *Publications include:* Gullible's Travels 1982. *Address:* c/o Tickety-boo Ltd, 2 Triq il-Barriera, Balzan, BZN 1200, Malta (office). *Telephone:* 21556166 (office). *Fax:* 21557316 (office). *E-mail:* tickety-boo@tickety-boo.com (office). *Website:* www.tickety-boo.com (office); www.billyconnolly.com.

CONNOR, Dean A., HBA; Canadian business executive; *President and CEO, Sun Life Financial Inc.;* ed Richard Ivey School of Business, Univ. of Western Ontario; with Mercer Human Resource Consulting 1978–2006, most recently as Pres. for the Americas –2006; joined Sun Life as Exec. Vice-Pres. with responsibility for UK and Reinsurance operations, strategic int. activities and corp. functions 2006–08, Pres. of Sun Life's Canadian operations 2008–10, COO with responsibility for Canadian and UK operations, MFS, Marketing, Human Resources, Information Tech. and other shared business services 2010–11, mem. Bd of Dirs, Pres. and CEO Sun Life Financial Inc. 2011–; mem. Ivey Advisory Bd; Dir Canadian Life and Health Insurance Asscn; Trustee, Univ. Health Network, Toronto; Fellow, Soc. of Actuaries, Canadian Inst. of Actuaries. *Address:* Sun Life Financial Inc., 150 King Street West, Toronto, ON M5H 1J9, Canada (office). *Telephone:* (416) 979-9966 (office). *Fax:* (416) 597-9108 (office). *E-mail:* boarddirectors@sunlife.com (office). *Website:* www.sunlife.com (office).

CONNORS, James Scott (Jimmy); American tennis player; b. 2 Sept. 1952, East St. Louis, Ill.; s. of James Scott Connors I and the late Gloria Thompson Connors; m. Patti McGuire 1978; one s. one d.; ed Univ. of California, Los Angeles; amateur player 1970–72, professional since 1972; Australian Open Champion 1974; Wimbledon Champion 1974, 1982; US Open Champion 1974, 1976, 1978, 1982, 1983; SA Champion 1973, 1974; WCT Champion 1977, 1980; Grand Prix Champion 1978; commentator for NBC; played Davis Cup for USA 1976, 1981; ranked World Number 1 for a record 157 weeks; won 109 tournament titles; joined BBC tennis commentary team for 2005 Wimbledon championships; coached Andy Roddick 2006–08; BBC Overseas Sports Personality 1982; inducted into International Tennis Hall of Fame 1998. *Leisure interest:* golf. *Address:* Tennis

Management Inc., 109 Red Fox Road, Belleville, IL 62223; RHB Ventures, 1320 18th Street, NW, Suite 100, Washington DC 20036, USA.

CONQUEST, (George) Robert (Acworth), (J. E. M. Arden, Victor Grey, Ted Pauker), CMG, OBE, MA, DLitt, FBA, FRSL; British/American writer, academic and fmr diplomatist; *Senior Research Fellow, Hoover Institution, Stanford University*; b. 15 July 1917, Malvern, Worcs., England; s. of Robert Folger W. Conquest and Rosamund A. Acworth; m. 1st Joan Watkins 1942 (divorced 1948); two s.; m. 2nd Tatiana Milhailova 1948 (divorced 1962); m. 3rd Caroleen Macfarlane 1964 (divorced 1978); m. 4th Elizabeth Neece 1979; one step-d.; ed Winchester Coll., Univ. of Grenoble and Magdalen Coll., Oxford; mil. service 1939–46; HM Foreign Service 1946–56; Sydney and Beatrice Webb Research Fellow, LSE 1956–58; Visiting Poet, Univ. of Buffalo 1959–60; Literary Ed. The Spectator 1962–63; Sr Fellow, Russian Inst., Columbia Univ. 1964–65; Fellow, Woodrow Wilson Int. Center, Washington, DC 1976–77; Sr Research Fellow, Hoover Inst., Stanford Univ. 1977–79, 1981–; Distinguished Visiting Fellow, Heritage Foundation 1980–81; Fellow, British Interplanetary Soc., American Acad. of Arts and Sciences; mem. Soc. for the Promotion of Roman Studies; Presidential Medal of Freedom 2005, Order of Yaroslav Mudryi (Ukraine) 2006, Cross of Terra Mariana (Estonia) 2008, Commdr's Cross and Officer's Cross, Order of Merit of the Repub. of Poland 2009; Alexis de Tocqueville Award 1992, Jefferson Lectureship 1993, Michael Braude Award for Light Verse, American Acad. of Arts and Letters 1997, Richard Weaver Award for Scholarly Letters 1999, Peter Shaw Memorial Award, Nat. Assocn of Scholars 2001, Nagrody Przegladu Wschodniego (Warsaw) 2003, Fondazione Liberal Career Award 2004, Dan David Prize 2012. *Television:* presenter, Red Empire (Granada TV) 1991. *Publications:* A World of Difference 1955, Poems 1955, Common Sense About Russia 1960, Soviet Deportation of Nationalities 1960, Power and Policy in the USSR 1961, Courage of Genius: The Pasternak Affair 1961, Between Mars and Venus 1962, Russia after Khrushchev 1965, The Egyptologists (with Kingsley Amis) 1965, The Great Terror: Stalin's Purge of the Thirties 1968, Arias from a Love Opera 1969, The Nation Killers 1970, Where Marx Went Wrong 1970, V.I. Lenin 1972, Kolyma: The Arctic Death Camps 1978, Present Danger 1979, Forays 1979, The Abomination of Moab 1979, Coming Across 1979, We and They: Civic and Despotic Cultures 1980, What To Do When the Russians Come (with Jon Manchip White) 1984, Inside Stalin's Secret Police: NKVD Politics 1936–1939 1985, The Harvest of Sorrow: Soviet Collectivization and the Terror-Famine 1986, New and Collected Poems 1988, Tyrants and Typewriters: Communiqués in the Struggle for Truth 1989, Stalin and the Kirov Murder 1989, The Great Terror: A Reassessment 1990, Stalin: Breaker of Nations 1991, History, Humanity, and Truth 1993, Demons Don't 1999, Reflections on a Ravaged Century 1999, The Dragons of Expectation: Reality and Delusion in the Course of History 2005, The Great Terror: 40th Anniversary 2008, Penultimata 2009, Blokesongs and Blokelore 2012. *Address:* Hoover Institution, Stanford University, Stanford, CA 94305-6010 (office); 52 Peter Coutts Circle, Stanford, CA 94305-2506, USA (home). *Telephone:* (650) 723-1647 (office). *Fax:* (650) 723-1687 (office). *E-mail:* conquest@stanford.edu (office). *Website:* www .hoover.org/fellows/9765 (office).

CONRAD, (Gaylord) Kent, AB, MBA; American fmr politician; b. 12 March 1948, Bismarck, ND; m. Lucy Calautti 1987; one d.; ed Univ. of Missouri, Stanford Univ. and George Washington Univ.; Asst to Tax Commr, State of ND Tax Dept, Bismarck 1974–80, Tax Commr 1981–86; Senator from North Dakota 1987–2013 (retd), Chair. Budget Cttee Jan. 2001, June 2001–03, 2007–13; mem. Nat. Comm. on Fiscal Responsibility and Reform (Simpson-Bowles comm.) 2010; mem. Bd of Dirs Genworth Financial Inc. 2013–; Democrat. *Address:* c/o Board of Directors, Genworth Financial Inc., 6620 West Broad Street, Richmond, VA 23230, USA.

CONRAD, Kevin M., BS, MBA; Papua New Guinea/American diplomatist and international organization official; *Executive Director, Coalition of Rainforest Nations;* m.; ed Ukarumpa High School, Eastern Highlands Prov., Papua New Guinea, Univ. of Southern California, USA, London Business School, UK, Columbia Univ., New York, USA; grew up in Arapesh tribe nr Wewak, East Sepik Prov., Papua New Guinea; worked in investment banking; serves as Special Envoy and Amb. for Environment and Climate Change for Papua New Guinea; on faculty, School for Int. and Public Affairs, Columbia Univ., Exec. Dir Coalition for Rainforest Nations, has been instrumental in establishment of World Bank's Forest Carbon Partnership Facility and UN's UN-REDD (Reducing Emissions from Deforestation and Forest Degradation in developing countries) programme; has advised govts in Africa, Asia, Latin America and the Pacific on sustainable devt, econ. reform and investment incentive programmes; named by Time magazine No. 1 in 'Leaders & Visionaries' category of Heroes of the Environment 2008, named 'Champion of the Earth' by UNEP 2009. *Address:* Coalition for Rainforest Nations, 370 Lexington Avenue, 26th Floor, New York, NY 10017, USA (office). *Telephone:* (212) 854-8181 (office). *Fax:* (212) 504-2622 (office). *E-mail:* kconrad@rainforestcoalition.org (office). *Website:* www.rainforestcoalition.org (office).

CONRADO, Dan, MBA, MBA; Brazilian business executive; *Chairman, Vale;* ed Universidade Dom Bosco, Mato Grosso do Sul, COPPEAD/Universidade Fed. do Rio de Janeiro, Instituto de Ensino e Pesquisa em Administração (INEPAD); CEO Previ (pension fund of the employees of Banco do Brasil) 2012–; CEO Valepar 2012–; mem. Bd of Dirs and Chair. Vale 2012–; mem. Bd of Dirs FRAS-LE SA 2010–; Alt. mem. Bd of Dirs BRASILPREV SA Jan.–March 2010, Aliança do Brasil SA 2010–11, Mapfre BBSH2 Participações SA 2011–; Dir for Marketing and Communications, Banco do Brasil SA 2009, also served as Dir of Distribution 2010–11, and Vice-Pres. for Retail, Distribution and Operations 2011–12; mem. Fiscal Council, Centrais Elétricas de Santa Catarina SA 2000–02, WEG SA 2002–05. *Address:* Vale, Av. Graça Aranha, 26, 20030-900 Rio de Janeiro RJ, Brazil (office). *Telephone:* (21) 3814-4477 (office). *Fax:* (21) 3814-4040 (office). *E-mail:* info@vale.com (office). *Website:* www.vale.com (office).

CONRAN, Jasper Alexander Thirlby, OBE; British fashion designer; *Chairman and Chief Creative Director, The Conran Shops;* b. 12 Dec. 1959, London; s. of Sir Terence Conran (q.v.) and Shirley Conran; ed Bryanston School, Dorset, Parsons School of Art and Design, New York; Fashion Designer, Man. Dir Jasper Conran Ltd 1978–, Chair. and Chief Creative Dir, The Conran Shops; designer of lines for Debenhams 1997–; theatre costumes, Jean Anouilh's The Rehearsal, Almeida Theatre 1990, My Fair Lady 1992; Sleeping Beauty, Scottish Ballet 1994,

The Nutcracker Sweeties, Birmingham Royal Ballet 1996, Edward II 1997, Arthur 2000; Fil d'Or (Int. Linen Award) 1982, 1983, British Fashion Council Designer of the Year Award 1986–87, Fashion Group of America Award 1987, Laurence Olivier Award for Costume Designer of the Year 1991, British Collections Award (in British Fashion Awards) 1991. *Address:* Jasper Conran Ltd, 1–7 Rostrevor Mews, Fulham, London, SW6 5AZ, England. *Telephone:* (20) 7384-0800. *Fax:* (20) 7384-0801. *E-mail:* info@jasperconran.com. *Website:* www.jasperconran.com.

CONRAN, Sir Terence Orby, Kt, FCSD; British designer and retail executive; b. 4 Oct. 1931, Esher, Surrey; s. of Rupert Conran and Christina Halstead; m. 1st Brenda Davison (divorced); m. 2nd Shirley Conran (divorced 1962); two s.; m. 3rd Caroline Herbert 1963 (divorced 1996); two s. one d.; m. 4th Vicki Davis 2000; ed Bryanston School and Cen. School of Art and Design, London; Chair. Conran Holdings Ltd 1965–68; Jt Chair. Ryman Conran Ltd 1968–71; Chair. Habitat Group Ltd 1971–88, Habitat/Mothercare PLC 1982–88; Chair. Habitat France SA 1973–88, Conran Stores Inc. 1977–88, J. Hepworth & Son Ltd 1981–83 (Dir 1979–83), Richard Shops 1983; Chair. Storehouse PLC 1986–90, CEO 1986–88, non-exec. Dir 1990; Chair. The Conran Shop Ltd 1976–, Conran Roche 1980–, Jasper Conran 1982–, Butlers Wharf 1984–90, Bibendum Restaurant 1986–, Benchmark Ltd 1989–, Blueprint Café 1989–, Terence Conran Ltd 1990–, Conran Holdings 1990–, The Conran Shop SNC 1990–, Le Pont de la Tour 1991–, Quaglino's Restaurant Ltd 1991–, The Butler's Wharf Chop House Ltd 1992–; CD Partnership 1993–, Conran Restaurants Ltd 1994–, Bluebird Store Ltd 1994–, Mezzo Ltd 1995–, Conran Shop Marylebone 1995–, Conran Shop Germany 1996–, Coq d'Argent Ltd 1997–, Orrery Ltd 1997–; Vice-Pres. FNAC 1985–89; Dir Conran Ink Ltd 1969–, The Neal Street Restaurant 1972–89, Electra Risk Capital 1981–84, Conran Octopus Ltd 1983–, Heal & Son Ltd 1983–87, Savacentre 1986–88, British Home Stores 1986–88, Michelin House Investment Co. Ltd 1989–; f. Conran Foundation, Butler's Wharf; launched Content by Conran range of furniture for Christie Tyler 2003; mem. Royal Comm. on Environmental Pollution 1973–76; mem. Council, Royal Coll. of Art 1978–81, 1986–; mem. Advisory Council, Victoria & Albert Museum 1979–83, Trustee 1984–90; Trustee Design Museum 1989–, Chair. 1992–; mem. Creative Leaders' Network; Dr hc (RCA) 1996, Hon. DLitt (Portsmouth) 1996; RSA Bicentenary Medal 1982, Commdr Ordre des Arts et des Lettres 1991 and other awards for design. *Publications include:* The House Book 1974, The Kitchen Book 1977, The Bedroom & Bathroom Book 1978, The Cook Book (with Caroline Conran) 1980, The New House Book 1985, The Conran Directory of Design 1985, The Soft Furnishings Book 1986, Plants at Home 1986, Terence Conran's France 1987, Terence Conran's D.I.Y. by Design 1989, D.I.Y. in the Garden 1991, Terence Conran's Toys and Children's Furniture 1992, Terence Conran's Kitchen Book 1993, The Essential House Book 1994, Terence Conran on Design 1996, The Essential Garden Book 1998, Easy Living 1999, Chef's Garden 1999, Terence Conran on Restaurants 1999, Terence Conran on London 2000, Q and A: A Sort of Autobiography 2001, Terence Conran on Small Spaces 2001, How to Live in Small Spaces 2006, Outdoors: The Garden Design Book for the Twenty-First Century (with Diarmuid Gavin) 2007, Terence Conran's Inspiration 2009. *Leisure interests:* gardening, cooking. *Address:* 22 Shad Thames, London, SE1 2YU, England. *Telephone:* (20) 7378-1161. *Fax:* (20) 7403-4309. *Website:* www.conran.com.

CONROY, (Donald Patrick) Pat, BA; American writer; b. 26 Oct. 1945, Atlanta, Ga; s. of Col Donald Conroy and Frances (Peg) Dorothy Conroy; m. 1st Barbara Bolling 1969 (divorced 1977); m. 2nd Lenore Gurewitz 1981 (divorced 1995), m. 3rd Cassandra King 1997; one s. five d.; ed The Citadel; mem. Authors Guild of America, PEN, Writers Guild; Ford Foundation Leadership Devt Grant 1971, Nat. Endowment for the Arts Award for Achievement in Educ. 1974, SC Hall of Fame, Acad. of Authors 1988, Golden Plate Award, American Acad. of Achievement 1992, Ga Comm. on the Holocaust Humanitarian Award 1996, Lotos Medal of Merit for Outstanding Literary Achievement 1996 and many others, elected mem. South Carolina Hall of Fame. *Film screenplays:* Invictus 1988, The Prince of Tides (with Becky Johnson) 1991, Beach Music 1997. *Publications:* non-fiction: The Boo 1970, The Water is Wide 1972, The Pat Conroy Cookbook 2004, My Reading Life 2010; novels: The Great Santini 1976, The Lords of Discipline 1980, The Prince of Tides 1986, Beach Music 1995, My Losing Season 2002, South of Broad 2009. *Address:* Marly Rusoff and Associates, PO Box 524, Bronxville, NY 10708, USA (office). *Telephone:* (914) 961-7939 (office). *E-mail:* mra_queries@rusoffagency.com (office). *Website:* www.rusoffagency.com (office); www.patconroy.com.

CONSIDINE, Frank William; American business executive; b. 15 Aug. 1921, Chicago; s. of Frank J. Considine and Minnie Regan; m. Nancy Scott 1948; ed Loyola Univ., Chicago; Partner, F. J. Hogan Agency, Chicago 1945–47; Asst to Pres. Graham Glass Co. Chicago 1947–51; Prin., F. W. Considine Co., Chicago 1951–55; Vice-Pres. Metro Glass Div. Kraftco, Chicago 1955–60; Vice-Pres. and Dir Nat. Can Corpn (now American Nat. Can Co.), Chicago 1961–67, Exec. Vice-Pres. 1967–69, Pres. 1969–88, CEO 1973–88, Chair. 1983–90, Hon. Chair. and Chair. Exec. Cttee 1990–; Vice-Chair. Triangle Industries Inc. (parent corpn) 1985–88; Vice-Pres. Lyric Opera of Chicago; mem. Bd of Dirs Encyclopaedia Britannica, First Chicago Corpn, First Nat. Bank of Chicago, Helene Curtis Industries Inc., Ill. Power Co., Schwitzer Inc., Scotsman Industries, Maytag Co., Tribune Co., IMC Fertilizer Group Inc.; Chair. Bd of Trustees Loyola Univ., Chicago –1999, Loyola Univ. Health System; Hon. LLD (Loyola Univ.) 1986; Hon. LHD (Northwestern Univ.) 1987.

CONSTANT, Paule, DèsSc; French author; b. 25 Jan. 1944, Gan; d. of Yves Constant and Jeanne Tauzin; m. Auguste Bourgeade 1968; one s. one d.; ed Univ. of Bordeaux and Univ. of Paris (Sorbonne); Asst Lecturer in French Literature, Univ. of Abidjan 1968–75; Maître-assistant, then Maître de conférences in French Literature and Civilization, Univ. of Aix-Marseille III 1975–90, Inst. of French Studies for Foreign Students 1986–95; Prof. Université Aix–Marseille III 1995–; diarist, Revue des Deux Mondes, Paris 1990–92; Founder and Pres. Centre des Ecrivains du Sud - Jean Giono; Chevalier, Légion d'honneur, Ordre de l'Educ. Nat. de Côte d'Ivoire. *Television includes:* L'Education des Jeunes Filles de la Légion d'Honneur 1992, Mon héros préféré: La Princesse de Clèves 1996, Les grands fleuves racontés par des écrivains: L'Amazone 1997, Galilée: Paule Constant sur les traces de Jean Giono 2001. *Publications:* novels: Ouregano 1980 (Prix Valery Larbaud), Propriété privée 1981, Balta 1983, White Spirit 1989 (Prix François Mauriac, Prix Lutèce, Prix du Sud Jean-Baumel, Grand Prix du Roman, Acad.

Française), Le Grand Ghâpal 1991, La Fille du Gobernator 1994, Confidence pour confidence 1998 (Prix du roman France-Télévision, Prix Goncourt Un monde à l'usage des demoiselles (essay) 1987 (Grand Prix de l'Essai, Acad. Française 1987), Sucre et Secret 2003 (Prix du roman, Amnesty international), La Bête à Chagrin 2007. *Leisure interest:* bibliophile (18th and 19th century works on educ.). *Address:* Institut d'études françaises pour étudiants étrangers, 23 rue Gaston de Saporta, 13100 Aix-en-Provence (office); 29 rue Cardinale, 13100 Aix-en-Provence, France. *Telephone:* 4-42-38-45-08 (office). *Fax:* 4-42-23-02-64 (office). *Website:* www .pauleconstant.com.

CONSTANTINE, David John, BA, PhD, FRSL; British poet, writer and translator; b. 4 March 1944, Salford, Lancs.; m. Helen Frances Best 1966; one s. one d.; ed Wadham Coll., Oxford; Lecturer to Sr Lecturer in German, Durham Univ. 1969–81; Fellow in German, The Queen's Coll., Oxford 1981–2000; Co-Ed. (with Bernard O'Donoghue) Oxford Poets anthologies 2000–11, (with Helen Constantine) Modern Poetry in Translation magazine 2004–12; mem. Poetry Soc., Soc. of Authors; Hon. DLitt (Durham) 2009; Alice Hunt Bartlett Prize 1984, Runciman Prize 1985, Southern Arts Literature Prize 1987, European Poetry Trans. Prize 1998, BBC Nat. Short Story Award 2010, Frank O'Connor Int. Short Story Award 2013. *Publications:* poetry: A Brightness to Cast Shadows 1980, Watching for Dolphins 1983, Mappi Mundi 1984, Madder 1987, Selected Poems 1991, Caspar Hauser 1994, Sleeper 1995, The Pelt of Wasps 1998, Something for the Ghosts 2002, Collected Poems 2004, A Poetry Primer 2004, Nine Fathom Deep 2009; fiction: Davies 1985, Back at the Spike 1994, Under the Dam (short stories) 2005, The Shieling (short stories) 2009, Tea at the Midland (short story) (BBC Nat. Short Story Prize 2010), Tea at the Midland and Other Stories 2012; non-fiction: The Significance of Locality in the Poetry of Friedrich Hölderlin 1979, Early Greek Travellers and the Hellenic Ideal 1984, Hölderlin 1988, Friedrich Hölderlin 1992, Fields of Fire: A Life of Sir William Hamilton 2001, A Living Language 2004; translator: Hölderlin: Selected Poems 1996, Henri Michaux: Spaced, Displaced (with Helen Constantine) 1992, Philippe Jaccottet: Under Clouded Skies/ Beauregard (with Mark Treharne) 1994, Goethe: Elective Affinities 1994, Kleist: Selected Writings 1998, Hölderlin's Sophocles 2001, Hans Magnus Enzensberger: Lighter Than Air 2002, Goethe: Faust 2005, 2009; ed.: German Short Stories 2 1972, Goethe: Werther. *Leisure interest:* walking. *Address:* The Queen's College, Oxford, OX1 4AW (office); 1 Hill Top Road, Oxford, OX4 1PB, England (home). *Telephone:* (1865) 244701 (office). *E-mail:* david.constantine@queens.ox.ac.uk (office).

CONSTANTINE II, King of the Hellenes; b. 2 June 1940; m. Princess Anne-Marie of Denmark 1964; three s. two d.; ed Anavryta School and Law School, Athens Univ.; mil. training 1956–58, graduated from three mil. acads (army, navy, air force); visited USA 1958, 1959; succeeded to throne March 1964; left Greece Dec. 1967; deposed June 1973; monarchy abolished by Nat. Referendum Dec. 1974; deprived of Greek citizenship, remaining property in Greece nationalized April 1994; won ruling in European Court of Human Rights for compensation; returned to live in Greece 2013; Gold Medal, Sailing (Dragon Class), Olympic Games, Rome 1960, Beppe Croce Trophy in recognition of outstanding voluntary contrib. to sport of sailing, Int. Sailing Fed. (ISAF) 2010. *Address:* 15 Grosvenor Square, London, W1K 6LD, England (office). *Website:* www.greekroyalfamily.org (home).

CONSTANTINESCU, Emil, PhD, DSc; Romanian politician, jurist, geologist and fmr head of state; *President, Romanian Foundation for Democracy;* b. 19 Nov. 1939, Tighina (now Repub. of Moldova); s. of Ion Constantinescu and Maria Constantinescu; m. Nadia Ileana Bogorin; one s. one d.; ed Bucharest Univ.; practising lawyer 1960–61; Lecturer and Sr Lecturer, Bucharest Univ. 1966–90, Prof. of Mineralogy 1990–, Vice-Rector 1990–92, Rector 1992–96, Hon. Pres. of Senate 1996–, Prof. of Mineralogy-Crystallography 2001–; Visiting Prof., Duke Univ., NC, USA 1991–92; Chair Nat. Romanian Council of Univ. Rectors 1992–96; mem. Steering Cttee of European Univs Assoc. (CRE) 1992–98, Int. Assoc. of Univ. Presidents 1994–96, Founder-mem. Univ. Solidarity 1990; Pres. Civic Acad. 1990–92; Acting Chair. Romanian Anti-Totalitarian Forum 1991; Pres. Democratic Convention 1992–96; Pres. of Romania 1996–2000; currently Pres., Romanian Foundation for Democracy, Romanian Academic Forum; Gen. Sec. Romanian Geological Soc. 1987–93, 1990–93; Co-Chair. World Justice Project (sponsored by ABA, European Bar Asscn, World Bar Asscn) 2007–; mem. A Global Forum on New Democracies, Taipei 2008; mem. Balkan Political Club 2001–, East West Inst., Victims of Communism Memorial Foundation, Washington, DC, High Council Int. Org. of Francophony 2004–; Int. Centre for Democratic Transition, Budapest 2006–; Fellow, World Acad. of Art and Science; Hon. Citizen of Athens, Prague, Budapest, San Francisco and Helsinki; Hon. mem. Geological and Mineralogical Socs of America, UK, Germany, SA, Japan, Greece; Hon. mem. Nat. Geographical Soc. of USA and Geographical Soc. of France; numerous int. decorations including Grand Croix, Légion d'honneur, Order of Merit (Austria), Stara Planina with Ribbon (Romania), White Rose of Finland with Collar, Great Cross of St Olaf (Norway), State Decoration (Turkey), St Andrew Order, Patriarchy of Constantinople, Orthodox Order of the Holy Grave with Collar, Orthodox Patriarchy in Jerusalem, Collar of Dom Infante Henrique (Portugal), Great Cross of High Order of St Michael and St George (UK), Kt, Order of the Elephant (Denmark); Hon. DSc (Univs of Athens, Liège, Montréal, Delhi, Beijing, Ankara, Chişinău, Astana, Maribor, Bangkok, Sofia, Ecole Nationale Supérieur, Paris); numerous awards including Romanian Acad. Award in Geology 1980, Aristide Calvany Award for Peace, Democracy and Human Devt Paris 1997, Award for Democracy of Democratic Center, Washington, DC 1998, European Statesman of the Year Award, New York 1998, European Coudenhove-Kalergi Award for Contrib. to Devt of Europe and Free Movt of Ideas, Bern 1998, Bethleem 2000 Medal, Nat. Palestinian Authority 2000; awards and medals from Acad. des Sciences, Inst. de France, Univs of Paris-Sorbonne, Prague, Amsterdam, Bratislava, Szeged, São Paulo. *Publications:* 12 books and more than 60 articles in scientific journals and more than 100 articles, speeches and essays on political, econ., social, educational, cultural and environmental issues; Time of Tearing Down, Time of Building (four vols) *Address:* 050093 Bucharest, Splaiul Independenţei 17/101, Romania. *Telephone:* (21) 3160397 (office). *Fax:* (21) 3160399 (office). *E-mail:* emil@constantinescu.ro (home); cabinet_ec@ constantinescu.ro (office). *Website:* www.frd.org.ro (office); www.constantinescu.ro (home).

CONSTAS, Dimitri, LLB, PhD; Greek academic, research institute director and fmr government official; *Professor of International Relations, Institute of International Relations;* ed Panteion Univ., Univ. of Thessaloniki, Carleton Univ., Canada, Tufts Univ., USA; Rector, Panteion Univ. 1990–95; Interim Minister for Press and Mass Media 1996; Perm. Rep. to Council of Europe, Strasbourg 1997–99; Head of Task Forces on Euro-Mediterranean Co-operation, Middle East Peace Process, Greek role in Int. Conflict Resolution 2000; Founder and Prof. of Int. Relations, Inst. of Int. Relations, Panteion Univ., Athens 1989; Pres. Hellenic Soc. of Int. Law and Int. Relations 1989–91; Vice-Pres. Foundation for Hellenic Culture 1994–95; Fellow, Woodrow Wilson Int. Center for Scholars 1998; International Relations Scholar, Minda de Gunzburg Center for European Studies, Harvard Univ. 2011; Fulbright Scholar 1976–79, MacJannet Fellow, Institut des Hautes Etudes Internationaux 1978, Robert Schumann Fellow in European Integration 1979, Noted Scholar, Univ. of British Columbia 1996, Sr Fulbright Scholar, Princeton Univ. 1996. *Publications include:* The Greek–Turkish Conflict in the 1990s (ed.) 1991, Modern Diasporas in World Politics: the Greeks in Comparative Perspective (co-ed.) 1993, Greece Prepares for the Twenty-First Century (co-ed.) 1995, Greek and European Foreign Policy (1991–99), Diplomacy and Politics 2003. *Address:* Institute of International Relations, 3–5 Hill Street, Athens 10558, Greece (office). *Telephone:* (21) 13312325 (office). *Fax:* (21) 13313575 (office). *E-mail:* constas@idis.gr (office). *Website:* www.idis.gr (office).

CONSUNJI, David Mendoza, BS; Philippine civil engineer and business executive; *Founder and Chairman, D.M. Consunji Inc.;* b. 1921; m. Fredesvinda Consunji; eight c.; ed De La Salle Univ., Manila; f. D.M. Consunji Inc. (construction firm) 1954, currently Chair. DMCI Holdings Inc.; Sec., Dept of Public Works, Transportation and Communications 1971–75; Chair. Dacon Corpn, Semirara Mining Corpn; fmr Chair. Contractors Licensing Bd, Philippine Domestic Construction Bd, Philippine Overseas Construction Bd; Hon. LLD (Univ. of the Philippines) 1993; Civil Engineer Diamond Jubilee Award, Univ. of the Philippines Alumni Engineers 1985, Meralco Award in Eng and Applied Sciences 1994. *Address:* DMCI Holdings Inc., 3rd Floor, Dacon Building, 2281 Don Chino Roces Avenue, Makati City 1231, Philippines (office). *Telephone:* (2) 8883000 (office). *Fax:* (2) 8167362 (office). *Website:* www.dmciholdings.com (office).

CONTAMINE, Claude Maurice; French television executive; b. 29 Aug. 1929, Metz, Moselle; s. of the late Henry Contamine and Marie-Thérèse Dufays; m. Renée Jaugeon (deceased); one s.; ed Lycée Malherbe, Caen, Facultés de Droit, Caen and Paris and Ecole Nat. d'Admin; public servant until 1997; Asst Dir-Gen. ORTF and Dir of TV 1964–67; Pres. Dir-Gen. Union générale cinématographique (UGC) 1967–71; Consul-Gen. Milan 1971–72; Asst Dir-Gen. in charge of external affairs and co-operation, ORTF 1973–74; Minister plenipotentiary 1974; mem. Haut Conseil de l'Audiovisuel 1973–80; Pres. France-Régions (FR3) 1975–81; Conseiller Maître, Cour des Comptes 1981; Pres. Télédiffusion de France (TDF) 1986; Pres. Dir-Gen. Soc. nat. de programme Antenne 2 1986–89; Rapporteur général European TV and Film Forum 1990–2000; Pres. Conservatoire Européen d'Ecriture Audiovisuelle 1996–2002; mem. Conseil Supérieur de la Magistrature 1998–2002, Comm. nationale consultative des droits de l'homme 2002–12; Commdr, Légion d'honneur 2003, Commdr, Ordre nat. du Mérite, Officier des Arts et des Lettres. *Address:* 12 rue de Bassano, 75116 Paris, France (home).

CONTAMINE, Philippe, DèsSc; French historian and academic; *Professor Emeritus of Medieval History, Université Paris-Sorbonne;* b. 7 May 1932, Metz; s. of Henry Contamine and Marie-Thérèse Dufays; m. Geneviève Bernard 1956; two s. one d.; ed Lycée Malherbe, Caen, Lycée Louis-le-grand, Paris, Sorbonne; history and geography teacher, Lycée, Sens 1957–60, Lycée Carnot, Paris 1960–61; Asst Prof. of Medieval History, Sorbonne 1962–65; Asst Lecturer, Lecturer then Prof. of Medieval History, Univ. of Nancy 1965–73; Prof. of Medieval History, Univ. of Paris (Nanterre) 1973–89; Prof. of Medieval History, Univ. of Paris (Sorbonne) 1989–2000, Prof. Emer. 2000–; Dir Dept of History 1976–79; Sec. to Soc. de l'histoire de France 1984–; Pres. Nat. Soc. of Antique Dealers 1999; mem. Institut de France (Acad. des Inscriptions et Belles-Lettres, Pres. 2000) 1990, Academia Europaea 1993; Corresp. Fellow Royal Historical Soc. 1993; Pres. Soc. Nat. des Antiquaires de France 1999; Chevalier Légion d'honneur, Commdr des Palmes académiques, Officier des Arts et Lettres. *Publications:* La Guerre de cent ans 1968, Guerre, Etat et Société à la fin du Moyen Age 1972, La Vie quotidienne en France et en Angleterre pendant la guerre de cent ans 1976, La guerre au Moyen Age 1980, La France aux XIVe et XVe siècles 1981, La France de la fin du XVe siècle (co-ed.) 1985, L'Etat et Les Aristocraties (ed.) 1989, L'histoire militaire de la France 1992, Des pouvoirs en France 1300–1500 1992, L'Economie Mediévale 1993, De Jeanne d'Arc aux guerres d'Italie 1994, La Noblesse au royaume de France de Philippe Le Bel à Louis XII 1997, Guerre et concurrence entre les Etats européens du XIVe au XVIIIe siècle (ed.) 1998, Autour de Marguerite d'Ecosse: reines, princesses et dames du XVe siècle (ed.) 1999, Les enceintes urbaines XIIIe-XVIe (jtly) 2002, Histoire de la France politique 2002. *Address:* 11–15 rue de l'Amiral Roussin, 75015 Paris, France.

CONTE, Fernando, BSc, MBA; Spanish airline executive; *Chairman and CEO, Iberia Group;* b. 28 Feb. 1950, Mérida, Mexico; m.; two d.; ed Instituto Catolico de Artes e Industrias, Instituto de Empresa (pvt. business school); worked for Asea Brown Boveri 1974–2003, positions included Sales Engineer/Product Man., Madrid, Regional Man. for Cen. America/Caribbean, Asea AB, Guatemala City, Industrial Div. Man. for Asea in Venezuela, Cen. Region Man., Asea Eléctrica, Madrid, Man. Power Transmission and Distribution Div., ASEA/ABB Energía, Madrid, Gen. Man. ABB Subestaciones, Madrid, Gen. Man. ABB Trafo, Madrid, Segment Vice-Pres. Asea Brown Boveri, SA, Madrid, Exec. Vice-Pres. and CEO Asea Brown Boveri, SA, Madrid, mem. Bd ABB Portugal, mem. ABB Ltd Group Exec. Team, Zürich; ind. Bd mem. Iberia 2001–03, Chair. and CEO Iberia Group 2003–; ind. Bd mem. Amadeus 2000–03; Chair. oneworld (airline alliance) 2005–06, Audit Cttee IATA 2005–, Asscn of European Airlines 2007–; Javier Benjumea Prize, Coll. Asscn of Engineers–ICAI 2005. *Address:* Iberia Aéreas de España, Velázquez 130, 28006 Madrid, Spain (office). *Telephone:* (91) 587-87-87 (office). *E-mail:* presidencia@iberia.es (office). *Website:* www.iberia.es (office).

CONTEH, Maj. (Alfred) Palo, LLB (Hons), LLM; Sierra Leonean army officer (retd) and government official; *Minister of Defence;* ed Univs of London and East London, UK; served in Sierra Leone army 1976–92, rose to rank of Maj. and CO of the Mil. Police; went to UK on leave to pursue legal studies 1986; Court Liaison

Officer and Prosecution Sec., Dept for Work and Pensions for the investigation service in London –2007; Minister of Defence 2007–. *Address:* Ministry of Defence, State Avenue, Freetown, Sierra Leone (office). *Telephone:* (22) 227369 (office). *Fax:* (22) 229380 (office).

CONTI, Fulvio; Italian business executive; *CEO and General Manager, Enel SpA;* b. 28 Oct. 1947, Rome; m.; one s.; ed Univ. of Rome 'La Sapienza'; joined Mobil Group 1969, Chief of Finance for Europe 1989–90; Head, Accounting, Finance and Control Dept Montecatini 1991–93; Head of Finance Montedison-Compart 1993–96; Gen. Man. and Chief Financial Officer Italian Nat. Railways 1996–98; also held important positions in other cos, including Metropolis and Grandi Stazioni; Vice-Chair. Eurofima 1997; Gen. Man. and Chief Financial Officer Telecom Italia 1998–99, also held important positions in other cos of the group, including Finsiel, TIM, Sirti, Italtel, Meie and STET International; Chief Financial Officer Enel SpA 1999–2005, CEO and Gen. Man. 2005–; Chair. Eurelectric 2011–13; Deputy Chair. Endesa, Research Dept of Confindustria; mem. Bd of Dirs Barclays plc, AON Corpn, RCS MediaGroup SpA; Dir, Nat. Acad. of Santa Cecilia, Italian Tech. Inst.; Cavaliere del Lavoro della Repubblica Italiana 2009, Officier, Légion d'honneur 2009. *Address:* Enel SpA, Viale Regina Margherita 137, 00198 Rome, Italy (office). *Telephone:* (06) 83057866 (office). *Fax:* (06) 83053472 (office). *E-mail:* secireteriaad@enel.it (office). *Website:* www.enel.it (office); www.enel.com (office).

CONTI, Most Rev. Mario Joseph, PhL, STL, FRSE; British ecclesiastic; *Archbishop of Glasgow;* b. 20 March 1934, Elgin; s. of Louis Joseph Conti and Josephine Quintilia Panicali; ed Blairs Coll., Aberdeen, Pontifical Scots Coll. and Gregorian Univ., Rome; ordained priest 1958; apptd Curate, St Mary's Cathedral, Aberdeen 1959, apptd Parish Priest, St Joachim's Wick 1962; Bishop of Aberdeen 1977–2002; Archbishop of Glasgow 2002–; Apostolic Admin. Diocese of Paisley 2004–05; Pres.-Treas. Scottish Catholic Int. Aid Fund 1978–84; Pres. Nat. Liturgy Comm. 1981–85, Nat. Comm. for Christian Doctrine and Unity 1985–; Vice-Pres. Comm. for Migrant Workers and Tourism 1978–84, Scottish Catholic Heritage Comm. 1980–; mem. Council for Promotion of Christian Unity (Rome) 1984–, Int. Comm. for English in the Liturgy 1978–87, Pontifical Comm. for Cultural Heritage of the Church, Rome 1994–2004; Convener, Action of Churches Together in Scotland 1990–93; Co-Moderator of Jt Working Group, RC Church and WCC 1995–2008; Prin. Chaplain to British Asscn of the Order of Malta 1995–2000, 2005–, Conventual Chaplain Grand Cross 2001–; mem. Historic Buildings Council of Scotland 1995–2000; Order of Merit of the Italian Repub. 1982; Kt Commdr of Holy Sepulchre 1989, Grand Official of the Order of the Star of Italian Solidarity (Italian Repub.) 2007; Hon. DD (Aberdeen) 1989, (Glasgow) 2010. *Publications:* Oh Help! The Making of an Archbishop 2003; occasional articles and letters in nat. and local press. *Leisure interests:* walking, travel, swimming, music and the arts. *Address:* Curial Offices, 196 Clyde Street, Glasgow, G1 4JY (office); 40 Newlands Road, Glasgow G43 2JD, Scotland (home). *Telephone:* (141) 226-5898 (office). *Fax:* (141) 225-2600 (office). *E-mail:* curia@rcag.org.uk (office). *Website:* www.rcag.org.uk (office).

CONTI, Tom; British actor and director; s. of Alfonso Conti and Mary McGoldrick; m. Kara Wilson 1967; one d.; ed Royal Scottish Acad. of Music; West End Theatre Mans' Award, Royal Television Soc. Award, Variety Club of Great Britain Award 1978, Tony Award of New York 1979. *London theatre includes:* Savages (Christopher Hampton) 1973, The Devil's Disciple (Shaw) 1976, Whose Life is it Anyway? (Brian Clarke) 1978, They're Playing Our Song (Neil Simon/Marvin Hamlisch) 1980, Romantic Comedy (Bernard Salde), An Italian Straw Hat 1986, Two Into One, Treats 1989, Jeffrey Bernard is Unwell 1990, The Ride Down Mt. Morgan 1991, Present Laughter (also dir) 1993, Chapter Two 1996, Jesus My Boy 1998. *Films include:* Flame, Full Circle, Merry Christmas Mr. Lawrence, Reuben, American Dreamer, Saving Grace, Miracles, Heavenly Pursuits, Beyond Therapy, Roman Holiday, Two Brothers Running, White Roses, Shirley Valentine, Someone Else's America, Crush Depth, Something to Believe In 1996, Out of Control 1997, The Enemy 2000, Derailed 2005, Rabbit Fever 2006, Paid 2006, Almost Heaven 2006, O Jerusalem 2006, Dangerous Parking 2007, A Closed Book 2010, The Tempest 2010, Rekindle 2011, StreetDance 2 2012, City Slacker 2012. *Television work includes:* Madame Bovary, Treats, The Glittering Prizes, The Norman Conquests, The Beate Klarsfield Story, Fatal Dosage, The Quick and the Dead, Blade on the Feather, The Wright Verdicts, Deadline, Friends 1998, Deadline 2000–01, I Was a Rat 2001, Donovan 2004, Deeply Irresponsible 2007, Four Seasons (mini-series) 2008–09. *Directed:* Last Licks, Broadway 1979, Before the Party 1980, The Housekeeper 1982, Treats 1989, Present Laughter 1993, Last of the Red Hot Lovers 1999. *Publication:* The Doctor (novel) 2004. *Leisure interest:* music. *Address:* Artists Independent Network, 32 Tavistock Street, London, WC2E 7PB, England. *Telephone:* (20) 7352-7722.

CONTOGEORGIS, George, MA, PhD; Greek political scientist and professor of political science; *Professor of Political Science, Panteion University of Athens;* b. 14 Feb. 1947, Letkas; s. of Dimitri Contogeorgis and Elia Contogeorgis; m. Catherine Kampourgiannidou 1972; two d.; ed Univ. of Athens, Univ. of Paris II, Ecole Pratique des Hautes Etudes, Ecole des Hautes Etudes en Sciences Sociales; Prof. of Political Science, Panteion Univ. of Athens 1983–, Rector 1984–90; Gen. Dir ERT SA (Hellenic Broadcasting Corpn) 1985, Pres.-Gen. Dir 1989; Minister, Ministry of the Presidency (State Admin., Communication, Media), Govt Spokesman 1993; Founding mem. European Political Science Network (EPSNET); Dir European Masters Programme in Political Science; Founder-mem. and Sec.-Gen. Greek Political Sciences Asscn 1975–80; fmr Dir of Research, CNRS, France; leader writer in Athenian daily newspapers; mem. High Council and Research Council, European Univ., Florence 1986–94; mem. High Council, Univ. of Europe, Paris and Centre of Regional Studies, Montpellier; Visiting Prof., Inst. d'Etudes Politiques, Paris, Univ. Libre de Bruxelles, Univ. Catholique de Louvain, Univs of Montpellier, Tokyo, IEP Bordeaux, Lille etc.; Prof., Franqui Chair., Univ. of Brussels; Prof. of European Studies, Univ. of Siena; mem. Council Pôle Sud, Political Science Review, Revue Internationale de Politique Comparée, Journal of Southern Europe; Corresp. mem. Int. Acad. of Culture (Portugal); mem. French Political Science Asscn, IPSA and other int. asscns; Chevalier des Palmes académiques, titulaire de la chair Franqui. *Publications include:* The Theory of Revolution in Aristotle 1975, The Popular Ideology: Socio-political Study of the Greek Folk Song 1979, Political System and Politics 1985, Social Process and

Political Self-government: The Greek City-State Under the Ottoman Empire 1982, History of Greece 1992, Système de communication et système d'échange: La télévision 1993, After Communism (in collaboration) 1993, Greek Society in the 20th Century 1995, Democracy in the Technological Society 1995, Society and Politics 1996, New World Order 1998, Identité cosmosystémique ou identité nationale? Le Paradigme hellénique 1999, Le Citoyen dans la cité (Typology of Citizenship) 2000, Modernity and Progress 2001, Work and Freedom 2003, Citizenship and State, Concept and Typology of Citizenship 2004, The Authoritarian Phenomenon 2004, Nation and Modernity 2006, The Hellenic Cosmosystem: Vol. 1, The Statocentric Period 2006, Democracy as Freedom. Democracy and Representation 2007, Youth, State and Freedom 2009, The 'Hellenic Democracy' of Rhigas Feraios 2009, Economic Systems and Freedom 2010, On the Nation and the Greek Continuity 2010, L'Europe et le Monde. Civilization et Pluralisme Culturel 2011, De l'Europe politique 2011, Partitocracy and Dynastic State 2012. *Leisure interest:* water sports. *Address:* Panteion University of Athens, 136 Sygrou Avenue, Athens 17671 (office); 37 Dafnomili Street, Athens 11471, Greece (home). *Telephone:* (210) 9201743 (office); (210) 6399662 (home); (210) 6081780 (home). *Fax:* (210) 9201743 (office). *E-mail:* gdc14247@gmail.com (office). *Website:* www.panteion.gr (office).

CONWAY, Craig A., BSc; American business executive (retd); b. 17 Oct. 1954, Fort Wayne, Ind.; m. Tina Conway; two c.; ed State Univ. of NY, Brockport; began career as Exec. Vice Pres. of Marketing, Sales and Operations, Oracle Corpn; fmr Pres. and CEO TGV Software; Pres. and CEO One Touch Systems –1999; joined PeopleSoft Inc. May 1999, Pres. and CEO 1999– 2004; mem. Bd of Dirs Salesforce.com 2005–, Kazeon Systems, Inc. 2006–, Unisys Corpn 2007–. *Address:* 170 Olive Hill Lane, Woodside, CA 94062, USA.

CONWAY, Jill Ker, AC, BA, PhD; Australian/American historian, author, academic and company director; b. 9 Oct. 1934, Hillston, NSW, Australia; m. John Conway (died 1995); ed Abbotsleigh School, Univ. of Sydney, Harvard Univ., USA; moved to USA 1960; taught at Univ. of Toronto, Canada 1964–75, Vice-Pres. of Internal Affairs 1973–75; Pres. Smith Coll., Mass, USA 1975–85, Pres. Emer. 1985–; Visiting Scholar, Program in Science, Technology and Society, MIT 1985–2008; mem. Bd of Dirs ImagineNations Group; fmr mem. Bd of Dirs Nike Inc., Colgate-Palmolive Co., Merrill Lynch & Co., Lend Lease Corpn (Chair. 2000–03); mem. Bd of Trustees Mount Holyoke Coll. 1991–2001; Dr hc (Concordia Univ.) 2003; Nat. Humanities Medal 2012. *Publications include:* Merchants and Merinos 1960, Women Reformers and American Culture 1870–1930 1972, The Female Experience in 18th- and 19th-Century America 1982, Women Reformers and American Culture 1987, Utopian Dream or Dystopian Nightmare? Nineteenth Century Feminist Ideas about Equality 1987, Learning About Women (co-author) 1989, The Road from Coorain (memoir) (LL Winship/PEN New England Award 1989) 1989, Autobiographies of American Women: An Anthology 1992, The Politics of Women's Education (co-author) 1993, True North: A Memoir 1995, Inventing the Truth: The Art and Craft of Memoir (co-author) 1995, Written by Herself (as ed.) 1995, Written by Herself Vol. 2: Autobiographies from Britain, Africa, Asia and the US 1996, Modern Feminism: An Intellectual History 1997, When Memory Speaks 1998, In Her Own Words: Women's Memoirs from Australia, New Zealand, Canada and the United States 1999, Overnight Float (co-author) 2000, Earth, Air, Fire, Water: Humanistic Studies of the Environment 2000, Women on Power: Leadership Redefined 2001, A Woman's Education 2001, Felipe the Flamingo 2006.

CONWAY, John Horton, MA, PhD, FRS; British mathematician and academic; *John von Neumann Distinguished Professor of Mathematics, Princeton University;* b. 26 Dec. 1937, Liverpool; m. Diana Conway; three s. four d.; ed Gonville and Caius Coll., Cambridge; Lecturer in Pure Math., Cambridge Univ. –1973, Reader in Pure Math. and Math. Statistics 1973–83, Prof. of Math. 1983–87; John von Neumann Distinguished Prof. of Math., Princeton Univ. 1986–; Fellow Sidney Sussex Coll., Cambridge 1964–70, Gonville and Caius Coll., Cambridge 1970–87; Hon. Fellow Gonville and Caius Coll. 1999; Hon. DSc (Liverpool) 2001; Polya Prize London Math. Soc. 1987, Frederic Esser Nemmers Prize, Northwestern Univ. 1999, Steele Prize, American Math. Soc. 1999, Joseph Priestley Award, Dickinson Coll. 2001. *Publications:* Regular Algebra and Finite Machines 1971, On Numbers and Games 1976, Winning Ways for Your Mathematical Plays (vol 2) 1982, 2003, Atlas of Finite Groups 1985, Sphere Packings, Lattices and Groups 1987, The Book of Numbers 1996, The Sensual Quadratic Form 1997, On Numbers and Games 2000, Winning Ways for You Mathematical Plays (vol 1) 2001, On Quaternions and Octonions, Winning Ways for Your Mathematical Plays (vol 3) 2003, Winning Ways for Your Mathematical Plays (vol 4) 2004. *Leisure interests:* puzzles, games, knots, knowlege. *Address:* Department of Mathematics, Fine Hall, Princeton University, Washington Road, Princeton, NJ 08544 (office); 71 Patton Avenue, Princeton, NJ 08540, USA (home). *Telephone:* (609) 258-6468 (office); (609) 683-0206 (home). *Fax:* (609) 921-0353 (home). *Website:* www.math.princeton.edu/menusa/index0.html (office).

COOGAN, Stephen (Steve) John; British actor, comedian, impressionist, producer and writer; b. 14 Oct. 1965, Middleton, Lancs., England; m. Caroline Hickman 2002 (divorced 2005); partner, Anna Cole; partner China Chow 2008–11; partner Elle Basey 2011–; one c.; ed ; began career working as a voice artist on satirical puppet show Spitting Image 1987; began creating original comic characters early 1990s; Co-founder and Chair. Baby Cow Productions 1999–; Perrier Award, Edinburgh Festival Fringe 1992. *Films:* Resurrected 1989, Steve Coogan: Live 'n' Lewd (video) 1994, The Indian in the Cupboard 1995, The Wind in the Willows 1996, Add-On Alan... with Alan Partridge (video short) 1997, The Revengers' Comedies 1998, Steve Coogan: The Man Who Thinks He's It (video) 1998, The Parole Officer 2001, 24 Hour Party People 2002, Coffee and Cigarettes (segment 'Cousins?') 2003, Ella Enchanted (voice) 2004, Around the World in 80 Days 2004, Happy Endings 2005, A Cock and Bull Story 2005, Alan Partridge Presents: The Cream of British Comedy (video) 2005, Lies & Alibis 2006, Marie Antoinette 2006, Night at the Museum 2006, Hot Fuzz (uncredited) 2007, For the Love of God (short) 2007, Hamlet 2 2008, Finding Amanda 2008, Tropic Thunder 2008, Tales of the Riverbank 2008, In the Loop (Chlotrudis Award for Best Cast 2010) 2009, What Goes Up 2009, Night at the Museum 2 2009, Pigsy Doodle (short) 2009, Steve Coogan Live: As Alan Partridge and Other Less Successful Characters (video) 2009, Percy Jackson & the Lightning Thief 2010, Marmaduke (voice) 2010,

The Other Guys 2010, The Trip 2010, Marvin (short) (voice) 2010, Our Idiot Brother 2011, Darkwood Manor 2011, Ruby Sparks 2012, What Maisie Knew 2012, The Look of Love 2013, Despicable Me 2 (voice) 2013, Alan Partridge: Alpha Papa 2013, Philomena (with Jeff Pope, Best Screenplay, Venice Film Festival, Best Movie About Women, Women Film Critics Circle) 2013, Northern Soul 2013, The Trip to Italy 2014. *Television:* Spitting Image (series) 1987–93, Sean's Show (series) (voice) 1992, The Smell of Reeves and Mortimer (series) 1993, Thatcherworld (short) (voice) 1993, Harry (series) 1993, Paul Calf's Video Diary (short) 1993, A Christmas Night with the Stars (series) 1994, Pauline Calf's Wedding Video (short) 1994, The Day Today (series) 1994, Knowing Me, Knowing You with Alan Partridge (series) (Best Male TV Performer, British Comedy Awards) 1994–95, Coogan's Run (series) 1995, Alan Partridge's Country Ramble (short) 1995, Tales from the Crypt (series) – The Kidnapper 1996, The Tony Ferrino Phenomenon (film) 1997, Introducing Tony Ferrino: Who and Why? A Quest (film) 1997, The Friday Night Armistice (series) 1997, The Fix (film) 1997, I'm Alan Partridge (series) (Best TV Comedy Actor, British Comedy Awards 1998, BAFTA Awards for Best Comedy Performance and Best Comedy (Programme or Series) 1998) 1997–2002, Bob and Margaret (series) 1998, Alice Through the Looking Glass (film) 1998, Live from the Lighthouse (film) 1998, The End of the Year Show (series) 1998, Mrs. Merton and Malcolm (series) 1999, Hooves of Fire (short) (voice) 1999, Comic Relief: Say Pants to Poverty (film) 2001, A Small Summer Party (film) 2001, Dr. Terrible's House of Horrible (series) 2001, Combat Sheep (film) (voice) 2001, Legend of the Lost Tribe (short) (voice) 2002, Cruise of the Gods (film) (Best TV Comedy Actor, British Comedy Awards 2003) 2002, Paul and Pauline Calf's Cheese and Ham Sandwich (short) 2003, Anglian Lives: Alan Partridge (film) 2003, The Private Life of Samuel Pepys (film) 2003, Monkey Trousers (film) 2004, I Am Not an Animal (series) 2004, Comic Relief: Red Nose Night Live 05 (film) 2005, Monkey Trousers (series) 2005, Little Britain (series) 2006, Saxondale (series) 2006–07, Curb Your Enthusiasm (series) 2007, Sunshine (series) 2008, Neighbors from Hell (series) 2010, Chekhov Comedy Shorts (series) – The Dangers of Tobacco 2010, The Trip (series) (BAFTA for Best Male Comedy Performance 2011) 2010, Mid Morning Matters with Alan Partridge (series) 2010–11, Comic Relief: Red Nose Day 2011 (film) 2011, The Jonathan Ross Show (series) 2011, Documental (film) 2011, The Simpsons (series) (voice) 2012, Alan Partridge on Open Books with Martin Bryce (film) 2012, Moone Boy (series) 2012, Uncle Wormsley's Christmas (film) 2012, Alan Partridge: Welcome to the Places of My Life (BAFTA for Best Male Comedy Performance 2013) 2012, Doubt (film) 2013. *Address:* Baby Cow Productions Ltd, 33 Foley Street, London, W1W 7TL, England. *Telephone:* (20) 7612-3370. *Fax:* (20) 7612-3352. *E-mail:* info@babycow.co.uk. *Website:* www.babycow.co.uk.

COOK, Alastair Nathan, MBE; British professional cricketer; *Captain, England National Cricket Team;* b. 25 Dec. 1984, Gloucester, Glos., England; s. of Graham Cook and Stephanie Cook; m. Alice Hunt 2011; ed Bedford School; opening batsman; left-hand batsman; right-arm slow bowler; plays for Bedfordshire 2002, Essex 2003–, MCC 2004–07, England Under-19s and England Lions 2000–06, England 2006– (Capt. One-Day Int. (ODI) Team 2011–, Capt. Test side 2012–); played for the Essex Acad. aged 15, debut (First-class) for the first XI 2003; Test debut: India v England, Nagpur 1 March 2006; ODI debut: England v Sri Lanka, Old Trafford, Manchester 28 June 2006; T20I debut: England v West Indies, The Oval 28 June 2007; has played in 102 Tests and scored 8,047 runs (25 hundreds and 35 fifties), highest score 294, average 46.51; ODI career: 77 matches, 2,825 runs (5 hundreds and 18 fifties), highest score 137, average 38.17; mem. England Ashes-winning team against Australia 2009, 2010/11, 2013 (Capt.); captained ODI series-winning team against Sri Lanka 2011; youngest Englishman to reach 1,000, 2,000, 3,000, 4,000, 5,000 Test runs (second youngest player behind Sachin Tendulkar) and youngest ever player to score 8,000 Test runs, making centuries in his first Test matches against India, Pakistan, West Indies and Bangladesh; only Englishman to score seven Test centuries before his 23rd birthday; set England record partnership in Australia, world record partnership and innings at The Gabba, Brisbane (329 with Jonathan Trott, 235 not out) Nov. 2010; world record time spent batting in a five-Test series, second most series runs by an Englishman (36 hours 11 minutes, 766 runs) Jan. 2011; captained England to first Test series victory on Indian soil since 1984–85 2012, broke record for most Test centuries for England (23) and became the first captain score a century in each of his first five Tests in charge, England's highest run scorer in India (866 runs) Dec. 2012; Pres. The Young Lord's Taverners (charity); Hon. Life mem. Maldon Cricket Club; Freeman of the City of London 2011; NBC Denis Compton Award 2003, 2004, 2005, 2006, CWC Young Cricketer of the Year 2005, PCA Young Cricketer of the Year 2005, 2006, ICC Test Player of the Year 2011, ICC World Test XI Opening Batsmen 2011, Wisden Cricketer of the Year 2012, ICC World Test XI Opening Batsmen 2012, ICC World ODI XI Opening Batsmen 2012, ICC World Test XI Captain 2013. *Leisure interest:* playing the clarinet, piano and saxophone. *Address:* c/o Essex County Cricket Club, The Ford County Ground, New Writtle Street, Chelmsford, Essex, CM2 0PG, England (office). *Telephone:* (1245) 252420 (office). *Fax:* (1245) 254030 (office). *E-mail:* info@essexcricket.org.uk (office). *Website:* www.essexcricket.org.uk (office).

COOK, Barbara; American singer and actress; b. 25 Oct. 1927, Atlanta, Ga; d. of Charles Bunyan and Nell Cook (née Harwell); m. David LeGrant 1952 (divorced 1965); one s.; Broadway debut as the ingenue lead in the musical Flahooley 1951; came to prominence after starring in Candide 1956 and The Music Man 1957; continued performing mostly in theatre until mid-1970s; then began a second career as a cabaret and concert singer; recognized as one of the "premier interpreters" of musical theatre songs and standards, especially those of Stephen Sondheim; numerous recordings. Honoree, 34th Annual Kennedy Center Honors 2011. *Broadway productions:* Flahooley 1951, Oklahoma! 1953, Carousel 1954, 1957, Plain and Fancy (Theatre World Award 1955) 1956, Candide 1957, The Music Man (Tony Award for Best Featured Actress in a Musical 1958) 1961, The Gay Life 1962, She Loves Me 1964, Any Wednesday 1964, Something More! 1964, Little Murders 1967, The Grass Harp 1971, Enemies 1972, Barbara Cook: A Concert for the Theatre (Drama Desk Award Outstanding One Person Show 1987) 1987, Angela Lansbury – A Celebration (benefit) 1996, Mostly Sondheim 2002, Something Good 2002, Barbara Cook's Broadway! 2004, Children and Art (benefit) 2005, Sondheim on Sondheim 2010. *Films include:* Thumbelina (voice) 1994. *Television includes:* Studio One (series) 1950, Armstrong Circle Theatre (series) –

Mr. Bemiss Takes a Trip 1952, Golden Windows (series) 1954, Producers' Showcase (series) – Bloomer Girl 1956, The Yeomen of the Guard (film) 1957, Kraft Television Theatre (series) (Kelly 1950, The Man Who Couldn't Say No 1957), Hallmark Hall of Fame (series) – The Yeoman of the Guard 1957, Alfred Hitchcock Presents (series) – A Little Sleep 1957, Hansel and Gretel (film) 1958, The Chevy Show (series) – O'Halloran's Luck 1961, The Dinah Shore Chevy Show (series) – O'Halloran's Luck 1961, Play of the Week (series) – In a Garden 1961, The United States Steel Hour (series) – The Go-Between 1962. *Music includes:* solo: Songs of Perfect Propriety 1958, Barbara Cook Sings 'From the Heart' (The Best of Rodgers & Hart) 1959, At Carnegie Hall 1975, As Of Today 1977, It's Better With a Band 1981, The Disney Album 1988, Dorothy Fields: Close as Pages in a Book 1993, Live from London 1994, Oscar Winners: The Lyrics of Oscar Hammerstein II 1997, All I Ask of You 1999, The Champion Season: A Salute to Gower Champion 1999, Have Yourself a Merry Little Christmas 2000, Sings Mostly Sondheim: Live at Carnegie Hall 2001, Count Your Blessings 2003, Barbara Cook's Broadway! 2004, Tribute 2005, Barbara Cook at The Met 2006, No One Is Alone 2007, Rainbow Round My Shoulder 2008; albums: Cheek to Cheek: Cook & Feinstein 2011, You Make Me Feel So Young: Live at Feinstein's 2011; cast and studio cast recordings: Flahooley 1951, Plain and Fancy 1955, Candide 1956, The Music Man (Grammy Award for Best Original Cast Album) 1957, Hansel and Gretel (TV soundtrack) 1958, The Gay Life 1961, Show Boat (studio cast) 1962, She Loves Me (Grammy Award for Best Score From An Original Cast Show Album) 1963, The King and I (studio cast) 1964, Show Boat (Lincoln Center cast) 1966, The Grass Harp 1971, The Grass Grows Green 1972, Follies in Concert 1985, The Secret Garden (world premiere recording) 1986, Carousel (studio cast) 1987, Thumbelina (motion picture soundtrack) 1994, Lucky in the Rain 2000, Sondheim on Sondheim 2010; compilations: The Broadway Years: Till There Was You 1995, Legends of Broadway – Barbara Cook 2006, The Essential Barbara Cook Collection 2009. *Address:* c/o Jeff Berger Management, 301 West 53rd Street, Suite 10J, New York, NY 10019, USA (office). *Telephone:* (212) 586-4978 (office). *Fax:* (212) 247-2724 (office). *E-mail:* jeffnooyawkagent@yahoo.com (office); barbara@barbaracook.com. *Website:* www.barbaracook.com.

COOK, Christopher Paul, BA, MA; British artist, poet and academic; *Reader in Painting, University of Plymouth;* b. 24 Jan. 1959, Great Ayton, N Yorks., England; s. of E. P. Cook and J. Leyland; m. Jennifer Jane Mellings 1982; two s.; ed Univ. of Exeter, Royal Coll. of Art, Accademia di Belle Arti, Bologna, Italy; Italian Govt Scholar, Accad. di Belle Arti, Bologna 1986–89; Fellow in Painting, Exeter Coll. of Art 1989–90; guest artist, Stadelschule, Frankfurt 1991; Visiting Fellow, Ruskin School, Univ. of Oxford 1992–93; Distinguished Visiting Artist, Calif. State Univ., Long Beach 1994; Visiting Artist to Banaras Hindu Univ., Varanasi, India 1994, 1996; Reader in Painting, Univ. of Plymouth 1997–; Artist in Residence, Eden Project, Cornwall 2001–03; Resident Artist, Univ. of Memphis 2004; Yokohama Museum residency, Japan 2005; Artist-in-Residence, Savannah Coll. of Art and Design, Atlanta, USA 2009; Resident Artist, Langgeng Foundation, Jogjakarta, Indonesia 2011; Prizewinner, John Moores Univ., Liverpool XXI 1999, Arts Council of England Award 2000, British Council Award to Artists 2003, Daiwa Award 2005, AHRC Award 2005, British Council Award, Beijing 2006, 2007, Phillips Award, British School at Rome 2009. *Film:* Journey 2007. *Publications:* Dust on the Mirror 1997, For and Against Nature 2000, A Thoroughbred Golden Calf 2003, Notes to the Graphites 2009. *Leisure interest:* the outdoors. *Address:* c/o Ryan Lee Gallery, Inc., 527th West 26th Street, New York, NY 10001, USA (office). *Telephone:* (212) 397-0742 (home). *Fax:* (212) 397-0742 (office). *E-mail:* c1cook@plymouth.ac.uk (home). *Website:* www.cookgraphites.com (office).

COOK, Gordon Charles, MD, DSc, MRCS, FRCP, FRCPE, FRACP, FLS; British physician specialising in tropical medicine and infectious diseases and medical historian; *Visiting Professor, University College London;* b. 17 Feb. 1932, Wimbledon, England; s. of Charles F. Cook and Kate Cook (née Kraninger, then Grainger); m. Elizabeth J. Agg-Large 1963; one s. three d.; ed Wellingborough, Kingston-upon-Thames, Raynes Park Grammar Schools and Royal Free Hosp. School of Medicine, Univ. of London; jr appointments, Royal Free Hosp., Brompton Hosp. and Royal Northern Hosp. 1958–60; medical specialist, captain, RAMC and Royal Nigerian Army 1960–62; Lecturer in Medicine, Royal Free Hosp. School of Medicine 1963–65, 1967–69, Makerere Univ. Coll., Uganda 1965–67; Prof. of Medicine, Univ. of Zambia 1969–74, Univ. of Riyadh, Saudi Arabia 1974–75; Visiting Prof. of Medicine, Univs of Basrah and Mosul, Iraq 1976; Sr Lecturer in Clinical Tropical Medicine, London School of Hygiene and Tropical Medicine 1976–97; Consultant Physician, Univ. Coll. London Hosps and Hosp. for Tropical Diseases, London 1976–97; Prof. of Medicine and Chair. Clinical Sciences Dept, Univ. of Papua New Guinea 1978–81; Hon. Sr Lecturer in Medicine, Univ. Coll. London 1981–2002, Visiting Prof. 2002–; Hon. Consultant Physician, St Luke's Hosp. for the Clergy 1988–2009; Visiting Prof. of Medicine, Doha, Qatar 1989; Hon. Lecturer in Clinical Parasitology, Medical Coll. of St Bartholomew's Hosp., London 1992–; Sr Research Fellow, Wellcome Centre for the History of Medicine 1997–2002; Founder and Chair. Erasmus Darwin Foundation, Lichfield 1994–2011, Vice-Pres. 2011–; Chair. Medical Writers Group, Soc. of Authors 1997–99; Vice-Pres. Royal Soc. of Tropical Medicine and Hygiene 1991–93, Pres. 1993–95; Vice-Pres. History of Medicine Section, Royal Soc. of Medicine 1994–96, Pres. 2003–04; Vice-Pres. Fellowship of Postgraduate Medicine 1996–2000, Pres. 2000–07; mem. Council, Galton Inst. 2005–09; mem. Cttee, Friends of the Florence Nightingale Museum 2005–09 (Vice-Chair. 2006–10); Examiner, Royal Coll. of Physicians, Univs of London and Makerere, Uganda; Ed. Journal of Infection 1995–97; mem. Editorial Bd, The Postgraduate Medical Journal; mem. Jt Cttee on Higher Medical Training, Exec. Cttee and Examiner Faculty of History and Philosophy of Medicine and Pharmacy, The Worshipful Soc. of Apothecaries 1997–; mem. of Council, History of Medicine Section, Royal Soc. of Medicine 1999–; mem. Code of Practice Cttee, Asscn of British Pharmaceutical Industry; mem. Asscn of Physicians of GB and Ireland 1973–; mem. numerous other medical and scientific socs; Trustee Overseas Devt Admin., Bookpower (fmrly Educational Low-Priced Sponsored Texts—ELST) 1996–2011; Hon. Research Assoc., Greenwich Maritime Inst. 2003–; Hon. Archivist, Seamen's Hosp. Soc. 2002–, Life Gov. 2008–; Charlotte Brown Prize, Cunning and Legg Awards, Royal Free Hosp. School of Medicine, Frederick Murgatroyd Memorial Prize, Royal Coll. of Physicians, London 1973, Hugh L'Etang Prize, Royal Soc. of Medicine 1999, Monckton Copeman Lecturer, Soc. of Apothecaries 2000, Denny Lecturer, Barbers Co. 2003. *Publications:* Acute

Renal Failure (jtly) 1964, Tropical Gastroenterology 1980, Communicable and Tropical Diseases 1988, Parasitic Disease in Clinical Practice 1990, From the Greenwich Hulks to Old St Pancras: A History of Tropical Disease in London 1992; 100 Clinical Problems in Tropical Medicine (co-ed.) 1987, 1998, Travel-associated Disease (ed.) 1995, Gastroenterological Problems from the Tropics (ed.) 1995, Manson's Tropical Diseases (ed.) (20–22nd edns) 1994–2009, Victorian Incurables: A History of the Royal Hospital for Neuro-Disability, Putney 2004, John MacAlister's Other Vision: A History of the Fellowship of Postgraduate Medicine 2005, The Incurables Movement: An Illustrated History of the British Home 2006, Tropical Medicine: An Illustrated History of the Pioneers 2007, Twenty-Six Portland Place: The Early Years of the Royal Society of Tropical Medicine and Hygiene 2011, Torrid Disease: Memoirs of a Tropical Physician in the Late Twentieth Century 2011, Origin of a Medical Specialty: The Seamen's Hospital Society and Tropical Medicine 2012, The Tropical Disease that Never Existed: a History of 'Sprue' 2013, The Rise and Fall of a Medical Specialty: London's Clinical Tropical Medicine 2014, National Service 50 Years Ago: Life of a medical conscript in West Africa 2014; more than 500 papers on physiology, gastroenterology, tropical medicine, nutrition and medical history. *Leisure interests:* cricket, walking, medical and scientific history, African and Pacific artefacts. *Address:* 11 Old London Road, St Albans, Herts., AL1 1QE, England (home). *Telephone:* (1727) 869000 (home).

COOK, Peter, CBE, BSc (Hons), MSc, PhD, DSc, FTSE; Australian geologist, academic and consultant researcher; *Professorial Fellow, University of Melbourne;* b. 15 Oct. 1938, UK; s. of John Cook and Rose Cook; m. Norma Cook; two s.; ed Durham Univ., UK, Australian Nat. Univ., Univ. of Colorado, USA; fmr Exec. Dir Petroleum CRC; fmr Dir British Geological Survey; fmr Pres. EuroGeoSurveys; fmr Assoc. Dir, Bureau of Mineral Resources; fmr Sr Research Fellow, ANU; est. GEODISC programme, and subsequently Co-operative Research Centre for Greenhouse Gas Technologies (CO2CRC), Chief Exec. 2003–11, Prin. Adviser 2011–; Professorial Fellow, Univ. of Melbourne 2011–; co-ordinating lead author of Special IPCC volume on CO_2 Capture and Storage; Fellow, Australian Acad. of Technological Sciences; Chevalier, Ordre nat. du Mérite; John Coke Medal, Centennial Medal, Lewis G. Weeks Medal, Leopold von Buch Medal, Greenman Award. *Publications:* Clean Energy Climate and Carbon 2012; numerous books and scientific papers on greenhouse issues, including carbon capture and storage, sedimentary geology, phosphate deposits, Australian geology and palaeogeography. *Leisure interests:* skiing, walking, history, small-scale farming. *Address:* CO2CRC, GPO Box 463, Canberra, ACT 2601, Australia (office). *Telephone:* (2) 6210-1600 (office); 419-490044 (mobile). *Fax:* (2) 6273-7181 (office). *E-mail:* pjcook@co2crc.com.au (office). *Website:* www.co2crc.com.au (office).

COOK, Sir Peter Frederick Chester, Kt, AADip, RIBA, BDA, FRSA, MEASA; British architect and academic; b. 22 Oct. 1936, Southend-on-Sea; s. of late Maj. Frederick William Cook and Ada Alice Cook (née Shaw); m. 1st Hazel Aimée Fennell 1960 (divorced 1990); m. 2nd Yael Reisner 1990; one s.; ed Bournemouth Coll. of Art, Architectural Assn (A.A.), London; Architectural Asst, James Cubitt & Partners, London 1960–62; Asst Architect, Taylor Woodrow Design Group, London 1962–64; taught at A.A. 1964–89; Partner, Archigram Architects 1964–75, Cook and Hawley Architects, London 1976–; Bartlett Prof. of Architecture, Bartlett School of Architecture and Planning, Univ. Coll. London 1990–2005, also Chair. Bartlett School of Architecture; Prof. of Architecture, HBK Frankfurt, Germany 1984–; visiting critic many schools of architecture USA and abroad; Visiting Prof. Oslo Architecture School 1982–83, RI School of Design 1981, 1984; Architect of 'Plug-in-City', 'Instant City', etc., of the Lutlowplatz Housing, Berlin 1990 (with Christine Hawley) and the Kunsthaus, Graz (with Colin Fournier), under construction; works featured in several books; Graham Foundation Award 1970, Monte Carlo Competition 1st Prize 1970, Landstuhl Housing Competition 1st Prize 1980, LA Prize (AIA) 1988, Int. Competition for Historic Museum 1st Prize, Austria 1995, Jean Tschumi Prize (U.I.A.) 1996, Int. Competition for Kunsthaus, Graz 1st Prize, Austria 2000, Grand Prize of the Buenos Aires Biennale 2001, Royal Gold Medal of the Royal Inst. of British Architects (RIBA) 2000 (as mem. of Archigram). *Publications:* Primer 1996, The Power of Contemporary Architecture 1999, The Paradox of Contemporary Architecture 2001, The City as Inspiration 2001. *Leisure interests:* listening to music, talking to young architects, restaurants. *Address:* 54 Compayne Gardens, London, NW6 3RY, England (home). *Telephone:* (20) 7372-3784 (home).

COOK, R. James, BSc, MSc, PhD; American plant pathologist, soil scientist and academic; *Professor Emeritus of Plant Pathology and Crop and Soil Sciences, Washington State University;* b. 1937, Minn.; m. Beverly Cook; four c.; ed North Dakota State Univ., Univ. of California, Berkeley; Research Plant Pathologist with US Dept of Agric. (USDA) Agricultural Research Service, Washington State Univ. 1965–98, R. James Cook Endowed Chair in Wheat Research 1998–2003, Interim Dean, Coll. of Agricultural, Human and Natural Resource Sciences 2003–05, Prof. Emer. of Plant Pathology and Crop and Soil Sciences 2005–; Chief Scientist, USDA's Nat. Research Initiative Competitive Grants Program 1993–96; Citizen trustee, Board Authority of Washington State's Life Sciences Discovery Fund; Past Pres. Washington State Acad. of Sciences; mem. NAS 1993; Fellow, American Phytopathological Soc., Crop Science Soc. of America, American Soc. of Agronomy, AAAS; Dr hc (North Dakota State Univ.); Superior Service Award, Distinguished Service Award, Agricultural Research Service Distinguished Scientist of the Year, ARS Science Hall of Fame (all from USDA); Award of Distinction and Ruth Allen Award, American Phytopathological Soc., recognition from grower orgs include Washington Crop Improvement/O.A. Vogel Award, Pioneer Direct Seeder Award, Pacific Northwest Direct Seed Asscn, and No-till Innovator Award for Research and Teaching, Nat. No-till Conf.; Wolf Prize in Agric. (Israel) (co-recipient) 2011. *Publications:* Biological Control of Plant Pathogens (co-author), Wheat Health Management (co-author); more than 200 peer-reviewed papers in professional journals on soil-borne plant diseases. *Address:* Department of Plant Pathology, PO Box 646430, Washington State University, Pullman, WA 99164-6430, USA (office). *Telephone:* (509) 592-0086 (office). *E-mail:* plpath@wsu.edu (office). *Website:* plantpath.wsu.edu/people/faculty/emeritus (office).

COOK, Sarah, PhD; British economist and UN official; *Director, United Nations Research Institute for Social Development;* ed Univ. of Oxford, London School of Econs, Harvard Univ., USA; has carried out int. academic research and has taught in field of devt studies; has undertaken policy and advisory work for int. governmental and non-governmental devt agencies; spent more than 12 years living in China, and has also worked in India, East Africa, Cambodia and Mongolia; with Inst. of Devt Studies, Univ. of Sussex, Brighton –2009, Ford Foundation China 2000–05; Dir UN Research Inst. for Social Devt 2009–. *Publications:* numerous articles on social policy, social protection in Asia, social welfare in China, the informalization of employment and the gender impacts of econ. reform. *Address:* United Nations Research Institute for Social Development (UNRISD), Palais des Nations, 1211 Geneva 10, Switzerland (office). *Telephone:* (22) 917-3060 (office). *Fax:* (22) 917-0650 (office). *E-mail:* director@unrisd.org (office). *Website:* www.unrisd.org (office).

COOK, Stephen Arthur, OM, PhD, FRS, FRSC; American/Canadian computer scientist and academic; *University Professor Emeritus, Department of Computer Science, University of Toronto;* b. 1939, Buffalo, NY; s. of Gerhard A. Cook and Lura Cook; m. Linda Cook 1968; two s.; ed Univ. of Michigan and Harvard Univ.; Asst Prof. of Math., Univ. of California, Berkeley 1966–70; Assoc. Prof. of Computer Science, Univ. of Toronto 1970–75, Prof. 1975–85, Univ. Prof. 1985–, now Prof. Emer.; E.W.R. Staecie Memorial Fellowship 1977–78; Killam Research Fellow, Canada Council 1982–83; mem. NAS, American Acad. of Arts and Science; Turing Award, Asscn for Computing Machinery 1982, Killam Prize 1997, CRM/Fields Inst. Prize 1999. *Publications:* numerous articles in professional journals on theory of computation. *Leisure interest:* sailing. *Address:* Department of Computer Science, 10 King's College Road, Sandford Fleming Building, Room SF2303C, University of Toronto, Toronto, ON M5S 3G4, Canada (office). *Telephone:* (416) 978-5183 (office). *E-mail:* sacook@cs.toronto.edu (office). *Website:* www.cs.toronto.edu/~sacook (office).

COOK, Timothy (Tim) D., BS, MBA; American computer industry executive; *CEO, Apple Computer Inc.;* b. 1 Nov. 1960, Robertsdale, Ala; ed Robertsdale High School, Auburn Univ., Duke Univ. (Fuqua Scholar); spent 12 years with IBM, most recently as Dir of North American Fulfillment; fmr COO Reseller Div., Intelligent Electronics; Vice-Pres. of Corp. Materials, Compaq Computer Corpn 1998; joined Apple Computer as Sr Vice-Pres. for Worldwide Operations 1998, Sr Vice-Pres., Worldwide Operations, Sales, Service and Support 2000–02, Exec. Vice-Pres., Worldwide Sales and Operations 2002–05, COO 2002–11, served as CEO (during absence on sick leave of CEO Steve Jobs) 2004, 2009, CEO 2011–; mem. Bd of Dirs (ind.) Nike, Inc.; ranked by Forbes magazine amongst The World's Most Powerful People (58th) 2011, (35th) 2012, (19th) 2013. *Leisure interests:* hiking, cycling, going to the gym. *Address:* Apple Computer Inc., 1 Infinite Loop, Cupertino, CA 95014, USA (office). *Telephone:* (408) 996-1010 (office). *Fax:* (408) 974-2113 (office). *E-mail:* media.help@apple.com (office). *Website:* www.apple.com (office).

COOK, William Alfred, BSc; American medical device industry executive; *Chairman, Cook Group Incorporated;* b. 1931; m. Gayle Cook; one s.; ed Northwestern Univ.; Founder and Chair. Cook Inc., Bloomington, Ind. (manufacturer of medical devices and supplies) 1963, now Cook Group Inc. *Address:* Cook Group Inc., PO Box 489, Bloomington, IN 47402-0489, USA (office). *Telephone:* (812) 339-2235 (office). *Website:* www.cookgroup.com (office).

COOK-BENNETT, Gail C. A., BA, PhD; Canadian business executive and academic; ed Carleton Univ., Univ. of Michigan, USA; fmr Exec. Vice-Pres. C.D. Howe Inst., Montreal; fmr Prof., Dept of Political Economy, Univ. of Toronto; mem. Bd of Dirs Manulife Financial Corpn 1978–2013, mem. Man. Resources and Compensation Cttee, Vice-Chair. 2007–08, Chair. (first woman) 2008–13; Chair. Canada Pension Plan Investment Bd 1998–2008, Chair. and mem. Investment Cttee, mem. Governance Cttee; Vice-Chair. Bennecon Ltd –1998; mem. Bd of Dirs Petro-Canada 1991– (Chair. Pension Cttee, mem. Audit, Finance and Risk Cttee), Transcontinental Inc. (also known as Groupe Transcontinental GTC Ltée; fmr mem. Audit Cttee), Cadillac Fairview Inc., Enbridge Consumers Gas Co., Mackenzie Financial Corpn, Emera Inc. (mem. Audit Cttee, Nominating and Corp. Governance Cttee), Nova Scotia Power Inc. (mem. Nominating and Corp. Governance Cttee); Fellow, Inst. of Corp. Dirs; Order of Canada 2010; Hon. LLD (Carleton Univ., York Univ.). *Address:* c/o Manulife Financial Corpn, 200 Bloor Street East, NT 11, Toronto, ON M4W 1E5, Canada. *E-mail:* info@manulife.com.

COOKE, Dominic, CBE; British theatre director and playwright; *Artistic Director, Royal Court Theatre;* b. 1966; partner Alexi Kaye Campbell; Asst Dir RSC 1992–93, Assoc. Dir 2002–06; Assoc. Dir Royal Court Theatre 1999–2002, Artistic Dir 2007–; Hon. DLitt (Warwick) 2013; Int. Theatre Inst. Award for Excellence in Int. Theatre 2013. *Productions include:* Royal Court Theatre: Other People 2000, Fireface 2000, Spinning into Butter 2001, Redundant 2001, Fucking Games 2001, Plasticine, The People are Friendly, This is a Chair (co-dir) 2002, Identical Twins 2002, The Pain and the Itch 2007, Rhinoceros 2007, War & Peace/Fear & Misery 2008, Wig Out! 2008, Now or Later 2008, Seven Jewish Children 2009, The Fever 2009, Aunt Dan & Lemon 2009, Clybourne Park 2010, The Comedy of Errors 2011, Chicken Soup with Barley 2011, In Basildon 2012, Choir Boy 2012, Ding Dong The Wicked 2012, In the Republic of Happiness 2013, The Low Road 2013; RSC: The Malcontent 2002, Cymbeline 2003, Macbeth 2004, As You Like It 2005, Postcards From America 2005, The Winter's Tale, Pericles, The Crucible (Gielgud; Best Dir and Best Revival, Laurence Olivier Awards 2007) 2006; other: Arabian Nights (Old Vic and on tour) (TMA/Equity Award for Best Show for Young People) 1998, Noughts and Crosses 2007, By the Bog of Cats (Wyndham's), The Eccentricities of a Nightingale (Gate, Dublin), The Weavers, Hunting Scenes From Lower Bavaria (Gate), The Bullet (Donmar Warehouse), Afore Night Come, Entertaining Mr Sloane (Clwyd), The Importance of Being Earnest (Atlantic Theatre Festival, Canada), Caravan (Nat. Theatre of Norway), My Mother Said I Never Should (Oxford Stage Col/Young Vic), Kiss of the Spider Woman (Bolton Octagon), Of Mice and Men (Nottingham Playhouse), Autogeddon (Assembly Rooms) (Fringe First Award). *Opera include:* The Magic Flute (Welsh Nat. Opera), I Capuleti e i Montecchi, La Bohème (Grange Park Opera). *Radio:* directed a version of Plasticine; currently adapting his version of Arabian Nights for BBC Radio 4. *Publications:* Arabian Nights (adaptation) 1998, Noughts and Crosses (adaptation) 2007. *Address:* Royal Court Theatre, Sloane Square, London, SW1W 8AS, England (office). *Telephone:* (20) 7565-5050 (office). *Fax:* (20) 7565-5001 (office). *E-mail:* info@royalcourttheatre.com (office). *Website:* www.royalcourttheatre.com (office).

COOKSON, (Michael) Brian, OBE; British sports administrator and fmr cyclist; *President, Union Cycliste Interntionale (International Cycling Union);* b. 22 June 1951, Lancs., England; m. Sian Cookson; three s.; Exec. Dir (Regeneration), Pendle Borough Council –2013; competed in road racing, track, cyclo-cross and MTB; won Lakeland Division Road Race championship 1971; completed the Pyrenees Coast to Coast ride 2011; Chair. Pendle Cycle Fest which included the Nat. Road Championships, Colne GP circuit race, Pendle Pedal sportive; Div. Road Race Sec., British Cycling Fed. (BCF) 1981–85, Div. Vice-Chair. 1984–87, Div. Chair. 1993–97, mem. Racing and Exec. Cttees 1984–93, mem. Bd Exec. Cttee and Bd, BCF 1996–2013, Pres. British Cycling 1997–2013, qualified as UCI Int. Commissaire (judge/referee) 1986, represented cycling at British Olympic Asscn since 1996; elected to Union Cycliste Internationale (UCI—Int. Cycling Union) Man. Cttee 2009, Pres. UCI Cyclo-Cross Comm. 2009–11, Pres. UCI Road Comm. 2011–13, Pres. UCI 2013–; mem. Exec. Cttee, British Olympic Asscn 2005–; Hon. Fellow, Univ. of Central Lancashire 2009. *Address:* Union Cycliste Internationale (UCI), Ch. de la Mêlée 12, 1860 Aigle, Switzerland (office); c/o British Cycling Federation, Stuart Street, Manchester, M11 4DQ, England (office). *Telephone:* (24) 4685811 (office). *Fax:* (24) 4685812 (office). *E-mail:* brian@briancookson.org (office); admin@uci.ch (office). *Website:* www.uci.ch (office); www.briancookson.org.

COOLEY, Denton Arthur, BA, MD; American surgeon; *Surgeon-in-Chief, Texas Heart Institute;* b. 22 Aug. 1920, Houston, Tex.; s. of Ralph C. Cooley and Mary Fraley Cooley; m. Louise Goldsborough Thomas 1949; five d.; ed Univ. of Texas and Johns Hopkins Univ. School of Medicine; Intern, Johns Hopkins School of Medicine, Baltimore 1944–45, Instructor in surgery 1945–50; Sr Surgical Registrar in Thoracic Surgery, Brompton Hospital for Chest Diseases, London 1950–51; Assoc. Prof. of Surgery, Baylor Univ. Coll. of Medicine, Houston 1954–62, Prof. 1962–69; Founder and Surgeon-in-Chief, Texas Heart Inst., Houston 1962–; Clinical Prof. of Surgery, Univ. of Texas Medical School, Houston 1975–; served as Capt., Chief Surgical Service, US Army Medical Corps, Linz, Austria 1946–48; has performed numerous heart transplants; mem. numerous socs and asscns; Hon. Doctorem Medicinae (Turin) 1969; Hon. Fellow, Royal Coll. of Physicians and Surgeons 1980, Royal Coll. of Surgeons 1984, Royal Australasian Coll. of Surgeons 1986; Kt Commdr, Order of Merit of Italian Repub., Order of the Sun, Peru and others; Hoktoen Gold Medal 1954, Grande Médaille, Univ. of Ghent, Belgium 1963, René Leriche Prize, Int. Surgical Soc. 1965–67, Billings Gold Medal, American Medical Asscn 1967, Semmelweis Medal 1973, St Francis Cabrini Gold Medal (first recipient) 1980, Theodore Roosevelt Award, Nat. Collegiate Athletic Asscn 1980, Presidential Medal of Freedom 1984, Nat. Medal of Tech., US Dept of Commerce 1999, Grand Hamdan Int. Award for Medical Science 2000. *Achievements include:* implanted first artificial heart 1969. *Publications:* Surgical Treatment of Congenital Heart Disease 1966, Techniques in Cardiac Surgery 1975, 1984, Techniques in Vascular Surgery 1979, Essays of Denton A. Cooley—Reflections and Observations 1984; over 1,000 scientific articles. *Leisure interests:* golf, ranching. *Address:* Texas Heart Institute, PO Box 20345, 1101 Bates Street, Houston, TX 77225-0345, USA (office). *Telephone:* (832) 355-4900 (office). *Fax:* (832) 355-3424 (office). *E-mail:* dcooley@heart.thi.tmc.edu (office). *Website:* www.texasheartinstitute.org (office).

COOLIDGE, Martha; American film director and producer; b. 17 Aug. 1946, New Haven, Conn.; d. of Robert Tilton Coolidge and Jean McMullen; one s.; ed Rhode Island School of Design, Columbia Univ. and New York Univ. Inst. of Film and TV Grad. School; producer, dir and writer of documentaries including Passing Quietly Through, David: Off and On, Old Fashioned Woman; wrote and produced daily children's TV show Magic Tom, Canada; Pres. Dirs Guild Asscn 2002–03; Blue Ribbon Award, American Film Festival (Not a Pretty Picture), Independent Spirit Award, Best Dir (Rambling Rose), Crystal Award, Women in Film, Breakthrough Award, Method Fest, Robert Aldrich Award, Dirs Guild Award. *Films include:* Valley Girl 1983, City Girl 1984, Joy of Sex 1984, Real Genius 1985, Plain Clothes 1988, Rambling Rose 1991, Lost in Yonkers 1993, Angie 1994, Three Wishes 1995, Out to Sea 1997, The Prince and Me 2004, Material Girls 2006. *Television includes:* The Twilight Zone, Sledge Hammer (pilot), House and Home (pilot), Trenchcoat in Paradise (film), Bare Essentials, Crazy in Love, Introducing Dorothy Dandridge 1999, If These Walls Could Talk II 2000, The Ponder Heart 2000, The Flamingo Rising 2001, Leap Years 2001, Sex and the City (two episodes) 2002, Girls Club (series) 2002, The Twelve Days of Christmas Eve (film) 2004, Tribute (film) 2009. *Leisure interest:* breeding Paso-Fino horses. *Address:* c/o Beverly Magid Guttman Associates, 118 South Beverly Drive, Suite 201, Beverly Hills, CA 90212, USA. *Telephone:* (310) 246-4600 (office). *Website:* www.marthacoolidge.com (office).

COOMARASWAMY, Radhika, BA, LLM, JD; Sri Lankan lawyer and UN official; ed Yale, Columbia and Harvard Univs and UN Int. School, New York, USA; Special Rapporteur on Violence Against Women 1994–2003; Chair. Sri Lanka Human Rights Comm. 2003–06; Dir Int. Centre for Ethnic Studies, Colombo; Special Rep. of the Sec.-Gen. for Children and Armed Conflict, UN 2006–12; mem. Global Faculty, New York Univ. School of Law; teaches a summer course at New Coll., Oxford, UK every July; title of 'Deshamanya' conferred on her by Pres. of Sri Lanka 2005 (only female recipient); Hon. PhD (Amherst Coll.), (Univ. of Edinburgh), (Univ. of Essex); ABA Int. Law Award, Human Rights Award, Int. Human Rights Law Group, Bruno Kreisky Award 2000, Special Jury Prize, Fondation Chirac 2012, Leo Ettinger Human Rights Prize, Univ. of Oslo, Cesar Romero Award, Univ. of Dayton, William J. Butler Award, Univ. of Cincinnati, Robert S. Litvack Award, McGill Univ. *Publications:* two books on constitutional law and numerous articles on ethnic studies and the status of women. *Address:* c/o Office of the Special Representative of the Secretary-General for Children and Armed Conflict, United Nations, Room S-3161, New York, NY 10017, USA.

COOMBER, John R., BSc; British insurance executive; *CEO, Pension Insurance Corporation;* b. 7 Feb. 1949; m.; ed Univ. of Nottingham; began career with Phoenix Insurance Co.; joined Swiss Re 1973, specialized in life reinsurance, Company Actuary 1983–90, Head of Life Div. 1987, Head of UK Operations 1993, apptd mem. Exec. Bd 1995, Head of Life and Health Div. 1995–2000, mem. Exec. Bd Cttee 2000–03, CEO Swiss Reinsurance Co. (first non-Swiss person in position) 2003–05 (retd), Dir (non-exec.) 2006–; Dir, Pension Insurance Corpn 2008–; Chair. Climate Group, Climatewise, MacTavish; mem. Deutsche Bank Climate Change Advisory Bd; fmr mem. Supervisory Bd Euler Hermes, Bd of Telent plc. *Address:*

Pension Insurance Corporation, 14 Cornhill, London, EC3V 3ND, England (office). *Telephone:* (20) 7105-2000 (office). *Fax:* (20) 7105-2001 (office). *Website:* www.pensioncorporation.com (office).

COOMBS, Stephen; British pianist; *Director of Instrumental Studies, Blackheath Conservatoire of Music and the Arts;* b. 11 July 1960; s. of Geoffrey Samuel Coombs and Joan Margaret Jones; ed Royal Northern Coll. of Music, RAM; debut at Wigmore Hall 1979; has given concerts and masterclasses in UK, France, Germany, Italy, Hungary, Portugal, Switzerland, Scandinavia, Korea, Thailand, the Philippines, Hong Kong, USA; has appeared in festivals at Cheltenham, Salisbury, Snape Maltings Proms, Henley, the Three Choirs, Radley, Bath, Lichfield, Cardiff, Spoleto, Italy, St Nazaire, France, Sintra, Portugal; Visiting Lecturer, Univ. of Cen. England 1994–96; Founder and Artistic Dir 'Pianoworks' Int. Piano Festival, London 1998–99; Dir of Instrumental Studies, Blackheath Conservatoire of Music and the Arts 2001–; Gold Medal, First Int. Liszt Concourse, Hungary 1977, Worshipful Co. of Musicians/Maisie Lewis Award 1986 and numerous other awards and prizes. *Recordings include:* Two Piano Works of Debussy 1989, Ravel Works for Two Pianos 1990, Mendelssohn Two Double Piano Concertos 1992, Arensky Piano Concerto in F Minor and Fantasy on Russian Folk Songs 1992, Bortkiewicz Piano Concerto No. 1 1992, Arensky Suites for Two Pianos 1994, Glazunov Complete Piano Works (four vols) 1995, Glazunov Piano Concertos Nos 1 & 2 1996, Goedicke Concertstück 1996, Reynaldo Hahn Piano Concerto 1997, Massenet Piano Concerto 1997, Bortkiewicz Piano Works 1997, Liadov Piano Works 1998, Milhaud Works for Two Pianos 1998, Arensky Piano Works 1998, Scriabin Early Piano Works 2001, Hahn Piano Quintet 2001, Verne Piano Quintet 2001. *Leisure interests:* genealogy, pubs, reading. *Address:* The Conservatoire, 19–21 Lee Road, Blackheath, London, SE3 9RQ; c/o Hyperion Records Ltd, 19–20 Chiltonian Industrial Estate, Manor Lane, London, SE12 0TX, England. *Website:* www.conservatoire.org.uk.

COONS, Christopher Andrew (Chris), BA, MA, JD; American lawyer and politician; *Senator from Delaware;* b. 9 Sept. 1963, Greenwich, Conn.; s. of Ken Coons and Sally Coons; m. Annie Lingenfelter 1996; two s. one d.; ed Tower Hill School, Amherst Coll. (Truman Scholarship), Univ. of Nairobi, Kenya, Yale Univ. Law School and Yale Divinity School; worked for Investor Responsibility Research Center, Washington, DC, wrote a book on S Africa and US divestment movement; then worked as volunteer for S African Council of Churches and as relief worker in Kenya, before returning to USA to work for Coalition for the Homeless, New York; worked as clerk for Judge Jane Richards Roth on US Court of Appeals for the Third Circuit; then worked for Nat. I Have a Dream Foundation, New York; In-house Counsel for W.L. Gore & Assocs, Inc., Newark, Del. (makers of Gore-Tex fabrics and other high-tech materials) 1996–2004; served on New Castle Co. Council, Del. 2001–05, Co. Exec. New Castle Co. 2005–10; Senator from Del. (special election to term ending 3 Jan. 2015, seat previously held by apptd Senator Edward E. Kaufman) 2010–, mem. Budget, Foreign Relations, Judiciary, and Energy and Natural Resources Cttees 2010–; mem. Bd First State Innovation, Bear/Glasgow Boys & Girls Club, Delaware Coll. of Art & Design, Wilmington Riverfront Devt Corpn, Better Business Bureau, First State Innovation, Hearts and Minds Film Org.; Democrat; Hon. Commdr 166th Air Wing of Delaware Air Nat. Guard, Hon. Life mem. Minquadale Fire Co.; Gov.'s Outstanding Volunteer Award for his work with I Have a Dream Foundation, Gov.'s Mentoring Council and United Way of Delaware 1999, Aspen-Rodel Fellow, Aspen Inst. Rodel Fellowships in Public Leadership 2009. *Address:* 127A Russell Senate Office Building, Washington, DC 20510, USA (office). *Telephone:* (202) 224-5042 (office). *Fax:* (202) 228-3075 (office). *Website:* coons.senate.gov (office).

COOPER, Alice; American singer; b. (Vincent Damon Furnier), 4 Feb. 1948, Detroit; s. of the late Mick Furnier and of Ella Furnier; m. Sheryl Goddard; one s. two d.; ed Cortez High School, Phoenix, Ariz.; mem. of band Alice Cooper, adopted this name after band split; first to stage theatrical rock concert tours; among first to film conceptual rock promotional videos (pre-MTV); considered among originators and greatest hard rock artists; host on Virgin Radio Classic Rock 2005–; mem. BMI, NARAS, SAG, AFTRA, AFofM; Foundations Forum Lifetime Achievement Award 1994, inducted into Rock and Roll Hall of Fame 2011. *Film appearances:* Sextette 1978, Sgt. Pepper's Lonely Hearts Club Band 1978, Leviatán 1984, Prince of Darkness 1987, Freddy's Dead: The Final Nightmare 1991, The Attic Expeditions 2001, Suck 2009, Dark Shadows 2012. *Recordings include:* with band Alice Cooper: Pretties For You 1969, Live At The Whisky 1969, Easy Action 1970, Love It To Death 1971, Killer 1971, School's Out 1972, Billion Dollar Babies 1973, Muscle of Love 1973, Alice Cooper's Greatest Hits 1974; solo: Welcome To My Nightmare 1975, Alice Cooper Goes To Hell 1976, Lace And Whiskey 1977, Alice Cooper Show (live) 1977, From The Inside 1978, Flush The Fashion 1980, Special Forces 1981, Zipper Catches The Skin 1982, Dada 1982, Constrictor 1986, Raise Your Fist And Yell 1987, Trash 1989, Prince Of Darkness 1989, Hey Stoopid 1991, The Last Temptation 1994, Fistful Of Alice (live) 1997, He's Back 1997, Science Fiction 2000, Brutal Planet 2000, Alice Cooper Live 2001, Take 2 2001, Dragontown 2001, Eyes Of Alice Cooper 2003, Hell Is 2003, Dirty Diamonds 2005, Along Came a Spider 2008, Welcome to My Nightmare 2 2010. *Address:* Alive Enterprises, PO Box 5542, Beverly Hills, CA 90211, USA (office). *Website:* www.alicecooper.com.

COOPER, Alison J., BSc, ACA; British business executive; *Chief Executive, Imperial Tobacco Group PLC;* with PricewaterhouseCoopers –1999, worked with Imperial Tobacco in several areas, including acquisitions; joined Imperial Tobacco 1999, Dir of Finance and Planning and mem. Chief Exec.'s Cttee 2001–05, Sales and Marketing Regional Dir for Western Europe 2005–07, mem. Bd of Dirs and Corp. Devt Dir 2007–09, mem. Altadis acquisition team, COO 2009–10, Chief Exec. 2010–; Dir (non-exec.) Inchcape plc 2009–; ranked by Fortune magazine amongst the 50 Most Powerful Women in Business outside the US (seventh) 2012. *Address:* Imperial Tobacco Group PLC, 121 Winterstoke Road, Bristol, BS3 2LL, England (office). *Telephone:* (117) 963-6636 (office). *Fax:* (117) 966-7405 (office). *E-mail:* info@imperial-tobacco.com (office). *Website:* www.imperial-tobacco.com (office).

COOPER, Bradley Charles, BA (Hons), MFA; American actor; b. 5 Jan. 1975, Philadelphia, Pa.; s. of Charles J. Cooper and Gloria Cooper (née Campano); m. Jennifer Esposito 2006 (divorced 2007); one s. one d.; ed Germantown Acad., Villanova Univ., Georgetown Univ., spent six months as an exchange student in Aix-en-Provence, France, Actors Studio Drama School at The New School, New

York; worked at the Philadelphia Daily News while a student; began his professional acting career on TV Sex and the City 1999; also served as a presenter for Globe Trekker; film debut in Wet Hot American Summer 2001; own production co. 22 & Indiana Pictures; Int. Man of the Year Award, GQ magazine (UK) 2011, named by People magazine as the Sexiest Man Alive 2011. *Films include:* Wet Hot American Summer 2001, My Little Eye 2002, Bending All the Rules 2002, Stella Shorts 1998–2002 (video) 2002, Wedding Crashers 2005, Failure to Launch 2006, The Comebacks 2007, American Evil 2008, The Rocker 2008, The Midnight Meat Train 2008, Bang Blow & Strike (video short) 2008, Yes Man 2008, New York, I Love You 2009, He's Just Not That Into You 2009, The Hangover 2009, Case 39 2009, All About Steve 2009, Valentine's Day 2010, The A-Team 2010, Limitless 2011, The Hangover Part II 2011, Kaylien (short) 2011, The Words 2012, Hit and Run 2012, The Place Beyond the Pines 2012, Silver Linings Playbook 2012, The Hangover Part III 2013, American Hustle (Screen Actors Guild Award for Outstanding Performance by a Cast in a Motion Picture 2014) 2013, Serena 2013, Guardians of the Galaxy (voice) 2014. *Television includes:* Sex and the City (series) 1999, Treks in a Wild World (series) 2000, Wall to Wall Records (film) 2000, The $treet (series) 2000–01, The Last Cowboy (film) 2003, Miss Match (series) 2003, The Reality of Love (film) 2004, Touching Evil (series) 2004, Jack & Bobby (series) 2004–05, Law & Order: Special Victims Unit (series) 2005, Law & Order: Trial by Jury (series) 2005, Alias (series) 2001–06, Kitchen Confidential (series) 2005–06, Nip/Tuck (series) 2007–09, Cubed (series) 2010. *Address:* c/o Dave Bugliari, Creative Artists Agency, 2000 Avenue of the Stars, Los Angeles, CA 90067, USA (office). *Telephone:* (424) 288-2000 (office). *Fax:* (424) 288-2900 (office). *Website:* www.caa.com (office).

COOPER, Chris; American actor; b. 9 July 1951, Kansas City, Mo.; s. of Charles Cooper and Mary Ann Cooper; m. Marianne Leone 1983; one s.; ed Univ. of Missouri; studied ballet at Stephens Coll., Mo.; entered US Coast Guard Reserves following high school graduation; studied theatre acting under Stella Adler and Wynn Handman, NY 1976; first Broadway appearance in Of the Fields Lately 1980; Best Actor Award, Cowboy Hall of Fame 1991, Peter J. Owens Award, San Francisco International Film Festival 2004. *Films include:* Bad Timing 1980, Matewan 1987, Non date da mangiare agli animali 1987, Guilty by Suspicion 1991, Thousand Pieces of Gold 1991, City of Hope 1991, This Boy's Life 1993, Money Train 1995, Pharaoh's Army 1995, Boys 1996, Lone Star 1996, A Time to Kill 1996, Great Expectations 1998, The Horse Whisperer 1998, The 24 Hour Woman 1999, October Sky 1999, American Beauty (Screen Actors Guild Award 2000) 1999, Me, Myself & Irene 2000, The Patriot 2000, Interstate 60 2002, The Bourne Identity 2002, Adaptation (Best Supporting Actor, Acad. Awards 2004, Golden Globe Awards, Nat. Bd of Review, San Francisco Film Critics, Toronto Film Critics, San Diego Film Critics, Broadcast Film Assocn, LA Critics Assocn) 2002, Seabiscuit 2003, Silver City 2004, Syriana 2005, Capote 2005, Jarhead 2005, Breach 2007, The Kingdom 2007, Married Life 2007. *Television includes:* Lonesome Dove (miniseries) 1989, Return to Lonesome Dove (miniseries) 1993, My House in Umbria 2003. *Stage appearances include:* Of the Fields Lately 1980, The Ballad of Soapy Smith 1983, A Different Moon 1983, Cobb, The Grapes of Wrath, Sweet Bird of Youth, Love Letters. *Address:* Paradigm Talent Agency, 10100 Santa Monica Boulevard, Suite 2500, Los Angeles, CA 90067 (office); c/o PMK, 8500 Wiltshire Boulevard, Suite 700, Beverly Hills, CA 90211-3105, USA (office).

COOPER, Imogen, CBE; British pianist; b. 28 Aug. 1949, London; d. of the late Martin Du Pré Cooper and of Mary Stewart; ed Paris Conservatoire and in Vienna with Alfred Brendel; TV debut at Promenade Concerts, London 1975, has appeared regularly since then; first British pianist and first woman pianist in South Bank Piano series, Queen Elizabeth Hall, London; broadcasts regularly for BBC; performs with New York, Berlin, Vienna and LA Philharmonic orchestras and with Boston, London, Sydney, Melbourne and Concertgebouw Symphony orchestras; gives solo recitals world-wide; Hon. MusD (Exon) 1999; Paris Conservatoire Premier Prix 1967, Mozart Memorial Prize 1969, Royal Philharmonic Soc. Award for Best Instrumentalist 2008. *Recordings include:* Schubert's Schwanengesang, Winterreise, Die Schöne Mullerin and Schumann's Heine Lieder and Kerner Lieder (with Wolfgang Holzmair), Mozart's Concerto for two pianos K.365 (with Alfred Brendel), Schubert four-hand piano music (with Anne Queffélec) 1996, Imogen Cooper and Friends (solo, chamber and lieder) 2004, The Last Six Years of Schubert's piano music 2005, Mozart Concertos (with the Northern Sinfonia) 2006, 2008, 2010, Schubert's Piano Sonata in G Major D. 894 2009. *Leisure interests:* visual arts, reading, walking, architecture. *Address:* c/o Avie Records, 103 Churston Drive, Morden, Surrey, SM4 4JE, England (office). *Telephone:* (20) 8542-4866 (office). *Fax:* (20) 8542-4854 (office). *E-mail:* info@avierecords.com (office). *Website:* www.avie-records.com (office).

COOPER, Jilly, OBE; British writer; b. 21 Feb. 1937, Hornchurch, Essex; d. of Brig. W. B. Sallitt, OBE and Mary Elaine Whincup; m. Leo Cooper 1961; one s. one d.; ed Godolphin School, Salisbury; reporter, Middx Independent 1957–59; account exec.; copy writer; publr's reader; various temporary roles 1959–69; columnist, The Sunday Times 1969–82, Mail on Sunday 1982–87; British Book Awards Lifetime Achievement Award 1998; Hon. DLitt (Univ. of Gloucester) 2009; Dr hc (Anglia Ruskin Univ.) 2011. *Publications:* How to Stay Married 1969, How to Survive from Nine to Five 1970, Jolly Super 1971, Men and Super Men 1972, Jolly Super Too 1973, Women and Super Women 1974, Jolly Superlative 1975, Emily 1975, Super Men and Super Women 1976, Bella 1976, Harriet 1976, Octavia 1977, Work and Wedlock 1977, Superjilly 1977, Imogen 1978, Prudence 1978, Class 1979, Intelligent and Loyal 1980, Supercooper 1980, Violets and Vinegar (co-ed with Tom Hartman) 1980, The British in Love (ed) 1980, Love and Other Heartaches 1981, Jolly Marsupial 1982, Animals in War 1983, Leo and Jilly Cooper on Rugby 1984, The Common Years 1984, Riders 1985, Hotfoot to Zabriskie Point 1985, How to Survive Christmas 1986, 1996, Turn Right at the Spotted Dog 1987, Rivals 1988, Angels Rush In 1990, Polo 1991, The Man Who Made Husbands Jealous 1993, Araminta's Wedding 1993, Appassionata 1996, Score! 1999, Pandora 2002, Wicked! 2006, Jump! 2010. *Leisure interests:* merry-making, mongrels, music, wild flowers, greyhounds. *Address:* c/o Vivienne Schuster, Curtis Brown Ltd, Fourth Floor, Haymarket House, 28–29 Haymarket, London, SW1Y 4SP, England (office). *Telephone:* (20) 7393-4400 (office). *Fax:* (20) 7393-4401 (office). *E-mail:* cb@curtisbrown.co.uk (office). *Website:* www.curtisbrown.co.uk (office).

COOPER, Leon, DSc, PhD; American scientist and academic; *Thomas J. Watson, Sr Professor of Physics, Brain Science Program, Brown University;* b. 28 Feb. 1930, New York; s. of Irving Cooper and Anna Zola; m. Kay Anne Allard 1969; two d.; ed Columbia Univ.; mem. Inst. for Advanced Study 1954–55; Research Assoc., Univ. of Ill. 1955–57; Asst Prof., Ohio State Univ. 1957–58; Assoc. Prof., Brown Univ. 1958–62, Prof. 1974–, Thomas J. Watson, Sr Prof. of Science 1974–, Dir Center for Neural Science 1978–90, Inst. for Brain and Neural Systems 1991–, Brain Science Program 2000–; Visiting Lecturer, Varenna, Italy 1955; Visiting Prof., Brandeis Summer Inst. 1959, Bergen Int. School of Physics, Norway 1961, Scuola Internazionale Di Fisica, Erice, Italy 1965, L'Ecole Normale Supérieure, Centre Universitaire Int., Paris 1966, Cargèse Summer School 1966, Radiation Lab., Univ. of Calif., Berkeley 1969, Faculty of Sciences, Quai St Bernard, Paris 1970, 1971, Brookhaven Nat. Lab. 1972; consultant for various industrial and educational orgs; Chair. of Math. Models of Nervous System Fondation de France 1977–83; mem. Conseil supérieur de la Recherche Univ. René Descartes, Paris 1981–88; mem. Defence Science Bd 1989–93; NSF Post-doctoral Fellow 1954–55; Alfred P. Sloan Foundation Research Fellow 1959–66; John Simon Guggenheim Memorial Foundation Fellow 1965–66; Fellow, American Physical Soc., American Acad. of Arts and Sciences; Sponsor, American Fed. of Scientists; mem. NAS, American Philosophical Soc.; Hon. DSc (Columbia, Sussex), 1973, (Illinois, Brown) 1974, (Gustavus Adolphus Coll.) 1975, (Ohio State Univ.) 1976, (Univ. Pierre et Marie Curie, Paris) 1977; Comstock Prize, NAS 1968, Nobel Prize for Physics 1972, Award in Excellence, Columbia Univ. 1974; Descartes Medal, Acad. de Paris, Univ. René Descartes 1977, John Jay Award, Columbia Coll. 1985. *Publications:* An Introduction to the Meaning and Structure of Physics 1968, Structure and Meaning 1992, How We Learn, How We Remember 1995; numerous scientific papers. *Leisure interests:* skiing, music, theatre. *Address:* Department of Physics and Neuroscience, Box 1843, Barus & Holley, Room 718, Brown University, Providence, RI 02912-1843, USA (office). *Telephone:* (401) 863-2585 (office). *E-mail:* Leon_Cooper@brown.edu (office). *Website:* physics/userpages/faculty/ Leon_Cooper/cooper.htm (office); www.physics.brown.edu/people/detail.asp?id=5 (office); www.brainscience.brown.edu (office).

COOPER, Richard Newell, PhD; American economist, academic and fmr public official; *Maurits C. Boas Professor of International Economics, Harvard University;* b. 14 June 1934, Seattle, Wash.; s. of Richard W. Cooper and Lucile Newell; m. 1st Carolyn Cahalan 1956 (divorced 1980); m. 2nd Ann Lorraine Hollick 1982 (divorced 1994); m. 3rd Jin Chen 2000; two s. two d.; ed Oberlin Coll., London School of Econs, UK, Harvard Univ.; Sr Staff Economist, Council of Econ. Advisers, The White House 1961–63; Deputy Asst Sec. of State for Monetary Affairs, US State Dept, Washington, DC 1965–66; Prof. of Econs, Yale Univ. 1966–77, Provost 1972–74; Under-Sec. of State for Econ. Affairs, 1977–81; Maurits C. Boas Prof. of Int. Econs, Harvard Univ. 1981–; Chair. Nat. Intelligence Council 1995–97; mem. Bd of Dirs Fed. Reserve Bank of Boston 1987–92, Chair. 1990–92; mem. Bd of Dirs Rockefeller Brothers Fund 1975–77, Schroders Bank and Trust Co. 1975–77, Warburg-Pincus Funds 1986–98, Center for Naval Analysis 1992–95, Phoenix Cos 1983–2005, Circuit City Stores 1983–2004, CNA Corpn 1997–, Inst. for Int. Econs 1983–; consultant to US Treasury, Nat. Security Council, World Bank, IMF, USN; Marshall Scholarship (UK) 1956–58; Fellow, American Acad. of Sciences 1974; Hon. LLD (Oberlin Coll.) 1958; Dr hc (Paris II) 2000; Nat. Intelligence Distinguished Service Medal 1996, USN Medal for Superior Public Service 2006. *Publications:* The Economics of Interdependence 1968, Economic Policy in an Interdependent World 1986, The International Monetary System 1987, Stabilization and Debt in Developing Countries 1992, Boom, Crisis and Adjustment (co-author) 1993, Environment and Resource Policies for the World Economy 1994, Trade Growth in Transition Economies (ed.) 1997, What The Future Holds (ed.) 2002, Rebalancing the Global Economy (co-author) 2010; more than 300 articles. *Address:* Center for International Affairs, Harvard University, 1737 Cambridge Street, Cambridge, MA 02138 (office); 33 Washington Avenue, Cambridge, MA 02140, USA (home). *Telephone:* (617) 495-5076 (office). *Fax:* (617) 495-8292 (office). *E-mail:* rcooper@harvard.edu (office). *Website:* www.economics.harvard.edu (office).

COOPER, Sir Robert Francis, Kt, KCMG, CMG, MVO, BA, MA; British diplomatist; *Counsellor, European External Action Service;* b. 28 Aug. 1947, Brentwood, Essex, England; partner Dame Mitsuko Uchida; ed Delamere School, Nairobi, Worcester Coll., Oxford, Univ. of Pennsylvania, USA; joined FCO 1970, worked at various embassies abroad, including Tokyo and Bonn, Head of Policy Planning Staff, FCO 1989–93, seconded to Bank of England and spent a period in the Cabinet Office as Deputy Sec. for Defence and Overseas Affairs, UK Special Rep. in Afghanistan –2002; Dir-Gen. for External and Politico-Mil. Affairs, Gen. Secr. of the Council of the EU 2002–10, mem. European Council on Foreign Relations 2007–, mem. Steering Cttee that drew up proposals for the European External Action Service (EEAS), Counsellor, EEAS 2010–; fmr Adviser to UK Prime Minister Tony Blair; Thouron Award, listed amongst the top 100 in Prospect magazine's Global Intellectuals Poll 2005, listed by EurActiv (European media network) as the 28th out of 40 "most influential Britons on EU policy" 2012. *Publications include:* The Post-Modern State and the World Order 2000, The Post-Modern State, in Mark Leonard (ed.) Re-Ordering the World: The Long-Term Implications of September 11 (Foreign Policy Centre: London) 2002, The Breaking of Nations: Order and Chaos in the Twenty-First Century (Orwell Prize for Political Writing) 2003. *Address:* European External Action Service, Triangle Building, 1046 Brussels, Belgium (office). *Telephone:* (2) 584-11-11 (office). *Website:* eeas.europa.eu (office).

COOPER, Yvette; British politician; *Shadow Secretary of State for the Home Department (Shadow Home Secretary);* b. 20 March 1969, Inverness, Scotland; d. of Tony Cooper and June Cooper; m. Ed Balls 1998; one s. two d.; ed Balliol Coll., Oxford, Harvard Univ., USA, London School of Econs; fmr Econ. Researcher for John Smith; fmr Policy Adviser, Bill Clinton Presidential Campaign, USA; fmr Policy Adviser to Labour Treasury Team on public spending; econs columnist and leader writer, The Independent (daily newspaper); MP (Labour) for Pontefract and Castleford 1997–2010, for Normanton, Pontefract and Castleford 2010–; Parl. Under-Sec. of State for Public Health 1999–2002, Parl. Sec. at Lord Chancellor's Dept 2002–03, in Office of Deputy Prime Minister 2003–05, Minister of State (Minister for Housing and Planning), Dept for Communities and Local Govt 2005–07, Minister for Housing 2007–08, Chief Sec. to Treasury 2008–09, Sec. of

State for Work and Pensions 2009–10 (with Ed Balls, first married couple to serve together in UK cabinet); Shadow Minister for Women and Equalities 2010–, Shadow Sec. of State for Work and Pensions May–Oct. 2010, Shadow Foreign Sec. 2010–11, Shadow Sec. of State for the Home Dept (Shadow Home Sec.) 2011–. *Address:* House of Commons, Westminster, London SW1A 0AA (office); 1 York Street, Castleford, West Yorks., WF10 IJS, England (office). *Telephone:* (20) 7219-5080 (London) (office); (1977) 553388 (Castleford) (office). *Fax:* (20) 7219-0912 (London) (office); (1977) 559753 (Castleford) (office). *E-mail:* coopery@parliament .uk (office). *Website:* www.yvettecooper.com (office).

COOR, Lattie Finch, PhD; American academic; *President Emeritus, Arizona State University;* b. 26 Sept. 1936, Phoenix, Ariz.; s. of Lattie F. Coor and Elnora Coor (née Witten); m. Elva Wingfield 1994; three c. from a previous marriage; ed Northern Arizona Univ., Washington Univ., St Louis, American Coll., Greece; Admin. Asst to Gov. of Mich. 1961–62; Asst to Chancellor, Washington Univ., St Louis 1963–67, Asst Dean, Grad. School of Arts and Sciences 1967–69, Dir Int. Studies 1967–69, Asst Prof. of Political Science 1967–76, Vice-Chancellor 1969–74, Univ. Vice-Chancellor 1974–76; Pres., Univ. of Vt, Burlington 1976–89; Pres. Ariz. State Univ. 1990–2002, Pres. Emer. 2002–, Prof. and Ernest W. McFarland Chair in Leadership and Public Policy, School of Public Affairs 2002–; Chair. and CEO Center for the Future of Arizona 2002–; consultant for Dept of Health, Educ. and Welfare; special consultant to US Commr for Educ. 1971–74; Chair., Cttee on governmental relations, American Council on Educ. 1976–80; Dir New England Bd of Higher Educ. 1976–; mem. Pres.'s Comm., Nat. Coll. Athletic Asscn, Nat. Asscn State Univs and Land Grant Colls (Chair. Bd 1991–92). *Address:* Downtown Center B5, Arizona State University, 541 E Van Buren, Phoenix, AZ 85004, USA (office). *Telephone:* (480) 727-5005 (office). *E-mail:* lattie.coor@asu.edu (office).

COORS, Peter H., BEng, MBA; American business executive; *Chairman, Molson Coors Brewing Company;* b. 20 Sept. 1946, Golden, Colo; great-grand s. of Adolph Coors, founder of the Golden brewery in 1873; ed Phillips Exeter Acad., NH, Cornell Univ., NY, Univ. of Denver; joined Adolph Coors Co. 1971, held several exec. and man. positions, including Dir Coors and Coors Brewing Co. 1973–2005, Exec. Vice-Pres. and Chair. brewing div. of Coors (before being organized as Coors Brewing Co.) –1993, interim Treas. and Chief Financial Officer Coors 1993–95, Vice-Chair. and CEO Coors Brewing Co. 1993, Chair. Coors Brewing Co. and Pres. and CEO Adolph Coors Co. 2000–02, Chair. Adolph Coors Co. and Coors Brewing Co. 2002–05, Chair. Coors Brewing Co. and Vice-Chair. Molson Coors Brewing Co. 2005–08, Chair. MillerCoors (following merger of Miller Brewing Co. and Coors Brewing Co.) 2008–, Chair. Molson Coors Brewing Co. 2008–; Chair. Univ. of Colorado Hosp. Foundation 2006–; mem. Bd of Dirs Energy Corporation of America 1996–, H.J. Heinz Co. 2001–; mem. Int. Chapter of Young Presidents Org., Denver Univ.'s Daniels School of Business Advisory Bd; mem. Exec. Cttee Nat. Western Stock Show Asscn; fmr Nat. Pres. and Chair. Ducks Unlimited; Trustee and mem. Exec. Bd Denver Area Council of the Boy Scouts of America; Trustee Seeds of Hope Foundation, Univ. of Northern Colorado; serves on bds of several conservation groups; Dr hc (Regis Univ.) 1991, (Wilberforce Univ.) 1992, (Johnson & Wales Univ.) 1997. *Leisure interests:* outdoor pursuits, wildlife conservation. *Address:* Molson Coors Brewing Co., 1225 17th Street, Suite 3200, Denver, CO 80202, (office), MillerCoors LLC, 250 South Wacker Drive, Suite 800, Chicago IL 60606-5888 USA (office). *Telephone:* (312) 496-2700 (Chicago) (office); (303) 927-2337 (Denver) (office). *Fax:* (303) 277-5415 (Denver) (office). *E-mail:* mcbcmedia@molsoncoors.com (office). *Website:* www.molsoncoors.com (office); www.millercoors.com (office).

COOTE, Alice; British singer (mezzo-soprano); b. 10 May 1968, Frodsham, Cheshire; ed Guildhall School of Music and Drama, London, Royal Northern Coll. of Music and Nat. Opera Studio; concerts include oratorio with London and Liverpool Philharmonic Orchestras, Bergen Philharmonic, London Mozart Players, appearances at the BBC Proms 1997, 2002, 2003, recitals at Cheltenham and Edinburgh Festivals, on BBC Radio 3, and at the Wigmore Hall, London; roles include Cherubino in Figaro, Dorabella in Così fan tutte, Penelope in The Return of Ulysses, Kate Pinkerton in Madama Butterfly, Suzy in La Rondine, the Page in Salome, Glycère in Cherubini's Anacréon ou l'amour fugitif, Fortuna and Valletto in Poppea, Hanna Kennedy in Mary Stuart; season 1998–99 included her debut at Opéra Bastille in Parsifal, the title role in Rape of Lucretia at Nantes, Tamyris in Il Re Pastore for Opera North, Ruggiero in Alcina at Stuttgart; season 2002–03 included Covent Garden debut as Dryade in Ariadne auf Naxos, Ruggiero in Alcina at San Francisco, Octavian in Der Rosenkavalier for ENO, Strauss' Composer in Chicago, Dido in Les Troyens for San Francisco Opera, Turnspit in Rusalka and Orlando at Covent Garden; Rinaldo at Göttingen, Der Komponist in Ariadne auf Naxos for Welsh Nat. Opera 2004; Idamante in Idomeneo, San Francisco 2008; Lucrezia Borgia, Bayerische Staatsoper 2009; Ariadne auf Naxos, Toronto, Bayerische Staatsoper, Lyric Opera of Chicago 2011; Prince Charming in Cendrillon, Royal Opera House 2011; Hansel and Gretel, Met Opera 2011–12; Octavian in Der Rosenkavalier, Geneva 2012; numerous performances with pianist Julius Drake; Brigitte Fassbaender Award for Lieder Interpretation, Decca-Kathleen Ferrier Prize 1992. *Recordings include:* Vaughan Williams' Hugh the Drover 1994, Rossini's Ricciardo e Zoraide 1997, Great Operatic Arias 2002, Verdi's Falstaff 2002, Handel's The Choice of Hercules 2002, Songs 2003, Walton's Gloria, The Choice of Hercules, Orfeo, Elgar's The Dream of Gerontius (Gramophone Award for Best Choral Recording 2009). *Address:* c/o Stefania Almansi, IMG Artists, The Light Box, 111 Power Road, London, W4 5PY, England (office). *Telephone:* (20) 7957-5800 (office). *Fax:* (20) 7957-5801 (office). *E-mail:* salmansi@ imgartists.com (office). *Website:* www.imgartists.com (office).

COPA CONDORI, Nilda; Bolivian trade unionist and politician; *Minister of Justice;* b. 4 Oct. 1977, La Quebrada; joined trade union aged 16; Sec. of Women's Affairs, Huayllajara Dist 1998–99; Health and Educ. Sec., Cen. Provincial Ass. 2000–03; Policy Sec., Nat. Confed. of Rural Indian Bolivian Women 'Bartolina Sisa', Sucre 2003–08, Sec.-Gen. 2008–10; mem. Asamblea Legislativa (Parl.) for Tarija 49th Dist 2006–; mem. Bolivian Constituent Ass. 2006–07; Minister of Justice 2010–. *Address:* Ministry of Justice, Avenida 16 de Julio (El Prado) 1769, La Paz, Bolivia (office). *Telephone:* (2) 212-4725 (office). *Fax:* (2) 231-5468 (office). *E-mail:* ministerio@justicia.go.bo (office). *Website:* www.justicia.gob.bo (office).

COPAKEN KOGAN, Deborah; American author and journalist; b. 11 March 1966, Boston, Mass; d. of Richard Daniel Copaken and Marjorie Ann Copaken (née

Schwartz); m. Paul M. Kogan; three c.; ed Harvard Univ.; worked as photojournalist 1988–92; television producer, ABC and NBC networks 1992–98; contrib. to many publs including Time, Newsweek, New York Times, The New Yorker, The Nation, Elle, More, Slate, Paris Match, O, Financial Times. *Publications include:* Shutterbabe 2001, Between Here and April 2008, Hell is Other Parents 2009, The Red Book 2012. *Address:* c/o David McCormick, McCormick & Williams, 37 West 20th Street, New York, NY 10011, USA (office). *Telephone:* (212) 691-9726 (office). *E-mail:* dm@mccormickwilliams.com (office). *Website:* www.mccormickwilliams.com (office); www.deborahcopakenkogan.com (home).

COPE, George A., BBA; Canadian telecommunications executive; *CEO, Bell Canada Enterprises (BCE) Inc;* b. 1961, Scarborough, Ont.; ed Univ. of Western Ont.; Pres. and CEO Clearnet Communications Inc. 1987–2000 (acquired by TELUS Mobility 2000), Pres. and CEO TELUS Mobility 2000–05; Pres. and CEO Bell Canada 2005–08, CEO Bell Canada Enterprises (BCE) Inc. 2008–; Dir BMO Financial Group, NII Holdings Inc.; mem. Advisory Bd Richard Ivey School of Business, Univ. of Western Ont.; Canada's Top 40 Under 40 Award 1996. *Address:* Bell Canada Enterprises Inc., 1 Carrefour Alexander Graham Bell Building A, 4th Floor, Verdun, Montreal, PQ H3E 3B3, Canada (office). *Telephone:* (1 888 932-6666 (office). *Fax:* (514) 766-5735 (office). *E-mail:* bcecomms@bce.ca (office). *Website:* www.bce.ca (office).

COPÉ, Jean François; French politician; *General Secretary, Union pour un Mouvement Populaire;* b. 5 May 1964, Boulogne-Billancourt (Hauts-de-Seine); s. of Prof. Roland Copé and Monique Ghanassia; m. 1st (divorced); two s. one d.; m. 2nd; one d.; ed École Active Bilingue Jeannine Manuel, Lycée Victor Duruy, Science-Po, École nationale d'Admin; joined Caisse des dépôts et consignations until 1991, worked as Head of Cabinet for CEO at Dexia until 1993; also taught Local Economy and Finance at Science-Po at same time; involved within RPR from 1993, Deputy Gen. Sec. 2001–02; Assoc. Prof. of Economy and Finance, Univ. of Paris VIII 1997–2002; returned to Caisse des dépôts et consignations 1997–99; joined Supervisory Bd of Dexia 2000–02; Sec. of State for Relationships with Parl. and Govt Spokesman 2002–04; Deputy (Union pour un Mouvement Populaire—UMP), Nat. Ass. for Seine-et-Marne 1995–97, 2002–, Pres. UMP Group 2007–; Minister delegated to the Interior and Govt Spokesman March–Nov. 2004; Minister of Budget, Budget Reform and Govt Spokesman 2004–05, of Budget, State Reform and Govt Spokesman 2005–07; Regional Councillor of Île-de-France 1998–2007 (resgnd); Municipal Councillor of Meaux 1995–, Mayor of Meaux 1995–2002 (resgnd), 2005–, Deputy Mayor of Meaux 2002–05; Pres. and mem. Communauté d'agglomération du Pays de Meaux 2003–; Gen. Sec. UMP 2010–. *Publications:* Finances locales – Economica 1990, Ce que je n'ai pas appris à l'ENA : L'aventure d'un maire 1999, Devoir d'inventaire. Le dépôt de bilan de Lionel Jospin 2002, Promis, j'arrête la langue de bois 2006. *Address:* UMP, TSA 41557, 75901 Paris Cedex 15, France (office). *Telephone:* 1-40-76-60-00 (office). *E-mail:* info@u-m-p.org (office). *Website:* www.u-m-p.org (office).

COPE, Jonathan, CBE; British ballet dancer (retd) and répétiteur; b. 1963, Crediton, Devon; m. Maria Almeida, one s. one d.; ed Royal Ballet School; joined Royal Ballet 1982, Soloist 1985–86, Prin. 1987–90, 1992–2005 (retd), Répétiteur 2005–; est. property dev business 1990–92; South Bank Show Dance Award 2003, Critics' Circle/Nat. Dance Awards, Best Male Dancer 2004. *Leading roles (with Royal Ballet) include:* Prince in Swan Lake, The Sleeping Beauty and The Nutcracker, Romeo and Juliet (partnering Sylvie Guillem and Darcey Bussell), Solor in La Bayadère, Albrecht in Giselle, Le Baiser de la Fée, The Prince of the Pagodas, Cinderella, Palemon in Ondine, Serenade, Agon, Apollo, Opus 19/The Dreamer, The Sons of Horus, Young Apollo, Galanteries, The Planets, Still Life at the Penguin Café, The Spirit of Fugue, Concerto, Gloria, Requiem, A Broken Set of Rules, Pursuit, Piano, Grand Pas Classique, Monotones, Crown Prince Rudolph in Mayerling, Woyzeck in Different Drummer, Second Friend in The Judas Tree, Beliaev in A Month in the Country, Birthday Offering, La Valise, Air Monotones II, Fox in Renard, Fearful Symmetries, Symphony in C (partnering Sylvie Guillem), Duo Concertant, If This Is Still a Problem, Des Grieux in Manon, Illuminations. *Address:* The Royal Ballet, Royal Opera House, Bow Street, Covent Garden, London, WC2E 9DD, England. *Telephone:* (20) 7240-1200. *Fax:* (20) 7212-9121. *Website:* info.royaloperahouse.org/ballet.

COPE, Wendy Mary, OBE, MA, FRSL; British writer; b. 21 July 1945, Erith, Kent, England; d. of Fred Stanley Cope and Alice Mary Cope (née Hand); m. Lachlan Mackinnon; ed Farringtons School, St Hilda's Coll., Oxford, Westminster Coll. of Educ., Oxford; primary school teacher, London 1967–86; freelance writer 1986–; mem. Soc. of Authors (mem. Man. Cttee 1992–95); Hon. Fellow, Goldsmiths, Univ. of London 2013; Hon. DLitt (Winchester) 2000, (Oxford Brookes) 2003; Cholmondeley Award for Poetry 1987, Michael Braude Award for Light Verse, American Acad. of Arts and Letters 1995. *Publications include:* Across the City 1980, Hope and the 42 1984, Making Cocoa for Kingsley Amis 1986, Poem from a Colour Chart of House Paints 1986, Men and Their Boring Arguments 1988, Does She Like Wordgames? 1988, Twiddling Your Thumbs 1988, The River Girl 1990, Serious Concerns 1992, If I Don't Know 2001; editor: Is That the New Moon? – Poems by Women Poets 1989, The Orchard Book of Funny Poems 1993, The Funny Side 1998, The Faber Book of Bedtime Stories 2000, Heaven on Earth – 101 Happy Poems 2001, George Herbert: Verse and Prose (a selection) 2002, Two Cures for Love: Selected Poems 2008, Family Values 2011; contribs to newspapers and reviews. *Leisure interest:* playing the piano. *Address:* c/o Faber and Faber, Bloomsbury House, 74–77 Great Russell Street, London, WC1B 3DA, England (office). *Telephone:* (20) 7927-3800 (office). *Website:* www.faber.co.uk (office).

COPPA, HE Cardinal Giovanni, PhD; Italian ecclesiastic; b. 9 Nov. 1925, Alba; s. of Paolo Viberti and Maria Viberti; ed Catholic Univ. of Milan; ordained priest 1949; began working at the Vatican in what was known as the Apostolic Chancery; served as Latinist at Second Vatican Council and worked in Vatican Sec. of State, which had taken over duties of Apostolic Chancery; Assessor of the Secr. of State 1975–79; apptd Titular Archbishop of Serta and Del. of the Apostolic Nunciatures 1979; Apostolic Nuncio to Czechoslovakia 1990–93, to Czech Repub. 1993–2001 (also accred to Slovakia 1993–94 (resgnd); cr. Cardinal (Cardinal-Deacon of S. Lino) 2007; Gratias Agit Award, Ministry of Foreign Affairs, Prague, Poland. *Publications include:* Problemi del Concilio 1966, S. Ambrosii de Mysteriis 1974, S. Ambrogio, Esposizione del Vangelo secondo Luca 1978, Origene-Gerolamo (homilies) 1993, Opere de San Ambrogio 1996, Budte Verni (homilies) 1998; articles in L'osservatore romano, Latinitas, Studi Romani and Diplomatic Life of Prague. *Address:* Palazzo della Canonica, 00120 Vatican City, Italy.

COPPENS, Yves; French professor of palaeoanthropology and prehistory; *Professor Emeritus, Collège de France;* b. 9 Aug. 1934, Vannes; s. of René Coppens and Andrée Coppens; m. Françoise Le Guennec 1959; ed Univ. of Rennes, Univ. of Paris (Sorbonne); Research Asst, CNRS, Paris 1956–69; Assoc. Prof., then Prof., Nat. Museum of Natural History 1969–83; Prof. of Palaeoanthropology and Prehistory, Collège de France 1983, now Prof. Emer.; mem. Acad. of Sciences 1985–, Nat. Acad. of Medicine 1991–, Royal Acad. of Sciences (Belgium) 1992–; Chevalier, Légion d'honneur, Officier, Ordre Nat. du Mérite, Officier des Palmes Académiques, Officier, des Arts et Lettres, Officier, Ordre Nat. Tchadien; Dr. hc (Bologna) 1988, (Liège) 1992; Le prix Edmond Hébert 1963, Le prix André C. Bonnet 1969, La médaille d'or de l'Empereur d'Éthiopie 1973, Le grand prix Jaffé de l'Académie des Sciences 1974, Le grand prix scientifique de la Fondation de France 1975, La médaille Fourmarier de la Société Géologique de Belgique 1975, Le prix Glaxo 1978, La médaille d'argent du CNRS 1982, Le prix Kalinga de l'UNESCO 1984, La médaille Vandenbroeck de la Société belge de géologie, de paléontologie et d'hydrologie 1987, La médaille André Duveyrier de la Société de Géographie 1989, La médaille d'or de l'encouragement au progèrsicence 1991. *Documentary film:* Homo sapiens 2005. *Publications:* Le Singe, l'Afrique et l'homme 1983, Préhistoire de l'art occidental (with Brigitte Delluc, André Leroi-gourhan) 1990, Origines de la bipédie (with Brigitte Senut) 1992, La plus belle histoire du monde 1996, Le genou de Lucy 1999, Pré-ambules : les premiers pas de l'homme 1999, Grand entretien 2001, Aux origines de l'humanité 2001, Les origines de l'homme T 1 et T 2 (with Pascal Picq) 2002, L'Odyssée de l'espèce 2003, Homo sapiens 2004; over 400 scientific papers. *Address:* Collège de France, 3, rue d'Ulm, 75231 Paris, Cedex 5; Musée de l'Homme, Palais de Chaillot, place du Trocadéro, 75116 Paris (office); 4 rue du Pont-aux-Choux, 75003 Paris, France (home). *Telephone:* 1-44-27-10-23. *E-mail:* yves.coppens@college-of-france.fr. *Website:* www.college-de-france.fr/site/pal_pre/p998923969623.htm.

COPPERFIELD, David; American magician; b. (David Kotkin), 1956, Metuchen, NJ; ed Fordham Univ.; Prof. of Magic, New York Univ. 1974; appeared in musical Magic Man 1974; presenter, The Magic of ABC; performer, dir, producer, writer, The Magic of David Copperfield 1978–; Founder and Chair. Project Magic 1982–; Founder Int. Museum and Library of Conjuring Arts, Nev. 1991; Owner Musha Cay resort, Bahamas; performs more than 550 shows per year world-wide; Dr hc (Fordham Univ.); Chevalier, Ordre des Arts et des Lettres; Golden Rose Award, Montreux Film Festival 1987, Bambi Award 1993, 19 Emmy Awards. *Film:* Terror Train 1980. *Achievements include:* illusions include levitating across Grand Canyon 1984, walking through Great Wall of China 1986, escaping from Alcatraz prison 1987, making Statue of Liberty disappear 1989, going over Niagara Falls 1990, making Orient Express disappear 1991; introduced flying illusion 1992; escaped from burning ropes 13 storeys above ground, Caesar's Palace 1993. *Publications:* Tales of the Impossible. *Website:* www.davidcopperfield.com.

COPPERWHEAT, Lee; British fashion designer; s. of Terence Copperwheat and Diana Frances Brooks; ed Tresham Coll., Northampton, London Coll. of Fashion; fmrly tailor with Aquascutum; est. design room and fmr man. of sampling and production Passenger sportswear; freelance design projects for numerous clients; fmr teacher menswear tailoring Brighton Univ.; fmr Lecturer, St Martin's School of Art, London; est. Copperwheat Blundell with Pamela Blundell; Young Designer of the Year 1994 (with Pamela Blundell).

COPPOLA, Francis Ford; American film director, film producer and screenwriter; b. 7 April 1939, Detroit, Mich.; s. of the late Carmine Coppola and Italia Coppola; m. Eleanor Neil; two s. (one deceased) one d. Sofia Coppola (q.v.); ed Hofstra Univ., Univ. of California; theatre direction includes Private Lives, The Visit of the Old Lady, San Francisco Opera Co. 1972; founder and Artistic Dir Zoetrope Studios 1969–; Owner, Niebaum-Coppola Estate (winery), Napa Valley; f. Zoetrope Argentina, Buenos Aires; Commdr, Ordre des Arts et des Lettres; Cannes Film Award for The Conversation 1974; Dir's Guild Award for The Godfather; Acad. Award for Best Screenplay for Patton, Golden Palm (Cannes) 1979 for Apocalypse Now, also awarded Best Screenplay, Best Dir and Best Picture Oscars for The Godfather Part II; US Army Civilian Service Award, Irving G. Thalberg Memorial Award, Acad. of Motion Picture Arts and Sciences 2010; Praemium Imperiale Award, Japan Arts Foundation 2013. *Films directed include:* The Playgirls and the Bellboy 1962, Tonight for Sure 1962, Dementia 13 1963, You're a Big Boy Now 1966, Finian's Rainbow 1968, The Rain People 1969, The Godfather 1972, The Conversation 1974, The Godfather: Part II 1974, Apocalypse Now 1979, One from the Heart 1982, The Outsiders 1983, Rumble Fish 1983, The Cotton Club 1984, Captain EO 1986, Peggy Sue Got Married 1986, Gardens of Stone 1987, Tucker: The Man and His Dream 1988, New York Stories 1989, The Godfather: Part III 1990, Dracula 1992, Jack 1996, The Rainmaker 1997, Youth Without Youth 2007, Tetro 2009, Twixt Now and Sunrise 2011; also numerous screenplays and films produced including American Graffiti. *Address:* Zoetrope Studios, 916 Kearny Street, San Francisco, CA 94133; Niebaum Coppola, POB 208, Rutherford, CA 94573; c/o CAA, 9830 Wilshire Boulevard, Beverly Hills, CA 90212, USA. *Website:* www.zoetrope.com; www.inglenook.com.

COPPOLA, Sofia; American actress, film director, screenwriter, film producer and photographer; b. 14 May 1971, New York; d. of Francis Ford Coppola (q.v.) and Eleanor Coppola; m. Spike Jonze 1999 (divorced 2003); pnr Thomas Mars; two d.; cr. pop-culture magazine show Hi-Octane 1994; fmr designer, Milkfed fashion label; photography has appeared in Interview, Paris Vogue and Allure; mem. Writers Guild of America. *Films include:* Frankenweenie 1984, Peggy Sue Got Married 1986, Anna 1987, The Godfather: Part III 1990, Inside Monkey Zetterland 1992, Ciao L.A. 1994, Lick the Star (dir, producer and writer) 1998, The Virgin Suicides (dir and writer) 1999, Star Wars: Episode I: The Phantom Menace 1999, CQ 2001, Lost in Translation (dir, producer and writer) (Acad. Award for Best Original Screenplay 2004, Golden Globe Awards for Best Picture, Best Screenplay 2004, Independent Spirit Awards for Best Screenplay, Best Dir, Best Picture 2004, Cesar Award for Best Foreign Feature 2005) 2003, Marie-Antoinette (dir, producer and writer) 2006, Somewhere (Golden Lion Award, Venice Film Festival) 2010, The Bling Ring (dir and writer) 2013. *Address:* c/o Bart Walker, Cinetic Media LLC, 555 West 25th Street, 4th Floor, New York, NY 10001, USA.

COPPS, Sheila Maureen, PC, BA; Canadian consultant and fmr politician; *President, Sheila Copps and Associates;* b. 27 Nov. 1952, Hamilton, Ont.; d. of Victor Kennedy Copps and Geraldine Florence Copps (née Guthro); m. Austin Thorne; one d.; ed Univ. of Western Ontario, Univ. of Rouen, France, McMaster Univ.; journalist, Ottawa Citizen 1974–76, Hamilton Spectator 1977; Constituency Asst to Leader Liberal Party, Ont. 1977–81; mem. Ont. Legis. Ass. for Hamilton Centre 1981–84; mem. House of Commons (Parl.) 1984–2004, Deputy Leader of Opposition, Fed. Liberal Party 1991; Deputy Prime Minister 1993–97, Minister of the Environment 1993–96, Minister of Canadian Heritage 1996–2004; currently Pres. Sheila Copps and Assocs, Ottawa; Achievement Award, Canadian Council for the Arts 2003. *Publications:* Nobody's Baby 1986, Worth Fighting For 2004. *Address:* Sheila Copps and Associates, 589 Rideau Street, Suite 212, Ottawa Ont., K1N 6A1, Canada (office). *Telephone:* (613) 355-0004 (office). *Fax:* (877) 832-2613 (office). *E-mail:* sheilacopps1@gmail.com (office). *Website:* www.sheilacopps.ca (office).

CORBAT, Michael L., BA (Econ); American banking executive; *CEO, Citigroup Inc.;* ed Harvard Univ.; has been at Citigroup and its predecessor cos since graduation in 1983, worked in Fixed Income Sales Dept in Atlanta and worked in New York and London, held several positions at Salomon Brothers (predecessor of Citigroup) including Man. Dir roles in Emerging Markets, High Yield and Derivatives, later Head of Global Emerging Markets Debt, Citigroup, then Head of the Global Corp. Bank and Global Commercial Bank –2008, CEO Global Wealth Man., CEO Citi Holdings, Inc. 2009–11, CEO Europe, Middle East and Africa, Citigroup Jan.–Oct. 2012, CEO Citigroup Inc. Oct. 2012–; Dir British American Business, Inc.; mem. Bd of Dirs Swedish American Chamber of Commerce; mem. Bd of Trustees, Salisbury School. *Address:* Citigroup Inc., 399 Park Avenue, New York, NY 10043, USA (office). *Telephone:* (212) 559-1000 (office). *Fax:* (212) 793-3946 (office). *E-mail:* info@citigroup.com (office). *Website:* www.citigroup.com (office).

CORBETT, Gerald Michael Nolan, MA, MSc; British business executive; *Chairman, Britvic PLC;* b. 7 Sept. 1951, Hastings, Sussex; s. of the late John Michael Nolan Corbett and of Pamela Muriel Corbett (née Gay); m. Virginia Moore Newsum; one s. three d.; ed Tonbridge School, Pembroke Coll. Cambridge, London Business School, Harvard Business School; with Boston Consulting Group 1975–82; Group Financial Controller Dixons Group PLC 1982–86, Corp. Finance Dir 1986–87; Group Finance Dir Redland PLC 1987–94, Grand Metropolitan PLC 1994–97; Dir (non-exec.) MEPC PLC 1995–98, Burmah Castrol PLC 1998–2000; CEO Railtrack PLC 1997–2000; Chair. Woolworths Group PLC 2001–07, Health Club Holdings, Holmes Place 2003–, SSL Int. 2005–, Britvic PLC 2005–, Moneysupermarket.com Group Ltd; Chair. Bd of Govs Abbots Hill School 1997–2002, Royal Nat. Inst. for the Deaf (RNID) 2007–; Foundation Scholar, Pembroke Coll., Cambridge 1972–75, William Pitt Prize 1974, London Business School Prize 1979. *Leisure interests:* golf, country pursuits. *Address:* Britvic PLC, Britvic House, Bloomfield Road, CM1 1TU, Chelmsford, Essex, UK (office). *Telephone:* (1245) 261871 (office). *Fax:* (1245) 267147 (office). *Website:* www.britvic.co.uk (office).

CORBETT, Roger Campbell, AM, BComm; Australian business executive; b. 1944; m.; ed Univ. of NSW; began career working on dock, Woolworths Store, Chatswood; fmr Dir of Operations and mem. Bd Dirs, David Jones (Australia) Pty Ltd; fmr Merchandising and Stores Dir and mem. Bd Dirs Grace Brothers; Man.-Dir Big W (gen. merchandise discount stores), Woolworths Ltd (Australia) 1990–97, apptd Exec. Dir Woolworths Ltd (Australia) 1990, Man.-Dir of Retail 1997–98, COO 1998–99, CEO, Group Man.-Dir and mem. Bd Dirs 1999–2006 (retd); mem. Bd Dirs Wal-Mart Stores Inc. 2006–, Reserve Bank of Australia, Fairfax Media Ltd, Outback Stores; Chair. ALH Group Pty Ltd; fmr Chair. CIES Food Business Forum, France; Deputy Chair. PrimeAg Australia; mem. Advisory Council, Australian Grad. School of Man., Univ. of New South Wales; B'nai B'rith (Australia-NZ) Gold Medal. *Address:* ALH Group Pty Ltd., Ground Floor, 16-20 Claremont Street, South Yarra, Vic. 3141, Australia (office). *Telephone:* (3) 9829-1000 (office). *Website:* www.alhgroup.com.au (office).

CORBETT, Ronald Balfour (Ronnie), CBE, OBE; British actor and comedian; b. 4 Dec. 1930, Edinburgh, Scotland; s. of William Balfour Corbett and Annie Elizabeth Corbett (née Main); m. Anne Hart 1965; one s. (deceased) two d.; ed Royal High School, Edinburgh; performed in amateur theatricals at a church youth club; first job with Ministry of Agric.; Nat. Service with RAF; moved to London to act and began career by playing schoolboy roles in films. *Films include:* You're Only Young Twice 1952, Fun at St. Fanny's 1956, Rockets Galore! 1958, Casino Royale 1967, Some Will, Some Won't 1970, The Rise and Rise of Michael Rimmer 1970, No Sex Please: We're British 1975, By the Sea 1982, Fierce Creatures 1997, Burke and Hare 2010. *Radio includes:* starred in two series of the BBC Radio 4 sitcom When The Dog Dies 2010–11. *Television includes:* The Frost Report (series) 1966–67, The Corbett Follies (series) 1969, Hark at Barker (series) 1969, The Ronnie Barker Yearbook (film) 1971, The Two Ronnies (series) – The Two Ronnies Old Fashioned Christmas Mystery 1973, The Prince of Denmark (series) 1974, All This and Corbett Too (series) 1975, Ronnie Corbett's Saturday Special (series) 1977, The Ronnie Corbett Special (series) 1979, The Two Ronnies in Australia (series) 1987, The Ronnie Corbett Show (series) 1987, Christmas Night with the Two Ronnies (film) 1987, Sorry! (series) 1981–88, Timbuctoo (series) 1998, The Two Ronnies Sketchbook 2005, Piers Morgan's Life Stories 2009, The One Ronnie 2010, Ronnie Corbett's Supper Club 2010, Ronnie Corbett's Comedy Britain 2011. *Leisure interest:* beekeeping, golf, Crystal Palace Football Club and Heart of Midlothian Football Club. *Address:* c/o Artists' Mail, BBC Television Centre, Wood Lane, London, W12 7RJ (office); c/o Prime Performers Ltd, 1–2 Faulkners Alley, Cowcross Street, London, EC1M 6DD, England (office). *Telephone:* (20) 7251-8222 (Prime Performers) (office). *E-mail:* info@primeperformers.co.uk (office). *Website:* www.primeperformers.co.uk (office).

CORBETT, Thomas Wingett (Tom), Jr, BA, JD; American lawyer, business executive, politician and state governor; *Governor of Pennsylvania;* b. 17 June 1949, Phila, Pa; s. of Thomas Wingett Corbett and Mary Bernadine Corbett (née Diskin); m. Susan Jean Manbeck 1972; one s. one d.; ed Lebanon Valley Coll., St Mary's Univ. Law School, San Antonio; employed as 9th grade teacher for one year; served in 28th Infantry Div., Pa Army Nat. Guard 1971–84, attained rank of Capt.; called to the Bar in Pa 1976, US Dist Court (Western Dist), Pa 1976, US Court of

Mil. Appeals 1979, US Supreme Court 1984; began legal career as Asst Dist Attorney, Allegheny Co., Pittsburgh, Pa 1976–80; Asst US Attorney for Western Dist of Pa 1980–83; went into pvt. law practice for several years; Assoc., Rose, Schmidt, Hasley & DiSalle 1983–86, Partner 1986–89, Thorp, Reed & Armstrong, Pittsburgh 1993–95, 1997–98; won first election as township commr in Pittsburgh suburb of Shaler Township; re-entered public arena when apptd to monitor Allegheny Co. jail while it was under court's supervision 1988; US Attorney for Western Dist of Pa 1989–93 (resgnd), mem. US Attorney Gen.'s Advisory Cttee 1991–93, Chair. 1992–93; returned to pvt. practice and also served as adviser to successful gubernatorial campaign of Tom Ridge; served on several state comms, including Pennsylvania Comm. on Crime and Delinquency (Chair.); Attorney Gen. of Commonwealth of Pa 1995–97, 2005–11; Asst Gen. Counsel for Govt Affairs, Waste Management Inc., Pittsburgh 1998–2002; Partner, Thomas Corbett & Assocs 2002–05; Gov. of Pennsylvania 2011–; del., Republican Nat. Convention 2000; mem. Gov.'s Partnership for Safe Children 1995–2003, Pennsylvania Weed & Seed Program 1995–2003, Pennsylvania Comm. on Crime and Delinquency 1995–2003; Pres. St Mary's Parent-Teacher Guild, Glenshaw; mem. Shaler Township Republican Cttee 1984–89, Allegheny Co. Republican Cttee 1985–89; mem. ABA, Allegheny Co. Bar Asscn, Pennsylvania Bar Asscn, Ancient Order of Hibernians, Nat. Rifle Asscn; Republican. *Leisure interests:* skiing, golf, reading. *Address:* Office of the Governor, 225 Main Capitol Building, Harrisburg, PA 17120, USA (office). *Telephone:* (717) 787-2500 (office). *Fax:* (717) 772-8284 (office). *Website:* www.governor.state.pa.us (office); www.tomcorbettforgovernor.com.

CORBO, Vittorio, PhD; Chilean economist, academic, business executive and fmr central banker; *President, ING Seguros de Vida SA;* b. 22 March 1943, Iquique; s. of Gerardo Corbo and Maria Lioi; m. Veronica Urzua 1967; one s. one d.; ed Universidad de Chile and Mass Inst. of Tech.; Asst Prof., Concordia Univ. 1972–81, Prof., Inst. of Econs, Pontificia Univ. Católica de Chile 1981–84, 1991–; Sr Adviser, IBRD 1984–87, Div. Chief. 1987–91; Chief, Macroeconomic Devt and Growth Div., World Bank 1984–91, mem. Chief Economist Advisory Council 2004–; Economic Adviser to Santander Group in Chile 1991–2003, 2008–, mem. Bd of Dirs Banco Santander-Chile 1995–2003; Chair. Cen. Bank of Chile 2003–07; Pres. ING Seguros de Vida SA (insurance co.), Santiago 2008–; Vice-Chair. Inmobiliaria Simonetti 2008–; mem. Bd of Dirs Global Devt Network 1999–2003, Universia-Chile 2000–03, Chilean Pacific Foundation 2000–, Cruz Verde Pharmacies 2008–; Prof. of Econs, Concordia Univ., Canada 1972–81; Visiting Prof., Georgetown Univ., Washington, DC 1984–91; Vice-Pres. Int. Econ. Asscn 1998–2002; mem. Man. Council, Global Devt Network 1993–2003, Int. Advisory Council, Center for Social and Econ. Research (CASE), Warsaw, Poland, Advisory Bd, Stanford Center for Int. Devt 1999–; Sr Research Fellow, Research Center for Econ. Devt and Policy Reform, Stanford Univ. 1999; Visiting Sr Scholar, Research Dept, IMF 2000, 2003; mem. editorial cttee Journal of Development Economics, Journal of Applied Economics; Economist of the Year, El Mercurio newspaper 2003. *Publications include:* Inflation in Developing Countries 1974, Monetary Policy in Latin America in the 1990s 2000. *Leisure interest:* skiing. *Address:* ING Seguros de Vida SA, Ave Succecia #211 Santiago, Piso 7, Santiago, Chile (office). *Telephone:* (2) 252-1464 (office). *Website:* www.ingvida.cl (office).

CORDANI, David M.; American business executive; *President and CEO, CIGNA Corporation;* ed Texas A&M Univ., Univ. of Hartford; chartered financial consultant; joined CIGNA Corpn 1991, Sr Vice-Pres., Customer Segments and Marketing, CIGNA HealthCare 2004–05, Pres. CIGNA HealthCare 2005–08, Pres. and COO CIGNA Corpn 2008–09, mem. Bd of Dirs Oct. 2009–, Pres. and CEO Dec. 2009–; mem. Bd of Dirs Nat. Asscn of Mfrs, Cigna Foundation. *Address:* CIGNA Corpn, 2 Liberty Place, 1601 Chestnut Street, Philadelphia, PA 19192, USA (office). *Telephone:* (215) 761-1000 (office). *Fax:* (215) 761-5515 (office). *E-mail:* info@cigna.com (office). *Website:* www.cigna.com (office).

CORDEN, James Kimberley; British actor and television comedy writer; b. 22 Aug. 1978; s. of Malcolm Corden and Margaret Corden; m. Julia Carey 2012; one s. *Television includes:* Out of Tune 1996–98, Boyz Unlimited 1999, Fat Friends 2000–05, Teachers 2001–03, Little Britain 2004, Dalziel and Pascoe 2004, Gavin & Stacey (also co-writer) (British Comedy Awards Best Male Comedy Performer 2007, BAFTA Television Award for Best Male Comedy Performance 2008) 2007–10, Horne & Corden 2009, Doctor Who 2010–11, Stella 2012. *Films include:* Whatever Happened to Harold Smith? 1999, All or Nothing 2002, Heartlands 2002, Cruise of the Gods 2002, Pierrepoint 2005, Heroes and Villains 2006, The History Boys 2006, Starter for 10 2006, How to Lose Friends & Alienate People 2008, Lesbian Vampire Killers 2009, Telstar 2009, The Boat That Rocked 2009, Planet 51 (voice) 2009, Gullliver's Travels 2010, The Three Musketeers 2011. *Theatre includes:* The History Boys (Lyttelton Theatre, London, then touring) 2006, A Respectable Wedding (Young Vic, London) 2007, One Man, Two Guvnors (Lyttelton Theatre, London, Adelphi Theatre, London, Music Box Theatre, New York City) (Tony Award, Leading Role in a Play 2012) 2011–12. *Address:* c/o United Agents, 12-26 Lexington Street, London, W1F 0LE, England (office). *Telephone:* (20) 3214-0800 (office). *Fax:* (20) 3214-0801 (office). *E-mail:* info@unitedagents.co.uk (office). *Website:* unitedagents.co.uk/james-corden (office).

CORDEN, Warner Max, AC, MComm, MA, PhD, FBA, FASSA; Australian economist and academic; *Professorial Fellow, Department of Economics, University of Melbourne;* b. 13 Aug. 1927, Breslau, Germany (now Wrocław, Poland); s. of Ralph S. Corden; m. Dorothy Martin 1957; one d.; ed Melbourne Boys High School, Univ. of Melbourne and London School of Econs; Lecturer, Dept of Econs, Univ. of Melbourne 1958–61, Professorial Fellow 2002–; Nuffield Reader in Int. Econs and Fellow of Nuffield Coll., Oxford 1967–76; Professorial Fellow, ANU 1962–67, Prof. of Econs 1976–88; Chung Ju Yung Prof. of Int. Econs, Paul H. Nitze School of Advanced Int. Studies, Johns Hopkins Univ., Washington, DC, USA 1989–2002, Prof. Emer. of Int. Econs 2002–; Visiting Prof., Univ. of California, Berkeley 1965, Univ. of Minnesota 1971, Princeton Univ. 1973, Harvard Univ. 1986; Sr Adviser, IMF 1986–88; Pres. Econ. Soc. of Australia and New Zealand 1977–80; mem. Group of Thirty 1982–90; Foreign Hon. mem. American Econ. Asscn 1984, Distinguished Fellow, Econ. Soc. of Australia 1995; Dr hc (Melbourne) 1995; Bernard Harms Prize 1986. *Publications include:* The Theory of Protection 1971, Trade Policy and Economic Welfare 1974, 1997, Inflation, Exchange Rates and the World Economy 1977, 1985, Protection, Growth and Trade 1985, International Trade Theory and Policy 1992, Economic Policy, Exchange Rates and the

International System 1994, The Road to Reform 1997, Too Sensational: On the Choice of Exchange Rate Regimes 2002. *Address:* Department of Economics, University of Melbourne, Melbourne, Vic. 3010, Australia (office). *Telephone:* (3) 8344-5296 (office). *Fax:* (3) 8344-6899 (office). *E-mail:* m.corden@unimelb.edu.au (office). *Website:* www.economics.unimelb.edu.au/WHO/mcorden (office).

CORDES, Eckhard, MBA, PhD; German business executive; *Co-founder, Emeram Capital Partners GmbH;* b. 25 Nov. 1950, Neumünster; ed Hamburg Univ.; joined DaimlerChrysler Group 1976, Asst Plant Man. Sindelfingen Plant 1977–81, Sr Man. Investment Planning, Sindelfingen Plant 1981–83, Head, Product Control, New Commercial Vehicle P 1983–86, Dir Accounting and Control, Mercedes-Benz, Sao Paulo, Brazil 1986–89, Dir Control AEG, Frankfurt 1989–91, Sr Vice-Pres. Control, Corp. Planning and Mergers and Acquisitions 1991–94, Sr Vice-Pres. Corp. Planning and Control, Daimler-Benz AG 1994–95, Sr Vice-Pres. Corp. Devt 1995–96, mem. Man. Bd, Corp. Devt and Directly-Managed Businesses 1997, Corp. Devt and IT Man. and MTU/Diesel Engines and TEMIC Daimler-Chrysler AG 1998–2000 (after Daimler-Benz merged with Chrysler Corpn 1998), mem. Man. Bd, Corp. Devt and IT Man. DaimlerChrysler AG 2000–04, Commercial Vehicles Div. 2000–04, Head, Mercedes Car Group 2004–05; CEO and Chair. Man. Bd Franz Haniel & Cie. GmbH 2006–09; Chair. Supervisory Bd METRO AG 2006–07, Chair. Man. Bd 2007–11, Chief Human Resources Officer 2010–11; Co-founder Emeram Capital Partners GmbH 2011–. *Address:* Emeram Capital Partners GmbH, Mühlbaurstr. 1, 81679 Munich, Germany (office). *Telephone:* (89) 41999670 (office). *Fax:* (89) 419996710 (office). *E-mail:* emeram.capital@t-online -de.

CORDES, HE Cardinal Paul Josef; German ecclesiastic; *President Emeritus of the Pontifical Council 'Cor Unum';* b. 5 Sept. 1934, Kirchhundem; ed briefly studied medicine before entering the seminary, doctoral studies at Univ. of Mainz; ordained priest of Paderborn 1961; apptd Titular Bishop of Naissus and Auxiliary Bishop of Paderborn 1975, Titular Archbishop of Naissus 1995; Vice-Pres. Pontifical Council for the Laity 1980; Pres. Pontifical Council 'Cor Unum' 1995–2005, 2005–10, Pres. Emer. 2010–; cr. Cardinal (Cardinal-Deacon of S. Lorenzo in Piscibus) 2007. *Address:* Pontifical Council 'Cor Unum', Piazza S. Calisto 16, 00153 Rome, Italy (office). *Telephone:* (06) 6988-9411 (office). *Fax:* (06) 6988-7301 (office).

CÓRDOBA RUIZ, Piedad Esneda; Colombian lawyer and politician; b. 25 Jan. 1955, Medellín, Antioquia; d. of Zabulón Córdoba and Lía Ruiz; ed Universidad Pontificia Bolivariana, Medellín; began her political career working as community leader in several neighbourhoods in Medellín; Municipal Sub-controller 1984–86; Pvt. Sec. to Mayor William Jaramillo 1986; elected Councilwoman, Medellín 1988–90; cand. for Chamber of Reps of Colombia 1990; elected Deputy of Antioquia Dept Ass. 1990; Deputy, Chamber of Reps 1992–94; Mayor of Medellín 1994; mem. Senate 1994–2010; Senator and mem. Seventh Comm. of Congress 2006–, in charge of debating labour topics, previously worked on Third Comm. (Financial affairs), Fifth Comm. (Mining and Energy) and Second Comm. (Foreign Affairs), Pres. Senate's Human Rights Comm. and the Peace Comm.; leading figure of Latin American feminist movt in Colombia, represents minority groups as part of Poder Ciudadano Siglo XXI Movt; participated in Fourth World Conf. on Women, Beijing 1995; kidnapped by leader of paramilitary group United Self-Defense Forces of Colombia (AUC) 1999, eventually freed and exiled with her family in Canada, returned to Colombia in 2000; Pres. Liberal Nat. Directorate (Head of Partido Liberal Colombiano—Colombian Liberal Party) 2003; participated as official Govt mediator, along with Pres. Hugo Chávez of Venezuela, in humanitarian exchange discussions between Colombia Govt and Fuerzas Armadas Revolucionarias de Colombia (FARC) guerrilla group Aug.–Nov. 2007, banned from public office due to alleged ties to FARC 2010. *E-mail:* piedadcordobaruiz@gmail.com. *Website:* www .piedadcordoba.net.

CÓRDOVA, France Anne, BA, PhD; American astrophysicist, academic and university administrator; *Chairman of the Board of Regents, Smithsonian Institution;* b. Paris, France; m. Christian J. Foster; one s. one d.; ed Bishop Amat High School, La Puente, Calif., Stanford Univ., California Inst. of Tech.; early career at Los Angeles Times News Service 1971; Staff Scientist, Earth and Space Science Div., Los Alamos Nat. Lab. (LANL) 1979–89, Deputy Group Leader, Space Astronomy and Astrophysics Group 1989; Prof. of Astronomy and Astrophysics, Pennsylvania State Univ. 1989–96, Dept Head 1989–93; Chief Scientist, NASA 1993–96; Prof. of Physics, Univ. of California, Santa Barbara 1996–2002, Vice-Chancellor Research 1996–2002; Chancellor Univ. of California, Riverside 2002–07; Pres. Purdue Research Foundation 2007–12, Purdue Univ. 2007–12; fmr Chair. numerous NASA bds including Exceptional Scientific Achievement Medal Panel 1993–96, Science Council 1994–96, Search Cttee for Dir Astrobiology Inst. 1998, Science Working Group, Constellation X Mission 1998–2000, Hubble Space Telescope Time Allocation Cttee 2001, Strategic Roadmap Cttee on Educ. (Co-Chair.) 2004; Chair. Research Advisory Council, Earth and Environmental Sciences Div. (LANL) 1985–86, Geosciences Space Science and Astrophysics (GSSA) Category Team (LANL) 1986–88, Science and Eng Advisory Council (SEAC) 1988–89; Co-founder Int. Astronomical Union Working Group on Multi-Frequency and Multi-Facility Astrophysics 1988; Vice-Chair. High Energy Astrophysics Div., American Astronomical Soc. 1989, Chair. 1990, Vice-Pres. American Astronomical Soc. 1993–96; Chair.-Elect Comm. on Human Resources and Social Change, Nat. Asscn State Univs and Land-Grant Colls (NASULGC) 2005–07; mem. of numerous panels and bds including Scientific Program Cttee, AAAS 2000–, NRC Policy and Global Affairs Advisory Cttee 2001–, Univ. of California Mexico Comm. on Educ. Science Tech. 2002–, Univ. of California Pres.'s Council on Nat. Labs 2002–, Calif. Council on Science and Tech. 2003–, Belo 2013–, NAS Roundtable on Scientific Communication and Security 2003–, Edison International 2004–, Nat. Panel of Pres and Chancellors, Models for Flexible Tenure-track Faculty Career Pathways, American Council on Educ. (ACE) 2004–, Univ. California Long-Range Guidance Team 2005–, Nat. Science Bd 2008, Bd of Regents, Smithsonian Inst. 2009– (Chair. 2011–); Fellow, Asscn for Women in Science 1999, AAAS 2007, American Acad. of Arts and Sciences 2008; Hon. Prof., China Agricultural Univ. 2005; Dr hc (Loyola-Marymount Univ.) 1997, (Ben Gurion Univ. of the Negev) 2011, (Purdue Univ.) 2012; NASA Distinguished Service Medal 1996, Hispanic Achievement Award, Hispanic Magazine 1997, NASA Group Achievement Award for Outstanding Teamwork, Swift Midsize

Explorer Team 2000, Kilby Prize Laureate, Jack Kilby Int. Awards Foundation 2000, Nat. Assoc. of Nat. Acads 2002, named by Hispanic Business Magazine as one of the 80 Elite Hispanic Women 2002, nominated to Stanford Univ. Multicultural Alumni Hall of Fame 2008. *Publications include:* approx. 140 scientific reports and papers; ed.: Multiwavelength Astrophysics 1988, The Spectroscopic Survey Telescope 1990; contribs. to Mademoiselle magazine; fiction: The Women of Santo Domingo. *Leisure interests:* rock-climbing, canoeing, reading, writing. *Address:* c/o John K. Lapiana, Chief of Staff to the Regents, Office of the Regents, Smithsonian Institution, MRC 050, PO Box 37012, Washington, DC 20013-7012, USA (office). *Telephone:* (202) 633-5230 (office). *E-mail:* lapianaj@si.edu (office). *Website:* www.si.edu/Governance/Members (office).

CORDOVEZ, Diego; Ecuadorean diplomatist and lawyer; b. 3 Nov. 1935, Quito; s. of Luis Cordovez-Borja and Isidora Zegers de Cordovez; m. Maria Teresa Somavia 1960; one s.; ed Univ. of Chile; admitted to Bar 1962; served in Foreign Service of Ecuador until 1963; joined UN as Econ. Affairs Officer 1963; Political Officer on special missions to Dominican Repub. 1965, Pakistan 1971; Dir UN Econ. and Social Council Secr. 1973–78, Asst Sec.-Gen. for Econ. and Social Matters, UN 1978–81; Special Rep. of UN Sec.-Gen. on Libya–Malta dispute 1980–82; Sec.-Gen.'s rep. on UN Comm. of Inquiry on hostage crisis in Tehran 1980; Sr officer responsible for efforts to resolve Iran/Iraq war 1980–88; Under-Sec.-Gen. for Special Political Affairs 1981–1988; Special Envoy to Grenada 1983; UN Mediator, Afghanistan 1982–88, Rep. for implementation of Geneva Accords 1988–89; Minister for Foreign Affairs 1988–92; Pres. World Trade Center (Ecuador) 1993–98; Special Counsel, LeBoeuf, Lamb, Greene & Macrae 1993–98; Special Adviser to UN Sec.-Gen. for Cyprus 1997–99, for Latin American Affairs 1999–2005; Amb. and Perm. Rep. to UN, New York 2005–07; Agent of Rep. of Ecuador to the Int. Court of Justice 2007–09; Pres. Andean Centre for Int. Studies 2000; mem. American Soc. of Int. Law; Order of Merit (Ecuador); Légion d'honneur; Grand Cross (Spain, Portugal, Brazil, Argentina, Chile, Peru, Colombia, Venezuela); Grand Cross, Order of Distinguished Services (Peru). *Publications:* UNCTAD and Development Diplomacy 1971, Out of Afghanistan: The Inside Story of the Soviet Withdrawal (with Selig S. Harrison) 1995, Nuestra Propuesta Inconclusa (Ecuador–Perú: Del Inmovilismo al Acuerdo de Brasilia) 2000, El Mundo que he vivido – Memorias de Diplomacia, de Episodios y de Gente 2013. *Leisure interests:* reading, carpentry. *Address:* Calle Afganistán N41–90, El Bosque, Quito, Ecuador.

COREA, Chick; American musician (piano) and composer; b. (Armando Corea), 12 June 1941, Chelsea, Mass; m. Gayle Moran; one s. one d.; ed Juilliard School of Music; pianist with artists, including Mongo Santamaria 1962, Blue Mitchell 1965, Stan Getz 1966–68, Miles Davis 1969–71, Sarah Vaughan 1970; Founder mem., leader, pianist with group, Return To Forever 1971–; Founder The Elektric Band 1986–; Dr hc (Norwegian Univ. of Science and Technology) 2010; numerous magazine awards from Downbeat, Keyboard Magazine; Jazz Life Musician of World, Jazz Forum Music Poll 1974, Best Electric Jazz group 1990, Best Acoustic Pianist 1990, Top Jazz Pianist 1990, many Grammy Awardsincluding Best Improvised Jazz Solo (for 500 Miles High) 2012, Best Instrumental Composition (for Mozart Goes Dancing), Best Improvised Jazz Solo (with Gary Burton) (for Hot House) 2013. *Recordings include:* Piano Improvisations 1 and 2, Leprechaun, My Spanish Heart, Mad Hatter, Delphi 1, 2 and 3, Light As A Feather, Romantic Warrior, Hymn of The Seventh Galaxy, Music Magic, Voyage (with Steve Kujala) 1984, The Chick Corea Akoustic Band 1989, Elektric Band Inside Out 1990, Chick Corea Akoustic Band Alive! 1991, Elektric Band Beneath The Mask 1991, Time Warp 1995, Remembering Bud Powell 1997, Native Sense 1997, Standards 2000, Past Present and Futures 2001, Elektric Band: To The Stars 2004, The Ultimate Adventure (Grammy Awards for Best Jazz Instrumental Album, Individual or Group, for Best Instrumental Arrangement 2007) 2006, The Enchantment (with Béla Fleck) (Latin Grammy Award for Best Instrumental Album) 2007, The New Crystal Silence (with Gary Burton) (Grammy Award for Best Jazz Instrumental Album 2009) 2008, Five Peace Band-Live (with John McLaughlin Five Peace Band) (Grammy Award for Best Jazz Instrumental Album 2010) 2009, Forever (with Stanley Clarke and Lenny White) (Grammy Award for Best Jazz Instrumental Album 2012) 2011, Orvieto 2012, Further Explorations 2012, The Continents 2012, Hot House 2012, The Mothership Returns 2012, Mozart Goes Dancing (with Gary Burton) (Grammy Award for Best Instrumental Composition 2013) 2012. *Address:* Chick Corea Productions Inc., 411 Cleveland Street, No. 215, Clearwater, FL 33755, USA (office). *Telephone:* (727) 446-8100 (office). *E-mail:* writein@chickcorea.com (office). *Website:* www.chickcorea.com.

CORELL, Hans Axel Valdemar, LLB; Swedish lawyer, judge and diplomatist (retd); b. 7 July 1939, Västermo; s. of Alf Corell and Margit Norrman; m. Inger Peijfors 1964; one s. one d.; ed Univ. of Uppsala; court clerk, Eksjö Dist Court and Göta Court of Appeal 1962–67; Asst Judge, Västervik Dist Court 1968–72; Legal Adviser, Ministry of Justice 1972, 1974–79; Additional mem. and Assoc. Judge of Appeal, Svea Court of Appeal 1973; Asst Under-Sec. Div. for Constitutional and Admin. Law, Ministry of Justice 1979–81; Judge of Appeal 1980; Under-Sec. for Legal Affairs, Ministry of Justice 1981–84; Amb. and Under-Sec. for Legal and Consular Affairs, Ministry of Foreign Affairs 1984–94; mem. Perm. Court of Arbitration, The Hague 1990–2014; Under-Sec.-Gen. for Legal Affairs, The Legal Counsel of the UN 1994–2004; Sr Counsel, Mannheimer Swartling Advokatbyrå AB (law firm), Stockholm 2005–09; Chair. Bd of Trustees Raoul Wallenberg Inst. of Human Rights and Humanitarian Law 2006–12, Stockholm Centre for Int. Law and Justice 2013–; mem. Advisory Bd Int. Center for Ethics, Justice and Public Life, Brandeis Univ. 2005–; mem. Council Human Rights Inst., Int. Bar Assc 2005–; Counsellor, American Soc. of Int. Law 2006–09; mem. Int. Law Assn, ABA; Council mem.-at-large Int. Law Section 2009–(15); Hon. LLD (Stockholm) 1997, (Lund) 2007; William J. Butler Human Rights Medal, Univ. of Cincinnati Coll. of Law 2001, Cox Int. Humanitarian Award for Advancing Global Justice, Case Western Reserve Univ. 2005. *Music:* Sec.-Gen. Kofi Annan's Prayer for Peace, Hymn composed for the Great Highland Pipe 2004. *Publications include:* Sekretesslagen (co-author) 1992, Proposal for an International War Crimes Tribunal for the Former Yugoslavia (CSCE Report) (co-author) 1993; various legal publs. *Leisure interests:* art, music (Piper of the Caledonian Pipes and Drums of Stockholm 1975–84); ornithology. *Address:* Norr Mälarstrand 70, 112 35 Stockholm, Sweden. *Website:* www.havc.se.

COREY, Elias James, PhD; American chemist and academic; *Professor Emeritus of Chemistry, Harvard University;* b. 12 July 1928, Methuen, Mass.; s. of Elias J. Corey and Tina Hasham; m. Claire Higham 1961; two s. one d.; ed Mass. Inst. of Tech.; Instructor in Chem., Univ. of Ill. 1951–53, Asst Prof. of Chem. 1953–55, Prof. 1956–59; Prof. of Chem., Harvard Univ. 1959–68, Chair. Dept of Chem. 1965–68, Sheldon Emery Prof. 1968, currently Prof. Emer.; Alfred P. Sloan Foundation Fellow 1955–57, Guggenheim Fellow 1957, 1968–69; mem. American Acad. of Arts and Sciences 1960–68, NAS 1966; Hon. AM, Hon. DSc; Pure Chem. Award of ACS 1960, Fritzsche Award of ACS 1967, Intra-Science Foundation Award 1967, Harrison Howe Award, ACS 1970, Award for Synthetic Organic Chem. 1971, CIBA Foundation Award 1972, Evans Award, Ohio State Univ. 1972, Linus Pauling Award 1973, Dickson Prize in Science, Carnegie Mellon Univ. 1973, George Ledlie Prize, (Harvard) 1973, Remsen Award, Arthur C. Cope Award 1976, Nichols Medal 1977, Buchman Memorial Award (Calif. Inst. of Tech.) 1978, Franklin Medal 1978, Scientific Achievement Award Medal 1979, J. G. Kirkwood Award (Yale) 1980, C. S. Hamilton Award (Univ. of Nebraska) 1980, Chemical Pioneer Award (American Inst. of Chemists) 1981, Rosenstiel Award (Brandeis Univ.) 1982, Paul Karrer Award (Zurich Univ.) 1982, Medal of Excellence (Helsinki Univ.) 1982, Tetrahedron Prize 1983, Gibbs Award (ACS) 1984, Paracelsus Award (Swiss Chem. Soc.) 1984, V. D. Mattia Award (Roche Inst. of Molecular Biology) 1985, Wolf Prize in Chemistry (Wolf Foundation) 1986, Silliman Award (Yale Univ.) 1986, Nat. Medal of Science 1988, Japan Prize 1989, Nobel Prize for Chem. 1990, Priestley Medal of ACS 2004 and numerous other awards and honours. *Publications:* nearly 1,000 scientific publs. *Leisure interests:* outdoor activities and music. *Address:* Department of Chemistry, Harvard University, 12 Oxford Street, Cambridge, MA 02138-2902 (office); 20 Avon Hill Street, Cambridge, MA 02140, USA (home). *Telephone:* (617) 495-4033 (office); (617) 864-0627 (home). *Fax:* (617) 495-0376 (office). *E-mail:* corey@chemistry.harvard.edu (office). *Website:* www.chem.harvard.edu (office).

CORFIELD, Sir Kenneth (George), Kt, CE, FREng, FIEE, FIMechE; British business executive and engineer; b. 27 Jan. 1924, Rushall; s. of Stanley Corfield and Dorothy Elizabeth Corfield (née Mason); m. Patricia Jean Williams 1960; one d.; ed Elmore Green High School, South Staffs. Coll. of Advanced Tech.; Tech. Officer, ICI Ltd 1947–50; Chief Exec., KG Corfield Ltd, camera Mfrs 1950–61; Exec. Dir Parkinson Cowan Ltd 1962–67; Vice-Pres., Dir ITT Europe Inc. 1967–70; Man. Dir Standard Telephones and Cables Ltd 1970–85, Deputy Chair. 1974–79, Chair. and CEO 1979–85; Chair. Standard Telephones and Cables (NI) 1974–85; Vice-Pres. Int. Standard Electric Corpn, ITT Sr Officer in UK 1974–84; Chair. Nat. Econ. Devt Cttee for Ferrous Foundries Industry 1975–78; Vice-Chair. British Inst. of Man. 1978–84; Vice-Pres. Inst. of Marketing 1980–; Chair. Eng Council 1981–85, Distributed Information Processing Ltd 1987–, Octagon Investment Man. 1987–96, Gandolfi Ltd 1987–, Tanks Consolidated Investments 1990–, Linhof & Studio Ltd 1993–; Dir Midland Bank Group 1979–91, Britoil 1982–88, Vice-Pres. Eng Employers Fed. –1985; mem. Pres.'s Cttee and Council, CBI –1985; mem. Council, Inst. of Dirs. 1981–85 (Pres. 1984–85); mem. Advisory Council, Science Museum 1975–83, Trustee 1984–92; mem. Advisory Council for Applied Research and Devt 1981, Nat. Econ. Devt Cttee for Electronics 1981; Hon. FIEE; Hon. Fellow, Sheffield City Polytechnic 1983, Wolverhampton Polytechnic 1986; Dr hc (Surrey), (Open Univ.) 1985; Hon. DSc (City Univ.) 1981, (Bath) 1982, (Queen's, Belfast) 1982, (Loughborough) 1982, (Aston) 1985; Hon. LLD (Strathclyde) 1982; Hon. DSc (Eng) Univ. of London 1982; Hon. DEng (Bradford) 1983. *Publications include:* Report on Product Design for NEDC 1979, No Man an Island 1982, Patterns of Change: Collected Essays 1983. *Leisure interests:* photography, cinema, music.

CORKER, Robert Phillips (Bob), Jr, BS; American business executive and politician; *Senator from Tennessee;* b. 24 Aug. 1952, Orangeburg, SC; m. Elizabeth Corker 1987; two d.; ed Univ. of Tennessee, Knoxville; moved to Tenn. aged 11; worked for four years as construction supt then f. own construction co., Bencor, sold in 1990; purchased two largest real estate cos in Chattanooga 1999, sold most of these holdings 2006; cand. for US Senate 1994; Commr of Finance and Admin for State of Tennessee 1995–2001; Mayor of Chattanooga 2001–05; Senator from Tenn. 2007–; Republican; inducted into Entrepreneurial Hall of Fame, Univ. of Tennessee at Chattanooga. *Address:* 185 Dirksen Senate Office Building, Washington, DC 20510, USA (office). *Telephone:* (202) 224-3344 (office). *Fax:* (202) 228-0566 (office). *Website:* corker.senate.gov (office).

CORKUM, Paul Bruce, OC, BSc, MSc, PhD, FRS, FRSC; Canadian physicist; *Director of the Attosecond Science Program, National Research Council of Canada;* b. 30 Oct. 1943, Saint John, NB; ed Acadia Univ., Wolfville, NS, Lehigh Univ., Bethlehem, Pa; Post-doctoral Fellow, Nat. Research Council of Canada 1973–, Dir Attosecond Science Program, Canada Research Chair in Attosecond Photonics; Adjunct Prof. of Chem., Univ. of Toronto; Adjunct Prof. of Physics, McMaster Univ., Univ. of British Columbia, Ottawa Univ.; mem. Int. Advisory Bd Max Planck Inst. for Quantenoptik, Garching, Germany 1996–, Advisory Bd for Advanced Synchrotron Sources, Brookhaven Nat. Labs 2001, Networks of Centres of Excellence: Canadian Inst. for Photonics Innovation and Team Leader for Ultrafast Dynamic Imaging Thrust; Program Chair. Conf. on Lasers and Electro-Optics/Int. Quantum Electronics Conf. 1996, Gen. Chair. 1998; Co-Chair. two Canadian workshops on femtosecond X-rays 2001–02; Program Chair. Int. Conf. on Ultrafast Optics 2001, Gen. Chair. 2003; Co-Chair. Gordon Conf. on Control of Light with Matter and Matter with Light 2003 (Chair. 2005), Dynamic Imaging Workshop, Sherbrooke, PQ 2003, Harvard-ITAMP Workshop on Attosecond Science 2003, 10th Int. Conf. on Multiphoton Processes 2005, Ultrafast Phenomena Conf. 2006; mem. Editorial Advisory Bd International Journal of Nonlinear Optics, Editorial Bd Journal of Physics B; mem. NAS; Hon. PhD (Acadia) 2006; Canadian Asscn of Physicists' Gold Medal for Lifetime Achievement in Physics 1996, Einstein Award, Soc. for Optical and Quantum Electronics 1999, LEOS Distinguished Lecturer 2001–03, Queen's Golden Jubilee Medal 2003, RSC Tory Medal 2003, Charles Townes Award, Optical Soc. of America 2005, IEEE Quantum Electronics Award 2005, Killam Prize for Physical Sciences 2006, Arthur Schawlow Award for Quantum Electronics, American Physical Soc. 2006, NSERC Polanyi Award 2008, NSERC Gerhard Herzberg Gold Medal for Science and Eng 2009, King Faisal Int. Prize for Science (co-recipient) 2013. *Publications:* more than 170 scientific papers in professional journals. *Address:* Steacie Institute for Molecular Sciences, National Research Council of Canada, 100 Sussex Drive,

Room 2063, Ottawa, ON K1A OR6, Canada (office). *Telephone:* (613) 993-7390 (office). *Fax:* (613) 991-3437 (office). *E-mail:* paul.corkum@nrc-cnrc.gc.ca (office). *Website:* www.jaslab.ca/corkum_e.html (office).

CORLĂŢEAN, Titus, PhD; Romanian lawyer and politician; *Minister of Foreign Affairs;* b. 11 Jan. 1968, Medgidia; m. Madalina Corlăţean; one c.; ed Univ. of Bucharest, Nat. Inst. for Public Admin, Paris, Nat. Defence Coll., Bucharest; Research Asst, Romanian Inst. of Int. Studies 1993–94; Co-agent of Romanian Govt before European Court of Human Rights 1997–2001; worked at Ministry of Foreign Affairs 1994–2001; Adviser to Prime Minister on Foreign Policy Issues 2001–03, Sec. of State for Romanian Diaspora 2003–04; mem. Chamber of Deputies for Braşov CUNY 2004–07, mem. European Affairs Cttee, European Integration Cttee; Senator for Braşov 2008–12, Chair. Foreign Policy Cttee; observer to European Parl. 2005–06, mem. 2007–08; Minister of Justice May–Aug. 2012, of Foreign Affairs Aug. 2012–; mem. Social Democratic Party 2002–. *Address:* Ministry of Foreign Affairs, 011822 Bucharest, Sector 1, Al. Alexandru 31, Romania (office). *Telephone:* (21) 3192108 (office). *Fax:* (21) 3196862 (office). *E-mail:* opinia_ta@mae.ro (office). *Website:* www.mae.ro (office); www.tituscorlatean.ro.

CORLEY, Elizabeth, FRSA, FCII; British business executive and author; *CEO, Allianz Global Investors AG;* b. Luton, Beds., England; m.; one step-d.; ed Post Grad. Diploma in Man. Studies; worked for several years in life and pensions sector; Partner, Coopers & Lybrand –1994; worked at Merrill Lynch Investment Managers (fmrly Mercury Asset Management) 1993–2004, became Man. Dir and Head of EMEA Asia Pacific Mutual Fund Business as well as mem. of various bds, including MLIM UK Ltd and Merrill Lynch International Investment Funds; joined Allianz 2005, later CEO Allianz Global Investors Europe, currently CEO Allianz Global Investors, mem. Exec. Cttee of Allianz Asset Management AG (financial holding co. for Allianz's asset man. businesses); Chair. Forum of European Asset Managers 2006–07, 2010–; mem. Advisory Council TheCityUK Ltd and its Int. Regulatory Strategy Group; Dir (non-exec.) Financial Reporting Council (UK) 2011–; mem. Crime Writers' Asscn (fmr Cttee mem. and Vice-Chair.), SvB of Euler Hermes, ESMA Stakeholder Group 2014–, Investment Comm. of the British Museum; Fellow, Chartered Insurance Inst.; Europamedaille (State of Bavaria) for special merits for Bavaria in Europe 2011; named Most Influential Woman in Asset Management 2009, named by Financial News as CEO of the Year 2011, ranked by Fortune magazine amongst the 50 Most Powerful Women in Business outside the US (23rd) 2012. *Publications:* crime novels: Requiem Mass 1998, Fatal Legacy 2000, Grave Doubts 2006, Innocent Blood 2008, Dead of Winter 2013. *Leisure interests:* travel, gardening, music. *Address:* Allianz Global Investors GmbH, Seidlstrasse 24–24A, 80335 Munich, Germany (office). *Telephone:* (89) 1220-70 (office). *Fax:* (89) 1220-7900 (office). *E-mail:* info@allianzgi.com (office). *Website:* www.allianzglobalinvestors.com (office); www.allianzam.com (office); www.fantasticfiction.co.uk/c/elizabeth-corley.

CORMACK, Baron (Life Peer); cr. 2010, of Enville in the County of Staffordshire; **Patrick Thomas Cormack,** BA, FSA, FRHistS; British politician, historian, journalist and author; *Chairman, Historic Lincoln Trust;* b. 18 May 1939, Grimsby, Lincs.; m. Kathleen Mary MacDonald 1967; two s.; ed Havelock School, Univ. of Hull; Second Master, St James's Choir School 1961–66; training and educ. officer with Ross Ltd 1966–67; Asst House Master, Wrekin Coll., Wellington 1967–69; Head of History, Brewood Grammar School 1969–70; contested Labour parl. seat of Bolsover in Gen. Election 1964, hometown seat of Grimsby in Gen. Election 1966; mem. Bow Group –1971; MP (Conservative) for Cannock 1970–74, for SW Staffs. 1974–83 (South Staffs. 1983–2010); Parl. Pvt. Sec. to Dept of Health and Social Security 1970–73; mem. Educ. Select Cttee 1979–83, Chair.'s Panel 1983–; Deputy Shadow Leader of House of Commons 1997–2000; unsuccessful cand. for Speaker of House of Commons (following retirement of Betty Boothroyd) 2000, 2010; Chair. NI Select Cttee 2005–10; Chair. Historic Lincoln Trust 2011–; consultant and adviser to FIRST (int. affairs org.) 1985–; Council mem. British Archaeology 1979–83; Ed., House Magazine 1982–2005, Life Pres. 2005–; mem. Worshipful Co. of Glaziers and Painters of Glass 1979–; Rector's Warden, St Margaret's, Westminster (Parl.'s parish church) 1978–90; Trustee, Churches Preservation Trust 1972–2004, Winston Churchill Memorial Trust 1983–93; Vice-Pres. Nat. Churches Trust 2004–; Vice-Pres. Tennyson Soc. 2009–; Pres. Prayer Book Soc. 2011; Freeman of the City of London 1980; Hon. Fellow, Historical Asscn; Hon. DLitt (Hull), Hon. LLD (Catholic Univ. of America). *Publications:* numerous books on subjects ranging from the history of parliament, British castles, English cathedrals, and a book on William Wilberforce. *Address:* House of Lords, Westminster, London, SW1A 0PW, England (office). *Telephone:* (20) 7219-5353 (office). *Fax:* (20) 7219-5979 (office).

CORMAN, Igor, PhD; Moldovan diplomatist and politician; *Chairman (Speaker), Parliament (Parlamentul);* b. 17 Dec. 1969, Ciulucani; m.; two c.; ed State Univ. of Moldova, Alexandru Ioan Cuza Univ., Romania, Ludwig Maximilian Univ., Germany, George Marshall Coll., Germany; Third, Second, First Sec., Political Analysis and Planning Dept, Ministry of Foreign Affairs 1995–97, Third, Second, First Sec., responsible for Political Affairs, Chargé d'affaires a.i., Embassy in Berlin 1997–2001, Dir of Gen. Dept for Europe and N America, Ministry of Foreign Affairs 2001–03, Amb. to Germany 2004–09; mem. Parl. (Democratic Party of Moldova in Alliance for European Integration coalition) 2009–, Chair. Cttee for Foreign Policy and European Integration, Chair. (Speaker) of Parl. May 2013–; Medal 'Civil Merit' from Pres. of Moldova 2006, Great Cross of Merit of FRG 2009. *Address:* Office of the Chairman, Parlamentul, 2073 Chişinău, bd. Ştefan cel Mare 105, Moldova (office). *Telephone:* (22) 26-82-44 (office). *Fax:* (22) 23-30-12 (office). *E-mail:* inform@parlament.md (office). *Website:* www.parlament.md (office).

CORMAN, Roger William, AB, AFM; American film director and film producer; *President, New Horizons Corporation;* b. 5 April 1926, Detroit; m. Julie Ann Halloran; two s. two d.; ed Stanford Univ., Calif., Univ. of Oxford, UK; founder and Pres. New World Pictures 1970–83, New Horizons Corpn 1983–; distributed films including: Cries and Whispers, Amarcord, Fantastic Planet, The Story of Adele H, Small Change, The Tin Drum; mem. Producers' Guild of America, Directors' Guild of America; Dr hc (American Film Inst.); Lifetime Achievement Award, LA Film Critics 1997, 1st Producers of Century Award, Cannes Film Festival 1998, Award of Venice Film Festival, PGA Lifetime Achievement Award, Hon. Acad. Award 2009. *Films directed include:* Swamp Women 1955, Apache Woman 1955, Five

Guns West 1955, Day the World Ended 1956, The Oklahoma Woman 1956, It Conquered the World 1956, Naked Paradise 1957, Carnival Rock 1957, Not of This Earth 1957, Attack of the Crab Monsters 1957, The Undead 1957, Rock All Night 1957, Teenage Doll 1957, Sorority Girl 1957, The Saga of the Viking Women 1957, I Mobster 1958, War of the Satellites 1958, Machine-Gun Kelly 1958, Prehistoric World 1958, She Gods of Shark Reef 1958, A Bucket of Blood 1959, Ski Troop Attack 1960, The Wasp Woman 1960, House of Usher 1960, The Little Shop of Horrors 1960, Last Woman on Earth 1960, Atlas 1961, Creature from the Haunted Sea 1961, Pit and the Pendulum 1961, The Premature Burial 1962, The Intruder 1962, Tales of Terror 1962, Tower of London 1962, The Young Racers 1963, The Raven 1963, The Terror 1963, The Haunted Palace 1963, Man with the X-Ray Eyes 1963, The Masque of the Red Death 1964, The Secret Invasion 1964, The Tomb of Ligeia 1965, The Wild Angels 1966, The St. Valentine's Day Massacre 1967, The Trip 1967, Target: Harry 1969, Bloody Mama 1970, Gas-s-s-s 1971, The Red Baron 1971, Frankenstein Unbound 1990. *Films produced include:* more than 300 films including The Fast and the Furious 1954, Attack of the Crab Monsters 1957, Teenage Cave Man 1958, Attack of the Giant Leeches 1959, The Premature Burial 1962, Queen of Blood 1966, Big Bad Mama 1974, Death Race 2000 1975, I Never Promised You a Rose Garden 1977, Saint Jack 1979, Rage and Discipline 2004, DinoCroc 2004, Scorpius Gigantus 2005. *Film appearances include:* The Silence of the Lambs, The Godfather Part II, Philadelphia, Apollo 13, Scream 3, The Independent, A Galaxy Far Far Away. *Publication:* How I Made 100 Films in Hollywood and Never Lost a Dime (autobiog.) 1990. *Address:* c/o New Horizons Corporation, 11600 San Vicente Blvd., Los Angeles, CA 90049, USA.

CORMANN, Mathias Hubert Paul, LLB; Australian (b. Belgian) politician; *Minister of Finance;* b. 20 Sept. 1970, Eupen, Belgium; m. Hayley Cormann; ed Notre Dame Univ., Namur, Catholic Univ. of Leuven; Chief of Staff to Minister for Family and Children's Services (WA) 1997–2000; Sr Adviser to State Premier of WA 2000–01; Adviser to Minister for Justice and Customs 2001–03; Health Services Man., HBF Health Insurance 2003–04, Acting Gen. Man. 2006–07, Gen. Man. Healthguard 2004–06; mem. Senate for W Australia 2007–; Minister of Finance 2013–; mem. Liberal Party of Australia. *Address:* Department of Finance and Deregulation, John Gorton Bldg, King Edward Terrace, Parkes, ACT 2600, Australia (office). *Telephone:* (2) 6215-2222 (office). *Fax:* (2) 6273-3021 (office). *E-mail:* feedback@finance.gov.au (office). *Website:* www.finance.gov.au (office); www.mathiascormann.com.au.

CORNEJO DÍAZ, René, MBA; Peruvian engineer and politician; *Prime Minister;* b. 1962, Arequipa; ed Universidad Nacional de Ingeniería, Pontificia Universidad Católica del Perú, Escuela de Administración de Negocios para Graduados, Univ. of California, Los Angeles, USA; served as Project Man. on various public-sector and pvt. infrastructure projects; Dir FONAFE (Nat. Fund for Financing State Enterprise Activity) 2000–02; Exec. Sec. MIVIVIENDA (Mortgage Housing Promotion Fund) 2002–04; Exec. Dir PROINVERSION (Agency for the Promotion of Private Investment) 2004–07; Minister of Housing, Construction and Sanitation 2011–14, Pres. Council of Ministers (Prime Minister) 2014–; mem. Partido democratico. *Address:* Office of the President of the Council of Ministers, Jirón Carabaya, cuadra 1 s/n, Anexo 1105-1107, Lima, Peru (office). *Telephone:* (1) 2197000 (office). *Fax:* (1) 4449168 (office). *E-mail:* atencionciudadana@pcm.gob.pe (office). *Website:* www.pcm.gob.pe (office).

CORNELIS, François; Belgian business executive; *Chairman, LBC Tank Terminals;* b. 25 Oct. 1949, Uccle, Brussels; m. Colette Durant 1973; two s. two d.; ed Collège Cardinal Mercier, Universite Catholique de Louvain; joined Petrofina SA as systems engineer, subsequently Co-ordinator of Supply and Refining Operations, Brussels, Supply and Shipping Man., Petrofina UK, London, Vice-Pres., Special Asst to Pres., American Petrofina, Dallas, Tex., USA 1983–84, Gen. Man. and Asst to Pres., Petrofina 1984–86, Exec. Dir, Office of the Chair. 1986–90, CEO and Vice-Chair. 1991–99, after merger with Total Vice-Chair. of Exec. Cttee, Totalfina and Sr Vice-Pres., Petrochemicals, Paints and US Operations (after merger with Total) 1999–2000, Exec. Vice-Pres. Chemicals Div., TotalFinaElf 2000, Vice-Chair. Exec. Cttee and Pres. of Chemicals, Total SA 1999–2011, Chair. Atofina 2000–03; Chair. LBC Tank Terminals 2013–, Bpost 2013–; Chair. European Chemical Industry Council 2006–08, Royal Automobile Club of Belgium 2002–; mem. Bd of Dirs Carmeuse Group 2013–, Equis 2012–; mem. Global Advisory Council of The Conference Board and Chair. European Steering Cttee. *Address:* LBC Tank Terminals, Schaliënhoevedreef 20 E, 2800 Mechelen, Belgium (office). *E-mail:* info@lbctt.com (office). *Website:* www.lbctt.com (office).

CORNELIUS, James M., BA, MBA; American pharmaceutical industry executive; *Chairman, Bristol-Myers Squibb;* b. Kalamazoo, Mich.; m.; two c.; ed Michigan State Univ.; Pres. and CEO IVAC Corpn 1980–82; Chief Financial Officer, mem. Bd of Dirs and Exec. Bd Lilly 1983–95; Chair. Guidant Corpn 1994–2000, Chair. (non-exec.) 2000–05, Chair. and Interim CEO 2005–06, Chair. Emer. 2006–; mem. Bd of Dirs Bristol-Myers Squibb 2005–, Interim Chief Exec. 2006, CEO 2006–10, Chair. 2008–, Chair. Mead Johnson Nutrition 2009–; Pres. Cornelius Family Charitable Foundation. *Leisure interest:* American football. *Address:* Bristol-Myers Squibb, 345 Park Avenue, New York, NY 10154-0037, USA (office). *Telephone:* (212) 546-4000 (office). *Fax:* (212) 546-4020 (office). *E-mail:* info@bms.com (office). *Website:* www.bms.com (office).

CORNELL, Eric Allin, BS, PhD; American physicist and academic; *Professor Adjoint, Department of Physics, University of Colorado;* b. 1961, Palo Alto, Calif.; s. of Allin Cornell and Elizabeth Cornell (née Greenberg); m. Celeste Landry; two d.; ed Stanford Univ., Massachusetts Inst. of Tech.; Research Asst, Stanford Univ. 1982–85, MIT 1985–90; Teaching Fellow, Harvard Extension School 1989; Postdoctoral research, Jt Inst. for Lab. Astrophysics, Boulder 1990–92, Fellow 1994–; Asst Prof. Adjoint, Dept of Physics, Univ. of Colorado at Boulder 1992–95, Prof. Adjoint 1995–; Sr Scientist, Nat. Inst. of Standards and Tech., Boulder 1992–, Fellow 1994–; Fellow, American Physical Soc. 1997–, Optical Soc. of America 2000–; mem. NAS 2000–; numerous awards including Dept of Commerce Gold Medal 1996, Fritz London Prize in Low Temperature Physics 1996, King Faisal Int. Prize in Science 1997, I. I. Rabi Prize 1997, Lorentz Medal, Royal Netherlands Acad. of Arts and Sciences 1998, Benjamin Franklin Medal in Physics 1999, Nobel Prize in Physics (jt recipient) 2001. *Address:* Joint Institute for Laboratory Astrophysics, University of Colorado, Campus Box 440, Boulder, CO 80309-0440,

USA (office). *Telephone:* (303) 492-6281 (office). *Fax:* (303) 492-5235 (office). *E-mail:* cornell@jila.colorado.edu (office). *Website:* jilawww.colorado.edu/bec/CornellGroup/index.html (office); jilawww.colorado.edu (office).

CORNILLAC, Clovis; French actor; b. 16 Aug. 1967, Lyon (Rhône); s. of Roger Cornillac and Myriam Boyer; two twin d.; acted in Peter Brooke's Mahabharata 1984–86; Commdr, Ordre des Arts et des Lettres 2005; César Award for Best Supporting Actor 2005. *Films include:* Hors-la-loi (aka Outlaws) 1985, Il y a maldonne 1988, The Unbearable Lightness of Being 1988, Les années sandwiches 1988, Suivez cet avion 1989, Le trésor des îles chiennes 1990, Trois nuits 1991, Traverser le jardin 1993, Pétain 1993, Les Mickeys 1994, Les amoureux 1994, Bons baisers de Suzanne 1995, Marie-Louise ou la permission 1995, Ouvrez le chien 1997, La mère Christain 1998, Karnaval 1999, Tea Time 2001, Grégoire Moulin contre l'humanité 2001, Bois ta Suze 2002, Une affaire privée 2002, Carnages 2002, Maléfique 2002, Une affaire qui roule (aka A Great Little Business) 2003, À la petite semaine (aka Nickel and Dime) 2003, Après la pluie, le beau temps 2003, Mariées mais pas trop (aka The Very Merry Widows) 2003, Vert paradis (aka Les cadets de Gascogne, TV title) 2003, Je t'aime, je t'adore 2003, Malabar Princess 2004, Doo Wop 2004, Grossesse nerveuse 2004, La femme de Gilles 2004, Mensonges et trahisons et plus si affinités... 2004, Un long dimanche de fiançailles (A Very Long Engagement) 2004, Close-Up 2005, Brice de Nice 2005, Au suivant! 2005, Les chevaliers du ciel (Sky Fighters) 2005, Le cactus 2005, Les brigades du Tigre 2006, Poltergay 2006, Le serpent 2007, Scorpion 2007, Astérix at the Olympic Games 2008. *Television includes:* Le village sur la colline (mini-series) 1982, Tu peux toujours faire tes bagages 1984, Les cadavres exquis de Patricia Highsmith: Légitime défense (episode) 1990, Les dessous de la passion 1991, Bonne chance Frenchie (mini-series) 1992, Van Loc: un grand flic de Marseille – La Grenade (episode) 1993, Le juge est une femme: Aux marches du palais (episode) 1993, Le JAP, juge d'application des peines: Chacun sa gueule (episode) 1993, Navarro: En suivant la caillera (episode) 1994, Un été à l'envers 1994, La bavure 1994, Les cordier, juge et flic: Un si joli témoin (episode) 1995, Billard à l'étage 1996, L'échappée 1998, Les vilains 1999, Sam 1999, L'amour prisonnier 2000, L'île bleue 2001, Orages 2003, Central nuit (aka Night Squad) episodes: Nuit de chien 2001, La petite fille dans le placard 2001, Vol à la poussette 2004; Gris blanc 2005.

CORNILLET, Thierry Pierre Fernand, DèsScPol; French politician and international organization official; *President, Association Internationale des Régions Francophones;* b. 23 July 1951, Montélimar, Drôme; s. of Col Jean-Baptiste Cornillet and Inès Genoud; m. Marie-France Rossi 1983; one s. one d.; ed Lycée Alain Borne, Montélimar, Univs of Lyon II, Lyon III and Paris I–Panthéon Sorbonne; Head of Dept, Office of Dir of Civil Security at Ministry of Interior 1977–81; Head of Dept, Office of Minister of External Trade, then of Admin. Reform 1980–81; Export Man., Lagarde SA, Montélimar 1981–83; Dir Office of Deputy Mayor of Nancy 1983–85; Legal Adviser to Jr Minister, Ministry of Interior 1985–86, Chef de Cabinet 1986–88; Head of Dept, Cie nationale du Rhône 1988–93; Municipal Councillor, Montélimar 1983, Mayor 1989–99; mem. Gen. Council of Drôme 1985–93, Vice-Chair. 1992–93; mem. and Sec. Regional Council of Rhône-Alpes 1986, Vice-Pres. 1999–; mem. Assemblée nationale (UDF) from Drôme 1993–97; Vice-Chair. Parti Radical 1988–97, Chair. 1997–, mem. European Parl. 1999–, Vice-Chair. EU Jt Parl. Ass. on Africa, Caribbean, Pacific; Pres. Association Internationale des Régions Francophones; Chevalier Ordre nat. du Mérite. *Address:* European Parliament, Bât. Altiero Spinelli, 09G103, 60, rue Wiertz, 1047 Brussels, Belgium; Rhône-Alpes Regional Council, Groupe UDF, 78 route de Paris, BP 19, 69751 Charbonnières-les-Bains, France. *E-mail:* thierry.cornillet@europarl.europa.eu. *Website:* www.rhonealpes.fr; www.regions-francophones.com; www.cornillet.net.

CORNISH, (Robert) Francis, CMG, LVO, FRSA; British business executive and diplomatist (retd); *Vice Chairman, Taunton Town Centre Company;* b. 18 May 1942, Bolton; m. Alison Jane Dundas 1964; three d.; ed Charterhouse, Royal Mil. Acad., Sandhurst; commissioned 14th/20th King's Hussars and served in Libya, UK and Germany, becoming Adjutant 1966; joined HM Diplomatic Service 1968, served in Kuala Lumpur and Jakarta before becoming Head of Greek Desk, London; First Sec. (EEC), Bonn 1976–80; apptd Asst Pvt. Sec. to Prince of Wales 1980, also worked for Princess of Wales 1980–83; High Commr to Brunei 1983–86; Dir of Public Diplomacy, Washington, DC and Head of British Information Services, New York 1986–90; Head of News Dept, FCO and Spokesman for Foreign Sec. 1990–93, Sr British Trade Commr, Hong Kong 1993, first Consul-Gen. Hong Kong 1997; Sr Directing Staff, Royal Coll. of Defence Studies 1998; Amb. to Israel 1998–2001; Chair. South West Tourism Ltd 2003–2009; Chair. Taunton Town Centre Co. Ltd 2005–13, currently Vice Chair.; Dir Grosshill Properties 2002–11, Sydney & London Properties 2003–11. *Leisure interests:* farming, theatre, riding, hill walking. *Address:* Taunton Town Centre Company, Orchard, Unit 12F, First Floor, Fore Street, Taunton, TA1 3TP, England (office). *E-mail:* info@tauntontowncentre.co.uk (office).

CORNISH, William Rodolph, CMG, LLD, BCL, FBA; British/Australian barrister (retd) and academic; *Professor Emeritus of Law, University of Cambridge;* b. 9 Aug. 1937, S Australia; s. of Jack R. Cornish and Elizabeth E. Cornish; m. Lovedy E. Moule 1964; one s. two d.; ed St Peter's Coll., Adelaide and Adelaide Univ., Australia, Univ. of Oxford, UK; Lecturer in Law, LSE 1962–68; Reader in Law, Queen Mary Coll., London 1969–70; Prof. of English Law, LSE 1970–90; Prof. of Law, Univ. of Cambridge 1990–95, Dir Centre for Euro Legal Studies 1991–94, Herchel Smith Prof. of Intellectual Property Law, Univ. of Cambridge 1995–2004, Prof. Emer. 2004–; Fellow, Magdalene Coll., Cambridge 1990–, Pres. 1998–2001; Academic Dir British Law Centre, Warsaw Univ., Poland 1992–2005; External Academic mem. Max Planck Inst., Intellectual Property 1990–; Hon. QC 1997, Bencher Gray's Inn 1998; Hon. LLD (Edinburgh) 2005. *Publications:* The Jury 1968, Intellectual Property 1981–2010, Encyclopaedia of UK and European Patent Law (with others) 1978, Law and Society in England 1750–1950 1989, Oxford History of the Laws of England (Vols XI–XIII); numerous articles in legal periodicals. *Address:* Magdalene College, Cambridge, CB3 0AG, England (office). *Telephone:* (1223) 330062 (office). *Fax:* (1223) 330055 (office). *E-mail:* wrc1000@cam.ac.uk (office). *Website:* www.law.cam.ac.uk (office).

CORNWALL, HRH The Duchess of, GCVO; British b. (Camilla Rosemary Shand), 17 July 1947, London, England; d. of the late Maj. Bruce Shand and Hon. Rosalind Cubitt; m. 1st Andrew Parker Bowles 1973 (divorced); one s. one d.; m.

2nd HRH The Prince of Wales 2005; ed Dumbrells School, Sussex, Queen's Gate School, South Kensington, Mon Fertile, Switzerland, Institut Britannique, Paris; made debut in London 1965; Patron, Animal Care Trust, Cornwall Community Foundation, Friends of Westonbirt Arboretum, London Chamber Orchestra, New Queen's Hall Orchestra, Public Catalogue Foundation's Cornish Catalogue, Soc. of Chiropodists and Podiatrists, St John's Smith Square Charitable Trust, Unicorn Theatre for Children, Wiltshire Bobby Van Trust, Youth Action Wiltshire; Pres. Nat. Osteoporosis Soc., Scotland's Gardens Scheme. *Address:* Clarence House, St James's Palace, London, SW1A 1BA, England. *Website:* www.princeofwales.gov.uk.

CORNWELL, Andrew, BSc, MSc; British politician and journalist; *Councillor and Executive Member for Finance, London Borough of Islington;* b. 30 Sept. 1966, London; ed London School of Econs; financial journalist 1988–98; mem. Bd London Pensions Fund Authority 2001–06; European Media Officer BOND (British Overseas NGOs for Devt) 2001; Green Party cand in Gen. Election 2001; Chair. Green Party of England and Wales 2002–03; Vice-Chair. Green Liberal Democrats 2004–; Councillor and Exec. Mem. for Finance, London Borough of Islington 2006–. *Address:* London Borough of Islington, Town Hall, Upper Street, London, N1 2UD, England (office). *Telephone:* (20) 7527-2986 (office). *E-mail:* andrew.cornwell@islington.gov.uk (office). *Website:* www.islington.gov.uk (office).

CORNWELL, Bernard, (Susannah Kells), OBE, BA; British writer; b. 23 Feb. 1944, London; m. Judy Acker 1980; ed Univ. of London. *Publications include:* Redcoat 1987, Wildtrack 1988, Sea Lord (aka Killer's Wake) 1989, Crackdown (aka Murder Cay) 1990, Stormchild 1991, Scoundrel 1992, Stonehenge 2000 BC 1999, The Archer's Tale 2001, The Last Kingdom 2004, The Pale Horseman 2005, Lords of the North Country 2006, Agincourt 2008, The Burning Land 2009, The Fort 2010; Starbuck Chronicles series: Rebel 1993, Copperhead 1994, Battle Flag 1995, The Bloody Ground 1996; Arthur series: The Winter King 1995, Enemy of God 1996, Excalibur 1997; Sharpe series: Sharpe's Eagle 1981, Sharpe's Gold 1981, Sharpe's Company 1982, Sharpe's Sword 1983, Sharpe's Enemy 1984, Sharpe's Honour 1985, Sharpe's Regiment 1986, Sharpe's Siege 1987, Sharpe's Rifles 1988, Sharpe's Revenge 1989, Sharpe's Waterloo 1990, Sharpe's Devil 1992, Sharpe's Battle 1995, Sharpe's Tiger 1997, Sharpe's Triumph 1998, Sharpe's Fortress 1999, Sharpe's Trafalgar 2000, Sharpe's Prey 2001, Sharpe's Skirmish (short story) 2002, Sharpe's Havoc 2003, Sharpe's Escape 2004, Sharpe's Fury 2006; Grail Quest series: Harlequin 2000, Heretic 2003; as Susannah Kells: A Crowning Mercy 1983, The Fallen Angels 1984, Coat of Arms 1986, The Aristocrats 1987. *Address:* Toby Eady Associates Ltd, Third Floor, 9 Orme Court, London, W2 4RL, England (office). *Telephone:* (20) 7792-0092 (office). *Fax:* (20) 7792-0879 (office). *E-mail:* toby@tobyeady.demon.co.uk (office). *Website:* www.tobyeadyassociates.co.uk (office); www.bernardcornwell.net (office).

CORNWELL, David John Moore, (John le Carré), BA; British writer; b. 19 Oct. 1931, Poole, Dorset, England; s. of Ronald Thomas Archibald Cornwell and Olive Glassy; m. 1st Alison Ann Veronica Sharp 1954 (divorced 1971); three s.; m. 2nd Valerie Jane Eustace 1972; one s.; ed St Andrew's Preparatory School, Pangbourne, Sherborne School, Berne Univ., Switzerland and Lincoln Coll., Oxford; teacher, Eton Coll. 1956–58; in Foreign Service (Second Sec., Bonn, then Political Consul Hamburg) 1959–64; Hon. Fellow, Lincoln Coll., Oxford 1984–; Commdr des Arts et des Lettres 2005; Hon. DLitt (Exeter) 1990, (St Andrews) 1996, (Southampton) 1997, (Bath) 1998, (Berne Univ., Switzerland) 2008, (Oxford) 2012; Somerset Maugham Award 1963, MWA Edgar Allan Poe Award 1965, James Tait Black Award 1977, CWA Gold Dagger 1978, MWA 'Grand Master Award' 1986, Premio Malaparte 1987, CWA Diamond Dagger 1988, Nikos Kazantzakis Prize 1991, CWA 'Dagger of Daggers' 2005, Sunday Times Award for Literary Excellence 2010, Goethe Medal (Germany) 2011. *Publications:* Call for the Dead 1961, Murder of Quality 1962, The Spy Who Came in from the Cold 1963, The Looking Glass War 1965, A Small Town in Germany 1968, The Naive and Sentimental Lover 1971, Tinker, Tailor, Soldier, Spy 1974, The Honourable Schoolboy 1977, Smiley's People 1979, The Quest for Karla (collected edn of previous three titles) 1982, The Little Drummer Girl 1983, A Perfect Spy 1986, The Russia House 1989, The Secret Pilgrim 1991, The Night Manager 1993, Our Game 1995, The Tailor of Panama 1996, Single and Single 1999, The Constant Gardener (British Book Awards Play.com TV & Film Book of the Year 2006) 2000, Absolute Friends 2004, The Mission Song 2006, A Most Wanted Man 2008, Our Kind of Traitor 2010, A Delicate Truth 2013. *Address:* c/o Curtis Brown Ltd, 28–29 Haymarket, London, SW1Y 4SP, England (office). *Telephone:* (20) 7393-4400 (office). *Fax:* (20) 7393-4401 (office). *E-mail:* cb@curtisbrown.co.uk (office). *Website:* www.curtisbrown.co.uk (office); www.johnlecarre.com (office).

CORNWELL, Patricia Daniels, BA; American writer; b. 9 June 1957, Miami, Fla; ed Davidson Coll.; police reporter, Charlotte Observer, NC 1979–81; computer analyst, Office of the Chief Medical Examiner, Richmond, Va 1985–91; mem. Authors Guild, Int. Asscn of Identification, Int. Crime Writers Asscn, Nat. Asscn of Medical Examiners; Investigative Reporting Award, North Carolina Press Asscn 1980, Gold Medallion Book Award, Evangelical Christian Publishers Asscn 1985, Edgar Award 1990, Prix du Roman d'Aventure 1991, Gold Dagger Award 1993, Sherlock Holmes Award 1999. *Publications include:* non-fiction: A Time of Remembering: The Story of Ruth Bell Graham 1983 (re-issued as Ruth: a Portrait 1997); fiction: Postmortem (John Creasey Award, British Crime Writers' Asscn 1991, Anthony Award, Boucheron Award, World Mystery Convention, MacAvity Award, Mystery Readers Int) 1990, Body of Evidence 1991, All That Remains 1992, Cruel and Unusual 1993, The Body Farm 1994, From Potter's Field 1995, Cause of Death 1996, Hornet's Nest 1996, Unnatural Exposure 1997, Point of Origin 1998, Southern Cross 1999, Black Notice 1999, The Last Precinct 2001, Isle of Dogs 2001, Portrait of a Killer: Jack the Ripper 2002, Blow Fly 2003, Trace 2004, Predator 2005, At Risk 2006, Book of the Dead (British Book Award for Best Crime Thriller 2008) 2007, Scarpetta 2008, The Front 2008, The Scarpetta Factor 2009, Port Mortuary 2010, Red Mist (RBA Int. Thriller Prize) 2011, The Bone Bed 2012, Dust 2013. *Address:* c/o Don Congdon Associates Inc., 156 5th Avenue, Suite 625, New York, NY 10010-7002, USA. *Website:* www.patriciacornwell.com.

CORNYN, John, LLM; American politician; *Senator from Texas;* b. 2 Feb. 1952, Houston, Tex.; s. of John Cornyn and Gale Cornyn; m. Sandy Cornyn; two d.; ed Trinity Univ. and St Mary's School of Law, San Antonio, Univ. of Virginia Law School; Dist Court Judge, San Antonio 1984–90; elected to Tex. Supreme Court

1990, re-elected 1996; Attorney-Gen. of Tex. 1997–2003; Senator from Tex. 2003–, fmr Vice-Chair. Senate Republican Conf., Chair. Nat. Republican Senatorial Cttee 2008–, mem. Finance, Judiciary, Armed Services, and Budget Cttees; mem. Bush-Cheney Transition Advisory Cttee 2000; St Mary's Distinguished Law School Grad. 1994; Trinity Univ. Distinguished Alumnus 2001; Outstanding Texas Leader Award, John Ben Shepperd Foundation of Texas 2000, James Madison Award, Freedom of Information Foundation of Texas 2001, Border Texan of the Year Award 2005, Children's Champion Award, Nat. Child Support Enforcement Asscn, Friend of Farm Bureau Award, American Farm Bureau Fed., Fighter for Free Enterprise Award, Texas Asscn of Business, Guardian of Small Business Award, Nat. Fed. of Ind. Business, Latino Leadership Award, Nat. Coalition of Latino Clergy and Christian Leader (CONLAMIC), Int. Leadership Legis. Award, Texas Asscn of Mexican American Chambers of Commerce, amongst others. *Address:* 517 Hart Senate Office Building, Washington, DC 20510, USA (office). *Telephone:* (202) 224-2934 (office). *Fax:* (202) 228-2856 (office). *Website:* cornyn .senate.gov (office).

CORONEL, Sheila S., BA, MA; Philippine journalist and academic; *Toni Stabile Professor of Professional Practice in Investigative Journalism, Columbia University;* b. 1958, Manila; ed Univ. of the Philippines, London School of Econs, UK; began as cub reporter for Philippine Panorama 1983; reporter for The Manila Times, Manila Chronicle; Co-founder and Exec. Dir Philippine Center for Investigative Journalism 1989–2006; Dir, Toni Stabile Center for Investigative Journalism, Columbia Univ., currently Toni Stabile Prof. of Professional Practice in Investigative Journalism; Ramón Magsaysay Award for Journalism 2003, Presidential Teaching Award, Columbia Univ. 2011. *Publications:* more than 12 books, including Coups, Cults and Cannibals, The Rulemakers, Pork and Other Perks. *Address:* Toni Stabile Center for Investigative Journalism, School of Journalism, Columbia University, 2950 Broadway, New York, NY 10027, USA (office). *Telephone:* (212) 854-5748 (office). *E-mail:* ssc2136@columbia.edu (office). *Website:* www.stabilecenter.org (office).

COROPCEAN, Div. Gen. Ion; Moldovan army officer; *Chief of General Staff, Commander of the National Army of the Republic;* b. 11 March 1960, Liveden' vill; s. of Ştefan Coropcean; m. Valentina Coropcean; one s. one d.; ed Poltava Mil. Air Defence High School, Mil. Air Defence Acad.; cadet 1977–81, Air Defence Platoon Commdr 1981–84, Air Defence Battery Commdr 1984–87, Air Defence Bn Commdr 1987–88, Air Defence Acad. 1988–91, Chief of Staff and Deputy Commdr Air Defence Regt 1991–92, Deputy Commdr Air Defence Brigade 1992–97, Commdr Mil. Coll. 1997–98, Chief of Gen. Staff Nat. Army and Deputy Minister of Defence 1998–2006, Chief of Gen. Staff, Commdr Nat. Army 2006–; Medal of Courage, Medal of Mil. Merit, Award for Allegiance to the Motherland. *Publications:* The Foreign Policy of the Republic of Moldova in the Context of Integration Processes: Interests and Priorities. *Leisure interests:* books, football, literature. *Address:* ŞOS. Hinceşti 84, 2021 Chişinău (office); str. Alba Julia 200/1, Ap. 100, 2071 Chişinău, Republic of Moldova (home). *Telephone:* (2) 252444 (office); (2) 514874 (home). *Fax:* (2) 234434 (office). *E-mail:* coropcei@md.pims.org (office); ion .coropcean@army.md (home). *Website:* www.army.md (office).

CORREA, Charles M., BArch, MArch; Indian architect and planner; b. 1 Sept. 1930, Secunderabad, AP; s. of Carlos Marcos Correa and Ana Florinda de Heredia; m. Monika Sequeira 1961; one s. one d.; ed Univ. of Bombay, Univ. of Michigan and Massachusetts Inst. of Tech., USA; Prin., Charles Correa Assocs, Mumbia (pvt. practice) 1958–; Chief Architect Navi Mumbai 1971–74, mem. Bd of Dirs CIDCO (Navi Mumbai) 1975–89; Consulting Architect, Govt of Karnataka 1975–78; Chair. Housing Urban Renewal and Ecology Bd, Mumbai 1975–83; Chair. Nat. Comm. on Urbanization 1985–88; Pres. World Soc. of EKISTICS, Athens 1996–98; Consulting Architect, Govt of Goa 1999–; Farwell Bernis Prof., MIT, USA 2001–; Chair. Delhi Urban Arts Comm. 2005–08; Founder-mem. Indian Nat. Trust for Art and Cultural Heritage 1983, Trust for Urban Design Research Inst. 1984; Fellow, Indian Inst. of Architects 1964–; mem. Council of Architecture 1974–; Hon. FAIA 1979; Hon. FRIBA 1993; Hon. Fellow, Acad. d'Architecture Français 1985, Int. Acad. of Architecture, Sofia, Bulgaria 1987, United Architects of the Philippines 1990, Finnish Asscn of Architects 1992, American Acad. of Arts and Sciences 1993, Royal Inst. of Architects of Ireland 1997, American Acad. of Arts and Letters 1998, Trinidad Inst. of Architects 1999, Royal Architectural Inst. of Canada 2002; Dr hc (Univ. of Michigan) 1980; Padma Shri, Pres. of India 1972, Padma Vibhushan, Pres. of India 2006; RIBA Gold Medal 1984, Gold Medal, Indian Inst. of Architects 1987, Gold Medal, Int. Union of Architects 1990, Praemium Imperiale for Architecture, Japan Art Asscn 1994, Aga Khan Award for Architecture 1998. *Major works include:* Mahatma Gandhi Memorial Museum, Sabarmati Ashram, Ahmedabad, Kovalam Beach Devt, Kerala, Kanchanjunga apartments, Mumbai, Cidade de Goa, Dona Paula, New India Centre, Delhi, Performing Arts Centre, Kala Acad., Goa, Previ low-income housing, Peru, Bharat Bhavan, Bhopal, Jawahar Kala Kendra, Jaipur, Nat. Crafts Museum, Delhi, British Council, Delhi, IUCCA, Pune Univ. *Publication:* The New Landscape 1985, Housing and Urbanisation 1999. *Leisure interests:* model railways, old films, swimming. *Address:* Charles Correa Associates, 9 Mathew Road, Mumbai 400 004 (office); Sonmarg, Nepean Sea Road, Mumbai 400 006, India (home). *Telephone:* (22) 23633307 (office); (22) 23633306 (home). *Fax:* (22) 23631138 (office). *E-mail:* cmc@charlescorrea.net (office). *Website:* www.charlescorrea.net (office).

CORREA DELGADO, Rafael, MSc, PhD; Ecuadorean economist, politician and head of state; *President;* b. 6 April 1963, Guayaquil; ed Universidad Católica de Santiago de Guayaquil, Catholic Univ. of Louvain, Belgium, Univ. of Illinois, USA; teaching asst, Econs Faculty, Universidad Católica de Santiago de Guayaquil 1983–85, Assoc. Prof. 1988–1989; Industrial Specialist, Centre of Industrial Devt 1984–87; volunteer in Mission of the Salesian Fathers, Zumbahua, Cotopaxi 1987–88; Admin. Dir in charge of educational projects financed by IDB 1992–93; Head Prof., Dept of Econs, Universidad San Francisco de Quito 1993–2005; Minister of the Economy following overthrow of Lucio Gutierrez April–Aug. 2005 (resgnd); Founder, Alianza PAIS (Patria Altiva i Soberana); Pres. of Ecuador 2007–. *Publications:* El Reto del Desarrollo: ¿Estamos Preparados para el Futuro? 1996, La Vulnerabilidad de la Economía Ecuatoriana 2004; numerous journal contribs. *Address:* Office of the President, Palacio Nacional, García Moreno 1043, Quito (office); Diego de Almagro N32-27 y Whimper, Edif. Torres Whimper, Of. 501, Quito, Ecuador. *Telephone:* (2) 221-6300 (office); (2) 600-0630; (2) 600-1029.

E-mail: info@rafaelcorrea.com. *Website:* www.presidencia.gov.ec (office); www .rafaelcorrea.com.

CORREIA, Carlos; Guinea-Bissau politician; b. 6 Nov. 1933; mem. Partido Africano da Indepêndencia da Guiné e Cabo Verde (PAIGC) –1999; fmr Minister of State for Rural Devt and Agric.; Prime Minister of Guinea-Bissau 1991–94, 1997–98, Aug.–Dec. 2008; fmr Perm. Sec. Council of State; fmr Gov. for Guinea Bissau, African Devt Bank. *Address:* c/o Office of the Prime Minister, Av. Unidade Africana, CP 137, Bissau, Guinea-Bissau.

CORRELL, A(lston) D(ayton) (Pete), MS; American paper industry executive; *Chairman Emeritus, Georgia–Pacific Corporation;* b. 28 April 1941, Brunswick, Ga; s. of Alston Dayton Correll and Elizabeth Correll (née Flippo); m. Ada Lee Fulford 1963; one s. one d.; ed Univs of Georgia and Maine; tech. service engineer, Westvaco 1963–64; instructor, Univ. of Maine (Orono) 1964–67; various positions in pulp and paper man., Weyerhaeuser Co. 1967–77; Div. Pres., Paperboard, Mead Corpn 1977–80, Group Vice-Pres. 1980–83, Sr Vice-Pres., Forest Products 1983–88; Sr Vice-Pres., Pulp and Printing Paper, Georgia–Pacific Corpn 1988–89, Exec. Vice-Pres., Pulp and Paper 1989–91, Pres., COO 1991–93, CEO 1993–2005, Chair. 1993–2006, Chair. Emer. 2006–; mem. Bd of Dirs Univ. of Maine Pulp and Paper Foundation (Vice-Pres.), Engraph Inc., Trust Co. Bank of Atlanta, Trust Co. of Ga, Atlanta Chamber of Commerce, Atlanta Symphony Orchestra, Robert W. Woodruff Arts Center; Nat. Brotherhood Award 1991, Distinguished Alumnus Award, Univ. Georgia Terry Coll. of Business 1994, Salute to Greatness Award, The King Center 1999, Atlanta Urban League Distinguished Community Service Award 2001, Oglethorpe Sword, British American Business Group 2002, Silver Hope Award, Nat. Multiple Sclerosis Soc. 2003, CEO of the Year, Business to Business Magazine 2004, Paperloop CEO of the Year 2005; elected Business Hall of Fame, Georgia State Univ. 2005. *Address:* Georgia-Pacific Corporation, PO Box 105605, 133 Peachtree Street, NE, Atlanta, GA 30303-1808, USA (office). *Telephone:* (404) 652-4000 (office). *Fax:* (404) 230-1674 (office). *Website:* www.gp.com (office).

CORRIGAN, E(dward) Gerald, BS, MA, PhD; American banker and economist; *Partner and Managing Director, Goldman Sachs & Co.;* b. 3 June 1941, Waterbury, Conn.; m. Cathy Minehan; ed Fairfield and Fordham Univs; Group Vice-Pres. (Man. and Planning) Fed. Reserve Bank of New York 1976–80, Pres. 1985–93; Special Asst to Chair., Bd of Govs Fed. Reserve System, Washington, DC 1979–80; Pres. Fed. Reserve Bank of Minneapolis 1981–84; Chair. Basel Cttee on Banking Supervision 1991–93; Chair. Int. Advisers, Goldman Sachs & Co. 1994–96, Man. Dir 1996–, now Partner and Man. Dir, Chair. GS USA (bank holding co.) 2008–, Co-Chair. firm-wide Risk Man. Cttee, Vice-Chair. firm-wide Business Practices Cttee, mem. firm-wide Commitments Cttee; Chair. Russian-American Enterprise Fund 1993; Chair. Counterparty Risk Man. Policy Group 1999–; Pres. BRI 1991–; mem. Trilateral Comm. 1986–, Group of Thirty Consultative Group on Int. Econ. and Monetary Affairs, Inc. (G-30), Washington, DC; Trustee, Macalester Coll. 1981–, Jt Council for Econ. Educ. 1981–, Fairfield Univ. 1985–; chair., trustee or mem. of several non-profit orgs; Fellow, American Acad. of Arts and Sciences 2005; Alumni Professional Achievement Award, Fairfield Univ. 1981, Risk Man. of the Year, Global Asscn of Risk Professionals 2006. *Address:* Goldman Sachs & Co., 200 West Street, New York, NY 10282, USA (office). *Telephone:* (212) 902-1000 (office). *Website:* www2.goldmansachs.com (office).

CORRIGAN, (Francis) Edward, MA, PhD (Cantab.), FRS; British mathematician and academic; *Professor of Mathematics and Head of Department, University of York;* b. 10 Aug. 1946, Birkenhead, Merseyside, England; s. of the late Anthony Corrigan and Eileen Corrigan (née Ryan); m. Jane Mary Halton 1970; two s. two d.; ed St Bede's Coll., Manchester, Christ's Coll., Cambridge; Addison Wheeler Fellow, Durham Univ. 1972–74; CERN Fellow, CERN, Geneva 1974–76; Lecturer, Durham Univ. 1976, Reader 1987, Prof. of Math. 1992–99, Visiting Prof. 1999–2007, Prof. of Math. and Prin. of Collingwood Coll. 2008–11; Prof. of Math., Univ. of York 1999–2007, 2011–, Head of Dept 1999–2004, 2005–07, 2011–; Visiting Prof., Centre for Partide Theory, Kyoto Univ. 2005; Visiting Research Assoc., ENS-Lyon 2005, Univ. of Bologna 2005; Life mem. Clare Hall, Cambridge 1992–; Ed.-in-Chief, Journal of Physics A 1999–2003; Adrian-Daiwa Prize 1998. *Publications:* more than 95 articles in learned journals and conf. proceedings. *Leisure interests:* music, squash, walking. *Address:* University of York, Department of Mathematics, Heslington, York, YO10 5DD (office); Panmure Cottage, Gate Helmsley, Yorks., YO41 1NE, England (home). *Telephone:* (1904) 433074 (office). *Fax:* (1904) 323071 (office). *E-mail:* edward.corrigan@york.ac.uk (office). *Website:* maths.york.ac.uk/www/ec9 (office).

CORSEPIUS, Uwe; German economist and international organization official; *Secretary General, Council of the European Union;* b. 9 Aug. 1960, Berlin; m.; two c.; ed Univ. of Erlangen-Nuremberg, Kiel Inst. for World Econs; Research Fellow, Kiel Inst. for World Econs 1985–89; Economist, Int. Econ. Policy Div., Fed. Ministry of Econs 1990; Economist, Policy Dept, IMF, Washington, DC 1992–94; several positions with German Fed. Chancellery including Economist, Directorate for Gen. Econ. Questions 1991–92, Div. for Gen. Econ. Policy 1994–96, Private Sec. to Dir-Gen. 1995, Head of Div. for Econ. Issues relating to European Integration 1997–99, Head of Div. for G8, IMF, WTO and International Financial Market Issues 1999–2003, Head of Group for European Policy Coordination, Econ. Aspects of European Integration 2003–05, Dir-Gen., European Policy Adviser to Fed. Chancellor 2006–11, G8-Sherpa Feb.–June 2011; Sec.-Gen. Council of the EU, Brussels 2011–. *Address:* Council of the European Union, 175 rue de la Loi, 1048 Brussels, Belgium (office). *Telephone:* (2) 281-61-11 (office). *Fax:* (2) 281-69-34 (office). *Website:* www.consilium.europa.eu (office).

CORSTENS, Geert J. M., PhD; Dutch judge; *President, Supreme Court of the Netherlands;* b. 1 Feb. 1946, Helvoirt; m. Madeleine Mignot; three d.; ed Radboud Univ., Nijmegen, Univ. of Amsterdam; Asst Public Prosecutor, Amsterdam 1973–1975; Law Clerk, Dist Court of Amsterdam 1975–1976; lawyer, Goudsmit & Branbergen (law firm), Amsterdam 1976–1977; Public Prosecutor, Arnhem 1977–1981; Prof. of Criminal Law, Catholic Univ., Nijmegen, 1982–1995; Visiting Prof., Univ. of Poitiers 1986; Justice, Supreme Court of the Netherlands 1995–2006, Vice-Pres. 2006–08, Pres. 2008–; Pres. Advisory Bd Nat. Research Project on Criminal Procedure 1998–2003, on the Quality of Criminal Judgements

2005–; mem. Bd and Pres. Advisory Bd, Dutch Law Asscn 1983–86, Nat. Cttee for the Reform of Criminal Procedure 1989–93; mem. Bd of Int. Advisors, Int. Judicial Acad., Washington, DC 2001–; mem. and Pres. Editorial Bd Nederlands Juristenblad 1995–2005; Pres. Network of Presidents of Highest Judicial Courts in the EU; Appointing Authority, Iran–US Claims Tribunal; Officier, Ordre des Palmes académiques, Chevalier, Légion d'honneur; Dr hc (Antwerp) 2011. *Publications:* several books, including European Criminal Law (with Jean Pradel) 2002, Droit pénal européen (third edn) 2009, Het Nederlands strafprocesrecht (seventh edn) 2011; more than 350 contribs to nat. and int. and legal journals. *Address:* Hoge Raad der Nederlanden, PO Box 20303, 2500 EH The Hague, Netherlands (office). *Telephone:* (70) 3611237 (office). *Fax:* (70) 7530347 (office). *E-mail:* president@hogeraad.nl (office). *Website:* www.hogeraad.nl (office).

CORT, Errol; Antigua and Barbuda politician, economist and lawyer; *Minister of National Security and Labour;* m.; c.; ed trained as economist and attorney; Attorney-Gen. of Antigua and Barbuda 1999–2001; elected mem. Parl. for St John's E; Minister of Finance, Econ. Devt and Planning 2004–09, of Nat. Security and Labour 2009–. *Address:* Ministry of National Security and Labour, Government Office Complex, Parliament Drive, St John's, Antigua (office).

CORTAZZI, Sir (Henry Arthur) Hugh, Kt, GCMG, MA (Hons); British diplomatist (retd); b. 2 May 1924, Sedbergh, Yorks. (now Cumbria), England; s. of F. E. M. Cortazzi and M. Cortazzi; m. Elizabeth Esther Montagu 1956; one s. two d.; ed Sedbergh School, Univs of St Andrews and London; served in RAF 1943–48; joined Foreign Office 1949; Third Sec., Singapore 1950–51; Second Sec., Tokyo 1951–54; Foreign Office, London 1954–58; First Sec., Bonn 1958–60, Tokyo 1961–65 (Head of Chancery 1963); Foreign Office 1965–66; Counsellor (Commercial), Tokyo 1966–70; Royal Coll. of Defence Studies 1971; Minister (Commercial), Washington, DC 1972–75; Deputy Under-Sec. of State, FCO 1975–80; Amb. to Japan 1980–84 (retd); apptd Dir Hill Samuel and Co. Ltd (later Hill Samuel Bank Ltd) 1984–91, Foreign and Colonial Pacific Investment Trust 1984–98, G.T. Japan Investment Trust 1984–99, Thornton Pacific Investment Trust SA 1986–2002; Adviser to Mitsukoshi Dept Store, Tokyo, Japan 1984–2004; Sr Adviser, NEC Corpn, Japan 1992–98, Dai-Ichi Kangyo Bank, Japan 1992–99, Bank of Kyoto 1992–99, Wilde Sapte, solicitors 1992–99; mem. Econ. and Social Research Council 1984–90; Hon. Fellow, Robinson Coll., Cambridge 1988; Grand Cordon, Order of the Sacred Treasure (Japan) 1995; Hon. DUniv (Stirling) 1988, Hon. DLitt (East Anglia) 2006; Yamagata Banto Prize, Osaka 1990. *Publications include:* trans. of Japanese short stories by Keita Genji 1972, A Diplomat's Wife in Japan: Sketches at the Turn of the Century (ed.) 1982, Higashi No Shimaguni, Nishi No Shimaguni 1984, Dr Willis in Japan (1862–1877) 1985, Mitford's Japan (ed.) 1985, Zoku Higashi No Shimaguni, Nishi No Shimaguni (ed.) 1987, Victorians in Japan: In and Around the Treaty Ports 1987, Kipling's Japan (ed.) 1988, The Japanese Achievement, A Short History of Japan and Japanese Culture 1990, A British Artist in Meiji Japan (ed.) 1991, Building Japan 1868–1876 1991, Modern Japan: A Concise Survey 1993, Caught In Time: Japan (ed.) 1995, Japan and Back and Places Elsewhere: A Memoir 1998, Japan Experiences (ed.) 2001, Britain and Japan: Biographical Portraits Vol. IV (ed.) 2002, Vol. V (ed.) 2004, Vol. VI (ed.) 2007, Vol. VII (ed.) 2010, Vol. VIII (ed.) 2012, British Envoys in Japan 1859–1972 (ed.) 2004, The Thames and I: A Memoir by the Crown Prince of Japan (trans.) 2007, Britain and the Re-opening of Japan: The Treaty of Yedo of 1858 and the Elgin Mission 2008, Japan in Late Victorian London, The Japanese Village in Knightsbridge and the Mikado 1857 2009, Images of Japan 1885–1912 2011, Scenes, Tales and Flowers 2011, Miscellany of Japanese Sketchbooks and Print Albums 2013. *Leisure interests:* the arts, literature, Japanese studies. *Address:* Ballsocks, Vines Cross, Heathfield, East Sussex, TN21 9ET, England (home).

CORTES, Joaquín; Spanish dancer and actor; b. 22 Feb. 1969, Córdoba; joined Spanish Nat. Ballet 1985, Prin. Dancer 1987–90; f. Joaquín Cortés Flamenco Ballet 1992; now appears in own shows, blending gypsy dancing, jazz blues and classical ballet; appeared in Pedro Almodóvar's film The Flower Of My Secret and Carlos Saura's film Flamenco; launched Stop Anti-Gypsyism campaign 2000; apptd Amb. for the Roma people to EU 2007. *Films include:* Flamenco (de Carlos Saura) 1995, Flor de mi secreto, La 1995, Gitano 2000, Vaniglia e cioccolato 2004. *Television includes:* Sabadabada (series) 1981, Hola Raffaella! (series) 1992. *Address:* C/ Alcalá, 155. E.Izda. 2ºC, Madrid, Spain. *Telephone:* (91) 7580350. *Fax:* (91) 5595245.

CORTINA DE ALCOCER, Alfonso, BEng; Spanish business executive; *President, Fundación Repsol;* b. 13 March 1944, Madrid; ed Univ. of Madrid; Vice-Pres. Sociedad Hispano Hipotecario 1981–84; Vice-Pres. Cementera Portland Valderrivas 1984–93, Pres. 1993–96; CEO Repsol YPF 1996–2004, Pres. Fundación Repsol 2004–; Chair. Inmobiliaria Colonial 2005–06; Vice Chair. Rothschild Europe and Sr Adviser for Spain and Latin America and mem. European Advisory Council, Rothschild; Sr Adviser Texas Pacific Group, Madrid 2007–; mem. Exec. Cttee Foundation for Technological Innovation; mem. Bd of Dirs Mutua Madrileña Automovilística Sociedad de Seguros a Prima Fija, Recoletos Grupo de Comunicación SA; mem. Int. Advisory Bd and Jt Advisory Council, Allianz Companies; mem. Advisory Cttee Altamar Private Equity; mem. Trilateral Comm. *Address:* Fundación Repsol, Velázquez, 166, 28002 Madrid, Spain. *Telephone:* (91) 3489079. *Fax:* (91) 3489370. *E-mail:* fundacion@fundacion.repsolypf.org.

CORVALÁN MENDOZA, Jorge Raúl, MSc; Paraguayan economist and central banker; *President, Banco Central del Paraguay;* b. 23 April 1969, Asunción; ed Univ. Nacional de Asunción, Univ. of Illinois, Urbana - Champaign, USA; Prof., Inst. of Devt, Univ. Nacional de Asunción 2002–; Gen. Coordinator, devt project financed by Japanese Govt and World Bank, Carapeguá and Nemby municipalities 2006–08; Dir-Gen., Minister's Technical Cabinet, Ministry of Industry and Commerce 2006; Dir, Int. Econs Dept, Banco Central del Paraguay 2001–05, Pres. Banco Central del Paraguay 2008–. *Address:* Office of the President, Banco Central del Paraguay, Avda Federación Rusa y Cabo 1º Marecos, Casilla 861, Barrio Santo Domingo, Asunción, Paraguay (office). *Telephone:* (21) 60-8011 (office). *Fax:* (21) 619-2328 (office). *E-mail:* informaciones@bcp.gov.py (office). *Website:* www.bcp.gov.py (office).

CORY, Suzanne, AC, PhD, FAA, FRS; Australian biochemist, geneticist and academic; *Research Professor, Molecular Genetics of Cancer Division, The Walter and Eliza Hall Institute, University of Melbourne;* b. 11 March 1942, Melbourne;

m. Dr Jerry McKee Adams; two d.; ed Canterbury Girls' Secondary School, Univ. High School, Univ. of Melbourne, MRC Laboratory of Molecular Biology, UK; Postdoctoral Fellow, Univ. of Geneva, Switzerland 1969–71; Queen Elizabeth II Fellow, Univ. of Melbourne Walter and Eliza Hall Inst. of Medical Research 1971–74, Roche Fellow 1974–76, Research Fellow 1977, Sr Research Fellow 1978–83, Prin. Research Fellow 1984–88, NHMRC Sr Prin. Research Fellow and Jt Head, Molecular Genetics of Cancer Div. 1988–96, Research Prof. of Molecular Oncology, Univ. of Melbourne 1993–96, Dir Walter and Eliza Hall Inst. 1996–2009, currently Research Prof., Molecular Genetics of Cancer Div., also Vice-Chancellor's Fellow; Int. Research Scholar, Howard Hughes Medical Inst. 1992–97; Pres. Australian Acad. of Science 2010–; Dir Bio21 Australia Ltd; mem. Bd CSIRO 2002–; mem. Knowledge, Innovation, Science and Eng Council of Victorian Govt, Council of The Cancer Council Victoria, Cttee for Melbourne Bd, Bd of Man. of CRC for Cellular Growth Factors, Council of Australian Acad. of Science; Foreign mem. NAS; Assoc. Foreign mem. Acad. des Sciences; Fellow, Royal Soc. of Victoria 1997, Inaugural Class of the AACR Acad.; Hon. mem. American Asscn for Immunology, The Japan Acad.; Foreign Hon. mem. American Acad. of Arts and Sciences; Chevalier, Légion d'honneur 2009; David Syme Prize, Univ. of Melbourne 1982, Charles S. Mott Prize, General Motors Cancer Research Foundation (jtly) 1988, Avon Australia Spirit of Achievement Award 1992, Lemberg Medal, Australian Soc. for Biochemistry and Molecular Biology 1995, Burnet Lecturer, Australian Acad. of Science 1997, Australia Prize 1998, L'Oreal-UNESCO Women in Science Award 2001, Royal Medal, Royal Soc. 2002, Pearl Meister Greengard Prize 2009, Colin Thomson Medal 2011, Australian Eureka Prize for Leadership in Science 2012. *Publications:* numerous articles in scientific journals. *Leisure interests:* hiking, reading, music, photography. *Address:* The Walter and Eliza Hall Institute of Medical Research, 1G Royal Parade, Parkville, Vic. 3050, Australia (office). *Telephone:* (3) 9345-2492 (office). *Fax:* (3) 9347-0852 (office). *E-mail:* cory@wehi.edu.au (office). *Website:* www.wehi.edu.au (office).

CORYDON, Bjarne Fog; Danish politician; *Minister of Finance;* b. 1 March 1973, Kolding; m. Nina Eg Hansen 1998; four c.; ed Univ. of Aarhus; mem. Socialdemokraterne (Social Democrats—SD) 1992–, political and econ. adviser to SD leadership, Christiansborg 2000–05, Chief of Staff to SD Chair. Helle Thorning-Schmidt 2005–11, Leader, SD Analysis and Information Div. 2005; mem. Folketing (Parl.) for S Jutland constituency 2011–; Minister of Finance 2011–. *Address:* Ministry of Finance, Christiansborg Slotspl. 1, 1218 Copenhagen K, Denmark (office). *Telephone:* 33-92-33-33 (office). *Fax:* 33-32-80-30 (office). *E-mail:* fm@fm.dk (office). *Website:* www.fm.dk (office); bjarnecorydon.dk.

CORZINE, Jon Stevens, MBA; American business executive and fmr politician; b. 1 Jan. 1947, Taylorville, Ill.; s. of Roy Allen Corzine and Nancy June Corzine (née Hedrick); m. Joanne Dougherty 1968 (divorced 2003); two s. one d.; ed Univs of Chicago and Illinois; bond officer, Continental Illinois Nat. Bank 1970; Asst Vice-Pres. BancOhio Corpn 1974–75; joined Goldman, Sachs & Co. 1975, Vice-Pres. 1977, Pnr 1980–98, man. consultant 1985–94, Co-Head, Fixed Income Div. 1988–94, Sr Pnr and Chair. Man. Cttee, CEO 1994–99; Senator from NJ 2001–05, mem. Foreign Relations Cttee; Gov. of NJ 2005–10; Chair. and CEO MF Global Holdings Ltd, New York 2010–11 (resgnd); Operating Pnr, J.C. Flowers & Co. LLC 2010–11; John L. Weinberg/Goldman Sachs and Co. Visiting Prof., Woodrow Wilson School of Public and Int. Affairs, Princeton Univ. 2010–11; fmr mem. Bd of Dirs New York Philharmonic 1996, now Dir Emer., Public Securities Asscn (Vice-Chair. 1985, Chair. 1986). *Address:* c/o MF Global, 717 Fifth Avenue, New York, NY 10022, USA.

COSBY, William (Bill) H., Jr, MA, EdD; American comedian and actor; b. 12 July 1937, Philadelphia, Pa; s. of William Cosby and Anna Cosby; m. Camille Hanks 1964; five c. (one s. deceased); ed Temple Univ. and Univ. of Massachusetts; served in USNR 1956–60; Pres. Rhythm and Blues Hall of Fame 1968–; mem. Bd of Dirs Sickle Cell Anemia Foundation, United Negro Coll. Fund, Operation PUSH; Hon. MusD, Berklee Coll. of Music 2004; recipient of four Emmy Awards and eight Grammy Awards, Bob Hope Humanitarian Award, Acad. of TV Arts and Sciences 2003; named to Hall of Fame, Acad. of TV Arts and Sciences 1994, to Nat. Asscn for the Advancement of Colored People Image Awards Hall of Fame 2007, Mark Twain Prize for American Humor 2009. *Films include:* Hickey and Boggs 1972, Man and Boy 1972, Uptown Saturday Night 1974, Let's Do It Again 1975, Mother, Jugs and Speed 1976, Aesop's Fables, A Piece of Action 1977, California Suite 1978, Devil and Max Devlin 1979, Leonard: Part VI 1987, Ghost Dad 1990, The Meteor Man 1993, Jack 1996. *Television includes:* The Bill Cosby Show 1969, 1972–73, I Spy, The Cosby Show 1984–92, Cosby Mystery Series 1994–; recitals include: Revenge, To Russell, My Brother, With Whom I Slept, Top Secret, 200 M.P.H., Why Is There Air, Wonderfulness, It's True, It's True, Bill Cosby is a Very Funny Fellow: Right, I Started Out as a Child, 8:15, 12:15, Hungry, Reunion 1982, Bill Cosby:Himself 1983, Those of You With or Without Children, You'll Understand; Exec. Producer A Different World (TV series) 1987–93; Presenter Kids Say the Darndest Things 1998–, As I Was Saying 1997. *Publications include:* The Wit and Wisdom of Fat Albert 1973, Bill Cosby's Personal Guide to Power Tennis, Fatherhood 1986, Time Flies 1988, Love and Marriage 1989, Childhood 1991, Little Bill Series 1999, Congratulations! Now What? 1999, Friends of a Feather (juvenile). *Address:* c/o William Morris Endeavor Entertainment, 9601 Wilshire Blvd., Beverly Hills, CA 90210; c/o The Brokaw Co., 9255 Sunset Blvd, Los Angeles, CA 90069, USA. *E-mail:* pughufoma@yahoo.com. *Website:* billcosby.com.

COSENZA JIMENEZ, Luis, BS, PhD; Honduran engineer, development banker, politician and academic: *Hewlett Visiting Fellow for Public Policy, Kellogg Institute for International Studies, University of Notre Dame;* ed Univ. of Notre Dame, USA; worked for Empresa Nacional De Energía Eléctrica (state-owned power utility) becoming CEO 1976; Energy Specialist, IDB 1981–89; Prin. Power Engineer responsible for east Africa and much of central American region, World Bank 1989; campaign man. for Ricardo Maduro (Arriba Honduras cand.) during presidential election in 2000; Minister of the Presidency 2002–05; Exec. Dir for Belize, Costa Rica, El Salvador, Guatemala, Honduras and Nicaragua, IDB 2005–06; Visiting Fellow, Kellogg Inst. for Int. Studies, Univ. of Notre Dame 2006–07, Hewlett Visiting Fellow for Public Policy 2008–; mem. Bd of Advisors Concern Yourself, Inc.; fmr Exec. Pres. Honduran Foundation for Investment and Promotion of Exports (FIDES). *Address:* Kellogg Institute for International Studies, University of Notre Dame, 130 Hesburgh Center, Notre Dame, IN 46556, USA (office).

Telephone: (574) 631-6580 (office). *Fax:* (574) 631-6717 (office). *Website:* kellogg.nd .edu (office).

COSGRAVE, Liam; Irish politician; b. 13 April 1920, Templeogue, Co. Dublin; s. of William T. Cosgrave (Pres. of the Exec. Council of the Irish Free State 1922–32) and Louise Flanagan; m. Vera Osborne 1952; two s. one d.; ed Synge Street Christian Brothers' Schools, Dublin, St Vincent's Coll., Castleknock, Co. Dublin and Kings Inns; called to the Bar 1943; SC 1958; served in army; TD, Dublin Co. 1943–48, Dún Laoghaire and Rathdown 1948–81; Leader, Fine Gael Party 1965–77; Parl. Sec. to the Prime Minister and to Minister for Industry and Commerce 1948–51; Minister for External Affairs 1954–57; Prime Minister 1973–77; Minister for Defence 1976; Chair. and Leader of first Irish Del. to UN Gen. Ass. 1956; Kt Grand Cross of Pius IX (Ordine Piano); Hon. LLD (Duquesne Univ., St John's Univ.) 1956, (De Paul Univ.) 1958, (Nat. Univ. of Ireland and Univ. of Dublin) 1974. *Address:* Beechpark, Templeogue, Co. Dublin, Ireland.

COSGROVE, Art, BA, PhD; Irish historian, academic, barrister and fmr university president; b. 1 June 1940, Newry, Co. Down, NI; m. Emer Sweeney 1968; nine c.; ed Abbey Christian Brothers School, Newry, Co. Down, NI and Queen's Univ., Belfast, NI; mem. academic staff, Univ. Coll. Dublin 1963–94, Sr Lecturer, Dept of Medieval History 1976, Assoc. Prof. and Acting Head of Dept 1990, apptd Chair. Combined Depts of History 1991, Pres. Univ. Coll. Dublin 1994–2003; mem. Bd of Dirs racecaller.com; Visiting Prof., History Dept, Univ. of Kansas 1974; Hon. LLD (Queen's Univ., Belfast) 1995. *Publications:* Studies in Irish History presented to R. D. Edwards (jtly) 1979, Late Medieval Ireland 1370–1541 1981, Parliament and Community (jtly) 1981, Marriage in Ireland 1985, A New History of Ireland II: Medieval Ireland 1169–1534 1987, Dublin Through the Ages 1988. *Website:* www.racecaller.com.

COSGROVE, Gen. Peter John, AM, MC; Australian army officer (retd) and government official; *Governor-General;* b. 28 July 1947; m. Lynne Cosgrove; three s.; ed Waverley Coll., Royal Mil. Coll., Duntroon; joined Australian Army 1965, served with 1st Bn, Royal Australian Regt (RAR) in Malaysia and with 9th Bn, RAR in Viet Nam 1969, Commdr, 1st Bn, RAR 1983–84, 1st Div. 1998–99, led int. forces in East Timor peacekeeping mission (INTERFET) 1999–2000, Chief of Army 2000–02, Chief of Defence Force 2002–05, retd from army 2005; Chancellor, Australian Catholic Univ. 2010–14; Gov.-Gen. of Australia 2014–; Dir Qantas 2005–14; attained rank of Lt 1968, Col 1989, Lt-Gen. 2000, Gen. 2002; Officier, Légion d'honneur, Commdr, Legion of Merit (USA); numerous awards including Mil. Cross 1971, Vietnam Medal, Nat. Medal 1980, Australian of the Year 2001. *Publication:* My Story (autobiography) 2006. *Address:* Government House, Canberra, ACT 2600, Australia (office). *Telephone:* (02) 6283 3533 (office). *Fax:* (02) 6281 3760 (office). *Website:* www.gg.gov.au (office).

ĆOSIĆ, Dobrica; Serbian writer and politician; b. 29 Dec. 1921, Velika Drenova; m. Božica Ćosić; one d.; ed Belgrade Univ., Higher Party School; war service 1941–45; worked as journalist, then as freelance writer; corresp. mem. Serbian Acad. of Arts and Sciences 1970, mem. 1976; left League of Communists of Yugoslavia (LCY), prosecuted; resumed active political activity 1980s; Pres. of Repub. of Yugoslavia 1992–93. *Publications:* The Sun is Far 1951, Roots 1954, Sections 1961, Fairy Tale 1965, The Time of Death (Vols 1–4) 1972–79, The Time of Evil: Sinner (Vols 1–4) 1985, Apostate 1986, Believer 1990, The Time of Power 1995, Kosovo; studies and essays: Hope and Fear 2001, Real and Possible 2001, Serbian Question (Vols 1–4) 2002, Writer's Notes (Vols 1–4) 2002. *Address:* Serbian Academy of Sciences and Arts, Knez Mikhailova Str. 35, Belgrade (office); Branka Djonovića 6, Belgrade, Serbia (home). *Telephone:* (11) 3342400 (office); (11) 663437 (home). *E-mail:* sasapres@bib.sanu.ac.yu (office).

COŞKUN, Ali, MSc; Turkish politician and business executive; b. 1939, Kemaliye, Erzincan; m.; two c.; ed Faculty of Electrical Eng, Yildiz Tech. Univ., Wirtschaft Academie, Hamburg, Germany; fmr Pres. Admin. Bd, Ihlas Finance Inst. and Bisan Bicycle Industry and Commerce; fmr Deputy Pres. Istanbul Chamber of Commerce; fmr Pres. Turkish Union of Chambers and Commodities Exchanges (TOBB); fmr Deputy Pres. Islamic Countries Union of Chambers; mem. Parl. (ANAP) for Istanbul Constituency 1995–2005, Chair. Nat. Defense Comm., mem. Plan and Budget Comm., Industry, Trade, Energy and Technology Comm.; Minister of Industry and Commerce 2005–07; Hon. Pres. TOBB; Hon. mem. Ass. of İstanbul Chamber Industry, Ass. of Ankara Chamber of Trade, Ass. of Turkish Exporters. *Publication:* Energy Problems of Turkey and Solutions 1986. *Address:* Öğretmenler Cad. Usta Apt. A Blok 1/1, 06140, Çukurambar, Ankara, Turkey. *Telephone:* (312) 2857037. *Fax:* (312) 2857034. *E-mail:* bilgi@alicoskun.com.tr. *Website:* www.alicoskun.com.tr.

COSMOS, Jean; French playwright; b. (Jean Louis Gaudrat), 14 June 1923, Paris; s. of Albert Gaudrat and Maria Maillebuau; m. Alice Jarrousse 1948; one s. two d.; ed Inst. St Nicholas, Igny, Coll. Jean-Baptiste Say, Paris; songwriter 1945–50, writer for radio 1952–60, for TV 1964–; mem. Comm. Soc. des auteurs dramatiques 1971–; co-librettist Goya 1996 (opera); Chevalier, Légion d'honneur, Officier des Arts et des Lettres; Soc. des auteurs et compositeurs prizes 1970. *Plays:* author or adapter of numerous plays for the theatre including la Fille du roi 1952, Au jour le jour 1952, les Grenadiers de la reine 1957, Macbeth 1959, 1965, le Manteau 1963, la Vie et la Mort du roi Jean 1964, Arden de Faversham 1964, Monsieur Alexandre 1965, la Bataille de Lobositz 1969, Major Barbara 1970, le Marchand de Venise 1971, Sainte Jeanne des Abattoirs 1972, Ce sacré Bonheur 1987; author of numerous TV plays including les Oranges (Albert Ollivier prize) 1964, le Pacte 1966, Un homme, un cheval 1968, la Pomme oubliée (after Jean Anglade), l'Ingénu (after Voltaire), Bonsoir Léon, la Tête à l'envers, le Trêve, le Coup Monté, Aide-toi, Julien Fontanes, magistrat (TV Series 1980–89), La Dictée 1984; with Jean Chatenêt: 16 à Kerbriant, Ardéchois coeur fidèle (Critics' choice) 1975, Les Yeux Bleus, la Lumière des Justes (after Henri Troyat); with Gilles Perrault: le Secret des dieux, la Filière, Fabien de la Drôme, seven-part serial of Julien Fontanes, Magistrat, regular contrib. to the Cinq dernières minutes. *Films include:* Bonjour toubib 1959 La vie et rien d'autre 1989, Le Colonel Chabert 1994, La fille de d'Artagnan 1994, Capitaine Conan 1996, Le bossu 1997, Laissez-passer 2002, Effroyables jardins 2003, Fanfan la tulipe 2003, Agents secrets 2004, Aurore 2006, Le Grand Meaulnes 2006, Michou d'Auber 2007, Dialogue avec mon jardinier 2007. *Address:* c/o Artmédia, 20 avenue Rapp, 75007 Paris (office); 57 rue

de Versailles, 92410 Ville d'Avray, France (home). *Telephone:* 1-43-17-33-00 (office). *E-mail:* info@artmedia.fr (office).

COSSART, Pascale, MSc, PhD; French bacteriologist and academic; *Director of Cell Biology and Infection Department, Institut Pasteur;* ed Lille Univ., Georgetown Univ., USA, Univ. of Paris VII; Asst, Univ. Inst. Tech., Lille; Fellow, Georgetown Univ. 1970–71; Prof., Royal School of Medicine, Laos 1974–75; joined Institut Pasteur, Paris 1972, Head of Listeria Molecular Genetics Lab. 1991–94, Prof. and Head of Bacterial-Cellular Interactions Unit 1994, Dir Cell Biology and Infection Dept 2006–; Int. Research Scholar, Howard Hughes Medical Inst. 2000–; mem. Scientific Advisory Bd at Research Centre for Infectious Diseases, Würzburg Univ., Germany 2000–, at Biozentrum, Univ., Basel, Switzerland 2002–; mem. Scientific Council, Ville de Paris 2003–, Nat. Ethics Consultative Cttee 2003, EMBO Course and Workshop Cttee 1999–2004, Chair. 2001–04; mem. Scientific Council, Institut Pasteur 2002–06, Pres. 2003–05; mem. Scientific Council, CNRS 2005–06, Soc. Francaise de Microbiologie 1977–, American Soc. for Microbiology 1987, American Soc. for Cell Biology 1993–, Soc. Francaise de Biologie Cellulaire 2007–, Soc. Francaise de Biochimie et de Biologie Moléculaire 2007–; mem. Cttee de Pilotage, Agence Nat. pour la Recherche 2006–; mem. editorial bds of several journals; mem. Deutsche Akad. der Naturforscher Leopoldina, Acad. des Sciences 2002–, American Acad. of Microbiology 2004; Chevalier, Légion d'honneur 1998, Officier 2007, Officier, Ordre National du Mérite 2002; UNESCO Carlos Finlay Prize 1995, Louis Rapkin Award 1997, Richard Lounsbery Prize, L'Oreal-UNESCO Women in Science Award 1998, Louis Pasteur Gold Medal, Swedish Soc. of Medicine 2000, Nestle Prize 2000, Valade Senior Price, Fondation de France 2003, INSERM Prize of Fundamental Research 2005, Glaxo Smith Kline Int. Mem. of the Year Award 2007, Robert Koch Prize 2007. *Publications:* numerous publns in scientific journals. *Address:* Institut Pasteur, 25–28 rue du Dr Roux, 75015 Paris, France (office). *Telephone:* 1-45-68-80-00 (office). *E-mail:* pcossart@pasteur.fr (office). *Website:* www.pasteur.fr (office).

COSSÉ, Steven A., BA, JD; American oil company executive; ed Southeastern Louisiana Univ., Loyola Univ.; Gen. Counsel, Ocean Drilling & Exploration Co. (ODECO, subsidiary of Murphy Oil Corpn) 1983–91, Vice-Pres. Murphy Oil Corpn 1993, Sr Vice-Pres. 1994–2005, also served as Chief Financial Officer, later Vice-Pres. and Gen. Counsel, Murphy Exploration & Production Co. USA (subsidiary of Murphy Oil Corpn), General Counsel 1991–2011, Exec. Vice-Pres. Murphy Oil Corpn 2005–11, Dir 2011–, Pres. and CEO 2011–13; Dir Simmons First Nat. Corpn 2004–, Simmons First Nat. Bank, Simmons First Bank of El Dorado, NA, Nat. Asscn of Mfrs, SHARE Foundation, Medical Center of South Arkansas; mem. Advisory Bd Union County Rape and Family Violence Center; mem. American Corp. Counsel Asscn, Louisiana Bar Asscn, Union County Bar Asscn; fmr Chair. South Arkansas Chapter of American Red Cross. *Address:* Murphy Oil Corpn, PO Box 7000, El Dorado, AR 71731-7000 (office); Murphy Oil Corpn, 200 Peach Street, El Dorado, AR 71730, USA (office). *Telephone:* (870) 862-6411 (office). *Fax:* (870) 864-6373 (office). *E-mail:* info@murphyoilcorp.com (office). *Website:* www .murphyoilcorp.com (office).

COSSONS, Sir Neil, Kt, OBE, MA, FSA; British foundation executive; b. 15 Jan. 1939, Nottingham, Notts., England; s. of Arthur Cossons and Evelyn Cossons (née Bettle); m. Veronica Edwards 1965; two s. one d.; ed Henry Mellish Grammar School, Nottingham, Univ. of Liverpool; Curator of Tech., Bristol City Museum 1964; Deputy Dir, City of Liverpool Museums 1969; Dir Ironbridge Gorge Museum 1971; Dir Nat. Maritime Museum, Greenwich 1983; Dir Science Museum, London 1986–2000; Commr Historic Buildings and Monuments Comm. for England (English Heritage) 1989–95, 1999–2000, Chair. 2000–07; Pres. Royal Geographical Soc. 2003–06; mem. RCA Council 1989–, Pro-Provost and Chair. of Council 2007–; mem. Design Council 1990–94, British Waterways Bd 1995–2001; Pres. European Museum Forum 2001–08; Fellow and Past Pres. of the Museums Asscn; mem. Comité Scientifique, Conservatoire Nat. des Arts et Métiers 1991–2000; Hon. Fellow, RCA; Hon. Companion, Royal Aeronautical Soc. 1996; Hon. mem. Soc. of Chemical Industry 2002; Hon. FRIBA 2002; Hon. DSocSc (Birmingham) 1979; Hon. DUniv (Open Univ.) 1984, (Sheffield Hallam) 1995, (York) 1998; Hon. DLitt (Liverpool) 1989, (Bradford) 1991, (Nottingham Trent) 1994, (Univ. of the West of England) 1995, (Bath) 1997, (Greenwich) 2004; Hon. DSc (Leicester) 1995, (Nottingham) 2000; Hon. DArts (De Montfort) 1997; Norton Medlicott Medal, Historical Asscn 1991, Pres.'s Medal, Royal Acad. of Eng 1993. *Publications:* Industrial Archaeology of the Bristol Region (with R. A. Buchanan) 1968, Industrial Archaeology 1975, Transactions of the First International Congress on the Conservation of Industrial Monuments (ed.) 1975, Rees's Manufacturing Industry (ed.) 1975, Ironbridge – Landscape of Industry (with H. Sowden) 1977, The Iron Bridge – Symbol of the Industrial Revolution (with B. S. Trinder) 1979, The Management of Change in Museums (ed.) 1985, Making of the Modern World (ed.) 1992, Perspectives on Industrial Archaeology (ed.) 2000, England's Landscape (eight-vol. series, gen. ed.) 2006, Liverpool: Seaport City (with M. Jenkins) 2011. *Leisure interests:* travel, design, industrial archaeology. *Address:* The Old Rectory, Rushbury, Shropshire, SY6 7EB, England. *Telephone:* (1694) 771603. *E-mail:* nc@cossons.org.uk (office).

COSTA, Antonio; Portuguese lawyer and politician; *Mayor of Lisbon;* b. 17 July 1961; s. of Orlando da Costa and Maria Antónia Palla; m.; two c.; ed Univ. of Lisbon; mem. Municipal Ass. of Lisbon 1982–93; Deputy Ass. of Repub. 1991–2007, mem. Partido Socialista, Pres. Parl. Group 2002–04; Sec. of State for Parl. Affairs 1995–97; Govt Rep. Expo '98 1997–98; Minister of Justice 1999–2002; MEP 2004–05, Vice-Pres. European Parl.; Minister of State and Internal Admin 2005–07; Mayor of Lisbon 2007–. *Address:* Câmara Municipal de Lisboa, Paços do Concelho -Praça do Município, 1100-365 Lisbon, Portugal (office). *Telephone:* (21) 3227000 (office). *Fax:* (21) 3227008 (office). *E-mail:* geral@cm-lisboa.pt (office). *Website:* www.cm-lisboa.pt (office).

COSTA, Antonio Maria, PhD; Italian economist and fmr UN official; b. 16 June 1941, Mondovi; s. of Francesco Costa and Maria Costa; m. Patricia Agnes Wallace 1971; two s. one d.; ed Univ. of California, Berkeley, Acad. of Sciences of the USSR and Univ. of Turin; Visiting Prof. of Econs, Moscow Univ. and Acad. of Sciences of the USSR 1965–67; Instructor of Econs, Univ. of Calif., Berkeley 1968–70; Sr economist UN Dept of Int. Econs and Social Affairs 1969–83; Prof. of Econs, New York Univ. 1976–83; Sr Econ. Adviser to the UN 1970–83; Special Counsellor in Econs to the Sec.-Gen. of OECD 1983–87; Dir Gen. Econ. and Financial Affairs, EC

1987–92; Sec.-Gen. EBRD, London, UK 1992–2001; Exec. Dir UN Office on Drugs and Crime (fmrly UN Office for Drug Control and Crime Prevention), Vienna, Austria 2002–10, also Dir-Gen. UN Office at Vienna (UNOV) 2002–10. *Publications:* articles on econs and politics. *Leisure interest:* work. *Address:* c/o United Nations Office on Drugs and Crime, Vienna International Centre, PO Box 500, 1400 Vienna, Austria.

COSTA, Enrico, PhD; Italian astrophysicist and research institute director; *Director of Research, Institute of Space Astrophysics and Planetology, National Institute of Astrophysics;* b. 1944, Sassari, Sardinia; ed Univ. of Rome; family moved to Rome 1954; participated in rocket experiments with X-ray detectors at Istituto di Astrofisica Spaziale (IAS), Rome; joined IAS and worked on balloon experiments 1976, later involved in BeppoSAX (Italian X-ray astronomy satellite); part of team of Livio Scarsi that proposed the construction of the satellite for X-ray detection 1981, currently Dir of Research, Inst. of Space Astrophysics and Planetology, Nat. Inst. of Astrophysics; Shaw Prize in Astronomy (co-recipient) 2011. *Achievements include:* developed X-ray detector for Italian X-ray/gamma-ray satellites AGILE 1999, which started in 2007; developed X-ray polarimeters. *Publications:* numerous papers in professional journals. *Address:* Instituto di Astrofisica e Planetologia Spaziali, Room 1B04, Via del Fosso del Cavaliere 100, 00133 Rome, Italy (office). *Telephone:* (06) 4993-4004 (office). *E-mail:* enrico.costa@iasf-roma.inaf.it (office). *Website:* www.iasf-roma.inaf.it/indexen.htm (office).

COSTA, Francisco; Brazilian fashion designer; *Creative Director, Calvin Klein Collection for Women, Calvin Klein Inc.;* b. 1969; fmr designer for Gucci, Balmain and Oscar de la Renta; joined Calvin Klein 2002, Design Dir for Womenswear (following sale of co. to Phillips-Van Heusen and retirement of Calvin Klein as Design Dir) 2003–, debut collection at NY Fashion Week 2003. *Address:* Calvin Klein Inc., 205 West 39th Street, New York, NY 10018, USA (office).

COSTA, Gabriel Arcanjo Ferreira da, BLL; São Tomé and Príncipe politician, lawyer and diplomatist; *Prime Minister;* b. 11 Dec. 1954; lawyer and magistrate; mem. Parl. (Juventude Movimento Libertação de São Tomé e Príncipe) in first Ass. following nat. independence 1975–98; Counsellor for Legal and Political Affairs to Pres. Trovoada 1991–95, Head of Cabinet of Pres. 1996–98; State Minister of Justice, Admin. Reform and Local Admin –1998; Special Rep. of Exec. of CPLP for Guinea-Bissau 1998–2000; Amb. to Portugal, Morocco and Spain 2000–02; Prime Minister of São Tomé e Príncipe March–Oct. 2002, 2012–; mem. Movimento de Libertação de São Tomé e Príncipe—Partido Social Democrata. *Address:* Office of the Prime Minister, Rua do Município CP 302, São Tomé, São Tomé and Príncipe (office). *Telephone:* 223913 (office). *Fax:* 224679 (office). *E-mail:* gpm@cstome.net (office).

COSTA, Jean-Paul, LLM, PhD; French judge; b. 3 Nov. 1941, Tunis, Tunisia; ed Inst. of Political Studies, Nat. School of Man., Paris; clerk, Council of State 1966, Advisor, Judicial Section 1966–71, 1977–80, 1987–89, Assessor of Sub-section of Judicial Section 1989–93, Pres. of Sub-section of Judicial Section 1993–98; Political Sec. to Minister of Educ. 1981–84; Assoc. Prof., Orléans Univ. 1989–98, Panthéon-Sorbonne Univ. 1992–98; Judge, European Court of Human Rights 1998–, Vice-Pres. 2001–07, Pres. 2007–11. *Address:* c/o Office of the President, European Court of Human Rights, Council of Europe, 67075 Strasbourg, France.

COSTA, Manuel Pinto da; São Tomé and Príncipe politician and head of state; *President and Commander-in-Chief of the Armed Forces;* b. 5 Aug. 1937, Agua Grande; f. Movt for the Liberation of São Tomé e Príncipe (MLSTP) 1972; Sec.-Gen. MLSTP, based in Gabon 1972–75, Pres. 1978; Pres. of São Tomé e Príncipe and C-in-C of the Armed Forces 1975–91, 2011–; Minister of Agric., Land Reform and Defence 1975–78, of Labour and Social Security 1977–78, of Territorial Admin. 1978–82, of Defence and Nat. Security 1982–86, fmr Minister of Planning and Econs; Prime Minister 1978–88; Dr hc (Berlin); José Marti Medal, Cuba. *Address:* Palácio Presidêncial, CP 38, São Tomé, São Tomé e Príncipe (office). *Website:* www .presidencia.st (office).

COSTA, Pedro; Portuguese film director and writer; b. 3 March 1959, Lisbon; s. of dir and writer Luís Filipe Costa; ed Univ. of Lisbon, Escola Superior de Teatro e Cinema. *Films:* E Tudo Invenção Nossa (also producer) 1984, Um Adeus Português (asst dir) 1986, Uma Rapariga no Verão (asst dir) 1986, Agosto (August) (asst dir) 1987, O Sangue (The Blood) (also writer) 1989, Casa de Lava (Down to Earth) (also writer) (Special Artistic Achievement, Thessaloniki Film Festival 1994, Grand Prix for Best Foreign Film, Entrevues Film Festival 1994) 1994, Ossos (Bones) (also writer) (Grand Prix for Best Foreign Film, Entrevues Film Festival 1997) 1997, No Quarto da Vanda (In Vanda's Room) (also cinematographer) (Don Quixote Award (Special Mention), Special Mention, and Youth Jury Award, Locarno Int. Film Festival 2000, FIPRESCI Prize (Int. Competition), Yamagata Int. Documentary Festival 2001, France Culture Award for Cineaste of the Year, Cannes Film Festival 2002) 2000, 6 Bagatelas (video) 2001, Ne change rien 2005, Juventude Em Marcha (Colossal Youth) (also writer and cinematographer) (Independent/Experimental Film and Video Award, Los Angeles Film Critics Association Awards 2007) 2006, O Estado do Mundo (State of the World) (segment Tarrafal) (also cinematographer) 2007. *Television:* Cinéma, de notre temps (episode Danièle Huillet/Jean-Marie Straub: Où gît votre sourire enfoui?) (also cinematographer) 2001.

COSTA-GAVRAS, Constantin; French (b. Greek) film director and screenwriter; b. (Constantin Gavras), 13 Feb. 1933, Arcadia; s. of Panayotis Gavras and Panayota Gavras; m. Michele Ray 1968; three c.; ed Sorbonne and Institut de Hautes Etudes Cinématographiques, Paris; worked as asst to film dirs Yves Allegret, Jacques Demy, René Clair, René Clément; Pres. Soc. des Réalisateurs Français 1973–75, Cinémathèque Française 1982–87, Festival Paris-Cinéma 2003–; Chevalier, Légion d'honneur; Commdr, des Arts et des Lettres, Officier, Ordre nat. du Mérite; Prix Académie Française for Life Achievement 1998. *Films directed include:* The Sleeping Car Murder (also writer) (MWA Award) 1965, Un Homme de Trop (Moscow Film Festival Prize) 1966, Z (co-writer) (Jury Award, Cannes, Award for Best Foreign-Language Film) 1969, L'Aveu (co-writer) 1970, State of Siege (co-writer) (Louis Delluc Prize) 1973, Section Spéciale (co-writer) (Best Dir, Cannes) 1975, Clair de Femme (writer) 1979, Missing (co-writer) (Gold Palm, Cannes, Academy Award, best screenplay, British Acad. best screenplay) 1982, Hanna K (co-writer) 1983, Family Business (writer) 1985, Betrayed (ACLUF Award) 1988, Music Box (Golden Bear, Berlin) 1989, The Little Apocalypse (dir

and co-writer) 1993, Mad City 1996, Amen 2001, Parthenon (short) 2003, Le Couperet 2005, Eden à l'Ouest 2009; directed opera Il Mondo della Luna (Joseph Haydn), Teatro San Carlo, Naples 1994. *Publication:* Etat de Siège: The making of the film. *Leisure interests:* theatre, opera, books, films. *Address:* 244 rue Saint-Jacques, 75005 Paris (office); c/o Artmédia, 20 avenue Rapp, 75007, Paris, France. *Telephone:* 1-44-41-13-73 (office). *Fax:* 1-44-41-13-74 (office). *E-mail:* kgprod@wanadoo.fr (office).

COSTA PEREIRA, Renato Claudio; Brazilian aviation official and international organization official; b. 30 Nov. 1936; m.; ed Brazilian Air Force Acad.; Personnel Commdr, Belo Horizonte Air Force Base 1961–67; Officer, Brazilian Air Force Gen. Personnel Command 1967–70, Instructor Officer, Brazilian Air Force Improvement Officer School 1970–74; Pilot Instructor, Brazilian Air Force Acad. 1974–77; Man. and Co-ordinator of Research and Devt project 1978–84; Dir Flight Protection Inst. 1984–85; Logistics Adviser to Minister of Aeronautics 1985–87; Chief, Brazilian Air Comm., London, England 1987–89; Sec. of Planning and Contracting, Secr. of Econ. and Finance, Ministry of Aeronautics 1989–90; Dir Operations Sub-Dept, Civil Aviation Dept 1990–92, Dir Planning Sub-Dept 1990–94; Pres. Latin American Comm. of Civil Aviation 1990–97, responsible for establishing the basis for the enlargement of the Comm. to a Pan-American body in 1997; Pres. Brazilian Govt agency for int. air navigation affairs 1990–97; Sec.-Gen. ICAO 1997–2003. *Address:* c/o International Civil Aviation Organization, 999 University Street, Montreal, PQ H3A 5H7, Canada (office).

COSTEDOAT, Lt.-Gen. Pierre-Jacques; French army officer and consultant; b. 27 Jan. 1942, Casablanca, Morocco; s. of René Costedoat and Marguerite Bosc; m. Anne-Marie Delamare 1965; four d.; ed Saint-Cyr-Coëtquidan Mil. Acad.; Second Lt, 74th Artillery Regt 1964, Lt 1966; Capt., 1st Artillery Regt 1972, then Battery CO; Maj., 11th Artillery Regt 1977, Lt-Col 1981, Col 1984; attended as auditeur Centre des hautes études militaires and Institut des hautes études de défense nationale 1987–88; CO 93rd Mountain Artillery Regt, then Staff 1988–89, at Direction Générale de la Sécurité extérieure 1989–95; Brig. 1992; CO Saint-Cyr Coëtquidan Mil. Acad. 1995–98; rank of Maj.-Gen. 1995, later Lt-Gen.; Asst Gen. Sec. of Nat. Defence 1998–2000; Gen. de corps 1998–2000; Mil. Gov. of Paris, Commdr of Ile-de-France, Officer Gen. Paris Zone of Defence 2000–02; Advisor to Pres. of Sécurité Sans Frontières (risk prevention and man. consultancy) 2003–; Officier Légion d'honneur, Commdr Ordre nat. du Mérite. *Leisure interests:* skiing, tennis, golf, hiking. *Address:* c/o Office of the President, Sécurité Sans Frontières, Sofema Groupe, 58 avenue Marceau, 75008 Paris France. *Website:* www.securite-sf.com.

COSTELLO, Elvis; British singer and songwriter; b. (Declan Patrick Aloysius McManus), 25 Aug. 1954, London, England; s. of Ross McManus and Lillian McManus (née Costello); m. 1st Mary Costello 1974; one s.; m. 2nd Cait O'Riordan 1986 (divorced 2003); m. 3rd Diana Krall 2003; twin s.; fmr mem. Flip City; formed Elvis Costello and the Attractions 1977–; Dir South Bank Meltdown 1995; Hon. DMus, (New England Conservatory) 2013; BAFTA Award for Best Original Television Music (for G.B.H.) 1992, MTV Video Award for Best Male Video 1989, Rolling Stone Award for Best Songwriter 1990, two Ivor Novello Awards, Nordoff-Robbins Silver Clef Award, ASCAP Founders Award 2003. *Films include:* Americathon 1979, No Surrender 1985, Straight to Hell 1987, Prison Song 2001, De-Lovely 2004. *Television includes:* Scully (Granada TV for Channel 4) 1984, The Juliet Letters 1993, presenter, Spectacle: Elvis Costello With... (Sundance Channel) 2008–. *Recordings include:* albums: My Aim Is True 1977, This Year's Model 1978, Armed Forces 1979, Get Happy 1980, Trust 1980, Almost Blue 1981, Taking Liberties 1982, Imperial Bedroom 1982, Punch The Clock 1983, Goodbye Cruel World 1984, The Best Of 1985, Blood and Chocolate 1986, King of America 1986, Spike 1989, Mighty Like A Rose 1991, The Juliet Letters (with the Brodsky Quartet) 1993, Brutal Youth (with Steve Nieve, Pete Thomas, Bruce Thomas and Nick Lowe) 1994, The Very Best of Elvis Costello and The Attractions 1995, Kojak Variety 1995, Deep Dead Blue, Live At Meltdown (with Bill Frisell) 1995, All This Useless Beauty 1996, Extreme Honey 1997, Terror and Magnificence 1997, Painted From Memory (Grammy Award 1999) 1998, The Sweetest Punch: The Songs of Costello 1999, Best of Elvis Costello 1999, For The Stars (with Anne-Sofie von Otter) 2001, When I Was Cruel 2002, North 2003, My Flame Burns Blue 2006, The River in Reverse (with Allen Toussaint) 2006, Momofuku 2008, Secret, Profane and Sugarcane 2009, National Ransom 2010, Wise Up Ghost 2013. *Address:* c/o Macklam Feldman Management, Suite 200, 1505 West 2nd Avenue, Vancouver, V6H 3Y4, Canada (office). *Telephone:* (604) 630-3199 (office). *E-mail:* gilmour@mfmgt.com (office). info@mfmgt.com (office). *Website:* www.mfmgt.com (office); www.elviscostello.com.

COSTELLO, Peter Howard, BA, LLB; Australian politician; b. 14 Aug. 1957; s. of R. J. Costello and M. A. Costello; m. Tanya Costello 1982; one s. two d.; ed Carey Grammar School, Monash Univ.; solicitor, Mallesons, Melbourne 1981–84; tutor (part-time) Monash Univ. 1984–86; mem. Victorian Bar 1984–90; MP for Higgins, Victoria, 1990–2007; Shadow Minister for Corp. Law Reform and Consumer Affairs 1990–92; Shadow Attorney-Gen. and Shadow Minister for Justice 1992–93, for Finance 1993–94; Deputy Leader of the Opposition and Shadow Treas. 1994–96; Deputy Leader Liberal Party 1996–2007, Commonwealth of Australia Treas. 1996–2007; mem. Liberal Party. *Publication:* Arbitration in Contempt (jtly) 1986; articles for periodicals and journals. *Leisure interests:* swimming, football, reading. *Address:* c/o Liberal Party of Australia, Federal Secretariat, cnr Blackall and Macquarie Streets, Barton, ACT 2600, Australia.

COSTELLOE, Paul; Irish fashion designer and artist; b. 23 June 1945, Dublin; m. 1982; six s. one d.; ed Blackrock Coll., Dublin, design coll. in Dublin and Chambre Syndical Paris; Design Asst Jacques Esterel, Paris 1969–71; Designer, Marks & Spencer 1972; Chief House Designer, A. Rinascente, Milan 1972–74; Designer, Anne Fogerty, New York, Pennaco, New York and Trimfit, Philadelphia 1974–79; established own design house, Paul Costelloe Int. Ltd in conjunction with business pnr Robert Eitel 1979; merchandise sold in UK, Ireland, Europe, Scandinavia and N America under Paul Costelloe Collection and Dressage labels; opened flagship store, Knightsbridge 1994; designer of British Airways uniform 1994; Hon. DLitt (Ulster) 1996; Fil d'Or award, Int. Linen Council, 1987, 1988, 1989; British Designer of the Year 1989 and other awards. *Leisure interests:* rugby, tennis, golf. *Address:* Main Road, Moygashel, Dungannon, County Tyrone, BT71 7QR, Ireland; c/o Signature Brands Group plc, 4 Fitzhardinge Street, London, W1H 6EG, England. *Website:* www.paulcostelloe.com.

COSTNER, Kevin; American actor and film director; b. 18 Jan. 1955; m. 1st Cindy Silva (divorced); one s. two d.; one s. by Bridget Rooney; m. 2nd Christine Baumgartner 2004; one s.; ed California State Univ., Fullerton; directing debut in Dances with Wolves 1990 (Acad. Award for Best Picture 1991); mem. band, Modern West. *Films include:* Malibu Hot Summer 1981, Chasing Dreams 1982, Night Shift 1982, Frances (uncredited) 1982, Table for Five 1983, Stacy's Knights 1983, The Big Chill 1983, Testament 1983, Fandango 1985, Silverado 1985, American Flyers 1985, Shadows Run Black 1986, The Untouchables 1987, No Way Out 1987, Bull Durham 1988, Field of Dreams 1989, The Gunrunner 1989, Revenge 1989, Dances with Wolves 1990, Robin Hood: Prince of Thieves 1991, JFK 1991, The Bodyguard 1992, A Perfect World 1993, Wyatt Earp 1994, The War 1994, Waterworld 1995, Tin Cup 1996, The Postman 1997, Message in a Bottle 1998, For Love of the Game 1999, Play It to the Bone 1999, Thirteen Days 2000, 3000 Miles to Graceland 2001, The Road to Graceland (short) 2001, Dragonfly 2002, Open Range 2003, The Upside of Anger 2005, Rumor Has It… 2005, The Guardian 2006, Mr. Brooks 2007, Swing Vote 2008, The New Daughter 2009, The Company Men 2010, Field of Dreams 2: Lockout (short) 2011, Man of Steel 2013; co-producer Rapa Nui, China Moon 1993, exec. producer Rapa Nui 1994. *Television includes:* Amazing Stories (series) 1985, Hatfields & McCoys (mini-series) (Emmy Award for Best Lead Actor in a Miniseries or Movie 2012, Golden Globe Award for Best Performance by an Actor in a Mini-Series or Motion Picture Made for Television 2013) 2012. *Recording:* album: with Modern West: Untold Truths 2008. *Leisure interest:* golf. *Address:* c/o J.J. Harris, One Entertainment, 9220 Sunset Blvd, Suite 306, Los Angeles, CA 90069 (office); c/o J.J. Harris, One Entertainment, 12 West 57th Street, Penthouse, New York, NY 10019, USA (office); c/o Rick Nicita, Creative Artists Agency, 2000 Avenue of the Stars, Los Angeles, CA 90067, USA; TIG Productions, Producers' Building 5, 4000 Warner Boulevard, Burbank, CA 91522-0001, USA. *Telephone:* (212) 974-3900 (New York) (office); (424) 288-2000. *Fax:* (424) 288-2900. *E-mail:* rnicita@caa.com. *Website:* www.caa.com; www .kevincostner.com; kevincostnermodernwest.com.

COSTOLO, Richard (Dick) W., BS; American internet business executive; *CEO, Twitter Inc.;* b. 10 Sept. 1963; m. Lorin Costolo; ed Univ. of Michigan; served eight years as Sr Man., Andersen Consulting; Co-founder Burning Door Networked Media; Co-founder and CEO SpyOnIt.com (internet monitoring co.); Co-founder and CEO FeedBurner (internet man. co.) 2004–07; Group Product Man., Google, Inc. 2007–09; Chief Operating Officer, Twitter, Inc. 2009–10, CEO 2010–; fmr Sr Man., Eagle Advanced Tech. Group; mem. Nat. Security Telecommunications Advisory Cttee 2011. *Address:* Twitter, Inc., 1355 Market Street, Suite 900, San Francisco, CA 94103, USA (office). *Telephone:* (415) 222-9670 (office). *Website:* twitter.com (office).

COT, Jean-Pierre; French politician, international organization official and academic; *Judge, International Tribunal for the Law of the Sea;* b. 23 Oct. 1937, Geneva, Switzerland; s. of Pierre Cot and Luisa Phelps; m.; three c.; Prof., then Dean, Faculty of Law, Amiens 1968; Prof. of Int. Law and Political Sociology, Univ. of Paris I (Panthéon-Sorbonne) 1969, Dir Disarmament Research and Study Centre (CEREDE); mem. Steering Cttee, Parti Socialiste (PS) 1970, 1973, mem. Exec. Bureau 1976; Mayor of Coise-Saint-Jean-Pied-Gauthier 1971–95; Deputy (Savoie) to Nat. Ass. 1973–81; Gen. Councillor, Savoie 1973–81; PS Nat. Del. for matters relating to the EC 1976–79; mem. European Parl. 1978–79, 1984–99, Pres. Budget Cttee 1984–87, Chair. Socialist Group 1989–94, Vice-Pres. 1997–99; Judge, Int. Tribunal for the Law of the Sea 2002–; Minister-Del. for Co-operation, attached to Minister for External Relations 1981–82; mem. Exec. Council UNESCO 1983–84. *Publication:* A l'épreuve du pouvoir: le tiers-mondisme, pour quoi faire? 1984 and numerous works on int. law and political science. *Address:* Coise-Saint-Jean-Pied-Gauthier, 73800 Montmélian, France (home).

COTE, David M., BBA; American business executive; *Chairman and CEO, Honeywell International Inc.;* ed Univ. of New Hampshire; various man. positions with General Electric –1996, Corp. Sr Vice-Pres., Pres. and CEO General Electric Appliances 1996–99; Pres., CEO and Chair. TRW, Cleveland 1999–2002; Pres. and CEO Honeywell International Inc. Feb.–July 2002, Chair. and CEO July 2002–; mem. Bd of Dirs JP Morgan Chase; adviser to Kohlberg Kravis Roberts & Co.; mem. Nat. Security Telecommunications Advisory Cttee; one of 10 US CEOs invited to serve on US-India CEO Forum est. by Pres. George W. Bush and Indian Prime Minister Manmohan Singh 2005, Co-Chair. 2009; named by Pres. Barack Obama to serve on bipartisan Nat. Comm. on Fiscal Responsibility and Reform 2010; Vice-Chair. Business Roundtable 2011, Chair. Energy and Environment Cttee; one of several CEOs from major global corpns to join USAID Admin. Henrietta Fore on her public pvt. partnership earthquake relief mission to Sichuan Prov., China following the earthquake May 2008; Hon. Prof., Beihang Univ. Aeronautics and Astronautics, Beijing 2009; Hon. LLD (Graziadio School of Business and Man., Pepperdine Univ.) 2001, Hon. DHumLitt (Univ. of New Hampshire) 2011; Corporate Social Responsibility Award, Foreign Policy Asscn 2007, Peter G. Peterson Award for Business Statesmanship, Cttee for Econ. Devt 2011, 2012, Distinguished Achievement Award, B'nai B'rith International 2011, Global Leadership Award, Asia Soc. 2012, named CEO of the Year by Chief Executive magazine 2013, recognized as one of the World's Best CEOs by Barron's magazine 2013. *Address:* Honeywell International Inc., 101 Columbia Road, Morristown, NJ 07962-1057, USA (office). *Telephone:* (973) 455-2000 (office). *Fax:* (973) 455-4807 (office). *Website:* www.honeywell.com.

COTILLARD, Marion; French actress and singer; b. 30 Sept. 1975, Paris; d. of Jean-Claude Cotillard (actor, playwright and dir) and Niseema Theillaud (actress and drama teacher); ed Conservatoire d'Art Dramatique, Orléans; raised in Orléans; made acting debut as child with role in one of her father's plays; cinema debut with film L'Histoire du garçon qui voulait qu'on l'embrasse 1994; first prominent screen role was in Taxi 1998, reprised role as Lili Bertineau in two sequels; only second actress to win Best Actress Academy Award performing in a language other than English (along with Sophia Loren in La Ciociara 1960); Chevalier, Ordre des Arts et des Letters 2010. *Films include:* L'Histoire du garçon qui voulait qu'on l'embrasse 1994, Snuff Movie 1995, Comment je me suis disputé… (ma vie sexuelle) (aka My Sex Life… or How I Got Into an Argument, USA) 1996, La belle verte 1996, Taxi 1998, La guerre dans le Haut Pays (aka War in the Highlands) 1999, L'Appel de la cave 1999, Du bleu jusqu'en Amérique (aka Blue Away to America) 1999, Quelques jours de trop 2000, Le Marquis 2000, Taxi 2

2000, Heureuse 2001, Boomer 2001, Lisa 2001, Les jolies choses (aka Pretty Things) 2001, Une affaire privée (aka A Private Affair) 2002, Taxi 3 2003, Jeux d'enfants (aka Love Me If You Dare) 2003, Big Fish 2003, Innocence 2004, Un long dimanche de fiançaille (aka A Very Long Engagement) (César Award for Best Supporting Actress) 2004, Edy 2005, Cavalcade 2005, Ma vie en l'air 2005, Mary 2005, Sauf le respect que je vous dois 2005, La boîte noire 2005, Toi et moi 2006, Fair Play 2006, A Good Year 2006, played and sang role of Edith Piaf in La Môme (retitled 'La Vie en Rose' in USA) (Academy Award for Best Actress 2008, César Award for Best Actress 2008, BAFTA Award for Best Actress in a Leading Role 2008, Golden Globe Award 2008, Czech Lion Award for Best Actress 2008, Los Angeles Film Critics' Asscn Award 2008, London Critics' Circle Film Award 2008, Boston Soc. of Film Critics Award 2008, Palm Springs Int. Film Festival Award 2008, Cabourg Romantic Film Festival Award 2008) 2007, Public Enemies 2009, Le Dernier Vol 2009, Nine 2009, Forehead Tittaes (video short) 2010, Lady Blue Shanghai (short) 2010, Inception 2010, Little White Lies 2010, Lady Grey London (short) 2011, Midnight in Paris 2011, Contagion 2011, L.A.dy Dior (short) 2011, Rust & Bone 2012, The Dark Knight Rises 2012. *Television:* Extrême limite (series) 1994, Chloé 1996, Interdit de vieillir 1998, Les redoutables (series) 2001, Une femme piégée 2001. *Address:* c/o Creative Artists Agency, 4th Floor, Space One, 1 Beadon Road, London, W6 0EA, England. *E-mail:* info@cotillard.net. *Website:* www.cotillard.net.

COTLER, Irwin, OC; Canadian lawyer, politician and professor of law; b. 8 May 1940, Montreal; Prof. of Law, McGill Univ., Dir Human Rights Programme, Chair. InterAmicus Int. Human Rights Advocacy Centre (on leave); fmr Visiting Prof., Harvard Law School; fmr Woodrow Wilson Fellow, Yale Law School; MP 1999–, mem. Standing Cttee on Foreign Affairs, Sub-cttee on Human Rights and Int. Devt, Cttee on Justice and Human Rights; Special Advisor to Minister of Foreign Affairs on Int. Criminal Court 2000–03; Minister of Justice and Attorney-Gen. 2003–06; Chair. Int. Comm. of Inquiry into the Fate and Whereabouts of Raoul Wallenberg, Comm. on Econ. Coercion and Discrimination. *Address:* House of Commons, 491 West Block, Ottawa, ON K1A 0A6, Canada (office). *Telephone:* (613) 995-0121 (office). *Fax:* (613) 992-6762 (office). *E-mail:* cotlei@parl.gc.ca (office). *Website:* www.irwincotler.ca (office).

COTTA, Michèle, LèsL; French journalist; *Vice-President, IDF1;* b. 15 June 1937, Nice; d. of Jacques Cotta and Hélène Scoffier; m. 1st Claude Tchou (divorced); one s. (deceased) one d.; m. 2nd Phillipe Barret 1992; ed Lycée de Nice, Faculté de Lettres de Nice and Inst. d'études politiques de Paris; journalist with L'Express 1963–69, 1971–76; Europ I 1970–71, 1986; political diarist, France-Inter 1976–80; Head of political service, Le Point 1977–80, Reporter 1986; Chief Political Ed. RTL 1980–81; Pres. Dir-Gen. Radio France 1981–82; Pres. Haute Autorité de la Communication Audiovisuelle 1982–86; Producer Faits de Soc. on TF1 1987, Dir of Information 1987–92, Pres. Sofica Images Investissements 1987; producer and presenter La Revue de presse, France 2 1993–95; political ed. Nouvel Economiste 1993–96; producer and presenter Polémiques, France 2 1995–99, Dir-Gen. France 2 1999–2002 (retd); editorial writer, RTL 1996–99; apptd Dir-Gen. JLA Groupe 2002; currently Vice-Pres., TV channel IDF1; mem. Conseil économique et social; Officier, Légion d'honneur, Officier, Ordre nat. du mérite. *Publications:* La collaboration 1940–1944, 1964, Les elections présidentielles 1966, Prague, l'été des Tanks 1968, La Vième République 1974, Les miroirs de Jupiter 1986, La Sixième République 1992, Les Secrets d'une Victoire 1999, Politic Circus 2004, Cahiers secrets of the Fifth Republic (Vol. 1) 1965–1977 2007, Cahiers secrets of the Fifth Republic (Vol. 2) 1977–1986 2008, Cahiers secrets of the Fifth Republic (Vol. 3) 1986–1997 2009, Cahiers secrets of the Fifth Republic (Vol. 4) 1997–2007 2010, Le rose et le gris 2013. *Address:* JLA Productions, 7 rue des Bretons, 93210 Saint-Denis la Plaine, France (office). *Telephone:* (1) 49-17-27-27 (office). *E-mail:* michele .cotta@groupe-jla.com (office).

COTTE, Bruno; French judge; *Judge, International Criminal Court;* b. 10 June 1945, Lyons; s. of André Cotte and Hélène Perol; m. Catherine Mathieu; three d.; ed Univ. of Lyons, Ecole Nationale de la Magistrature, Bordeaux; studies in Paris; Teaching Asst in Criminology, Faculty of Law, Univ. of Paris II 1970; Magistrate in Ministry of Justice and Head, Office of Dir of Criminal Affairs and Pardons 1970–73; Deputy Public Prosecutor, Tribunal de Grande Instance de Lyon (Lyons Dist Court) 1973–75; Head of Prosecution Bureau, Directorate of Criminal Affairs and Pardons, Ministry of Justice with competence in econ., financial and social criminal matters 1975–80; Lecturer, French Nat. School for Judiciary, Bordeaux 1975–80; Special Asst to First Pres. of Supreme Court of Appeal (judicial competence of First Pres.) 1980–81; Special Asst to Attorney Gen., Paris Court of Appeal, serving as Sec.-Gen. of Public Prosecutor's Dept 1981–84; Deputy Dir of Criminal Justice, Directorate of Criminal Affairs and Pardons, Ministry of Justice 1983–84, Dir for Criminal Affairs and Pardons 1984–90; Attorney Gen. to Versailles Court of Appeal May–Sept. 1990; Public Prosecutor in Tribunal de Grande Instance de Paris (Paris Dist Court) 1990–95; Counsel for Prosecution to Supreme Court of Appeal (Criminal Chamber) 1995–2000; Lecturer in Criminal Procedure to mems of Prefectural Police, Ministry of the Interior 1995–2000; Pres. of jury that confers rank of judicial police officers to student inspectors of Nat. Police Force, Ministry of the Interior 1996–2000; Pres. Criminal Chamber of Supreme Court of Appeal 2000–08; Lecturer in Criminal Procedure, Nat. School for the Judiciary, Paris 2000–07; Acting First Pres. Cour de Cassation (Supreme Court of Appeal) March–May 2007; Judge, Int. Criminal Court, The Hague 2008–; mem. Paris Aide aux Victimes, amongst others; Chevalier du Mérite agricole 1979, Commdr, Ordre nat. du Mérite 2001, Commdr, Légion d'honneur 2005; Penitentiary Medal. *Address:* International Criminal Court, PO Box 19519, 2500 CM The Hague, The Netherlands (office). *Telephone:* (70) 515-9920 (office). *Fax:* (70) 515-8789 (office). *E-mail:* bruno.cotte@icc-cpi.int (office). *Website:* www.icc-cpi.int (office).

COTTI, Flavio; Swiss politician; b. 18 Oct. 1939, Muralto; m. Renata Naretto; one d.; ed Univ. of Freiburg; barrister and public notary in Locarno 1965–75; mem. Locarno Communal Council 1964–75; mem. of cantonal Parl. of Ticino 1967–75; mem. of Govt, canton of Ticino, Head of Dept of Home Affairs, Econ. Affairs, Justice and Mil. Matters 1975–83; mem. Nat. Council 1983–86; mem. Fed. Council 1987–99; Head of Fed. Dept of Home Affairs 1987–93, Dept of Foreign Affairs 1994–99, Pres. of Swiss Confed. 1991 and 1998, Vice-Pres. 1990, 1997; Pres. Bd of Dirs Ticino Cantonal Tourist Office 1976–84; Pres. Christian Democratic People's

Party (CDPP) of Ticino 1981, CDPP of Switzerland 1984; Chair. OSCE 1996; Chair. Int. Advisory Bd Credit Suisse Group –2007; mem. Bd of Dirs Fiat SpA 2000–05, Jakobs Foundation (and trustee) 1999–2010, Georg Fischer Ltd 2000–10, Intier Automotive Inc. 2002–04; mem. Foundation Bd World Econ. Forum 1999–2010. *Address:* c/o Christlichdemokratische Volkspartei der Schweiz—Parti démocrate-chrétien suisse (Christian Democratic People's Party), Klaraweg 6, Postfach 5835, 3001 Bern, Switzerland.

COTTINGHAM, Robert; American artist; b. 26 Sept. 1935, Brooklyn, New York; s. of James Cottingham and Aurelia Cottingham; m. Jane Weismann 1967; three d.; ed Brooklyn Tech. High School, Pratt Inst.; served in US army 1955–58; Art Dir with Young and Rubicam Advertising Inc., New York 1959–64, Los Angeles 1964–68; left advertising to paint 1968–; taught at Art Centre Coll. of Design, Los Angeles 1969–70; moved to London 1972–76; returned to USA 1976; Nat. Endowment for the Arts 1974–75; numerous solo exhbns; works in many public galleries in USA and also in Hamburg Museum, Tate Gallery, London and Utrecht Museum; MacDowell Colony Residencies 1993, 1994; Walter Gropius Fellowship, Huntington Museum of Art 1992; mem. Nat. Acad. of Design. *Publications:* numerous print publs (lithographs, etchings). *Leisure interests:* travel, music, history. *Address:* PO Box 604, Blackman Road, Newtown, CT 06470; c/o Forum Gallery, 730 5th Avenue, Suite 201, New York, NY 10019, USA.

COUCEIRO PIZARRO BELEZA, Luís Miguel, PhD; Portuguese economist and banker; b. 28 April 1950, Porto; s. of José Júlio Pizaro Beleza and Maria dos Prazeres Couceiro da Costa Pizarro Beleza; m.; two c.; ed Massachusetts Inst. of Tech., USA; fmr Asst Prof., then Assoc. Prof., Faculty of Econs, Univ. Nova de Lisboa; econ. adviser and consultant Bank of Portugal 1979–87, mem. Bd 1987–90, Gov. 1992–94, mem. Advisory Bd 1994–; adviser, IMF 1984–87; Minister of Finance 1990–91; fmr adviser, Banco Comercial Português; fmr Visiting Prof., Brown Univ., Univ. dos Açores, INSEAD, Fontainebleau; Dir Banco Expresso Atlântico Lisbon, Siemens Portugal; consultant and Ed. Economia journal (Univ. Católica Portuguesa); Grand Cross, Nat. Order, Cross of the South (Brazil), Grand Cross, Order of Merit. *Publications:* numerous articles in journals. *Address:* c/o Advisory Board, Banco de Portugal, R. Francisco Ribeiro 2, 1150-165 Lisbon, Portugal (office). *Telephone:* (21) 3213200 (office). *Fax:* (21) 3128115 (office). *E-mail:* info@bportugal.pt (office). *Website:* www.bportugal.pt (office).

COUCHEPIN, François; Swiss lawyer; b. 19 Jan. 1935, Martigny; s. of Louis Couchepin and Andrée Couchepin; m. Anne Marie Cottier 1957; six c.; ed Univ. of Lausanne; legal practitioner at Rodolphe Tissières 1959–64; own legal practice in Martigny 1964–; elected to Cantonal Council of Canton Valais 1965, re-elected 1969, 1973, 1977; Sec. Radical Group 1965–77, Pres. 1977–79; Head of French Section, Cen. Language Service, Fed. Chancellery 1980; Vice-Chancellor responsible for gen. admin. of Fed. Chancellery 1981; Chancellor of the Swiss Fed. 1991–99; mem. Defence Staff. *Address:* c/o Federal Chancellery, Bundeshaus-West, 3003 Berne; Avenue Ruchonnet 41, 1003 Lausanne, Switzerland (home).

COUCHEPIN, Pascal; Swiss politician and fmr head of state; b. 5 April 1942, Martigny; m.; three c.; ed Lausanne Univ.; elected mem. local council Martigny 1968; Deputy Mayor of Martigny 1976, Mayor 1984–98; elected to the Nat. Council 1979; Chair. Parl. Group, Liberal Democrat Party (LDP) 1989–96; fmr Chair. Nat. Council's Cttee for Science and Research; fmr Chair. Fed. Dept of Justice and Police section of the Control Cttee; elected to Fed. Council 1998; Vice-Pres. of the Swiss Confed. 2002, 2007, Pres. of the Swiss Confed. 2003, 2008; Head of Fed. Dept of Econ. Affairs 1998–2002, of Home Affairs 2003–09 (resgnd); fmr Gov. IBRD, EBRD; Officier de la Légion d'honneur 2011; Dr hc (Kaslik, Lebanon 2008). *Address:* Av. du Grand St-Bernard 37, 1920 Martigny, Switzerland (office).

COUCHER, Iain, MBA; British transport industry executive; *CEO, Network Rail;* m.; two c.; ed Imperial Coll., London and Open Univ.; worked for EDS 1983–99, positions included Head of Mergers and Acquisitions; CEO TubeLines 1999–2002, seconded as CEO to TranSys consortium 1996–98; Man. Dir Network Rail 2002, Deputy CEO 2002–07, CEO 2007–. *Address:* Network Rail, 40 Melton Street, London, NW1 2EE England (office). *Telephone:* (20) 7557-8000 (office). *Fax:* (20) 7557-9000 (office). *Website:* www.networkrail.co.uk (office).

COUGHLAN, Mary, B.Soc.Sc; Irish politician; b. 1965, Co. Donegal; d. of the late Cathal Coughlan; m. David Charlton; one s. one d.; ed Ursuline Convent, Sligo, Univ. Coll., Dublin; early career in social work; mem. Co. Donegal Co. Council 1986–2001; mem. North Western Health Bd 1987–2001; mem. Fianna Fáil; mem. Dáil (TD) for Donegal SW 1987–2011; Chair. Oireachtas Jt Cttee on Irish Language 1993–95; Minister of State, Dept of Arts, Heritage, Gaeltacht and the Islands 2000–02, Minister for Social, Community and Family Affairs 2002–04, Minister for Agric. and Food 2004–08, Tánaiste (Deputy Prime Minister) 2008–11, Minister for Enterprise, Trade and Employment 2008–10, Minister for Educ. and Skills 2010–11, also for Health and Children 2011; mem. Co. Donegal Vocational Educ. Cttee 1986–99 (Chair. 1991–92); Chair. Bd of Man. Abbey Vocational School, Donegal Town; mem. Bd of Man. Tourism Coll., Killybegs; fmr mem. Comhchoiste na Gaeilge (Chair. 1993–94); Pres. Killybegs Coast and Cliff Rescue Service; Hon. Sec. Fianna Fáil Party 1995. *Address:* c/o Department of Education and Skills, Marlborough Street, Dublin 1, Ireland (office). *Telephone:* (1) 8896400 (office). *Fax:* (1) 8892367 (office). *Website:* www.education.ie (home).

COUGHLIN, Cathy M., BA, MS; American telecommunications industry executive; *Senior Executive Vice-President and Global Marketing Officer, AT&T Inc.;* b. St Louis, Mo.; ed Northwestern Univ., St Louis Univ.; began communications career at Southwestern Bell Telephone Co., St Louis 1979; has held sr man. roles in sales, marketing, operations and advertising; Pres. and CEO AT&T Midwest –2007, Sr Exec. Vice-Pres. and Global Marketing Officer, AT&T Inc. 2007–; mem. Bd of Dirs Northwestern Univ., Girl Scouts of the USA; mem. Bd of Trustees, American Film Inst.; named by RCR Wireless to the list of Top Ten Women in Wireless 2012. *Address:* AT&T Inc., 175 East Houston, San Antonio, TX 78205-2233, USA (office). *Telephone:* (210) 821-4105 (office). *Fax:* (210) 351-2071 (office). *E-mail:* info@att.com (office). *Website:* www.att.com (office).

COULIBALY, Tiéna, BS, MS; Malian economist and politician; b. 1952, Boré, Douentza Dist; m.; four c.; ed Laval Univ., Canada, Purdue Univ., USA; Technical Adviser, Ministry of Livestock 1981–87; Asst Dir-Gen., Libyan-Malian Livestock Devt Co. 1987–88; Minister of Finance and Trade 1988–91; arrested and charged

following revolution 1991, later acquitted; Technical Adviser, Mission de restructuration du secteur coton (cotton restructuring body) 2001; CEO Compagnie malienne de développement des textiles (state cotton co.) 2008–12; Minister of the Economy, Finance and the Budget 2012–13, of Commerce and Industry 2013. *Address:* c/o Ministry of Commerce and Industry, Bamako, Mali.

COUMAKOYE, Kassiré Delwa, DenD; Chadian politician; b. 31 Dec. 1949, Bongor; ed Ecole Nat. d'Admin, Chad, Inst. Int. d'Admin Publique, Paris, Univ. de Paris I and II; Minister of Justice 1981–82, of Public Works, Housing and Town Planning 1987–88, of Justice 1988–89, of Posts and Telecommunications 1989–90, of Higher Educ. and Scientific Research 1989–90, of Communications and Liberties, of Justice June–Nov. 1993; Govt Spokesperson April–June 1993; Gen. Inspector of Admin 1987–; Prime Minister of Chad 1993–95, 2007–08; mem. and Pres. Rassemblement nat. pour la démocratie et le progrès 1992–; also Leader, Convention de l'opposition démocratique (alliance of opposition parties); sentenced to three months' imprisonment for possessing illegal weapons 1996; Chevalier Ordre de Mérite Centrafricain 1976, Commdr Ordre nat. du Tchad 1994. *Achievements include:* Cen. African champion in 3,000m. steeple chase 1965 (record unbroken). *Address:* Rassemblement Pour La Démocratie et Le Progrès, N'Djamena, Chad (office).

COUPLES, Frederick Stephen (Fred); American golfer; b. 3 Oct. 1959, Seattle, Wash.; m. Thais Couples; one s. one d.; ed Univ. of Houston; turned professional 1980; mem. US Ryder Cup Team 1989, 1991, 1993, 1995, 1997, Asst Capt. 2012; mem. President's Cup Team 1994, 1996, 1998, Capt. 2009; won Kemper Open 1984, Tournament Players Championship 1984, Byron Nelson Golf Classic 1987, Nissan Los Angeles Open 1990, Federal Express St Jude Classic BC Open, Johnnie Walker World Championship 1991, Nissan Los Angeles Open, Nestlé Int., Masters 1992, Honda Classic 1993, Buick Open 1994, World Cup 1994, Dubai Desert Classic, Johnnie Walker Classic 1995, The Players' Championship 1996, Bob Hope Chrysler Classic 1998, Memorial Tournament 1998, Shell Houston Open 2003; won maiden sr major at Senior Players Championship 2011; won Senior British Open Championship 2012; mem. Bridgestone Golf Tour Staff 2005–; PGA Tour Player of the Year 1991, 1992, Arnold Palmer Award 1992, inducted into World Golf Hall of Fame 2013. *Leisure interests:* tennis, all sports, antiques, bicycling, vintage cars. *Address:* c/o PGA Tour, 100 Avenue of the Champions, P.O. Box 109601, Palm Beach Gardens, FL 33410, USA. *Website:* www.bridgestonegolf.com/tour/fred-couples.

COURANT, Ernest David, PhD; American (naturalized) physicist and academic; *Distinguished Scientist Emeritus, Brookhaven National Laboratory;* b. 26 March 1920, Göttingen, Germany; s. of Richard Courant and Nina Runge; m. Sara Paul 1944; two s.; ed Swarthmore Coll. and Univ. of Rochester, USA; Scientist, Nat. Research Council (Canada), Montreal 1943–46; Research Assoc. in Physics, Cornell Univ. 1946–48; Physicist, Brookhaven Nat. Lab., Upton, NY 1948–60, Sr Physicist 1960–89, Distinguished Scientist Emer. 1990–; Prof. (part-time), Yale Univ. 1961–67, State Univ. of NY, Stony Brook 1967–85; Visiting Prof., Univ. of Mich. 1989–; Hon. Prof., Univ. of Science and Tech. of China, Hefei 1994; mem. NAS 1976; Fellow, AAAS 1981; Hon. DSc (Swarthmore Coll.) 1988; Pregel Prize, New York Acad. of Sciences 1979, Fermi Award 1986, R. R. Wilson Prize 1987. *Achievements include:* co-discoverer of Strong-focusing principle, particle accelerators. *Publications:* various articles; contrib. to Handbuch der Physik 1959, Annual Review of Nuclear Science 1968. *Address:* 40 West 72nd Street, New York, NY 10023, USA (home). *Telephone:* (212) 580-1006 (home). *E-mail:* ecourant@msn.com (home).

COURIC, Katherine (Katie); American broadcast journalist; b. 7 Jan. 1957, Arlington, Va; m. Jay Monahan (deceased); two d.; ed Univ. of Virginia; began career as desk asst for ABC news bureau, Washington, DC 1979; Assignment Ed., CNN 1980, later Assoc. Producer, Atlanta, later Producer of Take Two; worked at WTVJ, Miami for three years; joined NBC Network News 1989, later Nat. Corresp., The Today Show, Washington, DC, Co-Anchor 1991–2006; Anchor and Man. Ed. CBS Evening News 2006–11, also contrib. to 60 Minutes and other CBS News specials; hired by ABC to produce and host a syndicated daytime talk show; Global Anchor, Yahoo News 2013–; Co-host, NBC's morning coverage of Summer Olympics, Barcelona 1992, Co-host, Now with Tom Brokaw and Katie Couric 1993–94, Contributing Anchor, Dateline NBC 2005; six Emmy Awards, named Best in the Business by Washington Journalism Review 1993, ranked by Forbes magazine amongst The World's 100 Most Powerful Women (57th) 2004, (47th) 2005, (54th) 2006, (63rd) 2007, (62nd) 2008, (22nd) 2010. *Address:* c/o Yahoo! Inc., 701 First Avenue, Sunnyvale, CA 94089, USA. *Website:* news.yahoo.com.

COURIER, Jim; American business executive and fmr professional tennis player; b. 17 Aug. 1970, Sanford Fla; m. Susanna Lingman 2010; ed Nick Bollettieri Tennis Acad.; coached by José Higueras; winner, French Open 1991, 1992, Indian Wells (doubles) 1991; runner-up, US Open 1991, ATP World Championship 1991; winner, Australian Open 1992–93, Italian Open 1993; runner-up, French Open 1993, Wimbledon 1993; winner of 23 singles titles and six doubles titles and over $16 million in prize money at retirement in May 2000; now plays Delta Tour of Champions 2004–; Founding Partner, InsideOut Sports & Entertainment, LLC 2004–; Capt. US Davis Cup team 2010–; f. Raymond James Courier's Kids (inner-city youth tennis program); mem. Bd of Dirs First Serve, Gullikson Foundation; mem. Advisory Bd Falconhead Capital; elected to Int. Tennis Hall of Fame 2005. *Address:* InsideOut Sports & Entertainment LLC, 401 Lafayette, Suite 600, New York, NY 10003, USA (office). *Telephone:* (646) 367-2770 (office). *Fax:* (646) 367-2780 (office). *E-mail:* info@insideoutse.com (office). *Website:* www.insideoutse.com (office).

COURT, Rev. Margaret, AO, MBE, PhD; Australian ecclesiastic and fmr tennis player; *Senior Pastor, Victory Life Centre;* b. 16 July 1942, Albury, NSW; d. of Lawrence Smith and Maud Smith; m. Barry Court 1967; one s. three d.; ed St Augustines, Wodonga, Vic.; amateur player 1960–67; professional 1968–77; Australian champion 1960, 1961, 1962, 1963, 1964, 1965, 1966, 1969, 1970, 1971, 1973; French champion 1962, 1964, 1969, 1970, 1973; Wimbledon champion 1963, 1965, 1970; US champion 1962, 1965, 1969, 1970, 1973; held more major titles in singles, doubles and mixed doubles than any other player in history; won two Grand Slams, in mixed doubles 1963 and singles 1970; played Federation Cup for Australia 1963, 1964, 1965, 1966, 1968, 1969, 1971; ordained a Pentecostal minister in 1991, f. the Victory Life Centre, Perth 1996, currently Sr Pastor; elected to Int. Tennis Hall of Fame 1979, Australian Tennis Hall of Fame 1993, Australian Sports Medal 2000, Centenary Medal 2001, Show Court One at Melbourne Park renamed Margaret Court Arena on eve of Australian Open Jan. 2003, Western Australia Greatest Ever Tennis Player 2005, Western Australia Greatest Ever Female Sports Star 2005, Philippe Chatrier Award 2006, Golden Racket Award, Italian Tennis Fed. 2007. *Publications:* The Margaret Smith Story 1964, Court on Court 1974, Winning Faith (with Barbara Oldfield) 1993, Winning Words 1999, Our Winning Position 2003. *Address:* Victory Life Centre, PO Box 20, Osborne Park, WA 6917, Australia (office). *Telephone:* (8) 9202-7111 (office). *Fax:* (8) 9201-1299 (office). *E-mail:* court.margaret@victorylifecentre.com.au (office); reid.marylyn@victorylifecentre.com.au (office). *Website:* www.victorylifecentre .com.au (office).

COURTENAY, Sir Thomas (Tom) Daniel, Kt, KBE; British actor; b. 25 Feb. 1937; s. of the late Thomas Henry Courtenay and Annie Eliza Quest; m. 1st Cheryl Kennedy 1973 (divorced 1982); m. 2nd Isabel Crossley 1988; ed Kingston High School, Hull, Univ. Coll. London, Royal Acad. of Dramatic Art; started acting professionally 1960; Fellow, Univ. Coll. London; Hon. DLitt (Hull); Best Actor Award, Prague Festival 1968, TV Drama Award (for Oswald in Ghosts) 1968, Golden Globe Award for Best Actor 1983, Drama Critics' Award and Evening Standard Award 1980, 1983, BAFTA Award for Best Actor 1999. *Films include:* The Loneliness of the Long Distance Runner 1962, Private Potter 1962, Billy Liar 1963, King and Country 1964, Operation Crossbow 1965, King Rat 1965, Doctor Zhivago 1965, The Night of the Generals 1967, The Day the Fish Came Out 1967, A Dandy in Aspic 1968, Otley 1969, One Day in the Life of Ivan Denisovich 1970, Catch Me a Spy 1971, The Dresser 1983, The Last Butterfly 1990, Redemption (TV) 1991, Let Him Have It 1991, Old Curiosity Shop (TV) 1995, The Boy from Mercury 1996, A Rather English Marriage (TV) 1998, Whatever Happened to Harold Smith 1999, Last Orders 2002, Nicholas Nickleby 2002, Ready When You Are Mr. McGill (TV) 2003, Flood 2006, The Golden Compass 2007, Quartet 2012. *Plays include:* Billy Liar 1961–62, The Cherry Orchard 1966, Macbeth 1966, Hamlet 1968, She Stoops to Conquer 1969, Charley's Aunt 1971, Time and Time Again (Variety Club of GB Stage Actor Award) 1972, Table Manners 1974, The Norman Conquests 1974–75, The Fool 1975, The Rivals 1976, Clouds 1978, Crime and Punishment 1978, The Dresser (Drama Critics Award and Evening Standard Award for Best Actor) 1980, 1983, The Misanthrope 1981, Andy Capp 1982, Jumpers 1984, Rookery Nook 1986, The Hypochondriac 1987, Dealing with Clair 1988, The Miser 1992, Moscow Stations, Edinburgh 1993, London 1994, New York 1995, Poison Pen, Manchester 1993, Uncle Vanya, New York 1995, Art, London 1996, King Lear, Manchester 1999. *Television includes:* She Stoops to Conquer 1971, I Heard the Owl Call My Name 1973, Me and the Girls 1985, Absent Friends 1985, Redemption 1991, The Adventures of Young Indiana Jones: Treasure of the Peacock's Eye 1995, The Old Curiosity Shop 1995, A Rather English Marriage 1998, Ready When You Are Mr. McGill 2003, Little Dorrit (mini-series) 2008, The Royle Family 2008. *Publication:* Dear Tom: Letters from Home (memoirs) 2000. *Leisure interests:* playing the flute, watching sport. *Address:* c/o Jonathan Altaras Associates, 11 Garrick Street, London, WC2E 9AR, England (office). *Telephone:* (20) 7836-8722 (office).

COURVILLE, Isabelle, BEng, BCL; Canadian engineer, lawyer and business executive; *President, Hydro-Québec Distribution;* ed École Polytechnique de Montréal, McGill Univ.; has spent most of her career in the telecommunications industry, with Bell Canada, where she held several exec.-level positions, also led the team responsible for managing Stentor's nat. and int. alliances as Vice-Pres., Alliances and Legal Services at Stentor Resource Centre, later Sr Vice-Pres., Supply Chain and Capital Man., later Pres. and CEO Bell Nordiq Group (Télébec-NorthernTel), later Pres., Enterprise, Bell Canada; currently Pres. Hydro-Québec Distribution; mem. Bd of Dirs Sainte-Justine Hosp. Foundation; fmr mem. Conseil des gouverneurs associés de l'Université de Montréal; fmr mem. Bd of Dirs Conf. Bd of Canada, Montréal International; mem. Ordre des ingénieurs du Québec, Barreau du Québec, Canadian Bar Assocn; twice awarded Canada's Most Powerful Women: Top 100 Award in the Corp. Execs category, Women's Exec. Network (WXN), ranked by Fortune magazine amongst the 50 Most Powerful Women in Business outside the US (39th) 2012. *Address:* Hydro-Québec, 75 René-Lévesque Blvd West, 19th Floor, Montréal, PQ H2Z 1A4, Canada (office). *Telephone:* (514) 289-2211 (office). *E-mail:* info@hydroquebec.com (office). *Website:* www .hydroquebec.com (office).

COUSIN, Ertharin, BA, JD; American diplomatist, government official and UN official; *Executive Director, United Nations World Food Programme;* b. 1957, Chicago, Ill.; d. of Anne Cousin; ed Univ. of Illinois, Chicago, Univ. of Georgia School of Law; fmr Asst Attorney Gen., State of Illinois, Chicago; Deputy Chief of Staff, Democratic Nat. Cttee, Washington, DC 1993–94; White House liaison, US Dept of State 1994–96; Exec. Dir Pres. Clinton Re-election Campaign Team for Illinois 1997; Vice-Pres. Govt, Community and Political Affairs, Presidential Inaugural Cttee 1997; Vice-Pres. for Govt and Community Affairs, Jewel Food Stores 1997–99; Vice-Pres. of Public Affairs, Albertsons Foods 1999–2001, Sr Vice-Pres. for Public and Govt Affairs 201–04, also served as Pres. and Chair. of co.'s corp. foundation; Exec. Vice-Pres. and COO Feeding America (fmrly America's Second Harvest) 2004–06; Founder and Pres. The Polk Street Group (nat. public affairs firm), Chicago 2007–09; Commr Bd for Int. Food and Agricultural Devt, USAID 1997–2001; Amb. and Perm. Rep. to UN Agencies for Food and Agric., Rome 2009–12; Exec. Dir UN World Food Programme, Rome 2012–; ranked by Forbes magazine amongst The World's 100 Most Powerful Women (69th) 2012, (49th) 2013. *Address:* United Nations World Food Programme, Via C.G.Viola 68, Parco dei Medici, 00148 Rome, Italy (office). *Telephone:* (06) 65131 (office). *Fax:* (06) 6590632 (office). *Website:* www.wfp.org (office).

COUSINS, Richard J., BSc, MSc; British food services industry executive; *Group Chief Executive, Compass Group PLC;* ed Univs of Sheffield and Lancaster; began career with Cadbury Schweppes PLC; joined BTR PLC 1984, becoming Corp. Planning Man., Newey & Eyre (subsidiary co.); joined BPB Group (plasterboard mfr) 1990, apptd Group Financial Controller 1992, served as Gen. Man. then Man. Dir for Packaging, Pres. (Canada) 1998–2000, Group CEO 2000–05; mem. Bd of Dirs and Group Chief Exec. Compass Group PLC 2006–, mem. Corp. Responsi-bility and Exec. Cttees; Dir (non-exec.) Reckitt Benckiser Group plc; fmr Dir (non-

exec.) P&O plc, HBOS plc. *Address:* Compass Group PLC, Compass House, Guildford Street, Chertsey, Surrey, KT16 9BQ, England (office). *Telephone:* (1932) 573000 (office). *Fax:* (1932) 569956 (office). *E-mail:* info@compass-group.com (office). *Website:* www.compass-group.com (office).

COUSTEAU, Jean-Michel; French explorer, oceanographer, environmentalist activist, educator and film producer; *President, Ocean Futures Society;* b. 8 May 1938; first s. of ocean explorer Jacques-Yves Cousteau and Simone Melchior; one s. one d.; pnr, Nancy Marr; Exec. Vice-Pres. The Cousteau Soc. for nearly 20 years; est. Ocean Futures Soc., Santa Barbara, Calif. (non-profit marine conservation and educ. org.) 1999, now offices in France, Brazil and Italy; has served as spokesman on water issues at UN World Summit on Sustainable Devt in Johannesburg, at 3rd World Water Forum in Kyoto, at Dialogues on Water for Life and Security in Barcelona; spokesperson for US Pavilion at Expo '98, Lisbon, Portugal 1998; merged Jean-Michel Cousteau Inst. with Free Willy Keiko Foundation to continue research and care for Keiko (captive killer whale) 1999; mem. Bd of Dirs Athens Environmental Foundation for Athens 2004 Olympic Games; launched Sustain-able Reefs Program (package of materials including CD-ROM, cartoon book and video on sustainable man. of coral reef systems) 2004; Hon. DHumLitt (Pepperdine Univ.) 1976; DEMA Reaching Out Award 1994, NOGI Award, Acad. of Underwater Arts and Sciences 1995, SeaKeepers Award, Showboats International 1996, John M. Olguin Marine Environment Award, Cabrillo Marine Aquarium 1996, Envir-onmental Hero Award, White House Nat. Oceans Conf. 1998, first Oceana Ocean Hero Award 2003, inducted into Int. Scuba Diving Hall of Fame 2003, Poseidon/ Lifetime Achievement Award, Reef Check 2006, Emmy Award, Peabody Award, 7 d'Or, Cable Ace Award. *Achievements include:* first person to represent the Environment in Opening Ceremony of Olympic Games, Salt Lake City 2002. *Films:* has produced more than 75 films, including Jean-Michel Cousteau's Ocean Adventures (three-year series of HD TV specials on PBS and internationally) (exec. producer), Sharks 3D, Return to the Amazon 2008, Dolphins and Whales 3D: Tribes of the Ocean 2008; appears in IMAX documentary film Coral Reef Adventure; also appeared in documentary-type special feature on DVD version of Spongebob Squarepants Movie; did similar feature for DVD of Disney/Pixar movie Finding Nemo. *Publications include:* Water Culture (ed. and contributing author), My Father, the Captain 2004, America's Underwater Treasures (co-author) 2006. *Address:* Ocean Futures Society, 325 Chapala Street, Santa Barbara, CA 93101, USA (office). *Telephone:* (805) 899-8899 (office). *E-mail:* contact@oceanfutures.org (office). *Website:* www.oceanfutures.org (office).

COUTARD, Raoul; French cinematographer and film director; b. 16 Sept. 1924, Paris; with French mil. Information Service, Vietnam, subsequently civilian photographer for Time and Paris-Match; worked in photographic labs during World War II; f. production co. making documentary films; head of photography for French New Wave directors including Godard and Truffaut; later with Costa-Gavras; Preis Film Kritik, Munich 1961, Prix de la photographie conjoint avec Henri Decaë, Mar del Plata Festival 1963, Prix de la Commission Supérieur Technique, Festival de Cannes 1982, Best Director of Photography, 30 Dernières Années dans la CEE, Festival de Brussel 1988, Int. Award, American Soc. of Cinematographers 1996, Prix Imago 1997, Marburger Kamerapreis 2001, Camera d'Or Manki Brother, Macedonia 2002. *Films include:* La Passe du diable 1958, Ramuntcho 1959, Pêcheur d'Islande 1959, Petit jour 1960, Au bout de souffle 1960, Shoot the Pianist 1960, Les Grandes personnes 1961, Lola 1961, Une femme est une femme 1961, Chronique d'un été 1961, Et satan conduit le bal 1962, Jules et Jim 1962, L'Amour à vingt ans 1962, La Poupée 1962, Vivre sa vie 1962, Le Petit soldat 1963, Als twee druppels water 1963, Baie des Anges, Les Carabiniers 1963, Vacances portugaises 1963, Le Mépris 1963, La Peau Douce 1964, Baisers 1964, La Difficulté d'être infidèle 1964, Bande à part 1964, Les Plus belles escroqueries du monde 1964, Une femme mariée 1964, Un monsieur de compagnie 1964, Scruggs 1965, L'Avatar botanique de Mlle Flora 1965, Alphaville 1965, Je vous salue mafia 1965, Pierrot Le Fou 1965, La 317ème Section 1965, The Defector 1966, Made in USA 1966, Horizon 1967, Two or Three Things I Know About Her 1967, Weekend 1967, Sailor from Gibraltar 1967, Rocky Road to Dublin 1968, The Bride Wore Black 1968, Z 1969, The Southern Star 1969, L'Aveu 1970, Hoa Binh (Prix Jean Vigo, Prix de la premiere oeuvre, Cannes, Bell Ring Scholastic Award, London Film Festival) 1970, La Liberté en croupe 1970, L'Explosion 1970, Êtes-vous fiancée à un marin grec ou à un pilote de ligne? 1971, Les Aveux les plus doux 1971, Embassy 1972, The Jerusalem File 1972, Le Trèfle à cinq feuilles 1972, Le Gang des otages 1973, L'Emmerdeur 1973, Comme un pot de fraises 1974, Le Crabe-Tambour (Cesar de la photographie) 1977, Passion 1982 (Prix de la photographie, Biennale de Venise 1983), Carmen 1983, Dangerous Moves 1984, La Garce 1984, Parachute 1985, Max mon amour 1986, Blanc de Chine 1988, Brennende Betten 1988, Let Sleeping Cops Lie 1988, Nachbarschaft 1990, Kaffeeklatsch 1990, Bethune: The Making of a Hero 1989 (Genie Awards, Canada 1991), Gemini Awards, Canada 1992), Les Enfants Volants 1990, La Femme Fardée 1990, Maigret et les Plaisirs de la Nuit 1991, La Vie Crevee 1992, The Birth of Love 1994, À Naissance De L'Amour 1994, Faut pas rire du bonheur 1994, Le Coeur Fantome 1996, Sauvage innocence 2001. *Publication:* L'Impériale de Van Su - Ou comment je suis entré dans le cinéma en dégustant une soupe chinoise (autobiography) 2007. *Address:* c/o Editions Ramsay, 91 bis rue de Cherche-Midi, 75006 Paris, France (office).

COUTO, Mia; Mozambican biologist, writer and journalist; b. (António Emílio Leite Couto), 5 July 1955, Beira; fmr Dir Mozambique Information Agency; columnist, Notícias daily newspaper, Tempo magazine; currently works as environmental biologist at Limpopo Transfrontier Park; Nat. Award for Litera-ture, Mozambican Nat. Journalistic Asscn 1991, Best of 1995 Award, Sao Paulo Art Critics Asscn 1996, Prémio Vergílio Ferreira 1999, Latin Union Prize for Literature 2007. *Publications include:* Raiz d'orvalho (poems) 1983, Vozes Anoitecidas (trans. as Voices Made Night) 1986, Cada homem e uma raca 1991 (trans. as Every Man is a Race 1994), Terra Sonambula 1992, Under the Frangipani 2001, Um Rio Chamado Tempo, Uma Casa Chamada Terra 2002, Vozes Anoitecidas 2002, Contos do Nascer da Terra 2002, The Last Flight of the Flamingo 2004, O fio das missangas 2002, A chuva pasmada 2004, Pensatempos 2005, O outro pé da Sereia 2006, Venenos de Deus, Remédios do Diabo 2008, Jesusalém 2009, A Confissão da Leoa 2012.

COUTTS, Ronald Thomson, PhD, DSc, FRSC; Canadian professor of medicinal chemistry; *Professor Emeritus of Psychiatry, University of Alberta;* b. 19 June 1931, Glasgow, Scotland; s. of Ronald Miller Coutts and Helen Alexanderina Crombie; m. Sheenah Kirk Black 1957; two s. one d.; ed Woodside Secondary School, Glasgow, Univ. of Strathclyde, Glasgow Univ. and Chelsea Coll., London; Lecturer in Medicinal Chem., Sunderland Tech. Coll., England 1959–63; Asst then Assoc. Prof., Univ. of Saskatchewan, Canada 1963–66; Prof., Univ. of Alberta 1966–97, Distinguished Univ. Prof. 1984–, Pres. Faculty Asscn 1978–79, mem. Bd of Govs 1982–85, Hon. Prof. of Psychiatry 1979–, Prof. Emer. 1997–; McCalla Prof., Univ. of Alberta 1985–86; Pres. Xenotox Services Ltd 1978–; Scientific Ed. Canadian Journal of Pharmaceutical Sciences 1967–72; mem. Ed. Bd Asian Journal of Pharmaceutical Sciences 1978–85; Ed. Journal of Pharmacological Methods 1984–98; Ed. Bd Chirality 1989–95; Pres. Asscn of Faculties of Pharmacy of Canada 1994–96; Fellow, Pharmaceutical Soc. of GB, Canadian Inst. of Chemistry, American Asscn of Pharmaceutical Scientists; McNeil Research Award 1982, Canadian Coll. of Neuropsychopharmacology Medal 1992, Innovation in Neuropsychopharmacology Research Award 1999. *Publications:* over 350 research manuscripts and reviews; several textbooks and chapters in textbooks. *Leisure interests:* golf, cross-country skiing, squash and music (playing and listening). *Address:* 4724 139 Street, NW, Edmonton, AB, Canada (home). *Telephone:* (780) 436-4313 (home).

COUTURE, Pierre-François; French business executive and civil servant; *Special Delegate for Economic Development in Ardennes;* b. 15 May 1946, Grenoble; s. of André Couture and Françoise Couture (née Dubourguez); brother of Xavier Couture (q.v.); m. 2nd Jocelyne Kerjouan; one s.; three c. from previous m.; ed Ecole Nat. d'Admin., Inst. d'Etudes Politiques, Paris, Univ. of Paris II; Dir Industry and Energy Dept, Ministry of the Econ. and Finance 1974–78, mem. Oil Co. Audit Programme 1979; Dir of Budgets Ministries of Finance and Justice and Office of the Prime Minister 1978–79; Gen. Sec. Exploration and Production Div., Cie Française des Pétroles 1979–81; Tech. Adviser Ministry of the Budget 1981–83; Tech. Adviser Ministry of Industry 1983–84, Dir of Gas, Electricity and Coal 1983–1990; Adviser to Chair. of La Poste 1996; Special Adviser to Industry Sec. in charge of Postal Services and Telecommunications, Ministry of the Economy, Finance and Industry 1997–99; Chair. Enterprise Minière et Chimique (EMC) 1999–2004; Head of Econ. and Financial Audit Programme, Ministry of Economy, Finance and Industry 2005–; Special Del. for Econ. Devt in Ardennes 2006–; mem. Bd of Dirs Charbonnages de France; Chair. Viet Nam Cttee, Medef Int; Chevalier, Ordre Nat. du Mérite, Légion d'honneur. *Leisure interests:* travel, mountain sports, golf. *Address:* Conseil Général des Ardennes, Hôtel du Département, 08011 Charleville-Mézières Cedex, France (office). *Telephone:* 3-24-59-60-60 (office). *Fax:* 3-24-37-76-76 (office). *E-mail:* conseil-general-ardennes@cg08.fr (office). *Website:* www.cg08.fr (office).

COUVREUR, Philippe; Belgian lawyer and international organization official; *Registrar, International Court of Justice;* b. 29 Nov. 1951, Schaerbeek; ed Collège Jean XXIII, Brussels, Facultés Notre-Dame de la Paix, Namur, Université Catholique de Louvain, King's Coll., London, UK, Universidad Complutense de Madrid, Spain; Intern, Legal Service, Comm. of EC 1978–79 (worked on accessions of Spain and Portugal to join EC); Special Asst in offices Registrar and Deputy-Registrar, Int. Court of Justice, The Hague 1982–86, Sec. 1986–94, First Sec. 1994–95, Prin. Legal Sec. 1995–2000, Registrar Int. Court of Justice, 2000– (re-elected 2007); Asst Prof., Centre d'études européennes and in Law Faculty of Université Catholique de Louvain 1976–82; Visiting Prof. in the Law of Int. Orgs, Univ. of Ouagadougou, Burkina Faso 1980–82; Professeur extraordinaire in Law of Nations and Comparative Constitutional Law, Ecole des Hautes études commerciales Saint-Louis, Brussels 1986–96; Guest Lecturer in Public Int. Law, Université Catholique de Louvain 1997–; Corresp. mem. Spanish Royal Acad. of Moral and Political Sciences; mem. various other learned socs; Netherlands Embassy Prize 1969. *Publications:* numerous publs and articles. *Address:* International Court of Justice, Peace Palace, Carnegieplein 2, 2517 KJ The Hague, The Netherlands (office). *Telephone:* (70) 302-23-23 (office). *Fax:* (70) 364-99-28 (office). *E-mail:* info@icj-cij.org (office). *Website:* www.icj-cij.org (office).

ČOVIĆ, Dragan, PhD; Bosnia and Herzegovina politician; *President, Croatian Democratic Union of Bosnia and Herzegovina;* b. 20 Aug. 1956, Mostar; m.; two d.; ed Univ. of Mostar, Sarajevo Univ.; with SOKO co., Mostar, holding sr managerial positions 1977–98; Assoc. Prof., then Prof., Univ. of Mostar 1996–; fmr mem. Croat Democratic Union; Deputy Prime Minister and Minister of Finance, Fed. of Bosnia and Herzegovina 1998–2001; elected to Tripartite Presidency 2002, Leader of Presidency 2003–04, dismissed by High Rep. of the Int. Community in Bosnia and Herzegovina Paddy Ashdown following indictment for financial corruption, before trial took place 29 March 2005; Vice-Pres., Croatian Democratic Union of Bosnia and Herzegovina 1998–2005, Pres. 2005–. *Address:* Croatian Democratic Union of Bosnia and Herzegovina, 88000 Mostar, Mostar-Zapad, Kneza Domagoja b.b, Bosnia and Herzegovina (office). *Telephone:* (36) 310701 (office). *Fax:* (36) 315024 (office). *E-mail:* hdzbih@hdzbih.org (office). *Website:* www.hdzbih.org (office).

ČOVIĆ, Željko, BSc, MSc; Croatian business executive; b. 9 Jan. 1953, Zagreb; ed Zagreb Univ., Int. Inst. of Man. Devt; joined PLIVA, Zagreb 1980, Dir Foodstuffs Div. 1985–86, Head of Sales, Foodstuffs Div. 1986–88, Head of Marketing and Sales 1988–91, Chair. and CEO PLIVA d.d. 1993–95, Pres. Man. Bd and CEO 1995–2008 (resgnd); CEO Genera Pharmaceuticals Ltd, Rakov Potok 2009–12; mem. Exec. City Council and Sec. for Econ. Affairs, City of Zagreb 1991–93, Advisor to Vice-Pres. of the Economy, Croatian Govt 1993; mem. American Chamber of Commerce, Croatian Nat. Council on Competitiveness (Pres. 2002–05), Croatian Employers' Asscn (Pres. 2001–02); Order of the Croatian Star 1995, Order of the Croatian Pleter 1995; Croatian Chamber of Commerce Golden Award 1994, Managers and Entrepreneurs Asscn Manager of the Year 1995, ING Barings and Emerging Markets CEO of the Year Award 1999. *E-mail:* zc9876@gmail.com (office).

COWELL, Simon Phillip; British television personality, television executive, record company executive and A&R consultant; b. 7 Oct. 1959, Lambeth, London; s. of the late Eric Cowell and Julie Brett (née Josie Dalglish); ed Dover Coll., Windsor Technical Coll., St Columba's Coll., St Albans; brought up in Elstree, Herts.; worked for EMI Music Publishing 1977–82; Founder Fanfare Records (with Iain Burton) 1982–89; A&R Consultant, BMG Records 1989; screen debut on TV

series Sale of the Century 1990; Founder and Co-Owner S Records 2001; first made a TV appearance on Pop Idol 2001, then on American Idol 2002; f. Syco record label (subsidiary of Sony BMG) 2002, artists include Westlife, Five, Robson & Jerome, Zig & Zag, Girl Thing, Will Young, Gareth Gates, Six, Il Divo, Steve Brookstein, Shayne Ward, Journey South, Paul Potts, Ray Quinn, Leona Lewis, Olly Murs, Rebecca Ferguson, Cher Lloyd, Susan Boyle, Little Mix, One Direction; Record Exec. of the Year 1998, 1999, A & R Man. of the Year 1999, Variety Club Showbusiness Personality of the Year 2005, BAFTA Special Award 2010, listed by New Statesman at No. 41 amongst The World's 50 Most Influential Figures 2010. *Television includes:* writer, producer and judge, Pop Idol (ITV) 2001–02, American Idol: The Search for a Superstar (Fox TV) 2002–10, Cupid 2003, The X Factor (ITV) 2004–10, (producer) 2011–, The Xtra Factor 2004–, America's Got Talent 2006–, Celebrity Duets 2006, American Inventor 2006–07, Grease Is the Word (ITV) 2007, Britain's Got Talent 2007– (ITV) (BAFTA Award for Best Entertainment Programme 2010), Britain's Got More Talent 2007–, Rock Rivals (ITV drama) 2008, Piers Morgan's Life Stories (special episodes) 2010–, Red or Black (ITV) 2011–, The X Factor USA 2011–, One Chance 2013–.

COWEN, Brian, BCL; Irish solicitor and politician; b. 10 Jan. 1960, Tullamore; s. of the late Bernard Cowen and of Mary Cowen; m. Mary Molloy 1990; two d.; ed Univ. Coll. Dublin and Inc. Law Soc. of Ireland; mem. Offaly Co. Council 1984–93; mem. Dáil for Laois-Offaly 1984–2011; Minister for Labour 1991–92, for Transport, Energy and Communications 1992–94, for Health and Children 1997–2000, for Foreign Affairs 2000–04, Jan.–Feb. 2011, for Finance 2004–08 (also Deputy Prime Minister), Taoiseach (Prime Minister) 2008–11, also Acting Minister of Defence Feb.–March 2010; Leader Fianna Fáil 2008–11 (resgnd), Leader Parl. Party 2008; fmr Opposition Spokesperson on Agric. and Food. *Leisure interests:* sport, reading, music. *Address:* Grand Canal House, William St, Tullamore, Co. Offaly, Ireland. *Telephone:* (57) 9321976. *Fax:* (57) 9321910. *E-mail:* barry.cowen@oireachtas.ie. *Website:* www.fiannafail.ie.

COWLEY, Alan Herbert, BS, MS, PhD, FRS; British chemist and academic; *Robert A. Welch Professor of Chemistry, University of Texas;* b. 29 Jan. 1934, Manchester; s. of the late Herbert Cowley and Dora Cowley; m. Deborah Elaine Cole 1975; two s. three d.; ed Univ. of Manchester; Postdoctoral Fellow, then Instructor, Univ. of Florida, USA 1958–60; Tech. Officer, Exploratory Group, ICI (Billingham Div.), UK 1960–61; Asst Prof. of Chem., Univ. of Texas at Austin 1962–67, Assoc. Prof. 1967–70, Prof. 1970–84, George W. Watt Centennial Prof. of Chem. 1984–88, Richard J.V. Johnson Regent's Prof. of Chem. 1989–91, Robert A. Welch Prof. of Chem. 1991–; Sir Edward Frankland Prof. of Inorganic Chem., Imperial Coll., London 1988–89; Vice-Chair. Bd of Trustees, Gordon Research Confs. 1993–94 (Chair. 1994–95) mem. Editorial Bd Inorganic Chemistry 1979–83, Chemical Reviews 1984–88, Polyhedron 1984–2000, Journal of American Chem. Soc. 1986–91, Journal of Organometallic Chemistry 1987–, Organometallics 1988–91, Dalton Trans 1997–2000, Inorganic Syntheses 1983–; Corresp. Mem. Mexican Acad. of Sciences 2004; Guggenheim Fellowship 1976–77; Chevalier, Ordre des Palmes Académiques 1997; Dr hc (Univ. of Bordeaux) 2003; Royal Soc. of Chem. Award for Main-Group Element Chem. 1980, Centenary Medal and Lectureship, Royal Soc. of Chem. 1986, ACS Southwest Regional Award 1986, Stiefvater Memorial Award and Lectureship, Univ. of Nebraska 1987, Chemical Pioneer Award, American Inst. of Chemists 1994, Von Humboldt Prize 1996. *Publications:* more than 450 articles in learned journals. *Leisure interests:* squash, sailing, classical music, literature. *Address:* Department of Chemistry and Biochemistry, WEL 4.330, University of Texas, Austin, TX 78712, USA. *Telephone:* (512) 471-7484 (office). *Fax:* (512) 471-6822 (office). *E-mail:* cowley@mail.utexas .edu (office). *Website:* www.cm.utexas.edu/alan_cowley (office); cowley.cm.utexas .edu/acowley (office).

COWLEY, Roger Arthur, FRS, FRSE, FRSC; British physicist and academic; *Professor Emeritus of Experimental Philosophy and Fellow Emeritus, Wadham College, University of Oxford;* b. 24 Feb. 1939, Essex, England; s. of C. A. Cowley; m. Sheila Joyce Wells 1964; one s. one d.; ed Brentwood School, Univ. of Cambridge; Fellow of Trinity Hall, Cambridge 1962–64; Research Officer, Atomic Energy of Canada Ltd 1964–70; Prof. of Physics, Univ. of Edinburgh 1970–88; Dr Lee's Prof. of Experimental Philosophy and Fellow of Wadham Coll., Oxford 1988–2007, Prof. Emer. and Fellow Emer. 2008–, Chair. of Physics Dept 1993–96, 1999–2002; Max Born Medal and Prize 1973, Holweck Medal and Prize 1990, Walter Hälg Prize and Medal 2003, Faraday Prize and Medal 2008. *Publications include:* more than 400 scientific publs in academic journals. *Leisure interests:* gardening, tennis, walking. *Address:* Oxford Physics, Clarendon Laboratory, Parks Road, Oxford, OX1 3PU (office); Tredinnock, Harcourt Hill, Oxford, OX2 9AS, England (home). *Telephone:* (1865) 272224 (office); (1865) 247570 (home). *Fax:* (1865) 272400 (office). *E-mail:* r.cowley@physics.ox.ac.uk (office). *Website:* www.physics.ox.ac.uk (office).

COWPER-COLES, Sir Sherard Louis, Kt, KCMG, LVO; British diplomatist; b. 8 Jan. 1955, London, England; s. of Sherard Hamilton Cowper-Coles and Dorothy Cowper-Coles (née Short); m. Bridget Cowper-Coles; four s. one d.; ed Tonbridge School, Hertford Coll., Oxford; joined FCO 1977; Third, then Second Sec., Cairo 1980–83; First Sec. Planning Office, FCO 1983–85, Pvt. Sec. to Perm. Under-Sec. of State 1985–87; First Sec., Washington, DC 1987–91; Asst Security Policy Dept, FCO 1991–93, Head Hong Kong Dept 1994–97; Counsellor, Paris 1997–99; Prin. Pvt. Sec. to Sec. of State for Foreign and Commonwealth Affairs 1999–2001; Amb. to Israel 2001–03, to Saudi Arabia 2003–07, to Afghanistan 2007–09; Foreign Sec.'s Special Rep. to Afghanistan and Pakistan 2009–10; Int. Business Devt Dir, BAE Systems 2010–; Hon. Fellow, Hertford Coll. Oxford 2002. *Publication:* From Defence to Security 2004. *Address:* Foreign and Commonwealth Office, King Charles Street, London, SW1A 2AH, England. *Telephone:* (20) 7008-1500 (office). *E-mail:* sherard.cowper-coles@fco.gov.uk (office). *Website:* www.gov.uk/government/organisations/foreign-commonwealth-office (office); www.baesystems.com.

COX, Barry Geoffrey, CBE, BA, FRTS; British journalist and television industry executive (retd); b. 25 May 1942, Guildford, Surrey, England; m. 1st Pamela Doran 1967 (divorced 1977); two s. two d. m. 2nd Kathryn Kay 1984 (divorced 1992); m. 3rd Fiona Hillary 2001; ed Tiffin School, Kingston, Surrey, Magdalen Coll., Oxford; reporter, The Scotsman 1965–67; feature writer, Sunday Telegraph 1967–70; Producer/Dir World in Action, Granada TV 1970–74; The London Programme,

London Weekend TV 1974–77, Head of Current Affairs 1977–81, Controller of Features and Current Affairs 1981–87, Dir of Corp. Affairs 1987–94, Special Adviser to Chief Exec. 1994–95; Dir Independent TV Asscn 1995–98; Deputy Chair. Channel 4 1999–2006; consultant to United Broadcasting and Entertainment 1998–2001, to Independent TV News 1998–2008; Chair. Digital TV Stakeholders Group 2002–04, Digital UK Ltd 2005–12, SwitchCo Ltd 2005, Oval House Theatre 2001–07; News International Visiting Prof. of Broadcast Media, Univ. of Oxford 2003; mem. Council Inst. of Educ. 2000–08; Chair. Digital Radio Working Group 2010. *Publications:* Civil Liberties in Britain 1975, The Fall of Scotland Yard 1977, Free For All: Public Service Television in the Digital Age 2004. *Leisure interests:* tennis, walking, theatre. *Address:* 72 Wilton Road, Victoria, London, SW1V 1DE, England. *E-mail:* barry.cox3@btopenworld.com.

COX, Brian Denis, CBE; British actor, director and writer; b. 1 June 1946, Dundee, Scotland; s. of Charles Mcardle Campbell Cox and Mary Ann Gillerine (née Mccann); m. 1st Caroline Burt 1968 (divorced 1987); one s. one d.; m. 2nd Nicole Ansari 2001; two s.; ed London Acad. of Music and Dramatic Art; Hon. LLD (Dundee) 2006; Hon. Dr of Drama (Royal Scottish Acad. of Music and Drama) 2006; Scottish BAFTA Award for Contrib. to Scottish Broadcasting 2004. *Stage appearances include:* debut at Dundee Repertory 1961; Royal Lyceum, Edinburgh 1965–66, Birmingham Repertory 1966–68, As You Like It, Birmingham and Vaudeville (London debut) 1967, Peer Gynt, Birmingham 1967, When We Dead Awaken, Edinburgh Festival 1968, In Celebration, Royal Court 1969, The Wild Duck, Edinburgh Festival 1969, The Big Romance, Royal Court 1970, Don't Start Without Me, Garrick 1971, Mirandolina, Brighton 1971, Getting On, Queen's 1971, The Creditors, Open Space 1972, Hedda Gabler, Royal Court 1972; Playhouse, Nottingham: Love's Labour's Lost, Brand, What The Butler Saw, The Three Musketeers 1972; Cromwell, Royal Court 1973; Royal Exchange, Manchester: Arms and the Man 1974, The Cocktail Party 1975; Pilgrims Progress, Prospect Theatre 1975, Emigres, Nat. Theatre Co., Young Vic 1976; Olivier Theatre: Tamburlaine the Great 1976, Julius Caesar 1977; The Changeling, Riverside Studios 1978; Nat. Theatre: Herod, The Putney Debates 1978; On Top, Royal Court 1979, Macbeth, Cambridge Theatre and tour of India 1980, Summer Party, Crucible 1980, Have You Anything to Declare?, Manchester then Round House 1981, Danton's Death, Nat. Theatre Co., Olivier 1982, Strange Interlude, Duke of York (Drama Magazine Best Actor Award 1985) 1984 and Nederlander, New York 1985, Rat in the Skull, Royal Court (Drama Magazine and Olivier Best Actor Awards 1985) 1984 and New York 1985, Fashion, The Danton Affair, Misalliance, Penny for a Song 1986, The Taming of the Shrew, Titus Andronicus 1987, The Three Sisters 1989, RSC and Titus Andronicus on tour, Madrid, Paris, Copenhagen (Olivier Award for Best Actor in a Revival and Drama Magazine Best Actor Award for RSC 1988) 1988, Frankie and Johnny in the Claire-de-Lune, Comedy 1989, Richard III, King Lear, nat. and world tour 1990–91, The Master Builder, Edinburgh 1993, Riverside 1994, St Nicholas, The Bush Theatre 1997, New York (Lucille Lortel Award 1998) 1998, Skylight, Los Angeles 1997, Dublin Carol, Old Vic and Royal Court 2000, Uncle Varrick, Royal Lyceum, Edinburgh 2004, Rock 'n' Roll, Royal Court Theatre. *Plays directed:* Edinburgh Festival: The Man with a Flower in his Mouth 1973, The Stronger 1973; Orange Tree, Richmond: I Love My Love 1982, Mrs Warren's Profession 1989; The Crucible, Moscow Art Theatre, London and Edinburgh 1989, The Philanderer, Hampstead Theatre Club (world premier of complete version) (Int. Theatre Inst. Award 1990) 1991. *Radio:* McLevy (BBC series). *Films include:* Nicholas and Alexandra 1971, In Celebration 1975, The Privilege (short) 1982, Manhunter 1986, Shoot for the Sun 1986, Hidden Agenda 1990, Deceptions 1992, L'oeil de Vichy (narrator of English version) 1993, Iron Will 1994, Prince of Jutland 1994, The Cutter 1994, I Was Catherine the Great's Stable Boy (short) 1994, Rob Roy 1995, Braveheart 1995, Chain Reaction 1996, The Glimmer Man 1996, The Long Kiss Goodnight 1996, Kiss the Girls 1997, The Boxer 1997, Desperate Measures 1998, Merchants of Venus 1998, Rushmore 1998, The Minus Man 1998, The Corruptor 1998, For Love of the Game 1999, The Invention of Dr. Morel (short) 2000, Complicity 2000, Mad About Mambo 2000, A Shot at Glory 2000, Saltwater 2000, Zulu 9 (short) (voice) 2001, The Legend of Loch Lomond (short) (narrator) 2001, Super Troopers 2001, L.I.E. 2001, Strictly Sinatra 2001, The Affair of the Necklace 2001, Bug 2002, The Rookie 2002, The Bourne Identity 2002, The Ring 2002, Adaptation 2002, 25th Hour 2002, The Reckoning 2003, X2 2003, Sin 2003, Troy 2004, The Bourne Supremacy 2004, Get the Picture (short) 2004, Match Point 2005, Red Eye 2005, The Ringer 2005, A Woman in Winter 2005, The Flying Scotsman 2006, Burns 2006, Running with Scissors 2006, Zodiac 2007, The Martyr's Crown (short) 2007, Battle for Terra (voice) 2007, The Water Horse 2007, Trick 'r Treat 2007, Shoot on Sight 2007, Red 2008, The Escapist 2008, Agent Crush (voice) 2008, Scooby-Doo and the Samurai Sword (video) (voice) 2009, Tell-Tale 2009, The Good Heart 2009, Fantastic Mr. Fox (voice) 2009, As Good as Dead 2010, Wide Blue Yonder 2010, Red 2010, Coriolanus 2011, Ironclad 2011, The Key Man 2011, The Veteran 2011, Rise of the Planet of the Apes 2011, Edwin Boyd 2011, Exit Humanity (narrator) 2011, Blumenthal 2012, Theatre of Dreams (as Matt Busby) 2012, The Campaign 2012. *Television includes:* The Wednesday Play 1965, Redcap (series) 1966, ITV Playhouse1967, The Gamblers (series) 1967, Theatre 625 1968, Z Cars (series) 1969, Thirty-Minute Theatre (series) 1969–71, When We Dead Awaken (film) 1970, ITV Sunday Night Theatre 1970, Doomwatch (series) 1970, Manhunt (series) 1970, Stage 2 (series) 1971, Ego Hugo (film) 1973, BBC Play of the Month – The Changeling 1974, Sutherland's Law (series) 1974, Churchill's People – The Wallace 1975, The Master of Ballantrae (short) 1975, Shades of Greene (series) 1975, Play for Today – Clay, Smeddum and Greenden 1976, Crown Court (series) 1976–82, Rooms (series) 1977, Target (series) 1977, Henry II in The Devil's Crown (series) 1978, Out (series) 1978, Thérèse Raquin (mini-series) 1980, BBC 2 Playhouse – Dalhousie's Luck 1980, Hammer House of Horror – The Silent Scream 1980, Bothwell 1980, The House on the Hill (series) 1981, Play for Today – A Cotswold Death 1982, Minder (series) 1982, King Lear (film) 1983, Jemima Shore Investigates (series) 1983, J.S. Bach in The Cantor of St Thomas's (film) 1984, Pope John Paul II 1984, Scotland's Story (series) 1984, Florence Nightingale (film) 1985, The Deliberate Death of a Polish Priest (film) 1986, The Fourth Floor (film) 1986, Shoot for the Sun (film) 1986, Unnatural Causes (series) 1986, The Modern World: Ten Great Writers (mini-series documentary) (voice of Henrik Ibsen) 1988, Beryl Markham: A Shadow in the Sun (film) 1988, Murder on the Moon (film) 1989, Secret Weapon (film) 1990, Perfect Scoundrels – The Milk of Human Kindness 1990, Red Fox (mini-series) 1991, Acting in Tragedy (BBC Masterclass) 1990, The Lost Language

of Cranes (film) 1992, The Cloning of Joanna May (film) 1992, Van der Valk (series) 1992, Screen Two – The Lost Language of Cranes 1992, Shakespeare: The Animated Tales (series) (voice of Macbeth) 1992, The Big Battalions (mini-series) 1992, Inspector Morse (series) 1993, Sharpe's Rifles (film) 1993, Sharpe's Eagle (film) 1994, Scene – Pig Boy 1993, Six Characters in Search of an Author (film) 1994, Grushko (series) 1994, The Negotiator (film) 1994, Witness Against Hitler (film) 1995, Blow Your Mind See A Play 1995, Red Dwarf (series) 1997, Superman (series) 1997, Great Performances – Henry V at Shakespeare's Globe (narrator) 1997, Food for Ravens (film) 1997, Family Brood (film) 1998, Poodle Springs (film) 1998, Longitude (film) 2000, Nuremberg (mini-series) (Emmy Award for Best Actor) 2000, Animated Tales of the World (series) (narrator) 2000, Smallpox 2002: Silent Weapon (film) (narrator) 2002, Frasier (series) 2002, The Biographer (film) 2002, Rasputin: The Devil in the Flesh (documentary) (narrator) 2002, French and Saunders (series) 2004, The Court 2002, Blue/Orange (film) 2005, Lost: The Journey (film) (narrator) 2005, The Strange Case of Sherlock Holmes & Arthur Conan Doyle (film) 2005, Danny Phantom (series) (voice) 2005, Deadwood (series) 2006, The Outsiders (film) 2006, Timewatch (series documentary) (narrator) 2007, The Secret of the Nutcracker (film) 2007, The Colour of Magic (film) (narrator) 2008, Lost & Found (film) 2009, Marple: They Do It with Mirrors (film) 2009, The Take (mini-series) 2009, Kings (series) 2009, Doctor Who (series) (voice) 2009, The Day of the Triffids (mini-series) 2009, On Expenses (film) 2010, The Big C (series) 2010, The Sinking of the Laconia (mini-series) 2010–11, The Straits (series) 2012. *Publications include:* Salem to Moscow: An Actor's Odyssey 1991, The Lear Diaries 1992. *Leisure interests:* keeping fit, tango. *Address:* c/o Nicola van Gelder, Conway van Gelder Grant Ltd, Third Floor, 8–12 Broadwick Street, London, W1F 8HW, England (office). *Website:* www.conwayvangeldergrant.com (office).

COX, Carrie S., BS; American pharmacist and business executive; *CEO, Humacyte, Inc.;* ed Massachusetts Coll. of Pharmacy and Health Sciences; held a variety of positions in market research, sales and product man. during a 10-year career with Sandoz Pharmaceuticals; Vice-Pres. Women's Health Care, Wyeth-Ayerst for seven years; Exec. Vice-Pres. and Pres. Global Prescription Business, Pharmacia Corpn (fmrly Pharmacia & Upjohn) 1997–2003; Exec. Vice-Pres. and Pres. Global Pharmaceuticals, Schering-Plough Corpn 2003–09 (until merger with Merck & Co., Inc.); mem. Bd of Dirs and CEO Humacyte, Inc. 2010–; mem. Bd of Dirs Texas Instruments Inc. 2004–, Cardinal Health, Celgene; ranked by Fortune magazine amongst the 50 Most Powerful Women in Business in the US 2001, (37th) 2005, (39th) 2006, (32nd) 2007–08, (23rd) 2009. *Address:* Humacyte, Inc., PO Box 12695, Durham, NC 27709 (office); Humacyte, Inc., 21 Davis Drive, Suite 140, Research Triangle Pa, NC 27709 (office); Humacyte, Inc., 7020 Kit Creek Road, Morrisville, NC 27560, USA (office). *Telephone:* (919) 806-4599 (office). *E-mail:* info@humacyte.com (office). *Website:* www.humacyte.com (office).

COX, Christopher, BA, MBA, JD; American lawyer, politician and fmr government official; *Partner, Bingham McCutchen LLP;* b. 16 Oct. 1952; m. Rebecca Gernhardt; three c.; ed Univ. of Southern California, Harvard Business School, Harvard Law School; fmr Ed. Harvard Law Review; Clerk US Court of Appeals 1977–78; Assoc. Latham & Watkins 1978–82, Pnr 1984–86; Lecturer in Business Admin, Harvard Business School 1982–83; Sr Assoc. Counsel to Pres., White House 1986–88; mem. US House of Reps from Calif. 1988–2005, Chair. House Cttee on Homeland Security, House Policy Cttee 1994–2005; Chair. SEC 2005–09 (resgnd); currently Partner, Bingham McCutchen LLP (law firm), Costa Mesa, Calif., also Pres. Bingham Consulting LLC. *Address:* Bingham McCutchen LLP, 600 Anton Boulevard, Suite 1800, Costa Mesa, CA 92626-7653, USA (office). *Telephone:* (714) 830-0606 (office). *Fax:* (714) 830-0700 (office). *E-mail:* chris.cox@bingham.com (office). *Website:* www.bingham.com (office).

COX, Sir David Roxbee, Kt, PhD, FRS, FRSC; British statistician; b. 15 July 1924, Birmingham, England; s. of Sam R. Cox and Lilian Cox (née Braines); m. Joyce Drummond 1948; three. one d.; ed Handsworth Grammar School, Birmingham and St John's Coll. Cambridge; with Royal Aircraft Establishment 1944–46; Wool Industries Research Asscn 1946–50; Statistical Lab., Univ. of Cambridge 1950–55; with Dept of Biostatistics, Univ. of North Carolina 1955–56, Birkbeck Coll., London 1956–66; Bell Telephone Labs 1965; Prof. of Statistics, Imperial Coll. of Science and Tech., London 1966–88; Warden, Nuffield Coll., Oxford 1988–94, Hon. Fellow 1994–; Science and Eng Research Council Sr Research Fellow 1983–88; Ed. Biometrika 1966–91; Pres. Int. Statistics Inst. 1995–97; Fellow, Imperial Coll., Birkbeck Coll., London; Hon. Fellow, St John's Coll. Cambridge, Inst. of Actuaries, British Acad.; Hon. Foreign mem. US Acad. of Arts and Sciences, Royal Danish Acad., NAS, American Philosophical Soc., Indian Acad. of Sciences, Finnish Statistical Soc.; Hon. mem. Portuguese Statistical Soc.; Hon. DSc (Reading, Bradford, Heriot Watt, Helsinki, Limburg, Queen's, Kingston, Ont., Waterloo, Neuchâtel, Padua, Minnesota, Toronto, Abertay Dundee, Crete, Bordeaux 2, Athens Univ. of Econs, Harvard, Elche, Rio de Janeiro, Leeds, Gothenburg, Glasgow); Guy Medals in silver and gold, Royal Statistical Soc., Weldon Medal, Univ. of Oxford, Deming Medal, ASQC, Kettering Medal and Prize, General Motors Cancer Research Foundation, Max Planck Prize, Copley Medal, Royal Soc. (co-recipient) 2010. *Publications:* several books on statistics, articles in Journal of the Royal Statistical Soc., Biometrika etc. *Address:* Nuffield Coll., Oxford, OX1 1NF, England (office). *Telephone:* (1865) 278690 (office). *Fax:* (1865) 278621 (office). *E-mail:* david.cox@nuffield.ox.ac.uk (office). *Website:* www.stats.ox.ac.uk/people/associate_staff/david_cox (office).

COX, Sir George Edwin, Kt, BSc; British business executive; b. 28 May 1940; s. of George Herbert Cox and Beatrice Mary Cox; m. 1st Gillian Mary Mannings (divorced 1996); two s.; m. 2nd Lorna Janet Peach 1996; two d.; ed Quintin School, Queen Mary Coll., Univ. of London; began career in aircraft industry, in factory man. and in precision eng; Man. Dir Butler Cox (IT consultancy and research group) 1977; Chief Exec. then Chair. PE Int.; fmr UK Chief Exec. Unisys UK, Head of Unisys Services Businesses across Europe; Dir-Gen. Inst. of Dirs 1999–2004; Chair. The Design Council 2004–07; fmr Chair. Merlin (Medical Emergency Relief Int.); mem. Bd of Dirs Shorts 2000–; fmr Dir Inland Revenue 1996–99, London Int. Financial Futures and Options Exchange (LIFFE) 1995–2002, Bradford & Bingley PLC; Visiting Prof., Man. School, Royal Holloway, Univ. of London 1995–; Pres. Royal Coll. of Speech Therapists 2004–; mem. Supervisory Bd Euronext 2003–; apptd mem. Advisory Bd Warwick Business School 2003, Chair. 2005, currently Pro-Chancellor and Chair of Council mem. Council Univ. of Warwick; Trustee VSO

2005–; Past Pres. Man. Consultancies Asscn; Past Master of Worshipful Co. of Man. Consultants; carried out Cox Review of Creativity in Business, commissioned by HM Govt 2005; Hon. Fellow, Queen Mary, London; Companion of Chartered Inst. of Man., Royal Aeronautical Soc.; Dr hc (Univ. of Middlesex) 2002, (Univ. of Wolverhampton) 2004, (Northumbria Univ.) 2007, (Univ. of Huddersfield) 2008. *Leisure interest:* rowing, history of aviation, theatre.

COX, Pat; Irish EU official and politician; b. 28 Nov. 1952; m.; six c.; ed Trinity Coll., Dublin; Lecturer, Dept of Econs, Inst. of Public Admin, Dublin and Univ. of Limerick (fmrly Nat. Inst. of Higher Educ.—NIHE) 1974–82; TV Current Affairs Reporter for 'Today Tonight' 1982–86; Gen. Sec. Progressive Democrats 1985–94, Deputy Leader 1990–94, MEP for Munster 1989–2004, served on Econ. and Monetary Affairs, Institutional Affairs, and Legal Affairs Cttees, Deputy Leader European Liberal Democrats (ELDR) 1994–98, Pres. 1998–2002; Pres. European Parl. 2002–04; TD (Irish Parl.) for Cork S Cen. and Progressive Democrats Spokesperson on Finance 1992–94; fmr mem. Jt Parl. Cttees to Sweden, Austria and Hungary, Parl. Del. to S Africa; mem. Bd Trustees Int. Crisis Group, Friends of Europe; Freeman of City of Limerick; honoured with highest nat. honours by Pres of Italy, Lithuania, Bulgaria and Romania; Dr hc (Nat. Univ. of Ireland, Trinity Coll. Dublin, American Coll. Dublin); Pres.'s Medal, Univ. of Limerick, MEP of the Year 2001, Campaigner of the Year, Brussels 2003, Special Diploma of Minister of Foreign Affairs (Poland) 2003, Polish Business Oscar 2003, Transatlantic Business Award of the Year, American Chamber of Commerce to the EU 2004, Int. Charlemagne Prize 2004. *Address:* Crawford Hall, Western Road, Cork, Ireland. *Telephone:* (21) 4975833. *Fax:* (21) 4975834. *E-mail:* pcoxmep@eircom.net (office). *Website:* www.patcox.ie (office).

COX, Paul; Dutch film director, screenwriter and author; *Chairman, Illumination Films;* b. 16 April 1940, Venlo, Limburg; s. of W. Cox; two s. one d.; ed Univ. of Melbourne, Univ. of Technology, Sydney, Australia; settled in Australia 1965; photographic exhbns in Australia, the Netherlands, Germany, Japan, India and USA; taught photography and cinematography for several years; f. Illumination Films (production co.) with Tony Llewellyn-Jones and Bernard Eddy 1977; Hon. Dr in Creative Arts; numerous awards and prizes. *Films directed:* feature length: The Journey 1972, Illuminations 1976, Inside Looking Out 1977, Kostas 1978, Lonely Hearts 1981, Man of Flowers 1983, Death and Destiny (A Journey into Ancient Egypt) 1984, My First Wife 1984, Cactus 1986, Vincent 1988, Island 1989, Golden Braid 1990, A Woman's Tale 1991, The Nun and the Bandit 1992, Exile 1993, Lust and Revenge 1996, The Hidden Dimension 1997, Molokai 1998, Innocence 1998, The Diaries of Vaslav Nijinsky 2001, Human Touch 2004, Salvation 2008; documentaries: Calcutta 1970, All Set Backstage 1974, For A Child Called Michael 1979, The Kingdom of Nek Chand 1980, Underdog 1980, Death and Destiny 1984, Handle with Care 1985, Kaluapapa Heaven 2007; shorts: Mantuta 1965, Time Past 1966, Skindeep 1968, Marcel 1969, Symphony 1969, Mirka 1970, Phyllis 1971, Island 1975, We are All Alone My Dear 1975, Ways of Seeing 1977, Ritual 1978; for Children's TV: The Paper Boy 1985, The Secret Life of Trees 1986. *Publications:* Home of Man: The People of New Guinea 1971, Human Still Lives of Nepal 1971, Mirka 1980, Vincent: The Life and Death of Vincent van Gough 1987, I Am 1997, Reflections 1998, Three Screenplays 1998, Tales from the Cancer Ward 2011. *Address:* Illumination Films, 1 Victoria Avenue, Albert Park, Vic. 3206, Australia (office). *Telephone:* (3) 9690-5266 (office). *Fax:* (3) 9696-5625 (office).

COX, Hon. Paula Ann, JP, BA; Bermudian politician and lawyer; d. of the late C. Eugene Cox MP, CBE, JP and Alinda Cox; m. Germain Nkeuleu; one s.; ed McGill Univ., Canada, Univ. of Manchester, UK; fmr Vice Pres. and Sr Legal Counsel, Global Funds Bank of Bermuda Ltd; Corp. Counsel, ACE Ltd 1996; mem. of Parl. 1996–2012, Minister of Labour, Home Affairs and Public Safety 1998–2001, Minister of Educ. and Devt 2001–02, Attorney-Gen. and Minister of Educ. 2003–04, Minister of Finance 2004–12, also Deputy Premier 2006–10, Premier of Bermuda 2010–12; Deputy Leader Progressive Labour Party; Dr hc (Wheelock Coll.) 2004; Most Effective Politician 2001, 2003. *Address:* c/o Office of the Premier, Cabinet Office, Cabinet Bldg, 105 Front Street, Hamilton, HM 12, Bermuda (office).

COX, Philip Sutton, AO, BArch, PhD, RIBA; Australian architect; *Director, Cox Architecture;* b. 1 Oct. 1939, Killara, Sydney; s. of Ronald Albert Cox and Lilian May Cox; m. Virginia Louise Gowing 1972; two d.; ed Sydney Church of England Grammar School, Sydney Univ.; worked in New Guinea 1962; apptd Tutor in Architecture, Univ. of Sydney 1963; est. Ian McKay & Philip Cox pvt. practice with Ian McKay 1963; est. Philip Cox and Assocs (later Cox Richardson Architects & Planners, now Cox Architecture) 1967; Architect Sydney Olympics, Stage I; Tutor in Architecture, Univ. of New South Wales 1971, 1973, 1978, Prof. 1989–; Founding mem. The Australian Acad. of Design 1990–; Life Fellow, Royal Australian Inst. of Architects, Chair. Educ. Bd, Fed. Chapter; Vice-Chair. Architecture and Design Panel, Visual Arts Bd, Australia Council; Fellow, Australian Acad. of Humanities; Hon. FAIA Commonwealth Scholarship 1956; numerous awards and prizes including Royal Australian Inst. of Architects Gold Medal and Merit Awards, Commonwealth Asscn of Architects Sir Robert Matthew Award, Blacket Award, Sir John Sulman Medal. *Major Artistic Works:* Darling Harbour, Freemantle Harbour, Emirates Univ. Uluru, Doya Stadium, Sydney Football Stadium, Sydney, Brisbane, Perth Exhbn Centres. *Publications:* several books including The Australian Homestead (with Wesley Stacey) 1972, Historic Towns of Australia (with Wesley Stacey) 1973, Restoring Old Australian Houses and Buildings, an Architectural Guide (with others) 1975, Australian Colonial Architecture (with Clive Lucas), The Functional Tradition (with David Moore) 1987, Cox Architects & Planners 1960–2010 (with others) 2008, Home, Evolution of the Australian Dream (with others) 2011. *Leisure interests:* gardening, swimming, walking, painting. *Address:* Cox Architecture, Level 2, 204 Clarence Street, Sydney, NSW 2000, Australia (office). *Telephone:* (2) 9267-9599 (office). *Fax:* (2) 9264-5844 (office). *E-mail:* sydney@cox.com.au (office); www .coxarchitecture.com.au (office).

COX, Robert Warburton, MA, FRSC; Canadian political scientist, academic and international civil servant; *Professor Emeritus, Department of Political Science, York University;* b. 18 Sept. 1926, Montreal, Quebec; s. of Geoffrey Cox and Edythe Mary Cox; m. Susan Margaret Cox; one d.; ed McGill Univ.; fmr Asst Dir-Gen. ILO; fmr Dir Int. Inst. for Labour Studies, Geneva, Switzerland; fmr Prof. of Political Science, Grad. Inst. of Int. Studies, Geneva; Prof. of Int. Org., Columbia Univ., New York 1972–77; Visiting Prof., Yale Univ., Univ. de Laval, Québec, Univ. of Toronto, Univ. of Denver; Programme Co-ordinator on Multilateralism and the UN System, UN Univ., Tokyo; currently Prof. Emer., Dept of Political Science, York Univ., Toronto. *Publications include:* The Anatomy of Influence 1975, Production, Power and World Order 1987, International Political Economy: Understanding Global Disorder 1995, Approaches to World Order 1996, The New Realism (ed.) 1997, Political Economy of a Plural World: Critical Reflections on Power, Morals and Civilizations 2002. *Address:* Office 210, Balsillie School of International Studies, Waterloo, ON N2L 6C2 (office); 82 McCarron Crescent, Waterloo, ON N2L 5N1, Canada (home). *Telephone:* (416) 574 5352 (mobile) (office); (416) 925-7307 (Toronto) (home). *Fax:* (416) 925-8892 (home). *E-mail:* rwcox@yorku.ca (office). *Website:* www.yorku.ca/polisci (office).

COX, Stephen Joseph; British artist; b. 16 Sept. 1946, Bristol; s. of Leonard John Cox and Ethel Minnie May McGill; m. Judith Atkins 1970; two d.; ed St Mary Redcliffe, Bristol, West of England Coll. of Art, Bristol and Cen. School of Art and Design, London; lives and practices near Ludlow, England as well as, Italy, India and Egypt; works held in collections of Tate Gallery, Victoria and Albert Museum, British Museum, South Bank Centre, Arts Council of GB, British Council, Walker Art Gallery, Liverpool, Henry Moore Centre for Sculpture, Leeds City Gallery, Southampton Museum, Fogg Museum, USA, Groningen Museum, Netherlands, Peter Ludwig Collection, FRG, Uffizi Gallery, Florence, Fattoria di Celle, Pistoia, Palazzo del Commune, Spoleto, Santa Maria della Scala, Siena, Regione di Aosta and pvt. collections in India, Egypt, USA and Europe; numerous public sculptures in England including Broadgate, Ludgate and Finsbury Square, London, St Paul's Church, Harringay, St Luke's, Chelsea, St Nicholas, Newcastle upon Tyne, Altar for St Anselm's Chapel, Canterbury Cathedral, Lincoln Coll. Oxford and British govt comms in Delhi, Cairo and Canberra; consultant sculptor, Rajiv Gandhi Samadhi, Delhi; Sr Research Fellow, Wimbledon School of Art 1995–96; Brian Montgomery Visiting Fellow in Sculpture, Lincoln Coll., Oxford 2009; subject of book The Sculpture of Stephen Cox by Stephen Bann 1995; Gold Medal Indian Triennale, Arts Council Major Awards 1978, 1980, British Council Bursaries 1978, 1979, Hakone Open Air Museum Prize, Japan 1985, Goldhill Sculpture Prize, Royal Acad. 1988, Arts & Business Award 1988, ACE (Art and Christianity Enquiry) Award 2007. *Television:* contributor The Divine Michelangelo (BBC) 2004. *Address:* Lower House Farm, Coreley, nr Ludlow, Salop., SY8 3AS, England (home). *Telephone:* (1584) 891532 (home). *E-mail:* coxstepstone@aol.com (home). *Website:* www.stephencox.info (home).

COX, Vivienne, BSc, MSc, MBA; British energy industry executive; *Chairman, Climate Change Capital Ltd;* b. 29 May 1959; m.; two d.; ed Univ. of Oxford and Institut européenne d'admin des affaires (INSEAD), Paris, France; joined BP Chemicals 1981, various sales and marketing posts 1981–85, moved to BP Exploration 1985, moved to BP Finance 1987, set up commodity derivatives group within oil trading 1990–93, took over responsibility for BP's share holding in Rotterdam refinery 1993–96, Man. New Business in Cen. and Eastern Europe, Vienna 1996–98, CEO Air BP 1998, Integrated Supply and Trading 2001, Group Vice-Pres. 2004; Exec. Vice-Pres. for Gas, Power and Renewables 2005–; CEO, Alternative Energy –2009; non-exec. Dir Vallourec SA 2009–; Sr Ind. Dir, Dept for Int. Devt, UK Govt 2009–; mem. Bd of Dirs (non-exec.) Eurotunnel PLC 2002–04, Rio Tinto plc 2005–, Climate Change Capital Ltd 2008– (Chair. 2009–), St Francis Hospice; Bd mem. INSEAD; Dr hc (Hull) 2009; ranked by Fortune magazine amongst the 50 Most Powerful Women in Business outside the US (19th) 2002, (19th) 2003, (15th) 2004, (12th) 2005, (15th) 2006, (16th) 2007, (19th) 2008, Harpers and Queen Businesswoman of the Year 2004, Veuve Clicquot Businesswoman of the Year 2006, ranked by the Financial Times amongst Top 25 Businesswomen in Europe (21st) 2005, (20th) 2006, (21st) 2007. *Address:* Climate Change Capital Ltd, 3 More London Riverside, London, SE1 2AQ, England. *Telephone:* (20) 7939-5000. *Fax:* (20) 7939-5030. *Website:* www .climatechangecapital.com.

COX, Warren Jacob, BA, MArch, FAIA; American architect; *Partner Emeritus, Hartman-Cox Architects;* b. 28 Aug. 1935, New York, NY; s. of Oscar Sydney Cox and Louise Bryson Cox (née Black); m. Claire Christie-Miller 1975; one s. one d.; ed The Hill School, Yale Univ., Yale Univ. School of Architecture; Partner, Hartman-Cox Architects, Washington, DC 1965–2011, Partner Emer. 2011–; Visiting Architectural Critic, Yale Univ. 1966, Catholic Univ. of America 1967, Univ. of Virginia 1976; Dir Center for Palladian Studies in America 1982–; Ed. Perspecta; mem. Editorial Bd Guide to the Architecture of Washington, DC 1965, 1974; fmr mem. Georgetown Review Bd, Comm. of Fine Arts; Dir Acad. Art Museum, Center for Palladian Studies in America; fmr Dir DC Preservation League; Chair. Council of Friends, Alibi Club; fmr Chair. Folger Shakespeare Library, Literary Soc., Cosmos Club; lecturer at numerous architectural schools and insts; juror for design awards programmes; AIA Architectural Firm Award 1988, AIA Nat. Honor Awards 1970, 1971, 1981, 1983, 1989, 1994, Louis Sullivan Prize 1972, Arthur Ross Award, Centennial Award, DC AIA, History of Art Prize, Yale Univ. School of Architecture Architecture, Henry Adams Prize, AIA Centennial Award D.C. for Service, and more than 120 other awards. *Publications:* Hartman-Cox Architects/Master Architects Series 1994, 2009, various books and periodicals. *Leisure interests:* architectural history, automobile racing, fishing, shooting, golden retriever and English springer spaniel dogs, farming, book collecting. *Address:* 3111 N Street NW, Washington, DC 20007 (home); Kennersley, PO Box 1, Church Hill, MD 21623, USA (home). *Telephone:* (202) 333-6446 (office); (202) 965-0615 (home). *Fax:* (202) 333-3802 (office). *E-mail:* wcox@hartmancox.com (office).

COX, Winston A., MSc (Econs); Barbadian banker and international organization official; *Executive Director for the Bahamas, Barbados, Guyana, Jamaica, and Trinidad and Tobago, Inter-American Development Bank;* m. Sylvia Potvin; five c.; ed Univ. of the West Indies, Inst. of Social Studies, Netherlands; joined Cen. Bank of Barbados 1974, Adviser to Gov. 1982–87, Gov. 1997; Dir of Finance, Ministry of Finance 1987–91; mem. Exec. Bd IBRD 1994–97; Gov. Cen. Bank of Barbados 1997–99; Deputy Sec.-Gen. (for Devt Co-operation) of the Commonwealth 2000–06; Alt. Exec. Dir for the Bahamas, Barbados, Guyana, Jamaica, and Trinidad and Tobago, IDB 2006–08, Exec. Dir 2008–; Gold Crown of Merit (GCM) 2009. *Address:* Inter-American Development Bank, 1300 New York Avenue, NW, Washington,

DC 20577, USA (office). *Telephone:* (202) 623-1039 (office). *Fax:* (202) 623-3611 (office). *E-mail:* winstonc@iadb.org (office). *Website:* www.iadb.org (office).

COX ARQUETTE, Courteney; American actress and film producer; b. 15 June 1964, Birmingham, Ala; d. of the late Richard Lewis and of Courteney Cox (née Bass-Copland); m. David Arquette 1999; one d.; modelling career in New York; appeared in Bruce Springsteen music video Dancing in the Dark 1984; Co-founder (with husband) Coquette Productions 2004. *Films include:* Down Twisted 1986, Masters of the Universe 1987, Cocoon: The Return 1988, Mr Destiny 1990, Blue Desert 1990, Shaking the Tree 1992, The Opposite Sex 1993, Ace Ventura, Pet Detective 1994, Scream 1996, Commandments 1996, Scream 2 1997, The Runner 1999, Alien Love Triangle 1999, Scream 3 2000, The Shrink Is In 2000, 3000 Miles to Graceland 2001, Get Well Soon 2001, Alien Love Triangle 2002, November 2004, Alpha Dog 2006, Barnyard (voice) 2006, Zoom 2006, The Tripper (also producer) 2006, The Monday Before Thanksgiving 2008, Bedtime Stories 2008, Web Therapy 2009, Scream 4 2011. *Television series:* Misfits of Science 1985–86, Family Ties 1987–88, The Trouble with Larry 1993, Friends 1994–2004, Dirt (also exec. producer) 2007–08, Scrubs 2009, Web Therapy (series) 2009, 2011, Cougar Town 2009–12. *Television films include:* Roxanne: The Prize Pulitzer 1989, Till We Meet Again 1989, Curiosity Kills 1990, Morton and Hays 1991, Topper 1992, Sketch Artist II: Hands That See 1995. *Address:* Coquette Productions, 8015 West 3rd Street, Los Angeles, CA 90048; c/o WME, 9601 Wilshire Blvd, Beverly Hills, CA 90210, USA. *Telephone:* (323) 801-1000 (Coquette).

COYIUTO, Robert R., Jr, BS; Philippine business executive; *President and Chief Operating Officer, Oriental Petroleum & Minerals Inc.;* b. 1953; s. of Robert Coyiuto; m. Rosie Ty-Coyiuto; ed San Beda Coll., Manila; Dir Oriental Petroleum & Minerals Inc. 1982–, Chair. 1991–93, Pres. and Chief Operating Officer 1994–; Chair. and CEO Coyiuto Group of Cos; Chair. and CEO Prudential Guarantee and Assurance (PGA) Inc.; f. PGA Cars Inc. 1996, currently Chair.; Chair. and Pres. Calaca High Power Corpn; Chair. and CEO PGA Sompo Japan Insurance Inc.; Chair. Manila Stock Exchange, Pioneer Tours Corpn, Coyiuto Foundation, Nissan North Edsa; Vice-Chair. First Guarantee Life Assurance Co. Inc., First Life Financial Co. Inc.; Dir Robinsons Land Corpn 1990–2008, Universal Robina Corpn 2002–, Interport Resources Corpn 2008–, Philippine Stock Exchange Inc., Canon Philippines Inc., Destiny Financial Plan Inc., R. Coyiuto Securities Inc.; fmr owner Manila Chronicle. *Address:* Oriental Petroleum & Minerals Corporation, 40th Floor, Robinsons Equitable Tower, Pasig City 1605, Philippines (office). *Telephone:* (2) 6371670 (office). *Fax:* (2) 3952586 (office). *Website:* www.opmc.com.ph (office).

COZ, Steve; American editor and publishing executive; *Editorial Director, Newsmax Media;* b. 26 March 1957, Grafton, Mass.; s. of Henry Coz and Mary Coz; m. Valerie Virga 1987; ed Harvard Univ.; freelance writer for various US publs 1979–82; reporter, Nat. Enquirer, Fla 1982–95, Ed.-in-Chief 1995, then Editorial Dir and Exec. Vice-Pres. American Media Inc.; Founder and Pres. Coz Media Group LLC; Co-founder and Man. Partner, MyReforma 2007, Editorial Dir Newsmax Media 2011–; American celebrity analyst BBC Radio 1995–96; Edgar Hoover Memorial Award for Distinguished Public Service 1996; Haven House Award of Excellence for Outstanding Reporting on Domestic Violence Issues 1996. *Address:* Newsmax Media, PO Box 20989, West Palm Beach, FL 33416, USA. *Website:* www.newsmax.com.

CRABTREE, Robert H., MA, DSc, DPhil; British/American chemist and academic; *Whitehead Professor of Chemistry, Yale University;* b. 17 April 1948, London, England; s. of Arthur Crabtree; m. Holly Darico; ed Brighton Coll. and Univs of Oxford and Sussex, UK; Attaché de Recherche, CNRS, France 1975–77; Asst Prof. of Chem., Yale Univ., USA 1977–82, Assoc. Prof. 1982–85, Prof. 1985–, now Whitehead Prof.; Fellow, American Acad. of Arts and Sciences; ACS Organometallic Chem. Award 1993, Dow Lecturer, Berkeley 2004, Williams Lecturer, Oxford 2004, Sabatier Lecturer, Toulouse 2006, Osborn Lecturer, Strasbourg 2009, Kosolapoff Award 2010, Stauffer Lecturer, Univ. of Southern California 2010, King Lecturer, Univ. of Georgia 2011, McElvain Lecturer, Univ. of Wisconsin 2013, Yale Postdoctoral Mentoring Award 2013, Siedle Lecturer, Indiana Univ. 2014, RSC Centenary Award 2014. *Publication:* The Organometallic Chemistry of the Transition Metals 2005 (sixth edn 2014). *Leisure interest:* travel. *Address:* Yale Chemistry Department, PO Box 208107, 225 Prospect Street, New Haven, CT 06520-8107 (office). *Telephone:* (203) 432-3925 (office). *Fax:* (203) 432-6144 (office). *E-mail:* robert.crabtree@yale.edu (office). *Website:* www.chem.yale .edu/faculty/crabtree.html (office); ursula.chem.yale.edu/~crabtree (office).

CRACE, Jim, BA; British writer and dramatist; b. 1 March 1946, Brocket Hall, Lemsford, Hertfordshire; m. Pamela Ann Turton 1975; one s. one d.; ed Birmingham Coll. of Commerce, Univ. of London; freelance writer and journalist 1976–87; Distinguished Writer-in-Residence, James Michener Center, Univ. of Texas, Austin 2008; Dr hc (Univ. of Central England) 2000; David Higham Award 1986, Guardian Prize for Fiction 1986, Whitbread Award 1986, 1997, Antico Fattore Prize, Italy 1988, GAP Int. Prize for Literature 1989, Soc. of Authors Travel Award 1992, RSL Winifred Holtby Memorial Prize 1995, E. M. Forster Award 1996, Nat. Critics' Circle Award, USA 2001. *Publications include:* Continent 1986, The Gift of Stones 1988, Arcadia 1992, Signals of Distress 1994, The Slow Digestions of the Night 1995, Quarantine 1997, Being Dead 1999, The Devil's Larder 2001, Genes 2001, Six 2003, Genesis 2003, The Pesthouse 2007, All That Follows 2010, Harvest 2013; short stories: Refugees 1977, Annie, California Plates 1977, Helter Skelter, Hang Sorrow, Care'll Kill a Cat 1977, Seven Ages 1980; other: radio plays. *Address:* 23 Mayfield Road, Mosely, Birmingham, B13 9HJ, England.

CRACKNELL, James, MBE; British oarsman; b. 5 May 1972, Sutton, Surrey; m. Beverley Turner 2002; two c.; ed Kingston Grammar School; int. debut in 1989 in coxed pair (finished tenth at Jr World Championships); won gold medal in coxless four at Jr World Championships 1990; sr int. debut in 1991 in coxless four (finished seventh in World Championships); won silver medal in the Eight at World Student Games 1993; part of British coxless four team 1997: gold medals at World Championships 1997–99, gold medals, FISA (Fédération Internationale des Sociétés d'Aviron) World Cup 1997, 1999, 2000, gold medals at Olympic Games, Sydney 2000, Athens 2004; with Matthew Pinsent won gold medals in the pair at World Championships 2001 and 2002 (also gold medal in coxed pair); qualified geography teacher; took a 12-month break from rowing 2004; currently presenter

for Channel 4 and ITV, also columnist for Daily Telegraph. *Publication:* The Crossing (with Ben Fogle) 2006. *Address:* c/o MTC (UK) Ltd, 20 York Street, London, W1U 6PU, England (office).

CRADDOCK, Gen. (Bantz) John, BA, MA; American army officer; b. 1950, West Union, Doddridge Co., W Va; m. Linda Craddock; one s. one d.; ed West Virginia Univ., Command and Gen. Staff Coll., US Army War Coll.; commissioned as Armour Officer; Tank Co. Commdr, 3rd Armoured Div.; Systems Analyst then Exec. Officer, Office of Program Man., Abrams Tank System, Warren, Mich. 1981; assumed command of 4th Bn 64th Armour 24th Infantry Div. (Mechanised), Fort Stewart, Ga 1989; Asst Chief of Staff, (Operations) for 24th Div.; assumed command of 194th Separate Armoured Brigade 1993–95, then Asst Chief of Staff (Operations) for III Corps, Fort Hood, Tex.; Asst Deputy Dir (Plans and Policy), Jt Staff at Pentagon 1996–98; Asst Divisional Commdr for Manoeuvre of 1st Infantry Div. (Mechanised), Germany 1998; Commanding Gen. 7th Army Training Command, US Army Europe, then assumed command of 1st Infantry Div. (Mechanised); Sr Mil. Asst to Sec. of Defense; Combatant Commdr US Southern Command –2004, led US Southern Command 2004–06; Supreme Allied Commdr Europe and Commdr US European Command, NATO 2006–09; served in Operation Desert Storm and Kosovo War; Valorous Unit Award, Defense Distinguished Service Medal, Distinguished Service Medal, Silver Star, Defense Superior Service Medal with 1 Oak Leaf Cluster, Legion of Merit with 2 Oak Leaf Clusters, Bronze Star. *Address:* c/o NATO Allied Commander Europe, NATO Headquarters, boulevard Léopold III, 1110 Brussels, Belgium.

CRAGG, Anthony (Tony) Douglas, CBE, BA, MA, RCA; British sculptor and professor; *Rektor, Düsseldorfer Kunstakademie;* b. 9 April 1949, Liverpool; s. of Douglas R. Cragg and Audrey M. Rutter; m. 1st Ute Oberste-Lehn 1977; two s.; m. 2nd Tatjana Verhasselt 1987; one s. one d.; ed Gloucester Coll. of Art and Design, Wimbledon School of Art, RCA; Lab. Technician, Nat. Rubber Producers Research Assen 1966–68; fmr Prof., Ecole des Beaux Arts de Metz; moved to Wuppertal 1977, first exhbns 1977; teacher, Düsseldorf Kunstakademie 1978–2001, Prof. 2005–, Co-Dir 2008, Rektor 2009–; Prof. Hochschule der Künste (HdK), Berlin 2001–05; Visiting Prof., Univ. of the Arts, London 2005; elected to Akademie der Künste, Berlin 2001, European Acad., Nordrhein-Westfalen Akademie der Wissenschaften und der Künste; over 300 solo exhbns in galleries and museums and numerous group exhbns 1977–2010; Hon. Prof., Budapest, Hon. Fellow, John Moores Univ. 2001; Chevalier des Arts et des Lettres 1992; Dr hc (Univ. of Surrey) 2001, (RCA) 2009; Mentione Speciale, Venice Biennale 1988, Von-der-Heydt Prize 1989, Turner Prize 1988, Shakespeare Prize 2001, Peipenbrock Prize for Sculpture 2002, First Prize, Beijing Biennale 2005, Praemium Imperiale 2007, Ehrenring der Stadt Wuppertal 2009. *Leisure interests:* walking, geology. *Address:* Lise-Meitner-Str. 33, 42119 Wuppertal Germany (home). *Telephone:* (202) 55-13-50 (home). *Fax:* (202) 55-13-512 (home). *E-mail:* jm@tony-cragg.com. *Website:* www.tony-cragg .com.

CRAIG, Daniel; British actor; b. 2 March 1968, Chester; s. of Timothy Craig and Carol Olivia Craig; m. Fiona Loudon 1992 (divorced); one d.; ed Guildhall School of Music and Drama. *Plays include:* A Steady Rain, Broadway 2009. *Films include:* The Power of One 1992, A Kid in King Arthur's Court 1995, Obsession 1997, Love and Rage 1998, Elizabeth 1998, Love Is the Devil: Study for a Portrait of Francis Bacon 1998, The Trench 1999, I Dreamed of Africa 2000, Some Voices 2000, Hotel Splendide 2000, Lara Croft: Tomb Raider 2001, Road to Perdition 2002, Ten Minutes Older: The Cello 2002, Occasional, Strong 2002, The Mother 2003, Sylvia 2003, Enduring Love 2004, Layer Cake 2004, The Jacket 2005, Sorstalanság 2005, Munich 2005, Renaissance (voice) 2006, Infamous 2006, Casino Royale (Evening Standard British Film Award for Best Actor 2007) 2006, The Invasion 2007, The Golden Compass 2007, Flashbacks of a Fool 2008, Quantum of Solace 2008, Defiance 2008, Cowboys and Aliens 2011, Dream House 2011, The Adventures of Tintin: The Secret of the Unicorn 2011, The Girl with the Dragon Tattoo 2011, Skyfall 2012. *Television includes:* Our Friends in the North 1996, Shockers: The Visitor 1999, Sword of Honour 2001, Copenhagen 2002, Archangel 2005. *Address:* c/o Creative Artists Agency, Inc., 9830 Wilshire Blvd., Beverly Hills, CA 90212-1825, USA. *Telephone:* (310) 288-4545. *Fax:* (310) 288-4800. *Website:* www.caa .com.

CRAIG, David Parker, AO, DSc, FRS, FRSA, FAA; Australian chemist and academic; *Professor Emeritus of Chemistry, Australian National University;* b. 23 Dec. 1919, Sydney, NSW; s. of Andrew Hunter Craig and Mary Jane Parker; m. Veronica Bryden-Brown 1948; three s. one d.; ed Univ. of Sydney, Univ. Coll. London, UK; Capt., Australian Imperial Force 1941–44; Lecturer in Chem., Univ. of Sydney 1944–46, Prof. of Physical Chem. 1952–56; Turner and Newall Research Fellow 1946–49; Lecturer in Chem., Univ. Coll. London 1949–52, Prof. 1956–67, Visiting Prof. 1968; Prof. of Chem., ANU 1967–85, Prof. Emer. 1985–, Dean, Research School of Chem. 1970–73, 1977–81; Firth Visiting Prof., Univ. of Sheffield, UK 1973; Visiting Prof., Univ. Coll. Cardiff, UK 1975–89; Visiting Foreign Prof., Univ. of Bologna, Italy 1984; part-time mem. Exec. CSIRO 1980–85; Pres. Australian Acad. of Science 1990–94; Fellow, Univ. Coll. London; Hon. FRSC; Hon. DSc (Sydney, Bologna), H.G. Smith Memorial Medal, Leighton Medal. *Publications include:* Excitons in Molecular Crystals – Theory and Applications (co-author) 1968, Molecular Quantum Electrodynamics: An Introduction to Radiation-Molecule Interactions (co-author) 1984; original papers on chemistry in scientific journals. *Leisure interest:* tennis. *Address:* 216 Dryandra Street, O'Connor, ACT 2602, Australia (home). *Telephone:* (2) 6125-2839 (office); (2) 6249-1976 (home). *Fax:* (2) 6125-3216 (office). *E-mail:* david.craig@anu.edu.au (office).

CRAIG, George; American publishing executive; Dir Production, Honeywell Computers Scotland 1965–74; Vice-Chair. and Group Man. Dir William Collins, UK 1974–87; Pres. and CEO Harper & Row Publrs Inc. (now HarperCollins Publrs), New York 1987–96; mem. Bd of Dirs The News Corpn Ltd; mem. Editorial Advisory Bd Publrs Weekly Int.

CRAIG, Ian Jonathan David, BSc, PhD; British astrophysicist and academic; *Professor, Department of Mathematics, University of Waikato;* b. 30 Aug. 1950, Sheffield; s. of Ronald W. Craig and Beatrice I. Craig; m. Fumiko Nishimura; one s. one d.; ed Chesterfield Coll. of Tech. and Westfield Coll. and Univ. Coll., London; Research Fellow, Dept of Astronomy, Univ. of Glasgow 1974–76, 1977–79; Research Assoc., Inst. for Plasma Research, Stanford Univ., USA 1976–77;

Lecturer in Math., Univ. of Waikato, NZ 1979–85, Sr Lecturer 1985–93, Assoc. Prof. 1993–2002, Prof. 2002–, Chair. of Dept 2002; Research Astronomer, Inst. for Astronomy, Univ. of Hawaii 1990–91; guest investigator on Skylab 1977; mem. Int. Astronomical Union. *Publications include:* Inverse Problems in Astronomy–A Guide to Inversion Strategies for Remotely Sensed Data (with J. C. Brown) 1986. *Leisure interests:* cycling, swimming, skiing, windsurfing; wood: growing it, working it and burning it. *Address:* Department of Mathematics, Room G3.21, University of Waikato, Private Bag, Hamilton (office); 25 Cranwell Place, Hamilton, New Zealand (home). *Telephone:* (7) 838-4466 (office). *Fax:* (7) 838-4466 (office). *E-mail:* i.craig@waikato.ac.nz (office). *Website:* www.math.waikato .ac.nz (office).

CRAIG, Larry Edwin, BA; American politician; b. 20 July 1945, Council, Ida; s. of Elvin Craig and Dorothy Craig; m. Suzanne Thompson 1983; two s. one d.; ed Univ. of Idaho and George Washington Univ.; farmer and rancher in Midvale, Ida area; mem. Ida Farm Bureau 1965–79; mem. Nat. Rifle Asscn, Future Farmers of America; Pres. Ida Young Republican League 1976–77; mem. Ida Republican Exec. Cttee 1976–78; mem. Ida Senate 1974–80; mem. US House of Reps from 1st Dist of Ida 1981–91; Senator from Idaho 1991–2009 (retd); Republican. *Leisure interest:* gardening.

CRAIG, Mary, MA; British author and broadcaster; b. 2 July 1928, St Helens, Lancs.; d. of William Joseph Clarkson and Anne Mary Clarkson; m. Francis John Craig 1952 (died 1995); four s. (one deceased); ed Notre Dame Convent, St Helens, Liverpool Univ., St Anne's Coll., Oxford; NW Organizer, Sue Ryder Trust 1962–68; TV Critic, Catholic Herald 1971–76; presenter and features writer (freelance) with BBC Radio 1969–77; interviewer, Thames TV, Southern TV (freelance); freelance journalist and book reviewer; Officer's Cross, Order of Polonia Restituta 1987; John Harriott Award 1993 and other awards. *Publications include:* Longford 1978, Woodruff at Random 1978, Blessings (The Christopher Book Award, USA 1979) 1979, Man from a Far Country 1979, Candles in the Dark 1983, The Crystal Spirit 1986, Spark from Heaven 1988, Tears of Blood: A Cry for Tibet 1992, Kundun: The Dalai Lama, His Family and His Times 1997, The Last Freedom: A Journal 1997, Waiting for the Sun: A Peasant Boy in Occupied Tibet 1999, His Holiness the Dalai Lama (anthology, ed.) 2001; for children: Pope John Paul II 1982, Mother Teresa 1984, Lech Wałęsa 1989. *Leisure interests:* reading modern history and biography, logic puzzles, listening to music, playing the piano, travel. *Address:* c/o PFD, Drury House, 34–43 Russell Street, London, WC2B 5HA, England (office); 1 Lodge Gardens, Penwood, Burghclere, nr Newbury, Berks., RG20 9EF, England (home). *Telephone:* (20) 7344-1000 (office). *Fax:* (20) 7836-9543 (office). *Website:* www.pfd .co.uk (office).

CRAIG-MARTIN, Michael, CBE, MFA, RA; Irish artist; *Professor Emeritus of Fine Art, Goldsmiths College;* b. 28 Aug. 1941, Dublin; s. of Paul F. Craig-Martin and Rhona Gargan Craig-Martin; m. Janice Hashey 1963 (divorced); one d.; ed The Priory School, Washington DC, Fordham Univ., NY, Yale Univ., Yale Univ. School of Art; family moved to USA 1946, returned to UK 1966; Lecturer, Bath Acad. of Art 1966–69; Artist in Residence, King's Coll., Cambridge 1970–72; Sr Lecturer, Goldsmiths Coll., Univ. of London 1974–88, Millard Prof. of Fine Art 1994–2000, now Prof. Emer.; Trustee, Tate Gallery 1989–99, The Art Fund 2004–; Hon. Fellow, Goldsmiths Coll.; Dr hc (San Francisco Art Inst.) 2001, (Christ Church Univ., Canterbury) 2012. *Address:* c/o Gagosian Gallery, 4–24 Britannia Street, London, WC1X 9JD, England. *Telephone:* (20) 7841-9960. *E-mail:* mcraigmartin@ gmail.com (office). *Website:* www.michaelcraig-martin.com.

CRAIG OF RADLEY, Baron (Life Peer), cr. 1991, of Helhoughton in the County of Norfolk; **Marshal of the RAF David Brownrigg Craig,** GCB, OBE, MA, DSc, FRAeS; British fmr air force officer; b. 17 Sept. 1929, Dublin, Ireland; s. of Maj. Francis Brownrigg Craig and Olive Craig; m. Elizabeth June Derenburg 1955; one s. one d.; ed Radley Coll. and Lincoln Coll., Oxford; commissioned in RAF 1951, Commanding Officer RAF Cranwell 1968–70; ADC to The Queen 1969–71; Dir Plans and Operations, HQ Far East Command 1970–71, Commanding Officer RAF Akrotiri 1972–73, ACAS (Ops) Ministry of Defence 1975–78, Air Officer Commanding No. 1 Group RAF Strike Command 1978–80, Vice-Chief of the Air Staff 1980–82, Air Officer, C-in-C, RAF Strike Command and C-in-C UK Air Forces 1982–85, Chief of Air Staff 1985–88, Chief of Defence Staff 1988–91; Air ADC to The Queen 1985–88; Chair. Council of King Edward VII Hosp. (Sister Agnes) 1998–2004; Deputy Chair. RAF Benevolent Fund 1996–2013; mem. (Crossbench), House of Lords 1991–, mem. Select Cttee on Science and Tech. 1993–99, House Cttee 2007–13, Liaison Cttee 2013–, Convenor Crossbench Peers 1999–2004; Pres. RAF Club 2002–12; Hon. Fellow, Lincoln Coll., Oxford 1984; Hon. DSc (Cranfield). *Leisure interests:* fishing, shooting. *Address:* House of Lords, Westminster, London, SW1A 0PW, England (office). *Telephone:* (20) 7219-2200 (office). *Fax:* (20) 7219-0147 (office). *E-mail:* craigd@parliament.uk (office). *Website:* www .parliament.uk/biographies/lords/lord-craig-of-radley/3385 (office).

CRAIGG, Wendy M., CBE, MA; Bahamian economist and central banker; *Governor and Chair, Central Bank of the Bahamas;* m. Anthony Craigg; ed St Augustine's Coll., Coll. of Mount St Vincent, New York, USA, Fordham Univ., New York; began career in Research Dept, Central Bank of the Bahamas 1978, mem. Bd of Dirs 1997–, Deputy Gov. 1997–2005, Gov. and Chair. 2005–; Deputy Chair. Securities Comm. of The Bahamas; mem. Exec. Cttee Caribbean Centre for Money and Finance, Trinidad and Tobago. *Publications:* numerous papers on econ. issues. *Address:* Office of the Governor, Central Bank of the Bahamas, Frederick Street, POB N-4868, Nassau, Bahamas (office). *Telephone:* 302-2600 (office). *Fax:* 322-4321 (office). *E-mail:* cbob@centralbankbahamas.com (office). *Website:* www .centralbankbahamas.com (office).

CRAIK, Fergus Ian Muirden, BSc, PhD, FRSC, FRS; British/Canadian psychologist and academic; *Senior Scientist, Rotman Research Institute;* b. 17 April 1935, Edinburgh; s. of George Craik and Frances Crabbe; m. Anne Catherall 1961; one s. one d.; ed George Watson's Boys' Coll., Edinburgh and Univs. of Edinburgh and Liverpool; mem. scientific staff, MRC Unit for Research on Occupational Aspects of Ageing, Univ. of Liverpool 1960–65; lecturer in Psychology, Birkbeck Coll. London 1965–71; Assoc. Prof. then Prof. of Psychology, Univ. of Toronto 1971–2000, now Univ. Prof. Emer., Chair. Dept of Psychology 1985–90; Sr Scientist, Rotman Research Inst., Baycrest Centre for Geriatric Care 2000–; Fellow, Killam Research Fellowship 1982–84; Guggenheim Fellowship 1982–83;

Fellow, Center for Advanced Study in Behavioral Sciences, Stanford Univ. 1982–83, Soc. of Experimental Psychologists, Canadian Psychological Asscn, American Psychological Asscn; Dr hc (Bordeaux) 2006; William James Fellow Award 1993, D. O. Hebb Award 1998, Killam Prize for Science 2000, Anderson Lifetime Achievement Award 2009. *Publications:* Levels of Processing in Human Memory (ed. with L. S. Cermak) 1979, Aging and Cognitive Processes (ed. with S. Trehub) 1982, Varieties of Memory and Consciousness (ed. with H. L. Roediger III) 1989, The Handbook of Aging and Cognition (ed. with T. A. Salthouse) 1992, The Oxford Handbook of Memory (ed. with E. Tulving) 2000, Lifespan Cognition (ed. with E. Bialystok) 2006. *Leisure interests:* reading, walking, tennis, music. *Address:* Rotman Research Institute, Baycrest Centre for Geriatric Care, 3560 Bathurst Street, Toronto, ON M6A 2E1, Canada (office). *Telephone:* (416) 785-2500 ext. 3526 (office). *Fax:* (416) 785-2862 (office). *E-mail:* fcraik@rotman-baycrest.on .ca (office). *Website:* www.rotman-baycrest.on.ca/content/people/profiles/craik .html (office).

CRANBROOK, 5th Earl of (cr. 1892), 5th Viscount (cr. 1878); **Gathorne Gathorne-Hardy,** MA, PhD, CBiol, DL; British biologist (retd); *Adjunct Senior Research Fellow, Monash University;* b. 20 June 1933, London, England; m. Caroline Jarvis 1967; two s. one d.; ed Eton Coll., Corpus Christi Coll., Cambridge and Univ. of Birmingham; Lecturer, Sr Lecturer in Zoology, Univ. of Malaya 1961–70; Ed. Ibis (journal of British Ornithologists' Union) 1973–80; mem. Royal Comm. on Environmental Pollution 1981–92; Trustee, Natural History Museum 1982–86; mem. Natural Environment Research Council 1982–88; mem. Nature Conservancy Council 1990–91; Chair. English Nature 1991–98, ENTRUST 1996–2002; Dir (non-exec.) Anglian Water 1989–98; mem. Broads Authority, Harwich Haven Authority 1988–98; mem. Bd Foundation for European Environmental Policy 1987–98, Chair. 1990–98; Vice-Pres. Nat. Soc. for Clean Air and Environmental Protection; also partner in family farming business in Suffolk; Chair. Inst. for European Environmental Policy 1990–98; Chair. Int. Trust for Zoological Nomenclature 2001–08; Adjunct Sr Research Fellow, Monash Univ., Australia 2014; Hon. Johan Bintang Sarawak (JBS) 1997, Hon. Panglima Negara Bintang Sarawak (PNBS) 2005; Hon. DSc (Aberdeen) 1989, (Cranfield) 1996. *Publications:* Mammals of Borneo 1965, Birds of the Malay Peninsula (co-author) 1974, Riches of the Wild: Mammals of South East Asia 1987, Belalong: A Tropical Rain Forest (co-author) 1994, Wonders of Nature in South East Asia 1997, Ballad of Jerjezang (co-author) 2001, Swiftlets of Borneo (co-author) 2002 (second edn 2014). *Leisure interest:* walking. *Address:* Glemham House, Great Glemham, Saxmundham, Suffolk, IP17 1LP, England (home). *Telephone:* 7775-755825 (mobile) (home). *Fax:* (1728) 663339 (home). *E-mail:* lordcranbook@ greatglemhamfarms.co.uk (office).

CRANDALL, Robert Lloyd, BA; American business executive; b. 6 Dec. 1935, Westerly, RI; s. of Lloyd Evans Crandall and Virginia Crandall (née Beard); m. Margaret Jan Schmults 1957; two s. one d.; ed William and Mary Coll., Univ. of Rhode Island, Wharton School, Univ. of Pennsylvania; Dir of Credit and Collections, then Vice-Pres. Data Services TWA 1967–73; COO American Airlines 1973–85, Sr Vice-Pres. (Finance) 1973–74, Sr Vice-Pres. Marketing 1974–80, Dir 1976–, Pres. 1980–95, Chair. and CEO 1985–98 (retd), Pres., Chair. and CEO AMR Corpn 1985–98, now Chair. Emer.; Chair. Celestica Inc. 2004–12; Chair. Pogo Jet Inc.; mem. Bd of Dirs Gogo, Inc; mem. US Fed. Aviation Admin Man. Advisory Cttee; Horatio Alger Award 1997, Wright Brothers Memorial Trophy, Nat. Aeronautic Asscn 2004, Eagle of Aviation Award, Embry-Riddle Aeronautical Univ. 2004. *Leisure interests:* skiing, tennis, running, reading. *Address:* Pogo Jet, Inc., 611 Access Road, Suite 105, Stratford, CT 06615, USA (office). *E-mail:* contact@flypogo.com (office). *Website:* www.flypogo.com (office).

CRANDALL, Roger W., BA, MBA; American insurance company executive; *Chairman, President and CEO, Massachusetts Mutual Life Insurance Company (MassMutual);* ed Univ. of Vermont, Wharton School of Business, Univ. of Pennsylvania; joined Massachusetts Mutual Life Insurance Co. (MassMutual) 1988, has held positions as Head of Corp. Bond Man., Public Bond Trading and Institutional Fixed Income, Chief Investment Officer, and Chair. Babson Capital 2005–08, Pres. and CEO Babson Capital Man. LLC 2006–08, Pres. and COO MassMutual 2008–09, Pres. and CEO Jan. 2010–, Chair. Dec. 2010–; mem. CFA Inst. *Address:* Massachusetts Mutual Life Insurance Co. (MassMutual), 1295 State Street, Springfield, MA 01111-0001, USA (office). *Telephone:* (413) 788-8411 (office). *Fax:* (413) 744-6005 (office). *E-mail:* info@massmutual.com (office). *Website:* www.massmutual.com (office).

CRANE, Christopher M.; American business executive; *President and CEO, Exelon Corporation;* ed New Hampshire Tech. Coll., Advanced Man. Program, Harvard Business School; worked in new plant start-up at Comanche Peak Nuclear Plant, Tex. and Palo Verde Nuclear Plant, Ariz.; served as Browns Ferry Nuclear site Vice-Pres. for the Tennessee Valley Authority; joined Exelon Corpn (utility holding co., then ComEd) 1998, Chief Nuclear Officer 2004–07, Pres. and COO Exelon Corpn and Pres. Exelon Generation 2008–12, Pres. and CEO Exelon Corpn 2012–; mem. Bd of Dirs Inst. of Nuclear Power Operations, Exec. Cttee Nuclear Energy Inst. (also served as Chair. New Plant Oversight Cttee and mem. Nuclear Strategic Issues Advisory Cttee, Nuclear Fuel Supply Cttee, Materials Initiative Group); Vice-Chair. World Nuclear Asscn; mem. Bd Foundation for Nuclear Studies. *Address:* Exelon Corpn, PO Box 805398, 48th Floor, 10 South Dearborn Street, Chicago, IL 60680-5398, USA (office). *Telephone:* (312) 394-7398 (office). *Fax:* (312) 394-7945 (office). *E-mail:* info@exeloncorp.com (office). *Website:* www.exeloncorp.com (office).

CRANE, Sir Peter Robert, Kt, PhD, FRS; British environmentalist, academic and plant scientist; *Carl W. Knobloch Jr Dean, School of Forestry and Environmental Studies, Yale University;* b. 18 July 1954, Kettering, Northants.; s. of Walter Robert Crane and Dorothy Mary Crane (née Mills); m. Elinor Margaret Hamer 1986; one s. one d.; ed Univ. of Reading; Lecturer, Dept of Botany, Univ. of Reading 1978–82; Post-doctoral Research Scholar, Dept of Biology, Indiana Univ. 1981–82; Curator Dept of Geology, The Field Museum, Chicago 1982–92, Vice-Pres. Center for Evolutionary and Environmental Biology 1992–93, Vice-Pres. Academic Affairs and Dir The Field Museum 1994–99; mem. Paleontological Soc. (Pres. 1998–2000); Dir Royal Botanic Gardens, Kew 1999–2005; Prof., Dept of Geophysical Sciences, Univ. of Chicago 2006–09; Carl W. Knobloch Jr Dean, School of Forestry and Environmental Studies, Yale Univ. 2009–; Foreign Assoc., NAS

2001; Foreign mem. Royal Swedish Acad. of Sciences 2002, German Acad. Leopoldina 2004; mem. American Acad. of Arts and Sciences 2008; Hon. DSc, (Cambridge) 2009; Bicentenary Medal, Linnean Soc. 1984, Schuchert Award, Paleontological Soc. 1993. *Publications:* The Origins of Angiosperms and their Biological Consequences (co-ed) 1987, The Evolution, Systematics and Fossil History of the Hamamelidae Vols 1 and 2 (co-ed) 1989, The Origin and Diversification of Land Plants (co-author) 1997, Ginkgo: The Tree That Time Forgot 2013. *Address:* Yale School of Forestry and Environmental Studies, 205 Prospect Street, New Haven, CT 06511, USA (office). *Telephone:* (203) 432-5109 (office). *Fax:* (203) 432-3051 (office). *E-mail:* peter.crane@yale.edu (office). *Website:* environment.yale.edu (office).

CRANFIELD, Rev. Charles Ernest Burland, MA, FBA; British academic; *Professor Emeritus of Theology, Durham University;* b. 13 Sept. 1915, London; s. of Charles Ernest Cranfield and Beatrice Mary Cranfield (née Tubbs); m. Ruth Elizabeth Gertrude Bole 1953; two d.; ed Mill Hill School, Jesus Coll., Cambridge and Wesley House, Cambridge; research in Basle until outbreak of World War II; Probationer in Methodist Church 1939; ordained 1941; Minister in Shoeburyness 1940–42; Chaplain to the Forces (from end of hostilities worked with German Prisoners of War, was first staff chaplain to POW Directorate in War Office) 1942–46; Minister in Cleethorpes 1946–50; admitted to Presbyterian Church of England (now part of United Reformed Church) 1954; Lecturer in Theology, Durham Univ. 1950–62, Sr Lecturer 1962–66, Reader 1966–78, Prof. of Theology (personal) 1978–80, Prof. Emer. 1980–; Jt Gen. Ed. new series of International Critical Commentary 1966–2005; Hon. DD (Aberdeen) 1980; Burkitt Medal for Biblical Studies 1989. *Publications:* The First Epistle of Peter 1950, The Gospel according to Saint Mark 1959, I and II Peter and Jude 1960, A Critical and Exegetical Commentary on the Epistle to the Romans, Vol. 1 1975, Vol. 2 1979, Romans: A Shorter Commentary 1985, The Bible and Christian Life: A Collection of Essays 1985, If God Be For Us: A Collection of Sermons 1985, The Apostles' Creed: A Faith to Live By 1993, On Romans and Other New Testament Essays 1998. *Address:* 30 Albert Street, Western Hill, Durham City, Durham, DH1 4RL, England (home). *Telephone:* (191) 384-3096 (home).

CRANFIELD, Thomas L., BA; Irish banker and civil servant; b. 3 Feb. 1945, Dublin; m.; three d.; ed Univ. Coll. Dublin; personal admin. in American biomedical eng co., Dublin 1970–73; Head of Div. EIB (Luxembourg) 1973–90; Deputy Registrar European Court of Justice (Luxembourg) 1990–2000; fmr Dir-Gen. Office for Official Publs of the EU; mem. Cttee of Experts Centre Virtuel de la Connaissance sur l'Europe (CVCE). *Address:* Centre Virtuel de la Connaissance sur l'Europe (CVCE), Château de Sanem, 4992 Sanem, Luxembourg.

CRANHAM, Kenneth Raymond; British actor; b. 12 Dec. 1944, Dunfermline, Scotland; s. of Ronald Cranham and Margaret McKay Ferguson; m. Fiona Victory; two d.; ed Tulse Hill School, London, Royal Acad. of Dramatic Art (RADA), Nat. Youth Theatre; Bancroft Gold Medal, RADA 1966, Christine Silver Memorial Prize, Herbert Tree Prize. *Plays include:* RSC: School for Scandal, Ivanov, The Iceman Cometh; Nat. Theatre: Flight, An Inspector Calls, Kick for Touch, The Cherry Orchard, Cardiff East, From Kipling to Vietnam, The Caretaker, Strawberry Fields, Love Letters on Blue Paper, The Passion, The Country Wife, Old Movies, Madras House, The UN Inspector; Royal Court: Saved, Ruffian on the Stair, Samuel Beckett's Play, Cascando, The London Cuckolds, Tibetan in Roads, Magnificence, Cheek, Owners, Geography of a Horse Dreamer; West End: Loot, Comedians, Entertaining Mr Sloane, The Novice, Doctor's Dilemma, Paul Bunyan (Royal Opera House), Endgame, Broadway: Loot, An Inspector Calls, Gaslight (Old Vic), The Homecoming, Little Malcolm and his Struggle Against the Eunuchs, Traverse, Edinburgh and European tour, A Month in the Country (Chichester Festival Theatre). *Radio includes:* The Barchester Chronicles, New Grub Street, Sons and Lovers, Hard Times, Answered Prayers, Earthly Powers, Barrack Room Ballads, Gilgamesh, The Complete Smiley, The Pantomine Life of Joseph Grimaldi, Dr Johnson. *Films:* Oliver! 1968, Otley 1968, All the Way Up 1970, Fragment of Fear 1970, Up Pompeii 1971, Brother Sun, Sister Moon 1972, Vampira 1975, Peer Gynt 1976, Robin and Marian 1976, Joseph Andrews 1977, Heart of the High Country 1985, Making Waves (short) 1987, Chocolate 1988, Stealing Heaven 1988, Hellbound: Hellraiser II 1988, Prospero's Books 1991, Under Suspicion 1991, Tale of a Vampire 1992, Bed of Roses 1996, Deep in the Heart 1996, The Boxer 1997, RPM 1998, Vigo: A Passion for Life 1998, Women Talking Dirty 1999, The Last Yellow 1999, Kevin & Perry Go Large (as Ken Cranham) 2000, Gangster No. 1 (as Ken Cranham) 2000, Born Romantic 2000, The Most Fertile Man in Ireland 2000, Shiner 2000, Two Men Went to War 2002, Man Dancin' 2003, Blackball 2003, Bible Mysteries – Revelation: The End of the World 2004, Trauma (as Ken Cranham) 2004, Layer Cake 2004, The Rising: Ballad of Mangal Pandey 2005, A Good Year 2006, Hot Fuzz 2007, The Curry Club (short) 2007, Valkyrie 2008, Running in Traffic 2009, Made in Dagenham 2010, Michael Stilton (as Ken Cranham), 5 Days of War 2011, Flying Blind 2012, Suspension of Disbelief 2012. *Television includes:* Ways with Words (series) 1967, City 68' – The Shooting War 1967, The Wednesday Play – Death of a Private 1967, – Sling Your Hook 1969, IPlayhouse – Rogues' Gallery: The Misfortunes of Lucy Hodges 1968, Boy Meets Girl (series) 1969, Thirty-Minute Theatre – Gangster 1969, Z Cars (series) 1970, ITV Playhouse – Private Lillywhite's Dead 1970, Omnibus (series documentary) 1970, A Family at War (series) 1971, Hadleigh (series) 1971, From a Bird's Eye View (series) 1971, Softly, Softly: Task Force (series) 1970–72, New Scotland Yard (series) 1972, Budgie (series) 1972, ITV Sunday Night Theatre – The Samaritan 1972, Thirty-Minute Theatre – The Chauffeur and the Lady 1972, Achilles Heel (film) 1973, BBC Play of the Month (series) 1974, Village Hall (series) 1975, Against the Crowd (series) 1975, Holding On (series) 1977, Danger UXB (series) 1979, Screenplay (series) 1979, Thérèse Raquin (mini-series) 1980, Enemy at the Door (series) 1980, Tis Pity She's a Whore (film) 1980, Cribb (series) 1980, Play for Today (series) 1978–81, Brideshead Revisited (mini-series) 1981, The Bell (series) 1982, The Bell (series) 1982, Crown Court (series) 1973–82, La ronde (film) 1982, Strangers (series) 1980–82, Reilly: Ace of Spies (mini-series) 1983, Summer Season (series) 1985, Shine on Harvey Moon (series) 1982–85, Dead Man's Folly (film) 1986, A Sort of Innocence (series) 1986, Inspector Morse (series) 1987, Normal Service (film) 1988, Just Another Secret (film) 1989, The Play on One (series) 1988–89, Theatre Night (series) 1985–89, Rules of Engagement (mini-series) 1989, Oranges Are Not the Only Fruit (mini-series) 1989, Boon (series) 1989, Casualty (series) 1990, Wales Playhouse (series) 1990, Dunrulin (film) 1990,

Bergerac (series) 1990, Van der Valk (series) 1991, Chimera (mini-series) 1991, Murder Most Horrid (series) 1991, El C.I.D. (series) 1990–92, Screenplay (series) 1988–92, The Young Indiana Jones Chronicles (series) 1992, Between the Lines (series) 1992, Minder (series) 1993, Lovejoy (series) 1993, Screen One – Royal Celebration 1993, Shooting to Stardom (short) 1993, Requiem Apache (film) 1994, On Dangerous Ground (film) 1996, Heartbeat (series) 1996, The Tenant of Wildfell Hall (mini-series) 1996, Midnight Man (film) 1997, Get Well Soon – Tucker's Gambit 1997, Our Mutual Friend (mini-series) 1998, Kavanagh QC – Dead Reckoning 1998, The Murder of Stephen Lawrence (film) 1999, Without Motive (series) 2000, Justice in Wonderland (film) 2000, Lady Audley's Secret (film) 2000, The Ancients (film) 2000, The Sins (mini-series) 2000, Hannibal: The Man Who Hated Rome (documentary) (narrator) 2001, NCS: Manhunt (film) 2001, Dalziel and Pascoe (series) 2001, Night Flight (film) 2002, Dickens (series) 2002, Believe Nothing (series) 2002, Pollyanna (film) 2003, Killing Hitler (documentary) 2003, Sparkling Cyanide (film) 2003, The Genius of Mozart (mini-series) 2004, M.I.T.: Murder Investigation Team (series) 2005, Genghis Khan (film) (voice of Genghis Khan) 2005, Rome (series) (as Pompey Magnus) 2005, The Lavender List (film) 2006, The Chatterley Affair (film) 2006, Hustle (series) 2006, Hannibal (film) (narrator) 2006, New Tricks (series) 2006, The Line of Beauty (mini-series) 2006, Afterlife (series) 2006, Doc Martin (series) 2006, Lilies – The Tallyman 2007, Lusitania: Murder on the Atlantic (documentary) 2007, The Last Detective – The Man from Montevideo 2007, Heroes and Villains (series documentary) – Napoleon 2007, Tess of the D'Urbervilles (mini-series) 2008, Merlin (series) 2008, Marple: A Pocket Full of Rye (film) (as Ken Cranham) 2008, Spanish Flu: The Forgotten Fallen (film) 2009, Midsomer Murders – Blood on the Saddle (film) 2010, The Night Watch (film) 2011, National Theatre Live – The Cherry Orchard 2011, Upstairs Downstairs (series) 2012. *Publication:* 50 Years at the Royal Court Theatre. *Leisure interests:* vernacular music, art, food, travel, some people, thinking on trains. *Address:* c/o Markham, Froggatt & Irwin, 4 Windmill Street, London, W1 2HZ, England (office). *Telephone:* (20) 7636-4412 (office). *Fax:* (20) 7637-5233 (office). *E-mail:* admin@markhamfroggattandirwin.com (office). *Website:* www .markhamfroggattandirwin.com (office).

CRANSTON, Bryan Lee; American actor, screenwriter and director; b. 7 March 1956, Canoga Park, Calif.; s. of Joseph L. 'Joe' Cranston and Peggy Sell; m. 1st Mickey Middleton 1977 (divorced 1982); m. 2nd Robin Dearden 1989; one d.; ed Canoga Park High School, Los Angeles Valley Coll.; began acting career in local and regional theatres, started at Granada Theatre, San Fernando Valley; numerous TV commercials; voice acting includes English dubbing of Japanese anime, under the name Lee Stone; original cast mem. ABC soap opera Loving; part-owner of ind. theatre Cinemas Palme d'Or in Palm Desert. *Films include:* Oritsu uchûgun Oneamisu no tsubasa (voice: English version) 1987, Amazon Women on the Moon 1987, The Big Turnaround 1988, Corporate Affairs 1990, Dead Space 1991, Morudaibā (video short) (voice: English version) 1993, The Super Dimension Century Orguss 02 (video short) (voice: English version) 1993, Erotique 1994, Clean Slate 1994, Macross Plus (video) (voice: English version) (as Lee Stone) 1994, Armitage III (video) (voice: English version) 1995, That Thing You Do! 1996, Street Corner Justice 1996, Strategic Command 1997, Armitage III: Poly Matrix (video) (voice) 1997, Time Under Fire (as Brian Cranston) 1997, Saving Private Ryan 1998, Last Chance (also dir) 1999, The Big Thing 2000, The Prince of Light 2000, Terror Tract 2000, Seeing Other People 2004, Illusion 2004, Magnificent Desolation: Walking on the Moon 3D (documentary short) (voice) 2005, Little Miss Sunshine 2006, Intellectual Property 2006, Hard Four 2007, Love Ranch 2010, The Lincoln Lawyer 2011, Detachment 2011, Drive 2011, Leave 2011, Larry Crowne 2011, Contagion 2011, Batman: Year One (video) (voice) 2011, Red Tails 2012, John Carter 2012, Madagascar 3: Europe's Most Wanted (voice) 2012, Rock of Ages 2012, Total Recall 2012, Argo (New York Film Critics Online for Best Ensemble Cast 2012) 2012, Get a Job 2013, Eye of Winter 2013, Cold Comes the Night 2013. *Television includes:* Seinfeld (series) 1994–97, Diagnosis Murder (series) 1996–98, From the Earth to the Moon (mini-series) 1998, Clerks: The Animated Series (series) (voice) 2000–01, Malcolm in the Middle (series) (also dir) 2000–06, 'Twas the Night (film) 2001, The Santa Claus Brothers (film) 2001, Thanksgiving Family Reunion (film) 2003, Lilo & Stitch: The Series (series) (voice) 2003–04, American Dad! (series) (voice) 2005–10, How I Met Your Mother (series) 2006–07, Fallen (mini-series) 2007, The Hollywood Quad (film) 2008, Breaking Bad (series) (also dir) (Primetime Emmy Award for Outstanding Lead Actor in a Drama Series 2008, 2009, 2010, Satellite Award for Best Actor in a Series (Drama) 2008, 2009, 2010, TV Critics Asscn Award for Individual Achievement in Drama 2009, Critics' Choice TV Award for Best Drama Actor 2012, Saturn Award for Best Actor on TV 2012, 2013, Screen Actors Guild Award for Outstanding Performance by a Male Actor in a Drama Series 2013, 2014, Primetime Emmy Award for Outstanding Drama Series (Producer) 2013, Golden Globe Award for Best Actor in TV Series, Drama 2014) 2008–13; dir: Special Unit (film) 2006, Big Day (series) 2006, Modern Family (series) 2012, The Office (series) 2012, 30 Rock 2012, The Simpsons 2013. *Leisure interests:* collector of baseball memorabilia, fan of the Los Angeles Dodgers. *Address:* c/o United Talent Agency, 9560 Wilshire Blvd, Suite 500, Beverly Hills, CA 90212-2401, USA (office). *Website:* www.unitedtalent.com (office).

CRANSTON, David Alan, CBE; British business executive and fmr army officer; b. 20 Oct. 1945, Windermere, Cumbria, England; s. of Stanley Cranston and Mary Cranston (née Fitzherbert); m. Pippa Ann Reynolds 1968; three d.; ed Strathallan School, Perthshire, Royal Mil. Acad., Sandhurst; served in army first in artillery and then as aviator 1966–95, retd with rank of Brig.; with Personal Investment Authority 1995–97, Royal Bank of Scotland Group 1997–2000; Dir-Gen. Nat. Asscn of Pension Funds 2000–02; Dir (non-exec.) Voller Energy Group PLC, Scandia UK, Austin Reed Group Pension Fund Ltd, WBB Minerals Pension Fund Ltd; Chair. British Biathlon Union 1996–2011; Chair. MRC Pension Scheme Trustee Bd. *Leisure interests:* gardening, reading, sport, qualified helicopter pilot. *Telephone:* 7833-472878 (mobile) (office).

CRAPO, Michael Dean (Mike), BA, JD; American lawyer and politician; *Senator from Idaho;* b. 20 May 1951, Idaho Falls, Bonneville Co., Ida; s. of George Lavelle Crapo and Melba Crapo (née Olsen); m. Susan Diane Hasleton 1974; two s. three d.; ed Idaho Falls High School, Brigham Young Univ., Univ. of Utah, Harvard Law School; called to Bar in Calif. 1977, in Idaho 1979; law clerk, US Ninth Circuit Court of Appeals, San Diego 1977–78; Assoc., Gibson, Dunn &

Crutcher (law firm) 1978–79; attorney, Holden, Kidwell, Hahn & Crapo 1979–92, Pnr 1983–92; mem. Idaho State Senate 1984–93, Asst Majority Leader 1987–88, Pres. Pro Tempore 1989–92; mem. US House of Reps from 2nd Idaho Dist 1992–99; Senator from Idaho 1999–, mem. Banking, Housing, and Urban Affairs Cttee, Budget Cttee, Environment and Public Works Cttee, Finance Cttee, Indian Affairs Cttee, Co-Chair. Canada-US Interparliamentary Group, Chair. Republican Capital Markets Task Force; Republican. *Leisure interests:* back-packing, skiing. *Address:* 239 Dirksen Senate Building, Washington, DC 20510, USA (office). *Telephone:* (202) 224-6142 (office). *Fax:* (202) 228-1375 (office). *Website:* crapo .senate.gov (office).

CRAVEN, Sir John Anthony, Kt, BA; Canadian/British merchant banker; b. 23 Oct. 1940; m. 3rd Ning Ning Chang 2005; three s. from 3rd m.; one s. one d. from 1st m.; ed Michaelhouse, S Africa, Jesus Coll., Cambridge, Queen's Univ., Kingston, Ont.; with Clarkson & Co., Toronto 1961–64, Wood Gundy Bankers 1964–67; Dir S. G. Warburg & Co. 1967–73, Vice-Chair. 1979; Chief Exec. White Weld & Co. Ltd 1973–78; Founder and Chair. Phoenix Securities Ltd 1981–89; CEO Morgan Grenfell Group 1987–89, Chair. 1989–97; mem. Bd Man. Dirs Deutsche Bank AG, Frankfurt 1990–96, Supervisory Bd Société Générale de Surveillance Holding, Geneva 1989–98; Chair. (non-exec.) Tootal Group 1985–91, Lonmin PLC 1997–2009; Dir Securities and Investment Bd 1990–93; Dir Rothmans Int. PLC 1991–99; Dir (non-exec.) Reuters 1997–2004, Robert Fleming Holdings Ltd 1999–2000; Dir Gleacher & Co. Ltd 2000–2003, Fleming Family & Pnrs Ltd 2000–2003, Chair. 2003–07; Ducati Motor Holdings SpA 1999–2000; mem. Ont. Inst. of Chartered Accountants, Canadian Inst. of Chartered Accountants. *Leisure interests:* hunting, shooting, skiing. *Address:* c/o Lonmin Plc, 4 Grosvenor Place, London, SW1X 7YL, England (office).

CRAVEN, Wes, MA; American director, screenwriter and actor; b. 2 Aug. 1939, Cleveland, Ohio; ed Wheaton Coll., Johns Hopkins Univ.; fmr Prof. of Humanities; began film career at film production house, became Asst to Co. Pres. working on post-production; Asst Ed. to Sena Cunningham; mem. Dirs Guild of America. *Films include:* The Last House on the Left (also screenplay and ed.) 1972, The Hills Have Eyes (also screenplay and ed.) 1976, You've Got to Walk It Like You Talk It or You'll Lose That Beat, Deadly Blessing (also co-writer) 1979, Swamp Thing (also screenplay) 1980, The Hills Have Eyes II (also screenplay) 1983, Invitation To Hell 1984, A Nightmare on Elm Street (also screenplay) 1984, Deadly Friend (co-writer) 1986, The Serpent and the Rainbow 1988, A Nightmare on Elm Street III (co-writer, co-exec. producer) 1986, Shocker (also screenplay and co-exec. producer) 1989, The People Under the Stars (also screenplay and co -exec. producer) 1991, Wes Craven's New Nightmare (also screenplay and actor) 1994, Vampire in Brooklyn 1995, The Fear (actor), Scream 1998, Scream 2 1999, Music of the Heart 1999 (dir), Scream 3, Carnival of Souls (exec. producer), Alice (producer), Red Eye (dir) 2005, Paris je t'aime (segment) 2006, Pulse (screenwriter) 2006, My Soul to Take (dir and writer) 2010, Scream 4 2011. *TV includes:* (films) A Stranger in our House (co-writer) 1978, Invitation to Hell 1982, Chiller 1983, Casebusters 1985, A Little Peace and Quiet 1987, Wordplay 1987, Chameleon 1987, Her Pilgrim Soul 1987, Shatterday 1987, Dealer's Choice 1987, The Road Not Taken 1988, Night Visions (also co-writer and exec. producer) 1990, Nightmare Café (exec. producer) 1991, Laurel Canyon (exec. producer), Body Bags (actor); (series) Twilight Zone, Crimebusters. *Address:* c/o William Morris Agency, 1 William Morris Place, Beverly Hills, CA 90212; c/o Joe Quenqua, PMK, 1775 Broadway, Suite 701, New York, NY 10019, USA.

CRAVID, Raul; São Tomé and Príncipe politician; fmr Dir Empresa de Agua e Electricidade (EMAE—electricity and water utility co.); Minister of Planning and Finance 2008, of Public Admin, State Reform and Territorial Admin 2008; Sec.-Gen. Movimento Democrático Força da Mudança (MDFM). *Address:* Movimento Democrático Força da Mudança (MDFM), São Tomé, São Tomé and Príncipe (office).

CRAWFORD, Cynthia (Cindy) Ann; American model; b. 20 Feb. 1966, DeKalb, Ill.; m. 1st Richard Gere (q.v.) 1991 (divorced); m. 2nd Rande Gerber 1998; one s. one d.; promoted Revlon (cosmetics) and Pepsi Cola; presented own fashion show on MTV (cable and satellite); has appeared on numerous covers for magazines; model for numerous fashion designers; has released several exercise videos; face of Kelloggs Special K 2000; spokesperson for eStyle.com, Omega watches, 24 Hr. Fitness (also Dir), EAS Health and Sports Products; signature fragrance collection launched 2002, Cindy Crawford Feminine launched 2003; f. Cindy Crawford Home collection. *Films include:* Fair Game 1995, 54 1998, The Simian Line 2000. *Publications:* Cindy Crawford's Basic Face 1996, About Face (for children) 2001. *Website:* www.cindy.com.

CRAWFORD, Sir Frederick William, Kt, DL, DEng, DSc, CCIM, FREng, FIEEE, FIET, FInstP, FIMA; British scientist; b. 28 July 1931, Birmingham, England; s. of William Crawford and Victoria Maud Crawford; m. Béatrice Madeleine Jacqueline Hutter 1963; one s. (deceased) one d.; ed George Dixon Grammar School, Birmingham, Univs of London and Liverpool; Research Trainee, J. Lucas Ltd 1948–52; scientist, Nat. Coal Bd Mining Research Establishment 1956–57; Sr Lecturer in Electrical Eng, Birmingham Coll. of Advanced Tech. 1958–59; Stanford Univ., Calif., USA 1959–82; Prof. (Research), Inst. for Plasma Research 1964–67, Assoc. Prof. 1967–69, Prof. 1969–82, Consulting Prof. 1982–84, Chair. 1974–80; Dir Centre for Interdisciplinary Research 1973–77; Visiting Prof., Math. Inst. 1977–78, Visiting Fellow, St Catherine's Coll., Oxford 1977–78, 1996–97; Vice-Chancellor of Aston Univ. 1980–96; Criminal Cases Review Comm. 1996–2003; Chair. US Nat. Cttee, Union Radio-Scientifique Internationale 1975–81, Int. Comm. 1978–81, UK Rep. 1982–84, Int. Scientific Cttee, Int. Conf. on Phenomena in Ionised Gases 1979–81; mem. US-UK Educ. Comm. 1981–84, British North-American Cttee 1987–2013, Franco-British Council 1987–98; Chair. Birmingham Civic Soc. 1983–88; High Sheriff, W Midlands Co. 1995; Freeman, City of London 1986; Hon. Fellow, Inst. of Linguists 1987; Master, Worshipful Co. of Engineers 1996, Co. of Information Technologists 2000; Hon. Bencher, Inner Temple 1996; Hon. DSc (Buckingham) 1996. *Publications:* numerous publs on higher educ. and plasma physics. *Address:* 47 Charlbury Road, Oxford, OX2 6UX, England (home). *E-mail:* f.w.crawford@btinternet.com (home).

CRAWFORD, James Richard, BA, DPhil, LLD, SC, FBA; Australian academic; *Whewell Professor of International Law, University of Cambridge;* b. 14 Nov. 1948,

Adelaide, SA; s. of James Crawford and Josephine Bond; m. 1st Marisa Luigina Ballini 1971 (divorced 1990); four d.; m. 2nd Patricia Hyndman 1992 (divorced 1998); m. 3rd Joanna Gomula 1998; one s.; ed Brighton High School and Univs of Adelaide and Oxford; Lecturer, then Sr Lecturer, Reader, Prof. of Law, Univ. of Adelaide 1974–86; mem. Australian Law Reform Comm. 1982–84, part-time 1984–90; Challis Prof. of Int. Law, Univ. of Sydney 1986–92, Dean, Faculty of Law 1990–92; Whewell Prof. of Int. Law, Univ. of Cambridge 1992–; Dir Lauterpacht Research Centre for Int. Law 1997–2003, 2006–10, Chair. Faculty Bd of Law 2003–06; barrister, SC (NSW, Australia) 1997; mem. UN Int. Law Comm. 1992–2001; mem. Matrix Chambers; Wolfgang Friedmann Memorial Award 2009, Nessim Habif World Prize for Int. Law 2010. *Publications:* The Creation of States in International Law 1979 (second edn 2006), The Rights of Peoples (ed.) 1988, Australian Courts of Law (third edn) 1993, The International Law Commission Articles on State Responsibility 2002, International Law as an Open System 2002, The Law of International Responsibility (ed.) 2010. *Leisure interests:* reading, cricket, walking. *Address:* Lauterpacht Research Centre for International Law, 5 Cranmer Road, Cambridge, CB3 9BL (office); 7 Archway Court, Barton Road, Cambridge, CB3 9LW, England (home). *Telephone:* (1223) 335358 (office). *Fax:* (1223) 311668 (office). *E-mail:* jrc1000@cam.ac.uk (office). *Website:* www.law.cam.ac.uk (office).

CRAWFORD, Lionel, BA, PhD, FRS, FRSE; British virologist and academic; ed Rendcomb Coll., Glos., Emmanuel Coll., Cambridge, Univ. of Cambridge; Nat. Service 1950–52; mem. scientific staff, MRC Inst. of Virology, Glasgow 1960–68; Head of Dept of Molecular Virology, Imperial Cancer Research Fund (ICRF, now Cancer Research UK), London 1968–88 (Chair. Cellular and Molecular Biology Groups 1968–70), Head of ICRF Tumour Virus Group, Pathology Dept, Univ. of Cambridge 1988–95; Visiting Research Fellow (Rockefeller Foundation Travel Fellowship), Virus Lab., Univ. of California, Berkeley 1958, Div. of Biology, California Inst. of Tech., Pasadena 1959; Co-organizer first Tumour Virus Workshops, Cold Spring Harbor 1969, European Molecular Biology Org. 1972; Ed. Journal of General Virology 1975–80, Oncogene Research 1986; expert in the field of DNA tumour viruses; Hon. mem. Biochemical Soc. 2004; Royal Soc. Gabor Medal 2005. *Publications include:* numerous scientific papers in professional journals on small DNA tumour viruses. *Address:* 18 Salters Road, Gosforth, Newcastle upon Tyne, NE3 1DJ, England (home).

CRAWFORD, Michael, CBE, OBE; British actor and singer; b. (Michael Dumbell-Smith), 19 Jan. 1942, Salisbury, Wilts., England; ed St Michael's Coll., Bexley, Oakfield School, Dulwich; actor 1955–; films for Children's Film Foundation; hundreds of radio broadcasts; appeared in original productions of Noyes Fludde and Let's Make an Opera by Benjamin Britten; has toured in UK, USA and Australia; Los Angeles Drama Critics Circle Award for Distinguished Achievement in Theatre (Lead Performance) 1990, named Showbusiness Personality of the Year by the Variety Club of GB, voted No. 17 in the 100 Greatest Britons poll sponsored by the BBC 2002. *Stage roles include:* Travelling Light 1965, The Anniversary 1966, No Sex Please, We're British 1971, Billy 1974, Same Time, Next Year 1976, Flowers for Algernon 1979, Barnum (Olivier Award for Best Actor in a Musical) 1981–83, 1984–86, Phantom of the Opera, London (Olivier Award for Best Actor in a Musical) 1986–87, Broadway (Tony Award for Best Actor in a Musical, Drama Desk Award for Outstanding Actor in a Musical, Outer Critics Circle Award for Best Actor in a Musical) 1988, Los Angeles 1989, The Music of Andrew Lloyd Webber (concert tour), USA, Australia, UK 1991–92, EFX, Las Vegas 1995–96, Dance of the Vampires (Broadway) 2002–03, The Woman in White (Outstanding Stage Performance Award, Variety Club of GB, Best Supporting Actor in a Musical, Theatregoers Choice Award voted by on-line readers of WhatsonStage.com) 2004–05, The Wizard of Oz (BroadwayWorld UK Award for Best Featured Actor in a Musical) 2011–12. *Films include:* Soap Box Derby 1950, Blow Your Own Trumpet 1954, Two Living One Dead 1962, The War Lover 1963, Two Left Feet 1963, The Knack 1965, A Funny Thing Happened on the Way to the Forum 1966, The Jokers 1966, How I Won the War 1967, Hello Dolly 1969, The Games 1969, Hello Goodbye 1970, Alice's Adventures in Wonderland 1972, Condorman 1981, Barnum 1986, Once Upon a Forest (voice) 1993, David Foster's Christmas Album 1993, Tony Palmer's Film About The Fantastic World of Michael Crawford 1996, My Favorite Broadway: The Love Songs 2001, The Ghosts of Christmas Eve 2001, WALL-E (archive footage from the film version of Hello Dolly!) 2008. *Television includes:* Sir Francis Drake (series) 1962, Some Mothers Do 'Ave 'Em (several series) 1973–78, Chalk and Cheese (series) 1979, Sorry (play) 1979, Barnum (film) 1986, Coronation Street 1998. *Publication:* Parcel Arrived Safely: Tied with String (autobiog.) 2000. *Address:* c/o Knight Ayton Management, 35 Great James Street, London, WC1N 3HB, England (office). *Telephone:* (20) 7831-4400 (office). *Fax:* (20) 7831-4455 (office). *E-mail:* info@knightayton.co.uk (office). *Website:* www.knightayton.co.uk (office).

CRAWFORD, Michael Hewson, MA, FBA; British historian and academic; *Professor Emeritus of Ancient History, University College, London;* b. 7 Dec. 1939, Twickenham, Middx; s. of Brian Hewson Crawford and Margarethe Bettina Crawford (née Nagel); ed St Paul's School, London and Oriel Coll. Oxford; Research Fellow, Christ's Coll. Cambridge 1964–69; Univ. Lecturer, Cambridge 1969–86; Jt Dir Excavations of Fregellae 1980–86, Valpolicesca Project 1987–94, Velleia Project 1994–95, S. Martino Project 1996–; Chair. British Epigraphy Soc. 1996–99; Visiting Prof. Pavia Univ. 1983, 1992, Ecole Normale Supérieure, Paris 1984, Padua Univ. 1986, Sorbonne, Paris 1989, San Marino Univ. 1989, Milan Univ. 1990, L'Aquila Univ. 1990, Ecole des Hautes Etudes, Paris 1997, Ecole des Hautes Etudes en Sciences Sociales, Paris 1999; Prof. of Ancient History, Univ. Coll. London 1986, now Prof. Emer.; Foreign mem. Istituto Lombardo, Reial Academia de Bones Lletres; mem. Academia Europaea; Joseph Crabtree Orator 2000; Trustee, Entente Cordiale Scholarships 2000; Officier des Palmes Académiques 2001; Archer Huntington Medal of the American Numismatic Society 2002. *Publications:* Roman Republican Coinage 1974, The Roman Republic 1978, La Moneta in Grecia e a Roma 1981, Sources for Ancient History 1983, Coinage and Money under the Roman Republic 1985, L'Impero romano e la struttura economica e sociale delle province 1986, Medals and Coins from Budé to Mommsen (with C. Ligota and J. B. Trapp) 1990, Antonio Agustín between Renaissance and Counterreform 1993, Roman Statutes (Ed.) 1995, Historia Numorum (with N.K. Rutter et al.) 2001. *Address:* 24 Gordon Square, Office B21, London, WC1H, England. *Telephone:* (20) 7679-7363. *E-mail:* imagines.italicae@sas.ac.uk.

CRAWFORD, Shawn; American sprinter; b. 14 Jan. 1978, Van Wyck, SC; ed Indian Land High School, Clemson Univ.; fmr 100m and 200m SC State Champion; Goodwill Games Champion 2001; Bronze Medal 200m, World Outdoor Championships 2001; Gold Medal 200m, World Indoor Championships 2001, US Outdoor Championships 2001, 2002, Athens Olympics 2004; Silver Medal 60m, World Indoor Championships 2004; Silver Medal 4×100m, Athens Olympics 2004; Gold Medal 60m, US Indoor Championships 2004; Silver Medal 200m, Beijing Olympics 2008; coach Bob Kersee. *Address:* c/o Kimberly N. Holland, Icon Management Inc., The Pinnacle Building, 3455 Peachtree Road, Suite 500, Atlanta, GA 30326, USA (office). *Telephone:* (404) 995-6730 (office). *Fax:* (404) 995-6878 (office).

CRAWLEY, Edward F., SB, SM, ScD; American engineer and academic; *Ford Professor of Engineering, Professor of Aeronautics and Astronautics and of Engineering Systems and Executive Director, Bernard M. Gordon-MIT Engineering Leadership Program, Massachusetts Institute of Technology;* ed Massachusetts Inst. of Tech.; Asst Prof., MIT 1980–84, Assoc. Prof. 1984–90, Dir Space Eng Research Center 1986–96, Prof. of Aeronautics and Astronautics 1990–, MacVicar Faculty Fellow 1992–2002, Prof. of Eng Systems 2000–, also Ford Prof. of Eng, Co-Dir Systems Design and Man. Program 1993–96, Dept Head of Aeronautics and Astronautics 1996–2003, Exec. Dir Cambridge MIT Inst. (jt venture with Univ. of Cambridge, UK) 2003–06, Exec. Dir Bernard M. Gordon-MIT Eng Leadership Program 2007–; Pres. Skolkovo Inst. of Science and Tech., Moscow (on leave); mem. Nat. Acad. of Eng, ASME, Soaring Soc. of America; Fellow, AIAA, AAAS, ACS; mem. Editorial Bd, NAS, NIH, NSF, RSC; Regional Soaring Champion 1991, 1995. *Publications:* numerous papers in professional journals. *Address:* Department of Aeronautics and Astronautics, Massachusetts Institute of Technology, Building 33-207, 77 Massachusetts Avenue, Cambridge, MA 02139, USA (office). *Telephone:* (617) 253-7510 (office). *E-mail:* crawley@mit.edu (office). *Website:* esd .mit.edu (office); systemarchitect.mit.edu (office).

CRAWLEY, Frederick William, CBE, FCIB, FRAeS; British banker; b. 10 June 1926, London; s. of William Crawley and Elsie Crawley; m. Ruth E. Jungman 1951 (deceased); two d.; entered Lloyds Bank 1942, Chief Accountant 1969, Asst Gen. Man. 1973, Exec. Dir Lloyds Bank Int. 1975, Asst Chief Gen. Man. 1977, Deputy Chief Gen. Man. 1978–82, 1983–84, Vice-Chair. and CEO Lloyds Bank Calif. 1982–83, Chief Gen. Man. Lloyds Bank PLC 1984–85, Deputy Group Chief Exec. 1985–87; Chair. Black Horse Agencies Ltd 1985–88; Deputy Chair. Girobank PLC 1991, Chair. 1991–94; Chair. Betta Stores PLC 1990–92, Alliance & Leicester Building Society 1991–94, Legal and General Recovery Investment Trust PLC 1994–98; Dir Lloyds Bank 1984–88, Lloyds Devt Capital Ltd 1987–92, FS Assurance Ltd 1988–89, FS Investment Mans. Ltd 1988–89, FS Investment Services Ltd 1988–89, Barratt Devts Ltd 1988–96, Alliance & Leicester Estate Agents Ltd 1988–92, Legal and General Bank Ltd 1997–2001; consultant, Anglo-Airlines Ltd 1988–92; Hon. Treas. RAF Benevolent Fund 1988–2004, Deputy Chair. RAF Benevolent Fund Enterprises Ltd 1988–2004; Chair. RAF Charitable Trust Enterprises 2005–10, Trustee RAF Charitable Trust 2005–; Fellow, St Andrew's Man. Inst. 1996–97; Assoc., Royal Aeronautical Soc. 1984, Fellow 2006; Freeman, Gapan 1992–, Liveryman, Gapan 2006, Freeman of the City of London 2006. *Leisure interests:* aviation, shooting, photography. *Address:* 4 The Hexagon, Fitzroy Park, London, N6 6HR, England (home). *Telephone:* (20) 8341-2279 (home). *Fax:* (20) 8341-2279 (home). *E-mail:* fredcrawleyis@yahoo.com (home).

CRAWLEY, Phillip, CBE; British/Canadian newspaper executive; *Publisher and CEO, The Globe and Mail;* b. 1944, Northumberland, England; m. Stephanie Crawley; three c., two step-c.; ed Univ. of Manchester; worked in various editorial roles for Thomson Regional Newspapers –1979; Ed. The Journal, Newcastle upon Tyne 1979–87; worked for Conrad Black as Northern Ed. The Daily Telegraph, London 1987–88; worked for Rupert Murdoch 1988–97, first as Ed. The South China Morning Post, Hong Kong 1988–93, then as Man. Dir The Times Supplements in London 1993–97; Man. Dir The New Zealand Herald 1997–98; Pres. and COO The Globe and Mail, Toronto 1998–99, Publr and CEO 1999–; Chair. of The Canadian Press; mem. Bd Audit Bureau of Circulation, Canadian Newspaper Asscn, World Asscn of Newspapers/IFRA; mem. Bd Sunnybrook Health Sciences Centre, Charter for Business (raises funds for the Duke of Edinburgh's Award in Canada), Royal Conservatory of Music, Sir Edmund Hillary Foundation; Hon. Consul for NZ in Toronto. *Address:* The Globe and Mail, 444 Front Street West, Toronto, ON M5V 2S9, Canada (office). *Telephone:* (416) 585-5000 (office). *Fax:* (416) 585-5150 (office). *E-mail:* pcrawley@globeandmail.com (office). *Website:* www.globeandmail.com.

CREAN, Hon. Simon Findlay, BEcons, LLB; Australian politician and trade union official; b. 26 Feb. 1949, Melbourne, Vic.; s. of Frank Crean and Mary Crean; m. Carole Lamb 1973; two d.; ed Middle Park Cen. School, Melbourne High School and Monash Univ.; Research Officer, Federated Storemen and Packers' Union of Australia 1970–74, Asst Gen. Sec. 1976–79, Gen. Sec. 1979–85; Jr Vice-Pres. Australian Council of Trade Unions 1981–83, Sr Vice-Pres. 1983–85, Pres. 1985–90; mem. House of Reps (for Hotham, Vic.) 1990–, Minister of Science and Tech. and Treas. 1990–91, of Primary Industries and Energy 1991–93, of Employment, Educ. and Training 1993–96; Man. Opposition Business, Shadow Minister for Industry and Regional Devt 1996–98, Shadow Treas. and Deputy Leader of the Opposition 1998–2001, Leader of the Opposition 2001–02, Shadow Treas. 2003–04, Shadow Minister for Regional Devt 2005–06, Shadow Minister for Trade and Regional Devt 2006–07, Fed. Minister for Trade 2007–10, Fed. Minister for Educ., Minister for Employment and Workplace Relations, Minister for Social Inclusion 2010; Minister for Regional Australia, Regional Devt and Local Govt 2010–13, for the Arts 2010–13; Deputy Leader of the Australian Labor Party 1998–2001, Leader 2001–02; Pres. Australian Council of Trades Unions 1985–90; mem. Econ. Planning Advisory Council, Nat. Labor Consultative Council, ILO Governing Body, Qantas Bd, Transport Industry Advisory Council, Business Educ. Council. *Leisure interest:* tennis, swimming, cycling, bushwalking. *Address:* 401 Clayton Road, Clayton, Vic. 3168, Australia (office). *Telephone:* (3) 9545-6211 (office). *Fax:* (3) 9545-6299 (office). *Website:* www.simoncrean.net.

CREECH, Rt Hon. Wyatt (W. B.), BA; New Zealand accountant, vintner and fmr politician; b. Oct. 1946, Oceanside, Calif., USA; m. Danny (Diana) Creech; three s.; ed Massey and Victoria Univs; mem. Martinborough Council 1980–86; MP for Wairarapa 1988–99; Minister of Revenue, Customs, in Charge of the Public Trust

Office and responsible for Govt Superannuation Fund 1990–91, Minister of Revenue, in Charge of the Public Trust Office and responsible for Govt Superannuation Fund and Sr Citizens, Assoc. Minister of Finance and Social Welfare 1991–93, Minister of Revenue and Employment, Deputy Minister of Finance 1993–96, Minister of Educ., for Courts, for Ministerial Services and Leader of the House 1996–98, Deputy Prime Minister 1998–99; Assoc. Spokesperson for Foreign Affairs and Trade; Deputy Leader Nat. Party 1997–2001; Chair. Cabinet Social Policy Cttee, Cabinet Legislation Cttee; mem. Nat. Party. *Leisure interests:* gardening, outdoor pursuits, wine tasting.

CREED, Martin; British artist; b. 21 Oct. 1968, Wakefield; s. of John Creed and Gisela Grosscurth; pnr Anouchka Grose; ed Slade School of Fine Art, London. *Dance:* Work No. 1020 (ballet), Sadler's Wells, London 2009. *Music:* released album 'nothing' with his band 'owada' 1995; now works as a solo artist. *Address:* c/o Hauser & Wirth London, 196a Piccadilly, London, W1J 9DY, England (office). *E-mail:* mail@martincreed.com (home). *Website:* www.martincreed.com (home).

CREEL, Michael A; American business executive; *President and CEO, Enterprise Products Partners LP;* Certified Public Accountant; Sr Vice-Pres. Enterprise Products GP, LLC (EPGP) (previous gen. partner of EPD) 1999–2001, Chief Financial Officer (CFO) EPGP 2000–07, Exec. Vice-Pres. 2001–07, mem. Bd of Dirs 2006–10, Pres. and CEO EPGP 2007–10, CFO Enterprise Products Co. (EPCO) 2000–07, COO 2005–07, mem. Bd of Dirs EPCO 2007–, Group Vice-Chair. and CFO EPCO 2007–10, Vice-Chair. EPCO 2010–, mem. Bd of Dirs, Pres. and CEO Enterprise GP 2005–07, Exec. Vice-Pres. and CFO DEP GP 2006–07, mem. Bd of Dirs Enterprise GP 2009–10, DEP Holdings, LLC (DEP GP) 2006–10, mem. Bd of Dirs, Pres. and CEO Enterprise Products Holdings LLC (current gen. partner of EPD (Enterprise GP) following merger of EPE with a subsidiary of EPD Nov. 2010–. *Address:* Enterprise Products Partners LP, 1100 Louisiana Street, Houston, TX 77002 (office); Enterprise Products Partners LP, PO Box 4324, Houston, TX 77210-4324, USA. *Telephone:* (713) 381-6500 (office). *E-mail:* info@epplp.com (office). *Website:* www.epplp.com (office).

CREEL MIRANDA, Santiago; Mexican lawyer and politician; b. 11 Dec. 1954, Mexico City; ed Univ. Nacional Autónoma de México, Univ. of Michigan, USA; lawyer, pvt. law firm; fmr Sec. Vuelta periodical; f. Este País magazine; fmr Prof. Autonomous Tech. Inst. of Mexico, Head Acad. Dept; Citizen Adviser to Gen. Council, Fed. Electoral Inst. 1994–96, Fed. Deputy 1997–; joined Partido Acción Nacional (PAN), cand. for Head of Govt of Fed. Dist 1999; Sec. of the Interior 2000–05; mem. Senado (Senate) 2006–; mem. Mexican Bar, Coll. of Lawyers, Mexican Acad. of Human Rights, Lawyers' Cttee for Human Rights. *Address:* Torre Azul Piso 20, Oficina A 20th floor, Reforma 136, Col. Juarez Del. Cuauhtémoc, 06600 México, DF, Mexico (office). *Telephone:* (55) 5345-3000, ext. 3493 (office). *E-mail:* santiago.creel@pan.senado.gob.mx (office). *Website:* www .senado.gob.mx (office).

CRENSHAW, William Edwin (Ed), BBA; American retail executive; *CEO, Publix Super Markets Inc.;* b. 1951, grandson of George Jenkins (founder of Publix); m. Denise Crenshaw; ed Baylor Univ.; joined Publix Super Markets Inc. 1974, becoming Dir of Retail Operations, Lakeland, Fla Div. 1984–90, Vice-Pres. Lakeland Div. 1990–91, Dir Publix Super Markets Inc. 1990–, Vice-Pres. Publix Atlanta Div. 1991–94, Exec. Vice-Pres. of Retailing 1994–96, Pres. 1996–2008, CEO 2008–; Vice-Chair. Food Marketing Inst.; mem. Advisory Bd Hankamer School of Business. *Address:* Publix Super Markets Corporate Office, 3300 Publix Corporate Parkway, Lakeland, FL 33811, USA (office). *Telephone:* (863) 688-1188 (office). *Fax:* (863) 284-5532 (office). *E-mail:* info@publix.com (office). *Website:* www .publix.com (office).

CRESSON, Édith; French politician; *President, Fondation des écoles de la deuxième chance;* b. (Édith Campion), 27 Jan. 1934, Boulogne-sur-Seine; d. of Gabriel Campion and Jacqueline Campion; m. Jacques Cresson 1959 (died 2001); two d.; ed Ecole de Haut Enseignement Commercial pour les Jeunes Filles (HECJF); Nat. Sec. Parti Socialiste; Youth Organizer, Parti Socialiste 1975; Mayor, Châtellerault 1983–97; Gen. Counsellor Châtellerault-Ouest 1982–97; mem. European Parl. 1979–81; Minister of Agric. 1981–83, of Foreign Trade and Tourism 1983–84, of Industrial Redeployment and Foreign Trade 1984–86, of European Affairs 1988–90; Prime Minister of France 1991–92; Pres. L'Asscn démocratique des français de l'étranger 1986; Pres. SISIE 1992–94; European Commr for Educ., Research, Science and Devt 1995–99; mem. Nat. Ass. for Vienne 1981, 1986–88; mem. Nat. Secr. Parti Socialiste 1974–90; Pres. Fondation des écoles de la deuxième chance 2002–; Pres. Inst. d'Études Européennes Univ. de Seine St Denis 1992; Chevalier, Légion d'honneur, Grand-Croix, Ordre nat. du Mérite; Dr hc (Weizmann Inst., Open Univ., UK, Technion, Israel). *Publications include:* Avec le soleil 1976, L'Europe à votre porte: manuel pratique sur les actions de la CEE intéressant les opérateurs économiques (co-author) 1989, Innover ou subir 1998, Histoires françaises 2006. *Address:* 21 boulevard de Grenelle, 75015 Paris, France (office). *Telephone:* 1-45-78-34-15 (office). *E-mail:* edith.cresson@wanadoo.fr (office).

CRESSWELL, Peter, BSc, MSc, PhD, FRS; British/American immunobiologist and academic; *Eugene Higgins Professor of Immunobiology and Professor of Cell Biology and Dermatology, School of Medicine, Yale University;* b. 6 March 1945, Mexborough, S Yorks., England; s. of Maurice Cresswell and Mary Cresswell; m. Ann K. Cooney 1969; two s.; ed Newcastle Univ., Univ. of London, Harvard Univ., USA; fmrly Chief Div. of Immunology, Duke Univ. Medical Center; Prof. of Immunobiology and Biology (now Eugene Higgins Prof. of Immunobiology and Prof. of Cell Biology and Dermatology), Yale Univ. School of Medicine 1991–; also currently Investigator, Howard Hughes Medical Inst., Chevy Chase, Md; The Newton-Abraham Visiting Prof., Univ. of Oxford 2007, Fellow of Lincoln Coll. 2007; mem. Scientific Advisory Bd, The Jane Coffin Childs Memorial Fund 2002–10, Center for HIV/AIDS Vaccine Immunology (CHAVI) 2005–; Assoc. Ed., Immunity 1994–; mem. Editorial Bd Traffic 1999–, PNAS 2001–, Immunological Reviews 2002–08, Tissue Antigens 2002–, Annual Review of Cell and Developmental Biology 2003–; mem. American Asscn of Immunologists 1976, American Soc. for Histocompatibility and Immunogenetics 1980, American Soc. for Cell Biology 1996, New York Acad. of Sciences 2000, NAS 2001, Inst. of Medicine, AAAS; Assoc. mem. European Molecular Biology Org. 1995; ASHI Rose Payne Distinguished Scientist Award 1995, Buchanan Medal, Royal Soc. 2010. *Publica-*

tions: numerous papers on the mechanisms regulating generation of complexes of peptides with Major Histocompatibility Complex (MHC) molecules, essential in the immune response. *Address:* Yale University School of Medicine, PO Box 208011, New Haven, CT 06520 (office); Howard Hughes Medical Institute, 4000 Jones Bridge Road, Chevy Chase, MD 20815-6789, USA (office). *Telephone:* (203) 785-5176 (Yale) (office). *Fax:* (203) 785-4461 (Yale) (office). *E-mail:* peter .cresswell@yale.edu (office). *Website:* medicine.yale.edu (office); www.hhmi.org (office).

CRETNEY, Stephen Michael, MA, DCL, FBA; British professor of law; *Fellow Emeritus, All Souls College, University of Oxford;* b. 25 Feb. 1936, Witney, Oxon.; s. of Fred Cretney and Winifred Cretney; m. Rev. Antonia L. Vanrenen 1973; two s.; ed Cheadle Hulme School, Magdalen Coll., Oxford; Parter, Macfarlanes (Solicitors), London 1964–65; Lecturer, Kenya School of Law, Nairobi 1966–67, Univ. of Southampton 1968–69; Fellow and Tutor in Law, Exeter Coll., Oxford 1969–78; mem. Law Comm. for England and Wales 1978–83; Prof. of Law, Univ. of Bristol 1984–93, Dean of Law Faculty 1984–88; Fellow, All Souls Coll. Oxford 1993–2001, Fellow Emer. 2001–; Hon. QC; Hon. LLD (Bristol). *Publications include:* Enduring Powers of Attorney (4th edn) 1996, Principles of Family Law (7th edn) 2002, Law, Law Reform and the Family 1998, Family Law (4th edn) 2000, Family Law in the 20th Century: A History 2003, Same Sex Relationships, from 'Odious Crime' to 'Gay Marriage' 2006.

CRIADO-PEREZ TREFAULT, Carlos; Argentine retail executive; *Executive Chairman, Dinosol Supermercados;* b. 1954, Buenos Aires; m.; three c.; with SHV Makro 1976–90, worked in Portugal, Brazil, and Taiwan 1990–97, also Exec. Dir; COO Int. Div. Wal-Mart Inc. 1997–99; COO Safeway PLC 1999, CEO 1999–2004; Exec. Chair. Dinosol Supermercados, Madrid 2004–; mem. Bd of Dirs X5 Retail Group N.V; Sr Advisor, UBS Bank 2007–; mem. Permira UK Advisory Bd; serves as adviser to Marks and Spencer's on int. expansion; Retail Personality of the Year, Retek 2001. *Leisure interests:* opera (Mozart), running marathons. *Address:* Dinosol Supermercados, Camino de la Zarzuela, 11, 28023 Madrid, Spain (office). *Website:* dinosol.es (office).

CRICKHOWELL, Baron (Life Peer), cr. 1987, of Pont Esgob in the Black Mountains and County of Powys; **(Roger) Nicholas Edwards,** PC, MA; British politician; b. 25 Feb. 1934; s. of Ralph Edwards and Marjorie Ingham Brooke; m. Ankaret Healing 1963; one s. two d.; ed Westminster School, Trinity Coll., Cambridge; mem. Lloyd's 1965–2002; MP (Conservative) for Pembroke 1970–87; Opposition Spokesman on Welsh Affairs 1975–79; Sec. of State for Wales 1979–87; mem. (Conservative) House of Lords 1987–; Chair. Nat. Rivers Authority 1989–96, ITNET PLC 1997–2004; Pres. Univ. of Wales, Cardiff 1988–98, Contemporary Art Soc. for Wales 1988–93; Dir HTV Ltd 1987–2002 (Chair. 1997–2002), Associated British Port Holdings PLC 1988–99; mem. Cttee Automobile Asscn 1997–98; Hon. LLD. *Publications:* Opera House Lottery 1997, Westminster, Wales and Water 1999, The Rivers Join 2009. *Leisure interests:* gardening, fishing. *Address:* House of Lords, Westminster, London, SW1A 0PW (office); 4 Henning Street, London, SW11 3DR, England (home); Y Cwt Mochyn, Manson Lane, Mon., NP25 5RD, Wales (home). *Telephone:* 7710-483682 (mobile). *E-mail:* crickhowelln@parliament .uk (office). *Website:* www.parliament.uk/biographies/lords/lord-crickhowell/1058 (office).

CRISP, Baron (Life Peer), cr. 2006, of Eaglescliffe in the County of Durham; **(Edmund) Nigel (Ramsay) Crisp,** KCB, MA; British civil servant; b. 14 Jan. 1952; s. of Edmund Theodore Crisp and Dorothy Shephard Crisp (née Ramsay); m. Siân Elaine Jenkins 1976; one s. one d.; ed Uppingham School and St John's Coll., Cambridge; Deputy Dir Halewood Community Council 1973; Production Man. Trebor 1978; Dir Cambs. Community Council 1981; Unit Gen. Man. E Berks. Health Authority 1986; Chief Exec. Heatherwood and Wexham Park Hosps 1988; Chief Exec. Oxford Radcliffe Hosps NHS Trust 1993–96; Regional Dir S Thames 1977–98, London 1999–2000; Perm. Sec. Dept of Health and Chief Exec. Nat. Health Service 2000–06 (retd). *Leisure interest:* the countryside. *Address:* House of Lords, London, SW1A 0PW, England. *Telephone:* (20) 7219-3873. *Website:* www .nigelcrisp.com.

CRIST, Charles Joseph (Charlie), Jr, BA, JD; American lawyer and politician; *Partner, Morgan & Morgan;* b. 24 July 1956, Altoona, Pa; s. of Charles Joseph Crist, Sr and Nancy Crist (née Lee); m. 1st Amanda Morrow 1979 (divorced 1980); m. 2nd Carole Rome 2008; ed St Petersburg High School, Fla, Wake Forest Univ., Florida State Univ., Cumberland School of Law, Birmingham, Ala; worked as intern in Fla State Attorney's Office before accepting position as Gen. Counsel for Nat. Asscn of Professional Baseball Leagues 1982–87; cand. for Fla State Senate 1986; began his govt service as State Dir for US Senator Connie Mack, Chair. Baseball Anti-Trust Advisory Cttee, mem. Fed. Judicial Advisory Comm. 1989–92; attorney, Wood & Crist law firm, Tampa 1987–; Fla State Senator 1993–99, Chair. Senate Ethics and Elections Cttee, Appropriations Criminal Justice Sub-cttee; cand. for US Senate 1998; Deputy Sec. Fla Dept of Business and Professional Regulation 1999–2000; Commr of Educ. 2001–03; State Attorney Gen. 2003–06; Gov. of Fla 2007–11; Partner, Morgan & Morgan, St Petersburg 2011–; mem. Domestic Security Oversight Bd, ABA Pres.'s Council, American Lung Asscn, Admin. Bd American Swiss Asscn Center Against Spouse Abuse, First United Methodist Church Ethics Cttee, Fla Bar Asscn, Bd Fla Conservation Asscn, Foundation for Fla's Future, Hillsborough Bar Asscn, Pinellas Park Chamber of Commerce, Rotary, St Petersburg Bar Asscn, St Petersburg Chamber of Commerce, Bd of Dirs Suncoasters Civic Club; Fellow, American Swiss Asscn; Pinellas Co. Fellow; Republican; Hon. Sheriff, Fla Sheriffs' Asscn, Police Benevolent Asscn 1995; Roll Call Award, Florida Chamber of Commerce 1993, Legislator Award, Pinellas School Admins 1993, Florida Asscn School Admins 1993, Florida Sheriffs Asscn 1994, 1996, named Conservationist Legislator of the Year, Florida Wildlife Fed. 1995, Govt Award, Urban League 1995, Senatorial Leadership Award, Florida Prosecuting Attorneys Asscn 1995, Legislator Conservation Award, Florida Conservation Asscn 1996, Distinguished Legislator Award, Florida Police Benevolent Asscn 1996, Phil Piton Award for service to MLB, Leadership St Petersburg. *Leisure interests:* water-skiing, reading, jogging. *Address:* Morgan & Morgan, Suite 150J, 695 Central Avenue, St Petersburg, FL 33701, USA (office). *Website:* www.forthepeople.com/charlie_crist.htm (office).

CRISTAS MACHADO DA GRAÇA, Maria da Assunção de Oliveira, PhD; Portuguese lawyer, academic and politician; *Minister of Agriculture, Sea, Environment and Spatial Planning;* b. 28 Sept. 1974, Luanda, Angola; m. Tiago Pereira dos Reis Machado da Graça; three c.; ed Univ. of Lisbon; Monitor, Faculty of Law, Univ. of Lisbon 1995–96, Asst Intern 1997–99; admitted to the Bar 1999; Deputy Minister of Justice April–Oct. 2002; Asst then Assoc. Prof. of Law, Universidade Nova de Lisboa 2005–09; legal consultant, Morais Leitão, Galvão Teles, Soares da Silva & Associados 2010–11; mem. Democratic and Social Centre–People's Party (CDS–PP) 2007–, now Vice-Pres.; mem. Ass. of the Repub. 2009–; Minister of Agric., Sea, Environment and Spatial Planning 2011–. *Address:* Praça do Comércio, 1149-010 Lisbon (office); c/o Morais Leitão, Galvão Teles, Soares da Silva & Associados, Rua Castilho 165, 1070-050 Lisbon, Portugal (office). *Telephone:* (213) 234600 (Ministry) (office), (213) 234652 (Ministry). *Fax:* (213) 234604 (Ministry) (office). *E-mail:* gabministra@mamaot.gov.pt (office); assuncaocristas@mlgts.pt (office). *Website:* www.min-agricultura.pt (office); www .portugal.gov.pt (office).

CRISTEA, Valerian; Moldovan politician and diplomatist; b. 1 Aug. 1950, Viprova, Orhei Co.; ed Polytechnic Inst., Chişinău; party instructor, Chisinau 1979–82; Chair. union of the State Enterprise 'Energoreparaţia' 1982–86; Chair. Republican Cttee of Trades Unions 'Sindenergo' 1986–94, Deputy Chairmanship of the Gen. Fed. of Trades Unions of Moldova 1994–98; mem. Parl. (CP of Moldova) 1998–2006, Chair. Perm. Comm. for Social Protection, Health and Family 1998–2001, Deputy Prime Minister 2001–06; Amb. to Czech Repub. 2007–09; Merit Prize of the Alliance War Against Trafficking (USA). *Address:* c/o Ministry of Foreign Affairs and European Integration, 2012 Chişinău, str. 31 August 1989 80, Moldova.

CRISTIANI, Mario; Italian gallery director; *Co-Director and Partner, Galleria Continua;* co-f., with Lorenzo Fiaschi and Maurizio Rigillo, Galleria Continua in San Gimignano, Tuscany 1990, other locations include Beijing 2004 and Boissy-le-Châtel, France 2007; represents several major artists, including Daniel Buren, Kendell Geers, Anish Kapoor and Hans Op de Beeck. *Address:* Galleria Continua, Via del Castello 11, 53037 San Gimignano, Italy (office). *Telephone:* (0577) 943134 (office). *E-mail:* info@galleriacontinua.com (office). *Website:* www.galleriacontinua .com (office).

CROCKER, Chester Arthur, BA, MA, PhD; American academic and fmr government official; *James R. Schlesinger Professor of Strategic Studies, Edmund A. Walsh School of Foreign Service, Georgetown University;* b. 29 Oct. 1941, New York, NY; s. of Arthur Crocker and Clare Crocker; m. Saone Baron 1965; three d.; ed Ohio State Univ., Johns Hopkins Univ.; editorial asst, Africa Report 1965–66, News Ed. 1968–69; Lecturer, American Univ. 1969–70; staff officer, Nat. Security Council 1970–72; Dir Master of Science, Foreign Service Program, Georgetown Univ. 1972–78, James R. Schlesinger Prof. of Strategic Studies, Edmund A. Walsh School of Foreign Service 1989–; Dir African Studies, Center for Strategic and Inst. Studies 1976–81; Asst Sec. of State for African Affairs 1981–89; Chair. African Working Group, Reagan Campaign 1980; Chair. US Inst. of Peace 1992–2004; work as int. consultant; mem. Bd of Dirs Global Leadership Foundation, US Inst. of Peace, Universal Corpn, G3 Good Governance Group Ltd, Housing for HIV Foundation; mem. Ind. Advisory Bd, World Bank; Hon. LLD (Rhodes Univ.) 2012; Presidential Citizen's Medal, Sec. of State's Distinguished Service Award, Vicennial Award for Service and John Carroll Medal, Georgetown Univ., Woodrow Wilson Award for Distinguished Public Service, Johns Hopkins Univ., Alumni Distinguished Achievement Award, Ohio State Univ. 2011. *Publications include:* South Africa's Defense Posture 1982, South Africa into the 1980s 1979, High Noon in Southern Africa 1992, African Conflict Resolution 1995, Managing Global Chaos 1996, Herding Cats: Multiparty Mediation in a Complex World 1999, Turbulent Peace: The Challenges of Managing International Conflict 2001, Taming Intractable Conflicts 2004, Grasping the Nettle: Analysing Cases of Intractable Conflict 2005, Leashing the Dogs of War: Conflict Management in a Divided World 2007, Rewiring Regional Security in a Fragmented World 2011; numerous articles. *Leisure interests:* music, tennis, fishing. *Address:* Room 801, Intercultural Center, Edmund A. Walsh School of Foreign Service, Georgetown University, Washington, DC 20057, USA (office). *Telephone:* (202) 687-5074 (office). *Fax:* (202) 687-2315 (office). *E-mail:* crockerc@georgetown.edu (office). *Website:* www.georgetown.edu/ sfs (office).

CROCKER, Ryan Clark, BA; American academic and diplomatist; b. 19 June 1949, Spokane, Wash.; s. of Carol Crocker; m. Christine Barnes; ed Univ. Coll. Dublin, Ireland, Whitman Coll., Walla Walla, Wash., Princeton Univ.; joined Foreign Service 1971, diplomatic positions in Iran 1972–74, Qatar 1974–76, Iraq 1978–80, Lebanon 1981–84; Deputy Dir Office of Arab-Israeli Affairs 1985–87; Political Counsellor, Embassy in Cairo 1987–90; Dir State Dept's Iraq-Kuwait Task Force 1990; Amb. to Lebanon 1990–93, to Kuwait 1994–97, to Syria 1998–2001, Deputy Asst Sec. of State for Near Eastern Affairs 2001–03, Interim Envoy to new Govt of Afghanistan 2002–04, rank of Career Amb. 2004, Amb. to Pakistan 2004–07, to Iraq 2007–09, to Afghanistan 2011–12; Int. Affairs Adviser, Nat. War Coll., Washington, DC 2003–04; Dean, Bush School of Govt and Public Service, Texas A&M Univ. 2010–11; Hon. Marine, US Marine Corps 2012; Hon. LLD (Whitman Coll.) 2001; Dr hc (Nat. Defense Univ.) 2010, (American Univ. of Afghanistan) 2013; Presidential Distinguished Service Award 1994, Dept of Defense Medal for Distinguished Civilian Service 1997, Presidential Meritorious Service Award 1999, 2003, State Dept Award for Valor, Three Superior Honor Awards, American Foreign Service Asscn Rivkin Award, State Dept Distinguished Honor Award 2004, Sec.'s Distinguished Service Award 2008, Presidential Medal of Freedom 2009. *Address:* Department of State, 2201 C Street NW, Washington, DC 20520 USA (office). *Telephone:* (202) 647-4000 (office). *Website:* www.state.gov (office).

CROCQUEVIEILLE, Hélène; French government official; *Director General, Customs and Excise;* ed École polytechnique, École nationale de la statistique et de l'admin économique, Institut d'études politiques de Paris (Sciences Po); began career as Head of Surveys, Directorate of Studies and Econ. Analysis, Institut Nat. de la Statistique et des Études Économiques (INSEE) 1992–95, Insp. Gen. INSEE; involved with management of Budget 1995–2003, including monitoring of fiscal policy in context of Econ. and Monetary Union, Deputy Dir of Budget Man. 2003–06, became head of the fourth sub-division in charge of ecology, energy, planning, transport policy, housing, urban policy, the Overseas culture, youth, sports and tourism 2006–09, Dir of Human Resources, Gen. Secr. Dept of Gender Equality and Housing (METL) and Ecology, Sustainable Devt and Energy (MEDDE) 2009–13; Dir Gen. Customs and Excise 2013–. *Address:* Douanes et Droits Indirects, 139 rue de Bercy, 75572 Paris Cedex 12, France (office). *Telephone:* 1-72-40-78-50 (office). *E-mail:* ids@douane.finances.gouv.fr (office). *Website:* www.douane.gouv.fr (office).

CROFF, Davide; Italian business executive; *Chairman, Permasteelisa SpA;* b. 1 Oct. 1947; ed in Venice, Pembroke Coll. Oxford; Asst Prof. of Political Econ., Univ. of Padua 1971–72; Research Dept Officer, Banca d'Italia, Rome 1974–79; Foreign and Financial Affairs Dept, Fiat SpA, Turin 1979–83, in charge of Int. Treasury Dept 1982, Finance Man. 1983–86, Sr Vice-Pres. 1986–89; CEO Finance and Int., Banca Nazionale del Lavoro, Rome 1989–90, Man. Dir 1990–2003; Chair. Permasteelisa SpA 2006–; Pres. la Biennale di Venezia 2004–; Chair. BPM 360 Gradi; Sr Adviser to Texas Pacific Group in Italy. *Address:* Permasteelisa SpA, Viale E. Mattei, 21/23, 31029 Vittorio Veneto (office); la Biennale di Venezia, Ca' Giustinian, 1364 San Marco, 30124 Venice, Italy. *Telephone:* (04) 38 505000 (office). *Fax:* (04) 38505125 (office). *E-mail:* info@permasteelisa.com (office). *Website:* www.permasteelisa.com (office); www.labiennale.org.

CROITORU, Lucian, DEcon; Romanian economist and politician; b. 13 Feb. 1957, Otopeni, Ilfov Co.; ed Academiei de Studii Economice (Acad. of Econ. Studies), Bucharest; Economist, Bucharest Well and Water Works 1982–84; Researcher, Inst. of Industrial Economy 1984–98; Expert, Govt Dept for Econ. Reform 1991–95; Consultant, Bucharest Investment Group 1995–96; Research Pnr, EU Phare Investment Programme 1996–97, 2001–02; Lecturer in Int. Macroeconomics, Faculty of Int. Econ. Relations, Academiei de Studii Economice 1998–2003; Chief Adviser to Finance Minister 1998; Adviser to Gov., Nat. Bank of Romania 1998–2003; Chief Adviser, IMF Exec. Directorate 2003–07; nominated by Pres. Traian Băsescu as Prime Minister Oct. 2009, nomination rejected by Parl. Nov. 2009; Comandor, Order of the Star of Romania 2000; Romanian Acad. Aurelian Prize 1995. *Publications:* several books and over 150 articles on econs. *Address:* c/o Banca Naţională a României, 030031 Bucharest 3, Str. Lipscani 25, Romania (office).

CROLL, Peter; German economist and research institute director; *Director, Bonn International Centre for Conversion;* early position at ECLA; held several positions with German Tech. Cooperation (devt org.), including Country Dir Kenya; facilitator, UNDP/FAO cross-border ecological programme in S Africa and other programmes in Africa and India; currently Dir Bonn Int. Centre for Conversion. *Address:* Bonn International Centre for Conversion, An der Elisabethkirche 25, Bonn, 53113, Germany (office). *Telephone:* (228) 911960 (office). *Fax:* (228) 241215 (office). *E-mail:* bicc@bicc.de (office). *Website:* www.bicc.de (office).

CROMBIE, Sir Alexander (Sandy), Kt, FFA; British insurance executive; *Chairman, Creative Scotland;* b. 1949, Leslie, Fife; joined Standard Life Insurance Co. 1966, various sr and man. positions including CEO Standard Life Investments (SLI) 1998–2004, Dir 2000–06, CEO Standard Life Assurance Co. 2004–06, Group Chief Exec. Standard Life PLC 2006–09; Vice-Chair. Royal Conservatoire of Scotland 2007–; Sr Ind. Dir, Royal Bank of Scotland PLC 2009–; Chair. Creative Scotland 2010–; mem. Chancellor of the Exchequer's high-level business group; mem. Bd Dirs Asscn of British Insurers 2002–09; The Prince's Amb. for Corp. Social Responsibility in Scotland 2007; Fellow, Faculty of Actuaries. *Address:* Creative Scotland, Waverley Gate, 2-4 Waterloo Place, Edinburgh, EH1 3EG, Scotland (office). *Telephone:* (330) 333-2000 (office). *Website:* www.creativescotland .com (office).

CROMME, Gerhard, DJur; German business executive; *Chairman of the Supervisory Board, Siemens AG;* b. 25 Feb. 1943, Vechta/Oldenburg; m.; four d.; ed Münster, Lausanne, Switzerland, Univ. of Paris, France and Harvard Univ., USA; joined Compagnie de Saint-Gobain 1971, latterly Deputy Del.-Gen. for FRG and Chair. Man. Bd VEGLA/Vereinigte Glaswerke GmbH, Aachen; Chair. Man. Bd Krupp Stahl AG, Bochum 1986; mem. Exec. Bd Fried. Krupp GmbH, Essen 1988 (now Fried. Krupp AG Hoesch-Krupp), CEO 1989–99; CEO ThyssenKrupp AG 1999–2001, Chair. Supervisory Bd 2001–; Chair. Supervisory Bd Siemens AG 2007–; mem. or fmr mem. Supervisory Bd Allianz SE, Axel Springer AG, Compagnie de Saint-Gobain (France); Chair. and mem. several supervisory bds and advisory councils. *Address:* Siemens AG, Wittelsbacherplatz 2, 80333 Munich (office); ThyssenKrupp AG, PO Box, 45063 Essen (office); ThyssenKrupp AG, ThyssenKrupp Allee 1, 45143 Essen, Germany (office). *Telephone:* (69) 797-6660 (Munich) (office); (201) 844-536212 (Essen) (office). *Fax:* (201) 844-536000 (Essen) (office). *E-mail:* info@siemens.com (office). *Website:* www.siemens.com (office); www.thyssenkrupp.com (office).

CRONENBERG, David, OC, FRSC; Canadian film director, producer and screenwriter; b. 15 March 1943, Toronto; ed Univ. of Toronto; fmr cinematographer and film editor; has directed fillers and short dramas for TV; Hon. Patron, Univ. Philosophical Soc., Trinity Coll., Dublin 2010; Chevalier, Légion d'honneur 2009. *Plays:* Opera version of The Fly, Théâtre du Châtelet, Paris 2008. *Films:* Transfer (writer, dir, producer) 1966, From the Drain (writer, dir) 1967, Stereo (writer, dir, producer) 1969, Crimes of the Future (writer, dir, producer) 1970, The Victim (dir) 1974, Shivers (writer, dir) 1974, Rabid (writer, dir) 1976, Fast Company (writer, dir) 1979, The Brood (writer, dir) 1979, Scanners (writer, dir) 1980, Videodrome (writer, dir) 1982, The Dead Zone (dir) 1983, Into the Night (actor) 1985, The Fly (writer, dir, actor) 1986, Dead Ringers (writer, dir, producer) 1988, Nightbreed (actor) 1990, Naked Lunch (writer, dir) 1991, Blue (actor) 1992, M. Butterfly (dir) 1993, Henry & Verlin (actor) 1994, Boozecan (actor) 1994, Trial by Jury (actor) 1994, To Die For (actor) 1995, Blood & Donuts (actor) 1995, Crash (writer, dir, producer) (Cannes Jury Special Prize 1997) 1996, The Stupids (actor) 1996, Extreme Measures (actor) 1996, I'm Losing You (exec. producer) 1998, Last Night (actor) 1998, Resurrection (actor) 1999, eXistenZ (writer, dir, producer) (Silver Berlin Bear 1999) 1998, Camera (writer, dir) 2000, Jason X (actor) 2001, Spider (dir, producer) 2002, A History of Violence (dir, producer) 2005, Chacun son cinéma (dir, segment) 2007, Eastern Promises (People's Choice Award, Toronto Int. Film Festival 2007) 2007, Drone (producer) 2008, A Dangerous Method (dir) 2011, Cosmopolis 2012. *Television:* Programme X (dir episode: Secret Weapons) 1970, Tourettes (film dir, writer) 1971, Letter from Michelangelo (film dir, writer)

1971, Jim Ritchie Sculptor (film dir, writer, prod.) 1971, Winter Garden (film dir, writer) 1972, Scarborough Bluffs (film dir, writer) 1972, Lakeshore (film dir, writer) 1972, In the Dirt (film dir, writer) 1972, Fort York (film dir, writer) 1972, Don Valley (film dir, writer) 1972, Peep Show (dir episodes: The Lie Chair, The Victim) 1975, Teleplay (writer, dir episode: The Italian Machine) 1976, Friday the 13th (dir episode: Faith Healer) 1987, Scales of Justice (dir episode: Regina vs Horvath) 1990, Moonshine Highway (actor) 1996, The Judge (actor) 2001. *Publications:* Crash 1996, Cronenberg on Cronenberg 1996. *Address:* David Cronenberg Productions Ltd, 217 Avenue Road, Toronto, ON M5R 2J3, Canada (office); c/o John Burnham, William Morris Agency, 151 South El Camino Drive, Beverly Hills, CA 90212, USA (office).

CRONIN, Anthony; Irish author; b. 23 Dec. 1928, Co. Wexford; s. of John Cronin and Hannah Barron; m. 1st Thérèse Campbell 1955; two d.; m. 2nd Anne Haverty 2003; ed Blackrock Coll., Univ. Coll., Dublin and Kings Inns, Dublin; Assoc. Ed. The Bell 1952–54; Literary Ed. Time and Tide 1956–58; Visiting Lecturer in English, Univ. of Montana, USA 1966–68; Writer-in-Residence, Drake Univ., Ia 1968–70; columnist, Irish Times 1973–80; cultural and artistic adviser to Prime Minister of Ireland 1980–83, 1987–92; Founding mem. Aosdána (arts asscn), elected Saoi 2003; Hon. DLitt (Trinity Coll., Dublin, Univ. of Ulster, Nat. Univ. of Ireland); Martin Toonder Award for contrib. to Irish literature 1983. *Publications:* Poems 1958, The Life of Riley 1964, A Question of Modernity 1966, Dead as Doornails 1976, Identity Papers 1980, New and Selected Poems 1982, Heritage Now 1982, An Irish Eye 1985, No Laughing Matter, The Life and Times of Flann O'Brien 1989, The End of the Modern World 1989, Relationships 1994, Samuel Beckett: The Last Modernist 1996, The Minotaur and Other Poems 1999, Anthony Cronin's Personal Anthology 2000, Collected Poems 2004, The Fall 2009. *Leisure interests:* reading, walking, travelling, watching horse-racing. *Address:* 30 Oakley Road, Dublin 6, Ireland (home). *Telephone:* (1) 4970490 (home). *Fax:* (1) 4970490 (home).

CRONIN, James Watson, PhD; American physicist and academic; *University Professor Emeritus of Astronomy and Astrophysics and Physics, Enrico Fermi Insitute, University of Chicago;* b. 29 Sept. 1931, Chicago, Ill.; s. of James Farley Cronin and Dorothy Watson Cronin; m. Annette Martin 1954; one s. two d.; ed Southern Methodist Univ., Univ. of Chicago; Nat. Science Foundation Fellow 1952–55; Assoc. Brookhaven Nat. Lab. 1955–58; Asst Prof. of Physics, Princeton Univ. 1958–62, Assoc. Prof. 1962–64, Prof. of Physics 1965–71; Prof. of Physics, Univ. of Chicago 1971, now Univ. Prof. Emer. of Astronomy and Astrophysics and Physics; Loeb Lecturer in Physics, Harvard Univ. 1976, lecturer Nashima Foundation 1993; mem. NAS, American Acad. of Arts and Sciences, American Physical Soc.; Hon. DSc (Leeds) 1996; Research Corpn Award 1968, Ernest O Lawrence Award 1977, John Price Wetherill Medal, Franklin Inst. 1975, shared Nobel Prize for Physics 1980 with Prof. Val Fitch (q.v.) for work on elementary particles, Nat. Medal of Science 1999. *Publications:* Fermi Remembered (ed.) 2004; numerous articles on physics. *Address:* Enrico Fermi Institute, University of Chicago, 5630 South Ellis Avenue, Chicago, IL 60637 (office); 5825 South Dorchester Avenue, Chicago, IL 60637, USA. *Telephone:* (773) 962-7102 (office). *Fax:* (773) 702-6645 (office). *E-mail:* jwc@hep.uchicago.edu (office). *Website:* efi .uchicago.edu (office).

CRONIN, Jeremy, MA; South African poet and politician; *Deputy Minister of Transport;* b. 12 Sept. 1949, Durban; s. of Denis Cronin and Freda Kemp; m. Gemma Paine; one s. one d.; ed Univ. of Cape Town and Sorbonne, Univ. of Paris; Lecturer in Philosophy and Political Science, Univ. of Cape Town 1974–76; imprisoned for seven years for his involvement with the African Nat. Congress (ANC) 1976; fmr Educ. Officer, United Democratic Front; spent time in exile in England and Zambia; Ed. African Communist, Umsebenzi; Deputy Minister of Transport 2009–; mem. cen. cttee South African Communist Party 1989–, Deputy Sec.-Gen. 1995–; mem. Nat. Exec. Cttee, ANC 1991–; mem. Parl. 1999–, Chair. Standing Cttee on Transport. *Publications include:* poetry: Inside (Ingrid Jonker Prize) 1983, Even the Dead 1997, Inside and Out 1999, More Than a Casual Contact 2006; non-fiction: Ideologies of Politics (co-ed.) 1976, 30 Years of the Freedom Charter (with R. Suttner) 1986, 50 Years of Freedom Charter (with R. Suttner) 2006. *Address:* Ministry of Transport, Private Bag X193, Pretoria 0001 (office); PO Box 1027, 2000 Johannesburg, South Africa (office). *Telephone:* (12) 3093000 (office). *Fax:* (12) 3285926 (office).

CROSBIE, John Carnell, PC, OC, QC, BA, LLB; Canadian politician and lawyer; b. 30 Jan. 1931, St John's, Newfoundland; s. of Chesley A. Crosbie and Jessie Crosbie (née Carnell); m. Jane Furneaux; two s. one d.; ed St Andrew's Coll., Aurora, Ont., Queen's Univ., Ont., Dalhousie Law School, Univ. of London, LSE; called to Newfoundland Bar 1957; Prov. Minister of Municipal Affairs and Housing 1966, mem. Newfoundland House of Ass. 1966, 1971–76; Minister of Finance, Econ. Devt, Fisheries, Inter-Govt Affairs, Mines and Energy and Pres. of the Treasury Bd, Leader of House of Ass. 1975; mem. House of Commons 1976–93; Minister of Finance 1979, of Justice and Attorney-Gen. of Canada 1984–86, of Transport 1986–89, of Int. Trade 1989–91, of Fisheries and Oceans and the Atlantic Canada Opportunities Agency 1991–93; Counsel to Patterson Palmer Law (now Cox and Palmer) 1994–2008; Chancellor Memorial Univ. of Newfoundland 1994–2008; Lt Gov. Newfoundland and Labrador 2008–13; mem. Progressive Conservative Party. *Publication:* No Holds Barred 1997. *Leisure interests:* reading, tennis, salmon and trout fishing. *Address:* PO Box 23119, St John's, Newfoundland, A1B 4J9, Canada (home). *Telephone:* (709) 895-3308 (home). *E-mail:* jane .crosbie@nf.sympatico.ca (home).

CROSBY, James Robert; British business executive; *Chairman, Misys plc;* b. 14 March 1956; m.; four c.; ed Lancaster Royal Grammar School and Brasenose Coll., Oxford; joined Scottish Amicable 1977, Investment Dir, Fund Man. 1983–, later Gen. Man. –1994; Man. Dir Halifax Life 1994–96, Financial Services and Insurance Dir Halifax PLC 1996–99, CEO Halifax Group PLC 1999–2001, Group CEO HBOS PLC (after merger of Halifax PLC and Bank of Scotland) 2001–06; Chair. Public Pvt. Forum on Identity Man., HM Treasury 2006; Chair. Misys plc 2009– (acquired by Vista Equity Partners 2012); mem. Bd of Dirs ITV plc 2002–, Financial Services Authority 2003–09 (Deputy Chair. 2004–09); Dir (non-exec.) Compass Group plc 2007–13 (resgnd); Trustee, Cancer Research UK; Fellow, Faculty of Actuaries 1980; appeared before the British Parl. Comm. on Banking Standards over his role as CEO during the collapse of HBOS Dec. 2012, formally stripped of his knighthood by the Honours Forfeiture Cttee June 2013. *Address:* Misys plc, One Kingdom Street, Paddington, London, W2 6BL, England (office). *Telephone:* (20) 3320-5000 (office). *Fax:* (20) 3320-1771 (office). *Website:* www .misys.com (office).

CROSBY, Sidney Patrick; Canadian professional ice hockey player; b. 7 Aug. 1987, Cole Harbour, Nova Scotia; s. of Troy Crosby and Trina Crosby; ed Shattuck-Saint Mary's Boarding School, Minn., USA; centre; played amateur ice hockey with Dartmouth Subways and Shattuck-Saint Mary's Sabres; leading scorer in Quebec Major Junior Hockey League 2004, 2005; first pick overall in Nat. Hockey League (NHL) Entry Draft 2005 by Pittsburgh Penguins; youngest player in NHL history to be named team capt., to record 100 points in a season, to record 200 career points, to have two consecutive 100 point seasons, to be named to All-Star Team; oungest player to win a World Championship scoring title; youngest team captain to win the Stanley Cup 2008/09; silver medal, World Junior Championships, Finland 2004, gold medal, USA 2005; gold medal (team), Olympic Winter Games, Vancouver 2010, Sochi 2014; Quebec Major Junior Hockey League: Michel Briere Trophy (most valuable player) 2004, 2005, Jean Béliveau Trophy (league leading scorer) 2004, 2005, Mike Bossy Trophy (best professional prospect) 2005, Paul Dumont Trophy (personality of the year) 2004, 2005, Guy Lafleur Trophy (playoff MVP) 2005, Michel Bergeron Trophy (offensive rookie of the year) 2004; Canadian Hockey League: Rookie of the Year 2004, Player of the Year 2004, 2005; NHL: Art Ross Trophy 2007, Lester B. Pearson Award 2007, Hart Memorial Trophy 2007, First Team All-Star 2007, Mark Messier Leadership Award 2007, Maurice Richard Trophy for most goals in a season 2010, Ted Lindsay Award (fmrly the Lester Pearson Award) for the 2012/13 season as the NHL's most outstanding player 2013. *Leisure interest:* watching movies. *Address:* c/o Pittsburgh Penguins, 1 Chatham Center, Suite 400, Pittsburgh, PA 15219-3447, USA. *Telephone:* (412) 642-1300. *Fax:* (412) 642-1859. *Website:* www .pittsburghpenguins.com; www.nhl.com/ice/player.htm?id=8471675; www .crosby87.com.

CROSS, George Alan Martin, PhD, FRS; British scientist and academic; *Professor and Head, Laboratory of Molecular Parasitology, Rockefeller University;* b. 27 Sept. 1942, Cheshire; s. of George Bernard Cross and Beatrice Mary Cross (née Horton); one d.; ed Cheadle Hulme School, Downing Coll. Cambridge; Scientist, Biochemical Parasitology, MRC 1969–77; Head, Dept of Immunochemistry and Molecular Biology, Wellcome Foundation Research Labs 1977–82; André and Bella Meyer Prof. of Molecular Parasitology, Rockefeller Univ. 1982–, Dean Grad. and Postgraduate Studies 1995–99; Leeuwenhoek Lecturer, The Royal Soc. 1998; Fleming Prize, Soc. for Gen. Microbiology 1978, Chalmers Medal, Royal Soc. of Tropical Medicine and Hygiene 1983, Paul Ehrlich and Ludwig Darmstaedter Prize 1984. *Leisure interests:* sailing, tennis. *Address:* The Rockefeller University, 1230 York Avenue, New York, NY 10021, USA (office). *Telephone:* (212) 327-7571 (office). *Fax:* (212) 327-7845 (office). *E-mail:* gamc@rockefeller.edu (office). *Website:* tryps.rockefeller.edu (office).

CROSSLEY, Paul Christopher Richard, CBE, MA; British concert pianist and music director; b. 17 May 1944, Dewsbury; s. of the late Frank Crossley and Myra Crossley (née Barrowcliffe); ed Silcoates School, Wakefield, Mansfield Coll., Oxford; has performed world-wide as concert pianist; dedicatee and first performer of works by Tippett, Henze, Berio, Takemitsu, Adams, Lindberg, Salonen, Knussen, Benjamin; Artistic Dir London Sinfonietta 1988–94; 15 major films on twentieth-century composers; Hon. Fellow, Mansfield Coll., Oxford 1991. *Recordings include:* complete piano music of Franck, Fauré, Debussy, Ravel, Poulenc, Janacek, Tippett, Takemitsu; works for piano and orchestra by Franck, Messiaen, Takemitsu, Lutoslawski, Stravinsky, Adams. *Leisure interests:* reading and mahjong. *Address:* Connaught Artists Management, 2 Molasses Row, Plantation Wharf, London, SW11 3UX, England (office). *Telephone:* (20) 7738-0017 (office). *Fax:* (20) 7738-0909 (office). *E-mail:* classicalmusic@connaughtartists.com (office).

CROW, Michael M., BA, PhD; American university administrator; *President, Arizona State University;* b. 11 Oct. 1955, San Diego; m. Sybil Francis; one s. two d.; ed Iowa State Univ.; Research Asst, Energy and Mineral Resources, Iowa State Univ. 1974–77, Assoc. Prof. of Man. 1988–91; Research Assoc., Inst. for Energy Research, Syracuse Univ. 1982–83, Sr Research Assoc., Maxwell School of Citizenship and Public Affairs, Syracuse Univ. 1983–87, Research Fellow 1987–89; Asst Prof. of Public Admin, Univ. of Kentucky 1984–85; Prof. of Science and Tech. Policy, School of Int. and Public Affairs, Columbia Univ. 1992–2002, Assoc. Vice Provost 1991–92, Vice Provost 1992–98, Exec. Vice Provost 1998–2002; Prof., School of Public Affairs, Arizona State Univ. 2002–, Pres. Arizona State Univ. 2002–; f. Center for Science, Policy and Outcomes, Washington, DC 1998; Fellow, Nat. Acad. of Public Admin 2006–. *Address:* Office of the President, Arizona State University, PO Box 877705, Tempe, AZ 85287–7705, USA (office). *Telephone:* (480) 965-8972 (office). *Fax:* (480) 965-0865 (office). *E-mail:* Michael .Crow@asu.edu (office). *Website:* president.asu.edu (office).

CROW, Sheryl; American singer, songwriter and musician (guitar); b. 11 Feb. 1962, Kennett, Mo.; two adopted s.; ed Univ. of Missouri; trained as classical pianist; worked as music teacher and part-time bar singer; fmr backing singer to Rod Stewart, Eric Clapton, Don Henley, Michael Jackson, Joe Cocker; solo artist mid-1980s–; BRIT Award for Best Int. Female Artist 1997, American Music Awards for Best Female Pop/Rock Artist 2003, 2004. *Film appearance:* De-Lovely 2004. *Recordings include:* albums: Tuesday Night Music Club (three Grammy Awards 1995) 1993, Sheryl Crow 1996, The Globe Sessions 1999, Sheryl Crow and Friends: Live in Central Park 1999, C'mon C'mon 2002, Sheryl Crow: Live At Budokan 2003, Wildflower 2005, Hits and Rarities 2007, Detours 2008, 100 Miles from Memphis 2010, Feels Like Home 2013. *Address:* c/o Stephen Weintraub (office); c/o A&M Records, 2220 Colorado Avenue, Santa Monica, CA 90404, USA (office). *E-mail:* wmgmt@aol.com (office); sheryl@sherylcrow.com (office). *Website:* www.sherylcrow.com.

CROW, Thomas, BA, MA, PhD; American art historian, critic and academic; *Rosalie Solow Professor of Modern Art, Institute of Fine Arts, New York University;* b. (Thomas Eugene Crow), 3 Jan. 1948, Oak Park, Ill.; m. Catherine Phillips; ed Pomona Coll., Univ. of California, Los Angeles; fmr Instructor, California Inst. of the Arts; Asst Prof. of History of Art, Univ. of Chicago 1978–80; Asst Prof. of Art and Archeology, Princeton Univ. 1980–86; Assoc. Prof. of History of Art, Univ. of

Michigan, Ann Arbor 1986–90; Prof. and Chair. in History of Art, Univ. of Sussex, UK 1990–96; Robert Lehman Prof. of History of Art, Yale Univ. 1996–2000; Dir Getty Research Inst. 2000–07; Rosalie Solow Prof. of Modern Art, New York Univ. Inst. of Fine Arts 2007–, Assoc. Provost for the Arts 2007–12; Contributing Ed. Artforum; mem. American Acad. of Arts and Sciences; Hon. DFA (Pomona Coll.) 2006. *Publications include:* Painters and Public Life in Eighteenth Century Paris (Eric Mitchell Prize in Art History, Charles Rufus Morley Book Award) 1985, Emulation: Making Artists for Revolutionary France 1995, The Rise of the Sixties: American and European Art in the Era of Dissent 1996, Modern Art in the Common Culture 1996, The Intelligence of Art 1999, Gordon Matta-Clark 2003, Comprendre Andy Warhol/Comprendre l'art contemporain 2013, The Long March of Pop: Art, Music and Design 1930–1995 2014. *Address:* The James B. Duke House, 1 East 78 Street, New York, NY 10075, USA (office). *Telephone:* (212) 992-5834 (office). *Fax:* (212) 992-5807 (office). *E-mail:* tc59@nyu.edu (office). *Website:* www.nyu.edu/gsas/dept/fineart/faculty/crow.htm (office).

CROWE, Martin David, MBE; New Zealand fmr professional cricketer; b. 22 Sept. 1962, Auckland; s. of David Crowe and Audrey Crowe; m. Simone Curtice 1991 (separated 1996); ed Auckland Grammar School; right-hand batsman, slip fielder; played for Auckland 1979/80–82/83, Cen. Dists 1983/84–89/90 (Capt. 1984/ 85–89/90), Somerset 1984–88, Wellington 1990/91–94/95 (Capt. 1993–94); Test debut: NZ v Australia, Wellington 26 Feb.–2 March 1982; One-Day Int. (ODI) debut: NZ v Australia, Auckland 13 Feb. 1982; played in 77 Tests for NZ 1981/ 82–95/96, 16 as Capt., scored 5,444 runs (average 45.36) with 17 hundreds, including NZ record 299 v Sri Lanka, Wellington, Feb. 1991; played in 143 ODIs, scored 4,707 runs (average 38.55, highest score 107 not out) and took 29 wickets; scored 19,608 first-class runs (average 56.02, 71 hundreds); toured England 1983, 1986, 1990 and 1994; Exec. Producer Sky TV cricket broadcasts; mem. Bd South Sydney Rabbitohs Rugby League Football Club; mem. man. team of Royal Challengers Bangalore; Wisden Cricketer of the Year 1985, NZ Sportsman of the Year 1991, selected as World Cup Champion Cricketer 1992. *Publication:* Out on a Limb 1996. *Leisure interests:* tennis, golf, wine. *Address:* PO Box 109302, Newmarket, Auckland, New Zealand. *E-mail:* rcbsupport@royalchallengers.com. *Website:* www.royalchallengers.com.

CROWE, Russell; New Zealand actor; b. 7 April 1964; m. Danielle Spencer 2003; two s.; singer, 30 Odd Foot of Grunts –2005, The Ordinary Fear of God 2006–. *Films include:* Romper Stomper (Seattle Int. Film Festival Award for Best Actor) 1992, The Crossing 1993, The Quick and the Dead 1995, Rough Magic 1995, Virtuosity 1995, Under the Gun 1995, Heaven's Burning 1997, Breaking Up 1997, LA Confidential 1997, Mystery Alaska 1999, The Insider (Best Actor, LA Film Critics Asscn, Nat. Bd of Review 1999, Nat. Soc. of Film Critics 1999) 1999, Gladiator (Acad. Award for Best Actor 2000) 2000, Proof of Life 2000, A Beautiful Mind (Golden Globe, BAFTA Award and Screen Actors' Guild Award for Best Actor) 2001, Master and Commander 2003, Cinderella Man 2005, A Good Year 2006, 3:10 to Yuma 2007, American Gangster 2007, Body of Lies 2008, Tenderness 2008, State of Play (Australian Film Inst. Award for Best Int. Actor) 2009, Robin Hood 2010, The Next Three Days 2010, The Man with the Iron Fists 2011, Les Misérables 2012, Man of Steel 2013. *Address:* WME, 9601 Wilshire Blvd, Beverly Hills, CA 90210, USA (office); Bedford & Pearke Management Ltd, PO Box 171, Cameray, NSW 2062, Australia (office).

CROZIER, Adam Alexander, BA; British business executive; *CEO, ITV plc;* b. 26 Jan. 1964, Bute; s. of Robert Crozier and Elinor Crozier; m. Annette Edwards 1994; two d.; ed Heriot-Watt Univ., Edinburgh; with Pedigree Petfoods, Mars (UK) Ltd 1984–86; with Daily Telegraph 1986–88; joined Saatchi & Saatchi 1988, Dir 1990, Media Dir 1992, Vice-Chair. 1994, Jt Chief Exec. 1995–99; Chief Exec. Football Asscn 2000–02; Chair. Group Exec. Team and Chief Exec. Royal Mail Group, Royal Mail Holdings PLC 2003–10; CEO ITV plc 2010–; mem. Bd of Dirs Debenhams PLC 2006–. *Leisure interests:* football, golf, music. *Address:* ITV plc, The London Television Centre, Upper Ground, London, SE1 9LT, England (office). *Telephone:* (20) 7157-3000 (office). *Website:* www.itv.com (office).

CRUICKSHANK, Sir Donald Gordon, Kt, MA, MBA, LLD, CA; British government official, financial administrator and business executive; b. 17 Sept. 1942; s. of Donald C. Cruickshank and Margaret Morrison; m. Elizabeth B. Taylor 1964; one s. one d.; ed Univ. of Aberdeen and Manchester Business School; consultant, McKinsey & Co. 1972–77; Gen. Man. Sunday Times, Times Newspapers 1977–80; Pearson PLC 1980–84; Man. Dir Virgin Group 1984–89; Chair. Wandsworth Health Authority 1986–89; CEO Nat. Health Service in Scotland 1989–93; Dir-Gen. UK Office of Telecommunications 1993–98; Chair. Action 2000 1997–2000; Chair. UK Banking Review 1998–2000; Chair. SMG PLC 1999–2004, London Stock Exchange 2000–03; mem. Financial Reporting Council 2002–08; mem. Bd of Dirs (non-exec.) and Chair. Taylor & Francis PLC 2004, mem. Bd of Dirs T&F Informa plc (formed by merger of Taylor & Francis and Informa) 2004–05; Chair. (non-exec.) Formscape Group Ltd 2003–06, Clinovia 2004–06; mem. Bd of Dirs Qualcomm, Inc. 2005–; mem. Inst. of Chartered Accountants of Scotland. *Leisure interests:* sport, golf, opera. *E-mail:* don.cruickshank@ btopenworld.com (office).

CRUICKSHANK, John; Canadian journalist and publisher; *Publisher, CBC News;* began career at Montreal Gazette and the Kingston Whig-Standard newspapers before holding several positions at The Globe and Mail 1981–95; beats included educ. and Queen's Park, then Vancouver bureau chief, editorial writer, Assoc. Ed., Man. Ed. 1992–95; Ed. The Vancouver Sun 1995–2000; Vice-Pres. Editorial and Co-Ed. Chicago Sun-Times 2000–03, Publr 2003–07, also COO Sun-Times Media Group; Publr CBC News, Toronto 2007–. *Address:* CBC News, 181 Queen Street, Station C, Ottawa, ON K1Y 1E4, Canada (office). *Telephone:* (613) 288-6000 (office). *E-mail:* webmaster@cbc.ca (office). *Website:* www.cbc.ca/ news (office).

CRUISE, Tom; American actor and film producer; b. (Thomas Cruise Mapother IV), 3 July 1962, Syracuse, New York; m. 1st Mimi Rogers 1987 (divorced 1990); m. 2nd Nicole Kidman 1990 (divorced 2001); one adopted s. one adopted d.; m. 3rd Katie Noelle Holmes 2006 (divorced 2012); one d.; Exec. Producer, United Artists Corpn 2006–; David di Donatello Lifetime Achievement Award 2005. *Films include:* Endless Love 1981, Taps 1981, All the Right Moves 1983, Losin' It 1983, The Outsiders 1983, Risky Business 1983, Legend 1985, Top Gun 1986, The Color of Money 1986, Rain Man 1988, Young Guns (uncredited) 1988, Cocktail 1989, Born on the Fourth of July 1989, Days of Thunder (also writer) 1990, Sure as the Moon 1991, Far and Away 1992, A Few Good Men 1992, The Firm 1993, Interview with the Vampire 1994, Mission: Impossible (also producer) 1996, Jerry Maguire 1996, Without Limits (producer) 1998, Eyes Wide Shut 1999, Magnolia 1999 (Golden Globe 2000), Mission: Impossible II (also producer) 2000, Vanilla Sky (also producer) 2001, Minority Report 2002, Narc (exec. producer) 2002, Space Station 3D (voice) 2002, Hitting It Hard (video) (producer) 2002, Shattered Glass (exec. producer) 2003, The Last Samurai (also producer) 2003, Collateral 2004, Ask the Dust (producer), Elizabethtown (producer) 2005, War of the Worlds 2005, Mission: Impossible III (also producer), Ask the Dust (producer) 2006, Lions for Lambs 2007, Tropic Thunder 2008, Valkyrie 2008, Knight and Day 2010, Mission Impossible: Ghost Protocol 2011, Rock of Ages 2012, Jack Reacher 2012, Oblivion 2013. *Television includes:* Fallen Angels (dir series episode The Frightning Frammis) 1993, hosted Nobel Peace Prize Concert 2004. *Address:* United Artists Corporation, 10250 Constellation Boulevard, Los Angeles, CA 90067 (office); Creative Artists Agency, 2000 Avenue of the Stars, Los Angeles, CA 90067, USA.

CRUMB, George, BM, MM, DMA; American fmr composer; b. 24 Oct. 1929, Charleston, WV; s. of George Henry and Vivian Reed; m. Elizabeth Brown 1949; two s. one d.; ed Mason Coll. of Music, Charleston, Univ. of Illinois, Univ. of Michigan at Ann Arbor, Hochschule für Musik, Berlin; Prof., Univ. of Colorado 1959–63; Creative Assoc., State Univ. of New York at Buffalo 1963–64; Prof. of Composition, Univ. of Pa 1971–83, Annenberg Prof. of the Humanities 1983–97, Emer. 1997–; mem. Nat. Inst. of Arts and Letters 1975–; Fulbright Scholarship 1955, Rockefeller Grant 1964, Guggenheim Grant 1967, 1973, Koussevitzky Int. Recording Award 1971, UNESCO Int. Rostrum of Composers Award 1971, Fromm Grant 1973, Ford Grant 1976, Prince Pierre de Monaco Prize 1989, Edward MacDowell Colony Medal, Peterborough 1995, Grammy Award (for Star Child) 2000. *Compositions include:* Two Duos for flute and clarinet 1944, Four Songs for voice, clarinet and piano 1945, Sonata for piano 1945, Four Pieces for violin and piano 1945, Poem 1946, Three Early Songs for voice and piano 1947, Gethsemane for orchestra 1947, Alleluja for chorus 1948, Sonata for violin and piano 1949, A Cycle of Greek Lyrics 1950, Prelude and Toccata 1951, Three Pastoral Pieces for oboe and piano 1952, String Trio 1952, Sonata for viola and piano 1953, String Quartet 1954, Sonata for cello 1955, Diptych for orchestra 1955, Variazioni for orchestra 1959, Five Pieces for piano 1962, Night Music I for soprano, piano and two percussionists 1963, Four Nocturnes for violin and piano 1964, Eleven Echoes of Autumn 1966, Madrigals, Books 1–4 1965–69, Songs, Drones and Refrains of Death 1968, Echoes of Time and the River (Pulitzer Prize for Music) 1968, Night of the Four Moons 1969, Ancient Voices of Children 1970, Black Angels for electric string quartet 1970, Vox Balaenae for three masked musicians 1971, Lux Aeterna 1971, Makrokosmos vols I–IV 1972–79, Dream Sequence for violin, cello, piano and percussion 1976, Star-Child for soprano, children's chorus and orchestra (Grammy Award for Best Contemporary Composition 2001) 1977, Apparition 1979, A Little Suite for Christmas 1979, Gnomic Variations for piano 1981, Pastoral Drone for organ 1982, Processional for piano 1983, A Haunted Landscape for orchestra 1984, The Sleeper 1984, An Idyll for the Misbegotten 1986, Federico's Little Songs for Children for soprano, flute and percussion 1986, Zeitgeist for two amplified pianos 1988, Easter Dawning for carillon 1991, Quest for guitar and ensemble 1994, Mundus Canis for guitar and percussion 1998, American Songbooks 2001–04, Unto the Hills 2001, A Journey Beyond Time 2002, Eine Kleine Mitternachtmusik 2002, Otherworldly Resonances 2002, River of Life 2003, Winds of Destiny 2004, Voices from a Forgotten World 2006, Voices from the Morning of the Earth 2007, The Ghosts of Alhambra for baritone, guitar and percussion 2009, Sun and Shadow for soprano, piano 2009, Voices from the Heartland 2010, The Yellow Moon of Andalusi, mezzo-soprano, piano 2013, Yester-Year 2013. *Leisure interest:* reading. *Address:* c/o Becky Starobin, Bridge Records, Inc., 200 Clinton Avenue, New Rochelle, NY 10801, USA (office). *Telephone:* (914) 654-9270 (office); (610) 565-2438 (home). *Fax:* (914) 636-1383 (office). *E-mail:* bridgerec@aol.com (office). *Website:* www.bridgerecords.com (office); www.georgecrumb.net.

CRUMPTON, Michael Joseph, CBE, PhD, FRS, FMedSci; British biochemist and immunologist; b. 7 June 1929; s. of Charles E. Crumpton and Edith Crumpton; m. Janet Elizabeth Dean 1960; one s. two d.; ed Poole Grammar School, Univ. Coll., Southampton and Lister Inst. of Preventive Medicine, London; joined scientific staff Microbiological Research Establishment, Porton, Wilts. 1955–60; Deputy Dir Research Labs., Imperial Cancer Research Fund Labs., London 1979–91, Dir 1991–93; Dir Imperial Cancer Research Tech. Ltd 1989–99 (COO 1993–94); Visiting Scientist Fellowship, NIH, Bethesda, Md, USA 1959–60; Research Fellow, Dept of Immunology, St Mary's Hosp. Medical School, London 1960–66; mem. scientific staff, Nat. Inst. for Medical Research, Mill Hill 1966–79, Head of Biochemistry Div. 1976–79; Visiting Fellow, John Curtin School for Medical Research, Australian Nat. Univ., Canberra 1973–74; mem. Cell Bd MRC 1979–83, Science Council, Celltech Ltd 1980–90, EMBO 1982–, WHO Steering Cttee for Encapsulated Bacteria 1984–91 (Chair. 1988–91), Sloan Cttee Gen. Motors Research Foundation 1986–88 (Chair. 1988), Council Royal Inst. 1986–90 (mem. Davy Faraday Lab. Comm. 1985–90, Chair. 1988–90), MRC 1986–90, Royal Soc. 1990–92, Scientific Advisory Comm., Lister Inst. 1986–91, MRC AIDS Directed Prog. Steering Cttee 1987–91, Scientific Cttee Swiss Inst. for Experimental Cancer Research 1989–96; Chair. Scientific Advisory Bd Biomedical Research Centre, Univ. of British Columbia 1987–91, Health and Safety Exec., Dept of Health Advisory Comm. on Dangerous Pathogens 1991–99; Dir (non-exec.) Amersham Int. PLC 1990–97, Amersham Pharmacia Biotech Ltd 1997–2001, Amersham Pharmacia Biotech Inc. 2001–02; mem. Governing Body British Postgraduate Medical Foundation 1987–95, Academia Europea 1994–, Governing Body Imperial Coll. 1994–98; mem. numerous Editorial Bds; Biochemistry Soc. Visiting Lecturer, Australia 1983; Trustee, EMF Biological Research Trust (fmr Chair.) 1995, Breakthrough Breast Cancer 1997–; Hon. FRCPath; Hon. Fellow, Inst. of Cancer Research, Breakthrough Breast Cancer; Hon. mem. American Asscn of Immunology 1995. *Publications:* numerous scientific papers. *Leisure interests:* gardening, reading. *Address:* c/o EMF Biological Research Trust, PO Box 23, South Croydon, CR2 7ZL (office); 8 Ticknell Piece Road, Charlbury, Oxon., OX7 3TW, England (home). *Telephone:* (1608) 811845 (home). *E-mail:* mikcrumpton@googlemail.com (home).

CRUTZEN, Paul Josef; Dutch professor of atmospheric chemistry; *Professor Emeritus, Max Planck Institute for Chemistry;* b. 3 Dec. 1933, Amsterdam; s. of the late Josef Crutzen and Anna Crutzen; m.; two c.; ed Stockholm Univ., Sweden; various computer consulting, teaching and research positions at Dept of Meteorology, Stockholm Univ. 1959–74; Post-doctoral Fellow, European Space Research Org., Clarendon Lab., Univ. of Oxford, UK 1969–71; Research Scientist, Upper Atmosphere Project, Nat. Center for Atmospheric Research (NCAR), Boulder, Colo, USA and Consultant at Aeronomy Lab., Environmental Research Labs, Nat. Oceanic and Atmospheric Admin, Boulder 1974–77; Sr Scientist and Dir Air Quality Div., NCAR 1977–80; Adjunct Prof., Atmospheric Sciences Dept, Colorado State Univ. 1976–81; Dir Atmospheric Chem. Div., Max Planck Inst. for Chem., Mainz, Germany 1980–2000, Exec. Dir Max Planck Inst. for Chem. 1983–85, currently Prof. Emer.; Prof., Dept of Geophysical Sciences, Univ. of Chicago, USA 1987–91; Prof., Scripps Inst. of Oceanography, Univ. of California, San Diego 1992–2000; Prof., Inst. for Marine and Atmospheric Sciences (IMAU), Utrecht Univ., Netherlands 1997–2000, Prof. Emer. 2000–; mem. Royal Swedish Acad. of Sciences 1991, Royal Swedish Acad. of Eng 1991, Deutsche Akademie der Naturforscher Leopoldina 1991, Accad. Nazionale dei Lincei 1997; mem. Council of Pontifical Acad. of Sciences 2001; Founding mem. Academia Europaea 1988; Foreign Assoc. NAS 1994; Corresp. mem. Royal Netherlands Acad. of Science 1990; Foreign mem. Russian Acad. of Sciences 1999; Fellow, American Geophysical Union 1986; Foreign Hon. mem. American Acad. of Arts and Sciences 1986; Hon. mem. American Meteorological Soc. 1997, European Geophysical Soc. 1997, Comm. on Atmospheric Chem. and Global Pollution 1998, Swedish Meteorological Soc. 2000, World Innovation Foundation 2002; Hon. Prof., Johannes Gutenberg Univ. of Mainz 1993; Hon. Chair. Climate Conference 2001, Utrecht 2001; Dr hc (York Univ., Canada) 1986, (Université Catholique de Louvain) 1992, (Univ. of East Anglia, UK) 1994, (Aristotle Univ., Thessaloniki, Greece) 1996, (Univ. of Liège, Belgium) 1997, (Univ. of San José, Costa Rica) 1997, (Tel-Aviv Univ.) 1997, (Oregon State Univ.) 1997, (Univ. of Chile) 1997, (Université de Bourgogne, Dijon, France) 1997, (Univ. of Athens, Greece) 1998, (Democritus Univ. of Thrace, Greece) 2001, (Nova Gorica Polytechnic, Slovenia) 2002, (Univ. of Hull, UK) 2002; Tyler Environment Prize 1989, Volvo Environmental Prize 1991, German Environmental Prize 1994, Max-Planck Research Prize 1994, Nobel Prize in Chem. 1995 (jt recipient), most cited author in the geosciences world-wide 2002. *Publications include:* Atmospheric Change; An Earth System Perspective (with T. E. Graedel) 1993. *Address:* Max Planck Institute for Chemistry, Joh.-Joachim-Becher-Weg 27, 55128 Mainz, Germany (office). *Fax:* (61) 31-305-511 (office). *E-mail:* paul.crutzen@mpic.de (office). *Website:* www.mpch-mainz.mpg.de/~air/crutzen (office).

CRUYFF, Johan; Dutch professional football manager and fmr professional footballer; *Head Coach, Catalonia national football team;* b. (Hendrik Johannes Cruijff), 25 April 1947, Amsterdam; m. Danny Coster 1968; one s. two d.; attacking midfielder, second striker; played for Ajax 1964–73 (made 240 appearances and scored 190 goals, top scorer in Dutch League with 33 goals 1967), FC Barcelona 1973–78 (made 143 appearances and scored 48 goals), Los Angeles Aztecs 1979–80, Washington Diplomats 1980–81, Levante, Spain 1981, Ajax 1981–83, Feyenoord 1983–84; with Ajax, won Eredivisie 1966, 1967, 1968, 1970, 1972, 1973, 1982, 1983, KNVB Cup 1967, 1970, 1971, 1972, 1983, European Cup 1971, 1972, 1973, Intercontinental Cup 1972, UEFA Super Cup 1972, 1973, Intertoto Cup 1968; with Barcelona won La Liga 1974, Copa del Rey 1978; with Feyenoord won Eredivisie 1984, KNVB Cup 1984; capped 48 times, scored 33 int. goals and captained Netherlands 1974 World Cup final; Man. Ajax 1985–88, winning European Cup Winners' Cup 1987; Man. FC Barcelona 1988–96, winning Cup Winners' Cup 1989, European Cup 1992, Spanish League title 1991, 1992, 1993, Spanish Super Cup 1992; Head Coach Catalonia nat. football team 2009–; currently Adviser to Ajax, FC Barcelona;; f. Cruyff Foundation 1997, Johan Cruyff Univ. (to assist retd sportspeople) 1998; European Footballer of the Year 1971, 1973, 1974, FIFA World Cup Golden Ball 1974, FIFA World Cup All-Star Team 1974, Don Balón Award for Foreign Player of the Year in La Liga 1977, 1978, Dutch Golden Shoe 1984, World Soccer Awards Manager of the Year 1987, Don Balón Award for Coach of the Year in La Liga 1991, 1992, Onze d'Or for Coach of the Year 1992, 1994, Dutch Supercup named Johan Cruijff-schaal in his honour 1996, voted European Player of the Century in election held by IFFHS 1999, came second behind Pelé in their World Player of the Century poll 1999, came third in vote organized by France Football magazine consulting their former Ballon d'Or winners to elect their Football Player of the Century 1999, Golden Player of the Netherlands (best player of past 50 years) 2003, gained sixth place in election of De Grootste Nederlander (The Greatest Dutchman) 2004, Lifetime Achievement Award, Laureus World Sports Awards 2006, Lifetime Achievement Award, Royal Netherlands Football Asscn 2006, Ajax retd the No. 14 shirt in his honour 2007. *Recording:* reached No. 21 in charts in the Netherlands with "Oei Oei Oei (Dat Was Me Weer een Loei)". *Address:* Johan Cruyff Institute for Sport Studies Barcelona, Pomaret 8 08017 Barcelona, Spain; Johan Cruyff Foundation, Olympisch Stadion 5, 1076 DE Amsterdam, Netherlands. *Telephone:* (93) 418-7868 (Barcelona); (20) 305-77-66 (Amsterdam). *Fax:* (20) 305-77-60 (Amsterdam). *E-mail:* info@cruyffinstitute.org (office). *Website:* www.cruyffinstitute.org; www.cruyff-foundation.org.

CRUZ, Avelino, Jr; Philippine lawyer and government official; ed Univ. of the Philippines Coll. of Law; Presidential Legal Counsel 2001–04; fmr mem. Cabinet Oversight Cttee on Internal Security; Sec. of Nat. Defense 2004–06 (resgnd), fmr mem. Nat. Security Council; currently adviser to Liberal Party Pres. Manuel Roxas II;. *Address:* c/o Liberal Party, 2nd Floor, Matrinco Bldg, Chino Roces Ave, Makati City, 1231 Metro Manila, Philippines.

CRUZ, Lourdes Jansuy, BS, MS, PhD; Philippines biochemist and academic; ed Univ. of the Philippines, Univ. of Iowa, USA; est. Rural Livelihood Incubator 2001; Outstanding Young Scientist Award, Nat. Acad. of Science and Tech. 1981, NRCP Achievement Award in Chem. 1982, Outstanding Women in Nation's Services Award (Biochemistry), Laureate for Asia Pacific, L'Oréal-UNESCO Awards for Women in Science 2013. *Publications:* more than 120 papers in professional journals. *Address:* c/o Nat. Acad. of Science and Tech., 3rd Level Philippine Science Heritage Centre, DOST Complex, Bicutan, Taguig, 1631 Metro Manila, The Philippines. *Telephone:* (632) 838-7739. *Fax:* (632) 837-3170. *E-mail:* secretariat@nast.ph.

CRUZ, Penélope; Spanish actress; b. 28 April 1974, Madrid; d. of Eduardo and Encarna Cruz Sánchez; m. Javier Bardem 2010; one s.; ed Nat. Conservatory, Madrid; Chevalier, Ordre des Arts et des Lettres 2006. *Films:* Live Flesh, Belle Epoque 1992, Jamón, Jamón 1992, La Celestina 1996, Open Your Eyes 1997, The Hi-Lo Country 1998, Talk of Angels 1998, The Girl of Your Dreams (Goya Award) 1998, All About My Mother 1999, Woman on Top 1999, All the Pretty Horses 2000, Captain Corelli's Mandolin 2001, Blow 2001, Vanilla Sky 2001, Fanfan La Tulipe 2003, Gothika 2003, Noel 2004, Head in the Clouds 2004, Non ti muovere (Don't Move) 2004, Bandidas 2006, Volver (Goya Award for Best Actress 2007) 2006, The Good Night 2007, Elegy 2007, Vicky Cristina Barcelona (BAFTA Award for Best Supporting Actress 2009, Acad. Award for Best Supporting Actress 2009) 2008, La concejala antropófaga 2009, Los abrazos rotos 2009, Nine 2009, Sex and the City 2 2010, Pirates of the Caribbean: On Stranger Tides 2011, To Rome with Love 2012. *Address:* c/o Kuranda Management International, 8626 Skyline Drive, Los Angeles, CA 90046, USA (office).

CRUZ, (Rafael Edward) Ted, BA, JD; American lawyer and politician; *Senator from Texas;* b. 22 Dec. 1970, Calgary, Alberta, Canada; s. of Rafael Cruz and Eleanor Darragh; m. Heidi Nelson Cruz; two d.; ed Faith West Acad., Katy, Texas, Second Baptist High School, Houston, Princeton Univ., Harvard Law School; fmr Ed. Harvard Law Review, fmr Exec. Ed. Harvard Journal of Law & Public Policy, Founding Ed. Harvard Latino Law Review; served as law clerk to William Rehnquist, Chief Justice of the US Supreme Court, and J. Michael Luttig of the US Court of Appeals for the Fourth Circuit; fmr Dir Office of Policy Planning, Fed. Trade Comm.; fmr Assoc. Deputy Attorney Gen., US Dept of Justice; fmr Domestic Policy Advisor Pres. George W. Bush on the 2000 Bush-Cheney campaign; Partner, Morgan, Lewis & Bockius law firm, led the firm's US Supreme Court and national appellate litigation practice; Solicitor Gen. of the State of Texas 2003–08; Adjunct Prof. of Law, Univ. of Texas School of Law, Austin 2004–09; Senator from Texas 2013–, Vice-Chair. Nat. Republican Senatorial Cttee 2012–; Republican; named by American Parl. Debate Asscn as Speaker of the Year and Team of the Year (with his debate partner, David Panton) 1992, Traphagen Distinguished Alumnus, Harvard Law School, named by Newsweek amongst 20 Young Hispanic Americans on the Rise 1999, named by National Law Journal amongst 50 Most Influential Minority Lawyers in America 2008, named by Chambers USA amongst America's Leading Lawyers for Business 2009, 2010, named by Texas Lawyer amongst 25 Greatest Texas Lawyers of the Past Quarter Century 2010. *Address:* United States Senate, Washington, DC 20510, USA (office). *Telephone:* (202) 224-3121 (office). *Website:* www.senate.gov (office).

CRUZ SEQUEIRA, Arturo José, MA, DPhil; Nicaraguan economist, politician, academic and diplomatist; *Professor, Instituto Centroamericano de Administración de Empresas (INCAE) Business School;* b. 1954; s. of Arturo José Cruz Porras and Consuelo Sequeira Ximénez; ed American Univ., Washington, DC and Paul H. Nitze School of Advanced Int. Studies, Johns Hopkins Univ., Univ. of Oxford, UK; supported Edén Pastora (fmr Sandinista commdr starting up rebel Democratic Revolutionary Alliance) 1982, then became involved with United Nicaraguan Opposition (rebel umbrella group) 1985, involved in exile politics of Contra rebels opposing Sandinista (FSLN) Govt 1987; Prof., Instituto Centroamericano de Administración de Empresas (INCAE) Business School, Managua –2007, 2009–; Visiting Prof., Advanced School of Econs and Business, San Salvador, El Salvador 2007; Amb. to USA 2007–09; fmr Bradley Fellow, Hudson Inst., Washington, DC. *Publications:* Memoirs of a Counter-Revolutionary, Nicaragua's Conservative Republic 1853–1893 2002 (translated and published in Spanish 2003), Varieties of Liberalism in Central America: Nation-States as Works in Progress (with Forrest Colburn) 2007; articles on the analysis of social, econ. and political trends in Latin America. *Address:* Instituto Centroamericano de Administración de Empresas (INCAE), Campus Francisco de Sola, Apartado 2485, Managua, Nicaragua (office). *Telephone:* (22) 658141 (office). *Fax:* (22) 658617 (office). *E-mail:* arturo.cruz@incae .edu (office). *Website:* www.incae.edu/ES/facultad/Arturo.Cruz (office).

CRVENKOVSKI, Branko; Macedonian politician, engineer and fmr head of state; b. 12 Oct. 1962, Sarajevo, Bosnia and Herzegovina; m. Jasmina Crvenkovska; one s. one d.; ed SS Cyril and Methodius Univ., Skopje; computer engineer, SEMOS Co. 1987–90; mem. Nat. Ass. 1990–2004; Chair. Social Democratic Alliance of Macedonia 1990–92, 2009–13, Pres. 1991–2004; Chair. Cabinet of Ministers (Prime Minister) 1992–98, 2002–04; Pres. of Fmr Yugoslav Repub. of Macedonia 2004–09; Hon. mem. Int. Raoul Wallenberg Foundation; Key of the City of Tirana on the occasion of his state visit to Albania. *Address:* Social Democratic Alliance of Macedonia (Socijaldemokratski sojuz na Makedonija), 1000 Skopje, Bihaćka 8, Former Yugoslav Republic of Macedonia (office). *Telephone:* (2) 3293100 (office). *Fax:* (2) 3293109 (office). *E-mail:* web@sdsm.org.mk (office). *Website:* www.sdsm.org.mk (office).

CRYSTAL, Billy; American actor and comedian; b. 14 March 1947, Long Beach, NY; s. of Jack Crystal and Helen Crystal; m. Janice Crystal (née Goldfinger); two d.; ed Marshall Univ., Nassau Community Coll., New York Univ.; mem. of the group 3's Company; solo appearances as a stand-up comedian; Emmy Award for Outstanding Writing 1991, Mark Twain Prize for American Humor 2007. *Television:* Soap (series) 1977–81, The Billy Crystal Hour 1982, Saturday Night Live 1984–85, The Love Boat, The Tonight Show; TV films include: Breaking up is Hard to do 1979, Enola Gay, The Men, The Mission, The Atomic Bomb 1980, Death Flight. *Stage appearances include:* 700 Sundays (one-man show) (Tony Award for special theatrical event 2005). *Films include:* The Rabbit Test 1978, This is Spinal Tap 1984, Running Scared 1986, The Princess Bride 1987, Throw Momma from the Train 1987, When Harry Met Sally 1989, City Slickers 1991, Mr Saturday Night (also dir producer, co-screen-play writer) 1993, Forget Paris 1995, Hamlet, Father's Day, Deconstructing Harry, My Giant 1998, Analyze This 1998, The Adventures of Rocky & Bullwinkle 2000, Monsters Inc. (voice) 2001, Mike's New Car (voice) 2002, Analyze That 2002, Howl's Moving Castle (voice) 2004, Cars (voice) 2006, Tooth Fairy 2010, Small Apartments 2012, Parental Guidance 2012. *Publications:* Absolutely Mahvelous 1986, I Already Know I Love You (juvenile) 2004, 700 Sundays (autobiog.) 2005. *Address:* c/o CAA, 2000 Avenue of the Stars, Los Angeles, CA 90067, USA.

CSABA, László, PhD, DrSci, DrHab; Hungarian economist and academic; *Professor of Economics and European Studies, Central European University;* b. 27 March 1954, Budapest; s. of Ede Csaba and Márta Biró; m. Gabriella Onody

1980; one s. one d.; ed Univ. of Budapest, Hungarian Acad. of Sciences; Fellow, Inst. for World Econs, Budapest 1976–87; economist/researcher, then Sr Economist, Kopint-Datorg Econ. Research 1988–2000; Hon. Prof. of Int. Econs, Coll. of Foreign Trade, Budapest Univ. of Econs 1991–97, Prof. 1997–; Prof. of Econs and European Studies, Cen. European Univ. 2000–; Head of Doctoral Programme, Univ. of Debrecen 1999–2004; Vice-Pres. European Asscn for Comparative Econs 1990–94, 1996–98, Pres. 1999–2000; mem. Econs Cttee Hungarian Acad. of Sciences 1986–, Co-Chair. 1996–99, 2000–02, Chair. 2003–05; Visiting Prof., Bocconi Univ., Milan 1991, Helsinki Univ. 1993, Europa Univ., Viadrina, Frankfurt 1997, Freie Univ., Berlin 1998–2000, Cen. European Univ. 1998; mem. Bd TIGER Inst., Poland, NORDI Inst., Finland; mem. editorial bd of various journals; Ministry of External Econ. Affairs Prize 1994, Bezeredi Prize for European Integration 2003, Nat. Bank of Hungary Prize 2004, Akademia Publishing House Best Economics Book Award 2005. *Publications:* Eastern Europe in the World Economy 1990, The Capitalist Revolution in Eastern Europe 1995, The New Political Economy of Emerging Europe 2005; ed. six books; over 190 articles and chapters in books published in 18 countries. *Leisure interests:* classical music, travel, soccer. *Address:* Department of International Relations and European Studies, Central European University, 1051 Budapest, Nador u. 9 (office); 1074 Budapest, Dohány u. 94, Hungary (home). *Telephone:* (1) 327-30-17 (office); (1) 322-05-19 (home). *Fax:* (1) 327-32-43 (office). *E-mail:* csabal@ceu.hu (office). *Website:* www.ceu.hu (office); www.csabal.com.

CSÁKY, Pál, MSc; Hungarian politician; *Chairman, Party of the Hungarian Coalition (Strana madarskej koalície);* b. 21 March 1956, Sahy; m.; four d.; ed Univ. of Pardubice, Czech Repub.; Chief Technologist, Levitex textile factory, Levice 1981–90; mem. Nat. Council of Slovak Repub. 1990–2010, mem. Jt Parl. Cttee Nat. Council of Slovak Repub. and European Parl. 1994–98; Deputy Chair. for Foreign Affairs, Hungarian Christian-Democratic Movt (HCDM) 1991–98, Chair. HCDM Parl. Group 1992–98; mem. Parl. Ass. of Council of Europe 1993–94; Deputy Prime Minister of Slovakia for Human Rights, Minorities, and Regional Devt 1998–2002, for European Affairs, Human Rights and Minorities 2002–06; Chair. Party of the Hungarian Coalition (Strana madarskej koalície/Magyar Koalíció Pártja) 2007–; Chair. Govt Council for Minorities and Ethnic Groups, Cttee of Ministers for European Affairs, Govt Council for Regional Policy and Control over Structural Operations, Govt Council for Third Sector, Govt Council for Sustainable Devt, Cttee of Ministers Against Drug Abuse and Drug Dependencies. *Publications include:* in Hungarian: Emlékek könyve (Book of Memoirs) 1992, Csillagok a falu felett (Stars Above the Village) 1993, Úton (On the Way) 1994, Magyarként Szlovákiában (Being a Hungarian in Slovakia) 1994, Két világ között (Between Two Worlds) 1998; more than 1,000 articles, political literature and fiction, mainly in Hungarian. *Leisure interests:* music, piano, literature, theatre, fitness, swimming. *Address:* Party of the Hungarian Coalition (Strana madarskej koalície), 811 05 Bratislava, Čajakova 8, Slovakia (office). *Telephone:* (2) 5249-5164 (office). *Fax:* (2) 5249-5264 (office). *E-mail:* karvai@smk.sk (office). *Website:* www.mkp.sk (office).

CSÁNYI, Sándor, BBA, MSc, PhD; Hungarian economist, banker and auditor; *Chairman and CEO, OTP Bank Plc;* b. 20 March 1953, Jászárokszállás; m.; five c.; ed Coll. of Finance and Accounting, Budapest Univ. of Econs; following graduation became a chartered accountant; first job at Ministry of Finance 1974–83; also worked for Ministry of Food and Agric. 1983–86 and at Hungarian Credit Bank 1986–89; Deputy CEO Commercial and Credit Bank (K&H) 1989–92; Chair. and CEO OTP Bank Plc 1992–; Vice-Pres. Bd Hungarian Oil and Gas Co. (MOL); mem. European Advisory Bd of Mastercard 2006–; Co-Chair. Nat. Asscn of Entrepreneurs and Employers (VOSZ), Chinese-Hungarian Business Council 2012–; mem. Institut Int. d'Études Bancaires; Pres. Hungarian Football Fed. 2010–; mem. Organizing Cttee for FIFA World Cup 2011–; First Vice-Chair. Nat. Asscns Cttee of UEFA 2013–; Hon. Prof., Univ. of Western Hungary 2004; Hon. Citizen, Budapest Corvinus Univ. 2005; Hon. Sign of Pres. of Bulgaria 2011; Honoris Causa Pro Scientia Gold Medal, Council of Nat. Scientific Students Asscn; Global Leader of Tomorrow, World Econ. Forum, Davos 1996, named by Global Finance as one of world's 600 most powerful financial players 1998, named by the Wall Street Journal Europe as one of the Top Ten Execs in Cen. Europe 1999, Entrepreneur of the Year (Hungary) 2000, Ernst & Young Entrepreneur of the Year 2003, Mercur Prize, Bd and Man. Collegium, Hungarian Acad. of Sciences 2006, voted Banker of the Year by banking professionals in Hungary 2006, Báthory Prize 2007, Kálmán Tódor Award 2007. *Leisure interests:* football, tennis, hunting, reading. *Address:* Nádor u. 16, 1051 Budapest, Hungary (office). *Telephone:* (1) 473-5000 (office). *Fax:* (1) 311-0072 (office). *E-mail:* csanyi.sandor@otpbank.hu (office). *Website:* www .otpbank.hu (office).

CSÁSZÁR, Ákos, PhD; Hungarian mathematician and academic; *Professor Emeritus, Eötvös Loránd University;* b. 26 Feb. 1924, Budapest; s. of Károly Császár and Gizella Szücs; m. Klára Cseley; ed Budapest Univ.; Prof., Eötvös Loránd Univ., Budapest 1957–94, Prof. Emer. 1994–; Dir Inst. of Math. 1983–86; Visiting Prof., Technische Universität, Stuttgart 1975, Università di Torino 1979, Technische Universität, Graz 1983; fmr mem. Editorial Bd Periodica Mathematica Hungarica, Studia Mathematica Hungarica; Chief Ed. Acta Mathematica Hungarica 1996, Annales Univ. Scientiarum Budapestinensis Sectio Mathematica; Gen. Sec. János Bolyai Mathematical Soc. 1966–80, Pres. 1980–90, Hon. Pres. 1990–; Corresp. mem. Hungarian Acad. of Sciences 1970, Full mem. 1979–, mem. St Stephen's Acad. 1999–; Hon. Dr and Prof. (Budapest) 2004; Kossuth Prize 1963, Bolzano Medal (Prague) 1981, Arany János Prize 1999, Gold Medal, Hungarian Acad. of Sciences 2009. *Publications:* Foundations of General Topology 1960, General Topology 1974, Valós analízis (Real Analysis) (two vols) 1983; articles in int. math. periodicals. *Leisure interests:* music, botany, bridge. *Address:* Párizsi utca 6/a, 1052 Budapest, Hungary (home). *Telephone:* (1) 318-5172 (home).

CSIKSZENTMIHALYI, Mihaly, BA, PhD; American psychologist and academic; *Distinguished Professor of Psychology, Claremont Graduate University;* b. 29 Sept. 1934, Fiume, Italy; s. of Alfred Csikszentmihályi and Edith Csikszentmihályi (née Jankovich de Jessenice); m. Isabella Selega 1961; two s.; ed Univ. of Chicago; emigrated to USA in 1956; Assoc. Prof. and Chair., Dept of Sociology and Anthropology, Lake Forest Coll. 1965–71; Prof. of Human Devt, Univ. of Chicago 1971, Chair. Dept of Behavioral Sciences 1985–87; Davidson Prof. of Man., Drucker School of Man., Claremont Grad. Univ. 1999, now Distinguished Prof. of

Psychology, also Dir Quality of Life Research Center; visiting professorships in Canada, NZ, Italy, Finland, UK and Australia; mem. Bd of Advisers, Encyclopaedia Britannica 1985–; Consultant, The JP Getty Museum, Malibu 1985–; Sr Fulbright Scholar, Brazil 1984, New Zealand 1990; Fellow, American Acad. of Arts and Sciences, American Acad. of Political and Social Sciences, Hungarian Acad. of Sciences, Nat. Acad. of Educ., Nat. Acad. of Leisure Sciences, World Econ. Forum, Center for Advanced Study in the Behavioral Sciences; Hon. DSc (Lake Forest Coll.) 1999, (Colorado Coll.) 2002, (Rhode Island School of Design) 2003, doctorates in Science and the Arts from several other univs; Research Awards from Nat. Endowment for the Arts, Nat. Inst. of Mental Health, Spencer Foundation, Templeton Foundation, The Atlantic Philanthropies, Don Clifton Prize, 2005, Szechenyi Prize 2011. *Publications:* Beyond Boredom and Anxiety 1975, The Creative Vision 1976, The Meaning of Things 1981, Being Adolescent 1984, Optimal Experience 1988, Flow–The Psychology of Optimal Experience 1990, Television and the Quality of Life 1990, The Art of Seeing 1990, Talented Teenagers 1993, The Evolving Self 1993, Creativity 1996, Finding Flow in Everyday Life 1997, Flow in Sport 1999, Becoming Adult 2000, Good Work 2001, Good Business 2003; contrib. to several other books. *Leisure interests:* mountain climbing, chess, history. *Address:* School of Behavioral and Organizational Sciences, Claremont Graduate University, 150 East 10th Street, Claremont, CA 91711 (office); 700 East Alamosa Drive, Claremont, CA 91711, USA (home). *Telephone:* (909) 607-3307 (office); (909) 621-7345 (home). *Fax:* (909) 621-8543 (office). *E-mail:* miska@cgu.edu (office). *Website:* www.cgu.edu/pages/154.asp (office).

CSOÓRI, Sándor; Hungarian poet and writer; b. 3 Feb. 1930, Zámoly, Co. Fejér; ed Lenin Inst., Budapest; contrib. to Irodalmi Újság (monthly) 1954–55, Uj hang (monthly) 1955–56; drama critic Mafilm Studio 1968; joined opposition movt 1980; participated in political discussions of Monor 1985 and Lakitelek 1987; Founding mem. Hungarian Democratic Forum 1987, presidium mem. 1988–92; Chair. Illyés Gyula Foundation 1990–94; Pres. World Fed. of Hungarians 1991–2000; Order of Merit (Hungary) 2000; Attila József Prize 1954, Cannes Film Festival Prize 1964, 1968, Herder Prize 1981, Istvan Bibo Prize 1984, Tibor Déry Prize 1987, Joseph Fitz Award 1989, Kossuth Prize 1990, Radnóti Biennial Poetry Prize 1990, Eeva Joenpelto Prize 1995, The Hungarian Book of the Year Award 1995, Karoli Gaspar Award 1995, Hungarian Heritage Award 1997, 2005, Hungarian Art Prize 2004, Balint Balassi Memorial Sword Award 2006, Prima Primissima Award 2008. *Films:* scriptwriter: Tízezer nap (Ten thousand days), Földobott kő (The thrown-up stone), 80 huszár (Eighty Hussars), Tüske a köröm alatt (A Thorn under the Fingernail), Hószakadás (Snow-Storm), Nincs idö (No Time Left). *Publications:* selected poems: Fölröppen a madár (The Bird Takes Wing) 1954, Ördögpille (Demon Butterfly) 1957, Menekülés a magánytól (Escape from Loneliness) 1962, Elmaradt lázálom (Postponed Nightmare) 1980, Knives and Nails 1981, Hóemléke (Memory of Snow) 1983, Várakozás a tavaszban (Waiting in the Spring) 1983, Hattyúkkal ágyútűzben (In Cannon Fire with Swans) 1995, Ha volna életem (If I Had a Life) 1996, Quiet Vertigo 2001, Before and After the Fall 2004; sociographies: Tudósítás a toronyból (Report From the Tower) 1963, Kubai utinapló (Cuban Travel Diary) 1965; essay volumes: Faltól falig (From Wall to Wall) 1968, Nomád napló (Nomadic Diary) 1979, Félig bevallott élet (Half Confessed Life) 1984, Készülődés a számadásra (Preparation for Final Reckoning) 1987, Nappali hold (Daytime Moon) 1991, Tenger és diólevél I. II. (The Sea and Nut Leaves) 1994, Száll a alá poklokra (Descent into Hell) 1997. *Address:* Benczúr u. 15, 1068 Budapest, Hungary.

CUARÓN, Alfonso; Mexican film director and producer; b. 28 Nov. 1961, Mexico City; m. 1st Mariana Elizondo 1980 (divorced 1993); one c.; m. 2nd Annalisa Bugliani 2001; two c.; ed Centro Universitario de Estudios Cinematográficos. *Films include:* Quartet for the End of Time (also writer) 1983, Who's Who Anyway (also screenplay) 1983, Cita con la muerte 1989, Sólo con tu pareja (also screenplay and producer) 1991, Camino largo a Tijuana (co-producer) 1991, A Little Princess 1995, Sistole Diastole (screenplay) 1997, Great Expectations 1998, Y tu mamá también (also screenplay and producer) 2001, Me la debes (exec. producer) 2001, Harry Potter and the Prisoner of Azkaban 2004, Temporada de patos (exec. producer) 2004, Crónicas (producer) 2004, The Assassination of Richard Nixon (producer) 2004, Black Sun (exec. producer) 2005, Paris, je t'aime (writer segment "Parc Monceau") 2006, Pan's Labyrinth (producer) (BAFTA Award for Best Film Not in the English Language) 2007, Children of Men (also screenplay) 2006, The Possibility of Hope (video documentary short) 2007, The Shock Doctrine (documentary short made with Naomi Klein) 2007, Rudo y Cursi (producer) 2008, Biutiful (assoc. producer) 2010, The Second Bakery Attack (short) (exec. producer) 2010, Gravity (also producer) (Golden Globe Award for Best Dir 2014, Outstanding Directorial Achievement in Feature Film, Dirs Guild of America 2014, BAFTA Award for Best Dir 2014, Academy Award for Best Dir, Academy Award for Best Film Editing (with Mark Sanger) 2014) 2013. *Television includes:* Hora Marcada 1988–90, Believe (series) 2013. *Address:* c/o WME Entertainment, 9601 Wilshire Blvd, Beverley Hills, CA 90210-5213, USA (office). *Telephone:* (310) 285-9000 (office). *Fax:* (310) 285-9010 (office). *Website:* www.wma.com (office).

CUBAS GRAU, Raúl; Paraguayan business executive, politician and fmr head of state; b. 23 Aug. 1943, Asunción; m. Mirta Gusinsky de Cubas; two d. (one deceased); ed Universidade Católica do Rio de Janeiro; worked as engineer for ANDE 1967–73; Commercial Dir CIE SRL 1977–79; Dir CONCRET-MIX SA 1970–88; Legal Rep. 14 de Julio SA 1980–1993; Dir COPAC VIAL SA 1987–91; Legal Rep. of consortium OCHO A SACI–14 Julio SA–CONPASA 1992; Exec. Minister of State for Ministry of Econ. and Social Planning and Devt 1994–96; Minister of Finance 1996; Pres. of Paraguay 1998–99.

CUBITT, Sir Hugh (Guy), Kt, CBE, JP, DL, FRICS, FRSA; British fmr business executive; b. 2 July 1928, London, England; s. of Col the Hon. Guy Cubitt and Rosamond M. E. Cholmeley; m. Linda I. Campbell 1958; one s. two d.; ed Royal Naval Coll., Dartmouth and Greenwich; served in RN 1949–53; Partner, Rogers, Chapman & Thomas 1958–67, Cubitt & West 1962–79; Chair. The Housing Corpn 1980–90, Lombard North Cen. PLC 1980–91; Commr English Heritage 1988–94; Chair. Anchor Group of Housing Assocs 1991–98; Chair. Rea Brothers Group PLC 1996–98; Dir PSIT PLC 1962–97; Dir National Westminster Bank 1977–90, mem. UK Advisory Bd 1990–91; Gov. Peabody Trust 1991–2003 (Chair. 1998–2003); mem. Westminster City Council 1963–78; Lord Mayor of Westminster 1977–78;

Hon. Steward, Westminster Abbey 1978–2002 (Chief Steward 1997–2002); Pres. London Chamber of Commerce 1988–91; High Sheriff of Surrey 1983–84; Hon. FRAM. *Leisure interests:* travel, photography, painting. *Address:* Chapel House, West Humble, Dorking, Surrey, RH5 6AY, England (home). *Telephone:* (1306) 882994 (home). *E-mail:* hughcubitt@btinternet.com (home).

CUCCHIANI, Enrico Tommaso, BA, MBA; Italian business executive; *Managing Director and CEO, Intesa Sanpaolo SpA;* b. 20 Feb. 1950, Milan; ed Bocconi Univ., Milan, Stanford Univ. and Harvard Univ., USA; began career working for Int. DE of a large US bank 1977–79; with McKinsey & Co., worked in Milan, London and New York 1979–85; Gen. Man. Gucci Group 1985–92; f. venture capital firm 1992–96; joined Lloyd Adriatico 1996, later, progressively, Gen. Man., CEO, mem. Exec. Cttee and Chair.; Chair. Allianz SpA and mem. Man. Bd Allianz SE, with responsibility for Italy, Spain, Portugal, Turkey, Greece and South America and of global strategic devt and restructuring programme for the Claims business and distribution system of the insurance group –2011; Man. Dir and CEO Intesa Sanpaolo SpA 2011–; mem. Gen. Council of Aspen Inst. in Italy, Advisory Council of Stanford Univ., Trilateral Comm. (Italy), Exec. Cttee of US-Italy Council; Cavaliere del Lavoro; Alumnus of the Year, Asscn of Bocconi Grads 2006. *Address:* Intesa Sanpaolo SpA, Piazza San Carlo 156, 10121 Turin, Italy (office). *Telephone:* (011) 5551 (office). *Fax:* (011) 5557007 (office). *E-mail:* info@intesasanpaolo.com (office). *Website:* www.group.intesasanpaolo.com (office).

CUEVAS, José Luis; Mexican painter; b. 26 Feb. 1934, México, DF; s. of Alberto Cuevas and María Regla; m. Bertha Riestra 1961; three d.; ed Univ. de México, School of Painting and Sculpture 'La Esmeralda', Mexico; over forty solo exhbns; group exhbns in N and S America, Europe, India and Japan; works are in Museum of Modern Art, Solomon R. Guggenheim Museum, Brooklyn Museum, Art Inst. Chicago, Phillips Collection, Washington, DC, Museums of Albi and Lyons, France, and others; First Int. Award for Drawing, São Paulo Bienal 1959, First Int. Award, Mostra Internazionale di Bianco e Nero de Lugano, Zürich 1962, First Prize, Bienal de Grabado, Santiago, Chile 1964, First Int. Prize for engraving, first Biennial of New Delhi, India 1968, Nat. Fine Arts Award Mexico 1981. *Publications:* Cuevas por Cuevas 1964, Cuevario 1973, Confesiones de José Luis Cuevas 1975, Cuevas por Daisy Ascher 1979; has illustrated following books: The Worlds of Kafka and Cuevas 1959, The Ends of Legends String, Recollections of Childhood 1962, Cuevas por Cuevas 1964, Cuevas Charenton 1965, Crime by Cuevas 1968, Homage to Quevedo 1969, El Mundo de José Luis Cuevas 1970, Cuaderno de Paris 1977, Zarathustra 1979, Les Obsessions Noirs 1982, Letters to Tasenda 1982. *Address:* c/o Adani Gallery, 16118 Shadybank Drive, Dallas, TX 75248, USA. *Telephone:* (972) 503-5662. *Fax:* (972) 503-7411.

CUEVAS ARGOTE, Javier Gonzalo, MBS; Bolivian government official; b. 1955, La Paz; ed Universidad Mayor de san Andrés, Universidad de Chile, Universidad Privada Boliviana, Florida Int. Univ., USA; director of numerous public and private finance insts; adviser to Pres. of Central Bank; Vice-Minister, Ministry of Finance, Minister of Finance 2003–06. *Address:* c/o Ministry of Finance, Edif. Palacio de Communicaciones, Avda. Mariscal Santa Cruz, La Paz, Bolivia (office).

ČUFER, Uroš, DrSc; Slovenian banker and politician; *Minister of Finance;* b. 1970; ed Université Paris IX – Dauphine, France; began career at Bank of Slovenia 1999, Dir Analysis and Research Dept 1999–2004; Dir Man. Centre for Financial Man., Nova Ljubljanska Banka 2004–13; Minister of Finance 2013–, also Gov. for Slovenia, EIB. *Address:* Ministry of Finance, 1502 Ljubljana, Župančičeva 3, Slovenia (office). *Telephone:* (1) 3695200 (office). *Fax:* (1) 3696659 (office). *E-mail:* uros.cufer@mf-rs.si (office). *Website:* www.mf.gov.si (office).

CUI, Naifu; Chinese politician (retired); b. 8 Oct. 1928, Beijing; s. of Cui Yu Lian and Chang Wei Fung Cui; m. 1955; one s. one d.; joined CCP 1948; Dir Propaganda Dept and Dean of Studies, Lanzhou Univ.; Vice-Chair. Lanzhou Univ. Revolutionary Cttee; Vice-Minister of Civil Affairs 1981, Minister 1982–93; mem. 12th Cen. Cttee CCP 1982–87, 13th Cen. Cttee CCP 1987–92, 14th Cen. Cttee 1992–97; mem. 8th NPC 1993–98, NPC Deputy Jiangxi Prov.; Deputy Head, Group for Resettlement of Ex-Servicemen and Retired Officers 1983–88, Head 1988–; Research Soc. for Theory of Civil Admin. and Social Welfare 1985; Chair. China Org. Comm. of UN Decade of Disabled Persons 1986; Hon. Pres. China Asscn of Social Workers 1991–; Deputy Dir China Org. Comm. of Int. Decade of Natural Disaster Reduction 1991–; Pres. China Charity Fed. 1994–; Hon. Dir China Welfare Fund for the Handicapped 1985–; Hon. Pres. China Asscn for the Blind and Deaf Mutes 1984. *Leisure interest:* calligraphy. *Address:* No. 9, Xi Huang Cheng Gen Street, Beijing 100032, People's Republic of China. *Telephone:* 66017240. *Fax:* 66017240.

CUI, Tiankai; Chinese diplomatist; *Ambassador to USA;* b. Oct. 1952, Shanghai; m.; one d.; ed Shanghai Normal Univ., Johns Hopkins Univ., USA; teacher, Shanghai Normal Univ. 1977–78; interpreter, UN HQ, New York 1981–84; began career at Ministry of Foreign Affairs with Dept of Int. Orgs and Confs, serving successively as Attaché, Third Sec., Deputy Dir, Dir, Counsellor 1984–96, Deputy Dir-Gen. Information Dept 1996–97, Minister Counselor, Perm. Mission to UN, New York 1997–99, Deputy Exec. Dir-Gen. Policy Research Office 1999–2001, Dir-Gen. Policy Research Office 2001–03, Dir-Gen. Dept of Asian Affairs 2003–06, Asst Minister of Foreign Affairs, responsible for Asian Affairs, Int. Orgs and Confs and Arms Control 2006–07, Amb. to Japan 2007–09, Vice-Minister of Foreign Affairs 2009–13, Amb. to USA 2013–. *Address:* Chinese Embassy, 3505 International Place NW, Washington, DC 20522, USA (office). *Telephone:* (202) 495-2000 (office). *Fax:* (202) 495-2138 (office). *E-mail:* chinaembpress_us@mfa.gov.cn (office). *Website:* www.china-embassy.org (office).

CUISIA, José L., Jr, BA, BS, MBA; Philippine business executive, central banker and diplomatist; *Ambassador to USA;* b. 16 July 1944, Manila; s. of Jose Cuisia and Magdalena Cuisia (née Lampe); m. Maria Victoria Jose Cuisia 1973; five d.; ed De la Salle Univ., The Wharton School, Univ. of Pennsylvania (Univ. Scholar), USA; served in several financial insts, including Philippine American Life & General Insurance Co., American International Group, Far East Bank & Trust Co., Insular Bank of Asia and America, Union Bank of the Philippines; CEO Filinvest Credit Corpn Jan.–Aug. 1980, Insular Bank of Asia and America 1980–84, Pres. and CEO 1984–85; Admin. Social Security System 1986–90; Chair. Barcelon Roxas Securities Inc. 1986, Union Bank of the Philippines 1986–90, Monetary Bd; Vice-Chair.

Century Bank 1986, Philippine Business for Social Progress; Gov. Central Bank and Chair. Monetary Bd and concurrently Chair. Philippine Deposit Insurance Corpn 1990–93; fmr Pres. and CEO/Admin. Social Security System and Dir Philippine Nat. Bank, Commr (representing the Employer's Group) Sept.–Dec. 2010; Amb. to USA 2011–; fmr mem. Bd of Dirs SM Prime Holdings, Phinma Corpn, Holcim Philippines Corpn, Manila Water Trust Co., San Miguel Corpn, Philippine Long Distance Telephone Trust Co., Philippine Airlines; Chair. Bd Paraclete Foundation; Gov. Cen. Monetary Authority; mem. Bd of Trustees, Asian Man. Inst., Makati Medical Center, Pres. Philippine Financial Exec. Inst. 1984, Philippine Man. Asscn 1984; numerous awards and accolades, including the Ten Outstanding Young Men Award for Domestic Banking, Distinguished La Sallian Award, Raul Locsin CEO of the Year Award 2004, Management Man of the Year, Management Asscn of the Philippines 2007, Joseph Wharton Award for Lifetime Achievement 2011, Manuel L. Quezon Award for Exemplary Governance. *Address:* Embassy of the Philippines, 1600 Massachusetts Avenue NW, Washington, DC 20036-2274, USA (office); 626 Adelfa Street, New Ayala Alabang Village, Muntinlupa, Manila, Philippines (home). *Telephone:* (202) 467-9300 (office). *Fax:* (202) 467-9417 (office). *E-mail:* info@philippineembassy-usa.org (office). *Website:* www.philippineembassy-usa.org (office).

CUKJATI, France, MD; Slovenian physician and politician; b. 15 Feb. 1943; m.; four c.; ed Jesuit Inst. of Philosophy, Zagreb, Croatia and Univ. of Ljubljana; practised medicine at Health Centre of Ljubljana-Šiška; fmr Dir Vrhnika Health Centre, entered pvt. practice 1994; mem. Državni zbor (Nat. Ass.) 2000–, Chair. (Speaker) 2004–08; Founding mem. and fmr Sec.-Gen. Slovenian Chamber of Medicine. *Address:* Office of the Speaker, Državni zbor, 1000 Ljubljana, Šubičeva 4, Slovenia (office). *Telephone:* (1) 4789400 (office). *Fax:* (1) 4789845 (office). *E-mail:* info@dz-rs.si (office). *Website:* www.dz-rs.si (office).

CULHANE, John Leonard, PhD, CPhys, FInstP, FRS; Irish physicist and academic; *Professor of Physics, University College London;* b. 14 Oct. 1937, Dublin; s. of the late John Thomas Culhane and Mary Agnes Culhane (née Durkin); m. Mary Brigid Smith 1961; two s.; ed Univ. Coll., Dublin, Univ. Coll., London; Lecturer in Physics, Univ. Coll. London 1967–69, 1970–76, Reader 1976–81, Prof. 1981–; research scientist, Lockheed Palo Alto Lab. 1969–70; Dir Mullard Space Science Lab., Univ. Coll. London 1983–2003, Head Dept of Space and Climate Physics 1993–2003; UK Del. and Vice-Pres. European Space Agency Science Programme Cttee 1989–94; Chair. British Nat. Space Centre Space Science Programme Bd 1989–92, COSPAR Comm. 1994–2002, European Space Science Cttee, European Science Foundation 1997–2002; mem. Advisory Panel European Space Agency Space Science Dept 1995–2000, UK Particle Physics and Astronomy Research 1996–2000; Foreign mem. Norwegian Acad. of Sciences and Letters 1996; Hon. DSc (Wrocław) 1996; Gold Medal, Royal Astronomical Soc. 2007. *Publications:* X-Ray Astronomy, over 350 papers on Solar and Cosmic X-Ray Astronomy, X-Ray Instrumentation and Plasma Spectroscopy. *Leisure interests:* music, motor racing. *Telephone:* (1483) 274111 (office). *Fax:* (1483) 278312. *E-mail:* jlc@mssl.ucl.ac.uk (office).

CULKIN, Macaulay; American actor; b. 26 Aug. 1980, New York; s. of Christopher "Kit" Culkin and Pat Culkin; m. Rachel Miner 1998; ed St Joseph's School of Yorkville, New York and George Balanchine's School of Ballet, New York. *Films include:* Rocket Gibraltar 1988, Uncle Buck 1989, See You In The Morning 1989, Jacob's Ladder 1990, Home Alone 1990, My Girl 1991, Only the Lonely 1991, Home Alone 2: Lost in New York 1992, The Nutcracker, The Good Son 1993, The Pagemaster 1994, Getting Even With Dad 1994, Richie Rich 1995, Body Piercer 1998, Saved! 2004, Jerusalemski sindrom 2004, Sex and Breakfast 2007. *Play:* Madame Melville, Vaudeville Theatre, London 2000. *Television includes:* Foster Hall 2004, Robot Chicken (series) 2005–10, Kings (series) 2009. *Publication:* Junior 2006. *Address:* c/o William Morris Agency, One William Morris Place, Beverly Hills, CA 90212, USA.

CULLEN, Sir Michael John, KNZM, MA, PhD; New Zealand fmr politician; *Chairman, New Zealand Post Group;* b. 1945, London, England; m. 1st Rowena Joy Knight; two d.; m. 2nd Anne Lowson Collins; ed Christ's Coll. Christchurch, Univ. of Canterbury and Univ. of Edinburgh, UK; Asst Lecturer, Univ. of Canterbury, Tutor Univ. of Stirling, Sr Lecturer in History, Univ. of Otago, Dunedin and Visiting Fellow, ANU 1968–81; MP for St Kilda 1981–96, for Dunedin South 1996–99, for Labour Party List 1999–2009; Sr Govt Whip 1984–87; Minister of Social Welfare 1987–90; Assoc. Minister of Finance 1987–89, of Health 1989–90, of Labour 1989–90; Opposition Spokesperson on Finance 1991, apptd Deputy Leader of Opposition 1996; Acting Minister for Accident Insurance 1999–2001; Minister of Revenue 1999–2005, of Finance 1999–2008; Leader of the House 1999–2008; Deputy Prime Minister 2002–08, Minister of Tertiary Educ. 2005–07, Minister in charge of Treaty of Waitingi Negotiations 2007–08, Attorney-Gen 2005, 2006–08; Shadow Leader of the House and Shadow Minister for Treaty of Waitingi Negotiations 2008; Chair. New Zealand Post Group 2009–; mem. Labour Party 1974–, mem. Party Exec. 1976–81, Party Council 1976. *Leisure interests:* music, reading, house renovation, golf. *Address:* Office of the Chairman, New Zealand Post Ltd, New Zealand Post House, 7 Waterloo Quay, Wellington Central, Wellington 6011, New Zealand (office). *Website:* www.nzpost.co.nz (office).

CULLINAN, Edward Horder, CBE, RA, RIBA; British architect; *Chairman, Edward Cullinan Architects;* b. 17 July 1931, London, England; s. of Edward Revil Cullinan and Dorothea Joy Horder; m. Rosalind Sylvia Yeates 1961; one s. two d.; ed Ampleforth Coll., Univ. of Cambridge, Architectural Asscn, Univ. of Calif., Berkeley, USA; with Denys Lasdun 1958–65; est. Edward Cullinan Architects 1965, currently Chair.; numerous professorships include Bannister Fletcher Prof., Univ. of London 1978–79, Graham Willis Prof., Univ. of Sheffield 1985–87, George Simpson Prof., Univ. of Edinburgh 1987–; currently Visiting Prof., Univ. of Nottingham; Chair. Urban Vision, N Staffordshire; Trustee, Sir John Soane's Museum, London, Construction Industry for Youth Trust, Building Experiences Trust, Koestler Award Trust; represented at RA Summer Exhbn and many others; Hon. Fellow, Royal Incorporation of Architects in Scotland; Financial Times Architecture at Work Award 1991, Special Commendation at Prince Philip Designers Prize 2005, RIBA Royal Gold Medal 2008, many other awards and prizes. *Publications:* Edward Cullinan Architects 1984, 1995, Master Plan for the University of North Carolina at Charlotte 1995, Ends Middles Beginnings 2005; contribs to journals. *Leisure interests:* horticulture, cycling, surfing, Arctic and

Sahara travel, history, building, geography. *Address:* 1 Baldwin Terrace, London, N1 7RU, England (office). *Telephone:* (20) 7704-1975 (office). *Fax:* (20) 7354-2739 (office). *E-mail:* eca@ecarch.co.uk (office). *Website:* www.edwardcullinanarchitects.com (office).

CULVER, Chester John (Chet), BA, MA; American teacher and politician; b. 25 Jan. 1966, Washington, DC; s. of fmr US Senator John Chester Culver and Ann Culver (née Cooper); m. Mariclare Thinnes Culver; one s. one d.; ed Bethesda-Chevy Chase High School, Md, Virginia Polytechnic Inst. and State Univ., Blacksburg, Drake Univ., Des Moines, Ia; worked as lobbyist 1989–90, clients included Ia Trial Lawyers' Asscn, Ia Beef Processors, Des Moines Univ.; began public service career as environmental and consumer advocate in Ia Attorney Gen.'s Office 1991–95; taught govt and history at Roosevelt High School and Hoover High School, Des Moines, also coached both football and basketball; Sec. of State for Ia (youngest Sec. of State in USA) 1999–2007, mem. Exec. Council, Chair. Exec. Council Insurance Advisory Cttee, Chair. State Voter Registration Comm., mem. State Records Man. Cttee; Gov. of Iowa 2007–11; Fed. Liaison for Democratic Govs' Asscn 2008–09; est. Iowa Student Political Awareness Club; mem. Nat. Asscn of Secs of State (mem. Elections and Voter Participation Cttee, Presidential Caucuses and Primaries Cttee, New Millennium Youth Initiative), Elections Task Force, Council of State Govts, Iowa State Educ. Asscn; Democrat; Fulbright Memorial Fund Teacher's Scholarship to Japan, Ia State Educ. Asscn 1997. *Address:* PO Box 6068, Des Moines, IA 50309, USA. *Telephone:* (515) 883-2010. *E-mail:* info@chetculver.com. *Website:* www.chetculver.com.

CUMING, Frederick George Rees, RA, ARCA, DLitt; British painter; b. 16 Feb. 1930; s. of Harold Cuming and Grace Cuming; m. Audrey Lee Cuming 1962; one s. one d.; ed Univ. School, Bexleyheath, Sidcup Art School, Royal Coll. of Art; travelling scholarship to Italy; exhbns in Redfern, Walker, New Grafton, Thackeray and Fieldborne Galleries; works in collections including Dept of the Environment, Treasury, Chantrey Bequest, RA, Kendal Museum, Scunthorpe Museum, Bradford, Carlisle, Nat. Museum of Wales, Brighton and Hove Museum, Maidstone Museum, Towner Gallery, Eastbourne, Monte Carlo Museum, Farringdon Trust, Worcester Coll. Oxford, St John's Coll. Oxford, W.H. Smith, Thames TV, Nat. Trust Foundation for Art; Assoc. RCA; mem. New English Art Club; Hon. DLitt (Univ. of Kent) 2004; Grand Prix, Art Contemporaine, Monte Carlo. *Publication:* A Figure in the Landscape, A Painter's Progress, Practical Art School. *Leisure interests:* tennis, golf, snooker, reading, music, travelling. *Address:* The Gables, Wittersham Road, Iden, Nr. Rye, East Sussex, TN31 7WY, England. *Telephone:* (1797) 280322. *E-mail:* gablesarithmited@googlemail.com (office). *Website:* www.fredcuming.com (office).

CUNLIFFE, Sir Jonathan Stephen, Kt, CB, MA; British civil servant and diplomatist; *Permanent Representative to EU;* b. 2 June 1953; s. of Ralph Cunliffe and Cynthia Cunliffe; m. Naomi Brandler 1984; two d.; ed St Marylebone Grammar School, Univs of London and Manchester; joined Civil Service 1980, various posts in Depts of Environment and Transport 1980–90; Head Public Sector Pay Div., HM Treasury 1990–92, Head Int. Financial Insts Div. 1992–94, Treasury Debt and Reserves Man. Div. 1994–96, Deputy Dir Macroeconomic Policy and Prospects and Head of Treasury European Monetary Union team 1996–98, Deputy Dir Macroeconomic Policy and Int. Finance 1998–2001, Man. Dir Finance Regulation and Industry, HM Treasury 2001–02, Man. Dir Macroeconomic Policy and Int. Finance 2002–05, Second Perm. Sec. 2005–07; Head of the European and Global Issues Secr. and Int. Econ. and EU Adviser to the Prime Minister, Cabinet Office 2007–11; Perm. Rep. to EU 2012–; Alt. Dir EBRD 1992–94; Alt. mem. EU Monetary Cttee responsible for Debt and Reserves Man. 1996–98. *Leisure interests:* tennis, cooking, walking. *Address:* Permanent Representation of the UK to the European Union, 10 Avenue d'Auderghem, 1040 Brussels, Belgium (office). *Telephone:* (2) 287-82-11 (office). *Fax:* (2) 287-83-33 (office). *E-mail:* debbie.chilcott@fco.gov.uk (office). *Website:* www.ukrep.be (office).

CUNNINGHAM, Edward Patrick, MAgrSc, PhD, MRIA; Irish academic, international public servant and scientific adviser; *Chief Scientific Adviser to Government of Ireland;* b. 4 Aug. 1934, Dublin; s. of Eugene Cunningham and Kathleen Moran; m. Catherine Dee 1965 (died 1998); four s. two d.; ed Clongowes Wood Coll., Univ. Coll. Dublin and Cornell Univ., Ithaca, NY, USA; Housemaster, Albert Agricultural Coll. Dublin 1956–57; Research and Teaching Asst, Univ. Coll. Dublin 1957–58, Cornell Univ. 1960–62; Research Officer, The Agricultural Inst., Dublin 1962, Head Dept of Animal Breeding and Genetics 1970, Deputy Dir Agricultural Inst. 1980–88; Prof. of Animal Genetics, Trinity Coll., Dublin 1974–; Dir Animal Production and Health Div., FAO, Rome 1990–93, Dir Screwworm Emergency Centre for N Africa 1990–92; Jt Founder and Chair. Identigen Ltd 1997–; Chief Scientific Adviser to Govt of Ireland 2007–; Visiting Prof., Agricultural Univ. of Norway 1968–69, Econ. Devt Inst., IBRD 1988; mem. Royal Swedish Acad. of Agriculture and Forestry, Royal Norwegian Acad. of Science and Letters, Russian Acad. of Agricultural Sciences, Acad. d'Agriculture de France; A. M. Leroy Fellowship 1991; Ordre du Mérite agricole; Hon. DAgric (Agric. Univ., Norway) 1997; Hon. DSc (Dublin Univ.) 1997, (Univ. Coll. Dublin) 2009; Golden Egg Int. Award, Verona 1983, Boyle Medal, Royal Dublin Soc. 1996. *Publications:* Animal Breeding Theory 1969, Development Issues in the Livestock Sector 1992. *Leisure interests:* farming, history. *Address:* Department of Genetics, Trinity College, Dublin 2 (office); Vesington House, Dunboyne, Co. Meath, Ireland (home). *Telephone:* (1) 6073047 (office); (1) 8255350 (home). *E-mail:* epcnnghm@tcd.ie (office); epcnnghm@tcd.ie (office); patrick.cunningham@chiefscientificadviser.ie (office). *Website:* www.tcd.ie (office); www.chiefscientificadviser.ie (office).

CUNNINGHAM, Michael, MA, MFA; American novelist and screenwriter; b. 6 Nov. 1952, Cincinnati, Ohio; ed Stanford Univ., Univ. of Iowa; fmr bartender; joined Univ. of Iowa Writers Workshop 1978; writer for Carnegie Corpn; fmr Adjunct Asst Prof., Columbia Univ.; Donald I. Fine Prof. in Creative Writing, Brooklyn Coll. 2001, Distinguished Prof. of English 2001, also head of MFA Writing Program, now Visiting Prof.; Guggenheim Fellowship 1993; Lambda Literary Award for Gay Men's Fiction 1995. *Screenplays include:* A Home at the End of the World 2004, Evening 2007. *Publications:* Golden States 1984, A Home at the End of the World 1990, Flesh and Blood 1995, The Hours (Pulitzer Prize, PEN/Faulkner Award for Fiction 1999) 1998, Specimen Days 2005, By Nightfall 2010. *Address:* Steven Barclay Agency, 12 Western Avenue, Petaluma, CA 94952, USA (office); English Department, 2308 Boylan Hall, Brooklyn College, 2900

Bedford Avenue, Brooklyn, NY 11210, USA (office). *Website:* www.barclayagency .com/cunningham.html (office); academic.brooklyn.cuny.edu/english (office). *Telephone:* (718) 951-5195 (office).

CUNNINGHAM, Ralph S., BS, MS, PhD; American engineer and business executive; *Chairman, TETRA Technologies Inc.;* ed Ohio State Univ., Auburn Univ.; began career in Exxon's refinery operations; held various exec. positions with Huntsman Corpn (Vice-Chair. 1994–95), Clark Oil and Refining, Tenneco, Inc.; Pres. Texaco Chemical Co. 1990–94; Pres. and CEO CITGO Petroleum Corpn 1995–97 (retd); Dir of Enterprise Products Co. (EPCO) 1987–97, 2006, Group Vice-Chair. 2007–10, Dir, Pres. and CEO EPE Holdings 2007–10, Group Exec. Vice-Pres. and COO EPGP 2005–07, Interim Pres. and Interim CEO June–Aug. 2007, Dir of Enterprise Products GP, LLC (EPGP) 1998–2005, 2006–10, DEP GP 2007–10, COO Enterprise Products GP LLC (gen. partner of Enterprise Products Operating LP) 2005–07, Interim Pres. and CEO June–July 2007, Group Exec. Vice-Pres. Enterprise Products GP LLC (gen. partner of Enterprise Products Partners LP) 2005–07, Pres. and CEO EPE Holdings, LLC (gen. partner of Enterprise GP Holdings LP) 2007–10, Dir of LE GP, LLC (gen. partner of Energy Transfer Equity, LP) 2009–10, mem. Bd of Dirs Enterprise Products Holdings LLC 2010–, Chair. 2010–13; Dir and Chair. Safety, Health and Responsibility Cttee Cenovus Energy Inc.; Chair. TETRA Technologies Inc. 2006–, Texas Eastern Products Pipeline Co., LLC (gen. partner of Teppco Partners LP) March–Nov. 2005, Dir 2005–06; Advisory Dir Pilko & Assocs; Ind. Dir Agrium Inc. 1996–2013, Tetra Technologies Inc. 1999–, Cenovus Energy Inc. 2009–, Reaction Design, Inc.; Corp. Dir of EnCana Corpn 2003–; mem. Auburn Univ. Chemical Eng Advisory Council, Auburn Univ. Eng Advisory Council, Univ. of Texas at Tyler Eng Advisory Council. *Address:* TETRA Technologies Inc., 24955 Interstate 45 North, The Woodlands, TX 77380, USA (office). *Telephone:* (281) 367-1983 (office). *E-mail:* corpsecretary@tetratec.com (office). *Website:* www.tetratec.com (office).

CUNNINGHAM, William Hughes, BA, MBA, PhD; American marketer, academic and fmr university administrator; *James L. Bayless Chair for Free Enterprise, McCombs School of Business, Department of Marketing, University of Texas;* b. 5 Jan. 1944, Detroit, Mich.; m. Isabella Cunningham; one s.; ed Michigan State Univ.; Asst Prof. of Marketing, Univ. of Texas, Austin 1971–73, Assoc. Prof. 1973–79, Prof. 1979–, Foley's/Sanger Harris Prof. of Retail Merchandising 1982–83, Dean, Coll. of Business Admin/Grad. School of Business 1983–85, Regents Chair in Higher Educ. Leadership 1985–92, James L. Bayless Chair. for Free Enterprise, McCombs School of Business, Dept of Marketing 1988–, Pres. Univ. of Texas at Austin 1985–92, Chancellor Univ. of Texas System 1992–2000, Lee Hage and Joseph D. Jamail Regents Chair in Higher Educ. Leadership 1992–2000, Fellow, IC² Inst.; mem. Bd of Dirs Lincoln Nat. Corpn (fmrly Jefferson-Pilot) 1985–, John Hancock Mutual Funds 1986–, Southwest Airlines 2000–, Pinnacle Foods Corpn 2000–03, Introgen Therapeutics 2000–09, Hicks Acquisition Co., Inc. 2007–09, Resolute Energy Corpn 2009–, LIN Television 2009–; mem. Bd of Dirs College Football Asscn 1988–89; mem. Econ. Advisory Cttee of US Dept of Commerce 1983–85; Hon. LLD (Michigan State Univ.) 1993; Outstanding Tex. Leader, John Ben Shepperd Leadership Forum 1987, Jewish Nat. Fund Tree of Life Award 1992, Distinguished Alumnus Award, Michigan State Univ. 1993, Presidential Citation, Univ. of Texas, Austin 2005, inducted into Univ. of Texas, Austin McCombs School of Business Hall of Fame 2011. *Publications:* with others: The Personal Force in Marketing 1977, Consumer Energy Attitudes and Behavior in the Southwest 1977, Effective Selling 1977, Métodos Efectivos de Ventas 1980, Marketing: A Managerial Approach 1987, Grondslagen van het Marketing Management 1984, Introduction to Business 1988, Business in a Changing World 1992 (fourth edn 1995), The Texas Way: Money, Power, Politics and Ambition at The University 2013. *Leisure interests:* golf, tennis, racquetball, horseback riding. *Address:* PO Box E, Austin, TX 78713 (office); 1412 Barton Creek Boulevard, Austin, TX 78735, USA (home). *Telephone:* (512) 232-7540 (office). *Fax:* (512) 232-7541 (office). *E-mail:* whc@po.utexas.edu (office).

CUNNINGHAM OF FELLING, Baron (Life Peer), cr. 2005, of Felling in the County of Tyne and Wear; **John A. (Jack) Cunningham,** PC, DL, PhD; British politician; b. 4 Aug. 1939, Newcastle upon Tyne; s. of Andrew Cunningham; m. Maureen Cunningham 1964; one s. two d.; ed Jarrow Grammar School and Bede Coll., Durham Univ.; fmr Research Fellow in Chem., Durham Univ.; fmr school teacher, trades union officer; MP for Whitehaven, Cumbria 1970–83, for Copeland 1983–2005; Parl. Pvt. Sec. to Rt Hon. James Callaghan 1972–76; Parl. Under-Sec. of State, Dept of Energy 1976–79; Opposition Spokesman on Industry 1979–83, on Environment 1983–89, Shadow Leader of the House and Campaigns Co-ordinator 1989–92, Opposition Spokesman on Foreign and Commonwealth Affairs 1992–94, on Trade and Industry 1994–95, on Nat. Heritage 1995–97; Minister of Agric., Fisheries and Food 1997–98, for the Cabinet Office and Chancellor of the Duchy of Lancaster 1998–99; DL (Cumbria) 1991; mem. Labour Party. *Leisure interests:* fell walking, fly-fishing, shooting, gardening, theatre, classical and folk music, reading, Newcastle United Football Club, listening to other people's opinions. *Address:* House of Lords, London, SW1A 0PW, England (office).

CUNY, Jean-Pierre, MSc; French business executive; *Chairman and CEO, Bigot Mécanique;* b. 8 April 1940, Menton; s. of Robert Cuny and Marie-Louise Marchal; m. Anne-Marie Fousse 1968; two d.; ed Ecole Centrale, Paris and Massachusetts Inst. of Tech., USA; engineer, Serete 1968–70; Data Processing Man. Firmin Didot 1970–73; Gen. Man. Dafsa Documentation 1973–76; Project Man. CGA 1976–77; Cost Controller Placoplatre 1977–78, Production Dir 1978–82, Sales and Marketing Dir 1982–85, CEO 1985–86, Chair. and CEO 1986–89, Dir BPB PLC (parent co. of Placoplatre) 1988–89, Deputy Chair. Gypsum Div. 1988–94, CEO BPB PLC 1994–99; Pres. Eurogypsum 1996–99; Chair. and CEO Bigot Mécanique 2002–, Sopram 2003–; Chevalier, Légion d'honneur. *Leisure interests:* skiing, theatre, reading, music, film. *Address:* Bigot Mécanique, 194 Chaussée Jules César, 95250 Beauchamp, France (office). *Telephone:* 1-39-95-60-47 (office). *E-mail:* jean-pierre .cuny@wanadoo.fr (office).

CUOMO, Andrew Mark, BA, JD; American lawyer, state governor and fmr government official; *Governor of New York;* b. 6 Dec. 1957, Queens, NY; s. of Mario Cuomo (q.v.) and Matilda Cuomo (née Raffa); m. Kerry Kennedy 1992 (divorced 2005); three d.; ed Archbishop Molloy High School, Fordham Univ., Albany Law School; Campaign Man., Mario Cuomo Gubernatorial Campaign, New York 1982; Special Asst to Gov. Mario Cuomo, State of NY, Albany 1983; Asst Dist Attorney,

Manhattan Dist Attorney's Office, New York City 1984–85; Partner, Blutrich, Falcone & Miller, NY 1985–88; Chair. New York City Comm. on the Homeless 1991–93; Asst Sec. for Community Planning and Devt, Dept of Housing and Urban Devt, Washington, DC 1993–97, Sec. of Housing and Urban Devt 1997–2001; unsuccessful cand. for Gov. 2002; Attorney Gen. of NY 2007–10; Gov. of New York State 2011–; f. H.E.L.P. – Housing Enterprise for the Less Privileged (now HELP USA) 1986, Co-Chair. 2001; Visiting Fellow, Harvard Univ. Inst. of Politics; Man of the Year Award, Coalition of Italian American Orgs 1988, Ed Sulzberger Award, Our Town – Manhattan Media LLC 1989, Public Service Award, Council of Jewish Orgs 1989, Distinguished Community Service award, New York University, 1991, Innovation award, Harvard University John F. Kennedy School Government, 1998. *Publication:* Crossroads: The Future of American Politics (ed.) 2003. *Address:* Office of the Governor, State Capitol Building, Albany, NY 12224-0341, USA (office); Washington Office of the Governor, State of New York, 444 North Capitol Street, Suite 301, Washington, DC 20001, USA (office). *Telephone:* (518) 474-7516 (office); (202) 434-7100 (DC) (office). *Fax:* (202) 434-7110 (DC) (office). *Website:* www.governor.ny.gov (office); www.andrewcuomo.com.

CUOMO, Mario Matthew, LLB; American lawyer, politician and fmr state governor; *Of Counsel, Corporate and Financial Services Department and Litigation Department, Wilkie Farr & Gallagher LLP;* b. 15 June 1932, Queen's County, NY; s. of Andrea Cuomo and Immaculata Cuomo; m. Matilda Raffa 1954; two s. (including Andrew Cuomo q.v.) three d.; ed St John's Coll. and St John's Univ.; admitted to New York Bar 1956, Supreme Court Bar 1960; Confidential Legal Asst to Hon. Adrian P. Burke, New York State Court of Appeals 1956–58; Assoc., Corner, Weisbrod, Froeb and Charles, Brooklyn 1958–63, Partner 1963–75; Sec. of State, NY 1975–79; Lt-Gov. of NY State 1979–82, Gov. 1983–95; Partner, Wilkie Farr & Gallagher LLP 1995, currently Of Counsel, Corp. and Financial Services Dept and Litigation Dept; Adjunct Prof., St John's Univ. Law School 1973–75; counsel to community groups 1966–72; mem. Bd of Eds, New York Law Journal; fmr Co-Chair. and mem. Bd of Dirs Partnership for a Drug-Free America; Democrat; New York Rapallo Award, Columbia Lawyers' Asscn 1976, Dante Medal, Italian Govt./American Asscn of Italian Teachers 1976, Silver Medallion, Columbia Coalition 1976, Public Admin. Award, C.W. Post Coll. 1977, American Acad. of Arts and Letters Medal 1999, Federal Bar Council's Emory Buckner Medal 2007. *Publications:* Forest Hills Diary: The Crisis of Low-Income Housing 1974, Maya 1984, Lincoln on Democracy (co-author) 1990, The New York Idea 1994, Common Sense 1995, Reason to Believe 1995, The Blue Spruce 1999, Why Lincoln Matters Today More Than Ever 2004, Lincoln Lessons: Reflections on America's Greatest Leader (contrib.) 2009. *Address:* Wilkie, Farr & Gallagher LLP, 787 7th Avenue, New York, NY 10019-6099 (office); 50 Sutton Place South, New York, NY 10022, USA. *Telephone:* (212) 728-8260 (office). *Fax:* (212) 728-9260 (office). *E-mail:* mcuomo@willkie.com (office). *Website:* www.willkie.com (office).

CUPITT, Rev. Don, MA; British ecclesiastic and university lecturer; b. 22 May 1934, Oldham, Greater Manchester, England; s. of Robert Cupitt and Norah Cupitt; m. Susan Marianne Day 1963; one s. two d.; ed Charterhouse, Trinity Hall, Cambridge, Westcott House, Cambridge; ordained 1959; Curate, St Philip's Church, Salford 1959–62; Vice-Prin. Westcott House, Cambridge 1962–65; Fellow, Emmanuel Coll., Cambridge 1965–96, Dean 1966–91, Life Fellow 1996–; Asst Lecturer, Univ. of Cambridge 1968–73, Lecturer in Divinity 1973–96; Fellow of the Jesus Seminar, Westar Inst., Ore., USA 2001; Hon. DLitt (Bristol) 1985. *Television documentaries:* Who Was Jesus? 1977, The Sea of Faith (series) 1984. *Publications:* Christ and the Hiddenness of God 1971, Crisis of Moral Authority 1972, The Leap of Reason 1976, The Worlds of Science and Religion 1976, Who Was Jesus? (with Peter Armstrong) 1977, The Nature of Man 1979, Explorations in Theology 1979, The Debate about Christ 1979, Jesus and the Gospel of God 1979, Taking Leave of God 1980, The World to Come 1982, The Sea of Faith 1984, Only Human 1985, Life Lines 1986, The Long-Legged Fly 1987, The New Christian Ethics 1988, Radicals and the Future of the Church 1989, Creation out of Nothing 1990, What is a Story? 1991, The Time Being 1992, After All 1994, The Last Philosophy 1995, Solar Ethics 1995, After God: The Future of Religion 1997, Mysticism after Modernity 1997, The Religion of Being 1998, The Revelation of Being 1998, The New Religion of Life in Everyday Speech 1999, The Meaning of It All in Everyday Speech 1999, Kingdom Come in Everyday Speech 2000, Philosophy's Own Religion 2000, Reforming Christianity 2001, Emptiness and Brightness 2001, Is Nothing Sacred? 2002, Life, Life 2003, The Way to Happiness: A Theory of Religion 2005, The Great Questions of Life 2006, The Old Creed and the New 2006, Radical Theology 2006, Impossible Loves 2007, Above Us It's Only Sky 2008, The Meaning of the West 2008, A New Method of Religious Enquiry 2008, Jesus and Philosophy 2009, Theology's Strange Return 2010, A New Great Story 2010, The Fountain 2010, Turns of Phrase 2011, The Last Testament 2012. *Leisure interest:* the arts. *Address:* Emmanuel College, Cambridge, CB2 3AP, England (office). *Telephone:* (1223) 334200 (office). *Fax:* (1223) 334426 (office). *E-mail:* susan.cupitt@gmail.com (home). *Website:* www.doncupitt.com.

CURA, José; Argentine singer (tenor), conductor, director and stage designer; *President, Cuibar Productions S.L.;* b. 5 Dec. 1962, Rosario, Santa Fe; m. Silvia Ibarra; two s. one d.; ed Rosario Univ., School of Arts, Teatro Colon, Buenos Aires; appearances at leading opera houses 1992–; debut at Royal Opera House, Covent Garden in Stiffelio 1995, at Vienna State Opera in Tosca 1996, at La Scala in La Gioconda 1997, at Teatro Colón, Buenos Aires and Metropolitan Opera 1999; Pres. Cuibar Productions; Prof. of Voice, RAM, London 2007–; Hon. Prof., CAECE Univ., Argentina 1999; Hon. Citizen of Rosario, Argentina 1999, of Veszprém, Hungary 2004; Hon. Founding mem. Portuguese Asscn against Leukaemia 2007; Chevalier, Ordre du Cedre (Lebanon) 2000; Premio Abbiati, Italian Critics' Award, Premio Carrara, Cultura Millenaria 1997, XII Premio Internazionale di Arte e Cultura Cilea 1997, Orphée d'Or, Acad. du Disque Lyrique 1998, ECHO Klassik Award: Singer of the Year, Deutsche Phono-Akad. 1999, Ewa Czeszejko Prize, Sochacka Foundation Award 2002, Giovanni Zanatello Prize for Best Artist of the Year, Arena di Verona 2005, Best Argentinian Opera Singer of the Year, Fundación Teatro Colón 2007, One of the Best 100 Argentinian Artists of the Last 10 Years, Fundación Konex 2009, Österreicher Kammersänger, Austrian Ministry of Culture 2010. *Address:* Cuibar Productions, Ronda de la Abubilla 30 bis, 28043 Madrid, Spain (office). *Telephone:* (91) 3000134 (office). *E-mail:* j.diez@cuibar.com (office). *Website:* www.cuibar.com (office); www.josesecura.com (home).

CURIGER, Beatrice (Bice) Gabriella Livia; Swiss art historian, critic and curator; *Director, Fondation Vincent van Gogh Arles;* b. 18 July 1948, Zurich; ed Univ. of Zurich; wrote art reviews for Zürich Tages-Anzeiger early 1980s; curated Saus & Braus, Stadtkunst exhbn 1980; co-curated Double Take with Lynne Cooke, Hayward Gallery, London; Co-founder (with Walter Keller, Jacqueline Burckhardt, Dieter von Graffenried and Peter Blum) and Ed.-in-Chief Parkett magazine 1984–; Publishing Dir Tate Etc magazine (produced by London's Tate Gallery) 2004–; Curator Zürich Kunsthaus 1993–2013; Dir Visual Arts Sector, with responsibility for curating the Venice Biennale 54th Int. Art Exhbn 2011; Dir Fondation Vincent van Gogh Arles 2014–; mem. Swiss Fed. Art Comm. 1984–94; mem. Council Univ. of Zurich 1999–2004; Rudolf Arnheim Prof., Humboldt Univ. of Berlin 2006–07; Chevalier des Arts et des Lettres 2013; Heinrich Wolfflin Medal 2007, Art Educator Award, City of Zurich 2009, SI Award, Swiss Inst., New York, ranked by ArtReview magazine amongst the ArtReview Power 100 (sixth) 2010, Kulturpreis des Kantons Zürich 2012, Meret Oppenheim Prize, Swiss Fed. 2012. *Publications:* Defiance in the Face of Freedom (monograph about Meret Oppenheim) 1982; author of various publs and catalogues of contemporary art. *Address:* Fondation Vincent van Gogh Arles, 20 rue de la Liberté, 13200 Arles, France (office). *Telephone:* (4) 90-93-08-08 (office). *Fax:* (44) 9244020 (Swiss office) (office). *E-mail:* b.curiger@parkettart.com (office); b.curiger@fvvga.org (office). *Website:* www.fondation-vincentvangogh-arles.org (office); www.parkettart.com (office).

CURRAN, Charles E., STD; American academic and ecclesiastic; *Elizabeth Scurlock University Professor of Human Values, Southern Methodist University;* b. 30 March 1934, Rochester, New York; s. of John F. Curran and Gertrude L. Beisner; ed St Bernard's Coll., Rochester, Gregorian Univ., Rome and Accad. Alfonsiana, Rome, Italy; ordained RC priest 1958; Prof. of Moral Theology, St Bernard's Seminary, Rochester, New York 1961–65; Asst Prof., then Assoc. Prof., then Prof. of Moral Theology, Catholic Univ. of America, Washington, DC 1965–89; Sr Research Scholar, Kennedy Center for Bio-Ethics, Georgetown Univ. 1972; External Examiner in Christian Ethics, Univ. of the West Indies 1982–86; Visiting Prof. of Catholic Studies, Cornell Univ. 1987–88; Visiting Brooks and Firestone Prof. of Religion, Univ. of Southern Calif. 1988–90; Visiting Eminent Scholar in Religion, Auburn Univ. 1990–91; Elizabeth Scurlock Univ. Prof. of Human Values, Southern Methodist Univ. 1991–; Pres. Catholic Theological Soc. of America 1969–70, Soc. of Christian Ethics 1971–72, American Theological Soc. 1989–90; mem. American Acad. of Arts and Sciences 2010; Dr hc (Charleston, W Va) 1987, (Concordia Coll., Portland, Ore.) 1992; J.C. Murray Award, Catholic Theological Soc. of America 1972, Building Bridges Award, New Ways Ministry 1992, Presidential Award, Coll. Theology Soc. 2003. *Publications include:* author, ed. co-ed. of more than 50 books, including Catholic Social Teaching 1891–Present: A Historical, Theological and Ethical Analysis, The Origins of Moral Theology in the United States: Three Different Approaches, The Catholic Moral Tradition Today: A Synthesis, The Moral Theology of Pope John Paul II, Catholic Moral Theology in the United States: A History (American Publr's Award for Professional and Scholarly Excellence in Theology and Religion 2008), The Social Mission of the U.S. Catholic Church: A Theological Perspective 2011, The Development of Moral Theology: Five Strands 2013; numerous articles, lectures and addresses. *Leisure interests:* reading, golf, swimming. *Address:* Southern Methodist University, 317 Dallas Hall, PO Box 750317, Dallas, TX 75275-0317 (office); 4125 Woodcreek, Dallas, TX 75220, USA (home). *Telephone:* (214) 768-4073 (office); (214) 352-8974 (home). *Fax:* (214) 768-4129 (office). *E-mail:* ccurran@mail.smu.edu (office). *Website:* www.smu.edu/theology (office).

CURRAN, Kevin; British trade union official; b. 1954, Stepney, London; s. of John Curran; m. June Curran; two c.; ed LSE; trained as welder in eng construction industry, Tipton, E Midlands; joined GMB (fmrly Boilermakers Union) as shop steward 1975, led disputes at Ford Motor Co., Dagenham and W Thurrock Power Station, Essex 1976, elected Br. Sec. Penge Boilermakers Br. 1978, GMB Safety Rep. 1978, elected Chair. London Dist Cttee of Boilermakers Soc. 1982, mem. GMB London Regional Council 1982, Regional Health and Safety Officer, London Region 1988–90, Regional Organiser, Southern Region 1990–96, Sr Organiser, Southern Region 1996–97, Regional Sec., Northern Region 1997–2003, est. North East Maritime Group (NEMG) to revitalise shipbuilding industry in NE 1997, Gen. Sec. GMB 2003–05; welding instructor in voluntary sector, London 1980–; apptd to Bd of Regional Devt Agency by Sec. of State 1998; mem. Working Group on productivity and industrial clusters devt policy, Dept of Trade and Industry 2001; mem. Treasury Cttee, TU(C)/CBI. *Leisure interests:* running (marathons), football, history.

CURRIE, James McGill, MA; British company director, civil servant and EU official; b. 17 Nov. 1941, Kilmarnock; s. of the late David Currie and Mary Currie (née Smith); m. Evelyn Barbara MacIntyre 1968; one s. one d.; ed St Joseph's High School, Kilmarnock, Blairs Coll., Aberdeen, Royal Scots Coll., Valladolid, Univ. of Glasgow; admin. trainee, Scottish Office, Edinburgh 1968–72; Prin. Scottish Educ. and Devt Depts 1972–77; Asst Sec. Scottish Industry Dept 1977–82; Transport and Environment Counsellor, UK Perm. Representation to EC 1982–86; Dir of Programmes Directorate-Gen. XVI Regional Policy 1987–88; Chief of Staff to Competition Policy Commr Sir Leon Brittan 1989–93; Deputy Head of Del., Washington, DC 1993–96; Dir-Gen. (Customs and Indirect Taxation), EC 1996–97, (Environment, Nuclear Safety and Civil Protection) 1997–2001; Visiting Prof. of Law, Georgetown Law Center, Washington, DC USA 1997–; Dir (non-exec.) Royal Bank of Scotland Group 2001–, British Nuclear Fuels plc 2002–05, Total UK Holdings; Int. Adviser, Eversheds LLP; Hon. DLitt (Glasgow) 2001. *Leisure interests:* golf, guitar, good food, tennis. *Address:* Flat 7, 54 Queens Gate Terrace, London, SW7 5PJ, UK (home). *E-mail:* jamesmcurrie@hotmail.com.

CURRIE, Lt-Col Nancy Jane, BA, MS, DEng; American astronaut; b. 29 Dec. 1958, Wilmington, Del.; d. of Warren Decker and Shirley Decker; m. David W. Currie (divorced); one d.; ed Ohio State Univ., Univ. of Southern California, Univ. of Houston; Neuropathology Research Asst, Coll. of Medicine, Ohio State Univ.; command 2nd Lt US Army 1981, helicopter instructor pilot, section leader, platoon leader, brigade flight standardization officer, master and aviator; flight simulation engineer, shuttle training aircraft, NASA Johnson Space Center, Houston 1987, astronaut 1991–, flight crew rep. for crew equipment, lead for remote manipulator system, spacecraft communicator; flight engineer mission specialist on STS-57

(Endeavour space shuttle) 1993, STS-70 (Discovery space shuttle) 1995, STS-88 (Endeavour space shuttle) 1998, STS-109 (Columbia space shuttle) 2002; chief astronaut robotics br.; currently Chief Engineer for NASA Eng and Safety Center, Johnson Space Center; mem. Army Aviation Asscn, Ohio State Univ. and ROTC Alumni Asscns, Inst. of Industrial Engineers, Human Factors and Ergonomics Soc.; NASA Flight Simulation Eng Award 1988, Defence Superior Service Medal 1993, Silver Order of St Michael, Army Aviation Award 1997, NASA Space Flight Medal 1993, 1995, 1998, 2002; inducted into Ohio Veterans Hall of Fame 1994, Troy Hall of Fame 1996, Ohio State Univ. Army ROTC Hall of Fame 1996. *Leisure interests:* weightlifting, running, swimming, scuba-diving, skiing. *Address:* NASA Lyndon B. Johnson Space Center, Houston, TX 77058, USA (office). *Website:* www .nasa.gov/centers/johnson/home/index.html.

CURRIE, Richard (Dick) J., OC, BS, MBA, LLD; Canadian business executive; b. St John, New Brunswick; m. Beth Currie; ed Univ. of New Brunswick, Tech. Univ. of Nova Scotia (TUNS), Harvard Business School, USA; began career with Atlantic Sugar Refineries; staff mem. McKinsey & Co., NY –1972; joined Loblaw Cos Ltd, Toronto 1972, Pres. 1976–96; Pres. and Dir George Weston Ltd 1996–2002; Dir Bell Canada Enterprises (BCE) Inc. 1995–2008, Chair. 2002–09; fmr Chair. (non-exec.) Telesat Canada; Chancellor Univ. of New Brunswick 2003–12, Chancellor Emer. 2013–; mem. Bd of Dirs CAE Inc., Staples Inc., Petro-Canada; mem. Int. Advisory Bd RJR Nabisco, Atlanta, USA, Jacobs Suchard, Zürich, Switzerland; fmr Chair. Food Marketing Inst., Washington DC; fmr Chair. Advisory Bd, Richard Ivey Business School, Univ. of Western Ontario; fmr mem. Visiting Cttee, Harvard Business School; Fellow, Inst. of Corp. Dirs 2004; Dr hc (Univ. of New Brunswick), (Univ. of Nova Scotia), (Dalhousie University) 2010; Golden Pencil Award, Rabb Award, Distinguished Retailer of the Year 1997, Canada's Outstanding CEO of the Year 2001, elected to Canadian Business Hall of Fame 2003, McGill Man. Achievement Award 2004, Retail Council of Canada Lifetime Achievement Award 2005, Business Leader of the Year, Richard Ivey School of Business, Univ. of Western Ontario 2009.

CURRIE OF MARYLEBONE, Baron (Life Peer), cr. 1996, of Marylebone, in the City of Westminster; **David Anthony Currie,** MSocSc, PhD, DSc, DLitt; British economist and company director; *Chairman, Competition and Markets Authority;* b. 9 Dec. 1946, London, England; s. of Kennedy Moir Currie and Marjorie Currie (née Thompson); m. 1st Shaziye Gazioglu 1965 (divorced); two s.; m. 2nd Angela Mary Piers Dumas 1995; ed Battersea Grammar School, Univs of Manchester, Birmingham and London; Economist, Hoare Govett 1971–72, Sr Economist, Econ. Models 1972; Lecturer in Econs, Queen Mary Coll., London 1972–79, Reader 1979–81, Prof. 1981–88; Houblon-Norman Research Fellow, Bank of England 1985–86, Visiting Scholar, IMF 1987; Prof. of Econs, London Business School 1988–2000, Dir Centre for Econ. Forecasting 1988–95, Research Dean 1989–92, Deputy Prin. 1992–95, Deputy Dean External Relations 1999–2000; Dean, City Univ.'s Cass Business School 2001–08; Chair. Office of Communications (Ofcom) 2002–09; mem. (Crossbench) House of Lords 1996–; mem. Advisory Bd to Research Councils 1992–93, Treasury's Panel of Ind. Forecasters 1992–95, OFGEM Man. Bd 1999–2001; Panel mem. Leveson Inquiry 2011–; Chair. Semperian PPP Investment Partners 2008–12; Chair. Independent Audit Ltd 2003–07, Int. Centre for Financial Regulation 2009–12, Council, Univ. of Essex 2011–13, Alacrity Foundation UK 2011–13; Chair. Competition and Markets Authority 2012–; mem. Bd of Dirs Abbey Nat. PLC 2001–02, Dubai Financial Services Authority 2004–, BDO 2008–12, Royal Mail 2009–12, IG Group 2010–12; Dir (non-exec.) London Philharmonic Orchestra 2007–12; Gov. London Business School 1989–95, 1997–2000, Inst. for Govt 2009–; Trustee, Joseph Rowntree Reform Trust 1991–2002. *Publications:* Advances in Monetary Economics 1985, The Operation and Regulation of Financial Markets (co-author) 1986, Macroeconomic Interactions Between North and South (co-author) 1988, Macroeconomic Policies in an Interdependent World (co-author) 1989, Rules, Reputation and Macroeconomic Policy Co-ordination (co-author) 1993, European Monetary Union: Problems in the Transition to a Single European Currency (co-author) 1995, North-South Linkages and International Macroeconomic Policy (co-author) 1995, The Pros and Cons of EMU 1997, Will the Euro Work? 1998. *Leisure interests:* music, literature, swimming. *Address:* House of Lords, Westminster, London, SW1A 0PW, England (office). *E-mail:* david.currie@cma.gsi.gov.uk (office). *Website:* www.parliament .uk/biographies/lords/lord-currie-of-marylebone/2727 (office).

CURRY, Ann, BA; American broadcast journalist and photographer; b. 19 Nov. 1956, Guam; d. of Robert Paul Curry and Hiroe Nagase; m. Brian Wilson Ross 1987; one s. one d.; ed Ernest J. King School on mil. base in Sasebo, Japan, Ashland High School, Ore., Univ. of Oregon School of Journalism; lived in Japan as a child for several years, later moved to Ashland, Ore.; began broadcasting career as an intern at the then NBC-affiliate KTVL, Medford, Ore. 1978, rose to become station's first female news reporter; reporter and anchor, NBC-affiliate KGW, Portland, Ore. 1980; reporter for KCBS-TV, Los Angeles, Calif. 1984–90; joined NBC News 1990, first as NBC News Chicago Corresp. then as anchor of NBC News at Sunrise 1991–96, also served as substitute anchor and news anchor for NBC news shows Today and Weekend Today, named co-anchor of Dateline NBC with Stone Phillips 2005–07, main anchor 2007–, has been one of the three anchors for Today's third hour 2007–, also substitute anchor for NBC Nightly News, news anchor, The Today Show 1997–2011, anchor, Dateline NBC 2005–11, Co-Anchor (with Matt Lauer) Today 2011–12, Nat. and Int. Corresp. and Anchor at Large, Today 2012–; Hon. Doctorate in Journalism (Southern Oregon Univ.) 2010, Hon. LHD (Wheaton Coll., Norton, Mass) 2010, hon. degree from Providence Coll., Providence, RI 2010; Emmy Award, Acad. of Television Arts and Sciences 1987, 1989, 2007, Golden Mike Award, Radio & Television News Asscn of Southern California 1986, 1987, 1989, Certificate of Excellence, Associated Press 1987, 1988, three Gracie Awards, The Foundation of American Women in Radio and Television, Excellence in Reporting, Nat. Asscn for the Advancement of Colored People (NAACP) 1989, voted Sexiest Newscaster and "Hottest MILF Newscaster" by readers of Ask Men magazine, awards from Save the Children, Anti-Defamation League as a Woman of Achievement, inducted into Hall of Achievement, Univ. of Oregon School of Journalism and Communication 2002, Americares Humanitarian Medal Award 2002, Nat. Journalism Award, Asian American Journalists Asscn 2003, Pioneer Award, Univ. of Oregon 2003, Simon Wiesenthal Medal of Valour for her extensive reporting in Darfur 2007, Common Wealth Award of Distinguished Service for outstanding achievements in mass communications, PNC Bank 2008, numerous awards for charity work, primarily for breast cancer research, ranked by Forbes magazine amongst The World's 100 Most Powerful Women (66th) 2011. *Leisure interest:* art history. *Address:* c/o Today Show, 30 Rockefeller Plaza, New York, NY 10112-0002, USA (office). *Telephone:* (212) 664-2555 (office). *Website:* today.msnbc.msn.com/id/4515786 (office).

CURTEIS, Ian Bayley, FSA; British dramatist; b. 1 May 1935, London; m. 1st Dorothy Joan Armstrong 1964 (died 2009); two s.; m. 2nd Joanna Trollope (q.v.) 1985; two step-d.; m. 3rd Lady Deirdre Grantley; two step-s.; ed Univ. of London; dir and actor in theatres throughout UK and BBC TV script reader 1956-63; BBC and ATV staff dir (drama) 1963-67; Chair. Cttee on Censorship, Writers' Guild of Great Britain 1981-85, Pres. of Guild 1998-2001. *Plays for TV:* Beethoven, Sir Alexander Fleming (BBC entry, Prague Festival 1973), Mr. Rolls and Mr. Royce, Long Voyage Out of War (trilogy), The Folly, The Haunting, Second Time Round, A Distinct Chill, The Portland Millions, Philby, Burgess and Maclean (British entry, Monte Carlo Festival 1978), Hess, The Atom Spies, Churchill and the Generals (Grand Prize for Best Programme of 1981, New York Int. Film and TV Festival), Suez 1956, Miss Morrison's Ghosts (British entry Monte Carlo Festival), BB and Lord D.; writer of numerous TV series; screenplays: La Condition humaine (André Malraux), Lost Empires (adapted from J. B. Priestley), Eureka, Graham Greene's The Man Within (TV) 1983, The Nightmare Years (TV) 1989, The Zimmerman Telegram 1990, The Choir (BBC 1), The Falklands Play 2002, More Love 2003, Yet More Love 2004, Miss Morrison's Ghosts 2004, The Bargain 2007, Boscobel 2008, The Last Tsar 2009; numerous articles and speeches on the ethics and politics of broadcasting. *Plays for radio:* Eroica 2000, Love 2001, After the Break, The Falklands Play 2002. *Publications:* Long Voyage Out of War (trilogy) 1971, Churchill and the Generals 1980, Suez 1956, 1980, The Falklands Play 1987. *Leisure interest:* avoiding television. *Address:* Markenfield Hall, North Yorks., HG4 3AD; 2 Warwick Square, London, SW1V 2AA, England. *Telephone:* (1765) 603411 (office); (20) 7821-8606 (home). *Fax:* (1765) 607195 (office). *E-mail:* info@markenfield.com (office).

CURTIS, David Roderick, AC, MB, BS, PhD, FRS, FRACP, FAA; Australian pharmacologist and academic; *Professor Emeritus, Australian National University;* b. 3 June 1927, Melbourne; s. of E. D. Curtis and E. V. Curtis; m. Lauris Sewell 1951; one s. one d.; ed Melbourne High School, Univ. of Melbourne and Australian Nat. Univ., Canberra; resident medical positions 1950-53; Research Scholar, ANU 1954-56, Research Fellow 1956-57, Fellow 1957-59, Sr Fellow 1959-62, Professorial Fellow 1962-65, Prof. of Pharmacology 1966-68, Prof. of Neuropharmacology 1968-73; Prof. and Head, Dept of Pharmacology, John Curtin School of Medical Research, ANU 1973-89, Dir and Howard Florey Prof. of Medical Research 1989-92, Univ. Fellow 1993-95, Prof. Emer. 1993-, Visiting Fellow 1995-2000; Burnet Lecturer 1983; Pres. Australian Acad. of Science 1986-90; Chair. Inaugural Australia Prize Cttee 1989-90. *Publications:* scientific papers on various topics concerned with neurophysiology and neuropharmacology. *Leisure interests:* reading. *Address:* 7 Patey Street, Campbell, ACT 2612, Australia. *Telephone:* (2) 6248-5664 (home).

CURTIS, Jamie Lee, Lady Haden-Guest; American actress and author; b. 22 Nov. 1958, Los Angeles, Calif.; d. of the late Tony Curtis and Janet Leigh; m. Christopher Guest; one s. one d.; ed Choate School, Conn., Univ. of the Pacific, Calif. *Films include:* Halloween, The Fog, Terror Train, Halloween II, Road Games, Prom Night, Love Letters, Trading Places, The Adventures of Buckaroo Banzai: Across the 8th Dimension, Grandview, USA, Perfect, 8 Million Ways to Die, Mother's Boys, Drowning Mona, Amazing Grace and Chuck, A Man in Love, Dominick and Eugene, A Fish Called Wanda, Blue Steel, My Girl, Forever Young, My Girl 2, True Lies 1994 (Golden Globe Award for Best Actress in a musical or comedy), House Arrest 1996, Fierce Creatures 1996, Halloween H20 1998, Virus 1999, The Tailor of Panama 2000, Daddy and Them 2001, Halloween: Resurrection 2002, True Lies 2 2003, Freaky Friday 2003, Christmas with the Cranks 2004, Beverly Hills Chihuahua 2008, You Again 2010, Little Engine That Could (voice) 2011. *Television includes:* She's In The Army Now, Dorothy Stratten: Death of a Centrefold, Operation Petticoat, The Love Boat, Columbo, Quincy, Charlie's Angels, Anything but Love, Money on the Side, As Summers Die, Anything but Love, Actor, The Heidi Chronicles, Nicholas' Gift. *Publications:* When I Was Little, A Four-Year-Old's Memoir of her Youth 1993, Tell Me Again About the Night I Was Born 1996, Today I Feel Silly and Other Moods That Make My Day 1999, Where Do Balloons Go? An Uplifting Mystery 2000, I'm Gonna Like Me Letting Off a Little Self-Esteem 2002, It's Hard To Be Five, Learning How To Work My Control Panel 2004, Is There Really a Human Race? 2006. *Leisure interests:* photography. *Address:* c/o Rick Kurtzman, CAA, 2000 Avenue of the Stars, Los Angeles, CA 90067, USA (office).

CURTIS, Penelope, BA, MA, PhD; British art gallery director; *Director, Tate Britain;* ed Corpus Christi Coll., Oxford, Courtauld Inst. of Art, Univ. of London; first Exhibitions Curator, Tate Liverpool 1988-94; Head of Henry Moore Centre for the Study of Sculpture, Leeds Museums and Galleries 1994-99, led its transformation into the Henry Moore Inst., Curator 1999-2010; Dir Tate Britain 2010-; mem. Turner Prize Jury 1997, British Council Cttee for the Venice Biennale 2008; mem. Advisory Cttee for the Govt Art Collection; mem. Advisory Cttee British School at Rome; mem. faculty Gulbenkian Museum. *Publications:* Sculpture 1900-1945 (in The Oxford History of Art 1999), Patio & Pavilion: The Place of Sculpture in Modern Architecture 2007. *Address:* Tate Britain, Millbank, London, SW1P 4RG, England (office). *Telephone:* (20) 7887-8888 (office). *E-mail:* pressoffice@tate.org.uk (office); visiting.britain@tate.org.uk (office). *Website:* www.tate.org.uk (office).

CURTIS, Richard Whalley Anthony, CBE, BA; British screenwriter, film director and film producer; b. 8 Nov. 1956, New Zealand; s. of Anthony J. Curtis and Glynness S. Curtis; two s. one d. by Emma Vallencey Freud; ed Harrow School, Christ Church, Oxford; Co-founder and Producer Comic Relief 1985-2000; BAFTA Fellowship 2007. *Films include:* Dead On Time 1983, The Tall Guy (writer) 1988, Four Weddings and a Funeral (writer, exec. producer) 1994, Bean (writer, exec. producer) 1997, Notting Hill (writer, exec. producer) 1999, Bridget Jones's Diary (screenplay) 2001, Love Actually (writer, dir) 2003, Bridget Jones: The Edge of Reason (screenplay) 2004, The Boat that Rocked (writer) 2009, War Horse (writer) 2011. *Television includes:* Not the Nine O'Clock News (series writer) 1979-82, The Black Adder (series writer) 1983, Spitting Image (series writer) 1984, Blackadder

II (series writer) 1986, Blackadder the Third (series writer) 1987, Blackadder's Christmas Carol (writer) 1988, Blackadder: The Cavalier Years (writer) 1988, Blackadder Goes Forth (series writer) 1989, The Robbie Coltrane Special (contrib.) 1989, Mr Bean (series writer) 1989-95, Bernard and the Genie (writer) 1991, Merry Christmas Mr Bean (writer) 1992, Rowan Atkinson Live (contrib.) 1992, The Vicar of Dibley (series writer, exec. producer) 1994-2007, Hooves of Fire (writer) 1999, French & Saunders Live (contrib.) 2000, Legend of the Lost Tribe (exec. producer) 2002, The Girl in the Café (writer and exec. producer) (Humanitas Prize 2006) 2005, The No.1 Ladies' Detective Agency 2008. *Leisure interests:* TV, films, pop music. *Address:* c/o Anthony Jones, United Agents, 12-26 Lexington Street, London, W1F 0LE, England (office); Portobello Studios, 138 Portobello Road, London W11 2DZ, England (office). *Telephone:* (20) 3214-0800 (office). *Fax:* (20) 3214-0801 (office). *E-mail:* dwalker@unitedagents.co.uk (office). *Website:* unitedagents.co.uk (office).

CUSACK, John; American actor; b. 28 June 1966, Evanston, Ill.; s. of Richard Cusack and Nancy Cusack; brother of Joan Cusack; mem. Piven Theatre Workshop, Evanston from age 9-19; f. New Criminals Theatrical Co., Chicago 1988; f. New Crime Productions 1992. *Films include:* Class 1983, Sixteen Candles 1984, Grandview USA 1984, The Sure Thing 1985, Journey of Natty Gann 1985, Better Off Dead 1985, Stand By Me 1985, One Crazy Summer 1986, Broadcast News 1987, Hot Pursuit 1987, Eight Men Out 1988, Tapeheads 1988, Say Anything 1989, Fatman and Little Boy 1989, The Grifters 1990, True Colors 1991, Shadows and Fog 1992, Roadside Prophets 1992, The Player 1992, Map of the Human Heart 1992, Bob Roberts 1992, Money for Nothing 1993, Bullets Over Broadway 1994, The Road to Wellville 1994, City Hall 1995, Anastasia 1997, Con Air 1997, Hellcab 1997, Midnight in the Garden of Good and Evil 1997, Grosse Pointe Blank (also dir, writer) 1997, High Fidelity (also screenwriter) 1997, This is My Father 1998, The Thin Red Line 1999, Pushing Tin 1998, Being John Malkovich 1999, The Cradle Will Rock (also screenwriter) 1999, America's Sweethearts 2001, Life of the Party 2000, Arigo (also prod.) 2000, Serendipity 2001, Max 2002, Adaptation 2002, Identity 2003, Runaway Jury 2003, The Ice Harvest 2005, Must Love Dogs 2005, The Contract 2006, Grace Is Gone 2007, 1408 2007, War, Inc. 2007, Martian Child 2007, Igor (voice) 2008, 2012 2009, Shanghai 2010, Hot Tub Time Machine (also prod.) 2010, The Factory 2011, The Raven 2012. *Address:* New Crime Productions, 555 Rose Avenue, Venice, CA 90291 (office); c/o William Morris Agency, 1 William Morris Place, Beverly Hills, CA 90212, USA.

CUSACK, Sinéad Moira; Irish actress; b. 18 Feb. 1948, Dalkey, Co. Dublin; d. of late Cyril Cusack and Maureen Kiely; m. Jeremy Irons (q.v.) 1977; two s.; acting at the Abbey Theatre in the 1960s; moved to England 1970s, debuted with the RSC at Stratford-on-Avon; numerous appearances in TV drama; played Paulina in The Winter's Tale, directed by Sam Mendes in the Bridge Project shared between the Brooklyn Acad. of Music, New York and the Old Vic, London 2009-12; Hon. DLitt (Univ. Coll. Dublin) 2013. *Theatre includes:* Lady Amaranth in Wild Oats, Lisa in Children of the Sun, Isabella in Measure for Measure, Celia in As You Like It, Evadne in The Maid's Tragedy, Lady Anne in Richard III, Portia in The Merchant of Venice, Ingrid in Peer Gynt, Kate in The Taming of the Shrew, Beatrice in Much Ado About Nothing, Lady Macbeth in Macbeth, Roxanne in Cyrano de Bergerac (all for RSC), Virago in A Lie of the Mind 2001, The Mercy Seat 2003, Oxford Festival, Gate Theatre, Dublin, Royal Court etc. *Films include:* Rocket to the Moon (uncredited) 1967, Alfred the Great 1969, The Rise and Rise of Michael Rimmer 1970, The Ballad of Tam Lin 1970, Revenge 1971, Hoffman 1971, A Likely Story 1973, The Last Remake of Beau Geste 1977, Rocket Gibraltar 1988, Venus Peter 1989, Waterland 1992, Bad Behaviour 1993, The Cement Garden 1993, Sparrow 1993, Uncovered 1995, Stealing Beauty 1996, The Nephew 1998, Passion of Mind 2000, My Mother Frank 2000, Dream 2001, I Capture the Castle 2003, Mathilde 2004, V for Vendetta 2005, The Tiger's Tail 2006, Eastern Promises 2007, Cracks 2009, Wrath of the Titans 2012. *Television includes:* Sanctuary – The Voice of His Calling 1967, ITV Playhouse – Square on the Hypotenuse 1969, David Copperfield (film) 1969, ITV Playhouse – A Sound from the Sea 1970, Armchair Theatre – The Dolly Scene 1970, The Sinners (mini-series) 1971, The Persuaders! (series) 1971, Scoop (series) 1972, Menace (series) 1973, Thriller (series) 1973, The Playboy of the Western World (film) 1974, The Protectors (series) 1974, Affairs of the Heart (series) 1974, Notorious Woman (mini-series) 1974, Quiller (series) 1975, BBC Play of the Month – Love's Labour's Lost 1975, – Trilby 1976, BBC 2 Play of the Week – The Kitchen 1977, Romance – The Black Knight 1977, Supernatural – Ghosts of Venice 1977, Twelfth Night (film) 1980, Cyrano de Bergerac (film) 1985, Screenplay – The Hen House 1989, God on the Rocks (film) 1990, Performance (series) 1992, Oliver's Travels (mini-series) 1995, Mirad (film) 1997, Have Your Cake and Eat It (mini-series) 1997, Food for Ravens (film) 1997, Winter Solstice (film) 2003, North & South (mini-series) 2004, Dad (film) 2005, The Strange Case of Sherlock Holmes & Arthur Conan Doyle (film) 2005, Summer Solstice (film) 2005, Home Again (series) 2006, A Room with a View (film) 2007, The Deep (mini-series) 2010, Camelot (series) 2011.

CUSHING, Sir Selwyn (John), KNZM, CMG, FCA; New Zealand business executive; b. 1 Sept. 1936; s. of Cyril John Cushing and Henrietta Marjory Belle Cushing; m. Kaye Dorothy Anderson 1964; two s.; ed Hastings High School, Univ. of New Zealand; pnr Esam Cushing and Co., Hastings 1960-86; Dir Brierly Investments Ltd 1986-93, Chair., CEO 1999-2001; Deputy Chair. Air New Zealand 1988, Chair. -2001; Chair. Carter Holt Harvey Ltd 1991-93, Electricity Corpn of NZ 1993-97, New Zealand Symphony Orchestra 1996-2005. *Leisure interests:* cricket, music. *Address:* c/o New Zealand Symphony Orchestra, POB 6640, Wellington 6001, (office); 1 Beaston Road, Hastings, New Zealand.

CUSHMAN, David W., PhD; American biochemist; ed Univ. of Illinois; began career as research assistant at Squibb Inst. for Medical Research (later the Bristol-Myers Squibb Pharmaceutical Research Inst.) 1969, Distinguished Research Fellow, Dept of Biochemistry -1994 (retd); Ciba Award For Hypertension Research 1983, Warren Alpert Foundation Prize 1991, Albert Lasker Award for Clinical Medical Research 1999, named by ACS one of 12 Heroes of Chemistry 2000. *Publications:* numerous publns in scientific journals. *Address:* c/o Bristol-Myers Squibb Pharmaceutical Research Institute, PO Box 4000, Princeton, NJ 08545-4000, USA (office). *Telephone:* (607) 252-4716 (office).

CUSSLER, Clive Eric, PhD; American novelist; b. 15 July 1931, Aurora, Ill.; s. of Eric Cussler and Amy Hunnewell; m. Barbara Knight 1955; three c.; ed Pasadena

City Coll., Orange Coast Coll., California State Univ.; Owner, Bestgen & Cussler Advertising, Newport Beach, Calif. 1961–65; Copy Dir Darcy Advertising, Hollywood, Calif. and Instructor in Advertising Communications, Orange Coast Coll. 1965–67; Advertising Dir Aquatic Marine Corpn, Newport Beach, Calif. 1967–79; Vice-Pres. and Creative Dir of Broadcast, Meffon, Wolff and Weir Advertising, Denver, Colo 1970–73; Chair. Nat. Underwater and Marine Agency; Fellow, New York Explorers Club, Royal Geographical Soc.; Lowel Thomas Award, New York Explorers Club. *Publications include:* The Mediterranean Caper 1973, Iceberg 1975, Raise the Titanic 1976, Vixen O-Three 1978, Night Probe 1981, Pacific Vortex 1982, Deep Six 1984, Cyclops 1986, Treasure 1988, Dragon 1990, Sahara 1992, Inca Gold 1994, Shock Wave 1995, Sea Hunters 1996, Flood Tide 1997, Clive Cussler and Dirk Pitt Revealed 1997, Serpent 1998, Atlantis Found 1999, Blue Gold 2000, Valhalla Rising 2001, Fire Ice (with Paul Kemprecos) 2002, Sea Hunters II 2002, The Golden Buddha (with Craig Dirgo) 2003, White Death 2003, Trojan Odyssey 2003, Black Wind (with Dirk Cussler) 2004, Sacred Stone 2005, Lost City (with Paul Kemprecos) 2006, Skeleton Coast 2006, Treasure of Khan (with Dirk Cussler) 2006, Dark Watch (with Jack Du Brul) 2007, The Chase 2007, Polar Shift 2007, Plague Ship 2008, Arctic Drift 2008, Corsair (with Jack du Brul) 2009, Medusa (with Paul Kemprecos) 2009, Spartan Gold (with Grant Blackwood) 2009, The Wrecker (with Justin Scott) 2009, The Silent Sea (with Jack du Brul) 2010, The Adventures of Hotsy Totsy 2010, The Spy (with Justin Scott) 2010, Lost Empire (with Grant Blackwood) 2010, Crescent Dawn (with Dirk Cussler) 2010, The Race (with Justin Scott) 2011, Devil's Gate (with Graham Brown) 2011, The Kingdom (with Grant Blackwood) 2011, The Jungle (with Jack Du Brul) 2011, Serpent (with Paul Kemprecos) 2011. *Leisure interests:* discovering shipwrecks, collecting classic cars. *Address:* c/o Penguin Group (USA) Inc., Putnam Publicity, 375 Hudson Street, New York, NY 10014, USA. *Website:* www.penguin.com.

CUTHBERT, Alan William, BPharm, BSc, MA, PhD, ScD, FRS, FMedSci; British academic; *Shield Professor Emeritus of Pharmacology, Department of Medicine, University of Cambridge;* b. 7 May 1932, Peterborough, Cambs., England; s. of the late Thomas William Cuthbert and Florence Mary Cuthbert (née Griffin); m. Harriet Jane Webster 1957; two s.; ed Deacons Grammar School, Peterborough, Leicester Coll. of Tech., Univs of St Andrews and London; Reader in Pharmacology, Univ. of Cambridge 1973–79, Shield Prof. of Pharmacology 1979–99, Prof. Emer. 1999–; Master, Fitzwilliam Coll. Cambridge 1991–99, Hon. Fellow 1999; Deputy Vice-Chancellor Univ. of Cambridge 1995–99; Gov. De Montfort Univ. 1998–2005; Chair. Editorial Bd British Journal of Pharmacology 1974–82; Vice-Pres. Ephar 1997–2002, Pres. 2002–04; Foreign Sec. British Pharmacological Soc. 1997–2000, Hon. mem. 2000; mem. Academia Europaea 2000, Acad. Royale de Médecine de Belgique; Fellow, Jesus Coll. Cambridge 1968–91, Hon. Fellow 1991–; Hon. Fellow, Academia Europaea 2004; Hon. DSc (De Montfort Univ., Aston Univ.), Hon. LLD (Dundee); Wellcome Gold Medal 2005. *Publications:* numerous articles on physiology, pharmacology and biology. *Leisure interests:* painting, sculpture, photography, gardening, travel. *Address:* Department of Medicine, University of Cambridge, Addenbrooke's Hospital, Hills Road, Cambridge, CB2 3QQ (office); 7 Longstanton Road, Oakington, Cambridge, CB4 5BB, England (home). *Telephone:* (1223) 336853 (office); (1223) 233676 (home). *Fax:* (1223) 336846 (office). *E-mail:* awc1000@cam.ac.uk (office). *Website:* www.med.cam.ac.uk (office).

CUTIFANI, Mark, BSc (Eng); Australian business executive; *Chief Executive, Anglo American plc;* ed Wollongong Univ.; held sr exec. positions with Normandy Group, Sons of Gwalia, Western Mining Corpn, Kalgoorlie Consolidated Gold Mines and CRA (Rio Tinto); COO Vale Inco, responsible for global nickel business –2007; CEO AngloGold Ashanti Ltd 2007–13; Chief Exec. Anglo American plc 2013–; mem. Bd of Dirs and Group Man. Cttee and Chair. De Beers 2013–; Pres. South African Chamber of Mines; mem. Int. Advisory Cttee, Kellogg Innovation Network (USA); mem. Exec. Cttee and Treas. Int. Council on Mining and Metals; mem. Mining & Metals Steering Bd and Gov., Mining and Metals Industry Programme, World Econ. Forum. *Address:* Anglo American plc, 20 Carlton House Terrace, London, SW1Y 5AN, England (office). *Telephone:* (20) 7968-8888 (office). *Fax:* (20) 7968-8500 (office). *E-mail:* info@angloamerican.com (office). *Website:* www.angloamerican.com (office).

CUTTAREE, Hon. Jayakrishna, BSc, MSc, PhD; Mauritian lawyer and politician; ed Univ. of Edinburgh, UK, Uppsala Univ., Sweden, Univ. of Cambridge, UK; called to the Bar, Lincoln's Inn, London, UK; fmr Asst Conservator of Forests, Ministry of Agric. and Natural Resources; fmr Gen. Man. Sugar Planters' Mechanical Pool Corpn; fmr Chief of Natural Resources Div., OAU, Addis Ababa, Ethiopia; fmr Programme Specialist (Research and Devt in Natural Resources), UNESCO, Paris, France; mem. Legis. Ass. 1982–; Minister of Labour and Industrial Relations 1982–83, Attorney-Gen. and Minister of Housing, Lands, Town and Country Planning 1991, of Industry, Industrial Tech., Scientific Research and Handicraft 1996, of Industry and Commerce 1996–97, of Industry, Commerce and Int. Trade 2000–03, of Foreign Affairs, Int. Trade and Regional Co-operation 2003–05; Deputy Leader, Mouvement Militant Mauricien; Spokesman, Pacific Common Market, Indian Ocean Comm. and Pacific Forum at WTO meeting, Doha, Qatar 2001; led negotiations between EU and African Pacific Caribbean countries under Cotonou Agreement 2002; Spokesman of African Union at WTO meeting, Cancun, Mexico 2003; Head of Mauritian Del. and Spokesman of the African Union at Africa Growth and Opportunity Act (AGOA) Conf., Washington, DC, 2003. *Address:* c/o Mouvement Militant Mauricien, 21 Poudrière St, Port Louis, Mauritius. *Telephone:* 212-6553. *Fax:* 208-9939. *Website:* mmm.mmmonline.org.

CUTTS, Simon; British artist, poet and publisher; *Director, Coracle Press;* b. 30 Dec. 1944, Derby; s. of George Tom Cutts and Elizabeth Purdy; m. 1st Annira Uusi-Illikainen (divorced 1973); one s.; m. 2nd Margot Hapgood (died 1985); ed Herbert Strutt Grammar School, Belper, Derbyshire, Nottingham Coll. of Art, Trent Polytechnic; travel and miscellaneous employment including The Trent Bookshop, Nottingham 1962–69; Jt Ed. Tarasque Press 1964–72; publishing, lecturing and writing 1972–74; Dir and Co-Partner Coracle Press Books (now Coracle Press) 1975–87, 1996–, Dir, Coracle Press Gallery 1983–86; Dir Victoria Miro Gallery 1985–; org. of exhbns in Europe and New York. *Publications:* Quelques Pianos 1976, Pianostool Footnotes 1983, Petits-Airs for Margot 1986, Seepages 1988, The Rubber Stamp Mini Printer 1993, 1995, After Frank O'Hara and Morton Feldman

(with Erica van Horn) 1996, The A. Goldsworthy Questionnaires 1997, A Smell of Printing 2000, Eclogues 2004, A English Dictionary of French Place Names 2004, Ceillets des Poètes 2005, Some Forms of Availability 2006, As If It Is At All 2007, Some More Notes on Writing & Drinking 2010, The Manifestation of the Poem 2011, 8 Old Irish Potatoes 2011, Six Jugs (co-author) 2011, Affinity 2011. *Leisure interests:* walking, running, cooking, eating, drinking and the nostalgia of innocence. *E-mail:* books@coracle.ie (office); coraclepress@eircom.net (office). *Website:* www.coracle.ie (office).

CVETKOVIĆ, Mirko, MA, PhD; Serbian economist and politician; b. 16 Aug. 1950, Zaječar; s. of Srboljub Cvetković and Stana Cvetković; m. Zorica Cvetković; two c.; ed Faculty of Econs, Univ. of Belgrade; began career as economist at Inst. of Mining and Inst. of Econs; consultant, CES MECON (advisory and research firm); fmr foreign consultant on World Bank projects in Pakistan, India and Turkey; Econ. Adviser, Inst. of Mining 1998–2001; Deputy Minister of Economy and Privatization 2001–04; Dir Privatization Agency 2003–04; apptd Special Adviser to CEO Intercom Consulting/CES MECON 2005; Minister of Finance 2007–08, 2011–12; Prime Minister 2008–12. *Publications:* several papers and articles on privatization published in Serbia and abroad. *Leisure interests:* playing piano, saxophone and clarinet. *Address:* c/o Office of the Prime Minister, 11000 Belgrade, Nemanjina 11, Serbia.

CVIJANOVIĆ, Željka, MA; Bosnia and Herzegovina academic and politician; *Prime Minister of Republika Srpska;* b. (Željka Grabovac), 1967, Teslić; m.; two c.; ed Faculty of Philosophy, Sarajevo, Faculties of Philosophy and of Law, Banja Luka; Prof. of English Language and Literature; worked as Sr Interpreter and later an Asst to EU Mission in Bosnia and Herzegovina, as an Adviser to Prime Minister of Republika Srpska for European Integration and Co-operation with Int. Orgs, as Head of Republika Srpska Co-ordination and European Integration Unit in Office of the Prime Minister, and as Chief of Staff to the Prime Minister of Republika Srpska; mem. Alliance of Ind. Social Democrats; mem. Nat. Ass. of Republika Srpska, mem. Expert Group to Cttee for European Integration and Regional Co-operation; Minister of Econ. Relations and Regional Co-operation –2013; Prime Minister of Republika Srpska 2013–. *Address:* Office of the Prime Minister of Republika Srpska, 78000 Banja Luka, trg Republike Srpske 1, Bosnia and Herzegovina (office). *Telephone:* (51) 339102 (office). *Fax:* (51) 339119 (office). *E-mail:* kabinet@vladars.net (office). *Website:* www.vladars.net (office).

CYPRIANO, Márcio Artur Laurelli, JD; Brazilian banker; b. 20 Nov. 1943; ed Mackenzie Presbyterian Univ.; began career with Banco da Bahia SA 1967; joined Banco Bradesco SA 1973, Dept Dir 1984–86, Asst Dir 1986–88, Man. Dir 1988–95, Dir and Vice-Pres. 1995–99, Pres. and CEO 1999–2009, mem. Exec. Cttee 2002–; Dir Fed. of Brazilian Banking Asscn (FEBRABAN) 2001–, Pres. of the Bd 2002–09; Dir Bradespar SA 2002–; Dir Serasa SA 1984–86, Empresas BCN 1998–99. *Address:* Banco Bradesco SA, Cidade de Deus, Predio Novo 4 andar, Sao Paulo 06029-900, Brazil (office). *Telephone:* (11) 3684-9229 (office). *Fax:* (11) 3684-4570 (office). *E-mail:* info@bradesco.com.br (office). *Website:* www.bradesco.com.br (office).

CYRULNIK, Boris; French doctor, ethologist, neurologist and psychiatrist; *Director of Teaching, Faculty of Arts and Social Sciences, Université du Sud – Toulon-Var;* b. 26 July 1937, Bordeaux; s. of Aaron Cyrulnik and Nadia Cyrulnik, orphaned and raised by a foster family; m. Florence Cyrulnik; one s. one d.; ed Univ. of Paris; escaped capture by Nazis in Bordeaux during World War II, then worked as a farm labourer until the end of the war; studied medicine; now Dir of Teaching, Faculty of Arts and Social Sciences, Univ. of the South, Toulon-Var; Prix Renaudot de l'essai 2008, Prix des Droits de l'Homme 2013. *Publications include:* author of several books on popular psychology, including La Naissance du sens 1992 (translated as The Dawn of Meaning 1998), Le Murmure des fantômes 2003 (translated as The Whispering of Ghosts: Trauma and Resilience 2005), Parler d'amour au bord du gouffre 2004 (translated as Talking of Love on the Edge of a Precipice 2007), Resilience: How Your Inner Strength Can Set You Free from the Past 2011. *Address:* UFR de Lettres et Sciences Humaines, Université du Sud – Toulon-Var, Campus de La Garde – Bâtiment Y, Avenue de l'Université, BP 20132, 83957 La Garde Cedex, France (office). *Telephone:* (4) 94-14-20-26 (office). *Fax:* (4) 94-14-20-90 (office). *E-mail:* info@univ-tln.fr (office); cyrulnik.boris@orange.fr (home). *Website:* www.univ-tln.fr (office).

CYWIŃSKA, Izabella, MA; Polish theatre producer and director; *Artistic Director, Athenaeum Theatre, Warsaw;* b. 22 March 1935, Kamień; d. of Andrzej Cywiński and Elżbieta Łuszczewska; m. Janusz Michałowski 1968; ed Warsaw Univ., State Acad. of Drama, Warsaw; Asst, Rural Architecture Faculty, Warsaw Univ. of Tech. 1956–58; Stage Dir, Theatre in Cracow-Nowa Huta 1966–68, Polski Theatre, Poznań 1966–68; Dir and Artistic Man. Wojciech Bogusławski Theatre, Kalisz 1969–73, Nowy Theatre, Poznań 1973–88; Vice-Pres. Understanding Cttee of Creative Circles, Poznań 1980–81; Minister of Culture and Art 1989–91; Founder and Vice-Pres. Culture Foundation 1991–93; Artistic Dir 50th Anniversary of the Revolt in the Warsaw Ghetto; currently Artistic Dir, Athenaeum Theatre, Warsaw; mem. Polish Stage Artists' Asscn, Presidential Council for Culture 1992–95, Gen. Ass. European Cooperation Foundation, Brussels; Minister of Culture and Art Award (Second class) 1977; Kts Cross of Polonia Restituta Order; All-Poland Drama Festivals, Kalisz 1970, 1973, 1980, Opole 1976, Wrocław 1976, Medal Kalos Kagathos, Gold Cross of Merit, Nat. Educ. Comm. Medal, Nat. Broadcasting Council of Poland Award 1999, Special Prix Europa Award 2000, Willy Brandt Award, Prix Europa Int. TV Festival, Berlin 2000. *Plays directed include:* Iphigenie auf Tauris 1968, The Morals of Mrs Dulska 1970, The Death of Tarelkin 1973, I giganti della montagna 1973, Lower Depths 1974, They 1975, Wijuny 1976, Bath-house 1978, Judas from Karioth 1980, The Accused: June '56 1981, Enemy of the People 1982, Dawn 1986, Virginity 1986, Cementeries 1988, Tartuffe 1989, Antygona in New York 1993, Hanemann 2002, Your Excellency 2006; also Dir in USA and USSR, I Leave You 2003. *TV films:* Frédéric's Enchantment (about Chopin) 1998, Purym's Miracle 1999. *Television productions include:* God's Lining (series) 1997, Beauty (TV theatre) (First Prize, Int. TV Festival, Plovdiv, Bulgaria 1997) 1998, Second Mother 1999, Touch (TV theatre) 2001, Marilyn Mongol (TV theatre) 2002, Bar World (TV theatre) 2003, God's Lining II (series) 2004, Lovers from Marona (feature film) 2004. *Publication:* Nagłe zastępstwo 1992. *Leisure interests:* foreign travel, politics. *Address:* ul. Jaracza 2, Warsaw (office); ul. Piwna 7A m. 5, 00-265 Warsaw, Poland (home). *Telephone:* (22)

635-32-33 (office). *Fax:* (22) 625-22-421; (22) 635-32-33 (home). *E-mail:* cywinska@hoga.pl (home); koordynacja@teatrateneum.pl.

CZIBERE, Tibor, Dr Ing; Hungarian engineer, politician and academic; *Professor Emeritus of Mechanical Engineering, University of Miskolc;* b. 16 Oct. 1930, Tapolca; s. of Jozsef Czibere and Maria Loppert; m. Gabriella Nagy 1956; two d.; ed Tech. Univ. of Heavy Industry, Miskolc; devt engineer at Ganz-MÁVAG Machine Works 1956; lecturer, Univ. of Miskolc 1963, Prof., Dept of Mechanical Eng 1968–88, Prof. Emer. 1989–, Dean of Mechanical Eng Faculty 1968–74, Rector 1978–86; Minister of Culture 1988–89; mem. Parl. 1983–85, 1988–90; Vice-Pres. Nat. Council of Patriotic People's Front 1985–89; mem. Local Editorial Council, Journal of Computational and Applied Mechanics; Corresp. mem. Hungarian Acad. of Sciences 1976, mem. 1985; Labour Order of Merit 1971, Star, Order of Merit, People's Repub. of Hungary 1986; Kossuth Prize 1962, Szetgyörgyi Albert Prize 1996, Szénchenyi Prize 2006. *Address:* Department of Fluid and Heat Engineering, University of Miskolc, 3515 Miskolc-Egyetemváros, Hungary (office). *Telephone:* (46) 365111 (office). *E-mail:* aramczt@gold.uni-miskolc.hu (office). *Website:* www.uni-miskolc.hu (office).

D

DA CÂMARA PESTANA, Carlos; Brazilian business executive; *Chairman, Itaúsa-Investimentos Itaú SA;* ed Universidade Clássica de Lisboa, Portugal; mem. Bd of Dirs Itaú Unibanco SA 1986–2003, Exec. Vice-Pres. 1986–90, CEO 1990–94, mem. Bd of Dirs Itaú Unibanco Holding SA 2003–08, Chair. Sept.–Nov. 2008, mem. Int. Advisory Bd 2003–09, Pres. Audit Cttee 2004–08, mem. Appointments and Compensation Cttee 2005–09, Pres. 2008–09, Vice-Chair. Itaúsa-Investimentos Itaú SA 2008–11, Chair. 2011–. *Address:* Itaúsa-Investimentos Itaú SA, Praça Alfredo Edydio de Souza Aranha 100, Torre Itaúsa, São Paulo 04344-902, SP, Brazil (office). *Telephone:* (11) 5019-1677 (office). *Fax:* (11) 5019-1114 (office). *E-mail:* info@itausa.com.br (office). *Website:* www.itausa.com.br (office).

DA COSTA, Zacarias; Timor-Leste politician; m. Milena Pires; served as Conselho Nacional da Resistência Timorense (CNRT) rep. to EU in Brussels, UN in Geneva –1999; fmr Vice-Pres. União Democrática Timorense; Co-founder Partido Social Democrata (PSD) 2000, held several posts including Gen.-Sec., Pres. Nat. Congress and Nat. Chair.; consultant for Asian Bank of Devt; Minister of Foreign Affairs 2007–12. *Address:* c/o Ministry of Foreign Affairs and Cooperation, GPA Building 1, Ground Floor, Rua Avenida Presidente Nicolau Lobato, PO Box 6, Dili, Timor-Leste (office).

DA COSTA FLORES, Ricardo José, BA, MBA; Brazilian business executive; *Chairman, Vale SA;* ed Escola de Administração de Empresas, Fundação Getulio Vargas, EBAP-FGV; mem. Bd Banco do Brasil SA 2009–, Vice-Pres., Credit, Accounting & Global Risk 2009–, served as its Vice-Pres. of Credit Controlling and Risk Man. and Dir of Insurance, Pensions and Capitalization; mem. Bd of Dirs and Chair. Vale SA 2010–; Pres. Federação Nacional de Capitalização (Fenacap); Vice-Pres. Confederação Nacional das Empresas de Seguros Gerais, Previdência Privada e Vida, Saúde Suplementar e Capitalização (CNSeg); Pres. Caixa de Previdência dos Funcionários do Banco do Brasil (PREVI—largest pension fund in Latin America); Head of Industry Rep. Group – FenaCap, Banco Bradesco SA; fmr mem. Bd of Exec. Officers Federação Brasileira de Bancos (Febraban); fmr Exec. Man. Assets Restructuring Unit and Dir of Operational Assets Restructuring of Ativos SA– Financial Credit Security, fmr Pres. Bd of Dirs; Chair. Brasilcap Capitalização SA; fmr Chair. Banco Nossa Caixa. *Address:* Vale SA, Av. Graça Aranha, 26, 20030-900 Rio de Janeiro RJ, Brazil (office). *Telephone:* (21) 3814-4477 (office). *Fax:* (21) 3814-4040 (office). *E-mail:* info@vale.com (office). *Website:* www.vale.com (office).

DA CRUZ VILAÇA, José Luís, LLM, PhD; Portuguese judge, lawyer and professor of law; *Partner, PLMJ – A.M. Pereira, Sáragga Leal, Oliveira Martins, Júdice e Associados;* b. 20 Sept. 1944, Braga; s. of Fernando da Costa Vilaça and Maria das Dores G. Cruz Vilaça; m. Marie-Charlotte Opitz 1995; two s. two d. (three c. from previous m.); ed Univ. of Coimbra, Univ. of Paris I, France, Univ. of Oxford, UK, Fordham Univ., New York, USA; Asst Faculty of Law, Univ. of Coimbra 1966, Prof. of Fiscal Law and Community Law 1979; mil. service, Naval Legal Dept 1969–72; mem. Parl. 1980–86; Sec. of State for Home Affairs 1980, for Presidency of Council of Ministers 1981, for European Affairs 1982; Advocate-Gen. Court of Justice of EC 1986–89; Full Prof. and Dir Inst. for European Studies, Lusiada Univ. Lisbon 1988–2000; Pres. Court of First Instance of EC 1989–95; Partner and Head of Competition Practice, PLMJ – A.M. Pereira, Sáragga Leal, Oliveira Martins, Júdice e Associados (law firm), Lisbon 1996–; Visiting Prof. Univ. Nova de Lisboa 2001–; Chair. Disciplinary Bd of EC 2003–07; Prof., Portuguese Catholic Univ., Lisbon 2004–; Pres. Portuguese Asscn of European Law (APDE) 2008–; Gran Croce, Ordine di Merito (Italy), Grand-Croix, Couronne de Chêne (Luxembourg), Officier, Légion d'honneur, Grã-Cruz, Ordem do Infante (Portugal). *Publications include:* À empresa cooperativa 1969, L'économie portugaise face à l'intégration économique européenne 1978, Introdução ao estudo da Economia 1979, Modelo económico da CEE e modelo económico português 1984, Y a-t-il des limites matérielles à la révision des traités? 1993, The Development of the Community Judicial System Before and After Maastricht 1994, La procédure en référé comme instrument de protection juridictionnelle des particuliers en droit communautaire 1998, Código da União Europeia 2001, On the Application of Keck in the Field of Free Provision of Services 2002, Código da Concorrência 2004, The Precautionary Principle in EC Law 2004, How Far Should National Courts Go in Drawing All the Necessary Inferences from the Last Sentence of Article 88(3) EC? 2005, Regional Selectivity and State Aid: The Azores Case 2006, Competition Law – Portuguese Law: An Overview 2007, Material and Geographical Selectivity in State Aid – Recent Developments: A Personal View 2009. *Leisure interests:* tennis, gardening, literature. *Address:* PLMJ – A.M. Pereira, Sáragga Leal, Oliveira Martins, Júdice e Associados, Avenida da Liberdade 224, 1250-148 Lisbon, Portugal (office). *Telephone:* (213) 197321 (office). *Fax:* (213) 197319 (office). *E-mail:* jcv@plmj.pt (office). *Website:* www.plmj.com (office).

DA GRAÇA VERÍSSIMO DA COSTA, Desidério; Angolan politician; b. 4 April 1934, Luanda; s. of Fernando Pascoal da Costa; m.; five c.; ed Montanuniversität Leoben, Austria, studies in Petroleum Man. in Cambridge, Mass, USA; went to school in Portugal and later sought refuge in FRG from prosecution by Polícia Internacional e Defesa do Estado secret police, prepared to study medicine, then served for several years as pres. of asscn of students from Portuguese colonies with seat in Morocco, before turning to study of petroleum eng; mem. Angolan Nat. Comm. for Restructuring the Petroleum Industry 1976–77; Gen. Deputy Dir Sonangol 1977–79; Nat. Dir of Petroleum 1982–84; Vice-Minister of Petroleum 1984–2002, Minister of Petroleum 2002–08; Chair. African Petroleum Producers Asscn 2005–06. *Address:* c/o Ministry of Petroleum, Av. 4 de Fevereiro, Luanda, Angola (office).

DA GRAÇA VIEGAS SANTIAGO, Ângela Maria, MSc; São Tomé and Príncipe politician; b. 14 Oct. 1961; ed Donetsk Univ., Ukraine, Bricham Int. Univ.; economist, Ministry of Econ. and Financial Affairs 1988–93; Dir Dept of Statistics and Econ. Studies, Banco Central de São Tomé e Príncipe 1997–98; prin. adviser to Minister of Planning and Finance 1999–2001; mem. Nat. Ass. 2002–, adviser to Prime Minister 2002–04; Minister of Finance and Planning 2008–10; mem. Movimento de Libertação de São Tomé e Príncipe–Partido Social Democrata

(MLSTP–PSD). *Address:* c/o Ministry of Planning and Finance, Largo Alfândega, CP 168, São Tomé, São Tomé and Príncipe (office).

DA SILVA, Luis Inácio (Lula) (see LULA DA SILVA, Inácio).

DA SILVA COSTA, Carlos; Portuguese economist and central banker; *Governor, Banco de Portugal;* b. 3 Nov. 1949; ed Oporto Univ., Univ. Paris I (Sorbonne) and Institut Européen d'Admin des Affaires (INSEAD), France; Lecturer, Faculty of Econs, Oporto Univ. 1973–86; joined Banco Português do Atlântico (now Banco Comercial Português) 1978, Head of Dept for Research on Portuguese Economy 1981–85; Coordinator, Econ. and Financial Affairs Dept, Perm. Mission to EU, Brussels, also mem. EU Econ. Policy Cttee 1986–92; Prof., European Studies Centre, Portuguese Catholic Univ. of Oporto 1986–2000; mem. Portuguese Higher Council for Reform of Financial System 1988–92; Head of Cabinet of European Commr João de Deus Pinheiro 1993–99, with responsibility for Communication, Culture and Audiovisual Policies 1993–94, for EU cooperation policy with Africa, the Caribbean and the Pacific 1995–99; Exec. Dir, Caixa Geral de Depósitos 2004–06, also Chair. Caixa Geral de Aposentações, Banco Nacional Ultramarino SA, Macao; Pres. Banco Caixa Geral (Spain) 2004–06; Vice-Pres. EIB 2006–10 (now Hon. Vice-Pres.); Gov. Banco de Portugal 2010–; Chair. Nat. Council of Financial Supervisors; Vice-Pres. European MANUFUTURE High Level Group 2005–06; Visiting Full Prof., Portuguese Catholic Univ. of Oporto, Univ. of Aveiro; mem. Governing Council and Gen. Council, European Central Bank; mem. Gen. Bd European Systemic Risk Bd; mem. Financial Stability Bd, Regional Consultative Group for Europe; mem. Bd of Dirs Unibanco Holdings SA, Brazil Jan.–Aug. 2005; Dir (non-exec.) Nat. Statistical Inst. 1990–92; Grand Officer, Order of Prince Henry the Navigator. *Address:* Office of the Governor, Banco de Portugal, Rua do Ouro 27, 1100-150 Lisbon, Portugal (office). *Telephone:* (21) 3213200 (office). *Fax:* (21) 3464843 (office). *E-mail:* info@bportugal.pt (office). *Website:* www.bportugal.pt (office).

DAAN, Serge, PhD, FRSC; Dutch biologist and academic; *Niko Tinbergen Professor of Behavioural Biology and Dean, Faculty of Mathematical and Natural Sciences, University of Groningen;* b. 11 June 1940, Mook; m. Ruth Hohe-Daan 1982; three c.; ed Gymnasium β, Deventer, Univ. of Amsterdam; Postdoctoral Fellow, Max Planck Inst. for Behavioural Physiology, Andechs, Germany; Postdoctoral Fellow, Stanford Univ., Calif., USA 1973–75; Sr Scientist, Zoological Lab., Univ. of Groningen 1975–85, Assoc. Prof. of Animal Ecology and Ethology 1985–90, Assoc. Prof. of Chronobiology 1994–96, Prof. of Ethology 1996–2004, Niko Tinbergen Prof. of Behavioural Biology 2003–, Vice-Dean for Research, Faculty of Math. and Natural Sciences 2001–04, Dean 2004–, Coordinator Topmaster programme in Behavioural and Cognitive Neurosciences; mem. Bd Earth and Life Sciences, Netherlands Org. for Scientific Research (NWO) 1997–2002, Chair. NWO program, Evolution and Behaviour 2002–; Pres. Dutch Soc. for Behavioural Biology 1996–2001; has served on numerous nat. and int. cttees and editorial bds; mem. Dutch Soc. of Sciences 1999; mem. Bd Dobberke Foundation for Biological Psychology, Amsterdam Advisory Bd, Institut für Vogelforschung, Wilhelmshaven Advisory Bd, Otto Creutzfeld Centre for Cognitive and Behavioural Neuroscience, Münster Editorial Bd, Journal of Biological Rhythms Editorial Bd, International Journal of Zoology; Chair. Leonardo da Vinci Foundation; Kt, Order of the Dutch Lion 2004; Victor and Erna Hasselblad Award 1982, Eighth Laurence Irving-Per Scholander Memorial Lecturer, Univ. of Alaska 1990, Prize of Dutch Soc. for Light Therapy 1992, Alexander von Humboldt Research Prize 1992, Niko Tinbergen Lecturer, London 1996, First Colin S. Pittendrigh Lecturer, Florida 1998, Int. Prize for Biology, Japan Soc. for the Promotion of Science 2006, Award for Eminent Scientists, Japan Soc. for the Promotion of Science 2008. *Achievements include:* contributed several key concepts and models, including 'circadian' (c. 24-h) rhythms of rest and activity, the regulation of human sleep, and the annual timing of reproduction. *Publications:* The Prudent Parent (with R. H. Drent) 1980; more than 250 scientific papers in professional journals on the temporal organization of behaviour in animals and humans. *Address:* Room 5161.0504, Faculty of Mathematics and Natural Sciences, University of Groningen, Nijenborgh 9, 9747 AG Groningen, The Netherlands (office). *Telephone:* (50) 363-46-15 (Sec.) (office). *E-mail:* s.daan@rug.nl (office). *Website:* www.rug.nl (office); www.rug.nl/biologie/onderzoek/onderzoekgroepen/gedragsbiologie/index (office).

DABBAGH, Amr Abdullah al-, BA; Saudi Arabian business executive; b. 1966; ed King Abdulaziz Univ., Jeddah, John F. Kennedy School of Govt, Harvard Univ. and Wharton School, Univ. of Pennsylvania, USA; CEO and Pres. Dabbagh Group 1991–2004; Gov. and Chair. Saudi Arabian Gen. Investment Authority 2004–12; Founding Chair. Global Competitiveness Forum, Stars Foundation 2001–; mem. World Econ. Forum, London Business School Middle East Regional Advisory Bd; fmr Chair. Jeddah Econ. Forum, Jeddah Marketing Bd; fmr mem. Bd Harvard Inst. for Social and Econ. Policy in the Middle East, Kennedy School of Govt; Arabian Business Magazine Man of the Year 2005, World Econ. Forum Global Leader of Tomorrow, 12th Arab Econ. Forum Leadership Award. *Address:* c/o Stars Foundation, 11 Belgrave Road, London, SW1V 1RB, England.

DABDOUB, Ibrahim Shukri; Palestinian banking executive; *CEO, National Bank of Kuwait;* b. 1938, Jerusalem; m. Hilda Dabdoub; one s. (deceased) one d.; ed Collège des Frères, Bethlehem, Middle East Tech. Univ. Ankara, Turkey, Stanford Univ., USA; joined Nat. Bank of Kuwait (NBK) 1961, Head of Credit 1969, Deputy CEO 1981, CEO 1983–, Group CEO 2008–; Chair. Nat. Bank of Kuwait Investment Management, London, Nat. Bank of Kuwait (Banque Privée Suisse) SA, Geneva, Nat. Bank of Kuwait (Lebanon) SAL, Beirut; Vice-Chair. Nat. Bank of Kuwait (International) PLC, London; Dir, Jordan Mobile Telephone Services Co., Centre for Contemporary Arab Studies, Georgetown Univ., Washington DC; mem. Int. Advisory Bd Council on Foreign Relations, Arab Thought Forum, Jordan; mem. Bd of Trustees Kuwait Maastricht Business School; mem. Arab Business Council, World Econ. Forum, Geneva; fmr Dir Inst. of Int. Finance, Washington, DC; Banker of the Year, Arab Bankers Asscn of N America 1995, Arab Banker of the Year, Union of Arab Banks 1997, Euromoney Award for Outstanding Contrib. to Devt of Financial Services in the Middle East 2005, The Banker (magazine) Lifetime Achievement Award 2009, ranked by Arabian Business amongst its

Power 500: The World's Most Influential Arabs (30th) 2012. *Leisure interests:* fishing, reading. *Address:* National Bank of Kuwait SAK, PO Box 95, 13001 Safat, Abdullah al-Ahmad Street, Kuwait City, Kuwait (office). *Telephone:* 22422011 (office). *Fax:* 22462469 (office). *E-mail:* webmaster@nbk.com (office). *Website:* www.nbk.com (office).

DABOUB, Juan José, PhD; Salvadorean politician and international organization official; led family-owned businesses for nearly a decade before joining Bd of CEL (electricity utility); fmr Pres. ANTEL (state-owned telecommunications co. which he privatized); served three different govts for 12 years and then returned to pvt. sector; fmr Chief of Staff to Pres. of El Salvador, co-ordinated donors and oversaw reconstruction of El Salvador after two earthquakes of 2001; Minister of Finance –2006; Man. Dir World Bank Group 2006–10. *Address:* c/o The World Bank Group, 1818 H Street, NW, Washington, DC 20433, USA. *Telephone:* (202) 473-1000. *E-mail:* pic@worldbank.org.

DĄBROWSKI, Waldemar; Polish arts administrator and fmr government official; *General Director, Teatr Wielki – Polish National Opera;* b. 23 Aug. 1951, Radzymin; ed Electronics Faculty, Warsaw Polytechnic, Exec. Programme for Leaders in Devt, Harvard Univ., USA; Founder and Dir, Riwiera-Remont student club 1973–78; Deputy Dir, Cultural Dept, City of Warsaw 1979–81; Co-Man., Warsaw Studio Art Centre 1982, produced more than 70 plays, co-f. Sinfonia Varsovia with Jerzy Maksymiuk and Yehudi Menuhin; Deputy Minister of Culture and Art and Head, Cttee of Cinematography 1990–94, Minister of Culture 2002–05; Pres. State Foreign Investment Agency 1994–98, conceived and created Vacation Festival of Stars in Miedzyzdroje (West Pomerania voivodship); Gen. Dir, Teatr Wielki – Polish Nat. Opera 1998–2002, 2008–; fmr Pres. Soc. for Encouragement of Fine Arts; fmr Vice-Pres. American-Polish-Israeli Foundation 'Shalom'; fmr Hon. Pres. Polish Golfing Asscn; Chevalier, Ordre des Arts et Lettres, Orderem Świętego Stanisława Pierwszej Klasy 2005; scholarships from British Council, Goethe Inst., US Dept of State; Merited for Warsaw Distinction, Warsaw City Council 2001. *Address:* Teatr Wielki–Opera Narodowa, Plac Teatralny 1, 00-950 Warsaw, Poland (office). *Telephone:* (22) 6920200 (office). *Fax:* (22) 8260423 (office). *E-mail:* office@teatrwielki.pl (office). *Website:* www.teatrwielki.pl (office).

DABWIDO, Sprent Jared; Nauruan politician and fmr head of state; b. 16 Sept. 1972; MP for Meneng constituency 2004–; Minister of Transport and Telecommunications 2007–11; Pres. of Nauru and Minister for Public Service, Police & Emergency Services, Home Affairs and Climate Changes 2011–13. *Address:* c/o Office of the President, Yaren, Nauru (office).

DACHEVILLE, Colette, (Stéphane Audran); French actress; b. 8 Nov. 1932, Versailles; d. of Corneille Dacheville and Jeanne Rossi; m. 1st Jean-Louis Trintignant; m. 2nd Claude Chabrol 1964; one s.; ed Lycée Lamartine, Paris, Cours Charles Dullin; studied drama under Tania Balachova and Michel Vitold; Commdr Légion d'honneur. *Films include:* Les bonnes femmes 1959, L'oeil du malin 1961, Landru 1962, Ligne de démarcation 1966, Champagne Murders 1966, Les biches 1968 (Best Actress, Berlin), La femme infidèle 1968, La peau de torpédo 1969, La dame dans l'auto avec les lunettes et un fusil 1969, Le boucher 1970 (Best Actress, San Sebastián), La rupture 1970, Aussi loin que l'amour 1970, Juste avant la nuit 1971, Without Apparent Motive 1971, Un meurtre est un meurtre 1972, Dead Pigeon on Beethoven Street 1972, Discreet Charm of the Bourgeoisie 1972 (Best Actress, Soc. of Film and TV Arts), Les noces rouges 1973, Comment réussir dans la vie quand on est con et pleurnichard 1973, Le cri du coeur 1974, Ten Little Indians 1974, B Must Die 1974, The Black Bird 1975, Vincent, François, Paul and Others 1975, Folies bourgeoises 1976, Silver Bears 1976, Devil's Advocate 1976, Violette Nozière 1978, Le Soleil en face 1979, The Big Red One 1980, Coup de Torchon 1981, Boulevard des assassins 1982, Le choc 1982, On ira tous au paradis, Le sang des autres 1983, Poulet au vinaigre 1984, Babette's Feast 1988 (Best Actress, Taormina), La Cage aux Folles III: The Wedding, Manika: The Girl Who Lived Twice 1989, Quiet Days in Clichy 1989, Betty 1991, The Turn of the Screw 1994, Au petit Marguery 1995, Maximum Risk 1996, Arlette 1997, Madeline 1998, Belle maman 1999, Le Pique-nique de Lulu Kreutz 2000, J'ai faim!!! 2001, Ma femme... s'appelle Maurice 2002, The Girl from Monaco 2008. *TV appearances in:* Brideshead Revisited 1981, Mistral's Daughter 1984, The Sun Also Rises 1984, Poor Little Rich Girl 1986, Tecx 1989, Cry No More My Lady 1992, Le Droit à l'oubli 1992, L'Évanouie 1994, Petit 1996, Un printemps de chien 1997, La Bicyclette bleue 2000, Sissi, l'impératrice rebelle 2004, La Battante 2005, Trois Femmes: un soir d'été 2005, The Condor Mystery (mini-series) 2005. *Address:* c/o 2F De Marthod, 11 rue Chanez, 75016 Paris, France.

DACI, Nexhat, MA, PhD; Kosovo politician and academic; *University Professor, University of Priština;* b. 26 July 1944, Tërnoc, Serbia and Montenegro (now in Kosovo); m. Zineta Daci; one s. two d.; ed Univs of Belgrade and Zagreb, also educated in UK and Belgium; Univ. Prof., Univ. of Priština 1983–; Pres. and Sec., Kosovo Acad. of Sciences and Arts 1995–2002; Pres. of Kosovo Ass. 2001–06; Acting Pres. of Kosovo Jan.-Feb. 2006; mem. Democratic League of Kosovo, European Acad. for the Environment, American Chem. Asscn. *Publications:* four text books, ten scientific projects and more than 100 scientific publs. *Address:* Velania 18/IV, Priština, Kosovo (home). *Telephone:* (38) 249303 (office); (38) 229964 (office). *Fax:* (38) 244636 (office). *E-mail:* ashak@ashak.org (office). *Website:* www.ashak.org (office).

DAČIĆ, Ivica; Serbian politician; *Minister of Foreign Affairs;* b. 1 Jan. 1966, Prizren, Kosovo; m. Sonja Dačić; one s. one d.; ed Faculty of Political Science, Univ. of Belgrade; Pres. Socialist Youth Brigade, Belgrade 1990; Deputy, Fed. Ass. of Yugoslavia 1992–2004; mem. Socialist Party of Serbia (SPS), Party Spokesman 1992–2000, Vice-Chair. 2000–03, Pres. 2006–; mem. Nat. Ass. of Serbia 2007–; mem. Parl. Ass., Council of Europe, Brussels 2003–04, 2006–, mem. Cttee on Culture, Science and Educ., on Equal Opportunities for Women, on Migration, Refugees and Population; unsuccessful cand. in Serbian presidential election 2004; Minister of Finance 2007–08; First Deputy Prime Minister 2008–12; Minister of Internal Affairs 2008–14; Prime Minister 2012–14; Minister of Foreign Affairs 2014–. *Address:* Ministry of Foreign Affairs, 11000 Belgrade, Kneza Miloša 24–26, Serbia (office). *Telephone:* ((11) 3616333 (office). *Fax:* (11) 2627170 (office). *E-mail:* mfa@mfa.rs (office). *Website:* www.mfa.gov.rs (office).

DACRE, Paul Michael, BA, FRSA; British newspaper editor; *Editor-in-Chief, Associated Newspapers;* b. 14 Nov. 1948, London, England; s. of Peter Dacre and Joan Dacre (née Hill); m. Kathleen Thomson 1973; two s.; ed Univ. Coll. School, London, Univ. of Leeds; reporter, feature writer, Assoc. Features Ed., Daily Express 1970–76, Washington and New York Corresp. 1976–79; New York Bureau Chief, Daily Mail 1980, News Ed., London 1981–85, Asst Ed. (News and Foreign) 1986, Asst Ed. (Features) 1987, Exec. Ed. 1988, Assoc. Ed. 1989–91, Ed. Daily Mail 1992–, Ed.-in-Chief Assoc. Newspapers 1998–; Ed. Evening Standard 1991–92; Dir Associated Newspaper Holdings 1991–; Daily Mail & General Trust PLC 1999–, Teletext Holdings Ltd 2000–02; Chair. Editors' Code of Practice Cttee 2008–; mem. Press Complaints Comm. 1998–2008, Press Bd of Finance 2004–, Govt Review into 30 Year Rule 2008; Amb. for Alzheimer's Soc. 2007; Hon. mem. Nat. Soc. for the Prevention of Cruelty to Children 2009; Cudlipp Lecturer, London Coll. of Commerce 2007. *Address:* Daily Mail, Northcliffe House, 2 Derry Street, London, W8 5TT, England (office). *Telephone:* (20) 7938-6000 (office). *Fax:* (20) 7937-7977 (office). *E-mail:* news@dailymail.co.uk (office). *Website:* www.dailymail.co.uk (office).

DADAE, Bob; Papua New Guinea politician; fmr Deputy Speaker of Parl.; Minister of Defence 2007–11; MP for Kabwum; Leader, United Party 2007, now mem. People's National Congress–. *Address:* c/o People's National Congress, POB 4172, Boroko, NCD, Papua New Guinea (office).

DADNADJI, Djimrangar Joseph, DEA; Chadian politician and fmr public servant; b. 1 Jan. 1954, Bebo-Pen, Mandoul Region; s. of Assingar Dadnadji and Lakoussal Sambaye; m.; 15 c.; ed Ecole Normale Supérieure d'Afrique Centrale, Fort-Lamy (now N'Djamena), Ecole Nat. d'Admin, N'Djamena, Univ. of N'Djamena, Univ. of Poitiers, France; joined civil service 1975, Head, Dept of Materials, Research and Legislation, Ministry of Interior and Security 1976–77, Acting Deputy Prefect, city of Kélo, Tandjilé Region 1977–79; Sec.-Gen. of Council, Koumra Town Hall 1980–82; Dir of Admin., Financial and Material Affairs, Ministry of Nat. Educ. 1988–91, Project Coordinator, Teacher Training Programme 1993–96, Dir-Gen., Ministry of Nat. Educ. 1996–2002; Minister of Planning, Devt and Cooperation 2002–03, of the Environment and Water 2003–04; Technical Adviser to Pres. for Legal and Admin. Affairs and Human Rights 2004–05; Sec.-Gen. of the Presidency 2005–08, 2009–10, Dir, Civil Cabinet of the Presidency 2008–09, 2012–13; Minister of Spatial Planning, Urban Planning and Housing 2010–11; Prime Minister Jan.–Nov. 2013; Founder mem. Nat. Union Party 1992; fmr univ. prof.; mem. Patriotic Salvation, mem. Nat. Political Bureau 2003–08, 2011–; Commdr, Ordre Nat. du Tchad, Chevalier des Palmes Académiques Françaises. *Address:* c/o Office of the Prime Minister, BP 463, N'Djamena, Chad.

DADOO, J. K., BA, MBA, LLB; Indian government official and civil servant; *Joint Secretary, Department of Commerce, Ministry of Commerce and Industry;* b. 10 Dec. 1957; ed St Stephen's Coll., Univ. of Delhi, Indian Inst. of Man., Ahmedabad, Indian Inst. of Foreign Trade, New Delhi; man. trainee, Procter & Gamble 1980–81; Br. Man., Core Parentals 1981–82; Sr Marketing Officer, Associated Cement Cos Ltd, Bombay 1983; joined Indian Admin. Service, AGMUT Cadre 1983, Sub-Divisional Magistrate, Delhi 1985–87, also functioned as Deputy Dir (Panchayat) and Admin. of Agricultural Produce Marketing Cttee of Najafgarh and Narela; Jt Sec., Planning and Devt, Govt of Arunachal Pradesh 1987–88; Deputy Commr in Lower Subansiri Dist 1988–89, Chair. Dist Rural Devt Agency and functioned as Dist and Sessions Judge; Sec., Gen. Admin, Personal Labour and Press in Arunachal 1990; Jt Sec. (Health), Delhi Admin 1990–91; Additional Commr, Sales Tax, Delhi 1991–94, also served as Dir Chit Funds; Additional Dir and Jt Sec. (Educ.), Govt of Delhi 1994–95; Sec. to Gov. of Goa with additional charge as Sec., Industry and Mines and Sec. (Power) (initiated process of privatization of power in Goa) 1995–96; Dir (Air Force), Dir (Resettlement) and Dir (Int. Co-operation), Ministry of Defence 1997–2000; Counsellor (Co-ordination), Embassy in Moscow 2000–04; Devt Commr for Daman Diu and Dadra Nagar Haveli, as Sec. of 14 Depts; Devt Commr of Goa 2005–06, Acting Chief Sec. of Goa on several occasions; Prin. Sec., Environment, Forests and Wildlife, Govt of Nat. Capital Territory of Delhi and also Chair. Delhi Pollution Control Cttee; Admin. of Union Territory of Lakshadweep 2009–11; Jt Sec., Dept of Commerce, Ministry of Commerce 2011–; Chair. Airfield Environment Man. Cttee of Delhi Airport, Sports Goods EPC; mem. various bds and insts, including High Court Cttee on Plastic Waste Man., Advisory Bd of The Energy Research Inst., Fed. of Indian Chambers of Commerce and Industry Task Force on Climate Change, Bd of Dirs of Bombay Suburban Electric Supply; mem. Bd, Delhi State Civil Supplies Corpn Ltd, Indian Inst. of Packaging, Indian Inst. of Foreign Trade, Nat. Centre for Trade Information, Export Promotion Councils of Computer Software, Telecom, Leather; mem. Governing Council, FIEO, Governing Council of Software Tech. Park of India (autonomous body under Dept of Electronics and Information Tech.), M-SIPS Appraisal Cttee of DeitY and Steering Cttee for Clusters of DeitY. *Address:* Department of Commerce, Ministry of Commerce and Industry, Udyog Bhawan, New Delhi 110 107, India (office). *Telephone:* (11) 23061971 (office). *Fax:* (11) 23063583 (office). *E-mail:* j.k.dadoo@nic.in (office). *Website:* commerce.nic.in (office).

DAERR, Hans-Joachim; German diplomatist; b. 22 Dec. 1943, Frankenstein, Schleswig; m. Alexa Daerr; two s.; ed Baccalauréat in Paris, France; nat. service in German Navy 1962–64, law studies in Tübingen, Bonn and Berlin 1964–68, Japanese studies, Tübingen 1969, joined Foreign Service 1970, Rep. to EC, Brussels 1970–71, posted to Consulate Gen., Osaka-Kobe 1973–76, NATO Dept, Foreign Office, Bonn 1976–79, Embassy in Tokyo 1979–83, Planning Staff, Foreign Office 1983–86, Head of Strategic Issues Opertions Staff 1986–87, Perm. Rep., Embassy in Lagos 1988–91, Head of S Africa Dept, Foreign Office 1991–95, Head of Subdivision 20 (NATO, WEU, OSCE, GASP, N America) and Deputy Political Dir 1995–98, Amb. to Pakistan 1998–2001, Rep. of Fed. Govt for Issues on Disarmament and Arms Control, Berlin 2001–02, Amb.-at-Large for Afghanistan 2001–02, Head of Dept for Global Issues, UN, Human Rights and Humanitarian Aid, Foreign Office, Berlin 2003–06, Amb. to Japan 2006–09. *Address:* c/o Embassy of Germany, 4-5-10, Minami Azabu, Minato-ku, Tokyo, 106-0047, Japan.

DAFA, Bader Omar ad-, MA; Qatari diplomatist and UN official; b. 2 Oct. 1950; m. Awatef Mohamed Al-Dafa; one s. two d.; ed Kalamazoo Community Coll., Western Michigan Univ., School of Advanced Int. Studies, Johns Hopkins Univ.,

USA; diplomatic attaché, Ministry of Foreign Affairs 1976–77, 1981–82; First Sec., Qatar Embassy, Washington, DC 1977–81; Amb. to Spain 1982–88, to Egypt (also Perm. Rep. to Arab League) 1988–93, to France (also accred to Greece and Switzerland) 1993–95, to Russia (also accred to Finland, Latvia, Lithuania and Estonia) 1995–98; Dir of European and American Affairs, Ministry of Foreign Affairs 1998–2000; Amb. to USA and Perm. Observer to OAS 2000–05, non-resident Amb. to Mexico 2002–07; Exec. Sec. UN Econ. and Social Comm. for Western Asia (ESCWA) 2007–10; mem. selection cttee, Takreem Arab Achievement Awards 2011–; Ordre nat. du Mérite. *Leisure interests:* reading, painting, music. *Address:* Selection Committee, TAKREEM Arab Achievement Awards, Asco Center, 5th floor, Sassine Square Ashrafieh, Beirut, Lebanon (office). *Telephone:* (1) 204787 (office). *Fax:* (1) 204789 (office). *E-mail:* info@takreemawards.com (office). *Website:* www.takreemawards.com (office).

DAFFA, Ali Abdullah ad-, BS, MS, PhD; Saudi Arabian mathematician and academic; *Professor, King Fahd University;* b. 1940, Unaizah; m.; four c.; ed Ohio Univ., Stephen F. Austin State Univ., Vanderbilt Univ., USA; Asst Prof. of Math., King Fahd Univ. of Petroleum and Minerals, Dhahran 1973–74, Chair. Dept of Math. 1974–77, Dean Coll. of Sciences 1977–84, Prof. of Math. and History of Pure Science 1980–; Visiting Prof., King Saud Univ., Riyadh 1979–82, Harvard Univ. 1981, Princeton Univ. 1991; Pres. Union of Arab Mathematicians and Physicists 1974–81, 1986–88, Supreme Council of Union of Arab Physicists and Mathematicians; mem. editorial Bd Encyclopedia of Islamic Civilization; mem. Int. Comm. on the History Science, Nat. Library Bd, Islamic Foundation for Science, Tech. and Devt, Bd of King Faisal for Islamic Research, Asscn of Muslim Scientist and Engineers, Asscn of Arab Scientists, The Arabic Acad. (Jordan), Islamic World Acad. of Science, Arabic Scientific Soc., American Math. Soc., British Soc. for History of Science; Hon. mem. Acad. of Arabic Language. *Publications:* 48 books and more than 250 articles on math. and history of science. *Address:* King Fahd University of Petroleum and Minerals, Dhahran 31261, Saudi Arabia (office). *Telephone:* (3) 860-0000 (office). *Fax:* (3) 860-3306 (office). *E-mail:* aldaffa@kfupm.edu.sa (office). *Website:* www.kfupm.edu.sa (office).

DAFOE, Willem; American actor; b. 22 July 1955, Appleton, Wis.; s. of William Dafoe; ed Univ. of Wisconsin; Lifetime Achievement Award, San Sebastian Film Festival 2005. *Films include:* The Loveless 1981, New York Nights 1981, The Hunger 1982, Communists are Comfortable (and three other stories) 1984, Roadhouse 66 1984, Streets of Fire 1984, To Live and Die in LA 1985, Platoon 1986, The Last Temptation of Christ 1988, Saigon 1988, Mississippi Burning 1989, Triumph of the Spirit 1989, Born on the 4th of July 1990, Flight of the Intruder 1990, Wild at Heart 1990, The Light Sleeper 1991, Body of Evidence 1992, Far Away, So Close 1994, Tom and Viv 1994, The Night and the Moment 1994, Clear and Present Danger 1994, The English Patient 1996, Basquiat 1996, Speed 2: Cruise Control 1997, Affliction 1997, Lulu on the Bridge 1998, eXistenZ 1998, American Psycho 1999, Shadow of the Vampire 2000, Bullfighter 2000, The Animal Factory 2000, Edges of the Lord 2001, Spider-Man 2002, Auto Focus 2002, Once Upon a Time in Mexico 2003, The Clearing 2004, The Reckoning 2004, The Life Aquatic with Steve Zissou 2004, The Aviator 2004, xXx: State of the Union 2005, Ripley Under Ground 2005, Manderlay 2005, Inside Man 2006, American Dreamz 2006, Paris, je t'aime 2006, The Walker 2007, Mr. Bean's Holiday 2007, Spider-Man 3 2007, Go Go Tales 2007, Anamorph 2007, Fireflies in the Garden 2008, Adam Resurrected 2008, I skoni tou hronou (The Dust of Time) 2008, Antichrist 2009, L'affaire Farewell 2009, My Son, My Son, What Have Ye Done 2010, The Hunter 2011, John Carter 2012. *Address:* c/o Widescreen Management, 270 Lafayette Street, Suite 402, New York, NY 10012; WME, 9601 Wilshire Blvd., Beverly Hills, CA 90210, USA.

DAFT, Douglas (Doug) N.; Australian business executive; b. 1944; joined Coca-Cola Co., Australia 1969, Pres. Cen. Pacific Div. 1984, N Pacific Div. 1988, Pres. Coca-Cola (Japan) Co. 1988, Pres. Pacific Group, Atlanta 1991, Head of Middle and Far East and Africa Groups, Head of Schweppes Div. 1999, Chair. and CEO 2000–04 (retd); mem. Bd of Dirs McGraw-Hill Ryerson Ltd 2003–, Wal-Mart Stores Inc. 2005–, Sistema-Hals; Chair. Advisory Bd Churchill Archives Center, Churchill Coll., Cambridge; mem. Advisory Bd Longreach, Inc., Tisbury Capital, Thomas H. Lee Partners; mem. European Advisory Council N.M. Rothschild & Sons Ltd; mem. Bd of Overseers Int. Business School, Brandeis Univ.; Patron American Australian Asscn; Trustee, Thunderbird School of Global Man., Cambridge Foundation. *Address:* c/o Board of Directors, Wal-Mart Stores Inc.,702 Southwest 8th Street, Bentonville, AR 72716, USA (office).

DAGAN, Maj.-Gen. (retd) Meir; Israeli army officer (retd), government official and business executive; *Chairman, Israel Ports Development and Assets Company;* b. (Meir Huberman), 1945, USSR; m.; three c.; family emigrated to Israel 1950; army officer, Head of Rimon undercover unit, Gaza Strip, early 1970s, mem. 143 Div., Yom Kippur War 1973, Commdr in S Lebanon 1982, Special Asst to Army Chief of Staff 1987–93, retd from army 1995; joined Mossad (Inst. for Intelligence and Special Operations) 1995, Deputy Dir 1995–97, Counter-Terrorism Adviser to Prime Minister 1997–2000, Head of Israeli negotiating team Nov. 2001, Dir Mossad 2002–10; Chair. Israel Ports Development and Assets Co. 2011–; several citations for bravery during army service. *Address:* Israel Ports Development and Assets Company, 74 Menachem Begin Road, Tel-Aviv -Jaffa, 67215, Israel. *Website:* eng.israports.co.il.

DAGHESTANI, Fakhruddin, PhD; Jordanian civil servant and engineer; b. 1936; m.; six c.; ed Univ. of Missouri, USA; Lecturer, Coll. of Eng, Univ. of Missouri 1961–67; Lecturer, IBM Rochester, Minn. 1968–71; Dir Mechanical Eng Dept, Royal Scientific Soc. 1971–76, Vice-Pres. 1976–83, Acting Pres. 1983–84, Pres. 1984–86, Adviser and Prin. Researcher 1986–91; Dir Centre for Int. Studies 1991–93, currently mem. Bd of Govs; Dir Gen. Natural Resources Authority 1993–96, Mineral Investment Co. 1998–; mem. Scientific Council Islamic Foundation for Science, Tech. and Devt 1984–86; mem. Exec. Cttee Org. of the Islamic Conf. Standing Cttee on Scientific and Technological Co-operation (COMSTECH) 1986–94; mem. Arab Fed. of Scientific Research 1983–86; Founding Fellow, Islamic Acad. of Sciences, mem. Council 1986–99; mem. Bd of Govs Telecommunications Corpn, Natural Resources Authority, Jordan Electricity Authority, Arab Potash Co., Nat. Petroleum Co., Jordan Phosphate Mining Co.; mem. Bd Faculties of Grad. Studies and Scientific Research, Jordan Univ.; mem. Editorial Bd Journal of the Islamic Academy of Sciences; fmr mem. Editorial Bd Islamic Thought and

Scientific Creativity (journal) 1990–95. *Publications:* ed. and co-ed. of 11 books, author of over 40 technical papers on applied mechanics. *Address:* c/o Royal Scientific Society, PO Box 1438, Al-Jubaiha 11941; PO Box 419, Al-Jubaiha 11941, Jordan (office).

DAGWORTHY PREW, Wendy Ann, OBE, BA; British fashion designer and academic; *Dean of the School of Material, Head of Fashion Programmes, Royal College of Art;* b. (Wendy Ann Dagworthy), 4 March 1950, Gravesend, Kent, England; d. of Arthur S. Dagworthy and Jean A. Stubbs; m. Jonathan W. Prew 1973; two s.; ed Medway Coll. of Design and Hornsey Coll. of Art; Founder, Designer and Dir Wendy Dagworthy Ltd (design co.) 1972–; Dir London Designer Collections 1982; consultant to CNAA Fashion/Textiles Bd 1982–; Course Dir Fashion BA Hons Degree, Central St Martin's Coll. of Art and Design 1989–, Prof. of Fashion 1998–; Prof. of Fashion and Head of Fashion Programmes, RCA 1998–, Dean of the School of Material 2011–; Judge, Royal Soc. of Arts Bd; judge of art and design projects for various mfrs; participating designer in Fashion Aid and many charity shows; exhibited seasonally in London, Milan, New York and Paris; Lecturer and External Assessor at numerous polytechnics and colls of art and design; frequent TV appearances; Hon. Fellow, Kent Inst. of Design, Univ. of the Creative Arts 2005; Fil d'Or Int. Linen Award 1986. *Leisure interests:* dining out, cooking, reading, painting, drawing. *Address:* Royal College of Art, Kensington Gore, London, SW7 2EU (office); 18 Melrose Terrace, London, W6 7RL, England (home). *Telephone:* (20) 7590-4444 (office); (20) 7602-6676 (home). *Fax:* (20) 7590-4360 (office). *E-mail:* wendy.dagworthy@rca.ac.uk (office). *Website:* www.rca.ac.uk (office).

DAHABI, Nader al-, MSc, MPA; Jordanian politician; b. 1946, Amman; m.; two s. one d.; ed Al Hussein Coll., Amman, Hellenic Air Force Acad., Tatoi, Greece, Cranfield Inst. of Tech., UK, Auburn Univ., USA; cadet in Royal Jordanian Air Force 1964, served 30 years becoming Asst Commdr for Logistics 1992–94; CEO Royal Jordanian Airlines 1994–2001; Minister of Transport 2001–03; Chief Commr Aqaba Special Econ. Zone Authority 2004–07; Prime Minister and Minister of Defence 2007–09 (resgnd); mem. Exec. Cttee Arab Air Carriers Org. (AACO), Chair. 1994–95; Chair. Royal Jordanian Air Falcons 1994–; Dir Royal Jordanian Acad.; mem. Higher Cttee Jerash Festival for Culture and Arts; mem. Higher Council of Tourism; Pres. IATA 1996–97, mem. Bd of Govs 1995–98. *Address:* c/o Office of the Prime Minister, POB 80, Amman 11180, Jordan (office).

DAHAL, Pushpa Kamal, (Prachanda), BSc (Agric.); Nepalese politician and fmr guerrilla leader; *Chairman, Unified Communist Party of Nepal (Maoist);* b. (Chhabilal Dahal), 11 Dec. 1954, Dhikure Pokhari, Kaski Dist; ed Inst. of Agric. and Animal Science, Rampur, Chitwan; once employed at rural devt project in Jajarkot sponsored by USAID; joined CP of Nepal (Fourth Convention) 1981, became Gen. Sec. (Leader) CP of Nepal (Mashal) 1989, later party renamed CP of Nepal (Maoist), lived underground after restoration of democracy in 1990, controlled clandestine wing of party, became internationally known (as Prachanda) as Leader of CPN (M), presiding over mil. and political wings 1996–, leader of Maoist insurgency 1996–2006, Chair. CPN (M) 2001–, negotiated with seven-party alliance, signed comprehensive peace agreement with Govt Nov. 2006, CPN (M) entered Parl. and Govt 2007, party merged with CPN (Unity Centre-Masal) to become Unified Communist Party of Nepal (Maoist) 2009; Prime Minister 2008–09 (resgnd). *Address:* Unified Communist Party of Nepal (Maoist), Central Office, Perishdanda-Koteshwor, Kathmandu, Nepal (office). *Telephone:* (1) 4602290 (office). *Fax:* (1) 4602289 (office). *E-mail:* ucpnminfo@gmail.com (office). *Website:* www.ucpnm.org.

DAHAN, René; Dutch business executive; *Chairman of the Supervisory Board, Royal Ahold NV;* b. 26 Aug. 1941; began career as process technician in refinery, Exxon Corpn, Rotterdam 1963, Man. Supply and Planning Dept, Esso Nederland 1973–74, Man. Refining Dept 1974–77, Head Corp. Planning Div., Esso Europe, London 1977–79, Man. Natural Gas Dept 1979-81, Deputy Man. Petroleum Products Dept, Exxon Corpn HQ, USA 1981–83, Exec. Vice-Pres. Esso BV, Breda 1983–85, Pres. and CEO Esso BV 1985–91, Exec. Vice-Pres. ECI 1991–92, Vice-Pres. Exxon Corpn 1992–95, Sr Vice-Pres. 1995–2001, Dir 1998–2001, Exec. Vice-Pres. Exxon Mobil Corpn 2001–04; Chair. Supervisory Bd Royal Ahold NV 2004–, Chair. Selection and Appointment Cttees; mem. Supervisory Bd VNU NV, TPG NV 2003–, Aegon NV; mem. Int. Advisory Bd, CVC Capital Partners, Inst. de Empresa; mem. Bd of Dirs, Jr Achievement Int.; mem. Bd Trustees, US Council for Int. Business. *Address:* Royal Ahold NV, Piet Heinkade 167–173, 1019 GM Amsterdam, The Netherlands (office). *Telephone:* (20) 509-51-00 (office). *Fax:* (20) 509-51-10 (office). *E-mail:* info@ahold.com (office). *Website:* www.ahold.com (office).

DAHL, Birgitta, BA; Swedish politician; b. 20 Sept. 1937, Råda; d. of Sven Dahl and Anna-Brita Axelsson; m. Enn Kokk; one s. two d.; ed Univ. of Uppsala; teacher, clerical officer, Scandinavian Inst. of African Studies, Uppsala 1960–65; Sr Admin. Officer, Dag Hammarskjöld Foundation 1965–68, Swedish Int. Devt Authority 1965–82; mem. Parl. 1968–2002; mem. Advisory Council of Foreign Affairs; del. to UN Gen. Ass.; mem. Exec. Cttee Social Democratic Party 1975–96; Minister with special responsibility for Energy Issues, Ministry of Energy 1982–86, for the Environment and Energy 1987–90, for the Environment 1990–91; Spokesperson on Social Welfare; Chair. Environment Cttee of Socialist Int. 1986–93, Confed. of Socialist Parties of EC 1990–94, Chair. High Level Advisory Bd on Sustainable Devt to Sec.-Gen. 1996–97; Speaker of Riksdag (Swedish Parl.) 1994–2002; Chair. Bd Swedish Coral Asscn 2002–05, Nat. Museum of Cultural History, Centre for Gender Research, Uppsala Univ.; Pres. UNICEF Sweden World Infections Foundation; Sr Adviser Global Environment Facility 1998–; mem. Panel of Eminent Persons on United Nations-Civil Society; mem. Bd Stockholm Environment Inst., Int. Inst. for Industrial Environment Econs, Lund Univ.; fmr mem. Bd of Dirs Nat. Housing Bd; Gran Condecoración de Honor del Senado (Chile) 2000, Grand Cross Order of the White Rose (Finland) 2002; Cross of Terra Mariana (Estonia) 2002, Das Grosse Goldene Ehrenzeichens am Bande für Verdienste (Austria) 2002, Illis Quorum Meruere Labores (Sweden) 2003, Medal of Merit (Algeria) 2006. *Publications:* contrib. numerous articles and chapters to magazines and books on democracy and human rights, peace and int. cooperation, sexual equality, children's rights, education and science, the environment and sustainable devt. *Address:* Idrottsgatan 12, 753 35 Uppsala, Sweden (home). *Telephone:* (18) 211793 (home). *Fax:* (18) 211793 (home). *E-mail:* 34dahl@telia.com (home).

DAHL, Lawrence F., BS, PhD; American chemist and academic; *Professor Emeritus, Department of Chemistry, University of Wisconsin;* b. 1929; ed Univ. of Louisville, Iowa State Univ.; R.E. Rundle Prof. of Chemistry, Univ. of Wisconsin 1978–, Hilldale Chair Prof. 1991, now Prof.; Emer. fmr Visiting Lecturer, Technische Universität, Munich, Germany 1965, Univ. of Louisville 1969, Univ. of Notre Dame 1987, Univ. of Illinois 1990, Texas A & M Univ. 1996, Bristol Univ., England 1997, Tulane Univ. 1998; mem. NAS 1988–; Guggenheim Fellow 1969-70; Fellow, NY Acad. of Sciences, 1975–, AAAS 1980–, American Acad. of Arts and Sciences 1992–; Hon. DSc (Univ. of Louisville) 1991; ACS Award in Inorganic Chemistry 1974, Alexander von-Humboldt-Stiftung Sr US Scientist Humboldt Award 1985, Hilldale Award in the Physical Sciences, Univ. of Wisconsin 1994, Amoco Distinguished Lecturer, Ind. Univ. 1996, ACS Willard Gibbs Medal 1999, American Inst. of Chemists Pioneer Award 2000. *Address:* University of Wisconsin, Department of Chemistry, Room 6375a, Chemistry Building, 1101 University Avenue, Madison, WI 53706, USA (office). *Telephone:* (608) 262-5859 (office). *Fax:* (608) 262-6143 (office). *E-mail:* dahl@chem.wisc.edu (office). *Website:* www.chem.wisc.edu (office).

DAHL, Sophie; British fmr model and author; b. 1978, granddaughter of the late Patricia Neal and the late Roald Dahl; m. Jamie Cullum 2010; began career as a model; gave up modelling to concentrate on writing career 2007; fmr long-term Contributing Ed. at Men's Vogue, currently a regular contrib. to both US and UK edns of Vogue, and to Waitrose Food Illustrated magazine; has also contributed to, amongst others, The Observer, The Guardian, The Saturday Times Magazine; wrote book chronicling her misadventures with food, Miss Dahl's Voluptuous Delights 2009; wrote and presented BBC 2 TV cookery programme, The Delicious Miss Dahl 2010; currently working on a documentary film project with Keo Films. *Publications:* The Man with the Dancing Eyes (illustrated novella) (Times bestselling book) 2003, Playing with the Grown Ups 2007, Miss Dahl's Voluptuous Delights 2009, From Season to Season 2011. *Address:* c/o Angela Becker, Becker Brown Management, 11 Knightsbridge, 3rd Floor, London, SW1X 7LY, England (office). *E-mail:* info@beckerbrown.com (office).

DAHLAN, Mohammed, BA; Palestinian politician; b. 1961, Gaza; m.; three c.; ed Islamic Univ. of Gaza; brought up in refugee camp in Gaza after fleeing 1948 war; grassroots organizer of Youth Br. of Fatah; arrested for subversive pro-Palestinian activities (ten times) 1981–86, deported to Jordan during intifada 1987; mem. Palestinian Liberation Org. (PLO) 1988–; involved in secret negotiations with Israel, leading to Oslo Peace Accords and creation of Palestinian Authority (PA) 1993–94; apptd Head of PA Preventative Security Force by Yasser Arafat 1994, resgnd June 2002; Minister of State for Security Affairs, PA April–Oct. 2003; visited UK to study English, returned to Gaza June 2004; Minister for Civil Affairs 2005–06; Nat. Security Adviser to Pres. Abbas 2006–07; mem. Fatah Party. *Address:* c/o Fatah, Ramallah, Palestinian Autonomous Areas. *E-mail:* fateh@fateh.org. *Website:* www.fateh.net.

DAHLBÄCK, Claes, MSc (Econs); Swedish business executive; b. 1947; Pres. and CEO Investor AB 1978–99, Exec. Vice-Chair. 1999–2001, Chair. 2002–05, Sr Adviser 2005–; Dir Stora 1990–98, Chair. 1997–98, Chair. Stora Enso Oyj (following merger of Stora and Enso 1998) 1998–2010; Vice-Chair. Skandinaviska Enskilda Banken 1997–2002, also Chair. Vin & Spirit AB 1991–2007, Gambro AB, EQT Funds; Dir (non-exec.) Goldman Sachs; Sr Advisor, Foundation Asset Management 2007–; mem. Bd Dirs ABB, Zürich, Switzerland 1991–96, Ericsson 1993–96. *Address:* c/o Investor AB, Arsenalsgatan 8, 111 47 Stockholm, Sweden.

DAHLFORS, John Ragnar, MCE; Swedish civil engineer; *Management Consultant, JD Management AB;* b. 31 Dec. 1934, Stockholm; s. of Mats Dahlfors and Astrid Dahlfors; m. 1st Anita Roger 1962 (divorced); one s. two d.; m. 2nd Ing-Britt Schlyter 1998; ed Royal Inst. of Tech., Stockholm; engineer with Gränges AB Liberia project 1962–66, Sales Man. Gränges Hedlund AB 1967–68, Pres. 1970–74, Tech. Man. Gränges Construction AB 1969, Pres. Gränges Aluminium AB 1974–78; Pres. Boliden AB 1978–86; fmr man. consultant Sevenco, currently consultant JD Man. AB. *Leisure interests:* sailing, golf, tennis, hunting. *Address:* Karlaplan 12, 115 20 Stockholm, Sweden (home). *Telephone:* (70) 889-85-77 (mobile); (8) 660-24-04 (home). *Fax:* (8) 660-24-04 (home). *E-mail:* john.dahlfors@telia.com.

DAHLIE, Bjorn; Norwegian fmr Olympic skier; b. 19 June 1967; pnr Vilde; two s.; winner of a record total of 29 medals (gold, silver and bronze) 1991–99, including eight Gold Olympic medals; Hon. Pres. Cross Country World Championships 2005; retd 2001; introduced Nordic skiwear collection 1996; majority stockholder Bj Sport AS. *Publication:* Gulljakten (autobiog.). *Leisure interest:* hunting. *Address:* Bj Sport AS, Adminbygget Hellerudsletta, 2013 Skjetten, Norway (office). *Telephone:* 45-28-03-33 (office). *Fax:* 63-84-16-70 (office). *E-mail:* info@bjsport.no (office). *Website:* www.bjorn-daehlie.com (office).

DAHOUL, Safwan, DFA; Syrian artist; b. 1961, Hama; ed Faculty of Fine Arts, Damascus Univ., Ecole Supérieure des Arts Plastiques et Visuels, Mons, Belgium; instructor, Faculty of Fine Arts, Damascus Univ.; regular participant in int. art fairs and solo and group exhbns throughout the Middle East, Europe and USA; best known works are oil/acrylic paintings in Hulum (Rêve/Dream) series; ranked by Arabian Business amongst the Power 500: The Worlds's Most Influential Arabs (48th) 2011, (81st) 2012. *Address:* c/o Ayyam Gallery, Mezzeh West Villas 30, Chile Street, Samawi Building, Damascus, Syria (office). *Telephone:* (11) 6131088 (office). *Fax:* (11) 6131087 (office). *E-mail:* info@ayyamgallery.com (office). *Website:* www.ayyamgallery.com (office); safwandahoul.com.

DAI, Bingguo; Chinese politician and diplomatist; *Member, State Council;* b. March 1941, Yinjiang Co., Guizhou Prov.; ed Foreign Affairs Coll., Sichuan Univ.; joined CCP 1973; Deputy Div. Chief, later Div. Chief, Dept of USSR and Eastern European Affairs, Ministry of Foreign Affairs 1973–85, Deputy Dir 1985–86, Dir 1986–89, Amb. to Hungary 1989–91, Asst Minister of Foreign Affairs 1991–93, Deputy Minister of Foreign Affairs 1993–95, 2003–07; Deputy Head Int. Liaison Dept of CCP Cen. Cttee 1995–97, Head 1997–2003; mem. 15th CCP Cen. Cttee 1997–2002, 16th CCP Cen. Cttee 2002–07, 17th CCP Cen. Cttee 2007–12; mem. State Council 2008–. *Address:* State Council, Beijing, People's Republic of China (office).

DAI, Hongjie, MS, PhD; American (b. Chinese) chemist and academic; *J.G. Jackson and C.J. Wood Professor in Chemistry, Stanford University;* b. 1966; ed Tsing Hua Univ., People's Repub. of China, Columbia Univ., Harvard Univ.; Postdoctoral Fellow, Harvard Univ. 1995–97; Postdoctoral Fellow, Rice Univ. 1997; Terman Fellow, Stanford Univ. 1998, Packard Fellow for Science and Eng 1999, Alfred P. Sloan Research Fellow 2001, Asst Prof. of Chem. 1997–2002, Assoc. Prof. 2002–05, Prof. of Chem. 2005–07, J.G. Jackson and C.J. Wood Prof. in Chem. 2007–; Founder, Molecular Nanosystems Inc. 2001; Changjian Visiting Professorship, Tsinghua Univ. 2005–08; Fellow, American Acad. of Arts and Sciences 2009–, AAAS 2011; mem. Editorial Bd several journals including Nano Letters, Chemical Physics Letters, International Journal of Nanoscience; Camille Dreyfus Teacher-Scholar Award 2002, ACS Pure Chem. Award 2002, Julius Springer Prize for Applied Physics 2004, American Physical Soc. James McGroddy Prize for New Materials 2006, Ramabrahmam and Balamani Guthikonda Award, Columbia Univ. 2009. *Publications:* more than 150 articles in profesional journals. *Address:* Stanford University, Department of Chemistry, Keck Chemistry Building, Room 125A, Stanford, CA 94305-5080, USA (office). *Telephone:* (650) 725-9156 (office). *Fax:* (650) 725-0259 (office). *E-mail:* hdai1@stanford.edu (office). *Website:* www.stanford.edu/dept/chemistry/faculty/dai/group (office).

DAI, Gen. (retd) Tobias Joaquim; Mozambican politician and fmr army officer; b. 25 Nov. 1950, Manica City; s. of Joaquin Dai and Beatriz Mucudo Dai; m.; two c.; ed João XXII and Pêro de Anaia Secondary Schools; joined Mozambique Armed Forces 1971; instructor and Commdr, Nachingweia 1971–76; Weapons Commdr, Vestrel de Moscovo Mil. Acad., USSR 1976–78; Commdr Mil. Garrison, City of Maputo 1978–80; several sr mil. positions including Vice-Commdt and Head of Mil. House of Pres. of the Repub., Prov. Mil. Commdr in Manica, Head of Directorate of Operations, and Commdr-in-Chief of Armed Forces 1980–95; Sec.-Gen. Ministry of Nat. Defence 1995–2000; Minister of Nat. Defence 2000–08; participated in Peace Negotiations 1993–94; elected to House of Reps 1987–94; mem. Frelimo Party; Veteran of the Struggle for Nat. Independence of Mozambique Medal. *Leisure interests:* sports, reading. *Address:* c/o Ministry of National Defence, Avda Mártires de Mueda 280, CP 3216, Maputo, Mozambique (office).

DAI, Weili, BA; American (b. Chinese) business executive; *Co-founder, Marvell Technology Group;* b. Shanghai, China; m. Sehat Sutardja; two c.; ed Univ. of California, Berkeley; involved in software devt and project man. at Canon Research Center America, Inc. –1995; Co-founder (with husband) Marvell Technology Group 1995, has served as Gen. Man., Exec. Vice-Pres. and COO Communications Business Group, also served as mem. Bd of Dirs Marvell Technology Group Ltd and Corp. Sec. of the Bd; mem. Bd Give2Asia; mem. Committee of 100; ranked by Forbes magazine amongst The World's 100 Most Powerful Women (89th) 2012, (88th) 2013. *Address:* Marvell Semiconductor, Inc., 5488 Marvell Lane, Santa Clara, CA 95054, USA (office). *Telephone:* (408) 222-2500 (office). *Fax:* (408) 988-8279 (office). *E-mail:* info@marvell.com (office). *Website:* www.marvell.com (office).

DAI, Xianglong; Chinese politician, banker and economist; *Chairman, National Council for Social Security Fund;* b. Oct. 1944, Yizheng City, Jiangsu Prov.; ed Cen. Inst. of Finance and Banking; mem. CCP 1973–; Deputy Section Chief, People's Bank of China (PBC), Jiangsu Prov. Br. 1978; Deputy Section Chief and Deputy Head of Dept Agricultural Bank of China (ABC), Jiangsu Br., Vice-Gov. 1983; Sec. CCP Group, Communications Bank of China (CBC), also Gen. Man. and Vice-Chair. Bd CBC 1989; Chair. Bd China Pacific Insurance Co. Ltd 1990–93; Vice-Gov. People's Bank of China 1993–95, Gov. 1995–2003; Alt. mem. 14th CCP Cen. Cttee 1992–97, 15th CCP Cen. Cttee 1997–2002, 16th CCP Cen. Cttee 2002–07, 17th CCP Cen. Cttee 2007–12; Acting Mayor Tianjin Municipality 2002–03, Vice-Mayor 2002–03, Mayor 2003–07, Deputy Sec. CCP Municipal Cttee 2003–07; Chair. Nat. Council for Social Security Fund 2007–. *Address:* National Council for Social Security Fund, Mailbox No.2, South Tower, Fortune Time, Building 11, Fenghuiyuan, Xicheng District, Beijing 100032, People's Republic of China (office). *Website:* www.ssf.gov.cn (office).

DAIANU, Daniel, PhD; Romanian economist, academic and politician; b. 30 Aug. 1952, Bucharest; ed Acad. of Econ. Studies, Bucharest, Acad. of Sciences, Bucharest and Harvard Business School, USA; Visiting Scholar, Russian Research Center, Harvard Univ. 1990–92; Deputy Minister of Finance Feb.–Aug. 1992; Chief Economist, Nat. Bank of Romania 1992–97; Minister of Finance 1997–98; currently Prof. of Econs, Acad. of Econ. Studies, Bucharest; Pres. Supervisory Bd Banca Comercială Română 2005–07; mem. European Parl. (Nat. Liberal Party) 2007–09; Visiting Scholar, Woodrow Wilson Center, Washington, DC 1992, IMF, Washington, DC 1993, UN/ECE; Visiting Sr Fellow, NATO Defense Coll., Rome 1995; Visiting Prof., Univ. of California, Berkeley 1999, Anderson School of Man., UCLA 2000–02, Univ. of Bologna 2000–02; Fellow, William Davidson Inst., Univ. of Michigan Business School; Chair. Romanian Econ. Soc.; Pres. European Asscn for Comparative Econ. Studies 2002–04, OSCE Econ. Forum 2001; Corresp. mem. Romanian Acad.; Pres. Junior Achievement Romania; mem. Aspen Inst. Romania; Hon. Pres. Romanian Acad. of European Studies; Acad. of Sciences Highest Award for Econs 1994. *Publications:* Economic Vitality and Viability – A Dual Challenge for European Security 1996, Transformation of Economies as a Real Process – An Insider's Perspective 1998, Romania—Winners and Losers: The Impact of Reform of Intergovernmental Transfers (research report, co-author) 1999, Balkan Reconstruction (co-ed.) 2001. *Leisure interests:* reading, football, basketball. *Website:* www.daniel-daianu.eu (office).

DAIBER, Hans Joachim, DPhil, DPhil.habil; German philologist and academic; *Professor Emeritus of Oriental Philology and Islam, University of Frankfurt am Main;* b. 1 April 1942, Stuttgart; s. of Otto Daiber and Martha Daiber; m. Helga Brosamler 1971; one s. one d.; ed Theological Seminaries of Maulbronn and Blaubeuren, Univs of Tübingen and Saarbrücken; Research Fellow, German Oriental Inst., Beirut, Lebanon 1973–75; Lecturer in Arabic, Univ. of Heidelberg 1975–77; Prof. of Arabic, Free Univ., Amsterdam 1977–95; Prof. of Oriental Philology and Islam, Univ. of Frankfurt am Main 1995–2010, Prof. Emer. 2010–; Special Visiting Prof., Univ. of Tokyo 1992; Visiting Prof., Int. Inst. of Islamic Thought and Civilization, Kuala Lumpur 2001; mem. Royal Netherlands Acad. of Arts and Sciences, German Oriental Inst., Beirut 1973–75; Ed. Aristoteles Semitico-Latinus, Islamic Philosophy, Theology and Science; Best Doctoral Thesis of the Year, Univ. of Saarbrücken 1967, Islamic Thought in the Middle Ages.

Studies in Text, Transmission and Translation, in honour of Hans Daiber 2008. *Publications include:* Die arabische Übersetzung der Placita philosophorum 1968, Das theologisch-philosophische System des Muammar Ibn Abbad as-Sulami 1975, Gott, Natur und menschlicher Wille im frühen islamischen Denken 1978, Aetius Arabus 1980, The Ruler as Philosopher: A New interpretation of al-Farabi's View 1986, Wasil Ibn Ata' als Prediger und Theologe 1988, Catalogue of Arabic Manuscripts in the Daiber Collection (Vol. I) 1988, (Vol. II) 1996, Neuplatonische Pythagorica in arabischem Gewande 1995, The Islamic Concept of Belief in the 4th/10th Century 1995, Bibliography of Islamic Philosophy (two vols) 1999, (Supplement) 2006, The Struggle for Knowledge in Islam: Some Historical Aspects 2004, Islamic Thought in the Dialogue of Cultures: Innovation and Mediation between Antiquity and The Middle Ages 2008; numerous articles in journals on Islamic philosophy, theology, history of sciences, Greek heritage in Islam. *Address:* Am Hüttenhof 10, 40489 Düsseldorf, Germany (home). *Telephone:* (211) 403714 (home); 17-24908395 (mobile). *Fax:* (211) 403725 (home). *E-mail:* daiber@em.uni -frankfurt.de (office).

DAILY, Gretchen C., BS, MS, PhD; American ecologist and academic; *Director, Center for Conservation Biology, Bing Professor of Environmental Science, Department of Biology and Senior Fellow, Woods Institute for the Environment, Stanford University;* b. 1964; ed Stanford Univ.; Research Asst, Worldwatch Inst., Washington, DC 1985–87; Research Asst, Ludwig Maximillian Univ., Munich, FRG 1988; Winslow/Heinz Postdoctoral Fellow, Energy and Resources Group, Univ. of California, Berkeley 1992–95; Bing Interdisciplinary Research Scientist, Dept of Biological Sciences, Stanford Univ. 1995–2002, Assoc. Prof. (Research), Dept of Biology and Sr Fellow, Inst. for Int. Studies 2002–05, Bing Prof. of Environmental Science 2005–, Dir Center for Conservation Biology, Dir Interdisciplinary Program in Environment and Resources; Sr Fellow, Woods Inst. for the Environment; Chair. The Natural Capital Project; mem. or fmr mem. Bd of Eds Ecological Applications, Ecological Economics, Ecosystems, Encyclopedia of Biodiversity; Fellow, American Acad. of Arts and Sciences 2003, NAS 2005, California Acad. of Sciences 2010; Einstein Professorship, Chinese Acad. of Sciences 2010; Frances Lou Kallman Award for Excellence in Science and Grad. Study 1992, Pew Fellow in Conservation and the Environment 1994, Fellow, Aldo Leopold Leadership Program 1999, 21st Century Scientist Award 2000, Smith Sr Scholar of The Nature Conservancy 2003, Sophie Prize 2008, Int. Cosmos Prize, The Expo '90 Foundation, Japan 2009, Environment and Energy Award for Thought Leadership, Aspen Inst. 2010, Heinz Award, The Heinz Family Philanthropies 2010, Midori Prize for Biodiversity, AEON Environmental Foundation, Ministry of the Environment, Japan, Secr. of the Convention on Biological Diversity and United Nations Univ. 2010, named amongst Women of Influence: 100 Leaders in The Silicon Valley, Silicon Valley/San Jose Business Journal 2011, Volvo Environment Prize 2012. *Achievements include:* has developed concepts of countryside biogeography, ecosystem services and conservation finance; works extensively with economists, lawyers, business people and govt agencies to incorporate environmental issues into business practice and govt policy. *Publications:* The Stork and the Plow: The Equity Solution to the Human Dilemma (coauthor) 1995, Nature's Services: Societal Dependence on Natural Ecosystems (ed.) 1997, The Encyclopedia of Biodiversity (co-ed.) 2001, The New Economy of Nature: The Quest to Make Conservation Profitable (with Katherine Ellison) 2002, Natural Capital: Theory & Practice of Mapping Ecosystem Services (co-ed.) 2011; more than 150 scientific papers and popular articles. *Address:* Department of Biology, Stanford University, 371 Serra Mall, Stanford, CA 94305-5020, USA (office). *Telephone:* (650) 723-9452 (office). *Fax:* (650) 725-1992 (office). *E-mail:* gdaily@stanford.edu (office). *Website:* www.stanford.edu/group/CCB/cgi-bin/ccb/content/gretchen-daily (office).

DAINBA, Gyaincan; Chinese government official; b. 1940, Lhasa, Tibet; joined CCP 1964; Mayor of Lhasa Municipality 1980–87. *Address:* Government of Xizang Autonomous Region, Lhasa City, People's Republic of China.

DAINTITH, Terence Charles, MA; British legal scholar; *Professor Emeritus of Law, University of London;* b. 8 May 1942, Croydon, Greater London, England; s. of Edward Daintith and Irene M. Parsons; m. Christine Bulport 1965; one s. one d.; ed Wimbledon Coll. and St Edmund Hall, Oxford; called to Bar, Lincoln's Inn 1966; Assoc. in Law, Univ. of California, Berkeley 1963–64; Lecturer in Constitutional and Admin. Law, Univ. of Edin. 1964–72; Prof. of Public Law, Univ. of Dundee 1972–83, Dir Centre for Petroleum and Mineral Law Studies 1977–83; Prof. of Law, European Univ. Inst., Florence, Italy 1981–87; Prof. of Law, Univ. of London 1988–2002, Prof. Emer. 2002–, Dir Inst. of Advanced Legal Studies 1988–95, Dean School of Advanced Study 1994–2001; Prof. of Law, Univ. of Western Australia 2002–; Visiting Prof. of Law, Univ. of Melbourne, Australia 2004–; Bencher, Lincoln's Inn 2000; Ed. Journal of Energy and Natural Resources Law 1983–92; mem. Academia Europaea (Chair. Law Cttee 1993–96, Social Sciences Section 1996–98); Hon. LLD (De Montfort) 2001; Kuntz Memorial Award, Univ. of Oklahoma 2010. *Publications:* The Economic Law of the United Kingdom 1974, United Kingdom Oil and Gas Law (with G. D. M. Willoughby) 1977 (third edn 2000), Energy Strategy in Europe (with L. Hancher) 1986, The Legal Integration of Energy Markets (with S. Williams) 1987, Law as an Instrument of Economic Policy 1988, Harmonization and Hazard (with G. R. Baldwin) 1992, Implementation of EC Law in the United Kingdom 1995, The Executive in the Constitution (with A. C. Page) 1999, Discretion in the Administration of Offshore Oil and Gas: A Comparative Study 2006, Finders Keepers? How the Rule of Capture Shaped the World Oil Industry 2010. *Address:* Institute of Advanced Legal Studies, 17 Russell Square, London, WC1B 5DR, England (office); Law School, University of Western Australia, Crawley, WA 6009, Australia (office). *Telephone:* (20) 7862-5800 (London) (office).

DALAI LAMA, The, former temporal and spiritual head of Tibet; Fourteenth Incarnation (Tenzin Gyatso); Tibetan; b. 6 July 1935, Taktser, Amdo Prov., NE Tibet; s. of Chujon Tsering and Tsering Dekyi; born of Tibetan peasant family in Amdo Prov.; enthroned at Lhasa 1940; rights exercised by regency 1934–50; assumed political power 1950; fled to Chumbi in S Tibet after abortive resistance to Chinese State 1950; negotiated agreement with China 1951; Vice-Chair. Standing Cttee CPPCC, mem. Nat. Cttee 1951–59; Hon. Chair. Chinese Buddhist Assocn 1953–59; Del. to Nat. People's Congress 1954–59; Chair. Preparatory Cttee for the 'Autonomous Region of Tibet' 1955–59; fled Tibet to India after suppression of

Tibetan national uprising 1959; Dr of Buddhist Philosophy (Monasteries of Sera, Drepung and Gaden, Lhasa) 1959; Supreme Head of all Buddhist sects in Tibet (Xizang); announced his retirement from active participation in Tibetan political affairs March 2011; Presidential Distinguished Prof., Emory Univ., USA 2007–; Hon. Citizen of Paris 2008; Memory Prize 1989, Congressional Human Rights Award 1989, Nobel Peace Prize 1989, Freedom Award (USA) 1991, Presidential Congressional Gold Medal (USA) 2007, ranked by Forbes magazine amongst The World's Most Powerful People (39th) 2009–10, (51st) 2011, Templeton Prize 2012. *Publications include:* My Land and People 1962, The Opening of the Wisdom Eye 1963, The Buddhism of Tibet and the Key to the Middle Way 1975, Universal Responsibility and the Good Heart 1977, Deity Yoga (with Jeffrey Hopkins) 1981, Four Essential Buddhist Commentaries 1982, Collected Statements, Interviews & Articles 1982, Advice from Buddha Shakyamuni 1982, Kindness, Clarity and Insight 1984, A Human Approach to World Peace 1984, Opening the Mind and Generating a Good Heart 1985, Opening of the Eye of New Awareness (translated by Donald S. Lopez with Jeffrey Hopkins) 1985, Kalachakra Tantra – Rite of Initiation (with Jeffrey Hopkins) 1985, Tantra in Tibet (with Jeffrey Hopkins) 1987, The Union of Bliss & Emptiness (translated by Dr Thupten Jinpa) 1988, Transcendent Wisdom (translated, edited and annotated by B. Alan Wallace) 1988, The Dalai Lama at Harvard (translated and edited by Jeffrey Hopkins) 1988, The Bodhgaya Interviews (edited by Jose Ignacio Cabezon) 1988, Ocean of Wisdom 1989, Policy of Kindness (compiled and edited by Sidney Piburn) 1990, The Nobel Peace Prize and the Dalai Lama (compiled and edited by Sidney Piburn) 1990, My Tibet (with Galen Rowell) 1990, The Global Community & the Need for Universal Responsibility 1990, Freedom in Exile (autobiog.) 1991, Path to Bliss 1991, Mind Science – an East-West Dialogue (with Herbert Benson, Robert A. Thurman, Howard E. Gardner and Daniel Goleman) 1991, Cultivating a Daily Meditation 1991, Gentle Bridges – Conversations with the Dalai Lama on the Sciences of the Mind (with Jeremy Hayward and Francisco Varela) 1992, Worlds in Harmony (with conf. participants) 1992, Generous Wisdom – Commentaries on the Jatakamala 1993, Words of Truth 1993, A Flash of Lightning in the Dark of Night 1994, The World of Tibetan Buddhism (translated, edited and annotated by Dr Thupten Jinpa) 1995, The Way to Freedom (edited by John Avedon and Donald S. Lopez) 1995, The Spirit of Tibet: Universal Heritage – Selected Speeches and Writings (edited by A. A. Shiromany) 1995, The Power of Compassion 1995, The Path to Enlightenment (translated and edited by Glenn H. Mullin) 1995, His Holiness the Dalai Lama Speeches Statements Articles Interviews from 1987 to June 1995 1995, Dimensions of Spirituality 1995, Dialogues on Universal Responsibility and Education 1995, Commentary on the Thirty Seven Practices of a Bodhisattva (translated by Acharya Nyima Tsering, edited by Vyvyan Cayley and Mike Gilmore) 1995, Awakening the Mind, Lightening the Heart (edited by John Avedon and Donald S. Lopez) 1995, The Good Heart – A Buddhist Perspective on the Teachings of Jesus 1996, Beyond Dogma 1996, Buddha Nature 1997, Sleeping, Dreaming and Dying (edited and narrated by Francisco Varela) 1997, Love, Kindness and Universal Responsibility 1997, The Joy of Living and Dying in Peace (edited by John Avedon & Donald S. Lopez) 1997, The Heart of Compassion 1997, Healing Anger – The Power of Patience from a Buddhist Perspective (translated by Dr Thupten Jinpa) 1997, The Gelug/Kagyu Tradition of Mahamudra (with Alexander Berzin) 1997, Spiritual Advice for Buddhists and Christians 1998, The Political Philosophy of His Holiness the Dalai Lama – Selected Speeches and Writings (edited by A. A. Shiromany) 1998, The Path to Tranquillity – Daily Meditations (compiled and edited by Renuka Singh) 1998, The Four Noble Truths (translated by Dr Thupten Jinpa, edited by Dominique Side and Dr Thupten Jinpa) 1998, The Art of Happiness (with Howard C. Cutler) 1998, Ethics for the New Millennium 1998, Violence and Compassion 1998, The Power of Buddhism (with Jean-Claude Carriere) 1999, Imagine All the People – The Dalai Lama on Money, Politics and Life as It Could Be (with Fabian Quaki) 1999, Introduction to Buddhism 1999, Training the Mind 1999, The Little Book of Buddhism (compiled and edited by Renuka Singh) 1999, The Heart of the Buddha's Path (translated by Dr Thupten Jinpa, edited by Dominique Side and Dr Thupten Jinpa) 1999, Consciousness at the Crossroads – Conversations with the Dalai Lama on Brain Science and Buddhism 1999, Ancient Wisdom, Modern World – Ethics for a New Millennium 1999, Essential Teachings 1999, The Path to Tranquility: Daily Wisdom 1999, Buddha Heart, Buddha Mind – Living the Four Noble Truths 2000, Dalai Lama's Book of Wisdom (edited by Matthew Bunson) 2000, Transforming the Mind: Eight Verses on Generating Compassion and Transforming Your Life (translated by Dr Thupten Jinpa, edited by Dominique Side and Dr Thupten Jinpa) 2000, The Little Book of Wisdom 2000, A Simple Path: Basic Buddhist Teachings by His Holiness the Dalai Lama 2000, The Meaning of Life – Bhuddist Perspectives on Cause and Effect (translated and edited by Jeffrey Hopkins) 2000, The Art of Living: A Guide to Contentment, Joy and Fulfillment 2001, The Transformed Mind – Reflections on Truth, Love and Happiness 2001, Stages of Meditation: Training the Mind for Wisdom (translated by Geshe Lobsang Jordhen, Lobsang Choephel Ganchenpa and Jeremy Russell) 2001, An Open Heart (edited by Nicholas Vreeland) 2001, Pocket Dalai Lama (compiled and edited by Mary Craig) 2002, Compassionate Life 2001, His Holiness the Dalai Lama: In My Own Words 2001, Illuminating the Path to Enlightenment 2002, Essence of the Heart Sutra 2002, How to Practice (translated and edited by Jeffrey Hopkins) 2002, The Spirit of Peace 2002, Advice on Dying (translated and edited by Jeffrey Hopkins) 2002, Healing Emotions – Conversation with the Dalai Lama on Emotions and Health 2003, Heart of Compassion 2003, 365 – Dalai Lama Daily Advice from the Heart (edited by Mathieu Ricard) 2003, Warm Heart Open Mind 2003, The Compassionate Life 2003, Destructive Emotions (with Daniel Goleman) 2004, Practicing Wisdom – The Perfection of Shantideva's Bodhisattva Way (translated by Geshe Tubten Jinpa) 2004, New Physics and Cosmology – Dialogues with the Dalai Lama (with Arthur Zajonc and Zara Houshmand) 2004, Dzogchen: Heart Essence of the Great Perfection 2004, The Wisdom of Forgiveness (with Victor Chan) 2004, Many Ways to Nirvana 2004, Path of Wisdom, Path of Peace – A Personal Conversation (with Felizitas Von Schoenborn) 2005, Lighting the Path, Teachings on Wisdom and Compassion (translated by Geshe Tubten Jinpa) 2005, Art of Happiness at Work (with and Howard C. Cutler) 2005, Widening the Circle of Love (translated and edited by Jeffrey Hopkins) 2005, The Universe in a Single Atom – The Convergence of Science and Spirituality 2005, Yoga Tantra – Paths to Magical Seats (with Dzong-ka-ba and Jeffrey Hopkins) 2005, Teachings on Je Tsong Khapa's Three Principal Aspects of the Path (translated by Ven. Lhakdor and edited by Jeremy Russell) 2006, Activating Bodhichitta and a Meditation on

Compassion 2006, Mind in Comfort and Ease – The Vision of Enlightenment in the Great Perfection 2007, How to See Yourself as You Really Are 2007, Dalai Lama at MIT (edited by Anne Harrington and Arthur Zajonc) 2008, In My Own Words – An Introduction to My Teachings and Philosophy (edited by Rajiv Mehrotra) 2008, Becoming Enlightened (translated and edited by Jeffrey Hopkins) 2009, Emotional Awareness (with Paul Ekman) 2009, Art of Happiness in a Troubled World (with Howard C. Cutler) 2009, All You Ever Wanted to Know about Happiness, Life and Living (compiled by Rajiv Mehrotra) 2009, Leaders's Way – Business, Buddhism and Happiness in an Interconnected World (with Laurens van den Muyzenberg) 2009, The Middle Way – Faith Grounded in Reason (translated by Thubten Jinpa) 2009, Toward a True Kinship of Faiths 2010, My Spiritual Journey (with Sofia Stril-rever) 2010. *Leisure interests:* gardening, mechanics. *Address:* The Office of His Holiness the Dalai Lama Thekchen Choeling, PO McLeod Ganj, Dharamsala 176219, Himachal Pradesh, India (office). *Telephone:* (1892) 221343 (office); (1892) 221879 (office). *Fax:* (1892) 221813 (office). *E-mail:* ohhdl@dalailama.com (office). *Website:* www.dalailama.com (office).

DALBERTO, Michel; French pianist; b. 2 June 1955, Paris; s. of Jean Dalberto and Paulette Girard-Dalberto; ed Lycée Claude Bernard, Lycée Racine, Conservatoire Nat. Supérieur de Musique, Paris with Vlado Perlemuter and Jean Hubeau; started professional career 1975; concerts in major musical centres and at int. festivals including Lucerne, Maggio Musicale Florence, Aix-en-Provence, Vienna, Edinburgh, Schleswig-Holstein, Roque d'Anthéron; has worked with conductors including Leinsdorf, Sawallisch, Dutoit, Masur, Davis and Dausgaard and with orchestras including Orchestre de Paris, Orchestre Nat. de France, Amsterdam Concertgebouw, Philharmonia, Santa Cecilia in Rome, Oslo Philharmonic, BBC Philharmonic, Orchestras of Beijing, Shanghai and Guangzhou, St Petersburg Philharmonic, Ensemble Orchestral de Paris, Orchestre Philharmonique de Liège; Artistic Dir, Acad.-Festival des Arcs 1991–; as chamber musician, has collaborated with artists including Henryk Szeryng, Lynn Harrell, Renaud and Gautier Capuçon, Dmitri Sitkovetsky, Boris Belkin, Vadim Repin, Yuri Bashmet and Truls Mørk; Pres. Jury, Clara Haskil Competition 1991–; Chevalier, Ordre nat. du Mérite; Clara Haskil Prize 1975; First Prize, Mozart Piano Competition, Salzburg 1975, Leeds Int. Pianoforte Competition 1978; Acad. Charles Cros Award 1980 and Acad. du Disque Français Award 1984 for recordings; Diapason d'Or Award for Best Concerto Recording 1991. *Recordings include:* albums: Grieg/Strauss 1992, French Melodies (with Barbara Hendricks), Debussy Preludes, Mozart Concerti 2000, Un Piano à l'Opéra (Gramophone Award, Classic FM Award, Diapason d'Or) 2004, Schubert Piano Music (complete recordings) 2006, Brahms Sonatas for cello and piano 2008, Fauré: Complete Chamber Music for Strings and Piano (ECHO Klassik Award for Chamber Music Recording of the Year 2012) 2011. *Leisure interests:* skiing, scuba diving, vintage cars. *Address:* c/o Agence Artistique Jacques Thélen, 15 Avenue Montaigne, 75008 Paris, France (office). *Telephone:* (1)-56-89-32-00 (office). *Fax:* (1)-56-89-32-01 (office). *E-mail:* thelen@wanadoo.fr (office). *Website:* www.jacquesthelen.com (office); www.micheldalberto.com.

DALBORG, Hans Folkeson, MBA, PhD; Swedish banker; *Honorary Chairman, Nordea Bank AB;* b. 21 May 1941, Säter; m. Anna Ljungqvist 1965; one s. two d.; ed Univ. of Uppsala and Stockholm School of Econs; teacher and admin., Stockholm School of Econs 1967–72; joined Skandia 1972, Deputy Man. Dir responsible for int. business 1981–83, Pres. and COO Skandia Int. Insurance Corpn 1983–89, Sr Exec., Vice-Pres., COO Skandia Group and CEO Skandia Int. Insurance Corpn 1989–91; Pres. and CEO Nordbanken AB 1991–97, Pres., Group CEO Merita-Nordbanken PLC 1998–99, Pres. and CEO Nordea Bank AB 2000–04, Chair. 2004–11, Hon. Chair. 2011–; Chair. Royal Swedish Opera 1997–2005, Royal Swedish Acad. of Eng Sciences (IVA) 2005–08, Swedish Code of Corp. Governance, Uppsala Univ.; mem. Bd of Dirs Axel Johnson AB, Stockholm Inst. of Transition Econs and East European Economies (SITE), Stockholm Inst. for Financial Research; mem. European Round Table of Financial Services (EFR). *Address:* Nordea Bank AB, Smålandsgatan 17, 105 71 Stockholm, Sweden. *Website:* www .nordea.com.

DALDRY, Stephen, CBE BA; British theatre and film director; b. 2 May 1960, Dorset; s. of the late Patrick Daldry and of Cherry Daldry (née Thompson); m. Lucy Daldry 2001; ed Huish Grammar School, Taunton, Univ. of Sheffield; trained with Il Circo di Nando Orfei, Italy; f. Metro Theatre Co., Artistic Dir 1984–86; Assoc. Artist, Crucible Theatre, Sheffield 1986–88; Artistic Dir Gate Theatre, London 1989–92; Artistic Dir English Stage Co., Royal Court Theatre, London 1992–99, Assoc. Dir 1999–; Dir Stephen Daldry Pictures 1998–; Cameron Mackintosh Visiting Prof. of Contemporary Theatre, Oxford Univ. 2002; Creative Dir of Ceremonies, London Olympic Games 2012; Int. Filmmaker Award, Palm Springs Int. Film Festival 2003. *Films include:* Eight 1998, Via Dolorosa 1999, Dancer (Dir) 2000, Billy Elliot (Dir) (BAFTA Award for Best British Film 2000) 2000, The Hours (Vancouver Film Critics Circle Award for Best Dir 2003) 2002, The Reader (Evening Standard British Film Award for Best Dir 2008) 2008, Extremely Loud & Incredibly Close 2011. *Theatre includes:* Billy Elliot (Dir, musical) 2004. *Producer:* Six Degrees of Separation, Oleanna, Damned for Despair (Gate) 1991, An Inspector Calls (Royal Nat. Theatre) 1992, (Aldwych) 1994, (Garrick) 1995, (NY) 1995, (Playhouse) 2001, Machinal (Royal Nat. Theatre) 1993, The Kitchen (Royal Court) 1995, Via Dolorosa (Royal Court) 1998, (NY) 1999, Far Away (Royal Court) 2000, (Albery) 2001, Judgement Day, Ingoldstadt, Figaro Gets Divorced, Rat in the Skull. *Address:* c/o Creative Artists Agency, 2000 Avenue Of The Stars, Los Angeles, CA 90067, USA.

DALE, Jim; British actor; b. (James Smith), 15 Aug. 1935; m.; three s. one d.; ed Kettering Grammar School; music hall comedian 1951; singing, compering, directing 1951–61; first film appearance 1965; appeared in nine Carry On films; later appeared with Nat. Theatre and Young Vic; appeared in London's West End in The Card 1973; host, Sunday Night at the London Palladium (TV show) 1973–74; with Young Vic appeared on Broadway in The Taming of the Shrew and Scapino 1974; Broadway appearances: Barnum (Tony Award) 1980, Joe Egg 1985, Me and My Girl 1987–88, Candide 1997; other stage appearances include: Privates on Parade (New York), Travels With My Aunt (off-Broadway) 1995, Fagin in Oliver! (London Palladium) 1995–97; lyricist for film Georgy Girl; Grammy Award for Best Spoken Word Album for Children (for Harry Potter and the Deathly Hallows) 2008. *Films include:* Lock Up Your Daughters, The Winter's Tale, The

Biggest Dog in the World, National Health, Adolf Hitler—My Part in his Downfall, Joseph Andrews, Pete's Dragon, Hot Lead Cold Feet, Bloodshy, The Spaceman and King Arthur, Scandalous, Carry On Cabby, Carry On Cleo, Carry On Jack, Carry On Cowboy, Carry On Screaming, Carry On Spying, Carry On Constable, Carry On Doctor, Carry On Don't Lose Your Head, Carry On Follow That Camel, Carry On Columbus 1992, Hunchback of Notre Dame 1997. *Address:* c/o Sharon Bierut, CED, 257 Park Avenue South, New York, NY 10010, USA; c/o Janet Glass, 28 Berkeley Square, London, W1X 6HD, England.

D'ALEMA, Massimo; Italian politician and journalist; *President, Fondazione Italianieuropei;* b. 20 April 1949, Rome; m. Linda Giuva; two s.; ed Univ. of Pisa; mem. Camera dei Deputati 1987–2004, 2006–, Chair. Parl. Cttee on Institutional Reform 1997; Dir L'Unità 1988–90; Sec. Partito Democratico della Sinistra, renamed Democratici di Sinistra (DS) 1998, Pres. 2000–07, mem. Partito Democratico (formed by merger of Democratici di Sinistra and Democrazia è Libertà) 2007–; Prime Minister of Italy 1998–2000; mem. European Parl. 2004–06; Deputy Prime Minister and Minister of Foreign Affairs 2006–08; Pres. Fondazione Italianieuropei 2000–, Foundation for European Progressive Studies 2010–; Chair. Parl. Cttee for the Intelligence and Security Services (COPASIR) 2010–; Vice-Pres. Socialist International 2003–. *Publications include:* Dialogo su Berlinguer (co-author) 1994, Un paese Normale: La Sinistra e il Futuro dell'Italia 1995, Progettare il Futuro 1996, La Sinistra nell'Italia che Cambia 1997, La Grande Occasione. L'Italia verso le Riforme 1997, Parole a Vista (co-author) 1998, Kosovo: Gli italiani e la Guerra (co-author) 1999, Oltre la Paura 2002, La Politica ai Tempi della Globalizzazione 2003, A Mosca l'Ultima Volta 2004, Il Mondo Nuovo 2009. *Address:* Fondazione Italianieuropei, piazza Farnese 101, 00186 Rome, Italy (office). *Telephone:* (06) 45508600 (office). *Fax:* (06) 45508698 (office). *E-mail:* segreteria@italianieuropei.it (office). *Website:* www.massimodalema.it.

DALES, Sir Richard Nigel, Kt, KCVO, CMG, MA; British diplomatist; b. 26 Aug. 1942, Woodford, Essex, England; s. of the late Maj. K. Dales and of O. M. Dales; m. Elizabeth M. Martin 1966; one s. one d.; ed Chigwell School, Essex and St Catharine's Coll. Cambridge; joined Foreign Office 1964; Third Sec. Yaoundé, Cameroon 1965–67; with FCO, London 1968–70; Second Sec., later First Sec., Copenhagen 1970–73; Asst Pvt. Sec. to Sec. of State for Foreign and Commonwealth Affairs 1974–77; Head of Chancery, Sofia 1977–81; FCO 1981–82; Head of Chancery, Copenhagen 1982–86; Deputy High Commr in Zimbabwe 1986–89; Head of Southern Africa Dept FCO 1989–91; seconded to Civil Service Comm. 1991–92; High Commr to Zimbabwe 1992–95; Dir (Africa and Commonwealth), FCO 1995–98; Amb. to Norway 1998–2002; Chair. Anglo-Norse Soc. 2003–; mem. Bd Norfolk and Norwich Festival 2003–06; mem. Council of Univ. of East Anglia 2004–; Chair. International Alert 2005–10. *Leisure interests:* music and the arts, walking, life in retirement. *Address:* 521 Bunyan Court, Barbican, London, EC2Y 8DH, England.

D'ALESSANDRO, Dominic, OC, BSc; Italian chartered accountant and financial services executive; b. 18 Jan. 1947, Molise; m. Pearl D'Alessandro; two s. one d.; ed Loyola Coll., Montreal, Canada; accountant, Coopers & Lybrand 1968–75; with Genstar Ltd 1975–81, Dir of Finance, Dhahran, Saudi Arabia, subsequently Gen. Man., Dhahran, later Vice-Pres. Materials and Construction Group, San Francisco; with Royal Bank of Canada 1981–88, Vice-Pres. and Controller, then Exec. Vice-Pres. for Finance –1988; Pres. and CEO Laurentian Bank of Canada 1988–94; mem. Bd Dirs, Pres. and CEO Manulife Financial Corpn 1994–2009; Dir American Council of Life Insurance; mem. Bd The Hudson's Bay Co., TransCanada PipeLines; mem. Business Council on Nat. Issues; fmr Chair. Bd Canadian Life and Health Insurance Asscn; mem. Advisory Cttee on the Public Service of Canada 2006–, North American Competitiveness Council of North American Free Trade Agreement (NAFTA) 2006–; Co-Chair. Corp. Fund for Breast Cancer Research Campaign 1996; Campaign Chair. for the Salvation Army, Ont. Cen. Div., for Greater Toronto United Way Campaign 1998; Fellow, Inst. Chartered Accountants 1993; Commendatore, Order of the Star of Italy 2008; Dr hc (Concordia Univ.) 1998, (York Univ.) 2006; Bronze Medal, Inst. of Chartered Accountants 1971, Man. Achievement Award, McGill Univ. 1999, Arbour Award, Univ. of Toronto 1999, CEO Award of Excellence in Public Relations, Canadian Public Relations Soc. 2001, named Canada's Outstanding CEO for 2002, voted Canada's Most Respected CEO 2004, Loyola Medal, Concordia Univ. 2004, honoured with Int. Horatio Alger Award 2005, Special Lifetime Man. Achievement Award, McGill Univ. 2005, Int. Distinguished Entrepreneur Award, Univ. of Manitoba 2007, Canadian Business Leader Award, Univ. of Alberta School of Business 2007, inducted into Insurance Hall of Fame 2008. *Address:* c/o Manulife Financial, 200 Bloor Street East, Toronto, ON M4W 1E5, Canada. *Telephone:* (416) 926-3000. *Fax:* (416) 926-5454. *E-mail:* info@manulife.com. *Website:* www .manulife.com.

DALEY, Richard Michael, BA, JD; American lawyer and politician; b. 24 April 1942, Chicago, Ill.; s. of the late Richard J. Daley and of Eleanor Guilfoyle; m. Margaret Corbett 1972; one s. (and s. deceased) two d.; ed De La Salle High School, Providence Coll. and DePaul Univ.; Asst Corpn Counsel, City of Chicago 1969; Del. Ill. Constitutional Convention 1970; Pnr, Simon and Daley (law firm) 1970–72, Daley, Riley & Daley 1972–80; mem. Ill. State Senate 1973–80; State's Attorney, Cook Co., Ill. 1980–89; Mayor of Chicago 1989–2011; mem. Chicago Bar Asscn, Illinois State Bar Asscn, ABA, Catholic Lawyers Guild; Democrat; numerous awards including Outstanding Leader, Ill. Asscn of Social Workers 1978, Public Official of Year, Governing magazine 1997, Politician of Year, Library Journal 1997, J. Sterling Morton Award, Nat. Arbor Day Foundation 1999, Nat. Trust for Historic Preservation Nat. Preservation Award, 2000, 2002, Lifetime Achievement Award, US Conference Mayors 2005, Kevin Lynch Award, MIT 2005. *Leisure interests:* cinema, reading. *Address:* c/o Office of the Mayor, City Hall, Room 507, 121 North LaSalle Street, Chicago, IL 60602–1202, USA (office).

DALEY, Thomas Robert (Tom); British diver; b. 21 May 1994, Plymouth, Devon; s. of Robert Daley and Debbie Daley; ed Eggbuckland Community Coll., Plymouth Coll.; began diving aged seven; spotted by a coach, taking part in regular diving lessons, and placed in competitive squad Sept. 2002; won his age-group at British Championships in 1m springboard, 3m springboard and platform 2004, 2005, 2006; won platform competition in Nat. Jr (under 18) group (youngest ever winner); competed as guest competitor in Australian Elite Jr Nationals 2005, placed first in platform and second in 3m springboard in 14–15 age group event;

also competed in 14–15 category at Aachen Jr Int. 2005, placed second in platform and third in 3m springboard; Under-18 British champion in platform and 3m springboard, placed second in 10m platform at Sr British Championships 2007; given special dispensation to compete at Australian Youth Olympic Festival aged 12 2007; now specializes in 10m platform event; won individual 10m platform event at British Championships 2008, 2009, European Championships 2008, 2012; represented GB at Olympics Games, Beijing 2008 where he was Britain's youngest competitor, the youngest competitor of any nationality outside the sport of swimming, and the youngest to participate in a final; participated in FINA Jr World Championships 2008, finished second in category 'B' platform competition (for 14- and 15-year-old boys), finished second in 3m springboard competition in same category; won individual 10m platform event at FINA World Championships, Rome 2009; ranked No. 1 for the ten-metre platform in FINA World Diving Rankings; won two gold medals in 10m synchro diving (with Max Brick) and 10m Individual Platform competition at Commonwealth Games, New Delhi 2010; bronze medal, 10m platform, Olympics Games, London 2012; mem. Plymouth Diving Club; celebrity supporter of ChildLine 2007–; head coach, Andy Banks; named Youngster of the Year by BBC South West 2005, named BBC South West Sports Personality of the Year, and Young Sports Personality of the Year 2009, named BBC Young Sports Personality of the Year 2007, 2009, 2010 (only person ever to win this award more than once), ranked 63rd in Time's edn of 100 Olympic Athletes To Watch 2008, LEN Magazine's Athlete of the Year Award for mens' divers, on behalf of European Swimming Fed. 2009. *Address:* Plymouth Life Centre, Mayflower Drive, Plymouth, PL2 3DG, England. *Telephone:* (1752) 606900. *E-mail:* andy@plymouthdiving.com. *Website:* www.plymouthdiving.com.

DALEY, William M., BA, JD; American lawyer, business executive and government official; b. 1948; s. of the late Richard J. Daley and of Eleanor Guilfoyle, brother of Richard Michael Daley; m. Loretta Daley; three c.; ed Loyola Univ., John Marshall Law School; called to Ill. Bar 1975; fmrly with Daley and George, Chicago; Pnr, Mayer, Brown and Platt; Vice-Chair. Amalgamated Bank, Chicago 1989, Pres., COO 1990–93; Sec. US Dept of Commerce, Washington, DC 1997–2000; Chair., Vice-Pres. Albert Gore's presidential election campaign 2000; Vice Chair. Evercore Capital Pnrs LP Jan.–Nov. 2001; Pres. SBC Communications 2001–04; Chair. Midwest Operations, J. P. Morgan Chase, Chicago 2004–11, also mem. Exec. Cttee, Operating Cttee and Int. Advisory Council; Chief of Staff to Pres. Barack Obama 2011–12 (resgnd); Co-Chair. Pres. Obama's 2012 campaign team, Chicago 2012–; fmr mem. Bd of Dirs Boeing Co., Abbott Laboratories 2004, Boston Properties Inc. 2003, Art Inst. of Chicago, Joffrey Ballet of Chicago, Loyola Univ. of Chicago, Northwestern Memorial Hosp., Northwestern Univ.; fmr Special Counsel to Pres. for North American Free Trade Agreement; mem. Council on Foreign Relations; St Ignatius Award for Excellence in the Practice of Law, World Trade Award, World Trade Center, Chicago 1994. *Address:* c/o Office of the President, The White House, 1600 Pennsylvania Avenue, NW, Washington, DC 20500, USA.

DALGARNO, Alexander, PhD, FRS, FInstP, MRIA; American (b. British) astronomer and academic; *Phillips Professor of Astronomy, Harvard University;* b. 5 Jan. 1928, London, England; s. of William Dalgarno and Margaret Dalgarno; m. 1st Barbara Kane 1957 (divorced 1972); two s. two d.; m. 2nd Emily Izsák 1972 (divorced 1987); ed Univ. Coll., London; mem. Faculty, Applied Math., Queen's Univ., Belfast 1951–67; Prof. of Astronomy, Harvard Univ. 1967–2012; Chair. Dept of Astronomy 1971–76, Dir Harvard Coll. Observatory 1971–72, Phillips Prof. of Astronomy 1977–; mem. Smithsonian Astrophysical Observatory 1967–; Ed. Astrophysical Journal Letters 1973–2002; Fellow, Univ. Coll. London, UMIST; mem. American Acad. of Arts and Science, NAS, Int. Acad. of Quantum Molecular Science; Fellow, American Geophysical Union, American Physical Soc.; Hon. DSc (Queen's Univ., Belfast) 1972, (York Univ., Canada) 2000; Medal of Int. Acad. of Quantum Molecular Science 1969, Hodgkins Medal, Smithsonian Inst. 1977, Davisson-Germer Prize, American Physical Soc. 1980, Meggers Award, Optical Soc. of America 1986, Gold Medal, Royal Astronomical Soc. 1986, Spiers Medal, Royal Soc. of Chem., Fleming Medal, American Geophysical Union 1995, Asteroid 6941 named in his honour 1998, Hughes Medal, Royal Soc. 2002, Benjamin Franklin Medal, Franklin Inst. 2013. *Publications:* numerous scientific papers in professional journals. *Address:* Harvard-Smithsonian Center for Astrophysics, B-324, 60 Garden Street, Cambridge, MA 02138 (office); 27 Robinson Street, Cambridge, MA 02138, USA (home). *Telephone:* (617) 495-4403 (office); (617) 354-8660 (home). *Fax:* (617) 495-5970 (office). *E-mail:* adalgarno@cfa.harvard.edu (office). *Website:* astronomy.fas.harvard.edu/people/alex-dalgarno (office).

DALGLISH, Kenneth (Kenny) Mathieson, MBE; British professional football manager and fmr professional footballer; b. 4 March 1951, Glasgow, Scotland; m. Marina Dalglish; four c.; deep-lying forward; played for Celtic 1969–77 (made 204 appearances and scored 112 goals), Scottish League champions 1972, 1973, 1974, 1977, Scottish Cup Winners 1972, 1974, 1975, 1977, Scottish League Cup winners 1975; played for Liverpool 1977–90 (made 355 appearances and scored 118 goals), European Cup winners 1978, 1981, 1984, European Super Cup 1984, FA Cup winners 1986, 1989, League Cup winners 1981, 1982, 1983, 1984, Charity Shield 1980, 1981, 1983, shared 1978, 1987, Man. 1985–91, Acad. Amb. (Int. Recruitment and Devt) 2009–11, Man. 2011–12, Football League Cup 2012; Man. Blackburn Rovers 1991–95, Newcastle United 1997–98; Dir of Football Operations, Celtic Feb.–June 2000; 102 full caps for Scotland, scoring 30 goals (both nat. records); Co-founder (with wife) The Marina Dalglish Appeal 2004; Freeman of the City of Glasgow 1986; Football Writers' Asscn Player of the Year 1979, 1983, PFA Players' Player of the Year 1983, Manager of the Year 1986, 1988, 1990, 1995, elected to Scottish Sports Hall of Fame 2001, Inaugural Inductee to English Football Hall of Fame 2002, Scottish Football Hall of Fame 2004, FIFA 100, First in Liverpool Football Club pool of 100 Players Who Shook The Kop 2006. *Publication:* My Liverpool Home (autobiog.) 2010. *Address:* c/o Liverpool Football Club, Anfield Road, Liverpool, L4 0TH; c/o The Marina Dalglish Appeal, 78 Seel Street, Liverpool, L1 4BH, England. *Telephone:* (151) 709-7079 (charity). *E-mail:* info@ liverpoolfc.tv; dianne@marinadalglishappeal.org. *Website:* www .marinadalglishappeal.org.

DALIBARD, Barbara, MA; French telecommunications executive; *Director General, SNCF Voyages;* b. (Barbara Ploux), 23 May 1958, Suresnes, Paris; m.; three c.; ed École Normale Supérieure, École Nationale Supérieure des

Télécommunications; began career with France Télécom SA in 1982, various man. positions in sales, Corp. Services Dir Orange France and Vice-Pres. Orange Business 2001–02, Exec. Vice-Pres. Corp. Solutions 2003–04, Exec. Vice-Pres. Enterprise Communications Services 2004–, Chair. Supervisory Bd Equant (now Orange Business Services—subsidiary of France Télécom) 2003–05 (mem. Strategy and Compensation Cttees), Pres. and CEO Equant SA 2005–10; Dir Gen. SNCF Voyages and mem. Man. Cttee SNCF (Soc. Nationale des Chemins de Fer Français) 2010–; Pres. Alcanet International SAS 1998, Sales Man. for New Operators, Alcatel CIT 1999, later Sales Man. for France; mem. Bd Eurostar; mem. Supervisory Bd Michelin SA (France), Supervisory Bd Wolters Kluwer (Netherlands); Chevalier, Légion d'honneur, Officier, Ordre nat. du Mérite; ranked by Fortune magazine amongst the 50 Most Powerful Women in Business outside the US (27th) 2004, (26th) 2005, (35th) 2006, (40th) 2007, (fifth) 2009. *Address:* SNCF Voyages, 2 place de la Défense, Cnit 1, 92053 Paris la Défense Cedex, France (office). *Telephone:* 1-74-54-01-02 (office). *E-mail:* barbara.dalibard@sncf.fr (office). *Website:* www.sncf.com (office).

DALIĆ, Martina, MSc; Croatian economist and politician; b. (Martina Štimac), 12 Nov. 1967, Velika Gorica; m.; two c.; ed Univ. of Zagreb; Asst, Faculty of Econs, Univ. of Zagreb 1991–95; joined Ministry of Finance 1995, Head of Macroeconomic Forecasting Dept 1995–97, Deputy Minister of Finance 1997–2000, Head of Cen. State Strategy Office 2004–05 (led Croatia-EU accession negotiations), Minister of Finance 2010–11; Chief Economist, Privredna banka dd, Zagreb 2000–04; Chair. Partner banka dd, Zagreb 2008; mem. Croatian Democratic Union. *Publications:* numerous papers and reports on economic issues. *Address:* c/o Ministry of Finance, 1000 Zagreb, ul. Katančićeva 5, Croatia (office). *Telephone:* (1) 4591300 (office). *Fax:* (1) 4922583 (office). *E-mail:* kabinet@mfin.hr (office). *Website:* www.mfin.hr (office).

DALLARA, Charles H., MA, PhD, MALD; American fmr government official and international organization official; *Managing Director, Institute of International Finance;* b. 1948, Spartanburg, NC; m. 1st Carolyn Gault; one s. one d.; m. 2nd Peixin Li; ed Univ. of S Carolina and Fletcher School of Law and Diplomacy; int. economist, US Treasury Dept 1976–79; Special Asst to Under-Sec. for Monetary Affairs 1979–80; Guest Scholar Brookings Inst. 1980–81; Special Asst to Asst Sec. for Int. Affairs 1981–82; Alt. Exec. Dir IMF 1982–83; Deputy Asst Sec. for Int. Monetary Affairs, US Treasury Dept 1983–85; Exec. Dir IMF 1984–89; Asst Sec. for Policy Devt and Sr Adviser for Policy 1988–89; Asst Sec. for Internal Affairs 1989–93; Man. Dir JP Morgan 1991–93; Man. Dir Inst. of Int. Finance 1993–. *Address:* Institute of International Finance, Inc., 1333 H Street, NW, Suite 800E, Washington, DC 20005-4770 (office); 12196 Goldenchair Court, Oak Hill, VA 20171, USA (home). *Telephone:* (202) 857-3604 (office). *Fax:* (202) 833-1194 (office). *E-mail:* cdallara@iif.com (office). *Website:* www.iif.com (office).

D'ALLEST, Frédéric Jean Pierre; French engineer; b. 1 Sept. 1940, Marseille; s. of Pierre d'Allest and Luce d'Allest; m. Anne-Marie Morel 1963; three s.; ed Ecole St Joseph and Lycée Thiers, Marseilles, Ecole Polytechnique and Ecole Nat. Supérieure d'Aéronautique; with Centre Nat. d'Etudes Spatiales (CNES) 1966–70, Head of Ariane Project 1973–76, Dir Ariane Programme 1976–82, Dir-Gen. CNES 1982–89; with Europa III project, European Launcher Devt Org. 1970–72; Pres. Soc. Arianespace 1980–90 (Hon. Pres. 1990–), Matra Transport 1992–, Matra Hachette 1993–; Dir-Gen. Groupe Matra 1990–93, Groupe Lagardère 1996–2000; f. Marseille Provence 1988; Officier, Légion d'honneur, Ordre nat. du Mérite; Prix de l'Aéronautique, IMechE James Watt Prize 1993. *Leisure interests:* sport, mountaineering. *Address:* 6 rue Marcel Allegot, 92190 Meudon, France. *E-mail:* frederic.dallest@orange.fr.

DALLI, Hon. John, FCCA, CPA, CIM; Maltese accountant, politician and international organization official; b. 5 Oct. 1948, Qormi; s. of Carmelo Dalli and Emma Bonnici; m. Josette Callus; two d.; ed Malta Coll. of Arts, Science and Tech.; posts in financial admin and gen. man., Malta and Brussels; Man. Consultant; MP, Nationalist Party 1987–; Parl. Sec. for Industry 1987–90; Minister for Econ. Affairs 1990–92, of Finance 1992–96, 1998–2003, of Finance and Econ. Affairs 2003–04, of Foreign Affairs and Investment Promotion 2004 (resgnd); Shadow Minister and Opposition Spokesman for Finance 1996–98; Commr for Health and Consumer Policy, EC, Brussels 2010–12; Exec. Chair. John Dalli and Assocs; mem. Inst. of Man., Malta, Nat. Asscn of Accountants, USA. *Address:* 2461 Blk 24, Portohaso, St Julians PTH01, Malta (home).

D'ALMEIDA, Armindo Vaz; São Tomé and Príncipe politician; Prime Minister 1995–96. *Address:* c/o Office of the Prime Minister, Praça Yon Gato, CP 302, São Tomé, São Tomé e Príncipe.

D'ALOISIO, Tony, BA, LLB (Hons); Australian barrister and business executive; *Chairman, Australian Securities and Investments Commission;* b. 6 Nov. 1946; ed Monash Univ.; admitted to practice as a barrister and solicitor in Vic., WA, Queensland and the ACT, and as a solicitor in NSW; Prin. legal officer with Commonwealth Attorney-Gen.'s Dept in Business and Consumer Affairs Div., Canberra –1977; joined Mallesons Stephen Jaques in 1977, practised as commercial lawyer 1977–92, Chief Exec. 1992, Chief Exec. Pnr, Mallesons 1992–2004; Man. Dir and CEO Australian Securities Exchange (ASX) 2004–06; Commr Australian Securities and Investments Comm. (ASIC) 2006–07, Chair. ASIC 2007–; mem. Business Council of Australia 1994–2006 (mem. Bd of Dirs 2003–06), Int. Legal Services Advisory Council 1998–2004 (Chair. Globalisation of Legal Services Cttee), Bd of Taxation 2002–04; mem. Bd of Dirs Australian Charities Fund 2001–, World Fed. of Stock Exchanges 2002–04, Boral Ltd 2003–04; Australian Law Awards Man. Pnr of the Year 2001, 2002, Australian Govt Centenary Medal for services to law and taxation 2000. *Address:* Australian Securities and Investments Commission, GPO Box 9827, Sydney, NSW 2001, Australia (office). *Telephone:* (2) 9911-2200 (office). *Fax:* (2) 9911-2333 (office). *E-mail:* infoline@asic.gov.au (office). *Website:* www.asic.gov.au (office).

DALRYMPLE, Frederick Rawdon, AO; Australian diplomatist; b. 6 Nov. 1930, Sydney, NSW; s. of Frederick Dalrymple and Evelyn Dalrymple; m. Ross E. Williams 1957; one s. one d.; ed Sydney Church of England Grammar School, Univ. of Sydney, Univ. of Oxford, UK; Lecturer in Philosophy, Univ. of Sydney 1955–57; joined Dept of External Affairs 1957, served in Bonn, London 1959–64; Alt. Dir Asian Devt Bank, Manila 1967–69; Minister, Djakarta 1969–71; Amb. to Israel 1972–75, to Indonesia 1981–85, to USA 1985–89, to Japan 1989–93; Chair. ASEAN

Focus Group Pty Ltd 1994–2001; Visiting Prof., Univ. of Sydney 1994–2002; Hon. Fellow, Univ. of Sydney 2003; Hon. DSc (Econ) (Sydney); NSW Rhodes Scholar, Univ. of Sydney 1952. *Publications include:* Looking East and West from Down Under 1992, Continental Drift: Australia's Search for a Regional Identity 2003. *Leisure interests:* reading, golf. *Address:* 13/8 Young Street, Paddington, NSW 2021, Australia (home). *Telephone:* (2) 9331-7738. *E-mail:* rdalrymp@ozemail.com .au.

DALRYMPLE, John (Jack), BS; American politician, state governor and business executive; *Governor of North Dakota;* b. 16 Oct. 1948, Minneapolis, Minn.; m. Betsy Wood 1971; four d.; ed Yale Univ.; early career working on family farm, Casselton, ND; worked with Casselton Jobs Devt Comm.; co-f. Share House, Inc. (welfare programme); mem. ND House of Reps for Cass Co. 1985–2000, fmr Chair. House Appropriations Cttee; Lt-Gov. of ND 2000–10, Gov. of North Dakota 2010–; Chair. Dakota Growers Pasta Co., Casselton; fmr Chair. Prairie Public Television; Republican; Ernst and Young Midwest Master Entrepreneur of the Year Award 2007. *Address:* Office of the Governor, 600 East Boulevard Avenue, Bismarck, ND 58505-0001 (office); Washington Office of the Governor, State of North Dakota, 500 New Jersey Avenue NW, Suite 400, Washington, DC 20001, USA (office). *Telephone:* (701) 328-2200 (Bismarck) (office); (202) 715-1256 (DC) (office). *Fax:* (701) 328-2205 (Bismarck) (office); (202) 478-0811 (DC) (office). *Website:* governor.nd.gov (office).

DALTON, Grant; New Zealand yachtsman; *Managing Director, Emirates Team New Zealand;* b. 1957; m. Nicki Dalton; one s. one d.; fmr accountant; trainee sailmaker 1977; first participation in Whitbread round the world race (now the Volvo Ocean Race) on board Dutch Flyer II 1981–82, Lion New Zealand 1985–86; skipper, Fischer & Peykel 1989–90, New Zealand Endeavour 1993–94 (race winner), Wor 60 1997–98 (Merit Cup), Club Med Catamaran, The Race (winner) March 2001, Nautor Challenge Team, Volvo Ocean Race 2001; other races include Sydney-Hobart race (four times), Fastnet Race (five times), Admirals' Cup 1985, Americas Cup, Fremantle, Australia 1987; Man. Dir Emirates Team New Zealand 2003–, won Louis Vuitton ACC Championship 2004, 2006; New Zealand Yachts-man of the Year 2001. *Address:* Emirates Team New Zealand, 141 Halsey Street, Freemans Bay, Auckland, New Zealand (office). *Telephone:* (9) 355-0900 (office). *Fax:* (9) 355-0901 (office). *E-mail:* info@emiratesteamnz.com (office). *Website:* www .emiratesteamnz.com (office).

DALTON, Timothy Peter; British actor; b. 21 March 1946, Colwyn Bay, Wales; ed Royal Acad. of Dramatic Art, London; joined Nat. Youth Theatre; first London appearance at Royal Court Theatre; toured with Prospect Theatre Co.; guest artist with RSC. *Stage appearances include:* King Lear, Love's Labour's Lost, Henry IV, Henry V (all with Prospect Theatre Co.), Romeo and Juliet (RSC), The Samaritan, Black Comedy and White Liars, The Vortex, The Lunatic, The Lover and the Poet 1980, The Romans 1980, Henry IV, Part I (RSC) 1981, Antony and Cleopatra 1986, The Taming of the Shrew 1986, A Touch of the Poet 1988, His Dark Materials (Royal Nat. Theatre) 2003–04. *Films include:* The Lion in Winter 1968, Wuthering Heights 1970, Cromwell 1970, The Voyeur 1970, Mary, Queen of Scots 1971, Permission to Kill 1975, Sextette 1978, The Man Who Knew Love 1978, Agatha 1979, Flash Gordon 1980, Chanel Solitaire 1981, The Doctor and the Devils 1985, role of Ian Fleming's James Bond in The Living Daylights 1987 and Licence to Kill 1989, Hawks 1988, Brenda Starr 1989, The King's Whore 1990, Rocketeer 1991, Naked in New York 1993, Salt Water Moose 1996, The Beautician and the Beast 1997, The Informant 1997, Made Men 1999, The Reef 1999, Bitter Suite 2000, American Outlaws 2001, Looney Tunes: Back in Action 2003, Tales from Earthsea (voice: English version) 2006, Hot Fuzz 2007, Toy Story 3 (voice) 2010, The Tourist 2010, Hawaiian Vacation (short) (voice) 2011, Small Fry (short) (voice) 2011, Tinker Bell: Secret of the Wings (video) (voice) 2012. *Television includes:* Sat'day While Sunday (series) 1967, The Three Princes (film) 1968, Judge Dee (series) 1969, BBC Play of the Month (series) – Five Finger Exercise 1970, – Candida 1971, Centennial (mini-series) 1978–79, Charlie's Angels (series) 1979, The Flame Is Love (film) 1979, Antony and Cleopatra (film) 1983, Jane Eyre (mini-series) 1983, The Master of Ballantrae (film) 1984, Mistral's Daughter (mini-series) 1984, Florence Nightingale (film) 1985, Faerie Tale Theatre (series) – The Emperor's New Clothes (narrator) 1985, Sins (mini-series) 1986, Tales from the Crypt (series) – Werewolf Concerto 1992, Framed (series) 1992, Lie Down with Lions (film) 1994, Scarlett (mini-series) 1994, Stories from My Childhood (series) – The Prince and the Swan (voice) 1998, Cleopatra (mini-series) 1999, Possessed (film) 2000, Dunkirk (documentary) (narrator) 2004, Hercules (film) 2005, Agatha Christie Marple: The Sittaford Mystery (film) 2006, Unknown Sender (series) 2008, Doctor Who (series) 2009–10, Chuck (series) 2010–11. *Address:* c/o Independent Talent Group Ltd, Oxford House, 76 Oxford Street, London, W1D 1BS, England. *Telephone:* (20) 7636-6565. *Fax:* (20) 7323-0101 (office). *E-mail:* info@ independenttalent.com. *Website:* www.independenttalent.com.

DALTREY, Roger Harry, CBE; British singer and actor; b. 1 March 1944, Hammersmith, London, England; m. Heather Daltrey; two d. two s. (one by previous m.); mem. rock group, The Detours, renamed The Who 1964–84 (various reunion tours and recordings); numerous festival appearances and tours; solo artist 1984–; Gold Ticket Madison Square Garden 1979, Ivor Novello Award for Outstanding Contribution to British Music 1982, BRIT Award for Outstanding Contribution to British Music 1988, Q Legend Award 2006, South Bank Show Award for Lifetime Achievement 2007, Kennedy Center Honor 2008. *Films include:* Tommy 1974, Lisztomania 1975, The Legacy 1979, McVicar 1980, Threepenny Opera 1989. *Recordings include:* albums: with The Who: My Generation 1965, A Quick One 1966, Happy Jack 1967, The Who Sell Out 1967, Magic Bus 1968, Tommy 1969, Live At Leeds 1970, Who's Next 1971, Meaty Beefy Big And Bouncy 1971, Quadrophenia 1973, The Who By Numbers 1975, The Story Of The Who 1976, Who Are You 1978, The Kids Are Alright (live) 1979, Face Dances 1981, Hooligans 1982, It's Hard 1982, Once Upon A Time 1983, Who's Last (live) 1984, Two's Missing 1987, Joined Together (live) 1990, Live At The Isle Of Wight Festival 1970 1996, The BBC Sessions 2000, Moonlighting 2005, Endless Wire 2006; solo: Daltrey 1973, Ride A Rock Horse 1975, One Of The Boys 1977, If Parting Should Be Painless 1984, Under A Raging Moon 1985, I Can't Wait To See The Movie 1987, Rocks In The Head 1992, McVicar 1996, Martyrs And Madmen 1997, Anthology 2002. *Address:* c/o Trinifold Management Ltd, 12 Oval Road,

London, NW1 7DH, England (office). *Telephone:* (20) 7419-4300 (office). *Fax:* (20) 7419-4325 (office). *E-mail:* trinuk@globalnet.co.uk (office).

DALY, Brendan; Irish fmr politician; b. 2 Feb. 1940, Cooraclare, Co. Clare; m. Patricia Carmody; two s. one d.; ed Kilrush Co. Boys' School; mem. Dáil 1973–89, 1997–2002; Minister of State, Dept of Labour 1980–81; Minister for Fisheries and Forestry March–Dec. 1982, for the Marine 1987–89, for Defence Feb.–Nov. 1991, for Social Welfare 1991–92; Minister of State, Dept of Foreign Affairs 1992–93; mem. Seanad Éireann 1993–97, 2002–07; mem. NI Peace Forum 1994; mem. Irish Parl. Foreign Affairs Cttee 1993–; mem. Fianna Fáil. *Address:* Cooraclare, Kilrush, Co. Clare, Ireland (home). *Telephone:* (65) 9059040 (home). *Fax:* (65) 9059218 (home).

DALY, John Patrick; American professional golfer; b. 28 April 1966, Carmichael, Calif.; m. Cherie Daly; two c.; ed Univ. of Arkansas; turned professional 1987; won Missouri Open 1987, Ben Hogan Utah Classic 1990, PGA Championship, Crooked Stick 1991, BC Open 1992, BellSouth Classic 1994, British Open 1995, Dunhill Cup 1993, 1998, BMW Int. Open 2001; f. John Daly Enterprises LLC 2000. *Recording:* My Life (album). *Leisure interests:* sports, writing lyrics, playing the guitar. *E-mail:* john@johndaly.com. *Website:* www.johndaly.com.

DALY, Robert (Bob) Anthony; American business executive; *President, Rule-maker Inc.;* b. 8 Dec. 1936, Brooklyn, New York; s. of James Daly and Eleanor Daly; m. Carole Bayer Sager; two s. one d.; one step-s.; ed Brooklyn Coll.; Dir Business Affairs, then Vice-Pres. Business Affairs, then Exec. Vice-Pres. CBS TV Network 1955–80; Pres. CBS Entertainment Co. 1977–80; Chair. and Co-CEO Warner Bros, Burbank, Calif. 1980, Chair., CEO 1982–99, Chair. and Co-CEO 1994; Chair. and Co-CEO Warner Music Group 1995–99 (resgnd); Man. Gen. Pnr, Chair. and CEO LA Dodgers professional baseball team 1999–2004; currently Pres. Rulemaker Inc. (investment consultancy), LA; Chair. Bd of Dirs American Film Inst. 2009–; mem. Bd of Dirs Museum of TV and Radio; mem. Acad. of Motion Picture Arts and Sciences, Nat. Acad. of TV Arts and Sciences; Chair. Save the Children Bd of Trustees 2005–10; Hon. DFA (American Film Inst.) 1999, Hon. DHumLitt (Trinity Coll.) 2001; Steven J. Ross/Time Warner Award from Univ. of Southern Calif. School of Cinema-TV 2004. *Address:* Rulemaker Inc., 10877 Wilshire Boulevard, Suite 610, Los Angeles, CA 90024, USA (office). *Telephone:* (310) 208-1555 (office). *E-mail:* bdaly@rulemakerinc.com (office).

DAM, Kenneth Willard, JD; American lawyer, academic and fmr government official; *Max Pam Professor Emeritus and Senior Lecturer, Law School, University of Chicago;* b. 10 Aug. 1932, Marysville, Kan.; s. of Oliver W. Dam and Ida L. Dam; m. Marcia Wachs 1962; one s. one d.; ed Univs of Kansas and Chicago; law clerk, Mr Justice Whittaker, US Supreme Court 1957–58; Assoc., Cravath, Swaine & Moore, New York 1958–60; Asst Prof., Univ. of Chicago Law School 1960–61, Assoc. Prof. 1961–64, Prof. 1964–71, 1974–76, Harold J. & Marion F. Green Prof. of Int. Legal Studies 1976–85, Max Pam Prof. of American and Foreign Law 1992–2001, Prof. Emer. 2001–, also Sr Lecturer 2003–; Provost, Univ. of Chicago 1980–82; Consultant, Kirkland & Ellis, Chicago 1961–71, 1974–80, 1993–; Exec. Dir Council on Econ. Policy 1973; Asst Dir for Nat. Security and Int. Affairs, Office of Man. and Budget 1971–73; Deputy Sec. of State 1982–85; Deputy Sec., US Treasury 2001–03; Vice-Pres., Law and External Relations, IBM Corpn 1985–92; Pres., CEO United Way America 1992; mem. Bd of Dirs Alcoa 1987–2001; Chair. German-American Academic Council 1999–2001; mem. American Acad. of Arts and Sciences, American Acad. of Diplomacy; mem. Bd Council on Foreign Relations 1992–2001, Chicago Council on Foreign Relations 1992–2001. *Publications include:* Federal Tax Treatment of Foreign Income (with L. Krause) 1964, The GATT: Law and International Economic Organization 1970, Oil Resources: Who Gets What How? 1976, Economic Policy Beyond the Headlines (with George P. Shultz) 1978, The Rules of the Game: Reform and Evolution in the International Monetary System 1982, Cryptography's Role in Securing the Information Society (co-ed.) 1996, The Rules of the Global Game: A New Look at US International Economic Policy 2001, The Law–Growth Nexus: The Rule of Law and Economic Development 2006, Technology, Policy, Law and Ethics Regarding US Acquisition and Use of Cyberattack Capabilities (co-ed.) 2009; numerous articles on legal and economic issues. *Address:* 5609 South Kenwood Avenue, Chicago, IL 60637, USA (home). *Telephone:* (773) 255-2428 (office). *E-mail:* kdam@law.uchicago.edu (office). *Website:* www.law.uchicago.edu (office).

DAM-JENSEN, Inger; Danish singer (soprano); b. 13 March 1964, Copenhagen; m. Morten Ernst Lassen; ed Royal Danish Acad. of Music, Danish Opera School, studied with Kirsten Buhl Møller; started career 1992, winner Cardiff Singer of the World Competition 1993; roles include Zdenka (Arabella), Ophelia (Hamlet), Norina (Don Pasquale), Sophie (Der Rosenkavalier), Adina (L'elisir d'amore), Susanna (Le Nozze di Figaro), Musetta (La Bohème), Gilda (Rigoletto), Cleopatra (Giulio Cesare), Despina (Così fan Tutte), Lisa (La Sonnambula), Blöndchen (Die Entführung aus dem Serail), Sifare (Mitridate), Pamina (Die Zauberflöte); concert appearances with numerous orchestras, including Danish Radio Symphony, New York Philharmonic, Berlin Philharmonic, Czech Philharmonic, Philharmonia Orchestra, Bastille Orchestra, Sydney Symphony Orchestra, Toronto Symphony Orchestra, Czech Philarmonic Orchestra and Gabrieli Consort; performed closing scene from Strauss' Daphne, London Proms 1999; has performed at Edin. Festival; winner, Cardiff Int. Singing Competition 1993. *Recordings:* Mahler's Fourth Symphony, Grieg's Peer Gynt, Brahms' Ein Deutsches Requiem. *Address:* Intermusica Artists' Management Ltd, 36 Graham Street, Crystal Wharf, London, N1 8GJ, England (office). *Telephone:* (20) 7608-9900 (office). *Fax:* (20) 7490-3263 (office). *E-mail:* mail@intermusica.co.uk (office); inger@danlassen.dk. *Website:* www.intermusica.co.uk (office).

DAMADIAN, Raymond V., BS, MD; American scientist and business executive; *CEO, Fonar Corporation;* b. 1936, Forest Hills, NY; ed Juilliard School of Music, New York, Univ. of WI, Albert Einstein School of Medicine, Yeshiva Univ., Israel; developed first Magnetic Resonance scanning machine named Indomitable 1977; est. Fonar Corpn 1978, now CEO; introduced first commercial MRI (Magnetic Resonance Imaging) scanner 1980; Prof., State Univ. of NY Health Science Center, Brooklyn, NY; Nat. Medal of Tech. 1988, inducted into Nat. Inventors Hall of Fame 1989, Lemelson-MIT Lifetime Achievement Award 2001. *Address:* Fonar Corpor-ation, 110 Marcus Drive, Melville, NY 11747, USA (office). *Telephone:* (631) 694-

2929 (office). *Fax:* (631) 753-5150 (office). *E-mail:* info@fonar.com (office). *Website:* www.fonar.com (office).

DAMANAKI, Maria, MSc; Greek chemical engineer, politician and international organization official; *Commissioner for Maritime Affairs and Fisheries, European Commission;* b. 31 May 1952, Aghios Nikolaos, Crete; d. of Theodore Damanaki and Eleftheria Damanaki; m. Dimitris Danikas (divorced); one s. two d.; ed Nat. Tech. Univ. of Athens, Lancaster Univ., UK; mem. Communist Youth of Greece (KNE); active in underground student opposition to the dictatorship in Greece 1970–74; took part in Athens Polytechnic Uprising Nov. 1973, voice of 'This is the Polytechnic' radio broadcast, calling on Greek citizens to support uprising; arrested, tortured and imprisoned by the dictatorship 1973–74; engineer, Pechiney Aluminum Industries 1974; Admin., Dept of Import-Export Planning, Ministry of Finance 1975–76; elected to Vouli (Parl.), Athens 1977–93, Vice-Pres. Vouli (first woman) 1986–90; mem. Communist Party of Greece (KKE), Tech. Chamber of Greece; Pres. Coalition of the Left (Synaspismos) 1991–93, resgnd from party 2003; cand. Mayor of Athens 1994, 1998, Head of Opposition in City Council; mem. Parl. (Panhellenic Socialist Movt—PASOK) 2000–09, Chair. Select Cttee on Foreign Affairs and Defence 2009, mem. Cttee on Culture, Science and Educ., Sub-cttee on Youth and Sport, Alt. mem. Cttee on Equal Opportunities for Women and Men, Sub-cttee on Equal Participation of Women and Men in Decision-making, Sub-cttee on Science and Ethics, PASOK Co-ordinator of Educ. and Culture Issues; Commr of Maritime Affairs and Fisheries, EC, Brussels 2010–; mem. Political Council of PASOK, responsible for Educ. 2004–06, Social Affairs 2006–07, and Culture 2008–09; mem. Group of the Unified European Left; Section Man., Dept of Energy and Waste Man., Helector S.A. 2003–04. *Publications include:* The Female Face of Power 1995, The Return of Politics 2001, Associative Democracy 2004, The University in Transition 2006. *Leisure interests:* cinema, reading. *Address:* European Commissioner for Maritime Affairs and Fisheries, European Commission, 200 rue de la Loi, 1049 Brussels, Belgium (office); Filothei 24, Thisseos Str., Athens, Greece (home). *Telephone:* (2) 295-03-75 (office); (2) 295-04-17 (office); (2) 295-08-60 (Asst) (office); (2) 299-11-11 (switchboard) (office); (210) 3707000; (2) 298-55-46 (Asst) (office). *Fax:* (2) 295-01-38 (office); (210) 3692170. *E-mail:* theodora.giouroukou@ec.europa.eu (office); anna.pilioura@ec.europa.eu (office); office@damanaki.net; natalia.manas-sentis@ec.europa.eu (office). *Website:* ec .europa.eu/commission_2010-2014/damanaki (office); www.damanaki.gr.

DAMASCENO ASSIS, HE Cardinal Raymundo; Brazilian ecclesiastic; *Archbishop of Aparecida;* b. 15 Feb. 1937, Capela Nova, Minas Gerais; ordained priest, Diocese of Brasília, DF 1968; Auxiliary Bishop of Brasília 1986–2004; Titular Bishop of Nova Petra 1986–; Archbishop of Aparecida, São Paulo 2004–; cr. Cardinal (Cardinal-Priest of Immacolata al Tiburtino) 2010; participated in Papal Conclave 2013. *Address:* Curia Metropolitana, Rua Barao do Rio Branco 412, C.P. 82, 12570-000 Aparecida, São Paulo, Brazil (office). *Telephone:* (12) 31052418 (office); (12) 31051055 (office). *Fax:* (12) 31051300 (office).

D'AMATO, Alfonse M., BA, LLB; American lawyer, business executive and fmr politician; *Founder, Park Strategies LLC;* b. 1 Aug. 1937, Brooklyn, New York; m. Penelope Ann Collenburg 1960 (divorced); two s. two d.; ed Syracuse Univ.; Receiver of Taxes, Town of Hempstead 1971–72, Supervisor, Hempstead 1972–78, Presiding Supervisor 1978–81; Senator from NY 1981–98, mem. Banking, Housing and Urban Affairs Cttee (Chair. 1995), Finance Cttee, Appropriations Cttee; Founder, Park Strategies LLC 1999–; mem. Bd of Dirs Computer Associates Int. Inc. 1999–. *Publications:* Power, Pasta and Politics (autobiog.) 1995. *Address:* Park Strategies LLC, 101 Park Avenue, Suite 2506, New York, NY 10178, USA (office). *Telephone:* (212) 883-5608 (office). *Website:* www.parkstrategies.com (office).

DAMAZER, Mark David, CBE, BA; British university administrator and fmr broadcasting executive; *Master, St Peter's College, Oxford;* b. 15 April 1955; s. of Stanislaw Damazer and Suzanne Damazer; m. Rosemary Jane Morgan 1981; one s. one d.; ed Gonville and Caius Coll., Cambridge, Harvard Univ., USA; trainee with ITN 1979–81; Producer BBC World Service 1981–83, TV-AM 1983–84, BBC Six O'Clock News 1984–86, Output Ed. Newsnight 1986–88, Deputy Ed., Nine O'Clock Main Evening News 1988–89, Ed. 1989–94, Ed. TV News 1994–96, Head of Current Affairs 1996–98, Head of Political Programmes 1998–2000, Asst Dir BBC News 1999–2001, Deputy Dir 2001–04, Controller BBC Radio 4 and BBC Radio 7 2004–10; Master, St Peter's Coll., Oxford 2010–; mem. Bd Inst. of Contemporary British History; Fellow, American Political Soc. 1978–79; Vice-Chair. and mem., Int. Press Inst.; Fellow, Radio Acad. 2008; Harkness Fellowship. *Publications:* articles in various newspapers and magazines. *Leisure interests:* opera, Tottenham Hotspur, Boston Red Sox, gardening, coarse tennis, Italian painting. *Address:* St Peter's College, New Inn Hall Street, Oxford, OX1 2DL, England (office). *Telephone:* (1865) 278900 (home). *Fax:* (1865) 278855 (office). *Website:* www.spc.ox.ac.uk (office).

D'AMBROSIO, Louis J., BS, MBA; American business executive; *Chairman, Sensus;* ed Pennsylvania State Univ. (Valedictorian), Harvard Business School; with IBM Corpn 1986–2002, held several exec. posts and was mem. Worldwide Man. Cttee, roles included leading strategy for Global Services, Sales and Marketing for Software, and Industry Operations for Asia Pacific; Group Vice-Pres., Avaya Global Services, Avaya Inc. 2002–03; Group Vice-Pres., Global Sales, Channels and Marketing 2004–05, Sr Vice-Pres. and Pres. Global Sales and Marketing 2005–06, mem. Bd of Dirs, Pres. and CEO Avaya Inc. 2006–08; Pres. and CEO Sears Holdings Corpn 2011–13; mem. Bd of Dirs Sensus 2010–, Chair. 2013–; fmr Chair. (non-exec.) Sensus (clean technology co.); Trustee, Jackson Laboratory, Walnut Street Theatre. *Address:* Sensus, 8601 Six Forks Road, Suites 300 & 700, Raleigh, NC 27615, USA (office). *Telephone:* (919) 845-4000 (office). *E-mail:* info@sensus.com (office). *Website:* www.sensus.com (office).

D'AMICO DE CARVALHO, Caterina; Italian film industry executive, screenwriter and academic; *CEO, RAI Cinema SpA;* b. Rome; d. of Fedele d'Amico and Suso Cecchi d'Amico; began career working as a theatre company dir, Rome 1972–76; Dean of Centro Sperimentale di Cinematografia (nat. film school) 1999–2007; CEO RAI Cinema SpA (film production and distribution arm of Govt-run Italian broadcaster RAI) 2007–; Founding mem. and Pres. Théatre des Italiens Foundation 1998–2003. *Films:* Luchino Visconti (consultant) 1999, My Voyage to Italy (assoc. producer) 2001. *Address:* RAI Cinema SpA, Piazza Adriana 12, 00193

Rome, Italy (office). *Telephone:* (06) 684701 (office). *E-mail:* info@raicinema.it (office). *Website:* www.raicinema.it (office).

DAMON, Matt; American actor; b. 8 Oct. 1970, Cambridge, Mass.; m. Luciana Barroso 2005; three d.; numerous awards for Good Will Hunting including Acad. Award for Best Writing, Screenplay written directly for Screen, Silver Berlin Bear Award for Outstanding Single Achievement 1997. *Films include:* Mystic Pizza 1988, Rising Son (TV) 1990, School Ties 1992, Geronimo: An American Legend 1993, The Good Old Boys (TV) 1995, Courage Under Fire 1996, Glory Daze 1996, Chasing Amy 1997, The Rainmaker 1997, Good Will Hunting (also co-writer) 1997, Saving Private Ryan 1998, Rounders 1998, Dogma 1999, The Talented Mr Ripley 1999, Titan A.E. (voice) 1999, All the Pretty Horses 1999, The Legend of Baggar Vance 2000, Finding Forrester 2000, Ocean's Eleven 2001, The Majestic (voice) 2001, Gerry (also writer) 2002, Spirit: Stallion of the Cimarron (voice) 2002, The Third Wheel 2002, The Bourne Identity 2002, Confessions of a Dangerous Mind 2003, Stuck on You 2003, Eurotrip 2004, Jersey Girl 2004, The Bourne Supremacy (Empire Film Award for Best Actor 2005) 2004, Ocean's Twelve 2004, The Brothers Grimm 2005, Syriana 2005, The Departed 2006, The Good Shepherd 2006, Ocean's Thirteen 2007, The Bourne Ultimatum 2007, The Informant! 2009, Invictus 2009, Green Zone 2010, 30 Rock 2010, Hereafter 2010, True Grit 2010, The Adjustment Bureau 2011, Contagion 2011, Margaret 2011, Happy Feet Two (voice) 2011, We Bought a Zoo 2011, Promised Land 2012, Behind the Candelabra 2013, Elysium 2013, The Monuments Men 2014. *Address:* WME, 9601 Wilshire Blvd., Beverly Hills, CA 90210, USA (office).

DANAILOV, Stefan, MA; Bulgarian actor and politician; *Minister of Culture;* b. Sept. 1942, Sofia; ed Krastyo Sarafov Nat. Acad. for Theatre and Film Arts; currently Prof., Nat. Acad. of Theatre and Film Arts; mem. Nat. Ass. 2001–, Chair. Parl. Cttee on Culture 2001–05; Minister of Culture 2005–; Order of Stara Planina, Commdr, l'Ordre des Arts et des Lettres 2006; Paisiy Hilendarsky (Ministry of Culture) 2002. *Plays:* prominent roles include Camille Demolen, The Danton Case (Psibishevska), Stylo, Banzy is Dead (Ethole Fewgard), Edmond, Long Day's Journey into the Night (Eugene O'Neill), Chadski, Blame His Misfortunes on His Wits (Griboedov), Hamlet (Shakespeare), Stavrogin, The Possessed (Dostoyevsky), Peer Gynt (Ibsen), Shylock, The Price (Arthur Miller), Alessandro Medici, Lorenzaccio (Alfred de Musset), Danton, Danton's Death (Buchner), Trigorin, The Seagull (Chekhov). *Television:* At Each Kilometer (series) 1969–71. *Films:* The Traces Remain 1956, The Inspector and the Night 1963, Quiet Paths 1967, The Sea 1967, Taste of Almonds 1967, The First Courier 1968, The Prince 1970, The Black Angels 1970, There Is Nothing Finer Than Bad Weather 1971, Affection 1972, Ivan Kondarev 1974, Houses Without Fences 1974, Glow Over the Drava River 1974, Life or Death 1974, The Weddings of King Ioan Assen 1975, A Real Man 1975, Beginning of the Day 1975, The Soldier of the Supply Column 1976, Guilt 1976, Amendment to the Defense-of-State Act 1976, RMS Five 1977, A Year of Mondays 1977, Warmth 1978, Moments in a Matchbox 1979, Something Out of Nothing 1979, The Porcupines' War 1979, The Blood Remains 1980, Ladies Choice 1980, The Queen of Turnovo 1981, Autumn Sun 1982, Crystals 1982, Twenty-Four Hours Raining 1982, The Odyssey in the Deliorman 1983, Balance 1983, Blood That Had to Be Shed 1985, The Conversion to Christianity & Discourse of Letters 1985, Manoeuvres on the Fifth Floor 1985, Misty Shores 1986, Transports of Death 1986, Three Marias and Ivan 1986, Ballad 1986, Dreamers 1987, A Sky for All 1987, The Mooncalf 1987, Protect the Small Animals 1988, Monday Morning 1988, The Carnival 1990, I Want Amerika 1991, The Berlin Conspiracy 1992, Crisis in the Kremlin 1992, Don Quixote Returns 1996, A Spanish Fly 1998, After the End of the World 1998, Vercingétorix 2001, The Lark Farm 2007, St. George Shoots the Dragon 2008. *Television:* Dying in the Worst 1978, Oncoming Traffic 1979, Time for Travelling 1987, Home for Our Children 1987, Big Game 1988, People Who Never Disappear 1988, The Black Frames 1989, Live Dangerously 1990, Fathers and Sons 1990, In fondo al cuore 1997, Racket 1997, Fine secolo 1999, About Love, Forgive Us 2003. *Address:* Ministry of Culture, 1040 Sofia, bul. A. Stamboliyski 17, Bulgaria (office). *Telephone:* (2) 940-08-63 (office). *Fax:* (2) 981-81-45 (office). *E-mail:* press@mc.government.bg (office). *Website:* www.mc.government.bg (office).

DANCE, Charles, OBE; British actor, writer and film director; b. 10 Oct. 1946, Rednal, Worcs., England; s. of the late Walter Dance and Eleanor Perks; m. Joanna Haythorn 1970; one s. one d.; worked in industry; with RSC 1975–80, 1981–92; Best Actor, Paris Film Festival 1996. *Theatre includes:* Coriolanus (title role) (RSC) 1989, Irma La Douce, Turning Over, Henry V, Three Sisters 1998, Good 1999, Long Day's Journey Into Night 2001, The Play What I Wrote 2002, Eh Joe (Sydney Theatre Festival), Shadowlands 2007–08 (London Theatre Critics Circle Best Actor Award 2008). *Films include:* For Your Eyes Only 1981, Plenty 1985, The Golden Child 1986, White Mischief 1987, Good Morning, Babylon 1987, Hidden City 1987, Pascali's Island 1988, La valle di pietra 1992, Alien 3 1992, Last Action Hero 1993, Century 1993, China Moon 1994, Kabloonak 1994, Desvío al paraíso 1994, Exquisite Tenderness 1995, Potemkin: The Runner's Cut (short) 1996, Space Truckers 1996, Michael Collins 1996, The Blood Oranges 1997, What Rats Won't Do 1998, Hilary and Jackie 1998, Chrono-Perambulator (short) 1999, Don't Go Breaking My Heart 1999, Jurij 2001, Dark Blue World 2001, Gosford Park 2001, Ali G Indahouse 2002, Black and White 2002, City and Crimes 2003, Swimming Pool 2003, Labyrinth 2003, Ladies in Lavender (writer and dir) 2004, Dolls (short) (narrator) 2006, Scoop 2006, Starter for 10 2006, Désaccord parfait 2006, Twice Upon a Time 2006, The Contractor (video) 2007, Intervention 2007, The Clerk's Tale (short) 2010, Paris Connections 2010, The Commuter (short) 2010, The Mapmaker (short) 2011, Ironclad 2011, There Be Dragons 2011, Your Highness 2011, The Door (short) 2011, Winds of Change 2011, Underworld: Awakening 2012, St George's Day 2012, Midnight's Children 2012, Viy. Vozvrashchenie 2013. *Radio:* The Heart of the Matter 2001, The Charge of the Light Brigade 2001. *Television appearances include:* Father Brown (series) 1974, Edward the Seventh (series) 1975, Raffles (series) 1977, Tales of the Unexpected (film) 1979, BBC2 Playhouse (series) – Fatal Spring (as Siegfried Sassoon) 1980, Nancy Astor (mini-series) 1982, Frost in May (mini-series) 1982, BBC Play of the Month (series) – Little Eyolf 1982, The Last Day (film) 1983, The Professionals (series) 1983, The Jewel in the Crown (mini-series) 1984, Play for Today (series) – Dreams of Leaving 1980, – Rainy Day Women 1984, The Secret Servant (series) 1984, Thunder Rock (film) 1985, This Lightning Always Strikes Twice (film) 1985, Screen Two (series) 1986, Out on a Limb (film) 1987, Tales of the Unexpected (series) 1987, Out of the

Shadows (film) 1988, First Born (mini-series) 1988, Goldeneye (film) 1989, The Lancaster Miller Affair (mini-series) 1990, The Phantom of the Opera (film) 1990, Undertow (film) 1996, Rebecca (film) 1997, In the Presence of Mine Enemies (film) 1997, Murder Rooms: Mysteries of the Real Sherlock Holmes (series) 2000, Justice in Wonderland (film) 2000, Randall & Hopkirk (Deceased) (series) 2000, The Life and Adventures of Nicholas Nickleby (film) 2001, Foyle's War (series) 2002, Trial & Retribution (series) 2003, Henry VIII (film) 2003, Looking for Victoria (film) 2003, When Hitler Invaded Britain (documentary) (narrator) 2004, Don Bosco (film) 2004, Last Rights (mini-series) 2005, Fingersmith (series) 2005, Titanic: Birth of a Legend (documentary) (narrator) 2005, To the Ends of the Earth (mini-series) 2005, Bleak House (mini-series) 2005, Marple: By the Pricking of My Thumbs (film) 2006, Fallen Angel (mini-series) 2007, Consenting Adults (film) 2007, Jam & Jerusalem (series) 2009, Merlin (series) 2009, Trinity (series) 2009, Going Postal (film) 2010, This September (series) 2010, Neverland (mini-series) 2011, Game of Thrones (series) 2011–12, Strikeback (series) 2012, Coup (series) 2012. *Address:* Angharad Wood, Tavistock Wood, 45 Conduit Street, London, W1S 2YN, England (office). *Telephone:* (20) 7494-4767 (office).

D'ANCONA, Matthew, BA, FRSA; British journalist, writer and editor; b. 1968, London; m. Sarah Schaefer; two s.; ed St Dunstan's Coll., Magdalen Coll., Oxford; fmrly worked for human rights magazine, Index on Censorship; trainee, news reporter, education correspondent The Times 1991–94, Asst Ed. 1994–95; Deputy Ed. comment section and political columnist The Sunday Telegraph 1996–98, Deputy Ed. 1998–2006, now political columnist; Ed. The Spectator 2006–09; political columnist, GQ magazine 2006–09; now Contributing Ed.; columnist, Evening Standard 2009–; mem. Bd of Dirs Centre for Policy Studies 1998–2006; Prize Fellow, All Souls Coll., Oxford 1989–96, now Quondam Fellow; mem. Advisory Council, Demos 1998–2006, Millennium Comm. 2001–06, Policy Advisory Bd, Social Market Foundation 2002–06, Puttnam Comm. on Parliament in the Public Eye 2004–05; Charles Douglas-Home Memorial Trust Prize 1995, British Press Award for Political Journalist of the Year 2004, Editor of the Year (Current Affairs), British Soc. of Magazine Editors 2007. *Publications include:* The Jesus Papyrus (non-fiction, with Carsten Peter Thiede) 1997, The Quest for the True Cross (non-fiction, with Carsten Peter Thiede) 2002, Going East (novel) 2004, Tabatha's Code (novel) 2006, Nothing to Fear 2008. *Address:* Evening Standard, Northcliffe House, 2 Derry Street, London, W8 5EE, England.

DANDA, Mahamadou; Niger politician; b. 25 July 1951, Tahoua; m.; six c.; ed Ecole Nat. d'Admin, Niamey; also studied in Bordeaux, France, Burkina Faso and Canada; Sub-Prefect of Niamey 1979–80, of Filingué 1983–87; Minister of Animal Resources and Hydraulics 1987–88; fmr Admin. Sec., Nat. Exec. Bureau, Mouvement nat. pour la société de développement; Chief Technical Adviser to Prime Minister for Institutional Issues 1997–99; Minister of Communication, Culture, Youth, and Sports, also Govt Spokesman April–Dec. 1999; Political Counsellor, Canadian Embassy, Niamey 2009–10; Prime Minister 2010–11. *Address:* c/o Office of the Prime Minister, BP 893, Niamey, Niger (office).

DANELIUS, Hans Carl Yngve; Swedish judge and diplomatist; b. 2 April 1934, Stockholm; s. of Sven Danelius and Inga Danelius (née Svensson); m. Hannah Schadee 1961; three s. one d.; ed Dept of Legal Studies, Stockholm Univ.; law practice in Swedish courts 1957–64; mem. Secr., European Comm. of Human Rights (ECHR), Strasbourg 1964–67, mem. ECHR 1983–99; Asst Judge, Svea Court of Appeal 1967–68; Adviser, Ministry of Justice 1968–71; Deputy Head, Legal Dept, Ministry for Foreign Affairs 1971–75, Head 1975–84, rank of Amb. 1977–84; Amb. to the Netherlands 1984–88; Judge, Supreme Court of Sweden 1988–2001; Pres. Council on Legislation 2001–03; Arbitrator, ICSID 1999–; mem. Perm. Court of Arbitration at The Hague 1982–; mem. Court of Conciliation and Arbitration, OSCE 1995–2007; mem. Constitutional Court of Bosnia and Herzegovina 1996–2002; Chief Ed. Svensk Juristtidning (Swedish Law Journal) 1973–84; Swedish and foreign decorations; Dr hc (Stockholm) 1988. *Publications:* The United Nations Convention Against Torture 1988, Mänskliga Rättigheter (Human Rights) (fifth edn) 1993, Mänskliga Rättigheter i Europeisk Praxis (Human Rights in European Practice) (third edn) 2007; numerous articles in Swedish and foreign journals. *Address:* Roslinvägen 33, 16851 Bromma, Sweden (home). *Telephone:* (8) 37-34-91 (home). *Fax:* (8) 37-34-91 (home). *E-mail:* hans .danelius@telia.com (home).

DANELIYA, Georgy Nikolayevich; Georgian film director; b. 25 Aug. 1930, Tbilisi; m. Galina Daneliya; one s. one d.; ed Moscow Inst. of Architecture, Higher Courses of Film Direction; worked at Inst. for City Designing; Prof. All-Russian Inst. of Cinematography 1975–85; film Dir studio Mosfilm; State Prizes of USSR and Russia; USSR People's Artist; more than 70 prizes in int. film festivals. *Films include:* Serezha 1960, I am Wailing About Moscow 1963, Thirty Three 1965, Don't Grieve 1969, Aphonya 1975, Mimino 1978 (Gold Prize Avelino Festival, Italy), Autumn Marathon 1979 (Grand Prix San Sebastián Festival, Spain, Grand Prix Chambourci Festival, France), Gentlemen of Luck 1981, Tears were Dropping 1982, Kin-Dza-Dza 1987, Passport 1989, White Dance 1992, Nastya 1993, Heads and Tails? 1995, Fortuna 2000. *Address:* 103062 Moscow, Makarenko 1/19 apt. 15, Russia. *Telephone:* (495) 921-43-74.

DANES, Claire Catherine; American actress; b. 12 April 1979, New York, NY; d. of Chris Danes and Carla Danes; m. Hugh Dancy 2009; ed performing arts school, NY and Lee Strasberg Studio; first acting roles in off-Broadway theatre productions: Happiness, Punk Ballet and Kids on Stage. *Plays include:* The Vagina Monologues (Westside Theatre) 2000, Christina Olson: American Model (Performance Space 122) 2005, Edith and Jenny (Performance Space 122) 2007, Pygmalion (American Airlines Theatre) 2007. *Films include:* Dreams of Love (debut) 1992, Thirty (short) 1993, The Pesky Suitor (short), Little Women 1994, Romeo and Juliet (Blockbuster Entertainment Award for Favorite Actress – Romance 1996, London Film Critics Circle Award for Actress of the Year 1996, MTV Movie Award for Best Female Performance 1996, YoungStar Award for Best Performance by a Young Actress in a Drama Film 1996) 1996, To Gillian on Her 37th Birthday (Young Artist Award for Best Performance in a Feature Film – Supporting Young Actress 1996) 1996, Polish Wedding, U-Turn 1997, The Rainmaker 1997, Les Misérables 1998, The Mod Squad 1999, Brokedown Palace 1999, Monterey Pop 2000, Dr T and the Women 2000, Flora Plum 2000, The Cherry Orchard 2002, Igby Goes Down 2002, The Hours 2002, Terminator 3: Rise of the Machines 2003, Stage Beauty 2004, Shopgirl 2005, The Family Stone 2005, Evening 2007, The Flock

2007, Stardust 2007, Me and Orson Welles 2008, As Cool as I Am 2013. *Television includes:* My So-Called Life (series) (Golden Globe Award for Best Actress – Television Series Drama 1994, Young Artist Award for Best Performance by a Youth Ensemble in a Television Series 1994), No Room for Opal (film), The Coming Out of Heidi Leiter, Temple Grandin (film) (Primetime Emmy Award for Outstanding Lead Actress in a Miniseries or a Movie 2011, Golden Globe Award for Best Performance by an Actress in a Mini-series or Motion Picture Made for TV 2011, Satellite Award for Best Actress – Miniseries or Television Film 2011, Screen Actors Guild Award for Outstanding Performance by a Female Actor in a Miniseries or Television Movie 2011) 2010, A Child's Garden of Poetry (film, voice) 2011, Homeland (series) (Golden Globe Award for Best Performance by an Actress in a Television Series – Drama 2012, 2013, Satellite Award for Best Actress – Television Series Drama 2012, Emmy Award for Best Lead Actress in a Drama 2012, 2013) 2011–. *Address:* c/o ICM, Constellation Boulevard, Los Angeles, CA 90067, USA (office). *Telephone:* (310) 550-4000 (office). *Website:* www.icmtalent .com (office).

DANESH JAFARI, Davoud, PhD; Iranian government official; b. 1954; ed Indian Univ. of Kashmir, Allameh Tabatabaei Univ., Tehran; expert Construction Jihad, Tehran Prov. 1979, later Commdr Eng Section, with Cen. HQ for Reconstruction 1983, Head, Logistics and Eng HQ, Construction Jihad 1984, mem. Cen. Council 1988; Man. Dir Inst. for Devt Jihad 1988; Deputy Minister of Construction Jihad for Reconstruction of Gilan and Zanjan Provs 1989, for Reconstruction of Palm Groves 1990, for Planning 1992; mem. Parl.; Minister of Econ. Affairs and Finance 2005–08; mem. High Monetary and Credit Council, High Council on Banks; Medal of Honour. *Address:* c/o Ministry of Economic Affairs and Finance, Sour Esrafil Avenue, Nasser Khosrou Street, Tehran 11149-43661, Iran (office).

DANEV, Bojidar, MSc, PhD; Bulgarian economist and business executive; *Chairman and Executive President, Bulgarian Industrial Association;* b. 5 Nov. 1939, Sofia; ed Tech. Univ., Sofia; began career at Inst. of Cybernetics, Bulgarian Acad. of Sciences, attained rank of Sr Research Assoc.; worked for two years at Univ. of Hanover, Germany; returned to Bulgaria 1980 to work as expert in Econ. Analysis Dept, Bulgarian Industrial Econ. Asscn (now Bulgarian Industrial Asscn) 1980–87, Vice-Pres. 1989–91, Chair. and Exec. Pres. 1993–; Vice-Chair. on financial issues, Cen. Cooperative Union 1987–89; Man. Sofia Stock Exchange 1991–97; Co-Chair. EU-Bulgaria Jt Consultative Cttee 1999–2004; Vice-Pres. Econ. and Social Council of Repub. of Bulgaria and of Nat. Council of Tripartite Cooperation 2006–, mem. European and Social Cttee and Head of working group on Lisbon Strategy; mem. Man. Cttee Bulgarian Acad. of Sciences; Vice-Pres. New Bulgarian Univ. Bd; Exec. Dir and mem. Man. Bd Interlease AD 1995–; mem. Man. Bd Solvay-Sodi AD, Industrial Holding Bulgaria, Doverie Insurance Company; and Chair., Industrial Holding Bulgaria AD; Chair. Man. Bd and Exec. Chair., Bulgarian Industrial Asscn. *Publications:* three books and more than 150 articles in scientific publications. *Address:* Bulgarian Industrial Association, 1000 Sofia, 16-20 Alabin Str., Bulgaria (office). *Telephone:* (2) 9800303 (office). *E-mail:* danev@bia-bg.com (office). *Website:* www.bia-bg.com (office).

DANFORTH, John Claggett, AB, BD, LLB; American politician, lawyer and diplomatist; *Partner, Bryan Cave LLP;* b. 5 Sept. 1936, St Louis, Mo.; s. of Donald and Dorothy Danforth; m. Sally B. Dobson 1957; one s. four d.; ed St Louis County Day (High) School, Princeton Univ., Yale Univ. Law School and Yale Divinity School; admitted to NY Bar 1963, Mo. Bar 1966; Davis Polk (law firm) 1963–66; Pnr Bryan Cave LLP (law firm) 1966–68, 1995–2004, 2005–; Attorney-Gen. of Mo. 1969–76; Senator from Missouri 1976–95; mem. Senate Cttees on Finance, Commerce, Science and Transportation, Select Cttee on Intelligence; Head of Special Envoy to Sudan 2001–04; US Perm. Rep. to UN, New York 2004 (resgnd); ordained priest, Episcopal Church 1964; asst or assoc. rector of churches in New York City, St Louis, Jefferson City; Assoc. Rector Church of the Holy Communion, Univ. City, Mo. 1995–; Hon. Assoc. St Alban's Church, Washington; awards include Presidential World Without Hunger Award, Legislative Leadership Award of Nat. Comm. against Drunk Driving, Brotherhood and Distinguished Missourian awards of Nat. Conf. of Christians and Jews. *Film appearance:* The Devil Came on Horseback 2006. *Publication:* Resurrection: The Confirmation of Clarence Thomas 1994. *Address:* Bryan Cave LLP, One Metropolitan Square, 211 North Broadway, Suite 3600, St. Louis, MO 63102-2750, USA. *Telephone:* (314) 259-2980 (office). *Fax:* (314) 552-8980 (office). *E-mail:* jcdanforth@bryancave.com (office). *Website:* www.bryancave.com (office).

DANGOTE, Aliko; Nigerian business executive; *Group President and CEO, Dangote Group;* b. 10 April 1957, Kano; s. of Mohammed Dangote and Mariya Sanusi Dantata; m.; two c.; ed Al-Azhar Univ., Egypt; began career trading in commodities including flour, sugar, rice and cement; Founder, Group Pres. and CEO Dangote Group (manufacturing conglomerate active in numerous fields including cement plants, sugar refineries, salt processing facilities, beverage manufacture) 1977–; Officer, Order of Niger 2000, Commdr, Order of Niger 2005; ZIK Award 1992, Int. Award of Sir Ahmadu Bello, Cross River State Roll of Honour Award 2002, Thisday Newspapers Award for CEO of the Year 2005; ranked by Forbes magazine amongst The World's Most Powerful People (64th) 2013. *Address:* Dangote Group, Union Marble House, 1 Alfred Rewane Road, PMB 40032, Falomo, Ikoyi, Lagos, Nigeria (office). *Telephone:* (1) 4480815 (office); (1) 4480816 (office). *Fax:* (1) 2702893 (office); (1) 2712231 (office). *E-mail:* communications@dangote -group.com (office). *Website:* www.dangote-group.com (office).

DANIEL, Sir John Sagar, Kt, OC, MA, MAEdTech, ATh, DèsSc; British/Canadian academic, university administrator and international organization official; b. 31 May 1942, Banstead, Surrey, England; s. of John Edward Daniel Sagar and Winifred Sagar; m. Kristin Anne Swanson 1966 (died 2011); one s. two d.; ed Christ's Hosp., Sussex and St Edmund Hall, Oxford, UK, Univ. of Paris, France, Concordia Univ., Montreal, Canada; Assoc. Prof., Ecole Polytechnique, Université de Montréal 1969–73; Dir des Etudes, Télé-Univ., Université de Québec 1973–77; Vice-Pres. Athabasca Univ., Alberta 1977–80; Academic Vice-Rector Concordia Univ. 1980–84; Pres. Laurentian Univ., Sudbury 1984–90; Vice-Chancellor Open Univ., UK 1990–2001; Pres. Open Univ., USA 1999–2001; Asst Dir-Gen. for Educ., UNESCO 2001–04; Pres. and CEO Commonwealth of Learning 2004–12; mem. Council of Foundation, Int. Baccalaureate 1992– (Vice-Pres. 1996–99), British North American Cttee 1995–; mem. Council, Open Univ., Hong

Kong 1996–, CBI 1996–; mem. Bd Canadian Council on Learning 2005–; Trustee, Carnegie Foundation for the Advancement of Teaching 1993–; Forum Fellow, World Econ. Forum, Switzerland 1998; Fellow, Open Univ. (UK); Sr Fellow, European Distance Educ. Network 2007; Hon. Fellow, St Edmund Hall, Oxford; Officier, Ordre des Palmes académiques; 32 hon. degrees, including Hon. DLitt (Indira Gandhi Nat. Open, India) 2003, (Thompson Rivers, Canada) 2005, (Netaji Subhas Open, India) 2005, (McGill Univ., Canada), (Univ. of South Africa) 2010, (Univ. of Ghana) 2013; Hon. DSc (Coll. Mil. Royal, Saint-Jean) 1988, (Open Univ. of Sri Lanka) 1994, (Univ. of Paris VI) 2001 (Univ. of Winneba, Ghana) 2006; Hon. DEd (Open Univ. Malaysia) 2009, (Empire State Coll., State Univ. of NY) 2011; Hon. LLD (Waterloo, Canada) 1993, (Univ. of Wales) 2002, (Laurentian Univ. Canada) 2006, (Univ. Canada West) 2008; Hon. DUniv (Univs of Athabasca, Portugal, Humberside, Anadolu Univ., Turkey, Sukhothai Thammathirat Open Univ., Thailand, Télé-université, Université du Québec, Canada, Univ. of Derby, Open Univ., Hong Kong, New Bulgarian Univ., Univ. of Montreal); Individual Award of Excellence, Commonwealth of Learning 1995, Morris T. Keeton Award, Council for Adult and Experiential Learning (USA) 1999, Queen's Jubilee Medal (Canada), Symons Medal, Asscn of Commonwealth Univs 2008, Frank H. Klassen Award of the Int. Council for Education for Teaching 2009, Educ. Master, Beijing DeTao Masters Acad. 2011. *Publications:* more than 320 articles and books, including Learning at a Distance: A World Perspective 1982, Developing Distance Education (co-author) 1988, Mega-universities and Knowledge Media: Technology Strategies for Higher Education 1996, Mega-Schools, Technology and Teachers: Achieving Education for All 2010. *Leisure interests:* walking, boating, reading. *E-mail:* odlsirjohn@gmail.com. *Website:* www.sirjohn.ca.

DANIEL, Patrick, BA (Hons), MPA; Singaporean journalist and newspaper executive; *Editor-in-Chief, English and Malay Newspapers Division, Singapore Press Holdings Ltd;* ed Univ. Coll., Oxford, UK, Kennedy School of Govt, Harvard Univ., USA; with Singapore Govt's Admin. Service, including post of Dir in Ministry of Trade and Industry –1986; Sr Leader/Feature Writer, The Straits Times Press Ltd 1975, Econs Ed., The Straits Times 1989, Man. Ed. 1990–92, Ed. The Business Times 1992–2002, Man. Ed. English and Malay Newspapers Div., Singapore Press Holdings Ltd 2002–06, Ed.-in-Chief 2006–. *Address:* Singapore Press Holdings Ltd, SPH News Centre, P2M, 1000 Toa Payoh North, Singapore City, 318994, Singapore (office). *Telephone:* 6319-5111 (office). *Fax:* 6319-8282 (office). *E-mail:* pdaniel@sph.com.sg (office). *Website:* www.sph.com.sg (office); www.straitstimes.com (office).

DANIEL, Paul Wilson, CBE; British conductor; *Music Director, Orchestre Nationale Bordeaux Aquitaine;* b. 5 July 1958, Birmingham; m. Joan Rodgers (q.v.) 1988; two d.; ed choir of Coventry Cathedral, King's Coll., Cambridge, Guildhall School of Music and Drama, London, studied with Franco Ferrara in Italy and with Adrian Boult and Edward Downes; mem. music staff, ENO, London 1982–87, Music Dir 1997–2005; Music Dir, Opera Factory 1987–90, Opera North, Leeds 1990–97; Prin. Conductor, English Northern Philharmonia 1990–97; Prin. Conductor and Artistic Adviser, West Australian Symphony Orchestra 2009–13; Principal Conductor and Artistic Dir, Royal Philharmonic Orchestra of Galicia, Santiago de Compostela 2013–; Music Dir, Orchestre Nat. Bordeaux Aquitaine 2013–; has conducted all the major London orchestras and most of the regional UK orchestras and orchestras in USA, Germany, Netherlands, France and Australia; Olivier Award for Outstanding Achievement in Opera 1997, Gramophone Award for English Music Series 1999. *Operas conducted include:* (ENO) The Mask of Orpheus, Akhnaten, Tosca, Rigoletto, Carmen, Figaro's Wedding, King Priam, Flying Dutchman, From the House of the Dead, Tales of Hoffmann, Falstaff, Manon, Othello, Boris Godunov, La Traviata, The Carmelites, Nixon in China, The Silver Tassie, War and Peace, Lulu, The Trojans, Twilight of the Gods, (Opera North) Ariane et Barbe-Bleue, Attila, King Priam, Don Giovanni, Der Ferne Klang, Boris Godunov (also at BBC Proms 1992), Rigoletto, Don Carlos, Wozzeck, Gloriana, Baa Baa Black Sheep (world premiere), Playing Away, Il Trovatore, Pelléas et Mélisande, Jenůfa, Luisa Miller; (Royal Opera Covent Garden) Mitridate; has also conducted opera productions in Nancy, Munich, Brussels, Geneva. *Address:* c/o Orchestre Nationale Bordeaux Aquitaine, Grand-Théâtre, Place de la Comédie, BP 90095, 33025 Bordeaux Cedex, France (office). *E-mail:* info@onb.fr (office). *Website:* www.onb.fr (office).

DANIEL, Hon. Wilmoth; Antigua and Barbuda politician and auctioneer; *Deputy Prime Minister and Minister of Works, Transportation and the Environment;* b. 18 Aug. 1948, Bolans; m.; one s. one d.; ed Hill Secondary School; fmr Man. Brysons Wholesale Dept, Bottling Plant and Building Supplies Dept; United Nat. Democratic Party cand. in St Phillip's South Constituency 1984; Senator in Upper House 1989–94; mem. Parl. for St Phillip's South 1994–99, 2004–; Deputy Prime Minister and Minister of Works, Transportation and The Environment 2004–; Co-founding mem. and currently Deputy Leader of United Progressive Party. *Address:* Ministry Public Works, Telecommunications and the Environment, New Administration Building, Queen Elizabeth Highway, St John's, Antigua (office). *Telephone:* 462-4625 (office); 462-0651 (office). *Fax:* 462-6398 (office); 462-2836 (office). *E-mail:* environment@antiguabarbuda.net (office). *Website:* www.ab .gov.ag/gov_v2/government/shared/bio_wilmothdaniel.html (office); www .uppantigua.com/leadership/daniel (office).

DANIELS, J(ohn) Eric, BA, MSc; American banker; b. 14 Aug. 1951, Mont.; ed Cornell Univ., Massachusetts Inst. of Tech.; joined Citibank 1975, Corp. Banking 1975–80 Panama City, Chief Financial Officer and Br. Man. of 15 brs in Argentina 1980–82, Business Man. Citibank, Chile 1982–85, Country Head, Citibank, Argentina 1985–88, Divisional Exec. Citibank Private Bank, London 1988–91, Head, Citibank Corp. Taskforce (charged with restoring bank's profitability) NY 1992, Pres. FSB Calif. (Citibank consumer franchise) San Francisco 1992–96, Regional Head, Citibank Consumer Bank Europe, Brussels 1996–97, COO Citigroup Consumer Bank NY 1998, Chair. and CEO Travelers Life & Annuity, Hartford, Conn. 1998–2000; Founder, Chair. and CEO Zona Financiera 2000–01; Group Exec. Dir UK Retail Banking Lloyds TSB 2001–03, Group Chief Exec. Lloyds TSB Group plc (renamed Lloyds Banking Group plc following acquisition of HBOS plc 2009) 2003–11; Dir (non-exec.) BT Group. *Address:* c/o Lloyds Banking Group plc, 25 Gresham Street, London, EC2V 7HN, England.

DANIELS, Jeff; American actor; *Executive Director, Purple Rose Theatre;* b. 19 Feb. 1955, Athens, Ga; m. Kathleen Treado; 3 c.; ed Cen. Mich. Univ.; apprentice Circle Repertory Theatre, New York; f. Purple Rose Theatre Co., Chelsea, Mich. *Theatre:* The Farm 1976, Brontosaurus 1977, My Life 1977, Feedlot 1977, Lulu 1978, Slugger 1978, The Fifth of July 1978, Johnny Got His Gun 1982 (Obie Award), The Three Sisters 1982–83, The Golden Age 1984, Redwood Curtain 1993, Short-Changed Review 1993, Lemon Sky. *Films include:* Ragtime 1981, Terms of Endearment 1983, The Purple Rose of Cairo 1985, Marie 1985, Heartburn 1986, Something Wild 1986, Radio Days 1987, The House on Carroll Street 1988, Sweet Hearts Dance 1988, Grand Tour 1989, Checking Out 1989, Arachnophobia 1990, Welcome Home, Roxy Carmichael 1990, Love Hurts 1990, The Butcher's Wife 1992, Gettysburg 1993, Speed 1994, Dumb and Dumber 1994, Fly Away Home 1996, Two Days in the Valley 1996, 101 Dalmatians 1996, Trial and Error 1997, Pleasantville 1998, All the Rage 1999, My Favorite Martian 1999, Chasing Sleep 2000, Escanaba in da Moonlight 2000, Super Sucker 2002, Blood Work 2002, The Hours 2002, Gods and Generals 2002, I Witness 2003, Imaginary Heroes 2004, Because of Winn-Dixie 2005, The Squid and the Whale 2005, Good Night and Good Luck 2005, RV 2006, Infamous 2006, The Lookout 2007, Space Chimp (voice) 2008, Traitor 2008, Arlen Faber 2009, State of Play 2009, Away We Go 2009, Paper Man 2009, Howl 2010, Quad 2011, Looper 2012. *Television includes:* A Rumor of War 1980, Fifth of July 1982, Invasion of Privacy 1983, The Caine Mutiny Court Martial 1988, No Place Like Home 1989, Disaster in Time 1992, Redwood Curtain 1995, Teamster Boss: The Jackie Presser Story, The Goodbye Girl 2004, The Five People You Meet in Heaven 2004, Sweet Nothing in My Ear (film) 2008, The Newsroom (series) (Emmy Award for Best Actor in a Drama 2013) 2012–. *Plays (author):* Shoeman 1991, The Tropical Pickle 1992, The Vast Difference 1993, Thy Kingdom's Coming 1994, Escanaba in da Moonlight 1995, Guest Artists 2005. *Address:* Purple Rose Theatre, 137 Park Street, Chelsea, MI 48118, USA (office). *Telephone:* (734) 433-7782 (office). *Fax:* (734) 475-0802 (office). *Website:* www .purplerosetheatre.org (office).

DANIELS, Mitchell (Mitch) Elias, Jr; American business executive, politician, fmr state governor and university administrator; *President, Purdue University;* b. 7 April 1949, Monongahela, Pa; s. of Mitchell Elias Daniels, Sr and Dorothy Mae Daniels (née Wilkes); m. Cheri Lynn Herman 1978 (divorced 1993, re-m. 1997); four d.; ed North Central High School, Indianapolis, Woodrow Wilson School of Public and Int. Affairs at Princeton Univ., Indiana Univ. School of Law, Georgetown Univ. Law Center; Chief of Staff to Richard Luger, Mayor of Indianapolis 1971–82; Exec. Dir Nat. Republican Senatorial Cttee 1983–84; political adviser and asst to Pres. Ronald Reagan and liaison with state and local officials, Washington, DC 1985–87; Exec. Vice-Pres. and COO Hudson Inst. 1987–90; also Pnr, Baker & Daniels (law firm); Vice-Pres. Corp. Affairs Eli Lilly and Co. 1990–93, Pres. N American Pharmaceutical Operations 1993–97, Sr Vice-Pres. of Corp. Strategy and Policy 1997–2001; Dir Office of Man. and Budget, Washington, DC 2001–03; Gov. of Indiana 2005–13; Pres. Purdue Univ. 2013–; Co-Chair. Nat. Research Council cttee to review and make recommendations on the future of the US human spaceflight programme 2013–14; mem. Bd of Dirs Energy Systems Network 2013–; Republican; eight hon. degrees, including Butler Univ., Rose-Hulman Inst. of Tech. and Wabash Coll.; Inaugural Medal for Distinguished Service to Educ., Woodrow Wilson Nat. Fellowship Foundation 2010, one of three recipients of the first Fiscy Award, Fiscy Awards Cttee, Real Leader Award, State Budget Solutions 2010, Friend of the Family Award Indiana Family Inst. 2011, Wetland Conservation Achievement Award, Ducks Unlimited 2011, Najeeb Halaby Award for Public Service, Arab-American Inst. 2011, Chancellor Award for Conservation and Wildlife Protection, Weatherby Foundation 2012, Theodore Roosevelt Award, Indiana Wildlife Fed. 2012, Woodrow Wilson Award, Princeton Univ. 2013, Bradley Prize, Lynde and Harry Bradley Foundation 2013, Excellence in Innovation Award, Centric's Indiana Innovation Network 2013. *Publications:* Notes from the Road 2004, Keeping the Republic: Saving America by Trusting Americans 2011. *Address:* Office of the President, Purdue University, Hovde Hall, Room 200, 610 Purdue Mall, West Lafayette, IN 47907-2040, USA (office). *Telephone:* (765) 494-4600 (office). *E-mail:* president@purdue.edu (office). *Website:* www.purdue.edu/president (office).

DANIELS, Ronald J., BA, LLM, JD; Canadian professor of law and university administrator; *President, Johns Hopkins University;* b. 16 Aug. 1959; m. Joanne Rosen; four c.; ed Univ. of Toronto, Yale Univ. Law School; Asst Prof., Faculty of Law, Univ. of Toronto 1988–93, Assoc. Prof. 1993–99, Dean and James M. Tory Prof. of Law 1995–2002; John M. Olin Visiting Fellow, Cornell Univ. Law School 1993; Visiting Prof. and Coca-Cola World Fellow, Yale Univ. Law School 2003–04; Prof., Univ. of Pennsylvania Law School 2005–08, Provost 2005–08; Pres. Johns Hopkins Univ. 2009–; Fellow, American Acad. of Arts and Sciences 2009–. *Address:* Office of the President, Johns Hopkins University, 242 Garland Hall, 3400 North Charles Street, Baltimore, MD 21218, USA (office). *Telephone:* (410) 516-8068 (office). *Fax:* (410) 516-6097 (office). *E-mail:* rjdaniels@jhu.edu (office); president@jhu.edu (office). *Website:* web.jhu.edu/administration/president (office).

DANIELS, William Burton, MS, PhD; American physicist and academic; *Unidel Professor Emeritus of Physics, University of Delaware;* b. 21 Dec. 1930, Buffalo, NY; s. of William C. Daniels and Sophia P. Daniels; m. Adriana A. Braakman 1958; two s. one d.; ed Univ. of Buffalo and Case Inst. (now Case-Western Reserve Univ.); Asst Prof. of Physics, Case Tech. 1957–59; Research Scientist, Union Carbide Corpn 1959–61; Asst Prof., Princeton Univ. 1961–63, Assoc. Prof. 1963–66, Prof. of Mechanical Eng 1966–72; Unidel Prof. of Physics, also of Astronomy, Univ. of Delaware 1972–2000, Unidel Prof. Emer. 2001–, Chair. Physics Dept 1977–80; Fellow, American Physical Soc.; John Simon Guggenheim Memorial Fellow 1976–77; Humboldt Sr Award 1982, 1992. *Publications:* more than 100 articles on the physics of solids at high pressures. *Leisure interests:* sailing, hiking. *Address:* Physics Department, University of Delaware, Newark, DE 19716 (office); Park Plaza Condos, 1100 Lovering Avenue, Wilmington, DE 19806, USA (home). *Fax:* (302) 384-8720 (home). *E-mail:* family_daniels@hotmail.com (home).

DANILOV, Yuri Mikhailovich; Russian judge; *Constitutional Court Judge;* b. 1 Aug. 1950, Mukachevo, Ukraine; m.; two s. one d.; ed Voronezh State Univ.; fmr metalworker in Lugansk; People's Judge, Povorinsk Dist Court, Voronezh Region 1971–80; mem. Voronezh Regional Court 1980–83, Chair. 1985–89; instructor, Voronezh Regional CP Cttee 1983–85; First Deputy Head of Dept of Gen. Courts, USSR Ministry of Justice 1989–91, Deputy Minister of Justice 1991–92; Chief Jurist, Vice-Pres. Int. Food Exchange 1992–93; Deputy Chair. State Cttee on Anti-

Monopoly Policy and Support of New Econ. Structures; Chair. Comm. on Stock Exchanges 1993–94; Judge Sec. Constitutional Court of Russian Fed. 1994–, mem. Second Chamber 1995–; Merited Jurist of Russian Fed.; Distinguished Jurist of the Russian Fed. *Address:* Constitutional Court of Justice of the Russian Federation, 103132 Moscow, Ilyinka str. 21, Russia (office). *Telephone:* (495) 206-16-29 (office). *Website:* www.ksrf.ru (office).

DANILOV-DANILYAN, Victor Ivanovich, DEcon; Russian politician; *Director, Institute of Aquatic Studies, Russian Academy of Sciences;* b. 9 May 1938, Moscow; m.; three s.; ed Moscow State Univ.; jr researcher, engineer, sr engineer, Computation Cen., Moscow State Univ. 1960–64; researcher, leading engineer, Head of lab., Cen. Inst. of Math. and Econs, USSR Acad. of Sciences 1964–76; Head of Lab., Prof., All-Union Research Inst. of System Studies, USSR Acad. of Sciences 1976–80; Head of lab., Chair. Acad. of Nat. Econ., USSR Council of Ministers 1980–91; Deputy Minister of Nature Man. and Environmental Control of USSR Aug.–Nov. 1991, Minister of Ecology and Natural Resources, Russian Fed. 1991–92, of Environmental Control and Natural Resources 1992–96; Chair. State Cttee for Environmental Control 1996–; Pres.-Rector Int. Industrial Ecology and Political Univ. (MNEPU) 1991–; mem. State Duma (parl.) 1993–96; founder and author, ecological programme of Kedr (Cedar) Movt 1994; Dir and corresponding mem., Inst. of Aquatic Studies, Russian Acad. of Sciences 2003–; mem. Russian Acad. of Natural Sciences. *Address:* Institute of Aquatic Studies, Russian Academy of Sciences, 119333 Moscow, 3 Gubkina Street (office); MNEPU, 117250 Moscow, Krasnokazarmennaya str. 14, Russia (office). *Telephone:* (499) 135-54-56 (office); (495) 273-55-48 (office). *Fax:* (499) 135-54-15 (office). *E-mail:* vidd@aqua.laser.ru (office). *Website:* www.iwp.ru (office).

DANIÑO ZAPATA, Roberto Enrique; Peruvian lawyer, politician and business executive; *Deputy Chairman, Hochschild Mining plc;* b. 2 March 1951, Lima; ed Catholic Univ. of Peru, Harvard Univ., USA; fmr Sec.-Gen. Ministry of Economy, Finance and Trade; fmr Pres. Foreign Investment and Tech. Agency, Chair. Foreign Public Debt Comm.; Founding Gen. Counsel Inter-American Investment Corpn, Washington, DC, Chair. Inter-American Devt Bank's External Review Group for Pvt. Sector Operations; Pnr, Wilmer, Cutler & Pickering, Head of Latin American Practice Group 1996–2001; Pres. Council of Ministers (Prime Minister) of Peru 2001–02; Sec.-Gen. Int. Centre for Settlement of Investment Disputes 2003–06 (resgnd); currently Deputy Chair. Hochschild Mining PLC; fmr mem. Bd Newbridge Andean Partners, Royal & Sun Alliance/Fenix, Cementos Pacasmayo, Sindicato Pesquero, Violy, Byorum & Partners, The Mountain Inst., The Infant Nutrition Fund; fmr mem. The Coca-Cola Co. Latin American Advisory Bd, Americas Soc. Chair.'s Council, Carnegie Endowment's G-50 Bd. *Address:* Hochschild Mining plc, Calle La Colonia No. 180, Urb. El Vivero Santiago de Surco, Lima 33, Peru (office).

DANISHEFSKY, Samuel J., BS, PhD; American chemist and academic; *Professor, Department of Chemistry, Columbia University;* b. 10 March 1936, Bayonne, NJ; ed Yeshiva and Columbia Univs, New York, Harvard Univ., Cambridge, Mass; Asst Prof., Univ. of Pittsburgh 1964–68, Assoc. Prof. 1968–71, Prof. 1971–79, Univ. Prof. 1978–79; Prof., Yale Univ. 1979–93, Chair. 1981–87, Eugene Higgins Prof. 1983–89, Sterling Prof. 1989–93; Dir Sloan-Kettering Inst. for Cancer Research, Lab. for Bioorganic Chem. 1991–, Kettering Chair 1993–; Prof., Dept of Chem., Columbia Univ. 1993–; mem. NAS 1986, Connecticut Acad. of Sciences 1987; Fellow, Japanese Soc. for the Promotion of Science 1980, AAAS 1985; Hon. DSc (Yeshiva Univ.) 1987; ACS Guenther Award 1980, Arthur C. Cope Scholar 1986, ACS Aldrich Award for Creative Work in Synthetic Organic Chem. 1986, Edgar Fahs Smith Award, Philadelphia Section, ACS 1988, Pfizer Grad. Training Award 1991, Cliff Hamilton Award Univ. of Nebraska 1994, Max Tishler Prize Lecturer, Harvard Univ. 1995, Wolf Prize in Chem. 1996, Tetrahedron Prize 1996, ACS Claude S. Hudson Award in Carbohydrate Chem. 1996, Allan Day Medal, Univ. of Pennsylvania 1997, ACS Cope Medal 1998, Paul Ehrlich Lecture Prize 1998, ACS Nichols Medal 1999, Nagoya Gold Medal 1999, ACS H.C. Brown Medal 2000, F.A. Cotton Medal 2001, New York City (Mayor's) Award for Science and Tech. 2003, Remsen Prize for Maryland Section, Johns Hopkins Univ. 2004, Benjamin Franklin Award in Chem. 2006, Bristol Myers Squibb Lifetime Achievement Award 2006, NAS Award in the Chemical Sciences 2006, ACS North Jersey Section Award for Creativity in Molecular Design and Synthesis 2006, ACS Roger Adams Award in Organic Chem. 2007, Inaugural Award for Chem. in Cancer Research, American Asscn for Cancer Research 2007. *Address:* Department of Chemistry, Columbia University, 3000 Broadway, MC 3106, New York, NY 10027; Department of Bioorganic Chemistry, Sloan-Kettering Institute, 1275 York Avenue, New York, NY 10021, USA (office). *Telephone:* (212) 854-6195 (Columbia); (212) 639-5502 (office). *Fax:* (212) 854-7142 (Columbia) (office); (212) 772-8691 (home). *E-mail:* sjd15@columbia.edu (office); s-danishefsky@ski.mskcc .org (office). *Website:* www.columbia.edu/cu/chemistry (office); www.ski.edu/lab (office).

DANJUMA, Lt-Gen. (retd) Theophilus Yakubu; Nigerian business executive and fmr army official; *Chairman, South Atlantic Petroleum Ltd;* b. 9 Dec. 1938, Takum, Taraba State; s. of Kuru Danjuma and Rufkatu Asibi; m.; ed Benue Provincial Secondary School; commissioned into Army as Second Lt and Platoon Commdr in the Congo, later joined UN peacekeeping force in Sante, Kataga Province in Congo; promoted to Capt. 1966, Lt Col 1967, Col 1971, Brig. and GOC 1975, Chief of Army Staff 1975–79 (retd); rep. to International Court Martial, Trinidad and Tobago 1970; f. NAL-Comet Group 1979; Minister of Defence 1999–2003; Founder-Chair. South Atlantic Petroleum Ltd 1995–, TY Danjuma Foundation 2008–; fmr Chair. Presidential Advisory Council; Grand Commdr, Order of Niger; Leadership Person of the Year 2011. *Address:* South Atlantic Petroleum Ltd, 11th and 12th Floor, South Atlantic Petroleum Towers, 1, Adeola Odeku Street, PO Box 73152, Victoria Island, Lagos, Nigeria (office). *Telephone:* (1) 2701906 (office). *Fax:* (1) 2701907 (office). *E-mail:* info@sapetro.com (office). *Website:* www.sapetro.com (office).

DANNATT, Baron (Life Peer), cr. 2011, of Keswick in the County of Norfolk; **(Francis) Richard Dannatt,** Kt, GCB, KCB, CBE, MC, BA, DL; British fmr army officer; *Constable of the Tower of London;* b. 23 Dec. 1950, Chelmsford, Essex, England; m. Philippa Margaret Gurney 1977; three s. one d.; ed Felsted School, Essex, St Lawrence Coll., Ramsgate, Hatfield Coll., Durham Univ.; fmr Pres. Durham Union Soc.; commissioned into The Green Howards 1971; has served with 1st Battalion in NI, Cyprus and Germany, Commdr in Airmobile role 1989–91; Commdr 4th Armoured Brigade in Germany and Bosnia 1994–96; Commdr 3rd (UK) Div. and Commdr British Forces in Kosovo 1999, Deputy Commdr, Operations of the Stabilisation Force (SFOR) 2000; Asst Chief of Gen. Staff, Ministry of Defence 2001–02; Commdr NATO Allied Rapid Reaction Corps 2002–05; C-in-C Land Command 2005–06; Chief of the Gen. Staff 2006–09; adviser on defence issues to Conservative Party 2009–10; Constable of the Tower of London 2009–; Sr Adviser, Control Risks plc (specialist risk consultancy) 2010–, Ricardo plc (technology, product innovation and strategic consulting) 2010–; writer, Telegraph Media Group; speaker, Celebrity Speakers Agency; Chair. Royal United Services Inst. 2009, Strategic Devt Bd Durham Global Security Inst.; Pres. Army Rifle Asscn, Army Rugby Union, Army Winter Sports Asscn, Soldiers' and Airmen's Scripture Readers Asscn; Vice-Pres. Armed Forces Christian Union; churchwarden, Keswick and Intwood, Norfolk; Trustee, Historic Royal Palaces, Royal Armouries, Windsor Leadership Trust; mem. (Crossbench) House of Lords 2011–; Queen's Commendation for Valuable Service 1999; Hon. DCL (Univ. of Kent at Medway) 2009. *Publication:* Leading from the Front: The Autobiography 2010. *Leisure interests:* cricket, rugby, tennis, skiing, shooting, fishing, reading. *Address:* The Tower of London, London, EC3N 4AB (office); House of Lords, Westminster, London, SW1A 0PW, England (office). *Telephone:* 0844-482-7777 (from UK) (office); (20) 3166-6200 (from outside UK) (office); (20) 7219-5353 (House of Lords) (office). *E-mail:* dannattr@parliament.com (office); richarddannatt8@ hotmail.com (home). *Website:* www.hrp.org.uk/TowerOfLondon (office).

DANNEELS, HE Cardinal Godfried; Belgian ecclesiastic; *Archbishop Emeritus of Mechelen-Brussels;* b. 4 June 1933, Kanegem, Bruges; ordained priest 1957; Bishop of Antwerp 1977; Archbishop of Mechelen-Brussels 1979–2010, Archbishop Emer. 2010–; Castrene Bishop of Belgium 1980–2010; participated in Papal Conclave 2005, 2013; Pres. Episcopal Conf. of Belgium, Pax Christi Int.; mem. Synod of Bishops, Sacred Congregation for Evangelization, Council for the Public Affairs of the Church, Congregation of Catholic Educ., Congregation of Divine Worship, Secr. for Non-believers, Congregation for the Oriental Churches; cr. Cardinal (Cardinal-Priest of Sant'Anastasia) 1983. *Address:* Aartsbisdom, Wollemarkt 15, 2800 Mechelen, Belgium. *Telephone:* (15) 216-501. *Fax:* (15) 209-485. *E-mail:* aartsbisdom@kerknet.be (office).

DANON, Laurence; French business executive; *Co-CEO, Leonardo & Co. France;* m. Pierre Danon; two c.; ed Ecole Normale Superieur and Corps des Mines; started carrier at Ministry of Industry; joined Elf group 1989, Gen. Man. Bostik (Ato Findley) 1996, merged with Total in 1999; joined Printemps in 2001, Chair. Man. Bd and CEO France Printemps 2002–07 (led buyout of Printemps from PPR); mem. Exec. Bd Edmond de Rothschild Corp. Finance 2007–13, Chair. 2009–13; Co-Pres. Exec. Bd Leonardo & Co. France 2012–13, Co-CEO 2013–; mem. Bd of Dirs Plastic Omnium 2003–10, Diageo plc 2006–, Experian Group Ltd 2007–10, Rhodia SA 2008–11; Officier, Légion d'honneur, ordre du Mérite; ranked by the Financial Times amongst Top 25 Businesswomen in Europe (19th) 2005, (19th) 2006. *Address:* Leonardo & Co. SAS, 32, rue de Lisbonne, 75008 Paris, France (office). *Telephone:* 1-73-44-44-00 (office). *Fax:* 1-73-44-44-02 (office). *E-mail:* mailto.fr@ leonardo-co.com (office). *Website:* www.leonardo-co.com (office).

DANSON, Ted; American actor; b. 29 Dec. 1947, San Diego, Calif.; s. of Edward Danson and Jessica McMaster; m. 1st Randall L. Gosch 1970 (divorced 1977); m. 2nd Cassandra Coates 1977 (divorced); two d.; m. 3rd Mary Steenburgen (1995); ed The Kent School, Connecticut and Stanford and Carnegie-Mellon Univs; teacher, The Actor's Inst. Los Angeles 1978; CEO Anasazi Productions (fmrly Danson/Fauci Productions). *Theatre includes:* The Real Inspector Hound 1972, Comedy of Errors. *Films include:* The Onion Field 1979, Body Heat 1981, Creepshow (segment Something To Tide You Over) 1982, Little Treasure 1985, Just Between Friends 1986, A Fine Mess 1986, 3 Men and a Baby 1987, Cousins 1989, Dad 1989, 3 Men and a Little Lady 1990, Made in America 1993, Getting Even with Dad 1994, Pontiac Moon 1994, Loch Ness 1996, Jerry and Tom 1998, Homegrown 1998, Saving Private Ryan 1998, Mumford 1999, Mrs. Pilgrim Goes to Hollywood 2002, Fronterz 2004, The Moguls 2005, Nobel Son 2007, Mad Money 2008, The Human Contract 2008, The Open Road 2009, Fight for Your Right Revisited (short) 2011, Jock (voice) 2011, Big Miracle 2012, Ted (uncredited) 2012. *Television includes:* Somerset (series) 1975–76, The Doctors (series) 1977, The Amazing Spider-Man (series) 1979, Mrs. Columbo (series) 1979, Trapper John, M.D. (series) (uncredited) 1979, The French Atlantic Affair (mini-series) (uncredited) 1979, B.J. and the Bear (series) 1979, Laverne & Shirley (series) 1980, Family (series) 1980, The Women's Room (film) 1980, Once Upon a Spy (film) 1980, Benson (series) 1981, Magnum, P.I. (series) 1981, Dear Teacher (film) 1981, Our Family Business (film) 1981, Taxi (series) 1982, Tucker's Witch (series) 1982, Cheers (series) 1982–93, Allison Sydney Harrison (film) 1983, Super Bowl XVII Pre-Game Show (film) (uncredited) 1983, Cowboy (film) 1983, Something about Amelia (film) 1984, When the Bough Breaks (film) 1986, We Are the Children (film) 1987, Mickey's 60th Birthday (film) 1988, The Simpsons (series) (voice) 1994, Frasier (series) 1995, Gulliver's Travels (film) 1996, Pearl (series) 1997, Ink (series) (also producer) 1996–97, Veronica's Closet (series) 1998, Becker (series) 1998–2004, Thanks of a Grateful Nation (film) 1998, Grosse Pointe (series) (voice) 2000, Curb Your Enthusiasm (series) 2000–09, Living with the Dead (film) 2002, Electric Playground (series) 2002, Gary the Rat (series) (voice) 2003, Surviving Love (film) 2004, Our Fathers (film) 2005, Knights of the South Bronx (film) 2005, Guy Walks Into a Bar (film) 2006, Bye Bye Benjamin (short) 2006, Heist (series) 2006, Help Me Help You (series) 2006–07, Damages (series) 2007–10, King of the Hill (series) 2008, Bored to Death (series) 2009–11, The Magic 7 (film) (voice) 2009, Tim and Eric Awesome Show, Great Job! (series) 2010, CSI: Crime Scene Investigation (series) 2011–12. *Address:* 10345 North Olympic Blvd, Suite 200, Los Angeles, CA 90054-2524, USA; c/o Josh Liberman, Creative Artists Agency, 2000 Avenue of the Stars, Los Angeles, CA 90067, USA (office). *Telephone:* (424) 288-2000 (office). *Fax:* (424) 288-2900 (office). *Website:* www.caa.com (office).

DANTICAT, Edwidge, BA, MFA; American writer; b. 19 Jan. 1969, Port-au-Prince, Haiti; m. Faidherbe Boyer 2002; ed Clara Barton High School, New York, Barnard Coll., New York and Brown Univ., Rhode Island; documentary film work with Jonathan Demme 1993–95; teacher at univs in Miami, New York and Texas; Pushcart Short Story Prize 1995, Granta's Best of American Novelists Citation 1996, American Book Award 1998, MacArthur Fellowship 2009, Langston Hughes

Medal 2011. *Films as associate producer:* Courage and Pain 1996, The Agronomist 2003. *Publications:* fiction: Breath, Eyes, Memory 1994, Krik? Krak! (short stories) 1995, The Farming of Bones 1998, Behind the Mountain 2002, The Dew Breaker 2004, Anacaona: Golden Flower, Haiti, 1490 2005; non-fiction: Odillon Pierre, Artist of Haiti (with Jonathan Demme) 1999, The Beacon Best of 2000: Great Writing by Women and Men of All Colors and Cultures (ed.) 2000, The Butterfly's Way: Voices from the Haitian Dyaspora in the United States (ed.) 2001, After the Dance 2002, Brother, I'm Dying (Nat. Book Critics' Circle Award for Autobiography 2007) 2007, Create Dangerously: The Immigrant Artist at Work (OCM Bocas Prize for Caribbean Literature 2011) 2010. *Address:* c/o Soho Press, 853 Broadway, No. 1903, New York, NY 10003, USA (office).

DANYLYSHYN, Bohdan Myhaylovich, DEcon; Ukrainian economist, academic and government official; b. 6 June 1965, Tserkivna, Dolyn dist, Ivano-Frankivsk Oblast; ed Ternopol State Pedagogical Inst.; Prof. of Econs 2003–; fmr Head of Council on Productive Forces Research, Nat. Acad. of Sciences of Ukraine; Minister of the Economy 2007–10; granted political asylum by Czech Repub. 2011 after charges of misusing public funds; Corresp. mem. Nat. Acad. of Sciences of Ukraine 2004–; State Prize of Ukraine in Science and Tech. *Publications include:* more than 150 scientific papers on regional policy, econs and exploration of nature resources.

DANYSZ, Magda; French art dealer and gallery director; *Owner/Director, Gallery Magda Danysz;* ed École Supérieure des Sciences Économiques et Commerciale (ESSEC); began in the art business early 1990s, opened first art space 1991; pursued a consulting career with Arthur Andersen 1997–2004, consultant for French retail group Carrefour; various posts with Ministry of Culture, Christie's, Theatre Marigny, Nantes Museum, the Louvre, others; Owner/Dir Gallery Magda Danysz, Paris 1999–; has participated in numerous art fairs world-wide; has taught cultural policies and economics at Sciences Po, Paris 2001–; mem. Bd multimedia cultural art centre Le Cube, Issy-les-Moulineaux; Co-founder contemporary art fair ShowOff, Paris 2006; apptd to direct Bund 18 gallery in Shanghai, China 2009; Vice-Pres. Fashion Group International of Paris 2009–; mem. Comité Professionnel des Galeries d'Art 2002–, French Art Dealers Cttee, Friends of the Palais de Tokyo 2005–; Young Leader, French American Foundation 2009–; mem. Compagnie Nat. des Experts, apptd expert in Chinese contemporary art and street art 2010–; Chevalier des Arts et des Lettres 2007; ESSEC Alumni 1998. *Publications include:* has published an extensive anthology about street art entitled From Style Writing to Art. *Address:* Gallery Magda Danysz, 78 rue Amelot, 75011 Paris, France (office); Gallery Magda Danysz, 188 Linqing Road, Shanghai, People's Republic of China (office). *Telephone:* 1-45-83-38-51 (Paris) (office). *E-mail:* info@magda-gallery.com (office). *Website:* www .magda-gallery.com (office).

DAOUDA, Idrissou L.; Benin economist and politician; ed Univ. de Paris IX Dauphine, France; fmr Econ. Adviser to Govt of Benin; Prin. Economist and Head of Treasury Div., Banque Centrale des Etats de l'Afrique de l'Ouest (BCEAO), Dakar, Senegal 1977–91, Deputy Dir of Issue and Financial Operations 1991–96, Head of Cotonou Br. 1996–98, Nat. Dir for Benin, BCEAO 1998–2006; Adviser to Provisional Authority, Regulation des Postes et Télécommunications de Benin 2007–10; Minister of Economy and Finance 2010. *Address:* c/o Ministry of the Economy and Finance, BP 302, Cotonou, Benin.

DAOUDI, Riad Rashad ad-, PhD; Syrian lawyer, professor of law, international arbitrator and university administrator; *President, Syrian Virtual University;* b. 22 July 1942, Damascus; s. of Rashad Daoudi and Adallat Fares; m. Viviane Collin 1978; two s. one d.; ed Institut des Hautes Etudes Internationales, Paris; Prof. of Int. Law, Damascus Law School 1978–91; Asst Dean for Academic Affairs, Faculty of Law, Univ. of Damascus 1980–82; lawyer, mem. Syrian Bar 1982–; Registrar, Judicial Tribunal OAPEC 1983, now lawyer and legal adviser, Registrar Judicial Tribunal OAPEC; Legal Adviser to Ministry of Foreign Affairs 1991–; mem. UN Int. Law Comm. 2001–06; currently Pres. Syrian Virtual Univ., Damascus; Lauréat, best doctoral thesis, Univ. of Paris 1977–78. *Publications:* Parliamentary Immunities: Comparative Study in Arab Constitutions (in Arabic) 1982, Peace Negotiations – Treaty of Versailles (textbook for law students, in Arabic) 1983, Arab Commission for Human Rights, An Encyclopedia of Public International Law (in English) 1985; articles and contribs to books on int. affairs and int. law. *Leisure interests:* tennis, reading. *Address:* c/o Syrian Virtual University, Ministry of Higher Education, BP 9251, place Mezzeh Gamarik, Damascus; Dam Zoukak Al Sakhar Salim Al Sharah Street, Hadjar Building, 3rd Floor, Damascus, Syria (home). *Telephone:* (11) 2149-9531. *E-mail:* rdaoudi@svuonline.org. *Website:* www .svuonline.org.

DAR, Muhammad Ishaq, BCom; Pakistani economist and politician; *Minister of Finance, Revenue, Economic Affairs and Statistics, and of Privatization;* ed Hailey Coll. of Commerce, Univ. of Punjab, Lahore; Minister of Commerce 1997–99, of Finance 1998–99, of Finance, Revenue, Econ. Affairs and Statistics, and of Privatization 2013–; Chair. Bd of Govs Islamic Devt Bank 1998–99; Senator (Pakistan Muslim League—Nawaz— PML-N) 2006–, also PML-N Parl. Leader; Minister of Finance and Minister for Econ. Affairs and Statistics 2008; Pres. Int. Affairs, Pakistan Muslim League—Nawaz; Pres. Lahore Chamber of Commerce and Industry; Fellow, Inst. of Chartered Accountants in England and Wales, Inst. of Chartered Accountants of Pakistan, Inst. of Public Finance Accountants of Pakistan. *Address:* Ministry of Finance, Block Q, Pakistan Secretariat, Islamabad (office); 7-H, Gulberg-III, Lahore, Pakistan. *Telephone:* (51) 9202576 (office). *Fax:* (51) 9206354 (office). *E-mail:* webmaster@finance.gov.pk (office). *Website:* www .finance.gov.pk (office).

DARABOS, Norbert, MA; Austrian politician; b. 31 May 1964, Vienna; m.; one s. one d.; ed Univ. of Vienna; Chief Exec. Dr.-Karl-Renner-Inst., Burgenland 1988–91; mem. Municipal Council of Nikitsch/Burgenland 1987–2003; Press Speaker for Gov. of Prov. of Burgenland Karl Stix 1991–98; mem. Diet of Burgenland 1999–2004, Pres. SPÖ Club 2000–03; Leader of Burgenland Prov. Social-Democratic Party of Austria—SPÖ 1998–2003, Sec.-Gen. Social Democratic Party of Austria 2003, Federal Man. 2013–; mem. Austrian Parl. 2004–; Minister of Defence 2007–13, also of Sports 2008–13; Grosses Goldenes Ehrenzeichen am Bande für die Verdienste um die Republik Österreich 2010. *Address:* Social Democratic Party of Austria, Löwelstraße 18, 1090 Vienna, Austria (office).

Telephone: (1) 534-27 (office). *Fax:* (1) 535-96-83 (office). *E-mail:* norbert.darabos@ spoe.at; direkt@spoe.at. *Website:* www.spoe.at (office).

DARAR HOUFFANEH, Hassan; Djibouti politician; *Minister of Defence;* b. 15 Oct. 1962, Wê'a, Arta Region; ed Ecole Nat. d'Admin, Paris, France; several years working in Ministry of Interior; fmr Second Deputy to Mayor of Djibouti, becoming First Deputy to Mayor of Djibouti; fmr Dir Population Office; Gov. Arta Region 1994; Minister of the Interior –2013, of Defence 2013–. *Address:* Ministry of Defence, BP 42, Djibouti, Djibouti (office). *Telephone:* 21352034 (office).

DARBINYAN, Armen Razmikovich, CandEcon; Armenian politician and university rector; *Rector and President, Russian-Armenian State University;* b. 23 Jan. 1965, Gyumri, Armenia; m.; one d.; ed Moscow State Univ.; Lecturer, Moscow State Univ. 1986–89; Sr Expert, Head of Dept, Perm. Mission of Armenia to Russian Fed., Plenipotentiary Rep., Intergovt Comm. on Debts of Vneshecono-nombank 1989–92; Dir-Gen. Armenian Foreign Trade Co. Armenintorg 1992–94; First Deputy Chair. Cen. Bank of Armenia 1994–97; Minister of Finance 1997, of Finance and Econs 1997–98; Prime Minister of Armenia 1998–99; Minister of Nat. Economy 1999–2000; Chair. Fund for Devt, Yerevan 2000–; Chair. Bd Trustees, Int. Center for Human Devt 2000–; Rector and Pres., Russian-Armenian State Univ. 2001–; mem. Russian Acad. of Natural Sciences; Commdr World Order of Science, Education and Culture 2002; Int. Socrates Award 2006. *Publications:* over 40 publs including Role of the State in Countries with Transition Economies, Economic Development: Prospects and Role of the Diaspora, From Stability to Economic Growth. *Leisure interests:* music and composing songs. *Address:* 19 str. Sayat Nova, 375001 Yerevan, Armenia. *Telephone:* (10) 28-97-00 (office). *Fax:* (10) 22-14-63 (office). *E-mail:* adarbinian@ichd.org (office). *Website:* www.ichd.org (office).

DARBOE, Ousainou N., LLB, BL, LLM; Gambian lawyer and politician; *Leader, United Democratic Party;* b. 8 Aug. 1948; ed Univ. of Ottawa, Canada, Fed. Law School, Lagos, Univ. of Lagos; State Counsel, Attorney Gen.'s Chambers, Banjul, Chief Prosecutor and Legal Adviser to Govt 1973–76, Acting Registrar-Gen. 1976–77; legal draftsman 1979–80; represented two-thirds of people detained under Govt's Emergency Powers regulations after 1981 abortive coup 1981–82, successfully defended leader of opposition Nat. Convention Party against charges of treason; pvt. legal practice, Banjul 1991–; mem. Bd of Dirs Gambia Public Transport Corpn 1987–92; mem. Nat. Advisory Cttee for nomination of judges to Int. Court of Justice 1992–, OAU Observer team in Eritrean referendum 1993–; Vice-Pres. Gambian Bar Asscn 1991–; Deputy Chair. Gambia Law Reform Comm. 1992–; Chair. Gambian Wrestling Fed. 1985–95, Bansang Yeriwa Kafo (charity) 1990–; First Vice-Pres. The Gambia Nat. Olympic and Sports Cttee 1989–; Leader United Democratic Party (UDP); unsuccessful cand. in presidential elections 1996, 2001, 2006, 2011. *Publications:* numerous articles in professional journals. *Address:* United Democratic Party, 1 ECOWAS Avenue, Banjul (office); Bansang Chambers, 18/19 Liberation Avenue, PO Box 688, Banjul, The Gambia (office). *Telephone:* 4227442 (office); 4228203 (office); 4222000 (office). *Fax:* 4224601 (office). *E-mail:* info@udpgambia.org (office).

DARBOVEN, Hanne; German artist, writer and musician; b. 29 April 1941, Munich; ed Hochschule für Bildende Künste, Hamburg; has participated in numerous group exhbns of contemporary art in galleries in Europe, USA, Canada and also São Paulo Biennale 1973 and Venice Biennale 1982. *Compositions:* series of pieces for solo instruments, chamber and full orchestra. *Publications:* books including: El Lissitzky, Hosmann, Hamburg und Yves Gevaert 1974, Atta Troll Kunstmuseum 1975, Baudelaire, Heine, Disecpolo, Maizi, Flores, Kraus: Pour écrire la liberté 1975, New York Diary 1976, Ein Jahrhundert, Vol. 1 1971–77, Schreibzeit 1999. *Leisure interest:* keeping goats. *Address:* Am Burgberg 26, 21079 Hamburg, Germany. *Telephone:* (40) 7633033.

D'ARCEVIA, Bruno; Italian painter and sculptor; b. 21 Oct. 1946, Arcevia, Ancona; s. of Benedetto Bruni and Amelia Filippini; m. Maria Falconetti 1972; one s. one d.; worked in France and Venezuela 1975–78; co-f. Nuova Maniera Italiana Movt 1982–83; one of 20 Italian artists included in ArToday review, London 1996; Commendatore Ordine della Repubblica Italiana; Gold San Valentino Award, named Marchigiano dell'Anno 1998. *Leisure interests:* underwater fishing. *Address:* Via dei Campi Sportivi 2A, 00197 Rome (office); Via Luigi Angeloni 29, 00149 Rome, Italy (home). *Telephone:* (06) 8070185 (office); (06) 5503637 (home). *Fax:* (06) 8070185. *E-mail:* info@brunodarcevia.net. *Website:* www.brunodarcevia .net.

DARCOS, Xavier, DèsL; French politician, scholar and civil servant; b. 14 Aug. 1947, Limoges (Haute-Vienne); s. of Jean-Gabriel Darcos and Anne-Marie Banvillet; m. 1st Marie-Lys Beaudry (deceased); one s. one d.; m. 2nd Laure Driant 1999; one s.; began career as teacher, Périgueux, at Lycée Montaigne, Bordeaux 1982–87, at Lycée Louis-le-Grand, Paris 1987–92; Insp.-Gen. of Educ. 1992–98; Assoc. Prof., Univ. de Paris-Sorbonne 1996; Counsellor, Ministry of Educ. 1993–94, 1995–97, Vice-Minister for School Educ. 2002–04, for Co-operation, Devt and Francophony 2004–05, Minister of Nat. Educ. 2007–09, of Labour, Social Relations, the Family and Solidarity 2009–10; Mayor of Périgueux 1997–2008; Senator for Dordogne 1998–2002, Vice-Pres. Senate Cultural Comm. 2001; Perm. Rep. to OECD 2005; mem. Acad. des sciences morales et politiques 2006, Acad. française 2013. *Publications:* Histoire de la littérature française 1992, Approches ovidiennes de la mort 1995, Mérimée 1998, Robert des grands écrivains de langue française (co-author), L'Art d'apprendre à ignorer 2000, Dictionnaire des mythes féminins (co-author) 2002, Lettre à tous ceux qui aiment l'école (co-author) 2003, Deux voix pour une école (co-author) 2004, L'École de Jules Ferry (Prix Louis Pauwels 2006) 2005, 2005-2005 2005, L'État et les Églises, la question laïque 2006, Tacite, ses vérités sont les nôtres 2007. *Address:* c/o Ministry of Labour, Social Relations, the Family and Solidarity, 127 rue de Grenelle, 75007 Paris, France.

D'ARCY, Margaretta Ruth; Irish playwright, writer, broadcaster and film maker; b. 14 June 1934, London, England; m. John Arden 1957; five s. (one deceased); Artistic Dir Corrandulla Arts and Entertainment Club 1973, Galway Women's Entertainment 1982, Galway Women's Sceal Radio, Radio Pirate-Woman 1986, Women in Media and Entertainment 1987; mem. Aosdána 1982; Arts Council Playwriting Award (with John Arden) 1972, Women's Int. News-gathering Service, Katherine Davenport Journalist of the Year Award 1998,

Documentary Award, Galway Film Fleadh 2005. *Plays produced:* The Happy Haven 1961, Business of Good Government 1962, Ars Longa Vita Brevis 1964, The Royal Pardon 1966, Friday's Hiding 1967, The Hero Rises Up 1969, The Island of the Mighty 1974, The Non-Stop Connolly Show 1975, A Pinprick of History 1977, Vandaleur's Folly 1978, The Little Gray Home in the West 1978, The Making of Muswell Hill 1979 (all with John Arden). *Films:* Circus Exposé 1987, Big Plane Small Axe (The Mis-Trials of Mary Kelly) 2005, Shell Hell 2005, Yellow Gate Women, Breda Lewis – A Portrait, Welcome to Our World. *Radio includes:* Keep Those People Moving 1972, The Manchester Enthusiasts 1984, Whose Is the Kingdom? 1988, A Suburban Suicide 1994 (all with John Arden). *Television documentary:* Profile of Sean O'Casey (with John Arden) 1973. *Publications:* Tell Them Everything (Prison Memoirs) 1981, Awkward Corners (with John Arden) 1988, Galway's Pirate Women, a Global Trawl 1996, Loose Theatre (Memoirs of a Guerrilla Theatre Activist) 2005. *Address:* c/o Casarotto Ramsay, 60-66 Wardour Street, London, W1V 3HP, England (office). *Telephone:* (91) 565430 (home). *Website:* www.margarettadarcy.com.

DARCY LILO, Gordon; Solomon Islands politician; *Prime Minister;* b. 28 Aug. 1965; ed Univ. of Papua New Guinea, Australian Nat. Univ.; fmr Perm. Sec. for Ministry of Finance, for Ministry of Forestry, Environment and Conservation; mem. Parl. (Peoples Alliance Party) for Gizo, Kolombangara 2001–, Leader Ind. Group in Parl. 2001–06; Minister for Nat. Planning and Aid Co-ordination –2006, of Finance and Treasury 2006–07, 2010–11, for Justice and Legal Affairs Nov. 2007, for Environment and Conservation Dec. 2007–10, Prime Minister 2011–; Chair. Forum Econ. Ministers Meeting 2006. *Address:* Office of the Prime Minister, PO G1, Honiara, Solomon Islands (office). *Telephone:* 21867 (office). *Fax:* 26088 (office). *Website:* www.pmc.gov.sb (office).

DARDARI, Abdullah ad-, DEcon; Syrian politician and fmr journalist; b. Damascus; fmr head of bureau of Alhayat pan-Arab daily in Syria; later the local deputy of UN Resident Rep.; fmr Chair. State Planning Comm.; Deputy Prime Minister, responsible for Econ. Affairs 2005–11 (resgnd with rest of cabinet at Pres.'s request following popular protests). *Address:* c/o State Planning Commission, Ibn Alnafees, Rukin Al Deen, Damascus, Syria.

DARDENNE, Jean-Pierre; Belgian film producer, director and screenwriter; b. (Carl Higgans), 21 April 1951, Liège; brother of Luc Dardenne; ed Arts Inst.; made several videos with his brother Luc about rough life in blue-collar small towns in the Wallonie 1970s; Pres. Jury Cannes Film Festival, Short Films 2000, Caméra d'Or 2006, Cinéfondation Jury 2012. *Films produced include:* Je pense à vous 1992, Faute de soleil (co-producer) 1995, L'héritier (exec. producer) 1999, Rosetta 1999, La devinière (documentary) (line producer) 2000, Le lait de la tendresse humaine (The Milk of Human Kindness) (co-producer) 2001, Le fils (The Son) 2002, Premier amour (First Love) 2002, Romances de terre et d'eau (documentary) 2002, Stormy Weather 2003, Le monde vivant (The Living World) (co-producer) 2003, Le soleil assassiné (The Assassinated Sun) 2003, Le couperet (The Ax) (co-producer) 2005, L'enfant (The Child) 2005, Mon colonel (The Colonel) 2006, Vous êtes de la police? (co-producer) 2007, Why We Can't See Each Other Outside When the Sun is Shining (documentary) 2007, Premier Jour (short) 2008, The Silence of Lorna 2008, The Front Line 2009, K.O.R. (documentary) 2010, The Kid with a Bike 2011, Beyond the Hills (co-producer) 2012. *Films directed include:* Le chant du rossignol (documentary) 1978, Lorsque le bateau de Léon M. descendit la Meuse pour la première fois (documentary short) 1979, Pour que la guerre s'achève, les murs devaient s'écrouter (documentary) 1980, R… ne répond plus (documentary) 1982, Leçons d'une université volante 1982, Regard Jonathan/Jean Louvet, son oeuvre (documentary) 1983, Il court, il court, le monde (short) 1987, Falsch 1987, Je pense à vous (I Think of You) 1992, La promesse (The Promise) (numerous awards in many festivals) 1996, Gigi, Monica… et Bianca (documentary) 1997, Rosetta (Palme d'Or, Cannes Festival 1999) 1999, Le fils (The Son) (Ecumenical Jury Prize, Cannes Festival 2002) 2002, L'enfant (The Child) (Palme d'Or, Cannes Festival 2005, Best Foreign Film and co-winner Best Dir, Toronto Film Critics Asscn 2006) 2005, Le Silence de Lorna (Best Screenplay, Cannes Festival) 2008, The Kid with a Bike (Grand Prix, Cannes Festival) 2011. *Television includes:* Brook by Brook (documentary) (co-producer) 2002. *Address:* Cinéfondation, 3 rue Amélie, 75007 Paris, France. *Telephone:* 1-53-59-61-00. *Fax:* 1-53-59-61-10. *E-mail:* cinefondation@festival-cannes.fr. *Website:* www.cinefondation.com; www.festival-cannes.fr.

DARDENNE, Luc; Belgian film producer, director and screenwriter; b. (Eric Higgans), 10 March 1954, Liège; brother of Jean-Pierre Dardenne; ed Arts Inst.; made several videos with brother Jean-Pierre about rough life in blue-collar small towns in Wallonie 1970s. *Films produced include:* Nous étions tous des noms d'arbres 1982, Je pense à vous 1992, Faute de soleil (co-producer) 1995, Rosetta 1999, Les siestes Grenadine 1999, Le lait de la tendresse humaine (The Milk of Human Kindness) (co-producer) 2001, Le fils (The Son) 2002, Premier amour (First Love) 2002, Romances de terre et d'eau (documentary) 2002, Stormy Weather 2003, Le monde vivant (The Living World) (co-producer) 2003, Le soleil assassiné (The Assassinated Sun) 2003, Le couperet (The Ax) (co-producer) 2005, L'enfant (The Child) 2005, Mon colonel (The Colonel) 2006, Vous êtes de la police? (co-producer) 2007, Why We Can't See Each Other Outside When the Sun is Shining (documentary) 2007, Premier Jour (short) 2008, The Silence of Lorna 2008, The Front Line 2009, K.O.R. (documentary) 2010, The Kid with a Bike 2011, Beyond the Hills (co-producer) 2012. *Films directed include:* Le chant du rossignol 1978, Lorsque le bateau de Léon M. descendit la Meuse pour la première fois 1979, Pour que la guerre s'achève, les murs devaient s'écrouter 1980, R… ne répond plus 1982, Leçons d'une université volante 1982, Regard Jonathan/Jean Louvet, son oeuvre 1983, Il court… il court le monde 1987, Falsch 1987, Je pense à vous (I Think of You) 1992, La promesse (The Promise) (numerous awards in many festivals) 1996, Rosetta (Palme d'Or, Cannes Festival 1999) 1999, Le fils (The Son) (Ecumenical Jury Prize, Cannes Festival 2002) 2002, L'enfant (The Child) (Palme d'Or, Cannes Festival 2005, Best Foreign Film and co-winner Best Dir Toronto Film Critics Asscn 2006) 2005, To Each His Own Cinema (segment Dans l'Obscurité) 2007, Le Silence de Lorna (Best Screenplay, Cannes Festival) 2008, The Kid with a Bike (Grand Prix, Cannes Festival) 2011. *Television includes:* Brook by Brook (co-producer) 2002.

DARE, Richard; American business executive and arts administrator; *CEO and Managing Director, Brooklyn Philharmonic Orchestra;* m. Kitty Dare; int.

investment strategist from San Francisco; f. own co., corp. air service WestJets, sold to Warren Buffet; fmr Head of Pacific Rim Partners pvt. investment firm; CEO and Man. Dir Brooklyn Philharmonic Orchestra 2011–. *Address:* Brooklyn Philharmonic Orchestra, 55 Washington Street, Suite 656, Brooklyn, NY 11201, USA (office). *Telephone:* (718) 488-5700 (office). *Fax:* (718) 488-5901 (office). *E-mail:* info@bphil.org (office). *Website:* bphil.org (office).

DARLING, Rt Hon. Alistair Maclean, PC, LLB; British politician and lawyer; b. 28 Nov. 1953, London; s. of Thomas Darling MP and Anna Darling; brief 1st m. in his youth; m. 2nd Margaret McQueen Vaughan 1986; one s. one d.; ed Loretto School, Musselburgh, East Lothian, Univ. of Aberdeen; Pres. Aberdeen Univ. Students Union; advocate 1978–82; admitted to Faculty of Advocates 1984; mem. Lothian Regional Council 1982–87 (Chair. Transport Cttee 1986–87), Lothian and Borders Police Bd 1982–86; Gov. Napier Coll., Edinburgh 1982–87; MP (Labour) for Edinburgh Cen. 1987–2005, for Edinburgh SW 2005–; Opposition Spokesman on Home Affairs 1988–92, on Treasury Affairs 1992–96; Shadow Chief Sec. to HM Treasury 1996–97; Chief Sec. to HM Treasury 1997–98; Sec. of State for Social Security 1998–2001, for Work and Pensions 2001–02, for Transport 2002–06, and for Scotland 2005–06, for Trade and Industry 2006–07; Chancellor of the Exchequer 2007–10. *Leisure interests:* listening to Pink Floyd, Coldplay, Leonard Cohen and US rock band The Killers. *Address:* House of Commons, Westminster, London, SW1A 0AA, England (office); 22A Rutland Square, Edinburgh, EH1 2BB, Scotland (office). *Telephone:* (131) 476-2552 (office). *Fax:* (131) 656-0368 (office). *E-mail:* darlinga@parliament.uk (office). *Website:* www.alistairdarlingmp.org.uk.

DARMAATMADJA, HE Cardinal Julius Riyadi, SJ, BPhil; Indonesian ecclesiastic; *Archbishop Emeritus of Jakarta;* b. 20 Dec. 1934, Muntilan, Magelang, Cen. Java; s. of Joachim Djasman Darmaatmadja (died 1973) and Maria Soepartimah (died 1966); ed Canisius Secondary School, Muntilan, St Peter Canisius Minor Seminary Nertoyudan, Magelang, St Stanislaus Coll., De Nobili Coll., Pontifical Athenaeum, Poona, India, St Ignatius Coll., Yogyakarta; entered St Stanislaus Novitiate of Soc. of Jesus, Giri Sonta-Klepu, Semarang 1957, took first vows 1959; teacher, St Peter Canisius Minor Seminary 1964–66, Vice-Prefect 1971–83, Rector 1977–81; ordained priest of Soc. of Jesus by Cardinal Justinus Darmojuwono, Archbishop of Semerang 1969; parish priest, Kalasan Parish, Yogyakarta 1971, Giri Sonta-Klepu 1971–73; Socius Magistri and House Minister, St Stanislaus Novitiate 1971–73; Socius Provincialis in Karangpanas 1973–77; Provincial of Indonesian Prov. of Soc. of Jesus 1981–83; Archbishop of Semarang 1983–96; Mil. Ordinary for Catholic Mems of Indonesian Armed Forces 1984–2006; Pres. Nat. Bishops' Conf. of Indonesia 1988–97, 2001; cr. Cardinal (Cardinal Priest of Sacro Cuore di Maria) 1994; Archbishop of Jakarta 1996–2010; participated in Papal Conclave 2005; Pres.-Del. Special Ass. for Asia, World Synod of Bishops 1998; del. to Ordinary Ass., World Synod of Bishops, Vatican 2001. *Address:* Archdiocese of Jakarta, Keuskupan Agung, Jl. Katedral 7, Jakarta 10710, Indonesia (office). *Telephone:* (21) 3813345 (office). *Fax:* (21) 3855681 (office).

DARNTON, Robert Choate, DPhil; American historian and academic; *Carl H. Pforzheimer Professor and Director of the University Library, Harvard University;* b. 10 May 1939, New York; s. of the late Byron Darnton and Eleanor Darnton; m. Susan Lee Glover 1963; one s. two d.; ed Harvard Univ., Oxford Univ., UK; reporter, The New York Times 1964–65; Jr Fellow, Harvard Univ., 1965–68; Asst Prof., subsequently Assoc. Prof., Prof., Princeton Univ. 1968–, Shelby Cullom Davis Prof. of European History 1984–2007, Dir Program in European Cultural Studies 1987–95; Carl H. Pforzheimer Prof. and Dir of Univ. Library, Harvard Univ. 2007–; fellowships and visiting professorships include Ecole des Hautes Etudes en Sciences Sociales, Paris 1971, 1981, 1985, Netherlands Inst. for Advanced Study 1976–77, Inst. for Advanced Study, Princeton 1977–81, Oxford Univ. (George Eastman Visiting Prof.) 1986–87, Collège de France, Wissenschafts-Kolleg zu Berlin 1989–90, 1993–94; Pres. Int. Soc. for Eighteenth-Century Studies 1987–91, American Historical Asscn 1999–2000; mem. Bd of Dirs, Voltaire Foundation, Oxford, Social Science Research Council 1988–91; mem. Bd of Trustees Center for Advanced Study in the Behavioral Sciences 1992–96, Oxford Univ. Press, USA 1993–, The New York Public Library 1994–; mem. various editorial bds; Fellow, American Acad. of Arts and Sciences, American Philosophical Soc., American Antiquarian Soc.; Adviser, Wissenschafts-Kolleg zu Berlin 1994–; Foreign mem. Academia Europaea, Acad. Royale de Langue et de Littérature Françaises de Belgique; Guggenheim Fellow 1970; Corresp. Fellow, British Acad. 2001; Officier Ordre des Arts et des Lettres 1995, Chevalier Légion d'Honneur 2000; Dr hc (Neuchâtel) 1986, (Lafayette Coll.) 1989, (Univ. of Bristol) 1991, (Univ. of Warwick) 2001, (Univ. of Bordeaux) 2005, (Yvelines-Saint Quentin) 2006, (Univ. of Paris IV-Sorbonne) 2006, (Univ. of St Andrews) 2010; Leo Gershoy Prize, American Historical Asscn 1979, MacArthur Prize 1982, Los Angeles Times Book Prize 1984, Prix Médicis 1991, Prix Chateaubriand 1991, Nat. Book Critics Circle Award 1996, Gutenberg Prize 2004, Lifetime Achievement Award, American Printing History Asscn 2005, Prix France-Amériques 2011, National Humanities Medal 2012. *Television series:* Démocratie (co-ed.), France 1999. *Publications include:* Mesmerism and the End of the Enlightenment in France 1968, The Business of Enlightenment 1979, The Literary Underground of the Old Regime 1982, The Great Cat Massacre 1984, The Kiss of Lamourette 1989, Revolution in Print (co-ed.) 1989, Edition et sédition 1991, Berlin Journal, 1989–1990 1991, Gens de lettres, gens du livre 1992, The Forbidden Best-Sellers of Pre-Revolutionary France 1995, The Corpus of Clandestine Literature 1769–1789 1995, Démocratie (co-ed.) 1998, J.-P. Brissot: His Career and Correspondence 1779–1787 2001, Poesie und Polizei 2002, Pour les Lumières 2002, George Washington's False Teeth: An Unconventional Guide to the 18th Century 2003, The Case for Books: Past, Present, and Future 2009. *Leisure interests:* squash, travel. *Address:* Office of the Director, Harvard University Library, Wadsworth House, 1341 Massachusetts Avenue, Cambridge, MA 02138, USA (office). *Telephone:* (617) 495-3551 (office); (617) 496-4587 (office); (609) 924-6905 (home). *Fax:* (617) 495-0370 (office). *E-mail:* robert_darnton@harvard.edu; administration@hulmail.harvard.edu (office). *Website:* hul.harvard.edu (office).

DARRAT, Ahmed Hussein al-; Libyan politician; mem. Nat. Transitional Council, Minister of the Interior (following overthrow of Mu'ammar Gaddafi) 2011. *Address:* c/o Ministry of the Interior, Tripoli, Libya (office).

DARROCH, Sir (Nigel) Kim, Kt, KCMG, CMG, BSc; British diplomatist; *National Security Adviser to Her Majesty's Government;* b. 30 April 1954, South

Stanley, Co. Durham; m.; one s. one d.; ed Durham Univ.; joined FCO 1976, served in Protocol Dept, Planning Staff and News Dept 1976–80, Desk Officer Channel Tunnel Project and Law of the Sea, Maritime, Aviation and Environment Dept 1985–86, Pvt. Sec. to Minister of State dealing with Middle East, Arms Control, Eastern Europe 1987–89, Asst then Deputy Head of EU Dept 1993–95, Head of Eastern Adriatic Dept 1995–97, Head of News Dept 1998, Dir EU Affairs 2000, Dir-Gen. EU Affairs 2003; EU Adviser to Prime Minister and Head of Cabinet Office European Secr. 2004; overseas postings include Third, then Second, then First Sec., Embassy in Tokyo 1980–84, First Sec., Embassy in Rome 1989–92, Counsellor, Perm. Mission to EU, Brussels 1997–98, Perm. Rep. to EU 2007–11; Nat. Security Adviser to HM Govt 2012–. *Address:* c/o Prime Minister's Office, 10 Downing Street, London, SW1A 2AA, England. *Telephone:* (20) 7276-1234. *E-mail:* NSAaction@cabinet-office.x.gsi.gov.uk (office). *Website:* www.cabinetoffice.gov.uk.

DARWAZAH, Samih T., BPharm, MPharm; Palestinian business executive and politician; *Founder and Chairman, Hikma Pharmaceuticals PLC;* b. 1930; m. Samira Fadli; four c.; ed American Univ. of Beirut, St Louis Coll. of Pharmacy, USA; worked at Eli Lilly 1964–76; f. Hikma Pharmaceuticals Ltd (now PLC), Jordan 1978, Chair. and CEO –2007, Chair. (non-exec.) 2007–; Minister of Energy and Mineral Resources, Jordan 1995–96; f. Jordan Trade Asscn; mem. Advisory Econ. Council to HM King Abdullah ibn al-Hussein; fmr mem. Jordanian Senate; Chair. Capital Bank of Jordan 2009–, Labatec Pharma SA; Dr hc (St Louis Coll. of Pharmacy) 2010; Ernst & Young Middle East Entrepreneur of the Year 2007, Distinguished Alumnus Award, American Univ. of Beirut 2012, Emerging Markets Leader, Scrip 100 2013. *Publication:* Building a Global Success (memoir) 2005. *Address:* Hikma Pharmaceuticals Building, Bayader Wadi Seer Area, PO Box 182400, Amman 11118, Jordan (office). *Website:* www.hikma.com (office).

DAS, Jatin; Indian artist and sculptor; b. Dec. 1941, Mayurbhanj, Orissa; ed Sir JJ School of Art, Bombay; Prof. Emer., Jamia Millia Islamia Univ. 2008–, Visiting Prof., Faculty of Fine Arts 2009–; Visiting Prof., Coll. of Art, Nat. School of Drama, Nat. Inst. of Design and School of Planning and Architecture; Founder Chair. JD Centre of Art, Bhubaneshwar; Founder Pres. Odissa Forum, Delhi, Mayurbhanj Cultural Devt Foundation; Founder mem. Poetry Soc. of India; Art Adviser, Housing and Urban Devt Corpn; Trustee, Delhi Blue Pottery Trust; Life Fellow, Royal Soc. of Arts, London; Cultural Amb. to Cabinet, UK; Life mem. Indian Nat. Trust for Art and Cultural Heritage; mem. Governing Bd Royal Soc. of Arts India; mem. Advisory Cttee Nat. Natural History Museum, Bhubaneshwar, Delhi Urban Art Comm., Rural India Complex 1972 (now Nat. Crafts Museum), Republic Day Parade Cttees; mem. India Int. Centre, Delhi, British Library, Chelsea Arts Club, London, Ghalib Memorial Movt, Delhi, Fan Circle Int., London, Soc. to Save Rocks, Hyderabad; Order of the Star of Italian Solidarity (Italy); Hon. DLitt (Utkal Univ. of Culture, Bhubaneswar) 2007; Utkala Award 2006, Bharat Nirman Award 2007. *Telephone:* (11) 26497504 (office). *Fax:* (11) 26492449 (home). *E-mail:* jatin@jatindas.com. *Website:* www.jatindas.com; www.jdcentreofart.org (office).

DAS, Maarten; Dutch lawyer and business executive; *Non-Executive Chairman, Heineken Holding NV;* b. 19 June 1948, Amsterdam; m.; three c.; ed Free Univ., Amsterdam, Parker School of Comparative Law, Columbia Univ., USA; attorney, Loyens & Loeff 1975–, Pnr 1980–; mem. Supervisory Bd Heineken NV 1994–95, Del. mem. Supervisory Bd 1995–, mem. Bd of Dirs Heineken Holding NV 1994–, Chair. (non-exec.) 2002–. *Address:* Heineken NV, PO Box 28, 1000 AA Amsterdam (office); Heineken NV, Tweede Weteringplantsoen 21, 1017 ZD Amsterdam, The Netherlands (office). *Telephone:* (20) 523-92-39 (office). *Fax:* (20) 626-35-03 (office). *E-mail:* info@heinekeninternational.com (office). *Website:* www.heinekeninternational.com (office).

DAS, Nandita, BA, MA; Indian actress and director; *Chairperson, Children's Film Society;* b. 7 Nov. 1969, New Delhi; d. of Jatin Das and Varsha Das; m. Saumya Sen 2002 (divorced 2009); m. 2nd Subodh Maskara 2010; one s.; ed Univ. of Delhi; started career with theatre group Jannatya Manch; teacher, Rishi Valley School; Chair. Children's Film Soc. 2009–; mem. main jury Cannes Film Festival 2005, Karlovy Vary Int. Film Festival 2007, Marrakech Int. Film Festival 2009; mem. South Asians for Human Rights; mem. Advisory Bd Alliance for a New Humanity; Chevalier, Ordre des Arts et des Lettres. *Films include:* Parinati 1989, Fire 1996, Earth 1996, Hazaar Chaurasi Ki Maa (Nat. Award 1997) 1998, Rockford 1999, Punaradhivasam (Best Foreign Feature Film, Atlantic Film Festival) 1999, Hari-Bhari (Nat. Award 1999) 1999, Bawandar (Best Actress, Santa Monica Film Festival 2001) 2000, Aks 2001, Aamaar Bhuvan (Best Actress, Cairo Film Festival 2002) 2002, Pitaah 2002, Lal Salaam 2002, Supari 2003, Bas Yun Hi 2003, Vishwa Thulasi (Golden Special Jury Award, World Fest Houston Int. Film Festival 2005) 2004, Fleeting Beauty 2005, Maati Maay (Best Actress, Madrid Int. Film Festival 2007) 2005, Podokkhep 2006, Before the Rains 2007, Provoked 2007, Ramchand Pakistani 2008, Firaaq (dir) (Best Film, Best Screenplay and Foreign Critics Award, Asian Festival of First Films, Singapore, Special Award Thessaloniki Int. Film Festival, Greece, Best Editor Dubai Int. Film Festival 2008, Best Film Kara Int. Film Festival 2009, Best Film, The Maverick Spirit Award, Cinequest Film Festival, San Jose, Special Jury Prize, Istanbul Film Festival 2009) 2008, I Am 2010; short films: Saanjh 1999, Fleeting Beauty 2003, Indo-Pak Music Film 2004, Saayey 2005, Rainwater Harvesting (dir), Education for All (dir), Learning is Child's Play (dir), Imprint in Clay (documentary) (dir). *Plays include:* Heads Ya Tails, The Spirit of Anne Frank, Moteram Ka Satyagrah, Mother, Equus. *Address:* Children's Film Society, Films Division Complex, 24, Dr.G.Deshmukh Marg, Mumbai 400 026, India (office). *Telephone:* (22) 23517148 (office). *Fax:* (22) 23522610 (office). *E-mail:* chairperson@cfsindia.org (office); contact@nanditadas.com. *Website:* www.cfsindia.org (office); www.nanditadas.com.

DAS NEVES CEITA BAPTISTA DE SOUSA, Maria; São Tomé and Príncipe economist and politician; b. 1958; two c.; ed Univ. of the East, Santiago de Cuba, Cuba; fmr economist at World Bank and UNICEF; mem. Movimento de Libertação de São Tomé e Príncipe—Partido Social Democrata; Minister of Trade, Industry and Tourism and Minister of the Economy –2002; Prime Minister of São Tomé e Príncipe (first woman premier in W Africa) 2002–04. *Address:* c/o Movimento de Libertação de São Tomé e Príncipe—Partido Social Democrata, Estrada Riboque, Edif. Sede do MLSTP, São Tomé, São Tomé e Príncipe (office).

DASCHLE, Thomas (Tom) Andrew, BA; American lawyer, government official and fmr politician; b. 9 Dec. 1947, Aberdeen, S Dakota; m. Linda Hall Daschle; one

s. two d.; ed S Dakota State Univ.; served as 1st Lt, USAF 1969–72; Chief Legis. Aide and then Field Co-ordinator to US Senator 1973–77; mem. 96th–97th Congresses from 1st S Dakota Dist, 98th Congress 1977–87; Senator from S Dakota 1987–2005, Senate Minority Leader Congress 1995–2001, 2002–05, Majority Leader 2001–02; Special Policy Advisor, Alston & Bird LLP, Washington, DC 2005–08; Distinguished Sr Fellow, Center for American Progress 2005–08; Visiting Prof., Public Policy Inst., Georgetown Univ. 2005–08; Co-founder Bipartisan Policy Center, Washington, DC 2007; Richard von Weizsäcker Distinguished Visitor, American Acad. in Berlin, Germany 2008; Democrat; numerous awards including Distinguished Service Award, Nat. Rural Electric Cooperation Asscn 2000. *Publications:* Critical: What We Can Do About the Health Care Crisis 2008, Getting It Done: How Obama and Congress Finally Broke the Stalemate to Make Way for Health Care Reform 2010. *Address:* c/o Bipartisan Policy Center, 1225 I Street, NW, Suite 1000, Washington, DC 20005, USA.

D'ASCOLI, Bernard Jacques-Henri Marc; French concert pianist; *Artistic Director, Piano Cantabile;* b. 18 Nov. 1958, Aubagne; one s.; ed Marseille Conservatoire; became blind 1962; took up music 1970; youngest Baccalauréat matriculate of France 1974; first public appearances on both piano and organ 1974; elected best young French talent of the year (Megève) 1976; began int. professional career 1982, following debuts at major London concert halls with Royal Philharmonic Orchestra and first recording; toured Australia with Chamber Orchestra of Europe 1983; debuts: Amsterdam Concertgebouw 1984, Houston Symphony 1985, Musikverein, Vienna 1986, Tokyo Casals Hall and Bunka Kaikan Hall 1988, Boston Symphony Orchestra 1992, Dresden Philharmonic 1998, Montreal Symphony 1999, English Chamber Orchestra 2004; festival appearances: BBC Proms, Sintra, Besançon, Oviedo, La Roque d'Anthéron, Sydney Olympics cultural festivities; Artistic Dir Piano Cantabile; First Prize, Int. Maria Canals competition, Barcelona 1979, Prizewinner, Marguerite Long, Paris, Leipzig Bach Competition, Warsaw Chopin Competition 1980, Chopin Prize, Santander, Third Prize, Leeds Int. Piano Competition 1981. *Radio:* numerous BBC Radio broadcasts in recital and as soloist with orchestra. *Television:* South Bank Show, Face the Music. *Recordings:* Liszt Sonata, Franck Prelude Chorale and Fugue 1982, Schumann and Chopin recordings 1988, 1989, Schumann Quintet with Schidlof Quartet 1999, Chopin Complete Nocturnes, Scherzi and Impromptus 2005, 2006. *Leisure interests:* reading, swimming, humane sciences. *Address:* c/o Eleanor Harris, Piano Cantabile, 350 Impasse du Baou, 13400 Aubagne, France (office). *Telephone:* (4) 42-84-02-36 (office). *E-mail:* eleaharr@orange.fr (office). *Website:* www.bernard-dascoli.com.

DASGUPTA, Sir Partha Sarathi, Kt, BSc, BA, PhD, FRS, FBA; Indian/British economist and academic; *Frank Ramsey Professor Emeritus of Economics, University of Cambridge;* b. 17 Nov. 1942, Dhaka, then in India, now in Bangladesh; s. of the late Prof. Amiya Dasgupta and Shanti Dasgupta; m. Carol M. Meade 1968; one s. two d.; ed Univs of Delhi and Cambridge; Lecturer in Econs, LSE 1971–75, Reader 1975–78, Prof. of Econs 1978–85; Prof. of Econs, Univ. of Cambridge 1985–2010, Frank Ramsey Prof. of Econs 1994–2010, Prof. Emer. 2010–, Fellow, St John's Coll. 1985–; Prof. of Econs and Prof. of Philosophy and Dir of Program on Ethics in Society, Stanford Univ., Calif., USA 1989–92; Andrew D. White Prof.-at-Large, Cornell Univ. 2007–13; Chair. Beijer Int. Inst. of Ecological Econs, Stockholm; Pres. European Econ. Asscn 1999, Royal Econ. Soc. 1998–2001, European Asscn of Environmental and Resource Economists 2008–09; Foundermem. Man. and Advisory Cttee South Asian Network for Devt and Environmental Econs 1999–; mem. Pontifical Acad. of Social Sciences 1997, Academia Europaea 2009; Foreign mem. Royal Swedish Acad. of Sciences 1991, American Acad. of Arts and Sciences 1991, American Philosophical Soc. 2005, Istituto Veneto di Scienze, Lettere ed Arti 2009; Foreign Assoc. NAS 2001; Fellow, Econometric Soc. 1975, Third World Acad. of Sciences 2001; Hon. Prof. of Environmental and Climate Econs, Univ. of Copenhagen 2008–10; Hon. Fellow, LSE 1994, Trinity Coll. Cambridge 2010; Distinguished Fellow CES, Univ. of Munich 2011; Dr hc (Wageningen) 2000, (Catholic Univ. of Louvain) 2007, (Faculté Universitaire Saint-Louis) 2009, (Bologna) 2010, (Tilberg) 2012, (Harvard) 2013; Stevenson Prize, Univ. of Cambridge 1967, Volvo Environment Prize 2002, John Kenneth Galbraith Award, American Agricultural Econs Asscn 2007, Erik Kempe Award in Environmental and Resource Econs, Kempe Foundation and the European Asscn of Environmental and Resource Economists (co-recipient) 2007, Zayed Int. Prize for the Environment (Category 2) 2011. *Publications include:* Guidelines for Project Evaluation (co-author) 1972, Economic Theory and Exhaustible Resources (co-author) 1979, The Control of Resources 1983, An Inquiry into Well-Being and Destitution 1993, Social Capital: A Multifaceted Perspective (co-ed.) 2000, Human Well-Being and the Natural Environment 2001, Economic Theory for the Environment: Essays in Honour of Karl-Göran Mäler (co-ed.) 2002, The Economics of Non-Convex Ecosystems (co-ed.) 2003, Ecosystems and Human Well-Being: Synthesis (co-author) (synthesised the findings of the Millennium Ecosystem Assessment, which has been awarded the Zayed International Prize 2005) 2005, Economics: A Very Short Introduction 2007 (translated into Arabic, Chinese, Japanese, Portuguese, Spanish, Italian and German), Poverta, Ambiente e Società (collected papers on poverty, environment and society, translated and edited by Elena Podrecca and Maurizio Zenezini) 2007, Selected Papers of Partha Dasgupta, Vols I & II, Vol. 1: Institutions, Innovations, and Human Values, Vol. 2: Poverty, Population, and Natural Resources 2010; books and articles on econs of environmental and natural resources, technological change, normative population theory, political philosophy, devt planning and the political economy of destitution. *Leisure interests:* cinema, theatre, reading. *Address:* Faculty of Economics and Politics, University of Cambridge, Sidgwick Avenue, Cambridge, CB3 9DD (office); 1 Dean Drive, Holbrook Road, Cambridge, CB1 7SW, England (home). *Telephone:* (1223) 335227 (office). *E-mail:* partha.dasgupta@econ.cam.ac.uk (office). *Website:* www.econ.cam.ac.uk/faculty/dasgupta (office).

DASH-YONDON, Budragchaagiin, PhD; Mongolian politician and diplomatist; b. 17 Feb. 1946, Huvsgul; s. of Jugnaa Budragchaa and Sengee Chogimoo; m. Choijamts Batjargal; one s. two d.; ed Mongolian State Univ., State Univ. of Kiev, USSR; Prof., Mongolian State Univ. 1968–74; officer at Scientific and Educational Dept, Mongolian People's Revolutionary Party (MPRP) Cen. Cttee 1978–79; Vice-Chancellor, Higher Party School, MPRP Cen. Cttee 1979–85; Deputy Head and Head of Dept, MPRP Cen. Cttee 1985–90; First Sec.-Gen., MPRP Ulan Bator City Party Cttee 1990–91; MPRP Sec.-Gen. 1991–96; apptd Political Adviser to Pres.

1997; fmr Amb. to Bulgaria. *Leisure interests:* reading, chess. *Address:* c/o Mongolian People's Revolutionary Party, Baga Toiruu 37/1, Ulan Bator, Mongolia (office). *Telephone:* (6) 50067805 (office). *E-mail:* contact@mprp.mn (office). *Website:* www.mprp.mn (office).

DASKALOPOULOS, Dimitris, BA, MBA; Greek business executive and art collector; b. 1957, Athens; ed Athens School of Man., Northwestern Univ., USA; Chair. and CEO Delta Holding SA –2007 (merged with Mechelany International SA, Goody's, Flocafé and several other cos to form Vivartia SA 2006), fmr Chair. Delta Dairy SA, Delta Ice Cream SA; fmr Vice-Chair. General Frozen Foods SA; mem. Bd of Dirs Nat. Bank of Greece, several cos listed on Athens Stock Exchange; Chair. Fed. of Hellenic Food Industries, Hellenic Fed. of Enterprises; mem. Bd Fed. of Greek Industries, American-Hellenic Chamber of Commerce; mem. Nat. Agricultural Policy Council, Asscn of Young Entrepreneurs of Greece, Greek Man. Asscn, Greek Inst. of Man., Euroglaces (European Ice Cream Asscn), Fed. of Greek Food Industries to CIAA (Confed. of the Food and Drink Industries of the EU), European Round Table of Industrialists, and many others; mem. Leadership Council of the New Museum, Tate's Int. Council; Trustee, Solomon R. Guggenheim Foundation; collection of modern art includes around 400 works, ranging from what is believed to be the last Marcel Duchamp urinal in pvt. hands to Christoph Büchel's 450m installation Unplugged (Simply Botiful) 2006–07. *Leisure interests:* adventure trips, mountain climbing, photography, collecting modern art. *Address:* c/o Vivartia SA, Ziridi 10, Marousi, Attica 15123, Greece. *Telephone:* (210) 349-4000. *E-mail:* info@vivartia.com. *Website:* www.vivartia.com.

DASSAULT, Olivier, BA, MA, PhD; French politician, business executive and fmr air force pilot; b. 1 June 1951, Boulogne-Billancourt (Hauts-de-Seine); s. of Serge Dassault and Nicole Dassault (née Raffel); grandson of Marcel Dassault; ed École de l'Air; qualified as professional IFR pilot 1975; Pres. Dassault Communications; Chair. Valmonde (publr); mem. Bd Journal des Finances financial newspaper; Admin. of Dassault subsidiary Socpresse; mem. Nat. Ass. (Union pour un Mouvement Populaire) for the first circonscription of Oise 2002–, mem. Comm. des finances; composer and musician and contributed several scores for well-known French films. *Achievements include:* set several world speed records: New York to Paris in Dassault Falcon 50 1977, New Orleans to Paris in Dassault Falcon 900 (both with Hervé Le Prince-Ringuet) 1987, Paris to Abu Dhabi in Falcon 900 EX 1996, Paris to Abu Dhabi in Falcon 900 EX (both with Guy Mitaux-Maurouard and Patrick Experton) 1996. *Publications:* has published several books of photos. *Leisure interest:* photography. *Address:* Assemblée nationale, 126 rue de l'Université, 75355 Paris 07 SP, France (office). *E-mail:* odassault@assemblee-nationale.fr (office). *Website:* www.assemblee-nationale.fr (office); www.olivierdassault.fr.

DASSAULT, Serge; French engineer, business executive and politician; *Chairman and CEO, Groupe Industriel Marcel Dassault SA;* b. 4 April 1925, Paris; s. of the late Marcel Dassault and Madeleine Minckès; m. Nicole Raffel 1950; three s. one d.; ed Lycée Janson-de-Sailly, Ecole Polytechnique, Ecole Nat. Supérieure de l'Aéronautique, Centre de Perfectionnement dans l'Administration des Affaires, Inst. des Hautes Etudes de la Défense Nationale; Dir of Flight Testing, Avions Marcel Dassault 1955–61, Export Dir 1961–63; Dir-Gen. Société Electronique Marcel Dassault 1963–67, Pres. Dir-Gen. 1967–86; Admin. Avions Marcel Dassault-Bréguet Aviation 1967, Pres. Dir-Gen. 1986–2000, Adviser, Hon. Pres. 2000–; currently Chair. and CEO Groupe Industriel Marcel Dassault SA, subsidiary cos include Dassault Aviation, Dassault Systemes, Socpresse; Vice-Pres. Société de Gestion de Participations Aéronautiques (SOGEPA); Admin. Dassault Belgique Aviation 1968; Town Councillor, Corbeil-Essonnes 1983–95, Mayor 1995–; Regional Councillor, Ile de France 1986–95; Gen. Councillor Essonne 1988–, Pres. Departmental Cttee RPR de l'Essonne 1998–; mem. Comité de direction du Groupement des industries électroniques 1968, Groupement des Industries Françaises Aéronautiques et Spatiales 1968; Hon. Pres. Fondation des Œuvres Sociales de l'Air 1968; Commissaire Général des Salons Internationaux de l'Aéronautique et de l'Espace 1974–93; Chief Engineer Armaments 1974; Pres. Asscn Française pour la Participation dans les Entreprises 1972; Chair. working group, Participation active dans l'entreprise, Nat. Council, Patronat Français 1985; Pres. of Section Asscn européenne des constructeurs de matériel spatial (AECMA) 1987–, Groupement des Industries Françaises Aéronautiques et Spatiales (Gifas) 1993–97, Council of French Defence Industry 1994–96; mem. Sénat 2004–; mem. Union pour un Mouvement Populaire (UMP); Chevalier, Légion d'honneur, Médaille de l'Aéronautique, Officier de l'Ordre national du Mérite ivoirien. *Publications:* La Gestion participative, J'ai choisi la vérité 1983. *Leisure interests:* golf, hunting, fishing. *Address:* Groupe Dassault, 9 rond-point des Champs-Elysées-Marcel Dassault, 75008 Paris (office); Mairie, place Galignani, 91100 Corbeil-Essonnes, France (office). *Telephone:* 1-53-76-93-00 (office). *Website:* www.dassault.fr (office); www.senat.fr/senfic/dassault_serge04055h.html.

DASSONVILLE, Yves, MEcon; French civil servant and government official; b. 1948; ed Ecole Nat. d'Admin, Paris; apptd Civil Admin. (2nd Class), Ministry of the Interior and Decentralization 1983; apptd Chief of Staff to Commr of Eure-et-Loire 1983; Deputy Sec.-Gen. of French Polynesia, Overseas Secr. 1984–86; Chief of Staff to Sec. of State to Minister in charge of South Pacific issues 1986; Sec.-Gen. Landes Pref. 1986–88; Civil Admin. (1st Class) and Deputy Prefect of Saint-Dizier 1988–92; Civil Admin. (unclassified), Sec.-Gen. for Regional Affairs of Languedoc and Sr Deputy Prefect 1992–95; Sec.-Gen. Pref. of Réunion 1995–98; Deputy Prefect of Lorient 1998–2001; Prefect Del. for Security and Defence to Prefect of the Southern Defence Zone 2001–02; Prefect of Jura 2002–04; Prefect (Commr) of Martinique 2004; Chief of Staff to Sec. of State for Overseas Territories 2004–07; High Commr of New Caledonia 2007–10; Chevalier de la Légion d'honneur, Chevalier de l'Ordre nat. du mérite. *Address:* c/o Office of the High Commissioner, Nouméa, New Caledonia (office).

DAUDA, Joseph Bandabla, LLB; Sierra Leonean lawyer and politician; *Minister of Internal Affairs;* b. 24 Dec. 1942, Bambawo; m.; two c.; ed Fourah Bay Coll., King's Coll., Univ. of London; teacher, St Edwards Secondary School, Freetown 1967–68; with Council of Legal Educ. 1969–72; called to the Bar, Middle Temple 1971; pvt. legal practice 1972–86, 1992–99; mem. and Legal Adviser to Man. Cttee Kenema Town Council 1980–86; mem. of Parl. 1986–92; Minister of State in Office of Attorney-Gen. and Minister of Justice 1987–88, Minister of Trade

and Industry 1988–91, Second Vice-Pres., Attorney-Gen. and Minister of Justice 1991–92, of Rural Devt and Local Govt 1999–2002, of Finance 2002–05, of Foreign Affairs and Int. Co-operation 2010–13, of Internal Affairs 2013–; Gov. for Sierra Leone, IBRD, IDA, IFC; mem. Sierra Leone People's Party (SLPP). *Address:* Ministry of Internal Affairs, Liverpool Street, Freetown, Sierra Leone (office). *Telephone:* (22) 226979 (office). *Fax:* (22) 227727 (office).

DAUDZAI, Mohammed Umar, MSc; Afghan diplomatist and government official; *Minister of Interior Affairs;* b. 12 Oct. 1957, Qarabagh Dist; ed Univ. of Manchester, UK; involved in mujahidin struggle against soviet occupation 1980–84; community mobilization team leader, Save the Children Fund (UK), Peshawar 1984–86, Man. Primary Health Care Programme 1986–88, Deputy Project Dir and Head Training Unit 1988–90, adviser to Field Dir 1992–93; Regional Dir Swedish Cttee for Afghanistan 1993–96; Programme Officer UNDP, Afghanistan 1996–99; Asst Resident Rep., UNDP, Islamabad 1999–2002; Area-based Devt Specialist, Switzerland 2000–03; Chief of Staff to Pres. Hamid Karzai 2003–05; Amb. to Iran and Perm. Rep. to Secr. of ECO 2005–07; Chief of Staff, Office of the Pres. 2007–11; Amb. to Pakistan 2011–13; Minister of Interior Affairs 2013–. *Address:* Ministry of Interior Affairs, Shar-i-Nau, Kabul, Afghanistan (office). *Telephone:* 799401540 (mobile) (office). *E-mail:* moiafghanistan@gmail.com (office). *Website:* www.moi.gov.af (office).

DAUDZE, Gundars; Latvian physician and politician; *Head of the Chancery of the President of Latvia;* b. 9 May 1965, Ventspils; ed Riga Medicine Inst.; mem. Saeima (Parl.) (Union of Greens and Farmers—ZZS list) for Kurzeme constituency, Chair. (Speaker) Saeima 2007–10, Deputy Speaker 2010–11; Head of the Chancery of the Pres. of Latvia 2011–; Chair. Nat. Security Cttee, mem. Foreign Affairs Cttee, Public Health Sub-cttee and Social Security Sub-cttee of Social and Employment Matters Cttee. *Leisure interests:* sailing, sport. *Address:* Rātslaukums 7, Rīga 1900, Latvia (office). *Telephone:* 67092106 (office). *Fax:* 67092158 (office). *E-mail:* gundars.daudze@president.lv (office). *Website:* www.president.lv (office); www.daudze.lv.

DAUGAARD, Dennis M., BS, JD; American lawyer, politician and state governor; *Governor of South Dakota;* b. 11 June 1953, Garretson, SDak; m. Linda Schmidt 1981; one s. two d.; ed Dell Rapids High School, Univ. of South Dakota, Northwestern Univ. School of Law, Chicago, Ill.; raised on family farm nr Garretson, SDak; called to Bar of South Dakota; attorney, Supena & Nyman 1978–79, Shand Morahan & Co. 1980–81; Vice-Pres. and Trust Officer, First Bank of South Dakota 1981–90; Devt Dir, Children's Home Soc., SDak 1990–2002, Exec. Dir 2003–09; mem. for Dist 9, SDak State Senate 1997–2003, Pres. SDak Senate, Chair. Workers' Compensation Advisory Council, served as mem. comm. that dealt with amendments to legislative article of SDak's Constitution, as chair. of state task force examining ways to reduce number of South Dakotans without health insurance; Lt Gov. of SDak 2003–11; Gov. of South Dakota 2011–; mem. South Dakota Planned Giving Council, Sioux Falls Estate Planning Council; mem. South Dakota Bar Asscn, Nat. Soc. of Fund Raising Execs, Rotary; Republican. *Address:* Office of the Governor, 500 East Capitol Avenue, Pierre, SD 57501, USA (office). *Telephone:* (605) 773-3212 (office). *Fax:* (605) 773-4711 (office). *Website:* sd.gov/governor (office).

DAUGHTRY, Christopher (Chris) Adam; American singer, songwriter and musician (guitar); b. 26 Dec. 1979, Roanoke Rapids, North Carolina; s. of Pete Daughtry and Sandra Daughtry; m. Deanna Robertson 2000; one s. one d. one step-d. one adopted s.; competitor on American Idol 2006; Founder mem. and lead singer Daughtry 2006–; American Music Awards for Breakthrough Artist, Best Adult Contemporary Artist 2007, People Choice Award for Best Rock Song (for Home) 2007, Billboard Music Awards for Top Artists (Pop Duo or Group), Top New Artist, Top Comprehensive Artist, Hot 100 Artists (Duo or Group), and Hot Adult Top 40 Artist 2007, World Music Awards for World's Best-Selling Rock Group of 2007, for World's Best-Selling New Artist of 2007. *Recordings include:* albums: with Daughtry: Daughtry (American Music Award for Best Pop/Rock Album 2007, Top Billboard 200 Album 2007) 2006, Leave this Town 2009, Break the Spell 2011, Baptized 2013; with Cadence: All Eyes on You 1999; with Absent Element: Uprooted 2005. *Address:* c/o 19 Entertainment, 8560 West Sunset Blvd, 9th Floor, West Hollywood, Los Angeles, CA 90069, USA (office). *E-mail:* inquiries@19entertainment.com (office). *Website:* www.daughtryofficial.com.

DAUKORU, Edmund Maduabebe, CON, PhD; Nigerian geologist, politician and international organization official; ed Imperial Coll. of Science and Tech., London, UK; Special Studies Geologist, Shell Int. Petroleum Co. 1978, held various positions in co. both in Nigeria and internationally, including Chief Geologist, apptd Div. Man. SPDC 1984; Group Man. Dir and CEO Nigerian Nat. Petroleum Corpn 1992–2003, Alt. Chair. 2003–; Special Adviser on Petroleum and Energy to Pres. of Nigeria 2003–05; Minister of State for Petroleum Resources 2005–06; Minister of Energy 2006–07; Sec.-Gen. OPEC and Pres. OPEC Conf. 2006–07; Chair. Solid Mineral Cttee for Bayelsa State; mem. Niger Delta Peace Forum, Ijaw Elder's Forum (Bayelsa State); Trustee Bayelsa State Devt Fund; apptd King Mingi XII Amanyanabo of Nembe Kingdom 2008. *Address:* c/o Ministry of Energy, Annex 3, Federal Secretariat Complex, Shehu Shagari Way, Central Area, PMB 278, Garki, Abuja, Nigeria (office).

DAUKŠYS, Kęstutis; Lithuanian politician; b. 31 Jan. 1960, Alytus; m.; two s.; ed Univ. of Vilnius and G. Plechanov Russian Acad. of Econs, Moscow; Asst. Political Economy Dept, Univ. of Vilnius 1983–85; Deputy Head of Planning Div., Furniture Design Construction Bureau 1985–87, Specialist of Foreign Trade Div. 1989–90; mil. service 1987–89; Dir UAB Balticum 1990–95, UAB Balticum grupė 1995–98, 2004; Dir Gen. AB Kilimai 1998–2003, Chair. 1999–2004;; mem. Seimas (Parl.) 2004–, mem. Cttee on Foreign Affairs 2008–, Nuclear Energy Comm. 2008–; Minister of the Economy 2005–06; mem. Darbo Partija (Labour Party). *Leisure interests:* music, fishing. *Address:* Seimas, Room I-438, Gedimino pr. 53, Vilnius 01109, Lithuania (office). *Telephone:* (5) 239-6958 (office). *E-mail:* Kestutis .Dauksys@lrs.lt (office). *Website:* www.lrs.lt (office).

DAUMAN, Philippe P., BA, JD; American lawyer and media executive; *President and CEO, Viacom;* b. 1 March 1954; m. Deborah Dauman; two c.; ed Yale Univ., Columbia Univ. Law School; Pnr, Shearman & Sterling (law firm), New York 1978–93, prin. outside counsel to Viacom, Sr mem. Mergers and Acquisitions Practice Group; mem. Bd of Dirs Viacom Inc. (predecessor of Viacom)

1987–, Gen. Counsel and Sec. 1993–98, Deputy Chair. 1996–2000, mem. Exec. Cttee and Exec. Vice-Pres. in charge of strategic transactions, legal and govt affairs, human resources and admin, supervising Paramount Entertainment, Showtime Networks and Simon & Schuster 1994–2000, mem. Bd of Dirs Viacom Jan. 2006–, Pres. and CEO Viacom Sept. 2006–; Co-founder, Co-Chair. and CEO DND Capital Pnrs LLC (pvt. equity firm) 2000–; mem. Bd of Dirs National Amusements, Inc., Lafarge North America Inc., CBS Corpn; mem. Bd Trustees, Museum of the City of New York; mem. Bd Visitors, Columbia Law School. *Address:* Viacom, 1515 Broadway, New York, NY 10036, USA (office). *Telephone:* (212) 258-6000 (office). *E-mail:* press@viacom.com (office). *Website:* www.viacom .com (office).

DAUNT, Sir Timothy Lewis Achilles, Kt, KCMG; British diplomatist; b. 11 Oct. 1935, Brecon, Powys, Wales; s. of L. H. G. Daunt and Margery Daunt (née Lewis Jones); m. Patricia Susan Knight 1962; one s. two d.; ed Sherborne School, St Catharine's Coll., Cambridge; mil. service with King's Royal Irish Hussars 1954–56; entered FCO 1959, Ankara 1960, Foreign Office 1964, Nicosia 1967, Pvt. Sec. to Perm. Under-Sec. of State, FCO 1970; with Bank of England 1973; mem. UK Mission, New York 1973; Counsellor OECD, Paris 1975; Head of S European Dept, FCO 1978–81; Assoc. Centre d'études et de recherches internationales, Paris 1982; Minister and Deputy Perm. Rep. to NATO, Brussels 1982–85; Asst Under-Sec. of State (Defence), FCO 1985–86; Amb. to Turkey 1986–92; Deputy Under-Sec. of State (Defence), FCO 1992–95; Lt-Gov. Isle of Man 1995–2000; Chair. British Inst., Ankara 1995–2006, Anglo-Turkish Soc. 2001–09, The Ottoman Fund Ltd 2005–10. *Address:* 20 Ripplevale Grove, London, N1 1HU, England. *Telephone:* (20) 7697-8177. *E-mail:* t.daunt@btinternet.com.

DAUTRY-VARSAT, Alice, DSci; French cell biologist and academic; b. 1950, Paris; ed Paris-Sud Univ., State Univ. of New York at Stony Brook, USA; training in solid-state physics and molecular biology, France and USA; joined Institut Pasteur, Paris 1977, currently Prof. and Dir Biology of Cell Interaction Unit, Pres. 2005–13; mem. Scientific Council, Life Sciences Dept, CNRS; Prof. École Polytechnique; fmr Visiting Scientist, MIT; mem. External Reference Group for Health Research Strategy, WHO; Trustee, Ecole Polytechnique, ISTA (Austria), DNDi (Switzerland); Chevalier Légion d'honneur. *Publications:* over 130 publs on receptors and infections by intracellular bacteria. *Address:* c/o Institut Pasteur, 25–28 rue du Dr Roux, 75724 Paris Cedex 15, France.

DAVENPORT, Lindsay; American professional tennis player; b. 8 June 1976, Palos Verdes, Calif.; d. of Wink Davenport and Ann Davenport; m. Jon Leach 2003; one s. two d.; ed Murriela Valley High School; turned professional 1993; has won 51 singles titles including Lucerne 1993, 1994, Brisbane 1994, singles and doubles (with Jana Novotna) Bausch & Lomb Championships 1997, Bank of the West 1998, Toshiba Classic 1998, Acura Invitational 1998, US Open 1998, European Championships 1998, Tokyo Pan Pacific 1998, 2001, 2003, Sydney Int. 1999, Wimbledon 1999 (singles and doubles), Advanta Championships, Philadelphia 1999, Chase Championships, New York 1999, Australian Open 2000, Indian Wells 2000; mem. Olympic Team 1996, gold medallist singles 2000; mem. US Fed. Cup Team 1993–2000, 2002; 86 career professional titles in total (35 doubles titles). *Leisure interests:* watching hockey, sports in general, music, crosswords, going to the beach. *Address:* c/o IMG Tennis, IMG Center, 1360 East 9th Street, Suite 100, Cleveland, OH 44114, USA.

DAVENPORT, Paul Theodore, OC, BA, MA, PhD; Canadian economist, academic and university administrator; b. 24 Dec. 1946, Summit; s. of Theodore Davenport and Charlotte Lomax Paul; m. Josette Brotons 1969; one s. two d.; ed Stanford Univ. and Univ. of Toronto; Prof., Dept of Econs McGill Univ. 1973–89, Assoc. Dean, Faculty of Grad. Studies and Research, 1982–86, Vice-Prin. (Planning and Computer Services) 1986–89; Pres. and Vice-Chancellor Univ. of Alberta 1989–94; Pres. Univ. of Western Ontario 1994–2009; Chair. Asscn of Univs and Colls of Canada 1997–99, Council of Ont. Univs 1999–2001; Chevalier Légion d'Honneur 2001; Hon. LLD (Alta) 1994, (Toronto) 2000, (Int. Univ. of Moscow) 2002. *Publications include:* Reshaping Confederation: The 1982 Reform of the Canadian Constitution (ed. with R. Leach) 1984, Universities and the Knowledge Economy in Renovating the Ivory Tower (ed. David Laidler) 2002. *Leisure interests:* biking, Impressionist painting, modern jazz, photography. *Address:* c/o Office of the President, University of Western Ontario, Natural Sciences Centre, Room 120A, London, ON N6A 5B9; 1836 Richmond Street, London, ON N5X 4B9, Canada (home).

DAVEY, Rt Hon. Edward (Ed) Jonathan, PC, BA, MSc (Econ), FRSA; British politician; *Secretary of State for Energy and Climate Change;* b. 25 Dec. 1965, Nottingham; m. Emily Gasson 2005; one s.; ed Nottingham High School, Jesus Coll., Oxford, Birkbeck Coll., London; worked in the Commons as economics researcher for Liberal Democrats 1989–93, later party's Sr Econs Adviser; left Parl. to work for Omega Partners 1993–97, specialized in consultancy in postal services sector; MP for Kingston and Surbiton 1997–2010, for Kingston and Surbiton (revised boundary) 2010–; Liberal Democrat: London Whip 1997–2000; Spokesperson for the Treasury (Public Spending and Taxation) 1997–99, for the Economy 1999–2001, for London 2000–03; Shadow Chief Sec. to the Treasury 2001–02; Spokesperson for Office of the Deputy Prime Minister 2002–05; Shadow Sec. of State for Educ. and Skills 2005–06, for Trade and Industry 2006; Chief of Staff to Sir Menzies Campbell as Leader of the Liberal Democrats 2006–07; Shadow Sec. of State for Foreign and Commonwealth Affairs 2007–10; Parl. Under-Sec. of State (Minister for Employment Relations, Consumer and Postal Affairs), Dept for Business, Innovation and Skills 2010–12; Sec. of State for Energy and Climate Change 2012–; mem. Fed. Policy Cttee 1994–95, Liberal Democrat Policy Group (Econs, Tax and Benefits and Transport), Asscn of Liberal Democrat Councillors; Chair. Campaigns and Communications Cttee 2006–09; Liberal Democrat; Royal Humane Soc. Bravery Award and commendation from Chief Constable of British Transport Police for rescuing a woman who had fallen onto the line before an oncoming train at Clapham Junction station 1995. *Publication:* contrib. to the Orange Book 2004. *Address:* Department of Energy and Climate Change, 3 Whitehall Place, London, SW1A 2AW (office); House of Commons, Westminster, London, SW1A 0AA (office); Constituency Office, Liberal Democrats, 21 Berrylands Road, Surbiton, KT5 8QX, England. *Telephone:* (300) 060-4000 (Dept) (office); (20) 7219-3512 (Westminster) (office); (20) 8288-0161 (Surbiton) (office). *Fax:* (20) 7219-0250 (Westminster) (office); (20) 8972-1088 (Surbiton) *E-mail:*

daveye@parliament.uk (office); correspondence@decc.gsi.gov.uk (office); edward@ edwarddavey.co.uk. *Website:* www.decc.gov.uk (office); www.edwarddavey.co.uk.

DAVEY, Grenville, BA; British sculptor, artist and academic; *Visiting Professor, University of the Arts, London;* b. 28 April 1961, Launceston, Cornwall; ed Exeter Coll., Goldsmiths Coll., London; currently Visiting Prof., Univ. of the Arts, London; Artist-in-Residence, Dept of Theoretical Physics, Queen Mary Coll., London, Isaac Newton Inst. of Math. Sciences, Cambridge 2010–12; Turner Prize, Tate Gallery 1992, Art and Architecture Award, Royal Soc. of Arts 1995. *Leisure interests:* work, walking. *Address:* University of East London, 4–6 University Way, London, E16 2RD, England (office). *Telephone:* (20) 8223-3433 (office).

DAVEY, Kenneth George, OC, PhD, FRSC, FESC; Canadian academic and scientist; *Distinguished Research Professor Emeritus of Biology, York University;* b. 20 April 1932, Chatham, Ontario; s. of William Davey and Marguerite Davey (née Clark); m. Jeannette Isabel Evans 1959 (separated 1989); one s. two d. (one deceased); ed McKeough Public School, Chatham, Chatham Collegiate Inst., Univ. of Western Ontario, Univ. of Cambridge, UK; NRC Fellow (Zoology), Univ. of Toronto 1958–59; Drosier Fellow, Gonville and Caius Coll., Cambridge 1959–63; Assoc. Prof. of Parasitology, McGill Univ., Montreal 1963–66, Dir Inst. of Parasitology 1964–74, Prof. of Parasitology and Biology 1966–74; Prof. of Biology, York Univ., Toronto 1974–84, Chair. of Biology 1974–81, Dean of Science 1982–85, Distinguished Research Prof. of Biology 1984–2000, Prof. Emer. 2000–, Vice-Pres. (Academic Affairs) 1986–91; Ed. International Journal of Invertebrate Reproduction and Development 1979–85, Canadian Journal of Zoology 1995–2004; Assoc. Ed. Encyclopedia of Reproduction 1996–; Vice-Chair. Canadian Science Publishing 2011–; mem. Bd of Dirs Huntsman Marine Lab. 1978–80, 1982–85, Pres. and Chair. of Bd 1977–80; Pres. Biological Council of Canada 1979–82, Canadian Soc. of Zoologists 1981–82; Sec. Acad. of Science, Royal Soc. of Canada 1979–85; mem. Council, Royal Canadian Inst. 1996– (Pres. 2000–02), mem. Nat. Council on Ethics in Human Research (Pres. 2002–03); Fellow, Entomological Soc. of Canada 1997; Hon. Fellow, Royal Entomological Soc. 2004; Queen's Jubilee Medal 1977, 2002, 2012; Hon. DSc (Western Ontario) 2002; Gold Medal, Entomological Soc. of Canada 1981, Fry Medal, Canadian Soc. of Zoologists 1987, Gold Medal, Biological Council of Canada 1987, Distinguished Biologist Award, Canadian Council of Univ. Biology Chairs 1992, Hitschfeld Award, Canadian Asscn Univ. Research Admins 1997, Wigglesworth Medal, Royal Entomological Soc., London 2004. *Publications include:* Reproduction in Insects 1964, Biology: Exploring the Diversity of Life (co-author) 2010; 200 articles on endocrinology of invertebrate animals. *Leisure interests:* handweaving, food and wine. *Address:* 96 Holm Crescent, Thornhill, ON L3T 5J3, Canada (home). *Telephone:* (905) 882-5077 (home). *E-mail:* davey@yorku.ca (office).

DAVID, Adelino Castelo; São Tomé and Príncipe economist, fmr central banker and government official; *Gov. Banco Central de São Tomé e Príncipe 1992–94;* Minister of Planning and Finance 1999–2001, 2004–05, Co-ordinator Centre de Recherche et d'Analyse des Politiques de Développement de São Tomé et Príncipe, Ministry of Planning and Finance 2007–. *Address:* Ministry of Planning and Finance, Largo Alfândega, BP 168, São Tomé, São Tomé e Príncipe (office). *Telephone:* 225467 (office). *E-mail:* adelinocd@yahoo.com (office).

DAVID, Cristian, PhD; Romanian politician; b. 26 Dec. 1967; ed Univ. of Bucharest and Romanian Nat. Defence Coll.; with TMUCB Bucharest (econ co.) 1986–90, Designer 1990–91; Co-ordinator Nat. Liberal Univ. Youth Org. 1990–93, Sec.-Gen. 1993–97; Adviser, Ministry of Youth and Sport 1997–98; mem. Standing Cttee, Nat. Liberal Party—Partidul Național Liberal 1991–93, Dir Foreign Relations Dept 1997–2004, mem. Nat. Rep. Del. 2002–04, Chair. Foreign Affairs Comm. 2004–05, mem. Cen. Standing Cttee 2005–06, mem. Cen. Political Bureau 2006–; Dir Van Soestbergen Import Export SRL 1992–94, Team Int. Import Export SRL 1995–96, Team Int. Consult SRL 1999–2004; Assoc. Lecturer, Dept of Statistics and Econ. Forecasting, Acad. of Econ. Studies 2001–04; mem. Senate 2004–, mem. Senate Human Rights, Cults and Minorities Comm. 2004–; Minister-Del. responsible for internationally financed projects 2004–07; Minister of the Interior and Admin. Reform 2007–08; mem. Romanian Asscn for Liberty and Devt 1997–2000; Founding mem. Liberal Studies Inst. 2006. *Publications include:* various articles on econs and statistics. *Address:* Senatul (The Senate), 050711 Bucharest 5, Calea 13 Septembrie 1–3 (office); National Liberal Party (NLP), 011866 Bucharest, Blvd Aviatorilor 86, Romania. *Telephone:* (21) 4021111 (office); (21) 2310795. *Fax:* (21) 3121184 (office); (21) 2310796. *E-mail:* dre@pnl.ro. *Website:* www.pnl.ro.

DAVID, François Paul; French civil servant; *Chairman, Coface;* b. 5 Dec. 1941, Clermont-Ferrand; s. of Jean David and Rose David (née Cabane); m. Monique Courtois 1967; two s.; ed French Lycée, London, Faculté de Lettres, Paris, Ecole nat. d'admin.; mem. staff Dept of Foreign Econ. Relations, Ministry of Finance 1969–73, Head Agric. Policy Office 1976–78; Commercial Counsellor, Embassy in the UK 1974–76; Tech. Adviser Office of Minister of Foreign Trade 1978–80; Asst Dir Ministry of Economy, Finance and Budget 1981–84, Deputy Dir 1984–86, Dir Office of Jr Minister in charge of Foreign Trade at Ministry of Economy, Finance and Privatization 1986–87, Dir Dept of Foreign Econ. Relations 1987–89; Dir-Gen. Int. Affairs, Aérospatiale 1990–94; Chair. Compagnie française d'assurance pour le commerce extérieur (Coface) 1994–; mem. Bd Dirs European Aeronautic Defence and Space Co. (EADS NV), Vinci; Censor of Rexel; Commdr, Légion d'honneur; Chevalier, Ordre nat. du Mérite; Officier du Mérite agricole; Officier, Ordre de Saint-Charles (Monaco). *Publications:* Le Mythe de l'exportation 1971, Autopsie de la Grande-Bretagne 1976, Le Commerce international à la dérive 1982, La Guerre de l'export 1987, Relations économiques internationales: La politique commerciale des grandes puissances face à la crise 1989, Jacques Cœur, l'aventure de l'argent 1990. *Leisure interests:* tennis, karate. *Address:* Coface, 12 cours Michelet, La Défense 10, 92065 Paris -la-Défense Cedex (office). *Telephone:* 1-49-02-13-00 (office). *Fax:* 1-49-02-14-21 (office). *E-mail:* francois_david@coface .com (office). *Website:* www.coface.com (office).

DAVID, George Alfred Lawrence, BA, MBA; American business executive; b. 7 April 1942, Bryn Mawr, Pa; s. of Charles Wendell David and Margaret Simpson; m. 1st Barbara Osborn 1965 (divorced 1997); one s.; m. 2nd 2003; two d.; ed Harvard Univ. and Univ. of Virginia; Asst Prof. of Va, Charlottesville 1967–68; Vice-Pres. Boston Consulting group 1968–75; Sr Vice-Pres. (Corp. Planning and Devt)

Otis Elevator Co., New York 1975–77, Sr Vice-Pres. and Gen. Man. Latin American Operations, West Palm Beach, Fla 1977–81, Pres. N American Operations, Farmington, Conn. 1981–85, Pres. and CEO Otis Elevator Co. 1985–89; Exec. Vice-Pres. and Pres. (Commercial/Industrial) United Technologies Corpn (parent co.) 1989–92, Pres. and COO 1992–94, CEO 1994–2008, Chair. 1997–2009 (retd); mem. Bd of Dirs Citigroup Inc., Nat. Acad. Foundation, Inst. Int. Econs, Washington 1996–; mem. The Business Council, The Business Roundtable; Trustee, Carnegie Hall Corpn, Inc.; Order of Friendship (Russia) 1999, Légion d'honneur 2002. *Address:* c/o United Technologies Corporation, 1 Financial Plaza, Suite 22, Hartford, CT 06103-2608, USA. *Telephone:* (860) 728-7000. *Website:* www.utc.com.

DAVID, Jacques-Henri; French business executive; *Chairman, Deutsche Bank (France);* b. 17 Oct. 1943, Ygrande (Allier); s. of André David and Suzanne Dupeyrat; m. Isabelle Lamy 1967; one d.; ed Lycée Louis-le-Grand, Paris, Ecole Polytechnique, Inst. d'Etudes Politiques, Paris and Ecole Nat. Supérieure de la Statistique et des Études Économiques (Insee), Paris; Admin. Insee 1967–68; Head, econometric studies service, Banque de France 1969–75; Deputy Sec.-Gen. Conseil Nat. du Crédit 1973–75; Prof. Inst. d'Etudes Politiques 1975; Insp. des Finances, Ministry of Econ. and Finance 1975–79; Adviser, Office of Minister of Econ. 1979, Deputy Dir 1980, Dir 1980–81; Sec.-Gen. Conseil Nat. du Crédit 1981–84; Finance Dir Cie Saint-Gobain 1984–86, Dir-Gen. 1986–89; Pres. Banque Stern 1989–92; Pres. Centre de Recherche pour l'expansion de l'économie (Rexecode) 1989–96; Dir-Gen. Compagnie Gen. des Eaux 1993–95; Pres. CEPME 1995–99, Sofaris 1996–99, Bank for Devt of Small and Medium-Sized Businesses (BDPME) 1997–99; mem. Deutsche Bank Group Social and Econ. Council 1996–1999; Chair. Deutsche Bank in France 1999–; Vice-Chair. Global Corporate Finance; Officier Légion d'honneur, Commdr Ordre du Mérite. *Publications:* La Politique monétaire 1974, Réévaluation et verité des bilans 1977, La Monnaie et la politique monétaire 1983, Crise financière et relations monétaires internationales 1985, Le Financement des opérations à risque dans les PME 1997. *Leisure interests:* skiing, yachting, golf. *Address:* Deutsche Bank, 3 avenue de Friedland, 75008 Paris, France (office). *Telephone:* 1-44-95-65-65 (office). *E-mail:* jacques-henri.david@db.com (office).

DAVID, Peter; Grenadian/Canadian politician; mem. House of Reps for St George 2003–; Gen. Sec., Nat. Democratic Congress Party; Minister of Foreign Affairs 2008–10, of Tourism and Civil Aviation 2010–12. *Address:* c/o Ministry of Tourism and Civil Aviation, Ministerial Complex, 4th Floor, Botanical Gardens, Tanteen, St George's, Grenada (office).

DAVID-WEILL, Michel; French business executive; *Chairman of the Supervisory Board, EURAZEO;* b. 23 Nov. 1932, Paris; s. of the late Pierre David-Weill and of Berthe Haardt; m. Hélène Lehideux 1956; four d.; ed Lycée français, New York and Inst. d'études politiques, Paris; Lazard Frères & Co. LLC, NY 1961–65, Chair. and Sr Pnr 1977–2005; Gen. Pnr Lazard Frères & Cie, Paris 1965, Maison Lazard & Cie 1976–2005; Gen. Pnr and Chair. Lazard Pnrs Ltd Partnership 1984–2005; Chair. Lazard Brothers & Co. Ltd, London 1990–92, Deputy Chair. 1992, Chair. Lazard LLC (after merger of Lazard Bros. Paris, London and NY offices) 2000–05; mem. Bd of Dirs EURAZEO 1972, now Chair. of Supervisory Bd; mem. Man. Bd, Sovac 1972–, Chair. 1982–95; mem. Bd of Dirs, Danone, later Vice-Chair.; mem. Man. Bd Publicis; Dir La France SA, La France IARD, La France-Vie, La France Participations et Gestion, SA de la Rue Impériale de Lyon, Fonds Partenaires-Gestion (FPG), Fiat SpA, Euralux, Exor Group, ITT Corp.; The Dannon Co. Inc.; fmr Dir Pearson PLC, NY Stock Exchange; Chair. Artistic Council, Réunion des Musées Nationaux, Paris, Metropolitan Museum Council, New York, New York Hosp. Morgan Library; mem. Inst. (Acad. des Beaux Arts, Paris); Grand Officier, Légion d'honneur 2007, Grand Croix 2011; Officier, Ordre nat. du Mérite; Commdr des Arts et des Lettres. *Publication:* L'esprit en fête 2007. *Address:* Institut de France, 23 quai Conti, 75006 Paris, France (office). *Telephone:* 1-44-15-89-34 (office). *Fax:* 1-47-66-43-72 (office). *E-mail:* staff@md-w.com (office). *Website:* www.eurazeo.com (office).

DAVIDE, Hilario G., Jr, BSc, BL; Philippine chief justice and diplomatist; b. 20 Dec. 1935, Barangay Colawin, Argao, Cebu; s. of Hilario P. Davide, Sr and Josefa L. Gelbolingo; m. Virginia (Gigi) Jimenea Perez; three s. two d.; ed Abellana Vocational High School, Univ. of the Philippines; Pvt. Sec. to Vice-Gov. then to Gov. of Cebu 1959–63; Faculty mem. Coll. of Law, Southwestern Univ., Cebu City 1962–68; Del. to Constitutional Convention 1971, Chair. Cttee on Duties and Obligations of Citizens and Ethics of Public Officials; Minority Floor Leader 1978–79; mem. interim Batasang Pambansa Ass. representing Region VII 1978–84; Chair. Comm. on Elections 1988–90, Presidential Fact Finding Comm. 1990–91; Assoc. Justice of the Supreme Court 1991–98, Sr Assoc. Justice Oct.–Nov. 1998, Chief Justice 1998–2005; Amb. and Perm. Rep. to UN, New York 2007–10, Vice-Chair. ECOSOC; Head of a truth comm. investigating important issues in The Philippines 2010–; mem. Advisory Council of Eminent Jurists, UNEP, Regional Office for Asia and the Pacific; Hon. Pres. World Jurist Asscn of the World Peace Through Law Centre; Hon. LLD (Southwestern Univ.) 1999, (Far Eastern Univ.) 2001, (Univ. of the Philippines) 2001, (Angeles Univ. Foundation) 2001, (De La Salle Univ.) 2001; Hon. DH (Univ. of Cebu) 2000, (Ateneo de Manila Univ.) 2001, (Univ. of the Visayas) 2001; Service to the Nation Award 1987, Outstanding Kts of Columbus Award 1995, Nat. Maagap Award, Organized Response for the Advancement of Soc. (ORAS) 1998, The Outstanding Filipino Award in Environmental Law 1999, Millennium Medal of Merit, Order of the Kts of Rizal 2000, Filipino of the Year Award, Philippine Daily Inquirer 2000, Rajah Humabon Award 2001, Grand Perlas Award, Philippine Foundation Inc. 2001, Chief Justice Techankee Foundation 2001, Chino Roces Foundation Freedom Award 2001, Rizal Peace Award, Univ. of S Philippines 2001, Rule of Law Award 2001, Ramon Magsaysay Award for Govt Service 2002, Man of the Year Award, Philippine Free Press 2003, Chief Justice Roberto Concepcion Award for Legal Aid, Integrated Bar of the Philippines 2003, Most Distinguished Alumnus Award, Univ. of the Philippines Alumni Asscn 2005, ABA Int. Rule of Law Award 2006. *Address:* c/o Department of Foreign Affairs, DFA Building, 2330 Roxas Blvd, Pasay City, 1330 Metro Manila, The Philippines (office). *Telephone:* (2) 8344000 (office). *Fax:* (2) 8321597 (office). *E-mail:* webmaster@dfa.gov.ph (office). *Website:* www.dfa.gov.ph (office).

DAVIDS, Willibrord Jacob Maria, LLM; Dutch judge; b. 17 Oct. 1938, Rotterdam; m. Marianne Baan; ed Roman Catholic Univ. of Nijmegen; worked at civil law notary office in Hilversum, Curaçao (Netherlands Antilles) and Groningen 1965; lectured in civil law, Groningen Univ. 1975–80; apptd judge, dist court, Assen 1980, Vice-Pres. 1984; apptd Justice, Supreme Court of the Netherlands 1986, Vice-Pres. 1998–2004, Pres. 2004–08; Pres. Benelux Court, Court of Appeal for Supervision of Standards of Certified Architects, Asscn of Dutch Architects; Chair. Advisory Cttee on assessment of Restitutions Applications for items of cultural value and the Second World War 2009; Chair. Cttee of Iraq Inquiry, The Netherlands 2009; mem. Coll. of Appeal, Benelux Asscn of Trade Mark Lawyers and Counsellors; Kt of the Order of the Dutch Lion 1995, Commdr, Order of Oranje Nassau, Grand Officier, Ordre Grand-Ducal de la Couronne de Chêne (Luxembourg) 2008, Grand Officier, Crown Order (Belgium) 2009. *Publications:* several books and articles on real estate law, corpn law and criminal law. *Address:* c/o De Hoge Raad der Nederlanden, PO Box 20303, 2500 EH The Hague, Netherlands (office). *E-mail:* kabinetpresident@HogeRaad.nl (office).

DAVIDSON, Janet Marjorie, ONZM, FRSNZ, MA, DSc; New Zealand archaeologist and ethnologist (retd); b. 23 Aug. 1941, Lower Hutt, Wellington, North Island; d. of Albert Dick Davidson and Christine Mary Davidson (née Browne); m. Bryan Foss Leach 1979; one d.; ed Hutt Valley High School, Univ. of Auckland; Field Assoc., Bernice P. Bishop Museum, Honolulu 1964–66; E. Earle Vaile Archaeologist, Auckland Inst. and Museum 1966–79; Rhodes Visiting Fellow, Lady Margaret Hall, Oxford, UK 1974–76; Hon. Lecturer in Anthropology, Univ. of Otago 1980–86; ethnologist, Nat. Museum of New Zealand 1987–91; Curator (Pacific Collections), Museum of New Zealand Te Papa Tongarewa 1991–2002, Hon. Research Assoc. 2002–; extensive archaeological field work in New Zealand and the Pacific. *Publications include:* Archaeology on Nukuaro Atoll 1971, The Prehistory of New Zealand 1984, Archaeology on Taumako: a Polynesian Outlier in the Eastern Solomon Islands (with B. F. Leach) 2008, numerous articles on the archaeology and prehistory of New Zealand and various Pacific Islands. *Leisure interests:* music, theatre, opera, ballet, cooking.

DAVIDSON, John Macdonald, AM, BArch, LFRAIA; Australian architect; *Principal, Catalyst Architecture;* b. 21 Oct. 1926, Sydney, NSW; s. of John H. Davidson and Daisy Macdonald; m. Helen M. King 1954; two s. one d.; ed Geelong Coll. and Univ. of Melbourne; Assoc. Godfrey and Spowers (architects) 1954–61, Pnr, later Dir 1961, Chair. Godfrey and Spowers Australia Pty Ltd 1979–91; Co-founder (with son Hugo Davidson) and Dir, Catalyst Design Group 1991–2004, Prin., Catalyst Architecture 2004–; Pres. Royal Australian Inst. of Architects 1978–79; mem. Expert Panel in Architecture (COPQ) 1978–; mem. Int. Council, Int. Union of Architects (UIA) 1981–85, Vice-Pres. UIA 1985–87; Chair. Metropolitan Strategy Consultative Cttee 1984–89, South Yarra Collaborative Pty Ltd 1983–89; Hon. FAIA 1985. *Publication:* The Awarding and Administration of Architectural Contracts 1961. *Leisure interests:* music, art, writing. *Address:* Catalyst Architecture, 453 Church Street, Richmond, Vic. 3121 (office); 502/633 Church Street, Richmond, Vic. 3121, Australia (home). *Telephone:* (3) 9428-6352 (office). *Fax:* (3) 9428-6897 (office). *E-mail:* jmd@catalyst.net.au (office). *Website:* www.catalyst.net.au (office).

DAVIDSON, Sir Martin Stuart, Kt, KCMG, CMG, MA, FRSA; British organization official; *CEO, British Council;* b. 14 Oct. 1955, Lowestoft, Suffolk, England; m.; three c.; ed St Andrew's Univ.; Admin. Officer, Hong Kong Govt 1979–83; with British Council, Peking 1984–87, Regional Officer, China 1987–89, Dir S China 1989–93, Asst Regional Dir E and S Europe 1993–95, Cultural Counsellor and Dir China 1995–2000, Regional Dir E Asia and the Americas 2000–03, Regional Dir Europe 2003–06, Deputy Dir Gen. 2006–07, CEO British Council 2007–; mem. Exec. Cttee GB China Centre; Trustee, Leonard Cheshire Disability; Gov., Goodenough Coll. *Leisure interests:* hill walking, flying. *Address:* British Council Customer Service UK, Bridgewater House, 58 Whitworth Street, Manchester, M1 6BB, England (office). *Telephone:* (161) 957-7755 (office). *E-mail:* general.enquiries@britishcouncil.org (office). *Website:* www.britishcouncil.org (office).

DAVIDSON, Ogunlade R., BEng, PEng, CEng; Sierra Leonean engineer, academic and international organization official; *Vice-Chairman, Intergovernmental Panel on Climate Change (IPCC);* ed Univ. of Sierra Leone, UMIST (now Univ. of Manchester) and Univ. of Salford, UK; chartered engineer 1993; Lecturer, Univ. of Sierra Leone 1978–83, Sr Lecturer 1983–93, first Dir of Research 1985–92, Head of Dept of Mechanical and Maintenance Eng 1993–2000, Prof. of Mechanical Eng 1993–, Dean of Faculty of Eng 1996–2000, 2003–05, currently Dean of Post-Grad. Studies; Prof. and Dir Energy and Devt Research Centre, Univ. of Cape Town, South Africa 2000–03; Minister of Energy and Water Resources 2010–12; Sr Fulbright Scholar, Univ. of California, Berkeley, USA 1987; MacArthur Scholar, Princeton Univ. and Lawrence Berkeley Lab., USA 1990–92; Visiting Prof., Univ. of Gothenburg, Sweden, ENDA-TM, Senegal, Riso Nat. Lab., Denmark; Co-Chair. Working Group III, Intergovernmental Panel on Climate Change (IPCC) 1997–2008, Vice-Chair. IPCC 2008–; Co-Chair. Steering Cttee of Global Network on Energy for Sustainable Devt; has worked as consultant in energy, tech., climate change and environment for several nat. and int. bodies, including UNESCO, UNIDO, ILO, UN Econ. Comm. for Africa, UNDP, UNEP, Global Environment Facility, UN Framework Convention on Climate Change, New Partnership for Africa's Devt (NEPAD), Arab Devt Bank, World Bank, Batelle Labs and Carnegie Corpn, New York; Corp. mem. Sierra Leone Inst. of Engineers 1979, Nigerian Soc. of Engineers 1985, Inst. of Energy (UK) 1993; Fellow, Univ. Research Council 1987, African Acad. of Sciences 1991, Sierra Leone Inst. of Engineers 2001. *Publications:* more than 300 publs, including books, book chapters, journal articles and conf. papers on African energy systems and policies, power sector reform, renewable energy policy, climate change-greenhouse gas mitigation and nat. climate change strategy. *Address:* Intergovernmental Panel on Climate Change, World Meteorological Organization, 7 bis, avenue de la Paix, CP 2300, 1211 Geneva 2, Switzerland (office). *Telephone:* (22) 730-82-08 (office). *E-mail:* IPCC-Sec@wmo.int (office); IPCC-Media@wmo.int (office). *Website:* www.ipcc.ch (office).

DAVIDSON, Richard K., BS; American business executive (retd); b. 1942, Allen, Kan.; m. Trish Davidson; three c.; ed Washburn Univ., Harvard Univ.; Conductor, Missouri Pacific Railroad 1960, Asst Trainmaster, Shreveport, LA 1966, later various operating positions in Fort Worth, Kansas City and N Little Rock, becoming Asst to Vice-Pres., Operations, St Louis 1975, Vice-Pres., Operations,

1976; joined Union Pacific Railroad (following merger with Missouri Pacific and Western Pacific) 1982, Vice-Pres., Operations 1986, Exec. Vice-Pres. 1989–91, Pres. and CEO 1991–2006, Chair. 1991–2006 (retd), Chair. Union Pacific Corpn 1997–2007; fmr Chair. Pres.'s Nat. Infrastructure Advisory Cttee; mem. Bd of Dirs Chesapeake Energy Corpn 2006–; Trustee and Dir Malcolm Baldrige Nat. Quality Award Foundation; fmr mem. US Strategic Command Consultation Cttee; mem. Horatio Alger Assen; mem. Bd of Advisors Thayer Capital Pnrs; fmr Trustee, Boy Scouts of America, Washburn Univ. Endowment Asscn, Strategic Air and Space Museum, Omaha; Dr hc (Washburn Univ.) 1984, (Bellevue Univ.) 2003, (Univ. of Nebraska, Kearney) 2003; Kan. Business Hall of Fame 2001, Horatio Alger Asscn of Distinguished Americans 2002, Light of Wellness Award 2003, Railway Age Railroader of the Year 2003, Neb. Business Hall of Fame 2004, Omaha Business Hall of Fame 2006.

DAVIES, A. Michael, MA, FCA; British business executive; b. 23 June 1934; s. of Angelo Henry Davies and Clarice Mildred Davies; m. Jane Priscilla Davies 1962; one s. (deceased) one d.; ed Shrewsbury School, Queens' Coll., Cambridge; Chair. Tozer Kemsley & Millbourne 1982–86, Bredero Properties 1986–94, Worth Investment Trust 1987–95, Calor Group 1989–97 (Dir 1987–97), Perkins Foods 1987–2001, Berk 1988–95, Wiltshier 1988–95, Nat. Express Group PLC 1991–2004, Simon Group 1993–2003, Corporate Services Group 1999–2002; Deputy Chair. T.I. Group 1990–93 (Dir 1984–93), Manpower 1987–91, AerFi 1993–2000; Dir Imperial Group 1972–82, Littlewoods Org. 1982–88, TV-am 1982–88, British Airways 1983–2002, Worcester Group 1991–92. *Address:* Little Woolpit, Ewhurst, Cranleigh, Surrey, GU6 7NP, England. *Telephone:* (1483) 277344. *Fax:* (1483) 277899. *E-mail:* amdavies@btinternet.com.

DAVIES, Sir David E. N., Kt, CBE, PhD, DSc, FRS, FREng; British electrical engineer and academic; *Board Member, Parliamentary Office of Science and Technology;* b. 28 Oct. 1935, Cardiff, Wales; s. of D. E. Davies and Sarah Samuel; m. 1st Enid Patilla 1962 (died 1990); two s.; m. 2nd Jennifer E. Rayner 1992; ed Univ. of Birmingham; Lecturer, then Sr Lecturer in Electrical Eng, Univ. of Birmingham 1961–67; Asst Dir Research Dept, British Railways Bd 1967–71; Visiting Industrial Prof. of Electrical Eng, Univ. of Loughborough 1969–71; Prof. of Electrical Eng, Univ. Coll. London 1971–88, Pender Prof. of Electrical Eng 1985–88, Vice-Provost Univ. Coll. 1986–88; Vice-Chancellor Loughborough Univ. of Tech. 1988–93; Chief Scientific Adviser, Ministry of Defence 1993–99; Chair. Defence Scientific Advisory Council 1992–93; Pres. IEE 1994–95; Vice-Pres. Royal Acad. of Eng 1995–96, Pres. 1996–2001; Chair. Railway Safety 2000–03; Chair. Hazards Forum 2002–10; Dir Strategy Ltd 1974–79, Gaydon Tech. 1986–88, Loughborough Consultants 1988–93, Inst. Consumer Ergonomics 1988–93, ERA Tech. 1997–, Lattice PLC 2000–02; Adviser to Bd, Nat. Grid plc 2003–08; mem. Defence Acad. Advisory Bd, Bd ERA Foundation 2002–07, Parl. Office of Science and Tech. 2010–; Foreign mem. Russian Acad. of Sciences 2004; Fellow, Learned Soc. of Wales 2010; Hon. Fellow, Univ. of Wales, Coll. of Cardiff 2001, Univ. Coll. London 2006; Hon. FIMechE; Hon. Fellow Inst. of Eng and Tech.; Hon. DSc (Birmingham) 1994, (Loughborough) 1994, (South Bank) 1994, (Bradford) 1995, (Surrey) 1996, (Warwick) 1997, (Bath) 1997, (Heriot-Watt) 1999, (UMIST) 2000, (Wales) 2002; Rank Prize for Optoelectronics 1984, IEEE Centennial Medal 1984, IEE Faraday Medal 1987, Royal Acad. of Eng Pres.'s Medal 2007. *Publications:* about 120 pubs on antennas, radar and fibre optics. *E-mail:* den@easonestates .freeserve.co.uk (office).

DAVIES, David Reginald Howell, DPhil; American (b. Welsh) X-ray crystal-lographer and researcher; *Scientist Emeritus, National Institutes of Health;* b. 22 Feb. 1927, Camarthen, Wales; s. of Theophilus Howell Davies and Gwladys Evelyn Evans Davies (née Hodges); m. 1st Cynthia Margaret Seaman 1951 (divorced 1981); two d.; m. 2nd Monica Walters 1985; ed Magdalen Coll., Oxford, UK, California Inst. of Tech., Pasadena; Research Assoc., Albright & Wilson Ltd, Birmingham, UK 1954–55; Visiting Scientist, NIH, Bethesda, Md 1955–61, Chief, Section on Molecular Structure, Lab. of Molecular Biology, Nat. Insts of Diabetes, Digestive and Kidney Diseases, NIH 1961–2012, Scientist Emer. 2012–; Visiting Scientist, MRC Lab. Molecular Biology 1963–64, Max Planck Inst., Heidelberg 1972–73; mem. NAS 1977, American Acad. of Arts and Sciences, American Soc. of Biological Chemists, American Crystallographic Asscn, Biophysical Soc. (Council 1960–65, 1973–78), Protein Soc.; Presidential Meritorious Exec. Award 1982, Presidential Rank Award 1988, Stein and Moore Award, Protein Soc. 1998, ASBMB Herb Tabor Award 2009. *Publications:* articles in scientific journals. *Leisure interests:* tennis, sailing. *Address:* Laboratory of Molecular Biology, Building 5, Room 338, NIDDK, National Institutes of Health, 9000 Rockville Pike, Bethesda, MD 20892 (office); 4224 Franklin Street, Kensington, MD 20895, USA (home). *Telephone:* (301) 496-4295 (office). *Fax:* (301) 496-0201 (office). *E-mail:* david.davies@nih.gov (office). *Website:* www-mslmb.niddk.nih.gov (office).

DAVIES, Edward Brian, BA, DPhil, FRS; British mathematician and academic; *Professor of Mathematics, King's College London;* b. 13 June 1944, Cardiff; m. Jane Christine Phillips 1968; one s. one d.; ed Oxford Univ.; Lecturer in Math., Oxford Univ. 1970–81; Prof. of Math., King's Coll., London 1981–; Fellow King's Coll. 1996; Sr Berwick Prize, London Math. Soc. 1998. *Publications:* Science in the Looking Glass 2003; four other academic books and more than 180 research papers. *Leisure interests:* philosophy, science. *Address:* Room 420, Strand Bldg, Department of Mathematics, King's College, Strand, London, WC2R 2LS, England (office). *Telephone:* (20) 7848-2698 (office). *Fax:* (20) 7848-2017 (office). *E-mail:* e.brian.davies@kcl.ac.uk (office). *Website:* www.mth.kcl.ac.uk/staff/eb_davies .html (office).

DAVIES, Gavyn, OBE, BS; British economist and business executive; *Founding Partner, Active Private Equity Advisory LLP;* b. 27 Nov. 1950; s. of W. J. F. Davies and M. G. Davies; m. Susan Jane Nye 1989; two s. one d.; ed St John's Coll., Cambridge and Balliol Coll., Oxford; Econ. Adviser, Policy Unit, 10 Downing Street 1974–79; economist, Phillips and Drew 1979–81; Chief UK Economist, Simon & Coates 1981–86; Chief UK Economist, Goldman Sachs 1986–93, Pnr 1988–2001, Head of Investment Research (London) 1991–93, Chief Int. Economist and Head of European Investment Research 1993–97, Chair. Investment Research Dept 1999–2001, Advisory Dir 2001–; Vice-Chair. BBC 2001, Chair. 2001–04 (resgnd); Founding Pnr, Active Private Equity Advisory LLP; Founder and Advisory Pnr, Prisma Capital Partners; Chair. Fulcrum Asset Management; Visiting Prof. of Econs, LSE 1988–98; Prin. Econs Commentator, The Independent

1991–99; mem. HM Treasury's Ind. Forecasting Panel 1993–97; Chair. Govt Inquiry into the Future Funding of the BBC 1999; Hon. Fellow, Aberystwyth Univ. 2002; Hon. DScS (Southampton) 1998; Hon. LLD (Nottingham) 2002; Dr hc (Middlesex). *Leisure interest:* Southampton Football Club. *Address:* Active Private Equity Advisory LLP, 5th Floor, 6 Chesterfield Gardens, London, W1J 5BQ, England (office). *Telephone:* (20) 7016-6480 (office). *Fax:* (20) 7016-6490 (office). *Website:* www.apeq.co.uk (office); www.prismapartners.com

DAVIES, Sir Graeme John, Kt, BE, MA, PhD, ScD, FRSE, FREng; British (b. New Zealand) university vice-chancellor; *Vice-Chancellor Emeritus, University of London;* b. 7 April 1937, Auckland, NZ; s. of Harry J. Davies and Gladys E. Davies; m. Florence I. Martin 1959; one s. one d.; ed Univ. of Auckland, Univ. of Cambridge; Lecturer, Univ. of Cambridge 1962–77, Fellow, St Catharine's Coll. 1967–76; Prof., Dept of Metallurgy, Univ. of Sheffield 1977–86; Vice-Chancellor Univ. of Liverpool 1986–91; Chief Exec. Univs' Funding Council 1991–93, Polytechnics' and Colls' Funding Council 1992–93, Higher Educ. Funding Council for England 1992–95; Prin. and Vice-Chancellor Univ. of Glasgow 1995–2003; Vice-Chancellor Univ. of London 2003–10, Vice-Chancellor Emer. 2010–; Free-man, City of London, Freeman and Burgess Holder, City of Glasgow; Hon. FRSNZ; Hon. Fellow, Trinity Coll. of Music 1995, School of Pharmacy 2012, Royal Veterinary Coll. 2012; Hon. DSc (Nottingham) 1995, (Edin.) 2003, (Ulster) 2004, (London South Bank) 2006; Hon. DMet (Sheffield) 1995; Hon. LLD (Liverpool) 1991, (Strathclyde) 2000, (London) 2012; Hon. DEng (Manchester Metropolitan) 1996, (Auckland) 2003; Hon. DUniv (Glasgow, Paisley) 2004; Hon. DLitt (Bath Spa) 2010. *Publications:* Solidification and Casting 1973, Textures and Properties of Materials 1976, Hot Working and Forming Processes 1980, Superplasticity 1981, Essential Metallurgy for Engineers 1985. *Leisure interests:* cricket, bird-watching, The Times crossword. *Address:* The Coach House, Fosse Road, Farndon, Newark, NG24 3SF, England (home). *Telephone:* (20) 7862-8006 (office); (1636) 673117 (home). *E-mail:* graeme.davies@lon.ac.uk (office).

DAVIES, Sir Howard John, Kt, MA, MSc; British academic administrator and business executive; *Professor of Practice, Institute of Political Studies, Sciences Po, Paris;* b. 12 Feb. 1951; s. of Leslie Davies and Marjorie Davies; m. Prudence Keely 1984; two s.; ed Manchester Grammar School, Merton Coll., Oxford and Stanford Grad. School of Business; Foreign Office 1973–74; Pvt. Sec. to British Amb. in Paris 1974–76; HM Treasury 1976–82; McKinsey & Co. Inc. 1982–87; Controller, Audit Comm. 1987–92; Dir GKN PLC 1990–95; Dir-Gen. Confed. of British Industry (CBI) 1992–95; Deputy Gov., Bank of England 1995–97, Dir (non-exec.) 1998–2003; Chair. Financial Services Authority (fmrly Securities and Investments Bd) 1997–2003; Dir LSE 2003–11 (resgnd), Nat. Theatre 2011–; Prof. of Practice, Inst. of Political Studies, Sciences Po, Paris 2011–; mem. NatWest Int. Advisory Bd 1992–95; mem. Bd Morgan Stanley 2004–, Paternoster UK Ltd 2006–10, Prudential Plc 2010–; mem. Int. Advisory Bd, Govt Investment Corpn of Singapore 2011–; Deputy Chair. Rowntree Cttee Enquiry 1993; Pres. Age Concern England 1994–98; Chair. Employers' Forum on Age 1996–2004; Chair. panel of judges Man Booker Prize 2007; Trustee, Tate Gallery 2002–10; Gov. RAM 2004–. *Publications:* Chancellors Tales 2006, Global Financial Regulation: The Essential Guide (with David Green) 2008, Banking on the Future (with David Green) 2010, The Financial Crisis: Who's to Blame 2010. *Leisure interests:* cricket, writing for publication. *Address:* c/o Sciences Po, PSIA, 28 rue des Saints Pères, 75006 Paris, France (office). *Website:* www.sciencespo.fr/en.

DAVIES, Jonathan, MBE; British sports commentator and fmr rugby player (rugby union and rugby league); b. 24 Oct. 1962, Trimsaran, Carmarthenshire; s. of the late Leonard Davies and of Diana Davies (née Rees); m. 1st Karen Marie Davies 1984 (died 1997); two s. one d.; m. 2nd Helen Jones 2002; ed Gwendraeth Grammar School; rugby union outside-half; played for the following rugby union clubs: Trimsaran, Neath, Llanelli; turned professional in 1989; with Cardiff 1995–97; played for Welsh nat. team (v. England) 1985, World Cup Squad (6 appearances) 1987, Triple Crown winning team 1988, tour NZ (2 test appearances) 1988, 29 caps, sometime Capt.; also played for Barbarians Rugby Football Club; rugby league career: played at three-quarters; Widnes (world record transfer fee) 1989, Warrington 1993–95 (free transfer); for Welsh nat. team; British nat. team, tour NZ 1990, 6 caps, fmr Capt.; reverted to rugby union 1995; retd from playing 1997; commentator on rugby union and league for Channel 4 Wales. *Publication:* Jonathan (autobiog.) 1989. *Leisure interest:* all sports. *Address:* c/o S4C, Parc Tŷ Glas, Llanishen, Cardiff, CF14 5DU, Wales.

DAVIES, Dame Kay Elizabeth, DBE, CBE, MA, DPhil, FRS, FRCPath, MRCP, FMedSci; British geneticist and academic; *Dr Lee's Professor of Anatomy and Associate Director (Development, Impact and Equality), Medical Sciences Division, University of Oxford;* b. 1 April 1951, Stourbridge, West Midlands, England; d. of Harry Partridge and Florence Partridge; m. Stephen Graham Davies 1973 (divorced); one s.; ed Somerville and Wolfson Colls, Oxford; Guy Newton Jr Research Fellow, Wolfson Coll., Oxford 1976–78; Royal Soc. European Postdoctoral Fellow, Service de Biochimie, Centre d'études nucléaires de Saclay, Gif-sur-Yvette, France 1978–80; Cystic Fibrosis Research Fellow, Biochemistry Dept, St Mary's Hosp. Medical School, London 1980–82, MRC Sr Research Fellow, 1982–84; MRC Sr Research Fellow, Nuffield Dept of Clinical Medicine, John Radcliffe Hosp., Oxford 1984–86, MRC External Staff 1986–89, Molecular Genetics Group, Inst. of Molecular Medicine 1989–92, MRC Research Dir, Royal Postgraduate Medical School 1992–94, Head of Molecular Genetics Group, Inst. of Molecular Medicine 1994–95; Prof. of Molecular Genetics, Univ. of London 1992–94; Prof. of Genetics, Dept of Biochemistry, Univ. of Oxford 1995–97, Dr Lee's Prof. of Anatomy and Assoc. Dir (Devt, Impact and Equality), Medical Sciences Div. 1998–; Hon. Dir MRC Functional Genetics Unit, Oxford 1999–; Co-Dir Oxford Centre for Gene Function 2001–; Univ. Research Lecturer, Nuffield Dept of Clinical Medicine, John Radcliffe Hosp. 1989–92; Fellow, Green Coll., Oxford 1989–92, 1994–95, Keble Coll., Oxford 1995–, Hertford Coll., Oxford 1997–; Gov., Wellcome Trust 2008–; Wellcome Trust Award 1996, SCI Medal 1999, Feldberg Foundation Prize 1999, Gaetano Conte Prize in Basic Myology 2002. *Publications:* more than 350 papers in scientific journals. *Leisure interests:* walking, music, gardening. *Address:* Depart-ment of Physiology, Anatomy and Genetics, University of Oxford, Parks Road, Oxford, OX1 3PT, England (office). *Telephone:* (1865) 285880 (office). *Fax:* (1865) 285878 (office). *E-mail:* kay.davies@dpag.ox.ac.uk (office). *Website:* www.dpag.ox .ac.uk (office).

DAVIES, Nicholas Barry, BA, DPhil, FRS; British biologist and academic; *Professor of Behavioural Ecology, Department of Zoology, University of Cambridge;* b. 23 May 1952, Liverpool, England; s. of Anthony Barry Davies and Joyce Margaret Davies; m. Jan Parr 1979; two d.; ed Merchant Taylors' School, Crosby, Pembroke Coll., Cambridge, Wolfson Coll., Oxford; Demonstrator in Zoology, Edward Grey Inst., Univ. of Oxford 1976–79; Jr Research Fellow, Wolfson Coll., Oxford 1977–79; Demonstrator, Dept of Zoology, Univ. of Cambridge 1979–84, Lecturer 1984–92, Reader 1992–95, Prof. of Behavioural Ecology 1995–, Fellow, Pembroke Coll. Cambridge 1979–; Pres. Int. Soc. for Behavioural Ecology 2000–02; Corresp. mem. German Ornithological Soc. 2000; Corresp. Fellow, American Ornithologists' Union 1999, Hon. Fellow 2004; Hon. mem. Spanish Ornithological Soc. 2004; Dr hc (Bielefeld) 2011; Scientific Medal, Zoological Soc. of London 1987, Cambridge Univ. Teaching Prize 1995, William Bate Hardy Prize, Cambridge Philosophical Soc. 1995, Medal of Asscn for Study of Animal Behaviour 1996, Frink Medal, Zoological Soc. of London 2001, Elliott Coues Award, American Ornithologists' Union 2005, Hamilton Prize Lecturer, Int. Soc. for Behavioural Ecology 2010. *Publications include:* Behavioural Ecology: an Evolutionary Approach (co-ed.) 1978 (fourth edn 1997), An Introduction to Behavioural Ecology (co-author) 1981 (fourth edn 2012), Dunnock Behaviour and Social Evolution 1992, Cuckoos, Cowbirds and Other Cheats (Best Book of the Year Award, British Trust for Ornithology 2000) 2000. *Leisure interests:* bird-watching, mountains, music. *Address:* Department of Zoology, University of Cambridge, Downing Street, Cambridge, CB2 3EJ, England (office). *Telephone:* (1223) 334405 (office). *Fax:* (1223) 336676 (office). *E-mail:* nbd1000@cam.ac.uk (office); n.b.davies@zoo.cam.ac.uk (office). *Website:* www.zoo.cam.ac.uk (office).

DAVIES, Omar, DEcon; Jamaican economist, academic and politician; *Minister of Transport, Works and Housing;* b. 28 May 1947, Clarendon; m.; three c.; ed Univ. of the West Indies, Northwestern Univ., USA; Asst Prof., Stanford Univ. 1973–76; Sr Lecturer, Univ. of the West Indies 1981–89; Dir-Gen. Planning Inst. of Jamaica 1989–93; mem. People's Nat. Party; with Office of the Prime Minister April–Aug. 1993; Minister without Portfolio responsible for Planning Devt Project Implementation Aug.–Nov. 1993; mem. Parl. 1993–; Chair. Public Accounts Cttee 2007–; Minister of Finance and Planning 1993–2007, of Transport, Works and Housing 2012–. *Address:* Ministry of Transport and Works, 138h Maxfield Avenue, Kingston 10, Jamaica (office). *Telephone:* 754-1900 (office). *Fax:* 960-2886 (office). *E-mail:* hm@mtw.gov.jm (office). *Website:* www.mtw.gov.jm (office).

DAVIES, Sir Peter Maxwell, Kt (see MAXWELL DAVIES, Sir Peter).

DAVIES, Rodney Deane, CBE, FRS, DSc, CPhys; British radio astronomer and academic; *Professor Emeritus of Radio Astronomy, University of Manchester;* b. 8 Jan. 1930, Balaklava, S Australia; s. of Holbin James Davies and Rena Irene Davies (née March); m. Valda Beth Treasure 1953; two s. (one deceased), two d.; ed Univs of Adelaide and Manchester; Research Officer, Radio Physics Div., CSIRO Sydney 1951–53; Lecturer, Univ. of Manchester 1953–63, Sr Lecturer 1963–67, Reader 1967–76, Prof. of Radio Astronomy 1976–97, Prof. Emer. 1997–; Sec., Royal Astronomical Soc. 1978–86, Pres. 1987–89; Dir Nuffield Radio Astronomy Labs, Jodrell Bank 1988–97. *Publications:* Radio Studies of the Universe (with H. P. Palmer) 1959, Radio Astronomy Today (with H. P. Palmer and M. I. Large) 1963. *Leisure interests:* fell-walking, gardening. *Address:* University of Manchester, Jodrell Bank Observatory, Jodrell Bank, Macclesfield, Cheshire, SK11 9DL (office); Parkgate House, Fulshaw Park South, Wilmslow, Cheshire, SK9 1QG, England (home). *Telephone:* (1477) 571321 (office); (1625) 523592 (home). *Fax:* (1477) 571618 (office). *E-mail:* rdd@jb.man.ac.uk (office). *Website:* www.jb.man.ac.uk (office).

DAVIES, Rt Hon. Ron(ald), PC; British politician; b. 6 Aug. 1946; s. of the late Ronald Davies; m. 1st Anne Williams; m. 2nd Christina Elizabeth Rees 1981; one d.; m. 3rd Lynne Hughes 2002; ed Bassaleg Grammar School, Portsmouth Polytechnic, Univ. Coll. of Wales, Cardiff; schoolteacher 1968–70; Workers' Educ. Asscn Tutor/Organizer 1970–74; Further Educ. Adviser, Mid-Glamorgan Local Educ. Authority 1974–83; mem. Rhymney Valley Dist Council 1969–84 (fmr Vice-Chair.); MP (Labour) for Caerphilly 1983–2001, Opposition Whip 1985–87, Labour Spokesman on Agric. and Rural Affairs 1987–92, on Wales 1992–97, Sec. of State for Wales 1997–98; elected leader of Labour Group in Nat. Ass. for Wales Sept. 1998, resgnd Oct. 1998; mem. Nat. Ass. for Wales for Caerphilly 1999–2003 (resgnd), Chair. Econ. Devt Cttee 1999–2003; joined Forward Wales party 2004, currently Policy Dir; Highest Order, Gorsedd of the Bards 1998. *Publications:* pamphlets on Welsh devolution. *Leisure interests:* walking, gardening, sport. *Address:* c/o Forward Wales HQ, 67 Regent Street, Wrexham, LL11 1PG, Wales (office). *Telephone:* (1978) 314085 (office).

DAVIES, Ryland; British singer (tenor); b. 9 Feb. 1943, Cwm Ebbw Vale, Monmouthshire (now Gwent); s. of Gethin and Joan Davies; m. 1st Anne Howells 1966 (divorced 1981); m. 2nd Deborah Jane Rees 1983; one d.; ed Royal Manchester Coll. of Music (Fellow 1971); voice teacher Royal Northern Coll. of Music (RNCM) 1987–94, Royal Coll. of Music, London 1999–, also Royal Acad. of Music; Dir Opera Productions RNCM Mananan Festival, Clonter Opera Trust; début as Almaviva in The Barber of Seville, Welsh Nat. Opera 1964; subsequent appearances including Tamino in The Magic Flute 1974, Yenick in Bartered Bride 1989; Glyndebourne Festival Chorus 1964–66, taking parts including Belmonte in The Abduction from the Seraglio, Ferrando in Così fan tutte, Flamand in Capriccio, Lysander in A Midsummer Night's Dream, The Prince in Love of Three Oranges, Lensky in Eugene Onegin, Tichone in Katya Kabanova, Basilio/Curzio in Le nozze di Figaro, Auctioneer in The Rake's Progress; appearances with Scottish Opera as Ferrando and as Fenton in Falstaff, Tamino in The Magic Flute and as Nemorino in L'Elisir d'Amore; with Sadler's Wells Opera as Almaviva, Essex in Britten's Gloriana; with Royal Opera as Hylas in The Trojans, Don Ottavio in Don Giovanni, Ferrando, Cassio in Otello, Nemorino in L'Elisir d'Amore, Ernesto in Don Pasquale, Lysander in A Midsummer Night's Dream and Almaviva; with English Nat. Opera as Eisenstein in Die Fledermaus, Basilio in Le nozze di Figaro, Rev. H. Adams in Peter Grimes, Albazar in Turk in Italy, L'Aumonier in Dialogues des Carmélites, Gaudenzio in La Bohème; overseas appearances include Salzburg Festival, at San Francisco, Chicago, Paris, at Metropolitan Opera, New York, Hollywood Bowl, Paris Opera, Geneva, Brussels, Lyons, Amsterdam, Mannheim, Israel, Buenos Aires, Stuttgart, Nice, Nancy, Philadelphia, Berlin, Hamburg; returned to Covent Garden 1994, 2002, Welsh Nat. Opera 1994, New York Metropolitan Opera 1994,

1995, 2001, Glyndebourne 1997, New Israeli Opera 1997, Chicago Lyric Opera 1998, 2003, Santa Fe Opera 1998, 1999, New Israeli Opera 1998, Netherlands Opera 1998, 1999, 2002, English Nat. Opera 1999, Houston Grand Opera 2002, Japan 2002, Florence 2002, Zauberflote/Monastatos Netherlands 2003, Covent Garden Monostatos 2003, Basilio, Chicago Lyric Opera 2003, Peter Grimes, London Symphony, Barbican and New York, Colin Davis 2004, A Midsummer Night's Dream, La Fenice, Venice 2004, Ein Hurt, La Scala, Milan 2007, 2009; Boise Mendelsohn Foundation Scholarship 1964; Fellow Welsh Coll. of Music and Drama 1996; Hon. Fellow Royal Manchester Coll. of Music 1971; Ricordi Opera Prize, Royal Manchester Coll. of Music 1963, Imperial League of Opera Prize, Royal Manchester Coll. of Music 1963, First John Christie Award, Glyndebourne 1965. *Recordings include:* The Abduction from the Seraglio, L'Amore dei Tre Re (Montemezzi), La Navarraise (Massenet), The Trojans, Saul, Così fan tutte, Thérèse (Massenet), Monteverdi Madrigals, Idomeneo, The Seasons (Haydn), Messiah, L'Oracolo (Leone), Judas Maccabaeus, Pulcinella, Il Matrimonio Segreto, Lucia di Lammamoor, Otello, Mozart's Requiem, C Minor Mass, Credo Mass, Coronation Mass, Messe Solonelle; Oedipus Rex (Shepherd), Il Trovatore (Ruiz), Don Carlo (Conte di Lerma), Le nozze di Figaro (Basilio/Curzio), Esclarmonde (Massenet). *Video films include:* Don Pasquale, A Midsummer Night's Dream, Die Entführung aus dem Serail, Love of Three Oranges, Trial by Jury, Katya Kabanova. *Television:* Merry Widow, Capriccio (BBC, Glyndebourne), A Goodly Manner for a Song (STV), On Wenlock Edge (BBC Wales), Dido and Aeneas (BBC), Mass in C Minor (BBC Wales). *Achievements:* played rugby for Wales Schoolboys, 2 caps 1957–58, Wales Boys Clubs under-18s 1959–60. *Leisure interests:* art, cinema, sport, reading. *Address:* Hazard Chase Ltd, 25 City Road, Cambridge, CB1 1DP, England (office); Elm Cottage, Loseberry Road, Claygate, Surrey, KT10 9DQ, England (home). *Telephone:* (1223) 213400 (office). *Fax:* (1223) 460827 (office). *E-mail:* info@hazardchase.co.uk (office); rylandtenore@hotmail.com (home). *Website:* www.hazardchase.co.uk (office); www.rylanddavies.info.

DAVIES, Stephen Graham, MA, DPhil; British chemist and academic; *Waynflete Professor of Chemistry, University of Oxford;* b. 24 Feb. 1950, Birmingham, England; s. of Gordon W. J. Davies and June M. Murphy; one s.; ICI Postdoctoral Fellow, Oxford 1975–77; NATO Postdoctoral Fellow, Oxford 1977–78; Attaché de Recherche, CNRS, Paris 1978–80; Fellow, New Coll., Oxford 1980–; Univ. Lecturer in Chem., Univ. of Oxford 1980–, currently Chair. of Chem. and Waynflete Prof. of Chem.; Dir Oxford Asymmetry Ltd 1991–; mem. of various cttees, editorial bds; Hickinbottom Fellowship 1984; Pfizer Award for Chem. 1985, 1988, Corday Morgan Medal 1984, RSC Award for Organometallic Chem. 1989, RSC Bader Award 1989, Tilden Lecture Award 1996, RSC Award in Stereochemistry 1997, Prize Lectureship, Soc. of Synthetic Organic Chemistry, Japan 1998, RSC Perkin Medal 2011. *Publications:* Organometallic Chemistry: Applications to Organic Chemistry 1982; more than 450 papers in learned journals. *Leisure interest:* chemistry. *Address:* Chemistry Research Laboratory, University of Oxford, Mansfield Road, Oxford, OX1 3TA, England (office). *Telephone:* (1865) 275695 (office). *Fax:* (1865) 275633 (office). *E-mail:* steve.davies@chem.ox.ac.uk (office). *Website:* research.chem.ox.ac.uk/steve-davies.aspx (office).

DAVIES, (Stephen) Howard, CBE, BA, FRSA; British theatre and film director; b. 26 April 1945; s. of the late Thomas Davies and (Eileen) Hilda Bevan; m. 1st Susan Wall (divorced); two d.; m. 2nd Clare Holman 2005; ed Christ's Hosp. and Univs of Durham and Bristol; Theatre Dir, Assoc. Dir Bristol Old Vic 1971–73; Founder-mem. Avon Touring Co.; Asst Dir RSC 1974, Assoc. Dir 1976–86; Founder and Dir The Warehouse RSC (productions include Piaf, Good, Les Liaisons Dangereuses) 1977–82; freelance dir 1974–76; Assoc. Dir Nat. Theatre 1989–. *Productions include:* RSC: Troilus and Cressida 1977, Bandits 1977, Bingo 1977, The Jail Diary of Albie Sachs 1979, Much Ado About Nothing 1980, Piaf 1983, Henry VIII 1983, Les Liaisons Dangereuses 1986; Nat. Theatre: The Shaughraun 1988, Cat on a Hot Tin Roof 1988, The Secret Rapture 1989, Hedda Gabler 1989, The Crucible 1990, A Long Day's Journey Into Night 1996, Mary Stuart 1996, Chips With Everything 1997, Flight 1998, Battle Royal 1999, All My Sons (Olivier Award for Best Dir 2001) 2000, Private Lives 2001, The Talking Cure 2003, Mourning Becomes Electra 2003, Cyrano de Bergerac 2004, The House of Bernarda Alba 2005, The Life of Galileo 2006, Philistines 2007, Present Laughter 2007, Never So Good 2008, Her Naked Skin 2008, Burnt by the Sun 2009, The White Guard (Evening Standard Award for Best Dir 2010) 2010, Blood and Gifts 2010; Almeida: Who's Afraid of Virginia Woolf 1996, The Iceman Cometh (Evening Standard and Olivier Awards for Best Dir) 1998, Conversations After a Burial 2000, Period of Adjustment 2006; other: Vassa (Albery) 1999, Private Lives (Albery) 2001, The Breath of Life (Haymarket) 2002, A Moon for the Misbegotten (Old Vic) 2006. *Film:* The Secret Rapture (dir) 1993. *Television:* Tales from Hollywood 1992, Armadillo (BBC) 2001, Copenhagen 2002, Blue/Orange 2005. *Leisure interests:* travel, hill-walking, watching rugby, film, painting. *Address:* Royal National Theatre, South Bank, London, SE1 9PX, England (office). *Telephone:* (20) 7452-3333 (office). *Fax:* (20) 7620-1197 (office). *Website:* www.nationaltheatre.org.uk (office).

DAVIES, Susan Elizabeth, OBE; British fmr gallery director; b. (Susan Adey), 14 April 1933, Iran; d. of Stanworth Adey and Joan Charlsworth; m. John R. T. Davies 1954 (deceased); two d.; ed Nightingale Bamford School, New York, Eothen School, Surrey and Triangle Secretarial Coll.; Municipal Journal 1953–54; Artists' Placement Group 1966–67; Inst. of Contemporary Arts 1967–70; Founder and Dir The Photographers' Gallery, London 1971–91; photography consultant and writer 1991–; Hon. FRPS 1986; Progress Medal, Royal Photographic Soc. 1982, Kulturpreis, German Photographic Soc. 1990. *Leisure interests:* jazz, gardening, grandchildren, great-grandchildren. *Address:* 57 Sandilands Road, Fulham, London, SW6 2BD, England. *Telephone:* (20) 7731-7262. *E-mail:* sue.ristic@btinternet.com.

DAVIES, Terence; British screenwriter and film director; b. 1945, Liverpool; ed Coventry Drama School and Nat. Film School; articled clerk in shipping office; later worked for 12 years in an accountancy practice. *Films:* Children 1977, Madonna and Child 1980, Death and Transfiguration 1983, Distant Voices, Still Lives (Int. Critics Prize, Cannes Film Festival) 1988, Movie Masterclass 1990, The Long Day Closes 1992, The Neon Bible 1995, The House of Mirth 2000, Of Time and the City (documentary) 2008, The Deep Blue Sea 2011. *Radio:* Travels in

Celluloid (BBC Radio 4 Book of the Week) 2000, The Walk to the Paradise Garden (BBC Radio 3) 2001. *Publications:* Hallelujah Now, A Modest Pageant.

DAVIES OF ABERSOCH, Baron (Life Peer), cr. 2009, of Abersoch in the County of Gwynedd; **E(van) Mervyn,** CBE, JP, FCIB; British banking executive and government official; *Vice-Chairman, Corsair Capital LLC;* b. 1952; s. of Richard Aled Davies and Margaret Davies; m. Jeanne Marie Gammie 1979; one s. one d.; ed Rydal School, North Wales, Harvard Business School; Man. Dir UK Banking and Sr Credit Officer, Citibank 1983–93; joined Standard Chartered Bank PLC with responsibility for Global Account Man. 1993, Head of Corp. and Investment Banking, Singapore –1997, mem. Bd Dirs 1997–2009, Group Exec. Dir responsible for Group-wide Tech. and Operations in Hong Kong, China and NE Asia 1997–2001, Group Chief Exec., London 2001–06, Chair. 2006–09 (resgnd); Minister for Trade Promotion and Investment 2009–10, also Labour Whip in House of Lords 2009–; Chair. Fleming Family & Partners, Nordic Windpower Ltd; Vice-Chair. Corsair Capital LLC 2010–; Dir (non-exec.) Tesco PLC 2003–, Breakingviews Ltd, Tottenham Hotspur Football Club, Trinity Ltd; mem. Advisory Cttee Corsair Capital LLC, UK India Business Council; Chair. Interim Exec. Cttee of Int. Centre for Financial Regulation 2007–, Business Council for Britain 2007–; Chair. Garden Bridge Trust 2013–; mem. Mayor of London's Int. Business Advisory Council, London; JP Hong Kong 2000; mem. Hong Kong Exchange Fund Cttee, Singapore British Business Council, UK-India Forum; mem. Exec. Cttee Hong Kong Community Chest –2001; fmr Chair. Hong Kong Youth Arts Festival, Hong Kong Asscn of Banks, Asia Youth Orchestra; Chair. Council of the Univ. of Wales; Dir Visa Int. Asia Pacific Regional Bd –2001; Chair. British Chamber of Commerce, Hong Kong 2000–01 (also fmr Chair.), The Roundhouse's Major Projects Bd, Corp. Bd of Royal Acad. of Arts; mem. Bd of Dirs Hong Kong Asscn 2007–; Gov. LSE; Trustee, Royal Acad. Trust, Sir Kyffin Williams Trust; Fellow, Inst. of Bankers. *Leisure interests:* sport, Welsh art, antiques, opera, music, reading. *Address:* Corsair Capital LLC, 53 Davies Street, London, W1K 5JH, England (office). *Telephone:* (20) 7152-6535 (office). *E-mail:* corsair@corsair-capital.com (office). *Website:* www.corsair-capital.com (office).

DAVIGNON, Viscount Etienne, LLD; Belgian diplomatist and business executive; *Vice-Chairman, Suez-Tractebel SA;* b. 4 Oct. 1932, Budapest, Hungary; m. Françoise de Cumont 1959; one s. two d.; joined Ministry of Foreign Affairs 1959, Attaché then Head of Office of Minister of Foreign Affairs Paul-Henri Spaak 1961–65; Political Dir 1969–76; Chair. Governing Bd, Int. Energy Agency 1974–77; Commr for Industry and Int. Markets, Comm. of European Communities 1977–81, Vice-Pres. for Industry, Energy and Research Policies 1981–85; joined Société Générale de Belgique 1985, 1988–2001, Exec. Chair. 1989–2001, Vice-Chair. 2001–03, Vice-Chair. Suez-Tractebel SA (subsidiary) 2003–; Co-founder Brussels Airlines 2006–; Chair. Palais des Beaux-Arts, Brussels, Compagnie Maritime Belge, Institut Catholique des Hautes Etudes Commerciales, Spaak Foundation; Vice-Chair. Union Minière 1993–; Pres. Friends of Europe (think tank), Brussels, CSR Europe, Brussels; mem. Bd of Dirs Accor, Suez, Sofina, Cumerio, Real Software, Royal Sporting Club d'Anderlecht; Hon. DHumLitt (American Coll. in Paris) 1988. *Leisure interests:* golf, skiing, tennis. *Address:* Suez-Tractebel SA, Place du Trône 1, 1000 Brussels (office); 12 Avenue des Fleurs, 1150 Brussels, Belgium. *Telephone:* (2) 507-03-82 (office). *Fax:* (2) 507-03-00 (office). *E-mail:* etienne.davignon@suez.com (office). *Website:* www.tractebel.be (office).

DAVIS, Adrian Derek; British economist and diplomatist; *Governor of Montserrat;* m. Sujue Davis; two c.; economist with Official Devt Assistance (ODA) 1974–77, First Sec. and Econ. Adviser, British High Comm. in Dhaka 1977–79, Econ. Adviser, South-East Asia Devt Div., Dept for Int. Devt (DFID)/ ODA, Bangkok 1980–83, First Sec. (Aid/Econ.), Embassy at Cairo 1984–87, Head UK 'Know-How-Fund' for Poland, Hungary, Czechoslovakia and Bulgaria, ODA 1989–91, UK Rep. Asian Devt Bank, Manila 1991–94, Head of East Asia and Pacific Dept, DFID London 1994–96, Head of Information Systems and Services Dept, DFID London and East Kilbride 1996–99, Head of Environmental Policy Dept, DFID London 1999–2003, DFID Country Dir for China, Beijing 2003–07, DFID Country Dir North and East Asia, Beijing 2007, Gov. of Montserrat 2011–. *Address:* Office of the Governor, 8 Farara Plaza, Brades, Montserrat (office). *E-mail:* govoffice.montserrat@fco.gov.uk (office). *Website:* ukinmontserrat.fco.gov .uk (office).

DAVIS, Sir Andrew, Kt, CBE; British conductor; *Musical Director, Chicago Lyric Opera;* b. 1944; m. Gianna Rolandi 1989; one s.; ed Royal Coll. of Music, King's Coll., Cambridge, studied conducting with Franco Ferrara, Rome; continuo player with Acad. of St Martin-in-the-Fields and English Chamber Orchestra; Festival Hall debut conducting BBC Symphony Orchestra 1970; Asst Conductor, Philharmonia Orchestra 1973–77; Prin. Guest Conductor, Royal Liverpool Philharmonic Orchestra 1974–77; Music Dir, Toronto Symphony 1975–88, Conductor Laureate 1988–; Musical Dir, Glyndebourne Festival Opera 1988–2002; Chief Conductor, BBC Symphony Orchestra 1989–2000, Conductor Laureate 2000–, tours with orchestra to Far East 1990, Europe 1992, Japan 1993, 1997, USA 1995, 1998, South America 2001, Far East and Australia 2002; Prin. Guest Conductor, Royal Stockholm Philharmonic 1995–99; Musical Dir, Chicago Lyric Opera 2000–; Chief Conductor and Artistic Dir, Melbourne Symphony Orchestra 2013–; has conducted London Philharmonic, London Symphony, Royal Philharmonic, Boston, Chicago, Cleveland, Los Angeles Philharmonic, New York Philharmonic, Pittsburg Symphony, Orchestre Nat. de France, Frankfurt Radio Orchestra, Royal Concertgebouw Orchestra, Tonhalle Orchestra, Stockholm Philharmonic Orchestra, Israel Philharmonic, Bavarian Radio Symphony and Berlin Philharmonic orchestras, London Sinfonietta, Dallas Symphony and Dresden Staatskapelle orchestras; has conducted at Glyndebourne Festival Opera, Covent Garden Opera, Metropolitan Opera, Washington, DC, Chicago Lyric Opera, Bavarian State Opera, Paris Opera, La Scala, Milan, Sir Henry Wood Promenade Concerts, maj. British and European music festivals; tours of People's Republic of China 1978, Europe 1983 with Toronto Symphony Orchestra. *Recordings include:* Duruflé's Requiem (Grand Prix du Disque 1978), cycle of Dvořák symphonies, Tippett's The Mask of Time (Gramophone Record of the Year Award 1987, Grand Prix du Disque 1988), Vaughan Williams symphony cycle. *Leisure interest:* medieval stained glass. *Address:* Columbia Artist Management Inc., 1790 Broadway, New York, NY 10019-1412, USA (office). *Telephone:* (212) 841-9500 (office). *Fax:* (212) 841-9744

(office). *E-mail:* cami@cami.com (office). *Website:* www.cami.com (office); www .lyricopera.org (office).

DAVIS, Carl, BA; American composer and conductor; *Principal Guest Conductor, Munich Symphony Orchestra;* b. 28 Oct. 1936, New York; s. of Isadore Davis and Sara Davis; m. Jean Boht 1971; two d.; ed New England Conservatory of Music, Bard Coll.; Asst Conductor, New York City Opera 1958; Assoc. Conductor London Philharmonic Orchestra 1987–88; Prin. Conductor Bournemouth Pops 1984–87; Prin. Guest Conductor Munich Symphony Orchestra 1990–; Artistic Dir and Conductor Royal Liverpool Philharmonic Orchestra, Summer Pops 1993–2000; Guest Conductor Hallé Orchestra, City of Birmingham Symphony Orchestra, Scottish Symphony Orchestra; Hon. Fellowship (Liverpool Univ.) 1992; Chevalier, Ordre des Arts et des Lettres 1983, Hon. CBE 2005; Hon. Dr of Arts (Bard, New York) 1994, Hon. DMus (Liverpool) 2002; Special Achievement Award for Music for Television and Film 2003. *Musical theatre:* Diversions (Obie Prize Best Review) 1958, Twists (Arts Theatre London) 1962, The Projector and Cranford (Theatre Royal Stratford East), Pilgrim (Edinburgh Festival), The Wind in the Willows, Peace (Opera North), Alice in Wonderland (Hammersmith) 1987, The Vackees (Haymarket) 1987, The Mermaid. *Incidental music for theatre includes:* Prospect Theatre Co., Nat. Theatre, RSC. *Ballet:* A Simple Man 1987, Lipizzaner 1988, Liaisons Amoureuses (Northern Ballet Theatre) 1988, Madly, Badly, Sadly, Gladly, David and Goliath, Dances of Love and Death (London Contemporary Dance Theatre), The Picture of Dorian Gray (Sadler's Wells Royal Ballet), A Christmas Carol (Northern Theatre Ballet) 1992, The Savoy Suite (English Nat. Ballet) 1993, Alice in Wonderland (English Nat. Ballet) 1995, Aladdin (Scottish Ballet) 2000, Pride and Prejudice: First Impressions (Central Ballet School Tour) 2002. *Music for TV includes:* The Snow Goose 1971, The World at War (Emmy Award) 1973, The Naked Civil Servant 1975, Our Mutual Friend 1978, Hollywood 1980, Churchill: The Wilderness Years 1981, Silas Marner 1985, Hotel du Lac 1986, The Accountant (BAFTA Award) 1989, The Secret Life of Ian Fleming 1989, Separate but Equal 1991, The Royal Collection 1991, A Year in Provence 1992, Fame in the 20th Century: Clive James 1992, Ghengis Cohn 1993, Thatcher: The Downing Street Years 1993, Pride and Prejudice 1995, Oliver's Travels 1995, Eurocinema: The Other Hollywood 1995, Cold War 1998–99, Goodnight Mr Tom 1998, The Great Gatsby 2000, The Queen's Nose, An Angel for May, Book of Eve 2003, Promoted to Glory 2003. *Operas for TV:* The Arrangement, Who Takes You to The Party?, Orpheus in the Underground, Peace. *Film music:* The Bofors Gun 1969, The French Lieutenant's Woman (BAFTA Award) 1981, Champions 1984, The Girl in a Swing 1988, Rainbow 1988, Scandal 1988, Frankenstein Unbound 1989, The Raft of the Medusa 1991, The Trial 1992, Voyage 1993, Widow's Peak 1994, Topsy Turvy 2000; series of Thames Silents including Napoleon 1980, 2000, The Wind, The Big Parade, Greed, The General, Ben Hur, Intolerance, Safety Last, The Four Horsemen of the Apocalypse 1992, Wings 1993, Waterloo 1995, Phantom of the Opera 1996, 6 Mutuals (Chaplin Shorts) 2004. *Concert works:* Music for the Royal Wedding, Variations on a Bus Route, Overture on Australian Themes, Clarinet Concerto 1984, Lines on London Symphony 1984, Fantasy for Flute and Harpsichord 1985, The Searle Suite for Wind Ensemble, Fanfare for Jerusalem 1987, The Glenlivet Fireworks Music 1988, Norwegian Brass Music 1988, Variations for a Polish Beggar's Theme 1988, The Pigeon's Progress 1988, Jazz Age Fanfare 1989, Everest 1989, Landscapes 1990, The Town Fox (text by Carla Lane) 1990, A Duck's Diary 1990, Paul McCartney's Liverpool Oratorio (with Paul McCartney) 1991. *Recordings include:* Napoleon 1983, Christmas with Kiri (with Kiri Te Kanawa) 1986, Beautiful Dreamer (with Marilyn Horne) 1986, The Silents 1987, Ben Hur 1989, A Simple Man 1989, The Town Fox and Other Musical Tales (text by Carla Lane) 1990, Paul McCartney's Liverpool Oratorio 1991, Leeds Castle Classics, Liverpool Pops at Home 1995. *Publications:* sheet music of television themes. *Leisure interests:* reading, gardening, playing chamber music, cooking. *Address:* c/o Hazard Chase, 72 Charlotte Street, London, W1T 4QQ, England (office). *Telephone:* (20) 3355-4535 (office). *Fax:* (20) 3355-4525 (office). *E-mail:* jeremy.woods@hazardchase.co.uk; admin@threefoldmusic.co.uk (office). *Website:* www.carl-davis.com.

DAVIS, Clive; American music company executive and producer; *Chief Creative Officer, Sony BMG Worldwide;* b. 4 April 1932, New York; lawyer CBS 1960, Vice-Pres. and Gen. Man. 1966; with Columbia Records –1973, joined Bell Records 1974, founder Arista Records 1975, later Pres.; Founder, Chair. and CEO J Records (Jt project with RCA Music Group) 2000–08; Chair. and CEO RCA Music Group 2000–08; Chair. and CEO BMG North America 2000–08; Chief Creative Officer Sony BMG Worldwide 2008–; producer for Dido, Aretha Franklin, Sarah McLachlan, Whitney Houston, Billy Joel, Janis Joplin, Alicia Keys, Carlos Santana, Patti Smith and Bruce Springsteen. *Publication:* Clive – Inside the Record Business (autobiography) 1974, The Soundtrack of My Life (autobiography) 2013. *Address:* Sony BMG, 550 Madison Avenue, New York, NY 10022-3211, USA (office). *Telephone:* (212) 833-8000 (office).

DAVIS, Sir Crispin Henry Lamert, Kt, MA; British business executive; b. 19 March 1949; s. of the late Walter Patrick Davis and of Jane Davis (née Lamert); m. Anne Richardson 1970; three d.; ed Charterhouse, Oriel Coll., Oxford; joined Procter & Gamble 1970, Man. Dir Procter & Gamble Co., Germany 1981–84, Vice-Pres. Food Div., Procter & Gamble USA 1984–90; European Man. Dir United Distillers 1990–92, Group Man. Dir 1992–94; CEO Aegis PLC 1994–99; Chief Exec. Reed Elsevier 1999–2009; mem. Finance Cttee, National Trust 2000–. *Leisure interests:* sport, gardening, art. *Address:* Hills End, Titlarks Hill, Sunningdale, Berks., SL5 0JD, England (home). *Telephone:* (1344) 291233 (home).

DAVIS, D. Scott, BSc, CPA; American business executive; *Chairman and CEO, UPS Inc.;* b. 1952, Medford, Ore.; s. of Darrell Davis and Rose Davis; ed Portland State Univ., Univ. of Pennsylvania Wharton School; began career with Arthur Andersen Accountants; fmr Chief Financial Officer and later CEO II Morrow Inc., Oregon –1986, joined UPS Inc. (following UPS purchase of II Morrow) 1986, Chief Financial Officer and mem. Man. Cttee 2001–, Dir 2006–, Vice-Chair. 2006–07, Chair. and CEO 2008–; CEO Overseas Partners Ltd, Bermuda 1998–2000; Deputy Chair. Fed. Reserve Bank of Atlanta 2007, Chair. 2007–09; mem. Bd Dirs Honeywell International Inc.; Chair. Georgia Council on Econ. Educ.; mem. Pres.'s Export Council 2010–, The Business Council, The Carter Center Bd of Councilors; Trustee, Annie E. Casey Foundation. *Address:* UPS Inc., 55 Glenlake Parkway

NE, Atlanta GA 30328, USA (office). *Telephone:* (404) 828-6000 (office). *Fax:* (404) 828-6562 (office). *E-mail:* info@ups.com (office). *Website:* www.ups.com (office).

DAVIS, Rt Hon. David (Michael), PC, MSc; British politician and business executive; b. 23 Dec. 1948; s. of Ronald Davis and Elizabeth Davis; m. Doreen Margery Cook 1973; one s. one d.; ed Warwick Univ., London Business School and Harvard Univ.; joined Tate & Lyle Transport 1974, Man. Dir Tate and Lyle 1980–82, Strategic Planning Dir Tate and Lyle PLC 1984–87, Dir (non-exec.) 1987–90; Conservative MP for Boothferry 1987–97, for Haltemprice and Howden 1997–; Asst Govt Whip 1990–93; Parl. Sec. Office of Public Service and Science, Cabinet Office 1993–94; Minister of State, FCO 1994–97; Chair. House of Commons Public Accounts Cttee 1997–; cand. Conservative Party leadership election 2001, 2005; Chair. Conservative Party 2001–02; Shadow Sec. of State for the Office of the Deputy Prime Minister 2002–03; Shadow Sec. of State for Home, Constitutional and Legal Affairs, Shadow Home Sec. 2003–08; Chair. Fed. of Conservative Students 1973–74; Chair. Financial Policy Cttee, Confed. of British Industry 1977–79. *Publications:* BBC Guide to Parliament, How to Turn Round a Business; numerous articles on business and politics. *Leisure interests:* writing, mountaineering. *Address:* House of Commons, Westminster, London, SW1A 0AA (office); Constituency Office, Spaldington Court, Spaldington, Howden, DN14 7NG, England (office). *Telephone:* (20) 7219-5900 (Westminster) (office); (1430) 430365 (Howden) (office). *Fax:* (20) 7219-4183 (Westminster) (office); (1430) 43025 (Howden) (office). *E-mail:* david.davis.mp@parliament.uk (office); davisdm@parliament.uk (office). *Website:* www.parliament.uk/biographies/commons/mr-david-davis/373 (office); www.daviddavismp.com.

DAVIS, Don H., Jr., MBA; American business executive (retd); ed Texas A&M Univ.; joined Allen-Bradley Co. 1963, Pres. 1989; fmrly Exec. Vice-Pres., COO Rockwell Automation and Semiconductor Systems, Pres. Automation, Rockwell Int. Corpn (later Rockwell Automation) 1993, Sr Vice-Pres. 1993, Pres., COO 1995–97, Pres. and CEO 1997–98, Chair. and CEO 1998–2004, Chair. 2004–05 (retd); mem. Bd of Dirs Illinois Tool Works, Inc. 2000–. *Address:* 4780 North Lake Drive, Milwaukee, WI 53211, USA (office).

DAVIS, Gareth, BA; British business executive; *Chairman, Wolseley PLC;* b. 13 May 1950, Bolton, Lancs.; m. Andrea Davis 1973; one d.; ed Beal Grammar School, Ilford, Essex, Univ. of Sheffield; joined Imperial Tobacco as man. trainee 1972, managed factory producing cigarettes in Newcastle upon Tyne 1973–79, Production Control Man., Bristol 1979–88, Man. Dir Int. Operations 1988–96, Chief Exec. Imperial Tobacco Group on demerger from Hanson 1996–2010, mem. Chief Exec.'s Cttee; Dir (non-exec.) Wolseley plc 2003–04, Sr Ind. Dir 2004–11, Chair. 2011–; Chair. William Hill plc 2010–; Dir (non-exec.) DS Smith plc 2010–. *Leisure interests:* cricket, golf, snooker, Bolton Wanderers Football Club. *Address:* Wolseley PLC, Parkview 1220, Arlington Business Park, Theale, West Berks., RG7 4GA (office); William Hill plc, Greenside House, 50 Station Road, Wood Green, London, N22 7TP, England (office). *Telephone:* (118) 929-8700 (Theale) (office); (20) 8918-3600 (London) (office). *Fax:* (118) 929-8701 (Theale) (office). *E-mail:* info@wolseley.com (office). *Website:* www.wolseley.com (office), www.williamhillplc.co.uk (office).

DAVIS, Geena, BFA; American actress; b. 21 Jan. 1957, Wareham, Mass.; m. 1st Richard Emmolo 1981 (divorced 1983); m. 2nd Jeff Goldblum (q.v.) (divorced 1990); m. 3rd Renny Harlin 1993 (divorced); m. 4th Reza Jarrahy 2001; one d. two s.; ed Boston Univ.; mem. Mount Washington Repertory Theatre Co.; worked as a model; f. Dads and Daughters - See Jane program; Chair. Calif. Comm. on the Status of Women and Girls; Dr hc (Bates Coll.) 2009. *Films include:* Tootsie 1982, Fletch 1984, Transylvania 6-5000 1985, The Fly 1986, Beetlejuice 1988, The Accidental Tourist 1988 (Acad. Award for Best Supporting Actress), Earth Girls are Easy 1989, Quick Change 1990, The Grifters, Thelma and Louise 1991, A League of Their Own 1992, Hero 1992, Angie 1994, Speechless (also producer) 1994, Cutthroat Island 1995, The Long Kiss Goodnight 1996, Stuart Little 1999, Stuart Little 2 2002, Stuart Little 3: Call of the Wild (voice) 2005, Accidents Happen 2009, In a World 2013. *TV appearances include:* Buffalo Bill (series) 1983, Sara (series) 1985, Secret Weapons 1985, The Geena Davis Show (series) 2000, Commander-in-Chief (series) 2005–06 (Golden Globe Award for Best Actress in a Drama TV Series 2006), Exit 19 (film) 2009, Coma (mini-series) 2012. *Address:* California Commission on the Status of Women and Girls, 901 P Street, Suite 142-A, Sacramento, CA 95814; 2401 Main Street, Santa Monica, CA 90405-3515; c/o Dads & Daughters - See Jane, 2 West 1st Street, Suite 101, Duluth, MN 55802, USA. *Website:* women.ca.gov.

DAVIS, Glyn, AC, BA, PhD, DUniv, FASSA; Australian university administrator; *Vice-Chancellor and Principal, University of Melbourne;* ed Univ. of New South Wales and Australian Nat. Univ.; Lecturer in Politics and Public Policy, Griffith Univ., Queensland 1985, Australian Research Council QE II Research Fellow 1988, Prof. 1998–2005, Vice-Chancellor 2002–04; Commr for Public Sector Equity in Queensland Public Sector Man. Comm. 1990–93, Dir Gen. Office of Cabinet 1995–96, Queensland Dept of Premier and Cabinet 1998–2002; Vice-Chancellor and Prin. Univ. of Melbourne 2005–, Foundation Chair. Australia and New Zealand School of Govt (ANZSOG) 2002–05; Dir Australia 21; fmr Chair. Universitas 21; Dir Menzies Centre for Australian Studies, King's Coll. London; mem. Sesquicentenary Cttee for Queensland; Dir, Melbourne Theatre Co., Grattan Inst., LH Martin Inst., Asialink; Harkness Fellowship to Univ. of California, Berkeley, Brookings Inst., Washington, DC and John F. Kennedy School of Govt, Harvard Univ. 1987–88, Boyer Lecturer 2010. *Publications:* The Future of Australian Governance: Policy Choices (co-ed.) 2000, Are You Being Served? State, Citizens and Governance (co-ed.) 2001, The Australian Policy Handbook (fourth edn, with Catherine Althaus and Peter Bridgman) 2007, The Republic of Learning: Higher Education Transforms Australia. *Address:* Office of the Vice-Chancellor, The University of Melbourne, 9th Floor, Raymond Priestley Building, Melbourne, Vic. 3010, Australia (office). *Telephone:* (3) 8344-6134 (office). *Fax:* (3) 9341-6060 (office). *E-mail:* vc@unimelb.edu.au (office). *Website:* www.unimelb.edu.au (office).

DAVIS, Gray, BA, JD; American lawyer and fmr politician; *Of Counsel, Loeb & Loeb LLC;* b. 26 Dec. 1942; m. Sharon Ryer 1983; ed Stanford Univ. and Columbia Univ. Law School; Chief of Staff to Gov. of California 1974–81, State Rep. 1982–86, State Controller 1986–94, Lt Gov. 1994–99, Gov. of California 1999–2003

(recalled); Of Counsel, Loeb & Loeb LLC, Los Angeles 2004–; mem. Southern Calif. Leadership Council; Distinguished Policy Fellow, UCLA School of Public Policy; f. Calif. Foundation for the Protection of Children. *Address:* Loeb & Loeb LLC, 10100 Santa Monica Boulevard, Suite 2200, Los Angeles, CA 90067-4120, USA (office). *Telephone:* (310) 282-2206 (office). *Fax:* (310) 510-6727 (office). *E-mail:* gdavis@loeb.com (office). *Website:* www.loeb.com/gdavis (office); www.gray-davis.com.

DAVIS, Ian, MA; British business executive; *Senior Partner, McKinsey & Company;* b. 10 March 1951, Kent, England; brother of Crispin Davis; m. Penny Davis; one s. one d.; ed Charterhouse, Balliol Coll., Oxford; began career with Bowater (paper manufacturing co.) 1972–79; joined McKinsey & Co. 1979, variety of positions in several countries with focus on consumer-related and retail industries, Head of London Office (with responsibility for Ireland and the Middle East) 1996–2003, Worldwide Man. Dir 2003–09, Sr Pnr 2010–; Chair. (non-exec.) Rolls-Royce plc 2013–; Dir (non-exec.) BP plc 2010–, Johnson & Johnson Inc. 2010–; Sr Adviser, Apax LLP 2010–; mem. (non-exec.) UK Cabinet Office 2011–; Trustee, Teach For All; Dir, Big Society Trust. *Leisure activities:* tennis, cricket, the Alps. *Address:* McKinsey & Co., 1 Jermyn Street, London, SW1Y 4UH, England (office). *Telephone:* (20) 7961-7085 (office). *Fax:* (20) 7961-5349 (office). *Website:* www.mckinsey.com (office).

DAVIS, John Horsley Russell, PhD, FBA; British social anthropologist and academic; *Honourary Fellow, All Souls College, University of Oxford;* b. 9 Sept. 1938; s. of William Russell Davis and Jean Davis (née Horsley); m. Dymphna Gerarda Hermans 1981; three s.; ed Univ. Coll., Oxford and Univ. of London; Lecturer, Sr Lecturer, Reader in Social Anthropology, then Prof. Univ. of Kent 1966–90, f. Centre for Social Anthropology and Computing 1983; Prof. of Social Anthropology, Univ. of Oxford 1990–95; Fellow, All Souls Coll. Oxford 1990–95, Warden 1995–2008, Hon. Fellow 2008–; Chair. European Asscn of Social Anthropologists 1993–94; Pres. Royal Anthropological Inst. 1997–2001. *Publications:* Land and Family in Pisticci 1973, People of the Mediterranean 1977, Libyan Politics: Tribe and Revolution 1987, Exchange 1992. *Leisure interests:* gardens, music. *Address:* c/o All Souls College, Oxford, OX1 4AL, England.

DAVIS, Judy; Australian actress; b. 23 April 1956, Perth; m. Colin Friels; one s. one d. *Films include:* My Brilliant Career, High Tide, Kangaroo, A Woman Called Golda, A Passage to India, Impromptu, Alice, Barton Fink, Where Angels Fear To Tread, Naked Lunch, Husbands and Wives, The Ref, The New Age, Children of the Revolution, Blood and Wine, Absolute Power, Deconstructing Harry, Celebrity, Gaudi Afternoon, The Man Who Sued God 2001, Swimming Upstream 2003, Marie Antoinette 2006, The Break-Up 2006. *Television includes:* Life with Judy Garland: Me and My Shadows (Golden Globe Award) 2001, The Reagans 2003, Coast to Coast 2004, The Starter Wife (Emmy Award for Best Supporting Actress in a Mini-series 2007) 2007–08, Diamonds (mini-series) 2008. *Address:* c/o Shanahan Management Pty Ltd, PO Box 478, King's Cross, NSW 2011, Australia.

DAVIS, Karen, BA, PhD; American economist and academic; *President, Commonwealth Fund;* b. 14 Nov. 1942, Okla; ed Rice Univ., Houston; Asst Prof. of Econs, Rice Univ. 1968–70; Research Assoc., Brookings Inst., Washington, DC 1970–74, Sr Fellow 1974–77; Visiting Lecturer on Econs, Harvard Univ. 1974–75; Deputy Asst Sec. of Planning and Evaluation/Health, Office of the Sec., US Dept of Health and Human Services, Washington, DC 1977–80; Admin., Health Resources Admin, Public Health Service, Hyattsville, Md 1980–81; Prof. of Econs, Johns Hopkins Univ. 1981–92, Chair. Dept of Health Policy and Man., School of Hygiene and Public Health 1983–92; Exec. Vice-Pres. Commonwealth Fund 1992–94, Pres. 1994–; mem. Kaiser Comm. on Medicaid and the Uninsured 1991–, Pres.'s Council, Health Policy Forum, United Hosp. Fund 1992–, New York Acad. of Medicine 1992–, Health Care Exec. Forum 1993–, Council on the Econ. Impact of Health Care Reform 1993–; mem. Bd of Dirs Geisinger Health System Foundation 2004–; mem. Panel of Health Advisors, Congressional Budget Office 2007–; mem. Bd of Trustees, Maumee Valley Country Day School; mem. NAS, Inst. of Medicine 1975, Nat. Acad. of Social Insurance 1991, American Acad. of Arts and Sciences 2009; Adam Yarmolinsky Medal, Inst. of Medicine 2007; Dr hc (Johns Hopkins Univ.) 2001, (Univ. of Maryland, Baltimore) 2009, (Newcastle Univ., UK) 2009; Health Achievement Award 1980, Distinguished Alumna Award, Rice Univ. 1991, Baxter-Allegiance Foundation Prize for Health Services Research 2000, AcademyHealth Distinguished Investigator Award 2006, Picker Award for Excellence in Advancement of Patient Centered Care 2006, BioMed San Antonio 2007, Healthcare Financial Man. Asscn Bd of Dirs Award 2009. *Publications include:* Net Income of Hospitals 1961–1969 1970, Community Hospitals: Inflation in the Pre-Medicare Period (co-author) 1972, National Health Insurance: Benefits, Costs and Consequences 1975, Health and the War on Poverty: A Ten Year Appraisal (co-author) 1978, Medicare Policy: New Directions for Health and Long-Term Care (co-author) 1986, Health Care Cost Containment (co-author) 1990; numerous articles in professional jounals. *Address:* Commonwealth Fund, One East 75th Street, New York, NY 10021, USA (office). *Telephone:* (212) 606-3825 (office). *E-mail:* kd@cmwf.org (office). *Website:* www.cmwf.org (office).

DAVIS, Leonard (Leon) Andrew, AO; Australian engineer and business executive; *President, Walter and Eliza Hall Institute of Medical Research;* b. 3 April 1939, Port Pirie, South Australia; s. of Leonard Harold Davis and Gladys Davis; m. Annette Brakenridge 1963; two d.; ed S Australian Inst. of Tech.; Man. Dir Pacific Coal 1984–89; Group Exec. CRA Ltd 1989–91; Mining Dir RTZ Corpn 1991–94; Man. Dir, Chief Exec. CRA Ltd 1994–95; Deputy Chief Exec., COO RTZ-CRA 1996; CEO Rio Tinto 1996–2000, Deputy Chair. 2000–05; Chair. Westpac Banking Corpn 2000–07 (retd); currently Pres. Walter and Eliza Hall Inst. of Medical Research; mem. Bd of Dirs Huysmans Pty Ltd, Trouin Pty Ltd; Gov., Ian Potter Foundation; Hon. DSc (Curtin) 1998, (Queensland) 2004, (South Australia) 2005; Centenary Medal (Australia) 2004. *Address:* Walter and Eliza Hall Institute of Medical Research, Royal Parade, Parkville, Vic. 3052, Australia (office). *Telephone:* (3) 9345-2555 (office). *E-mail:* information@wehi.edu.au (office). *Website:* www.wehi.edu.au (office).

DAVIS, Marc, SB, MS, PhD; American astronomer, physicist and academic; *Professor of Astronomy and of Physics, University of California, Berkeley;* b. 8 Sept. 1947, Canton, Ohio; ed Massachusetts Inst. of Tech., Princeton Univ.; Instructor of

Physics, Dept of Physics, Princeton Univ. 1973–74; Asst Prof., Dept of Astronomy, Harvard Univ. 1975–80, Assoc. Prof. 1980–81; Prof., Depts of Astronomy and Physics, Univ. of California, Berkeley 1981–, Chair. Dept of Astronomy 1988–92; mem. NAS 1991, American Acad. of Arts and Sciences 1992, American Astronomical Soc., Int. Astronomical Union; Fellow, AAAS 1988, American Physical Soc. 1989; Hon. PhD (Chicago) 2008; Alfred P. Sloan Foundation Fellowship 1975–79, Newton Lacy Pierce Prize, American Astronomical Soc. 1982, Miller Research Prof. 1986–87, 1999, Dannie Heineman Prize for Astrophysics, American Inst. of Physics and American Astronomical Soc. 2006, Cosmology Prize, The Gruber Foundation (co-recipient) 2011, among numerous other prizes and awards. *Achievements include:* collaborated with George Efstathiou, Carlos Frenk and Simon White (DEFW) to establish the validity of the 'cold dark matter' theory for the formation of galaxies and other cosmic structures during 1980s; led CfA (Harvard-Smithsonian Center for Astrophysics) galaxy survey that inspired the DEFW collaboration; helped organize and run an all-sky model of dust distribution in the Milky Way galaxy as well as the DEEP (Deep Extragalactic Evolutionary Probe) survey of 50,000 distant galaxies, conducted on the two ten-meter Keck telescopes in Hawaii. *Publications:* numerous papers in professional journals. *Leisure interest:* skiing. *Address:* Department of Astronomy, University of California, 517 Campbell Hall, MC 3411, Berkeley, CA 94720-3411, USA (office). *Telephone:* (510) 642-5156 (office). *Fax:* (510) 642-3411 (office). *E-mail:* mdavis@berkeley.edu (office). *Website:* astro.berkeley.edu/~marc (office); deep.ps.uci.edu (office).

DAVIS, Natalie Zemon, CC, BA, MA, PhD; Canadian/American historian and academic; *Professor Emerita of History, University of Toronto;* b. (Natalie Zemon) 8 Nov. 1928, Detroit, Mich., USA; d. of Julian Zemon and Helen Lamport; m. Chandler Davis 1948; three c.; ed Kingswood School, Cranbrook, Smith Coll., Radcliffe Coll., Harvard Univ., Univ. of Michigan; taught at Brown Univ. 1959–63; mem. Faculty, Univ. of Toronto, Canada 1963–71; mem. Faculty, Univ. of Calif., Berkeley 1971–77; mem. Faculty, Princeton Univ. 1978– 96, Henry Charles Lea Prof. of History 1981–96, Henry Charles Lea Prof. Emer. of History 1996–, Dir Shelby Cullom Davis Center for Historical Studies –1996, Northrop Frye Prof. of Literary Theory 1996; Adjunct Prof. of History and Anthropology, Sr Fellow in Comparative Literature and Prof. of Medieval Studies, Univ. of Toronto 1996, now Prof. Emer.; Pres. American Historical Asscn 1987; numerous hon. degrees; Holberg Int. Memorial Prize (Norway) 2010, Nat. Humanities Medal 2012. *Publications include:* Society and Culture in Early Modern France: Eight Essays 1975, The Return of Martin Guerre 1983, Fiction in the Archives: Pardon Tales and their Tellers in Sixteenth Century France 1987, Women on the Margins: Three Seventeenth-Century Lives 1995, Remaking Imposters: From Martin Guerre to Sommersby 1997, The Gift in Sixteenth-Century France 2000, Slaves on Screen: Film and Historical Vision 2002, Trickster Travels 2006; numerous articles. *Address:* History Department, University of Toronto, Sidney Smith Hall, 100 St George Street, Room 2074, Toronto, ON M5S 3G3, Canada (office). *Telephone:* (416) 978-3363 (office). *E-mail:* nz.davis@utoronto.ca (office). *Website:* www.history.utoronto.ca (office).

DAVIS, Sir Peter (John), Kt, FRSA; British business executive and university administrator; b. 23 Dec. 1941, Heswall, Cheshire, England; s. of John Stephen Davis and Adriaantje Davis (née de Baat); m. Susan J. Hillman 1968; two s. one d.; ed Shrewsbury School, Inst. of Marketing; man. trainee, The Ditchburn Org., Lytham, Lancs. 1959–65; Gen. Foods Ltd, Banbury, Oxon. 1965–72; Marketing Dir Key Markets 1973; Man. Dir David Grieg and Group Man. Dir Key Markets, David Grieg 1975–76; Departmental Dir (non-foods) J. Sainsbury PLC 1976, mem. Bd responsible for marketing 1977, Asst Man. Dir Buying and Marketing 1979–86; Dir then Deputy Chair. Homebase Ltd 1983–86; Group CEO J. Sainsbury PLC 2000–04, Chair. 2004; Dir Shaws Supermarkets, USA 1984–86, Chair. 2000–03; Deputy Chief Exec. Reed Int. PLC 1986, Chief Exec. 1986–94, Chair. 1990–94, CEO and Deputy Chair. of Reed Elsevier 1993 (following merger Jan. 1993), Co-Chair. 1993–94; Vice-Pres. Chartered Inst. of Marketing 1991–; Chair. Nat. Advisory Council for Educ. and Training Targets 1993–97, Basic Skills Agency 1991–97, Welfare to Work New Deal Task Force 1997–2000, Govt's Employer Task on Pensions 2004–05; mem. Bd Business in the Community 1991–2005, Deputy Chair. 1991–97, Chair. 1997–2001; Founder and Bd mem. Marketing Council 1994–2002; apptd mem. Curry Comm. on the Future of Farming and Food 2001, Implementation Group for Food and Farming Strategy 2002; Sr Adviser and mem. Advisory Bd Permira Advisers (pvt. equity co.) –2009; Dir (non-exec.) Granada Group 1987–91, British Satellite Broadcasting (BSB) 1988–90, Boots Co. 1991–2000, Prudential Corpn 1994–95 (Group Chief Exec. 1995–2000), UBS AG 2001–07; fmr mem. Supervisory Bd Aegon, Elsevier; mem. Bd of Dirs Royal Opera House 1999–2005, Trustee 1994–2005, also Chair. Royal Opera House Foundation –2005; Pro-Chancellor Univ. of Bangor 2007–11, Deputy Chair. of Govs 2012–; Chair. Int. Advisory Bd, Welsh Nat. Opera 2011–, mem. Bd WNO 2013–; Trustee, Victoria and Albert Museum 1994–96, Marie Curie Cancer Care Jan.–Sept. 2006 (Chair. 2006–11, Life Vice-Pres. 2011–); Fellow, Marketing Soc., City & Guilds 2004; Hon. LLD (Exeter) 2000; Gold Medal, Chartered Man. Inst. 2003. *Leisure interests:* sailing, opera, reading, wine.

DAVIS, Richard K.; American banking executive; *Chairman, President and CEO, U.S. Bancorp;* has held man. positions with U.S. Bancorp since joining Star Banc Corpn (a predecessor) as Exec. Vice-Pres. 1993, Vice-Chair. U.S. Bancorp (following merger of Firstar Corpn and U.S. Bancorp 2001) 2001–04, responsible for Consumer Banking, including Retail Payment Solutions (card services), assumed additional responsibility for Commercial Banking 2003–04, Pres. U.S. Bancorp 2004–, COO 2004–06, mem. Bd of Dirs and CEO 2006–, Chair. 2007–; mem. Bd of Dirs Xcel Energy Inc. 2006–; fmr Chair. Financial Services Roundtable; fmr Rep. for Ninth Dist of Fed. Reserve serving on its Financial Advisory Cttee. *Address:* U.S. Bancorp, U.S. Bancorp Center, 800 Nicollet Mall, Minneapolis, MN 55402-7014, USA (office). *Telephone:* (651) 466-3000 (office). *Fax:* (612) 303-0782 (office). *E-mail:* info@usbank.com (office). *Website:* www.usbank.com (office); www.usbancorp.com (office).

DAVIS, Roger J., MA, MPhil, PhD, FRS; British biologist/biochemist and academic; *H. Arthur Smith Chair and Professor, Program in Molecular Medicine, University of Massachusetts Medical School and Howard Hughes Medical Institute;* b. 26 March 1958; ed Queens' Coll., Cambridge; Research Fellow,

Univ. of Cambridge 1983; Damon Runyon-Walter Winchill Cancer Fund Fellow, Dept of Biochemistry and Molecular Biology, Univ. of Massachusetts Medical School, Worcester, MA, USA 1984–85, Asst Prof. 1985–90, Assoc. Prof., Program in Molecular Medicine 1990–93, Prof. 1993–, H. Arthur Smith Chair, Molecular Medicine 2002–; Asst Investigator, Howard Hughes Medical Inst., Chevy Chase, MD 1990–93, Assoc. Investigator 1993–97, Investigator 1997–; Established Investigator, American Heart Asscn 1990–95; mem. AAAS 1990–, Soc. for Microbiology 1990–; Open Entrance Scholarship Queens' Coll. 1976–78, Foundation Scholarship 1978–81, Science and Eng Research Council Scholarship 1979–82, Munro Studentship 1981–82, ranked 1st by Citation Index Inst. for Scientific Information 1996. *Publications:* more than 180 publs in scientific journals. *Address:* Program in Molecular Medicine, University of Massachusetts Medical School, Biotech II-Suite 309, 373 Plantation Street, Worcester, MA 01605, USA (office). *Telephone:* (508) 856-6054 (office). *Fax:* (508) 856-3210 (office). *E-mail:* Roger.Davis@umassmed.edu (office). *Website:* www.umassmed.edu (office); www.hhmi.org (office).

DAVIS, Steve, OBE; British professional snooker player; b. 22 Aug. 1957, Plumstead, London; s. of Harry George Davis and Jean Catherine Davis; m. Judith Lyn Greig 1990 (divorced 2005); two s.; ed Alexander McLeod Primary School, Abbey Wood School, London; began playing at Lucania Snooker Club, Romford, Essex; won English Under-19 Billiards Championship 1976; turned professional 1978; professional TV debut on Pot Black (BBC) playing against Fred Davis; has won 80 titles (28 ranking, 52 non-ranking) from 115 finals; in list of top 16 players for record 22 seasons; major titles include: UK Professional Champion 1980, 1981, 1984, 1985, 1986, 1987; Masters Champion 1981, 1982, 1988, 1997; Int. Champion 1981, 1983, 1984; World Professional Champion 1981, 1983, 1984, 1987, 1988, 1989; winner, Asian Open 1992, European Open 1993, Welsh Open 1994; 325 century breaks; mem. Bd World Professional Billiards and Snooker Asscn 1993–, Leyton Orient Football Club; regular snooker presenter on BBC TV; Hon. Pres. Snooker Writers' Asscn; BBC Sports Personality of the Year 1988, BBC TV Snooker Personality of the Year 1997, inducted into World Snooker Hall of Fame 2011. *Radio:* presents show on progressive rock and Canterbury scene on local radio station Phoenix FM 1996–. *Television:* Steve Davis and Friends (chat show), They Think It's All Over (guest team capt.) 2003–06. *Music:* joined musical duo Chas & Dave and other snooker stars, calling themselves The Matchroom Mob, on novelty record Snooker Loopy (UK Top 10 hit) 1986, follow-up single, Romford Rap 1987. *Publications:* Steve Davis, World Champion 1981, Frame and Fortune 1982, Successful Snooker 1982, Steve Davis: Snooker Champion 1983, Matchroom Snooker 1988, The Official Matchroom 1990, Simply Fix – The Steve Davis Interesting Cookbook No. 1 – Interesting Things to Do with Meat 1994, Simply Fix – The Steve Davis Interesting Cookbook No. 2 – Interesting Things to Make with Poultry 1994, Simply Fix – The Steve Davis Interesting Cookbook No. 3 – Interesting Things to Make Using Vegetables 1994, Steve Davis Plays Chess (with David Norwood) 1995, Grandmaster Meets Chess Amateur (with David Norwood) 1995. *Leisure interests:* collecting R & B and soul records, chess, Tom Sharpe books, Charlton Athletic Football Club. *Address:* 10 Western Road, Romford, Essex, RM1 3JT; Matchroom Sport Ltd, Mascalls, Mascalls Lane, Brentwood, CM14 5LJ, England. *Telephone:* (1277) 359911 (office). *Fax:* (1277) 359935 (office). *E-mail:* sharron.tokley@matchroom.com (office). *Website:* www.matchroomsport.com (office).

DAVIS, Rt Hon. Terence Anthony Gordon (Terry), CMG, PC, LLB, MBA; British politician and international organization official; b. 5 Jan. 1938, Stourbridge, West Midlands, England; s. of Charles Gordon Davis and Gladys Rose Davis; m. Anne Cooper 1963; one s. one d.; ed Univ. Coll., London, Univ. of Michigan, USA; Internal Auditor, Esso Oil Co. 1962–65; Man. Clarks Shoes 1965–68; Man. Chrysler Parts UK 1968–71; Sr Man. Leyland Cars 1974–79; joined Labour Party 1965; fmr local govt councillor; MP for Bromsgrove 1971–74, for Birmingham Stechford 1979–83, for Birmingham Hodge Hill 1983–2004, Opposition Whip 1979–80, Opposition Spokesman for Health, Finance and Economic Affairs, then for Trade and Industry 1980–87, mem. Public Accounts Cttee 1987–94, Public Records Advisory Cttee, Special Cttee of PCs; mem. WEU Ass. 1992–2004, Leader British Del. 1997–2002, Vice-Pres. 1997–2001; mem. Parl. Ass. of Council of Europe 1992–2004, Leader British Del. 1997–2002, Vice-Pres. Ass., mem. Bureau, Pres. Socialist Group 2002–04, Sec.-Gen. Council of Europe 2004–09; fmr Rapporteur, EBRD, North South Centre, OECD, Georgia's admission to Council of Europe; fmr Leader and mem. UK Del. to WEU Ass., fmr Vice-Pres. Ass., fmr Pres. Socialist Group, Rapporteur for several reports on defence and security issues; fmr mem. UK Del. to OSCE Ass., Leader of UK Del. to Parl. Ass.; fmr mem. Exec. Cttee of UK Br., IPU; fmr mem. UK Del. to UN Gen. Ass.; fmr Visiting Lecturer, Civil Service Coll.; Chair. Ind. Comm. of Inquiry into the Treatment of Elderly People in Birmingham 2001–02; attended two Parl. Confs for South East Europe Stability Pact; observed elections in Albania, Georgia, Latvia and Ukraine; mem. Amnesty International. *Address:* Hermitage, The Green, Adderbury, Oxon., OX17 3ND, England (home). *Telephone:* (1295) 810813 (home). *E-mail:* rthonterrydavis@gmail.com (home).

DAVIS, Viola; American actress; b. 11 Aug. 1955, St Matthews, SC; d. of Dan Davis and Mary Alice Davis; m. Julius Tennon 2003; one d., two step-s.; ed Cen. Falls High School, RI, Rhode Island Coll., Juilliard School; Dr hc (Rhode Island Coll.) 2002. *Stage credits include:* Seven Guitars, Broadway 1996, God's Heart 1997, Pericles 1998, Everybody's Ruby 1999, The Vagina Monologues 1999, King Hedley II, Broadway (Tony Award for Best Featured Actress in a Play 2001, Drama Desk Award for Outstanding Featured Actress in a Play 2001) 2001, Intimate Apparel (Drama Desk Award for Outstanding Actress in a Play 2004) 2004, Fences (Tony Award for Best Actress in a Play 2010, Drama Desk Award for Outstanding Featured Actress in a Play 2010) 2010. *Television includes:* NYPD Blue 1996, New York Undercover 1996, The Pentagon Wars 1998, Judging Amy 2000, Providence 2001, The Guardian 2001, Third Watch 2001, Law & Order: Criminal Intent 2002, The Division 2002, CSI: Crime Scene Investigation 2002, Hack 2003, The Practice 2003, Jesse Stone 2005–06, Threshold 2005, Without a Trace 2006, Brothers and Sisters 2008, The Andromeda Strain 2008, United States of Tara 2009; recurring roles in: City of Angels 2000, Law & Order: Special Victims Unit 2003–08, Century City 2004, Traveler 2007. *Films include:* The Substance of Fire 1996, Out of Sight 1998, Traffic 2000, The Shrink is In 2001, Kate & Leopold 2001, Far from Heaven 2002, Antwone Fisher 2002, Solaris 2002, Get Rich or Die

Tryin' 2005, World Trade Center 2006, The Architect 2006, Disturbia 2007, Nights in Rodanthe 2008, Doubt (Black Reel Award for Best Supporting Actress 2008, Nat. Bd of Review of Motion Pictures Award for Breakthrough Performance by an Actress 2008) 2008, Madea Goes to Jail 2009, State of Play 2009, Law Abiding Citizen 2009, Knight and Day 2010, Eat Pray Love 2010, It's Kind of a Funny Story 2010, Trust 2010, The Help (Black Reel Award for Best Actress 2011, NAACP Image Award for Outstanding Actress in a Motion Picture 2011), Screen Actors Guild Award for Outstanding Performance by a Female Actor in a Motion Picture 2011) 2011, Extremely Loud and Incredibly Close 2011, Beautiful Creatures 2012, Won't Back Down 2012. *Address:* c/o Principal Entertainment New York, 130 West 42nd Street, Suite 614, New York, NY 10036, USA (office). *Telephone:* (212) 997-9191 (office). *Fax:* (212) 997-9280 (office). *Website:* www.principalent.net (office).

DAVIS-BLAKE, Alison, BS, MOB, PhD; American professor of management and university dean; *Stephen M. Ross Professor of Business and Edward J. Frey Dean, Stephen M. Ross School of Business, University of Michigan;* d. of Prof. Gordon Davis; m.; two s.; ed Brigham Young Univ., Stanford Univ.; worked as an auditor in New York City office of Touche Ross & Co. 1979–80; Asst Prof. of Industrial Admin, Carnegie Mellon Univ. 1986–90; Asst Prof., later Assoc. Prof., later Prof., Univ. of Texas 1990–2006, Eleanor T. Mosle Fellow 1995, Co-Dir Exec. Master's Degree in Human Resource Devt Leadership 1995–2001, Chair. Dept of Man. 2002–03, Eddy C. Scurlock Centennial Prof. of Man. and Sr Assoc. Dean for Academic Affairs, McCombs School of Business 2003–06; Investors in Leadership Distinguished Chair in Organizational Behavior and Dean, Carlson School of Man., Univ. of Minnesota 2006–11; Leon Festinger Collegiate Prof. of Man., Stephen M. Ross Prof. of Business and Edward J. Frey Dean, Stephen M. Ross School of Business, Univ. of Michigan 2011–; mem. Editorial Bd Journal of Management, Academy of Management Review, Administrative Science Quarterly; mem. Bd Asscn to Advance Collegiate Schools of Business. *Publications:* numerous papers in professional journals on the effects of outsourcing on organizations and employees, organizational promotion systems, and determinants and consequences of contingent worker use and organizational wage structures. *Leisure interests:* musical theatre, global travel, spending time with her family. *Address:* Office of the Dean, Stephen M. Ross School of Business, University of Michigan, 701 Tappan Street, Ann Arbor, MI 48109-1234, USA (office). *Telephone:* (734) 763-3818 (office). *E-mail:* alisondb@umich.edu (office). *Website:* www.bus.umich.edu (office); rossblogs.typepad.com/deansblog (office).

DAVISON, Alan, BSc, PhD, DIC, FRS; British chemist and academic; *Professor of Chemistry, Massachusetts Institute of Technology;* b. 24 March 1936, Ealing; ed Univ. Coll. of Swansea, Imperial Coll. of Science and Tech.; lecturer in chem., Harvard Univ. 1962–64; Asst Prof. MIT 1964–67, Assoc. Prof. 1967–74, Prof. of Inorganic Chem. 1974–; Alfred P. Sloan Foundation Fellow 1967–69; Hon. Fellowship, Univ. Coll. of Swansea 1990; maj. research interests include Technetium and Rhenium chem., radiopharmaceutical chem. and bioinorganic chem.; Herbert M. Stauffer Award for Outstanding Laboratory Paper 1990, Paul C. Aebersold Award for Outstanding Achievement in Basic Science applied to Nuclear Medicine 1993. *Publications include:* numerous articles and papers in professional journals. *Address:* Department of Chemistry, Room 6-435, Massachusetts Institute of Technology, Cambridge, MA 02139 (office); 80 Cass Street, West Roxbury, MA 02132, USA (home). *Telephone:* (617) 253-1794 (office). *Fax:* (617) 258-6989 (office). *E-mail:* adavison@mit.edu (office). *Website:* www.mit.edu/chemistry (office).

DAVISON, Edward Joseph, BASc, MA, PhD, ScD, FIEEE, FRSC, ARCT, FCAE, P.Eng; Canadian electrical engineer and academic; *University Professor Emeritus, Department of Electrical Engineering, University of Toronto;* b. 12 Sept. 1938, Toronto, Ont.; s. of Maurice J. Davison and Agnes E. Quinlan; m. Zofia M. Perz 1966; four c.; ed Royal Conservatory of Music, Toronto, Univ. of Toronto, Univ. of Cambridge, UK; Asst Prof., Dept of Electrical Eng, Univ. of Toronto 1964–66, 1967–68, Assoc. Prof. 1968–74, Prof. 1974–2001, Univ. Prof. Emer. 2001–; Asst Prof., Univ. of California, Berkeley 1966–67; Pres. IEEE Control Systems Soc. 1983 (Distinguished mem. 1984–); Chair. Int. Fed. of Automatic Control (IFAC) Theory Cttee 1987–90, mem. IFAC Council 1991–93, 1993–96, Vice-Chair. IFAC Tech. Bd 1991–93, Vice-Chair. IFAC Policy Cttee 1996–99, Fellow, IFAC 2005; Dir Electrical Eng Assocs Ltd, Toronto 1977–, Pres. 1997–; Consulting Engineer, Asscn of Professional Engineers of Prov. of Ont. 1979–; mem. Russian Acad. of Nonlinear Sciences 1998–; Foreign mem. Nat. Acad. of Eng (USA) 2010; Hon. Prof., Beijing Inst. of Aeronautics and Astronautics 1986; Athlone Fellowship 1961, E.W.R. Steacie Research Fellowship 1974, Killam Research Fellowship 1979, 1981, IEEE Centennial Medal 1984, IFAC Quazza Medal 1993, IFAC Outstanding Service Award 1996, Hendrik W. Bode Lecture Prize, IEEE Control Systems Soc. 1997, Killam Prize in Eng, Canada Council 2003, inducted into Univ. of Toronto Eng Alumni Hall of Fame 2003, Canada Outstanding Engineer Award, IEEE (Canada) 2010. *Publications:* more than 500 research papers in numerous journals. *Leisure interests:* backpacking, skiing. *Address:* Department of Electrical Engineering, University of Toronto, Toronto, ON M5S 1A4, Canada (office). *Telephone:* (416) 978-6342 (office). *Fax:* (416) 978-0804 (office). *E-mail:* ted@control.utoronto.ca (office). *Website:* www.control.utoronto.ca/people/profs/ted/ted.html (office).

DAVISON, Ian Frederic Hay, CBE, BSc (Econ), FCA; British business executive and accountant (retd) and financial services regulator; b. 30 June 1931, Hillingdon, Middx; s. of the late Eric Hay Davison and Inez Davison; m. Maureen Patricia Blacker 1955; one s. two d.; ed Dulwich Coll., LSE and Univ. of Michigan, USA; mem. Inst. of Chartered Accountants (mem. Council 1975–99); Man. Partner Arthur Andersen & Co., Chartered Accountants 1966–82; Ind. mem. NEDC for Bldg Industry 1971–77; mem. Price Comm. 1977–79; Chair. Review Bd for Govt Contracts 1981; Chief Exec. and Deputy Chair. Lloyd's 1983–86; Dept of Trade Insp., London Capital Securities 1975–77; Insp. Grays Bldg Soc. 1978–79; Chair. Accounting Standards Cttee 1982–84; Chair. The Nat. Mortgage Bank PLC 1992–2000, Roland Berger Ltd 1996–98; Chair. Dubai Financial Services Authority 2002–04; Chair. Ruffer LLP 2002–11; Chair. (non-exec.) Northgate plc (fmrly McDonnell Information Systems) 1993–99, Newspaper Publrs 1993–94 (Dir 1986–94); Chair. Monteverdi Trust 1979–84, Sadler's Wells Foundation 1995–2003, Pro Provost RCA 1996–2007, Crédit Lyonnais Capital Markets 1988–91, Charterail 1991–92; Pres. Nat. Council for One-Parent Families

1991–2004; Dir Morgan Grenfell Asset Man. 1986–88, Midland Bank PLC 1986–88, Storehouse PLC 1988–96 (Chair. 1990–96), Chloride PLC 1988–98, Cadbury Schweppes PLC 1990–2000, CIBA PLC 1991–96; Dir and Trustee, Royal Opera House, Covent Garden 1984–86; Trustee, Victoria and Albert Museum 1984–93, SANE 1996– (Chair. 2000–02); Gov. LSE 1982–2006; Chair. Railway Heritage Cttee 1999–2004, Council, Exeter Cathedral 2002–08; Chair. Museum of East Asian Art, Bath 2012–13; Hon. Fellow, LSE 2004; Hon. DSc (Aston) 1985, Hon. LLD (Bath) 1998. *Publication:* Lloyd's: A View of the Room 1987. *Leisure interests:* music, theatre, bell-ringing. *Address:* 13 Catharine Place, Bath, BA1 2PR, England. *Telephone:* (1225) 445000; 7932-160482 (mobile). *E-mail:* ihdavison@aol.com.

DAVUTOGLU, Ahmed, PhD; Turkish academic and government official; *Minister of Foreign Affairs;* b. 1959, Konya; ed Bosphorus Univ.; fmr Chair. Dept of Int. Relations, Beykent Univ., Istanbul; began working at Marmara Univ. 1993, Prof. 1999–2003; Foreign Policy Adviser to the Prime Minister of Turkey 2003–09; Minister of Foreign Affairs 2009–. *Address:* Ministry of Foreign Affairs, Dişişleri Bakanlığı, Dr Sadık Ahmet Cad. 12, 06100 Balgat, Ankara, Turkey (office). *Telephone:* (312) 2921000 (office). *Fax:* (312) 2873869 (office). *E-mail:* webmaster@mfa.gov.tr (office). *Website:* www.mfa.gov.tr (office).

DAVYDOV, Mikhail Ivanovich, DrMed; Russian clinical oncologist; *Regional Co-ordinator for Russia and CIS, N.N. Blokhin Russian Cancer Research Center, Russian Academy of Siences;* b. 11 Oct. 1947, Konotop, Sumy region, Ukraine; s. of Ivan Ivanovich Davydov and Asmar Tamrazovna Davydova; m. Irina Borisovna Zborovskaya; one s.; ed Moscow 1st Sechenov Inst. of Medicine; researcher, Sr Researcher, Head of Lab., Head of Div., Deputy Dir Moscow Blokhin Oncological Scientific Center (now N.N. Blokhin Russian Cancer Research Center), Russian Acad. of Medicine, Dir Research Inst. of Clinical Oncology 1980, Prof. 1986, now Regional Co-ordinator for Russia and CIS; mem. Int. Soc. of Surgeons, American and European Soc. of Surgeons, New York Acad. of Sciences; Corresp. mem. Russian Acad. of Medicine; numerous decorations including Merited Worker of Science of Russia 1996. *Publications:* over 300 scientific publs on oncological surgery, including three monographs and six methodical films. *Leisure interests:* boxing, sports, hunting, classical and retro music. *Address:* N.N. Blokhin Russian Cancer Research Center, Russian Academy of Medical Sciences, 115478 Moscow, Kashirskoye shosse 24, Russia (office). *Telephone:* (495) 324-11-14 (office). *Fax:* (495) 323-57-77 (office). *E-mail:* davydov@eso.ru (office). *Website:* www.eso.ru (office).

DAWE, Donald Bruce, AO, MLitt, PhD; Australian writer; b. 15 Feb. 1930, Geelong; s. of Alfred James Dawe and Mary Ann Matilda Dawe; m. Gloria Desley Dawe (née Blain) 1964 (died 1997); two s. two d.; ed Northcote High School, Univs of Melbourne, New England and Queensland; Educ. Section, RAAF 1959–68; teacher, Downlands Sacred Heart Coll., Toowoomba, Queensland 1969–71; Lecturer, Sr Lecturer, Assoc. Prof., Faculty of Arts, Univ. of Southern Queensland 1971–93; Hon. Prof., Univ. of Southern Queensland 1995; Hon. DLitt (Univ. of Southern Queensland) 1995, (Univ. of NSW) 1997; Myer Poetry Prize 1965, 1968, Patrick White Award 1980, Christopher Brennan Award 1984, Paul Harris Fellowship, Rotary Int. 1990, Philip Hodgins Memorial Medal for Literary Excellence 1997, Australia Council for the Arts Emer. Writers Award 2001, Centenary Medal 2003. *Publications include:* poetry: No Fixed Address 1962, A Need of a Similar Name (Ampol Arts Award 1966) 1964, An Eye for a Tooth 1968, Beyond the Subdivisions 1969, Condolences of the Season: Selected Poems 1971, Over Here, Hark! and Other Stories 1983, Speaking in Parables 1987, The Side of Silence: Poems 1987–90 1990, Mortal Instruments: Poems 1990–95 1995, Sometimes Gladness: Collected Poems 1954–97 1997, A Poet's People 1999, Towards a War 2003; non-fiction: Essays and Opinions 1990; children's fiction: No Cat – and That's That 2002, The Chewing Gum Kid 2002, Luke and Lulu 2004, Smarty-Cat 2007. *Leisure interests:* gardening, watching Australian Rules football. *Address:* Authors, c/o Penguin Group (Australia), PO Box 701, Hawthorn 3122, Vic., Australia (office). *Website:* www.penguin.com.au (office).

DAWES, Kwame Senu Neville, BA, PhD; American/Ghanaian/Jamaican poet, playwright, critic and novelist; *Distinguished Poet-in-Residence and Louise Frye Scudder Professor of Humanities, University of South Carolina;* b. 28 July 1962, Accra, Ghana; s. of Neville Agustus Dawes and Sophia Dawes (née Tevi); m. Lorna Marie; three c.; ed Univ. of the West Indies, Univ. of New Brunswick; moved to Jamaica 1971; Chair. of the Division of Arts and Letters 1993–96; Asst Prof. in English, Univ. of S Carolina (USC) at Sumter 1992–96, Guest Lecturer, USC at Columbia 1994, Assoc. Prof. of English, USC 1996–2001, Prof. of English 2002–, currently Distinguished Poet-in-Residence and Louise Frye Scudder Prof. of Humanities, Dir MFA/Creative Writing program 2001–03; Series Ed. Caribbean Play Series, Peepal Tree Books, UK 1999–, Assoc. Poetry Ed. Peepal Tree Books 2006–; Criticism Ed. Obsidian II literary journal, Raleigh, NC 2000–05; programmer of annual Calabash Int. Literary Festival, Jamaica 2000–; Dir USC English Dept Spring Writers Festival 2002–03, S Carolina Poetry Initiative (founder) 2003–; Exec. Dir USC Arts Inst. 2005–; Faculty Mem., Pacific Univ. MFA program; mem. Nat. Book Critics' Circle, S Carolina Humanities Council (Bd mem.) 2000–07, S Carolina Book Festival (mem. Advisory Bd); Assoc. Fellow, Univ. of Warwick 1996; Hon. Fellow Univ. of Iowa Int. Writing Program 1986; Forward Poetry Prize for Best First Collection 1994, S Carolina Arts Comm. Individual Artist Fellowship 1996, Winner Poetry Business Chapbook Competition 2000, Ohio Univ. Press Hollis Summers Poetry Prize 2000, Pushcart Prize 2001, Hurston Wright Legacy Award for Fiction. *Plays:* In the Warmth of the Cold, And the Gods Fell, In Chains of Freedom, The System, The Martyr, It Burns and it Stings, Charity's Come, Even Unto Death, Friends and Almost Lovers, Dear Pastor, Confessions, Brown Leaf, Coming in from the Cold, Song of an Injured Stone (musical), In My Garden, Charades, Passages, A Celebration of Struggle, Stump of the Terebinth, Valley Prince, One Love 2001. *Writing for radio:* Salut Haiti (poem/drama), Samaritans (play), New World A-Comin' (play). *Publications:* poetry: Progeny of Air 1994, Resisting the Anomie 1995, Prophets 1995, Jacko Jacobus 1996, Requiem 1996, Shook Foil 1998, Wheel and Come Again: Reggae Anthology (ed.) 1998, Mapmaker (chapbook) 2000, Midland 2001, Selected Poems 2002, Bruised Totems 2004, Wisteria: Twilight Songs from The Swamp Country 2005, Brimming 2006, Gomer's Song 2007, Impossible Flying 2007; fiction: A Place to Hide (short stories) 2002, She's Gone (novel) 2007; non-fiction: Natural Mysticism:

Towards a New Reggae Aesthetic (literary criticism) 1998, Talk Yuh Talk: Interviews with Caribbean Poets 2000, Bob Marley: Lyrical Genius 2002, A Far Cry from Plymouth Rock (memoir) 2007; contrib. to numerous journals and periodicals, including Beat Magazine, Black Issues, Black Warrior Review, Bristol Evening Post, Calabash, Caribbean Writer, Dagens Nyheter (Sweden), Globe and Mail, Impact, Library Journal, Lines, Morning Star, Poetry London Newsletter, Poetry Review, Publishers Weekly, The Atlanta Journal/Constitution, The Brunswickan, The Courier, The Daily Gleaner, The Daily News, The English Review, The Guardian, The Herald, The London Times, The Observer, The State, The Sumter Item, The Telegraph Journal, The Voice, Time Out London, Venue, Wasafiri, Western Daily Press, World Literature Today, World Literature Written in English, Granta. *Address:* English Department, University of South Carolina, Columbia, SC 29208 (office); Alison Granucci, Blue Flower Arts LLC, PO Box 1361, Millbrook NY 12545, USA (office). *Telephone:* (803) 777-2096 (office). *Fax:* (803) 777-9064 (office). *E-mail:* alison@blueflowerarts.com (office); dawesk@mailbox.sc.edu (office). *Website:* www.kwamedawes.com (home); www.blueflowerarts.com (office).

DAWKINS, (Clinton) Richard, MA, DSc, FRS, FRSL; British biologist, academic and author; *Professorial Fellow, New College, University of Oxford;* b. 26 March 1941, Nairobi, Kenya; s. of Clinton John Dawkins and Jean Mary Vyvyan Dawkins (née Ladner); m. 1st Marian Stamp 1967 (divorced 1984); m. 2nd Eve Barham 1984 (died 1999); one d.; m. 3rd Hon. Lalla Ward 1992; ed Balliol Coll., Oxford; Asst Prof. of Zoology, Univ. of California, Berkeley, USA 1967–69; Lecturer, Univ. of Oxford 1970–89, Reader in Zoology 1989–96, Charles Simonyi Reader in the Public Understanding of Science 1995–96, Charles Simonyi Prof. 1996–2008 (retd), Professorial Fellow, New Coll., Oxford 1970–; Ed. Animal Behaviour 1974–78, Oxford Surveys in Evolutionary Biology 1983–86; Gifford Lecturer, Univ. of Glasgow 1988, Sidgwick Memorial Lecturer, Newnham Coll., Cambridge 1988; Kovler Visiting Fellow, Univ. of Chicago 1990; Nelson Lecturer, Univ. of California, Davis 1990; f. Richard Dawkins Foundation for Reason and Science 2006; Hon. Fellow, Regent's Coll., London 1988, Balliol Coll. 2004, Hon. Patron, Philosophical Soc., Trinity Coll. Dublin 2004; mem. Freedom From Religion Foundation's Hon. Bd of distinguished achievers 2010; Hon. DLitt (St Andrews) 1995, (ANU Canberra) 1996; Hon. DSc (Westminster) 1997, (Hull) 2001, (Sussex) 2005, (Durham) 2005, (Brussels) 2005; Hon. DUniv (Open Univ.) 2003; numerous awards including Silver Medal, Zoological Soc. 1989, Michael Faraday Award, Royal Soc. 1990, Nakayama Prize 1994, Int. Cosmos Prize 1997, Kistler Prize 2001, Bicentennial Kelvin Medal, Royal Soc. of Glasgow 2002, Richard Dawkins Award given annually by Atheist Alliance International to the atheist whose work has done most to raise public awareness of atheism 2003–, Shakespeare Prize for contribution to British Culture, Hamburg 2005, British Book Award for Author of the Year 2007, Nierenberg Prize for Science in the Public Interest 2009. *Television includes:* Nice Guys Finish First (BBC) 1985, The Blind Watchmaker (BBC) 1986, Break the Science Barrier (Channel 4) 1994, Royal Institution Christmas Lectures (BBC) 1992, Big Ideas in Science (Channel 5) 2004, The Root of All Evil? (Channel 4) 2006, The Enemies of Reason (Channel 4) 2007, The Genius of Charles Darwin (Channel 4) (Best TV Documentary Series, British Broadcast Awards 2008) 2008, Doctor Who: The Stolen Earth (as himself) 2008, Expelled: No Intelligence Allowed (as himself) 2008, The Purpose of Purpose – Lecture tour among American universities 2009, Faith School Menace? (More4) 2010, Beautiful Minds (BBC 4 documentary) 2012. *Publications include:* The Selfish Gene 1976, The Extended Phenotype 1982, The Blind Watchmaker (RSL Prize 1987, LA Times Literature Prize 1987) 1986, The Tinbergen Legacy (ed with M. Dawkins and T. R. Halliday) 1991, River Out of Eden 1995, Climbing Mount Improbable 1996, Unweaving the Rainbow: Science, Delusion and the Appetite for Wonder 1998, A Devil's Chaplain (essays) 2003, The Ancestor's Tale: A Pilgrimage to the Dawn of Life 2004, The God Delusion 2006, The Oxford Book of Modern Science Writing (ed) 2008, The Greatest Show on Earth: The Evidence for Evolution 2009, The Magic of Reality: How We Know What's Really True 2011; numerous articles in scientific journals. *Leisure interest:* human intercourse. *Address:* New College, Holywell Street, Oxford, OX1 3BN (office); Richard Dawkins Foundation for Reason and Science, Suite 184, 266 Banbury Road, Oxford, OX2 7DL, England (office). *E-mail:* contact@richarddawkins.net (office). *Website:* richarddawkins.net; www.richarddawkinsfoundation.org.

DAWKINS, Hon. John Sydney, AO, BEc, RDA; Australian politician, economist and business consultant; *Director, Government Relations Australia;* b. 2 March 1947, Perth; m. 1st (divorced); one s. one d.; m. 2nd Maggie Dawkins 1987; one d. one step-s.; ed Scotch Coll., Roseworthy Agricultural Coll., Univ. of W Australia; fmr mem. Senate, Univ. of W Australia; worked for Bureau of Agricultural Econs and Dept of Trade and Industry 1971–72; MP, House of Reps., Seat of Tangney, WA 1974–75, Seat of Fremantle, WA 1977–94; Minister for Finance and Minister Assisting the Prime Minister for Public Service Matters 1983–84, Minister for Trade and Minister Assisting the Prime Minister for Youth Affairs 1984–87, for Employment, Educ. and Training 1987–91, Treasurer 1991–93; Chair. Cairns Group of Agricultural Exporting Countries 1985–87, OECD Ministerial Council 1993, John Dawkins and Co. 1994–, Medical Corpn of Australasia 1997–2000, Elders Rural Bank Ltd 1998–2006; fmr mem. Bd Sealcorp Holdings, Fred Hollows Foundation, Indian Ocean Centre; mem. Nat. Exec., Australian Labor Party, Party Vice-Pres. 1982–83; Australian Govt Special Investment Rep. 1994–95; Press Officer, WA Trades and Labor Council 1976–77; Chair. Australian Qualification Framework Council; currently Dir Government Relations Australia (lobbying firm), Adelaide; Hon. DUniv (Univ. of S Australia, Queensland Univ. of Tech.) 1997, (Ballarat); Australia Centenary Medal. *Leisure interests:* farming, viticulture, travel. *Address:* Government Relations Australia, Level 2, 60 Hindmarsh Square, Adelaide, SA 5034, Australia (office). *Telephone:* (8) 8232-0344 (office). *Fax:* (8) 8359-3377 (office). *E-mail:* jdawkins@govrel.com.au (office). *Website:* www.govrel.com.au (office).

DAWOOD, Mohammad Hussain, BMet, MBA; Pakistani business executive; *Chairman, Dawood Hercules Corporation Limited;* s. of the late Ahmad Dawood; ed Salford Tech. Coll. and Sheffield Hallam Univ., UK, Northwestern Univ.–Kellogg School of Man., USA; Owner and Chair. Dawood Hercules Corpn Ltd, Chair. and CEO Dawood Hercules Chemicals Ltd, Dawood Cotton Mills and other cos within group; Chair. Engro Corpn Ltd, Hub Power Co. Ltd, Pakistan Poverty Alleviation Fund, The Dawood Foundation; mem. Bd of Dirs Dawood Bank Ltd;

Chair. Int. Advisory Council of the Cradle to Cradle Inst., San Francisco, Karachi Educ. Initiative's Karachi School for Business & Leadership; mem. Govt of Pakistan Educ. Task Force; Dir, Pakistan Business Council, Pakistan Centre for Philanthropy, Beaconhouse Nat. Univ.; Global Charter mem. The Indus Entrepreneurs (TiE); Hon. Consul of Italy in Lahore 2002; Ufficiale Ordine Al merito della Repubblica Italiana. *Address:* Dawood Centre, M.T. Khan Road, Karachi, Pakistan (office). *Telephone:* (21) 35686001 (office). *Fax:* (21) 35693416 (office). *E-mail:* info@dawoodhercules.com (office). *Website:* www.dawoodhercules.com (office).

DAWSON, Sir Daryl Michael, Kt, AC, KBE, CB, LLM, QC; Australian judge; *Professorial Fellow, University of Melbourne;* b. 12 Dec. 1933, Melbourne, Vic.; s. of Claude Charles Dawson and Elizabeth May Dawson; m. Mary Louise Thomas 1971; ed Canberra High School and Melbourne Univ. and Yale Univ., USA; admitted to Bar, Vic. 1957; Lecturer, Council of Legal Educ. 1962–74; mem. Ormond Coll. Council 1965–73 (Chair. 1992–93); QC 1971; mem. Victoria Bar Council 1971–74; admitted to Tasmania Bar 1972; Solicitor-Gen. State of Vic. 1974–82; mem. Australian Motor Sport Appeal Court 1974–86 (Chair. 1982–86); Judge, High Court of Australia 1982–97; Judge, Hong Kong Court of Final Appeal 1997–2003; Chair. Longford Royal Comm. 1998–99, Trade Practices Act Review Cttee 2002–03; Adjunct Prof., Monash Univ. 1998–2006; Professorial Fellow, Univ. of Melbourne 1998–; mem. Council Menzies Foundation (fmr Chair.); Fulbright Scholar 1955; Hon. LLD (Monash) 2006, (Melbourne) 2008. *Leisure interest:* gardening. *Address:* PO Box 147, East Melbourne, Vic. 8002, Australia (office). *Telephone:* (3) 9417-2818 (office). *Fax:* (3) 9417-4499 (office). *E-mail:* dawson.dl@hotkey.net.au (office).

DAWSON, Jill Dianne, BA, MA; British novelist, poet, editor and teacher; b. 1962, Durham, England; partner Meredith Bowles; two s.; ed Univ. of Nottingham, Sheffield Hallam Univ., Anglia Ruskin Univ.; Royal Literary Fund (RLF) Fellow, RLF Advisory Fellow; mem. Bd Writers Centre, Norwich; tutor at Univ. of East Anglia; mem. Nat. Asscn of Writers in Educ., Soc. of Authors; Hon. DLitt; Eric Gregory Award 1992, second prize, London Writers Short Story Competition 1994, Blue Nose Poet of the Year 1995, London Arts Board New Writers 1998, Fiction Uncovered Award 2011. *Publications include:* School Tales (ed) 1990, How Do I Look? (non-fiction) 1991, Virago Book of Wicked Verse (ed) 1992, Virago Book of Love Letters (ed) 1994, Wild Ways (co-ed with Margo Daly), White Fish with Painted Nails (poems) 1994, Trick of the Light (novel) 1996, Magpie (novel) 1998, Fred and Edie (novel) 2001, Gas & Air (co-ed with Margo Daly), Wild Boy (novel) 2003, Watch Me Disappear 2006, The Great Lover 2009, Lucky Bunny 2011; contrib. to anthologies and periodicals. *Address:* United Agents, 12–26 Lexington Street, London, W1F 0LE, England (office). *Telephone:* (20) 3214-0800 (office). *Fax:* (20) 3214-0801 (office). *E-mail:* cdawnay@unitedagents.co.uk (office). *Website:* www.jilldawson.co.uk.

DAWSON, Dame Sandra June Noble, DBE, BA, MA, FIPH, FCGI, CIMgt; British college principal and professor of management studies; *KPMG Professor of Management, Judge Business School and Master, Sidney Sussex College, University of Cambridge;* b. 4 June 1946, Bucks.; d. of Wilfred Denyer and Joy Denyer (née Noble); m. Henry R. C. Dawson 1969; one s. two d.; ed Dr Challoner's Grammar School, Amersham, Univ. of Keele; research officer, Govt Social Survey 1968–69; research officer, then Lecturer, Sr Lecturer, Industrial Sociology Unit, Dept of Social and Econ. Studies, Imperial Coll. of Science, Tech. and Medicine 1969–90, Deputy Dir Man. School 1987–94, Prof. of Organizational Behaviour, Man. School 1990–95; KPMG Prof. of Man. Studies, Univ. of Cambridge 1995–, Dir Judge Business School, 1995–2006, Fellow, Jesus Coll., Cambridge 1995–99; Master, Sidney Sussex Coll., Cambridge 1999–; Chair. Riverside Mental Health Trust 1992–95, Exec. Steering Cttee, Advanced Inst. of Man. 2007–; mem. Bd of Dirs (non-exec.) Riverside Health Authority 1990–92, Cambridge Econometrics 1996–2006, Fleming Claverhouse Investment Trust 1996–2003, Rand Europe (UK) 2002–03; Barclays PLC 2003–, Oxfam 2006–; mem. Research Strategy Bd, Offshore Safety Div., Health and Safety Exec. 1991–95, Strategic Review Group, Public Health Lab. Service 1994–99, Sr Salaries Review Body 1997–2003, Econ. and Social Research Council Research Priorities Bd 2000–03, UK-India Round Table; Fellow, City & Guilds of London Inst. 1999; Hon. Fellow, Jesus Coll. Cambridge; Hon. DSc (Keele Univ.), Hon. DLitt (Keele) 2000; Anglian Businesswoman of the Year 2000. *Publications include:* Analysing Organisations 1986, Safety at Work: The Limits of Self Regulation 1988, Managing the NHS 1995, Policy Futures for UK Health 2000, Future Health Organisations and Systems 2005, Engaging with Care (jtly) 2007; papers on man. in learned journals. *Leisure interests:* music, walking, family. *Address:* Judge Business School, University of Cambridge, Trumpington Street, Cambridge, CB2 1AG (office); Sidney Sussex College, Sidney Street, Cambridge, CB2 3HU, England (office). *Telephone:* (1223) 766331 (office); (1223) 338800 (office). *Fax:* (1223) 766332 (office). *E-mail:* s.dawson@jbs.cam.ac.uk (office). *Website:* www.jbs.cam.ac.uk (office); www.sid.cam.ac.uk.

DAWSON, Thomas C., II, AB (Econs), MBA; American economist; b. 9 March 1948, Washington, DC; s. of Allan Duval Dawson and Jane Dodge Dawson; m. Moira Jane Haley 1974; two s. one d.; ed Stanford Univ., Woodrow Wilson School of Public and Int. Affairs, Princeton Univ.; Financial Economist, Office of Investment Affairs, US Dept of State 1971–72, Staff Asst to Asst Sec. for Econ. Affairs 1972–73, Staff Asst to Under-Sec. for Econ. Affairs 1973–74, Economist, US Consulate Gen., Rio de Janeiro 1974–78; Consultant, McKinsey and Co. 1978–80; Deputy Asst Sec. for Developing Nations, US Treasury Dept 1981–84, Asst Sec. for Business and Consumer Affairs 1984–85; Deputy Asst to the Pres. and Exec. Asst to Chief of Staff, White House 1985–87; Exec. Vice-Pres. Regdon Associates 1987–89; Special Asst to Asst Sec. for Int. Affairs, US Treasury Dept 1989; US Exec. Dir IMF 1989–93, Dir External Relations Dept 1999–2006; First Vice-Pres. Merrill Lynch and Co. 1993–94, Dir Financial Insts Group 1993–99. *Address:* 50 Portland Road, Summit, NJ 07901, USA (home).

DAWUNI, Rocky; Ghanaian singer; s. of Koyatu Dawuni and Asibi Dawuni; m. Carry Dawuni; ed Univ. of Ghana; f. Rocky Dawuni Independence Splash (annual music festival); apptd Goodwill Amb. for Tourism, Ministry of Tourism 2011; mem. Bd of Advisors Jammin Java Corpn 2011–; often referred to as 'Ghana's Bob Marley'; Best African Artist, Int. Reggae and World Music Awards 2011. *Recordings include:* The Movement 1996, Crusade 1998, In Ghana (Reggae Song of the Year, Ghana Music Awards 2000) 1999, Awakening 2001, Book of Changes

2005, Hymns for the Rebel Soul 2010, Sun is Shining 2010. *Address:* Bob Dawuni, c/o Aquarian Records, POB 4151, Accra, Ghana (office). *Telephone:* (24) 2974303 (office). *E-mail:* bobdawuni@yahoo.com (office). *Website:* www.rockydawuni.com.

DAY, Catherine, MA; Irish EU official; *Secretary-General, European Commission;* b. 16 June 1954, Dublin; ed Univ. Coll., Dublin; loan officer, Investment Bank of Ireland 1974–75; EC Information Officer, Confed. of Irish Industry 1975–79; Admin., Directorate Gen. (DG) III 1979–82, mem. Cabinet of Richard Burke, in charge of Personnel and Admin 1982–84, Cabinet of Peter Sutherland, in charge of Competition 1985–89, Cabinet of Sir Leon Brittan, in charge of Competition and External Relations 1989–95, Deputy Chef de Cabinet to Sir Leon Brittan, in charge of External Relations 1995–96, Dir DG IA (External Relations) responsible for relations with the Balkans, Turkey and Cyprus 1996–97, Dir DG IA, subsequently DG Enlargement, responsible for relations with cand. countries of Cen. and Eastern Europe 1997–2000, Deputy Dir-Gen. DG for External Relations, responsible for relations with the Western Balkans, New Ind. States (NIS), Mediterranean including the Middle East 2000–02, Dir-Gen. DG Environment 2002–05, Sec.-Gen. EC 2005–; Hon. LLD (Nat. Univ. of Ireland) 2003. *Address:* Secretariat-General, European Commission, 1049 Brussels, Belgium (office). *Telephone:* (2) 2958312 (office). *Fax:* (2) 2993229 (office). *E-mail:* catherine.day@ec.europa.eu (office).

DAY, Christine, BA; Canadian business executive; *CEO, Lululemon Athletica;* m.; three c.; ed Central Washington Univ., Advanced Man. Program, Harvard Business School; spent 20 years at Starbucks in various capacities, including as Vice-Pres., Sales and Operations for Business Alliances and Sr Vice-Pres., North American Finance and Admin, sr man. positions, included Pres. of the Pacific Group of Starbucks Coffee International; joined Lululemon Athletica as Exec. Vice-Pres., Retail Operations 2008, oversaw Retail Operations in North America and internationally, as well as the Community Relations, Real Estate Devt, Guest Educ. Centre and Wholesale businesses, CEO Lululemon Athletica 2008–; mem. Bd of Dirs Rick Hansen Foundation, Vancouver; ranked by Fortune magazine amongst the 50 Most Powerful Women in Business outside the US (45th) 2012. *Leisure interests:* yoga, hiking the local mountains, biking on the seawall paths with her family. *Address:* Lululemon Athletica, Guest Education Centre, 105 – 5560 Trapp Avenue, Burnaby, BC V3N 5G4, Canada (office). *Telephone:* (877) 263-9300 (office); (604) 215-9300 (office). *E-mail:* gec@lululemon.com (office). *Website:* www.lululemon.com (office).

DAY, Sir Derek (Malcolm), Kt, KCMG; British diplomatist; b. 29 Nov. 1927, London, England; s. of Alan W. Day and Gladys Day; m. Sheila Nott 1955; three s. one d.; ed Hurstpierpoint Coll. and St Catharine's Coll., Cambridge; RA 1946–48; entered diplomatic service 1951; served in Tel-Aviv 1953–56, Embassy in Rome 1956–59, Embassy in Washington, DC 1962–66, Embassy in Nicosia 1972–75, Amb. to Ethiopia 1975–78, Asst Under-Sec. of State, FCO 1979, Deputy Under-Sec. of State 1980, Chief Clerk 1982–84, High Commr to Canada 1984–87; Commr Commonwealth War Graves Comm. 1987–92; Vice-Chair. British Red Cross 1988–94; Dir Monenco Ltd, Canada 1988–92; Chair. Crystal Palace Sports and Leisure Ltd 1992–97; mem. Defence Medical Services Clinical Research Cttee 1995–2003 (Chair. 1999); Gov. Hurstpierpoint Coll. 1987–97, Bethany School 1987–2000; Bronze Medal, Olympic Games 1952. *Address:* Pedlar's End, Goudhurst, Kent, TN17 1AD, England (home). *Telephone:* (1580) 211114 (home). *E-mail:* dands.day@virgin.net.

DAY, Doris; American actress and singer; b. (Doris Mary Anne von Kappelhoff), 3 April 1924, Cincinnati, Ohio; d. of Frederick Wilhelm and Alma Sophia von Kappelhoff; m. 1st Al Jorden 1941 (divorced 1943); one s.; m. 2nd George Weilder 1946 (divorced 1949); m. 3rd Marty Melcher 1951 (died 1968); m. 4th Barry Comden 1976 (divorced 1981); professional dancing appearances, Doherty and Kappelhoff, Glendale, Calif.; singer, Karlin's Karnival, radio station WCPO; singer with bands, Barney Rapp, Bob Crosby, Fred Waring, Les Brown; singer and leading lady, Bob Hope radio show (NBC) 1948–50; f. Doris Day Animal Foundation 1998; Founder and Pres. Doris Day Animal League; Laurel Award, Leading New Female Personality in Motion Picture Industry 1950, Top Audience Attractor 1962, American Comedy Lifetime Achievement Award 1991, Grammy Award for Lifetime Achievement 2008. *Achievements include:* oldest artist to achieve a UK Top 10 hit album featuring new material (My Heart), entering at No. 9 Sept. 2011. *Recordings:* albums: You're My Thrill 1949, Tea for Two 1950, Lullaby of Broadway 1951, On Moonlight Bay 1951, I'll See You in My Dreams 1951, By the Light of the Silvery Moon 1953, Young Man with a Horn 1954, Day Dreams 1955, Day in Hollywood 1955, Young at Heart 1955, Love Me or Leave Me 1955, Most Happy Fella 1956, Day by Day 1957, Hooray for Hollywood Vols I and II 1959, Cuttin' Capers 1959, Day by Night 1959, Boys and Girls Together 1959, Hot Canaries 1959, Lights Cameras Action 1959, Listen to Day 1960, Show Time 1960, What Every Girl Should Know 1960, I Have Dreamed 1961, Bright and Shiny 1961, You'll Never Walk Alone 1962, Duet 1962, The Best of Doris Day 2002, My Heart (compilation of previously unreleased recordings produced by her son, Terry Melcher, prior to his death in 2004) 2011; singles: Day by Day 1949, Sugarbush 1952, Secret Love 1954, The Black Hills of Dakota 1954, If I Give My Heart to You 1954, Ready Willing and Able 1955, Whatever Will Be Will Be (Que Sera Sera) 1956, Move Over Darling 1964. *Films include:* Romance on the High Seas 1948, My Dream is Yours 1949, Young Man with a Horn 1950, Tea for Two 1950, West Point Story 1950, Lullaby of Broadway 1951, On Moonlight Bay 1951, I'll See You in My Dreams 1951, April in Paris 1952, By the Light of the Silvery Moon 1953, Calamity Jane 1953, Lucky Me 1954, Yankee Doodle Girl 1954, Love Me or Leave Me 1955, The Pajama Game 1957, Teacher's Pet 1958, The Tunnel of Love 1958, It Happened to Jane 1959, Pillow Talk 1959, Please Don't Eat the Daisies 1960, Midnight Lace 1960, Lover Come Back 1962, That Touch of Mink 1962, Jumbo 1962, The Thrill of It All 1963, Send Me No Flowers 1964, Do Not Disturb 1965, The Glass Bottom Boat 1966, Caprice 1967, The Ballad of Josie 1968, Where Were You When the Lights Went Out? 1968, With Six You Get Egg Roll 1968, Sleeping Dogs, Hearts and Souls 1993, That's Entertainment III 1994. *Television includes:* Doris Day Show (CBS) 1952–53, 1968–72, The Governor & J.J. (series) 1970, The Pet Set 1972, Doris Day and Friends 1985–86, Doris Day's Best 1985–86. *Publication:* Doris Day: Her Own Story (autobiog., with A. E. Hotchner) 1975. *Address:* c/o Doris Day Animal Foundation, 8033 Sunset Boulevard, Suite 845, Los Angeles, CA 90046, USA. *Website:* www.dorisday.com.

DAY, Sir (Judson) Graham, Kt, ONS, QC, JD, LLD; Canadian/British lawyer and business executive; *Of Counsel, Stewart McKelvey;* b. 3 May 1933; s. of Frank C. Day and Edythe G. Day (née Baker); m. L. Ann Creighton 1958; one s. two d.; ed Queen Elizabeth High School, Halifax, NS and Dalhousie Univ., Halifax; pvt. law practice, Windsor, NS 1956–64; Canadian Pacific Ltd, Montreal and Toronto 1964–71; Deputy Chair. Org. Cttee for British Shipbuilders and Deputy Chair. and Chief Exec. desig., British Shipbuilders 1975–76; Prof. of Business Studies and Dir Canadian Marine Transportation Centre, Dalhousie Univ. 1977–81; Vice-Pres. Shipyards and Marine Devt, Dome Petroleum Ltd 1981–83; Chair. and CEO British Shipbuilders 1983–86; Chair. and CEO The Rover Group (fmrly BL) PLC 1986–91, CEO 1986–88; Dir Cadbury Schweppes PLC 1988–93, Chair. 1989–93 (retd); Deputy Chair. MAI 1989–93; Chair. British Aerospace 1991–92, PowerGen 1990–93 (retd), Sobeys Inc. 2001–04; currently Of Counsel, Stewart McKelvey LLP (law firm); Herbert Lamb Chair in Business Educ., Dalhousie Univ. Graduate Business School; Special Consultant to Ashurst Morris Crisp 1994–96; mem. Bd of Dirs Jacques Whitford, Extendicare Canada Inc., The Laird Group PLC 1985–98, NOVA Corpn of Alberta 1990–2000; Chair. Exec. Cttee Bank of NS (Canada) 1989–2004; Pres. Inc. Soc. of British Advertisers 1991–93; Dir (non-exec.) Ugland Int. Holdings (Deputy Chair. 1997–2000); Lead Dir DHX Media Ltd 2006; Dir (non-exec.) Scotia Investments Ltd 2004–11 (Chair. 2008–11), The CSL Group Inc. 2000–11; Hon. Fellow, Cardiff Univ. 1990; Hon. Col West Nova Scotia Regt 2005–11, Canadian Forces Legal Br. (JAG) 2011–; Dr hc (Humberside) 1992 and numerous other hon. degrees. *Television:* mem. original cast, later Musical Dir, Singalong Jubilee (CBC). *Leisure interests:* reading, lakeside chalet in Canada. *Address:* Stewart McKelvey, Suite 900, Purdy's Wharf Tower One, 1959 Upper Water Street, PO Box 997, Halifax, NS, B3J 2X2, Canada (office). *Telephone:* (902) 420-3376 (office). *Fax:* (902) 684-3880 (office). *E-mail:* sirgraham@win.eastlink.ca (office). *Website:* www.smss.com (office).

DAY, Julian, MA, MBA; British retail executive; *Chairman and CEO, Radio-Shack Corporation;* m.; two s.; ed Univ. of Oxford, London Business School; began career providing man. services for a variety of cos including Kohlberg, Kravis and Roberts; fmr Dir European Devt Chase Manhattan Bank; Pres. and CEO Bradley Printing Co. –1992; Exec. Vice-Pres. and Chief Financial Officer Safeway Inc. 1992–98; Exec. Vice-Pres. and Chief Financial Officer Sears, Roebuck and Co. 1999–2000, Exec. Vice-Pres. and COO 2000; Pres. and COO Kmart Holding Co. 2002–03, Pres. and CEO 2003–04, mem. Bd of Dirs Sears Holding Corpn (after meger of Kmart and Sears, Roebuck and Co.) 2004–06; Chair. and CEO RadioShack Corpn 2006–. *Leisure interests:* running, surfing, fitness. *Address:* RadioShack Corporation, 300 RadioShack Cir., Fort Worth, TX 76102, USA (office). *Telephone:* (817) 415-3011 (office). *Fax:* (817) 415-2647 (office). *Website:* www.radioshack.com (office).

DAY, Peter, MA, DPhil, FRS, FRSC, FInstP; British chemist and academic; *Professor Emeritus of Chemistry, University College London;* b. 20 Aug. 1938, Wrotham, Kent, England; s. of Edgar Day and Ethel Hilda Day (née Russell); m. Frances Mary Elizabeth Anderson 1964; one s. one d.; ed Maidstone Grammar School, Wadham Coll., Oxford; Cyanamid European Research Inst., Geneva 1962; Jr Research Fellow, St John's Coll., Oxford 1963–65, Tutor 1965–91; Departmental Demonstrator Univ. of Oxford 1965–67, Lecturer in Inorganic Chem. 1967–89; Oxford Univ. Prof. Associé de Paris-Sud 1975; Guest Prof., Univ. of Copenhagen 1978, Visiting Fellow, ANU 1980; Du Pont Lecturer, Indiana Univ. 1988; Sr Research Fellow, SRC 1977–82; mem. Neutron Beam Research Cttee Science and Eng Research Council 1983–88, Chem. Cttee 1985–88, Molecular Electronics Cttee 1987–88, Nat. Cttee on Superconductivity 1987–88, Materials Comm. 1988–90, Medicines Comm. 1998–2005; Vice-Pres. Dalton Div., Royal Soc. of Chem. 1986–88; Dir Inst. Laue-Langevin, Grenoble 1988–91; Dir Royal Inst. and Davy Faraday Research Lab. 1991–98, Fullerian Prof. of Chem. 1994–2008, Prof. Emer. 2008–; Visiting Prof., Univ. Coll., London 1991, Royal Inst. Research Fellow 1995–2008, Prof. Emer. of Chem. 2008–; mem. Academia Europaea, Treas. 2000–09; Fellow, IUPAC 2009; Hon. Foreign mem. Indian Acad. of Science, Materials Research Soc. of India, Hon. Fellow, Wadham Coll., Oxford 1991, St John's Coll., Oxford 1996, Univ. Coll. London 2002; Hon. DSc (Newcastle) 1994, (Kent) 1999; Royal Soc. of Chem. Corday-Morgan Medal 1971, Solid State Chem. Award 1986, Royal Soc. Blackett Memorial Lecturer 1994, Daiwa Adrian Prize 1999, Bakerian Lecturer 1999, Humphry Davy Lecturer 2002. *Publications:* Physical Methods in Advanced Inorganic Chemistry (co-author) 1968, Electronic States of Inorganic Compounds 1974, Emission and Scattering Techniques 1980, Electronic Structure and Magnetism of Inorganic Compounds (Vols 1–7) 1972–82, The Philosopher's Tree 1999, Nature Not Mocked 2005, Molecules Into Materials 2007, On the Cucumber Tree 2012; numerous papers on inorganic chem. in learned journals. *Leisure interest:* driving slowly through rural France. *Address:* Chemistry Department, University College London, 20 Gordon Street, London, WC1H 0AJ (office); 16 Dale Close, Oxford, OX1 1TU, England (home). *Telephone:* (20) 7679-7466 (office); (20) 7679-0072 (office). *Fax:* (20) 7670-2958 (office). *E-mail:* p.day@ucl.ac.uk (office); pday@ri.ac.uk (office). *Website:* www.ucl.ac.uk/chemistry/staff/emeritus/peter_day (office).

DAY, Peter Rodney, PhD; American (b. British) agricultural scientist (retd); b. 27 Dec. 1928, Chingford, Essex, England; s. of Roland Percy Day and Florence Kate (née Dixon); m. Lois Elizabeth Rhodes 1950; two s. one d.; ed Chingford County High School and Birkbeck Coll., Univ. of London; John Innes Inst. 1946–63; Assoc. Prof., Ohio State Univ., Columbus, USA 1963–64; Chief, Genetics Dept, Conn. Agricultural Experiment Station, New Haven 1964–79; Dir Plant Breeding Inst., Cambridge, UK 1979–87; Prof. of Genetics and Dir Biotechnology Center for Agric. and the Environment, Rutgers Univ. 1987–2001; Special Professorship, Univ. of Nottingham 1981–87; Sec. Int. Genetics Fed. 1984–93; Pres. British Soc. for Plant Pathology 1985; Chair. Cttee on Managing Global Genetic Resources, NAS, USA 1986–94; mem. Exec. Cttee, Norfolk Agricultural Station 1980–1987, Cttee on Genetic Experimentation, Int. Council of Scientific Unions 1984–93, Bd of Trustees, Int. Centre for Maize and Wheat Improvement, 1986–92, panel mem. Int. Food Biotechnology Council 1988–90; Fellow, American Phytopathological Soc.; Commonwealth Fund Fellow, Univ. of Wisconsin 1954–56; John Simon Guggenheim Memorial Fellow, Univ. of Queensland 1972; non-resident Fellow, Noble Foundation, Ardmore, Okla 1991–97; Visiting Fellow, Japan Soc. for the Promotion of Science 1998; Frank Newton Prize, Birkbeck Coll., Univ. of London 1950. *Publications:* Fungal Genetics (with J. R. S. Fincham) 1963,

Genetics of Host-Parasite Interactions 1974, Plant-Fungal Pathogen Interaction: A Classical and Molecular View (with Hermann Prell) 2001; more than 100 scientific papers. *Leisure interests:* music, Scottish country dancing, birdwatching. *Address:* 8200 Tarsier Avenue, New Port Richey, FL 34653-6559, USA (home). *Telephone:* (727) 372-6382 (home). *Fax:* (727) 372-6382 (home). *E-mail:* p1rd@verizon.net (home).

DAY, Hon. Stockwell Burt; Canadian consultant and fmr politician; *CEO, Stockwell Day Connex Limited;* b. 16 Aug. 1950, Barrie, Ont.; s. of Stockwell Day and Gwendolyn Day (née Gilbert); m. Valorie Martin 1971; three s.; auctioneer, Alberta 1972–74; Dir Teen Challenge Outreach Ministries, Edmonton, Alberta 1974–75; contractor, Commercial Interiors, Alberta 1976–78; School Admin., Asst Pastor, Bentley (Alberta) Christian Centre 1978–85; mem. Legis. Ass. Alberta, Edmonton 1986–2000; MP for Okanagan—Coquihalla 2000–11; Minister of Labour 1992–96, of Family and Social Services 1996–97; Prov. Treas., Ministry of Finance, Acting Premier 1997–2000; Leader, Official Opposition of Canada, Canadian Alliance 2000–02 (merged with Progressive Conservative Party of Canada to become Conservative Party of Canada 2003); Minister for Public Safety and Emergency Preparedness Canada 2006–08, for Int. Trade 2008–10, of Asia Pacific (Chair. Cabinet Cttee on Afghanistan), Pres. of the Treasury Bd 2010–11; Founder Stockwell Day Connex Ltd (consultancy); Sr Strategic Advisor, McMillan LLP; Dir, Telus, RCI Capital,WesternOne Equity, Eminata Group, Baylin Technologies, Canada-India Business Council; Vice-Chair. Canada-China Business Council; Distinguished Fellow, Asia Pacific Foundation; commentator, CBC Television; numerous publs; Hon. PhD (Trinity Western Univ.), (Univ. of St Petersburg). *Leisure interests:* marathon running, ocean kayaking, back-packing, reading, chess. *Address:* Stockwell Day Connex Ltd, Unit #112, 142-757 West Hastings Street, Vancouver, BC V6C 3M2, Canada (office). *Telephone:* (604) 800-9227 (office); (778) 214-0577 (office). *Fax:* (604) 685-7084 (office). *E-mail:* stockwellday@stockwellday.com (office).

DAY-LEWIS, Daniel; Irish actor; b. 29 April 1957, London, England; s. of Cecil Day-Lewis and Jill Balcon; m. Rebecca Miller 1996; two s.; one s. by Isabelle Adjani; ed Sevenoaks School, Sherington, SE London, Bedales and Bristol Old Vic Theatre School; Hon. DLit (Bristol) 2010; Berlinale Camera Award, Berlin Film Festival 2005. *Plays include:* Class Enemy, Funny Peculiar, Bristol Old Vic; Look Back in Anger, Dracula, Little Theatre, Bristol and Half Moon Theatre, London; Another Country, Queen's Theatre; Futurists, Nat. Theatre; Romeo, Thisbe, RSC, Hamlet 1989. *Films include:* Sunday Bloody Sunday (uncredited) 1971, Gandhi 1982, The Bounty 1984, My Beautiful Laundrette 1985, A Room with a View 1985, Nanou 1986, The Unbearable Lightness of Being 1988, Stars and Bars 1988, Eversmile, New Jersey 1989, My Left Foot (Acad. Award for Best Actor, BAFTA Award, Best Actor) 1989, The Last of the Mohicans 1992, The Age of Innocence 1993, In the Name of the Father 1993, The Crucible 1996, The Boxer 1997, Gangs of New York (Screen Actors Guild Award for Best Actor 2003, BAFTA Award for Best Actor in a Leading Role 2003) 2002, The Ballad of Jack and Rose 2005, There Will Be Blood (numerous awards, including Acad. Award for Best Actor 2008, Golden Globe for Best Actor in a Drama 2008, Outstanding Performance by a Male Actor in a Leading Role, Screen Actors Guild 2008) 2007, Nine 2009, Lincoln (Golden Globe Award for Best Actor in a Motion Picture – Drama 2013, BAFTA Award for Best Actor in a Leading Role 2013, Acad. Award for Best Actor 2013) 2012. *Television includes:* Shoestring (series) 1980, Thank You, P.G. Wodehouse (film) 1981, Artemis 81 (film) 1981, How Many Miles to Babylon? (film) 1982 Frost in May (mini-series) – Beyond the Glass 1982, BBC Play of the Month (series) – Dangerous Corner 1983, My Brother Jonathan (film) 1985, Screen Two (series) – The Insurance Man 1986. *Address:* c/o Victoria Belfrage, Julian Belfrage Associates, 3rd Floor, 9 Argyll Street, London, W1F 7TG, England (office). *E-mail:* email@julianbelfrage.co.uk (office). *Website:* www.julianbelfrage.com (office).

DAYAN, Edouard; French international organization official; Head of Air Transport Bureau 1984–86; held positions successively as Head Int. Mail Man. Dept, Int. Accounting Dept and Int. Partnership Strategy Dept, La Poste 1986–92, Deputy Dir of European and Int. Affairs 1993–97, Dir 1998–2005; Postal Expert, European Comm. 1992–93; Dir-Gen. UPU 2005–13; apptd Chair. European Social Dialogue Cttee 1994; Chair. Tech. Cooperation Action Group, UPU 2001, also Chair. Quality of Service Fund Cttee and Bd of Trustees; fmr mem. Bd of Man. PostEurop; Chevalier, Légion d'honneur, Ordre nat. du Mérite. *Address:* c/o Universal Postal Union, International Bureau, CP 13, 3000 Berne 15, Switzerland.

DAYANANDA, Mahendra; Sri Lankan business executive; *Chairman, B.P. de Silva Investments Limited;* Exec. Dir 1872 Clipper Tea Co. Ltd, B.P. De Silva Holdings Ltd; Dir Capital Suisse Asia, Risis Ltd, De Silva (Ceylon) Ltd; Chair. Tea Tang Ltd 1992–2006; Chair. B.P. de Silva Investments Ltd, Lewis Brown & Co. Ltd, Total Tea Concepts (Pvt.) Ltd, Indo Asia Teas (Pvt.) Ltd; Vice-Chair., then Chair. Colombo Tea Traders' Asscn; fmr Chair. and Deputy Chair. Ceylon Chamber of Commerce; Vice-Pres. Sri Lanka Japan Business Cttee; mem. Nat. Bd of Arbitrators; Ind. Dir (non-exec.) Nestlé Lanka PLC, Chair. Remuneration Cttee 2009–. *Address:* B.P. de Silva Investments Ltd, 18, Charles Drive, Colombo 03, Sri Lanka (office). *Telephone:* (11) 380150 (office). *Fax:* (11) 449352 (office). *Website:* www.bpdesilva.com (office).

DAYTON, Mark Brandt; American politician and state governor; *Governor of Minnesota;* b. 26 Jan. 1947, Minneapolis, Minn.; s. of Bruce Bliss Dayton and Gwendolen May Dayton (née Brandt); m. 1st Alida Rockefeller (divorced); two s.; m. 2nd Janice Haarstick (divorced); ed The Blake School, Minneapolis, Yale Univ.; science teacher, New York City Public Schools 1969–71; counsellor and admin. for social service agency, Boston 1971–75; legis. asst to Walter Mondale, Senator from Minn. 1975–77; mem. staff, Office of Minn. Gov. Rudy Perpich 1977–78; Commr of Econ. Devt, State of Minn. 1978–82, Commr of Energy and Econ. Devt 1982–86; cand. for Senate 1982; elected Minn. State Auditor 1990–94; held key positions in election campaign of Senator Paul Wellstone 1995–96; Senator from Minn. 2001–07, mem. Agric. Cttee, Armed Services Cttee, Rules Cttee, Governmental Affairs Cttee; Gov. of Minnesota 2011–; mem. Exec. Cttee Nat. Govs Asscn; mem. Minnesota Democratic–Farmer–Labor Party, affiliates with the nat. Democratic Party; Pres.'s Award, Nat. Asscn for the Advancement of Colored People (NAACP), Minnesota chapter 1995, Distinguished Citizen Award, Minnesota Veterans of Foreign Wars 1995, Golden Triangle, Minnesota Nat. Farmers Union 2002, 2003,

Legislator of the Year, American Ambulance Asscn 2003, Public Service award, Minnesota State Fed. Council for Exceptional Children 2003. *Address:* Office of the Governor, 130 State Capitol Building, 75 Rev. Dr Martin Luther King Jr Blvd, St Paul, MN 55155 (office); Washington Office of the Governor, State of Minnesota, 1017 8th Street NE, Washington, DC 20002, USA (office). *Telephone:* (651) 201-3400 (St Paul) (office); (202) 236-3717 (DC) (office). *Fax:* (651) 797-1850 (St Paul) (office). *E-mail:* mark.dayton@state.mn.us (office). *Website:* mn.gov/governor (office); www.markdayton.org.

DÉ, Shobhaa; Indian writer, journalist and editor; b. (Shobha Rajadhyaksha), 7 Jan. 1948, Satara, Maharashtra; m. 1st (divorced); m. 2nd Dilip Dé 1984; two s. four d.; ed Queen Mary's School, St Xavier's Coll., Mumbai; fmr model; later copywriter; launched India's first gossip magazine Stardust; also launched magazines Society, Celebrity and TV soap-opera Swabhimaan 1995; columnist, Times of India, Statesman, Sunday Observer; Publisher, Shobha Dé Books, Penguin India 2010–; Kelvinator GR8! Women Awards 2007. *Publications include:* Socialite Evenings 1989, Sisters 1992, Strange Obsessions 1993, Uncertain Liaisons 1993, Shooting From the Hip: Selected Writings 1994, Sultry Days 1994, Snapshots 1995, Small Betrayals (short stories) 1995, Second Thoughts 1996, Surviving Men 1998, Selective Memory: Stories From My Life 1998, Speedpost 1999, Socialite Evenings 2005, Sisters 2005, Starry Nights 2005, Spouse: The Truth about Marriage 2005, Superstar India 2008, Sandhya's Secret 2009, articles and columns in newspapers and magazines. *Leisure interests:* music, dancing, movies, reading. *Address:* c/o Marketing and Promotions Department, Penguin Books India Pvt. Ltd, 11 Community Centre, Panchsheel, Park, New Delhi 110 017, India (office). *E-mail:* publicity@in.penguingroup.com (office). *Website:* www.penguinbooksindia.com; shobhaade.blogspot.com.

DE ALVEAR, Helga; German-born art collector and gallery curator; *Director, Galería Helga de Alvear;* f. Galería Helga de Alvear, located in 700m space nr the Reina Sofia Nat. Museum Art Centre, Madrid, focuses on photography, video and installations, as well as other media used by conceptual and minimalist artists, artists represented include Helena Almeida, Slater Bradley, Angela Bulloch, James Casebere, José Pedro Croft, Ángela de la Cruz, Michael Elmgreen & Ingar Dragset, Alicia Framis, Katharina Grosse, Axel Hütte, Prudencio Irazabal, Isaac Julien, Jürgen Klauke, Imi Knoebel, Ester Partegás, Dan Perjovschi, Jorge Queiroz, Santiago Sierra, D.J. Simpson, Frank Thiel, Jane & Louise Wilson; endowed foundation in Cáceres with 2,500-strong collection of works by Flavin, Judd, Smithson and numerous contemporary int. and Spanish artists. *Address:* Galería Helga de Alvear, Doctor Fourquet 12, 28012 Madrid, Spain (office). *Telephone:* (91) 468-05-06 (office). *Fax:* (91) 467-51-34 (office). *E-mail:* galeria@helgadealvear.com (office). *Website:* www.helgadealvear.com (office).

DE ARAÚJO, Fernando; Timor-Leste politician and fmr acting head of state; *Speaker, National Parliament;* b. 1963; m. Jacqueline Aquino Siapno; fmr youth resistance leader; arrested for subversion 1991, imprisoned (with collaborator Xanana Gusmao) for six years in Cipinang Prison, Jakarta; f. Resistencia Nacional dos Estudantes de Timor-Leste (RENETIL); Founder and fmr Leader Partido Democrático (Democratic Party); unsuccessful cand. in presidential election 2007; mem. Nat. Parl. 2007–, Speaker 2007–; Acting Pres. Feb.–April 2008. *Address:* Partido Democrático, 1 Rua Democracia, Pantai Kelapa, Dili, Timor-Leste (office). *Telephone:* 3608421 (office). *E-mail:* flazama@hotmail.com (office).

DE AVILÉS, Victoria Marina Velásquez, LLD; Salvadorean judge and politician; *Minister of Labour and Social Security;* Sec. of Labour 1979–80; lawyer with Social Housing Fund 1983–93; Nat. Human Rights Procurator 1995–2011; Farabundo Marti Nat. Liberation Front cand. for presidency 1998; Judge, Civil Chamber of Supreme Court 2000–03, Constitutional Chamber 2003–09; Minister of Labour and Social Security 2009–. *Address:* Ministry of Labour and Social Security, Centro de Gobierno, Complejo Plan Maestro, Edifs 2 y 3, Alameda Juan Pablo II y 17 Avda Norte, San Salvador, El Salvador (office). *Telephone:* 2209-3700 (office). *Fax:* 2209-3756 (office). *E-mail:* informacion@mtps.gob.sv (office). *Website:* www.mtps.gob.sv (office).

DE BEAUCÉ, Thierry Martin; French fmr government official; b. 14 Feb. 1943, Lyon; s. of Bertrand Martin de Beauce and Simone de la Verpillère; two d.; ed Univ. of Paris and Ecole Nat. d'Admin; civil admin., Ministry of Cultural Affairs 1968–69; seconded to Office of Prime Minister 1969–73; Tech. Adviser, Pvt. Office of Pres. of Nat. Ass. 1974; seconded to Econ. Affairs Directorate, Ministry of Foreign Affairs 1974–76; Cultural Counsellor, Japan 1976–78; Second Counsellor, Morocco 1978–80; Vice-Pres. for Int. Affairs Société Elf Aquitaine 1981–86; Dir-Gen. of Cultural, Scientific and Tech. Relations, Ministry of Foreign Affairs 1986–87; State Sec. attached to Minister of Foreign Affairs 1988–91; Adviser to Pres. on African Affairs 1991–94; Vice-Pres. Conf. on Yugoslavia 1992; Amb. to Indonesia 1995–97; Dir of Int. Affairs, Vivendi 1997–2000; Chevalier, Légion d'honneur. *Publications:* Les raisons dangéreuses (essay) 1975, Un homme ordinaire (novel) 1978, L'Ile absolue (essay) 1979, Le désir de guerre 1980, La chute de Tanger (novel) 1984, Nouveau discours sur l'universalité de la langue française 1988, Le livre d'Esther 1989, La République de France 1991, La Nonchalance de Dieu 1995. *Address:* 45 rue de Richelieu, 75001 Paris, France.

DE BELOT, Jean Marie Louis, MA; French journalist and editor; b. 15 Dec. 1958, Neuilly-sur-Seine; s. of Philippe de Belot and Claude de Belot (née Vimal-Dessaignes); m. Frédérique Brunet 1983; two s. three d.; ed Univ. of Paris II-Panthéon Assas; journalist, La Tribune de l'economie 1984; journalist then Chief Econ. Reporter, Le Figaro 1985, Chief Reporter, Expansion Group 1987, Chief of Financial Services 1990, Editorial Dir 2000–04; Jt Chief Ed. Les Echos 1992, Chief Econ. Ed. 1998; Vice-Pres. and Partner Euro RSCG 2005–07; f. Aria Partners (public relations co.) 2007. *Publications:* La chute d'un agent de change: L'affaire Baudouin 1989. *Address:* Aria Partners, 3, Avenue Hoche, 75008 Paris, France. *Website:* www.aria-partners.com.

DE BENEDETTI, Carlo; Italian/Swiss business executive; *Chairman, Gruppo Editoriale L'Espresso SpA;* b. 14 Nov. 1934, Turin; m. Margherita Crosetti 1960; three s.; ed Turin Polytechnic; with Compagnia Italiana Tubi Metallici Flessibili 1959; Chair. and CEO Gilardini 1972–76; Dir Euromobiliare Finance Co. 1973–, Vice-Chair. 1977–; f. Compagnia Industriali Riunite (CIR) 1976, Vice-Chair. and CEO 1976–95, Chair. 1995–2009, Hon. Chair. 2009–; f. Finco 1976 (renamed Cofide–Compagnia Finanziaria De Benedetti 1985), Vice-Chair. and CEO

1976–91, Chair. 1991–; Vice-Chair. and CEO Olivetti & Co. SpA 1978–83, Chair. and CEO 1983–96, Hon. Chair. 1996–99; Dir SMI SpA 1983–; Chair. Cerus (Paris) 1986–; Chair. Sogefi; f. CDB Web Tech 2000, Exec. Chair. 2000–; f. Rodolfo Debenedetti Foundation 1998, Chair. 1998–; Vice-Chair. European Round Table of Industrialists, Brussels –2004; Vice-Pres. Confindustria 1984–; mem. Int. Council, Morgan Guaranty Trust 1980–; Chair. Fondiara 1989–; controlled Editore Arnoldo Mondadori 1990, half-share 1991–; f. Management & Capitali (investment firm) 2005; Chair. Gruppo Editoriale L'Espresso SpA 2006–; Co-Chair. Council for USA and Italy; mem. Supervisory Bd, Compagnie Financière Edmond de Rothschild Banque, Paris 2008–; mem. European Advisory Cttee, NY Stock Exchange 1985–2005; fmr mem. Int. Council, Centre for Strategic and Int. Studies, Int. Advisory Council, China Int. Trust and Investment Corpn, Beijing, Royal Swedish Acad. of Eng Science, Italian Council, European Inst. of Business Admin; Cavaliere del Lavoro 1983, Officier, Légion d'honneur 1987; Hon. LLD (Wesleyan Univ.) 1986. Publications: L'Avventura della Nuova Economia 2000, lectures and articles in business journals. Address: Gruppo Editoriale L'Espresso SpA, Via Cristoforo Colombo n. 98, 00147 Rome, Italy (office). Website: www.gruppoespresso .it (office).

DE BERNARDIS, Paolo, BSc, PhD; Italian astrophysicist and academic; Professor, Università di Roma 'La Sapienza'; b. 1 Feb. 1959, Florence; ed Università di Roma 'La Sapienza'; Researcher, Università di Roma 'La Sapienza' 1984–92, Assoc. Prof. 1992–2001, Full Prof. 2001–; Co-investigator, int. experiments Archeops, MAXIMA and BOOMERanG on the Cosmic Microwave Background; Co-investigator, High Frequency Instrument, ESA Planck Satellite, in charge of cryogenic pre-amplifiers of all Planck-HFI detectors; mem. ESA Astronomy Working Group 2002–04; fmr referee, Astrophysical Journal, Astronomy and Astrophysics, Nature; Ed. Journal of Cosmology and Astroparticle Physics, Memorie della Società Astronomica Italiana; Premio Feltrinelli, Accad. dei Lincei 2001, Balzan Prize for Observational Astronomy and Astrophysics 2006. Publications: more than 100 papers in scientific journals on experimental astrophysics and cosmology, especially the Cosmic Microwave Background. Address: Laboratori di fisica, Edificio E. Fermi, stanza 6, piano 1, Gruppi/Servizi G31, Università degli Studi di Roma 'La Sapienza', P. le Aldo Moro 5, Rome, 00185, Italy (office). Telephone: (06) 49914271 (office). Fax: (06) 4957697 (office). E-mail: debernardis@roma1.infn.it (office). Website: www.uniroma1.it (office); oberon .roma1.infn.it/boomerang/b2k (office).

DE BERNIÈRES, Louis, BA, MA, PGCE; British writer; b. (Louis Henry Piers de Bernière-Smart), 8 Dec. 1954, London; s. of Maj. Reginald Piers Alexander de Bernière-Smart; ed Bradfield Coll., Berkshire, Univ. of Manchester, Leicester Polytechnic, Inst. of Educ., Univ. of London; landscape gardener 1972–73; teacher and rancher, Colombia 1974; philosophy tutor 1977–79; car mechanic 1980; English teacher 1981–84; bookshop asst 1985–86; supply teacher 1986–93; mem. Antonius Players 2003–; mem. PEN; Hon. Fellow, Trinity Coll. of Music; Dr hc (Univ. of East Anglia, Deree Univ. of Athens, Univ. of Aberdeen, Inst. of Educ., London); Granta Best of Young British Novelists 1994, Author of the Year award 1997, Whittaker Platinum Award, Millepages Prize for Best Foreign Novel (France) 2006. Plays: Sunday Morning at the Centre of the World 2001, Mr Handel 2010. Publications: novels: (trilogy) The War of Don Emmanuel's Nether Parts 1990, Señor Vivo and the Coca Lord 1991, The Troublesome Offspring of Cardinal Guzman 1992, Captain Corelli's Mandolin (Commonwealth Writers' Prize, Eurasia region 1991) 1994, Red Dog 2001, Birds Without Wings 2004, A Partisan's Daughter 2008; short stories: Labels 1997, A Day Out for Mehmet Erbil 1999, Gunter Weber's Confession 2001; other: The Book of Job 1999, Notwithstanding 2009, Imagining Alexandria (poems) 2013; contrib. to Second Thoughts, Granta. Leisure interests: music, literature, golf, fishing, carpentry, gardening, cats. Address: Lavinia Trevor Agency, 29 Addison Place, London, W11 4RJ, England (office). Telephone: (1986) 788665 (office).

DE BLASIO, Bill, BA, MA; American politician; Mayor of New York City; b. (Warren Wilhelm, Jr), 8 May 1961, New York City; s. of Warren Wilhelm, Sr and Maria (De Blasio) Wilhelm; m. Chirlane McCray 1994; one s. one d.; ed New York Univ., Columbia Univ.; Political Organizer, Quixote Center (social justice org.) 1987; worked for non-profit org. aiming to improve healthcare in Central America; Aide to Deputy Mayor Bill Lynch, New York City 1989; Campaign Man., Hillary Clinton's successful Senate campaign 2000; Regional Dir, US Dept of Housing and Urban Devt 1996–99; City Councilman for Dist 39, New York City Council 2001–09, Chair. Gen. Welfare Cttee; Public Advocate, New York City 2010–; Mayor of New York City 2014–; Democrat. Address: Office of the Mayor, City Hall, New York, NY 10007, USA (office). Website: www1.nyc.gov/office-of-the-mayor (office).

DE BODINAT, Henri, MSc, PhD; French business executive; President, TIME Equity Partners; b. 15 July 1948, Paris; m. Clémence de Lasteyrie 1989; two s. two d.; ed Institut d'études politiques de Paris, Harvard Business School, USA; CEO, Sony Music, France 1985–93; Exec. Vice-Pres. Sony Software Europe 1993–94; fmr Man. Dir Saatchi & Saatchi PLC; Man. Dir, Club Mediterrannée 1994–98; Founder and Man. Dir Cantos Music 1999–2002; Vice-Pres. Arthur D Little 2003–08; Pres. TIME Equity Partners 2009–; mem. Bd of Dirs CCM Benchmark, Thema TV, iConcerts; Co-founder, Actuel magazine. Publications include: Influence in the Multinational Corporation 1977, The State: A Parenthesis in History? 1996. Address: TIME Equity Partners, 18 rue Bayard, 75008 Paris, France (office). Telephone: 1-40-73-87-30 (office). Fax: 1-40-73-78-00 (office). E-mail: hdebodinat@ time-ep.com (office); contact@time-ep.com (office). Website: www.time-ep.com (office).

DE BOECK, Karel, MEcon, MMechEng; Belgian business executive; Chairman of the Management Board and CEO, Dexia SA; ed Catholic Univ. of Leuven; worked at Generale Bank 1976–93, Gen. Man. Retail Marketing 1990–93; joined ASLK-CGER Bank 1993, Gen. Man. Marketing & Retail; apptd Man. Dir Fortis Bank 1999, CEO Commercial & Private Banking, Fortis AG and Fortis (B) SA 2005–06, Chair. Fortis Bank AŞ (fmrly Turk Dis Ticaret Bankasi AŞ) 2005–06, Man. Dir Fortis (a holding of Fortis Bank A.S.), Chief Risk Officer, Ageas SA/NV (fmrly Fortis SA/NV) –2007, CEO Fortis Holdings (UK) Ltd, ABN AMRO Holdings (UK) Ltd, Chief Risk Officer and Regional Co-coordinator of Europe Region of Fortis (B) SA, Regional Co-ordinator of Europe, Fortis AG, CEO Fortis Holding NV –2008, CEO Ageas NV (also called Fortis NV) 2008–09, Exec. Dir Fortis NV

2008–09; Vice-Chair. Man. Bd RBS Holdings NV (fmrly ABN AMRO Holding NV) 2007–08, mem. Man. Bd 2007–08; Chair. Man. Bd and CEO Dexia SA 2012–, CEO Dexia Crédit Local 2012–; Chair. European Financial Man. and Marketing Asscn 2003–06, Belgian Banking Asscn 1999–; Dir, ASLK-CGER Bank 1993–, Fortis Bank AŞ 2005–, Banca Intermobiliare di Investimenti e Gestioni SpA. Address: Dexia SA, Square de Meeûs 1, 1000 Brussels, Belgium (office). Telephone: (2) 213-57-00 (office). Fax: (2) 213-57-01 (office). E-mail: webmaster@dexia.com (office). Website: www.dexia.com (office).

DE BOER, Yvo; Dutch UN official; Executive Secretary, United Nations Framework Convention on Climate Change; b. 1954, Vienna, Austria; s. of a Dutch diplomatist; m.; three c.; ed boarding school in UK, tech. degree in social work in the Netherlands; involved in climate change policies since 1994; worked for UN Centre for Human Settlements (UN-HABITAT); served as Deputy Dir-Gen. for Environmental Protection, Ministry of Housing, Spatial Planning and Environment, as Head of Climate Change Dept; Dir for Int. Affairs, Ministry of Housing, Spatial Planning and Environment –2006; apptd by UN Sec.-Gen. as Exec. Sec. UN Framework Convention on Climate Change (UNFCCC) 2006–; helped prepare EU position in lead-up to negotiations on Kyoto Protocol, assisted in design of internal burden sharing of EU and led dels to UNFCCC negotiations; fmr Vice-Pres. Conf. of Parties to UNFCCC; fmr Vice-Chair. Comm. on Sustainable Devt; fmr mem. China Council for Int. Cooperation on Environment and Devt, Bureau of the Environment Policy Cttee of OECD, Advisory Group of the Community Devt Carbon Fund of the World Bank; fmr mem. Bd of Dirs Centre for Clean Air Policy. Address: UNFCCC, PO Box 260124, 53153 Bonn, Germany (office). Telephone: (228) 815-1000 (office). Fax: (228) 815-1999 (office). E-mail: ydeboer@unfccc.int (office); secretariat@unfccc.int (office). Website: unfccc.int (office).

DE BOER-BUQUICCHIO, Maud, LLD; Dutch lawyer and international organization official; b. 28 Dec. 1944, Hoensbroek; m. Gianni Buquicchio; two s.; ed Leiden Univ.; mem. Legal Secr., Applications Div., European Comm. on Human Rights (ECHR) 1969–71; mem. Pvt. Office of Sec.-Gen. of Council of Europe 1972–77; Prin. Legal Officer, Case Law and Research Div., ECHR Secr. 1977–90, Head of Div. 1990–92; Sec. to First Chamber of ECHR 1992–98; Deputy Registrar, European Court of Human Rights 1998–2002; Deputy Sec.-Gen. Council of Europe 2002–12 (retd); Pres. Missing Children Europe 2013–; mem. Exec. Bd and Man. Bd, Vienna 2012–; Cavaliere Grand'Ufficiale, Ordine Equestre di Sant'Agata (San Marino) 2007; Gold Medal of the Pres. of the Italian Repub. 2007. Publications include: Informationsfreiheit und die audio-visuelle Revolution (co-author) 1989, The Impact of the European Convention on Human Rights and the Rights of Children 1996, Council of Europe Convention to protect women against violence 2008; articles in professional journals and chapters in books on human rights and EU orgs. Address: European Union Agency for Fundamental Rights, Schwarzenbergplatz 11, 1040 Vienna, Austria (office). E-mail: information@fra.europa.eu (office). Website: fra.europa.eu (office).

DE BOGRÁN, María Antonieta Guillén; Honduran politician; First Vice-President; b. 13 July 1955, Tegucigalpa; m. Roberto Bográn Idiáquez; three c.; Dir Instituto Hondureño de Turismo 1990–94; fmr Univ. Prof.; fmr Consultant, Ricardo Ernesto Maduro Andreu Educ. Foundation; fmr Minister of the Presidency; First Vice-Pres. of Honduras 2010–; mem. Partido Nacional. Address: Office of the Vice-President, Palacio José Cecilio del Valle, Blvd Juan Pablo II, Tegucigalpa, Honduras (office).

DE BOISSIEU, Pierre; French economist, diplomatist and international organization official; b. 14 June 1945, Paris; grand-nephew of fmr French pres. Charles de Gaulle; ed École nationale d'Admin, Paris; fmr Amb. to EU; Deputy Sec.-Gen. Council of the EU 1999–2009, Sec.-Gen. 2009–11; Officier, Légion d'honneur 2002, Commandeur, Légion d'honneur 2010.

DE BONO, Edward Francis Charles Publius, DPhil, PhD; British author and academic; b. 19 May 1933; s. of the late Prof. Joseph de Bono and of Josephine de Bono (née O'Byrne); m. Josephine Hall-White 1971; two s.; ed St Edward's Coll., Malta, Royal Univ. of Malta and Christ Church, Oxford; Research Asst, Univ. of Oxford 1958–60, Jr Lecturer in Medicine 1960–61; Asst Dir of Research, Dept of Investigative Medicine, Univ. of Cambridge 1963–76, Lecturer in Medicine 1976–83; Dir Cognitive Research Trust, Cambridge 1971–; Sec.-Gen. Supranational Independent Thinking Org. 1983–; f. Edward de Bono Nonprofit Foundation; Chair. Council, Young Enterprise Europe 1998–; creator of two TV series: The Greatest Thinkers 1981, de Bono's Thinking Course 1982; apptd EU Amb. for Thinking for the Year of Creativity 2009; Hon. Registrar St Thomas' Hosp. Medical School, Harvard Medical School; Hon. Consultant Boston City Hosp. 1965–66; planet DE73 named edebono after him. Publications include: The Use of Lateral Thinking 1967, The Five-Day Course in Thinking 1968, The Mechanism of Mind 1969, Lateral Thinking: A Textbook of Creativity 1970, The Dog Exercising Machine 1970, Technology Today 1971, Practical Thinking 1971, Lateral Thinking for Management 1971, Children Solve Problems 1972, Po: Beyond Yes and No 1972, Think Tank 1973, Eureka: A History of Inventions 1974, Teaching Thinking 1976, The Greatest Thinkers 1976, Wordpower 1977, The Happiness Purpose 1977, The Case of the Disappearing Elephant 1977, Opportunities: A Handbook of Business Opportunity Search 1978, Future Positive 1979, Atlas of Management Thinking 1981, de Bono's Thinking Course 1982, Conflicts: A Better Way to Resolve Them 1985, Six Thinking Hats 1985, Letter to Thinkers 1987, I Am Right You Are Wrong 1990, Positive Revolution for Brazil 1990, Six Action Shoes 1991, Serious Creativity 1992, Teach Your Child to Think 1992, Water Logic 1993, Parallel Thinking 1994, Teach Yourself to Think 1995, Mind Pack 1995, Edward de Bono's Textbook of Wisdom 1996, How to be More Interesting 1997, Simplicity 1998, New Thinking for the New Millennium 1999, Why I Want to be King of Australia 1999, The Book of Wisdom 2000, The de Bono Code 2000, H+ (Plus) A New Religion 2006, Tactics: The Art and Science of Success 2007, How to Have Creative Ideas 2007, Six Frames for Looking at Information, Think–Before it is too late 2009, Reversed Quotations; numerous publs in Nature, Lancet, Clinical Science, American Journal of Physiology. Leisure interests: travel, toys, thinking. Address: L2 Albany, Piccadilly, London, W1V 9RR (office); Cranmer Hall, Fakenham, Norfolk, NR21 9HX, England (home). Website: www.edwarddebono .com.

DE BORTOLI, Ferruccio; Italian journalist; *Editor-in-Chief, Corriere della Sera, RCS MediaGroup;* b. 20 May 1953, Milan; s. of Giovanni De Bortoli and Giancarla Soresini; m. Elisabetta Cordani 1982; one s. one d.; ed Univ. of Milan; journalist 1973–; mem. editorial staff, Corriere d'Informazione 1975–78; Econs Corresp. Corriere della Sera, RCS MediaGroup 1978–85, Ed.-in-Chief, Econs Section 1987–93, Deputy Ed. 1993–96, Ed. 1997–2003, Ed.-in-Chief 2009–; Ed.-in-Chief, L'Europeo (magazine) 1985–86; apptd CEO RCS Libri 2003; apptd Pres. Flammarion 2003; Dir Il Sole 24 Ore 2005–09; Renato Fabrizi Benedict Award 2012. *Leisure interests:* reading, music, skiing. *Address:* RCS MediaGroup, Via Angelo Rizzoli 8, 20132 Milan (office); Via Donatello 36, 20131 Milan, Italy (home). *Telephone:* (02) 25841 (office). *Website:* www.rcsmediagroup.it (office).

DE BOTTON, Alain; Swiss writer; b. 20 Dec. 1969, Zürich; ed Gonville and Caius Coll., Cambridge; Chevalier, Ordre des Arts et des Lettres 2003. *Publications* include: Essays in Love (aka On Love) 1993, The Romantic Movement: Sex, Shopping, and the Novel 1994, Kiss and Tell 1995, How Proust Can Change Your Life: Not a Novel 1997, The Consolations of Philosophy 2000, The Art of Travel (Charles Veillon European Essay Prize, Switzerland 2003) 2002, Status Anxiety 2004; The Architecture of Happiness 2006, The Pleasures and Sorrows of Work 2009, A Week at the Airport: A Heathrow Diary 2009, Religion for Atheists 2012, Art as Therapy (co-author) 2013, The News: a User's Manual 2014; contrib. articles, book and television reviews to various periodicals. *Address:* c/o Caroline Dawnay, United Agents, 12–26 Lexington Street, London, W1F 0LE, England (office). *Telephone:* (20) 3214-0800 (office). *Fax:* (20) 3214-0801 (office). *E-mail:* ohunt@unitedagents.co.uk (office). *Website:* www.alaindebotton.com.

DE BRICHAMBAUT, Marc Perrin; French international organization executive; b. 29 Oct. 1948, Rabat, Morocco; m.; two c.; ed Ecole Normale Supérieur de Saint-Cloud, Institut d'Etudes Politiques and Ecole Nationale d'Admin, Paris; began his career at Conseil d'Etat, first as admin. judge, later as Conseiller d'Etat; posted to New York as Special Asst to UN Under-Sec.-Gen. for Int. Econ. and Social Affairs 1978; adviser to French Foreign Minister 1981–83; Chief of Staff, Ministry of European Affairs 1983–86, Ministry of Foreign Affairs 1984–86; Counsellor, Embassy in Washington, DC 1986–88; Prin. Adviser to Minister of Defence 1988–91; Head of French Del., CSCE (later became OSCE), Vienna 1991–94; Head, Legal Div., Ministry of Foreign Affairs 1994–98; Dir for Strategic Affairs, Ministry of Defence 1998–2005; Sec.-Gen. OSCE 2005–11; mem. Vienna Advisory Council, International Peace Inst. *Address:* c/o Conseil d'Etat, 1 Place du Palais-Royal, 75100 Paris 01 SP, France. *Website:* www.conseil-etat.fr (office).

DE BROGLIE, Prince Gabriel Marie Joseph Anselme; French administrator; *Chancellor, Institut de France;* b. 21 April 1931, Versailles; s. of Prince Edouard de Broglie and Princess Hélène Le Bas de Courmont; m. Diane de Bryas 1953; one s. one d.; ed Ecole Saint-Martin de France, Faculté de droit de Paris and Inst. d'études politiques; Auditor Conseil d'Etat 1960, Counsel 1967; Legal Adviser to Sec.-Gen., Interdepartmental Cttee on matters of European econ. co-operation 1964; Tech. Adviser, Ministry of Social Affairs 1966–68, to Prime Minister 1968–69, Minister of State for Cultural Affairs 1970; Sec.-Gen. Office de Radiodiffusion-Télévision Française 1971, Asst Dir-Gen. 1973; Dir Radio-France 1975–77, Dir-Gen. 1977–79; Pres. Inst. nat. de l'audiovisuel 1979–1981; mem. Haut Conseil de l'Audiovisuel 1972; Pres. Univ. Radiophonique et Télévisuelle Int. 1976–87, Hon. Pres. 1987; Vice-Pres., later Pres. TV Historical Cttee, Haute Autorité de l'Audiovisuel 1981–86 1980; Pres. Comm. Nat. de la Communication et des Libertés 1986–89; Pres. Soc. des Bibliophiles François, Soc. d'histoire diplomatique; Chancellor Institut de France 2006–; mem. Acad. des Sciences Morales et Politiques 1997, Acad. française 2001–, Roxburghe Club of London; Grand Croix de la Légion d'honneur; Chevalier, Ordre nat. du Mérite; Commdr des Arts et des Lettres, des Palmes académiques. *Publications* include: Le Général de Valence ou l'insouciance et la gloire 1972, Ségur sans cérémonie, ou la gaieté libertine 1977, L'histoire politique de la Revue des Deux Mondes 1979, L'Orléanisme, la ressource libérale de la France 1981, Une image vaut dix mille mots 1982, Madame de Genlis (Gobert Prize) 1985, Le français, pour qu'il vive 1986, Guizot (Amb.'s Prize) 1990, Le XIX[e]siècle, l'éclat et le déclin de la France 1995, Mac Mahon 2000. *Leisure interest:* books. *Address:* Institut de France, 23 quai Conti, 75006 Paris (office); 96 rue de Grenelle, 75007 Paris, France (home). *Telephone:* 1-44-41-43-30 (office). *Fax:* 1-44-41-44-34 (office). *E-mail:* secretariat_chancelier@institut-de-france.fr (office).

DE BRUM, Tony A.; Marshall Islands business executive and politician; *Minister of Foreign Affairs;* b. 1945, Likiep Atoll; ed Xavier High School, Micronesia; fmr mem. Ralik-Ratak Democratic Party; mem. Nitijela (Parl.) for Majuro 1984–2000, for Kwajalein Atoll 2007–; fmr Minister of Health and Environment, Minister of Finance 1998–99, of Foreign Affairs 2008, 2014–, Minister in Assistance to Pres. 2012–14; mem. Aelon Kein Ad (AKA) coalition 2007–. *Address:* Ministry of Foreign Affairs, POB 1349, Majuro, MH 96960, Marshall Islands (office). *Telephone:* (625) 3181 (office). *Fax:* (625) 4979 (office). *E-mail:* mofasec@ntamar.net (office).

DE CARLO, Massimo; Italian gallery owner; f. Galleria Massimo De Carlo in Milan 1987, opened in Via Panfilo Castaldi with exhbn of Olivier Mosset, moved to new space in Via Bocconi 1992, and to Viale Corsica 1998, moved to space in Via Ventura 2003, focuses on introducing Italian artists to European and American audiences and American and European artists to Italy; represents artists including John Armleder, Massimo Bartolini, Chris Burden, Maurizio Cattelan, Paul Chan, Spartacus Chetwynd, Steven Claydon, Dan Colen, George Condo, Roberto Cuoghi, Elmgreen & Dragset, Roland Flexner, Gelitin, Thomas Grünfeld, Carsten Höller, Christian Holstad, Rashid Johnson, Elad Lassry, Sol LeWitt, Nate Lowman, Matthew Monahan, Olivier Mosset, Matt Mullican, Steven Parrino, Diego Perrone, Paola Pivi, Jim Shaw, Josh Smith, Ettore Spalletti, Rudolf Stingel, Piotr Uklanski, Kelley Walker, Pei-Ming Yan and Andrea Zittel; opened London gallery 2009. *Address:* Galleria Massimo De Carlo Mdc S.R.L., Via Giovanni Ventura 5, 20134 Milan, Italy (office). *Telephone:* (02) 70003987 (office). *Fax:* (02) 7492135 (office). *E-mail:* info@massimodecarlo.it (office). *Website:* www .massimodecarlo.it (office).

DE CAROLIS, Patrick; French broadcasting executive, journalist, television producer and author; *Presenter, Des Racines et Des Ailes, France 3;* b. 19 Nov. 1953, Arles; s. of Dominique de Carolis and Lucette-Mary Mounier; m. Carol-Anne Hartpence 1980; four c.; ed École Supérieure de Journalisme de Paris; positions

with several TV channels, including TFI, M6, France 5; joined France 3 1974, presenter, Des racines et des ailes programme 1997–2005, 2013–, Le Grand Tour 2012–; Gen. Dir Figaro magazine 2001–04; CEO France Télévisions 2005–10; fmr Chair. Supervisory Bd France 24; f. own film production co., Anaprod 2010; Dir, Musée Marmottan Monet 2013–; mem. Acad. des beaux-arts 2010; Chevalier, Légion d'honneur, Ordre nat. du Mérite; Officier des Palmes académiques, Ordre des Arts et des Lettres; Commdr avec plaque, Ordre de Saint-Grégoire-le-Grand. *Publications:* Conversation (co-author) 2001, Les demoiselles de Provence 2005, Refuge pour temps d'orage 2009, La Dame du Palatin 2011. *Address:* France Televisions, 7 esplanade Henri de France, 75907 Paris Cedex 15, France (office). *Telephone:* 1-56-22-60-00 (office). *Website:* www.francetelevisions.fr (office).

DE CARVALHO, Col Celestino; Guinea-Bissau air force officer and politician; *Minister of National Defence and Fighters for the Country's Freedom;* b. 14 June 1955; s. of Domingos de Carvalho and Josefa Cabral; trained as mil. pilot; fmr Chief of Staff of Air Force; Adviser on Air Force Matters to Armed Forces Chief of Staff 2004; Dir Instituto Nacional de Defesa (Nat. Defence Inst.) –2012; mem. mil. command group which led coup d'état April 2012; Minister of Nat. Defence and Fighters for the Country's Freedom 2012–. *Address:* Ministry of National Defence, Amura, Bissau, Guinea-Bissau (office). *Telephone:* 223646 (office).

DE CASTELLA, (François) Robert, (Deek), MBE, BSc; Australian company director and fmr athlete; *Managing Director, SmartStart Pty Ltd;* b. 27 Feb. 1957, Melbourne; s. of Rolet François de Castella and Ann M. Hall; m. Gayelene J. Clews 1980 (divorced 1998); two s. one d.; m. Theresa de Castella 2003; one d.; ed Xavier Coll., Kew, Monash Univ. and Swinburne Inst. of Tech.; winner, Fukuoka Marathon (world's fastest for out-and-back course) 1981; Marathon Champion, Commonwealth Games, Brisbane 1982; winner Rotterdam Marathon 1983; World Marathon Champion, Helsinki 1983; winner Boston Marathon 1986; winner Commonwealth Games 1986; Dir Australian Inst. of Sport 1990–95; Chair. Health Promotions Bd ACT (Healthpact) 1996–; Man. Dir SmartStart (Australia) Pty Ltd 1997–; Chair. Leisure Australia Foundation 1999–2009; mem. Bd of Dirs Decorp Pty Ltd 1995–, Action Potential 1996–98, RWM Publs 1996–2000, Your Bread Co. Pty Ltd 2003–, Deeks Health Bakery & Cafes; mem. Bd Australian Sports Comm. –1999, Bd Sports Australian Hall of Fame 1997–; Dr hc (Univ. of Sunshine Coast) 2008, (Univ. of Canberra) 2008; Australian of the Year 1983, Sports Australia Hall of Fame, Athletics Australia Hall of Fame 2008. *Publications:* de Castella on Running 1984, Deek, Australia's World Champion 1984, Smart Sport 1996. *Leisure interests:* motorcycling, scuba diving, traditional Okinawian karate. *Address:* IMG, Level 3/480, St Kilda Road, Melbourne, Vic., 3004, Australia (office); SmartStart (Australia) Pty Ltd, PO Box 6127, Phillip DC, ACT 2606, Australia (office). *Telephone:* (3) 9864-1111 (office); (2) 6260-5750 (office). *Website:* www.imgworld.com (office); smartstart.com.au (office). *Fax:* (2) 6260-5799 (office). *E-mail:* deek@smartstart.com.au (office).

DE CASTRO, Manuel (Noli) Leuterio, Jr, BCom; Philippine politician and broadcaster; b. 6 July 1949, Pola, Oriental Mindoro; s. of Inay Nene; ed Pola Cen. School, Pola Catholic High School, Univ. of the East (UE), Manila; began career in broadcasting as field reporter for Johnny de Leon 1976; radio anchorman, DWW 1982–86; joined ABS-CBN 1986, hosted TV programmes Good Morning, Philippines, At Your Service 1986, Magandang Umaga 1987–98, Overseas Limited 1988, TV Patrol, Magandang Gabi... Bayan (Good Evening... Nation) 1998; hosted radio programme Kabayan, My Fellow Filipinos, DZMM (radio station of ABS-CBN); apptd Vice-Pres. DZMM and Head of Production TV Patrol 1999–2001; elected to Senate 2001; Vice-Pres. of the Philippines 2004–10, also Chair. Housing and Urban Devt Coordinating Council. *Address:* c/o Office of the Vice-President, 7th Floor, PNB Financial Center, President Diosdado Macapagal Boulevard, Pasay City 1300, Metro Manila, Philippines (office).

DE CECCO, Marcello, BA, LLB; Italian economist and academic; *Professor of History of Finance and Currency, Scuola Normale Superiore di Pisa;* b. 17 Sept. 1939, Rome; s. of Vincenzo de Cecco and Antonietta de Cecco; m. Julia Maud Bamford; two s.; ed Univ. of Parma, Univ. of Cambridge, UK; Asst Lecturer, Univ. of East Anglia, UK 1967–68; Prof. of Econs, Univ. of Siena 1968–79, European Univ. Inst., Florence 1979–86, Univ. of Rome 'La Sapienza' 1986, Prof. of Monetary Econs 1989; Prof. of History of Finance and Currency, Scuola Normale Superiore di Pisa 2003–; Exec. Dir Monte dei Paschi di Siena 1978–83; Dir Crediop, Rome 1979–81, Italian Int. Bank, London 1980–83; Visiting Scholar, IMF 1994; fmr mem. Inst. for Advanced Study, Princeton, NJ, USA, Center for Int. Affairs and Center for European Studies, Harvard Univ., USA, Wissenschaftskolleg zu Berlin, Germany. *Publications:* Money and Empire: International Gold Standard, 1890–1914 1975, International Economic Adjustment: Small Countries and the European Monetary System 1983, The International Gold Standard 1983, Changing Money 1985, Monetary Theory and Economic Institutions: Proceedings of a Conference Held by the International Economic Association at Fiesole, Florence, Italy (co-author) 1987, Changing Money 1987, A European Central Bank: Perspectives on Monetary Unification After Ten Years of the E.M.S. (co-author) 1989, Managing Public Debt: Index-linked Bonds in Theory and Practice 1997, Markets and Authorities: Global Finance and Human Choice (co-author) 2002. *Address:* Palazzo della Carovana, Piano 4, Studio 108, 56126 Pisa, Italy (office). *Telephone:* (05) 509877 (office). *E-mail:* m.dececco@sns.it (office). *Website:* www.sns.it (office).

DE CESARE, Vittorio; Italian accountant and business executive; *Chairman of the Supervisory Board, Premafin Finanziaria SpA;* b. 31 Aug. 1935, Naples; ed Univ. of Naples; substitute teacher of accounting and bookkeeping, Instituto Tecnico professionale alberghiero di Napoli 1965; employee with Naples shipping co. 1965; employee at major Italian chemical group with responsibility for Admin. Office (man. of corp. issues and tax) 1973–79; practised as Chartered Accountant in Milan 1980; Tech. Consultant for Judge, Civil Court of Milan; has acted as auditor to Supervisory Bd Napoletana Gas SpA; fmr Auditor, Premafin Finanziaria SpA, Chair. Supervisory Bd 2008–. *Address:* Premafin Finanziaria SpA, Via Daniele Manin 37, Milan 20121, Italy (office). *Telephone:* (02) 667041 (office). *E-mail:* info@ primafin.it (office). *Website:* www.premafin.it (office).

DE CHALENDAR, Pierre-André; French business executive; *Chairman and CEO, Compagnie de Saint-Gobain;* b. April 1958; ed École supérieure des sciences économiques et commerciales, École nat. d'admin, Strasbourg; Finance Insp., later

Deputy Dir-Gen. of Energy and Raw Materials, Ministry of Industry and Regional Devt –1989; Vice-Pres., Corp. Planning, Cie de Saint-Gobain 1989–92, Head of European Abrasives Div. 1992–96, also CEO Norton Abrasifs Europe (subsidiary co.) 1992–96, Pres. Worldwide Abrasives Div., N America 1996–2000, Gen. Del. for Saint-Gobain UK and Ireland 2000–02, CEO Meyer International (following acquisition by Saint-Gobain) 2000, Pres. Building Distribution Sector 2003–05, COO Compagnie de Saint-Gobain 2005–07, mem. Bd 2006–, CEO 2007–, Chair. 2010–; mem. Bd of Dirs Veolia Environnement, BNP Paribas; Chair. Entreprises pour l'Environnement 2012–. *Address:* Compagnie de Saint-Gobain, Les Miroirs, 18 avenue d'Alsace, 92400 Courbevoie, France (office). *Telephone:* 1-47-62-30-00 (office). *Fax:* 1-47-62-50-62 (office). *E-mail:* info@saint-gobain.com (office). *Website:* www.saint-gobain.com (office).

DE CHASSEY, Éric de Buretel; French art historian, art critic and professor of contemporary art; *Director, Académie de France à Rome;* b. 1965, Pittsburgh, Pa, USA; ed École Normale Supérieure; specialist on 20th century abstract art, on photography and on American art; Prof. of Contemporary Art, François Rabelais Univ., Tours; Dir Acad. de France à Rome, Villa Medici 2009–. *Address:* Académie de France à Rome, Villa Medici, Viale Trinità dei Monti 1, 00187 Rome, Italy (office). *Telephone:* (06) 67611 (office). *E-mail:* eric.dechassey@villamedici.it (office). *Website:* www.villamedici.it/en (office).

DE CHASTELAIN, Gen. (Alfred) John Gardyne Drummond, OC, CMM, CH, CD, BA; Canadian (b. British) army officer and diplomatist; b. 30 July 1937, Bucharest, Romania; s. of Alfred George Gardyne de Chastelain and Marion Elizabeth de Chastelain (née Walsh); m. Mary Ann Laverty 1961; one s. one d.; ed Fettes Coll., Edin., UK, Mount Royal Coll., Calgary, Royal Mil. Coll. of Canada, Kingston, British Army Staff Coll., Camberley, Surrey, UK; emigrated to Canada 1955, naturalized 1962; commissioned 2nd Lt, 2nd Bn, Princess Patricia's Canadian Light Infantry (PPCLI) 1960, Capt., ADC to Chief of Gen. Staff, Army HQ 1962–64, Co. Commdr, 1st Bn, PPCLI, FRG 1964–65, Co. Commdr, Edmonton, rank of Maj., later with 1st Bn, UN Force, Cyprus 1968; Brigade Maj., 1st Combat Group, Calgary 1968–70, Commdg Officer, 2nd Bn, PPCLI, Winnipeg 1970–72, rank of Lt-Col, Stagiare, Fed. Bicultural Program, Laval Univ., Quebec 1972–73, Sr Staff Officer, Quartier Gen. Dist, Quebec 1973–74, rank of Col, Commdr Canadian Forces Base, Montreal 1974–76, Deputy Chief of Staff, HQ UN Forces, Cyprus and Commdr Canadian Contingent 1976–77, rank of Brig.-Gen. and apptd Commdt, Royal Mil. Coll. of Canada, Kingston 1977–80, command of 4th Canadian Mechanized Brigade Group, FRG 1980–82, Dir-Gen. Land Doctrine and Operations, Nat. Defence HQ, Ottawa 1982–83, rank of Maj.-Gen. 1983, Deputy Commdr Mobile Command, St Hubert, Quebec 1983–86, rank of Lt-Gen. and apptd Asst Deputy Minister (Personnel) Nat. Defence HQ, Ottawa 1986–88, Vice-Chief, Defence Staff 1988–89, rank of Gen. and apptd Chief of the Defence Staff 1989–93; Amb. to USA 1993; re-apptd Chief of the Defence Staff 1994–95; mem. Int. Body on the Decommissioning of Arms in NI 1995–96, Chair. Business Cttee and Co-Chair. Strand Two Talks, NI Peace Process (leading to the Good Friday Agreement) 1996–98, Chair. Ind. Int. Comm. on Decommissioning (NI) 1997–2011; Col of the Regt, PPCLI 2000–03; Pres. Dominion of Canada Rifle Assen 1986–93; mem. Royal Canadian Legion; Past First Nat. Vice-Pres. Boy Scouts of Canada; mem. St Andrews Soc. of Montreal; Hon. Fellow, Lady Margaret Hall, Oxford 2006; Commdr and Canadian Forces Decoration 1968, Commdr, Order of Mil. Merit 1985, Commdr, Order of St John of Jerusalem (Kts of Malta) 1991, Commendation Medal of Merit and Honour (Greece) 1991, Commdr, US Legion of Merit 1995; Hon. DMilSc (Royal Mil. Coll. of Canada) 1996; Hon. LLD (Royal Roads Univ.) 2002, (Nipissing) 2006, (Carleton) 2006, (Queen's Univ., Kingston) 2007, (St Mary's, Halifax, NS) 2008, (Brock Univ.) 2011; Vimy Award 1992. *Publications:* articles on mil. affairs and int. diplomacy. *Leisure interests:* bagpipes, Scottish country dancing, fishing, painting. *Address:* 170 Acacia Avenue, Ottawa, ON K1M 0R3, Canada.

DE CHATEAUVIEUX, Jacques; French business executive; *Chairman, BOUR-BON;* b. 13 Feb. 1951; ed Institut Supérieur de Gestion, Paris, Columbia Univ., New York, USA; man. auditor, Union des Transports Aériens 1975–77; consultant, Boston Consulting Group (BCG) 1977–79; Chair. and CEO BOURBON 1979–2010, Chair. 2011–; mem. Supervisory Bd AXA Group 2005–, Chair. 2008–10, mem. Bd 2010–; Chair. and CEO JACCAR; Chair. SAPMER, SAGES SAS; mem. Bd of Dirs or Supervisory Bd SINOPACIFIC Shipbuilding Group (China); Non-Man. Partner, Michelin 2011. *Address:* BOURBON, 33 rue du Louvre, 75002 Paris, France (office). *Telephone:* 1-40-13-86-16 (office). *Fax:* 1-40-28-40-31 (office). *E-mail:* bourbon@bourbon-online.com (office). *Website:* www.bourbon-online.com (office).

DE CLERCK, Stefaan Maria Joris Yolanda; Belgian politician; *Mayor of Kortrijk;* b. 12 Dec. 1951, Kortryk; m.; two s. three d.; mem. Parl. (Flemish) 1990–95, (Chamber) 1998–2001; mem. Senate (Flemish) 2003–04, 2004–07, (Chamber) 2007–08; Minister of Justice 1995–98, 2008–11; Nat. Chair. Christelijke Volkspartij (CVP, renamed Christen-Democratisch en Vlaams—CD&V 2001) 1999–2003; Mayor of Kortrijk 2001–. *Publications:* Het bos en de bomen, justitie hervormen (The wood and the trees, reforming justice) 1997, Het open boek: Een boeiend verslag van wat leeft in de regio (The open book: a thrilling report on what lives in the region) (with Luc Martens) 1998–99, Hartslagen Christen-Democratische verkenningen (The heartbeats of Christian-Democrat observations) (co-author) 2000, Voor mensen en waarden (For people and values) 2003. *Address:* Damkaai, 8500 Kortryk, Belgium (home). *Fax:* (2) 542-80-00 (office). *Website:* www.stefaandeclerck.be.

DE CLERCQ, Peter; Dutch UN official; *Deputy Special Representative of the Secretary-General and UN Resident Coordinator and Humanitarian Coordinator, MINUSTAH;* b. 1959; m.; five c.; ed Clingendael, The Hague, Univ. of Tilburg; worked with UNHCR 1985–, held various positions in Geneva, Budapest, covered field assignments in Sudan, Zimbabwe, Angola, Pakistan, Special Adviser on Disarmament Demobilization and Reintegration, UN Org. Mission in Democratic Republic of the Congo (MONUC), Kinshasa, Democratic Republic of the Congo 2001–04, UNDP Senior Return, Reintegration and Recovery Adviser, S Sudan 2004–06, Head of Supply Man., UNHCR 2006–09, Resident Coordinator and Humanitarian Coordinator ad interim, Sudan –2012, Deputy Special Rep. of Sec.-Gen. for Somalia ad interim, UN Political Office for Somalia (UNPOS) 2012–13, Deputy Special Rep. of Sec.-Gen. and UN Resident Coordinator and Humanitarian Coordinator, United Nations Stabilization Mission in Haiti (MINUSTAH) 2013–.

Address: c/o Office of the Secretary-General, United Nations, New York, NY 10017, USA (office). *Telephone:* (212) 963-1234 (office). *Fax:* (212) 963-487 (office). *Website:* www.un.org (office).

DE CONCINI, Dennis, LLB; American lawyer and fmr politician; *Vice-President and Partner, Parry, Romani, De Concini & Symms Associates;* b. 8 May 1937, Tucson, Ariz.; s. of Evo and Ora De Concini; one s. two d.; ed Univ. of Arizona and Univ. of Arizona Coll. of Law; Committeeman, Pima Co. 1958–76; worked with family law practice 1963–65; special counsel to Gov. of Ariz. 1965, Admin. Asst to Gov. 1965–67; Pnr, DeConcini & McDonald, law firm 1968–73; Pima Co. Attorney 1972–76; Admin., Ariz. Drug Control Dist 1975–76; fmr mem. Ariz. Democratic Exec. Cttee, Vice-Chair. 1964, 1970; Senator from Arizona 1977–95, mem. Judiciary Cttee, Appropriations Cttee, Rules Cttee, Special Select Cttee on Indian Affairs, Veterans' Affairs Cttee; mem. Select Cttee on Intelligence, Senate Caucus on Int. Narcotics Control; Vice-Pres. and Pnr, Parry, Romani, De Concini & Symms Assocs., Washington, DC 1995–, DeConcini, McDonald, Yetwin & Lacy, Tucson 1995–; Dir Nat. Center for Missing and Exploited Children 1995–; mem. Académie Française 1993–; Chair. Comm. on Security and Co-operation in Europe; served US Army 1959–60, Judge Advocate Gen. Corps. 1964–67; mem. Arizona Board of Regents 2006–; mem. or fmr mem. Pima Co. Bar Assn, Ariz. Bar Assn, ABA, American Judicature Soc., American Arbitration Assn, Nat. District Attorneys' Assn; mem. Ariz. County Attorneys' and Sheriffs' Assn, Sec.-Treas. 1975, Pres. 1976. *Publication:* Senator Dennis DeConcini: From the Center of the Aisle 2007. *Leisure interests:* golf, boating, jogging. *Address:* Parry, Romani, De Concini & Symms Associates, 517 C Street, NE, Washington, DC 20002 (office); 2525 E Broadway, Suite 111, Tucson, AZ 85716, USA. *Telephone:* (202) 547-4000 (Washington) (office); (520) 325-9600 (Tucson) (office); (858) 459-5460 (LaJolla) (office). *Fax:* (202) 543-5044 (Washington) (office); (520) 327-9744 (Tucson) (office); (858) 459-5471 (LaJolla) (office). *E-mail:* prdands@aol.com (office); d.deconcini@atl .net (office). *Website:* www.lobbycongress.com (office).

DE CORTE, Frans; Belgian physicist and academic; Prof., Dept of Analytical Chem., Inst. for Nuclear Sciences, Univ. of Ghent –2007 (retd); mem. Int. Advisory Bd, Radiochemical Conf. (RadChem), Mariánské Lázně, Czech Repub. 2002; mem. Int. Union of Pure and Applied Chem.; Hevesy Medal 2000.

DE CREM, Pieter Frans Norbert Jozef Raymond; Belgian politician; *Deputy Prime Minister and Minister of Defence;* b. 22 July 1962, Aalter; m. Caroline Bergez; three c.; ed Univ. Catholique de Louvain, Univ. Libre de Bruxelles; worked for Roularta Media Group 1987–89; Pres. youth section of CVP (Christelijke Volkspartij), Gand-Eeklo 1989–95; Attaché, Cabinet of Prime Minister Wilfried Martens 1989–92, Cabinet of Minister of Defence 1992–93; Adviser to De fabrieken van de Gebroeders De Beukelaar 1993–94; elected Mayor of Aalter 1995, re-elected 2000, 2006; elected to Chamber of Reps for Gand-Eeklo (CVP) 1995, re-elected 1999, elected to Chamber of Reps for Flanders East (party renamed Christen-Democratisch en Vlaams—CD&V) 2003, re-elected 2007, Head, CD&V parl. group 2003–07, Pres. Interior Comm. 2007, mem. OSCE parl. cttee; Minister of Defence 2007–; Deputy Prime Minister 2013–; Officier, Ordre de Léopold. *Address:* Office of the Minister of Defence, Lambermont straat 8, 1000 Brussels, Belgium (office). *Telephone:* (2) 25-50-28-11 (office). *E-mail:* info@mod.mil.be (office). *Website:* www .pieterdecrem.be (office).

DE CUENCA Y CUENCA, Luis Alberto; Spanish philologist, poet, translator and writer; b. 1950, Madrid; ed Universidad Autónoma de Madrid; Prof. of Philology Inst. of Council for Scientific Research, then Publs Dir; literary critic for several publs including El País; Dir Biblioteca Nacional (Nat. Library) 1996–2000; Sec. of State for Culture 2000–04; Academician, Academia de Buenas Letras de Granada 2009–, Real Academia de la Historia 2010–; Gran Cruz de Isabel la Católica 2004; Premio de Cultura (Literatura), Madrid 2007. *Publications include:* Los Retratos 1971, Elsinore 1972, scholia 1978, Necrofilia 1983, Breviora 1984, La Caja de Plata 1985, Seis poemas por amor 1986, El otro sueño 1987, Poesía 1970–89 1990, Nausícaa 1992, El héroe y sus máscaras 1991, 77 Poemas 1992, Willendorf 1992, El hacha y la rosa 1993, El desayuno y otros poemas 1993, Los gigantes de hielo 1994, Animales domésticos 1995, Tres poemas 1996, Por fuertes y fronteras 1996, El bosque y otros poemas 1997, En el país de las maravillas 1997, Los mundos y los días 1998, Alicia 1999, Insomnios 2000, Mitologías 2001, Vamos a ser felices y otros poemas de humor y deshumor 2003, El enemigo oculto 2003, El puente de la espada: poemas inéditos 2003, Diez poemas y cinco prosas 2004, Ahora y siempre 2004, Su nombre era el de todas las mujeres y otros poemas de amor y desamor 2005, La vida en llamas 2006, Poesía 1979–1996 2006, A quemarropa 2006, Manantial 2007, Los mundos y los días: poesía 1970–2002 2007, Héroes y villanos del cómic 2007, En la cama con la muerte 25 poemas fúnebres 2011, Nombres propios 2011. *Address:* c/o Biblioteca Nacional, Paseo de Recoletos 22, 28001 Madrid, Spain.

DE ESCOBAR, Ana Vilma Albanez; Salvadorean economist and politician; b. 2 March 1954; m. Carlos Patricio Escobar; one d.; ed Universidad Centroamericana 'José Simeón Cañas'; fmr Product Man. USAID; fmr Prof. of French; Pres. Salvadorean Inst. of Social Security 1999–2003; Vice-Pres. of El Salvador 2004–09; mem. Asamblea Legislativa; mem. Trifinio Trinational Comm. *Address:* c/o Ministry for the Presidency, Avenida Cuba, Calle Darió González 806, Barrio San Jacinto, San Salvador, El Salvador.

DE FERRANTI, Sebastian Basil Joseph Ziani, DL; British electrical engineer; b. 5 Oct. 1927, Alderley Edge, Cheshire; s. of the late Sir Vincent de Ferranti MC and Dorothy H. C. de Ferranti (née Wilson); brother of the late Basil Ziani de Ferranti, MP, MEP; m. 1st Mona Helen Cunningham 1953 (died 2008); one s. two d.; m. 2nd Naomi Angela Rae 1983 (died 2001); m. 3rd Gillian Nadine Brown 2011; ed Ampleforth Coll.; served 4th/7th Dragoon Guards 1947–49; Brown Boveri, Switzerland and Alsthom, France 1948–50; Transformer Dept, Ferranti Ltd 1950, Dir 1954–82, Man. Dir 1958–75, Chair. 1963–82; Dir GEC PLC 1982–97; Pres. BEAMA 1969–70, Manchester and Region Centre for Educ. in Science, Educ. and Tech. 1972–78; Chair. Int. Electrical Assen 1970–73; Vice-Pres. RSA 1980–84; Commr Royal Comm. for Exhbn of 1851 1984–97; Dir Nat. Nuclear Corpn 1984–88; mem. Nat. Defence Industries Council 1969–77; Trustee, Tate Gallery 1971–78; Chair. North-West Civic Trust 1978–83; Chair. Hallé Concerts Soc. 1988–96, Pres. 1997–; High Sheriff of Cheshire 1988–89; Hon. mem. Royal Northern Coll. of Music 1997, mem. Bd of Govs 1988–2000; Hon. Fellow, UMIST; Granada Guildhall

Lecture 1966; Royal Inst. Discourse 1969; Louis Blériot Lecture, Paris 1970; Faraday Lecture 1970, 1971; DL; Hon. DSc (Cranfield Inst. of Tech.) 1973, (Salford Univ.), Hon. LLD (Manchester) 1998. *Address:* Henbury Hall, Macclesfield, Cheshire, SK11 9PJ, England (home). *Telephone:* (1625) 422101. *Fax:* (1625) 614361.

DE FONBLANQUE, John, CMG, MA, MSc,; British diplomatist; b. 20 Dec. 1943, Fleet, Hants; s. of Maj.-Gen. E. B. De Fonblanque and Elizabeth De Fonblanque; m. Margaret Prest 1984; one s.; ed Ampleforth School, King's Coll., Cambridge, London School of Econs; joined FCO 1968, Second Sec. Jakarta 1969–72, Second, later First Sec. to EC, Brussels 1972–77; Prin. HM Treasury 1977–80; FCO 1980–83; Asst Sec. Cabinet Office 1983–86; Head of Chancery, New Delhi 1986, Counsellor (Political and Institutional) Mission to EC, Brussels 1988, Asst Under-Sec. of State Int. Orgs, then Dir Global Issues 1994–98, Dir (Europe) FCO 1998–99, Head of Del. to OSCE with rank of Amb. 1999–2003; Dir Office of OSCE High Commr on Nat. Minorities 2004–06. *Leisure interest:* mountain walking.

DE GEUS, Aart; Dutch lawyer and international organization executive; *Chairman and CEO, Bertelsmann Foundation;* m.; three c.; ed Erasmus Univ., Rotterdam, Nijmegen Univ.; worked as lawyer in industry sector of Christian Trade Union –1988; mem. Exec. Bd Nat. Fed. of Christian Trade Unions 1988–98, Vice-Chair. Exec. Bd 1993–98; pnr in Amsterdam-based co. for strategy and man. 1998–2002; Minister of Social Affairs and Employment 2002–07; Chair. OECD Social Policy Ministerial Meeting 2005, has served in various functions at local, nat. and int. level, Deputy Sec.-Gen. OECD 2007–11, in charge of Political Economy of Reform, and preparations for Ministerial Council Meeting and Exec. Cttee in Special Session; mem. Bd Bertelsmann Foundation 2011–12, Chair. and CEO 2012–. *Address:* Office of the Chairman, Bertelsmann Foundation, Carl-Bertelsmann-Str. 256, 33311 Gütersloh, Germany (office). *Website:* www .bertelsmann-stiftung.de (office).

DE GIORGI, HE Cardinal Salvatore; Italian ecclesiastic; *Archbishop Emeritus of Palermo;* b. 6 Sept. 1930, Vernole; ordained priest 1953; Bishop 1973, Archbishop, See of Oria 1978, of Foggia 1981, of Taranto 1987, of Palermo 1996–2006 (retd), now Archbishop Emer.; elevated to Cardinal Priest of S. Maria in Ara Coeli 1998. *Address:* Curia Arcivescovile, Corso Vittorio Emanuele 461, 90134 Palermo, Italy (office). *Telephone:* (091) 6077248 (office). *Fax:* (091) 581069 (office). *E-mail:* arcivescovo@diocesipa.it (office). *Website:* www.diocesipa.it (office).

DE GLINIASTY, Jean; French diplomatist; *Ambassador to Russia;* b. 27 Sept. 1948; m.; three c.; ed Institut d'Etudes Politiques, Paris, Ecole Nationale d'Admin, Paris; with Cen. Admin (N Africa and Near East), Ministry of Foreign 1975–78, Econ. and Financial Affairs 1978–81, Asst to Chief of Centre of Analysis and Forecast 1981–82, Second Adviser with Perm. Representation of France to European Communities, Brussels 1982–85, with Cen. Admin (Econ. and Financial Affairs), delegated with functions of Deputy Man. 1985–86, N Africa and Middle East, delegated with functions of Deputy Man., N Africa 1986–89, Cultural, Scientific and Tech. Relations, Dir of Devt and Scientific, Tech. and Educational Co-operation 1989–91, Consul Gen. in Jerusalem 1991–95, with Cen. Admin (Political and Security Affairs), Dir UN and Int. Orgs 1995–99, Amb. to Senegal (also accred to The Gambia) 1999–2003, to Brazil 2003–06, with Cen. Admin, Dir of Africa and the Indian Ocean 2003–06, Amb. to Russia 2009–. *Address:* Embassy of France, 119049 Moscow, ul. B. Yakimanka 45, Russia (office). *Telephone:* (495) 937-15-00 (office). *Fax:* (495) 937-14-46 (office). *E-mail:* amba@ambafrance.ru (office). *Website:* www.ambafrance.org/russie (office).

DE GRAAF, Thom Carolus; Dutch politician and fmr civil servant; *Mayor of Nijmegen;* b. 11 June 1957, Amsterdam; m.; two c.; ed Catholic Univ. of Nijmegen; fmr Lecturer in Constitutional Law, Catholic Univ. of Nijmegen; civil servant, Ministry of Interior 1985–94; Deputy Dir for Police Affairs 1991–94; fmr Municipal Councillor, Leiden; mem. De Koning Cttee on Constitutional Reform 1992–93; joined Democraten 66 (D66) 1977, Sec. Nat. Bd 1986–90, Chair. D66 Parl. Group 1997; mem. Parl. 1994–2003; Deputy Prime Minister 2003–05, Minister of Govt Reform and Kingdom Relations 2003–05; Mayor of Nijmegen 2007–. *Leisure interests:* history, poetry, tennis, ice skating. *Address:* Municipality of Nijmegen, PO Box 9105, 6500 HG Nijmegen, Netherlands (office). *Telephone:* (24) 3292408 (office). *E-mail:* openhuis@nijmegen.nl (office). *Website:* www2.nijmegen.nl (office).

DE GRAVE, Franciscus (Frank) Hendrikus Gerardus, DJur; Dutch politician and organization official; *Chairman, Artis Zoo;* b. 27 June 1955, Amsterdam; m.; two c.; ed Univ. of Groningen; Int. Sec. JOVD youth org. 1977–78, Nat. Pres. 1978–80; mem. Volkspartij voor Vrihoid en Democratie (VVD) Parl. group 1977–81; Asst Sec. to Man. Bd AMRO bank 1980–82; Amsterdam City Councillor 1982–86; mem. First Chamber of Parl. 1982–90; Councillor for Finances and Deputy Mayor, Amsterdam City Council 1990–94, acting Mayor Jan.–June 1994; Sec. of State for Social Security and Employment 1996–98; Minister of Defence 1998–2002; Chief Financial Officer DSB Bank March–May 2009; Chair. Artis Zoo, Amsterdam 2008–; mem. Vaste Comm. for Defence 1982–86, Bd Vereniging Nederlandse Gemeenten; fmr Commr RAI, Bank Nederlandse Gemeenten and Amsterdam Arena. *Address:* Artis, Plantage Kerklaan 38-40, 1018 CZ Amsterdam, Netherlands (office). *Telephone:* (900) 2784796 (office). *Fax:* (20) 5233481 (office). *E-mail:* info@artis.nl (office). *Website:* www.artis.nl/international (office).

DE GUCHT, Karel; Belgian politician and international organization official; *Commissioner for Trade, European Commission;* b. 27 Jan. 1954, Overmere; m. Mireille Schreurs; two s.; ed Koninlijk Atheneum Aalst, Free Univ. Brussels; Chair. Liberal Students' Union Brussels 1974–75, Nat. Chair. 1975–77; MEP 1980–94; Vice-Chair. PVV party 1985–88; Senator 1994–95; Nat. Chair. Flemish Liberals and Democrats–Citizens' Party 1999; Minister of State 2002–04, Minister of Foreign Affairs 2004–07 (resgnd), 2007–09; Commr for Devt and Humanitarian Aid, EC 2009–10, Commr for Trade 2010–. *Publications:* De Tijd Wacht op Niemand (co-author; trans. Time and Tide Wait for No Man) 1990, Er Zijn Geen Eilanden Meer: Over Democratie, Vrijheid en Mensenrechten (co-author) 1999, Het Einde of the Pilaren: Een Toscaans Gesprek (co-author) 2001, De Toekomst is Vrij 2002, Vrijheid: Liberalisme in tijden van Cholera 2012. *Address:* European Commission, 200 rue de la Loi, 1049 Brussels, Belgium (office). *Telephone:* (2) 299-11-11 (office). *Fax:* (2) 298-08-99 (office). *Website:* ec.europa.eu (office).

DE GUILLENCHMIDT, Jacqueline, MLaw; French lawyer; *Member, Constitutional Council;* b. 25 Sept. 1943, Beijing, China; d. of Robert Barbara de Labelotterie and France Pasquet du Bousquet de Lauriere; m. Michel de Guillenchmidt 1966; ed Institut d'études politiques de Paris; barrister, Paris 1972–82; Magistrate High Court of Pontoise 1982–85; Judge, Dept of Justice 1985; Bureau Chief of the Commercial Law 1989–92, then in regulation in the conduct of civil affairs and Seal of the Dept of Justice 1992–93; Tech. Advisor to Minister of Justice 1993–94, Deputy Dir of cabinet of Minister of Justice 1994–95; State Councilor 1995; Chair. Comm. for Supervision and Control of Publications for Children and Adolescents 1995–99; Chair. Comm. for Support Fund for Expression Radio 1995–99; mem. Conseil supérieur de l'audiovisuel 1999–2004, Conseil Constitutionnel 2004–; Officier, Légion d'honneur, Ordre nat. du Mérite; Chevalier, Ordre des Palmes académiques, Ordre du Mérite agricole. *Address:* Conseil Constitutionnel, 2 rue de Montpensier, 75001 Paris, France (office). *Telephone:* 1-40-15-30-00 (office). *Fax:* 1-40-20-93-27 (office). *E-mail:* jacqueline .guillenchmidt@gmail.com (office). *Website:* www.conseil-constitutionnel.fr (office).

DE GUINDOS JURADO, Luis Miguel, BSc (Econs), PhD; Spanish economist, academic, business executive and government official; *Minister of Economic Affairs and Competitiveness;* b. 16 Jan. 1960, Madrid; m.; two c.; ed Universidad Complutense de Madrid; Counsellor, Ministry of Economy and Planning 1986, Asst Dir-Gen., Secr.-Gen. of Commerce 1987; Pnr and Dir AB Asesores 1988–96; Dir-Gen. for Econ. Policy and Defence of Competition, Ministry of Economy and Finance 1996–2000, Sec.-Gen. 2000–02, Sec. of State for Econ. Affairs 2002–04, Minister of Econ. Affairs and Competitiveness 2011–; Visiting Prof., Faculty of Econs, Univ. of Navarra 2005; CEO for Spain and Portugal, Lehman Brothers 2006–08; CEO Nomura Securities, Spain 2008; Sr Pnr, PricewaterhouseCoopers Spain 2008–10; Pres. Jury, III Jaime Fernández de Araoz Prize for Corp. Finance 2011. *Address:* Ministry of Economic Affairs and Competitiveness, Alcalá 9, Paseo de la Castellana 162, 28014 Madrid, Spain (office). *Telephone:* (91) 5958000 (office). *Fax:* (91) 5958486 (office). *E-mail:* informacion.alcala@meh.es (office). *Website:* www.meh.es (office).

DE HAVILLAND, Olivia Mary; American (b. British) actress; b. 1 July 1916, Tokyo, Japan; d. of Walter Augustus de Havilland and Lilian Augusta Ruse (stage name Lilian Fontaine); m. 1st Marcus Aurelius Goodrich 1946 (divorced 1953); one s.; m. 2nd Pierre Paul Galante 1955 (divorced 1979); one d.; ed Notre Dame Convent, Los Gatos Union High School; stage debut in A Midsummer Night's Dream 1934, film debut in screen version 1935; Pres. Cannes Film Festival 1965 (first woman); on lecture tours in USA 1971–80; Acad. of Motion Picture Arts and Sciences tribute to her career, Los Angeles 2006; mem. Bd of Trustees of American Coll. in Paris 1970–71, of American Library in Paris 1974–81; mem. Altar Guild, Lay Reader, American Cathedral in Paris 1971–81; Hon. Bd mem. American Library in Paris; Chevalier, Légion d'Honneur 2010; DHumLitt (American Univ. of Paris) 1994; Hon. DLitt (Univ. of Hertfordshire) 1998; numerous awards include Acad. Award 1946, 1949, New York Critics Award 1948, 1949, Look Magazine Award 1942, 1948, 1949, Exhibitor Laurel Award 1948, Winged Victory Award 1950, Women's Nat. Press Club Achievement Award for Outstanding Accomplishment in the Theatre 1950, Prix Femina Belge du Cinéma 1957, American Legion Humanitarian Medal 1967, Filmex Tribute 1978, American Acad. of Achievement Award 1978, American Exemplar Medal 1980, American Acad. of Achievement 25th Anniversary Salute to Excellence Statuette 1986, Golden Globe 1988, Birmingham Southern Coll. Gala XIV Women of Achievement Award 1999, John F. Kennedy Center for the Performing Arts Gold Medal 2005, Los Angeles County Museum Tribute 2006, Viennale: Vienna Int. Film Festival Tribute 2006, Nat. Medal of Arts 2008. *Films include:* Midsummer Night's Dream 1935, Captain Blood 1935, Anthony Adverse 1936, The Adventures of Robin Hood 1938, Gone with the Wind 1939, Hold Back the Dawn 1941, Princess O'Rourke 1942, To Each His Own (Acad. Award, Ciné-Revue Award, Belgium) 1946, The Dark Mirror 1946, The Snake Pit 1947 (Nat. Bd of Review of Motion Pictures Best Actress Award 1948, Brazilian Film Critics' Award 1948, New York Film Critics' Award 1948, Box Office Blue Ribbon Award 1948, San Francisco Film Critics' Award 1948, Silver Mask, Italian Film Critics' Award 1950), The Heiress (Acad. Award 1949, Golden Globe Award 1949, Venice Film Festival Award 1949, New York Film Critics' Award 1949, San Francisco Film Critics' Award 1949, Cité-Revue Award 1950) 1949, My Cousin Rachel 1952, Not as a Stranger 1954, The Proud Rebel 1957, The Light in the Piazza 1961, Lady in a Cage 1963, Hush Hush Sweet Charlotte 1964, The Adventurers 1968, Airport '77 1976, The Swarm 1978, The Fifth Musketeer 1979. *Plays include:* Romeo and Juliet 1951, Candida 1951–52, A Gift of Time 1962. *Television includes:* Noon Wine 1966, Screaming Woman 1972, Roots, The Next Generations 1979, Murder is Easy 1981, Charles and Diana: A Royal Romance 1982, North and South II (mini–series) 1986, Anastasia (Golden Globe Award) 1986, The Woman He Loved 1988. *Publications:* Every Frenchman Has One 1962, Mother and Child (contrib.) 1975. *Leisure interests:* crossword puzzles, reading tales of mystery and imagination, painting on Sunday. *Address:* BP 156-16, 75764 Paris Cedex 16, France.

DE HOOP, Adrianus Teunis, PhD; Dutch professor of electromagnetic theory and applied mathematics; *Lorentz Chair Professor Emeritus, Delft University of Technology;* b. 24 Dec. 1927, Rotterdam; ed Delft Univ. of Tech.; Research Asst, Delft Univ. of Tech. 1950–52, Asst Prof. 1953–56, Assoc. Prof. 1957–60, Prof. 1960–96, Lorentz Chair Prof. Emer. 1996–; Reserve Officer, Royal Netherlands Navy 1952–53; Research Asst, UCLA, USA 1956–57; Visiting Research Scientist, Philips Research Labs, Eindhoven 1976–77, Consultant 1977–89; mem. Royal Netherlands Acad. of Arts and Sciences 1989, Royal Flemish Acad. of Arts and Sciences of Belgium 1998; Hon. PhD (Ghent) 1982, (Vaxjo) 2008; Kt, Order of the Netherlands Lion 2003; awards from Stichting Fund for Science, Tech. and Research 1986, 1989, 1990, 1993, 1994, Gold Research Medal, Royal Inst. of Eng 1989, Heinrich Hertz Medal, IEEE 2001, URSI Balthasar van der Pol Gold Medal 2002. *Publications:* Handbook of Radiation and Scattering of Waves 1995; numerous articles in journals. *Leisure interest:* playing the piano. *Address:* Faculty of Electrical Engineering, Mathematics and Computer Science, Delft University of Technology, Mekelweg 4, 2628 CD Delft (office); Korenmolen 17, 2661 LE Bergschenhoek, Netherlands (home). *Telephone:* (15) 2785203 (office); (10) 5220049 (home). *Fax:* (15) 2786194 (office). *E-mail:* a.t.dehoop@tudelft.nl (office). *Website:* www.atdehoop.com.

DE HOOP SCHEFFER, Jakob Gijsbert (Jaap); Dutch politician and international organization official; *Pieter Kooijmans Chair for Peace, Law and Security, Leiden University;* b. 3 April 1948; m. Jeannine de Hoop Scheffer-van Oorschot; two c.; ed Leiden Univ.; fmr Reserve Officer in Air Force; fmr Sec. Del. of Netherlands to NATO, Brussels; Deputy Parl. Leader Christen-Democratisch Appèl (CDA – Christian Democrats) 1995–97, Leader 1997–2001; Minister of Foreign Affairs 2002–03; Sec.-Gen. NATO 2004–09; Pieter Kooijmans Chair. for Peace, Law and Security, Leiden Univ. 2009–. *Address:* c/o Leiden University, PO Box 9500, 2300 RA, Leiden, The Netherlands (office). *Telephone:* (71) 527-27-27 (office). *Fax:* (71) 527-31-18 (office). *E-mail:* j.g.de.hoop.scheffer@cdh.leidenuniv.nl (office). *Website:* www.leiden.edu (office).

DE JAGER, Cornelis (Kees); Dutch astrophysicist and academic (retd); b. 29 April 1921, Den Burg, Texel; s. of Jan de Jager and Cornelia Kuyper; m. Duotje Rienks 1947; two s. two d.; ed Univ. of Utrecht; Asst in Theoretical Physics, Univ. of Utrecht 1946; Asst in Astronomy, Univ. of Leiden; Asst Astronomy Inst., Utrecht; Assoc. Prof. of Stellar Astrophysics, Univ. of Utrecht 1957, Ordinary Prof. in Gen. Astrophysics 1960–86; Extraordinary Prof., Univ. of Brussels and Founder, Space Research Lab., Utrecht Astronomy Inst., Brussels 1961; Man. Dir Utrecht Astronomy Inst. 1963–78, Chair. Inst. Council 1978–83; Asst Gen. Sec. Int. Astronomical Union 1967–70, Gen. Sec. 1970–73; Pres. Netherlands Astronomy Comm. 1975–83; mem. Exec. Council Cttee on Space Research (COSPAR) 1970–72, Pres. 1972–78, 1982–86; mem. Exec. Council, ICSU 1970–82, Vice-Pres. 1976–78, Pres. 1978–80; Chair. Skepsis (for critical evaluation of the paranormal) 1987–97, European Council of Sceptical Orgs 1995–2001, Council of Chancellors of Global Foundation 2001–; Aggregate Prof., Univ. of Brussels 1970–86, currently Prof. Emer. of Space Research; mem. Royal Netherlands Acad. of Art and Sciences (Foreign Sec. 1985–90), Royal Belgium Acad. of Art and Sciences, Academia Europaea (Paris and London); Assoc. mem. Royal Astronomical Soc. (London); Corresp. mem. Soc. Royale de Science, Liège; mem. Int. Acad. Astronautics, Chair. Basic Sciences Section 1984–92; Foreign mem. Deutsche Akad. Leopoldina, Halle; Foreign Fellow, Indian Nat. Scientific Acad.; voluntary co-worker, Royal Netherlands Inst. for Sea Research; Hon. mem. Netherlands Soc. of Astronomy and Meteorology 1996; Kt, Order of the Dutch Lion 1983; Dr hc (Univ. of Wrocław, Poland) 1975, (Observatoire de Paris) 1976; Karl Schwarzschild Medal 1974, Yuri Gagarin Medal (USSR) 1984, J. Janssen Medal (France) 1984, Ziolkowski Medal, USSR Acad. of Sciences, Gold Medal, Royal Astronomical Soc., London 1988, Hale Medal, American Astronomical Soc. 1988, COSPAR Medal for Int. Co-operation in Space Science 1988, Silver Medal, Royal Netherlands Acad. Arts and Sciences, Gold Medal, Netherlands Soc. Astronomy and Meteorology, In Praise of Reason Award CSICOP, Buffalo, NY 1990, Von Karman Award, Int. Acad. of Astronautics 1993, Hon. Silver Medal, City of Utrecht 2003. *Publications:* about 550 publs including: The Hydrogen Spectrum of the Sun 1952, Structure and Dynamics of the Solar Atmosphere 1959, The Solar Spectrum 1965, Solar Flares and Space Research (with Z. Svestka) 1969, Sterrenkunde 1969, Reports on Astronomy 1970, 1973, Highlights in Astronomy 1970, Ontstaan en Levensloop van Sterren (with E. van den Heuvel) 1973 (second edn), Image Processing Techniques in Astronomy (with H. Nieuwenhuyzen) 1975, The Brightest Stars 1980, Instabilities in Evolved Super- and Hyper-Giants 1992, Bolwerk van de Sterren 1993, Tien Opmerkelijke Sterrekundige Ontdekkingen 1995, Kannibalen bij de grenzen van het heelal 1996, Solar Flares and Collisions Between Current-carrying Loops (co-author) 1996, Van het Clijf tot Den Hoorn (co-author) 1998. *Leisure interests:* birds, plants, jogging, history. *Address:* Molenstraat 22, 1791 DL Den Burg, Texel, Netherlands (home). *Telephone:* (620) 420611 (office); (222) 320816 (home). *E-mail:* info@cdejager.nl (office). *Website:* www.nioz.nl (office); www.cdejager.com.

DE JAGER, Jan Cornelis (Jan Kees), BBA, LLM; Dutch business executive and politician; b. 10 Feb. 1969, Kapelle; ed Nyenrode Univ., Erasmus Univ., Rotterdam; Co-founder Spyke Trading 1991, Dir and Man. Dir 1992–2010, Dir ISM BV 1997–2010 (renamed ISM eCompany 2004); State Sec. for Finance 2007–10, Minister of Finance 2010–12; mem. Christen Democratisch Appèl (CDA), mem. Bd CDA policy inst.; mem. Advisory Bd Centres for Work and Income, ICT-Office (IT org.). *Address:* c/o Ministry of Finance, Prinses Beatrixlaan 512, POB 20201, 2500 EE The Hague, Netherlands.

DE JESUS CASTELHANO MAURICIO, Amadeu; Angolan fmr central banker; fmr Chair. Unipetrol; Gov. Banco Nacional de Angola 2006–09; Gov Alternate IMF 2006. *Address:* c/o Banco Nacional de Angola, CP 1243, Av. 4 de Fevereiro 151, Luanda, Angola (office).

DE JONGH, Eduard S.; Dutch art historian and academic; *Professor Emeritus of Art History, University of Utrecht;* b. 7 June 1931, Amsterdam; m. Lammijna Oosterbaan 1977; two s. one d.; ed Baarns Lyceum and Univ. of Utrecht; journalist and art critic, Het Parool and Vrij Nederland 1954–74; Librarian, Inst. for Art History, Univ. of Utrecht 1963–66; Ed. Openbaar Kunstbezit (radio course) 1963–73; Ed. Simiolus (art history quarterly) 1966–77; mem. staff, Centrum Voortgezet Kunsthistorisch Onderzoek, Univ. of Utrecht 1966–73; Asst Prof., Inst. for Art History, Univ. of Utrecht 1973–76, Prof. of Art History 1976–89, Prof. Emer. 1989–; Ed. Kunstschrift 1990–; Visiting Scholar, Getty Center for History of Art and Humanities 1987; mem. Royal Netherlands Acad.; Foreign mem. Royal Belgian Acad.; Dr hc (Amsterdam) 2002; Karel van Mander Award 1987, De Gijselaar-Hintzenfondsprijs 2011. *Publications include:* Zinne- en minnebeelden in de schilderkunst van de zeventiende eeuw 1967, Tot Lering en Vermaak: Betekenissen van Hollandse genrevoorstellingen uit de zeventiende eeuw 1976, Still Life in the Age of Rembrandt 1982, Portretten van echt en trouw: Huwelijk en gezin in de Nederlandse kunst van de zeventiende eeuw 1986, Kunst en het vruchtbare misverstand 1993, Faces of the Golden Age: Seventeenth-Century Dutch Portraits 1994, Kwesties van betekenis: Thema en motief in de Nederlandse schilderkunst van de zeventiende eeuw 1995, Mirror of Everyday Life: Genre Prints in The Netherlands 1550–1700 (with Ger Luijten) 1997, Questions of Meaning: Theme and Motif in Dutch Seventeenth-Century Painting 2000, Dankzij de tiende muze: 33 Opstellen uit Kunstschrift 2000, Charles Donker, etser (with Peter Schatborn) 2002, Muziek aan de muur: Muzikale voorstellingen in de Nederlanden 1500–1700 2008, Peter Vos en Charles Donker (with J. P. Filedt Kok) 2010, Peter Vos, Metamorfosen (with J. P. Filedt Kok) 2013 (French edn Peter Vos, Métamorphoses 2013); numerous articles on iconological and art theoretical

subjects. *Address:* Frederik Hendrikstraat 29, 3583 VG Utrecht, Netherlands (home).

DE JONGH, John Percy, Jr, BA; American politician, state governor and business executive; *Governor of the US Virgin Islands;* b. 13 Nov. 1957, Brooklyn, NY; m. Cecile René Galiber 1986; two s. one d.; ed Catholic Central High School, Detroit, Mich., Antioch Coll., Yellow Spring, Ohio; fmr mem. Tri-Island Econ. Devt Council; then hired by Chase Manhattan Bank for six years, became first Country Consumer Man. responsible for all consumer banking products in the US Virgin Islands, British Virgin Islands and St Maarten; mem. Industrial Devt Comm. 1984–87; apptd Commr of Finance 1987; also served as Chair. Governing Bd Virgin Islands Water and Power Authority and Exec. Dir Virgin Islands Public Finance Authority; re-entered pvt. sector as Sr Man. Consultant for Public Financial Management, Inc. 1993; served as Pres., COO and Dir, Lockhart Companies Inc.; fmr Pres. St Thomas-St John Chamber of Commerce, Community Foundation of the Virgin Islands; unsuccessfull cand. for Gov. 2002; Gov. of the US Virgin Islands 2007–; Democrat. *Address:* Government House, 21–22 Kongens Gade, Charlotte Amalie, St Thomas, VI 00802, US Virgin Islands (office); Washington Office of the Governor of the US Virgin Islands, 444 North Capitol Street, Suite 305, Washington, DC 20001, USA (office). *Telephone:* (340) 774-0001 (St Thomas) (office); (202) 624-3560 (DC) (office). *Fax:* (340) 693-4309 (St Thomas) (office); (202) 624-3594 (DC) (office). *Website:* www.governordejongh.com (office).

DE JONGH-ELHAGE, Emily Saïdy; Curaçao politician; b. 7 Dec. 1946; Commr of Public Works and Public Housing of Curaçao 1998–99, Commr of Educ., Sport and Cultural Affairs 1999–2002; Minister of Educ. and Culture, Netherlands Antilles 2002–03; Commr of Public Enterprises and Public Housing of Curaçao 2004–05; Prime Minister and Minister of Gen. Affairs and Foreign Relations 2006–10 (last Prime Minister before dissolution of Netherlands Antilles); Leader, Partido Antia Restrukturá (Party for the Restructured Antilles—PAR) 2005–12. *Address:* c/o Partido Antía Restrukturá (PAR), Fokkerweg 26, Unit 3, Willemstad, Curaçao (office).

DE JUNIAC, Alexandre; French business executive; *Chairman and CEO, Air France-KLM Group;* b. 10 Nov. 1962; ed École Polytechnique de Paris, École Nationale d'Admin; Auditor, then Master of Petitions and Deputy Sec. Gen. of the Conseil d'Etat (Council of State) 1988–93; Tech. Adviser, then Asst Dir, responsible for issues related to communication in the cabinet of Nicolas Sarkozy, Dept of Budget 1993–95; Dir of Planning and Devt, Thomson SA 1995–97; Sales Dir, Sextant Avionics 1997–98, Dir of Econ. Interest Grouping, CNS Avionics (jt venture between Sextant Avionics and Dassault Electronics) 1998–99; Sec. Gen. Thomson-CSF (became Thales 2000) 1999–2004, Sr Vice-Pres. in charge of Aviation Systems Div. 2004–08, Gen. Man. for Asia, Africa, the Middle East and Latin America 2008–09; Pvt. Sec. to Christine Lagarde, Minister for the Economy, Industry and Employment 2009–11; Chair. and CEO Air France 2011–13, mem. Bd of Dirs Air France-KLM 2012–, Chair. and CEO 2013–; mem. Supervisory Bd Vivendi 2013–. *Address:* Groupe Air France, 45 rue de Paris, 95747 Roissy CDG Cedex, France (office). *Telephone:* 1-41-56-61-65 (office). *Fax:* 1-41-56-61-59 (office). *E-mail:* info@airfrance.fr (office). *Website:* www.airfrance.com (office).

DE KEERSMAEKER, Baroness; Anne Teresa; Belgian choreographer; b. 11 June 1960, Wemmel; one s. one d.; ed Mudra, School of Maurice Béjart, Brussels and Tisch School of the Arts, New York Univ., USA; presented first work, Asch, in Brussels 1980; Founder and Artistic Dir Rosas Dance Co. 1983–; Rosas became co.-in-residence, Théâtre de la Monnaie, Brussels with herself as resident choreographer 1992–2007; directed opera Bluebeard (Bartók) 1997; Artistic Dir at PARTS school 1995–; has also directed work for video; Officier, Ordre des Arts et des Lettres 2000, Commdr, Ordre des Arts et des Lettres 2008; Dr hc (Flemish Univ. of Brussels) 1995; Eugène Baie Prize 1996, City of Paris Médaille de Vermeil 2002, Gabriella Moortgat Stichting Award 2002, Flemish Govt Erepenning Medal 2002, Oost Vlaanderen Keizer Karelprijs 2004. *Choreographic works:* Asch 1981, Fase: four movements to music of Steve Reich 1982, Rosas danst Rosas (Bessie Award 1988) 1983, Elena's Aria 1984, Bartók/Aantekeningen 1986, Verkommenes Ufer/Medeamaterial/Landschaft mit Argonauten 1987, Mikrokosmos-Monument/Selbstporträt mit Reich und Riley (und Chopin ist auch dabei)/Im zart fliessender Bewegung-Quatuor Nr. 4 (Japanese Dance Award for Best Foreign Production 1989) 1987, Ottone, Ottone 1988, Stella (London Dance and Performances Award 1989) 1989, Achterland 1990, Erts 1992, Mozart/Concert Arias, un moto di gioia 1992, Toccata 1993, Kinok 1994, Amor Constante más allá de la muerte 1994, Erwartung/Verklärte Nacht 1995, Woud 1996, Just Before 1997, Three Solos for Vincent Dunoyer 1997, Duke Bluebeard's Castle 1998, Drumming (Golden Laurel Wreath, Sarajevo 1998) 1998, Quartett 1999, I Said I 1999, In Real Time 2000, Rain 2001, Small Hands (out of the lie of no) 2001, (but if a look should) April Me 2002, Repertory Evening 2002, Once 2002, Bitches' Brew/Tacoma Narrows 2003, Kassandra – Speaking in Twelve Voices 2004, Desh 2005, Raga for the Rainy Season/A Love Supreme 2005, D'un soir un jour 2006, Bartók/Beethoven/Schönberg Repertory Evening 2006, Steve Reich Evening 2007, Keeping Still 2007. *Films:* Hoppla! 1989, Achterland 1994, Rosas danst Rosas 1997, Tippeke 2000. *Address:* Rosas VZW, Van Volxemlaan 164, 1190 Brussels, Belgium (office). *Telephone:* (2) 344-55-98 (office). *Fax:* (2) 343-53-52 (office). *E-mail:* mail@rosas.be (office). *Website:* www.rosas.be (office).

DE KEPPER, Christophe; Belgian lawyer and international organization official; *Director-General, International Olympic Committee;* b. 1963, Uccle; ed Univ. of Louvain, Univ. of Brussels; fmr Asst to Legal Dir Belgian Olympic Cttee; Chief of Staff, Exec. Office of Pres., IOC 2002–11, Dir-Gen. IOC 2011–; fmr Dir European Olympic Cttee's liaison office with EU. *Address:* International Olympic Committee (IOC), Château de Vidy, 1007 Lausanne, Switzerland (office). *Telephone:* 216216111 (office). *Fax:* 216216216 (office). *Website:* www.olympic.org (office).

DE KLERK, F(rederik) W(illem), LLB; South African politician, lawyer and fmr head of state; b. 18 March 1936, Johannesburg; s. of J. de Klerk; m. 1st Marike Willemse 1959 (divorced 1998); two s. one d.; m. 2nd Elita Georgiadis 1998; ed Monument High School, Krugersdorp, Potchefstroom Univ.; in law practice 1961–72; mem. House of Ass. 1972; Information Officer Nat. Party, Transvaal 1975; Minister of Posts and Telecommunications and of Social Welfare and Pensions 1978, subsequently Minister of Posts and Telecommunications and of

Sport and Recreation 1978–79, of Mines, Energy and Environmental Planning 1979–80, of Mineral and Energy Affairs 1980–82, of Internal Affairs 1982–85, of Nat. Educ. and Planning 1984–89; Acting State Pres. of South Africa Aug.–Sept. 1989, State Pres. of South Africa 1989–94; Exec. Deputy Pres., Govt of Nat. Unity 1994–96; Leader of the Official Opposition 1996–97; mem. Nat. Party, Transvaal Leader 1982–89, Leader 1989–97; also fmr Chair. of the Cabinet and C-in-C of the Armed Forces; fmr Chair. Council of Ministers; seven hon. doctorates; shared Nobel Prize for Peace with Nelson Mandela 1993, jt winner Houphouet Boigny Prize (UNESCO) 1991, Asturias Prize 1992, Liberty Medal (SA) 1993, Order of Mapungube Gold 2002. *Publications:* The Last Trek: A New Beginning (autobiog.) 1999; various articles and brochures. *Leisure interests:* golf, reading. *Address:* PO Box 15785, 7506 Panorama, Cape Town, South Africa (office). *Telephone:* (21) 9200966 (office). *Fax:* (21) 9300995 (office). *E-mail:* fw@fwdeklerk.org (home). *Website:* www.fwdeklerk.org (office).

DE KORTE, Rudolf Willem, Dr rer. nat; Dutch politician and business executive; b. 8 July 1936, The Hague; m.; two c.; ed Maerlant Gymnasium, The Hague, Leiden Univ., Harvard Business School, USA; in various positions in Hong Kong 1964–66, in Ethiopia 1967–68; Gen. Sales Man. Unilever-Emery NV 1969–71, Dir 1972–77; Sec. People's Party for Freedom and Democracy (VVD) 1971–78; mem. Parl. 1977–86, 1989–95; Minister for Home Affairs March–July 1986, Deputy Prime Minister and Minister for Econ. Affairs 1986–89; mem. (VVD) Lower House of Parl. 1989; mem. Wassenaar Municipal Council 1978–82; Vice-Pres. Europese Investeringsbank 1995–2001. *Address:* c/o Volkspartij voor Vrijheid en Democratie (People's Party for Freedom and Democracy), Laan Copes van Cattenburch 52, POB 30836, 2500 GV The Hague, Netherlands.

DE LA BILLIÈRE, Gen. Sir Peter (Edgar de la Cour), Kt, KCB, KBE, DSO, MC, DL; British army officer (retd) and banker (retd); b. 29 April 1934, Plymouth; s. of Surgeon Lt-Commdr Claude Dennis Delacour de Labillière and Frances Christing Wright Lawley; m. Bridget Constance Muriel Goode 1965; one s. two d.; ed Harrow School, Staff Coll., Royal Coll. of Defence Studies; joined King's Shropshire Light Infantry 1952; commissioned, Durham Light Infantry; served Japan, Korea, Malaya (despatches 1959), Jordan, Borneo, Egypt, Aden, Gulf States, Sudan, Oman, Falkland Islands; Commdg Officer, 22 Special Air Service (SAS) Regt 1972–74; Gen. Staff Officer 1 (Directing Staff), Staff Coll. 1974–77; Commdr British Army Training Team, Sudan 1977–78; Dir SAS and Commdr SAS Group 1978–83; Commdr British Forces, Falkland Islands and Mil. Commr 1984–85; Gen. Officer Commdg Wales 1985–87; Col Commdt. Light Div. 1986–90; Lt-Gen. Officer commanding SE Dist 1987–90; Commdr British Forces in Middle East Oct. 1990–91; rank of Gen. 1991 after Gulf War, Ministry of Defence Adviser on Middle East 1991–92; retd from army June 1992; Pres. SAS Asscn 1991–96, Army Cadet Force 1992–99; mem. Council Royal United Services Inst. 1975–77; Chair. Jt Services Hang Gliding 1986–88; Cdre Army Sailing Asscn 1989–90; Commr Duke of York's School 1988–90; Freeman City of London 1991; Hon. Freeman Fishmongers' Co. 1991; Pres. Harrow School Asscn 2002–; Trustee Imperial War Museum 1992–99; Dir (non-exec.), Middle East and Defence Adviser, Robert Fleming Holdings 1992–99; Chair. Meadowland Meats 1994–2002; Jt Chair. Dirs FARM Africa 1995–2001 (mem. Bd 1992–2001); DL Hereford and Worcester 1993; Trustee Naval and Mil. Club 1999–2003, mem. Bd 1999–2003; Pres. Friends of Imperial War Museum 2003; Pres. Harrow Asscn 2002–; Meritorious Service Cross (Canada) 1991, Legion of Merit Chief Commdr (USA) 1993, Order of Abdul Aziz 2nd Class (Saudi Arabia) 1993, Kuwait Decoration of the First Class, Order of Qatar Sash of Merit; Hon. DSc (Cranfield) 1992; Hon. DCL (Durham) 1993. *Television:* Discovery: Clash of the Generals 2004. *Publications include:* Storm Command: a personal story of the Gulf War 1992, Looking for Trouble (autobiog.) 1994, Supreme Courage: Heroic Stories from 150 Years of the Victoria Cross 2004. *Leisure interests:* family, squash, apiculture, farming, sailing.

DE LA CROIX DE CASTRIES, Henri René Marie Augustin; French insurance business executive and fmr civil servant; *Chairman and CEO, AXA;* b. 15 Aug. 1954, Bayonne (Basses-Pyrénées); s. of François de La Croix de Castries and Gisèle de La Croix de Castries (née de Chevigné); m. Anne Millin de Grandmaison 1984; one s. two d.; ed Ecole Saint-Jean-de-Passy, Coll. Stanislas, Faculté de droit, Paris, École des Hautes Études Commerciales, Ecole Nat. d'Admin.; Deputy Insp., then Insp. of Finance, 2nd Class, Treasury 1984, Deputy Sec.-Gen. Interministerial Cttee on Industrial Restructuring 1984–85, Head, Office of Capital Goods 1985–88, of Foreign Exchange and Balance of Payments 1988–89; Man. Finance Dept, AXA (insurance group) 1989–90, Corp. Sec. 1991–93, Sr Exec. Vice-Pres. for Group's asset man., financial and real-estate businesses 1993–97, Chair. The Equitable Cos Inc. (now AXA Financial, Inc.) 1997–2000, mem. Exec. Cttee and Chair. Man. Bd AXA 2000–10, CEO 2000–, Chair. 2010–, Chair. AXA Assurances IARD Mutuelle, AXA Assurances Vie Mutuelle, AXA Financial, Inc. (USA); mem. Bd of Dirs AXA SA, AXA France IARD, AXA UK plc (UK), AllianceBernstein Corpn (USA), AXA Equitable Life Insurance Co. (USA), AXA America Holdings, Inc. (USA), MONY Life Insurance Co. (USA), MONY Life Insurance Co. of America (USA); mem. Bd of Dirs Nestlé; mem. Bd Asscn pour l'Aide aux Jeunes Infirmes, Musée du Louvre, Fondation Nationale des Sciences Politiques; Officier, Légion d'honneur 2009, Ordre nat. du Mérite; Commdr 2009, Ordre des Arts et des Lettres 2012. *Address:* AXA, 25 avenue Matignon, 75008 Paris (office); 17 rue du Cherche-Midi, 75006 Paris (home); Château de Gastines, 49150 Fougeré, France (home). *Telephone:* 1-40-75-57-00 (office). *Fax:* 1-40-75-46-96 (office). *E-mail:* henri.decastries@axa.com (office). *Website:* www.axa.com (office).

DE LA DEHESA ROMERO, Guillermo; Spanish business executive and government official; *International Adviser, Goldman Sachs Europe Ltd;* b. 19 July 1941, Madrid; ed Universidad Complutense de Madrid; govt economist 1968, served at Ministries of Trade, Industry and Energy and Economy and Finance, apptd Dir Gen. of Trade, Sec. Gen. of Industry and Energy 1978–80, Sec. Gen. of Trade, Deputy Sec. of Commerce at Ministry of Economy and Finance 1982–86, Sec. of State of Economy and Finance 1986–88 and Sec. of the Comm. for Econ. Affairs of Council of Ministers 1978–88; also worked at Bank of Spain as Man. Dir of Foreign Currency Assets Man. and Int. Relations 1980–82; participated in negotiations for accession of Spain to EU; later, mem. 113 Cttee and of ECOFIN; also served as mem. OECD Ministerial meetings, Deputy Gov. IMF and World Bank and Gov. of Inter American, Asian and African Devt Banks for several years;

CEO Banco Pastor, Chair. Gas Madrid 1988–91, Chair. Plus Ultra, Vice-Chair. Hullas de Coto Cortes and Dir Pastor-Aliance, Cubiertas y MZOV, Ibersuizas, Fondos Galicia, Plus Ultra); Ind. Dir (non-exec.) Campofrío Food Group SA, Madrid 1997–, Aviva PLC, London, UK 1999– (Chair. (non-exec.) Aviva Grupo Corporativo, SL and Aviva Vida y Pensiones, SA de Seguros y Reaseguros 2002–, Banco Santander 2002–, Unión Fenosa, Madrid, Amadeus IT Holding SA; apptd Vice-Chair. Goldman Sachs Europe Ltd 1988, currently Int. Adviser; Chair. Centre for Econ. Policy Research, London, European Cen. Bank Observatory, Madrid, Bd Instituto de Empresa, Madrid, Steering Cttee of Advisory Bd of ESCP-EAP (École Supérieure de Commerce de Paris merged with EAP-Ecole Européenne des Affaires to form ESCP-EAP European School of Man.), Paris, France, Governing Bd of Instituto de Empresa Business School, Madrid; mem. Euro 50 Group, Brussels, Belgium, Advisory Bd of CREI at Univ. Pompeu Fabra, Barcelona, Scientific Advisory Bd of Instituto de Estudios Europeos and of Instituto Elcano, Madrid; monetary expert, Econ. and Monetary Cttee of European Parl.; mem. Group of Thirty Consultative Group on Int. Econ. and Monetary Affairs, Inc. (G-30), Washington, DC; regular columnist for El País, Madrid, La Nación, Buenos Aires, Gazeta Mercantil, São Paulo and Reforma, Mexico. *Publications:* author of six books in Spanish and three books in English and co-author of 18 books in Spanish and 13 books in English on econs; more than 90 papers in econ. journals and more than 300 articles in newspapers and magazines. *Address:* Goldman Sachs Group Holdings (UK), 133 Fleet Street, London, EC4A 2BB, England (office). *Telephone:* (20) 7774-1000 (office). *E-mail:* info@goldmansachs.com (office). *Website:* www2.goldmansachs.com (office).

DE LA HOYA, Oscar; American boxer; b. 4 Feb. 1973, Los Angeles; s. of Joel De La Hoya and the late Cecilia De La Hoya; m. Millie Corretjer; fmr amateur boxer, 223 victories (163 knockouts), only 5 losses; turned professional after winning gold medal lightweight Barcelona Olympics 1992; Int. Boxing Fed. (IBF) lightweight title 1995; World Boxing Council (WBC) super lightweight title (over Julio César Chávez) 1996; WBC welterweight title (over Pernell Whitaker) 1997; lost WBC welterweight belt to Felix Trinidad in a majority decision in 1999; lost to Sugar Shane Mosley in 2000 in his 2nd career defeat; has won major titles in six weight divisions: 130, 135, 140, 147, 154 and 160 pounds; lost super welterweight title to Mosley 2003; won World Boxing Org. middleweight title June 2004 defeating Felix Sturm, lost it when defeated by Bernard Hopkins Sept. 2004; defeated WBC jr middleweight champion Ricardo Mayorga 2006, lost title to Floyd Mayweather, Jr. 2007; lost to Manny Pacquiao 2008; retd from boxing 2009; f. Oscar de la Hoya Foundation; Owner, Golden Boy Promotions LLC; WBC Boxer of the Decade 2001. *Album:* Oscar (topped Billboard's Latin Dance charts for several weeks). *Publication:* American Son (autobiography) 2008. *Address:* c/o Golden Boy Promotions, 626 Wilshire Blvd, Suite 350, Los Angeles, CA 90017, USA (office). *Telephone:* (213) 489-5631 (office). *Fax:* (213) 489-9048 (office). *E-mail:* info@goldenboyllc.com (office). *Website:* www.goldenboypromotions.com (office); www.oscardelahoya.com.

DE LA MARNIÈRE, Caroline; French business executive; *President, Capitalcom;* four c.; f. Ecocom 1994, acquired by Publicis Groupe 2001, CEO Publicis Consultants Ecocom 2001–05; Founder and Pres. Capitalcom communications agency 2005–; Prix du Jury de l'Assemblée Générale du CAC 40 2010. *Leisure interests:* trekking, yoga, skiing, 70s music, travel. *Address:* Capitalcom, 10 boulevard Malesherbes, 75008 Paris, France (office). *Telephone:* 1-45-49-93-37 (office). *Fax:* 1-45-51-33-72 (office). *E-mail:* info@capitalcom.fr (office). *Website:* www.capitalcom.fr (office).

DE LA NUEZ RAMÍREZ, Raúl; Cuban politician; fmr Vice-Minister, Basic Industry Ministry; Minister of Foreign Trade 2003–09. *Address:* c/o Ministry of Foreign Trade, Infanta 16, esquina 23, Vedado, Havana, Cuba (office).

DE LA QUADRA-SALCEDO Y FERNANDEZ DEL CASTILLO, Tomás, PhD; Spanish lawyer, politician and academic; b. 1946, Madrid; m.; two c.; ed Univ. Complutense of Madrid; Asst Lecturer in Admin. Law, Faculty of Law, Univ. Complutense of Madrid 1977–81 (Temporary Lecturer 1968), in Audiovisual Media, Information Sciences Faculty 1981–; mem. Lawyers' Asscn of Madrid 1968–; Minister of Territorial Admin. 1982–85; Pres. Council of State 1985–91; Minister of Justice 1991–93; currently Prof. of Admin. Law, Universidad Carlos III de Madrid. *Publications:* various articles and books. *Address:* c/o Department of Public State Law, Carlos III University of Madrid, Madrid Nª 126, 28903 Getafe Madrid, Spain. *Website:* www.uc3m.es.

DE LA RENTA, Oscar; Dominican Republic/American fashion designer; b. (Oscar Aristides Renta Fiallo), 22 July 1932, Santo Domingo; m. 1st Françoise de Langlade 1967 (died 1983); one adopted s.; m. 2nd Anne E. de la Renta 1989; ed Santo Domingo Univ., Academia de San Fernando, Madrid; staff designer, under Cristobal Balenciaga, AISA couture house, Madrid; Asst to Antonio Castillo, Lanvin-Castillo, Paris 1961–63; designer, Elizabeth Arden couture and ready-to-wear collection, New York 1963–65; designer and partner, Jane Derby Inc. New York 1965; after her retirement firm evolved into Oscar de la Renta, Inc. which was purchased by Richton Int. 1969; Chief Exec. Richton's Oscar de la Renta Couture, Oscar de la Renta II, Oscar de la Renta Furs, Oscar de la Renta Jewelry and mem. Bd of Dirs Richton Int. 1969–73; f. Oscar de la Renta, Ltd 1973, CEO 1973–; couturier for Balmain, Paris Nov. 1993–; produces about 80 different product lines including high-fashion clothing, household linens, accessories and perfumes for shops in USA, Canada, Mexico and Japan; owner, Oscar de la Renta shop, Santo Domingo 1968–; Caballero, Order of San Pablo Duarte, Order of Cristobal Colon; recipient of numerous fashion awards including CFDA Lifetime Achievement Award 1990. *Address:* Oscar de la Renta Ltd, 550 7th Avenue, 8th Floor, New York, NY 10018, USA. *Website:* www.oscardelarenta.com.

DE LA RÚA, Fernando; Argentine politician; b. 15 Sept. 1937, Córdoba; s. of Antonio de la Rúa and Eleonora Bruno de la Rúa; m. Inés Pertiné; two s. one d.; ed Liceo General Paz, Córdoba, Universidad Nacional de Córdoba; joined Unión Cívica Radical (UCR) as a student; mem. staff Ministry of Interior 1963–66; cand. for Vice-Pres. 1973, Senator for Fed. Capital 1973–76, 1983–96; visiting lecturer univs in USA, Mexico and Venezuela during mil. dictatorship; f. Centro de Estudios Para la República (now Fundación de estudios sobre temas políticos), Buenos Aires 1982; Mayor of Buenos Aires 1996–99; Leader ALIANZA coalition; Pres. of Argentina 1999–2001; Prof. of Criminal Law, Univ. of Buenos Aires; Founder mem. Consejo Argentino para las Relaciones Internacionales. *Leisure* *interests:* gardening, birds, nature, reading. *Address:* c/o Casa de Goberniero, Balcarce 50, 1064 Buenos Aires, Argentina (office).

DE LA TOUR, Frances; British actress; b. 30 July 1944, Bovingdon, Herts.; d. of Charles de la Tour and Moyra de la Tour (née Fessas); m. Tom Kempinski 1972 (divorced 1982); one s. one d.; ed Lycée français de Londres, Drama Centre, London; Hon. Fellow, Goldsmiths Coll., Univ. of London 1999. *Stage appearances include:* with RSC: As You Like It 1967, The Relapse 1969, A Midsummer Night's Dream 1971, The Man of Mode 1971, Antony and Cleopatra 1999; Small Craft Warnings (Best Supporting Actress, Plays and Players Award) 1973, The Banana Box 1973, As You Like It (Oxford Playhouse) 1974, The White Devil 1976, Hamlet (title role) 1979, Duet for One (Best Actress, New Standard Award, Best Actress, Critics Award, Best Actress, Soc. of West End Theatres—SWET Award) 1980, Skirmishes 1981, Uncle Vanya 1982, Moon for the Misbegotten (Best Actress, SWET Award) 1983, St Joan (Royal Nat. Theatre) 1984, Dance of Death (Riverside Studios) 1985, Brighton Beach Memoirs (Royal Nat. Theatre) 1986, Lillian 1986, Façades 1988, King Lear 1989, Chekhov's Women (Moscow Arts Theatre) 1990, When She Danced (Olivier Award) 1991, The Pope and the Witch 1992, Greasepaint 1993, Les Parents Terribles (Royal Nat. Theatre) 1994, Three Tall Women 1994–95, Blinded by the Sun (Royal Nat. Theatre) 1996, The Play About the Baby (Almeida Theatre) 1998, The Forest (Royal Nat. Theatre) 1998–99, Fallen Angels (Apollo) (Best Actress, Royal Variety Club) 2000–01, The Good Hope and Sketches by Harold Pinter (Royal Nat. Theatre) 2001–02, Dance of Death (Lyric) 2003, The History Boys (Nat. Theatre) 2004–05, (Broadway) (Tony Award for Best Supporting Actress) 2006, The Habit of Art (Nat. Theatre) 2009. *Films include:* Rising Damp (Best Actress, Standard Film Award) 1980, The Cherry Orchard 1998, Harry Potter and the Goblet of Fire 2005, The History Boys 2006, Alice in Wonderland 20108, Nutcracker: The Untold Story 2010, The Book of Eli 2010, Harry Potter and the Deathly Hallows: Part 1 2010, Hugo 2011. *Television appearances include:* Rising Damp 1974, 1976, Flickers 1980, Skirmishes 1982, Duet for One 1985, Clem 1986, A Kind of Living (series) 1987–88, Cold Lazarus 1996, Tom Jones 1997, The Egg 2002, Waking the Dead 2004, Poirot: Death on the Nile 2004, Sensitive Skin 2005, Agatha Christie: The Moving Finger 2005, 3 lbs 2006, Vicious (series) 2013–, Big School (series) 2013. *Address:* c/o Claire Maroussas, ICM, Oxford House, 76 Oxford Street, London, W1N 0AX, England (office).

DE LABOULAYE, Stanislas François Jean Lefebvre; French diplomatist and business executive; *Senior Vice-President, Sovereign Global Solutions;* b. 12 Dec. 1946, Beirut, Lebanon; m.; four c.; ed Collège Stanislas, Lycée Henri-IV, Univ. of Paris, Sorbonne, Vincennes Univ., Agrégé de l'Université, Ecole Nationale d'Admin; held teaching posts at Lycée de Garçons de Sfax, Tunisia 1970–72, Univ. of Manchester, UK 1972–76; joined Foreign Service 1980, served in several positions including Sec., Asia Div., Ministry of Foreign Affairs 1980–81, Econ. Div. 1981–84, Communications Dir 1991–95, Asst Sec.-Gen. and Political Dir 2002; First Sec., then Second Counsellor, Perm. Mission to EU, Brussels 1984–87, Second Counsellor, Embassy in Madrid 1987–91, Consul-Gen. in Jerusalem 1996–99, Amb. to Madagascar 2000–02, Sec.-Gen. and Dir-Gen. for Political Affairs and Security 2002–06, Amb. to Russia 2006–09, to the Holy See (Vatican City) 2009–12; Diplomatic Advisor to the Govt 2012; Sr Vice-Pres., Sovereign Global Solutions 2013–; Officier, Légion d'honneur 2008, Commdr, Ordre nat. du Mérite 2011. *Address:* Sovereign Global Solutions, 129 rue de l'Université, 75007 Paris, France (office). *Telephone:* 6-79-58-26-99 (mobile) (office). *E-mail:* sdelaboulaye@so-global.com (office). *Website:* www.so-global.com (office).

DE LADOUCETTE, Philippe, MA, DScS, DrSc (Econ); French company executive and government official; *President, Commission de régulation de l'énergie;* b. 15 March 1948, Paris; s. of Charles de Ladoucette; ed Ecole Nationale des Ponts et Chaussées; fmr civil engineer with Ministry of Equipment (responsible for state contracts with medium-sized towns) 1974–77; Commr for Industrialization, Ardennes 1977–83; responsible for industrial devt, DATAR 1983–86; tech. adviser, Ministry of Industry, Posts and Telecommunications and Tourism 1986–88; responsible for industrial matters, Secr.-Gen. of Channel Tunnel 1988–93; Asst Dir Office of Minister of Enterprise and Econ. Devt 1993–94; Chair. Houillères du Bassin du Centre et du Midi 1994–; CEO SNET 1996–2000; CEO Charbonnages de France 1996–2006; Pres. Commission de régulation de l'énergie 2006–; Chevalier, Légion d'honneur, Officier Ordre Nat. du Mérite. *Leisure interests:* swimming, jogging, cycling. *Address:* Commission de régulation de l'énergie, 2 rue du Quatre-Septembre, 75084 Paris cedex 02 (office); 40 avenue Marceau, 75008 Paris, France (home). *Website:* www.cre.fr (office).

DE LANGE, Titia, PhD; Dutch cell biologist, geneticist and academic; *Leon Hess Professor, Laboratory of Cell Biology and Genetics, The Rockefeller University;* b. 11 Nov. 1955, Rotterdam; ed Univ. of Amsterdam and Netherlands Cancer Inst.; Grad. Teaching Asst, Dept of Biochemistry, Univ. of Amsterdam 1981–85; Postdoctoral Fellow, Univ. of California, San Francisco 1985–90; Asst Prof., The Rockefeller Univ. 1990–94, Assoc. Prof. 1994–97, Prof. 1997–, Leon Hess Prof. 1999–, Assoc. Dir Anderson Center for Cancer Research 2006–11, Dir 2011–; American Cancer Soc. Research Prof. 2010–; Pres. Harvey Soc. 2000–01; mem. Editorial Bd, Molecular and Cellular Biology 1997–, Trends in Biological Science 2000–, PLoS Biology 2004–07, Genes and Development 2008–, Nucleus 2009–, Journal of Cell Biology 2010–, Current Opinion in Genetics and Development 2011–; mem. and Corresp., Royal Netherlands Acad. of Sciences 2000, Inst. of Medicine 2010; Foreign mem. European Molecular Biology Org. 2001; Foreign Assoc., NAS 2006; Fellow, New York Acad. of Sciences 2005, American Soc. for Microbiology 2006, American Acad. for Arts and Sciences 2007, AAAS 2007, American Acad. for Cancer Research 2014; Dr hc (Utrecht) 2003; Dr Catharine van Tussenbroek Award 1980, Christiaan and Constantijn Huygens Award 1985–87, Lucille P. Markey Trust Scholar Award 19987–95, Irma T. Hirschl-Monique Weill-Caulier Trust Award 1993–98, Rita Allen Award 1995–2000, Burroughs Wellcome Toxicology Scholar Award 1997–2002, New York Community Trust Cancer Research Award 1997–99, Ellison Medical Foundation Sr Scholar Award 2000–04, first Paul Marks Prize for Cancer Research (co-recipient) 2001, Charlotte Friend Memorial Award, American Asscn for Cancer Research (AACR) 2004, NIH MERIT Award (GM) 2005, NIH Dir's Pioneer Award 2005, Award for Excellence in Teaching, The Rockefeller Univ. 2007, Massachusetts Gen. Hosp. Cancer Center Prize 2008, AACR G.H.A. Clowes Memorial Award 2010, Vilcek Prize in

Biomedical Sciences 2011, Rosalind E. Franklin Award, Nat. Cancer Inst. 2012, Vanderbilt Prize in Biomedical Science 2012, Dr H.P. Heineken Prize for Biochemistry and Biophysics 2012, Breakthrough Prize in Life Sciences (co-recipient) 2013, Jill Rose Award, Breast Cancer Research Foundation 2013, Canada Gairdner Int. Award 2014. *Achievements include:* one of the first to isolate the telomeres of human chromosomes. *Publications:* more than 130 papers in professional journals. *Address:* Laboratory for Cell Biology and Genetics, The Rockefeller University, 1230 York Avenue, New York, NY 10065, USA (office). *Telephone:* (212) 327-8146 (office). *Fax:* (212) 327-7147 (office). *E-mail:* titia.de .lange@rockefeller.edu (office). delange@mail.rockefeller.edu (office). *Website:* www.rockefeller.edu/research/faculty/labheads/TitiadeLange (office); delangelab .rockefeller.edu (office).

DE LAROSIÈRE DE CHAMPFEU, Jacques Martin Henri Marie; French international civil servant; *Senior Adviser, BNP Paribas;* b. 12 Nov. 1929, Paris; s. of Robert de Larosière and Hugayte de Larosière (née de Champfeu); m. Franche du Bos 1960; one s. one d.; ed Lycée Louis-le-Grand, Paris Univ. and Ecole nat. d'Admin; Insp. adjoint 1958, Insp. des Finances 1960; Chargé de Mission in Inspectorate-Gen. of Finance 1961, External Finance Office 1963, Treasury 1965; Asst Dir Treasury 1967; Deputy Dir then Head of Dept, Ministry of Econs and Finance 1971; Prin. Pvt. Sec. to Valéry Giscard d'Estaing (then Minister of Econs and Finance) 1974; Under-Sec. of Treas. 1974–78; Pres. Group of Ten 1976–78; Dir-Gen. IMF 1978–87; Gov. Banque de France 1987–93, Hon. Gov. 1993–; Chair. Cttee of Govs, Group of Ten 1990–93; Pres. EBRD 1993–98; Sr Adviser BNP Paribas 1998–; Chair. Strategic Cttee of French Treasury 2000–; Insp. Gen. des Finances 1981; mem. Bd of Dirs Renault 1971–74, Banque nat. de Paris 1973–78, Air France and Soc. nat. de chemins de fer français (SNCF) 1974–78, Soc. nat. industrielle aérospatiale 1976–78, Power Corpn 1998–2001; Alstom 1998–2001, France Télécom 1998–2009, Stichting NYSE Euronext (the Dutch Foundation) 2007–; mem. AIG International Advisory Bd; Trustee Reuters 1999–2004; Censeur Banque de France 1974–78, Crédit nat. 1974–78, Comptoir des Entrepreneurs 1973–75, Crédit foncier de France 1975–78; Vice-Pres. Caisse nat. des Télécommunications 1974–78; mem. Acad. of Moral and Political Sciences 1993; Hon. mem. Soc. des Cincinnati de France; Commdr, Légion d'honneur; Chevalier, Ordre nat. du Mérite; Hon. KBE; numerous awards. *Address:* BNP Paribas, 3 rue d'Antin, 75078 Paris Cedex 02 (office); 10 bis, rue Paul Baudry, 75008 Paris, France (home). *Telephone:* 1-42-98-24-28 (office); 1-42-98-72-74 (office). *Fax:* 1-42-98-22-37 (office). *E-mail:* jacques.delarosiere@bnpparibas.com (office). *Website:* www.bnpparibas.net (office).

DE LIMA, Frank, BBA; Panamanian economist and politician; *Minister of the Economy and Finance;* ed Boston Univ., Georgetown Univ., Washington DC, Ciudad del Saber, Panamá; consultant specializing in issues of competitiveness, int. trade, strategic planning and public policy reform; led Panama team in negotiations with World Bank and UN, and at taxation agreements with several OECD countries; represented govt of Panama at Meso-American Council on Competitiveness; campaign spokesman and head of finance cttee, presidential campaign of Ricardo Martinelli 2009; Deputy Minister of Economy and Finance 2009–11, Minister of Economy and Finance 2011–; mem. Cambio Democrático. *Publications include:* articles on econ. issues and int. competitiveness in publs including La Prensa, Capital Finance, El Panama America. *Address:* Ministry of the Economy and Finance, Edif. Ogawa, Vía España, Calle del Santuario Nacional, Apdo 5245, Panamá 5, Panama (office). *Telephone:* 507-7000 (office). *E-mail:* prensa@mef.gob.pa (office). *Website:* www.mef.gob.pa (office).

DE LIMA MASSANO, José; Angolan accountant and central banker; *Governor, Banco Nacional de Angola;* b. 1971; ed City Univ., London, UK, Salford Univ., Manchester; Head of Technical Support Office and Accounting, Sonangol EP (state-owned oil firm) 1997–2000; Exec. Dir Banco Comercial Português 2000–05; Exec. Dir Banco Africano de Investimentos (BAI) 2005–06, Exec. Pres. 2006–10; Gov. Banco Nacional de Angola (central bank) 2010–; Pres. SADC Banking Asscn 2004–05, Angolan Asscn of Banks (ABANC) 2006–09. *Address:* Office of the Governor, Banco Nacional de Angola, Av. 4 de Fevereiro 151, CP 1298, Luanda, Angola (office). *Telephone:* 222333717 (also fax) (office). *E-mail:* bna.cri@ebonet .net (office). *Website:* www.bna.ao (office).

DE LIMA NETO, Antônio Francisco, BEcons, MBA; Brazilian banker; b. 13 June 1965; ed Univ. Fed. de Pernambucom, Fundacão Dom Cabral, Pontificia Universidade Catolica; joined Banco do Brasil SA as apprentice 1979, becoming Dir of Int. and Wholesale Business 2004–05, Man. Dir BB Leasing SA and BB Securities, Vice-Pres., Retail Div. 2006–07, Interim CEO 2006–07, Vice-Chair., Pres. and CEO Banco do Brasil SA 2007–09, also Counsellor, BB Securities Ltd; Regional Dir Associação Brasileira das Empresas de Leasing; Embassy of Brazil and Brazilian Chamber of Commerce in GB Personality of the Year 2007. *Address:* c/o Banco do Brasil SA, SBS Edificio, Sede III, 24º Andar, 70073-901 Brasília DF, Brazil. *Telephone:* (61) 3310-3400. *Fax:* (61) 3310-3735. *E-mail:* info@bb.com.br. *Website:* www.bb.com.br.

DE LUCCHI, Michele; Italian designer; b. 8 Nov. 1951, Ferrara; s. of Alberto De Lucchi and Giuliana Zannini; ed Liceo Scientifico Enrico Fermi, Padua, Faculty of Architecture, Univ. of Florence; Founder Mem., Cavart (avant-garde design and architecture group) 1973–76; Asst Prof., Univ. of Florence 1976–77; worked with Gaetano Pesce, Superstudio, Andrea Branzi, Ettore Sottsass 1977–80; Consultant, Centrokappa Noviglio, Milan 1978; Consultant, Olivetti Synthesis, Massa 1979–, Olivetti SpA, Ivrea 1984–; freelance designer, several furniture mfrs 1979–; founder mem., Int. Designer Group Memphis 1981. *Publication:* Architetture Verticali 1978. *Leisure interest:* travel photography. *Address:* Architetto Michele De Lucchi, srl 15 via Varese, 20121 Milan, Italy (office). *Telephone:* (02) 63786817 (office). *Fax:* (02) 63786814 (office). *Website:* www.micheledelucchi.com.

DE MADARIAGA, Isabel, PhD, FBA, FRHistS; British historian, academic and writer; *Professor Emerita of Russian Studies, School of Slavonic and East European Studies, University of London;* b. 27 Aug. 1919, Glasgow, Scotland; d. of Salvador de Madariaga and Constance Archibald; m. Leonard B. Schapiro 1943 (divorced 1976); ed Ecole Internationale, Geneva, Switzerland, Headington School for Girls, Oxford, Instituto Escuela, Madrid, Univ. of London; with BBC Monitoring Service 1940–43; with Cen. Office of Information London 1943–47, Econ. Information Unit, Treasury 1947–48; Editorial Asst, Slavonic and East

European Review 1951–64; Part-time Lecturer in History, LSE 1953–66; Lecturer in History, Univ. of Sussex 1966–68; Sr Lecturer in Russian History, Univ. of Lancaster 1968–71; Reader in Russian Studies, School of Slavonic and East European Studies, Univ. of London 1971–81, Prof. 1981–84, Prof. Emer. 1984–; Corresp. mem. Royal Spanish Acad. of History. *Publications:* Britain, Russia and the Armed Neutrality of 1780 1963, Opposition (with G. Ionescu) 1965, Russia in the Age of Catherine the Great 1981, Catherine II: A Short History 1990, Politics and Culture in Eighteenth-Century Russia 1998, Ivan the Terrible 2005; books translated into many languages including Turkish and Russian; many scholarly articles. *Leisure interest:* music. *Address:* 25 Southwood Lawn Road, London, N6 5SD, England (home). *Telephone:* (20) 8341-0862 (home).

DE MAESENEIRE, Baron Patrick; Belgian engineer and business executive; *CEO, Adecco Management & Consulting SA;* b. 1957; ed Solvay Brussels School of Econs and Man. (SBS-EM), Ghent Univ. London Business School, UK, Institut Européen d'Admin des Affaires (INSEAD), Fontainebleau, France; held exec. positions at Belgian TV station VTM, Sun International, Apple Computer, as well as sr positions at Wang in Belgium and Arthur Andersen Consulting 1986–97; held leading positions within Adecco Group, starting out as Country Man. for Benelux region then led Adecco Group's worldwide professional staffing business from New York 1998–2002, CEO Adecco 2009–; CEO Barry Callebaut (cocoa and chocolate products) 2002–09; title of Baron granted by King Albert II 2007. *Address:* Adecco Management & Consulting SA, Sägereistrasse 10, PO Box, 8152 Glattbrugg, Switzerland (office). *Telephone:* (44) 878-88-88 (office). *Fax:* (44) 829-88-88 (office). *E-mail:* info@adecco.com (office). *Website:* www.adecco.com (office).

DE MAIZIÈRE, Lothar; German lawyer and politician; b. 2 March 1940, Nordhausen; m.; three d.; mem. Christian Democratic Union, Leader 1989–90; Deputy Prime Minister and Spokesman on Church Affairs 1989–90; Prime Minister German Democratic Republic and Minister of Foreign Affairs March–Oct. 1990; Minister without Portfolio 1990–91, Deputy Chair. CDU, Chair Brandenburg CDU Oct.-Dec. 1990, 1991; leader Lutheran Church Council; resgnd as CDU deputy 1991. *Publication:* Anwalt der Einheit 1996. *Address:* Am Kupfergraben 6/6A, 10117 Berlin, Germany.

DE MAIZIÈRE, Thomas, DrJur; German lawyer and politician; *Federal Minister of the Interior;* b. 21 Jan. 1954, Bonn; s. of the late Ulrich de Maizière and Eva Werner; m. Martina de Maizière; three c.; ed Wilhelms-Univ. Münster, Univ. Freiburg; began career in office of Mayor of Berlin 1983–85; Leader, Grundsatzreferat (Basic Issues Div.), Senate Chancellery for Land of Berlin 1985–89; mem. W German del. to negotiations on German reunification 1990; Sec. of State in Ministry of Culture, Land of Mecklenburg-W Pomerania 1990–94, Chief of Staff of Chancellery, Mecklenburg-W Pomerania 1994–98; Adviser and Minister, later Chief of Chancellery, Land of Saxony 1999–2001, Minister of Finance, Saxony 2001–02, Prov. Minister of Justice 2002–04, of the Interior 2004–05, mem. Saxony Landtag (Prov. Ass.) 2004–05; Chief of Staff at Fed. Chancellor's Office and Fed. Minister for Special Affairs 2005–09, Fed. Minister of the Interior 2009–11, 2013–, of Defence 2011–13; mem. CDU 1971–; Cavaliere di Gran Croce (Italy) 2006. *Address:* Federal Ministry of the Interior, Alt-Moabit 101, 10559 Berlin, Germany (office). *Telephone:* (30) 186811002 (office). *Fax:* 30) 186811018 (office). *E-mail:* mb@bmi.bund.de (office). *Website:* www.bmi.bund.de (office); www .thomasdemaiziere.de.

(JACQUIN) DE MARGERIE, Christophe Gabriel Jean Marie; French oil company executive; *Chairman and CEO, Total Group;* b. 6 Aug. 1951, Mareuil-sur-Lay-Dissais (Vendée); s. of Pierre Rodocanachi and Colette Taittinger; adopted s. of Pierre-Alain Jacquin de Margerie; m. Colette Taittinger); m. Bernadette Prud'homme 1976; one s. two d.; ed Ecole Supérieure de Commerce, Paris; began career with Total (later Totalfina, then TotalFinaElf, then Total Group) in 1974 in Finance Div., responsible for Budget and Exploration-Production Depts, Group Treas. 1987–90, roles in Middle East Div. including Financial Dir, Asst Dir, Asst Dir-Gen. 1990–95, Dir-Gen. 1995–99, mem. Group Man. Cttee 1995–99, Exec. Cttee 1999–, Dir-Gen. Exploration-Production Div. 1999–2007, CEO 2007–, Chair. 2010–; mem. Supervisory Bd Vivendi; Chevalier, Légion d'honneur, Officier, Ordre nat. du Mérite. *Address:* Total SA, 2 place Jean Millier, La Défense 6, 92078 Paris La Défense Cedex, France (office). *Telephone:* 1-47-44-45-46 (office); 1-47-44-46-99 (office). *Fax:* 1-47-44-68-21 (office). *Website:* www.total.com (office).

DE MARIA, Walter, MFA; American artist; b. 1 Oct. 1935, Albany, Calif.; ed Univ. of California, Berkeley; participated in Happenings and theatrical productions in San Francisco area 1959–60; moved to NY, made first wooden box sculptures 1961; co-f. 9 Great Jones Street Gallery, NY 1963, presented first solo exhbn of sculpture 1963; drummer for rock group The Velvet Underground 1963; began 'invisible drawings' and composed music 1964; began making pieces from metal 1965; solo show at Cordier & Ekstrom, NY 1966; participated in Primary Structures, Jewish Museum, NY 1966; became leader of Earthworks Movt upon filling Galerie Heiner Friedrich with dirt, Munich, Germany 1968; created The Mile Long Drawing in the Desert in the Mojave Desert 1968; participated in Documenta, Kassel 1968; sculpture exhbn, Kunstmuseum Basel, Switzerland 1972; completed Three Continent Project 1972, Lightening Field, New Mexico 1977; recreated Earth Room, Heiner Friedrich Gallery, NY; Malter Sculpture Prize of Art Inst. of Chicago 1976, Baden-Württemberg Int. Fine Art Prize 1987. *Public Collections include:* Museum für Moderne Kunst (MKK), Frankfurt am Main (Germany), Museum für Gegenwartskunst, Basel (Switzerland), Dia Art Foundation, Chelsea, NY, Solomon R. Guggenheim Museum, NY, Gagosian Galleries in London, UK and USA. *Public Exhibitions include:* Walter de Maria – The 2000 Sculpture, Kunsthaus Zürich (Switzerland) 1999, Fernsehgalerie Gerry Schum, Kunsthalle Düsseldorf (Germany) 2003. *Publications:* essays on art, chapters in books. *Address:* c/o Gagosian Gallery, 456 North Camen Drive, Beverly Hills, CA 90210, USA.

DE MARIA Y CAMPOS, Mauricio, MA; Mexican economist, diplomatist and academic; *Director, Instituto de Investigaciones sobre Desarrollo Sustentable y Equidad Social (Research Institute for Sustainable Development and Social Equity), Universidad Iberoamericana Ciudad de México;* b. 13 Oct. 1943, Mexico DF; s. of Mauricio de María y Campos and Teresa Castello; m. Patricia Meade 1981; two s. one d.; ed Nat. Univ. of Mexico, Univ. of Sussex, UK; Head of Planning and Policy Unit, Mexican Nat. Science and Tech. Council 1971–72; Deputy Dir

Evaluation Dept Tech. Transfer Ministry of Trade and Industry 1973–74, Dir Gen. Foreign Investment 1974–77, Vice-Minister Industrial Devt 1982–89; Dir Gen. Tax Incentives and Fiscal Promotion Ministry of Finance 1977–82; Exec. Vice-Pres. Banco Mexicano SOMEX 1989–92; Deputy Dir Gen. UNIDO 1992–93, Dir Gen. 1993–97; Amb. at Large and Special Adviser on UN Affairs, Ministry of Foreign Affairs 1998–2001; Amb. to South Africa 2002–07; currently Dir Instituto de Investigaciones sobre Desarrollo Sustentable y Equidad Social (Research Inst. for Sustainable Devt and Social Equity), Universidad Iberoamericana; mem. Int. Club of Rome 1998– (Pres. of Mexican Chapter 1998–), Mexican Council on Foreign Relations (COMEXI); Grand Commendateur Ordre nat. du Mérite, Order of Francisco de Miranda (Venezuela); Great Decoration in Gold on the Sash (Austria); Grand Ordre du Mono (Togo). *Publications:* Challenges and Opportunities for Scientific and Technological Collaboration between the EEC and Mexico 1990, The Transformation of the Mexican Automobile Industry during the 1980s 1992; various publs on industrial and technological policy and on regional devt. *Leisure interests:* classical music, writing, reading, swimming, jogging, dancing, journalism. *Address:* Instituto de Investigaciones sobre Desarrollo Sustentable y Equidad Social (Research Institute for Sustainable Development and Social Equity), Edificio Q, 3er. piso, Universidad Iberoamericana Ciudad de México, Prolongación Paseo de la Reforma 880, Lomas de Santa Fe, México, C.P. 01219, Distrito Federal 01219 México DF, Mexico (office). *Telephone:* (55) 5950-4339 (office). *Fax:* (55) 5950-4195 (office). *E-mail:* mauricio.demaria@uia.mx (office). *Website:* www.uia.mx (office).

DE MELLO BRANDÃO, Lázaro; Brazilian economist and banking executive; *Chairman, Banco Bradesco SA;* b. 15 June 1926; joined Casa Bancária Almeida & Cie (renamed Banco Brasileiro de Descontos SA, then Banco Bradesco SA) 1942, various positions including Exec. Officer 1963–77, Deputy CEO 1977–81, Pres. 1981–99, Deputy Chair. 1982–1990, Chair. 1990–; Chair. Companhia Brasileira de Securitação (CIBRASEC) 1997–99, Bradespar SA 2004–; Chair. Man. Body and CEO Fundação Bradesco; mem. Bd of Dirs Banco Espírito Santo SA, Lisbon, Portugal, Nat. Housing Bank 1984–85; Chair. Credit Guarantor Fund (FGC) 1999–2001; Exec. Officer, Bank Trade Asscn in States of São Paulo, Paraná, Mato Grosso, Mato Grosso do Sul, Acre, Amazonas, Pará, Amapá, Rondônia and Roraima 1966–74, CEO 1974–83; Vice-Pres. Bd of Exec. Officers, Nat. Fed. of Banks (FENABAN) 1971–76, 1980–83, mem. Bd of Dirs 1983–91, 1994–2001; mem. Bd of Dirs Brazilian Fed. of Bank Asscns (FEBRABAN), Advisory Bd VBC Participações SA; Chair. and CEO Foundation Inst. for Digestive System and Nutrition Diseases (FIMADEN); Hon. Citizen of Joinville. *Address:* Banco Bradesco SA, Avenida Ipiranga 282, 10 andar, CEP 01046-920 São Paulo, Brazil (office). *Telephone:* (11) 3235-9566 (office). *Fax:* (11) 3235-9161 (office). *E-mail:* info@bradesco.com.br (office). *Website:* www.bradesco.com.br (office).

DE METZ, Robert; French business executive; *Chairman, Dexia SA;* ed Inst. of Political Studies, Paris, École Nat. d'Admin, Strasbourg; began career in Gen. Finance Inspectorate; joined Banque Indosuez 1983, held posts in Hong Kong and France before joining Demachy Worms & Cie; joined Paribas 1991, held numerous posts before being apptd to the Bd of Dirs, responsible from London for fixed income, forex and derivatives markets; Dir Cobepa 1993–99; Deputy Dir Gen. Vivendi Group in charge of mergers-acquisitions and strategy 2002–07; Chair. Dexia SA 2012–; Exec. Dir and mem. Accounts Cttee La Fayette Management Ltd; mem. Supervisory Bd Canal+ France; Dir, Média-Participations (Paris-Brussels), L.A. Finances (Paris); CEO Bee2Bees SA (Brussels); mem. Exec. Cttee Foundation Demeure Historique pour l'avenir du patrimoine. *Address:* Dexia SA, Square de Meeûs 1, 1000 Brussels, Belgium (office). *Telephone:* (2) 213-57-00 (office). *Fax:* (2) 213-57-01 (office). *E-mail:* webmaster@dexia.com (office). *Website:* www.dexia.com (office).

DE MEURON, Pierre, DipArch; Swiss architect; b. 1950, Basel; ed Fed. Tech. Univ. (ETH), Zurich; Asst to Prof. Dolf Schnebli, ETH, Zurich 1977; f. architectural practice Herzog & De Meuron (with Jacques Herzog q.v.) 1978; Prof. of Architecture and Design, ETH 1999–; Visiting Prof., Harvard Univ., Cambridge, Mass. 1989, Tulane Univ., New Orleans 1991; (all jtly with Jacques Herzog) Architecture Prize, Berlin Acad. of Arts 1987, Andrea Palladio Int. Prize for Architecture, Vicenza, Italy 1988, Pritzker Architecture Prize 2001, Praemium Imperiale 2007. *Principal works include:* Blue House, Oberwil 1979–80, Photostudio Frei, Weil am Rhein 1981–82, Sperrholz Haus, Bottmingen 1984–85, Apartment Bldg, Hebelstr. 11, Basel 1984–88, Wohn- und Geschäftshaus Schwitter, Basel 1985–98, Goetz Art Gallery, Munich 1989–92, Wohn- und Geschäftshaus Schützenmattstr., Basel 1992–93, Dominus Winery, Napa Valley, Yountville, Calif. 1995–97, Tate Gallery Extension (Tate Modern), Bankside, London (RIBA Gold Medal 2007) 1995–99, Cultural Centre and Theatre, Zurich 1996, Ricola Marketing Bldg, Laufen 1998, Laban Centre for Contemporary Dance (Stirling Prize) 2003, M. H. de Young Memorial Museum, San Francisco 2005, Walker Art Center expansion, Minneapolis, Minnesota 2005, Beijing Nat. Stadium, China (Lubetkin Prize 2009) 2008. *Works in progress include:* Prada Headquarters, New York, Miami Art Museum, São Paulo Companhia de Dança Brazil, Kolkata Museum of Modern Art, India, as well as projects in UK, France, Germany, Italy, Spain and Japan. *Address:* Herzog & De Meuron Architekten, Rheinschanze 6, Basel, 4056, Switzerland (office). *Telephone:* (61) 3855758 (office). *Fax:* (61) 3855757 (office). *E-mail:* info@herzogdemeuron.com (office).

DE MEY, Jozef; Belgian actuary and insurance industry executive; *Chairman, Ageas;* b. 1943; ed Univs of Gent and Louvain; began career at Insurance Control Authorities, Ministry of Econ. Affairs 1967; worked at Kredietbank Belgium 1969–71; joined John Hancock (financial services provider) 1971, held various positions –1990; joined Fortis 1990, served as Gen. Man. Fortis International, CEO Fortis AG, apptd mem. Exec. Cttee 2000, Chief Investment Officer within Exec. Cttee 2007, continued to hold several non-exec. bd memberships in Fortis operating cos, Chair. (non-exec.) Fortis (renamed Ageas April 2010) 2009–; Chair. Bd of Dirs Ageas, AG Insurance, Vice-Chair. Muang Thai Fortis Holding (Thailand), Muang Thai Life Insurance Co., De Eik NV, Credimo NV, Credimo Holding NV, Zinner NV, Festival van Vlaanderen Gent. *Address:* Ageas SA/NV, Rue du Marquis 1, 1000 Brussels, Belgium (office). *Telephone:* (2) 557-57-11 (office). *Fax:* (2) 557-57-51 (office). *E-mail:* info@ageas.com (office). *Website:* www .ageas.com (office).

DE MEZA, Mike Eric; Aruban business executive and politician; *Minister of Finance, Transportation and Utilities;* b. 13 May 1963; owner of an eng co.; mem. Arubaanse Volkspartij (AVP) (Aruba People's Party); currently mem. Staten (Parl.); Minister of Finance, Transportation and Utilities 2009–. *Address:* Ministry of Finance, Transportation and Utilities, Cumana 69, Oranjestad, Aruba (office). *Telephone:* 5880269 (office). *Fax:* 5880347 (office). *Website:* www.mikedemeza.com (office).

DE MICHELIS, Gianni; Italian chemist, academic and politician; b. 26 Nov. 1940, Venice; Prof. of Chem., Univ. of Padua; Lecturer in Chem., Univ. of Venice; Nat. Chair. Unione Goliardica Italiana 1962–64; Councillor, Venice 1964–76; mem. Cen. Cttee Italian Socialist Party (PSI) 1969–76, mem. Nat. Exec. 1976–; mem. Parl. for Venice 1976–; fmr Minister for State-owned Industries; Minister of Labour and Social Security 1986–87; Deputy Prime Minister 1988–89; Minister of Foreign Affairs 1989–92; Deputy Leader PSI 1992; charged with fraud May 1995; sentenced to two years' imprisonment for corruption; Founder and Sec. Partito Socialista 1996, merged to become Nuovo Partito Socialista Italiano 2001, Sec. 2001–07; currently mem. new Partito Socialista; mem. European Parl. 2004–09; Chair. Inst. for Relations between Italy and Africa, Latin America and the Middle East and Far East (IPALMO) 2002–. *Address:* c/o Partito Socialista (Socialist Party), Piazza S. Lorenzo in Lucina 26, 00186 Rome, Italy.

DE MIRANDA, João Bernardo; Angolan politician; b. 18 July 1951; m.; Dir of Information, Rádio Nacional de Angola 1977–80; Ed.-in-Chief Jornal de Angola newspaper 1980–84; Sec., Movimento Popular de Libertação de Angola (MPLA) Ideological Area (Prov. of Luanda); Head of Political and Legal Affairs Div., MPLA Cen. Cttee 1985–89, Head of Information and Propaganda Dept 1989–91; Vice-Minister of Information 1991; Vice-Minister of Foreign Relations 1991–99, Minister of Foreign Affairs 1999–2008; African Union Envoy to Guinea-Bissau 2009. *Publications include:* Nambuangongo. *Address:* Movimento Popular de Libertação de Angola, Luanda, Angola (office). *E-mail:* mpla@ebonet.net (office). *Website:* www2.ebonet.net/MPLA (office).

DE MISTURA, Staffan; Italian UN official and government official; *Under-Secretary of Foreign Affairs;* b. 25 Jan. 1947, Stockholm, Sweden; m.; two d.; ed Univ. of Rome; joined UN 1970, intern for UN WFP in Cyprus early 1970s, WFP project officer in Sudan 1971, led food aid and relief operations in Ethiopia, the Balkans and Rwanda, emergency relief officer in Chad 1973; Deputy Chef de Cabinet, FAO 1976–85; Dir WFP Operations in Sudan 1987; Dir of Fund-Raising and External Relations, UN Office of the Co-ordinator for Afghanistan 1988–91; Special Envoy of UN Sec.-Gen. to Albania 1990; UN Humanitarian Co-ordinator for Iraq March–Aug. 1997; Dir UN Information Centre, Rome –2000; Personal Rep. of UN Sec.-Gen. in S Lebanon 2001–05; Deputy Special Rep. of UN Sec.-Gen. in Iraq 2005–06, Special Rep. 2007–09; Dir UN Systems Staff Coll., Turin, Italy 2006–07; Deputy Exec. Dir for External Relations, UN WFP, Rome, Italy 2009–10; Special Rep. of UN Sec.-Gen. and Head of UN Assistance Mission in Afghanistan (UNAMA) 2010–11; Under-Sec. of Foreign Affairs in Italy's technocratic cabinet headed by Mario Monti 2011–. *Address:* Ministry of Foreign Affairs, Piazzale della Farnesina 1, 00194 Rome, Italy (office). *Telephone:* (06) 36911 (office). *Fax:* (06) 36918899 (office). *E-mail:* relazioni.pubblico@esteri.it (office). *Website:* www.esteri .it (office).

DE MOLINA, Alvaro G., BA, MBA; Cuban/American business executive; b. 13 July 1957, Cuba; ed Bergen Catholic High School, Oradell, NJ, Fairleigh Dickinson Univ., Rutgers Business School, Duke Univ. Advanced Man. Program; began career with PriceWaterhouse 1979; later served in lead financial role for emerging markets at J.P. Morgan; spent 17 years at Bank of America, served as Chief Financial Officer, also served as CEO Bank of America Securities, Pres. Global Corp. and Investment Banking, and Corp. Treas.; with Cerberus Capital Management June–Aug. 2007; COO GMAC Financial Services (renamed Ally Financial Inc. 2010) Aug. 2007–08, CEO 2008–09 (resgnd); mem. Bd Duke Univ. Fuqua School of Business, Foundation for the Carolinas, Florida International Univ., Financial Services Volunteer Corps. *Address:* c/o Ally Financial Inc., 200 Renaissance Center, Detroit, MI 48265-2000, USA. *Telephone:* (313) 556-5000. *E-mail:* info@ally.com. *Website:* www.ally.com.

DE MONTEBELLO, Comte Philippe, BA; French art historian and museum director; b. 16 May 1936, Paris; m. Edith Bradford Myles 1961; ed Harvard Univ., Inst. of Fine Arts, New York Univ., USA; Curatorial Asst, later Asst Curator, Assoc. Curator, Dept of European Paintings, Metropolitan Museum of Art, New York 1963–69, Vice-Dir for Curatorial and Educational Affairs 1974–77, Acting Dir 1977–78, Dir. 1978–99, Dir and CEO 1999–2008 (retd); Dir Museum of Fine Arts, Houston, Tex. 1969–74; Gallatin Fellow, New York Univ. 1981; Kt Commdr, Pontifical Order of St Gregory the Great 1984, Commendatore, Order of Merit (Italy) 1988, Orden de Isabel la Catolica (Spain) 1992, Officier de l'Ordre de Léopold (Belgium) 1994, Commdr de l'Ordre des Arts et Lettres 2001, Officier, Légion d'honneur 2005; Hon. LLD (Lafayette Coll.) 1979, (Dartmouth Coll.) 2004, Hon. DHumLitt (Bard Coll., New York) 1981, Hon. DFA (Iona Coll., New Rochelle) 1982, (Harvard) 2006, (New York) 2007; Nat. Inst. of Social Sciences Gold Medal 1989, Spanish Inst. Gold Medal Award 1992, National Council of Jewish Women, Rebekah Kohut Award 1993, Distinguished Alumnus Award, New York Univ. 1998, Mayoral Proclamation 2002, Celebration of twenty-five years as Dir of the Metropolitan Museum of Art, Nat. Endowment for the Arts, Nat. Medal of Arts 2003, Amigos del Museo del Prado Prize 2004, Conféd. Int. des Négociants en Oeuvres d'Art Prize 2005, and other awards. *Publications:* Peter Paul Rubens (monograph) 1968, articles in the Metropolitan Museum of Art Bulletin and the Bulletin, Museum of Fine Arts, Houston on topics from the Renaissance to the contemporary, more than 200 entries in the McGraw Hill Dictionary of Art 1967, including those on Velasquez, Murillo and Goya; The High Cost of Quality Museum News August 1984, The Met and the New Millennium: A Chronicle of the Past and a Blueprint for the Future 1994, introductions to numerous exhibition catalogues published by the Metropolitan Museum of Art. *Leisure interests:* chess, tennis, music. *Address:* 25 East 86th Street, 3E, New York, NY 10028, USA (home). *Telephone:* (212) 289-4475 (home).

DE MONTFERRAND, Bernard de Faubournet, LLB; French diplomatist; b. 6 Aug. 1945, Caudéran, Gironde; m. Catherine de Tavernost; three c.; ed Faculty of Law, Paris, Inst. of Political Studies, Paris, Ecole Nat. d'Admin.; Sec. of Foreign Affairs, Econ. and Financial Affairs Div., Ministry of Foreign Affairs 1974–79; Lecturer, then Dir of Studies, Inst. of Political Studies, Paris 1975–79; Counsellor for Econ., Financial and Admin. Affairs, French Mil. Govt in Berlin 1979–82; Deputy Dir and Jt Head of Personnel and Gen. Admin, Ministry of Foreign Affairs 1982–85; Consul-Gen. in San Francisco, USA 1985–86; Dir of Cabinet for Minister of Co-operation Michel Aurillac 1986–88; Amb. to Singapore 1989–93, to the Netherlands 1995–2000, to India 2000–02, to Japan 2002–06, to Germany 2007–11; Diplomatic Adviser to Prime Minister Edouard Balladur 1993–95; Founder and Pres. Centre int. de recherches préhistoriques de la vallée de la Couze; Pres. Fonds régional d'art contemporain d'Aquitaine 2007–; Officier, Légion d'honneur, Chevalier, Ordre nat. du Mérite. *Publications:* La France et l'Etranger 1987, La vertu des Nations 1993, Défendre l'Europe: la tentation suisse 1999, Diplomatie, des volontés françaises 2006. *Address:* Federal Ministry of Foreign Affairs, 11013 Berlin, Germany (office). *Telephone:* (30) 5000-0 (office). *Fax:* (30) 18173402 (office). *E-mail:* poststelle@auswaertiges-amt.de (office). *Website:* www.auswaertiges-amt.de (office).

DE MORAES, Antônio Ermírio; Brazilian business executive; b. 4 June 1928, São Paulo; s. of José Ermírio de Moraes; m. Maria Regina de Moraes; nine c.; ed Colorado School of Mines, USA; joined Grupo Votorantim 1949, apptd Pres. Admin. Council 1962, then Chair., now retd; f. Companhia Brasileira de Alumínio 1955; regular contrib. Folha de São Paulo (newspaper); Pres. Red Cross Brazil 1962–66; Pres. Brazilian Asscn of Ceramics 1963, 1966, 1969; Pres. Real e Benemérita Sociedade Potuguesa de Beneficência, São Paulo 1969; mem. São Paulo Acad. of Letters; Admin. Emer., Regional Admin. Council of São Paulo 1999; Grand Cross of the Nat. Order of Scientific Merit 2002; Engineer of the Year, São Paulo Inst. of Eng 1980, Personality of the Year in Agronomics, Instituto Agronômico de Campinas 2002. *Plays include:* Brasil S.A. 1996, Educação, pelo amor de Deus 1996, S.O.S. Brasil 2000, Acorda Brasil!. *Publications:* numerous newspaper articles. *Address:* c/o Grupo Votorantim, Rua Amauri 255, 01448-000 São Paulo, Brazil. *E-mail:* antonio.ermirio@antonioermirio.com.br. *Website:* www .votorantim.com.br; www.antonioermirio.com.br.

DE MORNAY, Rebecca; American actress; b. 29 Aug. 1959, Los Angeles, Calif.; m. Bruce Wagner 1989 (divorced 1991); ed in Austria and at Lee Strasberg Inst. in Los Angeles; apprenticed at Zoetrope Studios. *Theatre includes:* Born Yesterday 1988, Marat/Sade 1990. *Films include:* One from the Heart 1982, Risky Business 1983, Testament 1983, The Slugger's Wife 1985, Runaway Train 1985, The Trip to Bountiful 1985, Beauty and The Beast 1987, And God Created Woman 1988, Feds 1988, Dealers 1989, Backdraft 1991, The Hand that Rocks the Cradle (Best Actress, Cognac Crime Film Festival 1992), Guilty as Sin 1993, The Three Musketeers 1993, Never Talk to Strangers 1995, The Winner 1996, Thick as Thieves 1998, Table for One 1998, The Right Temptation 2000, Identity 2003, Raise Your Voice 2004, Lords of Dogtown 2005, Wedding Crashers 2005, Music Within 2007, American Venus 2007, Flipped 2010, Mother's Day 2010, Collar 2011, Apartment 1303 3D 2012. *Television appearances include:* The Murders in the Rue Morgue 1986, By Dawn's Early Light 1990, An Inconvenient Woman 1992, Blind Side 1993, Getting Out 1994, The Shining 1996, The Con 1997, Night Ride Home 1999, The Conversion (Dir) 1996, ER 1999, Night Ride Home 1999, Range of Motion 2000, A Girl Thing 2001, Salem Witch Trials 2002, Law and Order 2006, John from Cincinnati (series) 2007–09, Hatfields & McCoys (film) 2013.

DE NARVÁEZ, Francisco; Argentine (b. Colombian) business executive and politician; b. 22 Sept. 1953, Bogotá, Colombia; s. of Juan de Narváez and Doris Steur; m. 1st; three c.; m. 2nd Agustina Ayllón (fmr model); three c.; ed attended mil. acad. in Toronto, Canada; family moved to Buenos Aires, Argentina 1959; entered maternal grandfather's supermarket chain, Casa Tía 1970, took over man. of Casa Tía chain, along with brother Carlos 1980, attained Argentine citizenship 1983, apptd sole Man. Dir 1989, sold Casa Tía chain for US $638 million 1999; owner or main shareholder of: La Rural SA (exhbn and conf. centre in Buenos Aires), broadcaster América TV, Buenos Aires financial newspaper Ambito Financiero, radio station La Red; Co-founder Fundación Unidos del Sud (political think-tank) 2001; mem. Partido Justicialista (PJ, Peronists) 2002–; Nat. Deputy for Buenos Aires Prov. (first foreigner to be elected to congress in Argentina) 2005–, mem. 'El General' (anti-Kirchnerista Peronist group of PJ deputies and senators) 2006–; unsuccessful cand. for Gov. of Buenos Aires 2007; defeated fmr Pres. Néstor Kirchner in legis. mid-term elections in prov. of Buenos Aires June 2009. *Address:* Cámara de Diputados, Congreso de la nación, Av. Rivadavia 1864, C. P. C1033AAU, Ciudad Autónoma de Buenos Aires, Argentina (office). *Telephone:* (11) 6310-7100 (ext. 3117) (office); (800) 4444336. *Fax:* (11) 6313-6048 (office). *E-mail:* fdenarvaez@diputados.gov.ar (office); info@franciscodenarvaez .com. *Website:* www.diputados.gov.ar (office); www.franciscodenarvaez.com.

DE NIRO, Robert; American actor; b. 1943, New York, NY; s. of the late Robert De Niro and of Virginia Admiral; m. 1st Diahnne Abbott 1976; one s. one d.; two s. by Toukie Smith; m. 2nd Grace Hightower 1997; one s.; Founder and Pres. TriBeCa Productions 1989–; co-cr. We Will Rock You (musical) 2002; Co-owner Nobu restaurants; Pres. Jury, Cannes Film Festival 2011; Commdr, Ordre des Arts et des Lettres; Chevalier, Légion d'honneur; Lifetime Achievement Award, Gotham Awards 2001, American Film Inst. Lifetime Achievement Award 2003, Kennedy Center Honor 2009, Cecil B DeMille Award for Lifetime Achievement, Hollywood Foreign Press Asscn 2011. *Films include:* The Wedding Party 1969, Jennifer On My Mind 1971, Bloody Mama, Born to Win 1971, The Gang That Couldn't Shoot Straight 1971, Bang the Drum Slowly 1973, Mean Streets 1973, The Godfather, Part II 1974 (Acad. Award for Best Supporting Actor), The Last Tycoon, Taxi Driver 1976, 1900 1976, New York, New York 1977, The Deer Hunter 1978, Raging Bull (Acad. Award Best Actor) 1980, True Confessions 1981, The King of Comedy 1982, Once Upon a Time in America 1984, Falling in Love 1984, Brazil 1984, The Mission 1985, Angel Heart 1986, The Untouchables 1987, Letters Home from Vietnam, Midnight Run 1988, We're No Angels 1989, Stanley and Iris 1989, Goodfellas 1989, Jacknife 1989, Awakenings 1990, Fear No Evil 1990, Backdraft 1990, Cape Fear 1990, Guilty of Suspicion 1991, Mistress 1992, Night and the City 1992, Mad Dog and Glory 1992, This Boy's Life 1993, Mary Shelley's Frankenstein 1993, A Bronx Tale (also dir, co-produced) 1993, Sleepers 1996, The Fan 1996, Marvin's Room 1996, Great Expectations 1997, Jackie Brown 1998, Ronin 1998, Analyze This 1999, Flawless 1999 (also producer), The Adventures of Rocky and Bullwinkle (also producer) 1999, Meet the Parents (also producer) 2000,

Men of Honor 2000, 15 Minutes 2001, The Score 2001, Showtime 2002, City By the Sea 2002, Analyze That 2002, Godsend 2004, Shark Tale (voice) 2004, Meet the Fockers (also producer) 2004, The Bridge of San Luis Rey 2004, Hide and Seek 2005, Arthur and the Invisibles (voice) 2006, The Good Shepherd (also dir) 2006, Stardust 2007, What Just Happened? (also producer) 2008, Righteous Kill 2008, Everybody's Fine 2009, Machete 2010, Stone 2010, Little Fockers (also producer) 2010, Manuale d'amore 3 2011, The Ages of Love 2011, Limitless 2011, Killer Elite 2011, New Year's Eve 2011, Red Lights 2012, Being Flynn 2012, Crossfire 2012, Silver Linings Playbook 2012, The Big Wedding 2013, Killing Season 2013, Motel 2013, Malavita 2013; as producer Thunderheart 1992, Entrophy 1999, Conjugating Niki 2000, Prison Song 2001, About a Boy 2002, Stage Beauty 2004, Rent 2005, Warrior Queen 2010. *Television:* exec. producer: NYC 22 (series) 2012. *Address:* Tribeca Productions, 375 Greenwich Street, 8th Floor, New York, NY 10013 (office); c/o Creative Artists Agency, 2000 Avenue of the Stars, Los Angeles, CA 90067, USA (office). *Telephone:* (212) 941-2000 (office); (424) 288-2000 (office). *Fax:* (212) 941-2012 (office); (424) 288-2900 (office). *E-mail:* contactus@tribecafilm.com (office). *Website:* www.tribecafilm.com (office); www.caa.com (office).

DE NOINVILLE, Guillaume, LLM, MEcons, MBA; French business executive; *President-Director General, Electrolux France SAS;* b. 8 May 1960, Paris; s. of Christian Durey de Noinville and Béatrice Gallimard; m. Claire de Laguiche; three s. one d.; ed Inst. d'Etudes Politiques, Paris; Finance and Control Dept, Bull Group, Paris 1984–86; Treas. Electrolux France, Senlis 1986–92, Man. Dir Electrolux Financement (leasing co.), Senlis 1992–96, Chief Finance Officer Electrolux France 1994–2002, Electrolux Belgium 1998–2002, Pres.-Dir Gen. Electrolux France SA 2001–, Chief Admin. Officer, Western Europe, Electrolux Group 2003–. *Address:* Electrolux France SAS, BP 20139, 43 avenue Félix Louat, 60307 Senlis Cedex (office); 29 avenue de la Grande Armée, 75116 Paris, France (home). *Telephone:* (3) 44-62-26-39 (office). *Fax:* (3) 44-62-21-89 (office). *E-mail:* guillaume .de-noinville@electrolux.fr (office). *Website:* www.electrolux.com (office).

DE OLIVEIRA, Constantino, Jr; Brazilian business executive; *Chairman, Gol Linhas Aéreas Inteligentes SA;* b. 1969, Patrocínio, Minas Gerais; s. of Nenê Çonstantino de Oliveira; ed Univ. of the Fed. Dist, Brasília; mem. Exec. Bd Grupo Áurea 1994–2000; mem. Admin. Council, GOL 2001–, CEO 2001–12, Pres. and CEO Gol Linhas Aéreas Inteligentes SA (airline) 2004–12, Chair. 2012–; Admin. Emer., Regional Admin. Council of São Paulo 2006–; Exec. of Value, Valor Económico 2001, 2002, Exec. Leader, Gazeta Mercantil 2003, Federico Bloch Prize, Int. Asscn of Latin-American Air Transport 2005, Business Leader of the Year, Latin Trade Awards 2006. *Address:* Gol Linhas Aéreas Inteligentes SA, Rua Gomes de Carvalho, 1629, Vila Olímpia, 05457-006 São Paulo, Brazil (office). *Telephone:* (11) 3169-6800 (office). *Fax:* (11) 3169-6570 (office). *Website:* www .voegol.com.br (office).

DE OLIVEIRA MACIEL, Marco Antônio, LLB, MA; Brazilian lawyer and politician; b. 21 July 1940, Recife; s. of José do Rego Maciel and Carmen Sylvia Cavalcanti de Oliveira Maciel; m. Anna Maria Ferreira; one s. two d.; ed Catholic Univ. of Pernambuco, Pernambuco Univ.; adviser to Pernambuco State Govt 1964–66; Prof. of Public and Int. Law, Catholic Univ. of Pernambuco 1966–; State Deputy, Pernambuco Legis. Ass., Govt Leader 1967–71; Regional Sec. ARENA Party 1969–70, Second Nat. Sec. 1972, First Sec. 1974–75; Fed. Deputy 1971–79, Pres. Chamber of Deputies 1977–79; Gov. Pernambuco State 1979–82; Fed. Senator for PDS Party 1982; Minister for Educ. 1985–86; Minister Chief of Staff of Pres. 1986; Pres. Provisional Nat. Comm. Partido da Frente Liberal (PFL) 1984–85, Nat. Pres. 1987, Fed. Senator for PFL 1990, mem. Nat. Council, Leader PFL in Senate 1990; Minority Leader in Senate 1990, Govt Leader 1991–92; Vice-Pres. of Brazil 1994–2003; mem. Pernambuco Section Brazilian Bar Asscn, Brazilian Acad. of Political and Moral Sciences 1993–, Argentinian Law Asscn, Academia Brasileira de Letras 2003–; numerous honours including Grand Cross, Order of Rio Branco, Brasilia Order of Merit, Légion d'honneur (France), Grand Cross, Order of Infante Dom Henrique (Portugal), Grand Cross, Order of May (Argentina) 1979, Cross of Merit (FRG), Ordre nat. du Mérite (France), City of Recife Medal of Merit. *Publications:* numerous publs on politics and educ. *Address:* Senado Federal (Federal Senate), Anexo I, 5° andar, salas 1 a 6, Palácio do Congresso Nacional, Praça dos Três Poderes, 70165-900 Brasília, DF, Brazil (office). *Telephone:* (61) 3303-5710 (office). *Fax:* (61) 3303-5727 (office). *E-mail:* marco.maciel@senador.gov.br (office). *Website:* www.senado.gov.br (office).

DE ORIOL E YBARRA, Iñigo, LicenDer; Spanish business executive; b. 6 Aug. 1935, Madrid; s. of the late José María de Oriol y Urquijo; ed Univ. Complutense; began career as legal consultant, Hidroeléctrica Española (HE) 1959, mem. Supervisory Bd 1975, Chair. Man. Cttee, Pres. 1985–91; Chair. Iberdrola SA (following merger of HE and Iberduero 1991) 1991–2005 (retd); mem. Advisory Bd Cementos Molins –2004; Pres. Chamber of Commerce and Industry of Madrid 1968–78, UNESA (Employers' Assen of Electric Cos) 1987–89, 1996–98, 2002–04; fmr Pres. Spanish-Portuguese Chamber of Commerce; mem. Superior Council of Chambers of Spain; Hon. Pres. Asscn of Latin American Chambers of Commerce (AICO), Chamber of Commerce and Industry of Madrid; Gran Cruz de Alfonso X; Enterprise Leader of the Year, Spain-USA Chamber of Commerce 2001. *Address:* c/o Iberdrola SA, Cardenal Gardoqui 8, 48008 Bilbao, Spain. *Telephone:* (94) 415-1411. *Fax:* (94) 415-4579. *Website:* www.iberdrola.com.

DE PADT, Guido, LenD; Belgian politician; *Minister of the Interior;* b. 23 May 1954, Geraardsbergen; mem. Vlaamse Liberalen en Demokraten (VLD); Prov. Counsellor for E Flanders 1982–2003; Deputy Mayor of Geraardsbergen 1982–94, 2007–08, Mayor of Geraardsbergen 2001–06; Deputy for E Flanders 1994–2000; mem. Chamber of Reps 2003–; Minister of the Interior 2008–; Chair. Centre-Publique-d'Aide-Sociale for Geraardsbergen 2007–08. *Address:* Federal Public Service of the Interior, 1 rue de Louvain, 1000 Brussels, Belgium (office). *Telephone:* (2) 500-20-50 (Flemish) (office); (2) 500-20-48 (French) (office). *Fax:* (2) 500-20-39 (office). *E-mail:* info@ibz.fgov.be (office). *Website:* www.ibz.be (office).

DE PALMA, Brian, MA; American film director; b. 11 Sept. 1940, Newark, NJ; s. of Anthony Fredrick De Palma and Vivienne De Palma (née Muti); m. 1st Nancy Allen 1979 (divorced 1983); m. 2nd Gale Ann Hurd 1991 (divorced); one d.; m. 3rd Darnell Gregorio-De Palma 1997 (divorced) one c.; ed Sarah Lawrence Coll., Bronxville and Columbia Univ. *Films include:* (short films) Icarus 1960, 660124: The Story of an IBM Card 1961, Wotan's Wake 1962; (feature length) The Wedding

Party 1964, The Responsive Eye (documentary) 1966, Murder à la Mode 1967, Greetings 1968, Dionysus in '69 (co-Dir) 1969, Hi Mom! 1970, Get to Know Your Rabbit 1970, Sisters 1972, Phantom of the Paradise 1974, Obsession 1975, Carrie 1976, The Fury 1978, Home Movies 1979, Dressed to Kill 1980, Blow Out 1981, Scarface 1983, Body Double 1984, Wise Guys 1985, The Untouchables 1987, Casualties of War 1989, Bonfire of the Vanities 1990, Raising Cain 1992, Carlito's Way 1993, Mission Impossible 1996, Snake Eyes 1998, Mission to Mars 2000, Femme Fatale 2002, The Black Dahlia 2006, Redacted (Silver Lion, Venice Film Festival 2007) 2007. *Address:* Paramount Pictures, 5555 Melrose Avenue, W Hollywood, CA 90038, USA.

DE PAOLIS, HE Cardinal Velasio, CS, JCD, STL; Italian ecclesiastic and academic; *President Emeritus, Prefecture for the Economic Affairs of the Holy See;* b. 19 Sept. 1935, Sonnino, Prov. of Latina, Lazio region; ed Pontifical Gregorian Univ., Pontifical Univ. of St Thomas, La Sapienza Univ., Rome; professed as mem. of Congregation of the Missionaries of St Charles Borromeo 1958, ordained priest 1961; taught canon law at Pontifical Gregorian Univ.; Prof. of Canon Law, Pontifical Gregorian Univ. 1971–80, 1983–; Prof., Faculty of Canon Law, Pontifical Urban Univ. 1987–, Dean 1998–; Sec. Apostolic Signatura 2003–08, mem. 2010– (15); Titular Bishop of Thelepte 2003–08, Titular Archbishop 2008–; Pres. Pref. for the Econ. Affairs of the Holy See 2008–11, Pres. Emer. 2011–; Pontifical Del. for the Congregation of the Legionaries of Christ 2010–; cr. Cardinal (Cardinal-Deacon of Gesù Buon Pastore alla Montagnola) 2010; participated in Papal Conclave 2013. *Address:* Piazza Del Sant'Uffizio 11 00120 Vatican City, Italy (office). *Telephone:* (06) 69882074 (office). *E-mail:* v.depaolis@econaffr.va (office). *Website:* www.vatican.va/roman_curia/uffici/prefettura/index_en.htm (office).

DE PERETTI, Jean-Jacques; French politician; *Conseiller d'Etat, Conseil d'Etat;* b. 21 Sept. 1946, Clermont-Ferrand; three c.; ed Inst. des Hautes Etudes Internationales; Asst Lecturer, St-Maur Faculty of Law and Univs of Orléans and Paris I 1969–84; Chargé de Mission, Cabinet of Pierre Messmer 1972; Dir de Cabinet to Pres. of Paris Region 1974; Chargé de Mission to André Bord, Sec.-Gen. of Union des Démocrates pour la République (UDR) 1976; Chargé de Mission, Cabinet of Antoine Rufenacht, Sec. of State to Prime Minister; Sec. of State to Minister for Industry, Trade and Craft Trades; Man. Exec. IBM until 1986; Adviser to Prime Minister Jacques Chirac 1986; Mayor of Sarlat 1989–; fmr mem. Regional Council and Deputy to Nat. Ass. for Dordogne Dept's 4th constituency; Departmental Councillor for Dordogne 1992–; Nat. Sec. Rassemblement pour la République (RPR) 1990–93, Deputy Sec.-Gen. 1994–95; Minister for Overseas France May–Nov. 1995; Minister-Del. to Prime Minister with responsibility for Overseas France 1995–97; mem. Regional Council of Aquitaine; Conseiller, Conseil d'Etat; mem. Hudson Inst. 1969–; Legion d'Honneur. *Publications:* L'envol de la France dan les anées 80 (with Herman Khan and the Hudson Inst.) 1979, Gagner les Municipales 1988. *Address:* Hôtel de ville, 24200 Sarlat-la-Canéda, France (home). *Telephone:* (5) 53-31-53-30 (office); 1-47-53-80-53 (office). *Fax:* (5) 53-31-08-04 (office); 1-47-53-80-53 (office). *E-mail:* jjpc@wanadoo.fr (office). *Website:* jean-jacques.de-peretti@conseil-etat.fr (office).

DE PURY, Simon; Swiss auctioneer and art dealer; *Chairman, Phillips de Pury & Company;* b. 1951, Basel; ed Acad. of Fine Arts, Tokyo, Japan; worked at the Bern auctioneers, Kornfeld & Klipstein, and subsequently studied at Sotheby's Inst. before joining Sotheby's, working in London, Geneva and Monte Carlo; Curator Thyssen-Bornemisza collection, Lugano 1979–86; returned to Sotheby's first as Chair. Sotheby's Switzerland and then as Chair. of Sotheby's Europe and the co.'s Prin. Auctioneer 1986; conducted all of Sotheby's major sales in Europe which included the Thurn and Taxis sale in Geneva and Regensburg, the Margrave sales in Baden-Baden and, from 1994, all the major Impressionist sales in New York; co-f. (with Daniella Luxembourg) de Pury & Luxembourg Art (art advisory co.), Geneva 1997, merged with Phillips Auctioneers to become Phillips, de Pury and Luxembourg 2001, Chair. and majority shareholder of Phillips de Pury & Company 2004–. *Address:* Phillips de Pury & Company, 450 West 15th Street, New York, NY 10011, USA (office). *Telephone:* (212) 940-1200 (office). *Fax:* (212) 924-3306 (office). *E-mail:* info@phillipsdepury.com (office). *Website:* www .phillipsdepury.com (office).

DE QUEIROZ DUARTE, Sergio, BA, BL; Brazilian fmr diplomatist and fmr UN official; b. Rio de Janeiro; m.; two c.; ed Fed. Fluminense Univ., Rio de Janeiro, Brazilian School of Public Admin (Getúlio Vargas Foundation), Rio de Janeiro, Brazilian Diplomatic Acad. (Instituto Rio Branco), Rio de Janeiro; joined Foreign Service, apptd Third Sec. 1957, diplomatic appointments included Embassies in Rome 1961–63, in Buenos Aires 1963–66, in Washington, DC 1970–74, Perm. Mission to UN, Geneva 1966–68 (mem. Brazilian del. to 18-nation Disarmament Cttee); Alt. Rep., Office of Special Rep. of Brazil for Disarmament Affairs, Geneva 1979–86, Amb. to Nicaragua 1986–91, to Canada 1993–96, to People's Repub. of China 1996–99, to Austria 1999–2002 (also accred to Slovakia, Slovenia and Croatia and as Rep. to Int. Orgs, Vienna); Gov. for Brazil at Bd of Govs, IAEA, Chair. Bd Govs 1999–2000; Head of Personnel, Ministry of Foreign Affairs 1975–79, apptd Sec.-Gen. for Budget Control and Insp.-Gen. 1991, Exec. Sec.-Gen. 1991–92, Under-Sec.-Gen. for Foreign Service 1992–93, Amb.-at-Large for Disarmament and Non-Proliferation 2003–04; UN Under-Sec.-Gen. and High Rep. for Disarmament Affairs 2007–12; elected Pres. Review Conf. of Parties to Treaty Prohibiting the Emplacement of Nuclear Weapons on the Seabed and the Subsoil Thereof, Geneva 1988, VII Review Conf. of Parties to Treaty on the Non-proliferation of Nuclear Weapons, New York 2005.

DE QUERCIZE, Stanislas; French business executive; *CEO, Cartier;* extensive career within Richemont Group since 1989, worked with Montblanc, Alfred Dunhill, Cartier (Pres. Cartier North America Inc.), Pres. and CEO Van Cleef & Arpels SA 2005–12, CEO Cartier SA 2012–, mem. Man. Cttee Compagnie Financière Richemont SA. *Address:* Cartier SA, 33 rue Boissy d'Anglas, 75008 Paris, France (office); Compagnie Financière Richemont SA, 50 chemin de la Chênaie, 1293 Bellevue, Geneva, Switzerland (office). *Telephone:* 1-42-18-43-83 (Paris) (office); (22) 7153500 (Geneva) (office). *Fax:* (22) 7153550 (Geneva) (office). *E-mail:* customer.service@cartier.com (office); pressoffice@cfrinfo.net (office). *Website:* www.cartier.com (office); www.richemont.com (office).

DE RAAD, Ad, MSc; Dutch UN official; b. 7 Dec. 1952; ed Delft Univ. of Tech.; sr positions, UNDP Country Offices in Bangladesh 1980–84, Tanzania 1984–87;

various posts, Bureau for Finance and Admin, UNDP, New York 1987–93; Dir of Budget, UNDP, New York 1993–98; Deputy Exec. Coordinator UN Volunteers (UNV) programme, Bonn, Germany 1998–2003, Acting Exec. Coordinator 2003–04, Exec. Coordinator 2004–08. *Address:* c/o United Nations Volunteers, Postfach 260 111, 53153 Bonn, Germany (office).

DE RACHEWILTZ, Igor, PhD, FAHA; Italian historian, philologist and academic; *Fellow Emeritus, Australian National University;* b. 11 April 1929, Rome; s. of Bruno Guido and Antonina Perosio; m. Ines Adelaide Brasch 1956; one d.; ed St Gabriel's Coll., Rome Univ. and Australian Nat. Univ.; Research Scholar, ANU 1956–60, Sr Lecturer, Faculty of Asian Studies 1963–65, Fellow, Inst. of Advanced Studies 1965–67, Sr Fellow 1967–94, Visiting Fellow 1995–2008, Fellow Emer. 2009–; Lecturer in Asian Civilization, Canberra Univ. Coll. 1960–62; Visiting Prof., Univ. of Bonn 1979, Univ. of Rome 'La Sapienza' 1996, 1999, 2001, 2002; mem. Sonderforschungsbereich 12 1979–; Vice-Pres. International Asscn for Mongol Studies 1992–2002; Hon. Pres. International Centre for Genghis Khan Studies, Mongolia; Kt, Order of Merit of Italian Repub. 1998; Hon. DLitt (Univ. of Rome 'La Sapienza') 2001; Centenary Medal for Service to Australian Soc. and the Humanities in Asian Studies 2003, Gold Medal, Perm. International Altaistic Conf. 2004, Polar Star Medal (Mongolia) 2007, D. Sinor Medal, Royal Asiatic Soc., London 2007. *Publications include:* The Hsi-yu lu by Yeh-lü Ch'u-ts'ai 1962, Papal Envoys to the Great Khans 1971, Index to the Secret History of the Mongols 1972, The Preclassical Mongolian Version of the Hsiao-ching 1982, Repertory of Proper Names in Yüan Literary Sources 1988–96, text edn and word-index of Erdeni-yin tobci 1990–91, In the Service of the Khan 1993, Le matériel mongol du Houa ii iu de Houng-ou (1389): Commentaires 1995, The Mongolian Tanjur version of the Bodhicaryāvatāra 1996, The Secret History of the Mongols (new edn, Vol. 1, 2) 2004, (2nd edn, Vol. 3) 2006, Introduction to Altaic Philology: Turkic, Mongolian, Manchu (with Volker Rybatzki) 2010; more than 100 articles on Sino-Mongolian topics, medieval history and Altaic philology. *Leisure interests:* botany. *Address:* School of Culture, History and Language, College of Asia and the Pacific, Australian National University, Canberra, ACT 0200 (office); 9 Ridley Street, Turner, ACT 2612, Australia (home). *Telephone:* (2) 6125-3171 (office); (2) 6248-0557 (home). *Fax:* (2) 6125-5525 (office). *E-mail:* igor.derachewiltz@anu.edu.au (office). *Website:* www.anu.edu.au (office).

DE RIBEROLLES, Dominique, BEcons, MBA; Spanish business executive; *CEO, Compañía Española de Petróleos SA (CEPSA);* ed Polytechnic Univ. of Paris, Univ. of Washington, USA; began career as Admin. and Financial Man. of Lubricants Area, ELF Group, in charge of coordinating relations in Madrid between ELF and Compañía Española de Petróleos SA (CEPSA) 1990–96, Vice-Pres. CEPSA's Corp. Planning and Control Div. 1996–98, Sr Vice-Pres. 1998–2003, Exec. Dir 2003–06, CEO CEPSA 2006–. *Address:* Compañía Española de Petróleos SA, Campo de las Naciones, Avenida del Partenón 12, 28042 Madrid, Spain (office). *Telephone:* (91) 3376000 (office). *Fax:* (91) 7211613 (office). *E-mail:* webcepsa@cepsa.com (office). *Website:* www.cepsa.com (office).

DE RIVAZ, Vincent; French business executive; *CEO, Executive Director and Chairman of Executive Committee, EDF Energy (UK) Limited;* ed Ecole Nationale Supérieure d'Hydraulique, Grenoble; joined Electricité de France (EDF) SA's Centre for External Eng within Int. Affairs Dept 1977, Exec. Vice-Pres. of Far East 1985–92, Exec. Vice-Pres., Nat. Hydraulic Equipment Centre, Equipment Div. 1992–95, Asst Dir, Int. Div. 1995–96, Project Man. 1996–99, Operating Vice-Pres., Finance Div. 1999–2000, Exec. Vice-Pres. of Finance Strategy and Operations 2000–02, CEO, Exec. Dir and Chair. Exec. Cttee, EDF Energy (UK) Ltd 2002–, Dir, EDF Energy Networks (EPN) plc and EDF Energy Networks (LPN) plc; Dir, British Energy Group plc 2009–, South Eastern Power Networks Plc; named Nat. Amb. by HRH the Prince of Wales 2009; Hon. FIMechE 2009; Chevalier, Légion d'honneur; 71st Melchett Award, The Energy Inst. 2006. *Address:* EDF Energy (UK) Ltd, 40 Grosvenor Place, London, SW1X 7EN, England (office). *Telephone:* (20) 7242-9050 (office). *E-mail:* info@edfenergy.com (office). *Website:* www .edfenergy.com (office).

DE ROBIEN, Gilles, LenD; French politician; b. 10 April 1941, Cocquerel, Somme; began career as gen. insurance agent, Amiens 1965; Deputy in Nat. Ass. for 2nd Somme constituency 1986–, mem. Finance Cttee, Cttee of Enquiry into Causes, Consequences and Prevention of Floods, Vice Pres. Nat. Ass. 1993–98, architect of Robien Act on reform of working hours 1996; Mayor of Amiens 1989–2008; Minister for Capital Works, Transportation, Housing, Tourism and Maritime Affairs 2002, for Nat. Educ., Higher Educ. and Research –2007; Chair. Communauté d'Agglomération Amiens-Métropole; mem. Picardie Regional Council 1992; mem. Exec. Bureau and Steering Cttee, Republican Party 1990–; mem. Nat. Council and Political Cttee, Union pour la démocratie française (UDF) 1991–, Chair. UDF Group in Nat. Ass. 1995–97, mem. Political Bureau and Vice-Chair. UDF 1998–. *Address:* Union pour la Démocratie Française (UDF), 133 bis rue de l'Université, 75007 Paris, France. *Telephone:* 1-53-59-20-00. *Fax:* 1-53-59-20-59. *E-mail:* internet@udf.org. *Website:* www.udf.org.

DE ROMANET DE BEAUNE, Augustin; French financial industry executive; *Chairman and CEO, Caisse des Dépôts;* b. 2 April 1961, Boulogne-Billancourt; s. of Luc de Romanet de Beaune and Anne-Marie de Romanet de Beaune (née Lafont); m. Florence Burin des Roziers 1986; three c.; ed Inst. of Political Studies, Paris, Ecole Nationale d'Administration; began career in Budget Dept, Ministry of the Economy and Finance; Financial Attaché, Perm. Mission of France to EC, Brussels 1990–93, Head, Budget Office 1993–95; Chief of Staff to State Sec. for Budget and Special Adviser to Minister of Economy, Finance and Planning 1995–2002; Chief of Staff to the Minister responsible for Budget and Budget Reform and Deputy Chief of Staff to Minister of Economy, Finance and Industry 2002–04; Chief of Staff to the Minister of Employment, Work and Social Cohesion and Deputy Chief of Staff to Prime Minister 2004–05; Deputy Sec.-Gen. to the Presidency 2005; Deputy Dir for Finance and Strategy and mem. Exec. Cttee, Crédit Agricole SA 2006; Chair. and CEO Caisse des Dépôts 2007–; mem. Bd of Dirs Oddo et Compagnie 1999–, Man. Pnr, Oddo Pinatton Corp. 2000–; mem. Bd of Dirs Dexia SA 2007, Soc. Nat. Immobilière (SNI), Accor, Veolia, Icade, CNP Assurance 2007–; Chair. Bd, Fonds stratégique d'investissement 2008; Prof., Inst. of Political Studies, Paris 1986–90, Ecole Nationale d'Administration 1990–93; Chevalier, Légion d'honneur; Nat. Defence Medal. *Address:* Caisse des Dépôts, 56 rue de Lille, 75356 Paris 07 SP,

France (office). *Telephone:* 1-58-50-00-00 (office). *Website:* www.caissedesdepots.fr (office).

DE ROSNAY, Joël, DèsSc; French biologist and consultant; *CEO, Biotics International;* b. 12 June 1937, Mauritius; s. of Gaëtan de Rosnay and Natacha Koltchine; m. Stella Jebb 1959; one s. two d.; ed MIT; fmr Research Assoc., MIT; fmr Scientific Attaché, Embassy in Washington, DC; Scientific Dir European Enterprises Devt Co. (venture capital group) 1971–75; Dir of Applied Research, Inst. Pasteur 1975–84; Dir of Devt and Int. Relations, Cité des sciences et de l'industrie of La Villette 1988–97, Dir of Strategy 1997–99, Dir of Evaluation 1999–2002, Special Advisor to the Pres. 2002–; CEO Biotics International (consulting firm) 2004–; columnist, Europe 1 1987–95; Officier Légion d'honneur, Officier Ordre nat. du Mérite; Prix de l'Information Scientifique, Acad. des Sciences 1990. *Publications:* Les origines de la vie 1965, Le macroscope 1975, La révolution biologique 1982, Branchez-vous 1985, L'avenir du vivant 1988, L'avenir en direct 1989, Les rendez-vous du futur 1991, L'homme symbiotique 1995, La plus belle histoire du monde (contrib.) 1996. *Leisure interests:* skiing, surfing. *Address:* 146 rue de l'Université, 75007 Paris; Biotics International, 17 rue de l'Université, 75007 Paris, France. *Website:* www.cite-sciences.fr/derosnay.

DE ROSNAY, Tatiana; French journalist, novelist and screenwriter; b. 28 Sept. 1961, Neuilly-sur-Seine; d. of Joël de Rosnay and Stella Jebb; great-great-great-granddaughter of Isambard Kingdom Brunel; m. Nicolas Jolly 1992; one s. one d.; ed Univ. of East Anglia, Norwich, UK; raised in Paris and then in Boston, USA where her father taught at MIT in 1970s; moved to UK to study in early 1980s; returned to Paris 1984, worked as press officer for Christie's 1984; then served as Paris Ed. for Vanity Fair magazine –1993; currently writes for French ELLE; literary critic for Psychologies magazine; also worked on the series Family Affairs, including writing two episodes with PierreYves Lebert; named one of the top ten fiction writers in Europe 2009, ranked eighth by several French magazines amongst French novelists 2010, ranked fifth by Le Figaro out of the ten most read French authors 2011. *Film:* Sarah's Key (dir Serge Joncour) 2010. *Television:* Family Affairs (TF1) 2000, Ceremonia de clausura – 58 Festival Internacional de San Sebastián (film, as herself) 2010. *Publications:* novels: L'appartement témoin 1992, Maries, peres de famille: Romans d'adulteres 1995, Le diner des ex: Roman 1996, Le coeur d'une autre 1998, Le Voisin 2000, La Mémoire des Murs 2003, Spirales 2004, Sarah's Key 2006, A Secret Kept/Boomerang 2009, Moka 2009, Rose 2011, The House I Loved 2011, Russian Ink 2013. *Address:* c/o Pan Macmillan, 20 New Wharf Road, London, N1 9RR, England. *Website:* www.tatianaderosnay.com.

DE ROUSIERS, Gen. Patrick; French air force officer; *Inspector General of the Armed Forces;* b. 11 May 1955, Dijon; m.; five c.; ed Canadian Forces Coll., Toronto, Canada, Defence Staff Coll., Paris; 'Capitaine Duthoit' entry at Air Force Acad. 1975; fighter pilot's wings 1979; Deputy Commdr, then Commdr 02.004 'La Fayette' fighter Squadron, Luxeuil Air Base 1986–89; Chief of Operations, Deputy Commdr, then Commdr 33rd Recce Wing, Strasbourg Air Base 1990–93; Deputy then Chief of Planning, Plans and Budget Dept, Air Force Staff, Paris 1994–97; Chief of Planning Dept, Defence Staff, Paris 1997–99; Base Commdr, Nancy Air Base 1999–2002; Deputy to Vice-Chief of Defence Staff and Chief of Studies and Overall Mil. Strategy, Defence Staff, Paris 2002–04, Chief of Defence Euro-Atlantic Dept 2004–06; C-in-C Air Defence and Air Operations Command, Paris 2006; rank of Gen. 2006; Mil. Rep. to EU Mil. Cttee, Brussels 2008–10; Mil. Rep. to NATO, Brussels 2009–10; Insp. Gen. of the Armed Forces 2010–; Commdr, Légion d'honneur, Ordre nat. du Mérite; Medal of Aeronautics, Ehrenkreuz der Bundeswehr in Gold. *Address:* Inspection Générale des Armées, 5 bis Avenue de la Porte de Sevres, 75015 Paris, France (office). *Telephone:* 1-45-52-92-50 (office). *Website:* www.defense.gouv.fr (office).

DE RUITER, Hendrikus (Henny); Dutch business executive; b. 3 March 1934, The Hague; m. Theodora O. van der Jagt 1957; one s. two d.; ed Technological Univ. of Delft; Research Chemist, Koninklijke/Shell Laboratorium Amsterdam (KSLA) 1956; Chief Technologist, Berre Refinery, Compagnie de Raffinage Shell-Berre 1965–67; returned to KSLA 1967; joined Shell Int. Petroleum Co. Ltd (SIPC), London 1969; Man. Dir Shell Co. of Thailand and Pres. Société Shell du Laos 1972; Coal Production and Trading Co-ordinator, SIPC 1975; Pres. Shell Int. Trading Co. 1979; Dir Shell Internationale Petroleum Maatschappij BV 1981; Man. Dir NV Koninklijke Nederlandsche Petroleum Maatschappij; mem. Presidium, Bd of Dirs Shell Petroleum NV and Man. Dir The Shell Petroleum Co. Ltd 1983–94; mem. Supervisory Bd AEGON NV (Vice-Chair. 1993–2004, Heineken NV 1993–2004, Koninklijke Ahold NV (Chair.) 1994–2003, Wolters Kluwer NV (Chair.) 1994–2006, Royal Dutch Petroleum Co. 1994–2004, Beers NV (Chair) 1995–2002, Coris Group PLC (fmrly Hoogovens Group BV) (Vice-Chair.) 1995–2002, Koninklijke Vopak NV (fmrly Koninklijke Pakhoed NV) 1995–2002; Dir Shell Petroleum NV 1994–2004, The Shell Petroleum Co. Ltd 1994–2004, Chair. Univar NV (fmrly part of Koninklijke Vopak) 2002–04; Kt Order of the Netherlands Lion 1987. *Address:* c/o Royal Dutch Petroleum Company, Carel van Bylandtlaan 30, PO Box 162, 2501 AN The Hague, Netherlands.

DE SANCTIS, Roman William, MD; American cardiologist; b. 30 Oct. 1930, Cambridge Springs, Pa; s. of Vincent De Sanctis and Marguerita De Sanctis; m. Ruth A. Foley 1955; four d.; ed Univ. of Arizona, Harvard Medical School; Resident in Medicine, Mass. Gen. Hosp. 1958–60, Fellow in Cardiology 1960–62, Dir Coronary Care Unit 1967–80, Dir Clinical Cardiology 1980–98, Dir Emer. 1998–; Physician 1970–; mem. Faculty of Medicine, Harvard Medical School 1964–, Prof. 1973–98, James and Evelyn Jenks and Paul Dudley White Prof. of Medicine 1998–; Consultant to USN and Asst to Attending Physician to US Congress 1956–58; Master, American Coll. of Physicians 1995; Fellow, American Coll. of Cardiology, Inst. of Medicine; Hon. DSc (Wilkes Coll., Univ. of Ariz.); Distinguished Clinical Teaching Award, Harvard Medical School 1980; Gifted Teacher Award (American Coll. of Cardiologists), Glozny-Reisbeck Award, NY Acad. of Medicine 2003. *Publications:* author and co-ed. of over 130 scientific papers. *Leisure interests:* travel, music, golf. *Address:* Yawkey Building, Suite 5700, 55 Fruit Street, Boston, MA 02114 (office); 5 Thoreau Circle, Winchester, MA 01890, USA (home). *Telephone:* (781) 726-2889 (office); (617) 729-1453 (home). *Fax:* (617) 643-1615.

DE SAVARY, Peter John; British entrepreneur; b. 11 July 1944, Essex, England; m. 3rd Lucille Lana Paton; three d. (and two d. from previous m.); ed Charterhouse, Godalming, Surrey; commercial activities in finance, energy, leisure and property; British challenger for The Americas Cup 1983, 1987; Chair. The Carnegie Club, Scotland 1994–; Chair. Carnegie Abbey, Rhode Island; Chair. Cherokee Plantation, SC; Owner and Chair. Millwall Football Club 2005–06; Amb. for the Govt of Grenada for Inward Investment; Tourism Personality of the Year, English Tourist Bd 1988. *Leisure interests:* sailing, carriage driving, riding. *Address:* Azzurra Castle, Seaview Lane, L'Ance aux Epines, St Georges, Grenada. *E-mail:* info@desavary.com. *Website:* www.desavary.com.

DE SCHOUTHEETE DE TERVARENT, Baron Philippe; Belgian diplomatist (retd); b. 21 May 1932, Berlin, Germany; m. Bernadette Joos de ter Beerst 1956; two s.; ed Beaumont Coll., UK, Univ. of Louvain, Belgium; joined diplomatic service, served in Embassy in Paris 1959–61, Embassy in Cairo 1962–65, Embassy in Madrid 1968–72, Embassy in Bonn 1972–76, Chef de Cabinet to Minister of Foreign Affairs 1980–81, Amb. to Spain 1981–85, Political Dir, Ministry of Foreign Affairs 1985–87, Perm. Rep. to EU, Brussels 1987–97; Guest Prof., Univ. of Louvain la Neuve 1990–2000; Rep. of Order of Malta to EC 2000–12; Special Adviser EC 2000–04; Dir European Studies, Royal Inst. for Int. Relations, Brussels; Pres. Fund Inbev Baillet Latour 1999–2008; mem. Bd of Dirs Centre for European Policy Studies, Acad. Royale de Belgique; Grand Officer, Order of Leopold; Grand Cross, Order of Malta; Adolphe Bentinck Prize 1997, European Parl. Medal 1997. *Publications include:* La coopération politique européenne 1986, Une Europe pour tous 1997, The Case for Europe 2000. *Address:* Avenue de Broqueville 99, 1200 Brussels, Belgium. *E-mail:* deschoutheete@skynet.be.

DE SÈZE, Amaury; French business executive; ed Centre de Perfectionnenne dans l'Admin des Affaires, Stanford Grad. School of Business, USA; began career with Bull General Electric; fmr consultant, Towers Perrin Inc., Forster & Crosby; fmr Man. of Industrial Relations, Videocolor (Jt Venture Thomson-RCA); worked in Volvo Group holding various positions 1978–93, including Exec. Vice-Pres., Pres. and CEO Volvo France, Sr Vice-Pres. AB Volvo, Pres. Volvo European Corp. Office, one of four mems Group Exec. Cttee AB Volvo; mem. Man. Bd Compagnie Financière 1993, Bank Paribas 1998, Group Exec. Cttee BNP Paribas 1998, 2003; joined Paribas as Head of PAI 1993, Chair. and CEO PAI Partners 1998–2007; Vice-Chair. Power Corpn of Canada 2008–; mem. Supervisory Bd Carrefour SA 2005–08, Vice-Chair. 2006–08, Chair. Carrefour Group 2009–11, Lead Dir 2011–; mem. Bd of Dirs Power Corpn of Canada 2001–, Vice-Chair. 2008–; mem. Bd of Dirs Elis SA, Groupe Bruxelles Lambert SA 1994–, Suez Environnement SA, Atos Origin SA, French Postal Service, Fives-Lille, Schneider, Groupe Industriel Marcel Dassault SA, Poliet, Clemessy, Compagnie de Fives Lille, La Poste (France), Sema Group, IMS Int. Metal Service SA 1988–, Pargesa Holding SA (Switzerland) 2001–, Thales 2009–, GIB SA, United Biscuits Holding Ltd (UK), Imerys SA, PAI Partners srl (I), PAI Europe III General Partner Ltd (GG), PAI Europe IV UK General Partner Ltd (GB) (fmrly PAI Europe III UK General Partner Ltd), PAI Europe IV General Partner NC (GG), Vivarte SA (F), Paribas Santé SA (F), Sema plc (GB), Erbe SA (B), Gepeco SA, Novasaur SAS (F) 2005–, Bergesen Worldwide Ltd 2007–, Saeco Int. Group SpA, United Biscuits (Equity) Ltd; Rep. and Dir, NHG SAS; mem. Supervisory Bd Publicis Groupe SA (fmrly Saatchi & Saatchi PLC) 1998–, Gras Savoye SA; mem. Bd of Supervisors Publicis SA; mem. Strategic Cttee Imerys SA; fmr mem. Bd of Dirs SAS, UGC SA, United Biscuits Ltd, Corparex Int. SA (F), IMS SA (F), Eiffage SA 1993–2008, UGC SA (France), Cobepa SA, Novalis SAS (France); fmr mem. Supervisory Bd Gras Savoye SCA (France); fmr mem. Exec. Cttee BNP Paribas (France). *Address:* Groupe Carrefour, 26 Quai Michelet, TSA 20016, 92695 Levallois-Perret Cedex, France (office). *Telephone:* 1-55-77-91-00 (office). *Fax:* 1-55-77-91-02 (office). *E-mail:* info@carrefour.com (office). *Website:* www.carrefour.com (office).

DE SILGUY, Count Yves-Thibault Christian Marie; French construction industry executive and fmr diplomatist; *Vice-Chairman and Senior Director, Vinci;* b. 22 July 1948, Rennes; s. of Raymond de Silguy and Claude de Pompery; m. Jacqueline de Montillet de Grenaud (deceased); one s. one d.; ed Inst. Saint-Martin, Faculté de Droit et des Sciences Economiques, Rennes, Univ. de Paris I, Inst. d'Etudes Politiques de Paris and Ecole Nat. d'Admin; worked at Ministry of Foreign Affairs 1976–81, Deputy Chef de Cabinet to François-Xavier Ortoli, Vice-Pres. of EC Comm. 1981–85, Second Counsellor, Embassy in Washington, DC 1985–86; Adviser on European Questions and Int. Econs, Office of Prime Minister Chirac 1986–88; Dir, Int. Affairs Dept, Usinor-Sacilor 1988–90, Dir for Int. Affairs 1990–93; Sec.-Gen. Interdepartmental Cttee for Questions of Econ. Cooperation in Europe and Adviser for European Affairs to Prime Minister Balladur 1993–95; Commr for Econ. and Monetary Union, EC 1995–99; currently CEO, YTSeuropaconsultants; mem. Exec. Bd Suez Group 2000–, CEO 2001–02; Sr Exec. Vice-Pres. in charge of Int. Affairs and Relations 2001–06; Vice-Chair. Mouvement des entreprises de France (MEDEF) Int. 2000–; Chair. Vinci 2006–10, Vice-Chair. and Sr Dir 2010–; Commdr, Légion d'honneur, Officier du Mérite nat., Commdr des Arts et des Lettres. *Publications:* Le syndrome du diplodocus 1996, L'euro 1998, L'economie, fil d'Ariane de l'Europe 2000. *Leisure interests:* sailing, hunting. *Address:* Vinci, 1 cours Ferdinand-de-Lesseps, 92851 Rueil-Malmaison Cedex, France (office). *Telephone:* 1-47-16-35-00 (office). *Fax:* 1-47-51-91-02 (office). *E-mail:* yves-thibault.desilguy@vinci.com (office). *Website:* www.vinci.com (office).

DE SILVA, Asoka N.; Sri Lankan judge (retd); *Senior Legal Adviser to the President;* ed St Antony's Coll., Kandy, Univ. of Ceylon; enrolled as advocate of Supreme Court 1972; joined Attorney Gen.'s Dept as State Counsel 1974, rose to position of Sr Deputy Solicitor Gen. 1987; Judge, Court of Appeal 1995–2001, Pres. Feb.–Aug. 2001; Judge of Supreme Court Aug. 2001–, Chief Justice of Sri Lanka 2009–11; Sr Legal Adviser to the Pres. 2011–; served as a perm. judge of Int. Criminal Tribunal for Rwanda. *Address:* President's Secretariat, Republic Square, Colombo 1, Sri Lanka (office). *Telephone:* (11) 2324801 (office). *Fax:* (11) 2331246 (office). *E-mail:* priu@presidentsoffice.lk (office). *Website:* www.president.gov.lk (office).

DE SILVA, C(hitta) R(anjan); Sri Lankan lawyer and government official; *Chairman, Lessons Learnt and Reconciliation Commission;* ed Royal Coll., Colombo; joined Attorney-Gen.'s Dept as State Counsel 1976, promoted to Sr State Counsel 1983, Deputy Solicitor-Gen. 1992–96, Additional Solicitor-Gen. 1996–99, took silk 1997, Solicitor-Gen. 1999–2007, Attorney-Gen. 2007–09 (retd); currently Chair. Lessons Learnt and Reconciliation Comm.; mem. Sri Lanka dels the Human Rights Cttee under optional protocol to Int. Covenant on Civil and Political Rights and to UN Convention on the Elimination of All Forms of Racial Discrimination; fmr lecturer and examiner at Gen. Sir John Kotelawala Defence Univ.; examiner at Sri Lanka Law Coll.; mem. Law Comm. of Sri Lanka; fmr mem. Bd of Man. Child Protection Authority, Drug Control Bd, Post Grad. Inst. of Medicine. *Address:* Lessons Learnt and Reconciliation Commission, Lakshman Kadirgamar Institute of International Relations and Strategic Studies, No. 24, Horton Place, Colombo 7, Sri Lanka (office). *Telephone:* (11) 2673408 (office). *Fax:* (11) 2674637 (office). *E-mail:* llrc@sltnet.lk (office). llrcommission@gmail.com (office). *Website:* www.llrc.lk (office).

DE SMET, Bart; Belgian insurance executive; *CEO, Ageas;* b. 1957; ed Catholic Univ. of Louvain, diplomas in Math., Actuarial Sciences and Managerial Sciences; began career with Argenta 1982; Exec. Vice-Pres., Life Div., Nationale Suisse insurance co. 1985–93; joined ING Insurance Belgium 1994, mem. Exec. Cttee, responsible for individual and group life insurance, health insurance and banking activities; joined Fortis 1998, mem. Man. Cttee Fortis AG, responsible for Fortis Employee Benefits, took charge of Broker Channel at Fortis Insurance Belgium 2005–07, CEO Fortis Insurance Belgium 2007–09, CEO Ageas (renamed from Fortis Holding) 2009–; mem. Bd of Dirs Ageas, Ageas Insurance International, AG Insurance, Ageas UK, Tai Ping Life, Maybank Ageas Holding, IDBI Federal, Credimo. *Address:* Ageas SA/NV, Rue du Marquis 1, 1000 Brussels, Belgium (office). *Telephone:* (2) 557-57-11 (office). *Fax:* (2) 557-57-50 (office). *E-mail:* info@ageas.com (office). *Website:* www.ageas.com (office).

DE SOTO, Alvaro; Peruvian diplomatist; b. 16 March 1943, Argentina; s. of Alberto Soto de la Jara and Rosa Polar; divorced; two s. one d.; ed Int. School, Geneva, Catholic Univ. Lima, San Marcos Univ. Lima, Diplomatic Acad. Lima and Inst. of Int. Studies, Geneva; Acting Dir Maritime Sovereignty Div. Ministry of Foreign Affairs 1977–78; Deputy Perm. Rep. of Peru at UN, Geneva 1978–82; Special Asst to UN Sec.-Gen. 1982–86; Asst Sec.-Gen. and Exec. Asst to UN Sec.-Gen. 1987–91; Personal Rep. of UN Sec.-Gen. in El Salvador Peace Negotiations 1990–91; Asst Sec.-Gen. UN Office for Research and Collection of Information 1991; Sr Political Adviser to UN Sec.-Gen. 1992–94; Asst Sec.-Gen. for Political Affairs 1995–99, Under-Sec.-Gen., Special Adviser to Sec.-Gen. on Cyprus 1999–2004; UN Special Envoy for Myanmar 1995–99; Special Rep. of the Sec.-Gen. for Western Sahara and Chief of the UN Mission for the Referendum in Western Sahara (MINURSO) 2003–05; UN Special Coordinator for the Middle East Peace Process, Personal Rep. of the Sec.-Gen. to the Palestine Liberation Org. and the Palestinian Authority and Sec.-Gen.'s Envoy to the Middle East Quartet 2005–07; Invited Prof., Paris School of Int. Affairs, Sciences Po, Paris; mem. Global Leadership Foundation; mem. various advisory bds in New York and in Europe; mem. Bd of Advisors and Host, 'Conversations with Alvaro de Soto' series, Center for International Conflict Resolution, Columbia Univ.; Hon. LLD (St Joseph's Univ., Philadelphia) 1992; Orden de José Simeón Cañas, Libertador de los Esclavos, Gran Cruz (El Salvador) 2007. *Address:* Center for International Conflict Resolution, 1325 International Affairs Building, 420 West 118th Street, MC 3369, New York, NY 10027, USA. *Website:* www.cicr-columbia.org.

DE SOTO, Hernando; Peruvian economist; *President, Institute for Liberty and Democracy;* b. 2 June 1941, Arequipa; ed Institut Universitaire de Hautes Études Internationales, Geneva, Switzerland; fmr economist for GATT; fmr Pres. Exec. Cttee, Copper Exporting Countries Org. (CIPEC); fmr Man. Dir Universal Eng Corpn; fmr Prin. Swiss Bank Corpn Consultant Group; fmr Gov. Cen. Reserve Bank, Peru; Personal Rep. and Chief Adviser to Pres. Alberto Fujimori; currently Pres. Inst. for Liberty and Democracy, Lima; apptd rep. of Peru to USA on free trade agreement 2006; Co-Chair. UN High Level Comm. on Legal Empowerment for the Poor; Downey Fellow, Yale Univ., USA 2003; Most Admirable Order of the Direkgunabhorn (Fifth Class), Thailand 2004; Hon. DLitt (Buckingham, UK) 2005; Sir Antony Fisher Int. Memorial Award – Atlas 1990, 2001, one of five Leaders for the New Millennium chosen by Time magazine 1999, The Freedom Prize (Switzerland), Goldwater Award (USA) 2002, Adam Smith Award, Asscn of Pvt. Enterprise Educ. (USA) 2002, CARE Canada Award for Outstanding Devt Thinking 2002, inducted into Democracy Hall of Fame Int., Nat. Grad. Univ. 2003, Templeton Freedom Prize (USA) 2004, Milton Friedman Prize for Advancing Liberty (USA) 2004, Deutsche Stiftung Eigentum prize for Property Rights Theory 2004, IPAE Award, Peruvian Inst. of Business Admin 2004, Americas Award 2005, Acad. of Achievement Golden Plate Award, USA 2005, Forbes' Compass Award for Strategic Direction 2005. *Publications:* The Other Path 1986, The Mystery of Capital: Why Capitalism Triumphs in the West and Fails Everywhere Else 2000. *Address:* Instituto Libertad y Democracia, Av. Las Begonias 441, Oficina 901, San Isidro, Lima 27, Peru (office). *Telephone:* (1) 616-6100 (office). *Fax:* (1) 616-6190 (office). *E-mail:* hds@ild.org.pe (office). *Website:* www.ild.org.pe (office).

DE SOUZA, Wilfred Anthony, MB, BS, FRCS, FRCSE; Indian surgeon and politician; b. 23 April 1927, Anjuna, Bardez; s. of Tito Fermino and Alina Anamaria; m. Grace Goodwin; two c.; ed Grant Medical Coll., Univ. of Bombay; surgeon, Goa Medical Coll. Hosp. 1963–67; Consulting Surgeon, Hospicio Hosp., Margao and Asilo Hosp., Mapusa 1963–67; Consulting Surgeon, CMM Hosp., Panjim and Holy Cross Hosp., Mapusa 1969–96; elected to Goa, Daman and Diu Ass. 1974, 1980; elected to Legis. Ass. (after Goa became State in Repub. of India) 1989, 1994, 1999, 2002; Pres. Goa Pradesh Congress Cttee 1977–80; Minister for Public Health, Public Works Dept, Tourism and Fisheries, Govt of Goa 1981–83, Science and Tech. Planning 1990; Leader of Opposition 1990–91; Chair. Cttee of Privileges 1991–92, Deputy Chief Minister, Govt of Goa 1981–83, 1991–93, Chief Minister 1993–94, 1998; currently Deputy Chair. Planning Bd, Chair. Cttee on Public Undertakings; Pres. Rotary Club of Panjim 1970; fmr Pres. Goa unit, Nationalist Congress Party (resgnd from party 2009); Fellow, Asscn of Surgeons of India, Royal Coll. of Surgeons, UK, Royal Coll. of Surgeons, Edinburgh; Hon. Fellow, Int. Coll. of Surgeons; Commdr Grand Cross of the Order of Infante Dom Henrique (Portugal); Dr B. C. Roy Award for Eminent Medical Man and Statesman (India), Silver Elephant Award (India), Son of India Award, Jawaharlal Nehru Excellence Award, Indira Gandhi Solidarity Award, Rajiv Gandhi Excellence Award 1992, Int. Gold Star Award, Super Achievers of India Award, Glory of India Int. Award, Gold Award. *Leisure interests:* stamp collecting, numismatics, listening to classical music, reading. *Address:* 359 Bella Vista, Muddavaddi, Saligao, Bardez, Goa, India (home). *Telephone:* (832) 2224964 (office); (832) 2278000 (home); (832) 2409523. *Fax:* (832) 2409782 (home). *E-mail:* willie_goa@sancharnet.in; mla-sali.goa@nic.in.

DE SWAAN, Tom; Dutch banking executive; *Acting Chairman, Zurich Insurance Group Ltd;* b. 1946; joined De Nederlandsche Bank NV 1972, mem. Governing Bd 1986–98; mem. Man. Bd and Chief Financial Officer ABN AMRO Bank 1999–2006, Adviser to Man. Bd 2006–07; mem. Bd of Dirs Zurich Insurance Group Ltd and Zurich Insurance Co. Ltd 2006–, Vice-Chair. 2012–13, Acting Chair. 2013–; Chair. Amsterdam Financial Centre 1987–88, Banking Supervisory Sub-cttee of European Monetary Inst. 1995–97; mem. Basel Cttee on Banking Supervision 1991–96, Chair. 1997–98; Dir (non-exec.) Financial Services Authority (UK) 2001–06. *Address:* Zurich Insurance Group Ltd, 2 Mythenquai, PO Box, 8022 Zurich, Switzerland (office). *Telephone:* (44) 625-25-25 (office). *Fax:* (44) 625-02-99 (office). *E-mail:* info@zurich.com (office). *Website:* www.zurich.com (office).

DE TAVERNOST, Nicolas Bellet; French television executive, company director and fmr civil servant; *CEO and Chairman of the Executive Board, Métropole Télévision SA;* b. 22 Aug. 1950, Villefranche-sur-Saône; ed Collège Notre-Dame de Mongré, Lycée Saint-Joseph de Tivoli, Sciences-Po, Bordeaux; served at French Ministry of Int. Commerce 1974–76; Gen. Sec. French Chamber of Commerce, Zurich, Switzerland 1976–78; Head of Information and Public Relations, Ministry of Posts, Telegraphs and Telephones 1978–84, Head of Public Services Div., Video Communications Dept 1984–86; Dir of Audiovisual Business, Lyonnaise des Eaux 1986–87; Deputy Dir Gen. M6 (Métropole Télévision SA) channel 1987–90, Dir Gen. 1990–2000, CEO, Chair. Exec. Bd and mem. Exec. Cttee 2000–; Dir, Série Club, Nexans Hellas SA, TF6, Paris Premiere SA, SND, Extension TV SA, TF6 Gestion SA, Soc. Nouvelle de Distribution SA, Home Shopping Service SA, Tecipress, Antena 3, FRA Business Interactif, GL Events 2008–; Ind. Dir, Nexans SA 2007–, Nexans Maroc SA; mem. Supervisory Bd Ediradio RTL SA; Pres. Asscn of European Commercial Television; Admin. Girondins de Bordeaux club 1999–; Chevalier, Ordre nat. du Mérite 1994, Légion d'honneur 2003. *Address:* Métropole Télévision SA, 89 avenue Charles-de-Gaulle, 92575 Neuilly-sur-Seine, Île-de-France, France (office). *Telephone:* 1-41-92-66-66 (office). *Fax:* 1-41-92-66-10 (office). *E-mail:* marie-clotilde.perre@m6.fr (office). *Website:* www.m6.fr (office).

DE THÉ, Guy Blaudin, MD, PhD; French cancer research specialist and academic; *Professor Emeritus, Institut Pasteur;* b. 5 May 1930, Marseilles; s. of François Blaudin de Thé and Madeleine du Verne; m. Colette Pierrard de Maujouy 1958 (died 1991); one s. two d.; ed Faculty of Medicine, Marseilles, Univ. of Paris, Sorbonne; Research Asst Duke Univ. Medical Center, USA 1961–63; Visiting Scientist, Laboratory of Viral Oncology, Nat. Cancer Inst., NIH, USA 1963–65; Head of Unit of Electron Microscopy, CNRS 1965–67; Chief, Unit of Biological Carcinogenesis, WHO Int. Agency for Research on Cancer, Lyons 1967–78; Dir of Research Faculty of Medicine Alexis Carrel, Lyon and Cancer Research Inst., Villejuif, Paris 1979–90, CNRS 1990–; Head Unit of Epidemiology of Oncogenic Viruses and Prof. Pasteur Inst., Paris 1990–97, Prof. Emer. 1998–; Visiting Prof. Faculty of Public Health, Harvard Univ. 1981–85; Fogarty Scholar-in-Residence, NIH, Bethesda USA 1992–96; Gen. Sec., then Pres. Int. Asscn of Retrovirology 1998–99; mem. Scientific Council, Ligue nat. française contre le cancer 1972–74; mem. Nat. Acad. Médecine, Soc. française de Microbiologie, American Soc. for Cell Biology, American Asscn for Cancer Research, AAAS, European Asscn for Cancer Research; Corresp. mem. Inst. de France Acad. des Sciences; Scientific Prize, Acad. of Sciences 1971, Medical Research Foundation 1979, Collège de France 1981, Silver Medal, CNRS 1981, Life Sciences Inst. Paris 1991; Commandeur, Ordre National du Mérite. *Publications:* many publs on the cell virus relationship in avian and murine leukaemia viruses and role of viruses in human tumours (Burkitt's lymphoma in Africa, Nasopharyngeal carcinoma in South-East Asia); Retroviruses and Central Nervous Degenerative Diseases; Sur la piste du cancer (popular scientific book) 1984, Modes de vie et cancers 1988. *Leisure interest:* arts. *Address:* Institut Pasteur, Département des rétrovirus, Batiment Lwoff, 28 rue Docteur Roux, 75015 Paris (office); 14 rue Le Regrattier, 75004 Paris, France (home). *Telephone:* 1-45-68-89-30 (office); 1-43-54-01-22 (home). *Fax:* 1-45-68-89-31 (office); 1-40-51-05-15 (home). *E-mail:* dethe@pasteur.fr (office).

DE THUIN, Aude; French psychologist and business executive; *President, Thuin et Associés Consulting;* b. (Aude Le Roux), 18 Sept. 1950, Ploudaniel, Brittany; m. Hubert Ziesseniss 1989; six c.; cr. and managed Promotion Bourgogne (free newspaper in Burgundy) 1972; has f. several cos since 1981, including ADT Consultants sarl to edit La Semaine Internationale du Marketing Direct 1981 (acquired by CEP Exposium 1993), Compagnie Scheffer to organize two events, L'Art du Jardin flower show 1993–2003 and Créations et Savoir Faire (DIY fair) 1995–2003 (Compagnie Scheffer acquired by Hachette Filipacchi/Comexpo 2003), La Belle Ecole (first int. school devoted to the French art de vivre) 2003, PV Concept sarl (through its subsidiary Wefcos) to launched first edn of Women's Forum for the Economy and Society, Deauville 2005 (acquired by Publicis 2011); Founder and Pres. Thuin et Associés Consulting 2011–, publr of forum Dare France (to highlight French talent in all areas of industry, business science, research, education and the arts); Chevalier, Légion d'honneur, Officier, Ordre nat. du Mérite, Chevalier du Mérite agricole; EDC Ethique et Gouvernance Award 2012, Femme Entrepreneur Award, World Entrepreneurship Forum 2012. *Publications:* Le Livre Blanc du Marketing Direct 1985, En Direct 1993, Jardins Ephémères 1999, Femmes, si vous osiez (Women, If You Dare) 2012. *Address:* Thuin et Associés Consulting, 7 rue Scheffer, 75116 Paris, France (office). *Telephone:* 1-45-05-23-63 (office); 1-47-04-36-00 (office).

DE VABRES, Renaud Donnedieu; French politician and organization official; *Chairman, Atout France;* b. 13 March 1954, Neuilly-sur-Seine, Haut de Seine; grandson of Prof. Henri Donnedieu de Vabres; ed Institut d'Etudes Politiques, Paris and Ecole Nationale d'Admin; nat. service in navy on board patrol ship La Paimpolaise; Prin. Pvt. Sec. to Préfet of Indre-et-Loire; Sec.-Gen. Centre Region Police Admin 1980–81, Alpes de Hautes Provence 1981–82; Sous-Préfet Château-Thierry 1982–85; Sr Lecturer, Institut d'Etudes Politiques, Paris 1984–; mem. Conseil d'Etat 1985–; Deputy to Assemblé Nationale for Indre-et-Loire 1997–, Vice-Pres. Comm. for Foreign Affairs; mem. Tours Municipal Council 2001–; mem. Centre Regional Council 1986–2001, Chair. Union pour la démocratie française (UDF) Group and Gen. Rapporteur on the Budget and Planning 1986–93, Vice-Chair. and Gen. Rapporteur on the Budget 1993–98; Delegate-Gen. of Parti Républicain (PR) as mem. Political Bureau 1986–96; Special Asst to François Léotard, Minister of State, Minister of Defence 1993–95; Delegate-Gen. of UDF 1996–98, of Nouvelle UDF 1998–2002, and concurrently Prin. Pvt. Sec. to François Léotard (PR) 1986 and UDF 1996–98; fmr Minister Del. for European Affairs; Minister of Culture and Communication 2003–07; Vice-Pres. Indre-et-Loire Union pour un Mouvement Populaire (UMP) 2002–09, Spokesman for nat. Union pour un Mouvement Populaire 2003–04, Nat. Sec. in charge of cultural and artistic affairs 2009; Adviser, Group Allard (consulting firm) 2009–; Chair. Atout France (tourism agency) 2009–; Chevalier de la Legion d'Honneur 2009. *Address:* c/o Union pour un Mouvement Populaire, 55 rue La Boétie, 75384 Paris Cedex 08, France (office). *Website:* www.rddv.fr/blog.

DE VASCONCELOS, Álvaro; Portuguese research institute director; *Director, European Union Institute for Security Studies;* m. Maria do Rosário de Moraes Vaz; three d.; Co-founder and Head of Inst. of Strategic and Int. Studies (IEEI), Lisbon 1981–2007, launched several networks, including Euro-Latin American Forum and EuroMeSCo; Dir EU Inst. for Security Studies, Paris 2007–; regular columnist in Portuguese and int. press; Chevalier de la Légion d'honneur, Comendador do Ordem do Rio Branco (Brazil). *Publications:* author or co-ed. numerous books, articles and reports, notably in areas of EU Common Foreign and Security Policy, Euro-Mediterranean relations and on theme of world order, including Portugal: A European Story, La PESC: Ouvrir l'Europe au Monde, The European Union, Mercosul and the New World Order, and A European Strategy for the Mediterranean. *Address:* Institute for Security Studies, European Union, 43 avenue du Président Wilson, 75775 Paris Cedex 16, France (office). *Telephone:* 1-56-89-19-40 (office). *Fax:* 1-56-89-19-31 (office). *E-mail:* alvaro.vasconcelos@iss.europa.eu (office). *Website:* www.iss.europa.eu (office).

DE VASCONCELOS LIMA, José Jorge, MS; Brazilian politician; b. 18 Nov. 1944, Recife, Pernambuco; m.; two d.; ed Universidade Federal de Pernambuco, Univesidade Católica de Pernambuco, Univesidade Fed. do Rio de Janeiro, Universidad de Madrid, Spain; Prof., Universidade Fed. de Pernambuco in 1970s; Educ. Sec., Pernambuco 1975–79, Housing Sec. 1979–82; joined Partido da Frente Liberal—PFL (now Democratas) 1982, mem. Câmara dos Deputados 1982–98; Pres. PFL 1989–90, 1993–94; mem. Senado Fed. for Pernambuco 1999–2006, Minister of Mines and Energy 2001–02; unsuccessful PFL cand. for Vice Pres. 2006. *Address:* c/o Democratas, Senado Federal, Anexo 1, 26° andar, 70165-900 Brasília, DF, Brazil.

DE VASCONSELOS, Abraão F.; Timor-Leste economist and central banker; *Governor, Banco Central de Timor-Leste;* fmr Dir-Gen. Autoridade Bancária e de Pagamentos de Timor Leste; Chair. Investment Advisory Bd 2006–08; fmr Gen. Man. Banco Central de Timor-Leste, now Gov. *Address:* Office of the Governor, Banco Central de Timor-Leste, Av. Bispo Medeiros, POB 59, Dili, Timor-Leste (office). *Telephone:* 3313712 (office). *Fax:* 3313713 (office). *E-mail:* info@bancocentral.tl (office). *Website:* www.bancocentral.tl (office).

DE VAUCLEROY, Baron Gui, LLD, MEconSc; Belgian business executive; b. 28 Sept. 1933, Dendermonde; ed Univ. of Louvain; Research Asst Centre for Social Studies 1957–59; joined Delhaize Le Lion (later Delhaize Group) 1960, mem. Exec. Cttee 1967, Vice-Pres. Exec. Cttee 1984, CEO and Pres. Exec. Cttee 1990–98, Chair. of Bd of Dirs 1999–2004; Chair. Fed. of Enterprises in Belgium 1999–2002; Vice-Pres. Union of Industrial Employers Europe 2000–02; Commdr de l'Ordre de Léopold, Grand Officier de l'Ordre de Léopold II. *Address:* Avenue Baron Albert d'Huart 137, 1950 Kraainem, Belgium (home).

DE VIDO, Julio Miguel; Argentine politician; *Minister of Federal Planning, Public Investment and Services;* b. 26 Dec. 1949, Buenos Aires; ed Universidad de Buenos Aires; qualified architect; Dir-Gen. of Public Works, Inst. of Urban Devt, Santa Cruz 1988–90; Minister of Economy and Public Works of Santa Cruz 1991–99, Minister of Govt 1999–2003; elected Prov. Deputy, Santa Cruz 1997; adviser to presidential cand. Néstor Kirchner during election campaign 2003; Minister of Federal Planning, Public Investment and Services 2003–. *Address:* Ministry of Federal Planning, Public Investment and Services, Hipólito Yrigoyen 250, 11°, Of. 1112, C1086AAB, Buenos Aires, Argentina (office). *Telephone:* (11) 4349-5000 (office). *Website:* www.minplan.gov.ar (office).

DE VILLIERS, A(braham) B(enjamin); South African professional cricketer; *Captain of South African One Day International (ODI) and Twenty20 teams;* b. 17 Feb. 1984, Pretoria, Transvaal; s. of Dr Abraham Benjamin de Villiers and Millie de Villiers; ed Afrikaans Hoër Seunsskool, Pretoria; right-handed batsman; right-arm medium pace bowler; occasional wicketkeeper; played for Carrickfergus Cricket Club in NI as youngster; plays for Northerns 2003–04, Titans 2004–, S Africa 2004–, Delhi Daredevils 2008–10, Royal Challengers Bangalore 2011–, Africa XI; First-class debut: 2003/04; Test debut: S Africa v England, Port Elizabeth 17–21 Dec. 2004; One-Day Int. (ODI) debut: S Africa v England, Bloemfontein 2 Feb. 2005; T20I debut: S Africa v Australia, Johannesburg 24 Feb. 2006; Capt. South African ODI and T20I teams 2011–. *Achievements include:* became youngest and second fastest S African to reach 1,000 Test runs after Graeme Pollock; holds record for scoring most Test runs before getting out for a duck. *Leisure interest:* playing guitar. *Address:* c/o Titans Cricket, SuperSport Park, Centurion, Gauteng Province, South Africa. *Telephone:* (12) 663-1005. *Fax:* (12) 663-3329. *E-mail:* info@titans.co.za. *Website:* www.titans.co.za; www.abdevilliers.com.

DE VRIES, Gijs, MA; Dutch politician and international civil servant; *Member, European Court of Auditors;* b. 22 Feb. 1956, New York City, USA; m.; two c.; ed Univ. of Leiden; Lecturer in Int. Relations, Faculty of Law, Univ. of Leiden 1981–84; mem. Leiden City Council 1981–84; mem. European Parl. 1984–98, Leader, Liberal and Democratic Group 1994–98; Deputy Minister of Interior Affairs 1998–2002; Rep. of Netherlands at Convention of Future of EU, Brussels 2002–03; mem. Expert Cttee for Council of Europe's European Charter for Regional or Minority Languages 2003–04; Counter-Terrorism Co-ordinator, EU 2004–07; Chair. European Security Research and Innovation Forum 2007–08; Sr Fellow, Clingendael, Netherlands Inst. for Int. Relations 2008; mem. Bd Algemene Rekenkamer (Netherlands Court of Audit) 2008–10; mem. European Court of Auditors 2011–13; Commdr, Hellenic Order of Merit 1996. *Address:* European Court of Auditors, 12 rue Alcide de Gasperi, 1615 Luxembourg (office). *Telephone:* 4398-45236 (office). *Fax:* 4398-46202 (office). *E-mail:* gijs.devries@eca.europa.eu (office). *Website:* eca.europa.eu (office).

DE VRIES, Jan Egbert, PhD; Dutch immunologist and institute director; *Head, Novartis Institutes for BioMedical Research;* ed Univs of Utrecht and Amsterdam; Visiting Scientist, John Mendelsohn Lab., Univ. of California, San Diego 1977–79; Chair. Dept of Immunology, Nat. Cancer Research Inst., Amsterdam 1979–85; Dir of a biotechnology enterprise in Lyon, France (subsidiary of US pharmaceutical co. Schering Plough) 1985–88; moved with his research team to biotechnology enterprise DNAX, Palo Alto, Calif., USA (cr. by Nobel Laureates Paul Berg and Arthur Kornberg) 1988–97; joined Novartis as Global Head of Dermatology Disease Area, Novartis Research Inst., Vienna 1997, apptd Global Head of Auto-Immunity and Transplantation Disease Area with research activities in Vienna and Basel 2003, currently Head of Novartis Insts for BioMedical Research, Basel; Wilhelm Exner Medal, Austrian Asscn for SME (Oesterreichischer Gewerbeverein—OGV) (jtly) 2005. *Publications:* more than 300 scientific pubs and reviews in professional journals; 20 patents. *Address:* Novartis Institutes for BioMedical Research, Fabrikstrasse 2, 4002 Basel, Switzerland (office). *E-mail:* nibr .communications@novartis.com (office). *Website:* www.nibr.com (office).

DE WAART, Edo; Dutch conductor; *Music Director, Royal Flemish Philharmonic Orchestra;* b. 1 June 1941, Amsterdam; s. of M. de Waart and J. Rose; one s. one d.; ed Amsterdam Music Lyceum with Haakon Stotijn, Hilversum with Franco Ferrara; Co-Prin. Oboe, Amsterdam Philharmonic 1961, Concertgebouw Orchestra 1963; Asst Conductor, New York Philharmonic 1965–66, Concertgebouw Orchestra, Amsterdam 1966; Musical Dir Netherlands Wind Ensemble 1966; Conductor Rotterdam Philharmonic 1967, Musical Dir and Prin. Conductor 1973–79; Prin. Guest Conductor San Francisco Symphony Orchestra 1975–77, Music Dir 1977–85; Music Dir Minnesota Orchestra 1986–95; Artistic Dir Nederlandse Omroep Stichting (Dutch radio org.); Chief Conductor Netherlands Radio Philharmonic Orchestra 1989–; Prin. Guest Conductor Santa Fe Opera 1991–92; Artistic Dir and Chief Conductor Sydney Symphony Orchestra 1993–2003; Artistic Dir and Chief Conductor Hong Kong Philharmonic Orchestra 2004–12; Chief Conductor Santa Fe Opera 2007–09; Music Dir Milwaukee Symphony Orchestra 2009–; Artistic Partner, St Paul Chamber Orchestra 2010–; Music Dir Royal Flemish Philharmonic Orchestra 2012–; guest conductor with leading orchestras and at venues in USA and Europe and at festivals including Spoleto, Bayreuth and Holland; First Prize, Dimitri Mitropoulos Competition, New York 1964; Hon. AO 2005. *Address:* Harrison Parrott, 5–6 Albion Court, London, W6 0QT, England (office); deFilharmonie (Royal Flemish Philharmonic), Filharmonisch Huis, Braziliëstraat 15, 2000 Antwerp, Belgium (office). *Telephone:* (20) 7229-9166 (office); 32135420 (office). *Fax:* (20) 7221-5042 (office); 32135400 (office). *E-mail:* info@harrisonparrott.com (office); info@ defilharmonie.be (office). *Website:* www.harrisonparrott.com (office); www .defilharmonie.be (office).

DE ZOYSA, Tilak; Sri Lankan business executive; *Chairman, Carson Cumberbatch PLC;* Deputy Chair. and Man. Dir Associate Motorways Ltd 1993–; Chair. Carson Cumberbatch & Co. Ltd (now Carson Cumberbatch PLC 2001–; fmr Pres. Nat. Chamber of Commerce; fmr Chair. Ceylon Chamber of Commerce; Dir Bukit Darah Co. Ltd 2004–; Vice-Pres. Sri Lanka–France Business Council 2004–; mem. Monetary Bd of Sri Lanka; mem. Bd Dirs Taj Lanka Hotels Ltd; mem. Tariff Advisory Council; Hon. Consul for Croatia 1999–; Order of the Rising Sun, Gold Rays with Neck Ribbon, Japan. *Address:* Carson Cumberbatch PLC, 61 Janadhipathi Mawatha, Colombo 1, Sri Lanka (office). *Telephone:* (11) 4739200 (office). *Fax:* (11) 4739300 (office). *E-mail:* carsons@carcumb.com (office). *Website:* www.carsoncumberbatch.com (office).

DEACON, Richard, CBE, RA, MA; British sculptor; b. 15 Aug. 1949, Bangor, Wales; s. of the late Group Capt. Edward William Deacon and Joan Bullivant Winstanley; m. Jacqueline Poncelet 1977 (divorced 2001); one s. one d.; ed Somerset Coll. of Art, St Martin's School of Art, RCA, Chelsea School of Art; Prof., Ecole Nat. Supérieure des Beaux-Arts, Paris 1998–2009; Vice-Chair. Baltic Centre for Contemporary Art Trust 1999–2005; mem. British Council, Arts Council of England Architecture Advisory Group 1996–99; Visiting Prof., Chelsea School of Art 1992–; Prof., Kunstakademie Düsseldorf 2009–; Trustee, Tate Gallery 1992–97; Chevalier, Ordre des Arts et des Lettres 1997; Turner Prize 1987, Robert Jacobsen Prize 1995; Hon. DLitt (Leicester) 2005. *Works include:* What Could Make Me Feel This Way?, Struck Dumb, Doubletalk, Body of Thought No 2, The Back of My Hand, Distance No Object No 2, Dummy, Under My Skin, Breed, Skirt, Laocoon, After, Moor, Let's Not Be Stupid, No Stone Unturned, Building From the Inside, Can't See the Wood for the Trees, Out of Order, The Same But Different, Mountain, Another Mountain, Dead Leg, Nosotros Tres, Water Under The Bridge, Strut, Upper Strut. *Leisure interests:* swimming, walking. *Address:* c/o Lisson Gallery, 67 Lisson Street, London, NW1 5DA, England. *E-mail:* contact@ richarddeacon.net (office). *Website:* www.richarddeacon.net.

DEAL, (John) Nathan, BA, JD; American lawyer, politician and state governor; *Governor of Georgia;* b. 25 Aug. 1942; m. Sandra Dunagan; one s. three d.; ed Mercer Univ., Macon, Ga, Walter F. George School of Law; Capt., Judge Advocate Gen. Corps, US Army 1966–68; pvt. law practice 1979–82; Asst Dist Attorney, Northeast Circuit, Hall Co., Ga 1970–71, Judge, Juvenile Court 1971–72, attorney 1977–79; mem. from Dist 10, Georgia State Senate 1981–93, Pres. Pro Tempore 1991–93; originally a Democrat, elected to US House of Reps for 9th Congressional Dist of Ga 1993–2003 (switched to Republican Party 1995), 2007–10, for 10th Congressional Dist of Ga 2003–07 (resgnd from Congress to run in Ga gubernatorial election March 2010), mem. House Energy and Commerce Cttee 2007–10; Gov. of Georgia 2011–; mem. Congressional Boating Caucus, Congressional Caucus on Unfunded Mandates, Congressional Travel and Tourism Caucus, Congressional Vietnam-Era Veterans Caucus, Rural Health Care Coalition, Speaker's Immigration Task Force; mem. Bd of Trustees, Mercer Univ., Advisory Bd Honors Programs, North Georgia Coll. and Univ.; Republican. *Address:* Office of the Governor, 203 State Capitol, Atlanta, GA 30334 (office); Washington Office of the Governor, State of Georgia, 1455 Pennsylvania Avenue NW, Suite 400, Washington, DC 20004, USA (office). *Telephone:* (404) 656-1776 (Atlanta) (office); (202) 652-2299 (DC) (office). *Fax:* (404) 657-7332 (Atlanta) (office); (202) 347-1142 (DC) (office). *Website:* gov.georgia.gov (office).

DEAN, Christopher, OBE; British fmr ice skater; b. 27 July 1958, Nottingham; s. of the late Colin Dean and Mavis (née Pearson) Dean; m. 1st Isabelle Duchesnay 1991 (divorced 1993); m. 2nd Jill Ann Trenary 1994; two s.; police constable

1974–80; British Ice Dance Champion (with Jayne Torvill q.v., 1978–83, 1994; European Ice Dance Champion (with Jayne Torvill) 1981, 1982, 1984, 1994; World Ice Dance Champion (with Jayne Torvill) 1981–84, World Professional Champions 1984–85, 1990, 1995–96; Olympic Ice Dance gold medal (with Jayne Torvill) 1984, Olympic Ice Dance bronze medal (with Jayne Torvill) 1994; choreographed Encounters for English Nat. Ballet 1996, Stars on Ice in USA 1998–99, 1999–2000; Hon. MA (Nottingham Trent) 1994, BBC Sports Personality of the Year (with Jayne Torvill) 1984, Figure Skating Hall of Fame (with Jayne Torvill) 1989. *Ice Dance:* World tours with own and int. companies of skaters 1985, 1988, 1994, 1997, also tours of Australia and New Zealand 1984, 1991, UK 1992, 1997–98, Japan 1996, USA and Canada 1997–98. *Television:* Path to Perfection (ITV video) 1984, Fire & Ice (also video) 1986, Bladerunners (BBC documentary), The Artistry of Torvill & Dean (ABC TV) 1994, Face the Music 1995, Torvill & Dean, The Story So Far (biographical video) 1996, Bach Sixth Cello Suite (with Yo-Yo Ma) 1996, Dancing on Ice 2007–14 (followed by nat. tours). *Publications:* Torvill and Dean's Face the Music and Dance (with Jayne Torvill) 1993, Torvill and Dean: An Autobiography (with Jayne Torvill) 1994, Facing the Music (with Jayne Torvill) 1995. *Leisure interests:* theatre, ballet, fast cars. *Address:* c/o Sue Young, PO Box 32, Heathfield, East Sussex, TN21 0BW, England (office). *Telephone:* (1435) 867825 (office); (1273) 330798.

DEAN, Graham, BA; British artist; b. 5 Dec. 1951, Birkenhead, England; s. of Leslie Dean and Dorothy Dean; m. Denise Warr 1989; one s. one d.; ed Laird School of Art, Birkenhead, Bristol Polytechnic Faculty of Art and Design; artist since 1974 with over 100 solo exhbns and numerous mixed exhbns world-wide; Abbey Award in Painting, British School, Rome 1992, ICCD Studio Residency, Trivandrum, India 2000, Int. Fellowship, Vermont Studio Center, USA 2003. *Dance:* collaborations with Darshan Singh Bhuller, including No Go Zone, White Picket Fence. *Radio:* Painting by Radio (series), BBC Radio 4, 1984. *Films:* several ind. shorts and videos, including Solsbury Hill (with Peter Gabriel). *Publications:* The Green Room and Other Paintings 1995, Straight to Red 1999, Light Sweet Crude 2001, Shimmer 2004, Thinking Bodies 2005, White Noise 2007, Fragile Lessons 2008, Sleepers 2010, Fitter, Quicker, Longer 2012. *Leisure interests:* tennis, supporting Liverpool football club. *Address:* 17 Norfolk Road, Brighton, East Sussex, BN1 3AA (home); Waterhouse and Dodd, 26 Cork Street, London, W1S 3ND, England; Voc Palombaro, 32/37 San Vito, 05010 San Venanzo Terne, Umbria, Italy. *Telephone:* (20) 7734-7800 (office). *E-mail:* graham.dean1@virgin.net (home); jamie@ waterhousedodd.com (office). *Website:* www.modbritart.com; www.grahamdean .com.

DEAN, Howard, BA, MD; American politician; b. 17 Nov. 1948; s. of Howard Brush Dean and Andrea Maitland; m. Judith Steinberg; one s. one d.; ed Yale Univ. and Albert Einstein Coll. of Medicine; Intern, then resident in internal medicine, Medical Center Hosp. Vermont 1978–82; internal medicine specialist medical practice in Shelburne, Vt; mem. Vermont House of Reps 1983–86, Asst minority leader 1985–86; Lt Gov. State of Vermont 1986–91; Gov. of Vermont 1991–2003; sought Democratic Party presidential candidacy 2004; Chair. Democratic Nat. Cttee 2005–09. *Publications:* You Have the Power: How to Take Back our Country and Restore Democracy in America 2004, Howard Dean's Prescription for Real Healthcare Reform 2009. *Address:* 325 South Cove Road, Burlington, VT 05401-5447, USA (office). *Website:* www.democrats.org (office).

DEAN, Hon. John Gunther, PhD; American diplomatist; b. 24 Feb. 1926, Germany; s. of Dr Joseph Dean and Lucy Dean (née Aschkenazy); m. Martine Duphénieux 1952; two s. one d.; ed Harvard Coll., Harvard Univ. Graduate School and Univ. of Paris Law School, France; entered govt service 1950, diplomatic posts in France, Belgium, Viet Nam, Laos, Togo, Mali and in US Dept of State; Dir Pacification Program in Mil. Region 1, Viet Nam 1970–72; Deputy Chief Mission, Embassy in Laos 1972–74; Amb. to Khmer Repub. 1974–75, to Denmark 1975–78, to Lebanon 1978–81, to Thailand 1981–85, to India 1985–88; Personal Rep. of Dir-Gen. of UNESCO for Cambodia 1989–90; mem. bd Petroleum Inst. of Thailand 1991, Inst. Supérieur de Gestion 1991, General Mediterranean Holdings 1992, Maersk Line Shipping 1992–2007; numerous US and foreign decorations. *Publications:* The Oral History of John Gunther Dean, The Donation of Documents by Ambassador John Gunther Dean to the National Archives 2004, 2005, Danger Zones: A Diplomat's Fight for America's Interests 2009. *Address:* 29 boulevard Jules Sandeau, 75116 Paris, France (office); BP 1318, Chalet Crettaz-Cô, 1936 Verbier, Valais, Switzerland (home). *Telephone:* 1-45-04-71-84 (office); 277712917 (home). *Fax:* 1-45-04-78-57 (office). *E-mail:* johnmartinedean@aol.com (home).

DEAN, Stafford Roderick; British singer (bass); b. 20 June 1937, Surrey; s. of Eric E. Dean and Vera S. Bathurst; m. 1st Carolyn J. Lambourne 1963; four s.; m. 2nd Anne E. Howells 1981; one s. one d.; ed Epsom Coll., Royal Coll. of Music and privately with Howell Glynne and Otakar Kraus; Opera for All 1962–64; Glyndebourne Chorus 1963–64, Prin. début as Lictor in L'Incoronazione di Poppea 1963; under contract to Sadler's Wells Opera/English Nat. Opera 1964–70; Royal Opera House, Covent Garden 1969–, début as Masetto in Don Giovanni; int. début as Leporello in Don Giovanni, Stuttgart 1971; guest appearances with Metropolitan Opera, New York, Chicago Lyric, San Francisco, Berlin, Munich, Hamburg, Cologne, Frankfurt, Vienna, Paris, Turin operas etc.; specializes in Mozart bass repertoire; bass soloist in world premiere of Penderecki Requiem, Stuttgart 1984; concert appearances in choral works by Beethoven, Shostakovich, Verdi. *Leisure interests:* family life, garden.

DEAN, Tacita, OBE; British visual artist and filmmaker; b. (Tacita Charlotte Dean), 1965, Canterbury, Kent, England; ed Kent Coll., Canterbury, Falmouth School of Art, Slade School of Art; comms include Millennium Dome, London, Sadler's Wells Theatre, European City of Culture celebrations, Cork, Ireland; Deutscher Akademischer Austausch Dienst Scholarship, Berlin, Germany 2000; Aachen Art Prize 2002, Fondazione Sandretto Re Rebaudengo, Turin, Italy 2004, 51st Venice Biennale Sixth Benesse Prize 2005, Solomon R. Guggenheim Museum Hugo Boss Prize, New York 2006, Kurt Schwitters Prize 2009. *Films include:* The Story of Beard 1992, The Martyrdom of St Agatha (in several parts) 1994, Girl Stowaway 1994, How to Put a Boat in a Bottle 1995, A Bag of Air 1995, Disappearance at Sea 1996, Delft Hydraulics 1996, Foley Artist 1996, Disappearance at Sea II 1997, The Structure of Ice 1997, Gellért 1998, Bubble House 1999, Sound Mirrors 1999, From Columbus, Ohio, to the Partially Buried Woodshed 1999, Banewl 1999, Teignmouth Electron 2000, Totality 2000, Fernsehturm 2001,

The Green Ray 2001, Baobab 2002, Ztrata 2002, Section Cinema (Homage to Marcel Broodthaers) 2002, Diamond Ring 2002, Mario Merz 2002, Boots 2003, Pie 2003, Palast 2004, The Uncles 2004, Presentation Sisters 2005, Kodak 2006, Noir et Blanc 2006, Human Treasure 2006, Michael Hamburger 2007, Darmstädter Werkblock, 2007, Merce Cunningham Performs Stillness 2008, Amadeus 2008, Prisoner Pair 2008, Still Life 2009, Day for Night 2009, Craneway Event 2009, Manhattan Mouse Museum 2011, Edwin Parker 2011. *Publications include:* Teignmouth Electron 1999, Floh 2001, Seven Books 2003, Berlin Works 2005, Analogue 2006, Tacita Dean 2006, Die Regimentstochter 2006, Tacita Dean 2009, Film Works with Merce Cunningham 2009. *Address:* c/o Marian Goodman Gallery, 24 West 57th Street, New York, NY 10019, USA.

DEANE, Derek, OBE; British ballet dancer and choreographer; b. (Derek Shepherd), 18 June 1953, Redruth, Cornwall; s. of William Gordon Shepherd and Margaret Shepherd; ed Royal Ballet School; with Royal Ballet Co. 1972–89, reaching rank of Premier Dancer; Asst Dir Rome Opera 1990–92; Artistic Dir English Nat. Ballet 1993–2001. *Leisure interests:* tennis, gardening, reading, dinner parties, theatre, performing arts, travel. *Address:* c/o English National Ballet, Markova House, 39 Jay Mews, London, SW7 2ES, England.

DEANE, Seamus Francis, BA, MA, PhD, MRIA; Irish academic, poet and novelist; *Donald and Marilyn Keough Professor Emeritus of Irish Studies, University of Notre Dame, Indiana;* b. 9 Feb. 1940; s. of Winifred Deane and Frank Deane; m. 1st Marion Treacy 1963; three s. one d.; m. 2nd Emer Nolan; one d.; ed Queen's Univ., Belfast, Univ. of Cambridge; Fulbright and Woodrow Wilson Scholar, Visiting Lecturer, Reed Coll., Portland, Ore. 1966–67; Visiting Lecturer, Univ. of California, Berkeley 1967–68; Visiting Prof. 1978; Lecturer, Univ. Coll., Dublin 1968–77; Sr Lecturer 1978–80, Prof. of English and American Literature 1980–93; Visiting Prof., Univ. of Notre Dame, Indiana, USA 1977, Donald and Marilyn Keough Prof. of Irish Studies 1993–2005, Prof. Emer. 2005–; Walker Ames Prof., Univ. of Washington, Seattle 1987, Jules Benedict Distinguished Visiting Prof., Carleton Coll., Minn. 1988; Dir Field Day Theatre Co. 1980–; Ed. Field Day Review 2005–; Hon. DLitt (Ulster) 1999; Ireland/America Fund Literary Award 1988, South Bank Award for Literature 1997. *Publications:* Gradual Wars (AE Memorial Award for Literature 1972) 1972, Celtic Revivals 1985, Short History of Irish Literature 1986, Selected Poems 1988, The French Revolution and Enlightenment in England 1789–1832 1988, Field Day Anthology of Irish Writing 550–1990 1991, Reading in the Dark (Guardian Fiction Prize 1996, Irish Times Int. Fiction Prize 1997, Irish Times Irish Literature Prize 1997, Ruffino Antico Fattore Int. Literary Award 1998) 1996, Strange Country 1997, Foreign Affections: Essays on Edmund Burke 2005. *Address:* Field Day Publications, c/o O'Connell House, 58 Merrion Square, Dublin 2, Ireland (office). *E-mail:* deane.4@nd.edu (office).

DEANE, Hon. Sir William Patrick, AC, KBE, BA, LLB, QC; Australian fmr Governor-General and judge; b. 4 Jan. 1931, St Kilda; s. of the late C. A. Deane, MC and Lillian Hussey; m. Helen Russell 1965; one s. one d.; ed St Joseph's Coll. Sydney, Sydney Univ. and Trinity Coll. Dublin, Ireland; Teaching Fellow in Equity, Univ. of Sydney 1956–61; barrister 1957; Justice, Supreme Court, NSW 1977, Fed. Court of Australia 1977–82; Pres. Australian Trade Practices Tribunal 1977–82; Justice, High Court of Australia 1982–95; Gov.-Gen. of Australia 1996–2001; KStJ; Hon. LLD (Sydney, Griffith, Notre Dame, Trinity Coll., Univ. of NSW, Univ. of Tech. of Sydney, Univ. of Queensland); Hon. DUniv (Southern Cross, Australian Catholic Univ., Queensland Univ. of Tech., Univ. of W Sydney); Hon. DSacredTheol (Melbourne Coll. of Divinity). *Address:* c/o PO Box 4168, Manuka 2603, Australia. *Telephone:* (2) 6239-4716 (office). *Fax:* (2) 6239-4916 (office).

DEARLOVE, Sir Richard (Billing), Kt, KCMG, OBE, MA; British diplomatist and college principal; *Master, Pembroke College, Cambridge;* b. 23 Jan. 1945, Gorran Haven; m. Rosalind McKenzie 1968; two s. one d.; ed Monkton Combe School, Kent School, Conn., USA, Queens' Coll., Cambridge; joined the Foreign Office 1966, postings to Nairobi 1968–71, Prague 1973–76, FCO, London 1971–73, 1976–80, 1984–87, First Sec., Embassy in Paris 1980–84, Counsellor, UK Mission to the UN (UKMIS), Geneva 1987–91, Embassy in Washington, DC 1991–93; Dir of Personnel and Admin., Secret Intelligence Service 1993–94, Dir of Operations 1994–99, Asst Chief 1998–99, Chief 1999–2004; Master of Pembroke Coll., Cambridge 2004–; mem. Int. Advisory Bd AIG 2005–11; Sr Adviser, Monitor Group 2004–11; Chair. Ascot Underwriting 2006–; Chair. of Trustees, Cambridge Union Soc. 2007–; Dir Kosmos Energy 2013–; Gov. English Speaking Union 2008–10; Hon. Fellow, Queens' Coll., Cambridge 2004; Hon. LLD (Exeter) 2007. *Leisure interests:* painting, fly-fishing, the future of Cornwall. *Address:* The Master's Lodge, Pembroke College, Cambridge, CB2 1RF, England (office). *Telephone:* (1223) 338129 (office). *Fax:* (1223) 766395 (office).

DEBBASCH, Charles, DenD; French legal scholar and academic; *Professor of Law, Université d'Aix-Marseille III;* b. 22 Oct. 1937, Tunis, Tunisia; s. of Max Debbasch; m. 2nd Ivonne Chawki-Kamel; three s. three d.; tutorial asst 1957; Jr Lecturer, Law Faculty, Université d'Aix-Marseille III 1959–62; Prof. of Law, Grenoble Univ. 1962–63; Prof. of Law, Université d'Aix-Marseille II 1963–67, Chair of Public Law, Faculty of Law and Econ. Sciences 1967, Dir Centre of Research into Legal Admin. 1966–, Centre of Research and Study on Mediterranean Societies 1969–71; Head of Research Comm., Ministry of Educ. 1968–69; Dir Teaching and Research Unit attached to Faculty of Law and Political Sciences, Aix-Marseille Univ. 1966, Dean, Faculty of Law and Political Sciences 1971–73; Pres. Nat. Assen of Pres. of Univs Specializing in Law and Politics and Deans of Law Faculties 1971–78; Prof., Coll. of Europe, Bruges 1975–81; Pres. Consultative Cttee, Public Law Univs 1978; tech. adviser, Gen. Secr., French presidency 1978–81; Pres. Fondation Vasarely 1981–91; Dir and Dir-Gen. of Press Group, Dauphiné Libéré 1984–89; Pres. Agence générale d'information 1985–89, Supervisory Council of Dauphiné Libéré 1989–94, Observatoire int. de la démocratie 1994–; Dir Inst. Int. du droit des médias 1989–; Minister and Special Adviser to Pres. of Togo 2005–; Officier, Ordre nat. du Mérite, Chevalier, Légion d'honneur, Chevalier des Palmes académiques, Grand Officer of the Aztec Eagle (Mexico), Commdr, Order of Tunisian Repub., Officer of Merit, Senegal. *Publications include:* Procédure administrative contentieuse et procédure civile 1962, La République tunisienne 1962, Institutions administratives 1975, Le Droit de la radio et de la télévision 1970, L'Administration au pouvoir 1970, L'Université

désorientée 1971, Droit administratif 1973, La France de Pompidou 1974, Introduction à la politique 1982, Contentieux administratif 1985, Les Chats de l'émirat 1976, Institutions et droit administratifs (three vols) 1980–99, L'Elysée dévoilé 1982, Lexique de politique 1984, Les constitutions de la France 1983, Droit constitutionnel 1986, Les Associations 1985, La V^{e}République 1985, La Disgrace du socialisme 1985, La Cohabitation froide 1988, Le Droit de l'audiovisuel 1988, La société française 1989, Les grands arrêts du droit de l'audiovisuel 1991, Mémoires du Doyen d'Aix-en-Provence 1996, Droit des médias 1999, Droit administratif des biens 1999, La Constitution de la V^{e}République 2000, Un amour de Love 2001, Contes de nos animaux favoris 2004, La succession d'Eyadema 2006, L'entrée en Sarkozy 2008; contrib. to numerous other works. *Address:* 25 avenue Mozart, 75116 Paris, France (office). *Telephone:* 1-45-20-45-72 (home); 9-0042316 (Togo) (mobile) (office). *E-mail:* debbasch.charles@wanadoo.fr (home). *Website:* www .charlesarthur.space-blogs.com (office); www.charlesdebbasch.com.

DEBEN, Baron (Life Peer), cr. 2010, of Winston in the County of Suffolk; **Rt Hon. John Selwyn Gummer,** PC, MA; British politician; *Chairman, Sancroft International Ltd;* b. 26 Nov. 1939, Stockport, Greater Manchester, England; s. of the late Canon Selwyn Gummer and Sybille Gummer (née Mason); brother of Peter Selwyn Gummer, now Lord Chadlington (q.v.); m. Penelope J. Gardner 1977; two s. two d.; ed King's School, Rochester and Selwyn Coll., Cambridge; Ed., Business Publs 1962–64; Ed.-in-Chief, Max Parrish and Oldbourne Press 1964–66; Editorial Controller, BPC Publishing 1967–73; Dir Shandwick Publishing Co. 1966–81; Dir Siemssen Hunter Ltd 1973–80, Chair. 1979–80; Man. Dir EP Group of Cos 1975–81; Chair. Selwyn Sancroft Int. 1976–81; MP for Lewisham W 1970–74, Eye, Suffolk (now Suffolk Coastal) 1979–2010; Parl. Pvt. Sec. to Minister of Agric. 1972; Vice-Chair. Conservative Party 1972–74, Chair. 1983–85; Asst Govt Whip 1981, Lord Commr Treasury (Whip) 1982; Under-Sec. of State for Employment Jan.–Oct. 1983, Minister of State for Employment 1983–84, Paymaster-Gen. 1984–85; Minister of State at Ministry of Agric., Fisheries and Food 1985–88; Minister for Local Govt, Dept of Environment 1988–89; Minister of Agric. 1989–93; Sec. of State for the Environment 1993–97; Chair. Conservative Group for Europe 1997–2000, Sancroft International Ltd 1997–, Marine Stewardship Council 1998–2005, Valpak Ltd 1998–, Asscn of Professional Financial Advisers 2003–, Veolia Water UK 2004–13, Quality of Life Challenge 2006–07, Forewind (offshore wind co.) 2010–12, Corlan Hafren (energy co.) 2011–12, Cttee on Climate Change 2012–; mem. Gen. Synod of Church of England 1979–92 (resgnd); Pres. Globe International; mem. Bd of Dirs Prince Albert II of Monaco Foundation; Dir (nonexec.), Catholic Herald newspaper; Trustee, British Architectural Library Trust, Blue Marine Foundation, Theodore Trust; joined Roman Catholic Church 1994; The Ordre Saint-Charles 2012; Medal of Honour, Royal Soc. for the Protection of Birds 1998. *Publications:* When the Coloured People Come 1966, To Church with Enthusiasm 1969, The Permissive Society 1970, The Christian Calendar (with L. W. Cowie) 1971, Faith in Politics (with Alan Beith and Eric Heffer) 1987, Christianity and Conservatism 1990. *Leisure interests:* gardening, Victorian buildings. *Address:* Sancroft International Ltd, 46 Queen Anne's Gate, London, SW1H 9AP, England (office); House of Lords, Westminster, London, SW1A 0PW, England (office). *Telephone:* (20) 7960-7900 (office). *Fax:* (20) 7222-7536 (office). *E-mail:* secretariat@sancroft.com (office). *Website:* www.sancroft.com (office); www .parliament.uk/biographies/lords/lord-deben/4154 (office).

DEBONO, Giovanna, BA; Maltese politician; b. (Giovanna Attard), 25 Nov. 1956, Gozo; d. of the late Coronato Attard and Anna Attard (née Tabone); m. Anthony Debono; one s. one d.; ed Univ. of Malta; teacher, Educ. Dept 1981–87; MP (Nationalist Party) 1987–; Parl. Sec. Ministry for Social Devt 1995–96; Minister for Gozo 1998–2013. *Address:* Nationalist Party, Herbert Ganado Street, Pietà PTA 1541, Malta (office). *Telephone:* 21243641 (office). *Fax:* 21243641 (office). *E-mail:* admin@pn.org.mt (office). *Website:* www.pn.org.mt (office).

DEBRAY, (Jules) Régis; French writer and government official; b. 2 Sept. 1940, Paris; s. of Georges Debray and Janine Alexandre; m. Elisabeth Burgos 1968; one d.; ed Ecole normale supérieure de la rue d'Ulm; colleague of Che Guevara, imprisoned in Bolivia 1967–70; Co-ed. Comité d'études sur les libertés 1975; adviser on foreign affairs to François Mitterrand; responsible for Third World Affairs, Secr.-Gen. of Presidency of Repub. 1981–84, with Office of Pres. of Repub. 1984–85, 1987–88; Maître des requêtes, Conseil d'Etat 1985–93; Sec.-Gen. Conseil du Pacifique Sud 1984–85; Pres. Conseil scientifique de l'École nationale supérieure des sciences de l'information 1998–2002, Institut Européen en Sciences en Religions 2002–04; elected mem. Académie Goncourt (seventh seat) 2011. *Publications:* La Critique des armes 1973, La Guerilla du Che 1974, Entretiens avec Allende 1971, Les Epreuves du feu 1974, L'Indésirable 1975, La Neige brûle (Prix Fémina) 1977, Lettre aux communistes français et à quelques autres 1978, Le Pouvoir intellectuel en France 1979, Le Scribe 1980, Critique de la raison politique 1981, La Puissance et les rêves 1984, Les Empires contre l'Europe 1985, Comète, ma comète 1986, Eloges 1986, Les Masques, une éducation amoreuse 1988, Que vive la République 1988, A demain de Gaulle 1990, Cours de médiologie générale 1991, Christophe Colomb, le visiteur de l'aube: les traités de Tordesillas 1992, Vie et mort de l'image: une histoire du regard en Occident 1992, Contretemps: Eloge des idéaux perdus 1992, Ledannois 1992, L'Etat séducteur 1993, L'Oeil naïf 1994, Manifestes médiologiques 1994, Loués soient les seigneurs 1996, Par amour de l'art 1998, L'Abus monumental 1999, Croire, voir, faire 1999, L'Emprise 2000, i.f. suite et fin 2000, Introduction à la médiologie 2000, L'Enseignement du fait religieux dans l'école laïque 2002, L'Edit de Caracalla ou plaidoyer pour les Etats-Unis d'occident 2002, L'Ancien Testament à travers 100 chefs-d'œuvre de la peinture 2003, Le Nouveau Testament à travers 100 chefs-d'œuvre de la peinture 2003, Dieu, un itinéraire 2003, Haïti et la France: Rapport à Dominique de Villepin, ministre des Affaires étrangères 2004, Le siecle et la règle 2004, Ce que nous voile le voile 2004, La Mythologie gréco-latine à travers 100 chefs-d'oeuvres de la peinture 2004, L'Histoire ancienne à travers 100 chefs-d'oeuvres de la peinture 2004, Chroniques de l'idiotie triomphante 2004, Journal D'Un Petit Bourgeois Entre Deux Feux Et Quatre Murs 2004, Le Plan Vermeil 2004, Le Feu Sacré 2005, Julien Le Fidèle Ou Le Banquet Des Démons 2005, Sur le pont d'Avignon 2005, Aveuglantes Lumières 2006, Supplique Aux Nouveaux Progressistes Du Xxie Siècle 2006, Eloge des frontières 2010. *Address:* c/o Editions Gallimard, 5 rue Sébastien Bottin, 75007 Paris, France (office). *Website:* www .regisdebray.com.

DEBRÉ, Bernard André Charles Robert, DenM; French politician and surgeon; b. 30 Sept. 1944, Toulouse; s. of the late Michel Debré and Anne-Marie Lemaresquier; m. Véronique Duron 1971; three s. one d.; ed Lycée Janson de Sailly and Faculté de Médecine, Paris; hosp. doctor 1965–1980; hosp. surgeon 1980; Prof., Faculté de Médecine, Paris 1985; Head of Urology, Hôpital Cochin 1990; Deputy (RPR) to Nat. Assembly 1986–94, 2004– (joined UMP 2007); Mayor of Amboise 1992–2001; Minister of Cooperation 1994–95; Councillor, Paris XVI arrondissement 2008–; mem. of French Cttee of Ethics 1986–88; f. Pour Paris Asscn (cr. to oppose policies of incumbent Mayor of Paris, Betrand Delanoë) 2005; Chevalier, Légion d'Honneur and numerous foreign decorations. *Publications:* La France malade de sa santé 1983, Un traité d'urologie (4 vols) 1985, Le voleur de vie (la bataille du Sida) 1989, L'illusion humanitaire 1997, Le retour de Mwami 1998, La grande transgression 2000 (Prix Louis Pauwels 2001), Le suicide de France (jtly) 2002, Avertissement aux Malades, aux Médicins et aux Elus (ed.) 2002, De la mauvaise conscience en général et de l'Afrique en particulier 2003, Tant que nous t'aimerons (L'Euthanasie la loi impossible) 2004, Le Roman de Shangai 2005, La revanche du serpent ou la fin de l'homo sapiens 2005, La Véritable Histoire des génocides rwandais 2006, Et si l'on parlait d'elle? 2007, articles in French and foreign journals. *Leisure interests:* travel, collecting antique plates, sports. *Address:* Assemblée nationale, 126 rue de l'Université, 75355 Paris 07 SP (office); 30 rue Jacob, 75006 Paris, France (home). *Telephone:* 1-43-25-51-41 (home); 6-85-30-45-73. *Fax:* 1-58-41-27-55 (office). *E-mail:* bdebre@assemblee-nationale.fr (office); bdebre@yahoo.fr. *Website:* www.assemblee-nationale.fr (office).

DEBRÉ, Jean-Louis, DenD; French magistrate and politician; *President, Conseil Constitutionnel;* b. 30 Sept. 1944, Toulouse; s. of the late Michel Debré (fmr Prime Minister of France) and of Anne-Marie Lemaresquier; m. Ann-Marie Engel 1971; two s. one d.; ed Lycée Janson-de-Sailly, Inst. d'Etudes Politiques, Faculté de Droit, Paris and Ecole Nat. de la Magistrature; Asst Faculté de Droit, Paris 1972–75; Adviser, Office of Jacques Chirac 1974–76; Deputy Public Prosecutor, Tribunal de Grande Instance, Evry 1976–78; Magistrate, Cen. Admin. of Ministry of Justice 1978; Chef de Cabinet to Minister of Budget 1978; Examining Magistrate, Tribunal de Grande Instance, Paris 1979; RPR Deputy to Nat. Ass. 1986–95, 1997–2002, Pres. RPR Group 1997–2002; Town Councillor, Evreux 1989; Conseiller Général, Canton de Nonancourt 1992–2001; Deputy Sec.-Gen. and Spokesman for Gaullist Party 1993; Minister of the Interior 1995–97; Vice-Pres. Gen. Council of the Euro 1998–; Mayor of Evreux 2001–07; Pres. Nat. Ass. 2002–07; Pres. Conseil Constitutionnel 2007–; Chevalier du Mérite agricole, Grand-Croix, Ordre d'Isabelle la catholique (Spain) | Prix du Trombinoscope 2003, Marianne d'Or 2004. *Publications:* Les idées constitutionnelles du Général de Gaulle 1974, La constitution de la Ve République 1974, Le pouvoir politique 1977, Le Gaullisme 1978, La justice au XIXe 1981, Les républiques des avocats 1984, Le curieux 1986, En mon for intérieur 1997, Pièges 1998, Le Gaulisme n'est pas une nostalgie 1999, Qu'est-ce que l'Assemblée nationale? 2006. *Leisure interests:* riding, tennis. *Address:* Conseil Constitutionnel, 2 rue de Montpensier, 75001 Paris (office); 126 rue de l'Université, 75007 Paris, France (home). *Telephone:* 1-40-15-30-00 (office). *Fax:* 1-40-20-93-27 (office). *E-mail:* administration@conseil-constitutionnel.fr (office). *Website:* www.conseil-constitutionnel.fr (office).

DEBS, Richard A., BA, MA, PhD; American lawyer and business executive; *Advisory Director and Member of the International Advisory Board, Morgan Stanley & Company;* ed Colgate Coll., Harvard Law School and Advanced Man. Program at Harvard Business School, Princeton Univ. (Ford Foundation Fellow); fmr Fulbright Scholar in Egypt, subsequently held a jt Harvard-Princeton research fellowship; mem. NY Bar; served as COO Fed. Reserve Bank of New York, also Alt. mem. Fed. Open Market Cttee –1976; joined Morgan Stanley as Founding Pres. Morgan Stanley International 1976, currently Advisory Dir, Morgan Stanley and mem. Int. Advisory Bd; Chair. Bd of American Univ. of Beirut; Chair. Emer. Carnegie Hall; mem. Fulbright Asscn; mem. Emer. Group of Thirty Consultative Group on Int. Econ. and Monetary Affairs, Inc. (G-30), Washington, DC; Trustee, Carnegie Endowment for Int. Peace, Inst. of Int. Educ. 2001–; first recipient of Lifetime Achievement Award, Fulbright Asscn. *Address:* Morgan Stanley & Co. Inc., 1585 Broadway, New York, NY 10036, USA (office). *Telephone:* (212) 761-4000 (office). *Fax:* (212) 761-0086 (office). *E-mail:* info@morganstanley.com (office). *Website:* www.morganstanley.com (office).

DÉBY ITNO, Gen. Idriss; Chadian head of state; *President;* b. 1952, Zaghawa community; served in Army, trained as helicoptor pilot; fmr C-in-C of Armed Forces; fmr mil. adviser to Pres. Hissène Habré (q.v.), overthrew him in coup Dec. 1990; Chair. Interim Council of State, Head of State 1990–91; Pres. of Chad 1991–, also C-in-C of Armed Forces; mem. Mouvement patriotique du salut (MPS). *Address:* Office of the President, Palais rose, BP 74, N'Djamena, Chad (office). *Telephone:* 51-44-37 (office). *Fax:* 51-45-01 (office). *E-mail:* presidence@tchad.td (office).

DECAUX, Alain; French historian and television producer; b. 23 July 1925, Lille; s. of Francis Decaux and Louise Tiprez; m. 1st Madeleine Parisy 1957; one d.; m. 2nd Micheline Pelletier 1983; one s. one d.; ed Lycée Faidherbe, Lille, Lycée Janson-de-Sailly, Paris and Univ. of Paris; journalist 1944–; historian 1947–; cr. radio programme La tribune de l'histoire with André Castelot, Colin-Simard and later Jean-François Chiappe 1951; cr. TV programmes: La caméra explore le temps, with Stellio Lorenzi and André Castelot 1956, Alain Decaux raconte 1969, L'histoire en question 1981, Le dossier d'Alain Decaux 1985; f. magazine L'histoire pour tous 1960; Pres. Groupement syndical des auteurs de télévision 1965–66, 1971–72; Vice-Chair. Société des auteurs et compositeurs dramatiques 1965–67, 1969–71, Chair. 1973–75; Dir Société Técipress 1967–91; Vice-Chair. Syndicat nat. des auteurs et compositeurs 1968–73; Admin. Librairie Plon 1969–72; Dir Historia Magazine 1969–71; worked on various periodicals, including Les nouvelles littéraires, Le Figaro littéraire, Historia, Histoire pour tous, Miroir de l'histoire, Lecture pour tous; Chair. Centre d'animation culturelle des Halles et du Marais (Carré Thorigny) 1971–73; mem. Conseil supérieur des lettres 1974; mem. Man. Cttee, Centre nat. des lettres 1974–75; Minister of Francophone Affairs 1988–91; Policy Co-ordinator, French Overseas TV 1989; elected to Académie Française 1979; Chair. Centre d'action culturelle de Paris 1981–; Chair. Société des amis d'Alexandre Dumas 1971; Pres. Coll. des conservateurs du Château de Chantilly 1998–2009; Grand Officier, Légion d'honneur, Grand Croix, Ordre nat. du Mérite, Commdr des Arts et des Lettres; Prix d'histoire, Acad. française 1950, Grande médaille d'or, Ville de Versailles 1954, Grand prix du disque for Révolution française 1963, Prix Plaisir de lire 1968, Oscar de la télévision et de la radio 1968, 1973, Prix de la Création de Télévision 1972, Médaille de vermeil de la Ville de Paris 1973, Prix littéraire de la Paulée de Meursault 1973. *Publications:* Louis XVII 1947, Letizia, mère de l'empereur 1949, La conspiration du général Malet 1952, La Castiglione, dame de cœur de l'Europe 1953, La belle histoire de Versailles 1954, De l'Atlantide à Mayerling 1954, Le prince impérial 1957, Offenbach, roi de Second Empire 1958, Amours Second Empire 1958, L'énigme Anastasia 1960, Les heures brillantes de la Côte d'Azur, Les grands mystères du passé 1964, Les dossiers secrets de l'histoire 1966, Grands secrets, grandes énigmes 1966, Nouveaux dossiers secrets 1967, Les Rosenberg ne doivent pas mourir (play) 1968, Grandes aventures de l'histoire 1968, Histoire des Françaises (two vols) 1972, Histoire de la France et des Français (with André Castelot, 13 vols) 1970–74, Le cuirassé Potemkine (co-writer, play) 1975, Blanqui 1976, Les face à face de l'histoire 1977, Alain Decaux raconte (four vols) 1978, 1979, 1980, 1981, L'Histoire en question (two vols) 1982–83, Notre-Dame de Paris (co-writer, play) 1978, Danton et Robespierre (co-writer, play) 1979, Un homme nommé Jésus (co-writer, play) 1983, Victor Hugo (biog.) 1984, Les Assassins 1986, Le Pape pèlerin 1986, Destins fabuleux 1987, Alain Decaux raconte l'Histoire de France aux enfants 1987, L'Affaire du Courrier de Lyon 1987, Alain Decaux raconte la Révolution Française aux enfants 1988, La Liberté ou la mort (co-writer) 1988, La Révolution racontée aux enfants 1988, Alain Decaux raconte Jésus aux enfants 1991, Jésus était son nom (play) 1991, Le Tapis rouge 1992, Je m'appelais Marie-Antoinette (co-writer, play) 1993, Histoires Extraordinaires 1993, Nouvelles histoires extraordinaires 1994, L'abdication 1995, C'était le XXe siècle 1996, Alain Decaux raconte la Bible aux enfants 1996, Monaco et ses princes 1997, La course à l'abîme 1997, La Guerre absolue 1998, De Staline à Kennedy 1999, De Gaulle, celui qui a dit non (co-writer) 1999, Morts pour Vichy 2000, L'Avorton de Dieu: une vie de Saint Paul 2003, Tous les personnages sont vrais (Prix Saint-Simon 2005) 2004, La Révolution de la Croix – Néron et les Chrétiens 2007, Coup d'Etat à l'Elysée 2008, Dictionnaire amoureux d'Alexandre Dumas 2010. *Address:* 86 boulevard Flandrin, 75116 Paris, France (office). *Telephone:* 1-44-05-90-95 (office). *E-mail:* alain.decaux@noos.fr (office).

DECAUX, Jean-Claude; French advertising executive; *Chairman of the Supervisory Board, JC Decaux;* b. 1937; Founder and Chair. of Supervisory Bd, JC Decaux SA 1955–, Chair. Exec. Bd 1955–2000, Co-CEO 1955–2002; Prix France-Italie 2001. *Achievements include:* pioneered concept of street furniture providing cities with free bus shelters in return for advertising revenue 1964. *Address:* JC Decaux SA, Sainte Apelline, 78373 Plaisir Cedex, France (office). *Telephone:* 1-30-79-79-79 (office). *Fax:* 1-30-79-77-91 (office). *Website:* www.jcdecaux.com (office).

DECKER, Susan L., BSc, MBA; American business executive and accountant; ed Tufts Univ. and Harvard Business School; Chartered Financial Analyst; Publishing & Advertising Equity Securities Analyst, Donaldson, Lufkin & Jenrette 1986–98, Global Dir Equity Research 1998–2000; Chief Financial Officer, Yahoo! Inc. 2000–, Sr Vice-Pres. Finance and Admin 2000–02, Exec. Vice-Pres. Finance and Admin 2002–07, Pres. 2007–09; Entrepreneur-in-Residence, Harvard Business School 2009; mem. Bd of Dirs Costco Wholesale 2004–, Pixar Animation Studios 2004–06, Stanford Inst. for Econ. Policy Research 2005–07, Berkshire Hathaway, Intel Corpn; mem. Financial Accounting Standards Advisory Council 2000–04; ranked by Fortune magazine amongst 50 Most Powerful Women in Business in the US (48th) 2004, (40th) 2005, (20th) 2007, (39th) 2008, ranked by Forbes magazine amongst 100 Most Powerful Women (50th) 2008.

DECQ, Odile; French architect; *Partner, Studio Odile Decq;* b. 1955; ed School of Architecture, Rennes, Univ. of Paris School of Architecture at La Villette, Inst. of Political Studies, Paris; Founding Pnr (with Benoit Cornette), Odile Decq Benoit Cornette Architects (now Studio Odile Decq) 1985–; teacher, Ecole d'Architecture de Paris—La Villette 1984–86; Guest Prof., Univ. of Montréal, Canada 1992, Univ. of Kansas 1997, 2000, Technische Universität, Vienna 1998, University College, London, UK 1998–2000; Prof. of Architecture and Head of Dept, Ecole Spéciale d'Architecture, Paris 1992–99, Dir 2007–; taught at Columbia Univ., New York 2001–03, Akademie Künst, Vienna 2003, Kunst Akademie, Dusseldorf, Germany 2004, Southern California Inst. of Architecture, Los Angeles 2006; jury mem. Westminster Univ. and Bartlett School, London, UK; elected mem. Acad. d'Architecture; Int. Fellow, RIBA 2007–; Hon. mem. Nat. Soc. of Architects, Czech Repub. 2007–; Commdr, Ordre des Arts et Lettres, Chevalier, légion d'Honneur 2003; The Golden Lion Award, Architecture Biennale, Venice, Oscar du Design, Le Nouvel Economiste, Paris, Prix Plus Beaux Ouvrages de Construction Metallique, USINOR, Paris, Premier Award, Ninth Int. Prize for Architecture, London, DuPont Benedictus Commercial Award for Innovation in Architectural Laminated Glass, Premio Il Principe e l'Architetto, Museum of Contemporary Art, Rome 2003, Int. Architecture Award 2006, 2008, 2010, World Architecture Community Award 2008, MIPIM Future Project Award 2009, ECOLA Award 2012, Designer of the Year, Maison 2013. *Architectural works include:* Banque Populaire de l'Ouest, Rennes (received ten nat. and int. awards) 1990, Parc d'activités aéroportuaires, St Jacques de la Lande, Rennes 1994, Métafort, Aubervilliers 1995, Cité des Arts de Fort d'Aubervilliers 1995, Viaduct of Highway A14 and Highway Man. Centre, Nanterre 1996, French Pavilion, Venice Biennale 1996, A Third Bridge City, Rotterdam 1998, School of Econ. Sciences and Law Library, Univ. of Nantes 1998, Port de Gennevilliers 1999, Multiplex, Cambridge 1999, Collective Housing Project, Clichy 1999, Social Housing Complex, Paris 1999, Banque de France Office HQ, Montpellier, Vanishing black holes, (installation) Venice, Italy 2000, Ice skating rink, Bordeaux 2000, 2001, Renovation of the Conf. Hall, UNESCO, Paris 2001, Client Centre, Dunkerque, France 2001, Flat unlimited (installation), Beijing, China 2004, Lillle Italy (restaurant), Paris 2004, Il Tre (restaurant), Paris 2005, Boat Wally 141, Fano, Italy 2006 (Int. Show Boats Award 2007), social housing, Paris 2006. *Publications include:* The Architect's Journal 1997, 100 Red Candles for Reading 2007; articles in professional journals, exhibition catalogues, monologues. *Address:* Studio Odile Decq, 11 rue des Arquebusiers, 75003 Paris, France (office). *Telephone:* 1-42-71-27-41 (office). *Fax:* 1-42-71-27-42 (office). *E-mail:* office@odiledecq.com (office). *Website:* www.odiledecq.com (office).

DeCRANE, Alfred C., Jr; American lawyer and business executive; b. 11 June 1931, Cleveland, Ohio; s. of Alfred Charles DeCrane and Verona DeCrane (née Marquard); m. Joan Elizabeth Hoffman 1954; one s. five d.; ed Notre Dame and

Georgetown Univs; attorney, Texaco Inc., Houston and New York 1959, Asst to Vice-Chair. 1965, to Chair. 1967, Gen. Man. Producing Dept, Eastern Hemisphere 1968, Vice-Pres. 1970, Sr Vice-Pres. and Gen. Counsel 1976, mem. Bd of Dirs 1977–96, Exec. Vice-Pres. 1978–83, Pres. 1983–86, Chair. of Bd 1987–96, CEO 1993–96; Hon. Dir American Petroleum Inst.; mem. Bd of Dirs, Corn Products Int., Harris Corpn; mem. Advisory Bd Morgan Stanley Int.; mem. Bd of Trustees Univ. of Notre Dame; Hon. DHL (Manhattanville Coll.) 1990, Hon. JD (Univ. of Notre Dame) 2002. *Address:* c/o Texaco Inc., Two Greenwich Plaza, PO Box 1247, Greenwich, CT 06836, USA.

DEE, Elizabeth; American gallery owner and art dealer; est. Elizabeth Dee Gallery, New York; represents artists including Alex Bag, Mark Barrow, Eric Baudelaire, Philippe Decrauzat, Harry Dodge & Stanya Kahn, Lizzie Fitch & Ryan Trecartin, Renée Green, Gareth James, Kevin Landers, Miranda Lichtenstein, Virgil Marti, Ryan McNamarra, Josephine Meckseper, Amir Mogharabi, Carl Ostendarp, Adrian Piper, Meredyth Sparks, Mika Tajima/New Humans and Ryan Trecartin; Founder and mem. Advisory Bd X-Initiative (non-profit consortium of global art community to present exhbns and programming responding to the major philosophical and econ. shifts in contemporary art) 2009–; presented, with Darren Flook of London's Hotel gallery, Independent, an art fair that attracted participation from int. array of commercial galleries 2010. *Films:* has produced many of Trecartin's movies, including I-BE AREA 2007, K-Corea INC. K (Section A) 2009, Sibling Topics (Section A) 2009, P.opular S.ky (section ish) 2009. *Address:* Elizabeth Dee Gallery, 545 West 20th Street, New York, NY 10011, USA (office). *Telephone:* (212) 924-7545 (office). *Fax:* (212) 924-7671 (office). *E-mail:* edee@ elizabethdeegallery.com (office). *Website:* www.elizabethdeegallery.com (office). www.x-initiative.org.

DEECH, Baroness (Life Peer), cr. 2005, of Cumnor in the County of Oxfordshire; **Ruth Lynn Deech,** DBE, MA; British regulator and lawyer; *Chair, Bar Standards Board;* b. (Ruth Fraenkel), 29 April 1943, London, England; d. of Josef Fraenkel and Dora Rosenfeld; m. John Deech 1967; one d.; ed St Anne's Coll., Oxford and Brandeis Univ. USA; called to Bar, Inner Temple 1967, Bencher; Legal Asst, Law Comm. 1966–67; Asst Prof., Univ. of Windsor Law School, Canada 1968–70; Fellow and Tutor in Law, St Anne's Coll., Oxford 1970–91, Vice-Prin. 1988–91, Prin. 1991–2004; mem. Univ. of Oxford Hebdomadal Council 1986–2000; Chair. Univ. of Oxford Admissions Cttee 1993–97, 2000–03; Gov. Oxford Centre for Hebrew and Jewish Studies 1994–2000; Chair. Human Fertilization and Embryology Authority 1994–2002; Pro-Vice-Chancellor Univ. of Oxford 2001–04; Gresham Prof. of Law 2008–; Chair. Bar Standards Bd 2009–; mem. Human Genetics Comm. 2000–02; Rhodes Trustee 1997–2006; Visiting Prof., Osgoode Hall Law School, Canada 1978; Gov. BBC 2002–06; Ind. Adjudicator for Higher Educ. 2004–08; Freeman of the Drapers' Co. 2003, of the City of London 2003; Hon. Fellow, Soc. for Advanced Legal Studies 1997; Hon. Bencher, Inner Temple 1996–; Hon. QC 2013; Hon. LLD (Richmond American Int. Univ.) 2000, (Strathclyde) 2003; Hon. PhD (Ben Gurion Univ., Israel). *Publications:* Divorce Dissent 1994, From IVF to Immortality 1997; articles on family law, property law, autobiog. etc. *Leisure interests:* music, after-dinner speaking. *Address:* Bar Standards Board, 289–293 High Holborn, London, WC1V 7HZ (office); House of Lords, Westminster, London, SW1A 0PW, England. *Telephone:* (20) 7611-1444 (office). *Fax:* (20) 7831-9217 (office). *E-mail:* chair@barstandardsboard.org.uk (office); deechr@parliament .uk. *Website:* www.barstandardsboard.org.uk (office); www.parliament.uk/ biographies/lords/baroness-deech/3756.

DEEN, Mohamed Waheed; Maldivian business executive and government official; b. 3 March 1947, Malé; m. Aisha Sayed Mohamed; four s. eight d.; ed attended coll. in Sri Lanka; Vice-Pres. Maldives Chamber of Commerce and Industries; mem. Human Rights Comm. of the Maldives; Minister of Atolls Devt 2005–07, of Youth and Sports 2007–08; Vice-Pres. of the Maldives 2012–13; exec. mem. Maldives Tourism Advisory Bd; Exec. mem. Maldives Tourism Promotion Bd; Exec. mem. Sports Tourism Cttee; Exec. Vice-Pres. Commonwealth Bodybuilding Fed.; Exec. Vice-Pres. Asian Bodybuilding Fed.; Founder-mem. and Chair. Diabetes and Cancer Soc.; mem. Exec. Bd Maldives Asscn of Tourism Industry; Founder and Pres. Maldives Surfing Asscn; Man. Dir Orchid Holdings; Dir Thulhagiri Development, HPL Resorts; CEO Orchid Resorts Management Pvt. Ltd; Man. Dir Deens Orchid Agency; Presidential Commemoration for Nat. Service in recognition of service to the nation during terrorist attack of November 1988, Nat. Award in recognition of service to tourism industry 1993, Nat. Award in recognition of service to community devt 1997, Hon. Award from Ministry of Tourism in recognition of 25 years of distinguished service towards sustainable devt of tourism. *Leisure interests:* football, cricket, squash, badminton, health and fitness. *Address:* Orchid Resorts Management Pvt. Ltd, H. Deens Villa, Mihelli Goathé, Henveinu, Malé, The Maldives (office).

DEFAR, Meseret; Ethiopian athlete; b. 19 Nov. 1983, Addis Ababa; silver medal, 3,000m, World Youth Championships 1999; gold medal, 5,000m, African Championships, Bambous 2006, silver medal, 5,000m, Algiers 2000, Addis Ababa 2008, Nairobi 2010; silver medal, 5,000m, World Jr Championships 2000, gold medal, 3,000m, 5,000m. 2002; gold medal, 5,000m All-African Games 2003, 2007, Afro-Asian Games 2003; gold medal, 5,000m, Athens Olympics 2004, bronze medal, 5,000m, Beijing Olympics 2008, gold medal, 5,000m, London Olympics 2012; gold medal, 3,000m, World Indoor Championships, Budapest 2004, Moscow 2006, Valencia 2008, Doha 2010, silver medal, 3,000m, Istanbul 2012, bronze medal, 3,000m, Birmingham 2003; silver medal, 5,000m, World Championships, Helsinki 2005; gold medal, 5,000m, World Championships, Osaka 2007, bronze medal Berlin, 5,000m, Berlin 2009, Daegu 2011; gold medal, 5,000m, World Championships, Moscow 2013; Women's 5,000m Best Year Performance 2005–07, Women's 3,000m Best Year Performance 2006–07, Women's Track & Field Athlete of the Year 2007. *Address:* c/o Ethiopian Athletics Federation, PO Box 3241, Addis Ababa, Ethiopia. *Website:* www.ethiosports.com.

DEFLASSIEUX, Jean Sébastien; French banker; *Honorary Chairman, Crédit Lyonnais;* b. 11 July 1925, Cap d'Ail; s. of Alexis Deflassieux and Thérèse Dalmasso; m. 1st Christiane Orabona 1950 (deceased); one s.; m. 2nd Huguette Dupuy 2000; ed HEC, Law Faculty, Paris, London School of Econs, Ecole d'organisation scientifique du travail; analyst, Div. of financial studies, Crédit Lyonnais 1948–54; attached to Cabinet of Jean Filippi (Sec. of State for the Budget) 1956–57 and of Arthur Conte (Sec. of State for Industry) 1957; Insp. of

Paris br. offices, Crédit Lyonnais 1958; Sub-Dir Haute Banque 1959–69, Dir of External Commerce 1969–72, of Int. Affairs 1972, in charge of the Cen. Man. of Int. Affairs 1978–82; Adviser to Prime Minister Pierre Mauroy 1981–84; Gen. Admin. 1982, Chair. and CEO Crédit Lyonnais 1982–86, Hon. Chair. 1986–; Chair. Banque des Echanges Internationaux, Paris 1987–96; Monacrédit (Monaco) 1980–99, Banque AIG, Paris 1991–94; Dir Arab Banking Corpn Int. Bank PLC, London 1991–, and of other banks and cos; Del. Gen. Radio Alpazur NRJ Menton 1998; Pres. European League for Econ. Co-operation (French Section) 1983; Pres. (French Section) Int. Vienna Council (East–West) 1985–96; Commdr, Légion d'Honneur, Commdr Ordre Nat. du Mérite, Croix de Guerre 1939–45, Palmes Académiques. *Leisure interests:* history, economics, political philosophy. *Address:* 9 boulevard du Jardin exotique, 98000 Monaco (home); 41 rue Vineuse, 75116 Paris, France (home). *Telephone:* 7-93-50-06-28 (Monaco) (home); 1-47-04-37-10 (Paris) (home).

DEFORD, Frank, BA; American writer and commentator; b. 16 Dec. 1938, Baltimore, Md; m. Carol Penner 1965; one s. two d.; ed Princeton Univ.; Contributing Ed., Sports Illustrated 1962–69, 1998–, Vanity Fair 1993–96; writer and commentator, Cable News Network 1980–86, Nat. Public Radio 1980–89, 1991–, NBC 1986–89, ESPN 1992–96, Real Sports With Bryant Gumbel (HBO) 1996–; Ed.-in-Chief, The National 1989–91; writer, Newsweek Magazine 1991–93, 1996–98; Nat. Asscn of Sportswriters and Sportscasters Sportswriter of the Year 1982–88, Emmy Award 1988, Cable Ace 1996, Peabody Award 1999, Nat. Humanities Medal 2012. *Film screenplays:* Trading Hearts 1986, Four Minutes 2005. *Publications include:* Five Strides on the Banked Track 1969, Cut 'N' Run 1971, There She Is 1972, The Owner 1974, Big Bill Tilden: The Triumphs and the Tragedy 1977, Everyone's All-American 1981, Alex: The Life of a Child 1982, Spy in the Deuce Court 1987, World's Tallest Midget 1988, Casey on the Loose 1989, Love and Infamy 1993, The Best of Frank Deford 1999, The Other Adonis 2001, An American Summer 2002, The Old Ball Game 2005, The Entitled 2007, Bliss, Remembered 2010, Over Time: My Life as a Sportswriter 2012; contrib. to numerous magazines. *Address:* Sterling Lord Literistic Inc., 65 Bleecker Street, New York, NY 10012, USA (office).

DeGENERES, Ellen; American comedienne, actress and television presenter; b. 26 Jan. 1958, Metairie, La; d. of Elliott DeGeneres and Betty Jane DeGeneres (née Pfeffer); m. Portia DeGeneres (b. Amanda Lee Rogers) 2008; ed Grace King High School, Metairie, Atlanta High School, Univ. of New Orleans; left school to do clerical work in a law firm; held job selling clothes at chain store the Merry-Go-Round at Lakeside Shopping Center; also worked as waitress at TGI Friday's and another restaurant, as house painter, hostess and bartender; uses childhood and career experiences in her comedic work; began performing stand-up comedy at small clubs and coffee houses; emcee at Clyde's Comedy Club, New Orleans by 1981; cites Woody Allen and Steve Martin as her main influences at this time; began touring nationally early 1980s; appeared for first time on the Tonight Show with Johnny Carson 1986; TV and film work in late 1980s and early 1990s included roles on TV in Open House and in film Coneheads; named Showtime's Funniest Person in America 1982, Emmy Award for Outstanding Writing in a Comedy Series (Ellen: The Puppy Episode) 1997, Favorite Voice from an Animated Movie, Kids' Choice Awards 2004, People's Choice Awards: Favorite Funny Female Star 2005, 2006, 2007, 2008, Favorite Talk Show Host 2005, 2006, 2007, 2008, 2009, 2010, Favorite Yes I Chose This Star 2008; Pres.'s Medal, Tulane Univ. 2009, ranked by Forbes magazine amongst The World's 100 Most Powerful Women (tenth) 2010, (55th) 2011, (47th) 2012, (51st) 2013, Mark Twain Prize for American Humor 2012. *Films include:* Wisecracks 1991, Coneheads 1993, Mr Wrong 1996, Doctor Doolittle (voice) 1998, Goodbye Lover 1999, EdTV 1999, The Love Letter 1999, Reaching Normal 1999, Finding Nemo (voice) 2003, My Short Film 2005. *Television includes:* Women of the Night (as herself) 1988, Duet (series) 1988–89, Open House 1989, Laurie Hill 1992, Ellen 1994–98 (also producer), Roseanne 1995, Mad About You 1998, If These Walls Could Talk 2 (also exec. producer) 2000, On the Edge 2001, The Ellen Show (18 episodes) 2001–02, host Emmy Awards 2001, 2005, Ellen DeGeneres: Here and Now 2003, MADtv 2003, Ellen: The Ellen DeGeneres Show (Daytime Emmy Awards for Outstanding Talk Show 2004, 2005, 2006, 2007, Outstanding Talk Show Host 2005, 2006, 2007, 2008, Outstanding Special Class Writing 2005, 2006, 2007) 2003–, E! True Hollywood Story 2004, Six Feet Under 2004, Joey 2005, host Acad. Awards ceremony 2007, Ellen's Really Big Show 2007, Sesame Street (uncredited) 2007, Forbes 20 Richest Women in Entertainment 2007, The Bachelorette 2007, American Idol 2007–08 (Co-Judge 2009–10), Ellen's Even Bigger Really Big Show 2008, Ellen's Bigger, Longer & Wider Show 2009, So You Think You Can Dance (Guest Judge) 2009, The Simpsons (as herself in episode 'Judge Me Tender') 2010. *Recording:* Ellen DeGeneres: Taste This (stand-up comedy, live CD) 1996. *Publications:* My Point. . . And I Do Have One 1995, The Funny Thing Is. . . 2003. *Address:* c/o International Creative Management, 10250 Constellation Boulevard, Los Angeles, CA 90067, USA (office). *Telephone:* (310) 550-4000 (office). *E-mail:* comedy@icmtalent.com (office). *Website:* www.icmtalent.com (office).

DEGENHART, Elmar, Dipl-Ing, PhD; German business executive; *Chairman of the Executive Board, Continental AG;* b. 29 Jan. 1959, Dossenheim; ed Univ. of Stuttgart; fmr scientific employee, Fraunhofer Inst. for Manufacturing Eng and Automation IPA, Head of Dept of Handling and Industrial Robot Systems 1987–93; Dir of Operations, Brake Systems North America, ITT Automotive Europe GmbH 1993–98; Exec. Vice-Pres., Electronic Brake Systems, Continental AG and mem. Man. Bd Continental Teves AG & Co. oHG 1998–2003, Chair. Exec. Bd Continental AG, additionally responsible for Corp. Communications, Corp. Quality and Environment, Continental Business System, Continental Automotive Functions 2009–, additionally temporary responsibility for Div. Chassis & Safety Aug. 2013–; Pres. Chassis Systems, Robert Bosch GmbH 2004–05; CEO Keiper Recaro Group 2005–08; Pres. Schaeffler Group Automotive 2008–09. *Address:* Continental AG, Vahrenwalder Straße 9, 30165 Hanover, Germany (office). *Telephone:* (511) 938-01 (office). *E-mail:* info@conti-online.com (office). *Website:* www.conti-online.com (office).

DEGHATI, Reza; French (b. Iranian) photojournalist; *Founder, Webistan Photo Agency;* b. 26 July 1952, Tabriz, Iran; ed Univs of Tabriz and Tehran; photographer with Agence France Presse during Iranian revolution 1978; corresp. with Newsweek, Iran 1978–81, with Time Magazine 1983–88; consultant to UN

Humanitarian Programme, Afghanistan 1989–91; Reporter for UNICEF 1989–95, for National Geographic Magazine 1990–; f. Webistan Photo Agency 1991–; photographs have appeared in numerous int. magazines, including Der Spiegel, Paris-Match, Le Nouvel Observateur, The Observer, El País, Oggi, Newsweek, Life, etc.; regular corresp. for BBC Radio Persia and Radio France Int. Persia; Founder and Pres. Aïna (non-profit org.); Lecturer, George Washington Univ., Washington, DC, Stanford Univ., Beijing Univ., Sorbonne, Paris; mem. Advisory Bd National Geographic All Roads Film Project; mem. Exec. Cttee HSBC Bank Foundation; Sr Fellow, Ashoka Foundation 2008; Fellow, National Geographic; Chevalier, Ordre nat. du Mérite 2005; Dr hc (American Univ. of Paris) 2009; UNICEF Hope Prize for 'Portraits of Lost Children in Rwanda' 1996, Prince of Asturias Humanitarian Medal (Spain) 2006, Honor Medal, Univ. of Missouri (Columbia School of Journalism) 2006, Award of Recognition, Chicago Univ. 2006, Pictet Prize, Paris 2008, Lucie Award for Achievement in Documentary, Lucie Foundation 2009, Int. Center of Photography Infinity Award 2010. *Films:* National Geographic films: Into Forbidden Zone (Emmy Award 2002), Inside Mecca 2003, Reza: Shooting Back 2008, Afghan Warrior 2010. *Publications:* Paix en Galilee 1983, Bayan Ko! 1986, Paris-Pekin-Paris '87 1987, Around the World 1992, Kurdes: Les Chants Brules 1995, Massoud, des Russes aux Talibans 2001, Plus loin sur la Terre 2002, Le pinceau de Bouddha 2002, Eternités Afghanes 2002, Crossing Destinies 2003, Insouciances 2004, The Silk Road 2007, War Peace 2008, Reporters without Borders 2008, Sindbad 2009, Chemins parallèles 2009, Derrière l'Objectif 2010, Les âmes rebelles (Rebelling souls) 2010, L'Envol, La Conférence des Oiseaux (Soaring: The Conference of the Birds) 2010. *Address:* Webistan Photo Agency, 122 rue Haxo, 75019 Paris, France (office). *Telephone:* 1-53-19-83-83 (office). *Fax:* 1-53-19-83-02 (office). *E-mail:* reza@ainaworld.org (office); reza@webistan.com (office). *Website:* www.ainaworld.org (office); www.webistan.com (office).

DEGUARA, Louis, MD; Maltese physician and politician; b. 18 Sept. 1947, Naxxar; m. Maria Fatima Mallia; one s. one d.; ed St Aloysius Coll., Birkikara, Univ. of Malta; medical practitioner 1973; fmrly houseman, St Luke's, Sir Paul Boffa and Gozo Gen. Hosps, Prin. Medical Officer of Health, Northern Region; Gen. Practitioner 1977–; MP (Nationalist Party) 1981–2008; Parl. Sec., Ministry for Social Devt 1995–96; Shadow Minister and Opposition Spokesman for Health 1996–98; Minister of Health 1998–2008. *Address:* c/o Partit Nazzjonalista (Nationalist Party), Herbert Ganado Street, Pietà PTA 1541, Malta.

DEGUTIENĖ, Irena; Lithuanian politician; *Vice-Chairman (Deputy Speaker), Seimas (Parliament);* b. 1 June 1949, Šiauliai; m. Gedminias Degutis; one s. one d.; ed Vilnius Univ.; worked in Vilnius Red Cross Hosp. 1975–94; Deputy Minister of Health Care 1994–96; Minister for Social Security and Labour 1996–2000; mem. conservative Homeland Union—Lithuanian Christian Democrats; mem. Seimas (Parl.) 1996–, Deputy Chair. Cttee on Social Affairs and Labour 2000–04, Chair. (Speaker) Seimas (first woman) 2009–12, Vice-Chair. (Deputy Speaker) 2012–; mem. Cttee on Budget and Finance 2012–, Comm. of the Seimas of the Repub. of Lithuania and the Lithuanian World Community 2013–; Acting Prime Minister of Lithuania 4–18 May 1999, 27 Oct.–3 Nov. 1999. *Address:* Seimas (Parliament), Gedimino pr. 53, Vilnius 01109 (office). *Telephone:* (5) 239-6651 (office). *E-mail:* irena.degutiene@lrs.lt (office); irdegu@lrs.lt (office). *Website:* www.lrs.lt (office).

DEHAENE, Jean-Luc Joseph Marie, DrIur; Belgian (b. French) politician and business executive; b. 7 Aug. 1940, Montpellier, France; m. Celie Verbeke 1965; four c.; ed Univ. of Namur, Catholic Univ. of Louvain; began career as Asssen Sec. to Flanders' Scouting Fed. (Vlaams Verbond van Katholieke Scouts); mem. Research Dept, Christian Workers' Union (ACW) 1965; began political career in 1967, occupying several parl. and govt functions at fed. and European level; adviser to various govt ministries 1972–81; Minister of Social Affairs and Institutional Reforms 1981–88; Deputy Prime Minister and Minister of Communications and Institutional Reforms 1988–92; Prime Minister of Belgium 1992–99; Vice-Pres. of EU Special Convention on a European Constitution 2001–08; cand. (Christen-Democratisch en Vlaams Partij—CD&V) in Belgian elections 2003; mem. European Parl. (Group of the European People's Party (Christian Democrats)) 2004–; Ind. Dir and Chair. Dexia Group 2008–11, Chair. Appointment and Compensation Cttee, Strategy Cttee, also Chair. Dexia Crédit Local, Vice-Chair. Dexia Banque Belgique, Dir Dexia Banque International à Luxembourg; mem. or fmr mem. Bd of Dirs Inbev, Umicore, Lotus Bakeries, Novovil, Trombogenics 2006–; Chair. UEFA's Club Financial Control Panel 2009–; Pres. Admin. Council College of Europe 1999–2009; Vice-Chair. European Convention; fmr mem. Bd Govs of Fondation Roi Baudouin. *Address:* European Parliament, ASP 8F356, Wiertz-straat 60, 1047 Brussels, Belgium (office). *Telephone:* (2) 284-58-67 (office). *E-mail:* jean-luc.dehaene@europarl.europarl.eu (office). *Website:* www.europarl.europa .eu/meps/en/28256/Jean-Luc_DEHAENE.html (office); www.jean-lucdehaene.eu.

DEHAENE, Stanislas, PhD; French mathematician, neuroscientist, academic and author; *Director, INSERM-CEA Cognitive Neuroimaging Unit and Professor of Experimental Cognitive Psychology, Collège de France;* b. 12 May 1965, Roubaix; m. Ghislaine Dehaene-Lambertz; three s.; ed École Normale Supérieure, Paris, Univ. of Paris VI, École des Hautes Etudes en Sciences Sociales, Paris; Research Scientist, Cognitive Sciences and Psycholinguistics Lab., Institut Nat. de la Santé et de la Recherche Médicale (INSERM) 1989–99, Research Dir, INSERM 1997–2005, Dir INSERM-CEA Cognitive Neuroimaging Unit 2002–; Postdoctoral Fellow, Inst. of Cognitive and Decision Sciences, Univ. of Oregon, USA 1992–94; Prof. of Experimental Psychology, Collège de France 2005–; Assoc. Ed. Cognition 1999–2005, Frontiers in Neurosciences 2008–; mem. Editorial Bd, Mathematical Cognition 1991–97, Neuroimage 2001–, PLOS Biology 2003–, Mind Brain and Education 2006–, Trends in Cognitive Science 2011; mem. Bd of Reviewing Editors, Science 2008–; Editorial Advisor, Editions Odile Jacob, Paris 1996–; Action Ed., Cognitive Neuropsychology 1998–2003; mem. Acad. des sciences 2005, Pontifical Acad. of Sciences 2008, American Philosophical Soc. 2010, NAS 2010; Corresp. FBA 2010; Hon. Prof., East China Normal Univ., Shanghai 2010; Chevalier, Ordre nat. du Mérite 2008, Légion d'honneur 2011; Dr hc (Lisbon) 2011; Fanny Emden Prize, Acad. des sciences 1996, James S. McDonnell Foundation Centennial Fellowship (co-recipient) 1999, Villemot Prize, Acad. des sciences 2000, Jean-Louis Signoret Prize, IPSEN Foundation 2001, Pius XI Medal, Pontifical Acad. of Sciences 2002, Louis D. Prize (co-recipient), Institut de France 2003, Gold Medal, Asscn Arts-Sciences-Lettres 2007, Dr A.H. Heineken Prize for Cognitive

Science 2008. *Films:* La bosse des maths (documentary, ARTE/Transeurope Film) 2000, Dans le secret de nos émotions (documentary, ARTE/Transeurope Film) (Primé au festival int. Telecienca de Vila Real, Portugal 2003, Premier Prix, Festival Int. du Film de Santé de Liège, Belgique 2004, Prix de la réalisation, 17ème Festival Int. du Film Scientifique d'Orsay 2004) 2004. *Publications:* Numerical Cognition (ed.) 1993, Le Cerveau en action: l'imagerie cérébrale en psychologie cognitive (ed.) 1997, La Bosse des Maths (Jean Rostand Award) 1997, The Number Sense 1997 (second edn 2011), The Cognitive Neuroscience of Consciousness (ed.) 2001, From Monkey Brain to Human Brain (co-ed.) 2005, Vers une science de la vie mentale 2007, Les neurones de la lecture (Grand Prix RTL-Lire) 2007, Reading in the Brain 2009, Parole et musique: aux origines du dialogue humain (co-ed.) 2009, Space, Time and Number in the Brain: Searching for the Foundations of Mathematical Thought (co-author) 2011, Characterizing Consciousness: From Cognition to the Clinic? (co-ed.) 2011, Apprendre à lire. Des sciences cognitives à la salle de classe 2011; 39 book chapters and more than 220 papers in professional journals. *Address:* Inserm-CEA Cognitive Neuroimaging Unit, CEA/SAC/DSV/DRM/NeuroSpin, Bât 145, Point Courrier 156, 3, 91191 Gif-sur-Yvette, France (office). *Telephone:* 1-69-08-79-32 (office). *Fax:* 1-69-08-79-73 (office). *E-mail:* stanislas.dehaene@cea.fr (office). *Website:* www.college-de-france .fr/site/en-stanislas-dehaene (office); www.unicog.org/pm/pmwiki.php/Main/StanislasDehaene (office).

DEHECQ, Jean-François; French pharmaceuticals industry executive; *Chairman, Sanofi-Aventis SA;* b. 1 Jan. 1940, Nantes; ed Ecole Nat. Supériere des Arts et Métiers, Lille; began career as math. teacher, Lycée catholique Saint-Vincent de Senlis, Oise 1964; Man. Dir Sanofi (subsidiary of Elf-Aquitaine Group) 1973–98, Chair. and Man. Dir Sanofi-Synthélabo (following merger of Sanofi and Synthélabo 1998) 1999–2004, Chair. Sanofi-Aventis (following merger of Sanofi-Synthélabo and Aventis) 2004–; Pres. European Fed. of Pharmaceutical Industries and Asscns (EFPIA) 2001–02; Commdr, Légion d'honneur, Officier, Ordre nat. du Mérite agricole, Commdr du Mérite de l'Ordre souverain de Malte; Nessim Habif Prize, Congrès des Ingénieurs Arts et Métiers 2003. *Address:* Sanofi-Aventis, 174 Avenue de France, 75013 Paris, France (office). *Telephone:* 1-53-77-40-00 (office). *Fax:* 1-53-77-42-96 (office). *E-mail:* info@sanofi-synthelabo.com (office). *Website:* www.sanofi-synthelabo.com (office).

DEHGAN, Brig.-Gen. Hossein; Iranian politician and fmr air force officer; *Minister of Defence and Armed Forces Logistics;* b. 1957, Shahreza, Isfahan Prov.; ed Tehran Univ.; joined Iranian Revolution Guards Corps (IRGC) 1979, becoming Commdr, IRGC Tehran Div. 1980–82, Commdr Isfahan (Dist 2), Commdr IRGC in Syria and Lebanon 1982–83, Deputy Commdr, IRGC Air Force 1986–90, Commdr 1990–92, Gen. Man. IRGC Cooperatives Foundation 1996, Deputy Minister of Defence 1997–2003, Acting Minister of Defence 2003, Minister of Defence and Armed Forces Logistics 2013–; Deputy Pres. Bonyad Shadid (martyrs' foundation charitable trust) 2005, Pres. 2005–09; Deputy Head, Armed Forces Strategic Studies Centre 2009–10; Sec., Expediency Council Political, Defence and Security Cttee 2010–13; mem. Moderation and Devt Party. *Address:* Ministry of Defence and Armed Forces Logistics, Shahid Yousuf Kaboli Street, Sayed Khandan Area, Tehran, Iran (office). *Telephone:* (21) 26126988 (office). *E-mail:* info@mod.ir (office). *Website:* www.mod.ir (office).

DEHMELT, Hans Georg, Dr rer. nat; American physicist and academic; *Professor Emeritus of Physics, University of Washington;* b. 9 Sept. 1922, Görlitz, Germany; s. of Georg Dehmelt and Asta Klemmt; m. Diana Dundore 1989; one s. from a previous m.; ed Gymnasium Zum Grauen Kloster, Berlin, Breslau Tech. Univ., Göttingen Univ. and Inst. of Hans Kopfermann; served as private in German army 1940–45, POW 1945–46; Deutsche Forschungs-Gemeinschafts Fellow, Inst. of Hans Kopfermann 1950–52; postdoctoral work in microwave spectroscopy lab., Duke Univ., USA 1952–55; Visiting Asst Prof., Univ. of Washington, Seattle 1955–56, Asst Prof. 1956–58, Assoc. Prof. 1958–61, Prof. 1961–2002, Prof. Emer. 2002–; became US citizen 1961; Fellow, American Physical Soc.; mem. NAS, American Acad. of Arts and Sciences; Dr rer. nat hc (Ruprecht Karl Univ., Heidelberg) 1986, Hon. DSc (Chicago) 1987; Davisson-Germer Prize, American Physical Soc. 1970, Alexander von Humboldt Prize 1974, Award in Basic Research, Int. Soc. of Magnetic Resonance 1980, Count Rumford Prize, American Acad. of Arts and Sciences 1985, Nobel Prize in Physics 1989 for measurement on isolated subatomic particle and atomic particle at rest, Nat. Medal of Science 1995. *Achievements include:* co-discovered nuclear quadrupole resonance 1949; with others, achieved the most precise electron magnetic moment determination to date, through work on geonium. *Publication:* Radiofrequency Spectroscopy of Stored Ions 1967. *Address:* Department of Physics, Office C509, University of Washington, Seattle, WA 98195-1560 (office); 1600 43rd Avenue E, Seattle, WA 98112-3205, USA (home). *Telephone:* (206) 543-2779 (office). *E-mail:* dehmelt@phys.washington.edu (office). *Website:* www.phys.washington.edu/~dehmelt (office).

DEIGHTON, Len; British writer; b. 1929, London, England. *Publications:* The Ipcress File 1962 (also film), Horse under Water 1963, Funeral in Berlin 1964 (also film), Où est le Garlic 1965, Action Cook Book 1965, Cookstrip Cook Book (USA) 1966, Billion Dollar Brain 1966 (also film), An Expensive Place to Die 1967, Len Deighton's London Dossier (guide book) 1967, The Assassination of President Kennedy (co-author) 1967, Only When I Larf 1968 (also film), Bomber 1970 (also radio dramatization), Declarations of War (short stories) 1971, Close-Up 1972, Spy Story 1974 (also film), Yesterday's Spy 1975, Twinkle, Twinkle, Little Spy 1976, Fighter: The True Story of the Battle of Britain 1977, SS-GB 1978, Airshipwreck (co-author) 1978, Blitzkrieg 1979, Battle of Britain (co-author) 1980, XPD 1981, Goodbye Mickey Mouse 1982, Berlin Game 1983, Mexico Set 1984, London Match 1985, Winter: A Berlin Family 1899–1945 1987, Spy Hook 1988, ABC of French Food 1989, Spy Line 1989, Spy Sinker 1990, Basic French Cookery Course 1990, Mamista 1991, City of Gold 1992, Violent Ward 1993, Blood, Tears and Folly 1993, Faith 1994, Hope 1995, Charity 1996. *Address:* c/o Jonathan Clowes Ltd, 10 Iron Bridge House, Bridge Approach, London, NW1 8BD, England (office). *Telephone:* (20) 7722-7674 (office). *Fax:* 871-528-3647 (office). *E-mail:* admin@jonathanclowes .co.uk (office). *Website:* www.jonathanclowes.co.uk (office).

DEINEKIN, Gen. (retd) Piotr Stepanovich, DrMilSc; Russian army officer (retd); b. 14 Dec. 1937, Morozovsk, Rostov Region; m.; three c.; ed Balashov Military Aviation School, Yuri Gagarin Air Force Acad., Gen. Staff Acad.; pilot, army air force 1957–69, Commdr aviation regt, div. 1969–82, Deputy Commdr Army Air Force 1982–85, Commdr 1985–90, First Vice-C-in-C of USSR Air Force 1990, C-in-C and Deputy Minister of Defence of USSR (now Russia) 1991–97; Head Pres.'s Admin. Dept on the Cossack Problem 1998; Hero of Russian Fed. 1997. *Address:* Staraya pl. 4, entr. 1, Moscow, Russia. *Telephone:* (495) 206-35-73 (office).

DEISS, Joseph, PhD; Swiss economist, politician, UN official and business executive; *Chairman, Alstom (Schweiz) AG;* b. 18 Jan. 1946, Fribourg; m. Elizabeth Mueller; three s.; ed Coll. Saint-Michel, Fribourg, Univ. of Fribourg, King's Coll., Cambridge, UK; Lecturer (part-time) in Political Economy, Univ. of Fribourg 1973–83, Prof. Extraordinary 1984–99, Sr Faculty mem. Dept of Social and Econ. Science 1996–98, Prof. of Political Economy 2007–; Deputy, Great Council of Fribourg 1981–91, Pres. 1991, Nat. Adviser 1991–99; Vice-Pres. Comm. on Foreign Policy, Nat. Council 1995–96; Pres. Comm. on Revision of Fed. Constitution 1996; Head of Fed. Dept of Foreign Affairs 1999–2002; Head of Fed. Dept of Econ. Affairs 2003–06 (resgnd); Pres. of the Swiss Confed. 2004; Pres. 65th Session of the Gen. Ass., UN, New York 2010–11; Pres. Banque Raiffaisen du Haut-Lac 1996–99; Chair. Schumacher AG, Schmitten 1996–99; Chair. Alstom (Schweiz) AG 2012–; Vice-Chair. Advisory Council, Zurich Financial Services Int.; Bd mem. Emmi Group, Switzerland, Zurich Insurance Co., Ireland and South Africa; mem. Bd of Govs World Bank, EBRD; mem. Christlichdemokratische Volkspartei der Schweiz—Parti démocrate-chrétien suisse (Christian Democratic People's Party), Strategic Council, Saint Joseph Univ., Beirut; Hon. mem. Int. Raoul Wallenberg Foundation; Officier, Légion d'honneur 2007, Grand Cordon, Order of the Rising Sun (Japan) 2008; Dr hc (Univ. of Sofia, Bulgaria) 2001, (Univ. of Neuchâtel, Switzerland) 2007, (Business School of Lausanne, Switzerland) 2008. *Address:* Alstom (Schweiz) AG, Brown Boveri Strasse 7, 5401 Baden, Switzerland (office). *Telephone:* 562057733 (office). *Website:* www.alstom.com (office).

DEITCH, Jeffrey, MBA; American art dealer, art critic and exhibition organizer; *Director, Museum of Contemporary Art, Los Angeles;* ed Wesleyan Univ., Harvard Business School; art critic and exhbn curator since mid-1970s; fmr Asst Dir John Weber Gallery, New York; fmr Curator De Cordova Museum, Lincoln, Mass; Vice-Pres. Citibank, responsible for developing and managing the bank's art advisory and art finance businesses 1979–88; f. own art advisory firm 1988; first American Ed. Flash Art; first important curatorial project was Lives, a 1975 exhbn about artists who used their own lives as an art medium, presented in vacant office bldg in Tribeca, lower Manhattan; opened a public gallery, Deitch Projects 1996–2010; Dir, Museum of Contemporary Art, Los Angeles 2010–; mem. Art Dealers Asscn of America; mem. Bd Trustees Wesleyan Univ. 1982–85; Art Critic's Fellowship, Nat. Endowment for the Arts 1979. *Publications include:* numerous catalogue essays, including projects for the Museum of Modern Art, Paris, Stedelijk Museum, Amsterdam, Whitney Museum, New York; essay The Art Industry was included in catalogue for the Metropolis exhbn, Martin-Gropius-Bau, Berlin 1991; contrib. to Arts, Art in America, Artforum, and numerous other publs. *Address:* Museum of Contemporary Art, 250 South Grand Avenue, Los Angeles, CA 90012, USA (office). *Telephone:* (212) 626-6222 (office). *Fax:* (212) 620-8674 (office). *Website:* www.moca .org (office).

DEJEAN-ASSÉMAT, Anne, PhD; French molecular biologist and academic; *Permanent Scientist and Director, Laboratory of Nuclear Organization and Oncogenesis, Pasteur Institute and of the Molecular and Cellular Biology of Tumours Unit at French National Institute for Health and Medical Research (INSERM);* ed Université Pierre et Marie Curie, Paris; Researcher, INSERM (French Nat. Inst. for Health and Medical Research) 1985–91, Research Dir 1991–2003, Perm. Scientist and Dir Lab. of Nuclear Organization and Oncogenesis, Pasteur Inst. and of INSERM Research Unit of Molecular and Cellular Biology of Tumors 2003–; Corresp., Acad. des sciences 1999, mem. 2004; mem. European Molecular Biology Org. 2004; Hamdan Medicine Award 2000, Gagna & Van Heck Award 2003, Laureate for Europe, L'Oréal-UNESCO Awards for Women in Science 2010. *Publications:* numerous papers in professional journals on the molecular and cellular mechanisms involved in the development of human cancers. *Address:* Nuclear Organization and Oncogenesis Unit, Pasteur Institute, 28 rue du Docteur Roux, 75724 Paris Cedex 15, France (office). *Telephone:* 1-45-68-80-00 (office). *Fax:* 1-43-06-98-35 (office). *E-mail:* anne.dejean@pasteur.fr (office). *Website:* www.pasteur.fr (office).

DEKA, Ramesh C., MD; Indian physician and academic; *Distinguished Chair Professor, Medical Education and Research, Amity University;* b. 1 Oct. 1948, Assam; ed Gauhati Medical Coll. and Hosp., All India Inst. of Medical Sciences; Reader and Head, Dept of Otorhinolaryngology, Kasturba Medical Coll., Manipal 1976–79; with Jawaharlal Inst. of Postgraduate Medical Educ. and Research, Pondicherry 1979–81; joined faculty at All India Inst. of Medical Sciences 1981, Head of Dept of Otorhinolaryngology 1995–, Dean 2006–09, Dir All India Inst. of Medical Sciences 2009–13; Pres. Asscn of Otolaryngologists, Delhi 1988–89, mem. Governing Body 1993–94; Treasurer Neuro-otological and Equilibriometric Soc. 1981–82, Gen. Sec. 1982–90, Vice-Pres. 1991–92, Pres. 1993–94; Pres. All India Rhinology Soc. 2001–02, Asscn of Otolaryngologists 2002–03; Chair. Indian Acad. of Otolaryngology, Head and Neck Surgery 2002–10; Chair. Organizing Cttee Int. Asian Research Symposium in Rhinology, Mumbai 2004, Regional Consultation Meeting of WHO for SEA regional countries on Colombo for Prevention and Control of Deafness 2004; currently Distinguished Chair Prof., Medical Education and Research, Amity Univ.; Fellow, American Acad. of Otolaryngology 2004–, Int. Medical Sciences Acad. 2007–; mem. Int. Advisory Cttee Asian Research Symposium in Rhinology 2004–08; Chair. Editorial Bd Indian Journal of Otolaryngology, Head and Neck Surgery 1994–96; Editorial Chief Vertigo View Point; mem. Editorial Bd Indian Journal of Otolaryngology, Acta Otolaryngologica (Sweden), Otology and Neuro-otology (USA), Otolaryngology & HN Surgery, USA, Pakistan Journal of Otolaryngology (Pakistan); Hon. Sec., Asscn of Otolaryngologists, Delhi 1985–86; Dr R.A.F Copper (Gold Medal) Award, Asscn of Otolaryngologists 1975, NES India Research Award (Gold Medal), Neurotological Soc. of India 1984, G.D Birla Oration Award, Kashmir Univ. 1991, Rashtriya Ratan Award 1999, Best ENT Services Award, Jammu ENT Soc. 2000, Bharat Gaurav Award, Best Citizen Of India, Int. Publishing House 2007, Lifetime Achievement Award 2010. *Address:* Amity University, Sector 125, Noida, 201 303, India (office). *Telephone:* (12) 04713600 (office). *Website:* www.amity.edu (office); www.rameshcdeka.com.

DEKHEL, Turki al-; Saudi Arabian broadcaster and journalist; *Presenter, Al Arabiya News Network;* b. 1973, Riyadh; ed Imam Mohammed Univ., Riyadh; began career as mosque imam; fmr columnist with Al Hayat (daily newspaper), also fmr contributor to most major Saudi newspapers, including Al Riyadh, Al Sharq Al Awsat, Al Majala magazine; currently daily columnist, Al Watan newspaper; hosts own TV programme on Al Arabiya news network and radio show on Panorama radio channel. *Publications:* Memoirs of a Previously Obese Man (in Arabic). *Address:* c/o Middle East Broadcasting Center (MBC), POB 76267, Dubai, United Arab Emirates (office). *Telephone:* (4) 3919999 (office). *Fax:* (4) 3919900 (office). *E-mail:* infotv@mbc.ae (office). *Website:* www.mbc.net (office).

DEKKER, Cees, MSc, PhD; Dutch physicist and academic; *Distinguished University Professor, Department of Bionanoscience, Delft University of Technology;* b. 7 April 1959, Haren; ed Univ. of Utrecht; Research Asst, Univ. of Utrecht 1984–88, Perm. Scientific Staff 1988–93; Visiting Researcher, IBM Research, Yorktown Heights, USA 1990–91, Technion, Israel Inst. of Tech., Haifa 2000; Perm. Scientific Staff, Delft Univ. of Tech. 1993–99, Antoni van Leeuwenhoek Prof. 1999, Prof. of Molecular Biophysics 2000, Distinguished Univ. Prof. 2006–, Chair. Dept of Bionanoscience 2009–; Fellow, Inst. of Physics 2004–, American Physical Soc. 2006–; mem. Royal Netherlands Acad. of Arts and Sciences 2003–, New York Acad. of Sciences 2005–; Discover Award for Emerging Future Technologies 1999, Netherlands Org. for Scientific Research Pioneer Award 2000, European Physical Soc. Agilent Technologies Europhysics Prize 2001 (jt recipient), Julius Springer Prize for Applied Physics 2002, Netherlands Org. for Scientific Research Spinoza Prize 2003, Int. Montefiore Award 2005, Innovation in Nano Research Prize (Repub. of Korea) 2006. *Address:* Kavli Inst. of NanoScience, Delft University of Technology, Lorentzweg 1, 2628 CJ Delft, Netherlands (office). *Telephone:* (15) 2786094 (office). *Fax:* (15) 2781202 (office). *E-mail:* C.Dekker@ tudelft.nl (office). *Website:* www.ceesdekker.net.

DEKKER, Wout; Dutch business executive; *Chairman of the Supervisory Board, Rabobank Group;* b. 10 Nov. 1956; mem. Supervisory Bd Macintosh Retail Group NV, Randstad NV; mem. Taskforce Biodiversity and Natural Resources; mem. Advisory Council for Issuers, NYSE Euronext; mem. Supervisory Bd Rabobank Group 2010–, Chair. 2013–. *Address:* Rabobank Group, Postbus 17100, Croeselaan 18, 3500 HG Utrecht, Netherlands (office). *Telephone:* (30) 216-00-00 (office). *Fax:* (30) 216-26-72 (office). *E-mail:* info@rabobank.com (office). *Website:* www .rabobank.com (office).

DEKKERS, Marijn, PhD; Dutch/American business executive; *Chairman of the Board of Management, Bayer AG;* b. 22 Sept. 1957, Tilburg; m.; three d.; ed Univs of Nijmegen and Eindhoven; began career in research with General Electric in USA; moved to Honeywell 1995–2000; COO Thermo Electron Corpn (renamed Thermo Fisher Scientific, Inc. following acquisition of Fisher Scientific) 2000–02, Pres. and CEO 2002–10; mem. Bd of Man. Bayer AG Jan. 2010–, Chair. Oct. 2010–. *Address:* Bayer AG, Building W11, Kaiser-Wilhelm-Allee, 51368 Leverkusen, Germany (office). *Telephone:* (214) 301 (office). *Fax:* (214) 3066328 (office). *E-mail:* info@bayer.com (office). *Website:* www.bayer.com (office).

DEL CASTILLO, Michel Xavier Janicot, LèsL, LenP; French writer; b. 2 Aug. 1933, Madrid, Spain; s. of Michel Janicot and Isabelle del Castillo; ed Coll. des jésuites d'Ubeda, Spain, Lycée Janson-de-Sailly, Paris; mem. Soc. des gens de lettres, PEN; Chevalier, Légion d'honneur, Commdr des Arts et Lettres; Prix des Magots 1973, Grand Prix des libraires 1973, Prix Chateaubriand 1975, Prix Renaudot 1981, Prix Maurice Genevoix 1994, Prix Jacques Audiberti 2010. *Publications:* Tanguy 1956 (Prix des Neufs), La Guitare 1957, Le Colleur d'affiches 1958, Le Manège espagnol 1960, Tara 1962, Gerardo Laïn 1967, Le Vent de la nuit 1972, Le Silence des pierres 1975, Le Sortilège espagnol 1977, Les Cyprès meurent en Italie 1979, Les Louves de l'Escurial 1980, La nuit du décret 1981, La Gloire de Dina 1984, La Halte et Le Chemin 1985, Nos Andalousies 1985, Le Démon de l'oubli 1987, Mort d'un poète 1989, Une Femme en Soi 1991, Andalousie 1991, Le Crime des Pères 1993, Carlos Pradal 1993, Rue des Archives 1994, Mon frère l'idiot 1995 (Prix de l'Ecrit Intime), Le Sortilege Espagnol: Les Officiants De La Mort 1996, La Tunique d'infamie 1997, De père français 1998, Colette, une certaine France (Prix Femina 1999), L'Adieu au siècle 2000, Droit d'auteur 2000, Les Etoiles Froides 2001, Colette En Voyage 2002, Algerie, L'Extase Et Le Sang 2002, Les Portes Du Sang 2003, Le Jour Du Destin 2003, Sortie Des Artistes 2004, Le Dictionnaire Amoureux De L'Espagne (Prix Méditerranée) 2005, La Mémoire de Grenade (play) 2005, La Religieuse de Madrigal 2006, La Vie mentie (Prix des écrivains croyants 2008) 2007, Le Temps de Franco 2008, Mamita 2010. *Address:* Le Colombier, 7 avenue Camille Martin, 30190 La Calmette, France (home). *E-mail:* webmaster@micheldelcastillo.com (office). *Website:* www.micheldelcastillo .com.

DEL CASTILLO GÁLVES, Jorge Alfonso Alejandro; Peruvian lawyer and politician; b. 2 July 1950, Lima; ed Nat. Univ. of San Marcos, Lima, Pontifical Catholic Univ. of Peru; Mayor of Barranco Ward, Lima 1984–86, apptd Prefect of Lima 1985; mem. Partido Aprista Peruano—PAP, Sec.-Gen. PAP 1999–, Rep. of PAP before OAS; Mayor of Metropolitan Lima Oct. 1987–89; elected to Peruvian Congress of the Repub. for Lima 1995–, re-elected 2000, 2001, 2006; Pres. Council of Ministers (Prime Minister of Peru) 2006–08 (resgnd). *Address:* Partido Aprista Peruano, Avda Alfonso Ugarte 1012, Lima, Peru (office). *Telephone:* (1) 4281736 (office). *Website:* www.apra.org.pe (office).

DEL CID DE BONILLA, María Antonieta; Guatemalan fmr central banker and government official; Exec. Dir for Guatemala, IDB 1998; Minister of Public Finance 2004–08; fmr Vice-Pres. Banco de Guatemala (cen. bank), Pres. 2008–10. *Address:* c/o Banco de Guatemala, 7a Avda 22-01, Zona 1, Apdo 365, Guatemala City, Guatemala.

DEL GENIO, Anthony D., BS, MS, PhD; American atmospheric scientist and academic; *Physical Scientist, Goddard Institute for Space Studies, National Aeronautics and Space Administration;* b. 21 Feb. 1952, New York, NY; m.; one c.; ed Cornell Univ., Univ. of California, Los Angeles; Scientific Programmer/Analyst, Climate Group, GTE Information Systems, NASA/Goddard Inst. for Space Studies (GISS), New York June–Sept. 1976, Consultant 1976–77, Nat. Research Council (NRC) RRA 1978–80, Man. Planetary Group, Sigma Data Services 1980–85, Physical Scientist, NASA/GISS 1985–; Grad. Research Asst, Dept of Earth and Space Sciences, UCLA 1973–76, 1976–78; Coordinator, Columbia Univ. Grad.

Program in Atmospheric and Planetary Science 1984–; Lecturer, GISS/Columbia Univ. Summer Inst. on Planets and Climate 1980–85; Adjunct Asst Prof., Dept of Physics, Queensborough Community Coll., CUNY 1982–85; Adjunct Assoc. Prof., Dept of Environmental Science, Barnard Coll. 1993–99; Lecturer, Dept of Earth and Environmental Sciences, Columbia Univ. 1983–89, Adjunct Asst Prof. 1989–92, Adjunct Assoc. Prof. 1992–, Adjunct Prof. 1997–, Adjunct Prof., Dept of Applied Physics 1995–; Invited Lecturer, NATO ASI, Energy and Water Cycles in the Climate System, Glücksburg, Germany 1991, Int. Research Inst. for Climate Prediction, Applications and Training Pilot Project 1993, NCAR Summer School on Clouds and Climate 1993, NATO ASI, Remote Sensing of Energy and Water Cycles, Plon, Germany 1995, Goddard Earth Science and Tech. Summer Program 2003–04; Co-Investigator, Pioneer Venus Orbiter Cloud Photopolarimeter Experiment 1978–92; Pioneer Venus Dynamics and Structure Working Group 1979–80; Organizer, GISS/Columbia Univ. Summer Inst. on Planets and Climate 1983, 1985, 1987; Science Advisory Group, NASA Lidar Atmospheric Sensing Experiment 1988–97; Co-Investigator/Interdisciplinary, Earth Observing System 1989–99; Science Steering Group, GEWEX Water Vapor Project 1990; Prin. Investigator, Atmospheric Radiation Measurement Program 1993–; Team mem. Cassini Saturn Imaging Science Subsystem 1990–; Cassini/Huygens Atmospheric Working Group 1991–; mem. NASA/Goddard Space Flight Center (GSFC) Dir's Discretionary Fund Review Panel 1991–93; Science Team mem. NASA TRMM/GPM 1991–97, 1998–2001, 2003–; Prin. Investigator, First ISCCP Regional Experiment III 1995–98, Cttee 1995–98; mem. Science Team Exec. Cttee, Dept of Energy ARM Program 1996–2000, 2002–05, SGP Site Advisory Cttee 1995–98, Cloud Modeling Working Group Steering Cttee 2000–; Assoc. Ed. Journal of Climate 1996–2004, Ed. 2004–; mem. Drafting Panel, FIRE-IV: CRYSTAL Research Plan 1998–99; Prin. Investigator, Global Aerosol Climatology Project 1998–2002; Reviewer, NAS/NRC Report 'Understanding Climate Change Feedbacks'; Science Team mem. NASA Aqua AMSR-E 2003–07, CloudSat/CALIPSO 2007–; mem. Writing Panel, American Meteorological Soc. Statement on Climate Change 2007; mem. American Geophysical Union 1978, American Astronomical Soc. (Div. for Planetary Sciences) 1981, American Meteorological Soc. 1987 (Fellow 2007); NASA GISS Peer Award 1986, NASA Certificate of Outstanding Performance 1987, 1988, 1989, 1990, 1992, 1994, 1995, 1998, 2007, 2008, NASA GISS Best Publication Award 1989, 1990, 1993, 1994, 1997, 2000, 2002, 2003, 2006, 2007, Citation for Excellence in Reviewing, Icarus 1992, 1998, Outstanding Teacher Award, Columbia Univ. Dept of Earth and Environmental Sciences 1994, 2001, 2006, NASA Group Achievement Award, Cassini Imaging Science Subsystem 1998, NASA GSFC Earth Sciences Directorate Special Act Award 2004, 2005, 2006, NASA Exceptional Scientific Achievement Medal 2008. *Publications:* more than 100 scientific papers in professional journals on stratiform and cumulus cloud parameterization in general circulation models, hydrologic cycle feedbacks on climate, comparative dynamics of planetary atmospheres. *Address:* NASA Goddard Institute for Space Studies, 2880 Broadway, New York, NY 10025, USA (office). *Telephone:* (212) 678-5588 (office). *Fax:* (212) 678-5552 (office). *E-mail:* adelgenio@giss.nasa.gov (office); anthony.d.delgenio@nasa.gov (office). *Website:* www.giss.nasa.gov (office).

DEL NINNO, Giulio, BEng; Italian business executive; b. 12 June 1940, Milan; ed Politecnico di Milano; plant designer, Termosystem 1968–69; Researcher, Snia Viscose SpA 1969–73; Production Dir Garzanti SpA 1973–76; Tech. and Research Dir Montefibre (Montedison Group) 1976–79, Total Quality Dir 1986–88, Dir of Electrical Energy Sector, Edison SpA (Montedison Group) 1988–96, CEO Montedison SpA (now Edison) 2001–05, CEO Edipower SpA (subsidiary of Edison) 2003–08; Chair. Due Palme SpA 1979–86; mem. Bd of Dirs Prysmian SpA. *Address:* c/o Board of Directors, Prysmian SpA, Viale Sarca 222, 20126 Milan, Italy.

DEL PINO VEINTIMILLA, Eugenia Maria, PhD; Ecuadorean biologist and academic; *Professor of Biology, Pontifical Catholic University of Ecuador;* b. 19 April 1945, Quito; ed Pontifical Catholic Univ. of Ecuador, Quito, Vassar Coll., Emory Univ., Atlanta, Ga, USA; currently Prof. of Biology, Pontifical Catholic Univ. of Ecuador; Vice-Pres. for Ecuador, Darwin Foundation 1992–96, Vice-Pres. Gen. Ass. 1998–2001; Alexander von Humboldt Foundation Fellowship, Cancer Research Centre, Heidelberg, Germany 1984–85; Dept of Embryology, Fulbright Comm., Carnegie Inst., Washington, DC 1990; mem. Latin American Acad. of Sciences, Third World Acad. of Sciences (TWAS), American Acad. of Arts and Sciences, NAS; L'Oreal-UNESCO Award for Women in Science 2000, Sheth Distinguished Int. Alumni Award, Emory Univ. 2003, Medal of the Acad. of Science for the Developing World, TWAS 2005, Eugenio Espejo Award, City Council of Quito 2005. *Publications:* numerous publs in scientific journals. *Address:* Pontificia Universidad Católica del Ecuador, Quito, Ecuador (office). *Telephone:* (2) 299-1700 (office). *Fax:* (2) 299-1687 (office). *E-mail:* edelpino@puce .edu.ec (office). *Website:* www.puce.edu.ec (office).

DEL PONTE, Carla, LLM; Swiss lawyer, international organization official and diplomatist; b. 9 Feb. 1947, Lugano; one s.; ed Univs of Berne and Geneva; in pvt. practice, Lugano 1975–81; Investigating Magistrate, then Public Prosecutor, Lugano 1981–94; Attorney-Gen. and Chief Prosecutor of Switzerland 1994–2000, mem. Fed. Comm. on White-Collar Crime 1994–99; Chief Prosecutor, Int. Criminal Tribunals of Rwanda 1999–2003, of the Fmr Yugoslavia 1999–2007; Amb. to Argentina 2008–11; Dr hc (Liège) 2002, (Wales, Bangor) 2003, Hon. Dottore in Giurisprudenza (Genoa) 2004; 22nd Peace Prize, UNA (Spain) 2002, Goler T. Butcher Prize 2004. *Publications:* Madame Prosecutor (memoir) 2009. *Address:* c/o Embassy of Switzerland, Santa Fe 846, 10°, C1059ABP, Buenos Aires, Argentina. *E-mail:* carla.delponte@eda.admin.ch (office).

DEL REY, Lana; American singer and songwriter; b. (Elizabeth Woolridge Grant), 21 June 1986, New York, NY; d. of Robert Grant; ed Kent School, Conn., Fordham Univ.; early releases issued under name of Lizzy Grant; signed to Stranger Records 2011; signed to Next Model Management 2012; Q Awards Next Big Thing 2011, BRIT Award for Best Int. Breakthrough Act 2012, MTV Europe Music Award for Best Alternative 2012. *Recordings:* albums: Lana Del Rey AKA Lizzy Grant 2010, Born to Die 2012. *Address:* c/o Next Model Management, 15 Watts Street, 6th Floor, New York, NY 10013, USA (office). *Telephone:* (212) 925-5100 (office). *Fax:* (212) 925-5931 (office). *Website:* www.nextmodels.com (office); www.lanadelrey.com (office).

DEL TORO, Benicio; Puerto Rican actor, director and writer; b. 19 Feb. 1967, Santurce, Puerto Rico; s. of Gustavo Del Toro and the late Fausta Sanchez Del Toro; ed Univ. of California, San Diego, Circle in the Square Acting School, Stella Adler Conservatory. *Films include:* Big Top Pee-wee 1988, Christopher Columbus: The Discovery 1992, Fearless 1993, Money for Nothing 1993, China Moon 1994, The Usual Suspects 1995, Swimming With Sharks 1995, Cannes Man 1996, The Funeral 1996, Basquiat 1996, The Fan 1996, Joyride 1997, Excess Baggage 1997, Fear and Loathing in Las Vegas 1998, Snatch 2000, Traffic (Acad. Award for Best Supporting Actor) 2000, The Way of the Gun 2000, The Pledge 2001, Bread and Roses 2001, The Hunted 2002, 21 Grams 2003, Sin City 2005, Things We Lost in the Fire 2007, Che (Cannes Film Festival Best Actor Prize) 2008, The Wolfman 2010, Somewhere 2010, Savages 2012. *Address:* c/o IFA Talent Agency, 8730 Sunset Boulevard #490, Los Angeles, CA 90069, USA. *Website:* www .beniciodeltoro.com.

DEL TORO, Guillermo; Mexican film director, producer, screenwriter and novelist; b. 9 Oct. 1964, Guadalajara, Jalisco; m. Lorenza Newton; two d.; ed Centro de Investigación y Estudios Cinematográficos, Guadalajara; first got involved in film-making aged eight; spent ten years as make up supervisor; f. The Tequila Gang (production co.). *Films include:* Doña Lupe 1985, Doña Herlinda y su hijo (exec. producer) 1985, Geometria 1987, Un Embrujo (producer) 1988, Cronos (also writer) 1993, Mimic (also screenplay) 1997, Bullfighter (actor) 2000, El Espinazo del diablo (also writer and producer) 2001, Asesino en serio (exec. producer) 2002, Blade II 2002, Hellboy (also screenplay) 2004, Crónicas (producer) 2004, Caleuche: El llamado del mar (exec. producer) 2006, Pan's Labyrinth (also screenplay and producer, Best Film Nat. Soc. of Film Critics 2007, Goya Award for Best Original Screenplay 2007, BAFTA Award for Best Film not in the English Language 2007) 2006, The Orphanage (producer) 2008, Hellboy II: The Golden Army (also screenplay) 2008, Splice 2009, Biutiful (assoc. producer) 2010, Julia's Eyes (producer) 2010, Don't Be Afraid of the Dark (producer) 2010, Kung Fu Panda 2 (exec. producer) 2011, Puss in Boots (exec. producer) 2011, The Captured Bird (short) (exec. producer) 2012, Rise of the Guardians (exec. producer) 2012, The Hobbit: An Unexpected Journey (screenplay) 2012, Mama (exec. producer) 2013, Pacific Rim (dir) 2013. *Television includes:* Hora Marcada 1988. *Publications:* The Strain (with Chuck Hogan) 2009, The Fall (with Chuck Hogan) 2010, The Night Eternal 2011. *Address:* c/o Robert Newman, WME Entertainment, 9601 Wilshire Boulevard, Beverly Hills, CA 90210-5213, USA (office). *Telephone:* (310) 285-9000 (office). *Fax:* (310) 285-9010 (office). *Website:* www.wma.com (office).

DEL VALLE ALLIENDE, Jaime; Chilean lawyer and politician; b. 2 July 1931, Santiago; m. Paulina Swinburn Pereira; four c.; ed Escuela de Derecho de la Universidad Católica de Chile; taught at Catholic Univ. Law School from 1955, Dir 1969, Dean 1970; various posts in Supreme Court 1958–64; Public Prosecutor 1964–74; Pro-Rector, Pontificia Univ. Católica de Chile 1974; Dir-Gen. nat. TV channel 1975–78; mem. Bd Colegio de Abogados 1981–, Pres. 1982–83; Minister of Justice Feb.–Dec. 1983; Minister of Foreign Affairs 1983–87. *Address:* c/o Ministerio de Asuntos Exteriores, Palacio de la Moneda, Santiago, Chile.

DEL VECCHIO, Leonardo; Italian business executive; *Chairman and Chief Executive, Luxottica Group SpA;* b. 1935, Milan; m.; four c.; sent to orphanage aged seven; apprentice at factory that made moulds for automobile parts; opened his own moulding shop 1958; Founder and Chair. Luxottica (world's largest designer and manufacturer of high-quality eyeglass frames and sunglasses) 1961–; est. museum for one of world's oldest collection of spectacles, Agordo, Italy. *Leisure interests:* Medieval European antiques and paintings. *Address:* Luxottica Group SpA, Via C. Cantù 2, 20123 Milan, Italy (office). *Telephone:* (02) 863341 (office). *Fax:* (0437) 63223 (office). *Website:* www.luxottica.it (office).

DELACÔTE, Jacques; French conductor; s. of Pierre Delacôte and Renée Wagner Delacôte; m. Maria Lucia Alvares-Machado 1975; ed Music Conservatoire, Paris, Acad. of Music, with Prof. Hans Swarowsky, Vienna; was Asst to Darius Milhaud and Leonard Bernstein; among the orchestras conducted: Orchestre de Paris, Orchestre Nat. de France, New York Philharmonic, Vienna Philharmonic, Vienna Symphony, Israel Philharmonic, Orchestre Nat. de Belgique, London Symphony, San Francisco, Cleveland, Scottish Chamber, Scottish Nat. Opera, RIAS Berlin, WDR Cologne, SF Stuttgart, SWF Baden-Baden, Bavarian Radio, Munich, English Chamber, BBC, London, London Philharmonic, Royal Philharmonic, London, Japan Philharmonic, Yomiuri Symphony, Dresdner Staatskapelle, Royal Opera House, Covent Garden (including Far East tour, Korea and Japan), English Nat. Opera, Opernhaus Zürich, Teatro Real, Madrid, Teatro Liceo, Barcelona, La Fenice, Venice, Vienna State Opera, Deutsche Oper, Berlin, Pittsburgh Opera, Welsh Nat. Opera, Opéra de Paris, Teatro Colón, Buenos Aires, Canadian Opera Co., Royal State Opera, Copenhagen, State Opera, Hamburg, State Opera, Munich, Chicago Lyric Opera, Semper Oper, Dresden; also recordings with EMI, Philips London and Tring London; 1st Prize and Gold Medal Mitropoulos Competition, New York 1971. *Festivals include:* Flandernfestival, Macerata Festival, Klangbogen Vienna, Dresden Musiktage. *Leisure interest:* chess. *Address:* Paul Steinhauer Public Relations, Hermanngasse 3, 1070 Vienna, Austria (office); Praça Eugênio Jardim 34/602, Copacabana, 22061-040 Rio de Janeiro RJ, Brazil. *Telephone:* (1) 52496470 (office). *Fax:* (1) 52496475 (office). *E-mail:* office@paulsteinhauer.com (office). *Website:* www.paulsteinhauer.com (office); www.jacques-delacote.com.

DeLANEY, William J., BBA, MBA; American business executive; *President and CEO, Sysco Corporation;* ed Univ. of Notre Dame, Wharton Grad. Div., Univ. of Pennsylvania; Asst Treas., Sysco Corpn 1987–91, Treas. 1991–93, Vice-Pres. 1993–94, Chief Financial Officer (CFO), Sysco Food Services, Syracuse 1996–98, Sr Vice-Pres. 1998–2002, Exec. Vice-Pres. 2002–04, Pres. and CEO Sysco Food Services, Charlotte 2004–06, Sr Vice-Pres. of Financial Reporting 2006–07, Exec. Vice-Pres. and CFO 2007–09, Pres. and CEO 2010–, Chair. Employee Benefits Cttee, mem. Finance Cttee, Exec. Cttee. *Address:* Sysco Corporation, 1390 Enclave Parkway, Houston, TX 77077-2099, USA (office). *Telephone:* (281) 584-1390 (office). *Fax:* (281) 584-2721 (office). *E-mail:* info@sysco.com (office). *Website:* www .sysco.com (office).

DELANOË, Bertrand Jacques Marie; French politician; b. 30 May 1950, Tunis, Tunisia; s. of Auguste Delanoë and Yvonne Delanoë (née Delord); ed Inst. Sainte-Marie, Rodez, Univ. of Toulouse; mem. Conseil de Paris (18th arrondissement)

1977–83, 1986–2014, Socialist Deputy 1981–86, Senator 1995–2001, Mayor of Paris 2001–14; Pres. of Paris Socialist Group 1993–2001; mem. Cttee of Dirs, Parti Socialiste 1979–, Party Spokesman 1981–83, mem. Exec. Bureau 1983–87; Pres. France-Egypt Friendship Group 1981–86, Int. Asscn of French-speaking Mayors (AIMF) 2001–, World Org. of United Cities and Local Govts 2004–10, Founding Pres. of Honour 2010–; Hon. Citizen of Ouagadougou (Burkina Faso) 2012; Dr hc (Univ. of Quebec, Canada) 2006; Officier, Ordre nat. du Québec 2012. *Publications:* Pour l'honneur de Paris 1999, La Vie, passionnément (autobiog.) 2004, De l'audace (with Laurent Joffrin) 2008. *Address:* Hôtel de Ville, 75196 Paris RP, France (office). *Fax:* 1-42-76-53-43 (office). *Website:* www.paris.fr (office); bertranddelanoe.net.

DELATTRE, François Marie; French diplomatist; *Ambassador to USA ;* posted to Embassy in Bonn, in charge of environmental issues and econ. consequences of Germany's re-unification –1991, with Strategic, Security and Disarmament Dept, Ministry of Foreign Affairs 1991–93, adviser to Foreign Minister Alain Juppé 1993–95, mem. Pres. Jacques Chirac's Foreign Policy Team 1995–98, Press and Communications Dir, Embassy in Washington, DC 1998–2002, Deputy Dir Foreign Minister's Office 2002–04, Consul Gen. in New York 2004–08, Amb. to Canada 2008–11, to USA 2011–. *Address:* Embassy of France, 4101 Reservoir Road NW, Washington, DC 20007, USA (office). *Telephone:* (202) 944-6000 (office). *Fax:* (202) 944-6166 (office). *E-mail:* info@ambafrance-us.org (office). *Website:* www.ambafrance-us.org (office); www.info-france-usa.org (office).

DELAY, Florence; French writer, actress and university lecturer; b. 19 March 1941, Paris; d. of the late Jean Delay and of Marie Madeleine Delay (née Carrez); ed Lycée Jean de la Fontaine, Paris, Univ. of Paris (Sorbonne); Lecturer in Gen. and Comparative Literature, Univ. of Paris III 1972–; Theatre Critic, Nouvelle Revue française 1978–85; mem. Editorial Bd Critique magazine 1978–96, Reading Cttee Gallimard publrs 1979–86; mem. Acad. française 2000–; Commdr des Arts et des Lettres, Officier Légion d'honneur, Officier Ordre nat. du Mérite; Grand prix du roman de la Ville de Paris 1999. *Films:* Procès de Jeanne d'Arc 1962, Le Jouet criminel 1969, Mort de Raymond Roussel 1975, Écoute voir 1979. *Publications:* Minuit sur les jeux 1973, Le Aïe aïe de la corne de brume 1975, L'Insuccès de la fête 1980, Riche et légère (Prix Femina) 1983, Course d'amour pendant le deuil 1986, Petites formes en prose après Edison (essays) 1987, Partition rouge 1989 (jtly), Hexaméron 1989, Etxemendi (Prix François Mauriac) 1990, Semaines de Suzanne 1991, Catalina 1994, La Fin des temps ordinaires 1996, La Séduction brève (essays) 1997, Dit Nerval 1999, L'Evangile de Jean (trans. of Gospel of John) 2001, Trois désobéissances 2004, Graal Theatre 2005, Mon Espagne or et ciel (essays) 2008, Mes Cendriers 2010, Il me semble, mesdames 2012; several trans of Spanish dramatists including Fernando de Rojas, Pedro Calderón, Lope de Vega. *Address:* c/o Gallimard, 5 rue Sébastien Bottin, 75007 Paris, France (office).

DELAY, Tom; American fmr politician; b. 1947, Laredo, Tex.; m. Christine DeLay; one d.; ed Baylor Univ., Univ. of Houston; owned and operated small business in Tex. 1970s; elected to Texas House of Reps 1978; mem. US Congress from 22nd Dist, Texas, held various positions in House of Reps including Republican Conf. Sec., Deputy Whip, Chair. Republican Study Cttee, Majority Whip –2003, Majority Leader 2003–05 (resgnd after indictment by Tex. grand jury for money laundering, convicted 2010), mem. Appropriations Cttee; mem. Advisory Bd Child Advocates of Fort Bend Co.; Founder Grassroots Action and Information Network (GAIN) 2006–; Taxpayers Friend Award, Nat. Taxpayers Union; Golden Bulldog Award, Watchdog of the Treasury; Nat. Security Leadership Award, Peace Through Strength Coalition. *Publication:* No Retreat, No Surrender: One American's Flight (with Stephen Mansfield) 2007. *Website:* www.tomdelay.com.

DELCOURT, Guy; French editor and publisher; *Publisher, Editions Delcourt;* b. 1958; fmr Ed. Pilote magazine; Founder of Delcourt publishing house through merger of Charlie Mensuel and Pilote magazines 1986, now one of the largest publrs of comics and manga in France, produces some 480 comics annually; Chevalier, Ordre nat. du Mérite 2006. *Publications include:* Les Aventures de Sarkozix 3. N'en jetez plus!. *Address:* Editions Delcourt, 54 rue d'Hauteville, 75010 Paris, France (office). *Telephone:* 1-56-03-92-20 (office). *Fax:* 1-56-03-92-30 (office). *E-mail:* info@editions-delcourt.fr (office). *Website:* www.editions-delcourt.fr (office).

DELEBARRE, Michel Stéphane Henry Joseph; French politician; *Mayor of Dunkirk;* b. 27 April 1946, Bailleul (Nord); s. of Stéphane Delebarre and Georgette Deroo; m. Janine Debeyre 1969; one d.; Asst Sec.-Gen. Cttee for the Expansion of the Nord-Pas de Calais area 1968–71, Sec.-Gen. 1971–74; Cabinet Dir for Pres. of Nord-Pas de Calais Regional Council 1974–78; Gen. Del. for Devt for City of Lille 1977–80; Sec.-Gen. City of Lille 1980; Pres. regional fund for contemporary art 1982; mem. of Cabinet of Prime Minister 1981–82; Cabinet Dir 1982–84; unassigned prefect 1983; Minister of Labour, Employment and Professional Training 1984–86; Socialist mem. of Parl. for Nord 1986, 1988–93, 1997–98; mem. Exec. Bd Socialist Party 1987; Minister of Transport and Marine Affairs 1989; Minister of State, Minister of Town and Physical Planning 1990–91; Minister of State, Minister of Civil Service and Public Admin. Enhancement 1991–92; Adviser for Urban and Regional Planning; Chair. Cttee of Experts advising Lionel Jospin, Leader Socialist Party 1995; First Deputy Pres., Regional Council for Nord-Pas de Calais 1986–97, Pres. 1998–2001, regional counsellor 2001–02; Mayor of Dunkirk 1989–; Pres. Urban Community of Dunkirk 1995–, L'Union nationale des fédérations d'organismes d'HLM 1999–; mem. Nat. Council of Evaluation 1999–; Pres. Regional Cttees of EU 2006–. *Address:* Hôtel de Ville, place Charles Valentin, 59386 Dunkirk cedex 1, France (office). *Telephone:* 3-28-59-12-34 (office). *E-mail:* maire@ville-dunkerque.fr (office). *Website:* www.michel-delebarre.fr.

DELFIM DA SILVA, Fernando; Guinea-Bissau academic, public servant and politician; b. 13 May 1956, Bissau; ed St Petersburg State Univ., Russia, Lusíada Univ., Portugal; fmr Prof., Portuguese School of Bissau; Deputy Minister of Educ., Bafatá Region, also Dir Bafatá Secondary School 1974–81; Dir-Gen., Presidency of the Council of State 1980; with Technical Office of Studies and Planning, Ministry of Nat. Educ. 1986–87; fmr Sec. of State for Youth, Culture and Sports, later for Transport and Communications, becoming Minister of Nat. Educ.; Minister of Foreign Affairs, Int. Co-operation and Communities 1998, June–Dec. 2013. *Address:* c/o Ministry of Foreign Affairs, International Co-operation and Commu-

nities, Av. dos Combatentes da Liberdade da Pátria, Bissau, Guinea-Bissau (office).

DELGADO CAMPAÑA, Pedro Miguel; Ecuadorean economist and central banker; b. 10 Nov. 1962; ed INCAE Business School, Costa Rica; fmr Risk Man., Corporación Financiera Nacional; fmr Dir Intendente Nacional de Instituciones Financieras (financial supervisory body); Pres. Fideicomiso 'AGD CFN No Más Impunidad' (anti-corruption body); Dir Unidad de Gestión y Ejecución de Derecho Público (deposit insurance co.); Pres. Banco Central del Ecuador 2011–13 (resgnd).

DELGADO DURÁN, Norberto; Panamanian politician; ed Univ. de Panamá; Exec. Dir Multi Credit Bank 1990–98, fmr Vice-Pres. Commercial; Prof. Instituto de Microfinanzas 1998–; Vice-Minister of Finance 1999–2000, Minister of Finance and the Treasury 2000–04; mem. Bd of Dirs Panama Canal Authority (ACP) 2004–; Pres. Instituto Panameño Autónomo Cooperativo (IPACOOP) 1999; Pres. Bd of Dirs Fondo de Inversión Social 1999. *Address:* c/o Panama Canal Authority, PO Box 526725, Miami, FL 33152-6725, USA (office).

ĐELIĆ, Božidar, MA, MBA, MPA; Serbian economist and politician; b. 1 April 1965, Belgrade; m. Marie-Laure Đelić (divorced 2003); two d.; ed Institut d'Etudes Politiques de Paris, Ecole des Hautes Etudes Commerciales, Paris, Ecole des Hautes Etudes en Sciences Sociales, Harvard Business School and Kennedy School of Govt, Harvard Univ., USA; worked as expert adviser to several East European transition govts on issues of privatization, banking reform and macro-econ. reform, adviser to Leszek Balcerowicz in Poland (also helped establish Warsaw Stock Exchange) 1991–92, to Anatolii Chubais in Russia 1992–93, in Romania 1996; Pnr, McKinsey & Co. (consulting firm) 1991, returned on unpaid leave to Belgrade Nov. 2000; served as main negotiator with IMF, Paris Club and other financial insts; mem. Democratic Party; Minister of Finance 2001–04; withdrew from politics 2004–06; Man. for Southeastern Europe, Crédit Agricole 2005–06; returned to politics and became active in Democratic Party's election campaign late 2006, cand. for Prime Minister; Deputy Prime Minister, in charge of European Integration 2007–11, Minister of Science and Technological Devt 2008–11; won French nat. competitions for high-school students in history and econs 1980, 1981, named by Vreme as Person of the Year 2001, placed first on Blic's ranking list of politicians Dec. 2002, included in top 100 young leaders list of World EC Forum and Forbes magazine 2002. *E-mail:* office@djelic.net. *Website:* www.djelic.net.

DELIGNE, Vicomte Pierre René, PhD; Belgian mathematician and academic; *Professor Emeritus, School of Mathematics, Institute for Advanced Study;* b. 3 Oct. 1944, Etterbeek; ed Athénée Adolphe Max, Brussels, Univ. of Brussels, Université Libre de Bruxelles, Ecole Normale Supérieure, Paris, France; Jr Scientist, Fond Nat. de la Recherche Scientifique (FNRS), Brussels 1967–68; Guest Scientist, Institut des Hautes Etudes Scientifiques, Bures-sur-Yvette, France 1967–68, Visiting mem. 1968–70, Perm. mem. 1970–84; Prof., Inst. for Advanced Study, Princeton, NJ, USA 1984–2007, Prof. Emer. 2007–; mem. American Philosophical Soc. 2009; Foreign Assoc. mem. Acad. des Sciences, Paris 1978; Assoc. mem. Acad. Royale de Belgique 1994; Foreign mem. Accad. Nazionale dei Lincei 2003, Royal Swedish Acad. of Sciences 2009; Foreign Assoc. NAS 2007; Foreign Hon. mem. American Acad. of Arts and Sciences 1978; Dr hc (Flemish Univ. of Brussels) 1989, (Ecole Normale Supérieure) 1995; Francois Deruyts Prize, Acad. Royale de Belgique 1974, Henri Poincaré Medal, Acad. des Sciences (Paris) 1974, Quinquennal Prize 'Doctor A. De Leeuw-Damry-Bourlart', FNRS 1975, Fields Medal, Int. Congress of Mathematicians (Helsinki) 1978, Crafoord Prize (Stockholm) (co-recipient) 1988, Balzan Prize 2004, Wolf Prize in Math. (co-recipient) 2008, Abel Prize, Norwegian Acad. of Science and Letters 2013. *Publications:* Commensurabilities among Lattices in PU(1,n) 1993; more than 80 publs in math. journals. *Address:* Fuld Hall 210, School of Mathematics, Institute for Advanced Study, Einstein Drive, Princeton, NJ 08540, USA (office). *Telephone:* (609) 734-8391 (office). *E-mail:* deligne@ias.edu (office). *Website:* www.math.ias.edu (office).

DeLILLO, Don, BA; American writer; b. 20 Nov. 1936, New York, NY; m. Barbara Bennett 1975; ed Cardinal Hayes High School, Fordham Coll., New York; fmr advertising copywriter Ogilvy, Benson & Mather; American Acad. of Arts and Letters Award in Literature 1984, Jerusalem Prize for the Freedom of the Individual in Soc. 1999, William Dean Howells Medal 2000, PEN/Saul Bellow Award for Achievement in American Fiction 2010. *Plays:* The Day Room 1987, Valparaiso 1999, Love-Lies-Bleeding 2005. *Publications:* Americana 1971, End Zone 1972, Great Jones Street 1973, Ratner's Star 1976, Players 1977, Running Dog 1978, The Names 1982, White Noise 1985 (Nat. Book Award 1985), Libra 1988 (Irish Times Fiction Prize 1989), Mao II 1991 (PEN/Faulkner Award 1992), Underworld 1997, The Body Artist 2000, Cosmopolis 2003, Falling Man 2007, Point Omega 2010, The Angel Esmeralda: Nine Stories 2011. *Address:* c/o Wallace Literary Agency, 301 East 79th Street, 14-J, New York, NY 10075, USA (office). *Telephone:* (212) 570-9090 (office). *Fax:* (212) 772-8979 (office). *E-mail:* walliter@aol.com (office).

DELL, Anne, CBE, PhD, FRS, FRSC, FMedSci; Australian biochemist and academic; *Professor of Carbohydrate Biochemistry, Imperial College London;* currently Prof. of Carbohydrate Biochemistry, Imperial Coll., London; Chair. Biotechnology and Biological Sciences Research Council (BBSRC) Tools and Resources Strategy Panel (mem. BBSRC Strategy Bd, BBSRC Council), Royal Soc./Wolfson Lab. Refurbishment Grants Cttee, Royal Soc. Mercer Cttee; mem. Steering Cttee NIH Consortium for Functional Glycomics, 1851 Science Scholarships Cttee, Advisory Cttee Nat. Physical Lab., British Library Advisory Council; Advisory mem. Human Disease Glycomics Proteome Initiative; Chair. Glycobiology Gordon Conf., Ventura, Calif., USA 2001; mem. European Acad. of Science 2004; Tate & Lyle Medal, Royal Soc. of Chem. 1986, Whistler Award, Int. Carbohydrate Org. 2000, Haworth Memorial Medal and Lecture, Royal Soc. of Chem. 2003, Int. Glycoconjugate Award, Int. Glycoconjugate Org. 2005. *Publications:* numerous papers in professional journals. *Address:* Room 101B, Sir Ernst Chain Building, Imperial College London, South Kensington Campus, London, SW7 2AZ, England (office). *Telephone:* (20) 7594-5219 (office). *Fax:* (20) 7225-0458 (office). *E-mail:* ia.dell@imperial.ac.uk (office). *Website:* www3.imperial.ac.uk/people/a.dell (office).

DELL, Michael S.; American computer industry executive; *Chairman and CEO, Dell Inc.;* b. 23 Feb. 1965, Houston, Tex.; s. of Alexander Dell and Lorraine Dell; m. Susan Lieberman 1989; four c.; ed Univ. of Texas; Founder, Chair. and CEO Dell

Computer Corpn (fmrly PCs Ltd, now Dell Inc.), Austin, Tex. 1984–2004, Chair. 2004–, CEO 2007–; f. MSD Capital 1998; co-f., with his wife, The Michael & Susan Dell Foundation 1999; Vice-Chair. US Business Council; mem. Exec. Cttee of Int. Business Council, US Business Council, US Pres.'s Council of Advisors on Science and Tech., Tech. CEO Council, Governing Bd of Indian School of Business, Hyderabad; Bd mem.-elect of Catalyst; Hon. mem. Foundation Bd of World Econ. Forum; Entrepreneur of the Year Award, Inc. magazine 1990, JD Power Customer Satisfaction Award 1991, 1993, CEO of the Year, Financial World magazine 1993, Bower Award for Business Leadership 2013. *Publication:* Direct from Dell: Strategies that Revolutionized an Industry 1999. *Address:* Dell Inc., 1 Dell Way, Round Rock, TX 78682-0001 (office); MSD Capital, LP 645 Fifth Avenue, 21st Floor, New York, NY 10022-5910; Michael & Susan Dell Foundation, PO Box 163867, Austin, TX 78716, USA. *Telephone:* (512) 338-4400 (Round Rock) (office); (212) 303-1650 (New York). *Fax:* (512) 728-3653 (Round Rock) (office); (212) 303-1634 (New York); (512) 600-5501 (Austin). *E-mail:* webmaster@dell.com (office); info@msdf.org. *Website:* www.dell.com (office); www.msdcapital.com; www.msdf.org.

DELLA VALLE, Diego; Italian fashion designer and art collector; *President and CEO, Tod's SpA;* b. 30 Dec. 1953, Sant'elpidio a Mare, Ascoli Piceno; s. of Dorino della Valle, founder of the original Della Valle shoe makers 1940s; studied law in Bologna; brief work experience in USA 1975; joined his father in family business, leading role in definition of co. strategies and brand creation, Pres. and CEO Tod's SpA 2000–; mem. Bd IRI SpA, Banca Commerciale Italiana SpA; mem. Bd of Dirs Assicurazioni Generali, Banca Nazionale del Lavoro, LVMH, Ferrari, Maserati, Compagnia Immobiliare Azionaria, Confindustria; mem. Fundraising Cttee Umberto Veronesi Cancer Research; Pres. Bd of Dirs Della Valle Onlus Foundation; Hon. Pres. AC Fiorentina; degree hc in Business and Econs (Univ. of Ancona) 2000; Cavaliere del Lavoro 1996. *Address:* Tod's SpA, Via Filippo Della Valle 1, Sant'elpidio a Mare, Ascoli Piceno, Italy (office). *Telephone:* (0734) 871671 (office). *Website:* www.todsgroup.com (office).

DELLER, Jeremy; British artist; b. 1966, London, England; ed Courtauld Inst. of Art; acts as curator, producer or dir of broad range of projects, including orchestrated events, films and publs. *Works include:* Acid Brass (ongoing project and collaboration with The Williams Fairey Brass Band) 1997–, Fig. 1 2000, Folk Archive (ongoing project with Alan Kane investigating UK folk and vernacular art) 2000–, The Battle of Orgreave: The English Civil War Part II (co-production by Artangel/Channel 4, film by Mike Figgis) 2001, Social Parade (video), Five Memorials, This is US (CD produced in asscn with Bard Coll., Red Hook, USA) 2003, Memory Bucket (video documentary about Crawford, Texas—home town of George W. Bush—and Branch Davidian siege in nearby Waco) (Turner Prize 2004) 2003. *Address:* c/o Gavin Brown's Enterprise, 620 Greenwich Street, New York, NY 10014, USA (office). *E-mail:* gallery@gavinbrown.biz (office).

DELL'OLIO, Louis; American fashion designer; b. 23 July 1948, New York, NY; ed Parsons School of Design, New York; intern for Norman Norell 1965; asst designer to Dominic Rompello of Teal Traina, New York 1969–71; Chief Designer, Georgini div. of Originala, New York 1971–74; design collaborator with Donna Karan, Anne Klein & Co. 1974–79, Chief Designer following Karan's departure 1984–93; spent time working with Council of Fashion Designers of America's Fashion Targets Breast Cancer initiative 1993–96; cr. Dei Tre collection for Bergdorf Goodman, Neiman Marcus and Holt Renfrew 1996; launched outer-wear collection 1997; introduced exclusive collection for QVC 2000; mem. Fashion Designers of America; Parsons Gold Thimble Award 1969, Coty American Fashion Critics Awards (all with Donna Karan) 1977, 1982, 1984. *Address:* Louis Dell'Olio Co. Ltd, 435 Ocean Drive West, Stamford, CT 06902, USA.

DELON, Alain; French actor; b. 8 Nov. 1935, Sceaux; m. Nathalie Delon (divorced); one s.; one s. one d. by Rosalie Van Breemen; with French Marine Corps 1952–55; ind. actor-producer under Delbeau (Delon-Beaume) Productions 1964–; Pres. and Dir-Gen. Adel Productions 1968–87, Leda Productions 1987–; cr. Alain Delon Diffusion SA (specialising in luxury goods) 1978; Commdr des Arts et des Lettres, Officier, Ordre nat. du Mérite 1995, Officier, Légion d'honneur 2005. *Films include:* Christine 1958, Faibles femmes 1959, Le chemin des écoliers 1959, Purple Noon 1959, Rocco and His Brothers 1960, Eclipse 1961, The Leopard 1962, Any Number Can Win 1962, The Black Tulip 1963, The Love Cage 1963, L'insoumis 1964, The Yellow Rolls Royce 1964, Once a Thief 1964, Les centurions 1965, Paris brûle-t-il? 1965, Texas Across the River 1966, Les adventuriers 1966, Le samourai 1967, Histoires extraordinaires 1967, Diaboliquement votre 1967, Adieu l'ami 1968, Girl on a motorcycle 1968, La piscine 1968, Jeff 1968, Die Boss, Die Quietly 1969, Borsalino 1970, Madly 1970, Doucement les basses 1970, Le cercle rouge 1971, L'assassinat de Trotsky 1971, La veuve Couderc 1971, Un flic 1972, Le professeur 1972, Scorpio 1972, Traitement de choc 1972, Les granges brûlées 1973, Deux hommes dans la ville 1973, Borsalino & Co. 1973, Les seins de glace 1974, Creezy 1975, Zorro 1975, Le gitan 1975, Mr Klein 1975, Le gang 1977, Mort d'un pourri 1977, Armageddon 1977, L'homme pressé 1977, Attention, les enfants regardent 1978, Le toubib 1979, Trois hommes à abattre 1980, Pour la peau d'un flic 1981 (dir), Le choc 1982 (dir), Le battant 1983 (dir), Un Amour de Swann 1984, Notre Histoire (César, Best Actor 1985) 1984, Parole de flic 1985, Le passage 1986, Ne réveillez pas un flic qui dort, Nouvelle Vague 1989, Dancing Machine 1990, Le Retour de Casanova 1992, Un Crime 1993, L'Ours en peluche 1994, Le Jour et La Nuit 1996, Une Chance sur deux 1998, Les Acteurs 2000, Les Nouveaux refus 2004, Astérix at the Olympic Games 2008. *Stage performances:* 'Tis Pity She's a Whore 1961, 1962, Les yeux crevés 1967, Variations énigmatiques 1996. *Television:* Comme au Cinéma (series) 1988, Fabio Montale (series) 2001, Le Lion 2003, Frank Riva (series) 2003–4. *Leisure interests:* swimming, riding, boxing. *Address:* Alain Delon International Diffusion SA, 7 rue des Battoirs, 1205 Geneva, Switzerland (office). *Telephone:* 227021108 (office). *E-mail:* info@alaindelon.com (office). *Website:* www.alaindelon.com (office).

DELORS, Jacques Lucien Jean; French politician and economist; b. 20 July 1925, Paris; s. of Louis Delors and Jeanne Rigal; m. Marie Lephaille 1948; one s. (deceased) one d. (Martine Aubry (q.v.)); ed Lycée Voltaire, Paris, Lycée Blaise-Pascal, Clermont-Ferrand, Univ. of Paris, Centre d'Etudes Supérieur de Banque (IEP); Head of Dept, Banque de France 1945–62, attached to staff of Dir-Gen. of Securities and Financial Market 1950–62, mem. Gen. Council 1973–79; mem. Planning and Investments Section, Econ. and Social Council 1959–61; Head of

Social Affairs Section, Commissariat général du Plan 1962–69; Sec.-Gen. Interministerial Cttee for Vocational Training and Social Promotion 1969–72; Adviser to Jacques Chaban-Delmas 1969, Chargé de mission 1971–72; Assoc. Prof. of Co. Man., Univ. of Paris IX 1973–79; f. Club Echange et Projets 1974; Dir Labour and Soc. Research Centre 1975–79; Parti Socialiste Nat. Del. for int. econ. relations 1976–81; elected mem. European Parl. 1979, Chair. Econ. and Monetary Cttee 1979–81; Minister for the Economy and Finance 1981–84; for the Economy, Finance and Budget 1983–84; Mayor of Clichy 1983–84; Pres. Comm. of the European Communities (now European Commission) 1985–94; Pres. EMU Comm. 1988–89, Int. Comm. on Educ. for the Twenty-First Century, UNESCO 1992–99; Pres. Conseil d'admin. Collège d'Europe, Bruges 1995–99, Conseil de l'emploi, des revenus et de la cohésion sociale (CERC) 2000–08; Pres. Notre Europe 1996–2004; Officier, Légion d'honneur; hon. degrees from 30 univs in Europe, USA and Canada; Leonardo European Corporate Learning Award (first recipient) 2010. *Publications:* Les indicateurs sociaux 1971, Changer 1975, En sortir ou pas (jtly) 1985, La France par l'Europe (jtly) 1988, Le Nouveau concert Européen 1992, Our Europe 1993, L'Unité d'un homme 1994, Combats pour l'Europe 1996, Mémoires 2004, Europe tragique et magnifique 2006, Investir dans le social 2009; numerous articles; reports for UN on French planning (1966) and long-term planning (1969). *Address:* Notre Europe, Institut Jacques Delors, 19 rue de Milan, 75009 Paris, France (office). *Telephone:* 1-44-58-97-95 (office). *Fax:* 1-44-58-97-99 (office). *E-mail:* jdelors@notre-europe.eu (office). *Website:* www.notre-europe.eu (office).

DELPY, Julie; American (b. French) actress; b. 21 Dec. 1969, Paris; ed New York Univ. Film School. *Films include:* Detective 1985, Mauvais Sang 1986, La Passion Béatrice 1987, L'Autre Nuit 1988, La Noche Oscura 1989, Europa Europa 1991, Voyager 1991, Warszawa 1992, Young and Younger 1993, The Three Musketeers 1993, When Pigs Fly 1993, The Myth of the White Wolf 1994, Killing Zoe 1994, Mesmer 1994, Trois Couleurs Blanc 1994, Trois Couleurs Rouge 1994, Before Sunrise 1995, An American Werewolf in Paris 1997, The Treat 1998, LA Without a Map 1998, Blah, Blah, Blah (Dir), The Passion of Ayn Rand 1999, But I'm A Cheerleader 1999, Tell Me 2000, Sand 2000, Beginner's Luck 1999, Waking Life 2001, MacArthur Park 2001, Looking for Jimmy 2002, Cinemagique 2002, Notting Hill Anxiety Festival 2003, Before Sunset (Empire Film Award for Best Actress 2005) 2004, Frankenstein (TV) 2004, Broken Flowers 2005, 3 & 3 2005, The Legend of Lucy Keyes 2006, The Hoax 2006, The Air I Breathe 2007, Deux jours à Paris (Two Days in Paris) 2007, The Countess 2009, Les passages 2010. *Television includes:* ER 2001. *Address:* c/o The William Morris Agency, One William Morris Place, Beverly Hills, CA 90212, USA.

DELYAGIN, Mikhail G., DEcon; Russian economist; b. 18 March 1968, Moscow; ed Moscow State Univ.; mem. govt analytical expert group 1994–97; Head of Analytical Centre Kominvest, then Chief Analyst, Analytical Dept of the Presidency of the Russian Federation; adviser to the Deputy Chair. of the Govt 1997–99; adviser and Head of Motherland All-Russia 1997–99; Founder and Dir Inst. of Globalization Studies 1998–2002, Scientific Dir and Chair. Presidium 2002–06, Dir 2006–07; adviser to Prime Minister of Russian Fed. 2002–03; mem. Presidium Ideological Council of Rodina party 2004–06; mem. Presidium Congress of Russian Communities; mem. Political Conf., Drugaia Rossiya; mem. Council on Foreign and Defence Policy 1999–; mem. Bd of Dirs Russian Union of Taxpayers. *Publications include:* more than 350 publications in Russia and abroad, five monographs, including Economics of Nonpayments 1997, Ideology of Renaissance 2000, Practice of Globalization 2000. *Telephone:* (495) 510-57-71 (office). *E-mail:* iprog@iprog.ru (office). *Website:* deliagin.ru; www.iprog.ru/en (office).

DEMARCO, Richard, OBE, FRSA; British academic; *Professor Emeritus of European Cultural Studies, Kingston University;* b. 9 July 1930, Edinburgh; s. of Carmine Demarco and Elizabeth Valentine Fusco; m. Anne C. Muckle 1957; ed Holy Cross Acad., Edin. Coll. of Art, Moray House Coll. and Royal Army Educ. Corps; art master, Duns Scotus Acad., Edin. 1956–67; Vice-Chair. Founding Cttee and Vice-Chair. Bd Dirs Traverse Theatre, Edin. 1963–67; Dir Sean Connery's Scottish Int. Educ. Trust (SIET) 1972–74; Dir Richard Demarco Gallery 1966–, European Youth Parliament 1993–; Trustee, Kingston-Demarco European Cultural Foundation 1993–95, Dir Demarco European Art Foundation, Edinburgh 1993–; Prof. of European Cultural Studies, Kingston Univ. 1993–2000, Prof. Emer. 2001–; Artistic Adviser European Youth Parl. 1992–; Consultant to Ministries of the Environment and Culture, Malta 1999; mem. Royal Scottish Soc. of Painters in Watercolours; Hon. Fellow, Royal Incorporation of Architects; Cavaliere della Repubblica Italiana, Chevalier des Arts et des Lettres; Hon. LLD (Dundee). *Publications:* The Artist as Explorer 1978, The Road to Meikle Seggie 1978, A Life in Pictures 1994, Art = Wealth 1995. *Leisure interests:* exploring the road to Meikle Seggie in the footsteps of Roman legionnaires, Celtic saints and scholars, respectful of the Rule of St Benedict. *Address:* Demarco European Art Foundation, 11 Upper Gray Court, Edinburgh, EH4 6RQ (office); 23A Lennox Street, Edinburgh, EH4 1PY, Scotland (home). *Telephone:* (774) 896-1315 (office); (131) 343-2124 (home). *Fax:* (131) 557-5972 (office); (131) 343-3124 (home). *Website:* www.richarddemarco.org.

DEMBA DAHABA, Abubacar; Guinea-Bissau economist and politician; fmr Minister of Economy and Regional Integration; fmr Gov. Islamic Development Bank Group; Minister of Finance 1999–2000, 2003–04, 2012–13; mem. Partido Africano da Independência da Guiné e Cabo Verde (PAIGC). *Address:* c/o Ministry of Finance, Rua Justino Lopes 74a, CP 67, Bissau, Guinea-Bissau (office).

DEMBY, Albert Joe, PhD; Sierra Leonean politician; Vice-Pres. of Sierra Leone 1996–2002; Deputy Leader Sierra Leone People's Party. *Address:* Sierra Leone People's Party, 29 Rawdon Street, Freetown, Sierra Leone (office).

DEMEKSA, Kuma; Ethiopian politician; *Mayor of Addis Ababa;* fmr Minister of Internal Affairs; officially removed from presidency of Oromia State after he was dismissed from Oromo People's Democratic Org. for "abuse of power, corruption and anti-democratic practices"; absent from political scene until apptd State Minister of Capacity Building; Minister of Nat. Defence 2005–08; Mayor of Addis Ababa 2008–. *Address:* City Hall, PO Box 9137, Addis Ababa, Ethiopia (office). *Telephone:* (11) 562391 (office). *E-mail:* addisababac@ethionet.et (office).

DEMEL, Herbert H., PhD; Austrian business executive; *Executive Vice-President and Chief Strategy Officer, Magna International Inc.;* b. 14 Oct. 1953, Vienna; ed Vienna Tech. Univ.; with Robert Bosch GmbH, Stuttgart as Co-ordinator of Anti–Lock Braking Systems 1984–90, also responsible for gearbox control units 1989–90; joined Audi AG, Ingolstadt as Sr Man. 1990, mem. Man. Bd in charge of Research and Devt 1993, Speaker of Man. Bd and CEO responsible for Research and Devt and Sales and Marketing 1994, Chair. Man. Bd 1995–97; Pres. Volkswagen do Brasil 1997–2001; Pres. and CEO Magna Steyr AG, Oberwalters-dorf, Austria 2002–03; CEO Fiat Auto 2003–05; Pres. Magna Powertrain, Canada 2005–07, COO, Vehicles and Powertrain, Magna International Inc. 2007–10, Exec. Vice-Pres. Magna International Inc. 2010–, Chief Strategy Officer 2012–. *Address:* Magna International Inc., 337 Magna Drive, Aurora, ON L4G 7K1, Canada (office). *Telephone:* (905) 726-2462 (office). *Fax:* (905) 726-7164 (office). *E-mail:* info@magnaint.com (office). *Website:* www.magnaint.com (office); www.magna.com (office).

DEMETRIADES, Panicos O., BA, MA, PhD; Cypriot economist, academic and central banker; b. 9 Jan. 1959, Limassol; ed Univ. of Essex, Univ. of Cambridge, UK; Officer, Econ. Research Dept, Central Bank of Cyprus 1985–90, Gov. Central Bank of Cyprus 2012–14; Lecturer in Econs, Univ. of Keele, UK 1990–95, Sr Lecturer 1995–96, Reader in Econs 1996–97; Prof. of Financial Econs, South Bank Univ., London 1997–2000; Prof. of Financial Econs, Univ. of Leicester 2000–12, Head of Econs Dept 2002–05; with Research Dept, IMF 1994; Consultant, Co-operative Central Bank of Cyprus 1996–98; Gen. Ed. Cyprus Journal of Economics 1989–96; Ed. Ekonomia 1997–2007; mem. Governing Bd Cyprus Univ. of Tech. 2009–10. *Publications include:* numerous articles in academic journals. *Address:* c/o Central Bank of Cyprus, POB 25529, 80 Kennedy Avenue, 1076 Nicosia, Cyprus.

DEMETRIOU, Andreas, BA, PhD; Cypriot psychologist, academic and politician; b. 15 Aug. 1950, Strongylo, Famagusta; m. Julia Tsakalea; two s.; ed Aristotelian Univ. of Thessaloniki, Univ. of New South Wales, Australia; Research and Teaching Asst, Dept of Psychology and Educ., Aristotelian Univ. of Thessaloniki 1975–83, Lecturer in Developmental Psychology 1983–86, Asst Prof. of Developmental Psychology 1986–92, Prof. 1992–96, mem. Univ. Senate 1990–91, Head of Dept of Psychology 1991–92, Pres. School of Psychology 1993–95, mem. Research Cttee 1995–96; Visiting Asst Prof. of Psychology, Dept of Educ., Univ. of Thessaly 1988–90; Prof. of Psychology, Univ. of Cyprus 1996–, Head of Dept of Educational Science 1996–98, Vice-Rector 1999–2002, Acting Rector 2003, Dean of School of Humanities and Social Sciences 2004–06; Visiting Scholar, Univ. of New South Wales, Australia 1978, Stanford Univ. 1991; Consultant Visitor at Harvard, Yale, and Pittsburgh Univs 1985; Visiting Research Fellow, Univ. of Melbourne 1988; Visiting Prof., Univ. of Ljubljana 1995, Univ. of Porto 1998, Univ. of Marribor, Slovenia 2003; Distinguished Visiting Prof., Univ. of Fribourg 2001; Pres. First Conf. for Psychological Research 1989, Greek Psychological Soc. 1989–91, Sec.-Gen. 1991–93; Pres. Seventh Conf., Hellenic Psychological Soc. 1998, Interim Governing Bd, Technological Univ. of Cyprus 2004–08, Conf. of Rectors of the Univs of Cyprus 2007–08; Founding Ed. Psychology: The Journal of Greek Psychological Society 1992–96, mem. Editorial Bd 1997–; mem. Editorial Bd The European Journal of the Psychology of Education 1985–, Newsletter of the European Association for Research on Learning and Instruction 1987–91, Adult Development Series 1989–, Bulletin of the Didactics of Mathematics 1990–96, Developmental Science 1998–, The Child and the Adolescent: A Journal of Mental Health and Psychopathology 1999–, The Child and the Adolescent: The Journal of the Greek Association of Psychoanalytic Psychotherapy of Children 2001, MountainRise: An Electronic Journal Dedicated to Scholarship of Teaching and Learning 2004–; mem. Int. Programme Cttee, Third Conf. of European Asscn for Research on Learning and Instruction 1989, mem. Exec. Cttee 1989–93, Cttee for Oeuvre Award 2001, Conf. Pres. 2003–05; mem. Psychology Cttee, Inter-Univ. Center for Recognition of Foreign Degrees (Diapanepistimiako Kentro Anagnorisis Titlon Spoudon Allodapis—DIKATSA) 1989–92; mem. Psychological Practice Licencing Cttee, Ministry of Health and Social Services 1994–95; mem. Ad Hoc Cttee for Evaluation of Integrated Lyceum, Ministry of Educ.; mem. Governing Bd, Research Promotion Foundation 2000–03; Rep. to European Science Foundation 2001–03; Fellow, Int. Acad. of Educ. 2004–; Minister of Educ. and Culture 2008–11. *Publications:* numerous contribs to academic journals. *Address:* c/o Ministry of Education and Culture, Kimonos & Thoukydidou, Akropolis, 1434 Nicosia, Cyprus (home).

DEMIAN, Hani Qadri, BA, MIA; Egyptian economist and politician; *Minister of Finance;* ed Helwan Univ., School of Int. and Public Affairs, Columbia Univ., USA; joined Ministry of Finance 2004 as Sr Adviser and Dir, Macro-Fiscal Unit, Office of the Minister of Finance, becoming Deputy Minister of Finance 2007, First Deputy Minister 2012–13 (resgnd), Minister of Finance 2014–; Chair of Deputies, IMF Int. Monetary and Financial Cttee 2008; fmr dir several govt and non-govt insts including Egyptian Competition Authority, Nat. Telecommunication Regulatory Authority, Post Authority, Bd of Trustees, Egyptian Radio and TV Union, Misr-Bank Europe, Frankfurt. *Address:* Ministry of Finance, Ministry of Finance Towers, Cairo (Nasr City), Egypt (office). *Telephone:* (2) 23428886 (office). *Fax:* (2) 26861561 (office). *E-mail:* finance@mof.gov.eg (office). *Website:* www.mof.gov.eg (office).

DEMIN, Col.-Gen. Yuri Georgiyevich, DJur Sc; Russian lawyer; b. 1945, Voronezh; m.; one d.; ed Higher KGB School, USSR Council of Ministers; involved in drafting of Fed. Security Service law 1994–95; Head of Legal Dept, Fed. Security Service of Russian Fed. 1995–97; Deputy Prosecutor-Gen., Chief Mil. Prosecutor 1997–2000; First Deputy Minister of Justice 2000–. *Publications:* (monographs) Diplomatic Missions 1995, Status of Diplomatic Missions and their Personnel 1995 and numerous articles. *Address:* Ministry of Justice, B. Karetny per. IDA, 101434 Moscow, Russia (office). *Telephone:* (495) 209-77-44 (office). *Fax:* (495) 209-66-95 (office).

DEMING, Claiborne P., BA, JD; American lawyer and business executive; *Chairman, Murphy Oil Corporation;* m. Elaine Deming; four c.; ed Tulane Univ.; joined Murphy Oil Corpn as staff attorney 1979, held numerous exec. positions, including Pres. Murphy Oil USA, Inc. 1989–93, Exec. Vice-Pres. and COO 1993–94, mem. Bd of Dirs 1993–, Pres. and CEO 1994–2008, Chair. Exec. Cttee 2009–, Chair. of the Bd 2012–; mem. Bd of Dirs Entergy Corpn 2002–06; mem. Ark. State Bd of Educ. 1999–2002; Vice-Chair. Nat. Petroleum Council; Pres. El Dorado Educ. Foundation; Past Pres. 25 Year Club of the Oil and Gas Industry, South Ark. Symphony, United Way of Union Co.; mem. Tulane Law School Bd of Advisors,

A.B. Freeman School of Business of Tulane Univ. Bd of Advisors; mem. Bd of Dirs American Petroleum Inst.; mem. ABA, Ark. Bar Asscn, La Bar Asscn. *Address:* Murphy Oil Corporation, PO Box 7000, El Dorado, AR 71731-7000 (office); Murphy Oil Corpn, 200 Peach Street, El Dorado, AR 71730, USA (office). *Telephone:* (870) 862-6411 (office). *Fax:* (870) 864-6373 (office). *E-mail:* info@murphyoilcorp.com (office). *Website:* www.murphyoilcorp.com (office).

DeMINT, Jim, AB, MBA; American research foundation executive and fmr politician; *President, Heritage Foundation;* m. Debbie DeMint; four c.; ed Univ. of Tennessee, Clemson Univ.; est. marketing co.; mem. US House of Reps from S Carolina, 4th Dist 1998–2004, served as mem. House Educ. and Workforce Cttee, Transportation and Infrastructure Cttee, Small Business Cttee, Vice-Chair. Sub-Cttee on Employer and Employee Relations; Senator from S Carolina 2005–13 (resgnd), mem. Cttee on Commerce, Science and Transportation, Cttee on Banking, Housing and Urban Affairs, Cttee on Foreign Relations, Jt Econ. Cttee; Pres. Heritage Foundation 2013–; Friend of the Taxpayer Award, American for Tax Reform, Spirit of Enterprise Award, US Chamber of Commerce, 'A' Rating, Nat. Rifle Asscn, ranked by National Journal as the Senate's most conservative mem. 2012, ranked by Nat. Taxpayers Union as the No. 1 senator voting for responsible tax and spending policies 2012. *Address:* Heritage Foundation, 214 Massachusetts Avenue, NE, Washington, DC 20002-4999, USA (office). *Telephone:* (202) 546-4400 (office). *E-mail:* info@heritage.org (office). *Website:* www.heritage.org (office).

DEMIRCHIAN, Stepan; Armenian politician; *Chairman, People's Party of Armenia;* b. 7 June 1959, Yerevan; s. of Karen Demirchian (died 1999); m.; three d.; ed Yerevan Polytechnic Inst.; began career working at electrical eng plant; fmr dir of industrial machinery co.; elected Chair. People's Party of Armenia 1999, confirmed in post 2001–; Cand. in Presidential Election 2003; Head of Justice (Artarutiun) bloc (alliance of opposition parties) to contest legis. elections 2003. *Address:* People's Party of Armenia (Hayastani Zhoghovrdakan Kusaktsutyun—HzhK), 0002 Yerevan, Parpetsi Street, Armenia (office). *Telephone:* (10) 53-15-01 (office). *Fax:* (10) 53-77-01 (office). *E-mail:* npa_armenia@yahoo.com (office). *Website:* www.ppa.am (office).

DEMIREL, Süleyman; Turkish fmr head of state and engineer; b. 1924; ed Istanbul Tech. Univ.; researcher in irrigation and electrification, Bureau of Reclamation 1949–50; Engineer, Electrical Survey Admin.; Head of Dams Dept 1954–55; Exchange Fellowship scholar, several pvt. cos and public depts, USA 1954–55; Dir-Gen. Hydraulic Works, Turkey 1955–60; pvt. contractor, engineer and Lecturer, Middle East Tech. Univ. 1962–64; Chair. Justice Party (AP) 1965–80; Isparta Deputy 1965–80; Deputy Prime Minister Feb.–Oct. 1965; Prime Minister (led AP Govt) 1965–71, (four coalition govts) 1977–78; Opposition Leader 1978–80; Prime Minister 1979–80; banned from politics 1980–87; Chair. True Path Party (DYP) 1987–93; Deputy for Isparta 1987–93; Prime Minister 1991–93; Pres. of Turkey 1993–2000; Honoured Mem. Azerbaijan Nat. Acad. of Sciences. *Address:* c/o Office of the President, Cumhurbaş-Kanlığı Köşkü, Cankaya, Ankara, Turkey.

DEMJÁN, Sándor; Hungarian business executive; *Chairman, TriGranit Development Corporation;* b. 14 May 1943, Börvely; m.; ed Coll. for Trading and Catering, Budapest; Sr Man. Sales Dept AFÉSZ Gorsium, Székesfehérvár 1968–73; f. SKALA Dept Store Chain and SKÁLA-COOP, CEO SKÁLA Jt Venture 1973–86; Founder and Chair. Magyar Hitel Bank, CEO 1986–90; Founder and Pnr, Cen. European Devt Corpn 1990–91; Founder and Pres. Polus Investment Co. Inc., Toronto, Canada 1991–; f. Gránit Pólus Investment & Devt Co.; Founder and Co-Chair. Trigranit Devt Co. 1997–; f. WestEnd City Centre, Budapest 1999; Co-founder and Co-Chair. (with George Soros), Int. Man. Centre 1988; Chair. Bd United Way 1995–98; Co-Chair. Nat. Asscn of Enterpreneurs and Employers (Vosz) 1997, now Pres.; est. first corpn in fmr USSR (KAMAZ); adviser to Govt of Tatarstan; Pres. MLL Professional Football Sub-Alliance 2000; Man of the Year 1986, 1988, Entrepreneur of the Year 1996, Most Influential Businessman of the Decade 2000, Most Successful Real Estate Developer of the Year 2002, State of Hungary Award 1980, Planetary Consciousness, Hungarian Business Award 1998. *Leisure interests:* fishing, playing chess. *Address:* TriGranit Development Corporation, 1062 Budapest, Váci út 3, Hungary (office). *Telephone:* (1) 374-6502 (office). *Fax:* (1) 374-6505 (office). *E-mail:* info@trigranit.com (office). *Website:* www.trigranit.com (office).

DEMME, Jonathan; American director, producer and writer; b. 22 Feb. 1944, Rockville Center, NY; m. Joanne Howard; two c.; ed Univ. of Florida; worked in publicity Dept United Artists, Embassy Pictures, Pathe Contemporary Films; writer for Film Daily 1966–68. *Films directed:* Hot Box (also co-screenwriter), Caged Heat 1974, Crazy Mama 1975, Fighting Mad 1976, Citizens Band 1977, Last Embrace 1979, Melvin and Howard 1980, Swing Shift 1983, Something Wild 1986, Married to the Mob 1988, Swimming to Cambodia, The Silence of the Lambs (Acad. Award for Best Film 1992), Cousin Bobby 1992, Philadelphia 1993, Mandela 1996, That Thing You Do 1996, Beloved 1998, Storefront Hitchcock 1998, The Truth About Charlie 2002, The Agronomist 2003, Neil Young Heart of Gold 2006, Jimmy Carter Man from Plains 2007, Rachel Getting Married 2008, Neil Young Trunk Show (documentary) 2009, Neil Young Journeys (documentary) 2011, I'm Carolyn Parker (documentary) 2011; exec. producer Devil in a Blue Dress 1995; Who am I this Time (for TV) 1982, Stop Making Sense (documentary) 1984, Konbir (video) 1989, Konbir: Burning Rhythms of Haiti (recording) 1989; producer Miami Blues 1990. *Address:* c/o Bob Bookman, Creative Artists Agency, 9830 Wilshire Boulevard, Beverly Hills, CA 90212-1804; Clinica Estetico, 127 West 24th Street, #7, New York, NY 10011-1914, USA.

DEMPSEY, Gen. Martin E., BS, MA, MS; American army officer; *Chairman, Joint Chiefs of Staff;* b. 14 March 1952; one s. one d.; ed John S. Burke Catholic High School, Goshen, NY, US Mil. Acad., West Point, NY, Duke Univ., Nat. War Coll.; commissioned as an Armor officer 1974; first duty assignment in 2nd Armored Cavalry Regt, served as a Scout and Support Platoon Leader and Squadron Adjutant; completed Armor Officer Advanced Course, apptd Motor Officer for 1st Squadron, 10th Cavalry, Fort Carson, Colo 1979; later commanded Alpha and HQ Troops, 1st Squadron, 10th Cavalry, as well as serving as Squadron Operations Officer; assigned to English Dept, West Point 1984, performed duties as an instructor, Asst Prof. –1987; assigned to Command and Gen. Staff Coll., Fort Leavenworth, Kan.; reported to 3rd Armored Div., Friedberg, Germany 1988, served as Exec. Officer of 4th Bn, 67th Armor Regt, then as Operations Officer and later Exec. Officer for 3rd Brigade, 3rd Armored Div., deploying in support of Operations Desert Shield and Desert Storm; assumed command of 4th Bn, 67th Armored Regt, 1st Armored Div. 1991; assigned as Chief of Armor Br., US Total Army Personnel Command 1993; returned to Fort Carson to take command of 3rd Armored Cavalry Regt 1996; Asst Deputy Dir for Politico-Mil. Affairs Europe and Africa J5 and Special Asst to Chair. of Jt Chiefs of Staff, Washington, DC 1998–2001; Program Man., Saudi Arabian Nat. Guard Modernization Program, Saudi Arabia 2001–03; commanded 1st Armored Div. and deployed to Iraq in support of Operation Iraqi Freedom 2003–04; redeployed the div. to Germany and completed his command tour July 2005; returned to Iraq and assumed command of Multi-Nat. Security Transition Command-Iraq Aug. 2005–07; Deputy Commdr US Cen. Command 2007–08, Acting Commdr March–Oct. 2008; Commdr US Army Training and Doctrine Command 2008–11; Chief of Staff of the US Army April–Oct. 2011; Chair. Jt Chiefs of Staff Oct. 2011–; rank of 2nd Lt 1974, 1st Lt 1976, Capt. 1978, Maj. 1985, Lt Col 1991, Col 1995, Brig. Gen. 2001, Maj. Gen. 2004, Lt Gen. 2005, Gen. 2008; Defense Distinguished Service Medal (with one bronze Oak Leaf Cluster), Army Distinguished Service Medal (with two Oak Leaf Clusters), Defense Superior Service Medal, Legion of Merit (with two Oak Leaf Clusters), Bronze Star Medal with Oak Leaf Cluster and 'V' Device, Meritorious Service Medal (with two Oak Leaf Clusters), Joint Service Commendation Medal, Army Commendation Medal, Army Achievement Medal (with Oak Leaf Cluster), Joint Meritorious Unit Award (with Oak Leaf Cluster), Valorous Unit Award (with Oak Leaf Cluster), Army Superior Unit Award (with Oak Leaf Cluster), Nat. Defense Service Medal (with two bronze Service Stars), Southwest Asia Service Medal with three bronze Service Stars, Iraq Campaign Medal, Global War on Terrorism Expeditionary Medal, Global War on Terrorism Service Medal, Army Service Ribbon, Army Overseas Service Ribbon (with award numeral '4'), NATO Medal for Service with ISAF, Kuwait Liberation Medal (Saudi Arabia), Kuwait Liberation Medal (Kuwait), Combat Action Badge, Basic Parachutist Badge, Office of the Jt Chiefs of Staff Identification Badge, Army Staff Identification Badge, 7 Overseas Service Bars, 3rd Armored Cavalry Regt Distinctive Unit Insignia, 1st Armored Div. Combat Service Identification Badge. *Address:* Office of the Chairman of the Joint Chiefs of Staff, 9999 Joint Staff Pentagon, Washington, DC 20318-9999, USA (office). *Website:* www.jcs.mil (office).

DEMPSEY, Noel, BA, HDip in Ed; Irish politician and fmr teacher guidance counsellor; *Public Affairs Consultant, Noel Dempsey Consulting;* b. 6 Jan. 1953, Trim, Co. Meath; s. of Michael Dempsey and Maureen Dempsey (née Byrne); m. Bernadette Rattigan; two s. two d.; ed St Michael's Christian Brothers' School, Trim, Univ. Coll., Dublin, St Patrick's Coll., Maynooth (Diploma in Career Guidance, Diploma in Youth Leadership); fmr career guidance counsellor; Nat. Sec. Local Authority Members Asscn 1984–89; Chair. Meath Co. Council 1986–87; fmr mem. and Chair. Co. Meath Vocational Educ. Cttee; fmr Dir Midland East Regional Tourism Org.; fmr mem. numerous local govt cttees; mem. Dáil Éireann (Irish Parl.) 1987–2011, mem. Dáil Public Accounts Cttee 1987–89, 1990–92; fmr Opposition Spokesperson on Environment; Fianna Fáil Co-ordinator on Forum for Peace and Reconciliation; Nat. Treasurer Fianna Fáil; fmr Minister of State at Depts of the Taoiseach, Defence, and Finance; Govt Chief Whip 1992–94; Minister for the Environment and Local Govt 1997–2002, for Educ. and Science 2002–04, for Communications, Marine and Natural Resources 2004–07, for Transport 2007–11; Public Affairs Consultant, Noel Dempsey Consulting 2011–; European Road Safety Pin Award. *Leisure interests:* Gaelic football and hurling, reading, golf. *Address:* Newtown, Trim, Co. Meath, Ireland. *Telephone:* 86-7749999 (mobile). *E-mail:* noelmin@eircom.net (office).

DEMSZKY, Gábor; Hungarian politician, journalist, editor and sociologist; *Mayor of Budapest;* b. 4 Aug. 1952, Budapest; s. of Rudolf Demszky and Irén Király; m. Vera Révai (divorced); m. Anikó Németh; four c.; ed Eötvös Loránd Univ.; contrib. to periodical Világosság (Lucidity) 1977; founding mem. SZETA (fund to support poor) 1979; founder AB Független Kiadó (independent publr) 1981; Ed. illegal Hírmondó (Courier) 1983; founding mem. Network of Free Initiative and SZDSZ 1988; founding mem. Alliance of Free Democrats, mem. Exec. Bd 1989; mem. Parl. 1990 (resgnd), 1998; Chair. Cttee of Nat. Security 1990; mem. Exec. Bd Alliance of Free Democrats 1994–, Pres. of Alliance 2000–01; Founder Children's Rescue Soc.; negotiator in Moscow talks on Soviet troops withdrawal and on Hungary's leaving the Warsaw Pact; Mayor of Budapest 1990–; Vice-Pres. Standing Conf. of Local and Regional Authorities, Council of Europe 1992–94, Congress of Local and Regional Authorities 1994–96; mem., European Parl. 2004 (resgnd due to conflict of interest); founding mem. and Dir Asscn to Save the Children; Co-Pres. Budapest Bank for Budapest Foundation; Pres. Budapest Sports Asscn; Freedom to Publish Prize, Int. Asscn of Publishers, Vienna 1984. *Leisure interests:* jogging, sailing, riding, water-skiing, fishing. *Address:* Városház utca 9/11, 1052 Budapest, Hungary. *Telephone:* (1) 327-1022 (office). *Fax:* (1) 327-1819 (office). *E-mail:* demszkyg@budapest.hu (office). *Website:* www.budapest.hu (office).

DENCH, Dame Judith (Judi) Olivia, CH, DBE, FRSA; British actress; b. 9 Dec. 1934, York, England; d. of Reginald Arthur Dench and Eleanora Olave Dench (née Jones); m. Michael Williams 1971 (died 2001); one d.; ed The Mount School, York, Central School of Speech and Drama, London; performed in Old Vic seasons 1957–61, appearing in parts including Ophelia (Hamlet), Katherine (Henry V), Cecily (The Importance of Being Earnest), Juliet (Romeo and Juliet), appeared with Old Vic Co. at two Edin. Festivals, Venice, on tour to Paris, Belgium and Yugoslavia and on tour to USA and Canada; appearances with RSC 1961–62, including parts as Anya (The Cherry Orchard), Titania (A Midsummer Night's Dream), Dorcas Bellboys (A Penny for a Song), Isabella (Measure for Measure); on tour to W Africa with Nottingham Playhouse 1963; mem. Bd Nat. Theatre 1988–91; subsequent roles include Irina (The Three Sisters) and Doll Common (Alchemist), Oxford Playhouse 1964–65, title-role in Saint Joan and Barbara (The Astrakhan Coat), Nottingham Playhouse 1965, Amanda (Private Lives), Lika (The Promise) 1967, Sally Bowles (Cabaret) 1968, Grace Harkaway (London Assurance) 1970, 1972, Barbara Undershaft (Major Barbara) 1970; Assoc. mem. RSC 1969–, appearing as Bianca (Women Beware Women), Viola (Twelfth Night), Hermione and Perdita (Winter's Tale), Portia (Merchant of Venice), Duchess (Duchess of Malfi), Beatrice (Much Ado About Nothing), Lady Macbeth (Macbeth), Adriana (Comedy of Errors), also on tour with RSC to Japan and Australia 1970, Japan

1972; other performances include Vilma (The Wolf), Oxford and London 1973, Miss Trant (The Good Companions), 1974, Sophie Fullgarney (The Gay Lord Quex) 1975, Nurse (Too True to be Good) 1975, 1976, Millament (Way of the World) 1978, Cymbeline 1979, Juno and the Paycock 1980–81, Lady Bracknell (The Importance of Being Earnest) 1982, Deborah (A Kind of Alaska) 1982, Pack of Lies 1983, Mother Courage 1984, Waste 1985, Mr and Mrs Nobody 1986, Antony and Cleopatra 1987, Entertaining Strangers 1987, Hamlet 1989, The Cherry Orchard 1989, The Sea 1991, The Plough and the Stars 1991, Coriolanus 1992, The Gift of the Gorgon 1993, The Seagull (Royal Nat. Theatre) 1994, The Convent 1995, Absolute Hell (Royal Nat. Theatre) 1995, A Little Night Music (Royal Nat. Theatre) 1995, Amy's View (Royal Nat. Theatre) 1997, (New York) 1999, Filumena 1998, The Royal Family 2001, The Breath of Life (Theatre Royal, Haymarket) 2002, All's Well that Ends Well (Theatregoers' Award for Best Supporting Actress 2005) 2003–04, Madame de Sade (Donmar Warehouse) 2009, A Midsummer Night's Dream (Rose Theatre, Kingston) 2010, Peter and Alice (Noel Coward Theatre) 2013; Dir Much Ado About Nothing 1988, Look Back in Anger 1989, The Boys from Syracuse 1991; mem. Bd, Nat. Theatre 1988–; Hon. Fellow, Royal Holloway Coll., London, Lucy Cavendish Coll., Cambridge; Foreign Hon. Fellow, American Acad. of Arts and Sciences 2009; Freedom of the City of London 2011; Hon. DLitt (Warwick) 1978, (York) 1983, (Keele) 1989, (Birmingham) 1989, (Loughborough) 1991, (Open Univ.) 1994, (London) 1994, (Oxford) 2000; Dr hc (Surrey) 1996, (Mary Baldwin Coll., Va) 2004, (Juilliard Acad., New York) 2004, (Royal Acad. of Music and Drama, Glasgow), (Queen Margaret Univ. Coll., Edinburgh), (Univ. of East Anglia), (Univ. of Wales), (Leeds), (Hull), (St Andrews), (Nottingham Trent); numerous awards, including Paladino d'Argentino (Venice Festival Award for Juliet) 1961, Best Actress of Year (Variety London Critics for Lika in The Promise) 1967, Most Promising Newcomer (British Film Acad. for Four in the Morning) 1965, Best Actress of the Year (Guild of Directors for Talking to a Stranger) 1967, Soc. West End Theatre Award (for Lady Macbeth) 1977, Best Actress New Standard Drama Awards (for Juno and the Paycock) 1980, (for Lady Bracknell in The Importance of Being Earnest and Deborah in A Kind of Alaska) 1983, (for Cleopatra in Antony and Cleopatra) 1987, Olivier Award for Best Actress in Antony and Cleopatra 1987; BAFTA Award for Best Television Actress 1981, for Best Supporting Actress (for A Room with a View) 1987 and (for A Handful of Dust) 1988, Golden Globe and BAFTA Best Actress Award for Mrs Brown, Olivier Award for Outstanding Contrib. to Theatre 2004, Evening Standard Special Award for Outstanding Contrib. to British Theatre 2004, European Film Acad. Lifetime Achievement Award 2008, BFI Fellowship 2011, Sky Arts Award for Outstanding Achievement 2011, Crystal Globe for Outstanding Artistic Contrib. to World Cinema, 46th Int. Film Festival, Karlovy Vary, West Bohemia 2011, Praemium Imperiale Award, Japan Art Asscn 2011, Golden Seagull Award, Moscow Arts Theatre 2012. *Films include:* The Third Secret 1964, Four in the Morning 1965, A Study in Terror 1965, He Who Rides a Tiger 1965, A Midsummer Night's Dream (RSC Production) 1968, Luther 1974, Dead Cert 1974, Spaceship Earth (short) (4th edition narrator) 1982, Wetherby 1985, A Room with a View 1985, The Angelic Conversation (narrator) 1987, 84 Charing Cross Road 1987, A Handful of Dust 1988, Henry V 1989, Jack & Sarah 1995, GoldenEye 1995, Hamlet 1996, Mrs Brown 1997, Tomorrow Never Dies 1997, Shakespeare in Love (Acad. Award for Best Supporting Actress) 1998, The Bear (short) (narrator American version) 1998, Tea with Mussolini 1999, The World Is Not Enough 1999, Chocolat 2000, Iris (BAFTA Award for Best Actress 2002) 2001, The Shipping News 2001, The Importance of Being Earnest 2002, Die Another Day 2002, Home on the Range (voice) 2004, Disney Sing Along Songs: Home on the Range – Little Patch of Heaven (video short) 2004, The Chronicles of Riddick 2004, Ladies in Lavender 2004, A Dairy Tale (video short) (voice) 2004, Pride & Prejudice 2005, Angelina Ballerina: Angelina's Princess Dance (video) (voice) 2005, Mrs Henderson Presents 2205, Doogal (narrator) 2006, Angelina Ballerina: Angelina Sets Sail (voice) 2006, Casino Royale 2006, Notes on a Scandal 2006, Quantum of Solace 2008, Rage 2009, Nine 2009, James Bond Supports International Women's Day (short) (voice) 2011, Run for Your Wife (cameo) 2011, Jane Eyre 2011, Pirates of the Caribbean: On Stranger Tides 2011, My Week with Marilyn 2011, Friend Request Pending (short) 2011, J. Edgar 2011, The Best Exotic Marigold Hotel 2011, Skyfall 2012, Philomena 2013. *Television includes:* Hilda Lessways (series) 1959, The Terrible Choice (series) 1960, Armchair Theatre (series) – Pink String and Sealing Wax 1960, An Age of Kings (series) 1960, The Four Just Men (series) 1960, The Cherry Orchard (film) 1962, Z Cars (series) 1963, Festival (series) – August for the People 1964, Detective (series) 1964, The Troubleshooters (series) 1965, ITV Play of the Week (series) 1959–66, Court Martial (series) 1966, Talking to a Stranger (mini-series) 1966, Theatre 625 (series) 1964–66, BBC Play of the Month (series) – Days to Come 1966, Confession (series) 1970, Ooh La La! (series) 1973, 2nd House (series) – Frank's for the Memory 1974, Jackanory (series) (storyteller) 1968–78, The Comedy of Errors (film) 1978, A Performance of Macbeth (film) 1979, BBC 2 Play of the Week (series) – On Giant's Shoulders 1979, – Langrishe Go Down 1978, ITV Playhouse (series) – On Approval 1968, – Village Wooing 1979, Love in a Cold Climate (mini-series) 1980, BBC 2 Playhouse (series) – Going Gently 1981, The Cherry Orchard (film) 1981, Saigon: Year of the Cat (film) 1983, A Fine Romance (series) 1981–84, The Browning Version (film) 1985, Star Quality: Mr. and Mrs. Edgehill (film) 1985, Theatre Night (series) 1987, Behaving Badly (mini-series) 1989, Screen One (series) 1990, Absolute Hell (film) 1991, The Torch (mini-series) 1992, As Time Goes By (series) 1992–2005, Middlemarch (mini-series) 1994, 1914–1918 (series) – Total War (narrator as Dame Judi Dench) 1996, The Last of the Blonde Bombshells (film) 2000, Angelina Ballerina (series) 2001–07, Angelina Ballerina: The Show Must Go On (film) (voice) 2002, Cranford (mini-series) 2007–09, National Theatre Live (series) – 50 Years on Stage 2013. *Publications:* Judi Dench: A Great Deal of Laughter (biog.), Judi Dench: With a Crack in Her Voice 1998, Scenes from My Life 2005, And Furthermore 2010. *Leisure interests:* painting, drawing, swimming, sewing, catching up with letters. *Address:* c/o Julian Belfrage Associates, 3rd Floor, 9 Argyll Street, London, W1F 7TG, England (office). *E-mail:* info@julianbelfrage.com (office).

DENCKER, Nils, BSc, PhD; Swedish mathematician and academic; *Professor of Mathematics, Lund University;* b. 14 March 1953, Lund; m. Anna Dencker; two s. two d.; ed Lund Univ.; C.L.E. Moore Instructor, MIT, USA 1981–83; returned to Lund Univ. as Prof. of Math. 1983–, Dir of Studies, Dept of Math. 2001–03; Chair. Swedish Math. Soc. 2007–09; mem. Royal Swedish Acad. of Sciences, Swedish Nat. Cttee for Math.; Gaarding Prize, Royal Physiographic Soc., Lund 2003, Clay

Research Award, Clay Math. Inst. (co-recipient) 2005. *Achievement:* complete resolution of a conjecture made by F. Treves and L. Nirenberg in 1970. *Publications:* numerous papers in professional journals on micro-local analysis of partial differential equations and calculus of pseudo-differential operators. *Address:* Room 507, Center for Mathematical Sciences, Faculty of Science, Lund University, Box 118, 221 00 Lund, Sweden (office). *Telephone:* (46) 222-44-62 (office). *Fax:* (46) 222-42-13 (office). *E-mail:* dencker@maths.lth.se (office). *Website:* www.maths.lth.se (office).

DENDIAS, Nikolaos, LLM; Greek politician; *Minister of Public Order and Citizen Protection;* b. 7 Oct. 1959, Corfu; m.; two c.; ed Univ. of Athens, Univ. Coll. London, London School of Econs; called to Corfu Bar 1986; mem. Nea Dimokratia 1978–, mem. Parl. Group for the Control of Tourism 2002, Cttee for the Revision of the Constitution 2006; mem. Parl. for Corfu 2004–, mem. Perm. Cttee on Finance, Special Perm. Cttee on Nat. Budget and Cttee of Deontology 2007–, Vice-Pres. fact-finding Cttee for the Vatopedi Case 2008; apptd Minister of Justice 2009, of Public Order and Citizen Protection 2012–; mem. Centre for Political Research and Educ. 2006–; mem. Hellenic Cancer Soc. 2006–; currently Pres. Eptanission Politia Cultural Asscn. *Address:* Minister of Public Order and Citizen Protection, P. Khanellopoulou 4, 101 77 Athens, Greece (office). *Telephone:* (210) 6924558 (office). *Fax:* (210) 6929764 (office). *E-mail:* pressoffice@yptp.gr (office). *Website:* www.mopocp.gov.gr (office).

DENEUVE, Catherine; French actress; b. (Catherine Dorléac), 22 Oct. 1943, Paris; d. of Maurice Dorléac and Renée Deneuve; m. David Bailey (q.v.) 1965 (divorced); one s. by Roger Vadim; one d. by Marcello Mastroianni; ed Lycée La Fontaine, Paris; film début in Les petits chats 1959; Pres., Dir-Gen. Films de la Citrouille 1971–79; f. Société Cardeva 1983; UNESCO Goodwill Amb. for the Safeguarding of Film Heritage 1994–2005; Hon. Golden Bear, Berlin Film Festival, Arts de l'Alliance française de New York Trophy 1998, Bangkok Film Festival Lifetime Achievement Award 2006. *Films include:* Les portes claquent 1960, L'homme à femmes 1960, Le vice et la vertu 1962, Et Satan conduit le bal 1962, Vacances portugaises 1963, Les parapluies de Cherbourg 1963 (Palme d'Or, Festival de Cannes 1964), Les plus belles escroqueries du monde 1963, La chasse à l'homme 1964, Un monsieur de compagnie 1964, La Costanza della Ragione 1964, Repulsion 1964, Le chant du monde 1965, La vie de château 1965, Liebes Karusell 1965, Les créatures 1965, Les demoiselles de Rochefort 1966, Belle de jour 1967 (Golden Lion at Venice Festival 1967), Benjamin 1967, Manon 70 1967, Mayerling 1968, La chamade 1966, Folies d'avril 1969, Belles d'un soir 1969, La sirène du Mississippi 1969, Tristana 1970, Peau d'âne 1971, Ça n'arrive qu'aux autres 1971, Liza 1971, Un flic 1972, L'évènement le plus important depuis que l'homme a marché sur la lune 1973, Touche pas la femme blanche 1974, La femme aux bottes rouges 1975, La grande bourgeoisie 1975, Hustle 1976, March or Die 1977, Coup de foudre 1977, Ecoute, voir... 1978, L'argent des autres 1978, A nous deux 1979, Ils sont grands ces petits 1979, Le dernier métro 1980, Je vous aime 1980, Le choix des armes 1981, Hôtel des Amériques 1981, Le choc 1982, L'Africain 1983, The Hunger 1983, Le bon plaisir 1984, Paroles et musiques 1984, Le lieu du crime 1986, Pourvu que ce soit une fille 1986, Drôle d'endroit pour une rencontre 1989, La fleur blanche 1991, Indochine 1992 (César award for Best Actress 1993), Ma saison préférée 1993, La Partie d'Echecs 1994, The Convent 1995, Les Cent et une nuits 1995, Les Voleurs 1995, Généalogie d'un crime 1997, Place Vendôme 1998, Le Vent de la nuit 1999, Belle-Maman 1999, Pola x 1999, Time Regained 1999, Dancer in the Dark 2000, Je centre à la maison 2001, Absolument fabuleux 2001, 8 Femmes 2002, Au plus près du paradis 2002, Un film parlé 2003, Palais Royal! 2006, Le Concile de Pierre 2006, Le Héros de la famille 2006, Persepolis (voice) 2007, Un conte de Noël 2008, Je veux voir 2008, Mes stars et moi 2008, La fille dud RER 2009, Cyprien 2009, Bancs publics 2009, Mères et filles 2009, Potiche 2010, The Big Picture 2010, Les yeux de sa mère 2011, Beloved 2011. *Publication:* Close Up and Personal (autobiog.) 2005. *Address:* c/o Artmédia, 20 avenue Rapp, 75007 Paris, France.

DENG, Liqun; Chinese politician; b. 1914, Guidong Co., Hunan Prov.; m. Luo Liyun; one s.; ed Beijing No. 26 Middle School; mem. CCP 1936–; Dir Educ. Dept Marxism-Leninism Inst.; Dir Propaganda Dept CCP Jibei Pref. Cttee; Deputy Dir Gen. Office of Finance and Econ. Comm. of NE China; Dir Policy Research Office of CCP Liaoning Provincial Cttee; after founding of People's Repub. of China in 1949 served as Chair. Cultural and Educ. Cttee of Xinjiang Regional People's Cttee; Dir Propaganda Dept of Xinjiang Bureau under CCP Cen. Cttee; Ed. and Deputy Ed.-in-Chief, Red Flag; branded as counter-revolutionary revisionist and purged during Cultural Revolution; Vice-Pres. Acad. of Social Sciences 1978; Dir Policy Research Section under CCP Cen. Cttee 1981; Adviser to Soc. for Study of Econ. of Minority Areas 1981, to Soc. of Labour Science 1982, to Soc. for Study of Workers' Political and Ideological Work; Dir CCP Cen. Cttee Propaganda Dept 1982–85; mem. 12th CCP Cen. Cttee 1982–87, also mem. Secr. 1982–87; Vice-Chair. Nat. Cttee for Promoting Socialist Ethics 1983; Head, CCP Cen. Leading Group for Educ. of Cadres 1985; mem. CCP Cen. Advisory Comm. 1987; Deputy Head, CCP Cen. Cttee Party Bldg Group 1990–; Deputy Head, CCP Cen. Cttee Leading Group for Party History Work 1994–; Hon. Pres. Soc. for Studies on Party Mems 1991–. *Address:* c/o Central Committee of Chinese Communist Party, Beijing, People's Republic of China.

DENG, Nan; Chinese politician; *Vice-Chairman, China Association for Science and Technology;* b. Oct. 1945, Guang'an, Sichuan Prov.; d. of the late Deng Xiaoping (fmr Gen. Sec. CCP and fmr Chair. Gen. Mil. Comm., CCP) and of Zhuo Lin; ed Beijing Univ.; worker, Semiconductor Research Inst., Chinese Acad. of Sciences 1973; fmr Deputy Div. Chief, Policy Dept, State Science and Tech. Comm., later Deputy Dir, later Deputy Dir Science and Tech. Policy Dept, Dir 1989–91, Vice-Minister in charge of State Science and Tech. Comm. 1991–98; Vice-Minister of Science and Tech. 1998–2005; fmr Deputy Dir Environmental Protection Cttee of the State Council; joined CCP 1978; Del., CCP Nat. Congress 1992–97; mem. 17th CCP Nat. Cttee 2007–; Vice-Chair. China Assn for Science and Tech. 2005–; fmr Deputy Dir China Cttee of the Int. Decade for Natural Disaster Reduction; fmr mem. Exec. Cttee, All-China Women's Fed.; UN Boutros Boutros-Ghali Special Research Prize. *Address:* China Association for Science and Technology, 3 Fuxing Lu, Beijing 100032, People's Republic of China (office). *Website:* english.cast.org.cn (office).

DENG, Pufang; Chinese politician; b. 1943; s. of the late Deng Xiaoping and Zhuo Lin; ed Beijing Univ.; joined CCP 1965; fmr staff mem. Service Dept, Cen. Mil. Comm. of People's Repub. of China; Vice-Pres. Welfare Fund for Handicapped 1984, Pres. 1985–; Ed.-in-Chief Spring Breeze (Journal) 1984–; Vice-Chair. China Organizing Comm. of UN's Decade of Disabled Persons 1986–90, Chair. 1990–; Vice-Chair. Cttee for Coordination of Work for the Disabled; Chair. China Disabled Persons' Fed. 1988–; Adviser, China Asscn for Int. Friendly Contacts 1991–; Del., 14th CCP Nat. Congress 1992–97; Alt. mem. 15th CCP Cen. Cttee 1997–2002, 16th CCP Cen. Cttee 2002–07; mem. Standing Cttee, 9th CPPCC Nat. Cttee 1998–2003, Vice-Chair. 11th CPPCC Nat. Cttee 2008–13; Exec. Pres. Chinese Olympic Cttee 2003–; Rehabilitation International (RI) Presidential Awards, 15th RI World Ass. 1990, 17th RI World Ass. 1992, recipient of Testimonial from UN Sec.-Gen. 1998, UN Human Rights Award 2003. *Address:* China Welfare Fund for Handicapped, Beijing, People's Republic of China.

DENG, Qilin, MA; Chinese steel industry executive; *President, Wuhan Iron and Steel (Group) Corporation (WISCO);* ed Wuhan Iron and Steel Inst.; joined Wuhan Iron and Steel (Group) Corpn (WISCO) 1970, served as Dir WISCO No. 2 Smelting Plant, Chief of WISCO Production Dept and Asst to the Gen. Man. and Asst Gen. Man. WISCO, now Pres. and Vice-Sec. Party Cttee, currently Chair. Wuhan Iron and Steel Corpn Ltd of Consolidated Thompson Iron Mines Ltd, mem. Bd of Dirs and Chair. Wuhan Iron and Steel Co. Ltd 2005–; fmr Chair. China Iron and Steel Asscn. *Address:* Wuhan Iron and Steel (Group) Corporation, Changqian Qingshan District, Wuhan 430083, Hubei, People's Republic of China (office). *Telephone:* (27) 86892907 (office). *E-mail:* info@wisco.com.cn (office). *Website:* www.wisco.com.cn (office).

DENG, Yaping, MA, PhD; Chinese media executive and table tennis player (retd); *President, Jike.com;* b. 5 Feb. 1973, Zhengzhou, He'nan Prov.; m. Lin Zhigang 2007; one s.; ed Tsinghua Univ., Beijing, Univ. of Nottingham, UK; mem. Chinese women's table tennis team 1988; won over 20 gold medals in various world championships, including Barcelona Olympics 1992, Atlanta Olympics 1996; top-ranked female table tennis player 1991–98; retd 1997; mem. Sports Cttee of IOC; has co-chaired Chinese Olympic Cttee and Sports Asscn of China; mem. CPPCC; elected Deputy Sec. China Communist Youth League Beijing Cttee 2009; Deputy Sec. People's Daily (official newspaper of the CP of China), also Pres. Goso.cn (now jike.com) People's Daily news search engine 2010; Chinese Sports Personality of the Century 1999, mem. Laureus World Sports Acad. *Address:* Jike.com East Third Ring Road, Chaoyang District, One World Financial Center, 100020 Beijing, People's Republic of China (office). *Telephone:* (10) 57699999 (office). *Fax:* (10) 57699998 (office). *E-mail:* service@jike.com (office). *Website:* www.jike.com (office).

DENG, Youmei; Chinese writer; *Deputy Chairman, Chinese Writers' Association;* b. 1931, Tianjin; messenger in CCP-led New 4th Army 1945; entered Cen. Research Inst. of Literature 1952; in political disgrace 1957–77; Sec. Chinese Writers' Asscn 1985–96, Deputy Chair. 1996–. *Publications:* On the Precipice, Our Army Commander, Han the Forger, Tales of Taoranting Park, Snuff Bottles, Na Wu, Moon Over Liangshan Mountain. *Address:* Chinese Writers' Association, 25 Dongtucheng Road, Beijing 100013, People's Republic of China. *Telephone:* (10) 64261554.

DENG ATHORBEI, David; South Sudanese politician; ed Univ. of Khartoum; Minister of Transport and Roads in regional semi-autonomous Govt of South Sudan 2007, also fmr Minister of Finance; first Minister of Finance and Econ. Planning of South Sudan following independence 2011, Minister of Electricity and Dams –2013; mem. Sudan People's Liberation Movt. *Address:* c/o Ministry of Electricity and Dams, Juba, South Sudan.

DENG NHIAL, Nhial; South Sudanese lawyer and politician; ed Univ. of Khartoum; Minister of Regional Cooperation in regional semi-autonomous Govt of South Sudan 2007, also fmr Minister of Defence; mem. Sudan People's Liberation Movt (SPLM) Leadership Council and Political Bureau; led SPLM del. to Naivasha peace talks, Kenya 2002–05; first Minister of Sudan People's Liberation Army (SPLA) and Veteran Affairs of South Sudan following independence July–Aug. 2011, Minister of Foreign Affairs and Int. Co–operation 2011–13. *Address:* c/o Ministry of Foreign Affairs and International Co-operation, Juba, South Sudan.

DENHAM, Rt Hon. John Yorke, BSc, PC; British politician; b. 15 July 1953, Seaton, Devon, England; m. Ruth Eleanor Dixon (divorced); three c.; ed Univ. of Southampton; Head of Youth Affairs, British Youth Council 1979–83; responsible for public educ. and advocacy for War on Want (charity) 1984–88; Hants. Co. Councillor 1981–89; Southampton City Councillor 1989–93, Chair. Southampton City Housing Cttee 1989–93; MP (Labour) for Southampton Itchen 1992–; Minister of State at Home Office 2001–03, Chair. Home Affairs Select Cttee 2003–07, Sec. of State for Innovation, Univs and Skills 2007–09, for Communities and Local Govt 2009–10; Shadow Sec. of State for Communities and Local Government May–Oct. 2010, for Business, Innovation and Skills Oct. 2010–11; Parl. Pvt. Sec. to Ed Miliband 2011–; Vice-Pres. Local Govt Asscn 2010–; mem. AMICUS/MSF (trade union). *Leisure interests:* cookery, walking, music, Southampton Football Club. *Address:* House of Commons, Westminster, London, SW1A 2TT (office); Southampton Itchen Parliamentary Office, 20–22 Southampton Street, Southampton, SO15 2ED, England (office). *Telephone:* (20) 7219-4515 (London) (office); (23) 8033-9807 (Southampton) (office). *Fax:* (23) 8033-9907 (Southampton) (office). *E-mail:* denhamj@parliament.uk (office); john@johndenham.org.uk (office). *Website:* www.johndenham.org.uk (office).

DENHAM, Susan Jane, BA, LLB, LLM, SC, MRIA; Irish judge; *Chief Justice, Supreme Court of Ireland;* b. 22 Aug. 1945, Dublin; d. of Douglas Gageby and Dorothy Mary Gageby (née Lester); m. Brian Denham 1970; three s. one d. (and one s. deceased); ed Alexandra Coll. Dublin, Trinity Coll. Dublin, King's Inns, Dublin and Columbia Univ. New York; called to Irish Bar 1971; mem. Midland Circuit 1971–91; called to Inner Bar 1987; Bencher, King's Inns 1991–; Judge, High Court 1991–92, Supreme Court 1992–, Chief Justice 2011–; Pro-Chancellor Univ. of Dublin Trinity Coll. 1996–2010; Chair. Working Group on a Courts Comm. 1995–98, Chair. Courts Service 2001–04; Chair. Family Law Devt Cttee 1999–2001, Finance Cttee 2001–04; mem. Courts Service Bd 2004–08; Chair. Irish Sentencing Information System 2006–; Chair. Comm. on Court Practice and Procedures, Cttee on Videoconferencing, Working Group on Court of Appeal 2006–09; Chair. Courts Service 2011–, Finance Cttee 2011–, Cttee for Judicial

Studies 2011–, Judicial Appointments Advisory Bd 2011–, Superior Court Rules Cttee 2011–, Working Group for Renewal 2013–, Cttee on Judicial Induction and Mentoring 2012–, Courts Centenary Commemoration Cttee 2013–, Interim Judicial Council 2011–; Gov. of Marsh's Library, Dublin 2011–; Vice-Pres. Network of Presidents of the Supreme Judicial Courts of the EU, Asscn of Supreme Court Presidents and Chief Justices of EU Member States 2011–; Founding mem. European Network of Councils for the Judiciary; mem. ENCJ Steering Comm. 2004–07, Presidential Comm. of Ireland 2011–, Council of State of Ireland 2011–; Hon. Bencher, Middle Temple 2005; Hon. LLD (Queen's Univ., Belfast) 2002, (University of Ulster) 2013; Distinguished Fellowship Award, Griffith Coll., Dublin 2013. *Leisure interests:* Connemara ponies, gardens, reading. *Address:* Office of the Chief Justice, The Supreme Court, The Four Courts, Inns Quay, Dublin 7, Ireland (office). *Telephone:* (1) 8886540 (office). *E-mail:* supremecourt@courts.ie (office). *Website:* www.supremecourt.ie (office).

DENHARDT, David (Dave) Tilton, PhD, FRSC; American biologist and academic (retd); *Professor Emeritus of Cell Biology, Rutgers University;* b. 25 Feb. 1939, Sacramento, Calif.; s. of David B. Denhardt and Edith E. Tilton; m. Georgetta Louise Harrar 1961; one s. two d.; ed Swarthmore Coll., Pa and California Inst. of Tech., Pasadena; Instructor, Biology Dept, Harvard Univ. 1964–66, Asst Prof. 1966–70; Assoc. Prof. of Biochemistry Dept, McGill Univ., Montreal 1970–76, Prof. 1976–80; Dir Cancer Research Lab. and Prof. of Biochemistry, Microbiology and Immunology, Univ. of Western Ontario 1980–88; Chair. Biological Sciences, Rutgers Univ., NJ 1988–95, Dir Bureau of Biological Research 1988–95, Prof. of Biological Sciences 1988–2010, Prof. Emer. of Cell Biology 2010–, Chair. Biology Dept 1988–95; Ed. Journal of Virology 1977–87, GENE 1985–93, Experimental Cell Research 1994–2004; Assoc. Ed. Journal of Cell Biochemistry 1994–; mem. numerous bds; Fellow, American Acad. of Microbiology 1993. *Leisure interests:* travel, reading, canoeing, skiing, camping. *Address:* A301A Nelson Labs, Rutgers University, 604 Allison Road, Piscataway, NJ 08854-6999, USA (office). *Telephone:* (908) 704-0279 (home). *Fax:* (908) 704-0279 (home). *E-mail:* denhardt@biology.rutgers.edu (office). *Website:* lifesci.rutgers.edu/~denhardt/lab.html (office).

DENHOLM, Sir Ian (John Ferguson), Kt, CBE, JP, DL; British shipowner; b. 8 May 1927, Glasgow, Scotland; s. of Sir William Denholm and Lady Denholm (née Ferguson); m. Elizabeth Murray Stephen 1952; two s. two d.; ed Loretto School, Midlothian; Chair. Denholm Group of Companies 1974–98; Deputy Chair. P & O Steam Navigation Co. 1980–83; Pres. Chamber of Shipping of UK 1973–74; Chair. North of England Protecting & Indemnity Asscn 1976–78, Murray Group Investments Trusts 1985–93, Dir P & O 1974–83, Fleming Mercantile Investment Trust PLC 1984–94; Murray Man. Ltd 1985–92; Pres. Gen. Council of British Shipping 1988–89, BIFA 1990–91, BIMCO 1991–93; mem. Nat. Ports Council 1974–77, Scottish Transport Group 1975–82, London Bd of Bank of Scotland 1982–91, West of Scotland Bd of Bank of Scotland 1991–95; DL Renfrewshire 1980; Hon. Norwegian Consul in Glasgow 1975–97. *Leisure interest:* fishing. *Address:* Auchtertorr, Armadale Road, Rhu, Dunbartonshire, G84 8LG, Scotland. *Telephone:* (1436) 820333.

DENIS, Claire; French film director, writer and academic; *Professor of Film, European Graduate School;* b. 21 April 1948, Paris; ed Institut des Hautes Études Cinématographiques (now Ecole Nationale Supérieure des Métiers de l'Image et du Son); raised in colonial Africa (Burkina Faso, Somalia, Senegal and Cameroon), where her father was a French colonial administrator; following graduation, worked as an asst dir to Dušan Makavejev, Costa Gavras, Jacques Rivette, Jim Jarmusch and Wim Wenders; film debut with Chocolat 1988, a non-biographical account of post-colonialism; Prof. of Film, European Grad. School, Saas-Fee, Switzerland 2002–, also conducts an Intensive Summer Seminar; mem. jury, Venice Film Festival 2005. *Films include:* acted in: Mais où et donc Ornicar 1979, En avoir (ou pas) 1995, Le jour de Noël (short) 1998, Venus Beauty Salon 1999; directed: Chocolat (also writer) 1988, Man No Run (documentary) 1989, S'en fout la mort (also writer) 1990, Keep It for Yourself (short) (also writer) 1991, Contre l'oubli (segment 'Pour Ushari Ahmed Mahmoud, Soudan') 1991, Boom-Boom 1994, J'ai pas sommeil (also screenplay) 1994, À propos de Nice, la suite (segment 'Nice, Very Nice') 1995, Nénette et Boni (also writer) 1996, Beau travail (also writer) 1999, Trouble Every Day (also writer) 2001, Friday Night (also writer) 2002, Ten Minutes Older: The Cello (segment 'Vers Nancy') (also writer) 2002, The Intruder (also writer) 2004, Vers Mathilde (documentary) 2005, 35 Shots of Rum (also scenario) 2008, White Material (also scenario) 2009; writer: El Medina 1999. *Television includes:* Cinéma, de notre temps (series documentary) (Jacques Rivette – Le veilleur) 1990, Monologues (series short) (also writer; La robe à cerceau) 1993, Tous les garçons et les filles de leur âge . . . (series) (also writer) (US Go Home) 1994. *Address:* Media and Communication Division, European Graduate School, Alter Kehr 20, 3953 Leuk-Stadt, Switzerland (office). *Telephone:* (27) 4749917 (office). *Fax:* (27) 4749969 (office). *Website:* www.egs.edu/faculty/claire-denis/biography (office).

DENIS, Paul; Haitian politician; fmr mem. Democratic Convergence of Haiti; mem. Sénat 1995–99; mem. Tripartite Council (apptd following coup) 2004; Head, comm. of inquiry into misuse of public funds 2005; Leader, Organisation du Peuple en Lutte (OPL), unsuccessful OPL cand. for Pres. of Haiti 2006; Adviser to Pres. René Préval 2009; Minister of Justice and Public Security 2009–11 (resgnd). *Address:* c/o Ministry of Justice and Public Security, ave Charles Sumner 19, Port-au-Prince, Haiti (office).

DENISOV, Andrei Ivanovich; Russian politician and diplomatist; *First Deputy Minister of Foreign Affairs;* b. 3 Oct. 1952, Kharkov, Ukraine; m. Natalya Denisova; one d.; ed Moscow Inst. of Int. Relations; joined Ministry of Foreign Affairs 1992, various diplomatic posts in ministry and abroad, Dir Dept of Econ. Co-operation 1997–2000, Deputy Minister of Foreign Affairs responsible for int. econ. co-operation 2001–04; Amb. to Egypt 2000–01; Perm. Rep. to UN 2004–06; First Deputy Minister of Foreign Affairs 2006–. *Address:* Ministry of Foreign Affairs, 119200 Moscow, Smolenskaya-Sennaya pl. 32/34, Russian Federation (office). *Telephone:* (495) 244-16-06 (office). *Fax:* (495) 230-21-30 (office). *E-mail:* ministry@mid.ru (office). *Website:* www.mid.ru (office).

DENISSE, François-Jean; French astronomer; b. 16 May 1915, Saint-Quentin, Aisne; s. of Jean Julien Denisse and Marie Nicolas; m. Myriam Girondot 1948; two

d.; ed Ecole Normale Supérieure; teacher, Lycée, Dakar 1942–45; Attaché at CNRS 1946–47; Guest Worker, Nat. Bureau of Standards, USA 1948–49; Head of Research of CNRS at Ecole Normale Supérieure 1950–51, Dir of Studies, Inst. des Hautes Etudes, Dakar 1952–53; Asst Astronomer, Paris Observatory 1954–56, Astronomer 1956–63, Dir 1963–68; Chair. of Bd of Nat. Space Research Centre 1968–73; Dir Institut Nat. d'Astronomie et de Géophysique 1968–71; Pres. Bureau des Longitudes 1974–75; mem. Atomic Energy Comm. 1970–75, Head of Research at the Ministry of Univs 1976–81; Pres. Council of the European Southern Observatory 1977–81; Pres. Cttee for Space Research (COSPAR) 1978–82; mem. Acad. des Sciences 1967, Int. Acad. of Astronautics 1968–, Royal Astronomical Soc.; Commdr, Légion d'honneur, Commdr, Ordre national du Mérite. *Leisure interest:* golf. *Address:* 48 rue Monsieur Le Prince, 75006 Paris, France (home). *Telephone:* 1-43-29-48-74.

DENKTAŞ, Serdar; Turkish Cypriot politician; *Leader, Demokrat Parti;* b. 1959, Lefkoşa; s. of Rauf Denktaş; m.; three c.; ed Cardiff Coll., UK; est. Turkish Students Asscn of Cardiff Coll., N Cyprus Cultural Asscn 1986, Young Businessman Asscn 1989; Dir-Gen. Cyprus Credit Bank –1990; elected mem. 'Turkish Repub. of Northern Cyprus' Parl. for Lefkoşa 1990; Minister of Interior, Rural Affairs and Environment 1990–92; Dist Chair. for Lefkoşa, then Sec.-Gen. Demokrat Parti (fmrly Nine Movt) 1992–93, Leader 1996–2000, 2002–; elected mem. Parl. for Lefkoşa 1993; Minister of Youth and Sports 1994–95, of Tourism and Environment 2001–03; Deputy Prime Minister and Minister of Foreign Affairs 2003–06. *Address:* Demokrat Parti, Hasane Ilgaz Sok. 13a, Lefkoşa (Nicosia), Mersin 10, Turkey. *Telephone:* 2283795 (office). *Fax:* 2287130 (office). *E-mail:* yenidem@kktc.net (office). *Website:* www.demokratparti.net (home).

DENNARD, Robert (Bob) Heath, BS, MS, PhD; American electronic engineer; *IBM Fellow Emeritus, IBM Research Division;* b. 5 Sept. 1932, Terrell, Tex.; s. of Buford Dennard and Loma Dennard; m. Jane Bridges; ed Southern Methodist Univ., Carnegie Inst. of Tech. (now Carnegie Mellon Univ.); began career with IBM 1958, mem. research team on six-transistor memory cell, invented one-transistor dynamic random access memory (DRAM) 1967 and contrib. to MOS transistor scaling theory 1972, currently IBM Fellow Emer., IBM Research Div., Yorktown Heights, NY; mem. Nat. Acad. of Eng, American Philosophical Soc.; Fellow, IEEE; Hon. Dr of Science and Tech. (Carnegie Mellon Univ.) 2010; Nat. Medal of Tech. 1988, Industrial Research Inst. Achievement Award 1989, Harvey Prize, Technion, Israel 1990, inducted into Nat. Inventors Hall of Fame 1997, IEEE Edison Medal 2001, Aachener and Münchener Award for Tech. and Applied Natural Sciences 2001, Lifetime Achievement Award, Lemelson-MIT 2005, C&C Prize 2006, Benjamin Franklin Medal in Electrical Eng, The Franklin Inst. 2007, Charles Stark Draper Prize, Nat. Acad. of Eng 2009, IEEE Medal of Honor 2009, Kyoto Prize (co-recipient) 2013. *Achievements:* invention of the DRAM (Dynamic Random Access Memory) cell and contrib. to MOSFET scaling principles. *Publications:* Design of Ion-Implanted MOSFETs with Very Small Physical Dimensions 1974; more than 100 scientific papers; 64 US patents in semiconductors and microelectronics since 1965. *Leisure interests:* choral singing, Scottish country dancing. *Address:* Thomas J. Watson Research Center, PO Box 218, Yorktown Heights, NY 10598, USA (office). *Telephone:* (914) 945-1371 (office). *E-mail:* dennard@us.ibm.com (office). *Website:* researcher.ibm.com/researcher/view.php?person=us-dennard (office).

DENNEHY, Brian; American actor, producer and director; b. (Brian Manion Dennehy), 9 July 1938, Bridgeport, Conn.; m. 2nd Jennifer Dennehy; three c. from previous m.; ed Chaminade High School, Columbia and Yale Univs; served with US Marine Corps for five years; numerous stage appearances. *Films include:* Looking for Mr. Goodbar 1977, Semi-Tough 1977, F.I.S.T 1978, Foul Play 1978, Butch and Sundance: The Early Days 1979, 10 1979, Little Miss Marker 1980, Split Image 1982, First Blood 1982, Never Cry Wolf 1983, Gorky Park 1983, Finders Keepers 1984, The River Rat 1984, Cocoon 1985, Silverado 1985, Twice in a Lifetime 1985, F/X 1986, The Cheque Is in the Post 1986, Legal Eagles 1986, The Belly of an Architect 1987, Best Seller 1987, The Man from Snowy River II 1988, Miles from Home 1988, Cocoon: The Return (uncredited) 1988, Indio 1989, Seven Minutes 1989, Blue Heat 1990, Presumed Innocent 1990, F/X2 1991, Gladiator 1992, Tommy Boy 1995, The Stars Fell on Henrietta 1995, Romeo + Juliet 1996, Out of the Cold 1999, Silicon Towers 1999, Dish Dogs (video) 2000, Summer Catch 2001, Stolen Summer 2002, She Hate Me 2004, Assault on Precinct 13 2005, 10th & Wolf 2006, Everyone's Hero (voice) 2006, Ratatouille (voice) 2007, Welcome to Paradise 2007, War Eagle, Arkansas 2007, Cat City 2008, Righteous Kill 2008, Alleged 2010, Every Day 2010, Meet Monica Velour 2010, The Next Three Days 2010, The Big Year 2011, Twelfth Night 2012. *Television includes:* Kojak (series) 1977, Serpico (series) 1977, Johnny, We Hardly Knew Ye (film) 1977, Lanigan's Rabbi (series) 1977, M*A*S*H (series) 1977, Lucan (series) 1977, The Fitzpatricks (series) 1977, Lou Grant (series) 1977, It Happened at Lakewood Manor (film) 1977, The Tony Randall Show (series) 1978, Ruby and Oswald (film) 1978, A Death in Canaan (film) 1978, Dallas (series) 1978, Pearl (mini-series) 1978, A Real American Hero (film) 1978, Silent Victory: The Kitty O'Neil Story (film) 1979, The Jericho Mile (film) 1979, Dummy (film) 1979, Big Shamus, Little Shamus (series) 1979, The Seduction of Miss Leona (film) 1980, A Rumor of War (film) 1980, Knots Landing (series) 1980, Fly Away Home Dynasty (series) 1981, Once They Marched Through a Thousand Towns (film) 1981, Darkroom (series) 1981, Star of the Family (series) 1982, I Take These Men (film) 1983, Blood Feud (film) 1983, Cagney & Lacey (series) 1984, Pigs vs. Freaks (film) 1984, Hunter (series) 1984, The Ferret (film) 1985, The Last Place on Earth (mini-series) 1985, Evergreen (mini-series) 1985, Tall Tales & Legends (series) – Annie Oakley 1985, Acceptable Risks (film) 1986, Faerie Tale Theatre (series) – The Little Mermaid (narrator) 1987, Miami Vice (series) 1987, The Lion of Africa (film) 1988, Das Rattennest (film) 1988, Day One (film) 1989, Perfect Witness (film) 1989, Pride and Extreme Prejudice (film) 1990, Evidence of Love (film) 1990, Rising Son (film) 1990, In Broad Daylight (film) 1991, The Burden of Proof (film) 1992, To Catch a Killer (film) 1992, The Diamond Fleece (film) 1992, Teamster Boss: The Jackie Presser Story (film) 1992, Deadly Matrimony (film) 1992, Foreign Affairs (film) 1993, Murder in the Heartland (film) 1993, Prophet of Evil: The Ervil LeBaron Story (film) 1993, Final Appeal (film) 1993, Jack Reed: Badge of Honor (film) 1993, Birdland (series) 1994, Leave of Absence (film) 1994, Jack Reed: A Search for Justice (film) 1994, Midnight Movie (film) 1994, Deadly Justice (film) 1995, Shadow of a Doubt (film) 1995, Jack Reed: A Killer Among Us (film) 1996, A Season in Purgatory (film) 1996, Dead Man's Walk (mini-series) 1996, Undue Influence (film) 1996, Jack Reed: Death and Vengeance (film) 1996, Nostromo (mini-series) 1997, Indefensible: The Truth About Edward Brannigan (film) 1997, Thanks of a Grateful Nation (film) 1998, Voyage of Terror (film) 1998, NetForce (film) 1999, Too Rich: The Secret Life of Doris Duke (film) 1999, Sirens (film) 1999, Death of a Salesman (film) (Tony Award for Best Actor in a Drama) 2000, The American Experience (series documentary) – The Duel (voice) 2000, Fail Safe (film) 2000, Warden of Red Rock (film) 2001, The Fighting Fitzgeralds (series) 2001, Night Visions (series) 2001, Three Blind Mice (film) 2001, Great Performances (series) – Making 'The Misfits' (narrator) 2002, – The Girls in Their Summer Dresses and Other Stories 1981, A Season on the Brink (film) 2002, The Crooked E: The Unshredded Truth About Enron (film) 2003, The Agency (series) 2003, The Roman Spring of Mrs. Stone (film) 2003, Just Shoot Me! (series) 1998–2003, Behind the Camera: The Unauthorized Story of 'Three's Company' (film) 2003, Category 6: Day of Destruction (film) 2004, The Exonerated (film) 2005, The West Wing (series) 2005, Our Fathers (film) 2005, The 4400 (series) 2006, Law & Order: Special Victims Unit (series) – Scheherazade 2007, The Ultimate Gift 2006, Marco Polo (film) 2007, Masters of Science Fiction (mini-series) – The Discarded 2007, 30 Rock (series) 2008, Bunker Hill (film) 2009, Rules of Engagement (series) 2009, Rizzoli & Isles (series) 2010. *Address:* c/o Susan Smith and Associates, 121 North San Vicente Blvd, Beverly Hills, CA 90211, USA (office). *Telephone:* (213) 852-4777 (office).

DENNER, Volkmar, Dr rer. nat; German business executive; *Chairman of the Board of Management, Robert Bosch GmbH;* b. 30 Nov. 1956, Uhingen; m.; three c.; ed Univ. of Stuttgart; has held several positions in Bosch Group including in Semiconductors and Electronic Control Units Div. 1986–89, Dept Head in Power Semiconductor Tech. Devt 1989–91, Dept Head in Integrated Circuit Devt 1991–94, Dir of Sales, ECU Devt, and Systems Application, Gasoline Engine Man. Div. 1994–98, Dir Engine ECU Devt 1998–2003, Product Man. for Engine ECUs 2000–03, Exec. Vice-Pres., Sales and Devt, Pres. Semiconductors and Electronic Control Units Div., Automotive Electronics Div. 2003–12, mem. Bd of Man., Robert Bosch GmbH 2006–, Chair. Bd of Man. 2012–. *Address:* Robert Bosch GmbH, Postfach 106050, 70049 Stuttgart, Germany (office). *Telephone:* (711) 811-0 (office). *Fax:* (711) 8116630 (office). *E-mail:* info@bosch.com (office). *Website:* www .bosch.com (office).

DENNETT, Daniel Clement, BA, DPhil; American philosopher, academic and author; *University Professor, Austin B. Fletcher Professor of Philosophy and Co-Director, Center for Cognitive Studies, Tufts University;* b. 28 March 1942, Boston, Mass; s. of Daniel C. Dennett, Jr and Ruth M. Leck; m. Susan Bell 1962; one s. one d.; ed Phillips Exeter Acad., Wesleyan Univ., Harvard Univ., Univ. of Oxford; Asst Prof. of Philosophy, Univ. of California, Irvine 1965–70, Assoc. Prof. 1971; Assoc. Prof., Tufts Univ. 1971–75, Prof. 1975–85, Distinguished Arts and Sciences Prof. 1985–2000, Co-Dir Center for Cognitive Studies 1985–, Univ. Prof. 2000–, also Austin B. Fletcher Prof. of Philosophy; Visiting Prof., Harvard 1973–74, Pittsburgh 1975, Oxford 1979, Ecole Normale Supérieure, Paris 1985, Dept of Philosophy, Auburn Univ. 2011; Visiting Fellow, All Souls Coll., Oxford 1979; Writer-in-Residence, Bellagio Study and Conf. Centre, Italy 1990, 2001; Fellow, Center for Advanced Study in Behavioral Sciences 1979, American Acad. of Arts and Sciences 1987, Zentrum für Interdisziplinäre Forschung, Bielefeld, Germany 1990; Visiting Erskine Fellow, Univ. of Canterbury, Christchurch, NZ 1995; Distinguished Fellow, Centre for the Mind, Inst. for Advanced Study, ANU, Canberra 1998, Collegium Budapest, Hungary 2002; Fellow, SAGE Center, Univ. of California, Santa Barbara 2008; William Miller Fellow, Santa Fe Inst., NM 2010; Fellow, AAAS 2009; Hon. DHumLitt (Connecticut) 2003; Hon. DLitt (Edinburgh) 2007; Hon. DSc (McGill) 2007, (Bucharest) 2007; Dr hc (Amsterdam) 2012; Woodrow Wilson Fellow 1963, Guggenheim Fellow 1973, 1986, Santayana Fellowship, Harvard Univ. (hon.) 1974, Nat. Endowment for the Humanities Younger Humanist Fellowship 1974, Fulbright Fellow 1978, John Locke Lecturer, Oxford 1983, Gavin David Young Lecturer, Adelaide, Australia 1984, Jean Nicod Lecturer, Institut Nicod, Paris 2001, Daewoo Lecturer, Seoul, S Korea 2002, Petrus Hispanus Lecturer, Faculdade de Letras de Lisboa, Lisbon 2004, Patten Lecturer, Indiana Univ. 2006, Distinguished Fellow Award, Cognitive Science Soc. 2009, Erasmus Prize 2012. *Publications:* Content and Consciousness 1969, Brainstorms 1978, The Mind's I (with Douglas Hofstadter) 1981, Elbow Room 1984, The Intentional Stance 1987, Consciousness Explained 1991, Darwin's Dangerous Idea 1995, Kinds of Minds 1996, Brainchildren 1998, Freedom Evolves 2003, Breaking the Spell: Religion as a Natural Phenomenon 2006, Dove nascono le idée (translated by Francesca Garofoli) 2006, Science and Religion: Are They Compatible? (with Alvin Plantinga) 2011, Inside Jokes: Using Humor to Reverse-Engineer the Mind (with Matthew Hurley and Reginald B. Adams, Jr) 2011; numerous articles in professional journals. *Leisure interests:* sculpture, farming, cider-making, sailing, choral singing. *Address:* Center for Cognitive Studies, Tufts University, Medford, MA 02155-7059, USA (office). *Telephone:* (617) 627-3297 (office). *Fax:* (617) 627-3952 (office). *E-mail:* daniel.dennett@tufts.edu (office). *Website:* ase.tufts.edu/cogstud/incbios/dennettd/dennettdcv.htm (office).

DENNIS, Bengt, MA; Swedish banker; *Managing Director, Bengt Dennis Consulting AB;* b. 5 Jan. 1930, Grengesberg; m. Turid Stroem 1962; one s. one d.; ed Columbia Univ., New York, USA; econ. journalist 1959–67; Head of Dept, Ministry of Finance 1967–70; Under-Sec. of State, Ministry of Commerce 1970–76; Amb., Ministry of Foreign Affairs 1977–80; Ed.-in-Chief, Dagens Nyheter 1981–82; Gov. Cen. Bank of Sweden 1982–92; Chair. BIS 1990–93; Sr Adviser, Skandinaviska Enskilda Banken 1994–2001; Man. Dir Bengt Dennis Consulting AB 2002–. *Leisure interests:* sailing, skiing, skating. *Address:* Maria Sandels gränd 3, 112 69 Stockholm, Sweden (home). *Telephone:* 70-258-10-20 (mobile) (office); (8) 651-04-32 (home). *Fax:* (8) 505-88-529 (office). *E-mail:* bengt.dennis@bdco.biz (office).

DENNISON, Lisa, MA; American auction house executive and fmr art museum director; *Chairman, North and South America, Sotheby's;* m. Roderick Waywell 1983; two s.; ed Wellesley Coll., Brown Univ.; curatorial internships at Guggenheim Museum 1973, Fogg Art Museum, Harvard Univ. 1974–76, Museum of Fine Arts, Boston 1977–78; Exhbn Coordinator, Solomon R. Guggenheim Museum, New York 1978–81, Asst Curator 1981–90, Assoc. Curator 1990–91, Collections Curator 1991–94, Curator of Collections and Exhbns 1994–96, Deputy

Dir and Chief Curator 1996–2005, Dir and Chief Curator 2005–07, played key role in building Museum's perm. collections in New York and Bilbao, Spain; Chair. North and South America, Sotheby's, New York 2007–; fmr mem. Bd of Dirs American Assen of Museum Curators, Byrd-Hoffman Foundation; Founding mem. Creative Arts Advisory Bd, Brown Univ.; mem. New York Cttee, Wellesley Coll. Friends of Art, Nat. Advisory Council, Visual Arts, Wake Forest Univ., Int. Advisory Bd Louise T. Blouin Foundation; mem. ArtTable. *Publications:* numerous essays in exhbn catalogues. *Address:* Sotheby's, 1334 York Avenue at 72nd Street, New York, NY 10021, USA (office). *Telephone:* (212) 894-1424 (office). *Fax:* (212) 606-7105 (office). *E-mail:* lisa.dennison@sothebys.com (office). *Website:* www .sothebys.com (office).

DENNISS, Tom, PhD; Australian oceanographer, mathematician and business executive; *Executive Director and Chief Technology Officer, Oceanlinx Ltd;* fmr Lecturer in Math. and Oceanography, Univ. of New South Wales; spent five years in an investment bank; Founder and CEO Energetech Australia Pty Ltd (now called Oceanlinx Ltd) 1997–2006, Exec. Dir and Chief Tech. Officer 2006–; contrib. to marine tech. industry over many years through both academia and industry confs and cttees world-wide; several awards for pioneering work in wave power. *Address:* Oceanlinx Ltd, PO Box 116, Botany, NSW 1455, Australia (office). *Telephone:* (2) 9549-6300 (office). *Fax:* (2) 9549-6399 (office). *E-mail:* tom.denniss@ oceanlinx.com (office). *Website:* www.oceanlinx.com (office).

DENNY, Robyn (Edward M. F.), ARCA; British artist; b. 3 Oct. 1930, Abinger, Surrey, England; s. of Sir Henry Denny, Bt and Joan, Lady Denny; m. 1st Anna Teasdale (divorced); m. 2nd Marjorie Abéla; two s. one d.; ed Clayesmore School, Dorset, St Martin's School of Art and Royal Coll. of Art, London; first solo exhbns in London at Gallery One and Gimpel Fils 1958; has since given solo exhbns throughout Europe and USA; retrospective exhbn, Tate Gallery, London 1973; has represented UK at Biennales in Paris, Tokyo, Milan, Brussels, USA and Australia and at 33rd Venice Biennale; works in numerous public collections; has received many public commissions for site specific works; teaching assignments have included Slade School, Univ. of London and Minnesota Inst. of Fine Art; fmr adviser, Arts Council of GB, Inst. of Contemporary Arts, London; several awards and prizes. *Publications:* articles and criticism in int. publs.

DENOIX DE SAINT MARC, Renaud; French lawyer and civil servant; *Member, Conseil Constitutionnel;* b. 24 Sept. 1938, Boulogne-sur-Seine; s. of Henri Denoix de Saint Marc and Marie du Cheyron du Pavillon; m. Marie-Christine de Buchère de l'Epinois 1964; two c.; ed Ecole nationale d'admin, Institut d'études politiques de Paris; Auditor, Conseil d'État 1964, Maître des requêtes 1972, Govt Comm. Ass. of Conseil d'État 1974–78, 1983–86; Deputy Dir of Cabinet, Minister of Justice Alain Peyrefitte 1978–79; Dir of Civil Affairs and Seal 1979–82; State Councillor 1985; Secrétaire général du Gouvernement 1986–95; Vice-Pres. Conseil d'État 2005–06 (retd); mem. Acad. des sciences morales et politiques 2005, Conseil Constitutionnel 2007–, Acad. Nationale de Medecine 2009; Grand Croix de la Légion d'honneur 2008; Chevalier, Ordre nat. du Mérite, du Mérite agricole, des Palmes académiques; Croix de la Valeur militaire; Prix Edouard Bonnefous 2001. *Publications:* Leçons de droit public 1989, Le service public 1996, L'Etat 2004, Histoire de la loi 2008. *Address:* Conseil Constitutionnel, 2 rue de Montpensier, 75001 Paris (office); 1 rue du Capitaine Scott, 75015 Paris, France (home). *Telephone:* 1-40-15-30-00 (office); 1-45-48-75-67 (home). *Fax:* 1-40-20-93-27 (office). *E-mail:* relations-exterieures@conseil-constitutionnel.fr (office). *Website:* www .conseil-constitutionnel.fr (office).

DENT ZELEDÓN, Alberto; Costa Rican politician and banker; b. 11 Dec. 1945; m.; four c.; ed Calif. State Polytech. Univ., USA; Gen. Man. Dent and Sons Ltd 1973–84; Pres. Banex Bank Ltd 1980–84; Exec. Pres. BFA Financial Group 1984–96; Dir Costa Rican Bankers' Assen 1985–96, Pres. 1986–90; Adviser to Pres. of Costa Rica 1998–2000; Vice-Pres. Cen. Bank of Costa Rica 1998–2000; Minister of Agric. and Livestock 2000–01; Minister of Finance 2001–02, 2003–04 (resgnd); Pres. Consejo Nacional de Supervisión del Sistema Financiero (CONASSIF, financial system supervision council) April–July 2003, 2006–08. *Address:* c/o CONASSIF, Avda. Primera Edificio Banco Central, Piso 8, San José, Costa Rica.

DENTON, Charles Henry, BA, FRSA, FRTS; British television executive; b. 20 Dec. 1937; s. of Alan Charles Denton and Mary Frances Royle; m. Eleanor Mary Player 1961; one s. two d.; ed Reading School and Univ. of Bristol; worked as deckhand 1960; trainee advertising 1961–63; with BBC 1963–68; freelance TV producer Granada, ATV and Yorkshire TV cos 1969–70; Dir Tempest Films Ltd 1969–71; Man. Dir Black Lion Films 1979–81; Head of Documentaries ATV 1974–77, Controller of Programmes 1977–81; Dir of Programmes Cen. Ind. TV 1981–84; Dir Cen. Ind. Television PLC 1981–87; founder and Chief Exec. Zenith Productions 1984–93, Chair. Zenith North Ltd 1988–93; Head of Drama BBC 1993–96; Chair. Action Time Ltd 1988–93, Producers' Alliance for Cinema and TV (PACT) 1991–1993, Cornwall Film 2001; Gov. BFI 1992–99; mem. Arts Council of England 1996–98; mem. Bd Film Council 1999–2002; Fellow, Royal TV Soc., Royal Soc. of Arts. *Leisure interests:* walking, music.

DENTON, Derek Ashworth, AC, MB, BS, FRS, FAA, FRACP, FRCP; Australian research physiologist; *Honorary Professor of Physiology, University of Melbourne;* b. 27 May 1924, Launceston, Tasmania; s. of A. A. Denton; m. Margaret Scott 1953; two s.; ed Launceston Grammar School and Univ. of Melbourne; Haley Research Fellow, Walter & Eliza Hall Inst. of Medical Research 1948; Overseas Nat. Health and Medical Research Council (NH & MRC) Fellow, Cambridge 1952–53; Medical Research Fellow, later Sr Medical Research Fellow, Nat. Health and Medical Research Council 1949–63, Prin. Research Fellow, Admin. Head and Chief Scientist 1964–70; Dir and originating Bd mem. Howard Florey Inst. of Experimental Physiology and Medicine 1971–89, Emer. Dir 1990–; Visiting Prof., British Heart Foundation and Balliol Coll., Oxford, UK; Adjunct Scientist, Southwest Foundation for Biomedical Research, San Antonio, Tex., USA; Dir The David Syme Co. Ltd 1984–, Australian Ballet Foundation 1983–, Sydney Dance Co. 1994–; First Vice-Pres. Int. Union of Physiological Sciences 1983–89, Chair. Nominating Cttee of Council 1986–89, Chair. Cttee to Review Comms 1986–95; mem. Jury of Basic and Clinical Medical Awards, Albert and Mary Lasker Foundation 1979–89; OECD Examiner of Science and Tech. Policy of Govt of Sweden; Foreign Medical mem. Royal Swedish Acad. of Sciences; Foreign Assoc. NAS 1995, Acad. des Sciences 2000, Inst. of France 2000; Hon. Foreign Fellow,

American Acad. of Arts and Sciences 1986; Hon. Foreign mem. American Physiology Soc. 1987; Hon. Prof. of Physiology, Florey Neuroscience and Mental Health Insts, Univ. of Melbourne; Centenary Medal 2001; Hon. LLD (Melbourne) 2006. *Publications:* The Hunger for Salt 1982, The Pinnacle of Life 1993, Primordial Emotions: The Dawning of Consciousness 2006; 400 articles and reviews. *Leisure interests:* tennis, fishing, ballet, music, wine. *Address:* Office of the Dean, Faculty of Medicine, Dentistry and Health Sciences, University of Melbourne, 766 Elizabeth Street, Melbourne, Vic. 3010 (office); 816 Orrong Road, Toorak, Vic. 3142, Australia (home). *Telephone:* (3) 8344-5639 (office); (3) 9827-2640 (home). *Fax:* (3) 9347-0846 (office); (3) 9826-5457 (home). *E-mail:* ddenton@unimelb.edu.au (home).

DENTON, Frank Trevor, MA, FRSC; Canadian economist and academic; *Professor Emeritus of Economics, McMaster University;* b. 27 Oct. 1930, Toronto, Ont.; s. of Frank W. Denton and Kathleen M. Davies; m. 1st Marilyn J. Shipp 1953 (died 2002); three s. one d.; m. 2nd Helen R. Evans 2003; ed Univ. of Toronto; economist, Prov. Govt of Ont. 1953–54, Fed. Govt of Canada 1954–59, 1961–64, Philips Electronics Industries Ltd 1959–60, Senate of Canada Cttee staff 1960–61; Dir of Econometrics, Dominion Bureau of Statistics 1964–68; Consultant, Econ. Council of Canada 1964–68; Prof. of Econs, McMaster Univ. 1968–96, Prof. Emer. 1996–; Dir McMaster Program for Quantitative Studies in Econs and Population 1981–96; various other consulting appointments; Fellow, American Statistical Asscn; Hon. LLD (McMaster) 2008. *Publications:* Growth of Manpower in Canada 1970; co-author: Population and the Economy 1975, Working-Life Tables for Canadian Males 1969, Historical Estimates of the Canadian Labour Force 1967, The Short-Run Dynamics of the Canadian Labour Market 1976, Unemployment and Labour Force Behaviour of Young People: Evidence from Canada and Ontario 1980, Pensions and the Economic Security of the Elderly 1981, Independence and Economic Security in Old Age (co-ed.) 2000; numerous monographs, articles, technical papers in economics, statistics, demography. *Address:* Department of Economics, KTH 413, McMaster University, Hamilton, ON L8S 4M4 (office); 23 Pelham Drive, Ancaster, ON L9K 1L4, Canada (home). *Telephone:* (905) 525-9140 (ext. 23820) (office); (905) 304-9395 (home). *E-mail:* dentonf@mcmaster.ca (office). *Website:* www.economics.mcmaster.ca (office).

DENTON, Richard Michael, MA, PhD, DSc, FMedSci, FRS; British biochemist and academic; b. 16 Oct. 1941, Sutton Coldfield; s. of the late Arthur Benjamin Denton and Eileen Mary Denton (née Evans); m. Janet Mary Jones 1965; one s. two d.; ed Wycliffe Coll., Stonehouse, Glos., Christ's Coll., Cambridge; Lecturer in Biochemistry, Univ. of Bristol 1973–78, Reader 1978–87, Prof. (Personal Chair) 1987–2010, Head of Biochemistry Dept 1995–2000, Chair. Medical Sciences 2000–04, Dean of Medical and Veterinary Sciences 2003–04; MRC Research Fellowship 1984–88, mem. Council MRC 1999–2004, Chair. MRC Training and Career Devt Bd 2002–04; Founder-Fellow, Acad. of Medical Sciences 1998. *Publications:* more than 240 research papers in various int. research journals, with maj. topics the molecular basis of the control of metabolism by insulin and other hormones, and the role of calcium ions within mitochondria. *Leisure interests:* family, fell walking, keeping fit, cooking. *Address:* School of Biochemistry, Medical Sciences Building, University of Bristol, University Walk, Bristol, BS8 1TD, England (office). *Telephone:* (117) 331-2184 (office). *Fax:* (117) 331-2168 (office). *E-mail:* r.denton@bristol.ac.uk (office). *Website:* www.bch.bris.ac.uk (office).

DEOL, Abhay; Indian actor; b. 15 March 1976, Mumbai; s. of Ajit Deol and Usha Deol; f. Forbidden Films (production co.). *Films:* Socha Na Tha 2005, Ahista Ahista 2006, Honeymoon Travels Pvt Ltd 2007, Ek Chalis Ki Last Local 2007, Manorama Six Feet Under 2007 (Best Actor, MIAAC Festival, New York), Oye Lucky! Lucky Oye! 2008, Dev D 2009, Aisha 2010, Zindagi Na Milegi Dobara 2011, Shanghai 2012, Chakravyuh 2012, Raanjhanaa 2013. *Address:* Forbidden Films, B-31, Pandurang Wadi, Near Juhu Post Office, Juhu, Mumbai 400 049, India (office). *Telephone:* (22) 26184189 (office). *E-mail:* fqfilms@yahoo.com (office).

DÉON, Michel; French writer; b. 4 Aug. 1919, Paris; s. of Paul Déon and Alice de Fossey; m. Chantal d'Arc 1963; one s. one d.; ed Lycée Janson-de-Sailly and Faculty of Law, Paris; journalist with Action française, Marie-Claire 1942–56; Publr 1954; writer 1956–; mem. Acad. française 1978–, Acad. of Sciences, Portugal; Commdr, Légion d'honneur 2002, Officier des Arts et des Lettres; Dr hc (Nat. Univ. of Ireland); Prix Interallié 1970, Grand Prix du Roman 1973, Grand Prix Jean Giono 1996. *Plays:* Ma vie n'est plus un Roman, Ariane ou L'oubli. *Publications:* novels: Je ne veux jamais l'oublier 1950, La Corrida 1952, Le Dieu pâle 1954, Les trompeuses espérances 1956, Les gens de la nuit 1957, Tout l'amour du monde 1959, Un parfum de jasmin 1966, Les poneys sauvages 1970, Un taxi mauve 1973, Le jeune homme vert 1976, Mes arches de Noé 1978, Un déjeuner de soleil 1981, Louis XIV par lui-même 1983, Je vous écris d'Italie 1984, Bagages pour Vancouver 1985, La Montée du Soir, Ma Vie n'est plus un Roman (drama) 1987, Un Souvenir 1990, Le Prix de l'amour 1992, Parlons en… 1993, Ariane ou L'oubli (drama) 1992, Pages grecques (essays) 1993, Une longue amitié 1995, Je me suis beaucoup promené 1995, La Cour des Grands 1996, Madame Rose, Pages françaises 1999, Taisez-vous… J'entends venir un ange 2001, La chambre de ton père 2004, Cavalier passe ton chemin 2005. *Leisure interests:* shooting, sailing, bibliophile. *Address:* The Old Rectory, Tynagh, Co. Galway, Ireland; 5 rue Sébastien Bottin, 75007 Paris, France. *Telephone:* (90) 9745143 (Ireland). *Fax:* (90) 9745376 (Ireland). *E-mail:* chantaldeon@gmail.com (home).

DEPARDIEU, Gérard; French actor and vintner; b. (Gérard Xavier Marcel Depardieu), 27 Dec. 1948, Châteauroux (Indre); s. of René Depardieu and Alice Depardieu (née Marillier); m. Elisabeth Guignot 1970; one s. (deceased) one d.; ed Ecole communale, Cours d'art dramatique de Charles Dullin and Ecole d'art dramatique de Jean Laurent Cochet; Pres. Jury, 45th Cannes Int. Film Festival 1992; Chevalier, Ordre nat. du Mérite, Légion d'honneur, des Arts et des Lettres, Ordre Nat. du Québec 2002; Grand Prix Gérard Philippe, Jury des Grands Prix de la ville de Paris 1973, Prix ACIC (Asscn des Cadres de l'Industrie Cinématographique) for lifetime achievement 1983, Fellowship, British Film Inst. 1989, named Meilleur Acteur Etranger des années 1980–90, critique cinématographique américaine 1990, Piper-Heidseick Award, San Francisco Int. Film Festival 1994, Grand Prix Spécial des Amériques for his exceptional contrib. to cinema, Montréal World Film Festival 1995, Golden Camera (Germany) 1996, Prix Rudolph Valentino 1997, Lion d'Or for lifetime achievement, 54ème Mostra de

Venise XXIV 1997, Stanislavsky Prize, Moscow Int. Film Festival 2006, Jules Verne Award 2009, Prix Lumière 2011. *Plays include:* Boudu sauvé des eaux 1968, Les Garçons de la bande 1969, Une fille dans ma soupe 1970, Galapagos 1971, Saved 1972, Home 1972, Ismé 1973, Isaac 1973, La Chevauchée sur le lac de Constance 1974, Les Gens déraisonnables sont en voie de disparition 1977, Tartuffe (also Dir) 1983, Lily Passion 1986, Les portes du ciel 1999, Œdipus Rex 2001, Le Carnaval des animaux 2001. *Films include:* Le beatnik et le minet (short) 1967, Cry of the Cormoran 1970, Nathalie Granger (short) 1971, La vie sentimentale de Georges Le Tueur (short) 1971, Sunlight on Cold Water 1971, The Annuity 1972, Killer 1972, Nathalie Granger 1972, Hit Man 1972, At the Meeting with Joyous Death 1973, The Year 01 1973, The Dominici Affair 1973, Deux hommes dans la ville 1973, Rude journée pour la reine 1973, Les gaspards 1973, Les valseuses 1974, La femme du Gange 1974, Stavisky… 1974, Vincent, François, Paul… et les autres 1974, Maîtresse 1975, Pas si méchant que ça 1975, 7 morts sur ordonnance 1975, I Love You, I Don't 1976, The Last Woman 1976, 1900 1976, Barocco 1976, Rene the Cane 1977, The Lorry 1977, Baxter, Vera Baxter 1977, Dites-lui que je l'aime 1977, At Night All Cats Are Crazy 1977, Préparez vos mouchoirs 1978, Ciao maschio 1978, Violanta 1978, Die linkshändige Frau 1978, Le sucre 1978, L'ingorgo – Una storia impossibile 1979, Les chiens 1979, Buffet Froid 1979, Temporale Rosy 1980, My American Uncle 1980, Loulou 1980, The Last Metro 1980, Inspector Blunder 1980, Je vous aime 1980, Le choix des armes 1981, The Woman Next Door 1981, La chèvre 1981, The Return of Martin Guerre 1982, Le grand frère 1982, Danton 1983, The Moon in the Gutter 1983, Les compères 1983, Fort Saganne 1984, Le tartuffe (also dir) 1984, Rive droite, rive gauche 1984, Police 1985, A Woman or Two 1985, Tenue de soirée 1986, Jean de Florette 1986, Je hais les acteurs (uncredited) 1986, The Way Out 1986, Les fugitifs 1986, Under the Sun of Satan 1987, Strange Place for an Encounter 1988, Camille Claudel 1988, Deux 1989, Too Beautiful for You 1989, I Want to Go Home 1989, Cyrano de Bergerac 1990, Uranus 1990, Green Card 1990, 'Merci la vie' 1991, Mon père, ce héros 1991, Tous les Matins du Monde 1991, From Time to Time (short) 1992, 1492: Conquest of Paradise 1992, Oh, Woe Is Me 1993, Germinal 1993, My Father the Hero 1994, A Pure Formality 1994, Le colonel Chabert 1994, La machine 1994, Les cent et une nuits de Simon Cinéma 1995, Elisa 1995, The Horseman on the Roof (uncredited) 1995, Guardian Angels 1995, Le garçu 1995, Unhook the Stars 1996, Bogus 1996, The Secret Agent 1996, The Best Job in the World 1996, Hamlet 1996, XXL 1997, The Man in the Iron Mask, La parola amore esiste 1998, Bimboland 1998, Asterix and Obelix Take on Caesar 1999, Un pont entre deux rives (also dir) 1999, Mirka 2000, Tutto l'amore che c'è 2000, Vatel 2000, 102 Dalmatians 2000, The Envy of Gods 2000, The Closet 2001, Unfair Competition 2001, CQ 2001, Vidocq 2001, Witches to the North 2001, Asterix & Obelix: Mission Cleopatra 2002, I Am Dina 2002, A Loving Father 2002, Between Strangers 2002, City of Ghosts 2002, Blanche 2002, Le pacte du silence 2003, Crime Spree 2003, Bon voyage 2003, Nathalie… 2003, Shut Up! 2003, The Car Keys 2003, RRRrrrr!!! 2004, San Antonio 2004, New France 2004, 36 2004, Les temps qui changent 2004, La vie de Michel Muller est plus belle que la vôtre 2005, Je préfère qu'on reste amis 2005, Boudu 2005, How Much Do You Love Me? 2005, Olé! 2005, Last Holiday 2006, Paris, je t'aime (segment "Quartier Latin") 2006, Quand j'étais chanteur 2006, La vie en rose 2007, Michou d'Auber 2007, Asterix at the Olympic Games 2008, Vsyo mogut koroli 2008, Disco 2008, The Easy Way 2008, Babylon A.D. 2008, Mesrine: Killer Instinct 2008, Mesrine: Killer Instinct 2008, Bouquet final 2008, Hello, Goodbye 2008, Les enfants de Timpelbach 2008, Diamond 13 2009, In the Beginning 2009, Inspector Bellamy 2009, Coco 2009, Dumas 2010, Mammuth 2010, Glenn, the Flying Robot 2010, My Afternoons with Margueritte 2010, Potiche 2010, Pozdnyaya lyubov 2010, Je n'ai rien oublié 2010, Grenouille d'hiver (short) 2011, A Butterfly Kiss 2011, My Sinful Angel 2012, Le grand soir 2012, The Death of Ipu 2012, Life of Pi 2012, L'homme qui rit 2012, Astérix and Obélix: God Save Britannia 2012, Turf 2013, La marque des anges 2013, A Farewell to Fools 2013, Les boulistes 2013. *Television includes:* Nausicaa (film) 1970, Tango (film) 1970, Le cyborg ou Le voyage vertical (film) 1970, La pomme de son oeil (film) 1970, Rendez-vous à Badenberg (series) 1970, Les aventures de Zadig (film) 1970, Les enquêtes du commissaire Maigret (series) 1973, Un monsieur bien rangé (mini-series) 1973, Les gaspards 1974, L'inconnu (film) 1973, The Count of Monte Cristo (mini-series) 1999, Balzac (film) 1999, Les Misérables (mini-series) 2000, Bérénice (film) 2000, Napoléon (mini-series) 2002, Ruy Blas (film) 2002, Uboynaya sila (series) 2003, Volpone (film) 2003, The Lady Musketeer (film) 2004, A Cursed Monarchy (mini-series) 2005, L'abolition (film) 2008, Groland magzine (series) 2009, Le grand restaurant (film) 2010, Raspoutine (film) 2011. *Publication:* Lettres volées 1988. *Address:* c/o Bertrand De Labbey and Claire Blondel, Artmédia, 20 avenue Rapp, 75007 Paris, France (office). *Telephone:* 1-43-17-33-00 (office). *Fax:* 1-44-18-34-60 (office). *E-mail:* b.delabbey@artmedia.fr (office); c.blondel@artmedia.fr (office). *Website:* www.artmedia.fr (office).

DEPARDON, Raymond; French photographer; b. 6 July 1942, Villefranche-sur-Saône; s. of Antoine Depardon and Marthe Bernard; m. Claudine Nougaret 1987; two s.; ed primary school in Villefranche; apprentice to Louis Foucherand, Paris 1958, Asst 1959; copy then photographic reporter, Dalmas agency 1960; Co-founder Gamma agency 1967; mem. Magnum Agency, Paris and New York 1978; Artistic Dir Rencontres Int. d'Arles 2006; solo exhbn Correspondance new yorkaise, San Clemente, Paris 1984, Lausanne 1985. *Films include:* Jan Pallach, Tibesti Tou (short) 1974, Numéros zéro 1977, Reporters 1981, Faits divers: les Années déclic 1983, Empty Quarter 1985, Urgences 1987, La Captive du désert 1990, La Colline des Anges 1993, Délits flagrants 1994, Sida propos 1995, Afriques: Comment ça va avec la douleur 1995, Paris 1998, Muriel Leferle 1999, Profils paysans: l'approche 2001, Un homme sans l'Occident 2002, Quoi de neuf au Garet? 2004, Dixieme chambre - Instants d'audiences (Gold Plaque) 2004, Profils paysans: le quotidien 2005, Profils paysans: la vie moderne 2007, Le tour du monde en 14 jours 2008, Donner la parole 2008. *Publications include:* photographic albums: Tchad 1978, Notes 1979, Correspondance new yorkaise 1981, Le Désert américain 1983, San Clemente 1984, Les Fiancées de Saigon 1986, Hivers 1987, Depardon cinéma 1993, Return to Vietnam (with Jean-Claude Guillebaud) 1994, La Ferme du Garet 1995, La Porte des Larmes (with Jean-Claude Guillebaud) 1995, En Afrique 1995, Voyages 1998, Silence rompu 1998, Corse 2000, Détours (Nadar Prize) 2000, Errances 2000, Rêves de déserts 2000, À Tombeau Ouvert 2000, Désert: un Homme sans l'Occident 2002, Piemonte: Una Definizione Fotografica 2003, 06 Alpes Maritimes 2003, Paroles Prisonnières 2004, Jeux Olympiques 2004, Images politiques 2004, Paris Journal 2004, Afriques 2005, Photographies de

Personnalités Politiques 2006, La Solitude Heureuse du Voyageur 2006, Depardon-New York 2006. *Address:* Magnum, 19 rue Hégésippe Moreau, 75018 Paris (office); 18 bis rue Henri Barbusse, 75005 Paris, France (home). *Telephone:* 1-53-42-50-00 (office). *Fax:* 1-53-42-50-01 (office). *E-mail:* magnum@magnumphotos.fr (office). *Website:* www.magnumphotos.com (office).

DEPP, John (Johnny) Christopher; American actor; b. 9 June 1963, Owensboro, Ky; m. Lori Anne Allison 1983 (divorced 1985); partner Vanessa Paradis 1998–2012 (separated); one s. one d.; fmr rock musician; Co-founder and CEO Infinitum Nihil (production co.) 2004–; Actor of the Year, Hollywood Film Festival 2003, People's Choice Award for Favorite Male Movie Star 2005–08, La Grande médaille de Vermeil (France) 2006, Favorite Male Action Star 2007, Favorite Movie Actor 2010–12. *Films include:* A Nightmare on Elm Street 1984, Private Resort 1985, Platoon 1986, Cry Baby 1990, Edward Scissorhands 1990, Freddy's Dead: The Final Nightmare 1991, Benny and Joon 1993, What's Eating Gilbert Grape 1993, Arizona Dream 1993, Ed Wood 1994, Don Juan de Marco 1994, Dead Man 1995, Nick of Time 1995, The Brave 1997 (also writer and dir), Donnie Brasco 1997, Fear and Loathing in Las Vegas 1998, The Astronaut's Wife 1999, The Source 1999, The Ninth Gate 1999, Sleepy Hollow 1999, The Man Who Cried 2000, Before Night Falls 2000, Chocolat 2000, Blow 2001, From Hell 2001, Pirates of the Caribbean: The Curse of the Black Pearl (Screen Actors Guild Award Best Actor 2004) 2003, Once Upon a Time in Mexico 2003, Secret Window 2004, Finding Neverland 2004, The Libertine 2004, And They Lived Happily Ever After 2004, Charlie and the Chocolate Factory 2005, Corpse Bride (voice) 2005, Pirates of the Caribbean: Dead Man's Chest 2006, Pirates of the Caribbean: At World's End 2007, Sweeney Todd: The Demon Barber of Fleet Street (Golden Globe for Best Actor in a Musical or Comedy 2008) 2007, The Imaginarium of Doctor Parnassus 2009, Public Enemies 2009, Alice in Wonderland 2010, The Rum Diary 2010, The Tourist 2010, Rango (voice) 2011, Pirates of the Caribbean: On Stranger Tides 2011, Dark Shadows 2012, 21 Jump Street (uncredited) 2012. *Television includes:* Slow Burn 1986, 21 Jump Street (series) 1987–90, United States of Poetry (series) 1995, King of the Hill (episode, Hank's Back; voice) 2004, SpongeBob SquarePants (aka SpongeBob vs. the Big One) (episode) 2009. *Address:* c/o United Talent Agency, 9560 Wilshire Blvd, Suite 500, Beverly Hills, CA 90212-2401, USA (office); Infinitum Nihil, 9100 Wilshire Blvd, #275W, Beverly Hills, CA 90212. *Telephone:* (310) 273-6700 (office). *Fax:* (310) 247-1111 (office). *Website:* www.unitedtalent.com (office).

DERANT LAKOUÉ, Enoch; Central African Republic politician; fmr mem. Mouvement pour la Libération du Peuple Centrafricain (MLPC—Liberation Movt of the Cen. African People's Party); Founder and Pres. Parti social-démocrate (PSD) early 1990s; Prime Minister of Cen. African Repub. March–Oct. 1993; presidential cand. 1993, 1999; Minister of State in charge of the Economy, Planning and Int. Co-operation 2013; Founder Co-ordination of Opposition Political Parties; Dir BERETEC/CENTRAFRIQUE, Bangui. *Address:* c/o Ministry of the Economy, Planning and International Co-operation, BP 912, Bangui, Central African Republic (office).

DERBEZ BAUTISTA, Luis Ernesto, PhD; Mexican economist, politician and university administrator; *Rector, Universidad de las Américas Puebla;* b. 1 April 1947, Mexico City; ed San Luis Potosí Autonomous Univ., Univ. of Oregon and Iowa State Univ., USA; economist for IBRD, responsible for regional areas including Chile 1983–86, Cen. America 1986–89, Africa 1989–92, Western and Cen. Africa 1992–94, India, Nepal and Bhutan 1994–97 (also dir multilateral econ. assistance and structural adjustment programmes in Chile, Costa Rica, Honduras and Guatemala); ind. consultant, World Bank Group, Mexico City office and IDB, Washington, DC 1997–2000; Econ. Adviser and Co-ordinator of Econ. Affairs to Pres.-Elect of Mexico 2000; fmr Sec. for Economy; Sec. of State for Foreign Affairs 2003–06; Dir Gen. Centre for Globalization, Competitiveness and Democracy, Instituto Tecnológico de Monterrey 2007–; Sec. for Int. Affairs, Partido Acción Nacional 2007–; Rector, Universidad de las Américas Puebla 2008–; fmr Prof., Grad. School of Business Man., Instituto Tecnológico y de Estudios Superiores de Monterrey (also Dir Econometric Studies Unit and Econs Dept); fmr Vice-Rector Univ. of the Americas, Cholula, Mexico; fmr Visiting Prof., Johns Hopkins Univ. School of Int. Studies, USA. *Address:* Office of the Rector, Universidad de las Américas Puebla, Sta Catarina Mártir, Apdo Postal 100, 72820 Cholula, Puebla, Mexico (office). *Telephone:* (222) 229-2000 (office). *Fax:* (222) 229-2009 (office). *E-mail:* luisernesto.derbez@udlap.mx (office). *Website:* www.udlap.mx (office).

DERBYSHIRE, Sir Andrew George, Kt, MA (Cantab.), AADip (Hons), FRIBA, FRSA; British architect; b. 7 Oct. 1923, Sheffield, Yorks., England; s. of Samuel Reginald Derbyshire and Helen Louise Puleston Derbyshire (née Clarke); m. Lily Rhodes (née Binns); three s. one d.; ed Chesterfield Grammar School, Queens' Coll., Cambridge, Architectural Asscn, London; Admiralty Signals Establishment and Bldg Research Station 1943–46; Farmer and Dark (Marchwood and Belvedere power stations) 1951–53; W Riding Co. Architect's Dept 1953–55; Asst City Architect, Sheffield 1955–61; mem. Research Team, RIBA Survey of Architects' Offices 1960–62; mem. Robert Matthew, Johnson-Marshall and Partners 1961–, Chair. 1983–89, Pres. RMJM Group 1989–98; involved in Devt of Univ. of York 1962–, Cen. Lancs. New Town, NE Lancs. Impact Study, Univ. of Cambridge, W Cambridge Devt and New Cavendish Lab., Preston Market and Guildhall, London Docklands Study, Hillingdon Civic Centre, Cabtrack and Minitram feasibility studies, Suez Master Plan Study, Castle Peak Power Station, Hong Kong, Harbour reclamation and urban devt, Hong Kong; mem. RIBA Council 1950–72, 1975–81, Sr Vice-Pres. 1980–81; mem. Bldg Industry Communications Research Cttee 1964–66; mem. Ministry of Transport Urban Research and Devt Group 1967; mem. Inland Transport Research and Devt Council 1968; mem. Dept of the Environment Planning and Transport Research Advisory Council 1971–76; mem. Comm. on Energy and the Environment 1978–81; mem. (part-time) Cen. Electricity Generating Bd 1973–84; mem. of Bd, Property Services Agency 1975–79; mem. Bd London Docklands Devt Corpn and Chair. of Planning Cttee 1983–88; mem. Construction Industry Sector Group of NEDC 1988–92; mem. Construction Industry Council, Chair. Research Cttee 1989–94; Chair. Art for Architecture Project, RSA 1994–98; Hoffman Wood Prof. of Architecture, Univ. of Leeds 1978–80; External Prof., Dept of Civil Eng 1981–85; Gresham Coll. Prof. of Rhetoric 1990–92; Hon. Fellow, Inst. of Structural Eng 1992, Inst. of Advanced Architectural Studies, Univ. of York 1994; Hon. DUniv (York) 1972. *Publications:*

The Architect and His Office 1962; numerous articles on planning, energy conservation and scientific research, including from 1998 onwards papers on architecture, science and feedback, and the conservation of 20th century buildings. *Leisure interests:* family, garden. *Address:* 4 Sunnyfield, Hatfield, Herts., AL9 5DX, England (home). *Telephone:* (1707) 265903 (home); (1707) 265903 (office). *E-mail:* andrewderby@mailme.co.uk (office).

DEREVYANKO, Anatoly Panteleyevich, Dr His.; Russian scientist and archaeologist; *Director, Institute of Archaeology and Ethnography, Siberian Branch, Russian Academy of Sciences;* b. 9 Jan. 1943, Kozmo-Demyanovka Amurskaya oblast; m.; two c.; ed Blagoveshchensk Pedagogical Inst.; jr researcher, head of museum, Deputy Dir, Inst. of History, Dialectics and Philosophy at the Siberian branch of the Russian Acad. of Sciences 1965–76; Sec. of the Central Cttee of Comsomol 1976–79; Prof., Rector Novosibirsk Univ. 1980–83; Dir Inst. of Archaeology and Ethnography at the Siberian branch of the Russian Acad. of Sciences 1983–, currently also Chair. United Academic Council of Humanitarian Studies; specialist in the archaeology and ancient history of Siberia and the Far East; mem. Russian Acad. of Sciences (corresp. mem. 1979–87). *Publications include:* more than 400 scientific publications on general history; monographs include Palaeolithic of the Far East and Korea 1983, Palaeolithic of Japan 1984, Foreign Archaeology 1986. *Address:* Institute of Archaeology and Ethnography, Siberian branch of Russian Academy of Sciences, Academika Lavretyeva prosp. 17, Novosibirsk 630090, Russia (office). *Telephone:* (3832) 30-27-91 (office); (3832) 35-05-37 (office). *Fax:* (3832) 30-11-91 (office); (3832) 35-52-37 (office). *E-mail:* derev@archaeology.nsc.ru (office). *Website:* www.sati.archaeology.nsc.ru (office).

DERIPASKA, Oleg Vladimirovich; Russian business executive; *CEO and Chairman of the Management Board, United Company RUSAL;* b. 2 Jan. 1968, Dzerzhinsk, Gorkii (now Nizhnii Novgorod) Oblast; m. Polina Yumasheva; two c.; ed Moscow State Univ., Plekhanov Acad. of Nat. Econs; Financial Dir Jt Stock Mil. Investment and Trade Co. 1990–92; Dir Gen. Rosaluminprodukt 1992–93; Dir Krasnoyarskaluminprodukt 1993; Dir-Gen. Aluminprodukt 1993–94, Chief Financial Officer 1994–96; Dir Sayany Aluminium Plant 1996–2000; Pres. Sibirsky Aluminium Group 1997–2000; Dir-Gen. Russian Aluminium Corpn (RUSAL, formed from merger of aluminium smelters and alumina refineries of Sibirsky Aluminium Group and Sibneft oil co.) 2000–03, mem. Bd of Dirs 2006–, CEO and Chair. Man. Bd United Company RUSAL (formed from merger of RUSAL, SUAL Group and alumina assets of Glencore International AG 2007) 2009–; Founder and Chair. Supervisory Bd Basic Element LLC (holding group for RUSAL) 2001–, GAZ (automobile mfrs), Aviacor (aircraft mfrs), Ingosstrakh (insurance co.); Chair. Bd Russian Nat. Cttee of Int. Chamber of Commerce; mem. Entrepreneurship Council of Govt of Russian Fed.; mem. Business Advisory Council APEC 2004–, Chair. Russian section 2007–; Vice-Pres. Russian Union of Businessmen and Entrepreneurs 1999–; Trustee, Nat. Science Support Foundation, Bolshoi Theatre, Schools of Business Admin of Moscow State Univ. and St Petersburg State Univ.; Order of Friendship 1999; named by Vedomosti (business daily) Businessman of the Year 1999, 2006, 2007. *Address:* United Company RUSAL Corporate Headquarters, 109240 Moscow, ul. Nikoloyamskaya 13/1, Russia (office). *Telephone:* (495) 720-51-70 (office). *Fax:* (495) 745-70-46 (office). *E-mail:* rusal@rusal.ru (office). *Website:* www.rusal.com (office); www.basel.ru (office); www.deripaska.com (office).

DERMER, Ron, MA; Israeli diplomatist; *Ambassador to USA;* b. 1971, Miami Beach, Fla, USA; s. of Jay Dermer and Yaffa Rosenthal; m. Rhoda Pagano; five c.; ed Wharton School of Business, Univ. of Pennsylvania, Univ. of Oxford, UK; spent three years as columnist for Jerusalem Post; Econ. Affairs Minister, Embassy in Washington, DC 2005–08; Sr Adviser to Prime Minister Benjamin Netanyahu 2009–13; Amb. to USA 2013–. *Publication:* The Case For Democracy: The Power of Freedom to Overcome Tyranny and Terror (with Natan Sharansky) 2004. *Address:* Israeli Embassy, 3514 International Drive NW, Washington, DC 20008, USA (office). *Telephone:* (202) 364-5500 (office). *Fax:* (202) 364-5566 (office). *E-mail:* info@washington.mfa.gov.il (office). *Website:* www.israelemb.org (office).

DERN, Bruce MacLeish; American actor; b. 4 June 1936, Chicago, Ill.; s. of John Dern and Jean Dern (née MacLeish); ed The Choate School (now Choate Rosemary Hall) and Univ. of Pennsylvania. *Films:* Marnie 1964, Hush…Hush, Sweet Charlotte 1964, The Wild Angels 1966, The War Wagon 1967, The St. Valentine's Day Massacre 1967, The Trip 1967, Waterhole Three 1967, Will Penny 1968, Psych-Out 1968, Hang 'Em High 1968, Support Your Local Sheriff! 1969, Castle Keep 1969, Number One 1969, The Cycle Savages 1969, They Shoot Horses, Don't They? 1969, Bloody Mama 1970, The Rebel Rousers 1970, The Incredible 2-Headed Transplant 1971, Drive, He Said (Nat. Soc. of Film Critics Award for Best Supporting Actor) 1971, The Cowboys (Bronze Wrangler for Best Theatrical Motion Picture) 1972, Silent Running 1972, The King of Marvin Gardens 1972, Thumb Tripping 1972, An Investigation of Murder 1973, The Great Gatsby 1974, Posse 1975, Smile 1975, Family Plot 1976, Won Ton Ton: The Dog Who Saved Hollywood 1976, The Twist 1976, Black Sunday 1977, Coming Home 1978, The Driver 1978, Middle Age Crazy 1980, Tattoo 1981, That Championship Season (Silver Bear for Best Actor) 1982, Harry Tracy: Dead or Alive 1982, On the Edge 1986, The Big Town 1987, World Gone Wild 1988, 1969 1988, The 'Burbs 1989, After Dark, My Sweet 1990, Diggstown 1992, Mrs. Munck 1995, Wild Bill 1995, Down Periscope 1996, Last Man Standing 1996, Small Soldiers (voice) 1998, The Haunting 1999, If… Dog… Rabbit 1999, All the Pretty Horses 2000, The Glass House 2001, Masked and Anonymous 2003, Milwaukee, Minnesota 2003, Monster 2003, Madison 2005, Down in the Valley 2005, Believe in Me 2006, Walker Payne 2006, The Astronaut Farmer 2006, The Hard Easy 2006, The Cake Eaters 2007, Swamp Devil (Philadelphia Film Festival Jury Prize) 2008, The Golden Boys 2008, American Cowslip 2009, The Hole 2009, The Lightkeepers 2009, Choose 2010, Trim 2010, From Up on Poppy Hill (English version, voice) 2011, Inside Out 2011, Twixt 2011, Hitting the Cycle 2012, Django Unchained 2012, Coffin Baby 2013, Northern Borders 2013, Nebraska (Boston Society of Film Critics Award for Best Cast, Cannes Film Festival Best Actor Award, Dublin Film Critics Circle Award for Best Actor, Los Angeles Film Critics Asscn Award for Best Actor, Nat. Bd of Review Award for Best Actor) 2013, Fighting for Freedom 2013. *Television includes:* Stoney Burke (series) 1962–63, The Dick Powell Theatre (series) 1962–63, Wagon Train (series) 1963–65, The Fugitive (series) 1963–66, The Virginian (series) 1964–65, 12 O'Clock High (series) 1964–65, F.B.I. (series) 1965–68, Gunsmoke (series) 1965–69, The Long Hunt of April Savage (film) 1966,

Run for Your Life (series) 1966–67, The Big Valley (series) 1966–68, Lancer (series) 1968–69, Who Killed the Mysterious Mr. Foster? (film) 1971, Toughlove (film) 1985, Roses Are for the Rich (film) 1987, Uncle Tom's Cabin (film) 1987, Trenchcoat in Paradise (film) 1989, The Court-Martial of Jackie Robinson (film) 1990, Into the Badlands (film) 1991, Carolina Skeletons (film) 1991, It's Nothing Personal (film) 1993, Dead Man's Revenge (film) 1994, Amelia Earhart: The Final Flight (film) 1994, A Mother's Prayer (film) 1995, Comfort, Texas (film) 1997, When the Bough Breaks II: Perfect Prey (film) 1998, Hard Time: The Premonition (film) 1999, Hard Ground (film) 2003, Big Love (series) 2006–11, Unicorn Plan-It (series) 2012–13, Pete's Christmas (film) 2013. *Address:* c/o Creative Artists Agency, 2000 Avenue of the Stars, Los Angeles, CA 90067, USA (office). *Telephone:* (424) 288-2000 (office). *Fax:* (424) 288-2900 (office). *Website:* www.caa.com (office).

DERN, Laura Elizabeth; American actress, director and producer; b. 10 Feb. 1967, Los Angeles, Calif.; d. of Bruce Dern and Diane Ladd; m. Ben Harper 2005 (divorced 2010); ed Lee Strasberg Inst.; Royal Acad. of Dramatic Art, London, UK. *Films include:* Foxes 1980, Ladies and Gentlemen, The Fabulous Stains 1981, Teachers 1984, Mask 1985, Smooth Talk 1985, Blue Velvet 1986, Predator: The Concert 1987, Haunted Summer 1988, Fat Man and Little Boy 1989, Wild at Heart 1990, Rambling Rose 1991, Jurassic Park 1993, A Perfect World 1993, Devil Inside, Citizen Ruth 1996, Bastard Out of Carolina 1996, October Sky 1999, Dr T and the Women 2000, Daddy and Them 2001, Focus 2001, Novocaine 2001, Jurassic Park III 2001, I Am Sam 2001, Novocaine 2001, We Don't Live Here Anymore 2004, Happy Endings 2005, The Prize Winner of Defiance, Ohio 2005, Lonely Hearts 2006, Inland Empire 2006, Year of the Dog 2007, The Monday Before Thanksgiving (short) 2008, Tenderness 2009, Everything Must Go 2010, Little Fockers 2010, The Master 2012. *Television includes:* Happy Endings 1983, The Three Wishes of Billy Greer 1984, Afterburn (film) 1992, Fallen Angels (series) 1993, Down Came a Blackbird (film) 1995, Frasier (series) 1995, The Siege at Ruby Ridge (film) 1996, Ellen (series) 1997, The Baby Dance 1998, Hallmark Hall of Fame (series) 1999, A Season for Miracles 1999, Within These Walls (film) 2001, The West Wing (episode) 2002, Damaged Care (film) 2002, King of the Hill (series) 2002–03, Recount (Golden Globe Award for Best Supporting Actress in a Series 2009) 2008, Enlightened (series) (Golden Globe Award for Best Performance by an Actress in a Television Series – Comedy or Musical 2012) 2011; Dir The Gift 1994. *Address:* c/o Fred Specktor, Creative Artists Agency, 2000 Avenue of the Stars, Los Angeles, CA 90067, USA (office); c/o Wolf-Kasteler, 9350 Wilshire Blvd, Suite 450, Beverly Hills, CA 90212, USA (office). *Telephone:* (424) 288-2000 (office); (310) 205-0618 (office). *Fax:* (424) 288-2900 (office). *Website:* www.caa.com (office); www.wktpr .com (office).

DERNESCH, Helga; Austrian singer (soprano, mezzo-soprano); b. 3 Feb. 1939, Vienna; two c.; ed Vienna Conservatory; sang many operatic roles in Berne 1961–63, Wiesbaden 1963–66, Cologne 1966–69; freelance guest appearances at all major opera houses in Europe 1969–; regular appearances at Bayreuth Festival 1965–69, at Salzburg Easter Festival 1969–73; since 1979 has sung as mezzo-soprano; regular appearances at San Francisco Opera 1982–; debut Metropolitan Opera, New York 1985; has sung in operas and concerts throughout Europe, N and S America, Japan. *Leisure interests:* films, people, literature. *Address:* Salztorgasse 8/11, 1013 Vienna, Austria (home).

DERR, Kenneth T., MBA; American business executive; b. 1936; m. Donna Mettler 1959; three c.; ed Cornell Univ.; with Chevron Corpn (fmrly Standard Oil Co. of Calif.) 1960–1999, Vice-Pres. 1972–85, Pres. Chevron USA Inc. 1978–84, Head Merger Program, Chevron Corpn and Gulf Oil Corpn 1984–85, Vice-Chair. Chevron Corpn 1985–88, Chair. 1989–99, CEO 1989–99; Dir Calpine Corpn 2001–05, Chair. and Acting CEO 2005, Chair. 2005–08 (retd); mem. Bd of Dirs Citigroup Inc. 1987–2009, AT&T 1995–2005, Halliburton 2001–; Dir American Petroleum Inst. (fmr Chair.). *Address:* 345 California Street, Floor 3D, San Francisco, CA 94104-2638, USA (office).

DERSHOWITZ, Alan Morton, LLB; American lawyer and academic; *Felix Frankfurter Professor of Law, Harvard University;* b. 1 Sept. 1938, New York, NY; s. of Harry Dershowitz and Claire Ringel; m. Carolyn Cohen; two s. one d.; ed Brooklyn Coll. and Yale Univ.; admitted to DC Bar 1963, Mass Bar 1968, US Supreme Court 1968; law clerk to Chief Judge David Bazelon, US Court of Appeal 1962–63, to Justice Arthur Goldberg, US Supreme Court 1963–64; mem. Faculty, Harvard Coll. 1964–, Prof. of Law 1967–, Felix Frankfurter Prof. of Law 1993–; Fellow, Center for Advanced Study of Behavioral Sciences 1971–72; consultant to Dir Nat. Inst. for Mental Health 1967–69, Pres.'s Comm. on Civil Disorders 1967, Pres.'s Comm. on Causes of Violence 1968, Nat. Asscn for Advancement of Colored People Legal Defense Fund 1967–68, Pres.'s Comm. on Marijuana and Drug Abuse 1972–73, Ford Foundation Study on Law and Justice 1973–76; rapporteur, Twentieth Century Fund Study on Sentencing 1975–76; Guggenheim Fellow 1978–79; mem. Comm. on Law and Social Action, American Jewish Congress 1978; Dir American Civil Liberties Union 1968–71, 1972–75, Asscn of Behavioral and Social Sciences, NAS 1973–76; Chair. Civil Rights Comm. New England Region, Anti-Defamation League, B'nai B'rith 1980; Hon. MA (Harvard Coll.) 1967; Hon. LLD (Yeshiva) 1989. *Publications:* Psychoanalysis, Psychiatry and the Law (with others) 1967, Criminal Law: Theory and Process 1974, The Best Defense 1982, Reversal of Fortune: Inside the von Bülow Case 1986, Taking Liberties: A Decade of Hard Cases, Bad Laws and Bum Raps 1988, Chutzpah 1991, Contrary to Popular Opinion 1992, The Abuse Excuse 1994, The Advocate's Devil 1994, Reasonable Doubt 1996, The Vanishing American Jew 1997, Sexual McCarthyism 1998, Just Revenge 1999, The Genesis of Justice 2000, Letters to a Young Lawyer 2001, Shouting Fire: Civil Liberties in a Turbulent Age 2002, Why Terrorism Works 2002, Supreme Injustice: How the High Court Hijacked Election 2000 2002, America Declares Independence 2003, America on Trial 2004, Letters to a Young Lawyer 2005, The Case for Israel 2005, Rights from Wrongs: A Secular Theory of the Origins of Rights 2005, The Case for Peace: How the Arab-Israeli Conflict Can be Resolved 2006, Preemption: A Knife That Cuts Both Ways 2007, What Israel Means to Me 2007, Blasphemy 2008, The Case against Israel's Enemies 2008, Finding, Framing, and Hanging Jefferson 2009, The Case for Moral Clarity 2009, The Trials of Zion 2010, Israel on Trial 2011; contrib. articles to legal journals. *Address:* Harvard University Law School, Hauser Hall 520, 1575 Massachusetts Avenue, Cambridge, MA 02138-2801, USA (office). *Telephone:* (617) 495-4617

(office). *Fax:* (617) 495-7855 (office). *E-mail:* dersh@law.harvard.edu (office). *Website:* www.law.harvard.edu (office); www.alandershowitz.com.

DERVAN, Peter B, BS, PhD; American chemist and academic; *Bren Professor of Chemistry, California Institute of Technology;* b. 28 June 1945, Boston, Mass; ed Boston Coll., Yale Univ.; Postdoctoral Fellow, Stanford Univ. 1973; Asst Prof. of Chemistry, Calif. Inst. of Tech. 1973–79, Assoc. Prof. 1979–82, Prof. 1982–88, Bren Prof. of Chemistry 1988–, also Chair., Div. of Chemistry and Chemical Eng 1994–99; Visiting Prof. at several int. univs including Eidgenössische Technische Hochschule Zürich, Switzerland 1983, MIT 1987, Univ. of Cambridge, England 1989, Johann Wolfgang Goethe Univ., Frankfurt, Germany 1993, Univ. Catholique de Louvain, Belgium 1994; co-founder Gilead Sciences 1987, Gensoft; mem. Scientific Advisory Bd several biotechnology cos including Xencor Inc., Fluidigm; mem. Editorial Bd several journals including Chemical Reviews 1984–89, Journal of the American Chemical Society 1986–92, Journal of Medicinal Chemistry 1991–93, Bioorganic and Medicinal Chemistry 1993–; mem. NAS, American Acad. of Arts and Sciences, NAS Inst. of Medicine, American Philosophical Soc.; mem. several NSF Advisory Cttees; foreign mem. French Acad. of Sciences; Hon. DrSci (Boston Coll.) 1997 numerous awards including Willard Gibbs Medal 1993, Nichols Medal 1994, Kirkwood Medal 1998, Richard C. Tolman Medal 1999, Linus Pauling Award 1999, Tetrahedron Prize 2000, Harvey Prize 2002. *Address:* 351 Crellin, California Institute of Technology, Pasadena, CA 91125, USA (office). *Telephone:* (626) 395-6002 (office). *Fax:* (626) 5568-87443 (office). *E-mail:* dervan@caltech.edu (office). *Website:* chemistry.caltech.edu (office).

DERVİŞ, Kemal, BA, MA, PhD; Turkish economist, politician and UN official; *Vice-President and Director, Global Economy and Development, The Brookings Institution;* b. 10 Jan. 1949, Istanbul; m. Catherine Anne Derviş; ed London School of Econs, UK, Princeton Univ., USA; Lecturer in Econs, Middle Eastern Tech. Univ. 1973; adviser on issues of econ. and int. relations to Prime Minister Bülent Ecevit 1973–76; Lecturer in Int. Relations and Econs, Princeton Univ. 1977; mem. Research Dept, World Bank 1978–82, Head of Industrial Strategy and Policy, Global Industry Dept 1982–86, Sr Economist for Europe, Middle East and N African Affairs 1986–87, Head of Cen. Europe Div. 1987–96, Vice-Pres. in charge of Middle East and N Africa Region 1996–2000, Vice-Pres. in charge of Poverty Reduction and Econ. Man. 2000–01; returned to Turkey 2001; Minister of Econ. Affairs and the Treasury (without party affiliation) 2001–02 (resgnd); mem. Cumhuriyet Halk Partisi (CHP—Republican People's Party—centre-left) 2002–; mem. Parl. for Istanbul 2002–05, represented Turkish Parl. in Constitutional Convention on the Future of Europe, mem. Jt Comm. of Turkish and European Parls; Admin. UNDP and Chair. UN Devt Group 2005–09; Vice-Pres. and Dir Global Economy and Devt program, Brookings Inst., Washington, DC 2009–; was also active in Centre for Econ. and Foreign Policy Studies; active participant in various European and int. networks, including Global Progressive Forum, Progressive Governance Network; mem. Comm. on Growth and Devt (sponsored by World Bank and others), Comm. on the Measurement of Econ. Performance and Social Progress, Advisory Cttee Centre for Econ. and Foreign Policy Studies (EDAM), Advisory Cttee Turkish Econ. and Social Studies Foundation (TESEV); fmr mem. Int. Task Force on Global Public Goods, Special Comm. on the Balkans; adviser, Institut de Prospective Economique du Monde Méditerranéen. *Publications include:* General Equilibrium Models for Development Policy (co-author) 1982, A Better Globalization 2005, Recovery from the Crisis and Contemporary Social Democracy 2006; numerous papers in academic journals as well as current affairs publs on topics ranging from math. models of growth and social mobility and quantitative models of trade, to European enlargement and transatlantic relations (in English, Turkish, French and German). *Address:* The Brookings Institution, 1775 Massachusetts Avenue NW, Washington, DC 20036, USA (office); Türkiye Büyük Millet Meclisi, 06543 Ankara, Turkey (home). *Telephone:* (202) 797-6105 (office). *Fax:* (202) 797-6004. *E-mail:* communications@brookings .edu (office); kdervis@chp.org.tr (home). *Website:* www.brookings.edu (office).

DERWENT, Henry, CB; British civil servant and international organization official; *President and CEO, International Emissions Trading Association;* ed Berkhamsted School, Worcester Coll., Oxford; held several positions in Depts of Transport and Environment, covering roads, transport industries, vehicle licensing, finance, local government and other fields, also acted as Corp. Finance Exec. on loan to major int. investment bank; Dir Int. Climate Change, Energy and Environmental Risk, Dept for Environment, Food and Rural Affairs –2008, acted as Special Rep. to Prime Minister on Climate Change during UK Presidency of EU 2005; Pres. and CEO Int. Emissions Trading Asscn 2008–. *Address:* International Emissions Trading Association, 24 rue Merle d'Aubigné, 1207 Geneva, Switzerland (office). *Telephone:* (22) 737-05-09 (office); (788) 79-56-42 (mobile). *Fax:* (22) 737-05-08 (office). *E-mail:* derwent@ieta.org (office). *Website:* www.ieta.org (office).

DERYCKE, Erik, LLM; Belgian politician and lawyer; *Judge, Constitutional Court of Belgium;* b. 28 Oct. 1949, Waregem; m.; two c.; ed Rijksuniversiteit, Gent; barrister in Kortrijk 1972–; Provincial Councillor for W Flanders 1975–84; Rep. for Kortrijk, Belgian Chamber of Reps 1984; Municipal Councillor for Waregem 1989; Sec. of State for Science Policy 1990–91; Minister for Devt Aid and Deputy Minister for Science Policy 1991–92; Sec. of State for Devt Aid 1992–95; Minister for Foreign Affairs and Devt Co-operation March–June 1995; Minister for Foreign Affairs 1995–99; currently Judge, Constitutional Court of Belgium; Hon. Pres. Socialist Party of Waregem; mem. Socialist Party Bureau. *Address:* Constitutional Court of Belgium, 7 Place Royale, 1000 Brussels, Belgium.

DERZHAVIN, Mikhail Mikhailovich; Russian actor; b. 15 June 1936, Moscow; m. Roksana Babayan; one s.; ed Moscow Shchukin Theatre School; with Moscow Lenkom Theatre 1959–67; actor Malaya Bronnaya Theatre 1967–69; with Moscow Satire Theatre 1969–. *Films include:* Womanizer, Impotent. *Theatre roles include:* Master of Ceremonies in Goodbye, Master of Ceremonies, Bear in Ordinary Miracle, lead role in Tartuffe, A Piece for Two; two-man variety shows with A. Shirvindt (q.v.). *Leisure interest:* fishing. *Address:* Moscow Satire Theatre, 103050 Moscow, Triumphalnaya pl. 2, Russia (office). *Telephone:* (495) 299-63-05 (office).

DESAI, Anita, BA, FRSL; Indian writer and academic; *John E. Burchard Professor Emerita of Humanities, Massachusetts Institute of Technology;* b. 24 June 1937, Mussoorie; d. of Toni Nimé and D. N. Mazumdar; m. Ashvin Desai 1958; two s. two d.; ed Queen Mary's School, Delhi and Miranda House, Univ. of

Delhi; Elizabeth Drew Visiting Prof., Smith Coll., Mass, USA 1987–88; Purington Prof. of English, Mount Holyoke Coll. 1988–92; John E. Burchard Prof. of Humanities, MIT, Cambridge, Mass 1993–2002, now Prof. Emer.; Gildersleeves Prof., Barnard Coll.; Visiting Scholar, Rockefeller Foundation, Bellagio, Italy; Sidney Harman Visiting Prof. and Writer-in-Residence, Baruch Coll. 2003; mem. RSL, American Acad. of Arts and Letters, PEN, Sahitya Akademi, India; Hon. Fellow, Girton Coll., Cambridge 1988, Clare Hall, Cambridge 1991, Hon. mem. American Acad. of Arts and Letters; Royal Soc. of Literature Winifred Holtby Prize 1978, Sahitya Acad. Prize 1978, Fed. of Indian Publishers Award 1978, Guardian Prize for Children's Fiction 1983, Hadassah Prize, New York 1988, Padma Sri 1989, Literary Lion, New York Public Library 1993, Scottish Arts Council Neil Gunn Award for Int. Writing 1994, Alberto Moravia Prize for Literature, Italy 1999, Benson Medal for lifetime achievement, RSL 2003, Giuseppe de Lampedusa Award, Italy 2006, Padma Bhushan 2014. *Film screenplay:* In Custody 1994. *Television includes:* The Village By The Sea (BBC) 1994. *Publications include:* Cry, The Peacock 1963, Voices in the City 1965, Bye-Bye, Blackbird 1971, Where Shall We Go This Summer? 1973, Fire on the Mountain 1978, Games at Twilight 1979, Clear Light of Day 1980, The Village by the Sea 1983, In Custody 1984, Baumgartner's Bombay 1988, Journey to Ithaca 1995, Fasting, Feasting 1999, Diamond Dust and Other Stories 2000, The Zigzag Way 2004, The Artist of Disappearance 2011; children's books: The Peacock Garden, Cat on a Houseboat. *Address:* c/o Rogers, Coleridge & White, 20 Powis Mews, London, W11 1JN, England (office). *Telephone:* (20) 7221-3717 (office). *Fax:* (20) 7229-9084 (office). *E-mail:* info@rcwlitagency.com (office). *Website:* www.rcwlitagency.com (office).

DESAI, Baron (Life Peer), cr. 1991, of St Clement Danes in the City of Westminster; **Meghnad Jagdishchandra Desai,** PhD; British economist and academic; *Professor Emeritus of Economics, London School of Economics;* b. 10 July 1940, Baroda, India; s. of Jagdishchandra Desai and Mandakini Desai (née Majmundar); m. 1st Gail Wilson 1970 (divorced 2004); one s. two d.; m. 2nd Kishwar Rosha 2004; ed Univ. of Bombay, Univ. of Pennsylvania, USA; Assoc. Specialist, Dept of Agricultural Econs, Univ. of Calif., Berkeley, USA 1963–65; Lecturer, LSE 1965–77, Sr Lecturer 1977–80, Reader 1980–83, Prof. of Econs 1983–, now Prof. Emer., Head Devt Studies Inst. 1990–95, Dir Centre for the Study of Global Governance 1992–2003, Chair. Econ. Research Div. 1983–95; consultant at various times to FAO, UNCTAD, Int. Coffee Org., World Bank, UNIDO, UNDP, Ministries of Industrial Devt and Educ., Algeria, British Airports Authority and other bodies; Co-Ed. Journal of Applied Econometrics 1984–; mem. Editorial Bds Int. Review of Applied Econs and several other journals; mem. Council, Royal Econ. Soc. 1988; mem. Exec. Cttee Asscn of Univ. Teachers in Econs 1987– (Pres. 1987–90); mem. Univ. of London Senate representing LSE 1981–89; mem. Nat. Exec. of Council for Academic Freedom and Democracy 1972–83, Speaker's Comm. on Citizenship 1989–, Berndt Carlson Trust; mem. or fmr mem. Governing Body of Courtauld Inst., British Inst. in Paris, Cen. School of Arts, Polytechnic of N London; Chair. Holloway Ward (Islington Cen.) Labour Party 1977–80; Chair. Islington S and Finsbury Labour Party 1986–92, Pres. 1992–; Dr hc (Kingston Univ.) 1992; Hon. DSc (Econs) (E London) 1994; Hon. DPhil (London Guildhall) 1996; Hon. LLD (Monash Univ.) 2005; Pravasi Puraskar (Distinguished Diaspora Indian Award) 2004, Distinguished Alumnus Award, Wharton School of Finance 2004, Padma Bhushan 2008. *Films:* Life Goes On (cameo) 2009. *Publications:* Marxian Economic Theory 1974 (trans. in several languages), Applied Econometrics 1976, Marxian Economics 1979, Testing Monetarism 1981, Marx's Revenge 2001, Global Governance and Financial Crises 2003, Nehru's Hero: Dilip Kumar in the Life of India 2004, Development and Nationhood 2005, The Route to All Evil: Political Economy of Ezra Pound 2006, Rethinking Islamism 2006, Dead on Time (novel) 2009, The Rediscovery of India 2009; ed. several books; numerous papers and contribs to books and journals. *Leisure interests:* reading, politics. *Address:* House of Lords, London, SW1A 0AA (office); 3 Deepdene Road, London, SE5 8EG, England (home). *Telephone:* (20) 7219-5066 (office); (20) 7274-5561 (home). *Fax:* (20) 7219-5979 (office). *E-mail:* desaim@parliament.uk (office); lord.mdesai@gmail.com (home). *Website:* www.lse.ac.uk/Depts/global (office).

DESAI, Nitin Dayalji, BA, MA; Indian economist, civil servant and UN official; *Chairman, Board of Trustees, Oxfam International;* b. 5 July 1941, Bombay (now Mumbai); s. of Dayalji M. Desai and Shantaben Desai; m. Aditi Gupta 1979; two s.; ed St Xavier's High School and Elphinstone Coll., Mumbai, Univ. of Bombay, London School of Econs, UK; Lecturer in Econs, Univ. of Liverpool, UK 1965–67, Univ. of Southampton, UK 1967–70; consultant, Tata (India) Econ. Consultancy Services 1970–73; consultant/adviser, Planning Comm. Govt of India 1973–85; Sr Adviser, Brundtland Comm. 1985–87; Special Sec. Planning Comm. India 1987–88; Sec./Chief Econ. Adviser, Ministry of Finance 1988–90; Deputy Under-Sec.-Gen. UNCED, Geneva 1990–92, Under-Sec.-Gen. for Econ. and Social Affairs, UN 1992–2003, Under-Sec.-Gen. of Dept for Policy Co-ordination and Sustainable Devt 1993–97, Sec.-Gen. of Johannesburg Summit 2002, Special Adviser to the Sec.-Gen. for the World Summit on the Information Soc. 2003–05, Special Adviser to Sec.-Gen. for Internet Governance, Internet Governance Forum, UN 2003–10; mem. Advisory Bd IDEAcarbon; Chair. Cttee on Tech. Innovation and Venture Capital set up by Planning Comm., Govt of India 2006, Int. Working Group on Internet Governance; Co-Chair. (with Lord Chris Patten) India-UK Round Table; Finance Chair. The Poona Club Ltd; associated with Helsinki Process on Globalisation and Democracy, many academic orgs, research bodies and NGOs dealing with econ., social and environmental issues and also security and foreign policy; Distinguished Visiting Fellow, Centre for the Study of Global Governance, LSE 2003–04, Energy and Resources Inst.; fmr mem. Commonwealth Secretariat Expert Group on Climate Change; Chair. Bd of Trustees, Oxfam International 2013–; Hon. Fellow, LSE 2004. *Publications include:* several articles and papers on devt planning, regional econs, industry, energy and int. econ. relations; writes a monthly column for Business Standard (economic daily published from Delhi). *Address:* Oxfam International, Suite 20, 266 Banbury Road, Oxford, OX2 7DL, England (office). *Telephone:* (1865) 339100 (office). *Fax:* (1865) 339101 (office). *E-mail:* information@oxfaminternational.org (office); matt.grainger@oxfaminternational.org (office). *Website:* www.oxfam.org (office).

DESAILLY, Marcel David; French (b. Ghanaian) fmr professional footballer; b. (Odenke Abbey), 7 Sept. 1968, Nima-Accra, Ghana; m. Virginie Desailly; three s. one d.; defender/midfielder with Nantes Atlantique 1986–92, with Olympique de Marseille 1992–93 (won Champions League 1993), with AC Milan 1993–98 (won UEFA Champions League 1994, UEFA Super Cup 1994, Serie A 1994, 1996, Supercoppa Italiana 1994), with Chelsea 1998–2004 (Capt. 2000–04, won UEFA Super Cup 1998, FA Cup 2000, FA Charity Shield 2000), with Al-Gharafa, Qatar 2004–05 (won Qatari League 2005), with Qatar SC 2005–06; played for French nat. team 1993–2004 (made 116 appearances and scored three goals, Capt. 2000–04), winner World Cup 1998, European Football Championship 2000, Confederations Cup 2001, 2003; retd from int. football 2004; Chevalier, Légion d'honneur; Overall Team of the Decade – Premier League 10 Seasons Awards (1992/93–2001/02), ranked by FIFA amongst 100 greatest living players 2004. *E-mail:* contact_desailly@athleteline.com. *Website:* www.marcel-desailly.com.

DESALEGN, Hailemariam, BSc, MSc; Ethiopian civil engineer and politician; *Prime Minister;* b. 19 July 1965, Hombareka, Wolaita; ed Addis Ababa Univ.; began career as civil engineer, Arba Minch Water Tech. Inst. (renamed Arba Minch Univ. 2004) 1990, various positions including Registrar, Deputy Dean and Dean; Vice-Pres. Southern Nations, Nationalities and Peoples' Region 2003, Pres. 2004; Adviser on Social Affairs and Civic Orgs and Partnerships, Prime Minister's Office, Addis Ababa 2005–07; apptd Govt Whip, Fed. Parl. 2008; Chair. Privatization and Public Enterprises Supervisory Agency 2007; mem. and fmr Chair. Southern Ethiopian Peoples' Democratic Movt; Deputy Chair. Ethiopian People's Revolutionary Democratic Front 2010–12, Chair. 2012–; Minister of Foreign Affairs 2010–12, Deputy Prime Minister 2010–12, Acting Prime Minister (following death of Meles Zenawi) Aug.–Sept. 2012, Prime Minister 2012–; Chair. African Union Ass. 2013–14. *Address:* Office of the Prime Minister, POB 1013, Addis Ababa, Ethiopia (office). *Telephone:* (11) 1552044 (office). *Fax:* (11) 1552020 (office).

DESARIO, Vincenzo, BA; Italian banker; *Director-General, Banca d'Italia;* b. 11 June 1933, Barletta; m.; three c.; ed Univ. of Bari; joined Banca d'Italia (Bank of Italy), Foggia br. 1960; Banking Supervision Inspectorate, Bank of Italy head office, Rome 1968; Cen. Man. for Banking and Financial Supervision, Bank of Italy 1983; Bank of Italy Del. to Interbank Deposit Protection Fund 1991; Deputy Dir-Gen. Bank of Italy 1993–94, Dir-Gen. 1994–. *Address:* Banca d'Italia, Via Nazionale 91, 00184 Rome, Italy (office). *Telephone:* (06) 47921 (office). *Fax:* (06) 47922983 (office). *Website:* www.bancaditalia.it (office).

DESCHAMPS, Didier Claude; French fmr professional footballer; b. 15 Oct. 1968, Bayonne (Pyrénées-Atlantiques); m. Claude Deschamps; one s.; ed St Bernard pvt. school, Bayonne, Nantes Football Acad.; amateur player, Aviron Bayonnais; played for FC Nantes 1985–89, Olympique de Marseille (OM) 1989–90, FC des Girondins de Bordeaux 1990–91, OM 1989–94 (won Ligue 1 1990, 1992), Juventus, Turin, Italy 1994–99 (won UEFA Champions League 1993, 1996, Intercontinental Cup 1996, European Super Cup 1996, Italian Cup 1995, Italian Super Cup 1995, 1997, Serie A 1995, 1997, 1998), Chelsea, UK 1999–2000 (won FA Cup 2000), Valencia, Spain 2000–01; played for French nat. team 1989–2000 (made 103 appearances, nat. record) and scored four goals), Capt. and player, Euro 92, Tournoi de France 1997, Capt. of winning team of World Cup 1998 and Euro 2000; fmr Man. Club de Football de Concarneau; Sports Dir and Coach AS Monaco 2001–05, won Coupe de la Lique 2002, reached Champions' League final 2004; Head Coach Juventus, Italy 2006–07 (won Serie B 2007); consultant, Canal+ 2007–09; Head Coach, Olympique de Marseille 2009–; Chevalier, Légion d'honneur 1998; French Footballer of the Year 1996, Médaille de la ville de Bayonne 1998, ranked by FIFA amongst top 100 greatest living footballers 2004. *Address:* c/o Olympique de Marseille, Stade Vélodrome 3, Boulevard Michelet, 13008 Marseille, France. *Website:* www.om.net.

DESCHANEL, Zooey Claire; American actress, musician and singer-songwriter; b. 17 Jan. 1980, Los Angeles, Calif.; d. of Caleb Deschanel and Mary Jo Deschanel (née Weir); m. Ben Gibbard 2009 (divorce pending); ed French Woods Festival of the Performing Arts, attended Northwestern Univ.; guest role on TV series Veronica's Closet 1998; film debut in Mumford 1999; breakthrough role as Anita in Almost Famous 2000; performed in jazz cabaret act If All the Stars Were Pretty Babies with Samantha Shelton from 2001; released debut album Volume One (recorded with M. Ward as She & Him) 2008; follow-up album Volume Two 2010; often sings in her films. *Films include:* Mumford 1999, Almost Famous 2000, Manic 2001, The Good Girl 2002, Abandon 2002, Big Trouble 2002, The New Guy 2002, All the Real Girls 2003, It's Better to Be Wanted for Murder Than Not to Be Wanted at All 2003, Elf 2003, Eulogy 2004, The Hitchhiker's Guide to the Galaxy 2005, Winter Passing 2005, Failure to Launch 2006, Live Free or Die 2006, The Good Life 2007, The Go-Getter 2007, Bridge to Terabithia 2007, Flakes 2007, Surf's Up 2007 (voice) 2007, The Assassination of Jesse James by the Coward Robert Ford 2007, The Happening 2008, Gigantic 2008, Yes Man 2008, 500 Days of Summer 2009, Havin' a Summah (video short) 2010, Our Idiot Brother 2011, Your Highness 2011. *Television includes:* American Dad! (series) (voice) 2005, Once Upon a Mattress (film) 2005, Weeds (series) 2006–07, Tin Man (mini-series) 2007, The Simpsons (series) (voice) 2008, Bones (series) 2009, Drunk History (series) 2010, New Girl (series) 2011–. *Address:* c/o Christian Carino, Creative Artists Agency, 2000 Avenue of the Stars, Los Angeles, CA 90067, USA (office). *Telephone:* (424) 288-2000 (office). *Fax:* (424) 288-2900 (office). *Website:* www.caa.com (office).

D'ESCOTO BROCKMANN, Miguel; Nicaraguan politician and international organization official; b. 5 Feb. 1933, Hollywood, USA; s. of Miguel D'Escoto Muñoz and Rita Brockmann Meléndez; ed Instituto Pedagógico La Salle, Managua, Nicaragua, St Mary's Coll., Moraga, Calif., Manhattan Coll., New York, State Univ. of New York, Columbia Univ., Sur la ligne de Feu, New York; Sub-Dir Dept of Social Communications, Maryknoll, New York, USA 1962–63; worked for Brazilian and Mexican Church in slums of Belo Horizonte, Rio de Janeiro, Brazil and Mexico DF 1963–69, Dir 1970–79; Founder and Pres. Fundación Nicaragüense Pro-Desarrollo Comunitario Integral, León, Nicaragua 1973; became involved with Frente Sandinista de Liberación Nacional from 1975; f. Grupo de los 12, a group of professionals and intellectuals supporting the Sandinista Front 1977; Minister of Foreign Affairs 1979–90; Sr Adviser on Foreign Affairs to Pres. Daniel Ortega 2007–; Pres. 63rd UN Gen. Ass. 2008–09; elected mem. of Sandinista Ass. 1980. *Address:* United Nations, New York, NY 10017, USA. *Telephone:* (212) 963-1234 (office). *Fax:* (212) 963-4879 (office). *Website:* www.un.org (office).

DESHAPRIYA, Mahinda; Sri Lankan government official; *Election Commissioner;* ed Peradeniya Univ.; Class 1 Officer, Sri Lankan Admin. Service; Asst

Commr of Elections 1983–2006, Deputy Commr 2006–10, Additional Commr 2010–11, Commr 2011–. *Address:* Elections Secretariat, PO Box 02, Sarana Mawatha, Rajagiriya 10107, Sri Lanka (office). *Telephone:* (11) 2868441 (office). *E-mail:* election@slt.lk (office). *Website:* www.slelections.gov.lk (office).

DESHCHYTSYA, Andriy, BA, MA; Ukrainian diplomatist and politician; *Interim Minister of Foreign Affairs;* b. 22 Sept. 1965, Pervyatychi, Lviv region; ed Ivan Franko Lviv Nat. Univ., Univ. of Alberta, Canada; Press Sec., First Sec., Embassy in Warsaw 1996–99; Sr Co-ordinator, Polish-American-Ukrainian Co-operation Initiative 1999–2001; Counsellor, Embassy in Helsinki 2001–04, Counsellor, Minister-Counsellor, Embassy in Warsaw 2004–06, Spokesperson, Ministry of Foreign Affairs 2006–08, Amb. to Finland (also accred to Iceland) 2008–12, Amb.-at-Large 2012–, Special Rep. of OSCE Chairperson-in-Office for Conflict Resolution 2013–14; Acting Minister of Foreign Affairs 2014–. *Address:* Ministry of Foreign Affairs, 01018 Kyiv, pl. Mykhailivska 1, Ukraine (office). *Telephone:* (44) 238-15-50 (office). *Fax:* (44) 226-31-69 (office). *E-mail:* zsmfa@mfa .gov.ua (office). *Website:* www.mfa.gov.ua (office).

DESHPANDE, Shashi, BA, MA, BL; Indian writer; b. 19 Aug. 1938, Dharwad, Karnataka; d. of Adya Rangacharya and Sharada Adya; m. D. H. Deshpande 1962; two s.; ed Univs of Mumbai and Bangalore; fmrly worked for a law journal and magazine; full-time writer 1970–; mem. Sahitya Akademi Bd for English 1989–94; Thirumathi Rangammal Prize 1984, Padma Shri 2009. *Film script:* Drishti 1990. *Publications include:* The Dark Holds No Terrors (Nanjangud Thirumalamba Award) 1980, If I Die Today 1982, Come Up and Be Dead 1982, Roots and Shadows 1983, That Long Silence (Sahitya Akademi Award 1990) 1988, The Binding Vine 1993, A Matter of Time 1999, Small Remedies 2000, Moving On 2004, In the Country of Deceit 2008; short stories: The Legacy and Other Stories 1978, It Was Dark 1986, The Miracle and Other Stories 1986, It Was the Nightingale 1986, The Intrusion and Other Stories 1994, The Stone Women 2000, Collected Stories, Vol. I 2003, Vol. II 2004; non-fiction: Writing from the Margin and other essays 2003, Opening Scenes (trans. from Kannada of memoirs and a play), Deliverance (novel translated from Marathi). *Leisure interests:* reading, music. *Address:* c/o Alison M. Bond Agency, 155 West 72nd Street, New York, NY 10023, USA (office); 409 41st Cross, Jayanagar V Block, Bangalore 560 041, India (home). *Telephone:* (80) 26636228 (home). *Fax:* (80) 26641137 (home). *E-mail:* shashideshpande04@gmail .com (home).

DESJOYEAUX, Michel; French yachtsman; b. 16 July 1965; three c.; began racing at age 18; set fastest time ever and became first man to achieve a solo, non-stop navigation of the world in less than 100 days (93 days 4 hours approx.); Whitbread 1985–86, winner Triangle du Soleil 1986, Twostar (with Jean Maurel) 1992, Solitaire du Figaro 1992, 1998, 2007, Leg 2 of Mini Transat 1991, Transat AG2R 1992, Figaro French Championships 1996, 1998, Multihull Trophy 1994, Spi Ouest 1997, Leg 1 of Transat AG2R (with Frank Cammas) 1998, Grand Prix de Fécamp (with Alain Gautier) 1999, Grand Prix de la Trinité (with Alain Gautier) 2000, Vendée Globe 2001, 2009, transatlantic sprint Route du Rhum 2002, Transat 2004 and others; pioneered the swing keel early 1990s. *Publication:* L'enfant de la vallée des fous 2001, Coureur des océans, Vues de mer 2009. *Address:* Mer Agitée SARL, Port La Forêt, 29940 La Forêt Fouesnant, France (office). *Telephone:* 2-98-56-82-85 (office). *Fax:* 2-98-56-81-69 (office). *E-mail:* micheldesjoyeaux@meragitee .com (office). *Website:* www.meragitee.com (office).

DESLONGCHAMPS, Pierre, OC, OQ, BSc, PhD, DSc, FRS, FRSC, FCIC; Canadian chemist and academic; *Professeur-Associé of Chemistry, Laval University;* b. 8 May 1938, St-Lin, Québec; s. of Rodolphe Deslongchamps and Madeleine Magnan; m. 1st Micheline Renaud 1960 (divorced 1975); two s.; m. 2nd Shirley E. Thomas 1976 (divorced 1983); m. 3rd Marie-Marthe Leroux 1987; ed Univ. of Montréal, Univ. of New Brunswick; Post-doctoral Fellow, Harvard Univ. 1965–66; Asst Prof., Univ. of Montréal 1966–67; Asst Prof., Sherbrooke Univ. 1967–68, Assoc. Prof. 1968–72, Prof. of Chem. 1972–2005, Prof. Emer. 2006–; Professeur-Associé of Chem., Laval Univ. 2008–; Exec. Scientific Advisor, OmegaChem Inc.; mem. Canadian Cttee of Scientists and Scholars 1993–, Soc. française de Chimie 1995; Foreign Assoc. mem. Acad. des Sciences de Paris 1995; Fellow, AAAS and numerous other academic socs; Fellow, Guggenheim Foundation 1979, World Innovation Foundation (WIF), UK 2002; Dr hc (Université Pierre et Marie Curie, Paris VI) 1983, (Bishop's Univ., Lennoxville, Québec) 1984, (Univ. of Montreal) 1984, (Laval Univ.) 1984, (Univ. of New Brunswick) 1985, (Univ. of Moncton) 1995; A.P. Sloan Fellowship 1970–72, Scientific Prize of Québec 1971, E.W.R. Steacie Fellowship and Prize 1971–74, Médaille Vincent, Asscn francophone pour le savoir (ACFAS) 1975, Izaak Walton Killam Memorial Scholarships in Science 1976–77, Merck, Sharp and Dohme Lectures Award, Chemical Inst. of Canada 1976, ACFAS Médaille Pariseau 1979, Marie-Victorin Prize, Prov. of Québec 1987, Alfred Bader Award in Organic Chem., Canadian Soc. for Chem. (CSC) 1991, Canada Gold Medal for Science and Eng, Natural Sciences and Eng Research Council of Canada 1993, R.U. Lemieux Award for Organic Chem., CSC 1994, CSC Bernard Belleau Award 2011. *Publications:* Stereoelectronic Effects in Organic Chemistry 1983; more than 230 publs in the area of organic synthesis and devt of concept of stereoelectronic effects in organic chem. *Leisure interests:* reading, fishing, hunting. *Address:* Département de chimie, Faculté des sciences et de génie, Université Laval, 1045 avenue de la Médecine, Pavillon Alexandre-Vachon, Québec, QC G1V 0A6 (office); 69-B, St Louis Street, Apt 403, Lévis, QC G6V 4G2, Canada (home). *Telephone:* (418) 837-4444 (office); (418) 603-3753 (home). *Fax:* (418) 837-5196 (office). *E-mail:* pierre.deslongchamps@chm.ulaval.ca (office). *Website:* www.chm.ulaval.ca/sections/profs.html (office).

DESMARAIS, André, OC; Canadian business executive; *Deputy Chairman, President and Co-CEO, Power Corporation of Canada;* b. 1959; s. of Paul Desmarais, Sr; brother of Paul Desmarais, Jr (q.v.); m. France Chrétien; joined Power Corpn of Canada 1983, Deputy Chair., Pres. and Co-CEO 1996–; Co-Chair. Power Financial Corpn 1996–; mem. Int. Council J.P. Morgan Chase & Co. Inc. 2003–; Dir Great West Life Co. Inc., Investors Group Inc.; Officer of the Nat. Order of Québec 2009. *Address:* Power Corporation of Canada, 751 Victoria Square, Montreal, PQ H2Y 2J3, Canada (office). *Telephone:* (514) 286-7425 (office). *Fax:* (514) 286-7484 (office). *E-mail:* info@powercorporation.com (office). *Website:* www .powercorporation.com (office).

DESMARAIS, Paul, Jr, OC, BComm, MBA; Canadian business executive; *Chairman and Co-CEO, Power Corporation of Canada;* b. 1957; s. of Paul Desmarais, Sr (q.v.); brother of André Desmarais (q.v.); ed McGill Univ., Institut Européen d'Admin des Affaires (INSEAD), France; with S.G. Warburg & Co. Ltd, London 1979–80; Planning Man. Standard Brands Inc., NY 1980–81; Dir of Planning Power Corpn of Canada 1981–82, Vice-Pres. 1982–91, Vice-Chair. 1991–96; Vice-Pres. Power Financial Corpn 1984–86, Pres. and COO 1986–90, Vice-Chair. 1989–90, Chair. 1990–2005, Chair. Exec. Cttee 2005–, currently Co-Chair.; Chair. and Co-CEO Power Corpn of Canada (financial services and communications co.) 1996–; Chair. and CEO Parfinance, France 1993–98 (co. dissolved 1998); Dir and mem. Exec. Cttee IGM Financial Inc., Investors Group Inc., Mackenzie Inc., Great-West Lifeco Inc., The Great-West Life Assurance Co., Great-West Life & Annuity Insurance Co., London Insurance Group Inc., London Life Insurance Co., Pargesa Holding SA, Groupe Bruxelles Lambert SA; Dir Gesca Ltd, La Presse Ltd, Les Journaux Trans-Canada Inc. 1996, Suez, Total, Lafarge; mem. Strategic Cttee Imerys, then Vice-Chair. of the Bd; Chair. Advisory Bd SAGARD Private Equity Partners; Chair. HEC Int. Advisory Bd; mem. Bd of Dirs and Int. Council INSEAD; mem. Global Advisory Council Merrill Lynch; Hon. Chair. Faculty of Man., Int. Advisory Bd McGill Univ.; Canada 125 Medal 1992, Insigne d'Officier de l'Ordre de la Couronne (Belgium) 1994, Queen's Golden Jubilee Medal 2002, Officer of the Nat. Order of Québec 2009. *Leisure interests:* golf, skiing, hunting, fishing. *Address:* Power Corporation of Canada, 751 Victoria Square, Montreal, PQ H2Y 2J3, Canada (office). *Telephone:* (514) 286-7424 (office). *Fax:* (514) 286-7484 (office). *E-mail:* info@powercorporation.com (office). *Website:* www.powercorporation.com (office).

DESMAREST, Thierry Jean Jacques; French mining engineer and business executive; *Honorary Chairman, Total SA;* b. 18 Dec. 1945, Paris; s. of Jacques Desmarest and Edith Desmarest (née Barbe); m. Annick Geraux 1972; one s. two d.; ed École Polytechnique, Ecole Nat. Supérieure des Mines de Paris; qualified mining engineer; worked as engineer with Mines Directorate, New Caledonia 1971–73, Dir of Mines and Geology 1973–75; Tech. Adviser, Ministry of Industry 1975–78, of Econ. 1978–80; mem. Bd Dirs Total Algeria 1981–83, Dir for Latin America and W Africa 1983–87, for the Americas, France, Far East and Dir Man. and Econ. Div. 1988–89, CEO Total Exploration Production 1989–95, mem. Exec. Cttee 1989–95, Chair. and CEO Total 1995–99, Chair. and CEO TotalFina 1999–2000, Chair. and CEO TotalFinaElf 2000–03, Chair. and CEO Total SA 2003–07, Chair. Total SA 2007–10, Hon. Chair. 2010–; Dir Sanofi-Aventis, Air Liquide, Renault SA, Renault SAS, Bombardier; mem. Supervisory Bd Aveva; Officier, Légion d'honneur 2004; Man. of the Year 1999, Nouvel Economiste. *Leisure interest:* skiing. *Address:* Total SA, 2 place Jean Millier, La Défense 6, 92078 Paris La Défense Cedex, France (office). *Telephone:* 1-47-44-22-44 (office); 1-47-44-22-33 (office). *Fax:* 1-47-44-49-53 (office). *E-mail:* thierry.desmarest@total .com (office). *Website:* www.total.com (office).

DESMAZIÈRES, Érik; French cartoonist and writer; b. 1948, Rabat, Morocco; ed Institut d'Etudes Politiques de Paris; spent childhood in Morocco before coming to France to study 1967, graduated 1971; studied engraving with Jean Delpech, with the encouragement of Philippe Mohlitz; work includes drawings and etchings in collections world-wide; mem. Editorial Bd Nouvelles de l'estampe magazine; Pres. Soc. des peintres-graveurs français 2006–; elected to Acad. des beaux-arts 2008; Grand Prix des arts de la ville de Paris 1978. *Works include:* La Tentation de saint Antoine (the Caprices series), L'Atelier René Tazé, La Rue de Marignan, La Rue Charles-Nodier, Le Quai de Montebello, as well as views of Amsterdam (performed on the occasion of his exhbn at the Rembrandhuis), Voyage au centre de la bibliothèque 2012. *Publications include:* illustrated books: Benito Cereno of Herman Melville for Les Bibliophiles de France 1980, Le tremblement de terre du Chili, Heinrich von Kleist (translated by G. La Flize) for Les Bibliophiles d'Automobile Club de France 1986, Une invitation au voyage by Olivier Rolin (work commissioned by Nat. Library of France on the occasion of the restoration of the Globes de Coronelli) 2005, Le Prince Pluie by Maxime Préaud (illustrated with engravings in mezzotint) 2009. *E-mail:* info@erikdesmazieres.fr. *Website:* erikdesmazieres.fr.

DESMOND, Richard Clive; British publishing and media executive; *Chairman, Northern & Shell PLC;* b. 8 Dec. 1951; s. of Cyril Desmond and Millie Desmond; m. 1st Janet Robertson 1983 (divorced 2010); one s. m. 2nd Joy Canfield; Advertisement Exec. Thomson Newspapers 1967–68; Group Advertisement Man. Beat Publs Ltd 1968–74; f. Northern & Shell Network 1974 (later Northern & Shell PLC) Chair. 1974–; launched Int. Musician (magazine) 1974; Demonde Advertising 1976–89; Publr Next, Fitness, Cook's Weekly, Venture, Penthouse, Bicycle, Stamps, Electric Blue, Rock CD, Guitar, For Woman, Attitude, Arsenal, Liverpool; f. Fantasy Channel 1995, OK! Magazine 1993–, OK! TV 1999–; owner Express Newspapers 2000–, Channel 5 (UK TV station) 2010–. *Leisure interest:* drums. *Address:* Northern & Shell PLC, 10 Lower Thames Street, London, EC3R 6EN, England (office). *Telephone:* (871) 434-1010 (office). *Website:* www .northernandshell.co.uk (office).

DESMOND-HELLMANN, Susan, MD, MPH; American oncologist, academic, business executive and university administrator; *CEO, Bill & Melinda Gates Foundation;* b. Reno, Nev.; ed Univ. of Nevada, Reno and Univ. of California, Berkeley School of Public Health; Adjunct Assoc. Prof. of Epidemiology and Biostatistics, Univ. of Calif., San Francisco, fmr Asst Prof. of Hematology-Oncology; Assoc. Dir Clinical Cancer Research, Pharmaceutical Research Inst., Bristol-Myers Squibb –1995; Clinical Scientist, Genentech Inc. 1995, Chief Medical Officer 1996, Exec. Vice-Pres. Devt and Product Operations and mem. Exec. Cttee 1999–2004, Pres. Product Devt and mem. Exec. Cttee 2004–09; Chancellor, Univ. of Calif., San Francisco 2009–13, also Arthur and Toni Rembe Rock Distinguished Prof.; CEO Bill & Melinda Gates Foundation 2014–; mem. US Dept of Health and Human Services Advisory Cttee on Regulatory Reform 2002; mem. Bd of Dirs Affymetrix 2004–, Biotechnology Industry Org. 2001–09, American Asscn for Cancer Research 2005–08; spent two years as visiting faculty mem., Uganda Cancer Inst. studying AIDS and cancer; also spent two years in pvt. practice; ranked by Fortune magazine amongst 50 Most Powerful Women in Business in the US 2001, 2003, (24th) 2004, (23rd) 2005, (17th) 2006, (21st) 2007, (13th) 2008, ranked by Forbes magazine amongst 100 Most Powerful Women (81st) 2005, (61st) 2007, (87th) 2008, listed by The Wall Street Journal as one of its

Women To Watch 2004, 2005, named the Healthcare Businesswomens Asscn's Woman of the Year 2006; numerous honours and awards for work in oncology and AIDS research. *Address:* Bill & Melinda Gates Foundation, 500 5th Avenue North, Seattle, WA 98102, USA (office). *Telephone:* (206) 709-3100 (office). *Website:* www .gatesfoundation.org (office).

D'ESPAGNAT, Bernard, PhD; French theoretical physicist, academic, philosopher and author; b. 22 Aug. 1921, Fourmagnac, Lot; s. of Georges d'Espagnat and Marguerite de Ginestet; m. May de Schoutheete De Tervarent; two d.; ed Ecole Polytechnique, Institut Henri Poincaré, Univ. of the Sorbonne; spent most of his early years in Paris; researcher, CNRS 1947–57; worked with Enrico Fermi in Chicago, USA 1951–52, and on research project led by Niels Bohr at Inst. in Copenhagen, Denmark 1953–54; worked at CERN (European Org. for Nuclear Research), Geneva as a theoretical physicist 1954–59; Sr Lecturer, Faculty of Sciences, Univ. of the Sorbonne 1959–68; Prof. Univ. of Paris XI (Orsay) 1967–87, Dir Lab. of Theoretical Physics and Elementary Particles 1980–87; Visiting Prof., Univ. of Texas, Austin, USA 1977, Univ. of California, Santa Barbara, USA 1984; mem. Brussels Int. Acad. of the Philosophy of Science 1975, French Acad. of Moral and Political Sciences 1996; Templeton Prize for "work which acknowledges that science cannot fully explain the 'nature of being'" 2009. *Achievements include:* best known for his work on the nature of reality; developed concept of 'veiled reality'. *Publications include:* Conceptions de la physique contemporaine: les interprétations de la mécanique quantique et de la mesure 1965, Conceptual Foundations of Quantum Mechanics 1971, A la recherche du réel, le regard d'un physicien (In Search of Reality) 1979, Un atome de sagesse, propos d'un physicien sur le réel voilé 1982, Nonseparability and the Tentative Descriptions of Reality 1984, Une incertaine réalité: le monde quantique, la connaissance et la durée (Reality and the Physicist) 1985, Penser la science ou les enjeux du savoir 1990, Georges d'Espagnat 1990, Regards sur la matière des quanta et des choses (co-author) 1993, Le Réel voilé, analyse des concepts quantiques (Veiled Reality: An Analysis of Quantum Mechanical Concepts) 1994, Physique et réalité – un débat avec Bernard d'Espagnat 1997, Ondine et les feux du savoir – Carnets d'une petite sirène 1998, Traité de physique et de philosophie 2002 (translated as On Physics and Philosophy 2006), Candide et le physicien (Candide and the Physicist) (with Claude Saliceti) 2008. *Address:* 39 rue d'Assas, 75006 Paris, France.

DESSENS, C. W. M.; Dutch business executive; *Chairman of the Supervisory Board, GasTerra BV;* b. 30 Oct. 1947, Vlaardingen; ed Leiden Univ.; joined Directorate-Gen. for Industry and for Energy, Ministry of Econ. Affairs 1974, Dir-Gen. for Energy 1988–99; Dir-Gen. for Law Enforcement, Ministry of Justice 1999–2005; self-employed 2005–; mem. Supervisory Bd GasTerra BV (fmrly NV Nederlandse Gasunie) 2006–, Chair. 2007–, Chair. Cttee of Del. Mems; Chair. Stichting Aanpak Voertuigcriminaliteit (Foundation for Tacking Vehicle Crime); mem. Bd Meld Misdaad Anoniem; Chair. Exec. Bd CATO (CO2 Capture, Transport and Storage) project. *Address:* GasTerra BV, PO Box 477, 9700 AL Groningen (office); GasTerra BV, Rozenburglaan 11, 9727 DL Groningen, Netherlands (office). *Telephone:* (50) 364-86-48 (office). *Fax:* (50) 364-86-00 (office). *E-mail:* communicatie@gasterra.nl (office). *Website:* www.gasterra.com (office).

DESVIGNE, Michel; French landscape architect and author; b. 1958, Montbéljard (Doubs), Franche-Comté; m. Christine Dalnoky 1988; ed Univ. of Lyon-II, École Nationale Supérieure du Paysage, Versailles; led various projects, alone or in collaboration with Christine Dalnoky, Michel Corajoud and Alexandre Chemetoff 1983–86; resident in Villa Medici, Rome 1986–87; co-f. agency Desvigne & Dalnoky 1988; works with architects including Renzo Piano, Richard Rogers and Norman Foster; with Christine Dalnoky developed projects in Paris, Lyon, Avignon, Montpellier, Rome and Antwerp; collaborated on Greenwich Peninsula Masterplan, London with Richard Rogers; worked on gardens of Walker Art Center, Minneapolis with Herzog and De Meuron; central square of Almere, Belgium with Rem Koolhaas, Millau viaduct with Norman Foster; participated in Lyon Confluence 2004; has taught at École Nationale Supérieure du Paysage, Versailles 1985–95; Visiting Prof., Ecole Polytechnique Federale de Lausanne, Switzerland 1993, Architectural Inst., Geneva, Switzerland 1994–98, Harvard Univ., USA 1999, Architectural Asscn School of Architecture, London 2000; Chevalier des Arts et des Lettres 2003; numerous major prizes, including Lauréat du concours de l'Acad. de France à Rome (Architecture) 1986, 'Diploma com a Finalista', jury int. du prix européen du paysage Rosa Barba 2002, Civic Trust Award 2002, Medal of the Acad. of Architecture 2000, Grand Prix de l'urbanisme 2003, Lauréat du Grand Prix de l'urbanisme 2011. *Publications:* The Return of the Landscape (with Christine Dalnoky) 1997; several articles in L'architecture d'aujourd'hui. *Address:* DPLG, 23 rue du Renard, 75004 Paris, France (office). *Telephone:* 1-44-61-98-61 (office). *Fax:* 1-44-61-98-60 (office).

DESYATNIKOV, Leonid Arkadievich; Russian composer; b. 1955, Kharkov, Ukraine; ed Leningrad State Conservatory, studied with Boris Arapov and Boris Tishchenko; Music Dir, Bolshoi Theatre 2009–10; mem. Composers' Union 1979–; Golden Sheep Prize 2000. *Films:* as composer: Sunset 1990, Lost in Siberia 1991, Capital Punishment 1992, Touch 1992, Moscow Nights 1994, Katia Izmailova 1994, Hammer and Sickle 1994, Giselle's Mania 1995, The Prisoner of the Mountains 1996, The One Who is More Tender 1996, Moscow (Grand Prix, Int. Cinema Music Festival) 2000, His Wife's Diary 2000. *Works include:* opera: Poor Lisa, The Children of Rosenthal; ballet: Love Song in Minor; tango-operetta: Astor Piazzola's Maria de Buenos Aires; instrumental: The Right of Winter 1949, Sketches for Sunet, Russian Seasons; vocal: The Gift, Love and Death of a Poet, The Lead Echo. *Address:* c/o Bolshoi Theatre, 103009 Moscow, Teatralnaya pl. 1, Russia (office). *Website:* www.bolshoi.ru (office).

DETREKŐI, Ákos, DSc; Hungarian civil engineer and university rector; *UNESCO Chair in Continuing Engineering Education, Budapest University of Technology and Economics;* b. 27 Nov. 1939, Budapest; m.; two c.; ed Tech. Univ., Budapest; Asst Faculty of Civil Eng, Budapest Univ. of Tech. and Econs 1963–68, Sr Asst 1968–72, Lecturer, Dept of Geodesy 1963–78, Dept of Photogrammetry 1978–, Assoc. Prof. 1972–80, Prof. and Head of Dept 1980–, Dean Faculty of Civil Eng 1986–90, Rector 1997–, UNESCO Chair in Continuing Eng Educ. 2000–; Lecturer, Technische Univ., Dresden 1980–83; mem. Hungarian Acad. of Sciences (mem. Cttee of Geodesy 1975, Chair. 1990–97), Hungarian Council for Space Research 1995– (mem. Bd of Supervision); Hon. Pres. Hungarian Humboldt Soc., Hungarian Soc. of Surveying, Remote Sensing and Cartography 1994–; Fed.

Decoration of Germany, 1st Class 2002, Order of the Hungarian Repub. 2003; Fasching Antal Medal 1988, Lazar Deák Medal 1993, Albert Szent-Györgyi Prize 1996, Humboldt Medal 1996, Peter Pázmány Prize 2000. *Publications:* one book and numerous contribs and articles. *Leisure interest:* music. *Address:* Department of Photogrammetry and Geoinformatics, Budapest University of Technology and Economics, Müegyetem rkp. 9, 1111 Budapest (office); Naybányai ut 43/b, 1025 Budapest, Hungary (home). *Telephone:* (1) 4632471 (office). *Fax:* (1) 4632470 (office). *E-mail:* adetrekoi@epito.bme.hu (office). *Website:* www.fmt.bme.hu/fmt/ index.php (office).

DETTORI, (Lanfranco) Frankie; Italian professional flat race jockey; b. 15 Dec. 1970, Milan; s. of 13-times Italian champion jockey Gianfranco Dettori and Iris Maria Niemen; m. Catherine Allen 1997; has ridden races in England, France, Germany, Italy, USA, Dubai, Australia, Hong Kong and other countries in the Far East 1992–; 1,000 rides and 215 wins in UK 1995; horses ridden include Lamtarra, Barathea, Vettori, Mark of Distinction, Balanchine, Moonshell, Lochsong, Classic Cliché, Dubai Millennium, Daylami, Sakhee, Opinion Poll, Colour Vision; major race victories include St Leger (twice), The Oaks (twice), The Breeders Cup Mile, Arc de Triomphe (twice), French 2,000 Guineas (twice), English 1,000 Guineas, Queen Elizabeth II Stakes, Prix L'Abbaye, The Japan Cup (twice), The Dubai World Cup, Royal Ascot 2012; rode winners of all seven races at Ascot 1996; survived air crash 2000; launched signature range of food 2001; associated with Godolphin team 1994–2012; Team Capt., A Question of Sport, BBC TV 2002–04; Hon. MBE, Commendatore, Italy 2005; Jockey of the Year 1994, 1995, 2004, BBC Sports Personality of the Year 1996, Int. Sports Personality of the Year, Variety Club 2000. *Publications include:* A Year in the Life of Frankie Dettori 1996, Frankie: The Autobiography 2004, Frankie's: Recipes from an Italian Family (with Marco Pierre White) 2007. *Leisure interests:* golf, wine, cooking. *Address:* c/o Ray Cochrane, 10 Rectory Farm Road, Little Wilbraham, Cambridge, CB21 5LB, England.

DEUBA, Sher Bahadur, MA; Nepalese politician; *Leader, Nepali Congress;* b. 12 June 1946, Angra, Dadeldhura Dist; m. Dr Arju Rana Deuba; one s.; ed Tribhuvan Univ.; Chair. Far Western Students Cttee, Kathmandu 1965; served a total of nine years' imprisonment for political activities 1966–85; Founder-mem. Nepal Students' Union 1970; Research Fellow, LSE, UK 1988–90; active in Popular Movt for Restoration of Democracy in Nepal 1991; mem. Parl. 1991–; Minister of Home Affairs; Leader Parl. Party, Nepali Congress 1994; Prime Minister 1995–97, 2001–02, 2004–05; Minister of Foreign Affairs and Defence 2001–02; sentenced to two-year jail term for corruption July 2005, released Feb. 2006; fmr Pres. Nepali Congress Party (Democratic) (merged again with Nepali Congress under Girja Prasad Koirala as Nepali Congress 2007), Leader 2013–; Vice-Pres. Socialist International 2008. *Address:* Parliament of Nepal, Singha Durbar, Kathmandu (office); Nepali Congress (NC) Central Office, B.P. Smriti Bhawan, B.P.Nagar, Sanepa, Lalitpur, Nepal (office). *Telephone:* (1) 227480 (Parl.) (office); (1) 5555263 (NC) (office). *Fax:* (1) 4222923 (Parl.) (office); (1) 5555188 (NC) (office). *E-mail:* nparl@ntc.net.np (office); ncparty@wlink.com.np (office). *Website:* www .parliament.gov.np (office); www.nepalicongress.org (office).

DEUBET, Kalzeubé Pahimi; Chadian economist and politician; *Prime Minister;* m. Neldjikingar Madjimta; fmr teacher; fmr Gov. Chari-Baguirmi and Bahr el-Ghazal regions; fmr Minister of the Civil Service and of Communication; fmr Chef de cabinet to Pres.; Dir Gen. Société Cotonnière du Tchad –2013; Prime Minister 2013–; fmr mem. Rassemblement pour la Démocratie et le Progrès; mem. Mouvement patriotique du Salut. *Address:* Office of the Prime Minister, BP 463, N'Djamena, Chad (office). *Telephone:* 22-52-63-39 (office). *Fax:* 22-52-69-77 (office). *E-mail:* cpcprimt@intnet.td (office).

DEUTCH, John M., PhD; American chemist, academic and fmr government official; *Institute Professor, Department of Chemistry, Massachusetts Institute of Technology;* b. 27 July 1938, Brussels, Belgium; s. of Michael J. Deutch and Rachel Fischer Deutch; m. Pat Lyons; three s.; ed Amherst Coll. and Massachusetts Inst. of Tech.; Systems Analyst, Office of Sec. for Defense 1961–65; Fellow NAS/NRC, Nat. Bureau of Standards 1966–67; Asst Prof., Princeton Univ. 1967–70; mem. Faculty, MIT 1970–, Prof. of Chem. 1971–; Chair. Dept of Chem. 1976–77, Dean, School of Science 1982–85, Provost 1985–90, Inst. Prof. 1990–; Dir of Energy Research, Dept of Energy 1977–79, Acting Asst Sec. 1979, Under-Sec. 1979–80; UnderSec. for Acquisition and Tech. Dept of Defense 1993–94, Deputy Sec. 1994–95; Dir CIA 1995–96; mem. White House Science Council 1985–89; mem. Bd of Dirs Citigroup Inc. 1987–93, 1996–, Citibank NA 1987–93, 1996–98, Cummins Engine Co. 1997–, Raytheon Co. 1998–, Cheniere Energy Inc. 2007–; mem. ACS, American Physical Soc., American Acad. of Arts and Sciences, Council on Foreign Relations, President's Foreign Intelligence Advisory Cttee 1990–94, Trilateral Comm. 1991; Sloan Fellow 1969–71; Guggenheim Fellow 1974; Hon. DSc (Amherst Coll.) 1978; Hon. DPhil (Lowell) 1986; recipient of awards from Dept of State and Dept of Energy. *Publications:* research articles. *Address:* Department of Chemistry, Massachusetts Institute of Technology, 77 Massachusetts Avenue, Room 6-208, Cambridge, MA 02139, USA (office). *Telephone:* (617) 253-1479 (office). *Fax:* (617) 258-5700 (office). *E-mail:* jmd@mit.edu (office). *Website:* web.mit.edu/ chemistry/deutch (office).

DEUTSCH, David Elieser, MA, DPhil, FRS; British physicist, academic and author; *Non-stipendiary Visiting Professor, Centre for Quantum Computation, University of Oxford;* b. 1953, Haifa, Israel; with Centre for Quantum Computation, Clarendon Lab., Univ. of Oxford 1990–, becoming Non-stipendiary Visiting Prof.; Distinguished Fellow, British Computer Soc. 1998, Paul Dirac Prize and Medal, Inst. of Physics 1998, Fourth Int. Award on Quantum Communication for "theoretical work on Quantum Computer Science" 2002, Edge of Computation Science Prize, Edge Foundation, Inc. 2005. *Achievements include:* pioneered the field of quantum computers by being the first person to formulate a specifically quantum computational algorithm 1985; proponent of the many-worlds interpretation of quantum mechanics and of the multiverse hypothesis. *Publications include:* The Fabric of Reality 1997 (translated into German, Italian, Spanish, Japanese, Finnish, Brazilian Portuguese, Russian, Chinese, French and Polish), The Beginning of Infinity 2011; several scientific papers in professional journals on quantum computing, quantum theory and parallel universes. *Address:* Centre for Quantum Computation, The Clarendon Laboratory, Parks Road, Oxford, OX1 3PU, England (office). *Telephone:* (1865) 272400 (office). *Fax:* (1865) 272400 (office). *E-mail:* d.deutsch1@physics.ox.ac.uk. *Website:* daviddeutsch.physics.ox.ac .uk (office); oxfordquantum.org (office).

DEUTSCH, Tamás; Hungarian politician; b. 27 July 1966, Budapest; s. of György Deutsch and Julianna Takács; m. Agnes Sarolta Für (divorced); four s. two d.; ed Eötvös Loránd Univ., Budapest; Co-founder Alliance of Young Democrats (FIDESZ) 1988, mem. Nat. Steering Cttee 1988–90, campaign chief during 1990 local elections and 1998 parl. elections, party Vice-Pres. 1993–2003, Head of FIDESZ Budapest org. 2001–04, Leader Budapest FIDESZ-Hungarian Christian Democratic Alliance jt faction 2002–03, Deputy Leader Parl. Group 2006; mem. Nat. Ass. (Parl.) 1990–2009, Deputy Speaker 2004–06; Minister for Youth and Sport 1999–2002; MEP 2009–, Vice-Chair. Cttee on Budgetary Control; Vice-Chair. Hungarian Olympic Cttee 1999–2001; mem. Budapest Municipal Ass. 2002–03. *Publications:* contributing author to Jognak Asztalánál (Children at the Table of the Law) 1991. *Leisure interests:* film, football. *Address:* European Parliament, rue Wiertz, 1047, Brussels, Belgium (office). *E-mail:* tamas .deutsch@europarl.europa.eu (office). *Website:* www.europarl.europa.eu (office).

DEV, Kapil (see KAPIL DEV).

DEV SEN, Nabaneeta, BA, MA, AM, PhD; Indian writer and academic; b. 1938; d. of Narendra Dev and Radharani Devi; m. Amartya Sen (divorced); three d.; ed Calcutta (now Kolkata) Univ., Jadavpur Univ., Harvard Univ., Indiana Univ., USA; Bengali writer; Researcher, Newnham Coll., Cambridge 1961–64; Asst Prof. of Comparative Literature, Jadavpur Univ. 1970–72, Assoc. Prof. 1972–83, Prof. 1983–2002, Chair., Dept of Comparative Literature 1987–89; Maytag Prof. of Comparative Literature, Univ. of Colorado, USA 1988–89; Visiting Fellow, St Antony's Coll., Oxford 1997; Radhakrishnan Memorial Lecturer, Oxford Univ. 1996–97; Founder and Pres. West Bengal Women Writers Asscn; Vice-Pres. Indian Nat. Comparative Literature Asscn; mem. Bharatiya Jnanpith Award Language Advisory Cttee 1975–90, Advisory Bd Bengali, Sahitya Akademi 1978–82; Kavi Prize for Poetry 1976, Pratisuti Award for Literary Criticism 1979, Prasad Prize for Poetry 1985, Sisir Kumar Prize 1986, Kalkut Prize 1988, Celli Award 1993, Sanskritiki Award 1994, Saratchandra Award 1994, Archana Choudhury Memorial Prize 1998, Marwari Mitra Samsad Samman for Literature 1998, Harmony Award 1998, Shatabir Kanya Award 1999, Sahitya Akademi Award 1999, Bishwa Banga Sammelan Award 2000, Rajiv Gandhi Memorial Millennium Gold Medal 2000, Bharat Nirman Award 2000, Padma Shri 2000, Bimal Mitra Memorial Award 2001, Mahadevi Verma Memorial Award 2001, Shreyasi Samman for Literature 2001, Lifetime Achievement Award, Bangla Acad. 2003, Pratima Mitra Memorial Prize 2004, Narayan Gangopadhyay Smarak Puraskar 2006, Saratchandra Smriti Puraskar 2007, Bharatiya Bhasha Parishad Award, Gouridevi Memorial Award, Prasad Puraskar. *Publications include:* fiction: Ami Anupan 1978, Prabaase Doibera Bashe 1985, Swabhumi 1986, Sheet Saahasik Hemanta lok 1988, Ekti Dupur 1996, Baamaa Bodhini 1997, Deshaantar 1998, Thhikaanaa 1999, Maayaa Roye Gelo 2000, Shani-Rabi 2001, Paari 2002, Ural 2003, Dashti Upanyas 2003, Titli 2004, Albatross 2004, Ekati Iitibachak Premkahini 2005, Dwiragaman 2006, Ramdhan Mittir Lane 2006; juvenile fiction: Samudrer Sannyasini 1979, Icchamati 1995, Kayak 1996, Palachpurer Picnic 1997, Buddhi Bechaar Saudagar 1999, Chakum-chukum 2000, Saat Kanyer Desh 2000, Monkemoner Galpa 2002, Chhotoder Galpasangra 2005, Rankineer Rajyapat 2005, Sandesher Galpa 2006, Ek Dazan Roopkatha 2006; non-fiction: Karuna tomaar Kon Path Diye 1978, Ishwarer Pratidwandwi o Anyanya Prabandha 1978, Truckbahoney MacMahoney 1983, Hey Purna Taba Charaner Kachhe 1984, Birashaiba Santakabi ebang Birashaiba Sadhana 1987, Tin Bhubaner Parey 1990, Bhraamer Nabaneeta 2006; poetry: Pratham Pratyay 1959, Swaagata Debdut 1974, Shreshthha Kabita 1989. *Address:* 72 Hindustan Park, Kolkata 700 029, India (home). *Telephone:* (33) 24641603 (home).

DEVA, Prabhu; Indian actor, choreographer and director; *Chairman and Director, Prabhudeva's Dance Academy;* b. 3 April 1973, Mysore; s. of Mugur Sundar; m. Ramlath; three c. (one died 2008); currently Chair. and Dir Prabhudeva's Dance Acad., Singapore; launched dance school in Dubai 2009; Life mem. Int. Film and TV Research Centre, Asian Acad. of Film and TV. *Films include:* choreographer: Agni Nakshatram 1988, Vetri Vizha 1989, Raja Vikramarka 1990, Idhayam 1991, Kshana Kshanam 1991, Gharaana Mogudu 1992, Mechanic Alludu 1993, Rakshana 1993, Kadhalan 1994, Bombay 1995, Minsaara Kanavu (Nat. Award) 1997, Pukar 2000, Tappu Chesi Pappu Koodu 2002, Khushi 2003, Samba 2004, Lakshya (Nat. Award, Star Screen Award, Filmfare Award) 2004, Nuvvostanante Nenoddantana (also directed) (Filmfare Award) 2005, Jillunu Oru Kaadhal 2006, Sivaji 2007, Aegan 2008, Endhiran 2010; directed: Paurnami (also writer) 2006, Pokkiri (also writer) (Vijay Award, Mathubhumi Award) 2007, Shankardada Zindabad 2007, Villu 2009, Wanted 2009, Engeyum Kadhal 2010. *Address:* Prabhudeva's Dance Academy, 231 Mounbatten Road, Mounbatten center, Block G, 01-02, Singapore 397999, Singapore (office). *Telephone:* 62425835 (office). *E-mail:* register@prabhudeva.com.sg (office). *Website:* www.prabhudeva.com.sg (office).

DEVANEY, John Francis, CEng, FIEE, FIMechE; British business executive; *Chairman, Tersus Energy PLC;* b. 25 June 1946; s. of the late George Devaney and Alice Ann Devaney; two s. one d.; ed St Mary's Coll., Blackburn and Univ. of Sheffield; worked for Perkins Engines 1968–69, mfg positions in Peterborough 1968–76, Project Man., Ohio, USA 1976–77, Pres. 1983–88, Group Vice-Pres. European Components Group, Peterborough 1988, Group Vice-Pres. Enterprises Group, Toronto, Canada 1988–89; Chair., CEO and Group Vice-Pres. Kelsey-Hayes Corpn, Detroit, Mich., USA 1989–92; Dir Eastern Electricity PLC (later Eastern Group PLC) 1992, CEO 1993, Exec. Chair. 1995–98; Dir EXEL Logistics (formed from merger of Nat. Freight Corpn with Ocean Group) 1996, Chair. 2000–02; Chair. Marconi PLC (later Telent PLC) 2002–07; Founder and Chair. British Energy; Chair. Liberata –2002; Chair. Nat. Air Traffic Services (NATS) 2005–; Chair. Tersus Energy PLC 2005–; Dir and fmr Chair. EA Technology; Dir (non-exec.) HSBC (fmrly Midland Bank) 1994–, British Steel 1998–; Pres. Electricity Asscn 1994–95, Inst. for Customer Service 1998–; mem. Bd of Dirs Northern Rock 2007–. *Leisure interests:* skiing, golf, tennis, sailing. *Address:* Tersus Energy PLC, 343 Linen Hall, 162–168 Regent Street, London, W1B 5DT, England (office). *Telephone:* (20) 7038-0600 (office). *Fax:* (20) 7038-0605 (office). *E-mail:* power@tersusenergy.com (office). *Website:* www.tersusenergy.com (office).

DEVE GOWDA, Haradanahalli Dodde Gowda; Indian politician; *President, Janata Dal (Secular);* b. 18 May 1933, Haradan ahalli; s. of Dodde Gowda and Devamma Gowda; m. Chennamma; four s. two d.; ed Govt polytechnic inst.; trained as civil engineer; ran contracting business; mem. Congress Party 1953–62 (resigned 1962); mem. Karnataka State Legis. Ass. 1962–89, Leader of Opposition 1972–77; imprisoned during state of emergency in 1970s; Minister of Public Works and Irrigation, Karnataka –1980; Pres. Janata Dal 1994; Chief Minister of Karnataka 1994–96; fmr mem. Lok Sabha; Leader of multiparty United Front 1996; Prime Minister 1996–97, Minister of Home and Agric., Science and Tech., Personnel and Atomic Energy 1996–97; currently Pres. Janata Dal (Secular). *Address:* Janata Dal (Secular), 14A, Ferozeshah Road, New Delhi 110 001, India (office). *Telephone:* (11) 23321455 (office). *Fax:* (11) 23321455 (office). *E-mail:* info@ janatadalsecular.org.in (office); jdsecular@gmail.com (office). *Website:* www .janatadalsecular.org.in.

DEVEDJIAN, Patrick; French lawyer and politician; b. 26 Aug. 1944, Fontainebleau (Seine-et-Marne); ed Université Panthéon-Assas Paris II; fmr mem. Occident group; admitted to Paris Bar 1970; joined Gaullist movt 1971; helped establish RPR party 1976; elected Mayor of Antony (Hauts-de-Seine) 1983, re-elected 1989, 1995, 2001; mem. Assemblée Nat. for Hauts-de-Seine 1986, re-elected 1988, 1993, 1997, 2002, 2005; Vice-Pres. Mouvement européen (France) 2002; Minister for Local Liberties 2002–04, for Industry 2004–05, Minister in the Office of the Prime Minister, in charge of Implementation of the Econ. Stimulus Plan 2008–10; adviser to Nicolas Sarkozy during presidential bid 2007; Exec. Sec. Gen. Union pour un Mouvement Populaire (UMP) 2007–08; Pres. Conseil général des Hauts-de-Seine 2007–; as a lawyer, was involved in several cases defending mems of Armenian Secret Army for the Liberation of Armenia. *Address:* Union pour un Mouvement Populaire, 55 rue La Boétie, 75384 Paris Cedex 08, France (office). *Telephone:* 1-40-76-60-00 (office). *E-mail:* webmaster@u-m-p.org (office); information@patrickdevedjian.fr. *Website:* www.u-m-p.org (office); www .patrickdevedjian.fr.

DEVERS, Gail, BA; American athlete; b. 19 Nov. 1966, Seattle, Wash.; m. 1st Ron Roberts 1988 (divorced 1992); m. 2nd Mike Phillips; three d.; ed Univ. of California, Los Angeles; holds record for most World Championship gold medals won by a woman (five): 100m., (1993), 100m. hurdles (1993, 1995, 1999), 4x100m. relay (1997); Olympic champion 100m. (1992, 1996); Olympic gold medal 4x100m. relay (1996); won IAAF Grand Prix final 100m. hurdles 2000, 2002; won World Cup 100m. hurdles 2002; US champion 100m. hurdles (seven times); est. Gail Devers Foundation; inducted into Nat. Track & Field Hall of Fame 2011, United States Olympic Hall of Fame 2012; NCAA Silver Anniversary Award 2013. *Address:* c/o Gail Devers Foundation, 6555 Sugarloaf Parkway, Suite 307-137, Duluth, GA 30097, USA.

DEVESHWAR, Yogesh Chander; Indian business executive; *Chairman, ITC Limited;* b. 4 Feb. 1947, Lahore, British India; ed Indian Inst. of Tech., Delhi, Harvard Business School, USA, Cornell Univ., USA; joined ITC Ltd 1968, man. buyout adviser to corp. HQ, Kolkata 1974, Gen. Man. packaging and printing plant, Chennai 1978, mem. Bd of Dirs 1984–, Chair. Tobacco Div. 1991–94, Chair. ITC Ltd 1996–; Chair. and Man. Dir Air India 1991–94; apptd Pres. Confed. of Indian Industry 2005; mem. Bd of Govs Indian School of Business; fmr Chair. Bd of Govs Indian Inst. of Man.; Man. Entrepreneur of the Year, Ernst & Young 2001, Business Person of the Year Award, UK Trade and Investment 2006, Hall of Pride, Indian Science Congress 2006, Sustainable Asset Management/Sustainable Performance Group Sustainability Leadership Award 2007, Global Leadership Award, US-India Business Council, US Chamber of Commerce 2010, Padma Bhushan 2011. *Address:* ITC Ltd, 37 J. L. Nehru Road, Kolkata 700 071, India (office). *Telephone:* (33) 22889371 (office). *Website:* www.itcportal.com (office).

DEVGN, Ajay; Indian actor and film director; b. (Vishal Veeru Devgan), 2 April 1969, New Delhi; s. of Veeru Devgan and Veena Devgan; m. Kajol Devgan 1999; one s. one d.; ed Bappu School, Juhu, Mithibai Coll. *Films include:* Phool Aur Kaante (Filmfare Award) 1991, Jigar, Dil Hai Betaab 1992, Sangram 1993, Dhanwaan 1993, Dilwale 1994, Vijaypath 1994, Suhaag 1994, Hulchul 1995, Haqeeqat 1995, Diljale 1996, Jaan 1996, Itihaas 1997, Ishq 1997, Zakhm (Nat. Film Award) 1998, Major Saab 1998, Pyar To Hona Hi Tha 1998, Dil Kya Kare 1999, Kachche Dhaage 1999, Hum Dil De Chuke Sanam 1999, Lajja 2001, Deewane 2000, Raju Chacha (producer) 2000, Lajja 2001, Yeh Raaste Hain Pyaar Ke 2001, Company 2002, The Legend of Bhagat Singh (Nat. Film Award, Filmfare Critics Award) 2002, Deewangee (Filmfare Award) 2002, Bhoot 2003, Gangaajal 2003, LOC Kargil 2003, Khakee 2004, Raincoat 2004, Yuva 2004, Blackmail 2005, Apaharan 2005, Golmaal 2006, Omkara 2006, Cash 2007, Sunday 2008, U, Me aur Hum (producer, dir) 2008, Golmaal Returns 2008, London Dreams 2009, All the Best (Aprasara Award, Stardust Award) 2009, Rajneeti 2010, Once Upon a Time in Mumbai 2010, Aakrosh 2010. *Address:* Sea Cliff, 1st Floor, Gandhigram Road, Juhu, Mumbai (home); 5/6, Sheetal Apartments, Ground Floor, Opposite Chandan Cinema, Juhu, 400 049, India (home). *Telephone:* (22) 6200253 (home); (22) 6201977 (home). *Website:* www.ajaydevgn.com.

DEVINSKY, Ferdinand, DSc; Slovak medicinal chemist, academic and politician; b. 17 Aug. 1947, Bratislava; m.; two c.; ed Slovak Univ. of Tech., Bratislava; researcher, Slovakofoarma 1970–72; Lecturer, Comenius Univ., Bratislava 1972–2002, Rector 1997–2003, currently Rector Emer. and Head of Dept, Faculty of Pharmacy 1990–; research studies in UK 1986–87, 1991–2007, Belgium, USA, Germany 1991; currently mem. Parl., Chair. Cttee for Educ., Science, Sport, Youth, Culture and Media; mem. Slovak Democratic and Christian Union; mem. Steering Cttee European Univ. Asscn 2006–; mem. Governing Bd Slovak Academic Ranking and Rating Agency; Hon. Sr Research Fellow, King's Coll. London, UK; Stella Della Solidarieta Italiana (Commendatore) 2004; Jubilee Medal, Charles Univ., Prague 1998. *Publications include:* numerous scientific papers and textbooks. *Leisure interests:* tennis, any creative work. *Address:* Comenius University, Faculty of Pharmacy, Kalinciakova 8, 832 32 Bratislava (office); Národná rada Slovenskej republiky (National Council of the Slovak Republic), nám. Alexandra Dubčeka 1, 812 80 Bratislava, Slovakia (office). *Telephone:* (2) 50117331 (office). *Fax:* (2) 50117357 (office). *E-mail:* ferdinand_devinsky@nrsr.sk (office). *Website:* www.nrsr.sk (office).

DeVITO, Danny; American actor and director; b. 17 Nov. 1944, New Jersey; m. Rhea Perlman 1982; two s. two d.; ed American Acad. of Dramatic Arts, Wilfred Acad. of Hair and Beauty Culture; Co-founder and Co-Chair. Jersey Films (production co.); Golden Globe Award for Taxi 1979, Emmy Award 1981. *Stage appearances include:* The Man with a Flower in His Mouth, Down the Morning Line, The Line of Least Existence, The Shrinking Bride, Call Me Charlie, Comedy of Errors, Merry Wives of Windsor, Three by Pirandello, One Flew over the Cuckoo's Nest. *Films include:* Dreams of Glass 1970, Lady Liberty 1971, Hot Dogs for Gauguin 1972, Scalawag 1973, Hurry Up or I'll Be 30 1973, One Flew over the Cuckoo's Nest 1975, Deadly Hero 1976, The Money 1976, Car Wash 1976, The Van 1977, The World's Greatest Lover 1977, Goin' South 1978, Swap Meet 1979, Going Ape 1981, Terms of Endearment 1983, Romancing the Stone 1984, Johnny Dangerously 1984, Head Office 1985, Jewel of the Nile 1985, Wiseguys 1986, Ruthless People 1986, My Little Pony (voice) 1986, Tin Men 1987, Throw Momma from the Train (also dir) 1987, Twins 1988, War of the Roses (also dir) 1989, Other People's Money 1991, Batman Returns 1992, Hoffa (also producer, dir) 1992, Jack the Bear 1993, Look Who's Talking Now (voice) 1993, Renaissance Man 1994, Junior 1994, Get Shorty (also co-producer) 1995, Matilda (also dir, co-producer) 1996, Space Jam (voice) 1996, Mars Attacks 1996, The Rainmaker 1997, LA Confidential 1997, Living Out Loud (also producer) 1998, Man on the Moon (also producer) 1999, The Virgin Suicides 1999, The Big Kahuna 1999, Drowning Mona (also producer) 2000, Screwed 2000, Heist 2001, What's the Worst That Could Happen? 2001, Death to Smoochy (also dir) 2002, Duplex (voice, also dir) 2003, Anything Else 2003, Big Fish 2003, Family of the Year 2004, Catching Kringle (voice) 2004, Christmas in Love 2004, Marilyn Hotchkiss' Ballroom Dancing and Charm School 2005, Be Cool (also producer) 2005, The OH in Ohio 2006, Bye Bye Benjamin (exec. producer) 2006, Even Money 2006, Relative Strangers (also producer) 2006, Deck the Halls 2006, The Good Night 2007, Reno 911!: Miami 2007, Nobel Son 2007, Just Add Water 2008, House Broken, Solitary Man 2009, When in Rome 2010, Girl Walks Into a Bar 2011, The Lorax (voice) 2012. *Television includes:* Taxi (series, also dir), Mary (dir), Valentine, The Rating Game (dir), All the Kids Do It, A Very Special Christmas Party, Two Daddies? (voice), The Selling of Vince DeAngelo (dir), Amazing Stories (also dir), The Simpsons (voice), It's Always Sunny in Philadelphia (series) 2006–11. *Address:* c/o Fred Specktor, Creative Artists Agency, 2000 Avenue of the Stars, Los Angeles, CA 90067; Jersey Films, 10351 Santa Monica Blvd., Suite 200, Los Angeles, CA 90025, USA. *Telephone:* (310) 203-1000 (Jersey Films).

DEVLIN, Dean; American actor, screenwriter and producer; b. 27 Aug. 1962; George Pal Memorial Award 1998. *Film produced:* The Patriot 2000, Eight Legged Freaks 2002, Cellular 2004, Who Killed the Electric Car? 2006, Flyboys 2006. *Films written and produced:* Stargate 1994 (Best Picture, Acad. of Science Fiction, Fantasy and Horror Films, Readers' Choice Award, Sci-Fi Universe magazine), Independence Day 1996 (Best Picture, Acad. of Science Fiction, Fantasy and Horror Films, People's Choice Best Picture), Godzilla 1998. *Film screenplay:* Universal Soldier 1992. *Films acted in:* My Bodyguard 1980, The Wild Life 1984, Real Genius 1985, City Limits 1985, Martians Go Home 1990, Moon 44 1990, Total Exposure 1991. *TV series:* The Visitor (creator, exec. producer) 1997, Leverage (series) 2008–09. *TV appearances in:* North Beach 1985, Rawhide 1985, Hard Copy 1987, Generations 1989; guest appearances in: LA Law, Happy Days, Misfits of Science. *Address:* 11601 Wilshire Boulevard, Suite 2150, Los Angeles, CA 90025-0509, USA.

DEVLIN, Stuart Leslie, AO, CMG; Australian goldsmith, silversmith and designer; b. 9 Oct. 1931, Geelong; s. of Richard Devlin and Jesse Devlin; m. 1st Kim Hose 1962; m. 2nd Carole Hedley-Saunders 1986; ed Gordon Inst. of Tech., Geelong, Royal Melbourne Inst. of Tech. and Royal Coll. of Art; art teacher, Victoria Educ. Dept 1950–58, Royal Coll. of Art 1958–60; Harkness Fellow, New York 1960–62; Lecturer, Prahan Tech. Coll., Melbourne 1962; Inspector of Art in Tech. Schools, Victoria Educ. Dept 1964–65; working as goldsmith, silversmith and designer in London 1965–; exhbns of gold and silver in numerous cities in UK, USA, Australia, Middle East, etc.; has executed many comms for commemorative coins in gold and silver for various countries; designed and made cutlery for State Visit to Paris 1972, Duke of Edinburgh Trophy for World Driving Championship 1973, silver to commemorate opening of Sydney Opera House 1973, Grand Nat. Trophy 1975 and Regalia for Order of Australia 1975–76; Centrepiece for Royal Engineers to commemorate their work in Northern Ireland 1981; Bas-relief portrait HRH Princess of Wales for Wedgwood 1986; devised and executed Champagne Diamond Exhbn 1987; designed and made Sydney 2000 Olympic coins 1997; designed and made Millennium Commemorative dishes for Goldsmiths' Co. and Information Technologists' Co. 2000; granted Royal Warrant goldsmith and jeweller to HM Queen Elizabeth II 1982; mem. Court of Wardens, Goldsmiths' Co. 1992, Prime Warden 1996–97; Vice-Chair. Intergraph Graphics Users' Group, UK 1996–98; Dr hc (Royal Melbourne Inst. of Tech.) 2000. *Leisure interests:* work, computer graphics, swimming. *Address:* 72 Shippam Street, Roman Quarter, Chichester, PO19 1AG, England. *Telephone:* (1903) 858939. *E-mail:* stuart@stuart-devlin.co.uk.

DEVONSHIRE, 12th Duke of, cr. 1694, Baron Cavendish, Earl of Devonshire, Marquess of Hartington, Earl of Burlington, Baron Cavendish (UK); **Peregrine Andrew Morny Cavendish,** CBE; British horse racing executive and landowner; b. 27 April 1944; s. of 11th Duke of Devonshire and Hon. Deborah Vivian Freeman Mitford; m. Amanda Carmen Heywood-Lonsdale 1967; one s. two d.; ed Eton, Exeter Coll., Oxford; Sr Steward, Jockey Club 1989–94; Chair. British Horseracing Bd 1993–96; Dir Sotheby's Holdings Inc. 1994–; Deputy Chair. 1996–; HM's Rep. at Ascot 1997–; Trustee, Yorkshire Dales Nat. Park Millennium Trust. *Address:* Chatsworth, Bakewell, Derbyshire DE45 1PP, England (home). *Telephone:* (1246) 565300 (office). *Website:* www.chatsworth.org (office).

DEVRIES, William Castle, MD; American surgeon; b. 19 Dec. 1943, Brooklyn, New York; s. of Hendrik Devries and Cathryn L. Castle; seven c.; ed Univ. of Utah, Army Medical Dept Basic Officer program; Intern, Duke Univ. Medical Center 1970–71, Resident in Cardiovascular and Thoracic Surgery 1971–79; Asst Prof. of Surgery, Univ. of Utah 1979–84; Chief of Thoracic Surgery, Salt Lake Hosp. –1984; Pres. De Vries & Assocs 1988–99; Surgeon, Hardin Memorial Hosp., Elizabethtown, Ky 1999–; joined US Defense Department as medical contractor Walter Reed Army Medical Center, Washington, DC, joined US Army Reserve 2000–; Fellow,

American Coll. of Surgeons, American Coll. of Cardiology, American Coll. of Chest Physicians; mem. American Medical Asscn, Soc. of Thoracic Surgeons. *Achievements include:* implanted first permanent artificial heart 1982. *Address:* Devries and Associates, 7 Snowmound Court, Rockville, MD 20850, USA (office).

DEVROYE, Luc, BEng, PhD; Belgian/Canadian computer scientist and academic; *Professor of Computer Science, McGill University;* b. Tienen, Belgium; m. Bea Van Nuffel; ed Univ. of Leuven, Osaka Univ., Japan, Univ. of Texas at Austin, USA; Asst Prof., McGill Univ. 1977–81, Assoc. Prof. 1981–87, Prof. of Computer Science and Assoc. mem. Dept of Math. and Statistics 1987–, James McGill Prof. 2003–; working at Computational Geometry Lab., Carleton Univ., Ottawa 2006–; fmr mem. editorial bds of numerous Canadian and int. math. and computer science journals; Hon. mem. Belgian Statistical Soc. 1997; Dr hc (Catholic Univ. of Louvain) 2002; E.W.R. Steacie Memorial Fellowship 1987, Research Award, Alexander von Humboldt Foundation (Germany) 2004, Killam Prize, Canada Council for the Arts 2005. *Address:* School of Computer Science, McGill University, Office MC300N, 3480 University Street, Montreal, PQ H3A 2A7 (office); 3425 Redpath, Montreal, PQ H3G 2G2, Canada (home). *Telephone:* (514) 398-3738 (office); (514) 849-1564 (home). *E-mail:* lucdevroye@gmail.com (office). *Website:* www.cs.mcgill.ca (office); luc.devroye.org.

DEWAEL, Patrick; Belgian politician; b. 13 Oct. 1955, Lier; m. Marleen Van Doren; three c.; solicitor 1977–85; Sec., House of Reps 1985; mem. Parl. (Vlaamse Liberalen en Demokraten—VLD) for Tongeren-Maaseik Dist 1985–95, for Hasselt-Tongeren-Maaseik Constituency 1995–, Leader Liberal Party Group (VLD) 1992–99; Community Minister for Culture 1985–92; Mayor of Tongeren 1995–; Minister-Pres. of Govt of Flanders 1999–2001, Minister of Govt of Flanders for Finance, Budget, Foreign Policy and European Affairs, Minister-Pres. of Govt of Flanders 2001–03; Deputy Prime Minister and Minister of the Interior 2003–07 (resgnd), reappointed Minister of Interior Dec. 2007, resgnd March 2008; Pres. Chamber of Reps 2008–10. *Publications:* De warme hand 1991, Wederzijds respect. De gevaren van het Blok 2001, Vooruitzien 2001, Het Vlaams Manifest. Meer ruimte voor de regio's 2002, Eelt op mijn ziel 2007. *Address:* Chambre des Représentants, Place de la Nation, 1008 Brussels, (office); Office of the Mayor, Maastrichterstraat 10, 3700 Tongeren, Belgium. *E-mail:* steven.coenegrachts@stadtongeren.be. *Website:* www.dewael.com/NL.

DEWEY, John Frederick, MA, PhD, DSc, ScD, FRS, FGS; British professor of geology; *Distinguished Emeritus Professor, University of California, Davis and University College, Oxford;* b. 22 May 1937, London; s. of John Edward Dewey and Florence Nellie Mary Dewey; m. Frances Mary Blackhurst 1961; one s. one d.; ed Bancroft's School, Univ. of London; lecturer, Univ. of Manchester 1960–64, Univ. of Cambridge 1964–70; Prof. Univ. of Albany, NY 1970–82; Prof. Univ. of Durham 1982–86; Prof. of Geology, Univ. of Oxford 1986–2000, Fellow Univ. Coll. 1986–, Sr Research Fellow 2001–07, Emer. Fellow 2007–; Prof. of Geology, Univ. of Calif., Davis 2000–07, Distinguished Prof. 2001–, Distinguished Emer. Prof. 2007–; mem. Academia Europaea 1990; Foreign mem. NAS 1997; Hon. MRIA; T.N. George Medal, Univ. of Glasgow 1983, Lyell Medal, Geological Soc. of London 1984, Penrose Medal, Geological Soc. of America 1992, Arthur Holmes Medal, European Union of Geosciences 1993, Wollaston Medal, Geological Soc. of London 1999, Fourmarier Medal, Belgian Acad. of Sciences 2000. *Publications:* 138 papers in scientific journals. *Leisure interests:* skiing, tennis, cricket, model railways, watercolour painting, British, Irish and American music 1850–1950. *Address:* Department of Geology, One Shields Avenue, University of California, Davis, CA 95616-8605, USA (office); University College, Oxford, OX1 4BH (office); Sherwood Lodge, 93 Bagley Wood Road, Kennington, OX1 5NA, England (home). *Telephone:* (1865) 276640 (Oxford) (office); (1865) 735525 (home). *Fax:* (530) 752-0951 (Davis) (office). *E-mail:* jfdewey@ucdavis.edu (office). *Website:* www.geology.ucdavis.edu (office).

DeWINE, R. Michael (Mike), BS, JD; American academic and fmr politician; b. 5 Jan. 1947, Springfield, Ohio; s. of Richard DeWine and Jean DeWine; m. Frances Struewing 1967; four s. four d.; ed Miami Univ., Oxford, Ohio and Ohio Northern Univ.; admitted to Bar, Ohio 1972, US Supreme Court 1977; Asst Prosecuting Attorney, Green Co., Xenia, Ohio 1973–75, Prosecuting Attorney 1977–81; mem. Ohio State Senate 1981–82; mem. US House of Reps, Washington, DC 1983–90; Lt-Gov. of Ohio 1991–94; Senator from Ohio 1995–2007; Visiting Scholar, Center for Political Studies, Cedarville Univ. 2007; Co-Chair. Corp. Investigations Group, Keating Muething & Klekamp, Cincinnati 2007–; Republican. *Address:* 2587 Conley Road, Cedarville, OH 45314-9525, USA (home).

DeWOLFE, Richard B., BAS; American business executive; *Chairman, Manulife Financial Corporation;* ed Boston Univ., American Coll. of Corp. Dirs; Man. Partner, DeWolfe & Co. LLC; fmr Chair. and CEO The DeWolfe Companies, Inc. (acquired by Cendant Corpn 2002); Founder and fmr Chair. Reliance Relocations Services, Inc.; mem. Bd of Dirs Manulife Financial Corpn 2004–, Vice-Chair. 2012–13, Chair. 2013–; mem. Bd of Dirs Avantair, Inc.; Trustee, Boston Univ. (fmr Chair. Bd of Trustees); Hon. Dir The Boston Center for Community and Justice. *Address:* Manulife Financial Corpn, 200 Bloor Street East, NT 11, Toronto, ON M4W 1E5, Canada (office). *Telephone:* (416) 926-3000 (office). *Fax:* (416) 926-5410 (office). *E-mail:* info@manulife.com (office). *Website:* www.manulife.com (office).

DEWOST, Jean-Louis; French academic and government official; *President, Commission nationale de contrôle des interceptions de sécurité (CNCIS);* b. 6 Sept. 1937, Dunkirk; s. of Emmanuel Dewost and Colette Ruyssen; m. Agnès Huet 1967; one s. two d.; ed Univ. de Paris, Inst. d'Etudes Politiques de Paris and Ecole Nat. d'Admin; jr official, Conseil d'Etat 1967–69; Asst Man. Industrial Affairs, European Org. for Devt and Construction of Space Vehicle Launchers (CECLES/ELDO) 1962–72, Dir Finance and Econ. Planning 1972–73; Maître des Requêtes, Conseil d'Etat 1972, Conseiller d'Etat 1986, Pres. de la Section Sociale, 2001–03; legal adviser, EC Council Legal Service 1973–85, Jurisconsulte 1986–87; Dir-Gen. EC Legal Service 1987–2001; Pres. Comm. Nat. de contrôle des interceptions de sécurité (govt admin. authority) 2003–; Prof., Inst. d'Etudes Politiques (Sciences Po), Paris; Officier, Légion d'honneur, Officier, Ordre nat. du Mérite, Grand Officier, Order of White Rose of Finland, Grand Officier Order of the Falcon of Iceland. *Publications:* several publs on French public law and EU law. *Leisure interests:* swimming, opera. *Address:* Commission nationale de contrôle des interceptions de sécurité, 35 rue Saint-Dominique, 75007 Paris (office); Sciences

Po, 27 rue Saint-Guillaume, 75337 Paris Cedex 07 (office); 11 rue Sainte Anne, 75000, Paris, France (home). *Telephone:* 1-45-55-70-20 (office); 1-45-49-50-50 (office). *Fax:* 1-45-55-71-15 (office); 1-42-22-31-26 (office).

DEXTER, Hon. Darrell, BEd, LLB, MLA; Canadian politician; b. 1957, Halifax, NS; s. of Elvin Dexter and Florence Dexter; m. Kelly Wilson; one s.; ed Dalhousie Univ., Univ. of King's Coll., Halifax; served in Canadian Navy, attained rank of Sub-Lt; worked as lawyer in pvt. practice in Halifax; fmr Chair. Dartmouth Downtown Devt Corpn; elected Dartmouth City Councillor 1994; mem. Legis. Ass. (regional parl.) for Cole Harbour 1998–2013; mem. New Democratic Party, Leader 2001–; Premier of Nova Scotia 2009–13, also Pres. Exec. Council, Minister of Policy and Priorities, Minister of Intergovernmental Affairs, Minister of Aboriginal Affairs and Minister responsible for Mil. Relations. *Address:* c/o Nova Scotia New Democratic Party, 1660 Hollis Street, Halifax, NS B3J 1V7, Canada (office). *Website:* www.ns.ndp.ca (office).

DEXTER, (Norman) Colin, OBE, MA (Cantab.), MA (Oxon.); British author; b. 29 Sept. 1930, Stamford, Lincs., England; s. of Alfred Dexter and Dorothy Dexter (née Towns); m. Dorothy Cooper 1956; one s. one d.; ed Stamford School, Christ's Coll., Cambridge; nat. service (Royal Signals) 1948–50; taught Classics 1954–66; Sr Asst Sec. Oxford Delegacy of Local Examinations 1966–88; Fellow, St Cross Coll., Oxford; Freedom of the City of Oxford 2001; Gold Dagger, Crime Writers' Asscn (twice), Silver Dagger (twice), Cartier Diamond Dagger, ITV 3 Writer's Award for Classic TV Drama 2008. *Publications:* Last Bus to Woodstock 1975, Last Seen Wearing 1977, The Silent World of Nicholas Quinn 1977, Service of All the Dead 1979, The Dead of Jericho 1981, The Riddle of the Third Mile 1983, The Secret of Annexe 3 1986, The Wench is Dead 1989, The Jewel That Was Ours 1991, The Way through the Woods 1992, Morse's Greatest Mystery and Other Stories 1993, The Daughters of Cain 1994, Death is Now My Neighbour 1996, The Remorseful Day 1999, Book of 'Morse' Crosswords 2006, Cracking Cryptic Crosswords 2009. *Leisure interests:* reading, music, crosswords (fmr nat. crossword champion). *Address:* 456 Banbury Road, Oxford, OX2 7RG, England.

DGHAILI, Jalal al-; Libyan politician; mem. Nat. Transitional Council following overthrow of Mu'ammar Gaddafi, Minister of Defence 2011. *Address:* c/o Ministry of Defence, Tripoli, Libya (office).

DHALIWAL, Daljit, MA; British journalist; b. London; m. Lee Patrick Sullivan (divorced); ed Univ. of East London, Univ. of London; reporter for BBC, London 1990, NI Corresp. and Anchor, BBC World –1995; reporter ITN, London 1995, Anchor, World News for Public TV, Channel 4 News and World Focus 1996–2001; Anchor, Your World Today and World Report CNN (Cable Network News) Int., Atlanta, Ga USA 2002–04; Anchor, Wide Angle (Public Broadcasting System), New York, 2002, 2006–07, Anchor, Global Watch 2008, host, Foreign Exchange with Daljit Dhaliwal 2008–09; Anchor and Correspondent, Al-Jazeera 2010–; moderator and host, UN confs in New York and The Hague; Judge, Amnesty Int. Media Awards, BAFTA Awards; Dr hc (Univ. of East London). *Address:* HD Reps, 75 Rockefeller Plaza, 18th Floor, New York, NY 10019, USA (office). *Telephone:* (212) 710-1049 (office). *E-mail:* David@HDReps.com (office). *Website:* www.hdreps.com (office).

DHANABALAN, Suppiah, BA; Singaporean company director and fmr government official; b. 8 Aug. 1937; m. Tan Khoon Hiap; one s. one d.; ed Victoria School and Univ. of Malaya; Sr Industrial Economist, Deputy Dir (Operations and Finance) Econ. Devt Bd 1961–68; Vice-Pres., Exec. Vice-Pres. Devt Bank of Singapore (now DBS Group Holdings Ltd) 1968–78, Chair. 1998–2005; mem. Parl. 1976–96; Sr Minister of State 1978–80; Minister of Foreign Affairs 1980–88, Culture 1981–84, Community Devt 1984–86, Nat. Devt 1987–92, of Trade and Industry 1992–93; Chair. Parameswara Holdings 1994–2012; Sr Adviser, Nuri Holdings (S) Pte. Ltd 1994–99; Chair. Singapore Airlines Ltd 1996–98; Chair. Temasek Holdings (Pte.) Ltd (govt-owned investment co.) 1996–2013. *Leisure interests:* reading, golf. *Address:* c/o Temasek Holdings (Pte.) Ltd, 60B Orchard Road, #06-18, Tower 2, The Atrium@Orchard, Singapore 238891, Singapore (office).

DHANAPALA, Jayantha, BA, MA; Sri Lankan diplomatist and consultant; *President, Pugwash Conferences on Science and World Affairs;* b. 30 Dec. 1938, Colombo; s. of James Angus and Kumarihamy Dhanapala Ratemahatmaya; m. Maureen Elhart; one s. one d.; ed Univ. of Peradeniya, Univ. of London, UK, American Univ., Washington, DC, USA; corp. exec. in pvt. sector 1962–65; joined Foreign Service 1965, diplomatic appointments in People's Repub. of China, UK and USA 1965–77; Dir Non-Aligned Movt Div., Ministry of Foreign Affairs 1978–80, Dir Gen. and Additional Sec., Ministry of Foreign Affairs 1992–94; Deputy High Commr to India 1981–83; Amb. and Perm. Rep. to UN, Geneva, Switzerland 1984–87, Dir UN Inst. for Disarmament Research 1987–92; Amb. to USA (also accred to Mexico) 1995–97; apptd Pres. Review and Extension Conf. of Treaty on the Non-Proliferation of Nuclear Weapons 1995; UN Under-Sec.-Gen. for Disarmament Affairs 1998–2003; Sec.-Gen. Secr. for Co-ordinating the Peace Process 2004–05 (resgnd); Chief Negotiator in talks with LTTE 2004–05, Sr Adviser to Pres. 2005–07; Visiting Simons Prof., Simon Fraser Univ., Vancouver, Canada Jan.–April 2008; Overseas Visiting Scholar, St Johns Coll., Cambridge Univ. Oct.–Dec. 2009; Sr Visiting Scholar, US Inst. of Peace March–June 2010; Chair. UN Univ. Council 2006–08; Pres. Pugwash Confs on Science and World Affairs 2007–; Deputy Chair. Stockholm Int. Peace Research Inst. 2012–; Dir (non-exec.) Dialog Telekom 2007–, Cargils (Ceylon) Ltd 2008–; mem. Canberra Comm., Australia 1995–96; Diplomat-in-Residence, Center for Non-Proliferation Studies, Monterey Inst. of Int. Studies, Calif., USA 1997–98; mem. Advisory Bd, Geneva Centre for Democratic Control of Armed Forces 2003–12, Advisory Bd of Stimson Inst. for Int. Studies 2003–, Int. Advisory Bd of Bonn Int. Center for Conversion 2003–, Weapons of Mass Destruction Comm. 2004–06, Int. Advisory Group, ICRC 2004–07, Int. Advisory Bd, Center for Nonproliferation Studies, Monterey Inst. of Int. Studies 2006–; Dr hc (Univ. of Peradeniya) 2000, (Univ. of Sabaragamuwa) 2003, Dubna Int. Univ. of Nature, Society and Man, Russia 2009, Hon. DHumLitt (Monterey Inst. of Int. Studies) 2001, Hon. DSc in Social Sciences (Univ. of Southampton) 2003; Winner, Herald Tribune Essay Competition 1957, Jit Trainor Award for Distinction in the Conduct of Diplomacy, Georgetown Univ., USA 1995, Lifetime Achievement Award, Monterey Inst. for Int. Studies, USA 1998, Leadership in Crisis Award, Ploughshares Fund and Fourth Freedom Forum

2000, Pax Christi Ireland Peace Award 2002, Alan Cranston Peace Award, Global Security Inst., USA 2002, Mohamed Sahabdeen Award 2005, Mohamed Sahabdeen Award for Peace and Int. Understanding 2005, Sri Lankan of the Year, Lanka Monthly Digest 2006, Sean MacBride Peace Prize 2007, Simons Foundation Award for Distinguished Global Leadership in the service of Peace and Disarmament 2008, Sarvodaya Trust Fund Annual Nat. Award 2008. *Publications include:* China and the Third World 1984, Nuclear War, Nuclear Proliferation and Their Consequences (co-author) 1985, Multilateral Diplomacy and the NPT: An Insider's Account 2005. *Leisure interests:* reading, watching sports, theatre and film. *Address:* 25/6 Pepiliyana Road, Nugegoda, Sri Lanka (home). *Telephone:* (11) 2856297 (home). *E-mail:* jdhanapala@yahoo.co.uk (office). *Website:* www.jayanthadhanapala.com (home).

DHANARAJAN, Dato' Gajaraj (Raj), PhD; Malaysian educationalist; ed Univ. of Madras, India, Univ. of London, Univ. of Aston, UK; Research Officer and Lecturer, School of Biological Sciences, Univ. of Science, Malaysia, Assoc. Prof. of Distance Educ. and Deputy Dir Centre for Off-Campus Studies; Assoc. Dir (Academic) Open Learning Inst. of Hong Kong (now Open Univ. of Hong Kong) 1989–91, Dir 1991–95, Prof. 1992–95, Prof. Emer. 1995; Pres. and CEO The Commonwealth of Learning, Vancouver 1995–2004; Council Mem., United Nations University 2010–; fmr Sec.-Gen. Asian Asscn of Open Univs; fmr educational adviser, Int. Union for the Conservation of Nature; Hon. Fellow Coll. of Preceptors, London 1996–; several hon. degrees; Asian Asscn of Open Univs Meritorious Service Award 1997; Order of Chivalry, State of Penang 1994. *Address:* United Nations University, 5-53-70 Jingumae Shibuya-ku, Tokyo 150-8925, Japan (office). *Telephone:* (3) 5467-1212 (office). *Fax:* (3) 3499-2828 (office). *Website:* www.unu.edu.

D'HAUTERIVES, Arnaud Louis Alain; French artist; b. 26 Feb. 1933, Braine (Aisne); s. of Louis and Germaine (née Hincelin) d'Hauterives; m. Renée Delhaye 1959; two s. one d.; ed Ecole des Beaux Arts, Reims, Ecole Supérieure des Beaux Arts, Paris; started painting as a career 1957; illustrator of some art books; Jt Pres. Soc. Int. des Beaux Arts 1985, Hon. Pres. La Critique Parisienne 1984–; Pres. Acad. des Beaux Arts 1987–92, Life Sec. 1996–; mem. Inst. de France (Vice-Pres. 1987), Acad. des Sciences d'outre mer, Russian Acad. of Fine Arts (Dir 1998–); exhbns in France, Belgium, USA, China, Japan, Italy, Spain, USSR; academician Académie Royale des Beaux Arts de San Fernando; mem. Académie de Marseille; Hon. mem. Cercle de Lamer; Officier Légion d'honneur, des Palmes Académiques, Officier Ordre nat. du Mérite, Ordre des Arts et des Lettres; Premier Grand Prix de Rome 1957, Prix de la Critique 1967. *Leisure interests:* lithography, gliding. *Address:* c/o Institut de France, Académie des beaux-arts, 23 quai de Conti, 75006 Paris, France. *E-mail:* chantal.chevreux@academie-des-beaux-arts.fr.

DHAWAN, Neelam, MBA; Indian computer industry executive; *Managing Director, Hewlett Packard India;* m. Atul Dhawan; two c.; ed St Stephen's Coll., Delhi, Faculty of Man. Studies, Delhi Univ.; began career working for HCL Computers Technologies 1980s; Vice-Pres. Sales and Marketing, IBM India 1995–99; joined Compaq 1999, Vice-Pres. Customer Solutions Group, Hewlett Packard India (following HP and Compaq merger) –2005, Man. Dir Hewlett Packard India 2008–, also responsible for Tech. Solutions Group; Man. Dir Microsoft India 2005–08; named by Business Today magazine amongst the 25 Most Powerful Women in Indian Business 2006, 2008, named by Verve magazine amongst its 50 Power Women 2009, India Today Woman Awards 2009, ranked by Fortune magazine amongst the 50 Most Powerful Women in Business outside the US (37th) 2009, (36th) 2010, (35th) 2011. *Leisure interests:* puzzles and crosswords, cooking Sunday meals. *Address:* Hewlett-Packard India Sales Pvt. Ltd, 24 Salarpuria Arena, Adugodi Hosur Road, Bangalore 560 030, India (office). *Telephone:* (80) 2563-3555 (office). *Fax:* (80) 2563-3222 (office). *Website:* www.hp.com/country/in/en (office).

DHLAKAMA, Afonso Macacho Marceta; Mozambican politician; *President, Resistência Nacional Moçambicana (Renamo);* b. 1 Jan. 1953, Magunde; Chief of Logistics for Sofala Prov. of Forças Populares de Libertaçao de Moçambique 1975–77; Vice-Pres. Resistência Nacional Moçambicana (Renamo) (also known as Movimento Nacional de Resistência de Moçambique, fmr guerrilla group founded in 1976, in conflict with Govt 1976–82, obtained legal status 1994) and Vice-C-in-C of its armed forces 1977–79, Pres. and C-in-C 1979–92, Pres. of Renamo 1992–; unsuccessful presidential cand. 2004. *Address:* Resistência Nacional Moçambicana (Renamo), Av. Julius Nyerere 2541, Maputo, Mozambique (office). *Telephone:* 21493107 (office). *Website:* www.renamo.org.mz (office).

DHOININE, Ikililou, PhD; Comoran pharmacist, politician and head of state; *President;* b. 14 Aug. 1962, Djoiezi; m. Mrs Hadidja; two c.; ed univ. in Conakry, Guinea; trained as pharmacist, owner of pharmacy, Moheli; leader of several dels on funding, vaccination, etc to WHO; worked for several years in Ministry of Finance; Interim Pres. Nzwani island March 2008; Vice-Pres. of the Comoros 2008–11, responsible for Finance, Budget and Promotion of Women Entrepreneurs 2008–10, for Land Settlement, Infrastructure, Town Planning and Housing 2010–11, Pres. of the Comoros 2011–. *Address:* Office of the Head of State, Palais de Beit Salam, BP 521, Moroni, Comoros (office). *Telephone:* 7744808 (office). *Fax:* 7744829 (office). *E-mail:* presidence@comorestelecom.km (office). *Website:* www.beit-salam.km (office).

DHOLAKIA, Baron (Life Peer), cr. 1997, of Waltham Brooks in the Co. of West Sussex; **Rt Hon. Navnit Dholakia,** PC, OBE, DL, BSc; British politician; *Deputy Leader, Liberal Democrats Peers;* b. 4 March 1937, Tabora, Tanganyika (now Tanzania); m.; two d.; ed P.P. Inst., Bhavnagar, Gujerat, India, Brighton Tech. Coll.; fmr magistrate; fmr mem. Bd of Visitors, HM Prison Lewes; mem. (Liberal Democrat, House of Lords 1997–, Asst Whip 1997–2002, Deputy Leader, Liberal Democrat Peers 2004–; Pres. Liberal Democrat party 1999, 2002, Spokesperson on Home Affairs; Pres. Nat. Asscn for the Care and Resettlement of Offenders (NACRO); mem. Council, Howard League for Penal Reform; mem. Man. Bd, Policy Research Inst. on Ageing and Ethnicity; mem. Advisory Cttee on Business Appointments; Vice-Pres. Mental Health Foundation, Pallant House Gallery, Chichester; DL W Sussex 1999; Melvin Jones Fellowship, Lions Clubs International; Hon. DIur (Univ. of Hertfordshire) 2009, (York) 2010, (East London) 2010; Asian of the Year 2000, Bhartiya Samman Award (India) 2003. *Publications:* various articles on criminal justice matters. *Leisure interests:* photography, cooking, gardening, walking. *Address:* House of Lords, Westminster, London, SW1A 0PW, England (office). *Telephone:* (20) 7219-5203 (office). *Fax:* (20) 7219-3423 (office). *E-mail:* dholakian@parliament.uk (office). *Website:* www.parliament.uk/biographies/lords/lord-dholakia/2685 (office).

DHONI, Mahendra Singh; Indian professional cricketer; *Captain, Indian National Cricket Team;* b. 7 July 1981, Ranchi, Bihar (now in Jharkhand); s. of Pan Singh and Devaki Devi; m. Sakshi Singh Rawat 2010; wicket-keeper; right-handed batsman; right-arm medium pace bowler; plays for Bihar 1999–2005, Jharkhand 2004–, India Capt. One-Day Int. (ODI) side 2007–, Test side 2008–, Chennai Super Kings 2008–, Asia XI; First-class debut: 1999/2000; Test debut: India v Sri Lanka, Chennai 2–6 Dec. 2005; ODI debut: Bangladesh v India, Chittagong (MAA) 23 Dec. 2004; T20I debut: S Africa v India, Johannesburg 1 Dec. 2006; has played in 81 Tests and scored 4,342 runs (6 centuries, 28 fifties), highest score 224, average 38.76; ODIs: 242 matches, scored 7,999 runs, average 53.32, highest score 183 not out, took one wicket, average 14.00; First-class: 122 matches, 6,504 runs, average 37.16, highest score 224; mem. winning Indian team in ICC (Int. Cricket Council) World Twenty20 2007; Capt. winning Indian team of ICC Cricket World Cup 2011; maiden century against Pakistan in Faisalabad (148) is the fastest century scored by an Indian wicketkeeper; copartnered Akkineni Nagarjuna in buying bike racing team Mahi Racing Team India; Dr hc (De Montfort Univ.) 2011; MTV Youth Icon of the Year 2006, Idea NDTV Youth Icon 2006, MTV Most Stylish Person in Sports 2006, Rajiv Gandhi Khel Ratna Award 2007–08, ICC ODI Player of the Year 2008 (first Indian player) 2009, ICC World ODI XI 2008, 2009, 2010, 2011, 2012, 2013, ICC World Test XI 2009, 2010, 2013, Padma Shri 2009, ICC Spirit of Cricket Award 2011, included by TIME magazine in its Time 100 list of 100 most influential people of 2011, LG People's Choice Award 2013. *Leisure interests:* music, long drives, spending time with friends. *Address:* c/o Jharkhand State Cricket Association, Keenan Stadium, PO Box 68, Jamshedpur 831 001, Bihar, India. *Telephone:* (657) 2432722; (657) 2429578. *Fax:* (657) 2432722. *E-mail:* jsca_keenan@ediffmail.com; jsca_keenan@yahoo.co.in; jsca_keenan@sify.com. *Website:* www.cricjharkhand.org; www.dhoni.org.

DHUMAL, Prem Kumar; Indian politician and government official; b. 10 April 1944, Samirpur, Hamirpur; s. of Capt. Mahant Ram and Phulmu Devi; m. Smt. Sheela Devi 1972; two s.; ed Punjab Univ., Chandigarh, Guru Nanak Dev Univ., Amritsar; lectured at pvt. coll. in Punjab; Sec., Bhartiya Janata Yuva Morcha (BJYM) 1980–82, Vice-Pres. 1982–85; associated with many social orgs, including Bharat Vikas Parishad, Vivekanand Memorial Soc. and Himachal Hitkarini Sabha; State Sec. BJYM 1980, Vice-Pres. 1982–85; Gen. Sec. Bharatiya Janata Party (BJP) 1985–93, Pres. BJP 1993–98; contested parl. election 1984, elected MP to Lok Sabha (BJP) for Hamirpur constituency 1989, 1991, 2007, mem. Consultative Cttee Union Ministry of Communications 1989–96, Standing Cttee for Transport and Tourism and Railway Convention Cttee 1991–96, Nat. Council for Teachers' Educ. 1993–96, Alt. Chair. Estimates Cttee of Lok Sabha 1989–91; fmr Indian Rep. in Int. Parl. Union; Leader of Opposition in Himachal Pradesh State Legis. Ass. 2003–07; Chief Minister of Himachal Pradesh 1998–2003, 2007–12. *Leisure interests:* reading, writing short stories and articles for newspapers and magazines, listening to music. *Address:* Village and PO Samirpur, Teh. Bhoranj, Hamirpur Dist, 177 601, Himachal Pradesh, India (home). *Telephone:* (177) 2621384 (home); 98-68180104 (mobile). *Website:* www.premkumardhumal.com.

DI MONTEZEMOLO, Luca Cordero, LLM; Italian automotive industry executive; *Chairman, Fiat SpA;* b. 31 Aug. 1947, Bologna; s. of Massimo and Clotilde Cordero Lanza dei Marchese di Montezemolo; m. 1st Sandra Monteleoni (divorced); one s.; one d. (with Barbara Parodi); m. 2nd Ludovica Andreoni 2000; two d.; ed Univ. of Rome, Columbia Univ., New York, USA; began career working with the Chiomenti law firm, Rome, later joined Bergreen & Bergreen, New York; Team Man., Ferrari Formula One Racing Team and Asst to Chair. Enzo Ferrari 1973–77; Dir Public Affairs Dept, Fiat Group 1977–81; CEO ITEDI SpA (holding co. for Fiat Group's publishing interests) 1981–83; CEO Cinzano Int. SpA 1984–86; Gen. Man. Italia '90 Football World Cup Organising Cttee 1986–90; CEO RCS Video and Chair. RCS Home Video 1990–91; Chair. and CEO Ferrari SpA 1991–2006, Chair. 2006–; Chair. and CEO Maserati SpA 1997–2005; Chair. Fiat SpA 2004–; Pres. Confindustria 2004–08; mem. Bd of Dirs Pinault-Printemps-Redoute, La Stampa, Tod's, Poltrona Frau; Chair. Italian Asscn of Newspaper Publrs 2001–, Confindustria (Italian Employers' Asscn) 2004–; Pres. Modena Business and Industry Asscn 1996–2002, Bologna Int. Fair Org.; Pres. LUISS (Libera Università Internazionale degli Studi Sociali—Ind. Int. Univ. of Social Sciences), NTV (Nuovo Trasporto Viaggiatori), Industrialists of the Prov. of Modena 1996–2002, FIEG (Federazione Italiana Editori Giornali—Italian Newspaper Publrs Asscn)–2004; Vice-Pres. UNICE; mem. Gen. Council and Exec. Cttee Assonime; mem. Int. Advisory Bd Citi Inc.; Founder Charme (financial-entrepreneurial fund); Cavaliere del Lavoro, Chevalier, Légion d'honneur 2005; Hon. BEng (Modena Univ.) 2001, hon. degree in Business Man. (Univ. of Genoa) 2001, hon. degree in Industrial Design (Politecnico of Milan) 2001; voted Man of the Year by The Automobile magazine (USA), by Autocar magazine 2002, named by The Financial Times as one of the 50 Best Managers in the World. *Address:* Fiat SpA, 250 Via Nizza, 10126 Turin, Italy (office). *Telephone:* (011) 0061111 (office). *Fax:* (011) 0063798 (office). *E-mail:* info@fiatgroup.com (office). *Website:* www.fiatgroup.com (office).

DI PAOLA, Adm. Giampaolo; Italian naval officer and government official; b. 15 Aug. 1944, Torre Annunziata, Naples; m. Roberta di Paola; two d.; ed Naval Acad., Submarine School, NATO Defence Coll., Rome; served aboard conventional submarines Gazzana and Piomarta 1968–74; Commdr submarines Cappellini 1974–75, Sauro 1980–81; served as ASW and Undersea Warfare Programme Officer, Long Term Planning Br., SACLANT, Norfolk, Virginia, USA 1981–84; CO frigate Grecale 1984–86; Plans and Programmes Br. Chief, Gen. and Financial Planning Div., Navy Staff, Rome 1986–89; Capt. CO aircraft carrier Garibaldi 1989–90; Exec. Asst to Deputy Chief of Staff 1990–91; Chief of Naval Plans and Policy Br., Plans and Operations Div. 1991–92; Asst Chief of Staff for Plans and Operations 1993–94; Chief of Mil. Policy Div. 1994–98; Chief of the Cabinet, Ministry of Defence 1998–2001; Sec.-Gen. of Defence and Nat. Armaments Dir 2001–04; Chief of Defence Staff 2004–08; Chair. NATO Mil. Cttee, Brussels 2008–11; Minister of Defence (in Mario Monti's 'govt of technocrats') 2011–13; rank of Rear Adm. 1997, Adm. 2004; Kt Grand Cross, Order of Merit, Commdr, Ordre

nat. du Mérite, Kt Commdr, Order of St Gregory the Great, Grand Cross with Swords, Order of Merit of Malta, Kt of the Grand Cross of Merit of the Sacred Constantine Mil. Order of San Giorgio, Grand Officer, Order of Infante Dom Enrique (Portugal), Commdr, Legion of Merit (USA), Commdr, Légion d'honneur, Medal of the Order of St Maurice, Meritorious Long Command Gold Medal, Distinguished Award for Submariners, Sr Service Gold Cross, Bronze Medal for Sea-Duty Service in the Navy, Commemorative Medal of Sovereign Mil. Hospitaller Order of St John of Jerusalem, of Rhodes and of Malta, UN Medal for UN Peacekeeping Mission in Kosovo, NATO Afghanistan Medal. *Leisure interests:* arts, music, mountain climbing. *Address:* c/o Ministry of Defence, Palazzo Baracchini, Via XX Settembre 8, 00187 Rome, Italy.

DI PIETRO, Antonio; Italian lawyer and politician; *President, Italia dei Valori;* b. 2 Oct. 1950, Montenero di Bisaccia; m. 1st Isabella Ferrara; one s.; m. 2nd Susanna Mazzoleni 1995; ed Statale Univ. Milan, Pavia Univ.; studied law at evening classes; fmr factory hand, Germany; fmr police officer; fmr magistrate, Bergamo; Prosecutor, Milan 1984–94; uncovered bribery of officials in Milan 1992, led Operation Clean Hands exposing high levels of political corruption in Italy 1992–94; Chair. Penal Rights in Economy, Libero Istituto Universitario di Castellanza 1995–96; consultant, Parl. Comm. on Slaughter, on Co-operation with Developing Countries 1995–96; Minister of Public Works 1996–97; elected to Senate 1997; mem. European Parl. 1999–, Chair. Euro Parl. Del. for relations with S America, Cen. Asia and SA; Founder and Exec. Pres. Italia dei Valori party 2000–; Minister of Infrastructure 2006–08; Dr hc (Thrace Univ., Greece) 1995. *Publications:* Memoria 1999, Intervista su Tangentopoli 2000, Mani Pulite–La Vera Storia 2002. *Address:* Sede Nazionale, Italia dei Valori, Via Santa Maria in Via 12, 00187 Rome, Italy. *Telephone:* (06) 97848144 (office). *E-mail:* antoniodipietro@antoniodipietro.com (office). *Website:* www.antoniodipietro.com (office); italiadeivalori.antoniodipietro.com (office).

DI ROSA, Antonio, BSc; Italian journalist; b. 17 April 1951, Messina; s. of Calogero Rossetti and Anna Rossetti; partner; one s. two d.; began career at Giornale di Calabria 1974–78; moved to Gazzetta del Popolo 1978, Deputy Head Home News 1979–81, Head 1981–84; joined La Stampa 1984, Head Home News April–July 1988; Deputy Cen. Ed.-in-Chief Corriere della Sera 1988–93, Cen. Ed.-in-Chief 1993–96, Deputy Ed. 1996–2000; Ed. Il Secolo XIX 2000–04; Ed. La Gazzetta dello Sport 2004–06; Premio Senigallia 1983. *Leisure interests:* books, cinema, travel. *Address:* Via G. Morelli 1, Milan, Italy (home).

DI RUPO, Elio, DSc; Belgian politician; *Prime Minister;* b. 18 July 1951, Morlanwelz; ed Université de Mons; Researcher, Chef de Cabinet, Budget and Energy Minister, Walloon Region 1982–85; Communal Councillor, Mons 1982–2000; mem. Parl. 1987–89, mem. European Parl. 1989–91; Pres. Energy Comm.; Senator 1991–95; Minister of Educ. 1992–94; Deputy Prime Minister and Minister of Communications and Public Enterprises 1994–95, Deputy Prime Minister and Minister for Economy and Telecommunications 1995–99; Prime Minister 2011–; Minister-Pres. of Wallonia 1999–2000, 2005–07; Mayor of Mons 2001–; Pres. Socialist Party 2000–11. *Address:* Cabinet of the Prime Minister, 16 rue de la Loi, 1000 Brussels (office). *Telephone:* (2) 501-02-11 (office). *Fax:* (2) 512-69-53 (office). *E-mail:* info@premier.fed.be (office). *Website:* www.premier.be (office); www.belgium.be (office).

DIAB, Rashid, MFA, PhD; Sudanese artist and gallery director; b. 1 Jan. 1957, Wad Medani, Gezira Prov.; s. of Mubarak and Daralnaeem Diab; m. Mercedes Diab (divorced); one s. one d.; ed School of Fine and Applied Arts, Khartoum, Complutense Univ., Madrid, Spain; Teacher, Faculty of Fine Art, Complutense Univ., Madrid 1991–99; currently Owner and Dir, Medani Galería, Madrid; f. Rashid Diab Art Centre, Khartoum 2006; toured northern deserts of Sudan 2000; artistic adviser for presidential palace and govt offices, Sudan; works held in numerous public collections including OFID (OPEC Fund for Int. Devt) Collection, Vienna, Wifredo Lam Centre of Contemporary Art, Havana, Museum of Fine Arts, Alexandria, Modern Museum of Etching, Cairo, Arab World Inst., Paris, UNESCO, Paris. *Address:* Dara Art Gallery, PO Box 6554, Altakamul, Khartoum, Sudan. *E-mail:* daragallery@hotmail.com. *Website:* www.rashiddiabartscentre.net.

DIABRÉ, Zéphirin, MBA, PhD; Burkinabè international civil servant and business executive; *Chairman, Africa and Middle East Regions, International and Marketing Department, AREVA SA;* b. 26 Aug. 1959, Ouagadougou; ed Ecole Supérieure de Commerce, Bordeaux, France, Univ. of Bordeaux; Prof. of Business Admin. 1987–89; Man. Dir Burkina Brewery 1989–92; Minister for Trade, Industry and Mining 1992–94, for Economy, Finance and Planning 1994–96; Chair. Council of Econ. and Social Affairs 1996–97; Visiting Scholar, Harvard Inst. for Int. Devt, Fellow, Weatherhead Center for Int. Affairs, USA 1997–98; Assoc. Admin. UNDP, New York 1999–2006; Chair. Africa and Middle East Regions, Int. and Marketing Dept AREVA (Société des Participations du Commissariat à l'Energie Atomique) 2006–, also adviser to Chair.; Officier, Ordre nat. du Mérite, Burkina Faso, Chevalier, Légion d'honneur. *Address:* AREVA SA, 3 rue La Fayette, 75442 Paris Cedex 9, France (office). *Telephone:* 1-34-96-00-00 (office). *Fax:* 1-34-96-00-01 (office). *Website:* www.areva.com (office).

DIACK, Lamine; Senegalese international sports official and politician; *President, International Association of Athletics Federations (IAAF);* b. 7 June 1933, Dakar; m.; 15 c.; long jump record holder, France and W Africa 1957–60; football coach, Foyer France Senegal football team 1963–64; Pres. African Amateur Athletic Confed. (AAAC) 1963–64; Technical Dir Senegal Nat. Football Team 1964–68; Gen. Commr for State Sport 1969–70, Sec. of State for Youth and Sport 1970–73; mem. Exec. Cttee Supreme Council for Sport in Africa (SCSA) 1973–87; Pres. ASC DIARAAF football team 1974–78, 1994–; mem. Nat. Olympic Cttee of Senegal 1974–, Pres. 1985–; Gen. Sec. Senegalese Athletic Fed. 1974–78, Pres. 1974–78, Hon. Pres. 1978–; mem. Int. Olympic Cttee 1999–; Vice-Pres. Int. Asscn of Athletics Feds (IAAF) 1976–91, Sr Vice-Pres. 1991–99, Pres. 1999–; Chair. City Council (Mayor) of Dakar 1978–80; mem. Nat. Ass. of Senegal (Parl.) 1988–93, Sr Vice-Pres. (Deputy Speaker) 1988–93; Chief Insp. of Taxes and State Property 1995–2001; Chair. Bd Soc. Nat. des Eaux (SONES) 1995–2001; numerous honours, including Grand Cordon of the Order of the Rising Sun (Japan), Grand Officier de l'Etoile Equatoriale (Gabon), Commdr Order of Good Hope (S. Africa), Chevalier, Légion d'honneur, Chevalier de l'Ordre Nat. du Lion (Senegal), Officiale di Grancroce (Italy), Officier de la Médaille de la Reconnaissance Centrafricaine,

Médaille de l'Ordre du Nil de la République Arabe d'Egypte, Bernardo O'Higgins Medal, 1st Degree (Chile), Order of the Officer Cross Budapest (Hungary), Olympic Order, IAAF Order of Merit, ACNO Order of Merit, SCSA Order of Merit, CAF Order of Merit; Dr hc (Donetsk Nat. Univ.), (Beijing Sport Univ.). *Address:* Office of the President, International Association of Athletics Federations, 17 rue Princesse Florestine, BP 359, MC 98007, Monaco (office). *Telephone:* 9310888 (office). *Fax:* 93251082 (office). *E-mail:* secretariat-president@iaaf.org (office). *Website:* www.iaaf.org (office).

DIACONESCU, Cristian, LLB; Romanian judge and politician; b. 2 July 1959, Bucharest; m. Mariana Diaconescu; one d.; ed Univ. of Bucharest; mil. service, attained rank of 2nd Lt; judge, Court of Ilfov Agricultural Sector 1983–85, Court of Bucharest Fourth Dist and Tribunal of Bucharest 1985–89; Inspector Ministry of Justice 1989–90; mem. Perm. Mission to OSCE, then Perm. Mission to Int. Orgs, Vienna 1990–96; mem. OSCE Directorate, Ministry of Foreign Affairs 1996–97, Dir 1997, Gen. Dir, Gen. Directorate for Judicial and Consular Affairs 1998; Deputy Sec. Black Sea Org. for Econ. Cooperation 2000; Sec. of State for Bilateral Affairs, Ministry of Foreign Affairs 2000–04; mem. Senate for Constituency No. 42, Bucharest 2004–; Minister of Justice March–Dec. 2004, of Foreign Affairs 2008–09, Jan.–May 2012; Assoc. Prof., Chair of Int. Public Law, Hyperion Univ. 1993; mem. Nat. Defence Coll. Foundation 1995–, Prof. 1997–; Prof., Human Rights Inst. 1998–2000; mem. Partidul Social Democrat (PSD—Social Democratic Party) –2010; Ind. 2010–. *Address:* c/o Ministry of Foreign Affairs, 011822 Bucharest, Al. Alexandru 31, Romania. *Website:* mae@mae.ro; www .cristiandiaconescu.ro.

DIACONESCU, Dan; Romanian journalist, politician and TV presenter; *Founder, People's Party – Dan Diaconescu;* b. 9 Dec. 1968, Caracal; ed Faculty of Mechanical Eng, Univ. of Bucharest; Founder and Owner DDTV and OTV TV stations; Co-founder, with other OTV show presenters, People's Party – Dan Diaconescu 2011. *Address:* People's Party – Dan Diaconescu (Partidul Poporului – Dan Diaconescu), Bucharest, Romania (office). *Telephone:* (21) 3114199 (office). *E-mail:* mansimona@partidul.poporului.ro (office). *Website:* www.partidul .poporului.ro (office).

DIALLO, Cellou Dalein; Guinean economist and politician; *President, Union des forces démocratiques de Guinée;* b. 3 Feb. 1952, Labé; ed Faculty of Economics, Univ. of Conakry; worked at Cen. Bank of Guinea 1985–95; joined ministerial cabinet of Pres. Lansan Conté 1995; Minister of Transport, Communications, Tourism and Public Works 1997–99, of Public Works and Transport 1999–2004, of Fisheries 2004; Prime Minister of Guinea 2004–06; Pres. Union des forces démocratiques de Guinée 2007–; unsuccessful cand. in presidential election 2010. *Address:* Union des forces démocratiques de Guinée, BP 3036, Conakry, Guinea (office). *E-mail:* baggelmalal@yahoo.fr (office). *Website:* www.ufdg.org (office).

DIALLO, Gen. Mamadou Bailo; Guinean army officer; fmr Head of Ground Forces, Nat. Army of Guinea; Minister of Nat. Defence 2007–08. *Address:* c/o Ministry of National Defence, Camp Samory-Touré, Conakry, Guinea (office).

DIALLO NANDIGNA, Adiato; Guinea-Bissau politician; Minister of Culture, Youth and Sport 2007–09, of Foreign Affairs –Oct. 2009, of Social Communication and Parl. Affairs Oct. 2009; mem. Partido Africano da Independência da Guiné e Cabo Verde. *Address:* c/o Ministry of Social Communication and Parliamentary Affairs, Bissau, Guinea-Bissau (office).

DIAMOND, Abel J. (Jack), OC, MArch, DEng, FRAIC, ARIBA, RCA, MCIP, MAIP,; Canadian architect; *Principal and Founding Partner, Diamond and Schmitt Architects Inc.;* b. S. Africa; s. of Jacob Diamond and Rachel Zipporah Diamond (née Werner); m. Gillian Mary Huggins 1959; one s. one d.; ed Univs of Cape Town, Oxford, UK and Pennsylvania, USA; Asst Prof. of Architecture and Architectural Asst to Louis Kahn, Philadelphia 1963–64; Assoc. Prof., Univ. of Toronto 1964–69; Prof., Univ. of York 1969–72; Adjunct Prof., Univ. of Texas at Arlington 1980–81; Sr Pnr, A. J. Diamond, Donald Schmitt and Co. (now Diamond and Schmitt Architects Inc.) 1975–; Chair. Nat. Capital Comm., Design Advisory Comm., Ottawa; mem. Advisory Bd, School of Architecture, Univ. of Toronto 1987–; Commr Ont. Human Rights Comm. 1986–89; mem. Bd of Govs, Mount Sinai Hosp., Toronto 1987–; Graham Prof. of Architecture, Univ. of Pa 1996–; mem. Royal Acad. of Arts, Canada, RIBA, Canadian Inst. of Planners, American Inst. of Planners; Hon. FAIA; Hon. DEng (Dalhousie) 1996, Hon. LLD; numerous design prizes including Toronto Arts Award 1990, Royal Architectural Inst. Gold Medal 2001; Order of Ont. 1998. *Works include:* Ontario Medical Assen HQ 1970, Univ. of Alberta Long Range Plan 1970, Alcan HQ Office, Toronto 1972, Montreal 1978, Cleveland 1982, Queen's Univ. Housing, Kingston, Ont. 1976, Citadel Theatre, Edmonton, Alberta 1976 (with B. Myers and R. L. Wilkin), Nat. Ballet School Stage Training Facility, Toronto 1983, Burns Bldg Renovation, Calgary 1983, Berkeley Castle Renovation, Toronto 1983, Metro Toronto Central YMCA 1984, Ont. Arts Council HQ Offices, Toronto 1985, Four Seasons HQ Offices, Toronto 1985, Imperial Theatre, St John, NB 1988, Earth and Sciences Center, Univ. of Toronto 1988, Curtiss Hall, Toronto 1988, Sunny Brook Hosp., Newcastle Town Hall 1989, York Univ. Student Centre 1991, Lois Hancsey Aquatic Center 1991, Jerusalem City Hall 1992, Richmond Hill Cen. Library 1992, HQ Toronto Historic Bd 1993, Israeli Foreign Ministry, Jerusalem 1996, 'Alumbrera', Mustique 2000, Garland House, Toronto. *Leisure interest:* watercolour painting. *Address:* Diamond and Schmitt Architects Inc., 384 Adelaide Street West, Suite 300, Toronto, ON, M5V 1R7, Canada (office). *Telephone:* (416) 862-8800 (office). *Fax:* (416) 862-5508 (office). *E-mail:* ajd@dsai.ca (office). *Website:* www.dsai.ca (office).

DIAMOND, Douglas, AB, MA, MPhil, PhD; American economist and academic; *Merton H. Miller Distinguished Service Professor of Finance and Richard N. Rosett Faculty Fellow, Graduate School of Business, University of Chicago;* b. Oct. 1953; m.; two c.; ed Brown Univ., Yale Univ.; Teaching Fellow, Dept of Econs, Yale Univ. 1977–78, Prof. of Finance, Yale School of Org. and Man. 1987–88; Instructor, Univ. of Chicago 1979, Asst Prof. 1980–83, Assoc. Prof. 1983–86, Prof. of Finance 1988–93, 1986–87, Theodore O. Yntema Prof. of Finance 1993–2000, Merton H. Miller Distinguished Service Prof. of Finance and Richard N. Rosett Faculty Fellow, Grad. School of Business 2000–; Summer Research Assoc., Bd of Govs of the US Fed. Reserve System, summers of 1976–78; Assoc. Ed. Journal of Finance 1988–96, 2000–03, Journal of Financial Services Research 1993–, Journal of

Banking and Finance 1995–; Fellow, Econometric Soc. 1990–, American Acad. of Arts and Sciences 2001–, American Finance Assen 2004– (Pres. 2003). *Address:* University of Chicago Booth School of Business, 5807 South Woodlawn Avenue, Chicago, IL 60637-1610, USA (office). *Telephone:* (773) 702-7283 (office). *E-mail:* douglas.diamond@chicagobooth.edu (office). *Website:* faculty.chicagobooth.edu/ douglas.diamond (office).

DIAMOND, Jared Mason, BA, PhD; American biologist, physiologist, academic and writer; *Professor of Geography and Physiology, David Geffen School of Medicine, University of California, Los Angeles;* b. 10 Sept. 1937, Boston, Mass; s. of Louis K. Diamond and Flora K. Diamond; m. Marie Nabel Cohen 1982; twin s.; ed Harvard Coll., Univ. of Cambridge, UK; Fellow, Trinity Coll., Cambridge 1961–65, Jr Fellow, Soc. of Fellows, Harvard Univ. 1962–65; Assoc. in Biophysics, Harvard Medical School 1965–66; Assoc. Prof. of Physiology, David Geffen School of Medicine, Univ. of California Medical School, Los Angeles 1966–68, Prof. of Geography, UCLA 1968–; Research Assoc., Dept of Ornithology, American Museum of Natural History 1973–; US Regional Dir World Wide Fund for Nature; mem. Editorial Bd Skeptic Magazine; mem. NAS; Fellow, American Acad. of Arts and Sciences, American Physiological Soc., Biophysics Soc., American Philosophical Soc., American Soc. of Naturalists, American Ornithologists Union 1978; Hon. DLitt (Sejong Univ., S Korea) 1995; Dr hc (Katholieke Universiteit Leuven, Belgium) 2008; Prize Fellowship in Physiology, Trinity Coll., Cambridge 1961–65, Lederle Medical Faculty Award 1968–71, Distinguished Teaching Award, UCLA Medical Class 1972, 1973, Distinguished Achievement Award, American Gastroenterological Assen 1975, Kaiser Permanente/Golden Apple Teaching Award 1976, Nathaniel Bowditch Prize, American Physiological Soc. 1976, Franklin L. Burr Award, Nat. Geographic Soc. 1979, MacArthur Foundation 'Genius' Grant 1985, Archie Carr Medal 1989, MacArthur Foundation Fellow 1990, Tanner Lecturer, Univ. of Utah (and many other endowed lectureships) 1992, Royal Soc. Prizes for Science Books (Rhone-Poulenc Prize) 1992, 1998, Science Book Prize, New Scientist London 1992, Los Angeles Times Science Book Prize 1992, Zoological Soc. of San Diego Conservation Medal 1993, Randi Award, Skeptics Soc. 1994, Faculty Research Lecturer, UCLA 1996, Phi Beta Kappa Science Book Prize 1997, Elliott Coues Award, American Ornithologists' Union 1998, Gold Medal in nonfiction, California Book Awards 1998, Nat. Medal of Sciences 1999, Lannan Literary Award for Nonfiction 1999, Tyler Prize for Environmental Achievement 2001, Lewis Thomas Prize for Writing about Science 2002, Dickson Prize in Science 2006, Wolf Prize in Agric. 2013. *Television:* Guns, Germs and Steel (three-part PBS documentary) 2005. *Publications:* The Avifauna of the Eastern Highlands of New Guinea 1972, Ecology and Evolution of Communities (co-ed.) 1975, Birds of Karkar and Bagabab Islands, New Guinea (co-author) 1979, The Avifaunas of Rennell and Bellona Islands. The Natural History of Rennell Islands, British Solomon Islands 1984, Community Ecology (co-author) 1985, Birds of New Guinea (co-author) 1986, The Third Chimpanzee: The Evolution and Future of the Human Animal 1992, 2006, Why is Sex Fun? – The Evolution of Human Sexuality 1997, Guns, Germs, and Steel: The Fates of Human Societies (Pulitzer Prize 1998, Cosmos Prize 1998) 1998, The Birds of Northern Melanesia: Speciation, Ecology, & Biogeography (co-author) 2001, Guns, Germs, and Steel Reader's Companion 2003, Collapse: How Societies Choose to Fail or Succeed 2004, Natural Experiments of History (with James A. Robinson) 2010, The World until Yesterday: What Can We Learn from Traditional Societies? 2012; several hundred research papers on physiology, ecology and ornithology; contribs to Discover, Natural History, Nature. *Address:* 1251A Bunche Hall, University of California at Los Angeles, Los Angeles, CA 90095-1524, USA (office). *Telephone:* (310) 825-6177 (office). *Fax:* (310) 206-5976 (office). *E-mail:* jdiamond@geog.ucla.edu (office). *Website:* healthsciences.ucla.edu/dgsom (office); www.geog.ucla.edu (office); www .jareddiamond.org.

DIAMOND, Neil Leslie; American singer and composer; b. 24 Jan. 1941, Brooklyn, NY; m. Marcia Murphey 1975; two c. (and two c. from previous m.); m. Katie McNeil 2012; ed New York Univ.; fmr songwriter for publishing co.; numerous tours world-wide, television and radio broadcasts; mem. SESAC; inducted into Rock and Roll Hall of Fame 2011, Honoree, 34th Annual Kennedy Center Honors 2011. *Film scores:* Jonathan Livingston Seagull (Grammy Award) 1973, Every Which Way but Loose 1978, The Jazz Singer 1980; songs for many other films. *Film appearance:* The Jazz Singer 1980. *Recordings include:* albums: The Feel of Neil Diamond 1966, Just For You 1967, Velvet Gloves and Spit 1968, Brother Love's Travelling Salvation Show 1969, Touching You Touching Me 1969, Tap Root Manuscript 1970, Shilo 1970, Gold (live) 1970, Stones 1971, Hot August Night (live) 1972, Moods 1972, Serenade 1974, Beautiful Noise 1976, Love At The Greek (live) 1977, I'm Glad You're Here With Me Tonight 1977, Carmelita's Eyes 1978, You Don't Bring Me Flowers 1978, September Morn 1979, Voices Of Vista: Show # 200 1979, On The Way To The Sky 1981, Heartlight 1982, Song Sung Blue 1982, Primitive 1984, Headed For The Future 1986, Hot August Night II (live) 1987, The Best Years Of Our Lives 1989, Lovescape 1991, The Christmas Album 1992, Up On the Roof: Songs From The Brill Building 1993, The Christmas Album Vol. II 1994, Live In America 1994, Tennessee Moon 1996, Live In Concert 1997, The Movie Album: As Time Goes By 1998, Three Chord Opera 2001, 12 Songs 2005, Home Before Dark 2008, A Cherry Cherry Christmas 2009, Dreams 2010. *Address:* c/o Columbia Records, Sony BMG, 550 Madison Avenue, New York, NY 10022, USA. *Website:* www.neildiamond.com.

DIAMOND, Robert (Bob) Edward, Jr, BA, MBA; American business executive; b. 27 July 1951, Springfield, Mass; m.; two s. one d.; ed Colby Coll., Univ. of Connecticut Business School; began career as Lecturer at School of Business, Univ. of Connecticut 1976; held sr leadership roles at Credit Suisse First Boston in Tokyo and New York 1992–96, Morgan Stanley International; joined Barclays 1996, mem. Group Exec. Cttee 1997, Exec. Dir 2005–12, Pres. Barclays PLC and Chief Exec. of Corp. and Investment Banking, Barclays Wealth, comprising Barclays Capital, Barclays Corporate and Barclays Wealth, Pres. and Deputy Chief Exec. 2010–11, Chief Exec. 2011–12 (resgnd); Chair. Old Vic Productions Plc; mem. Bd BlackRock following integration of Barclays Global Investors; mem. Advisory Bd Judge Business School, Univ. of Cambridge, Bd The Diamond Family Foundation, International Advisory Bd British-American Business Council; Life mem. The Council on Foreign Relations; mem. The Atlantic Council; Chair. Bd of Trustees, Colby Coll.; Trustee, The Mayor's Fund for London; Republican; Hon. DHumLitt (Univ. of Connecticut) 2006, Hon. LLD (Colby Coll.) 2008. *Leisure* *interests:* supports Boston Red Sox in baseball, Chelsea in English football, the New England Patriots in American football and Boston Celtics in basketball. *Address:* c/o Barclays PLC, One Churchill Place, Canary Wharf, London, E14 5HP, England.

DIAMOND, Shelley; American advertising executive; *Worldwide Managing Partner, Young & Rubicam;* m. Richard Diamond; three c.; ed State Univ. of NY at Buffalo; began advertising career at Foote Cone & Belding; subsequently worked at Grey Advertising and Ted Bates Advertising; Man. Dir of New York office of Young & Rubicam 2007–09, Worldwide Man. Partner on the Dell, Campbell's Soup and Xerox accounts 2009–, also serves as a Dir on the global Young & Rubicam Bd; mem. Bd Students In Free Enterprise, Acad. of Urban Planning; mem. Bd of Dirs PAETEC Holding 2009–; mem. W.O.M.E.N in America, Fortune/State Dept's Vital Voice initiatives; named by YWCA as Woman of the Year 1995, Advertising Women of New York 2005, Advertising Working Mothers of the Year Award, recognized by Working Mother magazine as a trailblazer in the industry. *Address:* Young & Rubicam, 285 Madison Avenue, New York, NY 10016, USA (office). *E-mail:* info@yr.com (office). *Website:* www.yr.com (office); www.yrgrp.com (office).

DIANÉ, Elhadj Madifing; Guinean government official and fmr diplomatist; *Minister of Security and Civil Protection;* b. 1946, Kita, Mali; m.; ten c.; ed Acad. of Cairo, Egypt; Official, Directorate of State Security 1971–72; Foreign Auditor, Acad. of Algiers 1972–73; several years with Office of the Pres. including as Head, Central Bureau of Revenue 1973–78, First Counselor, responsible for Middle East and W Europe 1978–81, Dir of Safety Man. 1981–83; Head of Security, Labé City (attached to Office of the Pres.) 1983–84; Deputy Dir-Gen., Police Services 1984–85; Deputy Dir-Gen., Intelligence 1985–87; Adviser to Sec. of State for Security, responsible for external relations 1987–90; Dir, Office for Supervision of Police and Republican Guard 1990–93; Dir of Security, Kindia Region (responsible for security of presidential elections in Maritime Guinea) 1993–94; Dir of Security, Labé City (responsible for legislative and community elections in that region) 1994–96; Inspector-Gen. of Security Services 1996–2007; Technical Adviser, responsible for cooperation 2007–08; Minister of Security and Civil Protection Sept.–Dec. 2008, 2014–; Amb. to Senegal, Gambia, Mauritania and Cape Verde 2011–13; helped to open peace negotiations between Iraq and Iran under the auspices of Comité Islamique de Paix 1978–80; Vice-Pres. Asscn of Guinea–Arab Security 1981; Hero of the Liberation Struggle in Guinea-Bissau and Cape Verde 1972, White Cross Medal, Order of Merit of the Spanish Police Force. *Leisure interests:* reading, classical music. *Address:* Ministry of Security and Civil Protection, Coléah-Domino, Conakry, Guinea (office). *Telephone:* 300-41-45-50 (office).

DIANOV, Evgeny Mikhailovich; Russian physicist and academic; *Director, Fibre Optics Research Centre, Russian Academy of Sciences;* b. 31 Jan. 1936, Tula; m. Helen Zagorovskaya 1968; one s. one d.; ed Moscow State Univ.; researcher, Lebedev Inst. USSR (now Russian) Acad. of Sciences 1960–72, Sr researcher 1972–80, Head of Lab. 1980–83; Head of Lab. Gen. Physics Inst. of USSR (now Russian) Acad. of Sciences 1983–85, Head of Dept of Gen. Physics 1985–88; Prof., Physical-Technical Inst. 1985–88; Deputy Dir of Gen. Physics Inst., Russian Acad. of Sciences 1988–93, Dir Fibre Optics Research Centre, Gen. Physics Inst. 1993–2006, Dir Russian Acad. of Sciences Fibre Optics Research Center 2006–; Corresp. mem. USSR (now Russian) Acad. of Sciences 1987, mem. 1994; USSR State Prize 1974, Popov Prize, USSR Acad. of Sciences 1988, Russian Fed. State Prize 1998. *Publications:* over 700 papers on quantum electronics, fibre and integrated optics. *Leisure interests:* jogging, reading. *Address:* Fibre Optics Research Centre, Russian Academy of Sciences, 119333 Moscow, 38 Vavilova Street (office); 119071 Moscow, Leninsky Prospekt 13, Apt. 139, Russia (home). *Telephone:* (499) 135-05-66 (office); (495) 237-32-76 (home). *Fax:* (499) 135-81-39 (office). *E-mail:* dianov@fo.gpi.ru (office). *Website:* www.forc.gpi.ru (office).

DIARÉ, Mohamed; Guinean politician; *Minister of the Economy and Finance;* b. Kissidougou; ed Univ. de Conakry, IMF Inst., École nat. d'admin, France; Minister-Del. for the Budget 2011–14; Minister of the Economy and Finance 2014–. *Address:* Ministry of the Economy and Finance, Boulbinet, BP 221, Conakry, Guinea (office). *Telephone:* 300-45-17-95 (office). *Fax:* 300-41-30-59 (office).

DIARRA, Cheick Modibo, PhD; Malian astrophysicist and politician; *President, Rassemblement pour le Développement du Mali (RpDM);* b. 1952, Nioro du Sahel; son-in-law of Moussa Traoré (fmr Pres. of Mali); three c.; ed Université Pierre et Marie Curie, France, Howard Univ., USA; worked as interplanetary navigator at NASA Jet Propulsion Lab., collaborated in numerous space programs including Magellan probe to Venus, Ulysses probe to the sun, Galileo spacecraft to Jupiter, Mars Observer and Mars Pathfinder, also worked on Mars Exploration Program Educ. and NASA Public Outreach Program; Pres. Microsoft Africa 2006; est. solar energy research lab., Bamako 2002; Founder-Pres. Rassemblement pour le Développement du Mali (RpDM) 2011–; Prime Minister April–Dec. 2012; Pres. Africal Virtual Univ., Kenya –2005; Co-founder Université Numérique Francophone Mondiale 2005; Founder-Pres. African Science and New Tech. Summit; f. Fondation Pathfinder (educ. programme), Bamako 1999; Vice-Pres. UN World Comm. for the Ethics of Scientific Knowledge and Tech.; mem. Ind. Comm. on Africa and the Challenges of the Third Millennium; UNESCO Goodwill Amb. 2000–01; African Lifetime Achievement Award 1998. *Publication:* Navigateur interplanétaire (autobiography). *Address:* Rassemblement pour le Développement du Mali (RpDM), Rue 303, Porte 330, ACI 2000, Hamdallaye, Bamako, Mali (office). *Telephone:* 7619-3352 (office). *E-mail:* rpdm@rpdm.com (office). *Website:* www.rpdm-mali.com (office); www.cheickmodibodiarra.com (office).

DIARRA, Cheick Sidi; Malian diplomatist and UN official; b. 31 May 1957, Kayes; m.; two c.; ed Dakar Univ., Senegal; joined civil service in 1981, assigned to Ministry of Foreign Affairs and Int. Co-operation, Legal Adviser 1987–88; First Counsellor, Perm. Mission to UN, New York 1989–93, Perm. Rep. to UN, New York 1993–2007; UN Under-Sec.-Gen. and High Rep. for the Least Developed Countries, Landlocked Developing Countries and Small Island Developing States 2007–08, Special Adviser on Africa and Under-Sec.-Gen. and High Rep. for the Least Developed Countries, Landlocked Developing Countries and Small Island Developing States 2008–12; Chevalier, Ordre Nat. du Mali. *Address:* c/o Office of the High Representative for the Least Developed Countries, Landlocked Devel-

oping Countries and Small Island Developing States, United Nations, Room S-770, New York, NY 10017, USA.

DIARRA, Fatoumata Dembele, LLB; Malian judge and professor of law; *Judge, Constitutional Court of Mali;* b. 15 Feb. 1949, Koulikoro; m.; six c.; ed Ecole Nat. de la Magistrature, Paris, France, Ecole Nat. d'Admin, Bamako, Dakar Univ., Senegal; Investigative Judge, Jr Admin. Office, First Instance Tribunal of Bamako 1977–80; Trial Attorney, Office of the Prosecutor, Tribunal of Bamako 1980–81; Vice-Pres. Labour Court of Bamako 1981–82; Investigative Judge, Sr Investigation Office, Bamako 1984–86; Legis. Councillor Nat. Ass. of Mali 1986–91; Legal Adviser to Transition Cttee for the Reinstallation of Republican Inst., Office of the Head of State 1991; Gen.-Dir Malian Office for Intellectual Property and Copyright 1991–93; Official Rep. of Office of the Comm. for the Promotion of Women 1993–94; Appeal Court Adviser, Criminal Chamber 1994–96; Pres. Criminal Chamber, Bamako Appeal Court 1996–99; Nat. Dir Justice Admin 1999–2001; elected Judge ad litem Int. Criminal Tribunal for the Fmr Yugoslavia (ICTY) 2001; Judge, Int. Criminal Court 2003–, Judge, Pre-Trial Chamber II 2004–08, Pres., Pre-Trial Chamber III, Judge, Trial Chamber II Oct. 2008, First Vice-Pres. 2009–12; Judge, Constitutional Court of Mali 2013–; Prof. of Constitutional Law, Civil Law and Criminal Law, Cen. School for Industry, Trade and Admin (ECICA) 1986–91; Gen.-Sec. Asscn of Malian Women Lawyers 1986–88, Pres. 1988–95; Founding Pres. Legal Clinic for Women and Children Without Means 1993; Pres. Support Group for Legal Reform 1994, Observatory for the Rights of Women and Children (ODEF) 1995–, Legal Br. of Int. Council for French-speaking Women (CIFF) 1996–, Malian Electoral Support Network 1997–; Vice-Pres. Int. Fed. of Women with Legal Careers (FIFCJ) 1994–97, Fed. of African Women Lawyers (FJA) 1995–; mem. numerous working groups and parl. cttee on legal reform; frequent participant in UN Comm. on the Status of Women; Chevalier, Ordre nat. du Mali 2001, Chevalier, Légion d'honneur (France) 2009; Outstanding Achievement Award, Arizona State Univ., title of Pionnière, Fed. des Juristes Africaines. *Publications include:* numerous articles in professional journals on women's rights and int. law; special contribs on ICC-related issues, such as war crimes, crimes against humanity and genocide in particular in relation to women; other examples of individual criminal responsibility as foreseen in the Rome Statute, article 25. *Address:* Constitutional Court, Hamdallaye ACI 2000, Commune IV, BP E 213, Bamako, Mali (office). *Telephone:* 2022-5609 (office). *Fax:* 2023-4241 (office). *E-mail:* tawatybouba@yahoo.fr (office). *Website:* www.cc.insti.ml (office).

DIARRA, Seydou Elimane; Côte d'Ivoirian agronomist, diplomatist, politician and banker; b. 23 Nov. 1933, Katiola; m.; ed Lycée Fénelon, La Rochelle, France; won scholarship to study agric. in France; researcher, Office de la recherche scientifique et technique d'outre-mer (Orstom) 1961; apptd Dir Centre national de la mutualité agricole 1962; Commercial Dir Caisse de stabilisation du café et du cacao (Caistab) 1965, Rep. of Caistab in London; fmr head of state-run agric. co-operation and insurance body, Abidjan; Pres., Dir-Gen. Saco et Chocodi 1985; fmr head of govt org. in charge of cocoa; fmr African Rep. to Int. Coffee Org.; fmr Amb. to Brazil, EU and UK; Chair. Chamber of Commerce and Industry, Côte d'Ivoire 1992; Minister of State, responsible for Governmental Co-ordination and the Planning of Devt Jan.–May 2000; Prime Minister of Côte d'Ivoire May–Oct. 2000 (resgnd), 2003–05; Pres. Bd of Dirs Banque Internationale pour l'Afrique Occidentale, Cote d'Ivoire 2002; Chair. Banque Internationale pour le Commerce et l'Industrie de Cote d'Ivoire SA (BICICI) 2009. *Address:* c/o Banque Internationale pour le Commerce et l'Industrie de Cote d'Ivoire SA, 01 Avenue Franchet d'Esperey BP 1298, Abidjan 01, Côte d'Ivoire (office). *Telephone:* 20-20-16-00 (office). *Fax:* 20-20-17-00 (office). *E-mail:* michel.lafont@africa.bnpparibas.com (office). *Website:* www.bicicinet.net (office).

DIAS, HE Cardinal Ivan, PhD; Indian ecclesiastic; *Prefect Emeritus, Congregation for the Evangelization of Peoples;* b. 14 April 1936, Mumbai; s. of Carlo Nazaro Dias and Maria Martins; ed Pontifical Ecclesiastical Acad., Pontifical Lateran Univ., Rome; ordained priest 1958; Sec., Apostolic Nunciatures in Denmark, Sweden, Norway, Iceland, Finland, Indonesia, Madagascar, Réunion, Comoros, Mauritius 1965–73; Titular Archbishop of Rusubisir and Pro-Nuncio in Ghana, Togo and Benin 1982–87; pro-Nuncio in South Korea 1987–91, Apostolic Nuncio to Albania 1991–97; Archbishop of Mumbai (fmrly Bombay) 1996–2006; cr. Cardinal (Cardinal-Priest of Spirito Santo alla Ferratella) 2001; participated in Papal Conclave 2005, 2013; Prefect, Congregation for the Evangelization of Peoples, Vatican City 2006–11, Prefect Emer. 2011–; mem. Congregation for the Doctrine of the Faith, for Divine Worship and the Discipline of the Sacraments, for Catholic Educ.; mem. Pontifical Councils for Culture, for the Laity; of the Pontifical Comm. for the Cultural Heritage of the Church, of the Prefecture for Econ. Affairs of the Holy See; mem. Council of Cardinals for the Study of Organizational and Econ. Affairs of the Holy See. *Address:* Congregation for Evangelization of Peoples, 48 Piazza di Spagna, 00187 Rome, Italy (office). *Telephone:* (06) 69879299 (office). *Fax:* (06) 69880118 (office). *E-mail:* cepsegreteria@evangel.va (office); bombaydiocese@vsnl.com (office). *Website:* www.evangelizatio.org (office).

DIAS DIOGO, Luisa, MEconSc; Mozambican politician and international organization official; b. 11 April 1958, Dist of Mágoè, Tete; d. of Luís João Diogo and Laura Atanásia Dias; m. António Albana Silva; two s. one d.; ed Univ. Eduardo Mondlane, Univ. of London, UK; joined Ministry of Planning and Finance 1980, with Dept of Econs and Investment 1980–84, Assoc. Head of Dept 1984–86, Programme Officer Study Dept 1986–89, Head, Dept of Budget 1989–92, Nat. Dir of Budget 1993–94; Programme Officer IBRD, Maputo 1994; Vice-Minister of Planning and Finance 1994–2000; Minister of Planning and Finance 2000–05; Prime Minister of Mozambique 2004–10; Chair. Nat. Council of the Fight Against HIV/AIDS 2005–09; Co-Chair. High-level Panel on UN System-wide Coherence in the Areas of Development, Humanitarian Assistance and the Environment 2006; mem. UN High-level Panel on Global Sustainability 2010–; mem. Advisory Bd Brenthurst Foundation 2010–; mem. Advisory Council for Peace and Security, African Comm. 2010–; ranked by Forbes magazine amongst 100 Most Powerful Women (73rd) 2004, (96th) 2005, (83rd) 2006, (89th) 2007; Global Women's Leadership Award 2008. *Leisure interests:* reading, listening to music, spending time with family and friends. *Address:* c/o Global Sustainability Panel Secretariat, Room A-300, 866 United Nations Plaza, United Nations Headquarters, New York, NY 10017, USA (office).

DIAS FERREIRA LEITE, Maria Manuela, BEcons; Portuguese economist and politician; b. 3 Dec. 1940, Lisbon; d. of Carlos Eugénio Dias Ferreira and Julieta de Carvalho; ed Instituto Superior de Ciências Económicas e Financeiras, Tech. Univ. of Lisbon; researcher, Calouste Gulbenkian Foundation 1964–73; asst, Public Finance and Econs, Instituto Superior de Economia e Gestão 1966–79; Dir Dept of Statistics, Inst. of State Holdings 1975–77; Co-ordinator Finance Group, Research Bureau, Banco de Portugal 1977–86; Dir-Gen. Public Accounting, Ministry of Finance 1986–90; Sec. of State of Budget 1990–91; Sec. of State attached to Minister of Budget 1991–93; with Ministry of Educ. 1993–95; mem. Parl. 1991–95, 1995–2000; Vice-Pres. of Parl. Group, Social Democratic Party 1996–2001, Pres. Sept. 2001; Minister of State and of Finance 2002–04; consultant to Banco de Portugal 2004–; mem. Admin. Council, Banco Santander Totta 2006–. *Address:* c/o Banco de Portugal, Rua do Ouro 27, 1100-150 Lisbon; c/o Administrative Council, Banco Santander Totta, Rua de Ouro 88, 1100-061 Lisbon, Portugal. *E-mail:* info@bportugal.pt. *Website:* www.bportugal.pt; www.santandertotta.pt.

DIAZ, Cameron Michelle; American actress and fmr model; b. 30 Aug. 1972, San Diego, Calif.; d. of the late Emilio Diaz and of Billie Diaz (née Early); model with Elite Model Management 1988–93; rose to prominence during 1990s with roles in films including The Mask, My Best Friend's Wedding and There's Something About Mary. *Films include:* She's No Angel: Cameron Diaz (video short) 1992, The Mask 1994, The Last Supper 1995, Feeling Minnesota 1996, She's the One 1996, Head Above Water 1996, Keys to Tulsa 1997, My Best Friend's Wedding 1997, A Life Less Ordinary 1997, Fear and Loathing in Las Vegas 1997, There's Something About Mary 1998, Very Bad Things 1998, Being John Malkovich 1999, Invisible Circus 1999, Any Given Sunday 1999, Charlie's Angels 2000, Things You Can Tell Just by Looking at Her 2000, Shrek (voice) 2001, Vanilla Sky (Boston Soc. of Film Critics Best Supporting Actress 2001, Chicago Film Critics Best Supporting Actress 2002) 2001, The Sweetest Thing 2002, Gangs of New York 2002, Charlie's Angels: Full Throttle 2003, Shrek II (voice) 2004, In Her Shoes 2005, The Holiday 2006, Shrek the Third (voice) 2007, What Happens in Vegas 2008, My Sister's Keeper 2009, The Box 2009, Shrek Forever After (voice) 2010, Knight and Day 2010, The Green Hornet 2011, Bad Teacher 2011, What to Expect When You're Expecting 2012, Gambit 2013. *Television includes:* Trippin (documentary) 2005, Shrek the Halls (voice) 2007, Saturday Night Live 2008–09, Sesame Street 2009, Top Gear 2010, Scared Shrekless (short) (voice) 2010, The X Factor (French edn, guest judge) 2011. *Address:* c/o Creative Artists Agency, 2000 Avenue of the Stars, Los Angeles, CA 90067, USA (office). *Telephone:* (424) 288-2000 (office). *Fax:* (424) 288-2900 (office). *Website:* www.caa.com (office).

DÍAZ, Francisco Gil, BSc, PhD; Mexican economist, government official and telecommunications industry executive; *Executive President, Telefonica Moviles Mexico, SA De C V;* b. 2 Sept. 1943, Mexico City; m.; four c.; ed Instituto Tecnológico Autónomo de México (ITAM), Univ. of Chicago, USA; Prof., ITAM 1970–76, now Prof. Emer., Co-ordinator, ITAM Econs Program 1973–78; Prof., Colegio de México 1970–84; economist, Bank of Mexico 1973, Dir Gen. of Econ.-Treasury Studies, Secr. of Treasury 1976, Head of Org. and Analysis of Econ. Information 1977–78, Dir Gen. of Income Policy, Secr. of Treasury 1978–82; Asst Dir Bank of Mexico 1982–85, Dir of Econ. Research 1985–88; Under-Sec. of Revenue 1988–94 and later Gen. Man. for Econ. and Financial Studies, Finance and Public Credit Secr., then Gen. Dir of Revenue Policy; Gen. Man. Avantel SA (telecommunications co.) 1997–2000; Sec. of State for Finance and Public Credit 2000–06; Exec. Pres. Telefónica México and Central América (Telefonica Moviles Mexico) 2007–; mem. Bd of Dirs Corporacion Geo SAB de CV 2008–. *Address:* Telefonica Moviles Mexico, SA De C V, Prolg Paseo De La Reforma No 1200, Pisos 8-14, Santa Fe Cruz Manca, Cuajimalpa 05349 México DF, Mexico (office).

DIAZ, Illac Angelo, BA, MA, MBA; Philippine social entrepreneur and environmental campaigner; *Founder and Executive Director, MyShelter Inc.;* b. 1971; ed Ateneo de Manila Univ., De La Salle Univ., Manila, Asian Inst. of Man., Manila, Kennedy School of Govt, Harvard Univ., USA; Research Fellow, Special Program for Urban and Regional Studies, MIT, USA 2006; Co-founder USAP-KAMAY Program (support for deaf-mute students), Ateneo de Manila Univ. 1998–95; Founding Pres. Good Guys Inc. (support for law students) 1998–2003; Exec. Dir CentroMigrante (self-help housing community) 2003; Founder and Exec. Dir MyShelter Inc. 2005–; Founder and Exec. Dir Pier One Seafarers' Dormitories (sustainable shelter systems), Manila; Ernst & Young Entrepreneur of the Year 2006, named one of the 10 Outstanding Young Persons of the World by Jaycees Int. 2006. *Address:* Corte Real, Real cor. Solana Streets, Intramuros, Manila (office); 210 Loring St, Pasay City, Philippines. *Telephone:* (2) 301-0600 (office).

DIAZ, Miguel Humberto, BA, MA, PhD; American theologian, academic and diplomatist; *University Professor of Faith and Culture, University of Dayton;* b. 29 Sept. 1963, Havana, Cuba; m. Marian K Díaz 1993; four c.; ed St Thomas Univ., Univ. of Notre Dame, Ind.; Theology Instructor, Dept of Theology, Univ. of Notre Dame 1995–96; Asst Prof., Dept of Religious Studies, Univ. of Dayton, Ohio 1996–98; Asst Prof. in Systematic/Philosophical Theology, St Vincent de Paul Regional Seminary, Fla 1998–2001; Academic Dean, Vincent de Paul Seminary, Fla 2001–03; Assoc. Prof., Barry Univ., Fla 2003–04, Dept of Theology, Coll. of St Benedict/St John Univ., St John's School of Theology Seminary, St Joseph and Collegeville, Minnesota 2004–09, Prof. 2009; Amb. to the Holy See (Vatican City) 2009–12; Univ. Prof. of Faith and Culture, Univ. of Dayton 2012–; Chair. Multi-Cultural Cttee, St John's School of Theology Seminary 2007, Co-Chair. Intercultural Directions Council 2006; mem. Bd Voices for the Common Good, Catholic Theological Soc. of America 2008, Acad. of Catholic Hispanic Theologians, USA (Vice-Pres. 2005, Pres. 2006–08) 2001–08; mem. Steering Cttee Karl Rahner Soc. 2004–08; mem. Assessment Cttee, Dept of Theology 2006–07, Grad. Theological Studies Cttee 2005–06, Cttee of Latin American/Latino Studies Program at CSB/SJU 2004; Educational Trailblazer Theologian of the Year Award 2007. *Publications include:* From the Heart of Our People: Latino/a Explorations in Catholic Systematic Theology (co-ed) 1999, On Being Human: US Hispanic and Rahnerian Perspectives (Hispanic Theological Initiative Book of the Year Award, Princeton Theological Seminary 2002) 2002. *Address:* University of Dayton, HM 254, 300 College Park, Dayton, OH 45469, USA (office). *Telephone:* (937) 229-2105 (office). *Website:* www.udayton.edu (office).

DÍAZ-CANEL BERMUDEZ, Miguel Mario; Cuban politician; *First Vice-President, Council of State and Council of Ministers;* b. 20 April 1960, Santa Clara; mil. service with Fuerzas Armadas Revolucionarias 1982–85; early career as electrical engineer; Prof., Central Univ. of Las Villas 1985; various roles with Unión de Jóvenes Comunistas (communist youth league) from 1987; mem. Partido Comunista de Cuba (PCC—Communist Party of Cuba), PCC Rep. in Nicaragua –1989, elected to PCC Central Cttee 1991, PCC First Sec., Villa Clara Prov. 1994–2003, First Sec., Holguin Prov. 2003–08, elected to Political Bureau (youngest-ever mem.) 2003; Minister of Higher Educ. 2009–12; Vice-Pres., Council of Ministers, with responsibility for educ. issues 2012–13; First Vice-Pres., Council of State and Council of Ministers 2013–. *Address:* Consejo de Estado, Havana, Cuba (office).

DÍAZ RUEDA, Ruth Marina, LLD; Colombian lawyer and judge; *President, Supreme Court of Justice;* b. Socorro, Santander Dist; ed Univ. Santo Tomás de Aquino, Bucaramanga; started career as judge, Barichara, Santander 1978, later becoming judge, civil law court, Sorocco and municipal criminal, juvenile and circuit courts, San Gil (first woman); fmr Judge, Civil Court of the Circuit of Bogotá; Judge (first woman), Civil Appeal Chamber, Supreme Court of Justice 2006, Pres. 2007, 2010, Vice-Pres. Supreme Court of Justice 2012–13, Pres. (first woman) 2013–; fmr Prof. of law, Univ. Santo Tomás de Aquino, Bucaramanga, Univ. Libre, Bogotá, Fundación Universitaria de San Gil. *Address:* Supreme Court of Justice, Edif. de Palacio de Justicia, Calle 12, No 7-65, Bogotá, DC, Colombia (office). *Telephone:* (1) 562-2000 (office). *Website:* www.cortesuprema.gov.co (office).

DIBA, Farah (see PAHLAVI, Farah Diba).

DIBABA, Tirunesh; Ethiopian athlete; b. 1 June 1985, Bekoji, Arsi; d. of Dibaba Keneni and Gutu Tola; m. Sileshi Sihine; long distance track athlete; began athletics running aged 14; moved to Addis Ababa 2000; competed in and finished 5th, aged 15, in women's jr race at Int. Asscn of Athletics Feds (IAAF) World Cross Country Championships 2001; gold medal, 5,000m, World Championships, Paris 2003, 5,000m and 10,000m, Helsinki 2005, 10,000m, Osaka 2007, 10,000m, Moscow 2013; gold medal, Jr Race, World Cross Country Championships, Lausanne 2003, Short Course, Saint-Galmier 2005, Long Course, Saint-Galmier 2005, Long Course, Fukuoka 2006, Sr Race, Edinburgh 2008; silver medal, Jr Race, World Cross Country Championships, Dublin 2002, Short Race, Brussels 2004, Sr Race, Mombasa 2007; silver medal, 5,000m, World Jr Championships, Kingston 2002; bronze medal, 5,000m, Olympic Games, Athens 2004, gold medal, 5,000m and 10,000m (Olympic record), Beijing Olympics 2008, gold medal, 10,000m and bronze medal, 5,000m, London Olympics 2012; gold medal, 10,000m, African Championships, Addis Ababa 2008, Nairobi 2010, silver medal, 5,000m, Bambous 2006; first woman to win 10,000m/5,000m double at same championships, Helsinki 2005; won five out of six Golden League events (5,000m) in same season 2006; set a new 5,000m world record of 14 minutes 11.15 seconds at Oslo Golden League 2008; first ever woman to win both 5,000m and 10,000m at same Olympics 2008; Int. Asscn of Athletics Fed. Award 2005, 2008, Women's Track & Field Athlete of the Year 2008, Women's 5,000m Best Year Performance 2008–09, rank of Chief Supt conferred on her by her club The Prisons Police 2008, hosp. outside Addis Ababa named after her. *Address:* c/o Ethiopian Athletics Federation, PO Box 3241, Addis Ababa, Ethiopia. *Website:* www.ethiosports.com; www.tiruneshdibaba.net.

DIBANGO, Manu; Cameroonian musician (saxophone, piano); b. 12 Dec. 1934, Douala; ed piano lessons; moved to Paris 1949, then Brussels, Belgium 1956; residency at Black Angels Club, Brussels; joined band led by Joseph Kabsele, African Jazz 1960, played with African Jazz in Zaire –1963; returned to Cameroon to form own band 1963–65; studio musician, Paris 1965; backed musicians, including Peter Gabriel, Sinead O'Connor, Angélique Kidjo, Geoffrey Oryema, Ray Lema, Touré Kunda; solo artist 1968–; Pres., Francophone Diffusion; apptd UNESCO Artist for Peace 2004; Grammy Award for Best R&B Instrumental Performance of the Year 1973, Ronnie Scott Award for Services to Jazz 2007. *Compositions include:* commissioned by President Ahidjo to write song for Africa Cup football match 1971. *Recordings include:* albums: O Boso 1971, Soma Loba 1972, Soul Makossa 1973, Super Kumba 1974, Manu 76 1976, Afrovision 1976, Big Blow 1976, A L'Olympia 1977, Ceddo 1978, Gone Clear 1980, Ambassador 1980, Waka Juju 1982, Deliverence 1983, Sweet and Soft 1983, Melodies Africaines vols 1 and 2 1983, Deadline 1984, Electric Africa 1985, Afrijazzy 1986, Negropolitains Vol. 2 1993, Wakafrika 1994, Bao Bao 1996, Mboa' Su 2000, Voyage Anthologique 2004, Essential Recordings 2006, Lion of Africa 2008, Anthology 2009, Soft and Sweet 2010, African Woodoo 2010, From Africa 2011, Deliverance 2011, Bao Bao 2012. *Publications:* Trois Kilos de Café (autobiography) 1990. *Address:* c/o Global Mix Media Limited, PO Box 4702, Henley on Thames, RG9 9AA, England (office). *E-mail:* claire@manudibango.net (office). *Website:* www.manudibango.net (office).

DIBIAGGIO, John A., DDS, MA; American dentist and university administrator; *President Emeritus, Tufts University;* b. 11 Sept. 1932, San Antonio; s. of Ciro DiBiaggio and Acidalia DiBiaggio; m. Nancy Cronemiller 1989; one s. two d. (from previous marriage); ed Eastern Michigan Univ., Univ. of Detroit and Univ. of Michigan; gen. dentistry practice, New Baltimore, Mich. 1958–65; Asst Prof., School of Dentistry, Univ. of Detroit 1965–67; Asst Dean of Student Affairs, Univ. of Kentucky 1967–70; Prof., Dean School of Dentistry, Va Commonwealth Univ., Richmond 1970–76; Vice-Pres. for Health Affairs and Exec. Dir of the Health Center, Univ. of Conn., Farmington 1976–79; Pres. Univ. of Conn., Storrs 1979–85, Mich. State Univ., East Lansing 1985–92, Tufts Univ., Medford, Mass. 1992–2001, Pres. Emer. 2001–; mem. Bd American Automobile Asscn 1994–2002, Kaman Corpn 1984–2008; Trustee, American Cancer Soc. Foundation 1993– (Pres. 1999), Univ. of Massachusetts 2003–; 11 hon. degrees; Man of the Year, City of Detroit 1985, Pierre Fauchard Gold Medal Award 1989; Order of Merit (Italy). *Publications:* Applied Practice Management: A Strategy for Stress Control (with others) 1979; articles in professional journals. *Leisure interest:* tennis. *Address:* PO Box 5346, Snowmass Village, CO 81615-5346, USA.

DIBY, Charles Koffi, Côte d'Ivoirian economist and politician; *Minister of Foreign Affairs;* b. 7 Sept. 1957, Bouaké; m.; five c.; ed Nat. School of Man. and International Inst. of Public Admin, Paris; began career at Treasury 1984, responsible for Nat. Inst. for the Youth and Sports 1985–90, for Nat. Inst. for Professional Training 1990–91, Rep. for Cen. Agency for Public Spending 1991–93, Treasurer for Bondoukou Prov. 1993–94, Treas. for Daoukro Prov. 1994–97,

Accountant, Cen. Agency for Public Spending 1997–98, Paymaster-Gen. 1998–99, Deputy Dir-Gen. of the Treasury 1999–2000, Dir-Gen. 2001–07; Counsellor to Minister of the Economy and Finance 2000–01; Minister Del. of the Economy and Finance 2006–07; Minister of the Economy and Finance 2007–12; Minister of Foreign Affairs 2012–. *Address:* Ministry of Foreign Affairs and African Integration, Bloc Ministériel, blvd Angoulvant, BP V109, Abidjan, Côte d'Ivoire (office). *Telephone:* 20-22-71-50 (office). *Fax:* 20-33-23-08 (office). *E-mail:* infos@mae.ci (office). *Website:* www.mae.ci (office).

DICAPRIO, Leonardo Wilhelm; American actor and film producer; b. 11 Nov. 1974, Los Angeles, Calif.; s. of George DiCaprio and Irmelin DiCaprio; f. Appian Way production co.; Commdr des Arts et des Lettres; Platinum Award, Santa Barbara Int. Film Festival 2005. *Films:* Critters 3 1991, Poison Ivy 1992, This Boy's Life 1993, What's Eating Gilbert Grape 1993, The Foot Shooting Party (short) 1994, Les cent et une nuits de Simon Cinéma (uncredited) 1995, The Quick and the Dead 1995, The Basketball Diaries 1995, Total Eclipse 1995, Marvin's Room 1996, William Shakespeare's Romeo + Juliet 1996, Titanic 1997, The Man in the Iron Mask 1998, Celebrity 1998, The Beach 2000, Don's Plum 2001, Gangs of New York 2002, Catch Me If You Can 2002, The Aviator 2004, The Departed (Best Int. Actor, Irish Film and TV Awards 2007) 2006, Blood Diamond 2006, The 11th Hour (voice, producer) 2007, Body of Lies 2008, Revolutionary Road 2009, Shutter Island 2010, Inception 2010, J. Edgar 2011, Django Unchained 2012, The Great Gatsby 2013, The Wolf of Wall Street (Golden Globe Award for Best Actor in a Motion Picture, Comedy or Musical 2014) 2013. *Television:* The New Lassie (series) 1989, The Outsiders (series) 1990, Santa Barbara (series) 1990, Parenthood (series) 1990–91, Roseanne (series) 1991, Growing Pains (series) 1991–92. *Address:* c/o Special Artists Agency, 9465 Wilshire Blvd, Suite 890, Beverly Hills, CA 90212, USA (office); Appian Way, 9255 Sunset Blvd, Suite 615, West Hollywood, CA 90069; c/o Birken Productions Inc., PO Box 291958, Los Angeles, CA 90029, USA (office). *Telephone:* (310) 300-1390 (Appian Way). *Website:* www.leonardodicaprio.com (office).

DiCHRISTINA, Mariette, BS; American editor; *Editor-in-Chief, Scientific American;* b. 16 April 1964, North Tarrytown, NY; m. Carl John Gerosa 1989; two d.; ed Boston Univ.; reporter, Gannett-Westchester newspapers 1986–87; joined Popular Science magazine as copy ed., later becoming Assoc. Ed., Sr Ed. and Exec. Ed. 1987–2001; Exec. Ed. Scientific American 2001–09, Ed.-in-Chief 2009–; Adjunct Prof. in Science Writing, New York Univ.; Pres. Nat. Asscn of Science Writers 2009–10; adviser, Citizen Science Alliance, Origins Inst. at Arizona State Univ., Bulletin of Atomic Scientists; Fellow, AAAS 2011; Douglas S. Morrow Public Outreach Award 2001, Scientific American Nat. Magazine Award for General Excellence 2011. *Address:* Scientific American, Nature America, 75 Varick Street, 9th Floor, New York, NY 10013-1917, USA (office). *Telephone:* (212) 451-8200 (office). *E-mail:* mdichristina@sciam.com (office). *Website:* www.scientificamerican.com (office).

DICHTER, Avraham (Avi), BA, MBA; Israeli government official; b. 1952; m. Ilana Dichter; three c.; ed Bar Ilan Univ., Tel-Aviv Univ.; mil. service 1971–90, served in Sayeret Matkal commando unit; Head, Southern Dist (ISA), Israel Security Agency—ISA (Shabak) 1992–96, Head, Security and Protection Div. 1996–99, Deputy Dir ISA 1999–2000, Dir 2000–05; elected to Knesset 2006, Minister of Public Security 2006–09; Research Fellow, Brookings Inst., Washington, DC 2005; mem. Kadima party. *Address:* c/o The Knesset, HaKiryah, Jerusalem 91950, Israel (office).

DICHTER, Misha, BS; American concert pianist; b. 27 Sept. 1945, Shanghai, China; s. of Leon Dichter and Lucy Dichter; m. Cipa Dichter 1968; two s.; ed Juilliard School under Rosina Lhevinne; winner, Silver Medal, Tchaikovsky Int. Competition, Moscow 1966; since then has performed with leading orchestras and at festivals and given recitals worldwide; also performs with wife as piano duo; winner, Tchaikovsky Competition 1966, Grand Prix du Disque Liszt 1999. *Recordings include:* Beethoven Sonatas, Brahms Variations, music by Gershwin, Liszt, Mussorgsky, Stravinsky, Schumann, Tchaikovsky. *Publications:* articles in New York Times, Ovation and Keyboard magazines. *Leisure interests:* tennis, jogging, drawing, sketching. *Address:* Shuman Associates, 120 West 58th Street, New York, NY 10019, USA (office). *Telephone:* (212) 315-1300 (office). *Fax:* (212) 757-3005 (office). *E-mail:* shumanpr@cs.com (office). *Website:* mishadichter.com.

DICKERSON, Vivian M., MD; American physician and professor of obstetrics and gynaecology; one s.; ed Univ. of California, Santa Barbara, Univ. of California, San Diego School of Medicine; joined Peace Corps and worked in Togo, West Africa 1970s; completed residency training at UCLA Cedars-Sinai Medical Center; fmr Sr Research Analyst, Susan Samueli Center for Complementary and Alternative Medicine, Irvine, Clinical Prof. of Obstetrics and Gynecology, Univ. of California, Irvine (UCI) Medical Center –2006; apptd Exec. Medical Dir of Women's Health Programs and Care, Hoag Memorial Hosp. Presbyterian, Newport Beach, Calif. 2006; held numerous positions with American Coll. of Obstetricians and Gynaecologists (ACOG), including Chair. Dist IX (Calif.), Council of Dist Chairs, Cttee on Int. Relations, Grievance Cttee and Admin. Comm. 1984–2004, Pres. ACOG 2004–05; Chair. California Family Health Council 2000–04; Ed. in Chief The Female Patient (journal); mem. Advisory Bd Esprit Pharma Inc., Mirabel Medical Systems Ltd, Neomatrix LLC Inc.; ACOG Outstanding Dist Service Award, American Medical Women's Asscn Gender Equity Award 2000, UCI Coll. of Medicine, Golden Apple Award 2002. *Leisure interests:* hiking, skiing, scuba diving. *Address:* 615D E West View Drive, Orange, CA 92869, USA.

DICKIE, Brian James; British opera director (retd) and consultant; *Artistic Adviser, Bertelsmann Stiftung;* b. 23 July 1941, Newark, Notts., England; s. of the late Robert Kelso Dickie and of Harriet Elizabeth Dickie; m. 1st Victoria Teresa Sheldon (née Price) 1968; two s. one d.; m. 2nd Nancy Gustafson 1989; m. 3rd Elinor Rhys Williams 2002; one d.; ed Trinity Coll., Dublin; Admin. Asst, Glyndebourne Opera 1962–66; Admin. Glyndebourne Touring Opera 1967–81; Opera Man., Glyndebourne Festival Opera 1970–81, Gen. Admin. 1981–89; Artistic Dir Wexford Festival 1967–73; Artistic Adviser, Théâtre Musical de Paris 1981–87, Bertelsmann Stiftung; Gen. Dir Canadian Opera Co. 1989–93; Artistic Counsellor, Opéra de Nice 1994–97; Gen. Dir EU Opera 1997–99, Chicago Opera Theater 1999–2012; Chair. London Choral Soc. 1978–85, Theatres Nat. Cttee Opera Cttee 1976–85; Vice-Chair. Theatres Nat. Cttee 1980–85; Vice-Pres.

Theatrical Man. Asscn 1983–85; mem. Bd Opera America 1991–93. *Leisure interests:* cricket, photography, wine and food, travel, my blog. *Address:* 4 Bancroft Court, 35 Ackmar Road, London, SW6 4UR, England. *Telephone:* (20) 7736-1031; 7966-467512 (mobile). *E-mail:* briandickie@mac.com. *Website:* www.briandickie.com.

DICKIE, Lloyd Merlin, PhD, FRSC; Canadian ecologist and academic; *Research Scientist Emeritus, Department of Fisheries and Oceans;* b. 6 March 1926, Kingsport, Nova Scotia; s. of Ebenezer Cox Dickie and Pearl (née Sellars) Dickie; m. Marjorie C. Bowman 1952; one s. two d.; ed Acadia Univ., Yale Univ., Univ. of Toronto; research scientist, Fisheries Research Bd, NB 1951–62, Great Lakes Inst., Toronto 1962–65; Dir Marine Ecology Lab., Bedford Inst. Oceanography, Dartmouth, NS 1965–74; Chair. and Prof. of Oceanography, Dalhousie Univ., Halifax 1974–77, Dir Inst. of Environmental Studies, Dalhousie Univ. 1974–76; Research Scientist, Marine Ecology Lab. and Marine Fish Div., Bedford Inst. of Oceanography, Dartmouth, NS 1976–87; Sr Research Scientist, Biological Sciences Br., Dept of Fisheries and Oceans 1987–93, Research Scientist Emer. 1994–; participant in Ocean Production Enhancement Network 1991–92; mem. SPICES (Sr People of Int. Council for the Exploration of the Sea) Network; Oscar-Sette Memorial Award, American Fish Soc. 1991. *Publications:* Ad Mare: Canada Looks to the Sea (with R. W. Stewart) 1971, The Biomass Spectrum: A Predator-Prey Theory of Aquatic Production (co-author) 2001; more than 80 scientific papers. *Address:* 7 Lakewood Court, Dartmouth, NS B2X 2R6, Canada. *Telephone:* (902) 435-1545. *E-mail:* lloyd.dickie@eastlink.ca.

DICKINSON, Angie; American actress; b. (Angeline Brown), 30 Sept. 1931, Kulm, ND; ed Immaculate Heart Coll., Glendale Coll. *Films include:* Lucky Me 1954, Man With the Gun, The Return of Jack Slade, Tennessee's Partner, The Black Whip, Hidden Guns, Tension at Table Rock, Gun the Man Down, Calypso Joe, China Gate, Shoot Out at Medicine Bend, Cry Terror, I Married a Woman, Rio Bravo, The Bramble Bush, A Fever in the Blood, The Sins of Rachel Cade, Jessica, Rome Adventure, Captain Newman MD, The Killers, The Art of Love, Cast a Giant Shadow, The Chase, The Poppy is Also a Flower, Last Challenge, Point Blank, Sam Whiskey, Some Kind of a Nut, Young Billy Young, Pretty Maids All in a Row, The Resurrection of Zachary Wheeler, The Outside Man, Big Bad Mama, Klondike Fever, Dressed to Kill, Charlie Chan and the Curse of the Dragon Queen, Death Hunt, Big Bad Mama II, Even Cowgirls Get the Blues, The Maddening, Sabrina, The Sun, The Moon and The Stars, Pay It Forward, Sealed with a Kiss 1999, The Last Producer 2000, Duets 2000, Pay it Forward 2000, Big Bad Love 2001, Elvis Has Left the Building 2004. *Television series:* Police Woman, Cassie & Co. *Television films:* The Love War, Thief, See the Man Run, The Norliss Tapes, Pray for the Wildcats, A Sensitive Passionate Man, Overboard, The Suicide's Wife, Dial M for Murder, One Shoe Makes it Murder, Jealousy, A Touch of Scandal, Stillwatch, Police Story: The Freeway Killings, Once Upon a Texas Train, Prime Target, Treacherous Crossing, Danielle Steel's Remembrance, Mending Fences 2009; mini-series: Pearl, Hollywood Wives, Wild Palms. *Address:* 1715 Carla Ridge, Beverly Hills, CA 90210-1911, USA.

DICKSON, William Andrew; British diplomatist and business executive; *CEO, Independent (UK) Exports Limited;* b. 17 Dec. 1950, Glasgow, Scotland; s. of William Paul McBean Dickson and Isabella Dickson (née Goodwin); m. Patricia Ann Dickson (née Daniels) 2007; ed Univ. of Stirling, Northumbria Univ.; Training Dept, FCO 1969, on special unpaid leave (univ./Royal Marines) 1969–76, Vice-Consul, Embassy in Cairo 1976–79, Third Sec. (Commercial), High Comm. in Nairobi 1980–82, Second Sec. (Commercial), Embassy in Budapest 1982–85, Spokesperson, News Dept 1985–89, First Sec., IAEA, Vienna 1989–93, British Govt Spokesperson, Hong Kong 1994–98, Head of Atlantic and Oceans, Overseas Territories Dept, FCO 1998–2001, Acting Admin., Ascension Island 2000, Consul-Gen. and Admin., Tristan da Cunha 2001–04, Deputy Head of Information Man. Group 2005–07, Consul-Gen., Embassy in Erbil 2007–08, Amb. to Mongolia 2009–11; Dir of UK Operations, MongoliaNation; Dir, Orgill-Dickson Assocs 2011–, International Export Partners Ltd; CEO Independent (UK) Exports Ltd 2012–; Gov., Stalham High School. *Leisure interests:* boating, gardening. *Address:* 12 Trail Quay Cottages, Marsh Road, Hoveton, NR12 8UH, Norfolk, England (home). *E-mail:* shipwreckbt@hotmail.com (office).

DICTUS, Richard; Dutch UN official; *Executive Coordinator, United Nations Volunteers;* m.; three c.; ed Technical Univ. of Twente; Jr Professional Officer, UNIDO, South Yemen 1987; Asst Resident Rep. (Programme), UNDP, Sudan 1990–92, Lesotho 1992–94, Bangladesh 1994–98, Deputy Resident Rep., UNDP, Pakistan 1998–2000, Man. Adviser (Deputy Chief), Admin. Services Div., Bureau of Man., UNDP, New York 2000–01, Deputy Dir of Human Resources, Bureau of Man. 2001–05, UN Resident Coordinator and UNDP Resident Rep. in Fiji 2005–09, UN Resident Coordinator and UNDP Resident Rep. in Malawi 2009–12, Exec. Coordinator UN Volunteers 2013–. *Address:* United Nations Volunteers, Postfach 260 111, 53153 Bonn, Germany (office). *Telephone:* (228) 815-2000 (office). *Fax:* (228) 815-2001 (office). *Website:* www.unv.org (office).

DIDDY (see COMBS, Sean).

DIDI, Ali; Maldivian civil servant and diplomatist; joined civil service 1983, Dir Passport Office 2001–03, Controller of Immigration and Emigration March–Dec. 2003, Dir-Gen. Dept of Penitentiary and Rehabilitation, Ministry of Home Affairs and Environment 2004; Chair. Malé Municipality 2004–07; CEO Maldives Airports Co. 2007–08; High Commr to Sri Lanka 2008–11; Perm. Rep. to EU and Amb. to Belgium 2011–12. *Address:* Ministry of Foreign Affairs, Boduthakurufaanu Magu, Malé 20-077, Maldives (office). *Telephone:* 3323400 (office). *Fax:* 3323841 (office). *E-mail:* admin@foreign.gov.mv (office). *Website:* www.foreign.gov.mv (office).

DIDI, Maria Ahmed; Maldivian politician and lawyer; first qualified female lawyer in Maldives; fmr state prosecutor and Asst Exec. Dir, Attorney-Gen.'s Office; one of six women mems of People's Majlis (Parl.), non-aligned MP, mem. Maldivian Democratic Party 2005– (Chair. 2008), for Kaafu Atol 2005–, one of only two elected women (other four apptd by Pres.); organized first-ever women's rights rally in Maldives in 2006; co-recipient, first Int. Women of Courage Award, US Dept of State 2007. *Address:* Maldivian Democratic Party, H. Sharasha, 2nd Floor, Sosun Magu, Malé 20-059, Maldives (office). *Telephone:* 3340044 (office). *Fax:*

3322960 (office). *E-mail:* secretariat@mdp.org.mv (office). *Website:* www.mdp.org .mv (office).

DIDION, Joan, BA; American writer; b. 5 Dec. 1934, Sacramento, Calif.; d. of Frank Reese Didion and Eduene Didion (née Jerrett); m. John Gregory Dunne 1964 (died 2003); one d. (died 2005); ed Univ. of Calif., Berkeley; Assoc. Features Ed. Vogue magazine 1956–63; fmr columnist Esquire, Life, Saturday Evening Post, fmr contributor Nat. Review; freelance writer 1963–; mem. American Acad. of Arts and Letters, American Acad. of Arts and Sciences, Council on Foreign Relations; First Prize Vogue's Prix de Paris 1956, American Acad. of Arts and Letters Morton Dauwen Zabel Prize 1978, Edward McDowell Medal 1996, George Polk Award 2001, American Acad. of Arts and Letter Gold Medal for Belles Lettres 2005, Medal for Distinguished Contrib. to American Letters, Nat. Book Foundation 2007, Nat. Humanities Medal 2012. *Screenplays:* The Panic in Needle Park 1971, Play It as It Lays 1972, A Star is Born 1976, True Confessions 1981, Hills Like White Elephants 1991, Broken Trust 1995, Up Close and Personal 1996. *Publications include:* novels: Run River 1963, Play It as It Lays 1970, A Book of Common Prayer 1977, Telling Stories 1978, Democracy 1984, The Last Thing He Wanted 1996; essays: Slouching Towards Bethlehem 1969, The White Album 1978, After Henry 1992; non-fiction: Salvador 1983, Miami 1987, After Henry 1992, Political Fictions 2001, Where I Was From: A Memoir 2003, The Year of Magical Thinking (Nat. Book Award for Non-fiction; also screenplay) 2005, Blue Nights 2011. *Address:* Janklow & Nesbit, 445 Park Avenue, New York, NY 10022-2606, USA (office).

DIDO; British singer, musician (piano, violin) and songwriter; b. (Dido Florian Cloud de Bounevialle Armstrong), 25 Dec. 1971, London, England; sister of Rollo Armstrong; ed Guildhall School of Music, London; toured UK with classical music ensemble before joining pop groups aged 16; toured with brother Rollo's band, Faithless; signed solo deal with Arista Records, New York; BRIT Award for Best Female Solo Artist 2002, 2004, Ivor Novello Songwriter of the Year Award 2002, BAMBI Award for Best Int. Pop Act 2003, ASCAP Award for Songwriter of the Year 2008. *Recordings include:* albums: No Angel (BRIT Award for Best Album 2002) 1999, Life for Rent 2003, Safe Trip Home 2008, Girl Who Got Away 2013; singles: The Highbury Fields (EP) 1999, Here With Me 2001, Thank You 2001, Hunter 2001, All You Want 2002, Life for Rent 2003, White Flag (BRIT Award for Best British single 2004) 2003. *Website:* www.didomusic.com.

DIEDERICHSEN, Diedrich; German cultural critic and academic; *Professor of Theory, Practice and Communication of Contemporary Art, Academy of Fine Arts, Vienna;* b. 1957, Hamburg; m. Juliane Rebentisch; ed Univ. of Hamburg; Ed. Sounds (magazine) 1979–83; Ed. Spex (magazine) 1985–90; Prof. of Theory, Practice and Communication of Contemporary Art, Acad. of Fine Arts, Vienna, Austria 2008–; Prof. of Aesthetic Theory and Cultural Studies, Merz Acad., Stuttgart 1998–2007; Visiting Prof., Art Center Coll. of Design, Los Angeles, USA, Akad. der Bildenden Künste, Munich, Hochschule für Gestaltung, Offenbach, Bremen Univ., Bauhaus-Univ., Weimar, Justus-Liebig-Univ., Giessen, Univ. of Vienna; regular contrib. to Artforum, Texte Zur Kunst, Theater heute, tageszeitung; mem. Jury, Fed. Cultural Foundation of Germany 2002–05; mem. Advisory Bd, Zentrum für Medien und Interaktivität 2002, Arsenal der Freunde der Deutschen Kinemathek (cinema) 2005, Baden Württemberg Regional Art Bd 2008. *Publications include:* Sexbeat: 1972 bis heute 1985, Elektra 1986, Herr Dietrichsen 1987, 1500 Schallplatten 1989, Freiheit macht arm: Das Leben nach Rock'n'Roll 1990–93 1993, Politische Korrekturen 1996, Der lange Weg nach Mitte 1999, 2000 Schallplatten 1979–1999 2000, Musikzimmer: Avantgarde und Alltag 2005, Eigenblutdoping (Doping with Your Own Blood) 2008, On (Surplus) Value of Art 2008, Kritik des Auges 2008, Stein, Schere, Papier – Rock, Scissors, Paper (co-ed.) 2009, Utopia of Sound (co-ed.) 2010, Psicodelia y ready-made 2011, The Sopranos 2012. *Address:* Academy of Fine Arts, Schillerplatz 3, 1010 Vienna, Austria (office). *Telephone:* (1) 588-16-8200 (office). *Fax:* (1) 588-16-1898 (office). *E-mail:* d.diederichsen@akbild.ac.at (office). *Website:* www.akbild.ac.at (office). diedrich-diederichsen.de.

DIEKMANN, Kai; German newspaper executive; *Editorial Director and Editor-in-Chief, Bild Group;* b. 27 June 1964, Ravensburg; Parl. Corresp., Bild and Bild am Sonntag, Bonn 1987; Chief Reporter Bunte magazine, Munich 1989–91; Deputy Ed. B.Z., Berlin 1991–92, Deputy Ed. and Chief Political Corresp. Bild, Hamburg 1992–97; Chief Ed. Welt am Sonntag, Berlin 1998–2000, Ed.-in-Chief Bild and Publr Bild and Bild am Sonntag, Hamburg 2001–, Content Exec. bild.de 2007–; Editorial Dir Bild Group 2007–; Head, Bild hilft e.V. – Ein Herz für Kinder (charity org.) 2001–; External Bd mem. Hürriyet 2004–; non-Exec. Bd mem. Times Newspaper Holdings Ltd 2011–; Goldene Feder 2000, 2005, World Media Award 2002, German Media Exec. of the Year 2009. *Publications include:* Rita Süssmuth im Gespräch (co-author) 1994, Die neue Bundespräsident im Gespräch (co-author) 1994, Helmut Kohl. Ich wollte Deutschlands Einheit (co-author) 1996, Der große Selbstbetrug 2007, The Wall – Photographs 1961–1992 2009, Helmut Kohl – On the Path and In Past and Present 2010, Das BILD-Buch 2012. *Address:* Bild, Axel Springer AG, Axel-Springer-Straße 65, 10888 Berlin, Germany (office). *Telephone:* (30) 2591-0 (office). *Fax:* (30) 2591-76009 (office). *Website:* www.bild.de (office).

DIEKMANN, Michael; German business executive; *Chairman of the Board of Management and CEO, Allianz SE;* b. 23 Dec. 1954, Bielefeld; m.; three c.; ed Göttingen Univ.; Financial Dir Diekmann/Thieme GBR 1983–86, Pres. 1987–88; Exec. Asst to Head of Hamburg Regional Office, Allianz Versicherungs-AG 1988–89, Head of Sales, Hamburg Harburg Office 1990, Head of Hanover Office 1991–92, Head of Customer Relationship Man. for pvt. customers, Munich 1993, mem. Exec. Bd of Man. of regional office for N Rhine-Westphalia as Head of Sales 1994–95, Dir Allianz Insurance Man. Asia Pacific Pte Ltd, Singapore 1996–97, mem. Bd of Man. Allianz AG, Munich responsible for Asia-Pacific region 1998, responsible for Asia-Pacific, Cen. and Eastern Europe, Middle East, Africa and Group Man. Devt 2000, responsible for the Americas and Group Human Resources 2002–03, Chair. Bd of Man. and and CEO Allianz AG (renamed Allianz SE 2006) 2003–, also Chair. Allianz Deutschland AG, Allianz Global Investors AG, Vice-Chair. Allianz France SA, Allianz SpA; Vice-Chair. BASF SE, Linde AG; mem. Bd of Dirs Siemens AG, Allianz Deutschland AG. *Address:* Allianz SE, Königinstrasse 28, 80802 Munich, Germany (office). *Telephone:* (89) 3800-0 (office). *Fax:* (89) 3800-3810 (office). *E-mail:* michael.diekmann@allianz.com (office). *Website:* www .allianz.com (office).

DIEMU, Chikez; Democratic Republic of the Congo politician; mem. Parl. 1997–; Sec. for Strategic Planning 1997–99; Vice-Pres. in charge of organization of Govt 1999–2001; Vice-Minister of Interior 2001–04; Gen.-Sec. People's Party for Reconstruction and Democracy 2001–05; Vice-Gov. Katanga Prov. 2004–07; Minister of Defence, Demobilization and War Veterans' Affairs 2007–08. *Address:* c/o Ministry of Defence, Demobilization and War Veterans' Affairs, BP 4111, Kinshasa-Gombe, Democratic Republic of the Congo (office).

DIENER, Theodor Otto, DSc; American (b. Swiss) plant virologist and academic; *Distinguished University Professor Emeritus, Center for Biosystems Research, University of Maryland;* b. 28 Feb. 1921, Zurich, Switzerland; s. of Theodor E. Diener and Hedwig R. Baumann; m. Sybil Mary Fox 1968 (died 2012); three s. (from previous m.); ed Swiss Fed. Inst. of Tech. (ETH), Zurich; Plant Pathologist, Swiss Fed. Agricultural Research Station, Waedenswil 1948–49; Asst Prof. of Plant Pathology, Rhode Island State Univ., Kingston, USA 1950; Asst-Assoc. Plant Pathologist, Washington State Univ., Prosser 1950–59; Research Plant Pathologist, Plant Virology Lab., Agricultural Research Service, US Dept of Agric., Beltsville, Md 1959–88; Collaborator, Agricultural Research Service, US Dept of Agric., Beltsville, Md 1988–97; Prof., Center for Agric. Biotech. and Dept of Botany, Univ. of Md, College Park 1988–, Acting Dir Center for Agric. Biotech. 1991–92, Distinguished Univ. Prof. 1994–; Distinguished Prof., Univ. of Md Biotech. Inst. 1998–99, Distinguished Univ. Prof. Emer., Center for Biosystems Research 1999–; discovered and named viroids, smallest known agents of infectious disease; mem. NAS, American Acad. of Arts and Sciences, Leopoldina (German Acad. of Natural Scientists); Fellow, New York Acad. of Sciences, American Phytopathological Soc.; Campbell Award, American Inst. of Biological Sciences 1968, Superior Service Award, US Dept of Agric. 1969, Distinguished Service Award, US Dept of Agric. 1977, Alexander von Humboldt Award (FRG) 1975, Wolf Prize (Israel) 1987, E. C. Stakman Award, Univ. of Minn. 1988, Nat. Medal of Science (USA) 1987, Science Hall of Fame, Agricultural Research Service, US Dept of Agric. 1989, Circle of Discovery, Coll. of Chemical and Life Sciences, Univ. of Maryland 2007. *Publications:* Viroids and Viroid Diseases 1979, The Viroids (ed.) 1987; ed. numerous chapters in scientific books and more than 200 scientific papers. *Leisure interest:* private pilot. *Address:* PO Box 272, Beltsville, MD 20705, USA. *E-mail:* tod26@juno.com.

DIEPGEN, Eberhard; German lawyer and politician; b. 13 Nov. 1941, Berlin; m. Monika Adler 1975; one s. one d.; ed Free Univ. of Berlin; joined CDU 1962, later Chair., W Berlin CDU; mem. Berlin Chamber of Deputies 1971–81; mem. Bundestag (Parl.) as W Berlin Rep. 1980–81; Mayor of Berlin 1984–89, 1991–2001; Senator for Justice 1999–2001; Chair. Supervisory Bd Berlin Brandenburg Flughafen Holding GmbH 1996; currently attorney, Thümmel, Schütze & Partner, Berlin; Grosses Bundesverdienstkreuz mit Stern 1994. *Leisure interests:* soccer, European history. *Address:* Thümmel, Schütze & Partner, Berlin, Kurfürstendamm 31, 10719 Berlin, Germany (office). *Telephone:* (30) 8871700 (office). *Fax:* 930) 8850075 (office). *E-mail:* eberhard.diepgen@tsp-law.com (office). *Website:* www.tsp-law.com (office).

DIETRICH, Siegfried, PhD; German chemist and academic; *Director, Max-Planck-Institut für Metallforschung;* b. 1954, Singen; ed Univ. of Konstanz, Univ. of Munich; Research Assoc., Univ. of Washington, Seattle, USA 1982–83; Research Assoc., Ludwig-Maximilians-Universität, Munich 1983–86; Assoc. Prof., Univ. of Würzburg 1987–88, also Univ. of Mainz 1988; Full Prof., Univ. of Wuppertal 1989–90; Scientific mem. and Dir Max-Planck-Institut für Metallforschung 2002–; Chair. for Theoretical Solid State Physics, Univ. of Stuttgart; Fellow, Japan Soc. for the Promotion of Science 1997; mem. Int. Union of Pure and Applied Chem.; German Physical Soc. Walter-Schottky-Preis 1985, Max Born Medal and Prize 2002. *Address:* Max-Planck-Institut fur Metallforschung, Heisenbergstr. 3, 70569 Stuttgart, Germany (office). *Telephone:* (711) 689-1921 (office). *Fax:* (711) 689-1922 (office). *E-mail:* dietrich@mf.mpg.de (office). *Website:* www.mf.mpg.de/de (office).

DIEWERT, Walter Erwin, BA, MA, PhD, FRSC; Canadian economist and academic; *Professor of Economics, University of British Columbia;* b. 4 Dec. 1941, Vancouver, BC; s. of Ewald Diewert and Linda Diewert; m. Virginia Diewert; ed Univ. of British Columbia, Univ. of California, Berkeley; mem. Faculty of Econs, Univ. of Chicago 1968–70; mem. Faculty of Econs, Univ. of British Columbia 1970–, currently Prof. of Econs; Research Assoc., Nat. Bureau of Econ. Research; Chair. Statistics Canada Advisory Cttee on Prices, mem. Statistics Canada Services Advisory Cttee, Statistics Canada Advisory Group on Science and Tech.; mem. NAS Panel on Conceptual, Measurement and Other Statistical Issues in Developing Cost of Living Indexes, Washington, DC 1999–2000; Assoc. Ed. Macroeconomic Dynamics; Fellow, Econometric Soc., World Acad. of Productivity Science; Distinguished Fellow, American Economic Soc.; mem. UN Canberra Group on Capital Measurement, UN Ottawa Group on Price Measurement; consultant for OECD, ILO, IMF, World Bank, US Bureau of Econ. Analysis, US Bureau of Labor Statistics, NZ Treasury, Australian Bureau of Statistics; Killam Prize, Canada Council for the Arts 2003, Doug Purvis Memorial Prize, Canadian Econs Asscn 2005, Julius Shiskin Memorial Award for Econ. Statistics 2005. *Publications:* more than 260 publns in econ journals and books; numerous reports, including the report to NZ Business Roundtable, major contributor to 2004 Consumer Price Index Manual, 2004 Producer Price Index Manual and 2009 Export Import Price Index Manual. *Leisure interest:* tennis. *Address:* Department of Economics, University of British Columbia, Buchanan Tower 1009, #997-1873 East Mall, Vancouver, BC V6T 1Z1, Canada (office). *Telephone:* (604) 266-7300 (office). *Fax:* (604) 822-5915 (office). *E-mail:* diewert@econ.ubc.ca (office). *Website:* www.econ.ubc.ca/diewert/hmpgdie.htm (office).

DIFORIO, Robert George, BA; American publishing executive; *Principal, D4EO Literary Agency and Mandevilla Press;* b. 19 March 1940, Mamaroneck, NY; s. of Richard John Diforio, Sr and Mildred Kuntz; m. Birgit Rasmussen 1983; one s. one d.; ed Williams Coll., Williamstown, Mass and Harvard Business School's Advanced Man. Program; Vice-Pres. Kable News Co. 1970; Vice-Pres. and Sales Man. New American Library (NAL) 1977, Sr Vice-Pres. and Marketing Dir 1976, Pres. and Publr 1980–82, CEO and Chair. Bd NAL/E. P. Dutton 1983–89; Prin. D4EO Literary Agency 1991–, Mandevilla Press 2012–; helped launch paperback writing careers of Erica Jong, Stephen King, Robin Cook and Ken Follett. *Leisure interest:* golf. *Address:* 7 Indian Valley Road, Weston, CT 06883, USA (office). *Telephone:* (203) 544-7180 (office); (203) 544-7182 (home). *Fax:* (203) 544-7160 (office). *E-mail:* bob@d4eo.com (office). *Website:* www.d4eo.com (office); www.d4eoliteraryagency.com (office).

DIGUIMBAYE, Christian Georges; Chadian politician; s. of Georges Diguimbaye; Minister of Finance and the Budget 2011–13. *Address:* c/o Ministry of Finance and the Budget, BP 816, N'Djamena, Chad (office).

DIJKGRAAF, Henk G.; Dutch energy industry executive; b. 1946; ed Univ. of Delft, Massachusetts Inst. of Tech., USA; began career with Royal Dutch/Shell 1972, held various positions in Borneo, Kuala Lumpur, Gabon, Syria, London and The Hague; Dir Nederlandse Aardolie Maatschappij (NAM) 1992–95; CEO Shell Int. Gas and Shell Coal Int. 1995–99; Pres. Shell Nederland BV 1999–2003; Group CEO NV Nederlandse Gasunie 2004–05, CEO Gasunie Trade and Supply BV (after restructuring) 2005–06; mem. Bd of Dirs Eneco Holding, Royal Tropical Institute KIT, Sasol LTD ADR 2006–; Deputy Chair. Netherlands Inst. for the Near East. *Address:* c/o Board of Governors, Netherlands Institute for the Near East, P.O.Box 9515, 2300 RA Leiden, Netherlands.

DIJOUD, Paul Charles Louis; French fmr diplomatist and politician; b. 25 July 1938, Neuilly-sur-Seine; s. of Jules-Raoul Dijoud and Andrée Claquin; m. Catherine Cochaux 1968 (divorced 1983); one s. one d.; m. 2nd Maryse Dolivot 1988; ed Lycée Condorcet, Faculté de Droit de Paris, Ecole Nat. d'Admin., Inst. d'Etudes politiques de Paris; commercial attaché, Dept of External Econ. Relations in Ministry of Econ. and Finance; elected to Nat. Ass. 1967, 1968, 1973, 1978, defeated 1981; Asst Sec.-Gen. Ind. Republican Party 1967–69; Conseiller Général for Canton of Embrun 1968–88; Pres. Ind. Republican Exec. Cttee for Provence-Côte d'Azur 1968–88; Mayor of Briançon 1971–83; Sec. of State attached to Prime Minister's Office 1973–74, later to Minister of Cultural Affairs and the Environment, to Minister of Employment with Responsibility for Immigrant Workers 1974, Secretary of State for Sport 1977, for Overseas Depts and Territories 1978; Commercial Adviser to Cen. Admin., Ministry of Economy and Finance 1981; Man. Dir Cie Commerciale Sucres et Denrées 1982–84; Pres. Comidex 1984; Pres. Conseil d'admin du parc nat. des Ecrins 1973; Plenipotentiary Minister 1988; Amb. to Colombia 1988–91, to Mexico 1992–94; Minister of State with responsibility for the principality of Monaco 1994–97; Amb. to Argentina 1997–2003; Mayor of Les Orres, Hautes Alpes 2006–; Officier de la Légion d'honneur. *Address:* Town Hall, 05200 Les Orres, France (office). *Telephone:* 4-92-44-00-40 (office). *E-mail:* pauldijoudfr@hotmail.com (office).

DIJSSELBLOEM, Jeroen René Victor Anton, BEcons; Dutch politician; *Minister of Finance;* b. 29 March 1966, Eindhoven; two c.; ed Wageningen Univ., Univ. Coll. Cork, Ireland; began career as Asst to Partij van de Arbeid (PvdA—Labour Party) MEPs, Brussels 1992; joined staff of parl. PvdA, The Hague 1993, three years as policy officer in area of spatial planning (including environment, agric. and nature); mem. Wageningen municipal council 1994–97; Political-Admin. Adviser to Minister of Agric., Nature Man. and Fisheries 1996–98, Deputy Head, Ministry Advisory Section 1998–2000; mem. House of Reps (lower house of Parl.) 2000–02, 2002–12; Minister of Finance 2012–; mem. PvdA 1985–, Deputy Leader of Parl. party 2008–, mem. Electoral Programme Cttee 2010, 2012. *Address:* Ministry of Finance, Korte Voorhout 7, POB 20201, 2500 EE The Hague, Netherlands (office). *Telephone:* (70) 3428000 (office). *Fax:* (70) 3427900 (office). *E-mail:* webmaster@minfin.nl (office). *Website:* www.rijksoverheid.nl/ministeries/fin (office).

ĐIKIĆ, Ivan, MD, PhD; Croatian physician, medical scientist, academic and research institute director; *Director, Buchmann Institute for Molecular Life Sciences;* b. 28 May 1966, Zagreb; ed Univ. of Zagreb, New York Univ. School of Medicine, USA; Medical Doctor, Univ. of Zagreb 1986–91; worked at Inst. for Health Care of Mother and Child, New York 1991–92; Postdoctoral Fellow, New York Univ. School of Medicine 1995–97; Group Leader, Ludwig Inst. for Cancer Research, Uppsala, Sweden 1997–2002; Prof., Faculty of Medicine, Univ. of Split 2002–03, now Guest Prof.; Prof. C3, Inst. of Biochemistry II, Goethe Univ., Frankfurt, Germany 2002–08, Dir of Inst. 2009–; Scientific Dir, Buchmann Inst. for Molecular Life Sciences 2009–; mem. AAAS, New York Acad. of Sciences, World Asscn of Croatian Physicians, American Asscn for Cancer Research, European Molecular Biology Org., American Soc. for Biochemistry and Molecular Biology, Int. Union Against Cancer, German Soc. for Biochemistry and Molecular Biology; D. Perović Award for the Best Graduates in Medicine 1991, Chancellor's Award 1991, Award for Young Explorers 1997, Award for Young Leaders in Science 2002, AACR Award for Outstanding Achievements in Cancer Research 2006, Binder Award 2006, EACR Award for Cancer Research 2006, Ernst Jung Prize (co-recipient) 2013, Gottfried Wilhelm Leibniz Prize 2013. *Publications:* numerous papers in professional journals. *Address:* Buchmann Institute for Molecular Life Sciences, Max-von-Laue-Str. 15, 60438 Frankfurt am Main, Germany (office). *Telephone:* (69) 63015652 (office). *Fax:* (69) 63015577 (office). *E-mail:* ivan.dikic@biochem2.de (office). *Website:* www.biochem2.com/molsig/people.html (office). www.bmls.de/index.php?id=ivan_dikic1 (office).

DIKSHIT, Sheila, MA; Indian politician; *Governor of Kerala;* b. 31 March 1938, Kapurthala, Punjab; m. Vinod Dikshit (deceased); one s. one d.; ed Convent of Jesus and Mary School, Univ. of Delhi; mem. Parl. 1984–89; Minister of Parl. Affairs, Minister of State in the Prime Minister's Office 1986–89; Pres. Delhi Pradesh Congress Cttee 1998; Chief Minister, Govt of Nat. Capital Territory of Delhi 1998–2013; Gov. of Kerala 2014–; mem. Legis. Ass. 1998–2008; Sec. Indira Gandhi Memorial Trust; fmr Chair. Young Women's Asscn; represented India at UN Comm. on Status of Women 1984–89; Dr hc (Univ. of Delhi); Best Chief Minister of India, Journalist Asscn of India 2008, Politician of the Year, NDTV (news channel) 2009. *Address:* Office of the Governor, Kerala Raj Bhavan, Kerala Governor's Camp, Thiruvananthapuram 695 099, India (office). *Telephone:* (471) 2721100 (office). *Fax:* (471) 2720266 (office); (471) 2310720 (office). *E-mail:* keralagovernor@gmail.com (office). *Website:* www.rajbhavan.kerala.gov.in (office).

ĐILAS, Dragan; Serbian politician and business executive; *President, Democratic Party (Demokratska Stranka—DS);* b. 22 Feb. 1967, Belgrade; m. 1st Milica Delević 1994 (divorced 2007); two d.; m. 2nd Iva Đilas 2009; one s. one d.; ed Faculty of Mechanical Eng, Univ. of Belgrade; worked as journalist at Radio Index, merged with Ritam Srca radio programme to form Radio B92 (Founder) 1989, later news ed.; student leader/activist against rule of Slobodan Milošević, led student protests 1991, 1992; continued to participate in various anti-Milošević rallies 1996–2000; active in Serbian media market mid-1990s–; holds stake in limited-liability co. Multikom Group; Co-owner (through Multikom Group) Direct Media (closed jt stock media co.) 2001–; Dir People's Office of the Pres. 2004–07; Minister without Portfolio in charge of Nat. Investment Plan 2007–08; Mayor of Belgrade 2008–13; Pres. Democratic Party (Demokratska Stranka—DS) 2012–; Pres. Basketball Fed. of Serbia 2009–; Founder and Vice-Pres. Naša Srbija (humanitarian org. for Serbian children). *Address:* Democratic Party (Demokratska Stranka), 11000 Belgrade, Krunska 69, Serbia (office). *Telephone:* (11) 3443003 (office). *Fax:* (11) 2444864 (office). *E-mail:* info@ds.org.rs (office). *Website:* www.ds.org.rs (office).

DILAWARI, Noorullah, BS; Afghan central banker; *Governor, Da Afghanistan Bank (Central Bank of Afghanistan);* ed Univ. of California, Los Angeles, USA; Vice-Pres., Multinational Div., Lloyds Bank of California, LA, USA 1986–2002; Sr Adviser to Minister of Finance 2002; Pres. and CEO Afghan Investment Support Agency 2003–04, 2008–11; Gov. Da Afghanistan Bank (Cen. Bank of Afghanistan) 2004–08, 2011–. *Address:* Da Afghanistan Bank, Ibne Sina Wat, Kabul, Afghanistan (office). *Telephone:* (20) 2104146 (office). *Fax:* (20) 2100305 (office). *E-mail:* info@centralbank.gov.af (office). *Website:* www.centralbank.gov.af (office).

DILEITA, Dileita Mohamed; Djibouti politician and diplomatist; b. 12 March 1958, Tadjourah; ed Centre for Vocational Training (CFA), Médéa, Algeria; with Embassy in Paris 1990; Amb. to Ethiopia 1990, to Uganda 2000–01; Prime Minister of Djibouti 2001–13; Vice-Pres. Rassemblement populaire pour le progrès (RPP) 2003–. *Address:* c/o Office of the Prime Minister, BP 2086, Djibouti (office).

DILENSCHNEIDER, Robert, MA; American business executive; *Founder and Principal, The Dilenschneider Group;* b. 21 Oct. 1943, New York; s. of Sigmund J. Dilenschneider and Martha Witucki; m. Janet Hennessey 1969; two s.; ed Univ. of Notre Dame and Ohio State Univ.; Account Supervisor, Hill and Knowlton Inc., New York 1967–70, Vice-Pres. 1970–73, Sr Vice-Pres. 1973–80, Exec. Vice-Pres., Chicago 1980–84, Pres. and COO, Chicago 1984–86, Pres. and CEO Hill and Knowlton, New York 1986–91; Prin. The Dilenschneider Group Inc., New York 1991–; mem. US-Japan Business Council, Public Relations Soc. of America, Int. Public Relations Asscn; mem. Advisory Bd New York Hosp., Cornell Medical Center, Coll. of Business Admin. at Univ. of Notre Dame; New York's Big Apple Award. *Publications include:* Power and Influence: A Briefing for Leaders 1991, On Power 1993, Power and Influence: The Rules have Changed 2007, The AMA Handbook of Public Relations 2010. *Address:* The Dilenschneider Group Inc., 200 Park Avenue, MetLife Building, New York, NY 10166, USA (office). *Telephone:* (212) 922-0900 (office). *Fax:* (212) 922-0971 (office). *E-mail:* jma@dgi-nyc.com (office). *Website:* www.dilenschneider.com (office).

DILIBERTO, Oliviero; Italian politician and academic; *General Secretary, Partito dei Comunisti Italiani (Party of Italian Communists);* b. 13 Oct. 1956, Cagliari; s. of Marco Diliberto and Mariadonella Reale; m. Gabriella Serrenti 1997; ed in Cagliari, Rome, Frankfurt and Paris; Prov. Sec., Juvenile Fed. of Italian CP 1978; mem. Prov. Sec.'s Office, Italian CP 1982; mem. Nat. Sec.'s Office, Reconstructed CP 1994, Dir Liberazione (party journal) 1994, Leader Parl. Group 1995, Pres. Progressive Parl. Group, currently Gen. Sec., Partito dei Comunisti Italiani (Party of Italian Communists); fmrly mem. Third Perm. Cttee on Foreign and EC Affairs, Ninth Perm. Cttee on Transport, Post and Telecommunications; Minister of Justice 1998–2001; Prof. of Roman Law, Univ. of Cagliari; currently Prof. of Roman and Levantine Law, Univ. of Rome 'La Sapienza'. *Address:* Partito dei Comunisti Italiani (Party of Italian Communists), Piazza Augusto Imperatore 31, 00186 Rome, Italy (office). *Telephone:* (06) 686271 (office). *Fax:* (06) 68627230 (office). *E-mail:* direzionenazionale@comunisti-italiani.org (office). *Website:* www.comunisti-italiani.it (office).

DILKS, David Neville, BA, FRSL, FCGI; British historian, academic and university administrator; b. 17 March 1938, Coventry; s. of Neville Ernest and Phyllis Dilks; m. Jill Medlicott 1963; one s.; ed Royal Grammar School, Worcester, Hertford Coll. and St Antony's Coll., Oxford; Asst Lecturer, then Lecturer LSE 1962–70; Prof. of Int. History, Univ. of Leeds 1970–91, Chair. School of History 1974–79, Dean Faculty of Arts 1975–77; Vice-Chancellor Univ. of Hull 1991–99; Visiting Fellow, All Souls Coll., Oxford 1973; Chair. and Founder Commonwealth Youth Exchange Council 1968–73; mem. Advisory Council on Public Records 1977–85, Univs Funding Council 1988–91; Trustee Edward Boyle Memorial Trust 1982–96, Imperial War Museum 1983–91, Lennox-Boyd Trust 1984–91, Royal Commonwealth Soc. Library Trust 1987–91; Pres. Int. Cttee for the History of the Second World War 1992–2000; Freeman, Goldsmiths' Co. 1979, Liveryman 1984; Fellow, City and Guilds of London Inst.; Dr hc (Russian Acad. of Sciences) 1996; Curzon Prize, Univ. of Oxford 1960, Prix du rayonnement de la langue française 1994, Médaille de Vermeil, Acad. Française 1994. *Television:* historical adviser, The Gathering Storm (HBO/BBC) 2002, Winston Churchill at War (HBO/BBC) 2009. *Publications:* Curzon in India (Vols 1 & 2) 1969, 1970, The Diaries of Sir Alexander Cadogan (ed.) 1971, Retreat from Power (two vols, ed.) 1981, The Missing Dimension: Government and Intelligence Communities in the Twentieth Century (ed.) 1984, Neville Chamberlain: Pioneering & Reform, 1869–1929 1984, Barbarossa 1941, The Axis, The Allies and World War: Retrospect, Recollection, Revision (co-ed.) 1994, Grossbritannien und der deutsche Widerstand (co-ed.) 1994, The Great Dominion: Winston Churchill in Canada 1900–1954 2005, Churchill and Company 2012; and numerous articles in learned journals. *Leisure interests:* ornithology, steam railways, organ music, Bentley cars. *Address:* Wits End, Long Causeway, Leeds, LS16 8EX, West Yorks., England (home). *Telephone:* (113) 267-3466 (home).

DILLANE, Stephen; actor; b. 1957, London; pnr Naomi Wirthner; one c.; ed Univ. of Exeter, Bristol Old Vic Drama School; early career as journalist for Croydon Advertiser newpaper; attended drama school, then worked in repertory Coventry, Manchester and Chester; Tony Award for Best Leading Actor (The Real Thing) 2000. *Films include:* Business as Usual 1987, La Chance 1994, Two If by Sea 1996, Welcome to Sarajevo 1997, Firelight 1997, Déjà Vu 1997, Love and Rage 1998, The Darkest Light 1999, Ordinary Decent Criminal 2000, The Parole Officer 2001, Spy Game 2001, The Gathering 2002, The Truth About Charlie 2002, The Hours 2002, King Arthur 2004, Haven 2004, Nine Lives 2005, Goal! 2005, The Greatest Game Ever Played 2005, Klimt 2005, Goal II: Living the Dream 2006, Savage Grace 2007, Fugitive Pieces 2007, Freakdog 2008, Storm 2009, 44 Inch Chest 2009. *Television:*

Comeback 1987, The Secret Garden 1987, The One Game 1988, An Affair in Mind 1988, Christabel 1988, The Yellow Wallpaper 1989, Heading Home 1991, Achilles Heel 1991, Frankie's House 1992, Hostages 1993, You Me + It 1993, The Rector's Wife 1994, The Widowing of Mrs. Holroyd 1995, Anna Karenina (miniseries) 2000, The Cazalets (series) 2001, John Adams (series) 2008, God on Trial 2008, The Shooting of Thomas Hurndall 2008. *Plays:* (Royal Nat. Theatre) The Beaux's Strategem, Dancing at Lughnasa, Long Day's Journey into Night, Angels in America, Millennium Approaches, Perestroika; Hush (Royal Court); Endgame (Donmar Warehouse); Hamlet (Gielgud Theatre).

DILLARD, Annie, MA; American author; b. 30 April 1945, Pittsburgh, Pa; d. of Frank Doak and Gloria Lambert; m. 1st R. H. W. Dillard 1965; m. 2nd Gary Clevidence 1979 (divorced); m. 3rd Robert D. Richardson, Jr 1988; one d. two step-d.; ed Hollins Coll.; Contributing Ed. Harper's Magazine 1974–85; Scholar-in-Residence, Western Washington Univ. 1975–79; Distinguished Visiting Prof., Wesleyan Univ. 1979–83, Adjunct Prof. 1983, Writer-in-Residence 1987, now Prof. Emer., mem. Bd of Dirs Wesleyan Writers' Conf. 1984– (Chair. 1991–); Contributing Ed. Harper's magazine 1974–81, 1983–85; mem. Nat. Cttee on US–China Relations 1982–; Nat. Endowment for the Arts (Literature) Grant 1981, John Simon Guggenheim Memorial Grant 1985, Gov. of Connecticut's Award 1993, Campion Award 1994, Milton Prize 1994, American Arts and Letters Award in Literature 1998. *Publications include:* Tickets for a Prayer Wheel (poetry), Pilgrim at Tinker Creek (Pulitzer Prize 1975) 1974, Holy the Firm 1978, Living by Fiction 1982, Teaching a Stone to Talk 1982, Encounters with Chinese Writers 1984, An American Childhood 1987, The Writing Life 1989, The Living (novel) 1992, The Annie Dillard Reader 1994, Mornings Like This (poetry) 1995, For the Time Being 1999, The Maytrees (prose) 2007. *Leisure interests:* soup kitchens in Key West, Fla and Chapel Hill, NC. *Address:* c/o Will Lippincott, LMQ, 27 West 20th Street, Suite 305, New York, NY 10011, USA (office). *Telephone:* (212) 352-2055 (office). *Website:* www.anniedillard.com (office).

DILLER, Barry; American entertainment executive; *Chairman, IAC/InterActive Corporation;* b. 2 Feb. 1942, San Francisco; s. of Michael Diller and Reva (née Addison) Diller; Asst to Vice Pres. in charge of programming ABC-TV 1966–68, Exec. Asst to Vice Pres. in programming and dir of feature films, ABC, 1968, Vice Pres. Feature Films and Program Devt 1969–71, Vice Pres. Feature Films Circle Entertainment, div. of ABC) 1971–73, created TV movies of the week and miniseries, Vice-Pres. of prime-time TV, ABC network 1973; Chair. Bd and CEO Paramount Pictures Corpn 1974–84 (resgnd); Chair. and CEO 20th Century Fox Inc. 1984, Chair. and CEO Fox Inc. 1985–92 (resgnd); Chair. and CEO QVC Network 1992–95; Chair. and CEO Silver King Communications 1995–98, Chair. Home Shopping Network (HSN) 1995–98, Chair. and CEO USA Interactive (later IAC/InterActive Corpn) including USA Networks Inc., New York 1998–2001, Chair. 2001–, including Expedia, Inc. and Live Nation Entertainment 2010; Chair. and CEO Vivendi Universal Entertainment (VUE) 2002–03; mem. Bd of Dirs Washington Post Co., Coca-Cola Co., Conservation Int., Channel 13/WNET, Museum of TV and Radio; fmr mem. Bd of Dirs News Corpn Ltd; Trustee, New York Univ.; mem. Bd of Councilors Univ. of Southern Calif. School of Cinema-TV, Dean's Council Tisch School of the Arts, Exec. Bd for Medical Sciences UCLA, American Film Inst., Variety Clubs Int., Hollywood Radio and TV Soc., Acad. of Motion Picture Arts and Sciences. *Address:* IAC/InterActive Corporation, 152 West 57th Street, 42nd Floor, New York, NY 10019, USA (office). *Telephone:* (212) 314-7300 (office). *Fax:* (212) 314-7379 (office). *Website:* www.iac.com (office).

DILLER, Elizabeth, BArch; American architect and academic; *Principal, Diller Scofidio + Renfro;* b. Łodz, Poland; ed The Cooper Union School of Architecture; co-f. (with Ricardo Scofidio q.v.), Diller & Scofidio (now Diller Scofidio + Renfro), New York 1979, cr. installations and electronic media projects; taught at The Cooper Union School of Architecture 1981–90; Assoc. Prof. of Architectural Design, Princeton Univ. 1990, currently Prof. of Architectural Design, Dir Grad. Studies 1993–; jt recipient (with Ricardo Scofidio) fellowships from Graham Foundation for Advanced Study in the Fine Arts 1986, New York Foundation for the Arts 1986, 1987, 1989, Chicago Inst. for Architecture and Urbanism 1989, Tiffany Foundation Award for Emerging Artists 1990, Progressive Architecture Award (for Slow House) 1991, Chrysler Award for Achievement and Design 1997, National Design Award in Architecture from the Smithsonian 2005, chosen (with Ricardo Scofidio) by Time magazine amongst 100 Most Influential People in the World 2009. *Publications:* (with Ricardo Scofidio) Flesh 1995, Back to the Front: Tourisms of War. *Address:* 601 West 26th Street, Suite 1815, New York, NY 10001 (office); Princeton University School of Architecture, Princeton, NJ 08544-5264, USA (office). *Telephone:* (212) 260-7971 (New York) (home); (609) 258-3741 (Princeton) (office). *Fax:* (212) 260-7924 (New York) (office); (609) 258-4740 (office). *E-mail:* ediller@dillerscofidio.com (office); soa@princeton.edu (office). *Website:* www.dillerscofidio.com (office); www.princeton.edu (office).

DILLMAN, Linda M.; American retail executive; b. Fort Wayne, Ind.; ed Univ. of Indianapolis; with Hewlett-Packard 1987–92; joined Wal-Mart in 1992, served in several key information services man. positions including Applications Devt Man. for SAM'S CLUB and Applications Devt Man. for Wal-Mart Store Systems, Dir Applications Devt 1997–98, Vice-Pres. Applications Devt 1998, later Vice-Pres. Int. Systems, Sr Vice-Pres. Information Systems Div. 2002, Exec. Vice-Pres. and Chief Information Officer Wal-Mart Stores Inc. 2002–06, Exec. Vice-Pres. Risk Man. and Benefits Admin 2006–09; Sr Vice-Pres. 2009–12; Chief Information Officer, QVC Inc. 2012–, mem. Bd of Dirs 2010–; mem. Bd Network of Exec. Women, GS1 Global, Nat. Center for Women and Information Tech.; mem. Advisory Bd Univ. of Indianapolis; ranked by Fortune magazine amongst 50 Most Powerful Women in Business in the US (28th) 2003, (32nd) 2004, (29th) 2005, (29th) 2006, (33rd) 2007, Univ. of Indianapolis Distinguished Alumni Award 2003, David D. Lattanze Center at Loyola Coll. Information Systems Exec. of the Year 2004, Univ. of Michigan Stephen M. Ross School of Business Women in Leadership Award 2005, EMC Information Leadership Award, Computerworld 2006. *Leisure interests:* skiing, watching Formula 1 racing, travelling with college friends. *Address:* QVC Inc, 1200 Wilson Drive, West Chester, PA 19380, USA (office). *Telephone:* (484) 701-1000 (office). *Website:* www.qvc.com (office).

DILLON, David Brian, BA, LLB; American retail executive; *Chairman and CEO, The Kroger Company;* b. 30 March 1951, Hutchinson, Kan.; m. Dee A. Ehling 1973; one s. two d.; ed Hutchinson High School, Univ. of Kansas, Southern Methodist Univ.; various positions with family-owned business Dillon Cos including Head of Supermarket, Convenience Store and Mfg Operations, Vice-Pres. 1983–86, Pres. 1986–90; Exec. Vice-Pres. The Kroger Co. 1990–95, mem. Bd of Dirs 1995–, Pres. 1995–2000, Pres. and COO 2000–03, CEO 2003–04, Chair. and CEO 2004–; mem. Bd of Dirs Convergys Corpn 2000–02. *Address:* The Kroger Co., 1014 Vine Street, Cincinnati, OH 45202-1100, USA (office). *Telephone:* (513) 762-4000 (office). *Fax:* (513) 762-1160 (office). *E-mail:* info@kroger.com (office); kroger.investors@kroger.com (office). *Website:* www.kroger.com (office); www.thekrogerco.com (office).

DILLON, Matt; American actor; b. 18 Feb. 1964, New Rochelle, NY; s. of Paul Dillon and Mary Ellen Dillon. *Films include:* Over the Edge 1979, Little Darlings 1980, My Bodyguard 1980, Liar's Moon 1982, Tex 1982, The Outsiders 1983, Rumble Fish 1983, The Flamingo Kid 1984, Target 1985, Rebel 1985, Native Son 1986, The Big Town (The Arm) 1987, Kansas 1988, Drugstore Cowboy 1989, A Kiss Before Dying 1991, Singles 1992, The Saint of Fort Washington, Mr. Wonderful 1993, Golden Gate 1994, To Die For 1995, Frankie Starlight 1995, Beautiful Girls 1996, Grace of My Heart 1996, Albino Alligator 1996, In and Out 1997, Wild Things 1998, There's Something About Mary 1998, One Night at McCool's 2000, Deuces Wild 2000, City of Ghosts (also Dir) 2002, Employee of the Month 2004, Loverboy 2004, Crash 2005, Factotum 2005, Herbie Fully Loaded 2005, You, Me and Dupree 2006, Nothing But the Truth 2008, Old Dogs 2009, Armoured 2009, Takers 2010. *Address:* c/o CAA, 2000 Avenue of the Stars, Los Angeles CA 90067, USA.

DILNOT, Sir Andrew William, Kt, CBE, BA; British economist, broadcaster and fmr university administrator; *Chairman, UK Statistics Authority;* b. 19 June 1960; ed Olchfa Comprehensive School, Swansea, St John's Coll., Oxford; joined Inst. of Fiscal Studies 1981, Dir 1991–2002; Prin. St Hugh's Coll., Oxford 2002–12; Pro Vice-Chancellor, Univ. of Oxford 2005–12; Warden of Nuffield College, Oxford 2012–; visiting lecturer at numerous univs in UK and abroad; Chair. Statistics User Forum 2009–12, Comm. on Funding of Care and Support 2010–11, UK Statistics Authority 2012–; regular contrib. to broadcast and printed media, including BBC Radio 4 programmes Analysis and More or Less; mem. Social Security Advisory Cttee, Govt Evidence-Based Policy Panel, National Consumer Council; mem. Council, Royal Econ. Soc., Queen Mary and Westfield Coll.; fmr Trustee, Nuffield Foundation; Hon. Fellow, St John's Coll., Oxford, Queen Mary, Univ. of London, Swansea Inst. of Higher Educ., Inst. of Actuaries; Dr hc (City Univ., London). *Publication:* The Tiger That Isn't: Seeing Through a World of Numbers (with Michael Blastland) 2007. *Address:* UK Statistics Authority, 1 Drummond Gate, London, SW1V 2QQ (office); Office of the Warden, Nuffield College, New Road, Oxford, OX1 1NF, England (office). *E-mail:* authority.enquiries@statistics.gsi.gov.uk (office). *Website:* www.nuffield.ox.ac.uk (office).

DILSHAN, Tillakaratne Mudiyanselage, (Tuwan Mohammad Dilshan); Sri Lankan professional cricketer; b. 14 Oct. 1976, Kalutara; m. 2nd Manjula Thilini 2008; one s. from previous m.; wicketkeeper; right-handed batsman; right-arm off-break bowler; plays for Kalutara Town Club 1996–97, Singha Sports Club 1997–98, Sebastianites Cricket and Athletic Club 1998–2000, Sri Lanka 1999– (Capt. 2011–12), Bloomfield Cricket and Athletic Club 2000–, Basnahira South 2007–, Delhi Daredevils 2008–10, Royal Challengers Bangalore 2011–, Asia XI; First-class debut: 1993/94; Test debut: Zimbabwe v Sri Lanka, Bulawayo 18–22 Nov. 1999; One-Day Int. (ODI) debut: Zimbabwe v Sri Lanka, Bulawayo 11 Dec. 1999; T20I debut: England v Sri Lanka, Southampton 15 June 2006; mem. losing Sri Lankan team that reached final of ICC (Int. Cricket Council) Cricket World Cup against India, Mumbai 2 April 2011, top run scorer in tournament with 500 runs; developed batting stroke now called the Dilscoop after him during the ICC World Twenty20 held in England June 2009; Twenty20 Int. Performance of the Year, ICC Awards 2009. *Address:* c/o Sri Lanka Cricket, Sinhalese Sports Club, Colombo, Sri Lanka. *E-mail:* info@srilankacricket.lk. *Website:* www.srilankacricket.lk.

DIMAS, Pyrros; Greek army officer; *President, Hellenic Weightlifting Federation;* b. (Pirro Ohima), 13 Oct. 1971, Himarra, Albania; m. Anastasia Sdougkou; two d. one s.; ed Univ. of Athens; light-heavyweight lifter; emigrated to Greece 1991; gold medal Barcelona Olympic Games 1992, Atlanta Olympic Games 1996, Sydney Olympic Games 2000; World Championship title 1993, 1995, 1998; European Championship title 1995; world record in the snatch (85kg category); bronze medal, Athens Olympic Games 2004; Pres. Hellenic Weightlifting Fed. 2008–; serves as Major in the Greek army; Greek Athlete of the Year 1992, 1993, 1995, 1996; Top Athlete in the 1995 World Championship, Weightlifter of the Century Award, Int. Weightlifting Fed. 2005. *Leisure interests include:* video games, backgammon, cinema. *Address:* c/o The Hellenic Weightlifting Federation, 43 Sygrou Av., 117 43 Athens, Greece (office). *Telephone:* (210) 9231780 (office). *Fax:* (210) 9243875 (office). *E-mail:* info@weightlifting.gr (office); pyrros@pyrros.gr (home). *Website:* www.pyrros.gr (office).

DIMAS, Stavros, LLM; Greek politician and lawyer; b. 30 April 1941, Athens; ed Univ. of Athens, New York Univ., USA; lawyer, Sullivan & Cromwell law firm, New York 1969–70; lawyer for legal dept of Int. Finance Corpn, World Bank 1970–75; Deputy Gov. Hellenic Industrial Devt Bank 1975–77; mem. Parl. (New Democracy party) 1977–2004, Parl. Spokesman 1985–89; Deputy Minister of Econ. Co-ordination 1977–80; Minister of Trade 1980–81, of Agric. 1989–90, of Industry, Energy and Tech. 1990–91, of Foreign Affairs 2011–12; Sec.-Gen. New Democracy (Nea Demokratia) 1995–2000, Sr mem. Political Analysis Steering Cttee 2000–03, Head of Del. to Council of Europe 2000–04, Vice-Pres. 2010–; EU Commr for Employment and Social Affairs March–Oct. 2004, for Environment 2004–09; mem. negotiating cttee for accession of Greece to EEC 1977. *Address:* c/o Ministry of Foreign Affairs, Odos Sofias 1, 106 71 Kallithea, Athens, Greece. *E-mail:* mfa@mfa.gr.

DIMBLEBY, David, MA; British broadcaster and journalist; b. 28 Oct. 1938, Surrey; s. of the late Richard Dimbleby and of Dilys Thomas; m. 1st Josceline Gaskell 1967 (divorced 2000); one s. two d.; m. 2nd Belinda Giles 2000; one s.; ed Univs of Oxford, Paris and Perugia; presenter and interviewer, BBC Bristol 1960–61; Chair. Dimbleby and Sons Ltd 1986–2001, apptd Man. Dir 1967; currently commentator and presenter BBC; Pres. Dimbleby Cancer Care; Dr hc (Univ. of Essex) 2005; Richard Dimbleby Award, BAFTA 1998. *Television:* Quest (religious programme), What's New? (children's science), People and Power

1982–83, General Election Results Programmes 1979, 1983, 1987, 2001, various programmes for the Budget, by-elections, local elections etc.; Presenter, Question Time (BBC) 1994–, A Picture of Britain (BBC) 2005–, How We Built Britain (also writer) 2007–, Seven Ages of Britain (BBC 1) 2010–. *Films:* documentaries: Ku-Klux-Klan, The Forgotten Million, Cyprus: The Thin Blue Line 1964–65, South Africa: The White Tribe (Royal TV Soc. Supreme Documentary Award) 1979, US–UK Relations: An Ocean Apart 1988, The Struggle for South Africa (US Emmy Award, Monte Carlo Golden Nymph) 1990, David Dimbleby's India 1997; live commentary on many public occasions including: State Opening of Parliament, Trooping the Colour, Wedding of HRH Prince Andrew and Sarah Ferguson, HM The Queen Mother's 90th Birthday Parade (Royal TV Soc. Outstanding Documentary Award), Funeral of Diana, Princess of Wales 1997, memorial services including Lord Olivier (Royal TV Soc. Outstanding Documentary Award). *Publications:* An Ocean Apart (with David Reynolds) 1988, A Picture of Britain 2005, How We Built Britain 2007, Seven Ages of Britain 2010. *Address:* c/o Rosemary Scoular, United Agents, 12–26 Lexington Street, London, W1F 0LE, England (office). *Telephone:* (20) 3214-0894 (office). *Fax:* (20) 3214-0801 (office). *E-mail:* wmillyard@unitedagents.co.uk (office). *Website:* www.unitedagents.co.uk (office).

DIMBLEBY, Jonathan, BA; British broadcaster, journalist and writer; b. 31 July 1944, Aylesbury, Bucks.; s. of the late Richard Dimbleby and Dilys Thomas; m. 1st Bel Mooney 1968 (divorced); one s. one d.; m. 2nd Jessica Ray 2007; two d.; ed Univ. Coll. London; reporter BBC Bristol 1969–70, World at One (BBC Radio) 1970–71, This Week (Thames TV) 1972–78, 1986–88, TV Eye 1979, Jonathan Dimbleby in Evidence series (Yorkshire TV) 1980–84; Assoc. Ed./Presenter First Tuesday 1982–86; Presenter/Ed. Jonathan Dimbleby on Sunday (TV-am) 1985–86, On the Record (BBC TV) 1988–93, Charles: the Private Man, the Public Role (Central TV) 1994, weekly political programme Jonathan Dimbleby (ITV) 1995–2006; presenter Any Questions? and Any Answers? (both BBC Radio 4) 1987–; main presenter of Gen. Election coverage (ITV); Chair. Index on Censorship 2009–; Pres. Voluntary Service Overseas 1999–, Soil Assćn 1997–2009, Royal Soc. for the Protection of Birds 2001–04, Bath Festivals Trust 2003–06; Vice-Pres. Campaign for Protection of Rural England 1997–; Trustee Dimbleby Cancer Care; Richard Dimbleby Award 1974. *Publications:* Richard Dimbleby 1975, The Palestinians 1979, The Prince of Wales: A Biography 1994, The Last Governor 1997, Russia: A Journey to the Heart of a Land and its People 2008. *Leisure interests:* tennis, riding, music, rural life. *Address:* David Higham Associates Ltd, 5 Lower John Street, Golden Square, London, W1R 4HA, England (office). *Telephone:* (20) 7437-7888 (office).

DiMICCO, Daniel R.; American business executive; *Chairman, President and CEO, Nucor Corporation;* Vice-Pres. Nucor Corpn 1992–99, Exec. Vice-Pres. 1999–2000, mem. Bd of Dirs, Pres. and CEO 2000–, Vice-Chair. 2001–06, Chair. 2006–, Gen. Man. Nucor-Yamato Steel Co.; mem. Bd of Dirs Duke Energy Corpn 2007–; Chair. American Iron and Steel Inst. *Address:* Nucor Corporate Office, 1915 Rexford Road, Charlotte, NC 28211, USA (office). *Telephone:* (704) 366-7000 (office). *Fax:* (704) 362-4208 (office). *E-mail:* info@nucor.com (office). *Website:* www .nucor.com (office).

DIMITROV, Aleksander; Macedonian politician and lawyer; b. 29 Nov. 1949, Skopje; ed Skopje Univ.; mem. Man. Bd Air Service Skopje, Sec., Forum for Int. Relations; ed. Forum (newspaper) 1969–72, Mlad Borac (newspaper) 1972–78; Sec., Council for Foreign Relations 1979–82; Under-Sec., Cttee for Int. Relations 1982–92; Dir for Int. Affairs, Dir Office of Palair 1993–96; Minister of Foreign Affairs 1998–2001; joined New Alternative party 2007. *Address:* c/o Ministry of Foreign Affairs, Dame Grueva 14, 9100 Skopje, Macedonia.

DIMITROV, Martin; Bulgarian politician and economist; *Leader, Union of Democratic Forces;* b. 13 April 1977, Sofia; m.; mem. European Parl. (Group of the European People's Party–Christian Democrats and European Democrats) Jan.–June 2007, mem. Cttee on Budgets, Cttee on the Internal Market and Consumer Protection, Del. for Relations with the Mashreq Countries, Substitute mem. Cttee on Budgetary Control; Leader, Union of Democratic Forces (UDF); mem. Parl. for 24-Sofiya 2 constituency (Parl. Group of The Blue Coalition – UDF, DSB, The United Agrarians, BSDP, RDP) 2009–, Chair. Econ. Policy, Energy and Tourism Cttee, Friendship group Bulgaria–Estonia, Deputy Chair. Friendship group Bulgaria–Australia, Bulgaria–UK. *Address:* Union of Democratic Forces (Sayuz na Demokratichnite Sili), 1000 Sofia, bul. Rakovski 134, Bulgaria (office). *Telephone:* (2) 930-61-32 (office). *Fax:* (2) 930-61-22 (office). *E-mail:* dimitrovmartin@parliament.bg (office); dimitrovmartin@gmail.com (office); presscenter@sds.bg (office). *Website:* www.sds.bg (office); www.parliament.bg/en/MP/1018 (office); www.martindimitrov.com.

DIMITROV, Petar, DEcon; Bulgarian politician; b. 27 Jan. 1949, Klisura; ed Moscow Inst. of Econs and Statistics, Nottingham Trent Univ., UK 1994; Lecturer, Varna Univ. of Econs 1976–93, Deputy Rector 1989–93, Assoc. Prof. in Social Man. 1988, Head of Higher School of Man. 1990; mem. Nat. Ass. 1994–2009, Chair. Parl. Comm on Budget and Finance 2005–07, mem. Comm on Educ. and Science, on Econ. Policy, Budget and Finance; Minister of Economy and Energy 2007–09. *Address:* c/o Ministry of the Economy and Energy, 1000 Sofia, ul. Slavyanska 8, Bulgaria.

DIMITROV, Philip, JD; Bulgarian lawyer, politician, diplomatist, academic and author; *Deputy Speaker, National Assembly;* b. 31 March 1955, Sofia; s. of Dimitar Vassilev Dimitrov and Katherine Philipova Dimitrova; m. Elena Valentinova Gueorgieva-Dimitrova 1988; ed St Kliment Ohridsky Univ., Sofia; attorney 1979–1991, 2002–05;Vice-Pres. Union of Democratic Forces 1990, Pres. 1990–94; Prime Minister of Bulgaria 1991–92; mem. Parl. 1991–97; Vice-Chair. Jt Parl. Cttee, EU–Bulgaria 1995–97; Perm. Rep. to UN, New York 1997–98; Amb. to USA 1998–2002; Special Envoy of OSCE Pres. for Armenia and Azerbaijan 2004; Deputy Speaker, Nat. Ass. (Parl.) 2005–; MEP 2007–; Woodrow Wilson Center Public Policy Scholar, Washington, DC 2003; Adjunct Prof., American Univ. in Bulgaria 2003–; mem. Sofia Bar Asscn; Truman-Reagan Freedom Award for contrib. to overcoming communism 1999; Dimitrov Scholarships and Lectures, American Univ. in Bulgaria, Sofia inaugurated 2002. *Publications include:* The Myths of the Bulgarian Transition 2003, The New Democracies and the Transatlantic Link 2003; three historical novels, For They Lived, O Lord 1991, The True

Story of the Round Table Knights 1996, Light of Men 2003. *Leisure interest:* history. *Address:* Bulgarian National Assembly, 1 Batemberg Square, Sofia 1000 (office); American University in Bulgaria, 2700 Blagoevgrad, Bulgaria. *Telephone:* (2) 9873238 (office); (73) 888456. *Fax:* (2) 9805358 (office). *E-mail:* phd@parliament .bg (office). *Website:* www.parliament.bg (office).

DIMMELER, Stefanie, BSc, PhD; German biologist, biochemist and academic; *Professor of Experimental Medicine and Director, Institute of Cardiovascular Regeneration, University of Frankfurt;* b. 18 July 1967, Ravensburg; ed Univ. of Konstanz; completed a fellowship in Experimental Surgery at Univ. of Cologne; completed a fellowship in Molecular Cardiology at Univ. of Frankfurt, Head of Div. of Molecular Cardiology 1997–, Prof. of Experimental Medicine 2001–, Dir Inst. of Cardiovascular Regeneration 2008–; Visiting Prof., New York Medical Coll. 2006–08, Stanford Univ. 2009, Robert L. Krakoff International Lectureship in Cardiovascular Medicine 2010–; Hustinx Chair, CARIM, Univ. of Maastricht 2007–08; Chief Ed. EMBO Molecular Medicine 2010–; mem. Editorial Bd Circulation, Circulation Research, Basic Research in Cardiology, Journal of Molecular and Cellular Cardiology; mem. German Ethical Cttee (Deutscher Ethikrat) 2008–12; mem. Advisory Bd Lifeboat Foundation; Preis des Stifterverbandes für die Deutsche Wissenschaft 1991, Fritz Külz Prize, Deutschen Gesellschaft für Pharmakologie und Toxikologie 1994, Research Prize, Deutschen Stiftung für Herzforschung 1998, Herbert and Hedwig Eckelmann Foundation Prize 1999, Fraenkel Prize, Deutschen Gesellschaft für Kardiologie 2000, Alfried-Krupp-Förderpreis für junge Hochschullehrer 2002, Forßmann Prize, Ruhr-Universität Bochum 2004, Leibniz Prize 2005, Ernst Jung Prize, Jung-Stiftung für Wissenschaft und Forschung (co-recipient) 2007. *Achievements include:* responsible, together with Dr Zeiher, for scientific discoveries culminating in current clinical trial of human progenitor cells for cardiac repair. *Publications:* more than 120 scientific papers in professional journals on endothelial biology, including signal transduction, apoptosis, and renewal by circulating endothelial progenitor cells in health and disease. *Address:* Institute of Cardiovascular Regeneration, Centre for Molecular Medicine, Goethe-University Frankfurt, Theodor Stern Kai 7, 60590 Frankfurt am Main, Germany (office). *Telephone:* (69) 6301-7440 (office). *Fax:* (69) 6301-7113 (office). *E-mail:* Dimmeler@em.uni-frankfurt.de (office). *Website:* www.cardiovascular-regeneration.com (office).

DIMON, James (Jamie) L., MBA; American financial services industry executive; *Chairman and CEO, JPMorgan Chase & Company;* b. 13 March 1956, New York, NY; m. Judith Kent; three d.; ed The Browning School, New York, Tufts Univ., Harvard Univ.; Asst to Pres., American Express 1982–85; Pres. and COO Travelers Group 1991–98, also COO Smith Barney Inc. (subsidiary co.) –1996, Chair. and CEO 1996–97, Chair. and Co-CEO, Salomon Smith Barney Holdings Inc. (following merger) 1997–98; Pres. Citigroup 1998–2000; Chair. and CEO Bank One Corpn March 2000–04, Pres., COO and Dir JPMorgan Chase & Co. (after merger between Bank One Corpn and JPMorgan Chase & Co.) 2004–05, CEO and Pres. 2005–, Chair. 2006–; Vice-Chair. NYU School of Medicine Foundation Bd; Dir Tricon Global Restaurants Inc., Center on Addiction and Substance Abuse; Trustee, Mount Sinai-NYU Medical Center; mem. Council on Foreign Relations; ranked by Forbes magazine amongst The World's Most Powerful People (30th) 2009, (47th) 2010, (41st) 2011, (34th) 2012, (22nd) 2013. *Address:* JPMorgan Chase & Co., 270 Park Avenue, New York, NY 10017-2070, USA (office). *Telephone:* (212) 270-6000 (office). *Fax:* (212) 270-1648 (office). *E-mail:* joseph.evangelisti@jpmchase.com (office). *Website:* www.jpmorganchase.com (office).

DINARDO, HE Cardinal Daniel Nicholas, BA, MA, LicTheol; American ecclesiastic; *Archbishop of Galveston-Houston;* b. 23 May 1949, Steubenville, Ohio; ed Catholic Univ. of America, Washington, DC, Pontifical Gregorian Univ. and the Augustinianum, Rome; ordained priest in Pittsburgh 1977; staff mem. Vatican Congregation for Bishops 1984–90; also served as Dir of Villa Stritch (residence for American priests working at the Vatican); taught a theology seminar in methodology at Gregorian Univ.; held pastoral posts in Pittsburgh Diocese, where he taught in the ongoing formation programme for priests and was Asst Spiritual Dir at St Paul Seminary 1990–97; Coadjutor Bishop of Sioux City, Ia 1997–98, Bishop of Sioux City 1998–2004; Coadjutor Bishop of Galveston-Houston, Tex. Jan.–Dec. 2004, Coadjutor Archbishop of Galveston-Houston Dec. 2004–06, Archbishop of Galveston-Houston 2006–; cr. Cardinal (Cardinal-Priest of Sant'Eusebio) 2007; participated in Papal Conclave 2013; Vice Pres. US Conf. of Catholic Bishops 2013–; mem. Bd Trustees Catholic Univ. of America. *Address:* Chancery Office, Archdiocese of Galveston-Houston, PO Box 907, 1700 San Jacinto Street, Houston, TX 77001-0907, USA (office). *Telephone:* (713) 659-5461 (office). *Fax:* (713) 759-9151 (office). *E-mail:* info@diogh.org (office). *Website:* www.diogh.org (office).

DINARELLO, Charles A., MD; American professor of medicine; *Professor of Medicine and Immunology, School of Medicine, University of Colorado, Denver;* b. 22 April 1943, Boston, Mass; ed Yale Univ., Massachusetts Gen. Hosp.; Investigator, NIH, Bethesda, Md 1971–77; Prof. of Medicine and Immunology, School of Medicine, Univ. of Colorado, Denver 1996–; Prof. of Experimental Medicine, Radboud Univ., Nijmegen, The Netherlands; mem. Bd of Govs Weizmann Inst. of Science, Israel, Ben Gurion Univ., Israel; fmr Vice-Pres. American Soc. of Clinical Investigation; fmr Pres. International Cytokine Soc.; f. Interleukin Foundation (charity) 2009; mem. editorial bds of several scientific journals; mem. NAS 1998; Foreign mem. Royal Netherlands Acad. of Arts and Sciences 2011; hon. degrees from Univ. of Marseille (France), Weizmann Inst. of Science, Univ. of Frankfurth (Germany), Roosevelt Univ., Albany Medical Coll., Radboud Univ. (Netherlands), Trinity Coll. (Ireland); Squibb Award, Ernst Jung Prize in Medicine (Germany) 1993, Chirone Prize, Italian Nat. Acad. of Medicine, Carol Nachman Prize (Germany), Sheikh Hamdan bin Rashdid al Madktoum Award (UAE), Beering Prize, Bonfils-Stanton Prize, Bonazinga Award, Albany Prize in Medical Research (co-recipient) 2009, Craoford Prize, Royal Swedish Acad. of Sciences (co-recipient) 2009, Paul Ehrlich and Ludwig Darmstaedter Prize (Germany) 2010, Novartiz Prize in Clinical Immunology (Switzerland) (co-recipient) 2010. *Publications:* more than 600 original research articles and 250 reviews and book chapters on cytokines, particularly on Interleukin-1, Interleukin-18 and related cytokines. *Address:* Division of Infectious Diseases, 12700 East 19th Avenue, Box B168, Aurora, CO 80045, USA (office). *Telephone:* (303) 724-4922 (office). *E-mail:* charles

.dinarello@ucdenver.edu (office). *Website:* www.ucdenver.edu/academics/colleges/medicalschool (office).

DINDAR, Mohammad Naim, BS, Ing.Agric.; Afghan banker; *Director General of Internal Audit, Ministry of Finance;* b. 29 Sept. 1947, Khwabgah, Kabul City; s. of Mohammad Yasin and Zohra Begum; ed American Univ. of Beirut, Lebanon; Exchange Student, American Field Service 1964–65; Pres. Afghan Students' Asscn 1968–69; fmr Chief of Staff, Ministry of Finance, currently Dir Gen. of Internal Audit; fmr Pres., Int. Relations, Antinarcotic Comm.; Sr Agriculture Analyst, Office of Agricultural Affairs; Pres. and CEO Banke Millie Afghan 2005–09; Vice-Chair. Afghan Banking Asscn; mem. Bd Afghan Telecom, Ariana, Afghan Red Crescent. *Publications:* Afghan Marketing (co-author) 1975; contribs to Journal of Agriculture; several translations. *Address:* Internal Audit Dept, Ministry of Finance, Pashtunistan wat, Kabul, Afghanistan (office). *Telephone:* (20) 2103155 (office). *E-mail:* mohammed.dindar@mof.gov.af (office).

DINE, James; American artist; b. 16 June 1935, Cincinnati, Ohio; m. Nancy Minto 1957; three s.; ed Cincinnati Art Acad.; first solo exhbn at Reuben Gallery, New York 1960; work appears in many public collections including Guggenheim Museum, Moderna Museet, Stockholm, Museum of Modern Art, New York, Dallas Museum of Fine Arts, Tate Gallery and Whitney Museum of Modern American Art. *Publications:* Welcome Home, Lovebirds 1969 (also illustrator); co-author and illustrator The Adventures of Mr. and Mrs. Jim & Ron 1970; illustrator, The Poet Assassinated 1968, Drawing from the Glypothek 1993. *Address:* c/o Jonathan Novak Contemporary Art, 1880 Century Park East, Los Angeles, CA 90067, USA.

DING, Fengying; Chinese party official; *Vice-Chairman, Hubei Provincial Committee, Chinese People's Political Consultative Conference;* b. 1943, Luotian Co., Hubei Prov.; ed Huazhong Teachers Coll., Cen. China Teachers' Coll.; Sec. CCP CYLC and Chair. Women's Fed., Beifeng Commune, Luotian Co. 1960–69; Deputy Sec. and Sec. CCP Party Cttee, Beifeng Commune Fourth Brigade, Luotian Co. 1960–69; joined CCP 1961; Deputy Dir CCP Revolutionary Cttee, Luotian Co. 1969–71, Deputy Sec. CCP Co. Cttee 1969–71; Chair. Hubei Branch, Chinese Women's Fed. 1973; Vice-Chair. Revolutionary Cttee, Hubei Prov. 1978–79; Alt. mem. 12th CCP Cen. Cttee 1982–87; First Sec. CCP Cttee, Huangguang Pref. 1983–; Deputy Sec. CCP Cttee, Hubei Prov. 1986, mem. CCP 5th Hubei Prov. Cttee 1988–, Sec. Comm. for Discipline Inspection, Hubei Prov. 1988–; mem. CCP Cen. Discipline Inspection Comm. 1992–, 9th CPPCC Nat. Cttee 1998–2003; Vice-Chairman CPPCC Hubei Prov. Cttee 2003–. *Address:* Hubei Dangwei, 1 Beihuanlu Road, Shuiguohu, Wuchang City, Hubei Province, People's Republic of China. *Telephone:* 813351.

DING, Gen. Henggao; Chinese politician and scientist; b. 1931, Nanjing Co., Jiangsu Prov.; m. Nie Lili (d. of Marshal Nie Rongzhen); ed Nanjing Univ., Leningrad Inst. of Precision Machinery and Optical Instruments, USSR; joined CCP 1953; held posts of Section Chief, Deputy Inst. Dir, Deputy Bureau Dir and Research Fellow, Ministry of Defence 1960s–70s; Minister of State Comm. of Science, Tech. and Industry for Nat. Defence 1985–96, Party Cttee Sec. 1989–; rank of Lt-Gen. PLA 1988–94, Gen. 1994–; Alt. mem. 12th CCP Cen. Cttee 1982–87, mem. 13th CCP Cen. Cttee 1989–92, 14th CCP Cen. Cttee 1992–97; mem. State Leading Group for Science and Tech.; mem. Standing Cttee, 9th CPPCC Nat. Cttee 1998–2003; Pres. Chinese Soc. of Inertial Tech. 1995–; mem. Chinese Acad. of Eng 1994–; Hon. Pres. Chinese Astronautics Soc.; State Special Class Award for scientific and technological achievements for nat. defence 1994, Holeung Ho Lee Technological Science Prize 2006. *Address:* 1 South Building, Aimin Street, Xicheng District, Beijing 100034, People's Republic of China. *Telephone:* (10) 66056357. *Fax:* (10) 66738111. *E-mail:* engach@mail.cae.ac.cn (office).

DING, Shisun; Chinese university administrator and mathematician; b. 5 Sept. 1927, Shanghai; s. of Ding Rounong and Liu Huixian; m. Gui Linlin 1956; two s.; ed Tsinghua Univ., Asst Tsinghua Univ. 1950–52; joined China Democratic League 1952; joined staff Beijing Univ. 1952, promoted to Lecturer then Prof. of Math. 1979, Vice-Chair. Math. Dept 1978–80, Chair. 1981–82, Pres. Beijing Univ. 1984–89; Pres. Math. Soc. of Beijing 1986–88; Vice-Pres. Chinese Math. Soc. 1988–91; fmr Chair. Jiang Zehan Scholarship Fund Cttee; fmr Vice-Chair. Zhou Peiyuan Fund Cttee; fmr Vice-Pres. Chinese Educ. Asscn for Int. Exchanges; fmr Deputy Head, Math. Examination and Appraisal Group, Nat. Natural Science Foundation of China; fmr mem. 2nd Panel of Judges of State Academic Degrees Cttee, Exec. Council of China Overseas Exchanges Asscn, Exec. Council of China Soc. of Higher Educ., Council of Chinese People's Inst. of Foreign Affairs; visited Math. Dept, Harvard Univ., USA 1983; Exec. Vice-Chair. China Democratic League Cen. Cttee 1988–96, Chair. 1996–; mem. 7th CPPCC Nat. Cttee 1988–93, Standing Cttee of 8th CPPCC Nat. Cttee 1993–98; Vice-Chair. Educ. and Culture Cttee; Vice-Chair. Standing Cttee of 9th NPC 1998–2003, Standing Cttee of 10th NPC 2003–; Chair. Advisory Cttee American Studies Center, Peking Univ.; Pres. Western Returned Students' Asscn 1999–; mem. Macao Special Admin. Region Preparatory Cttee, Govt Del., Macao Hand-Over Ceremony 1999; Dr hc (Soka, Japan) 1985; Hon. DSc (Nebraska) 1988. *Publications:* Concise Textbook of Higher Algebra, Analytic Geometry and Orders of Linear Displacement Register; numerous math. papers on algebra and number theory. *Leisure interest:* classical music. *Address:* c/o Advisory Committee, American Studies Center, Main Library, 5th Floor, Peking University, Beijing, 100871, People's Republic of China.

DING, Gen. Wenchang; Chinese party official and army officer; b. 1933, Suxian Co., Anhui Prov.; ed PLA High Infantry School, Air Force Aviation School; joined CCP 1956; Chief, Political Dept, Air Force, PLA Services and Arms, Dir 1988, Political Commissar 1992–99, Party Cttee Sec.; rank of Maj.-Gen. 1988–90, Lt-Gen. of Air Force 1990–96, Gen. 1996–; Deputy, 7th NPC 1988–93; mem. 14th CCP Cen. Cttee 1992–97, 15th CCP Cen. Cttee 1997–2002. *Address:* Political Department of Air Force, Beijing, People's Republic of China.

DING, William, BSc; Chinese internet executive; *CEO, NetEase.com Inc.;* b. (Ding Lei), Oct. 1971, Ningbo City, Zhejiang Prov.; ed China Electronic Science and Tech. Univ., Chengdu; tech. engineer, Ningbo Telecom 1993–95; tech. support engineer, Sybase Guangzhou Co. 1995–96, Guangzhou Feijie Co. 1996–97; Founder and CEO NetEase.com Inc. (introduced first free e-mail service, online community and personalized information service in China) 1997–2000, Chief Tech. Officer 2000–01, Acting CEO and COO June–Sept. 2001, Chair. and Chief Tech. Officer

2001–, CEO 2005–; named one of the 10 most influential Internet celebrities in China 1999, named one of China's Top Ten IT Figures 2001, 2002. *Address:* NetEase.com, SP Tower D, 26th Floor, Tsinghua Science Park, Building 8, No. 1 Zhongguancun East Road, Haidian District, Beijing 100084 (office); 2nd Floor, Tower B, Keeven International R&D Centre, Beijing 100086, People's Republic of China. *Telephone:* (10) 82558163 (office). *Fax:* (10) 82618163 (office). *E-mail:* ir@service.netease.com (office). *Website:* ir.netease.com (office).

DING, Xiaqi; Chinese mathematician and research professor; *Professor, Center of Mathematical Sciences, Zhejiang University;* b. 25 May 1928, Yiyang Co., Hunan Prov.; m. Luo Peizhu 1957; three d.; ed Dept of Math., Wuhan Univ.; Research Asst, Assoc., Assoc. Prof., Prof., Inst. of Math., Acad. Sinica 1951–79; Research Prof., Inst. of Systems Sciences, Acad. Sinica 1979–91; Research Prof., Inst. of Applied Math., Academia Sinica 1991–; Prof. and Dir Wuhan Inst. of Math., Acad. Sinica 1985–94, Dr Wuhan Inst. of Math. Physics; Academician, Chinese Acad. of Sciences 1991–; currently Prof. Center of Mathematical Sciences, Zhejiang Univ. Hangzhou; mem. Cttee Math. Soc. of China; Standing mem. Cttee of Chinese Soc. of Systems Eng; Prize Award, Nat. Science Conf., Beijing 1978, Prize of Chinese Acad. of Sciences 1978, 1st Class Prize, Chinese Acad. of Science 1988, 2nd Class Prize Natural Science Prize of People's Repub. of China 1989, Holeung Ho Lee Mathematics Prize 2006. *Publications:* more than 80 papers on PDE, functions spaces, number theory and numerical analysis; 4 monographs. *Leisure interest:* mathematics. *Address:* Center of Mathematical Sciences, Zhejiang University, Hangzhou 310027, People's Republic of China (office). *Telephone:* (571) 87953030 (office). *Fax:* (571) 87953035 (office). *E-mail:* xqding@public.bta.net.cn (office). *Website:* www.cms.zju.edu.cn (office).

DING, Xuedong; Chinese government official; *Chairman and CEO, China Investment Corporation;* b. 1960, Jiangsu Prov.; ed Research Inst. for Fiscal Science, Ministry of Finance; fmr Dir-Gen., Dept of Property Rights; fmr Dir-Gen., Dept of Human Resources and Head of Gen. Office, State-owned Asset Admin Bureau; Dir, Agric. Dept, Ministry of Finance 2000–05, Dir, Educ., Science and Culture Dept 2005–06, Asst Minister of Finance 2006–08, Vice-Minister of Finance 2008–10; Deputy Sec.-Gen., State Council 2010–13; Chair. and CEO, China Investment Corpn (sovereign wealth fund) 2013–; Deputy Dir, Nat. Cttee for Disaster Reduction 2013; Deputy Dir, State Council Leading Group for Poverty Alleviation and Devt 2013–; mem. CCP 1984–, mem. Ministry of Finance CCP Leading Party Group 2006–10; ranked by Forbes magazine amongst The World's Most Powerful People (36th) 2013. *Address:* China Investment Corporation, New Poly Plaza, No.1 Chaoyangmen Beidajie, Dongcheng District, Beijing 100010, People's Republic of China (office). *Telephone:* (10) 8409 6277 (office). *Fax:* (10) 6408 6908 (office). *E-mail:* pr@china-inv.cn (office). *Website:* www.china-inv.cn/cicen (office).

DINGWALL, Bruce; British petroleum industry executive; b. 1959; began career as geophysicist with Exxon working in North Sea; Business Devt Man. for Asia, Vice-Pres. of Exploration for Indonesia and Exploration Man. for Pakistan, LASMO PLC –1997; Founder and CEO Venture Production (petroleum co.) 1997–2004; f. Ten Degrees North Energy Ltd (oil exploration co.), Trinidad 2005; Chair. MTEM 2005–07; Pres. UKOOA (UK Offshore Petroleum Operators Asscn) 2002; mem. Bd of Dirs Tullibardine Ltd (distiller) 2005–. *Address:* c/o Ten Degrees North Energy Ltd, 88-90 Lady Hailes Avenue, San Fernando, Trinidad and Tobago. *Telephone:* 653-7911. *Fax:* 653-1375.

DINI, Lamberto; Italian economist, politician and banker; b. 1 March 1931, Florence; m.; one d.; ed Univ. of Florence, Univs of Minnesota and Michigan, USA; economist, IMF, Washington, DC, then various posts to Deputy Dir Africa Dept 1959–76, mem. Bd Exec. Dirs 1976–78, now Alt. Gov. for Italy; joined Banca d'Italia (cen. bank) as Asst Gen. Man. 1979, later Gen. Man.; mem. Monetary Cttee of EU, Bd Dirs BIS; Minister of the Treasury 1994–95; Prime Minister of Italy 1995–96; Minister of Foreign Affairs 1996–2001; currently mem. Senate for Lazio, Deputy Speaker of Senate 2001–06; Pres. Liberal Democratici Riformisti (Liberal Democrats) 2007–08; Vice-Pres. European Liberal, Democrat and Reform Party; Fulbright Scholar. *Address:* Senato, Piazza Madama, 00186 Rome, Italy (office). *Telephone:* (06) 67062208 (office). *Fax:* (06) 67063611 (office). *E-mail:* dini_l@posta.senato.it (office). *Website:* www.senato.it (office).

DINKIĆ, Mlađan, BA, MSc; Serbian economist, academic, government official and fmr central banker; b. 20 Dec. 1964, Belgrade; s. of Dušan Dinkić and Milosinka Dinkić; m. Tatjana Dinkić; ed Univ. of Belgrade; research asst, Faculty of Econs, Univ. of Belgrade 1990–93, Assoc. Prof. 1994–; f. G17 (political party, later G17 Plus), Co-ordinator 1997–2001, Vice-Pres. 2001–06, Pres. 2006–, affiliated to United Regions of Serbia (Ujedinjeni regioni Srbije—URS) 2010–; Gov. Nat. Bank of Yugoslavia 2000–03, Gov. Nat. Bank of Serbia 2003–04; fmr econ. adviser to govt; Minister of Finance 2004–06, of the Economy and Regional Devt 2007–11, Deputy Prime Minister 2008–11; Minister of Finance and the Economy 2012–13; Euromoney Finance Minister of the Year, Euromoney Magazine 2007, Reformer of 2009 Award. *Publications:* Measuring Economic Efficiency 1994, The Economy of Destruction 1995, Final Account: Economic Consequences of NATO Bombing 1999. *Leisure interests:* music (has own rock band called Monetary Coup), guitar, piano. *Address:* c/o Ministry of Finance, 11000 Belgrade, Kneza Miloša 20, Serbia. *E-mail:* kontakt@mladjandinkic.com. *Website:* www.mladjandinkic.com.

DINKINS, David, BA, LLB; American lawyer, academic and fmr politician; *Professor in the Practice of Public Affairs and Senior Fellow, Center for Urban Research and Policy, School of International and Public Affairs, Columbia University;* b. 10 July 1927, Trenton, NJ; m. Joyce Burrows 1953; one s. one d.; ed Howard Univ., Washington, DC and Brooklyn Law School; served in US Marine Corps 1945–46; in pvt. law practice, New York 1956–75; mem. New York State Ass. 1966; Pres. Bd of Elections, New York City 1972–73; City Clerk, New York City 1975–85; Manhattan Borough Pres. 1986–89; Mayor of New York 1990–94; Prof. in Practice of Public Affairs and Sr Fellow, Center for Urban Research and Policy, Columbia Univ.'s School of Int. and Public Affairs 1993–; host, Dialogue with Dinkins radio public affairs program; mem. Council on Foreign Relations; mem. Bd of Govs American Stock Exchange; Democrat. *Leisure interest:* tennis. *Address:* School of International and Public Affairs, Columbia University, 420 West 118th

Street, New York, NY 10027, USA. *Telephone:* 212-854-4253. *E-mail:* dd98@columbia.edu. *Website:* www.sipa.columbia.edu.

DINKLAGE, Peter Hayden; American actor; b. 11 June 1969, Morristown, NJ; m. Erica Schmidt 2005; one d.; ed Bennington Coll.; Satellite Awards Special Achievement Award 2004, named by New York Times magazine as one of the Eight Actors Who Turn Television into Art Sept. 2011. *Theatre includes:* The Killing Act, Imperfect Love, Richard III. *Films include:* Living in Oblivion 1995, Safe Men 1998, Pigeonholed 1999, Never Again 2001, Human Nature 2001, 13 Moons 2002, Just a Kiss 2002, The Station Agent (Best Actor Award, Ourense Ind. Film Festival 2003) 2003, Tiptoes 2003, Elf 2003, Surviving Eden 2004, The Baxter 2005, Escape Artists 2005, Lassie 2005, Fortunes 2005, The Limbo Room 2006, Find Me Guilty 2006, Little Fugitive 2006, Penelope 2006, Death at a Funeral 2007, Ascension Day 2007, Underdog 2007, The Chronicles of Narnia: Prince Caspian 2008, Saint John of Las Vegas 2009, Death at a Funeral 2010, I Love You Too 2010, The Last Rites of Ransom Pride 2010, Pete Smalls Is Dead 2010, A Little Bit of Heaven 2011, Knights of Badassdom 2011, Ice Age: Continental Drift (voice) 2012. *Television includes:* The $treet (series) 2001, Third Watch (series) 2002, I'm with Her (series) 2004, Life As We Know It (series) 2005, Testing Bob (film) 2005, Ultra (film) 2006, Threshold (series) 2005-06, Nip/Tuck (series) 2006, 30 Rock (series) 2009, Game of Thrones (series) (Emmy Award for Best Supporting Actor in a Dramatic Series 2011, Golden Globe Award for Best Supporting Actor in a Series for Television 2012) 2011–12. *Address:* c/o Insight Entertainment, 1134 South Cloverdale Avenue, Los Angeles, CA 90019-6737, USA (office).

DION, Céline, CC, OQ; Canadian singer; b. (Marie Claudette Céline Dion), 30 March 1968, Charlemagne, Québec; d. of Adhémar Dion and Thérèse Tanguay; m. René Angélil 1994; three s.; recording artist 1981–; winner, Eurovision song contest, Dublin 1988; performed anthem The Power of the Dream at opening ceremony of Olympic Games, Atlanta 1996; Las Vegas show, A New Day 2002–07, Celine 2011–14; Taking Chances World Tour 2008–09; Medal of Arts (France) 1996, Légion d'honneur 2008; Dr hc (Laval Univ.) 2008; numerous awards including Gala de L'ADISQ Awards (Quebec) for Pop Album of the Year 1983, for Best Selling Record 1984, 1985, for Best Selling Single 1985, for Pop Song of the Year 1985, 1988, for Female Artist of Year 1983–85, 1988, for Discovery of the Year 1983, for Best Québec Artist Outside Québec 1983, 1988, Journal de Québec Trophy 1985, Spectrel Video Award for Best Stage Performance 1988, Juno Awards for Female Vocalist of the Year 1991–94, 1997, 1999, for Album of the Year 1991, 1995, 1999, for Single of the Year 1993, Acad. Award for Best Song Written for a Motion Picture or TV (for Beauty and The Beast duet with Peabo Bryson) 1992, Grammy Award (for Beauty and the Beast) 1993, (for My Heart Will Go On, from film Titanic) 1999, American Music Award for Best Adult Contemporary Artist 2003, World Music Diamond Award 2004. *Recordings include:* albums: Tellement J'ai D'Amour, Incognito, Unison 1990, Dion chante Plamondon 1991, Céline Dion 1991, The Colour of My Love 1993, Les Premières Années 1994, Des Mots Qui Sonnent 1995, Power Of Love 1995, The French Album 1995, D'eux 1995, Falling Into You 1996, Live à Paris 1996, Let's Talk About Love 1997, A l'Olympia 1998, Chansons En Or 1998, Céline Dion Vol. 2 1998, S'il Suffisait D'Aimer 1998, These Are Special Times (Grammy and Juno Awards 1999) 1998, Amour 1998, Au Coeur Du Stade 1999, Tout En Amour 2002, Let's Talk About Love 1999, All The Way – A Decade of Song 1999, A New Day Has Come 2002, One Heart 2003, 1 Fille & 4 Types 2003, Miracle 2004, Taking Chances 2007, My Love: Essential collection 2008, Taking Chances World Tour – The Concert 2010, Tournée mondiale Taking Chances: Le spectacle 2010, Sans attendre 2012, Loved Me Back to Life 2013. *Publications include:* Celine 1997, My Story, My Dreams 2001, Miracle (with Anne Geddes) 2004, For Keeps 2006. *Leisure interests:* architecture, fashion, philanthropy, photography, looking after sons, golf. *Address:* Les Productions Feeling, 2540 blvd Daniel-Johnson, Bureau 755, Laval, PQ H7T 2S3, Canada (office). *Telephone:* (450) 978-9555 (office). *Fax:* (450) 978-1055 (office). *E-mail:* info@feelingprod.com (office). *Website:* www.celinedion.com

DION, Hon. Stéphane, PC, BA, MA, PhD; Canadian politician and academic; b. 28 Sept. 1955, Quebec City; m. Janine Krieber; one d.; ed Laval Univ., Inst. d'études politiques de Paris, France; Asst Prof. of Political Science, Univ. of Moncton Jan.–May 1984; Asst Prof. of Political Science, Univ. of Montreal 1984–89, Assoc. Prof. 1989–95, Prof. 1995; MP (Liberal Party of Canada) for St-Laurent/Cartierville 1996–; Minister of Intergovernmental Affairs and Pres. Queen's Privy Council for Canada 1996–2003, Minister of Environment 2004–06, Leader Liberal Party of Canada 2006–08 (resgnd), also Leader of the Opposition; Pres. UN Climate Change Conference, Montreal 2005; Guest Scholar, Brookings Inst., Washington, DC 1990–91, Laboratoire d'économie publique de Paris 1994–95; Research Fellow, Canadian Centre for Man. Devt 1990–91; Co-Ed. Canadian Journal of Political Science 1990–93; mem. Aid to Scholarly Publs Cttee of Social Sciences Fed. of Canada, Advisory Council of Inst. of Intergovernmental Relations, Queen's Univ.; Dr hc (Carlos III Univ. of Madrid) 2002. *Address:* House of Commons, Room 301, Justice Building, Ottawa, ON, K1A 0A6, Canada (office). *Telephone:* (613) 996-5789 (office). *Fax:* (613) 996-6562 (office). *E-mail:* dions@parl.gc.ca (office). *Website:* www.stephanedion.parl.gc.ca (office).

DIOP, Abdoulaye; Senegalese politician; ed Lycée El Hadj Malick Sy de Thiès, Univ. of Dakar and Ecole Nat. d'Admin et de Magistrature; asst to Prin. Paymaster, Thiès 1980–81; rate collector, Commune de Fatick 1981–84, Commune de Mbour 1984–87, Commune de Pikine 1987–90; tax collector, Dakar Centre 1990–93; tax and rate collector, Ville de Dakar 1993–95, Dakar Urban Community 1993–95; Sr Banking Exec., Treasurer-Gen. and Dir of Treasury and Public Finance 1995–98; Minister Del., Ministry of Economy and Finance 2000; Minister of State, Minister of Economy and Finance 2001–12; mem. Observatoire des finances locales de Cotonou 1996–, Comm. de réforme des textes de la décentralisation; Pres. Tech. Cttee responsible for Reform of Local Finance in Senegal; Chevalier, Ordre nat. du Lion de la République du Sénégal 1996. *Address:* c/o Ministry of the Economy and Finance, rue René Ndiaye, BP 4017, Dakar, Senegal (office).

DIOP, Bécaye; Senegalese politician; b. 1945; m.; six c.; Minister Del. to the Minister of Educ. for Tech. Educ., Vocational Training, Adult Literacy and Nat. Languages 2000–01; Minister of the Armed Forces 2002–09, of the Interior, Local Communities and Decentralization 2009–10, Minister of State, Minister of Town Planning and Sanitation 2012; mem. Parti Démocratique Sénégalais (PDS).

Address: c/o Ministry of Town Planning, 54 ave Georges Pompidou X Raffenel, Immeuble Plazza, 1er étage, Dakar, Senegal (office).

DIOP, Bineta; Senegalese peace campaigner; *Founder and Executive Director, Femmes Africa Solidarité;* b. 1950; d. of Marèma Lô; m.; ed Coll. in Addis Ababa, Centre d'études stratégiques, Paris; Programme Coordinator, Int. Comm. of Jurists, Geneva 1981–96; Founder and Exec. Dir Femmes Africa Solidarité 1996–; campaigns for women's rights and social issues; mem. various dels to observe elections in post-conflict areas including Burundi, Congo and Liberia; Chair. UN Working Group on Peace, Geneva; Co-Chair. Civil Soc. Advisory Group on UN Security Council Resolution 1325 on Women, Peace and Security 2010–; Vice-Pres. African Union Women's Cttee; mem. African Union Women's Cttee for Peace and Devt; mem. Group of Int. Advisers to Int. Cttee of Red Cross; West African Women Asscn Award 2005, Int. Women Fed. for World Peace Leadership and Good Governance Award. *Address:* Femmes Africa Solidarité, PO Box 45077, Dakar Fann, Senegal (office). *Telephone:* 33 869 81 06 (office). *Fax:* 33 860 20 47 (office). *E-mail:* infodk@fasngo.org (office). *Website:* www.fasngo.org (office).

DIOP, Papa Bouba; Senegalese professional footballer; b. 28 Jan. 1978, Dakar; began career as midfielder with Espoir Dakar 1993–94, then Diaraaf Dakar 1994–95, Vevey-Sports 1995–96, Neuchâtel Xamax 1996–2000, Grasshoppers Zurich, Switzerland 2000–01, Racing Club de Lens, France 2002–04, Fulham FC, UK 2004–07, Portsmouth FC 2007–10 (won FA Cup 2008), AEK Athens 2010–; mem. Senegal nat. football team 1999– (has made 58 appearances and scored nine goals), took part in African Nations Cup 2002, top scorer for Senegal nat. football team in World Cup 2002. *Address:* c/o AEK Athens, 69–71 Grammou, Maroussi, 15124 Athens, Greece. *Telephone:* (210) 6121371. *Fax:* (210) 6121618. *E-mail:* info@aekfc.gr. *Website:* www.aekfc.gr.

DIOUF, Abdou, LenD, LèsL; Senegalese fmr head of state; *Secretary-General, La Francophonie;* b. 7 Sept. 1935, Louga; m. 1963; ed Lycée Faidherbe, St Louis, Dakar and Paris Univs; Dir of Tech. Co-operation and Minister of Planning Sept.–Nov. 1960; Asst Sec.-Gen. to Govt 1960–61; Sec.-Gen. Ministry of Defence June–Dec. 1961; Gov. Sine-Saloum Region 1961–62; Dir de Cabinet of Minister of Foreign Affairs 1962–63, of Pres. of Repub. 1963–65; Sec.-Gen. to Pres.'s Office 1964–68; Minister of Planning and Industry 1968–70; Prime Minister 1970–80; Pres. of Senegal 1981–2000, of Confed. of Senegambia 1982–89; Chair. OAU 1985–86; mem. Nat. Ass. for Longa Département 1973–; mem. Senegalese Progressive Union (UPS) 1961–, later Asst Sec.-Gen.; fmr Asst Sec.-Gen. Parti socialiste sénégalais (PS), now Chair.; currently Sec.-Gen. La Francophonie, Paris; Jt Winner Africa Prize for Leadership 1987. *Address:* La Francophonie, 28 rue de Bourgogne, 75007 Paris, France (office). *Telephone:* 1-44-11-12-50 (office). *Fax:* 1-44-11-12-76 (office). *E-mail:* oif@francophonie.org (office). *Website:* www.francophonie.org (office).

DIOUF, Jacques, BSc, PhD; Senegalese international civil servant and agronomist; b. 1 Aug. 1938, Saint-Louis; m. Aissatou Seye 1963; one s. four d.; ed Lycée Faidherbe, Saint-Louis, Ecole Nat. d'Agriculture, Paris/Grignon, Ecole Nat. d'Application d'Agronomie Tropicale, Paris/Nogent and Sorbonne, Paris; Dir European Office and Agricultural Programme of Marketing Bd, Paris and Dakar 1963–64; Exec. Sec. African Groundnut Council, Lagos 1965–71; Exec. Sec. West African Rice Devt Asscn, Monrovia 1971–77; Sec. of State for Science and Tech., Govt of Senegal, Dakar 1978–83; mem. Nat. Ass. 1983–84, Chair. Foreign Relations Cttee and elected Sec., Dakar 1983–84; Adviser to the Pres. and Regional Dir of International Development Research Centre, Ottawa 1984-85; Sec.-Gen. Banque centrale des états de l'Afrique de l'ouest, Dakar 1985–90; Special Adviser to the Governor, Banque centrale des etats de l'Afrique de l'ouest, Dakar 1990–91; Perm. Rep. of Senegal to UN 1991–93; Dir-Gen. FAO 1994–2011; led Senegalese dels to UN Confs on Science and Tech., Vienna 1979 (Chair. of 1st Comm.), Industrial Devt, New Delhi 1980, New and Renewable Energy Sources, Nairobi (Vice-Chair.) 1981, Peaceful Use of Space, Vienna 1982; African Rep., Consultative Group on Int. Agricultural Research, Washington; mem. Bd of Dirs ISNAR, The Hague, IITA Lagos, IIRSDA Abidjan, ICRAF, Nairobi, Int. Foundation for Science, Stockholm, African Capacity Building Foundation, Harare, World Inst. for Devt Econs Research, Helsinki, Council of African Advisers of the World Bank, Washington DC; Chair. SINAES, Dakar; mem. Consultative Cttee on Medical Research, WHO, Geneva; Grand Commdr, Order of the Star of Africa (Liberia) 1977, Commdr, Order of Agricultural Merit (Canada) 1995, Grand Cross, Order of Merit in Agric., Fisheries and Food (Spain) 1996, Order of Solidarity (Cuba) 1998, Commdr, Légion d'honneur 1998, Grand Cross, Order of May for Merit (Argentina) 1998, Two Niles Decoration (Sudan), 2000, Nat. Order of Merit for Co-Operation and Devt (Guinea Bissau) 2001, Distinguished Cross, Order of the Quetzal (Guatemala) 2001, Commdr, Order of St Charles (Monaco) 2002, Distinguished Cross (Peru) 2002, Kt Grand Cross (First Class) of the Most Exalted Order of the White Elephant (Thailand) 2003, Order of the Golden Fleece (Georgia) 2003, Golden Fortune Saint George Award 'Honour, Eminence, Labour' (First Grade) (Ukraine) 2003, Medal of Commdr, Nat. Order of Merit (Mauritania) 2003, Congressional Medal of Achievement (Philippines) 2004, Order of Vasco Nuñez de Balboa (Panama) 2004, Order of Ulises Rojas (Guatemala) 2004, Order of the Golden Heart, Rank of Grand Cross (Philippines) 2004, Grand Master Nat. Order (Madagascar) 2005, Order of Malta 2006, Commdr Grand Cross, Order of Merit of Repub. of Hungary 2007, Kt of Grand Cross of Equestrian Order of St Agatha (San Marino) 2009, Commdr, Nat. Order of Benin 2010, Grand Cross of Order of Independence (Equatorial Guinea) 2011; numerous hon. doctorates; Award for Services to Educ. (France) 1979, Hilal Award (Pakistan) 2005, European Football Leagues Asscn Special Award 2010, Action Against Hunger Humanitarian Award 2010, Khalifa Int. Date Palm Award 2011. *Publications include:* La détérioration du pouvoir d'achat de l'Arachide 1972, Les fondements du dialogue scientifique entre les civilisations Euro-occidentale et Négro-Africaine 1979, The Challenge of Agricultural Development in Africa 1989. *Leisure interests:* reading, music, sports. *Address:* c/o Food and Agriculture Organization of the United Nations, Viale delle Terme di Caracalla, 00153 Rome, Italy.

DIPICO, Manne Emsley, BA; South African civil servant and trade union official; *Regional Chairman, African National Congress, Northern Cape;* b. 21 April 1959, Kimberley; ed Univ. of Fort Hare; joined African Nat. Congress (ANC) 1982; Nat. Educ. Co-ordinator Nat. Union of Mineworkers; Azanian Students' Org. (AZASO) rep. for United Democratic Front (UDF) Exec. Border Region, AZASO

Treas. Univ. of Fort Hare; mem. UDF N Cape 1985–86; detained Ciskei 1984, detained under state of emergency Kimberley 1986, arrested and sentenced to five years for furthering the aims of a banned org. through terrorist activities 1987–90, released before end of sentence; Regional Sec. ANC 1991–92, Regional Chair. N Cape 1992–; Regional Elections Co-ordinator 1993–94; Premier N Cape Prov. Legislature 1994–2004. *Address:* c/o Private Bag X5016, Kimberley 8301 (office); 5248 Magashula Street, PO Mankurwane, Galeshawe-Kimberley 8345, South Africa (home). *Telephone:* (53) 8309300 (home). *Fax:* (53) 8332122 (office). *E-mail:* cmatlhacko@pancmail.ncape.gov.za (office).

DIPPENAAR, Lauritz (Laurie), MCom, CA; South African business executive; *Chairman, FirstRand Ltd;* b. 25 Oct. 1948; m.; three c.; ed Univ. of Pretoria; Investigating Accountant, Industrial Devt Corpn of South Africa Ltd 1973–76; Cofounder Rand Consolidated Investments (RCI) 1977, mem. Bd of Dirs 1977–84, Man. Dir Rand Merchant Bank (acquired by RCI 1985) 1988–92, Chair. 1992–98, currently Dir (non-exec.) RMB Holdings Ltd; est. FirstRand Ltd 1998, CEO 1998–2005, Chair. (non-exec.) 2008–; Chair. MMI Holdings 2010–11; Chair. (non-exec.) Discovery Holdings Ltd, OUTsurance, Momentum Group Ltd; mem. Business Trust. *Leisure interests:* cycling, canoeing, watching rugby. *Address:* FirstRand Ltd, PO Box 650149, Benmore, Johannesburg 2010, South Africa (office). *Telephone:* (11) 2821808 (office). *Fax:* (11) 2828088 (office). *Website:* www .firstrand.co.za (office).

DIRCEU DE OLIVEIRA E SILVA, José; Brazilian politician and lawyer; b. 16 March 1946, Passa Quatro; m. 1st Clara Becker (divorced); m. 2nd Maria Rita Garcia de Andrade; one s. two d.; ed Pontifical Catholic Univ. of São Paulo; fmr student leader; organized protest of 100,000 people against Brazilian mil. dictatorship 1967; jailed 1968, released 1969 in exchange for kidnapped US Amb. Charles Elbrick; went into exile in Cuba where he underwent plastic surgery to change his appearance and received guerrilla training; returned permanently to Brazil 1975; assumed false identity (Carlos Henrique Gouveia de Melo) in Cruzeiro do Oeste, Paraná, became a shopkeeper; amnestied 1979; co-founder (with Luiz Inácio Lula da Silva) Workers' Party (PT), later Gen. Sec., Leader 1994, Pres. 1995–; elected State Deputy 1986, Deputy Fed. Parl. 1990, 1997, 1999, 2001–; Gov. State of São Paulo 1994; Chief Adviser to Pres.-elect Luiz Inácio Lula da Silva (q.v.); Chief of Cabinet 2003–05 (resgnd); facing trial on charges of conspiracy and corruption 2007. *Address:* c/o Office of the Civilian Cabinet, Palácio do Planalto, 4° Andar, Praça dos Três Poderes, 70150 Brasília, DF, Brazil (office).

DIRKS, Nicholas, BA, MA, PhD; American historian, anthropologist, academic and university administrator; *Chancellor, University of California, Berkeley;* ed Wesleyan Univ., Conn., Univ. of Chicago; part-time Instructor in Cultural Anthropology, George Williams Coll. 1973; Instructor in Asian History, California Inst. of Tech., Pasadena 1978–80, Asst Prof. of History 1980–85, Assoc. Prof. of History, Div. of Humanities and Social Sciences 1986–87; Academic Visitor, Dept of Anthropology, LSE, UK Jan.–Dec. 1986; Assoc. Prof. of History, Univ. of Michigan 1987–90, Prof. of History and Anthropology 1990–97, Co-founder and Dir Interdepartmental Program in Anthropology and History, Univ. of Michigan 1988–97, Dir Center for South and Southeast Asian Studies 1992–95, Dir Advanced Study Center, Int. Inst. 1995–97; Directeur d'Études Associé, École des Hautes Études en Sciences Sociales, Paris Jan.–April 1992; Prof. of Anthropology and History, Columbia Univ., New York 1997–2000, Franz Boas Prof. of Anthropology and History 2000–12, Chair. Dept of Anthropology 1997–2003; Vice-Pres. Arts and Sciences and Dean of the Faculty, Univ. of California, Berkeley 2004–09, Exec. Vice-Pres. and Dean of the Faculty of the Arts and Sciences 2009–12, Chancellor Univ. of California, Berkeley 2013–; Sr Fellow, Council on Foreign Relations 2005–; Sr Research Fellow, American Inst. of Indian Studies, Smithsonian Inst. 1980; John D. and Catherine T. MacArthur Residential Fellow, Inst. for Advanced Study, Princeton 1989–90; Sr Fellow, Michigan Soc. of Fellows 1995–97; Old Dominion Fellow, Humanities Council and Dept of History, Princeton Univ. 2005; Trustee, Columbia University Press 2003–12, Series Ed., Cultures of History 2002–, Chair. Faculty Publs Bd 2003–05, mem. Faculty Bd 2001–03; Honours in Social Studies, Wesleyan Univ., Cum Laude in Gen. Scholarship, Wesleyan Univ., NDEA Title VI, 1972–73, 1973–74, Kent Fellow, The Danforth Foundation 1974–78, Fulbright-Hays Doctoral Dissertation Research Abroad Fellow 1975–76, Guggenheim Fellow 1989–91, Univ. of Michigan Faculty Recognition Award 1994, Julia Lockwood Certain Award, Univ. of Michigan 1995, Mellon Foundation, Sawyer Seminar Co-Convener (Michigan) 1996–97, Invited Mem., Center for Advanced Study in the Behavioral Sciences, Stanford, Calif. 1996, Mellon Foundation, Sawyer Seminar Convener (Columbia) 1999–2002. *Publications include:* Colonialism and Culture (ed.) 1992, Culture/Power/History: A Reader in Contemporary Social Theory (co-ed.) 1993, The Hollow Crown: Ethnohistory of an Indian Kingdom (second edn) 1993, In Near Ruins: Cultural Theory at the End of the Century (ed.) 1998, Castes of Mind: Colonialism and the Making of Modern India (Lionel Trilling Award for Best Book 2002) 2001, The Scandal of Empire: India and the Creation of Imperial Britain 2006; numerous papers in professional journals. *Address:* Office of the Chancellor, University of California, 200 California Hall #1500, Berkeley, CA 94720-1500, USA (office). *Telephone:* (510) 642-7464 (office). *Fax:* (510) 643-5499 (office). *E-mail:* chancellor@ berkeley.edu (office). *Website:* chancellor.berkeley.edu (office).

DISKIN, Yuval, BA, MA; Israeli state security official; *Director, Shin Bet;* b. 1956; m. 1st; four c.; m. 2nd; one d.; ed Bar Ilan Univ., Haifa Univ.; joined Shin Bet (Israel Security Agency) 1978, Co-ordinator Nablus Dist 1979–84, Dist Coordinator Nablus, Jenin, Tulkarm 1984–89, Dir Dept for Counter-terrorism, Arab Affairs Br. 1990, Deputy Dir Arab Affairs Br., Dir 1994, Dir Jerusalem, Judea and Samaria Region 1997–2000, Deputy Dir Shin Bet 2000–03, Dir 2005–. *Address:* c/o Ministry of Public Security, PO Box 18182, Building 3, Rinjat Hamemshala, Jerusalem 91181, Israel (office).

DISNEY, Anthea; British media executive; b. 13 Oct. 1946, Dunstable, Beds.; d. of Alfred Leslie and Elsie Wale; m. Peter Robert Howe 1984; ed Queen's Coll.; New York corresp., London Daily Mail 1973–75, Features Ed. 1975–77, New York Bureau Chief 1977–79; columnist, London Daily Express, New York 1979–84; Managing Ed. New York Daily News 1984–87; Ed. Sunday Daily News 1984–87; Ed. US magazine 1987–88; Ed.-in-Chief Self magazine 1988–89; magazine developer, Murdoch magazines 1989–90; Exec. Producer, A Current Affair, Fox TV 1990–91; Ed.-in-Chief TV Guide magazine 1991–95; Editorial Dir Murdoch

Magazines 1994–95; Pres. and CEO HarperCollins Publrs 1996–97; Chair. and CEO News America Publishing 1997–99; Exec. Vice-Pres. of Content, News Corpn 1999–2009; Founding Partner, Women's Enterprise Initiative; mem. Litchfield County Women's Network. *Address:* 50 East 89th Street, New York, NY 10128-1225; Women's Enterprise Initiative, PO Box 264, Litchfield, CT 06759-0264, USA (office).

DISSANAYAKE, Ariyawansa; Sri Lankan politician; *Leader, New Democratic Front;* unsuccessful cand. for Pres. (Democratic United Nat. Front) 1999; Leader, New Democratic Front. *Address:* New Democratic Front, 9/6 Jayanthi Mawatha, Pelawatta, Battaramulla, Sri Lanka (office).

DISSANAYAKE, Dayananda; Sri Lankan government official; apptd Asst Commr Dept of Elections 1983, Deputy Commr 2006, Additional Commr 2010, Commr 1995–2011; acted as Commonwealth Observer during elections in Guyana Aug. 2006. *Address:* c/o Office of the Commissioner of Elections, Elections Secretariat, PO Box 02, Sarana Mawatha, Rajagiriya 10107, Sri Lanka.

DITTUS, Peter, DEcon; German economist; *Secretary-General, Bank for International Settlements;* m., three c.; ed Saarbrücken Univ., Univ. of Mich.; worked as economist at World Bank and OECD; joined BIS as economist 1992, apptd Deputy Sec.-Gen. 2000, Sec.-Gen. 2005–, mem. Exec. Cttee. *Publications include:* Die Wahl der Geldverfassung 1987, A Macroeconomic Model for Debt Analysis of the Latin America Region and Debt Accounting Models for the Highly Indebted Countries (jtly) 1991, Trade and Employment: Can We Afford Better Market Access for Eastern Europe? (jtly) 1994, Corporate Governance in Central Europe: The Role of Banks 1994, Corporate Control in Central Europe and Russia: Should Banks Own Shares? (jtly) 1995, numerous papers on int. econs. *Address:* Bank for International Settlements, Centralbahnplatz 2, Basel 4002, Switzerland (office). *Telephone:* (61) 2808080 (office). *Fax:* (61) 2809100 (office). *E-mail:* peter.dittus@ bis.org (office). *Website:* www.bis.org (office).

DITZ, Johannes, DScS; Austrian industrial executive and politician; b. 22 June 1951, Kirchberg; m.; three c.; ed Vienna Univ. of Econs; employed at Industriellenvereinigung (Industrial Asscn) 1978–79; worked in Dept of Econ. Affairs, ÖVP (Österreichische Volkspartei—Austrian People's Party) fed. party leadership 1979–87; Sec. of State for Finance 1987–88, 1991–95; Deputy to Nat. Council 1988–93; took over leadership of Austrian People's Business Fed. in Econ. Chamber Austria, Exec. Sec. 1989–93; mem. Parl. Nov.–Dec. 1994, Jan.–March 1996; Fed. Minister for Econ. Affairs 1995–96 (resgnd); Chief Financial Officer Holding Post and Telekom Austria and Deputy Gen. Dir Post und Telekom AG 1996–99; apptd to Bd of Österreichische Industrieholding AG (Govt holding co.) 1999; mem. Supervisory Bd ESTAG 2003–05, Chair. 2004–05; CEO A-Tec Industries AG Feb. 2006; apptd Chair. Supervisory Bd Austrian Airlines 2001; fmr Chair. Supervisory Bd OMV (oil and gas co.); fmr Vice-Chair. Supervisory Bd Böhler-Uddeholm AG; returned to politics Sept. 2006; supported Chancellor Wolfgang Schüssel in election campaign 2006. *Address:* c/o Austrian Airlines, Fontanastr. 1, 1107 Vienna, Austria. *Telephone:* (1) 176-6. *Fax:* (1) 688-55-05. *E-mail:* public.relations@aua.com. *Website:* www.aua.com.

DIVUNGUI-DI-N'DINGE, Didjob; Gabonese engineer and politician; *Vice-President;* b. 5 May 1946, Alombié; m.; six c.; ed Ecole Nat. Supérieure des Arts et Métiers, Paris, France, Institut Nat. Polytechnique, Grenoble, France; fmr employers' rep. and Vice-Chair. Perm. Comm. to the Econ. and Social Council; Dir-Gen. Soc. d'Energie et d'Eau du Gabon 1974; Adviser to Pres. of Gabon for Electrical Energy and Water Resources 1975; Minister of Energy and Water Resources 1983; presidential cand. 1993; Vice-Pres. of Gabon 1997–; Grand Croix, Ordre Nat. de l'Etoile Equatoriale, Grand Croix, Ordre Nat. du Mérite Gabonais, Grand Officer, Ordre Nat. du Mérite Français, Commandeur, Ordre Nat. de Côte d'Ivoire. *Address:* Office of the Vice-President, Libreville, Gabon (office).

DIXIT, Avinash Kamalakar, BSc, BA, PhD; American economist and academic; *John J. F. Sherrerd '52 Professor of Economics, Princeton University;* b. 8 June 1944, Bombay (now Mumbai), India; s. of Kamalakar Ramachandra Dixit and Kusum Dixit; ed Bombay Univ., Univ. of Cambridge, UK, Massachusetts Inst. of Tech.; Research Asst, MIT 1965–67; Acting Asst Prof., Univ. of California, Berkeley 1968–69; Lord Thomson of Fleet Fellow and Lecturer in Econs, Balliol Coll., Oxford 1970–74; Prof. of Econs, Univ. of Warwick 1974–80; Prof. of Econs and Int. Affairs, Princeton Univ. 1981–85, Prof. of Econs 1985–89, John J.F. Sherrerd '52 Prof. of Econs 1989–; Visiting Research Assoc., MIT 1972, Visiting Prof. 1977, 1994; Visiting Scholar, IMF 1990, 2000; Visiting Scholar, Russell Sage Foundation 2002–03; Vice-Pres. American Econ. Asscn 2002, Pres. 2008; Fellow, Econometric Soc. 1977, Vice-Pres. 2000, Pres. 2001; Guggenheim Fellowship 1992; Fellow, American Acad. of Arts and Sciences 1992; mem. NAS. *Publications:* Theory of International Trade (co-author) 1980, Thinking Strategically (co-author) 1991, Investment under Uncertainty (co-author) 1994, Lawlessness and Economics 2004, The Art of Strategy (co-author) 2008. *Address:* Department of Economics, 212 Fisher Hall, Princeton University, Princeton, NJ 08544, USA (office). *Fax:* (609) 258-6419 (office). *E-mail:* dixitak@princeton.edu (office). *Website:* www .princeton.edu/~dixitak/home (office).

DIXON, Sir (David) Jeremy, Kt, AA Dip. (Hons), RIBA; British architect; *Principal, Dixon Jones Ltd;* b. 31 May 1939; s. of the late Joseph L. Dixon and Beryl M. Braund; m. Fenella Clemens 1964 (separated 1990); one s. two d.; pnr Julia Somerville; ed Merchant Taylors' School, Architectural Asscn School of Architecture, London; Tutor, Architectural Asscn 1974–83, RCA 1979–81; Prin., Jeremy Dixon (with Fenella Dixon) 1975–90, Jeremy Dixon BDP 1983–90; Chair. RIBA Regional Awards Group 1991–; Trustee, Midsummer Music and London Chamber Music Soc. 2012. *Works include:* int. competitions, First Prize: Northampton Co. Offices 1973, Royal Opera House 1983, Piazzale Roma, Venice 1990, Chelsea Barracks 2009; other competitions won: Tate Gallery Coffee Shop and Restaurant 1984, Study Centre Darwin Coll., Cambridge 1988, Robert Gordon Univ. Residence, Aberdeen 1991, Univ. of Portsmouth Science Bldg 1993, Nat. Portrait Gallery extension 1994, Saïd Business School, Oxford 1996, Magna Carta Building, Salisbury Cathedral 2001, Panopticon, Univ. Coll., London 2001, St Peter's Arcade, Liverpool 2001, Kings Place devt 2002, Exhibition Road Project 2004; other works: reconstruction of Tatlin Tower at RA 1971, 2012, London housing, St Mark's Road 1975, Compass Point, Docklands 1989, Henry Moore Sculpture Inst., Leeds 1988, Sainsbury's superstore, Plymouth 1991, Regent

Palace devt 2005. *Leisure interests:* walking in English landscape, contemporary sculpture and painting, music. *Address:* Dixon Jones Ltd, 2–3 Hanover Yard, Noel Road, London, N1 8YA, England (office). *Telephone:* (20) 7483-8888 (office). *Fax:* (20) 7483-8899 (office). *E-mail:* mail@dixonjones.co.uk (office). *Website:* www .dixonjones.co.uk (office).

DIXON, Kenneth Herbert Morley, CBE, DL, BA (Econs), FRSA; British business executive; b. 19 Aug. 1929, Stockport; s. of Arnold Morley Dixon and Mary Jolly; m. Patricia Oldbury Whalley 1955; two s.; ed Cranbrook School, Sydney, Univ. of Manchester, Harvard Business School, USA; joined Rowntree & Co. Ltd 1956, Dir 1970, Chair. UK Confectionery Div. 1973–78, Deputy Chair. Rowntree Mackintosh Ltd 1978–81, Group Chair. Rowntree Mackintosh PLC (now Rowntree PLC) 1981–89; Vice-Chair. Legal and General Group 1986–94; Deputy Chair. Bass PLC 1990–96; mem. Council Inc. Soc. of British Advertisers 1971–79, Council Cocoa, Chocolate and Confectionery Alliance 1972–79, Council Advertising Asscn 1976–79, CBI Cos Cttee 1979–84, Council CBI 1981–90, BIM Econ. and Soc. Affairs Cttee 1980–84, Food and Drink Fed. Exec. Cttee 1986–89 (mem. Council 1986–87); mem. Council York Univ. 1983–2001, Pro-Chancellor 1987–2001, Chair. 1990–2001; Trustee, Joseph Rowntree Foundation 1996–, Deputy Chair. 1998–2001, Chair. 2001–04; Morrell Fellow, Univ. of York 2007; Hon. DUniv (York) 1993, (Open) 1997. *Leisure interests:* reading, music, fell walking. *Address:* Low Hall, Askham Bryan, York, YO23 3QU, England.

DIXON, Richard Newland, PhD, ScD, FRS, CChem, FRSC; British chemist and academic; *Professor Emeritus of Chemistry and Senior Research Fellow, University of Bristol;* b. 25 Dec. 1930, Borough Green, Sevenoaks, Kent, England; s. of Robert T. Dixon and Lilian Dixon; m. Alison M. Birks 1954; one s. two d.; ed Judd School, Tonbridge, King's Coll. London and St Catharine's Coll. Cambridge; Scientific Officer, UKAEA, Aldermaston 1954–56; Postdoctoral Fellow, Univ. of Western Ont., Canada 1956–57, Nat. Research Council, Ottawa 1957–59; ICI Fellow, Univ. of Sheffield 1959–60, Lecturer in Chem. 1960–69; Prof. of Chem., Univ. of Bristol 1969–96, Alfred Capper Pass Prof. of Chem. 1990–96, Prof. Emer. 1996–, Leverhulme Fellow Emer. 1996–99, Univ. Sr Research Fellow 1996–, Dean, Faculty of Science 1979–82, Pro-Vice Chancellor 1989–92; Dir (non-exec.) United Bristol Healthcare NHS Trust 1994–2003, Vice-Chair. 1995–2003; Chair. Univ. of Bristol Alumni Foundation 1996–2009; Trustee, Charitable Trusts for United Bristol Hosps 2003–11, Chair. 2006–11; Sorby Research Fellow, Royal Soc. 1964–69; mem. Council, Faraday Div. Royal Soc. of Chem. 1985–98 (Vice-Pres. 1989–98), Cttees of Science and Eng Research Council 1980–83, 1987–90; Corday Morgan Medal, Royal Soc. of Chem. 1968, Spectroscopy Medal, Royal Soc. of Chem. 1985; Hallam Lecturer, Univ. of Wales 1988, Liversidge Lecturer, Royal Soc. of Chem. 1993, Harkins Lecturer, Univ. of Chicago, USA 1993, Rumford Medal, Royal Soc. 2004. *Publications:* Spectroscopy and Structure 1965, Theoretical Chemistry, Vol. I 1972, Vol. II 1974, Vol. III 1977; 220 research articles in scientific journals. *Leisure interests:* mountain walking, photography, gardening, theatre-going. *Address:* School of Chemistry, University of Bristol, Cantock's Close, Bristol, BS8 1TS (office); 22 Westbury Lane, Coombe Dingle, Bristol, BS9 2PE, England (home). *Telephone:* (117) 928-7661 (office); (117) 968-1691 (home). *Fax:* (117) 925-1295 (office). *E-mail:* r.n.dixon@bris.ac.uk (office). *Website:* www.chm .bris.ac.uk/staff/rdixon.htm (office).

DJA, Baciro; Guinea-Bissau politician; b. 1974; fmr Pres. Instituto de Defesa Nacional; Minister of Youth and Sport 2009, of Nat. Defence 2011–12; Vice-Pres. Nat. Comm. for UNESCO; mem. Partido Africano da Independência da Guiné e Cabo Verde. *Address:* c/o Ministry of National Defence, Amura, Bissau, Guinea-Bissau.

DJADALLAH, Gen. Bichara Issa; Chadian army officer and government official; Minister of Nat. Defence 2006–07; Gov. Ouaddaï region 2007–. *Address:* Gouverneur du Ouaddaï, Abéché, Chad (office).

DJAFFAR, Ahmed Ben Saïd; Comoran politician; fmr head of local devt charity funded by EU; Minister of External Relations and Co-operation, with responsibility for the Diaspora and Francophone and Arab Relations 2006–10. *Address:* c/o Ministry of External Relations and Co-operation, BP 428, Moroni, The Comoros (office).

DJALIL, Matori Abdul; Indonesian politician; b. 11 July 1942, Semarang, Jawa Tengah; ed Satya Wacana Christian Univ., Salatiga; previously Chair. Nat. Awakening Party; Sec. Gen. United Devt Party 1989–94; Deputy Chair. MPR RI 1999–2004; Minister of Defence 2001–04. *Address:* c/o Jalan Medan Merdeka Barat 13–14, Jakarta Pusat, Indonesia (office).

DJALÓ PIRES, Mamadu Saliu; Guinea-Bissau lawyer and politician; Pres. Supreme Court –1999; Minister of Justice –2011, Minister of Foreign Affairs, Int. Co-operation and Communities 2011–12. *Address:* c/o Ministry of Foreign Affairs, International Co-operation and Communities, Av. dos Combatentes da Liberdade da Pátria, Bissau, Guinea-Bissau (office).

DJANGONÉ-BI, Djessan Philippe, MA, PhD; Côte d'Ivoirian academic and diplomatist; b. 1 Jan. 1946; m. Martine Djangoné-Bi; two c.; ed Brandeis Univ., USA, Univ. of Abidjan, Sorbonne Univ., Paris, Univ. of Paris III, France; Second Asst to Dean of Faculty of Arts and Humanities, Nat. Univ. of Côte d'Ivoire 1979–82, Dir of English Dept 1980–82; Sr Lecturer, Dept of English, Univ. of Cocody, Abidjan; Head of Int. Co-operation Div., Ministry of Higher Educ. and Scientific Research 2000–01; Amb. and Perm. Rep. to UN, New York 2001–06, Amb. to UK 2007–11 (also accred to Ireland 2008–11); Chevalier de l'Ordre Nat. 2002. *Address:* Ministry of Foreign Affairs and African Integration, Bloc Ministériel, blvd Angoulvand, BP V109, Abidjan, Côte d'Ivoire (office). *Telephone:* 20-22-71-50 (office). *Fax:* 20-33-23-08 (office). *E-mail:* infos@mae.ci (office). *Website:* www.mae.ci (office).

DJEBAR, Assia; Algerian novelist, poet, dramatist, filmmaker and academic; *Silver Chair Professor of Francophone Literature and Civilization, New York University;* b. (Fatima-Zohra Imalhayène), 30 June 1936, Cherchell; d. of the late Tahar Imalhayène and Bahia Sahraoui; m. 1st Ahmed Ould-Roüis 1958 (divorced 1975); m. 2nd Malek Alloula 1981 (divorced 2005); one d.; ed Lycée Fénélon, Paris and École Normale Supérieure de Sèvres, France; taught history at Univ. of Algiers 1962–65, 1974–84; Foundation Distinguished Prof. and Dir Center for French and Francophone Studies, Louisiana State Univ., USA 1995–2001; Silver

Chair Prof. of Francophone Literature and Civilization, New York Univ. 2002–; mem. Acad. Royale de Langue Française de Belgique 2000–, Acad. Française 2005–; Dr hc (Concordia Univ., Montréal) 2002, (Osnabrück Univ.) 2005; Venice Film Festival Int. Critics' Prize 1979, Prix Maurice Maeterlinck 1995, Neustadt Int. Prize for Literature (USA) 1996, Yourcenar Prize 1997, Friedenspreis des Deutschen Buchhandels, Frankfurt 2000, Pablo Neruda Prize, Italy 2005, Grinzane Cavour Prize, Italy 2006. *Films include:* La Nouba des femmes du Mont Chenoua 1979, La Zerda ou les chants d'oubli 1982. *Publications include:* La Soif (trans. as The Mischief) 1957, Les Impatients 1958, Women of Islam 1961, Les Enfants du nouveau monde 1962, Les Alouettes naïves 1967, Poèmes pour l'Algérie heureuse 1969, Rouge l'aube (with Walid Garn) 1969, La Nouba des femmes du Mont Chenoua 1969, Femmes d'Alger dans leur appartement (trans. as Women of Algiers in their Apartment) 1980 (new edn 2002), L'Amour la fantasia (trans. as Fantasia: An Algerian Cavalcade) 1985, Ombre sultane (trans. as A Sister to Scheherazade) 1987, Loin de Médine (trans. as Far from Medina) 1991, Chronique d'un été algérien 1993, Le Blanc de l'Algérie (trans. as Algerian White) 1995, Vaste est la prison (trans. as So Vast the Prison) 1995, Oran, langue morte 1997, Les Nuits de Strasbourg 1997, Ces voix qui m'assiègent 1999, Filles d'Ismaël dans le vent et la tempête (musical drama in five acts) 2002, La Femme sans sepulture 2002, La Disparation de la langue française 2004, Nulle part dans la maison de mon père (ed Fayard) 2007. *Address:* Department of French, New York University, 13 University Place, Office 621, New York, NY 10003-4556, USA (office). *Telephone:* (212) 992-9509 (office). *E-mail:* assia.djebar@nyu.edu (office). *Website:* french.as.nyu.edu (office).

DJERASSI, Carl, AB, PhD; American/Austrian chemist, academic and author; *Professor Emeritus of Chemistry, Stanford University;* b. 29 Oct. 1923, Vienna, Austria; s. of Dr Samuel Djerassi and Dr Alice Friedmann; m. 1st Virginia Jeremiah (divorced 1950); m. 2nd Norma Lundholm (divorced 1976); one s. one d. (deceased); m. 3rd Diane W. Middlebrook 1985 (died 2007); ed Kenyon Coll., Univ. of Wisconsin; Research Chemist, Ciba Pharmaceutical Co., Summit, NJ 1942–43, 1945–49; Assoc. Dir of Research, Syntex, SA, Mexico City 1949–51, Research Vice-Pres. 1957–60, Pres. Syntex Research 1968–72; Assoc. Prof. of Chem., Wayne State Univ., Detroit 1952–54, Prof. 1954–59; Prof. of Chem., Stanford Univ. 1959–2002, Prof. Emer. 2002–; Pres. Bd Zoecon Corpn (renamed Sandoz Crop Protection Corpn) 1968–83, Chair. 1968–88; f. Djerassi Foundation Resident Artists Program; mem. Editorial Bd Journal of the American Chemical Society 1968–76, Journal of Organic Chemistry 1955–58, Tetrahedron 1958–92, Steroids 1963–2002, Proceedings of NAS 1964–70; mem. NAS Bd on Science and Tech. for Int. Devt 1967–76, Chair. 1972–76; mem. American Pugwash Cttee 1967–81; mem. NAS, NAS Inst. of Medicine, Brazilian Acad. of Sciences, American Acad. of Arts and Sciences; Foreign mem. German Acad. of Science (Leopoldina), Royal Soc. (London), Royal Swedish Acad. of Sciences 1973, Bulgarian Acad. of Sciences 1979, Royal Swedish Acad. of Eng Sciences 1984, Academia Europaea; Hon. Fellow, Royal Chemical Soc. 1968, American Acad. of Pharmaceutical Science; Austrian Cross for Culture and Science 1999, Grosse Goldene Ehrenzeichen für Verdienste um das Bundenland Niederösterreich 2002, Ehrenmedaille der Bundeshauptstadt Wien in Gold 2002, Great Merit Cross of Germany 2003, Great Merit Cross for Services to Austria 2008, Gold Honour Ring of Austrian Acad. of Sciences 2008; 26 hon. doctorates; Award in Pure Chem. 1958, Baekeland Medal 1959, Fritzsche Medal 1960, Royal Chemical Soc. Centenary Lecturer 1964, Royal Swedish Acad. of Eng Sciences 13th Chemical Lecturer 1969, Intra-Science Research Award 1969, Freedman Foundation Patent Award 1971, Swedish Pharmaceutical Soc. Scheele Lecturer 1972, Creative Invention Award 1973, Chemical Pioneer Award 1973, American Inst. of Chemists; Nat. Medal of Science 1973 (for synthesis of first oral contraceptive), Perkin Medal 1975, Wolf Prize in Chem. 1978, Bard Award in Medicine and Science 1983, Award in the Chem. of Contemporary Technological Problems 1983, Roussel Prize (Paris) 1988, Esselen Award for Chem. in the Public Interest, ACS 1989, NAS Award for the Industrial Application of Science 1990, Nat. Medal of Tech. 1991, Priestley Medal, ACS 1992, Nevada Medal 1992, Thomson Gold Medal, Int. Mass Spectrometry Soc. 1994, Prince Mahidol Award (Thailand) 1996, Willard Gibbs Medal 1997, Othmer Gold Medal, Chem. Heritage Foundation 2000, Erasmus Medal, Academia Europaea 2003, Gold Medal, American Inst. of Chemists 2004, on postage stamp, Austrian Post Office 2005, Serono Prize for Fiction, Rome 2005, Lichtenberg Medal, Göttingen Acad. of Sciences 2005, Edinburgh Medal 2011. *Plays:* An Immaculate Misconception 1998, Oxygen (with Roald Hoffmann) 2000, Calculus 2003, EGO 2003, Three on a Couch 2004, Phallacy 2005, Taboos 2006, Verrechnet (with Isabella Gregor) 2009, Foreplay 2011. *Radio:* five radio plays, BBC World Service, West German Radio (WDR), Austrian Radio (ORF), NPR (USA), Swedish Radio, Radio Prague; numerous broadcasts. *Publications:* (author or co-author) Optical Rotatory Dispersion 1960, Steroid Reactions 1963, Interpretation of Mass Spectra of Organic Compounds 1964, Structure Elucidation of Natural Products by Mass Spectrometry (two vols) 1964, Mass Spectrometry of Organic Compounds 1967, The Politics of Contraception 1979, 1981, The Futurist and Other Stories (fiction) 1988, Cantor's Dilemma (novel) 1989, Steroids Made It Possible (autobiog.) 1990, The Clock Runs Backward (poetry) 1991, The Pill, Pygmy Chimps and Degas' Horse (autobiog.) 1992, Bourbaki Gambit (novel) 1994, From the Lab into the World (collected essays) 1994, Marx, deceased (novel) 1996, Menachem's Seed (novel) 1997, NO (novel) 1998, This Man's Pill (memoir) 2001, Newton's Darkness: Two Dramatic Views (with David Pinner) 2003, Sex in an Age of Technological Reproduction 2008, Four Jews on Parnassus: A Conversation 2008, Foreplay 2011, Insufficiency 2011; numerous scientific articles, also poems, memoirs and short stories. *Leisure interests:* skiing, modern art, opera, theatre. *Address:* Department of Chemistry, Stanford University, Stanford, CA 94305-5080, USA (office). *Telephone:* (650) 723-2783 (office). *E-mail:* djerassi@stanford.edu (office). *Website:* www.djerassi.com.

DJEREJIAN, Edward P.; American diplomatist and business executive; *Independent Chairman, Occidental Petroleum Corporation;* served in US Foreign Service 1962–94, including as Special Asst to Pres. Ronald Reagan and Deputy Press Sec. for Foreign Affairs, White House 1985–86, Amb. to Syria 1988–91, Asst Sec. of State for Near Eastern Affairs 1991–93, Amb. to Israel 1993–94; Founding Dir James A. Baker III Inst. for Public Policy, Rice Univ.; Dir, Occidental Petroleum Corpn 1996–, Ind. Chair. 2013–, mem. Corp. Governance, Nominating and Social Responsibility Cttee; fmr mem. Bd of Dirs Global Industries, Ltd and

Chair. Governance Cttee; mem. Bd of Trustees, Carnegie Corpn of New York; Fellow, American Acad. of Arts and Sciences 2011; Presidential Distinguished Service Award, Dept of State's Distinguished Honor Award and numerous other honours, including the Ellis Island Medal of Honor, Anti-Defamation League's Moral Statesman Award; Asscn of Rice Alumni's Gold Medal. *Publication:* Danger and Opportunity: An American Ambassador's Journey through the Middle East 2008. *Address:* Occidental Petroleum Corporation, 10889 Wilshire Blvd, Los Angeles, CA 90024-4201, USA (office). *Telephone:* (310) 208-8800 (office). *Fax:* (310) 443-6690 (office). *E-mail:* info@oxy.com (office). *Website:* www.oxy.com (office).

DJINNIT, Said; Algerian politician, diplomatist and UN official; *Special Representative of the Secretary-General and Head, United Nations Office for West Africa (UNOWA);* b. 7 June 1954; ed Ecole Nationale d'Admin, Paris, France, Centre for Int. Relations Studies, Univ. of Brussels, Inst. of Political Affairs, Univ. of Algiers; served on various diplomatic missions, including as Chargé d'affaires, Embassy in Brussels and Deputy Head of Mission in Addis Ababa; also served in various capacities in OAU (now African Union), including as OAU Asst Sec.-Gen. for Political Affairs, also served as Chair. OAU Secr. Task Force on drafting of Constitutive Act of African Union 1999–2000; Commr for Peace and Security at African Union, with responsibility for issues including Darfur conflict –2008; Special Rep. of Sec.-Gen. and Head of UN Office for West Africa (UNOWA) 2008–. *Address:* UN Office for West Africa (UNOWA), Almadies Ouest, Lot 4, BP 23851, Dakar, Senegal (office). *Telephone:* (33) 8698585 (office). *Fax:* (33) 8204638 (office). *E-mail:* djinnitsaid@yahoo.com (home).

DJOJOHADIKUSUMO, Hashim, BA; Indonesian business executive; s. of Sumitro Djojohadikusumo; ed Pomona Coll., Calif., USA; grew up in exile in London; began career as mergers and acquisitions trainee, Lazard Frères & Co., Paris 1976; returned to Indonesia 1978; fmr Chair. and Pres. Nations Energy Ltd, Calgary, Canada; fmr Chair. and CEO Tirtamas Group, Pres. Tirtamas Comexindo (holding co.), Tirtamas Majutama, PT Kiani Kertas (pulp and paper co.), PT Semen Cibinong (cement co.); fmr Propr PT Bank Niaga; Chair. Indonesia Chess Federation; fmr Chair. Indonesia Polo Asscn. *Address:* c/o Indonesian Chess Federation, Kanselary KONI Pintu VI, Senayan, Jakarta, Indonesia.

DJOJONEGORO, Husain; Indonesian business executive; *Commissioner, ABC Group;* b. 1949; s. of Chandra Djojonegoro; m.; four c.; apptd Pres. ABC Group (family-owned co., conglomerate with diverse interests including batteries, sanitary products, toothpaste, consumer brand distribution) 1968, now Commr; fmr Commr PT Istana Pualam Kristal (PTIPK). *Address:* ABC Group, Jl. Rasak No. 7, Medan 20113, North Sumatra, Indonesia (office). *Telephone:* (61) 4566468 (office). *Fax:* (61) 4573124 (office). *E-mail:* hartini@abc-drycell.co.id (office). *Website:* www.abc-drycell.co.id (office).

DJOKOVIC, Novak; Serbian professional tennis player; b. (Novak Nikhil Ðoković), 22 May 1987, Belgrade, SFR Yugoslavia (now Serbia); s. of Srđan Djokovic and Dijana Djokovic; ed trained at Nikola Pilić's tennis acad., Munich, Germany; right-handed; two-handed backhand; turned professional 2003; winner, Dutch Open, Amersfoort 2006, Open de Moselle, Metz 2006, Next Generation Adelaide Int., Asscn of Tennis Professionals (ATP) Tour, Adelaide 2007, ATP Masters Series, Miami 2007, Estoril Open 2007, Masters Series Rogers Cup, Montreal 2007, 2011, BA-CA Tennis Trophy, Vienna 2007, Masters Series Pacific Life Open, Indian Wells, Calif. 2008, BNP Paribas Open, Indian Wells 2011, 2014, Masters Series singles title, Internazionali d'Italia, Rome 2008, Tennis Masters Cup, Shanghai 2008, ATP World Tour Masters 1000 Paris 2009, 2013, Basel 2009, Beijing 2009, 2010, Dubai 2009, 2011, 2013, Belgrade 2009, 2010, 2011, ATP World Tour Masters 1000, Indian Wells 2011, ATP World Tour Masters 1000, Miami 2011, 2012, 2014, ATP World Tour Masters 1000, Madrid 2011, ATP World Tour Masters 1000, Rome 2011, Shanghai Masters 2012, 2013, ATP World Tour Finals, London 2012, 2013, Monte Carlo Masters 2013, China Open 2013; Grand Slam results: winner, Australian Open 2008, 2011, 2012, 2013, Wimbledon 2011, US Open 2011, finalist, US Open 2007, 2010, 2012, 2013, French Open 2012, semifinalist, French Open 2007, 2008, 2011, 2013, Wimbledon 2007, 2010, 2012; bronze medal, Olympic Games, Beijing 2008; led Serbia to win the Davis Cup 2010; runner-up, Internazionali d'Italia, Rome 2012, French Open 2012; f. Novak Djokovic Foundation (previously Novak Fund) 2007; coached by Boris Becker (Head Coach) (along with Marian Vajda, Miljan Amanovic and Gebhard Phil-Gritsch) 2014; Order of Republika Srpska, Order of St Sava of I Class, Patriarch Irinej of Serbia 2011, Order of the Karađorđe's Star (First Degree) 2012; ATP Most Improved Player of the Year 2006, 2007, The Best Sportperson of Serbia Award 2007, 2010, DSL Sport Golden Badge 2007, 2010, 2011, Award for The Best Sportsman, Olympic Cttee of Serbia, Serbian Oscar Of Popularity Sportsman of the Year 2009, 2010, BBC Overseas Sports Personality of the Year 2011, ITF World Champion 2011, 2012, Golden Bagel Award 2011, US Sports Acad. Male Athlete of the Year 2011, GQ ACE of the Year 2011, Laureus World Sportsman of the Year 2012, Best Male Tennis Player ESPY Award 2012, US Open Series Champion 2012, Arthur Ashe Humanitarian of the Year 2012, Pride of the Nation Award, Serbia Tennis Fed. 2012, The Centrepoint GB Youth Inspiration Award from HRH Prince William, Duke of Cambridge, Vermillion Medal for Physical Educ. and Sports from Albert II, Prince of Monaco 2012. *Leisure interests:* golf, Internet, music, movies. *E-mail:* contact@novak-djokovic.com. *Website:* novakdjokovic.com.

DJOTODIA, Michel Am Nondroko; Central African Republic politician, fmr rebel leader and fmr head of state; b. 1949, Vakaga, Oubangui-Chari (now part of Central African Repub.); m. 1st; two d.; m. 2nd; ed studied in USSR; fmr Consul, Nyala, Sudan; fmr Pres. Union of Democratic Forces for Unity and Patriotic Action Group for the Liberation of the Central African Repub.; lived in exile in Cotonou, Benin; imprisoned 2006–08; leader of Séléka rebel coalition during Dec. 2012 rebellion; First Deputy Prime Minister and Minister of Nat. Defence, Restructuring of the Armed Forces, War Veterans and War Victims Feb.–March 2013; Pres. (self-declared, 24 March 2013, following overthrow of François Bozizé, confirmed by Nat. Transitional Council 13 April, re-designated Interim Pres. 18 July 2013, sworn in 18 Aug. 2013) and Minister of Defence 2013–14.

DJOUDI, Karim, BSc, MSc; Algerian banker and government official; b. 13 July 1958, Montpellier, France; ed Louis Pasteur Univ., Strasbourg and Univ. of Paris, Sorbonne, France; joined Central Bank of Algeria 1988, Central Dir 1990; Dir-Gen.

of the Treasury, Ministry of Finance 1999–2003; Minister Del. responsible for Promotion of Investment 2003–05, responsible for Financial Reform 2005–07; Minister of Finance 2007–14. *Address:* c/o Ministry of Finance, Immeuble Maurétania, place du Pérou, Algiers, Algeria.

DJUHAR, Sutanto; Indonesian (b. Chinese) business executive; b. 1928, Fujian Prov., People's Repub. of China; m.; five c.; co-f. Salim Group; f. PT Bogasari Flour Mills 1971, P.T. Indocement (cement mfg co.) 1985, numerous other cos in real estate sector; Commr PT Kartika Chandra; Chair. China Pacific Group; Dir First Pacific Co. Ltd 1981–2010, TPV Technology Ltd –2004, Pacific Industries and Devt Ltd; Pres. Lin's Group of Indonesia (jt venture co., Fuzhou, People's Repub. of China). *Address:* PT Bogasari Flour Mills, Jalan Raya Cilincing No.1, Tanjung Priok, Kunci Biru Building, Jakarta 14110, Indonesia (office).

DLAMINI, Absalom Themba; Swazi politician and business executive; *Managing Director, Tibiyo TakaNgwane;* served in various positions with Central Bank of Swaziland, Swazi National Provident Fund, Swaziland Industrial Development Co.; Prime Minister of Swaziland 2003–08; Chair. Royal Swaziland Sugar Corpn; Man. Dir Tibiyo TakaNgwane (co. owned by royal family); mem. Bd of Dirs Ubombo Sugar Co., Managa Sugar Packers, Royal Villas. *Address:* Office of the Chairman, Royal Swaziland Sugar Corporation, Simunye Sugar Estate, POB 1, Simunye L301, Swaziland. *Telephone:* 23134000. *Fax:* 23838171. *E-mail:* info@rssc.co.sz. *Website:* www.rssc.co.sz.

DLAMINI, Barnabas Sibusiso, BSc, MBA; Swazi politician and fmr chartered accountant; *Prime Minister;* b. 15 May 1942; ed Univ. of Wisconsin, Univ. of South Africa, New York Univ.; began career as chemist with Swaziland Iron Ore Devt Co. 1969–77; Accountant, Coopers & Lybrand Chartered Accountants Swaziland 1978–81, Partner 1983–84; Senator, Parl. of Swaziland 1978–83; Minister of Finance 1984–93; Exec. Dir IMF 1994–96; Prime Minister of Swaziland 1996–2003, 2008–; mem. King Mswati III's Advisory Council 2003–08; Hon. Life mem., Swaziland Inst. of Accountants 2007; Hon. LLD (Univ. of Swaziland) 1992; Chief Counsellor, Order of King Sobhuza II 1989, Brilliant Star with Cordon (Taiwan) 1989, mem., Order of the Royal Family, Swaziland 2003. *Address:* Office of the Prime Minister, Cabinet Offices, Hospital Hill, POB 395, Swazi Plaza, Mbabane, Swaziland (office). *Telephone:* 4042251 (office). *Fax:* 4043943 (office). *Website:* www.gov.sz (office).

DLAMINI, Lutfo Ephraim; Swazi politician; b. 7 July 1960; m. Thelma Ncane Smith-Dlamini; four c.; Minister of Enterprise and Employment 1998–2008, of Foreign Affairs 2008–11, of Labour and Social Security 2011–13; Chair. World Cup Facilitation Cttee. *Address:* c/o Ministry of Labour and Social Security, Mbabane, Swaziland (office).

DLAMINI, Mabili David, BA; Swazi politician and diplomatist; b. 10 April 1957, Mankayane; m.; three s.; ed Univ. of Botswana and Swaziland; fmr Amb. to Malaysia and Singapore; Minister of Foreign Affairs and Trade 2003–06, of Housing and Urban Devt 2006; Senator 2003–08. *Leisure interests:* golf, soccer. *Address:* c/o Senate, Mbabane, Swaziland.

DLAMINI, Martin Gobizandla; Swazi economist and fmr central banker; *Minister of Finance;* Man. Ed. Times of Swaziland group of newspapers –2009; Dir Smart Partnership Secretariat (based in Office of the Prime Minister) 2009–12; apptd Gov. Central Bank of Swaziland; Minister of Finance 2013–; apptd to Senate 2013. *Address:* Ministry of Finance, Mhlambanyatsi Road, POB 443, Mbabane, Swaziland (office). *Telephone:* 24048148 (office). *Fax:* 24043187 (office). *E-mail:* ps@finance.gov.sz (office). *Website:* www.gov.sz (office).

DLAMINI, Moses Mathendele; Swazi politician and diplomatist; fmr Amb. to Taiwan; fmr Pres. of the Senate; fmr Chair. Parl. Del. to UN; Minister of Foreign Affairs and Trade 2006–08; mem. Advisory Council (Liqoqo) to King Mswati III 2009–11; Order of Brilliant Star with Grand Cordon (Taiwan). *Address:* c/o Ministry of Foreign Affairs and Trade, POB 518, Mbabane, Swaziland.

DLAMINI, Obed Mfanyana; Swazi politician; *President, Ngwane National Liberatory Congress;* b. 4 April 1937, Mhlosheni Area, Shiselweni Dist; ed Swaziland Nat. High School, UNISA; teacher and Boarding Master, Manzini Nazarene High School 1961–64; cost clerk, later Asst Personnel Officer, Roberts Construction (Swaziland) (Pty) Ltd 1964–66; clerk, Standard Chartered Bank of Swaziland 1966, Asst Man. Admin. –1981; fmr Training and Ind. Relations Man. Swaziland Fruit Canners (Pty) Ltd; fmr Gen. Sec. Swaziland Fed. of Trade Unions, mem. Labour Advisory Bd, Training and Localization Council, Wages Advisory Bd, Man. Training Council, Regional Educ. Advisory Bd, Workers' Educ. Group; Prime Minister of Swaziland 1989–93; Senator 1993–; Pres. Ngwane Nat. Liberatory Congress (CNNLC); Chair. Swazi Democratic Alliance 1999–. *Leisure interests:* soccer, wrestling, tug-of-war, jazz, music. *Address:* Ngwane National Liberatory Congress, Ilanga Centre, Martin St, Manzini (office); The Senate, Mbabane, Swaziland. *Telephone:* 5053935 (office).

DLAMINI, Sotsha; Swazi politician; b. 1940; fmr Asst Police Commr –1984; Prime Minister of Swaziland 1986–89. *Address:* c/o Office of the Prime Minister, Mbabane, Swaziland.

DLAMINI-ZUMA, Nkosazana Clarice, BSc, MB ChB; South African politician, medical doctor and international organization official; *Chairperson, African Union Commission;* b. 27 Jan. 1949, Pietermaritzburg; d. of Willibrod Gweva Dlamini and Rose Dlamini; m. Jacob Zuma (divorced); four c.; ed Amanzintoti Training Coll., Univ. of Zululand, Univ. of Natal, Univs of Bristol and Liverpool, UK; Research Technician Medical School, Univ. of Natal 1972; Vice-Pres. South African Students Org. 1975–76; Chair. African Nat. Congress (ANC) Youth Section, Great Britain 1977–78; House Officer Frenchay Hosp., Bristol, England 1978–79; House Officer Canadian Red Cross Memorial Hosp., Berks., England 1979–80; Medical Officer (Pediatrics) Mbabane Govt Hosp., Swaziland 1980–85; Pediatric attachment Wittington Hosp. 1987–89; Vice-Chair. Regional Political Cttee of ANC Great Britain 1978–88, Chair. 1988–89; ANC Health Dept Lusaka, Zambia 1989–90; Research Scientist Medical Research Council, Durban 1991–94; Minister of Health 1994–99, of Foreign Affairs 1999–2009, of Home Affairs 2009–12; Chair. African Union Comm. 2012–; Dir Health Refugee Trust, Health and Devt Org., England 1988–90; Chair. S Natal Region Health Cttee of ANC 1990–92; Chair. S Natal Region ANC Women's League 1991–93; mem. ANC Nat. Exec. Cttee 1994–; apptd

Pres. World Conf. Against Racism 2001; mem. Exec. Cttee S Natal Region of ANC 1990–93; mem. Steering Cttee Nat. AIDS Co-ordinating Cttee 1992–; Bd mem. Centre for Social Devt Studies Univ. of Natal, Durban 1992–; Trustee, Health Systems Trust 1992–; Chancellor ML Sultan Technikon 1996; Hon. Prof., Belarusian State Univ.; Maitre de L'Ordre Nat. Republic of Mali 2002, Nat. Order of Luthuli in Gold Republic of South Africa 2013; Dr hc (Univ. of Natal) 1995, (Univ. of Bristol) 1996, (Univ. of Transkei) 1997, (Univ. of Rome) 2013; Tobacco Free World Award, WHO 1999, Women Who Make a Difference Award, Women In Film 2002, States Women of the Year Award, BBQ 2004, Int. Renaissance Women of the Year Award 2012, UN S-S Award for Global Leadership 2012, Chair.'s Award, Black Business Exec. Circle 2013, UN Women African Women's Pioneers Award 2013, Africa America Inst. Institutional Legacy Award 2013. *Telephone:* (11) 5182804/5 (office); (11) 5182919/2914 (office); (11) 5517700 (office). *E-mail:* kotannoul@africa-union.org (office); chairperson@africa-union.org (office). *Address:* African Union Commission, PO Box 3243, Roosvelt Street (Old Airport Area), W21K19 Addis Ababa, Ethiopia (office); 602 Stretten Bay, St Andrews Street, Durban 4001, South Africa (home). *Fax:* (11) 5517844 (office). *Website:* www .au.int (office).

DLOUHÝ, Vladimír, CSc, MBA; Czech economist and politician; b. 31 July 1953, Prague; m. 1st (divorced 1999); m. 2nd Eliška Břízoá 2001; one s. one d.; ed Prague School of Econs, Charles Univ., Prague and Catholic Univ., Louvain; fmr teacher, Prague School of Econs; researcher, Inst. of Econ. Forecasting, Czechoslovak Acad. of Sciences 1983–89, latterly Deputy Dir; Deputy Prime Minister and Chair. State Planning Comm. 1989–90; Minister of the Economy 1990–92; Minister of Trade and Industry of Czech Repub. 1992–97; Int. Advisor for Cen. and Eastern Europe, Goldman Sachs 1997–; Adviser to Exec. Man., ABB 1997–; currently teaches macroeconomics at Charles Univ., Prague; mem. Civic Democratic Alliance 1991–98, Vice-Pres. March–Oct. 1992, Deputy Chair. 1993–97; mem. State Defence Council 1993; Chair. Council of Customs Union 1994–97, Bd of Supervisors Stock Co. Unipetrol 1996–97; Deputy Chair. Bd of Supervisors, Volkswagen-Skoda Group, Mladá Boleslav 1994–95; mem. Parl. 1996–98; mem. Bd of Overseers, Illinois Inst. of Tech., Chicago; mem. Exec. Cttee Trilateral Comm.; mem. Bd of Supervisors, Foundation Bohemiae 1992–2001; mem. Bd of Dirs Cofinec 1997–2000; Grand-Croix, Ordre de Léopold II (Belgium). *Publications:* Ekonometrický model čs. obchodní bilance 1985, Models of Disequilibrium and Shortage in Centrally Planned Economies 1989; articles in Czechoslovak and int. econ. journals. *Leisure interest:* music. *Address:* c/o Goldman Sachs International, Peterborough Court, 133 Fleet St, London, EC4A 2BB, England; Pachtův palác, Anenské náměstí 4, 110 00 Prague 1, Czech Republic. *Telephone:* (2) 2163-5351. *Fax:* (2) 2163-5350.

DMITRIEV, Alexander Sergeevich; Russian conductor; b. 19 Jan. 1935, Leningrad; m.; one s.; ed Leningrad Choir School, Leningrad State Conservatory, Vienna Akad. für Musik und darstellende Kunst; Conductor Karelian Radio and TV Symphony Orchestra 1961, Prin. Conductor 1962–71; Prin. Conductor Maly Opera and Ballet Theatre, Leningrad (now St Petersburg) 1971–77, and Music Dir Symphony Orchestra of St Petersburg Philharmonia 1977–; Prin. Conductor Stavanger Symphony Orchestra (Norway) 1990–98; Merited Worker of Arts of Karelian ASSR 1967, People's Artist of Russia 1976, USSR People's Artist; Prize 2nd USSR Competition for Conductors 1966. *Recordings include:* Handel's Messiah, Haydn's Creation, Schubert's Symphony Nos. 1–9, Tchaikovsky's Symphonies 4, 5, 6, Rachmaninov's Symphony No. 2, Debussy's 3 Nocturnes, Ravel's Valses nobles et sentimentales, Ma Mère l'Oye, Saeverud's Peer Gynt, Symphony dolorosa, Balakirev's Piano Concerto, Medtner's Piano Concerto No. 1, Rachmaninov's Piano Concerto No. 3, Britten's Violin concerto, Sibelius Violin Concerto, Shostakovich and Tchaikovsky Violin Concertos, Shostakovich Symphony No. 7, Scriabin Symphony No. 3. *Address:* Symphony Orchestra, Rom Petersburg Philharmonic Society, Mikhailovskaya str. 2, St Petersburg 091011, Russia (office). *Telephone:* (812) 714-64-17 (home). *Fax:* (812) 571-21-26 (office). *E-mail:* dmitriev@mail.spbnit.ru (home). *Website:* www.philharmonia.spb.ru (office).

DMITRIYEVSKY, Anatoly Nikolayevich; Russian engineer; *Director, Oil and Gas Research Institute, Russian Academy of Sciences;* b. 6 May 1937; m.; one s. one d.; ed Gubkin Moscow Inst. of Oil and Gas; Sr teacher, Gubkin Moscow Univ. of Oil and Gas; Pro-rector and Chair. Algerian Nat. Inst. of Oil, Gas and Chem.; Dir Oil and Gas Research Inst., Russian Acad. of Sciences 1987–; Pres. Union of Scientific and Eng Orgs of Russia; mem. of Bd Int. Gas Union; mem. Russian Acad. of Sciences 1991; USSR State Prize 1986, State Prize of Russia 1998. *Publications include:* Lithological System and Genetic Analysis of Oil and Gas Sedimentary Basins 1982, Fundamental Basis of Oil and Gas Geology 1991. *Leisure interests:* tennis, mountain skiing, photography. *Address:* Oil and Gas Research Institute RAS, 119333 Moscow, 3 ul. Gubkina, Russia (office). *Telephone:* (495) 135-73-71 (office). *Fax:* (495) 135-54-65 (office). *E-mail:* a.dmitrievsky@ogri.ru (office).

DO, Muoi; Vietnamese politician; b. 2 Feb. 1917, Thanh Tri, Hanoi; joined movt against French colonial rule 1936; imprisoned by French; escaped in 1945 and took part in anti-Japanese uprising in Ha Dong Prov.; political and mil. leader in provs of Red River delta during struggle against French 1951–54; Alt. mem. Cen. Cttee, CP of Viet Nam 1955–60, mem. 1960–, Alt. mem. Political Bureau 1976–82, Sec. Gen. CP of Viet Nam 1991–97, Advisor to Party's Cen. Cttee 1997–2001; Deputy to Nat. Ass. 2nd, 4th, 5th, 6th, 7th and 8th Legislatures; Minister of Commerce 1969; Deputy Prime Minister and Minister of Building 1976–87; Vice-Chair. Council of Ministers in charge of Economy 1987–; Chair. Council of Ministers (Prime Minister) 1988–91; Vice-Chair. Nat. Defence Council 1989; Order of the October Revolution (USSR) 1987 and several Vietnamese decorations. *Address:* Communist Party of Viet Nam, 1 Hoang Van Thu, Hanoi, Viet Nam.

DO NASCIMENTO, Edson Arantes (see PELÉ).

DO SACRAMENTO E SOUSA, Lt-Col. Óscar Aguiar; São Tomé and Príncipe politician; *Minister of Defence and Interior; fmr* Minister of Agriculture; Vice-Pres. Chamber of Commerce 2002; Minister of Defence 2003–08, 2012–; Minister of Foreign Affairs 2004, 2006; Minister of Interior 2012–. *Address:* Ministry of Defence and Public Security, Avenue 12 de Julho, CP 427, São Tomé, São Tomé and Príncipe (office). *Telephone:* 222041. *E-mail:* midefesa@cstome.net.

DOBBINS, James Francis, BA; American diplomatist; *Special Representative for Afghanistan and Pakistan;* b. 31 May 1942, New York; m. Toril Kleivdal; two s.; ed Georgetown Univ. School of Foreign Service; US naval officer; mem. US Mission to OECD 1967–68, US Del. to Viet Nam Peace Talks 1968; Political Officer, US Embassy, Paris 1969; mem. Policy Planning Staff, State Dept, Washington, DC 1969–71, Deputy Asst Sec. 1982–85, Prin. Deputy Asst Sec. 1989–90, Acting Asst Sec. for European and Canadian Affairs 1991, Special Asst to Pres., Nat. Security Council Staff 1996–99, Special Adviser to Pres. for Kosovo and Dayton Implementation 1999–2000, Asst Sec. of State for European Affairs 2000–01; mem. US Mission to UN 1973–75, Political-Mil. Officer, US Embassy, London 1978–81; Deputy Chief of Mission, Bonn, FRG 1985–89; Amb. to the EC 1991–93; Special Envoy to Afghanistan 2001–03; Special Rep. for Afghanistan and Pakistan 2013–; Sr Fellow, RAND Corpn 1993, Dir Int. Security and Defense Policy Center 2003–; mem. Council on Foreign Relations 1995–96; two Superior Honor Awards, three Presidential Awards, six Sr Performance Awards, Dept of the Army Decoration for Dist Civilian Service, Armed Forces Expeditionary Medal, Nat. Defense Service Medal, Expeditionary Medal, Repub. of Viet Nam. *Publications include:* America's Role in Nation-Building: From Germany to Iraq (co-author) 2003, The UN's Role in Nation-Building: From the Congo to Iraq (co-author) 2005, The Beginner's Guide to Nation-Building (co-author) 2007, Europe's Role in Nation-Building: From the Balkans to the Congo (co-author) 2008, After the War: Nation-Building from FDR to George W. Bush (co-author) 2008, After the Taliban: Nation-Building in Afghanistan 2008, Occupying Iraq: A History of the Coalition Provisional Authority (co-author) 2009. *Address:* Department of State, 2201 C Street, NW, Washington, DC 20520 (office); International Security and Defense Policy Center, RAND Corporation, 1200 South Hayes Street, Arlington, VA 22202, USA (office). *Telephone:* (202) 647-4000 (Washington) (office); (703) 413-1100 (Arlington) (office). *Fax:* (202) 647-6738 (Washington) (office); (703) 414-4732 (Arlington) (office). *E-mail:* James_Dobbins@rand.org (office). *Website:* www.state.gov (office); www.rand.org (office).

DOBBS, Baron (Life Peer), cr. 2010, of Wylye in the County of Wiltshire; **Michael John Dobbs,** PhD, MALD, MA; British author, politician and broadcaster; b. Nov. 1948, Herts., England; m. Rachel Dobbs; four s.; ed Christ Church, Oxford and Fletcher School of Law and Diplomacy, USA; UK Govt Special Adviser 1981–87; Chief of Staff, UK Conservative Party 1986–87, Jt Deputy Chair. 1994–95; Deputy Chair. Saatchi & Saatchi 1983–91; BBC TV and radio presenter 1999–2009; mem. (Conservative) House of Lords 2010–. *Play:* The Turning Point 2009. *Television includes:* House of Cards (UK) 1990, House of Cards (USA) 2013. *Publications include:* House of Cards 1989, Wall Games 1990, Last Man to Die 1991, To Play the King 1992, The Touch of Innocents 1994, The Final Cut 1995, Goodfellowe MP 1997, The Buddha of Brewer Street 1998, Whispers of Betrayal 2000, Winston's War 2002, Never Surrender 2003, Churchill's Hour 2004, Churchill's Triumph 2005, First Lady 2006, The Lords' Day 2007, The Edge of Madness 2008, The Reluctant Hero 2010, A Sentimental Traitor 2011, A Ghost at the Door 2013. *Address:* House of Lords, Westminster, London, SW1A 0PW (office); Newton House, Wylye, Wilts. BA12 0QS, England (home). *E-mail:* michael@michaeldobbs .com (office); dobbsm@parliament.uk (office). *Website:* www.michaeldobbs.com.

DOBESCH, Gerhard, DPhil; Austrian historian and academic; *Professor of Roman History, Archaeology and Epigraphy, University of Vienna;* b. 15 Sept. 1939, Vienna; s. of Dr Carl Dobesch and Gustave Dobesch; ed Univ. of Vienna; Lecturer in Ancient History 1967–73; Prof. of Greek and Roman History, Univ. of Graz 1973–76; Prof. of Roman History, Archaeology and Epigraphy, Univ. of Vienna 1976–; Corresp. mem. Austrian Archaeological Inst. 1972–98 (mem. 1998–), Austrian Acad. of Sciences 1980–84 (mem. 1984–). *Publications:* Caesars Apotheose zu Lebzeiten und sein Ringen um den Königstitel 1966, Der Panhellen: Gedanke und der Philippos des Isokrates 1968, Wurde Caesar zu Lebzeiten in Rom als Staatsgott anerkannt? 1971, Nochmals zur Datierung des grossen Senatskonsultes 1971, Nikolaos von Damaskus und die Selbstbiographie des Augustus 1978, Die Kelten in Österreich nach den ältest 1980, Die Kimbern in den Ostalpen und die Schlacht bei Noreia 1982, Zu Caesars Sitzenbleiben vor dem Senat 1988, Zur Einwanderung die Kelten in Oberitalien 1989, Caesar als Ethnograph 1989, Zu zwei Daten d. Gesch. Galliens 1989, Europa in d. Reichskonzeption 1989, Autonomie des Menschen und Werthaftigkeit in der Antike 1990, Die Kelten als Nachbarn der Etrusker 1992, J. K. Newman u. Catull 1992, 100 Jahre Kleinasiat. Komm. 1993, Principis dignationem 1993; Vom äusseren Proletariat zum Kulturträger 1994, Phokion und der Korinthische Bund 1994, Aus der Vor-und Nachgeschichte der Markomannenkriege 1994, Das europäische 'Barbaricum' und die Zone der Mediterrankultur 1995, Der Ostalpenraum als Kultur- und Machtgrundlage in keltischer und römischer Zeit 1996, Würdigung Fritz Schachermeyr 1996, Die römische Kaiserzeit–eine Fortsetzung des Hellenismus? 1996; Zu Virunum als Namen der Stadt auf dem Magdalensberg 1997, Ende und Metamorphose des Etruskertums 1998, Der Weltreichsgedanke bei Caesar 1998, Mitherausgeber: Adolf Wilhelm, Kleine Schriften: Abt. II, Teil III 2000 Teil IV 2002, Teil V 2003, Einige merkwürdige Überlieferungen über Caesar 2000, Urgeschichtliches Eisen in der Sicht des Althistorikers 2000, Caesars monarchische Ideologie 2000, Ausgewählte Schriften (two vols) 2001, Caesars Volcae Tectosages in Mitteleuropa 2001, Caesar, Commentarii über den gallischen Krieg, Buch 1, Kapitel 1: eine Sensation, Wiener Humanistische Blätter 42 2001, Caesars Urteil über Ciceros Bedeutung – Gedanken über Cic. Brut. 253 und Plin. n. h., 117 2003, Caesar und der Hellenismus 2004, Zentrum, Peripherie und 'Barbaren' in der Urgeschichte und der Alten Geschichte 2004, Einige Beobachtungen zu Politik und Tod des Haeduers Diviciacus und seines Bruders Dumnorix 2005, Wassergrenzen oder Wasserwege aus urgeschichtlicher und römischer Sicht 2005, Das 'regnum Noricum' und die römische Okkupation 2006, Arverner aus Troja (Lucan b. c. 1, 427–428)? Kleine Überlegungen zur gallo-römischen Kultur 2006, Varro Atacinus und sein 'Bellum Sequanicum' 2006, Außenpolitische Strukturen der antiken Keltenstämme: Ein Überblick 2007, Die Römer in Niederösterreich 2008, Zwei Fragmente des Ephoros – Zwei Gedanken zur keltischen Religion 2007, Augustus, Tiberius, Caligula und Britannien 2007, Caesar as Ethnograph 2007, Politik zwischen Marbod und Rom 2009, Die Arverner in den Commentarii Caesars 2010, Zweierlei ferrum Noricum? 2011; numerous specialist articles. *Leisure interests:* literature, art history. *Address:* Universität Wien, Institut für Alte Geschichte, Universitätsring 1, 1010 Vienna (office); Spitalgasse 29/10, 1090 Vienna, Austria (home). *Telephone:* 4277-40520 (office); 40-9522 (home). *Fax:*

4277-9405 (office). *E-mail:* gerhard.dobesch@univie.ac.at (office); gerhard .dobesch@oeaw.ac.at (office).

DOBRETSOV, Nikolai Leontyevich, DGeol; Russian geologist; *Chief Research Scientist, Trofimuk Institute of Petroleum Geology and Geophysics, Siberia Branch, Russian Academy of Sciences;* b. 15 Jan. 1936, Leningrad (now St Petersburg); m.; five c.; ed Leningrad Inst. of Mines; chief of Altai Mining expedition, Jr then Sr Researcher; Head of Lab. Inst. of Geology and Geophysics, Siberian br. of USSR (now Russian) Acad. of Sciences in Novosibirsk; Head of Lab. Inst. of Tectonics and Geophysics, USSR Acad. of Sciences in Khabarovsk; Dir Buryat Inst. of Geology, Chair. Presidium of Buryat Research Cen. Siberian br. of USSR Acad. of Sciences, Dir-Gen. United Inst. of Geology, Geophysics and Mineralogy, Science Advisor, Inst. of Geology and Mineralogy, Siberian br. of Russian Acad. of Sciences (RAS) –2011, Chief Research Scientist, Trofimuk Inst. of Petroleum Geology and Geophysics, Siberian br. of RAS 2011–; Corresp. mem. USSR (now Russian) Acad. of Sciences 1984, mem. 1987, mem. Presidium 1991–, Pres. of Siberian br. 1997–2008, Vice-Pres. RAS; Pres. Asscn of Acads of Sciences in Asia (AASA) 2008–11; Order of Friendship 2006; Dr hc (St Petersburg Mining Technical Univ.) 2000; Labourer of the Red Banner 1986, State Prize of the Russian Fed. 1997, Demidov Prize 1999, A.N. Kossygin Prize 2003, Medal of Mongolian Acad. of Science 2006, Lavrentiev Prize 2007, Order of Merit for Fath 2007. *Publications include:* Introduction to Global Petrology 1980, Global Petrological Processes 1981, Deep-level Geodynamics 1994; papers on tectonics and petrography. *Leisure interests:* books, fishing. *Address:* Trofimuk Institute of Petroleum Geology and Geophysics, Siberian Branch of Russian Academy of Sciences, 630090 Novosibirsk, Prospect Acad. Koptyuga 3, Russia (office). *Telephone:* (383) 330-89-81 (office). *Fax:* (383) 333-23-01 (office). *E-mail:* dobr@ igm.nsc.ru (office). *Website:* www.sbras.ru (office); www.ipgg.nsc.ru (office).

DOBRIANSKY, Paula J., MA, PhD, BSFS; American diplomatist; *Senior International Affairs and Trade Advisor, Baker Hostetler;* b. 14 Sept. 1955, Alexandria, Va; ed Harvard Univ., Georgetown Univ. School of Foreign Service; early career positions include Dir European and Soviet Affairs, Nat. Security Council, The White House; Deputy Asst Sec. of State, Human Rights and Humanitarian Affairs; Assoc. Dir Policy and Programs, US Information Agency; Co-Chair Int. TV Council, Corpn for Public Broadcasting Sr Int. Affairs and Trade Advisor, Hunton and Williams; Sr Vice-Pres. and Dir, George F. Kennan Sr Fellow for Russian and Eurasian Studies, Washington Office, Council of Foreign Relations; Under-Sec. for Democracy and Global Affairs 2001–09, apptd Special Envoy for NI 2007; currently Sr Int. Affairs and Trade Advisor, Baker Hostetler; mem. Bd Western NIS Enterprise Fund, Nat. Endowment for Democracy (NED) (also Vice-Chair.), Freedom House, American Council of Young Political Leaders, ABA Cen. and E European Law Initiative, US Advisory Comm. on Public Diplomacy; Host, Freedom's Challenge (three years); Sr Fellow, John F. Kennedy Belfer Center for Science and Int. Affairs, Harvard Univ.; Co-host Worldwise (Nat. Empowerment TV); Ford and Rotary Foundation Fellow; Poland's Highest Medal of Merit, Grand Cross, Commdr of Order of Lithuanian Grand Duke Gediminas; Dr hc (Fairleigh Dickinson Univ., Flagler Coll., Roger Williams Univ.); State Dept Superior Honor Award, Dialogue on Diversity's Int. Award 2001, NED Service Medal, Georgetown Univ. Annual Alumni Achievement Award. *Address:* Baker Hostetler, Washington Square, Suite 1100, 1050 Connecticut Avenue NW, Washington, DC 20036-5304, USA (office). *Telephone:* (202) 861-1500 (office). *Fax:* (202) 861-1783 (office). *Website:* www.bakerlaw.com (office).

DOBRIȚOIU, Lt-Gen. (retd) Corneliu; Romanian army officer and politician; b. 18 Sept. 1955, Bucharest; ed Balcescu Army Acad., Sibiu, Acad. of Mil. Studies, Bucharest, NATO Coll., Rome, Italy, Naval Postgraduate School, Monterey, USA; officer in 1st Mechanized Regt, Bucharest platoon 1977–78, infantry co. commdr 1978–80, Deputy Chief of Research Bureau 1980–83; Bn Commdr, Inst. of Mil. Medicine, Bucharest 1983–87; apptd expert on human resource mobilization within a Territorial Command of Bucharest 1987; transferred to 3rd Mechanized Regt, Bucharest 1991; Head of Research Office, 2nd Mechanized Regt 1993; Deputy Chief of Bureau Research, 57th Tank Div., Bucharest 1993–94; expert on political-military analysis, Dept of Political-Mil. Analysis and International Mil. Relations, Ministry of Defence 1994–95; participated in defence training courses organized by Centre for European Security Studies, George C. Marshall Coll. of Strategic Studies and Defence Econs 1995; Chief of Mil. Liaison Team in Romanian-American cooperation programme; Head of International Office Contact Point, International Mil. Relations Directorate, Ministry of Defence 1995–96, Head of Dept of Evaluation International Mil. Relations, Directorate of International Mil. Relations 1996–98; Officer of the Directorate Staff, Regional Security Cooperation and the International Mil. Staff, NATO HQ, Brussels 1998–2000; attained rank of Brig. Gen. (one star) 2002, Maj. Gen. (two stars) 2004; Head of Euro-Atlantic Integration and International Relations, Ministry of Nat. Defence 2000–04, Deputy State Sec., Ministry of Nat. Defence and Head of Euro-Atlantic Integration Dept and Defence Policy 2004–06; attained rank of Lt-Gen. 2006 (retd); Minister of Nat. Defence Sept.–Oct. 2006, May–Dec. 2012; mem. Partidul Național Liberal (PNL) 2006–; Kt, Nat. Order 'Star of Romania' 2000. *Address:* Partidul Național Liberal (PNL), 011866 Bucharest, Bd. Aviatorilor 86, Sector 1, Romania (office). *Telephone:* (21) 2310795 (office). *Fax:* (21) 2310796 (office). *E-mail:* dre@pnl.ro (office). *Website:* www.pnl.ro (office).

DOBRODEYEV, Oleg Borisovich, CandHistSc; Russian television producer; *Chairman, All-Russian State Television-Radio Company (VGTRK);* b. 28 Nov. 1959, Moscow; m.; one s.; ed Moscow State Univ.; mem. of staff Inst. of USA and Canada 1982–83; Ed. TV programme Vremya, USSR Cen. TV, later Deputy Ed.-in-Chief 1983–90; Ed.-in-Chief news programme Vesti; Ed.-in-Chief Information TV Agency (ITA) 1990–91, Ostankino Co. 1991–93; Ed.-in-Chief Information Service, NTV Co., later Vice-Pres. 1993–2000, Dir-Gen. NTV Co. 1997–2000; Chair. All-Russian State TV-Radio Co. (VGTRK) 2000–; Order of Honour 1999. *Leisure interest:* reading people's memoirs. *Address:* All-Russian State TV-Radio Co., Yamskogo Polya 5th str. 19/21, 125040 Moscow, Russia (office). *Telephone:* (495) 234-8600 (office); (495) 214-4978 (office). *Fax:* (495) 214-2347 (office). *E-mail:* info@ rfn.ru (office); vgtrk2@space/ru (office). *Website:* www.vgtrk.com (office).

DOBRZAŃSKI, Stanisław; Polish business executive and government official; b. 22 March 1949, Hrubieszów; m.; two c.; ed Maria Skłodowska-Curie Univ., Lublin; Deputy Dir Polish Nat. Library, Warsaw 1982–85; Dept Dir Ministry of Culture

and Art; Dir Wschodni Bank Cukrownictwa; Under-Sec. of State, Office of the Council of Ministers 1993–96; Minister of Nat. Defence 1996–98; Pres. of Man. Bd Polskie Sieci Elektroenergetyczne SA (Polish Power Grid Co.) 2001–06; mem. Polskie Stronnictwo Ludowe (Polish People's Party). *Address:* c/o Polskie Stronnictwo Ludowe (Polish People's Party), 00-902 Warsaw, ul. Wiejska 4/6/8, Poland.

DOBSON, Christopher (Chris) Martin, BA, DPhil, FRS, FMedSci; British chemist, academic and college principal; *Master, St John's College, Cambridge;* b. 8 Oct. 1949; ed Keble Coll. and Merton Coll., Oxford; held research fellowships at Merton Coll. and Linacre Coll. before working at Harvard Univ., USA; returned to Oxford as Fellow of Lady Margaret Hall and Univ. Lecturer in Chem. 1980, later Reader, then Prof. in Chem.; John Humphrey Plummer Prof. of Chemical and Structural Biology, Univ. of Cambridge 2001–, Master of St John's Coll. 2007–; Presidential Visiting Scholar, Univ. of California, San Francisco 2001; Sammet Guest Prof., Johann Wolfgang Goethe Univ., Frankfurt, Germany 2007; mem. European Molecular Biology Org. 1999; Foreign Assoc., NAS 2013; Fellow, Int. Soc. of Magnetic Resonance 2008; Hon. mem. Nat. Magnetic Resonance Soc. of India 2004; Foreign Hon. mem. American Acad. of Arts and Sciences 2007; Hon. Fellow, Linacre Coll., Oxford 2008, Lady Margaret Hall, Oxford 2008, Merton Coll., 2009, Keble Coll., Oxford 2009, Chemical Council of India 2010; Hon. MD (Umeå Univ., Sweden) 2005, (Univ. of Florence, Italy) 2006; Dr hc (Univ. of Leuven, Belgium) 2001, (Univ. of Liège, Belgium) 2007; Hon. DSc (King's Coll. London) 2012; RSC Corday-Morgan Medal and Prize 1981, Howard Hughes Int. Research Scholar 1992, Brunauer Award, American Ceramic Soc. 1996, Dewey and Kelly Award, Univ. of Nebraska 1997, Nat. Lecturer, American Biophysical Soc. 1998, RSC Interdisciplinary Award 1999, Bijvoet Medal, Univ. of Utrecht, The Netherlands 2002, Silver Medal, Italian Soc. of Biochemistry 2002, Bakerian Lecturer, Royal Soc. 2003, Stein and Moore Award, The Protein Soc. 2003, Davy Medal, Royal Soc. 2005, Hans Neurath Award, The Protein Soc. 2006, Royal Medal, Royal Soc. 2009, RSC Khorana Award 2010. *Publications:* more than 550 papers in professional journals. *Address:* Department of Chemistry, University of Cambridge, Lensfield Road, Cambridge, CB2 1EW, England (office). *Telephone:* (1223) 763070 (office). *Fax:* (1223) 336362 (office). *E-mail:* cmd44@cam.ac.uk (office). *Website:* www.ch.cam.ac.uk (office).

DOBSON, Rt Hon. Frank (Gordon), PC, BSc (Econs); British politician; b. 15 March 1940; s. of the late James William Dobson and Irene Shortland Dobson; m. Janet Mary Alker 1967; two s. one d.; ed Archbishop Holgate Grammar School, York, LSE; admin. appointments with Cen. Electricity Generating Bd 1962–70, Electricity Council 1970–75; mem. Camden Borough Council 1971–76, Leader 1973–75; Asst Sec. Comm. for Local Admin. 1975–79; MP for Holborn and St Pancras South 1979–83, for Holborn and St Pancras 1983–; Opposition Spokesman on Educ. 1981–83, on Health 1983–87, on Energy 1989–92, on Employment 1992–93, on Transport and London 1993–94, on Environment and London 1994–97; Sec. of State for Health 1997–99; Labour candidate for Mayoralty of London 2000; Shadow Leader of the House of Commons 1987–89; Gov. LSE 1986–2003, Inst. of Child Health 1987–92; Gov. Royal Veterinary Coll. 2004–; mem. of Court, Univ. of York 2004–; mem. of Court, London School of Hygiene and Tropical Medicine 2009–. *Address:* House of Commons, London, SW1A 0AA (office); 22 Great Russell Mansions, Great Russell Street, London, WC1B 3BE, England (home). *Telephone:* (20) 7219-4452 (office); (20) 7242-5760 (home). *Fax:* (20) 7219-6956 (office).

DOBSON, Michael William Romsey, MA; British banking and finance executive; *CEO, Schroders plc;* b. 13 May 1952, London; s. of Sir Denis (William) Dobson; m. Frances de Salis 1998; two d.; ed Eton Coll., Trinity Coll. Cambridge; joined Morgan Grenfell 1973, with Morgan Grenfell New York 1978–80, Man. Dir 1984–85, Chief Exec. Morgan Grenfell Asset Management 1987–88, Deputy CEO Morgan Grenfell Group (now Deutsche Morgan Grenfell) 1988–89, CEO 1989–96; mem. Bd of Man. Dirs Deutsche Bank AG 1996–2000 (responsible for investment banking 1996–98, for asset man. 1998–2000), mem. Advisory Bd; f. Beaumont Capital Man. Ltd 2000 (acquired by Schroders PLC 2001); Dir (non-exec.) Schroders PLC April–Nov. 2001–, CEO 2001–. *Address:* Schroders plc, 31 Gresham Street, London, EC2V 7QA, England (office). *Telephone:* (20) 7658-6962 (office). *Fax:* (20) 7658-3476 (office). *E-mail:* michael.dobson@schroders.com (office). *Website:* www.schroders.com (office).

DOCHANASHVILI, Guram; Georgian writer and film industry executive; b. 1939, Tbilisi, Georgia; s. of Petre Dochanashvili and Gulnara Emukhvari; m.; one d.; ed Tbilisi State Univ.; worked in Dept of Archaeology, Inst. of History, Georgian Acad. of Sciences 1962–75; Head of Div. of Prose Mnatobi (magazine) 1975–85; Deputy Dir Gruzia Film Studio (now J.S.C Georgian Film) 1985–; Ivane Dzhavakhishvili Medal, Tbilisi State Univ. 1984, State Prize of Georgia 1994. *Publications include:* Besame 1989, Havaiuri valsi 1990. *Publications include:* There, Behind the Mountain 1966. *Address:* J.S.C Georgian Film, 10 A Akhmeteli ST, 0159 Tbilisi, Georgia (office). *Telephone:* (32) 43-30-30 (office). *Fax:* (32) 52-09-13 (office). *E-mail:* info@geofilm.ge (office). *Website:* www.geofilm.ge (office).

DOCHERTY, David, BA, PhD; British broadcasting executive and writer; *CEO, CSC Media Group;* b. 10 Dec. 1956, Scotland; s. of David Docherty and Anna Docherty; m. Kate Stuart-Smith 1992; two d.; ed Univ. of Strathclyde, London School of Econs; Research Fellow, Broadcasting Research Unit, London 1984–88; Dir of Research Broadcasting Standards Council 1988–89; Head of Broadcasting Analysis, BBC TV 1990–92, Head of TV Planning and Strategy, BBC Network TV 1992–96, Dir of Strategy and Channel Devt, BBC Broadcast 1996–97, Deputy Dir of TV BBC Broadcasting 1997, Dir New Services, BBC Bd of Man. 1999; Man. Dir of Broadband Content, Telewest Communications 2000–02; CEO iPublic div., YooMedia PLC's 2003–04; Group Chief Exec. YooMedia PLC 2004–05; CEO CSC Media Group 2005–; Chair. Living Health; Chair. Bd of Govs and Pro Vice-Chancellor, Univ. of Luton 2001–06; fmr mem. Bd BBC America UKTV; columnist, The Guardian; Hon. Fellow, Leeds Univ. *Publications:* The Last Picture Show?: Britain's Changing Film Audience 1987, Keeping Faith?: Channel 4 and Its Audience 1988, Running the Show: 21 Years of London Weekend Television 1990, Violence in Television Fiction 1991, The Spirit Death 2000, The Killing Jar 2002, The Fifth Season 2003, Fear Less 2005. *Leisure interest:* writing. *Address:* c/o Julian Friedmann, Blake Friedmann, 122 Arlington Road, London, NW1 7HP;

Serge Hill, Abbots Langley, Herts., WD5 0RY, England (home). *Telephone:* (20) 7284-0408. *Fax:* (20) 7284-0442. *E-mail:* info@blakefriedmann.co.uk.

DOCTOROW, Edgar Lawrence (E.L.), AB; American novelist, essayist, dramatist and academic; *Lewis and Loretta Gluckman Professor of American and English Letters, New York University;* b. 6 Jan. 1931, New York; s. of David Richard and Rose Doctorow (née Levine); m. Helen Esther Setzer 1954; one s. two d.; ed Kenyon Coll., Gambier, Ohio, Columbia Univ.; served with US army 1953–55; script reader, Columbia Pictures 1956–59; Ed. New American Library, New York 1960–64; Ed.-in-Chief Dial Press., New York 1964–69, Publr 1969; Writer-in-Residence, Univ. of Calif., Irvine 1969–70; mem. faculty, Sarah Lawrence Coll., Bronxville, NY 1971–78; Creative Writing Fellow, Yale School of Drama 1974–75; Creative Artists Program Service Fellow 1973–74; Visiting Sr Fellow, Council on Humanities, Princeton Univ. 1980–81; Adjunct Prof. of English, New York Univ. 1982–87, Lewis and Loretta Gluckman Prof. of American and English Letters 1987–; mem. Authors Guild, American PEN, Writers Guild of America East, Century Asscn, American Acad. of Arts and Letters, American Acad. of Arts and Sciences, American Philosophical Soc.; Guggenheim Fellow 1973; Hon. LHD (Kenyon Coll.) 1976, (Hobart Coll.) 1979, Hon. DLitt (William Smith Coll.) 1979, Hon. DHL (Brandeis Univ.) 1989; Arts and Letters Award (American Acad. and Nat. Inst. of Art) 1976, Nat. Book Critics Circle Award 1976, 1990, 2005, Guggenheim Fellow 1973, Nat. Book Award 1986, William Dean Howells Medal, American Acad. of Arts and Letters 1990, PEN/Faulkner Prize 1990, 2005, Nat. Humanities Medal 1998, Commonwealth Award 2000, PEN/Saul Bellow Award for Achievement in American Fiction 2012. *Publications:* Welcome to Hard Times 1960, Big as Life 1966, The Book of Daniel 1971, Ragtime 1975, Drinks before Dinner (play) 1978, Loon Lake 1980, Lives of the Poets: Six Stories and a Novella 1984, World's Fair 1985, Billy Bathgate 1989, Jack London, Hemingway and the Constitution: Selected Essays 1977–92 1993, The Waterworks 1994, The Best American Short Stories (ed. with Katrina Kenison) 2000, City of God 2000, Sweet Land Stories 2004, Reporting the Universe (lectures) 2004, The March 2006, Creationists: Selected Essays 1993–2006, Homer & Langley 2009, All the Time in the World: New and Selected Stories 2011. *Address:* c/o Amanda Urban, International Creative Management, 825 8th Avenue, New York, NY 10019, USA (office); English Department, New York University, 58 West 10th St, New York, NY 10011 (office); c/o Random House Publishers, 1745 Broadway, New York, NY 10019, USA (office). *Telephone:* (212) 556-5764 (office); (212) 998-8833 (office); (212) 572-2764 (office). *E-mail:* AUrban@icmtalent.com (office); JyMartin@randomhouse.com (office). *Website:* www.E.L.Doctorow.com (office).

DODD, Christopher (Chris) John, BA, JD; American lawyer, association executive and fmr politician; *Chairman and CEO, Motion Picture Association of America;* b. 27 May 1944, Willimantic, Conn.; s. of Thomas J. Dodd and Grace Mary Dodd (née Murphy); m. 1st Susan Mooney 1970 (divorced 1982); m. 2nd Jackie Clegg 1999; two d.; ed Providence Coll. and Univ. of Louisville School of Law, Ky; volunteer with US Peace Corps, Dominican Repub. 1966–68; admitted to Conn. Bar 1973; mem. US House of Reps, Washington, DC from 2nd Dist Conn. 1975–81; Senator from Conn. 1980–2011 (retd), Chair. Banking, Housing and Urban Affairs Cttee; Chair. and CEO Motion Picture Asscn of America 2011–; Democrat; numerous awards. *Address:* Motion Picture Association of America, 15301 Ventura Blvd, Sherman Oaks, CA 91403, USA (office). *Telephone:* (818) 995-6600 (office). *Fax:* (818) 285-4403 (office). *E-mail:* info@mpaa.org (office). *Website:* www.mpaa.org (office).

DODD, Lois; American artist; b. 22 April 1927, Montclair, NJ; d. of Lawrence Dodd and Margaret Vanderhoff; one s.; ed Montclair High School, Cooper Union Art School; Co-founder, Tanager Gallery 1952–62; mem. Bd of Govs Skowhegan School of Painting and Sculpture 1980– (Chair. 1986–88); mem. Nat. Acad. of Design 1988–, American Acad. of Arts and Letters 1998–; Hon. degree (Old Lyme Acad., Conn.); American Acad. and Inst. of Arts and Letters Award 1986, Hassam, Speicher, Betts and Symons Purchase Prize 1991, Nat. Acad. of Design Leonilda S. Gervas Award 1987, Henry Ward Ranger Purchase Award 1990, 2005, Augustus St Gaudens Award for Achievement from Cooper Union 2005. *Address:* 30 East 2nd Street, New York, NY 10003, USA (home).

DODGE, David A., OC, BA, PhD, FRSC; Canadian economist, academic, consultant, university administrator and fmr central banker and fmr politician; *Senior Advisor, Bennett Jones LLP;* b. 8 June 1943, Toronto, Ont.; m. Christiane Dodge; ed Queen's Univ., Princeton Univ., USA; fmr Asst Prof. of Econs, Queen's Univ.; Assoc. Prof. of Canadian Studies and Int. Econs, School of Advanced Int. Studies, Johns Hopkins Univ., USA; Dir Int. Econs Programme, Inst. for Research on Public Policy 1979–80; fmr fed. public servant, sr positions in Cen. Mortgage and Housing Corpn, Anti-Inflation Bd, Dept of Employment and Immigration, Dept of Finance; Deputy Minister of Health 1998–2001; fmr Deputy Minister of Finance; mem. Bd of Dirs Bank of Canada 1992–97, Gov. and Chair. 2001–08; currently Sr Advisor, Bennett Jones LLP; Chancellor Queen's Univ.; Dir, Scotiabank, Atco/CU Ltd. *Address:* Bennett Jones LLP, Suite 1900, World Exchange Plaza, 45 O'Connor Street, Ottawa, ON K1P 1A4, Canada (office). *Telephone:* (613) 683-2304 (office). *Fax:* (613) 683-2323 (office). *E-mail:* dodged@bennettjones.com (office). *Website:* www.bennettjones.com (office).

DODGE, Toby, BA, MSc, PhD; British research institute director and academic; *Reader, Department of International Relations, London School of Economics and Political Science;* ed SOAS, Univ. of London; fmr Lecturer on Int. Relations and Middle Eastern Politics, Dept of Political Studies, SOAS; Researcher, Middle E Programme, Royal Inst. of Int. Affairs (RIIA); currently Sr Research Fellow, Centre for the Study of Globalisation and Regionalisation, Univ. of Warwick; Dir of Gulf States Programme and Consulting Sr Fellow for Middle E, IISS, London 2003–; fmr Reader in Int. Politics, Dept of Politics, Queen Mary, Univ. of London; currently Reader, Dept of Int. Relations, London School of Econs and Political Science. *Publications include:* Globalisation and the Middle East, Islam, Economics, Culture and Politics (co-Ed.) 2002, Inventing Iraq: The Failure of Nation Building and a History Denied 2003; numerous research papers and scholarly articles. *Address:* Department of International Relations, London School of Economics and Political Science, Houghton Street, London, WC2A 2AE, England (office). *Telephone:* (20) 7955-6176 (office). *E-mail:* b.t.dodge@lse.ac.uk (office). *Website:* www.lse.ac.uk/middleEastCentre/people/TobyDodge.aspx (office).

DODIK, Milorad; Bosnia and Herzegovina politician; *President of Republika Srpska;* b. 12 March 1959, Banja Luka; m.; two c.; ed Univ. of Belgrade; Pres. Exec. Bd Municipal Ass. of Laktaši 1986–90; mem. Parl. Socialist Repub. of Bosnia and Herzegovina 1990; Rep. Nat. Ass. of Republika Srpska; Prime Minister 1998–2001, 2006–10; Pres. of Republika Srpska 2010–; Founder and Chair. Alliance of Ind. Social Democrats; Hon. Pres. Partizan Belgrade Basketball Club; Order of Republika Srpska, Order of Peter the Great (Russia), Order of St Sava (Serbian Orthodox Church), Holy Cross of the Guard of the Tomb of Christ (Patriarch of Jerusalem). *Address:* Office of the President of Republika Srpska, 78000 Banja Luka, Bana Milosavljevića 4, Bosnia and Herzegovina (office). *Telephone:* (51) 211178 (office). *Fax:* (51) 212018 (office). *E-mail:* info@predsjednikrs.net (office). *Website:* www.predsjednikrs.net (office).

DODIN, Lev Abramovich; Russian theatre director; *Artistic Director and General Manager, Maly Drama Theatre;* b. 14 May 1944, Leningrad; m. Tatyana Borisovna Shestakova (q.v.) 1972; ed Leningrad Theatre Inst.; lecturer in drama, Leningrad Theatre Inst. 1963–83; with Leningrad Youth Theatre 1967– (now Chief Dir), Artistic Dir and Gen. Man. Leningrad Maly Drama Theatre 1983–; Prof., St Petersburg Acad. of Dramatic Art; mem. Gen. Ass. of the Union of Theatres of Europe; USSR State Prize 1986, State Prize of Russia 1992, Triumph Prize 1992, Ubu Prize, Italy 1993, 1995, Stanislavsky Prize 1996, RSFSR Merited Artist 1986, People's Artist of Russian Fed., Golden Sofit Saint Petersburg Theatre Award 1996, Golden Mask National Theatre Award 1997, 1999, 2004, Abbiati Italian Critics' Award "for best opera staging" 1998, European Theatre Award 2000, Russian Presidential Award "for excellent service" in 2001, Tovstonogov's Award "for outstanding achievements in the art of theatre" 2002, Russian State Prize 2003, Chayka Moskow Theatre Award 2003, Pro Cultura Hungarica Hugary State Prize 2005; Order of Literature and Arts, France 1994. *Productions include:* The Robber (K. Čapek) 1974, The Gentle One (Dostoyevsky) 1980, The House (F. Abramov) 1980, Brothers and Sisters (F. Abramov) 1985, Lord of the Flies 1986, Stars in the Morning Sky (A. Galin) 1988, Gaudeamus 1990, The Demons (Dostoyevsky) 1992, Claustrophobia (V. Yerofeev) 1994, The Cherry Orchard (A. Chekhov) 1994, Play With No Title (A. Chekhov) 1966, Chevengur (A. Platonov) 1999, Molly Sweeney (Brian Friel) 2000. *Operas include:* Elektra (R. Strauss) 1995, Lady Macbeth of Mtsensk (Franco Abbiati Prize for best musical performance, Italy 1998) (D. Shostakovich) 1998, Mazeppa (Tchaikovsky) 1999, The Queen of Spades (Tchaikovsky) 1998–2001. *Address:* Maly Drama Theatre, Rubinstein Str. 18, St Petersburg, Russia. *Telephone:* (812) 113-21-08. *Fax:* (812) 113-33-66 (office). *E-mail:* levdodin@mdt.sp.ru (office). *Website:* www.mdt-dodin.ru (office).

DODON, Igor, DEcon; Moldovan economist, academic and government official; b. 18 Feb. 1975, Sadova, Straseni Dist; m.; one c.; ed Agrarian Univ. of Moldova, Acad. of Econ. Studies, Int. Inst. of Man.; worked at Moldovan Stock Exchange 1997–2005, positions included Sr Specialist in Clearing and Listing Depts, Man. of Electronic Systems of Negotiation, Dir of Marketing, Listing and Quotations Dept; Chair. Nat. Securities Depository 2001–05; Chair. Moldovan Commodity Exchange 2003–05; Deputy Minister of Economy and Trade 2005–06, Minister of Economy and Trade 2006–08, First Deputy Prime Minister and Minister of Economy and Trade 2008–09; fmr Prof., Acad. of Econ. Studies, Free Int. Univ. of Moldova, Int. Inst. of Man., State Univ. of Moldova. *Address:* c/o Ministry of the Economy and Trade, 2033 Chişinău, Piaţa Marii Adunări Naţionale 1, Moldova.

DOER, Hon. Gary Albert, OM; Canadian diplomatist and politician; *Ambassador to USA;* b. 31 March 1948, Winnipeg, Man.; m. Ginny Devine; two d.; first elected to Manitoba Legis. Ass. as MP for Concordia 1986, Minister of Urban Affairs 1986–88, of Crown Investments 1987–88, of Man. Telephone Systems 1987–88, also Minister responsible for Man. Liquor Control Comm.; Leader New Democrats 1988–2009, Leader of the Opposition 1988–99, Premier of Man. 1999–2009, Pres. Exec. Council and Minister of Fed.–Prov. Relations 1999–2009 (resgnd); Amb. to USA 2009–; Pres. Man. Govt Employees' Asscn 1979–86; fmr Deputy Supt, Vaughan Street Detention Centre; Vice-Pres. Man. Special Olympics, Pres. Boys' and Girls' Club of Winnipeg; mem. Bd Winnipeg Blue Bombers, Prairie Theatre Exchange, Niagara Inst., Univ. of Manitoba. *Leisure interest:* water skiing. *Address:* Canadian Embassy, 501 Pennsylvania Avenue NW, Washington, DC 20001, USA (office). *Telephone:* (202) 682-1740 (office). *Fax:* (202) 682-7678 (office). *E-mail:* washington-im-enquiry@international.gc.ca (office). *Website:* can-am.gc.ca/washington (office).

DOERIG, Hans-Ulrich, DEcon; Swiss academic, banker and business executive; *Senior Adviser to Board of Directors, Credit Suisse Group AG;* ed St Gallen Univ.; Research Assoc. and Lecturer, Univ. of Zurich and Swiss Banking School for over 10 years; man. training, Corp. Finance and Domestic Lending Business, J.P. Morgan, New York 1968; joined Credit Suisse, Zurich 1973, various man. positions in Int. Divs, Capital Markets, Interim CEO CS First Boston, London 1981–82, mem. Exec. Bd Credit Suisse, Zurich 1982, responsible for Multinational Div., Securities Trading, Capital Markets, Corp. Finance, Commercial Banking Asia, Vice-Chair. Credit Suisse, Zurich 1992–96, Chair. Credit and Finance Cttee and Audit Cttee, Pres. Exec. Bd 1996–97, Chair. and CEO Credit Suisse First Boston, Zurich 1997–98, instrumental in restructuring of Credit Suisse Group and merger of fmr Credit Suisse International and CS First Boston, Vice-Chair. Exec. Bd and Group Chief Risk Officer 1998–2002, Vice-Chair. Exec. Bd and Head Corp. Centre of Credit Suisse Group AG 2002–03, Vice-Chair. Credit Suisse Group AG and Chair. Risk Cttee 2003–09, Chair. Credit Suisse Group AG 2009–11, Sr Adviser to Bd of Dirs 2011–; mem. Bd of Dirs Bühler AG; Chair. Fondation Simón I. Patiño; mem. Bd and Vice-Chair. Univ. of Zurich (also its del. on Bd of Univ.-Hosp. Zurich); mem. Bd Red Cross Museum, Geneva. *Publications:* Universalbank – Banktypus der Zukunft (second edn) 1997, Operational Risks in Financial Services – An Old Challenge in a New Environment 2001, Neue Wege zur Hochschulfinanzierung (lead author) 2004, Strive for Credibility 2009; various other publns on finance, man. and educ. *Address:* Credit Suisse Group AG, PO Box 1, 8070 Zurich (office); Credit Suisse Group, Paradeplatz 8, 8001 Zurich, Switzerland (office). *Telephone:* (44) 212-16-16 (office). *Fax:* (44) 333-25-87 (office). *E-mail:* info@credit-suisse.com (office). *Website:* www.credit-suisse.com (office).

DOERR, L. John, BS, MS, MBA; American inventor and investment company executive; *Partner, Kleiner Perkins Caufield & Byers;* b. 29 June 1951, St Louis, Mo.; m. Ann Howland Doerr; two c.; ed Rice Univ., Harvard Univ.; joined Intel Corpn 1974, became one of Intel's most successful salespeople; Pnr, Kleiner

Perkins Caufield & Byers, Menlo Park, Calif. 1980–, has directed venture capital funding to several tech. cos, including Compaq, Netscape, Symantec, Sun Microsystems, drugstore.com, Amazon.com, Intuit, Google, Friendster, Go.com, myCFO; currently mem. Bd of Dirs Google, Amazon.com, Intuit, Homestore, Sun Microsystems (all public cos), Zazzle, Good Technology, Miasole, Purkinje, Segway Inc., Spatial Photonics (all pvt. ventures); helped found TechNet (lobbying org.); has also invested heavily in 'carbon trading'; Fellow, American Acad. of Arts and Sciences 2009–; listed in Forbes magazine's Midas List. *Achievements include:* holds patents for computer memory devices. *Leisure interests:* kids' stuff (trampolines and rock concerts), cycling, hiking, skiing, photography, surfing (the web), travelling, reading, music, messing around with computers/technology. *Address:* Kleiner Perkins Caufield & Byers, 2750 Sand Hill Road, Menlo Park, CA 94025, USA (office). *Telephone:* (650) 233-2750 (office). *Fax:* (650) 233-0300 (office). *E-mail:* johnd@kpcb.com (office). *Website:* www.kpcb.com (office).

DOGAN, Akhmed Demir, PhD; Bulgarian politician; b. 29 March 1954, Drundar, Varna Dist; two c.; ed Univ. of Sofia, Bulgarian Acad. of Sciences; f. underground resistance org. against so-called revival process (forcible re-naming of ethnic Turks in Bulgaria) 1985; arrested and sentenced for being leader of an anti-state org. (amnestied 1989); f. Movt for Rights and Freedoms party 1990, Chair. 1990–2013; elected Deputy, 7th Grand Nat. Ass. 1990, Chair. MRF Parl. Group; Deputy to 36th Nat. Ass. 1991–94, 37th Nat. Ass. 1994–97, Chair. Nat. Salvation Alliance (coalition) Parl. Group in 38th Nat. Ass. 1997–2001, 39th Nat. Ass. 2001–04, also Chair. MRF Parl. Group, Deputy to 40th Nat. Ass. 2005–09, 41st Nat. Ass. 2009–; Chair. Liberal Democratic Union 1998–99; Chair. Inst. for Integration Studies 1999; acquitted by Supreme Admin. Court of corruption charges brought by Parl. Comm. Oct. 2010. *Address:* Movement for Rights and Freedoms, 1301 Sofia, bul. A. Stamboliyski 45A, Bulgaria (office). *Telephone:* (2) 811-44-52 (office). *Fax:* (2) 811-44-53 (office). *E-mail:* press@dps.bg (office). *Website:* www.dps.bg (office).

DOĞAN, Aydın; Turkish media executive; *Chairman, Doğan Şirketler Grubu Holding A.Ş.;* b. 1936, Kelkit; m.; four c.; ed Istanbul High Economy and Commerce Acad.; started business operations while still at school, f. his first industrial co. 1974; currently Chair. Doğan Şirketler Grubu Holding A.Ş.; owner of eight newspapers including Hürriyet and Milliyet and two TV stations; fmr mem. Ass. and Admin. Bd Istanbul Chamber of Commerce; fmr Bd mem. Union of Chambers and Stock Markets; Chair. Newspaper Owners' Union 1986–96; Deputy Chair. World Asscn of Newspapers 2004–; f. Aydın Doğan Foundation 1996; Hon. DHumLitt (Girne American Univ.) 1999, Dr hc (Aegean Univ.) 2000; State Superior Services Medal 1999. *Address:* Doğan Şirketler Grubu Holding A.Ş., Oymacı Sok. No:15/1 Altunizade 34662, Üsküdar, İstanbul (office); Aydın Doğan Vakfi, Hürriyet Medya Towers, 34544, Güneşli, İstanbul, Turkey (office). *Telephone:* (212) 677-0760 (office). *Fax:* (212) 677-0762 (office). *E-mail:* advakfi@hurriyet.com.tr (office). *Website:* www.doganholding.com.tr (office).

DOGAR, Hon. Abdul Hameed, BSc, LLB; Pakistani judge; b. 22 March 1944, Gaarhi Mori, Khairpur Dist, Sindh Prov.; ed Punjab Univ., Int. Islamic Univ. Islamabad, Al-Azhar Univ., Cairo, Egypt, Macca and Madina Univ., Saudi Arabia; Justice of Sindh High Court 1995–2000, Justice of Supreme Court 2000–09 (retd), Chief Justice of Pakistan 2007–09 (took oath on Prov. Constitution Order (PCO) which replaced the Constitution 3 Nov. 2007, later took fresh oath according to Article 178 of the Constitution 15 Nov. 2007, Supreme Court Pakistan later declared that taking oath on PCO was not legal and held that Justice Dogar was never a Constitutional Chief Justice of Pakistan as office of Chief Justice of Pakistan was never vacant by *de jure* Chief Justice, hence treated him the *de facto* Chief Justice of Pakistan by protecting all his admin., financial acts and any oath made before him in ordinary course of affairs of office of Chief Justice of Pakistan 31 July 2009); Sec., Dist Bar Asscn, Khairpur 1973–74; Pres. 1987–88, 1989–90, 1991–92, 1993–94, 1994–95; Vice-Chair. Dist Council, Khairpur 1979–83; Jt Sec., High Court Bar Asscn, Sukkur Bench 1984–85; Chair. Bd Govs IBA March–April 2000; mem. Sindh Madresah Bd, Karachi 1980–83, Syndicate, Shah Abdul Latif Univ., Khairpur 1996–2000; mem. Bd Govs, Bd of Intermediate and Secondary Educ., Sukkur 1988–90, Nat. Univ. of Modern Languages, Islamabad 2003; Judge-in-Charge, Supreme Court Employees' Co-operative Housing Soc., Islamabad 2004; Acting Chief Election Commr July–Aug. 2004, Nov.–Dec. 2004, 2005–06; Chair. Supreme Judicial Council, Law and Justice Comm., Fed. Judicial Acad., Nat. Judicial Policy-making Cttee, Governing Body, Access to Justice Devt Fund; Hon. Sec. Dist Red Crescent Soc., Khairpur 1980–85. *Address:* c/o Supreme Court of Pakistan, Constitution Avenue, Islamabad, Pakistan. *Telephone:* (51) 9220581. *E-mail:* info@supremecourt.gov.pk. *Website:* www.supremecourt.gov.pk.

DOHERTY, Peter Charles, AC, MVSc, PhD; Australian immunologist and academic; *Laureate Professor, Department of Microbiology and Immunology, University of Melbourne;* b. 15 Oct. 1940, Oxley; s. of Eric Doherty and Linda Doherty; m. Penelope Stephens 1965; two s.; ed Indooroopilly High School, Univ. of Queensland and Univ. of Edinburgh, UK; following graduation, worked as rural veterinary officer in Queensland Dept of Agric. and Stock, later worked in Animal Research Inst., Yeerongpilly; worked in CSIRO and Serum Labs; Sr Scientific Officer, Dept of Experimental Pathology, Moredun Research Inst., Edinburgh 1967–71; Assoc. Prof., then Prof. Wistar Inst., Philadelphia, USA 1975–82; Head of Dept of Experimental Pathology, John Curtin School of Medical Research, Canberra, 1982–88; Michael F. Tamer Endowed Chair for Immunology Biomedical Research, Co-Leader of Infection and Host Defense Program and Chair. Dept of Immunology, St Jude Children's Research Hosp., Memphis, Tenn., USA 1988–2002, mem. Dept of Immunology 2002–; Adjunct Prof. of Pediatrics and Pathology, Univ. of Tennessee, Memphis 1992–2002; Laureate Prof., Dept of Microbiology and Immunology, Univ. of Melbourne 2002–; mem. Bd Int. Lab. for Research in Animal Diseases, Nairobi, Kenya 1987–92; mem. Scientific Review Bd, Howard Hughes Medical Inst. 1997–; Hon. DVSc (Queensland), Hon. DSc (Australian Nat. Univ., Edin., Tufts, Warsaw, Latrobe, Imperial Coll. London, Autonomous Univ. Barcelona, North Carolina State, Guelph, Pennsylvania, Michigan State, Illinois, of Technology, Sydney), Hon. DMSc (Rhodes), Hon. DPh (Kyorin); Paul Ehrlich Prize for Medicine, Germany 1983, Gairdner Int. Award for Medical Science, Canada 1986, Albert Lasker Basic Medical Research Award 1995, Nobel Prize in Medicine (jt recipient) 1996, Australian of the Year 1997. *Publications:* numerous publs in scientific journals, chapters in books and

review articles. *Leisure interests:* walking, reading. *Address:* Room 2.06A, Department of Microbiology and Immunology, University of Melbourne, Victoria 3010, Australia (office). *Telephone:* (3) 8344-7968 (office). *Fax:* (3) 9347-7990 (office). *E-mail:* pcd@unimelb.edu.au (office). *Website:* www.microbiol.unimelb.edu.au/people/doherty (office).

DOIG, Anne Frances, MD, LMCC, CCFP, FCFP; Canadian physician and organization official; m. Robert J. Cowan; five s. one d.; ed Coll. of Medicine, Univ. of Saskatchewan; in full-time family practice, City Centre Family Physicians PC Inc., Saskatoon 1978–; Clinical Assoc., Dept of Obstetrics and Gynecology, Univ. of Saskatchewan; mem. Active Staff, Saskatoon Regional Health Authority Practitioner Staff; mem. Bd Dirs Saskatchewan Blue Cross 1995–; Pres. Canadian Medical Asscn 2009–10; mem. Saskatoon Regional Medical Staff Asscn, Saskatchewan Medical Asscn, Coll. of Physicians and Surgeons of Saskatchewan, Coll. of Family Physicians of Canada, Soc. of Obstetricians and Gynecologists of Canada, Univ. of Saskatchewan Coll. of Medicine Alumni Asscn (Founding mem. and fmr Pres.), Univ. of Alberta Health Law Inst., Canadian Asscn of Medical Educ.; Pres. Swim Saskatchewan Inc.; represents Saskatchewan on Bd of Dirs Swimming/Natation Canada; mem. Bd of Dirs Canada Health Infoway Inc. 2010–, Third Avenue Centre 2012–, STARS Air Ambulance 2012–; fmr Pres. Saskatoon Goldfin Swim Club; Clinical Teacher of the Year in Family Medicine, Saskatoon City Hospital 1990, Excellence in Teaching Award, Asscn of Profs of Obstetrics and Gynecology 1996, Saskatchewan Centennial Leadership Award 2005. *Address:* City Centre Family Physicians, 514 Queen Street, Saskatoon, SK S7K 0M5, Canada (office). *Telephone:* (306) 244-3016 (office).

DOIG, Peter, MA; British painter and academic; b. 1959, Edinburgh; ed Chelsea School of Art, Wimbledon School of Art, St Martin's School of Art; grew up in Canada; moved to Trinidad 2002; Trustee, Tate Gallery 1995–2000; Prof., Düsseldorf State Acad. of Art 2005–. *Works include:* Architect's Home in the Ravine 1991, Blotter 1993, Olin MKIV Part II 1995–96, Daytime Astronomy 1997–98, 100 Years Ago 2001, Almost Grown 2001, Country Rock 2001, Black Orpheus 2003, Curious 2005. *Address:* c/o Victoria Miro Gallery, 16 Wharf Road, London N1 7RW, England (office). *Telephone:* (20) 7336-8109 (office). *E-mail:* info@victoria-miro.com (office). *Website:* www.victoria-miro.com (office).

DOJE, Cedain; Chinese government official; b. 1924; m. Gesang Zhuoga; ed Beijing Normal Univ.; Gov. of Xizang (Tibet) Autonomous Region 1983–85; Researcher, Inst. of Research on World Religions, Chinese Acad. of Social Sciences 1985–; adviser, United Front Work Dept under CCP Cen. Cttee 1986–; mem. Standing Cttee 6th NPC 1986–88, Standing Cttee 7th NPC 1988–93, 8th NPC 1993–97; Vice-Chair. Educ., Science, Culture and Public Health Cttee under the NPC 1986; Deputy Head China-Spain Friendship Group 1986; Gen. Sec. China Nat. Center for Tibetan Studies; Chair. Tibetan Folk Arts Asscn. *Publications:* Education in Tibet 1995, Tibet's Feudal Serfdom Society 2005. *Address:* c/o China National Center for Tibetan Studies, 3/F A2 Building (Rongfeng 2008), Blk 8, 305 Guang An Men Wai Street, Xuanwu District, Beijing, People's Republic of China.

DOJE, Cering; Chinese government official; *Chairman, Ethnic Affairs Committee, 10th National People's Congress;* b. 1939, Xiahe Co., Gansu Prov.; worked as clerk in Tibet 1959; joined CCP 1960; magistrate, Co. (Dist) People's Court, Nagarze Co. and Gyaca Co., Tibet 1962; mem. Tibet Autonomous Region CCP 1974–90; mem. Standing Cttee Tibet CCP 1977–90; First Sec. Xigaze Municipality CCP 1979–82; Vice-Chair. Tibet Autonomous Region 1983–85, Acting Adam. Head 1986–88, Chair. 1988–90; Deputy for Tibet Autonomous Region, 7th NPC 1988–; Vice-Minister of Civil Affairs 1990–93, Minister 1993–2003; Chair. 10th NPC Ethnic Affairs Cttee 2003–; Vice-Chair. China Cttee Int. Decade for Nat. Disaster Reduction 1998–; mem. 8th NPC 1993–97; mem. 14th CCP Cen. Cttee 1992–97, 15th CCP Cen. Cttee 1997–2002, 16th CCP Cen. Cttee 2002–07. *Address:* c/o Ministry of Civil Affairs, 147 Beiheyan Dajie, Dongcheng Qu, Beijing 100721, People's Republic of China (office).

DOKLE, Namik; Albanian politician; b. 1946, Durres; mem. Albanian Socialist Party (SP); Ed.-in-Chief Zeri Popullit (SP newspaper) 1991; Deputy Chair. of Parl. 1997–2001; Speaker of Parl. 2001–02; Deputy Prime Minister 2003–05.

DOKTOR, Martin, PhDr; Czech canoeist and sports coach; *Director of Sport, Czech Olympic Committee;* b. 21 May 1974, Polička; s. of Josef Doktor and Zuzana Doktorová; m. Kateřina Svobodová 2000; one s. one d.; ed Charles Univ., Prague; silver medals 500m and 1000m Canoeing World Championships, Duisburg, Germany; gold medals 500m and 1000m Olympic Games, Atlanta, USA 1996; silver medals 200m and 1000m, gold medal 500m Canoeing World Championships, Dartmouth, Canada 1997; silver medal 500m, gold medal 1000m European Championships, Plovdiv, Bulgaria 1997; World Cup winner 1998; gold medal 200m World Championships, Szeged, Hungary 1998, silver medal 1000m; World Cup winner 1999; silver medals 200m, 500m and 1000m European Championships, Zagreb, Croatia 1999; silver medal 200m and 500m, bronze medal 1000m Canoeing World Championships, Milan, Italy 1999; gold medal 1000m, bronze medal 200m European Championships 2000; World Cup winner 2000; bronze medal 1000m European Championships, Italy 2001; silver medal 1000m World Championships, Poland 2001; World Cup winner 2002, silver medal C1 200m and bronze medal C1 500m, World Championships, Gainesville, USA 2003; World Cup winner 2003, 2004, silver medal C1 200m European Championships, Račíce, Czech Repub. 2006; Head Coach of Czech nat. team 2008–; Coach in CS MV-ČR; Dir of Sport, Czech Olympic Cttee 2013–; mem. Bd Czech Fair Play Club, Czech Olympians; Best Czech Sportsman of the Year 1996, Gut Jarkovský Prize 1996. *Publications:* Story of the Defeated Champion 2000, Technique and Tactics of Paddling in Flat Water Canoes 2001. *Leisure interests:* skiing, music, cycling, golf. *Address:* Czech Olympic Committee, Benešovská 6, 101 00 Prague 10 (office); Sluneční 627, 533 04 Sezemice (home); Račíce 64, 411 08 Štětí, Czech Republic (home). *E-mail:* doktor@olympic.cz (home). *Website:* www.olympic.cz (office).

DOLAN, Charles F.; American cable television executive; *Chairman, Cablevision Systems Corporation;* b. 16 Oct. 1926, Cleveland, Ohio; m. Helen Burgess; three s. three d.; ed John Carroll Univ.; served in USAF; jtly with wife est. co. producing and distributing sports and industrial films; subsequently f. Teleguide Inc. (providing information services via cable to New York hotels) and Sterling Manhattan Cable (first urban cable TV co. in USA), Home Box Office Inc.; Founder and Chair. Cablevision Systems Corp. 1985–; Co-owner Madison Square Garden

Properties 1995–; Dir Cold Spring Harbor Lab., St Francis Hosp., Long Island; Chair. Nat. Acad. of TV Arts and Sciences; a Man. Dir of Metropolitan Opera, New York; Trustee, Fairfield Univ., Conn.; mem. Bd of Govs Nat. Hockey League. *Address:* Cablevision Systems Corporation, 1111 Stewart Avenue, Bethpage, NY 11714-3533, USA. *Telephone:* (516) 803-2300. *Fax:* (516) 803-2273. *Website:* www .cablevision.com.

DOLAN, James; American business executive; *President and CEO, Cablevision Systems Corporation;* s. of Charles F. Dolan and Helen Ann Dolan (née Burgess); m. Kristin Dolan; five c.; fmrly Asst Gen. Man. Cablevision Chicago, Vice-Pres. for Advertising Sales Cablevision; Man. WKNR-AM radio station, Cleveland; Corpn Dir Advertising Rainbow Programming Holdings, CEO 1992–95; CEO, Pres. Cablevision Systems Corpn 1995–; Chair. Madison Square Garden, New York 1999; named by Business Week magazine amongst The Most Influential People in the World of Sports 2007. *Leisure interests:* yachting, music. *Address:* Cablevision Systems Corporation, 1111 Stewart Avenue, Bethpage, NY 11714, USA (office). *Telephone:* (516) 803-2300 (office). *Fax:* (516) 803-2273 (office). *Website:* www .cablevision.com (office).

DOLAN, Peter Robert, BA, MBA; American business executive; b. 6 Jan. 1956, Salem, Mass; m. Katherine Lange 1981; two s.; ed Tufts Univ., Tuck School of Business, Dartmouth Coll.; with Gen. Foods 1980–88; Vice-Pres. of Marketing Bristol-Myers Products Div. 1988–90, Sr Vice-Pres. of Marketing and Sales 1990–91, Sr Vice-Pres. of Marketing, Sales and Operations 1991–92, Exec. Vice-Pres. 1992, Pres. 1993–94, Group Pres. Nutritionals and Medical Devices, Bristol-Myers Squibb Co. 1997–98, Pres. Europe and Worldwide Medicines 1998, Sr Vice-Pres. of Strategy 1998–2000, Pres. 2000–05, Chair. 2001–05, CEO 2001–06 (resgnd); mem. Bd of Dirs New York Botanical Garden, Nat. Center on Addiction and Substance Abuse, Columbia Univ.; Trustee Tufts Univ. *Address:* 4 Beach Avenue, Larchmont, NY 10538, USA (office).

DOLAN, HE Cardinal Timothy Michael, BA, LicSacredTheol; American ecclesiastic and academic; *Archbishop of New York;* b. 6 Feb. 1950, St Louis, Mo.; s. of the late Robert Dolan and of Shirley Dolan (née Radcliffe); ed St Louis Preparatory Seminary South, Shrewsbury, Cardinal Glennon Coll., Catholic Univ. of America, Pontifical North American Coll. and the Angelicum, Rome; ordained priest, Archdiocese of St Louis 1976; served as Assoc. Pastor at Immaculata Roman Catholic Parish, Richmond Heights –1979; doctoral studies at Catholic Univ. of America, Washington, DC; performed pastoral work in Mo. 1983–87; collaborated with Archbishop John May in reforming the archdiocesan seminary; Sec., Apostolic Nunciature, Washington, DC; appointed Vice-Rector Kenrick-Glennon Seminary 1992, also served as Spiritual Dir and taught Church history; fmr Adjunct Prof. of Theology, St Louis Univ.; rank of Mgr 1994; Rector, Pontifical North American Coll., Rome 1994–2001; taught at Pontifical Gregorian Univ. and the Angelicum; Auxiliary Bishop of St Louis and Titular Bishop of Natchesium 2001–02; Archbishop of Milwaukee, Wis. 2002–09; Apostolic Admin. of Green Bay, Wis. 2007–08; Archbishop of New York 2009–; cr. Cardinal (Cardinal-Priest of Nostra Signora di Guadalupe a Monte Mario) 2012; participated in Papal Conclave 2013; Chair. Catholic Relief Services –2010; Pres. US Conf. of Catholic Bishops 2010–, Chair. Priestly Life and Ministry Cttee, mem. Sub-cttee on the Church in Africa; mem. Bd of Trustees Catholic Univ. of America; Apostolic Visitor to Irish seminaries as part of Apostolic visitation to Ireland following publication of Ryan and Murphy Reports 2009; one of first mems of newly created Pontifical Council for Promotion of New Evangelisation 2011–, Pontifical Council for Social Communications 2011–. *Television:* co-hosted a programme with his brother called Living Our Faith. *Publications:* Called to Be Holy 2005, To Whom Shall We Go? Lessons from the Apostle Peter 2008, Priests for the Third Millennium 2009. *Address:* Archdiocese of New York, 1011 First Avenue, New York, NY 10022-4134, USA (office). *Telephone:* (212) 371-1000 (office). *Fax:* (212) 826-6020 (office); (212) 826-8379 (office). *E-mail:* communications@archny.org (office). *Website:* www.ny -archdiocese.org (office).

DOLCE, Domenico; Italian fashion designer; *CEO, Dolce & Gabbana;* b. 13 Aug. 1958, Polizzi Generosa, nr Palermo, Sicily; s. of Saverio Dolce; designer, father's atelier, then Asst in a Milan atelier; with Stefano Gabbana opened fashion consulting studio 1982, selected to take part in New Talents show, Milano Collezioni 1985; co-f. Dolce & Gabbana 1985, first maj. women's collection 1985, knitwear 1987, beachwear, underwear 1989, men's wear 1990, women's fragrance 1992, D&G line, men's fragrance 1994, eyewear 1995; est. Dolce and Gabbana Industria production units 1999–2000; acquired and renovated Cinema Metropol in Milan for fashion shows and exhibitions 2005; opened boutiques in major cities in Europe, America and Asia; with Steffano Gabanna, Woolmark Award 1991, Perfume Acad. Int. Prize for Best Feminine Fragrance of Year 1993, Best Masculine Fragrance of Year 1995, French "Oscar des Parfums", UK FHM Designers of the Year 1996, Footwear News Designers of the Year 1997, Russian Harper's Bizarre Style Award 1999, T de Telva Award for Best Designers of the Year 2002, US GQ Best Designers of the Year 2003, UK Elle Best Int. Designers 2004, Premio Resultati 2004, Russian GQ Best Int. Designers 2005. *Publications:* with Stefano Gabbana, 10 Years Dolce and Gabbana 1996, Wildness 1997, Dolce and Gabbana Mémoires de la Mode 1998, Holllywood 2003, Calcio 2004, Music 2004, 20 years Dolce and Gabbana 2006. *Leisure interests:* gym, travel, modern art. *Address:* Dolce & Gabbana, Via San Damiano 7, 20122 Milan, Italy (office). *Telephone:* (02) 774271 (office). *Fax:* (02) 76020600 (office). *Website:* www .dolcegabbana.it (office).

DOLE, Elizabeth Hanford, MA, JD; American fmr politician; b. 29 July 1936, Salisbury, N Carolina; d. of John Van Hanford and Mary E. Cathey; m. Robert J. Dole (q.v.) 1975; ed Duke and Harvard Univs, Univ. of Oxford, UK; called to DC Bar 1966; Staff Asst to Asst Sec. for Educ., US Dept of Health, Educ. and Welfare, Washington, DC 1966–67; practising lawyer, Washington, DC 1967–68; Assoc. Dir Legis. Affairs, then Exec. Dir Pres.'s Comm. for Consumer Interests 1968–71; Deputy Asst Office of Consumer Affairs, The White House, Washington, DC 1971–73; Commr Fed. Trade Comm. 1973–79; Asst to Pres. for Public Liaison 1981–83; Sec. of Transportation 1983–87; Sec. of Labor 1989–90; Pres. American Red Cross 1991–98; cand. for Republican presidential nomination 1999; Senator from N Carolina 2003–09; Trustee, Duke Univ. 1974–88; mem. Visiting Comm., John F. Kennedy School of Govt 1988–; mem. Comm. Harvard School of Public Health 1992–, Bd of Overseers, Harvard Univ. 1989–95; hon. doctorates from 40

colls and univs; Radcliffe Coll. Medal, Distinguished Service Award, Nat. Safety Council 1989, N Carolina Award 1991, Lifetime Achievement Award, Women Execs in State Govt 1993, named N Carolinian of the Year by NC Press Asscn 1993, Leadership Award, League of Women Voters 1994, Raoul Wallenberg Award for Humanitarian Service 1995, Churchwoman of the Year, Religious Heritage of America 1995, named one of the world's three most admired women in Gallup Poll 1998, inducted into Safety and Health Hall of Fame International 1998, Humanitarian Award, Nat. Comm. Against Drunk Driving 1998, Nat. Religious Broadcasters' Bd of Dirs Award 1999, Foreign Policy Asscn Medal, ranked by Forbes magazine amongst The World's 100 Most Powerful Women (30th) 2004, (58th) 2005. *Website:* www.elizabethdole.net.

DOLE, Robert Joseph (Bob); American lawyer and fmr politician; *Special Counsel, Alston & Bird LLP;* b. 22 July 1923, Russell, Kan.; s. of Doran R. Dole and Bina Dole; m. 1st Phyllis Holden 1948 (divorced 1972, died 2008); one d.; m. 2nd Elizabeth Hanford Dole (q.v.) 1975; ed Univ. of Kansas and Washbourn Municipal Univ.; mem. Kansas State Legislature 1951–53; Russell Co. Attorney 1953–61; mem. US House of Reps, Washington, DC 1960–68; Senator from Kansas 1969–96, Senate Majority Leader 1995–96, Senate Republican Leader 1987–96, Chair. Senate Finance Cttee 1981–84; Chair. Republican Nat. Cttee 1971–72; unsuccessful cand. for Vice-Pres. 1976, for Pres. 1996; mem. of Counsel, Verner, Liipfert, Bernhard, McPherson and Hand; Special Counsel, Alston and Bird LLP, Washington, DC 2003–; Pres. Bob Dole Enterprises, Inc.; Pres. Dole Foundation 1983–99; Dir Mainstream Inc.; Adviser, US Del. to FAO Conf., Rome 1965, 1974, 1977; mem. Congressional del. to India 1966, to Middle East 1967; mem. US Helsinki Comm., del. to Belgrade Conf. 1977; Chair. Int. Comm. on Missing Persons 1997–; Trustee, William Allen White Foundation, Univ. of Kan; mem. Nat. Advisory Cttee, The John Wesley Colls; mem. Nat. Advisory Cttee on Scouting for the Handicapped, Kan. Asscn for Retarded Children, Advisory Bd of United Cerebral Palsy, Kan.; mem. ABA; Republican; Hon. mem. Advisory Bd of Kidney Patients Inc.; Presidential Medal of Freedom 1997, Distinguished Service Award 1997, World Food Prize (shared with George McGovern) 2008. *Publications:* Great Political Wit (co-ed.) 1999, Great Presidential Wits 2001. *Leisure interests:* politics, watching the news. *Address:* 700 New Hampshire Avenue NW, Washington, DC 20037; Alston & Bird LLP, The Atlantic Building, 950 F Street NW, Washington, DC 20004-1404, USA (office). *Telephone:* (202) 756-3300 (office). *Fax:* (202) 756-3333 (office). *E-mail:* bdole@alston.com (office). *Website:* www.alston.com (office); www.bobdole.org.

DOLGEN, Jonathan L., JD; American film executive; b. 27 April 1945, NY; ed Cornell Univ., New York. Univ. Law School; lawyer Fried, Frank, Harris, Shriver & Jacobson 1969–76; Asst Gen. Counsel then Deputy Gen. Counsel Columbia Pictures Industries 1976–85, Sr Vice-Pres. World Business Affairs 1979, Exec. Vice-Pres. 1980; Pres. Columbia's Pay Cable & Home Entertainment Group 1983; Sr Exec. Vice-Pres. Fox Inc. 1985–90; Pres. TV Div. Twentieth Century Fox Inc. 1985–88, Pres. 1988–93; Chair. Twentieth TV 1988–90; Pres. Columbia Pictures 1990–94, Pres. Columbia Pictures, Culver City 1991–94; Chair. and CEO Viacom Entertainment Group 1994–2004; Sr Consultant ARTISTdirect Inc. 2006–; f. Friends of Cornell Univ. Arts Center, founder mem. Educ. First; mem. Alumni Council New York Univ. Law School; mem. City of Los Angeles Advisory Council, Los Angeles County Homeland Security Advisory Council, Cornell Univ. Major Gifts Cttee; Bd Dirs Sony Pictures, Charter Communications Inc., Expedia Inc.; Fellow Claremont Univ. Center and Grad. School. *Address:* ARTISTdirect Inc., 1601 Cloverfield Blvd S, Ste. 400, Santa Monica, CA 90404, USA (office). *Website:* www.ARTISTdirect.com.

DOLITTLE, W. Ford, BA, PhD, FRSC; Canadian microbiologist, geneticist and academic; *Professor Emeritus, Dalhousie University;* ed Harvard Coll., Stanford Univ., USA; USPH Postdoctoral trainee in Microbiology, Univ. of Illinois 1968–69; US Nat. Cancer Inst. Postdoctoral Fellow and Research Assoc., Nat. Jewish Hosp. and Research Center, Denver, Colo 1969–71; Asst Prof. (and MRC Scholar), Dept of Biochemistry, Dalhousie Univ. 1971–76, Assoc. Prof. 1976–82, Prof. 1982–2008, Prof. Emer. 2008–; Sabbatical Prof., Harvard Univ. 1977–78; Sabbatical Prof., Stanford Univ. 1985–86; Dir Canadian Inst. for Advanced Research Program in Evolutionary Biology 1986–2007; Canada Research Chair in Comparative Microbia Genomics 2001–08; mem. Editorial Bd Journal of Molecular Evolution 1984– (Assoc. Ed. 1992–), Molecular Biology and Evolution 1987–95, Environmental Microbiology 2000–, Archaea 2001–, Proceedings of the US National Academy of Sciences 2002–; mem. Advisory Bd Genome Biology 2000–; mem. Advisory Editorial Bd Trends in Microbiology 2000–; mem. Bd of Reviewing Eds Science 2006–; mem. NAS 2002; Fellow, AAAS 1985, Canadian Inst. for Advanced Research 1986, American Acad. of Microbiology 1999; Richard Ivey Fellow 2000; Hon. DSc (Ottawa) 2000; Nat. Merit Scholarship, Harvard Coll. 1959–63, NSF Predoctoral Fellowship, Stanford Univ. 1963–68 (declined), Young Scientist of the Year Award, Atlantic Provs Inter-Univ. Council on the Sciences 1978, Ayerst Award, Canadian Biochemical Soc. 1981, Max Forman Sr Faculty Award, Dalhousie Univ. 1982, Guggenheim Fellowship, Stanford Univ. 1985, Award of Excellence, Genetics Soc. of Canada 1991, Henry Friesen Award, Canadian Soc. for Clinical Investigation and Royal Coll. of Physicians and Surgeons of Canada 1996, Roche Diagnostics Prize for Biomolecular and Cellular Research, Canadian Soc. of Biochemistry and Molecular and Cellular Biology 2001, Herzberg Gold Medal 2014. *Publications:* 17 book chapters and more than 250 papers in professional journals on the evolution of genes and genomes. *Address:* Department of Biochemistry and Molecular Biology, Sir Charles Tupper Building, Room 8C, 5850 College Street, Halifax, NS B3H 1X5, Canada (office). *Telephone:* (902) 494-3569 (office). *Fax:* (902) 494-1355 (office). *E-mail:* w.ford.doolittle@dal.ca (office); ford@dal.ca (office). *Website:* www.biochem.dal.ca (office).

DOLLÉ, Guy; French steel industry executive; b. 1942; ed Ecole Polytechnique; began career with IRSID Steel Research Centre, Metz; Head of Plates and Tubes Div., Usinor 1980, Chair. GTS (subsidiary co.) 1985, Exec. Vice-Pres. Usinor Aciers 1986, Head of Production, Sollac N Region (following merger wih Usinor), Vice-Pres. Industrial Affairs 1987, Chair. and CEO Unimétal 1993-95, Exec. Vice-Pres. for Strategy, Usinor 1995–97, Head of Stainless Steel and Alloys Div. 1997–99, Sr Exec. Vice-Pres., Usinor 1999–2002, Chair. and CEO Arcelor SA (following merger of Aceralia, Arbed and Usinor groups) 2002–06; mem. Bd of Dirs Gaz de France

2004–06. *Address:* c/o Gaz de France, 23 rue Philibert-Delorme, 75840 Paris, France (office).

DOLLERY, Sir Colin (Terence), Kt, BS, MB, ChB, FRCP, FMedSci; British physician; b. 14 March 1931; s. of Cyril Robert Dollery and Thelma Mary Dollery; m. Diana Myra Stedman 1958; one s. one d.; ed Lincoln School and Univ. of Birmingham; House Officer, Queen Elizabeth Hosp. Birmingham, Hammersmith Hosp. and Brompton Hosp. 1956–58; Medical Registrar, Hammersmith Hosp. 1958–60, Sr Registrar and Tutor in Medicine 1960–62; Consultant Physician 1962–2000; Lecturer in Medicine, Royal Post grad. Medical School, Univ. of London 1962–65, Prof. of Clinical Pharmacology 1965–87, Prof. of Medicine 1987–91, Dean 1991–96, Pro-Vice-Chancellor for Medicine 1992–96; Sr Consultant Research and Devt, SmithKline Beecham PLC 1996–2000, GlaxoSmithKline 2001–; Dir (non-exec.) Larson-Davis, Inc. 1998–99, Discovery Partners, Inc. 2001–, Predict, Inc. 2001–; mem. MRC 1982–84, Univ. Funding Council (fmrly Univ. Grants Cttee) 1984–91; Fellow Imperial Coll. London 2003; fmr Pres. Int. Union of Pharmacology; Hon. mem. Asscn of American Physicians; Chevalier, Ordre Nat. du Mérite; British Pharmacological Soc. Wellcome Gold Medal. *Publications:* The Retinal Circulation 1971, Therapeutic Drugs 1991; papers in scientific journals. *Leisure interests:* travel, amateur radio, work. *Address:* c/o GlaxoSmithKline plc, 3rd Avenue, Harlow CM19 5AW (office); 101 Corringham Road, London, NW11 7DL, England (home). *Telephone:* (1279) 646154 (office). *E-mail:* colin-dollery-1@gsk.com (office).

DOLOGUELE, Anicet G.; Central African Republic politician; b. 17 April 1957, Bozoum; m.; three c.; ed Univ. de Bangui, Bordeaux Univ., France; fmr Finance and Budget Minister; Prime Minister, Minister of the Economy, Finance, Planning and Int. Co-operation 1999–2001; Chair. Banque de Développement des Etats de l'Afrique Centrale 2001–10; Grand Officier Ordre du Mérite Centrafricain, Commdr Ordre du Mérite Centrafricain, Médaille d'or Ordre du Mérite Centrafricain. *Address:* c/o Banque de Développement des Etats de l'Afrique Centrale, Place du Gouvernement, BP 1177, Brazzaville, Republic of the Congo (office).

DOMARKAS, Juozas; Lithuanian conductor; *Artistic Director and Chief Conductor, Lithuanian National Symphony Orchestra;* b. 28 July 1936, Plunge; m.; two s.; ed Klaipeda Simkus Coll. of Music, Lithuanian Acad. of Music, St Petersburg State Conservatory (conducting Symphony Orchestra and Opera, with Prof. Ilja Musin); Asst Conductor, Vilnius Band 1957–60; Artistic Dir and Chief Conductor, Lithuanian Nat. Symphony Orchestra 1964–; participated in numerous nat. and int. festivals; teacher, sr teacher, Assoc. Prof., Lithuanian Acad. of Music and Theatre 1968–93, Chair. and Prof. 1993–; mem. of jury for numerous int. competitions for symphony conducting in Russia, Poland and Finland; numerous recordings; Grand Cross, Order of the Lithuanian Grand Duke Gediminas 1998; People's Artist of the USSR 1986, Award of Govt of Lithuania for Merit to Lithuanian Culture 1997, Nat. Prize of Lithuanian Repub. 2000. *Address:* Lietuvos Nacionaline Filharmonija, Ausros Vartu 5, 01129 Vilnius (office); Zydu 4–15, 01131 Vilnius, Lithuania (home). *Telephone:* (5) 266-5210 (office); (5) 262-8461 (home). *Fax:* (5) 266-5266 (office); (5) 262-8461 (home). *E-mail:* info@filharmonija.lt (office); juozas.domarkas.1@gmail.com (home). *Website:* www .filharmonija.lt (office).

DOMBROVSKIS, Valdis; Latvian economist and politician; b. 5 Aug. 1971, Rīga; m.; ed Univ. of Latvia, Rīga Tech. Univ., Univ. of Mainz, Germany, Univ. of Maryland, USA; lab. asst, Inst. of Solid-State Physics, Univ. of Latvia 1991–93 (Asst 1997), Dept of Semiconductor Physics 1993–95, Inst. of Physics, Univ. of Mainz, Germany 1995–96; Research Asst, A. James Clark School of Eng, Univ. of Maryland, USA 1998; Macroeconomic Analyst, Monetary Policy Dept, Bank of Latvia 1998–99, Sr Economist 1999–2001, Chief Economist 2001–02; Foundermem. New Era Party (Jaunais laiks) 2002–11, mem. Bd 2002–04; mem. Parl. 2002–04, 2010–; Observer, Council of the EU 2003–04; Minister of Finance 2002–04; mem. European Parl. (Group of the European People's Party (Christian Democrats) and European Democrats) 2004–09; Minister for Children, Family and Integration Affairs March–July 2009; Prime Minister of Latvia 2009–13 (resgnd), also Minister for Regional Devt and Local Govt 2010–11; Founder and mem. Bd, Unity party 2011–; Int. Award from Friedrich August von Hayek Stiftung 2011, The Vašek and Anna Maria Polák Visiting Lecturer's Award 2012. *Publications:* How Latvia Came through the Financial Crisis (with A. Aslund) 2011; numerous publs on economics and politics in various periodicals, journals and electronic media. *Address:* c/o Office of the Cabinet of Ministers, Brīvības bulv. 36, Rīga 1520, Latvia. *E-mail:* birojs@valdisdombrovskis.lv. *Website:* valdisdombrovskis.lv.

DOMBROVSKIS, Vjačeslavs, BA, PhD; Russian/Latvian politician and economist; *Minister of the Economy;* b. 27 Dec. 1977, Rīga, Latvian SSR, USSR; ed Rīga 88th High School, Univ. of Latvia, Clarke Univ., USA; gained Latvian citizenship through naturalization process 1997; fmr researcher, Baltic Int. Econ. Policy Research Centre; fmr Assoc. Prof., Stockholm School of Econs; joined newly founded Zatlers' Reform Party 2011; mem. Parl. 2011–, Leader of Zatlers' Reform Party Parl. Group 2011–13, Chair. Econ., Agricultural, Environmental and Regional Policy Cttee; Minister for Educ. and Science 2013–14, of the Economy 2014–. *Address:* Ministry of the Economy, Brīvības iela 55, Rīga 1519, Latvia (office). *Telephone:* 6701-3101 (office). *Fax:* 6728-0882 (office). *E-mail:* pasts@em .gov.lv (office). *Website:* www.em.gov.lv (office).

DOMENICI, Pete V., BS, LLB; American fmr politician; b. 7 May 1932, Albuquerque; s. of Cherubino Domenici and Alda Domenici; m. Nancy Burk 1958; two s. six d.; ed Univs of Albuquerque, New Mexico, Denver; elected to Albuquerque City Comm. 1966, Chair. 1967; mem. Nat. League of Cities Revenue and Finance Steering Cttee and the Resolutions Cttee of 1969 Annual Conf. of Mayors; served on Gov.'s Policy Bd for Law Enforcement and on Middle Rio Grande Conf. of Govts; Senator from New Mexico 1972–2009 (retd), Chair. Senate Budget Cttee 1981, 1995–2001, Senate Indian Affairs Cttee; Republican; several hon. degrees; numerous awares including Public Sector Leadership Award 1996. *Leisure interests:* hunting, fishing.

DOMINGO, Eugene; Philippines theatre, film and television actress and comedienne; b. 23 July 1971; began career by enrolling in Theatre Arts Programme, Univ. of the Philippines, apprenticed as an actress, production and stage management staff under univ.'s theatre co. Dulaang UP; appeared in several

sitcoms, tele-series and drama anthologies on ABS-CBN and GMA Network; Filipino voice of Tagalog dubbed Cinderella of ABS-CBN as Fairy Godmother or Bb. Polette; best known for playing the role of Rowena in the Ang Tanging Ina series; Comedy Actress of the Year, Guillermo Mendoza Memorial Scholarship Foundation 43rd Box-Office Entertainment Awards 2012. *Films include:* Maricris Sioson: Japayuki 1993, Sa ngalan ng pag-ibig 1995, Ikaw pa rin ang iibigin 1998, Pagdating ng panahon 1998, Ms. Kristina Moran: Babaeng palaban 1999, Bullet 1999, Dito sa puso ko 1999, Mahal kita, walang iwanan 2000, Demons 2000, Laro sa baga 2000, Kung ikaw ay isang panaginip 2002, Pakisabi na lang... Mahal ko siya 2002, Lastikman 2003, Ang tanging ina 2003, Malikmata 2003, Volta 2004, Can This Be Love 2005, Bikini Open 2005, Tuli 2005, Kutob 2005, D' Lucky Ones! 2006, Kapag tumibok ang puso: Not Once, But Twice 2006, You Are the One 2006, Txt 2006, Reyna: Ang makulay na pakikipagsapalaran ng mga achucherva, achuchuva, achechenes... 2006, Shake Rattle and Roll 8 (segment 'LRT') 2006, The Promise 2007, Ang cute ng ina mo! 2007, Foster Child 2007, Paano kita iibigin 2007, Philippine Science 2007, Four in One 2007, Pasukob 2007, Shake, Rattle & Roll 9 (segment 'Bangungot') 2007, Katas ng Saudi 2007, Bahay kubo: A pinoy mano po! (Best Supporting Actress, Metro Manila Film Festival Philippines 2007) 2007, Pisay (Best Supporting Actress, Gawad Tanglaw Awards 2008) 2008, Foster Child (Best Supporting Actress, Gawad Tanglaw Awards 2008) 2008, Ploning 2008, Ikaw pa rin: Bongga ka boy! 2008, My Monster Mom 2008, 100 (Best Supporting Actress, Cinemalaya Ind. Film Festival 2008) 2008, I.T.A.L.Y. (I Trust and Love You) 2008, Ang tanging ina n'yong lahat 2008, Comedians (Bert Marcelo Award, Guillermo Mendoza Foundation Awards 2009) 2009, Kimmy Dora: Kambal sa kiyeme (Movie Actress of the Year, PMPC Star Awards for Movies 2010, Best Actress in a Comedy or Musical, Golden Screen Awards 2010) 2009, Soliloquy 2009, Nobody Nobody But Juan 2009, Shake Rattle & Roll XI (segment 'Diablo') (voice) 2009, Working Girls 2010, Here Comes the Bride 2010, Mamarazzi 2010, Petrang Kabayo 2010, Ang tanging ina mo: Last na 'to! (Best Supporting Actress, Metro Manila Film Festival 2010) 2010, RPG Metanoia (voice) 2010, My Valentine Girls (segment 'Gunaw') 2011, Who's That Girl? 2011, The Howl & the Fussyket (short) 2011, Ang babae sa septic tank (Best Actress, Cinemalaya 2011, People's Choice Award for Best Actress, Asian Film Awards 2012, Best Actress, Gawad Tanglaw for Films 2012) 2011, Zombadings 1: Patayin sa shokot si Remington 2011, Anatomiya ng Korupsiyon 2011 Wedding tayo, Wedding hindi! 2011, My Househusband: Ikaw na! (Best Supporting Actress, Metro Manila Film Festival 2011) 2011, Enteng ng Ina mo 2011, Shake Rattle Roll 13 (segment 'Rain Rain Go Away') 2011. *Television includes:* Kokey (series) 2001–07, Sa Dulo Ng Walang Hanggan (series) 2001, Buttercup (series) 2003, Tanging Ina (series) 2003, Marina (series) 2004, Kampanerang Kuba (series) 2005, Komiks (series) 2006, SineSerye (series) 2007, Love Spell (series) 2006–07, Volta (mini-series) 2008, Everybody Hapi (series) 2008, Ako si Kim Samsoon (series) 2008, Obra (series) 2008–10, Ang babaeng hinugot sa aking tadyang (series) 2009, Cool Center: Hello It's Me! (series) 2009, Adik sa'yo (series) 2009, First Time (series) 2010, Jejemom (series) 2010, Inday Wanda (series) 2010–11, Sa ngalan ng ina (series) 2011. *Address:* c/o ABS-CBN Corporation, Quezon City, The Philippines. *E-mail:* info@abs-cbn.com. *Website:* www.abs-cbn.com.

DOMINGO, Plácido, FRCM, FRNCM; Spanish singer (tenor) and conductor; *General Director, Los Angeles Opera;* b. 21 Jan. 1941, Madrid; s. of the late Plácido Domingo and Pepita Domingo (née Embil); m. Marta Ornelas; three s.; ed Nat. Conservatory of Music, Mexico City; operatic debut at Monterrey, Mexico 1961; with Israel Nat. Opera for over two years; debut at Metropolitan Opera, New York 1968; British debut in Verdi's Requiem at Royal Festival Hall 1969; Covent Garden debut in Tosca 1971, returned to sing in Aïda, Carmen 1973, La Bohème 1974, Un Ballo in Maschera 1975, La Fanciulla del West; has taken leading roles in about 120 operas; with New York City Opera 1965–; Artistic Dir Washington Nat. Opera 1994–2003, Gen. Dir 2003–11; Artistic Dir Los Angeles Opera 2000–03, Gen. Dir 2003–; engagements include Tosca (conducting), Romeo and Juliet at Metropolitan Opera, New York, Aïda, Il Trovatore in Hamburg, Don Carlos in Salzburg, I vespri siciliani and La forza del destino in Paris, Turandot in Barcelona, Otello in Paris, London, Hamburg and Milan, Carmen in Edinburgh, Turandot at the Metropolitan; New York stage debut in My Fair Lady 1988 (213 performances by 2000); Luigi in Il Tabarro at the Met 1989; Otello at Covent Garden 1990, Lohengrin at Vienna Staatsoper, Don José at Rio de Janeiro, Otello at the Met and Barcelona; Don Carlos at Los Angeles, Dick Johnson at Chicago, Riccardo in Un Ballo in Maschera at the 1990 Salzburg Festival; debut as Parsifal at the Met 1991 and 2001, Otello at Covent Garden 1992, Siegmund in Die Walküre at the Vienna Staatsoper 1992; 1997 season included Don José and Siegmund at the Met and Gabriele Adorno in Simon Boccanegra at Covent Garden; 1999 season Herman in the Queen of Spades at the Met, and at Covent Garden 2002; concert performance of Verdi's Battaglia di Legnano with the Royal Opera 2000; Canio in Pagliacci at Covent Garden 2003; Nero in premiere of Monteverdi's Poppea in Los Angeles 2003; Rasputin in premiere of Deborah Drattell's Nicholas and Alexandra, Los Angeles 2003; opened 2002/03 Los Angeles Opera season in Puccini's Fanciulla del West; Maurizio in Adriana Lecouvreur, Metropolitan Opera 2009; sang first baritone title role in Verdi's Simon Boccanegra at Berlin Staatsoper 2009, Covent Garden 2010, the Met 2010; cr. and performed at inaugural Plácido Domingo Festival, Spain 2012; Commdr, Légion d'honneur, Hon. KBE 2002, Medal of Freedom, Star of the Order of Merit (Hungary) 2005; Dr hc (Royal Coll. of Music) 1982, (Univ. Complutense de Madrid) 1989, Hon. DMus (Univ. of Oxford) 2003; 12 Grammy Awards, European Culture Foundation Culture Prize 2003, Classic FM Gramophone Listeners' Choice Award 2005, Opera News Award 2005, Classic BRIT Award for Lifetime Achievement 2006, Birgit Nilsson Prize 2009, Person of the Year, Latin Recording Acad. 2010, Wolf Foundation Prize in Music (shared with Sir Simon Rattle) 2012, Praemium Imperiale Award, Japan Art Foundation 2013. *Films include:* Madama Butterfly with von Karajan, La Traviata 1982, Carmen 1984, Otello 1986. *Recordings include:* has made well over 100 recordings, including Aïda, Un Ballo in Maschera, Tosca, Tannhäuser 1989, Die Frau ohne Schatten 1993, Gounod's Roméo et Juliette 1996, Merlin by Albeniz 2000, Tristan and Isolde (Critics' Choice Award, Classical Brit Awards 2006), Pasión Española (Latin Grammy Award for Best Classical Album) 2008; has made more than 50 videos. *Publications include:* My First Forty Years (autobiog.) 1983, My Operatic Roles 2000. *Address:* c/o Nancy Seltzer and Associates, 6220 Del Valle Drive, Los Angeles, CA 90048, USA (office). *Telephone:* (323) 938-3562 (office). *E-mail:* nseltzer@nsapr.com (office). *Website:* www.laopera.org; www.placidodomingo.com.

DOMINI, Amy, BA; American mutual fund company executive; *CEO and President, Domini Social Investments LLC;* b. 25 Jan. 1950, New York, NY; d. of Enzo Vice Domini and Margaret Cabot Domini (née Colt); m. Peter D. Kinder 1980 (divorced); two s.; ed Boston Univ.; stockbroker, Tucker Anthony & RL Day, Cambridge, Mass 1975–80, Moseley Securities, Cambridge 1980–85; portfolio man., Franklin R & D Corpn, Boston 1985–87; pvt. trustee, Loring, Wolcott & Coolidge 1987–; Chair. Bd Linder, Lydenberg, Domini & Co., Cambridge 1991–; f. Domino Social Equity Fund 1991; Founder, CEO and Pres. Domini Social Investments LLC, Boston 1996–; Chair. Pension Fund Episcopal Church, New York 1994–; mem. Governing Bd, Interfaith Center on Corp. Responsibility, New York 1985–95, Bd of Dirs, Social Investment Forum, Washington, DC 1994–, Westminster, London, SW1A 0PW, England (office). *Telephone:* (20) 7703-4573 (home). *Fax:* Security Analysis Soc.; Hon. DHumLitt (Berkeley Divinity School at Yale) 2007, Hon. DBA (Northeastern Univ. Law School) 2007; Accioniste Award, Accion International 1992, SRI (Socially Responsible Investing) Service Award 1996, Best Mutual Funds Award, Money Magazine 1998, Theodore M. Hesburgh Award for Business Ethics, Notre Dame Univ. 2005, citation from Pres. Bill Clinton for work with UN Foundation, 2005, ranked by Time magazine amongst the 100 Most Influential People in the World 2005. *Publications include:* Ethical Investing 1984, Challenges of Wealth 1988, The Social Investment Almanac 1992, Investing for Good 1993, Socially Responsible Investing: Making a Difference and Making Money 2001; several articles on ethical investment in professional journals. *Leisure interests:* day-sailing, gardening. *Address:* Loring, Wolcott & Coolidge, 230 Congress Street, Floor 12, Boston, MA 02110-2437 (office); 7 Dana Street, Cambridge, MA 02138, USA (home). *Telephone:* (617) 622-2240 (home); (617) 547-3236 (home). *Fax:* (617) 523-6531 (office). *E-mail:* adomini@domini.com (office). *Website:* domini.com (office).

DOMINIAN, Jacobus (Jack), MBE, DSc, FRCPE, FRCPsy; British psychiatrist; b. 25 Aug. 1929, Athens, Greece; s. of Charles Dominian and Mary Scarlato; m. Edith Mary Smith 1955; four d.; ed St Mary's School, Bombay, Stamford Grammar School, England, Fitzwilliam Coll., Cambridge, Exeter Coll., Oxford and Inst. of Psychiatry, London; Sr House Officer United Oxford Hosps 1955–58; Registrar Maudsley Hosp., London 1958–61, Sr Registrar 1961–64; Sr Consultant Psychiatrist Cen. Middx Hosp., London 1965–88, Hon. Consultant 1988–; Dir One Plus One (Marriage and Partnership Research) 1971–; Hon. DSc (Lancaster) 1976. *Publications:* Christian Marriage 1967, Marital Breakdown 1968, Depression 1976, Proposals for a New Sexual Ethic 1976, Authority 1976, Marital Pathology 1980, Marriage, Faith and Love 1981, The Capacity to Love 1985, Sexual Integrity: The Answer to AIDS 1987, Passionate and Compassionate Love – A Vision for Christian Marriage 1991, The Everyday God (with Edmund Flood) 1993, Marriage 1995, One Like Us: a psychological interpretation of Jesus 1998, Let's Make Love 2001. *Leisure interests:* swimming, theatre, music and reading. *Address:* 1 Benjamin Street, London, EC1M 5QG, England (office). *Telephone:* (20) 7553-9530.

DOMINO, Fats; American blues singer; b. (Antoine Domino), 26 Feb. 1928, New Orleans, La.; fmr factory worker; began singing career in local clubs; Hall of Fame Grammy Award 1997, Lifetime Achievement Grammy Award 1997, Nat. Medal of Arts 1998. *Singles include:* The Fat Man, Goin' Home, Going To The River, Please Don't Leave Me, Don't You Know, Ain't That A Shame, Bo Weevil, I'm In Love Again, My Blue Heaven, Blueberry Hill, Walking to New Orleans, My Girl Josephine, Let The Four Winds Blow, Red Sails In The Sunset. *Recordings include:* albums: Here Comes Fats Domino 1963, Southland USA 1965, Fats Domino 1966, Trouble in Mind, Fats is Back 1968, Sleeping on the Job 1978, The Fat Man 1995, Live at Gilleys 1999, Live! Collector's Edition 2000.

DOMLJAN, Žarko, PhD; Croatian editor and politician (retd); b. 14 Sept. 1932, Imotski; m. Iva Marjanovic; one d.; ed Zagreb Univ., Music Coll.; mem. Croatian Nat. Theatre Orchestra 1955–57; Ed.-in-Chief and Deputy Dir Editorial Dept, Lexicographical Inst. 1968–86; Ed.-in-Chief Yugoslav Encyclopedia of Art and Encyclopedia of Croatian Art 1985–96, Life of Art Journal 1967–73; research adviser, Inst. of Art History 1987–90; mem. and Pres. Sabor (Parl. of Croatian Repub.) 1990–92, Vice-Pres. 1992–2000; Chair. Foreign Policy Bd; mem. State Council of Defence and Nat. Security and of Presidential Council; Grand Order of King Petar Krešimir IV 1992. *Publications include:* Architect Hugo Ehrlich 1979, Modern Architecture in Yugoslavia 1986, Umjetnička topografija Hrvatske, Križevci – grad i okolica (Art Topography of Croatia, Križevci – The Town and its Environs) (co-ed.) 1993, Visoko podignimo zastavu (Let's Raise High the Flag) (autobiog.) 2010. *Leisure interests:* tennis, mountain trekking. *Address:* Kukuljevićeva 32, 10000 Zagreb, Croatia (home). *Telephone:* (1) 4822775 (home). *E-mail:* zarko.domljan@zg.t-com.hr (office).

DOMMISSE, Ebbe, MA, PhD; South African newspaper editor and author; b. 14 July 1940, Riversdal; s. of Jan Dommisse and Anna Dommisse; m. Daléne Laubscher 1963; two s. one d.; ed Univ. of Stellenbosch, Grad. School of Journalism, Columbia Univ., USA; reporter, Die Burger, Cape Town 1961, Chief Sub-Ed. 1968, News Ed. 1971; Asst Ed. and Political Commentator, Beeld, Johannesburg (Founder-mem. of new Johannesburg daily) 1974; Asst Ed. Die Burger 1979, Sr Asst Ed. 1984, Ed. 1990–2000; Dir Helpmekaarfonds; mem. Akad. vir Wetenskap en Kuns. *Publications:* with Alf Ries: Broedertwis 1982, Leierstryd 1990; Anton Rupert 2005, Sir David Graaff 2012. *Leisure interests:* reading, the arts, ecology, tennis. *Address:* 25 Chesterfield Road, Oranjezicht, Cape Town 8001, South Africa. *Telephone:* (21) 4651237. *E-mail:* edommisse@mweb.co.za.

DON MALAVO, Estanislao; Equatorial Guinean politician; *Minister of Labour and Social Security;* Deputy Minister of Finance and the Budget 2006–08, Minister of Finance and the Budget 2008, Minister of Labour and Social Security 2010–. *Address:* Ministry of Labour and Social Security, Malabo, Equatorial Guinea (office). *Telephone:* (09) 20-67 (office). *Website:* www.ceiba-guinea -ecuatorial.org/guineees/indexbienv1.htm (office); guinea-equatorial.com (office).

DONAGHY, Baroness (Life Peer), cr. 2010, of Peckham in the London Borough of Southwark; **Rita Margaret Donaghy,** CBE, OBE, BA, FRSA; British public servant; b. (Rita Margaret Willis), 9 Oct. 1944, Bristol, England; d. of William Scott Willis and Margaret Brenda Howard; m. 1st James Columba Donaghy 1968 (divorced 1985); m. 2nd Ted (Edward) Easen-Thomas; ed Durham Univ.; Asst Registrar, then Perm. Sec. of Students' Union, Univ. of London Inst. of Educ. 1968–2000; Pres. Nat. and Local Govt Officers' Asscn (NALGO) 1989–90, TUC

2000; mem. Low Pay Comm. 1997–2000; Chair. Advisory, Conciliation and Arbitration Service (ACAS) 2000–07; Dir (non-exec.) King's Coll. Hosp. 2005–09; mem. Cttee on Standards in Public Life (Kelly Cttee) 2000–07, Acting Chair. 2007; Chair., Dept of Work & Pensions Inquiry on Fatal Accidents in Construction; conducted Review of Women's Nat. Comm. for Dept of Communities & Local Govt 2007; mem. (Labour), House of Lords 2010–; ind. consultant on human resources and employment relations; Fellow, Chartered Inst. of Personnel and Devt 2002; Hon. DUniv (Open Univ.) 2002, (Keele Univ.) 2004; Hon. DBA (Greenwich) 2005. *Publication:* One Death is Too Many: Inquiry into the Underlying Causes of Construction Fatal Accidents (report to Sec. of State for Work and Pensions) 2009. *Leisure interests:* theatre, gardening, reading. *Address:* House of Lords, Westminster, London, SW1A 0PW, England (office). *Telephone:* (20) 7703-4573 (home). *Fax:* (20) 7703-4573 (home). *E-mail:* donaghyr@parliament.uk (office). *Website:* www .parliament.uk/biographies/lords/baroness-donaghy/4166 (office).

DONAHOE, Patrick R., BS (Econs), MS; American business executive; *Postmaster General and CEO, United States Postal Service;* b. Pittsburgh, Pa; m.; two c.; ed Univ. of Pittsburgh, Massachusetts Inst. of Tech. (Sloan Fellow); entered US Postal Service as a clerk in Pittsburgh, Pa, positions have included Vice-Pres. of Allegheny Area Operations, Sr Vice-Pres. of Human Resources, Sr Vice-Pres. of Operations, Exec. Vice-Pres., Deputy Postmaster Gen. and COO –2010, 73rd Postmaster Gen. of USA and CEO US Postal Service 2010–. *Address:* United States Postal Service, 475 L'Enfant Plaza SW, Washington, DC 20260-0010, USA (office). *Telephone:* (202) 268-2500 (office). *Fax:* (202) 268-4860 (office). *E-mail:* pmgceo@usps.gov (office). *Website:* www.usps.com (office).

DONAHUE, Timothy M., BA; American telecommunications industry executive (retd); ed John Carroll Univ.; Pres. Paging Div., McCaw Cellular Communications (now AT&T Wireless) 1986–89, Pres. US Cen. Region 1989–91, Pres. Northeast Region and Gen. Man. AT&T Wireless 1991–96; Pres. and COO Nextel Communications Inc. 1996–99, Pres. and CEO 1999–2005, Exec. Chair. Sprint Nextel Corpn 2005–06 (retd); Dir Eastman Kodak Co., NVR Inc., John Carroll Univ., Covidien, Tyco Healthcare 2007–. *Address:* c/o Board of Directors, Covidien, 15 Hampshire Street, Mansfield, MA 02048, USA (office).

DONALD, Sir Alan (Ewen), Kt, KCMG, BA, LLM; British fmr diplomatist; b. 5 May 1931, Inverurie, Aberdeenshire, Scotland; s. of Robert T. Donald and Louise Turner; m. Janet H. T. Blood 1958; four s.; ed Aberdeen Grammar School, Fettes Coll., Edinburgh and Trinity Hall, Cambridge; mil. service 1949–50; joined Foreign (later Diplomatic) Service 1954, Third Sec., Embassy in Beijing 1955–57, Pvt. Sec. to Parl. Under-Sec. of State, Foreign Office 1958–61, UK del. to NATO, Paris 1961–64, First Sec., Embassy in Beijing 1964–66, Counsellor, Embassy in Athens 1971–73; Political Adviser to Gov. of Hong Kong 1974–77; Amb. to Zaire, Rwanda and Burundi 1977–80, to People's Repub. of the Congo 1978–80, to Indonesia 1984–88, to People's Repub. of China 1988–91; Asst Under-Sec. (Asia/ Pacific), FCO 1980–84; Adviser on Chinese Affairs, Rolls-Royce 1991–99; Dir Fleming Far Eastern Investment Co. 1991–97, China Fund Inc. 1992–2003, Batey, Burn Ltd 1992–98, HSBC China Fund Ltd 1994–2004, Fleming Asian Investment Co. 1997–2001; Hon. LLD (Aberdeen) 1991. *Leisure interests:* music, military history, water colour sketching, films. *Address:* Applebys, Chiddingstone Causeway, Tonbridge, Kent, TN11 8JH, England (home). *Telephone:* (1892) 870598 (home). *E-mail:* alan.donald055@btinternet.com.

DONALD, Dame Athene Margaret, DBE, PhD, FRS; British physicist and academic; *Master, Churchill College, Cambridge;* b. (Athene Margaret Griffith), 15 May 1953, London, England; d. of Walter Griffith and Annette Marian Tylor; m. Matthew J. Donald 1976; one s. one d.; ed Camden School for Girls, London and Girton Coll., Cambridge; postdoctoral researcher, Cornell Univ., USA 1977–81; Fellow, Robinson Coll., Cambridge 1981–, Science and Eng Research Council Research Fellow, Univ. of Cambridge 1981–83, Royal Soc. Research Fellow 1983–85, Lecturer 1985–95, Reader 1985–98, Prof. of Experimental Physics 1998–, Deputy Vice-Chancellor 2009–, mem. Council Univ. of Cambridge 2009–, Gender Equality Champion, Master of Churchill Coll. 2014–; mem. Governing Council, Inst. of Food Research 1999–2003; mem. Biotechnology and Biological Sciences Research Council Research Bd 2003–04; mem. Royal Soc. Council 2004–06, 2012–, Chair. Royal Soc. Educ. Cttee 2010–; mem. Research Assessment Exercise panel E19 (2008 exercise), Scientific Council of the European Research Council 2013–; mem. Academia Europaea 2009; Trustee, Science Museum Group 2011–; Hon. FInstP 2013; Hon. ScD (East Anglia) 2012, (Exeter) 2012, (Sheffield) 2013; Samuel Locker Award in Physics, Univ. of Birmingham 1989, Charles Vernon Boys Prize, Inst. of Physics 1989, Rosenhain Medal and Prize, Inst. of Materials 1995, William Hopkins Prize, Cambridge Philosophical Soc. 2003, Mott Prize, Inst. of Physics 2005, Bakerian Lecturer, Royal Soc. 2006, L'Oréal-UNESCO Award For Women in Science (Europe) 2009, Faraday Medal, Inst. of Physics 2010, Lifetime Achievement Award, UKRC Women of Outstanding Achievement 2011. *Publications:* Liquid Crystalline Polymers (co-author) 1992, Starch: Structure and Function (co-author) 1997, Starch: Advances in Structure and Function (co-author) 2001; numerous articles in scientific journals. *Leisure interests:* music, walking. *Address:* Department of Physics, Cavendish Laboratory, University of Cambridge, JJ Thomson Avenue, Cambridge, CB3 0HE, England (office). *Telephone:* (1223) 337382 (office). *Fax:* (1223) 337000 (office). *E-mail:* amd3@cam.ac.uk (office). *Website:* www.phy.cam.ac.uk/people/donalda.php (office); www.bss.phy.cam.ac .uk/~amd3 (office).

DONALD, Luke Campbell, MBE; British professional golfer; b. 7 Dec. 1977, Hemel Hempstead, Herts., England; m. Diane Antonopoulos 2007; two d.; ed Royal Grammar School, High Wycombe, Bucks., Northwestern Univ., USA; played junior golf at Hazlemere Golf Club and Beaconsfield Golf Club (club champion twice); joined College Prospects of America and took golf scholarship at Northwestern Univ. 1997; won individual NCAA Div. I Men's Golf Championships men's title 1999; turned professional 2001; plays mainly on US-based PGA (Professional Golfers Asscn) Tour 2001–, also mem. of European Tour 2003–; winner Southern Farm Bureau Classic 2002, Scandinavian Masters by Carlsberg 2004, Omega European Masters 2004, Honda Classic 2006, Madrid Masters 2010, WGC-Accenture Match Play Championship 2011, BMW PGA Championship 2011, 2012, Barclays Scottish Open 2011, Children's Miracle Network Hospitals Classic 2011, Race to Dubai 2011, Transitions Championship 2012; other wins include Target World Challenge (unofficial money-list event) 2005, Gary Player Invitational (with Sally Little) 2007; results in major championships: tied for third at US Masters 2005, tied for fourth 2011, tied for third at PGA Championship 2006, tied for fifth at British Open 2009, 2012; mem. winning Ryder Cup teams representing Europe 2004, 2006, 2010, 2012, WGC-World Cup team representing England 2004 (winners), 2005; reached top ten in Official World Golf Rankings for first time 2006; briefly highest ranked European golfer Jan. 2007; first became No. 1 in World Rankings after winning BMW PGA Championship May 2011; first man to win both US and European money lists in one year after finishing third at Dubai World Championship Dec. 2011; Hon. Life mem. European Tour 2012; Fred Haskins Award 1999, PGA Tour leading money winner 2011, Vardon Trophy 2011, Byron Nelson Award 2011, PGA Player of the Year 2011, PGA Tour Player of the Year 2011, European Tour Race to Dubai winner 2011, European Tour Golfer of the Year 2011. *Leisure interests:* painting and drawing, collecting contemporary art, Tottenham Hotspur Football Club. *Address:* c/o IMG, McCormack House, Hogarth Business Park, Burlington Lane, Chiswick, London, W4 2TH, England.

DONALDSON, Roger; New Zealand (b. Australian) film director; b. 15 Nov. 1945, Ballarat, Australia; emigrated to NZ aged 19; established still photography business, then started making documentary films. *Television:* Winners and Losers (series of short dramas). *Films include:* Sleeping Dogs (also producer) 1977, Nutcase (1980, Smash Palace (also producer and writer) 1981, The Bounty 1984, Marie 1985, No Way Out 1987, Cocktail 1988, Cadillac Man (also producer) 1990, White Sands 1992, The Getaway 1994, Species 1995, Dante's Peak 1997, Thirteen Days 2000, The Recruit 2003, The World's Fastest Indian (also producer and writer) 2005, The Bank Job 2007, Seeking Justice 2011. *Address:* c/o CAA, 2000 Avenue of the Stars, Los Angeles, CA 90067, USA.

DONALDSON, Samuel (Sam) Andrew, BA; American broadcast journalist; b. 11 March 1934, El Paso, Tex.; s. of Samuel A. Donaldson and Chloe Hampson; m. 1st Billie K. Butler 1963; three s. one d.; m. 2nd Janice C. Smith 1983; ed Univ. of Texas, El Paso and Univ. of Southern California; radio and TV news reporter, anchorman, WTOP, Washington, DC 1961–67; Capitol Hill Corresp., ABC News, Washington, DC 1967–77, White House Corresp. 1977–89, Chief White House Corresp. 1998–99, News Contributor and Analyst 2010–; Pres. Advisory Board, Woodrow Wilson Int. Center for Scholars; Bd mem. Library of American Broadcasting, American Acad. of Achievement; Chair. Emer., Advisory Bd, H. Lee Moffett Cancer Center, Fla.; Broadcaster of the Year Award, Nat. Press Foundation 1998 and numerous other awards. *Television:* Anchor: World News Sunday 1979–89, Prime Time Live 1989–98, SamDonaldson@abcnews.com 1999–2001, The Sam Donaldson Show (ABC Radio Network) 2001–04, Politics Live 2004–10; Co-anchor: 20/20 Live (ABC Network) 1998–2000, This Week With Sam Donaldson and Cokie Roberts (ABC Network) 1996–2002, Politics Live (ABC News Now); panelist, This Week 1981–96, 2002–. *Publication:* Hold on Mr President 1987. *Address:* ABC News, 7 West 66th Street, New York, NY 20036, USA (office). *E-mail:* samdonaldson@abcnews.com (office). *Website:* www.abcnews.go.com (office).

DONALDSON, Sir Simon Kirwan, Kt, DPhil, FRS; British mathematician and academic; *Royal Society Research Professor, Imperial College London;* b. 20 Aug. 1957, Cambridge, England; s. of Peter Donaldson and Jane Stirland; m. Ana Nora Hurtado 1986; two s. one d.; ed Sevenoaks School, Kent, Pembroke Coll., Cambridge, Worcester Coll., Oxford; Jr Research Fellow, All Souls Coll., Oxford 1983–85; Wallis Prof. of Math., Univ. of Oxford 1985–98; Fellow, St Anne's Coll., Oxford 1985–98; Prof. of Pure Math., Imperial Coll., London 1998–, currently Royal Soc. Research Prof., Pres. Inst. of Math. Sciences 2003–; Foreign mem. Royal Swedish Acad. of Sciences 2010; Fellow, American Math. Soc. 2012; Hon. Fellow, Pembroke Coll., Cambridge 1992, St Anne's Coll., Oxford 1999; Junior Whitehead Prize, London Math. Soc. 1985, Fields Medal 1986, Crafoord Prize (with S-T Yau) 1994, King Faisal Int. Prize (with M. S. Narasimhan) 2006, Nemmers Prize, Northwestern Univ. 2008, Shaw Prize (with C. H. Taubes) 2009. *Publications:* The Geometry of Four-manifolds (with P. B. Kronheimer) 1990, Floer Homology Groups in Yang-Mills Theory 2002; numerous papers in math. journals. *Leisure interest:* sailing. *Address:* Room 674, Huxley Building, Department of Mathematics, Imperial College, 180 Queen's Gate, London, SW7 2BT, England (office). *Telephone:* (20) 7594-8559 (office). *Fax:* (20) 7594-8517 (office). *E-mail:* s.donaldson@imperial.ac (office). *Website:* www3.imperial.ac.uk/people/s.donaldson (office); www2.imperial.ac.uk/~skdona (office).

DONALDSON, William H., BA, MA, MBA, CFA; American business executive and fmr government official; m. Jane Donaldson; three c.; ed Yale Univ., Harvard Business School; rifle platoon Commdr and later aide-de-camp to Commanding Gen. 1st Provisional Marine Air Ground Task Force, US Marine Corps 1953–55; Co-Founder Donaldson, Lufkin & Jenrette, New York 1959, Chair. and CEO 1959–73, Sr Advisor 1996–2000; Under-Sec., US State Dept, Washington, DC 1973–75; Counsel to Vice-Pres. 1975; Dean and William S. Beinecke Prof. of Man., Grad. School of Man., Yale Univ. 1975–80; Chair. and CEO Donaldson Enterprises Inc. (investment co.), New York Chair. 1980–90, 2001–; Chair. and CEO New York Stock Exchange 1990–95; Chair., Pres. and CEO Aetna Inc. 2000–02; Chair. SEC, New York 2003–05; Chair. Carnegie Endowment for International Peace 1999–2003; mem. Pres.'s Econ. Recovery Advisory Bd 2009–; mem. Advisory Bd, Tokarz Group Advisers LLC; Founding Dean, Yale School of Man., Yale Univ. 1975, Chair. Bd of Advisors 1995–2003; Trustee, Ford Foundation 1968–80, Yale Univ. 1970–75.

DONDELINGER, Albert Marie Joseph, DJur; Luxembourg banker; b. 22 March 1934, Redange, Attert; s. of Jean Dondelinger and Simone Lamborelle; m. Francine Dondelinger-Gillen; three c.; ed Coll. St Michel, Brussels, Catholic Univ. of Louvain, Belgium; Alt. Gov. for Luxembourg, IBRD 1967–76; mem. European Monetary Cttee 1971–76, Bd of Belgium-Luxembourg Exchange Inst. 1972–76; Adviser to Group of Twenty and Assoc. mem. IMF Interim Cttee 1972–76; mem. Bd European Monetary Co-operation Fund and mem. Govs' Cttee, EEC Cen. Banks 1973–76; Govt Commr to State Savings Bank 1974–76; Co-Chair. Comm. for Financial Affairs of Conf. for Int. Econ. Co-operation (North-South Dialogue, Paris) 1975–76; Chair. Luxembourg Bankers' Assn 1977–78; Man. Dir and Chair. Exec. Bd, Banque Internationale à Luxembourg 1977–90, Hon. Chair. 1990–; ind. economic and business man. consultant 1990–; Pres. European League for Econ. Co-operation (Luxembourg Bureau); Vice-Pres. Foundation Prince Henri-Princesse Maria Teresa; Vice-Chair. SOS-Sahel; Pres. Cercle Artistique de

Luxembourg; mem. Bd Inst. Régional Intracommunautaire; mem. Inst. Int. d'Etudes Bancaires 1978–; Commdr Order of Couronne de Chêne (Luxembourg), Commdr Order of the Crown (Belgium), the Nat. Order (Ivory Coast), Officier, Ordre Nat. du Mérite, Order of Merit (Luxembourg). *Publication:* Le secret bancaire au Grand-Duché de Luxembourg 1972. *Leisure interests:* photography, bibliophily, golf, skiing, swimming.

DONDUKOV, Alexander Nikolayevich, DTechSc; Russian engineer and politician; b. 29 March 1954, Kuybyshev (now Samara); engineer, Sr engineer, leading constructor Moscow Machine Construction Bureau (designers' office), Moscow 1977–85; Deputy Chief Constructor 1985, Chief Constructor 1991, Head, Gen. Constructor Moscow Machine Construction factory Skorost' 1991–93; Chair. Bd of Dirs, Gen. Constructor A. S. Yakovlev Machine Designers' Office 1993–2000, 2001; mem. Govt Council for Industrial Policy 1994; mem. Congress of Russian Intelligentsia 1994–; Minister of Industry, Science and Tech., Russian Fed. 2000–02; mem. Fed. Council (representing Belgorod) 2002–03. *Address:* c/o A. S. Yakovlev Machine Designers' Bureau, Leningradsky prosp. 68, 123315 Moscow A–47, Russia (office).

DONE, Kenneth Stephen, AM; Australian artist; b. 29 June 1940, Sydney, NSW; s. of Clifford Wade Done and Lillian Maureen Done; m. Judith Ann Walker; one s. one d.; ed Katoomba and Mosman High Schools, Nat. Art School, Sydney; Creative Dir Advertising Samuelson Talbot, Sydney, J. Walter Thompson 1960–78; Chair. Ken Done Group of Cos 1979–; Goodwill Amb. for UNICEF Australia; Paul Harris Fellow, Rotary International; Hon. Fellow, Design Inst. of Australia 1999; NSW Tourism Award 1986, Rotary Award for Excellence 1993, Spirit of Australia Award 1993, Cannes Gold Lion Award, Export Hero Award, Westpac Banking Corpn 1999, Life Fellow, Medal Powerhouse Museum 2002. *Publications:* Ken Done: Paintings and Drawings 1975–87, Craftsman House 1992, Ken Done Paintings (1990–94) 1994, Ken Done: The Art of Design 1994, Ken Done's Sydney, 20 Years of Painting 1999, The Art of Ken Done, Craftsman House 2002. *Leisure interests:* golf, swimming, diving, travelling. *Address:* 1 Hickson Road, The Rocks, NSW 2000, Australia (office). *Telephone:* (2) 8274-4500 (office). *Fax:* (2) 8274-4545 (office). *E-mail:* kelly@done.com.au (office). *Website:* www.done.com.au (office).

DONEN, Stanley; American film producer and director; b. 13 April 1924, Columbia, SC; s. of Mortie Donen and Helen Donen; ed Univ. of South Carolina; Lifetime Achievement Award, Acad. of Motion Picture Arts and Sciences 1998, Golden Eddie Award, American Cinema Eds 1988, Lifetime Achievement Award, Palm Beach Int. Film Festival 1999. *Films include:* On the Town 1949, Royal Wedding 1951, Love Is Better Than Ever 1952, Singin' in the Rain 1952, Fearless Fagan 1952, Give a Girl a Break 1953, Seven Brides for Seven Brothers 1954, Deep in My Heart 1954, It's Always Fair Weather 1955, Funny Face 1957, The Pajama Game 1957, Kiss Them for Me 1957, Indiscreet 1958, Damn Yankees! 1958, Once More, with Feeling! 1960, Surprise Package 1960, The Grass Is Greener 1960, Charade 1963, Arabesque 1966, Two for the Road 1967, Bedazzled 1967, Staircase 1969, The Little Prince 1974, Lucky Lady 1975, Movie Movie 1978, Saturn 3 1980, Blame It on Rio 1984. *Television includes:* Love Letters 1999. *Address:* 146 Central Park West, #5D, New York, NY 10023, USA.

DONG, Kejun; Chinese woodcut artist; b. 18 Feb. 1939, Chongqing, Sichuan; s. of Dong Xueyuan and Gue Ximing; m. Lü Hengfen 1969; one s.; Dir of Chinese Artistic Asscn; Standing Dir Chinese Woodcut Asscn; Vice-Chair. Guizhou Artistic Asscn; Chair. Guiyang Artistic Asscn; Vice-Pres. Acad. of Painting and Calligraphy; mem. Standing Cttee of Guizhou Br. of CPPCC; Vice-Chair. Guizhou Prov. Br. Artists' Assoc. 1988–; Chair. Artists' Assoc. Guiyang Br. 1988–; Council mem. Artists' Assoc. 1988–; works on view at nat. exhbns 1965–, also in Japan, USA, France, Sweden, Germany, Africa and Australia; Prizewinner, 9th Nat. Woodcut Exhbn 1986; First Grade Nat. Artist. *Works include:* Spring Returns to the Miao Mountain 1979, A Close Ball 1979, An Illustration of the Continuation of Feng Xuefeng's Fables (a hundred pieces) 1980, Company 1981, Go Back Drunkenly 1982, Lively Spring 1983, The Miao Nat Sisters in Their Splendid Costume 1985, Contemporary Totem-1 1986, Mountain Breath 1986, A White Cottage 1987, Sunny Rain 1988, A Hundred Pieces of Coloured Inkwash Drawings 1991–92, The Big Sleep 1993, The Bird Market 1993, Illusion 1993, Eagle 1994, Man and Horse 1995, Going to Market 1995. *Publications:* Dong Kejun Woodcut Works, Selected Paintings of Dong Kejun 1992, Selected Chinese Coloured Inkwash Paintings 1995. *Leisure interests:* literature, music, film and dance. *Address:* Guiyang Artistic Asscn, 27 Road Shizi, Guiyang, Guizhou Prov., People's Republic of China.

DONG, Mingzhu; Chinese business executive; *Chairman and President, Gree Electric Appliances Inc.;* joined Gree Electric Appliances Inc. (then called Haili), Zhuhai 1990, later Business Man., later Departmental Man. of Business Dept, later Vice-Gen. Man., Gen. Man. 2001, Pres. –2012, Chair. and Pres. 2012–; Chair. Female Asscn of Entrepreneurs, Zhuhai City 2002–; Deputy Dir Chinese Household Appliances Asscn; mem. Female Asscn of Entrepreneurs, Guangdong, currently Vice-Chair.; mem. Standing Cttee Zhuhai Political Consultative Conf.; Del., 10th NPC 2003–; Nat. Excellent Woman Worker 1998, Guangdong Prov. Excellent Female Man. 1999, Nat. May 1 Labour Medal, elected one of Home Electric Appliance Top 10 Famous Individuals of the Year by Beijing Youth magazine 1999, received title of Excellent Woman in Guangdong Prov. 2000, Chinese Outstanding Woman 2001, elected one of Female Entrepreneurs of All Time in China 2002, one of Top 10 Businesswoman of China 2002, named as Excellent Woman and one of Nat. Successful Female Models by Nat. Women's Union 2003, named by first Global Chinese Women Conf. one of 10 Most Powerful Chinese Women 2003, named by MBA one of 10 Most Respected Innovative Entrepreneurs 2004, ranked by Fortune magazine amongst the 50 Most Powerful Women in Business outside the US (42nd) 2004, (48th) 2005, (48th) 2007, (33rd) 2008, (30th) 2009, (31st) 2010, (30th) 2012, named as one of Top 10 Chinese Marketing People 2004, named one of 10 Excellent Business Leaders and one of "10 Innovation People that influence the future development trend of Chinese household appliances" 2005, named one of Guangdong Top Ten Economically Influential People 2005, ranked by Forbes magazine amongst The World's 100 Most Powerful Women (93rd) 2007. *Publication:* Lay Out in the World (autobiog., adapted for TV by China-Central TV Station). *Address:* Gree Electric Appliances Inc., 6 West Jinji Road, Qianshan, Zhuhai 519070, Guangdong Province, People's

Republic of China (office). *Telephone:* (756) 8614883 (office). *Fax:* (756) 8614998 (office). *E-mail:* gree@gree.com (office). *Website:* www.gree.com.cn (office).

DONG, Wenbiao; Chinese economist and business executive; *Chairman, China Minsheng Banking Corporation Limited;* b. 1957; fmr Sec. CCP Cttee, Vice-Pres. and Pres. China Minsheng Banking Corpn Ltd, currently Chair.; Vice-Chair. All China Fed. of Industry and Commerce, China Civilian Chamber of Commerce; fmr Chair. and Pres. Haitong Securities Co. Ltd; fmr Man. Dir Zhengzhou Br. of Bank of Communications; fmr Dir, Bank of Communications; fmr Deputy Dean Henan Inst. of Financial Man.; mem. Standing Cttee 12th CPPCC Nat. Cttee; fmr Deputy Dir CPPCC Econ. Cttee, mem. CPPCC Nat. Cttee. *Address:* China Minsheng Banking Corporation Ltd, 2 Fuxingmennei Avenue, Beijing 100873, People's Republic of China (office). *Telephone:* (10) 68946790 (office). *E-mail:* webmaster@cmbc.com.cn (office). *Website:* www.cmbc.com.cn (office).

DONG, Zigang, MD, DrPH; biologist and academic; *Hormel-Knowlton Professor and Executive Director, Hormel Institute, University of Minnesota;* Guest Prof., The First Mil. Medical Univ., Guangzhou, China 2000–; Hon. Prof., The Fourth Mil. Univ., Xian, Shanxi, China 2000–; Hormel-Knowlton Prof. and Exec. Dir Hormel Inst., Univ. of Minn., also McKnight Presidential Prof. in Cancer Prevention 2006–; mem. NIG Reviewer Reserve 1997–, Study Section of Cancer Centers for NIH 2000–, Grant Review Panel of American Inst. for Cancer Research 2000–, Working Group for RAPID (Rapid Access for Preventive Intervention Devt) programme of Nat. Cancer Inst. 2002, Special Emphasis Study Section of NIH 2002; Hon. Prof., The Fourth Mil. Univ., Xian, China 2000–. *Publications:* numerous articles in scientific journals. *Address:* Hormel Institute, University of Minnesota, 801 16th Avenue, NE, Austin, MN 55912, USA (office). *Telephone:* (507) 437-5600 (office). *Fax:* (507) 437-9606 (office). *E-mail:* dongx004@umn.edu (office); zgdong@hi.umn.edu (office). *Website:* www.cancer.umn.edu/research/profiles/dong.html (office).

DONIGI, Peter Dickson, CBE, LLB; Papua New Guinea lawyer and diplomatist; *Consulting Lawyer, Warner Shand Lawyers;* b. 19 Dec. 1950, Wewak; m.; five c.; ed Univ. of Papua New Guinea; pvt. legal practice 1981–98; Amb. and Special Envoy to UN, New York 1991–92, apptd Perm. Rep. to UN, New York 1998; Amb. to Germany (also accred to Holy See) 1992–95; Lecturer in Int. Law, Univ. of Papua New Guinea; Consulting Lawyer, Warner Shand Lawyers, Boroko; mem. Council Commonwealth Lawyers' Asscn 1991–; fmr Pres. Papua New Guinea Law Soc.; Commonwealth Fellow 1991. *Publications:* Indigenous or Aboriginal Rights to Property: A Papua New Guinea Experience. *Address:* Warner Shand Lawyers, PO Box 1817, Boroko 111, Papua New Guinea (office). *Telephone:* 3215025. *Fax:* 3215079. *Website:* www.png-wealth-creation.com.

DONLEAVY, J(ames) P(atrick); Irish author; b. 23 April 1926, New York City; s. of Patrick Donleavy and Margaret Donleavy; m. 1st Valerie Heron (divorced 1969); one s. one d.; m. 2nd Mary Wilson Price (divorced 1989); one s. one d.; ed Preparatory School, New York and Trinity Coll., Dublin; served in USN during World War II; Evening Standard Drama Award 1960, Brandeis Univ. Creative Arts Award 1961–62, Citation, American Acad. and Nat. Inst. of Arts and Letters 1975, Worldfest Houston Gold Award 1992, Cine Golden Eagle Writer and Narrator 1993. *Publications include:* (novels) The Ginger Man 1955, A Singular Man 1963, The Beastly Beatitudes of Balthazar B 1968, The Onion Eaters 1971, A Fairy Tale of New York 1973, The Destinies of Darcy Dancer, Gentleman 1977, Schultz 1979, Leila 1983, Wrong Information is Being Given Out at Princeton 1998; (short stories and sketches) Meet My Maker the Mad Molecule 1964, An Author and His Image 1997; (novella) The Saddest Summer of Samuel S. 1966; also: The Unexpurgated Code: A Complete Manual of Survival and Manners 1975, De Alfonce Tennis, The Superlative Game of Eccentric Champions: Its History, Accoutrements, Rules, Conduct and Regimen, A Legend 1984, J. P. Donleavy's Ireland: In All Her Sins and in Some of Her Graces 1986, A Singular Country 1989, The History of the Ginger Man 1993, The Lady Who Liked Clean Rest Rooms 1995; (plays) The Ginger Man 1959, Fairy Tales of New York 1960, A Singular Man 1964, The Saddest Summer of Samuel S. 1968, The Plays of J. P. Donleavy 1972, The Beastly Beatitudes of Balthazar B. 1981, Are You Listening Rabbi Löw? 1987, That Darcy, That Dancer, That Gentlemen 1990. *Leisure interests:* De Alfonce Tennis, dry stone walling. *Address:* Levington Park, Mullingar, Co. Westmeath, Ireland (home). *Telephone:* (44) 9348903 (home). *Fax:* (44) 9348351 (home).

DONNELLAN, Declan; British theatre and opera director; b. 4 Aug. 1953, Manchester; ed Univ. of Cambridge; called to Bar (Middle Temple) 1978; freelance theatre productions include Don Giovanni (Scottish Opera Go Round), A Masked Ball (Opera 80), Rise and Fall of the City of Mahagonny (Wexford Festival), Macbeth and Philoctetes (Nat. Theatre of Finland); co-f. Cheek By Jowl (production co.) 1981, Artistic Dir 1981–; productions with Cheek By Jowl include Racine's Andromache, Corneille's The Cid, Twelfth Night, A Midsummer Night's Dream, Hamlet, As You Like It, Measure for Measure, Much Ado About Nothing 1998 and his own trans. of Musset's Don't Fool With Love and The Blind Men; also wrote and directed Lady Betty and Sara Sampson; Assoc. Dir Nat. Theatre (NT) 1989–97; work for NT includes Fuente Ovejuna 1989, Peer Gynt, Sweeney Todd 1993, Angels in America, Perestroika 1993, School for Scandal 1998; Dir Falstaff, Salzburg Festival 2001; Dir Le Cid by Corneille, Avignon Festival; Dir Boris Godunov and Twelfth Night, Russian Theatre Confed.; recipient of six Olivier Awards, Time Out Award (with Nick Ormerod) for Angels in America 1992, Observer Award for Outstanding Achievement, as well as awards in Paris, New York and Moscow. *Film:* Bel Ami 2012. *Publications:* The Actor and The Target. *Address:* Cheek by Jowl Theatre Company, The Barbican Centre, Silk Street, London, EC2Y 8DS, England. *Telephone:* (20) 7382-7281 (office). *Website:* www.cheekbyjowl.com (office).

DONNELLY, Christopher Nigel, CMG, TD, BA; British defence, security and foreign affairs specialist; *Director, The Institute for Statecraft;* b. 10 Nov. 1946, Rochdale, Lancs., England; s. of the late Anthony Donnelly and Dorothy M. Morris; m. Jill Norris 1971; one s. one d.; ed Cardinal Langley School, Middleton, Lancs. and Univ. of Manchester; Instructor, Royal Mil. Acad. Sandhurst (RMAS) 1969–72; Sr Lecturer, Soviet Studies Research Centre, RMAS 1972–79, Dir 1979–89; TA (Int. Corps) 1970–93; Adjunct Prof., Carnegie Mellon Univ. 1985–89, Georgia Tech. Univ. 1989–93; Special Adviser for Cen. and E European Affairs to Sec.-Gen. of NATO 1989–2003; Founder and Head of Advanced Research and Assessment Group, Defence Acad. of the UK 2003–07, Sr Fellow 2007–10; currently Dir Inst. for Statecraft, London; Commdr (Grand Cross), Order of the Grand Duke Gediminas (Lithuania) 2002. *Publications:* Red Banner 1989, War and the Soviet Union 1990, Gorbachev's Revolution 1991, Nations, Alliances and Security 2004; numerous articles on Russian and Eastern European defence and security issues. *Leisure interest:* field sports. *Address:* The Institute for Statecraft, 2 Temple Place, London, WC2R 3BD, England (office). *E-mail:* cdonnelly@statecraft.org.uk (office). *Website:* www.statecraft.org.uk (office).

DONNELLY, Joseph (Joe) Simon, Sr, BA, JD; American lawyer, politician and business executive; *Senator from Indiana;* b. 29 Sept. 1955, Massapequa, NY; m. Jill Donnelly; two c.; ed Univ. of Notre Dame and Notre Dame Law School, Washington and Lee Univ.; practised law –1996; ran campaign for Indiana Attorney Gen. 1988, lost at Democratic state convention; served on Indiana State Election Bd 1988–89; also ran unsuccessful campaign for Indiana State Senate 1990; opened Marking Solutions (printing and rubber stamp co.) 1996; served on local school bd 1997–2001, Pres. 2000–01; mem. US House of Reps for 2nd Congressional Dist of Indiana 2007–13, mem. Cttee on Financial Services, Cttee on Veterans' Affairs; Senator from Indiana 2013–; Democrat. *Address:* United States Senate, Washington, DC 20510, USA (office). *Telephone:* (202) 224-3121 (office). *Website:* www.senate.gov (office).

DONNER, Jörn Johan, BA; Finnish film director, writer, producer, politician and diplomatist; b. 5 Feb. 1933, Helsinki; s. of Dr Kai Donner and Greta von Bonsdorff; m. 1st Inga-Britt Wik 1954 (divorced 1962); m. 2nd Jeanette Bonnier 1974 (divorced 1988); m. 3rd Bitte Westerlund 1995; five s. one d.; ed Univ. of Helsinki; worked as writer and film dir in Finland and Sweden, writing own film scripts; contrib. and critic to various Scandinavian and int. journals; CEO Jörn Donner Productions 1966–; Dir Swedish Film Inst., Stockholm 1972–75, Exec. Producer 1975–78, Man. Dir 1978–82; Chair. Bd Finnish Film Foundation 1981–83, 1986–89, 1992–95; mem. Bd Marimekko Textiles and other cos; mem. Helsinki City Council 1969–1972, 1984–92; mem. Parl. 1987–95, Vice-Chair. Foreign Affairs Cttee 1991–95, Chair. Finnish EFTA Parliamentarians 1991–95; Consul-Gen. of Finland, Los Angeles, USA 1995–96; mem. European Parl. 1996–99; several literary awards. *Films include:* as dir: A Sunday in September (Venice Film Festival Best First Film 1963) 1963, To Love 1964, Adventure Starts Here 1965, Rooftree 1967, Black on White 1968, Sixty-nine 1969, Portraits of Women 1970, Anna 1970, Images of Finland 1971, Tenderness 1972, Three Scenes with Ingmar Bergman 1976, The Bergman File 1975–77, Men Can't Be Raped 1978, Dirty Story 1984, Letters from Sweden 1987, Ingmar Bergman, a Conversation 1998, The President 2000, The Interrogation 2009; numerous films as producer including: Fanny och Alexander (Fanny and Alexander) (Academy Award for Producer of Best Foreign Language Film 1984) 1982, The Faceless Man 1995, Abandoned Houses, Empty Homes 2000, Raja 1918 2007, Yksinteoin 2 2011. *Television:* host of talk shows (Sweden and Finland) 1974–95. *Publications:* 59 books, including Father and Son (Finlandia Prize 1985), Report from Berlin 1958, The Personal Vision of Ingmar Bergman 1962, Bergman: PM 2010, Notes on Marshal Mannerheim 2011. *Leisure interest:* fishing. *Address:* PO Box 214, 00171 Helsinki (office); Rauhankatu 3F11, 00170 Helsinki, Finland (home). *Telephone:* (9) 1356060 (home); 400-205606 (mobile) (office). *E-mail:* j.donner@surfnet.fi (home).

DONNER, Richard; American director and producer; b. 24 April 1930, New York; actor off-Broadway; collaborated with dir Martin Ritt on TV adaptation of Somerset Maugham's Of Human Bondage; moved to Calif. and began directing commercials, industrial films and documentaries. *Films include:* X-15 1961, Salt and Pepper 1968, Twinky 1969, The Omen 1976, Superman 1978, Superman II 1980, Inside Moves 1981, The Toy 1982, Ladyhawke 1985, The Goonies 1985, Lethal Weapon 1987, Scrooged 1988, Lethal Weapon 2 1989, Radio Flyer 1991, The Final Conflict (exec. producer) 1991, The Lost Boys (exec. producer) 1991, Delirious (exec. producer) 1991, Lethal Weapon 3 1992, Free Willy (co-exec. producer) 1993, Maverick 1994, Assassins 1995, Free Willy 3: The Rescue, Conspiracy Theory 1997, Double Tap (producer) 1997, Lethal Weapon 4 1998 (also producer), Made Men (producer) 1999, Any Given Sunday (producer) 1999, X-Men (producer) 2000, Blackheart (producer) 1999, Timeline (exec. producer) 2003, 16 Blocks 2006, X-Men Origins: Wolverine (exec. producer), Black & White in Colors (assoc. producer) 2012. *Television includes:* (films) Portrait of a Teenage Alcoholic, Senior Year, A Shadow in the Streets, Tales from the Crypt presents Demon Knight (co-exec. producer), Any Given Sunday 1999, X-Men 2000 (exec. producer); (series episodes) Have Gun Will Travel, Perry Mason, Cannon, Get Smart, The Fugitive, Kojak, Bronk, Lucas Tanner, Gilligan's Island, Man From U.N.C.L.E., Wild Wild West, Twilight Zone, The Banana Splits, Combat, Two Fisted Tales, Conspiracy Theory. *Address:* 8383 Wilshire Blvd, Suite 500, Beverly Hills, CA 90211, USA.

DONOGHUE, Denis, PhD; Irish literary critic and academic; *Henry James Professor of English and American Letters, New York University;* b. 1 Dec. 1928, Tullow, Co. Carlow; m. Frances Donoghue; three s. five d.; ed Univ. Coll., Dublin; Admin. Office, Irish Dept of Finance 1951–54; Asst Lecturer, Univ. Coll., Dublin 1954–57, Coll. Lecturer 1957–62, 1963–64, Prof. of Modern English and American Literature 1965–79; Visiting Scholar, Univ. of Pennsylvania 1962–63; Univ. Lecturer, Univ. of Cambridge and Fellow, King's Coll. 1964–65; Henry James Prof. of English and American Letters, New York Univ., USA 1979–; mem. Int. Cttee of Asscn of Univ. Profs of English; Hon. DLitt; BBC Reith Lecturer 1982. *Publications:* The Third Voice 1959, Connoisseurs of Chaos 1965, The Ordinary Universe 1968, Emily Dickinson 1968, Jonathan Swift 1969, Yeats 1971, Thieves of Fire 1974, Sovereign Ghost: Studies in Imagination 1978, Ferocious Alphabets 1981, The Arts Without Mystery 1983, We Irish: Essays on Irish Literature and Society 1987, Walter Pater: Lover of Strange Souls 1995, The Practice of Reading 1998, Words Alone: The Poet T. S. Eliot 2000, Adam's Curse: Reflections on Literature and Religion 2001, Speaking of Beauty 2003, The American Classics: A Personal Essay 2005, On Eloquence 2008, Irish Essays 2011; contribs to reviews and journals and ed. of three vols. *Address:* English Department, New York University, 726 Broadway (7th Floor), New York, NY 10003, USA (office); Gaybrook, North Avenue, Mount Merrion, Dublin, Ireland (home). *Telephone:* (212) 998-3954 (office). *E-mail:* dd1@nyu.edu (office).

DONOHO, David Leigh, BS, PhD; American professor of statistics; *Professor of Statistics and Anne T. and Robert M. Bass Professor in the Humanities and Sciences, Stanford University;* b. 5 March 1957, Los Angeles, Calif.; ed Princeton and Harvard Univs; mem. Faculty, Univ. of California, Berkeley 1984–90; Prof. of Statistics, Stanford Univ. 1990–, Anne T. and Robert M. Bass Prof. in the Humanities and Sciences 2002–; mem. NAS; Foreign Assoc., Acad. des sciences 2009; Fellow, American Acad. of Arts and Sciences 1992, Soc. for Industrial and Applied Math. (SIAM) 2009, American Math. Soc. 2012; Dr hc (Chicago) 2009; MacArthur Fellow 1990, COPSS Presidents' Award 1994, John von Neumann Prize, SIAM 2001, Norbert Wiener Prize in Applied Math., SIAM and American Math. Soc. 2010, Shaw Prize in Math. Sciences 2013. *Publications:* numerous papers in professional journals. *Address:* Statistics Department, Stanford University, Stanford, CA 94305, USA (office). *Telephone:* (650) 723-3350 (office). *Fax:* (650) 725-8977 (office). *E-mail:* donoho@stat.stanford.edu (office). *Website:* statweb.stanford.edu/~donoho (office).

DONOHOE, Amanda; British actress; b. 29 June 1962, London; ed Francis Holland School for Girls, London, Cen. School of Speech & Drama, London; mem. Royal Exchange Theatre, Manchester; Broadway debut, Uncle Vanya 1995. *Films include:* Foreign Body 1986, Castaway 1986, The Lair of the White Worm 1988, Tank Malling 1989, Diamond Skulls 1989, The Rainbow 1989, The Laughter of God 1990, Paper Mask 1990, The Madness of King George 1994, Liar Liar 1997, One Night Stand 1997, Stardust 1998, The Real Howard Spitz 1998, I'm Losing You 1998, Glory Glory 2000, Circus 2000, Wild About Harry 2000, Phoenix Blue 2001, Starship Troopers 3: Marauder 2008, The Calling 2009. *Television includes:* Star Quality 1985, Frankie and Johnnie 1985, An Affair in Mind 1988, Game, Set, and Match (series) 1988, L.A. Law (series) 1990–92, Shame 1992, It's Nothing Personal 1993, Briefest Encounter 1993, The Substitute 1993, A Woman's Guide to Adultery 1993, Shame II: The Secret 1995, Deep Secrets 1996, The Thorn Birds: The Missing Years 1996, A Knight in Camelot 1998, Batman Beyond: The Movie 1999, Rock the Boat 2000, In the Beginning 2000, Lucky Day 2002, Murder City (series) 2004, Bad Girls (series) 2006, Love Trap (series) 2007, Emmerdale (series) 2009. *Plays include:* The Graduate 2001.

DONOHOE, Peter Howard, CBE, BMus, ARCM, FRNCM; British pianist; b. 18 June 1953, Manchester; s. of Harold Donohoe and Marjorie Donohoe (née Travis); m. Elaine Margaret Burns 1980; one d.; ed Chetham's School of Music, Royal Manchester Coll. of Music, Univ. of Leeds, studied with Derek Wyndham and Yvonne Loriod, Paris; professional solo pianist 1974–; appears several times each season with major symphony orchestras in London and rest of UK and performs regularly at the Promenade Concerts 1979–; performances with the LA Philharmonic, Chicago, Boston, Pittsburgh, Cincinnati, Dallas, Detroit and Cleveland orchestras and in Europe with Berlin Philharmonic and Symphony, Leipzig Gewandhaus, Dresden Philharmonic, Vienna Symphony, Czech Philharmonic, Swedish Radio and Radio France Philharmonic orchestras and Maggio Musicale Fiorentino; has also performed at Edin. Festival, Schleswig-Holstein Music Festival, La Roque d'Anthéron, France, and Festival of the Ruhr; Founder and Artistic Dir British Piano Concerto Foundation; Vice-Pres. Birmingham Conservatoire of Music; Hon. DMus (Birmingham) 1992, (Univ. of Cen. England), Hon. DLitt (Warwick) 1996; jt winner, Moscow Int. Tchaikovsky Competition 1982, Grand Prix Int. du Disque (Liszt), Gramophone Concerto Award (Tchaikovsky). *Recordings include:* Messiaen's Turangalila Symphony 1986, Dominic Muldowney Piano Concerto 1986, Tchaikovsky's Piano Concerto No. 2 (Gramophone magazine's Concerto of the Year 1988) 1986, Brahms Piano Concerto No. 1, Liszt, Berg and Bartok Sonatas, Beethoven, Diabelli Variations and Sonata Opus 101, Rachmaninov Preludes, Four British Concertos with Northern Sinfonia, Foulds' Dynamic Triptych, pieces by Rawsthorne, Bliss, Darnton, Rowley, Ferguson, Gerhard, Alwyn, Pitfield and Harty. *Leisure interests:* golf, helping young musicians, jazz. *Address:* c/o EMI Classics, 27 Wrights Lane, London, W8 5SW, England (office). *Telephone:* (20) 7795-7000 (office). *Website:* www.emiclassics.co.uk (office).

DONOHUE, Craig S., BA, LLM, JD,; American lawyer and business executive; *CEO, CME Group Inc. (Chicago Mercantile Exchange);* b. 9 Oct. 1961; m.; three c.; ed Drake Univ., Illinois Inst. of Tech., John Marshall Law School, Northwestern Univ.; Assoc., McBride, Baker & Coles, Chicago; attorney, Chicago Mercantile Exchange (CME) 1989–95, Vice-Pres. and Assoc. Gen. Counsel CME Holdings 1995–97, Vice-Pres. Div. of Market Regulation 1997–98, Sr Vice-Pres. and Gen. Counsel CME 1998–2000, Man. Dir and Chief Admin. Officer CME 2001–, CME Holdings Aug. 2001, Exec. Vice-Pres. and Chief Admin. Officer, Office of the CEO, CME Holdings and of CME 2002–03, mem. Bd of Dirs and CEO CME Holdings and of CME 2004–06, CEO CME Group Inc. (following merger with Chicago Bd of Trade) 2006–; Vice-Chair. and Chair.-Elect Nat. Council on Econ. Educ.; mem. Bd of Dirs Execs' Club of Chicago, Chicagoland Chamber of Commerce; mem. Global Markets Advisory Cttee Commodity Futures Trading Comm., Advisory Council Youth Services of Glenview/Northbrook. *Address:* CME Group Inc., 20 South Wacker Drive, Chicago, IL 60606, USA (office). *Telephone:* (312) 930-1000 (office). *E-mail:* info@cme.com (office). *Website:* www.cme.com (office).

DONOVAN, Shaun L., BA, MA, MPA; American architect and government official; *Secretary of Housing and Urban Development;* b. 24 Jan. 1966, New York City; m. Liza Donovan (née Gilbert); two s.; ed Harvard Univ.; worked as an architect in New York and Italy; Asst Dir Community Preservation Corpn, New York City; Special Asst US Dept of Housing and Urban Devt, Washington, DC 1998–2000, Deputy Asst Sec. for Multifamily Housing 2000–01; acting Fed. Housing Admin Commr during the presidential transition 2000–01; Visiting Scholar, New York Univ.; consultant to Millennial Housing Comm., Washington, DC 2001–02; Man. Dir of FHA lending and affordable housing investments, Prudential Mortgage Capital Co. 2002–04; Commr New York City Dept of Housing Preservation and Devt 2004–08; US Sec. of Housing and Urban Devt, Washington, DC 2009–. *Address:* Department of Housing and Urban Development, 451 Seventh St, SW, Washington, DC 20410, USA (office). *Telephone:* (202) 708-1112 (office). *Fax:* (202) 708-0299 (office). *Website:* www.hud.gov (office).

DONSKOI, Sergei; Russian politician and government official; *Minister of Natural Resources and Ecology;* b. 13 Oct. 1968, Elektrostal, Moscow Oblast; ed Gubkin State Acad. of Oil and Gas; microprocessor-based systems lab engineer at Gazpriboravtomatika design bureau 1992–93; worked at financial cos Your Securities and SINT 1993–96; worked at Prema-Invest as dealer and analyst in Financial Instruments Dept, later Head of Information Analysis Section, leading analyst at Analysis and Marketing Dept 1996–98; adviser at Fuel and Energy Ministry, Deputy Head of Dept, then Head of Production Sharing Agreements Dept 1999–2000; worked at LUKoil's Main Dept for Investment and Finance and Main Dept for Corp. Financing and Investment 2000–01; Head of Dept at Zarubezhneft 2001–05; Head of Econs and Finance Dept, Ministry of Natural Resources 2005–08; Deputy Minister for Natural Resources and Environmental Protection 2008–11; Chief Exec. Rosgeologia (state geology holding co.) 2011–12; Minister of Natural Resources and Ecology 2012–. *Address:* Ministry of Natural Resources and Ecology, 123995 Moscow, ul. B. Gruzinskaya 4/6, Russia (office). *Telephone:* (495) 254-48-00 (office). *Fax:* (495) 254-43-10 (office). *E-mail:* admin@mnr.gov.ru (office); admin@cbi-mpr.ru (office). *Website:* www.mnr.gov.ru (office).

DOOCEY, Baroness (Life Peer), cr. 2010, of Hampton in the London Borough of Richmond upon Thames; **Elizabeth (Dee) Doocey,** OBE; British politician and business executive; *Chair, Economy, Culture and Sport Committee, London Assembly;* Dir of Finance and Admin, Liberal Party HQ late 1970s–early 1980s; fmr Group Man. Dir of an int. fashion co. with operations in London, Hong Kong and China; set up own co. DD Enterprises Management Consultancy; Councillor, London Borough of Richmond upon Thames 1986–94; Finance Dir of the Liberal Party for ten years; Financial Advisor to the Liberal Parl. Party for eight years; unsuccessful cand. for SW London constituency in London Ass. Elections 2004, elected as a London-wide mem. of London Ass. 2004–, Chair Economy, Culture and Sport Cttee 2004–10, 2011–, Chair London Ass. 2010–11, Deputy Chair 2011–; mem. Metropolitan Police Authority 2006–, Chair. Olympic and Paralympic Sub-cttee; mem. Home Office Olympic Security Bd, HM's Inspectorate of Constabulary External Reference Group, Advisory Bd, Asscn for Consultancy & Eng; Mayor's Rep., Bd of London Youth Games. *Address:* GLA, City Hall, The Queen's Walk, London, SE1 2AA (office); House of Lords, Westminster, London, SW1A 0PW, England. *Telephone:* (20) 7983-4797 (office); (20) 7219-5353. *E-mail:* dee.doocey@london.gov.uk (office). *Website:* www.london.gov.uk/profile/dee-doocey (office); www.parliament.uk/biographies/lords/elizabeth-doocey/47236; deedoocey.co.uk.

DOODY, Margaret Anne, BA, MA, PhD; Canadian academic and writer; *John and Barbara Glynn Family Professor of Literature, University of Notre Dame;* b. 21 Sept. 1939, St John, NB; d. of Rev. Hubert Doody and Anne Ruth Cornwall; ed Centreville Regional High School, NB, Dalhousie Univ., Halifax, Lady Margaret Hall, Oxford, UK; Instructor in English 1962–64; Asst Prof., English Dept, Univ. of Victoria, British Columbia 1968–69; Lecturer, Univ. Coll. of Swansea, UK 1969–77; Visiting Assoc. Prof. of English, Univ. of California, Berkeley 1976–77, Assoc. Prof. 1977–80; Prof. of English, Princeton Univ., NJ 1980–89, Stanley Kelley Jr Visiting Prof. for Distinguished Teaching 2008–09; Andrew W. Mellon Prof. of Humanities and Prof. of English, Vanderbilt Univ., Nashville, Tenn. 1989–99, Dir Comparative Literature 1992–99; John and Barbara Glynn Family Prof. of Literature, Univ. of Notre Dame, Ind. 2000–, Dir PhD Program in Literature 2001–07; Commonwealth Fellowship 1960–62, Canada Council Fellowship 1964–65, Imperial Oil Fellowship 1965–68, Guggenheim Foundation Fellowship 1978, Nat. Endowment for the Humanities Fellowship 2007; Hon. LLD (Dalhousie) 1985; Rose Mary Crawshay Prize 1986. *Play:* Clarissa (co-writer), New York 1984. *Publications:* non-fiction: A Natural Passion: A Study of the Novels of Samuel Richardson 1974, The Daring Muse 1985, Frances Burney: The Life in the Works 1988, Samuel Richardson: Tercentenary Essays (ed. with Peter Sabor) 1989, The True Story of the Novel 1996, Anne of Green Gables (co-ed. with Wendy Barry and Mary Doody Jones) 1997, Tropic of Venice 2007; Aristotle detective series: Aristotle Detective 1978, Aristotle and the Fatal Javelin (short story) 1980, Aristotle and Poetic Justice 2002, Aristotle and the Secrets of Life 2003, Poison in Athens (novel) 2004, Mysteries of Eleusis (novel) 2005, Aristotle and the Egyptian Murders 2010, also novella Annello di Bronzo; other fiction: The Alchemists (novel) 1980. *Leisure interests:* travel, looking at ancient buildings, paintings and mosaics, reading detective fiction, visiting Venice, swimming in the sea, music (Mozart, bluegrass). *Address:* c/o Donald Maass Literary Agency, Suite 801, 121 West 27th Street, New York, NY 10001, USA (office); English Department, 356 O'Shaughnessy Hall, University of Notre Dame, Notre Dame, IN 46556 (office); 435 Edgewater Drive, Mishawaka, IN 46545, USA (home). *Telephone:* (212) 727-8383 (office); (574) 257-7927 (home). *Fax:* (212) 727-3271 (office). *E-mail:* info@maassagency.com (office); mdoody@nd.edu (office); margaret.doody.1@nd.edu (office). *Website:* www.maassagency.com (office); www.nd.edu/~mdoody (office).

DOOKERAN, Winston, BA, MSc; Trinidad and Tobago economist and politician; *Minister of Foreign Affairs;* b. 24 June 1943, Trinidad and Tobago; m. Shirley Dookeran; one s.; ed Univ. of Manitoba, Canada, London School of Econs; Lecturer in Econs, Univ. of the West Indies 1971–81, 1981–86; MP for Chaguanas constituency 1981–91, MP for St Augustine 2002–; Minister of Planning and Mobilization, Vice-Chair. Nat. Planning Comm. 1986–91; Dir Price-Waterhouse Man. Consultants and to the Caribbean Govs 1992–95; Fellow, Center for Int. Affairs, Harvard Univ. 1993–95; Sr Economist UN ECLAC 1995–97; Gov. Cen. Bank of Trinidad and Tobago 1997–2002; Minister of Finance 2010–12, of Foreign Afairs 2012–; Visiting Scholar, Weatherhead Center for Int. Affairs Harvard Univ. 2002–03; Leader, United Nat. Congress 2005–06, Congress of the People 2006–; Hon. LLD (Univ. of Manitoba) 1991. *Publications include:* Choices and Change: Reflections on the Caribbean (ed.) 1996, The Caribbean Quest: Directions for Structural Reforms in a Global Economy (co-ed.) 1999, Uncertainty, Stability and Challenges 2006. *Address:* Ministry of Foreign Affairs, Tower C, Levels 10–14, Waterfront Complex, 1 Wrightson Rd, Port of Spain, Trinidad (office). *Telephone:* 623-4116 (office). *Fax:* 623-5853 (office). *E-mail:* communications@foreign.gov.tt (office); wdookeran@tstt.net.tt. *Website:* www.foreign.gov.tt (office); www.winstondookeran.com (home).

DOOKUN-LUCHOOMUN, Hon. Leela Devi, BSc, PGCE, PG Dip Educ.; Mauritian lecturer and politician; *Minister of Social Security, National Solidarity and Reform Institutions;* m.; two c.; ed Univ. of Delhi, India, Mauritius Inst. of Educ., Univ. of Brighton, UK; part-time Lecturer, Mauritius Inst. of Educ.; mem. Parl. 2000–, for No. 8 Moka/Quartier Militaire 2005–10, Parl. Pvt. Sec. 2000–04; Minister of Arts and Culture 2004–05, of Social Security, Nat. Solidarity and Reform Insts 2010–; Founder-mem. Soc. of Biology Teachers, fmr Sec. of Soc.; Vice-

Pres. Mouvement Socialiste Militant (MSM) party, Pres. Women's Wing of MSM. *Address:* Ministry of Social Security, National Solidarity and Reform Institutions, Level 13, Renganaden Seeneevassen Building, Port Louis, Mauritius (office). *Telephone:* 2083447 (office); 2106475 (office). *Fax:* 2136563 (office). *E-mail:* ldookun -luchoomun@mail.gov.mu (office). *Website:* www.gov.mu/portal/site/ssnssite (office).

DÖPFNER, Mathias, MA, PhD; German publishing executive; *CEO and Chairman, Axel Springer AG;* b. 15 Jan. 1963, Bonn; m.; journalist, Frankfurter Allgemeine Zeitung 1982; dir public relations agency 1988–90; fmr Asst to CEO, Gruner & Jahr, Hamburg; Ed.-in-Chief Wochenpost, Berlin 1994–96; Hamburger Morgenpost 1996–98; joined Axel Springer AG 1998, Ed.-in-Chief Die Welt 1998–2000, mem. Man. Bd, Multimedia Div. 2000–, Head of Newspapers Div. 2000–02, Chair. and CEO 2002–; mem. Bd of Dirs Time Warner 2006–, RHJ Int. 2008–; Axel Springer Prize for Young Journalists 1992, Golden Pen Award, Bauer Verlagsgruppe 2000, Journalism Award of German medium-sized businesses 2000, World Econ. Forum Global Leader of Tomorrow 2001, Berlin Order of Merit 2007, Leo Baeck Medal 2007, Jerusalem Award 2008, Global Leadership Award, American Inst. for Contemporary German Studies, New York 2008. *Publications:* Neue Deutsche Welle: Kunst oder Mode 1983, Erotik in der Musik 1986, Musikkritik in Deutschland seit 1945 1991, Brüssel: das Insider-Lexikon 1992, Axel Springer: Neue Blicke auf den Verleger (ed.) 2005, Ernst Cramer: Ich habe es erlebt (ed.) 2008. *Address:* Axel Springer AG, Axel-Springer-Straße 65, 10888 Berlin, Germany (office). *Telephone:* (30) 2591-0 (office). *Website:* www .axelspringer.com (office).

DORAN, Seán; Irish/Australian theatre director; b. 1958, Derry, Northern Ireland; m. Ruby Philogene; ed Univ. of East Anglia and Goldsmiths Coll., London; dir of music-theatre co., Bloomsbury, London 1988; Chief Exec. UK Year of Literature and Writing, Wales 1995; Artistic Dir Belfast Festival, NI 1997, 1998; Dir Perth Int. Arts Festival, Australia 2000–2003; Artistic Dir and Chief Exec. ENO, London 2003–05; Founder and Dir Insideworld Imagine Ltd.

DORDA, Abuzed Omar, BA; Libyan politician and diplomatist; b. 4 April 1944, Rhebat; m.; six c.; ed Benghazi Univ.; teacher 1965–70; Gov. Misurata Prov. 1970–72; Minister of Information and Culture 1972–74, Under-Sec., Ministry of Foreign Affairs 1974–76, Minister of Municipalities 1976–79, Sec.-Gen. People's Cttee for Economy 1979–82, for Agric. 1982–86, for the Municipality of Al-Jabal Al-Gharbi 1986–90, Sec. of the Gen. People's Cttee (Prime Minister) 1990–94, Asst Sec. 1994–95; Amb. and Perm. Rep. to UN, New York 1997–2003; Dir External Security Org. 2009–11. *Address:* c/o Secretariat for Foreign Liaison and International Co-operation, Tripoli, Libya.

DORDAIN, Jean-Jacques; French professor of fluid mechanics and international organization official; *Director-General, European Space Agency;* b. 14 April 1946; ed Ecole Centrale; researcher, Office nat. d'études et de recherches aérospatiales (ONERA) 1970–76, Co-ordinator of Space Activities 1976–86, Dir of Fundamental Physics 1983–86; Prof., Ecole Nationale Supérieure de l'Aéronautique et de l'Espace 1973–87; Sr Lecturer in Mechanical Eng, Ecole Polytechnique 1977–93; joined ESA 1986, Head of Space Station and Platforms Promotion and Utilisation Dept 1986, later Head of Microgravity and Columbus Utilization Dept, Assoc. Dir for Strategy, Planning and Int. Policy 1993–99, Dir Directorate of Strategy and Tech. Assessment 1999–2001, Dir of Launchers 2001–03, Dir-Gen. ESA 2003–; Exec. Sec. Evaluation Cttee of Japanese Space Agency 1997; mem. Académie des Technologies, Académie de l'Air et de l'Espace; Legion d'Honneur, Ordre National du Mérite. *Address:* European Space Agency, 8–10 rue Mario Nikis, 75738 Paris Cedex 15, France (office). *Telephone:* 1-53-69-76-54 (office). *Fax:* 1-53-69-75-60 (office). *Website:* www.esa.int (office).

DORÉ, Jean Marie; Guinean politician; ed studied law in France; veteran opposition leader and human rights activist; elected to Nat. Ass. 1995; Pres. Union pour le Progrès de la Guinée (UPG); unsuccessful presidential cand. (UPG) 1993, 1998; Leader, Forum des Forces Vives coalition 2009; Prime Minister, Repub. of Guinea Jan.–Dec. 2010. *Address:* c/o Office of the Prime Minister, BP 5141, Conakry, Guinea (office).

DORÉ, Ousmane; Guinean economist and politician; fmr Sr Economist, IMF Africa Dept, fmr IMF Rep. to Senegal and Guinea-Bissau; Minister of the Economy, Finance and Planning 2007–08. *Address:* c/o Ministry of the Economy and Finance, Boulbinet, BP 221, Conakry, Guinea (office).

DORE, Ronald Philip, CBE, BA; British fmr university professor; b. 1 Feb. 1925, Bournemouth; s. of Philip H. B. Dore and Elsie C. King; m. Nancy MacDonald 1957; one s. one d.; one s. with Maria Paisley; ed School of Oriental and African Studies, London Univ.; Asst Prof. then Assoc. Prof., Univ. of BC 1956–60; Reader, LSE 1961, Hon. Fellow 1980; Prof., LSE and SOAS 1964–69; Prof. of Welfare, Inst. of Devt Studies, Sussex Univ. 1970–81; Tech. Change Centre, London 1982–86; Dir Japan-Europe Industry Research Centre, Imperial Coll., London 1986–91; Research Assoc., Centre for Econ. Performance, LSE and Political Science 1991–2013; Visiting Prof. Imperial Coll. of Science, Tech. and Medicine, London Univ. 1982, of Sociology, Harvard Univ. 1987; Adjunct Prof., MIT 1989–94; President, Comparative Education Society 1982; mem. British Acad. 1975–; Foreign Hon. Fellow, American Acad. of Arts and Sciences 1978, Hon. Foreign Fellow Japan Acad. 1986–; Sr Fellow, Grad. Inst. for Policy Research, Tokyo 2013; Order of the Rising Sun (Third Class) Japan; Dr hc (Meiji Gakuin) 1989, (Doshisha) 2008, (Chuo Daigaku) 2010; Japan Foundation Prize 1977, Association of Asian Studies Distinguished Scholarship Award 1986, Academy of Management Eminent Scholar 2008. *Publications:* City Life in Japan 1958, Land Reform in Japan 1959, Education in Tokugawa Japan 1965, British Factory/Japanese Factory 1973, The Diploma Disease 1976, Shinohata Portrait of a Japanese Village 1978, Flexible Rigidities, Industrial Policy and Structural Adjustment in Japanese Economy 1986, Taking Japan Seriously: A Confucian Perspective on Leading Economic Issues 1987, Japan and World Depression, Then and Now (Essays) (Jt Ed.) 1987, How the Japanese Learn to Work (with Mari Sako) 1988, Corporatism and Accountability: Organized Interests in British Public Life (Jt Ed.) 1990, Will the 21st Century be the Age of Individualism? 1991, The Japanese Firm: the Source of Competitive Strength (Jt Ed.) 1994, Japan, Internationalism and the UN 1997, Stockmarket Capitalism, Welfare Capitalism: Japan and Germany versus the Anglo-Saxons 2000, Social Evolution, Economic Development and

Culture 2001, Selected Writings of Ronald Dore 2002, New Forms and Meanings of Work in an Increasingly Globalised World 2004, Dare No Tame No Kaisha Ni Suru Ka? (Whom Should Corporations Serve?) 2006, Hataraku to iu koto (On Working) 2006, Finanza Pigliatutto (Finance Takes All) 2009, Kinyu ga nottoru sekai keizai (Finance Hijacks the World Economy) 2011, Nihon no tenki: beichu no hazama de do ikinokoru ka (Turning Point for Japan: How to Survive, Squeezed Between the US and China) 2012. *Address:* 157 Surrenden Road, Brighton, East Sussex, BN1 6ZA, England. *Telephone:* (1273) 501370 (home).

DORENSKY, Sergey Leonidovich; Russian pianist and piano teacher; b. 3 Dec. 1931, Moscow; m. Nina Tserevitinova; one s.; ed Moscow State Conservatory (pupil of Grigory Ginzburg); winner, Int. Competitions Warsaw 1955, Rio de Janeiro 1958; concert tours in USSR, Brazil, Japan, Italy, Germany, Australia, New Zealand, S Korea; teacher, Special Piano Dept, Moscow P. I. Tchaikovsky Conservatory 1957–, Prof. 1981, Dean Piano Faculty 1978–97; Vice-Pres. Russian Chopin Soc., Russian Rachmaninov Soc.; mem. jury of more than 75 maj. int. competitions, including Tchaikovsky (Moscow), Van Cliburn (Fort Worth), Mozart (Salzburg), UNISA (Pretoria); mem. Russian Acad. of Arts 1995; People's Artist of Russia 1988, Order of Friendship 1997. *Address:* Moscow P. I. Tchaikovsky Conservatory, 125009 Moscow, Bolshaya Nikitskaya Street 13/6 (office); 103009 Moscow, Bryusov per. 8/10, Apt. 75, Russia (home). *Telephone:* (495) 229-22-24 (home). *E-mail:* spravka@mosconsv.ru (office). *Website:* www.mosconsv.ru (office).

DORFF, Stephen; American actor; b. (Stephen Dorff Jr), 29 July 1973, Atlanta, Ga; s. of composer Steve Dorff and the late Nancy Dorff; began acting aged nine. *Films:* The Gate 1986, The Power of One 1992, Rescue Me 1992, An Ambush of Ghosts 1993, Judgment Night 1993, Backbeat 1994, S.F.W. 1994, Les cent et une nuits de Simon Cinéma 1995, Innocent Lies 1995, Reckless 1995, I Shot Andy Warhol 1996, Space Truckers 1996, Blood and Wine 1996, City of Industry 1997, Blade 1998, Entropy 1999, Quantum Project (short) 2000, Cecil B. DeMented 2000, Deuces Wild 2002, Riders 2002, FeardotCom 2002, Cold Creek Manor 2003, Britney Spears: Greatest Hits - My Prerogative (video) (segment Everytime) 2004, Alone in the Dark 2005, Tennis, Anyone. . .? 2005, Shadowboxer 2005, World Trade Center 2006, .45 2006, Botched 2007, The Passage 2007, Felon 2008, Black Water Transit 2009, Public Enemies 2009, Somewhere 2010, Rites of Passage 2011, Bucky Larson: Born to Be a Star 2011, Immortals 2011, Carjacked 2011, Brake 2012, Boot Tracks 2011, The Motel Life 2012, Officer Down 2012, The Iceman 2012. *Television films:* In Love and War 1987, Mutts 1988, Hiroshima Maiden 1988, Quiet Victory: The Charlie Wedemeyer Story 1988, I Know My First Name Is Steven 1989, Do You Know the Muffin Man? 1989, A Son's Promise 1990, Always Remember I Love You 1990, Earthly Possessions 1999, Skip Tracer 2000. *Television series:* Still the Beaver 1985, Diff'rent Strokes 1985, Disneyland – The Absent-Minded Professor 1988, Empty Nest 1989, Married with Children 1989, Roseanne 1989, Father Dowling Investigates 1990, The Outsiders 1990, Blossom 1991, What a Dummy 1990-91, Covert One: The Hades Factor 2006, XIII: The Conspiracy (mini-series) 2008. *Address:* c/o ICM, 10250 Constellation Boulevard, Los Angeles, CA 90067, USA (office). *Telephone:* (310) 550-4000 (office). *Website:* www.icmtalent.com (office).

DORFMAN, (Vladimiro) Ariel; Chilean/American writer and academic; *Walter Hines Page Distinguished Professor of Literature and Latin American Studies, Duke University;* b. 6 May 1942, Buenos Aires, Argentina; s. of Adolfo Dorfman; m. Angélica Dorfman 1966; two s.; ed Univ. of Chile, Santiago; Teaching Asst, Univ. of Chile 1963–65, Asst Prof. of Spanish Literature and Journalism 1965–68, Assoc. Prof. 1968–70, Prof. 1970–73; exiled after Chilean coup 1973; Maître des Conférences Spanish-American Literature, Sorbonne Paris IV 1975–76; Head Scientific Research, Spanns Seminarium, Univ. of Amsterdam 1976–80; Visiting Prof., Univ. of Maryland 1983; Post-Doctoral Fellow and Consultant Latin American Council, Duke Univ., NC 1984, Visiting Prof. of Literature and Latin American Studies 1985–89, Research Prof. of Literature and Latin American Studies, 1989–96, Walter Hines Page Distinguished Prof. of Literature and Latin American Studies, Center for Int. Studies and Romance Studies 1996–; Research Scholar, Univ. of Calif., Berkeley 1968–69; Friedrich Ebert Stiftung Research Fellow 1974–76; Fellowship at Woodrow Wilson Int. Center for Scholars 1980–81; Visiting Fellow, Inst. for Policy Studies 1981–84; Fellow, American Acad. of Arts and Sciences; Dr hc (Ill. Wesleyan Univ.) 1989, (Wooster Coll.) 1991, (Bradford Coll.) 1993, (American Univ.) 2001; Time Out Award 1991, New York Public Library Literary Lion 1992, Dora Mavor Award 1994, Int. Poetry Forum Charity Randall Citation 1995, Writers' Guild of Great Britain Best Film for Television 1995, ALOA Prize, Denmark 2002, Lowell Thomas Silver Award for Travel Book 2004, O. Henry Award 2006, North American Congress on Latin America (NACLA) Award for Peace and Justice 2008. *Plays:* Widows (Kennedy Center New American Plays Award) 1988, Death and the Maiden (Olivier Award for Best Play, London 1992) 1991, Reader (Kennedy Center Roger L. Stevens Award) 1992, Who's Who (with Rodrigo Dorfman) 1998, Speak Truth to Power: Voices from Beyond the Dark 2000, Manifesto from Another World: Voices from Beyond the Dark 2004, Purgatorio 2005, Picasso's Closet 2006, The Other Side 2006, Dancing Shadows (with Eric Woolfson) 2007. *Film screenplays:* Death and the Maiden 1994, Prisoners in Time 1995, My House is on Fire 1997, A Promise to the Dead: The Exile Journey of Ariel Dorfman (Insight Award for Excellence in Writing, Nat. Asscn of Film and Digital Media Artists 2008) 2007. *Publications:* fiction: Hard Rain 1973, My House is On Fire 1979, Widows 1983, Dorando la pildora 1985, Travesía 1986, The Last Song of Manuel Sendero 1987, Máscara 1988, Konfidenz 1995, The Nanny and the Iceberg 1999, Blake's Therapy 2001, The Rabbit's Rebellion 2001, The Burning City (with Joaquin Dorfman) 2003, Americanos: Los Pasos de Murieta 2009; poetry: Missing 1982, Last Waltz in Santiago and Other Poems of Exile and Disappearance 1988, In Case of Fire in a Foreign Land: New and Collected Poems from Two Languages 2002; non-fiction: How to Read Donald Duck (with Armand Mattelart) 1971, The Empire's Old Clothes 1983, Some Write to the Future 1991, Heading South, Looking North: A Bilingual Journey 1998, Exorcising Terror: The Incredible Ongoing Trial of General Augusto Pinochet 2002, Desert Memories: Journeys Through the Chilean North 2004, Other Septembers, Many Americas: Selected Provocations, 1980–2004 2004, Feeding on Dreams: Confessions of an Unrepentant Exile 2011. *Address:* c/o Center for International Studies, Duke University, PO Box 90404, Durham, NC 27708, USA. *Fax:* (919) 684-8749 (office). *E-mail:* adorfman@duke.edu (office). *Website:* www .adorfman.duke.edu (office).

DORGAN, Byron Leslie, BS, MBA; American politician; *Senior Policy Advisor, Arent Fox LLP;* b. 14 May 1942, Dickinson, ND; s. of Emmett Patrick Dorgan and Dorothy Dorgan (née Bach); m. 1st; one s. one d. (deceased); m. 2nd Kimberly Olson; one s. one d.; ed Regent High School, Univ. of North Dakota, Univ. of Denver; Exec. Devt trainee, Martin Marietta Corpn, Denver 1966–67; Deputy Tax Commr, then Tax Commr, State of ND 1967–80; mem. 97th–101st Congress from N Dakota 1981–93, mem. Ways and Means Cttee 1981–93; Senator from N Dakota 1993–2011 (retd), Asst Democratic Floor Leader 1996–99, Chair. Democratic Policy Cttee 1999, mem. Cttee on Commerce, Science and Transportation, Cttee on Indian Affairs (Chair. 2007–11); Sr Policy Advisor and Co-Chair. Govt Relations Practice, Arent Fox LLP law firm, Washington, DC 2011–; Sr Fellow, Bipartisan Policy Center; Democrat. *Publications:* Electric Transmission Infrastructure and Investment Needs: Hearing Before the Committee on Energy and Natural Resources (ed.) 2003, Take This Job and Ship It: How Corporate Greed and Brain-Dead Politics Are Selling Out America 2006, Reckless! How Debt, Deregulation and Dark Money Nearly Bankrupted America (And How We Can Fix It!) 2009. *Address:* Arent Fox LLP, 1050 Connecticut Avenue NW, Washington, DC 20036-5339, USA (office). *Telephone:* (202) 857-6334 (office). *Fax:* (202) 857-6395 (office). *E-mail:* dorgan.byron@arentfox.com (office). *Website:* www.arentfox.com (office).

DÖRIG, Rolf, Dr iur; Swiss business executive; *Chairman, Adecco Management & Consulting SA;* b. 1957; m.; three s.; ed Univ. of Zurich, Harvard Business School, USA; called to the Bar, Zurich; joined Credit Suisse 1986, several exec. positions and in different geographical markets, Chief of Staff and Chief Communications Officer, Credit Suisse Group 1997–2000, mem. Exec. Bd responsible for Swiss corp. and retail banking 2000–02, also Chair. Switzerland, Credit Suisse Group 2002; Exec. Vice-Pres. Swiss Life Group (fmrly Swiss Life/Rentenanstalt), CEO 2002–08, Chair. 2009–, Chair. Swiss Life Holding 2009–; Chair. Danzer AG, Baar 2002–, Zurich Chamber of Commerce; mem. Bd of Dirs Adecco Management & Consulting SA 2007–, Chair. 2009–, mem. Nomination and Compensation Cttee 2007–08, Corp. Governance Cttee –2008; mem. Bd of Dirs Swiss Insurance Asscn, Kaba Holding AG (Vice-Chair. 2004–), economiesuisse, Zurich 2003–, Grasshopper-Club Zurich. *Address:* Adecco Management & Consulting SA, Sägereistrasse 10, 8152 Glattbrugg (office); Swiss Life, General Guisan-Quai 40, 8022 Zurich, Switzerland (office). *Telephone:* (44) 878-88-88 (Glattbrugg) (office); (43) 284-33-11 (Zurich) (office). *Fax:* (44) 829-88-88 (Glattbrugg) (office); (43) 281-20-80 (Zurich) (office). *E-mail:* info@adecco.com (office); info.com@swisslife.ch (office). *Website:* www.adecco.com (office); www.swisslife .com (office).

DORIN, Françoise Andrée Renée; French actress, novelist, playwright and songwriter; b. 23 Jan. 1928, Paris; d. of late René Dorin and of Yvonne Guilbert; m. Jean Poiret (b. Poiré) (divorced); one d.; at Théâtre des Deux-Ânes, then du Quartier Latin (Les Aveux les plus doux 1957), then La Bruyère (Le Chinois 1958); Presenter TV programme Paris-Club 1969; playwright and author 1967–; Chevalier, Légion d'honneur, Officier, Ordre nat. du Mérite, Arts et Lettres; Trophée Dussane 1973, Grand Prix du théâtre (for L'Etiquette) 1981. *Songs include:* Que c'est triste Venise 1965, La danse de Zorba 1965, Qu'est-ce que vous voulez que j'en fasse 1965, La bourse et la vie 1966, C'est ton nom 1966, C'est pas croyable 1966, Au coin de mes rêves 1966, Dieu que ça lui ressemble 1966, Une chanson comme on n'en fait plus 1967, Mais mon coeur est vide 1968, Il n'y a en que pour la rose 1968, Il a fallu 1968, Depuis le temps 1968, Quand on a notre âge 1968, Le reconnais-tu? 1968, Pourquoi je t'aime 1968, Les souvenirs que l'on a pas eus, Les filles et les roses, Mourir de soif, Pourquoi pas nous, Téléphoner à Sylvie, Les Fans de Mozart, Tout était pareil, Dis-moi, Oh non, ce n'est pas toi 1976, Tous les chemins mènent à l'homme, Le tournant, L'humour ensemble, Ma dernière chanson, N'avoue jamais, Faisons l'humour ensemble, Les miroirs truqués 1982, Et s'il n'en restait qu'une, je serai celle-là 2006, On s'est aimé à cause 2006. *Plays include:* Comme au théâtre 1967, La Facture 1968, Un sale égoïste, Les Bonshommes 1970, Le Tournant 1973, Le Tube 1974, L'Autre Valse 1975, Si t'es beau, t'es con 1976, Le Tout pour Le tout 1978, L'Intoxe 1980, La valise en carton 1986, Les Cahiers Tango 1987, Et s'il n'en restait qu'un 1992; lyrics for Vos gueules les mouettes 1971, Monsieur Pompadour 1972, L'Etiquette 1983, Les jupes-culottes 1984, La valise en carton (musical comedy) 1986, L'âge en question 1986, La Retour en Toupaine 1993, Monsieur de Saint-Futile (Vaudeville) 1996, Soins intensifs 2001, Vous avez quel âge? 2010. *Publications include:* novels include Virginie et Paul, La Seconde dans Rome, Va voir Maman, Papa travaille 1976, Les lits à une place 1980, Les miroirs truqués 1982, Les jupes-culottes 1984, Les corbeaux et les renardes 1988, Nini patte-en-l'air 1990, Au nom du père et de la fille 1992, Pique et Coeur 1993, La Moufflette 1994, Les Vendanges tardives 1997, La Courte paille 1999, Les Julottes 2001, La mouflette 2001, Le rêve party 2002, Tout est toujours possible 2004, Et puis...après 2005, En avant toutes 2007, Les lettres que je n'ai pas envoyées... 2009. *Address:* c/o Artmédia, 20 avenue Rapp, 75007 Paris, France.

DORIS, Ennio; Italian business executive; *Founder and CEO, Mediolanum SpA;* b. 3 July 1940, Tombolo; began career as salesman for Fideuram 1969; worked for Dival SpA 1971–82; started own fund man. co. Programma Italia 1982, expanded operations into banking and insurance, renamed co. Mediolanum SpA 1996, currently Chair. Banca Mediolanum SpA and CEO Mediolanum SpA; mem. Bd of Dirs Mediobanca SpA, Banca Esperia SpA, Fondazione S. Raffaele del Monte Tabor, Safilo SpA. *Address:* Mediolanum SpA, Palazzo Meucci, Via Francesco Sforza 15, 20080 Basiglio Milan 3, Italy (office). *Telephone:* (02) 90491 (office). *Fax:* (02) 90493434 (office). *E-mail:* info@mediolanum.it (office). *Website:* www .mediolanum.it (office).

DORJI, Damcho, BA, LLB, LLM; Bhutanese barrister; b. 1965, Chholing village, Gasa; ed Sherubtse Coll., Univ. of Bombay, India, Georgetown Univ. Law Center, Washington, DC, USA, Inst. of Social Studies, The Hague, Netherlands; began career as Deputy Registrar Gen. in High Court 1994; Chief Judge (Drangpon) in dist courts in Gelephu, Mongar, Wangduephodrang and Punakh 2000–06; Dir Office of Legal Affairs May–Aug. 2006, Attorney-Gen. Aug. 2006–07; currently mem. Parl. from Gasa; mem. People's Democratic Party. *Address:* c/o People's Democratic Party, Drizang Lam, Lower Motithang, Thimphu, Bhutan (office). *E-mail:* damchodorji@pdp.bt.

DORJI, Lt-Gen. Goongloen Gongma Lam; Bhutanese military officer (retd); b. 23 Oct. 1933, Haa; ed Indian Mil. Acad., Dehra Dun, India; Inspector-Gen. Royal Bhutan Police; Chief of Operations Royal Bhutan Army 1964–2005 (retd); Gen. Sec. Nat. Sports Asscn of Bhutan 1974–78; Druk Zhung Thugsay Medal 1969, Druk Yugyel Medal 1991, Drakpoi Wangyel Medal 2001. *Address:* c/o Royal Bhutan Army Headquarters, Lungtenphu, Bhutan.

DORJI, Dasho Karma; Bhutanese civil servant; ed St Joseph's Coll., Darjeeling, India, State Univ. of New York, USA; joined Ministry of Foreign Affairs 1974, various posts at missions to UN, USA and India, Amb. to Bangladesh (also accred to Maldives, Thailand and Repub. of Korea) 1989–93; Dir Dept of Power 1993–96, Jt Sec. for Power 1996–2000, Sec. Ministry of Trade, Industry and Power (now Ministry of Econ. Affairs) 2000–07; fmr Chair. State Trading Corpn of Bhutan; Man.-Dir Karma Group Org.; mem. Bd Bank of Bhutan, Bhutan Devt Finance Corpn, Bhutan Board Products Ltd; Pres. Bhutan Table Tennis Fed.; Nyekemship with Red Scarf and Sword of Honour 1998. *Address:* c/o Ministry of Economic Affairs, Tashichhodzong, PO Box 141, Thimphu, Bhutan. *Telephone:* (2) 322211. *E-mail:* kdorjee@druknet.bt. *Website:* www.moea.gov.bt.

DORJI, Lyonpo Kinzang, BA; Bhutanese politician, government official and fmr central banker; b. 1951, Chali, Mongar Dist; ed Kolkata, India; Zonal Admin. for Sarpang, Zhemgang, Trongsa and Bumthang 1989–91; Dir Gen. Ministry of Agric. 1991–93, Jt Sec. 1993–94, Sec. 1994–98, Deputy Minister 1998, Minister 1998–2003; elected Speaker Nat. Ass. 1997; Prime Minister, Chair. 2002–03; Minister of Works and Human Settlements 2003–07; Prime Minister 2007–08; Chair. Royal Monetary Authority (cen. bank) 2008–10, Dept of Planning, Tourism Council of Bhutan 2008–; Coronation Medal 1999. *Address:* Tourism Council of Bhutan, PO Box 126, Thimphu, Bhutan (office). *Telephone:* (2) 323251 (office). *Fax:* (2) 323695 (office). *E-mail:* dot@tourism.gov.bt (office). *Website:* www.tourism.gov .bt (office).

DORJI, Lyonpo Leki, BA; Bhutanese government official; b. 31 Dec. 1944, Rukubji, Wangduephodrang; ed Nanital Public School, India, Coll. of Mil. Eng, India, Victoria Univ. of Wellington, NZ; Third Sec. New York mission 1973–74; Second Sec., New Delhi mission 1974–75; Officer on Special Duty, Royal Secr. 1975–77; Head, Registration Dept 1978–80; Sec., Royal Secr. and to Ministry of Agric. 1980; Deputy Minister, Ministry of Agric. 1991–94; Deputy Minister, Ministry of Communications 1994, Minister of Information and Communications 2003–08; Red Scarf 1983, Orange Scarf 1991. *Address:* c/o Ministry of Information and Communications, POB 278, Thimphu, Bhutan. *Telephone:* (2) 327976. *Fax:* (2) 324860. *E-mail:* moic@druknet.bt. *Website:* www.moic.gov.bt.

DORJI, Lyonpo Namgay, BCom (Hons), LLB; Bhutanese politician; *Minister of Finance;* b. Ngada village, Draagteng-Langthil, Trongsa; m.; three c.; ed Sherubtse Coll., Bombay Univ., India; worked with Bhutan Devt Finance Corpn; cand. for People's Democratic Party 2008; Minister of Finance 2013–. *Address:* Ministry of Finance, Tashichhodzong, PO Box 117, Thimphu, Bhutan (office). *Telephone:* (2) 324867 (office). *Fax:* (2) 333976 (office). *E-mail:* wnorbu@mof.gov.bt (office). *Website:* www.mof.gov.bt (office).

DORJI, Lyonpo Rinzin, MA; Bhutanese politician; *Minister of Foreign Affairs;* b. Shingkhar, Zhemgang; m.; two c.; joined civil service 1988, became a Dzongda and worked in the planning comm. and the GNHC Secr. where he dealt with int. agencies and donors at different levels, headed SAARC Div. in GNH comm.; mem. People's Democratic Party 2013–; Minister of Foreign Affairs 2013–. *Address:* Ministry of Foreign Affairs, Convention Centre, PO Box 103, Gyalyong Tshokhang, Thimphu, Bhutan (office). *Telephone:* (2) 322781 (office). *Website:* www.mfa.gov.bt (office).

DORJI, Lyonpo Sangay Ngedup, BA; Bhutanese politician and fmr diplomatist; *President, People's Democratic Party;* b. 1953, Nobgang, Punakha Dist; m.; four c.; ed Dr Graham's Homes School, Kalimpong, St Stephen's Coll., New Delhi, India; joined Bhutanese Foreign Service 1976, served at Perm. Mission to UN, New York 1977, First Sec., New Delhi 1986, Amb. to Kuwait 1986–89; Dir of Trade and Industry, Ministry of Commerce and Industry 1989–92; Jt Sec., Planning Comm. 1991; Sec. of Health 1994–95, of Health and Educ. 1995–98, Deputy Minister of Health and Educ. 1998–99, Minister of Health and Educ. 1999–2003; Chair. Council of Ministers 1999–2000; Minister of Agric. 2001–05; Prime Minister 2005–06; Chair. People's Democratic Party 2007–09, currently Pres.; Chair. Exec. Cttee WHO 1996–99; mem. Bd of Dirs Global Alliance for Vaccines and Immunization (GAVI); responsible for establishing Health Trust Fund, Nat. Tech. Training Authority, Nat. Employment Bd, Royal Univ. of Bhutan, Inst. for Zorig Chusum, Trashiyangtse, Be Somebody movt, Educ. Staff Welfare Fund, Youth Counselling, Scouts Programme, Land Man. Campaign; Red Scarf 1987, Orange Scarf 1998, Druk Thuksay Medal (Heart Son of Bhutan) 1999, Coronation Medal 1999, numerous int. honours and awards. *Address:* People's Democratic Party, Drizang Lam, Lower Motithang, Thimphu, Bhutan (office). *Telephone:* (2) 335557 (office). *Fax:* (2) 335757 (office). *E-mail:* secretary@pdp.bt (office). *Website:* www.pdp.bt (office).

DORJI, Dasho Topgyal; Bhutanese business executive; *Co-Chairman, Tashi Group of Companies;* s. of the late Dasho Ugen Dorji; ed St Joseph's School, Darjeeling, India; Co-Chair. Tashi Group of Cos 2006–; Chair. Bhutan Carbide & Chemicals Ltd; Pres. Bhutan Chamber of Commerce and Industry 2009–. *Address:* Tashi Group of Companies, Corporate Head Office, Phuntsholing, Bhutan (office). *Telephone:* (5) 252109 (office). *Fax:* (5) 252110 (office). *E-mail:* tashi@tashigroup.bt (office). *Website:* www.tashigroup.bt (office).

DORJI, Dasho Tshering; Bhutanese government official and diplomatist; *Ambassador to Thailand;* fmr Sec.-Gen. Bhutan Chamber of Commerce and Industry; fmr Sec., Ministry of Works and Human Settlements; Amb. to Bangladesh (also accred to Sri Lanka) 2008–10, to Thailand (also accred to Australia, Singapore) 2010–. *Address:* Embassy of Bhutan, 375/1 Soi Ratchadanivej, Thanon Pracha-Uthit, Huay Kwang, Bangkok 10320, Thailand (office). *Telephone:* (2) 274-4740 (office). *Fax:* (2) 274-4743 (office). *E-mail:* bht_emb_bkk@yahoo.com (office).

DORJI, Dasho Ugen; Bhutanese politician and business executive; *Chairman, Lhaki Group of Companies;* served in Royal Court of HM the Third King of Bhutan –1972; ventured into business and laid foundation of Lhaki Group of Cos, pioneered dolomite mining industry in Bhutan; business concerns include cement, polymers, mining, polytex, steel, export, construction, ferro-alloys, in-bound travel services and hotels, IT, newspaper & media and real estate, currently Chair. Lhaki Group of Cos, Lhaki Cement, Lhaki Steels & Rolling Pvt. Ltd, Lhaki Construction, Jigme Polytex Pvt. Ltd, Jigme Mining Corpn Ltd, Jigme Industries Pvt. Ltd, Druk Ferro Alloys Ltd, Druk Mines & Mineral Ltd, Bhutan Polymers Corpn Ltd; mem. Bhutan Chamber of Commerce and Industry 1980–, Pres. 1992–2009; Chair. Bhutan Tourism Corpn Ltd, Bhutan Times Ltd, New Edge Technologies Pvt. Ltd, Citizens Initiative for Coronation and Centenary Celebrations; mem. or fmr mem. Bd Bank of Bhutan Ltd, Bhutan Nat. Bank Ltd, Bhutan Finance Devt Corpn Ltd, Royal Insurance Corpn Ltd, State Trading Corpn of Bhutan Ltd, Penden Cement Authority Ltd, and bds of cos under and co-promoted by the Lhaki Group; represented the business community in the Tshogdu Chenmo (Nat. Ass.) 1998, Deputy-Speaker 1998–2001, Speaker 2001–07; mem. Drafting Cttee of first draft constitution of Bhutan upon command of HM the Fourth King 2001–03. *Address:* Lhaki Group of Companies, Corporate Head Office, Lhaki Shopping Complex, Blocks 3 & 4, PO Box 179, Thimphu, Bhutan (office). *Telephone:* (2) 322570 (office). *Fax:* (2) 323916 (office). *E-mail:* info@lhakigroup.com (office). *Website:* www .lhakigroup.com (office).

DORJI, Dasho Wangchuk; Bhutanese business executive; *Co-Chairman, Tashi Group of Companies;* s. of the late Dasho Ugen Dorji; ed St Augustine's School, Kalimpong, India; Chair., Man. Dir and CEO Tai Industries Ltd, Kolkata, India 2005–; Co-Chair. Tashi Group of Cos 2006–; Man. Dir Bhutan Carbide Chemical Ltd; mem. Bhutan Mountain Biking Club. *Address:* Tashi Group of Companies, Corporate Head Office, Phuntsholing, Bhutan (office). *Telephone:* (5) 252109 (office). *Fax:* (5) 252110 (office). *E-mail:* tashi@tashigroup.bt (office). *Website:* www .tashigroup.bt (office).

DORJI, Yeshey; Bhutanese diplomatist and politician; *Minister of Foreign Affairs;* ed Univ. of Delhi, India, Royal Inst. of Man., Asian Inst. of Man., Columbia Univ. School of Int. and Public Affairs, USA; Policy Analyst and Programme Co-ordinator, Ministry of Econ. Affairs 2000–08; Diplomat and Sr Desk Officer, Regional Econ. Integration, Ministry of Foreign Affairs 2008–10, First Sec., Perm. Mission to the UN, New York 2010–12, Counsellor 2012–13; Minister of Foreign Affairs 2013–. *Address:* Ministry of Foreign Affairs, Convention Centre, PO Box 103, Gyalyong Tshokhang, Thimphu, Bhutan (office). *Telephone:* (2) 322781 (office). *Website:* www.mfa.gov.bt (office).

DORMAN, David W., BS; American telecommunications executive; *Non-Executive Chairman, CVS Caremark Corporation;* b. 1954, Ga; m. Susan Dorman; three c.; ed Georgia Inst. of Tech.; began career in software devt, sales and marketing; joined Sprint Business 1981, Pres. 1990–94; CEO Pacific Bell 1994–96, later becoming Exec. Vice-Pres. SBC Communications; Chair., Pres. and CEO PointCast Network 1996–99; CEO Concert (global jt venture between AT&T Corpn and British Telecom) 1999–2000; Pres. AT&T Corpn 2000–02, mem. Bd of Dirs Feb. 2002–, Chair. and CEO July 2002–05 (after acquisition of AT&T by SBC Communications, now AT&T Inc.), now consultant; Man. Dir and Sr Advisor, Warburg Pincus pvt. equity firm –2008; Chair. (non-exec.) Motorola, Inc. 2008–11, Lead Ind. Dir of the Bd Motorola Solutions, Inc. 2011–; Chair. (non-exec.) CVS Caremark Corpn 2011–; mem. Bd of Dirs 3Com Corpn, ETEK Dynamics Ltd, Sabre, Science Applications Int. Corpn, Scientific-Atlanta Inc., Yum! Brands, Inc., Atlanta Symphony Orchestra; mem. Int. Advisory Bd British American Business Council; mem. Pres. Clinton's Advisory Cttee on High Performance Computing and Communications, Information Tech. and Next Generation Internet. *Address:* CVS Caremark Corpn, 1 CVS Drive, Woonsocket, RI 02895, USA (office). *Telephone:* (401) 765-1500 (office). *Fax:* (401) 766-2917 (office). *E-mail:* storecomments@cvs.com (office). *Website:* info.cvscaremark.com (office); www.cvs .com (office).

DORMANDY, John Adam, MD, DSc, FRCS; British surgeon; *Consultant Vascular Surgeon, St. George's Hospital;* b. 5 May 1937, Hungary; s. of Paul Szeben and Clara Szeben; m. Klara Dormandy 1982; one s. one d.; ed St Paul's School, London and Univ. of London; Resident in Surgery, St George's Hosp. Medical School 1963–65, Lecturer in Applied Physiology 1970–74, Sr Lecturer in Surgery 1975–80, Prof. of Vascular Sciences 1995–; Consultant Vascular Surgeon, St James' and St George's Hosp. 1973–; Pres. of Section of Clinical Medicine, Royal Soc. of Medicine 1978; Pres. Venous Forum 1984; Chair. Int. Soc. of Haemorheol-ogy 1982; Examiner in Physiology, Royal Coll. of Surgeons 1984, Hunterian Prof. 1970; Hamilton Bailey Prize in Surgery 1973, Fahreus Medal 1983. *Publications:* numerous articles in books and scientific journals. *Leisure interests:* tennis, skiing. *Address:* St James' Wing, St George's Hospital, Blackshaw Road, London, SW17 0QT (office); 82 East Hill, London, SW18 2HG, England (home). *Telephone:* (20) 8767-8346 (office). *Fax:* (20) 8682-2550 (office). *E-mail:* dormandyjohn@aol.com (home).

DORMANN, Jürgen; German business executive; *Chairman, Sulzer AG;* b. 1940; ed Heidelberg Univ.; began career with Hoechst AG 1963, Finance and Accounting Dir 1987–94, Chair. Man. Bd 1994–2002, apptd Chair. Bd of Dirs 1999, oversaw merger of Hoechst AG with Rhône-Poulenc SA to create Aventis SA, CEO Aventis SA 1994–99, Chair. Man. Bd 1999–2002, Chair. Group Supervisory Bd 2002–04, Vice-Chair. Sanofi-Aventis 2004; Dir ABB (Asea Brown Boveri) Ltd 1998–, Chair. 2001–07, CEO 2002–04; Dir Adecco Management & Consulting SA 2004–08, Chair. 2007–08; Chair. Sulzer AG 2009–; Chair. V-ZUG AG, Metall Zug AG; Dir IBM 1996–2003 (mem. Audit Cttee), 2005–08; Dir (non-exec.) BG Group plc (UK); mem. Supervisory Bd Allianz AG 1999–; mem. European Chemical Industry Council 2000–. *Address:* Sulzer AG, Zürcherstrasse 14, Winterthur, 8401 Zürich, Switzerland (office). *Telephone:* (52) 262-11-22 (office). *Fax:* (52) 262-01-01 (office). *E-mail:* info@sulzer.com (office). *Website:* www.sulzer.com (office).

DORMENT, Richard, CBE, MA, MPhil, PhD; British (b. American) art critic; *Chief Art Critic, Daily Telegraph;* b. 15 Nov. 1946, Montclair, NJ, USA; s. of James Dorment and Marguerite Dorment (née O'Callaghan); m. 1st Kate S. Ganz 1970 (divorced 1981); one s. one d.; m. 2nd Harriet Mary Waugh 1985; ed Georgetown Prep. School, Princeton and Columbia Univs; Asst Curator European Painting Phila Museum of Art 1973–76; Curator Alfred Gilbert: Sculptor and Goldsmith Exhbn, RA, London 1985–86; art critic Country Life 1986; Co-Curator James McNeill Whistler Exhbn, Tate Gallery 1994–95; Chief Art Critic, Daily Telegraph

1987–; reviewer for New York Review of Books; contrib. to Burlington Magazine, Times Literary Supplement, Literary Review; Trustee, Watts Gallery 1996–, Wallace Collection, London 2004–14; mem. British Council Advisory Cttee 1996–, Govt Art Collection Advisory Cttee 1996–; mem. Reviewing Cttee on Export of Works of Art 1996–2002; mem. Judging Panel, Turner Prize 1989; Hawthornden Prize for Art Criticism in Britain 1992, Critic of the Year, British Press Awards 2000. *Publications:* Victorian High Renaissance (exhbn catalogue contrib.) 1976, Alfred Gilbert 1985, British Painting 1750–1900: A Catalogue of British Paintings in the Philadelphia Museum of Art 1986, Alfred Gilbert: Sculptor and Goldsmith 1986, James McNeill Whistler (with Margaret MacDonald) 1994, Manet and the Sea (exhbn catalogue contrib.) 2003, Pre-Raphaelite and Other Masters: The Andrew Lloyd Webber Collection (exhbn catalogue contrib.) 2003. *Address:* Flat 1, 63 Montagu Square, London, W1H 2LU, England. *Website:* www.telegraph.co.uk/journalists/richard-dorment.

D'ORMESSON, Comte Jean; French writer, journalist and international official; b. 16 June 1925; s. of Marquis d'Ormesson; nephew of Comte Wladimir d'Ormesson; m. Françoise Béghin 1962; one d.; ed Ecole Normale Supérieure; Deputy Sec.-Gen., Int. Council for Philosophy and Humanistic Studies (UNESCO) 1950–71, Sec.-Gen. 1971; mem. of staff of various Govt ministers 1958–66; Deputy Ed. Diogène (int. journal) 1952–72, mem. Man. Cttee 1971–; mem. Council ORTF 1960–62, Programme Cttee 1973; mem. Control Comm. of Cinema 1962–69; mem. Editorial Cttee Editions Gallimard 1972–74; Ed.-in-Chief and columnist, Le Figaro 1974–77, Dir-Gen. 1976, leader writer, columnist 1977–; mem. Acad. française 1973; Pres., Soc. des amis de Jules Romains 1974–; Grand Officier, Légion d'honneur, Commdr des Arts et des Lettres, Officier, Ordre nat. du Mérite, Chevalier des Palmes académiques. *Publications:* L'amour est un plaisir 1956, Du côté de chez Jean 1959, Un amour pour rien 1960, Au revoir et merci 1966, Les illusions de la mer 1968, La gloire de l'empire (Grand Prix du Roman, Acad. française) 1971, Au plaisir de Dieu 1974, Le vagabond qui passe sous une ombrelle trouée 1978, Dieu, sa vie, son oeuvre 1981, Mon dernier rêve sera pour vous 1982, Jean qui grogne et Jean qui rit 1984, Le vent du soir 1985, Tous les hommes en sont fous 1985, Bonheur à San Miniato 1987, Garçon de quoi écrire (co-author) 1989 (Prix de Mémorial 1990), Histoire du juif errant 1991, Tant que vous penserez à moi, entretien avec Emmanuel Berl 1992, La Douane de mer 1994, Presque rien sur presque tout 1996, Casimir mène la grande vie 1997, Une autre histoire de la littérature française 1997, Le rapport Gabriel (Prix Jean Giono) 1999, Voyez comme on danse 2001, C'était bien 2003, Une fête en Larmes 2005, La création du monde 2006, Odeur du temps 2007, La vie ne suffit pas 2007, Qu'ai-je donc fait 2008, Saveur du temps 2009, C'est une chose étrange à la fin que le monde 2010, La conversation 2011, Un jour je m'en irai sans en avoir tout dit 2013, Comme un chant d'espérance 2014; numerous articles in Le Figaro, Le Monde, France-Soir, Paris Match, etc. *Leisure interests:* skiing, sailing. *Address:* c/o Gallimard, 5 rue Gaston Gallimard, 75007 Paris, France.

DORN, Dieter; German theatre director; *Manager, Bayerisches Staatsschaus-piel;* b. 31 Oct. 1935, Leipzig; ed Theaterhochschule, Leipzig and Max-Reinhardt-Schule, Berlin; actor, producer and dir in Hanover 1958–68; Dir in Essen and Oberhausen 1968–70; Dir at Deutsches Schauspielhaus, Hamburg 1971, Burgth-eater, Vienna 1972, 1976; Dir at Staatliche Schauspielbühnen, Berlin 1972–75, Salzburg Festival 1974, 1982, 1986; Chief Dir Münchner Kammerspiele (produc-ing works by Lessing, Goethe, Büchner, Shakespeare etc.) 1976–83, Man. (Intendant) 1983–2001; Man. (Intendant) Bayerisches Staatsschauspiel 2001–; has also directed opera productions in Vienna, Munich, Kassel, New York and at Salzburg, Bayreuth and Ludwigsburg festivals; mem. Akademie der Künste, Berlin, Bayerische Akademie der Schönen Künste. *Address:* Bayerisches Staatsschauspiel, Max-Joseph-Platz 1, 80539 Munich, Germany (office). *Tele-phone:* (21) 852000 (office). *Fax:* (21) 852005 (office). *Website:* www .bayerischesstaatsschauspiel.de (office).

DORN, Ludwik, MA; Polish politician; b. 5 June 1954, Warsaw; m.; three c.; ed Warsaw Univ.; involved in anti-communist opposition; participated in ind. meetings of 1st Warsaw Scout's Czarna Jedynka; activist Workers' Defence Cttee; mem. editorial team underground newspaper Głos, Solidarity, KSR; f. Documen-tation and Analysis Centre; Ed. Wiadomości underground newspaper; mem., then Deputy Chair. Centre Accord party; Head of Analysis Team Chancellery of Pres. of Repub. of Poland 1991; co-f. Law and Justice party, currently Deputy Chair.; Deputy III and IV Sejm (Parl.); Chair. Parl. Club of Law and Justice Party 2002–; Deputy Prime Minister 2005–07; Minister of Interior and Admin 2005–07 (resgnd); Marshal Sejm (Parl. Ass.) 2007. *Publications:* translated novels by John Le Carré and Len Deighton; O śpiochu tłuściochu i psie Sabie (About the Fat Sleepyhead and Saba the Dog); numerous literary essays. *Leisure interests:* roller blading, connoisseur of fine wines and cuisine. *Address:* c/o Sejm, ul. Wiejska 4/6/8, 00-902 Warsaw, Poland. *E-mail:* zjablon@sejm.gov.pl.

DORONINA, Tatyana Vasiliyevna; Russian actress; *Artistic Director, Moscow Gorky Arts Theatre;* b. 12 Sept. 1933, Leningrad; d. of Vasiliy Ivanovich Doronin and Anna Ivanovna Doronina; m. Robert Dimitrievich Takhnenko; ed Studio School of Moscow Art Theatre; Leningrad Lenin Komsomol State Theatre 1956–59; Leningrad Maxim Gorky State Bolshoi Drama Theatre 1959–66; Moscow Art Theatre 1966–71; Moscow Mayakovski Theatre 1971–83; Moscow Arts Theatre 1983–, Artistic Dir Moscow Gorky Arts Theatre 1987–; works as actress and stage dir; People's Artist of the USSR 1981. *Theatre roles include:* Zhenka Shulzhenko (Factory Girl by Volodin), Lenochka (In Search of Happiness by Rozov), Sophia (Wit Works Woe by Griboyedov), Nadya Rozoyeva (My Elder Sister by Volodin), Nadezhda Polikarpovna (The Barbarians by Gorky), Lushka (Virgin Soil Upturned by Sholokov), Nastasya Filippovna (The Idiot by Dostoyevsky), Valka (Irkutsk Story by Arbuzov), Oxana (Loss of the Squadron by Korneichuk), Masha (Three Sisters by Chekhov), Grushenka (Brothers Karamazov by Dostoyevsky), Arkadina (The Seagull by Chekhov). *Films include:* Pereklichka 1965, Starshaya Sestra 1966, Yeshche Raz Pro Lyubov 1968, Tri Topolya Na Plyushchikhe 1969, Chudnyy Kharakter 1970, Machekha 1973, Kakaya U Vas Ulybka 1974, Na Yasnyy Ogon 1975, Kapel 1981, Valentin I Valentina 1985. *Address:* Moscow Gorky Arts Theatre, 119146 Moscow, 22 Tverskoi Blvd, Russia. *Telephone:* (495) 203-74-66.

DORR, Noel, MA, BComm, H.Dip.Ed; Irish fmr diplomatist; b. 1 Nov. 1933, Limerick; s. of John Dorr and Bridget Clancy; m. Caítríona Doran 1983; ed St

Nathy's Coll., Ballaghderreen, Nat. Univ. of Ireland, Georgetown Univ., Washington, DC, USA; Third Sec., Dept of Foreign Affairs, Dublin 1960–62, Embassy, Brussels 1962–64, First Sec., Embassy, Washington, DC 1964–70, Dept of Foreign Affairs, Dublin 1970–72, Counsellor (Press and Information) 1972–74, Asst Sec. and Political Dir 1974–77, Deputy Sec. and Political Dir 1977–80, Perm. Rep. to UN 1980–83; Amb. to UK 1983–87; Sec. Dept of Foreign Affairs 1987–95 (retd); Personal Rep. of Minister for Foreign Affairs, EU Intergovernmental Conf. 1996–97, 2000; Chair. Údarás na hOllscoile (Governing Authority), Nat. Univ. of Ireland, Galway 2005–08; Gov. The Irish Times Trust Ltd; Dr hc (Nat. Univ. of Ireland, Galway) 2001. *Leisure interests:* reading, swimming. *Address:* 19 Whitebeam Avenue, Clonskeagh, Dublin 14, Ireland (home). *Telephone:* (1) 2694086 (home). *E-mail:* ndorr@eircom.net (home).

DORRELL, Rt Hon. Stephen James, PC, BA; British politician; b. 25 March 1952; s. of Philip Dorrell; m. Penelope Anne Wears Taylor 1980; three s. one d.; ed Uppingham School, Brasenose Coll. Oxford; MP (Conservative) for Loughborough 1979–97, for Charnwood 1997–, Chair. Health Cttee 2010–; Parl. Pvt. Sec. to Sec. of State for Energy 1983–87, Asst Govt Whip 1987–88, a Lord Commr of Treasury 1988–90, Parl. Under-Sec. of State, Dept of Health 1990–92, Financial Sec. to Treasury 1992–94; Sec. of State for Nat. Heritage 1994–95, for Health 1995–97; Shadow Sec. for Educ. and Employment 1997–98. *Leisure interests:* walking, reading. *Address:* House of Commons, Westminster, London, SW1A 0AA, England (office). *Telephone:* (20) 7219-4472 (office). *E-mail:* stephen.dorrell.mp@parliament .uk (office); info@stephendorrell.org.uk (office). *Website:* www.parliament.uk/ biographies/commons/mr-stephen-dorrell/336 (office); www.stephendorrell.org.uk.

DORSAINVIL, Daniel, PhD; Haitian economist and government official; b. 25 Aug. 1959, Port-au-Prince; ed Univ. of Pennsylvania, USA; fmr official, USAID; Econ. Adviser to Pres. Préval –2006; Minister of the Economy and Finance 2006–09; Vice-Pres. Societe Haitienne De Promotion Immobilier SA 2010–; CEO Phareview SA 2010–.

DORSEN, Norman, BA, LLD; American professor of law, civil libertarian and educator; *Frederick I. and Grace A. Stokes Professor of Law and Counselor to the President, New York University;* b. 4 Sept. 1930, New York; s. of Arthur Dorsen and Tanya Stone; m. Harriette Koffler 1965; three d.; ed Bronx High School of Science, Columbia Coll., Harvard Law School and London School of Econs, UK; law clerk to Chief Judge Calvert Magruder, US Court of Appeals, First Circuit 1956–57, to Justice John M. Harlan, US Supreme Court 1957–58; pvt. law practice, New York 1958–60; Assoc. Prof. of Law, New York Univ. Law School 1961–65, Prof. 1965–78, Frederick I. and Grace A. Stokes Prof. of Law 1978–, Counselor to the Pres.; Co-Dir Arthur Garfield Hays Civil Liberties Program; mem. Bd of Dirs American Civil Liberties Union 1965–91, Gen. Counsel 1969–76, Pres. 1976–91; Founding Pres. Soc. of American Law Teachers 1972–74, Pres. US Asscn of Constitutional Law; Vice-Chair. US Dept of Health, Educ. and Welfare Review Panel on New Drug Regulation 1975–76, Chair. 1976–77; mem. Bd of Dirs Lawyers Comm. for Human Rights 1978–, Chair. 1995–2000, Thomas Jefferson Center for Protection of Free Expression 1990–; Dir Global Law School Program 1994–, Chair. 1996–2002; mem. Council on Foreign Relations; Chair., US Treasury Citizens' Panel on Allegations regarding Good O'Boys Round-up; consultant Americans for Religious Liberty; Fellow, American Acad. of Arts and Sciences; Founder and Editorial Dir I.CON, The Int. Journal of Constitutional Law; mem. Bd of Govs Int. Asscn of Law Schools; Hon. LLD (Ripon Coll., John Jay Coll. of Criminal Justice); Minister of Justice's Medal (France) 1983, Eleanor Roosevelt award for Human Rights, various awards for civil rights and as legal educator. *Publications include:* books: Political and Civil Rights in the US (with others) 1967, Frontiers of Civil Liberties 1968, ACLU Handbooks Series (Gen. Ed.) 1971–95, Disorder in the Court (co-author) 1973, The Evolving Constitution 1987, Human Rights in Northern Ireland (with others) 1991, Democracy and the Rule of Law (co-ed.) 2001, The Unpredictable Constitution (co-ed.) 2002, Comparative Constitutionalism 2003; articles on constitutional law and civil liberties. *Leisure interests:* country living, aerobics. *Address:* New York University School of Law, Vanderbilt Hall, 40 Washington Square South, Room 308, New York, NY 10012-1099 (office); 146 Central Park West, New York, NY 10023, USA (home). *Telephone:* (212) 998-6233 (office). *Fax:* (212) 995-4030 (office). *E-mail:* dorsen@juris.law.nyu.edu (office). *Website:* www.law.nyu .edu (office).

DORSEY, Jack; American internet industry executive; *Co-founder and Chairman, Twitter Inc.;* b. 19 Nov. 1976; s. of Tim Dorsey and Marcia Dorsey; ed Missouri Univ. of Science and Tech., New York Univ., Univ. of California, Berkeley; began career with dispatch co., Manhattan, New York 1999–2000; f. co. to dispatch couriers, taxis and emergency services using internet, Oakland 2000; Co-founder (with Isaac 'Biz' Stone) Obvious Corpn 2006 (spun off Twitter Inc. 2006); creator, Twitter.com 2006, Co-founder Twitter Inc., San Francisco 2007, CEO 2007–08, Chair. 2008–; Co-founder and CEO Square (iPhone-based payment system); mem. Advisory Bd Ustream.tv 2009–; named one of The World's Most Influential People, TIME magazine 2009, Technology's Best & Brightest Young Entrepreneurs, Business Week magazine; named to TR35, an outstanding innovator under the age of 35, MIT Technical Review. *Address:* Twitter Inc., 539 Bryant Street, Suite 402, San Francisco, CA 94107, USA (office). *Telephone:* (415) 896-2008 (office). *Website:* twitter.com (office); squareup.com (office).

DORST, Tankred; German writer; b. 19 Dec. 1925, Sonneberg; s. of Max Dorst and Elisabeth Dorst; m. Ursula Ehler-Dorst; ed Universität München; dir production of Wagner's Ring, Bayreuth Festival 2006; mem. German PEN Centre, Bayerische Akad. der schönen Künste, Deutsche Akad. der darstellenden Künste, Deutsche Akad. für Sprache und Dichtung; several prizes including Gerhart Hauptmann Prize, Georg-Büchner Prize 1990, Schiller Prize 2010, Faust Prize 2012. *Film as director and screenwriter:* Eisenhans. *Plays:* around 40 plays including Toller, Eiszeit, Merlin oder das wüste Land, Herr Paul, Was sollen wir tun, Fernando Krapp hat mir diesen Brief geschrieben, Ich Feuerbach, Die Legende vom Armen Heinrich, Karlos, Korbes, Ich bin nur vorübergehend hier 2007, Künstler 2008, Ich soll den eingebildet Kranken spielen 2009; several opera libretti; five plays for children; several plays in collaboration with Ursula Ehler. *TV films (writer and director):* Klaras Mutter, Mosch. *Publications:* Plays (Vols 1–8), Merlins Zauber, Die Reise nach Stettin, Der sickste Ort, Sich im Ordischen zü uben, Glück ist ein Vorübergehender Schwächezustand, Plays (Vol 8) 2008. *Address:* Suhrkamp Verlag, Pappelallee 78–79, 1043 Berlin; Karl Theodor Strasse

102, 80796 Munich, Germany (home). *Telephone:* (30) 7407440 (office). *Fax:* (89) 3073256 (home).

DORUK, Mustafa, PhD; Turkish engineer and academic; *Professor of Metallurgical Engineering, Middle East Technical University;* b. 23 Feb. 1932; ed School of Eng, Yildiz, Technische Hochschule, Darmstadt, Germany; Asst Prof., Dept of Metallurgical Eng, Middle East Tech. Univ., Turkey 1963–70, Assoc. Prof. 1970–76, Prof. 1976–, Chair. of Dept 1965–69, of Dept of Metallurgical and Materials Eng 1988–97; Asst Pres. and Acting Pres. Middle East Tech. Univ. 1974–77, Dean Faculty of Eng 1978–85; UN Scholar, UCLA, USA 1972–73; Visiting Prof. Technische Hochschule, Darmstadt 1979; mem. Structure and Materials Panel of NATO/AGARD, Int. Congress on Corrosion, Founding mem. Corrosion Asscn of Turkey; mem. Chamber of Turkish Metallurgical Engineers; Fellow, Islamic Acad. of Sciences; Hon. Senator, Technical Univ. Darmstadt. *Publications:* over 50 publs. *Address:* Middle East Technical University, Metallurgical and Materials Engineering Department, Room D-106, Ankara, Turkey (office); Islamic Academy of Sciences, PO Box 830036, Amman, Jordan (office). *Telephone:* (312) 2102516 (office). *Fax:* (312) 2102518 (office). *E-mail:* mdoruk@ metu.edu.tr (office). *Website:* www.mete.metu.edu.tr/home (office).

DOS ANJOS, Carlos Gustavo; São Tomé and Príncipe government official and diplomatist; *Ambassador to Belgium;* b. 1956; fmr foreign affairs adviser to the Pres.; Minister of Foreign Affairs, Co-operation and Communities 2006–07; currently Amb. to Belgium. *Address:* Embassy of São Tomé and Príncipe, Square Montgomery, 175 avenue de Tervueren, 1150 Brussels, Belgium (office). *Telephone:* (2) 734-89-66 (office). *Fax:* (2) 734-88-15 (office). *E-mail:* ambassade@ saotomeeprincipe.be (office).

DOS RAMOS, Américo d'Oliveira; São Tomé and Príncipe economist and politician; Minister of Finance and Int. Co-operation 2010–12. *Address:* c/o Ministry of Finance and International Co-operation, São Tomé, São Tomé and Príncipe.

DOS RAMOS, Manuel Salvador; São Tomé and Príncipe journalist and politician; b. 25 June 1956, Conceiçao; ed Int. Inst. for Journalism, Germany, Moscow State Univ., USSR, Agostino Neto Univ., Luanda, Angola; Ed., later Sr Ed., Radio Nationale de São Tomé and Príncipe 1977–83, Head of Programming 1983–84; joined Ministry of Foreign Affairs 1986, held numerous positions including Head of Political Affairs Dept 1985–91, Head of Int. Politics Dept 1986–87, Head of Press Office 1991–92, Head of Bilateral Affairs Dept, Political Affairs and Int. Legal Div. 1991–92, Adviser to Pres. on Diplomatic Affairs 1993–95, on Diplomatic and Political Affairs 1995–97, Amb. to Angola 1997, fmr Amb. to Gabon, Minister of Foreign Affairs and Communities 2010–12; Pres., Nat. Cttee for Celebration of 40th Anniversary of UN 1985. *Address:* c/o Ministry of Foreign Affairs and Communities, Av. 12 de Julho, CP 111, São Tomé, São Tomé and Príncipe.

DOS SANTOS, Carlos, BA, MSc; Mozambican diplomatist; *High Commissioner to UK;* b. 8 July 1961, Manhica, Maputo Prov.; m. Maria Isabel dos Santos; three c.; ed Univ. of Zimbabwe; joined Ministry of Foreign Affairs 1980, Protocol Officer 1980–82, Attaché, Perm. Mission to UN, New York 1982–84; Third Sec., Embassy in Harare, Zimbabwe 1985; Head of Political Dept, Africa and Middle East Div. 1990–91; Chef du Cabinet 1991–92; Counsellor and Pvt. Sec. to Pres. of Mozambique 1992–95; Perm. Rep. to UN, New York 1996–2002; High Commr to UK 2011–; Del. to UN, OAU, Non-Aligned Movt and other int. orgs; mem. African Asscn of Political Scientists. *Address:* Mozambique High Commission, 21 Fitzroy Square, London, W1T 6EL, England (office). *Telephone:* (20) 7383-3800 (office). *Fax:* (20) 7383-3801 (office). *E-mail:* sectorconsular@mozambiquehc.co.uk (office). *Website:* www.mozambiquehighcommission.org.uk (office).

DOS SANTOS, Fernando (Nandó) da Piedade Dias; Angolan politician; *Vice President;* b. 1952, Luanda; ed Instituto Industrial de Luanda; involved with Grupo Boa Esperança from 1970 (pro-independence); nat. service, Portuguese colonial army 1973–74, deserted to join guerilla forces of Movimento Popular de Libertação de Angola (MPLA); mem. staff FAPLA (Armed Forces of MPLA), rank of Maj. 1984, Col 1986, Maj.-Gen. 1992; Insp., Corpo do Polícia Popular de Angola—CPPA (People's Police Force of Angola) 1976–78, Head of 1st Command Div. 1978–79, Head of Political Dept and Personnel Section in Nat. Directorate 1979–81, Nat. Dir of People's Police 1984–86; Deputy Head Nat. Political Directorate, Ministry of the Interior 1981–84, Nat. Dir of Personnel 1982–84, Deputy Minister of State Security 1984, Deputy Minister of the Interior 1984, also Head of Information Services 1990, Deputy Minister of the Interior responsible for Internal Order 1995–99, Minister of the Interior 1999–2002; elected Deputy People's Ass. 1986–; Commdr-Gen. and Gen. Commr of Nat. Police (Polícia Nacional) 1995–; Co-ordinator Exec. Cttee of Inter-Ministerial Comm. of Process of Peace and Reconciliation 2001, Nat. Comm. for Social and Productive Reintegration of Demobilized Troops and Displaced Persons 2002; Prime Minister of Angola 2002–08; Speaker, Nat. Ass. 2008–10; Vice Pres. of Angola 2010–. *Address:* Office of the Vice President, Protocolo de Estado, Futungo de Belas, Luanda, Angola (office).

DOS SANTOS, Isabel; Angolan business executive; b. 1973, Baku, Azerbaijan; d. of José Eduardo dos Santos (Pres. of Angola) and Tatiana Kukanova; m. Sindika Dokolo 2003; f. Urbana 2000; f. Miami Beach Club (night club), Luanda 2006; worked for Ascorp diamond trading co.; Owner, Kento Holding Ltd; holds stakes in telecoms, diamonds and banking in Angola, also Portuguese media conglomerate Zon Multimedia, Banco Espírito Santo, Banco Português de Investimento, and energy co. Energias de Portugal. *Address:* Kento Holdings Ltd, 171 Old Bakery Street, Valletta VLT 1455, Malta. *Telephone:* 21235408.

DOS SANTOS, José Eduardo; Angolan head of state; *President;* b. 28 Aug. 1942, Luanda; s. of the late Eduardo Avelino dos Santos and Jacinta José Paulino; ed Liceu Salvador Correia; joined Movimento Popular de Libertação de Angola (MPLA) 1961; went into exile 1961 and was a founder mem. and Vice-Pres. of MPLA Youth based in Léopoldville, Congo (now Kinshasa, Democratic Repub. of Congo); first Rep., MPLA, Brazzaville 1961; sent with group of students for training in Moscow 1963; graduated as Petroleum Engineer, Inst. of Oil and Gas, Baku 1969; then mil. course in telecommunications; returned to Angola and participated in war against Portuguese 1970–74; Second in Command of

Telecommunications Services, MPLA Second Politico-Military Region, Cabinda; mem. Provisional Readjustment Cttee, Northern Front 1974; mem. MPLA Cen. Cttee and Political Bureau 1974–; Chair. MPLA; Minister of Foreign Affairs, Angola 1975; Co-ordinator, MPLA Foreign Relations Dept 1975; Sec. Cen. Cttee for Educ., Culture and Sport, then for Nat. Reconstruction, then Economic Devt and Planning 1977–79; First Deputy Prime Minister, Minister of Planning and Head of Nat. Planning Comm. 1978–79; Pres. of Angola 1979– and Chair. of Council of Ministers 1979–, also Prime Minister 1999–2002; C-in-C of FAPLA (Armed Forces of MPLA). *Address:* Office of the President, Protocolo de Estado, Futungo de Belas, Luanda, Angola (office). *Telephone:* 222370150 (office). *Fax:* 222370366 (office).

DOS SANTOS DINIZ, Abílio; Brazilian retail executive; *President, Companhia Brasileira de Distribuição;* b. 28 Dec. 1936, São Paulo; s. of Valentim Diniz; m.; two s. two d.; ed Getúlio Vargas Business Foundation, Columbia Univ., Ohio Univ., USA; joined Companhia Brasileira de Distribuição – Pão de Açúcar 1956, Vice Pres. 1989–96, CEO 1996–2002, Pres. Admin. Council 2000–; Admin. Emer. Regional Admin. Council of São Paulo 1983; f. São Paulo Supemarket Asscn; mem. Nat. Monetary Council 1979–89; mem. Superior Council Portuguese–Brazilian Community of São Paulo 2006–; Personality of the Year, Brazilian Asscn of Retail Mans 1971. *Address:* Grupo Pão de Açúcar, Avenida Brigadeiro Luís Antônio, 3126, Jardim Paulista, 01402-901 São Paulo, Brazil. *Website:* www.cbdri.com.br.

DOSBOL, Nur uulu, PhD; Kyrgyzstani politician; *Chairman, Jany Kyrgyzstan (New Kyrgyzstan) party;* b. 26 April 1948; ed Kyrgyz State Univ.; Jr Research Asst, History Inst. of Kyrgyz SSR Acad. of Sciences 1972–81, Intern-Researcher 1981–83, Sr Research Asst 1983–89, doctorate degree study 1989–92, Head of Dept, History Inst. 1993–95; Deputy of Zhogorku Kenesh (Parl.) 1995–2000; Minister of Educ., Science and Youth Policy 2005–07; Deputy Prime Minister 2007–08; State Sec. of Kyrgyzstan 2008–; Chair. Jany Kyrgyzstan (New Kyrgyzstan) party; fmr mem. Agrarian-Labor Party. *Address:* Jany Kyrgyzstan, 720000 Bishkek, Kiyevskaya 120, Kyrgyzstan (office). *Telephone:* (312) 21-19-61 (office). *Fax:* (312) 21-65-04 (office).

DOSS, Alan Claude, CMG; British UN official; b. 7 Jan. 1945, Cardiff, Wales; m. Soheir Doss; three d.; ed London School of Econs; held posts with UN in China, Kenya, Niger, Zaïre and Benin; fmr UN Resident Co-ordinator Regional Rep. of UNDP in Bangkok, Thailand; fmr Dir UN Border Relief Operation (Thai-Cambodia border); fmr Dir UNDP European Office, Geneva, Switzerland; Rep. of UNDP to Devt Assistance Cttee and OECD; Dir UN Devt Group (UNDG) –2001; Deputy Special Rep. of Sec.-Gen., UN Mission in Sierra Leone (UNAMSIL) 2001–04, Prin. Deputy Special Rep. of Sec.-Gen. for Côte d'Ivoire 2004–05, Special Rep. of Sec.-Gen. in Liberia 2005–07, in Democratic Repub. of the Congo (DRC) and Head of UN Org. Mission in DRC (MONUC, now MONUSCO), with rank of Under-Sec.-Gen. 2007–10; Nelson Mandela Africa Lecturer, Royal United Services Inst. 2009. *Address:* c/o United Nations Stabilization Mission in DRC (MONUSCO), PO Box Kinshasa BP 8811, 12 Avenue des Aviateurs, Kinshasa -Gombe, Democratic Republic of the Congo.

DOSTAM, Gen. Abdul Rashid; Afghan politician and military leader; *Chief of Staff to Commander-in-Chief of Armed Forces;* b. 1954, Khowja Dokoh, Juzjan Prov.; fmr plumber; with Oil and Gas Exploration Enterprise 1979; undertook mil. training in USSR 1980; Commdr pro-Soviet Jozjani Dostum Militia, N Afghanistan 1980–92; Defence Minister in Pres. Najibullah's Govt 1986–92; allied with Gulbuddin Hekmatyar's Pashtun warriors and Shi'a guerrillas following transition of power 1992; est. Itehad Shamal/Northern Unity org. which controlled most N Afghanistan provs 1993–97; fled to Turkey when Taliban occupied Mazar-i-Sharif 1997; returned to fight with Northern Alliance (NA) against Taliban 2001; Deputy Minister of Defence 2001–04; presidential cand. 2004; Chief of Staff to C-in-C of Armed Forces 2005–, temporarily suspended 2008; Leader, Junbesh-i Melli-i Islami (Nat. Islamic Movt), Uzbek mil. wing of NA –2005; mem. Jabhe-ye-Motahed-e-Milli (United Nat. Front) 2007–; f. Balkh Air (airline); awarded Hero of the Repub. of Afghanistan Medal by Pres. Najibullah. *Address:* c/o Ministry of Defence, Shash Darak, Kabul, Afghanistan. *Website:* www.jabhaemelli.com.

DOTÉ, Elie, PhD; Central African Republic politician and government official; b. Bangui; m.; six c.; with Ministry of Agric. and Animal Husbandry 1974–80; fmr mem. staff African Devt Bank (ADB), Chief of Agric. and Rural Devt 2001; Prime Minister and Head of Govt of Central African Repub. 2005–08 (resgnd), Minister of Finance 2006–08 (resgnd). *Address:* c/o Office of the Prime Minister, Bangui, Central African Republic (office). *Website:* www.kodro.net (office).

DOTRICE, Roy, OBE; British actor; b. 26 May 1925, Guernsey, Channel Islands; s. of Louis Dotrice and Neva Wilton; m. Kay Newman 1946; three d.; ed Dayton and Intermediate Schools, Guernsey; air gunner, RAF 1940; POW 1942–45; acted in repertory 1945–55; formed and directed Guernsey Theatre Co. 1955; TV Actor of the Year Award 1968. *Stage appearances include:* Royal Shakespeare Co. 1957–65 (playing Caliban, Julius Caesar, Hotspur, Firs, Puntila, Edward IV, etc.); World War 2½, New Theatre, London 1966; Brief Lives (one-man play), Criterion (over 400 performances, world record for longest-running solo performance) 1969; toured England, Canada, USA 1973, Mayfair (over 150 performances) 1974; Broadway season 1974; Australian tour 1975; Peer Gynt, Chichester Festival 1970; One At Night, Royal Court 1971; The Hero, Edinburgh 1970; Mother Adam, Arts 1971; Tom Brown's Schooldays, Cambridge 1972; The Hollow Crown, seasons in USA 1973 and 1975, Sweden 1975; Gomes, Queen's 1973; The Dragon Variation, Duke of York's 1977; Australian tour with Chichester Festival 1978; Passion of Dracula, Queen's 1978; Oliver, Albery 1979; Mr. Lincoln (one-man play), New York 1980, Fortune 1981, A Life, New York 1981, Henry V, Stratford, Conn. 1981, Falstaff (American Shakespeare Co.) 1982, Kingdoms, Broadway 1982, Churchill, Washington and Los Angeles 1983, The Genius, Los Angeles 1984, Enemy of the People, New York 1985, Hay Fever, New York and Washington 1985–86, The Homecoming 1991, New York, The Best of Friends, New York 1993, The Woman In Black, USA 1995, Moon for the Begotten (Tony Award) 2000. *Films include:* The Heroes of Telemark 1965, A Twist of Sand 1968, Lock up Your Daughters 1969, Buttercup Chain, Tomorrow, One of Those Things 1971, Nicholas and Alexandra 1971, Amadeus, The Corsican Brothers 1983, The Eliminators 1985, Shaka Zulu 1985, Young Harry Houdini 1986, Camila, L-Dopa, The Lady Forgets, The Cutting Edge, The Scarlet Letter, Swimming with Sharks, These Foolish Things 2006, Played 2006, Go Go Tales 2007, Hellboy II: The Golden Army 2008. *TV appearances include:* Dear Liar, Brief Lives, The Caretaker (Emmy Award), Imperial Palace, Misleading Cases, Clochemerle, Dickens of London, Stargazy on Zummerdown, Casualty 2005, Life Begins 2005–06, The Afternoon Play 2006, Heartbeat 2006; numerous American TV appearances including Remington Steele, Hart to Hart, Family Reunion, Magnum P.I., Fairy Tale Theatre, Beauty and the Beast, Tales of Gold Monkey, The Wizard, A Team, Tales from the Dark Side, Going to Extremes, The Good Policeman, Madigan Man. *Leisure interests:* baseball, fishing, riding. *Address:* 98 St Martin's Lane, London, WC2N 4AX, England. *Telephone:* (20) 7836-7054.

DOUANGCHAI, Maj.-Gen. Phichit; Laotian army commander and politician; *Deputy Prime Minister and Minister of National Defence;* fmr Mil. Chief of Staff; currently Deputy Prime Minister and Minister of Nat. Defence; mem. Politburo. *Address:* Ministry of National Defence, rue Phone Kheng, Ban Phone Kheng, Vientiane, Laos (office). *Telephone:* (21) 412803 (office). *Fax:* (21) 412801 (office).

DOUBANE, Charles-Armel, BS, MS; Central African Republic diplomatist and politician; *Permanent Representative, United Nations;* b. 12 Nov. 1966, Zamio; m.; ed Univ. of Paris-Sud 11, France, Univ. of Bangui; Minister for Relations with Parl. 1997–99; mem. Parl. (Alliance for Democracy and Progress, ADP) for Zemio constituency 1999; joined Public Service Gen. 2000; fmr Diplomatic Adviser to the Pres.; Minister of Educ., Literacy, Higher Educ. and Research 2006–08; Dir Chimie SARL 2008; Amb. and Perm. Rep. to UN, New York 2011–; apptd Minister of Foreign Affairs 2013 but did not take up post. *Address:* Permanent Mission of the Central African Republic to the United Nations, 866 United Nations Plaza, Suite 444, New York, NY 10017, USA (office). *Telephone:* (646) 415-9122 (office). *Fax:* (646) 415-9149 (office). *E-mail:* repercaf.ny@gmail.com (office). *Website:* www .pmcar.org (office).

DOUGAN, Brady W., BA (Econs), MBA; American banking executive; *CEO, Credit Suisse Group AG;* b. 1959; ed Univ. of Chicago, Ill.; began career in derivatives group of Bankers Trust; with Credit Suisse First Boston 1990–, fmr Co-Head, Global Debt Capital Markets Group and of Credit Suisse Financial Products marketing effort in the Americas, Head of Equities Div. 1996–2001, Global Head, Securities Div. 2001–02, Co-Pres. Institutional Securities 2002–04, mem. Exec. Bd, Chair. Man. Council and CEO, mem. Exec. Bd Credit Suisse Group AG 2004–07, CEO Credit Suisse Investment Bank 2004–07, CEO Credit Suisse Group AG 2007–; mem. Bd of Dirs Humacyte Inc. 2005–; mem. Bd of Trustees, Univ. of Chicago 2013–. *Address:* Credit Suisse Group AG, PO Box 1, 8070 Zurich (office); Credit Suisse Group AG, Paradeplatz 8, 8001 Zurich, Switzerland (office). *Telephone:* (44) 212-16-16 (office). *Fax:* (44) 333-25-87 (office). *E-mail:* info@ credit-suisse.com (office). *Website:* www.credit-suisse.com (office).

DOUGLAS, Barry, OBE; Irish pianist and conductor; b. 23 April 1960, Belfast, Northern Ireland; s. of Barry Douglas and Sarah Jane Douglas (née Henry); m. Deirdre O'Hara; two s. one d.; ed Royal Coll. of Music, London with John Barstow; pvt. study with Maria Curcio; London debut, Wigmore Hall 1981; toured Europe 1986–; regularly performs in USA; other concerts in Japan, USSR, Australia, Iceland, Czechoslovakia; recital debut in Carnegie Hall, New York 1988; Artistic Dir Camerata Ireland; winner of Tchaikovsky Piano Competition, Moscow 1986; tours in USA, S America, Russia, Europe, Australia; has given numerous premieres of contemporary music by Buckley, Wilson, McCabe, Penderecki and O'Leary; Hon. FRCM; Hon. DMus (Belfast); Diploma Royal Coll. of Music, Emmy Award for Concerto (Channel 4 TV programme) 1993, Diapason d'Or for Reger/ Strauss recording 1998. *Recordings include:* Tchaikovsky Concertos Nos 1, 2 and 3, Sonata in G, Brahms Concerto No. 1, Piano Quintet in F Minor, Liszt concertos and Sonata in B Minor, Beethoven, Mussorgsky, Prokofiev, Rachmaninov Concerto No. 2, Berg, Reger, Strauss, Debussy, Britten, Corigliano, Penderecki Piano Concerto (with composer conducting), Beethoven Piano Concertos. *Television:* Rhapsody in Belfast (BBC documentary) 1978, After the Gold (ITV) 1987, Playing for Peace (Sky Artsworld) 2001. *Leisure interests:* driving, reading, food, wine, theatre. *Address:* c/o IMG Artists, The Light Box, 111 Power Road, London, W4 5PY, England (office); c/o Opus 3 Artists, 470 Park Avenue South, 9th Floor North, New York, NY 10016, USA (office). *Telephone:* (20) 7957-5800 (office); (212) 584-7500 (office). *Fax:* (20) 7957-5801 (office); (646) 300-8200 (office). *E-mail:* lcoles@imgartists.com (office); info@opus3artists.com (office). *Website:* www .imgartists.com (office); www.opus3artists.com (office); www.camerata-ireland .com (office); www.barrydouglas.com (home).

DOUGLAS, Denzil Llewellyn; Saint Christopher and Nevis politician; *Prime Minister and Minister of Finance, Sustainable Development and Human Resource Development;* Leader Saint Kitts-Nevis Labour Party; Prime Minister of Saint Christopher and Nevis 1995–, also Minister of Finance, of Nat. Security, of Information, of Planning and of Foreign Affairs 1995–2001, Minister of Finance, Devt Planning and Nat. Security 2001–04, Minister of Finance, Sustainable Devt, Information and Tech. and Minister of Tourism, Sports and Culture 2004–2010, Minister of Finance, Sustainable Devt and Human Resource Devt 2010–; Chair. Bd Caribbean Devt Bank 2002–. *Address:* Office of the Prime Minister, Basseterre, Saint Christopher and Nevis (office).

DOUGLAS, Gabrielle (Gabby) Christina Victoria; American gymnast; b. 31 Dec. 1995, Virginia; d. of Timothy Douglas and Natalie Hawkins; started formal gymnastics training at Gymstrada at the age of six in 2002; Virginia State Champion 2004; begain training with coach Liang Chow in Ia; competed in Covergirl Classic, Chicago (ninth all-around in jr div.) 2010, Nastia Liukin Supergirl Cup (fourth all-around) 2010; silver medal, balance beam, Jr Nat. Championship 2010; won uneven bars title, gold medal (team), fifth, all-around, Pan American Championships 2010; made sr debut in 2011; seventh, all-around, Nat. Championship, Minn. 2011; gold medal (team), World Championships, Tokyo 2011; winner, AT&T American Cup 2012 (highest total all-around score); gold medal, uneven bars, silver medal, all-round, bronze medal, uneven bars, floor exercise Visa Championships 2012; gold medal, uneven bars, gold medal (team), Pacific Rim Championships 2012; gold medal, individual all-around, gold medal (team all-around), (first African-American woman to win the event), Olympic Games, London 2012; first American gymnast ever to win both team and individual all-around gold at same Olympics; mem. Chow's Gymnastics and Dance Inst. *Address:* c/o Chow's Gymnastics and Dance Institute, 2210 Park Drive, West Des Moines, IA 50265-5767, USA. *Website:* gabrielledouglas.com.

DOUGLAS, James Henry (Jim), AB; American politician, fmr state governor and academic; *Executive in Residence, Middlebury College;* b. 21 June 1951, Springfield, Mass; s. of Robert James Douglas and Cora Elizabeth Douglas (née Holley); m. Dorothy Foster 1975; two s.; ed East Longmeadow High School, Mass, Middlebury Coll., Vt; Gen. Man. Credit Bureau of Middlebury 1972–76; Exec. Dir United Way of Addison Co. 1976–79; mem. Vt House of Reps 1972–79, Majority Whip 1975–77, Majority Leader 1977–79; Exec. Asst to Gov. Richard A. Snelling of Vt 1979–80; Vt Sec. of State, Montpelier 1981–93; State Treas. 1994–2002; Gov. of Vt 2003–11; Exec. in Residence, Middlebury Coll. 2011–, also teaches course, Vermont Govt and Politics; Chair. Nat. Govs Asscn 2009–10; mem. Govs' Council, Bipartisan Policy Center, Washington, DC 2010–; mem. and fmr Pres. Nat. Asscn of Secs of State; fmr Pres. Addison Co. Chamber of Commerce, Porter Medical Center; mem. Republican Town Cttee; Nat. Order of Quebec (Canada) 2010. *Address:* Middlebury College, Munroe Hall 301, 427 College Street, Middlebury, VT 05753, USA (office). *Telephone:* (802) 443-5000 (office). *Website:* www .middlebury.edu (office).

DOUGLAS, Kirk, AB; American actor; b. 9 Dec. 1916, Amsterdam, NY; s. of Harry Danielovitch and Bryna Danielovitch (née Sanglel); m. 1st Diana Dill (divorced 1950); two s. including Michael Kirk Douglas; m. 2nd Anne Buydens 1954; two s. (one deceased); ed St Lawrence Univ. and American Acad. of Dramatic Arts; Pres. Bryna Productions 1955–; Dir Los Angeles Chapter, UN Asscn; Acad. Awards 1948, 1952, 1956; Commdr des Arts et Lettres 1979, Légion d'honneur 1985, Presidential Medal of Freedom 1981; New York Film Critics' Award, Hollywood Foreign Press Award, American Film Inst.'s Lifetime Achievement Award 1991, Kennedy Center Honors 1994, Hon. Acad. Award 1996, Lifetime Achievement Award Screen Actors' Guild 1999, Golden Bear, Berlin Film Festival 2000, Nat. Medal of Arts 2002. *Stage appearances include:* Spring Again, Three Sisters, Kiss and Tell, The Wind is Ninety, Alice in Arms, Man Bites Dog, The Boys of Autumn, Before I Forget. *Films include:* The Strange Love of Martha Ivers 1946, Out of the Past (aka Build My Gallows High) 1947, Mourning Becomes Electra 1947, I Walk Alone 1948, The Walls of Jericho 1948, My Dear Secretary 1949, A Letter to Three Wives 1949, Champion 1949, Young Man With a Horn 1950, The Glass Menagerie 1950, Along the Great Divide 1951, Ace in the Hole 1951, Detective Story 1951, The Big Trees 1952, The Big Sky 1952, The Bad and the Beautiful 1952, The Story of Three Loves 1953, The Juggler 1953, Un acte d'amour (Act of Love) 1953, 20,000 Leagues Under the Sea 1954, The Racers 1955, Ulisse (Ulysses) 1955, Man Without a Star 1955, The Indian Fighter 1955, Lust for Life 1956, Top Secret Affair 1957, Gunfight at the O.K. Corral 1957, Paths of Glory (also producer) 1957, The Vikings 1958, Last Train from Gun Hill 1959, The Devil's Disciple 1959, Spartacus (also exec. producer) 1960, Town Without Pity 1961, The Last Sunset 1961, Lonely Are the Brave 1962, Two Weeks in Another town 1962, The Hook 1963, The List of Adrian Messenger 1963, For Love or Money 1963, Strangers When We Meet, Seven Days in May 1964, In Harms Way 1965, Cast a Giant Shadow 1966, Paris brûle-t-il? (Is Paris Burning?) 1966, Grand Prix (producer) 1966, The Way West 1967, The War Waggon 1967, A Lovely Way to Die 1968, The Brotherhood (also producer) 1968, The Arrangement 1969, There Was a Crooked Man 1970, To Catch a Spy 1971, The Light at the Edge of the World (also producer) 1971, Gunfight 1971, Summertree (producer) 1971, The Special London Bridge Project 1972, Un uomo da rispettare (A Man to Respect) 1972, Cat and Mouse, Scalawag (also dir) 1973, Once Is Not Enough 1975, Posse (also dir and producer) 1975, Holocaust 2000 1977, The Fury 1978, The Villain 1979, Home Movies 1979, Saturn 3 1980, The Final Countdown 1980, The Man from Snowy River 1982, Eddie Macon's Run 1983, Tough Guys 1986, Oscar 1991, Welcome to Veraz 1991, Greedy 1994, Diamonds 1999, Family Jewels 2002, It Runs in the Family 2003, Illusion 2004. *Television work includes:* Tales of the Vikings (series, producer) 1960, Dr. Jekyll and Mr. Hyde 1973, Mousey 1974, The Moneychangers (mini-series) 1976, Victory at Entebbe 1976, Remembrance of Love 1982, Draw! 1984, Amos 1985, Queenie (mini-series) 1987, Inherit the Wind 1988, Two-Fisted Tales 1991, The Secret 1992, Take Me Home Again 1994, Touched by an Angel (series) 2000. *Publications:* The Ragman's Son: An Autobiography 1988, Dance with the Devil (novel) 1990, The Secret (novel) 1992, The Gift (novel) 1992, Last Tango in Brooklyn (novel) 1994, Climbing the Mountain: My Search for Meaning 1997, The Broken Mirror (novel) 1997, My Stroke of Luck 2002, Let's Face It 2007. *Address:* Warren Cowan Associates, 8899 Beverly Boulevard, Suite 412, Beverly Hills, CA 90048-2427 (office); The Bryna Company, 141 S El Camino Drive, Beverly Hills, CA 90212, USA (office). *Telephone:* (310) 274-5294 (office). *Fax:* (310) 274-2537 (office).

DOUGLAS, Michael Kirk, BA; American actor and film producer; b. 25 Sept. 1944, New Brunswick, New Jersey; s. of Kirk Douglas (q.v.) and Diana Douglas; m. 1st Diandra Mornell Luker 1977 (divorced); one s.; m. 2nd Catherine Zeta-Jones (q.v.) 2000; one s. one d.; appeared in TV series Streets of San Francisco; f. Further Films (production co.); Hon. DLit (Univ. of St Andrews, Scotland) 2006; Spencer Tracy Award 1999, UN Messenger of Peace 2000, Golden Globe Cecil B. DeMille Award 2004, Career Achievement Award, Nat. Bd of Review 2007, Lifetime Achievement Award, American Film Inst. 2009, David O. Selznick Achievement Award, Producers Guild of America 2009, Danny Kaye Humanitarian Peace Award 2014. *Film appearances include:* It's My Turn, Hail Hero! 1969, Summertime 1971, Napoleon and Samantha 1972, Coma 1978, Running 1979, Star Chamber 1983, Romancing the Stone (also producer) 1984, A Chorus Line 1985, Jewel of the Nile 1985, Fatal Attraction 1987, Wall Street (Acad. Award for Best Actor 1988) 1987, Heidi 1989, Black Rain 1989, The War of the Roses 1990, Shining Through 1990, Basic Instinct 1992, Falling Down 1993, Disclosure 1994, The American President 1995, The Ghost and the Darkness (also exec. producer) 1996, The Game 1997, A Perfect Murder 1998, One Day in September (voice) 1999, Traffic 2000, Wonder Boys 2000, One Night at McCool's (also producer) 2000, Don't Say a Word 2001, A Few Good Years 2002, It Runs in the Family 2003, Monkeyface 2003, The In-Laws 2003, The Sentinel (also producer) 2006, You, Me and Dupree 2006, King of California 2007, Beyond a Reasonable Doubt 2009, Ghosts of Girlfriends Past 2009, Solitary Man 2009, Wall Street: Money Never Sleeps 2010, Behind the Candelabra (Emmy Award for Best Actor in a Mini-series/Movie, Golden Globe Award for Best Actor in TV Mini-series or Movie, Screen Actors Guild Award for Outstanding Performance by a Male Actor in a TV Movie or Mini-series 2014) 2013. *Films produced include:* One Flew Over the Cuckoo's Nest (Academy Award for Best Film 1975), The China Syndrome, Starman (exec.

producer), Flatliners 1990, Stone Cold 1991, Eyes of an Angel (exec. producer) 1991, Radio Flyer 1992, Made in America (co-exec. producer) 1993, Face/Off (exec. producer) 1997, The Rainmaker 1997, Godspeed, Lawrence Mann 2002. *Address:* Further Films, 100 Universal City Plaza, Building 507-4G, Universal City, CA 91608, USA. *Telephone:* (818) 777-6700.

DOUGLAS, Hon. Sir Roger Owen, Kt; New Zealand politician and accountant; b. 5 Dec. 1937, Auckland, North Island; s. of Norman V. Douglas and Jennie Douglas; m. Glennis June Anderson 1961; one s. one d.; ed Auckland Grammar School, Auckland Univ.; entered House of Reps as Labour mem. for Manukau 1969 (now Manurewa); Minister of Broadcasting 1973–75, of the Post Office 1973–74, of Housing (with State Advances, Housing Corpn) 1974–75; Minister of Finance and Minister in Charge of the Inland Revenue Dept and of Friendly Socs 1984–87, of Finance 1988, of Police and Immigration 1989–90; MP for ACT Party List 2008–11; Dir Brierley Investments 1990–98 (Chair. (interim) 1998), John Fairfax Ltd 1997–99, Aetna Health (NZ) Ltd 1997–99, Tasman Inst. 1997–; fmr Pres. Auckland Labour Regional Council, Manukau Labour Cttee; Finance Minister of the Year, Euromoney Magazine 1985, Max Schmidheiny Freedom Prize, Switzerland 1995, Ludwig Erhard Foundation Prize, Germany 1997, Friedrich von Hayek Medal, Austria 2002, Turgot Freedom Prize, Paris 2008. *Publications:* There's Got to Be a Better Way 1980, Toward Prosperity 1987, Unfinished Business 1993, Completing the Circle 1996; several papers on int. and econ. affairs. *Leisure interests:* cricket, rugby, rugby league, reading, grandchildren. *Address:* 411 Redoubt Road, Totara Park, Auckland 2016, New Zealand (home). *Telephone:* (9) 2639596 (home). *E-mail:* rdouglas@xtra.co.nz (office). *Website:* www.rogerdouglas.org.nz (home).

DOURI, Izzat Ibrahim al-; Iraqi politician; b. 1942, al-Dour Shire; Ed. Voice of the Peasant 1968, Head Supreme Cttee for People's Work 1968–70; Minister of Agrarian Reform 1970–74; Vice-Pres. Supreme Agric. Council 1970–71, Head 1971–79; Minister of Agriculture 1973–74, of the Interior 1974–79; mem. Revolutionary Command Council, Vice-Pres. 1979–2003; Deputy Sec.-Gen. Regional Command of Arab Baath Socialist Party 1979–2003; mem. Nat. Command Arab Baath Socialist Party –2003, Leader Baath Party 2007–.

DOUSTE-BLAZY, Philippe Jean Georges Marie, DenM; French physician, politician and UN official; *Special Adviser to the Secretary-General on Innovative Financing for Development, United Nations;* b. 1 Jan. 1953, Lourdes; s. of Louis Douste-Blazy and Geneviève Béguère; m. Marie-Yvonne Calazel 1977; ed Lycée Pierre de Caousou, Toulouse and Univ. Paul Sabatier, Toulouse; Intern, Toulouse hosps 1976–82; Head of Cardiology Clinics and Asst to Toulouse hosps 1982–86; Univ. Prof. 1988–; Dir Arcol 1988–; Mayor of Lourdes 1989–2000, of Toulouse 2001–04; mem. European Parl. 1989–93; Regional Councillor for Midi-Pyrénées 1992; Deputy to Nat. Ass. (Union pour la démocratie française) 1993, 1997–2001; Minister of Social Affairs, of Health and the City 1993–95, of Culture 1995–97, of Health and Social Protection 2004–05, of Foreign Affairs 2005–07; Adviser to Pres. Nicolas Sarkozy 2007–08; Special Adviser to the Sec.-Gen. on Innovative Financing for Devt, UN 2008–; Pres. Union pour la démocratie française group, Nat. Ass. 1998–2004; mem. New York Acad. of Sciences and numerous medical orgs. *Leisure interests:* classical music, golf. *Address:* Office of the Secretary-General, United Nations, New York, NY 10017, USA (office); 1 rue de Bagnères, 65100 Lourdes, France (home). *Telephone:* (212) 963-1234 (office). *Fax:* (212) 963-4879 (office). *Website:* www.un.org/sg (office).

DOUVILLE, Jean; Canadian lawyer and business executive; *Chairman of the Board of Directors, National Bank of Canada;* b. Bedford, Quebec; ed Univ. of Ottawa; called to Québec Bar 1968; joined UAP Inc. 1971, Pres. 1981, CEO 1982, Chair. 1994–; mem. Bd of Dirs Nat. Bank of Canada 1991–, Chair. 2004–, fmr Chair. Audit and Risk Man. Cttee, Conduct Review and Corp. Governance Cttee; mem. Bd of Dirs Genuine Parts Co. 1990–, Richelieu's Hardware Ltd 2005–; Dir Leroux Steel Inc. 1999–2003, Van Houtte Inc. 1999–2003. *Address:* National Bank of Canada, National Bank Tower, 600 de la Gauchetière West, Montréal, PQ H3B 4L2, Canada (office). *Telephone:* (514) 394-5000 (office). *Fax:* (514) 394-8434 (office). *Website:* www.nbc.ca (office).

DOVE, Rita Frances, BA, MFA; American writer, poet and academic; *Commonwealth Professor of English, University of Virginia;* b. 28 Aug. 1952, Akron, Ohio; d. of Ray Dove and Elvira Dove (née Hord); m. Fred Viebahn 1979; one d.; ed Miami Univ., Ohio, Univ. of Tübingen, Germany and Univ. of Iowa; Asst Prof., Ariz. State Univ., Tempe 1981–84, Assoc. Prof. 1984–87, Prof. of English 1987–89; Prof., Univ. of Virginia, Charlottesville 1989–93, Commonwealth Prof. of English 1993–; Poet Laureate of the USA 1993–95, of the Commonwealth of Virginia 2004–06; Consultant in Poetry, Library of Congress 1993–95; Special Consultant in Poetry, Library of Congress Bicentennial 1999–2000; Assoc. Ed., Callaloo 1986–98, adviser and Contributing Ed. 1998–; adviser and Contributing Ed. Gettysburg Review 1987–, TriQuarterly 1988–, Meridian 1989–, Ploughshares 1992–, Georgia Review 1994–, Bellingham Review 1996–, Poetry Int. 1996–, Int. Quarterly 1997–, Mid-American Review 1998–, Hunger Mountain 2003–, American Poetry Review 2005–; Writer-in-Residence, Tuskegee Inst., Ala 1982; poetry panellist, Nat. Endowment for Arts, Washington, DC 1984–86 (Chair. 1985); judge, Pulitzer Prize in Poetry 1991 (Chair. of Jury 1997); mem. Bd of Dirs Associated Writing Programs 1985–88, Pres. 1986–87; mem. Jury, Anisfield-Wolf Book Awards; Chancellor Acad. of American Poets 2006–12; mem. Acad. of American Poets, Associated Writing Programs, Poetry Soc. of America, Poets and Writers, American Acad. of Arts and Sciences, American Acad. of Arts and Letters, American Philosophical Soc.; 24 hon. doctorates; Fulbright Fellow 1974–75, Nat. Endowment for the Arts grants 1978, 1989, Portia Pittman Fellow, Tuskegee Inst. 1982, Guggenheim Fellowship 1984, Rockefeller Foundation Residency in Bellagio, Italy 1988, Mellon Fellow, Nat. Humanities Center 1989, Fellow, Center for Advanced Studies, Univ. of Virginia 1989–92; numerous awards, including Acad. of American Poets Peter I. B. Lavan Younger Poets Award 1986, Callaloo Award 1986, Gen. Electric Foundation Award for Younger Writers 1987, Ohio Gov.'s Award 1988, Ohioana Library Book Awards 1990, 2000, NY Public Library Literary Lion Awards 1990, 1996, 2000, Nat. Book Award in Poetry 1991, NAACP Great American Artist Award 1993, American Acad. of Achievement Golden Plate Award 1994, Folger Shakespeare Library Renaissance Forum Award 1994, Charles Frankel Prize/Nat. Humanities Medal 1996, Heinz Award in the Arts and Humanities 1996, Barnes and Noble Writers Award 1997, Levinson Prize 1998, Duke Ellington Lifetime Achievement Award in the Literary Arts, Ellington Fund in Washington, DC 2001,

Commonwealth Award of Distinguished Service 2006, Library of Virginia Lifetime Achievement Award 2008, Fulbright Asscn Lifetime Achievement Medal 2009, Hurston/Wright Foundation Award for Poetry 2010, Amb.'s Award from Oklahoma Center for Poets and Writers 2010, Ohioana Book Award for Poetry 2010, Celebrating Black History Now: 40 Firsts In 40 Years, Essence Magazine 2010, 40th Anniversary Portfolio: Our 40 Favorite Poets, Essence Magazine 2010, Nat. Medal of Arts for 2011. *Publications:* poetry: Ten Poems 1977, The Only Dark Spot in the Sky 1980, The Yellow House on the Corner 1980, Mandolin 1982, Museum 1983, Thomas and Beulah (Pulitzer Prize in Poetry 1987) 1986, The Other Side of the House 1988, Grace Notes 1989, Selected Poems 1993, Lady Freedom Among Us 1994, Mother Love 1995, Evening Primrose 1998, On the Bus with Rosa Parks 1999, Best American Poetry (ed.) 2000, American Smooth 2004, Sonata Mulattica 2009, The Penguin Anthology of Twentieth-Century American Poetry (ed.) 2011; prose: Fifth Sunday (short stories) 1985, Through the Ivory Gate (novel) 1992, The Darker Face of Earth (verse play) 1994, The Poet's World (essays) 1995. *Leisure interests:* playing the viola da gamba, classical voice training, ballroom dancing. *Address:* 219 Bryan Hall, University of Virginia, PO Box 400121, Charlottesville, VA 22904-4121, USA (office). *Telephone:* (434) 924-6618 (office). *Fax:* (434) 924-1478 (office). *E-mail:* rfd4b@virginia.edu (office). *Website:* www.people.virginia.edu/~rfd4b (office).

DOWELL, Sir Anthony James, Kt, CBE; British director, producer and fmr ballet dancer; b. 16 Feb. 1943, London; s. of Arthur H. Dowell and Catherine E. Dowell; ed Hampshire School, Royal Ballet School; Prin. Dancer, The Royal Ballet 1966, Sr Prin. Dancer 1967–84, Asst to the Dir 1984, Assoc. Dir 1985–86, Dir 1986–2001 (retd); joined American Ballet Theatre 1978; cr. roles in the following ballets: The Dream 1964, Romeo and Juliet 1965, Shadow Play 1967, Monotones 1969, Triad 1972, Manon 1974, A Month in the Country 1976; narrator in Oedipus Rex, Metropolitan Opera House, New York 1981; cr. role of Prospero in Nureyev's The Tempest, Royal Opera House, London 1982; dir new productions of Swan Lake and The Sleeping Beauty for Royal Ballet; designed costumes for Thaïs pas de deux (Frederick Ashton), In the Night (Jerome Robbins) and Symphony in C (George Balanchine) for Royal Ballet; Queen Elizabeth II Coronation Award, Royal Acad. of Dancing 1994, Critics' Circle Award 2001, De Valois Award for Outstanding Achievement in Dance 2002. *Address:* c/o The Royal Ballet, Covent Garden, London, WC2E 7QA, England.

DOWELL, John Derek, PhD, FRS, CPhys, FInstP; British physicist and academic; *Professor Emeritus of Physics, University of Birmingham;* b. 6 Jan. 1935, Ashby-de-la-Zouch, Leics., England; s. of William E. Dowell and Elsie D. Dowell; m. Patricia Clarkson 1959; one s. one d.; ed Coalville Grammar School, Leics. and Univ. of Birmingham; Research Fellow, Univ. of Birmingham 1958–60; Research Assoc., CERN, Geneva 1960–62, Scientific Assoc. 1973–74, 1985–87, mem. Scientific Policy Cttee 1982–90, 1993–96, Research Bd 1993–96, Chair. LEP Cttee 1993–96; Lecturer, Univ. of Birmingham 1962–70, Sr Lecturer 1970–74, Reader 1974–80, Prof. of Elementary Particle Physics 1980–97, Poynting Prof. of Physics 1997–2002, Prof. Emer. 2002–; Visiting Scientist, Argonne Nat. Lab., USA 1968–69; Chair. Science and Eng Research Council (SERC) Particle Physics Cttee 1981–85; mem. European Cttee for Future Accelerators 1989–93, BBC Science Consultative Group 1992–94, DESY Extended Scientific Council 1992–98; Chair. ATLAS Collaboration Bd 1996–98; Lay Chair. Birmingham Children's Hosp. NHS Trust 2002–; mem. UK Particle Physics and Astronomy Research Council 1994–97; mem. Court of Univ. of Warwick 1993–2001, Council, Royal Soc. 1997–98 (also Vice-Pres.); mem. RAE Physics Panel, Higher Educ. Funding Council 2001; Fellow, American Physical Soc.; Rutherford Medal and Prize, Inst. of Physics 1988. *Publications:* numerous papers in physics journals. *Leisure interests:* piano, amateur theatre, golf. *Address:* School of Physics and Astronomy, University of Birmingham, Birmingham, B15 2TT (office); 57 Oxford Road, Moseley, Birmingham, B13 9ES, England (home). *Telephone:* (121) 414-4658 (office); (121) 449-3332 (home). *Fax:* (121) 414-6709 (home). *E-mail:* jdd@hep.ph.bham.ac.uk (office).

DOWLING, John Elliott, AB, PhD; American neuroscientist, neurobiologist and academic; *Gordon and Llura Gund Professor of Neurosciences, Harvard University;* b. 31 Aug. 1935, Rhode Island; s. of Joseph Leo Dowling and Ruth W. (Tappan) Dowling; m. 1st Susan Kinney (divorced 1974); two s.; m. 2nd Judith Falco 1975; one d.; ed Harvard Univ.; Instructor, Harvard Univ. 1961, Asst Prof. 1961–64, Prof. of Biology 1971–87, Assoc. Dean 1980–84, Master, Leverett House 1981–98, Prof. of Ophthalmology, Harvard Medical School 1986–, Maria Moors Cabot Prof. of Natural Science 1987–2001, Harvard Coll. Prof. 1999–2001, Pres., Corp. Marine Biological Lab. 1998–2007, Gordon and Llura Gund Prof. of Neurosciences 2001–, Head Tutor, Neurobiology, Harvard Univ. 2006–10; Assoc. Prof., Johns Hopkins Univ. 1964–71; mem. NAS, American Acad. of Arts and Sciences, American Philosophical Soc.; Hon. MD (Lund, Sweden) 1982; Hon. LLD Laws (Dalhousie, Canada) 2012; Friedenwald Medal 1970, Retinal Research Award 1981, Prentice Medal 1991, Von Sallman Prize 1992, Helen Keller Prize 2000, Llura Liggett Gund Award 2001, Paul Kayser Int. Eye Research Award 2008, Glenn A. Fry Medal in Physiological Optics 2009. *Publications:* The Retina: An Approachable Part of the Brain 1987 (revised edn 2012), Neurons and Networks 1992, Creating Mind: How the Brain Works 1998, The Great Brain Debate: Nature or Nurture? 2004; more than 250 publns in professional journals and ed. of five vols. *Leisure interests:* reading, golf and music. *Address:* The Biological Laboratories, Harvard University, 16 Divinity Avenue, Cambridge, MA 02138 (office); 135 Charles Street, Boston, MA 02114, USA (home). *Telephone:* (617) 495-2245 (office); (617) 720-4522 (home). *Fax:* (617) 496-3321 (office). *E-mail:* dowling@mcb.harvard.edu (office). *Website:* www.mcb.harvard.edu (office).

DOWLING, Patrick Joseph, CBE, BE, PhD, FICE, FCGI, FREng, FRS; Irish engineer, academic and university administrator; *Chairman, British Science Association;* b. 23 March 1939, Dublin; s. of John Dowling and Margaret McKittrick; m. Grace Lobo 1966; one s. one d.; ed Christian Bros. School, Dublin, Univ. Coll. Dublin and Imperial Coll. London; Sr Demonstrator in Civil Eng, Univ. Coll. Dublin 1960–61; Bursar in Structural Steelwork, Imperial Coll. London 1961–62, research on Steel Bridge Decks 1962–65; bridge engineer, British Constructional Steelwork Asscn 1965–68; Research Fellow, Imperial Coll. London 1968–74, Reader in Structural Steelwork 1974–79, Prof. of Steel Structures 1979–94, British Steel Prof. and Head, Dept of Civil Eng 1985–94; Vice-Chancellor

and Chief Exec., Univ. of Surrey 1994–2005 (retd), now Prof. Emer.; Pnr, Chapman and Dowling Consulting Engineers 1981–94; Chair. Surrey Satellite Tech. Ltd 1994–2005; currently Chair. British Science Asscn; fmr Chair. Eng Council, Steel Construction Inst., Daphne Jackson Trust, Surrey Research Park Exec.; Pres. Inst. of Structural Engineers 1994–95; fmr Pres. Asscn for Science Educ., City and Guilds Coll. Asscn; fmr Vice-Pres. Royal Acad. of Eng; Fellow, Imperial Coll., London 1997; DL Surrey 1999; Hon. LLD (Nat. Univ. of Ireland) 1995; Dr hc (Vilnius Tech. Univ., Lithuania) 1996, (Ulster) 1998; Telford Premium, ICE 1976, Gustave Trasenster Medal, Asscn des Ingénieurs Sortis de l'Univ. de Liège 1984; several awards from Inst. of Structural Engineers. *Publications:* Steel Plated Structures 1977, Buckling Shells in Offshore Structures 1982, Structural Steel Design 1988, Constructional Steel Design 1992; over 200 refereed papers. *Leisure interests:* travelling, sailing, reading, good company, modern art, theatre. *Address:* British Science Association, Wellcome Wolfson Building, 165 Queen's Gate, London, SW7 5HD, England (office). *Telephone:* (87) 0770-7101 (office). *Fax:* (87) 0770-7102 (office). *Website:* www.britishscienceassociation.org (office).

DOWNE, William (Bill) A., BA, MBA; Canadian banking executive; *President and CEO, BMO Financial Group (Bank of Montreal);* b. 1952, Montreal; m. Robin Downe; three s.; ed Wilfrid Laurier Univ., Univ. of Toronto; joined Bank of Montreal (BMO) 1983 as credit analyst, has held numerous sr man. positions in Corp. and Govt Banking, Houston and Denver, Sr Vice-Pres. US Corp. Banking 1992–96, Exec. Vice-Pres. North American Corp. Banking 1996–98, Head of Global Fixed Income Treasury 1998–99, Vice-Chair. Bank of Montreal 1999–2001, Deputy Chair. BMO Financial Group and CEO BMO Nesbitt Burns 2001–06, COO BMO Financial Group 2006–07, Pres. and CEO 2007–; Chair. Bd of Dirs St Michael's Hosp., Toronto; Rotman Distinguished Business Alumni Award, Joseph L. Rotman School of Man. 2003, Arbor Award, Univ. of Toronto 2005. *Address:* Bank of Montreal, 1 First Canadian Place, 100 King Street, West Toronto, ON M5X 1A1, Canada (office). *Telephone:* (416) 867-5000 (office). *Fax:* (416) 867-6793 (office). *E-mail:* info@bmo.com (office). *Website:* www.bmo.com (office).

DOWNER, Alexander John Gosse, BA; Australian politician, diplomatist and UN official; *High Commissioner to UK;* b. 9 Sept. 1951; s. of Sir Alexander Downer; m. Nicola Robinson 1978; one s. three d.; ed Geelong Grammar School, Victoria, Radley Coll. and Univ. of Newcastle-upon-Tyne, UK; mem. Australian Diplomatic Service 1976–81, Australian Mission to European Communities, Embassy in Belgium and Luxembourg 1977–80; Sr Foreign Affairs Rep., S Australia 1981; Political Adviser to Prime Minister 1982–83; Dir Australian Chamber of Commerce 1983–84; mem. House of Reps (Liberal) for Mayo, S Australia 1984–; Shadow Minister for Arts, Heritage and Environment 1987, for Housing, Small Business and Customs 1988–89, for Trade and Trade Negotiations 1990–92, for Defence 1992–93; Fed. Shadow Treas. 1993–94; Leader Liberal Party 1994–95; Shadow Minister for Foreign Affairs 1995–96; Minister for Foreign Affairs 1996–2007; Special Adviser to UN Sec.-Gen. on Cyprus 2008–14; High Commissioner to UK 2014–; Hon. DCL. *Leisure interests:* reading, music, tennis, golf. *Address:* Australian High Commission, Australia House, Strand, London, WC2B 4LA, England (office). *Telephone:* (20) 7379-4334 (office). *Fax:* (20) 7240-5333 (office). *Website:* www.uk.embassy.gov.au (office).

DOWNEY, James, OC, PhD; Canadian academic, university administrator and writer; b. 20 April 1939; s. of Ernest Downey and Mimy Ann Downey (née Andrews); m. Laura Ann Parsons 1964; one s. one d.; ed Memorial Univ. of Newfoundland, Univ. of London, UK; Asst Prof. of English, Carleton Univ. 1966–69, Assoc. Prof. 1969–75, Prof. 1975–80, Chair. Dept of English 1972–75, Acting Dean, Faculty of Arts 1975, Dean 1976–78, Vice-Pres. (Acad.) 1978–80, Pres. pro tempore 1979; Pres. and Vice-Chancellor Univ. of New Brunswick 1980–90, Prof. of English 1980; Pres. and Vice-Chancellor Univ. of Waterloo 1993–99, then Prof. of English, Founding Dir Centre for the Advancement of Co-operative Educ. 2002–05, now Pres. Emer.; Chair. Royal Mil. Coll. of Ontario 2005; Founding Pres. and CEO Higher Educ. Quality Council of Ontario 2005–09; Co-Chair. Comm. on Excellence in Educ. in NB 1991–92 Fellow, Univ. of Georgia 1985; Hon. DHumLitt (Maine) 1987, Hon. DLitt (Newfoundland) 1991, Hon. LLD (New Brunswick) 1991, Hon. LLD (Toronto) 1998, (McMaster) 1999, (Carleton) 2000; Symons Medal 2001, David Smith Award 2003. *Publications include:* The Eighteenth Century Pulpit 1969, Fearful Joy 1974 (co-ed.), Schools for a New Century 1993, Innovation: Essays by Leading Canadian Researchers 2002 (co-ed.), Lord Beaverbrook and the Kennedys 2012.

DOWNEY, Robert, Jr; American actor and singer; b. 4 April 1965, New York, NY; s. of Robert Downey and Elsie Ford; m. 1st Deborah Falconer (divorced 2004); one s.; m. 2nd Susan Levin 2005; first movie role in his father's film Pound 1970; joined cast of tv show Saturday Night Live for one season 1985–86; sentenced to probation for possession of cocaine; imprisoned for further drugs offence breaching terms of probation Dec. 1997; released to serve six months at rehabilitation centre 1998; imprisoned again Aug. 1999, freed Aug. 2000, charged with drugs possession Dec. 2000; f. Team Downey (production co.) 2010–. *Films include:* Pound (debut) 1970, Up the Academy (uncredited) 1980, Baby It's You 1983, Firstborn 1984, Deadwait 1985, Tuff Turf 1985, Weird Science 1985, To Live and Die in LA, America 1986, Back to School 1986, The Pick-up Artist 1987, Less Than Zero 1987, Johnny Be Good 1988, Rented Lips 1988, 1969 1988, That's Adequate 1989, True Believer 1989, Chances Are 1989, Air America 1990, Too Much Sun 1991, Soapdish 1991, Chaplin (BAFTA Award) 1992, Heart and Souls 1993, Short Cuts 1993, Hail Caesar 1994, Back to School, Soapdish, The Last Party (also writer) 1993, Natural Born Killers 1994, Only You 1994, Richard III 1995, Restoration 1995, Home for the Holidays 1995, Danger Zone 1996, One Night Stand 1997, Bliss Vision 1997, Two Girls and a Guy (also composed song 'Snakes') 1997, Hugo Pool (aka Pool Girl) 1997, The Gingerbread Man 1998, U.S. Marshals 1998, In Dreams 1999, Friends & Lovers (also composed song 'Carla') 1999, Bowfinger 1999, Black and White 1999, Wonder Boys 2000, Auto Motives 2000, Lethargy 2002, Whatever We Do 2003, The Singing Detective (also singer of 'In My Dreams') 2003, Gothika 2003, Eros 2004, Game 6 2005, Kiss, Kiss, Bang, Bang 2005, The Shaggy Dog 2006, A Scanner Darkly 2006, Goodnight, and Good Luck 2006, Fur: An Imaginary Portrait of Diane Arbus 2006, A Guide to Recognizing Your Saints 2006, Zodiac 2007, Lucky You 2007, Charlie Bartlett 2007, Iron Man 2008, Tropic Thunder 2008, The Soloist 2009, Sherlock Holmes (Golden Globe for best performance by an actor in a motion picture—comedy or musical 2010) 2009, Iron Man 2 2010, Due Date 2010, Sherlock

Holmes: A Game of Shadows 2011, Avengers Assemble 2012, Iron Man 3 2013. *Television includes:* Mussolini: The Untold Story (mini-series) 1985, Mr. Willowby's Christmas Tree 1995, as Larry Paul in Ally McBeal (series) 2000–01. *Recording:* album: The Futurist 2005. *Address:* CAA, 2000 Avenue of the Stars, Los Angeles, CA 90067, USA.

DOWNIE, Leonard, Jr, MA; American newspaper executive and academic; b. 1 May 1942, Cleveland, OH; s. of Leonard Downie, Sr and Pearl Evenheimer; m. 1st Barbara Lindsey 1960 (divorced 1971); two s.; m. 2nd Geraldine Rebach 1971 (divorced 1997); one s. one d.; m. 3rd Janice Galin 1997; ed Ohio State Univ.; joined The Washington Post 1964, became investigative reporter in Washington, specializing in crime, housing and urban affairs, helped to supervise coverage of Watergate affair, Asst Man. Ed. Metropolitan News 1974–79, London Corresp. 1979–82, Nat. Ed. 1982–84, Man. Ed. 1984–91, Exec. Ed. 1991–2008, Vice-Pres. at Large, The Washington Post Co. 2008–, Dir Los Angeles Times–Washington Post News Service 1991–2008, International Herald Tribune 1996–2002; Weil Family Prof. of Journalism, Walter Cronkite School of Journalism and Mass Communication, Arizona State Univ. 2009–; Founder and Bd mem. Investigative Reporters and Editors Inc.; Chair. Bd of Advisors, Kaiser Health News 2009–; mem. Bd of Dirs Investigative Reporters and Editors, Inc. Missouri School of Journalism 2009–, Center for Investigative Reporting 2009–; Fellow, Alicia Patterson Foundation 1971–72; Hon. LLD, Ohio State Univ.; two Washington-Baltimore Newspaper Guild Front Page Awards, American Bar Assen Gavel Award for legal reporting, John Hancock Award for business and financial writing, Ben Bradlee Editor of the Year Award, National Press Foundation 2008, Award for Editorial Leadership, American Society of News Editors 2009. *Publications:* Justice Denied 1971, Mortgage on America 1974, The New Muckrakers 1976, The News About the News (with Robert G. Kaiser) 2002, The Rules of the Game (novel) 2009. *Leisure interests:* ballet, classical music, travel, sports. *Address:* Room 389, Walter Cronkite School of Journalism, Arizona State University, 555 North Central Avenue, Phoenix, AZ 85004, USA. *Telephone:* (602) 496-7973 (office). *E-mail:* leonard.downie@asu.edu (office). *Website:* cronkite.asu.edu (office).

DOWNIE, Robert Silcock, MA, BPhil, FRSE, FRSA; British philosopher, academic and composer; *Professor Emeritus of Moral Philosophy, University of Glasgow;* b. 19 April 1933, Glasgow, Scotland; s. of Robert M. Downie and Margaret M. Brown; m. Eileen Dorothea Flynn 1958; three d.; ed Univ. of Glasgow, Queen's Coll., Oxford; Tutor, Worcester Coll., Oxford 1958–59; Lecturer in Moral Philosophy, Univ. of Glasgow 1959–68, Sr Lecturer 1968–69, Prof. 1969, now Prof. Emer. and Hon. Professorial Research Fellow; Visiting Prof., Syracuse Univ., USA 1963–64, Dalhousie Univ., NS, Canada 1976, Durham Univ. 2000. *Music:* choral music and songs composed, published and performed; chamber and piano music composed and performed. *Publications:* Government Action and Morality 1964, Respect for Persons 1969, Roles and Values 1971, Education and Personal Relationships 1974, Caring and Curing 1980, Healthy Respect 1987, Health Promotion: Models and Values 1990, The Making of a Doctor 1992, The Healing Arts 1994, Francis Hutcheson: Selected Writings 1994, Palliative Care Ethics 1996, Medical Ethics 1996, Clinical Judgement 2000, The Philosophy of Palliative Care 2006, End of Life Choices 2009. *Leisure interest:* music. *Address:* Department of Philosophy, University of Glasgow, Glasgow, G12 8QQ, Scotland (office). *Telephone:* (141) 339-8855 (office). *Fax:* (141) 330-4112 (office). *E-mail:* robert.downie@glasgow.ac.uk (office). *Website:* www.gla.ac.uk/schools/humanities/philosophy (office).

DOWSON, Duncan, CBE, BSc, PhD, DrSc, FRS, FRSE, FREng, FRSA, FCGI; British mechanical engineer and academic; *Professor Emeritus, School of Mechanical Engineering, University of Leeds;* b. 31 Aug. 1928, Kirbymoorside, N Yorks., England; s. of Wilfrid Dowson and Hannah Dowson; m. Mabel Strickland 1951; one s. (and one s. deceased); ed Lady Lumley's Grammar School, Pickering and Univ. of Leeds; Research Eng, Sir W.G. Armstrong Whitworth Aircraft Co. 1953–54; Lecturer in Mechanical Eng, Univ. of Leeds 1954, Sr Lecturer 1963–65, Reader 1965–66, Prof. of Eng Fluid Mechanics and Tribology 1966–93, Prof. Emer. 1993–; Hon. Fellow and Research Prof. 1998–2001; External Prof., Univ. of Loughborough 2001–, Dir Inst. of Tribology, Dept of Mechanical Eng 1967–87, Head, Dept of Mechanical Eng 1987–93, Pro-Vice-Chancellor 1983–85, Dean for Int. Relations 1987–93; Pres. IMechE 1992–93; Chair. Yorks. Region, Royal Soc. of Arts 1992–97; Foreign mem. Royal Swedish Acad. of Eng Sciences; Life Fellow, ASME; Hon. Prof., Univ. of Hong Kong 1992–, Univ. of Bradford 1996–; Hon. Fellow, American Soc. of Lubrication Engineers; Hon. FIMechE; Hon. DTech (Chalmers Univ. of Tech., Göteborg) 1979; Hon. DSc (Inst. Nat. des Sciences Appliquées, Lyon) 1991, (Liège) 1996; Hon. DEng (Waterloo, Canada) 2001, (Bradford) 2002, (Leeds) 2003, (Loughborough) 2005; James Clayton Fund Prize, Thomas Hawksley Gold Medal, Tribology Gold Medal 1979, James Alfred Medal 1988, Sarton Medal (Belgium) 1998, James Clayton Memorial Lecturer, IMechE 2000 and numerous other awards. *Publications:* Elastohydrodynamic Lubrication: the fundamentals of roller and gear lubrication (co-author) 1966, History of Tribology 1979, An Introduction to the Biomechanics of Joints and Joint Replacement (co-author) 1981, Ball Bearing Lubrication: The Elastohydrodynamics of Elliptical Contacts (co-author) 1981; numerous papers in professional journals. *Leisure interest:* genealogy. *Address:* Institute of Engineering Thermofluids, Surfaces and Interfaces, School of Mechanical Engineering, University of Leeds, Leeds, LS2 9JT (office); Ryedale, 23 Church Lane, Adel, Leeds, LS16 8DQ, England. *Telephone:* (113) 233-2153 (office); (113) 267-8933 (home). *Fax:* (133) 242-4611 (office); (113) 281-7039 (home). *E-mail:* d.dowson@leeds.ac.uk (office); DDRyedale@aol.com (home). *Website:* www.engineering.leeds.ac.uk/ietsi (office).

DOWSON, Sir Philip Henry (Manning), Kt, CBE, PPRA, RIBA; British architect (retd); b. 16 Aug. 1924, Johannesburg, S Africa; s. of Robert Dowson and Ina Cowen; m. Sarah Crewdson 1950; one s. two d.; ed Gresham's School, Univ. Coll., Oxford, Clare Coll., Cambridge; Lt, RNVR 1943–47; Cambridge 1947–50; Architectural Assen 1950–53; joined Ove Arup & Partners 1953; Founder, Architectural Partner, Arup Assocs 1963; Sr Partner, Ove Arup Partnership 1969–90, Consultant 1990–; Pres. Royal Acad. of Arts 1993–99; mem. Royal Fine Art Comm. 1971–97, Craft Advisory Cttee 1972–75; Gov. St Martin's School of Art 1975–80; Trustee, Thomas Cubitt Trust 1978–98, Royal Botanic Gardens, Kew 1983–95, The Armouries, HM Tower of London 1984–89, Nat. Portrait Gallery 1993–99, Coram Foundation 1993–99; Hon. FAIA; Hon. Fellow, Duncan of

Jordanstone Coll. of Art 1985, RCA 1989, Clare Coll., Cambridge 1992; Hon. Dr of Art (De Montfort Univ.) 2000; Royal Gold Medal, RIBA 1981. *Works include:* urban and univ. devt and coll. bldgs; Oxford, Cambridge, Birmingham, Leicester; housing; schools; new uses for old bldgs; bldgs for music and industrial and office devts. *Publications:* articles in the tech. press. *Leisure interest:* sailing. *Address:* c/o Royal Academy of Arts, Burlington House, Piccadilly, London, W1V 0DS, England.

DOYLE, James Edward (Jim), Jr, AB, JD; American lawyer and politician; *Of Counsel, Foley & Lardner LLP;* b. 23 Nov. 1945, Washington, DC; s. of James E. Doyle, Sr and Ruth Doyle (née Bachhuber); m. Jessica Laird 1966; two adopted s.; ed Madison West High School, Stanford Univ., Calif., Univ. of Wisconsin-Madison, Harvard Univ. Law School; worked as volunteer teacher, with his wife, in Tunisia, as part of US Peace Corps 1967–69; called to Bar: Ariz. 1973, Wis. 1975, US Dist Court, NM 1973, US Dist Court, Ariz. 1973, US Dist Court, Utah 1973, US Court of Appeals (10th Circuit) 1974, US Dist Court (Western Dist), Wis. 1975, Eastern Dist, Wis. 1976, US Court of Appeals (7th Circuit) 1985, US Supreme Court 1989; Attorney, DNA Legal Services, Navajo Indian Reservation, Chinle, Ariz. 1972–75; Partner, Jacobs & Doyle, Madison, Wis. 1975–77; Dist Attorney, Dane Co. 1977–82; Partner, Doyle & Ritz, Madison 1983–90; Of Counsel, Lawton & Cates, Madison 1990–91; Attorney-Gen. State of Wis. 1991–2002; Gov. of Wis. 2003–11; Of Counsel, Foley & Lardner LLP, Milwaukee 2011–; Past Pres. Nat. Assen of Attorneys Gen.; mem. ABA, Wis. Bar Assen (mem. Bd of Dirs Criminal Law section 1988), 7th Circuit Bar Assen (Chair. Criminal Law section 1988–89); Democrat. *Address:* Foley & Lardner LLP, Verex Plaza, 150 East Gilman Street, Madison, WI 53703, USA (office). *Telephone:* (608) 258-4301 (office). *Fax:* (608) 258-4258 (office). *E-mail:* jdoyle@foley.com (office). *Website:* www.foley.com (office).

DOYLE, Noreen, BA, MBA; American/Irish banker and international finance official; b. 1949; ed Coll. of Mount St Vincent, Tuck School of Business, Dartmouth Coll.; began career with Morgan Guaranty Trust; joined Bankers Trust 1974, Client Man., New York and Houston, Div. Man. for multinational cos, New York, Man. Dir for distribution of structured financings, New York, responsible for European affairs, London 1990–92; joined EBRD and set up syndication business 1992, responsible for credit and market risks 1997–2001, First Vice-Pres. and Head of Banking 2001–05 (retd), fmr mem. Exec. Cttee; mem. Bd of Dirs Credit Suisse 2004–, Newmont Mining Corpn 2005–, QinetiQ 2005–, Rexam PLC 2005–; Dame, American Assen of the Order of Malta; named by the Wall Street Journal as one of Europe's most successful women 2003. *Address:* c/o Board of Directors, Credit Suisse Group, Paradeplatz 8, 8070 Zurich, Switzerland.

DOYLE, Roddy; Irish writer and playwright; b. 1958, Dublin; m. Belinda Doyle; two s. *Play:* Brown Bread 1992, USA 1992. *Publications:* The Commitments 1987 (also screenplay with Dick Clement and Ian La Frenais 1991), The Snapper 1990 (screenplay 1992), The Van 1991, Paddy Clarke Ha Ha Ha (Booker Prize) 1993, The Woman Who Walked into Doors 1996, A Star Called Henry 1999, The Giggler Treatment 2000, Rory and Ita 2002, Oh, Play That Thing 2004, Paula Spencer 2006, Wilderness 2007, The Deportees (short stories) 2007, The Dead Republic 2010, A Greyhound of a Girl (children's book) 2012, The Guts 2013. *Address:* c/o John Sutton Management, Building Three, Kilmainham Square, Dublin 8, Ireland. *Website:* www.roddydoyle.ie.

DRABBLE, Dame Margaret, DBE, FRSL, BA; British author; b. 5 June 1939, Sheffield, Yorks., England; d. of the late J. F. Drabble and Kathleen Drabble (née Bloor); sister of A. S. Byatt; m. 1st Clive Swift 1960 (divorced 1975); two s. one d.; m. 2nd Michael Holroyd (q.v.) 1982; ed Newnham Coll., Cambridge; Ed. The Oxford Companion to English Literature 1979–2000; Chair. Nat. Book League 1980–82, Soc. of Authors 2008–09; Hon. Foreign mem. American Acad. of Arts and Letters 2002; Hon. Fellow, Sheffield City Polytechnic 1989; Hon. DLitt (Sheffield) 1976, (Bradford) 1988, (Hull) 1992; Dr hc (Manchester) 1987, (Keele) 1988, (East Anglia) 1994, (York) 1995, (Cambridge) 2006; James Tait Black Memorial Prize 1968, Book of the Year Award, Yorkshire Post 1972, E. M. Forster Award, American Acad. of Arts and Letters 1973, St Louis Literary Award 2003, Golden PEN Award 2011. *Publications:* fiction: A Summer Bird-Cage 1963, The Garrick Year 1964, The Millstone (John Llewelyn Rhys Memorial Prize 1966) 1965, Jerusalem the Golden 1967, The Waterfall 1969, The Needle's Eye 1972, The Realms of Gold 1975, The Ice Age 1977, The Middle Ground 1980, The Radiant Way 1987, A Natural Curiosity 1989, The Gates of Ivory 1991, The Witch of Exmoor 1996, The Peppered Moth 2001, The Seven Sisters 2002, The Red Queen 2004, The Sea Lady 2006, The Pure Gold Baby 2013; plays: Laura 1964, Isadora 1968, Thank You All Very Much 1969, Bird of Paradise 1969; non-fiction: Wordsworth 1966, Arnold Bennett: A Biography 1974, The Genius of Thomas Hardy (ed.) 1976, For Queen and Country: Britain in the Victorian Age 1978, A Writer's Britain 1979, The Oxford Companion to English Literature (co-ed.) 1985, 2000, The Concise Oxford Companion to English Literature (co-ed. with Jenny Stringer) 1987, Angus Wilson: A Biography 1995, The Pattern in the Carpet: A Personal History with Jigsaws (memoirs) 2009, A Day in the Life of a Smiling Woman: Complete Short Stories 2011. *Leisure interests:* walking and talking. *Address:* c/o United Agents, 12–26 Lexington Street, London, W1F 0LE, England (office). *Telephone:* (20) 3214-0800 (office). *Fax:* (20) 3214-0801 (office). *E-mail:* info@unitedagents.co.uk (office). *Website:* unitedagents.co.uk (office).

DRACH, Ivan Fyodorovich; Ukrainian politician and writer; b. 17 Oct. 1936, Telizhentsy, Kiev Oblast; m. Mariya Drach; one s. one d.; ed Univ. of Kiev, Moscow State Univ.; worked as school teacher; corresp. for Literaturnaya Ukraina and Witczyna newspapers 1961–87; scriptwriter, Dovzheniev Studio 1964–87; mem. Bd, Sec. Union of Ukrainian Writers 1989–92; joined CP 1959, resgnd 1990; Founder-mem. Narodny Rukh (Ukrainian nationalist opposition movt), Leader, then Co-Chair. 1989–92; Chair. Ukraina Soc. 1992–; mem. Ukrainian Supreme Soviet 1990–; mem. Ukrainian World Co-ordination Council 1992–99; Chair. State Cttee of Information Policy, TV and Radio 2001; Ukrainian State Prize 1976, USSR State Prize 1983, Yaroslav Mudry Order 1996. *Publications include:* Sun Flower 1962, Ballads of Everyday Life 1967, I Come to You 1970, Poems 1972, The Kievan Sky 1976, The Sun and the Word (poetry) 1978, Green Gates 1980, Dramatic Poems 1982, Grigory Skovoroda 1984, Temple of Sun 1988. *Address:* Gorky str. 18, Apt 7, 252005 Kiev, Ukraine. *Telephone:* (44) 228-87-69.

DRAGHI, Mario, PhD; Italian economist, civil servant, central banker and EU official; *President, European Central Bank;* b. 3 Sept. 1947, Rome; ed La Sapienza

Univ. of Rome, Massachusetts Inst. of Tech., USA; Prof. of Econs, Florence Univ., Italy 1981–91; Exec. Dir IBRD (World Bank), Washington, DC, USA 1984–90; Adviser to Bank of Italy 1990; Dir-Gen. Ministry of the Treasury and of the Budget 1991–2001; apptd mem. Econ. and Financial Cttee EEC (now EU) 1991 (Chair. 2000–01); Chair. Italian Cttee for Privatizations 1993; Dir ENI –2001; Vice-Chair. and Man. Dir Goldman Sachs Int., London, UK 2002–06; Gov. Banca d'Italia 2006–11; Pres. European Central Bank 2011–; Gov. for Italy, IBRD, Asian Devt Bank; Chair. Financial Stability Forum 2006–11 (renamed Financial Stability Bd 2009); mem. Group of Seven deputies 1991; mem. Group of Thirty Consultative Group on Int. Econ. and Monetary Affairs, Inc. (G-30), Washington, DC 2007; IOP Fellow, Kennedy School of Govt, Harvard Univ., USA; Trustee, Inst. for Advanced Study, Princeton, NJ, The Brookings Inst., Washington, DC 2003–; Chair. cttee that drafted legislation governing Italian financial markets ('Draghi Law'); Kt Grand Cross, Order of Merit of the Italian Repub. 2000; Dr hc (Padua) 2009; Hon. MBA (Centro Universitario di Organizzazione Aziendale Foundation, Vicenza) 2010; ranked by Forbes magazine amongst The World's Most Powerful People (12th) 2011, (eighth) 2012, (ninth) 2013. *Publications include:* several articles on int. and European monetary and financial issues. *Address:* European Central Bank, Eurotower, Kaiserstrasse 29, 60311 Frankfurt am Main, Germany (office). *Telephone:* (69) 13447455 (office). *Fax:* (69) 13447404 (office). *E-mail:* info@ecb .e.europa.eu (office). *Website:* www.ecb.europa.eu (office).

DRAGNEA, Liviu Nicolae; Romanian engineer and politician; *Deputy Prime Minister and Minister of Regional Development and Public Administration;* b. 28 Oct. 1962, Gratia, Teleorman Co.; m. Bombonica Dragnea; two c.; ed Faculty of Transport, Polytechnic Inst. of Bucharest, Intensive Course, School of Admin. Studies, Ministry of the Interior, Italy, Course in Man. of Local Public Admin, Bucharest Univ. of Econ. Sciences (ASE), Defence Coll., Univ. of Nat. Defence; Councillor, Turnu Magurele Local Council June–Dec. 1996; Prefect, Pref. of Teleorman Co. 1996–2000, Pres. Teleorman Co. Council 2000–12; mem. Congress of Local and Regional Authorities of Europe (CLRAE) 2001, Rapporteur of CLRAE for Water Resources Man. in River Basin project 2003, Rapporteur of CLRAE for Young People and Sustainable Devt project 2004; Chair. Nat. Union of Co. Councils of Romania 2004–12; mem./Alt. mem. Cttee of Regions 2007–13; mem. Social Democratic Party (PSD); fmr mem. Democratic Party (PD); Minister of Admin and Interior Jan.–Feb. 2009; mem. for Teleorman Co., Chamber of Deputies 2012–; Deputy Prime Minister and Minister of Regional Devt and Public Admin 2012–; Hon. Citizen of Leon Co., Fla, USA 2001; Oscar for Excellence, Teleorman County 2003, Diploma of Excellence, Fed. of Local Authorities from Romania 2004. *Address:* Ministry of Regional Development and Public Administration, 050741 Bucharest 5, Str. Apolodor 17, Romania (office). *Telephone:* (37) 2111506 (office). *Fax:* (37) 211337 (office). *E-mail:* ministru@mdrap.ro (office). *Website:* www.mdrap .ro (office).

DRĂGOI, Bogdan Alexandru; Romanian politician; *Minister of Public Finance;* b. 27 May 1980; s. of Dan Dragoi; ed Fletcher School of Law and Diplomacy, Tufts Univ., USA; Business Analyst, Inquam Ltd, UK 2002–03, Assoc. 2003–04; Vice-Pres. and Shareholder, FocusSat SA, Bucharest 2004–06; Adviser to Minister, Ministry of European Integration 2006; Sec. of State, Ministry of Finance 2006–07, 2009; Dir-Gen., Econ. Dept, Bucharest City Hall 2007–08; Minister of Public Finance 2012–; fmr Chair. Bd of Nominees, Fondul Proprietatea (govt compensation agency); mem. Democratic Liberal Party. *Address:* Ministry of Public Finance, 050741 Bucharest 5, Str. Apolodor 17, Romania (office). *Telephone:* (21) 3199759 (office). *Fax:* (21) 3122509 (office). *E-mail:* publicinfo@mfinante.gov.ro (office). *Website:* www.mfinante.gov.ro (office).

DRĂGUŢANU, Dorin; Moldovan central banker; *Chairman, Council of Administration and Governor, National Bank of Moldova;* b. 19 March 1974, Chişinău; m.; two c.; ed Alexandru Ioan Cuza Univ., Iaşi, Romania; extensive experience in fields of Int. Financial Reporting Standards, Int. Auditing Standards and Code of Ethics issued by Int. Fed. of Accountants (IFAC); led numerous audit missions in financial, banking and insurance sectors in Albania, Bulgaria, Montenegro, Romania and Serbia 2005–09, mem. PricewaterhouseCoopers (PwC) Serbia's tech. group for Financial Instruments in Central and Eastern Europe 2006–08, Dir responsible for risk management, Assurance Dept, PwC Serbia 2008–09; Chair. Council of Admin and Gov. Nat. Bank of Moldova 2009–. *Address:* National Bank of Moldova, Bulevardul Grigore Vieru nr 1, 2005 Chişinău, Moldova (office). *Telephone:* (22) 409006 (office). *Fax:* (22) 220591 (office). *E-mail:* official@bnm.md (office). *Website:* www.bnm.md (office).

DRAGUTINOVIĆ, Diana, MSc, PhD; Serbian economist and politician; b. 6 May 1958, Belgrade; m.; two c.; ed Univ. of Belgrade; Lecturer in Econs, Univ. of Belgrade 1999–; Special Adviser to Ministry of Finance and Economy 2001–02, to IMF 2002–04; Vice-Gov. Nat. Bank of Serbia 2004–08; Minister of Finance 2008–11; fmr Co-Ed. Economic Thought (journal); fmr mem. Int. Editorial Bd Economic Annals. *Publications:* numerous textbooks, 10 monographs and more than 50 studies, articles and journal contribs. *Address:* c/o Ministry of Finance, 11000 Belgrade, Kneza Miloša 20, Serbia. *Telephone:* (11) 3614007. *E-mail:* informacije@mfin.gov.rs.

DRAKE, Frank Donald, BEng (Phys), MA, PhD; American astronomer; *Director, Center for the Study of Life in the Universe, Search for Extraterrestrial Intelligence (SETI) Institute;* b. 28 May 1930, Chicago; s. of Richard C. Drake and Winifred Thompson Drake; m. 1st Elizabeth B. Bell 1953 (divorced 1977); three s.; m. 2nd Amahl Shakhashiri 1978; two d.; ed Cornell and Harvard Univs; served as Lt in USN 1947–55; Harvard Radio Astronomy Project 1955–58; Ewen-Knight Corpn 1957–58; scientist, Head Scientific Services and Telescope Operations on Nat. Radio Astronomy Observatory 1958–63; Chief, Lunar and Planetary Science Section, Jet Propulsion Lab., Pasadena, Calif. 1963–64; Prof. of Astronomy, Cornell Univ. 1964–85, Dir Arecibo Ionospheric Observatory 1966–68, Goldwin Smith Prof. of Astronomy 1976–85, Assoc. Dir Center for Radiophysics and Space Research 1967–75, Chair. Dept of Astronomy 1968–71; Dir Nat. Astronomy and Ionosphere Center 1971–81; Prof. of Astronomy, Univ. of Calif., Santa Cruz 1984–95, Prof. Emer. 1995–, Dean Div. of Natural Sciences 1984–88; Pres. SETI (Search for Extraterrestrial Intelligence) Inst. 1984–2000, Chair. Bd of Trustees 2000–02, Chair. Emer. 2002–, Dir Center for the Study of Life in the Universe 2005–; Pres. Astronomical Soc. of the Pacific 1988–90; mem. AAAS, NAS 1972–, The Explorers Club, Advisory Bd The World Book Encyclopedia, Int. Astronomical

Union, Int. Scientific Radio Union, American Astronomical Soc.; Fellow, American Acad. of Arts and Sciences. *Publications:* Intelligent Life in Space 1962, Murmurs of Earth 1979, (with Dava Sobel) Is Anyone Out There? 1992; and over 135 papers and articles. *Leisure interests:* snorkelling, horticulture, lapidary. *Address:* Center for the Study of Life in the Universe, SETI Institute, 515 North Whisman Road, Mountain View, CA 94043, USA (office). *Telephone:* (650) 961-6633 (office). *Fax:* (650) 961-7099 (office). *E-mail:* drake@seti.org (office). *Website:* www.seti.org (office).

DRAKE, Michael V., AB, MD; American ophthalmologist, academic and university administrator; *President, Ohio State University;* b. 9 July 1950, New York, NY; m. Brenda Drake; two s.; ed Stanford Univ., Univ. of California, San Francisco; grew up in Englewood, NJ, until moving with family to Sacramento, Calif.; mem. Faculty, Univ. of California, San Francisco (UCSF) School of Medicine from late 1970s, ultimately becoming Steven P. Shearing Prof. of Ophthalmology and Sr Assoc. Dean; Vice-Pres. for Health Affairs, Univ. of California 2000–05; Distinguished Prof. of Ophthalmology (School of Medicine) and of Educ. (School of Education), Chancellor Univ. of California, Irvine 2005–14; Pres. Ohio State Univ. 2014–; mem. Exec. Cttee and Div. I Bd Nat. Collegiate Athletic Asscn, Exec. and Membership Cttees of Asscn of American Univs; Trustee and Pres. Alpha Omega Alpha Honor Medical Soc.; Chair. Bd of Trustees, Asscn of Academic Health Centers; Fellow, Inst. of Medicine (Nat. Acads), American Acad. of Arts and Sciences; numerous honours and awards, including Burbridge Award for Public Service, Asbury Award (Clinical Science), Michael J. Hogan Award (Laboratory Science), UCSF School of Medicine Clinical Teaching Award, S.J. Kimura Teaching Award, UCSF School of Medicine Alumnus of the Year Award, Gold-Headed Cane Soc. Speaker's Cane, Asscn of American Medical Colls Herbert W. Nickens Award for promoting social justice, California Wellness Foundation's Champion of Diversity Award, inaugural Binational Health Pioneer Award, 18th Int. HIV/AIDS Conf., inducted into Stanford Univ. Multicultural Hall of Fame 2009. *Publications:* five textbooks; several book chapters and numerous articles in professional journals. *Address:* Office of the President, 205 Bricker Hall, 190 North Oval Mall, Columbus, OH 43210, USA (office). *Telephone:* (614) 292-2424 (office). *E-mail:* president@osu.edu (office). *Website:* president.osu.edu (office).

DRAPER, Kenneth, MA, RA; British painter and sculptor; b. 19 Feb. 1944, Killamarsh, Sheffield; s. of Albert Draper and Dorothy Rosa Anne Lamb; m. 1st Heather Lieven Beste 1965 (divorced); one s.; m. 2nd Nadiya Jinnah 1972 (divorced); m. 3rd Jean Macalpine; ed Chesterfield Coll. of Art, Kingston School of Art, RCA; solo exhbns include Redfern Gallery, London 1969, Warwick Arts Trust, London 1981, Galerie Nouvelles Images, Den Haag, Holland 1984, Austin Desmond, London 1991, Adelson Gallery, New York 1993, Friends Room, RA 1993, 2005, Hart Gallery, London 1994, 1996, 1998, Peter Bartlow Gallery, Chicago 1995; group exhbns include: British Sculptors 1972, RA 1972, Silver Jubilee Exhbn Contemporary British Sculpture, Battersea Park 1977, The British Art Show, Mappin, Sheffield 1980, British Sculpture in the Twentieth Century, Whitechapel Art Gallery 1981; work in public collections of Arts Council of GB, Contemporary Arts Soc., Courtauld Inst., London, Ashmolean Museum, Oxford, Usher Gallery, Lincoln; Mark Rothko Memorial Award 1971. *Leisure interests:* reading, chess, sport, travel. *Address:* Carrer Gran 55A, 07720 Es Castell, Minorca, Balearic Islands, Spain (home). *Telephone:* (971) 353457 (home). *Fax:* (971) 353457 (home). *E-mail:* drapermacalpine@terra.es (office). *Website:* www .kennethdraper.com (home).

DRAPER, William Henry, III, BA, MBA; American fmr government official; *General Partner, Draper Richards L.P.;* b. 1 Jan. 1928, White Plains, NY; s. of William Henry Draper and Katherine Baum; m. Phyllis Culbertson 1953; one s. two d.; ed Yale and Harvard Univs; with Inland Steel Co., Chicago 1954–59; Draper, Gaither & Anderson, Palo Alto, Calif. 1959–62; Pres. Draper & Johnson Investment Co. Palo Alto 1962–65; Founder and Gen. Pnr, Sutter Hill Capital Co., Palo Alto 1965–70, Sutter Hill Ventures, Palo Alto 1970–81; Pres. and Chair. Export-Import Bank US, Washington, DC 1981–86; Admin., CEO UNDP 1986–93; Man. Dir Draper Int., San Francisco 1994; currently Gen. Pnr Draper Richards L.P.; Trustee Yale Univ. 1991–98, George Bush Library Foundation 1993–; Chair. World Affairs Council, N Calif. 2000–02; Republican; Hon. LLD (Southeastern Univ.); SD Forum Vision Award, Dow Jones VC Hall of Fame 2005, Silicon Valley Fast 50 Lifetime Achievement Award 2006, IIE Distinguished Service Award, IBF Lifetime Achievement Award 2009, Commonwealth Club Lifetime Achievement Award 2009. *Address:* Draper Richards L.P., 50 California Street, Suite 2925, San Francisco, CA 94111 (office); 91 Tallwood Court, Atherton, CA 94027-6431, USA (home). *Telephone:* (415) 616-4050 (office). *Fax:* (415) 616-4060 (office). *E-mail:* bill@draperrichards.com (office). *Website:* www.draperrichards.com (office).

DRAŠKOVIĆ, Vuk; Serbian politician, journalist and writer; *President, Serbian Renewal Movement;* b. 29 Nov. 1946, Meda, Žitište municipality, Central Banat Region, Vojvodina; s. of Vidak Drašković and Stoja Drašković; m. Danica Bošković 1974; ed Univ. of Belgrade; moved to Herzegovina; as student took part in demonstrations 1968; mem. staff Telegraph Agency of Yugoslavia TANJUG 1969–78, worked in Lusaka, Zambia; dismissed from post of corresp. for disinformation 1978; Adviser Council of Trade Unions of Yugoslavia 1978–80; Ed. Rad (newspaper) 1980–85; freelance journalist and writer 1985–; Founder and Pres. Serbian Renewal Movt 1990–; cand. for presidency of SFR Yugoslavia 1990, 1992, of Serbia 1997; mem. Nat. Ass.; detained, released from detention July 1993; leader of mass protests against Pres. Milošević from Nov. 1996; Deputy Prime Minister of Yugoslavia 1998–99 (resgnd); Minister of Foreign Affairs of Serbia and Montenegro 2004–06. *Publications include:* novels: Judge, Knife, Prayer 1, Prayer 2, Russian Consul, Night of the General, Target, Polemics, Answers; numerous articles and collections of articles. *Address:* Serbian Renewal Movement (Srpski pokret obnove), 11000 Belgrade, Kneza Mihailova 48, Serbia (office). *Telephone:* (11) 2635281 (office); (11) 2626031 (office); (11) 3283620 (office). *Fax:* (11) 2628170 (office). *E-mail:* vuk@spo.rs (office). *Website:* www.spo.rs (office).

DRASKOVICS, Tibor, LLB; Hungarian banking executive and government official; b. 26 June 1955, Budapest; ed Eötvös Lóránd Univ. of Budapest; started career as legal expert Ministry of Finance 1979–84, Sec. to Minister 1984–86, Head of Legal Dept 1986, Head of Legal Div. 1988, Deputy State Sec. 1990–91, Admin. State Sec. 1994–98; Man. Dir Concordia Biztosítási (insurance brokers) 1991–93; tax consulting man. Arthur Andersen Ltd 1993–94; mem. Monetary Council, Nat.

Bank of Hungary 1995–98; CEO ABN-AMRO 1999; Deputy CEO K&H Bank 2001; Chief of Cabinet of the Prime Minister 2002; Minister of Finance 2004–05; Hungarian Power Companies Ltd. 2004–07; Vice-Pres., State Reform Comm. 2006; Minister without Portfolio 2007–08, Minister of Justice and Law Enforcement 2008–09; Order of Merit of the Hungarian Republic's Middle Cross. *Address:* c/o Ministry of Justice and Law Enforcement, 1055 Budapest, Kossuth Lajos tér 4, Hungary (office).

DRAVID, Rahul Sharad, BCom; Indian fmr professional cricketer; b. 11 Jan. 1973, Indore, MP; s. of Sharad Dravid and Pushpa Dravid; m. Vijeta Pendharkar; two s.; ed St Joseph's Boys' High School, Bangalore, St Joseph's Coll. of Commerce; right-handed batsman; right-arm off-break bowler; occasional wicketkeeper; plays for Karnataka 1990–, India 1996–2012 (Capt. 2005–07), Kent 2000, Scotland 2003, Royal Challengers Bangalore 2008–10, Canterbury, New Zealand 2009, Rajasthan Royals 2011–, Asia XI, ICC (Int. Cricket Council) World XI; First-class debut: 1990/91; Test debut: England v India, Lord's 20–24 June 1996; One-Day International (ODI) debut: India v Sri Lanka, Singapore 3 April 1996; has played in 164 Tests, taken 1 wicket and scored 13,288 runs (36 centuries and 63 half centuries), highest score 270, average 52.31, best bowling 1/18; played in 344 ODIs, took 4 wickets and scored 10,889 runs (12 centuries and 83 half centuries), highest score 153, average 39.16, best bowling 2/43; nicknamed The Wall; second Indian batsman, after Sachin Tendulkar, and fifth international player to have scored more than 11,000 runs in Test cricket; became sixth player in history of world cricket and third Indian, after Sachin Tendulkar and Sourav Ganguly, to score 10,000 runs in ODI cricket 14 Feb. 2007; first and only batsman to score a century in all ten Test-playing nations; currently holds world record for highest number of catches (more than 200) in Test cricket; has also been involved in more than 75 century partnerships with 18 different partners (world record); retd from international cricket 2012; Arjuna Award 1998, Ceat Cricketer of the 1999 World Cup 1999, one of five Wisden Cricketers of the Year 2000, inaugural ICC Player of the Year (Sir Garfield Sobers Trophy) and ICC Test Player of the Year 2004, Padma Shri 2004, MTV Youth Icon of the Year 2004, Capt. of ICC's Test Team 2006, Lifetime Achievement Award, NDTV Indian of the Year 2011, Don Bradman Award 2012, Padma Bhushan 2013. *Address:* Rajasthan Royals, 201-202 Windfall, Sahar Plaza Complex, Mathuradas Vasanji Road, J. B. Nagar, Andheri (East), Mumbai 400 059, India (office). *Website:* www.rajasthanroyals.com (office).

DRAVINS, Dainis, PhD; Swedish astronomer and academic; *Professor of Astronomy, Lund University;* b. 10 Sept. 1949, Lund; s. of Karlis Dravins and Velta Ruke-Dravina; m. Christina Dravins (née Hedqvist) 1982; one s.; ed Lund and Uppsala Univs and Calif. Inst. of Tech., USA; Prof. of Astronomy, Lund Univ. 1984–; mem. Royal Swedish Acad. of Sciences 1987; Foreign mem. Latvian Acad. of Sciences 1992. *Publications:* numerous articles on astronomy. *Address:* Lund Observatory, Box 43, 22100 Lund, Sweden (office). *Telephone:* (46) 2227297 (office); (46) 2227000 (office). *Fax:* (46) 2224614 (office). *E-mail:* dainis@astro.lu.se (office). *Website:* www.astro.lu.se/~dainis (office).

DRAZEN, Jeffrey M., BS, MD; American writer; *Editor-in-Chief, New England Journal of Medicine;* b. 19 May 1946, St Louis, Mo.; m.; two s.; ed Tufts Univ.; currently Prof. of Physiology, Harvard School of Public Health and Prof., Dept of Environmental Health, also Distinguished Parker B. Francis Prof. of Medicine, Harvard Medical School; currently also Sr Physician Brigham and Women's Hospital; Ed.-in-Chief, New England Journal of Medicine 2000–; fmr Assoc. Ed. Journal of Clinical Investigation, American Review of Respiratory Disease; Dr hc (Univ. of Ferrara, Italy), (Nat. and Kapodistrian Univ. of Athens, Greece). *Publications:* Five Lipoxygenase Products in Asthma (ed.) 1998; contribs to Genomic Medicine: Articles from the New England Journal of Medicine 2001. *Address:* New England Journal of Medicine, 10 Shattuck Street, Boston, MA 02115-6094, USA (office). *Telephone:* (617) 734-9800 (office). *Fax:* (617) 739-9864 (office). *E-mail:* jdrazen@nejm.org (office). *Website:* www.nejm.org (office).

DREIFUSS, Ruth; Swiss politician; *Chairperson of Commission on Intellectual Property Rights, Innovation and Public Health, World Health Organization;* b. 9 Jan. 1940, St Gall; ed Ecole d'Etudes Sociales, Geneva and Univ. of Geneva; Sec. 1958–59; Ed. Coopération, Swiss Union of Cooperatives, Basle 1961–64; Asst Sociologist, Centre Psycho-Social Universitaire, Geneva 1965–68; Asst in Nat. Accounting, Faculty of Econ. and Social Sciences, Univ. of Geneva 1970–72; civil servant, Swiss Devt Agency Fed. Ministry of Foreign Affairs 1972–81; Sec. Swiss Fed. of Trade Unions 1981–93; elected to Swiss Fed. Council 1993, Vice-Pres. 1998, Pres. of Swiss Confed. 1999; Head, Fed. Dept of Home Affairs 1994–2002; Chair. Comm. on Intellectual Property Rights, Innovation and Public Health, WHO; mem. Social Democratic Party; Dr hc (Haifa) 1999, (Jerusalem) 2000. *Address:* Secretariat for the Commission on Intellectual Property Rights, Innovation and Public Health, World Health Organization, 20 avenue Appia, 1211 Geneva 27, Switzerland (office). *Telephone:* (22) 7912764 (office). *Fax:* (22) 7914852 (office). *E-mail:* cipih@who.int (office). *Website:* www.who.int (office).

DRELL, Sidney David, AB, MA, PhD; American physicist and academic; *Professor Emeritus, SLAC National Accelerator Laboratory;* b. 13 Sept. 1926, Atlantic City, NJ; s. of Tulla and Rose White Drell; m. Harriet Stainback 1952; one s. two d.; ed Princeton Univ. and Univ. of Illinois; Research Assoc. Univ. of Illinois 1949–50; Research Assoc. MIT 1952–53, Asst Prof. 1953–56; Physics Instructor, Stanford Univ. 1950–52, Assoc. Prof. 1956–60, Prof. of Physics 1960–63, Lewis M. Terman Prof. and Fellow 1979–84, Prof. SLAC Nat. Accelerator Lab. 1963–98, Prof. Emer. 1998–, Deputy Dir 1998–98, Exec. Head of Theoretical Physics 1969–86, Co-Dir Stanford Center for Int. Security and Arms Control 1984–89; Sr Fellow, Hoover Inst. 1998–; Adjunct Prof., Dept of Eng and Public Policy, Carnegie Mellon Univ. 1989–96; Visiting Scientist and Guggenheim Fellow, CERN 1961–62; Visiting Prof. and Loeb Lecturer, Harvard Univ. 1962, 1970; consultant to Los Alamos Scientific Lab. 1956–, Office of Science and Tech., Exec. Office of the Pres. 1960–73; consultant Arms Control and Disarmament Agency 1969–81, Office of Tech. Assessment, US Congress 1975–91, Office of Science and Tech. Policy 1977–82, Nat. Security Council 1973–81; Consultant, Senate Select Cttee on Intelligence 1978–83; consultant to House Armed Services Cttee 1990–91, Senate Select Cttee on Intelligence 1990–93; Chair. Int. Advisory Bd Inst. of Global Conflict and Cooperation, Univ. of Calif. 1990–93; mem. High Energy Physics Advisory Panel to DOE 1974–86 (Chair. 1974–82); mem. JASON Div. (Mitre Corpn) 1960–; mem. Bd The Arms Control Asscn, Washington, DC 1971–93; mem.

Council on Foreign Relations 1980–2007; mem. Advisory Cttee MIT Physics Dept 1974–90; mem. Pres.'s Science Advisory Cttee 1966–70; Visiting Schrodinger Prof., Theoretical Physics, Univ. of Vienna 1975; mem. Bd of Trustees, Inst. for Advanced Study, Princeton, NJ 1974–83; Bd Gov. Weizmann Inst. of Science, Rehovoth, Israel 1970–; Bd Dir Annual Reviews Inc. 1976–97; mem. numerous advisory cttees and editorial bds including MIT Lincoln Lab. Advisory Bd 1985–90, Aspen Strategy Group 1984–91, Carnegie Comm. on Science, Tech. and Govt 1988–93, Scientific and Academic Advisory Cttee on Nat. Labs, Univ. of Calif. 1988–92, Pres.'s Foreign Intelligence Advisory Bd 1993–2001, Comm. on Maintaining US Nuclear Weapons Expertise 1999; Chair. Pres.'s Council on the Nat. Labs 1992–99; Fellow American Physical Soc. (Pres. 1986); mem. NAS, American Acad. of Arts and Sciences, American Philosophical Soc. 1987–, Academia Europaea 1995; Guggenheim Fellow, Rome 1972; Richtmeyer Memorial Lecturer to American Asscn of Physics Teachers 1978; Visiting Fellow, All Souls Coll., Oxford Univ. 1979; Danz Lecturer, Univ. of Washington 1983; I. I. Rabi Visiting Prof. Columbia Univ. 1984; Hans Bethe Lecturer, Cornell Univ. 1988, Brickwedde Lecturer, Johns Hopkins Univ.; Sr Advisory Group, LANL 2003–; External Gov. on Bd of Dirs, Los Alamos Nat. Lab. and Lawrence Livermore Nat. Lab. 2006–12; Hon. DSc (Univ. of Ill., Chicago Circle) 1981; numerous awards, including E.O. Lawrence Memorial Award 1972, Leo Szilard Award for Physics in the Public Interest 1980, MacArthur Fellowship Award 1984–89, Hilliard Roderick Prize in Science, Arms Control and Int. Security, AAAS 1993, co-recipient Ettore Majorana-Erice Science for Peace Prize 1994, Woodrow Wilson Award for Distinguished Achievement in the Nation's Service, Princeton Univ. 1994, Gian Carlo Wick Commemorative Award, ICSC World Lab. 1996, Distinguished Assoc. Award, US Dept of Environment 1997, I.Ya. Pomeranchuk Prize (Moscow) 1998, Linus Pauling Lecturer and Medallist, Stanford Univ. 1999–2000, Presidential Medal, Univ. of Calif. 2000, one of 10 scientists honoured by US Reconnaissance Office as Founders of Nat. Reconnaissance as a Space Discipline 2000, Enrico Fermi Award 2000, Nat. Intelligence Distinguished Service Medal 2001, Heinz R. Pagels Human Rights of Scientists Award 2001, Heinz Award for Public Policy 2005, American Acad. of Arts and Sciences Rumford Prize 2008, INSA Achievement Awards 2010, NNSA Gold Medal of Excellence 2012, Reykjavik Award, Fed. of American Scientists 2012, Public Service Award, Fed. of American Scientists 2012, 2011 Nat. Medal of Science presented by Pres. Barack Obama 2013. *Publications include:* Relativistic Quantum Mechanics, Relativistic Quantum Fields (both with J. D. Bjorken) and numerous papers on theoretical physics; Facing the Threat of Nuclear Weapons 1983 (updated 1989), The Reagan Strategic Defense Initiative: A Technical, Political and Arms Control Assessment (co-author) 1984, Sidney Drell on Arms Control 1988, Reducing Nuclear Danger (co-author) 1993, The New Terror: Facing the Threat of Biological and Chemical Weapons (co-ed.) 1999, New Mission for Nuclear Weapons? (co-author) 2003, The Gravest Danger: Nuclear Weapons (co-author) 2004, Nuclear Weapons, Scientists, and the Post-Cold War Challenge: Selected Papers on Arms Control 2007, What Are Nuclear Weapons For? (co-author) 2005, Implications of the Reykjavik Summit on Its Twentieth Anniversary 2007, Stevenson and the Comprehensive Test Ban Treaty (co-author) 2007, Reykjavik Revisited: Steps Toward a World Free of Nuclear Weapon (co-author) 2008, The Reality: A Goal of a World without Nuclear Weapons Is Essential (co-author) 2008, Technical Issues in Keeping the Nuclear Stockpile Safe, Secure, and Reliable (co-author) 2009, The nuclear state: a new start 2009, A World Free of Nuclear Weapons (co-author) 2009, A World Without Nuclear Weapons: End State Issues (co-author) 2009, The US Nuclear Stockpile and Ratification of the CTBT 2009, Working toward a World without Nuclear Weapons 2010, Ideas for a Better World in 2011 2010, Deterrence: Its Past and Future – Papers, Presented at Hoover Institution 2010 2011, Nuclear Deterrence in a World without Nuclear Weapons (co-author) 2010, Tribute to Andrei Sakharov 2011, Deterrence: Its Past and Future 2010 Summary Report (co-ed.) 2011, Realizing the Full Potential of the Open Skies Treaty (co-author) 2011, Modernize Open Skies (co-author) 2012, Nuclear Deterrence in a Changed World (co-author) 2012, A Safer Nuclear Enterprise (co-author) 2012, Reducing the Global Nuclear Risk (co-author) 2012, The Nuclear Enterprise: High-Consequence Accidents: How to Enhance Safety and Minimize Risks in Nuclear Weapons and Reactors (co-author) 2012, How to Detect a Nuclear Test on Your iPhone (co-author) 2013, Is it Illogical to Work Toward a World without Nuclear Weapons? 2013, Public Domain Treaty Compliance Verification in the Digital Age (co-author) 2013. *Leisure interests:* music, reading. *Address:* SLAC National Accelerator Laboratory, 2575 Sand Hill Road, Mail Stop 80, Menlo Park, CA 94025 (office); 620 Sand Hill Road, Apt 420–D, Palo Alto, CA 94304, USA (home). *Telephone:* (650) 926-2664 (office). *Fax:* (650) 926-4500 (office). *E-mail:* drell@slac.stanford.edu (office). *Website:* www.slac.stanford.edu (office).

DRENTH, Pieter Johan Diederik, PhD; Dutch academic; *Honorary President, European Network of Academies of Science (ALLEA);* b. 8 March 1935, Appelscha; s. of Gerrit Drenth and Froukje Wouda; m. Maria Annetta Elizabeth de Boer 1959; three s.; ed Vrije Univ., Amsterdam, New York Univ., USA; served in Royal Dutch Navy 1955–60; Research Fellow, Social Science Research Div., Standard Oil Co., New York 1960–61; Sr Lecturer in Psychometrics and Industrial Psychology, VU Univ., Amsterdam 1962–67, Prof. of Work and Organizational Psychology and Psychodiagnostics 1967–2000, Prof. Emer. 2000–, Rector Magnificus 1983–87, Dean Faculty of Psychology and Educ. 1998–2000; Visiting Prof., Washington Univ., St Louis 1966, Univ. of Washington, Seattle 1977; mem. Royal Netherlands Acad. of Arts and Sciences 1980–, Pres. 1990–96; Pres. ALLEA (European Network of Acads of Science) 2000–06, Hon. Pres. 2006–; mem. Supervisory Bd Shell-Nederland BV 1991–2011; Kt, Order of the Dutch Lion 1991, Commdr, Order of Oranje-Nassau 1996; Dr hc (Ghent) 1980, (Paris V) 1996; Heymans Award for Outstanding Contrib. to Psychology 1986, Aristotle Award for outstanding Contribs to European psychology 1995, IAAP Award for Distinguished Scientific Contribs to the Int. Advancement of Applied Psychology 2006. *Publications:* Mental Tests and Cultural Adaptation (ed.) 1972, Inleiding in de testtheorie 1976, Decisions in Organizations 1988, Advances in Organizational Psychology (ed.) 1988, New Handbook Work and Organizational Psychology (ed.) 1989, Testtheorie 1990 (revised edn 2006), Gardening in Science 1996; numerous scientific papers and psychological tests. *Leisure interests:* cycling, music, literature. *Address:* Pekkendam 6, 1081 HR Amsterdam, Netherlands. *Telephone:* (20) 6449109. *Fax:* (20) 6447938. *E-mail:* pjdd@xs4all.nl.

DRESSELHAUS, Mildred Spiewak, PhD; American physicist and academic; *Institute Professor and Professor Emerita of Physics and Electrical Engineering, Massachusetts Institute of Technology;* b. 11 Nov. 1930, New York; d. of Meyer Spiewak and Ethel Spiewak; m. Gene F. Dresselhaus 1958; three s. one d.; ed Hunter Coll. and Univ. of Chicago; mem. staff, Lincoln Lab., MIT, Lexington 1960–67, Prof. of Electrical Eng, MIT, Cambridge 1967–, Assoc. Head of Dept of Electrical Eng 1972–74, Abby Rockefeller Mauzé Chair. 1973–85, Dir Center for Materials Science and Eng 1977–83, Prof. of Physics 1983, Inst. Prof. 1985, now Prof. Emer.; Visiting Prof., Dept of Physics, Univ. of Campinas, Brazil 1971, Technion-Israel Inst. of Tech. 1972, 1990, Nihon and Aoyama Gakuin Univs, Japan 1973, IVIC, Caracas, Venezuela 1977; Graffin Lecturer, American Carbon Soc. 1982; mem. Energy Research Advisory Bd 1984–90; mem. Bd of Dirs The Alliance Fund, Rogers Corpn, Quantum Chem. Corpn; mem. Governing Bd Nat. Research Council 1984–87, 1989–90, 1992; Treas. NAS 1992–96; Pres. AAAS 1997; Hon. Fellowship, Inst. of Physics 2005; mem. Hall of Fame, Hunter Coll. 1972, Alumnae Medal (Radcliffe Coll., MA) 1973, Killian Faculty Achievement Award 1986–87, Nat. Medal of Science 1990, Nicholson Medal for Humanitarian Service 1999, L'Oréal Women in Science Award 2007, Oersted Medal 2008, Enrico Fermi Award (co-recipient) 2012, Kavli Prize 2012. *Publications include:* Physical Properties of Fullerenes; numerous contribs to professional journals. *Address:* Massachusetts Institute of Technology, Department of Physics, Building 6-113, Room 13–3005, 77 Massachusetts Avenue, Cambridge, MA 02139-4307, USA (office). *Telephone:* (617) 253-6864 (office); (617) 253-6867 (office). *Fax:* (617) 253-6827 (office). *E-mail:* millie@mgm.mit.edu (office). *Website:* web.mit.edu/physics (office).

DREW, John Sydney Neville, MA, AM, MBA; British academic, business executive and fmr diplomatist; *Chancellor, Regent's University, London;* b. 7 Oct. 1936, Hornchurch, Essex, England; s. of John Drew and Kathleen Wright; m. Rebecca Usher 1962; two s. one d.; ed King Edward's School, Birmingham, St John's Coll., Oxford, Tufts Univ., USA, London Business School; served in HM Diplomatic Service, First Sec. in Paris, Middle East Center for Arabic Studies, Kuwait, Bucharest 1960–73; Dir of Marketing and Exec. Programmes, London Business School 1973–79; Dir of Corp. Affairs, Rank Xerox 1979–84; Dir of European Affairs, Touche Ross International 1984–86; Head, UK Offices, Comm. of EC 1987–93; Dir Durham Inst., Visiting Prof. of European Business, Durham Univ. 1995–2003; Jean Monnet Prof. of European Business and Man., European Business School, London 2007–; Dir Inst. of Contemporary European Studies, Regent's Univ., London 2011–, Chancellor 2013–; Deputy Chair. Enterprise Support Group 1993–94; Dir, Europa Times 1993–94, Change Group International 1996–2003; Pres. Inst. of Linguists 1993–99, EUROTAS 1998–2003; Trustee, Thomson Foundation 1993–2007; Assoc. Fellow, Templeton Coll., Oxford 1982–86; Visiting Prof., Imperial Coll. London 1987–91, Open Univ. 1992–2001; Hon. Ed. European Business Journal 1987–2002; Hon. MBA (Northumbria) 1991. *Publications:* Doing Business in the European Community 1979, Networking in Organizations 1986, Developing an Active Company Approach to the European Market 1988, Readings in International Enterprise (ed.) 1995, Ways Through the Wall (ed.) 2005, The UK and Europe: Costs, Benefits, Options (ed.) 2013; articles on European integration and personal devt. *Leisure interests:* travel, golf, personal development. *Address:* 49 The Ridgeway, London, NW11 8QP, England (home). *Telephone:* (20) 8455-5054 (office). *E-mail:* profdrew@eurotas.org (office).

DREWS, Juergen, MD; German physician and business executive; b. 16 Aug. 1933, Berlin; s. of Walter Drew and Lotte Grohnert; m. Dr Helga Eberlein 1963; three d.; ed Univs of Berlin, Innsbruck, Austria, Heidelberg and Yale Univ., USA; Prof. of Medicine, Univ. of Heidelberg 1973–; Head of Chemotherapy Section, Sandoz Research Inst., Vienna 1976–79, Head of Sandoz Research Inst. 1979–82, Int. Pharmaceutical R&D, Sandoz, Basel 1982–85; Dir Pharmaceutical Research, F. Hoffmann-La Roche Ltd, Basel 1985–86, Chair. Research Bd and mem. Exec. Cttee 1986–90, Pres. Int. R&D and mem. Exec. Cttee Roche Group, Hoffmann-La Roche Inc., Nutley, NJ 1991–95, Pres. Global Research, mem. Exec. Cttee 1996–97; Chair. Int. Biomedicine Man. Partners, Basel 1997–2001; Man. Pnr, Bear Stearns Health Innoventures Man. LLC, New York 2001–04; Chair. Genomics Pharmaceutical Company, Munich; Chair. Genaissance Pharmaceuticals Inc –2005; fmr Chair. Supervisory Bd Tegenero Immuno Therapeutics AG; mem. Dean's Council, Yale Univ. School of Medicine 1993; mem. Bd of Dirs Human Genome Sciences, Inc., MorphoSys AG. *Publications:* Chemotherapie 1979, Immunpharmakologie, Grundlagen und Perspektiven 1986, Immunopharmacology 1990, Die verspielte Zukunft 1998, In Quest of Tomorrow's Medicines 1999; more than 200 scientific papers. *Leisure interests:* skiing, climbing, literature, piano. *Address:* c/o Board of Directors, MorphoSys AG, Lena-Christ-Strasse 48, 82152 Martinsried/Planegg, Germany.

DREXLER, Millard (Mickey) S.; American business executive; *Chairman and CEO, J. Crew Group, Inc.;* b. 1944, Bronx, New York; m. Peggy Drexler; two c.; Pres. and CEO Ann Taylor Co. 1980–83; Exec. Vice-Pres. of Merchandising and Pres. Gap Stores Div. Gap Inc., San Bruno, Calif. 1983–87; Pres. The Gap Inc. 1987–95, Pres. and CEO The Gap Inc., San Francisco 1995–2002; Chair. and CEO J. Crew Group Inc., New York 2003–; mem. Bd of Dirs Apple Inc. 1999–. *Leisure interest:* novels by John Grisham. *Address:* J. Crew Group Inc., 770 Broadway, New York, NY 10013, USA (office). *Telephone:* (212) 209-2500 (office). *Fax:* (212) 209-2666 (office). *Website:* www.jcrew.com (office).

DREYFUS, George, AM; Australian composer; b. 22 July 1928, Wuppertal, Germany; two s. one d.; ed Vienna Acad. of Music; Composer-in-Residence, Tienjin, China 1983, Shanghai 1987, Nanjing 1991; Grosses Bundesverdienstkreuz (Germany); Henry Lawson Award 1972, Prix de Rome 1976, 2004, Mishkenot Sha'ananim, Jerusalem 1980, Don Banks Fellowship 1992. *Compositions include:* Garni Sands, The Gilt-Edged Kid (operas); Symphonies Nos 1, 2 and 3; Symphonie Concertante 1977; Jingles ... & More Jingles; Reflections in a Glasshouse; The Illusionist; The Grand Aurora Australis Now Show; Galgenlieder; Songs Comic & Curious; Music in the Air; From within Looking out; The Seasons; Ned Kelly Ballads; Quintet after the Notebook of J.-G. Noverre; Sextet for Didjeridoo & Wind Instruments; Old Melbourne; several pieces for young people; The Sentimental Bloke (musical) 1985, Lifestyle 1988, Song of Brother Sun 1988 (choral pieces), Rathenau (opera) 1993, Die Marx Sisters (opera) 1994; more than 100 scores for film and TV including The Adventures of Sebastian the Fox 1963, Rush 1974,

Great Expectations 1986. *Television includes:* The Gilt-Edged Kid (Australian Broadcasting Corpn/ABC) 1975, Didjeridu in Deutschland (SBS) 1988, Bicycles and Bassoons (SBS) 1989, Life is Too Serious (ABC) 2000. *Publications:* The Last Frivolous Book (autobiog.) 1984, Being George – And Liking It! 1998, Don't Ever Let Them Get You 2009, Brush Off! 2011; numerous commercial CDs on the Move label. *Leisure interests:* swimming, gardening. *Address:* 3 Grace Street, Camberwell, Vic. 3124, Australia (home). *Telephone:* (3) 9809-2671 (home). *E-mail:* gdreyfus@bigpond.net.au.

DREYFUS, Gilles D., MD; French cardio-thoracic surgeon and academic; *Consultant and Professor of Cardiac Surgery, Royal Brompton & Harefield NHS Trust;* b. 24 May 1951, Paris; ed Paris V Universite, Rene Descartes Medical School; intern at Paris Hospitals 1978; Chef de Clinique, assistant des hopitaux 1982–86; univ. prof. 1989; Chief of Cardiothoracic Unit, Foch Hospital, Paris 1996–2001; Consultant and Prof. of Cardiac Surgery, Dept of Cardiac Surgery, Royal Brompton & Harefield NHS Trust 2001–; Prof., Imperial Coll. London; mem. European Asscn for Cardio-Thoracic Surgery, French Soc. for Thoracic and Cardiovascular Surgery, French Soc. for Cardiology, Soc. for Heart Valve Disease, American Asscn for Thoracic Surgery, Soc. of Thoracic Surgeons, Int. Soc. for Heart and Lung Transplantation, British Cardiac Soc.; Chevalier de la Légion d'honneur. *Leisure interests:* skiing, golf. *Address:* Royal Brompton & Harefield Hospital, Hill End Road, Harefield, Middx, UB9 6JH (office); 34 Queen's Gate Gardens, London SW7 5RR, England (home). *Telephone:* (1895) 828665 (office). *Fax:* (1895) 828666 (office). *E-mail:* g.dreyfus@rbht.nhs.uk (office); g.dreyfus@btinternet.com (home). *Website:* www.rbht.nhs.uk (office).

DREYFUS, Louis; French newspaper executive; *CEO, Le Monde Group;* Dir Les Inrockuptibles magazine and adviser to Owner and Pres., Matthieu Pigasse –2010; Chair. Man. Bd and CEO Le Monde Group 2010–, launched Le Huffington Post in collaboration with Les Nouvelles Editions Indépendants and The Huffington Post Media Group 2012. *Address:* Le Monde Group, 80 boulevard Auguste-Blanqui, 75707 Paris Cedex 13, France (office). *Telephone:* 1-42-17-20-00 (office). *Fax:* 1-42-17-21-21 (office). *E-mail:* lemonde@lemonde.fr (office). *Website:* www.lemonde.fr (office).

DREYFUSS, Richard Stephan; American actor; b. 29 Oct. 1947, New York; s. of Norman Dreyfuss and Gerry D. Student; m. Jeramie Dreyfuss 1983; two s. one d.; ed San Fernando Valley State Coll.; alternative mil. service Los Angeles County Gen. Hosp. 1969–71; mem. American Civil Liberties Union Screen Actors Guild, Equity Asscn, American Fed. of TV and Radio Artists, Motion Picture Acad. Arts and Sciences; Golden Globe Award 1978, Acad. Award for Best Actor in The Goodbye Girl 1978. *Stage appearances include:* Julius Caesar 1978, The Big Fix (also producer) 1978, Othello 1979, Death and the Maiden 1992, The Prisoner of Second Avenue 1999, Complicit 2008. *Films include:* American Graffiti 1972, Dillinger 1973, The Apprenticeship of Duddy Kravitz 1974, Jaws 1975, Inserts 1975, Close Encounters of the Third Kind 1976, The Goodbye Girl 1977, The Competition 1980, Whose Life Is It Anyway? 1981, Down and Out in Beverly Hills 1986, Stakeout 1988, Moon over Parador 1989, Let it Ride, Always 1989, Rosencrantz and Guildernstern are Dead, Postcards from the Edge 1990, Once Around 1990, Randall and Juliet 1990, Prisoners of Honor 1991, What About Bob? 1991, Lost in Yonkers 1993, Another Stakeout 1993, The American President, Mr Holland's Opus 1995, Mad Dog Time 1996, James and the Giant Peach (voice) 1996, Night Falls on Manhattan 1997, The Call of the Wild 1997, Krippendorf's Tribe 1998, A Fine and Private Place 1998, The Crew 2000, The Old Man Who Read Love Stories 2000, Who is Cletis Tout? 2001, Silver City 2004, Poseidon 2006, Signs of the Time 2008, W 2008, My Life in Ruins 2009. *Television includes:* Nuts 1987 (dir, producer) Oliver Twist 1997, Fail Safe 2000, Education of Max Bickford 2001–02, Day Reagan Was Shot 2001, Coast to Coast 2003, Copshop 2004, Ocean of Fear 2007, Tin Man 2007. *Publication:* The Two Georges (with Harry Turtledove) 1996. *Address:* William Morris Agency, 1 William Morris Place, Beverly Hills, CA 90212, USA (office). *Telephone:* (310) 859-4000 (office). *Fax:* (310) 859-4462 (office). *Website:* www.wma.com (office).

DRÈZE, Jacques H., PhD; Belgian economist and academic; *Professor Emeritus, Center for Operations Research and Econometrics (CORE);* b. 5 Aug. 1929, Verviers; m.; five s.; ed Univ. de Liège, Columbia Univ., USA; Research Fellow, Carnegie Inst. of Tech. 1954, Visiting Asst Prof. 1957–58; Lecturer, Université Catholique de Louvain 1958–62, Prof. 1962–89; Visiting Assoc. Prof., Northwestern Univ., USA 1962; Ford Foundation Prof., Univ. of Chicago, USA 1963–64, Prof. 1964–68; Titulaire de la Chaire Francqui Belge, Univ. de Bruxelles 1970–71, Katholieke Univ. Leuven 1982–83; Andrew D. White Prof.-at-Large, Cornell Univ. 1971–77; Chargé de recherche Univ. Libre de Bruxelles 1958–60; Research Assoc., Purdue Univ. 1957, Northwestern Univ. 1962, 1963, Univ. of Wisconsin 1964, MIT 1966, Stanford Univ. 1979; Research Dir Center for Operations Research and Econometrics (CORE), Louvain 1966–71, Pres. 1971–83, now Prof. Emer.; mem. CEPS Macroeconomic Policy Group 1984–85, Chair. 1986–87; Chair. Inst. of Man. Science 1961; Dir Int. Centre for Man. Science, Louvain 1966–71; Assoc. Ed. Econometrica 1963–64, Co-Ed. 1964–69; Vice-Pres. Econometric Soc. 1969, Pres. 1970; Pres. European Econ. Asscn 1985–86, Int. Econ. Asscn 1996–99; Co-ordinator European Unemployment Programme 1985–88; Corresp. FBA 1990; Foreign Assoc., NAS 1993; Corresp. mem. Acad. Royale des Sciences, des Lettres et de Beaux-Arts de Belgique 2000; mem. Academica Europaea 1989; Hon. mem. American Econ. Asscn 1976, Asociacion Argentina di Economica Politica 1998, Latin American and Caribbean Econ. Asscn 1999; Foreign Hon. mem. American Acad. of Arts and Science 1978, Royal Netherlands Acad. of Arts and Science 1980; Dr hc (Essex) 1980, (Sorbonne) 1980, (Montréal) 1982, (Liège) 1983, (Antwerp) 1985, (Norges Handelshoyskole, Bergen) 1986, (Bologna) 1988, (Geneva) 1988, (Basel) 1988, (Chicago) 1991, (Aix-Marseille) 1992, (Cergy-Pontoise) 1000, (Bolzano) 2000, (European Univ. Inst.) 2002, (Universidade Catolica Portuguesa) 2003, (Maastricht) 2005; Prix des Alumni, Fondation Universitaire, Brussels 1964, Prix Emile De Laveleye, Acad. Royale des Sciences, des Lettres et des Beaux-Arts de Belgique 1993, Prix, Accad. dei Lincei, Rome 1999. *Publications include:* numerous books and articles on econ. theory and policy, including Allocation under Uncertainty 1974, Essays on Economic Decisions under Uncertainty 1987, Labour Management, Contracts and Capital Markets 1989, Underemployment Equilibria 1991, Advances in Macroeconomics 2001. *Leisure interest:* sailing around the world with wife Monique. *Address:* Centre for Operations Research and Econometrics

(CORE), Université Catholique de Louvain, Voie du Roman Pays, 34, 1348 Louvain-la-Neuve, Belgium (office). *Telephone:* (10) 474347 (office). *Fax:* (10) 474301 (office). *E-mail:* jacques.dreze@uclouvain.be (office). *Website:* www.core.ucl.ac.be (office).

DRINFELD, Vladimir Gershonovich, PhD; Ukrainian mathematician and academic; *Harry Pratt Judson Distinguished Service Professor, Department of Mathematics, University of Chicago;* b. 14 Feb. 1954, Kharkov (now Kharkiv); ed Moscow Univ., Steklov Inst., Moscow; B. Verkin Inst. for Low Temperature Physics and Eng, Nat. Acad. of Sciences of the Ukraine 1981–98; Prof., Dept of Math., Univ. of Chicago 1999–2001, Harry Pratt Judson Distinguished Service Prof. 2001–; mem. Nat. Acad. of Sciences of the Ukraine 1992–, American Acad. of Arts and Sciences; Fields Medal, Int. Congress of Mathematicians, (Kyoto, Japan) 1990. *Publications:* Chiral Algebras (co-author) 2004 and numerous publs on quantum groups and number theory. *Address:* Department of Mathematics, University of Chicago, 5734 South University Avenue, Chicago, IL 60637, USA (office). *Telephone:* (773) 702-7100 (office). *Fax:* (773) 702-9787 (office). *Website:* www.math.uchicago.edu (office).

DRIVER, Minnie (Amelia); British actress; b. 31 Jan. 1970, London; d. of Charles Driver and Gaynor Churchward (née Millington); one s.; ed Bedales School, Hants.; Best Newcomer, London Circle of Film Critics 1997, Best Actress, London Circle of Film Critics 1998. *Plays include:* Sexual Perversity in Chicago, Comedy Theatre, London 2003. *Films include:* Circle of Friends 1995, Goldeneye 1995, Baggage 1996, Big Night 1996, Sleepers 1996, Grosse Pointe Blank 1997, Good Will Hunting 1997, The Governess 1998, Hard Rain 1998, At Sachem Farm 1998, Trespasser (voice) 1998, An Ideal Husband 1999, Tarzan (voice) 1999, South Park: Bigger, Longer and Uncut 1999, Slow Burn 2000, Beautiful 2000, Return to Me 2000, The Upgrade 2000, High Heels and Lowlifes 2001, D.C. Smalls 2001, Owning Mahoney 2003, Hope Springs 2003, Ella Enchanted 2004, Portrait 2004, The Phantom of the Opera 2004, The Virgin of Juarez 2006, Ripple Effect 2007, Motherhood 2009, Conviction 2010, Barney's Version 2010, Hunky Dory 2011. *Television includes:* God on the Rocks 1990, Mr Wroe's Virgins 1993, The Politician's Wife 1995, The Riches (series) 2007–08, Modern Family 2010, The Deep (mini-series) 2010, Hail Mary (film) 2011, Lady Friends (film) 2012. *Recordings:* albums: Everything I've Got in My Pocket 2004, Seastories 2008. *Address:* c/o Lou Coulson, First Floor, 37 Berwick Street, London, W1V 3LF, England.

DROGBA TÉBILY, Didier Yves; Côte d'Ivoirian professional footballer; b. 11 March 1978, Abidjan; m. Diakité Lalla; three c.; striker (centre forward); began career as youth player with French clubs Levallois 1996–97, Le Mans 1997–98 (professional debut aged 18); with Le Mans (64 appearances, 12 goals) 1998–2002, Guincamp (45 appearances, 20 goals) 2002–03, Olympique de Marseille (35 appearances, 35 goals) 2003–04, Chelsea FC (226 appearances, 157 goals) 2004–12 (won FA Premier League 2004–05, 2005–06, 2009–10, FA Cup 2006–07, 2008–09, 2009–10, 2011–12, Football League Cup 2004–05, 2006–07, FA Community Shield 2005, 2009, UEFA Champions League 2012), Shanghai Shenhua 2012–; mem. Côte d'Ivoire nat. football team (84 appearances, 54 goals) 2002–, team capt. during African Cup of Nations 2006; UNDP Goodwill Amb. 2007–; first player to score in four different FA Cup Finals, scoring the winner in Chelsea's 2–1 victory over Liverpool FC 5 May 2012; f. Didier Drogba Foundation (charity) 2009; Onze d'Or 2004, UEFA Cup Top Scorer 2004, Ligue 1 Goal of the Year 2004, Ligue 1 Team of the Year 2004, Ligue 1 Player of the Year 2004, Ivorian Footballer of the Year 2006, 2007, African Footballer of the Year 2006, 2009, Chelsea Players' Player of the Year 2007, Premier League Golden Boot 2007, 2010, PFA Team of the Year 2007, 2010, UEFA Team of the Year 2007, ESM Team of the Year 2007, FIFPro World XI 2007, BBC African Footballer of the Year 2009, West African Footballer of the Year 2010, Chelsea Player of the Year 2010, Time Top 100 2010, Côte d'Ivoire all-time Top Scorer, Levallois Sporting Club named its stadium after him 2010, Africa Cup Top Scorer 2012, African Cup Team of the Tournament 2006, 2008, 2012, UEFA Champions League Final Man of the Match 2012. *Address:* Shanghai Shenhua FC, Hongkou Football Stadium, 2600 Hu Nan Road, Pudong District, Shanghai 201315, People's Republic of China (office). *Telephone:* (21) 58128877 (office). *Fax:* (21) 68062550 (office). *E-mail:* tanxian.shenhuafc@gmail.com (office). *Website:* www.shenhuafc.com.cn (office); www.didierdrogba.com.

DRONKE, (Ernst) Peter (Michael), MA, FBA; British medieval Latin scholar and author; *Professor Emeritus of Medieval Latin Literature, University of Cambridge;* b. 30 May 1934; s. of A. H. R. Dronke and M. M. Dronke (née Kronfeld); m. Ursula Miriam Brown 1960; one d.; ed Victoria Univ., NZ and Magdalen Coll., Oxford; Research Fellow, Merton Coll., Oxford 1958–61; Lecturer in Medieval Latin, Univ. of Cambridge 1961–79, Reader in Medieval Latin Literature 1979–89, Prof. 1989–2001, Prof. Emer. 2001–, Fellow, Clare Hall 1964–2001; Visiting Prof. of Medieval Studies, Westfield Coll. London 1981–86; Carl Newell Jackson Lecturer, Harvard Univ., USA 1992; Corresp. Fellow, Real Academia de Buenas Letras, Royal Dutch Acad., Medieval Acad. of America, Austrian Acad. of Sciences, Fondazione Lorenzo Valla, Istituto Lombardo Acad. of Sciences and Letters; Co-ed. Mittellateinisches Jahrbuch 1977–2002; Hon. Pres., Int. Courtly Literature Soc.; Premio Internazionale Ascoli Piceno 1988, Premio Bettarini 2014. *Publications:* Medieval Latin and the Rise of European Love-Lyric (2 Vols) 1965–66, The Medieval Lyric 1968, Poetic Individuality in the Middle Ages 1970, Fabula 1974, Abelard and Heloïse in Medieval Testimonies 1976, Barbara et antiquissima carmina (with Ursula Dronke) 1977, Bernardus Silvestris, Cosmographia (ed.) 1978, Introduction to Francesco Colonna, Hypnerotomachia 1981, Women Writers of the Middle Ages 1984, The Medieval Poet and his World 1984, Dante and Medieval Latin Traditions 1986, Introduction to Rosvita, Dialoghi Drammatici 1986, A History of Twelfth-Century Western Philosophy (ed.) 1988, Hermes and the Sibyls 1990, Latin and Vernacular Poets of the Middle Ages 1991, Intellectuals and Poets in Medieval Europe 1992, Verse with Prose: From Petronius to Dante 1994, Nine Medieval Latin Plays 1994, Hildegard of Bingen, Liber divinorum operum (co-ed.) 1996, Sources of Inspiration 1997, Dante's Second Love (lectures) 1997, Introduction to Alessandro nel medioevo occidentale 1997, Growth of Literature: the Sea and the God of the Sea (with Ursula Dronke) 1998, Etienne Gilson's Letters to Bruno Nardi (ed.) 1998, Hildegard of Bingen: The Context of Her Thought and Art (co-ed.) 1998, Imagination in the Late Pagan and Early Christian World 2003, Forms and Imaginings 2007, The Spell of Calcidius

2008, Giovanni Scoto Eriugena, Periphyseon I (ed) 2012, II (ed) 2013, III (ed) 2014; essays in learned journals and symposia. *Leisure interests:* music, film and Brittany. *Address:* 6 Parker Street, Cambridge, CB1 1JL, England (home).

DROSDICK, John G. (Jack), BS, MS; American business executive; b. 9 Aug. 1943, West Hazelton, Pa; m. Gloria J. Shenosky; four c.; ed Villanova Univ., Univ. of Massachusetts; began career with Exxon Corpn 1968, various man. positions in NJ, Tex. and La; Pres. Tosco Corpn 1987–92; Pres. Ultramar Corpn 1992–96; Pres. and COO Sunoco Inc. 1996–2000, Chair., CEO and Pres. 2000–08, Chair. (non-exec.) July–Dec. 2008, Chair. Sunoco Partners LLC; Dir United States Steel (USS) Corpn 2003–, HJ Heinz Co., Lincoln Nat. Corpn; Chair. Bd of Trustees, Villanova Univ.; Trustee, Kimmel Center for the Performing Arts, Philadelphia Museum of Art (also Chair. Exec. Bd). *Address:* c/o Sunoco Inc., 1735 Market Street, Suite LL, Philadelphia, PA 19103-7583, USA. *E-mail:* info@sunocoinc.com.

DROSOS, Gina, BA, MBA; American business executive; *Group President, Global Beauty, Skin, Cosmetics, and Personal Care, Procter & Gamble Company;* ed Wharton School, Univ. of Pennsylvania; summer intern at Procter & Gamble's Spic and Span business, joined co. full time in 1987, began working on Olay skin care business 1992, promoted to positions of increasing responsibility until current position of Group Pres. Global Beauty, Skin, Cosmetics, and Personal Care, responsible for brands including Pantene, Head and Shoulders, Wella, Olay and Old Spice, additional responsibility for antiperspirants and deodorants 2011–; ranked by Fortune magazine amongst the 50 Most Powerful Women in Business in the US (39th) 2010, (31st) 2011. *Address:* Proctor & Gamble Company, 1 Procter & Gamble Plaza, Cincinnati, OH 43202-3315, USA (office). *Telephone:* (513) 983-1100 (office). *Fax:* (513) 983-9369 (office). *E-mail:* info@pg.com (office). *Website:* www.pg.com (office).

DROUTSAS, Dimitris P.; Greek lawyer, academic and politician; b. 5 Aug. 1968, Nicosia, Cyprus; m. Faye Karaviti; ed Univ. of Vienna School of Law, Austria; Asst Prof. of European Law, European Affairs Research Centre, Wirtschaftsuniversität Wien 1994–99; Legal Adviser to Austrian Minister of Foreign Affairs 1998–99; Special Adviser to Greek Foreign Minister, Athens 1999–2004; mem. Panhellenic Socialist Movt (PASOK), Dir of Diplomatic Cabinet of Pres. of PASOK (Georgios Papandreou) 2004–08, PASOK Spokesperson to int. news media 2008, PASOK Sec. for Foreign Policy and Int. Relations 2008; Alt. Minister of Foreign Affairs 2009–10, Minister of Foreign Affairs 2010–11. *Publications:* works on European law, int. and European commercial law, and foreign and defence policy published extensively in Greece and abroad. *Address:* c/o Ministry of Foreign Affairs, Odos Sofias 1, 106 71 Athens, Greece. *E-mail:* mfa@mfa.gr.

DROZDOVA, Margarita Sergeyevna; Russian ballerina; b. 7 May 1948, Moscow; ed Moscow Choreographic School, State Inst. of Theatre Art (GITIS); danced with Stanislavsky Musical Theatre Ballet Co., Moscow 1967–87, apptd teacher/repetiteur and balletmaster 1987; mem. CPSU 1980–91; Int. Competitions for Ballet Dancers in Varna 1972, in Moscow 1973, Anna Pavlova Award, Paris 1968; RSFSR State Prize 1980, People's Artist of USSR 1986. *Roles include:* Odette-Odile, Gayané, The Commissar (M. Bronner's 'Optimistic Tragedy'), Medora (A. Adam's 'Corsaire'), Swanilda (Delibes' 'Coppélia'), Cinderella (Prokofiev). *Address:* c/o Stanislavsky and Nemirovich Danchenko Musical Theatre, Bolshaya Dmitrovka 17, Moscow, Russia. *Telephone:* (495) 629-83-88; (495) 299-31-36 (home).

DRUBICH, Tatyana Lusienovna; Russian actress; b. 7 June 1960, Moscow; m. Sergey Soloviev (divorced); one d.; ed Third Moscow Medical Inst.; worked as a nurse then as a physician; actress 1972–; Head of Russian Rep. of German chemical factory Dr Weigert 1992–. *Films include:* 15th Spring (debut) 1972, 100 Days after Childhood 1975, Disarray 1978, Particularly Dangerous 1978, The Rescuer 1979, The Direct Heiress 1982, Selected 1983, Tester 1984, Black Monk 1986, Keep Me, My Talisman 1986, Assa 1987, Black Rose – An Emblem of Sorrow, White Rose – An Emblem of Love 1989, Hey, Fools 1996, Moscow 2000, O lyubvi (About Love) 2003, Gololed (Slippery Ice), Anna Karenina 2007, 2-Assa-2, ili vtoraya smert' Anny Kareninoy (2-Assa-2, or The Second Death of Anna Karenina) 2007, Posledniaya Skazka Riti (Nadya) 2011. *Address:* Seleznevskaya str. 30, korp. 3, Apt 77, 103473 Moscow, Russia. *Telephone:* (495) 281-60-82.

DRUCKER, Michel; French broadcast journalist and television producer; b. 12 Sept. 1942, Vire (Calvados); s. of Abraham Drucker and Lola Schafler; m. Danielle Savalle (Dany Saval) 1973; ed Lycée Emile-Maupas, Vire; sports reporter for ORTF 1964, presenter of variety programmes 1966, producer and presenter Sport en Fête, football commentator 1969; commentator, World Cup Football Championships 1970, 1974, 1978; presenter, (Radio-Télé-Luxembourg – RTL) C'est vous 1974–, Les Rendez-vous du dimanche 1975–1981, Stars 1981, Champs-Elysées 1982–85, (Europe 1) Studio 1 1983, (Antenne 2) Champs-Elysées, 1987–90, (TF1) Stars 90 1990–94, Ciné Stars 1991–94, (France 2) Studio Gabriel 1994–97, Faites la fête 1994–98, Drucker & Co., Stars & Co. 1997–98, Vivement dimanche, Vivement dimanche prochain, Tapis rouge 1998–2001, Tenue de soirée 2006–; acquired Production DMD from Canal+ 1998; Chevalier Légion d'honneur, des Arts et Lettres; Sports Journalist of the Year, Télémagazine 1971, 1972, 1973, Prix Triomphe de la télévision à la Nuit du cinéma 1973, 1987, 7 d'Or Award for Best Variety Programme Presenter, Prix Gémeaux de la francophonie, Quebec, Canada 2000. *Publications:* La Balle au bond (autobiog.) 1973, La Coupe du monde de football 1974, La Chaîne (novel) 1979, Novembre des amours 1984, Hors antenne, conversation avec Maurice Achard 1987, Les Numéros 1. Tous les grands du football français 1987, Stars 90 2000, Mais Qu'est-ce qu'on va faire de toi? 2007. *Leisure interests:* tennis, cycling, football, skiing, flying. *Address:* Production DMD, 21 rue Jean Mermoz, 75008 Paris (office); Pavillon Gabriel, 9 avenue Gabriel, 75008 Paris, France (home). *Telephone:* 1-40-76-00-89 (office). *Fax:* 1-45-63-61-42 (office).

DRUKER, Brian J., MD; American medical scientist and academic; *JELD-WEN Chair of Leukemia Research and Director, OHSU Knight Cancer Institute, Oregon Health and Science University;* b. 1955, Minn.; ed School of Medicine, Univ. of California, San Diego; completed residency in internal medicine at Washington Univ., St Louis, Mo.; held Oncology Fellowship at Dana-Farber Cancer Inst., Harvard Medical School; currently JELD-WEN Chair of Leukemia Research, Oregon Health and Science Univ., Dir OHSU Knight Cancer Inst. 2007–; named a Howard Hughes Medical Investigator 2002; mem. Inst. of Medicine of the Nat.

Academies 2003, American Assn of Physicians 2006, NAS 2007; Pres.'s Undergraduate Research Award, Univ. of California, San Diego, Lifetime Achievement Award, Leukemia and Lymphoma Soc., Medal of Honor, American Cancer Soc., Lasker-DeBakey Clinical Medical Research Award (co-recipient) 2009, Meyenburg Cancer Research Prize 2009, Hope Funds Award of Excellence for Clinical Research 2009, Japan Prize (co-recipient) 2012 and numerous other awards. *Achievements include:* developed, with Nicholas B. Lydon and Charles L. Sawyers, imatinib (or Gleevec) and dasatinib – targeted treatments for chronic myeloid leukemia. *Publications:* numerous papers in professional journals. *Address:* OHSU Knight Cancer Institute, Mail Code CR145, 3181 SW Sam Jackson Park Road, Portland, OR 97239-3098, USA (office). *Telephone:* (503) 494-5058 (office). *E-mail:* drukerb@ohsu.edu (office). *Website:* www.ohsu.edu/xd/health/services/cancer/about-us/druker (office).

DRURY, Very Rev. John Henry, MA; British ecclesiastic and university administrator; *Chaplain and Fellow, All Souls College, Oxford;* b. 23 May 1936, Clacton; s. of Henry Drury and Barbara Drury; m. Clare Nineham 1972 (died 2004); two d.; ed Bradfield Coll. and Trinity Hall, Cambridge; Curate, St John's Wood Church, London 1963; Chaplain, Downing Coll. Cambridge 1966; Chaplain and Fellow, Exeter Coll. Oxford 1969; Canon of Norwich Cathedral 1973; lecturer, Univ. of Sussex 1979; Dean, King's Coll. Cambridge 1981; Dean, Christ Church, Oxford 1991–2003; Hussey Lecturer Univ. of Oxford 1997; Chaplain and Fellow, All Souls Coll. Oxford 2003–; Hon. Fellow, Exeter Coll., Oxford 1992, Trinity Hall, Cambridge 1997, Hon. Student of Christ Church, Oxford 2003. *Television:* Painting the Word, Channel 5 (UK), 2002. *Publications:* Angels and Dirt 1972, Luke 1973, Tradition and Design in Luke's Gospel 1976, Parables in the Gospels 1985, Critics of the Bible 1724–1873 1989, The Burning Bush 1990, Painting the Word 1999. *Leisure interests:* drawing, walking, carpentry. *Address:* All Souls College, Oxford, OX1 4AL, England. *Telephone:* (1865) 279368. *Fax:* (1865) 279299. *E-mail:* john.drury@all-souls.ac.uk.

DRUT, Guy Jacques; French politician and fmr athlete; b. 6 Dec. 1950, Oignies (Pas de Calais); s. of Jacques Drut and Jacqueline Wigley; m. 2nd Véronique Hardy 1984; one d. and one d. by first m.; ed Lycée de Douai, Lycée d'Henin-Liétard, Lycée Roubaix, Ecole Normale Supérieure d'Educ. Physique et Sportive and Inst. Nat. des Sports; French Jr record-holder, 110m hurdles, pole vault and decathlon; French 110m hurdles champion 1970–76, 1981; European 100m hurdles champion, Rome 1974; European 110m hurdles record, Rome 1974, world record, Berlin 1975; silver medal, 110m hurdles, Munich Olympics 1972, gold medal, Montreal Olympics 1976; bronze medal, 50m hurdles, European Championships 1981; retd from competition 1981; Chief of Staff to Prime Minister Jacques Chirac 1975–76; mem. Nat. Council UDR, Cen. Cttee RPR; Deputy Mayor of Paris responsible for Youth and Sport 1985–89; Deputy (RPR) from Seine-et-Marne to Nat. Ass. 1986–95; Town Councillor, Meaux 1989–92; Mayor of Coulommiers 1992–; Minister of Youth and Sport May–Nov. 1995, Minister del. 1995–97; elected Deputy for Seine-et-Marne (Groupe du Rassemblement pour la République) 1997, re-elected (Groupe Union pour un Mouvement Populaire) 2002–07; mem. IOC 1996–2005 (resgnd); Chevalier, Ordre Nat. du Mérite. *Publications:* L'or et l'argent 1976, Jacques Chirac: la victoire du sport (co-author) 1988, J'ai deux mots à vous dire 1997. *Leisure interests:* golf, hunting. *Address:* Mairie, 77120 Coulommiers, France.

D'SOUZA, Baroness (Life Peer), cr. 2004, of Wychwood in the County of Oxfordshire; **Frances D'Souza,** DPhil; British anthropologist and politician; *Lord Speaker of the House of Lords;* ed St Mary's School, Princethorpe, Warwicks., Univ. Coll., London, Lady Margaret Hall, Oxford; worked for Nuffield Inst. of Comparative Medicine 1973–77, for Oxford Polytechnic (now Oxford Brookes Univ.) 1977–80; taught at LSE and Oxford Brookes Univ.; ind. research consultant for UN 1985–88; fmr consultant to REDRESS Trust; Exec. Dir ARTICLE 19 (human rights org.) for nine years; Convenor of the Crossbench Peers, House of Lords 2007–11, Lord Speaker of the House of Lords 2011–; Jt Pres. Commonwealth Parl. Assn (UK Br.) 2011–, British-American Parl. Group, Industry and Parl. Trust; Pres. Police Service Parl. Scheme; Co-Pres. Hansard Soc.; Trustee of several orgs; Hon. Pres. British Group, Inter-Parl. Union 2011–. *Address:* Office of the Lord Speaker, House of Lords, Westminster, London, SW1A 0PW, England (office). *Telephone:* (20) 7219-6444 (office). *Fax:* (20) 7219-2075 (office). *E-mail:* lordspeaker@parliament.uk (office). *Website:* www.parliament.uk/business/lords/lord-speaker (office).

DU, Daozheng; Chinese journalist; *Publisher, Yanhuang Chunqiu;* b. Nov. 1923, Dingxiang Co., Shanxi Prov.; s. of Du Xixiang and Qi Luaying; m. Xu Zhixian 1950; one s. four d.; ed Middle School, Dingxiang, Shanxi and Beijing Marx-Lenin Coll.; joined CCP 1937; Chief of Hebei and Guangdong Bureau, Xinhua News Agency 1949–56; Ed.-in-Chief Yangchen Wanbao 1956–69; Dir Home News Dept, Xinhua News Agency 1977–82; Ed.-in-Chief Guangming Daily 1982; Dir Media and Publs Office 1987–88; Deputy 7th NPC 1988–92; Dir State Press and Publs Admin. 1988–89; Founder and Publisher, Yanhuang Chunqiu (journal) 1991–; Hon. Pres. Newspaper Operation and Man. Assn 1988; Nat. News Prize 1979. *Publications:* Explore Japan (co-author), Interviews with Famous Chinese Journalists. *Leisure interest:* photography. *Address:* Yanhuang Chunqiu, Xicheng District, Yue Tan South Street No. 69, Beijing 100045, People's Republic of China (office). *Telephone:* (10) 68532048 (office). *Fax:* (10) 68532569 (office). *E-mail:* yhcqw01@126.com (office). *Website:* www.yhcqw.com (office).

DU, Ming-xin; Chinese composer and music editor; b. 19 Aug. 1928, Qianjiang Co., Hubei Prov.; m. 1966; one s. one d.; ed Yu Cai Music School and Tchaikovsky State Conservatoire, USSR; debut solo piano concert, Shanghai 1948; Prof. of Composition, Cen. Conservatory of Music 1978–; participated in the Asian Composers' Conf. and Music Festival, Hong Kong 1981; travelled to USA for performance of Violin Concerto No. 1, John F. Kennedy Center 1986, and gave lectures in music insts; Exec. Dir Chinese Musicians' Assn; mem. 11th CPPCC 1997–2002. *Compositions include:* Violin Concerto No. 1, Violin Concerto No. 2, Piano Concerto No. 1, Piano Concerto No. 2, Great Wall Symphony, Luoshen Symphony, Youth Symphony, The South Sea of My Mother Land (symphonic picture), The Goddess of the River Luo (symphonic fantasia), Flapping! the Flags of Army, The Mermaid (ballet suite), The Red Detachment of Women (ballet suite), Wonderful China (film soundtrack) 1982, piano trio, string quartet. *Address:*

Central Conservatory of Music, 43 Baojia Street, Beijing 100031, People's Republic of China.

DU, Qinglin, MA; Chinese politician; b. Nov. 1946, Panshi Co., Jilin Prov.; ed Northeast China Teachers' Univ., Jilin Univ.; joined CCP 1966; mem. Young Cadres Class, CCP Jilin City Cttee 1964–66; mem. and Deputy Group Leader Socialist Educ. Work Team, CCP Liuhe Co. Cttee, Jilin Prov., Yongji Co. Cttee, Jilin Prov., Shulan Co. Cttee, Jilin Prov. 1964–66; clerical worker, Publicity Dept, CCP Jilin City Cttee 1967–68; Sec. CCP Communist Youth League and Head of Workshop, No. 1 Automobile Works 1968–74, Deputy Chair. CCP Revolutionary Cttee 1974–78, Deputy Dir No. 1 Automobile Works 1974–78, Deputy Sec. CCP Party Br. 1974–78; Sec. CCP Communist Youth League, Jilin City Cttee 1978–79; Deputy Sec. Communist Youth League Jilin Prov. Cttee, mem. Communist Youth League Cen. Cttee 1979–84; Deputy Sec. CCP Changchun City Cttee 1984–85; Deputy Sec. CCP Jilin Prov. Cttee 1988–92; Deputy Sec. CCP Hainan Prov. Cttee 1992–98, Sec. 1998–2001; Alt. mem. 14th CCP Cen. Cttee 1992–97, mem. 15th CCP Cen. Cttee 1997–2002, 16th CCP Cen. Cttee 2002–07, 17th CCP Cen. Cttee 2007–12, 18th CCP Cen. Cttee 2012–, also 18th CCP Cen. Cttee Politburo Secr. 2012–; Chair. Standing Cttee, Hainan Prov. People's Congress 1993–2001; Minister of Agric. 2001–06; Sec. Sichuan CCP Prov. Cttee 2006–07; Head CCP Cen. Cttee United Front Work Dept 2007–12; Vice-Chair. 11th CPPCC Nat. Cttee 2008–13, 12th CPPCC Nat. Cttee 2013–. *Address:* Chinese People's Political Consultative Conference, Beijing, People's Republic of China (office).

DU, Shuanghua; Chinese business executive; *Chairman, Rizhao Steel Holding Group Co., Ltd.;* b. Hebei Prov.; m. Song Yahong (divorced); two s.; Man. Hengshui Jinghua Steel Pipe Co. Ltd; currently Chair. Rizhao Steel Holding Group Co. Ltd. *Address:* Rizhao Steel Holding Group Co., Ltd, 18F, No. 86, 276826 Rizhao, Shandong Province, People's Republic of China (office). *Telephone:* (633) 81800882 (office).

DU, Gen. Tiehuan; Chinese army officer; b. 1938, Anshan City, Liaoning Prov.; ed PLA Mil. Acad.; Asst Dir PLA Gen. Political Dept 1993–94; Political Commissar Ji'nan Mil. Region 1994–96; Political Commissar, Beijing Mil. Area Command 1996–97; mem. 15th CCP Cen. Cttee 1997–2002; rank of Lt-Gen. 1997–2000, Gen. 2000–. *Address:* c/o Political Commissar's Office, Beijing Military Area Command, Beijing, People's Republic of China (office).

DU, Yuzhou; Chinese textile engineer and government official; *Honorary President, China National Textile and Apparel Council;* b. 1942, Qiqihar, Heilongjiang; ed Tsinghua Univ.; joined CCP 1965; technician, Changde Textile Machinery Plant, Hunan 1968–70, Deputy Workshop Head, then Deputy Section Chief 1970–73; engineer, Deputy Dir then Dir Design Inst. of Ministry of Textile Industry 1978–85; Vice-Minister of Textiles 1985–93; Vice-Chair., Chair. Chinese Gen. Assn of Textile Industry, Dir State Admin. for the Textile Industry 1993–; Pres. China Nat. Garment Assn; Chair. of China Nat. Fed. of Textile Manufacturers; Hon. Pres. China Nat. Textile and Apparel Council. *Address:* State Administration for the Textile Industry, Huaye Internaional Center, No.39 Dongsihuan Zhonglu, Chaoyang, Beijing 100025, People's Republic of China (office). *Telephone:* (10) 85872528 (office). *Website:* www.ctei.gov.cn (office).

DU CANN, Rt Hon. Sir Edward Dillon Lott, PC, KBE, MA, FRSA; British politician and business executive; b. 28 May 1924, Beckenham; s. of C. G. L. du Cann and Janet du Cann (née Murchie); m. 1st Sallie Murchie 1962 (divorced 1989); one s. two d.; m. 2nd Jenifer Patricia Evelyn (Lady Cooke) (née King) 1990 (died 1995); ed Woodbridge School, Suffolk and St John's Coll., Oxford; served with RNVR 1943–46; MP 1956–87; Founder and Chair. Unicorn Group of Unit Trusts 1957–62, 1964–72; Founder-mem. Assn Unit Trust Mans. 1961, Chair. 1961; Econ. Sec. to the Treasury 1962–63; Minister of State, Bd of Trade 1963–64; Chair. of Conservative Party 1965–67, Pres. 1981–82; Chair. 1922 Cttee 1972–84; First Chair. Select Cttee on Public Expenditure 1971–73, Public Accounts Cttee 1974–79; mem. Cttee of Privileges 1972–87; First Chair. Treasury and Civil Service Cttee 1979–83, Liaison Cttee of Select Cttee Chairs 1979–83; Vice-Chair. British-American Parl. Group 1977–81; Pres. Conservative Parl. EC Reform Group 1985–87; Founder-Chair. All-Party Maritime Affairs Parl. Group 1984–87; Chair. Public Accounts Comm. 1984–87; led Parl. del. to USA 1978, 1979, first British Parl. del. to China 1982; Chair. Keyser Ullmann Ltd 1972–75, Cannon Assurance Ltd 1972–80, Lonrho PLC 1984–91 (Dir 1972–92), Sunshine Technology Group (China) 2006–; Dir Martins Bank 1967–69, Barclays Bank (London Bd) 1969–72; Visiting Fellow, Univ. of Lancaster Business School 1970–82; Patron Assn of Insurance Brokers 1973–77, Human Ecology Foundation 1987; Gov. Hatfield Coll., Durham Univ. 1988–92; Master Fruiterers Co. 1990; Pres. Inst. of Freight Forwarders 1988–89, Pres. Royal Naval Assn (Cyprus Br.) 2004–, Oxford Univ. Rugby League Club 2004–06, Oxford Soc. (Cyprus Br.) 2005–; Vice-Pres. St Margarets Hospice, Taunton 1984–, Limassol Hospice 2003–; Hon. Vice-Pres. British Insurance Brokers Assn 1978–; Chair. Templeton Foundation Awards Ceremony 1984 (mem. Panel of Judges 1984); mem. Man. Council of the GB-SasaKawa British-Japanese Foundation 1984–93; Adm., House of Commons Yacht Club 1974–87; Hon. Col 155 Regt (Wessex) Volunteers 1972–82; First Hon. Freeman, Borough of Taunton Deane 1977; Hon. Life mem. Inst. of RCT, Commonwealth Parl. Assn, Taunton Racecourse. *Publications:* Investing Simplified 1959, The Case for a Bill of Rights 1975, How to Bring Government Expenditure under Parliamentary Control 1979, A New Competition Policy 1984, Hoist the Red Ensign 1987, Two Lives 1995, The Wellington Caricatures 2000. *Leisure interests:* sailing, gardening, walking the dog. *Address:* Flat 7, 42 Great Smith Street, London, SW1P 3BU, England (home); Pervolia, Lemona, 8545 Paphos, Cyprus (home). *E-mail:* edwardducann@btinternet.com (home).

DU PLESSIS, Jan, BCom, LLB, CA (SA); South African chartered accountant and business executive; *Chairman, Rio Tinto plc;* b. Cape Town; m.; two s. one d.; ed Univ. of Stellenbosch; qualified as chartered accountant; joined Rembrandt Group 1981, moved to UK 1982, held various positions before co-founding Compagnie Financière Richemont SA (Swiss public co. formed following demerger of Rembrandt's non-South African interests 1988), Group Finance Dir 1988–2004; Finance Dir Rothmans International 1990–96; Dir (non-exec.) British American Tobacco (BAT) PLC 1999–2009, mem. Audit, Nominations and Remuneration Cttees, Chair. (non-exec.) BAT 2004–09 (resgnd), also Chair. Nominations Cttee; mem. Bd of Dirs Rio Tinto plc 2008–, Chair. 2009–; Chair. (non-exec.) RHM plc

2005–07; Dir (non-exec.) Lloyds TSB Group plc 2005–09 (Chair. Audit Cttee 2008–09), Marks & Spencer Group plc 2008– (Sr Ind. Dir (non-exec.) 2012–). *Address:* Rio Tinto plc, 2 Eastbourne Terrace, London, W2 6LG, England (office). *Telephone:* (20) 7781-2000 (office). *Fax:* (20) 7781-1800 (office). *Website:* www .riotinto.com (office).

DUAN, Qingshan, MBA; Chinese auditor and business executive; *Chairman of the Board of Supervisors, China Minsheng Banking Corporation Limited;* b. 1957; fmr Div. Dir Audit Div., Taiyuan Br., People's Bank of China; fmr Chief Financial Officer and Gen. Man. Human Resources Dept, China Minsheng Banking Corpn Ltd, fmr Man. Dir Taiyuan Br., fmr Deputy Head, then Head of Taiyuan Sub-br., currently Chair. Bd of Supervisors. *Address:* China Minsheng Banking Corporation Ltd, 2 Fuxingmennei Avenue, Beijing 100873, People's Republic of China (office). *Telephone:* (10) 68946790 (office). *E-mail:* webmaster@cmbc.com.cn (office). *Website:* www.cmbc.com.cn (office).

DUARTE, Cristina; Cape Verde politician, economist and international banker; *Minister of Finance and Planning;* Co-ordinator World Bank Growth and Competitiveness Project 2005–06; Minister of Finance and Planning 2006–. *Address:* Ministry of Finances and Planning, 107 Av. Amílcar Cabral, CP 30, Praia, Santiago, Cape Verde (office). *Telephone:* 2607400 (office). *E-mail:* aliciab@gov1 .gov.cv (office). *Website:* www.minfin.cv (office).

DUARTE FRUTOS, Oscar Nicanor, LicenFil, PhD; Paraguayan politician and fmr head of state; b. 11 Oct. 1956, Coronel Oviedo; m. María Gloria Penayo; six c.; ed Nat. Univ. of Asunción, Catholic Univ. of Asunción; journalist, Ultima Hora newspaper 1981–91; Minister of Educ. and Culture 1993–97, 1999–2001; Leader, Partido Colorado 2001–; Pres. of Paraguay 2003–08; fmr Prof. of Sociology and Ethics, Faculty of Philosophy, Nat. Univ. of Asunción. *Address:* Asociación Nacional Republicana—Partido Colorado, Casa de los Colorados, 25 de Mayo 842, Asunción, Paraguay (office). *Telephone:* (21) 44-4137 (office). *Fax:* (21) 49-7857 (office). *Website:* www.anr.org.py (office).

DUATO, Nacho; Spanish choreographer; *Chief Choreographer, Mikhailovsky Theatre;* b. (Juan Ignacio Duato Barcia), 8 Jan. 1957, Valencia; ed Maurice Bejart's Mudra School, Brussels, Belgium; began career by signing professional contract with Cullberg Ballet, Stockholm 1980–81; brought by Jiří Kylián to Nederlands Dans Theater 1981, a resident choreographer 1988–90; Artistic Dir Compania Nacional de Danza, Madrid 1990–2010; Chief Choreographer Mikhailovsky Theatre, St Petersburg (first foreigner to lead a Russian ballet co. in more than 100 years) 2011–; works have been featured in repertoires of major dance cos worldwide, including Paris Opera Ballet, American Ballet Theater, Deutsche Oper Ballet, Stuttgart Ballet, Les Grands Ballets Canadiens, Australian Ballet and Finnish Opera Ballet. *Address:* Mikhailovsky Theatre, 191186 St Petersburg, Arts Square 1, Russian Federation (office). *Telephone:* (812) 595-43-05 (office). *Fax:* (812) 595-43-19 (office). *E-mail:* info@mikhailovsky.ru (office). *Website:* www .mikhailovsky.ru (office).

DUBAI, Ruler of (see MAKTOUM, Rashid al-).

DUBENETSKY, Yakov Nikolayevich; Russian banker and economist; *Head of Centre of Investments, Institute of National Economic Forecasting;* b. 26 Oct. 1938, Stayki, Belarus; m.; one s.; ed Moscow State Univ.; Deputy Chair. Stroybank of the USSR 1985–87; First Deputy Chair. Bank for Industry and Construction of the USSR (Pomstroybank of the USSR) 1987–91; Chair. Bd Russian Jt Stock Investment and Commercial Bank for Industry and Construction (Pomstroybank of Russia) 1991–99; apptd Chair. Bank Asscn of Russia 1995; currently Head of Centre of Investments, Inst. of Nat. Econ. Forecasting, Russian Acad. of Sciences; Vice-Pres. Asscn of Russian Banks 1995–; Co-Chair. Round Table of Russian Business 2000–; mem. Political Consultative Council of Pres. of Russian Fed. 1996–, Nat. Banking Council 1996–, Int. Acad. of Man. 1997–, Bd for finance and economy, Rosneftegazstroi 2001–. *Address:* Institute of National Economic Forecasting, Russian Academy of Sciences, 47 Nakhimovskii prospect, 117418 Moscow, Russia (office). *Telephone:* (045) 129-34-22 (office). *Fax:* (045) 310-70-71 (office). *E-mail:* office@mail.ecfor.rssi.ru (office). *Website:* www.ecfor.rssi.ru (office).

DUBININ, Sergey Konstantinovich, DEcon; Russian business executive; *Chairman of the Supervisory Council, VTB Group;* b. 10 Dec. 1950, Moscow; m.; two c.; ed Moscow State Univ.; Docent, Researcher and Prof., Moscow State Univ. 1974–91; mem. Pres. Mikhail Gorbachev's admin 1991; Deputy Chair. Russian State Cttee for co-operation with CIS 1992–93; First Deputy Minister of Finance, Acting Minister of Finance 1993–94; First Deputy Chair. Exec. Bd Commercial Bank Imperial 1994–95; mem. Exec. Bd Jt Stock co. Gazprom 1995, Deputy Chair. Bd Gazprom Co. 1998–2001; Deputy CEO Unified Power Grids of Russia (RAO ES) 2001–04, mem. Man. Bd and Financial Dir 2005–08; currently Chair. Supervisory Council, VTB Group, mem. Bd of Dirs CJSC VTB Capital 2008–; Chair. Cen. Bank of Russia 1995–98; Russian Rep. to IBRD 1996–98; Chair. Interstate Monetary Cttee CIS 1996–98, Supervisory Bd Sberbank and Vneshtorgbank; 850th Anniversary of Moscow Govt Award 1998, Best Independent Dir of the Year, Aristos Award 2013. *Publications:* books on public, int. and corp. finance and finance markets; numerous articles on scientific research. *Leisure interests:* art, classical music, theatre, sports. *Address:* VTB Group, 123100 Moscow, 12 Presnenskaya Embankment, Russia (office). *E-mail:* info@vtb.ru (office). *Website:* www.vtb.com (office).

DUBOS, Jean-François; French lawyer, academic and business executive; *Chairman of the Management Board, Vivendi;* ed Univ. of Paris, Acad. of Int. Law, The Hague; fmr Lecturer, École Nationale d'Admin, Univ. of Paris I (Sorbonne), Paris X (Nanterre), Paris V (René Descartes), Institut d'Études Politiques, Aix-en-Provence; Co-head, Cabinet of Ministry of Defence 1981–84; full-time mem. Conseil d'Etat 1984–91; joined Compagnie Générale des Eaux (predecessor of Vivendi) as Deputy to the CEO 1991–94, Gen. Counsel 1994–99, CEO Carrousel du Louvre 1993–99, Exec. Vice-Pres., Gen. Counsel and Sec. of Man. and Supervisory Bds of Vivendi, Chair. Man. Bd 2012–; mem. Bd of Dirs Société des Eaux de Melun, CMESE; mem. Supervisory Bd Canal+, Groupe Canal+; Vivendi's Perm. Rep. on Bd of SFR; Gen. Sec. Aix-en-Provence Int. Opera Festival; Chair. Maison Européenne de la Photo, Centre de Musique Baroque de Versailles; Vice-Chair. Arles Int. Photography Festival; mem. Bd American Friends; Dir Amis de Mozart;

Dir and Treas. Théâtre du Châtelet; Hon. mem. Maître des Requêtes au Conseil d'Etat; Chevalier, Légion d'honneur, Ordre nat. du Mérite; Officier, Ordre des Arts et des Lettres, several other decorations. *Address:* Vivendi, 42 avenue de Friedland, 75380 Paris Cedex 08, France (office). *Telephone:* 1-71-71-10-00 (office). *Fax:* 1-71-71-11-79 (office). *E-mail:* info@vivendi.com (office). *Website:* www .vivendi.com (office).

DUBOWITZ, Victor, MD, PhD, FRCP, FRCPCH, DCH; British paediatrician and academic; *Professor Emeritus of Paediatrics, University of London;* b. 6 Aug. 1931, Beaufort West, S Africa; s. of Charley Dubowitz and Olga Schattel; m. Lilly M. S. Sebok 1960; four s.; ed Cen. High School, Beaufort West and Univs of Cape Town and Sheffield; intern, Groote Schuur Hospital, Cape Town 1955; Sr House Officer, Queen Mary's Hosp. for Children 1957–59; Research Assoc., Royal Postgraduate Medical School, Univ. of London 1958–59, Prof. of Paediatrics 1972–96, Prof. Emer. 1996–, Dir Jerry Lewis Muscle Research Centre 1975–96; Lecturer in Clinical Pathology, Nat. Hosp. for Nervous Diseases, London 1960; Lecturer in Child Health, Univ. of Sheffield 1961–65, Sr Lecturer 1965–67, Reader 1967–72; Research Assoc., Inst. for Muscle Disease and Asst Paediatrician, Cornell Medical Coll., New York 1965–66; Consultant Paediatrician, Hammersmith Hosp. 1972–96; Pres. European Paediatric Neurology Soc. 1994–97, World Muscle Soc. 1995–, Medical Art Soc. 1996–2000; Curator of Art, Royal Coll. of Paediatrics and Child Health; Dir of Therapeutic Studies, European Neuromuscular Centre, Netherlands 2000–03; Ed.-in-Chief Neuromuscular Disorders 1990–, European Journal of Paediatric Neurology 1996–2003; several awards. *Publications:* The Floppy Infant 1969, Muscle Biopsy: A Modern Approach (with M. Brooke) 1973, 1985, Gestational Age of the Newborn (with L. M. S. Dubowitz) 1977, Muscle Disorders in Childhood 1978, The Neurological Assessment of the Pre-term and Full-term Newborn Infant (with L. M. S. Dubowitz) 1981, 1999, A Colour Atlas of Muscle Disorders in Childhood 1989, A Colour Atlas of Brain Disorders in the Newborn (with L. de Vries, L. Dubowitz and J. Penock) 1990, Ramblings of a Peripatetic Paediatrician 2005, Muscle Biopsy: A Practical Approach (with Caroline Sewry) 2006, (new edition, with Caroline Sewry and Anders Oldfors) 2012. *Leisure interests:* sculpting, hiking, photography, antique glass. *Address:* 25 Middleton Road, Golders Green, London, NW11 7NR, England (home). *Telephone:* (20) 8455-9352 (home). *Fax:* (20) 8905-5922 (home). *E-mail:* v.dubowitz@imperial .ac.uk (home).

DUBRULLE, Christophe; French retail executive; joined Auchan 1965, mem. Bd of Dirs Groupe Auchan 1999–, Chair. Exec. Bd 1999–2010, also Man. Dir Hypermarkets –2010, Chair. E-Drive 2010–; Man. Dir Leroy Merlin 1982, later Chair. Bd of Admin.; Dir La Rinascente SpA. *Address:* Groupe Auchan, 200 rue de la Recherche, 59650 Villeneuve d'Ascq, France (office). *Telephone:* (3) 28-37-67-00 (office). *Fax:* (3) 20-67-55-20 (office). *E-mail:* info@auchan.com (office). *Website:* www.auchan.com (office).

DUBUC, Nancy; American media executive; *President of Entertainment and Media, A+E Networks;* began career at A+E Networks as Dir, Historical Programming for HISTORY, Sr Vice-Pres., Programming –2007, Pres. and Gen. Man. HISTORY and Lifetime Networks 2007–12, Pres. of Entertainment and Media, A+E Networks 2012–, oversees all content creation, brand development and marketing for the entire A+E Networks' portfolio including A&E Network, Lifetime and HISTORY and their affiliated brands, also oversees A+E Networks' Int. and Digital divs; named by Multichannel News and WICT as Wonder Woman 2007, Preserve America Presidential Award 2007. *Address:* A+E Networks, 235 East 45th Street, Suite 2, New York, NY 10017-3379, USA (office). *Telephone:* (212) 210-1400 (office). *E-mail:* info@aenetworks.com (office). *Website:* www.aenetworks .com (office); www.aetv.com (office).

DUBY, Jean Jacques, PhD; French mathematician and scientist; *President, Observatoire des Sciences et des Techniques;* b. 5 Nov. 1940, Paris; s. of Jean Duby and Lucienne Duby (née Lacomme); m. Camille Poli 1963; one d.; ed Ecole Normale Supérieure, Paris; research staff mem., Thomas J. Watson Research Center, USA 1963–64; Systems Engineer, IBM France 1965–66, Man. Application Systems, IBM Mohansic Lab. 1974–75, Exec. Asst to Vice-Chair. IBM Corpn 1975–76, Br. Office Man. IBM France 1977–78, special assignment, IBM Communications Div. 1979, Dir Switching Systems IBM Europe 1980–82, Dir Science and Tech., IBM France 1986–88, Group Dir Science and Tech., IBM Europe 1988–91; Man. Grenoble Scientific Centre 1967–69; Assoc. Prof., European Systems Research Inst. and Univ. of Geneva 1970–71; Project Man., Paris Stock Exchange 1972–73; Scientific Dir CNRS 1982–86; Scientific Dir Union d'assurances de Paris 1991–97; Pres. Inst. Nat. de recherche sur les transports et leur securité 1992–96; Chair. Bd of Dirs Ecole Normale Supérieure de Cachan 1994–2000; Dir-Gen. Ecole Supérieure d'Electricité 1995–2005; Professeur des universités 1999–; Chair. Scientific Council of Bouygues Telecom 2001–; Pres. Observatoire des Sciences et des Techniques 2002–; Scientific Council, Schneider Electric 2004–; Officier, Ordre nat. du Mérite, Chevalier, Ordre Nat. de la Côte d'Ivoire. *Leisure interests:* skiing, mountaineering. *Address:* Observatoire des Sciences et des Techniques, 93 rue de Vaugirard, 75006 Paris, France (office). *E-mail:* jean-jacques.duby@obs-ost.fr (office). *Website:* www.obs-ost.fr (office).

DUBYNA, Oleh; Ukrainian politician and engineer; *Chairman, Naftohaz Ukrainy;* b. 20 March 1959, Elizavetovka, Dnepropetrovsk region; m.; one s.; ed Dnieprodzerzhinsk Industrial Inst., Dnieprodzerzhinsk State Tech. Univ.; employee Dniepr Metallurgic plant 1976, master, Sr master, then engineer 1986–93, Head of Bureau, Deputy Head of Div., First Deputy Dir-Gen. 1996–98; teacher Dnieprodzerzhinsk Polytechnical Higher School 1985–86; Asst to Dir, then Deputy Dir-Gen. Dniepr br. of Intermontage Kam – Soviet-Swiss Joint Venture DEMOS 1993–96; Deputy Head, Chair. Bd of Dirs, Dir-Gen. Alchevsk Metallurgic plant 1998–99; Dir-Gen. Kryvoy Rog State Ore-Metallurgic plant, Krivorozhstal 1999–; Deputy Prime Minister for Econ. Policy 2000–01; First Deputy Prime Minister 2001–02; Adviser to Pres. Leonid Kuchma 2002–04; Pres. Ukrainian Nat. Energy Co. (Ukrenergo) 2004; CEO Dnieprodzerzhynsk metallurgical complex 2005–07; Chair. Naftohaz Ukrainy (Oil and Gas of Ukraine) 2007–. *Address:* Naftogaz Ukrainy (Oil and Gas of Ukraine), 01001 Kyiv, vul. B. Khmelnytskoho 6b, Ukraine (office). *Telephone:* (44) 461-25-37 (office). *E-mail:* ngu@naftogaz.net (office). *Website:* www.naftogaz.com (office).

DUCA, Gheorghe, DSci; Moldovan academic; *President, Academy of Sciences of Moldova*; b. 29 Feb. 1952, Sîngerei; ed State Univ. of Moldova, Inst. of Chemical Physics, Russian Acad. of Sciences, Univ. of Odessa; Head of Physical Chem. Dept, State Univ. of Moldova 1988–92, Dir Research Centre of Ecological and Applied Chem. 1991–98, Head of Industrial and Ecological Chem. Dept 1992–98, Dean of Faculty of Ecology 1992–95; Pres. Republican Cttee for awarding prizes to young researchers in science and tech. 1992–2006, Scientific Specialised Council for nomination of DrSci degree 1994–2006; Chair. Parl. Comm. for Culture, Science, Educ., and Mass Media 1998–2001; Pres. Moldovan Research and Devt Asscn 2000–06; Minister of Ecology, Construction and Territory Devt 2001–04; Pres. Acad. of Sciences of Moldova 2004–; Ed.-in-Chief Environment Journal 2002–04; Head of Editorial Bd Chemistry Journal of Moldova 2005–06; mem. Int. Editorial Bd Chemistry and Technology of Water Journal 2001–06, Editorial Advisory Bd Environmental Engineering and Management Journal 2002–06; Co-Pres. Moldo-Polish Intergovernmental Mixed Comm. for Commercial, Econ., Scientific and Tech. Co-operation 2001–05, Danube Convention 2003–04; Pres. Admin. Council of Concession Agreement of Redeco 2005–06, Admin. Council of Nat. Science Foundation of Moldova 2005–06; mem. ACS 1997–, Cen. European Acad. of Sciences and Arts 1999–, Int. Acad. of Informatics 1999–, Pedagogical Acad. of Russia 1999–; Order of St Sergius Radonezh of Holy Synod of Russian Orthodox Church 2003, Commdr, Cross of Honour (Poland) 2004, Gloria Muncii Order 2007, Order of the Repub. of Moldova 2011; Dr hc (Free Int. Univ., Moldova) 1993, (Gh. Asachi Univ., Romania) 2000, (Real-Humanist Univ. of Cahul) 2001, (Balkan Acad. of Sciences) 2004, (West Univ. V.Goldiş, Romania, State Univ. of Bălţi, Acad. of Economic Study, Moldova) 2006, (State Univ. of Tiraspol, State Univ. of Physical Educ. and Sport, Moldova, Russian Acad. of Sciences) 2011; State Prize for Youth in Science and Tech. 1983, State Prize for Science, Tech. and Production 1995, 2000, Om Emerit Medal, Repub. of Moldova 1996, Scientist of the Year, Acad. of Sciences of Moldova 2005, Medail d'Or 2005, Int. Socrates Prize, Oxford 2007, Nat. GALEX Prize for best founder of a library 2011. *Address:* Academy of Sciences of Moldova, 2001 Chisinau, 1 Bd. Stefan cel Mare, Moldova (office). *Telephone:* (22) 27-14-78 (office). *Fax:* (22) 27-60-14 (office). *E-mail:* duca@mrda.md (office); duca@asm.md (office). *Website:* www.duca.md (office).

DUCEPPE, Gilles, BA; Canadian politician; b. 22 July 1947, Montréal, Québec; s. of Jean Duceppe and Hélène Rowley; m. Yolande Brunelle; two c.; ed Collège Mont-Saint-Louis, Université de Montréal; Vice-Pres. Union générale des étudiants et étudiantes du Québec (UGEQ) 1968–69; Dir Quartier Latin journal 1970–71; with Company of Young Canadians –1977; Union Negotiator, Confed. of Nat. Trade Unions 1977; MP for Montreal's Laurier-Sainte-Marie riding (Bloc Québécois) 1990–2011, Interim Leader Bloc Québécois Jan.–Feb. 1996, Leader 1997–2011 (resgnd); Leader of the Opposition 1997.

DUCH-PEDERSEN, Alf, MSc; Danish banking executive; b. 15 Aug. 1946; began career with Danish Turnkey Dairies A/S 1973–84; various positions with APV Anhydro A/S 1984–87, APV Pasilac A/S 1987–91, APV PLC, London 1989–91; with Tryg-Baltica Forsikring, Skadesforsikringsselskab A/S 1991–97; mem. Bd Dirs Danisco 1994–97, CEO and Pres. Exec. Bd 1997–2006; mem. Bd Dirs Danske Bank Group 1999–11, Chair. 2003–11; Deputy Chair. Group 4 Securicor PLC (G4S) 2004–06, Chair. 2006–12; mem. Bd Dirs Tech. Univ. of Denmark, Denmark-America Foundation; mem. Cen. Bd Confed. of Danish Industries. *Address:* c/o Danske Bank Group, Holmens Kanal 12, 1092 Copenhagen K, Denmark (office).

DUCHAUFOUR-LAWRANCE, Noé; French architect and interior designer; ed École Nationale Supérieure des Arts Appliqués et des Métiers d'Art, Arts Décoratifs, Paris; began career designing Sketch Restaurant in London 2002; f. own studio; collaborates with publrs including Ceccotti Collezioni, Zanotta, Cinna, Baccarat; projects for Air France (in partnership with Brandimage), Paco Rabanne and Yves Saint Laurent; Tatler Restaurant Award Best Design: The Gallery for Restaurant Sketch, London 2002, Best Design, Theme Magazine for Restaurant Sketch, London 2003, Hotel and Restaurant Magazine Best Design Award for Restaurant Sketch, London 2003, Time Out magazine Eating and Drinking Award: Best Design for Restaurant Sketch, London 2003, Restaurant Senderens – Prix Fooding 2005, Meilleur restaurant avant l'amour 2005, Designer of the Year, Scènes d'intérieur, Maison & Objet, Paris 2007, Wallpaper Design Awards for the bed Buonanotte Valentina, CECCOTTI Collezioni 2009, Prix Elle Déco Int. Design Awards 2009, Lauréat de L'Empreinte de l'Année des Talents du luxe et de la création 2010, Gold Award for the Best of Neocon for the chair Corvo, Bernhardt Design 2010, Red Dot Award Product Design for the chair Corvo, Bernhardt Design 2011. *Address:* Noé Duchaufour Lawrance, 8 Passage de la bonne graine, 75011 Paris, France (office). *Telephone:* 1-43-14-99-59 (office). *Fax:* 1-43-14-48-68 (office). *E-mail:* contact@neonata.fr (office). *Website:* www.noeduchaufourlawrance.com (office).

DUCHESNEAU, François, Docteur d'état ès-lettres et sciences humaines; Canadian philosopher and academic; *Professor of Philosophy Emeritus, University of Montréal*; ed Univ. of Paris-I, France; taught at Univ. of Ottawa; Prof. of Philosophy, Univ. of Montréal 1979, currently Prof. Emer.; Visiting Prof., Catholic Univ. of Louvain, Belgium (Pulpit Draper) 1995, Univ. of Alberta 1997, École des Hautes Études en sciences sociales, Paris 1999; mem. RSC 1984–; Prix des sciences humaines, Asscn canadienne française pour l'avancement des sciences 1992, Killam Research Fellowship 1995–97, Killam Prize for Humanities, Canada Council for the Arts 2003. *Publications:* L'Empirisme de Locke 1973, La physiologie des lumières – Empirisme, modèles et théories 1982, Genèse de la théorie cellulaire 1987, Leibniz et la méthode de la science 1993, La dynamique de Leibniz 1994, Philosophie de la biologie 1997, Les modèles du vivant de Descartes à Leibniz 1998; more than 160 articles on the history of modern philosophy, the history and philosophy of science, empiricist theories of knowledge and the philosophy and scientific work of Leibniz. *Address:* Département de philosophie, Université de Montréal, CP 6128, succ. Centre-ville, Montréal, PQ H3C 3J7, Canada (office). *Telephone:* (514) 343-7373 (office). *Fax:* (514) 343-2098 (office). *E-mail:* francois.duchesneau@umontreal.ca (office). *Website:* philo.umontreal.ca/repertoire-departement/vue/duchesneau-francois/ (office).

DUCHOVNY, David; American actor; b. 7 Aug. 1960, New York; s. of Amram Duchovny and Meg Duchovny; m. Tea Leoni (q.v.) 1997; ed Yale and Princeton Univs; stage appearances include off-Broadway plays, The Copulating Machine of Venice, California and Green Cockatoo; writer and dir of various episodes of The X-

Files; Golden Globe for Best Actor in Drama Series 1996. *Films include:* Working Girl 1988, New Year's Day 1989, Bad Influence 1990, Julia Has Two Lovers 1990, The Rapture 1991, Don't Tell Mom the Babysitter's Dead 1991, Denial 1991, Beethoven 1992, Chaplin 1992, Red Shoe Diaries 1992, Ruby 1992, Venice, Venice 1992, Kalifornia 1993, Apartment Zero, Close Enemy, Loan, Independence Day, Playing God 1997, The X-Files 1998, Return To Me 2000, Evolution 2001, Zoolander 2001, Red Shoe Diaries 15: Forbidden Zone (video) 2002, Full Frontal 2002, XIII (voice) 2003, Connie and Carla 2004, House of D (also dir and writer) 2004, The X Files: Resist or Serve (voice) 2004, Area 51 (voice) 2005, Trust the Man 2005, The TV Set 2006, Queer Duck: The Movie (voice) 2006, Things We Lost in the Fire 2007, The X Files: I Want to Believe 2008, The Joneses 2009, Goats 2012. *Television includes:* Twin Peaks 1990, The X-Files 1993–2002, The X-Files: The Truth 2002, Life With Bonnie 2002, The TV Set 2006, Californication (series) 2007–. *Address:* ICM, 8942 Wilshire Blvd, Beverly Hills, CA 90211, USA.

DUCKWORTH, Marilyn, OBE; New Zealand writer; b. (Marilyn Rose Adcock), 10 Nov. 1935, Auckland; d. of Cyril John Adcock and Irene Robinson; sister of Fleur Adcock (q.v.); m. 1st Harry Duckworth 1955 (divorced 1964); m. 2nd Ian Macfarlane 1964 (divorced 1972); m. 3rd Daniel Donovan 1974 (died 1978); m. 4th John Batstone 1985; four d.; ed Queen Margaret Coll., Wellington and Victoria Univ., Wellington; ten writing fellowships 1961–96 including Katherine Mansfield Fellowship, Menton 1980, Fulbright Visiting Writer's Fellowship, USA 1987, Victoria Univ. Writing Fellowship 1990, Hawthornden Writing Fellowship, Scotland 1994, 2001, Sargeson Writing Fellowship, Auckland 1995, Auckland Univ. Literary Fellowship 1996; NZ Literary Fund Award for Achievement 1963, NZ Book Award for Fiction 1985. *Plays:* Home to Mother, Feet First. *Television:* Close to Home (series). *Publications:* 15 novels, including A Gap in the Spectrum 1959, The Matchbox House 1960, A Barbarous Tongue 1963, Over the Fence Is Out 1969, Disorderly Conduct 1984, Married Alive 1985, Pulling Faces 1987, A Message from Harpo 1989, Unlawful Entry 1992, Seeing Red 1993, Leather Wings 1995, Studmuffin 1997, Swallowing Diamonds 2003, Playing Friends 2007; short stories: Explosions on the Sun 1989; poems: Other Lovers' Children 1975; memoir: Camping on the Faultline 2000. *Leisure interest:* playing the violin. *Address:* 41 Queen Street, Mt Victoria, Wellington 6011, New Zealand. *Telephone:* (4) 384-9990. *E-mail:* marilynduckworth@paradise.net.nz.

DUCORNET, Erica (Rikki) Lynn, BA; American/French writer, artist and teacher; b. 19 April 1943, New York; d. of Gerard De Gré and Muriel Harris; m. Jonathan Cohen; one s.; apptd Novelist-in-Residence, Univ. of Denver 1988; has taught writing at Writers at Work, Bard Coll., Brown Univ., Naropa Univ., Vermont Studio Center, Centrum Writer's Workshop, Univ. of Trento; Writer-in-Residence Univ. of Louisiana, Lafayette 2007–09; mem. PEN; Lannan Literary Award in Fiction 1993, 2004, Critics Choice Award 1995, Charles Flint Kellogg Award in Arts and Letters 1998, Lannon Literary Fellowship 1998, Academy Award, American Acad. of Arts and Letters 2008. *Publications:* novels: The Stain 1984, Entering Fire 1986, The Fountains of Neptune 1989, Eben Demarst 1990, The Jade Cabinet 1993, The Butcher's Tales 1994, Phosphor in Dreamland 1995, The Word 'Desire' 1997, The Fan Maker's Inquisition (Los Angeles Times Book of the Year) 2000, Gazelle 2004, Netsuke 2011; short fiction: The Complete Butcher's Tales 1994, The Word 'Desire' 1997, The One Marvelous Thing 2008; poetry: From The Star Chamber 1974, Wild Geraniums 1975, Bouche a Bouche 1975, Weird Sisters 1976, Knife Notebook 1977, The Illustrated Universe 1979, The Cult of Seizure 1989; essay: The Monstrous and the Marvelous 1999. *Address:* c/o Coffee House Press, 79 Thirteenth Avenue NE, Suite 110, Minneapolis, MN 55413, USA (office). *E-mail:* rikki@rikkiducornet.com. *Website:* www.rikkiducornet.com (office).

DUCZMAL JAROSZEWSKA, Agnieszka; Polish conductor; *Artistic Director and Conductor, Amadeus Chamber Orchestra of Polish Radio;* b. 7 Jan. 1946, Krotoszyn; d. of Henryk Duczmal and Leokadia Surdyk Duczmal; m.; one s. two d.; ed Acad. of Music, Poznań; Founder, Artistic Dir and Conductor, Amadeus Chamber Orchestra of Polish Radio 1968–; Asst Conductor Poznań Nat. Philharmonic 1971–72, Conductor Poznań Opera 1972–81; performs in Europe, N and S America and Asia; over 46 recordings including live concerts for TV and performances for radio; Commdr's Cross, Order of Polonia Restituta 1998; won award at first Nat. Competition for Conductors, Katowice 1970, distinction, 4th Int. Herbert von Karajan Competition 1975, Silver Medal of Herbert von Karajan at the Meeting of Young Orchestras, West Berlin 1976, La Donna del Mondo Award of St Vincent Int. Culture Centre, Rome 1982. *Recordings:* J. S. Bach/Józef Koffler: Goldberg Variations (world premiere recording), Britten: A Midsummer Night's Dream (Polish premiere), Knittel: The Passion of Our Lord according to St Matthew, Op. 20 (world premiere recording), Alexandre Tansman: Chamber Music (world premiere recording); many other world premieres of Polish compositions. *Arrangements:* arrangements for string orchestra of Mussorgsky's Pictures at an Exhibition, and compositions by Chopin, Szymanowski, Brahms, Debussy, Paderewski. *Radio:* archive recordings for Polish Radio, BBC and NDR. *Television:* recordings for Polish, Japanese and French TV. *Leisure interests:* dogs, literary classics, gardening, mountaineering. *Telephone:* (61) 851-66-86 (office). *Fax:* (61) 851-66-87 (office). *E-mail:* agnieszka.duczmal@amadeus.pl (office). *Website:* www.amadeus.pl (office).

DUDAU, Nicolae; Moldovan politician and diplomatist; b. 19 Dec. 1945, Grineuts; m. Galina Dudau; one d.; ed Higher CPSU School, Moscow, Chişinău Tech. Univ.; worked at Chişinău tractor mfg factory 1963–75; army service 1964–67; various admin. posts in orgs in Chişinău 1975–90; Deputy Chair. Chişinău City Planning Cttee 1990–91; First Sec. Chişinău City CP Cttee 1990–91; Exec. Dir Int. Charity Foundation 1991–93; Minister-Counsellor, Embassy in Moscow 1993–94, Amb. to Uzbekistan, Tajikistan and Kyrgyzstan 1994–97, First Deputy Minister of Foreign Affairs 1997–98, Amb. to Belarus 1998–2001, Minister of Foreign Affairs 2001–04, Amb. to Italy 2004–07. *Address:* c/o Ministry of Foreign Affairs and European Integration, 2012 Chişinău, str. 31 August 80, Moldova.

DUDBRIDGE, Glen, PhD, FBA; British academic; *Emeritus Fellow, University College and Wolfson College, Oxford;* b. 2 July 1938, Clevedon, Somerset, England; s. of George Victor Dudbridge and Edna Kathleen Dudbridge (née Cockle); m. Sylvia Lo Fung-young 1965; one s. one d.; ed Bristol Grammar School, Magdalene Coll. Cambridge and New Asia Inst. of Advanced Chinese Studies, Hong Kong; Research Fellow, Magdalene Coll., Cambridge 1965; Lecturer in Modern Chinese,

Univ. of Oxford 1965–85; Prof. of Chinese, Univ. of Cambridge 1985–89; Shaw Prof. of Chinese, Univ. of Oxford 1989–2005 (retd); Fellow, Wolfson Coll., Oxford 1966–85, Emer. Fellow 1985–; Fellow, Magdalene Coll., Cambridge 1985–89; Fellow, Univ. Coll., Oxford 1989, now Emer. Fellow; Visiting Prof., Yale Univ., USA 1972–73, Univ. of California, Berkeley, USA 1980, 1998, Chinese Univ. of Hong Kong 2007; Hon. mem. Chinese Acad. of Social Sciences 1996. *Publications:* The Hsi-yu chi 1970, The Legend of Miao-shan 1978, The Tale of Li Wa 1983, Religious Experience and Lay Society in T'ang China 1995, Sanguo Dian Lüe Ji Jiao 1998, Lost Books of Medieval China 2000, Books, Tales and Vernacular Culture 2005, A Portrait of Five Dynasties China 2013. *Address:* University College, Oxford, OX1 4BH, England (office). *E-mail:* glen.dudbridge@univ.ox.ac.uk (office). *Website:* www.wolfson.ox.ac.uk/content/1150-prof-glen-dudbridge (office).

DUDERSTADT, James (Jim) Johnson, BEng, MS, PhD; American scientist, academic and fmr university administrator; *President Emeritus and University Professor of Science and Engineering, University of Michigan;* b. 5 Dec. 1942, Madison, Iowa; s. of Mack Henry Duderstadt and Katharine Sydney Johnson Duderstadt; m. Anne Marie Lock 1964; two d.; ed Yale Univ., California Inst. of Tech.; US Atomic Energy Comm. Postdoctoral Fellow, California Inst. of Tech. 1968; Asst Prof. of Nuclear Eng, Univ. of Michigan 1969, Assoc. Prof. 1972, Prof. 1976–81, Dean Coll. of Eng 1981, Provost and Vice-Pres. for Academic Affairs 1986, Pres. 1988–96, Pres. Emer. and Prof. of Science and Eng 1996–; Dir Millennium Project 1996–; mem. US Nat. Science Bd 1985–96 (Chair. 1991–94), Nat. Acad. of Eng Council 1997–2002, Advisory Councils of US Dept of Energy, Dept of Educ., NSF, Nat. Acads, MIT, Caltech, Georgia Tech; Co-Chair. Glion Colloquium; Dir Unisys; numerous hon. degrees and lectureships; Compton Award, American Nuclear Soc. 1985, E.O. Lawrence Award, US Dept of Energy 1986, Reginald Wilson Award, Nat. Medal of Tech., Nat. Acad. of Eng, American Acad. of Arts & Sciences, Duderstadt Center at Univ. of Michigan. *Publications:* Nuclear Reactor Analysis (with L. J. Hamilton) 1976, Transport Theory (with W. R. Martin) 1979, Inertial Confinement Fusion (with G. A. Moses) 1982, Intercollegiate Athletics and the American University 2000, A University for the 21st Century 2000, Higher Education in the Digital Age (co-author) 2003, Beyond the Crossroads: The Future of the Public University in America (co-author) 2003, Engineering Research and America's Future 2005, View from the Helm 2006, Globalization of Higher Education (co-author) 2008, Engineering for a Changing World 2008; numerous tech. publs on nuclear reactor theory, radiation transport, statistical mechanics and kinetic theory, plasma physics and computer simulation. *Address:* Millennium Project, 2001 Duderstadt Center, University of Michigan, 2281 Bonisteel Boulevard, Ann Arbor, MI 48109-2094, USA (office). *Telephone:* (734) 647-7300 (office). *Fax:* (734) 647-6814 (office). *E-mail:* jjd@umich.edu (office). *Website:* milproj.ummu.umich.edu/home/biography.html (office)

DUDLEY, Robert (Bob) Warren, BS, MIM, MBA; American oil company executive; *Group Chief Executive, BP plc;* b. 14 Sept. 1955, Queens, NY; m. Mary Dudley; two c.; ed Hinsdale Cen. High School, Chicago, Univ. of Illinois, Thunderbird School of Global Man., Southern Methodist Univ., Dallas, Tex.; joined Amoco Corpn 1979 (merged with BP 1998), held a variety of eng and commercial posts in USA and UK, worked on negotiation and devt of projects in South China Sea from 1987, later involved in restructuring of oil and gas research and devt activities in USA, based in Moscow working on corp. devt for both upstream and downstream businesses in Russia 1994–97, Gen. Man. for Strategy 1997–98, Gen. Man. for Strategy, BP plc 1999–2000, Exec. Asst to Group CEO 1999–2000, apptd Group Vice-Pres. for BP's renewables and alternative energy activities 2000, later Group Vice-Pres. responsible for BP's upstream businesses in Russia, the Caspian Region, Angola, Algeria and Egypt –2003, Pres. and CEO TNK-BP (jt venture between BP and Alfa, Access/Renova Group) 2003–08, Exec. Vice-Pres. and mem. Bd of Dirs BP plc 2009–, given oversight of co.'s activities in the Americas and Asia, assigned as Pres. and CEO in charge of Gulf Coast Restoration Org. responding to Deepwater Horizon oil spill June–Sept. 2010, mem. BP Exec. Man. Team, Group Chief Exec. 2010–; mem. Bd of Fellows, Thunderbird School of Global Man.; mem. Soc. of Petroleum Engineers; Hon. CBE 2009. *Address:* BP plc, International Headquarters, 1 St James's Square, London, SW1Y 4PD, England (office). *Telephone:* (20) 7496-4000 (office). *Fax:* (20) 7496-4630 (office). *E-mail:* info@bp.com (office). *Website:* www.bp.com (office).

DUDLEY, William C., BA, PhD; American banker, financier and economist; *President and CEO, Federal Reserve Bank of New York;* b. 1952; m. Ann E. Darby; ed New Coll., Sarasota, Fla, Univ. of California, Berkeley; Economist, Fed. Reserve Bd, Washington, DC 1981–83; Vice-Pres. Morgan Guaranty Trust Co. 1983–86; joined Goldman Sachs and Co. 1986, Chief US Economist 1995–2005, Partner and Man. Dir 1996–2006, Advisory Dir 2006; Exec. Vice-Pres. and Head of Markets Group, Fed. Reserve Bank of New York 2007–09, Pres. and CEO 2009–; Chair. Cttee on Payment and Settlement Systems of Cen. Banks of G-10 Countries hosted at BIS; Vice-Chair. and Perm. mem. Fed. Open Market Cttee 2009–; mem. Tech. Consultants Group to Congressional Budget Office 1999–2005. *Address:* Federal Reserve Bank of New York, 33 Liberty Street, New York, NY 10045, USA (office). *Telephone:* (212) 720-5000 (office); (646) 720-5000 (office). *E-mail:* general.info@ny .frb.org (office). *Website:* www.newyorkfed.org (office).

DUEA, Bradford D., BA, MBA, JD; American business executive; *Senior Vice-President, T-Mobile USA, Inc.;* ed Univ. of California, Santa Barbara, Univ. of Southern California, Univ. of San Diego; fmr corp. lawyer with O'Melveny and Myers LLP; Vice-Pres. Corp. Devt, PeopleSupport; Vice-Pres. Business Devt, Roxio, Vice-Pres. World-wide OEM Sales; Vice-Pres. Worldwide Business Devt, Roxio and Napster –2003, Pres. Napster Div., Roxio Inc. –2010; currently Sr Vice-Pres., Value Added Services, T-Mobile USA, Inc.; Ind. Dir, DTS, Inc.; mem. State Bar of California. *Address:* T-Mobile USA, Inc., 12920 Southeast, 38th Street, Bellevue, WA 98006, USA (office). *Telephone:* (425) 378-4000 (office). *Website:* www .t-mobile.com (office).

DUEÑAS, F. Tomás; Costa Rican business executive, politician and diplomatist; *President, Harsco Infrastructure Latin America;* m. Diana Chavarría; ed Univ. of Miami, Columbia Univ., Stanford Univ., Univ. of Pennsylvania; fmr CEO ESCO InterAmerica; fmr Chair. Bd of Dirs and Exec. Cttee Costa Rica Investment and Devt Bank; Procomer; Minister of Econs 2000, of Foreign Trade 2000–02, mem. Econ. Council; mem. Bd of Dirs La Nación newspaper and publishing group; fmr Chair. Bd of Trustees Costa Rican Cen. Bank Museums;

Vice-Chair. WTO Ministerial Meeting, Doha 2001; fmr Chief Negotiating Minister for a Free Trade Agreement of the Americas, as well as various other free trade agreements; Amb. to USA 2004–09; Pres. Harsco Infrastructure Latin America (oversees Harsco Infrastructure group operations in 10 Latin American countries from Mexico to Chile) 2009–; mem. Chair.'s Int. Advisory Council of the America's Soc./Council of the Americas 2010–; fmr Fellow, Aspen Inst. Leadership Program. *Achievements include:* credited with initiating process that led to Cen. American Free Trade Agreement with USA. *Address:* Harsco Infrastructure Mexico SA de CV, Prolongacion Sur 128: 52.55.2614.1410, Col. Jose Maria Pino Suarez, C.P. 01140, México, DF, Mexico (office). *Telephone:* (55) 2614-1410 (office). *Fax:* (55) 5516-0411 (office). *E-mail:* info@harsco-i.us (office). *Website:* www.harsco-i.us (office).

DUERR, Hans-Peter Emil, PhD; German physicist and academic; *Professor Emeritus, Max-Planck-Institut für Physik, University of Munich;* b. 7 Oct. 1929, Stuttgart; s. of Dr Rupert Duerr and Eva Duerr (née Kraepelin); m. Carol Sue Durham 1956; two s. two d.; ed Univs of Stuttgart and California, Berkeley; Research Asst Dept of Physics, Univ. of California, Berkeley 1956–57, Max-Planck Inst. für Physik, Göttingen and Munich 1958–62; Visiting Assoc. Prof., Univ. of California, Berkeley and Inst. of Math. Sciences, Madras, India 1962–63; Visiting Prof., Univ. of California, Berkeley 1968–69; Prof., Univ. of Munich 1969; mem. Directorate Max-Planck Inst. für Physik, Munich, Chair. 1971–72, 1977–80, 1987–92, Vice-Chair. 1981–86, 1993–95, Prof. Emer. 1997–; Man. Dir Max-Planck-Inst. für Physik und Astrophysik 1978–80; mem. Bd Vereinigung Deutscher Wissenschaftler 1980–86, mem. Advisory Bd 1986–91, Chair. Bd 1991–; Chair. Advisory Cttee Wissenschaftszentrum Munich 1984–; mem. Bd Greenpeace Germany 1985–91, Co-Chair. Exec. Cttee 1988–89; Chair. Bd Global Challenges Network 1987–; mem. Pugwash Council 1987–, Club of Rome 1991–; mem. Bd Int. Foundation for the Survival and Devt of Humanity 1988–93, Moscow, Chair. Bd German br., Munich 1988–93; mem. Bd and Scientific Advisory Cttee Internationale Akademie für Zukunftsfragen, Vienna 1990–; Chair. Kuratorium Umweltakademie-Umwelt und Man., Oberpfaffenhofen, 1990–; mem. Kuratorium E.F.-Schumacher-Gesellschaft 1980–, City Energy Cttee, Munich 1983–, Int. Advisory Council Econ. Devt of Hainan, China 1990–93, Council Int. Network of Engineers and Scientists for Global Responsibility, Hamburg 1991–, Ständiges Wissenschaftsforum der Sozialdemokratie, Bonn 1994–, Scientific Advisory Cttee Institut für Zukunftsstudien und Technologiebewertung, Berlin 1995– and other cttees and advisory bds; Pres. Bd of Trustees European Trust for Natural and Cultural Wealth, Prague; mem. Bd Dirs Bulletin of Atomic Scientists, Chicago 1993–, Academia Scientarium et Artium Europaea, Salzburg; Advisory Cttee Int. Judicial Org. for Environment and Devt (IJO) 1991–, Advisory Council Int. Center of Integrative Studies, New York 1993–, Scientific Advisory Bd Potsdam Inst. for Climate Impact Research; Trustee Muhammad Abdus Salam Foundation, London 1994–, Comm. on Globalization 2001; mem. Deutsche Akademie der Naturforscher Leopoldina; Grand Cross, Service Medal (Germany) 2004; Dr hc (Oldenburg) 2002; Award of Merit, Oakland 1956, Right Livelihood Award 1987, Waldemar von Knoeringen Award 1989, Ecology Prize Goldene Schwalbe 1990, Natura Obligat Medal 1991, Elise and Walter Haas Int. Award 1993, Nobel Peace Prize (awarded to Pugwash Conf.) 1995, 'München leuchtet' Gold Medal 1996, Hon. Citizen of Munich 2007, Int. Asscn for Human Values Ethics Award, Brussels 2008. *Publications:* Das Netz des Physikers 1988, De la Science à l'Éthique 1988, Respekt vor der Natur - Verantwortung fuer die Natur 1994, Die Zukunft ist ein unbetretener Pfad 1995, Gott, der Mensch und die Wissenschaft (co-author) 1997, Für eine zivile Gesellschaft 2000, Wir erleben mehr als wir begreifen (co-author) 2001, What is Life? (co-author) 2002, Auch die Wissenschaft spricht nur in Gleichnissen 2004, Potsdam Manifesto & Denkschrift (co-author) 2005, Lebensimpulse – Wege aus der Abhängigkeit (co-author) 2006, Liebe – Urquell des Kosmos (co-author) 2008, Warum es ums Ganze geht 2009, Geist, Kosmos und Physik 2010; more than 300 publs on nuclear physics, elementary particle physics, gravitation, epistemology, peace and disarmament, energy, ecology, econs, politics. *Address:* Max-Planck-Institut für Physik, Foehringer Ring 6, 80805 Munich (office); Grasmeierstrasse 14C, 80805 Munich, Germany (home). *Telephone:* (89) 32354280 (office); (89) 32197844 (home). *Fax:* (89) 3226704 (office); (89) 32197845 (home). *E-mail:* hpd@mppmu.mpg.de (office). *Website:* www.mppmu.mpg.de (office); www.gcn.de (office).

DUESBERG, Peter H., PhD; American (b. German) molecular biologist and academic; *Professor of Molecular and Cell Biology, University of California, Berkeley;* b. 2 Dec. 1936, Münster, Germany; s. of Richard Duesberg and Hilde Saettele; m. Sigrid Duesberg; one s. three d.; ed Univ. of Würzburg, Univ. of Basel, Switzerland, Univ. of Munich, Univ. of Frankfurt; Postdoctoral Fellow, Dept of Molecular Biology and Virus Lab., Max Planck Inst. for Virus Research, Tübingen, Germany 1963; Postdoctoral Fellow and Asst Research Virologist, Univ. of California, Berkeley 1964–68, Asst Prof. in Residence 1968–70, Asst Prof. 1970–71, Assoc. Prof. 1971–73, Prof. 1973–; Prof. of Molecular and Cell Biology 1989–; Fisher Distinguished Prof., Univ. of North Texas, Denton 1992; Guest Prof., Univ. of Heidelberg at the Medical School, Mannheim 1997, Aug.–Dec. 1998, July–Dec. 2000; mem. NAS 1986; mem. Int. Panel of Scientists invited by Pres. Thabo Mbeki and South African Govt to discuss the AIDS crisis, Pretoria 6–7 May 2000, Johannesburg 3–4 July 2000; Fogarty Scholar-in-Residence, NIH, Bethesda, Md 1986–87, Lichtfield Lecturer, Univ. of Oxford, UK 1988, C. J. Watson Lecturer, Abbott Northwestern Hosp., Minneapolis, Minn. 1990, Shaffer Alumni Lecturer, Tulane Univ., New Orleans, La 1992, Constance Ledward Rollins Lecturer, Univ. of New Hampshire, Durham, Distinguished Speaker, Dept of Biology, Univ. of Louisville, Ky; Merck Award 1969, Calif. Scientist of the Year Award 1971, First Annual American Medical Center Oncology Award 1981, NIH Outstanding Investigator Grant 1985–92, Wissenschaftspreis, Hanover, Germany 1988. *Achievements:* isolated the first cancer gene through work on retroviruses in 1970, and mapped the genetic structure of these viruses; came to public attention with claim that HIV is not the cause of AIDS 1987; based on experience with retroviruses, challenged virus-AIDS hypothesis in numerous medical and scientific journals and instead proposed hypothesis that various AIDS diseases are brought on by long-term consumption of recreational drugs and anti-HIV drugs; developed theory that cancers originate from normal cells with individual karyotypes, much like new species. *Publications:* AIDS: The Good News Is... (with John Yiamouyiannis) 1995, Infectious AIDS: Have We Been Misled?

(collection of 13 articles published in scientific journals 1987–96) 1995, AIDS: Virus or Drug Induced? (collection of 27 articles by scientists, independent scholars and investigative journalists from Australia, Europe and USA) 1996, Inventing the AIDS Virus 1996; numerous scientific papers in professional journals on genetic structure of retroviruses and aneuploidy of cancers. *Address:* Department of Molecular and Cell Biology, 353 Donner Lab #3206, University of California at Berkeley, 16 Barker Hall, Berkeley CA 94720-3206, USA (office). *Telephone:* (510) 642-6549 (office). *Fax:* (510) 643-6455 (office). *E-mail:* duesberg@berkeley.edu (office). *Website:* mcb.berkeley.edu/labs/duesberg (office); mcb.berkeley.edu/faculty/BMB/duesbergp.html (office); www.duesberg.com (office).

DUFF, Michael James, BSc, PhD, DIC, FRS, FInstP, FRSA; British physicist and academic; *Abdus Salam Professor of Theoretical Physics, Imperial College London;* b. 28 Jan. 1949, Manchester, England; s. of Edward Duff and Elizabeth Duff (née Kaylor); m. Lesley Yearling 1984; one s. one d.; ed De La Salle Coll., Salford, Queen Mary Coll. and Imperial Coll., London; Post-doctoral fellowships in Theoretical Physics, Int. Centre for Theoretical Physics, Trieste, Italy, Univ. of Oxford, King's Coll. and Queen Mary Coll., London Univ., Brandeis Univ., USA 1972–79; Faculty mem. Imperial Coll. London 1979–88, Prin. of Physical Sciences 2005–06, Abdus Salam Prof. of Theoretical Physics 2006–; Sr Physicist, CERN, Geneva 1984–87; Prof. of Physics, Texas A&M Univ., USA 1988–92, Distinguished Prof. of Physics 1992–99; Oskar Klein Prof. of Physics, Univ. of Michigan 1999–2005, Dir Michigan Center for Theoretical Physics 2000–05; Fellow, American Physical Soc.; Meeting Gold Medal, El Colegio Nacional, Mexico City 2004. *Publications:* Observations on Conformal Anomalies 1977, Kaluza-Klein Supergravity 1986, Strings Solitons 1994, The World in Eleven Dimensions 1999; numerous articles on unified theories of the elementary particles. *Leisure interests:* soccer, watercolours, golf. *Address:* Blackett Laboratory, Imperial College London, Prince Consort Road, London, SW7 2AZ (office); Yew Tree House, Church Lane, Milton, Oxon., OX14 4BL, England (home). *Telephone:* (20) 7594-8571 (office); (1235) 833511 (home). *Fax:* (20) 7594-7844 (office). *E-mail:* m.duff@imperial.ac.uk (office). *Website:* www3.imperial.ac.uk/people/m.duff (office).

DUFFEY, Joseph Daniel, PhD; American academic administrator and fmr government official; *Senior Vice-President, Laureate Education Inc.;* b. 1 July 1932, Huntington, W Va; s. of Joseph I. Duffey and Ruth Wilson Duffey; m. Anne Wexler 1974 (died 2009); four s.; ed Marshall Univ., Andover Newton Theological School, Yale Univ. and Hartford Seminary Foundation; Assoc. Prof. and Acting Dean, Hartford Seminary Foundation 1960–70; Adjunct Prof. and Fellow, Calhoun Coll. 1970–74; Gen. Sec. and Spokesman, American Assen of Univ. Profs, Washington, DC 1974–76; Asst Sec. of State, US State Dept 1977; Chair. Nat. Endowment for the Humanities 1977–82; US del. to UNESCO 1978–80; Chancellor Univ. of Mass. at Amherst 1982–91, also Pres. Univ. of Mass. System 1990–91; Pres. American Univ., Washington, DC 1991–93; Head of US Information Agency 1993–98; Sr Exec. Chair. Int. Univ. Project, Sylvan Learning Systems (now Laureate Education Inc.), Washington, DC 1999, now Sr Vice-Pres.; Public Policy Scholar, Woodrow Wilson Int. Center for Scholars 2003–04; mem. Bd of Visitors, Univ. of Maryland Univ. Coll.; mem. Council on Foreign Relations 1979–; Order of Leopold II (Belgium) 1979; 15 hon. degrees; Tree of Life Award, American Jewish Congress 1984. *Publications:* Lewis Mumford's Quest 1979, US Global Competitiveness 1988, Looking Back and Looking Forward: The US and the World Economy 1989. *Address:* Laureate Education Inc., 2801 New Mexico Avenue, NW, Washington, DC 20007, USA. *Telephone:* (202) 965-1044 (office). *Fax:* (202) 965-1098 (office). *E-mail:* www.jduffey@earthlink.net (office). *Website:* www.laureate-inc.com (office).

DUFFIELD, Dame Vivien Louise, DBE, CBE, MA; British philanthropist; *Campaign Chair, University of Oxford;* b. 26 March 1946; d. of Sir Charles Clore and Francine Halphen; m. John Duffield 1969 (divorced 1976); one s. one d.; ed Cours Victor Hugo, Paris, Lycée Français de Londres, Heathfield School, Lady Margaret Hall, Oxford; Dir Royal Opera House Trust 1985–2001, Royal Opera House 1990–2001; Vice-Chair. Great Ormond Street Hosp. Wishing Well Appeal 1987, Royal Marsden Hosp. Cancer Appeal 1990; currently Campaign Chair., Univ. of Oxford; mem. NSPCC Centenary Appeal Cttee 1983, Financial Devt Cttee 1985; mem. Royal Ballet Bd 1990–, Gov. Royal Ballet 2002–; Chair. Clore Duffield Foundation (after merger with Clore Foundation); Trustee, Dulwich Collection Picture Gallery 1993–2002; Gov. South Bank Bd 2002–; Hon. Mem. Royal Coll. of Music 1987, Hon. FRAM 2003; Hon. DLitt (Buckingham) 1990, Hon. DPhil (Weizmann Inst.) 1985, (Hebrew Univ.) 1998; Beacon Fellowship Prize 2006, Medal for Arts Philanthropy 2008. *Leisure interests:* skiing, opera, ballet, shooting. *Address:* c/o Clore Duffield Foundation, Studio 3, Chelsea Manor Studios, Flood Street, London, SW3 5SR, England. *Telephone:* (20) 7351-6061. *Fax:* (20) 7351-5308. *Website:* www.cloreduffield.org.uk.

DUFFUOR, Kwabena, BSc, MBA, MA, PhD; Ghanaian banking executive and politician; *Minister of Finance and Economic Planning;* ed Univ. of Ghana, Syracuse Univ., USA; with Ghana Commercial Bank 1969–1995, positions included Special Asst to Man. Dir, Chief Economist and Head of Research Dept; Deputy Gov. Bank of Ghana 1995–97, Gov. 1997–2001; Lecturer in Econs, Finance and Banking, Univ. Ghana 1982–91, mem. Advisory Bd Inst. of Social Statistical and Econ. Research; Minister of Finance and Econ. Planning 2009–; fmr Chair. Bd of Dirs UniBank Ghana Ltd; mem. Bd of Dirs Accra Brewery Ltd 1983–94, State Gold Mining Corpn 1984–91, Shell Ghana Ltd 1986–91, Ecobank, Cote d'Ivoire 1989–95, Ashanti Goldfields Co. Ltd 2000–01; mem. Econs Soc.; Fellow, Chartered Inst. of Bankers, Ghana. *Address:* Ministry of Finance and Economic Planning, POB M40, Accra, Ghana (office). *Telephone:* (21) 686100 (office). *Fax:* (21) 666205 (office). *E-mail:* promofep@mofep.gov.gh (office). *Website:* www.mofep.gov.gh (office).

DUFFY, British singer and songwriter; b. (Amy Ann Duffy), 1984, Nefyn, Wales; d. of John Duffy and Joyce Duffy (née Williams); solo artist 2007–; MOJO Award for Song of the Year (for Mercy) 2008, Q Award for Best Breakthrough Act 2008, BRIT Awards for Best British Breakthrough Act, for Best British Female Solo Artist 2009, Ivor Novello/PRS Award for Most Performed Work (for Mercy) 2009. *Recordings include:* album: Rockferry (Grammy Award for Best Pop Vocal Album 2009, BRIT Award for Best British Album 2009) 2008, Endlessly 2010. *Address:* c/o Rough Trade Records, 66 Golborne Road, London, W10 5PS, England. *Website:* www.roughtraderecords.com; www.iamduffy.com.

DUFFY, Carol Ann, CBE, BA, FRSL; British poet and dramatist; *Poet Laureate;* b. 23 Dec. 1955, Glasgow, Scotland; d. of Frank Duffy and May Black; one d.; ed St Joseph's Convent, Stafford and Univ. of Liverpool; Poetry Ed. Ambit 1983–; Lecturer in Creative Writing, then Prof. of Contemporary Poetry, Manchester Metropolitan Univ. 1996–; Poet Laureate 2009–; mem. Poetry Soc. (Vice-Pres.); C. Day-Lewis Fellowships 1982–84, Eric Gregory Award 1985, Cholmondeley Award 1992, Lannan Award (USA) 1995, Signal Poetry Award 1997, PEN Pinter Prize 2012. *Plays:* Take My Husband 1984, Cavern Dreams 1986, Grimm Tales 1994, More Grimm Tales 1997. *Publications include:* poetry: Fleshweathercock 1973, Standing Female Nude (Scottish Arts Council Award) 1985, Selling Manhattan (Scottish Arts Council Award, Somerset Maugham Award 1988) 1987, Home and Away 1988, The Other Country (Dylan Thomas Award) 1990, Mean Time (Whitbread Poetry Award, Forward Poetry Prize, Scottish Arts Council Book Award) 1993, Selected Poems 1994, The Pamphlet 1998, The World's Wife 1999, Time's Tidings 1999, Feminine Gospels 2001, Underwater Farmyard 2002, Out of Fashion (ed.) 2004, Rapture (T. S. Eliot Prize 2006) 2005, Another Night Before Christmas 2005, Selected Poems 2006, The Lost Happy Endings (with Jane Ray) 2006, The Hat (for children) 2007, Answering Back (ed.) 2008, New and Collected Poems for Children 2009, Another Night Before Christmas 2010, The Bees (Costa Book Award for Poetry 2011) 2011. *Leisure interest:* holidays. *Address:* Rogers, Coleridge and White, 20 Powis Mews, London W11 1JN, England (office); c/o Pan Macmillan Ltd, 20 New Wharf Road, London, N1 9RR, England (office). *Telephone:* (20) 7221-3717 (office). *Fax:* (20) 7229-9084 (office). *E-mail:* info@rcwlitagency.com (office). *Website:* www.rcwlitagency.co.uk (office).

DUFFY, Francis (Frank) Cuthbert, CBE, PhD, MArch, AADipl (Hons); British architect; *Senior Consultant with title of Founder, DEGW plc;* b. 3 Sept. 1940, Berwick-upon-Tweed; s. of the late John Austin Duffy and Annie Margaret Duffy (née Reed); m. Jessica Duffy; three d.; ed Architectural Assen School, London, Univ. of California, Berkeley and Princeton Univ., USA; Asst Architect, Nat. Bldg Agency 1964–67; consultant to JFN Assocs, New York 1968–70, est. JFN Assocs in London 1971–74; co-f. DEGW plc 1974, Partner 1974–89, Chair. 1989–99, Sr Consultant with title of Founder 1999–; Harkness Fellow 1967–71; Visiting Prof., MIT 2001–04, Univ. Coll. London, Univ. of Reading, Lancaster Univ.; Pres. RIBA 1993–95, Architects' Council of Europe 1994; est. DEGW's combination of major interior design and architectural work (e.g. Boots the Chemists, Nottingham, Apicorp, Saudi Arabia) and strategic workplace consultancy to int. corp. clients (e.g. BBC, BP, Google, GSK, Microsoft) as well as govt clients (e.g. UN, GSA, UK Treasury, Ministry of Defence, Home Office) and cultural insts (e.g. British Museum, Design Museum, Somerset House Trust, South Bank Centre); f. The Edge 1995; mem. Advisory Cttee on Restoration of Windsor Castle; Chair. Stratford City Design Review Panel, including Olympic Village, coordinated with the Design Review of Olympic venues and park, London 2010–11; Pres.'s Award for Lifetime Achievement from British Council of Offices 2004. *Publications:* Office Landscaping 1965, Planning Office Space 1966, The ORBIT Studies 1981–85, The Changing Workplace 1982, The Changing City 1989, RIBA Strategic Study 1992–95, The New Office 1997, Design for Change 1998, New Environments for Working 1998, Architectural Knowledge 1998, Work and the City 2008; numerous articles and papers in professional journals. *Leisure interests:* reading, writing, talking, drawing. *Address:* DEGW plc, MidCity Place, 71 High Holborn, London, WC1V 6QS (office); Threeways, The Street, Walberswick, nr Southwold, Suffolk, IP18 6UE, England (home). *Telephone:* (20) 7239-7777 (office); (1502) 723814 (home). *Fax:* (20) 7278-3613 (office). *E-mail:* fduffy@degw.com (office). *Website:* www.degw.com (office).

DUFFY, Maureen Patricia, (D. M. Cayer), BA, FRSL, FKC; British writer, poet and copyright consultant; b. 21 Oct. 1933, Worthing, Sussex, England; d. of Grace Rose Wright; ed Trowbridge High School for Girls, Sarah Bonnell High School for Girls, King's Coll., London; staged pop art exhbn with Brigid Brophy 1969; Chair. Greater London Arts Literature Panel 1979–81, Authors Lending and Copyright Soc. 1982–94, Copyright Licensing Agency 1996–99 (Vice-Chair. 1994–96); Pres. Writers' Guild of GB 1985–88 (Jt Chair. 1977–78); Co-founder Writers' Action Group 1972–79; Vice-Pres. European Writers Congress 1992–2003 (Pres. 2003–05), Beauty without Cruelty 1975–, British Copyright Council 1998–2003 (Vice-Chair. 1981–86, Chair. 1989–98, Hon. Pres. 2003); Fellow, King's Coll., London 2002, Royal Soc. of Literature 1985 (Vice-Pres. 2013–); Hon. Pres. Authors Lending and Copyright Soc. 2002, British Copyright Council; Hon. DLitt (Loughborough), (Kent); CISAC Gold Medal for Literature 2002, Benson Medal RSL 2004. *Plays:* Pearson (London Playwrights' Award), Rites (Nat. Theatre) 1969, A Nightingale in Bloomsbury Square (Hampstead Theatre) 1974, The Masque of Henry Purcell (Southwark Theatre) 1995, Sappho Singing 2009. *Radio:* The Passionate Shepherdess, Only Goodnight. *Television:* Upstairs Downstairs (Episode 11), Josie, Sanctuary. *Publications:* That's How It Was 1962, The Single Eye 1964, The Microcosm 1966, The Paradox Players 1967, Lyrics for the Dog Hour (poems) 1968, Wounds 1969, Love Child 1971, The Venus Touch 1971, The Erotic World of Faery 1972, I Want to Go to Moscow 1973, Capital 1975, Evesong (poems) 1975, The Passionate Shepherdess 1977, Housespy 1978, Memorials of the Quick and the Dead (poems) 1979, Inherit the Earth 1980, Gorsaga 1981, Londoners: An Elegy 1983, Men and Beasts 1984, Collected Poems 1949–84 1985, Change 1987, A Thousand Capricious Chances: Methuen 1889–1989 1989, Illuminations 1991, Occam's Razor 1992, Henry Purcell (biog.) 1994, Restitution 1998, England: The Making of a Myth from Stonehenge to Albert Square 2001, Alchemy 2004, Family Values 2008, The Orpheus Trail 2009, Environmental Studies 2013, In Times Like These 2013. *Address:* c/o Jonathan Clowes Ltd, 10 Ironbridge House, Bridge Approach, London, NW1 8BD, England (office); 18 Fabian Road, London, SW6 7TZ, England (office). *Telephone:* (20) 7722-7674 (office); (20) 7385-3598 (office). *Fax:* (871) 528-3647 (office); (20) 7385-2468 (office). *E-mail:* ann.evans@jonathanclowes.co.uk (office); 113714.1610@compuserve.com (office). *Website:* www.jonathanclowes.co.uk (office); www.maureenduffy.co.uk.

DUFFY, Terrence A.; American business executive; *Executive Chairman, CME Group Inc. (Chicago Mercantile Exchange);* ed Univ. of Wisconsin-Whitewater; Pres. TDA Trading, Inc. 1981–; mem. Chicago Mercantile Exchange Inc. (CME) 1981–, mem. Bd of Dirs CME 1995–, Vice-Chair. CME 1998–2002, served on exec., compensation, nominating, strategic planning and regulatory oversight cttees, Chair. 2002–06, Vice-Chair. Chicago Mercantile Exchange Holdings Inc. (CME Holdings) 2001–, Chair. 2002–06, Exec. Chair. CME Group Inc. (following merger with Chicago Bd of Trade) 2006–; mem. Nat. Saver Summit on Retirement Savings 2002–, Fed. Retirement Thrift Investment Bd 2003–; mem. Bd of Dirs World Business Chicago, Ill. Agricultural Leadership Foundation; mem. Bd of Regents, Mercy Home for Boys and Girls; Co-Chair. Mayo Clinic Greater Chicago Leadership Council; mem. Econ. Club of Chicago, Execs' Club of Chicago, Pres.'s Circle of Chicago Council on Global Affairs; Trustee Saint Xavier Univ.; recognized by Irish America Magazine as one of Top 100 Irish Business Leaders 2003, 2004, 2005. *Address:* CME, 20 South Wacker Drive, Chicago, IL 60606, USA (office). *Telephone:* (312) 930-1000 (office). *E-mail:* info@cme.com (office). *Website:* www .cme.com (office).

DUFLO, Esther, MA, PhD; French economist and academic; *Abdul Latif Jameel Professor of Poverty Alleviation and Development Economics and Director, Abdul Latif Jameel Poverty Action Lab, Massachusetts Institute of Technology;* b. 25 Oct. 1972; ed Ecole Normale Supérieure, Ecole Polytechnique and ENSAE, Paris, Massachusetts Inst. of Tech., USA; Asst Prof. of Econs, MIT 1999–2001, Castle Krob Career Devt Asst Prof. of Econs, on leave at Princeton Univ. 2001–02, Castle Krob Career Devt Asst Prof. of Econs, MIT 2002–04, Prof. of Econs and Dir Poverty Action Lab. 2004–05, Abdul Latif Jameel Prof. of Poverty Alleviation and Devt Econs and Dir Abdul Latif Jameel Poverty Action Lab 2005–, on leave at the Paris School of Econs Jan.–June 2007; Dir Devt Program, Center for Econ. Policy Research; Research Assoc., Nat. Bureau of Econ. Research; mem. Bd Bureau for Research and Econ. Analysis of Devt; Assoc. Ed. Journal of the European Economic Association 2002–06, Review of Economics and Statistics 2002–06, Journal of Economic Perspectives 2004–07; Co-Ed. Journal of Development Economics 2004–06, Review of Economics and Statistics 2005–07; Founding Ed. The American Economic Journal: Applied Economics 2007–; mem. Bd of Eds Annual Review of Economics 2007–; mem. Program Cttee European Econ. Asscn Annual Meeting 2003, Econometric Soc. Annual Meeting 2004, Econometric Soc. Ninth World Congress 2004, European Econ. Asscn Meetings 2007, American Econ. Asscn Meetings 2007; Review of Econ. Studies Tour 1999; mem. John D. and Catherine MacArthur Network on the Costs of Inequality 2001–06; Fellow, American Acad. of Arts and Sciences 2009; Alfred P. Sloan Doctoral Dissertation Fellowship 1998, John M. Olin Faculty Fellowship, Nat. Asscn of Scholars 2001–02, Alfred P. Sloan Research Fellowship 2002, Elaine Bennett Prize for Research 2003, Best Young French Economist Prize, Le Monde, Cercle des économistes 2005, CNRS Bronze Medal 2005, Best Advisor, Grad. Econs Asscn, MIT 2007–09, Inaugural holder of the chair 'Knowledge Against Poverty', Collège de France, Paris 2008, Prix Luc Durand-Reville, Acad. des Sciences Morale et Politiques (France) 2008, BBVA Foundation Frontiers of Knowledge Award for Devt Cooperation 2009, First recipient, Calvó Armengol Int. Prize, Barcelona Grad. School of Econs 2009, MacArthur Fellowship 2009, John Bates Clark Medal 2010. *Publications:* Expérience, science et lutte contre la pauvreté 2009; book chapters, reviews and numerous papers in professional journals. *Address:* Room 252G, Building E52, Department of Economics, Massachusetts Institute of Technology, 50 Memorial Drive, Cambridge, MA 02142-1347, USA (office). *Telephone:* (617) 258-7013 (office). *E-mail:* eduflo@mit.edu (office). *Website:* economics.mit.edu/faculty/eduflo (office).

DUFOIX, Georgina, DèsSc Econ; French politician; b. (Georgina Nègre), 16 Feb. 1943, Paris; d. of Alain Nègre and Antoinette Pallier; m. Antoine Dufoix 1963; two s. two d.; ed Lycée de Nîmes and Univs of Montpellier and Paris-Sorbonne; mem. Man. Cttee Parti Socialiste 1979; Sec. of State for Family Affairs 1981–83, for Family Affairs, Population and Immigrant Workers 1983–84; Govt Spokeswoman and Minister for Social Affairs and Nat. Solidarity 1984–86; Conseiller-gén. for Gard 1982, Socialist Deputy 1986–88; Sec. of State for Family Affairs, for Women's Rights and for Repatriates May–June 1988; Chargée de mission auprès du Président 1988–92; Pres. Admin. Council, French Red Cross 1989–92; Del. Fight against Drugs 1989–93; mem. Governing Bd UN Research Inst. for Social Devt, Geneva 1990–2000, Communications Co. Vera, Governing Bd War-torn Soc. Project, Geneva 1998–2008, Governing Bd InterPeace International, Geneva; Woman of the Year (France) 1989. *Leisure interest:* her vineyard. *Address:* Domaine de Montroche, Route de Saint Gilles, 30900 Nîmes, France (home). *Telephone:* (4) 66-29-80-00 (office). *E-mail:* gdufoix@free.fr (home).

DUFOUR, Bernard, MSc; French fmr aviation official; b. 14 Feb. 1933; s. of Jean Dufour and Denise Dufour (née Penot); m. Bernadette de Villepin 1956; five c.; ed Ecole Ozanam, Limoges, Lycée Janson de Sailly, Paris, Ecole Ste Geneviève, Ecole Polytechnique, Calif. Inst. of Tech., USA; engineer, Sud Aviation 1956–61, Dir helicopter production 1961–64, St Nazaire 1964–65, Toulouse 1965–76, Usine Belfort Alsthom 1977–89, GEC Alsthom (Electromechanical Div.) 1989–94; Dir Gen. ALSTOM Electromécanique 1989–94; Pres. and CEO SNECMA 1994–96; Phare (EU pre-accession programme) expert in Romania 1997–98; Chevalier, Ordre nat. du Mérite, Légion d'honneur; Tudor Vladiminescu (Romania); Médaille Aéronautique. *Leisure interests:* cycling, riding, sailing, skiing. *Address:* 4 rue Henri Heine, 75016 Paris, France (home). *Telephone:* 1-45-25-22-78 (home). *Fax:* 1-45-25-22-78 (home). *E-mail:* dufourbern@wanadoo.fr (home).

DUFOUR, Jean-Marie, BSc, MSc, MA, PhD, FRSC; Canadian economist and academic; *Professor of Economics, University of Montreal;* ed McGill Univ., Univ. of Montreal, Concordia Univ., Univ. of Chicago; Lecturer in Statistics, Univ. of Québec at Trois-Rivières 1972–73; Prof. of Math., Collège Édouard-Montpetit, Longueuil, Montréal 1973–75; Research Assoc., Inst. of Applied Econ. Research, Concordia Univ. 1978–79; Lecturer in Econs (full-time), Dept of Econ. Sciences, Univ. of Montreal 1978–79, Asst Prof. of Econs 1979–83, Assoc. Prof. of Econs 1983–88, Prof. of Econs 1988–, Chair. Dept of Econ. Sciences 1995–97, Holder of Canada Research Chair in Econometrics, Research Fellow, CIREQ (Centre interuniversitaire de recherche en economie quantitative, mem. research staff, Centre for Research in Econ. Devt 1979–85, Sr mem. research staff ('Chercheur régulier') and Dir research programme in econometrics and macroeconomics 1985–90, Dir Centre 1988–95, 1997–99; Lecturer in Econometrics, Univ. of Sherbrooke 1979, 1981; Lecturer in Quantitative Methods (Time Series), École des Hautes Études Commerciales, Montréal 1980, 1981; Fellow, CIRANO (Centre for Interuniversity Research and Analysis on Orgs, Montreal); Dir Canadian Econometrics Study Group; Project Leader Math. and Statistical Methods for Financial Modelling and Risk Man., MITACS (Math. of Information Tech. and Complex Systems) (Canadian network of centres of excellence); Consultant in Econs, Econ.

Council of Canada 1981, Office de Planification et de Développement économique du Québec 1982, Royal Comm. on the Econ. Union and Devt Prospects for Canada (McDonald Comm.), Ottawa 1983–84; Research Fellow, CORE (Centre for Operations Research and Econometrics), Université Catholique de Louvain, Belgium 1985–86; Invited Prof. of Econs, Université de Toulouse I, France 1983; Visiting Prof. of Econs, Univ. of Pennsylvania 1992, Stanford Univ. 1999, Univ. of Toronto 2000; Visiting Prof. of Econometrics, Univ. of Lausanne, Switzerland 1995, Institut d'Économie Industrielle, Université des sciences sociales de Toulouse, France 2002, École Nationale de la Statistique et de l'Admin Économique, Paris, France 2004; Visiting Prof. of Econometrics and Statistics, Institut Supérieur de Gestion, Université de Tunis III, Tunisia 1998; Visiting Scholar, Center for Computational Research in Econs and Man. Science, MIT 1980, Queen's Univ. 1986, CEPREMAP, Paris 1986, Université Libre de Bruxelles (Institut de statistique), Belgium 1988, 1989, 1990, 1993, Institut d'Économie Industrielle, Université des Sciences Sociales de Toulouse, France 1992, 1994, Institut für Statistik und Ökonometrie, Humboldt-Universität zu Berlin, Germany 1994, Institut Nat. de Statistique et d'Économie Appliquée, Rabat, Morocco 1997, École Nationale de la Statistique et de l'Admin Économique, Centre de Recherche en Économie et Statistique, Paris 1990, 1991, 1993, 1995, 1997, 2000, 2001, Centre for Econ. Research, Kaltholieke Universiteit Tilburg, Netherlands 2000, Faculty of Econs, Technische Universität Dresden, Germany 2000, Tinbergen Inst. and Dept of Actuarial Science and Econometrics, Universiteit van Amsterdam, Netherlands 1996, 1997, 1999, 2001, 2003, 2004, Deutsche Bundesbank, Frankfurt, Germany 2001, 2004, Institut für Wirtschaftsforschung, Halle, Germany 2005, 2006, 2007; mem. Bd Dirs Soc. canadienne de science économique 1984–87, Pres.-Elect 1998–99, Pres. 1999–2000; Vice-Pres. Canadian Econs Asscn 2000–01, Pres.-Elect 2001–02, Pres. 2002–03; mem. Int. Statistical Inst. 1990–; Assoc. Ed. Canadian Journal of Economics 1984–88, Cahiers du Centre d'Études de Recherche Opérationnelle 1989–, Econometric Theory 1991–93, Annales d'Économie et de Statistique 1990–, Econometric Reviews 1991–96, 1998–2003, Journal of Econometrics 1994–, Econometrica 1996–2002; Guest Ed. Empirical Economics 1993–94; mem. Editorial Bd Empirical Economics 1994–2003; Fellow, Centre for Operations Research and Econometrics, Université Catholique de Louvain, Belgium 1985–86; Benjamin Meaker Visiting Prof. of Econs, Univ. of Bristol, UK 1993, 1999; Killam Research Fellow, Canada Council for the Arts 1998–2000; Netherlands Org. for Scientific Research (Nederlandse Organisatie voor Wetenschappelijk Onderzoek, NWO) Visitor's Fellowship 2003–04; mem. American Econ. Asscn, Canadian Econs Asscn, Inst. of Math. Statistics, Int. Statistical Inst., Soc. Canadienne de Science Économique, Statistical Soc. of Canada; Fellow, Journal of Econometrics 1996–, Econometric Soc. 1998–, American Statistical Asscn 2005–; Officier, Ordre nat. du Québec 2006; Govt of Québec Doctoral Fellowship 1975–78, Canada Council Doctoral Fellowship 1975–78, Leave Fellowship from Social Sciences and Humanities Research Council of Canada 1985–86, Prize for Excellence in Research, Soc. Canadienne de Science Économique 1988, John Rae Prize for Outstanding Research, Canadian Econs Asscn 1994, Marcel Dagenais Prize for Excellence in Research, Soc. Canadienne de Science Économique 2000, Marcel-Vincent Prize pour les sciences sociales, Asscn francophone pour le savoir 2005, Konrad Adenauer Research Award, Alexander von Humboldt Foundation (Germany) 2005, Radio-Canada Personality of the week, La Presse/Radio-Canada 2006, Killam Prize for Social Sciences, Killam Trust and Canada Council for the Arts 2006, Guggenheim Fellow 2006–07. *Publications:* L'aide publique au financement des exportations (co-author) 1983, Government Assistance to Export Financing (English trans. of previous title) 1983, New Developments in Time Series Econometrics (co-ed.) 1993, Recent Developments in the Econometrics of Structural Change (co-ed.) 1996, Resampling Methods in Econometrics (co-ed.) 2006, Heavy Tails and Stable Paretian Distributions in Econometrics (co-ed.) 2007; more than 110 articles in professional journals on econometrics and statistics, macroeconomics, finance and public finance. *Address:* Université de Montréal, Département de sciences économiques 3150, rue Jean-Brillant, Room C-6030, bureau G6088 CP 6128, succursale Centre-ville, Montréal, PQ H3C 3J7 (office); 1060 Bernard Ouest, Apt. 5, Outremont, Montréal, PQ H2V 1V2, Canada (home). *Telephone:* (514) 343-2400 (office); (514) 273-0497 (home). *Fax:* (514) 343-5831 (office). *E-mail:* jean.marie.dufour@ umontreal.ca (office). *Website:* www.fas.umontreal.ca/SCECO/Dufour (office).

DUGAS, Richard J., Jr., BSc; American construction industry executive; *Chairman, President and CEO, Pulte Homes Inc.;* ed Louisiana State Univ.; held marketing and customer service postions with Exxon Co. 1986–89; worked in process improvement and plant operational efficiency, PepsiCo 1990–94; joined Pulte Homes Inc., Bloomfield Hills, Mich. 1994, has held numerous exec. positions including Vice-Pres. Process Improvement, City Pres. and Market Man., Atlanta Div., Coastal Region Pres., Exec. Vice-Pres. and COO 2002–03, Pres. and CEO 2003–, Chair. 2009–. *Address:* Pulte Homes Inc., 100 Bloomfield Hills Parkway, Suite 300, Bloomfield Hills, MI 48304, USA (office). *Telephone:* (248) 647-2750 (office). *Fax:* (248) 433-4598 (office). *Website:* www.pulte.com (office).

DUGGAL, Vinod Kumar; Indian civil servant; *Governor of Manipur;* b. 26 Nov. 1944; ed Nat. Defence Acad.; joined Indian Admin. Service 1968, served in various capacities including Municipal Commr of Delhi 1996–2000, Special Sec., Ministry of Environment and Forests, Sec., Water Resources Ministry, Home Sec. 2005–07; mem. numerous Comms and Cttees with rank of Minister of State, including mem., Nat. Disaster Man. Authority; Gov. of Manipur 2013–. *Address:* Office of the Chief Minister, Government of Manipur, Chief Minister's Secretariat, Imphal 795 001, India (office). *Telephone:* (385) 2220137 (office). *Fax:* (385) 2221398 (office). *E-mail:* cmmani@hub.nic.in (office). *Website:* manipur.gov.in (office).

DUGGER, John Scott; American artist and designer; b. 18 July 1948, Los Angeles, Calif.; s. of Dr James Attwood Dugger and Julian Marie Riddle; ed Loy Norrix High School, Kalamazoo, Mich., Gilmore Inst. of Art, Mich., School of the Art Inst. of Chicago; created Perennial (first Ergonic Sculpture), Paris 1970; Leader, Soc. for Anglo-Chinese understanding Del. to China 1972; Founder-Dir Banner Arts, London 1976; mem. Exec. Cttee Art Services Grants Ltd (Artists' Housing Charity) 1980–85; Chair. Asscn of Space Artists, London 1984, 1985; Vice-Chair. Int. Artists Asscn, UK Cttee 1986–87; major works include Documenta 5, People's ParticipatioStn Pavilion, Kassel, FRG 1972, Monumental Strip-Banner Installation, Trafalgar Square, London 1974, Sports Banner Exhbn, Inst. of Contemporary Arts, London 1980; Original Art Banners commissioned for HM the

Queen's 60th Birthday, Buckingham Palace 1986, Tibet Mountainscape Banner for His Holiness the XIV Dalai Lama—International Year of Tibet 1991; Int. Certified Master Fabric Craftsman, IFAI (Industrial Fabric Asscn) 1992; works on display at Arts Council of GB, Tate Gallery, London; Major Award, Arts Council of GB 1978, Calouste Gulbenkian Foundation Awards 1979, 1980, Int. Achievement Award 1993. *Leisure interests:* oriental art, mountaineering, martial arts. *Address:* c/o Steven Wolf Fine Arts, 49 Geary Street, Suite 411, San Francisco, CA 94108, USA.

DUHALDE MALDONADO, Eduardo Alberto; Argentine lawyer, politician and fmr head of state; b. 5 Oct. 1941, Lomas de Zamora, Prov. of Buenos Aires; s. of Tomás Duhalde and María Esther Maldonado; m. Hilda Beatriz González 1971; one s. four d.; ed Univ. of Buenos Aires; fmr mem. staff, Legal Dept, Lomas de Zamora Town Council; Pres. Exec. Cttee Partido Justicialista of Lomas de Zamora 1973; Mayor Lomas de Zamora 1974–76, removed from post following mil. coup, re-elected 1983; elected Nat. Deputy for Prov. of Buenos Aires 1987, First Vice-Pres. Chamber of Deputies 1987–89; Vice-Pres. of Argentina, Pres. Senate 1989–91; Gov. Prov. of Buenos Aires 1991–99; Partido Justicialista cand. in presidential elections 1999; Pres. Congreso Nacional del Partido Justicialista; Pres. of Argentina 2002–03; Unión Popular cand. in presidential elections 2011; Pres. MERCOSUR (Mercado Común del Sur) Reps Cttee 2005; f. Office for Drug Addiction Prevention and Assistance, Lomas de Zamora 1984, Comm. on Drug Addiction, Chamber of Deputies; Orden de Boyacá (Colombia), Orden Cruceiro do Sul (Brazil), Orden del Quetzal (Guatemala), Orden de Bernardo O'Higgins (Chile); Dr hc (Genoa) 1992, (Universidad Hebrea, Argentina) 1999, (Universidad del Salvador) 1999. *Publications:* La revolución productiva (with Carlos Saúl Menem q.v.) 1987, Los políticos y las drogas 1988, Hacía un mundo sin drogas 1994, Política, familia, sociedad y drogas 1997. *Leisure interests:* fishing, chess, folk music, reading, watching football. *Address:* c/o Partido Justicialista, Domingo Matheu 130, C1082ABD Buenos Aires, Argentina. *Telephone:* (11) 4954-2450. *Fax:* (11) 4954-2421. *E-mail:* contacto@pj.org.ar. *Website:* www.pj.org.ar.

DUHAMEL, Olivier, LLD; French academic; *Professor of Law and Political Science, University of Paris (Sciences Po);* b. 2 May 1950, Neuilly-sur-Seine; m. Evelyne Pisier; one s. one d.; ed Inst. of Political Studies, Paris; Founder and Ed. Pouvoirs magazine 1977–; Ed. TNS Sofres 1984–; currently Prof. of Law and Political Science, Univ. of Paris (Sciences Po); Adviser to Pres. of Constitutional Council 1983–95; mem. Consultative Comm. for the Revision of the Constitution 1992–93; Founder and Pres. REVE (Réflexion-Engagement-Vision pour l'Europe) 1994; founder mem. AGIR 1995–, SOS Europe (inter-parliamentary group) 1997–; Pres. Europartenaires 1997–2000; mem. European Parl. (Socialist Party) 1997–2004, mem. Cttee on Constitutional Affairs, Cttee on Citizens' Freedoms and Rights 1994–2001, on Justice and Home Affairs; mem. Bureau Party of European Socialists 2001–04; mem. Convention on Future of Europe 2002–03; fmr Visiting Prof., Univ. of Washington, New York Univ.; columnist, La Marseillaise 1997–; contrib. Valeurs actuelles, France Culture (radio), Europe 1 (radio), LCI (TV). *Television:* series: Les grandes batailles de la République (France 5), Democratie, democracy (France 5), Présidentielle, les surprises de l'Histoire (France 2), Petite histoire de la constitution européenne (Arte). *Publications:* Chili ou la tentative révolution 1974, Changer le PC? 1979, La Gauche et la 5ème République 1980, Histoire des idées politiques (co-author) 1982, Le nouveau Président (co-author) 1987, Le pouvoir politique en France 1991, Droit constitutionnel et politique 1994, Les Démocraties 1993, Histoire constitutionnelle de la France 1995, Petit Dictionnaire de l'Euro (co-author) 1998, Le Quinquennat 2000, La 5ème République (1958–2001) (co-author) 2001, Présidentielles: les surprises de l'historique (1965–95) 2001, Vive la VIème république 2002, Pour l'Europe 2003, La Constitution européenne 2004, Pour Europe: Le texte intégral de la constitution expliqué et commenté 2005, Des raisons du Non 2005, Matins d'un Européen 2005, Histoire des Présidentielles 2007, La Ve République (1985–2009) 2009, Droit constitutionnel et institutions politiques 2009. *Address:* Sciences Po, 27 rue Saint-Guillaume, 75007 Paris (office); 59 boulevard Raspail, 75006 Paris, France (home). *Telephone:* (6) 07-76-55-97 (home). *E-mail:* lolivier.d@wanadoo.fr (home). *Website:* www.sciences-po.fr (office).

DUIGAN, John, MA; Australian film director, screenwriter and author; b. 19 June 1949, Hartley Wintney, Hampshire, England; ed Univ. of Melbourne; fmr Lecturer, Univ. of Melbourne and Latrobe Univ.; Co-Dir Vietnam (TV mini-series); wrote and directed TV documentaries: Fragments of War: The Story of Damien Parer 1988, Bitter Rice 1989. *Films include:* The Firm Man (1975), Trespassers 1976, Mouth to Mouth 1978, Dimboola 1979, Winter of Our Dreams 1981, Far East 1982, One Night Stand 1984, The Year My Voice Broke 1987 (Australian Acad. Award for Best Dir), Romero 1989, Flirting 1991, Wide Sargasso Sea 1993, Sirens 1994, The Journey of August King 1995, The Leading Man 1996, Lawn Dogs 1997, Molly 1999, Paranoid 2000, The Parole Officer 2001, Head in the Clouds 2004. *Publications:* novels: Badge, Players, Room to Move. *Address:* c/o Creative Artists Management (CAA), 9830 Wilshire Blvd., Beverly Hills, CA 90212-1825, USA.

DUJARDIN, Jean; French actor, comedian, writer and director; b. 19 June 1972, Rueil-Malmaison, Paris; m. Alexandra Lamy 2009; two c.; cabaret performer during mid-1990s; fmr mem. cabaret group Nous C Nous. *Television includes:* Carré Blanc / Nous C Nous 1996-99, Farce Attaque (also writer) 1997-98, Un gars, une fille 1999–2003, Palizzi (also director) 2007. *Films include:* If I Were a Rich Man 2002, Toutes les filles sont folles 2003, Bienvenue chez les Rozes 2003, Le Convoyeur 2004, Les Dalton 2004, Brice de Nice 2005, L'Amour aux trousses 2005, Il ne faut jurer de rien! 2005, OSS 117: Cairo, Nest of Spies (Etoile D'Or Award 2006) 2006, OSS 117: Lost in Rio, Hellphone 2006, 99 francs (Raimu Award for Comedy 2007) 2007, Contre-enquête 2007, Ca$h 2008, A Man and His Dog 2009, OSS 117: Lost in Rio 2009, Lucky Luke 2009, Little White Lies 2010, Un balcon sur la mer (Swann d'Or for Best Actor) 2010, The Clink of Ice 2010, The Artist (Best Actor, Cannes Film Festival 2011, Golden Globe Award for Best Actor – Motion Picture Musical or Comedy 2012, Screen Actors Guild Best Actor Award 2012, BAFTA Best Actor Award 2012, Academy Award for Best Actor 2012) 2011, Les Infidèles (also co-writer and co-dir) 2012. *Address:* c/o WME, 9601 Wilshire Boulevard, Beverly Hills, CA 90210, USA (office). *Telephone:* (310) 285-9000 (office). *Fax:* (310) 285-9010 (office). *Website:* www.wmeentertainment.com (office).

DUKA, HE Cardinal Dominik Jaroslav, OP; Czech ecclesiastic and academic; *Archbishop of Prague;* b. 26 April 1943, Hradec Králové, Protectorate of Bohemia

and Moravia (now Hradec Králové, Czech Repub.); ed Theological Faculty of Litoměřice, Theological Faculty of St John the Baptist, Warsaw, Poland; professed Mem. Order of Friars Preachers (Dominicans) 1969; ordained Priest of Order of Friars Preachers 1970; worked in various parishes of Archdiocese of Prague for five years; deprived of state authorization for the sacred ministry, worked as designer in factories of Škoda Plzeň until collapse of Communism 1989; worked in secret in the Order as novice master and teacher of theology; jailed in Plzeň 1981–82; Provincial of the Dominicans in Bohemia and Moravia 1986–98; elected Fed. Pres. Conf. of Major Superiors 1989; Vice-Pres. Union of European Confs of Major Superiors 1992–96; Lecturer, Faculty of Theology, Palacký Univ., Olomouc 1990–99; Bishop of Hradec Králové 1998–2004; Apostolic Admin. of Litoměřice 2004–10; Archbishop of Prague 2010–; cr. Cardinal (Cardinal-Priest of Santi Marcellino e Pietro) 2012; participated in Papal Conclave 2013. *Address:* Archdiocese of Prague, Hradcanske nam. 16, 119 02 Prague 1, Czech Republic (office). *Telephone:* (2) 20392123 (office). *Fax:* (2) 20514647 (office). *E-mail:* info@apha.cz (office). *Website:* www.apha.cz (office).

DUKAKIS, Michael Stanley; American academic and fmr politician; *Distinguished Professor, Department of Political Science, Northeastern University;* b. 3 Nov. 1933, Brookline, Mass.; s. of Dr. Panos Dukakis and Euterpe Dukakis; m. Katharine Dickson; one s. two d.; ed Brookline High School, Swarthmore Coll., Harvard Law School; Army service in Korea 1955–57; mem. Town Meeting, Brookline 1959, Chair. Town Cttee 1960–62; Attorney Hill & Barlow, Boston 1960–74; alt. Del. Democratic Nat. Convention 1968; mem. Mass. House of Reps for Brookline 1962–70, later Chair. Cttee on Public Service and mem. Special Comm. on Low Income Housing; f. a research group for public information 1970; moderator of TV public affairs debate programme The Advocates; Gov. of Massachusetts 1975–79, 1983–91; teacher, Fla Atlantic Univ., Boca Raton 1992; Democratic cand. for US Pres. 1988; Lecturer and Dir of Inter-Governmental Studies, John F. Kennedy School of Govt, Harvard Univ. 1979–82; Distinguished Prof., Northeastern Univ., Boston; Vice Chair. AmTrack Reform Bd 1998; Gold Medal, City of Athens, Greece 1996. *Publication:* Creating the Future: Massachusetts comeback and its promise for America (with Rosabeth Moss Kanter) 1988. *Address:* Department of Political Science, Northeastern University, 327 Meserve Hall, Boston, MA 02115 (office); 650 Kelton Avenue, Apartment 302, Los Angeles, CA 90024, USA (home). *Telephone:* (617) 373-4396 (home). *Fax:* (617) 373-5311 (office). *E-mail:* m.dukakis@neu.edu (home). *Website:* www.polisci.neu.edu (office).

DUKAKIS, Olympia, MA; American actress, director, producer, teacher and activist and author; b. 20 June 1931, Lowell, Mass; m. Louis Zorich; two s. one d.; ed Arlington High School, Mass, Boston Univ.; London debut at Royal Nat. Theatre in Martin Sherman's one-woman play Rose 1999, followed by world premiere of Timberlake Wertenbaker's Credible Witness at Royal Court Theatre; appeared on BBC TV in film A Life for a Life and on BBC Radio starring in Hecuba; on Broadway, starred in Rose; starred as Clytemnestra in Agamemnon 2004; also performed at A.C.T. in The Mother (world premiere) by Gorky adapted by Constance Congdon; Founding mem. and Producing Artistic Dir of Whole Theatre, Montclair, NJ 1971–90, directed and appeared in many productions; Founding mem. The Actor's Company, Boston, Charles Playhouse, Boston; has appeared in more than 130 productions Off-Broadway and regionally, at venues including A.C.T., Shakespeare in the Park, Studio Arena in Albany, American Place Theatre, APA Phoenix, Circle Rep and Williamstown Summer Theatre Festival, where she also served as Assoc. Dir; taught acting at graduate school, New York Univ. for 15 years, currently teaches master classes at various colls and univs throughout USA; inducted into Arlington High School Hall of Fame, NJ Gov.'s Walt Whitman Creative Arts Award 1992. *Theatre includes:* A Man's A Man (Bertolt Brecht) (Obie Award), The Marriage of Bette and Boo (Christopher Durang), Joseph Papp's Public Theatre (Obie Award), Curse of the Starving Class (Sam Shepard), Titus Andronicus, Electra, and Peer Gynt. *Films include:* Twice a Man 1964, Lilith (uncredited) 1964, Stiletto 1969, John and Mary 1969, Made for Each Other 1971, Blood Sisters (uncredited) 1973, The Rehearsal 1974, Death Wish 1974, The Wanderers 1979, Rich Kids 1979, The Idolmaker 1980, National Lampoon's Movie Madness 1982, Walls of Glass 1985, Moonstruck (Academy Award for Best Supporting Actress 1988, New York Film Critics Award, the Los Angeles Film Critics Award, lden lobe Award) 1987, Working Girl 1988, Dad 1989, Look Who's Talking 1989, Steel Magnolias 1989, In the Spirit 1990, Look Who's Talking Too 1990, Over the Hill 1992, The Cemetery Club 1993, Digger 1993, Look Who's Talking Now 1993, I Love Trouble 1994, Mother (video) 1995, Jeffrey 1995, Mighty Aphrodite 1995, Mr Holland's Opus 1995, Jerusalem 1996, Milk & Money 1996, Never Too Late 1997, Balkan Island: The Last Story of the Century 1997, Picture Perfect 1997, Jane Austen's Mafia! 1998, Better Living 1998, Dead Badge 1999, Brooklyn Sonnet 2000, My Beautiful Son 2001, Ladies and The Champ 2001, And Never Let Her Go 2001, The Intended 2002, The Event 2003, Charlie's War 2003, The Great New Wonderful 2005, The Thing About My Folks 2005, 3 Needles 2005, Whiskey School 2005, Upside Out 2006, Jesus, Mary and Joey 2006, Away from Her 2006, Day on Fire 2006, In the Land of Women 2007, Hove (The Wind) (short) 2009, Dottie's Thanksgiving Pickle (short) 2010, Montana Amazon 2011, Birds of a Feather 2011, Cloudburst 2011, The Last Keepers 2012, Outliving Emily (short) 2012, Adventures of the Dunderheads 2012. *Television includes:* The Nurses (series) 1962, Dr. Kildare (series) 1962, Nicky's World (film) 1974, Great Performances (series) 1975, The Seagull 1975, The Andros Targets (series) 1977, F.D.R.: The Last Year (movie) 1980, Breaking Away (series) 1980, American Playhouse (series) – King of America 1982, One of the Boys (series) – His Cheatin' Heart 1982, The Neighborhood (movie) 1982, Search for Tomorrow (series) 1983, The Equalizer (series) – Shades of Darkness 1986, Lucky Day (film) 1991, The General Motors Playwrights Theater (series) – The Last Act Is a Solo (ACE Award) 1991, Fire in the Dark (film) 1991, Sinatra (film) 1992, Tales of the City (mini-series) – Episode 1.1 1993, Young at Heart (movie) 1995, Touched by an Angel (series) – A Joyful Noise 1996, Heaven Will Wait (film) 1997, A Match Made in Heaven (film) 1997, A Life for a Life (film) 1998, Scattering Dad (film) 1998, The Pentagon Wars (film) 1998, More Tales of the City (mini-series) 1998, Joan of Arc (film) 1999, The Last of the Blonde Bombshells (film) 2000, And Never Let Her Go (film) 2001, Ladies and the Champ (film) 2001, My Beautiful Son (film) 2001, Further Tales of the City (mini-series) 2001, Guilty Hearts (film) 2002, The Simpsons (series) 2002, Frasier (series) (voice) 2002, Mafia Doctor (film) 2003, It's All Relative (series) – Thanks, But No Thanks 2003, The Librarian: Quest for the

Spear (film) 2004, Center of the Universe (series) 2004–05, Numb3rs (series) – Hot Shot 2006, The Librarian: Return to King Solomon's Mines (film) 2006, Worst Week (series) 2008, Bored to Death (series) 2010–11, Law & Order: Special Victims Unit (series) – Pop 2011. *Publication:* Ask Me Again Tomorrow (memoir). *Telephone:* (212) 777-7786 (ext. 4) (office). *Address:* c/o Parseghian Planco LLP, 322 Eighth Avenue, Suite 601, New York, NY 10001; 684 Broadway #6E, New York, NY 10012, USA (home).

ĐUKANOVIĆ, Milo; Montenegrin politician and economist; *Prime Minister;* b. 15 Feb. 1962, Nikšić; s. of Radovan Đukanović and Stana Đukanović; m. Lidija Kuč; one s.; ed Faculty of Econs, Univ. of Montenegro, Podgorica; joined League of Communists of Yugoslavia (LCY) 1979 (mem. Cen. Cttee 1986–89), later named Democratic Party of Socialists of Montenegro (DPS), Deputy Chair. 1994–98, Chair. 1998–; Prime Minister 1991–98, 2003–06, 2008–10, 2012–; Pres. of Montenegro 1998–2002; Acting Minister of Defence June–Nov. 2006; mem. Skupština Crne Gore (Ass. of Montenegro) 2006–; Hon. mem. The Int. Raoul Wallenberg Foundation. *Address:* Office of the Prime Minister, 81000 Podgorica, Karadorđeva bb (office); Democratic Party of Socialists of Montenegro (Demok- ratska Partija Socijalista Crne Gore), 81000 Podgorica, Jovana Tomaševića bb, Montenegro (office). *Telephone:* (20) 242530 (Office of the PM) (office); (20) 242971 (DPS) (office). *Fax:* (20) 242329 (Office of the PM) (office); (20) 246356 (DPS) (office). *E-mail:* vojin.vlahovic@gov.me (office); predsjednik@dps.me (office). *Website:* www.gov.me (office); www.dps.me (office).

DUKE, Michael (Mike) Terry, BEng; American business executive; *President and CEO, Wal-Mart Stores, Inc. (Walmart);* b. 1949; m. Susan Duke; one s. two d.; ed Georgia Inst. of Tech.; spent 23 years working for various retailers including Federated Dept Stores and May Dept Stores; joined Wal-Mart Inc. 1995, Sr Vice- Pres. of Logistics 1995–2000, Sr Vice-Pres. of Distribution and Exec. Vice-Pres. of Logistics 2000, Exec. Vice-Pres. of Admin 2000–03, Pres. Wal-Mart Stores USA 2003–05, Vice-Chair. and Head of Walmart International 2005–09, mem. Bd of Dirs Wal-Mart Stores Inc. (now called Walmart) 2008–, Pres. and CEO 2009–; mem. Bd of Dirs The Consumer Goods Forum; mem. Exec. Bd Conservation International's Center for Environmental Leadership in Business, Exec. Cttee of Business Roundtable; mem. Bd of Advisors, Univ. of Arkansas, Advisory Bd Tsinghua Univ. School of Econs and Man., Beijing; mem. Nat. Acad. of Eng; ranked by Forbes magazine amongst The World's Most Powerful People (eighth) 2009, (25th) 2010, (27th) 2011, (17th) 2012, (tenth) 2013. *Address:* Walmart, 702 SW 8th Street, Bentonville, AR 72716-8611, USA (office). *Telephone:* (479) 273-4000 (office). *Fax:* (479) 277-1830 (office); (479) 277-4053 (office). *Website:* www.walmart .com (office); corporate.walmart.com (office).

DUKE, Robin Chandler; American diplomatist; b. 1923; m. Angier Biddle Duke (deceased); writer, New York Journal American newspaper during 1940s; fmr mem. Bd of Dirs American Home Products, Rockwell Int., Int. Flavors and Fragrances; mem. Bd of Trustees US–Japan Foundation; mem. Bd of Dirs Lucile and David Packard Foundation, UN Asscn of USA 2000–, The Worldwatch Institute 2005–; fmr Vice-Chair. and mem. Advisory Bd Inst. of Int. Educ.; Chair. Del. to 21st Session of UNESCO 1980, Amb. 1980; Amb. to Norway 2000–01; fmr Pres. NARAL Pro-Choice America; mem. Council on Foreign Relations; Fellow, Acad. of Arts and Social Sciences; f. Population Action International, now Chair. Emer. *Address:* c/o Population Action International, 1300 19th Street, NW, Suite 200, Washington, DC 20036-1624; 435 East 52nd Street, Apt 2E, New York, NY 10022-6445, USA.

DUKES, Alan Martin, MA; Irish banker, consultant and fmr politician; b. 22 April 1945, Dublin; s. of James Dukes and Margaret Moran; m. Fionnuala Corcoran 1968; two d.; ed Scoil Colmcille and Colaiste Mhuire, Dublin and Univ. Coll., Dublin; Chief Econ., Irish Farmers Asscn 1967–72; Dir Irish Farmers Asscn, Brussels 1973–76; Personal Adviser to Commr of EEC 1977–80; TD (Fine Gael) for Kildare 1981–2002; Opposition Spokesperson on Agric. March–Dec. 1982; Minis- ter of Agric. 1981–82, for Finance 1982–86, for Justice 1986–87; Leader and Pres. Fine Gael 1987–90; mem. Council of State 1987–90; Minister for Transport, Energy and Communications 1996–97; Opposition Spokesperson on Environment and Local Govt; Pres. Irish Council of the European Movt 1987–91, Chair. 1997–2000; Vice-Pres. Int. European Movt 1991–96; Adjunct Prof. of Public Admin, Man. Univ. of Limerick 1991; Dir-Gen. Inst. of European Affairs 2003–07; mem. Bd of Dirs Anglo Irish Bank 2008–, Chair. 2009–13; Chair. Irish Bank Resolution Corpn –2013; fmr Public Affairs Consultant, WHPR, Dublin; Vice-Pres. European People's Party 1987–96; Chair. Jt Oireachtas Cttee on Foreign Affairs 1995–96; judge, TG4 reality TV show Feirm Factor 2008–10; Officier, Légion d'honneur 2004, Commdr's Cross, Order of Merit (Poland) 2004. *Leisure interests:* reading, music, walking, horse riding, motor sport. *Address:* Tully West, Kildare, Co. Kildare, Ireland. *Telephone:* 87-6846274 (mobile). *E-mail:* alandukes@eircom .net.

ĐUKIĆ-DEJANOVIĆ, Slavica, MA, PhD; Serbian psychiatrist and politician; *Minister of Health;* b. 4 July 1951, Rača Kragujevačka; ed Medical Faculty, Univ. of Belgrade; joined Medical Faculty, Univ. of Kragujevac 1982, currently Prof. and Assoc. Dean for Int. Collaboration; Dir KBC Kragujevac Hosp. 1995–2001; Dir Centrum Neuropsychiatrii, Kragujevac; Minister for the Family 2000–01; mem. Socijalistička partija Srbije (Socialist Party of Serbia) 1990–, Vice-Pres. 1996–97, 2002–; mem. Narodna skupština Republike Srbije (Nat. Ass.), Pres. 2008–12; Acting Pres. of Serbia 5 April–31 May 2012; Minister of Health 2012–; Vice-Pres. Asscn of Psychiatrists of Serbia. *Publications:* more than 160 articles published in medical journals. *Address:* Ministry of Health, 11000 Belgrade, Nemanjina 22–26, Serbia (office). *Telephone:* (11) 3613734 (office); (11) 3616540 (office). *Fax:* (11) 2656548 (office). *E-mail:* kabinet@zdravlje.gov.rs (office); slavica1@eunet.rs (office). *Website:* www.zdravlje.gov.rs (office).

DULAIMI, Saadoun ad-, PhD; Iraqi government official, psychologist and statistician; *Minister of Culture and Acting Minister of Defence;* b. 1954, Ramadi; ed Univ. of Keele, UK; fmr army reserve officer; emigrated 1980s; has taught in Jordan and USA; returned to Iraq 2003; est. Centre for Research and Strategic Studies (polling firm) 2003; Minister of Defence 2005–06, Minister of Culture 2010–, also Acting Minister of Defence 2011–. *Address:* Ministry of Culture, POB 624, Qaba bin Nafi Sq., Sadoun St, Baghdad, Iraq (office). *Telephone:* (1) 538-3171 (office).

DULIĆ, Oliver, MD; Serbian physician and politician; *Minister of the Environ- ment and Spatial Planning;* b. 21 Jan. 1975, Belgrade; m. Andrea Dulić; ed Univ. of Belgrade; trained as orthopaedic surgeon, Belgrade; mem. Democratic Party (Demokratska Stranka) 1997–, Pres. Subotica br. 1997–2000, Vice-Pres. Vojvodina Prov. br. 2000–06, now mem. Exec. Cttee; mem. Narodna skupština Republike Srbije (Parl.) 2003–, Speaker 2007–08; Minister of the Environment and Spatial Planning 2008–. *Address:* Ministry of the Environment and Spatial Planning, Nemanjina 11, 11000 Belgrade, Serbia (office). *Telephone:* (11) 3617717 (office). *Fax:* (11) 3617722 (office). *E-mail:* info@ekoplan.gov.rs (office). *Website:* www .ekoplan.gov.rs (office).

DULLOO, Madan Murlidhar, LLB, DCL, SC, HSC; Mauritian lawyer and politician; b. 20 Sept. 1949, Port Louis; s. of Balram Bholanath Dulloo and Belwantee Lutchmee Gangaram; m. Indira Priyadarshani Dookun; three c.; ed Univ. of London, Inns of Court School of Law, Middle Temple, London, Univ. of Paris (Sorbonne); teacher 1970–71; lawyer 1976–86, 1994–2005; fmr Minister of Foreign Affairs and Emigration, Minister of Agric., Minister of Fisheries and Natural Resources; Minister of Justice and Attorney-Gen. 1986–94; Minister of Foreign Affairs, Int. Trade and Co-operation 2005–08; Leader, Mouvement Militant Socialiste Mauricien. *Leisure interests:* sports, yoga, religion, sun, sea, nature, anthropology. *Address:* c/o Ministry of Foreign Affairs, International Trade and Co-operation, New Government Centre, 5th Floor, Port Louis, Mauritius (office). *E-mail:* madan@wanadoo.mu (home).

DUMAS, Axel; French business executive; *CEO, Hermès International SA;* ed Sciences Po, Paris and Harvard Univ.; banking career with Paribas, now part of BNP Paribas, in Beijing and New York –1993; joined Hermès 1993, Commercial Dir for France, Head of Jewellery Dept before running leather goods div., Man. Dir of Operations, COO and Head of Operations & Sales, Hermès International SA 2011–13, Co-CEO June–Dec. 2013, CEO 2014–, CEO Hermes Logistik Gruppe Deutschland GmbH. *Address:* Hermès International SA, 24 rue du Faubourg- Saint-Honoré, 75008 Paris, France (office). *Telephone:* 1-40-17-49-20 (office). *Fax:* 1-40-17-49-94 (office). *E-mail:* info@hermes.com (office). *Website:* www.hermes .com (office).

DUMAS, Marlene; Dutch (b. South African) painter; b. 1953, Cape Town, South Africa; ed Univ. of Cape Town; with Atelier '63, Haarlem, Netherlands 1976–78, Psychological Inst., Univ. of Amsterdam 1979–80; Dr hc (Rhodes Univ., South Africa) 2010; Sandberg Prize 1989, Coutts Contemporary Art Foundation Coutts Award 1998, David Roell Prize/Prince Bernhard Cultural Prize for Visual Arts 1998, Rolf Shock Prize in the Visual Arts 2011, Johannes Vermeer Award 2012. *Address:* c/o Frith Street Gallery, 17-18 Golden Square, London, W1F 9JJ, England (office). *E-mail:* info@frithstreetgallery.com (office). *Website:* www .frithstreetgallery.com (office); www.marlenedumas.nl.

DUMASY, Lise, DèsL; French academic; *President, University Stendhal Grenoble III;* b. 18 June 1954, Taza, Morocco; d. of Marcel Queffélec and Paulette Haran; m. J.P. Dumasy; two s.; ed Ecole Normale Supérieure, Sèvres, Université Paris- Sorbonne-Paris IV; Visiting Asst, Princeton Univ., USA 1977–78; schoolteacher, 1978–80; Research Engineer CNRS 1980, seconded to Inst. de France 1984; teacher, Mannheim Univ. 1987–88; Sr Lecturer, Univ. Stendhal (Grenoble-III) then Prof. 1992–, Head of Dept of French Language, Literature and Civilization 1992–95, mem. Scientific Council 1997, Prin. 1999–2004, Pres. 2008–12; Officier, Ordre des Palmes académiques, Chevalier, Ordre nat, du Mérite. *Publications:* La querelle du roman-feuilleton 1999, Pamphlet, Utopie, Manifeste, XIX-XX (with C. Massol) 2001, Tocqueville, de la démocratie en Amérique, étude littéraire 2004, Stendhal, Balzac, Dumas: un récit romantique? (with C. Massol) 2007, Médecine, sciences de la vie et littérature en France et en Europe, de la Révolution à nos jours (three vols) 2012. *Leisure Interests:* music, reading, travel. *Address:* Office of the President, Université Stendhal (Grenoble III), BP 25, 38040 Grenoble Cedex 9, France (office). *Telephone:* (4) 76-82-43-01 (office). *E-mail:* presidence@u-grenoble3 .fr (office). *Website:* www.u-grenoble3.fr (office).

DUNAWAY, (Dorothy) Faye; American actress; b. 14 Jan. 1941, Bascom, Florida; d. of John Dunaway and Grace Dunaway; m. 1st Peter Wolf 1974; m. 2nd Terry O'Neill 1981; one s.; ed Univ. of Florida and Boston Univ.; spent three years with Lincoln Center Repertory Co. in New York, appearing in A Man For All Seasons, After the Fall and Tartuffe; Off-Broadway in Hogan's Goat 1965; appeared at the Mark Taper Forum, LA in Old Times, as Blanche du Bois in A Streetcar Named Desire 1973, The Curse of an Aching Heart 1982. *Films include:* Hurry Sundown 1967, The Happening 1967, Bonnie and Clyde 1967, The Thomas Crown Affair 1968, A Place For Lovers 1969, The Arrangement 1969, Little Big Man 1970, Doc 1971, The Getaway 1972, Oklahoma Crude 1973, The Three Musketeers 1973, Chinatown 1974, Three Days of the Condor 1975, The Towering Inferno 1976, Voyage of the Damned 1976, Network (Acad. Award Best Actress) 1976, The Eyes of Laura Mars 1978, The Champ 1979, The First Deadly Sin 1981, Mommie Dearest 1981, The Wicked Lady 1982, Supergirl 1984, Barfly 1987, Burning Secret 1988, The Handmaid's Tale 1989, On a Moonlit Night 1989, Up to Date 1989, Scorchers 1991, Faithful 1991, Three Weeks in Jerusalem, The Arrowtooth Waltz 1991, Double Edge, Arizona Dream, The Temp, Dun Juan DeMarco 1995, Drunks, Dunston Checks In, Albino Alligator, The Chamber, Fanny Hill 1998, Love Lies Bleeding 1999, Joan of Arc 1999, The Thomas Crown Affair 1999, The Yards 2000, Stanley's Gig 2000, Yellow Bird 2001, Changing Hearts 2002, The Rules of Attraction 2002, Mid-Century 2002, The Calling 2002, Blind Horizon 2003, Last Goodbye 2004, El Padrino 2004, Jennifer's Shadow 2004, Ghosts Never Sleep 2005, Cut Off 2006, Love Hollywood Style 2006, Rain 2006, Cougar Club 2007, Say It in Russian 2007, The Gene Generation 2007, Flick 2008, La Rabbia 2008, The Seduction of Dr. Fugazzi 2009, The Bait 2009, 21 and a Wake- Up 2009. *Television includes:* After the Fall 1974, The Disappearance of Aimee 1976, Hogan's Goat, Mommie Dearest 1981, Evita! – First Lady 1981, 13 at Dinner 1985, Beverly Hills Madame 1986, The Country Girl, Casanova, The Raspberry Ripple, Cold Sassy Tree, Silhouette, Rebecca, Gia 1998, Running Mates 2000, The Biographer 2002, Anonymous Rex 2004, Back When We Were Grownups 2004, Midnight Bayou (film) 2009, A Family Thanksgiving (film) 2010. *Publication:* Looking For Gatsby (autobiog., with Betsy Sharkey) 1995. *Address:* ICM, 10250 Constellation Blvd, Los Angeles, CA 90067, USA.

DUNAYEV, Arman G., PhD; Kazakhstani politician and economist; *Chairman, BTA Bank;* b. 1966; ed Kazakh State Univ., Moscow State Lomonosov Univ.; worked as consultant at NTO Service Centre, then as Sr Specialist and Head of Dept at office of Mayor of South Kazakhstan region; held exec. positions at KHK Astana Holdings and OJSC Bank Turan Alem; joined Ministry of Finance 2000, Vice-Minister of Finance 2001–04, Minister of Finance 2004–06; Chair. Regulation and Supervision of Financial Market and Financial Organizations Agency (FMSA) 2006–08; Chair. SC Kazyna Sustained Devt Fund 2008–09; Chair. BTA Bank 2009–. *Address:* BTA Bank, 97, Dzholdasbekov str., md Samal-2, 050051 Almaty, Kazakhstan (office). *Telephone:* (727) 250-01-11 (office). *Fax:* (727) 250-02-24 (office). *Website:* www.bta.kz (office).

DUNBAR, Adrian; British actor; b. Enniskillen, Northern Ireland; m. Anna Nygh 1986; one d., one step s.; ed Guildhall School of Music and Drama, London; Hon. DLit (Ulster) 2009. *Films include:* Sky Bandits 1986, Unusual Ground Floor Conversion 1987, The Dawning 1988, A World Apart 1988, My Left Foot 1989, Dealers 1989, Hear My Song 1991 (also writer), Force of Duty 1992, The Playboys 1992, The Crying Game 1992, Pleasure 1994, Widows' Peak 1994, Innocent Lies 1995, Richard III 1995, The Near Room 1995, The General 1998, The Wedding Tackle 2000, Wild About Harry 2000, How Harry Became a Tree 2001, Shooters 2002, Triggerman 2002, The Measure of My Days 2003, Mickybo and Me 2004, Monkey's Blood (dir) 2004, Against Nature 2005, Eye of the Dolphin 2006, The Last Confession of Alexander Pearce 2008. *Stage appearances include:* Ourselves Alone (Royal Court Theatre) 1985, King Lear (Royal Court), Girl with a Pearl Earring (Theatre Royal Haymarket) 2008. *Television appearances include:* After You've Gone 1984, The Englishman's Wife 1990, Drowning in the Shallow End 1990, Children of the North 1991, Force of Duty 1992, A Statement of Affairs (miniseries) 1993, A Woman's Guide to Adultery 1993, Pleasure 1994, The Blue Boy 1994, Cruel Train 1995, Melissa (miniseries) 1997, The Jump 1998, The Officer from France 1998, Relative Strangers (miniseries) 1999, Tough Love (series) 2000, Murphy's Law: Manic Munday 2003, Suspicion 2003, The Quatermass Experiment 2005, Child of Mine 2005, Ashes to Ashes (series) 2009, Mo 2010, A Touch of Frost 2010.

DUNCAN, Andy, BSc; British broadcasting executive and business executive; *CEO, H.R. Owen Plc;* b. 31 July 1962; ed Univ. of Manchester Inst. of Science and Tech.; joined Unilever in 1984, Chair. Van Den Bergh Foods Business Unit 1995–97, Van Den Bergh Foods Marketing Dir 1997–99, European Category Dir for Food and Beverages Div. and mem. Global Category Bd 1999–2001; Dir of Marketing and Communications, BBC 2001–03, Dir of Marketing, Communications and Audiences 2003–04, mem. Exec. Cttee BBC, Bd of Dirs BBC Commercial Holdings Ltd; CEO Channel 4 2004–09 (resgnd); CEO H.R. Owen Plc 2010–; Chair. Tea Council 1999; Grocer Magazine Overall Grand Prix Advertising Prize 1998, 1999, Marketer of the Year, Marketing Week Effectiveness Awards 2003, numerous IPA Effectiveness and other industry awards. *Address:* H.R. Owen Plc, Melton Court, Old Brompton Road, London, SW7 3TD, England (office). *Telephone:* (20) 7245-1122 (office). *E-mail:* info@hrowen.co.uk (office). *Website:* www.hrowen.co.uk (office).

DUNCAN, Arne, BA; American school administrator and government official; *Secretary of Education;* b. 6 Nov. 1964, Chicago; s. of Starkey Duncan and Sue Duncan (née Morton); m. Karen Duncan; two c.; ed Harvard Univ.; professional basketball player in Australia 1987–91; Dir Ariel Educ. Initiative, Chicago 1991–98; dir of magnet schools and Deputy Chief of Staff to CEO of Chicago Public Schools 1998–2001, CEO Chicago Public Schools 2001–08; US Sec. of Educ., Washington, DC 2009–; mem. Bd of Dirs Ariel Educ. Initiative, Chicago Cares, The Children's Center, Golden Apple Foundation, Illinois Council Against Handgun Violence, Jobs for America's Graduates, Junior Achievement, Nat. Asscn of Basketball Coaches' Foundation, Renaissance Schools Fund, Scholarship Chicago, South Side YMCA; mem. Bd of Overseers, Harvard Univ.; mem. Visiting Cttee Harvard Univ. Grad. School of Educ., Univ. of Chicago School of Social Service Admin; Fellow, Leadership Greater Chicago 1995; mem. Aspen Inst. Henry Crown Fellowship Program 2002; Dr hc (Illinois Inst. of Tech.), (National-Louis Univ.); Hon. LLD (Lake Forest Coll.) 2003; Citizen of the Year, City Club of Chicago 2006. *Achievements include:* was Co-captain of Harvard Univ. basketball team and was named first team Academic All-American. *Address:* Department of Education, 400 Maryland Ave, SW, Washington, DC 20202, USA (office). *Telephone:* (202) 401-2000 (office). *Fax:* (202) 401-0596 (office). *Website:* www.ed.gov (office).

DUNCAN, Daniel Kablan, Côte d'Ivoirian politician; *Prime Minister and Minister of Economy and Finance;* b. 1943, Ouelle; ed Inst. Commercial, Nancy and Inst. de Commerce Int. Paris; Ministry of Economy and Finance 1970; in-house training at IMF, Washington, DC 1973; joined Cen. Bank of W African States (BCEAO); with Caisse Nat. de Prévoyance Sociale; returned to BCEAO HQ, Dakar 1989; Minister Del. responsible for Econ., Finance and Planning, Office of Prime Minister 1990–93; Prime Minister of Côte d'Ivoire 1993–99, also Minister of Economy, Finance and Planning, Minister of Planning and Industrial Devt; left country for Paris after 1999 coup led by Gen. Robert Guéï, returned to Côte d'Ivoire 2000; Minister of Foreign Affairs 2011–12; Prime Minister and Minister of Economy and Finance 2012–; mem. Parti démocratique de la Côte d'Ivoire– Rassemblement démocratique africain. *Address:* Office of the Prime Minister, blvd Angoulvant, 01 BP 1533, Abidjan 01, Côte d'Ivoire (office). *Telephone:* 20-31-50-00 (office). *Fax:* 20-22-18-33 (office). *Website:* www.premierministre.ci (office).

DUNCAN, John Morris, BSc, PC; Canadian forester and politician; *Minister of State and Chief Government Whip;* b. 19 Dec. 1948, Winnipeg; ed Univ. of British Columbia; worked in coastal forest industry, BC 1972–93; MP for Vancouver Island N 1993–2006, 2008–; Pacific Region Adviser to Minister of Fisheries and Oceans 2006–07, Parl. Sec. to Minister of Indian Affairs and Northern Devt 2008–10, Minister of Indian Affairs (renamed Aboriginal Affairs May 2011) and Northern Devt, Federal Interlocutor for Métis and Non-Status Indians, and Minister of the Canadian Northern Econ. Devt Agency 2010–13, Minister of State and Chief Govt Whip 2013–; mem. Reform Party 1993–2000, Canadian Reform Conservative Alliance 2000–03, Conservative Party of Canada 2003–. *Address:* Conservative Party of Canada, 130 Albert Street, Suite 1204, Ottawa, ON K1P 5G4, Canada (office). *Telephone:* (613) 755-2000 (office). *Fax:* (613) 755-2001 (office). *Website:* www.conservative.ca (office).

DUNCAN, Lindsay Vere, CBE; British actress; b. 7 Nov. 1950, Edinburgh, Scotland; m. Hilton McRae; one s.; ed King Edwards VI High School for Girls, Birmingham, Cen. School of Speech and Drama, London; worked in theatre before TV productions during 1980s; created role of La Marquise de Merteuil in RSC production of Les Liaisons Dangereuses in Stratford, London and New York. *Theatre includes:* Don Juan (Hampstead Theatre Club) 1976, The Script (Hampstead Theatre Club) 1976, The Ordeal of Gilbert Pinfold (Royal Exchange Theatre, Manchester) 1977 (then Round House Theatre, London 1979), Plenty (Nat. Theatre, London), Comings and Goings (Hampstead Theatre Club) 1978, Julius Caesar (Riverside Studios, London) 1980, Top Girls (Royal Court Theatre, London, then New York Shakespeare Festival, Public Theatre) 1982, Les liaisons dangereuses (RSC, Ambassadors' Theatre, London) 1986 (then Music Box Theatre, New York) 1987, Cat on a Hot Tin Roof (Nat. Theatre, London) 1988, The Cryptogram (Ambassadors' Theatre, London) 1994, A Midsummer Night's Dream (Royal Court Theatre, then Lunt-Fontanne Theatre, New York) 1996, Ashes to Ashes (Royal Court Theatre, then Roundabout Theatre Company, Gramercy Theatre, New York) 1999, The Celebration, and Rose, The Room (double-bill) (Almeida Theatre, London then Laguardia Drama Theatre, New York) 2000, Private Lives (Olivier Award, Tony Award) 2001, Mouth to Mouth (RSC Jerwood Theatre Downstairs, Royal Court Theatre, then Albery Theatre, London) 2001; appeared as Daphne, Present Laughter, as Geraldine, What the Butler Saw, as Gladys, The Skin of Our Teeth, as Lucy, The Rivals, as Sally, Zack, and as Viola, Twelfth Night, all at Royal Exchange Theatre; appeared in title role, Berenice, as Natalie, The Prince of Homburg, and as Ruth, The Homecoming, all at Royal Nat. Theatre, London; appeared as Helen of Troy, Troilus and Cressida, and as Mistress Ford, The Merry Wives of Windsor, both with RSC; appeared as title role, Hedda Gabler, and in Don Juan and Incidents at Tulse Hill, all at Hampstead Theatre Club; also appeared as Anne, The Deep Blue Sea, Cambridge Theatre Co., Cambridge, as Barbara Boyle, Three Hotels, Tricycle Theatre, London, as Belinda, The Provok'd Wife, Nat. Theatre, as Ronnie, Progress, Bush Theatre, London, and as Sylvia, The Recruiting Officer, Bristol Old Vic Theatre and Edinburgh Festival; also appeared in productions at Southwold and Crewe; appeared in Ibsen's John Gabriel Borkman, Abbey Theatre, Dublin 2010. *Films include:* Loose Connections 1983, Samson and Delilah 1985, Prick Up Your Ears 1987, Manifesto (aka A Night of Love) 1988, The Child Eater 1989, Body Parts 1991, City Hall 1996, A Midsummer Night's Dream 1996, An Ideal Husband 1999, Star Wars: Episode I – The Phantom Menace (voice) 1999, Expelling the Demon (voice) 1999, Mansfield Park 1999, AfterLife 2003, Under the Tuscan Sun 2003, The Queen of Sheba's Pearls 2004, Starter for 10 2006, Burlesque Fairytales 2008, Alice in Wonderland 2010, Le Week-End (British Independent Film Award for Best Actress) 2013. *Television includes:* Further Up Pompeii! 1975, The New Avengers 1977, ITV Playhouse – The Winkler 1979, Dick Turpin 1980, BBC 2 Playhouse – Grown-Ups 1980, Muck and Brass (two episodes) 1982, BBC Play of the Month – On Approval 1982, Reilly: Ace of Spies – After Moscow 1983, Play for Today – Rainy Day Women 1984, Travelling Man (six episodes) 1984, Dead Head (three episodes) 1986, Kit Curran (six episodes) 1986, Colin's Sandwich (two episodes) 1988–90, Traffik (five episodes) 1989, The Reflecting Skin (aka L'enfant miroir) 1990, TECX – Getting Personnel 1990, Redemption 1991, G.B.H. (six episodes) 1991, The Storyteller: Greek Myths – Theseus & the Minotaur 1991, A Year in Provence (12 episodes) 1993, The Rector's Wife 1994, Just William 1995, Jake's Progress (six episodes) 1995, The History of Tom Jones, a Foundling (three episodes) 1997, Get Real (seven episodes) 1998, Letters to a Street Child 1999, Shooting the Past 1999, Oliver Twist (four episodes) 1999, Dirty Tricks 2000, Hamilton Mattress (voice) 2001, Perfect Strangers (aka Almost Strangers, USA) 2001, Witness of Truth: The Railway Murders (narrator) 2001, Agatha Christie: Poirot – The Mystery of the Blue Train 2005, Spooks (aka MI-5, USA) (two episodes) 2005–06, Rome (18 episodes) 2005–07, Longford 2006, Frankenstein 2007, Criminal Justice 2008, Lost in Austen (two episodes) 2008, Margaret 2009, Doctor Who – The Waters of Mars 2009, Marple: The Mirror Crack'd from Side to Side 2009, Come Fly with Me (series narrator) 2010–11, The Sinking of the Laconia (mini-series) 2011, Christopher and His Kind (film) 2011, White Heat (series) 2012. *Address:* c/o Independent Talent, Oxford House, 76 Oxford Street, London, W1D 1BS, England (office); c/o The Gersh Agency, 9465 Wilshire Blvd, 6th Floor, Beverly Hills, CA 90212, USA (office).

DUNCAN, Sam K.; American retail executive; *President and CEO, Supervalu Inc.;* b. Blytheville, Ark.; m. Sylvia Duncan; three d.; joined Albertson's Inc. 1969, positions including courtesy clerk, store man., Dir of Operations; Vice-Pres. Grocery Dept, Fred Meyer Inc. 1992–97, Exec. Vice-Pres. Food Div. 1997–98, Pres. 2001–02, Pres. Ralph's Supermarkets Div. 1998–2001, Pres. Fred Meyer Inc. 2001; Pres. and CEO Shopko Stores Inc. 2002–05; Chair. and CEO OfficeMax Inc. 2005–11; Pres. and CEO Supervalu Inc. 2012–; mem. Bd of Dirs Nash-Finch Co.; Trustee, North Central Coll. *Address:* Supervalu Inc., East View Innovation Center, 7075 Flying Cloud Drive, Eden Prairie, MN 55344, USA (office). *Telephone:* (952) 828-4000 (office). *Fax:* (952) 828-8998 (office). *E-mail:* info@supervalu.com (office). *Website:* www.supervalu.com (office).

DUNCAN, Tim, BA; American professional basketball player; b. 25 April 1976, St Croix, US Virgin Islands; s. of William Duncan and the late Ione Duncan; m. Amy Duncan 2001; two c.; ed Wake Forest Univ.; as a youth trained as swimmer; began playing organized basketball age 14; played college basketball at Wake Forest Univ. where he was elected All-American; selected by San Antonio Spurs in first round (first pick overall) in 1997 Nat. Basketball Asscn (NBA) draft; named NBA Finals Most Valuable Player 1999, 2003, 2005 as Spurs won NBA championship in those seasons; chosen for Team USA Team 1999, played 2004 Olympics (Athens) winning Bronze Medal; Founder and Pres. The Tim Duncan Foundation (educational charity) 2001–; Trustee, Children's Bereavement Center, Children's Center of San Antonio, Cancer Therapy and Research Center; John Wooden Award 1997, Naismith Coll. Player of the Year Award 1997, NBA Rookie of the Year 1998; NBA Most Valuable Player 2002, 2003; named to NBA All-Star Team 1997–98, 1999–2009, named to NBA All-Defensive Team 1997–2009, co-MVP NBA All-Star Game 2000; Home Team Community Service Award, Fannie Mae Foundation 2001. *Leisure interests:* video games, swimming, collecting knives and swords. *Address:* San Antonio Spurs, One SBC Center, San Antonio, TX 78219, USA (office). *Telephone:* (210) 444-5000 (office). *Website:* www.nba.com/spurs; www.slamduncan.com.

DUNCAN SMITH, Rt Hon. (George) Iain, PC; British politician; *Secretary of State for Work and Pensions;* b. 9 April 1954; s. of the late W. G. G. Duncan Smith and of Pamela Mary Duncan Smith (née Summers); m. Elizabeth Wynne Fremantle; two s. two d.; ed HMS Conway (Cadet School), Royal Mil. Acad. Sandhurst; served in Scots Guards 1975–81; Dir GEC (later Marconi) 1981–88, Bellwinch PLC 1988–89; Marketing and Devt Dir Jane's Defence Weekly, Jane's Fighting Ships 1989–92; Conservative Party cand. for Bradford W, gen. election 1987; Vice-Chair. Fulham Conservative Asscn 1991; MP for Chingford 1992–97, for Chingford and Woodford Green 1997–; mem. Select Cttee on Health 1994–95, on Standards and Privileges 1996–97; Vice-Chair. Conservative European Affairs Cttee 1996–97; Shadow Sec. of State for Social Security 1997–99, for Defence 1999–2001; Leader Conservative Party and Leader of the Opposition 2001–03; Sec. of State for Work and Pensions 2010–; Founder and Chair. Centre for Social Justice 2004–10, Patron 2010–; mem. Bd of Dirs Alyte Ltd 2007–; Freeman of the City of London. *Publications:* The Devil's Tune 2003, pamphlets on social security, European and defence issues. *Leisure interests:* family, painting, fishing, cricket, tennis, shooting, opera, reading. *Address:* Department for Work and Pensions, Caxton House, Tothill Street, London, SW1H 9DA (office); House of Commons, Westminster, London, SW1A 0AA; Parliamentary Association Office, 64A Station Road, Chingford, London, E4 7BE, England. *Telephone:* (20) 7219-3000 (Westminster); (20) 8524-4344 (Chingford); (20) 7219-1210 (home). *Fax:* (20) 7219-4867 (Westminster); (20) 8523-9697 (Chingford). *E-mail:* ministers@dwp.gsi.gov.uk (office); alambridesl@parliament.uk (office); cwgca@tory.org. *Website:* www.parliament.uk/biographies/commons/iain-duncan-smith/25640; www.dwp.gov.uk (office); www.iainduncansmith.org.

DUNDERDALE, Kathy; Canadian politician; b. Burin, Newfoundland; ed Memorial Univ. of Newfoundland; started public service career as town councillor, becoming Deputy Mayor of Burin; fmr Pres. Newfoundland and Labrador Fed. of Municipalities; fmr Dir Canadian Fed. of Municipalities; mem. House of Ass. (Prov. Parl.) for Virginia Waters 2003–, becoming Minister of Innovation, Trade and Rural Devt, also Minister Responsible for the Rural Secretariat 2003–06, Minister of Natural Resources and Minister Responsible for the Forestry and Agrifoods Agency 2006–10, also Minister Responsible for the Status of Women 2008–10, Deputy Premier 2008–10, Acting Premier Feb.–March 2010, Premier of Newfoundland and Labrador Dec. 2010–14; mem. Progressive Conservative Party (fmr Pres. Progressive Conservative Party of Newfoundland and Labrador). *Address:* House of Assembly, PO Box 8700, Saint John's, Newfoundland and Labrador, A1B 4J6, Canada (office). *E-mail:* ClerkHOA@gov.nl.ca (office). *Website:* www.assembly.nl.ca (office).

DUNFORD, Gen. Joseph F., Jr, MA; American army officer; *Commander, International Security Assistance Force (ISAF) and Commander, United States Forces Afghanistan (USFOR-A);* b. 1955, Boston, Mass; m. Ellen Dunford; one c.; ed St Michael's Coll., US Army War Coll., Ranger School, Amphibious Warfare School, Georgetown Univ., Fletcher School of Law and Diplomacy, Tufts Univ.; commissioned into US Marine Corps 1976, rank of 2nd Lt 1977; Platoon and Co. Commdr, 3rd Bn, 1st Marines 1978–81, Co. Commdr, 1st Bn, 9th Marines 1978–81, with Officer Assignment Br., US Marine Corps, Washington, DC 1982, Co. Commdr, L Co., 3rd Bn, 6th Marines 1985–87; Marine Officer Instructor, Coll. of Holy Cross, Mass 1988–91; mem. Commdt's Staff Group, later Sr Aide to Commdt, US Marine Corps, Washington, DC 1992–95; Regimental Exec. Officer, 6th Marines 1995–96, Commanding Officer, 2nd Bn 6th Marines 1996–98; Exec. Asst to Vice Chair., Global and Multilateral Affairs Div., Jt Staff, US Dept of Defense 1999–2001, Commanding Officer, 5th Marine Regt, Div. Chief of Staff and Asst Div. Commdr, 1st Marine Div. 2001–05 (led 5th Marine Regt during 2003 invasion of Iraq); Dir, Operations Div., US Marine Corps 2005–07, Vice Dir of Operations (J-3) 2007–08; rank of Lt-Gen. 2007; Deputy Commdt, Plans, Policies & Operations 2008–09; rank of Four-Star Gen. 2009; Commanding Gen., I Marine Expeditionary Force and Marine Forces Cen. Command 2009–10; Asst Commdt, US Marine Corps 2010–13; Commdr, US Forces Afghanistan (USFOR-A), Kabul, Afghanistan 2013–, also Commdr, Int. Security Assistance Force (ISAF), NATO, Kabul 2013–; numerous mil. awards including Defense Superior Service Medal, Legion of Merit, Navy Sea Service Deployment Ribbon, Global War on Terrorism Service Medal. *Address:* International Security Assistance Force (ISAF) Headquarters, Kabul, Afghanistan (office); Media Operations Center, NATO Headquarters, Blvd Leopold III, 1110 Brussels, Belgium (office). *E-mail:* moc.web@hq.nato.int (office). *Website:* www.nato.int/isaf (office).

DUNHAM, Archie W., BEng, MBA; American business executive (retd); b. 1938; m. Linda Dunham; three c.; ed Univ. of Oklahoma; served in US Marine Corps 1960–64; Pres. and CEO Conoco Inc. 1996–2002, Chair. 1999–2002, Chair. ConocoPhillips (following merger between Conoco and Phillips) 2002–04 (retd); mem. Bd of Dirs Union Pacific Corpn 2000–, Louisiana-Pacific Corpn, Phelps Dodge Corpn; fmr mem. Bd of Dirs American Petroleum Inst., Energy Inst. of the Americas, Nat. Bd, Smithsonian Inst., US–Russia Business Council, Greater Houston Partnership, Memorial Hermann Healthcare System; fmr Chair. Nat. Asscn of Mfrs; Chair. and fmr Pres. Houston Grand Opera; mem. Bretton Woods Cttee, Business Round Table, The Business Council; Gov. The Houston Forum; mem. Bd of Visitors M. D. Anderson Cancer Center; mem. Texas Gov.'s Business Council, Comm. on Nat. Energy Policy, Nat. Infrastructure Advisory Council, Marine Corps Heritage Foundation; Trustee, George Bush Presidential Library Foundation, Houston Symphony, United Way of the Texas Gulf Coast; Dr hc (Oklahoma) 1999; B'nai B'rith Int. Achievement Award 2000, Ellis Island Medal of Honor 2001, Horatio Alger Award 2001. *Address:* 141 Radney Road, Houston, TX 77024, USA (office).

DUNKEL, Gunter; German economist and banker; *Chairman of the Board of Management, Norddeutsche Landesbank (NORD/LB);* fmrly with McKinsey and Bayerische Hypotheken- und Wechselbank; mem. Bd of Man. Norddeutsche Landesbank (NORD/LB) 1997–, Deputy Chair. 2007–09, Chair. 2009–. *Address:* Norddeutsche Landesbank, Friedrichswall 10, 30159 Hanover, Germany (office). *Telephone:* (511) 361-0 (office). *Fax:* (511) 361-2506 (office). *E-mail:* info@nordlb.de (office). *Website:* www.nordlb.de (office).

DUNLOP, Frank, CBE, BA; British theatre director and festival director; *Director, Piccolo Theatre Company;* b. 15 Feb. 1927, Leeds, Yorks., England; s. of Charles Norman Dunlop and Mary Aaron; ed Kibworth Beauchamp Grammar School, Univ. Coll. London, Old Vic School, London; served in RAF 1946–49; Founder and Dir Piccolo Theatre Co. 1954–; Assoc. Dir Bristol Old Vic 1955–59; theatre dir, West End of London and Mermaid Theatre 1959–; theatre dir, Brussels, including Theatre Nat. Belge 1959–; Dir Nottingham Playhouse 1961–64; Founding Dir Pop Theatre 1966–; Assoc. Dir and Admin. Nat. Theatre, London 1967–71; Founder and Dir Young Vic Theatre 1970–78, 1980–83; theatre dir in New York and Los Angeles 1974–; Dir Edinburgh Festival 1983–91; Fellow, Univ. Coll., London 1979; Hon. DUniv (Heriot-Watt) 1989, (Edin.) 1990. *Publication:* Scapino 1975. *Leisure interests:* work and doing nothing. *Address:* Piccolo Theatre Co., 13 Choumert Square, London, SE15 4RE, England (office); c/o Miracle Management, 250 West 57th Street, Suite 1332, New York, NY 10107, USA (office). *Telephone:* (212) 265-8787 (office). *Fax:* (212) 265-8873 (office). *E-mail:* mirmgt@aol.com (office).

DUNMORE, Helen, BA; British poet and novelist; b. 1952, Yorkshire; m.; one s. one d. one step-s.; ed York Univ.; cttee mem. Soc. of Authors (Chair. 2005–); Hon. FRSL; winner, Nat. Poetry Competition (for The Malarkey) 2009. *Publications include:* poetry: The Apple Fall 1983, The Sea Skater (Poetry Soc. Alice Hunt Bartlett Award) 1986, The Raw Garden (Poetry Book Soc. Choice) 1988, Short Days, Long Nights: New & Selected Poems 1991, Secrets (Signal Poetry Award 1995) 1994, Recovering a Body 1994, Bestiary 1997, Out of the Blue: New and Selected Poems 2001, Glad of These Times 2007; fiction: Going to Egypt 1992, Zennor in Darkness (McKitterick Prize 1994) 1993, In the Money 1993, Burning Bright 1994, A Spell of Winter (Orange Prize for Women Writers of Fiction 1996) 1995, Talking to the Dead 1996, Your Blue-Eyed Boy 1998, With Your Crooked Heart 1999, The Siege 2001, The Silver Bead 2003, Ingo 2005, House of Orphans 2006, The Tide Knot 2006, The Deep 2007, Counting the Stars 2008, The Betrayal 2011; short stories: Love of Fat Men 1997, Ice Cream 2000, Mourning Ruby 2003. *Leisure interests:* family life and friendships. *Address:* c/o Caradoc King, AP Watt at United Agents LLP, 12–26 Lexington Street, London, W1F 0LE, England (office). *Telephone:* (20) 3214-0800 (office). *Fax:* (20) 3214-0801 (office). *E-mail:* info@unitedagents.co.uk (office). *Website:* www.apwatt.co.uk (office); www.helendunmore.com.

DUNN, Brian J.; American business executive; joined Best Buy Co. Inc. 1985, held positions as Store Man., Dist Man., Regional Man., Regional Vice-Pres. and Sr Vice-Pres., Exec. Vice-Pres. of Retail Sales 2002–04, Pres. of Retail Sales for N America 2004–06, Pres. and COO Best Buy Co. Inc. 2006–09, CEO 2009–12 (resgnd); mem. Bd of Dirs Dick's Sporting Goods Inc. 2007–; Dir Greater Twin Cities United Way. *Address:* c/o Best Buy Co. Inc., 7601 Penn Avenue South, Richfield, MN 55423, USA.

DUNN, Douglas Eaglesham, OBE, BA, FRSL; Scottish poet and academic; *Honorary Professor, University of St Andrews;* b. 23 Oct. 1942, Inchinnan; s. of William D. Dunn and Margaret McGowan; m. 1st Lesley B. Wallace 1964 (died 1981); m. 2nd Lesley Jane Bathgate 1985; one s. one d.; ed Univ. of Hull; full-time writer 1971–91; Writer-in-Residence, Duncan of Jordanstone Coll. of Art and Dundee Dist Libraries 1986–88; Fellow in Creative Writing, Univ. of St Andrews 1989–91, Prof. 1991–2008, Head School of English 1994–99, Dir St Andrews Scottish Studies Inst. 1992, now Hon. Prof.; Hon. Visiting Prof., Dundee Univ. 1987–89; mem. Scottish PEN; Hon. Fellow, Humberside Coll. 1987; Hon. LLD (Dundee) 1987; Hon. DLitt (Hull) 1995; Cholmondeley Award 1989. *Publications:* Terry Street (Somerset Maugham Award 1972) 1969, The Happier Life 1972, New Poems 1972–73 (ed.) 1973, Love or Nothing (Faber Memorial Prize 1976) 1974, A Choice of Byron's Verse (ed.) 1974, Two Decades of Irish Writing (criticism) 1975, The Poetry of Scotland (ed.) 1979, Barbarians 1979, St Kilda's Parliament (Hawthornden Prize 1982) 1981, Europa's Lover 1982, A Rumoured City: New Poets from Hull (ed.) 1982, To Build a Bridge: A Celebration of Humberside in Verse (ed.) 1982, Elegies (Whitbread Poetry Award and Whitbread Book of the Year 1986) 1985, Secret Villages (short stories) 1985, Selected Poems 1986, Northlight 1988, New and Selected Poems 1989, Poll Tax: The Fiscal Fake 1990, Andromache 1990, The Essential Browning (ed.) 1990, Scotland. An Anthology (ed.) 1991, Faber Book of Twentieth Century Scottish Poetry (ed.) 1992, Dante's Drum-Kit 1993, Boyfriends and Girlfriends (short stories) 1995, Oxford Book of Scottish Short Stories (ed.) 1995, The Donkey's Ears, The Year's Afternoon 2000, 20th Century Scottish Poems (ed.) 2000, The Faber Browning 2004. *Leisure interests:* playing the clarinet and saxophone, listening to jazz, gardening, philately. *Address:* School of English, Castle House, The University of St Andrews, St Andrews, Fife, KY16 9AL, Scotland (office). *Telephone:* (1334) 462666 (office). *Fax:* (1334) 462655 (office). *E-mail:* ded@st-andrews.ac.uk (office). *Website:* www.st-andrews.ac.uk/~www_se (office).

DUNN, John Montfort, BA, FBA, FSA, AcSS; British political theorist and academic; *Professor of Political Theory Emeritus, University of Cambridge;* b. 9 Sept. 1940, Fulmer; s. of Brig. Henry G. M. Dunn and Catherine M. Kinloch; m. 1st Susan D. Fyvel 1965; m. 2nd Judith F. Bernal 1971; m. 3rd Ruth Ginette Scurr 1997; two s. (one deceased) two d.; ed Winchester Coll., Millfield School, King's Coll., Cambridge and Harvard Univ., USA; Official Fellow in History, Jesus Coll., Cambridge 1965–66; Fellow, King's Coll., Cambridge 1966–, Coll. Lecturer, Dir of Studies in History 1966–72; Lecturer in Political Science, Univ. of Cambridge 1972–77, Reader in Politics 1977–87, Prof. of Political Theory 1987–2007, Prof. Emer. 2007–; Visiting Lecturer, Univ. of Ghana 1968–69; Chair. Section P. (Political Studies), British Acad. 1994–97, Bd of Consultants, Kim Dae-Jung Peace Foundation for the Asia-Pacific Region 1994–; Distinguished Visiting Prof., Tulane Univ., Univ. of Minnesota, Yale Univ.; mem. Council of British Acad. 2004–07; Hon. Foreign mem. American Acad. of Arts and Sciences 1991. *Publications include:* The Political Thought of John Locke 1969, Modern Revolutions 1972, Dependence and Opportunity (with A. F. Robertson) 1973, Western Political Theory in the Face of the Future 1979, Political Obligation in its Historical Context 1980, Locke 1984, The Politics of Socialism 1984, Rethinking Modern Political Theory 1985, The Economic Limits to Modern Politics (ed.) 1990, Interpreting Political Responsibility 1990, Storia delle dottrine politiche 1992, Democracy: The Unfinished Journey (ed.) 1992, Contemporary Crisis of the Nation State? (ed.) 1994, The History of Political Theory 1995, Great Political Thinkers (21 vols, co-ed.) 1997, The Cunning of Unreason 2000, Pensare la Politica 2002, Locke: A Very Short Introduction 2003, Setting the People Free: The Story of Democracy 2005, Exploring Utopian Futures of Politics (with Inwon Choue and John Ikenberry)

2008. *Leisure interests:* watching birds and animals, opera, travel. *Address:* King's College, Cambridge, CB2 1ST (office); The Merchant's House, 31 Station Road, Swavesey, Cambridge, CB4 5QJ, England (home). *Telephone:* (1223) 331258 (office); (1954) 231451 (home). *Fax:* (1223) 331315 (office). *E-mail:* jmd24@cam.ac .uk (office). *Website:* www.polis.cam.ac.uk (office).

DUNN, Baroness (Life Peer), cr. 1990, of Hong Kong Island in Hong Kong and of Knightsbridge in the Royal Borough of Kensington and Chelsea; **Lydia Selina Dunn;** British business executive; *Executive Director, John Swire & Sons Ltd;* b. 29 Feb. 1940; d. of Yenchuen Yeh Dunn and Chen Yin Chu; m. Michael David Thomas, CMG, QC 1988; ed St Paul's Convent School, Coll. of Holy Names, Oakland, Calif., USA and Univ. of California, Berkeley; Exec. Dir John Swire & Sons Ltd 1996–; Dir John Swire & Sons (HK) Ltd 1978–2003, Swire Pacific Ltd 1981–, Cathay Pacific Airways Ltd 1985–97 (Adviser to Bd 1997–2002), Volvo 1991–93 (mem. Int. Advisory Bd 1985–91), Christie's Int. PLC 1996–98, Christie's Fine Art 1998–2000, Marconi PLC (fmrly GEC) 1997–2002; Deputy Chair. Hong Kong & Shanghai Banking Corpn 1992–96 (Dir 1981–96), HSBC Holdings PLC (fmrly Hong Kong and Shanghai Banking Corpn) 1992–2008 (Dir 1990–2008); mem. Hong Kong Legis. Council 1976–88 (Sr mem. 1985–88); mem. Hong Kong Exec. Council 1982–95 (Sr mem. 1988–95); Chair. Lord Wilson Heritage Trust 1993–95; mem. Hong Kong/Japan Business Co-operation Cttee 1983–95, Chair. 1988–95; mem. Hong Kong/US Econ. Co-operation Cttee 1984–93; Chair. Hong Kong Trade Devt Council 1983–91; Pres. The Hong Kong LEP Trust 1993–; mem. Hong Kong Asscn (Chair. 2001–), Confucius Inst. for Business, London 2006–, Asia Task Force 2007–10, Advisory Bd Christie's Greater China 2009–; Hon. Fellow, London Business School 2000; Hon. LLD (Chinese Univ. of Hong Kong) 1984, (Univ. of Hong Kong) 1991, (Univ. of BC, Canada) 1991, (Leeds) 1994; Hon. DSc (Buckingham) 1995; Prime Minister of Japan's Trade Award 1987, US Sec. of Commerce's Award to Peace and Commerce 1988. *Publication:* In the Kingdom of the Blind 1983. *Leisure interests:* study of antiques, theatre, music, opera, ballet. *Address:* John Swire & Sons Ltd, Swire House, 59 Buckingham Gate, London, SW1E 6AJ, England (office). *Telephone:* (20) 7834-7717 (office). *Fax:* (20) 7630-0380 (office). *Website:* www.swire.com (office).

DUNNING, Thom H., BS, PhD; American chemist and academic; *Director, Oak Ridge National Laboratory Joint Institute for Computational Sciences and Distinguished Professor of Chemistry, University of Tennessee;* b. 3 Aug. 1943, Jeffersonville, IN; ed Univ. of Mo., Calif. Inst. of Tech., Pasadena; Research Fellow, Battelle Memorial Inst., Columbus, OH 1970–71; Scientist III, Jet Propulsion Lab., La Cañada, CA 1971; Research Fellow, Calif. Inst. of Tech., Pasadena 1971–73; Staff Mem., Laser Theory Group, Los Alamos Nat. Lab. 1973–78, Assoc. Group Leader 1975–76; Sr Scientist, Argonne Nat. Lab. 1978–89, Group Leader, Theoretical and Computational Chemistry Group 1978–79; Visiting Prof., Univ. of Colo 1989; Assoc. Dir Pacific Northwest Nat. Lab. 1989–94, Dir 1994–97, Battelle Fellow 1997–2001; Adjunct Prof., Washington State Univ. 1990–2001; Winslow Fellow, Univ. of Melbourne, Australia 1996; Asst Dir for Scientific Simulation, Office of Science, Washington, DC 1999–2001; Prof. of Chemistry, Univ. of NC Chapel Hill 2001–02; Vice Pres., High Performance Computing and Communications Div., MCNC Research 2001–02; Distinguished Scientist, Oak Ridge Nat. Lab., Computer Science and Mathematics Div. 2002–; Distinguished Prof. of Chemistry, Univ. of Tenn. 2002–, Dir Univ. of Tenn.–Oak Ridge Nat. Lab. Jt Inst. for Computational Sciences 2002–; mem. Editorial Bd Journal of Chemical Physics 1998–2001; mem. numerous advisory cttees; mem. American Physical Soc. (Fellow 1992–), AAAS (Fellow 1992–), ACS; US Dept of Energy E. O. Lawrence Award in Chemistry 1996. *Address:* Joint Institute for Computational Sciences, University of Tennessee – Oak Ridge National Laboratory, MS 6008, 1 Bethel Valley Road, Oak Ridge, TN 37831–6008, USA (office). *Telephone:* (865) 576-0750 (office). *Fax:* (865) 576-4368 (office). *E-mail:* dunning@jics.utk.edu (office). *Website:* www.chem.utk.edu/dunning.html (office).

DUNST, Kirsten Caroline; American actress; b. 30 April 1982, Point Pleasant, NJ; d. of Klaus Dunst and Inez Dunst; ed Notre Dame High School; began career aged four as model, Elite agency; first roles in TV commercials; has appeared in more than 40 films and 10 TV guest appearances; Female Star of the Year, ShoWest Awards 2007. *Films include:* The Bonfire of the Vanities 1990, High Strung 1991, Interview with the Vampire 1994 (MTV Award for Best Break-through Performance, Saturn Award for Best Young Actress), Little Women 1994, Jumanji 1995, Mother Night 1996, Wag the Dog 1997, Small Soldiers 1998, Strike! 1998, The Virgin Suicides 1999, Drop Dead Gorgeous 1999, Luckytown Blues 2000, Bring It On 2000, Crazy/Beautiful 2001, The Cat's Meow 2001, Spider-Man 2002, Mona Lisa Smile 2003, Levity 2003, Eternal Sunshine of the Spotless Mind 2004, Spider-Man 2 2004, Wimbledon 2004, Elizabethtown 2005, Marie Antoinette 2006, Spider-Man 3 2007, How to Lose Friends & Alienate People 2008, All Good Things 2010, Melancholia (Best Actress, Cannes Film Festival 2011) 2011, Bachelorette 2012. *TV appearances include:* Sisters 1991, Star Trek: The Next Generation 1993, ER (several episodes) 1996, The Outer Limits 1997, Stories From My Childhood 1998. *Address:* WME, 9601 Wilshire Blvd, Beverly Hills, CA 90210, USA (office).

DUNSTAN, (Andrew Harold) Bernard, RA; British fmr artist; b. 19 Jan. 1920, Teddington; s. of the late Dr A. E. Dunstan; m. Diana M. Armfield 1949; three s. (one died); ed St Paul's School, Byam Shaw School and Slade School; has exhibited at Royal Acad. since 1945; numerous solo exhbns; works in many public and pvt. collections including Museum of London, Nat. Portrait Gallery, Nat. Gallery of NZ; Past Pres. Royal West of England Acad.; mem. New English Art Club; Chair. Artists' Gen. Benevolent Inst. 1987–91; Trustee RA 1989–95. *Publications:* Learning to Paint 1970, Painting in Progress 1976, Painting Methods of the Impressionists 1976, The Paintings of Bernard Dunstan 1993, Ruskin's Elements of Drawing (ed.) 1991. *Leisure interest:* music. *Address:* 10 High Park Road, Kew, Richmond, Surrey, TW9 4BH, England (home). *Telephone:* (20) 8876-6633 (home).

DUNWOODY, (Thomas) Richard, MBE; British business executive and fmr professional jockey; b. 18 Jan. 1964, Belfast, Northern Ireland; s. of George Dunwoody and Gillian Dunwoody (née Thrale); m. (divorced); ed Rendcomb Coll.; rode winner of Grand Nat. (West Tip) 1986, (Minnehoma) 1994, Cheltenham Gold Cup (Charter Party) 1988, Champion Hurdle (Kribensis) 1990; Champion Nat. Hunt Jockey 1992–93, 1993–94, 1994–95; at retirement in 1999 held record for most wins (1,699, record later broken); Group Man. Pnr, Dunwoody Sports

Marketing 2002; Founder Richard Dunwoody Racing Associates Ltd 2004; Nat. Hunt Jockey of the Year 1990, 1992–95, Champion of Champions 2001. *Achievements include:* finished second in team race to magnetic North Pole; with Doug Stoup, the first to reach South Pole via route originally attempted by Sir Ernest Henry Shackleton. *Publications:* Hell For Leather (with Marcus Armytage) 1993, Dual (with Sean Magee) 1994, Hands and Heels (with Marcus Armytage) 1997, Obsessed 2000, Method in My Madness 2009. *Leisure interests:* motor sport, rugby, football, running. *Address:* Richard Dunwoody Racing Associates Ltd, PO Box 57190, London, SW6 4ZF, England (office). *E-mail:* richard.d@du-mc.co.uk (home). *Website:* www.richarddunwoody.co.uk.

DUPLAT, Jean-Louis; Belgian lawyer, judge and business executive; *Chairman, Aedifica NV;* b. 30 May 1937; of Univ. of Namur, Catholic Univ. of Louvain; practised law in Brussels; apptd First Deputy Prosecutor 1974; Pres. Tribunal de Commerce 1978–89; Chair. Belgian Banking and Finance Comm. 1989–2000, Hon. Chair. 2000–; Sr Adviser, Ernst & Young Special Business Services 2001–; Chair. Aedifica NV, Portolani SA; Chair. Vooruitzicht SA –2005; mem. Bd of Dirs Omega Pharma, Brantano NV; mem. Industry Expert Cttee Bencis Capital Pnrs; Pres. Child Focus 2007–; teacher, Faculty of Law, Univ. of Namur 2000–. *Address:* Office of the Chairman, Aedifica NV, Louizalaan 331-333, 1050 Brussels, Belgium (office). *Telephone:* (2) 626-07-70 (office). *Fax:* (2) 626-07-71 (office). *Website:* www .aedifica.be (office); www.childfocus.be.

DUPONT, Philippe, MBA; French business executive; b. 18 April 1951, Versailles; ed Lycée Hoche, Versailles, School Vendôme, Paris, Univ. of Paris-Dauphine; Head of Max Smith & Co. 1981–99; Chair. Advisory Cttee for Trade in Cereals and Feed (COCERAL) 1988–91, mem. Advisory Cttee for Cereals, Brussels 1988–94; mem. Bd of Dirs Banque populaire de la région Ouest de Paris 1983, Chair. (non-exec.) 1988–91, Vice-Pres. 1995–99, Vice-Pres. Caisse Centrale des Banques Populaires 1995–99, apptd Chair. Groupe Banque Populaire 1999, mem. Supervisory Bd Groupe BPCE (Banque Populaire Caisse d'Épargne, following merger of Banque Fédérale des Banques Populaires and Caisse Nationale des Caisses d'Epargne) 2008–, Chair. 2008–11; Pres. Fédération bancaire française (French Banking Fed.) 2003–; Sr Vice-Pres. French Asscn of Credit Insts and Investment Firms (Asscn française des établissements de crédit et des entreprises d'investissement—AFECEI); fmr mem. Supervisory Bd Fonds de garantie des dépôts (Fund Deposit Guarantee Bd), Conseil nat. du crédit et du titre (Nat. Council of Credit and Securities); Chevalier, Légion d'honneur. *Address:* Groupe BPCE, 50 avenue Pierre Mendès France, 75201 Paris Cedex 13, France (office). *Telephone:* 1-58-40-41-42 (office). *E-mail:* info@bpce.fr (office). *Website:* www.bpce .fr (office).

DUPUY, Albert, LenD; French diplomatist and government official; b. 1 Feb. 1947, Alicante, Spain; began career as academic inspector 1972–73; various civil service positions, including Préfecture Attaché 1973, Sr Attaché 1981, Head of Cabinet, Regional Commr, Nièvre Département 1982–83, Deputy Commr, Lesparre–Médoc 1983–84, Head of Cabinet, Minister of Foreign Affairs 1984–85, Sec. Gen., Haute–Corse Département 1985–86, Lot Préfecture 1986–87; Councillor, Admin. Tribunal, Montpellier 1989–91; Sub-Prefect, Dreux 1991–94; Sec. Gen., Haute–Savoie Préfecture 1994–95; Prefect, Pointe-à-Pitre, Guadeloupe 1998–2000; Sec. Gen., Gironde Préfecture 2000–05; Prefect, St Pierre and Miquelon 2005–06, Vosges Département 2007–08, Isère Département 2008–10; High Commr, New Caledonia 2010–13; Chevalier, Légion d'honneur, Chevalier, Ordre Nat. du Mérite. *Address:* c/o Haut-commissariat de la République en Nouvelle-Calédonie, 1 ave du Maréchal Foch, BP C5, 98844 Nouméa Cedex, New Caledonia (office). *Telephone:* 266300 (office). *Fax:* 272828 (office).

DUQUESNE, Jacques Henri Louis, LenD; French journalist and writer; b. 18 March 1930, Dunkerque; s. of Louis Duquesne and Madeleine Chevalier; m. Edith Dubois 1954; one s. one d.; ed Coll. Jean-Bart, Dunkirk, Faculté de Droit, Paris, Institut d'Études Politiques, Paris; reporter, La Croix 1957–64; Deputy Dir Panorama Chrétien 1964–70, head of investigations 1967; Asst Ed.-in-Chief, L'Express 1970–71; Co-founder and Asst Ed.-in-Chief, Le Point 1972–74, Ed.-in-Chief 1974–77, Pres.-Dir-Gen. 1985–90; Dir-Gen. La Vie Catholique group of publs 1977–79; news reporter, Europe No. 1 1969–97, La Croix 1983–, Midi Libre 1997–; Chair. Bd L'Express 1997–2005; mem. Jury, Prix Interallié 1986–; Chevalier, Légion d'honneur. *Publications:* L'Algérie ou la guerre des mythes 1959, Les 16–24 ans 1964, Les prêtres 1965, Les catholiques français sous l'occupation 1966, Demain une Eglise sans prêtres 1968, Dieu pour l'homme d'aujourd'hui 1970, La gauche du Christ 1972, Les 13–62 ans 1974, La grande triche 1977, Une voix, la nuit 1979, La rumeur de la ville 1981, Maria Vadamme 1983, Alice Van Meulen 1985, Saint-Eloi 1986, Au début d'un bel été 1988, les Vents du Nord m'ont dit 1989, Catherine Courage 1990, Jean Bart 1992, Laura C. 1994, Jésus 1994, Théo et Marie 1996, les Années Jean-Paul II 1996 (jtly), Le Dieu de Jésus 1997, Le Bonheur en 36 vertus, Panorama du Nord 1999, Les Héritières 2000, Pour comprendre la guerre d'Algérie 2001, Et pourtant nous étions heureux 2003, Marie 2004, Dieu malgré tout 2005, Judas, le deuxième jour 2007, Le mal d'Algérie 2011, François d'Assise 2014. *Address:* 13 rue de Poissy, 75005 Paris, France (home). *Telephone:* 1-43-54-32-41 (home).

DURACK, David Tulloch, MB, DPhil, FRCP, FRACP, FACP; American medical scientist and academic; *Vice-President of Corporate Medical Affairs, Becton Dickinson Technologies;* b. 18 Dec. 1944, W Australia; s. of Reginald W. Durack and Grace E. Tulloch; m. Carmen E. Prosser 1970; three s. one d.; ed Scotch Coll. Perth and Univs of W Australia and Oxford; Rhodes Scholar; intern, Radcliffe Infirmary, Oxford; further training at Royal Postgrad. Medical School, London; fmr Chief, Div. of Infectious Diseases and Int. Health, Duke Univ., NC 1977, Prof. 1982, now Consulting Prof.; Chair. Dept of Medicine and Chief, Div. of Infectious Diseases, Health Care Int., Scotland 1994–95; Worldwide Medical Dir Becton Dickinson Microbiology Systems, Baltimore 1995–99, Vice-Pres. Corp. Medical Affairs 1999–2005, Sr Vice-Pres. Corp. Medical Affairs 2005–; Fellow, American Coll. of Physicians, Royal Australasian Coll. of Physicians, American Infectious Diseases Soc., American Soc. for Clinical Investigation, American Fed. for Clinical Research. *Publications:* co-ed. of medical textbooks; more than 200 articles and 30 textbook chapters. *Leisure interest:* flying (multi-engine, instrument-rated pilot). *Address:* Becton, Dickinson and Company, 1 Becton Drive, Franklin Lakes, NJ 07417-1880, USA. *E-mail:* david.durack@bd.com (office). *Website:* www.bd.com (office).

DURAFOUR, Michel André François, Diplômé de l'Ecole libre des Sciences Politiques; French politician and writer; b. 11 April 1920, Saint-Etienne, Loire; s. of Antoine Durafour and Olga Durafour (née Gaillard); m. Maryse Forissier 1973; one s. one d.; ed Lycée de Saint-Etienne, Law Faculty of Paris Univ., Ecole des Sciences Politiques; assignment in office of Minister of Information 1944–46; journalist, writer, Deputy Mayor 1947–65, Mayor of Saint-Etienne 1965–77; mem. Senate for Loire (Ind.) 1965–67; Deputy to Nat. Ass. for Saint-Etienne NE, NW 1967–68, 1973–74, 1978–81; Minister of Labour 1974–76, Minister attached to Prime Minister with responsibility for Econ. and Finance 1976–77, of the Civil Service and Admin. Reform 1988–91, of State 1989–91; mem. Secr. Parti Radical-Socialiste; mem. Nat. Bureau of Mouvement Réformateur 1971–; Chair. Groupe des Réformateurs (Social Democratic group) in Nat. Ass. 1973–74; Pres. Comm. de la Production et des Échanges de l'Assemblée Nat.; Assoc. Prof., Univ. of Paris IX 1980–81; Prof., Univ. of Lyon III 1981; Pres. Conseil Régional (Rhône-Alpes) 1980–81, Regional Councillor and Gen. Chair. Budget 1986–88; mem. Senate for Loire, Social Democratic group 1983–88; Vice-Pres. de la Comm. des Affaires Culturelles du Sénat 1985, de la Comm. des Finances du Sénat 1986–88; Ministre d'Etat in charge of civil service and admin. reforms 1988–91; Conseiller d'Etat (on special service) 1992–96. *Publications:* Les Démoniaques (Grand Prix du Théâtre) 1950, Notre rêve qui êtes aux cieux (film entitled Les fruits sauvages), Ajouter après Bettina Colonna 1951, Les hommes sont comme ça, Le juif du ciel, Les moutons du ciel, Agnès et les vilains Messieurs (under pseudonym Pierre Jardin) (Grand Prix du Roman d'Aventure) 1963, Dites-le avec des pastèques, Pascaline, La Baïonnette de Mirabeau and others. *Address:* 13 rue Elisée Reclus, 42000 Saint-Etienne, France (home).

DURAK, Osman Turgay, MSc; Turkish mechanical engineer and business executive; *CEO, Koç Holding AŞ;* b. 1952, Istanbul; ed Robert Coll., Istanbul, Northwestern Univ., USA; Design Engineer, Product Devt, Ford Otomotiv Sanayi AŞ 1976–77, Process Engineer, Manufacturing Eng 1977–78, Supervisor, Inönü Plant 1979–81, Project Coordination Man., Inönü Plant New Investment 1982–84, Project Coordination Group Man., New Investments 1984–86, Asst Gen. Man., Marketing 1986–87, Asst Gen. Man., Purchasing 1987–99, Deputy Gen. Man. Ford Otomotiv Sanayi AŞ 2000–01, Gen. Man. 2002–07, Automotive Group Cos Ford Otosan, Koç Holding AŞ 2006–07, Pres. Automotive Group 2007–09, Deputy CEO Koç Holding AŞ 2009–10, mem. Bd of Dirs and CEO Koç Holding AŞ 2010–. *Address:* Koç Holding AŞ, Nakkastepe, Azizbey Sok. No. 1, Kuzguncuk, 34674 Istanbul, Turkey (office). *Telephone:* (216) 5310272 (office). *Fax:* (216) 3414519 (office). *E-mail:* stephenk@koc.com.tr (office). *Website:* www.koc.com.tr (office).

DURÁN, José Luis; Spanish business executive; b. 1965; with Arthur Andersen 1987; Man. Auditor Pryca (subsidiary of Carrefour) 1991–94, Man. Auditor Southern Europe 1994–96, Americas 1996–97, Chief Financial Officer (CFO) Pryca 1997–99, CFO Carrefour Spain 1999–2001, CFO and Man. Dir of Org. and Systems, Carrefour SA 2001–05, mem. Exec. Cttee, Group Man. Dir 2005, Chair. Bd of Man. 2005–08, CEO 2008; mem. Bd of Dirs HSBC Holdings plc 2008–. *Address:* HSBC Holdings plc, 8 Canada Square, London, E14 5HQ, England (office). *Telephone:* (20) 7991-8888 (office). *E-mail:* info@hsbc.com (office). *Website:* www.hsbc.com (office).

DURÁN, Roberto; Panamanian fmr professional boxer; b. 16 June 1951, Chorrillo; m. Felicidad Durán; four c.; professional boxer March 1967–2002; first fighter to win world titles at four different weights; won world lightweight title from Ken Buchanan June 1972; equalled the record number of championship defences (12) before relinquishing title to box as welterweight from Feb. 1979; won World Boxing Council version of world welterweight title from Ray Leonard, Montreal June 1980: lost it to Leonard, New Orleans Nov. 1980, retained it 1989; won WBC version of world middleweight title against Ian Barkley, Atlantic City Feb. 1989, relinquished it to challenge Ray Leonard to WBC super-middleweight title: lost to Leonard, Las Vegas Dec. 1989. *Leisure interest:* cars. *Address:* c/o CMG Worldwide, 9229 West Sunset Blvd, Suite 820, West Hollywood, CA 90069, USA. *Website:* www.cmgww.com/sports/duran.

DURAND, Claude; French publisher; b. 9 Nov. 1938, Livry-Gargan (Seine-et-Oise); s. of Félix Durand and Suzanne Durand (née Thuret); m. Carmen Perea 1965; two s.; ed Ecole normale d'instituteurs de Versailles; fmr schoolteacher; Literary Dir Editions du Seuil 1965–78; Gen. Man. Editions Grasset 1978–80; Chair. and CEO Librairie Arthème Fayard 1980–2009, Librairie Stock 1991–98; Chair. Bd of Dirs Inst. Mémoire de l'édition contemporaine 1990–93, Deputy Chair. 1993–95; Pres. Pre-Production Revenues Comm., Centre National de la Cinématographie 2005–; Officier, Légion d'honneur, Chevalier, Ordre nat. du Mérite, Commdr des Arts et des Lettres. *Publication:* La Nuit zoologique (novel, Prix Médicis) 1979. *Address:* c/o Librairie Fayard, 13 rue du Montparnasse, 75006 Paris (office); 46 rue de Naples, 75008 Paris, France (home). *Telephone:* 1-45-49-82-00 (office). *E-mail:* presse@editions-fayard.fr (office). *Website:* www.fayard.fr (office).

DURANT, Isabelle; Belgian politician; b. 4 Sept. 1954, Brussels; ed Univ. Coll. London, UK; registered nurse; teacher 1981–89; mem. of Ecologist Party (ECOLO) 1989–, Attaché of Ecologist Party Parl. Group at Regional Council of Brussels 1992–94, Fed. Sec. and Spokeswoman for ECOLO 1994–99, mem. Fed. Office of ECOLO-AGALEV 1995–99, Co-Pres. ECOLO 2004–; Co-ordinator of Etats généraux de l'Ecologie politique (EGEP) 1996–; Deputy Prime Minister and Minister for Mobility and Transport 1999–2003 (resgnd); Senator 2003–. *Address:* Maison des Parlementaires, 21 rue de Louvain, Bureau 3213, 1009 Brussels, Belgium (office). *Telephone:* (2) 5499059 (office). *E-mail:* isabelle.durant@ecolo.be (home). *Website:* www.isabelledurant.be (office).

DURANTE, Nicandro; Brazilian/Italian business executive; *Chief Executive, British American Tobacco plc;* ed degrees in finance, econs and business admin; spent three years working in finance in two Brazilian cos; joined Souza Cruz (Brazilian subsidiary of British American Tobacco) 1981, seconded to UK head office as Marketing Finance Controller 1996–98, Finance Dir Hong Kong 1998–2002, Finance Dir Souza Cruz 2002, Pres. Souza Cruz April 2002–06, Regional Dir for Africa and the Middle East, British American Tobacco plc 2006–08, mem. Bd of Dirs and COO 2008–10, Chief Exec. Designate Sept.–March 2010, Chief Exec. March 2011–. *Address:* British American Tobacco plc, Globe House, 4 Temple Place, London, WC2R 2PG, England (office). *Telephone:* (20)

7845-1936 (office). *Fax:* (20) 7845-2184 (office). *E-mail:* info@bat.com (office). *Website:* www.bat.com (office).

DURANTE, Viviana Paola; Italian ballerina; b. 8 May 1967, Rome; m. Nigel Cliff; one s.; joined Royal Ballet Co., London 1984, became soloist 1987, Prin. Dancer 1989, left co. 2001; Prin. Dancer, American Ballet Theater 1999–2000; Prin. Guest Artist, La Scala, Milan 2001–03; Prin. Guest Artist, K-Ballet, Japan 2001–; juror, Prix de Lausanne and judge, Royal Ballet School's Ursula Moreton Choreographic Competition 2011; Patron, Hammond School; Prix de Lausanne 1985, Evening Standard Award 1989, Time Out Award 1989, Premio Positano Award (Italy) 1991, Olivier Award 1997, Premio Internazionale Gino Tani 1997, Premio Vignale Danza 2003, Premio Bucchi 2006, Premio Apulia 2007, Dancer of the Year in the UK, Japan, Italy, Chile. *Principal parts include:* Ondine, Juliet, Nikiya (La Bayadère), Odette-Odile (Swan Lake), Aurore (Sleeping Beauty), Cinderella, Princess Rose (Prince of Pagodas), Anastasia, Marie Vetsera (Mayerling), Excelsior 2001; also roles in My Brother and My Sisters, Requiem, Don Quixote, Manon, Nutcracker, Rhapsody, Capriccio, Anna Karenina, Carmen, Symphonic Variations. *Leisure interests:* yoga, reading, life. *Website:* www.viviana-durante.com.

DURÃO BARROSO, José Manuel, MPolSci; Portuguese academic, politician and international organization official; *President, European Commission;* b. 23 March 1956, Lisbon; m. Margarida Sousa Uva; three s.; ed Univs of Lisbon and Geneva; mem. Maoist party after revolution in Portugal 1974; Lecturer, Faculty of Law, Univ. of Lisbon, Dept of Political Science, Univ. of Geneva; mem. Parl. 1985–; fmr Sec. of State for Home Affairs and for Foreign Affairs and Co-operation; Minister of Foreign Affairs 1992–95; mem. Nat. Council Social Democratic Party (PSD), Leader 1999–; Vice-Pres. EPP 1999–; Prime Minister of Portugal 2002–04 (resgnd); Chair. Comm. for Foreign Affairs 1995–96; Pres. European Comm. 2004–; Head, Dept of Int. Relations, Univ. Lusíada 1995–99; Visiting Scholar, Georgetown Univ., Washington, DC, Visiting Prof. 1996–98; decorations from Brazil, Germany, Japan, Morocco, Netherlands, Portugal, Spain, UK; Hon. DUniv (Rhode Island) 2005, Hon. DH (Georgetown Univ.) 2006, Hon. Dr rer. pol (Genoa Univ.) 2006, Hon. DIur (Kobe Univ.) 2006. *Publications include:* Governmental System and Party System (co-author) 1980, Le Système Politique Portugais face à l'Intégration Européenne 1983, Política de Cooperação 1990, A Política Externa Portuguesa 1992–93, A Política Externa Portuguesa 1994–95, Uma Certa Ideia de Europa 1999, Uma Ideia para Portugal 2000; several studies on political science and constitutional law in collective works, encyclopaedias and int. journals. *Address:* European Commission, 200 rue de la Loi, 1049 Brussels, Belgium (office); Social Democratic Party, Rua de São Caetano 9, 1249-087 Lisbon Codex, Portugal (office). *Telephone:* (2) 298-18-00 (office); (21) 3952140 (Lisbon) (office). *Fax:* (2) 295-01-38 (office); (21) 3976967 (Lisbon) (office). *E-mail:* psd@psd.pt (office). *Website:* europa.eu (office); www.psd.pt (office).

DURBIN, Richard (Dick) Joseph, BS, JD; American lawyer and politician; *Senator from Illinois;* b. 21 Nov. 1944, East St Louis, Ill.; s. of William Durbin and Ann Durbin; m. Loretta Schaefer 1967; one s. two d. (one deceased); ed Georgetown Univ.; called to the Bar, Ill. 1969; legal practice 1969–; Chief Legal Counsel to Lt-Gov. Paul Simon of Ill. 1969–72; parliamentarian, Ill. State Senate 1969–77, staff minority leader, 1972–77; Pnr, Durbin & Lestikow, Springfield, Ill. 1979–82; mem. US House of Reps for 20th Ill. Dist, Washington, DC 1983–97; Senator from Illinois 1997–, Asst Minority Whip 2005–07, Majority Whip 2007–, mem. Judiciary, Appropriations, Foreign Relations and Rules Cttees; Chair. Democratic Nat. Cttee 2004; Assoc. Prof. of Medical Humanities, Southern Illinois Univ. 1978–; Democrat; Friend of Agric. Award, Illinois Farm Bureau 2000, Excellence in Immunization Award, Nat. Partnership for Immunization 2001, Ground Water Protector Award, Nat. Ground Water Asscn 2005, Leadership Award, Nat. Org. on Fetal Alcohol Syndrome 2005, Public Service Award, ACS 2005, Lifetime Achievement Award, American Lung Asscn. *Address:* 711 Hart Senate Office Building, Washington, DC 20510-0001, USA (office). *Telephone:* (202) 224-2152 (office). *Fax:* (202) 228-0400 (office). *E-mail:* dick@durbin.senate.gov (office). *Website:* durbin.senate.gov (office).

DURDYLYEV, Shamuhammet; Turkmenistani engineer and politician; *Deputy Chairman and Chief of the Government and Presidential Staff;* b. 1963, Ahal Prov.; ed Industrial and Residential Dept, Polytechnic Inst.; worked as occupational safety and construction technician at Baharden Mobile Mechanical Div. No. 3; construction engineer 1990–92; Head of Baharden self-financed construction field of AshgabatRemBytStroi, responsible for renovation of public amenity centres in Aşgabat 1992–93; briefly Head of Ahal Welayat Gas Production Asscn 1993; Construction Man., Baharden Dist Specialized Mobile Mechanical Div. No. 17 1993–94; Deputy Head of Baharly township 1994–95; worked for Baharden Water Man. Production Admin 1995–2002; Deputy Head, then Head of the Ahal 2002–07; Minister of Construction and Construction Materials Industry 2007–10; Gov. City of Aşgabat 2010–14; Deputy Chair. and Chief of the Govt and Presidential Staff 2014–. *Address:* Office of the President and the Council of Ministers, 744000 Aşgabat, Galkynyş köç. 20, Turkmenistan (office). *Telephone:* (12) 35-45-34 (office). *Fax:* (12) 35-51-12 (office). *E-mail:* nt@online.tm (office). *Website:* www.turkmenistan.gov.tm (office).

DURDYNETS, Gen. Vasyl Vasylyevich; Ukrainian lawyer and army officer; b. 27 Sept. 1937, Romochevytsya; m.; one d.; ed Lvov State Univ.; Sec., then First Sec., Lvov Regional Comsomol Cttee, Deputy Head of Section, Cen. Comsomol Cttee, Moscow, Head of Section, Cen. Cttee of Lviv Regional CP 1960–73; Deputy Head of Dept of Admin., CP Cen. Cttee 1973–78; Deputy Minister of Internal Affairs 1978–82, First Deputy Minister of Internal Affairs 1982–91; People's Deputy of Ukraine 1991–94, Head, Cttee of Defence and Nat. Safety 1991–92, mem. 1997–, First Deputy Speaker of Parl. 1992–94; First Deputy Head of Co-ordination Cttee for Fighting Corruption and Organized Crime 1994–95, Head 1995–99; Vice-Prime Minister of Ukraine 1995–96, First Vice-Prime Minister 1996–99, Acting Prime Minister June–July 1997; Dir Nat. Bureau of Investigations 1997–99; Minister for Emergency Situations and Protection of the Population from the Consequences of the Chernobyl Catastrophe 1999–2002; Amb. to Hungary 2002–03; mem. Supreme Econ. Council 1997; Hon. Prof. Acad. of Internal Affairs 1997; ICDO Medal, Int. Civil Defence Org. (Switzerland) 2000, 14 nat. awards. *Address:* c/o Ministry of Foreign Affairs, 01018 Kyiv, pl. Mykhailivska 1, Ukraine.

DURIE, Sir David Robert Campbell, Kt, KCMG, KStJ, KCFO, MA, CCMI, FRSA; British public affairs consultant, diplomatist, lecturer and fmr public servant; b. 21 Aug. 1944, Glasgow, Scotland; s. of the late F. R. E. Durie; m. Susan Frances Weller; three d.; ed Univ. of Oxford; served in various British Govt depts 1966–91; Minister and Deputy UK Perm. Rep. to EU 1991–95; Dir-Gen. for Enterprise and Regions, Dept Trade and Industry 1995–2000; Gov. and C-in-C Gibraltar 2000–03; Ind. Chair. Responsibility in Gambling Trust (fmrly Gambling Industry Charitable Trust) 2004–07; mem. Lord Chancellor's Advisory Council on Nat. Records and Archives 2006–; Ind. mem. Greater London Authority Standards Cttee 2008–12. *Leisure interests:* exercise, culture, family.

DURKAN, Mark; Irish politician; b. 26 June 1960, Derry, Northern Ireland; s. of Brendan Durkan and Isobel Durkan (née Tinney); m. Jackie Durkan; one d.; ed St Columb's Coll., Derry, Queen's Univ., Belfast, Magee Coll., Derry; Deputy Pres. Union of Students in Ireland 1982–84; Asst to John Hume, MP 1984–98; Chair. Social Democratic and Labour Party (SDLP) 1990–95, Leader 2001–10; Derry City Council 1993–2002; mem. NI Housing Council 1993–95, Western Health and Social Services Council 1993–2000; mem. Forum for Peace and Reconciliation, Dublin 1994–96; SDLP Negotiator in inter-party discussions 1996–98; mem. NI Ass. 1998–2010; Minister of Finance 1999–2001, Deputy First Minister 2001–02; MP for Foyle 2005–. *Address:* Constituency Office, 1st Floor, 23 Bishop Street, Derry, BT48 6PR, Northern Ireland (office); House of Commons, Westminster, London, SW1A 0AA, England (office). *Telephone:* (28) 7136-0700 (Derry) (office); (20) 7219-5096 (London) (office). *Fax:* (28) 7136-0808 (Derry) (office); (20) 7219-2694 (London) (office). *E-mail:* m.durkan@sdlp.ie (office); mark.durkan.mp@parliament.uk (office). *Website:* www.parliament.uk/biographies/commons/mark-durkan/1594 (office); www.markdurkan.net.

DURLACHER, Nicholas (Nick) John, CBE, BA (Cantab); British business executive; *Chairman, Xoserve Ltd;* b. 20 March 1946, Plaxtol, Kent; s. of John Sidney Durlacher and Alma Gabriel Adams; m. Mary McLaren 1971; one s.; ed Stowe School, Buckingham, Magdalene Coll., Cambridge; fmrly Chair. London Int. Financial Futures and Options Exchange; Chair. Securities and Futures Authority 1995–2001; Ennismore European Smaller Companies Fund 1998–; Chair. FFastFill PLC 2000–02; Chair. Elexon Ltd 2000–10, Quilter Global Enhanced Income Trust PLC 2000–05, Xoserve Ltd 2011–; Dir UFJ Int. PLC 2002–04; Chair. Allied Schools 2007–; Trustee Brain and Spine Foundation 2000–. *Leisure interests:* skiing, golf, tennis. *Address:* Xoserve Limited, 31 Homer Road, Solihull, West Midlands, B91 3LT (office); 10 Rutland Street, London, SW7 1EH, England (home). *Website:* www.xoserve.com (office).

DURLEŞTEANU, Mariana; Moldovan economist and diplomatist; b. 5 Sept. 1971; m.; two c.; ed Babeş-Bolyai Univ., Cluj-Napoca, Romania; fmr nat. gymnast; economist, later leading economist, Foreign Financing and External Debt Dept, Ministry of Finance 1995–96, Chief of External Debt Service Div. 1996–97, Head of Foreign Financing and External Debt Directorate 1997–2001, Deputy Minister of Finance 2001–02, First Deputy Minister of Finance 2002–05, Minister of Finance 2008–09; Gov. for Moldova, Black Sea Trade and Devt Bank (BSTDB) 2001–04; Alt. Gov. for Moldova, IMF 2001–04; Deputy Chair. Moldovagaz (jt venture) 2004–05; Chair. Savings Bank (Banca de Economii) 2004–05; Amb. to UK 2004–08; Labour Glory Decoration.

DURON, Willy; Belgian insurance industry executive (retd); b. 1945; ed Ghent Univ., Catholic Univ. of Louvain; joined ABB-Insurance (Assurantie van de Belgische Boerenbond) as actuary 1970, Chair. Exec. Cttee KBC Insurance (after merger of Kredietbank, CERA Bank and ABB Insurance) 2000–03, Pres. Exec. Cttee KBC Bank and Insurance Holding Co. 2003–05, CEO KBC Group NV 2005–06 (retd); mem. Bd of Dirs Agfa-Gevaert NV 2008–. *Address:* c/o Board of Directors, Agfa-Gevaert NV, Septestraat 27, 2640 Mortsel, Belgium (office).

DUROV, Lev Konstantinovich; Russian actor; b. 23 Dec. 1931, Moscow; m. Irina Nikolayevna Kirichenko; one d.; ed Studio School of Moscow Art Theatre; actor and stage dir, Cen. Children's Theatre 1954–63, Lenkom Theatre 1963–67, Malaya Bronnaya Theatre 1967–; Theatre-School of Contemporary Plays 1993–; as stage dir produced over 20 theatre productions; People's Artist of Russian Fed. 1982, USSR People's Artist 1990, laureate, Pegas Prize (Ne poslat li nam gontsa?), laureate, Khrustalnaya Turandot For Honour and Achievement 2006. *Plays include:* Chebutykin, Medvedenko, Molière, Sganarelle, Yago, Zhevakin, Alyosha. *Films include:* Visokosnyy god 1961, 9 dney odnogo goda 1961, Ya shagayu po Moskve 1963, Ko mne, Mukhtar! 1964, Lebedev protiv Lebedeva 1965, Na polputi k lune 1966, Chyort s portfelem 1966, Zhitiye i vozneseniye Yurasya Bratchika 1968, Spokoynyy den v kontse voyny 1970, Sluchay s Polyninym 1970, Stariki-razboyniki 1971, Zemlya, do vostrebovaniya 1972, Zayachiy zapovednik 1972, Ekhali v tramvaye Ilf i Petrov 1972, Chetvyortyy 1972, Chelovek na svoyom meste 1972, Moskva-Kassiopeya 1973, Kalina krasnaya 1973, Tsimbireli papa 1973, Vesenniye perevyortyshi 1974, Posledniy den zimy 1974, Otroki vo vselennoy 1974, Georgiy Sedov 1974, Shag navstrechu 1975, Potryasayushchiy Berendeev 1975, Okovani soferi 1975, Na yasniy ogon 1975, Brillianty dlya diktatury proletariata 1975, Suse, liebe Suse 1975, ...I drugie offitsialnye litsa 1976, Doverie 1976, Vooruzhyon i ochen opasen 1977, Veter 'Nadezhdy' 1977, Po semeynym obstoyatelstvam 1977, Alenkiy tsvetochek 1977, Troye iz Prostokvashino (voice) 1978), Veroy i pravdoy 1979, Pyos v sapogakh (voice) 1981, 34-y skoryy 1981, Skazka stranstviy 1982, Kolybelnaya dlya brata 1982, Shyol chetvyortyy god voyny 1983, Proshchanie s Matyoroy 1983, Zachem cheloveku krylya 1984, Uspekh 1984, Tufli s zolotymi pryazhkami 1984, Kak stat schastlivym 1985, Detstvo Bambi 1985, Yunost Bambi 1986, Kapitan 'Piligrima' 1986, God telyonka 1986, Dzhek Vosmyorkin, amerikanets 1987, Chelovek s bulvara Kaputsinov 1987, Esperanza 1988, Smirennoye kladbishche 1989, Bespredel 1989, Dinozavry XX veka 1990, Lyubov 1991, Gangstery v okeane 1991, Au, ograblenie poezda - Za vsyo nado platit 1991, Zvezda sherifa 1992, Ubiystvo v Sunshine Menor 1992, Tayna villy 1992, Sem sorok 1992, Gardemariny III 1992, Davayte bez fokusov! 1992, Serye volki 1993, Master i Margarita 1994, Gospoda artisty 1994, Bulvarnyy roman 1994, Tsvety provincyi 1994, Meshcherskie 1995, Koroli i kapusta 1996, Tango nad propastyu 1997, Noch pered Rozhdestvom (voice) 1997, Ne valyai duraka 1997, Na zare tumannoy yunosti 1997, Akh, zachem eta noch 1997, Sirota kazanskaya 1997, Afinskie vechera 1999, Lunoi byl polon sad (two times laureate, Int. Moscow Cinema Festival 2000) 2000, Zhizn dlinoyu v pesnyu, Rannyaya lyubov 2003, Vesegonskaya volchitsa 2004, Poslednii boi mayora Pugacheva 2005,

Angel-khranitel 2007. *Television includes:* Bumbarash 1971, Neschastnyy sluchay 1972, Bolshaya Peremena (miniseries) 1972, Semnadtsat mgnoveniy vesny (miniseries) 1973, Strannye vzroslye 1974, Kashtanka 1975, Nos 1977, Krasa-vets-muzhchina 1978, D'Artanyan i tri mushketyora 1978, Ne boysya, ya s toboy 1981, Ne zhdali, ne gadali 1982, Etyud dlya domino s royalem 1982, Gori, gori yasno 1983, Gde-to v gubernskom sadu (Koe-chto iz gubernskoy zhizni) 1983, Russia (miniseries) 1986, Klad 1988, Syn klouna 1989, Selo Stepanchikovo i yego obitateli 1989, Detstvo Nikity (Iz russkoy zhizni) (miniseries) 1992, Stranitsy teatralnoy parodii (miniseries) 1996, Grafinya de Monsoro (series) 1998, Banditskiy Peterburg: Krakh Antibiotika (miniseries) 2001, Russkie v Gorode Angelov (series) 2003, Operativnyy psevdonim (series) 2003. *Address:* Frunzenskaya nab. 3B, Apt 206, 119146 Moscow, Russia (home). *Telephone:* (495) 242-43-46 (home). *E-mail:* editor@levdurov.ru (home). *Website:* www.levdurov.ru (home).

ĐUROVIĆ, Dragan; Montenegrin politician; b. 31 Oct. 1959, Danilovgrad; m.; three c.; Legal Adviser and Sec., Agro-Econ. Inst. 1982–92; Dir Directorate for Regional Agricultural Devt 1992–93; Chair. Exec. Bd, Danilovgrad Municipality Ass. 1993–95; Dir Pobjeda publishing co. 1995–2001; Deputy Prime Minister of Montenegro with Responsibility for Political System and Internal Policy 2001–06, Minister of Interior Affairs 2003–06; acting Minister of Foreign Affairs 2002–03; acting Prime Minister 2002–03; currently Deputy, Parl. of Repub. of Montenegro, apptd Deputy, House of Citizens of Fed. Parl. twice, Deputy, Parl. of Repub. of Montenegro three times; fmr mem. Presidency of Democratic Party of Socialists; Chief Deputy, Democratic Party of Socialists Club; Pres. Danilovgrad basketball club. *Television:* Bjelopavlici (co-writer). *Address:* Democratic Party of Montenegrin Socialists (Demokratska Partija Socijalista Crne Gore), 81000 Podgorica, Jovana Tomašević 33 (office); 104/20 Bulevar Sv. Petar Cetinjski, 81000 Podgorica, Montenegro (home). *Telephone:* (82) 243735 (office); (82) 202060 (home). *Fax:* (82) 242101 (office). *E-mail:* webmaster@dps.cg.yu (office); dragandj@cg.yu (office). *Website:* www.dps.cg.yu (office).

ĐUROVIĆ, Gordana, MA, PhD; Montenegrin (b. Serbian) economist, academic and politician; *Professor of Economic Development, International Economic Relations and EU Enlargement Policy, University of Montenegro;* b. 2 March 1964, Novi Knezevac, Serbia; m.; two s.; ed Herceg-Novi Secondary School of Econs, Faculty of Econs, Univ. of Belgrade and Univ. of Montenegro, Podgorica; Assoc. Prof., Faculty of Econs, Univ. of Montenegro, Podgorica, Assoc. Vice-Dean for Scientific Research 1998–2000, Head of Dept of Econ. Policy 2000; project man. and assoc., Regional Devt in Montenegro 1998, Programme on Utility Services Usurpation in Montenegro 1999, Devt Strategy and Poverty Reduction in Montenegro 2000; Minister for Int. Econ. Relations and European Integration, Govt of Montenegro 2004–06; Deputy Prime Minister with responsibility for European Integration 2006–09, Minister for European Integration 2009–10; Full Prof. of Econ. Devt, Int. Econ. Relations and EU Enlargement Policy, Faculty of Econs, Univ. of Montenegro 2010–. *Publications include:* Economic Development (co-author) 1996, Alternative Development Concepts of the Economy of Montenegro (co-author) 2002, Integration in the European and Euro-Atlantic structures (ed.) 2010, EU and Montenegro: Goals of Economic, Social and Territorial Cohesion 2012, EU and Montenegro: Enlargement Policy 2012. *Leisure interests:* walking, Pilates. *Address:* Faculty of Economics, University of Montenegro, 81000 Podgorica, Jovana Tomašević 37, Montenegro (office). *Telephone:* (78) 113304 (office); (20) 241138 (home); 69-070452 (mobile) (home). *Fax:* (20) 241757 (office). *E-mail:* gordana@t-com.me (office). *Website:* www.ekonomija.ac.me (office).

DÜRR, Heinz; German business executive; *Chairman of the Supervisory Board, Dürr AG;* b. 16 July 1933, Stuttgart; s. of Otto Dürr; m. Heide Dürr; three d.; ed Tech. Hochschule, Stuttgart; Man. and Man. Dir Dürr AG (fmrly Otto Dürr GmbH), Stuttgart 1957–80, Chair. Supervisory Bd 1980–; Chair. Exec. Bd AEG AG, Berlin and Frankfurt 1980–90; mem. Exec. Bd Daimler-Benz AG, Stuttgart 1986–90; Chair. Exec. Bd Deutsche Bundesbahn, Deutsche Reichsbahn 1991–94, Deutsche Bahn AG 1994–97, Supervisory Bd Deutsche Bahn AG 1997–99, Carl-Zeiss-Stiftung (Commr) 1999–, Krone GmbH 1999–; Chair. Fed. of Metal Working Industries in Baden-Württemberg and mem. Presidium Fed. of Metal and Electrical Industry Employers' Assocns 1975–80; mem. European Advisory Bd, Schroder, Salomon, Smith Barney 2001 and seven supervisory bds; Hon. DrIng (Rhine-Westphalian Tech. Univ., Aachen) 1996; Verdienstorden des Landes Berlin 2002, Verdienstmedaille des Landes Baden-Württemberg 2009. *Leisure interests:* tennis, golf, theatre, jazz, cross-country skiing. *Address:* Dürr AG, Otto-Dürr-Strasse 8, 70435 Stuttgart (office); Charlottenstrasse 57, 10117 Berlin, Germany. *Telephone:* (711) 1360 (office). *Fax:* (711) 1361455 (office). *Website:* www.durr.com (office).

DURR, Hon. Kent D. Skelton; South African business executive, fmr politician and fmr diplomatist; b. 28 March 1941, Cape Town; s. of Dr John M. Durr and Diana Skelton; m. Suzanne Wiese 1966; one s. two d.; ed SA Coll. School, Cape Town Univ.; dir of family publishing co. 1966–68; Founder and later Man. Dir Durr Estates 1968–84; Chair. Clean Diesel Technologies Inc. 1995–97, Fuel-Tech NV 1995–97; Exec. Chair. Commonwealth Investment Guarantee Agency Ltd 1997; elected to Prov. Council of Cape 1974, MP for Maitland 1977–91, Deputy Minister (Trade and Industry) 1984–86, (Finance) 1984–88; Minister of Budget and Public Works 1988–89; Cabinet Minister of Trade and Industry and Tourism 1989–91; Amb. to UK 1991–94, High Commr in UK 1994–95; Chair. Commonwealth Investment Guarantee Agency 1995–99, Nasdaq Listed Cos, USA 1995–99; mem. Parl. and Senate (African Christian Democratic Party) 1999–; Chair. Darling Wildlife (Cattle and Game) 1999–2004; Freeman City of London 1995. *Leisure interests:* field sports, mountaineering, conservation, game farming. *Address:* Sonquasfontein Private Nature Reserve, Darling, Western Cape 7345, South Africa (home). *Telephone:* (21) 6853908 (home). *Fax:* (2245) 12352 (home); (21) 6853908.

DURRANI, Akram Khan, BA, LLB; Pakistani politician; b. 2 March 1960, Bannu Dist; s. of Ghulam Qadir Khan Durrani and Kalam Bibi; three s. one d.; ed Govt Coll., Nowshera; mem. NW Frontier Prov. (NWFP) Prov. (now Khyber Pakhtoonkhwa) Ass. 1990–93, 1997–99, 2002–; Chief Minister of NWFP 2002–07; mem. Nat. Security Council; mem. Jamiat-e-Ulema-e-Islam. *Address:* c/o Chief Minister's Secretariat, Peshawar, Khyber Pakhtoonkhwa; Frontier House, SAQ Road, Peshawar, Khyber Pakhtoonkhwa, Pakistan (home). *Telephone:* (91) 9211719; (91) 9211074 (home). *Fax:* (91) 9210409 (home).

DURRANT, Jennifer Ann; British artist; b. 17 June 1942, Brighton; d. of Caleb John Durrant and Winifred May Durrant (née Wright); m. William A. H. Henderson 1964 (divorced 1976); m. 2nd Richard Alban Howard Oxby 2000; ed Varndean Grammar School for Girls, Brighton, Brighton Coll. of Art and Crafts, Slade School of Fine Art, Univ. Coll., London; part-time art teacher various colls 1965–74 including St Martin's School of Art, London 1974–87, Chelsea School of Art 1987–89; part-time Lecturer on Painting, RCA 1979–2000, Royal Acad. Schools 1991–98; external assessor at various colls; Exhbn Selector, Northern Young Contemporaries, Whitworth Gallery, Manchester, TV SW Arts; Painting Faculty mem. The British School at Rome 1979–83; Artist-in-Residence, Somerville Coll., Oxford 1979–80; works in collections of Arts Council of GB, British Council, Contemporary Art Soc., Tate Gallery, Museum of Fine Arts, Boston, USA, Neue Galerie, Aachen and in pvt. collections; Abbey Minor Travelling Scholarship British School at Rome 1964, Arts Council Award 1976, Arts Council Major Award 1977, Greater London Arts Asscn Award 1980, Athena Art Award 1988, Independent on Sunday Artist of the Year 1996. *Leisure interests:* classical music, including opera, archaeology, visiting museums, looking at paintings and sculpture, the natural world. *Address:* La Vigna, Via Bondi 14, 06069 Tuoro sul Trasimeno, Italy. *Telephone:* 75829010.

DURRANT, (Mignonette) Patricia, CD, OJ, BA; Jamaican diplomatist and UN official; b. 30 May 1943; ed Univ. of the West Indies, Univ. of Cambridge, UK; Admin. Officer, Ministry of Agric. 1964–70; First Sec. Ministry of Foreign Affairs 1971–72, Prin. Asst Sec. 1972–74; Minister-Counsellor, Mission to OAS, Washington, DC 1974–77; Asst Dir Political Div., Ministry of Foreign Affairs 1977–81, Deputy Dir 1981–83; Deputy Perm. Rep. to UN, New York 1983–87, Perm. Rep. 1995–2002, Pres. UN High-Level Cttee on Tech. Co-operation among Developing Countries 1999–2001, Rep. of Jamaica to UN Security Council 2000–01, UN Ombudsman 2002–07; Chair. UN Preparatory Cttee for the Special Session on Children, Chair. Consultative Cttee for the UN UNIFEM, Vice-Chair. Preparatory Cttee for Special Session on Population and Devt 1999 and Vice-Chair. Open-Ended Working Group on the Reform of the UN Security Council; Amb. to FRG (also accred to Israel, the Netherlands, Switzerland and the Holy See) 1987–92; Dir-Gen. Ministry of Foreign Affairs and Foreign Trade 1992–95; Distinguished Grad. Award, Univ. of the West Indies 1998, Distinguished Achievement Award, World Asscn of Fmr UN Interns and Fellows. *Address:* Ministry of Foreign Affairs and Foreign Trade, 21 Dominica Drive, PO Box 624, Kingston 5, Jamaica (office). *Telephone:* 926-4220 (office). *Fax:* 929-5112 (office). *E-mail:* mfaftjam@cwjamaica.com (office). *Website:* www.mfaft.gov.jm (office).

DUȘA, Mircea; Romanian politician; *Minister of National Defence;* b. 4 Jan. 1955, Toplița, Harghita Co.; m.; two c.; ed Lucian Blaga Univ., Sibiu; mem. City Council, Toplița 1976–86, Vice-Pres. 1986–90; Sr Vice-Pres. Asscn of Towns in Romania 1996–2001; Prefect of Harghita city 2001–04; mem. Chamber of Deputies (Parl.) for Harghita 2004–08, Social Democratic Party Parl. group leader 2010–12; Minister for Relations with Parl. May–Aug. 2012, Minister of Admin and the Interior Aug.–Dec. 2012, of Nat. Defence Dec. 2012–. *Address:* Ministry of National Defence, 050561 Bucharest 5, Str. Izvor 3–5, Romania (office). *Telephone:* (21) 3195660 (office). *Fax:* (21) 3195864 (office). *E-mail:* secretariat_general@mapn.ro (office). *Website:* www.mapn.ro (office).

DUSAUTOIR, Thierry; French professional rugby union player; *Captain, French National Rugby Union Team;* b. 18 Nov. 1981, Abidjan, Côte d'Ivoire; ed graduate chemical engineer; began with judo as his sport; played rugby from age 16; plays as a flanker; played for Bordeaux-Bègles 2001–03, US Colomiers 2003–04, Biarritz 2004–06 (played in final of Heineken Cup losing to Munster 23–19 at Millennium Stadium, Cardiff 2006, won final of Top 14 40–13 against Toulouse 2006), Toulouse 2006–, France 2006– (Capt.). Test debut against Romania (62–14), Cotroceni Stadium, Bucharest 2006; played in subsequent Test against the Springboks at Newlands Stadium, Cape Town with France winning 36–26; captained France to a 27–22 win over New Zealand in Dunedin 2009; captained France through to final of Rugby World Cup, Eden Park, Auckland 2011; Man of the Match Award, Rugby World Cup Final 2011, Int. Rugby Bd (IRB) Int. Player of the Year 2011. *Achievements include:* well-known for his try against New Zealand in quarterfinal of World Cup in Cardiff in which he made 38 tackles, two more than the entire All Blacks side 2007. *Address:* Stade Toulousain, BP 42354, 31022 Toulouse Cedex 2 (office); c/o Fédération Française de Rugby, 3–5 rue Jean de Montaigu, 91463 Marcoussis Cedex, France. *Telephone:* (8) 92-69-31-15 (office); 1-69-63-64-65. *Fax:* (5) 34-42-24-21 (office). *E-mail:* info@stadetoulousain .fr (office); info@ffr.fr. *Website:* www.stadetoulousain.fr (office); www.ffr.fr.

DUSSAULT, René, BA, LLL, PhD, FRSC; Canadian lawyer and judge; *Counsel, Heenan Blaikie LLP;* b. 23 Nov. 1939, Québec City; s. of Daniel Dussault and Madeleine Pelletier; m. Marielle Godbout 1967; two s.; ed Petit Séminaire de Québec, Laval Univ. and London School of Econs and Political Science; called to Bar, Québec 1963; Lecturer in Law, Laval Univ. 1966–70; Legal Counsel, Québec Health and Welfare Inquiry Comm.; Special Adviser to Minister of Social Affairs of Québec 1970–73; Chair. Québec Professions Bd 1973–77; Deputy Minister of Justice, Québec 1977–80; Prof., École nationale d'administration publique 1981–89; Laskin Chair in Public Law, Osgoode Hall Law School 1983–84; fmr legal consultant, Kronström, McNicoll & Assocs, Québec City; Judge, Québec Court of Appeal 1989–2008; Counsel, Heenan Blaikie LLP, Québec City 2008–; associate editor of the Canadian Public Administration journal (1982-1989); Co-Chair. Royal Comm. on Aboriginal Peoples 1991–96; Hon. LLD (York) 1992, (Dalhousie) 1997; Québec Bar Asscn Medal 1987, Québec Interprofessional Council Prize 1991, Vanier Medal, Inst. of Public Admin. of Canada 1998, Bertha Wilson Touchstone Award, Canadian Bar Asscn 2001, Council of Canadian Admin. Tribunals Medal 2006, Gloire de l'Escolle Medal, Alumni Asscn of Université Laval 2009. *Publications:* Le contrôle judiciaire de l'administration au Québec 1969, Traité de droit administratif, Vols I & II 1974 (also co-author of subsequent vols), Administrative Law: A Treatise, Vols I-V 1985–90 (Walter Owen Award, Canadian Bar Asscn's Foundation for Legal Research, prix du Concours juridique, Québec Bar Foundation 1988). *Address:* Heenan Blaikie LLP, 900, boul. René-Lévesque Est, Bureau 600, Québec City, PQ G1R 2B5 (office); 1332 James-LeMoine Avenue, Sillery, PQ G1S 1A3, Canada (home). *Telephone:* (418) 649-5053 (office); (418) 527-6332 (home). *Fax:* (418) 524-1717 (office). *E-mail:* rdussault@heenan.ca (office). *Website:* www.heenanblaikie.com (office).

DUTHEILLET DE LAMOTHE, Olivier; French lawyer; *Member, Conseil Constitutionnel;* b. 10 Nov. 1949, Neuilly; s. of Alain Dutheillet de Lamothe and Suzanne Garnier; m. Marie-Caroline Sainsaulieu 1981; one s. one d.; ed Institut d'Etudes Politiques de Paris, Ecole Nationale d'Administration; held several posts at Council d'Etat, including Auditor 1975, Rapporteur Litigation Section 1975–77, Head Documentation Centre and Coordination 1977–79, Maitre des requetes 1979, Advocate General, Ass. of Litigation and other judicial panels 1981–86; Tech. Adviser to Minister of Health and Social Security 1979–81; Legal Adviser to Directorate Gen. of Civil Aviation 1985–86; Adviser to Minister of Social Affairs and Employment 1986–87; Dir of Labour Relations Ministry of Labour, Employment and Vocational Training 1987–95; State Councillor 1992; Social Adviser Presidency of the Repub. 1995–97, Deputy Sec.-Gen. of the Presidency 1997–2000; Rapporteur Litigation Section 2000–01; Prof., Institut d'Etudes Politiques de Paris 2001; Mem. Conseil Constitutionnel 2001–10; Global Distinguished Fellow, Hauser Global Law School Program, New York Univ. School of Law; Chevalier de l'Ordre national de la Légion d'Honneur, de l'Ordre national du Mérite, Conseiller d'Etat. *Publications:* Politique de l'emploi et dynamique des entreprises 2005. *Leisure interests:* cinema, skiing. *Address:* Conseil Constitutionnel, 2 rue de Montpensier, 75001 Paris, France (office). *Telephone:* 1-40-15-30-06 (office); 1-45-48-50-48. *Fax:* 1-40-20-93-27 (office). *E-mail:* odl@conseil-constitutionnel.fr (office). *Website:* www.conseil-constitutionnel.fr (office).

DUTKOWSKY, Robert M., BS; American computer industry executive; *CEO, Tech Data Corporation;* b. 2 Jan. 1955, Endicott, NY; m. Lorraine Dutkowsky; two c.; ed Cornell Univ., Ithaca, NY; worked at IBM 1977–97, served in sr man. positions including Exec. Asst to fmr CEO Lou Gerstner, Vice-Pres. for Distribution, Asia/Pacific; Exec. Vice Pres. Sales and Marketing EMC Corpn 1997–2000; Chair., Pres. and CEO GenRad Inc. 2000–02; Pres. Assembly Test Div. Teradyne Inc. 2001–02; Chair., Pres. and CEO JD Edwards Inc. 2002–03; Chair., Pres. and CEO Egenera Inc. 2004–06; mem. Bd of Dirs and CEO Tech Data Corpn 2006–; mem. Bd of Dirs Sepaton, Inc. *Address:* Tech Data Corpn, 5350 Tech Data Drive, Clearwater, FL 33760-3122, USA (office). *Telephone:* (727) 539-7429 (office). *Fax:* (727) 538-7803 (office). *E-mail:* info@techdata.com (office). *Website:* www.techdata .com (office).

DUTOIT, Charles E.; Swiss conductor and music director; *Artistic Director and Principal Conductor, Royal Philharmonic Orchestra, London;* b. 7 Oct. 1936, Lausanne; s. of Edmond Dutoit and Berthe Dutoit (née Laederman); one s. one d.; ed Conservatoires of Lausanne and Geneva, Accademia Musicale Chigiana, Siena, Italy, Conservatorio Benedetto Marcello, Venice, Italy and Berkshire Music Center, Tanglewood, USA; Assoc. Conductor Berne Symphony Orchestra 1964, Prin. and Artistic Dir 1966–78; Assoc. Conductor Tonhalle Orchestra, Zürich 1966; Conductor and Artistic Dir Zürich Radio Orchestra 1964; Artistic Dir Nat. Symphony Orchestra of Mexico and Göteborg Symphony Orchestra 1977–2002; Artistic Dir Montréal Symphony Orchestra 1977–2002; operatic debut Covent Garden (conducting Faust) 1983; Prin. Guest Conductor Minnesota Orchestra 1983–84, 1985–86; Artistic Dir and Prin. Conductor Philadelphia Orchestra summer season, Mann Music Center 1991–2001, Saratoga Springs 1991–2010; Music Dir Orchestre Nat. de France 1990–2001; Prin. Guest Conductor NHK Symphony Orchestra, Tokyo 1996–, Music Dir 1998–2003; Chief Conductor and Artistic Adviser Philadelphia Orchestra 2007–; Artistic Dir and Prin. Conductor Royal Philharmonic Orchestra 2009–; guest conductor of all major orchestras in USA, Europe, South America, Asia, Australia and Israel; Hon. Citizen of the City of Philadelphia 1991; Commdr, Ordre des Arts et des Lettres 1996, Hon. OC; Hon. PhD (Montreal) 1984, (Laval) 1985, (McGill); two Grammys, Grand Prix de l'Académie du disque français, High Fidelity Int. Record Critics' Award, Montreux Record Award, Japan Record Acad. Award, Musician of the Year, Canada Music Council 1982, two awards from Canadian Conf. of the Arts, Grand Prix du Président de la République (France). *Recordings:* over 125 recordings with various orchestras since 1980, winning over 40 int. awards and including Falla's Three Cornered Hat and El amor Brujo, The Planets, Tchaikovsky's 1st Piano Concerto, Saint-Saëns 3rd Symphony, Bizet's L'Arlésienne and Carmen Suites, Gubaidulina Offertorium with Boston Symphony, Symphonies by Honegger, Roussel's Symphonies with French Nat. Orchestra, Saint-Saëns Piano Concertos, Suppé Overtures, Berlioz' Les Troyens. *Address:* Royal Philharmonic Orchestra, 16 Clerkenwell Green, London, EC1R 0QT, England (office). *Website:* www.rpo.co.uk (office).

DUTRA, José Eduardo de Barros, BSc; Brazilian oil and gas industry executive and politician; b. 11 April 1957, Rio de Janeiro; s. of José Araújo Dutra and Clóvis de Barros Dutra; m. (separated); ed Univ. Fed. Rural do Rio de Janeiro; geologist, Geologia Sondagens (Geosol) Ltda 1980–81; geologist, Petrobrás Mineradora (Petromisa) 1983–90, Companhia Vale do Rio Doce 1990–94; Senator for state of Sergipe 1995–2003; Pres. and CEO Petróleo Brasileiro SA (Petrobras) 2003–05; Leader, Partido dos Trabalhadores (Workers' Party) 1996–97; unsuccessful candidate Senator for Sergipe 2006; also mem. PT Nat. Bd; Pres. Sindimina (regional miners' union) 1989–94; mem. Geologist Asscn of Sergipe; Geologist Asscn of Sergipe Geologist of the Year 1988. *Address:* c/o Partido dos Trabalhadores, Rua Silveira Martins 132, Centro, 01019–000 São Paulo SP, Brazil. *Telephone:* (11) 3243-1313. *Fax:* (11) 3243-1345. *E-mail:* presidencia@pt.org .br. *Website:* www.pt.org.br.

DUTREIL, Renaud, MA, DEA; French business executive and fmr politician; *Chairman, Brasil Beauté;* b. 12 June 1960, Chambéry; ed École Normale Supérieure, Institut d'Études Politiques de Paris, École des Hautes Études en Sciences Sociales, Ecole Nationale d'Admin; Maitre des Requêtes, Council of State 1989–, later Govt Commr; elected Deputy, Assemblée Nationale 1993, 1997, 2002; mem. Council Castle-Thierry (Aisne) 1995–2001, Charly-on-Marne, (Aisne) 2001–08; Sec. of State 2002–04; Minister for the Civil Service and Reform of the State 2004–05; Minister of Small and Medium-Sized Enterprises, Trade, Crafts and the Liberal Professions 2005–07; Founder and first Pres. Union pour un Mouvement Populaire 2000–02, Union pour la Majorité Présidentielle 2002; Founder Entreprise du Patrimoine Vivant 2004–08; Chair. LVMH Moët Hennessy Louis Vuitton Inc. 2008–12; Chair. Brasil Beauté (develops int. beauty brands in Brazil) 2012–; Founder and Chair. Duplo T 2012–; mem. Bd of Dirs LCapital 2008–13, AHAlife 2012–; mem. Bd New England, Parsons School of Design, Maison Française, Columbia Univ.; mem. Partnership for New York; Pres. Friends of

Institut des Hautes Études Scientifiques 2010–; Trustee, Museum of Art and Design, New York; Chevalier, Légion d'honneur. *Publications:* Le coq sur la paille 1993, La République des Ames mortes 2001. *Address:* Duplo T, 45 Rockefeller Plaza, Suite 2000, New York, NY 10111, USA (office). *E-mail:* contact@duplo-T.com (office). *Website:* www.duplot-t.com (office).

DUTT, Barkha, BA; Indian TV journalist; *Group Editor, English News, New Delhi Television;* b. 18 Dec. 1971, New Delhi; d. of S.P. Dutt and the late Prabha Dutt; ed St Stephen's Coll., Delhi Jamia Millia Islamia, Columbia Univ., USA; started journalism career with New Delhi TV, currently Group Ed., English News; Fellow, Asia Soc. 2006; writes column Third Eye for The Hindustan Times; Global Leader of Tomorrow Award, World Econ. Forum 2001, 2008, Commonwealth Broadcasters Award 2002, Broadcast Journalist of the Year, Indian Express 2005, Padma Shri 2008, Indian News Broadcasting Award for the Most Intelligent News Show Host 2008, Society's Young Achievers Award. *Address:* NDTV Convergence Limited, 207, Okhla Industrial Estate, Phase 3, New Delhi 110 020, India (office). *Telephone:* (11) 26446666 (office). *Website:* www.barkhadutt.tv.

DUTT, Shekhar; Indian government official; *Governor of Chhattisgarh;* ed Univ. of S Wales, Swansea, UK; fmr Indian Army officer; Prin. Sec., Depts of School Educ., Sports & Youth Welfare 1996–98; Prin. Sec., Dept of Tribal Welfare 1998–2001; Dir Gen. Sports Authority of India 2001–03; Sec., Ministry of Health 2003–04; Defence Sec. 2005–07; Deputy Nat. Security Adviser 2007–09; Gov. of Chhattisgarh 2010–; mem. Bd of Trustees, DeSales Univ. 2009–; Sena Medal (mil. decoration) 1971. *Address:* Office of the Governor, Raj Bhavan, Raipur 492 001, India (office). *Telephone:* (771) 2331102 (office). *Fax:* (771) 2331104 (office).

DUVAL, Charles Gaëtan Xavier Luc, BA, FCA; Mauritian chartered accountant and politician; *Deputy Prime Minister and Minister of Finance and Economic Development;* b. 28 Jan. 1958; m.; three c.; ed Univ. of Leeds, UK; Audit Man., Casson Beckman, UK 1980–86; Founding Pnr, Coopers & Lybrand (Mauritius); fmr pnr and business consultant, De Chazal Du Mée (Chartered Accountants); Sr Pnr, Nexia, Baker & Arenson 2000–05; Minister of Industry and Tourism 1994–95; Founder and Leader Parti Mauricien Xavier-Luc Duval 1989–; mem. Nat. Ass. 1999–; Minister of Industry, Commerce, Corp. Affairs and Financial Services 1999–2000, of Tourism, Leisure and External Communications 2005–10, Deputy Prime Minister 2005–10, Deputy Prime Minister and Minister of Social Integration and Econ. Empowerment 2010–, Minister of Finance and Econ. Devt 2011–. *Address:* Ministry of Finance and Economic Development, Government House, Ground Floor, Port Louis, Mauritius (office). *Telephone:* 201-1146 (office). *Fax:* 211-0096 (office). *E-mail:* mof@mail.gov.mu (office). *Website:* www.gov.mu/portal/site/MOFSite (office).

DUVAL, David Robert; American professional golfer; b. 9 Nov. 1971, Jacksonville, Fla; s. of sr PGA Tour golfer Bob Duval; ed Georgia Tech.; turned professional 1993; mem. Walker Cup team 1991, Pres.'s Cup team, 1996, 1998, Ryder Cup team 1999; winner Nike Wichita Open 1993, Nike Tour Championship 1993, Michelob Championship at Kingsmill 1997, 1998, Walt Disney World/Oldsmobile Classic 1997, the Tour Championship 1997, Tucson Chrysler Classic 1998, Shell Houston Open 1998, NEC World Series of Golf 1998, Mercedes Championship 1999, Bob Hope Chrysler Classic 1999, the Players Championship 1999, BellSouth Classic 1999, Ryder Cup 1999, Open Championship, Royal Lytham, UK 2001; f. Duval Designs (golf design and architectural firm) 2005; Collegiate Player of the Year 1993, Dave Williams Award 1993, Jasper Award, Jacksonville 1996. *Leisure interests:* reading, fly fishing, surfing, skiing, baseball. *Address:* c/o IMG Golf, IMG Center, 1360 East 9th Street, Suite 100, Cleveland, OH 44114, USA (office).

DUVALIER, Jean-Claude ('Baby Doc'); Haitian politician; b. 3 July 1951, Port-au-Prince; s. of the late Pres. François Duvalier and the late Simone Duvalier (née Ovide); m. Michele Bennett 1980 (divorced 1990); one s.; ed Coll. of St Louis de Gonzague, Port-au-Prince and Faculty of Law, Univ. of Haiti; named political heir to Pres. François Duvalier Jan. 1971; Life Pres. 1971–86 (overthrown in coup); living in Mougins, France; returned to Haiti 2011.

DUVALL, Robert; American actor; b. 5 Jan. 1931, San Diego, Calif.; s. of William H. Duvall; m. 1st Gail Youngs (divorced); m. 2nd Sharon Brophy 1991; ed Principia Coll. Ill.; student, Neighborhood Playhouse, New York; f. Butchers Run Films (production co.) 1992. *Films include:* To Kill a Mockingbird 1963, Captain Newman, MD 1964, The Chase 1965, Countdown 1968, The Detective 1968, Bullitt 1968, True Grit 1969, The Rain People 1969, M*A*S*H 1970, The Revolutionary 1970, The Godfather 1972, Tomorrow 1972, The Great Northfield, Minnesota Raid 1972, Joe Kidd 1972, Lady Ice 1973, The Outfit 1974, The Conversation 1974, The Godfather Part II 1974, Breakout 1975, The Killer Elite 1975, Network 1976, The Eagle Has Landed 1977, The Greatest 1977, The Betsy 1978, Apocalypse Now 1979, The Great Santini 1980, True Confessions 1981, Angelo My Love (actor and dir) 1983, Tender Mercies (Acad. Award for Best Actor 1984) 1983, The Stone Boy 1984, The Natural 1984, The Lightship 1986, Let's Get Harry 1986, Belizaire the Cajun 1986, Colors 1988, Convicts, Roots in a Parched Ground, The Handmaid's Tale 1990, A Show of Force 1990, Days of Thunder 1990, Rambling Rose 1991, Newsies 1992, The New Boys 1992, Stalin 1992, The Plague, Geronimo, Falling Down 1993, The Paper 1994, Wrestling Ernest Hemingway 1994, Something To Talk About, The Stars Fell on Henrietta, The Scarlet Letter, A Family Thing (also co-producer), Phenomenon 1996, The Apostle 1997, Gingerbread Man 1997, Deep Impact, A Civil Action 1999, Gone In Sixty Seconds 2000, A Shot at Glory (also producer) 2000, The 6th Day 2000, Apocalypse Now: Redux 2001, John Q 2002, Assassination Tango (also producer and dir) 2002, Secondhand Lions 2003, Gods and Generals 2003, Open Range 2003, Kicking & Screaming 2005, Thank You for Smoking 2005, Lucky You 2007, We Own the Night 2007, Four Christmases 2008, The Road 2009, Get Low 2009, Crazy Heart 2009, Seven Days in Utopia 2011, Jayne Mansfield's Car 2012, Jack Reacher 2012; dir We're Not the Jet Set. *Television includes:* Lonesome Dove (mini-series) 1989, Broken Trail (mini-series; Emmy Award for Best Actor in a Mini-series 2007) 2006. *Stage appearances include:* A View from the Bridge 1965 (Obie Award), Wait Until Dark 1966, American Buffalo. *Address:* c/o ICM Partners, 10250 Constellation Boulevard, Los Angeles, CA 90067; Butchers Run Films, 100 Universal City Plaza Building 507, Suite 2D, Universal City, CA 91608, USA.

DUVALL, Shelley; American actress and producer; b. 7 July 1949, Houston, Tex.; f. TV production co. Think Entertainment. *Films include:* (actress): Brewster McCloud 1970, McCabe and Mrs. Miller 1971, Thieves Like Us 1974, Nashville 1975, Buffalo Bill and the Indians 1976, Three Women (Cannes Festival Prize 1977) 1977, Annie Hall 1977, The Shining 1980, Popeye 1980, Time Bandits 1981, Frankenweenie 1984, Roxanne 1987, Suburban Commando 1991, Underneath 1995, Portrait of a Lady 1996, Twilight of the Ice Nymphs 1997, Changing Habits 1997, Tale of the Mummy 1998, Home Fries 1998, The 4th Floor 1999, Dreams in the Attic 2000, Big Monster on Campus 2000, Manna From Heaven 2002. *Television includes:* (actress): Bernice Bobs Her Hair, Lily, Twilight Zone, Mother Goose Rock 'n' Rhyme, Faerie Tale Theatre (Rumpelstiltskin, Rapunzel), Tall Tales and Legends (Darlin' Clementine); (exec. producer): Faerie Tale Theatre, Tall Tales and Legends, Nightmare Classics, Dinner at Eight (film), Mother Goose Rock 'n' Rhyme, Stories from Growing Up, Backfield in Motion (film), Bedtime Stories, Mrs. Piggle-Wiggle. *Address:* POB 1660 Blanco, TX 78606, USA.

DUWAISAN, Khalid Abdulaziz al-, BA (Comm); Kuwaiti diplomatist; *Ambassador to UK and Dean of the Diplomatic Corps;* b. 15 Aug. 1947; s. of Abdulaziz Saud al-Duwaisan and Sabeka Abdullah al-Duwaisan; m. Dalal al-Humaizi 1980; one s. one d.; ed Cairo Univ., Univ. of Kuwait; joined Ministry of Foreign Affairs 1970, Diplomatic Attaché 1974, Embassy, Washington, DC 1975; Amb. to Netherlands 1984 (also accred to Romania 1988); Chair. Kuwaiti del. for supervision of demilitarized zone between Iraq and Kuwait and Chief Co-ordinator Comm. for Return of Stolen Property 1991; Amb. to UK (also accred to Norway, Sweden and Denmark) 1993–, (also accred to Ireland 1995–), Dean of the Diplomatic Corps; mem. Advisory Bd, Centre of Near and Middle East Studies, SOAS 1998–; participant, Workshop on Int. Diplomacy in the New Century, Kuwait Foundation for the Advancement of Sciences and John F. Kennedy School of Govt, Univ. of Harvard, USA 2007; Hon. GCVO (UK) 1995; Freedom of the City of London 2001; Hon. Certificate (Harvard Univ.) 2005; Dr hc (Univ. of East Anglia) 2012; Award of Excellence for Services to Anglo-Kuwaiti Relations, British Business Forum and British Amb. to Kuwait 2009, Diplomat Magazine Lifetime Contrib. to Diplomacy in London Award 2009, Three Faiths Forum Gold Medallion 2010, UN Assn's Annual Award for Exceptional Service to the Int. Community 2011, Ben TV Diplomatic Award in recognition of Lifetime Achievement as a Diplomat 2011. *Leisure interests:* tennis, swimming. *Address:* Kuwaiti Embassy, 2 Albert Gate, London, SW1X 7JU (office); 22 Kensington Palace Gardens, London, W8 4QQ, England (home). *Telephone:* (20) 7590-3400 (office); (20) 7221-7374 (home). *Fax:* (20) 7823-1712 (office). *E-mail:* kuwait@dircon.co.uk (office); widad@btconnect.com (office); enquiries@kuwaitinfo.org.uk (office).

DVORAK, Harold Fisher, AB, MD; American pathologist; *Founding Director, Center for Vascular Biology Research, Beth Israel Deaconess Medical Center;* b. 20 June 1937, Milwaukee, Wis.; s. of Harold J. Dvorak and Laura Dvorak (née Fisher); m. Ann Marie Tompkins; one s. two d.; ed Princeton Univ., Harvard Univ.; Asst Pathologist, Massachusetts Gen. Hosp. 1969–75, Assoc. Pathologist 1975–78, Head, Immunopathology Unit 1976–80; Chief, Dept of Pathology, Beth Israel Hosp., Boston, Mass 1979–96, Founding Dir, Center for Vascular Biology Research, Chief, Dept of Pathology, Beth Israel Deaconess Medical Center 1996–2005 (retd); Mallinckrodt Prof. of Pathology, Harvard Medical School 1979–; Fellow, AAAS 1999; mem. American Asscn of Immunologists, American Soc. of Investigative Pathology (Vice-Pres. 1996); ASIP Rous-Whipple Award 2002, Nat. Foundation for Cancer Research Albert Szent-Gyorgyi Prize for Progress in Cancer Research 2006, Canada Gairdner Int. Award 2014. *Address:* Beth Israel Deaconess Medical Center, Department of Pathology, 330 Brookline Avenue, RN-227C, Boston, MA 02215, USA (office). *Telephone:* (617) 667-8529 (office). *Fax:* (617) 667-2913 (office). *E-mail:* hdvorak@bidmc.harvard.edu (office). *Website:* cvbr.hms.harvard.edu (office).

DVORKIN, Maj.-Gen. Vladimir, PhD; Russian naval officer (retd), defence and foreign affairs specialist and academic; *Principal Researcher, Institute of World Economy and International Relations, Russian Academy of Sciences;* b. 12 Jan. 1936, Leningrad (now St Petersburg); ed High Mil. Naval Coll.; worked at State Cen. Naval Testing Site; took part in first Soviet tests of nuclear-powered ballistic missile submarines and in first underwater test launches; worked in 4th Cen. Research Inst., Russian Defence Ministry 1962–2001, Head of Inst. 1993–2001; Sr Advisor at PIR Center and Carnegie Moscow Center; Prof. and Full mem. Russian Acad. of Missile and Artillery Sciences, Acad. of the Mil. Sciences, Russian Eng Acad., Int. Eng Acad., Acad. of Astronautics; made significant contrib. to formulating Soviet and Russia's position at negotiations on strategic offensive arms control and reduction; participating for many years as an expert in preparing SALT II, the INF Treaty, START I and START II; Merits marked with orders: 'For Merits to the Fatherland' (Fourth Degree), 'For Military Merits', 'Labor Red Banner', 'Red Star'; numerous medals; Honoured Worker of Science and Tech. of Russian Fed. *Publications:* co-author of all major documents related to Strategic Nuclear Forces and Strategic Missile Forces; more than 350 publs. *Address:* Institute of World Economy and International Relations (IMEMO), Profsoyushaya Str. 23, Moscow, B-71, GSP-7, 117997 (office); PIR Center, Na Trekhprudnom, Trekhprudny Per. 9, Bldg 1B, Moscow 103001, Russia. *Telephone:* (495) 120-52-36 (office); (495) 234-05-25. *Fax:* (495) 234-95-58. *E-mail:* imemoran@imemo.ru (office); info@pircenter.org. *Website:* www.imemo.ru (office); www.pircenter.org.

DVORKOVICH, Arkadii Vladimirovich, MA; Russian economist and politician; *Deputy Chairman of the Government;* b. 26 March 1972, Moscow; m. Zumrud Rustamova; two s.; ed Moscow State Univ., New Econ. School, Moscow, Duke Univ., USA; worked for Econ. Expert Group, Ministry of Finance 1994–2000, Head of Economic Expert Group 1997–2000; Adviser to Minister of Econ. Devt and Trade 2000–, Expert of the Strategic Research Centre 2000–01; Deputy Minister of Econ. Devt and Trade 2001–04; Head of Presidential Experts Directorate, Admin of the Pres. of Russian Fed. 2004–08, Aide to the Pres. 2008–12; Deputy Chair. of the Govt 2012–; Pres. Russian Investment and Finance Analysts' Guild; mem. Nation Banking Council; First Vice-Pres. Russian Chess Fed. 2007–; Order of Merit for the Fatherland (Fourth Class), Order of Honour, Medal (Second Class) of the Order of Merit for the Fatherland, Medal 'In Commemoration of the 1,000th Anniversary of Kazan', Officer of the Order of Merit of the Italian Repub. *Publications:* various articles on econs. *Address:* Office of the Chairman of the Government, Krasnopresnenskaya nab. 2, 103274 Moscow, Russia (office). *Telephone:* (495) 205-57-35 (office). *Fax:* (495) 205-42-19 (office). *E-mail:*

dvorkovich_AV@gov.ru (office). *Website:* www.premier.gov.ru (office); government .ru (office).

DVORSKÝ, Peter; Slovak singer (tenor); b. 25 Sept. 1951, Partizánske, Topoľčany Dist; s. of Vendelín Dvorský and Anna Dvorská; m. Marta Varšová 1975; two d.; ed State Conservatoire, Bratislava; studied with R. Carossi and M. di Luggo, Milan 1975–76; opera soloist, Slovak Nat. Theatre, Bratislava 1972–96, 1999; sang at Metropolitan Opera, New York 1977, Covent Garden, London 1978, Bolshoi Theatre, Moscow 1978, La Scala, Milan 1979; performs regularly at Bratislava, Vienna State Opera, Covent Garden, La Scala, New York Metropolitan Opera, Munich, Berlin, Prague, Geneva, Paris, Buenos Aires, Tokyo and in many other cities throughout the world; numerous radio and TV performances; many recordings; Chair. Council of Slovak Music Union 1991–; Pres. Harmony Foundation 1991–; Dir of Opera, State Theatre, Košice 2006–10, Slovak Nat. Theatre, Bratislava 2010–12; performed charity concerts after floods in Czech Repub. 2002; Pres. Dvořak Competition, Karlovy Vary, Czech Repub.; awards include Tchaikovsky Competition, Geneva (5th Prize 1974, 1st Prize 1975), Leoš Janáček Memorial Medal 1978, Giuseppe Verdi Medal 1979, Artist of Merit 1981, Nat. Artist 1984, Kammersänger, Vienna 1986, Francisco Cilea Prize 1991, Wilhelm Furtwängler Prize 1992. *Leisure interests:* hunting, music, piano, family. *Address:* J. Hronca 1A, 841 02 Bratislava, Slovakia. *Fax:* (2) 64287626.

DWEK, Raymond Allen, CBE, DPhil, DSc, FRS, FRSC, FSB, FRCP, CBiol, CChem; British scientist and academic; *Director, Glycobiology Institute, University of Oxford;* b. 10 Nov. 1941, Manchester, England; s. of Victor Joe Dwek and Alice Liniado; m. Sandra Livingstone 1964; two s. two d.; ed Carmel Coll., Univ. of Manchester, Lincoln Coll., Oxford, Exeter Coll., Oxford; Research Lecturer in Physical Chem., Christ Church, Oxford 1966–68, in Biochemistry 1975–76; Lecturer in Inorganic Chem., Christ Church, Oxford 1968–75, in Biochemistry, Trinity Coll., Oxford 1976–84; Fellow, Exeter Coll., Oxford 1974–88, Professorial Fellow 1988–; Dir Glycobiology Inst., Univ. of Oxford 1988–, Prof. of Glycobiology 1988–, Head of Dept of Biochemistry 2000–; Dir for Grad. Training 1998–; mem. Oxford Enzyme Group 1971–88; Founder-mem. Oxford Oligosaccharide Group 1983; Univ. of Oxford Dir (non-exec.) and Founder Glycosciences Ltd (fmrly Glycosystems Ltd); Dir and Founding Scientist, IgX, Oxford 1998; Dir United Therapeutics 2002–; Visiting Royal Society Research Fellow, Weizmann Inst., Rehovot, Israel 1969; Royal Society Locke Research Fellow 1974–76; Visiting Prof., Duke Univ., NC; Hon. Life/Founder-mem. Swedish Biophysical Soc. 1979–; Kluge Chair of Tech. and Soc., Kluge Center of the Library of Congress, Washington, DC 2007; Biomedical Research Council Distinguished Visitor, Singapore 2005; mem. European Molecular Biological Org. (EMBO) 1988–, Scientific Advisory Bd, Hepatitis Foundation USA 1994–, Inst. for Applied Biosciences, Ben-Gurion Univ. of the Negev, Israel (chair.) 2001–05, Commonwealth Project for Hepatitis Outreach, USA 2002–, Bd of Scientific Govs Scripps Research Inst., La Jolla, USA 2003– (Inst. Prof. 2008–), European Lipidonics Initiative 2004–, Bd of Govs Exec. Cttee, Ben-Gurion Univ., Israel 2005–, Int. Advisory Bd of NIBN, Israel 2005–; Pres. Inst. of Biology, London 2008–09; Judge, Millennium Fund Competition, The Daily Telegraph 1994; Scientific Adviser to the Pres., Ben Gurion Univ., Negev, Israel; Foreign mem. American Philosophical Soc. 2006, 2010; mem. Chancellors Court of Benefactors, Oxford, UK/Israel Life Sciences Council; Hon. mem. Inst. of Biochemistry, Bucharest 2000–, Hon. Fellow, Lincoln Coll., Oxford 2004; Hon. Fellow, Royal Soc. of Physicians 2007; Commdr Nat. Romanian Order for Merit 2000; Dr hc (Catholic Univ. of Louvain) 1996, (Cluj, Romania) 2006; Hon. PhD (Ben-Gurion Univ., Israel) 2001; Hon. DSc (Scripps Research Inst., La Jolla, Calif.) 2004,; The Wellcome Trust Award for Research in Biochemistry Related to Medicine 1994, Scientific Leadership Award, Hepatitis B Foundation, Philadelphia, Delaware Valley Coll. Centennial Award 1997, Boyce Thompson Distinguished Lecturer, Cornell Univ., USA 1997, Lemieux Lecturer, Univ. of Alberta, Canada 2003, Huxley Medal 2007. *Publications include:* Nuclear Magnetic Resonance (NMR) in Biochemistry 1973, Physical Chemistry Principles and Problems for Biochemists (co-author) 2002, NMR in Biology (co-author) 1977, Biological Spectrosocopy (co-author) 1984; numerous scientific articles and patents. *Leisure interests:* family, patent law, sport, listening to music. *Address:* Glycobiology Institute, South Parks Road, Oxford, OX1 3QU (office); Exeter College, Oxford, OX1 3DP, England (home). *Telephone:* (1865) 275344 (office). *Fax:* (1865) 275771 (home). *E-mail:* raymond.dwek@exeter.ox.ac.uk (office). *Website:* www.bioch.ox.ac.uk/glycob (office).

DWURNIK, Edward; Polish painter and illustrator; b. 19 April 1943, Radzymin; m.; one d.; ed Acad. of Fine Arts, Warsaw; over 150 one-man exhbns (retrospective) including Warsaw 1971, 1974, 1975, 1977, 1980, 1990, 1994–95, 1997, 1999, 2000, The Zacheta Gallery of Contemporary Art, Warsaw 2001, Toruń 1980, Wrocław 1987, Bydgoszcz 1997, Bytom 1997, PGS, Sopot 1999, Kraków 2000; exhbns abroad: Darmstadt 1977, Moscow 1978, Göteborg 1981, Kassel 1982, Fifth Biennale of Sydney 1984, Nouvelle Biennale de Paris 1985, Eindhoven 1986, Lingen 1986, Cologne 1986, London 1987, 1991–92, 19th Art Biennale, São Paulo 1987, Olympic Art Festival, Seoul 1988, Leipzig 1991, Vienna 1993, 1999–2000, Stuttgart (retrospective) 1994, Fassbender Gallery, Chicago 1996, Nevin Kelly Gallery, Washington, DC 2004; Cyprian Kamil Norwid Art Critics' Award for Exhbn Summer 80, Warsaw 1981, Solidarity Labour Union Cultural Award (for paintings from Warsaw series 1981) 1983, Coutts Contemporary Art Foundation Award, Zurich 1992; numerous Polish and int. awards. *Leisure interests:* driving, travelling, opera, films, music (heavy metal). *E-mail:* edward@dwurnik.pl. *Website:* www.dwurnik.pl.

DYADKOVA, Larissa; Russian singer; b. 9 March 1952, Zelenodolsk; m. Alexandre Kogan 1985; one d.; ed Leningrad Conservatory class of J. Levando; joined Kirov Opera Co., making debut as Valvya in Glinka's Ivan Susanin; guest soloist, Metropolitan Opera, La Scala, Communale Theatre, Florence, Deutsche Oper Berlin, Arena di Verona, San Francisco Opera, New Israeli Opera, Chicago Lyric Opera. *Concert appearances:* performs Verdi's Requiem in concerts, vocal series by Mussorgsky and Mahler, cantatas by Prokofiev; works with conductors Levine, Rostropovich, Mehta, Abbado, Temirkanov, Gergiev. *Address:* c/o IMG Artists, Carnegie Hall Tower, 152 West 57th Street, 5th Floor, New York, NY 10019, USA (office). *Telephone:* (212) 994-3500 (office). *Fax:* (212) 994-3550 (office). *E-mail:* atreuhaft@imgartists.com (office). *Website:* www.imgartists.com (office).

DYAKOV, Dumitru; Moldovan politician and journalist; *Chairman, Democratic Party of Moldova (Partidul Democrat din Moldova);* b. 10 Feb. 1952, Kargopole, Kurgan Region, Russia; m.; two d.; ed Belarus State Univ.; Sec. Comsomol Cttee, Moldovan State TV and Radio; corresp., Komsomolskaya Pravda in Moldova –1976; on Comsomol Cen. Cttee, on Moldovan CP Cen. Cttee; Head TASS Bureau in Romania 1989–93; Sec. Moldovan Embassy, Moscow 1993–94; mem. Parl. 1994–; Chair. Parl. Comm. on Foreign Policy 1994–95; Deputy Speaker 1995–97, Speaker 1998–2000; f. Alliance for Democratic and Flourishing Moldova 1998; Founder Chair. Democratic Party of Moldova 2000–. *Address:* Democratic Party of Moldova (Partidul Democrat din Moldova), 2001 Chişinău, str. Tighina 32, Moldova (office). *Telephone:* (22) 27-82-29 (office). *Fax:* (22) 27-82-30 (office). *E-mail:* pdm@mtc.md (office). *Website:* www.pdm.md (office).

DYANKOV, Simeon, MA, PhD; Bulgarian economist and politician; b. 13 July 1970, Sofia; m. Caroline Freund; two c.; ed Language High School, Lovech, Karl Marx Inst. of Econs (now Univ. of Nat. and World Economy), Univ. of Michigan, USA; Chief Economist on Finance and Pvt. Sector Affairs, World Bank 1995–2009, Prin. Author of annual review of the World Bank – World Development Report 2002; Assoc. Ed. Journal of Comparative Economics 2004–09; Deputy Prime Minister and Minister of Finance 2009–13; jtly est. Ideas42 think-tank (Harvard Univ.-Int. Finance Corpn venture); ranked amongst the 100 Most Cited Economists in the world according to IDEAS/RePEc. *Publications:* more than 70 specialized articles in int. econ. journals, including Quarterly Journal of Economics, American Economic Review, Journal of Finance, Journal of Financial Economics, Journal of Public Economics; creator of the annual Doing Business report, World Bank Group 2003. *Address:* c/o Ministry of Finance, 1000 Sofia, ul. G.S. Rakovski 102, Bulgaria.

DYBKJAER, Lone, MChemEng; Danish politician and fmr EU official; b. (Lone Vincents), 23 May 1940, Copenhagen; m. Poul Nyrup Rasmussen (q.v.); two d.; ed Rungsted Statsskole, Tech. Univ. of Denmark; Sec., Acad. of Tech. Sciences 1964–66, Medico-Tech. Cttee 1966–70; Head Information Secr., Tech. Univ. of Denmark 1970–77; Adviser, Geotechnical Inst. 1978–79; mem. Folketing (Parl.) 1973–77, 1979–94; Chair. Parl. Energy Cttee, 1984–87, Tech. Cttee 1984–88, Parl. nine-mem. Cttee on Tech. Bd 1986–88; Social Liberal Party Spokesperson on Energy, Labour Market and Environmental Questions 1979–87, 1990–94, on Foreign Affairs 1987–88; Minister of the Environment 1988–90; mem. European Parl. 1994–2004, First Vice-Chair. Cttee on Devt and Co-operation (responsible for human rights) 1999–2002, mem. Cttee on Women's Rights and Equal Opportunities 1999–2004, Cttee on Constitutional Affairs 2002–04, ACP-EU Ass. 2002–04; Bird Life Prize 1993, Cyclist of the Year 1989, Gold Medal for Conservation of Bldgs 1991. *Publications include:* Tête à tête with a Modern Politician 1998, Peculiar Parliament 1999, Digital Denmark 1999. *Leisure interests:* tennis, reading, family life. *Address:* Christiansborg, 1240 KBHK, Denmark (office); Allégade 6A, 2000 Frederiksberg, Denmark (home). *Telephone:* 33212585 (office). *Fax:* 33253960 (office). *E-mail:* rvlody@ft.dk (office). *Website:* www.lonedybkjaer .dk (office).

DYDUCH, Marek; Polish politician and lawyer; b. 27 Aug. 1957, Świdnica; s. of Hipolit Dyduch and Krystyna Dyduch; m. Dorota Dyduch; one d. one s.; ed Wrocław Univ.; Chair. Local Council 1982–83; Chair. City-Communal Exec. Bd Union of Polish Socialist Youth (ZSMP), Żarów 1982–83, Vice-Chair. Prov. Exec. Bd, Wałbrzych 1983–86, Chair. 1986–91; mem. Polish United Workers' Party (PZPR) 1982–; mem. Prov. Nat. Council, Wałbrzych 1984–88; Deputy to Sejm (Parl.) 1993–2005, Vice-Chair. Comm. of Justice, Co-Pres. Comm. of Codification for Penal Codes, mem. Social Policy Comm., Comm. for Health Insurance, Comm. for Social Insurance, Justice and Human Rights Comm., Extraordinary Comm. for the Reform of Public Admin, Extraordinary Comm. for Social Insurance; mem. Social Democracy of the Repub. of Poland (SdRP) 1990–99, Democratic Left Alliance (SLD, after party reorganization) 1999–, Chair. Lower-Silesian Prov. Bd, SLD, Wrocław 1999–2002, Sec.-Gen. SLD 2002–05, fmr mem. SLD Nat. Exec. Bd; Sec. of State, Ministry of the Treasury 2001–02; Founder Ferdinand Lassal Foundation, Wrocław; joined Polish People's Party (Polskie Stronnictwo Ludowe) 2008; Bronze Cross of Merit 1989. *Leisure interests:* tennis, skiing, local and global social phenomena, history, science-fiction. *Address:* c/o Polish People's Party (Polskie Stronnictwo Ludowe), 00-902 Warsaw, ul. Wiejska 4/6/8, Poland.

DYER, Alexander Patrick, BS, MBA; American business executive (retd); b. 30 Aug. 1932, Santa Rosa, Calif.; s. of John Dyer and late Amie M. Moore; m. Shirley Shine 1954; one s. (and one s. deceased); ed US Mil. Acad., West Point and Harvard Business School; Exec. Vice-Pres. Air Products and Chemicals, BOC Group PLC 1987–89, Man. Dir Gases and CEO 1989–93, Deputy Chair. 1993–96, CEO 1993–96 (retd); Chair. 1993–96, Bunzl PLC 1993–96, Deputy Chair. Bunzl 1996–2005; mem. Bd of Dirs BWAY Corpn 1995–2002. *Publications:* Hardball in the Boardroom (memoir) 2011. *Leisure interests:* golf, skeet, antique collecting, photography. *Address:* 2117 Kirkland Village Circle, Bethlehem, PA 18017, USA (home). *Telephone:* (610) 691-4618 (home). *E-mail:* apdyer1954@aol.com (home).

DYKE, Gregory (Greg), BA; British media executive and football executive; *Chairman, The Football Association;* b. 20 May 1947; s. of David Dyke and Denise Dyke; partner Sue Howes; one s. one d.; one step-s. one step-d.; ed Hayes Grammar School, Univ. of York and Harvard Business School, USA; reporter on local paper; researcher, London Weekend Television (LWT) 1977, later founding producer, The Six O'Clock Show; joined TV-AM 1983; Dir of Programmes, TVS 1984–87; Dir of Programmes, LWT 1987–90, Man. Dir 1990; Group Chief Exec. LWT (Holdings) PLC 1991–94; Chair. Ind. TV Asscn 1992–94; Chair. GMTV 1993–94; Chair. CEO Pearson TV 1995–99; Chair. Channel 5 Broadcasting 1997–99; Dir Gen. BBC 2000–04 (resgnd); Dir BSkyB 1995, Phoenix Pictures Inc., New York, Pearson PLC 1996–99 and others; Dir (non-exec.) Manchester United Football Club 1997–99; mem. Supervisory Bd ProSiebenSat.1 Media 2004–; adviser, Apax Partners Inc. 2004–, Chair. Sunshine Acquisition Ltd (acquisition vehicle formed by Apax) 2005–, Chair. HiT Entertainment (acquired by Sunshine Acquisition) 2005–; Chair. BFI 2008–, FC 2006–13, Football Asscn 2013–; Chancellor Univ. of York 2004–; Trustee, Science Museum 1996–, English Nat. Stadium Trust 1997–99; Royal TV Soc. Lifetime Achievement Award, Broadcasting Press Guild Award 2004. *Publication:* Memoirs 2004. *Leisure interests:* tennis, theatre, football, cinema. *Address:* The Football Association, Wembley Stadium, PO Box 1966,

London, SW1P 9EQ, England (office). *Telephone:* (844) 980-8200 (office); (800) 169-1863. *Website:* www.thefa.com (office).

DYLAN, Bob; American composer, musician (guitar, piano, harmonica, autoharp) and singer; b. (Robert Allen Zimmerman), 24 May 1941, Duluth, Minn.; m. Sarah Lowndes (divorced 1978); four c. one adopted d.; ed Univ. of Minn.; best known for composition and interpretation of pop, country and folk music; performer; numerous tours and concerts; devised and popularized folk-rock 1965; performed with The Band; f. new group The Traveling Wilburys 1988; host, Theme Time Radio Hour with Your Host Bob Dylan (XM Satellite Radio) 2006–; mem. American Acad. of Arts and Letters 2013–; Commdr, Ordre des Arts et des Lettres 1990, Chevalier de la Legion d'honneur 2013; Hon. DMus (Princeton Univ.) 1970, (Univ. of St Andrews) 2004; Tom Paine Award 1963, Dorothy and Lillian Gish Prize 1997, Polar Music Prize 2000, Acad. Award for Best Theme Song (for Things Have Changed, from The Wonder Boys) 2002, Grammy Award for Best Solo Rock Vocal Performance (for Someday Baby) 2007, Premio Príncipe de Asturias 2007, Pulitzer Prize Special Citation 2008, Nat. Medal of Arts 2009, Presidential Medal of Freedom 2012. *Films appearances:* Eat the Document, Pat Garrett and Billy the Kid, Renaldo and Clara (also directed), Hearts of Fire 1986, Concert for Bangladesh, Masked and Anonymous 2003. *Radio:* presenter weekly music programme (Deep Tracks Channel, XM) 2006–. *Recordings include:* albums: The Freewheelin' Bob Dylan 1964, Bringing It All Back Home 1965, Highway 61 Revisited 1965, Blonde On Blonde 1966, John Wesley Harding 1968, Nashville Skyline 1969, Self Portrait 1970, New Morning 1970, Planet Waves (with The Band) 1974, Before The Flood 1974, Blood On The Tracks (with The Band) 1975, Hard Rain 1976, Desire 1976, Street Legal 1978, Slow Train Coming 1979, Infidels 1983, Empire Burlesque 1985, Knocked out Loaded 1986, Down in the Groove 1988, Traveling Wilburys (with Traveling Wilburys) 1988, Dylan and the Dead (with Grateful Dead) 1989, Oh Mercy 1989, Under The Red Sky 1990 (Vol. 3) with Traveling Wilburys) 1990, The Bootleg Series 1990, Good as I Been to You 1992, World Gone Wrong 1993, Unplugged 1995, Time Out of Mind (Grammy Award 1998) 1997, Love and Theft 2001, Modern Times (Grammy Award for Best Contemporary Folk/Americana Album 2007) 2006, Together Through Life 2009, Christmas in the Heart 2009, Tempest 2012, The Bootleg Series (Vol. 10): Another Self Portrait 2013. *Publications include:* Tarantula 1966, Writings and Drawings 1973, The Songs of Bob Dylan 1966–1975 1976, Lyrics 1962–1985 1986, Drawn Blank 1994, Highway 61 Revisited (interactive CD-ROM), Chronicles: Volume One (memoir) (Quill Book Award for Best Biography or Memoir 2005) 2004, Lyrics 1962–2001 2005, Dylan's Inspirations 2006. *Address:* c/o Jeff Rosen, PO Box 870, Cooper Station, New York, NY 10276, USA (office); c/o Columbia Records, 550 Madison Avenue, New York, NY 10022, USA. *Website:* www.bobdylan.com.

DYNKIN, Alexander A., PhD; Russian economist, political scientist and academic; *Director, Institute of World Economy and International Relations (IMEMO), Russian Academy of Sciences;* b. 1948, Moscow; ed Moscow Aviation Inst., Inst. of World Economy and Int. Relations, Russian Acad. of Sciences; Research Fellow, then Sr Research Fellow and Dept Head, Inst. of World Economy and Int. Relations 1975–89, Deputy Dir 1989–91, First Deputy Dir 1991–2006, Dir 2006–, Prof. of Econs, Russian Acad. of Sciences 1989–, Academician Sec., Div. for Global and Int. Relations 2010–, Corresponding mem. Russian Acad. of Sciences 2000–, Full mem. 2006–, Presidium mem. 2010–; Econ. Advisor to Russian Fed. Prime Minister 1998–99; Chair. School of Econs, Moscow Int. Univ. 2001–; Chair. Scientific Council of Russian Council on Foreign Affairs; First Deputy Chair., Pugwash Continuing Cttee; mem. Bd of Dirs Russian Union of Industrialists and Entrepreneurs 2003–07, Acron 2008– (Advisor to CEO 2009–, currently Chair. Strategic Planning and Corp. Governance Cttee); mem. Bd of Trustees, Inst. of Contemporary Devt Foundation 2009–; mem. Council on Competitiveness and Entrepreneurship to Russian Govt 2004–08, High Scientific Attestation Comm. 2007–, Russian Presidential Council on Science, Tech. and Educ. 2008–, Econ. Council under Pres. of Russian Fed., Scientific Expert Council under Chairman of Fed. Council of Russian Fed. Ass., 'International Position of Russia: Economic Guidelines' Expert Group, Council on Grants of Russian Govt Tender Comm. on Selection of Programs for Devt of Univs, Scientific Council of Russian Fed. Security Council, Scientific Council to Minister of Foreign Affairs, Comm. attached to Pres. of Russian Fed. on devt strategy of fuel and energy complex and environmental safety; Order of Friendship, Order of Honour, medal in commemoration of Moscow's 850th birthday. *Publications include:* New Stage of Technological Revolution 1991, Innovation Economy 2001, Business Groups and Modernisation of Russian Economy 2001, The World at the Turn of the Millennium: The Forecast for the World Economy until 2015 2001, World Economy: Forecast Towards 2020 2008, Global Strategic Outlook 2030 2011. *Address:* Office of the Director, Institute of World Economy and International Relations, Russian Academy of Sciences, Moscow 117997, 23 Profsoyuznaya Street, V-71, GSP-7, Russia (office). *Telephone:* (499) 128-0514 (office). *Fax:* (495) 913-9660 (office). *E-mail:* dynkin@imemo.ru (office). *Website:* www.imemo.ru (office).

DYSON, Freeman John, FRS; American physicist and academic; *Professor Emeritus of Physics, Institute for Advanced Study;* b. 15 Dec. 1923, Crowthorne, England; s. of late Sir George Dyson and Lady Mildred Dyson (Atkey); m. 1st Verena Huber 1950 (divorced 1958); one s. one d.; m. 2nd Imme Jung 1958; four d.; ed Univ. of Cambridge, UK, Cornell Univ.; Fellow, Trinity Coll., Cambridge 1946; Warren Research Fellow, Birmingham Univ. 1949; Prof. of Physics, Cornell Univ. 1951–53; Prof., Inst. for Advanced Study, Princeton 1953–94, Prof. Emer. 1994–; Chair. Fed. of American Scientists 1962; mem. NAS 1964–; Foreign Assoc. Acad. des Sciences, Paris 1989; Hon. DSc (City Univ., UK) 1981, (Oxford) 1997; Gifford Lecturer, Aberdeen 1985, Heineman Prize, American Inst. of Physics 1965, Lorentz Medal, Royal Netherlands Acad. 1966, Hughes Medal, Royal Soc. 1968, Max Planck Medal, German Physical Soc. 1969, Harvey Prize, Israel Inst. of Tech. 1977, Wolf Prize (Israel) 1981, Matteucci Medal, Rome 1990, Fermi Award (USA) 1994, Templeton Prize 2000. *Publications include:* Disturbing the Universe 1979, Weapons and Hope 1984, Origins of Life 1986, Infinite in All Directions 1988, From Eros to Gaia 1992, Imagined Worlds 1997, The Sun, The Genome and the Internet 1999, The Scientist as Rebel 2006, A Many-Colored Glass 2007; papers in The Physical Review, Journal of Mathematical Physics, etc. *Address:* Institute for Advanced Study, Princeton, NJ 08540 (office); 105 Battle Road Circle, Princeton, NJ 08540, USA (home). *Telephone:* (609) 734-8055 (office). *Fax:* (609) 951-4489 (office). *E-mail:* dyson@ias.edu (office). *Website:* www.sns.ias.edu/~dyson (office).

DYSON, Sir James, Kt, CBE, FCSD, MDes; British designer and inventor; *Chairman, Dyson Appliances Ltd;* b. 2 May 1947; s. of Alec Dyson and Mary Dyson (née Bolton); m. Deirdre Hindmarsh 1967; two s. one d.; ed Gresham's School, Royal Coll. of Art; Dir Rotork Marine 1970–74; Man. Dir Kirk Dyson 1974–79; developed and designed Dyson Dual Cyclone vacuum cleaner 1979–93; Founder and Chair. Prototypes Ltd (now Dyson Research) 1979–, Dyson Appliances Ltd 1992–; Chair. Bath Coll. of Higher Educ. 1990–92, Design Museum 1999–2004; mem. Design Council 1997–, Council RCA 1998–; Founder and Pres. James Dyson Foundation 2002–; est. Dyson School of Design Innovation, Bath 2006; Fellow, Royal Acad. of Eng 2005; Hon. Fellow, Liverpool John Moores Univ., MEID (Inst. of Eng Designers) 1997; numerous hon. doctorates including Hon. DSc (Oxford Brookes) 1997, (Bath, Imperial Coll. London, RCA); numerous design awards and trophies; Royal Designer for Industry Royal Soc. of Arts 2005. *Publications include:* Doing a Dyson 1996, Against the Odds (autobiog.) 1997. *Leisure interests:* running, garden design, music, fishing, cricket, tennis. *Address:* Dyson Ltd, Tetbury Mill, Malmesbury, Wilts., SN16 0RP, England (office). *Telephone:* (1666) 827200 (office). *Fax:* (1666) 827321 (office). *E-mail:* laura.brock@dyson.com (office). *Website:* www.dyson.com (office).

DYVIK, Helge Julius Jakhelln, DPhil; Norwegian academic; *Professor of General Linguistics, University of Bergen;* b. 23 Dec. 1947, Bodø; s. of late Einar Dyvik and Harriet Dyvik (née Jakhelln); m. 1st Eva Sætre 1973 (divorced 1994); one s. one d.; m. 2nd Martha Thunes 2001; one s.; ed Univ. of Bergen, Univ. of Durham, UK; Research Asst (Old Norse), Univ. of Bergen 1974–75, Lecturer 1976, Project Asst (Old Norwegian syntax) 1976–81, Research Fellow (Vietnamese syntax project) 1981–83, Prof. of Gen. Linguistics 1983–; Pres. Nordic Asscn of Linguists 1993–1998; mem. Norwegian Language Council 2000–, Programme Cttee for Nordic Council of Ministers' Research Programme on Language Tech. 2000–05 (Chair. 2002–); Chair. Expert Cttee for Standardisation and Language Observation under the Norwegian Language Council 2007–; Fridtjof Nansen Award for Eminent Research, Norwegian Acad. of Letters and Science 1987. *Publications:* Grammatikk og Empiri 1981, Categories and Functions in Vietnamese Classifier Constructions 1983, Semantic Mirrors 1998. *Leisure interests:* play reading, choral singing. *Address:* Department of Linguistic, Literary and Aesthetic Studies, Linguistic Studies Section, University of Bergen, Sydnespl. 7, 5007 Bergen (office); Straumevn. 3A, 5151 Straumsgrend, Bergen, Norway (home). *Telephone:* 55-58-22-61 (office). *E-mail:* helge.dyvik@lili.uib.no (office). *Website:* www.hg.uib.no/i/lili/slf/ans/Dyvik (office).

DZAIDDIN BIN HAJI ABDULLAH, Tun Mohamed; Malaysian judge; *Chairman, Bursa Malaysia Berhad;* b. 16 Sept. 1937, Arau, Perlis; m. Puan Noriah Binti Tengku Ismael; two c.; ed Sultan Abdul Hamid Coll. Alor Setar; journalist, Malay Mail 1956; joined police service as Inspector; called to Bar, Middle Temple, London, UK 1966; admitted as advocate and solicitor in Kota Bharu and Kuala Lumpur 1967; juridical commr (part-time) 1979–82; apptd High Court Judge, Criminal Div. of Kuala Lumpur High Court 1982–84, Penang High Court 1984–92; Supreme Court Judge (renamed Fed. Court Judge) 1992–2000; Chief Justice of the Fed. Court 2000–03; Chair. Bursa Malaysia Berhad (fmrly Kuala Lumpur Stock Exchange) 2004–; apptd Dir (non-exec.) and Public Interest Dir by Minister of Finance 2004–; Chair. Deutsche Bank (Malaysia) Berhad, Tun Mohamed Suffian Foundation; fmr Chair. Royal Comm. to Enhance the Operation and Man. of the Royal Police Force, Kelantan Bar Cttee; Vice-Pres. Malaysian Bar Asscn 1981–82; Life mem. ASEAN Law Asscn of Malaysia, Pres. 1994–97, Pres. ASEAN Law Asscn 1997; Hon. LLD (San Beda Coll.) 2002; several awards including Seri Paduka Baginda Yang DiPertuan Agong of the Most Esteemed Order of Seri Setia Mahkota Malaysia. *Address:* Office of the Chairman, Bursa Malaysia Berhad, Tingkat 8 Exchange Square, Bukit Kewangan, 50200 Kuala Lumpur, Malaysia (office). *Website:* www.klse.com.my (office).

DZASOKHOV, Aleksandr Sergeyevich, CandHistSc; Russian politician; b. 3 April 1934, Ordzhonikidze, North Ossetian ASSR; m. Farisa Borissovna 1959; two s.; ed North Caucasian Mining-Metallurgical Inst. and CPSU Higher Party School; mem. CPSU 1957–91; First Sec. Ordzhonikidze Komsomol City Cttee 1957–61; Sec. of USSR Cttee of Youth Orgs 1961–64; leader of young Soviet specialists to Cuba 1964–65; First Sec., Pres. of USSR Youth Orgs 1965–67; Deputy Chair., Chair. of Soviet Cttee for Solidarity with Countries of Asia and Africa 1965–86; USSR Amb. to Syria 1986–88; First Sec. of North Ossetian CPSU Dist Cttee (Obkom) 1988–90; USSR People's Deputy 1989–91; Chair. Cttee of USSR Supreme Soviet on Int. Affairs 1990–91; mem., Sec. of Cen. Cttee CPSU, mem. of CPSU Politburo 1990–91; People's Deputy of Russia, mem. Supreme Soviet of Russian Fed. 1992–93; Chair. Sub-Cttee on Asia and the Pacific; mem. State Duma (Parl.) 1993–98; elected Pres. of Repub. of North Ossetia-Alania 1998–2005; Deputy Chair. Inter-Parl. Group of Russian Fed. 1993, Chair. 1996–2001; mem. Acad. of Creative Endeavours; mem. Bd Dirs Pervyi Kanal. *Publications:* several books on problems of post-colonialism in third-world countries, including Formation and Evolution of the Post-colonial World 1999. *Address:* c/o House of Soviets, Office of the President, Svobody pl. 1, 362038 Vladikavkaz, North Ossetia-Alania, Russia. *Telephone:* (8672) 53-35-24.

DZHEMILEV, Mustafa (Abdul-Dzhemil); Ukrainian activist; b. 14 Nov. 1943, Ayserez, Crimea; m. Safinar Dzhemileva; two s. one d.; imprisoned or exiled for dissident activity 1966–67, 1969–72, 1974–75, 1975–77, 1979–82, 1983–86; continued to organize Crimean Tatar protest actions in Cen. Asia and Moscow; returned to Crimea 1989; Chair. Crimean Tatar Majlis 1991–; Pres. Crimea Foundation 1991–; mem. Verkhovna Rada (Supreme Council) 1998–, Chair. Council of Reps 1999–; political observer, Business magazine; Dr hc (Seljuk Univ., Higher Tech. Inst. Gebze, Turkey); Nansen Medal UNHCR 1998, Pylyp Orlyk Int. Award 2000, Yaroslav Mudryi Medal 2001, Hon. Prize of Parliament of Ukraine 2002. *Leisure interest:* studying informative websites. *Address:* Verkhovna Rada (Supreme Council), 01008 Kyiv, vul. M. Hrushevskoho 5 (office); 6th Microrayon 100, Bakhchesaray, Crimea, Ukraine (home). *Telephone:* (44) 255-46-26 (office); (652) 5443758 (home). *Fax:* (44) 253-32-17 (office). *E-mail:* Dzhemiliev.Mustafa@rada.gov.ua (home). *Website:* www.rada.gov.ua (office).

DZHIGARKHANIAN, Armen Borisovich; Armenian/Russian actor; b. 3 Oct. 1935, Yerevan; m. Tatiana Vlasova 1967; one s.; ed Yerevan Theatre Inst.; actor with Stanislavsky Russian Drama Theatre in Yerevan 1955–67; with Moscow Lenin Komsomol Theatre 1967–69, with Mayakovsky Theatre 1969–96, with

Dzhigarkhanian Theatre 1996–; Armenian SSR State Prize 1975, 1979; RSFSR People's Artist 1973, USSR People's Artist 1985, Stanislavsky Award 2001. *Films:* has appeared in a number of films. *Roles include:* Levinson in Fadeev's Thunder, Stanley in Tennessee Williams' Streetcar Named Desire, Socrates and Nero in Radzinsky's Chats with Socrates and the Theatre in the time of Nero and Seneca, Big Daddy in Tennessee Williams' Cat on a Hot Tin Roof, Max in Pinter's Homecoming, Krapp in Beckett's Krapp's Last Tape, Domenic in E. D. Phillippo's Philoumena Marturano. *Leisure interests:* reading, listening to classical music, playing with pet Siamese cat. *Address:* 121002 Moscow, 37 Starokonysheny per., Apt. 9, Russia. *Telephone:* (495) 930-23-07 (office); (495) 203-30-79 (home); (214) 772-7464 (Dallas, USA). *Fax:* (495) 930-03-47 (office).

DZHUMALIYEV, Kubanychbek; Kyrgyzstani politician; fmr Chief of Staff to Pres. Askar Akayev; fmr Gov. Jalal-Abad Region; First Deputy Prime Minister and Minister of Transport and Communications 2005–06 (resgnd). *Address:* c/o Ministry of Transport and Communications, 720017 Bishkek, Isanova 42 Kyrgyzstan (office).

DZIUBA, Andrzej Franciszek, (Franciszek Wieczyński), DD; Polish ecclesiastic and academic; *Bishop of Łowicz;* b. 10 Oct. 1950, Pleszew; s. of Stanisław Dziuba and Ludwika Ślachciak; ed Primatial Priests' Seminary, Gniezno, Pontifical Theological Faculty, Poznań, Catholic Univ. Lublin, Acad. Alfonsiana, Rome and Univ. Italiana per Stranieri, Perugia; ordained priest, Gniezno 1975; Asst Parish Priest and Catechist, Łobżenica 1975–76; studies in Lublin 1976–79, Rome 1979–81; Sec. to Primate of Poland 1981–98, Dir Secr. 1984–98; Asst Parish Priest, St Martin's Church, Warsaw 1981–98, St Barbara's Church, Warsaw 1998, Bishop of Łowicz 2004–; Prof., Catholic Univ. Lublin 1989–, Acad. of Catholic Theology, Warsaw 1995–99, Primatial Priest's Seminary, Gniezno 1998–, Cardinal S. Wyszyński Univ. 1999–; Hon. Chaplain to the late Pope John Paul II 1990, Prelate 1996; Primate of Poland Foundation in GB 1991; Canon Metropolitan Chapter of Warsaw 1998; Theological Counsellor to Primate of Poland 1998–; Hon. Conventual Chaplain of Order of Malta 1998, Grand Cross 2005; Kt Commdr of Equestrian Order of Holy Sepulchre of Jerusalem 1998, Cross with Gold Star of Merit of Holy Sepulchre of Jerusalem 1996, Kt Ecclesiastical Grace of Sacred Mil. Constantinian Order 1999. *Publications:* Mikołaj z Mościsk, teolog moralista XVII w. 1985, Jan Azor, teolog-moralista 1988, Informator Katolicki 89/90 1990, Droga Krzyżowa 1991, Różaniec święty 1992, Kościół katolicki w Polsce. Informator 1993, Jezus nam przebacza. Przygotowanie do sakramentu pojednania 1994, Matka Boża z Guadalupe 1995, Kościół katolicki w Polsce. Informator 1995, Orędzie moralne Jezusa Chrystusa 1996, Dynamika wiary 1997, Kościół katolicki w Polsce. Informator 1997, Droga krzyżowa 1998, Biography of Cardinal Józef Glemp 1998, Cardinal Stefan Wyszyński Primate of Poland. A Life-Sketch 2000, U źródeł Bożej Madrości. Życie i nauka Jezusa Chrystusa 2000, Spowiedź małżeńska. Życie małżeńskie a sakramentalna posługa pokuty i pojednania 2002, Prestamé społeczne karolynats Stefana Wyczyniskiego, Prymosa Polski 2004; numerous articles on moral theology, church history, Catholic social sciences. *Address:* Diocese of Łowicz, Stary Rynek 20, 99-400 Łowicz, Poland (office). *Telephone:* (46) 8376615 (office). *Fax:* (46) 8374349 (office). *E-mail:* kuria@diecezja.lowicz.pl (office). *Website:* www.diecezja.lowicz.pl (office).

DZIUBA, Ivan Mykhailovych; Ukrainian literary critic and academic; b. 26 July 1931, Mykolaivka, Ukraine; s. of Mykhailo Dzyuba and Olga Dzyuba; m. Marta Lenets 1963; one d.; ed Donetsk Pedagogical Inst.; ed. various journals and publs published by Ukrainian State Publishing House; published An Ordinary Man or a Petit Bourgeois as well as numerous samizdat articles in 1960s; expelled from Writers' Union 1972 after publication of Internationalism or Russification? (numerous edns); arrested 1972, sentenced to 5 years' imprisonment 1973; recanted and released Nov. 1973; Writers' Union membership restored 1980s; Academician, Nat. Acad. of Sciences of Ukraine 1992–, mem. Presidium 1997–; Academician-Sec. Dept of Literature, Language and Arts 1996–2004; Minister of Culture Dec. 1992–94; Sr Researcher, T. Shevchenko Inst. of Literature 1994–; Ed.-in-Chief Suchasnist (magazine) 1991–2003, Encyclopaedia of Modern Ukraine 1998–; Head of Cttee Tazas Shevchenko Nat. Ukrainian Award; freelance literary corresp. 1982–; Order of Rising Sun (Japan) 2006; O. Biletski Prize 1987, Laureate, Shevchenko's Award 1991, Int. Antonovich Prize 1992, V. Zhabotinsky Prize 1996, Vernadsky Prize 2001. *Publications include:* 25 books including Between Politics and Literature 1998, Thirst 2001, Trap 2003; numerous articles on history and devt of Ukrainian literature and writers of former USSR. *Leisure interests:* gardening, mushrooming. *Address:* Presidium of the National Academy of Sciences of Ukraine, 01601 Kyiv 30, Vladimirskaya St., 54 (office); Shevchenko Institute of Literature, 01601 Kyiv 1, vul. M.Hrushevskoho, 4 (office); Antonova str. 7, Apt 60, Kiev 03186, Ukraine (home). *Telephone:* (44) 235-09-81 (office); (44) 229-10-84 (office); (44) 248-41-77 (home). *Website:* www.nas.gov.ua (office).

DZIWISZ, Cardinal Stanisław, ThD; Polish ecclesiastic; *Archbishop of Kraków;* b. 27 April 1939, Raba Wyżna; ed Primatial Priest Seminary, Kraków, Metropolitan Ecclesiastic Seminary, Kraków, Pontifical Acad. of Theology, Kraków; ordained priest, Kraków 1963; Asst Parish Priest, Maków Podhalański 1963–65; Chaplain to Archbishop of Kraków Karol Wojtyła (later Pope John Paul II)

1966–78; Lecturer, Higher Inst. of Catechism, Kraków 1966–78; Ed. Kraków Curie Notificationes e Curia Metropolitana Cracoviensi 1966–78; Personal Sec. to Pope John Paul II 1978–2005, Prelate 1985, Apostolic Protonotary, Canon of Cathedral Chapter, Lviv and Metropolitan Chapter, Kraków 1997; Titular Bishop of San Leone and Prefetto aggiunto (Prefecture of the Sacred Household) 1998–2005; Titulare Archbishop of San Leone 2003–05; Archbishop of Kraków 2005–; cr. Cardinal (Cardinal-Priest of Santa Maria del Popolo) 2006; participated in Papal Conclave 2013; Vice-Chair. John Paul II Foundation 1985. *Publications include:* Kult św. Stanisława biskupa w Krakowie do Soboru Trydenckiego (Cult of Saint Stanislaus, Bishop of Kraków until Council of Trent) 1978, Swiadectwo (Testimony) 2007, A Life with Karol 2008. *Address:* Archdiocese of Kraków, ul. Franciszkanska 3, 31 004 Kraków, Poland (office). *Telephone:* (12) 6288100 (office). *Fax:* (12) 4294617 (office). *E-mail:* kuria@diecezja.krakow.pl (office). *Website:* www.diecezja.pl (office).

DŽOMBIĆ, Aleksandar; Bosnia and Herzegovina banking executive and government official; b. 1968, Banja Luka; m.; one c.; ed Univ. of Banja Luka, Belgrade Univ.; worked in Banja Luka City Admin.; Head, Dept and Project Man., Kristal Bank, Banja Luka; Dir Agroprom Bank, Banja Luka; Exec. Dir Nova Banka, Bijeljina; Minister of Finance of Republika Srpska 2006–10, Prime Minister of Republika Srpska 2010–13; Alt. Gov. EBRD. *Address:* c/o Office of the Prime Minister, 78000 Banja Luka, trg Republike Srpske 1, Bosnia and Herzegovina. *E-mail:* kabinet@vladars.net.

DZUMAGULOV, Apas Dzumagulovich; Kyrgyzstani engineer, politician and diplomatist; b. 19 Sept. 1934, Arashan, Kyrgyz SSR; m.; three s.; ed Moscow Gubkin Inst. of Oil; mem. CPSU 1962–91; worked at Complex S., Geological Expedition USSR Acad. of Sciences 1958–59; sr geologist, oil field Changar-Tash, Head of Cen. Research Lab., Chief Geologist Drilling Div., Chief Engineer, Oil Co. Kyrghizneft Osh Dist 1959–73; Head of Industrial-Transport Div. Cen. Cttee CP of Kyrgyz SSR 1973–79; Sec., Cen. Cttee CP of Kirgyzia 1979–85; First Sec., Issyk-Kul Dist Cttee 1985–86; Chair. Council of Ministers Kyrgyz SSR 1986–91; Chair. Org. Cttee, then Chair. Regional Soviet of Deputies, Head of Admin. Chuysk Region 1991–93; Deputy to USSR Supreme Soviet 1984–89; USSR People's Deputy 1989–91; People's Deputy of Kyrgyzstan; mem. Revision Comm. CPSU 1986–91; Prime Minister of Kyrgyz Repub. 1993–97; Amb. to Germany, Scandinavian countries and the Holy See 1998–2003. *Address:* c/o Ministry of Foriegn Affairs, 59 Razzakov str., Bishkek 720040, Kyrgyzstan (office).

DŽUNOV, Todor, DSc; Macedonian professor of law and jurist; b. 11 Oct. 1931, Vatasha, Kavadarci; m. Granka Džunov 1958; ed Univ. of Cyril and Methodius, Skopje; Asst, Faculty of Law, Skopje 1956, Reader 1964, Assoc. Prof. 1969, Prof. 1974–94, Dean, Faculty of Law 1981–83; Rector, Univ. of 'Cyril and Metodius', Skopje 1985–88; Justice of the Constitutional Court 1994, Pres. 2000–03; Pres. Research Council of Macedonia 1973–80; mem. and Chief of dels of interstate bodies for scientific and tech. co-operation with Greece, USA and UK; mem. del. on succession issues on Fmr Repub. of Yugoslavia; 11th of October Award 1980, Gold Award, Faculty of Law, Skopje 2001, Gold Award, Faculty of Philosophy, Univ. of Cyril and Methodius, Skopje, State Medal for Labour, State Medal for People Merit. *Publications:* more than 100 titles including Private International Law (textbook), International Legal Regulation of the Use of Rivers and Lakes of Common Interest Out of Navigation 1964, International Regulation of the Use of Waters 1979, Collection of Laws on the Private International Law 1984, Foreign Policy of SFRY and Non-Alignment 1989. *Address:* Partizanski odredi No. 8/25, 1000 Skopje, Republic of Macedonia (home). *Telephone:* (2) 130163 (home).

DZURINDA, Mikuláš, PhD; Slovak politician; b. 4 Feb. 1955, Spišský Štvrtok; m. Eva Dzurindová; two d.; ed Univ. of Transport and Communications, Žilina; econ. researcher, Transport Research Inst., Žilina 1979–80; information tech. officer, Czechoslovak Railways Regional Directorate, Bratislava 1980–88, Head of Automated Control Systems Dept 1988–91; Deputy Minister of Transport and Postal Service of Slovak Repub. 1991–92, 1994; mem. Nat. Council of Slovak Repub. 1992–94, 1994–98, 2006–10; Vice-Chair. for Econ. Christian Democratic Movt 1993–2000; spokesman of Slovak Democratic Coalition 1997–98, Chair. 1998–; Jt Acting Pres. of Slovakia 1998–99; Prime Minister 1998–2002, 2002–06; Minister of Foreign Affairs 2010–12; f. Slovak Democratic and Christian Union (SDKÚ, merged with Democratic Party 2006) 2000, Chair. 2000–12; has lectured at N American and European univs; Hon. mem. The Int. Raoul Wallenberg Foundation; Vittorino Colombo Award (Italy) 2000. *Achievements:* has taken part in the Int. Peace Marathon (MMM) in Košice 13 times, ran the Lesser Carpathians Marathon (in personal best time of 2 hours, 54 minutes and 57 seconds) 1986, and the Rajec Marathon 1996, took part in the New York City Marathon 2001, and the London Marathon 2003. *Publication:* Where There's a Will There's a Way. *Leisure interests:* family, sport, marathon running. *Address:* Slovak Democratic and Christian Union-Democratic Party (Slovenská demokratická a kresčanská únia-Demokratická strana), Ružinovská 28, 827 35 Bratislava, Slovakia (office). *Telephone:* (2) 4341-4102 (office). *Fax:* (2) 4341-4106 (office). *E-mail:* sdku@ sdkuonline.sk (office). *Website:* www.sdku-ds.sk (office).

E

EAGLETON, Terence (Terry) Francis, PhD, FBA; British academic; *Distinguished Professor of English Literature, Lancaster University;* b. 22 Feb. 1943, Salford, Lancs.; s. of Francis Paul Eagleton and Rosaleen Riley; m. 1st Elizabeth Rosemary Galpin 1966 (divorced 1976); two s.; m. 2nd Willa Murphy 1996; one s. one d.; ed Trinity Coll., Cambridge; Fellow in English, Jesus Coll., Cambridge 1964–69; Tutorial Fellow, Wadham Coll., Oxford 1969–89; Lecturer in Critical Theory and Fellow of Linacre Coll., Oxford 1989–92; Thomas Warton Prof. of English Literature and Fellow of St Catherine's Coll., Oxford 1992–2001; fmr Prof. of Cultural Theory, Univ. of Manchester, John Edward Taylor Prof. of English Literature 2001–08; Distinguished Prof. of English Literature, Lancaster Univ. 2008–; Hon. DLitt (Salford) 1994, (Durham), (E Anglia), (Univ. of Cen. Lancashire), (Nova Scotia, Canada), (Sacred Heart Univ., USA); Dr hc (Nat. Univ. of Ireland) 1995, (Santiago di Compostela) 1997; Irish Sunday Tribune Arts Award 1990. *Film:* screenplay for Wittgenstein. *Plays:* St Oscar 1989, Disappearances 1998. *Publications:* Criticism and Ideology 1976, Marxism and Literary Criticism 1976, Literary Theory: an Introduction 1983, The Function of Criticism 1984, The Rape of Clarissa 1985, Against the Grain 1986, William Shakespeare 1986, The Ideology of the Aesthetic 1990, Ideology: An Introduction 1993, The Crisis of Contemporary Culture 1993, Heathcliff and the Great Hunger 1995, The Illusions of Postmodernism 1996, Literary Theory 1996, Crazy John and the Bishop and Other Essays on Irish Culture 1998, Scholars and Rebels in Ireland 1999, The Idea of Culture 2000, The Gatekeeper (autobiog.) 2001, Sweet Violence: The Idea of the Tragic 2002, Figures of Dissent (essays) 2003, After Theory 2003, The English Novel: An Introduction 2004, Holy Terror 2005, The Meaning of Life 2007, Trouble with Strangers: A Study of Ethics 2008, How to Read a Poem 2008, Reason, Faith and Revolution: Reflections on the God Debate 2009, On Evil 2010, Why Marx Was Right 2011; contribs to periodicals incl. London Review of Books. *Leisure interest:* Irish music. *Address:* Department of English and Creative Writing, County Coll., Lancaster University, Lancaster, LA1 4YD, England (office). *Website:* www.lancs.ac.uk/fass/english (office).

EAGLING, Wayne John; Canadian ballet dancer, choreographer and artistic director; s. of Eddie Eagling and Thelma Eagling; ed P. Ramsey Studio of Dance Arts, Royal Ballet School; Sr Prin., Royal Ballet 1975–91; Artistic Dir Dutch Nat. Ballet 1991–2003; Artistic Dir English Nat. Ballet, London 2005–12. *Ballet roles include:* danced lead roles in Sleeping Beauty, Swan Lake, Cinderella and other major classics; created roles include: Young Boy in Triad, Solo Boy in Gloria, Ariel in The Tempest, Woyzeck in Different Drummer; choreographed The Hunting of the Snark and Frankenstein, The Modern Prometheus, Ruins of Time 1993, Symphony in Waves 1994, Alma Mahler (for La Scala, Milan) 1994, Duet 1995, Lost Touch 1995, Nutcracker and Mouseking (with Toer van Schayk) 1996, The Last Emperor (for Hong Kong Ballet) 1998, Magic Flute (with Toer van Schayk) 1999, Le Sacré du Printemps 2000, Mary Stuart (Rome Opera) 2004. *Publication:* The Company We Keep (with Ross MacGibbon and Robert Jude) 1981. *Leisure interests:* golf, scuba diving.

EALET, Isabelle; French business executive; *Co-Head of Securities, Goldman Sachs;* m.; two c.; ed Institut d'Études Politiques de Paris (SciencesPo); began career trading barrels of crude oil for Total, Paris; joined Goldman Sachs & Co. 1991, ran oil products group, Man. Dir 1999, Partner 2000–, Head of European Trading 2002–07, led team that bought European energy plants once owned by Enron, Global Head of Commodities, Goldman Sachs, London, UK 2007–12, Co-Head of Securities 2012–, mem. Man. Cttee, Partnership Cttee, Risk Cttee; mem. Bd of Dirs Int. Petroleum Exchange, London 1999; ranked by Fortune magazine amongst the 50 Most Powerful Women in Business outside the US (35th) 2008, (32nd) 2009–11, (22nd) 2012, ranked by US Banker magazine amongst The 25 Most Powerful Women in Finance (15th) 2010. *Address:* Goldman Sachs International, Peterborough Court, 133 Fleet Street, London, EC4A 2BB, England (office). *Telephone:* (20) 7774-1000 (office). *E-mail:* info@goldmansachs.com (office). *Website:* www.goldmansachs.com (office).

EAMES, Baron (Life Peer), cr. 1995, of Armagh in the County of Armagh; **Most Rev. Robert Henry Alexander Eames,** LLD, PhD, OM, DD; British ecclesiastic; b. 27 April 1937; s. of William E. Eames and Mary E. T. Eames; m. Ann C. Daly 1966; two s.; ed Methodist Coll., Belfast, Queen's Univ., Belfast and Trinity Coll., Dublin; Research Scholar and Tutor, Faculty of Laws, Queen's Univ., Belfast 1960–63; Asst Curate, Bangor Parish Church 1963–66; Rector, St Dorothea's, Belfast 1966–74; Examining Chaplain to Bishop of Down 1973; Rector, St Mark's, Dunelda 1974–75; Bishop of Derry and Raphoe 1975–80; Bishop of Down and Dromore 1980–86; Archbishop of Armagh and Primate of All Ireland 1986–2006 (retd); Select Preacher, Oxford Univ. 1986–87, Cambridge Univ. 1989; Irish Rep., Anglican Consultative Council 1984, mem. Standing Cttee 1985; Chair. Archbishop of Canterbury's Comm. on Communion and Women in the Episcopate 1988–, Comm. on Inter-Anglican Relations 1988–, Anglican Int. Doctrinal Comm. (USA) 1991; Chair. Consultative Group on the Past (NI) 2007–08; Gov. Church Army 1985–; Hon. LLD (Queen's Univ. Belfast) 1989, (Trinity Coll. Dublin) 1992, (Lancaster) 1994, (Univ. of the South, Sewannee) 2010; Dr hc (Cambridge) 1994, (Open Univ.) 2008; Hon. DD (Exeter) 1999. *Publications:* A Form of Worship for Teenagers 1965, The Quiet Revolution: Irish Disestablishment 1970, Through Suffering 1973, Thinking through Lent 1978, Through Lent 1984, Chains to be Broken 1992; contribs to New Divinity, Irish Legal Quarterly, Criminal Law Review, Northern Ireland Legal Quarterly, Univ. Review and The Furrow. *Leisure interests:* sailing, rugby, football, reading. *Address:* House of Lords, London SW1A 0PW, England (office); 3 Downshire Crescent, Hillsborough, Co. Down, BT26 6DD, Ireland (home). *Telephone:* (28) 9268-9913.

EANES, Gen. António dos Santos Ramalho; Portuguese politician and army officer; b. 25 Jan. 1935, Alcains; s. of Manuel dos Santos Eanes and Maria do Rosario Ramalho; m. Maria Manuela Duarte Neto Portugal 1970; two s.; ed High School, Castelo Branco, Higher Inst. of Applied Psychology, Lisbon Faculty of Law; enlisted in Army School 1953; commissioned to Portuguese India 1958–60, Macao 1960–62, Mozambique 1962–64, Operations Officer of Light Infantry Battalion, Mozambique 1966–67, Information Officer, Portuguese Guinea (Guinea-Bissau) 1969–73, Angola 1973–74; Physical Education Instructor, Mil. Acad. 1968; Dir of Dept of Cultural and Recreational Affairs 1973; rank of Second Lt 1957, Lt 1959, Capt. 1961, Maj. 1970, Gen. 1978; involved in leadership of mil. movts finally contesting mil. apparatus and colonial wars 1968–74; after April Revolution named to first 'Ad-hoc' Cttee for mass media June 1974; Dir of Programmes of Portuguese TV June–Sept. 1974, Chair. of Bd of Dirs of TV co., resigned after accusation of 'probable implication' in abortive counter-coup March 1975, cleared after inquiry; rank of Lt-Col; mem. Cttee restructuring 5th Div., Gen. Staff Armed Forces; Army Chief of Staff (with temporary rank of Gen.) 1975–76; mem. of Mil. Cttee of Council of Revolution; responsible for Constitutional Law approved Dec. 1975; Col 1976; Pres. of Portugal 1976–86; Chair. of Council of Revolution; C-in-C of Armed Forces 1976–80, 1980–81; Leader, Portuguese Democratic Renewal Party 1986–87; mem. Conselho de Estado (Council of State); Degree of Kt of Mil. Order of Avis; War Cross 2nd class, Silver Medal for Distinguished Services with Palm, Silver Medal for Exemplary Behaviour, Commemorative Medal of the Portuguese Armed Forces. *Leisure interests include:* playing bridge. *Address:* c/o Círculo Português de Bridge, Avenida 5 Outobro, 4, 1200 Lisbon, Portugal.

EARL, Robert I.; British business executive; *Chairman and CEO, Planet Hollywood International Inc.;* b. 1952; f. President Entertainment (theme restaurants) 1977, sold co. to Pleasurama PLC, joined Pleasurama man. team, Man. Hard Rock Cafe PLC 1987–93; Co-founder, CEO and Dir Planet Hollywood Int. 1993–2000, now Chair. and CEO; Co-Chair. BHM Gaming Opportunities (owner of fmr Aladdin Casino hotel now Planet Hollywood, Las Vegas); became shareholder in Everton FC 2006, Dir 2007–. *Address:* Planet Hollywood International, Inc., 7598 West Sand Lake Road, Orlando, FL 32819, USA (office). *Telephone:* (407) 903-5500 (office). *Fax:* (407) 352-7310 (office). *E-mail:* general_information@planethollywood.com (office). *Website:* www .planethollywood.com (office).

EARLE, Steve; American singer, songwriter and musician (guitar); b. 17 Jan. 1955, Fort Monroe, Va; s. of Jack Earle and Barbara Earle; m. 1st Sandy Earle; m. 2nd Cynthia Earle; m. 3rd Carol-Ann Earle; m. 4th and 6th Lou-Anne Earle; m. 5th Teresa Ensenat; m. 7th Allison Moorer; moved to Nashville, where became bar room musician, staff writer for the publisher, Sunbury Dunbar, and songwriter; solo artist with own backing band, The Dukes 1982–; BBC Radio 2 Folk Award for Lifetime Achievement 2004. *Film and television appearances include:* Nashville 1975, The Wire (TV series) 2002, Slacker Uprising 2008, Leaves of Grass 2009, Treme (TV series) 2010. *Recordings include:* albums: Pink and Black (EP) 1982, Guitar Town 1986, Early Tracks 1987, Exit O 1987, Copperhead Road 1988, The Hard Way 1990, Shut Up And Die Like An Aviator 1991, Train A Comin' 1995, Fearless Heart 1996, I Feel Alright 1996, Angry Young Man 1996, El Corazón 1997, The Mountain 1999, Transcendental Blues 2000, Together At The Bluebird Cafe 2001, Sidetracks 2002, Jerusalem 2002, Just An American Boy 2003, The Revolution Starts... Now 2004, Live From Austin TX 2004, Washington Square Serenade (Grammy Award for Best Contemporary Folk/Americana Album 2008) 2007, Townes (Grammy Award for Best Contemporary Folk Album 2010) 2009, I'll Never Get Out of This World Alive 2011, The Low Highway 2013. *Publication:* Doghouse Roses (short stories) 2001. *Address:* c/o GoldVE, 260 West 35th Street, 13th Floor, New York, NY 10001, USA (office). *Telephone:* (212) 741-2400 (office). *Fax:* (212) 741-4871 (office). *E-mail:* info@goldve.com (office). *Website:* www.goldve .com (office); www.steveearle.com (office).

EARNHARDT, Dale, Jr; American racing driver; b. 10 Oct. 1974, Kannapolis, NC; s. of the late Dale Earnhardt; grandson of Ralph Earnhardt; began driving career aged 17; competed in street stock div., Concord (NC) Speedway; drives Budweiser No. 8 Chevrolet; winner of two Championships and 13 races in Busch Series 1998–2000; became first third-generation NASCAR Champion after winning Busch Series Title 1998, 1999; moved into NASCAR Nextel Cup Circuit 2000; raced Winston Cup circuit with father 2000; opened Daytona Speedweeks with father as mems of same team 2001; 15 victories in 183 Cup starts 2000–04; winner Atlanta, Bristol, Daytona and Tex. NASCAR Nextel Cups 2004, Budweiser Shootout 2004, The Winston 2004, USG Sheetrock 400 2005; Co-owner Chance2 Team, winning Busch Series Championships 2004; Founder and Owner, JR Motorsports LLC 2002–, Hammerhead Entertainment (TV and film production co.) 2006–; named amongst the Most Influential People in World of Sports, Business Week magazine 2007, 2008. *Publication:* Driver No. 8 2002. *Leisure interests:* collecting street cars and race cars, computer games. *Address:* JR Motorsports LLC, Mooresville, NC 28115, USA (office). *Telephone:* (704) 799-4800 (office). *Fax:* (704) 799-4801 (office). *E-mail:* Info@jrmotorsport.com (office). *Website:* www .jrmotorsport.com (office); www.hammerheadent.com.

EASLEY, Michael F., JD, BA; American state official; b. 23 March 1950, Rocky Mount, NC; m. Mary Pipines; one s.; ed Univ. of NC, NC Cen. Univ. School of Law; Dist Attorney, 13th Dist, NC 1982–91; pvt. practice, Southport, NC 1991–92; NC Attorney-Gen. 1993–2000; Gov. of NC 2000–09; Pres. NC Conf. of Dist Attorneys; mem. NC Dist Attorneys Asscn; Democrat; Public Services Award, US Dept of Justice 1984. *Leisure interests:* hunting, sailing, woodwork. *Address:* Democratic National Committee, 430 South Capitol Street, SE, Washington, DC 20003, USA (office). *Telephone:* (202) 863-8000 (office). *Fax:* (202) 863-8174 (office). *Website:* www.democrats.org (office).

EAST, Rt Hon. Paul Clayton, PC, QC, LLM; New Zealand politician, lawyer and diplomatist; b. 1946, Opotiki; s. of Edwin Cuthbert East and Edith Pauline Addison East; m. Marilyn Therese Kottmann 1972; three d.; ed Univ. of Virginia School of Law, Univ. of Auckland School of Law, King's Coll.; law clerk, Morpeth Gould & Co., Auckland 1968–70; Pnr, East Brewster Solicitors, Rotorua 1974–; fmr Rotorua City Councillor and Deputy Mayor; Nat. Party MP for Rotorua 1978–96; Attorney-Gen., Minister responsible for Serious Fraud Office and Audit Dept 1990–97, Leader of the House 1990–93, Minister of Crown Health Enterprises 1991–96, for State Services 1993–97, for Defence and War Pensions 1996–97, for Corrections 1996–97; High Commr in UK (also accred to Nigeria and Ireland) 1999–2002. *Leisure interests:* fishing, skiing, golf. *Address:* 23 Sophia Street, PO Box 608, Rotorua, New Zealand. *E-mail:* pauleastnz@hotmail.com (home).

EASTMAN, Dean Eric, PhD; American physicist, science policy consultant and academic; *Professor, Department of Physics and James Franck Institute, University of Chicago;* b. 21 Jan. 1940, Oxford, Wis.; m. Ella Mae Staley 1979; Research Staff mem. IBM, Yorktown Heights, NY 1963–74, Man. Surface Physics and Photo-emission 1971–82, Dir Advanced Packaging Tech. Lab. and Sr Man. III-V Semi-conductor Packaging Tech. & Systems Dept and GaAs Devices and Tech. Dept 1982–85, STD Dir of Devt and Product Assurance 1985–86, IBM Research Vice-Pres. of System Tech. and Science 1986–94, IBM Dir Hardware Devt Re-Eng 1994–95, IBM Server Group Vice-Pres. Devt Re-Eng and Tech. Strategy 1996–98; Prof., Dept of Physics and James Franck Inst., Univ. of Chicago 1998–; Fellow, American Physical Soc.; mem. NAS, Nat. Acad. of Eng; IBM Fellow 1974–; APS Oliver E. Buckley Prize 1980. *Publications:* numerous articles on solid state physics in professional journals. *Address:* Department of Physics, JFI Box 15 - RI 231, University of Chicago, 5801 South Ellis Avenue, Chicago, IL 60637 (office); 806 Pines Bridge Road, Ossining, NY 10562, USA (home). *Telephone:* (773) 834-0988 (office). *Fax:* (773) 834-3444 (office). *E-mail:* d-eastman@uchicago.edu (office). *Website:* physics.uchicago.edu (office).

EASTMAN, John L.; American lawyer and business executive; *CEO, MPL Communications, Inc.;* b. 1940, New York; s. of late Lee Eastman; brother of Linda McCartney (died 1998); m. Jodie Eastman; three c.; ed Stanford Univ. and New York Univ.; worked for Senate Commerce Cttee 1963; Office of US Attorney, New York; took part in Robert Kennedy's 1968 presidential election campaign; with father founded Eastman & Eastman (law firm); specializes in contract and copyright law; represents many leading showbusiness and media personalities; currently CEO MPL Communications (McCartney Productions Ltd), also lawyerman. of Paul McCartney; fmr Dir Apple Corps Ltd Linda McCartney Foods; Trustee, American Museum of Natural History; fmr Trustee Smith Coll. *Leisure interests:* collecting pictures, 19th-century English literature. *Address:* MPL Communications, Inc., 41 West 54th Street, New York, NY 10019, USA (office). *Telephone:* (212) 246-5881 (office). *Fax:* (212) 246-7852 (office). *E-mail:* contact@mplcommunications.com (office). *Website:* www.mplcommunications.com (office).

EASTON, David, MA, PhD, FRSC; Canadian political scientist and academic; *Distinguished Research Professor of Political Science, University of California, Irvine;* b. 24 June 1917, Toronto; s. of Albert Easton and Mary Easton; m. Sylvia Johnstone 1942 (died 1990); one s.; ed Univ. of Toronto and Harvard Univ.; Teaching Fellow, Dept of Govt, Harvard Univ. 1944–47; Asst Prof., Dept of Political Science, Univ. of Chicago 1947–53, Assoc. Prof. 1953–55, Prof. 1955–, Andrew MacLeish Distinguished Service Prof. 1969–82, Prof. Emer. 1982–; Sir Edward Peacock Prof. of Political Science, Queen's Univ., Kingston, Ont. 1971–80; Distinguished Prof. of Political Science, Univ. of California, Irvine 1981–, Distinguished Faculty Lectureship for Research 1997; Ford Rotating Research Prof., Univ. of California, Berkeley 1960–61; Pres. American Political Science Asscn 1968–69; mem. Int. Cttee on Social Science Documentation 1969–71; Chair. Bd Trustees Acad. of Ind. Scholars 1979–81; Co-Chair. Western Center, American Acad. of Arts and Sciences 1984–90, Vice-Pres. of Acad. 1984–90; Fellow, Center for Advanced Study in the Behavioral Sciences, Stanford 1957–58, American Acad. of Arts and Sciences 1962–; Hon. LLD (McMaster) 1970, (Kalamazoo) 1972; Hon. DPhil (Freie Universität, Berlin) 2001; Int. Alexander von Humboldt Research Prize 1995, Lauds and Laurels Distinguished Research Award, Univ. of Calif., Irvine 1995, David Easton Award est. by American Political Science Foundation (Foundations of Political Theory Section) 1996, Public Policy Studies Org. Thomas R. Dye Service Award 1997, Panunzio Award, Univ. of Calif. 2005–06. *Publications:* The Political System: An Inquiry into the State of Political Science 1953, A Framework for Political Analysis 1965, A Systems Analysis of Political Life 1965, Varieties of Political Theory (ed.) 1966, Children in the Political System: Origins of Political Legitimacy (with J. Dennis) 1969, The Analysis of Political Structure 1990, Divided Knowledge: Across Disciplines, Across Cultures (co-ed.) 1991, The Development of Political Science (co-ed.) 1991, Regime and Discipline (co-ed.) 1995; plus several reports of educ. cttees chaired by him. *Address:* University of California, Department of Political Science, 4251 Social Sciences Plaza B, Mail Code 5100, Irvine, CA 92697, USA (office). *Telephone:* (949) 824-6132 (office). *Fax:* (949) 824-8762 (office); (949) 824-5180 (office). *E-mail:* deaston@uci.edu (office). *Website:* www.polisci.uci.edu (office).

EASTON, Sheena; British singer and actress; b. (Sheena Shirley Orr), 27 April 1959, Bellshill, Scotland; m. 1st Rob Light 1985; m. 2nd Tim Delarm 1997; two c.; ed Royal Scottish Acad. of Music and Drama; singer Glasgow club circuit 1979; career launched by appearance on TV show, The Big Time (BBC 1) 1980; solo recording artist 1980–; numerous concerts and worldwide tours, TV appearances; Grammy Award for Best New Artist 1981, for Best Mexican/American Performance (with Luis Miguel) 1985, Emmy Award (for Sheena Easton... Act 1) 1983. *Stage appearances include:* Man of La Mancha (Chicago, then Broadway) 1991–92, The Colors of Christmas 2001. *Television appearances include:* Miami Vice (series) 1987–88, Body Bags 1993, The Highlander 1993, The Adventure of Brisco County Jr 1993, TekWar 1995, Gargoyles 1995–96, Outer Limits 1996, Road Rovers 1996, All Dogs go to Heaven 1996–97, Duckman 1997, Chicken Soup for the Soul 1999, The Legend of Tarzan 2001, Young Blades 2005, Phineas and Ferb (series) 2009. *Recordings include:* albums: Take My Time 1981, You Could Have Been With Me 1981, Madness, Money And Music 1982, Best Kept Secret 1983, A Private Heaven 1985, Do You 1985, The Lover In Me 1989, The Collection 1989, What Comes Naturally 1991, No Strings 1993, My Cherie 1995, Body And Soul 1997, Freedom 2000, Fabulous 2000. *Address:* c/o Harriet Wasserman Management, 15250 Ventura Blvd, Suite 1215, Sherman Oaks, CA 91403-3201, USA (office). *Website:* www.sheenaeaston.com.

EASTWOOD, Clint; American actor and film director; b. 31 May 1930, San Francisco, Calif.; s. of Clinton Eastwood and Ruth Eastwood; m. 1st Maggie Johnson 1953 (divorced); one s. one d.; one d. by Frances Fisher 1993; m. 2nd Dina Ruiz 1996; one d.; ed Los Angeles City Coll.; worked as lumberjack in Ore.; served in US Army; appeared in TV series Rawhide 1959–65; Owner, Malpaso Productions 1969–; Owner, Mission Ranch Resort, Carmel, Calif.; Co-Chair. UNESCO Campaign to protect the world's film heritage; mem. Nat. Arts Council 1973; Mayor of Carmel, Calif. 1986–88; Co-founder and Pnr, Tehama Inc. (sportswear co.) 1997–; Vice-Chair. Calif. State Parks and Recreation Comm.; Fellow, BFI 1993; Légion d'honneur, Commdr des Arts et des Lettres; Hon. DFA (Wesleyan)

2000, Hon. DLit (Univ. of Southern California) 2007; numerous awards including Irving G. Thalberg Award 1995, Lifetime Achievement Award, American Film Inst. 1996, Kennedy Center Honors, John F. Kennedy Center Performing Arts 2000, Lifetime Achievement Award, Screen Actors Guild 2003, Broadcast Film Critics Asscn 2004, Lifetime Achievement Award, Dirs Guild of America 2006, Jack Valenti Humanitarian Award, Motion Picture Asscn of America 2007, Nat. Medal of Arts 2009. *Films include:* Revenge of the Creature 1955, Francis in the Navy 1955, Lady Godiva 1955, Tarantula 1955, Never Say Goodbye 1956, The First Travelling Saleslady 1956, Star in the Dust 1956, Escapade in Japan 1957, Ambush at Cimarron Pass 1958, Lafayette Escadrille 1958, A Fistful of Dollars 1964, For a Few Dollars More 1965, The Good, the Bad and the Ugly 1966, The Witches 1967, Hang 'Em High 1968, Coogan's Bluff 1968, Where Eagles Dare 1969, Paint Your Wagon 1969, Kelly's Heroes 1970, Two Mules for Sister Sara 1970, The Beguiled 1971, Play Misty for Me (also dir) 1971, Dirty Harry 1971, Joe Kidd 1972, High Plains Drifter (also dir) 1973, Magnum Force 1973, Breezy (dir) 1973, Thunderbolt and Lightfoot 1974, The Eiger Sanction (also dir) 1975, The Outlaw Josey Wales (also dir) 1976, The Enforcer 1976, The Gauntlet (also dir) 1978, Every Which Way But Loose 1978, Escape from Alcatraz 1979, Bronco Billy (also dir) 1980, Any Which Way You Can 1980, Firefox (also dir) 1982, Honky Tonk Man (also dir) 1982, Sudden Impact (also dir) 1983, Tightrope 1984, City Heat 1984, Pale Rider 1985 (also dir), Heartbreak Ridge 1986 (also dir), Bird 1988 (Golden Globe Award for Best Dir 1989), The Dead Pool 1988, Pink Cadillac 1989, White Hunter, Black Heart (also dir) 1989, The Rookie (also dir) 1990, Unforgiven (also dir) (Acad. Awards for Best Film and Best Dir 1993) 1992, In the Line of Fire 1993, A Perfect World (also dir) 1993, The Bridges of Madison County (also dir, producer) 1995, The Stars Fell on Henrietta (co-producer), Absolute Power (also dir) 1997, True Crime 1998, Midnight in the Garden of Good and Evil (dir) 1997, Space Cowboys (dir) 2000, Bloodwork (also dir and producer) 2002, Mystic River (dir) 2003, Million Dollar Baby (also dir and composer) (Special Filmmaking Achievement Award, Nat. Bd of Review of Motion Pictures, Best Dir, Golden Globe Awards, Dirs Guild of America Awards 2005, Best Film, Best Dir, Acad. Awards 2005) 2004, Flags of Our Fathers 2006, Letters from Iwo Jima (Nat. Bd of Review of Motion Pictures Best Film 2006, Los Angeles Film Critics Asscn Best Film 2006) 2006, Changeling (dir) 2008, Gran Torino (also dir) 2008, Invictus (dir) 2009, Hereafter (dir) 2010, J. Edgar (dir) 2011, Trouble with the Curve 2012. *Address:* Malpaso Productions, c/o Warner Bros, 4000 Warner Blvd., Bldg 81, Burbank CA 91522, USA. *Telephone:* (818) 954-3367.

EASTWOOD, David, PhD, FRHistS; British historian, academic and university administrator; *Vice-Chancellor and Principal, University of Birmingham;* ed St Peter's Coll., Oxford; Research Fellow, Keble Coll. Oxford 1983–87; Fellow and Sr Tutor, Pembroke Coll. 1988–95, Hon. Fellow, St Peter's Coll., Oxford, Keble Coll., Oxford; Prof. of Modern History, Univ. of Wales, Swansea, also a Head of Dept, Dean and Pro-Vice-Chancellor, co-f. Nat. Centre for Public Policy; Chief Exec. Arts and Humanities Research Bd; Vice-Chancellor Univ. of East Anglia; Chief Exec. Higher Educ. Funding Council for England 2006–09; Vice-Chancellor and Prin. Univ. of Birmingham 2009–; Chair. Russell Group; Dir, Universities Superannuation Scheme; mem. Bd Universities UK (fmr Chair. Longer Term Strategy Group), Arts and Humanities Research Council, Advisory Bd of Higher Educ. Policy Inst., Marketing Birmingham; fmr Chair. Asscn of Univs of East of England, Supporting Professionalism in Admissions, Westminster Educ. Comm. 2009; Fellow, Royal Historical Soc. 1991, Literary Dir 1994–2000, Chair. Studies in History Bd 2000–04; mem. Research Support Libraries Group 2002–03, Roberts Review of Research Assessment Exercise, Tomlinson Group on 14–19 Educ. 2003–04, Council of John Innes Centre, Council of Sainsbury Lab., Bd of Quality Assurance Agency; Chair. Group of Universities 1994; Int. mem. Hong Kong Univ. Grants Cttee; fmr mem. UK Govt's Ind. Review Panel looking at Higher Educ. Funding and Student Finance; DL, West Midlands 2012–; Hon. Fellow, Swansea Univ. *Publications:* numerous articles on the history of the British state, the history of ideas and on electoral politics. *Leisure interests:* music, politics, walking, sport, good wine, writing on football. *Address:* Vice-Chancellor's Office, Aston Webb Building, University of Birmingham, Edgbaston, Birmingham, B15 2TT, England (office). *Telephone:* (121) 414-4536 (office). *E-mail:* l.wilden@bham.ac.uk (office). *Website:* www.birmingham.ac.uk (office).

EASTWOOD, Trevor, AM, BEng; Australian business executive; ed Univ. of Western Australia, Advanced Man. Program at Harvard Business School, USA; began career with Westralian Farmers Co-operative Ltd 1963, held several man. positions until retirement in 1992, including Man. Dir Wesfarmers Ltd 1984–92, mem. Bd of Dirs 1994–2008, Chair. (non-exec.) 2002–08; mem. Bd of Dirs The WCM Group Ltd; fmr Chair. West Australian Newspapers Holdings Ltd; fmr mem. Bd of Dirs Qantas Airways Ltd. *Address:* c/o Wesfarmers Ltd, 11th Floor, Wesfarmers House, 40 The Esplanade, Perth 6000, WA, Australia.

EATON, Ashton James, BA; American decathlete; b. 21 Jan. 1988, Portland, Ore.; s. of Roslyn Eaton and Terrance Wilson; ed Univ. of Oregon; won state high school 400m championship 2006; winner in decathlon, Nat. Collegiate Athletic Asscn (NCAA) Men's Outdoor Track and Field Championship 2008, 2009, 2010; winner in heptathlon, NCAA Indoor Championships 2009, 2010; second in decathlon, Outdoor Track and Field Championships 2009; silver medal in decathlon, IAAF World Championships in Athletics 2011; gold medal in heptathlon, IAAF World Indoor Championships 2012; gold medal in decathlon, Olympic Games, London 2012; second decathlete (after Roman Šebrle) to break 9,000 point barrier (9,039 points); mem. Oregon Track Club Elite team 2010–; Div. I Field Athlete of the Year Award 2009, Bowerman Award, Track and Field and Cross Country Coaches Asscn 2010, Fair Play Award 2012. *Address:* Oregon Track Club, PO Box 11364, Eugene, OR 97440, USA. *Website:* www.oregontrackclub.org.

EATON, Fredrik Stefan, OC, BA, LLD; Canadian business executive and fmr diplomatist; *Chairman, White Raven Capital Corporation;* b. 26 June 1938, Toronto; s. of the late John David Eaton and Signy Hildur Stephenson; m. Catherine Martin 1962; one s. one d.; ed New Brunswick Univ.; joined The T. Eaton Co. Ltd and held various positions in Victoria, London, Toronto 1962–67, Dir 1967–69, Chair., Pres., CEO 1977–88, Chair. 1988–91; Pres., Dir Eaton's of Canada (parent co. of the other Eaton cos) 1969–77, Chair. Exec. Cttee 1994–97; High Commr in UK 1991–94; Chancellor Univ. of New Brunswick 1993–2003; currently Chair. White Raven Capital Corpn; Chair. Bd of Trustees, Canadian

Museum of Civilization Corpn 2007–11; Order of Ontario 2001, Queen Elizabeth II Diamond Jubilee Medal 2012; Hon. LLD (New Brunswick) 1983; Man. Award, McGill Univ. 1987. *Leisure interests:* art, music, reading, shooting, yachting. *Address:* White Raven Capital Corporation, 55 St Clair Avenue West, Suite 260, Toronto, ON M4V 2Y7, Canada (office). *Telephone:* (416) 929-3942 (office). *Fax:* (416) 925-4339 (office).

EATON, George, FCCA; Irish chartered accountant; *Consultant, Eaton Neary;* b. 11 Jan. 1942, Cork; s. of Thomas J. V. Eaton and Catherine Hannon; m. Ellen Patricia O'Grady 1966; one d.; ed Christian Brothers Coll., Cork, Inst. of Chartered Accountants, Ireland; with Touche Ross, Chartered Accountants, Cork 1960–66; Chief Accountant, Seafield Fabrics, Youghal 1966–67; Deputy Man. Dir General Textiles 1967–75; Sr Pnr, Eaton Dowd (later Eaton Neary) 1976–2012, Consultant 2012–; Chair. Portuguese Irish Chamber of Commerce 1987–89; Pres. Chambers of Commerce of Ireland 1985–87; Hon. Consul of Hungary 1990–2010. *Publication:* Introducing Ireland 1989. *Leisure interests:* history, genealogy, reading, book collecting. *Address:* Custume Place, Athlone, Ireland (office). *Telephone:* (9064) 78531 (office). *Fax:* (9064) 74691 (office). *E-mail:* companies@eatonneary.ie (office).

EATON, Robert J., BS; American engineer and automobile industry executive (retd); b. 13 Feb. 1940, Arkansas City, Kansas; s. of Gene Eaton and Mildred Eaton; m. Connie Drake 1964; two s.; ed Univ. of Kansas; joined Gen. Motors (Chevrolet Motor Div.) 1963, transferred to eng staff 1971, Exec. Engineer 1974, Chief Engineer, Corp. Car Programs 1976, Asst Chief Engineer and Dir of Reliability at Oldsmobile 1979, Vice-Pres. in charge of Tech. Staffs 1986, Pres. Gen. Motors Europe 1988–92; COO Chrysler Motors Corpn 1992–93, Chair., CEO 1993–1998 (now Chair. Emer.), Co.-Chair., Co.-CEO Daimler Chrysler 1998–2000 (after 1998 merger of Chrysler with Daimler Benz); mem. Bd of Dirs Group Lotus 1986–, ChevronTexaco Corpn 2000–, Int. Paper Co.; mem. Industrial Advisory Bd Stanford Univ.; Fellow, Soc. of Automotive Engineers, Eng Soc. of Detroit; mem. Nat. Acad. of Eng; Chevalier du Tastevin 1989; Contemporary Honors Award, Kansas Business Hall of Fame 2005. *Leisure interests:* skiing, golf, hunting. *Address:* 9675 Mashie Court, Naples, FL 34106, USA.

EATWELL, Baron (Life Peer), cr. 1992, of Stratton St Margaret in the County of Wiltshire; **John Leonard Eatwell,** PhD; British economist and academic; *President, Queens' College, Cambridge;* b. 2 Feb. 1945; s. of Harold Jack Eatwell and Mary Eatwell; m. 1st Hélène Seppain 1970 (divorced); two s. one d.; m. 2nd Susan Elizabeth Digby 2006; ed Headlands Grammar School, Swindon, Queens' Coll., Cambridge, Harvard Univ., USA; Teaching Fellow, Grad. School of Arts and Sciences, Harvard Univ. 1968–69; Research Fellow, Queens' Coll. Cambridge 1969–70; Fellow, Trinity Coll., Cambridge 1970–96, Asst Lecturer, Faculty of Econs and Politics, Univ. of Cambridge 1975–77, Lecturer 1977, currently Prof. of Financial Policy, Pres. Queens' Coll. 1997–; Visiting Prof. of Econs, New School for Social Research, New York 1982–96; Econ. Adviser to Neil Kinnock, Leader of Labour Party 1985–92; Opposition Spokesman on Treasury Affairs and on Trade and Industry, House of Lords 1992–93, Prin. Opposition Spokesman on Treasury and Econ. Affairs 1993–97; Trustee, Inst. for Public Policy Research 1988–95, Sec. 1988–97, Chair. 1997–; Dir (non-exec.) Anglia TV Group 1994–2001, Cambridge Econometrics Ltd 1996–2007; Chair. Extemporary Dance Theatre 1990, Crusaid 1993–98, British Screen Finance Ltd 1997–2000 and assoc. cos; Gov. Contemporary Dance Trust 1991–95; Dir Arts Theatre Trust, Cambridge 1991–98, Bd, Securities and Futures Authority 1997–2001; mem. Bd Royal Opera House 1998–2006; Chair. Royal Ballet 1998–2001, Commercial Radio Cos Asscn 2000–04, British Library Bd 2001–06, Royal Opera House Pension Scheme 2007–, Consumer Panel, Classic FM 2007–; mem. Regulatory Decisions Cttee, FSA 2001–05, Econ. Affairs Cttee, House of Lords 2009–; Dir Cambridge Endowment for Research in Finance 2002–; Gov. Royal Ballet School 2003–06, Artsworks Ltd 2007–, SAV Credit Ltd 2008–. *Publications:* An Introduction to Modern Economics (with Joan Robinson) 1973, Whatever Happened to Britain? 1982, Keynes's Economics and the Theory of Value and Distribution (ed. with Murray Milgate) 1983, The New Palgrave: A Dictionary of Economics, 4 Vols 1987, The New Palgrave Dictionary of Money and Finance, 3 Vols 1992 (both with Murray Milgate and Peter Newman), Transformation and Integration: Shaping the Future of Central and Eastern Europe (jtly) 1995, Global Unemployment: Loss of Jobs in the '90s (ed.) 1996, Not "Just Another Accession": The Political Economy of EU Enlargement to the East (jtly) 1997, Global Finance at Risk: The Case for International Regulation (with L. Taylor) 2000, Hard Budgets, Soft States 2000, Social Policy Choices in Central and Eastern Europe 2002, International Capital Markets (with L. Taylor) 2002; numerous articles in scientific journals. *Leisure interests:* classical and contemporary dance, Rugby Union football. *Address:* The President's Lodge, Queens' College, Cambridge, CB3 9ET, England (home). *Telephone:* (1223) 335556 (home). *Fax:* (1223) 335555 (home). *E-mail:* president@queens.cam.ac.uk (office).

EBADI, Shirin, JD; Iranian lawyer, human rights activist and academic; b. 1947, Hamadan; d. of Mohammad Ali Ebadi; m.; two d.; ed Univ. of Tehran; apptd Judge (first and only woman) and Pres. of Tehran City Court 1974, forced to step down from bench after 1979 revolution, retd 1984; currently runs own law practice specializing in human rights; mem. Cttee for the Defence of Rights of the Victims of Serial Murders; Founder Soc. for Protecting the Rights of the Child, Centre for Defence of Human Rights; Lecturer in Law, Univ. of Tehran; Founding mem. Nobel Women's Initiative 2006; Hon. LLD (Brown Univ.) 2004, (Univ. of British Columbia) 2004; Dr hc (Univ. of Maryland, College Park) 2004, (Univ. of Toronto) 2004, (Simon Fraser Univ.) 2004, (Univ. of Akureyri) 2004, (Australian Catholic Univ.) 2005, (Univ. of San Francisco) 2005, (Concordia Univ.) 2005, (Univ. of York) 2005, (Université Jean Moulin, Lyon) 2005, (Loyola Univ., Chicago) 2007, (New School Univ.) 2007; Human Rights Watch Award 1996, Rafto Prize 2001, Nobel Peace Prize (first Iranian and first Muslim woman) 2003, International Democracy Award 2004, Lawyer of the Year Award 2004, ranked 99th by Forbes magazine amongst 100 Most Powerful Women 2004, UCI Citizen Peacebuilding Award 2005, The Golden Plate Award, Acad. of Achievement 2005. *Publications include:* The Rights of the Child: A Study of Legal Aspects of Children's Rights in Iran 1994, History and Documentation of Human Rights in Iran 2000, Iran Awakening 2006, Refugee Rights in Iran 2008, The Golden Cage 2009; numerous other books and journal articles. *Address:* Society for Protecting the Rights of the Child, 26 Tenth Street, Nobakht Street, Tehran, Iran (office). *Website:* www.irsprc.org (office).

EBANKS, Donovan W. F., MBE, JP; Cayman Islands politician and public servant; *Chairman, Civil Service Appeals Commission;* joined Public Works Dept 1975, Chief Engineer 1983; Deputy Chief Sec. of Cayman Islands 1994–2009, First Official Mem., Legis. Ass. (parl.) 2009–, Chief Sec. and Head of Civil Service 2009–12, also Minister of Internal and External Affairs 2009, Acting Gov. Dec. 2009–12; Chair. Civil Service Appeals Comm. 2013–; fmr Chair. Nat. Hurricane Cttee. *Address:* Government Administration Bldg, Elgin Ave, George Town, Grand Cayman, Cayman Islands (office).

EBDANE, Hermogenes, Jr., BSc, MSc, PhD; Philippine politician; *Governor of Zambales;* b. 30 Dec. 1948, Candelaria, Zambales; m. Alma Cabanayan; three c.; ed Philippine Mil. Acad.; fmr Nat. Security Adviser and Dir Gen., Nat. Security Council; fmr Vice-Chair. Anti-Terrorism Task Force; fmr Nat. Anti-Terrorism Coordinator; fmr Dir Human Resources, Philippine Nat. Police, fmr Deputy Chief of Admin, Chief 2002–04; Sec. of Public Works and Highways 2004–07, 2008–10, of Nat. Defense (acting) 2007; Gov. of Zambales Prov. 2010–; Philippine Legion of Honor, Distinguished Conduct Star, Bronze Cross Medal, numerous military honours. *Address:* Office of the Governor, Iba, Zambales Province, Philippines (office).

EBERHARTER, Stephan; Austrian skier (retd); b. 24 March 1969, Brixlegg, Tirol; Gold Medal, Super-G and Combined, World Championships, Saalbach 1991, Super-G, St Moritz, Switzerland 2003; Silver Medal, Super-G, World Championships, St Anton 2001; Silver Medal, Giant Slalom, Olympic Games, Nagano, Japan 1998; Gold Medal, Giant Slalom, Olympics Games, Salt Lake City, USA 2002, Silver Medal, Super-G, Bronze Medal, Downhill; World Cup ranking (Gen.): Third 1998, Fourth 1999, Sixth 2000, Second 2001, First 2002, 2003, Second 2004. *Leisure interests:* music, golf. *Address:* Stephan Eberharter, Dorfstrasse 21, 6272 Stumm i.Z., Austria. *E-mail:* wcroad@hotmail.com; designskiwcorg@hotmail.com. *Website:* www.steff.at.

EBERLE, Adm. Sir James Henry Fuller, GCB; British naval officer (retd); b. 31 May 1927, Bristol; s. of Victor Fuller Eberle, MC and Joyce Mary Eberle; m. Ann Patricia Thompson 1950 (died 1988); one s. two d.; ed Clifton Coll. and Royal Naval Coll., Dartmouth; served in Second World War at home, East Indies and Pacific 1944–45; served in Korean War, HMS Belfast and Fleet Staff Officer 1952–53; Sr officer, 100 Minesweeping Squadron 1958–59; Capt. HMS Intrepid 1968–70; Defence Fellow, Univ. Coll., Oxford 1970; promoted Rear-Adm. 1971; Flag Officer, Carriers and Amphibious Ships and Commdr NATO Striking Group Two 1975–76; mem. Admiralty Bd 1977–78; Commdr-in-Chief Fleet, Allied C-in-C Eastern Atlantic, C-in-C Channel 1979–80; C-in-C Naval Home Command 1981–82; retd 1983, rank of Adm.; Dir Royal Inst. of Int. Affairs 1984–90; Dir UK-Japan 2000 Group 1986–98; Chair. UK Asscn of Harriers and Beagles 1998–; mem. Bd Countryside Alliance 2002–; Hon. DLit (Bristol) 1989, (Sussex) 1992;Freeman of Bristol 1946, London 1982. *Publications:* Management in the Armed Forces 1972, Jim, First of the Pack 1982, Britain's Future in Space 1988. *Leisure interests:* tennis, field sports. *Address:* Homestead Farm, Houghton, Stockbridge, Hants., SO20 6LG, England (home). *Telephone:* (1264) 821659 (home). *E-mail:* admiraljim@lineone.net (home).

ÉBERT, Tibor, BA; Hungarian writer, poet and dramatist; b. 14 Oct. 1926, Bratislava, Czechoslovakia; m. Eva Gati 1968; one d.; ed Ferenc Liszt Acad. of Music, Eötvös Lóránd Univ., Budapest; Dramaturg József Attila Theatre, Budapest 1984–85; Ed.-in-Chief Agora Publrs, Budapest 1989–92; Ed. Hirvivo Literary Magazine 1990–92; mem. PEN Club, Asscn of Hungarian Writers, Literary Asscn Berzsenyi; Hon. mem. Franco-Hungarian Soc. 1980–; Order of Hungarian Repub. 1996; Bartók Prize 1987, Commemorative Medal, City of Pozsony-Pressburg-Bratislava 1991, Esterházy Prize 1993. *Plays:* Les Escaliers, Musique de Chambre, Demosthenes, Esterházy, Bartók, Attila, Le Rout Casimir et Olivier, Le Tableau. *Publications:* Mikrodrámák 1971, Rosarium 1987, Kobayashi 1989, Legenda egy fúvószenekarról 1990, Jób könyve 1991, Fagyott Orpheusz (poems) 1993, Eső 1996, Egy város glóriája 1997, Bartók 1997, Eredők 1998, Éltem 1998, Drámák 2000, Bolyongás 2001, Vecseruye 2001, Kaleidoszkóp 2002, Álmomban 2002, Feljegyzcések 2004, Tüzfalau 2006, Vár 2006, Örvényben 2011; contrib. numerous short stories, poems, dramas and essays to several leading Hungarian literary journals and magazines. *Address:* Csévi u 15c, 1025 Budapest, Hungary (home).

EBTEKAR, Massoumeh, MSc, PhD, DSc; Iranian scientist, academic and politician; *Associate Professor of Immunology, Tarbiat Modares University;* b. 21 Sept. 1960, Tehran; d. of the late Prof. Taghi Ebtekar and Fatima Barzegar; m.; two c.; ed Shahid Beheshti Univ. and Tarbiat Modares Univ., Tehran; Ed.-in-Chief Keyhan Int. (English daily newspaper) 1981–83; Editorial Dir Farzaneh Journal of Women's Studies and Research; Founding mem. Centre for Women's Studies and Research 1986–; Dir Women's NGO Co-ordination Office, Tehran 1994–; Pres. Network of Women's NGOs in the Islamic Repub. of Iran 1995–; Faculty mem. School of Medical Science, Tarbiat Modares Univ. 1989–95, Asst Prof. of Immunology 1995–2006, Assoc. Prof. 2006–; Vice-Pres. of Iran and Head of Dept of the Environment (first female Vice-Pres.) 1997–2005; Founder and Head, Centre for Peace and the Environment, Tehran 2005–; mem. Tehran City Council 2007–, est. and Head of Environment Cttee, currently runs 20 working groups on environmental issues; del., vice-chair. or chair. numerous int. confs on women; Champion of the Earth Award, UNEP 2006, Distinguished Researcher 2007. *Publications include:* book: Natural Peace and Ethics; The Grapes of Shahrivar (Farsi), Memoirs of the First Vice President of Iran 2009; contribs to Farzaneh Journal of Women's Studies and numerous int. journals. *Leisure interests:* swimming, reading, blogging. *Address:* Faculty of Medical Sciences, Tarbiat Modares University, Intersection of Chamran and Ale-Ahmad Highways, PO Box 14115-331, Tehran (office); City Council, Behesht Avenue, Tehran, Iran (office). *Telephone:* (21) 82883891 (office); (21) 55893613 (home). *Fax:* (21) 88013030 (office). *E-mail:* ebtekarm@modares.ac.ir (office); ebtekarm@gmail.com. *Website:* www.modares.ac.ir/med/Ebtekarm (office); ebtekarm.blogspot.com.

ECARMA, Maj.-Gen. (retd) Natalio C., III; Philippine UN official and fmr army officer; b. 3 June 1955, Manila; m. Dr Beverly Antonio; two s.; ed Philippines Mil. Acad., Marine Corp Univ., Nat. Defense Coll. of Philippines; joined Philippine Marine Corps 1977, held several posts including Commdr of the Presidential Guards Bn, Presidential Security Group, 3rd Marine Brigade, Combat and Service

Support Brigade; numerous staff appointments including Asst Chief of Staff for Intelligence, Philippine Marine Corps, Asst Supt, Marine Corps Training Center, Chief of Staff, Philippine Marine Corps, Deputy Commdt; Concurrent Commdr, Marine Forces; retd from mil. service 2011; Head of Mission and Force Commdr, UN Disengagement Observer Force (UNDOF) 2010–12; Fellow, AIM TeaM Energy Center for Bridging Leadership; two distinguished service stars, two bronze cross medals 2001, 17 mil. merit medals, six mil. commendation medals. *Address:* c/o United Nations Disengagement Observer Force (UNDOF), Department of Peace-keeping Operations, Room S-3727-B, United Nations, New York, NY 10017, USA.

ECCLESTON, Christopher; British actor; b. 16 Feb. 1964, Salford; s. of Joseph Ronald Eccleston and Elsie Lavinia Eccleston. *Films include:* Let Him Have It 1991, Shallow Grave 1995, Jude 1996, Elizabeth 1998, A Price Above Rubies 1998, Heart 1999, Old New Borrowed Blue 1999, Existenz 1999, Gone in 60 Seconds 2000, The Invisible Circus 2001, The Others 2001, I am Dina 2002, 28 Days Later 2002, The Seeker: The Dark Is Rising 2007. *Theatre includes:* Miss June 2000. *Television appearances:* Cracker 1993–94, Hearts and Minds 1995, Our Friends in the North 1996, Hillsborough 1996, Strumpet 2001, Flesh and Blood (Best Actor, Royal TV Soc. Awards 2003) 2002, The Second Coming (TV film) 2003, Doctor Who (BBC) 2005, Perfect Parents 2006, Heroes 2007. *Leisure interest:* supporting Manchester United Football Club. *Address:* c/o Claire Maroussas, Independent Talent Group, Oxford House, 76 Oxford Street, London, W1D 1BF, England (office). *Website:* www.independenttalent.com (office).

ECCLESTONE, Bernard (Bernie), BSc; British business executive; *CEO, Formula One Management Limited;* b. Oct. 1930; m. 1st; one d.; m. 2nd Slavica Ecclestone; two d.; ed Woolwich Polytechnic, London; est. car and motorcycle dealership, Midweek Car Auctions, Bexley, Kent; racing-car driver for short period (Formula 3); Owner Connaught racing team 1957; Man. Jochen Rindt; purchased Brabham racing team 1970 (sold 1990); CEO Formula One Admin. Ltd, CEO Formula One Management Ltd, mem. Bd of Dirs Delta Topco Ltd (holding co. –2014); Vice-Pres. Fed. Int. de l'Automobile (FIA) (racing's int. governing body); Grand Decoration of Honour (Austria), Medal of the First Degree (Bahrain), Keys to the Cities of São Paulo and Rio de Janeiro, Order of Merit of the Medium Cross (Hungary), Grand Officer, Order of Merit (Italy), Grand Officer, Equestrian Order of St Agata (San Marino); Bandeirante Medal (Sao Paulo), Silver gilt and Silver grade medals (Monaco), Motorsport Industry Asscn Business Achievement Award, British Racing Driver's Club inaugural Gold Medal. *Address:* Formula One Management Ltd, 6 Prince's Gate, London, SW7 1QJ, England. *Telephone:* (20) 7584-6668. *Fax:* (20) 7589-0311. *E-mail:* ckai@fomltd.com. *Website:* www.formula1.com.

ECHÁVARRI, Luis Enrique, MSc; Spanish business executive and international organization official; b. 17 April 1949, Bilbao; m.; two c.; ed Univ. of Basque Country, Univ. of Madrid; Project Man. for Lemóniz, Sayago and Almaraz nuclear power plants, Westinghouse Electric, Madrid; Tech. Dir and Commr, Consejo de Seguridad Nuclear (Spanish nuclear regulatory comm.); Dir-Gen. OECD Nuclear Energy Agency (NEA) 1997–2014; rep. of Spain at int. fora on nuclear energy, including Int. Atomic Energy Agency and EU; mem. INSAG-IAEA; represents NEA at Int. Energy Agency Governing bd. *Address:* c/o OECD Nuclear Energy Agency, Le Seine Saint-Germain, 12 Blvd des Iles, 92130 Issy-les-Moulineux, France.

ECHENOZ, Jean Maurice Emmanuel; French writer; b. 26 Dec. 1947, Orange, Vaucluse; s. of Marc Echenoz and Annie Languin; one s.; ed Univ. of Aix-en-Provence, Sorbonne and Univ. of Paris; professional writer 1979–; Grand Prix du roman de la Ville de Paris 1997, Grand Prix de littérature Paul Morand de l'Acad. française 2007. *Film:* Le Rose et le blanc (dir Robert Pansard-Besson) (co-script writer) (Prix Georges Sadoul) 1979. *Publications:* Le Méridien de Greenwich (Prix Fénéon 1980) 1979, Cherokee (Prix Médicis) 1983, L'Equipée malaise (trans. as Double Jeopardy) 1986, L'Occupation des sols 1988 (trans. as Plan of Occupancy), Lac (Grand Prix du Roman de la Société des Gens de Lettres 1990, European Literature Prize, Glasgow 1990) 1989, Nous trois 1992, Les Grandes blondes (trans. as Big Blondes) (Prix Novembre) 1995, Un An 1997, Je m'en vais (trans. as I'm Gone) (Prix Goncourt) 1999, Jérôme Lindon 2001, Josué, Samuel, Daniel, Maccabées (trans. of Bible, jtly) 2001, Au piano (trans. as Piano) 2003, Ravel 2006, Courir (trans. as Running) 2008, Des éclairs (trans. as Lightning) 2010, 14 2012. *Address:* c/o Editions de Minuit, 7 rue Bernard-Palissy, 75006 Paris, France. *Website:* www.leseditionsdeminuit.com.

ECHEVARRIA, Most Rev. Javier, PhD; Spanish ecclesiastic; *Prelate, Opus Dei;* b. 14 June 1932; ed Univ. of Madrid, Pontifical Univ. of St Thomas, Rome, Pontifical Lateran Univ., Rome; moved to Rome 1950; ordained priest 1955; Lecturer in Moral Theology, Collegio Romano della Santa Croce 1960, Collegio Romano di Santa Maria 1964; apptd. personal sec. to Josemaría Escrivá (Founder of Opus Dei) 1957, mem. Gen. Council Opus Dei 1966–75, Sec.-Gen. 1975–82, Vicar-Gen. 1982–94, Prelate of Opus Dei 1994–; consecrated Bishop 1995; Consultant, Sacred Congregation for the Clergy 1995–2003; mem. Supreme Tribunal of the Apostolic Signatura 2000–12, Sacred Congregation for the Causes of Saints 2002–12; apptd by Pope Benedict XVI as Synod Father for 13th Ordinary Gen. Ass. of the Synod of Bishops on the New Evangelization Oct. 2012. *Publications:* Memoria del Beato Josemaría Escrivá 2000, Itinerarios de vida cristiana 2001, Para servir a la Iglesia 2001, Getsemaní 2005, Eucaristía y Vida Cristiana 2005, Por Cristo, con Él y en Él 2007, Vivir la Santa Misa 2010. *Address:* Curia of the Prelature, 73 Viale Bruno Buozzi, 00197 Rome, Italy (home). *Telephone:* (06) 808961 (home). *Fax:* (06) 80896420 (home). *Website:* www.opusdei.org (office).

ECHEVERRI CORREA, Fabio, BEcons; Colombian business executive; *Chairman, Ecopetrol SA;* ed Gimnasio Moderno, Universidad Jorge Tadeo Lozano; Asst Man., later Gen. Man. Banco de Colombia, Medellín 1957–62; Gen. Man. Banco Comercial Antioqueño, Medellín 1962–66; CEO Siderurgica de Medellín SA 1969–74; CEO Hojalata y Laminados SA, led first investment jt venture in Colombia between Mitsubishi Corpn and Kawasaki Corpn; Pres. Liberal Party Directory, Antioquia Dept 1972–74, mem. Cttee, Gen. Policy Comm. of Liberal Party (Pres.) 1973–74; Pres. and CEO Colombian Asscn of Industrialists (ANDI), Bogotá 1974–91; adviser and consultant to several pvt. enterprises in Bogotá and Medellín 1992–2001; Campaign Pres. to Presidency of Alvaro Uribe Vélez 2001–02,

Pres. Converging Comm. during transition period, adviser to the Pres. 2002–04, Campaign Pres. and Man. re-election of Pres. Uribe 2005–06; CEO Shaio Clinic; Pres. AILA (Latin American Asscn of Industries), CONANDI (Andean Confed. of Industries); mem. Inter-American Council for Trade and Production; mem. Bd of Dirs Ecopetrol SA 2002–, currently Chair.; mem. Bd of Dirs Shaio Clinic, Chamber of Commerce, Medellín, Empresa de Telecomunicaciones – Telecom, Proexpo, San Vicente de Paul Hosp., Medellín, Siemens SA, Hoechst Colombiana SA, Seguros del Caribe, Tampa Airlines, SAM Airlines, Distral SA, Peldar SA, Siderúrgica de Medellín SA, Corporación Financiera de Boyacá; adviser and consultant, Drummond Coal Co. Inc., Birmingham, Ala, British American Tobacco, Mayaguez Group, Cine Colombia, Ogden SA, USA, Columbus American Discovery Group, USA; perm. writer and columnist, El Tiempo newspaper and Colprensa; columnist, El Espectador, El Colombiano, El Universal, El Mundo, Credencial magazine, Aces bulletin, National Association of Industrials magazine, Cambio 16 magazine, Presidencia magazine. *Publication:* The Industry – From the Times of Protectionism to the Foreign Trade Opening 1991. *Address:* Ecopetrol SA, Carrera 13 No. 36 – 24, Bogotá, DC, Colombia (office). *Telephone:* (1) 2344000 (office). *Fax:* (1) 2344099 (office). *E-mail:* info@ecopetrol.com.co (office). *Website:* www.ecopetrol.com.co (office).

ECHEVERRY GARZÓN, Juan Carlos, BA, PhD; Colombian economist and politician; *Minister of Finance and Public Credit;* b. 12 Sept. 1962, Ibagué, Tolima; m. Verónica Navas; three c.; ed Univ. de los Andes, Bogotá, New York Univ., USA, Kiel Inst. for the World Economy, Germany, Univ. Complutense de Madrid, Spain; fmr Dir Departamento Nacional de Planeación; consultant to Banco Interamericano de Desarrollo; Minister of Econ. Planning 2000–02; Dean of Econs, Univ. de los Andes 2002–06, now Assoc. Prof.; Minister of Finance and Public Credit 2010–; Pres. Econcept (financial consulting firm); writes weekly column for CNN en Español (news channel). *Address:* Ministry of Finance and Public Credit, Carrera 8, No 6-64, Of. 305, Bogotá DC, Colombia (office). *Telephone:* (1) 381-1700 (office). *Fax:* (1) 350-9344 (office). *E-mail:* atencioncliente@minhacienda.gov.co (office). *Website:* www.minhacienda.gov.co (office).

ECKEL, Keith W.; American business executive; *Chairman, Nationwide Mutual Insurance Company;* b. Scranton, Pa; ed Newton-Ransom High School, Clarks Summit, Pa, Keystone Junior Coll., Dickinson Coll., Pennsylvania State Univ.; fmr Dir Nationwide Financial Services, Inc.; mem. Bd of Dirs Nationwide 1996–, Chair. Nationwide Mutual Insurance Co. (parent co.) 2008–; fmr Chair. Gartmore Global Asset Man. Trust, Allied Group, Inc.; Owner Fred W. Eckel Sons, Pres. Eckel Farms, Inc.; mem. Bd Int. Food and Agricultural Devt, Pennsylvania Vegetable Growers Asscn; fmr mem. Bd Pennsylvania Agricultural Land Preservation; Pres. Pennsylvania Farm Bureau for 15 years; fmr Pres. Lackawanna Co. Co-operative Extension Asscn; fmr Vice-Pres. Pennsylvania Council of Cooperative Extension Asscns; fmr mem. Bd and Exec. Cttee American Farm Bureau Fed.; Trustee, Pennsylvania State Univ.; Master Farmer Award, Pennsylvania State Univ. 1982, Distinguished Service Award, American Farm Bureau Fed. 2009. *Address:* Nationwide Mutual Insurance Co., One Nationwide Plaza, Columbus, OH 43215-2220, USA (office). *Telephone:* (614) 249-7111 (office). *Fax:* (614) 249-7705 (office). *E-mail:* info@nationwide.com (office). *Website:* www.nationwide.com (office).

ECKHARDT, Sándor, MD, PhD, DSc; Hungarian oncologist and academic; *Professor of Clinical Oncology, Semmelweis Medical University;* b. 14 March 1927, Budapest; s. of Sándor Eckhardt and Irén Huszár; m. Mária Petrányi; three s.; ed Semmelweis Medical Univ. Budapest; began his career at Uzsoki Hosp., Budapest; worked at Nat. Inst. of Oncology, Budapest from 1953, Dir 1971–92, now Prof. Emer.; took training course of malignant diseases in children, Villejuif, France 1969; MRC Fellow, Chester Beatty Inst., London 1961; Eleanor Roosevelt Cancer Research Fellow, Bethesda, Md 1964–65; Chair. Drug Devt Program, Hungary 1966–70; Prof. of Clinical Oncology, Postgraduate Univ. Medical School, Univ. of Budapest 1977–; currently Prof. of Clinical Oncology, Semmelweis Medical Univ.; mem. Hungarian Acad. of Sciences 1985–; Chair. Trial Centre of East European countries and Program Co-ordinator of drug research 1979–98; mem. Union Int. Contre le Cancer (UICC) Exec. Cttee 1978–86, Treas. 1986–90, Pres. 1990–94, Past Pres. 1994–98; Sec. Gen. 14th Int. Cancer Congress 1982–86; adviser WHO Cancer Unit 1971–98; mem. Medical Advisory Cttee WHO Euro Office, Copenhagen 1974–82; mem. Scientific Council Int. Agency for Research on Cancer 1976–80, Chair. 1979–82; mem. American Asscn of Cancer Research 1976–, Medical Acad. of Moscow 1979–, European Soc. of Medical Oncology 1985–; American Soc. of Clinical Oncology 1987–, Chief Ed. Antitumour Drug Therapy, Budapest 1977–86; Clinical Ed. Oncology 1978–84, Onkologie 1980–86, Current Medical Chem. 2002; Labour Order of Merit 1975; State Prize 1985, Széchenyi Prize 1994. *Publications:* include Drug Therapy of Cancer (WHO Geneva) 1973, Dibromodulcitol 1982, Drug Development in Eastern Europe 1987, Co-Ed. Proceedings of the 14th International Cancer Congress, Budapest (13 vols) 1986, Cancer Surveys 1994, Ann. Oncol. 1999, 7 Surgical Oncology 2000, Current Medical Chemistry 2002. *Address:* National Institute of Oncology, Ráth György utca 7/9, 1122 Budapest, Hungary (office). *Telephone:* (1) 224-8751 (office). *Fax:* (1) 224-8620 (office); (1) 224-8741 (office). *E-mail:* eckhardt@oncol.hu (office).

ECKRODT, Rolf, DipEng; German automotive industry executive (retd); b. 25 Feb. 1942, Gronau, Westphalia; ed Univ. of Bochum; Quality Assurance Passenger Cars Dept, Daimler Benz AG 1966–68, Man., Passenger Cars 1968, Project Leader, Production Components 1981–83, Vice-Pres. Axle Production 1983–86, Exec. Asst to Head of Mercedes-Benz Passenger Car Div. 1986–87, Dir Planning and Production, Passenger Cars and Components 1987–90, Dir Worldwide Planning and Production 1990–92, Pres. Mercedes Benz do Brasil 1992–96, Exec. Vice-Pres. and Deputy CEO, Adtranz 1996–98, Pres. and CEO 1998–2001; Exec. Vice-Pres. and COO Mitsubishi Motors Corpn 2001–02, Pres. and CEO 2002–04 (retd);; Vice-Pres. German-Brazil Chamber of Commerce, São Paulo 1993–96; Chair. Union of European Railway Industries (UNIFE) 1999–2000; Hon. Consul of Brazil, Potsdam 1999–2001; mem. Exec. Cttee Asien-Pazifik-Forum Berlin e.V. *Address:* c/o Executive Committee, Asien-Pazifik-Forum Berlin e.V, c/o Berlin Partner GmbH, Fasanenstr. 85, 10623 Berlin, Germany.

ECO, Umberto, PhD; Italian writer and academic; *Professor, University of Bologna;* b. 5 Jan. 1932, Alessandria, Piedmont; s. of Giulio Eco and Giovanna Bisio; m. Renate Ramge 1962; one s. one d.; ed Liceo Plana, Alessandria, Univ.

degli Studi, Turin; cultural ed. Italian TV (RAI), Milan 1954–59; mil. service 1958–59; Sr Non-fiction Ed., Bompiani, Milan 1959–75; Asst Lecturer in Aesthetics, Univ. of Turin 1956–63, Lecturer 1963–64; Lecturer, Faculty of Architecture, Univ. of Milan 1964–65; Prof. of Visual Communications, Univ. of Florence 1966–69; Prof. of Semiotics, Milan Polytechnic 1970–71; Assoc. Prof. of Semiotics, Univ. of Bologna 1971–75, Prof. 1975–, Dir Inst. of Communications Disciplines 1993–, Pres. Scuola Superiore di Studi Umanistici, f. School of Arts 2000; Visiting Prof. New York Univ. 1969–70, 1976, Northwestern Univ. 1972, Yale Univ. 1977, 1980, 1981, Columbia Univ. 1978, 1984; Columnist on L'Espresso 1965; Ed. VS 1971–; mem. Academia Europaea 1998–, Accademia dei Lincei 2010–; Hon. Fellow, Kellogg Coll., Univ. of Oxford; Chevalier de la Légion d'honneur, Ordre pour le Mérite, Cavaliere di Gran Croce (Italy); Hon. DLitt (Glasgow) 1990, (Kent) 1992 and numerous other hon. academic degrees; Medici Prize 1982, McLuhan Teleglobe Prize 1985, Crystal Award (World Econ. Forum) 2000, Prince of Asturias Prize for Communication and the Humanities 2000, UCLA Medal 2005, Manzoni Prize 2008. *Publications:* Il Problema Estetico in San Tommaso (trans. as The Aesthetics of Thomas Aquinas) 1956, Sviluppo dell'Estetica Medioevale (trans. as Art and Beauty in the Middle Ages) 1959, Opera Aperta 1962, Diario Minimo 1963, Apocalittici e Integrati 1964, L'Oeuvre Ouverte 1965, La Struttura Assente 1968, Il Costume di Casa 1973, Trattato di Semiotica Generale 1975, A Theory of Semiotics 1976, The Role of the Reader 1979, Il Nome della Rosa (novel, trans. as The Name of the Rose) 1981, Semiotics and the Philosophy of Language 1984, Sette anni di desiderio 1977–83 1984, Faith in Fakes 1986, Il pendolo di Foucault 1988, The Open Work 1989, The Limits of Interpretation 1990, Misreadings 1993, How to Travel with a Salmon and Other Essays 1994, L'isola del giorno prima (novel, trans. as The Island of the Day Before) 1995, The Search for the Perfect Language 1995, Serendipities 1997, Kant and the Platypus 1999, Baudolino (novel) 2000, Experiences in Translation 2000, Five Moral Pieces 2001, Mouse or Rat?: Translation as Negotiation 2003, On Beauty: A History of a Western Idea (ed.) 2004, The Mysterious Flame of Queen Loana 2005, Turning Back the Clock: Hot Wars and Media Populism (essays) 2007, On Ugliness 2007, An Infinity of Lists: From Homer to Pynchon 2009, The Prague Cemetery 2011. *Address:* Scuola Superiore Studi Umanistici, Via Marsala 26, Bologna, Italy (office). *Telephone:* (051) 2917111 (office). *E-mail:* sssub@dsc.unibo.it (office).

EDANO, Yukio; Japanese lawyer and politician; b. 31 May 1964, Utsunomiya City, Tochigi Pref.; ed Univ. of Tohoku; passed Nat. Bar Examination 1988, registered as attorney 1991; mem. House of Reps for Saitama No 5 Dist (New Japan Party) 1993–96, for Proportional Kitakanto Block (Democratic Party of Japan, DPJ) 1996–2000, for Saitama No 5 Dist 2000–; Founder mem. DPJ 1996, Chair. DPJ Policy Research Council 2000, Research Comm. on the Constitution 2004, DPJ Sec.-Gen. March–Sept. 2010; Minister of State for Govt Revitalization 2010, Chief Cabinet Sec. and Minister of State for Okinawa and N Territories Affairs Jan.–Sept. 2011, Minister of Economy, Trade and Industry 2011–12, also Minister for Nuclear Incident Economic Countermeasures and Minister of State for the Corpn in Support of Compensation for Nuclear Damage 2011–12. *Address:* Democratic Party of Japan, 1-11-1, Nagata-cho, Chiyoda-ku, Tokyo 100-0014, Japan (office). *Telephone:* (3) 3595-9988 (office). *Fax:* (3) 3595-9961 (office). *E-mail:* dpjenews@dpj.or.jp (office). *Website:* www.dpj.or.jp (office).

EDBERG, Stefan; Swedish fmr professional tennis player; b. 19 Jan. 1966, Vastervik; m. Annette Edberg (née Olsen); one s. one d.; won Jr Grand Slam 1983, Milan Open 1984, San Francisco, Basle and Memphis Opens 1985, Gstaad, Basle and Stockholm Opens 1986, Australian Open 1986, 1987, Wimbledon 1988, 1990, finalist 1989, US Open 1991, Masters 1989, German Open 1992, US Open 1992; winner (with Anders Jarryd) Masters and French Open 1986, Australian and US Opens 1987; semi-finalist in numerous tournaments; mem. Swedish Davis Cup Team 1984, 1987; retd in 1996 having won 60 professional titles and more than US $20 million in prize money; joined ATP Champions Tour 2008; co-owner and mem. Bd of Dirs Case Asset Management (pvt. investment co.); f. Stefan Edberg Foundation to assist young Swedish tennis players; Adidas Sportsmanship Award (four times), inducted into Int. Tennis Hall of Fame 2004. *Leisure interest:* golf. *Address:* Case Asset Management, Box 5352, 102 49 Stockholm, Sweden (office). *Telephone:* (8) 662-06-90 (office). *Fax:* (8) 660-36-42 (office). *E-mail:* info@case.nu (office). *Website:* www.case.nu (office).

EDDERY, Patrick James John, OBE; Irish fmr professional jockey and race horse trainer; b. 18 March 1952, Newbridge, Co. Galway; s. of Jimmy Eddery and Josephine Eddery; m. Carolyn Jane (née Mercer) 1978; one s. two d.; winner of 4,632 races in UK (second only to Gordon Richards); first win on Alvaro at Epsom 1969; has ridden 100 winners in a year 28 times 1973–; first jockey in Britain to ride seven winners in a day 1992; rode for Peter Walwyn 1972–80; Champion Jockey 1974–77, 1986, 1988–91, 1996; Champion Jockey in Ireland 1982; rode winner of the Oaks 1974, 1979, 1996, 2002, the Derby, on Grundy 1975, on Golden Fleece 1982, Quest for Fame 1990, Prix de l'Arc de Triomphe 1980, 1985–87, St Leger (four times) retd 2003; owner of stud farm; racehorse trainer 2003–; Flat Jockey of the Year 1990, 1991, 1996. *Leisure interests:* tennis, golf, snooker, swimming. *Address:* Musk Hill Farm, Nether Winchendon, Aylesbury, Bucks., HP18 0DT, England (home). *Telephone:* (1844) 296153 (office); (1844) 291980 (home). *Fax:* (1844) 290280 (office). *E-mail:* simon@patedderyracing.com; ceddery@waitrose.com (home). *Website:* patedderyracing.com.

EDDINGTON, Sir Roderick (Rod) Ian, Kt, AO, BEng, DPhil; Australian business executive; *Chairman for Australia and New Zealand, JPMorgan;* b. 2 Jan. 1950, Perth, Western Australia; s. of Gilbert Maxwell Eddington and April Mary Eddington; m. Young Sook Park 1994; one s. one d.; ed Christ Church Grammar School, WA, Univ. of Western Australia, Univ. of Oxford, UK; taught at Univ. of Oxford, UK for two years; joined Cathay Pacific Airways Ltd 1979, various positions in Hong Kong, Korea and Japan, Deputy Man. Dir 1990–92, Man. Dir and CEO 1992–96; Dir News Ltd (Australian arm of News Corpn) 1997–2000, Deputy Chair. 1998–2000; Exec. Chair. Ansett Australia 1997–2000; CEO British Airways (BA) 2000–05, also mem. Bd of Dirs; Chair. Victorian Major Events Co. 2006–, Infrastructure Australia (govt body) 2008–; Chair. for Australia and New Zealand, JPMorgan 2006–; mem. Bd of Dirs John Swire & Sons Pty Ltd 1997–, News Corpn 1999–, Rio Tinto plc 2005–11, Lion Pty Ltd 2011– (Chair. 2012–); apptd by UK Treasury and Dept for Transport to write report on the future of Britain's transport system 2006; mem. Bd of Man. Fremantle Dockers Football

Club 1998–2000; business adviser to Labor Party of Australia 2007–; Deputy Chair. Growing Victoria Together Summit 2000; mem. Victoria Govt's Innovation Economy Advisory Bd 2002–07; Rhodes Scholar 1974. *Leisure interests:* cricket, bridge, football. *Address:* JPMorgan Australia & New Zealand, Level 31, 101 Collins Street, Melbourne, Vic. 3000, Australia (office). *Telephone:* (3) 9633-4079 (office). *E-mail:* rod.i.eddington@jpmorgan.com (office). *Website:* www.jpmorgan .com.au (office).

EDDY, Don, MFA; American artist; b. 4 Nov. 1944, Long Beach, Calif.; m. Leigh Behnke 1995; one d.; ed Fullerton Jr Coll., Univ. of Hawaii, Honolulu, Univ. of California, Santa Barbara; represented in numerous public collections; subject of two monographs and an electronic book about his work. *Address:* 543 Broadway, New York, NY 10012, USA (office). *Telephone:* (212) 925-3124 (office). *Fax:* (212) 925-2302 (office). *E-mail:* doneddyart@aol.com (office).

EDELMAN, Gerald Maurice, MD, PhD; American molecular biologist, neuroscientist and academic; *Professor and Chairman, Department of Neurobiology, Scripps Research Institute;* b. 1 July 1929, New York; s. of Edward Edelman and Anna Freedman Edelman; m. Maxine Morrison 1950; two s. one d.; ed Ursinus Coll., Univ. of Pennsylvania and The Rockefeller Univ.; Medical House Officer, Mass Gen. Hosp. 1945–55; Capt., US Army Medical Corps 1955–56; Asst Physician, Hosp. of The Rockefeller Univ. 1957–60; Asst Prof. and Asst Dean of Grad. Studies, The Rockefeller Univ, 1960–63, Assoc. Prof. and Assoc. Dean of Grad. Studies 1963–66, Prof. 1966–74, Vincent Astor Distinguished Prof. 1974–92, Assoc. Neurosciences Research Program, Scientific Chair. 1980, Dir Neurosciences Inst., Neurosciences Research Program 1981–; Prof., Scripps Research Inst., La Jolla, Calif., Chair. Dept of Neurobiology 1992–; mem. Biophysics and Biophysical Chemistry Study Section, NIH 1964–67, Scientific Council, Center for Theoretical Studies 1970–72, The Harvey Society 1974– (Pres. 1975–76); mem. NAS, American Acad. of Arts and Sciences, American Philosophical Soc., Genetics Soc., ACS, American Soc. of Biological Chemists, American Asscn of Immunologists, American Soc. for Cell Biology, Soc. for Developmental Biology, Alpha Omega Alpha Hon. Medical Soc., Council on Foreign Relations, AAAS; mem. Bd of Overseers Faculty of Arts and Sciences, Univ. of Pa; mem. Bd Scientific Overseers, Jackson Lab.; mem. Bd of Trustees, Carnegie Inst. of Washington, also mem. Advisory Cttee; mem. Advisory Bd, The Basel Inst. for Immunology 1970–77 (Chair. 1975–77); mem. Bd of Govs, Weizmann Inst. of Science, Israel; Trustee, Rockefeller Brothers Fund 1972–82; Fellow, New York Acad. of Sciences, New York Acad. of Medicine; Non-Resident Fellow and mem. Bd of Trustees, Salk Inst. for Biological Studies; Foreign mem. Acad. des Sciences; Hon. mem. Japanese Biochemical Soc., Pharmaceutical Soc. of Japan; Hon. DSc (Univ. of Pa) 1973, (Adolphus Coll., Minn.) 1975, (Georgetown) 1989, (Tulane) 1991, (Miami) 1995, (Adelphi) 1995; Hon. ScD (Ursinus Coll.) 1974, (Williams Coll.) 1976; Hon. MD (Siena) 1974; Dr hc (Paris, Cagliari) 1989, (Naples) 1990; Annual Alumni Award, Ursinus Coll. 1969, Eli Lilly Award in Biological Chem., ACS 1965, Spencer Morris Award, Univ. of Pa 1954, Nobel Prize for Physiology or Medicine 1972 (with R. Porter), Albert Einstein Commem. Award of Yeshiva Univ. 1974, Buchman Memorial Award, Calif. Inst. of Tech. 1975, Rabbi Shai Shaknai Memorial Prize in Immunology and Cancer Research, Hebrew Univ.-Hadassah Medical School, Jerusalem 1977, Regents Medal of Excellence, New York 1984, Cécile and Oskar Vogt Award (Düsseldorf) 1988, Distinguished Grad. Award, Univ. of Pa 1990, Medal of the Presidency of the Italian Repub. 1999 and many other awards and prizes. *Publications:* Neural Darwinism 1987, Topobiology 1988, The Remembered Present 1989, Bright Air, Brilliant Fire 1992, A Universe of Consciousness 2000, Second Nature: Brain Science and Human Knowledge 2007; over 500 articles in professional journals. *Leisure interests:* violin, chamber music. *Address:* Department of Neurobiology, SBR 14, The Scripps Research Institute, 10550 North Torrey Pines Road, La Jolla, CA 92037-1000, USA (office). *Telephone:* (858) 784-2600 (office). *Fax:* (858) 784-2646 (office). *Website:* www.scripps.edu/nb (office).

EDELSTEIN, Victor Arnold; French couturier and artist; b. 10 July 1945, London; m. Anna Maria Succi 1973; trainee designer Alexon 1962, Asst Designer and Pattern Cutter to Biba 1967, designer Salvador 1971, Christian Dior 1975; f. Victor Edelstein Ltd 1978–93; designed ballet of Rhapsody in Blue for Rambert Dance Co. 1989; pantomime Cinderella, Richmond Theatre 1991, black pas de deux, Swan Lake, Covent Garden 1991; exhbns include Sotheby's, London 1996, Hopkins Thomas Gallery, Paris 1999. *Leisure interests:* opera, gardening, collecting old master drawings, skiing.

EDELSTEIN, Yuli; Israeli (b. Ukrainian) politician; *Speaker of the Knesset;* b. 1958, Chernovitz, Ukraine; m.; two c.; ed Moscow Inst. for Teacher Training; fmr Hebrew teacher, Moscow; emigrated to Israel 1987; fmr teacher Melitz Centre for Jewish-Zionist Educ., School for Educational Inst., Jerusalem; Adviser to Opposition Leader Benjamin Netanyahu 1993–94; a founder of Yisrael Ba-Aliya Party 1996; headed party's election campaign; mem. Knesset (Parl.) 1996–, Minister of Immigrant Absorption 1996–99, Deputy Minister 2001–03; Deputy Speaker, Knesset 1999–2001, Speaker 2013; Minister of Public Diplomacy and the Diaspora 2009–13. *Address:* Office of the Speaker, Knesset, Kiryat Ben-Gurion, Jerusalem 91006 (office); Alon Shvut, Israel (home).

EDELSTENNE, Charles; French aviation industry executive; b. 9 Jan. 1938, Paris; s. of Simon Edelstenne and Ida Edelstenne (née Brutman); m. Adèle Edelhertz 1963; one s. one d.; Chief Financial Officer Avions Marcel Dassault-Bréguet Aviation 1960–71, Deputy Sec.-Gen. 1971–75, Sec.-Gen. 1975–86, Vice-Pres. 1986–89, Dir 1989–2000, Chair. and CEO Dassault Aviation 2000–13, f. Dassault Systèmes 1981, Man. Dir 1981–93, Chair. and CEO 1993–2002, Pres. Dassault Systèmes America 1992–2002, Chair. Dassault Falcon Jet Corpn 1978–, Pres. Dassault International USA 2001; Dir Société Anonyme Belge de Constructions Aéronautiques, Belgium, Groupe Industriel Marcel Dassault, Paris, Sogitec Industries, Thales Systems Aéroportes, Dassault Réassurance; Pres. Groupement des Industries Françaises Aéronautiques et Spatiales (GIFAS) 2005–; Dir French Aircraft Mfrs Asscn (Chair. Econ. Cttee 1987–); fmr Vice-Pres. Foundation for Defence Studies; Chair. French Defence Industries Council 2006–; Pres. Aero-Space and Defence Industries Asscn Europe 2006–07; Commdr, Légion d'honneur. *Address:* Dassault Aviation, 9 Rond-Point des Champs-Elysées, 75008 Paris, France (office). *Telephone:* 1-53-76-93-00 (office). *Fax:* 1-53-76-93-20 (office). *Website:* www.dassault-aviation.com (office).

EDGAR, David Burman, BA; British writer; b. 26 Feb. 1948, Birmingham; s. of Barrie Edgar and Joan Edgar (née Burman); m. Eve Brook 1979 (died 1998); two step-s.; partner Stephanie Dale; ed Oundle School, Manchester Univ.; Fellow in Creative Writing, Leeds Polytechnic 1972–74; Resident Playwright, Birmingham Repertory Theatre 1974–75, Bd mem. 1985–; Lecturer in Playwriting, Univ. of Birmingham 1975–78, Dir of Playwriting Studies 1989–, Prof. 1995–99; Founder Writers' Union 1970s; UK/US Bicentennial Arts Fellow resident in USA 1978–79; Literary Consultant, RSC 1984–88; Fellow, Birmingham Polytechnic 1991, Judith E. Wilson Fellow, Clare Hall, Cambridge 1996; Hon. Sr Research Fellow, Univ. of Birmingham 1988–92, Hon. Prof. 1992–; Hon. MA (Bradford) 1986; DUniv (Surrey) 1993, (Birmingham) 2002; Soc. of West End Theatres Best Play Award 1980, Tony Award for Best Play 1981, Plays and Players Award for Best Play 1983, Evening Standard Award for Best Play 1995. *Plays include:* Two Kinds of Angel 1970, Rent or Caught in the Act 1972, State of Emergency 1972, The Dunkirk Spirit 1974, Dick Deterred 1974, O Fair Jerusalem 1975, Saigon Rose 1976, Blood Sports 1976, Destiny (for RSC) 1976, Wreckers 1977, The Jail Diary of Albie Sachs (for RSC) 1978, Mary Barnes 1978–79, Teendreams 1979, The Adventures of Nicholas Nickleby (adaptation for RSC) 1980, Maydays (for RSC) 1983, Entertaining Strangers 1985, That Summer 1987, The Shape of the Table 1990, Dr Jekyll and Mr Hyde (adaptation for RSC) 1991, Pentecost 1994, Other Place 1994, Young Vic 1995, Albert Speer (adaptation for Nat. Theatre) 2000, The Prisoner's Dilemma 2001, Continental Divide 2003, Playing with Fire (Nat. Theatre, London) 2005, A Time to Keep 2007, Testing the Echo 2008, Arthur and George 2010, The Master Builder 2010, Written on the Heart (adaptation for Royal Shakespeare Company) 2011. *TV plays include:* I Know What I Meant 1974, Baby Love 1974, Vote for Them 1989, Buying a Landslide 1992, Citizen Locke 1994. *Radio:* Ecclesiastes 1977, A Movie Starring Me 1991. *Film:* Lady Jane 1986. *Publications include:* Destiny 1976, Wreckers 1977, Teendreams 1979, Maydays 1983, Plays One 1987, The Second Time as Farce 1988, Heartlanders 1989, Plays Two 1990, Plays Three 1991, Pentecost 1995, State of Play (ed.) 1999, Albert Speer 2000, The Prisoner's Dilemma 2001, Continental Divide 2004, Playing With Fire 2005, How Plays Work 2009. *Leisure interests:* fine art, cookery, writing letters. *Address:* c/o Sarah McNair, Alan Brodie Representation, 211 Piccadilly, London, W1J 9HF, England (office). *Telephone:* (20) 7917-2871 (office). *Fax:* (20) 7917-2872 (office). *E-mail:* sarah@alanbrodie.com (office); info@alanbrodie.com (office). *Website:* www.alanbrodie.com (office).

EDGAR, James (Jim); American academic and fmr politician; *Distinguished Fellow, Institute of Government and Public Affairs, University of Illinois;* b. 22 July 1946, Vinita, Okla; m. Brenda Smith; one s. one d.; ed Eastern Ill. Univ., Univ. of Ill. and Sangamon State Univ.; key Asst to Speaker, Ill. House of Reps. 1972–73; aide to Pres. Ill. Senate 1974, to House Minority Leader 1976; mem. Ill. House of Reps 1977–91; Dir Legis. Affairs, Gov. of Ill. 1979–80; Sec. of State of Ill. 1981–91; Gov. of Ill. 1991–99; Chair. Nat. Govt's Asscn Comm. Econ. Devt and Tech. Innovation 1991, Strategic Planning Review Task Force 1991; Distinguished Fellow, Inst. of Govt and Public Affairs, Univ. of Ill. 1999–; Republican. *Address:* 1927 Country Road 150 East, Seymour, IL 61875-9619; University of Illinois Institute of Government and Public Affairs, 1007 W Nevada Street, Apartment MC-037, Urbana, IL 61801, USA (office). *Telephone:* (217) 333-3340 (office). *Website:* www.igpa.uiuc.edu (office).

THE EDGE; Irish musician (guitar) and songwriter; b. (David Howell Evans), 8 Aug. 1961, Barking, Essex, England; ed Mount Temple School; founder mem. and guitarist, the Feedback 1976, renamed the Hype, finally renamed U2 1978–; major concerts include Live Aid Wembley 1985, Self Aid Dublin, A Conspiracy of Hope (Amnesty Int. Tour) 1986, Smile Jamaica (hurricane relief fundraiser) 1988, Very Special Arts Festival, White House, Washington, DC 1988; numerous tours worldwide; Order of Liberty (Portugal) 2005; U2 have won 22 Grammy awards including Album of the Year and Best Rock Performance by a Duo or Group with Vocal (for The Joshua Tree) 1987, Grammy awards for Best Rock Performance by a Duo or Group with Vocal (for Desire) and Best Performance Video, short form (for Where the Streets Have No Name) 1988, BRIT Awards for Best Int. Act 1988–90, 1992, 1998, 2001, Best Live Act 1993, Outstanding Contribution to the British Music Industry 2001, JUNO Award 1992, World Music Award 1992, Grammy Award for Best Rock Vocal by a Duo or Group (for Achtung Baby) 1992, Grammy Award for Best Alternative Music Album (for Zooropa) 1993, Grammy Award for Best Music Video, long form (for Zoo TV Live from Sydney) 1994, Grammy Award for Song of the Year, Record of the Year, Best Rock Performance by a Duo or Group with Vocal (all for Beautiful Day) 2000, Grammy Awards for Best Pop Performance by a Duo or Group with Vocal (for Stuck In A Moment You Can't Get Out Of), for Record of the Year (for Walk On), for Best Rock Performance by a Duo or Group with Vocal (for Elevation), for Rock Album of the Year (All That You Can't Leave Behind) 2001, American Music Award for Favorite Internet Artist of the Year 2002, Ivor Novello Award for Best Song Musically and Lyrically (for Walk On) 2002, Golden Globe for Best Original Song (for The Hands That Built America, from film Gangs of New York) 2003, Grammy Awards for Best Rock Performance by a Duo or Group with Vocal, Best Rock Song, Best Short Form Music Video (all for Vertigo) 2004, TED Prize Award 2005, Nordoff-Robbins Silver Clef Award for lifetime achievement 2005, Q Award for Best Live Act 2005, Digital Music Award for Favourite Download Single (for Vertigo) 2005, Meteor Ireland Music Award for Best Irish Band, Best Live Performance 2006, Grammy Awards for Song of the Year, for Best Rock Performance by a Duo or Group with Vocal (both for Sometimes You Can't Make it on Your Own), for Best Rock Song (for City of Blinding Lights), for Album of the Year and Best Rock Album of the Year (both for How to Dismantle an Atomic Bomb) 2006, Golden Globe Award for Best Original Song (Ordinary Love in Mandela: Long Walk to Freedom) 2014, Ambs of Conscience Award, Amnesty International 2006, Palm Springs Film Festival Sonny Bono Visionary Award 2014;. *Plays include:* Spider-Man: Turn Off The Dark (music and lyrics by Bono and The Edge), Broadway, New York 2011–14. *Films include:* Rattle and Hum 1988. *Recordings include:* albums: Boy 1980, October 1981, War 1983, Under a Blood Red Sky 1983, The Unforgettable Fire 1984, Wide Awake In America 1985, The Joshua Tree (Grammy Award for Album of the Year, Best Rock Performance by a Duo or Group with Vocal) 1987, Rattle and Hum 1988, Achtung Baby (Grammy Award for Best Rock Performance by a Duo or Group with Vocal 1992) 1991, Zooropa (Grammy Award for Best Alternative Music Album) 1993, Passengers (film soundtrack with Brian Eno) 1995, Pop 1997, The Best Of

1980–90 1998, All That You Can't Leave Behind (Grammy Award for Best Rock Album 2001) 2000, The Best Of 1990–2000 2002, How To Dismantle An Atomic Bomb (Meteor Ireland Music Award for Best Irish Album 2006, Grammy Awards for Album of the Year, for Best Rock Album 2006) 2004, No Line on the Horizon 2009; solo: Captive 1987. *Address:* c/o Principle Management, 30–32 Sir John Rogersons Quay, Dublin 2, Ireland (office). *E-mail:* nadine@numb.ie (office). *Website:* www.u2.com.

EDGERTON, V. Reggie, BS, MS, PhD; American medical scientist and academic; *Professor of Integrative Biology and Physiology, University of California, Los Angeles;* ed East Carolina Univ., Univ. of Iowa, Michigan State Univ.; Prof., Dept of Integrative Biology and Physiology (fmrly the Dept of Physiological Science), UCLA 1968–, mem. Brain Research Inst.; J. Allyn Taylor Int. Prize in Medicine, Robarts Research Inst. 2012. *Publications:* numerous papers in professional journals. *Address:* Life Sciences Building, Brain Research Institute, UCLA, Los Angeles, CA 90095, USA (office). *Telephone:* (310) 825-1910 (office). *Fax:* (310) 825-4780 (office). *E-mail:* vre@ucla.edu (office). *Website:* www.ibp.ucla.edu/research/edgerton (office).

EDGLEY, Michael Christopher, MBE; Australian business executive; *Chairman, Edgley Ventures Pty Ltd.;* b. 17 Dec. 1943, Melbourne; s. of the late Eric Edgley and of Edna Edgley (née Luscombe); divorced; two s. three d.; ed Trinity Coll., Perth; Chair. Edgley Ventures Pty Ltd 1962–, promoting a wide range of cultural, artistic and sporting events throughout Australia, NZ, UK, Asia and S Africa; Citizen of the Year Award for WA 1976. *Leisure interests:* jogging, tennis. *Address:* Edgley International, 2 Chapel Street, Richmond, Vic. 2121, Australia (office). *Telephone:* (3) 9428-7711 (office). *Fax:* (3) 9428-7712 (office). *E-mail:* headoffice@edgley.com.au (office). *Website:* www.edgley.com.au (office).

EDINBURGH, HRH The Duke of; (Prince Philip), (Prince of the United Kingdom of Great Britain and Northern Ireland, Earl of Merioneth, Baron Greenwich), KG, KT, OM, GBE; b. 10 June 1921, Corfu, Greece; s. of Prince Andrew of Greece and Denmark and Princess Alice of Battenberg; m. 20 Nov. 1947 HRH Princess Elizabeth (HM Queen Elizabeth II q.v.); children: Prince Charles Philip Arthur George, Prince of Wales (q.v.), b. 14 Nov. 1948, Princess Anne Elizabeth Alice Louise, The Princess Royal (q.v.), b. 15 Aug. 1950, Prince Andrew Albert Christian Edward, Duke of York (q.v.), b. 19 Feb. 1960, Prince Edward Antony Richard Louis, Earl of Wessex (q.v.), b. 10 March 1964; ed Cheam, Salem and Gordonstoun Schools, Royal Naval Coll., Dartmouth; renounced right of succession to thrones of Greece and Denmark, naturalized British subject 1947, adopting surname Mountbatten; served Royal Navy 1939–51, served in Indian Ocean, Mediterranean, North Sea, Pacific Ocean during Second World War; Personal ADC to King George VI 1948–52; PC 1951–; ranks of Adm. of the Fleet, Field Marshal, Marshal of the Royal Air Force, Captain-Gen. Royal Marines 1953–; Lord High Adm. of the Navy 2011–; Chancellor, Univs of Wales 1948–76, Edinburgh 1952–, Salford 1967–91, Cambridge 1977–2011; Pres., Patron or Trustee of numerous orgs including Nat. Playing Fields Asscn 1948–, Nat. Maritime Museum 1948–, London Fed. of Clubs for Young People (now called London Youth) 1948–, City & Guilds of London Inst. 1951–, Cen. Council of Physical Recreation 1951–, Design Council 1952–, RSA 1952–, English-Speaking Union of the Commonwealth 1952–, Outward Bound Trust 1952–, Trinity House 1952–, Guild of Air Pilots and Air Navigators 1952–, RCA 1955–, Commonwealth Games Fed. 1955–90, Duke of Edinburgh's Award Scheme 1956–, Duke of Edinburgh's Commonwealth Study Confs 1956–, Royal Agric. Soc. of the Commonwealth 1958–, Voluntary Service Overseas 1961–, World Wildlife Fund UK 1961–82, Int. Equestrian Fed. 1964–86, Maritime Trust 1969–, Royal Commonwealth Ex-Services League 1974–, Royal Acad. of Eng 1976–, British Trust for Ornithology 1987–; Pres. World Wide Fund for Nature 1981–96, Pres. Emer. 1997–; numerous decorations, hon. degrees and awards world-wide. *Publications:* 14 publs 1957–2004. *Address:* Buckingham Palace, London, SW1A 1AA, England. *Website:* www.royal.gov.uk.

EDLEY, Christopher, Jr, BA, JD.; American professor of law, university administrator and civil rights scholar; *Honorable William H. Orrick Jr. Distinguished Chair and Dean, Boalt Hall Law School, University of California, Berkeley;* b. 13 Jan. 1953, Boston; ed Swarthmore Coll., Pa, John F. Kennedy School of Government, Harvard Univ., Harvard Law School, Cambridge, Mass; called to Bar, Washington, DC 1980; Asst Dir White House Domestic Policy Staff (Carter Admin) 1978–79; Special Asst to Sec., US Dept of Health, Educ. and Welfare 1979–80; Assoc. Asst to the Pres., The White House 1980; Asst Prof., Harvard Law School 1981–87, Prof. 1987–2004; Assoc. Dir Office of Man. and Budget, Washington, DC 1993–95; Special Counsel to Pres., The White House 1995, also Dir White House Review of Affirmative Action, Sr Adviser to Pres. for Race Initiative 1997–99; Honorable William H. Orrick Jr. Distinguished Chair and Dean, Boalt Hall School of Law, Univ. of Calif., Berkeley 2004–, also Founder and Faculty-Co-Director Chief Justice Earl Warren Inst. on Race, Ethnicity and Diversity; Founding Co-Dir The Civil Rights Project; served in Dukakis presidential campaign as Nat. Issues Dir; Sr Adviser on Econ. Policy for Clinton–Gore Presidential Transition 1992; Sr Policy Adviser to Al Gore and mem. Democratic Policy Drafting Cttee during presidential campaign 2000; mem. US Comm. on Civil Rights 1999–2005; Comm. Task Force on the Future of the Common School (Century Foundation), Nat. Comm. on Fed. Electoral Reform, Council on Foreign Relations, Nat. Acad. of Public Admin; mem. Bd Nat. Immigration Forum, Bd on Testing and Assessment of the Nat. Research Council (NAS), Comm. on No Child Left Behind 2006–07; Founding mem. Advisory Bd for the Madison Soc.; mem. Exec. Cttee of Bd of People for the American Way; Adjunct Scholar, Urban Inst.; Fellow, Nat. Acad. of Public Admin, Council on Foreign Relations, American Law Inst., American Acad. of Arts and Sciences 2007–; Trustee, Russell Sage Foundation, The Century Foundation; fmr Vice-Chair. Congressional Black Caucus Foundation; fmr Ed. Harvard Review; fmr mem. Editorial Bd Washington Post; named amongst 100 Most Influential Lawyers by National Law Journal, 2006, named amongst 50 Most Influential Minority Lawyers in America 2008. *Publications include:* Administrative Law: Rethinking Judicial Control of Bureaucracy, Not All Black and White: Affirmative Action, Race and American Values. *Address:* Office of the Dean, 215 Boalt Hall, University of California, Berkeley, CA 94720-7200 (office); The Civil Rights Project, 125 Mount Auburn Street, 3rd Floor, Cambridge, MA 02138, USA (office). *Telephone:* (510) 642-1741 (Berkeley) (office);

(617) 496-6367 (Cambridge) (office). *Fax:* (617) 495-5210 (Cambridge) (office). *E-mail:* edley@law.berkeley.edu (office). *Website:* www.law.berkeley.edu (office).

EDMISTON, Baron (Life Peer), cr. 2011, of Lapworth in the County of Warwickshire; **Robert Norman Edmiston,** FCMA; British motor industry executive and philanthropist; *Chairman, I.M. Group;* b. 1946; m.; three c.; began career as a bank clerk; Finance Dir at sports car manufacturer Jensen Motors –1974; est. International Motors 1976, acquired UK franchise for Subaru and Isuzu cars, later branched out into property and vehicle finance, est. I.M. Group (car importer) and I.M. Properties; f. Christian Vision (int. evangelical charity), Coleshill, Warwicks. 1988; sponsor of three secondary schools within English acad. programme, Grace Acad., Coventry, Grace Acad., Solihull, Grace Acad., Darlaston, Chair. Bd Govs of all three acads. *Address:* I.M. Group Ltd, I.M. House, South Drive, Coleshill, B46 1DF (office); House of Lords, Westminster, London, SW1A 0PW, England (office). *Telephone:* (121) 747-4000 (Coleshill) (office); (20) 7219-5353 (House of Lords) (office). *Fax:* (20) 7219-5979 (House of Lords) (office). *E-mail:* info@imgroup.co.uk (office). *Website:* www.imgroup.co.uk (office); www.christianvision.com.

EDMONDS, David, CBE, BA; British company director and fmr business executive; *Chairman, Legal Services Board;* b. 6 March 1944, Grapenhall; s. of Albert Edmonds and Gladys Edmonds; m. Ruth Edmonds (née Beech) 1964; two s. two d.; ed Helsby Co. Grammar School, Univ. of Keele; with Ministry of Housing 1966–70, with Dept of the Environment 1970–84; Chief Exec. The Housing Corpn 1984–91; Man. Dir Group Services NatWest Group 1991–98; Dir-Gen. Oftel (Office of Telecommunications) 1998–2004; Chair. NHSDirect 2004–08; Chair. Legal Services Bd 2008–; mem. Bd of Dirs Wincanton PLC 2004–11, Deputy Chair. 2007–08, Chair. 2008–11; mem. Bd of Dirs Hammerson plc 2003–11, William Hill plc 2005–, English Partnerships 2000– (Chair. Property, Planning and Projects Cttee 2000–); mem. Council and Treas. Keele Univ. 1997–; Dir-Gen. Oftel 1998–2003, mem. Bd Office of Communications (Ofcom) 2004–; mem. Bd London Legacy Devt Corpn 2009–, Barchester Healthcare 2012–; Gov. Kingston Univ. 2012–; Hon. DLitt (Keele) 2004. *Leisure interests:* opera, golf, art, walking. *Address:* Legal Services Board, Victoria House, Southampton Row, London, WC1B 4AD, England (office). *Telephone:* (20) 7271-0050 (office). *Fax:* (20) 7271-0051 (office). *Website:* www.legalservicesboard.org.uk (office).

EDMONDS, John Walter, MA; British academic and fmr trade union official; *Visiting Senior Research Fellow, King's College London;* b. 28 Jan. 1944, London; s. of Maude Rose Edmonds and Walter Edgar Edmonds; m. Janet Linden 1967; two d.; ed Oriel Coll. Oxford; Research Asst, GMB (fmrly Gen., Municipal and Boilermakers' Union) Trade Union 1965, Deputy Research Officer 1967, Regional Organizer 1968, Nat. Officer 1972, Gen. Sec. 1986–2003; fmr mem. Royal Comm. on Environmental Pollution, Council Advisory, Conciliation and Arbitration Service (ACAS), Forestry Comm.; mem. Nat. Employment Panel (fmrly New Deal Task Force)–2002; Dir (non-exec.) Carbon Trust 2002–, Environment Agency 2003–, Salix Finance 2005–; Visiting Sr Research Fellow, King's Coll. London 2003–; Chair. Inland Waterways Advisory Council 2006–; Hon. Trustee, Nat. Soc. for the Prevention of Cruelty to Children; Hon. Fellow, Society for the Environment 2006; Hon. DIur (Sussex) 1993. *Leisure interests:* cricket, carpentry. *Address:* 50 Graham Road, Mitcham, Surrey, CR4 2HA, England (home). *Telephone:* (20) 8648-9991 (home). *E-mail:* johnedmonds1@hotmail.com (home).

EDWARD, Sir David Alexander Ogilvy, Kt, KCMG, PC, QC, MA, LLD, FRSE; British advocate, judge and professor of European institutions; *Professor Emeritus, University of Edinburgh;* b. 14 Nov. 1934, Perth, Scotland; s. of John O. C. Edward and Margaret I. MacArthur; m. Elizabeth Young McSherry 1962; two s. two d.; ed Sedbergh School, Univ. Coll., Oxford and Univ. of Edinburgh; advocate 1962–, Clerk Faculty of Advocates 1967–70, Treas. 1970–77; Pres. Consultative Cttee, Bars and Law Socs of the EEC 1978–80; Salvesen Prof. of European Insts and Dir Europa Inst., Univ. of Edinburgh 1985–89, Prof. Emer. 1989–; Judge of the Court of First Instance of the European Communities 1989–92, Judge, Court of Justice of the EC 1992–2003; Hon. Pres. Scottish Arbitration Centre; fmr Specialist Adviser to House of Lords Select Cttee on the EEC; fmr Chair. Continental Assets Trust PLC; fmr Dir Adam & Co. PLC, Harris Tweed Asscn Ltd; mem. Scottish Advisory Cttee, British Council, Panel of Arbitrators, Int. Centre for Settlement of Investment Disputes, Comm. on a Bill of Rights; fmr mem. Law Advisory Cttee; fmr mem. Gründungssenat, Europa-Univ. Viadrina, Frankfurt/ Oder; Trustee, Trier Acad. of European Law, Industry and Parl. Trust, Carnegie Trust for the Univs of Scotland; fmr Trustee, Nat. Library of Scotland; Hon. Bencher, Gray's Inn; Hon. Fellow, Univ. Coll., Oxford; Hon. LLD (Edinburgh) 1993, (Aberdeen) 1997, (Napier) 1998, (Glasgow) 2003; Hon. DIur (Saarland) 2001, (Münster) 2001; Hon. DUniv (Surrey) 2003. *Publications:* The Professional Secret: Confidentiality and Legal Professional Privilege in the EEC 1976, European Community Law: an introduction (with R. C. Lane) 1995; articles in legal journals. *Address:* 32 Heriot Row, Edinburgh, EH3 6ES, Scotland.

EDWARDES, Sir Michael (Owen), Kt, BA, FBIM; British business executive; b. 11 Oct. 1930, South Africa; s. of Denys Owen Edwardes and Audrey Noel Edwardes (née Copeland); m. 1st Mary Margaret Finlay 1958 (divorced, died 1999); three d.; m. 2nd Sheila Ann Guy 1988; ed St Andrew's Coll., SA, Rhodes Univ., SA; joined Chloride Group in SA as management trainee 1951, mem. Man. Bd 1969, Chief Exec. 1972, Exec. Chair. 1974–77, Deputy Chair. (non-exec.) 1977–82, Chair. (non-exec.) 1982–88 (acting Chief Exec. 1985–87); Chair. and Chief Exec. British Leyland Ltd. 1977–82; Dir (non-exec.) Hill Samuel Group PLC 1980–87, Standard Securities 1984–87, Minerals and Resources Corpn 1984–, Flying Pictures Ltd 1987–; Chair. Mercury Communications Ltd 1982–83, ICL PLC 1984; Chair. and Chief Exec. Dunlop Holdings 1984–85; Chair. Charter Consolidated PLC 1988–96, Tryhorn Investments Ltd 1987–, Porth Group PLC 1991–95, ARC Int. Ltd 1991–93; Exec. Dir Minorco 1984, Syndicated Services Co. Inc. 1995–; Group Deputy Chair. R. K. Carvill Int. Holdings Ltd (now Carvill Group) 1988, now Dir; Dir (non-exec.) Int. Man. Devt Inst., Washington, DC 1978–94, Hi-Tec Sports 1993–, Strand Partners Ltd 1994–; Pres. Comité des Constructeurs d'Automobiles du Marché Commun 1979–80; Trustee, Thrombosis Research Inst. 1991–; mem. Nat. Enterprise Bd 1975–77, CBI Council 1974 (mem. President's Cttee 1981–), Review Cttee for Queen's Award for Industry; Hon. Fellow, Inst. of Mechanical Engineers; Hon. DIur (Rhodes Univ., SA) 1980; Young Businessman of the Year

1975. *Publication:* Back From the Brink 1983. *Leisure interests:* water skiing, sailing, squash, tennis.

EDWARDS, Anthony; American actor; b. 19 July 1962, Santa Barbara, Calif.; ed Royal Acad. of Dramatic Art, London; joined Santa Barbara Youth Theatre, in 30 productions aged 12–17; working in commercials aged 16; stage appearance in Ten Below, New York 1993; Screen Actors Guild Award 1996, 1998, 1999, Golden Globe 1998. *Films include:* Fast Times at Ridgemont High 1982, Heart Like a Wheel 1982, Revenge of the Nerds 1984, The Sure Thing 1985, Gotcha! 1985, Top Gun 1985, Summer Heat 1987, Revenge of the Nerds II 1987, Mr. North 1988, Miracle Mile 1989, How I Got into College 1989, Hawks 1989, Downtown 1990, Delta Heat, The Client 1994, Us Begins with You 1998, Don't Go Breaking My Heart 1999, Jackpot 2001, Northfork 2003, Thunderbirds 2004, The Forgotten 2004, Zodiac 2007, Motherhood 2009. *Television includes:* (series) It Takes Two 1982–83, Northern Exposure 1992–93, ER 1994–2008, Soul Man, Rock Story 2000; (films) The Killing of Randy Webster 1981, High School USA 1983, Going for the Gold: The Bill Johnson Story 1985, El Diablo 1990, Hometown Boy Makes Good 1990, In Cold Blood 1996; (specials) Unpublished Letters, Sexual Healing. *Address:* c/o United Talent Agency, 9560 Wilshire Boulevard, Suite 500, Beverly Hills, CA 90212, USA.

EDWARDS, Sir Christopher Richard Watkin, Kt, MD, FRCP, FRCPE, FMedSci, FRSE; British physician and university vice-chancellor; b. 12 Feb. 1942; s. of Thomas Archibald Watkin Edwards and Beatrice Elizabeth Ruby Watkin Edwards; m. Sally Amanda Kidd 1968; two s. one d.; ed Marlborough Coll., Christ's Coll. Cambridge; Lecturer in Medicine, St Bartholomew's Hosp., London 1969–75, Sr Lecturer and MRC Sr Research Fellow 1975–80, Hon. Consultant Physician 1975–80; Moncrieff Arnott Prof. of Clinical Medicine, Univ. of Edinburgh 1980–95, Dean Faculty of Medicine 1991–95, Provost Faculty Group of Medicine and Veterinary Medicine 1992–95; Prin. and Prof. of Medicine Imperial Coll. of Science and Medicine, Univ. of London 1995–2000; Vice-Chancellor Univ. of Newcastle 2001–07; Dir (non-exec.), Chelsea and Westminster Hosp. 2007–; Vice-Chair. (non-exec.), Cluff Geothermal Ltd; mem. MRC 1991–95; Fellow, Imperial Coll. London 2003; Gov. Wellcome Trust 1994–; Co-founder FMedSci 1998; Hon. DSc (Aberdeen) 2000. *Publications include:* Clinical Physiology (Ed.) 1984, Essential Hypertension as an Endocrine Disease 1985, Endocrinology 1986, Recent Advances in Endocrinology and Metabolism, Vol. 3 (Ed.) 1989, Davidson's Principles and Practice of Medicine (Ed.) 1995; over 400 scientific papers and communications. *Leisure interests:* running, reading, golf, skiing, painting. *Address:* Cluff Geothermal Ltd, 15 Carteret Street, St. James, SW1H 9DJ (office); Chelsea and Westminster Hospital, 369 Fulham Road, London, SW10 9NH, England. *Telephone:* (20) 7584-0328; (20) 8746-8000. *E-mail:* info@ cluffgeothermal.com. *Website:* www.cluffgeothermal.com; www.chelwest.nhs.uk.

EDWARDS, Gareth Owen, MBE, CBE; British business executive and fmr rugby union player; b. 12 July 1947; s. of Thomas Granville Edwards and Annie-Mary Edwards; m. Maureen Edwards 1972; two s.; ed Pontardawe Tech. School, Millfield School, Cardiff Coll. of Educ.; Welsh Secondary Schools Rugby int. 1965–66; English Schools 200 yards hurdles champion 1966 (UK under-19 record-holder); Welsh nat. team: 53 caps 1967–78, Capt. 13 times, youngest captain (aged 20) 1968; played with following clubs: Cardiff 1966–78, Barbarians 1967–78, British Lions 1968, 1971, 1974; Jt Dir Euro-Commercials (South Wales) Ltd 1982–, Players (UK) Ltd 1983–88; Chair. Hamdden Ltd 1991–; Chair. Regional Fisheries Advisory Cttee, Welsh Water Authority 1983–89. *Publications:* Gareth – An Autobiography 1978, Rugby Skills 1979, Rugby Skills for Forwards 1980, Gareth Edwards on Fishing 1984, Gareth Edwards on Rugby 1986, Gareth Edwards' 100 Great Rugby Players 1987. *Leisure interests:* fishing, golf. *Address:* 211 West Road, Nottage, Porthcawl, Mid-Glamorgan, CF36 3RT, Wales. *Telephone:* (1656) 785669 (Porthcawl).

EDWARDS, Huw, BA; British broadcaster, journalist and author; *Presenter, BBC News at Ten;* b. 18 Aug. 1961, Bridgend, Wales; s. of the late Prof. Hywel Teifi Edwards and of Aerona Protheroe; m.; five c.; ed Univ. Coll. of Wales, Cardiff; began career as a reporter with local radio station Swansea Sound; joined BBC training scheme 1984, becoming parl. reporter, Political Corresp. BBC News, London 1988, Chief Political Corresp., London 1997–99, BBC News 24, Presenter BBC One O'Clock, Six O'Clock and Breakfast News 1994–99, Six O'Clock News 1999–2003, BBC News at Ten (BAFTA Award for News Coverage – Madrid Bombing 2004, BAFTA Award for News Coverage (London Bombings) 2005, BAFTA Award for Best Coverage of a Live Event (Royal Wedding) 2012, Royal TV Soc. Award 2005, 2008, 2009) 2003–, BBC News at Five 2006–; Pres. London Welsh Asscn 2008–; Pro Chancellor, Cardiff Univ. 2009–; Hon. Fellow, Univ. of Wales, Cardiff 2003, Lampeter 2006, Swansea 2007, Newport 2007, Swansea Metropolitan 2007, Bangor 2013; Hon. Prof. of Journalism, Cardiff Univ. 2006; Dr hc (Univ. of Glamorgan) 2007; Paul Harris Fellow, Rotary International, BAFTA Wales Presenter of the Year 2001, 2002, 2003, 2004, 2009, 2012. *Other television and radio work includes:* Newsnight, Panorama, Songs of Praise, classical music programmes on BBC Two, BBC Radio 3 and Radio 4, The Story of Welsh (BBC Wales) 2002, Bread of Heaven (BBC Wales) 2004, Lloyd George the People's Champion (BBC Wales) 2007, The Prince and the Plotter (BBC Wales) 2009, The Story of Wales (BBC Wales) 2012, State Opening of Parliament, Trooping the Colour, Festival of Remembrance (all for BBC 1), The Royal Wedding (BAFTA Award for Best Sport & Live Event 2012) 2011, The Queen's Diamond Jubilee 2012, London Olympics Opening and Closing Ceremonies 2012. *Publication:* Capeli Llanelli: A History of Nonconformist Worship 2009. *Address:* c/o Jeremy Lee, JLA, 80 Great Portland Street, London, W1W 7NW, England (office); BBC, New Broadcasting House, London, W1A 1AA, England (office). *Telephone:* (20) 7907-2800 (office); (20) 7580-4468 (office). *E-mail:* jeremylee@jla.co.uk (office). *Website:* www.jla.co.uk (office); www.bbc.co.uk (office).

EDWARDS, John Coates, MA, CMG; British diplomatist; b. 25 Nov. 1934, Tunbridge Wells, Kent; s. of Herbert J. Edwards and Doris M. Edwards (née Starzacher); m. Mary Harris 1959 (died 2006); one s. one d.; ed Skinners' Co. School, Tunbridge Wells and Brasenose Coll. Oxford; Lt RA 1953–55; Colonial Office 1960–62; Nature Conservancy Council 1962–64; Ministry of Overseas Devt 1965–68, 1976–78; First Sec. Bangkok and Perm. Rep. to ECAFE 1968–71; Head, E Africa Devt Div. British High Comm. Nairobi 1972–75; Head, British Devt Div. in the Caribbean, Barbados and UK; Dir Caribbean Devt Bank 1978–81; Head, W

Indian and Atlantic Dept FCO 1981–84; Deputy High Commr in Kenya 1984–88; High Commr in Lesotho 1988–91, in Botswana 1991–94; Head UK Del., EC Monitoring Mission in fmr Yugoslavia 1995–99; JP, Kent 2000–04; Chair. Kenya Soc.; mem. council Royal Overseas League. *Leisure interests:* birdwatching, fishing, visual arts, walking, local history. *Address:* Fairways, Back Lane, Ightham, Sevenoaks, TN15 9AU, England (home). *Telephone:* (1732) 883556 (home). *E-mail:* johncoatesedward@aol.com.

EDWARDS, John Reid, BS, JD; American lawyer and fmr politician; b. 10 June 1953; s. of Wallace R. Edwards and Catherine Edwards; m. Mary Elizabeth Anania; one s. (deceased) two d.; ed Univ. of North Carolina at Chapel Hill; called to Bar, North Carolina 1977, Tenn. 1978; Assoc., Dearborn and Ewing, Nashville 1978–81; trial lawyer, Wade Smith 1981; Assoc., Tharrington Smith and Hargrove, Raleigh 1981–83, Partner 1984–92; Partner, Edwards and Kirby, Raleigh 1993–99; Senator from North Carolina 1999–2005; f. One America Cttee (political action cttee) 2001; unsuccessful pursuit of Democratic nomination for US presidency 2004, Democratic cand. for Vice-Pres. 2004; Dir Center on Poverty, Work and Opportunity, Univ. of North Carolina School of Law 2005–06; Sr Advisor, Fortress Investment Group LLC 2005; unsuccessful cand. for Democratic nomination for Pres. of US 2007–08; Dir Urban Ministries, Raleigh 1996–97; mem. North Carolina Acad. of Trial Lawyers (Vice-Pres. Bd of Govs), North Carolina Bar Assocn, Banking, Housing and Urban Affairs, Governmental Affairs, Small Business and Y2K Cttees; Fellow, American Coll. of Trial Lawyers; indicted for alleged campaign finance violations 2011. *Publications include:* Four Trials 2003, Home: The Blueprints of Our Lives 2006, Ending Poverty in America 2007.

EDWARDS, Jonathan, CBE; British fmr athlete; b. 10 May 1966, London; s. of Andrew David Edwards and Jill Caulfield; m. Alison Joy Briggs 1990; two s.; ed West Buckland, Devon; bronze medal, World Championships 1993; gold medal, Fifth Athletics World Championships, Gothenburg 1995 (twice breaking own world record for triple jump, clearing 18.29m), Edmonton 2001; silver medal, Olympic Games, Atlanta 1996, World Championships 1997, 1999; gold medal European Championships 1998, European Indoor Championships 1998, Goodwill Games 1998, Olympic Games 2000, World Championships 2001, Commonwealth Games 2002; retd after World Championships 2003; currently athletics commentator BBC; Sports Fellowship, Univ. of Durham 1999; British Sportsman of the Year 1995, IAAF Athlete of the Year 1995, BBC Sports Personality of the Year 1995, British Male Athlete of the Year 1995, 2000, 2001. *Publication:* A Time to Jump 2000. *Address:* c/o Jonathan Marks, MTC, 20 York Street, London, W1U 6PU, England. *Telephone:* (20) 7935-8000. *Fax:* (20) 7935-8066. *E-mail:* info@mtc-uk.com (office). *Website:* www.mtc-uk.com (office).

EDWARDS, Jorge; Chilean writer and diplomatist; *Ambassador to France;* b. 29 July 1931, Santiago; m. Pilar de Castro Vergara; two c.; ed Univ. of Chile, Princeton Univ., USA; joined diplomatic service 1954, Sec., Embassy in Paris 1962, Head of Eastern Europe Div. 1967, Amb. to Cuba 1970, Advisory Minister in Paris 1971–73, Amb. to UNESCO, Paris 1994–96, Amb. to France 2010–; mem. Academia Chilena de la Lengua; Literary Prize of the City of Santiago 1961, 1991, Atenea Prize of Univ. of Concepción (Chile), Essay Prize of the City of Santiago 1991, Cervantes Prize 1999. *Publications include:* (novels) El patio 1952, Gente de la ciudad 1962, Las máscaras 1967, Temas y variaciones 1969, Fantasmas de carne y hueso 1992, El peso de la noche 1965, Las máscaras 1967, Temas y variacones 1969, Persona non grata 1973, Desde la cola del dragón 1977, Los convidados de piedra 1978, El museo de cera 1981, La mujer imaginaria 1985, El anfitrión 1988, Cuentos completos 1990, Adiós poeta 1990, El regalo 1991, Fantasmas de carne y hueso 1993, El whisky de los poetas 1994, El origen del mundo 1996, El sueño de la Historia 2000, Diálogos en un tejado 2003, El inútil de la familia 2004, La casa de Dostoievsky (Premio Iberoamericano Planeta–Casa de América de Narrativa) 2008, La muerte de Montaigne 2011. *Address:* Embajada de Chile, 2 ave de la Motte-Picquet, 75007 Paris, France (office); c/o Alfaguara, Torrelaguna 60, 28043 Madrid, Spain. *Telephone:* 1-44-18-59-60 (office). *Fax:* 1-44-18-59-61 (office). *E-mail:* echile@amb-chili.fr (office). *Website:* chileabroad.gov.cl/francia (office).

EDWARDS, Kenneth John Richard, PhD; British university vice-chancellor (retd); b. 12 Feb. 1934; s. of John Edwards and Elizabeth M. Edwards; m. Janet M. Gray 1958; two s. one d.; ed Market Drayton Grammar School, Univ. of Reading and Univ. Coll. of Wales, Aberystwyth; Fellow, Univ. of Calif. 1961–62; ARC Fellow, Welsh Plant Breeding Station, Aberystwyth 1962–63, Sr Scientific Officer 1963–66; Lecturer in Genetics, Univ. of Cambridge 1966–84, Head, Dept of Genetics 1981–84; Lecturer, St John's Coll. Cambridge 1971–84, Fellow 1971–87, Tutor 1981–84; Sec.-Gen. of Faculties, Univ. of Cambridge 1984–87; Vice-Chancellor, Univ. of Leicester 1987–99; Chair. Cttee of Vice-Chancellors and Prins 1993–95; mem. Marshall Aid Commemoration Comm. 1991–98, Council ACU 1994–99; Chair. Governing Body, Inst. of Grassland and Environmental Research 1994–99; Pres. Asscn of European Univs 1998–2001; Visiting Lecturer, Birmingham 1965; Visiting Prof., Buenos Aires 1973; Leverhulme Research Fellow, Univ. of Calif. 1973; Hon. LLD (Belfast) 1994, (Leicester) 1999; Hon. DSc (Reading) 1995, (Loughborough) 1995, (Warwick) 2000; Dr hc (Cluj, Romania) 1997, (Maribor, Slovenia) 1999, (Olomouc, Czech Repub.) 2002. *Publications:* Evolution in Modern Biology 1977; articles on genetics in scientific journals. *Leisure interests:* music, gardening. *Address:* 10 Sedley Taylor Road, Cambridge, England. *Telephone:* (1223) 245680 (home). *E-mail:* kenneth.edwards@ntlworld.com (home).

EDWARDS, N. Murray, BComm, LLB (Hons), JD; Canadian lawyer and business executive; *Chairman, Magellan Aerospace;* b. Regina, Sask.; m. Heather Bala; one c.; ed Univs of Saskatchewan and Toronto; moved to Calgary in 1983 and became lawyer and later Partner, Burnet, Duckworth & Palmer; Owner and Pres. Edco Financial Holdings Ltd (merchant bankers) 1988–; leading investor in and Man. Dir and Exec. Chair. of numerous publicly traded cos, including Canadian Natural Resources Ltd (CNRL), Ensign Resource Service Group Inc., Magellan Aerospace Corpn, Penn West Petroleum Ltd and Resorts of the Canadian Rockies Inc.; Dir and Co-owner of Nat. Hockey League's Calgary Flames; fmr Dir of Business Devt, Bank of Canada; mem. Bd Govs The Canadian Unity Council; mem. Council of Champions, Calgary Children's Initiatives, Banff Centre; mem. Bd of Dirs Canadian Council of Chief Execs, Canada West Foundation. *Address:*

Office of the Chairman, Magellan Aerospace, 3160 Derry Road East, Mississauga, ON L4T 1A9, Canada (office). *Website:* www.magellan.aero (office).

EDWARDS, Peter Philip, PhD, FRS, FRSC; British scientist and academic; *Professor and Head of Inorganic Chemistry, University of Oxford;* b. 30 June 1949; s. of the late Ronald Goodlass and of Ethel Mary Edwards; m. Patricia Anne Clancy 1970; two s. one d.; ed Univ. of Salford; Fulbright Scholar and NSF Fellow, Baker Lab. of Chem., Cornell Univ., USA 1975–77; Science and Eng Research Council/NATO Fellow and Ramsay Memorial Fellow, Inorganic Chem. Lab., Univ. of Oxford 1977–79; demonstrator in Inorganic Chem., Jesus Coll., Cambridge 1979–81, Dir of Studies in Chem. 1979–91, Lecturer, Univ. Chem. Labs 1981–91; Visiting Prof., Cornell Univ. 1983–86; Nuffield Science Research Fellow 1986–87; Co-Founder and Co-Dir Interdisciplinary Research Centre in Superconductivity 1988; BP Venture Research Fellow 1988–90; Prof. of Inorganic Chem., Univ. of Birmingham 1991–2003, of Chem. and of Materials 1999–2003, Head of School of Chemistry 1996–99; Prof. and Head of Inorganic Chem., Univ. of Oxford 2003–; Royal Soc. Leverhulme Trust Sr Research Fellow 1996–97; Vice-Pres. Dalton Div. Royal Soc. of Chem. 1995; Corday Medal 1985, Tilden Medal 1992, Liversidge Medal 1999, Hughes Medal 2003, Bakerian Lecturer 2012. *Publications include:* The Metallic and Non-Metallic States of Matter (jtly) 1985, Metal-Insulator Transitions Revisited 1995. *Leisure interests:* exercise, sports. *Address:* Inorganic Chemistry Laboratory, University of Oxford, South Parks Road, Oxford, OX1 3QR, England (office). *Telephone:* (1865) 272646 (office). *Fax:* (1865) 272656 (office). *E-mail:* peter.edwards@chem.ox.ac.u (office). *Website:* www.chem.ox.ac.uk/icl (office).

EDWARDS, Philip Walter, PhD, FBA; British academic; b. 7 Feb. 1923, Barrow-in-Furness; s. of the late R. H. Edwards and B. Edwards; m. 1st Hazel Valentine 1947 (died 1950); m. 2nd Sheila Wilkes 1952; three s. one d.; ed King Edward's High School, Birmingham, Univ. of Birmingham; Lecturer in English, Univ. of Birmingham 1946–60; Prof. of English Literature, Trinity Coll. Dublin 1960–66; Visiting Prof., Univ. of Mich. 1964–65; Prof. of Literature, Univ. of Essex 1966–74; Visiting Prof., Williams Coll., Mass. 1969; Visiting Fellow, All Souls Coll., Oxford 1970–71; King Alfred Prof. of English Literature, Univ. of Liverpool 1974–90; Visiting Prof., Univ. of Otago, New Zealand 1980, Int. Christian Univ., Tokyo 1989. *Publications:* Sir Walter Raleigh 1953, The Spanish Tragedy (ed.) 1959, Shakespeare and the Confines of Art 1968, Massinger, Plays and Poems (ed. with C. Gibson) 1976, Pericles Prince of Tyre (ed.) 1976, Threshold of a Nation 1979, Hamlet Prince of Denmark (ed.) 1985, Shakespeare: A Writer's Progress 1986, Last Voyages 1988, The Story of the Voyage 1994, Sea-Mark: The Metaphorical Voyage, Spenser to Milton 1997, The Journals of Captain Cook (ed.) 1999, Pilgrimage and Literary Tradition 2005. *Leisure interest:* calligraphy. *Address:* High Gillingrove, Gillinggate, Kendal, Cumbria, LA9 4JB, England (home). *Telephone:* (1539) 721298 (home).

EDWARDS, Robert, BS, MBA; American business executive; *President and CEO, Safeway Inc.;* ed Brigham Young Univ.; fmr sr exec. at Maxtor Corpn, Imation Corpn and Santa Fe Pacific Corpn; joined Safeway in 2004, Exec. Vice-Pres. and Chief Financial Officer 2004–12, Pres. and CEO Safeway Inc. 2012–; Dir, KKR Financial Holdings, LLC, Blackhawk Network Holdings, Inc. (subsidiary of Safeway Inc.). *Address:* Safeway Inc., 5918 Stoneridge Mall Road, Pleasanton, CA 94588-3229, USA (office). *Telephone:* (925) 467-3000 (office). *Fax:* (925) 467-3321 (office). *E-mail:* info@safeway.com (office). *Website:* www.safeway.com (office).

EDWARDS, (Roger) Nicholas (see Crickhowell, Baron).

EDWARDS, Sir Samuel (Sam) Frederick, Kt, FRS, FInstP, FIMA, FRSC, CChem, CPhys, CMath; British physicist and administrator; *Cavendish Professor Emeritus of Physics, University of Cambridge;* b. 1 Feb. 1928, Swansea; s. of Richard and Mary Jane Edwards; m. Merriell E. M. Bland 1953; one s. three d.; ed Swansea Grammar School, Gonville and Caius College, Cambridge, Harvard Univ.; member, Inst. for Advanced Study, Princeton 1952–53; staff mem. Univ. of Birmingham 1953–58, Univ. of Manchester 1958–72; Prof. of Theoretical Physics, Univ. of Manchester 1963–72; John Humphrey Plummer Prof. of Physics, Univ. of Cambridge 1972–84, Cavendish Prof. 1984–95, Prof. Emer. 1995–, Pro Vice-Chancellor 1992–95; mem. Council, Inst. of Physics 1967–73, Vice-Pres. of Inst. 1970–73, Chair. Publ Div. 1970–73; mem. Science Bd, Science Research Council 1970–73, mem. Physics Cttee 1968–70, Polymer Science Cttee 1968–73, Chair. Physics Cttee 1970–73, Science Research Council 1973–77; Dir Lucas Industries 1981–93, Steetley PLC 1985–92; mem. Council European Physical Soc. 1969–71, Univ. Grants Cttee 1971–73, Scientific Advisory Council, Min. of Defence 1973–81, 1988– (Chair. 1978–81), Advisory Bd for the Research Councils, Dept of Ed. and Science 1973–77, Metrology and Standards Requirements Bd, Dept of Industry 1974–77, Advisory Council on Research and Devt, Dept of Energy 1974–77 (Chair. 1983–88), UK Del. NATO Science Cttee 1974–78, Senatsausschuss für Forschungspolitik und Forschungsplanung der Max Planck Gesellschaft 1975–77, Council Inst. of Math. and its Applications 1976– (Pres. 1980–81), European Council for Research and Devt 1975–79, Scientific Advisory Cttee Allied Corpn 1980–84; Chair. Council BAAS 1977–82, Pres. 1988–89, Council Royal Soc. 1981–83 (Vice-Pres. 1982–83); Chief Scientific Adviser, Dept of Energy 1983–88; Chair. Sr Advisory Group of Unilever PLC 1992–96; mem. Research Advisory Group BP 1993–97; Fellow, Gonville and Caius Coll., Cambridge 1972–; Foreign mem. Acad. des Sciences 1989, NAS 1996; Hon. Fellow, Inst. of Physics, French Physical Soc., BAAS 2002; Hon. mem. European Physical Soc.; Hon. DTech (Loughborough) 1975; Hon. DSc (Edin., Salford, Bath, Birmingham, Wales, Strasbourg, Sheffield, Dublin, Leeds), (Swansea) 1994, (E Anglia) 1995, (Cambridge) 2001, (Mainz) 2002, (Tel-Aviv) 2006; Maxwell, Guthrie Medals and Prizes, Inst. of Physics 1974, 1987, Founders' Polymer Prize 2001, American Physical Soc. Prize for High Polymer Physics 1982, Davy Medal, Royal Soc. 1984, Gold Medallist, Inst. of Math. 1986, Gold Medallist Rheology Soc. 1990, LVMH Science pour l'Art Prize 1993, Boltzmann Medal, IUPAP 1995, Royal Medal, Royal Soc. 2001, Dirac Medal 2005. *Publications:* Technological Risk 1980, Theory of Polymer Dynamics (with M. Doi) 1986, Networks of Liquid Crystal Polymers (with S. Aharoni) 1994. *Address:* Cavendish Laboratory, Cambridge, CB3 9LU (office); 7 Penarth Place, Cambridge, CB3 9LU, England (home). *Telephone:* (1223) 337259 (office); (1223) 366610 (home). *Fax:* (1223) 337000 (office). *E-mail:* sfe11@phy.cam.ac.uk (office). *Website:* www.poco.phy.cam.ac.uk/~sfe11/Welcome.htm (office).

EDWARDS, Sian; British conductor; b. 27 Aug. 1959; ed Royal Northern Coll. of Music, Manchester; studied with Sir Charles Groves, Norman Del Mar and Neeme Järvi and with Prof. I.A. Musin, Leningrad Conservatoire 1983–85; won first Leeds Conductors' Competition 1984; has worked with many leading orchestras in UK including London Philharmonic (LPO), Royal Liverpool Philharmonic, Royal Scottish Orchestra, City of Birmingham Symphony, Hallé, BBC Philharmonic, English Chamber orchestras and London Sinfonietta; also with LA Philharmonic Orchestra, The Cleveland Orchestra, The Ensemble Modern, Rotterdam Philharmonic Orchestra and other orchestras; operatic debut, Mahagonny, Scottish Opera 1986; other operatic productions include La Traviata and L'Heure Espagnole (Glyndebourne) 1987–88, Katya Kabanova, New Year (Glyndebourne Touring Opera) 1988–90, The Knot Garden, Rigoletto, Il Trovatore (Royal Opera House, Covent Garden) 1988–91, world premiere Greek (Mark Anthony Turnage), Munich Biennale 1988, Edin. Festival 1988, The Gambler (ENO) 1990, Khovanshchina (ENO) 1994, Mahagonny 1995, La Clemenza di Tito 1998, Eugene Onegin 2000, Peter Grimes (ENO) 2001, Don Giovanni, Danish Royal Opera 2001, The Death of Klinghoffer, La Damnation de Faust, Finnish Nat. Opera 2001; Music Dir ENO 1993–95. *Recordings include:* Tchaikovsky orchestral music (Royal Liverpool Philharmonic Orchestra) and Peter and the Wolf, Young Person's Guide to the Orchestra, Tchaikovsky's Fifth symphony (LPO). *Address:* c/o Ingpen & Williams, 7 St George's Court, 131 Putney Bridge Road, London, SW15 2PA, England (office). *Telephone:* (20) 8874-3222 (office). *Fax:* (20) 8877-3113 (office). *E-mail:* info@ingpen.co.uk (office).

EELSEN, Pierre Henri Maurice, LenD; French administrator and business executive; b. 12 July 1933, Montmorency, Val-d'Oise; s. of Maurice Eelsen and Jacqueline Robert; m. 1st; two s. one d.; m. 2nd Danièle Mesle, 1980; one s.; ed Lycée Jacques-Decour, Paris, Univ. de Paris; at Renault 1958–84, responsible for econ. studies Renault Eng 1959, attached to Dir of Relations 1965, Head Dept Agric. Machinery 1967, attached to Gen. Secretariat 1969, Asst to Sec.-Gen. 1971, Jt Sec.-Gen. 1975, Gen. Del. 1979, mem. Exec. Cttee 1981; Head Dept Int. Affairs Chambre syndicale des constructeurs d'automobiles 1962; mem. European Econ. and Social Cttee 1982–84; Pres. Nat. Asscn for Devt of Overseas depts 1982–85; Admin. Ecole nat. d'admin. 1983; Pres.-Dir-Gen. Air Inter 1984–90; Pres. Agence Nationale pour le Développement de l'Education Permanente (ADEP) 1985–91, Centre national d'enseignement à distance 1988–, Admin. council Institut régional d'admin. de Nantes 1988, French Div. of Centre européen de l'entreprise publique 1989, Chambre Syndicale des Transporteurs Aériens 1986–90; Pres. Nord-Pas de Calais Développement 1991–94, Observatoire Nat. du Tourisme 1991–96, L'Institut européen de recherche et de formation supérieure du tourisme 1992–94; Man. Ed Consultants 1994–; Vice-Pres. Airport Div. SEN (Vinci Group) 1999–2002; Chair. Sogindo 2002–06; Commdr, Ordre nat. du Mérite, Officier, Légion d'honneur. *Address:* 33 rue Lhomond, 75005 Paris (home); Domaine de Camarat, 83350 Ramatuelle, France (home). *Fax:* 1-43-31-20-37 (home).

EFI, HH Tuiatua Tupua Tamasese, (O le Ao o le Malo of Samoa); b. 1 March 1938; s. of Tupua Tamasese Mea'ole and Noue Irene Gustava Ta'isi Nelson; m. HH Masiofo Filifilia Imo; ed St Joseph's Coll., Apia, Western Samoa and Victoria Univ., Wellington, NZ; elected to Western Samoan Parl. 1965–91; Minister of Works, Civil Aviation, Marine and Transport 1970–73; Prime Minister (as the Hon. Ta'isi Tupuola Tufuga Efi) 1976–82, fmr Minister of Foreign Affairs, Local and Dist Affairs and Police; Deputy Prime Minister 1985–88; Jt Leader Samoa Nat. Devt Party; mem. Council of Deputies 2007; elected Head of State (O le Ao o le Malo) of Samoa 15 June 2007, re-elected 20 July 2012. *Address:* Government House, Vailima, Apia, Samoa (office). *Website:* www.govt.ws (office).

EFIMOV (see YEFIMOV).

EFSTATHIOU, George Petros, BA, PhD, FRS; British astrophysicist; *Professor of Astrophysics and Director, Kavli Institute for Cosmology, University of Cambridge;* b. 2 Sept. 1955, London, England; s. of Petros Efstathiou and Christina Parperi; m. 1st Helena Jane Smart 1976 (divorced 1997); m. 2nd Yvonne Nobis 1998; three s. one d.; ed Somerset Comprehensive School, London, Keble Coll., Oxford, Univ. of Durham; Research Asst, Univ. of Calif., Berkeley 1979–80; Research Asst, Univ. of Cambridge 1980–84, Jr Research Fellow, King's Coll., Cambridge 1980–84, Sr Research Fellow 1984–88, Asst Dir of Research, Inst. of Astronomy, Cambridge 1984–88, Savilian Prof. of Astronomy and Fellow, New Coll., Oxford 1988–97; Prof. of Astrophysics and Fellow, King's Coll. Cambridge 1997–, Dir Inst. of Astronomy 2004–08; Dir Kavli Inst. for Cosmology, Cambridge 2008–; Vainu Bappu Prize, Astronomical Soc. of India 1990, Maxwell Medal and Prize, Inst. of Physics 1990, Bodossaki Foundation Prize for Astrophysics 1994, Robinson Prize in Cosmology, Royal Soc. 1997, Heineman Prize for Astrophysics (jtly), American Inst. of Physics 2005, Group Award (2dF Galaxy Survey), Royal Astronomical Soc. 2008, Gruber Cosmology Prize (co-recipient), Peter and Patricia Gruber Foundation 2011, Nemitsas Prize in Physics 2013. *Publications:* articles in astronomical journals. *Leisure interests:* running, playing guitar, football. *Address:* Kavli Institute for Cosmology, University of Cambridge, c/o Institute of Astronomy, Madingley Road, Cambridge, CB3 0HA, England (office). *Telephone:* (1223) 337530 (office); (1223) 574001 (home). *Fax:* (1223) 337523 (office). *E-mail:* gpe@ast.cam.ac.uk (office). *Website:* www.ast.cam.ac.uk (office); www.kicc.cam.ac.uk (office).

EFUMAN, Santiago Nsobeya; Equatorial Guinean politician; Minister of Foreign Affairs, Int. Co-operation and Francophone Affairs 2001–03; Govt Spokesman, Ministry of Information, Culture and Tourism 2006–. *Address:* Ministry of Information, Culture and Tourism, Malabo, Equatorial Guinea (office).

EGAN, Christopher F., BS, MPA; American business executive and diplomatist; *President, Carruth Capital LLC;* b. Boston, Mass; m. Jean Egan; three c.; ed Univ. of Massachusetts Amherst, Kennedy School of Govt at Harvard Univ.; Pres. and Founding mem. Carruth Capital, LLC (commercial real estate investment and devt firm); Co-founder and Dir 'Break the Cycle of Poverty'; Trustee, Egan Family Foundation; mem. Bd of Dirs Fallon Community Health Plan (fmr Chair. Finance Cttee); fmr mem. Bd of Dirs MassDevelopment; fmr mem. Cen. Mass Regional Competitiveness Council; fmr Dir Corridor Nine Chamber of Commerce; Co-founder and mem. Bd Arc of Innovation/I-495 Initiative; TV commentator for numerous networks; op-ed. contrib. and documentary maker; Amb. to OECD 2007–09; fmr Trustee, Univ. of Massachusetts Memorial Health Care. *Television:*

Eclipsed by the Sun (documentary) 2004. *Address:* Carruth Capital LLC, 116 Flanders Road, Suite 2000, Westborough, MA 01581, USA (office). *Telephone:* (508) 898-3800 (office). *E-mail:* info@carruthcapital.com (office). *Website:* www.carruthcapital.com (office).

EGAN, HE Cardinal Edward Michael, DD, JCD; American ecclesiastic; *Archbishop Emeritus of New York;* b. 2 April 1932, Oak Park, Ill.; s. of Thomas J. Egan and Genevieve Costello Egan; ed St Mary of the Lake Seminary, Mundelein, Ill., Pontifical N American Coll., Vatican City, Pontifical Gregorian Univ., Rome, Italy; ordained priest 1957; curate at Holy Name Cathedral Parish 1958, later Asst Chancellor Archdiocese of Chicago and Sec. to HE Cardinal Albert Meyer; Asst Vice-Rector and Repetitor of Moral Theology and Canon Law, Pontifical N American Coll., Vatican City 1960; Sec. to HE Cardinal John Cody 1964, later Co-Chancellor Archdiocese of Chicago; Judge, Tribunal of the Sacred Roman Rota 1971–85; fmr Prof. of Canon Law, Vatican City, Pontifical Gregorian Univ., Rome; fmr Prof. of Civil and Criminal Procedure, Studium Rotale; fmr Commr Congregation for the Sacraments and Divine Worship; fmr Consultor Congregation of the Clergy; consecrated Bishop 1985; Auxiliary Bishop of New York and Vicar for Educ. 1985; Third Bishop of Bridgeport 1988–2000; Archbishop of New York 2000–09, Emer. 2009–; cr. Cardinal 2001; Pres. and Chair. Bd Trustees Catholic Near East Welfare Asscn; Trustee Ratisbonne Inst., Jerusalem, Israel, St Thomas More Coll., NH, Sacred Heart Univ., Fairfield, CT, Nat. Shrine of the Immaculate Conception, Washington, DC, Catholic Univ. of America, Washington, DC 2000–; Dr hc (St John's Univ., New York, Thomas More Coll., Western Connecticut State Univ.). *Address:* Archdiocese of New York, 1011 First Avenue, New York, NY 10022-4134 (office); 324 East 33rd Street, New York, NY 10016, USA (home). *Telephone:* (212) 371-1000 (office); (212) 213-6027 (home). *Fax:* (212) 826-6020 (office); (212) 213-9136 (home). *E-mail:* cardegan@archny.org (office). *Website:* www.ny-archdiocese.org (office).

EGAN, Sir John Leopold, Kt, MSc Econ, DL, FRAeS, FIC, FIMI, FCIT, FCIPS; British business executive; b. 7 Nov. 1939, Rawtenstall, Lancs.; s. of James Edward Egan; m. Julia Emily Treble 1963; two d.; ed Bablake School, Coventry, Imperial Coll., London, London Business School; petroleum engineer, Shell Int. 1962–66; Gen. Man. AC-Delco Replacement Parts Operation, Gen. Motors Ltd 1968–71; Man. Dir Unipart, Parts and Service Dir, Leyland Cars 1971–76; Corp. Parts Dir Massey Ferguson 1976–80; Chair. Jaguar Cars Ltd 1980–84, Chair and Chief Exec., Chief Exec. and Man. Dir Jaguar PLC 1984–85, Chair. and Chief Exec. Jaguar PLC 1985–90; Chief Exec. BAA PLC 1990–99, Dir 1990–; Dir Legal & Gen. Group 1987–97, Vice-Chair. 1993–97, Pres. 1998–; Chair. MEPC PLC 1998–2000, Inchcape PLC 2000–05, Harrison Lovegrove Ltd 2000–05, Qinetiq 2001–02, Asite 2001–05, Severn Trent PLC 2005–10; Deputy Pres. CBI 2001–02, Pres. 2002–2004; mem. Bd of Dirs Warwick Castle Park Trust Ltd; fmr mem. Bd of Dirs Foreign and Colonial Investment Trust, British Tourist Authority, Owners Group LLP, Borwick Group Ltd; Bd Mentor Criticaleye; Pres. Inst. of Man. 2000–01; Chancellor Coventry Univ. 2007–; Sr Fellow, RCA; Hon. Prof., Dept of Eng., Univ. of Warwick 1990; Dr hc (Cranfield Inst.) 1986, Hon. DTech (Loughborough) 1987, Hon. LLD (Bath) 1988; Castrol Gold Medal, Inst. of Motor Industry Award 1982, Int. Gold Medal, Inst. of Production Engineers, City and Guilds of London Hon. Insignia Award for Tech. 1987 and several other awards. *Leisure interests:* skiing, squash, walking, music.

EGASHIRA, Toshiaki; Japanese insurance industry executive; *Representative Director, President and CEO, MS&AD Insurance Group Holdings, Inc.;* fmr Dir in Pres.'s Office, fmr Chief Dir of China, Chief Dir of Kanagawa & Shizuoka, later Man. Exec. Officer and CEO Mitsui Sumitomo Insurance Co. Ltd, later Pres., Exec. Pres. and Rep. Dir, Rep. Dir, Pres. and CEO Mitsui Sumitomo Insurance Group Holdings, Inc. 2008–10, Rep. Dir, Pres. and CEO MS&AD Insurance Group Holdings, Inc. (following merger of Mitsui Sumitomo Insurance Group Holdings, Inc., Aioi Insurance Co. Ltd and Nissay Dowa General Insurance Co. Ltd April 2010) 2010–. *Address:* MS&AD Insurance Group Holdings, Inc., Yaesu First Financial Building, Yaesu 1-3-7, Chuo-ku, Tokyo 103-0028, Japan (office). *Telephone:* (3) 6202-5268 (office). *Fax:* (3) 6202-6882 (office). *E-mail:* info@ms-ad-hd.com (office). *Website:* www.ms-ad-hd.com (office).

EGELAND, Jan, MA; Norwegian international organization official and fmr UN official; *Europe Director and Deputy Executive Director, Human Rights Watch;* m. Anne Kristin Sydnes; two d.; ed Univ. of Oslo, Univ. of Calif., Berkeley, USA; State Sec., Ministry of Foreign Affairs 1990–97; Special Adviser to UN Sec.-Gen. on Colombia 1999–2002; Sec.-Gen. Norwegian Red Cross 2002–03; UN Under-Sec.-Gen. for Humanitarian Affairs and Humanitarian Relief Coordinator 2003–06, then Special Advisor to Sec.-Gen. 2007; Dir Norwegian Inst. of Int. Affairs (Norsk Utenrikspolitisk Institutt) 2007–11; Europe Dir and Deputy Exec. Dir, Human Rights Watch, New York 2011–; Prof., University of Stavanger; fmr Dir Int. Dept Norwegian Red Cross; fmr Chair. Amnesty Int. (AI) Norway and Vice-Chair. AI Int. Exec. Cttee; fmr Head of Devt Studies, Henry Dunant Inst., Geneva; fmr Fellow, Int. Peace Research Inst., Oslo and Truman Inst. for the Advancement of Peace, Jerusalem; fmr radio and TV int. news reporter, Norwegian Broadcasting Corpn. *Achievements include:* co-organized Norwegian channel between Israel and Palestinian Liberation Organisation leading to Oslo Accord 1993; directed Norwegian facilitation of UN-led peace talks leading to ceasefire agreement between Guatemalan govt and Unidad Revolucionaria Nacional Guatemalteca guerrillas 1996. *Publications include:* reports, studies and articles on conflict resolution, humanitarian affairs and human rights. *Address:* Human Rights Watch, 350 Fifth Avenue, 34th Floor, New York, NY 10118-3299, USA (office). *Telephone:* (212) 290-4700 (office). *Website:* www.hrw.org (office).

EGGERS, Dave; American writer; m. Vendela Vida 2003; Ed. Might magazine 1994–97, Timothy McSweeney's Quarterly Concern, or 'McSweeney's', journal and publrs 1998–; LA Times Innovators Award 2009. *Publications:* A Heartbreaking Work of Staggering Genius (memoir) 2000, You Shall Know Our Velocity (novel) 2003, The Future Dictionary of America (with Jonathan Safran Foer and Nicole Krauss) 2004, The Best of McSweeney's: Volume 1 (ed.) 2004, Volume 2 (ed.) 2005, How We Are Hungry 2005, What is the What: The Autobiography of Valentino Achak Deng: A Novel (Prix Médicis Étranger 2009) 2006, Zeitoun (LA Times Book Prize, Dayton Literary Peace Prize for Non-Fiction 2010) 2009, The Wild Things 2009, A Hologram for the King 2012; contrib. to periodicals. *Address:* McSweeney's, 849 Valencia Street, San Francisco, CA 94110, USA (office). *E-mail:* letters@ mcsweeneys.net (office). *Website:* www.mcsweeneys.net (office).

EGGLESTON, William; American photographer and academic; b. 27 July 1939, Memphis, Tenn.; Lecturer in Visual and Environmental Studies, Carpenter Center, Harvard Univ. 1974; Researcher in Color Video, MIT 1978; Guggenheim Fellow 1974; Fellow, American Acad. of Arts and Sciences 2009–; Photographic Soc. of Japan Master Photographers of 1960–1979 Award 1989, Univ. of Memphis Distinguished Achievement Award 1996, Hasselblad Award 1998, Nat. Arts Club Gold Medal for Photography, New York 2003, Getty Images Lifetime Achievement Award 2004, Photoespana Award 2004. *Address:* Eggleston Artistic Trust, 3251 Poplar Avenue #110, Memphis TN 38111, USA (office). *Telephone:* (901) 323-7575 (office). *Fax:* (901) 323-7557 (office). *E-mail:* info@egglestontrust.com (office). *Website:* www.egglestontrust.com (office).

EGGLETON, Hon. Arthur C. (Art), PC; Canadian politician; b. 29 Sept. 1943, Toronto; fmr accountant; mem. Toronto City Council and Metropolitan Toronto Council 1969–93; Mayor of Toronto 1980–91; MP for York Centre 1993–2004; Pres. Treas. Bd and Minister responsible for Infrastructure 1993–96; Minister for Int. Trade 1996–97, of Nat. Defence 1997–2002; mem. Bd of Dirs Luxell Technologies Inc. 2005–, Skylink Group; mem. Senate 2005–, Chair. Standing Cttee on Social Affairs, Science and Tech., mem. Standing Cttee on Nat. Finance; Voluntary Chair. Rebuilding Lives Campaign, St John's Rehabilitation Hosp.; Civic Award of Merit, Toronto 1992. *Address:* The Senate of Canada, Ottawa, ON K1A 0A4, Canada. *Telephone:* (613) 995-4230 (office). *Fax:* (613) 995-4237 (office). *E-mail:* egglea@sen.parl.gc.ca (office). *Website:* www.seatorartgggleton.ca (office).

EGILSSON, Ólafur; Icelandic diplomatist and lawyer; b. 20 Aug. 1936, Reykjavik; s. of Egill Kristjánsson and Anna Margrjet Thurídur Ólafsdóttir Briem; m. Ragna Sverrisdóttir Ragnars 1960; one s. one d.; ed Commercial Coll. of Iceland and Iceland Univ.; journalist with newspapers Vísir 1956–58, Morgunbladid 1959–62; Publishing Exec. 1963–64; Head, NATO Regional Information Office, Reykjavik 1964–66; Gen.-Sec. Icelandic Asscn for Western Co-operation 1964–66; Political Div., Icelandic Foreign Ministry 1966–69; First Sec., then Counsellor, Icelandic Embassy, Paris 1969–71; Deputy Perm. Rep. OECD, UNESCO and Council of Europe 1969–71; Deputy Perm. Rep. N Atlantic Council, Deputy Head, Icelandic Del. to EEC, Counsellor, Embassy in Brussels 1971–74; Counsellor, then Minister Counsellor, Political Div. of Foreign Ministry 1974–80; Chief of Protocol (with rank of Amb.) 1980–83; Acting Prin. Pvt. Sec. to Pres. of Iceland 1981–82; Deputy Perm. Under-Sec. and Dir-Gen. for Political Affairs, Foreign Ministry 1983–87; Amb. to UK (also accred to Ireland, Netherlands and Nigeria) 1986–89; Amb. to USSR, later Russia 1990–94; Amb. to Denmark (also accred to Japan, Italy, Israel, Lithuania and Turkey) 1994–96; in charge of Arctic co-operation 1996–98 (also accred to Holy See, Turkey, Australia and NZ); Amb. to China (also accred to Australia, Japan, Repub. of Korea, NZ and Viet Nam) 1998–2002, to Cambodia, Indonesia, Malaysia, Thailand and Singapore (non-resident) 2002; Chair. Bd of Govs Icelandic Int. Devt Agency 1982–87; Exec. mem. Bible Soc. of Iceland 1977–87, History Soc. 1982–88; Commdr Icelandic Order of the Falcon 1981 and decorations from Finland, France, Norway, Spain, Sweden and Luxembourg. *Publications:* Co-author: Iceland and Jan Mayen 1980, NATO's Anxious Birth – The Prophetic Vision of the 1940s 1985; Ed. Bjarni Benediktsson 1983. *Leisure interests:* history, walking, music (classical, opera). *Address:* Valhúsabraut 35, 170 Saltjarnarnes, Iceland (home). *Telephone:* (354) 551 5411 (home). *Fax:* (354) 551 5411 (home). *E-mail:* olegice@simnet.is (home).

EGLINTON, Geoffrey, PhD, DSc, FRS; British organic geochemist and academic; *Emeritus Professor, University of Bristol;* b. 1 Nov. 1927, Cardiff; m. Pamela J. Coupland 1955; two s. one d. (deceased); ed Sale Grammar School and Univ. of Manchester; Post-doctoral Fellow, Ohio State Univ. 1952; Lecturer in Organic Chem., Univ. of Glasgow 1954–64; Visiting Fellow, Univ. of Calif., Berkeley 1964; Sr Lecturer in Organic Chem., Univ. of Glasgow 1964–67, Reader 1967; Sr Lecturer in Organic Geochem. and Head, Organic Chem. Unit, Univ. of Bristol 1967, Reader in Organic Geochem. 1968–73, Prof. and Head of Organic Geochem. Unit 1973–93, Prof. Emer. 1993–, Dir Biogeochemistry Centre 1991–97, Sr Research Fellow 1995; H. Burr Steinbach Visiting Scholar, Woods Hole Oceanographic Inst., Mass 1986, Adjunct Scientist 2000–; Adjunct Prof. Dartmouth Coll., NH 2003, Visiting Prof. 2006–; Melvin Calvin Lectureship (Univ. of Calif., Berkeley) 1985; Geochemistry Fellow, Geochemical Soc. and European Asscn for Geochemistry 1996; NASA Gold Medal 1973, Hugo Muller Silver Medal, Chem. Soc. 1974, Alfred E. Treibs Medal Geochemical Soc. 1981, Major Edward Fitzgerald Coke Medal of the Geological Soc. 1986, Harold C. Urey Award, European Asscn of Geochemists 1997, Royal Medal, Royal Soc. 1997, Martin Gold Medal, Chromatographic Soc. 1999, Goldschmidt Medal, Geochemical Soc. 2000, Wollaston Medal, Geological Soc. 2004, Dan David Prize 2008. *Publications:* over 500 articles and books. *Leisure interests:* hiking, sailing.

EGON, Nicholas; British painter; b. 15 Nov. 1921, Brno, Czechoslovakia; m. 1st Diana Horton 1948; m. 2nd Matti Xylas 1980; ed pvt. tutors, Birkbeck Coll., London Univ., Oxford Univ.; served with army in Middle East 1942–46; taught painting and history of art, Sir John Cass Coll., lectured at Nat. Gallery, London and Oxford and Cambridge 1946–50; portraits, landscapes and abstracts in nat., royal and pvt. collections in USA, UK, France, Italy, Greece, Spain, Jordan, Saudi Arabia, Morocco, Oman and Switzerland; Chair. of Patrons, Centre for Hellenic Studies, King's Coll., London Univ. 1989–. *Publications:* Some Beautiful Women (portraits) 1952, Paintings of Jordan 1986. *Leisure interests:* travel, history, music, archaeology. *Address:* Villa Aëtos, Katakali, 20100 Corinthia (Studio) (home); Deinokratous 81, 115 21 Athens, Greece (home); 34 Thurloe Square, London, SW7 2SR, England (home). *Telephone:* (20) 7935-2020 (London secretary) (office); (27410) 33442 (Corinthia) (home); (20) 7589-0700 (London) (home); (210) 7291774 (Athens) (home). *Fax:* (27410) 33640 (Corinthia) (home); (210) 7291774 (Athens) (home); (20) 7589-0620 (London) (home). *E-mail:* egon@faroship.com (office); egon@seirios.com.gr (home).

EGOROV, Mikhail P., PhD; Russian chemist and academic; *Director, N.D. Zelinsky Institute of Organic Chemistry, Russian Academy of Sciences;* currently Dir N.D. Zelinsky Inst. of Organic Chem., Russian Acad. of Sciences; Corresp. mem. Russian Acad. of Sciences. *Publications:* numerous papers in professional journals. *Address:* N.D. Zelinsky Institute of Organic Chemistry, Russian Acad-

emy of Sciences, 119991 Moscow, Leninsky Prospekt 47, Russia (office). *Telephone:* (095) 137-2944 (office). *Fax:* (095) 135-5328 (office). *E-mail:* secretary@ioc.ac.ru (office); mpe@cacr.ioc.ac.ru (office). *Website:* www.ioc.ac.ru (office).

EGOYAN, Atom, OC, BA; Canadian film director; b. 19 July 1960, Cairo, Egypt; s. of Joseph Egoyan and Shushan Devletian; m. Arsinée Khanjian; one c.; ed Univ. of Toronto; Dir Ego Film Arts, Toronto 1982–; Chevalier, Ordre des Arts et des Lettres; Dr hc (Trinity Coll., Univ. of Toronto, Univ. of Victoria, Brock Univ., Ont., Coll. of Art and Design, Univ. of British Columbia); Best Dir, Irish Times 2007, Dan David Prize for Creative Rendering of the Past 2008. *Exhibitions:* Return to the Flock, Irish Museum of Modern Art 1996, Early Development, Le Fresnoy, USA 1997, Notorious, Museum of Modern Art, Oxford 1999, Venice Biennale, Close, Venice Biennale 2001, Steenbeckett, Museum of Mankind, London 2002, Hors d'Usage, Musée d'Art Contemporain de Montréal 2002. *Films:* writer, dir and producer feature films: Next of Kin (Gold Ducat award, Mannheim Int. Film Week 1984) 1984, Family Viewing (Int. Critics Award 1988, Best Feature Film Award, Uppsala, Prix Alcan, Festival du Nouveau Cinéma, Montreal) 1987, Speaking Parts (Best Screenplay Prize, Vancouver Int. Film Festival) 1989, The Adjuster (Special Jury Prize, Moscow Film Festival, Golden Spike Award, Valladolid Film Festival) 1991, Calendar (prize at Berlin Int. Film Festival) 1993, Exotica (Int. Film Critics Award, Cannes Film Festival 1994, Prix de la Critique award for Best Foreign Film 1994) 1994, The Sweet Hereafter (Grand Prix, Int. Critics Prize, Cannes Film Festival 1997) 1997, Elsewhereless 1998, Dr Ox's Experiment 1998, Felicia's Journey 1999, Krapp's Last Tape 2000, Ararat 2002, Where the Truth Lies 2005, Adoration 2008, Chloe 2009, Devil's Knot 2013. *Operas:* Salome, Canadian Opera Co. 1996, Houston Grand Opera 1997, Elsewhereless 1998, Dr Ox's Experiment 1998, Salome (new production), Canadian Opera Co. 2002, 2013, Die Walküre, Canadian Opera Co. 2004, 2006, Così fan tutte, Canadian Opera Co. 2014. *Play:* Eh Joe (interpretation of Samuel Beckett's teleplay for the stage, Dublin and London) 2006, Cruel and Tender (Canadian Stage Co., Toronto) 2012. *Leisure interest:* classical guitar. *Address:* Ego Film Arts, 80 Niagara Street, Toronto, ON M5V 1C5, Canada. *Telephone:* (416) 703-2137 (office). *Fax:* (416) 504-7161 (office). *E-mail:* questions@egofilmarts.com (office). *Website:* www .egofilmarts.com (office).

EGUIAGARAY UCELAY, Juan Manuel, BA, PhD; Spanish politician and think tank director; *Director, Fundación Alternativas;* b. 25 Dec. 1945, Bilbao; m.; one s.; ed Univ. of Deusto, Univ. of Nancy, France; Prof. of Econs, Univ. de Deusto 1970–82; joined PSE-PSOE (Workers' Socialist Party of Spain) 1977, mem. Exec. Cttee 1979, Fed. Sec. for the Economy (34th Fed. Congress of PSOE), fmrly PSOE Nat. Parl. Spokesman and PSOE Nat. Parl. Spokesman for Econ. Affairs, Sec. PSOE Fed. Exec. Comm. 1990; councillor, Town Council, Bilbao 1979, Prov. Deputy, Vizcaya 1979–81, mem. Juntas Generales Vizcaya 1979–83, Deputy and Spokesman for Socialist Party of Basque Parl. 1980–88, Vice-Sec. Gen. Basque Socialists 1985–88, Govt Del. for Autonomous Community of Murcia, then for Autonomous Community of the Basque Country 1988–89; Minister for Public Admin 1991–93, of Industry and Energy 1993–96; Nat. Deputy for Murcia 1996–2001; currently Dir of Studies, Fundación Alternativas (think tank), Madrid; Pres. Solidaridad Internacional (NGO); mem. Bd of Dirs European Aeronautic Defence and Space Co. (EADS NV); mem. Advisory Bd Cap Gemini Spain, FoundationGroup EP. *Address:* Fundación Alternativas, Zurbano 29, 3° Izq., 28010 Madrid, Spain (office). *Telephone:* (91) 3199860 (office). *Fax:* (91) 3192298 (office). *Website:* www.falternativas.org/en (office).

EHLE, Jennifer; British/American actress; b. 29 Dec. 1969, Winston-Salem, N Carolina, USA; d. of John Ehle and Rosemary Harris; m. Michael Ryan 2001; one s. one d.; ed North Carolina School of the Arts, Cen. School of Speech and Drama, London, UK; stage debut as a toddler in a Broadway revival of A Streetcar Named Desire 1973; spent her childhood between the UK and USA, attending 18 different schools including the Interlochen Arts Acad. *Plays include:* Summerfolk (Royal Nat. Theatre), The Relapse (RSC), The Painter of Dishonour (RSC), Richard III (RSC) 1996, Tartuffe (Playhouse) (Ian Charleson Award) 1991, The Real Thing (Albery) (Tony Award for Best Lead Actress in a Play 2000, Variety Club Award 2000) 1999, (Broadway) 2000 (Tony Award for Best Actress 2000), The Philadelphia Story (Old Vic, London) 2005, The Coast of Utopia (Lincoln Centre, New York) (Tony Award for Best Performance by a Featured Actress in a Play 2007) 2006. *Films include:* Backbeat 1994, Paradise Road 1997, Wilde 1997, Bedrooms and Hallways 1998, This Year's Love 1999, Sunshine (Golden Satellite Award for Best Supporting Actress in a Motion Picture Drama 2001) 1999, Possession 2002, The River King 2005, Alpha Male 2006, Michael Clayton 2006, Before the Rains 2007, Pride and Glory 2008, The Greatest 2009, The King's Speech (Screen Actors Guild Award for Outstanding Performance by a Cast in a Motion Picture 2010) 2010, The Adjustment Bureau 2011, The Ides of March 2011, Zero Dark Thirty 2012. *Television includes:* The Camomile Lawn (mini-series) (Radio Times Award for Best Newcomer 1992) 1992, Micky Love (film) 1993, The Maitlands (film) 1993, Self Catering (film) 1994, Pleasure (film) 1994, Beyond Reason (film) 1995, Pride and Prejudice (mini-series) (BAFTA Award for Best Actress 1996) 1995, Melissa (mini-series) 1997, The Russell Girl (film) 2008, A Gifted Man (series) 2011–12. *Address:* c/o Independent Talent Group, 76 Oxford Street, London, W1N 0AX, England. *Telephone:* (20) 7636-6565. *Fax:* (20) 7323-0101. *Website:* www.independenttalent.com.

EHLERMANN, Claus-Dieter, DrIur; German lawyer and international organization official; *Senior Counsel, Wilmer Cutler Pickering Hale and Dorr LLP;* b. 15 June 1931, Scheessel; s. of Kurt Ehlermann and Hilde Ehlermann (née Justus); m. Carola Grumbach 1959; two d.; ed Univs of Marburg/Lahn and Heidelberg, Univ. of Michigan Law School; Research Asst Fed. Constitutional Court, Karlsruhe 1959–61; Legal Adviser, Legal Service of the Comm. of European Communities 1961–73, Dir and Deputy Financial Controller 1973–77, Dir-Gen. of the Legal Service 1977–87; Spokesman of the Comm. of the European Communities and of its fmr Pres. Jacques Delors (q.v.) 1987–90, Dir-Gen. of Directorate-Gen. for Competition 1990–95; fmr Prof. of Econ. Law, European Univ. Inst., Florence; fmr mem. Appellate Body of WTO, Geneva 1995–2001, Chair. 2001; Sr Counsel, Wilmer, Cutler & Pickering (law firm), Brussels 2002–, Co-Chair. Antitrust and Competition Dept 2005–08; Hon. Prof., Univ. of Hamburg; Hon. Bencher, Gray's Inn, London; Hon. DrIur 1999. *Publications:* numerous documents on the European Community and its legal order. *Leisure interests:* reading, skiing.

Address: Wilmer Cutler Pickering Hale and Dorr LLP, Bastion Tower, Place du Champ de Mars, Marsveldplein 5, 1050 Brussels, Belgium (office). *Telephone:* (2) 285-49-02 (office). *Fax:* (2) 285-49-49 (office). *E-mail:* claus-dieter.ehlermann@wilmerhale.com (office). *Website:* www.wilmerhale.com/claus-dieter_ehlermann (office).

EHLERS ZURITA, Freddy; Ecuadorean journalist, politician and international organization official; *Minister of Tourism;* b. 1945, Quito; ed Cen. Univ. of Ecuador; fmr host, TV programme La Televisión; Dir Bd of Cartagena Agreement's Andean TV Program 1980–88; unsuccessful cand. for Pres. of Ecuador 1996, 1998; mem. Andean Parl. for Ecuador 2002–06, Vice-Pres. 2003–04, mem. Cttee on Educ., Culture, Science, Tech. and Communication; Sec.-Gen. Andean Community of Nations (Comunidad Andina de Naciones) 2007–10; currently Minister of Tourism. *Address:* Ministry of Tourism, Avda Eloy Alfaro N32-300 y Carlos Tobar, 2°, Quito, Ecuador (office). *Telephone:* (2) 399-9333 (office). *Fax:* (2) 222-9330 (office). *E-mail:* info@turismo.gov.ec (office). *Website:* www.turismo.gov.ec (office).

EHRLICH, Paul Ralph, MA, PhD, FRS; American entomologist, population biologist and academic; *Bing Professor of Population Studies and President, Center for Conservation Biology, Stanford University;* b. 29 May 1932, Philadelphia, Pa; s. of William Ehrlich and Ruth Ehrlich (née Rosenberg); m. Anne Fitzhugh Howland 1954; one d.; ed Univs of Pennsylvania and Kansas; Field Officer, Northern Insect Survey (Canadian Arctic and Sub-arctic) summers of 1951 and 1952; Research Asst, DDT Resistance Project, Dept of Entomology, Univ. of Kansas 1952–54, Kansas Univ. Fellow 1954–66, NSF Pre-Doctoral Fellow 1955–57, Assoc. Investigator, USAF research project, Alaska and Univ. of Kansas 1956–57, Research Assoc., Chicago Acad. of Sciences and Univ. of Kansas Dept of Entomology 1957–59; Asst Prof. of Biological Sciences, Stanford Univ. 1959–62, Assoc. Prof. of Biological Sciences 1962–66, Prof. of Biological Studies 1966–, Dir Grad. Studies, Dept of Biological Sciences 1966–69, 1974–76, Bing Prof. of Population Studies 1977–, Pres. Center for Conservation Biology 1988–; NSF Sr Post-Doctoral Fellow, Univ. of Sydney 1965–66; Assoc., Center for the Study of Democratic Insts, Santa Barbara, Calif. 1969–72; Sec. Lepidopterists' Soc. 1957–63, mem. Exec. Council 1968; Corresp. NBC News 1989–92; Pres. Zero Population Growth 1969–70 (Hon. Pres. 1970–), Zero Population Growth Fund 1972–73, The Conservation Soc. 1972–73, American Inst. of Biological Sciences 1989, Assc'n for Tropical Lepidoptera 2001; Vice-Pres. Soc. for the Study of Evolution 1970; Co-Chair. Research Cttee, Rocky Mountain Biological Lab. 1973–75, Trustee 1971–86; Mem.-at-Large, Governing Bd American Inst. of Biological Sciences 1969–70; mem. Advisory Council, Friends of the Earth 1970–, Scientific Advisory Cttee, Sierra Club 1972–, Council, Soc. for the Study of Evolution 1974–76; mem. and Active Cttee mem., Int. Assc'n for the Study of Ecology 1969–70; mem. Bd Dirs Common Cause 1972; mem. Bd of Consultants, Lizard Island Research Station 1975–78; mem. Bd of Govs Soc. for Conservation Biology 1986–88; mem. Editorial Bd Systematic Zoology 1964–67, International Journal of Environmental Sciences 1969–71, American Naturalist 1974–76, Oecologia 1981–85, 1991–, Revista de Biologia Tropical, Universidad de Costa Rica 1996–; Sr Assoc. Ed. American Naturalist 1984; Advisory Ed. Human Nature 1977–79; mem. NAS 1985, American Philosophical Soc. 1990, European Acad. of Sciences and Arts 1992; Elective mem. American Ornithologists' Union 1989; Foreign mem. Russian Acad. of Natural Sciences 1997–; Fellow, California Acad. of Sciences 1961, AAAS 1978, American Acad. of Arts and Sciences 1982, Entomological Soc. of America 1987; Hon. Life mem. American Humanist Assc'n 1989, British Ecological Soc. 1989, Int. Soc. for Philosophical Enquiry 1991; Sigma Xi-Resa Grant-in-Aid of Research done in Alaska and NW Canada 1955, First Prize, Mitchell Foundation 1979, John Muir Award, Sierra Club 1980, Humanist Distinguished Service Award, American Humanist Assc'n 1985, First Distinguished Achievement Award, Soc. for Conservation Biology 1987, Gold Medal, World Wildlife Fund Int. 1987, AAAS/Scientific American Gerard Piel Award for Service to Science in the Cause of Humankind 1989, UN Global 500 Roll of Honour 1989, Crafoord Prize in Population Biology and the Conservation of Biological Diversity, Royal Swedish Acad. of Sciences 1990, Distinguished Service Citation, Univ. of Kansas 1991, MacArthur Prize Fellowship 1990–95, Major Achievement Award, New York City Audubon Soc. 1991, Volvo Environment Prize 1993, World Ecology Medal, Int. Center for Tropical Ecology 1993, UNEP Sasakawa Environment Prize 1994, Heinz Award for the Environment 1995, Distinguished Peace Leader, Nuclear Age Peace Foundation 1996, Tyler Prize for Environmental Achievement 1998, Dr A.H. Heineken Prize for Environmental Sciences 1998, Nat. Audubon Soc., One Hundred Champions of Conservation 1998, Blue Planet Prize, Asahi Glass Foundation (Japan) 1999, Distinguished Scientist Award, American Inst. of Biological Sciences 2001, Eminent Ecologist Award, Ecological Soc. of America 2001. *Publications include:* How to Know the Butterflies 1960, Process of Evolution 1963, The Population Bomb 1968, 1971, Population Resources, Environment: Issues in Human Ecology (with A. H. Ehrlich) 1970, 1972, How to Be a Survivor (with R. L. Harriman) 1971, The Race Bomb (with S. Feldman) 1977, Extinction: The Causes and Consequences of the Disappearance of Species (with A. H. Ehrlich) 1981, The Golden Door: International Migration, Mexico and the United States (with D. L. Bilderback and A. H. Ehrlich) 1981, The Cold and the Dark: The World After Nuclear War (with Carl Sagan, Donald Kennedy and Walter Orr Roberts) 1984, Earth (with A. H. Ehrlich) 1987, Science of Ecology (with Joan Roughgarden) 1987, New World, New Mind (with R. Ornstein) 1988, The Birder's Handbook: A Field Guide to the Natural History of North American Birds (with David S. Dobkin and Darryl Wheye) 1988, The Cassandra Conference: Resources and the Human Predicament 1988, The Population Explosion (with A. H. Ehrlich) 1990, Healing the Planet: Strategies for Resolving the Environmental Crisis (with A. H. Ehrlich) 1991, Birds in Jeopardy: The Imperiled and Extinct Birds of the United States and Canada, Including Hawaii and Puerto Rico (with David S. Dobkin and Darryl Wheye) 1992, The Stork and the Plow (with A. H. Ehrlich and G. C. Daily) 1995, A World of Wounds: Ecologists and the Human Dilemma 1997, Betrayal of Science and Reason: How Anti-Environment Rhetoric Threatens Our Future (with A. H. Ehrlich) 1998, Human Natures: Genes, Cultures, and the Human Prospect 2002, One With Nineveh: Politics, Consumption and the Human Future (with A. H. Ehrlich) 2004, The Dominant Animal: Human Evolution and the Environment (with A. H. Ehrlich) 2008; co-ed.: Man and the Ecosphere: Readings from Scientific American (with J. P. Holdren and R. W. Holm) 1971, Global Ecology (with J. P. Holdren) 1971, Human Ecology: Problems and Solutions (with A. H. Ehrlich and J. P. Holdren) 1973, Introductory Biology 1973, Ark II (with D. Pirages) 1974, The Process of Evolution (with R. W. Holm and D. R. Parnell) 1974, The End of Affluence (with A. H. Ehrlich) 1974, Biology and Society (with R. W. Holm and I. Brown) 1976, Ecoscience: Population, Resources, Environment (with A. H. Ehrlich and J. P. Holdren) 1977, Introduction to Insect Biology and Diversity (with H. V. Daly and J. T. Doyen) 1978, Machinery of Nature 1986, Wild Solutions 2001, Butterflies: Ecology and Evolution taking Flight (with Carol Boggs and Ward Watt) 2003, On the Wings of Checkerspots: A Model System for Population Biology (with Ilkka Hanski) 2004, The Dominant Animal (with Anne Ehrlich) 2008, Humanity on a Tightrope (with Robert E.Ornstein) 2010; numerous scientific and popular articles. *Leisure interest:* collecting primitive art. *Address:* Department of Biology, HERRIN 409, Stanford University, Stanford, CA 94305-5020, USA (office). *Telephone:* (650) 723-3171 (office). *Fax:* (650) 723-5920 (office). *Website:* www.stanford.edu/group/CCB/Staff/Ehrlich.html (office).

EHRLICH, Robert L., Jr, BA, JD; American lawyer and fmr politician; *Attorney at Law, Womble Carlyle Sandridge & Rice PLLC;* b. 25 Nov. 1957, Arbutus, Md; s. of Bob Ehrlich and Nancy Ehrlich; m. Kendel Sibiski; one c.; ed Gilman School, Princeton Univ., Wake Forest Univ. Law School; Assoc., Ober, Kaler, Grimes and Shriver (law firm) 1982–92, Of Counsel 1992–94; mem. Md House of Dels 1987–95; mem. US House of Reps, Washington, DC 1995–2003; Gov. of Md 2003–07; Attorney at Law, Womble Carlyle Sandridge & Rice PLLC, Baltimore 2007–; co-host (with wife) talk show on WBAL radio; unsuccessful cand. for Gov. of Md 2010; Republican; Outstanding Young Marylander, Md Jaycees 1995, Legislator of the Year, Biotechnology Industry Org., Spirit of Enterprise Award, US Chamber of Commerce, Guardian of Small Business, Nat. Fed. of Ind. Business 1987–90, Fed. Official of the Year, Nat. Industries for the Blind. *Address:* Womble Carlyle Sandridge & Rice PLLC, 250 West Pratt Street, Baltimore, MD 21201, USA (office). *Telephone:* (410) 545-5807 (office). *Fax:* (410) 694-0872 (office). *E-mail:* Robert.Ehrlich@wcsr.com (office). *Website:* www.wcsr.com (office).

EHRLICH, Thomas, BA, LLB; American lawyer, academic and fmr university president; b. 4 March 1934, Cambridge, Mass; s. of William Ehrlich and Evelyn Seltzer; m. Ellen Rome Ehrlich 1957; two s. one d.; ed Harvard Coll. and Harvard Law School, Cambridge, Mass; law clerk, US Court of Appeals, New York 1959–60; Assoc., Foley, Sammond & Lardner (law firm), Milwaukee, Wis. 1960–62; Special Asst to Legal Adviser, US Dept of State, Washington, DC 1962–65, to Under-Sec. of State George W. Ball 1964–65; Prof., Stanford Univ. Law School, Stanford, Calif. 1965–71, Dean and Richard E. Lang Prof. 1971–75; Pres. Legal Services Corpn, Washington, DC 1976–79; Dir Int. Devt Co-operating Agency, Washington, DC 1979–80; Guest Scholar, The Brookings Inst. 1981; Provost and Prof. of Law, Univ. of Pa, Phila 1982–87; Pres. Ind. Univ. 1987–94; Distinguished Univ. Scholar, Calif. State Univ., San Francisco 1995–2000; Sr Scholar, Carnegie Foundation for the Advancement of Teaching 1997–2010; Visiting Prof., Stanford Univ. School of Educ. 2009–; fmr Dir, Public Welfare Foundation; fmr Trustee, Univ. of Pennsylvania, Bennett Coll., Mills Coll. and many other orgs; mem. American Acad. of Arts and Sciences; Hon. LLD (Villanova) 1979, (Notre Dame) 1980, (Univ. of Pennsylvania) 1987, (Indiana), (Univ. of the Pacific) 2003. *Publications:* The International Legal Process (with Abram Chayes and Andreas F. Lowenfeld), (three vols) 1968, Supplement 1974, New Directions in Legal Education (with Herbert L. Packer) 1972, International Crises and the Role of Law, Cyprus 1958–67 1974, International Law and the Use of Force (with Mary Ellen O'Connell) 1993, The Courage to Inquire 1995, The Future of Philanthropy and the Nonprofit Sector in a Changing America (co-ed. with Charles T. Clotfelter) 1999, Higher Education and Civic Responsibility 2000, Educating Citizens (with Anne Colby, Elizabeth Beaumont and Jason Stephens) 2003, Reconnecting Education and Foundations: Turning Good Intentions into Educational Capital 2007, Educating for Democracy (with Anne Colby, Elizabeth Beaumont and Josh Corngold) 2007, Rethinking Undergraduate Business Education: Liberal Learning for the Profession (with Anne Colby, William Sullivan and Jonathan Dolle) 2011, Civic Work, Civic Lessons (with Ernestine Fu) 2013; numerous articles, reviews and other publs. *Address:* Stanford University, School of Education, CERAS, Room 226, 520 Galvez Mall, Stanford, CA 94305, USA (office). *Telephone:* (650) 721-2500 (office). *Fax:* (650) 723-7578 (office). *E-mail:* tehrlich@stanford.edu (office). *Website:* www.stanford.edu (office).

EHRLING, Marie, BSc (Econs); Swedish business executive; *Vice-Chairman, Nordea Bank AB;* b. 1955; m.; one s.; ed Stockholm School of Econs; Financial Analyst 4th Swedish Nat. Pension Fund 1977–79, Information Officer Ministry of Education 1979–80, Ministry of Finance 1980–82; Deputy CEO, SAS Group, also COO SAS Airlines and other exec. positions within SAS Group 1982–2002; Pres. TeliaSonera Sweden 2003–06; mem. Bd of Dirs Securitas AB 2006–, Nordea Bank AB 2007– (Vice-Chair. 2013–), Oriflame Cosmetic SA 2007–, Schibsted ASA 2007–, Safegate AB 2007–, Loomis AB 2008–, World Childhood Foundation, Royal Swedish Acad. of Eng Sciences; Chair. Norwegian Swedish Chamber of Commerce; ranked by Fortune magazine amongst 50 Most Powerful Women in Business outside the US (27th) 2003, (21st) 2004, (21st) 2005, ranked by Forbes magazine amongst 100 Most Powerful Women (85th) 2006, ranked by the Financial Times amongst Top 25 Businesswomen in Europe (18th) 2005, (15th) 2006.

EHRMAN, Sir William Geoffrey, KCMG; British diplomatist; b. 28 Aug. 1950; m. Penelope Anne Le Patourel; one s. three d.; ed Eton Coll., Trinity Coll., Cambridge; joined FCO 1973; language study, Hong Kong 1973–76; Third Sec., later Second Sec. Beijing 1976–78; First Sec. Perm. Mission to UN, New York 1979–83; First Sec. Beijing 1983–84; Hong Kong and Security Policy Depts, FCO 1985–89, Political Adviser Hong Kong 1989–93, Head Near East and North Africa Dept, FCO 1993–94; mem. Bosnia Contact Group 1994–95; Prin. Pvt. Sec. to Foreign Sec. 1995–97; with Unilever China 1997–98; Amb. to Luxembourg 1998–2000; Dir of Int. Security, FCO 2000–02, Dir-Gen. of Defence and Intelligence 2002–04; Chair. Jt Intelligence Cttee, Cabinet Office 2004–05; Amb. to People's Repub. of China 2006–10; mem. Locarno Group (supports devt and implementation of FCO foreign policy) 2012–. *Address:* Foreign and Commonwealth Office, King Charles Street, London, SW1A 2AH, England (office). *Telephone:* (20) 7008-1500 (office). *E-mail:* fcocorrespondence@fco.gov.uk (office). *Website:* www.gov.uk/government/organisations/foreign-commonwealth-office (office).

EHSAS, Mohammad Qasim; Afghan trade union official; fmr mem. Parcham (leftist party); fmr Deputy Minister of Commerce; cand. in elections 2005; fmr Pres. of Cen. Council Nat. Union of Afghanistan Employees; adviser to Workers' Del., 95th Session of ILO Conf., Geneva 2006. *Address:* c/o Central Council of National Union of Afghanistan Employees, Aryana Square in front of Urdu Puplication Department, Shashdarak, POB 756, Kabul, Afghanistan.

EIBL-EIBESFELDT, Irenäus, DrPhil; Austrian zoologist and academic; *Head of Human Ethology Film Archive, Max-Planck Institute, Andechs;* b. 15 June 1928, Vienna; s. of Anton Eibl-Eibesfeldt and Maria Eibl-Eibesfeldt (née von Hauninger); m. Eleonore Siegel 1950; one s. one d.; ed Univ. of Vienna, Univ. of Munich, Germany; Research Assoc., Biology Station, Wilhelminenstr, nr Vienna 1946–48, Max Planck Inst. of Behavioural Physiology 1951–69; Head of ind. research unit on human ethology, Max Planck Inst. 1970–96, Emer. Researcher and Head Human Ethology Film Archive 1996–; Lecturer, Univ. of Munich 1963, Prof. 1970; Hon. Scientific Dir Int. Inst. for Submarine Research, Vaduz 1957–70; Head of Ludwig-Boltzmann-Inst. for Urban Ethology, Vienna 1992–; mem. Humanwissenschaftliches Zentrum, Ludwig-Maximilians-Univ., Munich 1997, Deutsche Akad. der Naturforscher 1977; Founding mem. and Pro-Dekan European Acad. of Arts and Sciences; Pres. Int. Soc. for Human Ethology 1985–93; Corresp. mem. Deutsche Akad. der Naturforscher Leopoldina, Fellow, Animal Behavior Soc.; Bundesverdienstkreuz (Germany) 1995, Bayerischer Verdienstorden 1997, Österreichisches Ehrenkreuz für Wissenschaft und Kunst 1998; Dr hc (Salamanca) 1994; Wilhelm Bölsche Gold Medal 1971, Burda Prize for Communications Research 1980, Philip Morris Research Prize 1988, Gold Medal of Honour (City of Vienna) 1989, Schwenk'scher Umweltpreis 1996, Haackert Medal for Research on Human Ethology 1997, Jahrespreis von STAB, Zurich 1997, Premio Nonino 2011 and many others. *Publications:* Galapagos, die Arche Noah im Pacific 1960, Im Reich der tausend Atolle 1964, Grundriss der vergleichenden Verhaltensforschung 1967, Liebe und Hass 1970, Die ko-Buschmanngesellschaft 1972, Der vorprogrammierte Mensch 1973, Menschenforschung auf neuen Wegen 1976, Der Hai: Legende eines Mörders (with H. Hass) 1977, Die Malediven. Paradies im Indischen Ozean 1982, Die Biologie des menschlichen Verhaltens, Grundriss der Humanethologie 1984, Der Mensch – das riskierte Wesen 1988, Human Ethology 1989, Das verbindende Erbe 1991, Und grün des Lebens goldner Baum 1992, Im Banne der Angst (co-author) 1992, Wider die Misstrauensgesellschaft 1994, In der Falle des Kurzzeitdenkens 1998, Weltsprache Kunst (co-author) 2007. *Leisure interests:* skin diving, skiing, arts. *Address:* Humanethologisches Filmarchiv in der Max Planck Gesellschaft, Von-der-Tann-Strasse 3-5, 82346 Andechs (office); Fichtenweg 9, 82319 Starnberg, Germany (home). *Telephone:* (8152) 373157 (office); (8152) 373159 (office); (8151) 746607 (home). *Fax:* (8152) 373170 (office). *E-mail:* eibl@orn .mpg.de (office). *Website:* erl.ornithol.mpg.de/~fshuman/index.html (office).

EICHEL, Hans; German politician; b. 24 Dec. 1941, Kassel; m.; two c.; ed Univs of Marburg and Berlin; fmr schoolmaster; mem. Kassel City Council 1968–75, Chair. Social Democratic Party (SDP) Group 1970–75; mem. Nat. Exec. of Young Socialists 1969–72; Chief Mayor of Kassel 1975–91; mem. SDP Nat. Exec. and Spokesman on Local Govt 1984; Chair. SDP Asscn Hesse 1989; Minister-Pres. of Hesse 1991–99; Federal Minister of Finance 1999–2005. *Address:* Pappenheimstraße 10, 34119 Kassel, Germany (home). *Telephone:* (561) 9371170 (office), (561) 9885091 (home). *Fax:* (561) 9371172 (office), (561) 9885092 (home). *E-mail:* hans.eichel@t-online.de. *Website:* www.hans-eichel-kassel.de.

EICHELBAUM, Rt Hon. Sir (Johann) Thomas, GBE, PC; New Zealand lawyer and judge (retd); b. 17 May 1931, Koenigsberg, Germany; s. of Dr Walter Eichelbaum and Frida M. Eichelbaum; m. Vida Beryl Franz 1956; three s.; ed Hutt Valley High School and Victoria Univ. Coll.; admitted solicitor 1953, barrister 1954; Partner, Chapman Tripp & Co. 1958–78; QC 1978; barrister 1978–82; Pres. NZ Law Soc. 1980–82; Judge, High Court of NZ 1982; Chief Justice of NZ 1989–99; Judge of Appeal, Fiji 1999–2007; Non-Perm. Judge, Court of Final Appeal Hong Kong 2000–09; Privy Councillor 1989–; Chair. Royal Comm. on Genetic Modification 2000–01; Hon. LLD (Vic. Univ. of Wellington) 1998. *Publications:* Mauet's Fundamentals of Trial Techniques (Ed.-in-Chief) 1989, Introduction to Advocacy (Consulting Ed.) 2000. *Leisure interests:* reading, walking. *Address:* Raumati Beach, New Zealand. *E-mail:* thoseich@xtra.co.nz.

EICHHORN, Lisa; American actress; b. 2 April 1952, Glen Falls, NY; ed Queen's Univ. Ontario, St Peter's Coll., Oxford and Royal Acad. of Dramatic Art UK. *Films include:* Yanks 1979, The Europeans 1979, Why Would I Lie? 1980, Cutter and Bone (Cutter's Way) 1981, The Weather in the Streets 1983, Wildrose 1984, Opposing Force (Hell Camp) 1986, Grim Prairie Tales 1990, Moon 44 1990, Grim Prairie Tales 1990, King of the Hill 1993, The Vanishing 1993, Mr 247 1994, A Modern Affair 1995, Sticks and Stones 1996, First Kid 1996, Judas Kiss 1998, The Talented Mr Ripley 1999, Goodbye Lover 1999, Boys and Girls 2000, Things Left Unsaid 2000, Things I Don't Understand 2012. *Television includes:* Diana: A Tribute to the People's Princess 1998, My Neighbor's Daughter 1998, Kenneth Tynan: In Praise of Hardcore 2005, Cracker 2006. *Stage appearances include:* roles in British Shakespearean productions, A Doll's House, A Golden Boy, The Speed of Darkness, The Summer Winds, The Common Pursuit, The Hasty Heart, Pass/Fail, Arms and the Man, Misfits 1996.

EICHLER, Ralph, PhD; Swiss physicist, academic and research institute director; *President, Swiss Federal Institute of Technology (ETH Zurich);* b. 31 Dec. 1947, Guildford, Surrey, England; m.; three c.; ed Swiss Fed. Inst. of Tech. (ETH Zurich); Postdoctoral Fellow, Stanford Univ., USA 1977–79; Scientist, Deutsches Elektronen Synchrotron (DESY), Hamburg 1979–82; Scientist, Inst. for Medium-Energy Physics, ETH Zurich 1982–86, Project Leader 1988–90, Assoc. Prof. of Physics 1989–91, Prof. 1993–, Pres. ETH Zurich 2007–; Deputy Dir Paul Scherrer Inst. 1998–2002, Dir 2002–07. *Address:* ETH Zurich, HG F 59, Rämistrasse 101, 8092 Zurich, Switzerland (office). *Telephone:* (44) 632-20-17 (office). *Fax:* (44) 632-10-01 (office). *E-mail:* ralph.eichler@sl.ethz.ch (office). *Website:* www.sl.ethz.ch/people/eichler/index_EN (office).

EICK, Karl-Gerhard, PhD; German business executive; *Chairman of the Management Board and CEO, Arcandor AG;* b. 1954; ed Univ. of Augsburg; worked in various positions for BMW AG, Munich, including as Head of Controlling in Chair.'s Div. –1988; Head of Controlling, WMF AG 1989–91; Head of Controlling, Planning and IT Div., Carl Zeiss Group 1991–93; worked with Franz Haniel & Cie GmbH, Duisburg 1993–99, mem. Bd of Man. Haniel Group co. Gehe AG, Stuttgart 1993–98, mem. Man. Bd Franz Haniel & Cie GmbH 1998–99; mem. Bd of Man. Deutsche Telekom AG 2000–, Head of Finance Div., Deputy Chair. 2004–; Chair. Man. Bd and CEO Arcandor AG 2009–. *Address:* Arcandor AG, Theodor-Althoff-Strasse 2, 45133 Essen, Germany (office). *Telephone:* (201) 727-1 (office). *Fax:* (201) 727-5216 (office). *E-mail:* info@arcandor.com (office). *Website:* www.arcandor.com (office).

EIDE, Espen Barth, CandPolit; Norwegian politician; b. 1 May 1964; m.; three s.; ed Univ. of Oslo, Autonomous Univ. of Barcelona; Sr Researcher, Norwegian Inst. of Int. Affairs 1993–99, Dir, Dept of Int. Politics 2002–05; Sec. of State, Ministry of Foreign Affairs 2000–01, Deputy Minister 2010–11; Sec. of State, Ministry of Defence 2005–10, Minister of Defence 2011–12, Minister of Foreign Affairs 2012–13; several assignments for UN, including expert adviser to High-Level Panel on UN Reform 2005; mem. Presidency, Party of European Socialists 2001–; mem. Det norske Arbeiderparti. *Address:* c/o Ministry of Foreign Affairs, 7 juni place, POB 8114 Dep., 0032 Oslo, Norway (office).

EIFMAN, Boris Yakovlevich; Russian choreographer; *Artistic Director, St Petersburg Ballet Theatre Boris Eifman;* b. 22 July 1946, Rubtsovsk, Altai Region; s. of Yankel Borisovich Eifman and Klara Markovna Kuris; m. Valentina Nikolayevna Morozova; one s.; ed Kishinev School of Choreography, Leningrad State Conservatory; Balletmaster, Leningrad School of Choreography 1970–77; concurrently ballet productions in professional theatres including Firebird (Kirov Theatre 1975); Founder and Artistic Dir Leningrad Ensemble of Ballet (now St Petersburg Ballet Theatre Boris Eifman) 1977; Chevalier des Arts et des Lettres 1999; People's Artist of Russia 1995, Golden Baton Prize 1995, 1996, 1997, 2001, 2005, Triumph Prize 1996, Golden Mask Prize 1996, 1999, Russian State Prize 1999, Best Choreographer, Benois de la Dance 2006. *Ballets include:* Before Firebird – Gayaney 1972, Idiot (Tchaikovsky's 6th Symphony) 1980, Marriage of Figaro 1982, The Legend 1982, Twelfth Night 1984, The Duel (after Kuprin) 1986, Master and Margarita (after Bulgakov) 1987, Thérèse Raquin 1991, Requiem (Mozart) 1991, Tchaikovsky 1993, Don Quixote or Madman's Fantasy (Minkus) 1994, Brothers Karamazov (after Dostoyevsky) 1995, Red Giselle 1997, My Jerusalem 1998, Russian Hamlet 1999, Don Juan 2001, Who is Who? 2003, Musagete 2004, Anna Karenina 2005, The Seagull 2007, Rodin 2011. *Address:* St Petersburg Ballet Theatre Boris Eifman, 197198 St Petersburg, ul. Liza Chaikina 2, Russia (office). *Telephone:* (812) 232-23-70 (office). *Fax:* (812) 232-18-62 (office). *E-mail:* eifman@inbox.ru (home). *Website:* eifmanballet.ru (office).

EIGEN, Manfred, Dr rer. nat; German physical chemist and academic; b. 9 May 1927, Bochum; s. of Ernst Eigen and Hedwig Feld; m. Elfriede Müller; one s. one d.; ed Georg-August-Univ. zu Göttingen; Max-Planck Inst. of Physical Chem., Göttingen, as Asst, later as Head of Dept 1953–, Dir 1964; Hon. Prof., Technical Univ., Braunschweig 1965–; Pres. Studienstiftung des Deutschen Volkes 1983–; mem. Akad. der Wissenschaften, Göttingen; Foreign Assoc. mem. NAS; Foreign mem. Royal Soc., UK, Acad. Française 1978; Foreign hon. mem. American Acad. of Arts and Sciences; Dr hc (Univ. of Washington, St Louis), (Harvard Univ.), (Cambridge Univ.) and numerous other hon. degrees; Otto Hahn Prize 1967; Nobel Prize for Chem. (jt recipient). *Achievements include:* investigated extremely rapid chemical reactions by means of disturbing the (molecular) equilibrium by the action of very short energy pulses 1967. *Address:* Max Planck Inst. for Biophysical Chemistry, Am Fassberg 11, 37077 Göttingen, Germany (office). *Telephone:* (551) 2011432 (office). *Fax:* (551) 2011435 (office). *Website:* www.mpibpc.mpg.de (office).

EIJK, HE Cardinal Willem Jacobus, MDiv, PhD, SDL; Dutch ecclesiastic and academic; *Archbishop of Utrecht;* b. 22 June 1953, Duivendrecht, North Holland; ed Coll., Univ. of Amsterdam, Seminary of Rolduc, Kerkrade, Univ. of Leiden, Pontifical Univ. of St Thomas Aquinas (Angelicum) and Pontifical Lateran Univ., Rome; ordained priest, Diocese of Roermond 1985; work as a curate in Parish of St Anthony of Padua, Venlo Blerick; taught moral theology at seminary of Rolduc; Prof. of Moral Theology, Pontifical Faculty of Theology, Lugano, Switzerland 1997–99; mem. Int. Theological Comm. 1997–2002; Bishop of Groningen-Leeuwarden 1999–2007; Archbishop of Utrecht 2008–; cr. Cardinal (Cardinal-Priest of San Callisto) 2012; participated in Papal Conclave 2013; mem. Congregation for the Clergy 2008–, Congregation of Catholic Educ., Pontifical Acad. for Life. *Publications:* De zelfgekozen dood naar aanleiding van een dodelijke en ongeneelijke ziekte 1987, The Ethical Problems of Genetic Engineering of Human Beings 1990, Handboek katholieke medische ethiek (co-ed.) 2010; contrib. of articles in books, periodicals and newspapers. *Leisure interest:* organ-playing. *Address:* Aartsbisdom, PO Box 14019, 3508 SB Utrecht (office); Aartsbisdom, Maliebaan 38–40, 3581 CR Utrecht, The Netherlands (office). *Telephone:* (30) 233-80-30 (office). *Fax:* (30) 231-19-62 (office). *E-mail:* aartsbisschop@aartsbisdom.nl (office). *Website:* www.aartsbisdom.nl (office).

EINARSSON, Sveinn, PhD; Icelandic theatre director and author; b. 18 Sept. 1934, Reykjavik; s. of Einar Ól Sveinsson and Kristjana Thorsteinsdóttir; m. Thora Kristjánsdóttir 1964; one d.; ed Univ. of Stockholm, Univ. of Paris, Sorbonne, Univ. of Iceland; Artistic Dir Reykjavik Theatre Co. 1963–72 (Hon. mem. 1991); Prin. Reykjavik Theatre School 1963–70; Gen. Man. and Artistic Dir Nat. Theatre of Iceland 1972–83; Head of Programme Production, Icelandic State TV 1989–93; Counsellor, Ministry of Culture 1983–89, 1993–2004; Chair. Icelandic Nat. Comm. for UNESCO 1995–; Artistic Dir Reykjavik Arts Festival 1998–2001; Vice-Pres. Int. Theatre Inst. 1979–81; mem. (part-time) Faculty, Univ. of Iceland 1970–; now freelance director and author; has directed over 90 productions (including opera) on stage and TV in Iceland, the Nordic countries, UK and Germany; productions also presented in Venezuela, Canada, the Baltic States and Korea (Theatre of Nations); several appointments with the Council of Europe: Chair. several cultural cttees; Vice-Pres. Nordic Theatre Union 1975–82; mem. Exec. Bd UNESCO 2001–05; hon. mem. of several socs etc.; Paul Harris Fellow Rotary Club of Reykjavik 2004, Hon. mem. The Nordic Theatre Union 2008; Officer, Order of White Rose of Finland, Order of Merit (Norway), Commdr, Swedish Nordstjärnan, Commdr, Ordre des Arts et Lettres (France) 2004; Children's Book of Year Award 1986, Clara Lachmann Prize 1990, First Prize, Short Story Competition, 50th Anniversary of Repub. of Iceland 1994, Jón Sigurdsson Prize 1997, Best Theatre Production Award 2003, Hon. Award for Lifetime Achievement in the Theatre 2003. *Plays:* Egg of Life 1983, I'm Gold and Treasures 1984, Bukolla 1991, Bandamannasaga 1992, The Amlodi Saga 1996, The Daughter of the Poet 1998,

Edda 2000. *Television:* (plays) A Stop on My Way 1971, Time is in No Harmony with Me 1993. *Publications include:* on theatre: Theatre By the Lake 1972, My Nine Years Down There 1987, Íslensk Leiklist (History of Icelandic Theatre) Vol. I 1991, Vol. II 1996, My Eleven Years Up There 2000, A People's Theatre Comes of Age 2007, Leiklisten i veröldinni (The Theatre in the World) 2007; novel: The Electricity Man 1998; children's books: Gabriella in Portugal 1985, Dordingull 1994. *Leisure interests:* music, skiing, forestry. *Address:* Ministry of Culture, Solvholsgata 4, 101 Reykjavik (office); Tjarnargata 26, 101 Reykjavik, Iceland (home). *Telephone:* 551-4032 (home); 545-9500 (office). *Fax:* 562-3068 (office). *E-mail:* sveinn.einarsson@mrn.stjr.is.

EINAUDI, Luigi R., AB, PhD; American international organization official, diplomatist and academic; m. Carol Peacock 1958; two s. two d.; ed Harvard Univ.; served in US Army 1957–59; Teaching Fellow, Harvard Univ. 1960–61; instructor, Wesleyan Univ. 1961–62; researcher, RAND Corpn, Santa Monica, Calif. 1962–73; Visiting Prof., UCLA 1964–73; mem. Policy Planning Staff, Office of Sec. of State, Washington, DC 1974–77, Dir Inter-American Regional Planning Office 1977–89, Sr Advisor, Policy Planning Staff 1993–97, Acting Dir 1994; Amb. to OAS, Washington, DC 1989–93; US Special Envoy to Ecuador–Peru Peace Talks 1995–98; worked on multilateral governance and conflict resolution at Inter-American Dialogue, Washington, DC 1998–2000; Asst Sec.-Gen. OAS 2000–04, Sec.-Gen. 2004–05, Special Rep. of OAS Sec.-Gen. in Honduras–Nicaragua boundary dispute 1999; mem. Council on Foreign Relations; recipient of decorations from Pres. of Ecuador and Peru; recipient of awards from Presidents Jimmy Carter, Ronald Reagan, George Bush and Secretaries of State Henry Kissinger, Madeleine Albright, Frasure Award for Peace-keeping 1997, seven other medal citations from US Depts of State and Defense; Terry Woods Memorial Award, OAS 2005. *Publications include:* Beyond Cuba, Latin America Takes Charge of Its Future 1974; numerous articles and monographs. *Address:* c/o Organization of American States, 17th and Constitution Avenue, NW, Washington, DC 20006, USA (office).

EINHORN, Jessica P., MA, PhD; American academic and fmr government official; *Dean, Paul H. Nitze School of Advanced International Studies (SAIS), Johns Hopkins University;* b. 1948; ed Barnard Coll., Columbia Univ., Paul H. Nitze School of Advanced Int. Studies (SAIS), Princeton Univ. LSE, London, Brookings Inst., Harvard Univ.; various roles with US Treasury, US State Dept and Int. Devt Cooperation Agency of USA –1992; Vice-Pres. and Treasurer, World Bank 1992–96, Man. Dir 1996-98; Visiting Fellow, IMF 1998–99; Consultant, Clark & Weinstock, Washington 1999–2002; Dean, Paul H. Nitze School of Advanced Int. Studies (SAIS), Johns Hopkins Univ. 2002–; Trustee Rockefeller Brothers Fund; Dir Council on Foreign Relations, Inst. for Int. Econs, Center for Global Devt; Dir Pitney Bowes Inc. 1999–; Chair. Global Advisory Bd J.E. Robert Cos; mem. Cttee Trilateral Comm.; fmr Trustee German Marshall Fund. *Publications:* Expropriation Politics 1974; various articles. *Address:* Paul H. Nitze School of Advanced International Studies, 1740 Massachusetts Avenue, NW, Washington, DC 20036, USA (office). *Telephone:* (202) 663-5624 (office). *Fax:* (202) 663-5621 (office). *E-mail:* jeinhorn@jhu.edu (office). *Website:* www.sais-jhu.edu (office).

EINIK, M. Michael, MBA; American organization official and fmr diplomatist; *Deputy Executive Director, Partnering and Sustainability Department, International Science and Technology Center;* b. 1949, New York; ed Univ. of Miami, George Washington Univ., Washington, DC; joined Dept of State 1972; Econ./Commercial Officer Brasilia, then San Salvador; with Bureau of Econ. and Business Affairs, Dept of State; staff Asst to Asst Sec. of State; worked in Office of Fuels and Energy during 1970s oil crisis; Petroleum Officer, Embassy, Nigeria 1981; served in Econ. Section, Moscow; Prin. Officer, Consulate-Gen., Zagreb representing US in both Croatia and Slovenia 1988–92; Chief of Personnel, European Bureau 1992–94; Deputy Chief of Mission, Bucharest; Amb. to Macedonia 1999–2002; Chair. AMGAZ SA 2002–07; Pres. Netcare Healthcare Central Europe (Netcare CE) 2004; Exec. Dir Project on Ethnic Relations (PER) Regional Center for Cen., Eastern and Southeastern Europe, Bucharest, Romania 2005–07; Chair. and Pnr, Ratz De Nagylak (ecologically friendly hotel village under development in Transylvania) 2006; Pnr, Cube Consulting, Romania 2007–; Deputy Exec. Dir Partnering and Sustainability Dept, International Science and Technology Center, Moscow, Russia 2009–; mem. Bd of Dirs Bulgarian American Business Center. *Address:* International Science and Technology Center, 127473 Moscow, Krasnoproletarskaya 32-34, Russia (office). *Telephone:* (495) 982-3200 (office). *Fax:* (499) 982-3201 (office). *E-mail:* istcinfo@istc.ru (office). *Website:* www.istc.ru (office).

EISELE, Lt-Gen. Manfred S.; German army officer; b. 17 March 1938, Wilhelmshaven; s. of Wilhelm Eisele and Gertrud Eisele-Meyer; m. Elke Krümpelmann 1962; two d.; ed Blankenese High School, Mil. Acad., Gen. Staff Acad., Hamburg, USA Command and Gen. Staff Coll. and Royal Coll. of Defence Studies; Commdg Officer, Artillery-Bn 125, Bayreuth 1977–78; Chef de Cabinet/Chief of Gen. Staff, Bonn 1978–80; Head of Public Information, Ministry of Defence 1980–81; Commdg Officer, Mechanized Infantry Brigade 17, Hamburg 1984–88; Chief, Combat Requirements Brigade, Supreme HQ Allied Forces Europe (SHAPE), Mons, Belgium 1988–91; Dir Politico-Military Affairs, Ministry of Defence, Bonn 1991–92; Commdg Officer, 12th Panzer Div. Würzburg 1992–94, Armed Forces Office, Bonn 1994; Asst Sec.-Gen. UN Dept of Peace-Keeping Operations 1994; Bundesverdienstkreuz, Legion of Merit, USA, Grand Cross, Rider of Vadar, Bulgaria; Dag Hammarskjöld Medal. *Publications:* Die Vereinten Nationen und das Internationale Krisenmanagement (preface by Kofi Annan) 2000. *Leisure interests:* international politics, history, music, sport. *Address:* Ravensburgstrasse 2B, 97209 Veitshöchheim, Germany. *Telephone:* (931) 9500055. *Fax:* (931) 9500042. *E-mail:* E.u.M.Eisele@t-online.de (home).

EISEN, Herman Nathaniel, AB, MD; American immunologist, microbiologist and academic; *Professor Emeritus of Immunology, Massachusetts Institute of Technology;* b. (Nathan H. Eisen), 15 Oct. 1918, Brooklyn, NY; s. of Joseph M. Eisen and Lena M. Eisen (née Karush); m. Natalie Aronson 1948; three s. two d.; ed New York Univ., Washington Univ. in St Louis; Prof. of Medicine (Dermatology), Washington Univ., St Louis 1955–61, Prof. of Microbiology and Head of Dept 1961–73; Dermatologist-in-Chief, Barnes Hosp. 1955–61; Prof. of Immunology, MIT 1973–89, Whitehead Inst. Prof. of Immunology 1982–89, Prof. Emer. 1989–;

mem. Bd Scientific Advisers Mass Gen. Hosp., Boston 1977–, Boston Children's Hosp. 1976–, Howard Hughes Medical Inst., Merck Sharp & Dohme Research Labs, Rahway 1976–; Consultant to Surgeons-Gen. of Public Health Service, Dept of the Army; Chair. Study Section for Allergy and Immunology, NIH 1964–68; mem. Advisory Bd/Visiting Comm., Harvard School of Public Health, Yale Medical School; mem. Editorial Bd Journal of Immunology, Bacteriological Reviews, Physiological Reviews, Proceedings of the NAS; mem. American Soc. for Clinical Investigation (Vice-Pres. 1963–64), American Asscn of Immunologists (Pres. 1968–69), American Soc. for Biological Chemists, American Asscn of Physicians, Inst. of Medicine, NAS, American Acad. of Arts and Sciences; Hon. ScD (Washington Univ.) 2003; Harvey Soc. Lecturer 1965, New York Univ. Medical Science Achievement Award 1978, Dupont Award, Clinical Ligand Soc. 1987, Outstanding Investigator Award, Nat. Cancer Inst. 1986, Lifetime Achievement/Service Award, American Asscn of Immunologists 1991, Behring-Heidelberger Award, American Asscn of Immunologists 1993. *Publications:* Methods in Medical Research Vol. 10 (ed.) 1964, Microbiology (co-author) 1967–90, Immunology 1974–90 (four edns), Contemporary Topics in Molecular Immunology Vol. 5 (ed.) 1976; more than 230 scientific articles. *Leisure interest:* landscape gardening. *Address:* Center for Cancer Research, Massachusetts Institute of Technology, Room E17-128, 77 Massachusetts Avenue, Cambridge, MA 02139-4307 (office); 9 Homestead Street, Waban, MA 02168, USA (home). *Telephone:* (617) 253-6406 (office). *Fax:* (617) 258-6172 (office). *E-mail:* hneisen@mit.edu (office). *Website:* mit.edu/biology/www/facultyareas/facresearch/eisen.html (office).

EISENBERG, David S., AB, DPhil; American biochemist, biophysicist and academic; *Professor, University of California, Los Angeles;* b. 15 March 1939, Chicago, Ill.; ed Harvard Univ., Univ. of Oxford, UK (Rhodes Scholar); Postdoctoral Researcher, Princeton Univ. 1964–66, California Inst. of Tech. 1966–69; Prof., Dept of Chem. and Biochemistry, UCLA 1969–, Prof., Dept of Biological Chem., UCLA Medical School, Dir UCLA-DOE Inst. for Genomics and Proteomics 1993–, mem. California NanoSystems Inst.; Investigator, Howard Hughes Medical Inst. 2001–; Pres. Protein Soc. 1988–89; Ed. Advances in Protein Chemistry 1988–; mem. NAS 1989, American Acad. of Arts and Sciences 1991; Fellow, AAAS 2001; Hon. Fellow, The Queen's Coll., Oxford 2010; L.J. Henderson Prize 1961, Harvard Coll. Honorary Scholarships 1958–60, Career Devt Award, US Public Health Service 1972–77, UCLA Distinguished Teaching Award 1975, McCoy Award, UCLA Dept of Chem. and Biochemistry 1982, Pierce Award, Immunotoxin Soc. 1992, Stein & Moore Award, Protein Soc. 1996, ACS Repligen Corpn Award in Chem. of Biological Processes 1998, Amgen Award, Protein Soc. 2000, Seaborg Medal, UCLA 2004, Westheimer Medal, Harvard Univ. 2005, Harvey Prize (Human Health) (co-recipient) 2008, ACS Nobel Laureate Signature Award for Grad. Educ. in Chem. 2008, Emily Gray Award, Biophysical Soc. 2009, Sr Scientist Award, Int. Soc. for Computational Biology 2013. *Publications:* numerous papers in professional journals. *Address:* Department of Chemistry and Biochemistry, University of California, 201A Boyer Hall, 611 Charles Young Drive East, Los Angeles, CA 90095-1569, USA (office). *Telephone:* (310) 825-3754 (office). *Fax:* (310) 206-3914 (office). *E-mail:* david@mbi.ucla.edu (office). *Website:* www.doe-mbi.ucla.edu/People/Eisenberg (office).

EISENBERG, Jesse Adam; American actor; b. 5 Oct. 1983, New York; s. of Barry Eisenberg and Amy Eisenberg; ed The New School, New York. *Television includes:* Get Real 1999, Lightning: Fire from the Sky 2001. *Films include:* Roger Dodger (San Diego Film Festival Award for Most Promising New Actor) 2002, The Squid and the Whale 2005, The Hunting Party 2007, Adventureland 2009, Zombieland 2009, Solitary Man 2010, Camp Hope 2010, The Social Network (Boston Soc. of Film Critics Award for Best Actor, Nat. Bd of Review Best Actor, Toronto Film Critics Asscn Award for Best Actor, Nat. Soc. of Film Critics Award for Best Actor) 2010, To Rome With Love 2012, Now You See Me 2013, The Double 2013. *Address:* ICM Los Angeles, 10250 Constellation Boulevard, Los Angeles, CA 90067, USA (office). *Telephone:* (310) 550-4000 (office). *Fax:* (310) 550-4100 (office).

EISENMAN, Peter David, BArch, MS, MA, PhD, FAIA; American architect and academic; *Charles Gwathmey Professor in Practice, Yale School of Architecture;* b. 11 Aug. 1932, Newark, NJ; s. of Herschel I. Eisenman and Sylvia H. Heller; m. 1st Elizabeth Henderson 1963 (divorced 1990); one s. one d.; m. 2nd Cynthia Davidson 1990; one s.; ed Cornell Univ., Columbia Univ., Univ. of Cambridge, UK; Founder Inst. of Architecture and Urban Studies, New York 1967, Dir 1967–82; Architect-in-Residence, American Acad., Rome 1976; with Eisenman/Robertson Architects, New York 1980–88; Eisenman Architects 1988–; commissioned to design Berlin Holocaust Memorial; Kea Prof., Univ. of Maryland 1978; apptd Charlotte Davenport Prof., Yale Univ. 1980, Louis I. Kahn Prof. of Architecture 2001, currently Charles Gwathmey Prof. in Practice, Yale School of Architecture; Arthur Rotch Prof., Harvard Univ. 1982–85; apptd Irwin S. Chanin Distinguished Prof. 1986; Louis H. Sullivan Research Prof. of Architecture, Univ. of Illinois 1987–93; John Williams Prof. of Architecture, Univ. of Arkansas 1997; Frank H.T. Rhodes Class of '56 Prof., Cornell Univ. 2008–; mem. American Acad. of Arts and Sciences, American Acad. of Arts and Letters; Hon. DFA (Univ. of Illinois, Pratt Inst., New York, Syracuse Univ.), (Accad. delle Belle Arti di Brera, Milan) 2012; Hon. DArch (Università La Sapienza, Rome) 2003; Arnold W. Brunner Memorial Prize in Architecture, American Acad. and Inst. of Arts and Letters 1984, Medal of Honor, New York Chapter of AIA 2001, Cooper-Hewitt Nat. Design Award in Architecture, Smithsonian Inst. 2001, Golden Lion for Lifetime Achievement, Venice Biennale 2004, Wolf Foundation Prize in the Arts (Architecture) (jtly) 2010. *Principal works include:* Pvt. Residences Princeton, NJ, Hardwick, Vt, Lakeville and Cornwall, Conn. 1968–76, Housing, Koch-Friedrichstrasse, Berlin 1980–86, Wexner Center for Visual Arts, Columbus, Ohio 1983–89, Columbus Convention Centre 1988–93, Univ. of Cincinnati Coll. of Design, Art, Architecture and Planning 1988–96, Koizumi Sangyo Bldg, Tokyo 1989–90, Emory Univ. Art Centre 1991–95, Rebstock Park, Frankfurt, Germany 1991–95, Max Reinhardt Haus, Berlin 1992–, Haus Immendorff, Düsseldorf, Germany 1993–94, Jewish Museum, San Francisco 1996–, Library UN Complex, Geneva 1996–, Staten Island Inst. of Arts and Sciences 1997–2001, Holocaust Memorial, Berlin 1998–2005, City of Culture, Santiago de Compostela, Spain 1999–, Spree Dreieck Tower, Berlin 2000–, Deportivo La Coruña, Spain 2001–, Il Giardino dei Passi Perduti, Verona, Italy 2003, New Hamburg Library, Germany 2005, Univ. of Phoenix Stadium for the Arizona Cardinals (named by Popular Science magazine one of the top five innovators of 2006), Pompei Stazione Santuario, Pompei, Italy 2006–, Sheikh

Zayed Nat. Museum, Abu Dhabi, UAE 2007, Pozzuoli Waterfront Masterplan, Pozzuoli, Italy 2009–. *Publications include:* Written Into the Void: Selected Writings, 1990–2004 2007, Ten Canonical Buildings, 1950–2000 2008. *Address:* Eisenman Architects, 41 West 25th Street, New York, NY 10010-2043, USA (office). *Telephone:* (212) 645-1400 (office). *Fax:* (212) 645-0726 (office). *E-mail:* info@eisenmanarchitects.com (office). *Website:* www.eisenmanarchitects.com (office).

EISGRUBER, Christopher Ludwig, AB, MLitt, JD; American lawyer, constitutional scholar, academic and university administrator; *President, Princeton University;* b. 24 Sept. 1961, Corvallis, Ore.; m. Lori A. Martin; one s.; ed Princeton Univ., Univ. of Oxford (Rhodes Scholar), UK, Univ. of Chicago Law School; grew up in Ore. and Ind.; Ed.-in-Chief of the law review, Univ. of Chicago Law School; clerked for US Court of Appeals Judge Patrick Higginbotham and US Supreme Court Justice John Paul Stevens; taught at New York Univ. School of Law 1990–2001; joined Princeton Faculty as Dir Program in Law and Public Affairs and Laurance S. Rockefeller Prof. of Public Affairs, Woodrow Wilson School of Public and Int. Affairs and Univ. Center for Human Values 2001, directed Princeton's Program in Law and Public Affairs 2001–04, acting Dir Program in Ethics and Public Affairs 2002–03, served as a Faculty Rep. on Alumni Council Exec. Cttee and taught in Alumni Studies programme, Provost 2004–13, Gen. Deputy to Pres. and Chair. Academic Planning Group, Priorities Cttee, Exec. Cttee of Council of Princeton Univ. Community, Pres. Princeton Univ. 2013–. *Publications include:* Constitutional Self-Government 2001, Global Justice and the Bulwarks of Localism: Human Rights in Context (co-ed.) 2005, Religious Freedom and the Constitution (with Lawrence G. Sager) 2007, The Next Justice: Repairing the Supreme Court Appointments Process 2007. *Leisure interest:* supports Chicago Cubs baseball team. *Address:* Office of the President, 1 Nassau Hall, Princeton University, Princeton, NJ 08544, USA (office). *Telephone:* (609) 258-6100 (office). *Fax:* (609) 258-1615 (office). *Website:* www.princeton.edu/president/eisgruber (office).

EISNER, Michael Dammann, BA; American business executive; b. 7 March 1942, Mount Kisco, NY; s. of Lester Dammann and Margaret Dammann; m. Jane Breckenridge 1967; three s.; ed Lawrenceville School, Denison Univ.; Sr Vice-Pres. Prime-Time Production and Devt, ABC Entertainment Corpn 1973–76; Pres. and COO Paramount Pictures Corpn 1976–84; Chair. and CEO The Walt Disney Co. 1984–2004, CEO 2004–05, mem. Bd of Dirs 2005–06; fmr mem. Bd of Dirs Calif. Inst. of the Arts, Denison Univ., American Hosp. of Paris Foundation, UCLA Exec. Bd for Medical Sciences, Nat. Hockey League (ice hockey); mem. Business Steering Cttee of the Global Business Dialogue on Electronic Commerce, The Business Council; est. Eisner Foundation; host, Conversations with Michael Eisner (CNBC) 2006; Founder Tomante LLC 2005–, Dir Veoh Networks Inc. 2006–; Chevalier, Légion d'honneur. *Address:* Tornante LLC, 233 South Beverly Drive, Beverly Hills, CA 90212-3896; c/o Veoh Networks, Inc., 7220 Trade Street, Suite 115, San Diego, CA 92121, USA (office). *Telephone:* (310) 274-2550 (Tornante). *E-mail:* admin@tornante.com. *Website:* www.tornante.com; www.veoh.com (office).

EITEL, Bernhard, Dr rer. nat habil.; German professor of geography and university administrator; *Rector, University of Heidelberg;* b. 1959, Karlsruhe; ed Univs of Karlsruhe and Stuttgart; Lecturer, Dept of Geography, Univ. of Stuttgart 1989–95; Prof. of Physical Geography, Univ. of Passau 1995–2001; Prof. of Physical Geography, Univ. of Heidelberg 2001–, also Head of Geography Dept, Rector, Univ. of Heidelberg 2007–; mem. Exec. Comm. of the Int. Asscn of Geomorphologists 2002–; mem. German Acad. of Science and Eng (acatech) 2008, German Acad. of Sciences Leopoldina 2010; Corresp. mem. German Archaeological Inst. 2009; Chevalier, Ordre des Palmes académiques 2011. *Publications:* numerous scientific papers in professional journals. *Address:* Office of the Rector, University of Heidelberg, Grabengasse 1, 69117 Heidelberg, Germany (office). *Telephone:* (6221) 542315 (office); (6221) 542316 (office). *Fax:* (6221) 542147 (office). *E-mail:* rektor@rektorat.uni-heidelberg.de (office). *Website:* www.uni-heidelberg.de/institutions/rectorate/bernhard_eitel.html (office).

EJETA, Gebisa, BSc, MS, PhD; Ethiopian/American plant breeder, geneticist and academic; *Distinguished Professor of Plant Breeding and Genetics, Purdue University;* b. west central Ethiopia; ed Alemaya Coll. of Agric., Ethiopia, Purdue Univ., USA; Prin. Plant Breeder, Sorghum at ICRISAT 1979–83; Asst Prof. of Plant Breeding and Genetics, Purdue Univ. 1984–88, Assoc. Prof. of Plant Breeding and Genetics 1988–92, Prof. of Plant Breeding and Genetics 1992–2007, Distinguished Prof., Plant Breeding and Genetics 2007–; mem. Science Council of CGIAR (fmrly Consultative Group on Int. Agricultural Research) 2008–10, mem. CGIAR Consortium Bd 2010–; mem. Bd Sasakawa Africa 2010–; apptd by Pres. Barack Obama to Bd for Int. Food and Agricultural Devt 2011; Fellow, Crop Science Soc. of America 1994, American Soc. of Agronomy 1995, AAAS 2005; silver plaque for Outstanding Contrib. to Agric. of the Sudan, Sudan Agricultural Research Corpn 1983, Int. Service in Crop Science Award, Crop Science Soc. of America 1994, Int. Service in Agronomy Award, American Soc. of Agronomy 1997, Distinguished Scientific Career Award, African Crop Science Congress 1997, Purdue School of Agric. Dean's Interdisciplinary Team Mem. Award 1998, Distinguished Career Achievement Award, INTSORMIL 2002, Outstanding Research Paper of the Year on Plant Genetic Resources, Crop Science Soc. of America 2005, Certificate of Recognition from Govt of Ethiopia 2007, World Food Prize (co-recipient) 2009, Nat. Hero Award, Govt of Ethiopia 2009, P.E. Nelson Prize for Innovation, State of Indiana 2009, Commemoration by Indiana Gen. Ass. 2009, Dow Agro-Sciences Award for Outstanding Contrib. to Global Agric. 2009, Presidential Award, Crop Science Soc. of America 2009, Indiana Hero Award, Indiana Pacers 2010, Henry Bennett Fellow, School of Int. Studies, Oklahoma State Univ. 2010, Outstanding Scientific Achievement Award, Soc. of Ethiopians in Diaspora 2010, Special Advisor to USAID Admin. 2010, US Govt Agricultural Science Envoy 2010. *Publications:* Integrating New Technologies for Striga Control: Towards Ending the Witch-hunt (co-ed.) 2007; numerous papers in professional journals. *Address:* Department of Agronomy, Purdue University, Lilly Hall of Life Sciences 2-363, 915 West State Street, West Lafayette, IN 47907-2054, USA (office). *Telephone:* (765) 494-4320 (office). *Fax:* (765) 496-2926 (office). *E-mail:* gejeta@purdue.edu (office). *Website:* ag.purdue.edu/agry/Pages/gejeta .aspx (office).

EJIOFOR, Chiwetel, OBE; British actor; b. 10 July 1977, Forest Gate, London, England; s. of Arinze Ejiofor and Obiajulu Ejiofor; ed Dulwich Coll., Nat. Youth Theatre; stage debut in Othello (title role), Bloomsbury Theatre, London 1995; film debut in Deadly Voyage (TV film) 1996. *Theatre includes:* Macbeth 1997, Sparkleshark 1999, Blue/Orange (Jack Tinker Award for Most Promising Newcomer, Critics' Circle Theatre Awards 2000, London Evening Standard Theatre Award for Outstanding Newcomer 2000) 2000, Romeo and Juliet 2000, Peer Gynt 2000, The Vortex (Donmar Warehouse, London) 2002, The Seagull 2007, Othello (Laurence Olivier Award for Best Actor) 2007. *Films include:* Amistad 1997, G:MT Greenwich Mean Time 1999, It Was an Accident 2000, My Friend Soweto 2001, Dirty Pretty Things (British Ind. Film Award for Best Actor, San Diego Film Critics Soc. Award for Best Actor, Evening Standard British Film Award for Best Actor) 2002, 3 Blind Mice 2003, Love Actually 2003, She Hate Me 2004, Red Dust 2004, Melinda and Melinda 2004, Four Brothers 2005, Serenity 2005, Slow Burn 2005, Kinky Boots 2005, Inside Man 2006, Children of Men 2006, Talk to Me 2007, American Gangster (Screen Actors Guild Award) 2007, Redbelt 2008, Slapper (short, writer and dir) 2008, Endgame 2009, 2012 2009, Salt 2010, Columbite Tantalite (short, writer and dir) 2013, Savannah 2013, 12 Years a Slave (BAFTA Award for Best Actor in a Leading Role 2014) 2013, Half of a Yellow Sun 2013. *Television:* Deadly Voyage (film) 1996, Mind Games (film) 2001, Murder in Mind (series) 2001, Trust (series) 2003, Twelfth Night, or What You Will (film) 2003, Canterbury Tales (mini-series) 2003, Tsunami: The Aftermath (film) 2006, Masterpiece Contemporary (series) 2009, The Shadow Line (series) 2011, Dancing on the Edge (series) 2013, Phil Spector (film) 2013. *Address:* c/o Markham, Froggatt and Irwin, 4 Windmill Street, London, W1T 2HZ, England (office). *Telephone:* (20) 7636-4412 (office). *Fax:* (20) 7637-5233 (office). *E-mail:* admin@markhamfroggattirwin.com (office). *Website:* www.markhamfroggattirwin.com (office).

EKE, 'Aisake Valu, BA, MBA, CPA; Tongan politician and fmr civil servant; *Minister of Finance and National Planning;* m.; ed Univ. of South Queensland, Australia; civil servant 1986–2010, positions included Sec. for Finance 1994, Acting Commr of Revenue, posted to World Bank 2002, Acting Minister of Finance 2006; mem. Bd of Dirs Nat. Reserve Bank 2009; Chair. Tonga Devt Bank 2009; mem. Legis. Ass. (parl.) for Tongatapu No. 5 2010–; Minister of Finance and Nat. Planning 2014–; mem. Tupou High School Advisory Cttee 2001; fmr mem. Democratic Party, currently ind. *Address:* Ministry of Finance and National Planning, POB 87, Treasury Bldg, Vuna Rd, Nuku'alofa, Tonga (office). *Telephone:* 23066 (office). *Fax:* 26011 (office). *E-mail:* info@finance.gov.to (office). *Website:* www.finance.gov.to (office).

EKÉUS, Carl Rolf; Swedish diplomatist; *Commissioner, International Commission on Missing Persons;* b. 7 July 1935, Kristinehamn; m. Christina C. Oldfelt 1970; three s. three d.; ed Univ. of Stockholm; law practice, Karlstad 1959–62; Legal Div. Ministry of Foreign Affairs 1962–63; Sec. Swedish Embassy, Bonn 1963–65; First Sec. Nairobi 1965–67; Special Asst to Minister of Foreign Affairs 1967–73; First Sec., Counsellor, Perm. Mission to UN, New York 1974–78; Counsellor, The Hague 1978–83; Amb. and Perm. Rep. to Conf. on Disarmament, Geneva 1983–89, Chair. Cttee on Chemical Weapons 1984, 1987; Amb. and Head of Swedish Del. to CSCE, Vienna 1989–93; Chair. Cttee on Principles Chapter of Charter of Paris 1991; Exec. Chair. UN Special Comm. on Iraq 1991–97; Amb. to USA 1997–2000; Chair. Stockholm Int. Peace Research Inst. 2000–10; OSCE High Commr on Nat. Minorities 2001–07; Commr of the International Comm. on Missing Persons (ICMP) 2005–; mem. Supervisory Council Int. Luxembourg Forum on Preventing Nuclear Catastrophe, Canberra Comm. on the Elimination of Nuclear Weapons, Advisory Bd Centre for Non-Proliferation, Monetary Inst., Tokyo Forum on Non-Proliferation and Disarmament; mem. Exec. Bd, European Leadership Network 2011–; mem. Advisory Bd UN Sec.-Gen. on Disarmament Matters 1999–2004, Bd of Dirs Nuclear Threat Initiative 2001, Bd Axel and Margaret Ax:son Johnson Foundation 2001–11; mem. Royal Acad. of War Science, Stockholm 2001–, European Council for Foreign Relations 2011–; Hon. LLD (California Lutheran Univ.) 1999; Wateler Peace Prize, Carnegie Foundation 1997. *Publications include:* reports as Special Investigator on the submarine question 1980–2001, Sweden's security policy 1969–89 2002; several articles on foreign policy, int. economy, nuclear non-proliferation, disarmament and arms control, chemical weapons, European security, Iraq and weapons of mass destruction. *Leisure interests:* piano playing, tennis. *Address:* International Commission on Missing Persons, Alipašina 45A, 71000 Sarajevo, Bosnia and Herzegovina (office); Rådmansgatan 57, 113 60 Stockholm, Sweden (home). *Telephone:* (33) 280800 (office); (8) 313653 (home). *Fax:* (33) 280900 (office). *E-mail:* rekeus@gmail.com (home); icmp@ic-mp.org (office). *Website:* www.ic-mp .org (office).

EKREN, Nazim, PhD; Turkish politician; b. 1956, Istanbul; m.; two c.; ed Uludağ and Marmara univs, Manchester Business School, UK; fmr Dir Türkiye Vakıflar Bankasi; fmr Dir Banking and Insurance Inst., Univ. of Marmara; mem. of Grand Nat. Ass., representing Istanbul 2002–; Deputy Prime Minister and State Minister for Economy 2007–09; Co-founder, Bd Mem. and Deputy Chair. (Econ. Affairs), AKP (Adalet ve Kalkınma Partisi/Justice and Devt Party). *Address:* c/o Deputy Prime Ministers' Office, Başbakan Yard, ve Devlet Bakani, Bakanliklar, Ankara, Turkey (office).

EKWUEME, Alex Ifeanyichukwu, BArch, LLB, MA, PhD; Nigerian architect, lawyer and politician; b. 21 Oct. 1932, Oko; s. of the late Lazarus Ibeabuchi Ekwueme and Agnes Nkwodumma Ekwueme; ed King's Coll., Lagos, Univ. of Washington, Seattle, Univ. of Strathclyde, Glasgow, Nigerian Law School, Lagos; est. Ekwueme Associates (architects) 1958; fmr Pres. Nigerian Inst. of Architects, Architectural Registration Council of Nigeria; Vice-Pres. of Nigeria 1979–83; detained 1983, released July 1986; fmr mem. Nat. Exec. of banned Nat. Party of Nigeria; mem. Nat. Constitutional Conf. 1994–95; Chair. All-Nigeria Politicians Summit Conf. 1995; Founding Chair. and Chair. Bd of Trustees People's Democratic Party 1998; Fulbright Scholar 1952; Grand Commdr Order of the Niger 1988–; several hon. doctorates. *Leisure interests:* reading, lawn tennis. *Address:* Oko, Anambra State, Nigeria. *Telephone:* (42) 454815. *Fax:* (42) 456667; (42) 254757 (office).

EL-BADRI, Abdalla Salem, BS; Libyan oil industry executive and international organization official; *Secretary-General, Organization of the Petroleum Exporting*

Countries (OPEC); b. 25 May 1940, Ghemmines; m.; five c.; ed Univ. of Southern Florida, USA; began career at Esso-Libya 1965, Asst Accountant and Co-ordinator, Man. Information Systems, then Asst Controller; Chair. Waha Oil Co. 1980–83; Chair. Nat. Oil Corpn 1983–90, 2000, 2004–06, Sec. Gen. People's Cttee of Petroleum 1990–92, Sec. Gen. People's Cttee of Energy 1993–2000, Deputy Sec. Gen. People's Cttee for Services 2000–02, Deputy Sec. Gen. People's Cttee 2002–04; Sec.-Gen. OPEC 1994, 2007–; Pres. OPEC Conf. 1994, 1996–97; Pres. OAPEC 1998; Chair. Bd of Dirs Arab Petroleum Services Co. 1987–90; mem. Bd Libya Oil Invest (Tamoil), Chair. 2005–06; mem. Bd of Dirs Umm Al-Jawabi Oil Co. 1977–80; ranked 53rd by Forbes magazine amongst The World's Most Powerful People 2010. Address: Organization of the Petroleum Exporting Countries (OPEC), Helferstorferstrasse 17, 1010 Vienna, Austria (office). Telephone: (1) 211-12-0 (office). Fax: (1) 216-43-20 (office). Website: www.opec.org (office).

EL-BAZ, Farouk, BS, MS, PhD; Egyptian/American scientist and academic; Director, Center for Remote Sensing, Boston University; b. 2 Jan. 1938, Zagazig, Egypt; s. of the late El-Sayed El-Baz and of Zahia Hammouda; m. Catherine Patricia O'Leary 1963; four d.; ed Ain Shams Univ., Cairo, Asyut Univ., Missouri School of Mines and Metallurgy, Univ. of Missouri, Massachusetts Inst. of Tech., Heidelberg Univ., Germany; Demonstrator, Geology Dept, Asyut Univ. 1958–60; Lecturer, Mineralogy-Petrography Inst., Univ. of Heidelberg 1964–65; exploration geologist, Pan-American UAR Oil Co., Cairo 1966; Supervisor, Lunar Science Planning and Operations, BellComm, Bell Telephone Labs., Washington, DC for Apollo Program, NASA HQ 1967–72; Research Dir, Center for Earth and Planetary Studies, Nat. Air and Space Museum, Smithsonian Inst., Washington, DC 1973–82; Science Adviser to Pres. Anwar Sadat of Egypt 1978–81; Vice-Pres. for Science and Tech. and for Int. Devt, Itek Optical Systems, Lexington, Mass. 1982–86; Dir Center for Remote Sensing, Boston Univ. 1986–; Research Prof., Depts of Archeology and Electronic and Computer Eng, Boston Univ.; Adjunct Prof., Faculty of Science, Ain Shams Univ., Cairo, Egypt; pioneering work in the applications of space photography to understanding of arid terrain; Pres. Arab Soc. of Desert Research; mem. Bd of Dirs, USA Civilian R&D Foundation, Mantor Arabia; mem. Advisory Bd, EXPEC-ARC, Aramco, Saudi Arabia; numerous radio interviews, especially on NPR, TV interviews on Al-Jazeerah and other Arab stations; mem. US Nat. Acad. of Eng, Academia Bibliotheca Alexandrina, the African, Arab, Islamic, Palestine, Hassan II (Moroccan) Acad. of Science, TWAS (Acad. of Science for the Developing World); Order of Merit, First Class (Arab Repub. of Egypt); Hon. DSc (New England Coll., NH) 1989, Hon. PhD (Mansoura Univ.), Hon. LLD (American Univ. of Cairo), Hon. DEng (Univ. of Missouri-Rolla), (American Univ. of Beirut); numerous honours and awards, including from NASA: Apollo Achievement Award, Certificate of Merit for contribs to Manned Space Flight, Exceptional Scientific Achievement Medal and Special Recognition Award; from AAAS: Award for Public Understanding of Science and Tech. 1992, Apollo-Soyuz Test Project Experiment Team Award 1992; Golden Door Award, Int. Inst. of Boston, Nevada Medal, Arab Thought Foundation Pioneer Award, Texas Dawa Award; World Water Masters Award 2009. Publications: Say It in Arabic 1968, Astronaut Observations from the Apollo-Soyuz Mission 1977, Egypt as Seen by Landsat 1979, Desert Landforms of Southwest Egypt 1982, Deserts and Arid Lands 1984, The Geology of Egypt 1984, Physics of Desertification 1986, The Gulf War and the Environment 1994, Atlas of Kuwait from Satellite Images 2000, Wadis of Oman: Satellite Image Atlas 2002, Development Corridor: Securing a Better Future for Egypt 2007, Remote Sensing in Archaeology 2007. Leisure interests: reading history, travel, swimming. Address: Center for Remote Sensing, Boston University, 725 Commonwealth Avenue, Boston, MA 02215-1401, USA (office). Telephone: (617) 353-9709 (office). Fax: (617) 353-3200 (office). E-mail: farouk@bu.edu (office). Website: www.bu.edu/remotesensing/faculty/el-baz (office).

ELACHI, Charles, MS, MBA, PhD, FIEEE; American (b. Lebanese) electrical engineer and academic; Director, Jet Propulsion Laboratory, California Institute of Technology; b. (Charles Asshur Al-Wadad Elachi), 18 April 1947, Rayak, Lebanon; m. Valerie Gifford; two d.; ed Collège des Apôtres, Jounieh, École Orientale, Zahlé, Joseph Fourier Univ., Grenoble and Grenoble Inst. of Tech., France, California Inst. of Tech. (Caltech), Pasadena, Univ. of Southern California, Univ. of California, Los Angeles; joined Jet Propulsion Lab. 1970; taught The Physics of Remote Sensing at Caltech 1982–2000, now Prof. of Electrical Eng and Planetary Science, Vice-Pres. Caltech 2001–; Dir Space and Earth Science, Jet Propulsion Lab. late 1980s–90s, Dir Jet Propulsion Lab. 2001–; Prin. Investigator or Co-Investigator on numerous research and devt studies and flight projects sponsored by NASA including Shuttle Imaging Radar series (SIR-A 1981, SIR-B 1984, SIR-C 1994), Magellan Imaging Radar, Rosetta Comet Nucleus Sounder Experiment; Team Leader Cassini Titan Radar Experiment; participated in several arche-ological expeditions in Egyptian Desert, Arabian Peninsula and Western Chinese Desert in search of old trading routes and buried cities using satellite data; lecturer and keynote speaker at numerous nat. and int. confs and univs in China, Japan, Australia, France, UK, Netherlands, Denmark, Austria, Switzerland, Norway, Germany, Italy, Greece, Egypt, Kenya, India, Morocco, and Brazil; mem. Univ. of Arizona Eng School Advisory Cttee, Boston Univ. Center of Remote Sensing Advisory Council, UCLA Science Bd of Visitors; fmr Chair. several nat. and int. cttees that developed NASA road-maps for exploration of neighbouring solar systems 1995, our solar system 1997, Mars 1998; mem. Univ. Advisory Bd King Fahd Univ. of Petroleum and Minerals, Saudi Arabia, 2010–, Bd King Abdullah Univ. of Science and Tech., Saudi Arabia; Chair. Bd of Trustees, Lebanese American Univ., Beirut; mem. Nat. Acad. of Eng (NAE) 1989–, NAE 4th Decadal Cttee 1993–95, NAE Membership Cttee 1995; mem. Int. Acad. of Astronautics; Fellow, AIAA; Order of Cedars (Lebanon) 2006, Chevalier, Légion d'honneur 2010; numerous awards including ASP Autometric Award 1980, 1982, NASA Exceptional Scientific Medal 1982, W.T. Pecora Award 1985, IEEE Geoscience and Remote Sensing Distinguished Achievement Award 1987, Asteroid 1982 SU was renamed 4116 Elachi in recognition of his contrib. to planetary exploration 1989, IEEE Medal of Eng Excellence 1992, NASA Outstanding Leadership Medal 1994, Nevada Medal 1995, COSPAR Nordberg Medal 1996, NASA Distinguished Service Medal 1999, Dryden Award 2000, UCLA Dept of Earth and Space Science Distinguished Alumni Award 2002, Wernher Von Braun Award 2002, NASA Outstanding Leadership Medal 2002, Takeda Award 2002, Space Flight Award, American Astronautical Soc. 2005, Bob Hope Distinguished Citizen Award, Nat. Defense Industrial Asscn 2005, NASA Exceptional Service

Medal 2005, Massey Award, Royal Soc. of London 2006, Philip Habib Award for Distinguished Public Service, American Task Force for Lebanon 2006, Nat. Acad. of Eng Arthur M. Bueche Award 2011, Gen. James E. Hill Lifetime Space Achievement Award, Space Foundation 2011, ranked by Arabian Business amongst the Power 500: The World's Most Influential Arabs (21st) 2012, (13th) 2013. Publications: three textbooks and more than 230 publs and patents in the fields of remote sensing, planetary exploration, Earth observation from space, electromagnetic theory and integrated optics. Leisure interests: skiing, woodworking, history, travel. Address: Jet Propulsion Laboratory, 4800 Oak Grove Drive, Pasadena, CA 91109, USA (office). Telephone: (818) 354-4321 (office). Website: www.jpl.nasa.gov (office).

ELAHI, Chaudhry Pervez; Pakistani politician; b. 1 Nov. 1945; s. of Chaudhry Manzoor Elahi; ed Forman Christian Coll., Univ. of London, UK; mem. Punjab Prov. Ass. 1985–, Deputy Leader, then Leader of the Opposition 1993–96, Speaker 1997–99; Minister of Local Govt and Rural Devt, Punjab 1985–86, 1988–1990, 1990–93; Chief Minister of Punjab 2002–07; Deputy Prime Minister and Minister Responsible for Defence Production and for Industries 2012–13; Pres. Pakistan Muslim League (Q) party in Punjab; mem. Nat. Security Council. Address: 30C, Ch. Zahur Elahi Rd, Gulberg-II, Lahore, Pakistan (home). E-mail: info@pml.org .pk (office). Website: www.pml.org.pk (office).

ELALAMY, Moulay Hafid; Moroccan business executive; President and Director-General, Saham Group; b. 1960, Marrakech; ed Univ. of Sherbrooke, Canada; began career as Sr Adviser to Ministry of Finance of Quebec, Canada 1980; Head of Information Systems, Saint-Maurice (Canadian insurance co.); Man. Dir Compagnie Africaine d'Assurance 1988; f. Saham Group 1995, currently Pres. and Dir-Gen., also Chair. and Man. Dir CNIA SAADA Assurance; Pres. Gen. Confed. of Enterprises of Morocco 2006–09; Vice-Pres. Moroccan Fed. of Insurance Cos and Reinsurance; Dir Investment Cttee, Caisse Interprofessionnelle Marocaine de Retraite (also mem.); Dir and Treas., Lalla Salma Asscn; mem. Bd of Dirs Colina Holdings Ltd. E-mail: contact@saham.ma (office). Website: www.sahamgroup.com (office).

ELBA, Idris; British actor and hip-hop artist; b. (Idrissa Akuna Elba), 6 Sept. 1972, Hackney, London; s. of Winston Elba and Eve Elba; m. Kim Elba (divorced); one d.; ed Nat. Youth Music Theatre; started own DJ co. 1987; night shift at Ford factory in Dagenham 1989–90; worked in nightclubs under DJ nickname Big Driis 1991; worked at Nat. Youth Music Theatre; best known for playing Russell 'Stringer' Bell in The Wire (HBO) and title role of Detective John Luther in Luther (BBC 1); Anti-Crime Amb. 2009–; featured by Essence magazine as one of the Ten Hottest Men on the Planet April 2004, Nov. 2005, selected as one of People Magazine's annual 100 Most Beautiful People in the World 2007, Best Actor, BET Awards 2010, 2011. Films include: Belle maman 1999, Sorted 2000, Buffalo Soldiers 2001, One Love 2003, The Gospel 2005, Daddy's Little Girls 2007, The Reaping 2007, 28 Weeks Later 200, American Gangster 2007, This Christmas 2007, Prom Night 2008, RocknRolla 2008, The Human Contract 2008, The Unborn 2009, Obsessed (BET Award for Best Actor 2010) 2009, Legacy: Black Ops (also exec. producer) 2010, The Losers 2010, Takers (BET Award for Best Actor 2011) 2010, Thor 2011, Ghost Rider: Spirit of Vengeance 2011, Demons Never Die (exec. producer) 2011, Prometheus 2012, Pacific Rim 2013, Second Coming 2013, Thor: The Dark World 2013, Mandela: Long Walk to Freedom 2013, No Good Deed 2014. Music video: Lover of the Light, Mumford and Sons (producer and star) 2012. Television includes: Bramwell (mini-series) 1995, Space Precinct 1994, The Bill (series) 1994–95, Absolutely Fabulous 1995, Crucial Tales (mini-series) 1996, Crocodile Shoes II 1996, Family Affairs (series) 1997–98, Silent Witness (series) 1997, Ultraviolet 1998, Dangerfield 1999, In Defence 2000, The Inspector 2002, The Wire (series) 2002–04, Girlfriends (series) 2005, Sometimes in April (film) 2005, Jonny Zero (series) 2005, World of Trouble (film) 2005, All in the Game (film) 2006, Queens Supreme (series) 2007, The No. 1 Ladies' Detective Agency (series) 2008, The Office 2009, Luther (series) (also producer) (NAACP Image Award for Outstanding Actor in a Television Movie, Mini-Series, or Dramatic Special 2011, Golden Globe Award for Best Actor – Miniseries or Television Film 2012, Black Reel Award for Best Actor: TV Movie/Cable 2012) 2010–, Call of Duty: Modern Warfare 3 (video game) 2011, Idris Elba's How Clubbing Changed the World (presenter) 2012; exec. producer: Walk Like a Panther (series) 2010, How Hip Hop Changed the World (documentary) 2011. Recordings include: EPs: Big Man 2006, Kings Among Kings 2009, High Class Problems Vol. 1 2010. Address: c/o ICM, 3rd Floor, Marlborough House, 10 Earlham Street, London, WC2H 9LN, England (office). Telephone: (20) 7836-8564 (office). Website: www.icmtalent.com (office); www.driis.com.

ELBAZ, Alber; Israeli designer; Designer, Rive Gauche, Yves Saint Laurent; b. 1961, Casablanca, Morocco; ed Shenkar Coll. of Textile Tech. and Fashion, Tel-Aviv; moved to New York, USA 1980s; worked for cheap fashion firm for two years; worked for Geoffrey Beene, New York 1989–96; joined Guy Laroche, Paris, France 1997–98; designer of ready-to-wear, Yves Saint Laurent, Paris 1998–2000, Designer, Rive Gauche 2003–; designer for Krizia 2000–01; Creative Dir Lanvin 2001–03; Chevalier, Légion d'honneur 2007; named amongst the 100 Most Influential People in the World by Time magazine 2007. Address: Rive Gauche, Yves Saint Laurent, 38 rue du Faubourg, Saint-Honoré, 75008 Paris, France (office). Telephone: 1-42-65-74-59 (office). Fax: 1-42-65-23-16 (office). Website: www .ysl.com (office).

ELBEGDORJ, Tsakhiagiin, MA; Mongolian politician and head of state; President; b. 30 March 1963, Zereg Som, Hovd Prov.; m.; two c.; ed Harvard Univ., USA; machinist, Erdenet copper mine 1981–82; army service 1982; mil. reporter, Mil. School, Lvov, Ukraine 1983–88; journalist, Ulaan-Od (Ministry of Defence newspaper) 1988–90; mem. Co-ordinating Council of Mongolian Democratic Union (MDU) 1989, Leader 1990; Deputy to People's Great Hural 1990–92, also mem. State Little Hural; mem. State Great Hural 1992–94, 1996, Vice-Chair. 1996–; mem. Gen. Council Mongolian Nat. Democratic Party 1994, Leader 1996–, also Leader Democratic Union coalition in State Great Hural; Prime Minister of Mongolia April–Dec. 1998, 2004–06; Pres. of Mongolia 2009–. Address: State Palace, Ulan Bator 12 (office); Mongolian National Democratic Party, Chingisiyn Örgön Chölöö 1, Ulan Bator, Mongolia (office).

ELDER, Sir Mark Philip, Kt, BA, MA (Hons), CBE; British conductor; *Music Director, Hallé Orchestra;* b. 2 June 1947, Hexham; s. of John Elder and Helen Elder; m. Amanda Jane Stein 1980; one d.; ed Bryanston School and Corpus Christi Coll., Cambridge; music staff, Wexford Festival 1969–70; Chorus Master and Asst Conductor Glyndebourne 1970–71; music staff, Royal Opera House, Covent Garden 1970–72; Staff Conductor, Australian Opera 1972–74; Staff Conductor, ENO 1974–77, Assoc. Conductor 1977–79, Music Dir 1979–93; Prin. Guest Conductor London Mozart Players 1980–83, BBC Symphony Orchestra 1982–85, City of Birmingham Symphony Orchestra 1992–95; Music Dir Rochester Philharmonic Orchestra, NY 1989–94, Hallé Orchestra, Manchester, UK 2000–; Artistic Dir Opera Rara 2011–; Hon. FRNCM, Hon. Fellow, Corpus Christi Coll., Cambridge 2010, Hon. mem. Royal Philharmonic Soc. 2011; Dr hc (Manchester) 2003, (Sheffield) 2006, (Open Univ.) 2009, (RAM) 2012; Olivier Award for Outstanding Contrib. to Opera 1990, Royal Philharmonic Soc. Award for Conductor 2006. *Recordings include:* with Hallé Orchestra, Choir and Youth Chorus: Elgar: The Apostles (BBC Music Magazine Choral Award and Recording of the Year 2013, Gramophone Choral Award 2013). *Address:* c/o Ingpen & Williams, 7 St George's Court, 131 Putney Bridge Road, London, SW15 2PA (office); Hallé Concerts Society, The Bridgewater Hall, Manchester, M1 5HA, England (home). *Telephone:* (20) 8874-3222 (office). *E-mail:* info@ingpen.co.uk (office). *Website:* www.ingpen.co.uk (office); www.halle.co.uk (office).

ELDER, Murdoch George, DSc, MD, FRCS, FRCOG; British physician and academic; *Emeritus Professor of Obstetrics and Gynaecology, Imperial College London;* b. 4 Jan. 1938, Kolkata, India; s. of the late A. J. Elder and L. A. C. Elder; m. Margaret McVicker 1964; two s.; ed Edinburgh Acad. and Edinburgh Univ.; lecturer, Royal Univ. of Malta 1969–71; Sr Lecturer and Reader, Univ. of London, Charing Cross Hosp. Medical School 1971–78; Prof. of Obstetrics and Gynaecology, Univ. of London at Hammersmith Hosp. 1978–98; Dean, Royal Postgrad. Medical School Inst. of Obstetrics and Gynaecology 1985–95; Chair. Div. of Paediatrics, Obstetrics and Gynaecology, Imperial Coll. School of Medicine, Univ. of London 1996–98, Emer. Prof. 1998–; Visiting Prof. UCLA 1984, 1986, 1997, Univ. of Singapore 1987, Univ. of Natal 1988; consultant to WHO and other int. orgs; mem. WHO Scientific and Ethics Research Group; External Examiner to Univs of Edin., Cambridge, Oxford, London, Leeds, Bristol, Glasgow, Dundee, Malta, Malaya, Malaysia, Helsinki, Rotterdam, Cape Town, Singapore; Hon. Fellow Imperial Coll. School of Medicine 2001; Silver Medal, Hellenic Obstetrical Soc. 1984, Bronze Medal, Helsinki Univ., 1996. *Publications include:* Human Fertility Control (co-author) 1979, Preterm Labor (co-ed.) 1981 and 1996, Obstetrics and Gynaecology 2002; more than 240 original publns in field of biochemistry of reproduction and clinical high-risk obstetrics. *Leisure interests:* travel, golf. *Address:* Easter Calzeat, Broughton, Biggar, ML12 6HQ, Scotland. *Telephone:* (1899) 830359. *E-mail:* melder@eastercalzeat.fsnet.co.uk

ELDERFIELD, John, PhD; American art historian and museum curator; *Chief Curator Emeritus, Museum of Modern Art, New York;* ed Courtauld Inst. of Art, UK; various positions with Museum of Modern Art, New York 1975–, Chief Curator at Large –2003, Chief Curator of Painting and Sculpture 2003–08 (retd), Chief Curator Emer. 2008–, organizer of exhbns including The Wild Beasts: Fauvism and Its Affinities 1976, Kurt Schwitters 1985, Henri Matisse 1992, Bonnard 1998, Matisse Picasso 2003; Chevalier des Arts et des Lettres; Eric Mitchell Prize, Time Magazine 100 Most Influential People 2005. *Publications:* Modern Painting and Sculpture: 1880 to Present at the Museum of Modern Art, Henri Matisse: A Retrospective, Helen Frankenthaler, Language of the Body. *Address:* Museum of Modern Art, 11 West 53rd Street, New York, NY 10019-5497, USA (office). *Telephone:* (212) 708-9400 (office). *E-mail:* info@moma.org (office). *Website:* www.moma.org (office).

ELDIN, Gérard, Licence ès Lettres, Licence en Droit; French civil servant and banker; b. 21 March 1927, Cannes; s. of Charles Eldin and Elise Eldin; m. Marie-Cécile Bergerot 1960; two s. two d.; ed Bethany Coll., USA, Univ. d'Aix-en-Provence and Ecole Nat. d'Admin, Paris; Insp. of Finances 1954–58; served in the Treasury 1958–63; Adviser to Minister of Finance and Econ. Affairs 1963–65; Deputy Dir Dept of Planning 1965–70; Deputy Sec.-Gen. OECD 1970–80; Deputy Gov. Crédit Foncier de France 1980–86; Chair. Foncier-Investissement 1982–86, Crédit-Logement 1986–87, 1995–96; Chair. Banque centrale de compensation 1987–90; Chair. Foncier-court terme Sicav 1988–96; Chair. and CEO Soc. d'études immobilières et d'expertises foncières (Foncier-Expertise) 1990–96; Dir Compagnie foncière de France 1980–93, Soc. immobilière Paix-Daunou 1987–93, Soc. des Immeubles de France 1993–2000; Hon. Inspecteur Général des Finances; Chevalier, Légion d'honneur, Commdr, Ordre nat. du Mérite. *Publications:* Avenue des Broussailles, Souvenirs d'enfance et de jeunesse (1927–1951) 2009. *Leisure interests:* singing, local history. *Address:* 32 rue des Archives, 75004 Paris, France (home). *Telephone:* 1-44-54-09-83 (home). *E-mail:* eldingmc@wanadoo.fr.

ELDON, David Gordon, CBE, JP, FCIB; British business executive; *Senior Independent Non-Executive Director, Noble Group Ltd;* with HSBC Group, based in Middle and Far East 1968–2005, mem. Bd of Dirs HSBC Holdings and Chair. Hongkong and Shanghai Banking Corpn Ltd –2005 (retd); currently Sr Adviser, PricewaterhouseCoopers, Hong Kong; mem. Bd of Dirs Noble Group Ltd 2007–, later Ind. Chair. (non-exec.), currently Sr Ind. Dir (non-exec.); Chair. (non-exec.) Dubai Int. Financial Centre Authority; Deputy Chair. Hong Kong Jockey Club; mem. Bd of Dirs Mass Transit Railway Corpn, Hong Kong, Eagle Asset Man. Ltd, China Central Properties Ltd; fmr Chair. Hong Kong Gen. Chamber of Commerce; Founding mem. and Past Chair. Seoul Int. Business Advisory Council; Int. Council mem. Bretton Woods Cttee; Adviser to Unisys; Hon. Citizenship of Seoul 2005; Gold Bauhinia Star, Govt of Hong Kong Special Admin. Region 2004; Hon. DBA (City Univ. of Hong Kong); named DHL/SCMP Hong Kong Business Person of the Year 2003, Asian Banker Lifetime Achievement Award 2006. *Address:* Noble Group Ltd, 18th Floor, MassMutual Tower, 38 Gloucester Road, Hong Kong Special Administrative Region, People's Republic of China (office). *Telephone:* 2861-3511 (office). *Fax:* 2527-0282 (office). *E-mail:* noble@thisisnoble.com (office). *Website:* www.thisisnoble.com (office).

ELDON, Sir Stewart Graham, KCMG, OBE, CMG, MSc, MIEE; British diplomatist; *Senior Adviser on Defence and Security, Transparency International;* b. 18 Sept. 1953, Accra, Ghana; m. Christine Mason 1978; one s. one d.; ed Pocklington School, Yorks. and Christ's Coll., Cambridge; entered FCO 1976, UK Mission New York 1976, Asst Desk Officer, UN Dept, FCO 1977–78, Third (later Second) Sec., British Embassy, Bonn 1978–82, Head of Section, Repub. of Ireland Dept, FCO 1982–83, Minister of State, FCO 1983–86, First Sec., Chancery, UK Mission, New York 1986–90, Deputy Head, Middle East Dept, FCO 1990–91, seconded to Cabinet Office 1991–93, Fellow, Center for Int. Affairs, Harvard Univ. 1993–94, Political Counsellor, UK Del. to NATO/WEU 1994–97, Dir of Confs, FCO 1997–98, Deputy Perm. Rep., UK Mission to UN, New York 1998–2002; Visiting Fellow, Yale Univ. 2002; Amb. to Ireland 2003–06; UK Perm. Rep. to NATO, Brussels 2006–10, NATO Subject Matter Expert on Building Integrity 2010–; Sr Adviser on Defence and Security, Transparency International 2010–; Ind. mem. Parole Bd for England and Wales 2010–; Partner, The Ambassador Partnership 2010–; Sr Civil Adviser, UK Higher Command and Staff Course 2012–; mem. Advisory Council, Joint Services Command and Staff Coll. 2013–; Visiting Fellow, Yale Univ. 2002. *Publication:* From Quill Pen to Satellite: Foreign Ministries in the Information Age 1994. *Leisure interests:* travel, good food, reading science fiction, breaking computers. *Address:* Transparency International, CAN Mezzanine, 32-36 Loman Street, London, SE1 0EH, England (office). *Telephone:* (20) 7922-7906 (office). *Fax:* (20) 7922-7907 (office). *E-mail:* enquiries@stewarteldon.com (office). *Website:* www.transparency.org (office); www.stewarteldon.com.

ELENOVSKI, Lazar, BA; Macedonian politician; *President, Euro-Atlantic Council of Macedonia;* b. 19 March 1971, Skopje; s. of Aleksandar Elenovski and Mirusha Elenovski; m.; two c.; ed Faculty of Econs, Skopje; fmr Deputy CEO JSP (public transport co.); joined Social Democratic Alliance of Macedonia, f. Social Democratic Youth of Macedonia 1992, Sec.-Gen. 1996–99, Pres. 1999–2001; f. Young Europeans for Security (YES Macedonia) 1995; mem. Presidency, Social-Democratic Union of Macedonia 1997–2003; Sec.-Gen. Euro-Atlantic Club of Macedonia 2001–05; Pres. Euro-Atlantic Council of Macedonia 2005–; Co-founder Cen. and South Eastern European Security Forum (Balkan Mosaic); Minister of Defence 2006–08; mem. Atlantic Treaty Asscn, Vice-Pres. 2011–. *Publications:* numerous articles on the Euro-Atlantic integration process, the Balkan region, and security sector reforms. *Leisure interest:* philosophy. *Address:* Euro-Atlantic Council of Macedonia, 22/1/15 Makedonija Str., 1000 Skopje, Former Yugoslav Republic of Macedonia (office). *Telephone:* (2) 3162221 (office). *Fax:* (2) 3162221 (office). *Website:* www.atamacedonia.org.mk (office).

ELFMAN, Danny; American film music composer and musician (guitar); b. 29 May 1953, Amarillo, Tex.; lead singer, rhythm guitarist and songwriter eight-piece rock band, Oingo Bongo; numerous songs and scores for films, TV programmes and computer games. *Music for film:* Forbidden Zone 1980, Fast Times at Ridgemont High 1982, Bachelor Party 1984, Surf II 1984, Beverly Hills Cop 1984, Weird Science 1985, Pee-Wee's Big Adventure 1985, Wisdom 1986, Something Wild 1986, Back to School 1986, Summer School 1987, Hot to Trot 1988, Big Top Pee-Wee 1988, Beetlejuice 1988, Midnight Run 1988, Scrooged 1988, Batman 1989, Ghostbusters II 1989, Dick Tracy 1990, Nightbreed 1990, Darkman 1990, Edward Scissorhands 1990, Pure Luck 1991, Batman Returns 1992, Article 99 1992, Army of Darkness 1993, Sommersby 1993, The Nightmare Before Christmas 1993, Black Beauty 1994, Dolores Claiborne 1995, To Die For 1995, Dead Presidents 1995, Mission: Impossible 1996, The Frighteners 1996, Freeway 1996, Extreme Measures 1996, Mars Attacks! 1996, Men In Black 1997, Flubber 1997, Good Will Hunting 1997, Scream 2 1997, A Simple Plan 1998, A Civil Action 1998, My Favorite Martian 1999, Instinct 1999, Anywhere But Here 1999, Sleepy Hollow 1999, The Family Man 2000, Proof of Life 2000, Spy Kids 2001, Planet of the Apes 2001, Heartbreakers 2001, Mazer World 2001, Novocaine 2001, Spider-Man 2002, Men in Black II 2002, Red Dragon 2002, Chicago 2002, Hulk 2003, Big Fish 2003, Spider-Man 2 2004, Charlie and the Chocolate Factory 2005, Charlotte's Web 2006, Spider-Man 3 2007, Hellboy II: The Golden Army 2008, Wanted 2008, Standard Operating Procedure 2008, Milk 2008, Notorious 2009, Terminator Salvation 2009, Taking Woodstock 2009, The Wolf Man 2009, Men in Black III 2012, Dark Shadows 2012, Promised Land 2012, Hitchcock 2012, Oz the Great and Powerful 2013. *Music for television:* Amazing Stories 1985, Alfred Hitchcock Presents 1985, Fast Times 1986, Sledge Hammer! 1986, Pee-Wee's Playhouse 1986, Tales from the Crypt 1989, The Simpsons 1989, Beetlejuice 1989, The Flash 1990, Batman 1992, Family Dog 1993, Weird Science 1994, Perversions of Science 1997, Dilbert 1999, Desperate Housewives 2004. *Recordings:* albums with Oingo Boingo: Only A Lad 1981, Nothing To Fear 1982, Good For Your Soul 1983, Dead Man's Party 1985, Boingo 1986, Skeletons In The Closet 1989, Dark At The End Of The Tunnel 1990, Article 99 1992. *Address:* c/o Blue Focus Management, 15233 Ventura Boulevard, Suite 200, Sherman Oaks, CA 91403, USA (office).

ELIADES, Demetris J.; Cypriot lawyer and politician; b. 1947, Lefkoniko, Famagusta Dist; m. Angeliki Hadjisavva; one s. one d.; ed Lefkoniko Greek Gymnasium, Univ. of Athens; in legal practice 1980–; mem. House of Reps 1985–2001, Chair. Parl. Environment Cttee, mem. Law Cttee; Minister of Agric., Natural Resources and Environment 2010–11, of Defence 2011–13; mem. Bd of Dirs Hellenic Bank 2005–10; mem. Exec. Cttee Commonwealth Parl. Asscn; mem. European Exec. Cttee Commonwealth Parl. Asscn of Legislation 1990–; mem. European Asscn of Legislation 1990–. *Address:* c/o Ministry of Defence, 4 Emmanuel Roides Avenue, 1432 Nicosia, Cyprus (office).

ELIAS, Rt Hon. Dame Sian, PC, LLB, QC; New Zealand lawyer; *Chief Justice;* m. Hugh Fletcher; ed Auckland Univ., Stanford Univ., USA; worked for Turner Hopkins & Partners 1972–75; barrister 1975–88; QC 1988; Law Commr and Chair. ICI Cttee of Inquiry 1989–90; apptd High Court Judge 1995; involved in litigation concerning Treaty of Waitangi 1987; sat on Court of Appeal 1998–99; Chief Justice 1999–; Acting Gov.-Gen. March–April 2001, Aug. 2006, Aug. 2011; mem. Motor Sports Licensing Appeal Authority 1984–88, Working Party on the Environment 1984; Commemorative Medal for Services to the Legal Profession 1990, Dame Grand Companion, New Zealand Order of Merit. *Address:* Chief Justice's Chambers, PO Box 1091, Wellington, New Zealand (office). *Telephone:* (4) 9188399 (office). *Fax:* (4) 4963985 (office). *E-mail:* lynette.maru@justice.govt.nz (office). *Website:* www.courtsofnz.govt.nz (office).

ELIASSON, Jan Kenneth Glenn, MA; Swedish diplomatist, politician and UN official; *Deputy Secretary-General, United Nations;* b. 17 Sept. 1940, Göteborg; s. of John H. Eliasson and Karin Eliasson (née Nilsson); m. Kerstin Englesson 1967; one s. two d.; ed School of Econs, Göteborg; entered Foreign Service 1965; Swedish OECD Del., Paris 1967; at Swedish Embassy, Bonn 1967–70; First Sec. Swedish

Embassy, Washington 1970–74; Head of Section, Political Dept, Ministry for Foreign Affairs, Stockholm 1974–75; Personal Asst to the Under-Sec. of State for Foreign Affairs 1975–77; Dir Press and Information Div., Ministry for Foreign Affairs 1977–80, Asst Under-Sec., Head of Div. for Asian and African Affairs, Political Dept 1980–82; Foreign Policy Adviser, Prime Minister's Office 1982–83; Under-Sec. for Political Affairs, Stockholm 1983–87; Perm. Rep. of Sweden to UN, New York 1988–92; Chair. UN Trust Fund for SA 1988–92; Personal Rep. to UN Sec.-Gen. on Iran-Iraq 1988–92; Vice-Pres. ECOSOC 1991–92; Under-Sec.-Gen. for Humanitarian Affairs, UN 1992–94; Chair. Minsk Conf. on Nagornyi Karabakh 1994; State Sec. for Foreign Affairs 1994–2000; Amb. to USA 2000–05; Pres. 60th UN General Ass. 2005–06; Minister of Foreign Affairs April–Oct. 2006; Special Envoy of the UN Sec.-Gen. for Darfur 2006–08; Sr Visiting Scholar, US Inst. of Peace 2008–; Deputy Sec.-Gen. UN 2012–; Sec. to Swedish Foreign Policy Advisory Bd 1983–87; Expert, Royal Swedish Defence Comm. 1984–86; Dir Inst. for East–West Security Studies, New York 1989–93, Int. Peace Acad. 1989–2001; currently Visiting Prof., Uppsala Univ.; currently also Chair. WaterAid, Sweden; mem. of UN Sec.-Gen.'s Advocacy Group of the Millennium Development Goals; Dr hc (American Univ. Washington, DC) 1994, (Gothenburg) 2001, (Bethany Coll., Kansas) 2005, (Uppsala) 2006. *Leisure interests:* art, literature, sports. *Address:* United Nations, New York, NY 10017, USA (office). *Telephone:* (212) 963-1234 (office). *Fax:* (212) 963-4879 (office). *Website:* www.un.org (office).

ELIASSON, Olafur; Danish artist; b. 1967, Copenhagen; ed Royal Danish Acad. of Fine Arts, Copenhagen; est. Studio Olafur Eliasson as a lab. for spatial research in Berlin 1995; represented Denmark at 50th Venice Biennale 2003; installed The Weather Project in Turbine Hall of Tate Modern, London 2003; Prof., Berlin Univ. of the Arts, f. Institut für Raumexperimente (Inst. for Spatial Experiments) 2009; lives and works in Copenhagen and Berlin. *E-mail:* studio@olafureliasson.net. *Website:* www.olafureliasson.net.

ELIZABETH II, HM Queen (Elizabeth Alexandra Mary), (Queen of Great Britain and Northern Ireland and of Her other Realms and Territories), (see Reigning Royal Families section for full titles); b. 21 April 1926, London; d. of HRH Prince Albert, Duke of York (later HM King George VI) and Duchess of York (later HM Queen Elizabeth The Queen Mother); succeeded to The Throne following Her father's death 6 Feb. 1952; married 20 Nov. 1947, HRH The Prince Philip, The Duke of Edinburgh (q.v.), b. 10 June 1921; children: Prince Charles Philip Arthur George, Prince of Wales (q.v.) (heir apparent), b. 14 Nov. 1948; Princess Anne Elizabeth Alice Louise, The Princess Royal (q.v.), b. 15 Aug. 1950; Prince Andrew Albert Christian Edward, Duke of York (q.v.), b. 19 Feb. 1960; Prince Edward Antony Richard Louis, Earl of Wessex, b. 10 March 1964. *Address:* Buckingham Palace, London, SW1A 1AA; Windsor Castle, Berkshire, SL4 1NJ, England; Balmoral Castle, Aberdeenshire, AB35 5TB, Scotland; Sandringham House, Norfolk, PE35 6EN, England; Palace of Holyroodhouse, Edinburgh, Scotland. *Website:* www.royal.gov.uk.

ELIZONDO BARRAGÁN, Fernando, LicenDer, MJ; Mexican lawyer, politician and business executive; b. 1949, Monterrey, Nuevo León; m. Verónica Ortiz Salinas; ed Centro Univ. Monterrey (CUM), Univ. of Nuevo León, New York Univ., USA; laywer, Monterrey 1972–79, 1986–94; various positions in legal div., Grupo Industrial Alfa 1979–89; Co-ordinator CANACO Monterrey, CAINTRA Nuevo León and COPARMEX Nuevo León 1988–92; mem. Civic Council of Nuevo León 1988–92; Exec. Pres. Grupo Salinas y Rocha 1995–97; Sec. of Finance and the Treasury, State of Nuevo León 1997–2003; Gov. (interim) of State of Nuevo León 2003–04; Sec. of Energy of Mexico and Chair. Petróleos Mexicanos (PEMEX) 2004–05; elected to Senate 2006–; del. to numerous int. confs and orgs. *Address:* Senado de la Republica, Xicotencatl 9, col. Centro, CP, 06000 México, DF, Mexico (office).

ELKANN, John Jacob Philip; American/Italian automotive industry executive; *Chairman, Fiat Group;* b. 1 April 1976, New York, NY, USA; s. of Alain Elkann and Margherita 'Daisy' Agnelli de Pahlen; grandson of the late Gianni Agnelli, fmr Chair. of Fiat; m. Donna Lavinia Borromeo 2004; two s. one d.; ed Lycée Victor Duruy, Paris, Politecnico di Torino; spent his childhood travelling with his parents and siblings between UK, Brazil and France; mem. Bd of Dirs Fiat 1997–; analyst, Gen. Electric Co. 2000, later mem. Corp. Audit Group 2001–02; returned to Turin to work with Fiat family business 2002, Vice-Chair. Fiat Group 2004–10, Chair. 2010–, Investment Man. IFIL SpA (investment co., one of Agnelli-family holding cos) 2003–06, Vice-Chair. 2006–; Chair. and CEO EXOR SpA; Chair. IFI SpA 2007–, Giovanni Agnelli e C. Sapaz 2010–; Chair. Itedi SpA (publr of La Stampa); mem. Bd RCS Mediagroup, Le Monde, The Economist Group, Gruppo Banca Leonardo SpA; Vice-Chair. Fondazione Giovanni Agnelli, Italian Aspen Inst.; mem. Confindustria, Fondazione Italia-Cina; mem. Bd of Dirs Le Monde, News Corp 2013–. *Leisure interest:* Juventus football club. *Address:* Fiat SpA, Via Nizza 250, 10126 Turin (office); EXOR, Corso Matteotti 26, 10121 Turin, Italy (office). *Telephone:* (011) 006-1111 (office). *Fax:* (011) 006-3798 (office). *E-mail:* governance@exor.com (office). *Website:* www.fiatspa.com (office); www.exor.com (office).

ELLEMANN-JENSEN, Uffe, MA; Danish politician and international organization official; *Chairman, Baltic Development Forum;* b. 1 Nov. 1941; s. of Jens Peter Jensen; m. Alice Vestergaard 1971; two s. two d.; ed Univ. of Copenhagen; Danish Defence staff 1962–64; Sec., Meat Producers' Asscn 1964–67; journalist on Berlingske Aftenavis 1967–70; econ. and political corresp. Danish TV 1970–75; Ed.-in-Chief and mem. Bd daily newspaper Borsen 1975–76; mem. Parl. 1977–2001 (Liberal), Party Spokesperson, Political Affairs 1978–82, Chair. Parl. Market Cttee 1978–79; mem. Exec. Cttee Liberal Party 1979, Chair. 1984–98; mem. Bd Cen. Bank 1978–81, 1996–99, Index Figures' Bd 1979–81, Inter-Parl. Union 1979–82; Minister of Foreign Affairs 1982–93; Vice-Pres. European Liberal Party 1985–95, Pres. 1995–2000; Co-founder and Chair. Baltic Devt Forum 1998–; Chair. Foreign Policy Soc., Denmark 1993–, Danish Centre for Int. Studies and Human Rights 2002–06, BankInvest (investment and venture capital firm) 2003–; Adjunct Prof., Copenhagen Business School 2006–; Dir Reuters Founders Share Co. Ltd 2000–; Trustee, Int. Crisis Group 1999–; mem. Bd Royal Theatre 2004, The Vaccine Fund 2005; Dr hc (Univ. of Gadansk) 2002; Robert Schuman Prize 1987, Hansa Prize 1993. *Publications:* De nye millionaerer (The New Millionaires) 1971, Det afhaengige samfund (The Dependent Society) 1972, Hvad gør vi ved Gudenåen (We Ought to Do Something About Gudenåen) 1973, Den truede velstand (The

Threatened Wealth) 1974, Økonomi (Economy) 1975, Da Danmark igen sagde ja til det falles (When Denmark Repeated its Yes to Europe) 1987, Olfert Fischer 1991, Et lille land – og dog (A Small Country – And Yet) 1991, Din egen dag er kort (Short is Your Own Day) 1996, Ude med snøren (Going Fishing) 2001, Østen for solen (East of the Sun) 2002, Fodfejl (Foot Fault) 2004, Fodfejl: Da Danmark svigtede om den kolde krig 2005, og Vejen jeg valgte 2007; numerous articles in newspapers and periodicals. *Leisure interests:* fishing, hunting, opera. *Address:* Baltic Development Forum, Nygade 3, 5th Floor, PO Box 56, 1002 Copenhagen K, Denmark (office). *Telephone:* 7020-9394 (office). *Fax:* 7020-9395 (office). *E-mail:* bdf@bdforum.org (office); uffe@ellemann.dk (home). *Website:* www.bdforum.org (office).

ELLER, Timothy, BS; American building industry executive; *Vice Chairman, Pulte Homes Inc.;* b. 1948; ed Univ. of Nebraska; joined Centex Homes, Ill. 1973, Project Man. 1975, Vice-Pres. Minn. Div. 1977, Pres. 1981, Exec. Vice-Pres. Centex Real Estate Corpn/Centex Homes 1985–90, Pres. and COO 1990–91, Pres. and CEO Centex Homes 1991–98, Chair. 1998–2003, Exec. Vice-Pres. Centex Corpn 1998, Pres. and COO 2002, mem. Bd of Dirs 2002–, Chair. and CEO 2004–09, Vice-Chair. Pulte Homes Inc., Bloomfield Hills, Mich. (after merger of Centex and Pulte) 2009–; Chair. High Production Home Builders Council; mem. Exec. Cttee Jt Center for Housing Studies, Harvard Univ.; Life Trustee, Nat. Housing Endowment; mem. Bd of Trustees Nature Conservancy of Tex. *Address:* Pulte Homes Inc., 100 Bloomfield Hills Pkwy, Suite 300, Bloomfield Hills, MI 48304, USA (office). *Telephone:* (248) 647-2750 (office). *Fax:* (248) 433-4598 (office). *Website:* www.pulte .com (office).

ELLINGSRUD, Geir, CandReal, PhD; Norwegian mathematician, academic and fmr university rector; *Professor of Mathematics, University of Oslo;* b. 29 Nov. 1948; ed Univ. of Oslo, Stockholm Univ., Sweden; Asst Lecturer, Univ. of Oslo 1973–80, Assoc. Prof. 1985–89, Prof. of Math. 1992–; Rector Univ. of Oslo 2006–09; Guest Prof., Univ. of Strasbourg, France 1980–81, Univ. of Nice, France 1982–83; Lecturer, Stockholm Univ. 1983–84; Prof. of Math., Univ. of Bergen 1989–92. *Address:* University of Oslo, PO Box 1072, Blindern, 0316 Oslo, Norway (office). *Telephone:* 22-85-58-88 (office). *E-mail:* ellingsr@math.uio.no (office). *Website:* www.math.uio.no (office).

ELLIOTT, Rev. Charles Middleton, MA, DPhil; British ecclesiastic and academic; *Associate, Prison Research Centre, University of Cambridge;* b. 9 Jan. 1939, Wakefield; s. of Joseph William Elliott and Mary Evelyn Elliott; m. 1st Hilary Margaret Hambling 1962 (divorced 2003); three s. one d. (deceased); m. 2nd Virginia Clare Greany 2004; ed Repton, Lincoln and Nuffield Colls Oxford and Scholae Cancellarii, Lincoln; lecturer in Econs Univ. of Nottingham 1962–65; Reader in Econs Univ. of Zambia 1965–69; Asst Sec. Jt Cttee on Soc., Devt and Peace, Vatican/WCC, Geneva 1969–72; Sr Lecturer in Econs Univ. of E Anglia 1972–77; Prof. of Devt Studies, Univ. of Wales 1977–82; Dir Christian Aid 1982–84; Benjamin Meaker Prof. Univ. of Bristol 1985–86; Visiting Prof. King's Coll. London 1987–88; Prebendary of Lichfield Cathedral 1987–96; Fellow, Chaplain and Dean, Trinity Hall, Cambridge 1990–2001, now Dean Emer., also Affiliated Lecturer in Theology, Univ. of Cambridge 1991–2001, in Social and Political Sciences 1993–2001, Assoc. of Prison Research Centre 1995–; Sec. Inst. of Contemporary Spirituality 1988–92; Pres. Feed the Minds 1991; Chair. Univ. Bd of Electors to Livings 1997; Collins Religious Book Prize 1985. *Publications:* Patterns of Poverty in the Third World 1975, Praying the Kingdom 1985, Praying through Paradox 1987, Comfortable Compassion 1987, Signs of Our Times 1988, Sword and Spirit: Christianity in a Divided World 1989, Memory and Salvation 1995, Strategic Planning for Churches: An Appreciative Approach 1997, Locating the Energy for Change: An Introduction to Appreciative Inquiry 1999; numerous articles in learned journals. *Leisure interests:* walking, gardening, fly-fishing, sailing. *Address:* Old Forge, Colney, Norwich, NR4 5TW, England (home). *Telephone:* (1603) 454606 (home); (7944) 023886. *E-mail:* charleselliott9988@gmail.com (home).

ELLIOTT, Sir John Huxtable, Kt, FBA; British historian and academic; b. 23 June 1930, Reading, Berks.; s. of Thomas Charles Elliott and Janet Mary Payne; m. Oonah Sophia Butler 1958; ed Eton Coll. and Trinity Coll., Cambridge; Asst Lecturer in History, Univ. of Cambridge 1957–62, Lecturer 1962–67; Prof. of History, King's Coll., Univ. of London 1968–73; Prof., School of Historical Studies, Inst. for Advanced Study, Princeton, NJ 1973–90; Regius Prof. of Modern History, Univ. of Oxford and Fellow, Oriel Coll., Oxford 1990–97; Fellow, Trinity Coll., Cambridge 1954–67; mem. Scientific Cttee, Prado Museum 1996; Fellow, Royal Acad. of History, Madrid, American Acad. of Arts and Sciences, American Philosophical Soc., King's Coll., Univ. of London 1998, Accad. Naz. dei Lincei 2003, Accad. delle Scienze di Torino 2009, Académico de honor, Real Academia de Buenas Letras de Sevilla 2009; Hon. Fellow, Trinity Coll. Cambridge 1991, Oriel Coll. Oxford 1997; Commdr, Order of Alfonso X El Sabio 1984, Commdr, Order of Isabel la Católica 1987, Grand Cross of Order of Alfonso X, El Sabio 1988, Grand Cross of Order of Isabel la Católica 1996, Cross of Sant Jordi (Catalonia) 1999; Dr hc (Universidad Autónoma de Madrid) 1983, (Genoa) 1992, (Portsmouth) 1993, (Barcelona) 1994, (Warwick) 1995, (Brown) 1996, (Valencia) 1998, (Lleida) 1999, (Madrid Complutense) 2003, (Coll. of William and Mary) 2005, (London) 2007, (Carlos III, Madrid) 2008; Visitante Ilustre of Madrid 1983, Leo Gershoy Award, American Historical Asscn 1985, Wolfson Literary Award for History and Biography 1986, Medal of Honour, Universidad Int. Menéndez y Pelayo 1987, Gold Medal for Fine Arts (Spain) 1991, Eloy Antonio de Nebrija Prize (Univ. of Salamanca) 1993, Prince of Asturias Prize in Social Sciences 1996, Gold Medal, Spanish Inst., New York 1997, Balzan Prize for History 1500–1800 1999. *Publications:* Imperial Spain, 1469–1716 1963, The Revolt of the Catalans 1963, Europe Divided, 1559–1598 1968, The Old World and the New, 1492–1650 1970, The Diversity of History (co-ed. with H. G. Koenigsberger) 1970, A Palace for a King (with J. Brown) 1980 (revised edn 2003), Memoriales y Cartas del Conde Duque de Olivares 1978–80, Richelieu and Olivares 1984, The Count-Duke of Olivares 1986, Spain and Its World 1500–1700 1989, The Hispanic World (ed.) 1991, The World of the Favourite (co-ed.) 1999, The Sale of the Century (with J. Brown) 2002, Empires of the Atlantic World (Francis Parkman Prize 2007) 2006, Spain, Europe and the Wider World 1500–1800 2009. *Leisure interest:* looking at paintings. *Address:* 122 Church Way, Iffley, Oxford, OX4 4EG, England. *Telephone:* (1865) 716703. *E-mail:* john.elliott@history.ox.ac.uk (office).

ELLIOTT, Marianne, OBE, DPhil, FRHistS, FBA; Irish historian and academic; *Blair Chair of Irish Studies and Director, Institute of Irish Studies, University of Liverpool;* b. 25 May 1948, Northern Ireland; d. of Terence J. Burns and Sheila O'Neill; m. Prof. Trevor Elliott 1975; one s.; ed Dominican Convent, Fort William, Belfast, Queen's Univ. Belfast and Lady Margaret Hall, Oxford; French Govt research scholar in Paris 1972–73; other research in Ireland, UK, France, Netherlands and USA; Lecturer in History, West London Inst. of Higher Educ. 1975–77; Research Fellow, Univ. Coll. Swansea 1977–82; Visiting Prof., Iowa State Univ. 1983, Univ. of South Carolina 1984; Research Fellow, Univ. of Liverpool 1984–87; Simon Fellow, Univ. of Manchester 1988–89; Lecturer, Birkbeck Coll., Univ. of London 1991–93; Andrew Geddes and John Rankin Prof. of Modern History, Univ. of Liverpool 1993–2008, Dir Inst. of Irish Studies 1997–, Blair Chair of Irish Studies 2008–; mem. Int. Opsahl Comm. on the Conflict in NI 1993, Encounter 1998–; Fellow, British Acad. 2000, section mem. of Modern History; Leo Gershoy Award for History 1983, Sunday Independent/Irish Life Award for Biography 1989, James Donnelly Sr Award for History (American Conf. for Irish Studies) 1991, Ford's Lecturer, Univ. of Oxford 2005. *Publications:* Partners in Revolution: The United Irishmen and France 1982, Watchmen in Sion: The Protestant Idea of Liberty 1985, The People's Armies (translation) 1987, Wolfe Tone: Prophet of Irish Independence 1989, A Citizens' Inquiry: The Report of the Opsahl Commission on Northern Ireland 1993, The Catholics in Ireland: A History 2000, The Long Road to Peace in Northern Ireland (ed.) 2001, Robert Emmet: The Making of a Legend 2003, When God Took Sides. Religion and Identity in Ireland, Unfinished History 2009. *Leisure interests:* running, swimming, hill-walking, following the tangleweed of Northern Irish identities. *Address:* Institute of Irish Studies, University of Liverpool, 1 Abercromby Square, Liverpool, L69 7WY, England (office). *Telephone:* (151) 794-3831 (office). *Fax:* (151) 794-3836 (office). *E-mail:* melliott@liverpool.ac.uk (office); irishstudies@liv.ac.uk (office). *Website:* www.liv.ac.uk/irish (office).

ELLIOTT, Sir Roger James, Kt, MA, DPhil, FRS; British physicist and publisher; b. 8 Dec. 1928, Chesterfield, Derbyshire; s. of James Elliott and Gladys Elliott (née Hill); m. Olga Lucy Atkinson 1952; one s. two d.; ed Swanwick Hall School, Derbyshire, New Coll., Oxford; Research Assoc., Univ. of California, Berkeley, USA 1952–53; Research Fellow, Atomic Energy Research Establishment, Harwell 1953–55; Lecturer, Univ. of Reading 1955–57; Lecturer, Univ. of Oxford 1957–65, Reader 1965–74, Fellow, St John's Coll. 1957–74 (now Hon. Fellow), New Coll. 1974–96 (now Hon. Fellow), Wykeham Prof. of Physics 1974–89, Prof. of Physics 1989–96, Prof. Emer. 1996–; Del., Oxford University Press 1971–88, Sec. to Dels and Chief Exec. 1988–93, Chair. Computer Bd 1983–87; mem. Bd Blackwell Ltd 1996–, Chair. 1999–2002; Visiting Prof., Univ. of California, Berkeley 1960–61; Miller Visiting Prof., Univ. of Illinois, Urbana, USA 1966; Visiting Distinguished Prof., Florida State Univ. 1981, Michigan State Univ. 1997–2000; Physical Sec. and Vice-Pres. Royal Soc. (London) 1984–88; Treas. Publrs Assocn 1990–92, Pres. 1992–93; Chair. ICSU Press 1997–2002, Disability Information Trust 1998–2001; mem. Bd (part-time) UKAEA 1988–94, British Council 1990–98, Mexican Acad. of Science 2003; Fellow, Inst. of Physics; Treas. ICSU 2002, Academia Europaea 2009; Hon. DSc (Paris) 1983, (Bath) 1991, (Essex) 1993; Maxwell Medal (Physical Soc.) 1968, Guthrie Medal 1989. *Publications:* Magnetic Properties of Rare Earth Metals 1972, Solid State Physics and its Applications 1973; articles in academic journals. *Address:* 11 Crick Road, Oxford, OX2 6QL, England (home). *Telephone:* (1865) 273997 (office). *Fax:* (1865) 273947 (office). *E-mail:* r.elliott1@physics.ox.ac.uk (office).

ELLIS, Bret Easton, BA; American writer; b. 7 March 1964, Los Angeles; ed Bennington Coll.; mem. Authors Guild. *Publications:* Less Than Zero 1985, The Rules of Attraction 1987, American Psycho 1989, The Informers (short stories) 1994, Glamorama 1998, Lunar Park 2005, Imperial Bedrooms 2010; contrib. to Rolling Stone, Vanity Fair, Elle, Wall Street Journal, Bennington Review. *Address:* c/o Amanda Urban, ICM Partners, 730 Fifth Avenue, New York, NY 10019, USA (office). *Website:* www.randomhouse.com/kvpa/eastonellis/#/home (office).

ELLIS, Gavin Peter; New Zealand journalist and academic; b. 6 March 1947, Auckland; s. of Peter Fisher Dundass Ellis and Catherine Ellis (née Gray); m. 1st Janine Laurette Sinclair 1969; m. 2nd Jennifer Ann Lynch 1991; one s.; ed Mount Roskill Grammar School and Univ. of Auckland; on staff of Auckland Star paper 1965–70; public relations consultant 1970–71; joined New Zealand Herald 1972, Asst Ed. 1987–96, Ed. 1996–99, Ed.-in-Chief 1999–2005; Sr Lecturer, Univ. of Auckland 2006–12; currently media consultant; presenter, Media with Gavin Ellis, Radio New Zealand; Harry Brittain Memorial Fellow 1980; fmr Chair. NZ Section, Commonwealth Press Union; mem. New Zealand Knowledge Wave Trust; mem. NZ Council for Security Co-operation Asia-Pacific; Astor Award for Press Freedom, Commonwealth Press Union 2005. *Leisure interests:* medieval history, opera. *Address:* c/o Radio New Zealand, PO Box 123, Wellington, New Zealand. *E-mail:* ninetonoon@radionz.co.nz.

ELLIS, George Francis Rayner, FRAS, PhD, FRS; British/South African professor of astrophysics and applied mathematics; *Professor Emeritus, Mathematics Department, University of Cape Town;* b. 11 Aug. 1939, Johannesburg; s. of George Rayner Ellis and Gwen Hilda Ellis (née MacRobert); m. 1st Sue Parkes 1963; one s. one d.; m. 2nd Mary Wheeldon 1978; ed Michaelhouse, Univ. of Cape Town, Univ. of Cambridge, UK; Fellow, Peterhouse, Cambridge 1965–67; Asst Lecturer, then Lecturer, Univ. of Cambridge 1967–73; Prof. of Applied Math., Univ. of Cape Town 1974–88, 1990–2005, Prof. Emer. 2005–; Prof. of Cosmic Physics, SISSA, Trieste 1988–92; G.C. MacVittie Visiting Prof. of Astronomy, Queen Mary Coll., London 1987–; Chair. GR10 Scientific Cttee 1988; mem. Int. Cttee on Gen. Relativity and Gravitation; Pres., Int. Soc. of Gen. Relativity and Gravitation 1989–92; mem. Cttee (and Vice-Pres.) Royal Soc. of SA 1990–, Pres. 1992–96; Founding mem. and fmr mem. Council, Acad. of Science of SA; Fellow, Univ. of Cape Town, Inst. of Math. and its Applications, Third World Acad. of Science 2004–; Jt Ed.-in-Chief International Journal of General Relativity and Gravitation 2006–; Chair. Quaker Service, West Cape 1976–86, 1990–, Quaker Peacework Cttee 1978–86, 1990–95, SA Inst. of Race Relations, West Cape 1985–87; Clerk SA Yearly Meeting of Quakers 1986–88; Fellowship of Univ. of Cape Town; mem. Bd of Dirs, Asscn for Educational Transformation, Early Learning Resource Unit, Philani Child Health and Nutrition Project; Hon. Fellow,

Royal Soc. of SA 2008–; Order of Mapungubwe (Silver) 2006; Hon. DSc (Haverford Coll.) 1996, (Natal Univ.) 1998, (Queen Mary, Univ. of London) 2004, (Univ. of Cape Town) 2009; Herschel Medal of Royal Soc. of SA, Gravity Research Foundation 1st Prize 1979, Templeton Prize 2004, Science-for-Society Gold Medal, Acad. of Science of South Africa 2005. *Publications:* The Large Scale Structure of Space-Time (with S. W. Hawking) 1973, The Squatter Problem in the Western Cape (with J. Maree, D. Hendrie) 1976, Low Income Housing Policy (with D. Dewar) 1980, Flat and Curved Space-Times (with R. Williams) 1988, Before the Beginning 1993, The Renaissance of General Relativity and Cosmology (co-ed.) 1993, The Dynamical Systems Approach to Cosmology (co-ed.) 1996, The Density of Matter in the Universe (with P. Coles) 1996, On the Moral Nature of the Universe: Cosmology, Theology and Ethics (with N. Murphy) 1996. *Leisure interests:* climbing, gliding. *Address:* Department of Mathematics and Applied Mathematics, University of Cape Town, Rondebosch 7701, Cape Town (office); 10 Brabant Court, Marna da Gama, Cape Town 7945, South Africa (home). *Telephone:* (21) 6502339 (office); (21) 7888387 (home). *Fax:* (21) 6502334 (office). *E-mail:* george.ellis@uct.ac.za (office); gfrellis@gmail.com (home). *Website:* www .mth.uct.ac.za/~ellis (office).

ELLIS, Adm. (retd) James (Jim) Oren, Jr, MSc; American naval officer (retd) and aerospace engineering; *President and CEO, Institute of Nuclear Power Operations (INPO);* b. 20 July 1947, Spartanburg, SC; m. Paula Matthews (died 2008); ed US Naval Acad., Georgia Inst. of Tech., Univ. of West Florida, Harvard Univ., US Naval Aviator Training, US Naval Test Pilot School, US Naval Nuclear Power Training; Naval Aviator 1971, carrier-based tours with Fighter Squadron 92, USS Constellation (CV 64) and Fighter Squadron 1, USS Ranger (CV 61); first CO of Strike/Fighter Squadron 131, USS Coral Sea (CV 43); served as experimental/operational test pilot, in Navy Office of Legis. Affairs, and F/A-18 Program Coordinator, Deputy Chief of Naval Operations (Air Warfare); served as Exec. Officer of USS Carl Vinson (CVN 70) and CO of USS LaSalle (AGF 3); assumed command of USS Abraham Lincoln (CVN 72) and participated in Operation Desert Storm while deployed during her maiden voyage 1991; Inspector Gen. US Atlantic Fleet, served as Dir for Operations, Plans and Policy on staff of C-in-C US Atlantic Fleet 1993; Commdr Carrier Group Five/Battle Force Seventh Fleet 1995–96; Deputy Commdr and Chief of Staff, Jt Task Force Five (counter-narcotics force for US C-in-C in the Pacific); Deputy Chief of Naval Operations (Plans, Policy and Operations) 1996–98; C-in-C US Naval Forces, Europe, London, UK and C-in-C Allied Forces, Southern Europe, Naples, Italy 1998; C-in-C US Strategic Command, Offutt Air Force Base, Neb. 1998–2004; Pres. and CEO Inst. of Nuclear Power Operations (INPO) 2005–12; mem. Bd of Dirs Lockheed Martin Corpn, Level 3 Communications, Inc. 2005–; Advisor to Bd, Inmarsat 2004, Bd of Dirs Inmarsat PLC 2005–; US Presidential appointee, Foreign Intelligence Advisory Bd 2006–09; Order of Merit (Hungary), Grand Order of Merit (Italy), Star of Merit and Honor (Greece); Defense Distinguished Service Medal (three awards), Navy Distinguished Service Medal, Legion of Merit (four awards), Defense Meritorious Service Medal, Meritorious Service Medal (two awards), Navy Commendation Medal; inducted into Georgia Inst. of Tech. Eng Hall of Fame. *Leisure interests:* running, cycling, hiking, fly-fishing, reading. *Address:* Institute of Nuclear Power Operations, 700 Galleria Parkway SE, Suite 100, Atlanta, GA 30339-5943 (office); 3150 Shumard Way, Marietta, GA 30064, USA (home). *Telephone:* (770) 644-8000 (office); (770) 427-8960 (home). *Fax:* (770) 644-8549 (office); (770) 427-0245 (home). *E-mail:* ellisjo@inpo.org (office); joellisjr@comcast.net (home). *Website:* www.inpo .info (office).

ELLIS, John Martin, BA, PhD; American academic; *Professor Emeritus of German Literature, University of California, Santa Cruz;* b. 31 May 1936, London, England; s. of John Albert Ellis and Emily Ellis; m. Barbara Rhoades 1978; two s. two d. one step-d.; ed City of London School and Univ. Coll., London; Royal Artillery 1954–56; Tutorial Asst in German, Univ. of Wales, Aberystwyth 1959–60; Asst Lecturer in German, Univ. of Leicester 1960–63; Asst Prof. of German, Univ. of Alberta, Canada 1963–66; Assoc. Prof. of German Literature, Univ. of Calif., Santa Cruz 1966–70, Prof. 1970–94, Prof. Emer. 1994–, Dean Graduate Div. 1977–86; Literary Ed. Heterodoxy 1992–2000; Sec.-Treas. Asscn of Literary Scholars and Critics 1994–2001; Pres. Calif. Asscn of Scholars 2007–; Guggenheim Fellowship, Nat. Endowment for the Humanities Sr Fellowship; Nat. Asscn of Scholars' Peter Shaw Memorial Award (for Literature Lost). *Publications include:* Narration in the German Novelle 1974, The Theory of Literary Criticism: A Logical Analysis 1974, Heinrich von Kleist 1979, One Fairy Story Too Many: The Brothers Grimm and Their Tales 1983, Against Deconstruction 1989, Language, Thought and Logic 1993, Literature Lost: Social Agendas and the Corruption of the Humanities 1997. *Leisure interests:* birdwatching, golf. *Address:* 144 Bay Heights, Soquel, CA 95073, USA (home). *Telephone:* (831) 476-1144 (home). *Fax:* (831) 476-1188 (home). *E-mail:* johnellis2608@att.net (office).

ELLIS, (Jonathan Richard) John, CBE, MA, PhD, FRS, FInstP; British physicist and academic; *Clerk Maxwell Professor of Theoretical Physics, King's College London;* b. 1 July 1946, Hampstead, London, England; s. of Richard Ellis and Beryl Lilian Ellis (née Ranger); m. Maria Mercedes Martinez Rengifo 1985; one s. one d.; ed Highgate School, King's Coll., Cambridge; Post-doctoral Research Fellow, Stanford Linear Accelerator Center, USA 1971–72; Richard Chase Tolman Fellow, California Inst. of Tech., USA 1972–73; Research Fellow, CERN, Geneva, Switzerland 1973–74, staff mem. 1974–, Leader, Theoretical Physics Div. 1988–94, Sr Staff Physicist 1994–, also Adviser to CERN Dir-Gen. on relations with nonmem. states; currently Clerk Maxwell Prof. of Theoretical Physics, King's Coll. London; Hon. Fellow, King's Coll. Cambridge 2006; Dr hc (Southampton) 1994; Maxwell Medal, Royal Soc. 1982, Dirac Medal and Prize, Inst. of Physics 2005. *Publications:* more than 800 scientific publs in professional journals. *Leisure interests:* literature, music, travel, hiking, cinema. *Address:* Department of Physics, King's College London, The Strand, London, WC2R 2LS, England (office); Theory Division, CERN, 1211 Geneva 23 (office); 5 Chemin du Ruisseau, Tannay, 1295 Mies, Vaud, Switzerland (home). *Telephone:* (20) 7848-2148 (London) (office); (22) 7674142 (Geneva) (office); (22) 7764858 (Geneva) (home). *Fax:* (20) 7848-2420 (London) (office); (22) 7673850 (Geneva) (office); (22) 7764858 (Geneva) (home). *E-mail:* john .ellis@cern.ch (office). *Website:* www.cern.ch (office).

ELLIS, Reginald John, PhD, FRS; British biologist and academic; *Professor Emeritus of Biological Sciences, University of Warwick;* b. 12 Feb. 1935, Newcastle-under-Lyme, Staffs.; s. of Francis Gilbert Ellis and Evangeline Gratton Ellis; m. Diana Margaret Warren 1963; one d.; ed Highbury Grove Grammar School, London and King's Coll., London; Agricultural Research Council Fellow, Dept of Biochemistry, Univ. of Oxford 1961–64; Lecturer, Depts of Botany and Biochemistry, Univ. of Aberdeen 1964–70; Sr Lecturer, Univ. of Warwick 1970–73, Reader 1973–76, Prof. of Biological Sciences 1976–96, Prof. Emer. 1996–, f. Molecular Chaperone Club; Sr Research Fellow, Science and Eng Research Council 1983–88; mem. European Molecular Biology Org. 1986–; Sr Visiting Research Fellow, St John's Coll. Oxford 1992–93; Academic Visitor, Oxford Centre for Molecular Sciences 1996–2000; Tate & Lyle Award 1980, International Gairdner Foundation Award 2004, Cell Stress and Chaperones Int. Medal 2007, Royal Soc. Croonian Lecture Prize 2011. *Publications:* Chloroplast Biogenesis (ed.) 1984, Molecular Chaperones (ed.) 1990, The Chaperonins (ed.) 1996, Molecular Chaperones Ten Years On (ed.) 2000, Protein Misfolding and Human Disease (ed.) 2004, How Science Works: Evolution 2010; 165 papers on plant and microbial biochemistry. *Leisure interests:* landscape photography, fell walking.

ELLIS, Richard Salisbury, CBE, DPhil, FRS, FRAS, FInstP; British astronomer and academic; *Steele Professor of Astronomy, California Institute of Technology;* b. 25 May 1950, Colwyn Bay, Wales; s. of the late Capt. Arthur Ellis and of Marion Ellis; m. Barbara Williams 1972; one s. one d.; ed Univ. Coll., London, Univ. of Oxford; researcher, Durham Univ. 1974–81, Lecturer 1981–83, Prof. of Astronomy 1985–93, Visiting Prof. 1994–; Plumian Prof., Univ. of Cambridge 1993–99, Visiting Prof. 2000–03, Dir Inst. of Astronomy 1994–99, Professorial Fellow, Magdalene Coll. Cambridge 1994–99; Prof. of Astronomy, California Inst. of Tech., USA 1999–2002, Steele Prof. of Astronomy 2002–, Dir Palomar Observatory 2000–02, Caltech Optical Observatories 2002–05; Royal Soc. Prof., Univ. of Oxford 2008–09, Professorial Fellow, Merton Coll., Oxford 2008–09; Sr Research Fellow, Royal Greenwich Observatory 1983–85; Visiting Prof., Univ. Coll. London 2004–; mem. American Astronomical Soc.; Fellow, Univ. Coll. London 1998; Hon. DSc (Durham) 2002; Bakerian Prize, Royal Soc. 1998, Gruber Cosmology Prize 2007, Gold Medal, Royal Astronomical Soc. 2011. *Publications:* numerous articles in scientific journals; Observational Tests of Cosmological Inflation 1991, Large Scale Structure in the Universe 1999. *Leisure interests:* skiing, photography, travel. *Address:* Astronomy Department, Mail Stop 249-17, California Institute of Technology, Pasadena, CA 91125, USA (office). *Telephone:* (626) 395-2598 (office); (626) 676-5530 (home). *Fax:* (626) 568-9352 (office). *E-mail:* rse@astro.caltech.edu (office). *Website:* www.astro.caltech.edu/~rse (office).

ELLISON, Harlan Jay; American author and screenwriter; b. 27 May 1934, Cleveland, OH; s. of Louis Laverne Ellison and Serita (née Rosenthal) Ellison; m. 1st Charlotte Stein 1956 (divorced 1959); m. 2nd Billie Joyce Sanders 1961 (divorced 1962); m. 3rd Lory Patrick 1965 (divorced 1965); m. 4th Lori Horwitz 1976 (divorced 1977); m. 5th Susan Toth 1986; ed Ohio State Univ.; part-time actor, Cleveland Playhouse 1944–49; f. Cleveland Science-Fiction Soc. 1950 and Science-Fantasy Bulletin; served US Army 1957–59; ed. Rogue magazine, Chicago 1959-60, Regency Books, Chicago 1960–61; lecturer at colls and univs; voice-overs for animated cartoons; book critic, LA Times 1969–82; Editorial Commentator Canadian Broadcasting Co. 1972–78; Instructor Clarion Writers Workshop, Michigan State Univ. 1969–77; Pres. The Kilimanjaro Corpn 1979–; TV writer for Alfred Hitchcock Hour, Outer Limits, The Man from U.N.C.L.E., Burke's Law; film writer for The Dream Merchants, The Oscar, Nick the Greek, Best By Far, Harlan Ellison's Movie; scenarist: I, Robot 1978, Bug Jack Barron 1982–83; creative consultant, writer and dir The Twilight Zone 1984–85; conceptual consultant, Babylon 5 1993–98; mem. American Writers' Guild and American Science Fiction Writers; Hugo Awards 1967, 1968, 1973, 1974, 1975, 1977, 1986, Special Achievement Awards 1968–72, Certificate of Merit, Trieste Film Festival 1970, Edgar Allan Poe Award, Mystery Writers 1974, 1988, American Mystery Award 1988, Bram Stoker Award, Horror Writers Asscn 1988, 1990, 1994; World Fantasy Award 1989, Georges Méliès Award for cinematic achievement 1972, 1973, PEN Award for journalism 1982; Americana Annual American Literature: Major Works 1988, World Fantasy 1993 Life Achievement Award, two Audie Awards, Audio Publishers Asscn 1999 and numerous other awards. *Publications include:* Web of the City 1958, The Deadly Streets 1958, Sex Gang 1959, A Touch of Infinity 1960, The Sound of a Scythe 1960, Spider Kiss 1961, Children of the Streets 1961, Gentleman Jackie 1961, Ellison Wonderland 1962, Paingod 1965, I Have No Mouth and I Must Scream 1967, From the Land of Fear 1967, Dangerous Visions (ed.) 1967, Doomsman 1967, Love ain't Nothing but Sex Mispelled 1968, The Beast that Shouted Love at the Heart of the World 1969, Over the Edge 1970, The Glass Teat 1970, De Helden van de Highway 1973, Approaching Oblivion 1974, Deathbird Stories 1975, No Doors, No Windows 1975, The Other Glass Teat 1975, A Boy and His Dog 1975, Strange Wine 1978, Shatterday 1980, Stalking the Nightmare 1982, An Edge in My Voice 1985, Demon with a Glass Hand 1986, Night and the Enemy 1987, The Essential Ellison 1987, Angry Candy 1988, Harlan Ellison's Watching 1989, Vic and Blood 1989, The Harlan Ellison Hornbook 1990, Harlan Ellison's Movie 1990, All the Lies that are my Life 1991, Run for the Stars 1991, Mefisto in Onyx 1993, Mind Fields (33 stories inspired by the art of Jacek Yerka) 1994, Robot: The Illustrated Screenplay 1994, City on the Edge of Forever (screenplay) 1995, Jokes without Punchlines 1995, Slippage 1996, Harlan Ellison's Dream Corridor 1996, Edgeworks: The Collected Ellison (four vols) 1996–97, Repent, Harlequin 1997, Troublemakers 2001. *Leisure interests:* shooting pool, supporting progressive and environmental agendas and causes. *Address:* c/o The Harlan Ellison Recording Collection, PO Box 55548, Sherman Oaks, CA 91413-0548, USA (office). *Website:* harlanellison.com.

ELLISON, Lawrence (Larry) J.; American software industry executive; *CEO, Oracle Corporation;* b. 1944, Bronx, New York; divorced; two c.; ed Univs of Illinois and Chicago; started as technician with Firemans' Fund, Wells Fargo Bank; with Ampex built databases; co-f. Software Devt Labs (later Oracle Corpn) 1977, CEO 1977–, Pres. 1978–96, mem. Bd of Dirs and Chair. 1990–92, 1995–2004; mem. Bd of Dirs Apple Computer Inc. 1997; ranked by Forbes magazine amongst The World's Most Powerful People (58th) 2013. *Leisure interests:* racing sail boats, flying aeroplanes, playing tennis and guitar. *Address:* Oracle Corpn, 500 Oracle Parkway, Redwood City, CA 94065-1675, USA (office). *Telephone:* (650) 506-7000 (office). *Fax:* (650) 506-7200 (office). *E-mail:* info@oracle.com (office). *Website:* www .oracle.com (office).

ELLMAN, Michael, MSc(Econ), PhD; British economist and academic; *Professor of Economics, University of Amsterdam;* b. 27 July 1942, Ripley, Surrey; m. Patricia Harrison 1965; one s. one d.; ed Univ. of Cambridge and London School of Econs; Lecturer, Glasgow Univ. 1967–69; Research Officer then Sr Research Officer, Dept of Applied Econs, Univ. of Cambridge 1969–75; Assoc. Prof., Univ. of Amsterdam 1975–78, Prof. of Econs 1978–; Fellow, Tinberg Inst.; Kondratieff Prize 1998. *Publications:* Planning Problems in the USSR 1973, Socialist Planning 1989, The Destruction of the Soviet Economic System (ed. with V. Kontovovich) 1998, Russia's Oil and Natural Gas: Bonanza or Curse? (ed.) 2006. *Leisure interests:* walking, cycling. *Address:* Department of Economics, Universiteit van Amsterdam, Roetersstraat 11, 1018 WB Amsterdam, Netherlands (office). *Telephone:* (20) 5254235 (office). *Fax:* (20) 5254254 (office). *E-mail:* m.j.ellman@uva.nl (office). *Website:* www.feb.uva.nl (office).

ELLROY, James; American writer; b. (Lee Earle Ellroy), 4 March 1948, Los Angeles, Calif.; m. 1st Mary Doherty 1988 (divorced 1991); m. 2nd Helen Knode 1991; ed John Burroughs Junior High School and Fairfax High School, Los Angeles. *Films include:* Dark Blue 2002, Street Kings (screenplay and story) 2008. *Publications:* Brown's Requiem 1981, Clandestine 1982, Blood on the Moon (Lloyd Hopkins series) 1983, Because the Night (Lloyd Hopkins series) 1984, Killer on the Road 1986, Silent Terror 1986, Suicide Hill (Lloyd Hopkins series) 1986, The Black Dahlia (LA series) 1987, The Big Nowhere (LA series) 1988, LA Confidential (LA series) 1990, White Jazz (LA series) 1992, Hollywood Nocturnes (essays and stories) 1994, American Tabloid (Underworld USA series) (Time Magazine Novel of the Year) 1995, My Dark Places (memoir) (Salon.com Book of the Year) 1996, LA Noir 1998, Crime Wave (essays and stories) 1999, The Cold Six Thousand (Underworld USA series) 2001, Destination: Morgue (essays and stories) 2003, Blood's a Rover 2009, The Hilliker Curse: My Pursuit of Women 2010. *Address:* Sobel Weber Associates Inc, 146 East 19th Street, New York, NY 10003-2404, USA (office). *Telephone:* (212) 420-8585 (office). *Website:* www.sobelweber.com (office).

ELLWOOD, David T., PhD; American economist and academic; *Scott M. Black Professor of Political Economy and Dean, John F. Kennedy School of Government, Harvard University;* b. Minnesota; m. Marilyn Ellwood; two d.; ed Harvard Univ.; Research Asst, Cttee on Costs and Benefits of Auto Air Emission Controls, Nat. Bureau of Econ. Research 1974, Research Asst 1978–80, Research Assoc. 1988–; Research Asst to A. Mitchell Polinsky, Harvard Univ. 1974–75, to Prof. Martin S. Feldstein 1974–75, 1977, Teaching Fellow, Labor Econs 1977–79; Research Assoc., Health Policy Program, Univ. of California, San Francisco 1975–76; Asst Prof. of Public Policy, John F. Kennedy School of Govt, Harvard Univ. 1980–84, Assoc. Prof. of Public Policy 1984–88, Prof. of Public Policy 1988–92, Co-Dir Malcolm Wiener Center for Social Policy 1992–93, Academic Dean, 1992–93, 1995–97, Malcolm Wiener Prof. of Public Policy 1992–93, 1995–98, Dir Multidisciplinary Program in Inequality and Social Policy 1998–99, Lucius N. Littauer Prof. of Political Economy 1998–2003, Scott M. Black Prof. of Political Economy 2003–, Dean John F. Kennedy School of Govt 2004–; Asst Sec. for Planning and Evaluation, US Dept of Health and Human Services, Washington, DC 1993–95; Faculty Affiliate, Jt Center for Poverty Research, Northwestern Univ. and Univ. of Chicago 1997–; Sr Research Affiliate, Nat. Poverty Center, Gerald R. Ford School of Public Policy, Univ. of Michigan 2003–; mem. Nat. Acad. of Social Insurance 1990–, Nat. Acad. of Public Admin 2000–; mem. of Review Panel, Work and Welfare Demonstration, Manpower Demonstration Research Corpn 1985–; mem. Bd of Dirs Malcolm Hewitt Wiener Foundation 2000–, Abt Assocs 2001–; Morris and Edna Zale Award for Outstanding Distinction in Scholarship and Public Service, Stanford Univ., David Kershaw Award for Outstanding Contribution to Policy Analysis and Man., Asscn of Public Policy Analysis and Man. *Publications:* A Working Nation?: Workers, Work and Government in the New Economy (co-ed.) 2000; contribs to The Economic Journal, Harvard Business Review, New England Economic Review, Bulletin of the New York Academy of Medicine, The American Prospect, Journal of Economic Perspectives, The New York Times, Washington Post, Los Angeles Times, Boston Globe; books: Poor Support: Poverty and the American Family 1988. *Address:* Office of the Dean, John F. Kennedy School of Government, Harvard Kennedy School, 79 John F. Kennedy Street, Cambridge, MA 02138, USA (office). *Telephone:* (617) 495-1122 (office). *Fax:* (617) 495-9118 (office). *E-mail:* david_ellwood@Harvard.edu (office). *Website:* www.hks.harvard .edu (office).

ELLWOOD, Sir Peter Brian, Kt, CBE, FCIB, FRSA; British business executive; *Chairman, Rexam PLC;* b. 15 May 1943, Bristol; s. of the late Isaac Ellwood and Edith Ellwood (née Trotter); m. Judy Ann Windsor 1968; one s. two d.; ed King's School, Macclesfield; joined Barclays Bank 1961; worked in London and Bristol; Chief Exec. Barclaycard 1985; Dir Barclays Bank (UK) Ltd; Chief Exec. Retail Banking, TSB Bank PLC, Dir TSB Group PLC 1990–95, Chief Exec. 1992–95, Deputy Chief Exec. Lloyds TSB Group PLC 1995–97, Chief Exec. 1997–2003; Chair. ICI PLC 2004–08, mem. Supervisory Bd Akzo Nobel NV (after acquisition of ICI) 2008–; Chair. (non-exec.) Rexam PLC 2008–; Chair. Royal Parks Advisory Bd 2003, Royal Parks Foundation 2003; Deputy Chair. Royal Coll. of Music 2003; Chair. Visa Europe, Middle East and Africa 1992–96, Visa International 1994–99; Dir (non-exec.) Sears PLC 1994–96, Royal Philharmonic Orchestra 1996–; mem. Court Univ. Coll., Northampton (fmrly Nene Coll.) 1989–; Hon. LLD (Leicester) 1994; Dr hc (Univ. of Central England) 1995. *Leisure interests:* music, theatre. *Address:* Rexam PLC, 4 Millbank, London, SW1P 3XR, England (office). *Telephone:* (20) 7227-4100 (office). *Fax:* (20) 7227-4109 (office). *Website:* www.rexam .com (office).

ELLWOOD, Susie, BSE; American publishing and media executive; *Executive Vice-President and General Manager, USA TODAY;* b. Ark.; m. Bill Ellwood; six c.; ed Arkansas State Univ., Jonesboro; fmr Dir Sales and Marketing, National Investors Life Insurance Co., Little Rock, Ark.; Vice-Pres. and Dir of Marketing, Arkansas Gazette (newspaper), Little Rock 1984–91; Vice-Pres. Market Devt, Detroit Media Partnership 1991–2004, Exec. Vice-Pres. and Gen. Man. Detroit Media Partnership 2006–09, CEO 2009–11; Vice-Pres. Market Devt, Gannett's Newspaper Div. 2004–06, Exec. Vice-Pres. and Gen. Man. USA TODAY 2011–; mem. Bd of Dirs Int. Newsmedia Marketing Asscn North America 2011–; mem. Bd Detroit Regional Chamber, Detroit Econ. Club, Inforum Center for Leadership, Make-A-Wish Foundation of Michigan, CATCH, Sparky Anderson's Charity for Children; mem. Int. Women's Forum; recipient of Newspaper Asscn of America's

Distinguished Marketing Award and Lifetime Achievement Award, named Gannett's Manager of the Year 2009, nine-time winner of Gannett's President Ring. *Address:* USA TODAY, 7950 Jones Branch Drive, McLean, VA 22108-0605, USA (office). *Telephone:* (703) 854-3400 (office). *Fax:* (703) 854-2139 (office). *E-mail:* sellwood@usatoday.com (office). *Website:* www.usatoday.com (office).

ELMAN, Richard Samuel; British business executive; *Non-Executive Chairman, Noble Group Ltd;* arrived in Asia from England mid-1960s; Regional Dir of Asia Operations, Phibro, New York, USA 1976–86, mem. Bd of Dirs for two years; Founder and CEO Noble Group Ltd (global commodity merchant) from 1986, Exec. Dir 1994–, Chair. –2010, Chair. Emer. Sept.–Nov. 2010, Chair. (non-exec.) Nov. 2010–, Acting CEO 2011–12; Dir (non-exec.) Consolidated Minerals Ltd 2002–07; mem. Bd of Dirs Territory Resources Ltd June–Dec. 2008; mem. Hong Kong Inst. of Dirs. *Address:* Noble Group Ltd, 18th Floor, MassMutual Tower, 38 Gloucester Road, Hong Kong Special Administrative Region, People's Republic of China (office). *Telephone:* 2861-3511 (office). *Fax:* 2527-0282 (office). *E-mail:* richard@thisisnoble.com (office). *Website:* www.thisisnoble.com (office).

ELMANDJRA, Mahdi, PhD; Moroccan academic; *Professor, University Mohamed V;* b. 13 March 1933, Rabat; s. of M'Hamed Elmandjra and Rabia Elmrini; m. Amina Elmrini 1956; two d.; ed Lycée Lyautey, Casablanca, Putney School, Vermont, USA, Cornell Univ., London School of Econs and Faculté de Droit, Univ. de Paris; Head of Confs, Law Faculty, Univ. of Rabat 1957–58; Adviser, Ministry of Foreign Affairs and to Moroccan Del. to UN 1958–59; Dir-Gen. Radiodiffusion Télévision Marocaine 1959–60; Chief of African Div., Office of Relations with Mem. States, UNESCO 1961–63; Dir Exec. Office of Dir-Gen. of UNESCO 1963–66; Asst Dir-Gen. of UNESCO for Social Sciences, Human Sciences and Culture 1966–69; Visiting Fellow, Centre of Int. Studies, LSE 1970; Asst Dir-Gen. of UNESCO for Pre-Programming 1971–74; Special Adviser to Dir-Gen. of UNESCO 1975–76; Prof., Univ. Mohamed V, Rabat 1977–; Co-ordinator, Conf. on Tech. Co-operation between Developing Countries (UNDP) 1979–80; Sr Adviser, UN Int. Year of Disabled Persons 1980–81; mem. Consultative Cultural Council of the Inst. of the Arab World (Paris); fmr Pres. World Future Studies Fed. (WFSF), Futuribles Int.; mem. Club of Rome, Acad. of the Kingdom of Morocco; Vice-Pres. Asscn Maroc-Japon; mem. World Acad. of Art and Science, Exec. Cttee, Soc. for Int. Devt, Exec. Cttee, African Acad. of Sciences, Pugwash Confs, Founding Pres. Moroccan Asscn of Human Rights, Acad. of the Kingdom of Morocco; Officier des Arts et des Lettres (France), Order of the Rising Sun (Japan) and numerous other decorations; Master Jury Aga Khan Award for Architecture 1986, Albert Einstein Int. Foundation Medal for Peace 1990. *Television:* various programmes for French, Moroccan, Spanish, Japanese and Arab channels. *Publications:* Africa 2000 1980, The New Age of Culture and Communication 1981, The Future of Humor 1982, Maghreb 2000 1982, L'Interpellation du Tiers Monde 1982, Les Aspects économiques du dialogue Euro-Arabe 1982, Information and Sovereignty 1983, The Conquest of Space: Political, Economic and Socio-Cultural Implications 1984, Casablanca 2000 1984, Development and Automation 1985, Communications, Information and Development 1985, Tomorrow's Habitat 1985, Learning Needs in a Changing Society 1986, Media and Communications in Africa 1986, The Future of International Cooperation 1986, The Financing of Research and Development in the Third World 1986, Maghreb et Francophonie 1988, Three Scenarios for The Future of International Cooperation 1988, The Place of Arab Culture in the World of Tomorrow 1988, Social Change and Law 1988, China in the 21st Century 1989, Fusion of Science and Culture: Key to the 21st Century 1989, Human Rights and Development 1989, How to Construct a Positive Vision of the Future 1990, Gulf Crisis: Prelude to the North-South Confrontation 1990, Western Discrimination in the Field of Human Rights 1990, Africa: The Coming Upheaval 1990, La Première Guerre Civilisationnelle 1991, Retrospective des Futurs 1992, Nord-Sud: Prélude à l'Ere Post-coloniale 1992, The Agreements Concerning Gaza and Jericho 1993, Biodiversity: Cultural and Ethical Aspects 1994, Cultural Diversity: Key to Survival in the 21st Century 1994, The New Challenges Facing the United Nations 1995, Dialogue de la Communication 1996, Al Quds (Jerusalem): Symbole et mémoire 1996, La décolonisation culturelle: défi majeur du 21ᵉsiècle 1996, Immigration as a Cultural Phenomenon 1997, The Path of a Mind 1997, Communication Dialogue 2000, Reglobalization of Globalization 2000, Intifadate 2000, Humiliation 2003. *Leisure interests:* reading, swimming, music, writing. *Address:* University Mohamed V, BP 53, Rabat, Morocco (office). *Telephone:* (37) 774-258 (office). *Fax:* (37) 757-151 (office). *E-mail:* elmandjra@elmandjra.org (home). *Website:* www.elmandjra.org (home).

ELMER, Michael B.; Danish lawyer and judge; *President, Iraq and Afghanistan Inquiry;* b. 26 Feb. 1949, Copenhagen; s. of Poul Chr. B. Elmer and Etly Elmer (née Andersson); m. Annette Elmer; one d.; ed Univ. of Copenhagen; civil servant, Ministry of Justice 1973–76, 1977–82, Head of Div. 1982–87, 1988–91, Deputy Perm. Sec., Head of Community Law and Human Rights Dept 1991–94; Assoc. Prof., Univ. of Copenhagen 1975–85; Deputy Judge, Hillerød 1976–77; Asst Public Prosecutor 1980–81; Judge, Court of Ballerup 1981–82; external examiner, Danish law schools 1985–; High Court Judge (a.i.), Eastern High Court, Copenhagen 1987–88; Vice-Pres. (a.i.) Danish Maritime and Commercial High Court, Copenhagen 1988, Vice-Pres., Pres. of Chamber 1997–2012; Pres. Iraq and Afghanistan Inquiry 2012–; Rep. EC Court of Justice, Luxembourg 1991–94; Advocate-Gen. EC Court of Justice 1994–97; mem. Governing Council UNIDROIT, Rome 1999–2013; int. commercial arbitrator; Chair. and mem. numerous govt and int. orgs and cttees; Kt (First Degree), Order of the Dannebrog, Grand Cross, Order of Merit (Luxembourg). *Publications:* several books and articles on civil law, penal law, community law and the law on aliens. *Leisure interests:* travelling, collecting antiques, Leica photography. *Address:* Holbergsgade 6, 1057 Copenhagen K (office); Skovalléen 16, 2880 Bagsvaerd, Denmark (home). *Telephone:* 41-18-50-10 (office). *E-mail:* michael@elmer.eu (home).

ELMI, Mohamed Hashi; Somali civil engineer and politician; *Minister of Finance, 'Somaliland';* b. 1938; fmr Mayor of Hargeisa; Minister of Commerce and Industry, 'Somaliland' 2005, Minister of Finance 2010–; Deputy Chair. Qaran (political grouping) (imprisoned for five months for involvement with banned group 2007). *Address:* Ministry of Finance, Hargeisa, Somalia (office). *Telephone:* 252-225-3605 (office). *Website:* www.somalilandgov.com (office).

ELOP, Stephen, BEngMgt; Canadian engineer and business executive; *Executive Vice-President, Devices Group, Microsoft Corporation;* b. 31 Dec. 1963, Ancaster,

Ont.; m. Nancy Elop; five c. (including triplets and one adopted d.); ed McMaster Univ., Hamilton, Ont.; Chief Information Officer, Boston Chicken, Inc. 1992–98, Einstein Brothers Bagels, Inc. 1994–97; joined Macromedia 1998, held numerous sr positions, including COO, Exec. Vice-Pres. of Worldwide Field Operations, Gen. Man. eBusiness Div. and Pres. and CEO –2005, joined Adobe following acquisition of Macromedia Inc. 2005, Pres. Worldwide Field Operations 2005–06; COO Juniper Networks 2007–08; Pres. Microsoft Business Div., Microsoft Corpn 2008–10, mem. sr leadership team that set overall strategy and direction for Microsoft, oversaw the Information Worker, Microsoft Business Solutions and Unified Communications Groups, Exec. Vice-Pres. Microsoft Devices Group 2014–; Pres. and CEO Nokia Corpn (first non-Finn) 2010–13, Nokia Leadership Team mem. 2010–13, Chair. 2010–13, mem. Bd of Dirs 2011–13, Exec. Vice-Pres., Devices & Services (until his transfer to Microsoft following sale of business in Sept. 2013) 2013–14; Chair. NAVTEQ Corpn; Hon. LLD (McMaster Univ.). *Address:* Microsoft Corporation, 1 Microsoft Way, Redmond, WA 98052, USA (office). *Telephone:* (425) 882-8080 (office). *Fax:* (425) 706-7329 (office). *Website:* www.microsoft.com (office).

ELRINGTON, Wilfred, SC; Belizean lawyer and politician; *Minister of Foreign Affairs and Foreign Trade;* mem. United Democratic Party; contested Pickstock constituency as an ind. 2002; Minister of Foreign Affairs and Foreign Trade 2008–, Attorney-Gen. 2008–10; Pnr, Pitts and Elrington (law firm). *Address:* Ministry of Foreign Affairs and Foreign Trade and of Tourism, Information and NEMO, New Administration Building, PO Box 174, Belmopan, Belize (office). *Telephone:* 822-2167 (office). *Fax:* 822-2854 (office). *E-mail:* belizemfa@btl.net (office). *Website:* www.mfa.gov.bz (office).

ELS, Theodore Ernest (Ernie); South African professional golfer; b. 17 Oct. 1969, Johannesburg; s. of Nils Els and Hettie Els; m. Leizl Els; one s. one d.; wins include South African Open 1992, 1996, US Open, 1994, 1997, Toyota World Matchplay Championships 1994, 1995, 1996, South African PGA Championship 1995, Byron Nelson Classic 1995, Buick Classic 1996, 1997, Johnnie Walker Classic 1997, Bay Hill Invitational 1998, Nissan Open 1999, Int. presented by Quest 2000, Standard Life Loch Lomond 2000, Open Championship 2002, 2012, Genuity Championship 2002, sixth World Match Play title 2004, Mercedes Championship 2003; mem. Dunhill Cup Team 1992–2000, World Cup Team 1992, 1993, 1996, 1997, 2001; mem. President's Cup 1996, 1998, 2000; f. Ernie Els and Fancourt Foundation 1999; South African Sportsman of the Year 1994, Lifetime Membership European Tour 1998. *Leisure interests:* movies, reading, sport. *Address:* 46 Chapman Road, Klippoortjie 1401, South Africa. *E-mail:* info@ernieels .com. *Website:* www.ernieels.com.

ELSTEIN, David Keith, MA; British broadcasting executive; *Chairman, open Democracy;* b. 14 Nov. 1944; ed Haberdashers' Aske's School, Gonville and Caius Coll. Cambridge; producer (BBC) The Money Programme, Panorama, Cause for Concern, People in Conflict 1964–68; (Thames TV) This Week, The Day Before Yesterday, The World At War 1968–72; (London Weekend) Weekend World 1972; Ed. This Week (Thames TV) 1974–78; f. Brook Productions 1982; Exec. Producer A Week in Politics 1982–86, Concealed Enemies 1983; Man. Dir Primetime TV 1983–86; Dir of Programmes, Thames TV 1986–92; Head of Programmes BSkyB 1993–96; Chief Exec. Channel 5 Broadcasting 1996–2000; Chair. Nat. Film and TV School 1996–2002, British Screen Advisory Council 1997–2008, Broadcasting Policy Group 2003–, Commercial Radio Cos Asscn 2004–06, Screen Digest 2004–10, XSN PLC 2004–08, Sparrowhawk Investments Ltd 2004–07, DCD Media PLC 2005–11, Luther Pendragon Holdings 2006–10, open Democracy 2009–; Vice-Chair. Kingsbridge Capital Advisors Ltd 2004–; Dir Virgin Media Inc. 2003–08; Visiting Prof., Univ. of Stirling 1995–2000, Univ. of Oxford 1999, Univ. of Westminster 2000–05. *Publications:* The Political Structure of UK Broadcasting 1949–1999 (Oxford Lectures) 1999, Beyond The Charter: The BBC After 2006 (Broadcasting Policy Group) 2004. *Leisure interests:* theatre, cinema, bridge, politics, reading. *E-mail:* elsteindavid@aol.com (home).

ELSTONE, Robert G., BA (Hons), MA (Econ), MCom; Australian investment banker and business executive; *Managing Director and CEO, Australian Stock Exchange Ltd (ASX);* ed Univs of London and Manchester, UK and Univ. of Western Australia, Sr Exec. Devt Programs at Harvard and Stanford Grad. Schools of Business, USA; career has spanned investment banking in 1980s, public co. CFO roles in 1990s, aviation and global resource materials sectors, and wholesale financial markets and risk man. in 2000s; managed Australian office of Paribas' int. capital markets activities in Paris, London and New York 1980s; Man. Dir and CEO SFE Corpn (holding co. for Sydney Futures Exchange prior to its merger with Australian Stock Exchange Ltd (ASX)) 2000–06, Man. Dir and CEO ASX 2006–; Dir (non-exec.) Nat. Australia Bank (also Chair. Risk Cttee of the Bd); mem. Bd Guardians Commonwealth Govt's Future Fund; mem. Bd of Dirs SFE Clearing Corpn Ltd, Austraclear Ltd, Australian Clearing House Pty Ltd, ASX Settlement and Transfer Corpn Pty Ltd; Chair. Financial Sector Advisory Council; Adjunct Chair (Professorial Fellow), Finance Faculty, School of Econs and Business, Univ. of Sydney; Hon. Fellow, Finance and Treasury Asscn. *Address:* ASX Ltd, Exchange Centre, 20 Bridge Street, Sydney, NSW 2000, Australia (office). *Telephone:* (2) 9338-0000 (office). *Fax:* (2) 9227-0885 (office). *E-mail:* info@asx.com.au (office). *Website:* www.asx.com.au (office).

ELTIS, Walter Alfred, MA, DLitt; British economist; *Fellow Emeritus, Exeter College, Oxford;* b. 23 May 1933, Warnsdorf, Czechoslovakia; s. of Rev. Martin Eltis and Mary Schnitzer; m. Shelagh M. Owen 1959; one s. two d.; ed Wycliffe Coll., Emmanuel Coll. Cambridge and Nuffield Coll. Oxford; Research Fellow in Econs, Exeter Coll., Oxford 1958–60; Lecturer in Econs, Univ. of Oxford 1961–88; Fellow and Tutor in Econs, Exeter Coll. Oxford 1963–88, Fellow Emer. 1988–; Econ. Dir Nat. Econ. Devt Office 1986–88, Dir-Gen. 1988–92; Chief Econ. Adviser to the Pres. of Bd of Trade 1992–95; Visiting Reader in Econs, Univ. of Western Australia 1970–71; Visiting Prof., Univ. of Toronto 1976–77, European Univ. Florence 1979, Univ. of Reading 1992–2004; Gresham Prof. of Commerce, Gresham Coll. London 1993–96; mem. Reform Club (Chair. 1994–95), Political Economy Club, European Soc. for the History of Econ. Thought (Vice-Pres. 2000–04). *Publications:* Growth and Distribution 1973, Britain's Economic Problem: Too Few Producers (with R. Bacon) 1976, The Classical Theory of Economic Growth 1984, Keynes and Economic Policy (with P. Sinclair) 1988, Classical Economics, Public Expenditure and Growth 1993, Britain's Economic Problem Revisited 1996, Condillac:

Commerce and Government (co-ed. with S. M. Eltis) 1998, Britain, Europe and EMU 2000. *Leisure interests:* chess, music. *Address:* Danesway, Jarn Way, Boars Hill, Oxford, OX1 5JF, England (home). *Telephone:* (1865) 735440 (home).

ELTON, Sir Arnold, Kt, KB, CBE, MS, FRCS, FRSM, FICS; British surgeon; *Health Adviser, Hospital Corporation of America Group of Hospitals;* b. 14 Feb. 1920; s. of the late Max Elton and Ada Elton; m. Billie Pamela Briggs 1952; one s.; ed Univ. Coll., London, Univ. Coll. Hosp. Medical School, London; House Surgeon, House Physician, Casualty Officer, Univ. Coll. Hosp. 1943–45; Sr Surgical Registrar, Charing Cross Hosp. 1947–51; Consultant Surgeon, Harrow Hosp. 1951–70, Mount Vernon Hosp. 1960–70, Wellington Hosp.; Consultant Surgeon, Northwick Park Hosp. and Clinical Research Centre 1970–85 (now Consulting Surgeon); Surgeon Emer. Clementine Churchill Hosp.; First Chair. Medical Staff Cttee Northwick Park Hosp., Chair. Surgical Div. and Theatre Cttee; Health Adviser, Wellington Hosp. 2000–; mem. Ethical Cttee Northwick Park Hosp., Govt Working Party on Breast Screening for Cancer 1985–; Surgical Tutor, Royal Coll. of Surgeons 1970–82; Nat. Chair. Conservative Medical Soc. 1975–92, Chair. European Group and Pres. 1992–97, Pres. Emer. 1997–, European Rep. 1994–, Ed. European Bulletin 1994–, also Chair. Educ. and Research Div.; Examiner, Gen. Nursing Council, Royal Coll. of Surgeons 1971–83; Medical Adviser Virgin Fitness Clubs, Adviser, Hospital Corpn of America Group of Hosps 2009–; Exec. Dir Healthy Living (UK) Ltd, Healthy Living (Durham) Ltd, Universal Lifestyle Ltd, Medical Consulting Services Ltd; Chair. Int. Medical and Scientific Fundraising Cttee, British Red Cross, Medical and Science Div., World Fellowship Duke of Edinburgh Award; Fellow, Asscn of Surgeons of GB, Int. Coll. of Surgeons; Founding mem. British Asscn of Surgical Oncology; mem. Court of Patrons Royal Coll. of Surgeons 1986–, Int. Medical Parliamentarians Org. (Chair UK Div.), European Soc. of Surgical Oncology, World Fed. of Surgical Oncological Socs (adviser on int. affairs), European Fed. of Surgeons, Tricare Europe Preferred Provider Network (US Armed Forces and Families), Breast and Thyroid Surgery 1997–; Devt Consultant, Ridgeford Properties Ltd 2001; Health Exec. Bovis Lend Lease Ltd 2000–; Medical Consultant and Adviser, Keltbray Ltd 2003–; Health Consultant and Adviser, Clipfine, BDL; mem. Nat. Events Cttee of Imperial Cancer Research Fund; Gosse Research Scholarship; Health Consultant and Adviser to Sir Robert McAlpine Ltd; mem. Apothecaries and Carmen Liveries; Queen's Jubilee Medal for Community Services; Freeman, City of London. *Publications:* various medical publs. *Leisure interests:* tennis, music, cricket. *Address:* The Consulting Rooms, Wellington Hospital, Wellington Place, London, NW8 9LE (office); 58 Stockleigh Hall, Prince Albert Road, London, NW8 7LB, England (home). *Telephone:* (20) 7483-5275 (office). *Fax:* (20) 7722-6638 (office).

ELTON, Benjamin (Ben) Charles, BA; British writer and performer; b. 3 May 1959; s. of Prof. Lewis Richard Benjamin Elton and Mary Elton (née Foster); m. Sophie Gare 1994; ed Godalming Grammar School, S Warwicks. Coll. of Further Educ., Univ. of Manchester; first professional appearance at Comic Strip Club 1981; numerous tours as stand-up comic 1986–; British Acad. Best Comedy Show Awards 1984, 1987, Best New Comedy Laurence Olivier Award 1998. *Film:* Much Ado About Nothing (actor) 1993, Maybe Baby (writer and dir) 2000. *Television:* writer: Alfresco 1982–83, The Young Ones (jtly) 1982–84, Happy Families 1985, Filthy Rich and Catflap 1986, Blackadder II (jtly) 1986, Blackadder the Third (jtly) 1987, Blackadder Goes Forth (jtly) 1989, The Thin Blue Line (jtly) 1995–96, Blessed 2005, The Wright Way 2013; writer and performer: South of Watford (jtly, documentary series) 1984–85, Saturday Live 1985–87, Friday Night Live 1988, Ben Elton Live 1989, 1993, 1997, The Man from Auntie 1990, 1994, Stark 1993, The Ben Elton Show (jtly) 1998, Get a Grip 2007. *Theatre:* Gasping 1990, Silly Cow 1991, Popcorn 1996, Blast from the Past 1998, The Beautiful Game (musical, book and lyrics) 2000, We Will Rock You (story to musical) 2002, Tonight's the Night (story to musical) 2003, Love Never Dies 2010. *Recordings:* albums: Motormouth 1987, Motorvation 1989. *Publications:* novels: Bachelor Boys 1984, Stark 1989, Gridlock 1992, This Other Eden 1993, Popcorn 1996, Blast from the Past 1998, Inconceivable 1999, Dead Famous 2001, High Society 2002, Past Mortem 2004, The First Casualty 2005, Chart Throb 2006, Blind Faith 2007, Meltdown 2009, Two Brothers 2012. *Leisure interests:* walking, reading, socializing. *Address:* Phil McIntyre Entertainments, 3rd Floor, 85 Newman Street, London, W1T 3EU, England (office).

ELTON, 2nd Baron, cr. 1934, of Headington; **Rodney Elton,** TD, MA; British politician and company director; *Backbench and Select Committee Member, House of Lords;* b. 2 March 1930, Oxford, England; s. of Godfrey Elton, 1st Baron and Dedi Hartmann; m. 1st Anne Frances Tilney 1958 (divorced 1979); one s. three d.; m. 2nd Susan Richenda Gurney, DCVO 1979; ed Eton Coll. and New Coll., Oxford; fmr Capt. Queen's Own Warwicks. and Worcs. Yeomanry; fmr Maj. Leics. and Derbyshire Yeomanry; farming 1957–73; Asst Mastership in History, Loughborough Grammar School 1962–67, Fairham Comprehensive School for Boys 1967–69; contested Loughborough div. of Leics. 1966, 1970; Lecturer, Bishop Lonsdale Coll. of Educ. 1969–72; joined House of Lords May 1973, Opposition Whip 1974–76, an Opposition Spokesman 1976–79, a Deputy Chair. of Cttees 1997–2008, Deputy Speaker 1999–2008, mem. House of Lords Select Cttee on the Scrutiny of Delegated Powers 1994–97, Select Cttee on the Constitution 2002–06, Ecclesiastical Cttee (of both houses) 2002–, Procedure Cttee 2005–09, Conventions (Jt Cttee) 2006, EU Sub-cttee B – Internal Market, Infrastructure and Employment 2012–13; Parl. Under-Sec. of State for NI 1979–81, Dept of Health and Social Security 1981–82, Home Office 1982–84, Minister of State 1984–85; Minister of State Dept of Environment 1985–86; Chair. Financial Intermediaries' Mans' and Brokers' Regulatory Asscn (FIMBRA) 1987–90; Dir Andry Montgomery Ltd 1977–79, Deputy Chair. 1978–79, 1986–99; Dir Overseas Exhbns Ltd 1977–79, Bldg Trades Exhbn Ltd 1977–79; mem. Panel on Takeovers and Mergers 1987–90; Chair. Ind. Inquiry into Discipline in Schools (Report 1989), Intermediate Treatment Fund 1990–93; Chair. DIVERT Trust 1993–2000, Pres. 2000–2002; Deputy Chair. Asscn of Conservative Peers 1986–93; Vice-Pres. Inst. of Trading Standards Admins 1990–; mem. Council Rainer Foundation 1990–96, City and Guilds of London Inst. 1991–97 (mem. Quality and Standards Cttee 1999–2004); Licensed Lay Minister, Oxford Diocese, Church of England 1999–; fmr Trustee, City Parochial Foundation and Trust for London; Conservative; Hereditary Peer 1999; Hon. Vice-Pres. Inst. of Trading Standards Officers; Hon. Fellow, City and Guilds Inst. of London. *Leisure interest:* painting. *Address:* House of Lords, Westminster, London, SW1A 0PW, England (office). *Telephone:* (20)

7219-3165 (office). *Fax:* (20) 7219-5979 (office). *E-mail:* eltonr@parliament.uk (office). *Website:* www.parliament.uk/biographies/lords/lord-elton/2812 (office).

ELVERDING, Peter A. F. W.; Dutch business executive; *Chairman of the Supervisory Board, ING Groep NV;* b. 1948; Chair. Man. Bd of Dirs Royal DSM NV –2007; Vice-Chair. Supervisory Bd De Nederlandsche Bank NV (Dutch Cen. Bank) –2007; mem. Supervisory Bd ING Groep NV 2007–, Chair. 2009–, Chair. Nomination Cttee and Corp. Governance Cttee, mem. Remuneration Cttee; Chair. Supervisory Bd Océ NV, Oostwegel Holding BV, Maastricht Univ.; Vice-Chair. Supervisory Bd Q-Park NV; mem. Bd Stichting Instituut GAK; mem. Supervisory Bd SHV Holdings NV, Koninklijke FrieslandCampina NV, cross-border Univ. of Limburg. *Address:* ING Groep NV, ING House, Amstelveenseweg 500, 1081 KL Amsterdam, The Netherlands. *Telephone:* (20) 541-54-11 (office). *Fax:* (20) 541-54-97 (office). *E-mail:* info@ing.com (office). *Website:* www.ing.com (office).

ELWES, Cary; British actor; b. 26 Oct. 1962, London; s. of Dominic Elwes and Tessa Kennedy; ed Harrow School; stage debut in Equus 1981. *Films include:* Another Country 1984, Oxford Blues 1984, The Bride 1985, Lady Jane 1986, Maschenka 1987, The Princess Bride 1987, Glory 1989, Days of Thunder 1990, Hot Shots! 1990, Leather Jackets 1991, Bram Stoker's Dracula 1992, Robin Hood: Men in Tights 1992, The Crush 1993, Rudyard Kipling's Jungle Book 1994, The Chase 1994, Twister 1996, Liar Liar 1997, Kiss the Girls 1997, The Informant 1997, Quest for Camelot (voice) 1998, Cradle Will Rock 1999, Shadow of the Vampire 2000, Wish You Were Dead 2000, Saw 2004, Ella Enchanted 2004, The Bard's Tale (voice) 2004, Neo Ned 2005, Edison 2005, Pucked 2006, Walk the Talk 2007, Georgia Rule 2007, The Alphabet Killer 2008, A Christmas Carol (voice) 2009. *Television includes:* Race Against Time 2000, The X Files (series) 2001–02, The Riverman 2004, Pope John Paul II 2005, Haskett's Chance 2006, Law & Order 2007. *Address:* c/o Michael Gruber, William Morris Agency, 1 William Morris Place, Beverly Hills, CA 90212, USA.

ELZUBAIR, Mohammad Khari, BSc, MA, PhD; Sudanese economist, government official and central banker; *Governor, Central Bank of Sudan;* ed Univ. of Khartoum, Univ. of Wales, UK; Financial Insp., Loans and Int. Aid Admin, Ministry of Finance and Nat. Economy 1968–73, First Insp., Ministry of Finance and Econ. Planning 1975–79, Dir of Commodity Aid 1983–86, Dir of External Loans, Econ. Planning Agency 1986–98, First Under-Sec. for Planning 1989–93, State Minister for Planning 1993–96; Chair. and Gen. Man. Sudanese Devt Corpn 1996–98; State Minister for Finance, Ministry of Finance and Nat. Economy 1998–2000, Minister of Finance and Nat. Economy 2000–01; Vice-Pres., Bank of Sahel and Sahara Community 2002–09; Gov. Cen. Bank of Sudan 2011–. *Address:* Central Bank of Sudan, Mogran, PO Box 313, Khartoum, Sudan (office). *Telephone:* (1) 83774420 (office). *Fax:* (1) 83780273 (office). *E-mail:* governor@ cbos.gov.sd (office). *Website:* www.cbos.gov.sd (office).

EMADI, Ali Shareef, BFin; Qatari banking executive and politician; *Minister of Finance;* ed Univ. of Arizona, USA; began career at Qatar Nat. Bank 1990, held various positions, including in Banking Control Dept 1990–98, Sr Man. of Retail Banking 1998–2001, Asst Gen. Man. Credit 2001–05, Gen. Man. Risk Dept 2005, Acting CEO, then apptd Group CEO Qatar Nat. Bank SAQ 2005; Pres. Commr, PT Bank QNB Kesawan Tbk 2011; Vice-Chair. Nat. Mobile Telecommunications Co. (KSC); Minister of Finance 2013–; Deputy Chair. Qatar Telecom (Q-TEL) (QSC), Dir 1999; mem. Bd of Dirs Wataniya Telecom; ranked by Arabian Business amongst the Power 500: The Worlds's Most Influential Arabs (34th) 2012. *Address:* Ministry of Economy and Finance, POB 83, Doha, Qatar (office). *Telephone:* 44461608 (office). *Fax:* 44413617 (office). *E-mail:* qatfin@mof.gov.qa (office). *Website:* www.mof.gov.qa (office).

EMAN, Jan Hendrik Albert (Henny); Aruban politician and lawyer; b. 20 March 1948; s. of Shon A Eman and Blanche Eman-Harthogh; brother of Michiel Godfried (Mike) Eman; ed Leiden Univ., Netherlands; fmr Leader, Arubaanse Volkspartij (AVP); Prime Minister of Aruba and Minister of Gen. Affairs 1986–89, 1993–2001; Orden Francisco de Miranda, Orden del Libertador (Venezuela), Officier in de orde van de Nederlandse Leeuw (Netherlands). *Address:* c/o Arubaanse Volkspartij, Oranjestad, Aruba (office).

EMAN, Michiel Godfried (Mike), LLB; Aruban lawyer and politician; *Prime Minister and Minister of General Affairs;* b. 1 Sept. 1961, Oranjestad; s. of Albert (Shon A.) Eman and Blanche Eman-Harthogh; brother of Jan Hendrik Albert (Henny) Eman; ed Univ. of the Netherlands Antilles; worked in pvt. law practise 1992–2001; mem. Arubaanse Volkspartij, Vice-Pres. 2001–03, Leader 2003–; mem. Staten (Parl.), Leader of the Opposition 2005–09, Prime Minister and Minister of Gen. Affairs 2009–. *Address:* Office of the Prime Minister, Government Offices, L. G. Smith Blvd 76, Oranjestad, Aruba (office). *Telephone:* 5880300 (office). *Fax:* 5880024 (office). *Website:* www.avparuba.net (office). mikeeman.com (office).

EMANUEL, Elizabeth Florence, MA, DesRCA, FCSD; British fashion designer; *Founder and Creative Director, Art of Being Limited;* b. 5 July 1953, London, England; d. of Samuel Charles Weiner and Brahna Betty Weiner; m. David Leslie Emanuel 1975 (divorced 2009); one s. one d.; ed City of London School for Girls, Harrow Coll. of Art, Royal Coll. of Art; opened London salon 1978; co-designed wedding gown for HRH Princess of Wales 1981, costumes for Andrew Lloyd Webber's Song and Dance 1982, sets and costumes for ballet Frankenstein, The Modern Prometheus, Royal Opera House London, La Scala Milan 1985, costumes for Stoll Moss production of Cinderella 1985, costumes for film The Changeling 1995, Ros Beef 2004, uniforms for Virgin Atlantic Airways 1990, Britannia Airways 1995; launched int. fashion label Elizabeth Emanuel 1991; launched Bridal Collection for Berkertex Brides UK Ltd 1994; launched bridal collection in Japan 1994; opened new shop and design studio 1996; launched own brand label (with Richard Thompson) 1999; f. Art of Being (couture label) 2005; Founder and Creative Dir new luxury fashion co. Art of Being Ltd in Little Venice studio 2013. *Dance:* Frankenstein, The Modern Prometheus. *Films:* Middletons Changeling, Ros Beef. *Publication:* Style for All Seasons (with David Emanuel) 1982, A Dress for Diana (with David Emanuel) 2006. *Leisure interests:* ballet, cinema, writing, environmental and conservation issues. *Address:* Garden Studio, 51 Maida Vale, Little Venice, London, W9 1SD, England (office). *Telephone:* (20) 7289-4545 (office). *Fax:* (20) 7289-7584 (office). *E-mail:* elizabeth@elizabethemanuel.co.uk (office). *Website:* www.elizabethemanuel.co.uk (office).

EMANUEL, Kerry Andrew, PhD; American meteorologist and academic; *Professor of Meteorology, Massachusetts Institute of Technology;* b. 21 April 1955, Cincinnati; ed Massachusetts Inst. of Tech.; Adjunct Asst Prof. then Asst Prof., UCLA 1978–81; Postdoctoral Fellow, Univ. of Oklahoma Cooperative Inst. for Mesoscale Meteorological Studies 1979; Asst Prof., Dept of Meterology and Physical Oceanography, MIT 1981–83, Asst Prof. then Assoc. Prof. Center for Meteorology and Physical Oceanography and Dept of Earth, Atmospheric and Planetary Sciences 1983–87, Prof. 1987–, Dir 1989–97; mem. NAS 2007–; Carl-Gustaf Rossby Research Medal, named one of Time 100 influential people of 2006. *Achievements include:* researcher in atmospheric dynamics, has specialized in atmospheric convection and mechanisms acting to intensify hurricanes. *Publications:* Atmospheric Convection 1994, Divine Wind: The History and Science of Hurricanes 2005, What We Know About Climate Change 2007; numerous scientific papers in professional journals. *Address:* Room 54-1620, Department of Earth, Atmospheric and Planetary Sciences, Massachusetts Institute of Technology, 77 Massachusetts Avenue, Cambridge, MA 02139-4307, USA (office). *Telephone:* (617) 253-2462 (office). *Fax:* (617) 253-6208 (office). *E-mail:* emanuel@mit.edu (office). *Website:* wind.mit.edu/~emanuel/home.html (office).

EMANUEL, Rahm Israel, BA, MA; American banking executive and politician; *Mayor of Chicago;* b. 29 Nov. 1959, Chicago; ed Sarah Lawrence Coll., Northwestern Univ.; mem. campaign team for Paul Simon's election to US Senate 1984; nat. campaign dir for Democratic Congressional Campaign Cttee 1988; Sr Adviser and chief fundraiser for Richard M. Daley's campaign for Mayor of Chicago 1988–89; Nat. Financial Dir Clinton/Gore Campaign 1991–92; Asst to Pres. Bill Clinton, also Dir of Political Affairs and Deputy Dir of Communications, The White House, Washington, DC 1993–95, Dir of Special Projects and Sr Adviser for Policy and Strategy 1995–98; Man. Dir Wasserstein Perella (now Dresdner Kleinwort), Chicago 1999–2002; mem. US House of Reps from Fifth Illinois Dist 2003–09, Chair. Democratic Congressional Campaign Cttee 2005–07, House Democratic Caucus 2007–08; Chief of Staff, The White House, Washington, DC 2009–10 (resgnd); Mayor of Chicago 2011–; mem. Bd of Dirs Fed. Home Loan Mortgage Corpn (Freddie Mac) 2000–01. *Publication:* The Plan: Big Ideas for Change in America (with Bruce Reed) 2009. *Address:* Office of the Mayor, City Hall, Room 507, 121 North LaSalle Street, Chicago, IL 60602-120, USA (office). *Telephone:* (313) 744-3300 (office). *Website:* www.ci.chi.il.us (office).

EMBUREY, John Ernest; British professional cricket coach and fmr professional cricketer; *Head Coach, Middlesex County Cricket Club;* b. 20 Aug. 1952, Peckham, London; s. of John Emburey and Rose Emburey (née Roff); m. 2nd Susan Elizabeth Ann Booth 1980; two d.; ed Peckham Manor Secondary School; right-hand late-order batsman, off-break bowler, slip or gully fielder; teams: Middx 1973–95, Western Prov. 1982–84, Northants. 1996–98 (player/chief coach and man.), England 1978–95 (Capt. 1988); played in 64 Tests (two as Capt.), scored 1,713 runs (average 22.53, highest score 75) and took 147 wickets (average 38.04), best bowling 7/78; scored 12,021 first-class runs (seven hundreds) and took 1,608 wickets, best bowling 8/40; toured Australia 1978–80, 1986–87, West Indies 1981, 1986, India 1981/82, 1992/93, Pakistan 1987, NZ 1988, Sri Lanka 1982, 1993; 61 One-Day Ints (ODIs, seven as Capt.); mem. seven County Championship winning teams with Middx 1976, 1977, 1980, 1982, 1985, 1990, 1993, Gillette Cup 1977, 1980, Benson and Hedges Cup 1983, 1986, Sunday League Winners' Trophy 1991, Natwest Trophy 1994, 1998; retd from playing 1997; coached Northamptonshire Co. Cricket Club; Head Coach Middx Co. Cricket Club 2001–, Ahmedabad Rockets (Indian Cricket League) 2008–; Sky TV commentator; Wisden Cricketer of the Year 1984. *Publications:* Emburey – A Biography 1987, Spinning in a Fast World 1989. *Leisure interests:* golf, fishing, reading. *Address:* c/o Middlesex County Cricket Club, Lord's Cricket Ground, London, NW8 8QN, England. *Telephone:* (20) 7289-1300. *Website:* www.middlesexccc.com.

EMERSON, Hon. David L., PC, OBC, PhD; Canadian public servant, politician and business executive; *CEO, Emerson Services Limited;* b. 17 Sept. 1945, Montreal, PQ; s. of Bernard Emerson and Beulah Emerson; m. Theresa Emerson; one s. one d.; ed Univ. of Alberta, Queen's Univ.; Researcher, Econ. Council of Canada, Ottawa 1972; Deputy Minister of Finance, BC 1984, 1990, later Deputy Minister to Premier; fmr Pres. BC Trade Devt Corpn; Pres. and CEO Western and Pacific Bank of Canada, Vancouver 1986–90; Pres. and CEO Vancouver Int. Airport Authority 1992; Pres. and CEO Canfor Corpn 1998; CEO Emerson Services Ltd; mem. Conservative Party of Canada; MP (Vancouver Kingsway) 2004–08; Minister of Industry 2004, of Int. Trade and Minister for the Pacific Gateway and the Vancouver-Whistler Olympics 2006–08, Acting Minister for Foreign Affairs May–June 2008, Minister of Foreign Affairs 2008; Order of BC. *Address:* Emerson Services Ltd, Suite 2833, Bentall Three, 595 Burrard Street Vancouver, BC V7X 1B8, Canada (office). *Telephone:* (604) 569-0237 (office). *Fax:* (604) 263-9852 (office). *E-mail:* emerson.services@shaw.ca (office).

EMERSON, E. Allen, BS, PhD; American computer scientist and academic; *Endowed Professor, Department of Computer Sciences, University of Texas at Austin;* ed Univ. of Texas at Austin, Harvard Univ.; currently Endowed Prof., Dept of Computer Sciences, Univ. of Texas at Austin; mem. editorial bds of leading formal methods journals and conf. programme cttees; Kanellakis Prize, Asscn for Computing Machinery (ACM) 1998, CMU Newell Prize, IEEE LICS'06 Test-of-Time Award, ACM A.M. Turing Award 2007, an Information Sciences Inst. Highly Cited Researcher. *Publications:* Methods for Mu-calculus Model Checking: A Tutorial 1995; several book chapters and numerous scientific papers in professional journals on model checking, decision procedures and algorithmic methods of program synthesis. *Address:* Department of Computer Sciences, Taylor Hall 2.124, University of Texas at Austin, Austin, TX 78712, USA (office). *Telephone:* (512) 471-9537 (office); (512) 471-7316 (Sec.) (office). *Fax:* (512) 471-8885 (office). *E-mail:* emerson@cs.utexas.edu (office). *Website:* www.cs.utexas.edu/~emerson (office).

EMERTON, Rev. John Adney, MA, DD, FBA; British ecclesiastic and academic; *Regius Professor Emeritus of Hebrew, University of Cambridge;* b. 5 June 1928, Winchmore Hill; s. of Adney Spencer Emerton and Helena Mary Emerton (née Quin); m. Norma Elizabeth Bennington 1954; one s. two d.; ed Minchenden Grammar School, Southgate, Corpus Christi Coll., Oxford and Wycliffe Hall, Oxford; ordained deacon 1952, priest 1953; Asst Lecturer in Theology, Univ. of Birmingham 1952–53; curate, Birmingham Cathedral 1952–53; Lecturer in Hebrew and Aramaic, Univ. of Durham 1953–55; Lecturer in Divinity, Univ. of Cambridge 1955–62; Visiting Prof., Trinity Coll., Univ. of Toronto 1960; Fellow, St Peter's Coll. and Reader in Semitic Philology, Univ. of Oxford 1962–68; Regius Prof. of Hebrew, Univ. of Cambridge 1968–95, Prof. Emer. 1995–; Fellow, St John's Coll. Cambridge 1970–; Sec. Int. Org. for Study of Old Testament 1971–89, Pres. 1992–95; Hon. Canon, St George's Cathedral, Jerusalem 1984–; mem. Ed. Bd Vetus Testamentum 1971–97; Visiting Fellow, Inst. for Advanced Studies, Hebrew Univ. of Jerusalem 1983; Corresp. mem. Göttingen Akad. der Wissenschaften 1990; Hon. DD (Edin.) 1977; Burkitt Medal for Biblical Studies, British Acad. 1991. *Publications:* The Peshitta of the Wisdom of Solomon 1959, The Old Testament in Syriac – The Song of Songs 1966; articles in journals. *Address:* St John's College, Cambridge CB2 1TP (office); 34 Gough Way, Cambridge, CB3 9LN, England (home). *Telephone:* (1223) 363219 (home).

EMERY, Alan Eglin Heathcote, MD, PhD, DSc, FRCP, FRCPE, FACMG, FLS, FRSE; British physician and professor of human genetics; *Professor Emeritus, University of Edinburgh;* b. (Alan Eglin Heathcote-Emery), 21 Aug. 1928, Manchester, England; s. of Harold Heathcote Emery and Alice Eglin; m. 2nd Marcia Lynn Miller 1988; three s. three d. from previous m.; ed Manchester Central Grammar School, Chester Coll., Univ. of Manchester, Johns Hopkins Univ., USA; Postdoctoral Research Fellow, Johns Hopkins Univ., Baltimore 1961–64; Lecturer, then Reader in Medical Genetics, Univ. of Manchester 1964–68; Foundation Prof. and Chair., Dept of Human Genetics, Univ. of Edinburgh 1968–83, Prof. Emer. 1983–, Hon. Fellow 1990–; Research Dir European Neuromuscular Centre and Chair. Research Cttee 1990–99, Chief Scientific Adviser 1999–2012; Pres. British Clinical Genetics Soc. 1980–83; Visiting Prof., Univs of New York, Heidelberg, UCLA, Padua, Beijing, Duke, Cape Town, Warsaw, Royal Postgraduate Medical School, London, etc.; Harveian, Boerhaave, Jenner Lecturer etc.; mem. Scientific Cttee Int. Congress on Neuromuscular Diseases 1990, 1994, 1998, 2000; mem. Exec. Cttee Research Group on Neuromuscular Diseases of World Fed. of Neurology 1996–, Exec. Bd World Muscle Soc. 1999–; Adviser, Asian and Oceanian Myology Centre, Tokyo 2000–; Vice-Pres. Muscular Dystrophy Campaign of Great Britain 1999–; Pres. Section Medical Genetics, Royal Soc. of Medicine 2001–04 (Council mem. 2004–, Trustee 2007–08); Fellow, American Coll. of Medical Genetics; Hon. Prof., Peninsula Medical School Exeter; Hon. FRS (SA); Hon. Fellow, Green Templeton Coll., Oxford 1985, Gaetano Conte Acad. (Italy) 1991, Royal Soc. of Medicine; Hon. mem. Dutch Soc. of Genetics 1999, Asscn of British Neurologists 1999; Hon. MD (Naples, Würzburg, Athens); Int. Award for Genetic Research (USA), Gaetano Conte Prize for Clinical Research 2000, Pro Finlandiae Gold Medal for contribs to Neuroscience 2000, Lifetime Achievement Award, WFN 2002, Doubleday Award and Cockcroft Medal, School of Medicine, Univ. of Manchester 2007, Int. Honouree Award, Int. Congress on Neuromuscular Diseases 2010, Wall of Honour, Royal Soc. of Medicine 2010, Int. Award for Excellence in Educ., American Soc. of Human Genetics 2012, Lifetime Achievement Award, Muscular Dystrophy Campaign (UK) 2012. *Publications:* Psychological Aspects of Genetic Counselling 1984, Methodology in Medical Genetics (second edn) 1986, Principles and Practice of Medical Genetics (second edn) 1991, Elements of Medical Genetics (eighth edn) 1992, The History of a Genetic Disease: Duchenne Muscular Dystrophy or Meryon's Disease 1995, Introduction to Recombinant DNA (second edn with S. Malcolm) 1995, Diagnostic Criteria for Neuromuscular Disorders (second edn) 1997, Neuromuscular Disorders: Clinical and Molecular Genetics 1998, The Muscular Dystrophies 2001, Medicine and Art (with M. L. H. Emery) 2003, Duchenne Muscular Dystrophy (third edn) 2003, Surgical & Medical Treatment in Art (with M. L. H. Emery) 2006, Mother & Child Care in Art 2007, Muscular Dystrophy: The Facts (third edn) 2008, The History of a Genetic Disease (with M. L. H. Emery) (second edn) 2011; several books of poetry, including haiku, 400 scientific papers. *Leisure interests:* Ancient Greek history, oil painting, writing poems. *Address:* Green Templeton College, Woodstock Road, Oxford, OX2 6HG (office); 2 Ingleside Court, Budleigh Salterton, Devon, EX9 6NZ, England (home). *Telephone:* (1395) 445847 (home). *Fax:* (1395) 445847 (home). *E-mail:* alan.emery@gtc.ox.ac.uk (home).

EMERY, Lin; American sculptor; b. New York City, NY; d. of Cornell Emery and Jean Weill; m. S. B. Braselman 1962 (deceased); one s.; ed Univs of Chicago and Sorbonne, Paris; worked in studio of Ossip Zadkine, Paris 1950; 54 solo exhbns in US museums and galleries 1957–2006; int. exhbns in Tokyo, Hong Kong, Manila, Sofia, Paris, London, Berlin, Brisbane, Kyoto and Frankfurt 1961–98; public sculpture erected in Civic Center, New Orleans 1966–70, Fidelity Center, Oklahoma City 1972, Humanities Center, Columbia, SC 1974, Federal Plaza, Houma, La. 1997, Marina Centre, Singapore 1986, City of Oxnard, Calif. 1988, Osaka Dome, Japan 1997, Mitre Corpn, Alexandra, Va 2001, Schiffer Publishing Co., Atglen, Pa 2002, Sterling Corpn, Las Colinas, Tex. 2002, etc.; Visiting Prof., Tulane School of Architecture, New Orleans 1969–70, Newcomb School of Art, New Orleans 1980; Visiting Artist and Lecturer, Art Acad. of Cincinnati, Louisiana State Univ., Univ. of New Orleans, Univ. of Texas at Austin, Univ. of Maine 1985–88; Chair. 9th Int. Sculpture Conf. 1976, Co-Chair. Mayor's Steering Cttees, New Orleans 1979–80; Studio Chair. Coll. Art Assen 1979; Chair. Int. Sculpture Symposium, New Orleans 2004; mem. Bd Contemporary Arts Center, New Orleans 1997–; mem. Loyola Univ. Visiting Cttee 1996–99; adviser, Artists Guild, New Orleans 1997–99; mentor, Center for Creative Arts, New Orleans 1998; mem. Nat. Acad. of Design 2003–, Int. Women's Forum 2003–, Century Asscn, New York; Order of St Lazarus Companionate of Merit 2004; Hon. LHD (Loyola Univ) 2004; Mayor's Award for Achievement in the Arts, La 1980, Lazlo Aranyi Award for Public Art, Va 1990, Delgado Award for Artistic Excellence, La. 1997, Grand Prix for Public Sculpture (Japan) 1997, Gov.'s Arts Award, La. 2001, S. Simon Award, Nat. Acad. 2005. *Address:* 7520 Dominican Street, New Orleans, LA 70118, USA (home). *Telephone:* (504) 866-7775 (home). *Fax:* (504) 866-0144 (home). *E-mail:* lin@linemery.com (office).

EMIN, Tracey, CBE, RA; British artist; b. 1964, Margate, Kent, England; ed John Cass School of Art, London, Maidstone Coll. of Art, Royal Coll. of Art; f. Tracey Emin Museum, London 1996; Int. Award for Video Art, Baden-Baden 1997, Video Art Prize, Südwest Bank, Stuttgart 1997. *Art work:* 'The Roman Standard' (commissioned by the BBC for Art05 Festival, Upper Duke Street, Liverpool) 2005. *Films include:* Why I Never Became a Dancer, Top Spot (dir) 2004. *Publications:* Exploration of the Soul 1995, Always Glad to See You 1997, Tracey Emin: Holiday Inn 1998, Tracey Emin on Pandaemonium 1998, Absolute Tracey 1998, Strangeland 2005. *Leisure interests:* writing poetry, watching sunsets. *Address:* c/o White Cube, 48 Hoxton Square, London, N1 6PB, England (office). *Telephone:* (20) 7930-5373 (office). *Website:* www.whitecube.com/artists/emin (office).

EMINEM, (Slim Shady); American rap artist and musician; b. (Marshall Bruce Mathers III), 17 Oct. 1972, St Joseph, Mo.; m. Kim Mathers (divorced); one d.; moved to Detroit aged 12; dropped out of high school to join local rap groups Basement Productions, D12; released debut album The Infinite on ind. label FBT; after releasing Slim Shady EP, made guest appearances with Kid Rock and Shabbam Shadeeq, leading to deal with Dr Dre's Aftermath Records; collaborations with artists, including Dr Dre, D12, Missy Elliott, Dido; Founder and Owner Slim Shady record label 1999–, Eight Mile Style publishing co.; f. Marshall Mathers Foundation (charity); MTV Annual American Music Awards Best Hip Hop Artist 2000, 2002, three Grammy Awards 2001, Best Pop/Rock Male Artist 2002, MTV Europe Music Awards for Best Male Act 2002, 2009, for Best Hip Hop Act 2002, 2013, for Global Icon 2013, BRIT Award for Best Int. Male Solo Artist 2003, 2005, American Music Awards for Best Male Pop/Rock Artist, Best Male Hip Hop/R&B Artist 2003, Acad. Award for Best Music (for Lose Yourself, from film 8 Mile) 2004, Grammy Award for Best Male Rap Solo Performance (for Lose Yourself) 2004, Grammy Award for Best Rap Song (for Lose Yourself) 2004, Grammy Award for Best Rap Performance by a Duo or Group (for Crack a Bottle with Dr Dre and 50 Cent) 2010, Grammy Award for Best Rap Solo Performance (for Not Afraid) 2011, Echo Award for Best Int. Hip Hop Artist, Germany 2005, Smash Hits Award for Best Hip-Hop Act 2005, American Music Award for Favorite Male Rap/Hip-Hop Artist 2005, 2006. *Film:* 8 Mile 2002. *Recordings include:* albums: The Infinite 1997, The Slim Shady LP 1999, The Marshall Mathers LP (MTV Award for Best Album) 2000, The Eminem Show (MTV Award for Best Album 2002, Grammy Award for Best Rap Album, BRIT Award for Best Int. Album, American Music Awards for Best Pop/Rock Album, Best Hip Hop/R&B Album 2003) 2002, Eminem Is Back 2004, Encore 2004, Curtain Call 2005, Eminem Presents The Re Up 2006, Relapse (Grammy Award for Best Rap Album 2010) 2009, Relapse 2 2009, Recovery (Grammy Award for Best Rap Album 2011) 2010, The Marshall Mathers LP 2 2013. *Publications:* Angry Blonde 2000, The Way I Am (auto-biog.) 2008. *Address:* c/o Paul Rosenberg, Goliath Artists, 151 Lafayette Street, New York, NY 10013, USA (office). *Telephone:* (212) 324-2410 (office). *Fax:* (212) 324-2415 (office). *Website:* www.shadyrecords.com; www.eminem.com.

EMMANUELLI, Henri Joseph; French politician; *Chairman, Conseil général des Landes;* b. 31 May 1945, Eaux-Bonnes, Pyrénées-Atlantiques; s. of the late Louis Emmanuelli and of Julie Chourre; m. Antonia Gonzalez 1967; one s. one d.; ed Lycée Louis-Barthou, Pau, Institut d'études politiques de Paris; mem. staff Banque de l'Union Parisienne, then Compagnie financière de banque 1969–78; Deputy for Landes 1978–82, 1986–93, 1993–97, 2000–; Chair. Conseil général, Landes 1982–98, 2000–; Sec. of State for Overseas Territories and Depts 1981–83, for Budget 1983–86; Chair. Finance Comm. of Nat. Ass. 1991–93, Pres. Nat. Ass. 1992–93, Pres. Comm. for Finances, Gen. Econs and Planning 1997, 2000–; mem. Nat. Secr. Parti Socialiste 1987–, Leader 1994–95. *Publications:* Plaidoyer pour l'Europe 1992, Citadelles interdites 2000. *Leisure interests:* skiing, swimming. *Address:* Assemblée nationale, 75355 Paris; Parti Socialiste, 10 rue de Solférino, 75333 Paris Cedex, France; 22–24 rue Victor Hugo, 40000 Mont-de-Marsan (office). *E-mail:* presidence@cg40.fr (office); hemmanuelli@assemblee-nationale.fr (office).

EMMERICH, Roland; film director, screenwriter and film producer; b. 10 Nov. 1955; film produced as student Das Arche Noah Prinzip (The Noah's Ark Principle) shown at 1984 Berlin Film Festival and sold to more than 20 countries; f. Centropolis Film Productions. *Films include:* Franzmann 1979, Das Arche Noah Prinzip 1984, Joey 1985, Hollywood-Monster 1987, Moon 44 1990, Eye of the Storm (producer) 1991, Universal Soldier 1992, Stargate 1994, The High Crusade (producer) 1994, Independence Day 1996, Godzilla 1998, The Thirteenth Floor (producer) 1999, The Patriot 2000, Eight Legged Freaks (producer) 2002, The Day After Tomorrow 2004, 10,000 BC 2008, 2012 2009. *TV:* (series) The Visitor (producer) 1997. *Address:* c/o Creative Artists Agency, 9830 Wilshire Boulevard, Beverly Hills, CA 90212, USA.

EMMERT, Mark A., BA, MPA, PhD; American political scientist, academic and university administrator; *President, University of Washington;* b. 16 Dec. 1952, Tacoma, Wash.; m. DeLaine S. Emmert; one s. one d.; ed Univ. of Washington, Maxwell School, Syracuse Univ.; various public service roles 1976–80; Univ. Fellow and Research Asst, Maxwell School, Syracuse Univ. 1980–83; Research Assoc., Center for Governmental Studies, then Asst Prof., Dept of Political Science, Northern Illinois Univ. 1983–85; held faculty and admin. positions at Univ. of Colorado, including Assoc. and Asst Prof., Grad. School of Public Affairs, Assoc. Dean Grad. School of Public Affairs, Assoc. Vice-Chancellor for Academic Affairs, Univ. of Colorado, Denver and Pres.'s Office, Boulder and Denver Campuses 1985–92; Prof. of Political Science, Provost and Vice-Pres. for Academic Affairs, Montana State Univ. 1992–95; Prof. of Political Science, Chancellor and Provost Univ. of Connecticut 1995–99; Prof., E.J. Ourso Coll. of Business Admin and Chancellor Louisiana State Univ. 1999–2004; Prof., Evans School of Public Affairs and Pres. Univ. of Washington 2004–, mem. Univ. of Washington Medicine Bd; Guest of Ministry of Educ., People's Repub. of China; Visiting Scholar and Guest of Monash Univ., Melbourne, Australia; lectured and conducted training programs in Hong Kong, Okinawa, Panama City, Guam, US Micronesia, Germany, France and Mexico; consultant and trainer, Asscn of Governing Bds, San Antonio Art Inst., Colorado State Univ., Vision Hispanica, Colorado Gov.'s Business-Educ. Summit, Educ.-Policy Fellowship Program for the Inst. for Educational Leadership, Univ. of Oklahoma, Minnesota State Univ. System, Rochester Inst. of Tech.; Chair. Louisiana Univs Marine Consortium 2002; Chair. Pres.'s Council Southern Univs Research Asscn 2001–02; Co-Chair. Prosperity Partnership 2005–; mem. New England Council of Pres 1994–99, New England Asscn of Schools and Colls 1998–99, Educ. Comm. of the States, Commr for Louisiana 2000–04, Univ. Research Asscn (Pres Council 2000–04), Cttee Exec. Southeastern Conf. 2002–04, Exec. Council Southern Asscn of Schools and Colls 2000–04, Nat. Visiting Cttee Arizona State Univ. 2004–, American Asscn of Colls and Univs 2005–, Asscn of American Univs, Nat. Security Higher Educ. Advisory Bd 2005–, Asscn of Governing Bds of Univs and Colls Council of Pres 2005–, Nat. Asscn of State Univs and Land-Grant Colls (Co-Chair. Bd on Oceans and Atmosphere), American

Council on Educ., Council of Fellows, Comm. on Leadership and Institutional Effectiveness, Nat. Collegiate Athletic Asscn Presidential Task Force on the Future of Intercollegiate Athletics Fiscal Responsibility Sub-cttee, Pac-10 Conf. of CEOs 2005–; Charter mem. Asscn of Pacific Rim Univs 2005–; fmr Dir Josephson Inst. of Ethics Bd, Louisiana Research Park Corpn, Shaw Center for the Arts, Baton Rouge Chamber of Commerce; Leadership mem. and Campaign Cabinet, Capital Area United Way; mem. Organizing Cttee Summer Nat. Sr Games 2001; mem. Advisory Bd Policy Consensus Center, Seattle Community Devt Roundtable 2005–, Gov.'s Global Competitiveness Council 2005– (mem. Research and Innovation Sub-cttee), Puget Sound Partnership; fmr mem. Bd of Dirs Baton Rouge Center for World Affairs; Trustee Greater Seattle Chamber of Commerce 2006–; mem. Conn. Acad. of Arts and Sciences; American Council on Educ. Fellow, J. W. Fulbright Admin. Fellow, Germany 1991, J.W. Fulbright Sr Admin. Seminar, Germany 1994, Gambit Magazine Baton Rouge Citizen of the Year 2000, Good Growth Award, Baton Rouge Business Report and Growth Council 2003, Marketer of the Year, Sales and Marketing Execs Asscn 2003. *Publications:* numerous journal articles, monographs, book chapters and tech. reports. *Leisure interests:* boating, golf, scuba diving, fly-fishing, skiing, reading. *Address:* Office of the President, University of Washington, 301 Gerberding Hall, Box 351230, Seattle, WA 98195-1230, USA (office). *Telephone:* (206) 543-5010 (office). *Fax:* (206) 616-1784 (office). *E-mail:* emmert@u.washington.edu (office). *Website:* www.washington.edu (office).

EMMOTT, William (Bill) John, BA; British journalist; b. 6 Aug. 1956, Hammersmith, London; s. of Richard Emmott and Audrey Emmott; m. 1st Charlotte Crowther 1982 (divorced); m. 2nd Carol Barbara Mawer 1992; ed Latymer Upper School, Hammersmith and Magdalen and Nuffield Colls, Oxford; Brussels Corresp., The Economist 1980–82, Econs Corresp. 1982–83, Tokyo Corresp. 1983–86, Finance Ed. 1986–89, Business Affairs Ed. 1989–93, Ed.-in-Chief 1993–2006, Editorial Dir Economist Intelligence Unit May–Dec. 1992; Chair., London Library 2009–, PeerIndex 2010–; Trustee, IISS 2010–; Hon. Fellow, Magdalen Coll. Oxford 2002; Hon. LLD (Warwick) 1999, (Northwestern) 2009; Hon. DLitt (City) 2001. *Publications:* The Pocket Economist (with R. Pennant-Rea) 1983, The Sun Also Sets 1989, Japanophobia 1993, Kanryo no Taizai 1996, 20:21 Vision: The Lessons of the 20th Century for the 21st 2003, Hiwa Mata Noboru 2006, Japan's New Golden Age - of the next ten years 2006, Nihon no sentaku 2007, Sekai Choryu no Yomikata 2008, Rivals: How the Power Struggle between China, India and Japan will Shape our Next Decade 2008, Forza, Italia: Come Ripartire dopo Berlusconi 2010. *Leisure interests:* cricket, dog-walking, journalism. *Address:* PO Box 23, Dulverton, TA22 9WW, England (office). *E-mail:* bill@billemmott.com (office). *Website:* www.billemmott.com.

EMOTO, Kanji; Japanese steel industry executive; *Adviser, JFE Holdings Incorporated;* Chair. Kawasaki Steel Corpn –2003, Chair., Co-CEO and Rep. Dir JFE Holdings, Inc. (formed from merger of Kawasaki Steel Corpn with Nihon Kôkan Kabushiki-gaisha 2002) –2005, Adviser 2005–; Dir Energy Conservation Center, Tokyo. *Address:* JFE Holdings Inc., 2-2-3 Uchisaiwaicho, Chiyoda-ku, Tokyo 100-0011, Japan (office). *Telephone:* (3) 3597-4321 (office). *Website:* www.jfe-holdings.co.jp (office).

EMOVON, Emmanuel Uwumagbuhunmwun, PhD; Nigerian chemist, academic and fmr politician; b. 24 Feb. 1929, Benin City; s. of late Gabriel A. Emovon and Oni Emovon; m. Princess Adesuwa C. Akenzua 1959; three s. three d.; ed Baptist School, Benin City, Edo Coll., Benin City, Univ. Coll., Ibadan, Univ. Coll., London Univ., UK; Lecturer in Chem., Univ. Coll. Ibadan 1959; Prof. of Chem., Univ. of Benin 1971; Vice-Chancellor Univ. of Jos 1978; Fed. Minister of Science and Tech. 1985–89; Co-ordinator, Sheda Science and Tech. Complex 1990–98 (retd); invested Chief Obayagbona of Benin 1991; fmr mem. numerous govt cttees and bds; fmr external examiner; Fellow Science Asscn of Nigeria, Nigerian Acad. of Science; nat. mem. ICSU 1986. *Publications:* numerous scientific papers. *Leisure interests:* photography, gardening, tennis, table tennis, cricket and football. *Address:* c/o Sheda Science and Technology Complex, Ministry of Science and Technology, P.M.B. 186, Garki, Abuja, Nigeria.

EMPEY, Baron (Life Peer), cr. 2011, of Shandon in the City and County of Belfast; **Reginald Norman Morgan (Reg) Empey,** Kt, OBE, BSc; British politician; *Chairman, Ulster Unionist Party;* b. 26 Oct. 1947, Belfast, Co. Antrim, Northern Ireland; s. of Samuel Frederick Empey and Emily Winifred Empey (née Morgan; m. Stella Ethna Donnan 1977; one s. one d.; ed The Royal School, Armagh, Queen's Univ., Belfast; Publicity Officer, Ulster Young Unionist Council 1967–68, Vice-Chair. 1968–72; Chair. Vanguard Unionist Party 1974–75; mem. E Belfast NI Constitutional Convention 1975–76; mem. Belfast City Council 1985–; Deputy Lord Mayor 1988–89, Lord Mayor of Belfast 1989–90, 1993–94; mem. NI Ass. for Belfast East 1998–2002 (Ass. suspended Oct. 2002, restored May 2007), 2007–; Minister of Enterprise, Trade and Investment 1999–2002; Acting First Minister of Northern Ireland July–Nov. 2001; Minister for Employment and Learning 2007–10; Deputy Leader United Ulster Unionist Party 1977–84; mem. Ulster Unionist Party (UUP), Deputy Leader UUP in NI Ass. 2003–05, Leader UUP 2005–10 (resgnd), Chair. 2012–; mem. Ulster Unionist Council 1987– (Hon. Sec. 1990–96, Vice-Pres. 1996–); Vice-Pres. Inst. of Export; Bd mem. Police Authority for NI 1992–, European Cttee of the Regions for NI 1994; mem. Orange Order (lodge, Eldon LOL 7); mem. (Conservative) House of Lords 2011–. *Leisure interests:* gardening, walking. *Address:* Ulster Unionist Party, 1st Floor, 174 Albertbridge Road, Belfast, BT5 4GS, Northern Ireland (office); House of Commons, Westminster, London, SW1A 0AA, England. *Telephone:* (28) 9046-3200 (office); (20) 7219-8482. *Fax:* (28) 9045-6899 (office). *E-mail:* empeyr@parliament.uk (office); uup@uup.org (office). *Website:* www.uup.org (office); www.parliament.uk/biographies/lords/lord-empey/4216.

EMSIS, Indulis, PhD; Latvian politician and biologist; b. 2 Jan. 1952, Salacgrīva, Limbazi Dist; m.; one d.; ed Rīga First Secondary School, Univ. of Latvia, Moscow Scientific Research Inst.; Head, Lab. of Environmental Protection 1978–89; Deputy Chair. Nature Preservation Cttee 1989–90; mem. Supreme Council, Chair. Latvian Environmental Protection Cttee 1990–93; Minister of State, Ministry for Environmental Protection and Regional Devt 1993–98; Deputy Chair. SIA Eirokonsultants 1998–2000, Dir-Gen. SIA Eiroprojekts 2000–02; mem. Rīga City Council 2000–02, Deputy Chair. Devt Cttee; mem. 6th Saeima (Parl.) 1993–98, 8th Saeima 2002–04, 9th Saeima 2006–, Speaker 2006–07; Prime

Minister of Latvia March–Dec. 2004; mem. Latvian Green Party (part of Greens' and Farmers' Union) 1990–, currently Co-Chair.; Three Star Order (Third Degree) 1996; Award of the Baltic Sea Foundation for Outstanding Contribs to Protection of the Marine Environment, Certificate of Merit of the Cabinet of Ministers of the Repub. of Latvia. *Address:* c/o Office of the Speaker, Saeima, Jekaba iela 11, Rīga 1811, Latvia. *Telephone:* 7087-111. *E-mail:* Indulis.Emsis@saeima.lv (office). *Website:* www.saeima.lv (office).

ENCINAS RODRÍGUEZ, Alejandro, BEcons; Mexican politician; b. 13 May 1954, Mexico City; ed Univ. Nacional Autónoma de México; mem. Cámara Federal de Diputados (Partido Revolucionario Institucional—PRI) 1985–88, mem. (Partido de la Revolución Democrática—PRD) 1991–94; adviser, ECLAC 1990, Inter-American Inst. for Co-operation on Agric. 1991; Head, Mexico City Govt 2005–06. *Address:* Partido de la Revolución Democrática, Avda Benjamín Franklin 84, Col. Escandón, 11800 México DF, Mexico (office). *Telephone:* (55) 1085-8000 (office). *Fax:* (55) 1085-8144 (office). *E-mail:* comunicacion@prd.org (office). *Website:* www .prd.org.mx (office).

ENDERBY, Sir John Edwin, Kt, KB, CBE, PhD, DSc, FRS; British scientist and academic; *Chairman, Melys Diagnostics Ltd;* b. 16 Jan. 1931, Grimsby, Lincs.; s. of the late Thomas Edwin Enderby and Rheita Rebecca Enderby (née Hullinshead); m. Susan Bowles; one s. two d.; one s. (deceased) one d. from previous m.; ed Chester Grammar School, Westminster Coll., Birkbeck Coll., Univ. of London; Lecturer then Reader, Univ. of Sheffield 1960–69; Prof. and Head of Dept, Univ. of Leicester 1969–76; Prof. of Physics, Univ. of Bristol 1976–81, H.H. Wills Prof. 1981–96, Prof. Emer. 1996–, Head of Dept and Dir H.H. Wills Lab. 1981–94; Directeur-Adjoint, Inst. Laue-Langevin, Grenoble, France (on secondment) 1985–88; Ed. Proceedings of the Royal Society 'A' 1989–93; Ed.-in-Chief Journal of Physics: Condensed Matter 1997–2001; Physical Sec. and Vice-Pres. Royal Soc. 1999–2004; Pres. Inst. of Physics 2004–06, Hon. FInstP 2011; Chair. Melys Diagnostics Ltd 2004–; mem. Council Particle Physics and Astronomy Research Council 1994–98; Chief Scientific Adviser, Inst. of Physics Publishing 2002; Distinguished Argonne Fellow (USA); Foreign mem. Royal Holland Acad. of Science and Humanities 2001; Hon. Fellow, Birkbeck Coll., Univ. of London 2001; Hon. DSc (Loughborough) 1998, (Leicester) 2006, (Bristol) 2006, (Sheffield) 2007, (East Anglia) 2007, (Kent) 2008, (Huddersfield) 2011, (Chester) 2012; Guthrie Medal and Prize, Inst. of Physics 1995. *Publications:* numerous papers on liquids in academic journals. *Leisure interests:* travel, woodwork, music, reading. *Address:* Melys Diagnostics Ltd, Whitland Abbey, Whitland, Carmarthenshire, SA34 0LG, Wales (office); H.H. Wills Physics Laboratory, University of Bristol, Tyndall Avenue, Bristol, BS8 1TL (office); 7 Cotham Lawn Road, Bristol, BS6 6DU, England (home). *Telephone:* (1994) 240265 (Whitland) (office); (117) 928-8737 (Bristol) (office); (117) 973-3411 (home). *Fax:* (1994) 241176 (Whitland) (home); (117) 925-5624 (Bristol) (home). *E-mail:* susan.enderby01@btinternet.com (home). *Website:* www.melysdiagnostics.com (office); www.iop.org.

ENDERS, Thomas (Tom), PhD; German aeronautics industry executive; *CEO, European Aeronautic Defence and Space Co. (EADS) NV;* b. 21 Dec. 1958; ed Univ. of Bonn, Univ. of California, Los Angeles, USA; served with 1st Airborne Div., Bundeswehr 1977–78, completed officer training, Maj. in Army Reserve Forces 1978–83; Asst. Fed. Parl., Bonn 1982–85; Research Assoc., Research Inst. of Konrad Adenauer Foundation, St Augustin 1985–87; Research Inst. of German Council on Foreign Affairs, Bonn 1988–89; Sr Research Assoc., IISS, London, UK 1989–90; mem. Planning Staff, Minister of Defence 1989–91; joined aeronautics mfr MBB (later Dasa and now part of EADS) 1991, served in various marketing posts 1991–95, Corp. Sec. and Head of Office of Chair. 1995–96, Dir of Corp. Devt and Tech. 1996–2000, apptd Head of Defence and Security Systems Div. 2000; mem. Exec. Cttee and CEO Defence and Security Systems Div., European Aeronautic Defence and Space Co. (EADS) NV 2000–05, Co-CEO EADS 2005–07, CEO Airbus SAS (subsidiary of EADS) 2007–12, CEO EADS 2012–; Pres. German Aerospace Industries Asscn (BDLI) 2005–; Chair. Atlantik-Brücke e.V. 2005–. *Achievement:* performed a paradrop from the A400M Nov. 2010. *Address:* European Aeronautic Defence and Space Co. (EADS) NV, Mendelweg 30, 2333 CS Leiden, Netherlands (office). *Telephone:* (71) 524-56-00 (office). *E-mail:* info@ eads.com (office). *Website:* www.eads.com (office).

ENDICOTT, Timothy Andrew Orville, AB, MPhil, LLB, DPhil; Canadian lawyer and academic; *Professor of Legal Philosophy and Dean, Faculty of Law, University of Oxford;* ed Harvard Coll., USA, Univ. of Oxford, UK, Univ. of Toronto; barrister and solicitor, Osler, Hoskin & Harcourt LLP (law firm), Toronto 1988–91; Tutor in Law, Univ. of Oxford 1994–, Stipendiary Lecturer, Jesus Coll. 1994–95, Stipendiary Lecturer, St Anne's Coll. 1995–96, Lecturer, St Catherine's Coll. 1996–99, Fellow 1998–99, Fellow, Balliol Coll. 1999–, Dir of Grad. Studies, Faculty of Law 2004–, Prof. of Legal Philosophy 2006–, Dean, Faculty of Law 2007–; Rhodes Scholar, Univ. of Oxford 1983–85. *Publications:* Vagueness in Law 2000, Properties of Law (co-ed.) 2006, Administrative Law 2009. *Address:* Balliol College, University of Oxford, Oxford, OX1 3BJ, England (office). *Telephone:* (1865) 277754 (office). *E-mail:* timothy.endicott@law.ox.ac.uk (office). *Website:* www.law.ox.ac.uk (office).

ENDO, Akira, BA, PhD; Japanese biochemist and academic; *Director, Biopharm Research Laboratories, Inc.;* b. 14 Nov. 1933, Akita; ed Faculty of Agric., Tohoku Univ.; joined Sankyo Co. Ltd 1957, later Head of Lab. of Fermentation Research Labs; fmr Research Assoc., Albert Einstein Coll. of Medicine; Assoc. Prof., Dept of Agricultural Chem., Faculty of Agric., Tokyo Univ. of Agric. and Tech. 1979–86, Prof. 1986–97; Dir Biopharm Research Laboratories Inc. 1997–; Young Investigator Award in Agricultural Chem. (Japan) 1966, Heinrich Wieland Prize for the discovery of the HMG-CoA reductase inhibitors (FRG) 1987, Toray Science and Tech. Prize (Japan) 1988, Warren Alpert Foundation Prize, Harvard Medical School, USA) 2000, Massry Prize, Keck School of Medicine, Univ. of Southern California 2006, Japan Prize, The Science and Tech. Foundation of Japan 2006, Lasker-DeBakey Clinical Medical Research Award 2008. *Achievements include:* discovered first cholesterol-lowering statin drug. *Publications:* numerous scientific papers in professional journals. *Address:* Biopharm Research Laboratories, Inc., 3-41-3, 501 Shimorenjaku, Mitaka, Tokyo, Japan (office). *E-mail:* info@ biopharmgroup.com (office). *Website:* www.biopharmgroup.com (office).

ENDO, Nobuhiro; Japanese business executive; *President and Representative Director, NEC Corporation;* b. 8 Nov. 1953; ed Grad. School of Science and Eng, Tokyo Inst. of Tech.; joined NEC Corpn 1981, Gen. Man. Mobile and Wireless Div. 2003–05, Sr Gen. Man. Mobile Network Operations Unit 2005–06, Assoc. Sr Vice-Pres. and Exec. Gen. Man. 2006–09, Sr Vice-Pres. April–June 2009, Sr Vice-Pres. and mem. Bd of Dirs June 2009–, Pres. and Rep. Dir 2010–. *Address:* NEC Corporation, 7-1, Shiba 5-chome, Minato-ku, Tokyo 108-8001, Japan (office). *Telephone:* (3) 3454-1111 (office). *Fax:* (3) 3798-1510 (office). *E-mail:* info@nec.com (office). *Website:* www.nec.com (office).

ENDZIŅŠ, Aivars, DrIur; Latvian lawyer and politician; b. 8 Dec. 1940, Rīga; m.; two s.; ed Univ. of Latvia, Moscow State Univ.; Lecturer, then Assoc. Prof., Univ. of Latvia 1972–90, 1996–97; Assoc. Prof., Police Acad. 1998–, Prof. 2002–; mem. Supreme Council, Presidium Supreme Council 1990–93; mem. Saeima (Parl.), Vice-Chair. Legal Affairs Cttee 1993–96; Acting Chair., then Chair. Constitutional Court 1996–2007; unsuccesful cand. (Harmony Centre party) in presidential elections 2007; mem. Parl. Ass., Council of Europe 1995–96; Assoc. mem. Democracy Through Law Comm. (Venice Comm.) 1992–95, mem. 1995–, mem. Bureau 1991–2001; Order of Three Stars 2001, Grand Officer Repub. of Italy 2004. *Publications:* more than 60 academic publs. *Leisure interests:* fishing, hunting. *Address:* c/o Harmony Centre (Saskaņas Centrs/Tsentr soglasiya), Jūra Alunana 8/3, Rīga 1010 (office); No. 31 Drustu St, Rīga 1002, Latvia (home). *Telephone:* 793-4654 (home).

ENESTAM, Jan-Erik, MPolSci; Finnish politician; b. 12 March 1947, Västanfjärd; m. Solveig V. Dahlqvist 1970; three c.; tourism researcher, Åland Provincial Govt 1972–74; researcher, Finnish Tourist Bd 1974; Head of Office, Åland Provincial Govt 1974–78; Municipal Man. Västanfjärd 1978–83; Project Man. Nordic Council of Ministers 1983–91; mem. Regional Policy Advisory Bd 1987–91; mem. Parl. 1991–; Chair. Västanfjärd Municipal Council 1989–96; Special Adviser to Minister of Defence 1990–91; Minister of Defence and Minister at Ministry of Social Affairs (Equality) and Health Jan.–April 1995; Minister of the Interior 1995–99, of Defence, Nordic Co-operation and Foreign Affairs (Adjacent Areas) 1999–2003, of the Environment and Foreign Affairs (Nordic Co-operation) 2003–07; Deputy Chair. Cen. Fed. of Fishing Industry 1986–94; Vice-Pres. Svenska Folkpartiet (SFP—Swedish People's Party) Parl. Group 1991–94, Chair. SFP 1998–2006; Sec.-Gen. Nordic Council 2007–13; Commdr, Order of the White Rose of Finland 1996, Kt (Third Class), Order of Grand Duke Gediminas (Lithuania) 1997, Cross of Merit with Clasp, Armour Guild; Medal for Mil. Merit 1995, Medal of Merit, Cen. Chamber of Commerce of Finland. *Leisure interests:* literature, cross-country skiing, swimming, football, canoeing, cooking. *E-mail:* jee@kitnet.fi.

ENGEL, Klaus, Dr rer. nat; German business executive; *Chairman of the Executive Board and CEO, Evonik Industries AG;* b. 21 April 1956, Duisburg; ed Ruhr Univ., Bochum; with Chemische Werke Hüls AG, Marl 1984–89, VEBA AG, Düsseldorf 1989–94, Hüls AG, Marl 1994–98; Man. Dir Creanova Spezialchemie GmbH, Marl 1998; with Stinnes AG, Mülheim an der Ruhr 1998; mem. Exec. Bd Brenntag AG, Mülheim an der Ruhr 1999–2006, Chair. 2001–06, Chief Exec. Dir Brenntag Man. GmbH 2004–06; mem. Exec. Bd RAG AG, Essen 2006–07; Chair. Exec. Bd Degussa AG, Düsseldorf 2006–08, Chair. Bd of Man., Evonik Degussa GmbH, Essen 2007–08; mem. Exec. Bd Evonik Industries AG, Essen 2007–, Chair. and CEO 2009–. *Address:* Evonik Industries AG, Rellinghauser Straße 1–11, 45128 Essen, Germany (office). *Telephone:* (201) 177-01 (office). *Fax:* (201) 177-3475 (office). *E-mail:* info@evonik.com (office). *Website:* www.evonik.com (office); corporate.evonik.com (office).

ENGELBRECHT, Jüri; Estonian physicist, mathematician and academic; *Professor, Institute of Cybernetics, Tallinn Technical University;* b. 1 Aug. 1939, Tallinn; m.; two c.; ed Tallinn Tech. Univ.; part-time assoc., then Prof., Tallinn Tech. Univ. 1974–92, 1994–, Head of Dept, Inst. of Cybernetics 1986–; mem. Estonian Acad. of Sciences 1990, Pres. 1994–2004, Vice-Pres. 2004–; Chair. Estonian Cttee for Mechanics 1991–; Adjunct Prof., Helsinki Univ. of Tech.; Visiting Prof., Czech Technical Univ. 1967–68, Newcastle-upon-Tyne Univ. 1979–80, 1986, Univ. of Messina 1981, 1987, Budapest Technical Univ. 1989, Univ. of Cambridge 1989, 1994, Univ. of Paris VI 1991, RWTH Aachen 1992, 1995, Univ. of Torino 1996, Univ. of Duisburg-Essen 2003; Pres. ALLEA (European Fed. of Nat. Acads of Sciences and Humanities) 2005–; For Ed.-in-Chief Proceedings of the Estonian Academy of Sciences 1991–95; Ed. Research Reports in Physics 1988–93; mem. Ed. Bd Prikladnaya Mekhanika and several other journals; mem. Estonian Soc. for Physics, Academia Scientiarum et Artium Europaea 1996–, Accad. Peloritana dei Pericolanti, Italy; Foreign mem. Latvian Acad. of Sciences 1996–, Gothenburg Royal Soc. of Sciences and Arts 1998–, Hungarian Acad. of Sciences 1998–, Bulgarian Acad. of Sciences 2007–; Fellow, World Innovation Foundation 2001–, Academia Europaea 2004–; Kt White Rose 1st Class (Finland) 1999, Coat of Arms 4th Class (Estonia) 1999, Lion Grand Cross (Finland) 2001, Chevalier des Palmes Académiques 2003, Order of Merit (No 1) of Ministry of Educ. and Research 2004, Cavalier Cross of the Order of Merit (Poland) 2005, Order of the Nat. Coat of Arms 3rd Class 2007; Dr hc (Budapest) 1999; Estonian Science Prize 1992, Humboldt Research Award 1993, Medal of the Baltic Acads 2000, Marin Drinov Medal, Bulgarian Acad. of Sciences 2004, Nikolai Alumäe Medal, Estonian Acad. of Sciences 2005. *Publications:* Nonlinear Deformation Waves 1981, Nonlinear Wave Processes of Deformation in Solids 1983, Nonlinear Evolution Equations 1986, An Introduction to Asymmetric Solitary Waves 1991, Nonlinear Dynamics and Chaos 1993, Nonlinear Wave Dynamics: Complexity and Simplicity 1997, and more than 200 scientific articles. *Address:* Estonian Academy of Sciences, Kohtu 6, 10130 Tallinn (office); Centre for Nonlinear Studies, Institute of Cybernetics, Tallinn Technical University, Akadeemia tee 21, 12618 Tallinn, Estonia (office). *Telephone:* (2) 644-20-13 (office). *Fax:* (2) 645-18-05 (office). *E-mail:* J.Engelbrecht@akadeemia.ee (office). *Website:* www.akadeemia.ee (office); www .allea.org.

ENGELL, Hans; Danish politician, columnist, author and newspaper editor; b. 8 Oct. 1948, Copenhagen; s. of Knud Engell Andersen; m. Pernille Kongsoe; ed Coll. of Journalism; journalist for Berlingske newspaper consortium 1968–78; Head of Press Service of Conservative People's Party 1978–82; mem. Parl. 1984–2000; Minister for Defence 1982–87, of Justice 1989–93; Chair. Conservative Parl. Group 1987–89; Leader Conservative People's Party 1995–97; Ed.-in-Chief Ekstra Bladet

2000–07; Commdr, Order of Dannebrog, Grand Commdr Order of Benemerencia p.p. *Address:* Puggaardsgade 13, 1573 Copenhagen, Denmark (home). *Telephone:* 33-13-09-13 (office). *E-mail:* hans.engell@eb.dk (office).

ENGELL, Mikaela, MA; Danish government official; *High Commissioner of Greenland;* b. 4 Oct. 1956, Copenhagen; d. of Maj.-Gen. Hans Christian Blæsenborg Engell; four c.; ed Univ. of Copenhagen; teacher, Head of Dept, Greenland Teacher Training Coll. and Greenland Business School 1984–93; Head of Section, Greenland Home Rule Ministry of Health and the Environment 1993–95, Pvt. Sec. to the Minister 1995–99, Head of Office, Foreign Affairs, Greenland Home Rule 1999–2001 Acting Perm. Sec. 2001–03, Perm. Sec. for Foreign Affairs 2003–05, Counsellor, Danish Ministry of Foreign Affairs 2005–11, High Commr of Greenland (Danish External Territory) 2011–; mem. Danish-Greenland Cultural Foundation. *Address:* The High Commissioner of Greenland, PO Box 1030, 3900 Nuuk, Greenland (office). *Telephone:* 321001 (office). *Fax:* 324171 (office). *E-mail:* riomgr@gl.stm.dk (office). *Website:* www .rigsombudsmanden.gl (office).

ENGEN, Travis, BS; American business executive (retd); b. 1944, Calif.; m.; one d.; ed MIT; held various man. positions at Bell Aerospace including dir of electronics; Dir Marketing Republic Electronic Industries Group 1976–79; Dir Govt Avionics, Bendix Avionics Div. 1980–83; Vice-Pres. and Gen. Man., Bendix Gen. Aviation Avionics Div. 1983–85; Pres. and Gen. Man. ITT Avionics 1985–1986, Pres. and CEO ITT Defence, Exec. Vice-Pres. ITT Corpn 1991–94, CEO ITT Industries, 1995; Dir Alcan Inc. 1996–2006, Pres. and CEO 2001–06 (retd); Dir Lyondell Chemical Co., Int. Aluminium Inst., Canadian Council of Chief Execs; mem. US Govt Defense Business Practice Implementation Bd; Chair. World Business Council for Sustainable Devt 2006–08; apptd Chair. Prince of Wales Int. Business Leaders Forum 2005, now mem. Int. Advisory Bd; SAM/SPG Sustainability Leadership Award 2006. *Leisure interest:* racing vintage cars. *Address:* c/o International Advisory Board, The Prince of Wales International Business Leaders Forum (IBLF), 15–16 Cornwall Terrace, Regent's Park, London, NW1 4QP, England (office).

ENGIBOUS, Thomas (Tom) J., MSc; American electronics industry executive (retd); ed Purdue Univ.; joined Texas Instruments Inc. (TI) 1976, Exec. Vice-Pres. 1993–96, Pres. Semiconductor group 1993–96, Pres. and CEO TI 1996–2004, mem. Bd of Dirs 1996–, Chair. 2004–08 (retd); Chair. Catalyst org.; Dir J. C. Penney Co. Inc., Dallas Citizens Council, Southwest Medical Foundation, US–Japan Business Council, Nat. Center for Educational Accountability; mem. Eng Visiting Cttee, Purdue Univ.; mem. Nat. Acad. of Eng, Inst. of Electrical and Electronics Engineers; Trustee Southern Methodist Univ.; Hon. DEng (Purdue Univ.) 1997. *Address:* 20 Shady Bend Drive, Melissa, TX 75434, USA.

ENGL, Walter L., Dr rer. nat, FIEEE; German professor of engineering; b. 8 April 1926, Regensburg; ed Technical Univ. of Munich; Siemens Instrument and Control Div. 1950–63, latterly Head of Research Div.; Prof., Tech. Univ. of Aachen 1963–91, Dean Faculty of Eng 1968–69; Visiting Prof., Univ. of Arizona 1967, Stanford Univ. 1970, Univ. of Tokyo 1972, 1980; mem. Acad. of Science of North Rhine-Westphalia; mem. Int. Union of Radio Science; Foreign Assoc. mem. Eng Acad. of Japan; Hon. Prof., Univ. of Kiel 1992; VDE-Ehrenring (highest award of German Electrical Engineers Soc.). *Publications include:* 100 publs. *Address:* Zum Heider Busch 5, 52134 Herzogenrath, Germany (home). *E-mail:* w.l.engl@web.de.

ENGLAND, Philip Christopher, BSc DPhil; British geophysicist and academic; *Professor of Geology, Department of Earth Sciences, University of Oxford;* ed Univ. of Bristol, Univ. of Oxford; NATO Postdoctoral Fellow, Norwegian Seismic Array, Kjeller, Norway 1976; NERC Research Fellow, Dept of Geodesy and Geophysics, Univ. of Cambridge 1977–79, Jr Research Fellow, Darwin Coll. 1978–80, IBM Research Fellow, Dept of Earth Sciences, Cambridge 1979–81; Asst and Assoc. Prof., Dept of Geological Sciences, Harvard Univ., USA 1981–86; Lecturer in Geophysics, Dept of Earth Sciences, Univ. of Oxford 1986–2000, Prof. of Geology 2000–; Fellow, Univ. Coll. Oxford. *Address:* Department of Earth Sciences, University of Oxford, Parks Road, Oxford, OX1 3PR, England (office).

ENGLAND, Richard, BArch; Maltese architect, academic, artist and poet; *Director, England & England, Architects;* b. 3 Oct. 1937, Sliema; s. of Edwin England Sant Fournier and Ina Desain; m. Myriam Borg Manduca 1962; one s. one d.; ed St Edward's Coll., Univ. of Malta, Politecnico, Milan, Italy; student-architect in Gio Ponti's studio, Milan 1960–62; Dir England & England, Architects 1962–; Dean Faculty of Architecture, Head, Dept of Architecture, Univ. of Malta 1987–89; Prof., Int. Acad. of Architecture 1987–, Academician 1991–, Vice-Pres. 2009–; Visiting Prof., Univ. of Malta; Fellow, Inst. of Professional Designers, London, Foundation of Int. Studies, Malta, Royal Society of Arts, UK; Hon. Prof., Univ. of Georgia, Inst. of Advanced Studies, New York Univ., Univ. of Buenos Aires; Hon. Fellow, Univ. of Bath (UK); Hon. FAIA 1999; Hon. mem. World Forum of Young Architects, Colegio de Arquitectos, Jalisco, Mexico; Officer, Nat. Order of Merit (Malta) 1993; Dr hc (Univ. of Architecture, Civil Eng and Geodesy, Sofia, Bulgaria), (Spiru Haret Univ., Romania); Interarch 1985, 1989, 1991, 1993 and 1995 Laureate Prizes, Commonwealth Architects Regional Awards 1985, 1987, Gold Medal City of Toulouse 1985, Comité des Critiques d'Architecture Silver Medal 1987, USSR Biennale Laureate Prize 1988, IFRAA Prize (USA) 1991, Int. Prize, Costa Rica Biennale 1996, Gold Medal, Belgrade Architectural Biennale 2000, Grand Prix, Int. Acad. of Architecture 2006, Annual Prize, Int. Acad. of Architecture 2012. *Works include:* Manikata Church, Univ. of Malta Extension, Cen. Bank of Malta, Malta Parl., Millennium Chapel, St James Cavalier Centre for Creativity, Valletta; various commercial bldgs, hotels and banks in Malta and the Middle East. *Publications include:* Walls of Malta 1973, White is White 1973, Contemporary Art in Malta 1974, Carrier-Citadel Metamorphosis 1974, Island: A Poem for Seeing 1980, Uncaged Reflections: Selected Writings 1965–80, In Search of Silent Spaces 1983, Octaves of Reflection (with Charles Camilleri) 1987, Eye to I (selected poems) 1994, Sacri Luoghi 1995, Mdina, Citadel of Memory (with Conrad Thake) 1996, Fraxions 1996, Gozo – Island of Oblivion 1997, Transfigurations: Places of Prayer (with Linda Schubert) 2000, Viaggio in Italia: Travel Sketches 2000, Gabriel Caruana Ceramics 2001, The Palette, Paintings of John Borg Manduca 2005, Norbert Attard 2007, Sanctuaries: Collected Poems 2007, Clavichords: Collected Poems 2009, Between Shadow & Stone: A Visual Exploration of Richard England's Architecture with Timmy Gambin 2011, Tapestries: Collected

Poems 2012. *Leisure interests:* music and art in general. *Address:* England & England Architects, 26/1 Merchants Street, Valletta, VLT10 (office); 8 Oleander Street, The Gardens, St Julians, STJ 1912, Malta (home). *Telephone:* 27350171 (home); 21350171 (home). *E-mail:* richardengland@onvol.net (office). *Website:* www.richardengland.com (office).

ENGLE, Robert F., BS, MS, PhD; American economist and academic; *Michael Armellino Professor in the Management of Financial Services, Leonard Stern School of Business, New York University;* b. 10 Nov. 1942, New York; ed Williams Coll., Cornell Univ.; Asst Prof., MIT 1969–74, Assoc. Prof. 1974–77; Assoc. Prof., Univ. of Calif., San Diego 1975–77, Prof. 1977–, Chair. Dept of Econs 1990–94, Chancellor's Assocs Chair. in Econs 1993–; Michael Armellino Prof. in the Man. of Financial Services, New York Univ. Stern School of Business 2000–, also Dir Volatility Inst.; Prin. Robert F. Engle Econometric Services; Co-Founding Pres. Soc. for Financial Econometrics; Nat. Bureau of Econ. Research Assoc. 1987–; Fellow, Econometric Soc. 1981– (mem. Council 1994–), AAAS 1995–, Inst. For Quantitative Research in Finance; Roger F. Murray Prize, Inst. for Quantitative Research in Finance 1991, Nobel Prize in Econs 2003 (jt recipient). *Publications include:* more than 100 academic papers and three books. *Address:* Kaufman Management Center, 44 West 4th Street, KMC 9-62, New York, NY 10012-1126, USA (office). *Telephone:* (212) 998-0710 (office). *Fax:* (212) 995-4220 (office). *E-mail:* rengle@stern.nyu.edu (office). *Website:* www.stern.nyu.edu/~rengle (office).

ENGLER, John Mathias, JD; American lawyer, politician, fmr state official and association executive; *President and CEO, National Association of Manufacturers;* b. 12 Oct. 1948, Mount Pleasant, Mich.; s. of Mathias Engler and Agnes Neyer; m. Michele Engler; three d.; ed Mich. State Univ. and Thomas M. Cooley Law School; mem. Mich. House of Reps 1971–78; mem. Mich. Senate 1979–90, Republican leader 1983, majority leader 1984–90; Gov. of Mich. 1990–2003; Pres. and CEO Nat. Asscn of Mfrs 2004–; Hon. LLD (Alma Coll.) 1984, (W Mich.) 1991. *Address:* National Association of Manufacturers, 1331 Pennsylvania Avenue, NW, Washington, DC 20004-1790, USA (office). *Telephone:* (202) 637-3106 (office). *Fax:* (202) 637-3460 (office). *E-mail:* john.m.engler@nam.org (office). *Website:* www.nam.org (office).

ENGLERT, Baron; François, DèsSc; Belgian physicist and academic; *Professor Emeritus of Physics, Université Libre de Bruxelles;* b. 6 Nov. 1932, Etterbeek; m. Mira Nikomarow; one s. four d.; ed Université Libre de Bruxelles; Asst, Université Libre de Bruxelles 1959–60, Chargé de cours 1961–64, Prof. of Physics 1964–98, Co-Dir Theoretical Physics Group 1980–98, Prof. Emer. 1998–; Research Assoc., Cornell Univ., USA 1959–60, Asst Prof. 1960–61; Perm. Sackler Fellow and Sr Prof. by Special Appointment, Tel-Aviv Univ. 1992–, Visiting Prof., Inst. for Quantum Studies, Chapman Univ. 2011–; Hon. mem. Solvay Insts 2006; Dr hc (Université de Mons-Hainaut) 2004, (Vrije Universiteit Brussels) 2005; Prix de Sciences Mathematiques et Physiques, Acad. Royale de Belgique 1977, First Award of the Int. Gravity Contest (with R. Brout and E. Gunzig) 1978, Prix Franqui 1982, European Physical Soc. High Energy and Particle Physics Prize (with R. Brout and Peter W. Higgs) 1997, Wolf Prize in Physics (with R. Brout and Peter W. Higgs) 2004, J.J. Sakurai Prize (co-recipient), American Physical Soc. 2010, Nobel Prize in Physics (co-recipient with Peter W. Higgs) 2013. *Publications include:* more than 115 articles in scientific journals. *Address:* Institute for Quantum Studies, Chapman University, One University Drive, Orange, CA 92866, USA (office); Service de physique théorique, Université Libre de Bruxelles, Campus de la Plaine, CP 225, 2 Boulevard du Triomphe, 1050 Brussels, Belgium (office). *Telephone:* (714) 997-6815 (Chapman); (2) 650-55-80 (office); (2) 375-46-49 (home). *Fax:* (2) 650-59-51 (office). *E-mail:* fenglert@ulb.ac.be (office). *Website:* www.chapman.edu/research-and-institutions/quantum-studies (office); web.me.com/fenglert (office).

ENGLISH, Hon. Bill, BA, BComm; New Zealand politician; *Deputy Prime Minister, Minister of Finance and Minister for Infrastructure;* b. 1961; m.; six c.; ed Otago Univ., Victoria Univ. of Wellington; fmr policy analyst and farmer; MP for Wallace 1990–93, for Clutha-Southland 1993–; Parl. Under-Sec. for Health and Crown Health Enterprises 1993–96, Minister of Crown Health Enterprises, Assoc. Minister of Educ., Minister of Health 1996–99 and Assoc. Minister of Revenue 1997–99, Minister of Finance (including Responsibility for Govt Superannuation Fund) and of Revenue 1999, Assoc. Treas. 1998–99; Leader New Zealand Nat. Party 2001–03, Deputy Leader 2006–, Leader of the Opposition 2001–03, Nat. Party Spokesman for Education 2003–08; Deputy Prime Minister, Minister of Finance and Minister for Infrastructure 2008–. *Leisure interests:* rugby, running, cycling. *Address:* Parliament Buildings, Wellington, New Zealand (office). *Telephone:* (4) 817-6801 (office). *Fax:* (4) 817-6501 (office). *E-mail:* b.english@ministers .govt.nz (office). *Website:* www.billenglish.co.nz.

ENGLISH, Edmond J. (Ted), BA; American business executive; *CEO, Bob's Discount Furniture LLC;* b. 1954; ed Northeastern Univ. Coll. of Business Admin; joined TJC Companies Inc. 1983, held various merchandising positions 1983–95, Sr Vice-Pres. Merchandising 1995–97, Exec. Vice-Pres. Merchandising, Planning and Allocation, Marmaxx Group 1997–98, Sr Vice-Pres. and Group Exec. 1998–99, COO TJX 1999–2000, Chair. Marmaxx Group 2000–01, Pres. 1999–2005, CEO 2000–05 (resgnd); CEO Bob's Discount Furniture LLC, Manchester, Conn. 2006–; mem. Bd of Dirs Citizens Financial Group, BJ's Wholesale Club, Inc. 2006–; Hon. Dr of Law, Framingham State Coll. 2002; Sir Ernest Shackleton Award, Shackleton Schools 2002, named Business Leader of the Year, MetroWest Chamber of Commerce 2003, named one of America's Most Powerful People, Forbes 2000. *Address:* Bob's Discount Furniture LLC, 428 Tolland Turnpike, Manchester, CT 06040-1715, USA (office). *Telephone:* (860) 645-3208 (office). *Fax:* (860) 645-4056 (office). *Website:* www.mybobs.com (office).

ENGLISH, Joseph Thomas, MD; American psychiatrist; *Professor and System Chairman, Department of Psychiatry and Behavioral Sciences, St. Vincent Catholic Medical Centers of New York;* b. 21 May 1933, Philadelphia, Pa; s. of Thomas J. English and Helen Gilmore English; m. Ann Carr Sanger 1969; two s. one d.; ed Jefferson Medical Coll.; intern, Jefferson Medical Coll. Hosp., Philadelphia 1958–59; Resident in Psychiatry, Inst. of Pa Hosp., Philadelphia 1959–61, Nat. Inst. of Mental Health, Bethesda, Md 1961–62; Chief Psychiatrist, US Peace Corps, Washington, DC 1962–66; Deputy Asst Dir of Health Affairs,

Office of Econ. Opportunity 1966, Asst Dir 1966–68; Admin., Health Services and Mental Health Admin., US Dept of Health, Educ. and Welfare 1968–70; Pres. New York City Health and Hosps Corpn 1970–73; Chair.; Prof. and System Chair. Dept of Psychiatry and Behavioral Sciences, St Vincent Catholic Medical Centers of New York 1973–; Prof. of Psychiatry, New York Medical Coll. 1979–, Assoc. Dean 1979–; Adjunct Prof., Cornell Univ. School of Medicine 1975–; Lecturer in Psychiatry, Harvard Univ. 1978–89; Visiting Fellow, Woodrow Wilson Nat. Fellowship Foundation 1979–; Trustee, Sarah Lawrence Coll. 1986–90, Menninger Foundation 1993–; Pres. American Psychiatric Asscn 1992–93; mem. World Psychiatric Soc. (Chair. section on religion and psychiatry 1994–), American Medical Asscn, New York Psychiatric Soc., Hosp. Soc. of New York, Asscn for Acad. Psychiatry, New York State Medical Soc., American Asscn of Gen. Hosp. Psychiatrists, Group Advancement Psychiatry, American Coll. of Mental Health Admins, American Hosp. Asscn, Greater New York Hosp. Asscn (Chair. Mental Health and Substance Abuse Services Cttee 1975–), Catholic Health Asscn; mem. Joint Comm. Accreditation Hosps 1984–86, Vice-Chair. 1986–88, Chair. 1988–89, Commr 2002–; numerous awards. *Address:* Department of Psychiatry and Behavioral Sciences, St Vincent's Hospital and Medical Center, 203 West 12th Street, New York, NY 10011-7762, USA (office). *Telephone:* (212) 604-8252 (office). *Fax:* (212) 604-8794 (office). *Website:* www.svcmc.org (office).

ENGLISH, Sir Terence Alexander Hawthorne, Kt, KBE, MA, FRCS, FRCP; British cardiac surgeon (retd); *Patron, Primary Trauma Care Foundation;* b. 3 Oct. 1932, Pietermaritzburg, South Africa; s. of Arthur Alexander English and the late Mavis Eleanor Lund; m. 1st Ann Margaret Smart Dicey; two s. two d.; m. 2nd Judith Milne 2002; ed Witwatersrand Univ. and Guy's Hosp. Medical School, London; Intern, Demonstrator in Anatomy, Jr Surgical Registrar, Guy's Hosp. 1962–65; Resident Surgical Officer, Bolingbroke Hosp. 1966; Surgical Registrar, Brompton Hosp. 1967; Sr Surgical Registrar, Nat. Heart and London Chest Hosps 1968–72; Research Fellow, Cardiac Surgery, Univ. of Ala 1969; Consultant Cardiothoracic Surgeon to Papworth and Addenbrooke's Hosps 1973–95; Dir British Heart Foundation Heart Transplant Research Unit, Papworth Hosp. 1980–89; Consultant Cardiac Adviser, Humana Hosp. Wellington, London 1983–89; Master of St Catharine's Coll. Cambridge 1993–2000; Pres. Int. Soc. for Heart Transplantation 1984–85, Royal Coll. of Surgeons 1989–92; mem. Jt Consultants Cttee 1989–92, Standing Medical Advisory Cttee 1989–92, Audit Comm. 1993–99; Pres. BMA 1995–96; Gov. The Leys School 1993–2001; Trustee, Medical Aid for Palestinians, Steering Group, Healthcare Professionals for Assisted Dying, Dignity in Dying; Patron, Primary Trauma Care Foundation; Hon. Fellow, St Catharine's Coll., Cambridge, St Hugh's Coll., Cambridge, Worcester Coll., Oxford, King's Coll., London; Hon. FRCP and Hon. FRCS (Canada); Hon. FRACS; Hon. FRCA; Hon. FACS; Hon. FRCS (Ireland); Hon. FRCS (Glasgow); Hon. DSc (Sussex, York); Hon. MD (Nantes), (Mahidol, Bangkok, Witwatersrand, S Africa); Man. of the Year, Royal Asscn for Disability and Rehabilitation 1980, Clement Price Thomas Award, Royal Coll. of Surgeons 1986, Lifetime Achievement Award, Soc. for Cardiothoracic Surgery of GB and Ireland 2009. *Achievement:* performed Britain's first successful heart transplant in 1979. *Publications:* Follow Your Star from Mining to Heart Transplants – A Surgeon's Story 2011; more than 100 articles in scientific journals. *Leisure interests:* reading, hill walking, South African history. *Address:* 28 Tree Lane, Oxford, OX4 4EY, England (home). *Telephone:* (1865) 717708 (home). *E-mail:* tenglish@doctors.org.uk (home).

ENHSAYHAN, Mendsayhany, PhD; Mongolian economist and politician; early work as an economist; fmr Chief of Staff to Pres. Ochirbat; Prime Minister of Mongolia 1996–98; Pres. Premier Int. Inc. 1998; mem. Democratic Alliance. *Address:* Pease Avenue 11A, Ulan Bator 210648, Mongolia (office). *Telephone:* (1) 321733 (home).

ENKHBAYAR, Jadambaagiin; Mongolian lawyer and politician; *Minister of Defence;* b. 16 Feb. 1973, Ulan Bator; s. of Shagalyn Jadambaa; ed Nat. Univ. of Mongolia, Maastricht School of Man., Netherlands; Dir-Gen. Gazar LLC 1992–2000; Head of Dept, Petroleum and Customs Authority 2000–02; Head of Dept and Vice-Chair., Ulan Bator Customs Authority 2002–03; Adviser, Customs Gen. Authority 2004–06; Vice-Chair. State Professional Inspection Authority 2006–08, Head of Secr. 2008; mem. Mongolian Great Khural (Parl.) for Govi–Altai 2008–, mem. Standing Cttee on Environment, Food and Agric.; Minister of Defence 2012–; mem. Mongolian People's Party (fmrly Mongolian People's Revolutionary Party). *Address:* Ministry of Defence, Government Bldg 7, Dandaryn Gudamj 51, Bayanzürkh District, Ulan Bator, Mongolia (office). *Telephone:* (51) 264818 (office). *E-mail:* mdef@mdef.pmis.gov.mn (office). *Website:* www.mdef.pmis.gov.mn (office).

ENKHBAYAR, Nambaryn; Mongolian politician and writer; b. 1 June 1958, Ulan Bator; s. of Baljinnyam Nambar and Radnaa Budkhand; m. Onon Tsolmon 1986; four c.; ed High School No. 23, Ulan Bator, Literature Inst., Moscow, Leeds Univ., UK; Ed. and Interpreter, Exec. Sec. and Head of Dept, Asscn of Mongolian Writers 1980–90; Vice-Pres. and Ed., Mongolian Interpreters' Union 1990–92; First Vice-Pres. Culture and Art Devt Cttee 1990–92; Minister of Culture 1992–96; Leader of the Opposition 1997–2000; mem. Great Hural (Parl.) 1992–, Speaker 2004–05; Prime Minister of Mongolia 2000–04; Pres. of Mongolia 2005–09, also C-in-C of Armed Forces; Leader, Mongolian People's Revolutionary Party (MPRP) 1997–; World Bank Adviser on Asian Culture and Buddhist Religion 1998–; Chair. Mongolia-India Friendship Asscn; Head Nat. Council of Museums 1995–; Int. Pres. Alliance of Religions and Conservation 2003–; Govt of Mongolia Polar Star 1996; MPRP Politician of the Year 1997; Govt of Mongolia Star of the Flag for Work Achievements 2001. *Publications:* translated several classic Russian novels; About Mongolian Arts, Literature and Emptiness 1989, On the Indicators of Development from the Buddhist Point of View 1998, Some Thoughts on the Relationship between Buddhist Philosophy and Economics 1998, To Develop or Not to Develop 1998. *Leisure interests:* reading, tennis, basketball, volleyball. *Address:* c/o State Palace, Ulan Bator 12 (office); Ikh Tenger, Suite 50-3, Ulan Bator, Mongolia (home).

ENKHBOLD, Mieyeegombo; Mongolian politician; *Chairman, Mongolian People's Party;* b. 1964; ed Mongolian Nat. Univ.; joined Mongolian People's Revolutionary Party (MPRP) 1990, Chair. MPRP Council, Ulan Bator 1997, Chair. MPRP (now Mongolian People's Party—MPP) 2005–07, 2013–; elected Mayor of Ulan Bator 1999–2006; Prime Minister of Mongolia 2006–07 (resgnd); Deputy

Prime Minister 2007–12. *Address:* Mongolian People's Party (MPP), Palace of Independence, Ulan Bator, Mongolia (office). *Telephone:* (77) 444167 (office). *Fax:* (77) 444167 (office). *E-mail:* contact@mpp.mn (office). *Website:* www.mpp.mn (office).

ENKHBOLD, Nyamaa, MA; Mongolian politician; *Deputy Chairman, State Great Hural (Parliament);* b. 1957; m.; two c.; ed Press Inst. of Moscow, Russia, Political Inst., Moscow, Univ. of Sydney, Australia; mem. Mongolian People's Revolutionary Party; Economist, Ministry of Culture 1979–80, Expert, Planning Dept 1980–86; Deputy Dir State Printing House 1986–90; Gen. Dir Mongol Hevlel Corpn 1990–93; Adviser to Deputy Prime Minister 1993–95; Head of Press and Public Relations Dept, Office of the Pres. 1997–2000; mem. State Great Hural (Parl.) 2000–, Deputy Chair. 2008–; Minister of Foreign Affairs 2006–07; Head of Govt Affairs Directorate 2007–08. *Address:* State Great Hural (Parliament), State Palace, Sükhbaataryn Talbai 1, Ulan Bator, Mongolia (office). *Telephone:* (11) 329889 (office). *Fax:* (11) 329889 (office). *E-mail:* enkhbold@parliament.mn (office).

ENKHSAIKHAN, Jargalsaikhany, DrIur; Mongolian diplomatist and researcher; *Ambassador-at-Large, Ministry of Foreign Affairs;* b. (Enkhee), 2 Sept. 1950, Ulan Bator; s. of Jargalsaikhan Bayaryn and Martha Tserengiin; m. 1st Tuul Myagmarjavyn 1976 (divorced 1993); m. 2nd Batgerel Budjavyn 1994; two s. four d.; ed Moscow State Inst. for Int. Relations; has held numerous positions at Ministry of Foreign Affairs, including Third, then Second Sec., Treaty and Legal Affairs Dept 1974–79, Third, then Second Sec. Perm. Mission to UN, New York 1979–86, Acting Head, Policy Planning Dept and Treaty and Legal Affairs Dept 1986–88, Deputy Chief of Mission, Embassy in Moscow 1988–92; Foreign Policy and Legal Adviser to Pres. of Mongolia 1992–93; Exec. Sec. Nat. Security Council 1993–96; Mongolian Rep. at UN Conf. on Law of the Sea 1976–82; Perm. Rep. to UN, New York 1996–2003, Rapporteur Legal (Sixth) Cttee of UN Gen. Ass. 1983, Vice-Chair. 1984, Chair. 1998, Vice-Chair. Special Cttee on Non-Use of Force in Int. Relations 1983, Chair. Group of Land-Locked States 1997, Vice-Pres. 52nd session UN Gen. Ass. 1997, Vice-Chair. Disarmament Comm. 1997; Exec. Dir Mongolian Nat. Coalition for Int. Criminal Court 2004–06; Adviser and Lead Researcher, Inst. for Strategic Studies, Nat. Security Council 2007; Adviser to Minister of Foreign Affairs 2007–08; Focal Point and Co-ordinator of Mongolia's nuclear-weapon-free status 2008–; Amb. to Austria and Amb. and Perm. Rep. to UN, Vienna 2008–13 (also accred as Amb. to Italy 2009–12, to Croatia 2010–12), Perm. Rep. to FAO, Rome 2009–12, to OSCE 2012–13; Advisor, Ministry of Foreign Affairs 2013, Amb.-at-Large 2013–; Gov. of Mongolia, Bd Govs, IAEA 2009–11, Pres. 54th Gen. Conf. of IAEA Sept. 2010; Chair. Working Group A, Comprehensive Test Ban Treaty Preparatory Comm. (CTBTO Prepcom) 2011–12; Hon. Prof. of Int. Relations 2006; Mongolian State Order of the Polar Star 1991, Mongolian Order of the Labour Red Banner 2012. *Publications:* articles on int. relations, int. law, foreign policy, democratic reforms in Mongolia, increasing role of civil society in Mongolia, etc. *Leisure interest:* reading. *Address:* Ministry of Foreign Affairs, 7A Peace Avenue, 14210 Ulan Bator, Mongolia (office). *Telephone:* (51) 262085 (office); 9931-3661 (mobile). *Fax:* (11) 322127 (office). *E-mail:* enkhsaikhanj@mfa.gov.mn (office). *Website:* www.mfa.gov.mn (office).

ENNACEUR, Mohamed, PhD; Tunisian lawyer, diplomatist and politician; *Minister of Social Affairs;* b. 21 March 1934, El Djem; m. Siren Möenstre; three s. two d.; ed Univ. of Tunis, Univ. of Paris (Sorbonne); early career as lawyer; Attaché, Ministry of Public Health and Social Affairs 1959–61, Chef du Cabinet 1961–64; Head of Transport Div., Ministry of Social Affairs 1964–67; Dir-Gen., Office for Professional Training and Employment 1967–72; Gov. of Sousse 1972–73; Minister of Labour and Social Affairs 1974–77, 1979–85, Minister of Social Affairs 2011–; Pres. Econ. and Social Council of Tunisia 1985–91; Perm. Rep. to UN and other int. orgs, Geneva 1991–96; barrister 1997–; consultant 2000–; Co-ordinator, UN Pacte Mondial agreement in Tunisia 2005–; Chair. World Employment Conf. (ILO) 1976, 71st session of Int. Labour Conf. (ILO) 1985, 49th session of Human Rights Comm. (UN) 1993; Pres. Inst. Social-Consult; Ed. Tunisian Social Law Review; Hon. KBE; Grand Cordon of Order of Independence, Order of the Repub., Ordre de Léopold (Belgium), Ordre d'Orange-Nassau (Netherlands), Ordre du Grand-Duché (Luxembourg), Ordre National du Mérite (France), Ordre National du Mérite (Côte d'Ivoire), Commdr, Order of Merit (Germany). *Publications:* Human Rights after the Vienna Conference 1993; articles on labour law, human rights and social policy in Int. Studies Review, Tunisian Social Law Review, Int. Review of the Red Cross and other publs. *Leisure interests:* sports, music. *Address:* Ministry of Social Affairs, 27 ave Bab Benat, 1019 Tunis (office); 10 rue du Mali, 1002 Tunis, Tunisia (home). *Telephone:* (71) 567-502 (office); (1) 741-127 (home). *Fax:* (71) 568-722 (office). *E-mail:* masste@rnas.gov.tn (office); med.ennaceur@gnet.tn (home). *Website:* www.social.tn (office).

ENNIS-HILL, Jessica, CBE, MBE, BSc; British track and field athlete; b. 28 Jan. 1986, Sheffield, Yorks., England; d. of Vinnie Ennis and Alison Powell; m. Andy Hill 2013; ed Univ. of Sheffield; competed at World Youth Championship, Sherbrooke 2003, World Junior Championship, Grosseto 2004; winner European Athletics Junior Championship, Kaunas 2005; bronze medal, Summer Universiade, Izmir 2005; bronze medal (heptathlon), Commonwealth Games, Melbourne 2006; bronze medal (100m hurdle), European Under-23 Championship, Debrecen 2007; finished sixth at European Indoor Championship (pentathlon), Birmingham 2007; finished fourth at World Championship, Osaka 2007; gold medal (heptathlon), World Championship, Berlin 2009; winner Int. Asscn of Athletics Feds (IAAF) World Combined Events Challenge, Desenzano del Garda 2009; gold medal (heptathlon), European Championship, Barcelona 2010; gold medal (pentathlon), World Indoor Championship, Doha 2010; winner (60m hurdle), five team int. meeting, Glasgow 2010; winner (heptathlon), Hypo-Meeting, Götzis 2010; seventh position (javelin throw), Diamond League, Gateshead 2010; silver medal (heptathlon), World Championship, Daegu 2011; winner (60m hurdle), Aviva Int. meeting, Glasgow 2011; winner (heptathlon), Hypo-Meeting, Götzis 2011; finished seventh (100m hurdle), eighth position (long jump), Diamond League, New York 2011; silver medal (pentathlon), World Indoor Championship, Istanbul 2012 (nat. record of 4,965 points); winner (heptathlon), IAAF World Combined Events Challenge, Götzis 2012; gold medal (heptathlon), Olympic Games, London 2012 (British and Commonwealth record of 6,995 points); double World Champion, first British woman to win world titles both indoors and outdoors; writes a column for The Times newspaper; Amb. for the Jaguar Acad. of Sport; Patron Sheffield

Children's Hosp., Wells Sports Foundation; advertising campaigns for Aviva, Powerade, BP, Adidas, Omega watches and Olay 'Essentials;' featured on the cover Cosmopolitan magazine Aug. 2012; a 'new face' of Santander UK's advertising campaign Feb. 2013; Hon. DLitt (Sheffield) 2010; Women's European Athletics Rising Star of the Year 2007, Sportswoman of the Year, British Sports Journalists Asscn 2009, 2010, Sportswoman of the Year, Ultimate Woman of the Year Awards, Cosmopolitan Magazine 2009, 2010, British Athlete of the Year, British Athletics Writers Asscn 2009, 2010, 2011, Outstanding Female Athlete, Commonwealth Sports Awards 2010, Dame Marea Hartman Award 2010, Most Inspirational Sportswoman of the Year, Jaguar Acad. of Sport Annual Awards 2010, Sportswoman of the Year, Glamour Magazine 2012, Sunday Times Sportswoman of the Year Award 2012, Women's European Athlete of the Year 2012, Laureus World Sportswoman of the Year 2012. *Publication:* Jessica Ennis: Unbelievable – From My Childhood Dreams to Wi 2012. *Leisure interests:* cooking, shopping, listening to music, Sheffield United Football Club. *Address:* c/o United Kingdom Athletics, Athletics House, Alexander Stadium, Walsall Road, Perry Barr, Birmingham, B42 2BE, England. *Website:* www.jessicaennis.net.

ENO, Brian Peter George St John Baptiste de la Salle; British composer, artist, keyboard player and producer; b. 15 May 1948, Woodbridge, Suffolk; s. of the late William Arnold Eno and of Maria Alphonsine Eno (née Buslot); m. 1st Sarah Grenville 1967; one d.; m. 2nd Anthea Norman-Taylor 1988; two c.; ed St Mary's Convent, St Joseph's Coll., Ipswich School of Art, Winchester Coll. of Art; Founder-mem. Roxy Music 1971–73; worked with guitarist Robert Fripp 1975–76; invented 'ambient music' 1975; Visiting Prof., RCA 1995–; Hon. Prof. of New Media, Berlin Univ. of Art 1998–; f. Long Now Foundation 1996; mem. PRS, BAC&S; Hon. DTech (Plymouth) 1995; Dr hc, Royal Coll. of Art 2007; Q Magazine Award for Best Producer (with others) 1993, BRIT Awards for Best Producer 1994, 1996, Inspiration Award (with David Bowie) 1995, Grammy Awards for Producer of Best Record of the Year 2000, 2009. *Recordings include:* albums: Here Come The Warm Jets 1974, Taking Tiger Mountain (By Strategy) 1974, Another Green World 1975, Discreet Music 1975, Before and After Science 1977, Music For Films 1978, Ambient 1: Music For Airports 1978, After the Heat 1978, My Life in the Bush of Ghosts (with David Byrne) 1981, Ambient 3: Day of Radiance 1981, Empty Landscapes 1981, Ambient 4: On Land 1982, Music For Films Vol. 2 1983, Apollo: Atmospheres and Soundtracks 1983, Begegnungen 1984, Thursday Afternoon 1985, Begegnungen II 1985, Music For Films Vol. 3 1988, Wrong Way Up 1990, Nerve Net 1992, The Shutov Assembly 1992, Neroli 1993, Headcandy 1994, Spinner 1995, The Drop 1997, Extracts from Music for White Cube 1997, Kite Stories 1999, I Dormienti 1999, Music for Onmyo-Ji 2000, Music for Civic Recovery Center 2000, Drawn From Life 2001, January 07003: Bell Studies for The Clock 2003, Another Day on Earth 2005; with Robert Fripp: No Pussyfooting 1975, Evening Star 1976, The Equatorial Stars 2004, The Cotswold Gnomes 2006, Beyond Even 1992–2006 2007, Everything that Happens will Happen Today (with David Byrne) 2008, Small Craft on a Milk Sea 2010, Lux 2012; numerous albums as producer, co-producer, collaborations, guest appearances on albums, and remixes including: U2, Coldplay, Paul Simon, David Bowie, David Byrne. *Publications include:* A Year with Swollen Appendices 1995, The Margin: A Canongate Diary for 2007 (ed.). *Address:* c/o Shakedown Records Ltd, Regent House, 1 Pratt Mews, London, NW1 0AD, England (office). *Telephone:* (19082) 70546 (office). *E-mail:* orders@shakedownrecords.com (office). *Website:* www .enoshop.co.uk (office).

ENOKSEN, Hans; Greenlandic politician; b. 1956; mem. Siumut Party, Chair. 2001–09; mem. Parl. 1995–; Minister for Fisheries, Hunting and Settlements 2001–02; Prime Minister, Greenland Home Rule Govt 2002–09; Greenland Home Rule Nersonaat in Gold 2003. *Address:* Inatsisartut, PO Box 1060, 3900 Nuuk, Greenland (office). *Telephone:* 345000 (office). *Fax:* 325002 (office). *E-mail:* hes@ kni.gl (office); inatsisartut@inatsisartut.gl (office). *Website:* www.inatsisartut.gl (office); www.nanoq.gl (office).

ENQUIST, Per Olov, MA; Swedish novelist, playwright, journalist and poet; b. 1934, Hjoggböle; m. 2nd Lone Bastholm; ed Univ. of Uppsala; Visiting Prof. UCLA 1973; Nordic Council literary prize 1968, August Award 1999, Independent Foreign Fiction Prize 2003, Augustpriset 2008, Nordic Prize, Swedish Academy 2010. *Publications include:* Kristallögat 1961, Färdvägen 1963, Magnetisörens Femte Vinter 1964, Bröderna Casey 1964, Hess 1966, Sextiotalskritik 1966, Legionärerna 1968, Sekonden 1971, Katedralen i München 1972, Berättelser Från de Inställda Upprorens Tid (short stories) 1974, Tribadernas Natt 1975, Chez Nous (with Anders Ehnmark) 1976, Musikanternas Uttåg 1978, Mannen På Trottoaren 1979, Till Fedra 1980, Från Regnormarnas Liv 1981, En Triptyk 1981, Doktor Mabuses Nya Testamente (with Anders Ehnmark) 1982, Strindberg Ett Liv 1984, Nedstörtad Ängel 1985, Två Reportage om Idrott 1986, I Lodjurets Timma 1988, Kapten Nemos Bibliotek 1991, Hamsun (screenplay) 1996, Bildmakarna (play) 1998, Livläkarens Besök (The Visit of the Ryal Physician) 1999, Systrarna (play) 2000, Lewis Resa (Lewi's Journey) 2001, Boken om Blanche och Marie (The Story of Blanche and Marie) 2004, Et Annat Liv 2008; contrib. to literary criticism in newspapers, including Uppsala Nya Tidning, Svenska Dagbladet, Expressen. *Address:* c/o Norstedts, Tryckerigatan 4, Box 2052, 103 12 Stockholm, Sweden (office).

ENRILE, Juan Ponce (see PONCE ENRILE, Juan).

ENSIGN, John E., DMV; American politician and fmr veterinarian; *Senator from Nevada;* b. 25 March 1958, Roseville, Calif.; s. of Mike Ensign and Sharon Ensign; m. Darlene Sciaretta; one s.; ed Ore. State Univ., Colo State Univ.; owner of animal hosp. in Las Vegas; Gen. Man. Gold Strike Hotel and Casino 1991, Nevada Landing Hotel and Casino 1992; mem. US Congress from 1st Dist, Nev. 1994–98, mem. Ways and Means Cttee, Sub-Cttee on Health, Sub-Cttee on Human Resources, Comm. on Resources 1995–98; cand. for Senate 1998–99; Senator from Nevada 2000–. *Address:* 119 Russell Senate Office Building, Washington, DC 20510, USA (office). *Telephone:* (202) 224-6244 (office). *Fax:* (202) 228-2193 (office). *Website:* ensign.senate.gov (office).

ENSLER, Eve; American playwright; b. 25 May 1953, New York City; m. Richard McDermott (divorced); ed Middlebury Coll.; best known for play The Vagina Monologues, translated into nearly 50 languages and performed in over 140 countries; toured 20 North American cities with play The Good Body 2005–06; regular contrib. to Glamour Magazine, The Guardian, Marie Claire, Huffington Post, Washington Post, Utne Reader, O Magazine; Co-founder and Artistic Dir V-Day (global activist movt to stop violence against women and girls) 1998; Hon. DLit (Middlebury Coll.) 2003; Hon. DHumLitt (Manhattanville Coll.) 2005; Hon. Dr of Communications (Simmons Coll.) 2006; numerous awards including Guggenheim Fellowship Award in Playwriting 1999, Amnesty International Media Spotlight Award for Leadership 2002. *Films include:* The Vagina Monologues 2002, What I Want My Words to Do to You: Voices From Inside a Women's Maximum Security Prison 2003, Until the Violence Stops 2004. *Publications:* Plays: Conviction, Lemonade, The Depot, Floating Rhoda and the Glue Man, Extraordinary Measures, The Vagina Monologues (Obie Award for Best New Play 1996) 1996, The Good Body, Necessary Targets, The Treatment, Here 2010; Books: Vagina Warriors 2005, A Memory, A Monologue, A Rant and A Prayer 2006, Insecure at Last: Losing It in Our Security Obsessed World 2006, The Good Body, Necessary Targets, I Am An Emotional Creature 2010. *E-mail:* tech@vday.org (office). *Website:* www.vday.org (office).

ENSOUR, Abdullah, PhD; Jordanian politician; *Prime Minister and Minister of Defence;* b. 1939, Salt, Transjordan (now Jordan); ed American Univ. of Beirut, Univ. of Paris, France; elected Deputy to Parl. 1989, re-elected 1992; Minister of Planning 1984, 1985, of Educ. 1989–91, of Foreign Affairs 1991–93, of Industry and Trade 1993–96, of Higher Educ. 1996–97; Deputy Prime Minister and Minister of Admin. Devt 1997–98; Deputy Prime Minister and Minister of Information 1998–2001; Senator in Jordanian Parl. –2001; Prime Minister and Minister of Defence 2012–; Chair. Bd of Trustees, Al-Zaytoonah Univ. of Jordan –2001; fmr Gov. of Jordan to the World Bank, Deputy to IMF and Deputy Perm. Del. to UNESCO; mem. Bd Arab African Bank, Nuackchott (Pres.), Univ. of Jordan (Vice-Pres.), French Univs' Grads in Jordan (Hon. Pres.); Ind. *Address:* Office of the Prime Minister, PO Box 80, Amman 11180, Jordan (office). *Telephone:* (6) 4641211 (office). *Fax:* (6) 4642520 (office). *E-mail:* info@pm.gov.jo (office). *Website:* www.pm .gov.jo (office).

ENTHOVEN, Marius, MSc; Dutch civil servant and international organization official; *Vice-Chairman, Energy Council;* b. 23 Nov. 1940, Baarn; s. of Emil S. Enthoven and Anna G. Schouten; m. Lidwine Kolfschoten 1965; four d.; ed Delft Tech. Univ., Princeton Univ., USA; scientist with Dutch Aerospace Labs (NLR) 1967–72; Head of Noise Abatement Dept, Ministry for Environment 1972–77, Dir Scientific Affairs 1977–80, Chief Insp. Environmental Protection 1980–88, Dir-Gen. Environmental Protection 1988–94; Dir-Gen. Environment, Nuclear Safety and Civil Protection, Directorate-Gen. XI, European Comm. 1994–97; Special Adviser to Sec.-Gen., European Comm. 1997–98; Dir NIB Capital Bank NV, Netherlands 1998–2004, also Exec. Dir Research Inst.; mem. Energy Council (ind. advisory body that advises Dutch govt and parl. on energy policy) 2002–, currently Vice-Chair.; Kt Order of the Dutch Lion. *Publications:* books and articles on environmental man. issues. *Leisure interests:* literature, theatre, music, tennis. *Address:* c/o Energy Council, Adelheidstraat 8, PO Box 11723, 2502 AS The Hague, Netherlands (office). *Telephone:* (70) 3924001 (office). *Fax:* (70) 3652836 (office). *E-mail:* info@energieraad.nl (office). *Website:* www.algemene-energieraad.nl (office).

ENTHOVEN, Raphaël, PhD; French philosopher, academic and television producer; *Producer, Philosophie, ARTE France;* b. 9 Nov. 1975, Paris; s. of Jean-Paul Enthoven and Catherine David; m. Justine Lévy 1995; one s. with Carla Bruni; one c. with Chloé Lambert; ed École Normale Supérieure; taught for two years at Jean Moulin Univ. Lyon 3, then at Univ. of Paris VII-Jussieu, then at Université populaire de Caen 2002–03; Co-producer of radio show Les vendredis de la philosophie on France Culture; now teaches at École Polytechnique and Sciences Po; adviser to Ed. of Philosophie Magazine; producer of Philosophy programme, broadcast on Sundays on ARTE France 2008–. *Publications:* Un jeu d'enfant: la philosophie 2007, L'Endroit du décor 2009, Lectures de Proust 2013, Matière Première 2013. *Address:* Philosophie, ARTE France, 8 rue Marceau, 92785 Issy-les-Moulineaux Cedex 9, France (office). *Telephone:* 1-55-00-77-77 (office). *Fax:* 1-55-00-77-00 (office). *Website:* www.arte.tv/fr/accueil/2235074.html (office).

ENTOV, Revold Mikhailovich, PhD; Russian economist; *Professor, University of Moscow;* b. 23 March 1931, Kiev; m. Galina Gorvitz 1962; one s. one d.; ed Kharkov Univ. and Inst. for World Econ. and Int. Relations (IMEMO); Asst Prof., Bashkirian Agricultural School 1954–57; research worker, IMEMO 1961, now Head of Section; Prof., Univ. of Moscow 1970–; mem. Comm. Evaluating Projects of Econ. Reform in USSR (now Russia) 1990–91; mem. Russian Acad. of Sciences 1994; mem. Editorial Bd Mirovaya ekonomika i mezhdunarodnye otnosheniya (The World Economy and International Relations), Ekonomika i matematicheskie metody (The Economy and Mathematical Methods); USSR State Prize 1977, Adam Smith Prize 1999, Zolotaya Vyshka Prize 2004. *Publications include:* Public Credit of the U.S. 1967, Theories of Prices 1982, Movements of Capital and the Profit Rate 1987, The Distribution of Wealth 1992, Corporate Management and the Protection of Property Rights: Empirical Analysis and Actual Reform Tendencies (with A. D. Radygin) 2001; numerous articles on econ. theory and the US economy. *Leisure interest:* history of psychology. *Address:* Institute for World Economy and International Relations, Profsoyuznaya 23, 117859 Moscow (office); Azovskaya 4, Apt 44, 113149 Moscow, Russia (home). *Telephone:* (495) 128-29-07 (office); (495) 310-17-67 (home).

ENTRECANALES DOMECQ, José Manuel, Licenciado en Ciencias Económicas; Spanish business executive; *Chairman, Endesa SA;* b. 1 Jan. 1963, Madrid; ed Universidad Complutense de Madrid; Assoc., Merrill Lynch Europe Ltd Capital Markets, London and New York 1986–90; mem. Bd of Dirs Sefinco Ltd New York 1990–92; Finance Dir Acciona SA 1992–2004, Chair. 2004–; Man. Dir Vodafone España 1994–2000, Chair. 2000–07, also Chair. Vodafone Foundation; Chair. Endesa SA 2007–; mem. Bd of Dirs Agropecuaria El Cijaral, SA, Grupo Entrecanales, SA, Tivafen, SA, Servicios Urbanos Integrales, SA, Osmosis Internacional, SA; mem. Bd Conferencia Española de Fundaciones, Guggenheim Foundation, Spanish Red Cross, Universal Library, Cotec Foundation for Technological Innovation, Reina Sofía Higher School of Music, Business and Society Foundation, Inst. of Family Business, Spanish-US Chamber of Commerce, Spanish Institutional Foundation; Patron Pro CNIC Foundation, Carolina Foundation, Prince of Asturias Foundation, Family Enterprise Inst. *Address:* Endesa SA, Ribera de Loira 60, 28042 Madrid, Spain (office). *Telephone:* (91) 2131000 (office).

Fax: (91) 5645496 (office). *E-mail:* info@endesa.es (office). *Website:* www.endesa.es (office).

ENTREMONT, Philippe; French pianist and conductor; b. 7 June 1934, Reims; s. of Jean Entremont and Renée Entremont (née Monchamps); m. Andrée Ragot 1955; one s. one d.; ed Inst. Notre-Dame à Reims, Conservatoire Nat. Supérieur de Musique de Paris; has performed with all major orchestras of world 1953–; Pres. of Acad. Int. de Musique Maurice Ravel, Saint-Jean-de-Luz 1973–80; Musical Dir and Permanent Conductor, Vienna Chamber Orchestra 1976–; Dir New Orleans Symphony Orchestra 1980–86; Prin. Conductor Denver Symphony Orchestra 1986–88, Paris Orchestre Colonne 1987–90, Netherlands Chamber Orchestra 1993–2002, Israel Chamber Orchestra 1995–; Dir American Conservatory Fontainebleau 1994; f. Santo Domingo Biennial Festival 1997; Prin. Guest Conductor Shanghai Broadcasting Symphony Orchestra 2001–; Prin. Guest Conductor Munich Symphony Orchestra 2005–06, Prin. Conductor 2006; Conductor Super World Orchestra, Tokyo 2006; Officier Ordre nat. du Mérite, Officier, Légion d'honneur, Commdr des Arts et Lettres, Österreichisches Ehrenkreuz für Wissenschaft und Kunst (Arts and Sciences Cross of Honour, Austria); Harriet Cohen Piano Medal 1951, Grand Prix Int. Concours Marguerite Long-Jacques Thibaud 1953, four Grand Prix du Disque Awards, Edison Award 1960, Grammy Award 1972;. *Leisure interest:* golf. *Address:* c/o Tim Fox, Columbia Artists Management Inc., 1790 Broadway, New York, NY 10019-1412, USA; c/o Bureau de concerts Dominique Lierner, 17 rue du 4 septembre, 75002 Paris (office); 10 rue de Castiglione, 75001 Paris, France. *Telephone:* 1-42-86-06-08. *Fax:* 1-42-86-86-61 (home).

ENTWISTLE, George Edward, BA; British media executive; b. 8 July 1962, Yorks., England; m. Jane Porter; one s. one d.; ed Durham Univ.; began career as writer and magazine ed., Haymarket Magazines 1984–89; joined BBC as Broadcast Journalism trainee 1989, Asst Producer, Panorama 1990–92, Producer, On The Record 1993–94, Asst Ed. and later Deputy Ed., Newsnight 1994–99, Deputy Ed., Tomorrow's World 1999–2001, Ed., Newsnight 2001–04, Exec. Ed. of Topical Arts on BBC Two and BBC Four 2004, Head and Commissioning Ed. of TV Current Affairs 2005, Acting Controller of BBC Four 2007, Controller of Knowledge Commissioning 2008–11, also Controller of Editorial Standards for BBC Vision, Dir, BBC Vision 2011–12, Dir-Gen. BBC Sept.–Nov. 2012 (resgnd); Advisory Chair. Edinburgh Int. TV Festival 2011. *Address:* c/o Office of the Director-General, Broadcasting House, Portland Place, London, W1A 1AA, England.

ENTWISTLE, John Nicholas McAlpine, OBE; British solicitor and consultant; *Tribunal Judge, Tribunal Service – Criminal Injuries Compensation;* b. 16 June 1941, Southport, Lancs.; s. of Sir Maxwell Entwistle and Lady (Jean) Entwistle; m. Phillida Burgess; one s. one d.; ed Uppingham School, Rutland; qualified as solicitor 1963; Asst Attorney, Shearman & Sterling, New York, USA 1963–64; Pnr, Maxwell Entwistle & Byrne 1966–91; mem. Liverpool City Council 1968–71; Nat. Vice-Chair. The Bow Group 1967–68; Parl. cand. (Conservative) for Huyton 1970; Consultant Solicitor, Davies Wallis Foyster 1992–2004; Lloyds underwriting mem. 1971–2000; Founder-Dir Merseyside TEC 1990–91; Dir (non-exec.) Rathbone Brothers PLC 1992–98; Deputy Dist Chair. Appeals Service 1992–; Chair. Liverpool Chamber of Commerce & Industry 1992–94; Founder-Chair. NW Chambers of Commerce Assen 1993–97; Pres. British Chambers of Commerce 1998–2000; mem. Chancellor of Exchequer's Standing Cttee on preparation for EMU 1998–2000, Council of Britain in Europe 1999–2004; Home Sec.'s rep. for appointments to Merseyside Police Authority 1994–2000; Chair. several pvt. property cos; mem. Nat. Trust NW Regional Cttee 1992–98, Parole Bd 1994–2000, Disciplinary Cttee, Mortgage Compliance Bd 1999–2004, Criminal Injuries Compensation Appeals Panel 2000–; currently Tribunal Judge, Tribunal Service – Criminal Injuries Compensation; part-time asylum adjudicator 2000–05, part-time immigration judge 2005–10; Trustee, Nat. Museums & Galleries on Merseyside 1990–97, Royal Acad. of Arts Trust 2006–; DL for Merseyside 1992–2002; Hon. Fellow, Liverpool John Moores Univ. 2010. *Leisure interests:* collecting and painting pictures, gardening, shooting. *Address:* Low Crag, Crook, nr Kendal, Cumbria, LA8 8LE, England (home). *Telephone:* (15395) 68715 (office); (15395) 68268 (home). *Fax:* (15395) 68769 (office). *E-mail:* jentwistle@onetel.net (office).

ENWEZOR, Okwui, BA; American (b. Nigerian) art critic; *Dean of Academic Affairs and Senior Vice President, San Francisco Art Institute;* b. 1963, Calabar, Cross River State; ed Jersey City State Coll.; began curatorial career at Solomon R. Guggenheim Museum, New York; Founder and Ed. Nka Journal of Contemporary African Art (critical art journal) 1994; Artistic Dir 2nd Johannesburg Biennale 1996–97; Adjunct Curator of Contemporary Art, Art Inst. of Chicago 1998–2000; Artistic Dir Documenta 11, Kassel, Germany 1998–2002; currently Dean of Academic Affairs and Sr Vice Pres., San Francisco Art Inst.; fmr Visiting Prof. in Art History, Univ. of Pittsburgh, Columbia Univ., New York, Univ. of Illinois, Urbana-Champaign, Univ. of Umea, Sweden; fmr Artistic Dir Bienal Internacional de Arte Contemporaneo de Sevilla, Spain; mem. numerous juries, advisory bodies and curatorial teams including Carnegie Int. 1999, Venice Biennale, Hugo Boss Prize, Foto Press, Barcelona, Carnegie Prize, Int. Center for Photography Infinity Awards, Young Palestinian Artist Award, Ramallah, Cairo, Istanbul, Sharjah and Shanghai Biennales; curator, seventh Gwangju Biennale, Repub. of Korea 2008; awards from Prince Claus Fund for Culture and Devt, Ford Foundation, Rockefeller Foundation, Int. Art Critics Assen, Peter Norton Curatorial Award, Bard Coll. Award for Curatorial Excellence 2009. *Publications include:* Reading the Contemporary: African Art from Theory to the Marketplace (co–ed.) 1999, The Postcolonial Constellation: Contemporary Art in a State of Permanent Transitions, Archaeology of the Present: The Postcolonial Archive, Photography and African Modernity. *Address:* San Francisco Art Institute, 800 Chestnut Street, San Francisco, CA 94133, USA (office). *Telephone:* (415) 771-7020 (office). *Website:* www.sfai.edu (office).

ENYA; Irish singer, composer and musician (piano); b. (Eithne Ní Bhraonáin), 17 May 1961, Gweedore, Co. Donegal; d. of Leon Ó Braonáin and Máire Bean Uí Bhraonáin; keyboard and vocals with family group, Clannad (trad-itional Irish music) 1980–82; formed Aigle Music (with producer and sound engineer Nicky Ryan and man. and lyricist Roma Ryan) 1982; performed at the Queen's 50th Wedding Anniversary, birthday celebrations of King Gustav of Sweden and privately for Pope John Paul II; numerous other live appearances,

including the Acad. Awards 2002; Ivor Novello Int. Achievement Award 1998, six World Music Awards including Best-Selling Artist in the World 2001, Japanese Grand Prix Award for New Artist of the Year, Hot Press Best Irish Solo Artist, Academy of Achievement of America Golden Plate Award, Billboard Artist Award, Echo Award (for Only Time), BMI Special Citation of Achievement (for Only Time, for Orinoco Flow, I Don't Wanna Know), Las Vegas Film Critics' Soc. Award for Best Original Song (for May It Be), Phoenix Film Critics' Award for Best Original Song (for May It Be), Broadcast Film Critics' Award for Best Song (for May It Be). *Recordings include* albums: with Clannad: Crann Ull 1980, Fuaim 1982; as Enya: Enya 1987, Watermark (IFPI Platinum European Award) 1988, Shepherd Moons (IFPI Platinum European Award, Grammy Award, Billboard Music Award, NARM Best-Selling Album Award) 1991, The Celts 1992, The Memory of Trees (Grammy Award) 1995, Paint the Sky with Stars (Japanese Grand Prix Album of the Year) 1997, A Day Without Rain (Grammy Award, Japanese Grand Prix Album of the Year) 2000, Amarantine (Grammy Award for Best New Age Album 2007) 2005, And Winter Came 2008. *Address:* Treesdale, Church Road, Killiney, Co. Dublin, Ireland (office). *Website:* www.enya.com.

ENZENSBERGER, Hans Magnus, (Andreas Thalmayr), DPhil; German poet and writer; *Artistic Director, Renaissance Theatre Berlin;* b. 11 Nov. 1929, Kaufbeuren; m. 1st Dagrun Averaa Christensen; one d.; m. 2nd Maria Alexandrowna Makarowa 1986; m. 3rd Katharina Bonitz; one d.; ed Univs of Erlangen, Freiburg im Breisgau, Hamburg and Paris; Third Programme Ed., Stuttgart Radio 1955–57; Lecturer, Hochschule für Gestaltung, Ulm 1956–57; Literary Consultant to Suhrkamp's (publrs), Frankfurt 1960–; mem. 'Group 47', Ed. Kursbuch (review) 1965–75, Publr 1970–90; Ed. TransAtlantik (monthly magazine) 1980–82; Publr and Ed., Die Andere Bibliothek 1985–2005; Artistic Dir Renaissance Theatre Berlin 1995–; Ordre pour le Mérite 2000; Hugo Jacobi Prize 1956, Kritiker Prize 1962, Georg Büchner Prize 1963, Premio Pasolini 1982, Heinrich Böll Prize 1985, Kultureller Ehrenpreis der Stadt München 1994, Heinrich Heine Prize, Düsseldorf 1997, Príncipe de Asturias 2002, Griffin Trust for Excellence in Poetry's Lifetime Recognition Award 2009, and others. *Publications:* poetry: Verteidigung der Wölfe 1957, Landessprache 1960, Blindenschrift 1964, Poems for People Who Don't Read Poems (English edn) 1968, Gedichte 1955–1970 1971, Mausoleum 1975, Gedichte 1950–2005 2006; essays: Clemens Brentanos Poetik 1961, Einzelheiten 1962, Politik und Verbrechen 1964; also: Deutschland, Deutschland unter Anderen 1967, Das Verhör von Habana (play) 1970, Freisprüche 1970, Der kurze Sommer der Anarchie (novel) 1972, Gespräche mit Marx und Engels 1973, Palaver 1974; Ed. Museum der Modernen Poesie 1960, Allerleirauh 1961, Andreas Gryphius Gedichte 1962, Edward Lears kompletter Nonsense (trans.) 1977, Raids and Reconstruction (essays, English edn), Der Untergang der Titanic (epic poem) 1978, Die Furie des Verschwindens 1980, Politische Brosamen 1982, Critical Essays 1982, Der Menschenfreund 1984, Ach Europa! 1987, Mittelmass und Wahn 1988, Requiem für eine romantische Frau 1988, Der Fliegende Robert 1989, Zukunftsmusik (poems) 1991, Die grosse Wanderung 1992, Aussichten auf den Bürgerkrieg 1993, Diderots Schatten 1994, The Palace (libretto) 1994, Civil War (English edn) 1994, Selected Poems (English edn) 1994, Kiosk (poems 1995 (English edn 1997), Voltaires Neffe (play) 1996, Der Zahlenteufel 1997, The Number Devil (English edn) 1998, Zickzack 1997, Wo warst du, Robert? (novel) 1998, Where were you, Robert? (English edn) 2000, Leichter als Luft (poems) 1999 (English edn 2001), Mediocrity and Delusion (English edn) 1992, Die Elixiere der Wissenschaft (essays and poems) 2002, Nomaden im regal (essays) 2003, Die Geschichte der Wolken (poems) 2003, Dialoge (prose) 2005, Hammerstein oder der Eigensinn 2008; as Andreas Thalmayr: Heraus mit der Sprache 2005. *Leisure interests:* early 17th century Flemish art, mathematics. *Address:* c/o Suhrkamp-Verlag, Lindenstr. 29, 60325 Frankfurt am Main, Germany (home).

ENZI, Michael (Mike) Bradley, MBA; American politician; *Senator from Wyoming;* b. 1 Feb. 1944, Bremerton, Wash.; s. of Elmer Enzi and Dorothy Bradley; m. Diana Buckley 1969; one s. two d.; ed George Washington Univ. and Denver Univ.; staff sergeant, Wyoming Air Nat. Guard 1967–73; Pres. NZ Shoes Inc., Gillette, Wyo. 1969–96, NZ Shoes of Sheridan Inc., Wyo. 1983–91; Acting Man. Dunbar Well Services, Gillette 1985–97; Chair. First Wyoming Bank, Gillette 1978–88; Dir, Black Hills Corpn 1992–96; Mayor of Gillette 1975–82; mem. Wyo. House of Reps, Cheyenne 1987–91, Wyo. State Senate 1991–96; Senator from Wyo. 1997–, mem. Foreign Relations Cttee, Co-founder and Chair. USAF Caucus; Pres. Wyoming Assen of Municipalities 1980–82; mem. Energy Council Exec. Cttee 1989–93, 1994–96, Educ. Comm. of the States 1989–93; Commr Western Interstate Comm. for Higher Educ. 1995–96; Republican; Distinguished Eagle Scout. *Publication:* Harvard Journal on Legislation 1998. *Leisure interests:* fishing, fly tying, canoe making, reading. *Address:* 379A Russell Senate Office Building, Washington, DC 20510 (office); 431 Circle Drive, Gillette, WY 82716, USA (home). *Telephone:* (202) 224-3424 (office). *Fax:* (202) 228-0359 (office). *E-mail:* senator@enzi.senate.gov (office). *Website:* enzi.senate.gov (office).

EÖRSI, Mátyás, PhD; Hungarian lawyer and politician; b. 24 Nov. 1954, Budapest; s. of Gyula Eörsi and Marianna Eörsi; m. Katalin Eörsi; three c.; ed Eötvös Loránd Univ., Budapest; Founding mem. Alliance of Free Democrats (SZDSZ) and mem. Nat. Cttee.; also Legal Rep. 1988, mem. Nat. Governing Cttee 1991, 2003–, Chair. SZDSZ Goodwill and Ethics Cttee 1993–98, Foreign Affairs Spokesman 1994–, Deputy Leader Parl. Group 2002–06, Leader Parl. Group 2007–; mem. Exec. Office Liberal Int. 1997–, Vice-Pres. 2002–; foreign trade lawyer 1981 and worked as legal adviser and at int. trading co.; est. Eörsi and Pnrs 1987; following regime change became regular mem. Council of Europe Parl. Ass.; Head of Hungarian del. with observer status Ass. of WEU and Head of del. to Parl. Ass. of Cen. European Initiative; mem. Nat. Ass. 1990–, Chair. Foreign Affairs Cttee 1994–97, Vice-Chair. Foreign Affairs Cttee 2002–06, Chair. European Affairs Cttee 2004–, Chair. Foreign Affairs and Hungarian Minorities Abroad Cttee 2006–; State Sec. for Policy, Ministry of Foreign Affairs 1997–98; mem. Hungarian Parl. del. to Council of Europe 1998–; Leader, Liberal faction, Council of Europe Parl. Ass. 2001–09; mem. OSCE. *Address:* Hungarian National Assembly, 1357 Budapest, Kossuth tér 1–3, Hungary (office). *Telephone:* (1) 441-5000 (office); (1) 441-5765 (office). *Fax:* (1) 441-5952 (office). *Website:* www.parlament.hu (office).

EÖTVÖS, Peter; German (b. Hungarian) composer, conductor and academic; b. 2 Jan. 1944, Székelyudvarhely, Hungary; s. of László Eötvös and Ilona Szücs; m. 1st Piroska Molnár 1968; one s.; m. 2nd Pi-Hsien Chen 1976; one d.; m. 3rd Maria Mezei 1995; ed Budapest Music Acad., Musikhochschule, Cologne; played in Stockhausen's Ensemble, Cologne 1968–76; composer and producer at WDR Electronic Music Studio, Cologne 1971–79; Conductor and Musical Dir Ensemble Intercontemporain, Paris 1979–91; Prin. Guest Conductor BBC Symphony Orchestra, London 1985–88, Gothenburg Symphony Orchestra 2003–07; First Guest Conductor, Budapest Festival Orchestra 1992–95, ORF Radio Symphony Orchestra, Vienna 2009–12; Chief Conductor Netherlands Radio Chamber Orchestra 1994–2005; Prof., Musikhochschule Karlsruhe, Germany 1992–98, 2002–08, Cologne 1998–2001; f. Peter Eötvös Contemporary Music Foundation 1991; mem. Akad. der Künste, Berlin, Szechenyi Acad. of Art, Budapest, Sächsische Akad. der Künste, Dresden, Royal Swedish Acad. of Music, Stockholm; Commdr, Ordre des Arts et des Lettres 2003; Bartók Award, Budapest 1997, Stephan Kaske Prize, Munich 2000, Kossuth Prize, Hungary 2002, Royal Philharmonic Soc. Music Award 2002, Midem Classical Award 'Living Composer', Cannes 2004, European Composing Prize 2004, Frankfurt Music Prize 2007, Prince Pierre de Monaco Prize in Musical Composition 2008, Golden Lion Award for Lifetime Achievement 2011, ECHO Klassik Award for Choral Recording of the Year – 20th/21st Century (for Ligeti Requiem) 2012, Gramophone Recording of the Year 2013, Echo Klassik Prize 2013. *Compositions include:* for orchestra: Chinese Opera, Shadows, Psychokosmos, Atlantis, Ima, Jet Stream, CAP-KO, Zeropoints, Two Monologues, Replica, Konzert für zwei Klaviere, Levitation; for ensemble: Intervalles-Intérieurs, Windsequenzen, Steine, Triangel, Octet, Sonata per sei; for string quartet: Korrespondenz, Encore, Da Capo; for vocal ensemble: Three comedy madrigals, Schiller: energische Schönheit; for percussion: Psalm 151, Speaking Drums; for violin: Seven (Prix de Composition Musicale, Fondation Prince Pierre de Monaco 2008), Doremi; for violoncello: Cello Concerto Grosso; for musical theatre/opera: Radames, Harakiri, Three Sisters, As I Crossed a Bridge of Dreams, Le Balcon, Angels in America, Lady Sarashina, Love and Other Demons, Die Tragödie des Teufels, Paradise Reloaded. *Leisure interests:* pipe, jazz, walking. *Address:* c/o Harrison Parrott, 5–6 Albion Court, Albion Place, London, W6 0QT, England (office). *Telephone:* (20) 7229-9166 (office). *Fax:* (20) 7221-5042 (office). *E-mail:* info@harrisonparrott.co.uk (office); eotvos@eotvospeter.com (home). *Website:* www.harrisonparrott.com (office); www.eotvospeter.com (home).

EPHREM, Gen. Sebhat; Eritrean politician and army officer; *Minister of Defence;* b. 5 Sept. 1950, Asmara; m. Ruth Halle; three c.; ed Haile Selassie Univ., Ethiopia, Open Univ., UK; served in Eritrean Armed Forces, rank of Gen.; currently Minister of Defence; Grand Officiale, Italy 1997. *Leisure interests:* reading, football. *Address:* Ministry of Defence, POB 629, Asmara (office); Marsa Teklay St., 17, Asmara, Eritrea (home). *Telephone:* (1) 160552 (office); (1) 122572 (home). *Fax:* (1) 124920 (office); (1) 1244548 (home). *E-mail:* asmeromht@yahoo .com (office).

EPSTEIN, Emanuel, BS, MS, PhD; American professor of plant nutrition and plant physiologist; *Edward A. Dickson Professor Emeritus, University of California, Davis;* b. 5 Nov. 1916, Duisburg, Germany; s. of Harry Epstein and Bertha Epstein (née Löwe); brother of Gabriel Epstein (q.v.); m. Hazel M. Leask 1943; two c. (one deceased); ed Univ. of California, Davis, Univ. of California, Berkeley; served in US Army 1943–46; Plant Physiologist, US Dept of Agric., Beltsville, Md 1950–58; Lecturer and Assoc. Plant Physiologist, Univ. of California, Davis 1958–65, Prof. of Plant Nutrition and Plant Physiologist 1965–87, Research Prof. 1987–, Prof. of Botany 1974–87, Research Prof. 1987–, Edward A. Dickson Emer. Prof. 2009; Faculty Research Lecturer 1980; consultant to govt agencies, private orgs and publrs at various times; mem. NAS; Fellow, AAAS, Pres. Pacific Div. 1990–91; Guggenheim Fellow 1958, Fulbright Sr Research Scholar 1965–66, 1974–75; Gold Medal, Pisa Univ., Italy 1962, Charles Reid Barnes Life Membership Award, American Soc. of Plant Physiologists 1986, Univ. of California, Davis Coll. of Agricultural and Environmental Sciences Award of Distinction 1999, Cal Aggie Alumni Asscn Citation for Excellence 1999, Award of Honor, American Soc. of Agronomy, Calif. Chapter 2002. *Publications:* Mineral Nutrition of Plants: Principles and Perspectives 1972 (second edn, with A. J. Bloom 2005), The Biosaline Concept: An Approach to the Utilization of Underexploited Resources (co-ed.) 1979, Saline Agriculture: Salt-Tolerant Plants for Developing Countries (co-ed.) 1990; research papers, reviews and articles. *Leisure interests:* hiking, photography and history. *Address:* Department of Land, Air and Water Resources, Soils and Biogeochemistry, University of California, Davis, CA 95616-3630, USA (office). *Telephone:* (530) 752-0197 (office). *Fax:* (530) 752-1552 (office). *E-mail:* eqepstein@ucdavis.edu (office). *Website:* lawr.ucdavis.edu (office).

EPSTEIN, Gabriel, AADip (Hons), FRIBA, SADG; British architect, planning consultant and teacher; *Professor Emeritus, University of Stuttgart;* b. 25 Oct. 1918, Duisburg, Germany; s. of Harry Epstein and Bertha Epstein (née Löwe); brother of Emanuel Epstein (q.v.); m. Josette A. Glonneau 1955; two s. one d.; ed schools in Germany, Belgium and Israel and Architectural Assen School of Architecture, London; officer in Royal Engineers in World War II; Partner, Shepheard, Epstein & Hunter 1955–86; Prof. of Architecture and Dir Inst. of Public Bldgs and Design, Univ. of Stuttgart 1978–88, Prof., Centre for Infrastructure Planning, Univ. of Stuttgart 1984–2006, Prof. Emer. 2006–; consultant and mem. competition juries London, Stuttgart, Paris, Brussels, Leipzig, Berlin, Munich, etc. 1992–96; Pres. Architectural Assen, London 1963–64, Franco-British Union of Architects 1976–77; mem. Berlin Acad. of Arts and Letters, Soc. Française des Architectes; Hon. DLit (Lancaster); four Civic Trust Awards for Univ. and Housing Work 1966–82, two Ministry Medals for Good Design in Housing 1968, 1976, Int. Prize for Architecture for London Housing 1983. *Publications:* Planning Forms for Twentieth Century Cities 1976, Well-Being In Cities: The Low Energy City 1979, Energy Use and City Form 1981, Living-Places 2004, Sustainable Urban Growth 2013. *Leisure interest:* sketching/painting. *Address:* 3 rue André Mazet, 75006 Paris, France. *Telephone:* 1-43-25-89-59. *Fax:* 1-43-26-57-42.

EPSTEIN, Matthew A., BA; American opera administrator and academic; b. 23 Dec. 1947, New York, NY; ed Univ. of Pennsylvania; Vice-Pres. Columbia Artists Man. 1973–99, now Dir Columbia Artists Vocal; Artistic Dir Brooklyn Acad. of Music 1987–90; consultant, Santa Fe Opera 1980–; Artistic Dir Welsh Nat. Opera 1991–94; mem. Faculty, Voice and Vocal Piano, Music Acad. of the West, Santa Barbara, Calif. 1997–; Artistic Dir Lyric Opera of Chicago 1999–2005; Vice-Pres., Dir of Vocal Divisions, Columbia Artists Management Inc. 2005–10; Artistic Dir Kennedy Center Gala honouring George London 1981; Dir Rossini 200th Birthday Celebration Gala, Lincoln Center 1990; Artistic Consultant 'Celebration of the American Musical', Lincoln Center 1997. *Address:* Music Academy of the West, 1070 Fairway Road, Santa Barbara, CA 93108-2899, USA. *Telephone:* (805) 969-4726. *Fax:* (805) 969-0686. *Website:* www.musicacademy.org.

EPSTEIN, Sir (Michael) Anthony, Kt, CBE, MA, MD, DSc, PhD, FRCPath, FRS; British virologist and academic; *Honorary Fellow, Wolfson College, Oxford;* b. 18 May 1921, London, England; ed St Paul's School, London, Trinity Coll., Cambridge, Middlesex Hosp. Medical School, London; House Surgeon, Middlesex Hosp. and Addenbrooke's Hosp., Cambridge 1944; commissioned RAMC 1945–47; Asst Pathologist, Bland Sutton Inst., Middlesex Hosp. Medical School 1948–65; Berkeley Travelling Fellow and French Govt Exchange Scholar, Inst. Pasteur, Paris 1952–53, Visiting Investigator, Rockefeller Inst., New York 1956; Reader in Experimental Pathology, Middlesex Hosp. Medical School and Hon. Consultant in Experimental Virology, Middlesex Hosp. 1965–68; Prof. of Pathology, Univ. of Bristol 1968–85, Head of Dept and Hon. Consultant Pathologist, Avon Area Health Authority (Teaching) 1968–82, Prof. Emer. 1985–; Prof., Nuffield Dept of Clinical Medicine, Univ. of Oxford 1985–2012; Extraordinary Fellow, Wolfson Coll., Oxford 1986–2001, Hon. Fellow 2001–; mem. MRC Cell Bd 1979–84, Chair. 1982–84; Chair. CRC/MRC Jt Cttee for Inst. of Cancer Research 1982–87; mem. MRC 1982–86, Chair. MRC Tropical Medicine Research Bd 1985–88, Medical and Scientific Advisory Panel, Leukaemia Research Fund 1982–85, Council of Royal Soc. 1983–85, 1986–91; mem. UK Co-ordinating Cttee on Cancer Research 1983–87, Scientific Advisory Cttee, The Lister Inst. of Preventive Medicine 1984–86; Scientific Adviser, Charing Cross Medical Research Centre 1984–87; Foreign Sec. and Vice-Pres. Royal Soc. 1986–91, MRC Assessor 1987–91; mem. Expert Working Party on Bovine Spongiform Encephalopathy, Dept of Health 1988, mem. Exec. Bd Int. Council of Scientific Unions 1990–93, Chair. Cttee for Science in Cen. and Eastern Europe 1992–95; mem. Exec. Council European Science Foundation 1990–93; Special Rep. of Dir-Gen., UNESCO, for Science in Russia, Moscow 1992; mem. Programme Advisory Group, World Bank China Key Studies Project 1992–96; Hon. Prof., Zhongshan Medical Univ., People's Repub. of China 1981, Chinese Acad. of Preventive Medicine 1988; Hon. Fellow Queensland Inst. of Medical Research 1983, Royal Coll. of Pathologists of Australasia 1995, Cancer Research UK 2004, Univ. of Bristol 2006; Hon. mem. Belgian Soc. for Study of Cancer 1979, Pathological Soc. 1987; Hon. FRSE 1991; Hon. FRCP 1986; Hon. MD (Edinburgh) 1986, (Charles Univ., Prague) 1998; Hon. DSc (Birmingham) 1996; Leeuwenhoek Prize Lecturer, Royal Soc. 1983; Markham Skerritt Prize (Univ. of Bristol) 1977, Paul Ehrlich and Ludwig Darmstaedster Prize and Medal (Frankfurt) 1973, Bristol-Myers Award (New York) 1982, Prix Griffuel (Paris) 1986, Gairdner Foundation Int. Award (Toronto) 1988, S. Weiner Distinguished Visitor Award (Univ. of Manitoba) 1988, Royal Medal, The Royal Soc. 1991. *Scientific achievements include:* discovered the Epstein-Barr virus (EBV) (first human cancer virus) 1964. *Publications includes:* more than 240 scientific papers in int. journals; numerous studies on EBV and other viruses; author and ed. of five scientific books; Jt Founder-Ed., Int. Review of Experimental Pathology 1962–86, Vols 1–28, Academic Press Inc., New York and London. *Address:* Wolfson College, University of Oxford, Linton Road, Oxford, OX2 6UD, England (office). *Telephone:* (1865) 250885 (office). *E-mail:* anthony.epstein@wolfson.ox.ac.uk (office).

ERAKAT, Saeb, BA, MA, PhD; Palestinian politician and journalist; b. 1955, East Jerusalem; m. two s. two d.; ed San Francisco State Univ., USA and Bradford Univ., UK; fmr journalist, Al Quds daily; Lecturer in Political Science, An-Najah Univ. 1983, fmr Sec.-Gen. Arab Studies Soc.; mem. negotiating team Oslo Peace Process 1995; Head of Palestinian Negotiation Steering and Monitoring Cttee 1996–2011, Chief Palestinian Peace Negotiator 1995–2003 (resgnd), 2003–11; elected mem. Palestinian Legis. Council, Jericho 1996; Minister of Negotiation Affairs, Palestinian Nat. Authority (PNA) 2004–06; Hon. PhD (Peru) 2004. *Publications include:* eight books and numerous articles on foreign policy. *Address:* c/o Fatah, Ramallah, Palestinian Autonomous Areas (office). *E-mail:* fateh@fateh .org. *Website:* www.fateh.net.

ERBSEN, Claude Ernest, BA; American journalist; *Senior Consultant, Innovation International Media Consultancy Group;* b. 10 March 1938, Trieste, Italy; s. of Henry M. Erbsen and Laura Erbsen; m. 1st Jill J. Prosky 1959; m. 2nd Hedy M. Cohn 1970; two s. one d.; ed Amherst Coll. Mass.; reporter and printer, Amherst Journal Record 1955–57; staff reporter, El Tiempo, Bogotá 1960; with Associated Press (AP) in New York and Miami 1960–65; reporter to Chief of Bureau, AP Brazil 1965–69; Exec. Rep. for Latin America, AP 1969–70; Business Man. and Admin. Dir AP-Dow Jones Econ. Report, London 1970–75; Deputy Dir AP World Services, New York 1975–80, Vice-Pres., Dir 1987–2003; Vice-Pres., Dir AP-Dow Jones News Services 1980–87; fmr Dir, Innovation Int. Media Consultancy Group, currently Sr Consultant; mem. Bd of Dirs World Press Inst. St Paul; mem. Int. Press Inst., Council on Foreign Relations; San Giusto d'Oro Award, City of Trieste 1995. *Publications:* Her Job: Planning Meals for 200! 1963. *Leisure interests:* reading, travel, folk art. *Address:* Innnovation, 27 Stratton Road, Scarsdale, NY 10583-7556, USA (office). *Telephone:* (914) 725-1809 (office). *E-mail:* erbsen@ innovation-mediaconsulting.com (office); headquarters@innovation -mediaconsulting.com (office). *Website:* www.innovation-mediaconsulting.com (office).

ERÇEL, Gazi; Turkish fmr central banker and consultant; *President, Erçel Global Advisory;* b. 20 Feb. 1945, Gelibolu; m. Zeynel Erçel; one d.; ed Ankara Univ., Vanderbilt Univ., Tenn.; bank examiner, Ministry of Finance 1967–77; Deputy Dir-Gen. of Treasury 1977–82; Asst to Exec. Dir IMF, Washington DC 1982–86; Dir-Gen. of Treasury and Foreign Trade 1987–89; Gov. Cen. Bank of Turkey 1996–2001; Founder and Pres. Erçel Global Advisory 2002–; mem. Policy and Econs Council, Gerson Lehrman Group; Cen. Banker of the Year Award, Global Finance, Prague 2000. *Address:* Erçel Global Advisory, Abdi Ipekçi Caddesi No. 32/7, Nisantasi 80200, Istanbul, Turkey (office). *Telephone:* (212) 2919565 (office). *Fax:* (212) 2919566 (office). *E-mail:* gazi.ercel@erceladvisory.com (office). *Website:* www.erceladvisory.com (office).

ERDEI, Tamás; Hungarian banker; b. 1954; one c.; fmr Gen. Man. Br. Office Nat. Savings Bank; Chief Officer in Banking Supervision, Ministry of Finance 1981–83; Chief Accountant Hungarian Foreign Trade Bank (MKB) 1983–85, Exec. Dir 1985–90, Deputy Chief Exec. 1990–94, CEO 1994–97, Chair. and CEO 1997–2012; Pres. Hungarian Banking Asscn 1997. *Address:* c/o Hungarian Foreign Trade Bank MKB, Váci u. 38, Budapest V, Hungary (office).

ERDENEBAT, Badarchiin, DEcon; Mongolian politician; b. 1959, Hövsgöl prov.; m. Sergelen; ed Novosibirsk Higher School of Geodesy and Cartography, Mongolian State Univ., Inst. of Econ. and Political Studies, Russian Acad. of Sciences; f. Erel Group (interests in banking, investment, mining and construction) 1989, Dir-Gen. –2000; f. Mongolian Democratic New Socialist Party (now Motherland Party) 1998, currently Chair.; mem. Mongolian Great Khural (Parl.) 2000–; Minister of Defence 2004–06, of Fuel and Power 2006–07. *Address:* Motherland Party, Erel Co, Bayanzürkh District, Ulan Bator, Mongolia (office).

ERDENECHULUUN, Luvsangiin, MA; Mongolian diplomatist and politician; *Director, Human Security Policy Studies Centre;* b. 10 Oct. 1948, Ulan Bator; s. of Sonomyn Luvsan and Lhamsurengiin Baimanhand; m. Sukh-Ochiryn Solongo 1969; two s. one d.; ed State Inst. of Int. Relations, Moscow and Diplomatic Acad. Moscow; officer, Dept of Int. Relations, Ministry of Foreign Affairs 1972–80; First Sec., Perm. Mission to UN, New York 1980–84; Head of Press and Information Dept Ministry of Foreign Affairs 1985–86, Head of Dept of Int. Orgs 1988–90; Deputy Perm. Rep. to UN, New York 1990, Perm. Rep. 1992–96; Adviser to Pres. of Mongolia 1996–97; Minister of Foreign Affairs 2000–04; Dir Human Security Policy Studies Centre 2003–; mem. Exec. Bd of UNESCO 2007–; mem. Mongolian People's Party; Distinguished Service Medal, Order of Polar Star, Medal of Service Merit, Order of Friendship Among Nations (Russian Fed.), Order of Red Banner of Service Excellence. *Address:* Chingeltei District, 1st khoroo, M-100, 442, Ulan Bator, Mongolia (home). *Telephone:* 70110216 (office); 379151 (home). *Fax:* 70110215 (office). *E-mail:* hspsc@mongol.net (office); echuluun.unesco@yahoo .com (home). *Website:* www.hspsc.mn (office).

ERDŐ, HE Cardinal Péter, DCL, D'Theol; Hungarian ecclesiastic; *Archbishop of Esztergom-Budapest;* b. 25 June 1952, Budapest; ed Seminary of Esztergom, Theological Acad. of Budapest, Pontifical Lateran Univ., Rome; ordained priest by Bishop László Lékai 1975; Parish Priest, Parish of Dorog; Prof. of Theology and Canon Law, Seminary of Esztergom 1980–88; Prof., Faculty of Canon Law, Pontifical Gregorian Univ., Rome 1986–2002; Invited Prof., Faculty of Theology, Peter Pazmany Catholic Univ., Budapest 1988–2003, Rector 1998–2002; Auxiliary Bishop of Szekesfekhervar 1999; Titular Bishop of Puppi 1999; consecrated by Pope John Paul II, Vatican City 2000; Archbishop of Esztergom-Budapest 2002–; cr. Cardinal (Cardinal-Priest of Santa Balbina) 2003; participated in Papal Conclave 2005, 2013; Pres. Hungarian Catholic Bishops' Conf. 2005–, Consilium Conferentiarum Episcopaliae Europae 2006–; mem. Hungarian Acad. of Sciences 2007; Galileo Galilei Prize, Italian Rotary Club 1999. *Publications:* 30 books, 400 articles.

ERDOES, Mary Callahan, BS, MBA; American business executive; *CEO, Asset Management, JPMorgan Chase & Company;* b. 13 Aug. 1967, Winnetka, Ill.; d. of Patrick Joseph Callahan Jr and Patricia Ann Callahan (née Henebry); m. Philip Erdoes; three d.; ed Georgetown Univ. and Harvard Business School; worked at Bankers Trust in corp. finance, merchant banking and high yield debt underwriting; Vice-Pres. with Meredith, Martin & Kaye –1996; Head of Fixed Income Group, J.P. Morgan Investment Management 1996–99, Head of Investment Man. and Alternative Solutions for the Pvt. Bank 1999, assumed responsibility for global suite of investment solutions and investment strategy for pvt. banking clients world-wide following J.P. Morgan/Chase merger 2000, CEO J.P. Morgan's Pvt. Bank 2005–08, Chair. and CEO Global Wealth Man., J.P. Morgan (comprises Pvt. Bank, Pvt. Wealth Man., Bear Stearns Pvt. Client Services) 2008–, CEO, Asset Man., JPMorgan Chase & Co. 2009–, also mem. JPMorgan Chase & Co.'s Exec. Cttee and Operating Cttee; mem. Bd of Dirs US Fund for UNICEF 2005–; ranked by Forbes magazine amongst The World's 100 Most Powerful Women (100th) 2005, 2009, (84th) 2010, (74th) 2011, (95th) 2012, (86th) 2013, featured by US Banker magazine amongst the 25 Most Powerful Women in Banking 2009, ranked by Fortune magazine amongst the 50 Most Powerful Women in Business in the US (30th) 2010, (24th) 2011–12, included in the 50 Most Influential list of Bloomberg Markets Magazine 2012. *Leisure interests:* running, Dora the Explorer games, Ring Around the Rosie or whatever her daughters request. *Address:* JPMorgan Chase & Co., 270 Park Avenue, New York, NY 10017 (office); 41 River Terrace, New York, NY 10282-1113, USA. *Telephone:* (212) 270-6000 (office). *Fax:* (212) 270-1648 (office). *Website:* www.jpmorgan.com (office).

ERDOGAN, Recep Tayyip, BA; Turkish politician; *Prime Minister;* b. 1954, Rize; m.; four c.; ed Marmara Univ., Istanbul; professional footballer 1969–80; elected Chair. Nat. Salvation Party Youth Org. early 1970s; Chair. Istanbul Br. Welfare Party 1985; Mayor of Metropolitan Istanbul 1994–98, tenure of office ended by court decree 1998, convicted of having read a provocative poem in public, imprisoned for four months and banned for life from holding public office; mem. Virtue Party 1998–2001; Founder and Chair. AK Partisi – AKP (Justice and Development Party), ruling party in Turkey following 2002 elections, constitutional ban preventing him from holding public office overturned Jan. 2003; Prime Minister of Turkey March 2003–; Founder Democratization and Action Movt; European of the Year 2004, Agricola Medal, UN Food and Agric. Org. 2007, ranked by Forbes magazine amongst The World's Most Powerful People (48th) 2011. *Address:* Office of the Prime Minister, Başbakanlik, Bakanliklar, Ankara (office); AK Partisi, Genel Merkezi Ceyhun Atif Kansu Cad., No. 202 Balgat, Ankara, Turkey (office). *Telephone:* (312) 4189056 (office). *Fax:* (312) 4180476 (office). *E-mail:* info@basbakanlik.gov.tr (office). *Website:* www.basbakanlik.gov.tr (office); www.akparti.org.tr (office).

ERDŐS, André; Hungarian diplomatist; *Senior Adviser, International Centre for Democratic Transition, Budapest;* b. 18 May 1941, Algiers, Algeria; s. of Gusztáv Erdős and Márta Czeichner; m. Katalin Pintér 1965; one d.; ed Moscow State Inst. for Int. Relations, Budapest School of Political Sciences; joined Ministry of Foreign Affairs 1965, attaché, Morocco 1968–72, staff mem., CSCE Dept Ministry of Foreign Affairs 1972–78, assigned to Perm. Mission to UN, New York 1978–83, del. to UN Gen. Ass. 1984, 1985, 1989, Adviser to Minister of Foreign Affairs of

Hungary 1984–86, Head of Hungary's del. to Vienna CSCE follow-up meeting 1986–89, Amb. and Perm. Rep. to UN, New York 1990–94, 1997–2002, Pres. UN Disarmament and Int. Security Comm. 2001–02, Hungarian Rep., UN Security Council 1992–93, Deputy State Sec. for Multilateral Affairs, Ministry of Foreign Affairs 1994–97, Amb. to France 2002–06, currently Sr Adviser Int. Centre for Democratic Transition, Budapest; Prof., Corvinus Univ., Budapest; Chair. Supervisory Bd, Hungarian Atlantic Council; Vice-Pres. Hungarian UN Asscn; mem. Prime Minister's Council on Foreign and Security Policy 2007–09; Hon. Prof., Budapest Inst. for Grad. Int. and Diplomatic Studies 1999; Commdr's Cross, Order of Merit (Hungary), Order of Duke Branimir with Ribbons (Croatia), Commdr, Légion d'honneur (France), Grand Croix, Ordre nat. du Mérite (France). *Television:* Face to Face with History (Duna TV series) 2008–10. *Publications:* Co-operation in the United Nations between Socialist and Developing Countries 1981, Soviet-German Relations 1939–41 1984, The Circumstances of the Birth of the 1941 Soviet-German Non-Aggression Pact 1987, Geography vs. Political Reality at the United Nations 2001, Sorsfordító Esztendők (Crucial Years) 2004, Additions to the history of Hungarian foreign policy during the system change 2009; numerous articles on int. affairs. *Leisure interests:* philately, numismatics, collecting postcards, making video movies. *Address:* International Centre for Democratic Transition, Budapest 1022, Arvacska u. 12, Hungary (office). *Telephone:* (1) 438-0820 (office). *Fax:* (1) 438-0821 (office). *E-mail:* a.erdos@icdt.hu (office). *Website:* www.icdt.hu (office).

ERDRICH, (Karen) Louise, MA; American writer and poet; b. 7 June 1954, Little Falls, MN; d. of Ralph Louis Erdrich and Rita Joanne (Gourneau) Erdrich; m. Michael Anthony Dorris 1981 (died 1997); six c. (one s. deceased); ed Dartmouth Coll., Johns Hopkins Univ.; Visiting Poetry Teacher, ND State Arts Council 1977–78; Teacher of Writing, Johns Hopkins Univ., Baltimore 1978–79; Communications Dir, Ed., Circle-Boston Indian Council 1979–80; Textbook Writer Charles Merrill Co. 1980; mem. PEN (mem. Exec. Bd 1985–90); Guggenheim Fellow 1985–86; Nelson Algren Award 1982, Pushcart Prize 1983, Nat. Magazine Fiction Award 1983, 1987, First Prize O. Henry Awards 1987. *Publications include:* fiction: Love Medicine (Nat. Book Critics' Circle Award for best work of fiction) 1984, The Beet Queen 1986, Tracks 1988, The Crown of Columbus (with Michael Anthony Dorris) 1991, The Bingo Palace 1994, The Bluejay's Dance 1995, Tales of Burning Love 1996, The Antelope Wife 1998, The Birchbark House 1999, The Last Report on the Miracles at Little No Horse 2001, The Master Butcher's Singing Club 2003, Four Souls 2004, The Painted Drum 2005, The Plague of Doves 2008, The Red Convertible: Selected and New Stories 1978–2008 2009, Shadow Tag 2010, The Round House 2012; poetry: Jacklight 1984, Baptism of Desire 1989; non-fiction: Imagination (textbook) 1980; contrib. short stories, children's stories, essays and poems to anthologies and journals, including American Indian Quarterly, Atlantic, Frontiers, Kenyon Review, Ms, New England Review, New York Times Book Review, New Yorker, North American Review, Redbook. *Address:* The Wylie Agency, 250 West 57th Street, Suite 2114, New York, NY 10107, USA (office). *Telephone:* (212) 246-0069 (office). *Fax:* (212) 586-8953 (office). *E-mail:* mail@wylieagency.com (office). *Website:* www.wylieagency.com (office); www.harpercollins.com/authors/2905/Louise_Erdrich/index.aspx (office).

EREDIAUWA, Omo N'Oba N'Edo Uku-Akpolokpolo, Oba of Benin, BA; Nigerian traditional monarch; b. 24 June 1923; ed Edo Coll., Benin, Govt Coll., Ibadan, Yaba Coll., Lagos, Cambridge Univ., England; career in Civil Service, retd 1973 as Perm. Sec. in Fed. Ministry of Health; Civil Commr for Bendel State 1975–77; Oba of Benin Kingdom 1979–; mem. Council of State 1979–. *Address:* The Palace, Box 1, Benin City, Bendel State, Nigeria. *Telephone:* (52) 240001.

EREN, Halit, MA, PhD; Turkish institute director and academic; *Director-General, Research Centre for Islamic History, Art and Culture (IRCICA);* b. 1953, Gümülcine (Komotini); m.; two s. one d.; ed Inst. of Social Sciences and Inst. of Turkic Studies, Marmara Univ., Istanbul; apptd Sr Researcher and Head of Library and Documentation Dept, Research Centre for Islamic History, Art and Culture (IRCICA) 1981, Deputy Dir-Gen. 1984–2005, Co-ordinator/mem. Organizing Cttee of IRCICA's congresses and symposiums relating to Caucasia, Cen. Asia and the Balkans, participated in Islamic Summit Confs, Islamic Confs of Ministers of Foreign Affairs, Culture, and Information, and other confs and cttees of OIC, Dir-Gen. IRCICA 2005–; Founder and Admin. Turkish-Islamic Asscn of England 1979–81; mem. Exec. Bd Cen. Office of the Solidarity Asscn of Western Thrace Turks, Istanbul 1984–94, Pres. 1992–94; Sec.-Gen. Foundation for Research on Islamic History, Art and Culture, Istanbul 1990–; Founding mem. Turkish Soc. for the History of Science 1989–, Rumeli (Eastern Europe) Foundation for Educ., Istanbul 1993–; mem. Preparatory Cttee Seventh Devt Plan of Turkey 1993; Second Pres. Cultural and Solidarity Asscn of East European Turks 1997–2001; Founding mem. Western Thrace Foundation for Educ., Culture and Health, Istanbul 1996, Vice-Pres. 1996–98, 2002–04; Founding mem. and Chair. (BALMED Asscn) Centre for Balkan Civilization 2007–; mem. Exec. Bd and Second Chair. Cultural and Solidarity Foundation of East European Turks 2001–; Adviser on Balkan Affairs to Minister of State of Repub. of Turkey 1997; Founder and Ed.-in-Chief Bati Trakya'nin sesi (The Voice of Western Thrace) journal 1987–94, Gen. Co-ordinator 1994–97; Ed. Rumeli kültürü journal 2002–; Hon. Prof., UFA Bashkir State Univ., Bashkortostan 2010; Sultan Qaboos Order for Culture, Science and Art of the First Degree (Oman) 2012; Dr hc (Sh. Marjany History Inst. of Tatarstan Acad. of Sciences) 2006, (Tatarstan Repub. Kazan Federal Univ.) 2010; Russian Fed. State Medal 2006. *Publications include:* World Bibliography of Translations of the Meanings of the Holy Quran: 1515–1980 (compiler, jtly with Ismet Binark) 1986, Bati Trakya Türkleri (Western Thrace Turks) 1997; numerous articles in professional journals. *Address:* Research Centre for Islamic History, Art and Culture (IRCICA), PO Box 24, Beşiktaş, 80692 İstanbul, Turkey (office). *Telephone:* (212) 2591742 (office). *Fax:* (212) 2584365 (office). *E-mail:* ircica@ircica.org (office). *Website:* www.ircica.org (office).

ERESMAN, Randall K. (Randy), BSc; Canadian petroleum engineer and energy industry executive; *President and CEO, EnCana Corporation;* b. Medicine Hat, Alberta; m. Shelly Eresman; two c.; ed Northern Alberta Inst. of Tech., Edmonton, Univ. of Wyoming; joined Alberta Energy Co. (AEC) 1980, Vice-Pres. AEC Oil and Gas 1994–99, Pres. AEC Oil and Gas Partnership 1999–2002, Exec. Vice-Pres. EnCana Corpn (after merger of AEC and PanCanadian Energy Corpn), responsible for Onshore N America Div. Jan.–Dec. 2002, COO 2002–06, Pres. and CEO

2006–; mem. Asscn of Professional Engineers, Geologists and Geophysicists of Alberta, Young Pres' Org., Canadian Council of Chief Execs; mem. Nat. Advisory Bd of Univ. of Wyoming's Coll. of Eng, Nat. Petroleum Council (an Oil and Natural Gas Advisory Cttee to US Sec. of Energy). *Address:* EnCana Corpn, 1800 855 2nd Street SW, PO Box 2850, Calgary, Alberta, T2P 2S5, Canada (office). *Telephone:* (403) 645-2000 (office). *Fax:* (403) 645-3400 (office). *E-mail:* info@encana.com (office). *Website:* www.encana.com (office).

ERGEN, Charles (Charlie) W., BS, MBA; American communications industry executive; *Chairman and CEO, EchoStar Communications Corporation;* b. 1 March 1953, Oak Ridge, Tenn.; m.; five c.; ed Univ. of Tenn., Babcock Grad. School, Wake Forest Univ.; f. EchoStar Communications Corpn 1980, now Chair. and CEO, f. Dish Network (subsidiary of EchoStar Communications Corpn) 1996, Chair. and CEO 1998–; Home Satellite TV Asscn Star Award 1988, Rocky Mountain News Business Person of the Year 1996, 2001. *Address:* EchoStar Communications Corporation, 100 Inverness Terrace, Englewood, CO 80112, USA (office). *Telephone:* (303) 723-1000 (office). *Fax:* (303) 723-1399 (office). *Website:* www.echostar.com (office); www.dishnetwork.com (office).

ERGIN, Mehmet, PhD; Turkish professor of physical chemistry; *Fellow and Vice-President, Islamic World Academy of Sciences;* b. 25 May 1936, Yozgat; m.; two c.; ed Ankara Gazi High School, Ankara Univ., Univ. of Glasgow, UK; researcher, Nuclear Chem. Lab., Atomic Energy Comm., Acting Dir 1963–66, fmr Pres.; research and training at IAEA Labs, Vienna; researcher, Inst. for Physics and Chem., Asscn for Meat Research, FRG, then Dept of Chem., Univ. of Glasgow; Lecturer, Asst Prof., then Prof. of Physical Chem., Dept of Chem., Hacettepe Univ.; Exec. Sec. Eng Dept, Turkish Scientific and Research Council (TUBITAK) 1974, Deputy Sec. Gen. for Planning and Coordination 1985–87, Pres. 1987–90; Fellow, Islamic World Acad. of Sciences, Vice-Pres. 1986–99, 2009–, Sec. Gen. 1999–2009; mem. Bd of Trustees and Lecturer, Fatih Univ., Istanbul. *Address:* Islamic World Academy of Sciences, PO Box 830036, Amman, Jordan (office). *Telephone:* 5522104 (office). *Fax:* 5511803 (office). *E-mail:* secretariat@ias-worldwide.org (office). *Website:* www.ias-worldwide.org (office).

ERGMA, Ene, CandSci, DrSci; Estonian astrophysicist, academic and politician; *President (Speaker), Riigikogu (State Assembly);* b. 29 Feb. 1944, Rakvere; ed Viljandi Carl Robert Jakobson Secondary School No. 1, Secondary School, Lomonosov Moscow State Univ., Russia, Tartu Univ., Inst. of Space Research, Moscow; jr research assoc., Inst. of Physics and Astronomy, Estonian Acad. of Sciences 1972–74; jr research assoc., Exec. Sec., Sr and Leading Research Assoc., Astronomical Council, USSR Acad. of Science 1974–88; Prof. of Theoretical Physics and Astrophysics, Tartu Univ. 1988–92, Prof. of Astrophysics 1992–, Head of Theoretical Physics Inst. 1993–96, Head of Physics Dept 1993–98; fmr Vice-Chair. Educ. and Culture Cttee, Tartu City Council; Pres. (Speaker), Parl. of Estonia (Riigikogu) 2003–06, 2007–, Vice-Pres. (Deputy Speaker) 2006–07; Gauss Prof., Göttingen Acad. of Sciences 1994; Guest Prof., Univ. of Amsterdam 1997; Guest Researcher, Univ. of Helsinki 2000; Descartes Grand Jury 2002–, Pres. 2003–05; mem. European Astronomical Union, Int. Astrophysical Union, Estonian Astronomical Cttee, Tartu Observatory Science Council, Estonian Physical Soc. Cttee, Estonian Acad. of Sciences 1997 (Vice-Pres. 1999–), Euroscience; Assoc. mem. Royal Astronomical Soc. 2001; Foreign mem. Royal Swedish Acad. of Eng Sciences; Order of the White Star, Fourth Class (Estonia) 2001, Grand Cross, Order of Infante Dom Henrique (Portugal) 2003, Grand Cross, Order of Merit (Italy) 2004, Commdr's Cross, Order of Repub. of Poland 2005, Royal Order of the North Star, First Class (Sweden) 2007, Order of Merit for Services Grand Gold Decoration of Austria 2007, Badge of Honour 'Jüriöö Star' 2007, Order of the Nat. Coat of Arms, Second Class 2008, Grand Cross, Order of Orange-Nassau (Netherlands) 2008, Grand Cross, Order of Crown (Belgium) 2008; Medal of the Baltic Ass., Estonian Repub. Science Award in Exact Sciences 2002, Grand Medal of Estonian Acad. of Sciences 2004. *Publications include:* more than 100 scientific articles in professional journals and articles in Estonian press and encyclopaedias. *Leisure interest:* tennis. *Address:* Office of the Speaker, Riigikogu (State Assembly), Lossi plats 1A, 15165 Tallinn, Estonia (office). *Telephone:* 631-6301 (office). *E-mail:* ene.ergma@riigikogu.ee (office). *Website:* www.riigikogu.ee (office).

ERIAN, Mohamed El-, MA, DPhil; French/Egyptian/American business executive and investment analyst; *Chairman, US President's Global Development Council;* b. 19 Aug. 1958, New York, NY, USA; ed schools in Cairo, New York, Paris and UK, Univs of Cambridge and Oxford, UK; lived in Egypt as a young child, family moved back to New York 1968, accompanied his diplomat father on postings abroad, settled in USA 1983; worked at IMF, Washington, DC 1983–98; Man. Dir, Citigroup, London, UK 1998–99; joined Pacific Investment Management Co. LLC (PIMCO) 1999, Sr mem. PIMCO's portfolio man. and investment strategy group, left co. 2005, re-joined PIMCO 2007, CEO and Co-Chief Information Officer –2014; apptd by Pres. Barack Obama as Chair. US Pres.'s Global Devt Council 2012–; Pres. and CEO Harvard Management Co. 2005–07; fmr mem. of Faculty, Harvard Business School; served on several bds and cttees, including US Treasury Borrowing Advisory Cttee, Int. Center for Research on Women, IMF's Cttee of Eminent Persons, Peterson Inst. for Int. Econs; mem. Bd Carnegie Endowment for Peace, Nat. Bureau of Econ. Research, Cambridge in America; writes a monthly column in Foreign Policy; regular op-ed contrib. to Project Syndicate; Dr hc (American Univ. in Cairo); named to Foreign Policy's list of Top 100 Global Thinkers 2009, 2010, 2011, inducted into Fixed Income Analysts Soc. Hall of Fame 2011, included in the top four of Investment Advisor's annual IA 25 list 2012, Creative Leadership Award, Louise Blouin Foundation 2012, ranked by Arabian Business amongst the Power 500: The World's Most Influential Arabs (61st) 2012, (28th) 2013. *Publications include:* When Markets Collide (New York Times and Wall Street Journal bestseller, Financial Times/Goldman Sachs Business Book of the Year 2008, named a book of the year by The Economist and one of the best business books of all time by the Independent) 2008; columns have appeared in The Atlantic, Bloomberg, The Economist, Financial Times, Fortune, Newsweek, The Wall Street Journal, The Washington Post, The Financial Express, and other publs. *Leisure interests:* sports, supports NY Jets football team. *Address:* Global Development Council, 1600 Pennsylvania Ave, NW, Washington, DC 20500, USA (office). *Telephone:* (202) 456-1414 (office). *Website:* www.whitehouse.gov (office).

ERIKSEN SØREIDE, Ine Marie, Cand. jur; Norwegian politician; *Minister of Defence;* b. 2 May 1976, Lørenskog, Akershus; d. of Egil Eriksen and Wenche Irene

Hansen; m. Øystein Eriksen Søreide; ed Univ. of Tromsø; mem. Tromsø City Council 1995–99; Presenter, Metropol TV 2001; mem. Storting (Parl.) for Oslo 2005–, Chair. Standing Cttee on Educ., Research and Church Affairs 2005–09, Standing Cttee on Foreign Affairs and Defence, Enlarged Foreign Affairs Cttee 2009–13; Minister of Defence 2013–; mem. Conservative Party (Høyre), Chair., Young Conservatives in Norway 2000–04, mem. Conservative Party Central Exec. Cttee 2000–. *Address:* Ministry of Defence, Glacisgt. 1, POB 8126 Dep., 0032 Oslo, Norway (office). *Telephone:* 23-09-80-00 (office). *Fax:* 23-09-60-51 (office). *E-mail:* postmottak@fd.dep.no (office). *Website:* www.regjeringen.no/fd (office).

ERIKSSON, Per, MSc, PhD; Swedish telecommunications engineer and university administrator; *Vice-Chancellor, Lund University;* b. 22 June 1949; ed Lund Univ.; Pres. and Chair. of several consultancies in signal processing and acoustics 1980–79; Asst Prof. of Telecommunications and Signal Processing, Faculty of Eng, Lund Univ. 1981, Prof. of Signal Processing 2007–, Dir of Undergraduate Studies in Electrical Eng 1981–87, Dean and Chair. of Undergraduate Studies 1983–88, Vice-Chancellor Lund Univ. 2009–; Founding Pres. Blekinge Inst. 1989–2000; Dir Gen. Swedish Govt Agency for Innovation Systems (Vinnova) 2001–08; mem. Royal Swedish Acad. of Eng Sciences; Royal Inst. of Tech. Janne Carlsson Prize for Academic Leadership 1999, Telecom City Prize of Honour 2001. *Address:* Office of the Vice-Chancellor, Lund University, PO Box 117, 221 00 Lund, Sweden (office). *Telephone:* (46) 222-70-01 (office). *Fax:* (46) 222-47-20 (office). *E-mail:* per.eriksson@rektor.lu.se (office); rektor@rektor.lu.se (office). *Website:* www.lunduniversity.lu.se/about-lund-university/vice-chancellor-and-management (office).

ERIKSSON, Per-Olof, MSc (Eng); Swedish business executive; *Chairman, Ferronordic Machine AB;* b. 1 March 1938, Seglora; s. of Gunhild Eriksson and Herbert Eriksson; m. Helena Eriksson Joachimsson 1962; two s. one d.; ed Royal Inst. of Tech., Stockholm; Dir and Head of Production and Materials Control, Sandvik Coromant 1975; Pres. Seco Tools AB 1976; Pres. and CEO Sandvik AB 1984–94; Chair. Ferronordic Machine AB, Odlander, Fredriksson & Co. AB; mem. Bd Biotage AB, Kamstrup AB, Öresund Investment AB, Södersjukhuset AB, Fed. Swedish Bridge; Hon. DTech. *Leisure interests:* orienteering, skiing, hunting, golf, bridge. *Address:* Hedåsvägen 57, 811 61 Sandviken, Sweden. *Telephone:* 26-27-02-02. *Fax:* 26-27-02-02. *E-mail:* per-olof.eriksson@ofco.se (office).

ERIKSSON, Sven-Göran; Swedish professional football manager; b. 5 Feb. 1948, Sunne; m. Ann-Christine Petterson 1977 (divorced); two c.; raised in Torsby, Värmland; player (right back) with Torsby IF 1966–71, SK Sifhälla 1971–73, KB Karlskoga 1973–75, Degerfors 1975, Asst Coach 1976, Coach 1977–78; Coach, IFK Gothenburg 1979–82 (won Swedish Cup 1979, Swedish League Champions 1981 1982, UEFA Cup 1982), Benfica 1982–84, 1989–92 (won Portuguese League Championship and Cup 1983, Portuguese League Championship 1984), AS Roma 1984–87 (won Italian Cup 1986), AC Fiorentina 1987–89, Sampdoria 1992–97 (won Italian Cup 1994), Lazio 1997–2001 (won Italian Cup 1998, Italian Super Cup 1998, UEFA Cup 1999, UEFA Super Cup 1999, Italian League Champions 2000); Coach, England Nat. Team 2001–06; Man. Manchester City Football Club 2007–08; Head Coach, Mexican Nat. Team 2008–09; Dir of Football, Notts County FC 2009–10; Head Coach, Côte d'Ivoire Nat. Team 2010; Man. Leicester City 2010–11; Tech. Dir BEC Tero 2012, Al Nasr 2013; Man. Guangzhou R&F, People's Repub. of China 2013–; Prince's Plaque (Swedish Govt Award) 2001, BBC Sports Coach of the Year 2001. *Publications:* Sven-Goran Eriksson on Football 2001, Sven: My Story 2013. *Address:* c/o Athole Still, Athole Still Ltd, Foresters Hall, 25–27 Westow Street, London, SE19 3RY, England (office). *Telephone:* (20) 8771-5271 (office). *Fax:* (20) 8771-8172 (office). *E-mail:* enquiries@atholestill.co.uk (office). *Website:* www.atholestill.co.uk (office); sven.speaksup.com; www.gzrffc.com.cn.

ERJAVEC, Karl Viktor; Slovenian politician and government official; *Deputy Prime Minister and Minister of Foreign Affairs;* b. 21 June 1960, Aiseau, Belgium; m.; two d.; ed Univ. of Ljubljana; worked in pvt. business sector –1990; mem. Kranj Urban Municipality Ass. Exec. Council 1990–95, apptd Sec. for Gen. Admin and other Legal Affairs 1990; fmr Head, Office of Human Rights Ombudsman, Repub. of Slovenia 1995–2000; fmr Dir Expert Service; State Sec. for Judicial Admin, Ministry of Justice 2001–04, Minister of Defence 2004–08, of the Environment and Physical Planning 2008–10, Deputy Prime Minister and Minister of Foreign Affairs 2012–; Pres. Democratic Party of Pensioners of Slovenia 2005–. *Publications:* numerous articles on human rights and judicial system functions. *Leisure interests:* painting, sports. *Address:* Ministry of Foreign Affairs, 1001 Ljubljana, Prešernova 25, Slovenia (office). *Telephone:* (1) 4782231 (office). *Fax:* (1) 4782340 (office). *E-mail:* karl.erjavec@gov.si (office). *Website:* www.mzz.gov.si (office).

ERKEBAEV, Abdyganu Erkibayevich, DPhilSci; Kyrgyzstani politician; b. 9 Sept. 1953, Kara-Tent, Osh Oblast; m.; two s. one d.; ed Kyrgyz State Univ.; jr researcher, Inst. of World Literature, USSR Acad. of Sciences 1976–82; sr teacher, Kyrgyz Women's Pedagogical Inst. 1982–85; Deputy Ed. Kyrgyzstan Madanyaty (newspaper), Dir Inst. of Language and Literature, Kyrgyz Acad. of Sciences 1985–90; Deputy, Supreme Soviet, Kyrgyz SSR 1990–91; Minister of Press and Information, Kyrgyz Repub. 1991–92; Vice-Prime Minister 1992–93; Head, Osh Oblast Admin. 1993–95; mem. Zhogorku Kenesh (Parl.), Chair. Cttee on Social Problems 1995–, Zhogorku Kenesh 2000–05; Chair. Interparl. Cttee of Russia, Belarus, Kazakhstan, Kyrgyzstan (Union of Four); Co-Chair. Union of Democratic Forces; mem. Nat. Acad. of Sciences, Kyrgyz Repub.; Dank Medal. *Publications:* eight books and more than 150 articles and reviews on problems of literature, arts and politics. *Leisure interest:* reading. *Address:* Zhogorku Kenesh, ul. Abdymomunov 207, 720003 Bishkek, Kyrgyzstan (office). *Telephone:* (312) 61-16-04 (office); (312) 550408 (home). *Fax:* (312) 62-50-12 (office). *E-mail:* zs@kenesh.gov.kg (office). *Website:* www.kenesh.kg (office).

ERLANDE-BRANDENBURG, Alain; French museum curator; b. 2 Aug. 1937, Luxeuil-les-Bains; s. of Gilbert Erlande and Renée Pierra; m. Anne-Bénédicte Mérel 1980; four c.; ed École des Chartes, École du Louvre section supérieure, École pratique des hautes études (IVe section); Curator Musée de Cluny and Musée d'Ecouen 1967, Chief Curator 1981; Dir of Studies École pratique des hautes études 1975; Prof., École du Louvre; Assoc. Prof., École Nationale des Chartes 1991–2000; Asst Dir, Musées de France 1987–92; Head of Musée Nat. du Moyen-Age 1991–94; Curator Musée Nat. de la Renaissance, Château d'Ecouen

1998–2005; Dir of Studies, L'Institut d'Etudes Supérieures des Arts 2005–07; Pres. Soc. française d'archéologie 1985–94; Dir French Archives, Ministry of Culture and the French Language 1994–98; Pres. French Soc. of Archaeology 1985–94, Nat. Soc. of French Antique Dealers 1995; Commdr, Ordre nat. du Mérite, Officier, Légion d'honneur, Commdr des Arts et des Lettres, Officier du Lion (Sénégal). *Publications:* Paris monumental 1974, Le roi est mort 1975, Les rois retrouvés 1977, La dame à la licorne 1978, La cathédrale d'Amiens 1982, L'abbaye de Cluny 1982, L'art gothique 1984, Chartres 1986, La conquête de l'Europe 1260–1380 1987, La cathédrale 1989, Notre-Dame de Paris 1991, Quand les cathédrales étaient peintes 1993, Histoire de l'architecture française: Du Moyen Age à la Renaissance 1995, De pierre, d'or et de feu: la création artistique au Moyen Age 1999, Trois abbayes cisterciennes en Provence, Senanque, Silvacane, Le Thoronet 2000, Le Sacre de l'artiste. La création au Moyen Age 2000, Royaumont 2004, L'art gothique 2004, Qu'est-ce qu'une église? 2010, Cathédrales d'Europe 2012, Saint-Germain-des-Prés. An 1000 2012, La révolution gothique 2012, La cathédrale de Rouen 2012. *Address:* 14 rue de Rennes, 75006 Paris (home); Impasse de l'abbaye, 77120 Beautheil, France (home). *Telephone:* 1-44-45-95-38 (home). *E-mail:* alain .brandenburg@gmail.com.

ERLEN, Hubertus, Dr-Ing; German business executive; *Vice-Chairman, Supervisory Board, Bayer Schering Pharma AG;* b. 7 June 1943, Troppau; ed Tech. Univ., Berlin; joined pharmaceutical manufacturing arm of Schering AG 1972, moved to Electroplating Div. 1981, Tech. Dir Feucht plant, Nuremberg 1981–84, mem. Div. Bd 1984–85, mem. Bd 1986–, CEO Schering AG 2001–06, Vice-Chair. Supervisory Bd Bayer Schering Pharma AG 2006–; mem. Supervisory Bd Celesio AG, Invest in Germany GmbH; Chair. Robert Koch Foundation; Vice-Chair. Schering Foundation. *Address:* Supervisory Board, Bayer Schering Pharma AG, Friedrichstr. 81–82, 10117 Berlin, Germany (office). *Telephone:* (30) 46814041 (office). *Website:* www.bayerscheringpharma.de (office).

ERMAKOVA, Nadezhda Andreevna; Belarusian central banker and fmr local government official; *Chair, National Bank of the Republic of Belarus;* b. 19 April 1953, Mogilev Region; divorced; two d.; ed Pinsk Accounting Coll. of the State Bank of the USSR, V. V. Kuibyshev Belarusian State Inst. of Nat. Economy (now Belarus State Econ. Univ.), Minsk; Credit Inspector, later Chief Credit Inspector and Deputy Head, Khotimsk Br., Belarusian Republican Office of State Bank of USSR 1971–79, Deputy Head, Kirawsk Br. 1979–83, Head, Skłoŭ Br. 1983–84; Deputy Chair., Skłoŭ Town Municipal Exec. Cttee and Head of Planning Comm. 1984–90, Head, Financial Div. 1990–94; Head, Skłoŭ Br., Severo-Zapad Commercial Bank 1994; Head, Skłoŭ Br., JSCB Belagroprombank 1994–95; Deputy Chair., later Chair., JSC JSSB Belarusbank 1996–2011; mem. Bd Nat. Bank of Repub. of Belarus (central bank) 2006–10, Chair. 2011–; mem. Council of Repub. (upper house of parl.) 1996–2008; mem. Nat. Council for Gender Policy under Council of Ministers; Chair. Belarusian Union of Women 1999–; Honoured Economist of Repub. of Belarus, Honorary Worker of the Banking System of Repub. of Belarus, Order of Honour and two Certificates of Merit of Nat. Assembly, Certificate of Merit of Presidential Admin of Repub. of Belarus. *Address:* National Bank of the Republic of Belarus, 220008 Minsk, pr. Nezavisimosti 20, Belarus (office). *Telephone:* (17) 328-59-13 (office). *Fax:* (17) 227-48-79 (office). *E-mail:* email@ nbrb.by (office). *Website:* www.nbrb.by (office).

ERMITA, Eduardo; Philippine politician and fmr army officer; b. 13 July 1935, Balayan, Batangas; m. Elivra Ermita (née Ramos); one s. three d.; ed Naval Postgraduate School, Monterey, Calif., Kennedy Center, Fort Bragg, N Calif., Airborne School, Fort Benning, Ga, USA; Sr Mil. Asst, Office of the Under-Sec. of Nat. Defence 1976–85; Commdg Gen., Civil Relations Service, Armed Forces of the Philippines (AFP) 1985–86; Deputy Chief of Staff, AFP 1986–88, Vice Chief of Staff 1988; Under-Sec., Dept of Nat. Defence 1988–92; Vice-Chair. Govt Peace Panel Negotiations with Moro Nat. Liberation Front 1992–96; Acting Sec. of Nat. Defence 2001; Presidential Adviser on Peace Process 2001–03; Chair. Govt Peace Negotiating Panel in Talks with Moro Islamic Liberation Front 2003; resgnd from AFP, rank of Gen. 2003; Sec. of Nat. Defence 2003–04; Exec. Sec. 2004–10; Prov. Chair. LAKAS-NUCD, Prov. of Batangas 1992–; Regional Chair. LAKAS-NUCD, Region IV 1992–; Chair. Inter-Agency Cttee for the Relief, Rehabilitation and Devt 2001; Chair., Vice-Chair. or mem. numerous Govt and Legis. Cttees 1992–2001; mem. Nat. Unification Comm. 1993–94; Pres. Repub. of Philippines Golf Asscn (RPGA) 1994–2000; Commdr, Legion of Honour (Philippines) 1988; Mil. Merit Medals, Outstanding Achievement Medal 1986, Distinguished Service Star 1986, Gold Cross Medal 1987, Distinguished Conduct Star 1988. *Address:* c/o Secretariat of National Defence, DND Building, 3rd Floor, Camp Aguinaldo, Quezon City, Metro Manila, Philippines (office).

ERMOTTI, Sergio P.; Swiss banking executive; *Group CEO, UBS AG;* b. 11 May 1960; ed Advanced Man. Programme, Univ. of Oxford, UK; began career with Merrill Lynch 1987, held various positions in equity derivatives and capital markets, Co-Head of Global Equity Markets and mem. Exec. Man. Cttee for Global Markets and Investment Banking 2001–03; joined UniCredit as Head of Markets and Investment Banking Div. 2005–07, Deputy CEO UniCredit Group with responsibility for strategic business areas, Corp. and Investment Banking and Pvt. Banking 2007–10; mem. Group Exec. Bd April 2011–, Chair. and CEO UBS Group Europe, Middle East and Africa April–Nov. 2011, Acting Group CEO UBS AG Sept.–Nov. 2011, Group CEO Nov. 2011–; Dir (non-exec.) London Stock Exchange Group plc. *Address:* UBS AG, Bahnhofstrasse 45, 8021 Zurich, Switzerland (office). *Telephone:* (44) 234-11-11 (office). *Fax:* (44) 239-91-11 (office). *E-mail:* info@ubs .com (office). *Website:* www.ubs.com (office).

ERNAUX, Annie; French writer; b. (Annie Duchesne), 1 Sept. 1940, Lillebonne, Seine-Maritime; d. of the late Alphonse Duchesne and Blanche Dumenil; m. Philippe Ernaux 1964 (divorced); two s.; ed Lycée Jeanne-d'Arc, Rouen, Univs of Rouen, Bordeaux and Grenoble; lived in Yvetot, Normandy as a child; turned from fiction to concentrate on autobiography early in her career; teacher of literature 1966–2000. *Publications:* Les armoires vides 1974, Ce qu'ils disent ou rien 1977, La femme gelée 1981, La place (Prix Renaudot 1984) 1984, Une femme 1989, Passion simple 1991, Journal du dehors 1993, La honte 1997, Je ne suis pas sortie de ma nuit 1997, La Vie Extérieure: 1993–1999 2000, L'événement 2000, Se perdre 2001, L'occupation 2002, L'écriture comme un couteau 2003, L'usage de la photo 2005, Les Années 2008, L'autre fille 2011, L'atelier noir 2011, Écrire la vie 2011.

Address: 23 rue des Lozères, 95000 Cergy, France (home). *E-mail:* annie.ernaux@ tiscali.fr (home).

ERNI, Hans; Swiss painter; b. 21 Feb. 1909, Lucerne; m. Doris Kessler 1949; one s. two d.; ed Académie Julien, Paris and Vereinigte Staatsschulen für freie und angewandte Kunst, Berlin; mem. Groupe Abstraction-Création, Paris; mem. SWB;. Int. Prize at the Biennale del Mare 1953. *Publications:* Wo steht der Maler in der Gegenwart? 1947, Erni en Valais 1967, Israel Sketchbook 1968. *Website:* www.hans-erni.ch.

ERNST, Richard R., DrScTech; Swiss chemist and academic; *Professor Emeritus, Laboratory of Physical Chemistry, Eidgenössischen Technischen Hochschule (ETH) Zürich;* b. 14 Aug. 1933, Winterthur; s. of Robert Ernst and Irma Brunner; m. Magdalena Kielholz 1963; one s. two d.; ed Edgenössische Technische Hochschule, Zürich; Scientific Collaborator, Physical-Chem. Lab., ETH, Zürich 1962–63; Scientist, Varian Associates, Palo Alto, Calif., USA 1963–68; tutor, then Asst Prof., Assoc. Prof., ETH, Zürich 1968–76, Prof. of Physical Chem. 1976–98, now Prof. Emer.; mem. editorial bd various journals on magnetic resonance; Pres. Research Council of ETH, Zürich 1990–94; Vice-Pres. Bd Spectrospin AG, Fällanden 1989–; Fellow American Physical Soc.; mem. Schweizer Chemikerverband, Int. Soc. of Magnetic Resonance, Schweizerische Chemische Gesellschaft, Deutsche Akad. der Naturforscher Leopoldina, Academia Europaea, Schweizerische Akad. der Technischen Wissenschaften, NAS, Royal Soc. London; Dr hc (ETH-Lausanne) 1985, (Zürich) 1994, (Antwerp) 1997, (Babes-Bolyai) 1998, (Montpellier) 1999, (Allahabad) 2000, (Prague) 2002; Hon. Dr rer. nat (Munich Tech. Univ.) 1989; several awards including Benoist Prize 1986, John Gamble Kirkwood Medal, Yale Univ. 1989, Ampere Prize 1990, Wolf Prize for Chem., Jerusalem 1991, Nobel Prize for Chem. 1991. *Leisure interests:* music, Tibetan art. *Address:* Laboratorium für Physikalische Chemie, ETH Zürich, Wolfgang Paulistr. 10, HCI, 8093 Zürich (office); Kurlistr. 24, 8404 Winterthur, Switzerland (home). *Telephone:* (52) 2427807 (home); (1) 6324368 (office). *Fax:* (1) 6321257 (office). *E-mail:* ernst@nmr.phys.chem.ethz.ch (office). *Website:* www.chab.ethz.ch (office).

EROĞLU, Derviş, PhD; Turkish-Cypriot politician; *President, 'Turkish Republic of Northern Cyprus';* b. 1938, Ergazi Magosa Dist; m.; four c.; ed Univ. of Istanbul; fmr urologist, Ankara; mem. Parl. 1976–; Chair. Ulusal Bırlık Partisi (Nat. Unity Party) 1981–; Prime Minister 'Turkish Repub. of Northern Cyprus' 1985–93, 1996–2003, 2009–10, Pres. 2010–. *Address:* Office of the President, Şht Selahattin Sonat Sok., Lefkoşa (Nicosia), Mersin 10; National Unity Party, 9 Atatürk Meydanı, Lefkoşa (Nicosia), Mersin 10, 'Turkish Republic of Northern Cyprus' (office). *Telephone:* 2283141 (office); (22) 73972. *Fax:* 2277225 (office). *E-mail:* info@ kktcbasbakanlik.org (office). *Website:* www.kktcbasbakanlik.org (office).

EROKHIN, Vladimir Petrovich; Russian business executive; *Chairman, OJSC Surgutneftegas;* b. 1949; Deputy Gen. Dir on Drilling, Surgutneftegas (now OJSC Surgutneftegas) 2003–07, Chair. 2007–. *Address:* OJSC Surgutneftegas, Surgut 628415, ul. Kukuyevitskogo 1, Tyumen, Russia (office). *Telephone:* (3462) 42-61-33 (office). *Fax:* (3462) 33-32-35 (office). *E-mail:* secret_b@surgutneftegas.ru (office). *Website:* www.surgutneftegas.ru (office).

EROPKIN, Dmitriy P.; Russian economist and banker; *President, Rossiyskiy Kredit Bank;* b. 1970, Moscow; ed Moscow Aviation Univ., Financial Acad. to Govt of Russian Fed.; economist, JSC Rossiyskiy Kredit Bank 1994–95, Man. Int. Transfers Area, Int. Settlement Dept April–June 1995, Deputy Head of Int. Settlement Dept June–Sept. 1995, Deputy Dir Int. Settlement Div. and Head of Int. Settlement Dept Sept. 1995–, also Head of Financial Trade and Documentary Business Dept March 1996–, Dir Int. Settlement and Corresp. Relations Div. and Vice-Pres. JSC Rossiyskiy Kredit Bank responsible for devt programmes of rep. offices and subsidiary banks in UK, Switzerland, Hungary, China, Viet Nam and Bahrain 1996–97, Deputy Chair. and Dir Int. Div. 1997–2001, Chair. and Pres. Rossiyskiy Kredit Bank 2006–07, Pres. 2007–; Chair. JSC Impexbank 2001–04, Chair. and Pres. 2004–06; Pres. and Chair. Supervisory Bd Unicor man. co.; mem. Presidium of Council of Asscn of Russian Banks; mem. Cttee on Financial Markets and Credit Orgs, Chamber of Trade and Industry of Russian Fed.; Hon. Diploma, Asscn of Russian Banks 2004. *Address:* Rossiyskiy Kredit Bank, 26/9 Smolenskii Blvd, Moscow 119002, Russia (office). *Telephone:* (495) 967-34-43 (office). *Fax:* (495) 247-39-39 (office). *E-mail:* web-adm@roscredit.ru (office). *Website:* www .roscredit.ru (office).

ERRÁZURIZ OSSA, HE Cardinal Francisco Javier; Chilean ecclesiastic; *Archbishop Emeritus of Santiago de Chile;* b. 5 Sept. 1933, Santiago; ed German School of the Congregation of the Divine Word, Catholic Univ., Univ. of Fribourg, Switzerland; ordained priest 1961; first Superior of Secular Inst. of Schoenstatt (German-based Marian movt) in Chile, Spain and Ecuador 1965, Superior Gen. in Germany 1971–87; Sec. Vatican Congregation for Consecrated Life and Socs of Apostolic Life, Rome 1990; Titular Archbishop of Hólar 1990; Archbishop (Personal Title) of Valparaíso 1996–98, of Santiago de Chile 1998–2010, Archbishop Emer. 2010–; Pres. Chilean Bishops' Conf. 1998; cr. Cardinal (Cardinal-Priest of Santa Maria della Pace) 2001; participated in Papal Conclave 2005, 2013. *Address:* Archdiocese of Santiago de Chile, Casilla-30 D, Erasmo Escala 1884, Santiago, Chile (office). *Telephone:* (2) 6963275 (office); (2) 2744830 (home). *Fax:* (2) 6989137 (office); (2) 2092251 (home). *Website:* www.iglesiadesantiago.cl (office).

ERRERA, Gérard, CVO; French fmr diplomatist and business executive; *Chairman (France), The Blackstone Group;* b. 30 Oct. 1943, Brive; s. of Paul Errera and Bella Montekio; m. Virginie Bedoya; three c.; ed Inst. d'Etudes Politiques and Ecole Nat. d'Admin. Paris; First Sec. Washington, DC 1971–75; Special Adviser to Minister of Foreign Affairs 1975–77, 1980–81; Political Counsellor, Madrid 1977–80; Consul-Gen. San Francisco 1982–85; Dir of Int. Relations, French Atomic Energy Comm. and Gov. for France, IAEA 1985–90; Amb. to Conf. on Disarmament, Geneva 1991–95; Amb. and Perm. Rep. to NATO, Brussels 1995–98; Dir-Gen. of Political Affairs, Ministry of Foreign Affairs 1998–2002; Amb. to UK 2002–07; Sec.-Gen. Ministry of Foreign Affairs 2007–09; Dir, Areva, EDF 2007–09, Asscn des Arts Décoratifs 2012–; Sr Adviser to The Blackstone Group 2009–, Chair. (France) 2012–; mem. Huawei Int. Advisory Bd 2010–; Officier, Légion d'honneur, Ordre nat. du Mérite. *Leisure interests:* skiing, tennis, guitar. *Address:* The Blackstone Group International Partners LLP, 127 avenue des Champs-Élysées, 3rd Floor, 75008 Paris, France (office). *Telephone:* 1-

56-69-16-30 (office). *Fax:* 1-56-69-16-31 (office). *E-mail:* gerard.errera@blackstone .com (office). *Website:* www.blackstone.com (office).

ERRÓ, Gudmundur, (pseudonym of Gudmundur Gudmundsson); Icelandic artist; b. 19 July 1932, Olafsvik; s. of Gudmundur Einarsson and Soffia Kristiansdottir; m. Bat Yosef 1958 (divorced 1969); one c.; ed Reykjavik, Oslo, Ravenna and Florence Art Acads; painter since 1956, over 135 personal exhbns worldwide (six retrospective including Jeu de Paume, Paris 1999) and has participated in over 250 group exhbns; works in perm. public collections in Betzalel Museum, Jerusalem, Tel-Aviv Museum of Modern Art, Moderna Museet, Stockholm, Samlung Ludwig, Aachen, Musée Nat. d'Art Moderne, Centre Georges Pompidou, Paris, Musée d'Art Moderne de la Ville de Paris, Nat. Museum of Iceland, Reykjavik, Musée Municipal, Reykjavik, Museo Nacional, Havana, Luisiana Museum, Denmark, Museum of Modern Art, New York, Nat. Gallery, Berlin, Kunstmuseum, Berne, Hara Museum, Tokyo, Stadische Galerie im Lenbachhaus, Munich, Nat. Air and Space Museum, Washington, DC, Musée des Deux Guerres Mondiales aux Invalides, Paris, Musée de Grenoble, Musée Hedendaagse Kunst, Utrecht, Bibliothèque Nationale, Paris, Fandation Maeght, St Paul de Vence, Musée de Dunkerque, Musée Cantini, Marseille, La Donation Lintas, Musée de Nîmes, FRAC Rhône-Alpes, FRAC, Ile de la Réunion, Musée Bertrand, Chateauroux, Musée d'Art Moderne, Saint-Etienne, Fonds Nat. d'Art Contemporain, Musée Picasso, Antibes, Konstmuseet Arkiv for Decorativ Kunst, Lund, Sweden, Randes Kunstmuseum, Denmark, Hôtel de Ville, Lille, La Villette, Cité des Sciences et de l'Industrie, Paris, Göteborg Kunstmuseum, Museum of Contemporary Art, Seoul, Fondation Van Gogh, Arles, FDAC Val-de-Merne, Conseil Géné; public comms include Angoulême (Ma campagne) 1982, Ministère de la Culture, ADEA 1982, Hommage à la Bande Dessinée 1982, Réalisation d'un autobus peint 1985, Commande de Samurval, Valencienne 1985, Hôtel de Ville, Lille, salle de Conseil Municipal (L'Histoire de Lille, Commande de la Mairie de Lille) 1988, La Cité des Sciences et de l'Industrie la Villete, Paris (La science et les ingénieurs, Commande de la Cité des Sciences et du Ministère de la Culture) 1989, Réalisation d'une sérigraphie pour le Bicentenaire de la Révolution Française (Commande du Ministère de la Culture) 1989, Auditorium Des Halles, Paris (Music Scape, Commande de la Ville de Paris) 1997; Officier des Arts et Lettres; Gold Medal (Sweden), Falcon Medal (Iceland). *Publications:* Sjalfsdadledsla (Mecapoème 1959) 1991, Easy is Interesting 1993, The Discontinued Story: Se Non E Vero E Ben Trovato (catalogue) 1996. *Leisure interests:* travelling (Far East), food, Cuban cigars, wine. *Address:* 39 rue Fondary, 75015 Paris, France; c/o Galleri GKM, Stora Nygatan 30, 211 37 Malmö, Sweden. *Telephone:* 1-45-75-26-33. *Fax:* 1-45-75-26-33.

ERSEK, Hikmet; Turkish-American business executive; *President and CEO, The Western Union Company;* ed Wirtschaftsuniversität, Vienna, Austria; began career in financial services at Europay/MasterCard, Austria 1986, held a variety of progressively responsible roles in sales, marketing and banking relationships; with General Electric (GE) Capital 1996–99, responsible for retailer sales, finance and the card business, also represented GE Corpn as Nat. Exec. in Austria and Slovenia; joined Western Union 1999, has held exec. roles of increasing responsibility, including as Regional Vice-Pres. for Southeastern Europe, Sr Vice-Pres., Europe, Middle East, Africa and South Asia 2004–06, Exec. Vice-Pres. 2006–08, assumed overall responsibility for EMEA-APAC region 2008, COO The Western Union Co. 2008–10, Pres. and CEO 2010–. *Address:* The Western Union Co., 12500 East Belford Avenue, Englewood, CO 80112, USA (office). *Telephone:* (720) 332-1000 (office). *Fax:* (720) 332-4753 (office). *Website:* corporate.westernunion.com (office).

ERSHAD, Lt-Gen. Hossain Mohammad; Bangladeshi politician and fmr army officer; *Chairman, Jatiya Dal;* b. 1 Feb. 1930, Rangpur; s. of the late Maqbul Hussain and of Begum Majida Khatun; m. Raushan Ershad 1956; one s. one adopted d.; ed Univ. of Dhaka, Officers' Training School, Kohat, Pakistan; first appointment in 2nd E Bengal Regt 1952; several appointments in various units including Adjutant, E Bengal Regt Centre, Chittagong 1960–62; completed staff course, Quetta Staff Coll. 1966; promoted Lt-Col 1969; Commdr 3rd E Bengal Regt 1969–70, 7th E Bengal Regt 1971–72; Adjutant-Gen. Bangladesh Army; promoted Col 1973; attended Nat. Defence Coll., New Delhi, India 1975; promoted Brig. 1975, Maj.-Gen. 1975; Deputy Chief of Army Staff 1975–78, Chief 1978–86; rank of Lt-Gen. 1979; led mil. takeover in Bangladesh March 1982; Chief Martial Law Admin. and Pres. Council of Ministers 24 March 1982, adopted title of Prime Minister Oct. 1982, of Pres. of Bangladesh Dec. 1983, elected Pres. of Bangladesh Oct. 1986, resigned Dec. 1990; also Minister of Defence 1986–90, of Information 1986–88; fmrly in charge of several ministries including Home Affairs; Chief Adviser Bangladesh Freedom Fighters' Asscn; Chair. Bangladesh Olympic Asscn, Bangladesh Lawn Tennis Fed.; UN Population Award 1987; sentenced to ten years' hard labour on charges of keeping unlicensed firearms, acquitted after appeal 1995; sentenced to a further ten years' imprisonment for illegally amassing money 1992, to seven years' imprisonment for graft 1993, to five years' imprisonment for misappropriation of funds 2000, to six months' imprisonment for attempting to influence the proceedings in a corruption case 2002, to two years' imprisonment for corruption 2006, acquitted of several corruption charges from the previous decade 2006, sentenced to two years' imprisonment on corruption charges 2006, sentence suspended due to time already served 2007; Chair. Jatiya Dal 2009–. *Leisure interests:* golf, writing poems, art, literature, oriental music. *Address:* Jatiya Dal, c/o Jatiya Sangsad, Dhaka, Bangladesh (office). *E-mail:* ershad@dhaka.agni.com (office). *Website:* www.jatiyaparty.org (office).

ERSKINE, Peter; British business executive; *Chairman, Ladbrokes Plc;* fmr European Vice-Pres. of Sales and Customer Service, Mars; fmr Sr Vice-Pres. of Sales and Marketing, UNITEL; sr positions with British Telecommunications (BT) 1993–, including Dir BT Mobile, Pres. and CEO Concert and Man. Dir BT Cellnet 1998–2001; CEO mmO2 2001–08, mem. Bd of Dirs Telefónica SA (parent co.) 2008–; mem. Bd of Dirs Ladbrokes Plc Jan. 2009–, Chair. May 2009–; mem. Advisory Bd Univ. of Reading Business School. *Address:* Ladbrokes Plc, Imperial House, Imperial Drive, Rayners Lane, Harrow, HA2 7JW, England (office). *Telephone:* (20) 8868-8899 (office). *Fax:* (20) 8868-8767 (office). *Website:* www .ladbrokesplc.com (office).

ERTL, Gerhard, Dr rer. nat, Dipl. Phys; German chemist and academic; *Professor Emeritus, Department of Physical Chemistry, Fritz-Haber-Institut der* Max-Planck-Gesellschaft, Berlin; b. 10 Oct. 1936, Stuttgart; m. Barbara Ertl; one s. one d.; ed Tech. Univ. of Stuttgart, Univ. of Paris, Ludwig-Maximilians Univ., Munich; Asst and Lecturer, Tech. Univ. of Munich 1965–68; Prof. and Dir, Inst. for Physical Chem., Tech. Univ., Hanover 1968–73; Prof. and Dir, Inst. for Physical Chem., Ludwig-Maximilians Univ., Munich 1973–86; Visiting Prof., Dept of Chemical Eng, Calif. Inst. of Tech., Pasadena, Calif., USA 1976–77; Visiting Prof., Dept of Physics, Univ. of Wis., Milwaukee 1979; Visiting Prof., Dept of Chem., Univ. of Calif., Berkeley 1981–82; Dir, Dept Physical Chem., Fritz-Haber-Institut der Max-Planck-Gesellschaft, Berlin 1986–2004, Prof. Emer. 2004–; mem. German Acad. of Sciences Leopoldina 1986–, Academia Europaea 1992–, Berlin-Brandenburg Acad. of Sciences 1998–; Foreign Assoc. NAS 2002–; Foreign Hon. mem. American Acad. of Arts and Sciences 1993; Hon. FRSE 1985; Dr hc (Ruhr Univ. of Bochum) 1992, (Univ. of Münster) 2000, (Aarhus Univ.) 2003, (Univ. of Leuven) 2003, (Chalmers Univ. of Tech.) 2003 and six others; numerous awards, including E.W. Muller Award, Univ. of Wisconsin, Milwaukee 1979, C.F. Gauss Medal, Scientific Soc. of Braunschweig 1985, RSC Centenary Medal 1985, ACS Langmuir Lecturer 1986, Liebig Medal, German Chemical Soc. 1987, RSC Bourke Medal 1991, Prize of Science and Tech. Foundation of Japan 1992, Wolf Prize in Chem. 1998, Nobel Prize in Chem. 2007, Otto Hahn Prize 2007. *Address:* Physical Chemistry Department, Fritz-Haber-Institut der Max-Planck-Gesellschaft, Faradayweg 4–6, 14195 Berlin, Germany (office). *Telephone:* (30) 8413-5100 (office). *Fax:* (30) 8413-5106 (office). *E-mail:* ertl@fhi-berlin.mpg.de (office). *Website:* www .rz-berlin.mpg.de/pc/Ertl.html (office).

ERTUĞRULOĞLU, Tahsin, BA; Turkish-Cypriot politician; b. 17 Aug. 1953, Lefkosa (Nicosia); m.; two c.; ed Univs of Arizona and Minnesota, USA; joined Ministry of Foreign Affairs and Defence 1983, Head of Political Affairs, 'Turkish Republic of Northern Cyprus' London Rep.'s Office 1986–91; Under-Sec. to Prime Minister 1991–94, re-apptd 1996–98; Counsellor, Office of the Prime Minister, Legis. Ass. 1994–96; Humphrey Fellowship, Univ. of Minnesota 1995–96; mem. Parl. for Lefkosa 1998–; Minister of Foreign Affairs and Defence 1998–2004; Chair. Bayrak Radio and TV Exec. Cttee; Chair. Nat. Unity Party (UBP) 2006–08, rejoined UBP 2013–; ind. cand. in presidential election 2010; Founder and Chair. Democracy and Trust Party 2011–12; Having Served the Turkish Nation, Ankara 2002. *Leisure interests:* football, travelling, music. *Address:* 28 Kasım Street No 8, KKTC via Mersin 10, Köşklüçiftlik, Lefkoşa, Cyprus (office). *Telephone:* (392) 228-5033 (office). *Fax:* (392) 228-5714 (office). *E-mail:* tahsin99@gmail.com (office).

ERWA, Lt-Gen. Elfatih Mohamed; Sudanese diplomatist and business executive; *CEO and Managing Director, Zain Sudan;* b. 11 May 1950, Khartoum; m. Kawther Amin Mohamed 1973; seven c.; ed Sudan Military Coll.; fmr pilot; joined Nat. Security Services 1976; served as Consul General in Embassies in Moscow and Addis Ababa 1977–84; Nat. Security Adviser to Pres. 1989–95; State Minister for Nat. Defence 1995–96; Perm. Rep. to UN 1996–2006; consultant 2006–08; CEO and Man. Dir Zain Sudan 2008–; Order of Bravery. *Leisure interests:* flying, reading, computers. *Address:* c/o Zain Group Head Office Bldg, Airport Road, Shuwaikh, PO Box 22244, 13083 Safat, Kuwait (office). *Website:* www.zain.com (office).

ERWIN, Alexander (Alec), BEcons; South African politician, academic and trade union official; b. 17 Jan. 1948; m.; ed Durban High School, Univ. of Natal; Lecturer, Dept of Econs, Univ. of Natal 1971–78; visiting lecturer, Centre of Southern African Studies, Univ. of York 1974–75; Gen. Sec. Trade Union Advisory and Co-ordinating Council 1977–79; Gen. Sec. Fed. of SA Trade Unions 1979–81; Br. Sec. Nat. Union of Textile Workers 1981–83; Educ. Sec. Fed. of SA Trade Unions 1983–85; Educ. Sec. Congress of SA Trade Unions 1986–88; Nat. Educ. Officer Nat. Union of Metalworkers 1988–93; Interim Exec. mem. ANC S Natal Region 1989; Exec. mem. ANC Western Areas Br. 1990–91; fmr mem. Devt and Reconstruction Cttee, Natal Peace Accord; fmr Congress of SA Trade Unions rep. at Nat. Econ. Forum; fmr Ed. ANC Reconstruction and Devt Programme; Deputy Minister of Finance 1994; Minister of Trade and Industry 1996–99, 1999–2004, of Public Enterprises 2004–08 (resgnd); Dr hc 1997. *Address:* African National Congress, 54 Sauer Street, Johannesburg 2001, South Africa. *Telephone:* (11) 3761000 (office). *Fax:* (11) 3761134 (office). *E-mail:* nmtyelwa@anc.org.za (office). *Website:* www.anc .org.za (office).

ERWIN, Tami; American business executive; *Vice-President and Chief Marketing Officer, Verizon Wireless;* ed Pacific Union Coll.; began career as a customer service rep. for US WEST, Bellevue, Wash. 1987, later held a series of man. assignments in outbound calling, tech. operations, call centre admin, activations and service inquiries, also worked on an int. team responsible for implementing cellular service in Hungary; fmr Pres., Southwest Region, and Vice-Pres., Customer Service for the West Area, Verizon Wireless, later Pres., Wash./Baltimore/Va Region, later West Area Pres., currently Vice-Pres. and Chief Marketing Officer, Verizon Wireless; mem. Verizon Foundation Bd, Forbes Exec. Women's Bd, Paley Center for Media; cr. and leads a Women's Leadership Conf. to develop women for professional growth and advancement; three-time winner Verizon Pres.'s Cabinet Award for sales achievement, Women of Excellence Award in Community Service, Nat. Asscn of Female Execs 2011. *Address:* Verizon Wireless Corporate Office and Headquarters, 15 Federal Road, Brookfield, CT 06804, USA (office). *Telephone:* (203) 269-8858 (office). *E-mail:* info@verizonwireless.com (office). *Website:* www .verizonwireless.com (office).

ERZAN, Ayse, BA, PhD; Turkish physicist; *Professor of Physics, Istanbul Technical University;* b. 2 May 1949, Ankara; m. Orhan Silier; ed Bryn Mawr Coll. and State Univ. of NY at Stony Brook, USA; worked at univs and research inst. in Switzerland, Portugal, Germany, the Netherlands and Italy –1990; currently Prof. of Physics, Istanbul Tech. Univ.; specialization in condensed matter physics, phase transitions and scaling behaviour in complex systems; recently involved in investigating math. models of evolution and biological networks; mem. Turkish Acad. of Sciences, Palestinian Acad. for Science and Tech., TWAS (fmrly Third World Acad. of Sciences), Editorial Bd, Journal of Statistical Physics 2002–; L'Oréal UNESCO Award for Women in Science 2003. *Address:* Department of Physics, Faculty of Sciences and Letters, Istanbul Technical University, Maslak, 34 469 Istanbul, Turkey (office). *Telephone:* (212) 2853277 (office). *Fax:* (212) 2856386 (office). *E-mail:* erzan@itu.edu.tr (office). *Website:* atlas.cc.itu.edu.tr/~erzan (office).

ERZEN, Jale Nejdet, MFA, PhD; Turkish art historian, painter and writer; *Professor of History of Art and Aesthetics, Middle East Technical University*; b. (Adile Jale Erzen), 12 Jan. 1943, Ankara; d. of Necdet Erzen and Selma Erzen; ed Art Center Coll. of Design, Los Angeles, USA, Istanbul Tech. Univ.; taught part-time at various univs in Turkey; lectured widely in USA, Italy and France; mem. staff, Faculty of Architecture, Middle East Tech. Univ. 1974–; Prof. of History of Art and Aesthetics 1992–; Visiting Prof., Univ. Bologna, Italy 1999–; Founder and Ed. Boyut Fine Arts Journal 1980–85; Founder and Pres. SANART Asscn of Aesthetics and Visual Culture; Gen. Sec. Int. Asscn of Aesthetics 1995–98, currently Vice-Pres.; adviser, Int. Asscn for Applied Aesthetics 1998–2001; work in collections in Europe, USA and in nat. and pvt. collections in Turkey; consultant, Istanbul Biennale 1992, Istanbul Contemporary Museum 1992–93, Ankara Contemporary Museum 2000–01; Fullbright Fellow, Lawrence Univ., Wis. 1985; Japan Soc. for the Promotion of Science Fellowship 2003–; Organizer of Int. Congress of Aesthetics in Ankara 2007; also consultant for various architectural journals; Chevalier, Ordre des Arts et des Lettres 1991; Best Author Award 2000, Best Critic Award, Istanbul Art Fair 2000, Contribution to Architecture Award, Turkish Chamber of Architects 2008. *Video:* Exhbn of Suleiman the Magnificent, Grand Palais, Paris (with Stephane Yerasimos) 1989. *Publications:* books on Ottoman architect Sinan, and Turkish artists Sabri Berkel, Erol Akyavas, Mehmet Aksoy; various articles on aesthetics, modern art, Ottoman architecture, environmental aesthetics, competitive aesthetics. *Leisure interests:* gardening, horse riding, poetry. *Address:* Faculty of Architecture, Middle East Technical University, Inönu blvd, 06531 Ankara (office); Sanart, Kenedi Cad. 42, Kavaklidere, 06660 Ankara, Turkey (home). *Telephone:* (312) 2102215 (office); (312) 4464761 (home). *Fax:* (312) 2101249 (office). *E-mail:* erzen@arch.metu.edu.tr (office). *Website:* www.metu.edu.tr (office).

ESAKI, Leona, PhD; Japanese scientist, academic and university administrator; *President, Yokohama College of Pharmacy*; b. 12 March 1925, Osaka; s. of Soichiro Esaki and Niyoko Ito; m. 1st Masako Araki 1959; one s. two d.; m. 2nd Masako Kondo 1986; ed Univ. of Tokyo; with Sony Corpn 1956–60, conducted research on heavily-doped germanium and silicon which resulted in the discovery of tunnel diode; with IBM Corpn, USA 1960–92, IBM Fellow 1967–92, IBM T. J. Watson Research Center, New York, 1960–92, Man. Device Research 1962–92; Dir IBM-Japan 1976–92, Yamada Science Foundation 1976–; Pres. Univ. of Tsukuba, Ibaraki, Japan 1992–98, Chair. Science and Tech. Promotion Foundation of Ibaraki 1998; Dir-Gen. Tsukuba Int. Congress Center 1999; Pres. Shibaura Inst. of Tech. 2000–05; Pres. Yokohama Coll. of Pharmacy 2006–; Sir John Cass Sr Visiting Research Fellow, London Polytechnic 1981; mem. Japan Acad. 1975, American Philosophical Soc. 1991, Max-Planck Gesellschaft 1984; Foreign Assoc. NAS 1976, American Nat. Acad. of Engineering 1977; Order of Culture 1974, Grand Cordon Order of Rising Sun (First Class) 1998; Nishina Memorial Award 1959, Asahi Press Award 1960, Toyo Rayon Foundation Award 1961, Morris N. Liebmann Memorial Prize 1961, Stuart Ballantine Medal, Franklin Inst. 1961, Japan Acad. Award 1965, Nobel Prize for Physics 1973, US-Asia Inst. Science Achievement Award 1983, American Physical Soc. Int. Prize for New Materials (jtly) 1985, IEEE Medal of Honor 1991, Japan Prize 1998. *Achievements include:* at IBM pioneered (with co-workers) research on superlattices and quantum wells, triggering wide spectrum of experimental and theoretical investigations leading to emergence of new class of transport and optoelectronic devices. *Publications:* numerous articles in professional journals. *Address:* Office of the President, Yokohama College of Pharmacy, 601 Matanocho, Totsuka-ku, Yokohama, Kanagawa 245-0066; 12-6 Sanban-cho, Chiyoda-ku, Tokyo 102, Japan (home). *Telephone:* (1) 2076-8089 (office); (3) 3262-1788 (home). *Website:* hamayaku.jp (office).

ESCHENBACH, Christoph; German conductor and concert pianist; *Music Director, National Symphony Orchestra*; b. 20 Feb. 1940, Breslau (now Wrocław, Poland); ed Musikhochschulen, Cologne and Hamburg; Musical Dir of Philharmonic Orchestra, Ludwigshafen 1979–83; Chief Conductor Tonhalle Orchestra, Zürich 1982–86; Co-Artistic Dir Pacific Music Festival 1992–98; Artistic Dir Schleswig-Holstein Music Festival 1999–2002; Musical Dir Houston Symphony Orchestra 1988–99 (Conductor Laureate 1999–), Ravinia Festival 1994–2003; Prin. Conductor NDR Symphony Orchestra 1998–2004; Musical Dir Orchestre de Paris 2000–10, Philadelphia Orchestra 2003–08; Music Dir, Nat. Symphony Orchestra, includes role as Music Dir, Kennedy Center 2010–; has appeared as conductor Boston Symphony, Chicago Symphony, Houston Symphony, LA Philharmonic, New York Philharmonic, Philadelphia Orchestra, San Francisco Symphony (US conducting debut 1975), Berlin Philharmonic, Danish Nat. Radio Orchestra, Hamburg NDR Symphony Orchestra, Kirov Orchestra, all five London orchestras, Orchestre de Paris, Vienna Philharmonic; as pianist with Atlanta Symphony, Radio Orchestras of Munich and Stuttgart, Israel Philharmonic and Israel Chamber Orchestras, NHK Orchestra Tokyo; operatic engagements include Bayreuth, Houston Grand Opera, NY Metropolitan Opera, Hessian State Theatre, Darmstadt (operatic conducting debut 1978); festivals include Bayreuth, Ravinia Festival and Schleswig-Holstein Musical Festival; Officer's Cross with Ribbon, German Order of Merit 1990, Commdr's Cross 1993, Officer's Cross with Star of the German Order of Merit 2002, Chevalier de la Légion d'honneur 2002; 1st Prize, Steinway Piano Competition 1952, Munich Int. Competition 1962, Clara Haskil Competition 1965, Leonard Bernstein Award 1993. *Address:* Opus 3 Artists, 470 Park Avenue South, 9th Floor North, New York, NY 10016, USA (office). *Telephone:* (212) 584-7500 (office). *Fax:* (646) 300-8200 (office). *E-mail:* info@opus3artists.com (office). *Website:* www.opus3artists.com (office); www.christoph-eschenbach.com.

ESCHENMOSER, Albert, DrScNat; Swiss chemist and academic; *Professor Emeritus, Swiss Federal Institute of Technology (ETH) Zurich*; b. 5 Aug. 1925, Erstfeld; s. of Alfons Eschenmoser and Johanna Eschenmoser (née Oesch); m. Elizabeth Baschnonga 1954; two s. one d.; ed Collegium Altdorf, Kantonsschule St Gallen, Swiss Federal Inst. of Tech. (ETH), Zürich; Privatdozent, Organic Chem., ETH Zurich 1956, Assoc. Prof. of Organic Chem. 1960, Prof. 1965–92, Prof. Emer. 1992–; Prof., Skaggs Inst. for Chemical Biology, La Jolla, Calif., USA 1996–2009; mem. Deutsche Akad. der Naturforscher Leopoldina (Halle) 1976, Pontifical Acad. (Vatican) 1986; Foreign Assoc. NAS 1973; Foreign mem. American Acad. of Arts and Sciences (Boston) 1966, Royal Soc. (London) 1986, Akad. der Wissenschaften (Göttingen) 1986, Academia Europaea (London) 1988, Croatian Acad. of Sciences

and Arts 1994; Foreign Hon. mem. American Acad. of Arts and Sciences 1966, Pharmaceutical Soc. for Japan 1999; Hon. FRSC (London) 1981; Hon. mem. Gesellschaft Oesterreichischer Chemiker, Vienna 1997, Swiss Chemical Soc. 2009; Orden pour le mérite für Wissenschaften und Künste (Berlin) 1992, Österreich. Ehrenzeichen für Wissenschaft und Kunst (Vienna) 1993; Hon. Dr rer. nat (Fribourg) 1966; Hon. DSc (Chicago) 1970, (Edin.) 1979, (Bologna) 1989, (Frankfurt) 1990, (Strasbourg) 1991, (Harvard) 1993, (TSRI, La Jolla) 2000, (Innsbruck) 2010; ETH Kern Award 1949, Werner Award, Swiss Chemical Soc. 1956, ETH Ruzicka Award 1958, ACS Fritzsche Award 1966, Marcel Benoist Prize (Switzerland) 1973, R.A. Welch Award in Chem., Houston, Texas 1974, Kirkwood Medal, Yale 1976, A.W.v. Hofmann-Denkmünze, GDCh 1976, Dannie-Heinemann Prize, Akad. der Wissenschaften, Göttingen 1977, Davy Medal, Royal Soc., London 1978, Cliff S. Hamilton Award and Medal, Lincoln 1980, Tetrahedron Prize, Pergamon Press 1981, G. Kenner Award, Univ. of Liverpool 1982, ACS Arthur C. Cope Award 1984, Wolf Prize in Chem. (Israel) 1986, M.-M. Janot Medal (France) 1988, Cothenius Medal, Akad. Leopoldina 1991, Ciba-Drew Award, Madison 1994, H.H. Inhoffen Medal, Braunschweig 1995, Nakanishi Prize, Chemical Soc. of Japan 1998, Paracelsus Prize, New Swiss Chemical Soc. 1999, Grande Médaille d'Or, Acad. des Sciences, Paris 2001, A.I. Oparin Medal, Int. Soc. for the Origin of Life 2002, ACS Roger Adams Award 2003, Kitasato Microbial Chemistry Medal, Tokyo 2003, F.A. Cotton Medal, Texas A&M Univ. 2004, F. Westheimer Medal, Harvard Univ. 2004, RSC D.H.R. Barton Medal 2004, Benjamin Franklin Medal in Chem., Philadelphia 2008, Paul Karrer Medal, Univ. of Zurich 2009. *Publications:* numerous articles on organic synthesis and bio-organic chemistry in professional journals. *Address:* Laboratorium für Organische Chemie, ETH Hönggerberg HCI-H309, 8093 Zürich (office); Bergstrasse 9, 8700 Küsnacht (ZH), Switzerland (home). *Telephone:* (44) 6322893 (office); (44) 9107392 (home). *Fax:* (44) 6321043 (office). *E-mail:* eschenmoser@org.chem.ethz.ch (office).

ESCHWEY, Helmut Ludwig, DSc; German business executive; *Chairman of the Advisory Board, Atreus Interim Management*; b. 25 July 1949, Heidenheim/Brenz; m.; two s.; ed Freiburg Univ.; various man. roles with Henkel KGaA, Düsseldorf, Veith Pirelli AG, Höchst/Odenwald and Freudenberg Group, Weinheim 1975–92; mem. Man. Bd Battenfeld Holding 1992, Chair. 1993; mem. Man. Bd SMS Kunststofftechnik AG 1994, Pres. Plastics Tech. Group 1994–2003, mem. Advisory Bd; Chair. Bd of Man. Heraeus Holding GmbH 2003–08; Chair. Advisory Bd Atreus Interim Management 2008–; Dir Inst. of Plastics Processing (IKV), Rheinish-Westphalian Tech. Univ. (RWTH); mem. Supervisory Bd Altana AG 2007–12; fmr Chair. Plastics and Rubber Machinery Div., Verband Deutscher Maschinen- und Anlagenbau eV (VDMA, German Eng Fed.); Dir, Novelis Inc. 2005–07; mem. Bd of Trustees, Business Ethics Inst. of the European Business School. *Address:* Atreus GmbH, Landshuter Allee 10, 80637 Munich, Germany (office). *Telephone:* (89) 452249-0 (office). *E-mail:* eschwey@atreus.de (office). *Website:* www.atreus.de (office).

ESCOBAR CERDA, Luis, MPA; Chilean economist and academic; *Professor of Economics, University of Chile*; b. 10 Feb. 1927, Santiago; m. 2nd Helga Koch 1973; five c.; ed Univ. de Chile and Harvard Univ.; Dir School of Econs, Univ. de Chile 1951–55, Dean of Faculty of Econs 1955–64; Minister of Econ. Devt and Reconstruction 1961–63; mem. Inter-American Cttee for Alliance for Progress 1964–66; Exec. Dir IMF 1964–66, 1968–70, IBRD 1966–68; Special Rep. for Inter-American Orgs, IBRD 1970–75; Trustee of Population Reference Bureau 1968–73; mem. OAS Advisory Cttee on Population and Devt 1968–73; mem. Council Soc. for Int. Devt 1969–72; Deputy Exec. Sec. Jt Bank/Fund Devt Cttee 1975–79; Prof., Georgetown Univ. 1975–79, George Washington Univ. 1977, Dept of Econs, American Univ. 1978–79; CEO at pvt. banks 1979–84; Minister of Finance 1984–85; Amb. to UN and Int. Orgs, Geneva 1986–90; int. consultant on econ. and financial matters 1990–; Prof., Univ. of Chile 1990–, Dean, Faculty of Business Admin., Iberoamerican Univ. for Sciences and Tech. 1997–2001, Acad. mem. for Life and Extraordinary Prof.; Prof., Univ. del Pacifico 2002–09; Vice-Pres. Partido Radical Social Demócrata 1994–95; Gold Medal for Best Graduate in Econs and Honor Medal, Univ. of Chile; recognition for contribution to teaching and research in econs 1996. *Publications:* The Stock Market 1959, Organization for Economic Development 1961, A Stage of the National Economic Development 1962, Considerations on the Tasks of the University 1963, Organizational Requirements for Growth and Stability 1964, The Role of the Social Sciences in Latin America 1965, The Organization of Latin American Government 1968, Multinational Corporations in Latin America 1973, International Control of Investments 1974, External Financing in Latin America 1976, 1978, Mi Testimonio 1991, Financial Problems of Latin American Economic Integration 1992, Globalization and Challenges of Globalization 2000–01; contrib. of articles to newspapers and reviews. *Leisure interests:* reading, tennis, skiing. *Address:* 2979 Los Tulipanes, Providencia, Santiago, Chile. *Telephone:* (2) 7618635. *E-mail:* escobarcerda@yahoo .com. *Website:* lecchile.wordpress.com.

ESCOVAR SALOM, Ramón; Venezuelan politician and fmr diplomatist; b. 1926, Lara State; mem. Nat. Congress 1947; Minister of Justice; Rep. to Lara State Legis. Ass.; mem. Senate; Sec.-Gen. of the Presidency 1974–75; Minister of Foreign Affairs 1975–77; Amb. to France 1986–89; Attorney-Gen. of Venezuela 1989–93; Prosecutor Int. Tribunal investigating crimes committed in Fmr Yugoslavia 1993–94; Minister of the Interior 1994; Perm. Rep. to UN 1999–2001. *Address:* c/o Ministry of Foreign Affairs, Edif. MRE, Avda Urdaneta, Esq. Carmelitas, Caracas 1010, Venezuela.

ESCUDERO DURÁN, Lorena, PhD; Ecuadorean academic and politician; *Secretary for Migration*; b. 1965; ed Univ. of Cuenca, Nat. Autonomous Univ. of Mexico and Univ. of Alicante, Spain; Dir Centre for Latinamerican Social and Political Studies, Univ. of Cuenca 2002–07, Coordinator of Postgraduate Studies 2003–07; Minister of National Defence Feb.–Aug. 2007; Sec. for Migration 2007–. *Publications:* numerous articles in professional journals. *Address:* Secretariat for Migration, Palacio Nacional, García Moreno 1043, Quito, Ecuador (office). *Telephone:* (2) 221-6300 (office).

ESHAQ, Mohammad; Afghan radio and television administrator and engineer; fmr Man. Dir Afghan News (English-language daily) 1985–96; Deputy Minister of Aviation and Tourism 1985–96; fmr Man. Dir Payam-e Mojahed (weekly publ. of Jamiat-e Eslami—Islamic Society); rep. of Northern Alliance in Washington, DC 2000–02; Dir-Gen. Radio-Television Afghanistan 2002–04; mem. Bd Int. Acad. of

TV Arts and Sciences 2003–. *Address:* c/o Radio-Television Afghanistan, St 10, Lane 2, Wazir Akbar Khan, POB 544, Kabul, Afghanistan. *E-mail:* mohammadeshaq@hotmail.com.

ESKÉNAZI, Gérard André, MBA; French business executive; b. 10 Nov. 1931, Paris; s. of Roger Eskénazi and Léone Blanchard; m. Arlette Gravelin 1964; three s. one d.; ed studies in law and business admin; joined Banque de Paris et des Pays-Bas (now Banque Paribas) 1957, Pres. Cie Financière de Paribas 1978–82; Chair. of Bd and Chair. Exec. Cttee of Pargesa SA 1985–90; Deputy Chair. and Pres. Groupe Bruxelles Lambert SA 1982–90; Chair. Parfinance 1986–90; Deputy Chair. Banque Bruxelles Lambert 1982–90; Deputy Chair. Banque Internationale à Luxembourg 1984–90; Chair. Compagnie Industrielle Pallas (COMIPAR) 1991–95; Chair. Naviter 1999–; mem. Bd Schneider 1981–97, Petrofina 1986–90, Cie Financière Paribas 1988–90; Chevalier, Légion d'honneur and Ordre nat. du mérite. *Leisure interest:* horse riding. *Address:* Naviter, 68 rue de Faubourg Saint-Honoré, 75008 Paris (office); 7 rue Maurice Ravel, 92210 Saint-Cloud, France (home). *Telephone:* 1-53-05-28-30 (office).

ESKEW, Michael L., BEng; American business executive (retd); b. 28 June 1949, Vincennes, Ind.; m.; four c.; ed Purdue Univ.; joined UPS 1972, Industrial Eng Man., Ind. 1972, various man. positions including roles with UPS Germany and UPS Airlines, Corp. Vice-Pres., Industrial Eng 1994–96, Group Vice-Pres. for Eng 1996–99, Dir UPS 1998–, Exec. Vice-Pres. 1999–2002, also Vice-Chair. 2000–02, Chair. and CEO 2002–07 (retd); mem. Bd of Dirs 3M Corpn 2003–, IBM Corpn 2005–, Eli Lilly Inc. 2008–; Trustee, The UPS Foundation, The Annie E. Casey Foundation; mem. Pres.'s Export Council, Business Roundtable. *Address:* 4505 Club Drive, Atlanta, GA 30319, USA.

ESKIN, Alex, BS, PhD; American mathematician and academic; *Professor of Mathematics, University of Chicago;* b. 19 May 1965, Moscow; ed UCLA, MIT, Stanford Univ., Princeton Univ.; Dickson Instructor, Univ. of Chicago 1994–96, Assoc. Prof. of Math. 1997–98, Prof. 1998–; research interests include lie groups, ergodic theory, geometric group theory, rational billiards; DOE Scholarship 1991, Sloan Fellowship 1992, Packard Fellowship 1997–2002, Clay Research Prize 2007. *Publications:* numerous papers in academic journals. *Address:* Department of Mathematics, University of Chicago, 5734 University Avenue, Chicago, IL 60637-1514, USA (office). *Telephone:* (773) 702-7380 (office). *Fax:* (773) 702-9787 (office). *E-mail:* eskin@math.uchicago.edu (office). *Website:* www.math.uchicago.edu (office).

ESKINDAROV, Mikhail A., DEcon; Russian economist, academic and university rector; *Rector, Finance Academy of the Government of the Russian Federation;* currently Rector, Finance Acad. of Govt of Russian Fed.; co-f. Earmarked Capital Endowment; mem. Bd of Dirs VTB group. *Address:* The Finance Academy, Moscow 125993, 49–55 Leningradsky Prospect, Russia (office). *Telephone:* (495) 943-98-55 (office). *Fax:* (495) 157-70-70 (office). *E-mail:* academy@fa.ru (office). *Website:* www .fa.ru (office).

ESKOLA, Antti Aarre, PhD; Finnish academic; *Professor Emeritus of Social Psychology, University of Tampere;* b. 20 Aug. 1934, Urjala; m. Riti Laakso 1958; one s. one d.; ed Univ. of Helsinki; Prof. of Sociology, Univ. of Turku 1965; Prof. of Social Psychology, Univ. of Tampere 1966–97, Prof. Emer. 1997–; Research Prof., Acad. of Finland 1982–87; mem. Finnish Acad. of Science and Letters 1983; Hon. DScS (Lapland) 2004. *Publications:* Social Influence and Power in Two-Person Groups 1961, Blind Alleys in Social Psychology 1988; several other studies, textbooks, essay collections and a novel. *Address:* Tammelan puistokatu 30–32 A 16, 33100 Tampere, Finland (home).

ESMAHAN D'AUBUISSON, Ricardo; Salvadorean politician; *Minister of the Economy;* Exec. Sec., Inter-party Comm. to Support the Peace Process 1989–92; Dir-Gen. Directorate Gen. for Consumer Protection 1994–95; Pres. El Savador Chamber of Agric. and Agro-industry (CAMAGRO) 2003–08, Cen. American Fed. of Agric. and Agro-industry (FECAGRO) 2003–07; adviser to Exec. Cttee Nat. Asscn of Pvt. Enterprise (ANEP) 2004–08; Minister of the Economy 2008–. *Address:* Ministry of the Economy, Edif. C1–C2, Centro de Gobierno, Alameda Juan Pablo II y Calle Guadalupe, San Salvador, El Salvador (office). *Telephone:* 2231-5600 (office). *Fax:* 2221-5446 (office). *E-mail:* webmaster@minec.gob.sv (office). *Website:* www.minec.gob.sv (office).

ESMATI, Zabiullah; Afghan government official and fmr airline executive; *Deputy Director, Project Coordination Unit, Emergency Irrigation Rehabilitation Project (Mazar Region), Ministry of Energy and Water;* fmrly lived in Calif., USA; Dir Gen. Ind. Admin of Anti-Bribery and Corruption –2007; Pres. Ariana Afghan Airlines 2007–09; Deputy Dir Project Coordination Unit, Emergency Irrigation Rehabilitation Project, Ministry of Energy and Water, Mazar Region 2009–. *Address:* Project Coordination Unit Regional Office, Emergency Irrigation Rehabilitation Project, Ministry of Energy & Water, Deputy Director PCU Regional Office, Mew Tasadi Bridge, Mazar e Sharif City, Afghanistan (office). *Telephone:* 79-5399864 (mobile) (office). *E-mail:* engzabi@eirp-afg.org (office).

ESMENARD, Francis; French publisher; b. 8 Dec. 1936, Paris; s. of Robert Esmenard and Andrée Michel; one s.; Pres. and Dir-Gen. Editions Albin Michel 1982–, Paris; Vice-Pres. Nat. Publishing Syndicat 1979–; Prés. du Directoire 1999–. *Leisure interests:* tennis, golf, skiing. *Address:* Editions Albin Michel, 22 rue Huyghens, 75014 Paris, France (office). *Telephone:* 1-42-79-10-00 (office). *Fax:* 1-43-27-21-58 (office). *E-mail:* virginie.caminade@albin-michel.fr (office). *Website:* www.albin-michel.fr (office).

ESONO EDJO, Melchor; Equatorial Guinean economist and politician; *Minister of Finance and the Budget;* nephew of Pres. Teodoro Obiang Nguema Mbasogo; ed studied econs in Morocco; State Paymaster Gen. 1992–2001, Sec. of State for the Treasury 2001; apptd Pres. Bd of Dirs Ecuato Guineana de Aviación (airline co.) 2002; Minister of Finance and the Budget 2010–; mem. Partido Democrático de Guinea Ecuatorial; Hon. Pres. Liste Mouvement Int. pour la Paix. *Address:* Ministry of Finance and the Budget, Malabo, Equatorial Guinea (office). *Website:* www.ceiba-guinea-ecuatorial.org/guineees/indexbienv1.htm (office).

ESPADA, Rafael, MD; Guatemalan/American cardiac surgeon, academic and politician; *Vice-President of Guatemala;* b. 14 Jan. 1944, Guatemala City; ed Universidad San Carlos, Guatemala City, Baylor Coll. of Medicine, Tex., specialist training from LeClub Mitrale, France; performed surgery internship residency training in gen. and thoracic surgery at Baylor Coll. of Medicine, Houston 1970–76, Instructor, Asst and Assoc. Prof. of Surgery 1977–97, Prof. of Cardiothoracic Surgery 1997–, joined Methodist DeBakey Heart Center, Houston 1977, Deputy Chief of Cardiothoracic Surgery 2005–07; Founder and Medical Dir Unidad de Cirugía Cardiovascular de Guatemala (UNICAR) (cardiovascular hosp.), Guatemala City 1995–; Vice-Pres. of Guatemala 2008–; mem. Unidad Nacional de la Esperanza (UNE); Hon. Prof., Universidad LaSalle, Mexico; Dr hc (Univ. of Francisco Marroquin, Guatemala) 1992; Chest Foundation Gov.'s Award, Int. Rotary Soc. Paul Harris Award, Methodist Hosp. Humanitarian Award 2006, among others. *Achievements include:* believed to have been one of first surgeons ever to perform successfully a cardiac autotransplant. *Address:* Vicepresidencia de la República de Guatemala, 6 Avenida, 4-19, Zona 1, Casa Presidencial, Guatemala City (office); c/o UNICAR, 9 avenida, 8-00, Zona 11, Guatemala City, Guatemala. *Telephone:* 2238-0106 (office). *E-mail:* webmastervice@vicepresidencia.gob.gt (home). *Website:* www.vicepresidencia.gob.gt (office).

ESPERSEN, Lene Feltmann, MSc; Danish politician; b. 26 Sept. 1965, Hirtshals; d. of Ole Peter Espersen and Inger Tanggaard Espersen; m.; two s.; ed Hirtshals Municipal School, Hjørring Upper Secondary School, Lester B. Pearson United World Coll., Canada, Arhus Univ.; Vice-Chair. Denmark Conservative Students 1986–88; market analyst Aarhuus Stiftsbogtrykkerie 1991–92; systems designer Bankernes EDB Cen., Roskilde 1992–94; cand. for Conservative People's Party (DKF) in Ringkjøbing constituency 1993, Sæby constituency 1994; cand. for European Parl. 1994; mem. of Folketing (Parl.) for N Jutland Co. constituency 1994–; Political Spokesperson and mem. Parl. Party, DKF 1999–2001, Leader 2008–; Minister of Justice 2001–08, of Econ. and Business Affairs 2008–10, of Foreign Affairs 2010–11; Outstanding Young Person, The Outstanding Young Persons of the World, JCI Denmark 1996, Tingprisen 2004, alle tiders kvinde 2009, Årets nordjyske erhvervskvindepris 2009. *Publications include:* Stygge Krumpen (children's book) 2005, Det er et yndigt land (with Villy Søvndal) 2008. *Leisure interests:* running, fitness, swimming, Olympic distance triathlon. *Address:* Folketinget, Christiansborg, 1214 Copenhagen K, Denmark. *Telephone:* 33-37-55-00 (office). *E-mail:* kflees@ft.dk (office). *Website:* www .leneespersen.dk.

ESPINASSE, Jacques Paul, MBA; French business executive; b. 12 May 1943, Alès; s. of Gustave Espinasse and Andrée Bernadel; m. Daniele Samat 1964; one s. one d.; ed Univ. of Michigan, USA; financial analyst, London and Brussels 1967–70; Consultant, Science Man. Int. 1970–73; Head, Control Dept Renault Véhicules Industriels 1973–78, Commercial Man. in charge of export in Europe 1979; Head, Int. Treasury Dept Régie Renault 1980; Financial Officer, Sommer Allibert 1981–82; Chief Financial Officer CEP Communication 1982–85; Chief Financial Officer Havas 1985–87, Exec. Vice-Pres. 1987–93; Consultant 1994–; Dir-Gen. Télévision par satellite (TPS) 1999–2002; Chief Financial Officer (CFO), Vivendi Universal (now Vivendi) 2002–07, mem. Man. Bd 2005–07; mem. Supervisory Bd Canal+ Group; mem. Bd of Dirs SFR, Vivendi Games, Inc., Veolia Environnement, Vivendi Universal Net; currently Bd mem. Hammerson, AXA Belgium, AXA Bank Europe, SES, LBPAM; Chevalier, Légion d'honneur, Ordre nat. du Mérite; voted Institutional Investor's Best CFO (Media) 2005. *Leisure interest:* golf, skiing. *Address:* Avenue Louise 541, 1050 Brussels, Belgium (home). *Telephone:* (2) 649-47-10 (home). *Fax:* (2) 649-48-10 (home). *E-mail:* jacques@espinasse.eu (office).

ESPINOSA CANTELLANO, Patricia, MA; Mexican government official, politician and diplomatist; ed Ibero-American Univ.; mem. Partido Acción Nacional (PAN) 1987–, Head Secr. of Political Promotion of Women, mem. Nat. Exec. Cttee, Head of Sub-coordination for Culture, Educ. and Information, PAN Parl. Group; mem. 57th Legislature, Chamber of Deputies 1997–2000, mem. Equity and Gender Cttee; Chair. Querétaro Municipal Directive Cttee, Head State Secr. of Political Promotion of Women, Head Secr. of Social Devt, Municipality of Querétaro 2000–01; Pres. Nat. Women's Inst. of Mexico (Inmujeres) 2001–06; Sec. of Foreign Affairs 2006–12; participated in Non-Governmental Org. (NGO) Forums, Fourth World Conf. on Women, Beijing; Chair. of Bd, Regional Conf. on Women of Latin America and the Caribbean; mem. Mexican Asscn for the Integral Advancement of the Family. *Address:* Partido Acción Nacional (PAN), Avda Coyoacán 1546, Col. del Valle, Del. Benito Juárez, 03100 México, DF, Mexico (office). *Telephone:* (55) 5200-4000 (office). *E-mail:* correo@cen.pan.org.mx (office). *Website:* www.pan.org.mx (office).

ESPINOSA GARCÉS, Maria Fernanda, PhD; Ecuadorean anthropologist, diplomatist, government official and poet; *Minister of Defence;* b. 7 Sept. 1964, Quito; m. Galo Mora; ed Catholic Univ. of Ecuador, Facultad Latinoamericana de Ciencias Sociales (FLACSO) and Rutgers Univ., USA; fmr Adjunct Prof. of Politics and Political Ecology, FLACSO; Sr Adviser on Biodiversity and Indigenous Peoples, Int. Union for the Conservation of Nature (IUCN) 1995–2005, Regional Dir for South America 2005–07; Minister of Foreign Affairs 2007 (resgnd); Amb. and Perm. Rep. to UN, New York 2008–09; Minister Coordinator of Natural and Cultural Heritage 2009–12; Minister of Defence 2012–; research fellowships from Ford Foundation, Latin American Studies Asscn, Int. Soc. of Women Geographers, Rockefeller Foundation, Natura Foundation; Premio Nacional de Poesía 1990. *Publications include:* poetry: Caymándote 1990, Tatuaje de Selva 1992, Loba Triste 2000; numerous newspaper and journal articles on environmental, cultural and political issues. *Address:* Ministry of National Defence, Calle Exposición 208, La Recoleta, Quito, Ecuador (office). *Telephone:* (2) 295-1951 (office). *Fax:* (2) 258-0941. *E-mail:* comunicacion@midena.gob.ec (office). *Website:* www.midena.gob.ec (office).

ESQUIVEL, Rt Hon. Sir Manuel, Kt, KCMG, PC; Belizean politician and fmr teacher; *Senior Adviser, Office of the Prime Minister;* b. 2 May 1940, Belize City; s. of John Esquivel and Laura Esquivel; m. Kathleen Levy 1971; one s. two d.; ed Loyola Univ., USA, Univ. of Bristol, UK; teacher at St John's Jr Coll., Belize City –1984; f. United Democratic Party 1973, Chair. 1976–82; fmr Councillor, Belize City Council; mem. Senate 1979–84; Prime Minister of Belize 1984–89, 1993–98, also Minister of Finance, fmrly of Defence and of Econ. Devt; Leader of the Opposition 1989–93; Sr Financial Adviser to Govt with the rank of Minister 2008–; Chair. Cen. Bank of Belize; mem. Bd of Dirs Belize Telecommunication Ltd, Belize Sugar Industries Ltd, Belize Petroleum & Energy Ltd; Order of Belize; Dr hc

(Loyola Univ., USA) 1986. *Address:* Office of the Prime Minister, Belmopan (office); c/o United Democratic Party, South End Bel-China Bridge, PO Box 1898, Belize City, Belize. *Telephone:* 610-6198 (office); 227-2576. *Fax:* 227-6441. *E-mail:* manuel.esquivel@opm.gov.bz (office); unitedd@btl.net. *Website:* www.udp.org.bz.

ESSAAFI, M'Hamed; Tunisian diplomatist; b. 26 May 1930, Kelibia; m. Hedwige Klat 1956; one s. one d.; ed Sorbonne, Paris; First Sec., London 1956; Counsellor, then Minister Plenipotentiary, Ministry of Foreign Affairs 1960–64; Amb. to UK 1964–69; Sec.-Gen. Ministry of Foreign Affairs 1969–70, 1976–78; Amb. to USSR 1970–74, to FRG 1974–76, to Belgium, Luxembourg and EEC 1978–79; Perm. Rep. to UN Jan.–Aug. 1980; UN Sec.-Gen.'s Special Rep. for Humanitarian Affairs in SE Asia 1980–81; Chef de Cabinet of UN Sec.-Gen. Jan.–June 1982; UN Under-Sec.-Gen. and Disaster Relief Co-ordinator 1982–92; Grand Officier, Ordre de la République tunisienne; Chevalier, Ordre de l'Indépendance. *Address:* 41 Chemin Moise-Duboule, 1209 Geneva, Switzerland (home); rue de la Mosquée BH20, La Marsa, Tunis, Tunisia (home). *Telephone:* (71) 746-442 (Tunisia) (home); 227886462 (Switzerland) (home).

ESSAYDI, Lalla, BFA, MFA; Moroccan photographer; b. 1956; ed Ecole des Beaux Arts, Paris, Tufts Univ., USA, School of the Museum of Fine Arts, Boston; lives and works in New York; works held in numerous public collections including Brooklyn Museum of Art, Kodak Museum of Art, Rochester, NY, Williams Coll. Museum of Art, Williamstown, Mass, Longwood Center for the Visual Arts, Farmville, Va, Brooks Museum of Art, Memphis, Chicago Art Inst., Santa Barbara Museum of Art, Museum of Fine Arts, Boston, Kresge Art Museum, East Lansing, Mich., Columbus Museum of Art, Museum of Fine Arts Houston, Fries Museum, Leeuwarden, The Netherlands. *Address:* c/o Edwynn Houk Gallery, 745 Fifth Avenue, New York, NY 10151, USA (office). *Telephone:* (212) 750-7070 (office). *E-mail:* info@houkgallery.com (office). *Website:* www.houkgallery.com (office).

ESSEBSI, Béji Caïd; Tunisian lawyer, diplomatist and politician; b. 29 Nov. 1926, Sidi Bou Said; m.; two s. two d.; ed Univ. of Paris, France; called to bar, Tunisia 1952, worked as lawyer with Cour de cassation (Supreme Court of Judicature); active within Néo-destour Party (pro-independence political movt); joined govt following independence as adviser to Pres. Habib Bourguiba 1956; Dir Gen. Sûreté nationale (police authority) 1963; Minister of the Interior 1965–69, of Defence 1969–70; Amb. to France 1970–71, to Germany 1987–90; Ed. Democracy (opposition magazine) –1980; Minister-Del. to Prime Minister 1980, Minister of Foreign Affairs 1981–86; Speaker, Majlis al-Nuab (Chamber of Deputies) 1989–91; Prime Minister Feb.–Dec. 2011; fmr mem. Parti socialiste destourien (PSD); mem. Mouvement des démocrates socialistes (MDS) 1978–. *Address:* c/o Office of the Prime Minister, pl. du Gouvernement, La Kasbah, 1008 Tunis, Tunisia (office).

ESSENHIGH, Sir Nigel, Kt, KCB; British naval officer (retd) and business executive; *Chairman, NGC UK Ltd;* b. 1944; m. Susie Essenhigh; ed Royal Coll. of Defence Studies; joined Royal Navy 1963, qualified as Prin. Warfare Officer, specializing in navigation 1972, served in variety of ships, Commdr Type 42 Destroyers HMS Nottingham and HMS Exeter; Hydrographer of the Navy, Chief Exec. UK Hydrographic Office, with rank of Rear Adm.; several appointments at Ministry of Defence including Asst Chief of Defence Staff (Programmes); promoted to Adm., C-in-C Fleet; C-in-C E Atlantic (NATO) and Commdr Allied Naval Forces N (NATO); First Sea Lord and Chief of Naval Staff 2001–02; Chair. NGC UK Ltd (Northrop Grumman Corpn's UK holding co.); mem. Bd of Dirs Babcock International Group plc 2003–; Fellow, Nautical Inst., Royal Inst. of Navigation; mem. Hon. Co. of Master Mariners; Younger Brother Trinity House; ADC. *Address:* NGC UK Ltd, 100 New Bridge Street, London, WC4V 6JA, England (office). *Telephone:* (20) 7747-1931 (office). *E-mail:* nigel.essenhigh@euro.ngc.com (office). *Website:* www.northropgrumman.co.uk (office).

ESSEX, David, OBE; British singer, actor and composer; b. (David Albert Cook), 23 July 1947, London; s. of Albert Cook and Doris Cook (née Kemp); m. Maureen Annette Neal 1971; one s. one d.; ed Shipman Secondary School, E London; started in music industry 1965; TV debut on Five O'Clock Club; has since made numerous TV appearances in UK, Europe and USA, including own BBC series 1977, The River BBC1 Series 1988; appeared on stage in repertory and later in Godspell 1971, Evita 1978, Childe Byron, Mutiny! (also wrote music) 1985, with Sir Peter Hall's Co. in She Stoops to Conquer tour and Queen's Theatre, London 1993–94; wrote score for Russian All Stars Co.'s Beauty and the Beast 1995–96; first concert tour of UK 1974, subsequent tours 1975 (including Europe, USA and Australia), 1976, 1977, 1978, 1979 (including Europe and USA), 1980, 1987, 1988, 1989/90 (World Tour); Amb. for Voluntary Service Overseas 1990–92; Pres. Stanstead Park Cricket Club; numerous gold and silver discs for LP and single records in Europe and USA; voted Best Male Singer and Outstanding Music Personality in Daily Mirror poll 1976; Variety Club of GB Award for Show Business Personality of the Year (joint) 1978 ASCAP Award 1989, BASCA Award for Composer 1994. *Films include:* Assault, All Coppers Are . . . 1971, That'll Be The Day (Variety Club Award) 1973, Stardust 1974, Silver Dream Racer 1979, Shogun Mayeda 1991. *Albums include:* Rock On 1974, All the Fun of the Fair 1975, Out on the Street 1976, Gold and Ivory 1977, Imperial Wizard 1979, Hot Love 1980, Be Bop the Future 1981, Stage Struck 1982, The Whisper 1983, This One's For You 1984 (all solo); Under Different Skies (album of musicians from developing countries); War of the Worlds (with Jeff Wayne, Richard Burton and others), From Alpha to Omega (with Cat Stevens) 1978, Silver Dream Racer (film soundtrack: composer/producer) 1979, Centre Stage 1986, Touching the Ghost 1989, David Essex Greatest Hits 1991, Cover Shot 1993, Back to Back 1994, Living in England 1995, A Night at the Movies 1997, The Very Best of David Essex 1998, I Still Believe 1999, Thank You 2000, Wonderful 2001, Forever 2002, Sunset 2003, It's Gonna Be Alright 2004, Greatest Hits 2006, Beautiful Day 2006, Happily Ever After 2007, All the Fun of the Fair 2008, Unplugged 2009. *Publication:* A Charmed Life 2003. *Leisure interests:* motorcycling, cricket, squash, flying helicopters. *Address:* David Essex Management, PO Box 390, Billingshurst, West Sussex, RH14 4BE, England. *Website:* www.davidessex.com.

ESSIMI MENYE, Lazare; Cameroonian government official; *Minister of Agriculture and Rural Development;* b. Mfomakap; m.; four c.; ed Institut des Statistiques et d'Économie Appliquée, Morocco, Institut National des Sciences et Techniques Nucléaires, Saclay, France; UNDP adviser for Rwanda 1990–92; adviser to World Bank 1994; fmr govt adviser for IMF, Washington, DC; fmr

Minister-Del. in charge of the budget, Ministry of Finance and Economy, Minister of Finance and Economy 2007, currently Minister of Agriculture and Rural Development. *Address:* Ministry of Agriculture and Rural Development, Quartier Administratif, Yaoundé, Cameroon (office). *Telephone:* 2223-1190 (office). *Fax:* 2222-5091 (office).

ESSNER, Robert Alan, BA, MA; American pharmaceutical industry executive; b. 26 Oct. 1947; s. of Arthur Essner and Charlotte E. Levy; m. 1st Rosalind Essner (divorced); two c.; m. 2nd Anne Essner; three c.; ed Miami Univ., Oxford, Ohio and Univ. of Chicago; with Sandoz Pharmaceutical Corpn 1978–86, Vice-Pres. 1986–87; Pres. Sandoz Consumer HealthCare Group 1987; joined American Home Products (AHP) 1989, Pres. Wyeth-Ayerst Labs 1993–97, Pres. Wyeth-Ayerst Pharmaceuticals 1997–2000, Exec. Vice-Pres., mem. Bd of Dirs, AHP (now Wyeth) 1997–2007, Pres. and COO 2000–01, CEO 2001–07, Chair. 2003–08; mem. Bd Dirs Massachusetts Mutual Life Insurance Co.; Chair. Children's Health Fund Corp. Council; mem. Business Roundtable, Business Council; fmr Chair. Pharmaceutical Research & Mfrs of America. *Address:* c/o Wyeth, 5 Giralda Farms, Madison, NJ 07940-0874, USA. *Telephone:* (973) 660-5000.

ESSO, Laurent; Cameroonian magistrate and politician; *Minister of State and Secretary-General at the Presidency;* b. 1942, Douala; Minister of Justice 1996–2000, of Public Health 2000–01; Minister Del. at the Presidency in charge of Defence 2001–04; Minister of State in charge of External Relations 2004–06; Minister of State and Sec.-Gen. at the Presidency 2006–; mem. Rassemblement démocratique du peuple camerounais. *Address:* Office of the President, Palais de l'Unité, Yaoundé, Cameroon. *Telephone:* 2223-4025. *Website:* www.camnet.cm/celcom/homepr.htm.

ESSWOOD, Paul Lawrence Vincent, ARCM; British singer (countertenor) and conductor; b. 6 June 1942, Nottingham; s. of Alfred W. Esswood and Freda Garatt; m. 1st Mary L. Cantrill 1966 (divorced 1990); two s.; m. 2nd Aimée Désirée Blattmann 1990; one s. one d.; ed West Bridgford Grammar School and Royal Coll. of Music; Lay Vicar, Westminster Abbey 1964–71; Prof., Royal Coll. of Music 1973–85, Royal Acad. of Music 1985–; Co-founder Pro Cantione Antiqua – A Cappella 1967; opera debut in L'Erismena, Univ. of Calif., Berkeley 1968; debut at La Scala, Milan with Zürich Opera in L'Incoronazione di Poppea and Il Ritorno d'Ulisse 1978; Scottish opera debut in Dido and Aeneas 1978; world premiere in Penderecki's Paradise Lost, Chicago Lyric Opera 1979, Philip Glass's Akhnaton, Stuttgart 1984, Herbert Will's Schlafes Bruder, with Zurich Opera 1996; world première in Schnittke's Faust Cantata, Vienna, 1986; Handel's Riccardo Primo, Covent Garden, 1991; has appeared at many maj. int. festivals; specialist in performing baroque music and has made many recordings of works by Bach, Handel, Purcell, Monteverdi, Cavalli, Britten (Abraham and Isaac), folksongs, others; Prof. at 'Maîtrise de Notre Dame', Paris, conducting debut at Chichester Festival with Purcell's The Fairy Queen 2000, Kraków, Poland 2001; Hon. RAM 1990; Handel Prize (Germany) 1992. *Leisure interests:* gardening, apiculture. *Address:* Jasmine Cottage, 42 Ferring Lane, Ferring, West Sussex, BN12 6QT, England (home). *Telephone:* (1903) 504480 (home). *Fax:* (1903) 504480 (home). *Website:* www.themusickecompanye.com; www.esswood.co.uk.

ESSY, Amara, LLM; Côte d'Ivoirian diplomatist and international organization executive; *President, International Institute for Water and Environmental Engineering (2iE) Foundation;* b. 20 Dec. 1944, Bouake; m. Lucie Essy 1971; three s. three d.; ed Univ. of the Carnegie Endowment for Int. Peace; Chief of Div. of Econ. Relations 1970; First Counsellor, Embassy in Brazil 1971–73, Perm. Misson to UN, New York 1973–75; Perm. Rep. to the UN Office, Geneva 1975–81, to UNIDO, Vienna 1975–81; Amb. to Switzerland 1978–81; Perm. Rep. to UN (and non-resident Amb. to Argentina and Cuba), New York 1981–91; Pres. UN Security Council 1990–91; Minister of Foreign Affairs 1990–98; Pres. 49th Session UN Gen. Ass. 1994–95; Minister of State, Minister of Foreign Affairs in charge of Int. Co-operation 1998–99; Sec.-Gen. OAU Sept. 2001–02; Chair. (interim) African Union July 2002–03; currently Pres. Int. Inst. for Water and Environmental Eng (2iE) Foundation; fmr UN Special Envoy for Countries Affected by the War in the Democratic Repub. of the Congo; participated in the following UN confs: Law of the Sea (Caracas, Geneva, New York), Int. Women's Year (Mexico City), Econ. Co-operation among Developing Countries, UNCTAD (Nairobi, Manila) and of the codification of int. law; meetings of the Econ. and Social Council and Comm. on Human Rights; Grand Officier, Ordre Nat. (Côte d'Ivoire), Grand Croix, Ordre Nat. de Bolivar (Venezuela), Grand Officier, Ordre Nat. de San Carlos (Colombia), Grand Croix de Rio Branco (Brazil), Grand Croix, Ordre du Lion du Sénégal. *Address:* 2iE Foundation, rue de la Science, 01 BP 594, Ouagadougou 01, Burkina Faso (office). *Telephone:* 50-49-28-00 (office). *Fax:* 50-49-28-01 (office). *E-mail:* 2ie@2ie-edu.org (office). *Website:* www.2ie-edu.org (office).

ESTEFAN, Gloria Maria; American singer and songwriter; b. 1 Sept. 1957, Havana, Cuba; d. of Jose Fajardo and Gloria Garcia; m. Emilio Estefan 1979; one s. one d.; ed Univ. of Miami; went to USA 1959; f. Gloria Estefan Foundation 1997; hon. law degree (Barry Univ., Miami) 2002, Hon. DMus (Berklee Coll. of Music, Boston) 2007; American Music Award 1987, Billboard Latin Music Award for Best Female Tropical Airplay Track (for Tu Fotografía) 2005, Latin Grammy Award for Best Tropical Song (for Pintame de Colores) 2008, Billboard Spirit of Hope Award 2011. *Recordings include:* albums: Primitive Love 1986, Let it Loose 1987, Anything For You 1988, Cuts Both Ways 1989, Coming Out of the Dark 1991, Greatest Hits 1992, Mi Terra 1993, Hold Me, Thrill Me, Kiss Me 1994, Destiny 1996, Gloria! 1998, Santo Santo 1999, Alma Caribeño: Caribbean Soul 2000, Greatest Hits: Vol. 2 2001, Unwrapped 2003, 90 Millas (Latin Grammy Award for Best Traditional Tropical Album 2008) 2007, Miss Little Havana 2011. *Address:* Estefan Enterprises Inc., 6205 Bird Road, Miami, FL 33155, USA. *Website:* www.gloriaestefan.com.

ESTEPA LLAURENS, HE Cardinal José Manuel; Spanish ecclesiastic; *Archbishop Emeritus of Spain, Military;* b. 1 Jan. 1926, Andújar, Prov. of Jaén; ordained priest, Diocese of Madrid 1954; Auxiliary Bishop of Madrid 1972–83; Titular Bishop of Tisili 1972–83; Archbishop of Spain, Mil. 1983–2003, Archbishop Emer. of Spain, Mil. 2003–; Titular Archbishop of Velebusdus 1983–89; Titular Archbishop of Italica 1989–98; cr. Cardinal (non-voting) 20 Nov. 2010 (installed as Cardinal-Priest of S. Gabriele Arcangelo all'Acqua Traversa 2011). *Address:* Military Ordinariate of Spain, Calle Nuncio 13, 28005 Madrid, Spain (office).

Telephone: (91) 365-3654 (office). *Fax:* (91) 366-8225 (office). *E-mail:* info@arzobispadocastrense.com (office). *Website:* www.arzobispadocastrense.com (office).

ESTERHÁZY, Péter; Hungarian writer and essayist; b. 14 April 1950; s. of Mátyás Esterházy and Lili Mányoky; m. Gitta Reén; two s. two d.; ed Budapest Univ.; worked as a system supervisor; full-time writer 1978–; Füst Milán, Déry, Kossuth Prize 1996, József Attila, Krúdy, Aszu, Márai, Magyar Irodalini Díj, Vilenica awards, Österreichische Staatspreis für europäische Literatur, Grinzane Cavour Prize 2004, Frankfurt Book Fair Peace Prize 2004, Pro Europa Prize 2004, Premio Letterario Internazionale Pablo Neruda 2006, Angelus Prize 2008. *Publications:* short stories: Fancsikó és Pinta 1976, Pápai vizeken ne kalózkodj! 1977, Utazás a 16-os mélyére 2006; novels: Termelési regény 1979, Függő 1981, Ki szavatol a lady biztonságáért? 1982, Fuharosok 1983, Kis magyar pornográfia (trans. as A Little Hungarian Pornography) 1984, A sziv segédigéi 1985, Bevezetés a szépirodalomba 1986, Tizenhét hattyúk (trans. as Csokonai Lili) 1987, Hrabal könyve (trans. as The Book of Hrabal) 1990, Hahn-Hahn grófnő pillantása (trans. as The Glance of Countess Hahn-Hahn Down the Danube) 1991, Egy nő (trans. as She Loves Me) 1995, Harmonia caelistis (trans. as Celestial Harmonies) 2000, Semmi művészet (trans. as Not Art) 2008; essays: A kitömött hattyú 1988, Az elefántcsonttoronyból 1991, A halacska csodálatos élete 1991, Egy kékharisnya följegyzéseiből 1994, Egy kék haris 1996, A szabadság nehéz mámora 2003. *Leisure interests:* football, mathematics. *Address:* Emöd utca 20, 1031 Budapest, Hungary. *E-mail:* esterhazypeter@irolap.hu (office). *Website:* esterhazy.irolap.hu.

ESTES, Richard; American painter; b. 14 May 1932, Kewanee, Ill.; s. of William Estes and Maria Estes; ed Chicago Art Inst.; began career as commercial artist working in publishing and advertising 1956; moved to Spain 1962; began to paint full-time 1966; currently living and working in New York and Maine; MECA Award for Achievement as a Visual Artist, Maine Coll. of Art 1996. *Address:* c/o Marlborough Gallery, 40 West 57th Street, New York, NY 10019, USA (office). *Telephone:* (212) 541-4900 (office). *Fax:* (212) 541-4948 (office). *E-mail:* mny@marlboroughgallery.com (office). *Website:* www.marlboroughgallery.com (office).

ESTEVE-COLL, Dame Elizabeth, DBE, BA, FRSA; British university chancellor and fmr museum director; *Chancellor Emerita, University of Lincoln;* b. 14 Oct. 1938; d. of P. W. Kingdon and Nora Kingdon; m. José Alexander Timothy Esteve-Coll 1960 (died 1980); ed Birkbeck Coll., London; librarian, London Borough of Merton, Kingston Coll. of Art, Kingston Polytechnic 1968–77; Head, Dept of Learning Resources, Kingston Polytechnic 1977–82; Univ. Librarian Univ. of Surrey, Chair. Arts Cttee 1982–85; Chief Librarian, Nat. Art Library, Victoria & Albert Museum 1985–87; Dir Victoria & Albert Museum 1988–95; Vice-Chancellor Univ. of East Anglia 1995–97; Chancellor, Univ. of Lincoln 2001–10, Chancellor Emer. 2010–; Assoc. Library Assscn; Hon. LittD (E Anglia) 1997; Hon. DLitt (Hull) 1998. *Publication:* The Victoria and Albert Museum (with others) 1992. *Address:* c/o The Tabernacle, Millgate, Aylsham, Norfolk, NR11 6HR, England (home).

ESTEVES, (Maria da) Assunção; Portuguese judge and politician; *President, Assembleia da República (Assembly of the Republic);* b. 15 Oct. 1956, Valpaços; mem. Social Democratic Party (SDP), fmr Vice Pres., fmr mem. Nat. Political Cttee; mem. Assembleia da República (Assembly of the Republic) 1987–89, 2002–04, Chair. first Parl. Cttee 2002–04, Pres. Assembleia da República 2011–; Judge, Constitutional Tribunal 1989–98; mem. European Parl., Brussels 2004–09; Asst Prof. of Public Law, Univ. of Lisbon 1989–99; Pres. Nat. Council of the European Movt; Vice-Pres. Sá Carneiro Inst. *Address:* Palácio de S. Bento 1249-068 Lisbon, Portugal (office). *Telephone:* (21) 3919000 (office). *Fax:* (21) 3917440 (office). *E-mail:* correio.geral@ar.parlamento.pt (office). *Website:* www.en.parlamento.pt (office).

ESTEVEZ, Emilio; American actor and film director; b. 12 May 1962, New York; s. of Martin Sheen (q.v.); m. Paula Abdul (q.v.) 1992 (divorced 1994); one s. one d. *Television:* The West Wing (actor episode, Twenty Five) 2003, The Guardian (dir episodes, Hazel Park 2003, All is Mended 2004, The Watchers 2004), Cold Case (dir episodes, The Sleepover 2004, Wishing 2005), CSI:NY (dir episodes, The Closer, The Dove Commission 2005), Close to Home (dir episode, Baseball Murder 2005). *Films include:* Seventeen Going on Nowhere (actor) 1980, To Climb a Mountain (actor) 1981, In the Custody of Strangers (actor) 1982, Tex (actor) 1982, The Outsiders (actor) 1983, Nightmares (actor) 1983, Repo Man (actor) 1984, The Breakfast Club (actor) 1984, St Elmo's Fire (actor) 1984, That was Then, This is Now (actor, writer) 1985, Maximum Overdrive (actor) 1986, Wisdom (dir, actor, writer) 1986, Stakeout (actor) 1987, Young Guns (actor) 1988, Nightbreaker (actor) 1989, Young Guns II (actor) 1990, Men at Work (dir, actor, writer) 1989, Freejack (actor) 1992, The Mighty Ducks (actor) 1992, Loaded Weapon (actor) 1993, Another Stakeout (actor) 1993, Judgement Night (actor) 1993, D2: The Mighty Ducks (actor) 1994, Mission Impossible (actor) 1996, The War at Home (dir, actor, prod.) 1996, D3: Mighty Ducks (actor) 1996, Dollar for the Dead (actor) 1998, Late Last Night (actor) 1999, Rated X (dir, actor) 2000, Sand (actor) 2000, Los Reyes magos (voice) 2003, Culture Clash in AmeriCCa (dir) 2005, LA Riot Spectacular (actor) 2005, Bobby (dir, actor, writer) 2006, Arthur and the Invisibles (voice) 2006. *Address:* c/o UTA, 5th Floor, 9560 Wilshire Boulevard, Beverly Hills, CA 90212, USA.

ESTIER, Claude; French journalist, politician and writer; b. 8 June 1925, Paris; s. of Henri Ezratty and Lucie Bernerbe; m. Victoria Man; three d.; ed Lycée Carnot and Ecole des Sciences Politiques, Paris; Political Ed. Le Populaire 1947; Ed. L'Observateur, France-Observateur, then Le Nouvel Observateur 1950–; Ed. Le Monde 1955–58; Ed.-in-Chief Libération 1958–64, Dir 1968; mem. Nat. Assembly 1967–68, 1981–86; Pres. Comm. for Foreign Affairs 1983–86; mem. Paris City Council 1971–89; Nat. Press Sec. Socialist Party 1971–79; Editorial Dir L'Unité (Socialist Party Weekly) 1972–86; MEP 1979–81; Senator 1986; Chair. Senate Socialist Group 1988–2004; Hon. MP; Officier Légion d'honneur. *Publications:* Pour l'Algérie 1963, L'Egypte en révolution 1965, Journal d'un Fédéré 1969, La plume au poing 1977, Mitterrand Président 1981, Véridique histoire d'un Septennat (with Véronique Neiertz) 1987, De Mitterrand à Jospin: Trente ans de campagnes présidentielles 1995, Dix ans qui ont changé le monde 2000, Un combat centenaire 2005, J'ai tant vu (Memoires) 2008. *Address:* Palais du Luxembourg, 75291 Paris Cedex 06, France (office). *Telephone:* 1-42-34-45-12 (office).

ESTLEMAN, Loren Daniel, BA; American writer; b. 15 Sept. 1952, Ann Arbor, Mich.; s. of Leauvett C. Estleman and Louise A. Estleman; m. Deborah Ann Green 1993; one step-s. one step-d.; ed Eastern Mich., Univ.; police reporter, Ypsilanti Press 1972–73; Ed.-in-Chief, Community Foto News 1975–76; Special Writer, Ann Arbor News 1976; staff writer, Dexter Leader 1977–80; full-time novelist 1980–; Vice-Pres. Western Writers of America 1998–2000, Pres. 2000–02; Western Writers of America Spur Award, Best Historical Novel 1981, Spur Award, Best Short Fiction 1986, 1996, Private Eye Writers of America Shamus Award, Best Novel 1984, Shamus Award, Best Short Story 1985, 1988, Mich. Foundation of the Arts Award for Literature 1987, Mich. Library Asscn Authors Award 1997, Spur Award, Best Western Novel 1999, Western Heritage Award, Outstanding Western Novel 1998, 2001, Western Heritage Award, Outstanding Short Story 2000, Western Heritage Award for Outstanding Western Novel 2001, Shamus Award for Best Short Story 2003; Dr hc of Humane Letters, Eastern Mich. Univ. 2002. *Publications:* novels: The Oklahoma Punk 1976, The Hider, Sherlock Holmes vs. Dracula 1978, The High Rocks 1979, Dr. Jekyll and Mr. Holmes, Stamping Ground, Motor City Blue 1980, Aces and Eights, Angel Eyes, The Wolfer 1981, Murdock's Law, The Midnight Man 1982, Mister St John, The Glass Highway 1983, This Old Bill, Sugartown, Kill Zone, The Stranglers 1984, Every Brilliant Eye, Roses Are Dead, Gun Man 1985, Any Man's Death 1986, Lady Yesterday 1987, Bloody Season, Downriver 1988, Silent Thunder, Peeper 1989, Sweet Women Lie, Whiskey River 1990, Sudden Country, Motown 1991, King of the Corner 1992, City of Widows 1994, Edsel 1995, Stress 1996, Never Street, Billy Gashade 1997, The Witchfinder, Journey of the Dead, Jitterbug 1998, The Rocky Mountain Moving Picture Association 1999, The Hours of the Virgin 1999, White Desert 2000, The Master Executioner 2001, Sinister Heights 2002, Something Borrowed, Something Black 2002, Black Powder, White Smoke 2002, Poison Blonde 2003, Port Hazard 2004, Retro 2004, Little Black Dress 2005, The Undertaker's Wife 2005, Nicotine Kiss 2006, The Adventures of Johnny Vermillion, 2006, American Detective 2007, Amos Walker's Detroit 2007, Frames 2008, Gas City 2008, The Branch and the Scaffold 2009, Alone 2009, The Book of Murdock 2010, Amos Walker: The Complete Story Collection 2010, The Left-Handed Dollar 2010, Infernal Angels 2011, Burning Midnight 2012; non-fiction: The Wister Trace 1987, Writing the Popular Novel 2004; collections: General Murders 1988, The Best Western Stories of Loren D. Estleman 1989, People Who Kill 1993; anthologies: P.I. Files 1990, Deals with the Devil 1994, American West 2001. *Leisure interests:* collecting books, antiques, typewriters, records and old films on tape and DVD, movie posters. *Address:* c/o Tor/Forge Books, 175 Fifth Avenue, New York, NY 10010 (office); 5552 Walsh Road, Whitmore Lake, MI 48189, USA (home). *Website:* www.lorenestleman.com.

ESTRADA, Joseph Marcelo Ejercito (Erap); Philippine politician; b. 19 April 1937, Tondo, Manila; m. Dr Luisa Pimentel; three c.; film actor 1960–89; Mayor of San Juan 1969–85; mem. Senate 1987, Vice-Pres. 1992; fmr Chair. Partido ng Masang Pilipino (PMP), now Founding Pres. Puwersa ng Masang Pilipino; Pres. of the Philippines 1998–2001; impeached for corruption by Congress Nov. 2000, on trial in Senate 2002, sentenced to life imprisonment Sept. 2007, granted exec. clemency and released Oct. 2007; f. ERAP (Educ., Research and Assistance Program) Foundation 1998;. *Address:* c/o Puwersa ng Masang Pilipino, Metro Manila, Philippines. *Website:* erap.ph.

ESZTERHAS, Joseph (Joe) A.; American scriptwriter; b. 23 Nov. 1944, Csakanydoroszlo, Hungary; s. of Stephen Eszterhas and Maria Biro; m. 1st Geraldine Javer 1972 (divorced 1994); one s. one d.; m. 2nd Naomi Baka 1994; one s.; ed Ohio State Univ.; reporter, Plain Dealer, Cleveland; staff writer, Man. Ed. Rolling Stone, San Francisco 1971–75; screenwriter 1975–; writer and producer, Checking Out 1980, Betrayed 1989; recipient of various awards. *Film screenplays:* FIST 1978, Flashdance 1983, Jagged Edge 1985, Big Shots 1987, Betrayed 1988, Checking Out 1989, Music Box 1990, Hearts of Fire 1990, Basic Instinct 1992, Nowhere to Run 1993, Sliver 1993, Showgirls 1995, Jade 1995, Telling Lies in America 1997, An Alan Smithee Film: Burn Hollywood Burn 1997, Basic Instinct 2 2006, Szabadság, szerelem 2006. *Publications include:* novels: Thirteen Seconds: Confrontation at Kent State 1970, Charlie Simpson's Apocalypse 1974, Nark! 1974, Fist 1977; non-fiction: Hollywood Animal: A Memoir 2004, The Devil's Guide to Hollywood: The Screenwriter as God! 2006, Crossbearer: A Memoir of Faith 2008, Heaven and Mel 2012. *Leisure interest:* reading. *Address:* c/o St Martin's Press, 175 Fifth Avenue, New York, NY 10010, USA (office). *Telephone:* (646) 307-5151. *Website:* www.joeeszterhas.com.

ETAIX, Pierre; French film director and actor; b. 23 Nov. 1928, Roanne; s. of Pierre Etaix and Berthe Etaix (née Tacher); m. 2nd Annie Fratellini 1969 (deceased); ed Lycée de Roanne; apprenticed as stained-glass designer; asst film producer 1949–55; Chevalier, Ordre nat. du Mérite, Ordre des Arts et des Lettres. *Films include:* Pickpocket 1959, Une grosse tête 1961, Rupture (also dir and writer) 1961, Le Pèlerinage 1962, Heureux anniversaire (also dir, writer, producer, Acad. Award ('Oscar') for best short film 1963) 1962, Le Soupirant (also dir and writer) 1962, Yoyo (also dir and writer) 1965, Tant qu'on a la santé (also dir and writer) 1966, Le Grand amour (also dir and writer) 1969, Pays de cocagne (dir) 1971, The Day the Clown Cried 1972, Sérieux comme le plaisir 1975, Max mon amour 1986, L'Âge de Monsieur est avancé (also dir and writer) 1987, Nuit docile 1987, Henry & June 1990. *Television includes:* Show Pierre Etaix 1974, Lundi 1980, La Métamorphose 1983, L'Étrange château du docteur Lerne 1983, L'Aide-mémoire 1984, Les Idiots 1987, Souris noire (series writer and writer) 1987, Méliès 88: Rêve d'artiste (dir) 1988, Bouvard et Pecuchet 1989, J'écris dans l'espace (dir and writer) 1989. *Achievements include:* creator (with Amie Fratellini) of the first circus school in France 1973. *Publications:* Le carton à chapeau 1981, Dactilographisme 1982, Croquis de Jerry Lewis 1983, Stars System (jtly) 1986, Critiques la caméra 2001. *Address:* Editions du Seuil, 27 rue Jacob, 75261 Paris cedex 06, France (office). *E-mail:* od.crepin@wanadoo.fr.

ETCHEGARAY, HE Cardinal Roger, DIurUtr; French ecclesiastic; b. 25 Sept. 1922, Espelette; s. of Jean-Baptiste Etchegaray and Aurélie Dufau; ed Petit Séminaire, Ustaritz and Grand Séminaire, Bayonne; ordained priest 1947; served diocese of Bayonne 1947–60; Asst Sec., then Sec.-Gen. French Episcopal Conf. 1961–70, Pres. 1975–81; Archbishop of Marseilles 1970–84; Pres. Council of European Episcopal Confs 1971–79; Prelate, Mission of France 1975–81; Titular Bishop of Porto-Santa Rufina; cr. Cardinal 1979; Pres. Pontifical Council for

Justice and Peace 1984, now Pres. Emer.; Vice Dean Coll. of Cardinals 2005–; Pres. Council Cor Unum 1984–95; Special Papal Emissary to Togo 1993, to Bethlehem to try to help end the standoff between Israeli forces and Palestinian gunmen in Church of the Nativity 2002; Pres. Cttee for Grand Jubilee of Year 2000; Officier, Légion d'honneur, Commdr, Ordre nat. du Mérite, Grand Cross Nat. Order (FRG), Grand Cross Nat. Order of Hungary. *Publications:* Dieu à Marseille 1976, J'avance comme un âne 1984, L'évangile aux couleurs de la vie 1987, Jésus, vrai homme, vrai Dieu 1997. *Address:* Piazza San Calisto, Vatican City, Rome 00120, Italy.

ETCHEGARAY AUBRY, Alberto; Chilean civil engineer, politician and business executive; *Chairman, SalfaCorp Ingeniería Construcción Inmobiliaria SA;* b. 5 May 1945; s. of Alberto Etchegaray and Odette Etchegaray; m.; five s., two d.; ed Pontificia Universidad Catolica de Chile; Univ. Prof. of Business Admin.; Dir Dept of Studies, Unión Social de Empresarios Cristianos; co-ordinator of visit of Pope John Paul II to Chile; Dir Hogar de Cristo; mem. Council, Semanas Sociales de Chile (initiative of Episcopal Conf. of Chile); Minister of Housing and Urban Devt 1990–94; Pres. Nat. Council against Poverty 1994–98; Dir Cía. Seg. de Vida la Construcción SA; Pres. Fundación Nacional para la Superación de la Pobreza 1997–2000, Dir 2000–; Chair. SalfaCorp Ingeniería Construcción Inmobiliaria SA 2008–; Dir Banco del Desarollo. *Publication:* Poverty in Chile: The Challenge of Equity and Social Intergration. *Address:* SalfaCorp Ingeniería Construcción Inmobiliaria SA, 5335 Presidente Riesco Avenue, 11th Floor, Las Condes, Santiago, Chile (office). *Telephone:* (2) 476-0000 (office). *Fax:* (2) 476-0021 (office). *E-mail:* salfacorp@salfacorp.com (office). *Website:* www.salfacorp.com (office).

ETEKI MBOUMOUA, William Aurélien, LicenDroit; Cameroonian politician; *President, Cameroon Red Cross Society;* b. 20 Oct. 1933, Douala; s. of Joseph Mboumoua and Mana Katta; m. Naimi Bessy Eyewe; one s. one d.; ed Ecole Nat. de la France d'Outre-mer, Paris; Prefect for Nkam 1959, for Sanage Maritime 1960–61; Minister of Educ., Youth and Culture 1961–68; mem. Exec. Council, UNESCO 1962–68, Pres. of Conf., UNESCO 1968–70; Special Adviser, with rank of Minister, to Pres. of United Republic of Cameroon 1971–74, 1978–80; Minister charged with management of the Presidency 1978; Co-Minister in charge of Missions 1980–84, Minister of Foreign Affairs 1984–87; Sec.-Gen. OAU 1974–78; Special Rep. of UN Sec.-Gen. on Small Arms Proliferation in West Africa, mem. Eminent Persons Group on curbing illicit trafficking in Small Arms and Light Weapons 1999; Nat. Pres. Cameroon Red Cross Soc. 1994–; mem. Ind. Comm. for implementation of proposals in UNDP document Proposals for Africa in this Millennium 1999, Jury du Prix UNESCO Ville pour la Paix; Commdr des Palmes académiques, Grand Officier de l'Ordre de la Valeur and many other decorations. *Publications:* Un certain humanisme 1970, Démocratiser la culture 1974, Le pouvoir de l'humanité: un certain humanisme 2009; and many articles on education and African culture. *Leisure interests:* literature, poetry, painting, tennis, football, swimming. *Address:* Cameroon Red Cross Society, 2005 Rue Henri Dunant, BP 631, Yaoundé (office); PO Box 1155, Yaoundé, Cameroon (home). *Telephone:* 2224177 (office); 2202592 (home). *Fax:* 2224177 (office); 2202592 (home). *E-mail:* crol-Rcam@iccnet_cm (office).

ETHERINGTON, William (Bill) A., BEE; Canadian banking executive; b. 1942; ed Univ. of Western Ontario; joined IBM Canada 1964, held several sales, services and staff positions 1964–80, served successively as Vice-Pres. Western Region, Vice-Pres. Sales, Vice-Pres. Finance and Chief Financial Officer 1980–88, Asst Gen. Man. IBM Latin America 1988–91, Pres. and CEO IBM Canada Ltd 1991–95, Global Gen. Man., Large Enterprise Sales, IBM Corpn 1995–97, Gen. Man. IBM Europe, Middle E and Africa 1997–98, Sr Vice-Pres. and Group Exec., Sales and Distribution, IBM Corpn and Chair., Pres. and CEO IBM World Trade Corpn 1998–2001; Chair. Canadian Imperial Bank of Commerce 2003–09, mem. Bd of Dirs Canadian Imperial Bank (USA) 1994–2009; mem. Bd of Dirs Celestica Inc. 2001–, MDS Inc. 2001–, SS Technologies Holdings Inc. 2006–, Onex Corpn 2007–, Allstream Inc., Dofasco Inc. 2002–06, MDS Inc.; Head of United Way Campaign of Greater Toronto 1993; Hon. LLD (Univ. of Western Ont.). *Address:* c/o Canadian Imperial Bank of Commerce, Commerce Court, Toronto, ON M5L 1A2, Canada.

ETHERTON, Sir Terence Michael Elkan Barnet, Kt, QC; British barrister and judge; *Chancellor of the High Court;* b. 21 June 1951; ed St Paul's School, Corpus Christi Coll., Cambridge; called to the bar (Gray's Inn) 1974; Queen's Counsel 1990; worked as barrister, primarily at Chancery Bar; apptd a High Court Judge, Chancery Div. 2001; apptd a Lord Justice of Appeal 2008; Chancellor of the High Court (Pres. of the Chancery Div.) 2013–; Chair. The Law Comm. of England and Wales 2006–09; Pres. Council of the four Inns of Court 2009–12; Visiting Prof. of Law, Birkbeck, Univ. of London 2010; Chair. Trust Law Cttee 2012; Hon. Pres. Property Bar Asscn; Hon. Fellow, Royal Holloway Coll. 2005, Corpus Christi Coll., Cambridge 2007; Hon. Prof., Univ. of Kent 2011; Dr hc (City Univ., London) 2009. *Achievements include:* mem. British int. fencing team 1977–80, competed in World Championships 1977, 1978 and 1979. *Address:* High Court of Justice, The Royal Courts of Justice, Strand, London, WC2A 2LL, England (office). *Telephone:* (20) 7947-6000 (office). *Website:* www.justice.gov.uk (office).

ETIANG, Paul Orono, BA; Ugandan politician and diplomatist; *Director, Cairo International Bank;* b. 15 Aug. 1938, Tororo; s. of Kezironi Orono and Marikho Adacat Adeke Achom; m. Zahra A. Foum 1967; two s. two d.; ed Busoga Coll. and Makerere Univ. Coll.; Dist Officer, Prov. Admin 1962–64; Asst Sec., Ministry of Foreign Affairs 1964–65, Third Sec., Uganda Embassy, Moscow 1965–66, Second Sec. 1966–67; First Sec., Uganda Perm. Mission to UN, New York 1967–68; High Commr to UK 1968–71; Chief of Protocol and Marshal of Diplomatic Corps, Uganda 1971; Perm. Sec., Ministry of Foreign Affairs 1971–73, Acting Minister of Foreign Affairs May–Oct. 1973; Minister of State for Foreign Affairs 1973–76, of Transport, Works and Communications 1976–78, for Regional Co-operation 1988–89, for Commerce 1989–91, for Information 1991–96, Third Deputy Prime Minister and Minister of Labour and Social Services 1996–97, Third Deputy Prime Minister and Minister for Disaster Preparedness and Refugees 1997–98; mem. Parl. 1998–2001; Asst Sec.-Gen. OAU, Addis Ababa 1978–87; Chair. Tororo Rock FM Radio 2001–, Uganda Railways Corpn 2003–06; Dir Cairo Int. Bank 2004–. *Leisure interests:* billiards, badminton, music, theatre. *Address:* PO Box 7089, Kampala, Uganda (office).

ETO'O FILS, Samuel; Cameroonian professional footballer; b. 10 March 1981, Nkon; striker; teams played for include Real Madrid, Spain 1997–2000 (won Intercontinental Cup 1998), Leganes, Spain 1997–98 (on loan), Espanyol, Spain 1999 (on loan), Real Mallorca, Spain 1999–2004 (initially on loan and then part-owned by Real Madrid, won Copa del Rey 2003), FC Barcelona, Spain 2004–09 (won La Liga 2005, 2006, 2009, Supercopa de España 2006, 2007, UEFA Champions League 2006, 2009, Copa del Rey 2009), Internazionale, Italy 2009–11, Anzhi Makhachkala, Dagestan 2011–; plays for Cameroon Nat. Team 1996–, played in World Cups 1998, 2002, gold medal, Olympic Games, Sydney 2000, winner African Nations Cup 2000, 2002, currently Capt. of nat. team; leading scorer for Real Mallorca in 2003–04 Primera Liga season, won Copa del Rey 2003; Confed. of African Football Footballer of the Year 2003, African Cup of Nations Top Scorer 2006, 2008, African Player of the Year 2003, 2004, 2005, FIFPro World XI 2004–05, 2005–06, UEFA Champions League Best Forward 2006, UEFA Team of the Year 2005, 2006, Spanish La Liga Top Scorer 2006, World XI Striker 2004–05, 2005–06, Most Goals Scored in Domestic League for RCD Mallorca 54 Goals, African Cup of Nations Top Scorer of All Time with 16 Goals, Most Goals Scored in History of Cameroon Nat. Team, FIFA World Player of the Year (Third Place) 2005. *Address:* Dinamo Stadium, 367025 Makhachkala, Dakhadaev Street, 23, Dagestan, Russia. *Telephone:* (8722) 67-85-20. *Fax:* (8722) 68-20-08. *E-mail:* info@fc-anji.ru. *Website:* www.fc-anji.ru.

ETTL, Harald; Austrian trade union official and politician; b. 7 Dec. 1947, Gleisdorf, Styria; m.; three c.; ed Higher Fed. Teaching and Experimental Coll. for Textile Industry, Vienna; Asst to Works Man., Eybl carpet factory, Ebergassing; Sec. Textile, Clothing and Leather Workers' Union 1971–73, Cen. Sec. 1973–84, Pres. 1984–2000; Vice Pres. Metal-Textile Trade Union 2000–; Vice-Pres. Int. Textile, Clothing and Leather Workers' Asscn 2004–; Chair. Consumer Information Asscn 1993–; Minister for Health and the Civil Service 1989–92; MEP 1996–2009; Chair. Gen. Accident Insurance Scheme 1978–89; Pres. Accident Insurance Cttee, Fed. of Austrian Social Insurance Bodies 1978–89; Chair. Working Group for Integration in Austrian Trade Union Confed.; mem. Social Democratic Party. *Address:* c/o Metal-Textile Trade Union, Plössglasse 15, 1041 Vienna, Austria (office). *Telephone:* (1) 501-46-402 (office). *Fax:* (1) 501-46-400 (office). *E-mail:* harald.ettl@metaller.at (office). *Website:* www.metaller.at (office).

EUBANK, Chris; British fmr professional boxer; b. 8 Aug. 1966, Dulwich, London; m.; four c.; WBC Int. Middleweight Boxing Champion March–Nov. 1990 two defences; WBO Middleweight Boxing Champion Nov. 1990–Aug. 1991 three defences; WBO World Super-Middleweight Boxing Champion Sept. 1991–March 1995 fourteen defences, lost title to Steve Collins, Cork Sept. 1995, failed to regain title against Joe Calzaghe, Sheffield Oct. 1997; unsuccessful fights for WBO Cruiserweight title against Carl Thompson, Manchester April 1998, Sheffield July 1998; Patron Breakthrough; numerous UK television appearances; Amb. for the Int. Fund for Animal Welfare; spokesperson for the Nat. Soc. for the Prevention of Cruelty to Children.

EUGENIDES, Jeffrey, BA, MA; American novelist; b. 8 March 1960, Detroit, Mich.; m.; one d.; ed Brown Univ., Stanford Univ.; Fellow, Berliner Künstlerprogramm 2002; Guggenheim Foundation Fellowship, Nat. Foundation for the Arts Fellowship, American Acad. in Berlin Prize Fellowship 2000–01; teacher in Creative Writing Program, Princeton Univ. 1999–2000, Prof. of Creative Writing, Peter B. Lewis Center for the Arts 2007–; Whiting Writers' Award, American Acad. of Arts and Letters Harold D. Vursell Memorial Award. *Publications:* The Virgin Suicides 1993, Middlesex (Pulitzer Prize for Fiction 2003, WELT-Literaturpreis, Great Lakes Book Award) 2002, Air Mail 2005, My Mistress's Sparrow is Dead (Ed.) 2008, The Marriage Plot 2011; contrib. to The New Yorker, The Paris Review, The Yale Review, The Gettysburg Review, Best American Short Stories, Granta's Best of Young American Novelists. *Address:* New South Building, Floor 6, Princeton University, 185 Nassau Street, Princeton, NJ 08544, USA (office). *Telephone:* (609) 258-8561 (office). *Fax:* (609) 258-2230 (office). *E-mail:* jeugenid@princeton.edu (office). *Website:* www.princeton.edu/~visarts/cwr (office).

EUH, Yoon-dae, BA, MA, MBA, PhD; South Korean academic; *Professor of International Business and Finance, Korea University;* ed Korea Univ., Asian Inst. of Man., Univ. of Michigan, USA; Prof. of Int. Business and Finance, Korea Univ. 1979–, Chair. Dept of Int. Business and Trade 1982–86, Assoc. Dean Coll. of Business Admin 1986–89, Dean Academic Affairs 1991–93, Dir Inst. for Business Research and Educ. 1993–97, Dean Grad. School of Business Admin 1996–98, Pres. Korea Univ. 2003–06; Research Fellow, Inst. for Int. Commerce, Univ. of Michigan 1976–78; Visiting Prof., PAMI (Summer Program) Coll. of Business Admin, Univ. of Hawaii, USA 1982–87, Faculty of Commerce and Business Admin, Univ. of British Columbia, Canada 1989; Visiting Scholar, Inst. of Developing Economies, Japan 1985–86; Scholar, Faculty of Econs, Univ. of Tokyo, Japan 1990–91; adviser, Korea Inst. for Int. Econ. Policy 1997–, Korea Devt Inst. 1997–; Policy Advisor, Ministry of Foreign Affairs and Trade 1993–2004; Chair. Advisory Bd Ministry of Educ. and Human Resources 2003–05, Cttee for Future Korea, Ministry of Information and Communication 2006–; Co-Chair. Nat. Fed. for Cooperation between Univ. and Industry 2006–; Vice-Chair. Nat. Econ. Advisory Council 2005–; Founding Pres. Korea Center for Int. Finance 1999–2000; Dir (non-resident) Korea Inst. for Public Finance 1996–99; mem. Monetary Bd Bank of Korea 1992–95; mem. Bd of Dirs Korea Devt Bank 1996–97, Korea First Bank 1998–99, Hyundai Corpn 1998–2002, CJ Home Shopping 1999–2003; mem. (Minister) Public Fund Oversight Comm. 2001–03; Pres. Korean Acad. of Int. Business 1992–93, Korea Money and Finance Asscn 1995–96, Korean Academic Soc. of Business Admin 2002–03; Hon. Prof., Jilin Univ. 2005, Nanjing Univ. 2006; Hon. Fellow, Royal Holloway, Univ. of London 2005; Hon. LLD (Weseda Univ.) 2005; Hon. PhD (Yonsei Univ.) 2006; Hon. DUniv (Griffith Univ.); Asian Inst. of Man. Triple A Award, A Merit, Les Insignes de Chevalier de l'Ordre nat. du Mérite, Global CEO Award 2006. *Address:* College of Business Administration, University of Korea, Anam-dong, Sungbuk-gu, Seoul 136-701, South Korea (office). *Telephone:* (2) 3290-1916 (office). *Fax:* (2) 395-1976 (office). *E-mail:* ydeuh@korea.ac.kr (office). *Website:* www.korea.ac.kr (office).

EUSTACE, Arnhim Ulric; Saint Vincent and the Grenadines economist and politician; *President, New Democratic Party;* b. 1946; economist specializing in fiscal man.; fmr Minister of Finance; Prime Minister of Saint Vincent and the Grenadines 2000–01; Pres. New Democratic Party (NDP) 2000–. *Address:* New Democratic Party, Murray Road, PO Box 1300, Kingstown, Saint Vincent and the

Grenadines (office). *Telephone:* 456-2114 (office). *Fax:* 457-2647 (office). *E-mail:* ndp@caribsurf.com (office). *Website:* www.ndpsvg.com (office).

EUSTACE, Dudley Graham (D. G.), BA; British business executive; *Operating Partner, Tri-Artisan Capital Partners, LLC;* b. 3 July 1936; m. Carol Diane Zakrajsek; two c.; ed Univ. of Bristol; with John Barrit & Son, Hamilton, Bermuda 1962; with Int. Resort Facilities 1963; exec. positions with Alcan Aluminium Ltd in various locations including Montreal, Vancouver, Buenos Aires, Rio de Janeiro, Madrid and UK 1964–87; joined British Aerospace plc 1987, Financial Dir 1988–92; mem. Group Cttee, Royal Philips Electronics NV 1992–2001, Exec. Vice-Pres. and Chief Financial Officer 1993–97, Vice-Chair. Bd of Man. 1997–99; Deputy Chair. Smith & Nephew PLC 1999–2000, Chair. (non-exec.) 2000–06; mem. Supervisory Bd AEGON NV 1997–2010, Vice-Chair. –2005, Chair. 2005–10, fmr Chief Financial Officer AEGON Canadian NV; Operating Partner, Tri-Artisan Capital Partners, LLC; Exec. Vice-Pres. and mem. Corp. Exec. Bd Koninklijke Ahold NV (fmrly Royal Ahold) 2003–, Interim Chief Financial Officer March–June 2003; Chair. Supervisory Bd The Nielsen Company (mem. 2006–); Vice-Chair. Supervisory Bd Royal KPN NV 2001– (mem. 2000–), Hagemeyer NV (mem. 1999–); fmr Chief Financial Officer Hagemeijer NV, Royal KPN NV (fmrly Koninklijke KPN NV), Smith and Nephew PLC, Sendo Holdings PLC, Sonae.-com.SGPS, W&S Nederland BV; mem. Supervisory Bd KLM Royal Dutch Airlines 1999–, Hagemeyer NV 2001–, Stork NV 2007–, European Advisory Council of Rothschilds; mem. Export Guarantees Advisory Council, UK 1988, European Advisory Council for Rothschilds; mem. Bd Sonae.Com SGPS S.A. of Portugal, Council of Univ. of Surrey. *Address:* Tri-Artisan Capital Partners, LLC, 110 East 59th Street, 37th Floor, New York, NY 10022, USA (office). *Telephone:* (212) 610-1500 (office). *Fax:* (212) 610-1501 (office). *E-mail:* contact@tri-artisan.com (office). *Website:* www.tri-artisanpartners.com (office).

EVAN, Gerard, BA, MA, PhD, FRS, FMedSci; British/American biomedical scientist, cancer researcher and academic; *Sir William Dunn Professor of Biochemistry, University of Cambridge;* b. 17 Aug. 1955, London, England; s. of Robert Evan and Gwendoline Evan (née Groom); m.; one s. one d.; ed Univs of Oxford and Cambridge, UK, Univ. of California, San Francisco, USA; MRC Lab. of Molecular Biology, Univ. of Cambridge 1977–82, Research Fellowship, Downing Coll. Cambridge 1984–88, Asst Prof., Ludwig Inst. for Cancer Research, Cambridge 1984–88, Sir William Dunn Prof. of Biochemistry, Univ. of Cambridge 2009–, Fellow of Christ's Coll. 2010–; Dept of Microbiology and Immunology, Univ. of California, San Francisco 1982–84, Gerson and Barbara Bass Bakar Distinguished Prof. of Cancer Biology 1999–2009; Prin. Scientist, Imperial Cancer Research Fund 1988–99; Royal Soc. Napier Research Prof., Univ. Coll., London 1996–99, George Daniel Brooks Lectureship in Oncology 2010; mem. Scientific Advisory Bd EISAI London Research Labs 1994–97, Oxagen Inc. 1997–99, ESBA Tech 1998–2007, Genomic Health Inc.; Consultant Cantab Pharmaceuticals Ltd 1994–99, Ontogeny Inc., Boston 1998–2000, Cambridge Antibody Tech. Inc. 1998–99, Amersham/Nycomed 1998–99; mem. Scientific Review Bd DNAX 1998–2006, Oncology Advisory Bd Astra-Zeneca; mem. European Acad. of Sciences, European Molecular Biology Org.; Pfizer Prize in Biology 1995, Royal Soc. Napier Research Prof. of Cancer Biology 1996, Joseph Steiner Prize, Swiss Oncological Soc. 1997, Royal Soc. Wolfson Foundation Research Award 2009, Marguerite Vogt Lecturer, Salk Inst. 2010. *Radio includes:* participation in numerous science programmes for BBC. *Publications:* numerous academic publs. *Leisure interests:* sailing, music, white water rafting, hiking, skiing. *Address:* Sanger Building, Department of Biochemistry, 80 Tennis Court Road, Cambridge, CB2 1GA, England (office). *Telephone:* (1223) 765944 (office). *Fax:* (1223) 766082 (office). *E-mail:* gie20@cam.ac.uk (office). *Website:* www.bioc.cam.ac.uk/uto/evan .html (office).

EVANGELISTA, Linda; Canadian model; b. St Catharines, Ont.; m. Gerald Marie (divorced 1993); ome s. with Francois-Henri Pinault; face of L'Oréal, Paris; numerous catwalk fashion shows. *Address:* c/o dna Model Management, 520 Broadway, 11th Floor, New York, NY 10012, USA (office). *Telephone:* (212) 226-0080 (ext. 4) (office). *E-mail:* info@dnamodels.com (office). *Website:* www .dnamodels.com (office).

EVANGELOU, Alecos C., Barrister-at-Law; Cypriot lawyer; *Senior Partner, Alecos Evangelou and Co.;* b. 23 July 1939, Kato Lakatamia; s. of Costas Evangelou and Theano A. Tsiappa; m. Nicoulla Protopapa 1965; one s. two d.; ed English School, Nicosia and Gray's Inn, London; called to the Bar, Gray's Inn, London 1967; worked in Nicosia Dist Admin., later at Ministry of Finance 1957–72; law officer, Attorney, Office of Attorney-Gen. 1972–93; fmr Chair. Appropriate Authority for Intellectual Property; fmr Pres. Supreme Sports Tribunal; Minister of Justice and Public Order 1993–97; now Sr Partner Alecos Evangelou and Co. (law firm); del. to several UN, European and Commonwealth confs; Chair. two Commonwealth Ministerial Confs; fmr Chair. Cyprus Radio-TV Authority; Deputy Gov. American Biographical Inst., Inc. *Publications:* legal studies and manuals on matters of public and private law. *Leisure interest:* gardening. *Address:* PO Box 29238, Nicosia 1623, Cyprus (office). *Telephone:* (22) 879999 (office). *Fax:* (22) 879990 (office). *E-mail:* evangelou@evangelou.com.cy (office).

EVANS, Daniel Jackson, MS; American consultant and fmr politician; *Chairman, Daniel J. Evans Associates;* b. 16 Oct. 1925, Seattle, Wash.; s. of Daniel Lester and Irma Evans (née Ide); m. Nancy Ann Bell 1959; three s.; ed Roosevelt High School, Seattle and Univ. of Washington; USNR 1943–46; Lt on active duty Korean War 1951–53; Asst Man. Mountain Pacific, Assoc. Gen. Contractors 1953–59; State Rep. King County 1956–64; Pnr, Gray and Evans (structural and civil engineers) 1959–64; Gov. Washington State 1965–77; Chair. Western Govs Conf. 1968–69, Nat. Govs Conf. 1973–74; Senator from Washington 1983–89; mem. Advisory Comm. on Intergovernmental Relations 1972, Trilateral Comm. 1973; Keynote Speaker, Republican Nat. Convention 1968; mem. Pres.'s Vietnamese Refugee Comm. 1974; mem. Nat. Center for Productivity and Quality of Working Life 1975–76; mem. Carnegie Council on Policy Studies in Higher Educ. 1977; mem. Univ. of Washington Bd of Regents 1993–2005 (Pres. 1996–97); Trustee, Urban Inst. 1977, Carnegie Foundation for the Advancement of Teaching 1977; Pres. Evergreen State Coll. 1977–83; Chair. Daniel J. Evans Assocs (consulting firm), Seattle 1998–; mem. Bd of Dirs NIC Inc., Archimedes Technology Group, Costco Wholesale Corpn 2003–; mem. Univ. of Washington Bd of Regents 1993–2005, Vice-Pres. 1995–96, Pres. 1996–97; Republican; several hon. degrees;

Nat. Municipal League Distinguished Citizen Award 1977. *Leisure interests:* skiing, sailing, mountain climbing. *Address:* Daniel J. Evans Associates, 4000 NE 41st Street, Seattle, WA 98105-5428, USA. *Telephone:* (206) 525-9090.

EVANS, David (see (The) Edge).

EVANS, David Albert, AB, PhD, FRSC; American chemist and academic; *Arthur and Ruth W. Sloan Research Professor of Chemistry, Harvard University;* b. 11 Jan. 1941, Washington, DC; m. Selena Anne Welliver 1962; one d.; ed Oberlin Coll., California Inst. of Tech.; Asst Prof. of Chem., UCLA 1967–72, Assoc. Prof. 1972–73, Prof. 1974; Prof. of Chem., Calif. Inst. of Tech. 1974–83; Prof. of Chem., Harvard Univ. 1983–90, Abbott and James Lawrence Prof. of Chem. 1990–, Chair. Dept of Chem. and Chemical Biology 1995–98, Arthur and Ruth W. Sloan Research Prof. 1999–; Consultant, Upjohn Co. 1972–74, Eli Lilly Co. 1974–89, Merck Research Lab. 1989–2008, Oxford Asymmetry Ltd 1994–2001, UK 1994–2001, Bristol-Myers Squibb Pharmaceuticals Co. 1994–2002, Amgen 2002–; visiting lecturer at numerous int. univs; mem. NAS 1984–, American Acad. of Arts and Sciences 1988–; mem. Editorial Bd Journal of the American Chemical Society 1983–88, Topics in Stereochemistry 1989–, Chemical Reviews 1993–96, Organic Letters 1999–; Fellow, Alfred P. Sloan Foundation 1972–74, AAAS 1992–; Hon. MA (Harvard) 1983; numerous awards including Phila Organic Chemists Club Allen R. Day Award 1984, ACS Arthur C. Cope Scholar Award 1988, Ohio State Univ. Mack Award 1992, Univ. of Neb. C. S. Hamilton Award 1992, ACS Remsen Award 1996, Univ. of Tokyo Yamada Prize 1997, Royal Soc. of Chem. Robert Robinson Award 1998, Tetrahedron Prize 1998, Eidgenossische Technische Hochschule Prelog Medal 1999, ACS Arthur C. Cope Award 2000, Nagoya Medal, Nagoya Univ., Japan, 2003, Karl Ziegler Prize 2003, Willard Gibbs Award 2005, Ryoji Noyori Prize 2006, ACS Herbert C. Brown Award for Creative Research in Synthetic Methods 2007, Welch Prize in Chem. 2012, ACS Roger Adams Award 2013. *Address:* Department of Chemistry and Chemical Biology, Harvard University, 12 Oxford Street, Cambridge, MA 02138, USA (office). *Telephone:* (617) 495-2948 (office). *Fax:* (617) 495-1460 (office). *E-mail:* evans@chemistry.harvard .edu (office). *Website:* www2.lsdiv.harvard.edu/labs/evans (office); evans.harvard .edu/problems/index.cgi (office).

EVANS, Donald Louis, BEng, MBA; American oil industry executive and fmr government official; *Chairman, Energy Future Holdings Corporation;* b. 27 July 1946, Houston; m. Susie Marinis; three c.; ed Univ. of Texas; joined Tom Brown Inc. 1975, Pres. 1979, Chair. and CEO 1985–2001; advisor to George W. Bush's political campaigns, Nat. Finance Chair. 1999, Chair. Bush/Cheney campaign 2000; Sec. of Commerce 2001–05 (resgnd); CEO Financial Services Forum 2005–; Chair. Energy Future Holdings Corpn (fmrly TXU Corpn) 2007–; mem. Univ. of Tex. System Bd of Regents 1995–2001, Chair. 1997–2001; Chair. United Way of Midland 1981, Pres. 1989; Chair. Beefeaters Ball, Midland Cerebral Palsy Center; mem. YMCA of Midland Metropolitan Bd 1988–94, Bd of Govs, Bynum School; mem. Bd of Dirs The Gladney Fund 1992–96, Scleroma Research Foundation 1992–2000, Young Presidents Org., Omicron Delta Kappa Soc., Texas Cowboys; mem. Midland Chamber of Commerce; mem. Exec. Cttee Young Life, Bd; Trustee, Memorial Hosp. and Medical Center; Hon. DHumLitt (Univ. of South Carolina) 2001; Midland Jaycees Distinguished Service Award and Boss of the Year 1980, Univ. of Texas at Austin Distinguished Alumni Awards (School of Eng) 1997, 2002, (McCombs School of Business) 2002, Nat. Foreign Trade Council World Trade Award 2002. *Leisure interest:* golf. *Address:* Energy Future Holdings Corporation, Energy Plaza, 1601 Bryan Street, Dallas, TX 75201, USA (office). *Telephone:* (214) 812-4600 (office). *Website:* www.energyfutureholdings.com (office).

EVANS, Hon. Gareth John, AC, QC, LLB, MA; Australian international organization official and fmr politician; *Chancellor, Australian National University;* b. 5 Sept. 1944, Melbourne, Vic.; s. of the late Allan O. Evans and Phyllis Evans (née Le Boeuf); m. Merran Anderson 1969; one s. one d.; ed Univ. of Melbourne, Magdalen Coll., Oxford; Lecturer and Sr Lecturer in Law, Univ. of Melbourne 1971–76; mem. Australian Reform Comm. 1975; Barrister-at-Law 1977–; Senator for Victoria 1978–96; Shadow Attorney-Gen. 1980–83; Attorney-Gen. 1983–84; Minister for Resources and Energy, Minister Assisting the Prime Minister and Minister Assisting the Minister for Foreign Affairs 1984–87; Minister for Transport and Communications 1987–88, for Foreign Affairs 1988–96; Deputy Leader of Govt in the Senate 1987–93, Leader 1993–96; MP for Holt, Vic. 1996–99; Deputy Leader of Opposition, Shadow Treas. 1996–98; Pres. and Chief Exec. Int. Crisis Group 2000–09, Pres. Emer. 2009–; Professorial Fellow, Univ. of Melbourne 2009–12; Chancellor ANU 2010–; Co-Chair. Int. Comm. on Intervention and State Sovereignty 2000–01, Int. Comm. on Nuclear Non-Proliferation and Disarmament 2008–10; mem. UN Sec.-Gen.'s High Level Panel on Threat, Challenges and Change 2003–04, Weapons of Mass Destruction Comm. 2004–06; Hon. Fellow, Magdalen Coll., Oxford 2004–; Hon. FASSA 2012; Chilean Order of Merit (Grand Cross) 1999; Hon. LLD (Melbourne) 2002, (Carleton Univ., Canada) 2005, (Sydney) 2008, (Queen's Univ., Canada) 2010; Australian Humanist of the Year 1990, ANZAC Peace Prize 1994, Grawemeyer Award for Ideas Improving World Order 1995, Roosevelt Inst. Freedom from Fear Award 2010, cited by Foreign Policy magazine one of the Top 100 Global Thinkers for 2011. *Publications:* Labor and the Constitution 1972–75 (ed.) 1977, Law, Politics and the Labor Movement (ed.) 1980, Labor Essays 1980, 1981, 1982 (co-ed.), Australia's Constitution: Time for Change? (co-author) 1983, Australia's Foreign Relations (co-author) 1991, Co-operating for Peace 1993, The Responsibility to Protect 2008, Nuclear Weapons: The State of Play (co-ed.) 2013. *Leisure interests:* reading, writing, football, travel. *Address:* ANU House Level 11, 52 Collins Street, Melbourne, Vic. 3000, Australia (office). *Telephone:* (3) 9639-8197 (office). *Fax:* (3) 9639-8203 (office). *E-mail:* ge@gevans.org (office). *Website:* www.gevans.org (office).

EVANS, Sir Harold Matthew, Kt, KBE, MA; American (b. British) author, publisher, fmr newspaper editor and author; b. 28 June 1928, Manchester, England; s. of the late Frederick and Mary Evans; m. 1st Enid Parker 1953 (divorced 1978); one s. two d.; m. 2nd Tina Brown (q.v.) 1982; one s. one d.; ed St Mary's Road Central School, Loreburn Coll., Manchester, Durham Univ.; Commonwealth Fund Fellow, Univ. of Chicago 1956–57; Lecturer, Workers' Education Asscn 1959; Ed. Sunday Times, London 1967–81; The Times 1981–82; mem. Bd Times Newspapers Ltd, Dir 1978–82; Int. Press Inst. 1974–80; Dir Goldcrest Films and Television 1982–85; Visiting Prof., Duke Univ. 1983; Ed.-in-Chief Atlantic

Monthly 1984–86, Contributing Ed. 1986–, Editorial Dir and Vice-Chair. 1998–; Ed. Dir U.S. News and World Report 1984–86, Contributing Ed. 1986–, Editorial Dir and Vice-Chair. 1998, currently Editor at Large, The Week; Vice-Pres. and Sr Ed. Weidenfeld and Nicolson 1986–87; Adviser to Chair. Condé Nast Publications 1986–; Founding Ed.-in-Chief, Condé Nast Traveler 1986–90; Pres. and Publr Random House Adult Trade Group 1990–97; Editorial Dir Mortimer Zuckerman's media properties 1997–; Editorial Dir and Vice-Chair. New York Daily News Inc. 1998–99, Fast Co. 1998–; Poynter Fellow, Yale Univ.; author, Little, Brown and Co., NY 2000–; writer and presenter A Point of View (BBC Radio 4) 2005–; Fellow, Soc. Industrial Artists, Inst. of Journalists; Hon. Visiting Prof., Journalism City Univ. 1978; Dr hc (Stirling) 1982, (Teesside, London Inst.), Hon. DCL (Durham) 1998; Journalist of the Year Prize 1973, Int. Ed. of the Year Award 1975, Inst. of Journalists Gold Medal Award 1979; Design and Art Dir, Pres.'s Award 1981, Ed. of Year Award, Granada 1982, Hood Medal, Royal Photographic Soc. 1981, Press Photographers of GB Award 1986; Gold Award for Achievement, British Press Awards 2000, World Press Freedom Hero, Int. Press Inst. 2000. *Radio:* Point of View BBC; Breakfast at Barneys literary conversations. *Television:* They Made America (four-part series, WGBH), Shots in the America (four-part series, WGBH), Mayor of America (BBC), What the Papers Say. *Publications:* Active Newsroom 1964, Editing and Design, Newsman's English 1970, Newspaper Design 1971, Newspaper Headlines 1973, Newspaper Text 1973, We Learned to Ski (co-author) 1974, Freedom of the Press 1974, Pictures on a Page 1978, Suffer the Children (co-author), How We Learned to Ski 1983, Good Times, Bad Times 1983, Front Page History 1984, The American Century 1998, They Made America 2004, We the People 2007, My Paper Chase 2009. *Leisure interests:* music, table tennis, swimming. *Address:* Little, Brown and Co., 1271 Avenue of the Americas, New York, NY 10020, USA (office). *Telephone:* (646) 717-9543 (office); (212) 371-1193 (home). *Fax:* (212) 302-9671 (office); (212) 754-4273 (home). *E-mail:* cindyquillinan@gmail.com (office); harold371@aol.com. *Website:* sirharoldevans .com (office).

EVANS, Jill, BA (Hons), MPhil; British politician; *President, Plaid Cymru;* b. 8 May 1959, Ystrad Rhondda, Glamorgan, Wales; ed Tonypandy Grammar School, Univ. of Wales, Aberystwyth, Polytechnic of Wales, Trefforest (now Univ. of Glamorgan); worked as Research Asst at Polytechnic of Wales; Public Affairs Officer, Nat. Fed. of Women's Insts in Wales 1989–96; Wales Regional Organiser for CHILD – The Nat. Infertility Support Network 1997–99; elected to Rhondda Borough Council 1992–93, Mid-Glamorgan Co. Council 1993–96 and, following their abolition, to Rhondda Cynon Taf Council 1996–99; elected (Plaid Cymru) Alt. mem. Cttee of the Regions 1993–97; Chair. Plaid Cymru 1994–96, Vice-Pres. 2003–10, Pres. 2010–, Party Spokesperson for European and Int. Issues, Chair. CND Cymru; MEP (Plaid Cymru) for Wales 1999–, mem. Group of the Greens/ European Free Alliance (EFA), Pres. EFA and first Vice-Pres. Greens/EFA Group in European Parl., Vice-Chair. Cttee on Women's Rights and Equal Opportunities 1999–2004, mem. Cttee on the Environment, Public Health and Food Safety, Substitute mem. Cttee on Agric. and Rural Devt, Cttee on Women's Rights and Gender Equality, Del. for Relations with the Palestinian Legis. Council, Del. for Relations with Iraq; unsuccessful cand. in Rhondda constituency for Nat. Ass. for Wales election 2007; Assoc. mem. Glamorgan Women's Inst. *Leisure interests:* organic gardening, jigsaw puzzles. *Address:* European Parliament, Bâtiment Altiero Spinelli, 08H153, 60 rue Wiertz, 1047 Brussels, Belgium (office); 45 Heol Gelligaled, Ystrad, Rhondda Cynon Taf, CF41 7RQ, Wales. *Telephone:* (2) 284-51-03 (office). *Fax:* (2) 284-91-03 (office). *E-mail:* jill.evans@europarl.europa.eu (office). *Website:* www.europarl.europa.eu (home); www.plaidcymru.org (office); www.jillevans.net (office).

EVANS, John David Gemmill, MA, PhD, MRIA; British academic; *Professor of Logic and Metaphysics, Queen's University, Belfast;* b. 27 Aug. 1942, London; s. of John Desmond Evans and Babette Evans; m. Rosemary Ellis 1974; ed St Edward's School, Oxford, Queens' Coll., Cambridge; Research Fellow, Sidney Sussex Coll., Cambridge 1964–65, Fellow and Lecturer 1965–78; Visiting Prof., Duke Univ., NC 1972–73; Dean of Arts Faculty, Queen's Univ., Belfast 1986–89, Prof. of Logic and Metaphysics 1978–, Head of School of Philosophical Studies 2004–05; Dir of School of Philosophical and Anthropological Studies 1987–95; Bd mem. Arts Council of NI 1991–94; Council mem. Royal Inst. of Philosophy 1991–98; Chair. UK Nat. Cttee for Philosophy 1994–2003; mem. Exec. Cttee Int. Fed. of Philosophical Socs (FISP) 1988–, Aristotelian Soc. 1998–2001, Exec. Cttee British Philosophical Asscn 2003–05, Bureau Centrale, Asscn Int. des Professeurs de Philosophie 2000–. *Publications:* Aristotle's Concept of Dialectic 1977, Aristotle 1987, Moral Philosophy and Contemporary Problems 1987, Teaching Philosophy on the Eve of the Twenty-First Century 1997, Philosophy of Education (Proceedings of 21st World Congress of Philosophy vol. 4) 2006. *Leisure interests:* mountaineering, astronomy, travel, gardening. *Address:* School of Philosophical Studies, Queen's University, Room 101, 15 University Square, Belfast, BT7 1NN, Northern Ireland (office). *Telephone:* (28) 9097-3624 (office). *Fax:* (28) 9024-7895 (office). *E-mail:* jdg.evans@ qub.ac.uk (office). *Website:* www.qub.ac.uk/phil (office).

EVANS, Sir Jonathan, Kt, KCB; British government official; *Director General, Security Service (MI5);* b. 1958; ed Univ. of Bristol; joined Security Service (MI5) 1980, worked on counter-espionage investigations 1980–85, moved to Protective Security Policy Dept serving in posts related to Irish-related counter terrorism, Head of Security Service's Secr. and attachment to Home Office 1985–99, moved to Int. Terrorism Dept 1999, Dir of Int. Counter Terrorism 2001–05, Deputy Dir Gen. MI5 2005–07, Dir Gen. 2007–. *Address:* Office of the Director General, Security Service, PO Box 3255, London, SW1P 1AE, England (office). *Website:* www.mi5.gov .uk (office).

EVANS, Lloyd Thomas, AO, MAgrSci, DPhil, DSc, FRS; Australian botanist and agriculturist; b. 6 Aug. 1927, Wanganui, New Zealand; s. of Claude Evans and Gwendolyn Fraser; m. Margaret Newell 1954; two s. two d. (one deceased); ed Wanganui Collegiate School, Univ. of Canterbury, New Zealand and Brasenose Coll., Oxford; Rhodes Scholar 1951–54; Commonwealth Fund Fellow, Calif. Inst. of Tech. 1954–56; Research Scientist, Div. of Plant Industry, CSIRO 1956–, Chief 1971–78, now Hon. Research Scientist; NAS Pioneer Research Fellow, US Dept of Agric. 1963–64; Overseas Fellow, Churchill Coll., Cambridge 1969–70; Visiting Fellow, Wolfson Coll., Cambridge 1978; Pres. Australian Soc. of Plant Physiologists 1971–73, Australian and New Zealand Assen for the Advancement of Science

1976–77, Australian Acad. of Science 1978–82 (Fellow); mem. Bd of Trustees, Int. Foundation for Science, Stockholm 1982–87, Int. Rice Research Inst., Philippines 1984–89, Int. Centre for Improvement of Wheat and Maize 1990–95; mem. Norwegian Acad. of Science and Letters; Foreign Fellow, Indian Nat. Acad. of Agricultural Science; Hon. mem. Royal Soc., NZ, Royal Agric. Soc., England, Hon. Research Fellow, CSIRO Div. of Plant Industry 1992–; Hon. LLD (Canterbury) 1978; Bledisloe Medal 1974, Farrer Medal 1979, Adolph E. Gude Award and other awards and prizes. *Publications:* Environmental Control of Plant Growth 1963, The Induction of Flowering 1969, Crop Physiology 1975, Day-length and the Flowering of Plants 1975, Wheat Science – Today and Tomorrow 1981, Policy and Practice: Essays in Honour of Sir John Crawford 1987, Crop Evolution, Adaptation and Yield 1993, Feeding the Ten Billion: Plants and Population Growth 1998; over 200 research papers. *Leisure interests:* chopping wood, Charles Darwin, tennis. *Address:* 3 Elliott Street, Campbell, Canberra, ACT 2612, Australia. *Telephone:* (2) 477815. *E-mail:* Lloyd.Evans@csiro.au.

EVANS, Sir Martin John, Kt, PhD, ScD, FRS, FMedSci; British scientist and academic; *Chancellor, Cardiff University;* b. 1 Jan. 1941, Stroud, Glos., England; s. of Leonard Wilfred Evans and Hilary Joyce Evans (née Redman); m. Judith Clare Williams 1966; two s. one d.; ed St Dunstan's Coll. Catford and Christ's Coll. Cambridge; Research Asst Dept of Anatomy and Embryology, Univ. Coll. London 1963–66, Asst Lecturer 1966–69, Lecturer 1969–78; Univ. Lecturer, Dept of Genetics, Univ. of Cambridge 1978–91, Reader in Mammalian Genetics 1991, Prof. of Mammalian Genetics 1994–99; Prof. of Mammalian Genetics and Dir, School of Biosciences, Cardiff Univ. 1999–2007, Pres. Cardiff Univ. 2009–12, Chancellor 2012–; mem. Advisory Bd Faraday Inst. for Science and Religion 2009–; Hon. Fellow, St Edmund's Coll., Cambridge 2002, Hon. Mem. Biochemical Soc.; Hon. DSc (Mount Sinai School of Medicine) 2002; March of Dimes Prize in Developmental Biology 1999, Albert Lasker Basic Medical Research Award 2001, Miami Nature Biotechnology Winter Symposium Special Achievement Award 2003, Nobel Prize in Physiology or Medicine (with Mario Capecchi and Oliver Smithies) 2007, Copley Medal, Royal Soc. 2009, Gold Medal, Royal Soc. of Medicine 2009, UCL Prize Lecture in Clinical Science 2011, named amongst 10 Britons Who Changed Our World by The Independent newspaper, School of Biosciences building re-named the Sir Martin Evans Building in his honour 2013. *Publications:* more than 150 scientific publs. *Leisure interests:* family, golf. *Address:* Office of the Chancellor, Cardiff University, Main Building, Park Place, Cardiff, CF10 3AT, Wales (office). *Telephone:* (29) 2087-4879 (office). *E-mail:* EvansMJ@cardiff .ac.uk (office). *Website:* www.cardiff.ac.uk (office).

EVANS, Nicholas, BA; British author; b. Bromsgrove, Worcs., England; m. 2nd Charlotte Gordon Cumming; three s. one d.; ed Univ. of Oxford; previously journalist for Evening Chronicle, Newcastle upon Tyne and producer documentaries for London Weekend TV, writer and producer films for TV and cinema; now novelist. *Publications:* The Horse Whisperer 1995, The Loop 1998, The Smoke Jumper 2001, The Divide 2005, The Brave 2010. *Leisure interests:* tennis, skiing, books, cinema. *Address:* c/o AP Watt at United Agents LLP, 12–26 Lexington Street, London, W1F 0LE, England (office). *Telephone:* (20) 3214-0800 (office). *Fax:* (20) 3214-0801 (office). *E-mail:* info@unitedagents.co.uk (office); nicholas@ nicholasevans.com (office). *Website:* www.apwatt.co.uk (office); www .nicholasevans.com.

EVANS, Paul, BSc; British insurance industry executive; *CEO, AXA Sun Life;* b. 1965; m.; three c.; ed Imperial Coll., London; Dir PricewaterhouseCooper Insurance Div., London and Toronto, 1985–2000; joined AXA 2000, Group Finance Dir and mem. Bd AXA UK 2001–03, CEO AXA Sun Life 2003–; mem. Inst. of Chartered Accountants, Assen of British Insurers. *Address:* AXA Centre, POB 1810, Bristol BS99 5SN, England (office). *Website:* www.axa.co.uk (office).

EVANS, Sir Richard John, Kt, MA, DPhil, LittD, FBA, FRSL, FLSW, FRHistS; British historian and academic; *Regius Professor of History and President, Wolfson College, University of Cambridge;* b. 29 Sept. 1947, Woodford, Essex, England; s. of the late Ieuan Trefor Evans and of Evelyn Evans (née Jones); m. 1st Elín Hjaltadóttir 1976 (divorced 1993); m. 2nd Christine L. Corton 2004; two s.; ed Forest School, London, Jesus Coll., Oxford, St Antony's Coll., Oxford; Lecturer in History, Stirling Univ. 1972–76; Lecturer in European History, Univ. of East Anglia 1976–83, Prof. 1983–89; Prof. of History, Birkbeck Coll., London 1989–98, Vice-Master 1993–98, Acting Master 1997; Prof. of Modern History, Univ. of Cambridge 1998–, Regius Prof. of Modern History 2008–10, Regius Prof. of History 2010–, Chair. Faculty of History 2008–10, Fellow, Gonville and Caius Coll., Cambridge 1998–2010; Visiting Assoc. Prof. of European History, Columbia Univ., New York 1980; Fellow, Alexander von Humboldt Foundation, Free Univ. of Berlin 1981, Humanities Research Centre, ANU, Canberra, Australia 1986; Gresham Prof. of Rhetoric, Gresham Coll. 2009–; Pres. Wolfson Coll., Cambridge 2010–; Fellow, Learned Soc. of Wales; Hon. Fellow, Jesus Coll., Oxford 1998, Birkbeck Coll. 1999; Hon. LitD (London) 2012; Stanhope Historical Essay Prize 1969, Wolfson Literary Award for History 1987, William H. Welch Medal, American Assen for the History of Medicine 1988, Hamburg Civic Medal for Arts and Sciences 1993, Fraenkel Prize in Contemporary History 1994, History Honoree, Los Angeles Times Book Awards 2008, 2009. *Publications:* The Feminist Movement in Germany 1894–1933 1976, The Feminists 1977, Society and Politics in Wilhelmine Germany (ed.) 1978, Sozialdemokratie und Frauenemanzipation im deutschen Kaiserreich 1979, The German Family (co-ed.) 1981, The German Working Class (co-ed.) 1982, The German Peasantry (co-ed.) 1986, The German Unemployed (co-ed.) 1987, Death in Hamburg 1987, Comrades and Sisters 1987, Rethinking German History 1987, In Hitler's Shadow 1989, Kneipengespräche im Kaiserreich 1989, Proletarians and Politics 1990, Rituals of Retribution 1996, Rereading German History 1997, In Defence of History 1997, Tales from the German Underworld 1998, Lying about Hitler 2001, The Coming of the Third Reich 2003, The Third Reich in Power 2005, The Third Reich at War 2008, Cosmopolitan Islanders 2009; contrib. to scholarly journals, newspapers, magazines, radio and TV. *Leisure interests:* gardening, music (playing the piano), reading, travelling. *Address:* The President's Lodge, Wolfson College, Barton Road, Cambridge, CB3 9BB, England (office). *Telephone:* (1223) 335938 (office). *E-mail:* rje36@cam.ac.uk (office). *Website:* www.richardjevans.com.

EVANS, Robert J.; American actor and film producer; b. 29 June 1930, New York; s. of Josh Evans; m. 1st Ali McGraw (divorced); one s.; m. 2nd Phyllis George 1977

(divorced 1978); m. 3rd Catherine Oxenberg 1998 (annulled); m. 4th Leslie Ann Woodard 2002; child radio actor in more than 300 radio productions; partner in women's clothing firm Evan-Picone 1952–67; ind. producer at 20th Century-Fox 1966–76; Vice-Pres. (Production) Paramount Pictures Corpn 1966–69, Vice-Pres. (Worldwide Production) 1969–71, Exec. Vice-Pres. 1971–76 (resgnd); Prof. of Film, Brown Univ. 1976. *Films include:* as actor: The Man of 1000 Faces 1957, The Sun Also Rises 1957, The Fiend Who Walked the West 1958, The Best of Everything 1959; as producer: Chinatown 1974, Marathon Man 1976, Black Sunday 1977, Players 1979, Popeye 1980, Urban Cowboy 1980, Cotton Club 1984, The Two Jakes 1989, Sliver 1993, Jade 1995, The Phantom 1996, The Saint 1997, The Out of Towners 1999, How to Lose a Guy in 10 Days 2003. *Publication:* The Kid Stays in the Picture 1994.

EVANS, Robert John Weston, PhD, FBA; British historian and academic; *Regius Professor Emeritus of History, University of Oxford;* b. 7 Oct. 1943, Leicester; s. of T. F. Evans and M. Evans; m. Kati Robert 1969; one s. one d. (deceased); ed Dean Close School, Cheltenham and Jesus Coll., Cambridge; Research Fellow, Brasenose Coll., Oxford 1968–97, Univ. Lecturer in Modern History of East-Central Europe, Univ. of Oxford 1969–90, Reader 1990–92, Prof. of European History 1992–97, Regius Prof. of History 1997–2011, Emer. 2011–; Ed. English Historical Review 1985–95; Fellow, Hungarian Acad. of Sciences 1995, Austrian Acad. of Sciences 1997, Learned Soc. of Czech Repub. 2004; Ehrenkreuz für Kunst und Wissenschaft (Austria) 2010; Wolfson Literary Award for History 1980, Anton Gindely-Preis (Austria) 1986, František Palacký Medal (Czechoslovakia) 1991. *Publications:* Rudolf II and His World 1973, The Wechel Presses 1975, The Making of the Habsburg Monarchy 1979, The Coming of the First World War (co-ed) 1988, Crown, Church and Estates (co-ed) 1991, The Revolutions in Europe 1848–9 (ed.) 2000, Austria, Hungary, and the Habsburgs, c. 1683–1867 2006, Curiosity and Wonder from the Renaissance to the Enlightenment (co-ed) 2007, Czechoslovakia in a Nationalist and Fascist Europe 1918-48 (co-ed) 2007, Wales and the Wider World (co-ed) 2010, The Uses of the Middle Ages in Modern European States (co-ed) 2011, The Holy Roman Empire, 1495–1806 (co-ed) 2011. *Address:* Rowan Cottage, 45 Sunningwell, Abingdon, Oxon., OX13 6RD, England (home). *Telephone:* (1865) 736973 (office). *E-mail:* robert.evans@history.ox.ac.uk (office).

EVANS, Ronald M., BA, PhD; American biologist and academic; *March of Dimes Chair in Molecular and Developmental Biology, Professor and Director, Gene Expression Laboratory, Salk Institute for Biological Studies;* b. 17 April 1949, Los Angeles, Calif.; ed Univ. of California, Los Angeles; worked in Dept of Molecular Cell Biology, The Rockefeller Univ., New York 1975–78; Asst Research Prof., Tumor Virology Lab., Salk Inst. for Biological Studies, La Jolla, Calif. 1978–83, Assoc. Prof., Molecular Biology and Virology Lab. 1983–84, Sr Mem. 1984–86, Prof. and Dir Gene Expression Lab. 1986–, also March of Dimes Chair in Molecular and Developmental Biology, mem. Bd of Trustees 1990–94, 1996–99, Chair. Faculty 1993–94, 1997–98; Adjunct Prof., Dept of Biology, Univ. of California, San Diego 1985–, Adjunct Prof., Dept of Biomedical Sciences, School of Medicine 1989–, Adjunct Prof., Dept of Neuro-sciences 1995–; Investigator, Howard Hughes Medical Inst., Chevy Chase, MD 1985–; S. Richard Hill, Jr Visiting Prof., Univ. of Alabama 1995; Woodward Visiting Prof., Memorial Sloan-Kettering 1996; First Alvin Taurog Lectureship in Pharmacology, Southwestern Medical Center 1996; Burroughs Wellcome Visiting Prof., Univ. of Massachusetts 1998; Founder and Chair. Scientific Advisory Bd Ligand Pharmaceuticals 1988–; mem. Scientific Advisory Bd SIBIA 1983–, Nat. Advisory Cttee Pew Scholars Program in the Biomedical Sciences 1987–2000, External Scientific Advisory Bd Massachussets Gen. Hosp. 1996–, Scientific Advisory Bd Dana Farber Cancer Inst. 1996–, Scientific Advisory Bd Osaka Bioscience Inst. 1999–; Assoc. Ed. Molecular Brain Research 1985–93, Journal of Neuroscience 1985–90, Neuron 1987–93; Co-Ed. Current Opinion in Cell Biology 1993; Ed. Molecular Endocrinology 1993–97; mem. Editorial Bd Genes and Development 1992–, Hormones and Signalling (Academic Press series) 1996–; NIH Fellowship 1975–78; mem. NAS 1989, Inst. of Medicine 2004, American Asscn for Cancer Research, Harvey Soc., American Acad. of Microbiology, Soc. for Neuroscience, Soc. for Developmental Biology, Endocrine Soc.; Fellow, American Acad. of Microbiology 1993, American Acad. of Arts and Sciences 1997; Gregory Pincus Medal, Laurentian Soc. 1988, The Louis S. Goodman and Alfred Gilman Award, American Soc. for Pharmacology and Experimental Therapeutics 1988, Van Meter/Rorer Pharmaceuticals Prize, American Thyroid Asscn 1989, Eleventh C.P. Rhoads Memorial Award, American Asscn for Cancer Research 1990, Gregory Pincus Memorial Award, Worcester Foundation for Experimental Biology 1991, Rita Levi Montalcini Award, Fidia Research Foundation Neuroscience 1991, Osborne and Mendel Award, American Inst. of Nutrition 1992, Robert J. and Claire Pasarow Foundation Award for Cancer Research 1993, Edwin B. Astwood Lectureship Award, The Endocrine Soc. 1993, Transatlantic Medal, Soc. for Endocrinology 1994, California Scientist of the Year, California Museum of Science 1994, Dickson Prize in Medicine, Univ. of Pittsburgh 1994–95, Morton Lecture and Award, Biochemical Soc., Univ. of Liverpool, UK 1996, Gerald Aurbach Memorial Award, Asscn for Bone and Mineral Research 1997, Fred Conrad Koch Award, The Endocrine Soc. 1999, Bristol-Myers Squibb Award for Distinguished Achievement in Metabolic Research 2000, Lya and Harrison Latta Lecturer, UCLA 2000, Pezcoller International Award, American Asscn for Cancer Research 2001, Alfred P. Sloan Junior Prize, GM Cancer Research Foundation 2003, Albert Lasker Award for Basic Medical Research, Lasker Foundation 2004, Gairdner Foundation Int. Award 2006, Grande Médaille d'Or (France) 2005, Glenn T. Seaborg Medal 2005, Harvey Prize in Human Health 2006, Albany Medical Center Prize in Medicine and Biomedical Research (shared with Solomon H. Snyder and Robert J. Lefkowitz) 2007, Wolf Prize in Medicine 2012. *Publications:* more than 260 publs in scientific journals. *Address:* Salk Institute for Biological Studies, Howard Hughes Medical Institute, 10010 N Torrey Pines Road, La Jolla, CA 92037, USA (office). *Telephone:* (858) 453-4100 ext. 1302 (office). *Fax:* (858) 455-1349 (office). *E-mail:* evans@salk.edu (office). *Website:* www.salk.edu/faculty/evans.html (office).

EVANS, Stephen Nicholas, CMG, OBE, BA, MPhil; British diplomatist; b. 29 June 1950; s. of Vincent Morris Evans and Doris Mary Evans (née Braham); m. Sharon Ann Holdcroft 1975; one s. two d.; ed King's Coll., Taunton, Bristol Univ., Corpus Christi Coll., Univ. of Cambridge; Lt in Royal Tank Regt 1971–74; Third

Sec., FCO 1974–75, language student (Vietnamese), SOAS, London 1975, Second Sec., FCO 1976–78, First Sec., Hanoi 1978–80, FCO 1980–82, language training (Thai), Bangkok 1982–83, First Sec., Bangkok 1983–86, FCO 1986–90, First Sec. (Political), Ankara 1990, Counsellor (Econ., Commercial, Aid), Islamabad 1993–96, seconded to UN Special Mission to Afghanistan 1996–97, Counsellor and Head of OSCE and Council of Europe Dept, FCO 1997–98, Counsellor and Head of South Asian Dept 1998–2001, Chargé d'affaires, Kabul 2001–02, High Commr to Sri Lanka 2002–06, Amb. to Afghanistan 2006–07, Dir Afghanistan Information Strategy, FCO 2007–08, High Commr to Bangladesh 2008–11. *Leisure interests:* military, naval and South Asian history, cycling, golf. *Address:* Foreign and Commonwealth Office, King Charles Street, London, SW1A 2AH, England (office). *Telephone:* (20) 7008-1500 (office). *E-mail:* webmaster@fco.gov.uk (office). *Website:* www.gov.uk/government/organisations/foreign-commonwealth-office (office).

EVANS, Ted, AC, BEcon (Hons); Australian banking executive; *Chairman, Westpac Banking Corporation;* ed Queensland Univ.; began career in Postmaster-Gen.'s Dept, Ipswich, Queensland; joined Australian Treasury 1969, Deputy Sec. 1984–89, Sec. to Treasury 1993–2001, mem. Australian Perm. Del. to OECD, Paris 1976–79, Exec. Dir representing Australia, IMF 1989–93; Dir (Ind.) Westpac Banking Corpn 2001–, Chair. 2007–, Chair. Nominations Cttee; Dir Commonwealth Bank of Australia 1993–96, Reserve Bank of Australia 1993–2001, IBT Education Ltd 2004–08, Navitas Ltd; Hon. DUniv (Griffith). *Address:* Westpac Banking Corpn, Level 20, Westpac Place, 275 Kent Street, Sydney, NSW 2000, Australia (office). *Telephone:* (2) 8253-0390 (office). *Fax:* (2) 8253-1888 (office). *E-mail:* info@westpac.com.au (office). *Website:* www.westpac.com.au (office).

EVANS OF PARKSIDE, Baron (Life Peer), cr. 1997, of St Helens in the County of Merseyside; **John Evans;** British politician and engineer; b. 19 Oct. 1930; s. of the late James Evans and Margaret Evans (née Robson); m. Joan Slater 1959; two s. one d.; ed Jarrow Cen. School; apprentice marine fitter 1946–49, 1950–52; nat. service, Royal Engineers 1949–50; engineer, Merchant Navy 1952–55; joined Amalgamated Union of Eng Workers (later Amalgamated Eng Union) 1952; joined Labour Party 1955; worked as fitter in ship-building, steel and eng industries 1955–65, 1968–74; mem. Hebburn Union Dist Council 1962, Leader 1969, Chair. 1972; Sec./Agent Jarrow Co-operative Labour Party 1965–68; Labour MP for Newton 1974–83, for St Helens, North 1983–97; Asst Govt Whip 1978–79; Opposition Whip 1979–80; Parl. Pvt. Sec. to Leader of Labour Party 1980–83; Opposition Spokesman on Employment 1983–87; MEP 1975–78; Chair. Regional Policy, Planning and Transport Cttee 1976–78; mem. Labour Party Nat. Exec. Cttee 1982–96. *Leisure interests:* watching football, reading, gardening. *Address:* House of Lords, Westminster, London, SW1 0PW (office); 6 Kirkby Road, Culcheth, Warrington, Cheshire, WA3 4BS, England (home). *Telephone:* (20) 7219-6541 (office).

EVANS OF TEMPLE GUITING, Baron (Life Peer), cr. 2000, in the County of Gloucestershire; **Matthew Evans,** CBE, BSc Econs, FRSA; British publishing executive; b. 7 Aug. 1941; s. of the late George Ewart Evans and Florence Ellen Evans; m. 1st Elizabeth Amanda Mead 1966 (divorced 1991); two s.; m. 2nd Caroline Michel 1991; two s. one d.; ed Friends' School, Saffron Walden and LSE; bookselling 1963–64; with Faber & Faber 1964–, Man. Dir 1972–93, Chair. 1981; Chair. Nat. Book League 1982–84, English Stage Co. 1984–90; mem. Council, Publishers' Asscn 1978–84; Gov. BFI 1982–97, Vice-Chair. 1996–97; Chair. Library and Information Comm. 1995–99; Govt Whip, House of Lords 2002–07; Govt Spokesperson for Office of the Deputy Prime Minister 2002–03, Justice/Lord Chancellor's Dept (Scotland and Wales) 2003–07, Trade and Industry 2003–04, Work and Pensions 2005–07, Treasury 2005–07, Cabinet Office 2007, Culture, Media and Sport 2007, Trade and Industry/Business, Enterprise and Regulatory Reform 2007, Environment, Food and Rural Affairs 2007, Opposition Spokesperson for Culture, Media and Sport 2010–; Chair. EFG Private Bank; Chair. Museums, Libraries and Archives Council 2000–02; Dir Which? Ltd 1997–; Vice-Pres. Hay Literary Festival, Philip Larkin Soc.; mem. Arts Council Nat. Lottery Advisory Panel 1997–99, Univ. for Industry Advisory Group 1997, Royal Opera House Working Group 1997, Arts and Humanities Research Bd 1998–; mem. Franco-British Soc. 1981–; Founder mem. Groucho Club (Dir 1982–97); Hon. FRCA 1999; Hon. FLA 1999. *Leisure interest:* cricket. *Address:* c/o House of Lords, London SW1A 0PW, England (office). *Telephone:* (20) 7219-6631 (office). *E-mail:* evansm@parliament.uk (office).

EVATT, The Hon. Elizabeth Andreas, AC, LLB, LLM; Australian lawyer and human rights expert; *Commissioner, International Commission of Jurists;* b. 11 Nov. 1933, Sydney, NSW; d. of Clive R. Evatt and Marjorie H. Evatt (née Andreas); m. Robert Southan 1960; one d.; ed Univ. of Sydney and Harvard Univ.; called to Bar, Inner Temple; Chief Judge Family Court of Australia 1976–88; Deputy Pres. Conciliation and Arbitration Comm. 1973–89, Australian Industrial Relations Comm. 1989–94; Pres. Australian Law Reform Comm. 1988–93, mem. 1993–94; mem. UN Cttee on Elimination of Discrimination Against Women 1984–92, Chair. 1989–91; Chancellor, Univ. of Newcastle 1988–94; reviewed Aboriginal and Torres Strait Islander Heritage Protection Act 1984; Hearing Commr (part-time), Human Rights and Equal Opportunity Comm. 1995–98; mem. UN Human Rights Cttee 1993–2000, World Bank Admin. Tribunal 1998–2006, Commr Int. Comm. of Jurists 2003–; fmr Hon. Visiting Prof., Univ. of New South Wales Law School; fmr Chair. Public Interest Advocacy Centre, Sydney; Australian Human Rights Medal 1995. *Address:* Unit 2003, 184 Forbes Street, Darlinghurst, NSW 2010, Australia (home). *E-mail:* eevatt@bigpond.net.au (office).

EVE, Trevor John; British actor; b. 1 July 1951, Sutton Coldfield, Warwicks. (now West Midlands), England; s. of Stewart Frederick Eve and Elsie Eve (née Hamer); m. Sharon Patricia Maughan 1980; two s. one d.; ed Bromsgrove School, Kingston Art Coll., Royal Acad. of Dramatic Art; best known for playing the eponymous detective in BBC series Shoestring and for playing Detective Supt Peter Boyd in BBC series Waking the Dead; Patron, Childhope International. *Theatre includes:* Children of a Lesser God (Olivier Award for Best Actor 1982) 1981, The Genius 1983, High Society 1986, Man Beast and Virtue 1989, The Winter's Tale 1991, Inadmissible Evidence 1993, Uncle Vanya (Olivier Award for Best Supporting Actor 1997) 1996. *Films include:* Children (short) 1976, Dracula 1979, The Terence Davies Trilogy 1983, Scandal 1989, In the Name of the Father (short) 1992, Aspen Extreme 1993, Don't Get Me Started 1994, Soup (short) 1996, Next Birthday (short) 1998, The Tribe 1998, Appetite 1998, Possession 2002, Troy

2004, She's Out of My League 2010. *Television includes:* 2nd House (series) 1974, Hindle Wakes (film) 1976, Sunday Night Drama (series) 1977, London Belongs to Me (series) 1977, Shoestring (series) 1979–80, Jamaica Inn (film) 1983, A Brother's Tale (film) 1983, Lace (film) 1984, The Corsican Brothers (film) 1985, Shadow Chasers (series) 1985, A Wreath of Roses (film) 1987, Life on the Flipside (film) 1988, Beryl Markham: A Shadow on the Sun (film) 1988, Dear John USA (series) 1989, The Stone Age (film) 1989, A Sense of Guilt (series) 1990, Coup de foudre (series) 1990, Parnell & the Englishwoman (mini-series) 1991, Murder, She Wrote (series) 1992, A Doll's House (film) 1992, Jack's Place (series) 1992, The President's Child (film) 1992, Murder in Mind (film) 1994, The Politician's Wife (series) 1995, No Man's Land (film) 1995, Ivana Trump's For Love Alone (film) 1996, Heat of the Sun (mini-series) 1998, An Evil Streak (series) 1999, Doomwatch: Winter Angel (film) 1999, David Copperfield (film) 1999, Waking the Dead (series) 2000–11, Lawless (film) 2004, The Family Man (film) 2006, Hughie Green, Most Sincerely (film) 2008, Framed (film) 2009, Bouquet of Barbed Wire (series) 2010, Kidnap and Ransom (series) 2011–12, The Farmer (film) 2013. *Leisure interests:* golf, tennis, squash, painting. *Address:* c/o Independent Talent Group Ltd, Oxford House, 76 Oxford Street, London, W1D 1BS, England (office). *Telephone:* (20) 7434-1110 (office); (20) 7636-6565 (office). *Fax:* (20) 7323-0101 (office). *E-mail:* jojacob9@googlemail.com (office); info@independenttalent.com (office). *Website:* www.independenttalent.com (office).

EVENO, Bertrand; French publishing executive; b. 26 July 1944, Egletons; s. of Jean-Jacques Eveno and Suzanne Gavoille; m. 2nd Brigitte Pery 1984; five d. (three d. from previous m.); ed Lycée Condorcet and Law Faculty, Paris; Treasury Inspector 1973–77; Tech. Consultant to Health Minister 1977–78; Cabinet Dir for Minister of Culture and Communication 1978–81; mem. Atomic Energy Comm. Control Bd 1981–83; Deputy Gen. Man. André Shoe Co. 1984–86; Chair. Editions Fernand Nathan 1987–2000; Pres. Conseil d'admin., Fondation nationale de la photographie 1981–95, Gens d'Image 1986–2000; Chair. Larousse-Nathan Int. 1988–90, Le Robert dictionaries 1989–2000, Editions Masson 1995–98; Dir-Gen. Groupe de la Cité 1988–2000, Presses de la Cité 1991–95; Pres., Dir-Gen. Larousse-Bordas 1996–2000; Pres., Dir-Gen. Havas Educ. et Référence 1999–2000; Dir Anaya Groupe 1999–2000; Pres. Agence France Presse 2000–05; apptd Dir-Gen. Hachette Filipacchi Photos (includes agencies Gamma, Rapho, Hoa-Who, Keystone) (known as Eyedea 2007–10, taken over 2010) 2005; Pres. Literary Soc. of Friends of Emile Zola 2009–; Chair. Cttee on Cinema Arthouse, Nat. Centre for Cinematography 2009–. *Publication:* monograph on Willy Ronis in Les grands photographes 1983. *Address:* Committee on Cinema Arthouse, National Centre for Cinematography, 12 rue de Lubeck, 75116 Paris, France (office).

EVERED, David Charles, MD, FRCP, FIBiol; British scientific administrator and physician; b. 21 Jan. 1940, Beaconsfield; s. of the late Thomas C. Evered and Enid C. Evered; m. 1st Anne Lings 1964 (died 1998); one s. two d.; m. 2nd Sheila Pusinelli 2000; ed Cranleigh School, Surrey and Middlesex Hosp. Medical School; jr hosp. appointments London and Leeds 1964–70; First Asst in Medicine, Wellcome Sr Research Fellow and Consultant Physician, Univ. of Newcastle-upon-Tyne and Royal Vic. Infirmary 1970–78; Dir The Ciba Foundation, London 1978–88; Second Sec., MRC, London 1988–96, Consultant 1996–; mem. Council Int. Agency for Research into Cancer 1988–96, Royal Post grad. Medical School 1994–96, Bd Hammersmith Hosps Nat. Health Service (NHS) Trust 1995–96, numerous cttees, socs and other professional bodies; Chair. NOC NHS Trust 1998–2001; Special Adviser Int. Agency for Research on Cancer, WHO, Lyon, France 2001–03. *Publications:* Diseases of the Thyroid 1976, Atlas of Endocrinology (with R. Hall and R. Greene) 1979, Collaboration in Medical Research in Europe (with M. O'Connor) 1981; numerous papers in professional journals. *Leisure interests:* reading, history, tennis, music. *Address:* Old Rectory Farm, Rectory Road, Padworth Common, Berks., RG7 4JD, England (home). *E-mail:* david_evered@hotmail.com (home).

EVERETT, Rupert; British actor; b. 29 May 1960, Norfolk; ed Ampleforth School and Cen. School for Speech and Drama, London; apprenticed with Glasgow Citizen's Theatre 1979–82; has modelled for Versace, Milan; sometime image of Opium perfume for Yves Saint Laurent. *Stage appearances include:* Another Country 1982, The Vortex 1989, Private Lives, The Milk Train Doesn't Stop Here Anymore, The Picture of Dorian Gray 1993, The Importance of Being Earnest 1996, Some Sunny Day 1996. *Films include:* A Shocking Accident 1982, Another Country 1984, Dance with a Stranger 1985, The Right Hand Man 1985, Duet for One 1986, Chronicle of Death Foretold 1987, Hearts of Fire 1987, Haunted Summer 1988, The Comfort of Strangers 1990, Inside Monkey Zetterland 1992, Pret à Porter 1994, The Madness of King George 1995, Dunston Checks In 1996, My Best Friend's Wedding 1997, A Midsummer Night's Dream 1998, B Monkey 1998, An Ideal Husband 1999, Inspector Gadget 1999, The Next Best Thing 2000, Unconditional Love 2002, The Importance of Being Earnest 2002, To Kill a King 2003, Stage Beauty 2004, Separate Lies 2005, The Chronicles of Narnia: The Lion, the Witch and the Wardrobe (voice) 2005, Shrek the Third (voice) 2007, Stardust 2007, St Trinian's 2007, Wild Target 2010. *Television includes:* Arthur the King, The Far Pavilions 1982, Princess Daisy 1983, Mr Ambassador 2003, Sherlock Holmes and the Case of the Silk Stocking 2004, Boston Legal 2005, Who Do You Think You Are? 2010. *Publications:* Hello Darling, Are You Working? 1992, The Hairdressers of St Tropez 1995, Red Carpets and Other Banana Skins (autobiog.) 2006. *Address:* c/o William Stein, ICM, 8942 Wilshire Boulevard, Beverly Hills, CA 90211-1934, USA (office). *Telephone:* (310) 550-4000 (office). *E-mail:* film@icmtalent.com (office).

EVERITT, Anthony Michael, BA; British writer, academic and fmr arts organization administrator; b. 31 Jan. 1940, Hunstanton, Norfolk, England; s. of the late Michael Everitt and Simone Vergriette; ed Cheltenham Coll. and Corpus Christi Coll. Cambridge; Lecturer, Nat. Univ. of Iran, SE London Coll. of Further Educ., Birmingham Coll. of Art, Trent Polytechnic 1963–72; Art Critic, The Birmingham Post 1970–75, Drama Critic 1974–79, Features Ed. 1976–79; Dir Midland Group Arts Centre, Nottingham 1979–80, E Midlands Arts Asscn 1980–85; Chair. Ikon Gallery, Birmingham 1976–79, Birmingham Arts Lab. 1977–79; Vice-Chair. Council of Regional Arts Asscns 1984–85; mem. Drama Panel, Arts Council of GB 1974–78, Regional Cttee 1979–80; mem. Cttee for Arts and Humanities, Council for Nat. Academic Awards 1986–87, Performing Arts Cttee 1987–92; mem. Gen. Advisory Council, IBA 1987–90; Deputy Sec.-Gen. Arts

Council of GB 1985–90, Sec.-Gen. 1990–94; Visiting Prof. in Visual and Performing Arts, Nottingham Trent Univ. 1996–2006; Hon. Fellow, Dartington Coll. of Arts 1995; Companion, Liverpool Inst. of Performing Arts 2003. *Publications:* Abstract Expressionism 1974, In from the Margins 1997, Joining In 1997, The Governance of Culture 1997, The Creative Imperative 2001, Citizens – Towards a Citizenship Culture (contrib.) 2001, Cicero – A Turbulent Life 2000, Cicero – The Life and Times of Rome's Greatest Politician (USA), New Voices 2004, The First Emperor – Caesar Augustus and the Triumph of Rome 2006, Augustus – The Life of Rome's First Emperor (USA) 2006, Hadrian and the Triumph of Rome (USA) 2009, The Rise of Rome (USA) 2012; contribs to newspapers and journals. *Address:* Westerlies, Anchor Hill, Wivenhoe, Essex, CO7 9BL, England.

EVERLING, Ulrich, DJur; German judge and academic; *Honorary Professor of European Law, University of Bonn;* b. 2 June 1925, Berlin; s. of Emil Everling; m. Lore Schwerdtfeger 1953; two s. two d.; ed Zehlendorfer Gymnasium, Berlin and Univ. of Göttingen; lawyer, Fed. Ministry of Econs 1953–80, Dept of European Policy 1970–80; Lecturer, Hon. Prof. of European Law, Univ. of Münster 1971–80, Univ. of Bonn 1981–; Judge, Court of Justice of the European Communities 1980–88; Großes Verdienstkreuz der Bundesrepublik Deutschland 2013; Dr hc 2001. *Publications include:* Die europäische Wirtschaftsgemeinschaft: Kommentar zum Vertrag (co-author) 1960, Das Niederlassungsrecht im Gemeinsamen Markt 1964, Das europäische Gemeinschaftrecht im Spannungsfeld von Politik und Wirtschaft, Ausgewählte Aufsätze 1964–1984 1986, Buchpreisbindung im deutschen Sprachraum und Europäisches Gemeinschaftrecht 1997, Unterwegs zur Europäischen Union, Ausgewählte Aufsätze 1985–2000 2001; numerous articles on European law and policy. *Address:* Dahlienweg 5, 53343 Wachtberg, Germany. *Telephone:* (228) 324177. *Fax:* (228) 324898.

EVERT, Christine (Chris) Marie; American fmr professional tennis player; b. 21 Dec. 1954, Fort Lauderdale, Fla; d. of James Evert and Colette Evert; m. 1st John Lloyd 1979 (divorced 1987); m. 2nd Andy Mill 1988 (divorced 2006); m. 3rd Greg Norman 2008 (divorced 2010); three s.; ed St Thomas Aquinas High School, Fort Lauderdale; amateur player 1970–72; professional 1972–1989; Wimbledon Singles Champion 1974, 1976, 1981; French Champion 1974, 1975, 1979, 1980, 1983, 1985, 1986; US Open Champion 1975, 1976, 1977, 1978, 1980, 1982; Italian Champion 1974, 1975, 1980; South African Champion 1973; Colgate Series Champion 1977, 1978; World Champion 1979; played Wightman Cup for USA 1971–73, 1975–82, 1984–85; won 1,000th singles victory (first ever player) Australian Open Dec. 1984; played Federation Cup for USA 1977–82; ranked No. 1 in the world for seven years; won 1,309 matches in her career; won 157 singles titles and 18 Grand Slam titles (third best in history); Pres. Women's Tennis Asscn (WTA) 1975–76, 1983–91; Founder Chris Evert Charities for needy and drug-abusive mothers and their children 1989; Host and Organizer Annual Chris Evert Pro-Celebrity Tennis Classic 1989–; Pnr and coach, Evert Tennis Acad., Boca Raton, Fla; owner, Evert Enterprises/IMG, Boca Raton, Fla 1989–; Dir and mem. Bd Pres.'s Council on Physical Fitness and Sports 1991; NBC TV sports commentator and host for numerous TV shows; mem. Bd Ounce of Prevention Fund of Florida, Make-A-Wish Foundation of S Florida, Florida Sports Foundation, United Sports Foundation of America, Save the Children, American AIDS Asscn, Women's Sports Foundation, The Don Shula Foundation, Nat. Cttee to Prevent Child Abuse, The Buoniconti Fund, Palm Beach Co. Sports Authority; Sports Illustrated Sportsman of the Year Award 1976, WTA Sportsmanship Award 1979 and Player Service Award 1981, 1986, 1987, named Greatest Woman Athlete of the Last 25 Years (Women's Sports Foundation) 1985, voted by Korbel One of Top 10 Romantic People of 1989, Flo Hyman Award 1990, Providencia Award 1991, Nat. High School Hall of Fame 1992, March of Dimes Lifetime Achievement Award 1993, Madison Square Garden Walk of Fame 1993, Int. Tennis Hall of Fame 1995, bi-colour hybrid tea rose named for her by Spring Hill Nurseries Co. 1996, Int. Tennis Fed. Chartrier Award 1997, named by ESPN as One of Top 50 Athletes of the 20th Century 1999. *Publications:* Chrissie (autobiog.) 1982, Lloyd on Lloyd (with John Lloyd) 1985. *Leisure interests:* Visiting Paris and the Great Barrier Reef in Hamilton Island. *Address:* Evert Enterprises/IMG, 7200 West Camino Real, Suite 310, Boca Raton, FL 33433; Evert Tennis Academy, 10334 Diego Drive South, Boca Raton, FL 33428, USA. *Telephone:* (561) 394-2400 (office); (561) 488-2055 (office). *Website:* www.chrisevert.org (office); www.evertacademy.com (office).

EVERY, Bob, AO, BSc, PhD; Australian business executive; *Non-Executive Chairman, Wesfarmers Ltd;* b. 18 June 1945; m. Sheryl Every; two s. two d.; ed Univ. of New South Wales; mem. Bd of Dirs Wesfarmers Ltd 2006–, Chair. (non-exec.) 2008–, Chair. Remuneration and Nomination Cttees, mem. Audit Cttee; Man. Dir and CEO OneSteel Ltd –2005; Chair. Iluka Resources Ltd 2004–10, Sims Group Ltd 2005–07; Deputy Chair. Boral Ltd 2007, Chair. 2007–10, Chair. (non-exec.) 2010–; fmr Chair. Steel & Tube Holdings Ltd, NZ; fmr Man. Dir Tubemakers of Australia Ltd; fmr Pres. BHP Steel; Adjunct Prof. Australian School of Business; fmr adviser to Proudfoot Consulting; mem. or fmr mem. Bd of Dirs O'Connell Street Assocs Pty Ltd, OCA Services Pty Ltd, OneSteel Ltd, CARE Australia; fmr Chair. Malcolm Sargent Cancer Fund for Children in Australia Ltd (known as Redkite); Fellow, Australian Acad. of Technological Sciences and Eng, Australian Inst. of Co. Dirs; Centenary Medal of Australia. *Leisure interest:* golf. *Address:* Wesfarmers Ltd, 12th Floor, Wesfarmers House, 40 The Esplanade, Perth, WA 6000 (office); 6/28 Billyard Avenue, Elizabeth Bay, NSW 2011, Australia (home). *Telephone:* (8) 9327-4283 (office); (2) 9331-7551 (home). *Fax:* (8) 9327-4216 (office). *E-mail:* info@wesfarmers.com.au (office); bevery@wesfarmers.com.au (home). *Website:* www.wesfarmers.com.au (office).

EVES, Ernie, QC; Canadian investment banker and fmr politician; *Executive Chairman, Jacob Securities Inc.;* b. 1946, Windsor, Ont.; m. ; one s. (deceased) one d.; ed Univ. of Toronto, Osgoode Hall Law School, York Univ.; first elected as MPP for Parry Sound, Ont. Legislature 1981, fmr Vice-Chair. Priorities, Policy and Communications Bd of Cabinet, fmr Vice-Chair. Man. Bd of Cabinet, fmr Govt House Leader, fmr Minister of Community and Social Services, fmr Minister of Skills Devt, Deputy Premier and Minister of Finance, Ont. 1995–2001, Leader Ont. Progressive Conservative Party March 2002–Sept. 2004, MPP for Dufferin-Peel-Wellington-Grey 2002–05 (resgnd), Premier of Ont. April 2002–Oct. 2003; Leader of the Official Opposition Oct. 2003–Sept. 2004; Chair. Ont. Advisory Council on Int. Trade and Investment 2006–; fmr Vice Chair. and Sr Advisor, Credit Suisse First Boston (Canada); fmr Counsel, Borden Ladner Gervais, LLP;

Exec. Chair. Jacob Securities Inc (investment bank), Toronto 2007–; Founder and Sec. Treas. Big Brothers' Assen of Parry Sound; mem. Advisory Bd Embassy of Hope; Co-founder and Chair. Justin Eves Foundation 1995–. *Address:* Jacob Securities Inc., 199 Bay Street, Suite 2901, Commerce Court West, PO Box 322, Toronto, ON M5L 1G1, Canada (office). *Telephone:* (416) 866-8300 (office). *Fax:* (416) 866-8333 (office). *Website:* www.jacobsecurities.com (office).

EVIN, Claude, DIur; French politician and organization official; *President, Fédération hospitalière de France;* b. 29 June 1949, Le Cellier, Loire-Atlantique; s. of André Evin and Adrienne Lecommandeur; m. Françoise Guillet 1971; three d.; Sec. St-Nazaire Section, Parti Socialiste 1975–77, mem. Loire-Atlantique Fed. Cttee of Socialist Party 1975–, mem. Nat. Cttee 1991–; Mun. Councillor and Deputy Mayor of St-Nazaire 1977–; Deputy to Nat. Ass. 1978–88, 1997–; MP Ass. of Council of Europe; Chair. Nat. Ass. Cultural, Family and Social Affairs Cttee 1981–86; mem. Social Security Audit Comm. 1985; Vice-Pres. Nat. Ass. 1986–88; Minister-Del. attached to Minister of Social Affairs and Employment with responsibility for Social Protection May–June 1988; Minister of Solidarity, Health and Social Protection 1988–91; Conseiller régional Pays de la Loire 1992–98; mem. Econ. and Social Council 1994–97, Parl. Ass., Council of Europe 1997–2007; Pres. Fédération hospitalière de France 2004–; Chevalier, Légion d'honneur. *Address:* Fédération hospitalière de France, 1 bis rue Cabanis, 75014 Paris (office); 30 rue du Bois Savary, 44600 St-Nazaire, France. *Telephone:* 1-44-06-84-44 (office). *Fax:* 1-44-06-84-45 (office). *Website:* www.fhf.fr (office).

ÉVORA, Nelson; Portuguese (b. Côte d'Ivoirian) athlete; b. 20 April 1984, Côte d'Ivoire; triple jumper and long jumper; triple jump Olympic and World Champion; relocated to Portugal aged five; represented Cape Verde until June 2002, when became Portuguese citizen; still holds Cape Verdean records in both long jump (7.57m) and triple jump (16.15m); first coached by João Ganço; Gold Medal, triple and long jump, European Athletics Jr Championships, Tampere, Finland 2003; competed in triple jump at Athens Olympics 2004; Bronze Medal, triple jump, European Under-23 Championships 2005; finished first in long jump and second in triple jump, European Cup in Athletics, Thessaloniki 2006; finished sixth at Int. Assen of Athletics Feds (IAAF) World Indoor Championships 2006; finished fourth in triple jump and sixth in long jump at European Athletics Championships, Gothenburg 2006 (set Portuguese triple jump record of 17.23m during qualification); finished fifth at European Athletics Indoor Championships, Birmingham 2007; finished first in triple jump, European Cup in Athletics, Milan 2007; Gold Medal, World Championships, Osaka 2007 (set personal best, Portuguese nat. record and second-best world mark of the year at 17.74m); Bronze Medal, triple jump (17.27m), IAAF World Indoor Championships, Valencia 2008; Gold Medal, triple jump (17.67m), Olympic Games, Beijing 2008; competes for S.L. Benfica (sports club), Lisbon. *Address:* c/o Federação Portuguesa de Atletismo, 15-B Largo da Lagoa, 2799-538 Linda a Velha, Portugal. *Telephone:* (21) 4146020. *Fax:* (21) 4146021. *E-mail:* comunicacao@fpatletismo.pt. *Website:* www.fpatletismo.pt.

EVREN, Gen. Kenan; Turkish army officer and fmr head of state; b. 1918, Alaşehir, Manisa; s. of Naciye Evren and Hayrullah Evren; m.; three d.; ed Military Acad., War Coll.; Artillery Officer 1938; served in Korea; Chief of Staff of the Land Forces, then Deputy Chief of Staff of the Armed Forces; Commdr Fourth Army (Aegean Army), Izmir 1976; rank of Gen. 1974; Chief of the Land Forces 1977; Chief of Staff of the Armed Forces 1978; led coup deposing civilian Govt Sept. 1980; Head of State and Chair. Nat. Security Council 1980–82, Pres. of Turkey 1982–89; Head, Turkish mil. del. to USSR 1975; est. cultural foundation; numerous decorations. *Achievements include:* building Marmaris High School, opened 2000. *Leisure interests:* oil painting, education. *Address:* Beyaz Ev Sokak 27, Armutalan, Marmaris, Turkey (home). *Telephone:* (252) 4171300 (home). *Fax:* (252) 4171313 (home). *E-mail:* kev@marmariskoleji-kiz.com (office).

EWALD, François, PhD; French insurance expert and academic; *Professor, Conservatoire national des arts et métiers;* b. 29 April 1946, Boulogne-Billancourt; ed Sorbonne, Paris; Asst to Michel Foucault, Coll. de France 1975–84; expert on issues of risk and responsibility, the formation of an insured soc. and the devt of the French Social Security System; Professorial Chair. of Insurance, Conservatoire nat. des arts et métiers (CNAM) 1997–; Distinguished Visitor, Univ. of Connecticut Law School 2003; Founder and Pres. Michel Foucault Centre; mem. Acad. des Technologies. *Publications include:* L'Etat providence 1986, Naissance du Code civil 1989, Le problème français des accidents thérapeutiques 1992, Le principe de précaution (jtly) 2001. *Address:* c/o Fédération française des sociétés d'assurances, 26 boulevard Haussmann, 75 311 Paris, Cedex 09, France (office). *Telephone:* 1-42-47-93-51 (office). *E-mail:* ewald@academie-technologies.fr. *Website:* www.ffsa.fr (office).

EWANGO, Corneille E. N., BSc, MSc; Democratic Republic of the Congo botanist and conservationist; *Senior Botanist Researcher and Head of Botanical and Forest Ecology Programme, Democratic Republic of the Congo Programme, Wildlife Conservation Society;* ed Univ. of Kisangani, Univ. of Missouri, St Louis, USA, Wageningen Univ., the Netherlands; staff mem. Congolese Inst. for the Conservation of Nature and Wildlife Conservation Soc. (WCS)'s Democratic Repub. of Congo (DRC) programme, responsible for Okapi Faunal Reserve's botany programme, Ituri Rainforest 1996–2003; extensive research experience in DRC, Rwanda, Uganda and Cameroon; Dir WCS and Centre de Formation et de Recherche en Conservation Forestière (CEFRECOF), Ituri Landscape, DRC Programme 2006–07; Sr Botanist Researcher and Head of Botanical and Forest Ecology Programme, WCS-DRC Programme 2006–; PhD student, Forest Ecology and Forest Man. Group, Wageningen Univ., the Netherlands 2007–; Goldman Environmental Prize 2005, Emerging Explorers Award—Africa, Nat. Geographic Soc. 2007, Invited Speaker, TEDGlobal 2007 Conf., Africa: The Next Chapter, Arusha, Tanzania 2007. *Achievements include:* helped lead effort to protect and preserve Okapi Reserve during civil war in DRC; uncovered 270 species of lianas and 600 tree species in the area. *Publications:* several scientific papers in professional journals on forest dynamics, tropical forest structure and functional ecology, lianas, biodiversity conservation, biology of epiphytes, and plant taxonomy and systematics. *Address:* WCS Site Manager, 1725 Avenue Col. Mondjiba, Chanic Building, PO Box 240, Ngaelima, Kinshasa I, Democratic Republic of the Congo (office). *E-mail:* ewango_corneille@yahoo.com (office). *Website:* www.wcs.org/drcongo (office).

EWING, Maria Louise; American singer (soprano); b. 27 March 1950, Detroit; d. of Norman I. Ewing and Hermina M. Veraar; m. Sir Peter Hall 1982 (divorced 1989); one d.; ed Cleveland Inst. of Music; debut at Metropolitan Opera, New York singing Cherubino in The Marriage of Figaro 1976, closely followed by debuts with major US orchestras, including New York Philharmonic and at La Scala Milan; regular performances at Glyndebourne including the Barber of Seville, L'Incoronazione di Poppea and Carmen; repertoire also includes Pelléas et Mélisande, The Dialogues of the Carmelites, Così fan Tutte, La Perichole, La Cenerentola, The Marriage of Figaro (Susanna); performed Salome, Covent Garden 1988, Carmen, Earl's Court, London 1989, Tosca, Los Angeles 1989, Salome, Washington 1990, Madame Butterfly, Los Angeles, Tosca, Seville, Salome, Covent Garden 1992, Tosca, Los Angeles, Chicago, Salome, San Francisco, Madame Butterfly, Tosca, Vienna, The Trojans, Metropolitan, New York 1993–94; also appears as concert and recital singer; debut Promenade Concerts, London 1987, Lady Macbeth of Mtsensk with Metropolitan Opera 1994. *Leisure interests:* home and family. *Address:* c/o David Godfrey, Mitchell-Godfrey Management, 48 Gray's Inn Road, London, WC1X 8LT, England (office); c/o Herbert Breslin, 119 West 57th Street, Room 1505, New York, NY 10019, USA (office).

EWING, Rodney Charles, BS, MS, PhD; American geologist, materials scientist and academic; *Donald R. Peacor Collegiate Professor, Department of Geological Sciences, University of Michigan;* b. Abilene, Tex.; ed Texas Christian Univ., Stanford Univ. (NSF Fellowship); mem. Faculty, Dept of Earth and Planetary Sciences, Univ. of New Mexico 1974–97, Chair. Dept 1979–84, Regents' Prof. Emer. 1997–; Prof. Dept of Nuclear Eng and Radiological Sciences, Univ. of Michigan 1997–, responsible for programme in radiation effects and nuclear waste man., also holds appointments in Geological Sciences and Materials Science and Eng, currently Donald R. Peacor Collegiate Prof., Dept of Geological Sciences; Adjungeret Prof., Univ. of Arhus, Denmark; Councillor, Materials Research Soc. 1983–85, 1987–89, Sec. 1985–86; Pres. Mineralogical Soc. of America 2002, Int. Union of Materials Research Socs 1997–98, New Mexico Geological Soc. 1981; mem. Bd Dirs Caswell Silver Foundation 1980–84, Energy, Exploration, Education, Inc. 1979–84; Guest Scientist or Faculty mem. Battelle Pacific Northwest Labs, Oak Ridge Nat. Lab., Hahn-Meitner-Institut, Berlin, Dept of Nuclear Eng, Technion Univ., Haifa, Israel, Centre d'Études Nucléaires de Fontenay-Aux-Roses, Commissariat à l'Énergie Atomique (France), Charles Univ., Prague, Japan Atomic Energy Research Inst., Institut für Nukleare Entsorgungstechnik of Kernforschungszentrum Karlsruhe, Arhus Univ., Mineralogical Inst., Tokyo Univ., Khlopin Radium Inst., St Petersburg, Russia; mem. Bd of Radioactive Waste Man., Nat. Research Council, Nat. Research Council cttees for NAS that reviewed Waste Isolation Pilot Plant in NM 1984–96, Remediation of Buried and Tank Wastes at Hanford, Wash. and INEEL, Ida 1992–95, INEEL High-Level Waste Alternative Treatments 1998–99, sub-cttee on WIPP for the Environmental Protection Agency's Nat. Advisory Council on Environmental Policy and Tech. 1992–98; has served as invited expert to Advisory Cttee on Nuclear Waste of Nuclear Regulatory Comm.; fmr consultant to Nuclear Waste Tech. Review Bd; mem. Program Cttee, Materials Research Soc., Ed. or Assoc. Ed. proceedings vols for symposia on the 'Scientific Basis for Nuclear Waste Management', Berlin 1982, Boston 1984, Stockholm 1985, Berlin 1988, Strasbourg 1991, Kyoto 1994, Boston 1998, Sydney 2000; Fellow, Geological Soc. of America, Mineralogical Soc. of America; Dr hc (Université Pierre et Marie Curie) 2006; Guggenheim Fellowship 2002, Lomonosov Gold Medal, Russian Acad. of Sciences 2006. *Publications:* Radioactive Waste Forms for the Future (co-ed. and contributing author) 1988; ed. or co-ed. of seven monographs, proceedings vols or special issues of journals; author or co-author of more than 600 specialist research publs; holds patent for the development of a highly durable material for the immobilization of excess weapons plutonium. *Address:* Department of Geological Sciences, University of Michigan, 2534 C.C. Little Building, 1100 N University Avenue, Ann Arbor, MI 48109-1005, USA (office). *Telephone:* (734) 763-9295 (office). *Fax:* (734) 647-8531 (office). *E-mail:* rodewing@engin.umich.edu (office). *Website:* www.earth.lsa.umich.edu/relw/groupmembers/ewing/ewing.htm (office).

EWING, Rufus Washington, DM, MPH; Turks and Caicos physician and politician; *Premier;* b. 1972, Blue Hills, Providenciales Island; s. of Hilly Ewing and Jane Ewing; m. Dawn Perry 1993; one s.; ed Barbados Community Coll., Univ. of the West Indies, IWK Grace Health Center, Halifax, Canada, Johns Hopkins Univ. Bloomberg School of Public Health, Baltimore, USA; Deputy Chief Medical Officer, Turks and Caicos 2001–05, Chief Medical Officer and Dir of Health Services 2005–12; f. Omnicare (private medical practice), Providenciales 2001–; Pres. Civil Servants Assen (trade union) 2011–12; Leader, Progressive Nat. Party; Premier of Turks and Caicos (first since suspension of office by UK in 2009) 2012–; fmr Chair. Health Practitioners' Bd, Public and Environmental Health Bd, Nat. Insurance Medical Bd; fmr Dir Caribbean Health Research Council; Fellow Royal Coll. of Surgeons of Edinburgh 1998. *Address:* Office of the Premier, Government Square, Grand Turk, Turks and Caicos (office). *Telephone:* 946-2801 (office). *Fax:* 946-2777 (office). *Website:* www.rufusewing.com.

EYCKMANS, Luc A. F., MD, PhD; Belgian fmr professor of medicine; b. 23 Feb. 1930, Antwerp; s. of Robert Eyckmans and Alice van Genechten; m. Godelieve Cornelissen 1957; four s. three d.; ed Univ. of Leuven; Fellowship in Tropical Medicine, Antwerp 1956–57; Hosp. Physician, Kisantu (fmr Belgian Congo) 1957–60; Fellowship in Infectious Diseases, Dallas and Cornell, New York 1961–64, in Tropical Medicine, Bahia, Brazil 1964; Lector in Infectious Diseases and Physician, Univ. of Leuven 1965–72; Prof. of Medicine (Infectious Diseases), Univ. of Antwerp 1973–76, Dir Inst. of Tropical Medicine "Prince Leopold" 1976–95, Visiting Prof., Univ. of Antwerp 1977–95; Visiting Prof., Univ. of Leuven 1989–95; Exec. Dir and mem. Bd Francqui Foundation 1992–; mem. Royal Acad. of Overseas Sciences (Belgium), Acad. Europaea; Corresp. mem. Acad. Nat. de Médicine, Paris; Hon. Fellow, Royal Soc. of Tropical Medicine and Hygiene; Grand Officer, Order of the Crown (Belgium); Dr hc (Lille). *Publications:* 130 contributions to professional journals and chapters in scientific publs. *Leisure interest:* hiking. *Address:* Wildenhoge 26, 3020 Winksele, Belgium (home). *Telephone:* (16) 22-05-96 (home).

EYRE, Ivan; Canadian artist and academic; *Professor Emeritus of Drawing and Painting, University of Manitoba;* b. 15 April 1935, Tullymet, Sask.; s. of Thomas Eyre and Kay Eyre; m. Brenda Fenske 1957; two s.; mem. Faculty, Univ. of

Manitoba, Winnipeg 1959–93, Head, Drawing Dept 1974–78, Prof. of Drawing and Painting 1975–93, Prof. Emer. 1994–; works represented in permanent collections at Winnipeg Art Gallery, Nat. Gallery, Ottawa, Edmonton Art Gallery, Montreal Museum of Fine Arts, Assiniboine Park Pavilion Gallery, Winnipeg, Man. etc.; Canada Council Sr Fellow 1966–77; Founder mem. Winnipeg Art Gallery 1996; mem. Royal Canadian Acad. of Arts; subject of books 'Ivan Eyre' by George Woodcock, 'Ivan Eyre Drawings' by Tom Lovatt and of various documentary films; Queen's Silver Jubilee Medal 1977, Academic of Italy with Gold Medal 1980, Jubilee Award, Univ. of Manitoba Alumni Asscn 1982, Queen's Golden Jubilee Medal 2002, Order of Manitoba 2007. *Publications:* Ivan on Eyre (auto-biog.). *Address:* 1098 Des Trappistes Street, Winnipeg, Manitoba, R3V 1B8, Canada (home). *Fax:* (204) 275-6650 (home).

EYRE, Sir Richard, Kt, KBE, CBE, BA, FRSL; British theatre, film and television director; b. 28 March 1943, Barnstaple, Devon, England; s. of Commdr R. G. H. G. Eyre, RN, Minna Mary Jessica Royds; m. Sue Birtwistle 1973; one d.; ed Sherborne School, Peterhouse, Cambridge; directed his first production, The Knack, at Phoenix Theatre, Leicester 1965; Asst Dir Phoenix Theatre 1967; Assoc. Dir Royal Lyceum, Edinburgh 1967–70, Dir of Productions 1970–72; Artistic Dir Nottingham Playhouse 1973–78; Producer-Dir Play for Today for BBC 1978–80; Assoc. Dir Nat. Theatre (now called Royal Nat. Theatre) 1980–86, Artistic Dir 1988–97; BBC Gov. 1995–2004; Cameron Mackintosh Visiting Professorship, St Catherine's Coll. Oxford 1997; Visiting Prof. of Drama, Univ. of Warwick 1999, Univ. of Sheffield 2000; Emer. Fellow, St Catherine's Coll., Oxford 2003; Chair. Pearson Playwrights' Award 2010–; Hon. Fellow, Goldsmiths Coll. 1993, King's Coll. London 1994, Guildhall School of Music and Drama 1996, Peterhouse, Cambridge 2001; Officier des Arts et des Lettres 1998; Hon. DLitt (Nottingham Trent) 1992, (South Bank) 1994, (Liverpool) 2003; Hon. DUniv (Oxford Brookes Univ.) 2003, (Nottingham) 2008, (East Anglia) 2011; Hon. BA (Surrey) 1998; Hon. Dr of Drama (Royal Scottish Acad. of Drama) 2000; Patricia Rothermere Award 1995, STV Award for Best Dir 1969, 1970, 1971, Vittorio de Sica Award 1986, BAFTA Best Dir 1987, Special Award, Evening Standard Awards for Drama 1988, for Best Dir 1997, Special Award for running Nat. Theatre 1997, Critics Circle Award for Best Dir 1996, for Lifetime Achievement 1997, Laurence Olivier Awards for Best Dir 1982, 1997, 2005, for Outstanding Achievement 1997, South Bank Show Award for Outstanding Achievement 1997, Director's Guild Award for Outstanding Achievement 1997. *Plays directed include:* Hamlet (Royal Court) 1980, Guys and Dolls (Olivier 1982, Soc. of West End Theatres and Evening Standard Awards for Best Dir 1982), The Beggar's Opera, Schweyk in the Second World War (Nat. Theatre) 1982, The Government Inspector (Nat. Theatre) 1985, Futurists (Nat. Theatre) (Time Out Award for Best Dir) 1986, Kafka's Dick (Royal Court) 1986, High Society (West End) 1987, The Changeling 1988, Bartholomew Fair 1988, Hamlet 1989, The Voysey Inheritance 1989, Racing Demon 1990, Richard III (Nat. Theatre, also nat. and int. tour) 1990, Napoli Milionaria 1991, Murmuring Judges 1991, White Chameleon 1991, The Night of the Iguana 1992, Macbeth 1993, The David Hare Trilogy – Racing Demon, Murmuring Judges, The Absence of War 1993 (Racing Demon, New York 1995), Johnny on a Spot 1994, Sweet Bird of Youth 1994, Skylight 1995, 1996 (New York 1996), La Grande Magia 1995, The Prince's Play 1996, John Gabriel Borkman 1996, Guys and Dolls 1996, 1997, King Lear 1997, Amy's View 1997 (New York 1999), The Invention of Love 1997, The Judas Kiss 1998 (New York 1998), The Novice 2000, The Crucible (New York) 2002, Vincent in Brixton 2002, Mary Poppins 2004, Hedda Gabler (London 2005), Mary Poppins (New York) 2006, The Reporter (Nat. Theatre) 2007, The Last Cigarette (Chichester and West End) 2009, The Observer (Nat. Theatre) 2009, Private Lives (Theatre Royal Bath, Vaudeville) 2010, Toronto and Broadway) 2011, Welcome to Thebes (Nat. Theatre 2010), Flea in Her Ear (Old Vic) 2010, Betty Blue Eyes (Novello Theatre) 2011, The Last of the Duchess (Hampstead Theatre) 2011, Quartermaine's Terms (Wyndham's Theatre) 2013, The Pajama Game (Chichester) 2013, Liolá (Nat. Theatre), Ghosts (Almeida and Trafalgar Studios) 2013, Stephen Ward (Aldwych 2013. *Opera:* La Traviata, Covent Garden 1994, Le Nozze di Figaro, Aix-en-Provence, France 2001, Carmen, Metropolitan Opera 2009. *Films:* The Ploughman's Lunch (Evening Standard Award for Best Film) 1983, Loose Connections 1984, Laughterhouse (Venice Film Festival Award for Best Film) 1984, Iris (co-dir and co-writer) (Special Mention for Excellence in Filmmaking Award, Nat. Bd of Review (NBR) 2001, Humanitas Screenwriting Award for screenplay 2002, Efebo D'Oro Award) 2001, Stage Beauty (NBR Award, Jury Prize, Abbeville Film Festival) 2004, Notes on a Scandal (NBR Award, Rotten Tomatoes Award, Best Gay Film, Berlin Festival) 2006, The Other Man (Official Selection at Toronto, San Sebastian and London Film Festivals) 2008. *Radio:* Macbeth (BBC Radio 3) 2000, Angel (BBC Radio 4) 2001, Ghosts 2013. *Television includes:* producer: BBC Play For Today 1978, Just a Boy's Game, Long Distance Information, Chance of a Lifetime; director: Waterloo Sunset 1979, Comedians 1979, The Cherry Orchard 1980, The Imitation Game 1980, Pasmore (own adaptation) 1981, Country 1982, Loose Connections 1984, Laughterhouse (Venice Film Festival Award for Best TV Film) 1984, Past Caring (Venice TV Prize Special Mention) 1985, The Insurance Man (Tokyo World TV Festival Special Prize) 1985, 'V' (RTS Award) 1987, Tumbledown (Italia RAI Prize 1988, BAFTA Award for Best TV Single Drama, Royal TV Soc. Award for Best Single Drama 1989, BPG Award) 1987, Suddenly Last Summer (BBC) 1993, The Absence of War (BBC) 1995, King Lear (BBC) (Peabody Award 1998) 1998, The Three Kings (Sky TV) 2009, Henry IV Parts 1 and 2 2012. *Publications include:* Utopia and Other Places (memoirs) 1993 (revised edns 1994, 2003), The Eyre Review: The Future of Lyric Theatre in London 1998, Changing Stages (with Nicholas Wright) 2000, Iris (screenplay) 2002, National Service: Diary of a Decade (Theatre Book Award 2004) 2003, Hedda Gabler 2005, Talking Theatre: Interviews with Theatre People 2009. *Address:* c/o Judy Daish Associates Ltd, 2 St Charles Place, London, W10 6EG, England (office). *Telephone:* (20) 8964-8811 (office). *Fax:* (20) 8964-8966 (office). *E-mail:* judy@judydaish.com (office). *Website:* www.judydaish.com (office).

EYRE, Richard Anthony, CBE, MA; British media executive; *Chairman, Internet Advertising Bureau;* b. 3 May 1954; s. of Edgar Gabriel Eyre and Marjorie Eyre (née Corp); m. Sheelagh Colquhoun 1977; one s. one d.; ed King's Coll. School, Wimbledon, Lincoln Coll., Oxford; media buyer, Benton & Bowles 1975–79, media planner 1980–84; TV airtime salesman, Scottish TV 1979–80; Media Dir, Aspect 1984–86, Bartle Bogle Hegarty 1986–91; Chief Exec. Capital Radio PLC 1991–97, ITV 1997–2000, Pearson TV 2000–01; Dir of Strategy and Content, RTL Group

2000–01; Chair. (non-exec.), RDF Media 2001, GCap Media PLC 2007–08, Next 15; Adviser to 19 Group 2002–; Chair. Internet Advertising Bureau; Dir (non-exec.), MGt plc, Results International; mem. Bd Grant Thornton; Chair. Eden Project; fmr mem. Bd, Guardian Media Group; Mackintosh Medal 2013. *Address:* c/o Patricia Siakwang, Executive Assistant to the CEO, Internet Advertising Bureau, 14 Macklin Street, London, WC2B 5NF, England. *Telephone:* (20) 7050-6952. *E-mail:* patricia@iabuk.net. *Website:* www.iabuk.net/about/iab-team.

EYSKENS, Mark, Bac. Philo., LLD, DEcon, MA; Belgian politician, academic and author; *Chairman, PA Europe International Foundation;* b. (Marc Maria Frans Eyskens), 29 April 1933, Louvain; s. of Gaston Eyskens and Gilberte Eyskens; m. Ann Rutsaert 1962; two s. three d.; ed Catholic Univ. of Louvain, Columbia Univ., New York; Prof., Catholic Univ. of Louvain; Econ. Adviser, Ministry of Finance 1962–65; mem. of Parl. (Christian People's Party (Belgium), now called Christian Democratic and Flemish) 1977–2003; Sec. of State for the Budget and Regional Economy and Minister of Co-operation 1976–80; Minister of Finance 1980–81; Prime Minister April–Dec. 1981; Minister for Econ. Affairs 1981–85, for Finance 1985–88, of Foreign Affairs 1989–92, Minister of State 1998–; Chair. Council of EC Ministers of Finance 1987; Gov. IMF, IBRD 1980–81, 1985–88; mem. Council of Europe 1995–2003; fmr Pres. Royal Acad. of Sciences (now Hon. Pres.), Letters and Fine Arts, Centre for European Culture, Inst. for European Policy; Vice-Pres. Royal Inst. for Int. Relations, Ass. of WEU 1995–2003; Observer, European Convention 2002–; Chair. PA Europe Int. Foundation; Pres. Francqui Foundation, Music Festival of Flanders, Arenberg Foundation, Center European Culture; mem. Bd Int. Crisis Group, Itinera, several cos; numerous radio and TV interviews; numerous Belgian and foreign decorations; numerous Belgian and foreign awards, including Benelux-Europe Prize, J.M./Huyghe Prize, Scriptores Christiani Prize, Grande médaille d'or Acad. française des Arts, Sciences et Lettres. *Publications:* author of 50 books including Algemene economie 1970, Economie van nu en straks 1975, Ambrunise 1976, Une planète livrée à deux mondes 1980, La source et l'horizon, Le redressement de la société européenne 1985, Economie voor iedereen 1987, Vie et mort du Professeur Mortal 1989, Buitenlandse zaken 1992, Affaires étrangères 1992, Le Fleuve et l'océan 1994, De Reis naar Dabar 1996, De lust van de verbeelding 1996, L'Affaire Titus 1998, Democratie tussen Spin en Web 1999, Het verdriet van het werelddorp 2000, Leven in tijden van Godsverduistering 2001, Het hijgen van de geschiedenis 2003, Omdat wij van de avond nooit genzen 2004, De oude prof en de zee 2005, Le vieux prof et la mer 2006, Mijn levens 2008, Absurdistan 2009; Mes vies. A la recherche du temps vécu 2010, Vonken in het duister (e-book) 2010, 1001 quotes 2011, Het land van ergens 2012; has written more than 1,000 articles, prefaces, columns, poems and contribs. *Leisure interests:* painting, literature, music. *Address:* Royal Academy of Sciences and Arts, Hertogsstraat 1, 1000 Brussels (office); PA Europe, Franklin Street 106, 1000 Brussels, Belgium (office). *Telephone:* (2) 550-23-23 (Royal Acad.) (office); (2) 735-83-96 (PA Europe) (office). *Fax:* (1) 640-60-18 (home). *E-mail:* m.eyskens@skynet.be (office). *Website:* www.eyskens.com (home).

EYTON, Anthony John Plowden, RA, RWS, R.W.A.; British artist; b. 17 May 1923, Teddington, Middx; s. of the late Capt. John Seymour Eyton and Phyllis Annie Tyser; m. Frances Mary Capell 1960 (divorced); three d.; ed Twyford School, Canford School and Camberwell School of Art; part-time teacher, Camberwell Art School 1955–86, Royal Acad. Schools 1963–99; Resident Artist, Eden Project 1999–2009; mem. Royal Cambrian Acad., Royal Inst. Oil Painters (ROI); Hon. mem. Pastel Soc., Hon. Prof. and Fellow, Univ. of the Arts, London 2011; several awards and prizes. *Publications:* Indian Memories, Journal of P A Eyton (RA Publications) 1996, Eyton's Eye, a Life in Painting (by Jenny Perry, RA Publications) 2005. *Leisure interest:* gardening. *Address:* c/o Browse and Darby Ltd, 19 Cork Street, London, W1X 1HB, England (office).

EYYUBOV, Yagub Abdulla oğlu; Azerbaijani politician; b. 28 Nov. 1945, Baku; ed Azerbaijan Technical Univ.; Deputy Prime Minister 1999–2003, First Deputy Prime Minister 2003–; Head of Azeri-Saudi Inter-governmental Econ. Comm. *Address:* c/o Office of the Prime Minister, Lermontov küç. 63, 1066 Baku, Azerbaijan (office). *Telephone:* (12) 492-66-23 (office). *Fax:* (12) 492-91-79 (office).

EYZAGUIRRE GUZMAN, Nicolás, PhD; Chilean economist, international organization official and politician; *Minister of Education;* b. 1954, Santiago; ed Univ. of Chile, Harvard Univ., USA; worked at Cen. Bank of Chile 1990–97, positions included Adviser, Man. and Dir of Studies, also prin. adviser to the Pres. 1990–97; Exec. Dir IMF 1998; Minister of Finance 2000–06; Pres. Chilean Competitiveness Council 2006–; Minister of Educ. 2014–; fmr mem. Bd of Dirs Banco Estado; mem. Latin American Advisory Bd Deutsche Bank AG 2008–; mem. Partido Por la Democracia—PPD;. *Publication:* The Macroeconomy of Quasi-Fiscal Operations in Chile (with Osvaldo Larrañaga) 1990. *Address:* Ministry of Education, Alameda 1371, 7°, Santiago, Chile (office). *Telephone:* (2) 2406-6000 (office). *E-mail:* consultas@mineduc.cl (office). *Website:* www.mineduc.cl (office).

EZRA, Baron (Life Peer), cr. 1983, of Horsham in the County of West Sussex; **Derek Ezra,** Kt, MA, MBE; British business executive; b. 23 Feb. 1919, Australia; s. of David Ezra and Lillie Ezra; m. Julia Elizabeth Wilkins 1950; ed Monmouth School and Magdalene Coll., Cambridge; mil. service 1939–47; rep. of Nat. Coal Bd at Cttees of OEEC and ECE 1948–52; mem. UK Del. to High Authority of European Coal and Steel Community 1952–56; Regional Sales Man. Nat. Bd 1958–60, Dir-Gen. of Marketing 1960–65; mem. Nat. Coal Bd 1965, Deputy Chair. 1965–71, Chair. 1971–82; Chair. British Inst. of Man. 1976–78, Vice-Chair. 1978; Chair. British Coal Int.; Chair. British Nationalised Industries Chairmen's Group 1980–81, Pres. Nat. Materials Handling Centre 1978; Pres. Coal Industry Soc. 1981–86, British Standards Inst. 1983–86, Econ. Research Council 1985–2000, Inst. of Trading Standards Admin. 1987–92; Dir Redland PLC 1982–89; Chair. Associated Heat Services PLC 1966–2000, British Iron and Steel Consumers Council 1983–86, Petrolex PLC 1982–85, Sheffield Heat and Power Ltd 1985–2000, Associated Gas Supplies Ltd 1987–95, Energy and Tech. Services Group 1990–2000, Micropower Ltd 2000–; Industrial Adviser to Morgan Grenfell 1982–88; Chair. Throgmorton Trust 1984–90; mem. British Overseas Trade Bd 1972–82, Bd, Solvay, Belgium; Hon. Fellow, Inst. of Civil Engineers 1986; Hon. LLD (Leeds) 1982; Order of Merit, Italy, Commdr Order of Merit, Luxembourg, Officier, Légion d'honneur. *Publications:* Coal and Energy 1978, The Energy Debate 1983. *Address:* House of Lords, Westminster, London, SW1A 0PW, England. *Telephone:* (20) 7219-3180.

F

FABIUS, Laurent; French politician; *Minister of Foreign Affairs;* b. 20 Aug. 1946, Paris; s. of André Fabius and Louise Fabius (née Strasburger-Mortimer); m. Françoise Castro (divorced); ed Lycées Janson-de-Sailly and Louis-le-Grand, Paris, Ecole normale supérieure and Institut d'études politiques, Paris, Ecole nat. d'admin, Strasbourg; Auditor, Council of State 1973; apptd First Deputy Mayor of Grand-Quevilly 1977, apptd Mayor 1995; Deputy (Seine-Maritime) to Nat. Ass. 1978–81, 1986–, Pres. 1988–92, 1997–2000, 2002–07, 2007–12; Nat. Sec. Parti Socialiste, in charge of press 1979–81, 1991–92, First Sec. 1992–93, Pres. Groupe Socialiste in Nat. Ass. 1995–97; Minister-Del. for the Budget, attached to Minister of Econ. and Finance 1981–83; Minister of Industry and Research 1983–84, of Econs, Finance and Industry 2000–02; Prime Minister 1984–86; Minister of Foreign Affairs 2012–; Pres. Regional Council, Haute Normandie 1981–82; Pres. Syndicat intercommunal à vocations multiples (Sivom) 1989–2000; mem. Gen. Council, Seine-Maritime 2000–; Grand Cross, Royal Norwegian Order of Merit, Kt Grand Cross, Order of Merit of the Italian Repub. 1990, Commdr, Ordre nat. du Mérite, Grand Cross, Order of the Star of Romania, Grand Officier, Ordre de la Légion d'honneur. *Publications:* La France inégale 1975, Le coeur du futur 1985, C'est en allant vers la mer 1990, Les blessures de la vérité (Prize for Best Political Book 1996) 1995, Cela commence par une balade 2003, Une certaine idée de l'Europe 2005. *Address:* Ministry of Foreign Affairs, 37 quai d'Orsay, 75351 Paris Cedex 07 (office); Assemblée Nationale, Casier de la Poste, Palais Bourbon, 75355 Paris 07, France (office). *Telephone:* 1-43-17-53-53 (Ministry) (office). *Fax:* 1-43-17-52-03 (Ministry) (office). *E-mail:* lfabius@assemblee-nationale.fr (office). *Website:* www.diplomatie.gouv.fr (office); www.assemblee-nat.fr/12/tribun/fiches_id/1268 .asp (office); www.laurent-fabius.net.

FABRE, Jan; Belgian artist, playwright and stage designer; b. 1958, Antwerp; ed Decorative Arts Inst., Royal Acad. of Fine Arts; began career as decorator and set designer; wrote a series of plays and produced black and white films 1970s; became active in the field of performance art 1976–81; produced a series of chamber plays 1980s; Founder and Artistic Dir Troublyn (creative work asscn) 1986–; fmr Artist-in-Residence, Museum of Natural History, London; decorated the Hall of Mirrors at the Royal Palace at the invitation of the Queen of Belgium 2003; productions have been staged in Europe, the USA, Japan and Australia; contrib. to numerous European museums and galleries including deSingel arts centre, Antwerp, Centre for Contemporary Art, Warsaw, Gallery of Modern and Contemporary Art, Bergamo; solo exhbn at Louvre (Angel of Metamorphosis) 2008. *Drawings include:* The Flying Cock, The Road from the Earth to the Stars is not Smooth, Hour of the Blue. *Sculptures include:* House of Flames III, Scissors' House. *Stage works include:* Body, Body on a Wall. *Plays include:* This is the Theatre One Should have Awaited and Expected 1982, The Power of Theatrical Frenzy (staged at Venice Biennial) 1984, Sweet Temptations, Universal Copyrights 1 & 9, Luminous Icons, The End Comes a Little Bit Earlier This Century. But Business as Usual 1998, The Values of Night 1999, Requiem für eine Metamorphose 2007, Another Sleepy Dusty Delta Day 2008, Orgy of Tolerance 2008. *Opera includes:* Glass in the Head will be Made of Glass (Flemish Opera House, Antwerp) 1990. *Ballet includes:* Sound of One Clapping Hand 1989, The Four Temperaments 1997. *Address:* Troubleyn/Jan Fabre VZW, Pastorijstraat 23, 2060 Antwerp, Belgium (office). *Telephone:* (3) 201-13-00 (office). *Fax:* (3) 233-15-01 (office). *E-mail:* info@troubleyn .be (office). *Website:* www.troubleyn.be (office).

FÁBREGA, Jorge, ML, DLaw; Panamanian lawyer, judge and academic; b. (Jorge Fábrega Ponce), 19 April 1922, Santiago; s. of Luis Ramon Fábrega and Maria Fábrega; m. Gloria de Fábrega 1960; two s. two d.; ed Univ. of Southern California and Univ. of Pennsylvania, USA, Univ. of Panama; Alt. Justice Court of Appeals 1960–68, Supreme Court of Panama 1970–80, 1989, 1999–2005; Co-founder and mem. Moreno y Fabrega (law firm), Panamá 1960–; Prof. of Law, Univ. of Panama 1967; Pres. Govt Comm. drafting Labour Code 1969–71, mem. Govt Comm. drafting new Judicial Code 1970–74, Constitutional Comm. 1983, Panamanian Bar Asscn 1982–83; mem. Panamanian Acad. of Law, Panamanian Acad. of Labour Law, Iberoamerican Inst. of Procedural Law, Interamerican Asscn of Procedural Law; Hon. mem. Spanish Bar Asscn, American Foreign Law Asscn; Brazilian Labour Judicial Order. *Publications:* Enriquecimiento sin causa 1960, Institutes of Civil Procedure 1972, Casación 1978, Estudios Procesales 1984, Código de Trabajo Anotado 1970, 1971, 1986, Estudios Procesales 1988, Instituciones de Derecho Procesal 1998, Procesos Civiles 1999, Medios de Prueba, Casación Civil, Teoría General de la Prueba 2000, Judges and Lawyers in the World Literature 2001. *Leisure interests:* reading, travel. *Address:* Edificio P.H., Plaza 54, Segundo Piso, Oficina 2A, Aveni da Samuel Lewis, Urbanización Obarrio, Panamá (office); Moreno y Fabrega, PO Box 0816-02883, Panamá, (office); Las Cumbres, Vía El Peñón, Panamá, Panama (home). *Telephone:* 269-6412 (office); 269-6621 (home). *Fax:* 264-3933 (office). *E-mail:* fabregam@ morenoyfabrega.com (office).

FABRIZI, Pier Luigi, BEcons; Italian professor of finance and banker; *Professor of Financial Markets, Bocconi University;* b. 23 April 1948, Siena; s. of Francesco Fabrizi and Bianca Corradeschi; m. Patrizia Vaselli; two c.; ed Università degli Studi di Siena; Asst Prof. of Banking, Università degli Studi di Parma 1974–82, Assoc. Prof. of Financial Markets 1982–87, Full Prof. of Banking 1987–89, Full Prof. of Financial Intermediaries 1990–93, Dean Faculty of Econs 1990–93; Full Prof. of Financial Markets, Bocconi Univ., Milan 1993–; mem. Bd of Dirs Banca Monte dei Paschi di Siena SpA 1997–2006, Chair. 1998–2006; mem. Bd of Dirs S. Paolo IMI SpA 1998–99, Olivetti SpA 1999–2001, Banca Monte Parma SpA 1999–2003, Banca Agricola Mantovana SpA 1999–2006, Banca Nazionale del Lavoro SpA 2001–06, Unipol Assicurazioni SpA 2001–07; Chair. Gruppo Monte Paschi Asset Management SGR SpA 1999–2000, MPS Finance SpA 2000–01, CartaSi SpA 2006–09, SiHolding SpA 2006–09; Grande Ufficiale dell' Ordine al Merito. *Publications:* Il credito al consumo 1975, Il credito fondiario e il credito edilizio 1977, La politica degli investimenti in titoli nelle banche di deposito 1982, L'attività in titoli con clientela nelle banche di deposito (ed.) 1986, La gestione dei flussi finanziari nelle aziende di credito (ed.) 1990, La gestione integrata dell'attivo e del passivo nelle aziende di credito (ed.) 1991, Nuovi modelli di gestione dei flussi finanziari nelle banche (ed.) 1995, La formazione nelle banche e nelle assicurazioni

1998, Il futuro del sistema bancario italiano: atrasigie e modelli organizzativi 2000, La gestione del risparmio privato (ed.) 2000, La crisi finanziaria globale: teoria e realtà a confronto 2009, Economia del mercato mobiliare (ed.) 2011. *Address:* Department of Finance, Università Bocconi, Via Roentgen 1, 2nd Floor, 20136 Milan (office); Via Adelaide Coari 11, 20141 Milan, Italy. *Telephone:* (02) 58365901 (office). *Fax:* (02) 58365920 (office). *E-mail:* pierluigi.fabrizi@unibocconi .it (office).

FADDEEV, Ludvig Dmitriyevich, PhD; Russian mathematician and physicist; *Director, Euler International Mathematical Institute, St Petersburg Branch, V.A. Steklov Mathematical Institute;* b. 23 March 1934, Leningrad; m.; two d.; ed Leningrad Univ.; Sr Research Fellow, Leningrad Br., Inst. of Math., USSR (now Russian) Acad. of Sciences 1965–; mem. staff, Leningrad State Univ. 1967–, Prof. at Math.-Mechanical Faculty 1969–; Dir Int. Math. Inst., St Petersburg Br. of V.A. Steklov Math. Inst. 1976–99, now Dir Euler Math. Inst.; Pres. Int. Math. Union 1986–90; mem. USSR (now Russian) Acad. of Sciences 1976, mem. Presidium 1991, Academician-Sec. Dept of Math.; mem. American Acad. of Arts and Sciences, Boston 1979; Foreign mem. nat. acads of USA, France, Sweden, China, Finland, Poland, Brazil and European Acad.; Hon. Citizen of St Petersburg 2010; Soviet orders; Red Banner, Lenin, Friendship and Russian Repub. Orders of Merit (Fourth and Third degrees), Order for Scientific Merit (Brazil); D. Heinemann Prize, American Physical Soc. 1975, USSR State Prize 1971, Max Planck Gold Medal 1995, Russian Repub. Prize 1995, 2004, Demidov Prize 2002, Poincaré Prize 2006, ICTP Dirac Medal and Prize 2008, Shaw Prize (co-recipient) 2008, Euler Gold Medal, Karpinski Prize. *Publication:* 40 Years in Mathematical Physics, Vol. 2, World Scientific series in 20th century mathematics 1995. *Address:* International Mathematical Institute, St Petersburg Branch of V.A. Steklov Mathematical Institute, Nab. Fontanka 27, D-11, 191023 St Petersburg, Russia (office). *Telephone:* (812) 571-43-95 (office); (812) 433-77-07 (home). *Fax:* (812) 310-53-77 (office). *E-mail:* faddeev@pdmi.ras.ru (office). *Website:* eimi.imi.ras.ru/eng/perso/ faddeev.php (office).

FADEYECHEV, Alexei Nikolayevich; Russian ballet dancer; b. 16 Aug. 1960, Moscow; s. of Nikolay Fadeyechev (q.v.) and Nina Fetisova; m. Rastozguyeva Tatyana; ed Bolshoi Choreographic School; Prin. Dancer, Bolshoi Ballet 1978, Artistic Dir 1998–2000; co-f. (with Nina Ananiashvili q.v.) ballet co. Moscow Theatre of Dance 2000; has performed with Mariinsky (fmrly Kirov) Ballet, Royal Danish Ballet, Royal Swedish Ballet, Nat. Ballet of Netherlands, Nat. Ballet of Finland, Nat. Ballet of Portugal, Birmingham Royal Ballet, Boston Ballet, Tokyo Ballet and numerous others; People's Artist of Russia. *Performances as a dancer include:* Frantz in Coppelia, Prince Siegfried in Swan Lake, Prince Desire in The Sleeping Beauty, Prince in The Nutcracker, Jean de Brienne in Raimonda, Basil in Don Quixote, Albrecht in Giselle, title roles in Spartacus, Ivan the Terrible, Macbeth, Romeo and Juliet, Cyrano de Bergerac, Prince of the Pagodas, leading roles in Les Sylphides, Paquita. *Address:* Karetny Ryad str. 5/10, Apt 20, 103006 Moscow, Russia (office). *Telephone:* (495) 419-35-31 (home).

FADEYECHEV, Nikolay Borisovich; Russian ballet dancer; b. 27 Jan. 1933; m. 1st Nina Fetisova; m. 2nd Irina Kholina; two s.; ed Bolshoi Theatre Ballet School; Bolshoi Theatre Ballet Co. 1952–76, coach, Bolshoi Theatre 1971–; People's Artist of USSR 1976. *Chief roles:* Siegfried (Swan Lake), Albert (Giselle), Jean de Brienne (Raimonde), Harmodius (Spartacus), Frondoso (Laurensia), Danila (Stone Flower), Romeo (Romeo and Juliet), Prince Desire (Sleeping Beauty), José (Carmen Suite), Karenin (Anna Karenina), Prince (Nutcracker), Illiys (Giselle), Vatslav. *Address:* Viktorenko str. 2/1, Apt 19, 125167 Moscow, Russia (home). *Telephone:* (495) 157-33-22 (home).

FADUL, Francisco José, BA, MA, PhD; Guinea-Bissau lawyer, politician and academic; *President, Partido para a Democracia, Desenvolvimento e Cidadania (PADEC);* b. 15 Dec. 1953, Mansoa; s. of Ângelo Fadul and Adelina da Silva Gonçalves; m. Jóia Albino Ialá Fadul; five s. four d.; fmr adviser to Gen. Ansumane Mane; Prime Minister of Guinea-Bissau 1998–2000; Leader Partido Unido Social Democrático (PUSD) 2002–06 (resgnd); unsuccessful PUSD presidential cand. 2005; Personal Counsellor to Pres. of the Repub. 2005–06 (resgnd); Pres. Partido para a Democracia, Desenvolvimento e Cidadania (Party for Democracy, Devt and Citizenship—PADEC) 2007–; Pres. Tribunal of Accounts 2009–12; barred by Supreme Court as PADEC cand. in presidential election on the grounds that he was still Pres. of Tribunal of Accounts 2009; mem. UNESCO Int. Comm. for Peace Research; Amb. for Peace of Universal Peace Fed. *Publication includes:* O Desenvolvimento do Continente Africano na Era da Mundialização 2005. *Leisure interests:* literature, music, cinema, sport, gymnastics. *Address:* Partido para a Democracia, Desenvolvimento e Cidadania (PADEC), Apartado 415, 1032 Bissau Codex, Guinea-Bissau (office). *Telephone:* 92-5263801 (Portugal, mobile) (office). *E-mail:* fjfadul@hotmail.com (office).

FAECKE, Peter; German journalist, writer and editor; b. 3 Nov. 1940, Grunwald, Silesia; ed Univs of Göttingen, Berlin, Hamburg, Paris; Lecturer, Univ. of Texas, Austin, USA; Dir Edition Köln, PEN-Centre Germany; awards include stipend of Villa Massimo, Rome and literature prizes of Lower Saxony, North-Rhine-Westphalia and City of Cologne. *Publications:* Die Brandstifter (novel) 1962, Der Rote Milan (novel) 1965, Postversand-Roman (novel) (with Wolf Vostell) 1970, Gemeinsam gegen Abriss: Ein Lesebuch aus Arbeitersiedlungen 1974, Das Unaufhaltsame Glück der Kowalskis 1982, Flug ins Leben (novel) 1988, Der Mann mit den besonderen Eigenschaften (novel) 1993, Grabstein für Fritz (documentary film) 1993, Als Elizabeth Arden Neunzehn war (novel) 1994, Eine Liebe zum Land (film script) 1994, Ankunft eines Schüchternen im Himmel (novel) 2000, Das Kreuz des Südens (reports) 2001, Vom Überfliessen der Anden, Reportagen aus Peru 2001, Hochzeitsvorbereitungen auf dem Lande (novel) 2003, Die geheimen Videos des Herrn Vladimiro (novel) 2004, Lima die Schöne-Lima die Schreckliche (reports) 2005, Wenn bei uns ein Gratis stirbt... (reports) 2005, Der Kardinal, ganz in Rot und frisch gebügelt (novel) 2007, Die Tango-Sängerin (novel) 2008, Dem alten Mann seine Kiste (novel) 2009. *Address:* Edition Köln, Mevissenstr. 16, 50668 Cologne; Pohlstadtsweg 414, 51109 Cologne, Germany (home). *Telephone:* (221) 726207 (home). *Fax:* (221) 1794149 (office).

E-mail: edition.koeln@t-online.de (office); peterfaecke@t-online.de (home). *Website:* www.peterfaecke.de (home).

FAGERNÄS, Peter, LLM; Finnish investment banker and business executive; *Managing Partner, Hermitage & Co Oy;* b. 1952; ed Univ. of Helsinki; Founder and Chair. Conventum Oyj (investment bank); Chair. Pohjola Group PLC 2001–03; Man. Pnr, Hermitage & Co. Oy and Chair. Oy Hermitage Ab 2003–; Chair. Fortum Corpn 2004–09 (resgnd); mem. Supervisory Bd Finnlines PLC, Trigon Capital; fmr mem. Bd of Dirs Merita Bank, Kansallis-Osake-Pankki; Vice-Chair. Helsinki Stock Exchange. *Address:* Hermitage & Co Oy, Erottajankatu 11 A 16, 00130 Helsinki, Finland (office). *Telephone:* (9) 6818180 (office). *Fax:* (9) 68181880 (office). *Website:* www.hermitage.fi (office).

FAGIN, Claire Muriel Mintzer, PhD, RN; American nurse; b. 25 Nov. 1926, New York, NY; d. of Harry Mintzer and Mae Mintzer (née Slatin); m. Samuel Fagin 1952; two s.; ed Wagner Coll., Teachers' Coll., Columbia Univ. and New York Univ.; staff nurse, Sea View Hosp., Staten Island, NY 1947, Clinical Instructor 1947–48; Bellevue Hosp., New York 1948–50; Psychiatric Mental Health Nursing Consultant, Nat. League for Nursing 1951–52; Asst Chief, Psychiatric Nursing Service Clinical Center, NIH 1953–54, Supt 1955; Research Project Co-ordinator, Children's Hosp., Dept of Psychiatry, Washington, DC 1956; Instructor in Psychiatric-Mental Health Nursing, New York Univ. 1956–58, Asst Prof. 1964–67, Dir Grad. Programs in Psychiatric-Mental Health Nursing 1965–69, Assoc. Prof. 1967–69; Prof. and Chair. Nursing Dept, Herbert H. Lehman Coll. 1969–77; Dir Health Professions Inst., Montefiore Hosp. and Medical Center 1975–77; Dean, School of Nursing, Univ. of Pennsylvania, Philadelphia 1977–92, Prof. 1992–96, interim Pres. 1993–94, Dean Emer., Prof. Emer. 1996–; mem. Task Force, Jt Cttee on Mental Health of Children 1966–69, Gov.'s Cttee on Children, New York 1971–75, Inst. of Medicine, NAS (Governing Council 1981–83), Comm. on Human Rights 1991–94, American Acad. of Nursing (Governing Council 1976–78), Expert Advisory Panel on Nursing, WHO 1974, Nat. Advisory Mental Health Council, Nat. Inst. of Mental Health 1983–87, Bd of Health Promotion and Disease Prevention 1990–94; Pres. American Orthopsychiatric Asscn 1985; Dir Salomon Inc. 1994–97; mem. Bd of Dirs Radian 1994–2002, Visiting Nurse Service of NY; Program Dir, Building Academic Geriatric Nursing Capacity Program, John A. Hartford Foundation 2000–05; Sr Advisor to Univ. of California, Davis School of Nursing; Pres. Nat. League for Nursing 1991–93; Sr Advisor to Jonas Center for Nursing; consultant to numerous foundations, public and pvt. univs, health-care agencies; speaker on radio and TV; Hon. Fellow, Royal Coll. of Nursing 2002; Hon. DSc (Lycoming Coll., Cedar Crest Coll., Univ. of Rochester, Medical Coll. of Pennsylvania, Univ. of Maryland, Loyola Univ., Wagner Coll., Case Western Reserve 2002); Hon. LLD (Pennsylvania); Hon. DHumLitt (Hunter Coll., Rush Univ., Johns Hopkins 2003), Hon. DrIur (Toronto) 2004, (Syracuse) 2010, (New York Univ.) 2011; numerous awards and distinctions including American Acad. of Nursing Living Legend 1998, New York Univ. Pres.'s Medal 1998, American Nurses Asscn Nightingale Lamp Award 2002, named to American Nurses Asscn Hall of Fame 2010. *Publications:* numerous books including Nursing Leadership: Global Strategies (ed.) 1990, Essays in Nursing Leadership 2000, When Care Becomes a Burden 2001, and over 100 articles on nursing and health policy. *Leisure interests:* theatre, opera, art, sailing, snorkeling, gardening. *Address:* 200 Central Park South, Apartment 12E, New York, NY 10019-1415, USA (home). *Telephone:* (212) 581-4752 (office). *Fax:* (212) 581-4752 (office). *E-mail:* cfagin1@nyc.rr.com (office).

FAGIOLO, Silvio, LLB; Italian diplomat and academic; *Professor of International Relations, Libera Università Internazionale degli Studi Sociali Guido Carli;* b. 15 July 1938, Rome; m. Margret Klauth; two c.; ed Univ. La Sapienza, Rome; joined diplomatic service 1969; foreign missions to Moscow 1972–76, Detroit, USA 1976–79, Bonn, W Germany 1982–86; Deputy Chief, Embassy in Washington, DC 1991–95; Amb. to Germany 2001; Adviser for European and Security Affairs, Ministry of Foreign Affairs, Head of Cabinet 1997–2000; mem. EU Group that organized Intergovernmental Conf. that led to Maastricht Treaty; Personal Rep. of Italian Foreign Minister at Intergovernmental Confs that led to Treaty of Amsterdam 1996, Treaty of Nice 2002; Perm. Rep. to EU 2001; currently mem. Faculty of Political Science and Prof. of Int. Relations, Libera Università Internazionale degli Studi Sociali Guido Carli, Rome; contrib. Il Sole 24 Ore 2006–09. *Publications:* I gruppi di pressione in URSS 1977, L'operaio americano 1980, La Russia di Gorbaciov 1987, La pace fredda 1998, L'Idea dell'Europa nelle relazioni internazionali 2009. *Leisure interests:* sports, music. *Address:* Faculty of Political Science, Libera Università Internazionale degli Studi Sociali Guido Carli in Roma, Viale Romania 32, 00198 Rome (office); Via Casalvecchio Siculo 4, 00133 Rome, Italy (home). *Telephone:* (06) 45472990 (home). *Fax:* (06) 45472990 (home). *E-mail:* s.fagiolo@hotmail.it (home). *Website:* www.luiss.it/scienzepolitiche (office).

FAHEY, Hon. John Joseph, AC; Australian politician and lawyer; b. 10 Jan. 1945, New Zealand; s. of Stephen Fahey and Annie Fahey; m. Colleen McGurran 1968; one s. two d.; ed St Anthony's Convent, Picton and Chevalier Coll. Bowral, Sydney Univ. Law Extension; mem. Parl. of NSW 1984–95; Minister for Industrial Relations and Employment and Minister Assisting Premier of NSW 1988–90; Minister for Industrial Relations, Further Educ., Training and Employment, NSW 1990–92; Premier and Treas. of NSW 1992; Premier and Minister for Econ. Devt of NSW 1993–95; Fed. mem. for Macarthur and Minister for Finance 1996–2001, for Admin. 1997–2001; consultant, adviser, dir 2002–; Chair. Sydney 2000 Olympic Bid Co. 1992–93. *Leisure interest:* keen sports follower. *Address:* Ashford, 39 Hurlingham Avenue, Burradoo, NSW 2576, Australia (home). *E-mail:* faheyj@bigpond.com (home).

FAHIM, Makhdoom Muhammad Amin, BA; Pakistani politician; b. 4 Aug. 1939, Hala Taluka; s. of Makhdoom Muhammmad Zaman 'Talib-ul-Mola', spiritual leader of Sarwari Jammat of Pakistan and a founding mem. Pakistan Peoples Party (PPP); ed Sindh Univ.; elected mem. Nat. Ass. from southern Thatta dist of Sindh Prov. 1970 (re-elected 1977, 1988, 1990, 1993, 1997, 2002), boycotted non-party elections of 1985 held by Gen. Muhammad Zia ul-Haq-led mil. regime; Minister of Communications 1988–90, of Railways 1988–89, for Housing and Works 1994–96; Vice-Chair. PPP, Leader PPP Parliamentarians faction to contest elections 2002, currently Leader Parl. Group; Acting Chair. Alliance for the Restoration of Democracy 2003, currently Chair.; Minister of Commerce 2008–13; leader of spiritual group 'Sarwari Jamaat', with more than 6 million people world-

wide. *Leisure interests:* reading and writing poetry. *Address:* c/o Ministry of Commerce, Block A, Pakistan Secretariat, Islamabad (office); 11-A, 2nd Sun Set Street, DHA, Karachi, Pakistan (home). *Website:* www.ppp.org.pk.

FAHIM, Sulaiman Abdul Kareem Mohammad al-, MBA, PhD; United Arab Emirates business executive; *President and Chairman, Arab Union for Real Estate Development;* b. 1977, Dubai; ed American Univ., Washington, DC, Kogod School of Business; Founder and CEO Hydra Properties (real estate co.) 2005–09; Pres. and Chair. Arab Union for Real Estate Devt 2009–; Rep., Abu Dhabi United Group for Devt and Investment (sovereign wealth fund), involved in takeover of Manchester City Football Club 2008; Chair. Portsmouth Football Club 2009–10; creator and host Hydra Executives (reality TV series) 2008–; Founder Intergovernmental Inst. for the use of Micro-algae Spirulina Against Malnutrition (IIMSAM) and IIMSAM's Amb. to the Kingdom of Spain; Dir Intergovernmental Renewable Energy Org. 2010; Pres. UAE Chess Asscn; has been at the forefront of many green social housing initiatives in Saudi Arabia; Visionary Award, Middle East CEO magazine 2007, ranked 20th by Arabian Business Magazine amongst 100 Most Powerful Arabs 2010, also ranked amongst the Power 500: The Worlds's Most Influential Arabs (112th) 2011, (87th) 2012. *Address:* Arab Union for Real Estate Development, Abu Dhabi, United Arab Emirates (office).

FAHIYE, Husayn Elabe; Somali politician; *Minister of Reconstruction;* Minister of Nat. Planning 2000–07, of Human Rights 2004–07, of Foreign Affairs 2007, of Trade, Industry and Tourism 2008–09, of Reconstruction 2009–. *Address:* Ministry of Reconstruction, Mogadishu, Somalia.

FAHRENSCON, Georg; German economist, politician and banking executive; *Chairman of the Board of Administration, Bayerische Landesbank;* b. 8 Feb. 1968, Munich; m.; two c.; ed Univ. of Augsburg; involved in Youth Union (Jungen Union—JU) 1985–2003, including as mem. Fed. JU Germany, Dist Chair. Upper JU; mem. Christian Social Union (CSU) 1987–, Deputy Dist Chair. CSU, Munich-Land 1999–, Dist Treas. Upper Bavaria CSU 2003–, Deputy Chair. CSU Policy Comm. 2006–08, Chair. CSU (Econ.) 2008–; Councillor Neuried 1990–2002, Second Mayor of Neuried 2002; mem. Co. Council for Munich-Land 1996–; mem. Bundestag 2002–07; State Sec., Bavarian State Ministry of Finance 2007–08, Minister of Finance 2008–; Chair. Bd of Admin Bayerische Landesbank 2010–; Alt. mem. Federalism Comm. II 2007–; mem. Cen. Cttee of German Catholics 2004–, Presidium of Ecumenical Church Congress, Munich 2010 2007–, Sudeten Germans 2008–; Founding mem. Soc. and mem. Bd of Trustees, air rescue 'Christoph 1' eV 2005–. *Address:* Bayerische Landesbank Girozentrale, Brienner-strasse 18, 80333 Munich, Germany (office). *Telephone:* (89) 2171-01 (office). *Fax:* (89) 2171-23-578 (office). *E-mail:* info@bayernlb.de (office). *Website:* www.bayernlb .de (office); www.georg-fahrenschon.de.

FAHRHOLZ, Bernd, LLB; German lawyer and banking executive; *Partner, Dewey & LeBoeuf LLP;* b. 4 Aug. 1947, Oldenburg, Lower Saxony; ed Univ. of Hamburg; joined Dresdner Bank as legal adviser 1977, with Domestic Corp. Customer Div. 1985–89, Man. Corp. Finance Div. 1989, later Co-Head, Int. Activities, Sr Gen. Man. Head of Global Finance, Investment Banking Div. 1997, mem. Bd of Man. Dirs 1998–2003, Chair. 2000–01, also Man. Dir Corp. Centre, Corp. Communications, Econs, Gen. Sec., Group Devt, Group Strategy, Human Resources and Legal Services, CEO 2000–03 (after acquisition of Dresdner Bank by Allianz AG forming Allianz-Dresdner AG); currently Pnr, Dewey & LeBoeuf LLP (law firm), Frankfurt; also currently Chair. Supervisory Bd Smartrac NV, Amsterdam; mem. Supervisory Bd Fresenius Medical Care AG; mem. Frankfurt Bar Asscn; Hon. Prof., Johann Wolfgang Goethe Univ. *Address:* Dewey & LeBoeuf LLP, Skyper, Taunusanlage 1, 60329 Frankfurt, Germany (office). *Telephone:* (69) 36393550 (office). *Fax:* (69) 36393333 (office). *E-mail:* bfahrholz@dl.com (office). *Website:* www.deweyleboeuf.com (office).

FAHRNI, Fritz, PhD; Swiss academic and business executive; *Chairman, u-blox Ltd;* b. 7 Sept. 1942; m.; two d.; ed Swiss Fed. Inst. of Tech. (ETH), Zürich, Illinois Inst. of Tech., Chicago and Harvard Business School, USA; research worker, Ill. Inst. of Tech., NASA 1967–70; Team Leader, Research, Eng, Devt and Production Processes, CIBA-GEIGY 1971–76; Head, Research and Devt Gas Turbine Dept Sulzer Brothers 1976–80, Head, Gas Turbine Dept 1980–82, Head, Textile Machinery Group 1982–87, Pres. and CEO Sulzer Corpn 1988–99; Chair. Bd, Universität St Gallen, Institut für Technologiemanagement (ITEM-HSG) 1999–2007, Prof. of Practice in Tech. Man. and Entrepreneurship, ETH Zürich and Universität St Gallen 2000–07; Chair. LEM SA, Switzerland 1998–2004, u-blox Ltd 2007–; mem. Bd of Dirs in four orgs (two industrial, one hosp. and one pvt. equity); Hon. mem. Swiss American Chamber of Commerce; Int. Entrepreneurial Leadership Award, Ill. Inst. of Tech. 2000; several times winner of 'Entrepreneur of the Month' and 'E of the Year' Awards, Switzerland. *Leisure interests:* sport, mountaineering, reading, music, garden. *Address:* Universität St Gallen, Institut für Technologiemanagement, Dufourstrasse 40A, 9000 St Gallen (office); ETH Zentrum, Kreuzplatz 5, 8032 Zürich, Switzerland (office). *Telephone:* (71) 224-72-01 (office), (44) 632-05-50 (office); (44) 390-25-95 (home). *Fax:* (71) 224-73-21 (office). *E-mail:* fritz.fahrni@unisg.ch (office); ffahrni@ethz.ch (office). *Website:* www.item.unisg.ch (office); www.tmu.ethz.ch (office).

FAINSILBER, Adrien, DPLG; French urban designer and fmr architect; b. 15 June 1932, Le Nouvion; s. of Sigismond Fainsilber and Fanny Moscovici; m. Julia Berg 1961; two s. one d.; ed Ecole Nationale Supérieure des Beaux Arts; architect, Univ. of Villetaneuse 1969–70, Univ. of Tech. of Compiègne 1973, Evry Hosp. 1980, La Géode, Parc de la Villette, Paris 1984, Cité of Science and Industry, Paris 1985, Water Treatment Plant, Valenton 1987, Museum of Beaux Arts, Clermont-Ferrand 1992, Town Hall, La Flèche 1994, HQ Unedic, Paris 1994, master plan and housing for Zac Richter, Port Marianne, Montpellier 1995, Montsouris Mutual Inst. Psychiatric Centre for Adolescents, Paris 1996, Museum of Modern and Contemporary Art, Strasbourg 1997, Children's Hosp., Purpan, Toulouse 1998, Courthouse Avignon 2000, Municipal Library, Marseille 2003, Extension, Water Treatment Plant, Valenton 2005, Obstetrical and Gynaecological Hospital, Lyons 2007; co. seat for Haut-Rhin 2004; mem. Int. Acad. of Architecture; Chevalier, Légion d'honneur 1987, Officier des Arts et des Lettres 1997; Bronze Medal, Soc. d'Encouragement à l'Art et à l'Industrie 1973, Silver Medal, Acad. of Architecture 1986, UIA Prix Auguste Perret 1990, Prix de Construction Metallique 2004. *Publications:* La Virtualité de l'Espace: Projets et Architecture 1962–1988, Adrien

Fainsilber & Associés 1986–2002 by Christine Desmoulins. *Leisure interests:* swimming, travel. *Address:* 9 rue de Monttessuy, 75007 Paris, France. *Telephone:* 1-45-51-34-33. *E-mail:* adrienfainsilber@free.fr.

FAIRBANK, Richard (Rich) D., BEcons, MBA; American banking executive; *Chairman and CEO, Capital One Financial Corporation;* b. 1950, Northampton, Mass.; m.; four c.; ed Stanford Univ., Stanford Grad. School of Business; consultant, Strategic Planning Assocs (later Mercer Management) 1981–87; Chair. and CEO Capital One Financial Corpn 1994–; mem. US Region Bd of Dirs MasterCard 1995–2004 (Chair. 2002–04), mem. MasterCard International Global Bd of Dirs 2004–; Washingtonian Magazine Business Leader of the Year, Institutional Investor magazine Best CEO in specialty finance, American Banker magazine Banker of the Year Award 2006. *Address:* Capital One Financial Corporation, 1680 Capital One Drive, McLean, VA 22102-3407, USA (office). *Telephone:* (703) 720-1000 (office). *Fax:* (703) 720-2306 (office). *E-mail:* info@capitalone.com (office). *Website:* www.capitalone.com (office).

FAIREY, Michael Edward, ACIB; British banker (retd); b. 17 June 1948, Louth, Lincs.; s. of Douglas Fairey and Marjorie Fairey; m. Patricia Ann Dolby 1973; two s.; ed King Edward VI Grammar School; Asst Dir Watford Group, Barclays Bank 1967–86, Operations Dir Barclaycard 1986–88, Exec. Dir Barclays Card Services 1988–92; Dir Retail Credit and Group Credit Dir TSB Group 1992, Group Dir Credit Operations 1993–96, Information Tech. and Operations Dir 1996–97, Group Dir, Cen. Services, Lloyds TSB Group 1997–98, Deputy Group Chief Exec. 1998–2008 (retd); Pres. British Quality Foundation; Chair. Race for Opportunity. *Leisure interests:* tennis, opera, football. *Address:* Churchfields House, Hitchin Road, Codicote, Herts., SG4 8TH, England (home). *Telephone:* (1438) 821710 (home). *Fax:* (1438) 821079 (home).

FAIRHEAD, Rona, CBE, BL, MBA; British business executive; *Chief Executive, Financial Times Group;* m. Tom Fairhead; three c.; ed Univ. of Cambridge, Harvard Business School, USA; worked for Bain & Co. and Morgan Stanley; sr exec. in aerospace industry, working for Bombardier/Shorts Aerospace and British Aerospace –1995; Exec. Vice-Pres. Strategy and Group Financial Control and mem. Exec. Bd ICI PLC 1995–2001; Deputy Finance Dir, Pearson 2001–02, Chief Financial Officer 2002–06, Chief Exec. Financial Times Group 2006–, mem. Bd and Man. Cttee Pearson; Chair. Interactive Data Corpn 2007–10; Dir (non-exec.) HSBC Holdings plc 2004–. *Address:* The Financial Times Group, One Southwark Bridge, London, SE1 9HL, England (office). *Telephone:* (20) 7873-3000 (office). *Website:* www.ft.com (office).

FAISAL, Ameen; Maldivian politician; *National Security Adviser;* grand-s. of Mohamed Ameen Didi, first Pres. of the Maldives; m. Aminath Mubarik; four c.; mem. Maldivian Democratic Party (MDP), mem. MDP Nat. Council and Pres. of MDP Malé Dhaairaa constituency 2007–08; arrested and detained for several weeks following Addu Boat Crisis Nov. 2006; arrested while attending funeral of Hussein Salah and detained in solitary confinement in Dhoonidhoo Prison April 2007; Shadow Defence Minister –2008; Minister of Defence and Nat. Security 2008–10; Nat. Security Adviser 2010–; currently Chair. Nat. Crime Prevention Cttee. *Address:* Ministry of Defence and National Security, Ameer Ahmed Magu, Malé 20-126, Maldives (office). *Telephone:* 3322607 (office). *Fax:* 3332689 (office). *E-mail:* admin@defence.gov.mv (office). *Website:* www.defence.gov.mv (office).

FAITHFULL, Marianne; British singer; b. 29 Dec. 1946, Ormskirk, Lancs.; d. of Glynn Faithull and Eva Faithull; m. 1st John Dunbar; one s.; m. 2nd Ben Brierley; m. 3rd Giorgio della Terza; made first recording (As Tears Go By) aged 17; Commdr, Ordre des Arts et des Lettres 2011. *Films:* I'll Never Forget Whatsisname 1967, Girl on a Motorcycle 1968, Hamlet 1969, Lucifer Rising 1972, Ghost Story 1974, Assault on Agathon 1975, When Pigs Fly 1993, The Turn of the Screw 1994, Shopping 1994, Moondance 1995, Crimetime 1996, Intimacy 2001, Far From China 2001, Alone in the Dark 2003, A Letter to True 2003, Nord-Plage 2004, Paris, je t'aime 2006, Marie Antoinette 2006, Irina Palm 2007. *Television:* Anna 1967, The Door of Opportunity 1970, The Stronger 1971. *Stage appearances:* Three Sisters (London) 1967, Seven Deadly Sins (St Ann's Cathedral, New York) 1990, The Threepenny Opera (Gate Theatre, Dublin) 1992. *Recordings include:* albums: Come My Way 1965, Marianne Faithfull 1965, Go Away From My World 1966, North Country Maid 1966, Faithfull Forever 1966, Love in a Mist 1967, Dreaming My Dreams 1977, Faithless (with the Grease Band) 1978, Broken English 1979, Dangerous Acquaintances 1981, A Child's Adventure 1983, Summer Nights 1984, Music for the Millions 1985, Strange Weather 1987, Rich Kid Blues 1988, Blazing Away 1990, A Secret Life 1995, 20th Century Blues 1997, The Seven Deadly Sins 1998, Vagabond Ways 1999, Stranger On Earth 2001, Kissin' Time 2002, Before the Poison 2004, Easy Come Easy Go 2009. *Publications:* Faithfull (autobiog.) 1994, Marianne Faithfull Diaries 2002. *E-mail:* assistante@mac.com (office). *Website:* www.mariannefaithfull.org.uk.

FAIVRE d'ARCIER, Bernard, LèsL; French civil servant and culture consultant; *CEO, BFA-Conseil;* b. 12 July 1944, Albertville; s. of Guy Faivre d'Arcier and Geneviève Teilhard de Chazelles; m. 1st Sylvie Dumont 1966; one s.; m. 2nd Madeleine Lévy 1991; m. 3rd Ophélie Orecchia 2012; ed Hautes études commerciales, Inst. d'études politiques and Ecole nat. d'admin; Civil Admin., Ministry of Culture 1972–79; Dir Festival d'Avignon 1979–84, Artistic Dir 1992–2003; Tech. Adviser to the Prime Minister's Cabinet 1984–86; Pres. la SEPT (TV Channel) 1986; Consultant, UNESCO 1987–88; Adviser to the Pres. of the Nat. Ass. 1988; Head of Dept of Theatre, Ministry of Educ. and Culture 1992–; Dir Nat. Centre for Theatre 1992; CEO BFA-Conseil (man. consultants); Commdr des Arts et des Lettres, Officier, Ordre nat. du Mérite, Officier, Légion d'honneur. *Leisure interests:* art, theatre. *Address:* 27 rue Michel Le Comte, 75003 Paris, France (home). *Telephone:* 1-42-78-72-13 (home). *E-mail:* bernard.faivre-darcier@orange.fr.

FAIZULLAEV, Alisher, (Alisher Faiz), PhD, DSc; Uzbekistani diplomatist and social and political scientist; *Director of Negotiation Laboratory and Professor, Department of Practical Diplomacy, University of World Economy and Diplomacy;* b. 10 Jan. 1957, Tashkent; s. of Omonulla Faizullaev and Nasiba Ashrapkhanova; m. Shakhnoz Faizullaeva; two s. two d.; ed Tashkent State Univ. and Inst. of Psychology, USSR Acad. of Sciences, Moscow; Lecturer, Uzbekistan Acad. of Sciences, Tashkent 1979–80, Sr Lecturer 1983–86; Visiting Fellow, Inst. of Psychology, USSR Acad. of Sciences 1986–87; Sr Lecturer, Tashkent State Univ.

1987–88; Head of Dept, Exec. Training Inst., Tashkent 1988–91; Intern, City Council of San Diego, CA 1989; Head of Dept, Inst. of Political Sciences and Man., Tashkent 1991–92; Distinguished Visiting Scholar, Western Washington Univ., Bellingham, USA 1992; Dir Inst. of Man., Univ. of World Economy and Diplomacy, Tashkent 1992–93, First Vice-Rector 2003–05; currently Dir of Negotiation Laboratory and Prof., Dept of Practical Diplomacy; Consultant on Political Affairs, then Chief Consultant on Int. Affairs and Foreign Econ. Relations, Office of the Pres. of Uzbekistan 1993–94; Deputy Minister of Foreign Affairs 1994–95; Amb. to Belgium and Head of Missions to EU and Euro-Atlantic Partnership Council/ NATO 1995–98, concurrently Amb. to the Netherlands and Luxembourg with residence in Brussels 1997–98; State Adviser to Pres. of Uzbekistan on Int. Affairs and Foreign Econ. Relations 1998–99; First Deputy Minister of Foreign Affairs Feb.–Dec. 1999; Amb. to UK 1999–2003; Visiting Scholar, Centre of Int. Studies and Visiting Fellow, New Hall Coll., Cambridge 2005, Jesus Coll., Cambridge 2007; Fulbright Scholar, Fletcher School of Law and Diplomacy, Tufts Univ. and Inst. for the Study of Diplomacy, School of Foreign Service, Georgetown Univ. 2011–12; USSR Young Social Scientists Prize 1987. *Publications:* Motivational Self-Regulation of Personality (in Russian) 1987, Human Being, Politics, Management (in Russian and Uzbek) 1995, Tabula rasa (short stories in Russian) 2004, Krugovorot (short stories in Russian) 2006, Diplomatic Negotiations (in Russian) 2007, As Power to Power: Politics of Interpersonal Relations (in Russian) 2010; numerous articles on behavioural, social and political sciences in academic journals. *Leisure interests:* tennis, fencing. *Address:* University of World Economy and Diplomacy, 54 Buyuk Ipak Yuli, Tashkent 100113, Uzbekistan (office). *Telephone:* (71) 2676769 (office). *Fax:* (71) 2670900 (office). *E-mail:* negolab@gmail .com (office). *Website:* www.uwed.uz (office); www.alisher-faiz.net; sites.google .com/site/negolab.

FAKHFAKH, Elyès; Tunisian engineer and politician; b. 1972, Tunis; ed Institut Nat. des Sciences Appliquées, Lyons, France; began career as engineer with Total France (petroleum co.), worked in Europe, USA and Asia, becoming Dir of new Total industrial plant in Poland 2004–06; fmr Deputy Dir Gen. Cortrel (Tunisian automotive parts mfr); Minister of Tourism 2011–12, of Finance 2012–14; mem. Forum démocratique pour le travail et les libertés (Ettakatol). *Address:* c/o Ministry of Finance, pl. du Gouvernement, La Kasbah, 1008 Tunis, Tunisia (office).

FAKHFAKH, Mokhtar, BS; Tunisian banker; b. 10 Aug. 1930, Sfax; s. of Ahmed B. Abdessalem Fakhfakh and Fatouma Hamouda; m. Samira Fakhfakh; one s. one d.; ed law studies; Pres. and Gen. Man. Soc. Hotelière et Touristique de Tunisie 1961–67; Dir of Commerce, Ministry of Finance and Commerce 1967–69; Pres. and Gen. Man. Banque du Sud 1969–71; Gen. Man. Banque de Développement Economique de Tunisie 1971–78; Pres. and Gen. Man. Cie Financière Immobilière et Touristique de Tunisie 1978–80, Banque Int. Arabe de Tunisie 1980, then Pres., now Hon. Chair.; special adviser on banking affairs to Pres. Zine el Abedine Ben Ali 2001–; mem. Bd of Dirs Société Frigorifique et Brasserie de Tunis SA; Commdr, Ordre de la République; African Banker of Year 1994. *Address:* c/o Banque International Arabe de Tunisie, 70–72 Avenue Habib Bourguiba, BP 520, 1001 Tunis, Tunisia. *Website:* www.biat.com.tn (office).

FAKI MAHAMAT, Moussa; Chadian politician; *Minister of External Relations and African Integration;* b. 21 June 1960; early career as Prof. of Law, Chad Univ.; Dir-Gen. Nat. Sugar Soc. 1996–99; Minister of Transport and Public Works 2002; Prime Minister of Chad 2003–05; Minister of External Relations and African Integration 2008–. *Address:* Ministry of External Relations, BP 746, N'Djamena, Chad (office). *Telephone:* 251-80-50 (office). *Fax:* 251-45-85 (office). *E-mail:* tchaddiplomatie@gmail.com (office). *Website:* www.tchad-diplomatie.org (office).

FAKUDZE, Mtiti, BAgr; Swazi politician; ed Univ. of Swaziland; mem. House of Ass. (Parl.) for Dvokodvweni constituency; Minister of Agric. and Co-operatives 2003–08, of Public Service and Information 2008–11, of Foreign Affairs 2011–13. *Address:* c/o Ministry of Foreign Affairs, POB 518, Mbabane, Swaziland (office).

FALCAM, Leo A.; Micronesian fmr head of state; b. 20 Nov. 1935; ed Univ. of Hawaii, Princeton Univ., USA; Political Affairs Officer, Office of the US Trust Territory of the Pacific Islands High Commr 1962–64, Asst Dist Admin. for Ponape Dist 1964–65, Exec. Officer, Office of the High Commr 1966–72, Dist Admin. for Ponape Dist 1972–76; Gov. of Pohnpei 1979–83; Post Master Gen. 1984–87; Senator-at-Large for Pohnpei State 1987–97; Vice-Pres. of Micronesia 1997–99, Pres. 1999–2003; Chair. Standing Cttee for the Pacific Islands Conf. of Leaders 2001; fmr Pres. FSM Bank; fmr Trustee, Pohnpei Agric. and Trade School, PATS PEACE Foundation.

FALCO, Edith (Edie); American actress; b. 5 July 1963, Brooklyn, New York; d. of Frank Falco and Judith Loney; one adopted s.; ed State Univ. of New York at Purchase. *Television includes:* The Sunshine Boys (film) 1995, Oz (series) 1997–99; The Sopranos (series – Emmy Award for Outstanding Lead Actress in a Drama Series 2000, 2003, Golden Globe Award for Best Performance by an Actress in a Drama Series 2000, SAG Award for Outstanding Performance by a Female Actor in a Drama Series 2000, 2008) 1999–2007, Jenifer (film) 2001, Fargo (film) 2003, 30 Rock 2007–08, Nurse Jackie 2009–13. *Films include:* The Unbelievable Truth 1989, Trust 1990, Laws of Gravity 1992, Time Expired 1992, Bullets Over Broadway 1994, Rift 1995, The Addition 1995, Breathing Room 1996, Hurricane 1997, Private Parts 1997, Cop Land 1997, Trouble on the Corner 1997, Cost of Living 1997, A Price above Rubies 1998, Judy Berlin 1999, Stringer 1999, Random Hearts 1999, Overnight Sensation 2000, Death of a Dog 2000, Sunshine State 2002, Family of the Year 2004, The Girl from Monday 2005, The Great New Wonderful 2005, The Quiet 2005, Freedomland 2006, Three Backyards 2009. *Plays:* 'night, Mother 2005. *Address:* c/o ICM, 10250 Constellation Boulevard, Los Angeles, CA 90067, USA (office).

FALCO, Randel (Randy) E., MBA; American fmr media executive; b. 26 Dec. 1953; m. Susan Falco; three c.; ed Iona Coll.; joined NBC 1975, several positions in Finance, Tech. Operations, Corp. Strategic Planning, Vice-Pres. Finance and Admin, NBC Sports 1986–91, Pres. Broadcast and Network Operations Div., NBC 1993–98, COO Olympics, Barcelona Olympics 1992, Atlanta Olympics 1996, Sydney Olympics 2000, Salt Lake City Olympics 2002, Pres. NBC TV Network 1998–2003, Group Pres. 2003–04, Pres. NBC Universal TV Networks Group 2004–06; Chair. and CEO AOL LLC (div. of Time Warner) 2006–09; mem. Bd of

Dirs Ronald McDonald House; Dr hc (Iona Coll.) 2001; six Emmy Awards. *Address:* c/o AOL LLC, 22000 AOL Way, Dulles, VA 20166, USA (office).

FALCONER OF THOROTON, Baron (Life Peer), cr. 1997, in the County of Nottinghamshire; **Charles Leslie Falconer,** QC; British lawyer and politician; b. 19 Nov. 1951; s. of the late John Falconer and Anne Falconer; m. Marianna Hildyard 1985; three s. one d.; ed Trinity Coll., Glenalmond, Queen's Coll., Cambridge; called to the Bar 1974, took silk 1991; Solicitor-Gen. 1997–98; Minister of State Cabinet Office 1998–2001; Minister with responsibility for Millennium Dome 1998–2001; Minister of State for Housing and Planning 2001, for the Criminal Justice System 2002–03; Lord Chancellor 2003–07; also Sec. of State for Justice May–June 2007; Labour; Chair. John Smith Memorial Trust 2007–, Amicus Horizon Housing Group 2008–; Visitor Queens Coll., Cambridge 2008–; Chair Ravensbourne Coll. 2011–; Chair. Comm. on Assisted Dying 2012–; Trustee, Roy Castle Lung Cancer Foundation 2007–. *Address:* House of Lords, London, SW1A 0PW, England (office). *Telephone:* (20) 7219-3000 (office). *Website:* www .parliament.uk (office).

FALCONES JAQUOTOT, Baldomero, MBA; Spanish business executive; *Chairman and Managing Director, Fomento de Construcciones y Contratas SA;* b. 1946, Majorca; ed IESE Business School of Univ. of Navarra; Founding Pnr, Magnum Industrial Partners; mem. Bd of Dirs MasterCard International Worldwide 1997–2007, Vice-Chair. 2003–07, Chair. 2003–07; fmr Chair. Santander Central Hispano, Seguros y Reaseguros SA; Exec. Vice-Chair. and CEO Fomento de Construcciones y Contratas SA 2007–08, Chair. and Man. Dir 2008–; mem. Bd of Dirs Unión Fenosa; fmr Dir for Spain at RWE; fmr Gen. Man. and mem. Exec. Cttee, Banco Santander Central Hispano; Chair. Plan Foundation (Spain); mem. Econ. Cttee, Fundación Albéniz. *Address:* Fomento de Construcciones y Contratas SA, Calle Federico Salmón, Madrid 28010 (office); Fomento de Construcciones y Contratas SA, Calle Balmes 36, 08007 Barcelona, Spain (office). *Telephone:* (93) 496-4900 (office). *Fax:* (93) 487-8892 (office). *E-mail:* info@fcc.es (office). *Website:* www.fcc.es (office).

FALCONÍ BENÍTEZ, Fander, MSc, PhD; Ecuadorean economist, academic and politician; *National Secretary, Secretaría Nacional de Planificación y Desarrollo;* ed Pontifical Catholic Univ. of Ecuador, Latin-American Faculty of Social Sciences, Autonomous Univ. of Barcelona; econs ed. for Punto de Vista newspaper 1987–91; econs analyst for Hoy newspaper 1987–89; adviser to Nat. Energy Inst. 1989–91; Tech. Asst Dept of Energy Planning and Dept for Subregional Andean Oil Integration Project, Latin American Energy Org. 1991–93; researcher, Ecuador Chamber of Commerce and Industry, Germany 1993–96; consultant to Petróleos del Ecuador SA 1995; Financial Man. Petróleos y Servicios 1995–96; Presidential adviser to Nat. Telecommunications Council 1996; UNDP adviser, Ministry of the Environment 2001; adviser to Fundación Natura 2001–02; Prof., Latin-American Faculty of Social Sciences 2001–; Prof. of Agricultural Econs and Rural Devt, Central Univ. of Ecuador 2001–04; Prof., Nat. Polytechnic School 2002–04; Nat. Sec. for Planning and Devt 2007–08; Minister of External Relations, Trade and Integration 2008–10 (resgnd); currently Nat. Sec., Secretaría Nacional de Planificación y Desarrollo (govt. agency); Visiting Prof., San Simón Univ. 2003, Centro Bartolomé de las Casas 2004, Univ. of Guadalajara, Mexico 2004. *Address:* Secretaría Nacional de Planificación y Desarrollo, Edif. CFN, 8°, Avda Juan León Mera 130 y Avda Patria, Quito, Ecuador (office). *Telephone:* (2) 397-8900 (office). *E-mail:* senplades@senplades.gob.ec (office). *Website:* www.senplades.gob.ec (office).

FALDO, Sir Nicholas (Nick) Alexander, Kt, MBE; British professional golfer, golf course designer and television commentator; b. 18 July 1957, Welwyn Garden City, Herts.; one s. three d.; ed Sir Francis Osborne School, Welwyn Garden City; won England Boys' Int. 1974, England Youth Int. 1975, Herts. Co. Championship, Berkshire Trophy, Scrutton Jug, S African Golf Union Special Stroke Championship, was Co. Champion of Champions, mem. GB Commonwealth team, Sr England Int. 1975–; became professional 1976; won Skol Lager Int., Rookie of the Year (Best British Newcomer) 1977, Colgate PGA Championship 1978, 1980, 1981, five titles on PGA European Tour, Golf Writers' Asscn Trophy and Harry Vardon Trophy 1983, Open Championship, Muirfield 1987, French Open and Volvo Masters, Valderrama 1988, Masters, Augusta, Ga, USA 1989, French Open 1989, US Masters 1989, 1990, 1996, Open Championship, St Andrew's 1990, Irish Open 1991, 1992, 1993, Open Championship, Muirfield 1992, Toyota World Match Play Championship 1992, Scandinavian Masters 1992, European Open 1992, Johnnie Walker World Championship 1992, (seven tournament victories 1992), Alfred Dunhill Belgian Open 1994, Doral Ryder Open, USA 1995; World No. 1 1992–94, Johnnie Walker Asian Classic 1993, Los Angeles Open, USA 1997, World Cup 1998; named Capt. European Ryder Cup team beginning 2008; involved in Faldo Design, an int. golf course architectural co. 1991–; lead analyst for Golf Channel and CBS TV PGA tour coverage; BBC Sports Personality of the Year 1989, PGA Award for Outstanding Services to Golf 2003. *Publications:* In Search of Perfection (with Bruce Critchley) 1995, Faldo – A Swing for Life 1995, Life Swings: The Autobiography 2004. *Leisure interests:* fly fishing, helicopter flying, golf course design. *Address:* c/o Faldo Enterprises, 18–20 Sheet Street, Windsor, Berks., SL4 1BG, England (office). *Telephone:* (1753) 829711 (office). *Fax:* (1753) 829712 (office). *Website:* www.nickfaldo.com (office).

FALIH, Khalid A. al-, BS, MBA; Saudi Arabian business executive; *President and CEO, Saudi Arabian Oil Company (Saudi Aramco);* b. 1960, Riyadh; m. Dr Najah Al-Garawi; two s. three d.; ed Texas A&M Univ., USA, King Fahd Univ. of Petroleum and Mineral Resources, Dhahran; joined Saudi Arabian Oil Co. (Saudi Aramco, fmrly Aramco) 1979, held various man. positions including Pres. Petron Corpn (jt venture with Philippine Nat. Oil Co.) 1999, Sr Vice-Pres. of Gas Operations and Industrial Relations, Head of New Business Devt 2003, Dir Aramco 2004–, Exec. Vice-Pres. for Operations 2007–08, Pres. and CEO Saudi Aramco 2009–; fmr Chair. South Rub' al-Khali (exploration co.), Dammam City Municipal Council; Dir Saudi Nat. Program for Devt of Industrial Clusters; mem. Saudi Arabian Supreme Council of Petroleum and Mineral Affairs, American Soc. of Mechanical Engineers, Int. Asscn for Energy Econs, Oxford Energy Policy Club; mem. Bd of Dirs US-Saudi Arabian Business Council; mem. Asia Business Council, JP Morgan International Council; Founding mem. Bd of Trustees, King Abdullah Univ. of Science and Tech. 2008–; ranked by Arabian Business amongst the Power 500: The World's Most Influential Arabs (eighth) 2012, (ninth) 2013. *Address:*

Saudi Aramco, PO Box 5000, Dhahran 31311, Saudi Arabia (office). *Telephone:* (3) 872-0115 (office). *Fax:* (3) 873-8190 (office). *Website:* www.saudiaramco.com (office).

FALIK, Yuri Aleksandrovich; Russian composer and conductor; b. 30 July 1936, Odessa; s. of Aleksander Yefimovich Falik and Yevgeniya Mikhailovna Bochko; m. Valentina Alexandrovna Papkova; one s. one d.; ed Odessa Specialized School, Leningrad State Conservatory as cellist (teachers A. Shtrimer and M. Rostropovich), as composer (B. Arapov); teacher, Leningrad (now St Petersburg) Conservatory 1965–88, Prof. of Composition and Instrumentation 1988–; toured as conductor with orchestras in Russia and USA; First Prize, Int. Cellists Competition Helsinki 1962, Merited Worker of Arts of Russia 1981, People's Artist of Russia 2002. *Compositions:* for musical theatre: Orestea (choreographic tragedy) 1968, Scapin Antics (opera) 1981; comic opera: Plutin Skapena 1984; ballet: Oresteya 1968; for symphony orchestra: Symphony No. 1 1963, No. 2 (Kaddish) 1993, Light Symphony 1971, Concertos 1967, 1977, Mass over Igor Stravinsky 1975, Symphonietta for strings 1984, Canto in memoria: Symphony No 3 2005; for instruments with orchestra: Concertino for oboe 1961, Violin Concerto 1971, Chamber Concerto for three flutes 1983, Concertino for bassoon 1987, Concerto della Passione for cello 1988, Lyrical Concertino for viola and orchestra 2005; vocal-symphony works: Five Poems by Anna Akhmatova for soprano and chamber orchestra 1978, Ringaday for mezzo-soprano and orchestra 1986, Polly and Dinosaurs (musical fairy-tale over Geraldine Freund) 1989, Mass 1996; works for choir a cappella, including Liturgy Chants 1992; chamber ensembles, including, "Buffoons", a Concerto for Winds and Percussion 1966, Eight Quartets 1955–2001, Brass quintet 2003; romances, instrumental pieces; Four Concertos for chorus a capella 1979–98, Elegies: Concerto for soprano solo and chorus a capella 2001, Miraculous images, cycle for chorus a capella 2004. *Address:* Finlyandsky prospekt 1, Apt 54, 194044 St Petersburg, Russia (home). *Telephone:* (812) 542-63-06 (home). *Fax:* (812) 311-58-11 (home). *E-mail:* afalik2000@mail.ru (home).

FALK, Thomas J., BCom, MSc; American business executive; *Chairman and CEO, Kimberly-Clark Corporation;* b. 1958, Waterloo, Ia; m. Karen Falk; one s.; ed Univ. of Wisconsin, Stanford Univ. Grad. School of Business; accountant, Alexander Grant & Co. –1983; joined Audit Dept, Kimberly-Clark Corpn 1983, various man. positions, including Sr Auditor 1984, Sr Financial Analyst 1986, Dir of Corp. Strategy Analysis 1987, Operations Man. for Infant Care, Beech Island, SC 1989, Vice-Pres. Operations Analysis and Control 1990, Sr Vice-Pres. of Analysis and Admin 1991–93, Group Pres., Infant and Child Care 1993–95, Group Pres. N America Consumer Products 1995–98, Group Pres. Global Tissue and Paper 1998–99, COO 1999, Pres. 1999–2002, Dir 1999–, CEO 2002–, Chair. 2003–; mem. Bd of Dirs Lockheed Martin, Catalyst, Univ. of Wisconsin Foundation; Nat. Gov. Boys and Girls Clubs of America. *Address:* Kimberly-Clark Corpn, 351 Phelps Drive, Irving, TX 75038, USA (office). *Telephone:* (972) 281-1200 (office). *Fax:* (972) 281-1490 (office). *E-mail:* info@kimberly-clark.com (office). *Website:* www.kimberly-clark.com (office).

FALKENGREN, Annika; Swedish business executive; *President and Group CEO, SEB AB;* b. (Annika Bolin), m.; one c.; ed Univ. of Stockholm; joined SEB (Skandinaviska Enskilda Banken) AB as trainee in Stockholm br. 1987, Head, Corp. & Insts Div. 2001–05, Deputy CEO SEB AB 2005, Pres. and Group CEO 2005–; mem. Bd of Dirs Securitas AB; mem. Supervisory Bd Volkswagen Group 2011–, Munich RE 2011–; named by Veckans Affärer magazine as the most powerful woman in Swedish business 2005, ranked by Financial News Online 68th amongst "the 100 most influential people in European capital markets", ranked by Fortune magazine amongst the 50 Most Powerful Women in Business outside the US (13th) 2006, (11th) 2007, (seventh) 2008–09, (eighth) 2010, (tenth) 2011, (ninth) 2012, ranked by the Financial Times amongst Top 25 Businesswomen in Europe (20th) 2005, (14th) 2006, (ninth) 2007, ranked by Forbes magazine amongst The World's 100 Most Powerful Women (65th) 2010. *Leisure interests:* golf, reading. *Address:* SEB AB, Kungsträdgårdsg 8, 106 40 Stockholm, Sweden (office). *Telephone:* (771) 62-10-00 (office). *E-mail:* seb@seb.se (office). *Website:* www.seb.se (office).

FALL, Sir Brian James Proetel, GCVO, KCMG, MA, LLM; British diplomatist (retd); b. 13 Dec. 1937, London; s. of John William Fall and Edith Juliette Fall (née Proetel); m. Delmar Alexandra Roos 1962; three d.; ed St Paul's School, Magdalen Coll. Oxford, Univ. of Michigan Law School, USA; joined HM Foreign (now Diplomatic) Service 1962, UN Dept, Foreign Office 1963, Moscow 1965, Geneva 1968, Civil Service Coll. 1970, Eastern European and Soviet Dept and Western Orgs Dept, Foreign Office 1971, New York 1975, Harvard Univ. Center for Int. Affairs 1976, Counsellor, Embassy in Moscow 1977–79, Head of Energy, Science and Space Dept, FCO 1979–80, Head of Eastern European and Soviet Dept, FCO 1980–81, Prin. Pvt. Sec. to Sec. of State for Foreign and Commonwealth Affairs 1981–84, Dir Cabinet Sec.-Gen. of NATO 1984–86, Asst Under-Sec. of State (Defence), FCO 1986–88, Minister, Embassy in Washington, DC 1988–89, High Commr to Canada 1989–92; Amb. to Russia (also accred to several mems of CIS) 1992–95; Prin. Lady Margaret Hall, Oxford 1995–2002; British Govt Special Rep. for S Caucasus 2002–12; Chair. MC Russian Market Fund 1996–2002; Adviser, Rio Tinto 1996–2012; Gov. St Mary's School, Calne 1996–2006; Hon. Fellow, Lady Margaret Hall 2002; Hon. LLD (York Univ., Toronto) 2002. *Leisure interest:* France. *Address:* 2 St Helena Terrace, Richmond, Surrey, TW9 1NR, England (home).

FALL, Cheikh Ibrahima, MSc (Econ), MBA; Senegalese international civil servant and banker; b. 1 Oct. 1947, Louga; m. Marième Diouma Faye 1972; two s. one d.; financial analyst, Operations Dept Banque Ouest-Africaine de Développement (BOAD) 1978–79, Rural Devt and Infrastructural Operations Dept 1979–81, Officer-in-Charge of Dept 1981, Dir of Dept 1981–85, Dir Loans and Equity Dept 1985–86; Dir Office of Pres. of African Devt Bank (ADB) 1986–92, Dir Co. Programmes, S Region Dept 1992–95, Officer-in-Charge of Admin. and Gen. Services and ADB restructuring exercise 1995–96, Sec.-Gen. ADB 1996–99, 2004–06; Vice-Pres. and Corp. Sec. World Bank 1999–2004. *Leisure interests:* music, golf, reading.

FALL, François Lonseny, LLM; Guinean politician and diplomatist; *Minister of Foreign Affairs and Guineans Abroad;* b. 21 April 1949; m.; four c.; ed Univ. of Conakry; Asst Prof., Faculty of Law, Univ. of Conakry 1977–79; First Counsellor,

Embassy in Cairo 1982–85, Abuja 1985–89, Paris 1989–90, Mission to UN, New York 1990–93; Head, Div. of Consular Affairs, Ministry of Foreign Affairs 1993, Deputy Dir of Legal and Consular Affairs 1995–96, Dir 1996–2000; Perm. Rep. to UN, New York 2000–02, Vice-Pres. 55th Session of UN Gen. Ass. 2000; Minister at the Presidency, in charge of Foreign Affairs 2002–04, Del. to UN Security Council during debate over US mil. action in Iraq, acted as Pres. of UN Security Council March 2003; Prime Minister Feb.–April 2004 (resgnd); mem. UN Cttee for the Elimination of Racial Discrimination 2000–02, Econ. Community of West African States (ECOWAS) Ministerial Cttee for Security and Mediation 2002–04; UN Sec.-Gen.'s Special Rep. for Somalia and Head of UN Political Office for Somalia (UNPOS), Nairobi, Kenya 2005–07, Special Rep. for Cen. African Repub. (CAR) and Head of UN Peace-building Office in CAR (BONUCA—Bureau de l'Organisation des Nations Unies en République Centrafricaine) 2007–09; Minister of Foreign Affairs and Guineans Abroad 2012–. *Address:* Ministry of Foreign Affairs and Guineans Abroad, face au Port, ex-Primature, BP 2519, Conakry, Guinea (office). *Telephone:* 30-45-12-70 (office). *Fax:* 30-41-16-21 (office). *Website:* www .mae.gov.gn (office).

FALL, Ibrahima D., LLM, PhD; Senegalese international organization official, politician and academic; *Resident Coordinator and Resident Representative, Deputy Special Representative of the Secretary-General and Humanitarian Coordinator for Burundi, United Nations Development Programme (UNDP);* b. 1942, Tivaouane, Thies; s. of Momar Khoudia Fall and Seynabou (Diakhate) Fall; m. Déguène Fall; five c.; ed Univ. of Dakar, Inst. of Political Science, Paris, Faculty of Law, Univ. of Paris, Acad. of Int. Law, The Hague, Netherlands; Prof. of Int. Law and Int. Relations, Cheikh Anta Diop Univ., Dakar 1972–81, Dean of Faculty of Law 1975–81; Minister of Higher Educ. 1983–84, of Foreign Affairs 1984–90; Adviser, Supreme Court of Senegal; Asst Sec.-Gen. for Human Rights and Dir UN Centre for Human Rights, Geneva 1992–97; Sec.-Gen. UN World Conf. on Human Rights, Vienna 1993; Asst Gen. Sec. UN Dept of Political Affairs 1997–2000, Special Envoy of UN Sec.-Gen. to Côte d'Ivoire 2000–02, Special Rep. for the Great Lakes Region 2002–08, currently Resident Coordinator and Resident Rep., Deputy Special Rep. of UN Sec.-Gen. and UNDP Humanitarian Coordinator for Burundi, Bujumbura; consultant, UNESCO; Founding-mem. and Hon. Pres. Senegalese Asscn for African Unity; mem. African Council for Higher Educ. *Publications:* articles on int. public law, constitutional law and political science in professional journals. *Address:* UNDP Office in Burundi, Bujumbura, Burundi (office); Sicap Fenêtre Mermoz, Dakar, Senegal (home). *Telephone:* 228108 (office). *Fax:* 215213 (office). *E-mail:* ibrahima.fall@undp.org (office); fall5@un.org (office). *Website:* www.undp.org (office).

FALLIN, Mary, BS; American politician and state governor; *Governor of Oklahoma;* b. 9 Dec. 1954, Warrensburg, Mo.; d. of Joseph Newton Copeland and Mary Jo Copeland (née Duggan); m. 1st; one s. one d.; m. 2nd Wade Christensen; four c.; ed Tecumseh High School, Oklahoma Baptist Univ., Shawnee, Univ. of Cen. Oklahoma, Edmond, Oklahoma State Univ.; business man., Oklahoma Dept of Securities, Oklahoma City 1979–81; State Travel Coordinator, Oklahoma Dept of Tourism 1981–82; sales rep., Associated Petroleum 1982–83; Marketing Dir, Brian Head Hotel & Ski Resort, UT 1983–84; Dir of Sales, Residence Inn Hotel, Oklahoma City 1984–87; Dist Man., Lexington Hotel Suites 1988–90; Real Estate Assoc., Pippin Properties, Inc. 1990–94; mem. Oklahoma House of Reps 1990–94; Lt Gov. of Okla (first Republican and first woman) 1995–2007; mem. US House of Reps for 5th Congressional Dist of Okla 2007–11; Gov. of Okla (first woman) 2011–; fmr Chair. Nat. Conf. of Lt Govs; mem. and del., Oklahoma Fed. of Republican Women; mem. American Legis. Exchange Council, Nat. Conf. of State Legislatures; fmr mem. Bd United Way of Oklahoma City, YWCA; mem. Advisory Bd Trail of Tears; fmr Co-Chair. Festival of Hope; mem. Aerospace States Asscn (Chair. 2003–05); Republican; fmr Hon. Chair. Organ Donor Network; fmr Hon. Co-Chair. Indian Territory Arts and Humanities Council; Legislator of the Year 1993, Woman of the Year in Govt 1998, Women in Communication's Woman in the News Award, inducted into Okla Women's Hall of Fame and Okla Aviation Hall of Fame, Clarence E. Page Award, recognized by American Legis. Exchange Council as Legislator of the Year, named Guardian of Small Business by Nat. Fed. of Ind. Business. *Address:* Office of the Governor, State Capitol Building, 2300 North Lincoln Blvd, Room 212, Oklahoma City, OK 73105, USA (office). *Telephone:* (405) 521-2342 (office). *Fax:* (405) 521-3353 (office). *Website:* www.gov.ok/governor (office); www.maryfallin.org.

FALLON, James (Jimmy) Thomas, BA; American actor, comedian, singer, musician and television host; b. 19 Sept. 1974, Brooklyn, NY; s. of James W. Fallon and Gloria Fallon; m. Nancy Juvonen 2007; one d.; ed Saugerties High School, NY, The Coll. of Saint Rose, Albany, NY; began career as stand-up comedian, after college did stand-up tours across USA; took improvisation classes with The Groundlings, Los Angeles; played at Caroline's Comedy Club, New York City; joined cast of Saturday Night Live as featured player 1998–2004, Weekend Update co-anchor with Tina Fey 2000–04; host, MTV Movie Awards 2001 (with Kirsten Dunst), 2005, MTV Video Music Awards 2002, Emmy Awards 2010; host, Late Night with Jimmy Fallon (NBC) 2009–14; host, The Tonight Show (NBC) 2014–; Dr hc (The Coll. of Saint Rose) 2009; chosen for People Magazine's 50 Most Eligible Bachelors, chosen by People Magazine as one of the 50 Most Beautiful People in the World 2002. *Films include:* Almost Famous 2000, Anything Else 2003, The Entrepreneurs 2003, Taxi 2004, The Perfect Catch 2005, Doogal (voice) 2006, Arthur et les Minimoys (voice: English version) 2006, Factory Girl 2006, The Year of Getting to Know Us 2008, Whip It 2009, Arthur and the Great Adventure (voice) 2009, Arthur 3: The War of the Two Worlds (voice) 2010. *Television includes:* Saturday Night Live (series) 1998–2004, 2011, Band of Brothers (mini-series) 2001, Saturday Night Live Christmas 2002 (film) (writer) 2002, Just for Laughs (series) (writer) 2009, Late Night with Jimmy Fallon (series) (writer) 2009–14, Guys with Kids (series) (writer and exec. producer) 2012–13. *Recordings:* albums: The Bathroom Wall 2002, Blow Your Pants Off 2012; singles: Idiot Boyfriend 2002, Car Wash for Peace 2008, Drunk On Christmas (featuring John Rich) 2010. *Address:* The Tonight Show, NBC Studios, 30 Rockefeller Plaza, New York, NY 10112, USA (office). *Website:* www.nbc.com/the-tonight-show (office).

FALLON, John, BA; British publishing executive; *CEO, Pearson PLC;* m.; two c.; ed Univ. of Hull; held sr public policy and communications roles in British and UK local govts; fmr Dir of Corp. Affairs, Powergen plc, mem. Exec. Cttee; Dir of

Communications, Pearson PLC 1997–2003, Pres. Pearson Inc. 2000–03, CEO of Pearson's educational publishing businesses for Europe, Middle East and Africa 2003–08, Chief Exec. Int. Educ. Businesses 2008–12, mem. Pearson Man. Cttee, mem. Bd of Dirs and CEO Pearson PLC 2013–. *Address:* Pearson PLC, 80 Strand, London, WC2R 0RL, England (office). *Telephone:* (20) 7010-2300 (office). *Fax:* (20) 7010-6601 (office). *E-mail:* marjorie.scardino@pearson.com (office). *Website:* www .pearson.com (office).

FALLON, Martin (see Patterson, Harry).

FALLON, Adm. William Joseph, MA; American military officer (retd); b. 30 Dec. 1940, East Orange, NJ; ed Naval War Coll., Newport, RI, Nat. War Coll., Washington, DC, Old Dominion Univ., Norfolk, Va, Villanova Univ., Pa; received comm. through USN ROTC Program, designated naval flight officer upon completion of training 1967; began Naval Aviation service flying RA-5C Vigilante with a combat deployment to Viet Nam; served in flying assignments with Attack Squadrons and Carrier Air Wings with deployment to the Mediterranean Sea, Atlantic, Pacific and Indian Oceans, in USS Saratoga, USS Ranger, USS Nimitz, USS Dwight D. Eisenhower, USS Theodore Roosevelt; Commdr Carrier Air Wing Eight, Operation Desert Storm 1991, Battle Force Sixth Fleet, Operation Deliberate Force, Bosnia 1995, other command posts included Attack Squadron Sixty Five on USS Dwight D. Eisenhower, Medium Attack Wing One at NAS Oceana, Va, Carrier Group Eight, Theodore Roosevelt Battle Group; Commdr, Second Fleet and Commdr, Striking Fleet Atlantic 1997–2000; shore duties have included Deputy Dir for Operations, Jt Task Force, Southwest Asia, Deputy Dir, Aviation Plans and Requirements, Staff of the Chief of Naval Operations, Washington, DC; flag officer assignments included Asst Chief of Staff, Plans and Policy, NATO Supreme Allied Commdr, Atlantic, Deputy and Chief of Staff, US Atlantic Fleet, Deputy C-in-C and Chief of Staff, US Atlantic Command; Vice-Chief of Naval Operations 2000–03; Commdr US Fleet Forces Command and US Atlantic Fleet 2003–05; Commdr US Pacific Command 2005–07; Commdr US Cen. Command (first naval officer to hold the position) 2007–08 (resgnd); Defense Distinguished Service Medal, Distinguished Service Medal, Defense Superior Service Medal, Legion of Merit, Bronze Star, Meritorious Service Medal, Air Medal, Navy Commendation Medal. *Address:* c/o US Central Command, 7115 South Boundary Boulevard, MacDill AFB, Tampa, FL 33621-5101, USA (office).

FÄLTHAMMAR, Carl-Gunne, PhD; Swedish scientist and academic; *Professor Emeritus of Plasma Physics, Alfvén Laboratory, Royal Institute of Technology;* b. 4 Dec. 1931, Markaryd; s. of Oskar Fälthammar and Ingeborg Fälthammar; m. Ann-Marie Sjunnesson 1957; one s. one d.; ed Royal Inst. of Tech. (KTH), Stockholm; Asst Prof., KTH 1966–69, Chair. Dept of Plasma Physics 1967–97, Prof. of Plasma Physics 1975–, now Emer.; mem. Swedish Nat. Cttee for Radio Science 1970–96, Swedish Nat. Cttee for Geodesy and Geophysics 1973–96; Chair. Swedish Geophysical Soc. 1978–80; mem. Royal Swedish Acad. of Sciences, Int. Acad. of Astronautics, Academia Europaea; other professional affiliations; Hon. PhD (Oulu) 1989; Basic Sciences Award, Int. Acad. of Astronautics 1996, Golden Badge Award, European Geophysical Union 1996, Hannes Alfvén Medal, European Geophysical Soc. 1998. *Publications:* Cosmical Electrodynamics (with H. Alfvén) 1963, Magnetospheric Physics (with B. Hultqvist) 1990; papers in plasma physics and space physics. *Address:* Royal Institute of Technology (KTH), Teknikringen 31, Floor 4, Room 1515, 100 44 Stockholm (office); Bovägen 35, 18143 Lidingö, Sweden (home). *Telephone:* (8) 790-76-85 (office); (8) 7650862 (home). *E-mail:* carl -gunne.falthammar@ee.kth.se (office); carl-gunne.falthammar@telia.com (home). *Website:* www.ee.kth.se/profile/cgf (office).

FALTINGS, Gerd, PhD; German mathematician and academic; *Professor and Member of the Board of Scientific Members, Max-Planck-Institut für Mathematik;* b. 28 July 1954, Gelsenkirchen-Buer; ed Westphalian Wilhelm Univ. of Münster; Postdoctoral Research Fellow, Harvard Univ., Cambridge, Mass, USA 1978–79; Prof. of Math., Univ. of Wuppertal 1979–85; mem. Faculty, Princeton Univ., NJ, USA 1985; currently Prof. and mem. Bd Scientific Mems, Max-Planck-Institut für Mathematik, Bonn; Danny Heineman Prize, Akad. der Wissenschaften, Göttingen 1983, Fields Medal, Int. Congress of Mathematicians, Berkeley, Calif. 1986, Leibniz Prize, Germany 1996, von Staudt Prize, Erlangen 2008. *Publications:* numerous publs in math. journals. *Address:* Max-Planck-Institut für Mathematik, PO Box 7280, 53072 Bonn (office); Max-Planck-Institut für Mathematik, Vivatsgasse 7, 53111 Bonn, Germany (office). *Telephone:* (228) 402228 (office). *Fax:* (228) 402277 (office). *E-mail:* gerd@mpim-bonn.mpg.de (office). *Website:* www .mpim-bonn.mpg.de (office).

FALTLHAUSER, Kurt, BEcons, Dr rer. pol; German politician; b. 13 Sept. 1940, Munich; m.; two c.; ed Univ. of Munich; leader, Gen. Student Council, Univ. of Munich 1964–65; mem. Bavarian Landtag 1974–80, 1998–2008; State Minister and Head, Bavarian State Chancellery 1995–98, State Minister of Finance 1998–2007; mem. Bundestag 1980–95; Chair. Finance and Budget Committee, Christian Social Union (CSU); Financial Spokesman CDU/CSU Parl. Group., also Deputy Chair.; Parl. State Sec. to the Fed. Minister of Finance; Chair. Bd of Admin Bayerische Landesbank; Lecturer and Hon. Prof., Faculty of Econs, Univ. of Munich. *Address:* Maximilianeum, 81627 Munich, Germany. *Telephone:* (89) 41260 (home). *E-mail:* info@faltlhauser.de (home).

FÄLTSKOG, Agnetha Åse; Swedish singer and actress; b. 5 April 1950, Jönköping; m. 1st Björn Ulvæus 1971 (divorced 1979); m. 2nd Tomas Sonnenfeld; solo recording artist aged 17; actress, Jesus Christ Superstar, Sweden; mem. pop group ABBA 1973–82; winner, Eurovision Song Contest 1974; world-wide tours; concerts include Royal Performance, Stockholm 1976, Royal Albert Hall, London 1977, UNICEF concert, New York 1979, Wembley Arena 1979; reunion with ABBA, Swedish TV This Is Your Life 1986; solo artist 1982–90, 2004–; World Music Award, Best Selling Swedish Artist 1993. *Films:* ABBA: The Movie 1977, Nöjesmaskinen 1982, Rakenstam 1983. *Recordings:* albums: with Abba: Waterloo 1974, Abba 1976, Greatest Hits 1976, Arrival 1976, The Album 1978, Voulez-Vous 1979, Greatest Hits Vol. 2 1979, Super Trouper 1980, The Visitors 1981, The Singles: The First Ten Years 1982, Thank You For The Music 1983, Absolute Abba 1988, Abba Gold 1992, More Abba Gold 1993, Forever Gold 1998, The Definitive Collection 2001; solo: Eleven Women In One Building 1975, Wrap Your Arms Around Me 1983, Eyes of a Woman 1985, I Stand Alone 1987, My Colouring Book 2004, A 2013; singles include: with Abba: Ring Ring 1973, Waterloo 1974, Mamma

Mia 1975, Dancing Queen 1976, Fernando 1976, Money Money Money 1976, Knowing Me Knowing You 1977, The Name Of The Game 1977, Take A Chance On Me 1978, Summer Night City 1978, Chiquitita 1979, Does Your Mother Know? 1979, Angel Eyes/Voulez-Vous 1979, Gimme Gimme Gimme (A Man After Midnight) 1979, I Have A Dream 1979, The Winner Takes It All 1980, Super Trouper 1980, On and On and On 1981, Lay All Your Love On Me 1981, One Of Us 1981, When All Is Said and Done 1982, Head Over Heels 1982, The Day Before You Came 1982, Under Attack 1982, Thank You For The Music 1983; solo: I Was So In Love, The Heat Is On, Can't Shake You Loose, I Wasn't The One (Who Said Goodbye), If I Thought You'd Ever Change Your Mind 2004, My Colouring Book 2004, My Very Best 2008. *Address:* Warner Music Sweden, Besöksadress Rehnsgatan 20, 102 44 Stockholm, Sweden. *E-mail:* webmaster@agnetha.net (office). *Website:* www.abbasite.com; www.agnetha.net.

FALUSI, Adeyinka Gladys, PhD; Nigerian geneticist and academic; *Professor of Haematology and Head of Genetic and Bioethics Research Unit, Institute for Medical Research and Training, College of Medicine, University of Ibadan;* m. A. O. Falusi; c.; has served as Visiting Scientist at numerous hosps including Hammersmith Hosp., London, UK 1983–84, John Radcliffe Hosp., Oxford, Memorial Sloan Kettering Cancer Center, New York, USA 1994–95, Humboldt Univ. Inst. for Tropical Medicine, Berlin 1998; currently Prof. and Head of Genetic and Bioethics Research Unit, Inst. for Advanced Medical Research and Training, Coll. of Medicine, Univ. of Ibadan, Acting Dir of Inst. 2001–02, Dir 2002–05, Chair. Univ. of Ibadan/Univ. Coll. Hosp. Institutional Review Cttee 2001–05; Country Coordinator for Nigeria, Networking for Ethics of Biomedical Research in Africa 2005–06; Founder and Vice-Pres. Sickle Cell Asscn of Nigeria; Founding Chair. Nigerian Bioethics Initiative; Fellow, Nigerian Acad. of Science 2009–; Trustee, Sickle Cell Hope Alive Foundation (currently Pres.); Nat. Productivity Order of Merit 2005; L'Oréal-UNESCO Women in Science Award 2001, CEDPA/Nigerian News Rare Gems Award 2003, Vocational Excellence Award for Impact in Science 2004. *Address:* College of Medicine, University of Ibadan, Ibadan, Nigeria (office). *Website:* com.ui.edu.ng (office).

FALZON, Michael, BArch; Maltese architect and politician; *Chairman, Water Services Corporation;* b. 17 Aug. 1945, Gzira; m. Mary Anne Aquilina; one s.; ed the Lyceum and Univ. of Malta; practised as architect; mem. Nat. Exec. Nationalist Party 1975, fmr Sec. of Information; Ed. The Democrat (weekly newspaper) 1975; mem. Parl. 1976–96; Shadow Minister for Information and Broadcasting 1976–81, for Industry 1981–87, Minister for Devt of Infrastructure 1987–92, for Environ-ment 1992–94, for Educ. and Human Resources 1994–96; Ed. The People and People on Sunday (newspapers) 1997–98; Chair. Water Services Corpn 1998–. *Address:* Water Services Corporation, Qormi Road, Luqa, LQA 9043, Malta. *Telephone:* 22443309 (office). *Fax:* 22443900 (office). *E-mail:* water@wsc.com.mt (office); micfal@maltanet.net (home). *Website:* www.wsc.com.mt (office).

FAMA, Eugene F., BA; American economist and academic; *Robert R. McCormick Distinguished Service Professor of Finance, University of Chicago;* b. 14 Feb. 1939, Boston, Mass; m. Sally Fama; four c.; ed Tufts Univ.; Asst Prof. of Finance, Univ. of Chicago Grad. School of Business 1963–65, Assoc. Prof. 1966–68, Prof. 1968–73, Theodore O. Yntema Prof. of Finance 1973–84, Theodore O. Yntema Distinguished Prof. of Finance 1984–93, Robert R. McCormick Distinguished Service Prof. of Finance 1993–; Visiting Prof., Catholic Univ. of Leuven, Belgium 1975–76, Anderson Grad. School of Man., UCLA 1982–95; Assoc. Ed. Journal of Finance 1971–73, 1977–80, American Economic Review 1975–77, Journal of Monetary Economics 1984–96; Fellow, American Acad. of Arts and Sciences 1989, American Finance Assoc., Econometric Soc.; Hon. LLD (Leuven) 1985, (Rochester) 1987, (DePaul) 1989; Hon. DSc (Tufts) 2002; Deutsche Bank Prize in Financial Econs 2005, Nicholas Molodovsky Award 2006, Morgan Stanley American Finance Asscn Award for Excellence in Finance 2007, Onassis Prize in Finance 2009, Nobel Prize in Econs (with Lars Peter Hansen and Robert Shiller) 2013. *Leisure interests:* windsurfing, golf, tennis, biking, old movies, opera. *Address:* 5807 South Woodlawn Avenue, Chicago, IL 60637-1610, USA (office). *Telephone:* (773) 702-7282 (office). *E-mail:* eugene.fama@chicagobooth.edu (office). *Website:* www .chicagobooth.edu/faculty/directory/f/eugene-f-fama (office).

FAN, Gen. Changlong; Chinese army officer and politician; *Vice-Chairman, Central Military Commission;* b. 1947, Donggang City, Liaoning Prov.; ed Beijing Mil. Acad.; sent to countryside to do manual work during Cultural Revolution 1968–69; joined PLA 1969, soldier, Ground Force 1969–71, Platoon Leader 1971–72, Political Dir, PLA Company Command 1973–76, Chief of Staff, Regt Command 1976–82, Chief of Staff, Div. Command 1985–90, Div. Commdr (Army) 1990–93, Chief of Staff, 16th Army Group 1993–95, Army Commdr, 16th Army Group 1995–2000, Chief of Staff, Shenyang Mil. Region 2000–03, Asst to Chief of PLA Gen. Staff 2003–04, Commdr, Jinan Mil. Region 2004–12; Vice-Chair., 18th CCP Cen. Cttee Cen. Mil. Comm. 2012–; Vice-Chair., Cen. Mil. Comm. of the PRC 2013–; joined CCP 1969, alt. mem. 16th CCP Cen. Cttee 2002–07, mem. 17th CCP Cen. Cttee 2007–12, 18th CCP Cen. Cttee 2012–, also mem. Politburo 2012–; attained rank of Maj.-Gen. 1995, Lt-Gen. 2002, Gen. 2008. *Address:* Central Military Commission, 20 Jingshanqian Jie, Beijing 100009, People's Republic of China (office). *Telephone:* (10) 66730000 (office). *E-mail:* chinamod@chinamil.com .cn (office). *Website:* www.mod.gov.cn (office).

FAN, Jixiang; Chinese business executive; *Chairman, Power Construction Corporation of China (PowerChina);* Group Pres. Sinohydro Corpn, Chair. Sinohydro Group Ltd; Chair. Power Construction Corpn of China (PowerChina, state-owned corpn) 2011–. *Address:* Power Construction Corporation of China, No. 7 & 8 Building, Beijing Xiyuan Hotel, 1 Sanlihe Road, Haidian District, Beijing 100040, People's Republic of China. *Telephone:* (10) 58382266 (office); (10) 88358715 (office). *Fax:* (10) 58382888 (office). *E-mail:* infocenter@powerchin.com (office). *Website:* www.powerchin.com; en.powerchina.cn (office).

FAN, Maj.-Gen. Zhilun; Chinese army official; b. 1935, Fushun Co., Sichuan Prov.; s. of Fan Ximing and Fan Zhougshi; m. Ding Xin 1966; one s. one d.; Deputy Commdr and Chief of Staff Chinese People's Armed Police Force 1985; Deputy Pres. Mil. Educ. Coll. and Mil. Staff Coll. 1991–; Deputy Chief of Staff, Beijing Mil. Region of PLA 1993–. *Leisure interests:* climbing, swimming, calligraphy. *Address:* Headquarters of the Beijing Military Region, No. Jia 1, Badachu, Western Hill, Beijing, People's Republic of China.

FAN HSU, Rita, CBE, JP, BA, MScS; Chinese politician; b. 20 Sept. 1945, Shanghai, People's Repub. of China; m. Stephen Fan Sheung-tak; two c.; ed St Stephen's Girls' Coll., Univ. of Hong Kong; mem. Legis. Council 1983–92, Exec. Council 1989–92; Chair. Bd of Educ. 1986–89, Educ. Comm. 1990–92; mem. Preliminary Working Cttee of the Preparatory Cttee for the Hong Kong Special Admin. Region (HKSAR) 1993–95, Preparatory Cttee for the HKSAR 1995–97; Deputy to the 9th NPC, People's Repub. of China 1998–2003, 10th NPC 2003–08, 11th NPC 2008–; Pres. Provisional Legis. Council 1997–98, First Legis. Council of HKSAR 1998–2000, Second Legis. Council 2000–04, Third Legis. Council 2004–08; Supervising Adviser, Hong Kong Fed. of Women; Hon. Advisor, Jr Chamber Int. Hong Kong; Gold Bauhinia Star 1998, Grand Bauhinia Medal 2007; Hon. LLD (China Univ. of Political Science and Law) 2003; Hon. DScS (City Univ. of Hong Kong) 2005, (Hong Kong Univ.) 2009. *Website:* www.npcfan.hk.

FANG, Shouxian; Chinese nuclear physicist; *Director, Beijing Electron Positron Collider National Laboratory;* b. 27 Oct. 1932, Shanghai; m. 1st Run Moyin (died 1965); m. 2nd Yao Mayli 1968, two d.; ed Fudan Univ., Shanghai; Prof. of Research, Nuclear Physics Inst., Academia Sinica 1982–; Project Dir, Beijing Electron Positron Collider (BEPC, first high energy accelerator in China) 1986, Dir Inst. of High Energy Physics 1988, Dir BEPC Nat. Lab. 1992–; mem. Chinese Acad. of Sciences 1991–; Hon. Nat. Natural Science Award 1990, Ho Leung Ho Lee Foundation Prize 1997, Asian Cttee for Future Accelerators Lifetime Prize 2013. *Address:* Institute of High Energy Physics, 19B YuquanLu, Shijingshan District, Beijing 100049, People's Republic of China (office). *Telephone:* (10) 88233093 (office). *Fax:* (10) 882333744 (office). *Website:* english.ihep.cas.cn (office).

FANG, Weizhong; Chinese economist; *Chairman, Chinese Macroeconomics Society;* b. 11 March 1928, Dongfeng Co., Jilin Prov.; three s.; ed Dongbei Univ., Northeast China Univ., Northeast China Teachers' Univ.; joined CCP 1950; Sec. Publicity Dept, CCP Northeast Bureau 1950–52; Deputy Dir Research and Editing Div., State Devt and Reform Comm. 1952–61; Researcher, General Office, CCP Cen. Cttee 1961–65; Vice-Minister, State Devt and Reform Comm. 1977–93; Prof., Beijing Univ., People's Univ. of China, Beijing; Deputy Ed. China Econ. Yearbook; Chief Ed. Chronicle of Major Econ. Events; Alt. mem. 12th CCP Cen. Cttee 1982–87; mem. 13th CCP Cen. Cttee 1987–92; Alt. mem. 14th CCP Cen. Cttee 1992–97; mem. CPPCC 8th Nat. Cttee 1993–98, 9th Nat. Cttee 1998–2003, Chair. Economy Sub-Cttee 1993–2003; Chair. Chinese Macroeconomics Soc. 1995–; Vice-Chair. China Planning Soc., China Enterprise Man. Asscn; mem. Council of People's Bank of China 1974–; Chief Ed. Chronicle of Major Economic Events. *Leisure interest:* calligraphy. *Address:* Chinese Macroeconomics Society, 18th Floor B, Hua Zun Mansion, 29 Beisanhuan Zhonglu, Xicheng District, Beijing 100029, People's Republic of China (office). *E-mail:* Eng@macrochina.com.cn.

FANG, Gen. Zuqi; Chinese army officer; b. 1935, Jingjiang, Jiangsu Prov.; joined PLA 1951, took part in Korean War 1952; joined CCP 1956; worked as Asst, Cadre Dept, Army (or Ground Force), PLA Services and Arms, later Deputy Chief of Div. Org. Section; Deputy Regt Political Commissar, Army (or Ground Force), PLA Services and Arms 1969–70; fmr Dir Political Dept, PLA Shenyang and Beijing Mil. Area Command; Political Commissar, Nanjing Mil. Region 1993–2000; rank of Maj.-Gen. Group Army, PLA Services and Arms 1988–93, Lt-Gen. 1993–98, Gen. 1998–; mem. 15th CCP Cen. Cttee 1997–2002. *Address:* c/o Political Commissar's Office, Nanjing Military Region, Nanjing, Jiangsu Province, People's Republic of China.

FANGIONO, Ciliandra, BA, MA; Indonesian business executive; *CEO, President and Director, First Resources Ltd;* b. 1976; s. of Martias Fangiono; m.; two c.; ed Univ. of Cambridge, UK; with Investment Banking Div., Merrill Lynch, Singapore 1999–2001; CEO First Resources Ltd (family palm oil plantation co.) 2002–, Pres. and Dir 2003–, Dir 2007–. *Address:* First Resources Ltd, Wisma 77, 7th Floor, Jalan Letjend, S. Parman Kav. 77, Slipi, Jakarta 11410, Indonesia (office). *Telephone:* (21) 53670888 (office). *Fax:* (21) 53671888 (office). *Website:* www.first -resources.com (office).

FANJUL, Oscar, PhD; Spanish business executive; *Vice-Chairman and CEO, Omega Capital;* b. 20 May 1949, Santiago, Chile; m. Curra Orozco; two c.; ed Founder, Chair. and CEO Repsol SA 1985–96, now Hon. Chair.; fmr Chair. Hidroeléctrica del Cantábrico; currently Vice-Chair. and CEO Omega Capital; Vice-Chair. Lafarge, mem. Bd of Dirs The Marsh and McLennan Companies and Acerinox; fmr mem. Bd of Dirs Unilever, BBVA, London Stock Exchange, Areva; mem. Trilateral Comm.; Chair. British-Spanish Tertulias; Trustee, International Financial Reporting Standards (IFRSs); Vice-Chair. Fundación de Amigos del Museo del Prado; Orden de Isabel la Católica, Ordre de la Couronne Belge. *Publications:* several articles on industrial and financial matters. *Address:* Omega Capital, Paseo de la Castellana 28, Madrid 28046, Spain (office). *Telephone:* (91) 7027991 (office). *Fax:* (91) 3195733 (office). *E-mail:* ofanjul@omega-capital.com (office).

FANZHI, Zeng; Chinese artist; b. 1964, Wuhan, Hubei; ed Hubei Fine Arts Inst. *Publications:* Raw Beneath the Mask 2001, I, We 2003, Scapes – The Paintings of Zeng Fanzhi 1989–2004 2005, The Paintings of Zeng Fanzhi 2007, Idealism 2007, Tai Ping you xiang 2008. *Address:* c/o ShanghART Gallery, 50 Moganshan Road, Bldg 16, Shanghai, 200060, People's Republic of China (office). *Telephone:* (21) 6359-3923 (office). *Fax:* (21) 6359-4570 (office). *E-mail:* info@shanghartgallery.com (office). *Website:* www.shanghartgallery.com (office).

FAOURI, Refaat al-, PhD; Jordanian university rector, international organiza-tion executive and academic; *Director-General, Arab Administrative Development Organization (ARADO);* ed Saint Louis Univ., Mo., USA; occupied several positions at Yarmouk Univ., including researcher and teaching asst, School of Econs, Asst Teacher, Public Relations Div., Co-teacher in Public Relations Div., Asst Dean of Faculty of Economy and Admin. Sciences, mem. Bd of Dirs Consulting and Community Service Centre, Refugees and Immigrants Centre, Dean of Faculty of Economy and Admin. Sciences, Vice-Chair. Admin. Affairs, Chair. Refugees, Immigrants and Expatriation Centre, Chair. Jordanian Studies Centre, currently Deputy Rector Yarmuk Univ. for Quality Affairs; fmr Lecturer, Saint Univ.; has held numerous admin. posts, including mem. Bd of Dirs Public Admin Inst., Amman-Jordan, Dir Trust Council, Ministry of Higher Educ. and Scientific Research, Dir at Distinction Centre for Jordanian Office Services, mem. Informa-tive Cttee for the Creativity and Distinction Fund Program, Ministry of Admin.

Devt, Jordan; Dir-Gen. Arab Admin. Devt Org. (ARADO) 2007–. *Publications:* several books, including Management of Organizational Innovation; 36 research papers on business admin. *Address:* Arab Administrative Development Organization, 2 El Hegaz Street, PO Box 2692 al-Horreia, Heliopolis, Cairo, Egypt (office). *Telephone:* (2) 4175410 (office). *Fax:* (2) 4175407 (office). *E-mail:* arado@idsc.gov.eg (office); info@arado.org.eg (office). *Website:* www.arado.org.eg (office).

FARACI, John V.; American forest products industry executive; *Chairman and CEO, International Paper Company;* b. 1950; joined International Paper Co. in 1974 as financial analyst, various positions in Planning, Gen. Man. and Finance Depts, Vice-Pres. 1989, CEO and Man. Dir Carter Holt Harvey (subsidiary co.) 1995–99, Sr Vice-Pres. and Chief Financial Officer, International Paper Co. 1999–2000, Exec. Vice-Pres. and Chief Financial Officer 2000–03, Pres. Feb.–Nov. 2003, Chair. and CEO Nov. 2003–; mem. Bd of Dirs United Technologies Corpn 2005–, Grand Teton Nat. Park Foundation, Nat. Park Foundation; mem. Citigroup Int. Advisory Bd; mem. Business Round Table, Sustainable Forestry Bd; Trustee, Denison Univ. *Address:* International Paper Company, 6400 Poplar Avenue, Memphis, TN 38197, USA (office). *Telephone:* (901) 419-9000 (office). *Fax:* (901) 214-9682 (office). *E-mail:* corporatesecretary@ipaper.com (office). *Website:* www.internationalpaper.com (office).

FARAH, former Empress of Iran (see Pahlavi).

FARAH, Ali Abdi; Djibouti politician; b. 16 Feb. 1947; mem. Rassemblement Populaire pour le Progrès (RPP); fmr Minister for Industry, Energy and Minerals and Acting Minister for Public Works and Housing; Minister of Foreign Affairs, Int. Co-operation and Parl. Relations 1999–2005, of Communication and Culture 2005; fmr Govt Spokesperson. *Address:* c/o Office of the President, Djibouti. *E-mail:* sggpr@intnet.dj. *Website:* www.presidence.dj.

FARAH, Col. Hassan Abshir; Somali government official, diplomatist and politician; b. 20 June 1945; m.; c.; ed Mil. Acad., Cairo, Egypt., Somali Nat. Univ.; Dist Commr of Mogadishu 1970–71, Vice-Mayor of Mogadishu 1971–73, Gov. and Mayor of Mogadishu 1973–76, 1982–87; Gov. of Middle Shabelle and Bakol 1976–82; Amb. to Germany (also accred to Austria) 1989–98; Minister of Internal Affairs and Security, Puntland Regional Govt 1998–2000; Minister of Water and Mineral Resources 2000–01; Chair. Somali Peace Conf. 2000; Prime Minister of Somalia 2001–03; Minister of Fishery and Marine Resources 2004–06; mem. Transitional Parl. 2006–. *Address:* c/o Transitional Parliament, Mogadishu, Somalia. *Website:* www.hassanabshir.net.

FARAH, Mohamed (Mo), CBE; British (b. Somali) track and field athlete; b. 23 March 1983, Mogadishu, Somalia; s. of Muktar Farah; m. Tania Nell 2010; twin d. one step-d.; ed Feltham Community Coll., London; arrived in UK aged eight and grew up in West London; began cross country running in early teens; ran for Newham and Essex Beagles athletics club; finished ninth in English schools cross country 1996, then won first of five English school titles 1997; trained at St Mary's Univ. Coll., Twickenham 2001–11; started professional career 2005; relocated to Oregon, USA to further training with coach Alberto Salazar 2011; gold medal (individual), European Cross Country Championships, San Giorgio su Legnano 2006; silver medal, 5,000m, European Championships, Göteborg 2006; silver medal (individual), bronze medal (team), European Cross Country Championships, Brussels 2008; gold medal, 5,000m, European Team Championships, Leiria 2009; gold medal, 3000m, European Indoor Championships, Torino 2009; silver medal (individual, team), European Cross Country Championships, Dublin 2009; won 5,000m, Super Grand Prix, London 2009; gold medal, 5,000m, 10,000m, European Championships, Barcelona 2010 (became the fifth man in history of European Championships to win both 5,000m and 10,000m and the first in 20 years); ran 5,000m in 12:57.94, Diamond League, Zurich 2010 (became first British athlete to run under 13 minutes); winner, 5,000m, Diamond League, Birmingham 2011, Monaco 2011; also won 10,000m (in 26:46.57, new British and European record), Diamond League, Eugene 2011; gold medal, 3,000m, European Indoor Championships, Paris 2011; gold medal, 5,000m, European Championships, Helsinki 2012; gold medal, 5,000m, silver medal, 10,000m IAAF World Championships, Daegu 2011; gold medal, 5,000m, 10,000m, Olympic Games, London 2012; winner, 5,000m, Diamond League, Eugene 2012; gold medal, 5,000m, 10,000m, IAAF World Championships, Moscow 2013; est. Mo Farah Foundation 2011; Sponsor Muslim Writers' Awards; Male Athlete of the Year, British Athletics Writers' Asscn 2006, 2010, 2011, 2012, British Sr Athlete of the Year, UK Aviva Athletics Awards 2010, inducted into London Youth Games Hall of Fame 2010, Track-and Field Athlete of the Year, British Olympic Asscn 2010, European Athlete of the Year Award 2011, 2012, Premier Inn Celebrity Dad of the Year 2013; ranked by Arabian Business amongst the Power 500: The World's Most Influential Arabs (third) 2013. *Leisure interests:* spending time with his family, music. *E-mail:* info@mofarahfoundation.org.uk. *Website:* www.mofarah.com; www.mofarahfoundation.org.uk.

FARAH, Nuruddin; Somali writer; b. 24 Nov. 1945, Baidoa; s. of Farah Hassan and Fatuma Aleli; m. Amina Mama 1992 (divorced 2007); one s. one d.; ed Panjab Univ., Chandigarh, India, Univs of London and Essex, UK; Lecturer, Nat. Univ. of Somalia, Mogadishu 1971–74; Assoc. Prof., Univ. of Jos, Nigeria 1981–83; Writer-in-Residence, Univ. of Minn. 1989, Brown Univ., USA 1991; Prof., Makerere Univ., Kampala 1990; Rhodes Scholar St Antony's Coll., Oxford 1996; Visiting Prof., Univ. of Texas at Austin 1997; now full-time writer; mem. Union of Writers of the African People, PEN Int., Somali-Speaking PEN Centre; Hon. DLitt (Univ. of Kent at Canterbury) 2000; English-speaking Union Literary Prize 1980, Tucholsky Award 1991, Premio Cavour Award 1992, Zimbabwe Annual Award 1993, Neustadt Int. Literary Prize 1998, Festival Étonnant Voyageur St Malo, France 1998. *Plays include:* The Offering 1976, Yussuf and his Brothers 1982. *Publications include:* From a Crooked Rib 1970, A Naked Needle 1976, Sweet and Sour Milk 1979, Sardines 1981, Close Sesame 1983, Maps 1986, Gifts 1992, Secrets 1998, Yesterday, Tomorrow: Voices from the Somali Diaspora 1999, Links 2004, Knots 2007, Crossbones 2011; contrib. to Guardian, New African, Transition Magazine, New York Times, Observer, TLS, London Review of Books. *Address:* c/o Deborah Rogers, Rogers, Coleridge & White, 20 Powis Mews, London, W11 1JN, England (office).

FAREMO, Grete, LLB; Norwegian lawyer, business executive and politician; b. 16 June 1955, Byglandsfjord, Setesdal; d. of Osmund Faremo and Tora Aamlid;

partner Magne Lindholm; one d.; ed Univ. of Oslo; with Ministry of Finance, Norwegian Agency for Devt Co-operation; Head of Div. Ministry 1984, Minister of Devt Co-operation 1990–92, of Justice 1992–96, of Oil and Energy 1996, of Defence 2009–11, of Justice and Public Security 2011–13; mem. Stortinget (Parl.) 1993–97; Dir Storebrand Insurance Co. 1997–98, Pres. 1997–2003; Dir of Legal and Corp. Affairs, Microsoft Northern Europe 2003–08; mem. Bd Labour Party Forum for Art and Culture 1989–90, Int. Analysis 1997; mem. Bd of Dirs Norsk Hydro 2006–; Chief Negotiating Officer Aker Eiendom 1986; fmr Dir (of Cultural Affairs) Aker Brygge (business and leisure complex), Norsk Arbeiderpresse; Chair. Norsk Folkehjelp 2003–08; mem. European Group, Trilateral Comm. 1998–2002. *Address:* c/o Ministry of Justice and Public Security, Gullhaug Torg 4A, PO Box 8005 Dep, 0030 Oslo, Norway (office).

FARES, Farouk Saleh, BAgr, DEA, PhD; Syrian soil scientist, institute director and academic; *Director-General, Arab Centre for the Study of Arid Zones and Dry Lands (ACSAD);* b. 1945; m.; three c.; ed Damascus Univ., Paris Univ. VI in cooperation with the Nat. Agricultural Inst.-Nat. Higher School for Agric., Paris, INA-ENSA and ORSTOM, Nancy Univ. (France) in cooperation with Soil Research Centre (CNRS), Nancy, Nuclear Studies Centre (France), Nat. Inst. for Polytechnic, Lorraine and Biological Soil Research Centre (CNRS), Nancy, Pennsylvania State Univ., USA (Fulbright Scholarship), Environmental Resources Research Inst.; Dir-Gen. Arab Centre for the Study of Arid Zones and Dry Lands (ACSAD), Damascus, Syria 2004–. *Address:* Arab Centre for the Study of Arid Zones and Dry Lands (ACSAD), PO Box 2440, Damascus, Syria (office). *Telephone:* (11) 5743039 (office). *Fax:* (11) 5743063 (office). *E-mail:* acsad@net.sy (office). *Website:* www.acsad.org (office).

FARES, Issam M.; Lebanese politician and business executive; b. 1937, Bayno, Akkar; m. Hala Fares; four c.; ed Tripoli Coll.; began as businessman in Arabian Gulf, then moved to investment; f. numerous major business corpns in USA, Europe and Middle E including The Wedge Group; f. The Fares Foundation; mem. Parl.; Deputy Prime Minister –2005; Chair. numerous governmental cttees; serves on bds of int. orgs, major business corpns and univs and insts of higher learning; lectures frequently at home and abroad; Order of the Prince Yaroslav the Wise, Second Rank (Ukraine), Grand Officer of the Nat. Order (Lebanon), Grand Cordon de Jean Baptiste (Antiochian Orthodox Church), Grand Cordon of Archon Depoutatos (Patriarchate of Constantinople), Grand Cordon of St Daniel (Patriarchate of Moscow and All Russia), Grand Officier de la Légion d'honneur (France), Grand Cross of the Phoenix (Greece), Grand Commdr Makarios the Third (Cyprus), Order of 'Stara Platina', First Rank (Bulgaria); Dr hc (Diplomatic Acad., Moscow, Tufts Univ., Mass, USA); Medal of Sts Peter and Paul (Antiochian Orthodox Patriarchate), World Maronite Foundation Gold Decoration, Antiochian Orthodox Christian Archdiocese of NY and N America Gold Medal of Merit, Maronite Cen. Council Gold Medal (Lebanon), Prize of the Int. Foundation for the Unity of Orthodox Nations (Patriarchate of Moscow and All Russia), UNESCO Gold Medal of Acropole, Alahd Nat. Merit (Algeria), Ministry of Youth and Sports Hon. Golden Medal (Bulgaria). *Address:* Sofil Center, Charle Malek Avenue, Achrafieh, Beirut (office); POB 16-5169, Beirut, Lebanon. *Telephone:* (1) 201755 (office). *Fax:* (1) 203999 (office). *E-mail:* dpmissam@fares.org.lb (office). *Website:* www.issam-fares.org (office).

FARHADI, Asghar, BA, MA; Iranian film director and screenwriter; b. 1 Jan. 1972, Khomeyni Shahr County, Esfahan Prov.; m. Parisa Bakhtavar; two c.; ed Tehran Univ., Tarbiat Modares Univ.; joined Iranian Young Cinema Soc. as student; began career working as screenwriter and dir for state broadcaster IRIB; mem. jury, 62nd Berlin Int. Film Festival 2012. *Television includes:* (as dir) A Tale of a City. *Films include:* Low Heights (screenwriter) 2001, Dancing in the Dust (Best Dir and Best Screenplay, Asia Pacific Film Festival 2003) 2003, The Beautiful City (Grand Prix, Warsaw Int. Film Festival 2004, Golden Peacock, Int. Film Festival of India 2004, FIPRESCI Prize, Split Film Festival 2005) 2004, Fireworks Wednesday 2006, About Elly (Silver Bear for Best Dir, Berlin Int. Film Festival 2009) 2009, Nader and Simin: A Separation (Acad. Award for Best Foreign Language Film 2012, Golden Globe for Best Foreign Film 2012, Golden Bear for Best Film, Berlin Int. Film Festival 2011) 2011. *Address:* c/o United Talent Agency, 9336 Civic Center Drive, Beverly Hills, CA 90210, USA (office). *Website:* www.unitedtalent.com (office).

FARHANG, Mohammad Amin, PhD; Afghan government official, economist and academic; b. 1940, Kabul; s. of Mir Mohammad Sediq Farhang; ed Esteqlal High School, Kabul Univ., Köln Univ., Germany; Prof. of Econs, Kabul Univ. and Dir Nat. Economy Inst. 1974–78; imprisoned because of opposition to Communist regime 1978–82; emigrated to Germany 1982; fmr Prof., Ruhr Univ., Co-ordinator Afghanistan Archive; returned to Afghanistan 2001; Minister of Reconstruction 2001, of Economy 2005–06, of Commerce and Industry 2006–08. *Publications:* numerous articles. *Address:* c/o Ministry of Commerce and Industry, Darulaman Wat, Kabul, Afghanistan. *Telephone:* 70-0225718 (mobile). *E-mail:* fawad.it@commerce.gov.af.

FARINA, HE Cardinal Raffaele, PhD, SDB; Italian ecclesiastic; *Archivist Emeritus of the Vatican Secret Archives;* b. 24 Sept. 1933, Buonalbergo; ed Pontifical Gregorian Univ.; professed as mem. of Salesians of Saint John Bosco 1954; ordained priest of Salesians of Saint John Bosco 1958; Prof., Pontifical Salesian Univ., Rome for several years before becoming Dean of the Theology Faculty, Rector Pontifical Salesian Univ. 1977–83, 1992–97; Under-Sec. Pontifical Council for Culture 1983–92; Prefect of Vatican Library 1997–2007, Librarian of the Vatican Library and Archivist of the Vatican Secret Archives 2007–12, Archivist Emer. 2012–; Titular Bishop of Opitergium 2007–; cr. Cardinal (Cardinal-Deacon of San Giovanni della Pigna) 2007; participated in Papal Conclave 2013. *Address:* Vatican Secret Archives, 00120 Città del Vaticano, Italy (office). *Telephone:* (06) 6988-3314 (office). *Fax:* (06) 6988-5574 (office). *E-mail:* info@vatican.va (office). *Website:* www.vatican.va/library_archives/vat_secret_archives/index.htm (office).

FARISH, William; American business executive, race horse owner and fmr diplomatist; b. 1938, Houston, Tex.; m. Sarah Sharp; one s. three d.; ed Univ. of Virginia; f. investment firm W. S. Farish & Co.; f. Lane's End Farm, Versailles, Ky (thoroughbred horse farm) 1978; Chair. Exec. Cttee Breeders Cup Ltd; Vice-Chair. US Jockey Club; Dir Thoroughbred Breeders and Owners Asscn; Chair. Bd

Churchill Downs Inc., Ky; US Amb. to UK 2001–04; Trustee Keeneland Asscn 2006–. *Leisure interests:* horse breeding, hunting quail, polo. *Address:* c/o Lane's End, POB 626, Versailles, KY 40383; W. S. Farish & Co., Houston, Texas, USA (office). *E-mail:* bfarish@aol.com.

FARIZ, Ziad, PhD; Jordanian economist, fmr government official and central banker; *Governor, Central Bank of Jordan;* b. 1943, Salt; ed Univ. of Baghdad, Arab Inst. for Planning, Kuwait, Keele Univ., UK; Minister of Planning 1989, 1991, of Industry and Trade 1989–91; Chair. Bd Bank of Export and Finance 1995; Gov. Cen. Bank of Jordan 1996–2001, 2012–; CEO Arab Banking Corpn 2001–05; Deputy Prime Minister and Minister of Finance 2005–07 (resgnd); Chair. Capital Bank 2007–09; Chair. First Investment Group, Amman 2009–12; fmr mem. Advisory Bd UNDP Regional Bureau for Arab States, Arab Human Devt Report. *Address:* Central Bank of Jordan, POB 37, King Hussein St, Amman 11118, Jordan (office). *Telephone:* (6) 4630301 (office). *Fax:* (6) 4638889 (office). *E-mail:* info@cbj.gov.jo (office). *Website:* www.cbj.gov.jo (office).

FARLEY, Carole, MusB; American singer (soprano); b. 29 Nov. 1946, Le Mars, Ia; d. of Melvin Farley and Irene Farley (née Reid); m. José Serebrier 1969; one d.; ed Indiana Univ. and Hochschule für Musik, Munich (Fulbright Scholar); operatic debut in USA in title role of La Belle Hélène, New York City Opera 1969; debut at Metropolitan Opera as Lulu 1977; now appears regularly in leading opera houses of the world and in concert performances with major orchestras in USA and Europe; Metropolitan Opera premiere of Shostakovich's Lady Macbeth of Mtsensk (Katerina Ismailova); Wozzeck (Marie), Toulouse Opera, Teatro Colón; mem. American Guild of Musical Artists; numerous awards and prizes including Grand Prix du Disque for Les Soldats Morts (by A. Lemeland) 1995 and Diapason d'Or (France) 1997, Abbiati Prize for Best Production of an Opera in Italy (for Berg's Lulu, Turin). *Recordings include:* Le Pré aux Clercs, Behold the Sun, French songs by Chausson, Duparc, Satie and Fauré, Prokofiev songs, Poulenc's La Voix Humaine, Menotti's The Telephone, Britten's Les Illuminations, Prokofiev's The Ugly Duckling, Kurt Weill songs, Milhaud songs (with John Constable), Strauss Songs and the Four Last Songs, Strauss Final Scenes from Daphne and Capriccio, Tchaikovsky opera arias, Delius songs with orchestra, Les Soldats Morts 1995 (Grand Prix du Disque), Grieg songs with orchestra, Serebrier Symphony No. 3, Ned Rorem Songs with Ned Rorem, Piano, Der Wampyr by Marschner, Songs of William Bolcom, Classic American Love Songs. *Roles include:* Monteverdi's Poppea, Massenet's Manon, Mozart's Idomeneo, Don Giovanni, Entführung, Die Zauberflöte, Verdi's La Traviata, Puccini's La Bohème, Tosca, Lehar's The Merry Widow, Strauss' Zigeunerbaron, Berg's Lulu, Wozzeck, Weill's Mahagonny, Offenbach's Tales of Hoffmann, La Belle Hélène, Strauss's Salome, Capriccio, Die Frau ohne Schatten, Elektra, Shostakovich's Lady Macbeth of Mtsensk, Wagner's Parsifal, Die Walküre, Schönberg's Erwartung, Janáček's Macropoulos Case, Jenůfa, Katya Kabanova. *Leisure interests:* skiing, jogging, swimming, dancing, cooking, entertaining, reading. *Address:* c/o Robert Lombardo Associates, Suite 6F, 61 West 62nd Street, New York, NY 10023, USA (office). *Telephone:* (212) 586-4453 (office). *Fax:* (212) 581-5771 (office). *Website:* www.rlombardo.com (office); www.carolefarley.com. *E-mail:* carole@carolefarley.com (home).

FARMER, Bill, AO, BA, MSc; Australian fmr diplomatist; b. 10 June 1947; m. Rev. Elaine Farmer; ed Univ. of Sydney, London School of Econs, UK; joined Foreign Service 1969; served in Embassy in Cairo 1969–71, in London 1971–75; Deputy High Commr to Fiji 1979–82; Minister, Perm. Mission to UN, New York 1984–87, Deputy Rep. of Australia on Security Council 1985–86; Amb. to Mexico (also accred to Cen. American countries and Cuba) 1987–89; High Commr to Papua New Guinea 1993–95, to Malaysia 1996–97; Deputy Sec., Dept of Foreign Affairs and Trade 1997–98, Sec., Dept of Immigration and Multicultural Affairs 1998–2001, Sec., Dept of Immigration and Multicultural and Indigenous Affairs 2001–05, also Sec., Dept of Reconciliation and Aboriginal and Torres Strait Islander Affairs; Amb. to Indonesia 2005–10; Centenary Medal 2003. *Address:* c/o Embassy of Australia, Jalan H. R. Rasuna Said, Kav. C15–16, Kuningan, 12940 Jakarta, Indonesia.

FARMER, Paul, MD, PhD; American physician, medical anthropologist and academic; *Kolokotrones University Professor, Harvard Medical School;* b. 1959; m.; three c.; ed Harvard Medical School and Harvard Univ.; worked amongst dispossessed peasants in Haiti 1990s; fmr Maude and Lillian Presley Prof. of Medical Anthropology, Dept of Social Medicine, Harvard Medical School, Co-dir Program in Infectious Diseases and Social Change, also Kolokotrones Univ. Prof. 2010–; divides his clinical time between Brigham and Women's Hosp. (Div. of Infectious Disease), where he is an attending physician, and Clinique Bon Sauveur charity hosp. in rural Haiti, where he serves as Medical Co-dir; Founding Dir Partners in Health 1987; UN Deputy Special Envoy to Haiti 2009–12, Special Adviser to UN Sec.-Gen for Community Based Medicine and Lessons From Haiti 2012–; visiting prof. at insts throughout USA as well as in France, Canada, Peru, Netherlands, Russia and Central Asia; has worked in communicable disease control in Americas for over a decade and is an authority on tuberculosis treatment and control; mem. Int. Scientific Cttee's Int. Conf. on AIDS, AIDS DOTS-Plus Working Group for the Global Tuberculosis Programme of WHO, Scientific Cttee of WHO Working Group on DOTS-Plus for MDR-TB, Commonwealth of Mass Bureau of Communicable Disease Control; Coordinator Int. Working Group on Multidrug-Resistant Tuberculosis; Chief Advisor, Tuberculosis Programs of the Open Soc. Inst.; Chief Medical Consultant, Tuberculosis Treatment Project in the Prisons of Tomsk (Siberia) for Public Health Research Inst.; has served on Scientific Review Bds of ten Int. Confs on AIDS; Fellow, American Acad. of Arts and Sciences 2009–; Duke Univ. Humanitarian Award, Margaret Mead Award, American Anthropological Asscn, Outstanding Int. Physician Award, American Medical Asscn, Heinz Humanitarian Award, John D. and Catherine T. MacArthur Foundation Genius Award 1993. *Publications:* more than 75 publs including AIDS and Accusation 1992, The Uses of Haiti 1994, Infections and Inequalities 1998, Pathologies of Power 2003; Co-Ed.: Women, Poverty, and AIDS 1996, The Global Impact of Drug-Resistant Tuberculosis 1999. *Address:* Department of Social Medicine, Harvard Medical School, 641 Huntington Avenue, Boston MA 02115, USA (office). *Telephone:* (617) 432-1707 (office). *Website:* www.hms.harvard.edu/dsm (office).

FARMER, Richard Gilbert, MS, MD, MACP, MACG; American physician and professor of medicine; *Professor of Medicine, Division of Gastroenterology, University of Rochester Medical Center;* b. 29 Sept. 1931, Kokomo, Ind.; s. of

Oscar I. Farmer and Elizabeth J. Gilbert Farmer; m. Janice M. Schrank 1958; one s. one d.; ed Indiana Univ., Univ. of Maryland, Milwaukee Co. Hosp. (Marquette Univ.), Mayo Foundation, Rochester, Minn. and Univ. of Minnesota; mil. service 1960–62; staff, Cleveland Clinic Foundation and Cleveland Clinic Hosp. 1962–91, Chair. Dept of Gastroenterology 1972–82, Chair. Div. of Medicine 1975–91; Asst and Assoc. Clinical Prof., Case Western Reserve Univ. School of Medicine 1972–91; Sr Medical Adviser, Bureau for Europe, USAID 1992–94; consultant in health care, Eastern Europe and Soviet Union 1994–96; consultant, American Medico-Legal Foundation 1996–2003, Inst. for Health Policy Analysis 1996–2004; Clinical Prof. of Medicine, Georgetown Univ. Medical Center 1992–2004; Medical Dir Quality Health Int. 1997–98, Eurasian Medical Educ. Program (Russia) 1998–2004; medical consultant, Scandinavian Care Consultants, Stockholm 1998–2003; Prof. of Medicine and Chief of Digestive and Liver Disease Unit, Univ. of Rochester Medical Center, New York 2004–; mem. Inst. of Medicine, Nat. Advisory Bd, Nat. Foundation for Ileitis and Colitis, Nat. Comm. on Digestive Diseases 1977–79; Gov. for Ohio, American Coll. of Physicians 1980–84, Regent 1985–91; Chair. Health and Public Policy Comm. 1986–88; Pres. American Coll. of Gastroenterology 1978–79, Asscn of Program Dirs in Internal Medicine 1977–79; Interstate Postgraduate Medical Asscn 1983–84; mem. council to assess quality of care in the Medicare program, Gen. Accounting Office, US House of Reps, Washington, DC 1986–89; Special Citation, American Coll. of Physicians 1984, Mastership American Coll. of Gastroenterology 1991, American Coll. of Physicians 1993, mem. Int. Org. for Study of Inflammatory Bowel Disease (Deputy Chair. 1982–86); Founder's Award, Asscn of Program Dirs in Internal Medicine 1993, Jubilee Medal, Charles Univ. of Prague, Czech Repub. 1998, Mentor Award, American Gastroenterological Asscn 2007. *Publications:* author or co-author of 260 publs in the medical literature, primarily relating to digestive diseases with a specific interest in inflammatory bowel disease and health care in Eastern Europe and the fmr Soviet Union; author of six books and contrib. to others. *Leisure interests:* squash, tennis, running and reading (history and current events). *Address:* School of Medicine and Dentistry, Gastroentrology Division, University of Rochester Medical Center, 601 Elmwood Avenue, ACF 4-2071A, Rochester, NY 14642 (office); 9126 Town Gate Lane, Bethesda, MD 20817, USA (home). *Telephone:* (585) 275-7432 (office); (301) 365-5828 (home). *Fax:* (301) 365-6202 (home). *E-mail:* richard_farmer@urmc.rochester.edu (office). *Website:* www.urmc .rochester.edu (office).

FARNHAM, John Peter, AO; Australian (b. British) singer and entertainer; b. 1 July 1949, Essex, UK; m. Jillian Farnham 1973; two s.; ed Lyndale High School; settled in Australia 1959; apprenticed as plumber; lead singer for Strings Unlimited 1965; began recording 1967; television appearances including nature series Survival with Johnny Farnham for ABC; f. John Farnham Band 1978; lead singer for Little River Band 1982–85; 12 Gold Record Awards; Australian of the Year, Bicentennial 1998. *Recordings include:* Sadie the Cleaning Lady 1967 (3 Gold Records), Friday Kind of Monday 1968, Rose Coloured Glasses 1968, One 1969, Raindrops Keep Falling on My Head 1969, Comic Conversation 1970, Rock Me Baby 1972, Don't You Know It's Magic 1973, Everything is Out of Season 1973, Uncovered 1980, The Net 1982, Playing to Win 1984, Whispering Jack 1986, Chain Reaction 1990, Full House 1991, Jesus Christ Superstar: The Album 1992, Then Again 1992, Romeo's Heart 1996, Anthology Series I, II and III 1997, 33$\frac{1}{3}$ 2001, The Last Time 2002, I Remember When I was Young 2005, Jack 2010. *Website:* www.johnfarnham.com.au.

FARNISH, Christine, CBE, BSc, MSc; British financial executive; *Group Director of Public Policy, Barclays PLC;* b. 21 April 1950, Ipswich, Suffolk; m. 1st; three s.; m. 2nd John Hayes; one d.; ed Ipswich High School, Univ. of Manchester; with Countryside Comm. 1972–76; London Borough of Lewisham 1983–86; London Research Centre 1986–88; joined Cambridge City Council 1988, Asst Chief Exec. –1994; Dir Consumer Affairs, Oftel 1994–98, Deputy Dir-Gen. 1998; Dir Consumer Div., Financial Services Authority (FSA) 1998–2002; Chief Exec. Nat. Asscn of Pension Funds 2002–06; Group Dir of Public Policy, Barclays PLC 2006–; Chair. Family and Parenting Inst. 2010–, Consumer Focus 2010–; Dir (non-exec.) Papworth NHS Trust 1998–2002, Office of Fair Trading 2003–06; Dir, ABTA 2010–; mem. Council Advertising Standards Authority 2002–08; Trustee, FSA Pension Plan 1998–2002. *Address:* Barclays PLC, 1 Churchill Place, London, E14 5HP, England (office). *Telephone:* (20) 7116-1000 (office). *Fax:* (20) 7116-7542 (office). *E-mail:* christine.farnish@barclays.com (office). *Website:* www.barclays .com (office).

FAROOQ, Qazi Muhammad, BL; Pakistani judge (retd) and government official; b. 6 Jan. 1938, Abbottabad; ed Dennys High School, Rawalpindi, Gordon Coll., Rawalpindi, Univ. Law Coll., Lahore, Nat. Inst. of Public Admin, Lahore, Inst. of Shariah and Legal Profession, Islamabad, Islamic Univ., Madina Munawwara; lawyer in Abbottabad –1967; joined PCS (Judicial Br.) 1967, worked as Civil Judge in Charsadda, Lakki Marwat, Bannu and as Sr Civil Judge, Mardan 1967–74, promoted as Additional Dist and Session Judge 1974, served at Haripur, Abbottabad and Mansehra 1974–77, promoted as Dist and Session Judge 1977, served at Mansehra, Bannu and Peshawar 1977–82; Prov. Election Commr NW Frontier Prov. 1982–88; Registrar Peshawar High Court 1988–91, Judge of Peshawar High Court 1991–99, Chief Justice Peshawar High Court 1999–2000; Judge, Supreme Court of Pakistan 2000–03; Judge-in-Charge, Fed. Judicial Acad., Islamabad 2000–03; Chief Election Commr 2006–09; Chair. Cttee of Admin, Al-Mizan Foundation 2005–; mem. Law Reforms Comm. 2000–03, Law and Justice Comm. of Pakistan 2005–. *Address:* c/o Election Commission of Pakistan Secretariat, Election House, Constitution Ave G-5/2, Islamabad, Pakistan.

FAROOQI, Hamidullah, MA; Afghan banker, economist, academic and government official; ed Faculty of Econs, Kabul Univ., Int. Inst. of Foreign Trade, New Delhi, India, Queens Coll., City Univ. of New York, USA; fmr Prof. of Econs, Kabul Univ., currently Lecturer; Chair. Banke Millie Afghan (Afghan Nat. Bank) 2003–05; Pres. and CEO Afghanistan Int. Chamber of Commerce 2005–; Founder and Prin. Int. Model School (pvt. primary school teaching exclusively through English) 2005–08; Co-founder and Chair. Brishna (think tank) 2007–; Co-founder Mesbah Inst. 2008–; mem. Microfinance Investment Support Facility for Afghanistan 2006–, Afghanistan-Pakistan Peace Jerga 2007–; mem. Advisory Bd Kabul Center for Strategic Studies 2007–; Minister of Transport and Civil Aviation 2009. *Address:* c/o Ministry of Transport and Civil Aviation, Ansari Wat, Kabul,

Afghanistan. *Telephone:* (20) 2103064. *E-mail:* arasikh@motca.gov.af; info@kabulcenter.org.

FAROOQI, Khaled; Afghan politician; *Leader, Hizb-i Islami Afghanistan (Islamic Party of Afghanistan);* Leader of Hizb-i Islami (Islamic Party) in Paktika Prov., led breakaway faction that claimed to renounce violence and support US-trained Afghan Nat. Army, higher educ. for women, free elections and moves to disarm pvt. militias 2001, Leader, Hizb-i Islami Afghanistan (Islamic Party of Afghanistan) 2006–; mem. Parl. (Paktika Prov.) 2005–, Chair. Cttee on Communication, Urban Devt, Water, Power and Municipal Affairs 2005–. *Address:* Hizb-i Islami Afghanistan (Islamic Party of Afghanistan), Area A, Khushal Mena, Kabul, Afghanistan. *Telephone:* (79) 9421474.

FAROOQUI, Dewan M. Yousuf; Pakistani business executive; *Chairman, Dewan Mushtaq Group;* b. 13 March 1963, Karachi; Sindh Prov. Minister for Local Govt, Transport, Labour, Industries, Housing and Town Planning 2000–03; currently Chair. and Chief Exec. Dewan Mushtaq Group, and CEO Dewan Farooqui Motors Ltd, responsible for overseeing Dewan Motorcycles, Dewan Sugar Mills Ltd, Dewan Textile Mills Ltd, Dewan Salman Fiber Ltd; Chair. Pakistan Textile City 2004–09; Co-Chief Patron Pakistan-Korea Business Forum; mem. Bd of Dirs Pakistan Industrial Tech. Assistance Centre; mem. Pakistan Automotive Mfrs Asscn, Pakistan-France Business Alliance, Young Pres. Org., Int. Chamber of Commerce, Pakistan-India Business Forum; Pres. Sindh Squash Asscn; Sitara-i-Imtiaz Award for Public Service (Highest Industrial Investor), Pres. of Pakistan. *Address:* Dewan Mushtaq Group, Dewan Centre, 7th Floor Block A, Finance & Trade Centre, Shahrah-e-Faisal, Karachi, Pakistan (office). *Telephone:* (21) 35857862 (home); (21) 111364463 (office). *Fax:* (21) 35630814 (office). *E-mail:* dewanyousuf@dewangroup.com.pk (office). *Website:* www.dewangroup.com.pk (office).

FARQUHAR, John William, AB, MD, FAHA; American/Canadian physician and academic; *Professor Emeritus of Medicine and Health Research and Policy, Stanford University;* b. 13 June 1927, Winnipeg, Man., Canada; s. of John Giles Farquhar and Marjorie Victoria Roberts; m. Christine Louise Johnson 1968; one s. one d. (and two s. from previous m.); ed Univ. of California, Berkeley, Univ. of California, San Francisco, London School of Hygiene and Tropical Medicine, UK; Intern, Univ. of California Hosp., San Francisco 1952–53, Resident 1953–54, 1957–58; Postdoctoral Fellow 1955–57; Resident, Univ. of Minn. 1954–55; Research Assoc., Rockefeller Univ., New York 1958–62; Asst Prof. of Medicine, Stanford Univ. 1962–66, Assoc. Prof. 1966–73, Prof. 1973–97, C.F. Rehnborg Prof. in Disease Prevention 1989–99, Prof. Emer. of Medicine and Health Research and Policy 1999–, Dir Stanford Center for Research in Disease Prevention (now Stanford Prevention Research Center) 1973–98, Assoc. Chief of Staff for Health Promotion, Stanford Univ. Hosp. 1994–97; Dir Collaborating Center for Chronic Disease Prevention, WHO 1985–99; Pres. Soc. of Behavioral Medicine 1990–92; mem. NAS Inst. of Medicine Cttee on Preventing the Global Epidemic of Cardiovascular Disease, US Del., German-American Scientific Treaty and the German Cardiovascular Project; mem. NAS Inst. of Medicine, American Soc. of Clinical Investigation, Acad. of Behavioral Medicine, American Soc. of Preventive Cardiology; Order of St George for Service to Autonomous Govt of Catalonia 1996; James D. Bruce Award 1983, Myrdal Prize 1986, Charles A. Dana Foundation Award for Pioneering Achievements in Health 1990, Nat. Cholesterol Award for Public Educ. 1991, Research Achievement Award, American Heart Asscn 1992, Joseph Stokes Preventive Cardiology Award, American Soc. of Preventive Cardiology 1999, American Heart Asscn Ancel Keys Lectureship 2000, Fries Award for the person who most improved the public's health 2005. *Publications include:* The American Way of Life Need Not Be Hazardous to Your Health 1978, The Last Puff (with G. Spiller) 1990, The Victoria Declaration for Heart Health 1992, The Catalonia Declaration: Investing in Heart Health 1996, Worldwide Efforts to Improve Heart Health 1997, The Singapore Declaration: Forging the Will for Heart Health in the Next Millennium, Diagnosis: Heart Disease (with G. Spiller) 2000; contribs to professional journals. *Leisure interests:* 20th century history, global health policy, classical music, ornithology, Scottish history, Canadian history, languages. *Address:* 649 Cabrillo Street, Stanford, CA 94305 (home); School of Medicine, Stanford Prevention Research Center, MSOB, 251 Campus Drive, Stanford, CA 94305-5411, USA. *Telephone:* (650) 690-6190 (mobile) (office); (650) 327-1177 (home). *Fax:* (650) 498-4828 (office); (650) 498-7623 (office). *E-mail:* john.farquhar@stanford.edu (office). *Website:* www.prevention.stanford.edu (office).

FARQUHAR, Robin Hugh, PhD; Canadian academic and university administrator; *Professor Emeritus, School of Public Policy and Administration, Carleton University;* b. 1 Dec. 1938, Victoria, BC; s. of Hugh E. Farquhar and Jean MacIntosh; m. Frances Caswell 1963; three d.; ed Victoria High School, Victoria Coll., Univ. of British Columbia, Univ. of Chicago; teacher, Counsellor and Coach, Edward Milne Secondary School, Sooke, BC 1962–64; Assoc. Dir and Deputy Dir, Univ. Council for Educational Admin 1966–71; Chair., Dept of Educational Admin, Asst Dir, Ont. Inst. for Studies in Educ. and Assoc. Prof., then Prof., School of Grad. Studies, Univ. of Toronto 1971–76; Dean of Educ. and Prof., Univ. of Sask., Saskatoon 1976–81; Pres., Vice-Chancellor and Prof., Univ. of Winnipeg 1981–89, Pres. Emer. 1989–; Pres., Vice-Chancellor and Prof., Carleton Univ., Ottawa 1989–96, Prof. of Public Policy and Admin 1996–2004, now Prof. Emer.; int. consultant, higher educ. policy and man. 2004–, mem. Int. Advisory Cttee, Salzburg Seminar Univs Project, Institutional Evaluation Experts Pool, European Univ. Asscn, mem. General Council, Univ. of Madeira; mem. Bd of Dirs Academics Without Borders Canada; Fellow, Commonwealth Council for Educational Admin; Hon. mem. World Innovation Foundation; Hon. Citizen, City of Winnipeg; Hon. Scout, Scouts Canada; 125th Anniversary of the Confed. of Canada Commemorative Medal; Hon. Diploma in Adult Educ.; Award of Merit, Canadian Bureau for Int. Educ., Ottawa–Carleton Partnership Award of Excellence for Leadership. *Publications:* numerous books and articles on educational admin. *Leisure interests:* jogging, golf, music. *Address:* 64 Queen Elizabeth Drive, Ottawa, ON K2P 1E3, Canada. *Telephone:* (613) 230-4735. *Fax:* (613) 230-1094. *E-mail:* rfarquha@connect.carleton.ca.

FARR, David N., BS, MBA; American business executive; *Chairman and CEO, Emerson Electric Company;* b. 1955; m.; two c.; ed Wake Forest Univ., Vanderbilt Univ.; joined Corp. Staff Dept, Emerson Electric Co. (later Emerson) 1981,

becoming Man., Investor Relations, Vice-Pres., Corp. Planning and Devt, Pres. Ridge Tool Div., Group Vice-Pres. for Industrial Components and Equipment, Pres. Emerson Electric Asia-Pacific, Hong Kong 1994–97, Exec. Vice-Pres. Emerson 1997–99, Sr Exec. Vice-Pres. and COO 1999–2000, CEO 2000–, mem. Bd of Dirs and Chair. 2004–, Pres. 2005–10; mem. or fmr mem. Bd of Dirs Delphi Corpn, United Way of Greater St Louis (Chair. annual fund-raising campaign 2007, Chair. of its de Tocqueville Soc. 2010), US-China Business Council; mem. Exec. Bd Municipal Theatre Asscn of St Louis (The Muny at Forest Park), Boy Scouts of America (Greater St Louis Area Council); mem. Civic Progress (current Pres.), The Business Council, Washington DC; Trustee, Webster Univ.; ranked by Institutional Investor magazine amongst the best CEOs in America 2008, 2009, 2010, 2011, St Louis Citizen of the Year 2011, Semper Fidelis Award, Marine Scholarship Foundation 2012. *Address:* Emerson Electric Co., PO Box 4100, 8000 West Florissant Avenue, PO Box 4100, St Louis, MO 63136-8506, USA (office). *Telephone:* (314) 553-2000 (office). *Fax:* (314) 553-3527 (office). *E-mail:* info@emerson.com (office). *Website:* www.emerson.com (office).

FARRAKHAN, Louis; American religious leader; *Leader, Nation of Islam;* b. (Louis Eugene Wolcott), 11 May 1933, New York City; m. Betsy Wolcott; nine c.; ed Winston-Salem Teachers Coll.; joined Nation of Islam 1955, Leader and Nat. Spokesman, Nation of Islam Mosque, New York 1965–75; f. reorganized Nation of Islam 1977, Leader 1977–;. *Achievements include:* organizer of Million Man March, Washington, DC 1995, Million Family March 2000. *Address:* Nation of Islam, 7351 South Stony Island Avenue, Chicago, IL 60649, USA. *Telephone:* (773) 324-6000 (office). *Website:* www.noi.org (office).

FARRANT, Jill, MSc, PhD; South African plant physiologist, molecular biologist and academic; *Research Chair in Molecular Physiology of Plant Desiccation Tolerance, University of Cape Town;* mem. Faculty, Univ. of Cape Town (UCT), initiated work on resurrection plants, Head of Molecular and Cell Biology Dept 2004–07, Research Chair in Molecular Physiology of Plant Desiccation Tolerance 2007–, mem. UCT Coll. of Fellows 2009–; Pres. South African Asscn of Botanists; Harry Oppenheimer Memorial Trust Fellowship Award 2009, awarded an A-rating by the Nat. Research Foundation (first female researcher at UCT) 2009, Distinguished Woman in Science Award, Dept of Science and Tech. 2010, L'Oréal-UNESCO For Women in Science Award (Africa and the Arab States) (for the elucidation of mechanisms by which plants overcome drought conditions) 2012. *Publications:* numerous papers in professional journals. *Address:* Molecular and Cell Biology Department, University of Cape Town, Private Bag, Rondebosch 7701, South Africa (office). *Telephone:* (21) 6504496 (office). *Fax:* (21) 6897573 (office). *E-mail:* jill.farrant@uct.ac.za (office). *Website:* www.mcb.uct.ac.za/Staff/JMF (office).

FARRELL, Andrew (Andy), OBE; British rugby football coach and fmr rugby football player; b. 30 May 1975, Wigan, Lancs.; s. of Peter Farrell; m. to Colleen Farrell; loose forward, second row, prop forward or stand off; signed for Wigan Warriors 1992–2004 (sr debut versus Keighley Nov. 1991); became youngest player to win a Wembley final in 1993 aged 17 years and 11 months; won Harry Sunderland Trophy for Man of the Match in 1996 and 1997 Premiership finals (both against St Helens)—only Wigan player to have won the award twice; Super League record of 11 goals in a match versus St Helens 1997, repeated feat versus Paris St Germain 1997; highest Super League point scorer 1997; passed 3,000 points for Wigan in 2004 (second-highest total for the club); five caps for GB Acad., one cap for GB Under-21s, full GB debut versus Australia 1993 (youngest forward to win GB cap), 34 caps in total (fifth highest); GB Capt. 1998–2003 on 29 occasions (record); five caps for England; rep. Lancashire in 2003 Origin Match; awarded Wigan testimonial season 2001; retd from rugby league and joined Saracens in Rugby Football Union 2005–09 (retd), Skills and Backs Coach 2009–; eight caps for England 2007, mem. runner-up team in Rugby World Cup, France 2007; Man of Steel 1995, 2004, selected for Super League Dream Team 2003, 2004, Rugby League World Golden Boot Award 2004 (only second British player to win prize). *Address:* c/o Saracens Ltd, Kingsley House, Unit 3, Sandridge Park, Porters Wood, St Albans, AL3 6PH, England. *Telephone:* (1727) 792800. *Fax:* (1727) 792801. *Website:* www.saracens.com.

FARRELL, Colin; Irish actor; b. 31 May 1976, Castleknock, Dublin; s. of Eamon Farrell and Rita Farrell (née Monaghan); ed Gaiety School of Drama, Dublin. *Films include:* Drinking Crude 1997, Falling for a Dancer (TV) 1998, The War Zone 1999, Ordinary Decent Criminal 2000, Tigerland (Boston Soc. of Film Critics Best Actor Award) 2000, American Outlaws 2001, Hart's War (Shanghai Int. Film Festival Best Actor Award) 2002, Minority Report 2002, Phone Booth 2002, The Recruit 2003, Daredevil 2003, Veronica Guerin 2003, S.W.A.T. 2003, Intermission 2003, A Home at the End of the World 2004, Alexander 2004, The New World 2005, Ask the Dust 2006, Miami Vice 2006, Cassandra's Dream 2007, In Bruges (Golden Globe Award for Best Actor in a Musical or Comedy 2009) 2008, Pride and Glory 2007, The Imaginarium of Doctor Parnassus 2009, Ondine (Irish Film & TV Award for Best Actor) 2010, London Boulevard 2010, Total Recall 2012, Seven Psychopaths 2012. *Television includes:* Ballykissangel 1996, Love in the 21st Century 1999, Scrubs 2005. *Address:* c/o Creative Artists Agency, 9830 Wilshire Boulevard, Beverly Hills, CA 90212-1825, USA. *Telephone:* (310) 288-4545 (office). *Fax:* (310) 288-4800 (office). *Website:* www.caa.com (office).

FARRELL, Norman, BA, LLB, LLM; Canadian lawyer and international organization official; *Chief Prosecutor, Special Tribunal for Lebanon;* ed Queen's Univ., Kingston, Ont., Columbia Univ., USA; admitted to Law Soc. of Upper Canada, Ont. 1988; Crown Counsel (Criminal Div.) with Attorney Gen. for Prov. of Ont. 1988–96; held several positions in ICRC, including as Del. and Co-ordinator in charge of dissemination of int. humanitarian law in Bosnia and Herzegovina, Legal Adviser on int. humanitarian law in Ethiopia, Adviser on int. criminal law and int. humanitarian law in Switzerland 1996–99; Appeals Counsel, Int. Criminal Tribunal for the Fmr Yugoslavia 1999–2002, Head of Appeals Section and Sr Appeals Counsel 2002–05, Prin. Legal Officer, Office of the Prosecutor 2005–08, Deputy Prosecutor 2008–12, Head of Appeals Section and Sr Appeals Counsel, Int. Criminal Tribunal for Rwanda 2002–03, Chief Prosecutor, Special Tribunal for Lebanon 2012–; Lecturer on Int. Criminal Law, Faculty of Law, Queen's Univ. 2004–11, Int. Studies Centre, Herstmonceux, UK 2004–14. *Address:* Special Tribunal for Lebanon, PO Box 115, 2260 AC Leidschendam, Netherlands (office). *Telephone:* (70) 8003400 (office). *E-mail:* stl-pressoffice@un.org (office). *Website:* www.stl-tsl.org (office).

FARRELL, Patrick (Pat) M.; Irish business executive and fmr politician; *Head of Communications and Government Affairs, Bank of Ireland;* b. 30 Aug. 1957, Leitrim; s. of Bill Farrell and Mamie Casey; m. Margaret Logan 1988; one s. one d.; ed Management Coll., Carrick-on-Shannon, Inst. of Public Admin.; Hosp. Admin., Sligo 1981–86; CEO Galvia Hosp., Galway 1986–91; Gen. Sec. Fianna Fáil 1991–98; fmr Chair. Irish Council of the European Movt; mem. of Senate 1992; CEO Irish Banking Fed. 2004–13; Head of Communications and Government Affairs, Bank of Ireland 2013–; mem. Bd of Friends of Fianna Fáil Inc., USA; Fellow, Inst. of Bankers. *Leisure interests:* current affairs, reading, writing. *Address:* Bank of Ireland, 40 Mespil Road, Dublin 4, Ireland (office). *E-mail:* Pat .Farrell@boi.com (office). *Website:* www.bankofireland.com (office).

FARRELL, Suzanne; American ballerina; *Artistic Director, Suzanne Farrell Ballet;* b. 16 Aug. 1945; ed School of American Ballet; fmr Prin. Dancer with New York City Ballet –1989; also danced with Béjart Ballet, Brussels; appeared in numerous Balanchine ballets choreographed for her including Mozartiana, Chaconne, Meditation, Vienna Waltzes; staged seven Balanchine ballets at John F. Kennedy Center for Performing Arts, Washington, DC 1995 and many other stagings of Balanchine's works; Founder-Artistic Dir Suzanne Farrell Ballet Co., Kennedy Center for the Performing Arts 2000–; repetiteur for Balanchine Trust, including Kirov Ballet, Royal Danish Ballet and Paris Opéra Ballet; mem. Advisory Panel Princess Grace Foundation, Sr Advisory Bd of Arthritis Foundation; EPPES Prof. of Dance, Florida State Univ.; trains ballet dancers in camp in The Adirondacks; several hon. degrees; Nat. Medal of the Arts 2003, Kennedy Center Honor 2005, Capezio Dance Award 2005. *Television:* Suzanne Farrell: Elusive Muse (documentary). *Publication:* Holding On To The Air (autobiography) 1990. *Address:* Suzanne Farrell Ballet, Kennedy Center for the Performing Arts, 2700 F Street, NW, Washington, DC 20566, USA (office). *Website:* www.kennedy -center.org/programs/ballet/farrell (office).

FARRELL, Sir Terence (Terry), Kt, CBE, MCP, MArch, MRTPI, RIBA, FCSD, FRSA; British architect; *Principal, Terry Farrell & Partners;* b. 12 May 1938; s. of Thomas Farrell and Molly Farrell (née Maguire); m. 1st Angela Rosemarie Mallam 1960; two d.; m. 2nd Susan Hilary Aplin 1973; two s. one d.; ed St Cuthbert's Grammar School, Newcastle-upon-Tyne, Newcastle Univ., Univ. of Pennsylvania, USA; Harkness Fellow, Commonwealth Fund, USA 1962–64; Pnr, Farrell Grimshaw Partnership 1965–80, Terry Farrell Partnership 1980–87; Prin. Terry Farrell & Partners 1987–; Visiting Prof., Univ. of Westminster 1998–2001; Hon. FAIA; Hon. DCL (Newcastle) 2000; Hon. DArts (Lincoln) 2003. *Major projects include:* Vauxhall Cross (MI6 Bldg), London, The Peak, Hong Kong, Charing Cross Station Redevelopment, London, Edinburgh Int. Conf. Centre, British Consulate and British Council Bldgs, Hong Kong, Dean Centre Art Gallery, Edin., Int. Centre for Life, Newcastle, Transportation Centre for Inchon Int. Airport, Seoul, The Deep 'Submarium' (aquarium), Hull, British Library masterplan, London 2009–, West Kowloon Cultural District. Hong Kong 2009–12, Kingkey 100, Shenzhen (Shenzhen's tallest building) 2011, Embassy Gardens, Wandsworth, London (under construction). *Publications:* Architectural Monograph 1985, Urban Design Monograph 1993, Ten Years, Ten Cities: The work of Terry Farrell and Partners, 1991–2001 2002, Place 2005; articles in numerous journals. *Leisure interests:* walking, swimming. *Address:* Terry Farrell & Partners, 7 Hatton Street, London, NW8 8PL, England (office). *Telephone:* (20) 7258-3433 (office). *Fax:* (20) 7723-7059 (office). *E-mail:* tfarrell@terryfarrell.co.uk (office). *Website:* www.terryfarrell.co.uk (office).

FARRELL, Thomas Francis, II, BA, JD; American lawyer and business executive; *Chairman, President and CEO, Dominion;* b. 1954; m. Anne Garland Farrell (née Tullidge); two s.; ed Univ. of Va; Pnr, McGuire Woods Beatle & Booth (law firm) 1981–95; joined Dominion Resources Inc. (now Dominion), Richmond 1995, Sr Vice-Pres. and Gen. Counsel 1995–97, Sr Vice-Pres. for Corp. Affairs 1997–99, Exec. Vice-Pres. 1999–2003, Pres. and COO 2002–05, Pres. and CEO 2006–07, Chair., Pres. and CEO 2007–, also CEO Va Power, Dominion Generation Inc., Pres. and COO Consolidated Natural Gas Co. (subsidiaries of Dominion); mem. Bd of Dirs Virginia Electric and Power Co., Inst. of Nuclear Power Operations; mem. Va Bar Assen, Va Law Foundation; Rector, Bd of Visitors, Univ. of Va 2005–. *Address:* Dominion, 120 Tredegar Street, Richmond, VA 23219, USA (office). *Telephone:* (804) 819-2000 (office). *Fax:* (804) 819-2233 (office). *E-mail:* thomas_farrell@dom.com (office). *Website:* www.dom.com (office).

FARRINGTON, David Philip, OBE, MA, PhD, FBA, FMedSci; British psychologist, academic and criminologist; *Professor Emeritus of Psychological Criminology, Institute of Criminology, University of Cambridge;* b. 7 March 1944, Ormskirk, Lancs.; s. of William Farrington and Gladys Holden Farrington; m. Sally Chamberlain 1966; three d.; ed Univ. of Cambridge; mem. staff, Inst. of Criminology, Univ. of Cambridge 1969–, Prof. of Psychological Criminology 1992–2012, Prof. Emer. 2012–; Pres. European Assen of Psychology and Law 1997–99; Visiting Fellow, US Nat. Inst. of Justice 1981; Chair. Div. of Criminological and Legal Psychology, British Psychological Soc. 1983–85; mem. Parole Bd for England and Wales 1984–87; Vice-Chair. US Nat. Acad. of Sciences Panel on Violence 1989–92; Visiting Fellow, US Bureau of Justice Statistics 1995–98; Co-Chair. US Office of Juvenile Justice and Delinquency Prevention Study Group on Serious and Violent Juvenile Offenders 1995–97; Pres. British Soc. of Criminology 1990–93, Pres. American Soc. of Criminology 1998–99; Co-Chair. US Office of Juvenile Justice and Delinquency Prevention Study Group on Very Young Offenders 1998–2000; Chair. UK Dept of Health Advisory Cttee for the Nat. Programme on Forensic Mental Health 2000–03; mem. Bd of Dirs Int. Soc. of Criminology 2000–09; Pres. Acad. of Experimental Criminology 2001–03; Co-Chair. Campbell Collaboration Crime and Justice Group 2000–04; Sellin-Glueck Award of American Soc. of Criminology 1984, Sutherland Award of American Soc. of Criminology 2002, Joan McCord Award, Acad. of Experimental Criminology 2005, Beccaria Gold Medal, Criminology Soc. of German-Speaking Countries 2005. *Publications:* many books and over 420 articles on criminology and psychology. *Address:* Institute of Criminology, University of Cambridge, Sidgwick Avenue, Cambridge, CB3 9DA (office); 7 The Meadows, Haslingfield, Cambridge, CB3 7JD, England (home). *Telephone:* (1223) 335360 (office); (1223) 872555 (home). *Fax:*

(1223) 335356 (office). *E-mail:* enquiries@crim.cam.ac.uk (office). *Website:* www .crim.cam.ac.uk (office).

FARROW, Mia Villiers; American actress; b. 9 Feb. 1945, Calif.; d. of John Villiers Farrow and Maureen O'Sullivan; m. 1st Frank Sinatra 1966 (divorced 1968); m. 2nd André Previn 1970 (divorced 1979); 14 c.; stage début in The Importance of Being Earnest, New York 1963; French Acad. Award for Best Actress 1969, David Donatello Award (Italy) 1969, Rio de Janeiro Film Festival Award 1969, San Sebastian Award. *Stage appearances in London:* Mary Rose, The Three Sisters, House of Bernarda Alba 1972–73, The Marrying of Ann Leete (RSC) 1975, The Zykovs 1976, Ivanov (RSC) 1976; appeared in Romantic Comedy (Broadway) 1979. *Films include:* Guns at Batasi 1964, Rosemary's Baby 1968, Secret Ceremony 1969, John and Mary 1969, See No Evil 1970, The Great Gatsby 1973, Full Circle 1978, A Wedding 1978, Death on the Nile 1978, The Hurricane 1979, A Midsummer Night's Sex Comedy 1982, Zelig 1983, Broadway Danny Rose 1984, Purple Rose of Cairo 1985, Hannah and Her Sisters 1986, Radio Days 1987, September 1988, Another Woman 1988, Oedipus Wrecks 1989, Crimes and Misdemeanors 1989, Alice 1990, Shadows and Fog 1992, Husbands and Wives 1992, Widow's Peak 1994, Miami Rhapsody 1995, Private Parts 1997, Reckless 1995, Coming Soon 2000, Purpose 2002, The Omen 2006, Arthur and the Invisibles 2006, The Ex 2007, Be Kind Rewind 2007, Dark Horse 2011. *Television appearances:* Peyton Place 1964–66; Johnny Belinda 1965, Peter Pan 1975, Goodbye Raggedy Ann (film), Miracle at Midnight, The Secret Life of Zoey (film) 2002, Samantha: An American Girl Holiday (film) 2004. *Publication:* What Falls Away (autobiog.) 1996. *Leisure interests:* reading, mind wandering, listening to music and certain people. *Address:* International Creative Management, c/o Sam Cohn, 40 West 57th Street, New York, NY 10019, USA. *Website:* www.mia-farrow .com.

FARUQUE, Mohammad, BEng; Pakistani industrialist; *Chairman, Ghulam Faruque Group;* b. 14 Jan. 1930, Magpur, India; s. of Ghulam Faruque and Zulfara Faruque; two s. one d.; ed Univ. of Southern California, USA; Chair. Ghulam Faruque Group, conglomerate which includes Cherat Cement Co. Ltd, Mirpurkhas Sugar Mills Ltd, Greaves Pakistan (Pvt.) Ltd. *Leisure interests:* cricket, golf, reading. *Address:* Ghulam Faruque Group, Modern Motors House, Beaumont Road, Karachi 75530, Pakistan (office). *Telephone:* (21) 5682565 (office); (21) 5888889 (home). *Fax:* (21) 5682839 (office). *E-mail:* faruque@fascom.com (office). *Website:* www.gfg.com.pk (office).

FASCETTO, Jorge E.; Argentine journalist and fmr international organization official; ed La Plata Nat. Univ.; apptd. Gen. Man. El Día newspaper, La Plata 1967, Chair. 1980, Chair. Diario Popular (after split from El Día) 2009–; Vice-Pres. Exec. Cttee Asociacíon de Diarios del Interior de la República Argentina 1985, Asociacíon de Entidades Periodísticas Argentinas 1986; Dir and mem. Exec. Cttee and Advisory Council Inter-American Press Assen (IAPA), Pres. IAPA Tech. Center 1989; Chair. Int. Press Inst. 2002–04; *Website:* www.popularonline.com.ar.

FASE, Martin M. G., PhD; Dutch banker, economist and academic; *Professor Emeritus of Monetary Economics, University of Amsterdam;* b. (Martinus Maria Gerard), 28 Dec. 1937, Skoop; s. of A. P. Fase and G. J. M. de Groot; m. Lida E. M. Franse 1965; two s.; ed Univ. of Amsterdam; Research Assoc., Inst. of Actuarial Sciences and Econometrics, Amsterdam 1965–69; Ford Foundation Fellow, Dept of Econs, Univ. of Wisconsin, Madison, USA 1969–71; with De Nederlandsche Bank 1971–2001, Deputy Dir 1985–2001; Extraordinary Prof. of Business Statistics, Erasmus Univ., Rotterdam 1978–86; Extraordinary Prof. of Monetary Econs, Univ. of Amsterdam 1986–2003, Prof. Emer. 2003–; Man. Ed. De Economist 1998–2008, Chair. Editorial Bd 2003–08; Fellow, Royal Netherlands Acad. of Arts and Sciences 1987, Royal Hollandsche Maatschappij der Wetenschappen 1989; mem. Maatschappi der Nederlandse Letterkunde 2001; Officer, Order of Orange Nassau 1995; N.G. Pierson Medal 1996. *Publications include:* An Econometric Model of Age-Income Profiles: A Statistical Analysis of Dutch Income Data 1970, The Monetary Sector of the Netherlands in 50 Equations: A Quarterly Monetary Model for the Netherlands 1970–79, In Analysing the Structure of Econometric Models (ed. J. P. Ancot) 1984, Seasonal Adjustment as a Practical Problem 1991, Demand for Money and Credit in Europe 1999, Tussen behoud en vernieuwing 2000; articles in European Economic Review, Journal of International Economics and other journals; several monographs. *Leisure interests:* Dutch literature, hiking. *Address:* Ruysdaelweg 3B, 2051 EM Overveen, Netherlands (home). *Telephone:* (23) 527-17-00 (home). *E-mail:* mmg.fase@wxs.nl.

FASQUELLE, Jean-Claude; French publisher; *Chairman of the Board, Éditions Grasset et Fasquelle;* b. 29 Nov. 1930, Paris; s. of Charles Fasquelle and Odette Cyprien-Fabre; m. 1st Solange de la Rochefoucauld; one d.; m. 2nd Nickla Jagher 1966; ed Ecole des Roches, Verneuil-sur-Avre, Sorbonne and Faculté de Droit, Paris; Pres.-Dir-Gen. Société des Editions Fasquelle 1953–60, Editions du Sagittaire 1958–; Admin.-Dir-Gen. Editions Grasset et Fasquelle 1960, Pres.-Dir-Gen. 1980–2000, Chair. of Bd 2000–; Dir Le Magazine littéraire (monthly) 1970–2004. *Address:* Editions Grasset et Fasquelle, 61 rue des Saintes-Pères, 75006 Paris (office); 13 Square Vergennes, 75015 Paris, France (home). *Telephone:* 1-44-39-22-00 (office). *Fax:* 1-44-39-22-18 (office). *E-mail:* jcfasquelle@wanadoo.fr (home). *Website:* www.edition-grasset.fr (office).

FASSBENDER, Michael; Irish/German actor; b. 2 April 1977, Heidelberg, Baden-Württemberg, Germany; s. of Josef Fassbender and Adele Fassbender; ed St Brendan's Coll., Killarney, Drama Centre, London, UK; raised in Killarney, Co. Kerry, south west Ireland, where his family moved in 1979; moved to London to study acting 1996; toured with Oxford Stage Co. performing Chekov's Three Sisters; lives in London. *Films:* 300 2006, Angel 2007, Hunger 2008, Eden Lake 2008, Fish Tank 2009, Blood Creek 2009, Centurion 2010, Jonah Hex 2010, Jane Eyre 2011, X-Men: First Class 2011, A Dangerous Method 2011, Shame 2011, Haywire 2011, Prometheus 2012, 12 Years a Slave 2013, The Counsellor 2013, Frank 2014, X-Men: Days of Future Past 2014, Slow West 2014. *Television includes:* Band of Brothers (mini-series) 2001, Carla (film) 2003, Gunpowder, Treason & Plot (film) 2004, Julian Fellowes Investigates: A Most Mysterious Murder – The Case of Charles Bravo (film) 2004, A Bear Named Winnie (film) 2004, Sherlock Holmes and the Case of the Silk Stocking (film) 2004, Hex (series) 2004–05, Our Hidden Lives (film) 2005, Trial & Retribution (series) 2006-07, Wedding Belles (film) 2007, The Devil's Whore (mini-series) 2008. *Leisure interest:*

Formula 1 motor racing. *Address:* c/o Conor McCaughan, Troika Talent Agency, Cosmopolitan House, 10A Christina Street, London, EC2A 4PA, England (office); c/o Michael Cooper, Creative Artists Agency, 2000 Avenue of the Stars, Los Angeles, CA 90067, USA (office). *Telephone:* (20) 7336-7868 (London) (office); (424) 288-2000 (Los Angeles) (office). *Fax:* (424) 288-2900 (Los Angeles) (office). *E-mail:* info@troikatalent.com (office); info@caa.com (office); www.troikatalent .com (office); www.caa.com (office); michael-fassbender-online.net.

FASSI, Abbas al-; Moroccan politician; b. 18 Sept. 1940, Berkane; m.; four c.; ed Univ. Mohammed V, Rabat; apptd Sec.-Gen. Moroccan Human Rights League 1972; mem. Exec. Cttee Istiqlal Party 1974–, Gen. Sec. 1998–; Minister of Housing 1977–81, of Handicrafts and Social Affairs 1981–85, of Social Devt, Solidarity, Employment and Professional Training 2000–02, Minister of State 2002–07; Prime Minister of Morocco 2007–11; Amb. to Tunisia and Perm. Rep. to League of Arab Nations 1985–90; Amb. to France 1990–94; mem. Bd of Dirs Caisse Nat. de Sécurité Sociale, Entraide Nationale, Social Devt Agency; Grand Officier, Order National de Mérite (France), Commandeur, Ordre de la République (Tunisia). *Address:* c/o Office of the Prime Minister, Palais Royal, Touarga, Rabat, Morocco (office).

FASSI-FIHRI, Ahmed, LenD; Moroccan civil servant and diplomatist; b. 6 Aug. 1936, Oujda; m. Touria El Ouazzani; two s. two d.; pvt. sec. of Minister of Interior 1956; Head of Office, Dept of Minerals and Geology 1958; Head, Office of Minister of Foreign Affairs 1959; Chargé d'affaires, Moroccan Embassy, Berne 1960; Pres. Melnes Municipality 1963; founder and Dir Nat. Documentation Centre 1967–98, Information Science School 1974, Multimedia Centre 1993; Order of Ridha. *Publications:* articles in field of information science in Arabic and French. *Leisure interests:* listening to Arabic and classical music, reading of the Arabic intellectual literary productions. *Address:* c/o Centre National de Documentation, Boulevard Hadj Ahmed Cherkaoui, Rabat, Morocco.

FASSI-FIHRI, Taieb, PhD; Moroccan government official; b. 9 April 1958, Casablanca; m.; two c.; ed Lycée Descartes, Rabat, Institut Nat. de la Statistique et d'Economie Appliquée, Rabat, Université Panthéon-Sorbonne, Paris, Institut d'Etudes Politiques, Paris; Lecturer, Univ. of Paris VII, also Chargé d'Etudes at Institut Français des Relations Internationales 1983–84; attached to Dept of Planning, Ministry of Planning 1984, in charge of special duties in Cabinet of Minister in charge of relations with the EEC 1985–86; Chief of Div., Ministry of Foreign Affairs and Co-operation in charge of relations with EC 1986–89; Dir Office of the Minister of State in charge of Foreign Affairs and Co-operation 1989–93; Sec. of State for Foreign Affairs and Co-operation 1993–98; Head of Mission at Royal Cabinet 1998–99; Sec. of State for Foreign Affairs 1999–2000, for Foreign Affairs and Co-operation 2000–02, Coordinator, responsible for negotiation of free trade agreement between Morocco and USA 2002, Minister Del. for Foreign Affairs and Co-operation 2002–07, Minister of Foreign Affairs and Co-operation 2007–11; Officer, Wissam Al Arch Order 2001. *Address:* c/o Ministry of Foreign Affairs and Co-operation, avenue Franklin Roosevelt, Rabat, Morocco.

FASSINO, Piero Franco Rodolfo, BSc; Italian politician; *Mayor of Turin;* b. 7 Oct. 1949, Avigliana; m.; local councillor Turin 1975–80, 1985–90, Prov. Councillor 1980–85; various posts within Turin Fed. of Partito Comunista Italiano (PCI) 1971–83, Prov. Sec. 1983–87, elected to PCI Exec. 1983, Co-ordinator Nat. Secr. 1987, then Head of party org. during transition to Partito Democratico della Sinistra (PDS), mem. Nat. Secr. and Int. Sec. PDS 1991–96, PDS Rep. to Socialist Int. 1992, PDS re-named Democratici di Sinistra (DS) 1998, Leader (Nat. Sec.) DS 2001–07, mem. Partito Democratico (formed after merger between Democratici di Sinistra, Democrazia è Libertà—La Margherita and other left-wing and centrist parties); Pres. Cen. and Western Europe Cttee Socialist Int. 1993, Chair. Cttee for Peace, Democracy and Human Rights 2004; fmr Vice-Pres. Socialist Group, Council of Europe; mem. Chamber of Deputies from Liguria (PDS) 1994–96, from Piedmont 1996–11; Mayor of Turin 2011–; Under-Sec. Ministry for Foreign Affairs 1996–98; Minister for Foreign Trade 1998–2000, for Justice 2000–01; mem. Parl. Assćn for Cen. Europe Initiative; Vice-Pres. Italian-Israeli Parl. Friendship Assćn 1995; Chevalier, Légion d'honneur; Grand Medal of Merit, Gala Dinner Dance and Awards Ceremony. *Publication:* Per Passione 2003. *Address:* Piazza Palazzo di Città, 1, Turin, Italy (office). *Telephone:* (011) 4423000 (office). *Fax:* (011) 5625580 (office). *E-mail:* segreteria.sindaco@comune.torino.it (office). *Website:* www .comune.torino.it (office); www.pierofassinosindaco.it.

FAST, The Hon. Edward (Ed) Daniel, PC; Canadian lawyer and politician; *Minister of International Trade and Minister for the Asia-Pacific Gateway;* b. 18 June 1955, Winnipeg; m. Annette Fast; four c.; ed Univ. of British Columbia; f. Linley Welwood (legal practice), Abbotsford, BC 1983; mem. Abbotsford School Bd 1985–90; mem. Abbotsford City Council 1996–2005; fmr Deputy Mayor of Abbotsford; MP for Abbotsford 2006–; Minister of Int. Trade and Minister for the Asia-Pacific Gateway 2011–; mem. Conservative Party of Canada. *Address:* Department of Foreign Affairs and International Trade Canada, Lester B. Pearson Building, 125 Sussex Drive, Ottawa, ON K1A 0G2, Canada (office). *Telephone:* (613) 944-4000 (office). *Fax:* (613) 996-9709 (office). *E-mail:* ed.fast@parl.gc.ca (office). *Website:* www.international.gc.ca (office); www.edfast.ca.

FATTOUH, Rawhi, (Abu Wisam), BA; Palestinian politician; b. 23 Aug. 1949; m.; one d. two s.; ed Damascus Univ.; Speaker of Palestinian Parl. 2004–06; Acting Exec. Pres. Palestinian (Nat.) Authority 2004–05; aide to Pres. Mahmoud Abbas –2008. *Publications:* several articles in Arabic about the Middle East. *Address:* c/o Office of the President, Ramallah, Palestinian Autonomous Areas, via Israel (office).

FAU, Yamandú; Uruguayan academic and politician; mem. Parl. 1984–2000; Minister of Educ. and Culture 2000; elected Senator 2000; Minister of Nat. Defence 2002–05; mem. Partido Colorado de Uruguay. *Address:* c/o Ministry of National Defence, Edif. General Artigas, Avda 8 de Octubre 2628, Montevideo, Uruguay (office).

FAUCI, Anthony Stephen, MD; American medical researcher; *Director, National Institute of Allergy and Infectious Diseases;* b. 24 Dec. 1940, Brooklyn, New York, NY; s. of Stephen Fauci and Eugenia Fauci; m. Christine Grady 1985; three d.; ed Coll. of the Holy Cross, Cornell Univ. Medical Coll.; Instructor in Medicine, Cornell Medical Coll. 1971–72; Medical Dir US Public Health Service

1968–70, 1972; Clinical Assoc., Lab. of Clinical Investigation, Nat. Inst. of Allergy and Infectious Diseases (NIAID) 1968–71, Sr Staff Fellow, Lab. of Clinical Investigation 1970–71, Sr Investigator 1972–74, Head of Physiology Section 1974–80, Deputy Clinical Dir NIAID 1977–84, Dir 1984–; Chief Resident in Medicine, New York Hosp., Cornell Univ. Medical Center 1971–72; Chief Lab. of Immunoregulation 1980–; Dir Office of AIDS Research and Assoc. Dir Nat. Inst. of Health for AIDS Research 1988–94; consultant, Naval Medical Center, Bethesda, Md 1972–; mem. NAS, American Philosophical Soc., Royal Acad. of Medicine (Spain), Royal Danish Acad., Inst. of Medicine, Asscn of American Physicians, American Soc. for Clinical Investigation, Infectious Diseases Soc. of America, Int. AIDS Soc., American Fed. for Clinical Research, American Soc. for Cell Biology, American Soc. for Virology, American Asscn of Immunologists; numerous awards, including Squibb Award, Infectious Diseases Soc. of America 1983, Bristol Award, Infectious Diseases Soc. of America 1999, Int. Prize for Scientific Research, Fondazione PISO 1999, Frank Berry Prize in Fed. Medicine 1999, Timely Topics Award Lecture of the US and Canadian Acad. of Pathology 1999, Frank Annunzio Humanitarian Award, Christopher Columbus Fellowship Foundation 2001, Ellis Island Family Heritage Award, Statue of Liberty-Ellis Island Foundation 2003, Lifetime Achievement Award, American Asscn of Immunologists 2005, Nat. Science Medal, NSF 2007, Mary Woodard Lasker Award for Public Service 2007, Presidential Medal of Freedom 2008. *Leisure interests:* jogging, tennis. *Address:* NIAID/NIH, 31 Center Drive MSC 2520, Bethesda, MD 20892-0001 (office); 3012 43rd Street NW, Washington, DC 20016, USA (home). *Telephone:* (301) 496-2263 (office). *Fax:* (301) 496-4409 (office). *E-mail:* afauci@niaid.nih.gov (office). *Website:* www.niaid.nih.gov (office).

FAUCON, Bernard; French photographer; b. 12 Sept. 1950, Apt; ed Lycée d'Apt, Univ. of Aix en Provence, Sorbonne, Paris; Grand Prix Nat. 1989. *Publications:* Les Grandes Vacances 1980, Les Papiers qui Volent 1986, Les Chambres d'Amour 1987, Tables d'Amis 1991, Les Idoles et les Sacrifices 1991, Dernier Portrait 1991, Les Ecritures 1993, Jours d'Image 1995, La Fin de l'Image 1997, Chambres d'Amour, Chambres d'Or 1998, La Peur du Voyage 1999, Le Plus Beau Jour de ma Jeunesse 2000, La Plus Belle Route du Monde 2000, Une Singulière Gourmandise 2003, Atelier Faucon à Pingyao 2004, Catalogue Raisonné 2005, Le Tour de Monde 2008, Eté 2550 2009. *Leisure interests:* cookery, travelling. *Address:* 6 rue Barbanègre, 75019 Paris, France (home). *Telephone:* 1-40-05-99-70 (home). *E-mail:* info.contact@bernardfaucon.net (office). *Website:* www.bernardfaucon.net.

FAUGÈRE, Jean-Paul; French civil servant, government official and business executive; *Chairman, CNP Assurances SA; b,* 12 Dec. 1956; ed Ecole Polytechnique, Institut d'Etudes Politiques de Paris, Ecole Nationale d'Admin; insurance commr and controller 1980–81; Auditor to Council of State 1983; Rapporteur for Special Pensions Appeal Cttee and Cen. Cttee for Social Assistance 1983–86; Maître des requêtes (Counsel) to Council of State 1986; Govt Commr for CCAS 1986–87; Deputy Sec.-Gen., Council of State 1986–87; tech. adviser to Minister of Infrastructure, Transport and Housing 1987–88; Govt Commr for Council of State's litigation ass. 1988–90, adviser to Gen. Admin. 1990, then Finance Dir Atomic Energy Comm. 1991–94; Dir of Civil Liberties and Legal Affairs, Ministry of Interior 1994–97; Prefect for Loir et Cher 1997–2001, for La Vendée 2001–02; State Councillor 1998; Head of François Fillon's Office (fmr Minister of Social Affairs, then Minister of Nat. Educ.) 2002–05; Prefect for Alsace-Bas Rhin region 2005–07; Head of Prime Minister's Office 2007–12; Chair. CNP Assurances SA 2012–. *Address:* CNP Assurances SA, 4 place Raoul Dautry, 75716 Paris Cedex 15, France (office). *Telephone:* 1-42-18-88-88 (office). *Fax:* 1-42-18-93-66 (office). *E-mail:* edmond.alphandery@cnp.fr (office). *Website:* www.cnp.fr (office).

FAUJOUR, Olivier; French business executive; *President, Yoplait International, and Vice-President, General Mills;* ed Lycée Hoche, Versailles, ESCP Europe Grad. School, Paris; worked for 12 years for Procter & Gamble, holding various marketing roles in Europe and Latin America, including as Marketing Dir in Brazil; worked for seven years for Danone, held various leadership positions at nat. and global levels, participated in the expansion of Danone in China, f. commercial and industrial operations in S Korea; joined General Mills as Vice-Pres. and Man. Dir for General Mills France, Benelux and Southern Europe Nov. 2010, led devt of Häagen-Dazs, Old El Paso and Green Giant, currently Vice-Pres., General Mills and Pres., Yoplait International, oversees the global Yoplait (yogurt) business outside USA, mem. Bd of Dirs, Yoplait Joint Venture with Sodiaal. *Address:* Number One General Mills Boulevard, Minneapolis, MN 55426-1347, USA (office). *Telephone:* (763) 764-76002 (office). *Fax:* (763) 764-8330 (office). *E-mail:* info@generalmills.com (office). *Website:* www.generalmills.com (office).

FAULKNER, John, BA, DipEd; Australian politician; b. 12 April 1954, Leeton, NSW; ed Macquarie Univ.; mem. NSW Admin. Cttee, Australian Labor Party (ALP) 1978–89, Asst Gen. Sec. 1980–89, mem. ALP Nat. Exec. 1989–, Nat. Pres. ALP 2007–08; research officer for NSW Minister for Sport and Recreation 1980; mem. Senate 1989–, Man. of Govt Business 1993–96, Leader of Opposition 1996–2004; Minister for Veterans' Affairs and Minister for Defence Science and Personnel 1993–94, for Sport and Territories March 1994, for Environment, Sport and Territories 1994–96; Shadow Minister for Social Security 1996–97, for Public Admin and Govt Services 1997–2001, for Territories 1997–98, for Olympic Coordination and Centenary of Fed. 1998–2001, for Public Admin and Home Affairs 2001–03, for Public Admin and Accountability 2003–04, for Defence 2009–10; Special Minister of State, Cabinet Sec. and Vice-Pres. of the Exec. Council 2007–09; mem. Macquarie Univ. Council 1984–92. *Publications:* True Believers (co-author). *Address:* c/o Department of Defence, Russell Offices, Russell Drive, Campbell, Canberra, ACT 2600, Australia.

FAULKS, Sebastian, CBE, MA, FRSL; British writer; b. 20 April 1953, Newbury, Berks.; s. of Peter Faulks and Pamela Lawless; m. Veronica Youlten 1989; two s. one d.; ed Wellington Coll. and Emmanuel Coll., Cambridge; reporter, Daily Telegraph newspaper 1979–83, feature writer, Sunday Telegraph 1983–86; Literary Ed. The Independent 1986–89, Deputy Ed. The Independent on Sunday 1989–90, Assoc. Ed. 1990–91; columnist, The Guardian 1992–97, Evening Standard 1997–99, Mail on Sunday 1999–2000; invited to write new James Bond 007 novel to celebrate centenary of Ian Fleming's birth 2008; Hon. Fellow, Emmanuel Coll., Cambridge 2007; Hon. DLitt (Tavistock Clinic, Univ. of East London). *Radio:* Panelist, The Write Stuff, BBC Radio 4 1998–. *Television:* Churchill's Secret Army 2000, Faulks on Fiction 2011. *Publications:* A Trick of the

Light 1984, The Girl at the Lion d'Or 1989, A Fool's Alphabet 1992, Birdsong 1993, The Fatal Englishman 1996, Charlotte Gray 1998, On Green Dolphin Street 2001, Human Traces 2005, Pistache 2006, Engleby 2007, Devil May Care (writing as Ian Fleming) (British Book Award for Popular Fiction 2009) 2008, A Week in December 2009, Faulks on Fiction 2011, A Possible Life 2012. *Leisure interests:* wine, sport. *Address:* c/o Aitken Alexander Associates Ltd, 18–21 Cavaye Place, London, SW10 9PT, England (office). *Telephone:* (20) 7373-8672 (office). *Fax:* (20) 7373-6002 (office). *E-mail:* reception@aitkenalexander.co.uk (office). *Website:* www .aitkenalexander.co.uk (office); www.sebastianfaulks.com.

FAURE, Danny; Seychelles politician; *Vice-President, Minister of Information Technology and Public Administration;* b. 1962; early career as teacher, Seychelles Polytechnic and Nat. Youth Service; fmr Chair. Seychelles People's Progressive Front; Leader of Govt Business, Nat. Ass. 1993–98; Minister for Educ. and Youth 1998–2006; Minister of Finance and Designated Minister 2006–10, Vice-Pres., Minister of Finance, Trade, Information Tech. and Public Admin 2010, now Minister of Information Technology and Public Administration. *Address:* Office of the Vice-President, State House, POB 1303, Victoria, Seychelles (office). *Telephone:* 4286800 (office). *Fax:* 4225152 (office). *E-mail:* jbelmont@statehouse.gov.sc (office).

FAURE, Philippe René Jean-Paul Yves; French fmr diplomatist; b. 13 June 1950, Toulouse; s. of Maurice Faure; ed École Nationale d'Admin; Sec. of Foreign Affairs, Ministry of Foreign Affairs 1976–77, Asst Dir Cabinet of Sec.-Gen. 1977–79, tech. adviser to Minister of Foreign Affairs Jean François-Poncet 1979–81; served as Second Counsellor and Head of Press, Embassy in Washington, DC 1981–87, First Counsellor, Embassy in Madrid 1987–89; Dir-Gen., then Co-Pres. Cecar (insurance co.) 1990–97; Pres. Marsh McLennan France 1997–2000, Gault et Millau 1997–2000; Sec.-Gen. Ministry of Foreign Affairs 2006–08; Admin. AREVA and EDF (Électricité de France) public energy groups 2006–08; Amb. to Mexico 2000–04, to Morocco 2004–06, to Japan 2008–11; Officier, Légion d'honneur, Ordre nat. du Mérite, Commdr, Ordre d'Isabelle la Catholique (Spain), Commdr du Mérite de la République fédérale d'Allemagne, Commdr du Wissam Al Alaoui (Morocco), Grand officier de l'Aigle Aztèque (Mexico). *Address:* c/o Embassy of France, 4-11-44 Minami-Azabu, Minato-ku, Tokyo 106-8514, Japan (office).

FAURE, Roland; French journalist; b. 10 Oct. 1926, Montelimar; s. of Edmond Faure-Geors and Jeanne Gallet; m. Véra Hitzbleck 1956; three s.; ed Enclos Saint-François, Montpellier and Faculté de Droit, Aix-en-Provence; journalist, Méridional-la France, Marseilles 1947; del. in America, Asscn de la presse latine d'Europe et d'Amerique 1951, Sec.-Gen. 1954–; Founder and Ed.-in-Chief, Journal français du Brésil, Rio de Janeiro 1952–53; Diplomatic Ed. L'Aurore 1954, Head of Diplomatic Service 1959, Ed.-in-Chief 1962, Dir and Ed.-in-Chief 1968–78; attached to Cabinet of Minister of Public Works 1957–58; Dir Toutes les nouvelles de Versailles 1954–86; mem. Admin. Bd Antenne 2 1975–79; Dir of Information, Radio-France 1979–81; Founder and Dir Radio CVS 1982; Pres. Dir-Gen. Société Nat. de programme Radio France 1986–89, Société Nat. de Radiodiffusion; Pres. Université radiophonique et télévisuelle int. (URTI) 1987–97, Communauté des radios publiques de langue française (CRPLF) 1987; Pres. Admin. Council Fondations Marguerite Long-Jacques Thibaud 1991–2007; Pres. Club DAB 1991–; mem. Conseil Supérieur de l'Audiovisuel (CSA) 1989–97; Officier, Légion d'honneur, Officier, Ordre Nat. du Mérite, des Arts et des Lettres. *Publications:* Brésil dernière heure 1954; articles in newspapers and journals. *Address:* 94 boulevard de la Tour Maubourg, 75007 Paris, France (home).

FAUST, (Catharine) Drew Gilpin, BA, MA, PhD; American historian, academic and university president; *President, Harvard University;* b. 18 Sept. 1947, Clarke Co., Va; d. of McGhee Tyson Gilpin and Catharine Gilpin; m. 1st Stephen Faust (divorced); m. 2nd Charles E. Rosenberg; two d.; ed Concord Acad., Bryn Mawr Coll. and Univ. of Pennsylvania; Asst Prof. of History, Dept of American Civilization, Univ. of Pennsylvania 1976–80, Assoc. Prof. 1980–84, Prof. 1984–88, Stanley Sheerr Prof. of History 1988–89, Annenberg Prof. of History 1989–2000, Chair. Dept of American Civilization 1990–95, Dir Women's Studies Program 1996–2000; Dean, Radcliffe Inst. for Advanced Study, Harvard Univ. 2001–07, Lincoln Prof. of History 2003–07, Pres. Harvard Univ. (first woman) 2007–; Chair. Presidential Cttee on Univ. Life, Univ. of Pennsylvania 1988–90; mem. American Acad. of Arts and Sciences, American Philosophical Soc., Southern Historical Assscn (Pres. 1999–2000), American Historical Assscn (Vice-Pres. 1992–96), Exec. Bd Org. of American Historians 1999–2002, Exec. Bd Soc. of American Historians 1999–2002, Educational Advisory Bd Guggenheim Foundation, Pulitzer Prize for History jury 1986, 1990, 2004 (Chair.); Trustee, Bryn Mawr Coll. 1997–, Nat. Humanities Center 2002–, Andrew W. Mellon Foundation 2003–; Hon. DHumLitt (Bowdoin Coll.) 2007; Dr hc (Univ. of Pennsylvania) 2008; Hon. DH (Yale Univ.) 2008; Hon. LLD (Princeton Univ.) 2010; Dread Void of Uncertainty named one of ten best history essays of 2005 by Org. of American Historians, named amongst the TIME 100 2007, ranked by Forbes magazine amongst 100 Most Powerful Women (47th) 2007, (76th) 2008, (83rd) 2009, 2011, (63rd) 2012, (43rd) 2013, selected by the Nat. Endowment for the Humanities for the Jefferson Lecture (US Fed. Govt's highest honour for achievement in the humanities) 2011. *Publications:* A Sacred Circle: The Dilemma of the Intellectual in the Old South 1977, The Ideology of Slavery: Proslavery Thought in the Antebellum South, 1830-1860 1981, James Henry Hammond and the Old South: A Design for Mastery 1985, The Creation of Confederate Nationalism: Ideology and Identity in the Civil War South 1989, Southern Stories: Slaveholders in Peace and War 1992, Mothers of Invention: Women of the Slaveholding South in the American Civil War (Soc. of American Historians' Francis Parkman Prize 1997) 1996, This Republic of Suffering – Death and the American Civil War (American History Book Prize 2008, Bancroft Prize, Columbia Univ. 2009) 2008. *Address:* Office of the President, Harvard University, Massachusetts Hall, Cambridge, MA 02138, USA (office). *Telephone:* (617) 495-1502 (office). *Fax:* (617) 495-8550 (office). *E-mail:* president@harvard.edu (office). *Website:* (office).

FAVIER, Jean, DèsL; French historian and academic; b. 2 April 1932, Paris; m. Lucie Calisti 1956; four s.; ed Faculté des Lettres, Paris and Ecole nationale des chartes; mem. Ecole française de Rome 1956–58; Curator, Nat. Archives 1956–61; Researcher, CNRS 1962–64; taught at Lycée d'Orléans 1961–62; Lecturer, Faculté des lettres, Univ. of Brest 1964–66, Rouen 1966–69; Dir of Studies, Ecole pratique des hautes études 1965–1997; Prof. of Medieval Econ. History, Univ. of Paris-

Sorbonne 1969–97; Dir Inst. of History, Sorbonne 1971–75; Dir Revue Historique 1973–97; Dir-Gen. Archives de France 1975–94; Curator Château de Langeais 1995–; Hon. mem. Soc. of Antiquaries, London, Soc. Nat. des Antiquaires de France, Pres. 1993; Pres. Conseil d'admin, Ecole normale supérieure 1988–97; Pres. Nat. Library of France 1994–96, Asscn des lauréats du concours général 1990–2001, French Comm. for UNESCO 1997–; mem. Acad. des Inscriptions et Belles-Lettres, Medieval Acad. of America, Acad. Royale des Sciences, des Lettres et des Beaux-Arts, Belgium; mem. Cttee for Nat. Celebrations 1998–; Hon. mem. Belgium and Luxembourg Acad., Acads of Lyon, Reims and Rouen; Grand Officier, Légion d'honneur; Grand Croix, Ordre Nat. du Mérite; Commdr des Arts et des Lettres; Commdr des Palmes académiques, and decorations from Belgium, Germany, Luxembourg, Spain and Poland; several prizes including Prix des Ambassadeurs 1978 and Grand Prix Gobert (Acad. française) 1981. *Publications:* Un conseiller de Philippe-le-Bel: Enguerran de Marigny 1963, Les Finances pontificales à l'époque du grand schisme d'Occident 1966, De Marco Polo à Christophe Colomb 1968, Les contribuables parisiens à la fin de la guerre de cent ans 1970, Finance et fiscalité au bas moyen age 1971, Paris au XVe siècle 1974, Le trafic fluvial dans la région parisienne au XVe siècle 1975, Philippe-le-Bel 1978, La guerre de cent ans 1980, François Villon 1982, Le Temps des principautés 1984, Chronicle of the French Revolution 1788–1789 (co-ed.) 1988, L'univers de Chartres 1988, les Grandes découvertes d'Alexandre à Magellan 1991, les Archives de la France (ed.) 1992, Dictionnaire de la France médiévale 1993, Paris, deux mille ans d'histoire 1997, Charlemagne 1999, Louis XI 2001, De l'or et des épices: naissance de l'homme d'affaires au Moyen-Âge 2004, Les Plantagenêts 2004, Un roi de marbre 2005, Les papes d'Avignon 2006. *Leisure interests:* organ, photography. *Address:* Institut de France, 23 quai de Conti, 75006 Paris (office); 9 rue Reiter, 94100 St-Maur-des-Fossés, France (home).

FAVILA, Peter B., BSc; Philippine banker and government official; b. 27 Aug. 1948, Manila; m. Alice Arnaldo Favilo; two c.; ed Univ. of Santo Tomas; fmr positions include Sr Vice-Pres. Metropolitan Bank and Trust Co., Pres. Security Bank, Allied Bank, Philippine Nat. Bank; Chair. Philippine Stock Exchange –2005, Securities Clearing Corpn of the Philippines –2005; Presidential Adviser on Infrastructure Finance, Econ. Adviser to Speaker of House of Reps –2005; Sec. of Trade and Industry 2005–10; fmr Dir ASEAN Chamber of Commerce and Industry, Philippine Airlines, Bankers Asscn of the Philippines; mem. Advisory Council, Asian Bankers Asscn; mem. Bd of Advisors, Asian Inst. of Man. Policy Forum, Bd of Trustees Alay sa Kawal Foundation; mem. Man. Asscn of the Philippines, Philippine Chamber of Commerce and Industry, Rotary Club of Makati South. *Address:* c/o Department of Trade and Industry, Industry and Investments Building, 385 Sen. Gil J. Puyat Avenue, Buendia, Makati City, 3117 Metro Manila, Philippines (office).

FAVRE, Brett Lorenzo; American professional football player; b. 10 Oct. 1969, Gulfport, Miss.; s. of the late Irvin Favre and Bonita Favre; m. Deanna Tynes 1996; two d.; ed Hancock North Cen. High School, Univ. of Southern Miss.; quarterback; drafted out of coll. by Nat. Football League (NFL) Atlanta Falcons 1991 (33rd pick overall); traded to Green Bay Packers 1992–2007 (retd) but returned to play with New York Jets 2008 (retd); led Packers to seven div. championships 1995, 1996, 1997, 2002, 2003, 2004, 2007, four NFC Championship Games 1995, 1996, 1997, 2007, winning two 1996, 1997, and two Super Bowl appearances, winning one, Super Bowl XXXI 1997; came out of retirement for second time and signed with Minnesota Vikings Aug. 2009, 30–23 victory over fmr team, Green Bay Packers, on 5 Oct. made him first quarterback in NFL history to defeat every one of league's 32 franchises since NFL first expanded to 32 franchises in 2002 and game was most-viewed TV programme, sports or otherwise, in history of cable TV, drawing a 15.3 rating and having 21.8 million viewers; selected Nat. Football Conf. (NFC) Pro Bowl squad 1992–2007, youngest quarterback in Nat. Football League (NFL) history to play in a Pro Bowl; set record of 38 touchdown passes 1995; holds record for consecutive starts with 282 (304 including playoffs), most consecutive starts by a position player (NFL) with 282, most career regular-season victories by a starting quarterback with 180 (regular-season record: 180-102), most career passing touchdowns with 491, most career passing yards with 68,468, most career pass completions with 6,015, most career pass attempts with 9,713, most career interceptions thrown with 316, most career games with at least three touchdown passes with 70, most career games with at least four touchdown passes with 22, most seasons with at least 30 touchdown passes with eight, most consecutive seasons with at least 30 touchdown passes with five, most seasons with at least 3,000 passing yards with 18, most consecutive seasons with at least 3,000 passing yards with 18, most AP NFL MVP awards with three (tied with Peyton Manning), most career playoff interceptions thrown with 28 (tied with Jim Kelly), most career playoff losses as starting quarterback with 10 (tied with Dan Marino); f. Brett Favre Forward Foundation 1996; Favre family owns and operates the Brett Favre's Steakhouse, Green Bay, Wis.; NFL Most Valuable Player (MVP) 1995, 1996, 1997 (jtly with Detroit Lions' Barry Sanders, only player to win AP MVP three consecutive times), Green Bay Chamber of Commerce's Community Service Award 1997, Sports Illustrated Sportsman of the Year 2007, selected to play in Pro Bowl ten times in his career, a six-time First- or Second-team All-Pro selection, named to NFL 1990s All-Decade Team. *Film:* Reggie's Prayer 1996. *Publications:* For the Record (with Chris Havel) 1997, Most Valuable Player (with Marc Serota) 1999, Favre (with Bonita Favre and Chris Havel) 2004. *Leisure interest:* golf. *Address:* c/o The Brett Favre Forward Foundation, 1 Willow Bend, Hattiesburg, MS 39402, USA. *E-mail:* info@officialbrettfavre.com. *Website:* www .officialbrettfavre.com; www.vikings.com.

FAVRHOLDT, David Cornaby, DPhil; Danish philosopher and professor of philosophy; *Professor Emeritus, University of Southern Denmark;* b. 24 April 1931, Oregon, USA; s. of Elias Favrholdt and Bertha Cornaby; m. 1st Nina Fønss 1961; m. 2nd Anne Birch 1968; ed Copenhagen Univ.; Asst Prof. in Philosophy, Copenhagen Univ. 1961–66; Prof. of Philosophy and Head of Dept, Odense Univ. 1966–2001; currently Prof. Emer., Univ. of Southern Denmark; mem. Danish Research Council for Humanities 1985–91; mem. Royal Danish Acad. of Science and Letters, Academia Europaea; Århus Univ. Gold Medal 1958, Fyens Stiftstid Research Prize 1972. *Publications:* An Interpretation and Critique of Wittgenstein's Tractatus 1964, Philosophy and Society 1968, Chinese Philosophy 1971, The List of Sins 1973, Lenin: His Philosophy and World View 1978, Niels Bohr's Philosophical Background 1992, Studies in Niels Bohr's Philosophy 1994, Philosophical Codex 1999; trans. of Wittgenstein and John Locke; Niels Bohr: Collected Works, Vol. 10 Complementarity Beyond Physics (ed.) 1999, Aesthetics and Philosophy 2000, Niels Bohr, the Philosopher 2009; articles on Niels Bohr. *Leisure interests:* piano, classical music. *Address:* University of Southern Denmark, Campusvej 55, 5230 Odense M (office); Oehlenschlaegersvej 57, 5230 Odense M, Denmark (home). *Telephone:* 65-50-33-20 (office). *E-mail:* d.favrholdt@webspeed .dk (office). *Website:* www.sdu.dk (office).

FAWCETT, Amelia Chilcott, DBE, BA, JD; British/American lawyer, investment banker and company director; *Chairman, Hedge Fund Standards Board;* b. 16 Sept. 1956, Boston, Mass; d. of Frederick John Fawcett II and Betsey Sargent Chilcott; ed Wellesley, Univ. of Virginia School of Law; worked for Sullivan & Cromwell law firm, New York 1983–85, Paris 1986–87; joined Morgan Stanley 1987, Vice-Pres. 1990, Exec. Dir 1992, Man. Dir and Chief Admin. Officer for European Operations 1996–2002, Vice-Chair. and COO, Morgan Stanley International Ltd 2002–06; Chair. Pensions First Group LLP 2007–10; Chair., London Int. Festival of Theatre 2002–, Hedge Fund Standards Bd 2011–, Prince of Wales' Charitable Foundation 2012–; mem. Bd of Dirs (non-exec.), State Street Corpn 2006–, Guardian Media Group 2006–13 (Chair. 2009–13), Business in the Community 2005–09; mem. Financial Services Practitioner Forum 1999–2001, Court of Dirs Bank of England (Chair. Audit Cttee) 2004–09, Council of Univ. of London (Chair. Audit Cttee) 2002–08; Trustee and Deputy Chair. Nat. Portrait Gallery 2002–11; Gov. London Business School 2009–; Dir Project Hope (UK) 2009–; Commr US–UK Fulbright Comm. 2010–; mem. Advisory Bd Cambridge Programme for Sustainability Leadership; mem. London Employers Coalition 1998–2002, Competitiveness Council (Dept of Trade and Industry) 1999–2000, New Deal Task Force, Nat. Employment Panel 1999–2005; Companion of the Chartered Management Inst.; Dr hc (American Univ. in London); ranked by Fortune magazine amongst 50 Most Powerful Women in Business outside the US (43rd) 2003, (40th) 2004, (43rd) 2005, (49th) 2006, Prince of Wales Amb. Award 2004, ranked by the Financial Times amongst Top 25 Businesswomen in Europe (16th) 2005, (14th) 2006. *Leisure interests:* fly fishing, sailing, hill walking, reading, farm in Wales. *Address:* Hedge Fund Standards Board, Central Court, 25 Southampton Buildings, London, WC2A 1AL, England (office). *Telephone:* (20) 3178-2753 (office). *E-mail:* info@hfsb.org (office). *Website:* www.hfsb.org (office).

FAXON, Roger, BA; American entertainment business executive; *CEO, EMI Music Group;* ed Johns Hopkins Univ.; fmrly Sr Staff mem. US Congress; COO LUCASFILM Ltd 1980–84; Founding Pnr The Mount Company 1984–86; worked at Tri-Star and Columbia Pictures 1986–90, rising to Sr Exec. Vice-Pres. Columbia Pictures Entertainment; fmrly COO Sotheby's North and South America, CEO Sotheby's Europe, Man. Dir Sotheby's –1994; Sr Vice-Pres. of Business Devt and Strategy EMI Music 1994–99, Exec. Vice-Pres. and Chief Financial Officer EMI Music Publishing 1999–2002, Chief Financial Officer EMI Group PLC 2002–05, Bd mem. 2002–05, 2006–, Pres. and COO EMI Music Publishing 2005–06, Jt CEO 2006–07, Chair. and CEO 2007–10, CEO EMI Music Group 2010–; mem. Bd of Dirs ASCAP. *Address:* EMI Music Group, 150 Fifth Avenue, New York, NY 10011, USA (office). *Telephone:* (212) 786-8000 (office). *Website:* www.emimusic.com (office).

FAYE, Jean Pierre; French writer; *President, European University of Research;* b. 19 July 1925, Paris; m. Marie-Odile Demenge 1952; one s. one d.; ed Univ. de Paris à la Sorbonne; teacher, Lycée de Reims 1951–54; Exchange Fellow, Univ. of Chicago 1954–55; Asst Prof., Univ. of Lille 1955–56, Univ. de Paris (Sorbonne) 1956–60; Research, CNRS 1960 (Dir of Research 1983); Founder of the Collectif Change and Centre d'Analyse et de Sociologie des Langages (CASL); Founder and Pres. High Council, Coll. Int. de Philosophie; Founder and Pres. The European Philosophical Univ.; Pres. European Univ. of Research, Paris 1985–90, 1993–, Inst. for Foundation of the European City of Culture 1997; Ed. Change (review) 1968–85; Hon. Pres. European City of Récollets, Paris 2004; Chevalier Légion d'honneur, Commdr des Arts et des Lettres; Prix Renaudot 1964, Int. Essay Prize, Weimar Cultural Capital of Europe 2000, Int. Literature Prize, Novi Sad 2007. *Artistic achievements:* art exhbns: paintings, books and catalogues of Titus-Carmel, Erro, Fromanger, Velickovic, Vieira da Silva, Henri Maccheroni, Kienholz, Arman; plays: Le Centre, directed by Polieri, Hommes et Pierres, directed by Roger Blin, Vitrine, directed by Jacques Mauclair; radio: 15 lectures on Nietzsche 2000; television: debate on Nietzsche 2002. *Publications:* novels: Entre les rues 1958, La cassure 1961, Battement 1962, Analogues 1964, L'écluse 1964, Les Troyens 1970, Inferno versions 1975, L'ovale 1975, Yumi, visage caméra 1983, La Grande Nap 1992; poems: Fleuve renversé 1959, Théâtre 1964 (produced at Odéon, Théâtre de France by Roger Blin and Jean-Louis Barrault 1965), Couleurs pliées 1965, Verres 1977, Syeeda 1984; essays: Le récit hunique 1967, Langages totalitaires, Théorie du récit 1972, La critique du langage et son économie 1973, Migrations du récit sur le peuple juif 1974, Les Grandes Journées du Père Duchesne 1981, Dictionnaire Politique, essai de Philosophie Politique 1982, La raison narrative 1990, Le livre de Lioube 1992, Ode Europe 1992, La déraison antisémite et son langage 1993, Le piège: La philosophie heideggerienne et le nationalsocialisme 1993, Didjla, le Tigre 1994, Le langage meurtrier 1995, le Siècle des idéologies 1996, Qu'est-ce que la philosophie? 1997, Guerre trouvée 1997, Le vrai Nietzsche 1998, Le livre du vrai 1998, Nietzsche et Salomé 2000, Court traité sur le transformat 2000, Introduction aux langages totalitaires 2003, Journal de voyage absolu 2003, La philosophie désormais 2004, Le transformat, le littoral, in Jean-Pierre Faye et la philosophie 2004, Eclat Rançon 2007, Les voies neuves de la philosophie 2008. *Address:* European University of Research, 1 rue Descartes, 75005 Paris (office); 1B rue Vaneau, 75007 Paris, France (home). *Telephone:* 1-4705-1803 (home).

FAYED, Mohamed al-; Egyptian business executive; *Honorary Chairman, Harrods Holdings;* b. 27 Jan. 1933, Alexandria; s. of Aly Aly Fayed; m. 1st Samira Khashoggi 1954 (divorced 1958); one s. (died 1997); m. 2nd Heini Wathen; four c.; f. co. in Alexandria 1956; involved in shipping, property, banking, oil and construction; Chair. and owner Ritz Hotel, Paris 1979–; Chair. Harrods Ltd, London 1985–2010, Harrods Holdings PLC 1994–2010, Hon. Chair. 2010–; owner Fulham Football Club, London 1997–; Hon. mem. Emmanuel Coll., Cambridge; Commdr Order of Merit (Italy) 1990, Officier, Légion d'honneur 1993; La Grande Médaille de la Ville de Paris 1985, Plaque de Paris 1989. *Address:* Harrods Holdings, 87-135 Brompton Road, Knightsbridge, London, SW1X 7XL, England (office). *Telephone:*

(20) 7730-1234 (office). *Fax:* (20) 7581-0470 (office). *Website:* www.harrods.com (office).

FAYEZ, Eid al-, BA; Jordanian politician; b. 1945; ed Beirut Arab Univ.; Dir-Gen. Jordanian-Iraqi Transport Co. 1983–86; Dir-Gen. Jordanian Ports Corpn, Aqaba 1986–90; Sec.-Gen. Ministry of Youth 1990–93; Adviser, Royal Hashemite Court 1993–99; Minister of Labour 1999–2002, also of Youth and Sports 2001–02, of the Interior 2005–07, 2007–09. *Address:* c/o Ministry of the Interior, POB 100, Amman, Jordan (office).

FAYEZ, Faisal al-, BSc, MA; Jordanian diplomatist and government official; b. 1952; ed Univ. of Cardiff, UK, Boston Univ., USA; joined Ministry of Foreign Affairs upon graduation; fmr diplomat, Embassy in Brussels; fmr Deputy Dir of Royal Protocol, Royal Court, Chief of Royal Protocol and Minister of the Royal Court 2003; Prime Minister and Minister of Defence 2003–05; Minister of the Royal Court of Jordan 2003–05; Speaker, House of Reps (Parl.) 2010–. *Address:* Office of the Speaker, House of Representatives, PO Box 72, Amman 11118, Jordan (office). *Website:* www.representatives.jo.

FAYEZ, Mohamed Baha-Eldin, PhD; Egyptian chemist and academic; *Research Professor Emeritus, National Research Centre;* b. 4 Feb. 1927, Cairo; ed Alexandria Univ. and Univ. of Glasgow, UK; scientist Nat. Research Centre (NRC), Cairo, f. Dept of Chem. of Natural Products, Dir NRC 1984–87, now Research Prof. Emer.; six industrial inventions including a urinary tract medicine; Science and Tech. Exec., Egyptian Acad. of Scientific Research and Tech., later Vice-Pres.; Founder and Dir UNDP Knowledge Transfer Programme in Egypt 1980; Chair. UN Intergovernmental Cttee on Science and Tech. for Devt, UNCTAD Cttees on Transfer of Tech. and Reverse Transfer of Tech.; consultant to UN on tech. policies and tech. devt, adviser on tech. devt to UNCTAD in Zimbabwe; Egyptian del. to int. and UN groups on tech. transformation and tech. transfer for developing countries; Founding Fellow, Islamic Acad. of Sciences 1986; State Prize for Chem. (Egypt) 1966, Prize for Islamic Medicine, Kuwait Foundation for the Advancement of Science 1982, Prize for Outstanding Invention of the Year, WIPO 1984, State Prize of Merit in Sciences (Egypt) 1990. *Address:* National Research Centre, Dokki, Cairo 12622, Egypt; 14 Tahrir Street, Dokki, Cairo, Egypt. *E-mail:* fayez.mohd@ yahoo.com.

FAYEZ, Nora bint Abdullah Al-, BA, MA; Saudi Arabian educationalist, academic and politician; *Deputy Minister of Women's Education;* m.; three s. two d.; ed King Saud Univ., Utah State Univ., USA; served as Dir-Gen. of Girls' Schools at Kingdom Schools; Lecturer and Head of Training Techniques Centre, women's section of Inst. of Public Admin 1984–88, Dir-Gen. women's section 1993–2009; Assoc. Prof. in Educ. Techniques, Coll. of Educ., King Saud Univ. 1989–95; Controller of Educ. Techniques, Inst. of Pvt. Educ., Ministry of Educ. 1989–93, apptd to Council of Ministers (first woman) as Deputy Minister for Women's Educ. 2009–; Head of Women's Cttee of Human Resources Devt Forum under Human Resources Devt Fund, Riyadh 2004; mem. Women's Organizing Cttee of Janadriya Festival 1991, 1992, Bd of Dirs Coll. of Literature at Gen. Presidency of Girls Educ. 1994–2000, Cultural Advisory Cttee of Janadriya Festival 1995, Women's Cttee for King Abdul Aziz Museum (Darah) 1997–99, Consultative Council of Nat. Museum 1999–, Consultative Council of Supreme Comm. for Tourism 2001–03, Women's Cttee of King Abdul Aziz Foundation for Gifted Persons 2002–07, Women's Cttee of First Riyadh Econ. Forum 2003, Women's Science Cttee for the Cultural Season of the World Ass. of Muslim Youth 2005; adviser, Prince Salman Social Center 1998–2001, King Abdul Aziz Women's Charity Soc., Qassim 2000–03; has attended several nat. and int. seminars and courses, including The Effective Training Man. Workshop Course, Brussels, Belgium 1985, Man. Communication for Devt, Washington, DC, USA 1994, Distance Educ., Salzburg, Austria 1997, Man. Work Conf., Denver, USA 1997, Women in Man., Dubai 1998, The Art of Leadership, Advanced Management, Euromatech, Amsterdam, Netherlands 2003, Oxford Advanced Man. and Leadership Programme, Oxford Man. Centre, London, UK 2008; Dr hc (Utah State Univ.) 2012. *Address:* Ministry of Education, PO Box 3734, Airport Road, Riyadh 11148, Saudi Arabia (office). *Telephone:* (1) 404-2888 (office). *Fax:* (1) 401-2365 (office). *E-mail:* webmaster@moe.gov.sa (office). *Website:* www .moe.gov.sa (office).

FAYMANN, Werner; Austrian politician; *Federal Chancellor;* b. 4 May 1960, Vienna; m.; two c.; ed Univ. of Vienna; consultant, Zentralsparkasse 1985–88; Prov. Chair. Socialistic Youth Vienna 1985–94; mem. State Parl. and Municipal Council of Vienna 1994–2007, Exec. City Councillor for housing, housing construction and urban renewal; fmr Pres. Viennese Fund for Provision of Property and Urban Renewal; fmr Vice-Pres. Viennese Business Agency; Fed. Minister for Transport, Innovation and Tech. 2007–08; Federal Chancellor 2008–; Exec. Chair. Social Democratic Party of Austria (SPÖ) 2008–. *Address:* Office of the Federal Chancellor, Ballhauspl. 2, 1014 Vienna (office); Social Democratic Party of Austria, Löwelstr. 18, 1014 Vienna, Austria (office). *Telephone:* (1) 531-15-0 (office); (1) 534-27-0 (SPÖ) (office). *Fax:* (1) 535-03-38-0 (office); (1) 535-96-83 (SPÖ) (office). *E-mail:* post@bka.gv.at (office); werner.faymann@spoe.at (office). *Website:* www.bka.gv.at (office); www.spoe.at (office); www.das-ist-faymann.at.

FAYYAD, Salam Khaled Abdullah, BSc, MBA, PhD; Palestinian economist and politician; b. 1952, Tulkarm, West Bank; m.; three c.; ed American Univ. of Beirut, Lebanon, Univ. of Texas, USA; fmr Lecturer in Econs, Yarmuk Univ., Jordan; fmr official, US Fed. Reserve Bank, St Louis; joined IMF, Washington, DC 1987, various sr positions including Resident Rep. to Palestinian Authority (PA), Jerusalem 1995–2001; Regional Man. of West Bank–Gaza, Arab Bank 2001–02 (resgnd); Minister of Finance 2002–05 (resgnd), 2007–12, also of Foreign Affairs 2007–08; Prime Minister of Palestinian Autonomous Areas 2007–13 (resgnd). *Publications include:* numerous research papers on Palestinian economy. *Address:* c/o Ministry of Foreign Affairs, POB 1336, Ramallah, Palestinian Autonomous Areas.

FAZIO, Antonio, BSc; Italian fmr central banker; b. 11 Oct. 1936, Alvito, Frosinone; s. of the late Eugenio Fazio and Maria Giuseppa Persichetti; m. Maria Cristina Rosati; one s. four d.; ed Univ. of Rome, Massachusetts Inst. of Tech., USA; Research Fellow, Research Dept, Banca d'Italia 1960, Consultant in Research Dept 1961–66, Deputy Head, then Head, Econometric Research Office 1966, Deputy Dir Research Dept's Monetary Section 1972, Head, Research Dept 1973–79, Cen. Man. for Econ. Research 1980, Deputy Dir-Gen. Banca d'Italia

1982–93, Gov. 1993–2005 (resgnd); Asst Prof. of Demography, Univ. of Rome 1961–66; Chair. Italian Foreign Exchange Office 1993–2005; mem. Bd of Dirs Bank for Int. Settlements 1993–2005; mem. Governing Council, European Cen. Bank (fmrly European Monetary Inst.), 1993–2005; Paul Harris Fellow, Rotary International; Hon. mem., Circolo St Thomas Aquinas, Aquino (Italy); Kt Grand Gross, Order of Merit of the Italian Repub.; Hon. DEcon (Bari) 1994; Hon. DLitt (Johns Hopkins) 1995; Hon. Dr rer. pol (Macerata) 1996; Hon. LLB (Cassino) 1999; Hon. Dr Statistics and Econs (Milan) 1999; Hon. Dr Computer Eng (Lecce) 2000; Hon. Dr Banking Econs (Verona) 2002; Hon. LLD (St John's) 2002; Hon. PhD (Catania) 2002; Hon. Dr Moral Theol. (Pontificia Salesiana) 2003; Ezio Tarantelli Prize for most original theory in Economic Policy, Club dell'economia 1995, Euromoney Cen. Banker of the Year 1996, St Vincent Prize for Econs 1997, 'Pico della Mirandola' Prize for Econs, Finance and Business 1997–98, Int. Award in the Humanities, Accad. di Studi Mediterranei 1999, Keynes Sraffa Prize (London) 2003, Fiaccola d'oro Award, Circolo San Tommaso d'Aquino 2012. *Publications include:* Econometric Model of the Italian Economy; Razionalità economica e solidarietà 1996, Globalizzazione: politica economica e dottrina sociale 2008, Enciclica Caritas in Veritate: prospettiva storica e attualità; Sviluppo e declino demografico in europa e nel mondo 2012; texts dealing mainly with monetary theory, econ. policy and monetary policy issues. *Address:* Bank of Italy, Via Nazionale 91, 00184 Rome, Italy (office). *Telephone:* (06) 47921 (office).

FEARON, Douglas Thomas, BA, MD, FRCP, FAAS, FRS, FMedSci; American immunologist, academic and physician; *Senior Group Leader, Cancer Research UK Cambridge Research Institute, University of Cambridge;* b. 16 Oct. 1942, Brooklyn, NY; s. of the late Henry Dana Fearon and of Frances Fearon (née Eubanks); m. 2nd Clare M. Wheless 1977; one s. one d.; ed Williams Coll., Johns Hopkins Univ. School of Medicine; residency, Johns Hopkins Hosp. 1968–70; US Army Medical Corps 1970–72; Post-doctoral Fellowship, Harvard Medical School 1972–75, Instructor, Harvard Medical School 1975–76, Asst Prof. of Medicine 1976–79, Assoc. Prof. 1979–84, Prof. of Medicine 1984–87; Prof. of Medicine, Johns Hopkins Univ. School of Medicine 1987–93; Prof., Wellcome Trust Immunology Unit, Univ. of Cambridge, UK 1993–, Fellow, Trinity Coll., Cambridge 2001–, Sheila Joan Smith Prof. of Immunology 2004–11, Emer. 2011–, Sr Group Leader, Cancer Research UK Cambridge Research Inst. 2011–; mem. NAS 2001; Hon. Consultant, Addenbrooke's Hosp. Cambridge 1993–; Bronze Star (US Army); Lee C. Howley Prize, Arthritis Foundation. *Publications:* more than 100 articles in scientific journals. *Leisure interest:* golf. *Address:* Li Ka Shing Centre, Robinson Way, Cambridge, CB2 0RE, England (office). *Telephone:* (1223) 404473 (office). *Fax:* (1223) 404573 (office). *E-mail:* dtf1000@cam.ac.uk (office). *Website:* www.trin.cam .ac.uk (office).

FEAST, Michael William, PhD, DSc, FRSSA, ARCS; South African astronomer and academic; *Senior Research Associate, South African Astronomical Observatory;* b. 29 Dec. 1926, Deal, Kent, England; s. of Frederick Feast and Dorothy Feast (née Knight); m. Elizabeth Constance Maskew 1962; one s. two d.; ed Imperial Coll., London; Postdoctoral Fellow, Nat. Research Council of Canada 1949–51; astronomer, Radcliffe Observatory 1952–74; astronomer, South African Astronomical Observatory 1974–92, Dir 1977–92, now Sr Research Assoc.; Royal Soc. Guest Fellow, Inst. of Astronomy, Cambridge 1992–93; Pres. Int. Astronomical Union Comm. on Stellar Spectra 1967–70, on Variable Stars 1970–76; Pres. Astronomical Soc. of SA 1957–58, 1979–80; mem. Int. Astronomical Union, Vice-Pres. 1979–85; Founder-mem. South African Acad. of Science 1995–; Hon. FRAS; Hon. Prof. of Astronomy, Univ. of Cape Town 1993–; Hon. DSc (Cape Town) 1993; Gill Medal, Astronomical Soc. of SA 1983, de Beers' Gold Medal, S African Inst. of Physics 1992. *Publications:* more than 300 astronomical and physics papers, mainly in Royal Astronomical Soc. monthly notices. *Address:* Department of Astronomy, University of Cape Town, Rondebosch 7701, South Africa (office). *Telephone:* (21) 6502396 (office). *Fax:* (21) 6503342 (office). *E-mail:* mwf@ast.uct.ac .za (office). *Website:* www.ast.uct.ac.za (office).

FEDERER, Roger; Swiss professional tennis player; b. 8 Aug. 1981, Binningen, nr Basel; s. of Robert Federer and Lynette Federer (née Durand); m. Miroslava (Mirka) Vavrinec 2009; two s. (twins) two d. (twins); world rank No. 1 as jr 1998, won Wimbledon jr title that year; turned professional 1998; semi-finalist, men's singles, Olympic Games, Sydney 2000; singles titles: Milan 2001, Hamburg TMS 2002, 2005, Sydney 2002, Vienna 2002, 2003, Marseille 2003, Tennis Masters Cup, Houston 2003, 2004, 2006, 2007, Wimbledon 2003, 2004, 2005, 2006, 2007, 2009, 2012, Halle 2003, 2004, 2005, 2006, 2008, 2013, Vienna 2002, 2003, Munich 2003, Dubai 2003, 2004, 2005, 2007, 2012, 2014, Australian Open 2004, 2006, 2007, 2010, Bangkok 2004, 2005, Canada AMS 2004, Gstaad 2004, Hamburg AMS 2004, 2007, Indian Wells AMS 2004, 2005, 2006, Toronto 2004, 2006, US Open 2004, 2005, 2006, 2007, 2008, Cincinnati 2005, 2007, 2010, Doha 2005, 2006, Miami 2005, 2006, Rotterdam 2005, Basel 2006, 2007, 2008, Madrid 2006, 2009, 2012, Tennis Masters Cup, Shanghai 2006, 2007, Tokyo 2006, Estoril 2008, French Open 2009, Barclays ATP World Tour Finals, London 2010, 2011, BNP Paribas Masters Open 2011, 2012, ABN AMRO World Tennis Tournament, Rotterdam 2012; runner-up, French Open 2006, 2007, 2008, 2011, Wimbledon 2008, Australian Open 2009, US Open 2009; eight doubles titles: Rotterdam 2001 (with Jonas Bjorkman), 2002 (with Max Mirnyi), Gstaad 2001 (with Marat Safin), Moscow 2002 (with Mirnyi), Vienna 2003 (with Yves Allegro), Miami TMS 2003 (with Mirnyi), Halle 2005 (with Yves Allegro), Beijing Olympics 2008 (with Stanislas Wawrinka); first player to be ranked World No. 1 for four consecutive (non-calendar) years 2004–08; won silver medal, Olympic Games, London 2012; top ranked player on ATP computer for a record 237 consecutive weeks 2 Feb. 2004–17 Aug. 2008; first player to be ranked World No. 1 for 237 consecutive weeks; became sixth man to complete a Career Grand Slam after winning French Open 7 June 2009; became first man to win 15 Grand Slam titles and break Pete Sampras's record of 14 titles after winning Wimbledon 5 July 2009; reached a record 32nd Grand Slam semi-final and a record 33rd consecutive Grand Slam quarter-final at Wimbledon 2012; also holds the record for most match wins in Grand Slam tournaments (244); broke Sampras's record of 286 weeks as World No. 1 top ranked player July 2012; coached by Peter Lundgren 1999–2003, Tony Roche (part-time) 2005–07, José Higueras 2008, Darren Cahill 2009, Paul Annacone 2010–; ITF Jr World Champion 1998, ATP European Player of the Year 2003, 2004, Swiss Sportsman of the Year 2003, 2004, 2006, 2007, Swiss Personality of the Year 2003, Michael-Westphal Award 2003, ITF World Champion 2004, 2005, 2006, 2007, ATP Player of the Year 2004, 2005,

2006, 2007, 2008, BBC Sports Personality of the Year 2004, Laureus World Sportsman of the Year 2005, 2006, 2007, 2008, ESPY Best Male Tennis Player 2005, 2006, 2007, 2008, BBC Sports Personality of the Year (Overseas Personality) 2006, 2007, Stefan Edberg Sportsmanship Award 2008, 2009, ATPTennis.com Fan's Favourite 2008, Swiss Team of the Year (with Stanislas Wawrinka as "golden team FedRinka") 2008, ATPWorldtour.com (fmrly ATPTennis.com) Fan's Favourite 2009. *Leisure interests:* golf, soccer, skiing, playstation, music, playing cards. *Address:* c/o Lynette Federer, PO Box 209, 4103 Bottmingen, Switzerland; IMG Tennis, IMG Center, 1360 East 9th Street, Suite 100, Cleveland, OH 44114, USA. *Telephone:* (61) 4215712. *Fax:* (61) 4215719. *E-mail:* management@ rogerfederer.com. *Website:* www.rogerfederer.com.

FEDEROVSKI, Vladimir; Russian/French writer, academic and fmr diplomatist; *Professor of History, Hautes Etudes Commerciales;* b. 1950, Moscow; ed Inst. of Int. Relations, Moscow; attaché, Soviet Embassy in Nouakchott, Mauritius 1972; interpreter for Leonid Brezhnev, Sec.-Gen. of CP during 1970s; counsellor, Soviet Embassy in Paris 1985; Spokesperson, Movt for Democratic Reform 1985–91; attained French citizenship 1995; currently Prof. of History, Hautes Etudes Commerciales (HEC), Paris; adviser on Cold War history, Mémorial de Caen; Officier des Arts et des Lettres. *Publications include:* Histoire de la diplomatie française 1985, Histoire secrète d'un coup d'État 1991, Les Égéries russes 1993, Les Égéries romantiques 1995, Le Département du diable 1996, Les Deux Soeurs ou l'art d'aimer 1997, Le Triangle russe 1999, Les Tsarines: Les Femmes qui ont fait la Russie 1999, L'Histoire secrète des ballets russes 2002, Le roman de Saint-Petersbourg 2002, Le Roman du Kremlin 2004, Le Roman de la Russie insolite 2004, Paris-Saint-Petersbourg 2005, Le Roman de l'Orient-Express 2006, Regards sur la France 2006, Le Fantôme de Staline 2007. *Address:* 22C av. des Courlis, 78110 Le Vésinet, France.

FEDERSPIEL, Thomas Holger, CBE; Danish lawyer; b. 25 Oct. 1935, Hellerup; s. of Per Torben Federspiel and Elin Federspiel (née Zahle); m. 1st Benedicte Buhl 1965 (divorced 1984); two s.; m. 2nd Bettina Hage 1997; ed Krebs Skole, Rungsted Statsskole, Copenhagen Univ.; Assoc. Jonas Bruun 1961–66, Slaughter and May, London, Davis Polk & Wardwell 1966–67; Partner Per Federspiel 1968, Gorrissen & Federspiel (now Gorrissen Federspiel Kierkegaard) 1989–2004; admitted to Court of Appeal 1964, Supreme Court 1969; F. Gorrissen & Federspiel 1989; Chair. Danish Bar Council Cttee on Pvt. Int. Law 1971–81; Pres. Int. Bar Ass400 1980–82; mem. Council Int. Bar Ass400 1971–84; mem. Bd Queen Margrethe's and Prince Henrik's Foundation; Chair. and mem. bd various cos and charitable foundations; Hon. mem. ABA 1981, Int. Bar Ass400 1984; Hon. Legal Adviser to the British Embassy; Kt of the Order of Dannebrog, Insignia of Honour of the Order of Dannebrog. *Leisure interests:* tennis, skiing, shooting, reading. *Address:* 12 H.C. Andersens Boulevard, 1553 Copenhagen (office); Rungsted Strandvej 22, 2950 Vedbaek, Denmark (home). *Telephone:* 33-41-41-41 (office); 45-86-13-42 (home). *Fax:* 33-41-41-33 (office). *E-mail:* tf@gfklaw.dk (office).

FEDIN, Vladimir, DChemSci; Russian chemist and academic; *Director, Nikolaev Institute of Inorganic Chemistry;* b. 5 Sept. 1954, Pensa; ed Russian Acad. of Sciences and Univ. of Moscow; currently Prof. and Dir Nikolaev Inst. of Inorganic Chem., Siberian Br. of Russian Acad. of Sciences; Prof. and Head of Chair of Inorganic Chem., Novosibirsk State Univ. *Publications:* numerous articles in professional journals. *Address:* Nikolaev Institute of Inorganic Chemistry, Siberian Branch of Russian Academy of Sciences, 3 Acad. Lavrentiev Avenue, Novosibirsk 630090, Russia (office). *Telephone:* (383) 330-94-90 (office), (383) 330-58-42 (home). *Fax:* (383) 330-94-89 (office). *E-mail:* cluster@niic.nsc.ru (office). *Website:* www.niic.nsc.ru (office).

FEDOR, Martin, MEconSc; Slovak politician; b. 4 March 1974, Považská Bystrica; ed Comenius Univ., Dublin European Inst., Ireland; Head of Cabinet 1998; Dir Int. Relations Section, SDKÚ 2000–02, Head of Dept of Foreign Policy and Integration 2000–, Deputy Chair. New Generation (SDKU Youth Org.) –2002; State Sec., Ministry of Defence 2003–06, Minister of Defence 2006; mem. Slovak Nat. Council 2006–. *Address:* Krajská agentúra SDKÚ-DS Trenčín, Elektrická 17, 911 00 Trenčín, Slovakia (office). *Telephone:* (32) 744-4708 (office). *Website:* www .martinfedor.sk.

FEDOROV, Alexey Innokentevich; Russian manufacturing executive; *President, Irkut Corporation;* b. 14 April 1952, Irkutsk; ed Oklahoma City Univ. Business School, USA; design engineer, Irkutsk Aviation Industrial Assen, Irkutsk, Siberia, USSR 1974, Pres. 1998–2005, Chair. 2005–; Pres. Irkut Corpn (biggest producer of mil. and civilian aircraft in Russia) 2000–, outlets in Russia, USA, Europe, India, SE Asia, annual contracts exceed US $4 billion; Gen. Dir and Gen. Constructor Russian Aviation Construction Corpn MiG 2004–; Pres. United Aviation Construction Corpn 2004–; Order Merit to Fatherland (Fourth Degree), Badge of Honour, Peter the Great Golden Symbol. *Address:* Irkut Corporation, 68 Leningrad Prospect, 125315 Moscow, Russia (office). *Telephone:* (495) 777-21-01 (office). *Fax:* (495) 777-21-01 (office). *E-mail:* inbox@irkut.com (office). *Website:* www.irkut.com (office).

FEDOROV, Igor B., DrTech; Russian university administrator; *Rector, Moscow Bauman Technical University;* b. 1940; m.; one d.; ed Moscow Bauman Tech. Univ.; engineer, asst, Docent, Head of Dept, Prorector for Scientific Work, Moscow Bauman Tech. Univ. –1991, Rector 1991–; mem. Int. Acad. of Informatization, Int. Acad. of Eng, Assen of Rectors of Europe, Eurasian Assen of Univs, Russian Acad. of Natural Sciences, Int. Acad. of Higher Educ. Problems; Merited Worker of Science and Tech.; Prize of USSR Ministry of Educ. 1991. *Publications include:* more than 140 scientific papers on higher education problems; five monographs and 15 patents. *Address:* Moscow Bauman Technical University, 2nd Baumanskaya str. 5, 105005 Moscow, Russia (office). *Telephone:* (495) 261-17-43 (office). *E-mail:* bauman@bmstu.ru (office). *Website:* www.bmstu.ru (office).

FEDOROV, Valentin Petrovich, DEcon; Russian politician and research institute director; *Deputy Director for Research, Institute of Europe, Russian Academy of Sciences;* b. 6 Sept. 1939, Zhatai, Yakutia; m.; two d.; ed G. Plekhanov Moscow Inst. of Nat. Econ., Inst. of World Econ. and Int. Relations, USSR Acad. of Sciences; worked in State Planning Cttee Yakutia 1964–78; jr researcher, Head of Div. and Corresp., Journal of Inst. of World Economy and International Relations in West Germany 1978–84; Pro-Rector on Int. Relations, Prof. G. V. Plekhanov Moscow Inst. of Nat. Econ., 1987–90; Gov. of Sakhalin Region, opposed transfer of

S Kuril Islands to Japan 1990–93; People's Deputy of Russia 1990–93; Deputy Minister of Econ. 1993–94; Prime Minister of Sakhá (Yakutia) Repub. 1997–98; mem. Political Council Movt for Democratic Reforms, Co-Chair. Duma of Russian Nat. Sobor; Vice-Pres. Russian Union of Industrialists and Entrepreneurs 1994–2001; Pres. Asscn of Road-Builders 1996–; Deputy Dir for Research, Inst. of Europe, Russian Acad. of Sciences, Moscow 2000–; mem. Russian Acad. of Natural Sciences, Russian Eng Acad. *Publications:* FRG: Country and People; several plays, collections of poems, monographs on econs. *Address:* Institute of Europe, 125993 Moscow, 11-3B Mokhovaya str., Russia (office). *Telephone:* (495) 629-59-18 (office). *Fax:* (495) 629-92-96 (office). *E-mail:* europe@ieras.ru (office); vpfyodorov@mail.ru. *Website:* www.ieras.ru (office).

FEDOSEYEV, Vladimir Ivanovich; Russian conductor; *Artistic Director, Tchaikovsky Academy Symphony Orchestra;* b. 5 Aug. 1932, Leningrad; s. of Ivan Fedoseyev and Elena Fedoseyeva; m. Olga Dobrokhotova; two c.; ed conductors' class of Moscow Musical Pedagogical Inst., Moscow Conservatoire; mem. CPSU 1963–91; Artistic Dir and Chief Conductor Moscow Radio Symphony Orchestra of USSR Radio Network (now Tchaikovsky Acad. Symphony Orchestra) 1974–; concurrently Music Dir Vienna Symphony Orchestra 1997–; first Perm. Guest Conductor Tokyo Philharmonic Orchestra 1996–, Radio France Orchestra 2001–; Perm. Guest Conductor Zürich Opera 1997–; works with Bolshoi and Mariinsky Theatres, opera productions and concerts abroad, including Italy, France, Austria, Germany, Japan, Switzerland, Spain, UK, USA; People's Artist of USSR 1980, RSFSR State Prize 1989, Crystal Award of Asahi Broadcasting Corpn, Osaka 1989, Golden Orpheus, for recording of opera May Night, Gold Medal, Int. Gustav Mahler Soc. 2007. *Recordings:* Symphonies by Beethoven, Mahler, Shostakovich, Mussorgsky, Sviridov, Russian operas. *Address:* Malaya Nikitskaya 24, 121069 Moscow, Russia (home). *Telephone:* (495) 229-57-68 (Moscow) (home); (495) 690-64-52 (Moscow) (home); (1) 503-84-77 (Vienna) (home). *Fax:* (495) 291-82-43 (Moscow) (office). *E-mail:* tsom@fedoseyev.com (office); vdedyukhin@fedoseyev.com (office). *Website:* www.fedoseyev.com (office); www.bso.ru (office).

FEDOSOV, Yevgeny Aleksandrovich, DTechSc; Russian automation and avionics specialist; *Director of Science & Technology, State Research Institute of Aviation Systems (GosNIIAS);* b. 14 May 1929, Moscow; s. of Alexander Yefimovitch Fedosov and Nadezhda Anempodistovna Smirnova; m. Lydia Petrovna Vasilyeva; one d.; ed Bauman Tech. Inst.; post-grad. work at Inst. 1953–56; mem. CPSU 1959–91; Research Fellow, Head of Dept, Deputy Dir State Research Inst. of Aviation Systems (GosNIIAS) 1956–70, Dir Research and Tech. 1970–2001, Gen. Dir GosNIIAS 2001–06, Scientific Dir 2006–; simultaneously Head of Dept Physico-Tech. Inst. 1970–; Prof. 1969; Corresp. mem. USSR (now Russian) Acad. of Sciences 1979, mem. 1984–; Lenin Prize 1976, Hero of Socialist Labour 1983, B.N. Petrov Gold Medal, Acad. of Sciences 1989, Honoured Scientist of Russian Fed. 1996. *Publications:* works on analysis and synthesis of complex multi-level operational systems. *Leisure interests:* tennis, gardening. *Address:* State Research Institute of Aviation Systems (GosNIIAS), Viktorenko str. 7, 125319 Moscow, Russia (office). *Telephone:* (499) 157-70-47 (office). *Fax:* (499) 943-86-05 (office). *E-mail:* info@gosniias.ru (office). *Website:* www.gosniias.ru (office).

FEDOTOV, Maxim Viktorovich; Russian violinist and academic; *Professor and Head, Violin and Viola Department, Russian Gnesin Academy of Music;* b. 24 July 1961, Leningrad (now St. Petersburg); s. of Viktor Andreyevich Fedotov and Galina Nikolayevna Fedotova; m. Galina Yevgenyevna Petrova, pianist; one d.; ed Specialized Music School for Gifted Children in Leningrad, Moscow State Conservatory (with D. Tsyganov and I. Bezrodny); concert tours since 1975; Prof., Moscow State Conservatory 1987–2001; Prof. and Head, Violin and Viola Dept, Russian Gnesin Acad. of Music 2003–; Artistic Dir and Chief Conductor, Russian Symphony Orchestra 2003–; as soloist plays with G. Petrova, regular recitals in Moscow and St Petersburg; performed in Madrid, Berlin, Leipzig, Frankfurt, Cologne, Milan, Chicago and other cities; took part in music festivals in Salzburg, Oakland, Bergen, Dresden, Klagenfurt; toured Australia, New Zealand, Korea, Turkey; Pres. Asscn of Laureates of P.I. Tchaikovsky Int. Competition 2002–; mem. Peter the Great's Arts and Sciences Acad., St Petersburg; prizewinner, All-Union Music Competition Riga 1981, N. Paganini Competition, Genoa 1982, Vercelli 1984, P. Tchaikovsky, Moscow 1986, Tokyo 1986 (First Prize), People's Artist of Russia. *Address:* Gnesin Academy of Music, 121069 Moscow, Povarskaya, 38 (office); 121596 Moscow, Tolbukhin str. 8, korp. 1, Apt. 6, Russia. *Telephone:* (495) 291-3855 (office); (495) 447-25-60 (home). *Fax:* (495) 291-3102 (office). *E-mail:* mailbox@gnesin-academy.ru (office). *Website:* www.gnesin-academy.ru (office).

FEDOTOV, Mikhail Aleksandrovich, DJur; Russian politician and lawyer; b. 18 Sept. 1949, Moscow; m. 3rd Maria Fedotova; one s. one d; ed Moscow State Univ., All-Union Inst. of Law; teacher of law, All-Union Inst. of Law 1973–90; Deputy Minister of Press and Mass Information of Russia 1991–92, Minister 1992–93; represented Pres. Yeltsin in Constitutional Court trial against CPSU 1992; Dir-Gen. Russian Agency of Intellectual Property (RAIS) Feb.–Dec. 1992; Russian rep. at UNESCO, Paris 1993–97; Sec. Russian Union of Journalists 1998–; Laureate Prize, Union of Journalists of the USSR 1990, UNESCO Medal in honour of the 50th anniversary of the Universal Declaration of Human Rights 1999. *Publications:* more than 100 books and essays on human rights and constitutionalism, intellectual property and int. humanitarian co-operation. *Address:* Russian Union of Journalists, Zubovskiy blvd 4, 119021 Moscow, Russia (office). *Telephone:* (495) 201-44-47 (office). *E-mail:* ruj@ruj.ru (office). *Website:* www.ruj.ru (office).

FEDOTOV, Yury Victorovich; Russian diplomatist and UN official; *Executive Director, United Nations Office on Drugs and Crime and Director General, United Nations Office at Vienna;* b. 14 Dec. 1947, Moscow; m. Elena Fedotova; one s. one d.; ed Moscow State Inst. of Int. Relations; entered diplomatic service 1971, served in various posts in Ministry of Foreign Affairs and abroad (Algeria 1974–80, India 1983–88), Deputy Head, Dept of Int. Relations, Ministry of Foreign Affairs 1991–93, Deputy Perm. Rep. and Acting First Deputy Perm. Rep. to UN, New York 1993–99, Dir Dept of Int. Orgs, Ministry of Foreign Affairs 1999–2002, Deputy Minister of Foreign Affairs 2002–05, mem. Bd of Dirs 2000–05, Amb. to UK 2005–10; Exec. Dir UN Office on Drugs and Crime (UNODC) 2010–, also Dir Gen. UN Office at Vienna (UNOV) 2010–; Order of Friendship; Certificate of Appreciation, President of the Russian Fed. *Address:* United Nations Office on Drugs and Crime, Vienna International Centre, PO Box 500, 1400 Vienna, Austria (office).

Telephone: (1) 26060-0 (office). *Fax:* (1) 26060-5866 (office). *E-mail:* unodc@unodc.org (office); yfedotov@mid.ru (office). *Website:* www.unodc.org (home).

FEFFER, Marc-André (Patrice), M.Droit pub; French television executive and lawyer; *Director General, La Poste;* b. 22 Dec. 1949, Neuilly-sur-Seine; s. of Jacques Feffer and Marie-Jeanne Thirlin; m. Hélène Cataix 1976; three d.; ed Lycée Condorcet and Faculté de Droit, Inst. d'Etudes Politiques and Ecole Nat. d'Admin, Paris; official Conseil d'Etat 1976, Counsel 1980, now mem.; Sec.-Gen. Comm. des Sondages 1980; Adviser Office of Pres. of EEC 1981–84; Dir Centre Mondial Informatique et Ressource Humaine 1984; Head of Information (Legal and Tech.), Prime Minister's Staff 1985–88, Sr Defence Counsel, Information 1986–88; Sec.-Gen. Canal+ 1988–94, Gen. Man. 1994–95, Dir Exec. Cttee 1994, Exec. Vice-Pres. 1995–2003, Deputy Chair. Exec. Bd and Gen. Council 2000–03; Dir-Gen. La Poste 2004–; Chair. Bd of Dirs Poste Immo 2007–; Chevalier, Légion d'honneur, Commdr Ordre des Arts et des Lettres. *Leisure interests:* sailing, windsurfing. *Address:* La Poste, 44 boulevard de Vaugirard, 75757 Paris Cedex 15, France (office). *Telephone:* 1-55-44-00-00 (office). *Fax:* 1-55-44-22-62 (office). *E-mail:* service.presse@laposte.fr (office). *Website:* www.laposte.fr (office).

FEFFERMAN, Charles, PhD; American mathematician and academic; *Herbert Jones University Professor of Mathematics, Princeton University;* b. 18 April 1949, Washington, DC; ed Univ. of Maryland and Princeton Univ.; child prodigy, graduated aged 17, doctorate aged 20, professor aged 22; Lecturer in Math., Priceton Univ. 1969–70, Prof. 1973–84, Herbert Jones Univ. Prof. of Math. 1984–, Chair. and Prof., Dept of Math. 1999–2002; Asst Prof. of Math., Univ. of Chicago 1970–71, Prof. 1971–73 (youngest full prof. ever appointed in USA); Wilson Elkins Visiting Professorship, Univ. of Maryland; Visiting Prof., Calif. Inst. of Tech., Courant Inst. of Math. Sciences, New York Univ., Univ. of Paris, France, Mittag-Leffler Inst., Djursholm, Sweden, Weitzmann Inst., Rehovot, Israel, Bar-Ilan Univ., Ramat-Gan, Israel Univ. of Madrid (Autónoma), Spain; mem. American Acad. of Arts and Sciences 1972, NAS 1979, American Philosophical Soc. 1989; mem. Editorial Bd Communications in Partial Differential Equations, Advances in Mathematics, Re-vista Mat. Iberoamericana, Journal of Fourier Analysis and Applications, Proceedings of the National Academy of Sciences, Journal d'Analyse; 1979 Hon. PhD (Univ. of Maryland) 1979, (Knox Coll.) 1981, (Bar-Ilan Univ.) 1985, (Univ. of Madrid (Autónoma)) 1990; NSF Fellowship 1966–69, Alfred P. Sloan Foundation Fellowship 1970, Nato Postdoctoral Fellowship 1971, Salem Prize 1971, First Recipient Alan T. Waterman Award 1976, Fields Medal, Int. Congress of Mathematicians, Helsinki 1978, American Math. Soc. Colloquium Lecturer 1983, Bergman Prize 1992. *Publications:* Renewing U.S. Mathematics – A Plan for the Nineties (co-author); more than 80 publs in math. journals on multivariable complex analysis, partial differential equations and harmonic analysis. *Address:* 1102 Fine Hall, Department of Mathematics, Washington Road, Princeton University, Princeton, NJ 08544-1000, USA (office). *Telephone:* (609) 258-4200 (office). *Fax:* (609) 258-1367 (office). *E-mail:* cf@math.princeton.edu (office). *Website:* www.math.princeton.edu (office).

FEGAN-WYLES, Sally, BA, MS; Irish international civil servant and UN official; *Director a.i., United Nations Institute for Training and Research;* b. 1954, Dublin; m. John Wyles; ed Trinity Coll., London School of Econs and Political Science, UK, Harvard Univ., USA; Health Economist, then Programme Officer, UNICEF 1980–98, Rep. in Uganda 1986–91, Rep. in Zimbabwe 1991–95, Adviser on Change Man., New York 1995–98; UN Resident Coordinator and Resident Rep., UNDP, Tanzania 1998–2001; Dir UN Devt Group Office 2004–08; Sr Adviser on Peacebuilding, Office of UN Sec.-Gen. 2008–09, Sr Adviser on System-Wide Coherence, Office of Deputy Sec.-Gen., UN 2009–10, Sr Adviser on Transition, UN Women 2010–11; Asst Sec.-Gen. and Dir a.i., UNITAR 2012–. *Address:* United Nations Institute for Training and Research, Palais des Nations, 1211 Geneva 10, Switzerland (office). *Telephone:* (22) 9178400 (office). *Fax:* (22) 9178047 (office). *E-mail:* info@unitar.org (office). *Website:* www.unitar.org (office).

FEHER, George, PhD; American physicist and academic; *Professor of Physics, University of California, San Diego;* b. 29 May 1924, Czechoslovakia; s. of Ferdinand Feher and Sylvia Feher (née Schwartz); m. Elsa Rosenvasser Feher 1961; three d.; ed Univ. of California, Berkeley; Research Physicist, Bell Telephone Labs, NJ 1954–60; Visiting Assoc. Prof., Columbia Univ., New York 1956–60; Prof. of Physics, Univ. of Calif., San Diego 1960–; Visiting Prof., MIT 1967–68; mem. American Physical Soc., Biophysical Soc. (Nat. Lecturer 1983), mem. Bd of Dirs Technion-Israel Inst. of Tech., Haifa, Israel 1968; mem. Bd of Govs Weizmann Inst. of Science, Rehovot 1988; Fellow, AAA, Int. EPR/ESR Soc. 1996, Biophysical Soc. 2000; mem. NAS, American Acad. of Arts and Sciences; Hon. DPhil (Hebrew Univ. of Jerusalem) 1994; American Physical Soc. Prize for origination and devt of Electron Nuclear Double Resonance (ENDOR) technique and for applying it to solid state and nuclear research problems 1960, Oliver E. Buckley Solid State Physics Prize 1976, Biophysics Prize 1982, Inaugural Annual Award, Int. Electron Spin Resonance Soc. 1991, Bruker Lectureship, Oxford Univ., UK 1992, Rumford Medal, American Acad. of Arts and Sciences 1992, Zavoiski Award 1996, Wolf Prize in Chemistry 2007. *Publications:* over 200 articles in numerous specialist scientific journals, reviews, symposia. *Leisure interests:* photography, sports. *Address:* Department of Physics 0319, University of California, San Diego, 9500 Gilman Drive, La Jolla, CA 92093-0319, USA (office). *Telephone:* (858) 534-4389 (office). *E-mail:* gfeher@physics.ucsd.edu (office). *Website:* physics.ucsd.edu/~raifeher (office).

FEHRENBACH, Franz, BEng; German business executive; *Chairman of the Supervisory Board, Robert Bosch GmbH;* b. 1 July 1949, Kenzingen, Breisgau; m.; three s.; ed Univ. of Karlsruhe; trainee, Robert Bosch GmbH 1975–76, Man. Office of the Exec. Man., Electrical and Electronic Engine Equipment Div. 1976–78, Dir Material Planning and Logistics Dept 1978–80, Commercial Plant Man., Hildesheim 1980–82, Vice-Pres., Corp. Dept Planning and Control 1982–85, Commercial Plant Man., Robert Bosch Corpn, Automotive Group, USA 1985–88, Exec. Vice-Pres. 1988–89, Exec. Vice-Pres., Finance and Admin, Starters and Alternators Div. 1989–94, Pres., Starters and Alternators Div. 1994–96, Exec. Vice-Pres., Finance and Admin, Diesel Systems Div. 1996–97, Pres. Diesel Systems Div. 1997–99, Deputy mem. Bd of Man. 1999–2001, mem. 2001–03, Chair. 2003–12, Chair. Supervisory Bd 2012–, also Man. Partner, Robert Bosch Industrietreuhand KG 2003–; mem. Supervisory Bd BASF SE, Linde AG; mem. Advisory Bd of Stihl Holding AG & Co. K.G, Man. Bd VDA (German Asscn of the

Automotive Industry), US Bd of Presiding Cttee of BDI (Fed. of German Industries), Asia Pacific Cttee of German Business, BBUG (Baden-Baden Entrepreneurs' Conf.); mem. Senate of Max Planck Soc.; Eco-Man. of the Year (cos category), WWF Deutschland and Capital magazine 2006, Honorary Golden Steering Wheel Prize, awarded to outstanding personalities by a German newspaper 2008, 'Yellow Angel' Personality of 2009 award, ADAC (German automobile asscn) 2009, environment award presented by BAUM (German Environmental Management Asscn) 2009, Award for Understanding and Tolerance of the Jewish Museum, Berlin 2009, Greentech Manager of the Year 2011 Award, Capital magazine 2012. *Address:* Robert Bosch GmbH, Postfach 106050, 70049 Stuttgart, Germany (office). *Telephone:* 400-40990 (office). *Fax:* 400-40999 (office). *E-mail:* kontakt@bosch.de (office). *Website:* www.bosch.com (office).

FEI, Maj.-Gen. Junlong; Chinese astronaut; b. 1965, Suzhou, Jiangsu; m. 1991; one s.; joined PLA Air Force 1982, served as fighter pilot; selected to be astronaut, Shenzhou Program 1998; shortlisted to fly on board Shenzhou 5 (China's first manned space mission) 2003; debut space flight on board Shenzhou 6, with astronaut Nie Haisheng, launched from Jiuquan Satellite Launch Centre, Gobi Desert (China's second space mission) 12 Oct. 2005; asteroid 9512 Feijunlong named after him; rank of Maj.-Gen. 2011. *Address:* c/o China National Space Administration, Beijing, People's Republic of China.

FEIFFER, Jules Ralph; American cartoonist, writer and dramatist; b. 26 Jan. 1929, New York, NY; s. of David Feiffer and Rhoda Davis; m. 1st Judith Sheftel 1961 (divorced 1983); one d.; m. 2nd Jennifer Allen 1983; two c.; ed Art Students' League, Pratt Inst.; asst to syndicated cartoonist Will Eisner 1946–51; cartoonist, author, syndicated Sunday page, Clifford, engaged in various art jobs 1953–56; contributing cartoonist Village Voice, New York 1956–97; cartoons published weekly in The Observer (London) 1958–66, 1972–82, regularly in Playboy (magazine); sponsor Sane; US Army 1951–53; mem. Dramatists' Guild (council 1970); currently Adjunct Prof., Program in Writing and Literature, Stony Brook Southampton Coll.; fmr teacher Yale School of Drama, Northwestern Univ.; fmr Sr Fellow, Columbia Univ. Nat. Arts Journalism Program; mem. American Acad. of Arts and Letters 1995–; Hon. Fellow, Inst. for Policy Studies 1987; Dr hc (Southampton Coll., Long Island Univ.) 1999; Acad. Award for Animated Cartoon (for Munro) 1961, Special George Polk Memorial Award 1962, Best Foreign Play, English Press (for Little Murders) 1967, Outer Critics Circle Award (Obie) 1969, (The White House Murder Case) 1970, Pulitzer Prize for Editorial Cartooning 1986, Writers Guild of America, East's Ian McLellan Hunter Award for Lifetime Achievement in Writing 2004, Nat. Cartoonist Soc. Milton Caniff Lifetime Achievement Award 2004, Benjamin Franklin Creativity Laureate Award 2006. *Plays:* Crawling Arnold 1961, Little Murders 1966, God Bless 1968, The White House Murder Case 1970, Feiffer on Nixon: The Cartoon Presidency 1974, Knock Knock 1975, Grown Ups 1981, A Think Piece 1982, Carnal Knowledge 1988, Anthony Rose 1989, Feiffer The Collected Works (vols 1, 2, 3) 1990, A Bad Friend 2003. *Screenplays:* Little Murders 1971, Carnal Knowledge 1971, Popeye 1980, I Want to Go Home (Best Screenplay, Venice Film Festival) 1989, I Lost My Bear 1998, Bark, George 1999. *Publications:* Sick, Sick, Sick 1959, Passionella and Other Stories 1960, The Explainers 1961, Boy, Girl, Boy, Girl, 1962, Hold Me! 1962, Harry, The Rat With Women (novel) 1963, Feiffer's Album 1963, The Unexpurgated Memoirs of Bernard Mergendeiler 1965, The Great Comic Book Heroes 1967, Feiffer's Marriage Manual 1967, Pictures at a Prosecution 1971, Ackroyd (novel) 1978, Tantrum 1980, Jules Feiffer's America: From Eisenhower to Reagan 1982, Marriage is an Invasion of Privacy 1984, Feiffer's Children 1986, Ronald Reagan in Movie America 1988, Elliott Loves (also play) 1990, The Man in the Ceiling (juvenile) 1993, A Barrel of Laughs, A Vale of Tears (juvenile) 1995, A Room with a Zoo (juvenile), The Daddy Mountain (juvenile), Explainers 2008, Backing into Forward: A Memoir 2010. *Address:* Royce Carlton Inc., 866 United Nations Plaza, New York, NY 10017, USA (office). *Telephone:* (212) 355-7700 (office). *Fax:* (212) 888-8659 (office). *E-mail:* info@roycecarlton.com (office); info@julesfeiffer.com (office). *Website:* www.roycecarlton.com (office); www.julesfeiffer.com.

FEINENDEGEN, Ludwig E., DrMed; German professor of nuclear medicine; *Professor Emeritus, Department of Nuclear Medicine, University Hospital, Heinrich Heine University;* b. 1 Jan. 1927, Garzweiler; s. of Ludwig Feinendegen and Rosa Klauth; m. Jeannine Gemuseus 1960; two s.; ed Univ. of Cologne; Asst Physician and Scientist, Medical Dept, Brookhaven Nat. Lab., Upton, New York, USA 1958–63; Scientific Officer, Euratom, Brussels and Paris 1963–67; Dir Inst. of Medicine Research Center, Jülich GmbH and Prof. for Nuclear Medicine, Heinrich Heine Univ., Dept of Nuclear Medicine, Univ. Hosp., Düsseldorf 1967–93, Prof. Emer. 1993–; Scientist, Brookhaven Nat. Lab., USA 1993–98, Research Collaborator 2000–; Assignee, Dept of Energy, Washington, Wash., DC 1994–98; Fogarty Scholar, NIH, Bethesda 1998–99; mem. Advisory Council, Fed. Ministries of Interior Environment and Defence; mem. Cttee for meetings of Nobel Laureates 1978–2005; mem. Rhine Westfalian Acad. of Sciences (Vice-Pres. 1978–79); mem. Int. Comm. on Radiation Units and Measurements 1982–2006; Dist Gov. Rotary Int. 1992–93; Bundesverdienstorden, Ehrenkreuz Gold Deutsche Bundeswehr; numerous nat. and int. awards. *Publications include:* more than 600 publns in nat. and int. scientific journals and books on nuclear medicine and radiation biology. *Address:* Biosciences Department, Brookhaven National Laboratory, Upton, NY 11973, USA (office); Wannental 45, 88131 Lindau, Germany (home). *Telephone:* (8382) 277310 (Germany) (office); (631) 344-3715 (USA) (office); (8382) 75673 (home). *Fax:* (8382) 947626 (home). *E-mail:* feinendegen@gmx.net (home).

FEINGOLD, Russell (Russ) Dana, BA, BA (Oxon.), JD; American lawyer and politician; *Founder, Progressives United;* b. 2 March 1953, Janesville, Wis.; s. of Leon Feingold and Sylvia Feingold (née Binstock); m. 1st Susan Levine 1977 (divorced 1986); two d.; m. 2nd Mary Speerschneider 1991 (divorced 2005); two step-c.; ed Joseph A. Craig High School, Univ. of Wisconsin-Madison, Magdalen Coll., Oxford, UK (Rhodes Scholar), Harvard Univ. Law School; Assoc., Foley & Lardner (law firm), Madison 1979–82, LaFollette, Sinykin, Andeson & Munson, Madison 1983–85, Goldman & Feingold 1985–88; State Senator 1983–92; Senator from Wis. 1993–2011, mem. Foreign Relations Cttee; Founder Progressives United (a Political Action Cttee) 2011–; teaches at Marquette Univ. Law School, Milwaukee 2011–; Democrat; John F. Kennedy Profile in Courage Award. *Address:* PO Box 620062, Middleton, WI 53562 (office); 8383 Greenway Boulevard,

Middleton, WI 53562, USA. *Telephone:* (608) 831-7877 (office). *Fax:* (608) 831-3192 (office). *E-mail:* info@progressivesunited.org (office). *Website:* www.progressivesunited.org (office).

FEINSTEIN, Dianne Goldman Berman; American politician; *Senator from California;* b. 22 June 1933, San Francisco, Calif.; d. of Leon Goldman and Betty Goldman (née Rosenburg); m. 1st Bertram Feinstein 1962 (deceased); one d.; m. 2nd Richard C. Blum 1980; ed Stanford Univ.; Intern in Public Affairs, Coro Foundation, San Francisco 1955–56; Asst to Calif. Industrial Welfare Comm., Los Angeles, also San Francisco 1956–57; Vice-Chair. Calif. Women's Bd Terms and Parole 1962–66; Chair. San Francisco City and Co. Advisory Comm. for Adult Detention 1967–69; Supervisor City and Co. of San Francisco 1970–78; Mayor of San Francisco 1978–88; served on Trilateral Comm. 1980s; Senator from California 1992–; mem. Council on Foreign Relations; Democrat; numerous hon. degrees; named by City and State Magazine the nation's Most Effective Mayor 1987, Woodrow Wilson Award for Public Service 2001, Nat. Distinguished Advocacy Award, American Cancer Soc. 2004, ranked by Forbes magazine amongst 100 Most Powerful Women (50th) 2004, (42nd) 2005, Women of Achievement Award, Century City Chamber of Commerce 2004, Funding Hero Award, Breast Cancer Research Foundation 2004, Outstanding Mem. of the US Senate Award, Nat. Narcotic Officers Asscns Coalition 2005, William Penn Mott Jr Park Leadership Award for singular outstanding achievement on behalf of Nat. Park protecting 2006, League of California Cities Congressional Leader of the Year Award 2006, Grammy on the Hill Award, Recording Acad. 2006, Charles Dick Medal of Merit, California Nat. Guard 2007, Legislator of the Year Award, California Co. Supts Educational Services Asscn 2007, Outstanding Int. Public Service Award, World Affairs Council 2012. *Address:* 331 Hart Senate Office Building, Washington, DC 20510-0001, USA (office). *Telephone:* (202) 224-3841 (office). *Fax:* (202) 228-3954 (office). *Website:* feinstein.senate.gov (office).

FEIREISS, Kristin; German art gallery director and writer; *Director, Aedes West;* b. 1942; Founder and Dir (with partner Hans-Jürgen Commercell) Aedes West Gallery (first pvt. forum for architecture in Germany), West Berlin 1980–, est. office in East Berlin 1995, over 250 exhbns shown including work of Peter and Alison Smithson, Peter Cook, Rem Koolhas, John Hejduk, over 200 catalogues published; Dir Netherlands Architecture Inst. 1996–2001; Bundesverdienstkreutz, Germany 1994; Literaturpreis für Baukultur, German Asscn of Architects and Engineers 1995. *Publications include:* Josef Paul Kleihues 1983, John Hejduk 1984, Fehling und Gogel 1986, Also Rossi 1989, Frank Gehry 1989, Nalbach und Nalbach 1990, Shin Takamatsu 1991, Syskowitz und Kowalski 1991, Zaha Hadid 1992, Hilde Léon Konrad Wohlhage 1992, Gustav Peichl: von der Skizze zum Bauwerk 1992, Sauerbruch und Hutton 1992, Daniel Libeskind: Erweiterung des Berlin Museums mit Abteilung Jüdisches Museum 1992, Ben van Berkel 1994, Christoph Mäckler 1995, Architekten Grüntuch/Ernst 1997, The Netherlands Architecture Institute 1999, Clorindo Testa 2001, Andre Poitiers 2002. *Address:* Aedes am Pfefferberg, Christinenstr. 18-19, 10119 Berlin, Germany. *Telephone:* (30) 282-7015 (office). *Fax:* (30) 2839-1466 (office). *E-mail:* aedes@baunetz.de (office). *Website:* www.aedes-arc.de (office).

FEITH, Pieter Cornelius, LicenPolSci, MA; Dutch diplomatist and international organization official; *Special Representative in Kosovo, European Union;* b. 9 Feb. 1945, Rotterdam; m.; three d.; ed Univ. of Lausanne, Switzerland, Fletcher School of Law and Diplomacy, Medford, USA; performed mil. service as reserve officer of Netherlands Marine Corps; with diplomatic service 1970–95, posted to Damascus, Bonn, New York (Mission to UN), Khartoum and Netherlands Mission to NATO and WEU, Brussels, also Chair. first UN Conf. of States Parties to the Chemical Weapons Convention, The Hague 1997; Personal Rep. of NATO Sec.-Gen. Lord Robertson for Yugoslavia, Dir of Crisis Man. and Operations Directorate, Head of NATO Balkans Task Force and Political Adviser to Commdr IFOR Bosnia-Herzegovina 1995–2001; Gen. Secr. of Council of EU, Deputy Dir-Gen. for Politico-Mil. Affairs 2001–; Personal Rep. of EU High Rep., Javier Solana, for Sudan/Darfur 2004; Head of EU Expert Team for Iraq 2005; Head of EU-led Aceh Monitoring Mission (AMM) in Indonesia 2005–06; Civilian Operations Commdr for all civilian ESDP Crisis Man. Operations, Acting Dir of EU Civilian Planning and Conduct Capability 2007; led team of EU officials and approved the Constitution of the Repub. of Kosovo April 2008, EU Special Rep. in Kosovo 2008–. *Leisure interest:* playing tennis. *Address:* International Civilian Office —EU Special Representative, Blue Building, St Ahmet Krasniqi PN (100 metres south of Hotel Adria), 10000 Pristina, Kosovo (office). *Telephone:* (38) 2044100 (office). *Fax:* (38) 2044210 (office). *E-mail:* office@ico-kos.org (office). *Website:* www.ico-kos.org (office).

FEKTER, Maria, DIur; Austrian politician; b. 1 Feb. 1956; ed Linz Univ.; Municipal Counsellor, Attnang-Puchheim 1986–90; State Sec., Fed. Ministry of Econ. Affairs 1990–94; mem. Nat. Council (Parl.) 1994–2007, Sec. 2004–07; Fed. Minister of the Interior 2008–11, of Finance 2011–13; mem. Exec. Cttee Österreichischer Wirtschaftsbund 1990–2002; Großes Silbernes Ehrenzeichen am Bande für Verdienste um die Republik Österreich 1994, Großes Goldenes Ehrenzeichen am Bande für Verdienste um die Republik Österreich 2011. *Address:* c/o Federal Ministry of Finance, Hintere Zollamtstr. 2b, 1030 Vienna, Austria (office).

FELCHT, Utz-Hellmuth, PhD; German chemist and business executive; *Chairman of the Supervisory Board, Deutsche Bahn AG;* b. 8 Jan. 1947, Iserlohn; ed Univs of Mainz, Saarbrücken and Kaiserslautern; Scientific Asst, Univ. of Kaiserslautern 1977–; various man. positions at Hoechst AG Inc. 1977–91, mem. Bd Hoechst AG 1991–98; Head of Div. Coordination, Corp. Staff Dept, Dir Cen. Research 2 and Deputy Head of Corp. Planning Dept, Ruhrkohle AG, Essen 1995–96; fmr Exec. Vice-Pres. and Pres. Advanced Tech. Group, Hoechst Celanese Corpn, Chatham, NJ, USA, responsible for Celanese Mexicana SA; Chair. Man. Bd SKW Trostberg AG 1998–2000; Chair. Man. Bd Degussa-Hls AG 2000–01, CEO Degussa AG, Chair. Man. Bd 2001–06, Chair. Man. Bd Degussa (China) Co. Ltd 2002–; Partner, One Equity Partners LLC 2007–, One Equity Partners Europe GmbH, Munich, currently a Man. Dir based at firm's Frankfurt office; Chair. Supervisory Bd Deutsche Bahn AG 2010–; Chair. Man. Bd Essen, Wiesbaden, SKW Metallurgie AG, Ruetgers AG, Goldschmidt AG, SKW Stickstoffwerke Piesteritz GmbH; mem. Bd of Dirs Sued-Chemie AG, CRH plc, CIBA Specialty Chemicals Holding, Inc.; mem. Man. Bd Ruetgers AG 2003–, Goldschmidt AG,

Ph.Holzmann AG; mem. and Chair. Supervisory Bd Gerling-Group Globale Rückversicherungs AG, Gerling-Konzern Globale Rückversicherungs AG, Degussa Corpn (USA), Süd-Chemie AG, Munich 2008–; mem. Supervisory Bd SGL CARBON AG 1992–, Chair. 1992–2004; mem. Advisory Bd Hapag-Lloyd AG; fmr mem. Supervisory Bd RAG Coal International AG, fmr mem. Man. Bd Rag AG; fmr Chair. Gesellschaft für Chemische Technik und Biotechnologie (DECHEMA); mem. Atlantic Bridge Asscn, Presidium of German Acad. of Science and Eng (Acatech); Hon. Prof., Tech. Univ. of Munich, Jilin Univ., Changchun, People's Repub. of China; Dr hc (Univ. of Rostock); DECHEMA Medal 2004. *Address:* Deutsche Bahn AG, Potsdamer Platz 2, 10785 Berlin (office); One Equity Partners Europe, Taunusanlage 21, 60325 Frankfurt am Main, Germany. *Telephone:* (30) 297-0 (Berlin) (office); (69) 5060-747-0 (Frankfurt) (office). *Fax:* (30) 297-61919 (Berlin) (office); (69) 5060-747-40 (Frankfurt) (office). *E-mail:* info@deutschebahn .com (office); oep.info@oneequity.com (office). *Website:* www.deutschebahn .com (office); www.bahn.de (office); www.oneequity.com (office).

FELD, Eliot; American dancer and choreographer; b. 5 July 1942, Brooklyn, New York; s. of Benjamin Feld and Alice Posner; ed High School of Performing Arts, New York; debut as Child Prince in Nutcracker, New York City Ballet 1954; mem. cast, West Side Story, Broadway 1958 (also appeared in film), I Can Get It For You Wholesale, Broadway 1962 and Fiddler on the Roof, Broadway; dancer and choreographer, American Ballet Theater 1963–68; Founder, Prin. Dancer and Choreographer, American Ballet Co. 1968–71; freelance choreographer, N America and Europe 1971–73; Founder, Artistic Dir and Choreographer, Feld Ballets, New York; Founder, The New Ballet School 1977, The Joyce Theater 1982, Ballet Tech 1996; Co-founder, Lawrence A. Wien Center for Dance & Theater 1986; has choreographed over 140 ballets since 1967 including Nodrog Doggo 2000, Coup de Couperin 2000, Organon 2001, Pacific Dances 2001, Skandia 2002, Pianola 2002, Lincoln Portrait 2002, Behold the Man 2002; Guggenheim Fellow; Dance Magazine Award 1990; Dr hc (Juilliard) 1991. *Address:* c/o Ballet Tech, 890 Broadway, 8th Floor, New York, NY 10003-1211, USA (office). *Telephone:* (212) 777-7710 (office). *Fax:* (212) 353-0936. *Website:* www.ballettech.org.

FELDBAEK, Ole, MA, DPhil; Danish academic; *Professor of Economic History, University of Copenhagen;* b. 22 July 1936, Copenhagen; s. of Commdr Henri Feldbaek and Kathy Feldbaek; m. Inge Kjaergaard 1976; one s. one d.; ed Univ. of Copenhagen; Lecturer in Econ. History, Univ. of Copenhagen 1968, Prof. 1981–; Fellow, Royal Danish and Royal Norwegian Acads, Academia Europaea; Amalienborg Prize 2001. *Publications include:* The Battle of Copenhagen: Nelson and the Danes and numerous books and articles on 18th century European and Asian history (econ., political and mil.). *Address:* 12 Sagaparken, 2920 Charlot-tenlund, Denmark (home).

FELDMAN, Jerome Myron, MD; American physician, medical scientist and academic; *Professor Emeritus, Division of Endocrinology, Metabolism and Nutrition, Duke University Medical Center;* b. 27 July 1935, Chicago, Ill.; s. of Louis Feldman and Marian Feldman (née Swichkow); m. Carol B. Feldman; one s. two d.; ed Northwestern Univ., Michael Reese, Chicago and Duke Univ.; Chief, Endocrinology and Metabolism, Durham Veteran's Admin. Hosp. 1971–2000, Staff Internist 1971–; Assoc. Prof. of Medicine, Duke Univ. 1972–98, Prof. of Medicine 1998–, now Prof. Emer., Dir Clinical Research Unit Core Lab. 1984; mem. Duke Comprehensive Cancer Center 1982–; Ed. Journal of Clinical Endocrinology and Metabolism 1983–89. *Publications:* 218 research articles, book chapters and reviews dealing with hormone-secreting tumours, endocrinology and metabolism. *Leisure interests:* music, art. *Address:* c/o Duke University Medical Center, Box 2963, Durham, NC 27710, USA (office). *Telephone:* (919) 286-0411 (office). *E-mail:* feld002@duke.edu (office). *Website:* endocrine.duke.edu/home .asp?divisionID=46 (office).

FELDMAN, Michael, PhD; Israeli biologist and academic; *Professor Emeritus, Department of Immunology, Weizmann Institute of Science;* b. 21 Jan. 1926, Tel-Aviv; m. Lea Noyfeld 1946; one s. one d.; ed Herzlia High School, Tel-Aviv, Hebrew Univ., Jerusalem; British Council Scholar, Inst. of Animal Genetics, Edinburgh, Scotland 1953–55; joined Weizmann Inst. of Science, Rehovot 1955, Head, Dept of Cell Biology, Weizmann Inst. 1961–90, Chair. Scientific Council 1962–64, Dean, Feinberg Grad. School 1966–72, Dean, Faculty of Biology 1983–85, now Prof. Emer., Dept of Immunology; with Dept of Virology, Univ. of Calif., Berkeley, USA 1960–61; Visiting Scientist, Nat. Cancer Inst., NIH, Bethesda, Md, USA 1961; Visiting Prof., Stanford Medical School, Stanford, Calif., USA 1976–77; Scholar-in-Residence, John F. Fogarty Int. Center, NIH, Bethesda 1978–79; Visiting Prof., Memorial Sloan Kettering Cancer Inst., New York 1990–91; mem. Israel Acad. of Sciences and Humanities 1980–; Hon. Fellow, Open Univ. of Israel 2000; Dr hc (Ben-Gurion Univ.) 1988; Griffuel Prize, Paris 1984, Rothschild Prize, Jerusalem 1986, San Marino Prize for Medicine 2000. *Publications:* numerous publs on cancer research immunology and developmental biology, in Scientific American, Nature, Nature Medicine, Journal of Experimental Medicine and other int. journals. *Leisure interests:* the arts, art history. *Address:* c/o The Weizmann Institute of Science, P.O. Box 26, Rehovot 76100, Israel. *Telephone:* 8-9344073 (office); 8-9472763 (home). *Fax:* 8-9344125 (office). *Website:* www.weizmann.ac.il/ immunology (office).

FELDMAN OF ELSTREE, Baron (Life Peer), cr. 2010, of Elstree in the County of Hertfordshire; **Andrew Feldman;** British politician, business executive and fmr barrister; *Chairman of the Party Board and Co-Chairman, Conservative Party;* m.; three c.; ed Haberdashers' Aske's School, Elstree, Herts., Brasenose Coll., Oxford; worked as man. consultant at Bain & Co. 1989–91; called to the Bar 1991; commercial barrister at chambers of Lord Grabiner QC 1991–95; left the Bar to take over running of family textile manufacturing and retail business 1995; acted as Treas. for and helped to run David Cameron's successful Conservative Party leadership campaign 2005; Deputy Treas. Conservative Party and Chair. Leaders Group 2005–08, Chief Exec. Conservative Party 2008–10, Chair. Party Bd and Co-Chair. Conservative Party 2010–; Dir, Jayroma (London) Ltd, Conservative Party Foundation Ltd (endowment fund), C & UCO Properties Ltd, C & UCO Management Ltd, C & UCO Services Ltd. *Address:* House of Lords, Westminster, London, SW1A 0PW, England (office). *Telephone:* (20) 7219-3000 (office). *Fax:* (20) 7219-5979 (office). *E-mail:* chairman@conservatives.com (office). *Website:* www .conservatives.com (office).

FELDMANN, Sir Marc, Kt, MB BS, PhD, FRS, FRCP, FRCPath, FMedSci, FAA; Australian immunologist and rheumatologist; *Head of Kennedy Institute of Rheumatology, University of Oxford;* b. 2 Dec. 1944, Lvov, Poland; ed Univ. of Melbourne, Walter and Eliza Hall Inst. of Medical Research; family moved to France 1945, emigrated to Australia aged eight; Resident Medical Officer, Professorial Dept of Medicine and Surgery, St Vincent's Hosp., Melbourne 1968; Postdoctoral C.J. Martin Fellow, Dept of Zoology, Imperial Cancer Research Fund Tumour Immunology Unit, Univ. Coll. London, UK 1972–73, Sr Staff mem. 1974, Special Appointment Grade 1977; Deputy Dir and Head, Immunology Unit, Charing Cross Sunley Research Centre 1985–92; Prof. of Cellular Immunology, Univ. of London 1986; Wellesley Visiting Prof. and Distinguished Lecturer, Toronto, Canada 1988; mem. Scientific Advisory Bd and Consultant, Xenova PLC, Slough, UK 1989–99, Syntex Research (now Roche Bioscience), Palo Alto, Calif., USA 1991–, Centocor, Inc., Malvern, Pa, USA 1991–; Consultant, Sandoz, Basel, Switzerland 1991–98, Canji, Inc., La Jolla, Calif. 1994–, Alza Inc., Palo Alto 1994–, Ferring AS, Copenhagen, Denmark 1996–2000, Wyeth (fmrly Genetics Inst.), Boston, Mass, USA 1997–, Boehringer-Ingelheim 1999–, Novartis, Canfite, Inc., Receptor Biologix, Inc., Novo Nordisk 2003–; Head of Div., Imperial Coll. School of Medicine, Kennedy Inst. of Rheumatology 2000–11, Head of Kennedy Inst. of Rheumatology when it joined Univ. of Oxford 2011–, Head of Dept of Cytokine Biology and Cellular Immunology 2000–11; Founder and Consultant, Synovis Ltd 2001–; Founder-mem. and Jr Councillor, Int. Cytokine Soc.; mem. British Soc. for Rheumatology (currently Pres), British Soc. of Immunologists, American Asscn of Immunologists, Autralian Immunology Soc.; mem. Research Sub-cttee, Arthritis Research Council, UK 1984–88 (mem. Scientific Consultative Cttee 2000–05), Oliver Bird Cttee, Nuffield Foundation 1991–96, Medical Research Advisory Cttee, Multiple Sclerosis Soc., UK 1991–2000 (Chair. 1999–2000), Scientific Advisory Bd, Jenner Inst. 2000–05, Scientific Advisory Cttee, Deutsches RheumaForschungs-Zentrum, Berlin, Germany 2002–06; Transmitting Ed. International Immunology 2001–; mem. Editorial Bd Journal of Experimental Pathology 1997–, Cytokines, Cytokine and Growth Factor Reviews, Journal of Autoimmunity, European Cytokine Network, Medical Immunology; mem. European Molecular Biology Org. 2005; Hon. mem. Scandinavian Soc. of Immunology, Polish Immunology Soc.; Hon. MD (Technical Univ., Munich) 2002; Univ. of Melbourne awards: Robert Gartley Healey Prize in Medicine, Hubert Sydney Jacobs Prize in Clinical Gynaecology, Sandoz Prize in Clinical Obstetrics, Fulton Scholarship, Clara Myers Prize in Surgical Pediatrics, Robert Garley Healey Prize in Surgery, Beaney Scholarship, Mead Johnson Prize in Pediatrics, Grieve Memorial Prize in Pediatrics; other awards: Margaret Ryan Prize in Surgery, Royal Australian Coll. of Surgeons, Marshall-Allen Prize in Obstetrics, Royal Coll. of Obstetricians and Gynaecologists, Michael Ryan Prize in Medicine Royal, Australian Coll. of Medicine, Watson-Smith Lecturer, Royal Coll. of Physicians (London) 1994, Canada Trust Distinguished Lecturer in Immunology (Toronto, Canada) 1998, Carol-Nachman Prize for Rheumatology Research (Germany) 1999, EULAR Prix Courtin-Clarins (jtly) 1999, Crafoord Prize (jtly), Royal Swedish Acad. 2000, Albert Lasker Clinical Medical Research Award (jtly) 2003, Cameron Prize, Univ. of Edinburgh (jtly) 2004, European Inventor of the Year, Lifetime Achievement Award, European Patent Office 2007, Curtin Medal, ANU 2008, Dr Paul Janssen Award for Biomedical Research 2008, Ernst Schering Prize (jtly) 2010, Croonian Lecturer, Royal Coll. of Physicians 2012, Canada Gairdner Int. Award (jtly) 2014. *Publications:* more than 600 publs in scientific journals and 90 patents. *Leisure interests:* tennis, hiking. *Address:* The Kennedy Institute of Rheumatology, University of Oxford, Roosevelt Drive, Headington, Oxford, OX3 7FY, England (office). *Telephone:* (1865) 612600 (office). *Fax:* (1865) 612601 (office). *E-mail:* marc .feldmann@kennedy.ox.ac.uk (office). *Website:* www.kennedy.ox.ac.uk/research/ teams/feldmann/feldmann1.html (office).

FELDSTEIN, Martin Stuart (Marty), AB, BLitt, MA, DPhil; American economist and academic; *George F. Baker Professor of Economics, Harvard University;* b. 25 Nov. 1939, New York, NY; s. of Meyer Feldstein and Esther Feldstein (née Gevarter); m. Kathleen Foley 1965; two d.; ed South Side High School, Rockville Centre, New York, Harvard Univ., Univ. of Oxford, UK; Research Fellow, Nuffield Coll. Oxford, UK 1964–65, Official Fellow 1965–67, Lecturer in Public Finance 1965–67, Hon. Fellow 1998–; Asst Prof. of Econs, Harvard Univ. 1967–68, Assoc. Prof. 1968–69, Prof. 1969–, George F. Baker Prof. of Econs 1984–; Research Assoc., Nat. Bureau of Econ. Research 1977–, Pres. and CEO 1977–82, 1984–2008, Pres. Emer. 2008–; Chair. Pres.'s Council of Econ. Advisers 1982–84; mem. Pres.'s Foreign Intelligence Advisory Bd 2006–09, Pres. Obama's Econ. Recovery Advisory Bd 2009–11; mem. Advisory Bd Congressional Budget Office, New York Fed. Reserve Bank, Boston Fed. Reserve Bank; mem. JP Morgan Int. Council 1984–93, 2001–; mem. Bd Dirs American International Group (AIG) 1988–2009, Eli Lilly 2001–; mem. Bd of Contribs, Wall Street Journal; mem. American Econ. Asscn Exec. Cttee 1980–82, Vice-Pres. 1988–89, Pres.-Elect 2003, Pres. 2004, Distinguished Fellow 2005; mem. Bd of Dirs Smith-Richardson Foundation 2007–; mem. Council on Foreign Relations 1986–, Dir 1998–, Trustee 1999–2007, 2009–, mem. Exec. Cttee 2002–; mem. Trilateral Comm. 1984– (mem. Exec. Cttee 1990–), Nat. Cttee on US-China Relations (Dir) 2001–, Group of Thirty Consultative Group on Int. Econ. and Monetary Affairs, Inc. (G-30), Washington, DC 2002– (mem. Exec. Cttee 2007–), Academic Advisory Council American Enterprise Inst. 2008–, Corpn of Massachusetts Gen. Hosp., New York Economic Club; mem. Bd of Contribs The Wall Street Journal; mem. Inst. of Medicine, NAS 1971–, American Philosophical Soc. 1989–; Foreign mem. Austrian Acad. of Sciences 1996; Fellow, Econometric Soc. 1970, American Acad. of Arts and Sciences 1977, Nat. Asscn of Business Economists 1980, European Econ. Asscn 2004; Corresp. Fellow, British Acad. 1998; Distinguished Fellow, Center for Naval Analysis 2009–; Hon. LLD (Univ. of Rochester) 1984, (Marquette) 1985, (Bentley Coll.) 1988, (Adelphi Univ.) 1991, (Dartmouth Coll.) 2009; Elizabeth Morgan Prize, Univ. of Chicago 1976, John Bates Clark Medal, American Econ. Asscn 1977, Fisher-Shultz Lecture, Econometric Soc. 1980, Joseph Schumpeter Prof., Univ. of Vienna March 1981, Distinguished Public Service Award, The Tax Foundation 1983, 1999, John R. Commons Prize, Omicron Delta Epsilon 1989, Jan Tinbergen Lecture, Netherlands Royal Econ. Soc. 1992, Adam Smith Lecturer, Nat. Asscn for Business Econs 1993, Bernhard Harms Prize, Weltwirtschafts Institut (Germany) 1994, Schumpeter Lecturer, European Econ. Asscn 1994, Richard Ely Lecturer, American Econ. Asscn 1996, Int. Prize of INA, Accad. Nazionale dei Lincei (Italy) 1997, Frank Geary Lecture, Econ. and Social Research Inst. (Ireland) 2001, Corp.

America's Outstanding Directors Award, Year 2000 (Dir's Alert) 2000, Daniel M. Holland Award, Nat. Tax Asscn 2003, Money Marketeers Lifetime Achievement Award. *Publications:* more than 360 research articles in econs; regular contrib. to the Wall Street Journal. *Address:* National Bureau of Economic Research, 1050 Massachusetts Avenue, Cambridge, MA 02138 (office); 147 Clifton Street, Belmont, MA 02478, USA (home). *Telephone:* (617) 868-3905 (office). *Fax:* (617) 868-7194 (office). *E-mail:* mfeldstein@harvard.edu (office); msfeldst@nber.org (office). *Website:* www.nber.org (office).

FELDT, Kjell-Olof, PhD; Swedish politician; b. 18 Aug. 1931, Holmsund; m. Birgitta von Otter; three c.; ed Univs of Uppsala and Lund; Budget Sec., Ministry of Finance 1962–64, Budget Dir 1965, Under-Sec. 1967–70; Minister of Trade 1970–75, of Finance 1983–90; Minister without Portfolio 1975–76; mem. Parl. 1971–90; mem. Exec. Cttee Social Democratic Party 1978–90; Chair. Bank of Sweden 1967–70, 1994–99, Swedish Road Fed. 1992–, Vin & Sprit AB 1991–93; mem. Bd of Dirs Nordbanken 1991–94, Sandrew Theatre Co. 1990–. *Publication:* Memoirs 1991.

FELICI, Claudio; San Marino politician; *Secretary of State for Finance and Budget;* b. 10 March 1960; m.; one c.; ed Università di Bologna; worked in eng design for 10 years; mem. Consiglio Grande e Generale (Parl.) 1998–; Sec. of State for Industry 2002–03, 2003–06, for Finance, the Budget, Postal Services and Relations with the Azienda Autonoma di Stato Filatelica e Numismatica 2013–; mem. Del. to Council of Europe; mem. Partito Democratico Cristiano Sammarinese. *Address:* Secretariat of State for Finance, the Budget, Postal Services and Relations with the Azienda Autonoma di Stato Filatelica e Numismatica, Palazzo Begni, Contrada Omerelli, 47890 San Marino (office). *Telephone:* 0549 882661 (office). *Fax:* 0549 882244 (office). *E-mail:* lbeccari@finanze.sm (office). *Website:* www.finanze.sm (office).

FELIX, Allyson Michelle; American track and field athlete; b. 18 Nov. 1985, Los Angeles; d. of Paul Felix and Marlean Felix; ed Los Angeles Baptist High School, North Hills, Univ. of Southern California; competes internationally for USA, primarily in 200m but also at 100m and 400m; gold medal, 100m, World Athletics Youth Championships, Budapest 2001; gold medal, 4×100m relay, bronze medal, 200m, Pan American Games, Santo Domingo 2003; silver medal, 200m, Olympic Games, Athens 2004, gold medal, 4×400m relay, silver medal, 200m, Olympic Games, Beijing 2008, gold medal, 200m, 4×100m relay, 4×400m relay, Olympic Games, London 2012; World Athletics Championships: gold medal, 200m (youngest ever gold medallist sprinter), Helsinki 2005, gold medal, 200m, 4×100m relay, 4×400m relay, Osaka 2007, gold medal, 200m, 4×400m relay, Berlin 2009, gold medal, 4×100m relay, 4×400m relay, silver medal, 400m, bronze medal, 200m, Daegu 2011; World Athletics Final: gold medal, 200m, Monte Carlo 2005, gold medal, 200m, bronze medal, 100m, Stuttgart 2006; gold medal, 4×400m relay, World Indoor Athletics Championships, Doha 2010; personal bests: 60m 7.10s, Fayetteville, Ark. 2012, 100m 10.89s, London, UK 2012, 200m 21.69s, Eugene 2012, 300m 36.23s, Fayetteville, Ark. 2007, 400m 49.59s, Daegu, South Korea 2011; participant in US Anti-Doping Agency's 'Project Believe' programme; coached by Bobby Kersee 2005–; named by Track and Field News the nat. girls' High School Athlete of the Year 2003, Women's 200m Best Year Performance 2003, 2005, 2007, Women's Track & Field ESPY Award 2006, Jesse Owens Award 2007, 2010. *E-mail:* info@theevolveagency.com (office); allyson@allysonfelix.com. *Website:* www.theevolveagency.com (office); www.allysonfelix.com.

FELL, Sir David, Kt, KCB, BSc, DUniv, FIB; British business executive, banker and fmr government official; *Chairman, Goldblatt McGuigan;* b. 20 Jan. 1943, Belfast, Northern Ireland; s. of Ernest Fell and Jessie McCreedy; m. Sandra J. Moore 1967; one s. one d.; ed Royal Belfast Academical Inst. and Queen's Univ. Belfast; Sales Man. Rank Hovis McDougall Ltd 1965–66; teacher 1966–67; Research Assoc. 1967–69; Dept of Agric. 1969–72, Asst Sec. 1971–81; Dept of Commerce 1972–82, Under-Sec. 1981–82; Deputy Chief Exec. Industrial Devt Bd 1982–84; Perm. Sec. Dept of Econ. Devt 1984–91; Second Perm. Under-Sec. NI Office and Head, NI Civil Service 1991–97; Chair. Northern Bank Ltd (subsidiary of Nat. Australia Bank) 1998–2005, Boxmore Int. PLC 1998–2000, Nat. Irish Bank Ltd 1999–2005; Dir Nat. Australia Group Europe Ltd 1998–, Dunloe Ewart PLC 1998–2002, Fred Olsen Energy ASA 1999–2003, Chesapeake Corpn 2000–08; Chair. Prince's Trust, NI 1999–, Harland & Wolff Group PLC 2001–02, Titanic Properties Ltd 2001–, Titanic Quarter Ltd 2001–, Goldblatt McGuigan 2005–, Novenso Ltd 2010–; Pro Chancellor Queen's Univ., Belfast 2005–. *Leisure interests:* music, reading, golf, rugby. *Address:* Goldblatt McGuigan, Alfred House, 19 Alfred Street, Belfast, BT2 8EQ, Northern Ireland (office). *Telephone:* (28) 9031-1113 (office). *Fax:* (28) 9031-0777 (office). *E-mail:* sirdavid@goldmac.com (office). *Website:* www.goldblattmcguigan.com (office).

FELLAG, Mohamed Said; Algerian actor and comedian; b. 1950, Kabylie; began career as classical actor; fmr Dir Théâtre Régional, Bougie; moved to Paris 1995; Prince Claus Award 1999. *Films include:* Liberté, la nuit 1983, Le Gone du chaâba 1998, Inch'Allah dimanche 2001, Fleurs de sang 2002, Momo mambo 2003, Voisins, voisines 2005, Rue des figuiers (TV) 2005, Michou d'Auber 2007, L'ennemi intime 2007, Il faut sauver Saïd (TV) 2008, La veuve tatouée (TV) 2008, Les barons 2009, Monsieur Lazhar 2011. *Shows include:* The Adventures of Tchop 1986, Khorotov Cocktail 1989, Djurdjurassic Bled 1998. *Website:* www.fellag.fr.

FELLEGI, Tamás László, PhD, JurD; Hungarian politician, jurist, political scientist and business executive; *Minister without Portfolio, responsible for Liaison with certain International Financial Organizations;* b. 7 Jan. 1956, Budapest; m. Ágnes Szokolszky; two s.; ed Agoston Trefort high school, Budapest, Eötvös Loránd Univ. (ELTE), Budapest, Univ. of Connecticut, USA; Research Fellow, Inst. of Social Sciences (Társadalomtudományi Intézet), Hungarian Socialist Workers' Party 1981–87; Teaching Asst, then Adjunct, Dept of State and Law Theories, Faculty of Law and State, ELTE 1981–87, Dozent, Dept of Political Science 1993–97; Research Fellow, Harvard Univ., USA 1985–86; Int. Fellow and Teaching Asst, Univ. of Connecticut 1987–92; Sr Post-Doctoral Fellow, Univ. of Rochester 1992–93; Head of Advisory Body of Party Chair., Viktor Orbán, Fidesz 1993–94; Co-owner and Dir of Public Affairs, Press & Inform Public Relations Ltd; mem. Edelman Public Relations Worldwide 1994–95; Exec. Dir and Man. Partner, EuroAtlantic Business Development and Communication Consulting Ltd 1995–96, 2000–; Br. Dir, then Chief Officer for Govt Relations, Regulatory

and Public Affairs, Magyar Telekom (then Matáv Rt., subsidiary of Deutsche Telekom) 1996–2000, Perm. Invitee of Man. Bd; Man. Dir Kapsch Telematic Services Hungary 2007–09; Minister of Nat. Devt 2010–11; Minister without Portfolio, responsible for Liaison with certain Int. Financial Orgs 2011–; Chair. American Chamber of Commerce, Budapest, Telecommunications Task Force Studies 1998–2000; mem. Supervisory Bd, M-RTL Television Corpn (jt venture of Bertelsmann AG, RTL Television, Pearson Technologies and Magyar Telekom) 1997–; Rep. of Magyar Telekom, Trans-Atlantic Business Dialogue (Brussels-Washington, DC) 1998–2000; mem. Presidium, Joint Venture Asscn 2000–06. *Publications:* several book chapters and numerous articles in professional journals. *Address:* c/o Office of the Prime Minister, 1055 Budapest, Kossuth Lajos tér 4 (office); c/o Office of the Prime Minister, 1357 Budapest, Budapest, Pf. 6, Hungary (office). *Telephone:* (1) 795-6978 (office). *Fax:* (1) 795-0381 (office). *E-mail:* webszerkeszto@meh.gov.hu (office). *Website:* www.kormany.hu/en/prime-minister -s-office (office).

FELLNER, Eric, CBE; British film producer; b. 10 Oct. 1959; four s. one d.; ed London Guildhall; Co-Chair. Working Title Films; four Academy Awards and 18 BAFTA Awards, Empire Film Award for outstanding contribution to British cinema (jtly) 2005. *Films include:* Sid and Nancy 1986, Pascali's Island 1988, The Rachel Papers 1989, Hidden Agenda 1990, A Kiss Before Dying 1991, Liebstraum 1991, Wild West 1992, Posse 1993, Romeo is Bleeding 1993, Four Weddings and a Funeral 1994, The Hudsucker Proxy 1994, Loch Ness 1995, French Kiss 1995, Dead Man Walking 1995, Fargo 1996, Bean 1997, The Borrowers 1997, Elizabeth 1998, The Big Lebowski 1998, Notting Hill 1999, Plunkett & Macleane 1999, O Brother, Where Art Thou? 2000, Billy Elliot 2000, Bridget Jones's Diary 2001, Captain Corelli's Mandolin 2001, The Man Who Wasn't There 2001, About a Boy 2002, The Guru 2002, 40 Days and 40 Nights 2002, Ali G Indahouse 2002, Long Time Dead 2002, My Little Eye 2002, Love Actually 2003, Calcium Kid 2003, Ned Kelly 2003, Shape of Things 2003, Johnny English 2003, Thirteen 2003, Shaun of the Dead 2004, Thunderbirds 2004, Wimbledon 2004, Bridget Jones: The Edge of Reason 2004, Gettin' Square 2004, Inside I'm Dancing 2004, Mickybo and Me 2005, The Interpreter 2005, Pride and Prejudice 2005, Nanny McPhee 2005, Middle of Nowhere 2006, Smokin' Aces 2006, United 93 (Best British Producer, London Film Critics' Circle Awards 2007) 2006, Hot Fuzz 2007, Atonement 2007, Elizabeth: The Golden Age 2007, Definitely Maybe 2008, Wild Child 2008, Burn After Reading 2008, Frost/Nixon 2009, The Boat that Rocked 2009, The Soloist 2009, A Serious Man 2009, Green Zone 2010, Nanny McPhee and the Big Bang 2010, Senna 2011, Paul 2011, Johnny English Reborn 2011, Tinker Tailor Soldier Spy 2011, Les Miserables 2012, I Give It a Year 2013, Closed Circuit 2013, About Time 2013, Rush 2013, Anna Karenina 2013. *Address:* Working Title Films, 26 Aybrook Street, London, W1U 7AN, England (office); Working Title Films, 4th Floor, 9770 Wilshire Blvd, Beverly Hills, CA 90212, USA (office). *Telephone:* (20) 7307-3000 (London) (office); (310) 777-3100 (USA) (office). *Fax:* (20) 7307-3001 (London) (office); (310) 777-5243 (USA) (office). *Website:* www.workingtitlefilms.com (office).

FELLNER, Peter John, PhD; British pharmaceuticals and biotechnology executive; *Chairman, Vernalis PLC;* b. 31 Dec. 1943; s. of the late Hans Julius Fellner and essica Fellner (née Thompson); m. 1st Sandra Head (née Smith) 1969; one d. one step-s.; m. 2nd Jennifer Mary Zabel (née Butler) 1982; two step-s.; ed Univ. of Sheffield and Trinity Coll. Cambridge; Post-doctoral Research Fellow, Univ. of Strasbourg, France 1968–70, Assoc. Prof. 1970–73; Sr Research Investigator, Searle UK Research Labs 1973–77, Dir of Chem. 1977–80, Dir of Research 1980–84; Dir of Research Roche UK Research Centre 1984–86, Man. Dir Roche UK 1986–90; CEO Celltech PLC 1990–99, CEO Celltech Group (fmrly Celltech Chiroscience) PLC 1999–2003; Chair. Vernalis PLC (fmrly British Biotech PLC), Chair. (non-exec.) Celltech Group PLC 2003–, Ionix Pharmaceuticals Ltd, Astex Technology 2002–; Chair. Premier Research Group PLC 2007–; Dir (non-exec.) Colborn Dawes Ltd 1986–90, Synaptica Ltd 1999–2002, Qinetiq Group PLC 2004–, UCB SA 2005–, Evotec AG 2005–, Bespak PLC 2005–; mem. MRC 2000–07. *Leisure interest:* country walking. *Address:* Vernalis PLC, Oakdene Court, 613 Reading Road, Winnersh, RG41 5UA, England (office). *Telephone:* (118) 989-9312 (office). *Fax:* (118) 989–9369 (office). *Website:* www.vernalis.com (office).

FELLS, Ian, CBE, MA, PhD, FRSE, FREng, FIE, FIChemE; British professor of energy conversion; *Principal Consultant, Fells Associates;* b. 5 Sept. 1932, Sheffield, Yorks.; s. of Dr H. Alexander Fells and Clarice Fells; m. Hazel Denton Scott 1957; four s.; ed King Edward VII School, Sheffield and Trinity Coll. Cambridge; Lecturer and Dir of Studies, Dept of Fuel Tech. and Chemical Eng, Univ. of Sheffield 1958–62; Reader in Fuel Science, King's Coll., Durham Univ. 1962; Prof. of Energy Conversion, Univ. of Newcastle-upon-Tyne 1975–; mem. Science Consultative Group, BBC 1976–81, Electricity Supply Research Council 1979–90; Exec., David Davies Inst. of Int. Affairs 1975–; Pres. Inst. of Energy 1978–79; Scientific Adviser, World Energy Council 1990–98; Life Vice-Pres. Int. Centre for Life 1995–; Chair. New and Renewable Energy Centre, Northumberland 2002–05; Prin. Consultant, Fells Associates; Adviser to House of Commons and House of Lords Select Cttee; numerous other professional appointments; Hatfield Memorial Prize 1974, Beilby Memorial Medal and Prize 1976, Royal Soc. Faraday Medal and Prize 1993, Melchett Medal 1999, John Collier Memorial Medal 1999, Kelvin Medal 2002. *Television series:* Young Scientist of the Year, The Great Egg Race, Men of Science, Earth Year 2050, Take Nobody's Word For It, What If the Lights Go Out?, Murphy's Law, Dr Priestley and the Breath of Life. *Radio:* extensive radio contribs. *Publications:* UK Energy Policy Post-Privatization 1991, Energy for the Future 1995, World Energy, 1923–1998 and Beyond 1998, Turning Point, An Independent Review of UK Energy Policy 2001, A Pragmatic Energy Policy for the UK 2008. *Leisure interests:* cross-country skiing, sailing, swimming. *Address:* Fells Associates, 29 Rectory Terrace, Newcastle upon Tyne, NE3 1YB, England (office). *Telephone:* (870) 321-1661 (office); (191) 285-5343 (home). *Fax:* (191) 285-5343 (home). *E-mail:* ian@fellsassociates.com (office). *Website:* www.fellsassociates.com (office).

FELS, Gerhard, Dr rer. pol; German economist, academic and business executive; b. 1939, Baumholder; ed Univs of Bonn, Saarbrücken and the Saar; worked for Institut für Weltwirtschaft Kiel, Vice-Pres. 1976–83; Man. Dir and mem. Presidium, Institut der deutschen Wirtschaft, Cologne 1983; Prof., Univ. of Cologne 1985–2004; mem. German Expert Council on Overall Econ. Devt 1976–82, UN Cttee for Devt Planning 1978–82; currently serves on supervisory bds of several major corpns; mem. Group of Thirty Consultative Group on Int. Econ. and Monetary Affairs, Inc. (G-30), Washington, DC 1988 (now mem. Emer.); Hon. Prof., Univ. of Kiel 1974–85. *Publications:* has written widely on applied econs and econ. policy. *Address:* c/o The Group of Thirty, 1726 M Street NW, Suite 200, Washington, DC 20036, USA.

FELSENSTEIN, Joseph (Joe) Hua, BS, PhD; American geneticist and academic; *Professor, Department of Genome Sciences and Department of Biology, University of Washington;* b. 9 May 1942, Philadelphia, Pa; ed Central High School, Philadelphia, Univ. of Wisconsin, Nat. Insts of Health Trainee (Genetics Training Grant), Univ. of Chicago; NIH Postdoctoral Research Fellow, Inst. of Animal Genetics, Univ. of Edinburgh, UK 1967–68; Asst Prof., Dept of Genetics, Univ. of Washington, Seattle 1967–73 (on leave 1967–68), Assoc. Prof. 1973–78, Prof. 1978–2001, Prof., Dept of Genome Sciences 2001–, Adjunct Prof., Dept of Statistics 1981–, Adjunct Prof., Dept of Zoology 1990–2002, Prof. 2002–03 (on jt basis with Genome Sciences), Prof., Dept of Biology 2003– (on jt basis with Genome Sciences), Adjunct Prof., Dept of Computer Science and Eng 2003–; Co-ordinator, Program in Computational Molecular Biology, Univ. of Washington 2001–06; Assoc. Ed. Theoretical Population Biology 1975–86, 1995–98, 2003–, Journal of Classification 1984–; mem. Editorial Bd, Molecular Phylogenetics and Evolution 1992–, Journal of Molecular Evolution 1993–, Journal of Computational Biology 1994–; Pres. Soc. for Study of Evolution 1993; mem. American Acad. of Arts and Sciences 1992, NAS 1999, Washington State Acad. of Sciences 2008–, Soc. for Study of Evolution, Soc. of Systematic Biology, Soc. of Molecular Biology and Evolution; Hon. mem. Editorial Bd, Evolutionary Bioinformatics 2005–; Hon. DSc (Edinburgh) 2005; Sewall Wright Award, American Soc. of Naturalists 1993, Weldon Memorial Prize, Univ. of Oxford 2000, Pres.'s Award for Excellence in Systematics, Soc. of Systematic Biology 2002, Darwin-Wallace Medal, Linnean Soc. of London 2009, John J. Carty Award for the Advancement of Science, NAS 2009, Distinguished Scientist Award, American Inst. of Biological Sciences 2009, Int. Prize for Biology, Japan Soc. for the Promotion of Science 2013. *Publications:* more than 110 research papers in professional journals. *Address:* Department of Genome Sciences, University of Washington, Box 357730, Seattle, WA 98195-7730, USA (office). *Telephone:* (206) 543-0150 (office); (206) 543-8751 (office). *Fax:* (206) 543-0754 (office). *E-mail:* joe@gs.washington.edu (office). *Website:* www.gs .washington.edu (office); evolution.genetics.washington.edu (office).

FELTHEIMER, Jon, BA; American entertainment industry executive; *Co-Chairman and CEO, Lions Gate Entertainment Corporation;* b. 2 Sept. 1951, Brooklyn, NY; m.; three c.; ed Washington Univ., St Louis; moved to LA to become musician; joined New World Entertainment 1983, held various exec. positions including Pres. and CEO, Dir of Domestic and Int. Distribution Businesses, Man. New World TV Div., Marvel Productions and Learning Corpn of America Units; joined Sony Pictures Entertainment (SPE) 1991, launched interactive TV business 1996, cr. TriStar TV, Head of Columbia TriStar TV Group and Exec. Vice-Pres. SPE –2000; CEO Lions Gate Entertainment Corpn, Vancouver, Canada 2000–, Co-Chair. 2005–. *Address:* Lions Gate Entertainment Corporation, 1055 West Hastings Street, Suite 2200, Vancouver, BC V6E 2E9, Canada (office). *Telephone:* (604) 983-5555 (office). *Fax:* (604) 983-5554 (office). *Website:* www.lionsgatefilms .com (office).

FELTUS, Alan Evan, MFA; American artist and academic; b. 1 May 1943, Washington, DC; s. of Randolph Feltus and Anne Winter; m. Lani H. Irwin 1974; two s.; ed Tyler School of Fine Arts, Pa, Cooper Union for Advancement of Science and Art, NY, Yale Univ., Conn.; instructor, School of Dayton Art Inst., Ohio 1968–70; Asst Prof., American Univ., Washington, DC 1972–84; full-time artist 1984–, represented by Forum Gallery, New York 1973–; exhibits regularly in USA; occasional teaching workshops and lectures; resident in Italy since 1987; Rome Prize Fellowship, American Acad. in Rome 1970–72, Nat. Endowment for Arts Fellowship 1981, Louis Comfort Tiffany Foundation Grant in Painting 1980, Pollock-Krasner Foundation Grant in Painting 1992, 2005, Thomas B. Clarke Prize, Nat. Acad. of Design 1984, Benjamin Altman Prize 1990, Joseph S. Isidor Memorial Medal 1995, Raymond Neilson Prize 2001. *Address:* c/o Forum Gallery, 730 Fifth Avenue, New York, NY 10019, USA; Porziano 68, 06081 Assisi, Perugia, Italy (home). *Telephone:* (212) 355-4545. *Fax:* (212) 355-4547. *E-mail:* alan@feltus .com (home); gallery@forumgallery.com. *Website:* www.forumgallery.com; www .alanfeltus.com.

FENBY, Jonathan Theodore Starmer, CBE; British writer and journalist; *Director, China Research, Trusted Sources;* b. 11 Nov. 1942, London; s. of the late Charles Fenby and June Fenby (née Head); m. Renée Wartski 1967; one s. one d.; ed King Edward's School, Birmingham, Westminster School and New Coll. Oxford; corresp. and ed. Reuters World Service, Reuters Ltd 1963–77; corresp. (France and Germany), The Economist 1982–86; Home Ed. and Asst Ed. The Independent 1986–88; Deputy Ed. The Guardian 1988–93; Dir Guardian Newspapers 1990–95; Ed. The Observer 1993–95; Ed. South China Morning Post 1995–99; Ed. Netmedia Group; Assoc. Ed. Sunday Business 2000–01; Ed. Business Europe 2000–01; Ed. www.earlywarning.com 2004–06; currently Dir China Research, Trusted Sources; mem. Bd European Journalism Centre, Belgian–British Colloquium; Chevalier, Ordre du Mérite (France) 1992. *Radio:* broadcasts on BBC, CBC and French and Swiss radio. *Television:* broadcasts on BBC, CNN, CNBC, Channel Four, FR2, Sky, Bloomberg. *Publications:* The Fall of the House of Beaverbrook 1979, Piracy and the Public 1983, The International News Services 1986, On the Brink: The Trouble with France 1998 (new edn 2002), Comment peut-on être Français? 1999, Dealing With the Dragon: A Year in the New Hong Kong 2000, Generalissimo: Chiang Kai-shek and the China He Lost 2003, The Sinking of the Lancastria 2005, Alliance: The Inside Story of How Roosevelt, Stalin and Churchill Won One War and Began Another 2007, The Penguin History of Modern China: The Fall and Rise of a Great Power (1850–2008) 2008, The General: Charles De Gaulle and the France He Saved 2010; contrib. to newspapers and magazines in Europe, USA, Asia. *Leisure interests:* walking, jazz, belot. *Address:* Trusted Sources, 48 Charlotte Street, London, W1T 2NS (office); 101 Ridgmount Gardens, Torrington Place, London, WC1E 7AZ, England (home). *Telephone:* (20) 3008-5764 (office). *E-mail:* jtfenby@ hotmail.com (home). *Website:* www.trustedsources.co.uk (office).

FENCHEL, Tom Michael, DSci; Danish marine biologist and academic; *Professor Emeritus of Marine Biology, University of Copenhagen;* b. 19 March 1940, Copenhagen; s. of W. Fenchel and Käte Fenchel (née Sperling); m. 1st Anne

Thane 1964; m. 2nd Hilary Adler 1978 (divorced 1989); one s. one d.; m. 3rd Ilse Duun 1995; ed Univ. of Copenhagen; Lecturer in Marine Biology, Univ. of Copenhagen 1964–70, Prof. of Marine Biology 1987–2010, Prof. Emer. 2010–; Prof. of Ecology and Zoology, Univ. of Aarhus 1970–87; mem. Danish Royal Soc. of Science and Letters, Royal Swedish Acad. of Science, Royal Soc., London, NAS, American Acad. of Microbiology; Hon. mem. Soc. for Gen. Microbiology; Gold Medal, Univ. of Copenhagen 1964, Ecology Inst. Prize 1987, Huntsmann Award for Oceanography 1987, A.G. Hutsman Award for Exellency in Oceanography, America Soc. of Limnology and Oceanography, Alfred C. Redfield Lifetime Achievement Award. *Publications:* Theories of Populations in Biological Commu-nities (with F. B. Christiansen) 1977, Bacteria and Mineral Cycling (with T. H. Blackburn) 1979, Ecology of Protozoa 1987, Ecology and Evolution in Anoxic Worlds (with B. J. Finlay), Bacterial Biochemistry (co-author), Bacterial Biogeochemistry (with G. M. King and T. H. Blackburn) 1998, Origin and Early Evolution of Life 2002. *Address:* Marine Biological Laboratory, University of Copenhagen, Strandpromenaden 5, 3000 Helsingor, Denmark (office). *Telephone:* 35-32-19-60 (office). *Fax:* 35-32-19-51 (office). *E-mail:* tfenchel@bi.ku.dk (office). *Website:* www.mbl.ku.dk (office).

FENDER, Sir Brian Edward Frederick, Kt, CMG, PhD; British chemist, academic and business consultant; *President, Institute of Knowledge Transfer;* b. 15 Sept. 1934, Barrow, Cumbria, England; s. of the late George Clements Fender and of Emily Goodwin; m. 1st 1956; one s. three d.; m. 2nd Ann Linscott 1986 (died 2011); ed Carlisle and Sale Grammar Schools, Imperial Coll., London; Research Instructor, Univ. of Washington, Seattle, USA 1959–61; Sr Research Fellow, Nat. Chemical Lab., Teddington 1961–63; Fellow, St Catherine's Coll., Oxford 1963–84, Lecturer in Inorganic Chem. 1965–80; Asst Dir Inst. Laue-Langevin, Grenoble 1980–82, Dir 1982–85; Vice-Chancellor, Keele Univ. 1985–95; Chief Exec. Higher Educ. Funding Council for England 1995–2001; Chair. BTG PLC 2003–08; Pres. and Chair. Inst. of Knowledge Transfer 2005–11, Pres. 2011–; mem. Science and Eng Research Council 1985–90; Pres. Nat. Foundation for Educational Research 1999–2007; Chair. New Victoria Theatre, Staffs. 2003–, London Waterways Partnership, Canal & River Trust 2011–; Hon. Fellow, St Catherine's Coll. Oxford, Imperial Coll. London, Cardiff Univ. *Publications:* scientific articles on neutron scattering and solid state chemistry. *Leisure interests:* theatre, gardens, cooking. *Address:* Bishops Offley Manor, Bishops Offley, Stafford, ST21 6ET, England (home). *Telephone:* (1785) 280401 (office). *E-mail:* fenderbrian1@gmail.com (home); chair.london@canalrivertrust.org.uk (office).

FENECH, Tonio, BCom, BA (Hons); Maltese accountant, auditor and politician; b. 5 May 1969; s. of the late Carmel V. Fenech and of Helen Fenech (née Zarb); m. Claudine Ellul 1998; one s. one d.; ed St Aloysius' Coll., Birkirkara, Manoel Theatre Acad. of Dramatic Arts, Univ. of Malta; gained early work experience during school summer holidays at Multi Packaging Ltd; mem. Youth Fellowship 1987–96; with Price Waterhouse (later PricewaterhouseCoopers) 1993–2004, later became man. in audit practice, subsequently Sr Consultant in man. consultancy practice, several int. work experiences in Italy and Libya, including Instituto per le Opere Religiose (IOR), Vatican Bank; mem. Partit Nazzjonalista (Nationalist Party), mem. Exec. Cttee Nationalist Party Coll. of Councillors 1998–99, Sec.-Gen. Nationalist Party Coll. of Councillors 1999–2003, mem. Nationalist Party Exec. Cttee 1999–; elected as local councillor for Birkirkara 1996–98, Mayor of Birkirkara 1998–2003; MP from 8th Dist 2003–, apptd observer to European Parl. 2003–04; Parl. Sec., Ministry of Finance 2004–08 (participated in Malta's accession to EuroZone), Minister of Finance, Economy and Investment 2008–13; mem. Housing Authority Bd 1998–2003, e-Malta Comm. 2001–03. *Address:* Nationalist Party, Herbert Ganado Street, Pietà PTA 1541, Malta (office). *Telephone:* 21243641 (office); 79927302 (home); 27327302 (home). *Fax:* 21243640 (office). *E-mail:* admin@pn.org.mt (office); fenechtonio@gmail.com (home). *Website:* www.pn.org.mt (office); www.toniofenech.com (home).

FENECH-ADAMI, Edward, KUOM, BA, LLD; Maltese politician, lawyer and fmr head of state; b. 7 Feb. 1934, Birkirkara; s. of Luigi Fenech Adami and Josephine Pace; m. Mary Sciberras 1965; four s. one d.; ed St Aloysius Coll., Univ. of Malta; entered legal practice 1959; Ed. Il-Poplu (weekly) 1962–69; mem. Nat. Exec. Nationalist Party 1961, Asst Gen. Sec. 1962–75, Pres. Gen. and Admin. Councils 1975–77, Leader 1977–2004; mem. Parl. 1969–2004; Leader of Opposition 1977–82, 1983–87, 1996–98; Prime Minister 1987–96, 1998–2004; Pres. of Malta 2004–09; Vice-Pres. European Union of Christian Democrat Parties 1979–99; Nat. Order of Merit. *Address:* c/o President's Office, The Palace, Valletta CMR02, Malta (office).

FENEUILLE, Serge Jean Georges, PhD; French academic and company director; *Member, French Academy of Technologies;* b. 16 Nov. 1940, Rheims; s. of Georges Feneuille and Marguerite Lemoine; m. Jeannine Large 1960; ed Coll. Moderne de Rheims, Ecoles Normales d'Instituteurs de Chalons-sur-Marne and Nancy, Ecole Normale Supérieure de St-Cloud; Maître-Asst, Univ. of Paris 1964–69; Maître de Recherche CNRS 1969–74, Dir of Research 1974–, Dir-Gen. CNRS 1986–88; Prof., Univ. Paris-Sud 1979–98; Dir of Research, Lafarge Coppée 1981–85, Scientific Dir and mem. Exec. Cttee 1985–86, Asst Dir-Gen. 1988–89, Dir-Gen. and Head of Research, Tech. and Strategy 1989–94, Special Adviser to Chair. and CEO 1995–2000; Man. Dir Centre Expérimental du Bâtiment et des Travaux Publiques 1998–2000; Pres. Admin. Council Ecole Normale Supérieure de Lyon 1986–94; Chair. Orsan (subsidiary of Lafarge Coppée) 1992–94, Innovation and Research Comm., Conseil Nat. du Patronat Français (CNPF) 1993–97; mem. Archaeological mission in Saggarah 2002–; mem. Sudanese Antiquities (French section) 2003–; Chair. High Council of Science and Tech. 2006–09; mem. French Acad. of Tech. 2000–; Hon. Prof.; Officier, Ordre nat. du Mérite, des Palmes académiques, Chevalier Légion d'honneur; Prix Daniel Guinier de la Soc. Française de Physique, Bronze Medal, CNRS, Prix Servant de l'Acad. des Sciences, Prix Jaffé de l'Institut de France. *Publications:* Paroles d'éternité 2007, Pensées égytiennes in Philosophies d'ailleurs (ed. R.-P. Droit) 2009, Paroles d'amour 2010, Paroles de sagesse 2012; numerous articles in scientific journals. *Leisure interests:* egyptology, painting, literature. *Address:* 25 avenue du Maréchal Maunoury, 75016 Paris, France (office). *Telephone:* 1-45-27-14-50 (home); 6-12-97-49-28 (mobile) (home). *E-mail:* serge.feneuille@orange.fr (home).

FENG, Duan; Chinese physicist; *Professor of Physics, Nanjing University;* b. 27 April 1923, Suzhou City, Jiangsu Prov.; s. of Feng Zhou-bai and Yan Su-qing; m.

Chen Lianfang 1955; three d.; ed Nat. Cen. Univ., Nanjing; Prof. of Physics, Nanjing Univ. 1978–; Dir of Grad. School of Nanjing Univ. 1984–88; Dir Nat. Lab. of Solid State Microstructures 1986–95; mem. Chinese Acad. of Sciences 1980–; Pres. Chinese Physical Soc. 1991–95; Fellow, the Third World Acad. of Sciences 1993–; State Prize for Natural Sciences 1982, 1995, 2003, 2004, State Prize for Progress of Science and Tech. 1997, 1998, Tan Kah Kee Prize in Math. and Physics 1999. *Publications:* Physics of Metals (Vols 1–4) 1987–99, New Perspective on Condensed Matter Physics 1992, Introduction to Condensed Matter Physics, Vol. I 2005. *Leisure interest:* literature. *Address:* Institute of Solid State Physics, Nanjing University, Nanjing 210008, Jiangsu Province, People's Republic of China. *Telephone:* (25) 83593705 (office); (25) 83592906 (home). *Fax:* (25) 83590535 (office); (25) 83300535. *E-mail:* duanf@netra.nju.edu.cn (home).

FENG, Gong; Chinese actor and film director; b. Dec. 1957, Tianjin; joined China Railway Art Work Troupe 1980; actor, China Broadcasting Art Troupe 1984–; performs comic dialogues with Niu Qun; numerous prizes. *Films include:* Xiao po qing wang 1987, Li hun he tong 1990, Zhanzhi luo bie paxia 1993, Meishi touzhe le (Steal Happiness) 1998, Shui shuo wo bu zai hu (The Marriage Certificate) 2001, Eat Hot Tofu Slowly 2005, Getting Home 2007, A Simple Noodle Story 2009, Just Call Me Nobody 2010, The Founding of a Party 2011, The Grandmasters 2012. *Address:* China Broadcasting Art Troupe, Beijing, People's Republic of China.

FENG, He; Chinese sculptor; b. 12 Nov. 1931, Peixian, Jiangsu Prov.; s. of Feng Zigu and Chen Jiechen; m. Zhou Ji 1965; one s.; ed Cen. Inst. of Fine Arts; mem. Sculpture Research Studio, Inst. of Fine Arts, Deputy Dir 1981–84, Vice-Dir 1988–; specialized in ceramics and animal sculpture; exhibited work China Art Gallery 1979, 1981, also in France and Burma. *Works include:* Woman's Head 1958, The Master of the Land 1964, Doe 1964, Bellicose Goat 1978, Buffalo 1979, You are Always in Our Hearts Dear Premier Zhou 1979, Ah Bing the Blind Man 1979, Buffalo and the Leopard 1985, Moonlight 1985, Winter 1986, Monument of Juvenile Heroes, The Song of the Young Pioneer 1990, Dream 1990, 12 Animals, Young Pioneer Park 1991. *Leisure interest:* drama. *Address:* Central Institute of Fine Arts, East Beijing 100730, People's Republic of China (office). *Telephone:* 55-4731 (ext. 391) (office).

FENG, Jicai; Chinese writer and artist; *Director, Feng Jicai Research Institute of Arts and Literature;* b. 9 Feb. 1942, Tianjin, Zhejiang Prov.; s. of Feng Jifu and Ge Changfu; m. Gu Tongzhao; ed Tianjin Middle School; painter, Tianjin Calligraphic and Painting Studio 1962; writer, Tianjin Municipal Writers' Asscn 1978; joined China Asscn for Promoting Democracy 1983, currently Vice-Chair. 10th Cen. Cttee; Exec. Vice-Chair. China Fed. of Literary and Art Circles 1988, 2001–, Chinese Writers' Asscn 1986 (mem. Council 1986), Chinese Soc. for the Study of Folk Literature and Art 1986, UNESCO Int. Folk Arts Org.; Chair. Fiction Soc. of China 2000–; Dir Feng Jicai Research Inst. of Arts and Literature and Hon. Dean School of Social Sciences and Foreign Languages, Tianjin Univ. 2001–; Ed.-in-Chief Free Forum on Literature 1986; Ed. Artists; mem. 6th CPPCC Nat. Cttee 1983–88, 7th CPPCC Nat. Cttee 1988–93, 8th CPPCC Nat. Cttee 1993–98, Standing Cttee 9th CPPCC Nat. Cttee 1998–2003. *Publications:* Magic Whip 1984, Gratitude to Life 1991, Legend of Magic Lamp, Tall Woman and Her Dwarf Husband, Sculpted Pipe, Crysanthemums and other stories. *Address:* Tianjin Municipal Federation of Literary and Art Circles, Tianjin, People's Republic of China (office). *Website:* fengjicai.artron.net.

FENG, Lanrui; Chinese economist; b. 17 Sept. 1920, Guiyang, Guizhou Province; d. of Feng Shaotang and Xie Guangyu; m. Li Chang 1946; two s. two d.; ed Senior Party School of the CCP Cen. Cttee; Sr Research Fellow, Inst. of Marxism-Leninism and Mao Zedong Thought, Chinese Acad. of Social Sciences 1980–, Deputy Dir 1980–82, Adviser 1983–86; mem. Editorial Cttee, Encyclopedia of People's Repub. of China, for vol. Scientific Socialism 1980–93, A Comprehensive Dictionary of Economics, for vol. Population, Labour and Consumption 1983–92; Sr Adviser, Economy in the Special Zone 1989–; mem. Cttee of Specialists, Social Security in China 2002–; Sec.-Gen. China Council of Econ. Asscns 1981–91; mem. Standing Cttee Chinese People's Friendship Asscn 1988–93; Sun Yefang Prize for econ. article of 1984, Xinhya Digests Prize for Most Impressive Article of the Year 1998. *Publications include:* Labour: Payment and Employment (collected articles) 1982, Regarding the Principle – To Each According to his Work, Chinese Research on Employment Theory 1982, Urban Employment and Wages in China (co-author) 1982, On the Relationship between Employment and Economic Growth (co-author) 1983, The Worldwide New Industrialization and China's Socialist Modernization (co-author) 1984, On Letting Some People Get Rich Ahead of Others 1984, The Incomplete Form of Distribution According to Work at the Initial Stage of Socialism 1985, Overcome Egalitarianism and Let Some People Get Rich Ahead of Others 1985, The Double Hundred Policy and Science Associations 1986, Distribution According to Work, Wage and Employment 1988, Employment at the Initial Stage of Socialism (co-author) 1988, On the Ageing of the Chinese Population 1989, The Labour Market of China 1991, Actively Foster the Labour Market 1995, Can Inflation be Reduced under 10% for the Current Year?, Unemployment in China: 21% by the year 2000? 1996 (Impressive Article of the Year 1998), The Restructuring of China's Social Security System 1997, Selected Works on Economics of Feng Lanrui (two vols) 1999, Forward in the Same Ship: A Suggestion for Amending the PRC Constitution 2002, Living in the People's Heart 2006 and numerous articles on the market economy including contribs to China Economics Daily, Studies in the Market Economy, Hu Yaobong. *Leisure interest:* literature. *Address:* 34 Dongzongbu Hutong, Beijing 100005, People's Republic of China (home). *Telephone:* 65124654 (home).

FENG, Mengbo; Chinese pop artist; b. 1966, Beijing; ed Print-Making Dept, Cen. Acad. of Fine Arts, Beijing; work consists of computer animations and paintings which resemble video-game screens; has exhibited at galleries in Germany, London, Sydney, Taipei and Hong Kong and at 45th Venice Biennale 1993; Interactive Art award, Prix Ars Electronica (Austria) 2004. *Works include:* Game Over: The Long March 1994, My Private Album (interactive installation) 1997, Q4U 2002, Taking Mount Doom by Strategy, Phantom Tales, Streetfighter (painting series), Long March Restart 2009. *Leisure interest:* collecting industrial antiques. *Address:* c/o Art So Close, No 7, Tianwei 4th Street, Tianzhu Airport Industrial Zone A Shunyi, Beijing 101312, People's Republic of China.

FENG, Xiaogang; Chinese screenwriter, director and actor; b. 1958, Beijing; m. Xu Fan 1999; ed Beijing Broadcasting Acad.; art designer Beijing TV Art Centre 1985; began writing film and TV screenplays 1989; Hundred-Flower Award for Party A, Party B. *Films:* Zaoyu jiqing (Unexpected Passion) (writer) 1991, After Separation 1992, Yong shi wo ai (Lost My Love) (writer) 1994, The Funeral of a Famous Star, Living in Dire Strait, Jiafang yifang (The Dream Factory) (actor, dir) 1997, Bu jian bu san (Be There or Be Square) (writer, dir) 1998, Sorry, Baby 1999, Yi sheng tan xi (A Sigh) (writer, dir) 2000, Baba (Father) (actor) 2000, Da wan (Big Shot's Funeral) (writer, dir) 2001, Shui shuo wo bu zai hu (The Marriage Certificate) (actor) 2001, Shou ji (dir, producer) 2003, Ka la shi tiao gou (Cala, My Dog!) (exec. producer) 2003, Tian xia wu zei (A World Without Thieves) (writer, dir) 2004, Gong fu (actor) 2004, The Banquet 2006, The Assembly 2007, Trivial Matters (actor) 2007, The Nobles (writer, dir) 2008, If You Are the One 2008, Aftershock 2010, If You Are the One 2 2010. *Television:* Lend Me a Little Love, A Beijing Man in New York (TV Gold Eagle Award). *Publications:* After Separation 1992, A Born Coward 1994, Stories in the Editorial Office. *Address:* Beijing Television Art Centre, Beijing, People's Republic of China (office).

FENG, Ying; Chinese ballet dancer; *Director and Artistic Director, National Ballet of China;* b. 28 Feb. 1963, Harbin; m. James Y. Ho 1989; one d.; ed Beijing Dance Acad.; Paris Opera Ballet School 1982–83; apptd Prin. Dancer, Cen. Ballet of China 1980; leading role in many classical and Chinese ballets; Guest Artist, 2nd Paris Int. Ballet Competition 1986; toured USA, UK, Russia, Japan, Singapore, Hong Kong, Taiwan; left stage 1997 to concentrate on training new generation of dancers; Deputy Dir, Nat. Ballet of China 2004–09, Dir and Artistic Dir 2009–; mem. Chinese Dancers' Asscn 1982, China Ballet Art Soc. 1992; Leader Cen. Corps de Ballet 2008; First Prize Pas de Deux, Nat. Ballet Competition 1987, award at 5th Japan World Ballet Competition 1987, First Class Dancer of the State 1987. *Address:* Central Ballet of China, 3 Taiping Street, Beijing 100050, People's Republic of China. *Website:* www.ballet.org.cn/en (office).

FENIC, František (Fero); Slovak producer, writer and media executive; *Director, FEBIO s.r.o.;* b. 20 March 1951, Nižná Šebastová; ed Comenius Univ., Bratislava, FAMU/Acad. of Musical Arts, Prague, Czech Repub.; mil. service 1978–79; Dir Studio of Short Films, Slovak Film Production, Bratislava 1979–83, 1985–86, Barrandov Film Studio Prague 1984; film-making interrupted for political reasons March 1984; freelance tourist guide, Youth Travel Agency 1986–92; f. FEBIO s.r.o. 1991, Dir 1992–; '1 June 1953' Journalism Award. *Films include:* over 20 documentary films and full-length films, including Vlak dospelosti, Praha slzám neverí, Noc, kdy se rospadl stát, Dzusový román (also screenwriter) 1984, Zvlástní bytosti (also screenwriter) 1990, Ceská soda 1998. *Television includes:* GEN, GENUS, OKO, VIP – Influential People, Czech Soda, The Way We Live. *Publication:* Encyclopedia of Slovak Dramatic Arts 1989. *Leisure interest:* travel. *Address:* FEBIO s.r.o., Ruzová 13, 110 00 Prague 1 (office); Vejvodova 4, 11000 Prague 1, Czech Republic (home). *Website:* www.ferofenic.cz.

FENN, Sir Nicholas M., GCMG, MA; British fmr diplomatist; b. 19 Feb. 1936, London; s. of the late Rev. Prof. J. E. Fenn and Kathleen Fenn (née Harrison); m. Susan Clare Russell 1959; two s. one d.; ed Kingswood School, Bath and Peterhouse, Cambridge; Flying Officer, RAF 1954–56; Third Sec., Mandalay, then Rangoon 1959–63, Asst Pvt. Sec. to Sec. of State for Foreign Affairs 1963–67, First Sec. British Interests Section, Swiss Embassy, Algiers 1967–69, First Sec. and Spokesman, UK Mission to the UN, New York 1969–72, Deputy Head of Energy Dept FCO 1972–75, Counsellor, Embassy in Beijing 1975–77, Royal Coll. of Defence Studies 1978, Head of News Dept and Foreign Office Spokesman 1979–82; Amb. to Burma 1982–86, to Ireland 1986–91; High Commr in India 1991–96; Chief Exec. Marie Curie Cancer Care 1996–2000, Chair. 2000–06, Vice-Pres.; Jt Chair. Encounter 1998–2003; Trustee Sight Savers Int. 1996–2005, Vice-Pres. 2005–; Trustee, Guide Dogs for the Blind 2002–06; Gov. Kingswood School, Bath 1996–2006, Jawaharlal Nehru Memorial Trust 1998–2006; Churchwarden, Parish Church of St Michael and All Angels, Marden, Kent 2001–06; Patron, Arpana India, Village Service Trust India, Catriona Hargreaves Charitable Trust, Safe Anaesthesia Worldwide, Marden Heritage Centre; Hon. Fellow, Peterhouse, Cambridge. *Leisure interests:* grandchildren. *Address:* c/o Oxford and Cambridge Club, 71 Pall Mall, London, SW1Y 5HD, England.

FENTENER VAN VLISSINGEN, Annemiek M.; Dutch business executive; *Chairman of the Supervisory Board, SHV Holdings NV;* b. 14 April 1961; ed Univ. of Groningen; fmr Man. of Strategy and Business Devt, SHV Holdings NV, currently Chair. Supervisory Bd; mem. Supervisory Bd Draka Holding NV 2001– (Deputy Chair. 2006–), Flint Holding NV, Heineken NV 2006–; fmr mem. Bd of Dirs Ubbink/Buco; mem. Supervisory Bd Stadsherstel Amsterdam 2009–; mem. NPM Capital NV, Audit and Governance Cttee, Remuneration and Nomination Cttee. *Address:* SHV Holdings NV, Rijnkade 1, 3511 LC Utrecht, Netherlands (office). *Telephone:* (30) 233-88-33 (office). *Fax:* (30) 233-83-04 (office). *E-mail:* info@shv.nl (office). *Website:* www.shv.nl (office).

FENTIE, Dennis G.; Canadian politician and business executive; b. 8 Nov. 1950, Edmonton, Alberta; Owner and Man. Francis River Construction Ltd; elected MLA (New Democratic Party) for Watson Lake, Yukon Territory 1996–; joined Yukon Party May 2002–, Leader June 2002–; Premier of the Yukon 2002–11; fmr Dir Watson Lake Chamber of Commerce; fmr Commr Yukon Forest Comm.; fmr Dir Asscn of Yukon Forests. *Leisure interests:* baseball, hockey, history, current affairs. *Address:* c/o Government of Yukon, Box 2703, Whitehorse, Yukon Y1A 2C6, Canada (office).

FENTON, James Martin, MA, FRSL, FRSA, FSA; British poet, writer and journalist; b. 25 April 1949, Lincoln; s. of Rev. Canon J. C. Fenton and Mary Hamilton Ingoldby; ed Durham Choristers School, Repton School, Magdalen Coll., Oxford; Asst Literary Ed., New Statesman 1971, Editorial Asst 1972, Political Columnist 1976–78; freelance corresp. in Indo-China 1973–75; German Corresp., The Guardian 1978–79; Theatre Critic, Sunday Times 1979–84; Chief Book Reviewer, The Times 1984–86; Far East Corresp. The Independent 1986–88, columnist 1993–95; Prof. of Poetry, Univ. of Oxford 1994–99, Trustee, Nat. Gallery London 2002, Visitor, Ashmolean Museum 2003; Hon. Fellow, Magdalen Coll., Oxford 1999; Antiquary to the RA 2002; Queen's Gold Medal for Poetry 2007. *Publications include:* Our Western Furniture 1968, Terminal Moraine 1972, A Vacant Possession 1978, A German Requiem 1980, Dead Soldiers 1981, The

Memory of War 1982, You Were Marvellous 1983, Children in Exile 1984, Poems 1968–83 1985, The Fall of Saigon (in Granta 15) 1985, The Snap Revolution (in Granta 18) 1986, Cambodian Witness: The Autobiography of Someth May (ed.) 1986, Partingtime Hall (poems, with John Fuller) 1987, All the Wrong Places: Adrift in the Politics of Asia 1989, Manila Envelope 1989, Underground in Japan, by Rey Ventura (ed.) 1992, Out of Danger (poems) 1993, Collected Stories by Ernest Hemingway (ed.), Leonardo's Nephew: Essays on Art and Artists 1998, The Strength of Poetry: Oxford Lectures, An Introduction to English Poetry 2002, A Garden from a Hundred Packets of Seed, The Love Bomb & Other Musical Pieces 2003, Selected Poems 2006, Yellow Tulips: Poems 1968-2011 2012; trans.: Verdi's Rigoletto 1982, Simon Boccanegra 1985, Tamar's Revenge 2004; libretti: Haroun and the Sea of Stories (composer Charles Wuorinen) 2004, Tsunami Song Cycle (composer Dominic Muldowney) 2009; theatre: Pictures from an Exhibition 2009. *Address:* c/o United Agents, 12–26 Lexington Street, London, W1F 0LE, England (office). *Telephone:* (20) 3214-0800 (office). *Fax:* (20) 3214-0801 (office). *E-mail:* info@unitedagents.co.uk (office). *Website:* www.unitedagents.co.uk (office); www .jamesfenton.com (home).

FENTY, Adrian Malik, BA, JD; American lawyer and politician; b. 6 Dec. 1970, Washington, DC; s. of Philip Fenty and Jan Fenty; m. Michelle Cross; twin s. one d.; ed Mackin Catholic High School, Oberlin Coll., Howard Univ. School of Law, Washington, DC; passed DC Bar; worked as intern for Senator Howard Metzenbaum (Democrat-OH), Del. Eleanor Holmes Norton (Democrat-DC), and Rep. Joseph P. Kennedy II (Democrat-Mass) before becoming involved in local politics; served as ANC 4C Commr and Treas. and Pres. 16th Street Neighborhood Civic Asscn; lead attorney and Counsel for Washington, DC City Council's Cttee on Educ., Libraries and Recreation –2000; mem. Washington, DC City Council representing Ward 4 2001–07 (re-elected 2004), Chair. Cttee on Human Services, overseeing Dept of Youth Rehabilitation Services, Child and Family Services Agency, Dept of Human Services, and Office on Aging; Mayor of Dist of Columbia (youngest ever mayor) 2007–11; signed with Greater Talent Network (speakers bureau) 2011; outside adviser, Rosetta Stone Inc. 2011–; mem. 16th Street Neighborhood Civic Asscn (fmr Pres.), Bd Lamond-Riggs Recreation Center, Friends of Upshur Recreation Center; Democrat; named to Power 150, Ebony magazine 2008, Commitment to Social Justice Award, DC Acorn, Courageous Community Service Award, Fed. of Citizens. *Leisure interest:* takes part regularly in triathlons and other races in DC and throughout region. *Address:* Rosetta Stone, 1919 North Lynn Street, 7th Floor, Arlington, VA 22209, USA (office); c/o Greater Talent Network Speakers Bureau, 437 Fifth Avenue, New York, NY 10016, USA (office). *Website:* www.rosettastone.com (office); www.greatertalent.com (office). *Telephone:* (212) 645-4200 (office). *Fax:* (212) 627-1471 (office). *E-mail:* info@greatertalent.com (office).

FÉRAUD, Pierre; French retail executive; ed École des Hautes Etudes Commerciales, Institut d'Etudes Politiques, Paris; fmrly with UIC-SOFAL (commercial bank) and GMF (insurance co.); joined Groupe Euris 1991, apptd Pres. Foncière Euris SA 1991, Pres. and CEO –2010, Admin. 2010–, Perm. Rep. of Euris on Bd of Dirs of Finatis; Chair. Carpinienne de Participations, Marigny Belfort, Matignon Marne La Vallée SAS, Mermoz Kléber SAS, Centre Commercial de l'Ile Saint-Denis, Marigny Concorde, Marigny Elysées, Marigny Expansion, Marigny Foncière, Marigny Participations, Marigny Percier, Marigny Valbréon, Marigny Tours, Matignon Abbeville, Matignon Bail, Matignon Corbeil Centre, Les Moulins à Vent, Matignon Meylan, Matignon Moselle; Dir, Casino Guichard Perrachon & Cie SA –2009, Rallye Group SA 1995–2010, Mercialys 2006–; Vice-Chair. Supervisory Bd Les Nouveaux Constructeurs SA 2006–; Man. Centrum NS Sarl, Alexanderplatz Voltairestrasse GmbH, Alexa Holding GmbH, amongst others. *Address:* Foncière Euris SA, 83 rue du Faubourg Saint-Honoré, 75008 Paris, France (office). *Telephone:* 1-44-71-14-00 (office). *Fax:* 1-44-71-14-50 (office). *E-mail:* info@fonciere-euris.fr (office). *Website:* www.fonciere-euris.fr (office).

FERGESA, Siraj; Ethiopian politician; *Minister of Defence;* Minister of Fed. Affairs 2005–08, of Defence 2008–; mem. South Ethiopian People's Democratic Movt. *Address:* Ministry of Defence, POB 1373, Addis Ababa, Ethiopia (office). *Telephone:* (11) 5511777 (office). *Fax:* (11) 5516053 (office).

FERGUS-THOMPSON, Gordon, FRCM; British pianist; *Professor of Piano, Royal College of Music;* b. 9 March 1952, Leeds, Yorks., England; s. of the late George Thompson and Constance Webb; ed Temple Moor Grammar School, Leeds and Royal Northern Coll. of Music; debut at Wigmore Hall 1976; has appeared as soloist with orchestras including Orchestra of the Hague, Gothenburg Symphony Orchestra, Royal Liverpool Philharmonic, The Philharmonia, City of Birmingham Symphony, Hallé, BBC Symphony; extensive tours in Europe, N America, Australia, Far East and S Africa; Prof. of Piano, Royal Coll. of Music 1996–; Gulbenkian Foundation Fellowship 1978; MRA Prize for Best Instrumental Recording of the Year 1991, 1992. *Recordings include:* The Rachmaninov Sonatas 1987, Balakirev and Scriabin Sonatas 1987, Complete Works of Debussy (five vols), Complete Works of Scriabin (five vols) 1990–2001, Rachmaninov's Etudes-Tableaux 1990, Bach Transcriptions 1990, Complete Works of Ravel (two vols) 1992, Headington: Piano Concerto 1997. *Leisure interests:* art, chess, cooking, tennis, humour. *Address:* 44 Courtfield Rise, West Wickham, BR4 9BH, Kent, England (home). *Telephone:* 7590-515645 (mobile) (office). *E-mail:* gfergusthompson@rcm.ac.uk (office). *Website:* www.gordonfergusthompson.com.

FERGUSON, Sir Alexander (Alex) Chapman, Kt, CBE, OBE; British fmr professional football manager and fmr football player; b. 31 Dec. 1941, Govan, Glasgow, Scotland; s. of the late Alexander Beaton Ferguson and Elizabeth Hardy; m. Catherine Holding 1966; three s.; ed Govan High School; amateur player (striker) with Queen's Park 1958–60, professional player with St Johnstone 1960–64 (won Scottish First Div. 1962–63), Dunfermline Athletic 1964–67, Glasgow Rangers 1967–69, Falkirk 1969–73 (won Scottish First Div. 1969–70), Ayr United 1973–74 (two Scottish League caps); managed the following clubs: East Stirling 1974, St Mirren 1974–78 (First Div. Champions 1976–77), Aberdeen 1978–86 (winners UEFA European Cup Winners' Cup 1983, UEFA Super Cup 1983, Scottish Premier Div. Champions 1980, 1984, 1985, Scottish FA Cup 1982, 1983, 1984, 1986, Scottish League Cup 1986), Scottish Nat. Team (Asst Man.) 1985–86, Manchester United 1986–2013 (winners FA Cup 1990, 1994, 1996, 1999, 2004, League Cup 1992, 2006, 2009, 2010, UEFA European Cup Winners' Cup 1991, UEFA Super Cup 1991, FA Premier League Championship 1992/93, 1993/94,

1995/96, 1996/97, 1998/99, 1999/2000, 2000/01, 2002/03, 2006/07, 2007/08, 2008/09, 2010/11, 2012/13, League and FA Cup double 1994 and 1996 (new record), UEFA Champions League European Cup 1999, 2008, FA Charity/Community Shield 1990 (shared), 1993, 1994, 1996, 1997, 2003, 2007, 2008, 2010, 2011, European-S American Cup 1999, FIFA Club World Cup 2008, announced retirement May 2013, now a Dir and Amb. for the club; Vice-Pres. Nat. Football Museum, Preston, Lancs.; mem. Exec. Cttee League Mans Asscn (LMA); only man. to win top league honours and Double north and south of England-Scotland border (winning the Premiership with Manchester United and Scottish Premier League with Aberdeen); won 49 trophies as a manager, making him the most successful British football manager in history; Freeman, Cities of Aberdeen, Glasgow and Manchester; Hon. MA (Salford) 1996, (Manchester) 1997; Hon. LLD (Robert Gordon) 1997, (St. Andrews) 2002; Jt Hon. MSc (Manchester Metropolitan), (UMIST) 1998; Hon. DLitt (Glasgow Caledonian) 2001; Hon. DUniv (Glasgow) 2001, (Stirling) 2011, (Manchester) 2011; Hon. DBA (Manchester Metropolitan) 2009; Hon. DSc (Ulster) 2012; Man. of the Year Scotland 1983–85, Man. of the Year England 1993–94, 1996, World Soccer Magazine World Manager of the Year 1993, 1999, 2007, 2008, Football Writers' Asscn Tribute Award 1996, Onze d'Or Coach of the Year 1999, 2007, Mussabini Medal 1999, voted Best Coach in Europe, UEFA Football Gala 1999, UEFA Champions League Manager of the Year 1998–99, LMA Man. of the Year 1998–99, 2007–08, 2010–11, 2012–13, BBC Sports Personality of the Year Coach Award 1999, BBC Sports Personality of the Year Team Award 1999, IFFHS Club Coach of the Year 1999, LMA Manager of the Decade 1990s, Laureus World Sports Award for Team of the Year 2000, BBC Sports Personality of the Year Lifetime Achievement Award 2001, an inaugural inductee into English Football Hall of Fame 2002, inaugural recipient of FA Coaching Diploma 2003, Professional Footballers' Assn Merit Award 2007, UEFA Team of the Year 2007, 2008, Premier League 10 Seasons Awards (1992/93–2001/02) (Manager of the Decade and Most Coaching Appearances — 392 games), Premier League Manager of the Year 1993–94, 1995–96, 1996–97, 1998–99, 1999–2000, 2002–03, 2006–07, 2007–08, 2008–09, 2010–11, LMA Special Merit Award 2011, Old Trafford North Stand officially renamed the Sir Alex Ferguson Stand in honour of his 25 years as manager 2011, bronze statue designed by Scottish sculptor Philip Jackson, and named after Ferguson, unveiled outside Old Trafford Nov. 2012. *Publications:* A Light in the North 1985, Alex Ferguson: Six Years at United 1992, Just Champion 1993, A Year in the Life: The Manager's Diary 1995, Alex Ferguson: 10 Glorious Years 1996, A Will to Win (co-author) 1997, Managing My Life: My Autobiography (co-author) 1999, The Unique Treble 2000, My Autobiography 2013. *Leisure interests* golf, snooker, horse racing, fine wine. *Address:* Manchester United FC, Old Trafford, Manchester, M16 0RA, England (office). *Telephone:* (161) 868-8103 (office). *Fax:* (161) 868-8807 (office). *Website:* www.manutd.com (office); www.mufcinfo.com/manupag/managers/mangers_pages/ferguson_alex.html.

FERGUSON, Iain, CBE; British business executive; *Chairman, Wilton Park Departmental Board and Advisory Council;* m. Catherine Ferguson; one d.; ed Univ. of St Andrews; Graduate Trainee, Unilever from 1977, various roles in operations, sales, industrial marketing, Chair. Plant Breeding International 1988–92, Chair. Unilever Plantation Group 1992–95, Exec. Chair. Birds Eye Walls 1995–2001, Sr Vice-Pres. Corp. Devt 2001–03; CEO Tate & Lyle PLC 2003–09; Chair. Wilton Park Departmental Board and Advisory Council 2009–; Commr Govt Comm. on the Future of Farming and Food 2001–02; fmr Pres. Food & Drink Fed., Inst. of Grocery Distribution; non-Exec. Dir Greggs PLC, Balfour Beatty PLC, Berendsen PLC, Rothamsted Research Ltd 1996–2005, Sygen International PLC 2002–06; mem. DEFRA Supervisory Bd; fmr mem. Dept of Trade and Industry Foresight Panel, Bd of Companies House; Hon. Vice-Pres. British Nutrition Foundation; Forbes magazine European Businessman of the Year 2004. *Address:* Wilton Park, Wiston House, Steyning, West Sussex, BN44 3DZ, England (office). *Telephone:* (1903) 817766 (office). *Fax:* (1903) 815931 (office). *E-mail:* iain .ferguson@wiltonpark.org.uk (office). *Website:* www.wiltonpark.org.uk (office).

FERGUSON, John, BCom, CA; Canadian chartered accountant and business executive; *Chairman, Suncor Corporation;* ed Univ. of Alberta; Founder and Chair. Princeton Developments Ltd, Princeton Ventures Ltd, Edmonton, Alberta; mem. Bd of Dirs Suncor Corpn 1995–, Chair. 2007–; mem. Bd of Dirs Fountain Tire Ltd, Royal Bank of Canada, Strategy Summit Ltd; Dir, C.D. Howe Inst., Alberta Bone and Joint Inst.; Advisory mem. Canadian Inst. for Advanced Research; Chancellor Emer. and Bd Govs Chair. Emer., Univ. of Alberta, mem. Business Advisory Council, School of Business; mem. World Presidents' Org.; Fellow, Alberta Inst. of Chartered Accountants, Inst. of Corp. Dirs; Hon. Lt Col, South Alberta Light Horse; Mem. of the Order of Canada 2011; Hon. LLD (Univ. of Alberta) 1996; Commemorative Medal for 125th Anniversary of Confed. of Canada 1992, inducted into Jr Achievement Alberta Business Hall of Fame 2001, Golden Jubilee Medal 2003, Alberta Centennial Medal 2005. *Address:* Suncor Energy Inc., PO Box 2844, 150 – 6 Avenue SW, Calgary, Alberta, T2P 3E3, Canada (office). *Telephone:* (403) 296-8000 (office). *Fax:* (403) 296-3030 (office). *E-mail:* info@suncormail.com (office). *Website:* www.suncor.com (office).

FERGUSON, Niall Campbell, MA, DPhil; British historian, writer, academic and television presenter; *Laurence A. Tisch Professor of History, Harvard University;* b. 18 April 1964, Glasgow, Scotland; s. of James Campbell Ferguson and Molly Hamilton; m. 1st Susan M. Douglas 1994 (divorced 2011); two s. one d.; m. 2nd Ayaan Hirsi Ali 2011; one s.; ed Univ. of Oxford; Fellow, Christ's Coll., Cambridge 1989–90, Peterhouse, Cambridge 1990–92, Jesus Coll. Oxford 1992–2013; Houblon Norman Fellowship, Bank of England 1998–89; Prof. of Political and Financial History, Univ. of Oxford 2000–02; Herzog Prof. of Financial History, Stern School of Business, New York Univ. 2002–04; Laurence A. Tisch Prof. of History, Harvard Univ. 2004–, William Ziegler Prof. of Business Admin, Harvard Business School 2006–11; Sr Fellow, Hoover Inst., Stanford Univ. 2003–; Founder Chimerica Media Ltd 2006–, Greenmantle LLC 2011–; Philippe Roman Visiting Prof., LSE 2010–11; consultant, GLG Partners (hedge fund) 2007–11; Sr Adviser, Morgan Stanley 2007–09; Trustee Museum of Financial History, New York 2008–, New York Historical Soc. 2009–, American Acad. in Berlin 2011–; Bd mem. Centre for Policy Studies, London 2009–; GetAbstract Int. Book Award 2009, Benjamin Franklin Award for Public Service 2010, Hayek Lifetime Achievement Award 2012, BBC Reith Lecturer 2012, Estoril Global Issues Distinguished Book Prize 2013, Ludwig Erhard Prize for Economic Journalism 2013. *Film:* Kissinger (Best Documentary, New York Film Festival 2011) 2011. *Television:* Empire: How

Britain Made the Modern World 2003, American Colossus 2004, The War of the World 2006, The Ascent of Money (International Emmy for Best Documentary 2009) 2008, Civilization: Is the West History? 2011, China: Triumph and Turmoil 2012. *Publications:* Paper and Iron: Hamburg Business and German Politics in the Era of Inflation 1897–1927 1995, (ed.) Virtual History: Alternatives and Counterfactuals 1997, The World's Banker: A History of the House of Rothschild (Wadsworth Prize for Business History 1998) 1998, The Pity of War 1998, The Cash Nexus: Money and Power in the Modern World 2001, Empire: How Britain Made the Modern World 2003, Colossus: the Price of America's Empire 2004, The War of The World: History's Age of Hatred 2006, The Ascent of Money: A Financial History of the World 2008, High Financier: The Lives and Times of Siegmund Warburg 2010, Civilization: The West and the Rest 2011, The Great Degeneration: How Institutions Decay and Economies Die 2012. *Leisure interests:* reading, hiking, playing the double bass, surfing, skiing. *Address:* Harvard University, Minda de Gunzberg Center for European Studies, Adolphus Busch Hall, 27 Kirkland Street, Cambridge, MA 02138, USA (office). *Telephone:* (617) 495-4303 (office). *Fax:* (617) 496-9594 (office). *E-mail:* nfergus@fas.harvard.edu (office). *Website:* www.ces.fas.harvard.edu (office); www.niallferguson.com.

FERGUSON, Rodwell; Belizean politician; MP for Stann Creek West Area; fmr Minister of State for Tourism, Nat. Devt and Educ.; Minister of Defence, Youth and Sports 2007–08; fmr Vice-Pres. Belize Nat. Comm. for UNESCO; mem. People's United Party. *Address:* c/o People's United Party, 3 Queen Street, Belize City, Belize. *Telephone:* 223-2428. *Fax:* 223-3476. *Website:* www.pupbelize.bz.

FERGUSON, Roger Walter, Jr, BA, JD, PhD; American business executive; *President and CEO, TIAA-CREF;* b. 28 Oct. 1951, Washington, DC; m. Annette Nazareth; two c.; ed Harvard Univ.; attorney with Davis Polk & Wardwell, New York 1981–84; Assoc. and Partner, McKinsey & Co. 1984–97, Dir of Research and Information Services; mem. Bd Govs US Fed. Reserve, Washington, DC 1997–2006, Vice-Chair. 1999–2006 (resgnd); Chair. America Holding Corpn and Head of Financial Services, Swiss Re 2006–08; Pres. and CEO TIAA-CREF (Teachers Insurance and Annuity Asscn-Coll. Retirement Equities Fund), New York 2008–, Overseer and TIAA Trustee 2008–; Co-Chair. Nat. Research Council panel on the Long-Run Macro-Econ. Effects of the Aging US Population 2010–; mem. Bd of Dirs Partnership for New York City; mem. Council on Foreign Relations, Econ. Club of New York, Group of Thirty Consultative Group on Int. Econ. and Monetary Affairs, Inc. (G-30), Washington, DC, Pres. Obama's Econ. Recovery Advisory Bd 2009–, Business Higher Educ. Forum, Comm. on the Future of Grad. Educ.; mem. Bd of Overseers, Harvard Univ. (Pres. 2008–09), Bd of Dirs Harvard Alumni Asscn; mem. Bd of Trustees, Nat. Bureau of Econ. Research, Inst. for Advanced Study, Carnegie Endowment for Int. Peace, New America Foundation, Memorial Sloan-Kettering Cancer Center; Treas. Friends of Educ. (a Trustees' Cttee of The Museum of Modern Art); Trustee, Cttee for Econ. Devt 2008–, Co-Chair. 2011–; Hon. Fellow, Pembroke Coll. Cambridge; Dr hc (Lincoln Coll., Webster Univ.); Distinguished Service Award, Bond Market Asscn 2002, Econs in Government Distinguished Lecturer sponsored by Soc. of Govt Economists and American Econ. Asscn 2004, The George Mitchell Payments Systems Excellence Award, NACHA—The Electronic Payments Asscn (fmrly the Nat. Automated Clearing House Asscn) 2005, The William F. Butler Memorial Award, New York Asscn for Business Econs 2006, The Renaissance Award, Abyssinian Devt Corpn 2006, The Frederick Heldering Global Leadership Award, Global Interdependence Center 2006, first GAIM/CERF Global Financial Policy Award for significant contribs to effective governance of global capital markets, Global Alternative Investment Man. Forum (GAIM) and Cambridge Endowment for Research in Finance (CERF) 2007, Good Scout Award, Nat. Capital Area Boy Scout Council 2007, Visionary Award, Council for Econ. Educ. 2009, Good Scout Award, Greater New York Boy Scout Councils 2009, Nat. Council of ISACs Critical Infrastructure Protection Award 2010, Business Achievement Award, African American Chamber of Commerce of NJ 2011, Leadership Award, St Aloysius School for outstanding public service and commitment to improving the lives of New York City's children and families 2011. *Publications include:* International Financial Stability, Geneva Report No. 9 (co-author) 2007, The Structure of Financial Supervision: Approaches and Challenges in a Global Marketplace (co-author) 2008. *Address:* TIAA-CREF, 730 Third Avenue, New York, NY 10017, USA (office). *Telephone:* (212) 916-6240 (office). *Fax:* (212) 916-6230 (office). *E-mail:* trustees@tiaa-cref.org (office). *Website:* www.tiaa-cref.org (office).

FERGUSON-McHUGH, Mary Lynn, BS, MBA; American business executive; *Group President, Western Europe and Global Discounter & Pharmacy Channels, Proctor & Gamble;* b. 1 Oct. 1959, Oakland, Calif.; ed Univ. of the Pacific, Univ. of Pennsylvania Wharton School; with Doubleday & Co. 1981–84; joined Proctor & Gamble (P&G) 1986, Brand Asst to Asst Brand Man., Vicks NyQuil 1986–88, Asst Brand Man., Vicks 1988–90, Brand Man. 1990–91, Brand Man., Vicks NyQuil/DayQuil 1991–93, Marketing Dir Global Speed Teams, Egham, UK 1993–94, Marketing Dir Managed Care Team 1994–95, Marketing Dir PHC US (Respiratory/GI) 1995–99, Gen. Man., North America, Personal Health Care 1999–2001, Vice-Pres. 2001–03, Vice-Pres. Global Personal Health Care 2003–05, Vice-Pres. North America, Family Care 2005–07, Pres. Family Care 2007–10, Group Pres. Global Family Care 2010–11, Group Pres. Western Europe and Global Discounter & Pharmacy Channels, P&G 2011–; mem. Advisory Bd, Center for Brand and Product Man., Univ. of Wisconsin; fmr Treas., New York City PanHellenic; fmr mem. Bd of Trustees, Art Acad. of Cincinnati; fmr mem. United Way of Greater Cincinnati; fmr Mentor with Cincinnati Youth Collaborative; fmr mem. Bd of Dirs YWCA; ranked by Fortune magazine amongst the 50 Most Powerful Women in Business outside the US (29th) 2012. *Address:* The Procter & Gamble Co., Rutistrasse 26, 8952 Schlieren, Switzerland (office). *Telephone:* (58) 0046111 (office). *Website:* www.pg.com/fr_CH (office); www.pg.com/de_CH (office).

FERGUSON-SMITH, Malcolm Andrew, MB ChB, MA, FRS, FRSE, FRCPath, FRCP (Glas), FRCOG, FMedSci; British professor of pathology; *Research Professor Emeritus, Department of Veterinary Medicine, University of Cambridge;* b. 5 Sept. 1931, Glasgow, Scotland; s. of John Ferguson-Smith and Ethel May Ferguson-Smith (née Thorne); m. Marie Eva Gzowska 1960; one s. three d.; ed Stowe School, Univ. of Glasgow; Registrar in Lab. Medicine, Dept of Pathology, Western Infirmary, Glasgow 1958–59; Fellow in Medicine and Instructor, Johns Hopkins Univ. School of Medicine 1959–61; Lecturer, Sr Lecturer, then Reader in Medical

Genetics, Univ. of Glasgow 1961–73, Prof. 1973–87; Prof. of Pathology, Univ. of Cambridge 1987–98, Research Prof. Emer., Dept of Veterinary Medicine 1998–; Fellow, Peterhouse Coll., Cambridge 1987–98; Dir West of Scotland Medical Genetics Service 1973–87, East Anglian Regional Clinical Genetics Service 1987–95; Pres. Clinical Genetics Soc. 1979–81, European Soc. of Human Genetics 1997–98, Int. Soc. for Prenatal Diagnosis 1998–2002, Asscn of Clinical Cytogeneticists 2003–05; Ed. Prenatal Diagnosis 1980–2006; mem. Johns Hopkins Univ. Soc. of Scholars; mem. BSE Inquiry Cttee 1997–2000; Foreign mem. Polish Acad. of Science 1988, Nat. Acad. of Medicine Buenos Aires 2002; Hon. Consultant in Medical Paediatrics, Royal Hosp. for Sick Children, Glasgow 1966–73, in Clinical Genetics, Yorkhill and Assoc. Hosps 1973–87, in Medical Genetics, Addenbrooke's Hosp., Cambridge 1987–98; Hon. Assoc., Royal Coll. of Veterinary Surgeons 2002; Hon. DSc (Strathclyde) 1992, (Glasgow) 2002; Bronze Medal, Univ. of Helsinki 1968, Makdougall-Brisbane Prize of Royal Soc. of Edinburgh 1984–86, San Remo Int. Prize for Research in Genetics 1990, Mauro Baschirotto Award for achievements in human genetics 1996, Sir James Y. Simpson Award 1998, J.B.S. Haldane Medal 2000, McLaughlin-Gallie Professorship, Royal Coll. of Physicians and Surgeons of Canada 2001, Pruzansky Lecture, American Coll. of Medical Genetics 2008. *Publications:* Early Prenatal Diagnosis (ed.) 1983, Essential Medical Genetics (co-author) 1984 (sixth edn 2011), Prenatal Diagnosis and Screening (co-ed.) 1992; papers on cytogenetics, gene mapping, human genetics, comparative genomics, evolutionary biology and prenatal diagnosis in medical and scientific journals. *Leisure interests:* swimming, sailing, fishing. *Address:* Department of Veterinary Medicine, University of Cambridge, Madingley Road, Cambridge, CB3 0ES, England (office). *Telephone:* (1223) 766496 (office). *Fax:* (1223) 766496 (office). *E-mail:* maf12@cam.ac.uk (office). *Website:* www.vet.cam.ac.uk/genomics (office).

FERGUSSON, Sir Ewen Alastair John, GCMG, GCVO, MA; British diplomatist (retd); b. 28 Oct. 1932, Singapore; s. of the late Sir Ewen MacGregor Field Fergusson and Lady (Winifred Evelyn) Fergusson; m. Sara Carolyn Montgomery Cuninghame (née Gordon Lennox) 1959; one s. two d.; ed Rugby and Oriel Coll., Oxford; 2nd Lt 60th Rifles (KRRC) 1954–56; Foreign (Diplomatic) Service 1956–92; Asst Pvt. Sec. to Minister of Defence 1957–59; British Embassy, Addis Ababa 1960; FCO 1963; British Trade Devt Office, New York 1967; Counsellor and Head of Chancery, Office of UK Perm. Rep. to EEC 1972–75; Pvt. Sec. to Foreign and Commonwealth Sec. 1975–78, Asst Under-Sec. of State 1978–82; Amb. to SA 1982–84, to France 1987–92; Deputy Under-Sec. of State 1984–87; Chair. (non-exec.) Coutts & Co. 1993–99, Savoy Hotel Group 1995–98 (Dir 1993–98); Dir (non-exec.) BT 1993–99, Sun Alliance 1993–96; Chair. Rugby School 1995–2002 (Gov. 1985–2002); Trustee, Nat. Gallery 1995–2002, Henry Moore Foundation 1998– (Chair. 2001–07); Hon. Fellow, Oriel Coll. Oxford 1988; Grand Officier, Légion d'honneur 1992, King of Arms 1996–2007; Hon. LLD (Aberdeen) 1995. *Achievements:* played rugby for Oxford Univ. 1952–53, for Scotland (five caps) 1954 and for the Barbarians 1954. *Address:* 111 Iverna Court, London, W8 6TX (office); 22 Iverna Gardens, London, W8 6TN, England (home). *Telephone:* (20) 7937-2240 (office); (20) 7937-5545 (home). *Fax:* (20) 7938-1136 (office); (20) 7376-0418 (home). *E-mail:* sir.ewenfergusson@btinternet.com (office).

FERIANTO, Djaduk; Indonesian composer and musician; b. 19 July 1964, Java; s. of Bagong Kussudiardja; brother of Butet Kertaredjasa; Founder and leader of group Kua Etnika 1996–; f. Padepokan Seni Bagong K Foundation. *Compositions include:* Kompi Susu (Milk Brigade), Brigade Mailing (Thieves' Brigade). *Address:* c/o Padepokan Seni Bagong K Foundation, Jogjakarta, Indonesia.

FERLAND, E. James, BSc, MBA; American energy industry executive (retd); b. 19 March 1942, Boston; ed Univ. of Maine, Univ. of New Haven, Harvard Grad. School of Business Admin; began career as engineer, The Hartford Electric Light Co., CT 1964–67; mem. operating staff Millstone Nuclear Power Station 1967–76, Station Superintendent 1976–78; Dir of Rate Regulatory Project, Corp. HQ, Northeast Utilities 1978–80, Exec. Vice-Pres. and Chief Financial Officer 1980–83, Pres. and COO 1983–86; Chair., Pres. and CEO Public Service Enterprise Group Inc. (PSEG) 1986–2007; Chair. and CEO Public Service Electric and Gas Co. (PSE&G) 1986–91, Pres. 1986–91; Chair. and CEO PSEG Energy Holdings LLC 1989–2007; fmr mem. Bd of Dirs Vermont Yankee Nuclear Power Corpn, Yankee Atomic Electric Co., Maine Yankee Atomic Power Co., The HSB Group Inc., Foster Wheeler Corpn; fmr mem. Bd Cttee for Econ. Devt; fmr Chair. NJ State Chamber of Commerce, Metro Newark Chamber of Commerce, Public Affairs Research Inst. of NJ, Inst. of Nuclear Power Operations, Electric Power Research Inst.; fmr mem. Bd NJ Performing Arts Center, Edison Electric Inst., Nuclear Energy Inst., American Gas Asscn, Asscn of Edison Illuminating Cos, NJ Utilities Asscn, The United Way of Tri-State. *Address:* c/o Public Service Enterprise Group Inc., 80 Park Plaza, Newark, NJ 07102, USA.

FERLINGHETTI, Lawrence, MA, PhD, DUniv; American writer and painter; b. 24 March 1920, Yonkers, New York; s. of Charles Ferlinghetti and Clemence Mendes-Monsanto; m. Selden Kirby-Smith 1951; one s. one d.; ed Columbia Univ., Univ. of Paris; served as Lt Commdr in USNR in World War II; co-f. (with Peter D. Martin) the first all-paperback bookshop in USA, City Lights Bookstore, San Francisco 1953; f. City Lights publishing co. 1955; arrested on obscenity charges following publ. of Allan Ginsberg's 'Howl' 1956 (later acquitted); participant One World Poetry Festival, Amsterdam 1980, World Congress of Poets, Florence 1986; First Poet Laureate of San Francisco 1998–99; Ed. City Lights Books; mem. Nat. Acad. of Arts and Letters 2003; Commdr, French Acad. of Arts and Letters 2007; Poetry Prize, City of Rome 1993, Premio Internazionale Fliano, Italy 1999, Premio Internazionale di Camaiore, Italy 1999, Premio Cavour, Italy 2000, Los Angeles Times Book Festival Lifetime Achievement Award 2001, Poetry Soc. of America Robert Frost Medal 2003, Nat. Book Foundation Literarian Award 2005, Douglas MacAgy Distinguished Achievement Award, San Francisco Art Inst. 2012. *Publications include:* Pictures of the Gone World (poems) 1955, Selections from Paroles by Jacques Prévert, A Coney Island of the Mind (poems) 1958, Berlin 1961, Her (novel), Starting from San Francisco (poems) 1961, Where is Vietnam? 1965, An Eye on the World 1967, After the Cries of the Birds 1967, Unfair Arguments with Existence (seven plays), Routines (plays), The Secret Meaning of Things (poems) 1969, Tyrannus Nix? (poem) 1969, The Mexican Night (travel journal) 1970, Back Roads to Far Places (poems) 1971, Open Eye, Open Heart (poems) 1973, Who Are We Now? 1976, Northwest Ecolog 1978, Landscapes of Living and Dying (poems) 1979, Literary San Francisco: A Pictorial History from the Beginnings to the Present (with Nancy J. Peters) 1980, Leaves of Life: Drawings from the Model 1983, The Populist Manifestos 1983, Over All the Obscene Boundaries (poems) 1984, Endless Life: Selected Poems 1984, Seven Days in Nicaragua Libre 1984, Inside the Trojan Horse 1987, Love in the Days of Rage (novel) 1988, When I Look at Pictures (poems and paintings) 1990, These Are My Rivers: New and Selected Poems 1993, A Far Rockaway of the Heart 1997, How to Paint Sunlight: New Poems 2001, Americus (Book One) 2004, Poetry as Insurgent Art (prose and poetry) 2007, At Sea 2011. *Address:* City Lights Bookstore, 261 Columbus Avenue, San Francisco, CA 94133, USA (office). *Telephone:* (415) 362-8193 (office). *Fax:* (415) 362-4921 (office). *Website:* www.citylights.com (office).

FERNALD, Ivan Christiaan; Suriname government official; fmr Dir Inst for Econ. Administrative Secondary Educ. (IMEAO); Minister of Defence 2005–10. *Address:* c/o Ministry of Defence, Kwattaweg 29, Paramaribo, Suriname (office).

FERNANDES, Anthony (Tony) Francis; Malaysian airline executive and fmr music industry executive; *Group CEO, AirAsia;* b. 1964, Kuala Lumpur; ed boarding school in England, LSE; started as auditor London accountancy firm 1987; fmr Financial Analyst, Virgin, Financial Controller Virgin TV Div. 1987–89; joined Warner Music 1989, youngest ever Man. Dir Warner Music (Malaysia), Vice-Pres. ASEAN Region, 1999–2001; co-founder Tune Air; bought Air Asia Sept. 2001, CEO AirAsia (Asia's first 'no frills' airline) and Tune Air (parent co. of AirAsia) 2001–; awarded title Setia Mahkota Selangor by HRH King of Malaysia Sultan Salahuddin Abdul Aziz Shah 1999; Joint Winner CEO of the Year 2003 American Express Corp. Services/Business Times, Emerging Entrepreneur of the Year 2003 Ernst & Young. *Address:* AirAsia Sdn Bhd, Lot N1, Level 4, Main Terminal Building, Kuala Lumpur International Airport, 64000 KLIA, Sepang, Selangor, Malaysia (office). *Telephone:* (3) 8660-4274 (office). *Fax:* (3) 8776-0222 (office). *E-mail:* tonyfernandes@airasia.com (office). *Website:* www.airasia.com (office).

FERNANDES, George; Indian trade union official, politician and journalist; b. 3 June 1930, Mangalore, Karnataka; s. of John Fernandes and Alice Fernandes; m. Leila Kabir 1971; one s.; ed St Peter's Seminary, Bangalore; joined Socialist Party of India 1949, mem. Nat. Cttee 1955–77, Treas. 1964, Chair. 1971–77; Ed. Konkani Yuvak (Konkani Youth) monthly in Konkani language 1949, Raithavani weekly in Kannada language 1949, Dockman weekly in English 1952–53, also New Society; fmr Chief Ed. Pratipaksha weekly in Hindi; trade union work in S Kanara 1949, 1950, in Bombay (now Mumbai) and Maharashtra 1950–58; Founding Pres. All-India Radio Broadcasters and Telecasters Guild, Khadi Comm. Karmachari Union, All-India Univ. Employees' Confed.; Pres. All-India Railwaymen's Fed. 1973–77; organized nat. railways strike 1974; Treas. All-India Hind Mazdoor Sabha 1958; formed Hind Mazdoor Panchayat 1958, Gen. Sec. for over 10 years; Convenor, United Council of Trade Unions; fmr mem. Gen. Council of Public Services Int., Int. Transport Workers' Fed.; Founder-Chair. New India Co-operative Bank Ltd (fmrly Bombay Labour Co-operative Bank Ltd); Gen. Sec. Samyukta Socialist Party of India 1969–70; mem. Bombay Municipal Corpn 1961–68; mem. Lok Sabha for Bombay City 1967–77; went underground on declaration of emergency 1975; mem. Janata Party 1977, Gen. Sec. 1985–86; mem. Lok Sabha for Muzzafarpur, Bihar, Lok Sabha 1977–79, also elected to Lok Sabha 1980, 1989, 1991, 1996, 1998, unsuccessfully contested 15th Lok Sabha elections as ind. cand. after being denied a ticket by his party Janata Dal—United 2009; Minister of Communications March–July 1977, of Industry 1977–79 (resgnd from Govt 1979), for Railways 1989–90, for Kashmir Affairs 1990–91, of Defence 1998–2001, 2001–04; Deputy Leader Lok Dal 1980–; mem. Standing Parl. Cttee on Finance 1993–96, also Consultative Cttee on Home Affairs, mem. Standing Parl. Cttee on External Affairs 1996, also Consultative Cttee on Human Resources Devt; Pres. Samata Party 1994–2000, 2002–04; fmr Pres. and Sr Leader Janata Dal—United; Chair. Editorial Bd Pratipaksh (Hindi monthly); Ed. The Other Side (English language monthly); Pres. Hind Mazdoor Kisan Panchayat; Chair. India Devt Group, London 1979, Schumacher Foundation 1979; fmr mem. Press Council of India; mem. Amnesty International, People's Union for Civil Liberties; involved in anti-nuclear and environmental campaigns. *Publications:* What Ails the Socialists: The Kashmir Problem, The Railway Strike of 1974, George Fernandes Speaks (autobiography). *Leisure interests:* music, reading. *Address:* 3 Krishna Menon Marg, New Delhi 110 011 (home); 30 Leonard Rd, Richmond Town, Bangalore 560 025, India. *Telephone:* (80) 22214143; (11) 23015403 (home); (11) 23793397 (home).

FERNANDES DE ARAÚJO, HE Cardinal Serafim; Brazilian ecclesiastic; *Archbishop Emeritus of Belo Horizonte;* b. 13 Aug. 1924, Minas Novas; ordained priest 1949; Auxiliary Bishop of Belo Horizonte, Minas Gerais, 1959–82, Coadjutor Archbishop 1982–86, Archbishop of Belo Horizonte 1986–2004, Archbishop Emer. 2004–; Titular Bishop of Verinopolis 1959; Cardinal-Priest of S. Luigi Maria Grignion de Montfort 1998–. *Address:* c/o Archdiocese of Belo Horizonte, Cúria Metropolitana, Av. Brasil 2079, CP 494, 30140-002 Belo Horizonte, MG, Brazil. *Telephone:* (31) 261-3400. *Fax:* (31) 261-5713.

FERNÁNDEZ, Alberto Angel; Argentine politician; b. 2 April 1959, Buenos Aires; m.; one s.; ed Universidad de Buenos Aires; Prof., Dept of Penal Rights, Universidad de Buenos Aires; Pres. Asociacíon de Superintendentes de Seguros de América Latina 1989–92; Exec. Vice-Pres. Grupo Banco Provincia 1997; mem. Parl. for Buenos Aires 2000; Cabinet Chief 2003–08 (resgnd); Industrialist of the Year in Insurance 1997, Millennium Prize for Industrialist of the Century 2000. *Address:* c/o Avenida Pte Julio A. Roca 782, 1067 Buenos Aires, Argentina (office).

FERNÁNDEZ, Aníbal Domingo; Argentine accountant and politician; b. 9 Jan. 1957, Quilmes; m.; one s.; ed Universidad Nacional de Lomas de Zamora; adviser to Budget Cttee, Buenos Aires Prov. Senate 1983–85, Admin. Sec., Peronista bloc 1985–91, Senator 1995; Mayor of Quilmes 1991–95; Asst to Minister of Govt and Justice, Govt of Buenos Aires 1997–99; Sec. of Labour 1999–2001, Minister of Labour 2001–02; Sec.-Gen. to the Presidency Jan.–Oct. 2002; Minister of Production 2002–03, of the Interior 2003–07, of Justice and Human Rights 2007–09; Cabinet Chief 2009–11; Senator, Upper House of Parl. 2011–; mem. Alianza Frente para la Victoria; Senator of the Year 1996. *Address:* Senate, Hipólito Yrigoyen 1849, 1089 Buenos Aires, Argentina (office). *Telephone:* (11) 4010-3000 (office). *E-mail:* anibal.fernandez@senado.gov.ar (office).

FERNÁNDEZ, Carlos Rafael, BEcons; Argentine economist and politician; b. 1954, Ciudad de la Plata; ed La Plata Nat. Univ.; Nat. Dir of tax coordination for provs 1989–97; Sub-Sec., tax coordination and policy for Buenos Aires prov. govt 1997, Under-Sec. for Fiscal Policy, Buenos Aires Prov. 2002–03, interim Prov. Minister of Economy 2007; Treasury Sec. 2006; Under-Sec. for Relations with the Provinces, Ministry of Economy 2007; Sub-Sec of the Budget Dec. 2007–March 2008; Dir Administración Fed. de Ingresos Públicos (tax agency) March–April 2008; Minister of Economy and Production 2008–09. *Address:* c/o Ministry of Economy and Production, Hipólito Yrigoyen 250, C1086AAB Buenos Aires, Argentina (office).

FERNANDEZ, Dominique, DèsSc; French writer; b. 25 Aug. 1929, Neuilly-sur-Seine; s. of Ramon Fernandez and Liliane Chomette; m. Diane Jacquin de Margerie (divorced); one s. one d.; ed Lycée Buffon, Paris and Ecole Normale Supérieure; Prof. Inst. Français, Naples 1957–58; Prof. of Italian, Univ. de Haute-Bretagne 1966–89; literary critic, L'Express 1959–84, Le Nouvel Observateur 1985–; music critic, Diapason 1977–85, Opera International 1978, Classical Repertoire 2000–; elected mem. Académie française 2007; mem. Reading Cttee, Editions Bernard Grasset 1959–; Chevalier, Légion d'honneur, Commdr, Ordre nat. du Mérite, Cruzeiro do Sul (Brazil); Prix Médicis 1974, Prix Goncourt 1982, Grand Prix Charles Oulmont 1986, Prix Prince Pierre de Monaco 1986, Prix Méditerranée 1988, Prix Oscar Wilde 1988. *Publications:* Le roman italien et la crise de la conscience moderne 1958, L'écorce des pierres 1959, L'aube 1962, Mère Méditerranée 1965, Les Evènements de Palerme 1966, L'échec de Pavèse 1968, Lettre à Dora 1969, Les enfants de Gogol 1971, Il Mito dell'America 1969, L'arbre jusqu'aux racines 1972, Porporino 1974, Eisenstein 1975, La rose des Tudors 1976, Les Siciliens 1977, Amsterdam 1977, L'étoile rose 1978, Une fleur de jasmin à l'oreille 1980, Le promeneur amoureux 1980, Signor Giovanni 1981, Dans la main de l'ange 1982, Le volcan sous la ville 1983, Le banquet des anges 1984, L'amour 1986, La gloire du paria 1987, Le rapt de Perséphone (opera libretto) 1987, Le radeau de la Gorgone 1988, Le rapt de Ganymede 1989, L'Ecole du Sud 1991, Porfirio et Constance 1992, Séville 1992, L'Or des Tropiques 1993, Le Dernier des Médicis 1994, La Magie Blanche de Saint-Pétersbourg 1994, Prague et la Bohème (jtly) 1995, La Perle et le croissant 1995, Le Musée idéal de Stendhal 1995, Saint-Pétersbourg 1996, Tribunal d'honneur 1997, Le musée de Zola 1997, Le voyage d'Italie 1998, Rhapsodie roumaine 1998, Palerme et la Sicile 1998, Le loup et le chien 1999, Les douze muses d'Alexandre Dumas 1999, Bolivie 1999, Nicolas 2000, Errances solaires 2000, L'amour qui ose dire son nom 2001, Syrie 2002, La Course à l'abîme 2003, Dictionnaire amoureux de la Russie 2004, Rome 2004, Sentiment indien 2005, Sicile 2006, Jérémie! Jérémie! 2006, l'Art de raconter 2007, Place rouge 2008, Ramon 2009, Avec Tolstoï 2010, Pise 1951 2011, Transsibérien 2012, Dictionnaire amoureux de Stendhal 2013. *Leisure interest:* operatic music. *Address:* 14 rue de Douai, 75009 Paris (home); c/o Editions Bernard Grasset, 61 rue des Saints-Pères, 75006 Paris, France (office).

FERNÁNDEZ, Gonzalo; Uruguayan lawyer and politician; Sec. of Presidency 2005–08; Minister of Foreign Affairs 2008–09, of Defence 2009–10; mem. Partido Socialista del Uruguay. *Address:* c/o Ministry of National Defence, Edif. General Artigas, Avda 8 de Octubre 2628, Montevideo, Uruguay (office).

FERNANDEZ, Manuel (Manny) A., BEE; American business executive; *Executive Chairman, Sysco Corporation;* b. 22 April 1946; ed Univ. of Florida; began his career in engineering positions with Fairchild and Harris Corpn, fmr Group Exec. Vice-Pres., Fairchild Semiconductor; fmr Pres. and CEO Dataquest, Inc., Gavilan Computer Corpn, Zilog Inc.; Co-founder and Man. Dir SI Ventures 1996–; Chair., Pres. and CEO Gartner, Inc. (information tech. research and consulting co.) –2001, Chair. Emer. 2001–; mem. Bd of Dirs Sysco Corpn 2006–, Chair. (non-exec.) 2009–12, Exec. Chair. 2012–; mem. Bd of Dirs Brunswick Corpn, Flowers Foods, Inc., The Black & Decker Corpn, Florida Research Consortium and several pvt. cos and foundations; apptd by Pres. George W. Bush to serve on Pres.'s Information Tech. Advisory Cttee; Chair. Bd of Trustees, Univ. of Florida. *Address:* Sysco Corpn, 1390 Enclave Parkway, Houston, TX 77077-2099 (office); SI Ventures, 12600 Gateway Boulevard, Fort Myers, FL 33913, USA (office). *Telephone:* (281) 584-1390 (Houston) (office); (239) 561-4760 (Fort Myers) (office). *Fax:* (281) 584-2721 (Houston) (office); (239) 561-4916 (Fort Myers) (office). *E-mail:* info@sysco.com (office). info@siventures.com (office). *Website:* www.sysco.com (office); www.siventures.com (office).

FERNÁNDEZ, Margarita Cedeño de, LLD, LLM; Dominican Republic lawyer; *First Lady;* b. 1 May 1965, Santo Domingo; d. of Luis Cedeño and Margarita Cedeño; m. Leonel Antonio Fernández Reyna (Pres. of Dominican Repub.) 2003; one d.; two c. from previous marriage; ed Universidad Autónoma de Santo Domingo, Pontificia Universidad Católica Madre y Maestra; Assoc., Dr Abel Rodríguez del Orbe and Fernández y Asociados (law firms); legal adviser to Pres. 1996–2000; fmr consultant and Dir Legal Man. and Investment Bd, Office for the Promotion of Foreign Investment; First Lady of Dominican Repub. 2004–, acts as head of govt's social programmes centred on educ., tech., social solidarity and family devt; Founding mem. Digital Solidarity Fund, Geneva 2005; FAO Goodwill Amb. 2009–; primary cand. of Partido de la Liberación Dominicana for presidential election 2011; Honorary Pres. 40th Nat. Congress of Paediatrics 2009; Grande Ufficiale, Ordine della Stella della Solidarietà Italiana 2009; Dr hc (Univ. Centre of Brasília) 2005; ITU Union World Information Soc. Award 2007, Latin Pride Nat. Awards Woman of the Year 2009. *Address:* c/o Office of the President, Palacio Nacional, Avda México, esq. Dr Delgado, Gazcue, Santo Domingo, DN; Partido de la Liberación Dominicana (PLD), Avda Independencia 401, Santo Domingo DN, Dominican Republic (office). *Telephone:* 685-3540 (PLD) (office). *Fax:* 685-3540 (PLD) (office). *E-mail:* pldorg@pld.org.do (office). *Website:* www.pld.org.do (office). www.presidencia.gob.do (office).

FERNÁNDEZ AMUNATEGUI, Mariano, LLB; Chilean diplomatist, editor and UN official; b. 21 April 1945, Santiago; m. María Angélica Morales; two s. one d.; ed Universidad Católica de Santiago, Bonn Univ., Germany; joined Chilean Foreign Service 1967; Third Sec., Embassy in Germany 1971–74; in exile, Bonn, Germany 1974–82; Ed. Development and Cooperation (magazine) and Chief Ed. IPS-Dritte Welt Nachrichtenagentur (news agency) 1974–82; Chief Ed. Handbuch der Entwicklungshilfe 1974–76; returned to Chile 1982; Researcher and mem. Exec. Cttee Centre of Studies for Devt (CED) 1982–90; Amb. to EC 1990–92, to Italy (also accred to Malta) 1992–94, to Spain (also accred to Andorra) 2000–02, to UK

2002–06, to USA 2006–09; Under-Sec. of Foreign Affairs 1994–2000, Minister of Foreign Affairs 2009–10; Special Rep. of Sec.-Gen. for Haiti, UN 2011–13; Head UN Stabilization Mission in Haiti 2011–13; Pres. Int. Council of Latin-American Centre for Relations with Europe (CELARE), Santiago 1996–98; Vice-Pres. European-Latin American Relations Inst. (IRELA), Madrid, Spain 1992, Pres. 1992–94; Vice-Chair. Italian-Latin-American Inst. 1992–94; Commr Int. Whaling Comm. 2003–07; mem. Exec. Cttee Jacques Maritian Inst., Rome, Italy 1994–96; mem. Bd of Dirs Fintesa Financial Agency (Banco del Desarrollo) 1982–84, Radio Cooperativa 1982–90; mem. Editorial Bd Mensaje (magazine) 1984–86, Fortin Mapocho (newspaper) 1986–88, Apsi (magazine) 1986–89; mem. Political Science Asscn of Chile, Acad. Int. du Vin; Hon. Pres., Chilean Asscn of Sommeliers; Grand Cross (Argentina, Brazil, Colombia, Ecuador, Finland, Germany, Holy See, Italy, Mexico, Panama, Peru, Spain), Grand Officer (Croatia, Germany, Sweden). *Address:* c/o Special Representative of United Nations Secretary-General for Haiti, United Nations, New York, NY 10017, USA.

FERNÁNDEZ BERMEJO, Marjano, LicenDer; Spanish lawyer, professor of law and politician; b. 10 Feb. 1948, Ávila; ed Complutense Univ.; Public Prosecutor, Prov. Court of Santa Cruz de Tenerife 1974–76, Territorial Court of Cáceres 1976–81; Deputy Chief Prosecutor, Prov. Court of Segovia 1981–84, Chief Prosecutor 1984–86; exec. adviser to Ministry of Justice 1986–89; Prosecutor, Tribunal Supremo (Supreme Court) 1989–92, Chief Prosecutor, Chamber for Admin. Proceedings 2004–07; Chief Prosecutor, Madrid High Court of Justice 1992–2003; Minister of Justice 2007–09 (resgnd); Interim Adjunct Prof. of Criminal Law, Extremadura Univ. 1977–80; Prof., Nat. Univ. of Distance Learning (UNED) 1980–81; San Raimundo de Penafort Cross of Honour, Silver Cross Order of Merit of the Civil Guard; Jesús Vicente Chamorro Prize 2003, Political Merit Medal. *Publications:* El concepto de desamparo 1987, Líneas generales de la Reforma del Derecho del Menor 1988, Adopción y acogimientos familiares 1988, El menor de edad en la legislación española 1994, La Mediación como solución alternativa al proceso y su significación respecto a la víctima 2000, La protección de los Derechos Humanos en los colectivos sociales marginales 2001, Contra la especulación del suelo 2003. *Address:* c/o Ministry of Justice, San Bernardo 45, 28015 Madrid, Spain (office).

FERNÁNDEZ DE KIRCHNER, Cristina Elisabet; Argentine politician, lawyer and head of state; *President;* b. 19 Feb. 1953, La Plata, Buenos Aires; m. Néstor Carlos Kirchner (died 2010); one s. one d.; ed Universidad Nacional de La Plata; began political career in Tendencia Revolucionaria faction of Partido Justicialista 1970s; elected prov. rep. in Patagonian prov. of Santa Cruz 1989–95, Chair. Constitutional Affairs, Authorities and Regulations Cttee, Santa Cruz House of Reps 1989–95, First Vice-Chair. 1990; elected to represent Santa Cruz in Senate 1995–97, 2001–05, in Chamber of Deputies 1997, Senator representing Prov. of Buenos Aires (Front for Victory faction of party) 2005–07; Pres. of Argentina (first elected female pres.) 2007–; mem. Congress Partido Justicialista 1985, mem. Nat. Congress 1995, Pres. Congress Partido Justicialista 2004; ranked by Forbes magazine amongst The World's 100 Most Powerful Women (13th) 2008, (11th) 2009, (68th) 2010, (17th) 2011, (16th) 2012, (26th) 2013. *Address:* General Secretariat to the Presidency, Balcarce 50, C1064AAB, Buenos Aires, Argentina (office). *Telephone:* (11) 4344-3674 (office). *Fax:* (11) 4344-2647 (office). *E-mail:* dgi@presidencia.gov.ar (office). *Website:* www.secretariageneral.gov.ar (office); www.cristina.com.ar.

FERNÁNDEZ DE LA VEGA, María Teresa; Spanish lawyer, judge and politician; b. 15 June 1949, Valencia; d. of Wenceslao Fernández de la Vega Lombán; ed Complutense Univ. of Madrid, Barcelona Univ.; started career as legal sec.; one of first women judges in Justicia Democrática movement during transition to democracy; served in Ministry of Justice 1980s; magistrate 1989; Sec. of State for Justice 1994; Deputy for Jaén, Congress of Deputies 1996–2000, for Madrid 2000–08, for Valencia 2008–10; First Deputy Prime Minister, Minister of the Presidency and Govt Spokesperson 2004–10; Assoc. Prof. Barcelona Central Univ., Complutense Univ. of Madrid; tutor, UNED Perm. mem. Consejo de Estado 2010–; fmr Sec.-Gen., Socialist Group in Congress; Tomás y Valiente Award 2006. *Address:* c/o Prime Minister's Chancellery and Ministry of the Presidency, Complejo de la Moncloa, 28071 Madrid, Spain.

FERNÁNDEZ DE SOTO VALDERRAMA, Guillermo; Colombian politician, international organization official and diplomatist; *Vice-Chairman, Inter-American Juridical Committee, Organization of American States;* b. 1956; m. 1st Consuelo Camacho, three c.; m. 2nd Alexandra Kling Mazuera, one s.; ed Univ. of Bogotá, Georgetown Univ., USA; Asst to Mayor of Santafé de Bogotá 1972–73; Exec. Sec. Circulo de Investigaciones para el Desarollo Económico y Social 1972–77; Gen. Man. Consultant, Corporación Financiera Popular 1973–76; Exec. mem. Esguerra Fernandez de Soto y Asociados 1976–77; Minister, Ministry of Foreign Affairs 1985–86; Consultant, UNDP 1987–91; Founder and Exec. Dir Int. Studies Center, Inter-American Forum 1988–91; Exec. Dir Presidential Campaign for Rodrigo Lloreda Caicedo 1990; Adviser to Minister of Foreign Affairs 1990–92; Pres. Chamber of Commerce of Bogotá and Pres. Colombian Cttee Int. Chamber of Commerce 1993–98; Minister of Foreign Affairs 1998–2002; f. Groupe de Contadora; Intermediate Sec. Groupe de Rio; Sec.-Gen. Andean Community of Nations 2002–03; Amb. to Netherlands 2004–09; mem. Inter-American Juridical Committee, OAS, Rio de Janeiro, Brazil 2008–, Vice-Chair. 2009–; Founder and Pres. Center for Colombian Studies, Washington, DC; Ordre nat. du Mérite 1985. *Address:* Inter-American Juridical Committee, Avenida Marechal Floriano, 196-3 andar, Palacio de Itamaraty, Centro 20080-002, Rio de Janeiro, R.J., Brazil (office). *Telephone:* (21) 2206-9903 (office). *Fax:* (21) 2203-2090 (office). *E-mail:* cjioea.trp@terra.com.br (office). *Website:* www.oas.org/CJI (office).

FERNÁNDEZ DIAZ, Jorge; Spanish engineer and politician; *Minister of the Interior;* b. 6 April 1950, Valladolid; m.; two c.; ed Escuela Técnica Superior de Barcelona, Escuela Superior de Marketing y Administración de Empresas, Barcelona; trained as industrial engineer; Deputy Del., later Del. of Ministry for Labour Affairs in Barcelona 1979–80; Civil Gov. of Asturias 1980–81, of Barcelona 1981–82; Councillor, Barcelona City Council 1983–84; mem. Regional Parl. of Catalonia 1984–89; Sec. of State for Regional Authorities 1996–99, for Educ., Univs, Research and Devt 1999–2000, for Parl. Relations 2000–04; mem. Congreso de los Diputados (Parl.) for Barcelona 1989–96, 2004–, Third Vice-Pres. (Deputy Speaker) 2008–11; Minister of the Interior 2011–; mem. Partido Popular, mem.

Nat. Exec. Cttee. *Address:* Ministry of the Interior, Paseo de la Castellana 5, 2046 Madrid, Spain (office). *Telephone:* (91) 5371111 (office). *Fax:* (91) 5371003 (office). *E-mail:* estafeta@mir.es (office). *Website:* www.mir.es (office).

FERNÁNDEZ ESTIGARRIBIA, José Félix; Paraguayan lawyer, diplomatist, international organization official and academic; *Minister of Foreign Affairs;* ed Nat. Univ. of Asuncion, Universidad Católica, Int. Law Acad., The Hague, Netherlands; fmr Amb. to Mexico (also accred to Guatemala and the Dominican Repub.), fmr Amb. to the UN, New York; fmr Deputy to Nat. Ass., later Senator of the Nation; fmr Minister of Foreign Affairs and mem. Advisory Council of the Chancellor; fmr Prof. of Int. Relations and Int. Law, Faculty of Juridical and Diplomatic Sciences, Universidad Católica; fmr Prof. of Int. Law, Faculty of Law and Social Sciences, Nat. Univ. of Asuncion; fmr Prof. of Contemporary Int. System, Diplomatic and Consular Acad., Ministry of Foreign Affairs; taught at XVIII and XXIX Course on Int. Law, OAS, Rio de Janeiro, Brazil; served as Pres. Bar Asscn of Paraguay, Latin American Asscn of Lawyers for Human Rights (Paraguay Br.); fmr mem. Bd Diplomatic Acad. of Paraguay; Paraguayan Referee, Schedule for the Settlement of Disputes in MERCOSUR Protocol of Brasilia, mem. MERCOSUR Council of Inst. for European-Latin American Relations (IRELA); Sec.-Gen. Latin American Integration Asscn (Asociación Latinoamericana de Integración—ALADI) 2009–11; Minister of Foreign Affairs 2012–. *Publications include:* co-author: The International Society and the Authoritarian State of Paraguay, The Transnational in Paraguay, International Politics, Economy and Integration, Legislation Paraguaya. *Address:* Ministry of Foreign Affairs, Edif. Benigno López, Palma, esq. 14 de Mayo, Asunción, Paraguay (office). *Telephone:* (21) 49-3872 (office). *Fax:* (21) 49-3910 (office). *E-mail:* sistemas@mre.gov.py (office). *Website:* www.mre.gov.py (office).

FERNÁNDEZ-FAINGOLD, Hugo; Uruguayan diplomatist and fmr politician; b. 1 March 1947, Montevideo; m.; seven c.; ed Columbia Univ., Georgetown Univ., USA; fmr Prof., Univ. of the Repub., Montevideo; Dean, School of Social Sciences, Nat. Univ. Costa Rica 1974–76; fmr consultant to several int. orgs including UNDP, ILO, Inter-American Inst. for Cooperation in Agriculture, Inter-American Devt Bank; mem. Nat. Convention and Montevideo Convention, Colorado Party 1985–, Sec. Gen. Colorado Party Nat. Exec. Cttee 1995–2000; Minister of Labor and Social Security 1985–89; mem. Senate 1995–2000; Dir El Dia (daily newspaper) 1997–98; Vice-Pres. of Uruguay and Pres. of Gen. Ass. 1998–2000; Amb. to USA 2000–05. *Publications:* more than 70 articles and papers. *Leisure interests:* soccer, fencing. *Address:* c/o Ministry of Foreign Affairs, Avda 18 de Julio 1205, 11100 Montevideo, Uruguay (office).

FERNÁNDEZ FIGUEROA, Rosario del Pilar; Peruvian lawyer and politician; b. 9 Nov. 1955, Lima; d. of Joffre Fernandez Veldivieso; m. Ernest Coz; two d.; ed Pontifical Catholic Univ. of Peru; Pnr, Fernández, Heraud & Sánchez (law firm) 1988–2007; Vice-Chair. Lima Stock Exchange 1988–91; Treas. Lima Bar Asscn 1993–94; Minister of Justice 2008–09, 2010–11; Pres. Council of Ministers (Prime Minister) March–July 2011. *Address:* c/o Office of the President of the Council of Ministers, Jirón Carabaya, cuadra 1 s/n, Anexo 1105-1107, Lima, Peru (office).

FERNÁNDEZ ORDÓÑEZ, Miguel Ángel, LicenDer, LicenCienEcon; Spanish politician, fmr central banker and academic; b. 3 April 1945, Madrid; ed Universidad Complutense de Madrid; mem. Socialist Workers' Party; Prof. of Political Economy Universidad Complutense de Madrid 1970–72; Chief of Section, Coyuntura de la Comisaría del Plan de Desarrollo 1970–72; economist, Dept of Econ. Studies, OECD 1973; Chief of Co-ordination Service, Ministry of Planning and Devt 1974–75; econ. consultant, Ministry of Finance 1976; Deputy Dir-Gen. of Conjunctural Analysis, Ministry of the Economy 1977; consultant to Exec. Dir World Bank 1978–80; Sec. Cttee of Public Investments, Ministry of the Economy 1980–82; Sec. of State for the Economy and Planning 1982–86; elected Deputy for Madrid 1986–88; Sec. of State for Commerce 1987–88; Exec. Dir IMF 1988–90; Pres. Icopostal, Sociedad de Valores y Bolsa 1990–91; mem. Council of Admin Banco Argentaria and Pres. Fundación Argentaria 1991–92; Pres. Court of Defence of Competition 1992–95; Pres. Comm. of Nat. Electric System 1995–99; econ. columnist, El País y Cinco Días, collaborator on TV programme Economía a Fondo, CNN+ and Dir radio programme Economía de los Negocios, SER 2000–03; Sec. of State for Internal Revenue 2004–06; Counsellor, Banco de España and mem. Exec. Comm. March–July 2006, Gov. Banco de España July 2006–12; mem. Cuerpo de Técnicos Comerciales and State Economists. *Publications include:* La Competencia; numerous articles on political economy, regulation, liberalization, privatization, defence of competition and the financial system. *Address:* c/o Banco de España, Alcalá 48, 28014 Madrid, Spain.

FERNÁNDEZ RETAMAR, Roberto, Dr en Fil; Cuban writer; b. 9 June 1930, Havana; s. of José M. Fernández Roig and Obdulia Retamar; m. Adelaida de Juan 1952; two d.; ed Univ. de la Habana, Univ. de Paris à la Sorbonne and Univ. of London; Prof., Univ. de la Habana 1955–; Visiting Prof., Yale Univ. 1957–58; Dir Nueva Revista Cubana 1959–60; Cultural Counsellor of Cuba in France 1960; Sec., Union of Writers and Artists of Cuba 1961–65; Ed. Casa de las Américas 1965–, now Pres.; Visiting Lecturer, Columbia Univ. 1957, Univ. of Prague 1965; Felix Varela Order of first grade 1981, Orden de Mayo, Argentina 1998; Nat. Prize for Poetry, Cuba 1952, Rúben Dario Latin American Prize 1980, Int. Prize for Poetry Nikola Vaptsarov, Bulgaria 1989, Nat. Literary Award, Cuban Book Inst. 1989, Int. Prize for Poetry, Pérez Bonalde, Argentina 1989, Official Medal of Arts and Letters (France) 1998. *Publications:* poetry: Elegía como un Himno 1950, Patrias 1952, Alabanzas, Conversaciones 1955, Vuelta de la Antigua Esperanza 1959, Con las Mismas Manos 1962, Poesía Reunida 1948–1965 1966, Buena Suerte Viviendo 1967, Que veremos arder 1970, A quien pueda interesar 1970, Cuaderno paralelo 1973, Juana y otros temas personales 1981, Aquí 1995; studies: La Poesía contemporánea en Cuba 1954, Idea de la Estilística 1958, Papelería 1962, Ensayo de otro mundo 1967, Introducción a Cuba: la historia 1968, Caliban 1971, Lectura de Martí 1972, El son de Vuelo popular 1972, Introducción a Martí 1978. *Leisure interests:* reading, swimming. *Address:* Casa de las Américas, 3ra y G Street, El Vedado, Havana, Cuba (office). *E-mail:* webmaster@casa.cult.cu (office). *Website:* www.casadelasamericas.com (office).

FERNÁNDEZ REYNA, Leonel, DIur; Dominican Republic politician and fmr head of state; *President, Partido de la Liberación Dominicana;* b. 26 Dec. 1953, Santo Domingo; s. of the late José Antonio Fernández Collado and of Yolanda

Reyna Romero; m. Margarita Cedeño; one c. (two c. from previous m.); ed Universidad Autónoma de Santo Domingo; joined Partido de la Liberación Dominicana 1973, Pres. 2002–; cand. for Vice-Pres. 1994; Pres. 1996–2000, 2004–12. *Address:* Partido de la Liberación Dominicana, Avda Independencia 401, Santo Domingo, Dominican Republic (office). *Telephone:* 685-3540 (office). *Fax:* 687-5569 (office). *E-mail:* pldorg@pld.org.do (office). *Website:* www.pld.org.do (office).

FERNÁNDEZ SAAVEDRA, José Gustavo; Bolivian politician and diplomatist; b. 24 Sept. 1941, Cochabamba; m.; three c.; ed San Simón Univ.; Exec. Sec., Secr. of Integration, La Paz 1969–70; Head Legal Dept, Comm. on Cartagena, Lima, Peru 1970–76; Dir of Consultation and Latin American Co-ordination, Caracas, Venezuela 1976–77; Consulting Dir-Gen. Coprinco y Asociados Consultores 1977–78, Pres. 1979–80, 1982–83; Minister of Integration 1978, of Foreign Affairs 1979, 1984–85, 2001–02; Consultant to UNCTAD 1980–83, 1987–89, 1993–98; Rep. of Ministries of Industry and Foreign Affairs, Quito, Ecuador 1980–81, Geneva, Switzerland 1985–87; Amb. to Brazil 1983–84; Exec. Dir Muller y Asociados Consultores 1987–89, Network of Advising and Man. SA 1993; Vice-Presidential cand. 1989; Minister of the Presidency 1989–93; Co-ordinator, Nat. Dialogue 1997; Rep. Andean Corpn of Promotion in Peru 1998–99; Gen. Consul of Bolivia in Chile 2000–01; Special Rep. of the OAS Sec.-Gen. and Head, Misión Especial de Acompañamiento al Proceso Democrático y Electoral de la República de Nicaragua (Special Mission Accompanying the Democratic Process and Elections of Repub. of Nicaragua) 2006, Head of OAS Election Observation Mission (EOM) to El Salvador 2013–14. *Address:* Casilla 7ll, La Paz, Bolivia (home). *Telephone:* (2) 278-2614 (home). *Fax:* (2) 278-6793 (home). *E-mail:* gustavof@acelerate.com (home).

FERNANDO, Merrill Joseph; Sri Lankan tea planter and business executive; *Founder and Chairman, Dilmah Tea;* b. 6 May 1930, Negombo; s. of P. Harry Fernando and Lucy Fernando; m.; two s.; ed Maris Stella Colles, Negombo; selected for training as tea taster, travelled to Mincing Lane, London, UK; worked in UK tea co. before returning to Sri Lanka; joined A. F. Jones & Co., becoming Man. Dir within two years, bought out British shareholders and ran business with another pnr; supplied first ever consignment of Ceylon tea direct to then USSR 1950s; est. Merrill J. Fernando & Co. Ltd, supplied bulk tea to most of world's major tea brands 1960s–70s; lost tea plantation to nationalization 1970s, sold business with intention of emigrating from Sri Lanka, remained in Sri Lanka and est. M. J. F. Exports Ltd 1974; registered trademark DILMAH in face of opposition from bulk tea customers early 1980s; DILMAH Tea launched in Australia 1988, thereafter in NZ and to date in 94 countries world-wide; est. The Merrill J. Fernando Charitable Foundation. *Address:* Dilmah (MJF Group), POB 1630, Colombo 10, Sri Lanka (office). *Telephone:* (11) 2933070 (office). *Fax:* (11) 2933080 (office). *E-mail:* info@dilmahtea.com (office). *Website:* www.dilmahtea.com (office); www.mjffoundation.org.

FERNANDO, Most Rev. Nicholas Marcus, BA, PhL, STD; Sri Lankan ecclesiastic; *Archbishop Emeritus of Colombo;* b. 6 Dec. 1932; s. of W. Severinus Fernando and M.M. Lily Fernando; ordained priest 1959; Rector, St Aloysius Minor Seminary 1965–73; Archbishop of Colombo 1977–2002 (resgnd), Archbishop Emer. 2002–; mem. Sacred Congregation for the Evangelization of Peoples 1989; Pres. Catholic Bishops' Conf. of Sri Lanka 1989–95. *Address:* c/o Archbishop's House, 976 Gnanartha Pradeepaya Mawatha, Colombo 8, Sri Lanka.

FERNANDO, Rear Adm. Sarath Palitha, PC, LLB, LLM, LLM; Sri Lankan lawyer, naval officer and government official; *Attorney General;* ed Royal Coll., Colombo, Sri Lanka Law Coll., Univ. of Colombo, Univ. of Bristol, UK; captained the Coll. English and Sinhala debating teams, served as Student Chair. Coll. English Literary Asscn and Gen. Sec. Sinhala Literary Asscn; Pres. Young Zoologists' Asscn of Sri Lanka 1976; joined Attorney Gen.'s Dept as acting State Counsel 1980–89, Sr State Counsel 1989–97, Deputy Solicitor Gen. 1997–2004; apptd Judge Advocate of Sri Lanka Navy, as a Cdre in the Volunteer Naval Force to head the legal br. 2004, served as prosecutor and Judge Advocate at several Courts Martial of all three Services, Solicitor Gen. 2011–12, Acting Attorney Gen. June–July 2012, Attorney Gen. July 2012–; attained rank of Rear Adm. in Volunteer Naval Force; Visiting Lecturer, Open Univ. of Sri Lanka; Faculty mem. Bandaranaike Centre for Int. Studies; mem. Pres.'s Council; Prize for Commercial Law and Hector Jayawardena Gold Medal, Sri Lanka Law Coll. *Address:* Attorney General's Department, Colombo 12 (office); Supreme Court, Superior Court Complex, PO Box 01200, Colombo 12, Sri Lanka (office). *Telephone:* (11) 2436421 (Attorney General) (office). *Website:* www.supremecourt.lk (office).

FERNEYHOUGH, Brian John Peter, ABSM, ARAM, FRAM, FBC, DMus; British composer and academic; *William H. Bonsall Professor in Music, Stanford University;* b. 16 Jan. 1943, Coventry, West Midlands, England; s. of Frederick George Ferneyhough and Emily May Ferneyhough (née Hopwood); m. 4th Stephanie Hurtik 1990; ed Birmingham School of Music, Royal Acad. of Music, Sweelinck Conservatory, Amsterdam, Music Acad., Basle; composition teacher, Musikhochschule, Freiburg, Germany 1973–78, Prof. of Composition 1978–86; Prin. Composition Teacher, Royal Conservatory of The Hague 1986; Prof. of Music, Univ. of California, San Diego 1987–99; Leader of Master Class in Composition, Civica Scuola di Musica, Milan 1982–86, Fondation Royaumont, France 1990–; Visiting Artist, DAAD, Berlin 1976–77; Guest Prof., Musikhögskolan, Stockholm 1980, 1981, 1982, 1985; Visiting Prof., Univ. of Chicago 1986; Lecturer in Composition, Darmstadt Int. Courses 1976–96, 2008–; Guest Prof. of Poetics, Mozarteum, Salzburg, Austria 1995; mem. Akad. der Künste, Berlin 1996; William H. Bonsall Prof. in Music, Stanford Univ. 2000–; Visiting Prof., Harvard Univ. 2007–08, S. L. Lee Visiting Professorial Fellow, Univ. of London 2012; Hon. DMus (Goldsmiths College) 2011; Chevalier, Ordre des Arts et des Lettres 1984; Koussevitzky Prize 1979, Grand Prix du Disque 1978, 1984, Ernst von Siemens Prize for Lifetime Achievement 2007, and other awards and prizes. *Works include:* Sonatas for String Quartet 1967, Firecycle Beta 1969–71, Transit 1972–74, Time and Motion Study III 1974, La Terre Est Un Homme 1976–79, Second String Quartet 1979–80, Lemma-Icon-Epigram 1981, Carceri d'Invenzione 1981–86, 3rd String Quartet 1987, Kurze Schatten II 1988, La Chute d'Icare 1988, Fourth String Quartet 1989–90, Allgebrah 1991, Bone Alphabet 1991, Terrain 1992, On Stellar Magnitudes 1994, String Trio 1995, Incipits 1995–96, Flurries 1997, Unsichtbare Farben 1999, Doctrine of Similarity 2000, Opus Contra Naturam

2000, Stele for Failed Time 2001, Shadowtime (opera) 2004, Plötzlichkeit 2005, Fifth String Quartet 2006, Dum transisset I–IV 2007, Exordium 2008, Chronos-Aion 2008, Renvois/Shards 2008, Sisyphus Redux 2008, Sixth String Quartet (Royal Philharmonic Soc. Chamber-scale Composition Prize 2011) 2009, Liber Scintillarum 2012, Finis Terrae 2012, Quirl 2013, Schatten aus Wasser und Stein 2013, Silentium 2013. *Publications include:* Complete Writings on Music 1994, Collected Writings 1996; various articles published separately. *Leisure interests:* reading, cats, wife, wine (not in that order). *Address:* Office 231A, Department of Music, Braun Music Center, Stanford University, 541 Lasuen Mall, Stanford, CA 94305-3076, USA (office). *Telephone:* (650) 725-3102 (office). *Fax:* (650) 725-2686 (office). *E-mail:* brian.ferneyhough@stanford.edu (office). *Website:* music.stanford .edu (office).

FERRAGAMO, Ferruccio; Italian business executive; b. 9 Sept. 1945, Fiesole, Florence; s. of the late Salvatore Ferragamo and Wanda Ferragamo; m. Amanda Collingwood; five c.; began career working on production side of family business Salvatore Ferragamo Italia SpA, later involved in worldwide management of Ferragamo stores; finance and admin. from 1983, currently CEO Salvatore Ferragamo Italia SpA; Vice-Pres. Polimoda, Florence; mem. Bd Società Gaetano Marzotto & Fratelli, La Fondaria Assicurazioni, Banca Mercantile, Florence, Centro di Firenze per la Moda Italiana. *Leisure interests:* golf, shooting, sailing, tennis. *Address:* Salvatore Ferragamo Italia, SpA, Palazzo Feroni Via dei Tornabuoni, 2, Florence 50123 Italy (office). *Telephone:* (055) 33601 (office). *Fax:* (055) 3360444 (office). *Website:* www.salvatoreferragamo.it (office).

FERRARA, Abel; American film director and actor; b. 12 May 1951, Bronx, NY; m. Nancy Ferrara; two d.; began making short films while at school; has used pseudonym Jimmy Laine; television work includes episodes of Miami Vice and pilot for NBC's Crime Story. *Films include:* Nicky's Film 1971, The Hold Up 1972, Could This Be Love? 1973, Nine Lives of a Wet Pussy 1976, Not Guilty: For Keith Richards 1977, Driller Killer (also acted) 1979, Ms.45 (also acted) 1981, Fear City 1984, China Girl 1987, Cat Chaser 1989, The King of New York 1990, Bad Lieutenant 1992, Body Snatchers 1993, Dangerous Game 1993, The Addiction 1995, The Funeral 1996, California 1996, The Blackout 1997, New Rose Hotel 1998, 'R Xmas 2001, Mary (Venice Film Festival Special Jury Prize) 2005, Go Go Tales 2007, Chelsea on the Rocks 2008, Napoli, Napoli, Napoli 2009, The Bad Lieutenant: Port of Call–New Orleans 2009 (writer). *Address:* c/o William Morris Agency, 151 S El Camino Drive, Beverly Hills, CA 90212, USA.

FERRARA, Napoleone, MD; Italian/American molecular biologist and academic; *Distinguished Professor of Pathology, University of California, San Diego;* b. Italy; ed Univ. of Catania Medical School, Univ. of California, San Francisco; Univ. Postdoctoral Research, Univ. of California, San Francisco; Internship, The Oregon Health Sciences; worked at Genentech, Inc., San Francisco 1988–2013; Distinguished Prof., Univ. of California, San Diego 2013–; Sr Deputy Dir for Basic Science, Moores Cancer Center; mem. NAS 2006; Dr hc (Univ. of Eastern Piedmont, Italy) 2007; Discover Magazine Award 2004, Italian Asscn for Research and Therapy of Eye Disorders (AIRCMO) Prize 2004, American-Italian Cancer Foundation Prize 2004, Lefoulon-Delelande-Institut-de-France Prize 2005, AACR Bruce F. Cain Memorial Award 2005, Passano Award 2006, General Motors Cancer Research Award 2006, C. Chester Stock Award Lecturer, Memorial Sloan-Kettering Cancer Center 2007, Special Recognition for Scientific Achievement, Biotech Hall of Fame 2007, ASCO Science of Oncology Award 2007, Arnall Patz Award, Macula Soc. 2008, Pezcoller Foundation-AACR Int. Award 2009, Macula Soc.-Michaelson Symposium Award 2010, Lasker–DeBakey Clinical Medical Research Award 2010, Special Recognition, ARVO/AFER 2011, Dr Paul Janssen Award for Biomedical Research 2012, The Economist Innovation Award (Bioscience) 2012, Breakthrough Prize in Life Sciences 2013, Canada Gairdner Int. Award (jtly) 2014. *Publications:* numerous papers in professional journals. *Address:* Department of Pathology, University of California, San Diego, 9500 Gilman Drive, La Jolla, CA 92093, USA (office). *Telephone:* (858) 534-0455 (office). *E-mail:* nferrara@ucsd.edu (office). *Website:* pathology.ucsd.edu/faculty/ferrara .htm (office).

FERRARI, Margaret Hughes, BL; Saint Vincent and the Grenadines lawyer and fmr diplomatist; b. 1 Jan. 1948; m.; three c.; ed Univ. of London, UK; Sec. and Legal Exec. Hughes and Cummings law firm 1967–90, Partner 1990–; called to Bar, Lincoln's Inn, London, UK 1990; Pres. Bar Asscn of Saint Vincent and the Grenadines 1998–; Deputy Chair. Bd Saint Vincent Co-operative Bank Ltd; Dir Bottlers Ltd. (bottling co.); Perm. Rep. to UN, New York 2000–07. *Address:* c/o Ministry of Foreign Affairs, Foreign Trade and Consumer Affairs, Administrative Building, 3rd Floor, Bay Steet, Kingstown, Saint Vincent and the Grenadines.

FERRARI BRAVO, Luigi; Italian judge and legal scholar; *Professor of Law, University of Rome;* b. 5 Aug. 1933; ed Univ. of Naples; Asst Prof., Univ. of Naples 1956–61; Prof. of Int. Org., Univ. of Bari 1961–65, of Int. Law 1965–68, Full Prof. of Int. Law and Dir Inst. of Int. Law 1968–74; Prof. of Int. Law, Istituto Universitario Orientale, Naples 1962–68, Full Prof. of Int. Org. 1974–79, Dean, Dept of Political Science 1975–76; Prof. of EC Law, High School of Public Admin. Rome 1965–79, Full Prof. 1975; Full Prof. of EC Law, Faculty of Political Science, Univ. of Rome 1979–82, Full Prof. of Public Int. Law 1982–91; Full Prof. of EC Law, Faculty of Law, Univ. of Rome 1991–; Co-founder Uniform Law Foundation, The Hague 1996; Judge, Int. Court of Justice, Rome 1995–97; Lecturer, Hague Acad. of Int. Law 1975, 1982 and many other univs and scientific insts; mem. Italian Bar, Int. Law Asscn, American Soc. of Int. Law, Soc. Française de Droit Int. *Publications:* articles in professional journals. *Address:* Faculty of Law, University of Rome, Piazzale Aldo Moro 5, 00185 Rome, Italy.

FERREIRA, G(errit) T(homas), BCom, BBA, MBA; South African business executive; *Chairman, RMB Holdings;* b. 6 April 1948; m.; two c.; ed Stellenbosch Univ.; Co-founder Rand Consolidated Investments (RCI) 1977, Man. Dir Rand Merchant Bank (RMB) (acquired by RCI 1985) 1985–88, later Chair., Chair. (non-exec.) RMB Holdings (RMBH) 1987–, Chair. (non-exec.) FirstRand 1998–2008; mem. Bd of Dirs Glenrand M.I.B Ltd, VenFin Ltd, Remgro Ltd, Open Soc. of South Africa; mem. of Council, Univ. of Stellenbosch; Open Soc. Foundation of South Africa; Trustee, Univ. of Stellenbosch 2000 Trust; owns Tokara vineyard; Business Leader, Cape Town Chamber of Business 2010. *Address:* RMB Holdings, 3rd Floor, 2 Merchant Place, Corner Fredman Drive, Rivonia Road, Sandton, Johannesburg

2196, South Africa (office). *Telephone:* (11) 2821824 (office). *Fax:* (11) 282 4210 (office). *Website:* www.rmbh.co.za (office).

FERREIRA, Murilo Pinto de Oliveira, BA, MBA; Brazilian business executive; *President and CEO, Vale;* ed Escola de Administração de Empresas, Fundação Getulio Vargas, EBAP-FGV; began career at Vale SA (Companhia Vale do Rio Doce—CVRD) as financial and econ. analyst 1977, Commercial and Financial Dir, Vale do Rio Doce Alumínio SA 1998, Aluvale (holding co. of CVRD that merged into CVRD 2003), held positions as Exec. Officer, Nickel Marketing & Sales of Copper & Aluminum and Exec. Dir, Nickel Business, Marketing and Sales of Copper and Aluminum, mem. Exec. Bd Vale SA (Companhia Vale do Rio Doce—CVRD), Exec. Dir, Holdings, Energy, Equities & Business Devt, Companhia Vale do Rio Doce (holding company of Vale Overseas Ltd) 2005–07, Pres. and CEO Vale Inc. (fmrly CVRD Inc. Ltd) (subsidiary of PT International Nickel Indonesia Tbk) 2007–08, Pres. and CEO Vale SA 2011–; worked at Albras – Aluminio Brasileiro SA as Man. of Int. Financial Dept 1980–89; consultant 1990–97, worked on projects involving mergers and acquisitions and restructuring, especially related to Cia. Paulista de Ferro Ligas, Sibra Eletrosiderurgica and Alunorte – Alumina do Norte do Brasil SA; fmr CEO Aluminio Brasileiro (Albras) and Alumina do Norte do Brasil (Alunorte); Chief Commr/Pres. Commr of Int. Nickel Indonesia tbk PT 2007–08, Commr–Dec. 2008; mem. Bd of Dirs Mineracao Rio do Norte, Valesul Aluminio. *Address:* Vale, Av. Graça Aranha, 26, 20030-900 Rio de Janeiro RJ, Brazil (office). *Telephone:* (21) 3814-4477 (office). *Fax:* (21) 3814-4040 (office). *E-mail:* info@vale .com (office). *Website:* www.vale.com (office).

FERREIRA BRUSQUETTI, Manuel Adolfo; Paraguayan economist and politician; ed Universidad Católica Nuestra Señora de la Asunción, Univ. of Essex, UK, Univ. of Massachusetts, Amherst, USA; Partner, MCS Consulting Group 1998–2012; Pres. Investor Casa de Bolsa SA 2010–12; Minister of Finance 2012–13; Founding mem. Desarrollo en Democracia (Dende). *Address:* c/o Ministry of Finance, Chile 252, entre Palma y Presidente Franco, Asunción, Paraguay (office).

FERREIRA DE OLIVEIRA, Manuel, PhD; Portuguese engineer and business executive; *Vice-Chairman and CEO, Galp Energia SGPS SA;* b. 21 Dec. 1948, Fajões; s. of Henrique Soares De Oliveira and Maria José Gomes Ferreira; m. Maria Teresa Ferreira De Oliveira; two s.; ed Faculdade de Engenharia da Universidade do Porto (FEUP), Univ. of Manchester, UK; exec. responsibilities in LAGOVEN SA (subsidiary of Petroleos de Venezuela SA– PDVSA), including responsibilities as CEO and mem. Bd BP Bitor Energy, Nynas Petroleum and Ruhr Oel 1980–95; Chair. and CEO PETROGAL – Petróleos de Portugal SA 1995–2000; Chair. and CEO UNICER – Bebidas de Portugal SGPS SA 2000–06; CEO Galp Exploração e Produção, Petrogal – Petróleos de Portugal, GDP – Gás de Portugal, Galp Power and Galp Energia SA 2006–, Exec. Dir and COO Galp Energia SGPS SA 2006–07, Vice-Chair. and CEO Galp Energia SGPS SA 2007–, Chair. Fundação Galp Energia 2009–; Order of Francisco de Miranda (Venezuela) 1995, Grã-Cruz, Order of Merit (Portugal) 2006; Dr hc (Technical Univ. of Lisbon) 2001. *Address:* Galp Energia SGPS SA, Rua Tomás da Fonseca, Torre A, Edifício Galp Energia, 1600-209 Lisbon, Portugal (office). *Telephone:* (21) 724-25-00 (office); (21) 724-19-69 (office). *Fax:* (21) 003-90-80 (office). *E-mail:* presidencia@galpenergia.com (office). *Website:* www.galpenergia.com (office).

FERRELL, John William (Will); American comedian and actor; b. 16 July 1967, Irvine, Calif.; s. of Lee Ferrell and Kay Ferrell; m. Viveca Paulin 2000; two s.; ed Univ. of Southern California; started as mem. The Groundlings (improvisation group), Los Angeles; Mark Twain Prize for American Humor 2011. *Films include:* Men Seeking Women 1997, Austin Powers: International Man of Mystery 1997, The Thin Pink Line 1998, A Night at the Roxbury 1998, The Suburbans 1999, Austin Powers: The Spy Who Shagged Me 1999, Dick 1999, Superstar 1999, Drowning Mona 2000, The Ladies Man 2000, Jay and Silent Bob Strike Back 2001, Zoolander 2001, Old School 2003, Elf 2003, Anchorman: The Legend of Ron Burgundy 2004, Melinda and Melinda 2004, The Wendell Baker Story 2005, Kicking and Screaming 2005, Bewitched 2005, Winter Passing 2005, The Producers 2005, Wedding Crashers 2005, Curious George (voice) 2006, Talladega Nights: The Ballad of Ricky Bobby 2006, Stranger Than Fiction 2006, Blades of Glory 2007, Semi-pro 2008, Step Brothers 2008, Land of the Lost 2009, The Other Guys 2010, Everything Must Go 2010, Tim and Eric's Billion Dollar Movie 2012, Casa de mi Padre 2012, The Campaign 2012. *Stage performance:* You're Welcome America. A Final Night with George W. Bush (Broadway) 2009. *Television includes:* cast mem. Saturday Night Live 1995–2002, Funny or Die Presents 2010–11, The Office 2011. *Address:* Creative Artists Agency, Inc., 9830 Wilshire Blvd, Beverly Hills, CA 90212-1825, USA. *Telephone:* (310) 288-4545. *Fax:* (310) 288-4800. *Website:* www.caa.com.

FERRER, David; Spanish professional tennis player; b. 2 April 1982, Xàbia, Alicante; right-handed (two-handed backhand); moved to Gandia aged 13, to Barcelona to attend Catalan Tennis Fed. aged 15; spent nine months at Equelite, Juan Carlos Ferrero's Acad. in Villena; coached by Javier Piles; turned professional 2000, finishing as World No. 419, winning in Poland F1 and Spain F3, runner-up in Spain F1; won first career Challenger title in Sopot 2001; winner, Bucharest 2002, Stuttgart 2006, Tokyo 2007, Bastad 2007, Auckland 2007, 2011, 2012, 2013, 's-Hertogenbosch 2008, 2012, Valencia 2008, 2010, 2012, Acapulco 2010, 2011, 2012, Buenos Aires 2012, 2013, Abierto Mexicano Telcell, Acapulco 2012, SkiStar Swedish Open 2012, BNP Paribas Masters, Paris 2012; runner-up, Tennis Masters Cup 2007; Grand Slam results: runner-up, French Open 2013, quarterfinalist, French Open 2005, 2008, Australian Open 2008, Wimbledon 2012, semifinalist, US Open 2007, 2012, Australian Open 2011, French Open 2012; finalist, ATP World Tour Finals 2007; mem. winning Spanish Davis Cup team 2008, 2009, 2011; doubles titles: Acapulco (with Santiago Ventura) 2005, Viña del Mar (with Ventura) 2005; first achieved a top-10 ranking 2006; lives in Valencia; Golden Bagel Award 2007. *Leisure interests:* soccer, basketball, supports Valencia Football Club, reading. *E-mail:* albert.molina@imgworld.com (office). *Website:* en .davidferrer.com.

FERRERO, Juan Carlos; Spanish professional tennis player; b. 12 Feb. 1980, Onteniente; s. of Eduardo Ferrero and the late Rosario Ferrero; world ranked 1st as a junior 1998, won Wimbledon junior title that year; turned professional 1998; 12 singles titles: Mallorca 1999, Barcelona 2001, Dubai 2001, Estoril 2001, Rome

Tennis Masters Series (TMS) 2001, Hong Kong 2002, Madrid TMS 2003, Monte Carlo TMS 2002, 2003, French Open 2003, Valencia 2003, Grand Prix Hassan II, Casablanca, Morocco 2009; runner-up French Open 2002, US Open 2003; ranked 4th Champions Race 2002, ranked 3rd in 2003; career winnings of more than US$12 million; nine Davis Cup ties 1999–; won Davis Cup with Spain in 2000; coached by Antonio Martinez and Samuel Lopez; f. Equalite J. C. Ferrero tennis school 2001; Asscn of Tennis Professionals Rookie of the Year 1999. *Leisure interests:* soccer, collecting cars and motorcycles. *Address:* c/o IMG, via Augusta, 200, 4th Floor, 08021 Barcelona, Spain. *Website:* www.juancarlosferrero.com.

FERRERO, Michele; Italian business executive; b. 1927, Alba; s. of Pietro Ferrero; m.; two s. (one deceased); joined family confectionery co. Ferrero SpA in 1950, later took control of co. and expanded throughout Europe and world-wide eventually becoming one of Europe's largest confectionery manufacturers; products include Nutella, Ferrero Rocher, Kinder, Tic Tacs, turned over control of co. to his sons 1997; Founder Fondazione Ferrero 1983. *Address:* Ferrero SpA, Via Maria Cristina 47, 10025, Pino Torinese (office); Fondazione Ferrero, Strada di Mezzo 41, Alba 12051, Italy. *Telephone:* (173) 2951 (office). *Fax:* (173) 363034 (office). *E-mail:* info@fondazioneferrero.it. *Website:* www.ferrero.com (office); www .fondazioneferrero.it (office).

FERRERO COSTA, Carlos; Peruvian politician; b. 7 Feb. 1941, Lima; m. Nina Ghislieri 1968; four c.; Congressional Speaker 2000–03; Prime Minister of Peru 2003–05 (resgnd); currently mem. Congreso (Perú Posible). *Address:* c/o Perú Posible, Avda Faustino Sánchez Carrión, Lima, Peru (office). *Telephone:* (1) 4620303 (office). *E-mail:* carfecos@gmail.com (office). *Website:* www.carlosferrero .org (office).

FERRERO-WALDNER, Benita Maria, DIur; Austrian politician and diplomatist; b. 5 Sept. 1948, Oberndorf, Salzburg; ed Univ. of Salzburg; export and sales managerial roles in German and US cos, Germany 1978–83; joined Diplomatic Service 1984, several posts in Ministry of Foreign Affairs, Vienna 1984–86, First Sec., Dakar, Devt Aid Dept, Vienna; Counsellor for Econ. Affairs, Deputy Head of Mission, Chargé d'affaires, Paris 1986–93; Deputy Chief of Protocol, Ministry of Foreign Affairs 1993; UN Chief of Protocol, Exec. Office of Sec.-Gen., New York 1994–95; State Sec., Ministry of Foreign Affairs 1995–2000, Minister of Foreign Affairs 2000–04; EU Commr for External Relations and European Neighbourhood Policy 2004–09, for Trade and European Neighbourhood Policy 2009–10; mem. Supervisory Bd of Munich Re 2010–; Mérite Européen Gold Medal. *Publications:* The Future of Development Co-operation, Setting Course in a Changing World. *Leisure interests:* reading, yoga, cycling. *Address:* c/o European Commission, 200 rue de la Loi, 1049 Brussels, Belgium (office).

FERRES, Veronica Maria; German actress; b. 10 June 1965, Cologne; m. Martin Krug 2001; one d.; ed Ludwig-Maximilian-Univ., Munich; several awards including Golden Camera Award, Germany 1998, 2002, Bavarian TV Award 2002. 2004, Romy Award, Austria 2002, Video Award, Germany 2004. *Films include:* The Mask of Desire (Bambi Best Actress Award) 1992, Lateshow, The Ladies Room, Schtonk 1992, Superwoman 1996, Rossini 1997, Honeymoon 1997, The Parrot 1997, The Second Homeland 1997, The Bride (Best Actress Award 9th Int. Film Festival, Pescara 1999) 1999, Klimt 2006, Die Wilden Hühner 2006, Bye Bye Harry! 2006, Die Wilden Hühner und die Liebe 2007, Adam Resurrected 2008, Die Wilden Hühner und das Leben 2009, Unter Bauern – Retter in der Nacht 2009, Das Leben ist zu lang 2010. *Plays include:* Gold 1998, The Casket 2000, The Geierwally 2000, Talking With 2000, The Bernauerin 2000, Ghostride 2000, Everyman 2002–04. *Television includes:* Jack's Baby, The Chaos Queen, The Naughty Woman, Dr Knock, Catherine the Great, Tatort Fatal Motherlove, The Mountain Doctor, Bobby 2002, Sans Famille 2002, Les Misérables 2002, The Manns (Golden Grimme Award, Emmy Award) 2002, Forever Lost 2003, Anna's Return 2003, Stronger Than Death 2003, The Return of the Dancing Master 2004, Stars Even Shine At Day 2004, No Heaven Over Africa 2005, Neger, Neger, Schornsteinfeger 2006, Mein alter Freund Fritz 2007, Die Frau vom Checkpoint Charlie (mini-series) 2007, Das Wunder von Berlin 2008, Das Geheimnis der Wale 2010, Das blaue Licht 2010, Die lange Welle hinterm Kiel 2011, Tsunami – Das Leben danach 2012. *Leisure interests:* horseriding, skiing, fencing, golf, scuba diving, dancing. *Address:* Ferres Management, Kurfürstenstr. 18, 80801 Munich, Germany (office). *Telephone:* (89) 34020927 (office). *Fax:* (89) 38398689 (office); (89) 4702198 (office); (89) 399744 (home).

FERRETTI, Alberta; Italian fashion designer and retailer; b. 1951; m. 1968 (separated); two s.; made clothes and opened first boutique The Jolly Shop, Cattolica 1968, launched first collection under the name Alberta Ferretti 1974; began mfg clothes for other designers in 1970s; launched Alberta Ferretti line 1981, Philosophy line 1984, lingerie, accessories and beachwear lines 2001; opened flagship store in Los Angeles 2008; Owner and Vice-Pres. Aeffe fashion design and mfg co.; Cavaliere del Lavoro 1998; Dr hc (Bologna); Alta Roma Career Awards 2005. *Leisure interests:* swimming, reading, sailing. *Address:* AEFFE Spa, via Delle Querce, 15, 47842 San Giovani in Marignana; Via Donizetti 48, 20122 Milan, Italy (office). *Telephone:* (2) 760591 (office). *Fax:* (2) 782373 (office). *E-mail:* info@ aeffe.com (office). *Website:* www.aeffe.com (office); www.albertaferretti.com (office).

FERRO, Marc; French historian and academic; *Director of Studies in Social Sciences, École des hautes études en sciences sociales;* b. 1924, Paris; noted for his studies of Russian and Soviet history as well as history of cinema; currently Dir of Studies in Social Sciences, École des hautes études en sciences sociales; Co-Dir French review Annales; Co-Ed. Journal of Contemporary History; Chevalier, Légion d'honneur. *Television:* directed and presented documentaries on the rise of the Nazis, Lenin and the Russian revolution and on the representation of history in cinema. *Publications include:* La Révolution de 1917 1967 (reprinted 1976, 1997) (English trans.: October 1917: A Social History of the Russian Revolution, translated by Norman Stone 1980), La Grande Guerre, 1914–1918 1968 (reprinted 1987) (English trans.: The Great War, 1914–1918, translated by Nicole Stone 1972), Cinéma et Histoire 1976 (reprinted 1993) (English trans.: Cinema and History, translated by Naomi Greene 1988), L'Occident devant la révolution soviétique 1980, Suez 1981, Comment on raconte l'histoire aux enfants à travers le monde 1983 (reprinted 1986), L'Histoire sous surveillance: science et conscience de l'histoire 1985 (reprinted 1987), Pétain 1987 (reprinted 1993, 1994), Les Origines de la Perestroïka 1990, Nicolas II 1991, Questions sur la Deuxième Guerre mondiale 1993, Histoire des colonisations, des conquêtes aux indépendances (XIIIe-XXe siècle) 1994, L'internationale 1996, Les sociétés malades du progrès 1999, Que transmettre à nos enfants (with Philippe Jammet) 2000, Les Tabous de l'histoire 2002, Le livre noir du colonialisme (ed.) 2003, Histoire de France 2003, Le choc de l'Islam 2003, Le Cinéma, une vision de l'histoire 2003, Les Tabous de L'Histoire, Pocket Vol. 11949 2004, Les individus face aux crises du XXe siècle-L'Histoire anonyme 2005, Mes histoires parallèles: Entretiens avec Isabelle Veyrat-Masson (Prix Saint-Simon 2011) 2011. *Address:* EHESS, 190–198 avenue de France, 75244 Paris Cedex 13, France (office). *Telephone:* 1-49-54-25-25 (switchboard) (office). *E-mail:* info@ehess.fr (office). *Website:* ehess.fr (office).

FERRY, Bryan, CBE; British singer and songwriter; b. 26 Sept. 1945, Washington, Co. Durham, England; s. of the late Frederick Charles Ferry and Mary Ann Ferry (née Armstrong); m. Lucy Margaret Mary Helmore 1982 (divorced 2003); three s. one d.; m. 2nd Amanda Sheppard 2012; ed Newcastle Univ.; formed Roxy Music 1971; official debut, Lincoln Festival 1972; first US concerts 1972; first British and European tours 1973; Ivor Novello Award for Outstanding Contrib. to British Music 2003, BMI Icon Award 2008. *Recordings include:* albums: with Roxy Music: Roxy Music 1972, For Your Pleasure 1973 (Grand Prix du Disque, Golden Rose Festival, Montreux 1973), Stranded 1973, Country Life 1974, Siren 1975, Viva Roxy Music 1976, Manifesto 1979, Flesh & Blood 1980, Avalon 1982, The Atlantic Years 1983, Street Life – 20 Great Hits 1986; solo: These Foolish Things 1973, Another Time Another Place 1974, Let's Stick Together 1976, In Your Mind 1977, The Bride Stripped Bare 1978, Boys And Girls 1985, Bete Noire 1987, The Ultimate Collection 1988, Taxi 1993, Mamouna 1995, Bryan Ferry and Roxy Music Video Collection 1996, Frantic 2002, Dylanesque 2007, Olympia 2010. *Address:* c/o Alistair Norbury, Studio One, Avonmore Place, London, W14 8RY, England (office). *E-mail:* info@denejesmond.co.uk (office); info@bryanferry.com (office). *Website:* www.bryanferry.com.

FERRY, Luc, Dr rer. pol; French philosopher, politician and academic; *President Delegate, Conseil d'analyse de la société;* b. 3 Jan. 1951, Colombes; s. of Pierre Ferry and Monique Faucher; m. Marie-Caroline Becq de Fouquières 1999; three d. (one from previous m.); ed Lycée Saint-Exupéry, Centre nat. de télé-enseignement, Sorbonne, Univ. of Heidelberg; Lecturer, Teacher Training Coll., Arras, Asst Lecturer, Univ. of Reims 1977–79; Asst Lecturer, Ecole Normale Supérieure, Paris 1977–79, 1980–82; Research Attaché Nat., CNRS 1980–82; Asst Lecturer, Univ. of Paris I-Panthéon Sorbonne and Paris X-Nanterre 1980–88; Prof. of Political Sciences, Inst. of Political Studies, Univ. of Lyon II–Lumière 1982–88; Prof. of Philosophy, Univ. of Caen 1989–97; Asst Lecturer, Paris I 1989; Prof. of Philosophy, Univ. of Paris VI-Jussieu 1996–; Founder-mem. and Sec.-Gen. Coll. of Philosophy 1974–; responsible for Ideas section then Editorial Adviser, L'Express 1987–94; Pres. Nat. Curriculum Council (CNP) 1994–2002; Minister for Nat. Educ., Research and Tech. 1997–2002; Minister of Youth, Nat. Educ. and Research 2002–04; mem. Comm. for UNESCO 1997–2002; Pres. Conseil d'analyse de la société 2004–; Dir Editions Grasset collection of Coll. of Philosophy; fmr mem. Saint-Simon Foundation; columnist for Le Point 1995–; Chevalier, Légion d'honneur, Ordre des Arts et des Lettres. *Publications include:* Philosophie politique (three vols 1984–85), la Pensée 68, le Nouvel ordre écologique: l'arbre, l'animal et l'homme (Prix Jean-Jacques Rousseau) 1992, Homo aestheticus – L'Intervention du goût à l'âge démocratique 1990 (Prix Médicis 1992), l'Homme Dieu ou le sens de la vie (Prix Littéraire des Droits de l'Homme) 1996, La Sagesse des Modernes (with Le Sens du Beau 1998, Philosopher à dix-huit ans (co-author) 1999, Qu'est-ce que l'homme? (co-author) 2000, Lettres à tous ceux qui aiment l'école (co-author) 2003, Le Religieux après la religion 2004, Comment peut-on être ministre? 2005, Vaincre les peurs 2006, Kant. Une lecture des trois Critiques 2006, Familles, je vous aime 2007, Kant. L'oeuvre philosophique expliquée 2008, Nietzsche. L'oeuvre philosophique expliquée 2008, La tentation du christianisme (co-author) 2009, Quel devenir pour le christianisme (co-author) 2009, Face à la crise 2009, La révolution de l'amour: Pour une spiritualité laïque 2010,La Politique de la jeunesse (co-author) 2011; numerous articles on philosophy. *Address:* Conseil d'analyse de la société, 113 rue de Grenelle, 75007 Paris, France (office). *Telephone:* 1-42-75-86-89 (office). *Fax:* 1-42-75-87-40 (office). *E-mail:* luc.ferry@yahoo.fr (office). *Website:* www.cas.gouv.fr (office); www.lucferry.fr.

FERSHT, Sir Alan Roy, Kt, MA, PhD, FRS, FMedSci; British chemist and academic; *Master and Life Fellow of Gonville and Caius College and Group Leader, MRC Laboratory of Molecular Biology, University of Cambridge;* b. 21 April 1943, London, England; s. of Philip Fersht and Betty Fersht; m. Marilyn Persell 1966; one s. one d.; ed Sir George Monoux Grammar School, Walthamstow, Gonville and Caius Coll., Cambridge; Research Fellow, Brandeis Univ., Waltham, Mass, USA 1968–69; Fellow, Jesus Coll., Cambridge 1969–72; mem. scientific staff, MRC Lab. of Molecular Biology, Cambridge 1969–77; Eleanor Roosevelt Fellow, Stanford Univ., Calif. 1978–79; Wolfson Research Prof. of Royal Soc. 1978–89; Prof. of Biological Chem., Imperial Coll., London 1978–88; Herchel Smith Prof. of Organic Chem., Univ. of Cambridge 1988–2010, Prof. Emer. 2010–, Dir Cambridge Interdisciplinary Research Centre for Protein Eng 1989–2010, Dir MRC Unit for Protein Function and Design 1989–2010, Group Leader, MRC Lab. of Molecular Biology 2010–; Professorial Fellow, Gonville and Caius Coll. Cambridge 1988–, Master 2012–; Co-founder and Sr Ed. Protein Engineering Design and Selection; Assoc. Ed. Proceedings of the National Academy Sciences; Co-founder Cambridge Antibody Technology 1989 (acquired by Astra-Zeneca 2006); Co-founder Cambridge Drug Discovery 1997 (acquired by Millennium Pharmaceuticals 2000); Co-founder Avidis (France) 2000; Pres. Cambridge Univ. Chess Club 1964–65; mem. European Molecular Biology Org. 1980, American Philosophical Soc. 2008 Foreign mem. Italian Nat. Acad.; Foreign Assoc. NAS 1993; Hon. Foreign mem. American Acad. of Arts and Sciences 1988; Hon. mem. Japanese Biochemical Soc. 2002; Hon. Fellow, Manchester Interdisciplinary Biocentre 2006; Hon. Prof., Sichuan Univ. 2006, Shanghai Inst. of Materia Medica 2008; Freeman of the Worshipful Co. of Clockmakers 2005; Hon. PhD (Uppsala) 1999, (Free Univ. of Brussels) 1999, (Weizmann Inst.) 2004, (Hebrew Univ.) 2006, (Arhus) 2008; Fed. of European Biochemical Socs Anniversary Prize 1980, Novo Biotech. Award 1986, Charmian Medal for Enzyme Chem., RSC 1986, Gabor Medal, Royal Soc. 1991, Max Tishler Prize, Harvard Univ. 1992, Harden Medal, Biochemical Soc. 1993, Feldberg Foundation Prize 1996, Davy Medal, Royal Soc. 1998, Anfinsen Award, The Protein Soc. 1999, Laureate, 'Chaire Bruylants', Louvain 1999, RSC Natural

Products Award 1999, Stein and Moore Award, The Protein Soc. 2001, ACS Bader Award 2005, Linderstrøm-Lang Prize and Medal 2005, Bijvoet Medal 2008, G.N. Lewis Medal, Berkeley 2008, Royal Medal, Royal Soc. 2008, Wilhelm Exner Medal, Austrian Asscn for SME (Oesterreichischer Gewerbeverein—OGV) (jtly) 2009. *Achievements:* Essex Co. Jr Chess Champion 1961, Half-Blue (Chess) 1965. *Publications include:* Enzyme Structure and Mechanism 1977, Structure and Mechanism in Protein Science 1999: A Guide to Enzyme Catalysis and Protein Folding, Jaques Staunton Chess Sets 1849–1939: A Collectors Guide 2007; papers in scientific journals. *Leisure interests:* chess, horology. *Address:* Gonville and Caius College, Cambridge, CB2 1TA (office); MRC Laboratory of Molecular Biology, MRC Centre, Hills Road, Cambridge, CB2 0QH (office). *Fax:* (1223) 402140 (office). *E-mail:* master@cai.cam.ac.uk (office); arf25@cam.ac.uk (office); alan@mrc-lmb.cam.ac.uk (office). *Website:* www.cai.cam.ac.uk/people/alan-fersht (office); www2.mrc-lmb.cam.ac.uk/group-leaders/a-to-g/alan-fersht (office); www.ch.cam.ac.uk/person/arf25 (office).

FERT, Albert, PhD; French physicist and academic; *Scientific Director, Unité Mixte de Physique, Centre National de la Recherche Scientifique-Thales;* b. 7 March 1938, Carcassonne; m.; two c.; ed Ecole Normale Supérieure, Paris, Université de Paris, Université Paris-Sud; Asst. Univ. of Grenoble 1962–64; Asst Prof., Université Paris-Sud (Orsay) 1966–76; Prof. of Physics, Université Paris-Sud 1976–; Scientific Dir Unité Mixte de Physique, CNRS-Thales (Orsay) 1995–; mem. French Acad. of Sciences 2004; Grand Officier, Ordre nat. du Mérite, Commdr, Légion d'honneur; American Physical Soc. New Materials Prize (co-recipient) 1994, IUPAP Magnetism Award (co-recipient) 1994, Grand Prix de Physique Jean Ricard, Soc. Française de Physique 1994, Hewlett-Packard Europhysics Prize (co-recipient) 1997, CNRS Gold Medal 2003, Japan Prize (co-recipient) 2007, Wolf Foundation Prize for Physics (co-recipient) 2007, Nobel Prize in Physics (co-recipient) 2007. *Achievements include:* discoverer (with Peter Grünberg) of giant magnetoresistance phenomenon, which has led to enormous increase in storage capacity of magnetic hard-disk drives and has triggered the devt of a new field of research and tech., spintronics, to which he has made seminal contribs. *Publications:* about 350 articles in scientific journals or chapters of books. *Leisure interests:* jazz, cinema, windsurfing, mountain-hiking. *Address:* UMR CNRS/Thales, TRT, 1 avenue A. Fresnel, 91767 Palaiseau, France (office). *Telephone:* 1-69-41-58-64 (office). *Fax:* 1-69-41-58-78 (office). *E-mail:* albert.fert@thalesgroup.com (office). *Website:* www.trt.thalegroup.com/ump-cnrs-thales (office).

FERZAT, Ali; Syrian political cartoonist; b. 22 June 1951, Hama; ed Damascus Univ. Faculty of Fine Arts; early work appeared in state-run newspapers including al-Thawra and Tishreen 1970s; gained int. recognition after cartoons were published in Le Monde (French newspaper) 1980; exhbn at Institut du Monde Arabe, Paris 1989; published satirical review Domari (Lamplighter) 2001–03 (forced to close when licence revoked); fmr Pres. League of Arab Cartoonists; Prins Claus Prize (Netherlands) 2002, EU Sakharov Prize 2011, Index on Censorship Freedom of Expression Award (Arts) 2012. *Website:* www.ali-ferzat.com (office).

FETISOV, Vyacheslav Aleksandrovich; Russian professional ice hockey coach and fmr professional ice hockey player; *Head, Federal Agency for Physical Culture and Sports;* b. 20 April 1958, Moscow; m. Lada Fetisova; one d.; played with Cen. Army Sports Club 1975–89; USSR champion 1975, 1979–89; seven times world champion with USSR teams 1977–91; Olympic champion 1984, 1988; played with Nat. Hockey League (NHL) New Jersey Devils 1989–95, Detroit Red Wings 1995–98 (team won Stanley Cup 1997); Asst Coach New Jersey Devils 1998–2001; Gen. Man. and Coach Russian Olympic hockey team Salt Lake City 2002 (won bronze medal); Chair. Fed. Agency on Physical Culture and Sports 2002–; mem. Council of Founders of World Anti-Doping Agency (WADA), Head, Cttee of Sportsmen of WADA; Soviet Honoured Masters of Sport Award 1984, 1986, 1990, inducted into Hockey Hall of Fame 2001, UNESCO Champion for Sport 2004. *Address:* Federal Agency of Physical Culture and Sport, Kazakova str. 18, 105064 Moscow, Russia (office). *Telephone:* (495) 105-72-50 (office). *Fax:* (495) 267-34-40 (office). *E-mail:* info@rossport.ru (office). *Website:* www.rossport.ru (office).

FETSCHER, Iring, (Edler von Goldeck), DPhil; German political scientist and academic; *Professor Emeritus, J. W. Goethe Universität;* b. 4 March 1922, Marbach/Neckar; s. of Prof. Rainer Fetscher; m. Elisabeth Götte 1957; two s. two d.; ed König-George-Gymnasium, Dresden, Eberhard-Karls-Universität, Tübingen, Université de Paris and Johann Wolfgang Goethe-Univ., Frankfurt; Ed. Marxismusstudien 1956–; radio commentator on political, philosophical and sociological questions; Prof. of Political Science, Johann Wolfgang Goethe-Univ., Frankfurt 1963–88, Prof. Emer. 1988–; Theodor-Heuss Prof. New School for Social Research, New York 1968–69; Guest Prof. Tel Aviv Univ. 1972; Fellow, Netherlands Inst. for Advanced Study in the Humanities and Social Sciences 1972–73; Inst. for Advanced Studies, ANU, Canberra; Extraordinary Prof. for Social and Political Philosophy, Catholic Univ. of Nijmegen 1974–75; Chair. of the Expert Comm. for Criminal Prevention at the Govt of Hessen 1993–2004, Hon. Chair. 2004–; Bundesverdienstkreuz (First Class) 1993; Chevalier Ordre des Palmes Académiques 1993, Order of Merit, Hessen 2003; Hon. DPhil 2004; Goethe Plakette (Frankfurt) 1992. *Publications include:* Von Marx zur Sowjetideologie 1956, Über dialektischen und historischen Materialismus (Commentary of Stalin) 1956, 1962, Rousseaus politische Philosophie 1960, 1968, 1975, Der Marxismus, seine Geschichte in Dokumenten Vol. I 1962, Vol. II 1964, Vol. III 1965, 4th edn in one vol. 1983, Marx-Engels Studienausgabe (5 vols) 1966–2008, Introduction to Hobbes' Leviathan 1966, Karl Marx und der Marxismus 1967, Der Rechtsradikalismus 1967, Der Sozialismus 1968, Der Kommunismus 1969, Hegel: Grösse und Grenzen 1971, Modelle der Friedenssicherung 1972, Wer hat Dornröschen wachgeküsst?–das Märchenverwirrbuch 1972, 1974, Marxistische Porträts Vol. I 1975, Herrschaft und Emanzipation 1976, Terrorismus und Reaktion 1981, Analysen zum Terrorismus, Ideologien und Strategien 1981, Vom Wohlfahrtsstaat zur neuen Lebensqualität, die Herausforderungen des demokratischen Sozialismus 1982, Der Nulltarif der Wichtelmänner, Märchen- und andere Verwirrspiele 1982, Arbeit und Spiel (essays) 1983, Handbuch der politischen Ideen (co-ed. with H. Münkler), Vols 1, 2, 3, 4, 5 1985–93, Überlebensbedingungen der Menschheit zur Dialektik des Fortschritts 1986 (enlarged edn) 1991, Die Wirksamkeit der Träume, literarische Skizzen eines Sozialwissenschaftlers 1987, Utopien, Illusionen, Hoffnungen-Plädoyer für eine politische Kultur in Deutschland 1990, Toleranz—von der Unentbehrlichkeit einer kleinen Tugend für die Demokratie 1990, Neugier und Furcht: Versuch, mein Leben (autobiog.) 1995, Joseph Goebbels im Berliner Sportpalast: 'Wollt ihr den totalen Krieg?' 1988, Marx 1999, Bertolt Brecht: Die Dreigroschenoper—Dreigroschenroman Kommentar 2001. *Leisure interests:* collecting autographed letters and manuscripts and first edns of philosophers and writers. *Address:* J.W. Goethe Universität, PO Box 111932, 60054 Frankfurt-am-Main, Germany (office). *Telephone:* (69) 79822300 (office); (69) 521542 (home). *Fax:* (69) 7988383 (office); (69) 510034 (home). *E-mail:* iefetscher@yahoo.de (home). *Website:* www.iring-fetscher.de.

FETTER, Trevor, BEcons, MBA; American business executive; *President and CEO, Tenet Healthcare Corporation;* b. 16 Jan. 1960, San Diego; m.; two c.; ed Stanford Univ., Harvard Business School; Investment Banker, Merrill Lynch Capital Markets –1988; Exec. Vice-Pres. and Chief Financial Officer Metro-Goldwyn-Mayer Inc. 1988–95; joined Tenet Healthcare Corpn 1995, Exec. Vice-Pres. and later Chief Financial Officer 1996–2000, Pres. 2002–03, Pres. and CEO 2003–, also mem. Bd of Dirs; Chair. Broadlane Inc. 2000–, also CEO 2000–02; Dir Fed. of American Hosps; fmr Dir Catalina Island Conservancy, Santa Barbara Zoological Gardens, Neighborhood Youth Asscn. *Address:* Tenet Dallas, 13737 Noel Road, Dallas, TX 75240, USA (office). *Telephone:* (469) 893-2200 (office). *Fax:* (469) 893-1321 (office). *Website:* www.tenethealth.com (office).

FETTIG, Jeff M., BA, MBA; American business executive; *Chairman and CEO, Whirlpool Corporation;* b. 1957, Tipton, Ind.; ed Indiana Univ.; began career as Operations Assoc., Whirlpool Corpn 1981, various man. positions in sales, planning, operations and product devt 1981–89, Vice-Pres. Marketing, KitchenAid Appliance Group 1989–90, Vice-Pres., Marketing, Philips Whirlpool Appliance Group, Whirlpool Europe BV 1990–92, Vice-Pres., Group Marketing and Sales, N American Appliance Group 1992–94, Exec. Vice-Pres. Whirlpool Corpn and Pres. Whirlpool Europe and Asia 1994–99, apptd Dir Whirlpool Corpn 1999, Pres. and COO 1999–2004, Chair., Pres. and CEO 2004–06, Chair. and CEO 2006–; mem. Bd Dirs Dow Chemical Co.; mem. Dean's Advisory Council, Ind. Univ. Kelley School of Business; Trustee, Midwest Region, Boys and Girls Club of America. *Address:* Whirlpool Corporation, 2000 North M-63, Benton Harbor, MI 49022-2692, USA (office). *Telephone:* (269) 923-5000 (office). *Fax:* (269) 923-5443 (office). *E-mail:* info@whirlpoolcorp.com (office). *Website:* www.whirlpoolcorp.com (office).

FETTING, Rainer, German painter and sculptor; b. 31 Dec. 1949, Wilhelmshaven; ed Hochschule der Künste, Berlin, with Prof. Jänisch; Co-founder Galerie am Moritzplatz with Helmut Middendorf, Salome, Bernd Zimmer, Anne Jud and Berthold Schepers, Luciano Castelli 1977; lived in New York and Berlin 1983–94, lives and works in Berlin 2006–; DAAD scholarship, Columbia Univ., New York 1978. *Works include:* Willy Brandt sculpture for Willy-Brandt-Haus, Berlin 1996. *Address:* Hasenheide 61/1, 10967 Berlin, Germany (home). *Telephone:* (30) 690-42-275 (home). *Fax:* (30) 694-19-83 (home). *E-mail:* privat@fetting.de. *Website:* www.fetting.de.

FETTWEIS, Alfred Leo Maria, DèsSc Appl., FIEEE; German communications engineer and academic; *Professor Emeritus, Ruhr-University Bochum;* b. 27 Nov. 1926, Eupen, Belgium; s. of Paul Fettweis and Helene Fettweis (née Hermanns); m. Lois Jane Piaskowski 1957; two s. three d.; ed Catholic Univ. of Louvain, Belgium, Columbia Univ., Polytechnic Inst. of Brooklyn, USA; Devt Engineer with Int. Telephone and Telegraph Corpn (ITT), Belgium 1951–54, 1956–63 and USA 1954–56; Prof. of Theoretical Electricity, Eindhoven Univ. of Tech. 1963–67; Prof. of Communications Eng Ruhr-Univ. Bochum 1967–92, Prof. Emer. 1992–; Visiting Distinguished Prof., Univ. of Notre Dame 1994–96; Vice-Pres. IEEE Circuits and Systems Soc., Region 8 1987; mem. Rheinisch-Westfälische Akad. der Wissenschaften und der Künste, Academia Europaea, Academia Scientiarum et Artium Europaea, Acatech Deutsche Akad. der Technikwissenschaften; Dr hc (Linköping) 1986, (Mons) 1988, (Leuven) 1988, (Budapest) 1995, (Poznań) 2004, (Paderborn) 2011; Prix Acta Technica Belgica 1963, Darlington Prize Paper Award 1980, Prix George Montefiore 1981, Verband der Elektrotechnik (VDE) Ehrenring 1984, IEEE Centennial Medal 1984, Tech. Achievement Award, IEEE Circuits and Systems Soc. (CASS) 1988, Karl-Küpfmüller-Preis of Informationstechnische Gesellschaft 1988, Basic Research Award of Eduard Rhein Foundation 1993, Peter-Johns Prize, International Journal of Numerical Modelling 1993, CASS Golden Jubilee Medal 1999, IEEE Millennium Medal 2000, Van Valkenburg Award 2001, (first) CASS Belevitch Award 2003, IEEE Gustav Robert Kirchhoff Award 2008. *Achievements include:* invention and comprehensive theory of the wave-digital method for filtering and numerical integration. *Publications:* two books, many tech. papers on circuits, systems, telecommunications, digital signal processing, numerical integration and related areas, physics fundamentals; about 30 patents. *Leisure interests:* hiking, biking, music. *Address:* Lehrstuhl für Nachrichtentechnik/Digitale Kommunikationssysteme, Ruhr-Universität Bochum, Universitätsstrasse 150, 44780 Bochum (office); Im Königsbusch 18, 44797 Bochum, Germany (home). *Telephone:* (234) 322-2497 (office); (234) 322-3063 (office); (234) 797922 (home). *Fax:* (234) 321-4100 (office). *E-mail:* alfred.fettweis@rub.de (office); alfred.fettweis@ruhr-uni-bochum.de (office). *Website:* www.nt.ruhr-uni-bochum.de (office).

FETTWEIS, Günter Bernhard Leo, DrIng; Austrian/German mining engineer and academic; *Professor Emeritus, Montanuniversität Leoben;* b. 17 Nov. 1924, Düsseldorf, Germany; s. of Ewald I. Fettweis and Aninhas M. Fettweis (née Leuschner-Fernandes); m. Alice Y. Fettweis 1949; one s. three d.; ed Univ. of Freiburg and Tech. Univ. of Aachen; Scientific Asst, Tech. Univ. of Aachen 1950–52; Jr Mining Inspector, Nordrhein-Westfalen 1953–54; worked in Ruhr coal-mining industry, then Production Man. of Osterfeld, Sterkrade and Hugo Haniel coal mines, B.A.G. Neue Hoffnung, Oberhausen/Ruhr 1955–59; Prof. and Head Dept of Mining Eng and Mineral Econs, Montanuniversität Leoben 1959–93 (now Prof. Emer.), Rector (Vice-Chair.) 1968–70; Vice-Pres., later Pres. Mining Soc. of Austria 1963–93; Vice-Pres. Austrian Soc. of Rock Mechanics 1968–81, Int. Organizing Cttee World Mining Congress 1976–2001; mem. Supervising Bd ÖBAG (Austrian State Mining Industry) 1988–95; Chair. Bd Inst. for Research about Mineral Resources 1983–87; Corresp. mem. Austrian Acad. of Sciences 1977, mem. 1983–; Foreign mem. Polish Acad. of Sciences 1991–, European Acad. of Sciences, Salzburg 1991–, Russian Acad. of Natural Sciences 1997–, Acad. of Mining Sciences 1998–; Hon. mem. Hungarian Acad. of Sciences 1990; Dr hc (Aachen), (Miskolc, Hungary), (Petrosani, Romania), (Moscow); Dr hc mit Laureate Assessor

des Bergfachs; Austrian State Award of Energy Research; nat. and int. medals (Austria, Germany, Poland, The Vatican). *Publications:* World Coal Resources, Methods of Assessment and Results 1976–79, Atlas of Mining Methods (3 vols, co-author) 1963–66, Mining in the Process of Change (ed.) 1988, Bergwirtschaft (mineral econs; co-author) 1990, Deponietechnik und Entsorgungsbergbau (waste disposal) (ed.) and about 250 other publs. *Leisure interests:* history, philosophy, cosmology, Africa, sailing. *Address:* Institut für Bergbaukunde, Borgtechnik und Bergwirtschaft der Montanuniversität Leoben, Franz-Josef-Strasse 18, 8700 Leoben (office); Gasteigergasse 5, 8700 Leoben, Austria (home). *Telephone:* (3842) 402/538 (office); (3842) 21190 (home). *Fax:* (3842) 402/530 (office); (3842) 21190 (home). *E-mail:* fettweis@unileoben.ac.at (office). *Website:* fettweis.at.

FEUILLÉE, Marc; French editor and newspaper executive; *Director-General, Le Figaro;* b. 1 Sept. 1962, Paris; ed secondary school in Dijon, Univ. of Paris I-Panthéon-Sorbonne, École des hautes études commerciales, Institut d'études politiques de Paris; Business Analyst, Hachette, Lagardère Group 1987–90; Financial Dir, L'Express 1990–98, Gen. Man. 1998–2006, CEO 2006–10; Vice-Pres. of Magazine Distribution, Libre Service Actualités 1996–98; Head of Syndicat de la presse magazine, SPM 2010–11; Dir-Gen. (CEO) Le Figaro newspaper 2011–; mem. Bd and Treas., OJD; mem. Supervisory Bd Presstalis; Pres. Syndicat de la presse quotidienne nationale. *Address:* Le Figaro, 14 blvd Haussmann, 75009 Paris, France (office). *Telephone:* 1-42-21-62-00 (office). *Fax:* 1-42-21-64-05 (office). *E-mail:* info@lefigaro.fr (office). *Website:* www.lefigaro.fr (office).

FEULNER, Edwin J., MBA, PhD; American research institute administrator; *Chairman, Asian Studies Center, Heritage Foundation;* m. Linda Claire Leventhal; one s. one d.; ed Regis Univ., Georgetown Univ., Univ. of Edinburgh and London School of Econs, UK; Pres. Heritage Foundation, Washington, DC 1973–2013, continues as Chair. Asian Studies Center, Chancellor, Heritage Foundation; Treasurer and Trustee, Mont Pelerin Soc. (also fmr Pres.); Trustee and fmr Chair. Intercollegiate Studies Inst.; Dir Nat. Chamber Foundation; adviser to several US govt depts and agencies; fmr Consultant for Domestic Policy to US Pres. Ronald Reagan; US Rep. to UN Special Session on Disarmament 1982; mem. numerous govt comms including Carlucci Comm. on Foreign Aid 1983, Pres.'s Comm. on White House Fellows 1981–83, Meltzer Comm. 1999–2000; mem. Bd of Visitors, George Mason Univ.; Trustee Acton Inst., Int. Republican Inst.; fmr Pres. Philadelphia Soc.; fmr Dir Sequoia Bank, Regis Univ., Council for Nat. Policy; regular contrib. to several publs including Chicago Sun Times, Chicago Tribune, New York Times, Washington Post; Dr hc (Nichols Coll.) 1981, (Univ. Francisco Marroquin, Guatemala) 1982, (Bellevue Coll.) 1987, (Gonzaga Univ.) 1992, (Grove City Coll.) 1994, (Pepperdine Univ.) 2000, (St Norbert Coll.) 2002, (Hillsdale Coll.) 2004, (Thomas More Univ.) 2005, (Edin.) 2006, (Hanyang Univ., Korea); Presidential Citizen's Medal 1989. *Publications include:* US–Japan Mutual Security: The Next Twenty Years (Ed.), China: The Turning Point (ed.), Looking Back 1981, Conservatives Stalk the House 1983, The March of Freedom 1998, Intellectual Pilgrims 1999, Leadership for America 2000, Getting America Right 2006. *Address:* Heritage Foundation, 214 Massachusetts Avenue, NE, Washington, DC 20002, USA (office). *Telephone:* (202) 546-4400 (office). *Fax:* (202) 544-0904 (office). *Website:* www.heritage.org (office).

FFOWCS WILLIAMS, John Eirwyn, MA, PhD, ScD (Cantab.), CEng, FREng, FRAeS, FInstP, FIMA, FRSA; British engineer and academic; b. 25 May 1935; m. Anne Beatrice Mason 1959; two s. one d.; ed Derby Tech. Coll., Univ. of Southampton; eng apprentice, Rolls-Royce Ltd 1951–55; Spitfire Mitchell Memorial Scholar to Southampton Univ. 1955–60 (Pres. Students' Union 1957–58); joined Aerodynamics Div., Nat. Physical Lab. 1960–62; with Bolt, Beranek & Newman, Inc. 1962–64; Reader in Applied Math., Imperial Coll. of Science and Tech. 1964–69, Rolls-Royce Prof. of Theoretical Acoustics 1969–72; Rank Prof. of Eng, Univ. of Cambridge 1972–2002, now Prof. Emer.; Master, Emmanuel Coll., Cambridge 1996–2002 (Professorial Fellow 1972–96, Life Fellow 2002); Chair. Concorde Noise Panel 1965–75, Noise Research Cttee, Airport Regions Conf. 1969–76, Topexpress Ltd 1979–89; Dir VSEL Consortium PLC 1987–95; Foreign Assoc. Nat. Acad. of Eng, USA 1995; Fellow, AIAA, Inst. of Acoustics, Acoustical Soc. of America; Hon. Prof. Beijing Inst. of Aeronautics and Astronautics 1992–, Foreign Hon. mem. American Acad. of Arts and Sciences 1989; Aero-Acoustics Medal, AIAA 1977, Rayleigh Medal, Inst. of Acoustics 1984, Silver Medal, Soc. Française d'Acoustique 1989, Gold Medal, Royal Aeronautical Soc. 1990, Per Bruel Gold Medal, ASME 1997, Sir Frank Whittle Medal, Royal Acad. of Eng. 2002. *Publications:* Sound and Sources of Sound (with A. P. Dowling) 1983, numerous articles in professional journals; film on Aerodynamic Sound (jtly). *Leisure interests:* friends and cigars. *Address:* University of Cambridge, Department of Engineering, Trumpington Street, Cambridge, CB2 1PZ; Emmanuel College, Cambridge, CB2 3AP, England. *Telephone:* (1223) 332629. *Fax:* (1223) 332662. *E-mail:* jewc@eng.cam.ac.uk. *Website:* www.eng.cam.ac.uk/~jefw.

FFRENCH-DAVIS MUÑOZ, Ricardo, PhD; Chilean economist; *Principal Regional Adviser, United Nations Economic Commission for Latin America and the Caribbean;* b. 27 June 1936, Santiago; m. Marcela Yampaglia 1966; ed Catholic Univ. of Chile, Univ. of Chicago; Researcher and Prof. of Econs, Econ. Research Cen., Catholic Univ. 1962–64; Prof. of Econs, Univ. of Chile 1962–73, 1984–; Deputy Man. Research Dept, Cen. Bank of Chile 1964–70; Research Dir Cen. on Planning Studies, Catholic Univ. 1970–75; Vice-Pres. and Dir Centre for Latin American Econ. Research (CIEPLAN), Santiago 1976–90; Research Dir Cen. Bank of Chile 1990; mem. Acad. Council, Latin American Program, The Woodrow Wilson Center, Washington, DC 1977–80; mem. UN Cttee on Econ. Planning 1990–92; mem. Exec. Cttee Latin American Studies Asscn 1992–94; Visiting Fellow, Univ. of Oxford 1974, 1979; Visiting Prof., Boston Univ. 1976; Pres. Acad. Circle, Acad. de Humanismo Cristiano, Chile 1978–81; Co-ordinator Working Group on Econ. Issues of Inter-American Dialogue 1985–86; Prin. Regional Adviser, Econ. Comm. for Latin America and the Caribbean (ECLAC) 2000–; mem. Editorial Bds Latin American Research Review, El Trimestre Economico and Colección Estudios Cieplan; Ford Foundation Grants 1971, 1975, 2001, Social Science Research Council Grant 1976, Inter-American Dialogue Grant 1985–86. *Publications:* Políticas Económicas en Chile: 1952–70 1973, El cobre en el desarrollo nacional (co-ed.) 1974, Economía internacional: teorías y políticas para el desarrollo 1979, 1985, Latin America and a New International Economic Order (co-ed.) 1981, 1985,

The Monetarist Experiment in Chile 1982, Relaciones financieras externas y la economía latinoamericana (ed.) 1983, Development and External Debt in Latin America (co-ed.) 1988, Debt-equity swaps in Chile 1990, Latin America and the Caribbean: Policies to Improve Linkages with the World Economy (ed.) 1998, Macroeconomics, Trade and Finance 2000, Financial Crisis in 'Successful' Emerging Economies (ed.) 2001, Economic Reforms in Chile: From Dictatorship to Democracy 2002; over 100 articles on int. econs, Latin-American econ. devt and Chilean econ. policies in 8 languages. *Address:* Economic Commission for Latin America and the Caribbean, Santiago, Chile (office); Casilla 179-D, Santiago, Chile (home). *Telephone:* (562) 210-2555 (office). *Fax:* (562) 208-1801 (office). *E-mail:* ricardo.ffrenchdavis@cepal.org (office). *Website:* www.eclac.cl (office).

FIASCHI, Lorenzo; Italian gallery director; *Co-Director and Partner, Galleria Continua;* co-f., with Mario Cristiani and Maurizio Rigillo, Galleria Continua in San Gimignano, Tuscany 1990, other locations include Beijing 2004 and Boissy-le-Châtel, France, 2007–; represents several major artists, including Daniel Buren, Kendell Geers, Anish Kapoor and Hans Op de Beeck. *Address:* Galleria Continua, Via del Castello 11, 53037 San Gimignano, Italy (office). *Telephone:* (0577) 943134 (office). *E-mail:* info@galleriacontinua.com (office). *Website:* www.galleriacontinua.com (office).

FICEAC, Bogdan; Romanian editor and newspaper executive; *Editor-in-Chief, România Liberă (Free Romania);* fmr Deputy Ed.-in-Chief, România Liberă (Free Romania), Bucharest, currently Ed.-in-Chief; Reuters Foundation Fellow, John S. Knight Fellowship, Stanford Univ. *Publications include:* Cenzura comunista 1999, Tehnici de manipulare 2004. *Address:* România Liberă, Piaţa Presei Libere 1, Corp. c, etaj 4, 013701 Bucharest, Romania (office). *Telephone:* (21) 2224770 (office). *Fax:* (21) 2232071 (office). *E-mail:* redactia@romanialibera.ro (office). *Website:* www.romanialibera.ro (office).

FICO, Robert, JUDr, CSc; Slovak politician and lawyer; *Prime Minister;* b. 15 Sept. 1964, Topolčany; m. Svetlana Ficová; one s.; ed Comenius Univ., Bratislava; mem. staff Inst. of Laws, Ministry of Justice 1986–91; mem. CP 1987–90; mem. Party of Democratic Left—SDL 1990–99, Vice-Chair. 1998–99; mem. Nat. Council 1992–2006, 2010–12; Head of Slovak del. to Parl. Meeting of European Council, Rep. to European Cttee for Human Rights and European Court for Human Rights 1994–2000; Founder and Chair. Direction Smer party 1999– (absorbed Party of Civic Understanding 2003, Social Democratic Alternative, Social Democratic Party of Slovakia and Party of Democratic Left 2004, renamed Direction—Social Democracy (Smer—Sociálna demokracia) 2004), Pres. Parl. Mems' Club 2002–; Observer on behalf of European Socialists' faction at European Parl. 2002–04; Prime Minister 2006–10, 2012–; unsuccessful cand. in 2014 presidential election. *Publication:* Trest smrti (Punishment of Death). *Leisure interest:* sport. *Address:* Office of the Government, nám. Slobody 1, 813 70 Bratislava (office); Direction—Social Democracy (Smer—Sociálna demokracia), Súmračná 25, 821 02 Bratislava, Slovakia (office). *Telephone:* (2) 5729-5111 (office). *Fax:* (2) 5249-7595 (office). *E-mail:* urad@vlada.gov.sk (office); generalny.manager@strana-smer.sk (office). *Website:* www.vlada.gov.sk (office); www.strana-smer.sk (office).

FIDAI, Muhammad Halim, MA, MBA; Afghan politician; *Governor of Wardak Province;* b. 28 Dec. 1970, Paktika Prov.; m. Samina Fidai; four c.; ed High Teachers' Inst., Peshawar, Pakistan; worked with several NGOs in Afghanistan since 1990s, including Dir Gen., American Center 1989–2002; Head of Media Dept, CARE International 1995–2003, also Ed.-in-Chief Pamlarana Magazine 1995–2003; Communication Man., Creative Associates 2003–05; Media and Communication Dir Counterpart Int. 2005–08; Country Dir in Afghanistan, South Asia Free Media Asscn 2007–08; Gov. Wardak Prov. 2008–. *Leisure interests:* reading and writing. *Address:* Office of the Governor, Maidan Shahr, Maidan Wardak Province, Afghanistan (office). *Telephone:* (799) 733-733 (office).

FIDALGO, José María; Spanish trade union official, orthopaedic surgeon and academic; b. 18 Feb. 1948, León; orthopaedic surgeon, Hosp. La Paz, Madrid; mem. trade union movt 1974–; mem. Confederación Sindical de Comisiones Obreras (CCOO) 1977–, Sec. of Institutional Policy 1987–2000, Gen.-Sec. 2000–08; Gen.-Sec. Fed. of Health Workers 1981–87; Dir Negocia, Negotiation and Mediation Centre, IE Law School, Madrid 2009–. *Address:* IE Law School, María de Molina, 11, 28006 Madrid, Spain (office). *Telephone:* (91) 5689600 (office). *Website:* www.ie.edu/IE/site/php/en/school_law.php (office).

FIELD, Sir Malcolm David, Kt; British business executive; b. 25 Aug. 1937, London; m. (divorced 1982); one d.; m. 2nd Rosemary Anne Charlton 2001; ed Highgate School and London Business School; joined W.H. Smith 1963, Wholesale Dir 1970–78, Man. Dir Retail Group 1978–82, Man. Dir 1982–93; Group Chief Exec. 1994–96; Chair. Civil Aviation Authority (CAA) 1996–2001; Policy Adviser to Dept of Transport, London and the Regions 2000–; mem. Bd of Man. Navy, Army and Air Force Insts (NAAFI) 1973–93, Chair. 1986–93; Dir (non-exec.) Marine Environment Protection Cttee 1989–99, Scottish & Newcastle PLC 1993–98, Phoenix Group 1994–97, The Stationery Office 1996–2001, Walker Greenbank PLC 1997–2001, Sofa Workshop Ltd 1998–2002, Beeson Gregory 2000–04, Odgers 2002–; Chair. (non-exec.) Tubelines Ltd 2003–06; Chair. Aricom PLC 2004–06; Sr Dir Hochschild Mining 2006–. *Leisure interests:* watching cricket, tennis, ballet, modern art, reading biographies, recreating garden in Devon. *Address:* 21 Embankment Gardens, London, SW3 4LW, England (office). *Telephone:* (20) 7351-7455 (office); (7740) 433744 (home). *Fax:* (20) 7351-7452 (office). *E-mail:* mdfield@netcomuk.co.uk (office).

FIELD, Sally; American actress and film producer; b. 6 Nov. 1946, Pasadena, Calif.; m. Alan Greisman 1984; three c.; ed Actor's Studio; co.-f. Fogwood Films Ltd (production co.) 1984. *Films include:* The Way West 1967, Stay Hungry 1976, Smokey and the Bandit 1977, Hooper 1978, Norma Rai (Cannes Film Festival Best Actress Award 1979, Acad. Award 1980) 1979, Beyond the Poseidon Adventure 1979, Smokey and the Bandit II 1980, Absence of Malice 1981, Places in the Heart (Acad. Award 1984) 1984, Murphy's Romance (also exec. producer) 1985, Punchline 1987, Steel Magnolias 1989, Not Without My Daughter 1991, Soapdish 1991, Dying Young (co-producer) 1991, Homeward Bound: The Incredible Journey (voice) 1993, Mrs Doubtfire 1993, Forrest Gump 1994, Eye for an Eye 1996, Homeward Bound II: Lost in San Francisco (voice) 1996, Where the Heart Is 2000, Time of Our Lives 2000, Say It Isn't So 2001, Legally Blonde 2: Red, White & Blonde 2003, Two Weeks 2006, The Amazing Spider-Man 2012, Lincoln 2012. *TV*

appearances include: Gidget (series) 1965, The Flying Nun (series) 1967–69, Maybe I'll Come Home In the Spring 1971, Marriage: Year One 1971, Home for the Holidays 1972, The Girl With Something Extra (series) 1973, Bridges 1976, Sybil (Emmy Award 1977) 1976, A Woman of Independent Means (mini-series) 1995, Merry Christmas, George Bailey 1997, From the Earth to the Moon (mini-series) 1998, A Cooler Climate 1999, David Copperfield 2000, ER (series) 2000–06, The Court (series) 2002, Conviction 2005, Brothers & Sisters (Emmy Award for Best Actress in a Drama Series 2007) 2006–09. *Address:* 9100 Wilshire Blvd, Suite 1000, Beverly Hills, CA 90212; c/o Creative Artists Agency (CAA), 2000 Avenue of the Stars, Los Angeles, CA 90067, USA.

FIELDING, Sir Leslie, Kt, KCMG, LLD, FRSA, FRGS; British fmr university vice-chancellor and diplomatist; b. 29 July 1932, London, England; s. of Percy Archer Fielding and Margaret Calder Horry; m. Sally Harvey 1978; one s. one d.; ed Emmanuel Coll., Cambridge, School of Oriental and African Studies, London, St Antony's Coll., Oxford; with HM Diplomatic Service (served Tehran, Singapore, Phnom Penh, Paris and London) 1956–73; Dir External Relations Directorate-Gen., European Comm., Brussels 1973–77; Visiting Fellow, St Antony's Coll., Oxford 1977–78; Head EC Del., Tokyo 1978–82; Dir-Gen. for External Relations, Brussels 1982–87; Vice-Chancellor Univ. of Sussex 1987–92; mem. Japan-EC Asscn 1988–98, UK-Japan 2000 Group 1993–2000; mem. House of Laity of Gen. Synod of Church of England 1990–92; Hon. Pres. Univ. Asscn for Contemporary European Studies 1990–2000; Hon. Fellow, Emmanuel Coll. Cambridge 1990–, Sussex European Inst. 1993; Grand Officer's Star, Order of St Agatha of San Marino 1987, White Rose of Finland 1988, Silver Order of Merit (Austria) 1989. *Publications:* Travellers' Tales (contrib.) 1999, More Tales from the Travellers' (contrib.) 2005, Before the Killing Fields: Witness to Cambodia and the Vietnam War 2008, Kindly Call Me God: The Misadventures of 'Fielding of the FO', Eurocrat Extraordinaire and Vice-Chancellor Semipotentiary 2009, Twilight over the Temples: The Close of Cambodia's Belle Epoque 2010, The Mistress of the Bees 2011, Mentioned in Despatches (Phnom Penh, Paris, Tokyo, Brussels): Is Diplomacy Dead? 2012. *Leisure interests:* country life, theology. *Address:* Wild Cherry Farm, Elton, nr Ludlow, Shropshire, SY8 2HQ, England. *E-mail:* fieldingleslie@aol.com.

FIELDS, Janice (Jan) L.; American business executive; *President, McDonald's USA, LLC;* m. Doug Fields; two c.; joined McDonald's as restaurant crew mem. 1978, worked in all facets of restaurant business, served as a Dir of Store Man. and Operations from 1978, apptd Regional Vice-Pres. Pittsburgh Region 1994, Vice-Pres. McDonald's Great Lakes Div. May 2000, Pres. Cen. Div., McDonald's USA –2006, Exec. Vice-Pres. and COO McDonald's USA, LLC 2006–10, Pres. 2010–, Exec. Sponsor for Career Devt Program; mem. Bd of Dirs Monsanto Co. 2008–; Chair. and mem. Advisory Bd Catalyst, Inc. (women's org.); Dir of Ronald McDonald House Charities, Chicago Urban League; McDonald's Pres.'s Award 1988, McDonald's Golden Arch Partners Award 1988, McDonald's Women Operators Network Recognition Award 2001, McDonald's Women's Leadership Award 2002, named to The Wall Street Journal's 50 Women to Watch list 2007, named to Crain's Chicago Business' list of 25 Women to Watch 2007, ranked by Fortune magazine amongst the 50 Most Powerful Women in Business in the US (48th) 2007, (36th) 2008, (32nd) 2009, (25th) 2010, (17th) 2011, (25th) 2012, ranked by Forbes magazine amongst The World's 100 Most Powerful Women (67th) 2008, (90th) 2009, (92nd) 2011, (88th) 2012. *Address:* McDonald's Corporation, 2111 McDonald's Drive, Oak Brook, IL 60523, USA (office). *Telephone:* (630) 623-3000 (office). *Fax:* (630) 623-5004 (office). *E-mail:* info@mcdonalds.com (office). *Website:* www.mcdonalds.com (office).

FIELDSEND, Sir John Charles Rowell, Kt, KBE, BA, LLB; British fmr judge and barrister; b. 13 Sept. 1921, Lincoln; s. of Charles Fieldsend and Phyllis Fieldsend; m. Muriel Gedling 1945 (died 2010); one s. one d.; ed Michaelhouse, Natal, Rhodes Univ. Coll., Grahamstown, SA; served in Royal Artillery 1943–45; called to the Bar, Southern Rhodesia 1947, QC 1959; advocate in pvt. practice 1947–63; Pres. Special Income Tax Court for Fed. of Rhodesia and Nyasaland 1958–63; High Court Judge, Southern Rhodesia 1963–68 (resgnd); Asst Solicitor, Law Comm. for England and Wales 1968–78; Sec., Law Comm. 1978–80; Chief Justice of Zimbabwe 1980–83; Chief Justice, Turks and Caicos Islands 1985–87; Pres. Court of Appeal, St Helena 1985–93; Judge, Court of Appeal, Falkland Islands and British Antarctic Territory 1985–96, Court of Appeal, Gibraltar 1985–97 (Pres. 1990); Prin. Legal Adviser, British Indian Ocean Territory 1984–87, Chief Justice 1987–98. *Leisure interest:* travel. *Address:* Great Dewes, Ardingly, Sussex, RH17 6UP, England (office).

FIENNES, Joseph Alberic; British actor; b. 27 May 1970, Salisbury; s. of Mark Fiennes and the late Jini Lash; brother of Ralph Fiennes (q.v.), Martha, Magnus, Sophie and Jacob Fiennes; m. María Dolores Diéguez 2009; one d.; ed Guildhall School of Music and Drama. *Theatre includes:* The Woman in Black, A Month in the Country, A View from the Bridge, Real Classy Affair, Edward II, Love's Labours Lost, Epitaph for George Dillon (Comedy Theatre, London) 2005–06, Cyrano de Bergerac (Chichester Festival Theatre) 2009. *RSC performances include:* Son of Man, Les Enfants Du Paradis, As You Like It, Troilus and Cressida, The Herbal Bed. *Television includes:* The Vacillations of Poppy Carew 1995, Animated Epics: Beowulf (voice) 1998, FlashForward 2009–10, Camelot (mini-series) 2011. *Radio:* Romeo and Juliet, Keith Douglas Poems. *Films include:* Stealing Beauty 1996, Shakespeare in Love 1998, Martha – Meet Frank, Daniel and Laurence 1998, Elizabeth 1998, Forever Mine 1999, Rancid Aluminium 2000, Enemy at the Gates 2001, Killing Me Softly 2001, Dust 2001, Leo 2002, Sinbad: Legend of the Seven Seas 2003, Luther 2003, Merchant of Venice 2004, Man to Man 2005, The Great Raid 2005, The Darwin Awards 2006, Running with Scissors 2006, Goodbye Bafana 2007, The Escapist 2007, Pretty/Handsome 2008, Spring 1941 2008, Against the Current 2009,. *Address:* c/o Tracy Brennan, Creative Artists Agency, 2000 Avenue of The Stars, Los Angeles, CA 90067, USA (office). *E-mail:* josephfiennesnet@gmail.com (office). *Website:* www.joseph-fiennes.net (office).

FIENNES, Ralph Nathaniel Twisleton Wykeham; British actor; b. 22 Dec. 1962, Ipswich, Suffolk, England; s. of the late Mark Fiennes and Jennifer (Jini) Lash; brother of Joseph Fiennes (q.v.); m. Alex Kingston 1993 (divorced 1997); partner Francesca Annis 1995–2006; ed St Kieran's Coll., Kilkenny and Newtown School, Co. Waterford, Ireland, Bishop Wordsworth's School, Salisbury, Chelsea

School of Art, Royal Acad. of Dramatic Art, London. *Theatre includes:* Open Air Theatre, Regent's Park: Twelfth Night, Ring Round the Moon 1985, A Midsummer's Night Dream 1985, 1986, Romeo and Juliet 1986; Royal Nat. Theatre: Six Characters in Search of an Author, Fathers and Sons, Ting Tang Mine 1987; RSC: King John, Much Ado About Nothing, title role of Henry VI in The Plantagenets 1988, Playing with Trains 1989, Troilus and Cressida, King Lear 1990, The Man Who Came to Dinner, Love's Labours Lost 1991; Almeida Theatre: Hamlet 1995, Ivanov 1997, Richard II 2000, Coriolanus 2000, Brand 2003, Oedipus 2008. *Films include:* Wuthering Heights 1992, The Baby of Mâcon 1993, Schindler's List (BAFTA Award for Best Actor in a Supporting Role) 1993, Quiz Show 1994, Strange Days 1995, The English Patient 1996, Oscar and Lucinda 1997, The Avengers 1998, The Prince of Egypt (voice) 1998, Onegin (also exec. producer) 1999, Sunshine 1999, The End of the Affair 1999, Spider 2002, The Good Thief 2002, Red Dragon 2002, Maid in Manhattan 2002, The Chumscrubber 2005, Chromophobia 2005, Harry Potter and the Goblet of Fire 2005, The Constant Gardener 2005, The White Countess 2005, Wallace & Gromit in the Curse of the Were-Rabbit (voice) 2005, Land of the Blind 2006, Harry Potter and the Order of the Phoenix 2007, Bernard and Doris 2007, In Bruges 2008, The Duchess 2008, The Hurt Locker 2008, The Reader 2008, Cemetery Junction 2009, Clash of the Titans 2009, Harry Potter and the Half-Blood Prince 2009, Harry Potter and the Deathly Hallows: Part 1 2010, Coriolanus (actor and dir (debut)) 2010, Wrath of the Titans 2012, Great Expectations 2012, Skyfall 2012, The Invisible Woman 2013, The Grand Budapest Hotel 2014. *Television includes:* Prime Suspect (film) 1991, Great Performances (series) – A Dangerous Man: Lawrence after Arabia 1992, Screen Two (series) – The Cormorant 1993, The Great War and the Shaping of the 20th Century (series) (voice of Wilfred Owen) 1996, How Proust Can Change Your Life (film) 2000, The Miracle Maker (voice) 2000, Freedom: A History of Us (series documentary) 2003, Page Eight (film) 2011, Rev. (series) 2011, Turks & Caicos 2014. *Address:* c/o Dalzell & Beresford Ltd, 26 Astwood Mews, London, SW7 4DE, England (office). *Telephone:* (20) 7341-9411 (office). *Fax:* (20) 7341-9412 (office). *E-mail:* mail@dbltd.co.uk (office). *Website:* www.dalzellandberesford.com (office).

FIENNES, Sir Ranulph Twisleton-Wykeham-, 3rd Bt, cr. 1916, OBE, DLitt; British travel writer, lecturer and explorer; b. 7 March 1944, Windsor; s. of Lt-Col Sir Ranulph Twisleton-Wykeham-Fiennes, DSO, 2nd Bt and Audrey Newson; m. 1st Virginia Pepper 1970 (died 2004); one d.; ed Eton; Lt Royal Scots Greys 1966, Capt. 1968, retd 1970; attached 22 SAS Regt 1966, Sultan of Muscat's Armed Forces 1968; Leader, British Expeditions to White Nile 1969, Jostedalsbre Glacier 1970, Headless Valley, BC 1971, (Towards) North Pole 1977; Leader, Transglobe Expedition (first polar circumnavigation of world on its polar axis) 1979–82; led first unsupported crossing of Antarctic continent and longest unsupported polar journey in history Nov. 1992–Feb. 1993; first man to reach both poles on land; discovered lost city of Ubar in Oman 1993; ran seven marathons on seven continents in seven days 2003; climbed north face of Mount Eiger 2007; climbed Mount Everest 2009; Exec. Consultant to Chair. of Occidental Petroleum Corpn 1984–90; Hon. mem. Royal Inst. of Navigation; Hon. DSc (Loughborough Coll.) 1986; Hon. DUniv (Univ. of Cen. England in Birmingham) 1995, (Univ. of Portsmouth) 2000, (Sheffield) 2005, (Univ. of Abertay, Dundee) 2007; Hon. DLitt (Glasgow Caledonian) 2002; Dhofar Campaign Medal 1969, Sultan's Bravery Medal 1970, Livingstone Medal, Royal Scottish Geographical Soc., Royal Inst. of Navigation 1977, Gold Medal of Explorers Club of NY 1983, Founders Medal Royal Geographical Soc. 1984, Polar Medal for Arctic and Antarctic, with Bars 1985, with clasp 1995, ITN Award for Int. Exploit of the Decade 1989, Explorers Club Millennium Award for Polar Exploration 2000, ITV1 Greatest Briton – Sportsman of the Year 2007. *Achievements include:* has raised £16 million for various charities (Just Giving Top Fundraiser 2011). *Films:* Killer Elite 2011 (based on The Feather Men). *Publications:* A Talent for Trouble 1970, Ice Fall in Norway 1972, The Headless Valley 1973, Where Soldiers Fear to Tread 1975, Hell on Ice 1979, To the Ends of the Earth 1983, Bothie – The Polar Dog (with Virginia Twisleton-Wykeham-Fiennes) 1984, Living Dangerously 1987, The Feather Men 1991, Atlantis of the Sands 1992, Mind over Matter 1993, The Sett 1996, Fit for Life 1998, Beyond the Limits 2000, The Secret Hunters 2001, Captain Scott 2003, Mad Bad and Dangerous to Know (auto-biog.) 2007, Mad Dogs And Englishmen 2009, My Heroes 2011, Cold 2013. *Leisure interests:* langlauf, photography. *Address:* Greenlands, Exford, Minehead, West Somerset, TA24 7NU, England (office). *Telephone:* (1643) 831350 (office).

FIERSTEIN, Harvey Forbes; American actor and screenwriter; b. 6 June 1954, Brooklyn, New York; s. of Irving Fierstein and Jacqueline Harriet Gilbert; ed Pratt Univ.; began acting career as founding mem. The Gallery Players, Brooklyn; professional acting debut in Pork 1971; Fund for Human Dignity Award 1983, GLAAD Award for Visibility 1994, Humanitas Prize (in Children's Animation category) 2000; also three Drama Desk Awards, Drama League Award, New York Magazine Award, a special Obie, Theater World and LA Drama Critics Circle Award. *Films include:* Garbo Talks 1984, Torch Song Trilogy (also writer) 1988, The Harvest 1993, Mrs. Doubtfire 1993, Bullets Over Broadway 1994, Dr. Jekyll and Ms. Hyde 1995, White Lies 1996, Independence Day 1996, Everything Relative 1996, Kull the Conqueror 1997, Mulan (voice) 1998, Safe Men 1998, Jump 1999, Playing Mona Lisa 2000, Death to Smoochy 2002, Duplex 2003, Mulan II (voice) 2004, Farce of the Penguins (voice) 2007; narrator The Times of Harvey Milk. *TV appearances include:* The Demon Murder Case (voice) 1983, Apology 1986, Tidy Endings 1988, In the Shadow of Love: A Teen AIDS Story 1992, Daddy's Girls (series) 1994, Happily Ever After: Fairy Tales for Every Child (voice) 1995, Stories from My Childhood (series, voice) 1998, X-Chromosome (series, voice) 1999, Double Platinum 1999, The Sissy Duckling (also writer, voice) 1999, Common Ground (also writer) 2000. *Plays:* Torch Song Trilogy (writer and actor) (four Tony Awards including Best Actor (Play) and Author of Best Play 1983) 1982, La Cage aux Folles (librettist) (Tony Award for Best Book (Musical) 1984) 1983, Legs Diamond (author) 1988, Hairspray (Best Actor (Musical) 2003) 2003, Fiddler on the Roof 2005, A Catered Affair (also co-author) 2007, Newsies (author) 2012, Kinky Boots (author) (Tony Award for Best Musical 2013) 2012. *Leisure interests:* gay rights activist, painting, gardening, cooking. *Address:* c/o William Morris Agency, 1325 Avenue of the Americas, New York, NY 10019, USA.

FIGEĽ, Ján, MSc, PhD; Slovak politician and research scientist; *Chairman, Christian Democratic Movement;* b. 20 Jan. 1960, Vranov nad Toplou; m.; four c.; ed Košice Tech. Univ., Georgetown Univ., USA, Universitaire Faculteiten Sint-Ignatius Antwerpen, Antwerp, Belgium, St Elisabeth Univ. of Health and Social Work, Bratislava; Research and Devt Scientist, ZPA Prešov 1983–92; mem. Parl. 1992–98, 2002–, mem. Foreign Affairs Cttee, Cttee for European Integration 1992–98, Chair. Foreign Affairs Cttee 2002–; mem. Christian Democratic Movt (Krestansko-demokratické hnutie—KDH) 1990–, mem. Party Presidium 1992–98, Deputy Chair. for Foreign Policy 1992–94, 1994–98, 2000–04, Chair. KDH 2010–; State Sec., Ministry of Foreign Affairs 1998–2002; Chief Negotiator for Slovakia's accession to EU 1998–2003; mem. Presidium Slovak Democratic Coalition 1998–2000; Vice-Chair. European People's Party (EPP) in Parl. Ass. 1998; mem. Convention on the Future of Europe 2002–03; Head, Standing Del. of Observers of European Parl. 2003–04; Presidency mem. EPP-ED fraction in European Parl. 2003–04; mem. European Parl. Cttee on Econ. Affairs and Devt 2003–04, Vice-Chair. 2004; EU Commr without Portfolio Jan.–Nov. 2004, for Educ., Training, Culture and Multilingualism 2004–06, for Educ., Training, Culture and Youth 2007–09; First Deputy Prime Minister and Minister of Transport, Posts and Telecommunications 2010–11, First Deputy Prime Minister and Minister of Transport, Construction and Regional Devt 2011–12; Lecturer in Int. Relations, Univ. of Trnava 1995–2000; mem. Cen. European Forum, Int. Cttee for Support of Democracy in Cuba; Pres. Pan-European Union in Slovakia; mem. Bd of Dirs Slovak Soc. for Foreign Policy, Anton Tunega Foundation, Foundation for the Support of Social Change; mem. Council Cen. European Inst. for Econ. and Social Reforms; Hon. Pres. Centre for European Policy, Kolping Work Slovakia; Hon. Citizen of Ustí nad Toplou 2005; Hon. Prof., Tech. Univ. of Cluj-Napoca, Romania 2007; Hon. Chair. Centre for European Policy, Kolping Soc. in Slovakia; Chevalier, Légion d'honneur 2004; Dr hc (Tech. Univ. of Košice) 2006, (Dimitri Cantemir Christian Univ., Bucharest) 2008, (Univ. of Trnava) 2009; Andrew Elias Prize, Czechoslovak Soc. of Arts and Science, Washington, DC 2004, Gold Medal, Int. Relations Council of Christians and Jews, Cambridge, UK 2006, Prešov Region Prize 2006, Freedom Prize, Int. Peace Centre, Sarajevo 2007. *Publications:* Slovakia on the Road to EU Membership (co-author) 2002, Slovakia on the Road to the European Union (with Miroslav Adam) 2003, Ageing Europe 2005, Return Home 2009. *Address:* Christian Democratic Movement (Krestansko-demokratické hnutie), Bajkalská 25, 821 01 Bratislava, Slovakia (office). *Telephone:* (2) 5823-3431 (office). *Fax:* (2) 5823-3434 (office). *E-mail:* sekretariat@kdh.sk (office). *Website:* www.kdh.sk (office).

FIGES, Orlando, PhD; British historian, writer and academic; *Professor of History, Birkbeck College, London;* b. 20 Nov. 1959; s. of John Figes and Eva Figes (née Unger); m. Stephanie Palmer 1990; two d.; ed Gonville and Caius Coll., Cambridge, Trinity Coll., Cambridge; Fellow, Trinity Coll., Cambridge 1984–89, Dir of Studies in History 1988–98, Lecturer in History, Univ. of Cambridge 1987–99; Prof. of History, Birkbeck Coll., Univ. of London 1999–. *Publications include:* Peasant Russia, Civil War: the Volga Countryside in Revolution 1917–21 1989, A People's Tragedy: the Russian Revolution 1891–1924 (Wolfson History Prize, WHSmith Literary Award, NCR Book Award, Los Angeles Times Book Prize) 1996, Interpreting the Russian Revolution (co-author) 1999, Natasha's Dance: a Cultural History of Russia 2002, The Whisperers: Private Life in Stalin's Russia 2007, Crimea: The Last Crusade 2010, Just Send Me Word: A True Story of Love and Survival in the Gulag 2012; numerous review articles and contribs to other published books. *Leisure interests:* football, wine, gardening. *Address:* School of History, Classics and Archaeology, Birkbeck College, Malet Street, London, WC1E 7HX, England (office). *Telephone:* (20) 7631-6299 (office). *Fax:* (20) 7631-6552 (office). *E-mail:* o.figes@bbk.ac.uk (office). *Website:* www.bbk.ac.uk/hca/staff/orlandofiges (office); www.orlandofiges.com.

FIGGIS, Brian Norman, PhD, DSc, FAA; Australian chemist and academic; *Professor Emeritus of Inorganic Chemistry, University of Western Australia;* b. 27 March 1930, Sydney; s. of John N. E. Figgis and Dorice B. M. Figgis (née Hughes); m. Jane S. Frank 1968; one s. one d.; ed Univs of Sydney and New South Wales; Research Fellow, then Lecturer, Univ. Coll., London, UK 1957–62; Reader, Univ. of Western Australia 1963–69, Prof. 1969, now Prof. Emer.; Visiting Prof., Univ. of Texas, USA 1961, Univ. of Arizona 1968, Univ. of Florence, Italy 1975, Univ. of Sussex, UK 1975; Visiting Scientist, Institut Laue-Langevin, France, Brookhaven Nat. Lab., Upton, NY, USA, Argonne Nat. Lab., Ill. 1984, 1991; Inorganic Award, Royal Australian Chemical Inst. 1985, Walter Burfitt Prize, Royal Soc. of NSW 1986, H.G. Smith Medal, Royal Australian Chemical Inst. 1989, Centenary Medal 2003. *Publications:* Introduction to Ligand Fields 1966, Ligand Field Theory and Its Applications 2000; Ed. Transition Metal Chemistry (Vols 8 and 9) 1984–85; 220 articles in scientific journals. *Leisure interest:* DIY. *Address:* 9 Hamersley Street, Cottesloe, WA 6011, Australia. *Telephone:* (8) 9384-3032. *E-mail:* bnf@cyllene.uwa.edu.au.

FIGGIS, Mike; British film director, writer and musician; b. 28 Feb. 1949, Carlisle; studied music, performing in band Gas Board; musician in experimental theatre group The People Show in early 1970s; made ind. films including Redheugh, Slow Fade, Animals of the City; made film The House for Channel 4 (UK); Inst. of Film Professionals (IFP) Ind. Spirit Award 1996, Nat. Soc. of Film Critics Award. *Films include:* Stormy Monday (also screenplay and music) 1988, Internal Affairs (also music) 1990, Liebestraum (also screenplay and music) 1991, Mr. Jones 1993, The Browning Version 1994, Leaving Las Vegas (also screenplay and music) 1995, One Night Stand 1997, Flamenco Women 1997, Miss Julie 1999, The Loss of Sexual Innocence 1999, Time Code 2000, Hotel 2001, The Battle of Orgreave 2001, Cold Creek Manor 2003, Co/Ma 2004 (also writer), The 4 Dreams of Miss X 2007, Love Live Long 2008. *Address:* c/o Robert Newman, William Morris Endeavor Entertainment, 9601 Wilshire Blvd., Beverly Hills, CA 90212, USA.

FIGO, Luis Filipe Madeira Caeiro; Portuguese fmr professional footballer; b. 4 Nov. 1972, Lisbon; m. Helene Svedin; three d.; attacking midfielder/winger; youth player for União de Pastilhas and Sporting Clube de Portugal (CP); sr player for Sporting CP 1989–95 (won Cup of Portugal 1995, Portuguese SuperCup 1995), Barcelona 1995–2000 (won La Liga 1998, 1999, Copa del Rey 1997, 1998, Spanish SuperCup 1996, UEFA Cup Winners' Cup 1997, UEFA Super Cup 1997), Real Madrid (signed for then world record transfer fee) 1995–2000 (won La Liga 2001, 2003, Supercopa de España 2001, 2003, UEFA Champions League 2002, UEFA Super Cup 2002, Intercontinental Cup 2002), Inter Milan 2005–09 (won Serie A 2006, 2007, 2008, 2009, Italian Cup 2006, Italian SuperCup 2005, 2006, 2008) (retd); 127 caps and scored 32 goals with Portugal nat. team 1991–2006 (FIFA World Cup, (Fourth Place) 2006, European Football Championship (runner-up) 2004, (Third Place) 2000, FIFA U-20 World Cup 1991); jt seat holder with Carlos Queirós for A1 Team Portugal in A1 Grand Prix 2005–06; owns fashionable bar in Algarve region; Portuguese Golden Ball 1994, Portuguese Footballer of the Year 1995, 1996, 1997, 1998, 1999, 2000, Don Balón Award for Foreign Player of the Year in La Liga 1999, 2000, 2001, Ballon d'Or for Best Player of the Year 2000, FIFA European Footballer of the Year 2000, FIFA World Player of the Year 2001, FIFA 100, UEFA Team of the Year 2003, FIFA World Cup All-Star Team 2006. *Leisure interests:* the beach, rock music, spending time with friends.

FIGUEIREDO MACHADO, Luiz Alberto, LLB; Brazilian diplomatist and politician; *Minister of Foreign Affairs;* b. 17 July 1955; ed State Univ. of Rio de Janeiro; served in Perm. Mission to UN, New York 1986–89, Embassy in Santiago 1989–92, Head, Sea, Antarctic and Outer Space Affairs Div., Ministry of Foreign Affairs 1995–96, served in Embassy in Washington, DC 1996–99, Embassy in Ottawa 1999–2002, Head, Environmental Policy and Sustainable Devt Div. 2002–04, served in Mission to UNESCO 2003–05, Dir, Dept for Environment and Special Affairs 2005–11, Under-Sec. for Environment, Energy, Science and Tech. 2011–13, Perm. Rep. to UN, New York 2013, Minister of Foreign Affairs 2013–; Exec. Sec. Rio +20 Nat. Comm.; served for many years as chief negotiator for Brazil at numerous int. confs on environmental issues. *Address:* Ministry of Foreign Affairs, Palácio do Itamaraty, Térreo, Esplanada dos Ministérios, Bloco H, 70170-900 Brasília DF, Brazil (office). *Telephone:* (61) 3411-8006 (office). *Fax:* (61) 3225-8002 (office). *E-mail:* imprensa@itamaraty.gov.br (office). *Website:* www.itamaraty.gov.br (office).

FIGUERES OLSEN, José María, MPA; Costa Rican/Spanish international organization official, business executive and fmr politician; *CEO, Concordia 21;* b. 24 Dec. 1954, San José; s. of José Figueres Ferrer (fmr Pres. of Costa Rica); two c.; ed US Mil Acad., West Point, NY, Kennedy School of Govt, Harvard Univ.; mem. Partido de Liberación Nacional; Minister of Agric. 1986–90; Pres. of Costa Rica 1994–98; Pres. Leadership for Environment and Devt (LEAD); Man. Dir World Econ. Forum 2000–03, Co-CEO 2003–04, CEO 2004; CEO Concordia 21, Madrid, Spain 2004–; Chair. Water Supply and Sanitation Collaborative Council 2004–; mem. Bd Global Fairness Initiative, BT Global Services Strategy & Marketing Advisory Bd, Abraaj Capital Advisory Bd, Grupo San Cristobal, Dubai Recycling Park, Talal Abu-Ghazaleh Org., Earth Council Geneva, DARA (non-profit org.), Fundación para las Relaciones Internacionales y el Diálogo Exterior (FRIDE); mem. Dean's Alumni Council, Harvard Univ.; Bd Fellow, Thunderbird School of Man.; Int. Adviser, Global Environmental Action; Order of José Matías Delgado Grand Silver Cross (El Salvador) 1999; first recipient of Global Prize from World Bank's Global Environmental Fund 1988, Liberty Prize, Max Schmidheiny Foundation and St Gallen Univ. 1998, Award of the Climate Inst., Washington, DC 1998, Sustainability Award in Switzerland 2003. *Address:* Concordia 21, C/ Felipe IV, 9 – 1°, Derecha, 28014 Madrid, Spain (office). *Telephone:* (91) 531-52-32 (office). *E-mail:* info@josemariafigueres.org (office). *Website:* www.josemariafigueres.org (office).

FIGUEROA, Adolfo, PhD; Peruvian economist, academic and international consultant; *Professor Emeritus and Senior Researcher, Centrum Buisness School, Catholic University of Peru;* b. 14 April 1941, Carhuaz; s. of José Manuel Figueroa and Modesta Figueroa; m. Yolanda Vásquez 1965; one s. one d.; ed Colegio Guadalupe (High School), Lima, San Marcos Univ., Lima, Vanderbilt Univ., Nashville, Tenn., USA; Prof. of Econs, Catholic Univ. of Peru, Lima 1970–2007, Head, Dept of Econs 1976–79, 1987–90, 1996–98, Dean Faculty of Social Sciences 2002–05, Prof. Emer. 2008–, also Sr Researcher, Centrum Business School 2008–; Dir Research Project on Productivity and Educ. in Agric. in Latin America, ECIEL Program 1983-85; Consultant to ILO, FAO, Inter-American Foundation, Ford Foundation, IFAD, IDB, World Bank; Visiting Prof., Univ. of Pernambuco, Brazil 1973, St Antony's Coll., Oxford 1976, Univ. of Ill., USA 1980, Econs Dept, Univ. of Nicaragua 1985, Univ. of Notre Dame, USA 1992, Univ. of Tex. 1997, Univ. of Wis. 2001; mem. Exec. Council Latin American Studies Asscn 1988–91, Editorial Advisory Bd, Journal of International Development 1988–92, World Devt 1997–, European Review of Latin American Studies 1997–2007, Journal of Human Devt and Capabilities 2008–; mem. Int. Network for Econ. Method; Award of Excellence in Grad. Teaching Univ. of Ill., USA 1980, Winner, Collaborative Research Grant Competition, MacArthur Foundation 1999, Winner, Tinker Professorship Competition, Univ. of Wis. 2001. *Publications:* Estructura del Consumo y Distribución de Ingresos en Lima 1968–1969 1974, Distribución del Ingreso en el Perú (co-author) 1975, La Economía Campesina de la Sierra del Perú 1981, Capitalist Development and the Peasant Economy in Peru 1984, Educación y Productividad en la Agricultura Campesina de América Latina 1986, Teorías Económicas del Capitalismo 1992, Crisis Distributiva en el Perú 1993, Social Exclusion and Inequality in Peru 1996, Reformas en sociedades desiguales 2001, La sociedad sigma: una teoría del desarrollo económico 2003, Nuestro mundo social, una introducción a la ciencia económica 2008, A Unified Theory of Capitalist Development 2009; articles in econ. journals on inequality and poverty, econ. growth, econ. devt, agric., labour markets, and econs of educ. *Leisure interests:* music, popular and classical guitar. *Address:* Centrum Business School Universidad Católica del Perú, Apartado 1761, Lima 1 (office); Jirón Robert Kennedy 129, Lima 21, Peru (home). *Telephone:* (1) 313-3400 (office); (1) 261-6241 (home). *Fax:* (1) 313-3417 (home). *E-mail:* afiguer@pucp.edu.pe (office). *Website:* macareo.pucp.edu.pe/~afiguer/afiguer.htm (office).

FIGUEROA SERRANO, Carlos; Chilean lawyer, politician and diplomatist; b. 28 Nov. 1930, Angol; s. of Carlos Figueroa and Isabel Serrano; m. Sara Guzmán 1953; seven c.; ed Colegio de los Sagrados Corazones, School of Law, Universidad de Chile; practising lawyer 1957–; served at Appeals Court, Santiago 1971–72; Prof. of Procedural Law, Catholic Univ. of Chile 1960–76; joined Partido Demócrata Cristiano (PDC) 1957; Under-Sec. for Agric. 1967–69; Minister of Economy 1969–70; Acting Minister of Foreign Relations and of Finance on various occasions 1967–70; Pres. PDC Political Cttee 1980; Del. for Providencia to Prov. Bd of Eastern Santiago 1984–87; Head of Communications and Publicity, Patricio Aylwin's presidential campaign 1989; Amb. to Argentina 1990–93; Dir Communications and Publicity, Eduardo Frei's presidential campaign 1993; Minister for Foreign Affairs March–Sept. 1994, for Interior 1994–99; mem. Bd of Dirs CIC SA

1971, Financiera Condell 1986–90, Pesquera Guafo SA 1987–89; Gen. Man. VEEP SA (bldg contractors) 1980–86; Pres. Asociación Radiodifusoras de Chile 1972–78; Counsellor, Asociación Iberamericana de Radiodifusión 1973–79, Sec. Bd of Dirs 1975–77.

FIKENTSCHER, Wolfgang, LLM, DJur; German professor emeritus of law; b. 17 May 1928, Nuremberg; s. of Erich Fikentscher and Elfriede Fikentscher (née Albers); m. Irmgard van den Berge 1956; three s. one d.; ed Univs of Erlangen and Munich and Univ. of Michigan Law School, USA; teacher of Labour Law, Trade Union Schools 1952–56; Prof. of Law, Univ. of Münster 1958–65, Univ. of Tübingen 1965–71, Univ. of Munich 1971–96, Prof. Emer. 1996–; Scientific mem. Max-Planck Inst. for Foreign and Int. Patent, Copyright and Competition Law (now Intellectual Property, Competition and Tax Law), Munich; Co-Dir Gruter Inst. for Law and Behavioral Research, Portola Valley, Calif. 1996–, also Dir Munich Office; Faculty mem., Parmenides Centre for the Study of Thinking, Elba, Italy and Munich 2004–; Visiting Prof., Univ. of Calif. Law School, Berkeley 1996–2000; Fellow, Netherlands Inst. for Advanced Study in the Social Sciences 1971–72, Santa Fe Inst. 1991–92, 1995–96, 2003; mem. Bavarian Acad. of Sciences Philosophical-Historical Class, Munich 1977–, Chair. Comm. for Studies in Cultural Anthropology 1996–; mem. Advisory Bd Center for Int. and Comparative Law, Univ. of Michigan Law School 1998–2003; Bundesverdienstkreuz, Bayerischer Verdienstorden 1992; Hon. DrJur (Zürich) 1995; Max-Planck Research Prize (jtly with Robert D. Cooter) 1994. *Publications:* Methoden des Rechts in vergleichender Darstellung (five vols) 1975–77, Wirtschaftsrecht (two vols) 1983, Modes of Thought 1995, Schuldrecht 1997, Die Freiheit und ihr Paradox 1997, numerous books and articles on civil and commercial law, antitrust law, int. law, anthropology and ethology of law. *Address:* Ringstrasse 15, 86911 Diessen-Riederau (home); Max-Planck-Institut für Geistiges Eigentum, Wettbewerbs- und Steuerrecht, Marstallplatz 1, 80539 Munich, Germany (office). *Telephone:* (8807) 206808 (home). *Fax:* (8807) 206808 (home). *Website:* www.gruterinstitute.org.

FILARDO, Leonor, MS; Venezuelan economist, banker and international finance official; b. 1944; d. of Jesus Filardo and Carmen Vargas de Filardo; m. (divorced); three d.; ed Caracas Catholic Univ., Surrey Univ.; worked for Cen. Bank of Venezuela 1970–75, Sr Vice-Pres. Int. Operations 1979–84; Sr Vice-Pres. of Int. Finance, Venezuelan Investment Fund 1975–79; Exec. Dir, World Bank Exec. Bd 1984–86; Alt. Exec. Dir IMF 1986–88, Exec. Dir 1988–90; Rep. Office, Washington DC 1990; Vice-Pres. Cen. Bank of Venezuela 1993–94; Minister Counsellor, Embassy in Washington, DC 1994; fmr Adviser to Cen. American and Venezuelan govts on stabilization and structural adjustment programmes, participant in negotiations with IMF for External Fund Facility for Venezuela; mem. Centro de Divulgación del Conocimiento Económico—CEDICE (think tank); mem. Exec. Cttee Youth Orchestra of the Americas; Francisco de Miranda Medal, (1st Class) Venezuela 1990. *Leisure interests:* art, music, opera, travel, workout. *Address:* CEDICE, Av. Andrés Eloy Blanco (Este 2), Edif. Cámara de Comercio de Caracas, Nivel Auditorio, Los Caobos, Caracas, Venezuela (office). *Telephone:* (212) 571-3357 (office). *E-mail:* cedice@cedice.org.ve (office). *Website:* www.cedice.org.ve (office).

FILARET (see Philaret).

FILARET, Denisenko M. A.; Ukrainian ecclesiastic; *'Patriarch of Kyiv and all Rus-Ukraine';* b. 1929, Donetsk Oblast; ed Odesa Seminary and Moscow Theological Acad.; monk and teacher from 1950; Rector Moscow Acad. 1954; moved to Saratov Seminary 1956, Kyiv Seminary 1957; fmr Chancellor Ukrainian Exarchate of Russian Orthodox Church – Moscow Patriarchate; apptd Bishop of Luga, Leningrad (now St Petersburg) Diocese 1962, Bishop of Vienna and Austria Nov. 1962, Bishop of Dmitrov, Moscow Diocese 1964; Rector Moscow's theological schools and Deputy Chair. Dept of External Church Relations 1964–66; Archbishop of Kyiv and Galicia 1966; Metropolitan of Kyiv 1968, dismissed May 1992; was instrumental in formation of self-styled 'Patriarchate of Kyiv and all Rus-Ukraine' June 1992, 'Patriarch of Kyiv and all Rus-Ukraine' 1995–. *Address:* Ukrainian Orthodox Church (Kyiv Patriarchate), 01004 Kyiv, vul. Pushkinska 36, Ukraine (office). *Telephone:* (44) 234-10-96 (office). *Fax:* (44) 234-30-55. *E-mail:* prescentr@gmail.com (office). *Website:* www.cerkva.info (office).

FILAT, Vladimir (Vlad); Moldovan business executive and politician; *President, Liberal Democratic Party of Moldova (Partidul Liberal Democrat din Moldova);* b. 6 May 1969, Lăpușna, Hîncești Dist; m. Nadejda Filat; one s. one d.; ed Co-operation Coll. (Kooperativny technikum), Chișinău, Alexandru Ioan Cuza Univ., Iași, Romania; served in Soviet army 1987–89; Man. Dir RoMold Trading SRL, Iași 1994–97; Pres. Admin. Council, Dosoftei Co., Iași 1997–98; Gen. Dir Dept of Privatization and State Property Admin, Ministry of Economy and Reform, Chișinău 1998–99; Minister of State, Ion Sturza Cabinet March–Nov. 1999; mem. Democratic Party of Moldova 1997–2007, Vice-Pres. 2000–07; mem. Parlamentul 1997–2007, Vice-Pres. Parl. Comm. for Security, Public Order and Defence 2005–09; unsuccessful cand. for Mayor of Chișinău 2007; Founder-mem. and Pres. Liberal Democratic Party of Moldova (PLDM) 2007–, party absorbed Our Moldova Alliance April 2011; Prime Minister 2009–13; Acting Pres. of Moldova 28–30 Dec. 2010. *Address:* Liberal Democratic Party of Moldova (Partidul Liberal Democrat din Moldova), 2012 Chișinău, str. București 88, Moldova (office). *Telephone:* (22) 81-51-54 (office). *Fax:* (22) 81-51-63 (office). *E-mail:* info@pldm.md (office). *Website:* www.pldm.md (office).

FILI, Sunia Manu, BA; Tongan lawyer and politician; *Minister of Finance and National Planning;* b. 1 Dec. 1965; m.; ed Univ. of the South Pacific; began career as lawyer and high school teacher before entering politics; mem. Legis. Ass. as People's Rep. for Eua 1999–; Minister of Finance and Nat. Planning 2011–; fmr mem. Human Rights and Democracy Movt. *Leisure interests:* tennis, reading, debating, swimming, gardening, walk-for-life. *Address:* Ministry of Finance and National Planning, Treasury Bldg, POB 87, Vuna Rd, Nuku'alofa, Tonga (office). *Telephone:* 23066 (office). *Fax:* 26011 (office). *E-mail:* info@finance.gov.to (office); sunia_fili@parliament.gov.to. *Website:* www.finance.gov.to (office).

FILI-KRUSHEL, Patricia (Pat), BS, MBA; American media executive; *Chairman, NBCUniversal News Group, NBCUniversal;* ed St John's Univ., Fordham Univ.; worked for ABC Sports in various positions; held several positions with Home Box Office, later Vice-Pres. of Business Affairs and Production; with Lifetime Television as both Group Vice-Pres. of Hearst/ABC-Viacom Entertainment Services (HAVES) and Sr Vice-Pres. of Programming and Production of Lifetime Television 1988–93; joined ABC 1993, Pres. ABC Daytime 1993–98, responsible for introducing daytime talk show The View, Pres. ABC Television Network 1998–2000, conceived and orchestrated SoapNet (24-hour soap opera cable network); CEO WebMD Health 2000–01; Exec. Vice-Pres. of Admin, Time Warner Inc. 2001–12; Exec. Vice-Pres. NBCUniversal, Chair. NBCUniversal News Group 2012–; mem. Bd Dollar General Corpn; mem. Bd of Trustees, The Public Theater of New York (mem. Exec. Cttee and Chair. Nominating Cttee), The Paley Center for Media; mem. Mayor Bloomberg's Comm. on Women's Issues; Women in Film Muse Award 1993, ranked by Fortune magazine amongst the 50 Most Powerful Women in Business in the US 1998, (41st) 2012, recognized by New York Women in Communications, Inc. through their Matrix Awards for her contribution to the field of broadcasting, inducted into Museum of Television & Radio's "She Made It" Collection 2006, Vision Award, Crystal Apple Award, City of New York. *Address:* NBCUniversal Media LLC, 30 Rockefeller Plaza, New York, NY 10112, USA (office). *Telephone:* (212) 664-4444 (office). *Fax:* (212) 664-4085 (office). *E-mail:* info@nbcuni.com (office). *Website:* www.nbcuni.com (office).

FILIMON, Valeria; Romanian journalist; b. 29 May 1949, Butimanu; d. of Ion Dumitrescu and Maria Dumitrescu; m. Vasile Filimon 1984; ed Univ. of Bucharest; freelance journalist for various Romanian dailies and literary magazines 1967–90; Assoc. Prof. 1970–90; journalist 1990–93; Ed.-in-Chief Femeia Moderna (magazine) 1993–98, Regala 1998–, Olimp 1999–; apptd Project Co-ordinator in Romania, International Fed. of Journalists 1996; Vice-Pres. Societatea Ziaristilor din Romania; Romanian Writers' Union Prize. *Publications:* Lyceum (collection of literary criticism in two vols) 1974. *Address:* Societatea Ziaristilor din Romania, Piata Presei Libere 1, Oficial Postal 33, 71341 Bucharest, Romania (office). *Telephone:* (21) 2228351 (office). *Fax:* (21) 2224266 (office).

FILIP, Vojtěch; Czech politician; *Chairman, Communist Party of Bohemia and Moravia (KSČM) (Komunistická strana Čech a Moravy);* b. 13 Jan. 1955, Jedovary, nr České Budějovice; m. Ludmila Filip 1979; one s. one d.; ed gymnasium in Trhové Sviny, Univ. of Jan Evangelista Purkyně, Brno (now Masaryk Univ.); work as lawyer for Sfinx Budweis, returned following mil. service in Prague 1979–90; opened own law firm 1993, first as commercial lawyer, then as attorney specializing in commercial and constitutional law, political parties and human rights; worked for Socialistický svaz mládeže (SSM—Socialist Union of Youth) 1970–86; mem. Communist Party of Czechoslovakia (KSČ) from 1983, Communist Party of Bohemia and Moravia (KSČM—Komunistická strana Čech a Moravy) 1990–, worked in Cen. Auditing Comm., later Chair. IP KSČM, České Budějovice and UV KSČM, mem. Exec. Cttee of Cen. KSČM from 1996, also worked as Chair. Comm. for legislation and human rights of UV KSČM, Vice-Chair. KSČM 2004–05, Chair. 2005–; mem. Municipal Cttee, České Budějovice 1984–90; mem. Fed. Ass. 1990–92; City Councillor, České Budějovice 1994–2002; mem. Parl. (KSČM) for South Bohemian Region 1996–2013, 2013–, Chair. Parl. Party 1996–2002, Vice-Pres. Chamber of Deputies 2002–06, 2006–10, 2013–; Prize for Human Rights, German Soc. for the Protection of Civil Rights and Human Dignity 2007. *Publications:* numerous articles in professional journals and proceedings on the liability of relations in civil, commercial, labour and criminal law. *Leisure interests:* music (especially rock), nature, fishing, travelling. *Address:* Communist Party of Bohemia and Moravia (Komunistická strana Čech a Moravy), Politických vězňů 9, 111 21 Prague 1, Czech Republic (office). *Telephone:* (2) 22897111 (office). *Fax:* (2) 22897207 (office). *E-mail:* info@kscm.cz (office). *Website:* www.kscm.cz (office).

FILIPACCHI, Daniel; French journalist and publisher; b. 12 Jan. 1928, Paris; s. of Henri Filipacchi and Edith Besnard; typographer, Paris-Match 1944, photographer 1948, head of information and dir of photographic service 1953; fashion photographer, Marie-Claire 1957; producer of radio transmissions, Europe No. 1 1955, 1960; Owner and Dir Jazz Magazine 1955, Cahiers du cinéma 1961–70; Founder and Dir Salut les copains (became Salut 1976) 1961, Lui, Mlle Age tendre (became OK Age tendre 1976), Pariscope 1965, Photo 1967, Le Monde des Grands Musées 1968, Ski 1969, Union 1972, Playboy France 1973–84, Girls 1982; editorial adviser to Newlook 1982, Penthouse 1984; Pres.-Dir-Gen. WEA Filipacchi Music SA 1971–84, Cogedipresse; Owner and fmr Dir Paris-Match 1976; mem. editorial Cttee Elle 1981; Vice-Pres. Hachette 1981–93, Pres.-Dir-Gen. Hachette Magazines Inc. (USA) 1990; Pres.-Dir-Gen. Filipacchi Médias SA 1993–97; Jt Man. Cogédipresse 1994–97; Admin. and Hon. Pres. Hachette Filipacchi Médias 1997–.

FILIPOVIĆ, Karlo; Bosnia and Herzegovina politician; *Executive Board President, Social Democratic Party of Bosnia and Herzegovina;* b. 1954, Solakovicima; s. of Jozo Filipović and Mara Filipović; m.; one d.; ed Univ. of Sarajevo; Pres. Council of Municipalities, Sarajevo City Ass. 1987–89; mem. Cen. Cttee Communist League of Bosnia and Herzegovina 1988–91, elected mem. of presidency 1989; mem. of presidency Socialist Party of Bosnia and Herzegovina 1991–92; mem. of presidency of Social Democratic Party of Bosnia and Herzegovina (SDP BiH) 1992–95, Sec. 1995–97, Sec.-Gen. 1997–2001, Pres. Exec. Bd 2001–; mem. House of Reps (Parl.) 1998–2001; Pres. Fed. of Bosnia and Herzegovina 2001–02, Vice-Pres. 2002–04. *Address:* Social Democratic Party of Bosnia and Herzegovina, Alipašina 41, 71000 Sarajevo, Bosnia and Herzegovina (office). *Telephone:* (33) 664044 (office). *Fax:* (33) 644042 (office). *E-mail:* predssednik-glavnog-odbora@sdp-bih.org.ba (office). *Website:* www.sdp-bih.org.ba (office).

FILIPPENKO, Aleksander Georgyevich; Russian actor; b. 2 Sept. 1944, Moscow; m. 2nd Marina Ishimbayeva; one d.; ed Moscow Inst. of Physics and Tech., Moscow, Shchukin Higher School of Theatre; Sr Engineer, Inst. of Geochemistry, USSR Acad. of Sciences 1967–69; actor in Amateur Theatre Nash Dom 1967–69, Taganka Theatre 1969–75, Vakhtangov Theatre 1975–94; Founder and actor, Experimental One-Man Theatre 1995–; staged Train to Chatanooga, Dead Souls, Fanbala; Merited Artist of Russia. *Films include:* Ostanovite Potapova! 1974, Kto zaplatit za udachu? 1980, Brosok 1981, Tam, na nevedomykh dorozhkakh 1982, Torpedonostsy 1983, Moy drug Ivan Lapshin 1984, Chyornaya strela 1985, Iz zhizni Potapova 1985, Oci ciornie 1987, Ubit drakona 1988, Es ist nicht leicht ein Gott zu sein 1989, Pod severnym siyaniyem 1990, The Inner Circle 1991, Ubiystvo v Sunshine Menor 1992, Anomaliya 1993, Master i Margarita 1994, Igra voobrazheniya 1995, Karera Arturo Ui 1996, Romanov: Ventsenosnaya semya 2000, Ledi na den 2002, Aziris nuna 2006, Aziris nuna 2006, Leningrad 2007. *Television includes:* Oshibka Toni vendisa 1981, Vizit k Minotavru 1987,

Prestuplenie lorda Artura 1991, Azbuka lyubvi 1992, Sledstvie vedut znatoki 23: Treteyskiy sudiya 2002, Bednaya Nastya 2003, Master i Margarita 2005, Zagovor 2007. *Address:* 103104 Moscow, Spiridonyevsky per. 8, Apt 17, Russia (home). *Telephone:* (495) 202-77-15 (home).

FILIPPETTI, Aurélie; French politician and novelist; *Minister of Culture and Communication;* b. 17 June 1973, Villerupt (Meurthe-et-Moselle); of Italian descent, family originates from Gualdo, Umbria; ed École normale supérieure de Fontenay–Saint-Cloud, agrégation in Classic Literature; fmr mem. Les Verts (Green Party), now mem. Parti socialiste (PS—Socialist Party); Tech. Adviser for Minister of Environment, Yves Cochet 2001–02; mem. (PS) Assemblée nationale for the Eight Dist of the Moselle département 2007–; Minister of Culture and Communication 2012–; Commdr, ordre des Arts et des Lettres 2012. *Publications include:* Les derniers jours de la classe ouvrière (novel) 2003, wrote the script for theatre production Fragments d'humanité 2003, Un homme dans la poche 2006, L'école forme-t-elle encore des citoyens? (co-author) 2008, Si nous sommes vivants - le socialisme et l'écologie (co-author) 2010, J'ai 20 ans qu'est-ce qui m'attend? (co-author) 2012. *Address:* Ministry of Culture and Communication, 3 rue de Valois, 75001 Paris (office); Assemblée nationale, 126 rue de l'Université, 75355 Paris Cedex 07, France (office). *Telephone:* 1-40-15-80-00 (Ministry) (office); 1-40-63-60-00 (Assemblée nationale) (office). *Fax:* 1-40-15-81-72 (Ministry) (office); 1-45-55-75-23 (Assemblée nationale) (office). *E-mail:* point.culture@culture.fr (office); afilippetti@assemblee-nationale.fr (office). *Website:* www.culture.gouv.fr (office); www.assemblee-nationale.fr (office); aureliefilippetti.free.fr.

FILIPPOV, Vladimir Mikhailovich, Dr Physics-Math; Russian government official, mathematician, academic and university rector; *Rector, Peoples' Friendship University of Russia;* b. 15 April 1951, Uryupinsk; m.; one s. one d.; ed Patrice Lumumba Peoples' Friendship Univ., Steklov Math. Inst. USSR Acad. of Sciences; Asst, Chair of Higher Math., Chair. Council of Young Scientists and Head, Dept of Science, Patrice Lumumba Peoples' Friendship Univ. 1973–85, Prof., Head, Chair of Math. Analysis, Dean, Faculty of Natural Sciences 1985–93, Rector 1993–98; Minister of Gen. and Professional Educ. of Russian Fed. 1998–2000; Minister of Educ. 2000–04, Aide to Prime Minister 2004–05; Rector Peoples' Friendship Univ. of Russia 2005–; Vice-Pres. Euro-Asian Asscn of Univs; Presidium mem. Russian Acad. of Educ.; Order of the Friendship of People 1995, Order of King's Crown (Belgium) 2000, Rank IV Order for Service to Fatherland 2001, Chevalier, Légion d'honneur 2002, Belgian Inventor Medal, Mérite de l'Invention 2003, Order of Francisco Paulo Santander 2008; Govt Award in Educ. 2000. *Publications:* more than 240 scientific and methodological publications. *Address:* Peoples' Friendship University of Russia, 117198 Moscow, 6 Miklukho-Maklaya str., Russia (office). *Telephone:* (495) 434-70-27 (office). *Fax:* (495) 433-73-79 (office). *E-mail:* rector@rudn.ru (office). *Website:* www.rudn.ru (office).

FILIU, Jean-Pierre, PhD; French scholar and academic; *Associate Professor, Institute of Political Studies (Sciences Po);* b. 1961, Paris; ed Inst. of Political Studies (Sciences Po), Paris, Institut national de langues et civilisations orientales; fmr diplomatist and ministerial adviser; specializes in contemporary Islam, with an emphasis on jihadi movements and Al-Qaeda; Assoc. Prof., Inst. of Political Studies (Sciences Po), Paris 2006–, teaches in French, English and Arabic at Gilles Kepel's Middle East Chair; Visiting Prof., Columbia Univ., New York, Georgetown Univ., Washington, DC, USA 2008; mem. Scientific Bd, Maison méditerranéenne des Sciences de l'homme, Steering Cttee, Annuaire de la Méditerranée; mem. CERI (Centre d'études et de recherches internationales) 2009–. *Publications:* Mitterrand et la Palestine 2005, Les frontières du jihad 2006, L'Apocalypse dans l'Islam (Augustin-Thierry Prize, Rendez-vous de l'Histoire, Blois 2008) 2008, Mai 68 à l'ORTF 2008, Les neuf vies d'Al-Qaida 2009, La Révolution arabe, dix leçons sur le soulèvement démocratique 2011, Best of Enemies (with David B.) 2012; articles on the adaptation of Islam to globalized modernity. *Address:* Sciences Po, 27 rue Saint-Guillaume, 75337 Paris Cedex 07, France (office). *Telephone:* 1-45-49-51-47 (office). *Fax:* 1-42-22-31-26 (office). *E-mail:* jeanpierre.filiu@sciences-po.org (office). *Website:* www.ceri-sciencespo.com/cerifr/cherlist/filiu.php (office); www.sciencespo.fr (office).

FILIZZOLA SERRA, Rafael, LLB; Paraguayan lawyer, academic and politician; b. 16 Feb. 1968, Asunción; m. Desirée Masi; ed Univ. Católica Nuestra Señora de la Asunción; Sec. Gen. Nat. Fed. of Univ. Students 1990–91; Founding mem. Asunción Para Todos (APT) and Constitución Para Todoa (CPT) (ind. political movts) 1991; Prof. of Political Law, Universidad Católica de Asunción; mem. Nat. Congress for Asunción 1998–2008; Founder and Pres. Partido Demcrática Progresista (PDP) 2007–; Minister of the Interior 2008–11. *Address:* c/o Ministry of the Interior, Estrella y Montevideo, Asunción, Paraguay (office).

FILLON, François-Charles Amand, MA, DEA; French politician; b. 4 March 1954, Le Mans; s. of Michel Fillon and Anne Soulet; m. Penelope Clarke 1980; four s. one d.; ed Univ. of Le Mans, Univ. René-Descartes, Paris; Parl. Asst to Joël Le Theule 1976–77; served in Office of Minister of Transport 1978–80, Office of Minister of Defence 1980–81; Head of Legis. and Parl. Work, Ministry of Industry 1981; Town Councillor, Sablé-sur-Sarthe, Mayor 1983–2001; Pres. Conseil Général of Sarthe 1992–98, of Sablé-sur-Sarthe Dist 2001–; Chair. Conseil Régional des Pays de la Loire 1998–2002; Municipal Councillor, Solesmes 2001–; RPR/UMP Deputy to Nat. Ass. 1981–1993, 1997–2002, 2007; Senator for Sarthe 2004–07; Spokesman, Exec. Comm. RPR 1998, Political Adviser 1999–2001; Founder mem. Union en Mouvement 2002; Political Adviser to Nicolas Sarkozy (Union pour un Mouvement Populaire—UMP) 2004–07; Pres. Comm. for Nat. Defence and Armed Forces 1986–88; Minister for Higher Educ. and Research 1993–95; Minister of Information Tech. and Post May–Nov. 1995, Minister del. for Post, Telecommunications and Space 1995–97; Minister of Social Affairs, Labour and Solidarity 2002–04; Minister for Nat. Educ., Higher Educ. and Research 2004–05; Prime Minister 2007–12; Minister of Ecology, Sustainable Devt, Transport and Housing February–May 2012; Grand Officier, Légion d'honneur, Grand Croix, Ordre nat. du Mérite. *Publication:* La France peut supporter la vérité 2006. *Leisure interests:* climbing, hiking, skiing, mountain biking, motor racing, running, cinema, reading. *Address:* c/o Office of the Prime Minister, Hôtel de Matignon, 57 rue de Varenne, 75007 Paris, France. *Website:* www.blog-fillon.com.

FILMON, Gary Albert, PC, MSc; Canadian engineer, politician and business executive; *Vice-Chairman, Wellington West Capital;* b. 24 Aug. 1942, Winnipeg,

Man.; s. of Albert Filmon and Anastasia Filmon (née Dosckocz); m. Janice Wainwright 1963; two s. two d.; ed Sisler High School, Univ. of Manitoba; consulting engineer, Underwood McLellan Ltd 1964–69; Pres. Success/Angus Commercial Coll. 1969–80; Winnipeg City Councillor 1975–79; mem. Legis. Ass. for River Heights 1979–81, for Tuxedo 1981–2000; Minister of Consumer and Corp. Affairs and Environment and Minister Responsible for Man. Housing and Renewal Corpn 1981; Leader Man. Progressive Conservative Party 1983–88; Premier of Manitoba 1988–99, also Pres. Exec. Council, Minister of Fed. Prov. Relations; currently Vice-Chair. Wellington West Capital Inc.; headed govt task force to evaluate emergency response to forest fires in BC 2004; Chair. Exchange Industrial Income Fund, Dir and Trustee, Arctic Glacier Income Fund, Pollard Banknote Income Fund; mem. Bd of Dirs F.W.S. Construction Ltd, Canadian Natural Resources Ltd, Manitoba Telecom Services Inc., Canada West Foundation, ParticipACTION Canada; mem. Security Intelligence Review Cttee 2001–, Chair. 2005–. *Address:* Wellington West Capital, 200 Waterfront Drive, Suite 400, Winnipeg, MB R3B 3P1, Canada (office). *Telephone:* (204) 925-2250 (office). *Website:* www.wellingtonwest.com (office).

FILO, David, BS, MS; American internet executive; *Chief Yahoo!, Yahoo! Inc.;* b. Moss Bluff, La.; ed Tulane Univ. and Stanford Univ., Calif.; co-created Yahoo! internet navigational guide 1994, co-founder, Chief Exec. Yahoo! Inc. 1994–. *Address:* Yahoo! Incorporated, 701 1st Avenue, Sunnyvale, CA 94089, USA (home). *Telephone:* (408) 349-3300 (office). *Fax:* (408) 349-3301 (office). *Website:* www .yahoo.com (office).

FILONI, HE Cardinal Fernando, PhD, DCL; Italian ecclesiastic and diplomatist; *Prefect, Congregation for the Evangelization of Peoples;* b. 15 April 1946, Manduria, Taranto; ed Pontifical Lateran Univ., Rome; ordained priest, Diocese of Nardò-Gallipoli 1970; served in Nunciatures of Sri Lanka 1982–83, Iran 1983–85, Brazil 1989–92, the Philippines (based in Hong Kong) 1992–2001; apptd Titular Archbishop of Volturnum 2001; Apostolic Nuncio to Iraq and Jordan 2001–06, to Philippines 2006–07; Substitute (Sostituto) of Secr. of State 2007–11; Prefect of Congregation for Evangelization of Peoples 2011–13, 2013–; Pres. Interdicasterial Comm. for Consecrated Religious 2011–; Grand Chancellor, Pontifical Urbaniana Univ. 2011–; cr. Cardinal (Cardinal-Deacon of Nostra Signora di Coromoto in San Giovanni di Dio) 2012; participated in Papal Conclave 2013. *Address:* The Congregation for the Evangelization of Peoples, Palazzo di Propaganda Fide, Piazza di Spagna 48, 00187 Rome, Italy (office). *Telephone:* (06) 69879299 (office). *Fax:* (06) 69880118 (office); (06) 69880137 (office). *E-mail:* segreteria@propagandafide.va (office). *Website:* www.vatican.va/roman_curia/congregations/cevang (office).

FINCHER, David; American film director; b. 28 Aug. 1962, Denver, Colo; s. of Jack Fincher; m. Donya Fiorentino 1990 (divorced); one d.; fmrly with Propaganda Films (video production co.) and Korty Films; worked at Industrial Light and Magic 1981–83; directed numerous music videos and commercials. *Films include:* Alien 3 1992, Se7en 1995, The Game 1997, Fight Club 1999, Panic Room 2002, Zodiac 2007, The Curious Case of Benjamin Button 2008, The Social Network (Golden Globe for Best Dir 2011, BAFTA Award for Best Dir 2011) 2010, The Girl with the Dragon Tattoo 2011. *Television includes:* House of Cards (Emmy Award for Best Dir in Drama Series) 2013. *Address:* Creative Artists Agency, 2000 Avenue of the Stars, Los Angeles, CA 90067, USA (office).

FINCK, August von, Jr; German business executive; b. 11 March 1930, Munich; s. of the late August von Finck, Sr; m. Francine von Finck; four c.; grandfather f. Allianz insurance co. and Bankhaus Merck, Finck & Co., Munich, sold to Barclay's Bank 1990, Deutsche Spar- & Kreditbank AG, Munich, 1999; moved to Switzerland and acquired stakes in Mövenpick Holding AG, Von Roll, Alusuisse-Lonza, Oerlikon, SGS, Hochtief; mem. Bd of Dirs Generali Holding Vienna AG, SGS United Kingdom Ltd. *Address:* c/o Board of Directors, SGS United Kingdom Ltd, Rossmore Business Park, Ellesmere Port, South Wirral, Cheshire, CH65 3EN, England.

FINDLAY, Paul Hudson Douglas, BA; British opera director; b. 26 Sept. 1943, New Zealand; s. of the late John Niemeyer Findlay and Aileen May Findlay (née Davidson); m. Françoise Christiane 1966; one s. one d.; ed Univ. Coll. School, London, Balliol Coll., Oxford, London Opera Centre; Production and Technical Man. New Opera Co. 1967; Dir London Sinfonietta 1967–; Stage Man. Glyndebourne Touring Opera and English Opera Group 1968; Asst Press Officer, Royal Opera House, Covent Garden 1968–72, Personal Asst to Gen. Dir 1972–76, Asst Dir 1976–87, Opera Dir 1987–93; Man. Dir Royal Philharmonic Orchestra 1993–95; Planning Dir European Opera Centre 1997; Arts Man. Kirov Ballet; Chair. Opera 80 1987; fmr Gen. Man. Mariinsky Theater, St Petersburg, Russia; Co-founder and Vice-Pres. Performing and Visual Arts, Global Music Network –2002, Vice-Pres. GMN Europe 1998–2001; mem. Bd of Dirs Nat. Youth Music Theatre, English Touring Opera, Arts Educational Trust, Arts Education London, Welsh National Opera; Cavaliere Ufficiale dell Ordine al Merito della Repubblica Italiana; Chevalier des Arts et des Lettres 1991. *Leisure interests:* tennis, gardening.

FINE, Anne, OBE, BA, FRSL; British writer; b. (Anne Laker), 7 Dec. 1947, Leicester; d. of Brian Laker and Mary Baker; m. Kit Fine 1968 (divorced 1991); two d.; ed Northampton High School for Girls and Univ. of Warwick; Children's Laureate 2001–03; mem. Soc. of Authors; Dr hc; Scottish Arts Council Writer's Bursary 1986, Scottish Arts Council Book Award 1986, Publishing News' British Book Awards Children's Author of the Year 1990, 1993, Nasen Special Educational Needs Book Award 1996, Prix Sorcière 1998, Prix Versele 1999, 2000, Boston Globe Horn Book Award 2003, Silver Medal, Nestlé Children's Book Prize 2007, Winner, Good Writing Award 2010. *Publications:* for older children: The Summer House Loon 1978, The Other Darker Ned 1978, The Stone Menagerie 1980, Round Behind the Icehouse 1981, The Granny Project 1983, Madame Doubtfire 1987, Goggle-Eyes (Guardian Children's Fiction Prize, Carnegie Medal 1990) 1989, The Book of the Banshee 1991, Flour Babies (Whitbread Children's Book of the Year, Carnegie Medal 1993) 1992, Step by Wicked Step 1995, The Tulip Touch (Whitbread Children's Book of the Year 1997) 1996, Very Different (short stories) 2001, Up on Cloud Nine 2002, Frozen Billy 2004, The Road of Bones 2006, The Devil Walks 2011; for younger children: Scaredy-Cat 1985, Anneli the Art Hater 1986, Crummy Mummy and Me 1988, A Pack of Liars 1988, Stranger Danger 1989,

Bill's New Frock (Smarties Prize 1990) 1989, The Country Pancake 1989, A Sudden Puff of Glittering Smoke 1989, A Sudden Swirl of Icy Wind 1990, Only a Show 1990, Design-a-Pram 1991, A Sudden Glow of Gold 1991, The Worst Child I Ever Had 1991, The Angel of Nitshill Road 1991, Poor Monty (picture book) 1991, The Same Old Story Every Year 1992, The Chicken Gave It to Me 1992, The Haunting of Pip Parker 1992, Press Play 1994, How to Write Really Badly 1996, Countdown 1996, Jennifer's Diary 1996, Care of Henry 1996, Loudmouth Louis 1998, Charm School 1999, Roll Over Roly 1999, Bad Dreams 2000, Ruggles (picture book) 2001, Notso Hotso 2001, How to Cross the Road and Not Turn into a Pizza 2002, The More the Merrier 2003, Ivan the Terrible 2007, Eating Things on Sticks 2009, Trouble in Toadpool 2012; Killer Cat series: The Diary of a Killer Cat 1994, The Return of the Killer Cat 2003, The Killer Cat Strikes Back 2006, The Killer Cat's Birthday Bash 2008, The Killer Cat's Christmas 2009; Jamie and Angus series: The Jamie and Angus Stories 2002, Jamie and Angus Together 2008, Jamie and Angus Forever 2009; adult fiction: The Killjoy 1986, Taking the Devil's Advice 1990, In Cold Domain 1994, Telling Liddy 1998, All Bones and Lies 2001, Raking the Ashes 2005, Fly in the Ointment 2008, Our Precious Lulu 2009; non-fiction: Telling Tales: an Interview with Anne Fine 1999. *Leisure interests:* reading, walking. *Address:* c/o David Higham Associates, 5–8 Lower John Street, London, W1R 4HA, England (office). *Telephone:* (20) 7434-5900 (office). *Fax:* (1833) 908127 (home). *Website:* www.annefine.co.uk.

FINE, Kit, BA, PhD, FBA, AAAS; British philosopher, mathematician and academic; *University Professor and Silver Professor of Philosophy and Mathematics, New York University;* b. 26 March 1946, Farnborough, Hants., England; s. of Maurice Fine and Joyce Cicely Woolf; two d.; ed Cheltenham Grammar School for Boys, Balliol Coll. Oxford, Univ. of Warwick; Prof., Univ. of Michigan, Ann Arbor, USA 1978–88; Prof., UCLA 1988–97; Univ. Prof. and Silver Prof. of Philosophy and Math., New York Univ. 1997–; Ed. Journal of Symbolic Logic 1978–87, Notre Dame Journal of Formal Logic 1984–87, Studies in Logic 1989–93; Guggenheim Fellow 1978–79; Fellow, American Council of Learned Socs 1981–82, American Acad. of Arts and Sciences; Corresponding Fellow, British Acad.; Dr hc (Bucharest). *Publications:* Worlds, Times and Selves (with A. N. Prior) 1977, Reasoning with Arbitrary Objects 1985, Limits of Abstraction 2002, Modality and Tense 2005, Semantic Relationism 2007. *Leisure interests:* music, gardening, cooking. *Address:* Department of Philosophy, New York University, 5 Washington Place, New York, New York, NY 10003, USA (office). *Telephone:* (212) 998-3558 (office). *Fax:* (212) 995-4179 (office). *E-mail:* kit.fine@nyu.edu (office). *Website:* philosophy.fas .nyu.edu (office).

FINE, Leon Gerald, MB, ChB, FRCP, FACP, FRCP (Glas), FMedSci; American physician and professor of medicine; *Dean, Faculty of Clinical Sciences, Royal Free and University College Medical School;* b. 17 July 1943, Cape Town, South Africa; s. of Matthew Fine and Jeanette Lipshitz; m. Brenda Sakinovsky 1966; two d.; ed Univ. of Cape Town; postgraduate clinical and research training, Albert Einstein Coll. of Medicine, New York 1972–76, Univ. of Miami 1976–78; Chief, Div. of Nephrology, UCLA 1978–91; Head, Dept of Medicine, Univ. Coll. London Medical School 1991–2002, Dean, Faculty of Clinical Sciences, Royal Free and Univ. Coll. Medical School 2002–; Ed.-in-Chief Nephron 2003–; numerous invited lectureships; Founding Fellow, Acad. of Medical Sciences, UK 1998–; mem. Bd of Dirs Nat. Inst. for Clinical Excellence 2002–. *Publications:* over 100 articles in the area of kidney disease and renal biology. *Leisure interest:* book collecting. *Address:* University College London, Faculty of Clinical Sciences, Drayton House, 30 Gower Street, London, WC1E 6BT, England (office). *Telephone:* (20) 7679-5486 (office); (20) 8342-9680 (home). *Fax:* (20) 7679-5484 (office); (20) 8342-9680 (home). *E-mail:* l.fine@ucl.ac.uk (office). *Website:* www.ucl.ac.uk/medicalschool.

FINEBERG, Harvey Vernon, MD, PhD; American physician and professional society administrator; *President, Institute of Medicine;* b. 15 Sept. 1945; s. of Saul Fineberg and Miriam Fineberg (née Pearl); m. Mary Elizabeth Wilson 1975; ed Harvard Univ.; Intern, Beth Israel Hosp., Boston 1972–73; Asst Prof., School of Public Health, Harvard Univ., Boston 1973–78, Assoc. Prof. 1978–81, Prof. 1981–2002, Dean 1984–97; Provost, Harvard Univ. 1997–2001; physician at E Boston Health Center 1974–76, Harvard St Health Center 1976–84; Trustee, Newton Wellesley Hosp., Mass. 1981–86; mem. Public Health Council, Mass. 1976–79; mem. Bd of Dirs American Foundation for AIDS Research 1986–97; mem. Inst. of Medicine 1983– (Pres. 2002–); Jr Fellow, Harvard Univ. 1974–75, Mellon Fellow 1976. *Address:* Institute of Medicine, 500 5th Street NW, Washington, DC 20001-2721 (office); 1812 Kalorama Square NW, Washington, DC 20008-4022, USA (home). *Telephone:* (202) 334-3300 (office). *Fax:* (202) 334-3851 (office). *Website:* www.iom.edu (office).

FINEMAN, S. David, BA, LLB; American lawyer and business executive; ed America Univ., George Washington Univ.; fmr Lecturer on Business Law, Temple Univ.; Co-founder and Man. Pnr, Fineman & Bach, PC (law firm), now Fineman, Krekstein & Harris, PC, Phila; served as Special Counsel to Phila Parking Authority, Sec. of Banking of Commonwealth of Pa, Insurance Commr of Commonwealth of Pa; fmr mem. Phila Planning Comm., Phila Mayor Edward Rendell's Intergovernmental Task Force, Mayor W. Wilson's Transition Team 1987; apptd Gov. US Postal Service by Pres. Bill Clinton 1995, Vice-Chair. Bd of Govs 2001–03, Chair. 2003–05; fmr mem. Industry Policy Advisory Cttee, US Secr. of Commerce, Bd Dirs Phila Chamber of Commerce, Free Library of Phila; apptd to Center City Advisory Bd, Jefferson Bank 1999; currently mem. Bar Asscns of Phila, Pa and USA; mem. Defense Research Inst. *Address:* Fineman, Krekstein & Harris, 30 South 17th Street, Suite 1800, Philadelphia, PA 19103, USA (office). *Telephone:* (215) 893-9300 (office). *Fax:* (215) 893-8719 (office). *Website:* www .finemanbach.com (office).

FINI, Gianfranco; Italian politician; *President, Camera dei Deputati;* b. Bologna; fmr journalist; mem. Movimento Sociale Italiano-Destra Nazionale (MSI) 1987–94, Alleanza Nazionale 1994–2008, Chair. 1994–2008; Vice-Pres. Council of Ministers (Deputy Prime Minister) 2001–04; Minister of Foreign Affairs 2004–06; Pres. Camera dei Deputati (Chamber of Deputies) 2008–; Co-founder Popolo della Libertà (People of Freedom) 2009, then Founder and Leader, Generazione Italia (Generation Italy) 2010–; Rep. to EU Special Convention on Pan-European Constitution 2002–06. *Address:* Camera dei Deputati, Palazzo di Montecitorio, Rome, Italy. *Telephone:* (06) 67603316 (office). *Fax:* (06) 6892953 (office). *E-mail:*

dlwebmast@camera.it (office). *Website:* www.camera.it (office); www .generazioneitalia.it.

FINIKASO, Taukelina T., LLB; Tuvaluan diplomatist and politician; *Minister of Foreign Affairs, Environment, Trade, Labour and Tourism;* ed Univ. of Sydney, Australia; High Commr to Fiji (non-resident to Papua New Guinea and Samoa) 2001–06; MP for Vaitupu 2006–; Minister of Works, Communications and Transport 2006–10, for Communications, Transport and Fisheries Sept.–Dec. 2010, Minister of Foreign Affairs, Environment, Trade, Labour and Tourism 2013–. *Address:* Ministry of Foreign Affairs, Vaiaku, Funafuti, Tuvalu (office). *Telephone:* 20102 (office). *Fax:* 20820 (office).

FINK, Bernarda; Slovenian singer (mezzo-soprano); b. 29 Aug. 1955, Buenos Aires; m.; two c.; ed Instituto Superior de Arte del Teatro Colón, Buenos Aires and studied with Michel Corboz in Europe; sang Rossini's Cenerentola at Buenos Aires 1986; concerts of Baroque music with Michel Corboz as conductor in Paris, Geneva, Berlin, Lisbon and Tokyo; sang Penelope in Monteverdi's Ulisse at Innsbruck 1993, Montpellier and Barcelona (also the Messenger in Orfeo); Amsterdam as Proserpina in Orfeo 1995; Cenerentola at the Berlin Staatsoper 1994; season 2000 as Dorabella at Aix-en-Provence and European tour as Gluck's Orpheus, with René Jacobs; recitals at Carnegie and Wigmore Halls, Paris, Vienna and Sydney Opera Houses; sang Cecilio in Lucio Silla at Theater an der Wien 2005–06, Sesto in a concert version of La Clemenza di Tito 2005; has worked with leading conductors including Blomstedt, Bychkov, Gardiner, Gergiev, Harnoncourt, Herreweghe, Jansons, Marriner, Minkowski, Muti, Norrington, Welser-Möst; festival appearances include Salzburg Festival and Mozartwochen, Wiener Festwochen, Schubertiade Schwarzenberg, Prague Spring Festival, Tokyo Summer Festival and the Montreux Festival. *Recordings include:* Caldara's Maddalena ai Piedi di Cristo (Gramaphone Award), Dvořák songs (solo recital) (Diapson d'Or), Rossini's Zelmira and Handel's Amadigi, Handel's Giulio Cesare and Flavio, Monteverdi's Orfeo and Ulisse, Messiah. *Address:* Impulse Art Management, PO Box 15401, MK Amsterdam, Netherlands (office). *Telephone:* (20) 626-69-44 (office). *Fax:* (20) 622-71-18 (office). *E-mail:* info@impulseartmanagement.nl (office). *Website:* www .impulseartmanagement.nl (office).

FINK, Gerald R., BA, MS, PhD; American geneticist and professor of genetics; *American Cancer Society Professor of Genetics, Massachusetts Institute of Technology;* b. 1 July 1940, Brooklyn, NY; s. of Rebecca Fink and Benjamin Fink; m. Rosalie Lewis 1961; two d.; ed Amherst Coll., Yale Univ.; Postdoctoral Fellow, NIH 1965–66, 1966–67; Instructor, NIH Grad. Program 1966; Instructor, Cold Spring Harbor Summer Program 1970; Asst Prof. of Genetics, Cornell Univ. 1967–71, Assoc. Prof. 1971–76, Prof. 1976–79, Prof. of Biochemistry 1979–82; Prof. of Molecular Genetics, MIT 1982–; American Cancer Soc. Prof. of Genetics 1979–; Founding mem. Whitehead Inst. for Biomedical Research 1982–, Dir 1990–2001; Sec. Genetics Soc. of America 1977–80, Vice-Pres. 1986–87, Pres. 1988–89; Fellow, American Acad. of Arts and Sciences; mem. NAS, American Philosophical Soc., Inst. of Medicine 1996, American Acad. of Microbiology 1996; Hon. DSc (Amherst Coll.) 1982, (Cold Spring Harbor) 1999; NAS-US Steel Prize in Molecular Biology 1981, Genetics Soc. of America Medal 1982, Yale Science and Eng Award 1984, Emil Christian Hansen Foundation Award for Microbiological Research 1986, Wilbur Lucius Cross Medal, Yale Univ. 1992, Bristol-Myers Squibb Infectious Disease Research Award 1993, Ellison Medical Foundation Sr Scholar Award 2001, George W. Beadle Award, Genetics Soc. of America 2001, Yeast Genetics and Molecular Biology Lifetime Achievement Award 2002, Genetics Prize, Peter and Patricia Gruber Foundation 2010. *Publications:* numerous scientific publs. *Address:* Department of Biology, Massachusetts Institute of Technology, 77 Massachusetts Avenue 68-132, Cambridge, MA 02139, USA (office). *Telephone:* (617) 258-5215 (office). *E-mail:* gfink@wi.mit.edu (office). *Website:* www.biology .mit.edu (office).

FINK, Jonathan, BA, PhD, FAAS; American volcanologist and academic; *Director, Center for Sustainability Science Applications, Arizona State University;* b. New York City; ed Colby Coll., Stanford Univ.; has held post-doctoral appointments in Dept of Applied Math., Weizmann Inst., Israel, and in Planetary Geology group, Arizona State Univ.; Post-doctoral researcher in Geology, Stanford Univ.; joined Arizona State Univ. 1979, Prof., School of Earth and Space Exploration, Coll. of Liberal Arts and Sciences and School of Sustainability 1982–, Chair. Geology Dept (now part of School for Earth and Space Exploration) –1997, Vice-Pres. for Research and Econ. Affairs 1997–2007, Julie A. Wrigley Dir Global Inst. of Sustainability 2007–09, Dir, Center for Sustainability Science Applications 2009–; also Univ. Sustainability Officer, Office of the Pres. 2007–09; has held an adjunct faculty position in Dept of Chemical Eng, Univ. of Colorado; Dir Geochemistry and Petrology Program, NSF 1992–93; fmr Visiting Fellow, Research School of Earth Sciences, ANU, Australia; fmr Visiting Scientist, Smithsonian Inst. Nat. Museum of Natural History; mem. Bd of Dirs The Nature Conservancy, Arizona; mem. Bd of Advisors, Smithsonian Institution National Museum of Natural History; Fellow, Geological Soc. of America 1997. *Publications:* numerous scientific papers in professional journals on fluid mechanics, remote sensing, isotope geochemistry to study volcanic eruptions on Earth and other planets, and problems of urban sustainability. *Leisure interests:* bicycling, skiing, swimming, hiking, bird-watching. *Address:* GIOS Building, Room 476, 800 S. Cady Mall, Box 875402, Mail Code: 5402, Tempe, AZ 85287-5502, USA (office). *Telephone:* (480) 965-4797 (office). *E-mail:* jonathan.fink@asu.edu (office). *Website:* www.asu.edu (office); cssa.asu.edu (office).

FINK, Laurence (Larry) Douglas, BA, MBA; American investment banker; *Chairman and CEO, BlackRock, Inc.;* ed Univ. of California, Los Angeles and UCLA Anderson School of Man.; began career in bond trading div. of The First Boston Corpn 1976, became one of first mortgage-backed securities traders on Wall Street, later Co-head, Taxable Fixed Income Div., started Financial Futures and Options Dept and headed Mortgage and Real Estate Products Group, mem. Man. Cttee and a Man. Dir The First Boston Corpn aged 28; f. BlackRock 1988, mem. Bd of Dirs 1999–, Chair. and CEO BlackRock, Inc. 1998–, Chair. Exec. Cttee, Man. Cttee, mem. Nominating and Governance Cttee, Chair. and CEO Blackrock Financial Management Inc., CEO and Dir BlackRock International Ltd, Chair. and CEO BlackRock Advisors, Chair. Nomura BlackRock Asset Man. (jt venture in Japan), Trustee and Pres. BlackRock Funds, Dir several of BlackRock's offshore funds and alternative investment vehicles; mem. Bd of Trustees New York Univ.,

Chair. Financial Affairs Cttee and mem. Exec. Cttee, Ad Hoc Exec. on Bd Governance, Cttee on Trustees; Co-Chair. and mem. Exec. Cttee Mount Sinai New York Univ. Health Bd of Trustees, New York Univ. Hosps Center Bd of Trustees (Chair. Devt/Trustee Stewardship Cttee and mem. Finance Cttee); mem. Bd Execs New York Stock Exchange (now NYSE Next), mem. an advisory panel 2003–; ranked by Forbes magazine amongst The World's Most Powerful People (16th) 2009, (48th) 2010, (52nd) 2011, (42nd) 2012–13. *Address:* Corporate Communications Department, BlackRock, Inc., 55 East 52nd Street, New York, NY 10055, USA (office). *Telephone:* (212) 810-5300 (office). *Fax:* (212) 810-8760 (home). *E-mail:* blackrockbod@blackrock.com (office). *Website:* www2.blackrock.com (office).

FINK, Baron (Life Peer), cr. 2011, of Northwood in the County of Middlesex; **Stanley Fink;** British banking and finance executive and philanthropist; *CEO, International Standard Asset Management;* b. 12 Sept. 1957; m. Barbara Fink; three c.; ed Manchester Grammar School, Trinity Hall, Cambridge; qualified as chartered accountant 1982; with Mars 1982–83; Vice-Pres. Citibank NA 1983–86; joined Man Group plc 1987, mem. Bd of Dirs with responsibility for planning, strategy and mergers and acquisitions 1988–91, Group Finance Dir 1991–96, led Man's initial public offering on London Stock Exchange 1994, Man. Dir most full man. business 1996–2000, Group Chief Exec. 2000–07, Deputy Chair. –2008; CEO International Standard Asset Management in partnership with Lord Levy 2008–; Chair. Earth Capital LLP; Chair. Absolute Return for Kids 2009–; Co-Treas. Conservative Party 2009–10, Treas. 2010–. *Address:* International Standard Asset Management, 52 Queen Anne Street, London, W1G 8HL (office); House of Lords, Westminster, London, SW1A 0PW, England (office). *Telephone:* (20) 7258-9940 (office); (20) 7219-3000 (House of Lords) (office). *Fax:* (20) 7258-9941 (office); (20) 7219-5979 (House of Lords) (office). *Website:* www.isamfunds.com (office).

FINKE, Nikki; American journalist; *Founder and Editor-in-Chief, Deadline;* b. 1953; m. Jeffrey W. Greenberg 1980 (divorced 1982); ed Wellesley Coll.; worked in Washington, DC for New York congressman Ed Koch; later joined the Associated Press (AP) and worked in Baltimore, Boston, the foreign desk at New York City headquarters, Moscow and London; later worked for The Dallas Morning News; joined staff of Newsweek as corresp. in Washington, DC and Los Angeles; later worked at Los Angeles Times as staff writer covering entertainment and features; West Coast Ed. for The New York Observer and then New York Magazine and wrote Hollywood business columns 1995–2000; has also written for The New York Times, Vanity Fair, Esquire, Harper's Bazaar, Elle, The Washington Post, Salon.com, Premiere and Los Angeles magazine; began writing LA Weekly column, Deadline Hollywood 2002, began Deadline (Deadline Hollywood Daily –2009) blog as daily online version of weekly column 2006–, Founder, Ed.-in-Chief and Gen. Man. Deadline.com; sold Deadline to Jay Penske's Mail.com Media Corpn under an agreement by which she continues as the writer and ed. of the website 2009; LA Weekly columns won First Place in the Alternative Weekly Awards for the category Media Reporting/Criticism, Circulation >50,000 2006, Los Angeles Press Club's Southern California Journalism Award for Entertainment Journalist of the Year 2007, Deadline won Second Place in AltWeekly Awards 2007, named by Elle magazine amongst the 25 Most Influential Women in Hollywood 2008, named to the Heeb Magazine 100 2008, ranked by Forbes magazine amongst The World's 100 Most Powerful Women (79th) 2010. *E-mail:* nikki@deadline.com (office). *Website:* www.deadline.com (office).

FINLAY, B. Brett, OC, BSc, PhD, FRSC; Canadian microbiologist and academic; *Peter Wall Distinguished Professor, University of British Columbia;* ed Univ. of Alberta, Stanford Univ. School of Medicine, USA; Assoc. Prof., Biotechnology Lab., Univ. of British Columbia 1989–96, Prof., Michael Smith Labs and Dept of Biochemistry and Molecular Biology and Dept of Microbiology and Immunology 1996–, Peter Wall Distinguished Prof. 2002–; Dir SARS Accelerated Vaccine Initiative; Co-founder Inimex Pharmaceuticals, Inc.; mem. several editorial and advisory bds; mem. Canadian Centres of Excellence for Bacterial Diseases 1989; Fellow, American Acad. of Microbiology 2003, Canadian Acad. of Health Sciences 2005; Hon. mem. Univ. of British Columbia Golden Key Int. Honour Soc. 2001; Distinguished Scientist Seminar Award, Univ. of Southern Alabama 1991, Howard Hughes Medical Inst. Int. Research Scholar 1991, 1997, 2000, 2001, Fisher Scientific Award, Canadian Soc. of Microbiologists 1991, Killam Research Prize, Univ. of British Columbia 1993, Soc. Scientist Award 1996, 21st Annual Joseph E. Smadel Lecturer, Infectious Diseases Soc. of America 1997, E.W. R. Steacie Prize 1998, Howard Hughes Medical Inst. Holiday Lectures Presenter (first non-American) 1999, Dr Cam Coady Foundation Lectureship 2001, CIHR Distinguished Investigator Award 2001, 3M Distinguished Lectureship, Univ. of Western Ontario 2001, Distinguished Lecture in Biochemistry Award and Plaque, Univ. of Alberta 2001, Celebrate Research citation, Univ. of British Columbia 2001–04, James W. McLaughlin Distinguished Speaker, Univ. of Texas Medical Br. at Galveston 2002, Nat. Merit Award, Ottawa Life Sciences Council 2003, chosen by Time Canada as one of five Best in Medicine 2003, British Columbia Biotechnology Award for Innovation and Achievement 2003, featured in Maclean's The 2003 Watch List 2003, Solutions Through Research Award, British Columbia Innovation Council 2004, Squibb Award, Infectious Diseases Soc. of America 2004, Michael Smith Prize in Health Research 2004, CIHR Partnership Award for Sars Accelerated Vaccine Initiative 2005, awarded $5.7 million from Genome Canada for the PREPARE (Proteomics for Emerging Pathogen Response) project 2005, Gates Foundation Award in Global Disease Fight 2005, Jacob Biely Faculty Research Prize, Univ. of British Columbia 2006, Killam Prize, Canada Council for the Arts 2006, RSC Flavelle Medal 2006. *Publications:* numerous scientific papers in professional journals on host–pathogen interactions at the molecular level. *Address:* Michael Smith Laboratories, Room #301, 2185 East Mall, University of British Columbia, Vancouver, BC V6T 1Z4, Canada (office). *Telephone:* (604) 822-2210 (office). *Fax:* (604) 822-9830 (office). *E-mail:* bfinlay@interchange.ubc.ca (office). *Website:* www.finlaylab.msl.ubc.ca (office).

FINLAY, Frank, CBE; British actor; b. 6 Aug. 1926, Farnworth, Lancs.; s. of Josiah Finlay and Margaret Finlay; m. Doreen Joan Shepherd 1954; two s. one d.; ed St Gregory the Great, Farnworth, Royal Acad. of Dramatic Art, London; repertory 1950–52, 1954–57. *Stage appearances include:* Belgrade, Epitaph for George Dillon 1958, Sugar in the Morning, Sergeant Musgrave's Dance, Chicken Soup with Barley, Roots, I'm Talking About Jerusalem, The Happy Haven,

Platonov, Chips with Everything 1958–62 (all at Royal Court, Clarence Derwent Best Actor Award 1962), St Joan, The Workhouse Donkey, Hobson's Choice 1963, Othello, The Dutch Courtesan 1964 (Best Actor Award, San Sebastian 1966), The Crucible, Much Ado About Nothing, Mother Courage 1965, Juno and the Paycock, The Storm 1966 (all at Nat. Theatre), After Haggerty (Aldwych, Criterion), Son of Man (Leicester Theatre, Round House) 1970, Saturday Sunday Monday, The Party 1973, Plunder, Watch It Come Down, Weapons of Happiness 1976, Amadeus 1982 (all at Nat. Theatre), Kings and Clowns (Phoenix), Filumena (Lyric) 1978, The Girl in Melanie Klein 1980, The Cherry Orchard 1983, Mutiny (Piccadilly) 1985, Beyond Reasonable Doubt 1987, Black Angel 1990, A Slight Hangover 1991, The Heiress 1992, The Woman in Black 1993–94, Capt. Hook/Mr Darling in Peter Pan 1994, Gaslight 1995, The Handyman 1996. Film appearances include: The Longest Day 1962, Private Potter 1962, Life for Ruth 1962, Loneliness of the Long Distance Runner 1962, The Comedy Man 1963, The Informers 1964, Hot Enough for June 1964, A Study in Terror 1965, Othello 1965, The Sandwich Man 1966, The Deadly Bees 1966, The Jokers 1967, I'll Never Forget What's 'is name 1967, Robbery 1967, The Shoes of the Fisherman 1968, Inspector Clouseau 1968, Twisted Nerve 1968, Cromwell 1970, The Molly Maguires 1970, Assault 1971, Danny Jones 1971, Gumshoe 1971, Shaft in Africa 1973, Van Der Valk and the Dead, The Three Musketeers 1973, The Ring of Darkness, The Wild Geese, The Four Musketeers 1974, Murder by Decree 1979, The Return of the Soldier 1982, The Ploughman's Lunch 1982, Enigma 1983, The Key 1983, 1919 (voice) 1985, Life Force 1985, King of the Wind 1989, The Return of the Musketeers 1989, Cthulhu Mansion 1990, Sparrow 1993, Gospa 1995, Romance and Rejection 1996, Limited Edition 1996, For My Baby 1997, Stiff Upper Lips 1998, So This Is Romance? 1998, Dreaming of Joseph Lees 1999, Ghosthunter 2000, The Martins 2001, The Pianist 2002, Silent Cry 2002, The Statement 2003, Lighthouse Hill 2004, The Waiting Room 2007. Television appearances include: Target Luna (series) 1960, The Compartment 1961, The Murderer 1966, Much Ado About Nothing 1967, Oldenberg 1967, Never Mind the Quality, Feel the Width 1967, Les Misérables 1967, This Happy Breed 1969, Julius Caesar 1969, Blood of the Lamb 1969, The Lie 1970, Casanova (mini-series) 1971, The Merchant of Venice 1972, The Adventures of Don Quixote 1973, Candide 1973, Voltaire, Van Der Valk and the Girl 1972, Van Der Valk and the Rich 1973, The Death of Adolf Hitler 1973, Pas de frontières pour l'inspecteur: Le bouc émissaire 1975, 84 Charing Cross Road 1975, Bouquet of Barbed Wire (mini-series) 1976, Another Bouquet (mini-series) 1977, Count Dracula 1977, The Thief of Baghdad 1978, Saturday Sunday Monday, Sakharov 1984, A Christmas Carol 1984, In the Secret State 1985, Arc de Triomphe 1985, The Last Campaign, Napoleon in Betzi, Dear Brutus, Tales of the Unexpected, Tales from 1001 Nights, Aspects of Love—Mona, Casanova 1987, Verdict on Erebus, Mountain of Diamonds 1991, Encounters, The Other Side, Stalin 1992, Charlemagne (mini-series) 1993, An Exchange of Fire 1993, Common as Muck (series) 1994, A Mind to Murder 1995, How Do You Want Me? (series) 1998, The Magical Legend of the Leprechauns 1999, Longitude 2000, The Sins (mini-series) 2000, In The Beginning (voice, uncredited) 2000, Station Jim 2001, The Lost Prince 2003, Eroica 2003, Prime Suspect 6 2003, Life Begins (series) 2004, Prime Suspect: The Final Act 2006, Four Seasons (mini-series) 2008–09. Leisure interests: reading, walking, the countryside. Address: c/o Ken McReddie Associates Ltd, 11 Connaught Place, London, W2 2ET, England (office). E-mail: email@kenmcreddie.com (office). Website: www.kenmcreddie.com (office); www.frankfinlay.net.

FINLAYSON, Chris, BA, LLM, LTCL; New Zealand lawyer and politician; Attorney-General, Minister in Charge of Treaty of Waitangi Negotiations and Minister for Arts, Culture and Heritage; b. 4 Dec. 1956, Wellington; ed Victoria Univ.; admitted to Bar 1981; Pnr, Brandon Brookfield (law firm) 1986–90; Lecturer in Law, Victoria Univ. 1987–2002; Law Soc. Rep., New Zealand Council of Law Reporting 1990–98, New Zealand Council of Legal Educ. 1992–98, High Court Rules Cttee 1999–2005; Pnr, Bell Gully 1991–2003; Barrister 2003–; mem. New Zealand Nat. Party 1974–, mem. Rules Cttee 1997–2001, Regional Chair. Lower North Island 2001–03, Electorate Chair. Mana Electorate 2003–05, Policy Chair. 2005–05; Assoc. Spokesman Treaty of Waitangi Issues and Maori Affairs 2005–06, Arts, Culture and Heritage 2005–06; Deputy Chair. Justice and Electoral Cttee 2005–08; Attorney-Gen., Minister in Charge of Treaty of Waitangi Negotiations and Minister for Arts, Culture and Heritage 2008–; Chair. Arts Board 1998–2001; Trustee Theatre Arts Charitable Trust, New Zealand Symphony Orchestra Foundation. Address: Office of the Attorney-General, Department of the Prime Minister and Cabinet, Executive Wing, Parliament Buildings, Wellington, New Zealand (office). Telephone: (4) 817-9700 (office). Fax: (4) 472-3181 (office). E-mail: admin@dpmc.govt.nz (office). Website: www.dpmc.govt.nz (office).

FINLAYSON, Max, BSc, PhD; Australian ecologist, academic and international organization official; Professor of Ecology and Biodiversity and Director, Institute for Land, Water and Society, Charles Sturt University; b. Mt Barker, WA; ed Univ. of Western Australia, James Cook Univ., Townsville; worked with CSIRO Irrigation Research at Griffith on aquatic weed control and using water plants to treat waste water 1980–83; worked at Office of the Supervising Scientist, Alligator Rivers Region, Kakadu, Northern Territory researching effects of uranium mining on floodplain environment 1983–89, research/managerial job 1993–2000; worked with Int. Waterbird and Wetland Research Bureau, Slimbridge, Glos., UK 1989–93, worked on wetlands conservation projects and capacity building in USSR, Eastern Europe, Eastern Africa and the Mediterranean; worked in S Africa arguing against expansion of mineral sands mining into St Lucia Nature Reserve; Dir Environmental Research Inst. for Office of Supervising Scientists, Darwin 2000–05; Prin. Researcher (Ecology), Int. Water Man. Inst., Colombo, Sri Lanka 2005–07; Prof. of Ecology and Biodiversity and Dir Inst. for Land, Water and Society, Charles Sturt Univ. 2007–; Pres. Supervisory Council Wetlands International 2001–07; mem. Scientific Advisory Council to Biological Station Tour Du Valat, Camargue, France 2007–; Recognition of Excellence, Ramsar Wetland Conservation Awards 2002. Publications: more than 200 book chapters, journal articles, reports, guidelines and proceedings on wetland ecology and management. Address: Institute for Land, Water and Society, Charles Sturt University, Albury-Wodonga (Thurgoona) Campus, Elizabeth Mitchell Drive, PO Box 789, Albury, NSW 2640, Australia (office). Telephone: (2) 6051-9779 (office). Fax: (2) 6051-9797 (office). E-mail: mfinlayson@csu.edu.au (office). Website: www .csu.edu.au/research/ilws (office).

FINLEY, The Hon. Diane, PC, BA, MBA; Canadian politician; Minister of Public Works and Government Services; b. 1957, Hamilton, Ont.; m. Doug Finley; ed Port Dover Composite School, Univ. of Western Ont.; fmr Admin. Univ. of Western Ont. French immersion school; positions in health care, transportation, agricultural equipment manufacturing, publishing, aviation; fmrly with Laidlaw Group of Cos; mem. Parl. for Haldimand—Norfolk 2004–; Official Opposition Critic for Agric. and Agri-food 2004; Minister of Human Resources and Skills Devt 2006–07, 2008–13, of Citizenship and Immigration 2007–08, of Public Works and Government Services 2013–. Address: Department of Public Works and Government Services, 11 rue Laurier, PDP III, Gatineau, QC K1A 0S5, Canada (office). Telephone: (819) 956-3115 (office). Fax: (819) 956-9062 (office). E-mail: questions@ tpsgc-pwgsc.gc.ca (office). Website: www.tpsgc-pwgsc.gc.ca (office).

FINLEY, Gerald Hunter, MA (Cantab.), ARCM, FRCM; Canadian singer (baritone) and conductor; b. 1960, Montreal, Quebec; s. of Eric Gault Finley and Catherine; m. 1st Louise Winter 1990 (divorced 2009); two s.; m. 2nd Heulwen Keyte 2010; ed Glebe Collegiate Inst., Ottawa, Univ. of Ottawa, Royal Coll. of Music (RCM), London, UK, Nat. Opera Studio, London, King's Coll., Cambridge; chorister, St Matthew's Church, Ottawa 1969–78; mem. Ottawa Choral Soc., Cantata Singers, Ont. Youth Choir 1977–78, Glyndebourne Festival Chorus, UK 1986–89; professional debut as opera soloist, Antonio (Le nozze di Figaro), Ottawa 1987 and Papageno (Die Zauberflöte), London 1989; debut at Glyndebourne with Glyndebourne Touring Opera as Kuligin (Katya Kabanova) 1988, Sid (Albert Herring) 1989, English Clerk (Death in Venice) 1989, Fiorello, Figaro (Il barbiere di Siviglia) 1989, Papageno 1990, with Glyndebourne Festival Opera as the Count Dominik (Arabella) 1989, Guglielmo 1990, 1992, Figaro at opening of new Glyndebourne opera house 1994, Owen Wingrave 1997, Olivier (Capriccio) 1998, Nick Shadow (The Rake's Progress) 2000, Agamemnon (Iphigénie en Aulide) 2002, Don Giovanni 2010, Hans Sachs (Meistersinger) 2011; debut at Canadian Opera Co. as Sid 1991, Figaro 1993; debut at Amsterdam as Demetrius (A Midsummer Night's Dream) 1993, Count 2001; debut at Covent Garden as Figaro 1995, Achilla (Giulio Cesare) 1997, Pilgrim (Pilgrim's Progress) 1997, Creonte (L'anima del filosofo) 2001, Forester (Cunning Little Vixen) 2003, Don Giovanni 2005, 2012, Count (Le nozze di Figaro) 2006, Yeletsky (Pique Dame) 2006, Golaud (Pélléas et Mélisande) 2008, Onegin (Eugene Onegin) 2008, Frank/Fritz (Die tote Stadt) 2009, Zurga (Les pêcheurs de perles) 2010, Howard K. Stern (Anna Nicole) 2011; debut at Opéra de Paris Valentin (Faust) 1997, Sharpless (Madama Butterfly) 1998, Papageno 2001, Figaro 2003, Don Giovanni 2003, Count Almaviva 2003; debut at Metropolitan Opera, New York as Papageno 1998; Papageno 2000, Marcello 2001, 2010, Don Giovanni 2005, Golaud 2010; Don Giovanni at Tel-Aviv 2000, Vienna 2006, Prague 2006, Budapest 2006, Rome 2006; debut at Los Angeles Opera as Figaro 1995, Belcore (L'elisir d'amore) 1996, Mr Fox (Fantastic Mr Fox) 1998; debut at ENO as Harry Heegan (The Silver Tassie) 2000, Onegin 2005, Balstrode (Peter Grimes) 2009; debut at San Francisco Opera as J. Robert Oppenheimer (Dr Atomic) 2005, Amsterdam 2007, Chicago 2008, Metropolitan Opera 2008, Atlanta 2008, ENO 2009; debut at Salzburg Festival as Conte (Nozze di Figaro) 2007, 2009, Don Giovanni 2011, Don Alfonso 2013; debut at Munich State Opera as Don Giovanni 2010, Escamillo (Carmen) 2011; Iago (Otello), London Symphony Orchestra, London 2009; Guillaume Tell, Accad. di Santa Cecilia 2010; concert soloist and lieder singer; Visiting Prof., RCM 2000–; John Christie Award, Glyndebourne 1989, Juno Award for Best Vocal Performance (Canada) 1998, 2011, Singer Award, Royal Philharmonic Soc. 2001, Opera News Award 2009, Grammy Award for Best Opera Recording (for Doctor Atomic with Alan Gilbert, Meredith Arwady, Richard Paul Fink, Sasha Cooke, Thomas Glenn, Eric Owens and Jay David Saks) 2012. Films include: Owen Wingrave 2001, L'amour de loin 2006, Doctor Atomic 2008. Recordings: albums include: Papageno, Guglielmo, Sid, Masetto, Haydn's Creation, Brahms' Requiem, Handel Messiah, Bach Weihnachtsoratorium, Silver Tassie, Pilgrim's Progress, Dido and Aeneas, Songs of Travel 1998, Schubert Complete Songs 1817–1821, Complete Songs of Henri Duparc 2002, Songs of Charles Ives 2005, 2008, Stanford – Orchestral Songs (Editor's Choice Award, Gramophone Awards) 2006, Barber – Songs (Gramophone Award for Best Solo Vocal 2008), Schumann – Dichterliebe, etc. (Gramophone Award for Best Solo Vocal Performance 2009), Ravel – Songs 2009, Opera Arias in English (Juno Award 2011) 2010, Otello 2010, Britten Songs & Proverbs of William Blake (Gramophone Award for Best Solo Vocal Recording) 2011, The Ballad Singer 2011. Radio: numerous recordings with BBC, CBC, ORF and BR. Leisure interests: wine, reading, ice skating. Address: c/o IMG Artists, The Light Box, 111 Power Road, London, W4 5PY, England (office); c/o IMG Artists, Carnegie Hall Tower, 152 West 57th Street, 5th Floor, New York, NY 10019, USA (office). Telephone: (20) 7957-5800 (London) (office); (212) 994-3500 (New York) (office). Fax: (20) 7957-5801 (London) (office); (212) 994-3550 (New York) (office). E-mail: salmansi@imgartists .com (office). Website: www.imgartists.com (office); www.geraldfinley.com; www .geraldfinley.info.

FINN, Maj.-Gen. Michael; Irish army officer and UN official; Head of Mission and Chief of Staff, United Nations Truce Supervision Organization; b. 1953, Aughavilla, Claremorris; m. Helen Cummins; three c.; ed Univ. Coll. Galway, Irish Command and Staff School; long career in Irish army and with UN peacekeeping forces, becoming mil. observer assigned to various UN operations including Observer Group Golan, UN Disengagement Observer Force 1993–95 and Observer Group Lebanon, UN Interim Force in Lebanon (UNIFIL), becoming Co. Commdr and Bn Operations Officer, UNIFIL, Commdr, first Irish infantry force with KFOR (Kosovo Force) mission, Kosovo 2003–04; Dir of Logistics, EU Mil. Staff, Brussels 2007–10; Gen. Officer commanding Second Infantry 2010–13; Head of Mission and Chief of Staff, UN Truce Supervision Org. 2013–. Address: United Nations Truce Supervision Organization (UNTSO), Government House, POB 490, Jerusalem 91004, Israel (office). Website: www.un.org/en/peacekeeping/missions/untso (office).

FINN, Pavel Konstantinovich; Russian scriptwriter; b. (Pavel Finn-Halfin), 28 June 1940, Moscow; m. Irina Chernova-Finn; one s.; ed All-Union State Inst. of Cinematography; fmr journalist, documentary maker; freelance script writer 1968–; Head of Higher Workshop Course of Scriptwriters; Chair. Cinema Dramaturgy Council, Moscow Union of Cinematographers 2001; apptd Deputy Chair. Russian Union of Cinematographers 2001; Distinguished Artist of the Russian SFSR 1991. Films include: Headless Horse Rider 1973, Armed and Very Dangerous 1977, 26 Days of Dostoyevsky's Life 1980, Icicle in a Warm Sea 1983,

Witness 1985, Lady Macbeth of Mtsensk Region 1989, Accidental Waltz 1989, Sunset 1990, Myth about Leonid 1991, A Big Concert of Peoples 1991, Shylock 1993, Jester's Revenge 1994, For What 1995, Career of Arthur Whui 1996, Break Point, We Are Your Kids, Moscow, Eve's Gates, Death of Tairov or Princess Brambilla, Secrets of Court Coups: Film Two 2000, Miracles, or Pike in the Moscow Style 2001, Ravine 2007, The Gift to Stalin 2008, There Was Never a Better Brother 2011. *Leisure interests:* buying books, reading. *Address:* 4th Rostovsky per. 2/1, Apartment 9, 119121 Moscow, Russia (home). *Telephone:* (495) 248-53-28 (home); (495) 334-59-34 (home). *E-mail:* pavelfinn@mtu-net.ru (home).

FINN, Victor Konstantinovich, DrSc; Russian philosopher, logician and computer scientist; b. 15 July 1933, Moscow; m. Irina Yevgenyevna Yavchunovskaya-Belova; one d.; ed Moscow State Univ.; researcher, Head of Sector, Lab. of Electromodelling, USSR Acad. of Sciences 1957–59; Head of Lab. All-Union Inst. for Scientific and Tech. Information (VINITI) 1959–; Lecturer, Moscow State Univ. 1967–69; Prof., Head Dept of Artificial Intelligence, Moscow State Inst. of History and Archives (now Russian Humanitarian Univ.) 1979–; mem. Acad. of Natural Sciences; mem. Bd int. journals Studia Logica, Foundation of Science; mem. Council Russian Asscn of Artificial Intelligence; Honoured Science Worker 2007. *Publications:* over 100 scientific papers and books including Logical Problems of Information Search 1976, Epistemological and Logical Problems of History (with K. Khvostova) 1995, Intellectual Systems and Society 2001. *Address:* 1st Miusskaya str. 20, Apt. 19, 125047 Moscow, Russia (home). *Telephone:* (495) 155-43-65 (office), (495) 251-08-99 (home). *Fax:* (495) 152-54-47 (office). *E-mail:* finn@viniti.ru (office); ira-finn@mtu-net.ru (home).

FINNBOGADÓTTIR, Vigdís; Icelandic politician and fmr head of state; b. 15 April 1930, Reykjavik; d. of Finnbogi Rutur Thorvaldsson and Sigridur Eiriksdóttir; m. (divorced); one adopted d.; ed Junior Coll., Menntaskólinn i Reykjavik, Univs of Grenoble and Sorbonne, France, Univ. of Iceland; press officer, Nat. Theatre of Iceland 1954–57, 1961–64; teacher at Reykjavík Grammar School 1962–67, Hamrahlíð Grammar School 1967–72; taught French at Jr Colls, Menntaskólinn i Reykjavik, Menntaskólinn vid Hamrahlid; fmr Head of Guide Training, Iceland Tourist Bureau; Dir Reykjavik Theatre Co. 1972–80; taught French drama, Univ. of Iceland; worked for Icelandic State TV; fmr Chair. Alliance Française; mem. Advisory Cttee on Cultural Affairs in Nordic Countries 1976–80, Chair. 1978–80; Pres. of Iceland 1980–96; UNESCO Goodwill Amb. for Languages 1998–; mem. Club of Madrid; Hon. GCMG 1982; Dr hc (Grenoble) 1985, (Bordeaux) 1987, (Smith Coll., USA) 1988, (Luther Coll., USA) 1989, (Manitoba) 1989, (Nottingham) 1990, (Tampere) 1990, (Gothenburg) 1990, (Gashuin, Tokyo) 1991, (Miami) 1993, (St Mary's, Halifax) 1996, (Leeds) 1996, (Memorial, St John) 1997, (Guelph) 1998, (Iceland) 2000. *Leisure interest:* theatre.

FINNEGAN, John D., BA, JD, MBA; American business executive; *Chairman, President and CEO, The Chubb Corporation;* b. 31 Jan. 1949, Jersey City, NJ; m. Kathleen Finnegan; two c.; ed Princeton, Rutgers and Fordham Univs; began career with General Motors (GM) 1976, various positions including Vice-Pres. GM and Pres. GM Acceptance Corpn 1997–99, Exec. Vice-Pres. GM and Pres. and Chair. GM Acceptance Corpn 1999–2002; apptd Dir The Chubb Corpn 2002, Pres. and CEO 2002–03, Chair., Pres. and CEO 2003–; mem. Bd United Negro Coll. Fund. *Address:* The Chubb Corporation, 15 Mountain View Road, Warren, NJ 07061-1615, USA (office). *Telephone:* (908) 903-2000 (office). *Fax:* (908) 903-3402 (office). *Website:* www.chubb.com (office).

FINNEY, Albert; British actor; b. 9 May 1936; m. 1st Jane Wenham (divorced); one s.; m. 2nd Anouk Aimée 1970 (divorced 1978); m. 3rd Pene Delmage 2006; ed Salford Grammar School and Royal Acad. of Dramatic Art; Birmingham Repertory Co. 1956–58; Shakespeare Memorial Theatre Co. 1959; Nat. Theatre 1965, 1975; formed Memorial Enterprises 1966; Assoc. Artistic Dir English Stage Co. 1972–75; Dir United British Artists 1983–86; Hon. LittD (Sussex) 1966; Lawrence Olivier Award 1986; London Standard Drama Award for Best Actor 1986, Dilys Powell Award, London Film Critics Circle 1999; BAFTA Fellowship 2001. *Plays include:* Julius Caesar, Macbeth, Henry V, The Beaux' Stratagem, The Alchemist, The Lizard on the Rock, The Party 1958, King Lear, Othello 1959, A Midsummer Night's Dream, The Lily-White Boys 1960, Billy Liar 1960, Luther 1961, 1963, Much Ado About Nothing, Armstrong's Last Goodnight 1965, Miss Julie 1965, Black Comedy 1965, Love for Love 1965, A Flea in Her Ear 1966, A Day in the Death of Joe Egg 1968, Alpha Beta 1972, Krapp's Last Tape 1973, Cromwell 1973, Chez Nous 1974, Loot (Dir) 1975, Hamlet 1976, Tamburlaine the Great 1976, Uncle Vanya 1977, Present Laughter 1977, The Country Wife 1977–78, The Cherry Orchard 1978, Macbeth 1978, Has 'Washington' Legs? 1978, The Biko Inquest (Dir) 1984, Sergeant Musgrave's Dance (Dir) 1984, Orphans 1986, J.J. Farr 1987, Another Time 1989, Reflected Glory 1992, Art 1996. *Films acted in include:* The Entertainer 1959, Saturday Night and Sunday Morning 1960, Tom Jones 1963, Night Must Fall 1963, Two for the Road 1967, Charlie Bubbles (also Dir) 1968, Scrooge 1970, Gumshoe 1971, Murder on the Orient Express 1974, Wolfen 1979, Loophole 1980, Looker 1980, Shoot the Moon 1981, Annie 1982, Life of John Paul II 1983, The Dresser 1983, Under the Volcano 1983, Orphans (also Dir) 1987, Miller's Crossing 1989, The Image 1989, The Playboys 1992, Rich in Love 1992, The Browning Version 1993, The Run of the Country 1995, Washington Square, Breakfast of Champions 1999, Simpatico 1999, Delivering Milo 1999, Erin Brockovich 2000, Big Fish 2003, A Good Year 2006, Amazing Grace 2006, The Bourne Ultimatum 2007, Before the Devil Knows You're Dead 2007, Skyfall 2012. *TV appearances include:* The Endless Game 1989, The Green Man (mini-series) 1990, Karaoke 1995, Nostromo 1997, My Uncle Silas 2001, 2003, The Lonely War 2002, The Gathering Storm (Emmy Award 2002, Golden Globe for Best Actor in a mini-series or TV movie 2003, BAFTA Award for Best Actor 2003) 2002. *Address:* c/o Michael Simkins LLP, Lynton House, 7–12 Tavistock Square, London, WC1H 9LT, England (office). *Telephone:* (20) 7874-5600 (office). *Fax:* (20) 7874-5601 (office).

FINNIS, John Mitchell, LLB, DPhil, FBA; Australian/British academic and barrister; *Emeritus Professor of Law and Legal Philosophy, University of Oxford;* b. 28 July 1940, Adelaide, South Australia; s. of the late Maurice M. S. Finnis and of Margaret McKellar Stewart; m. Marie Carmel McNally 1964; three s. three d.; ed St Peter's Coll., Adelaide, St Mark's Coll., Univ. of Adelaide, Univ. Coll., Oxford, UK; Fellow and Praelector in Jurisprudence, Univ. Coll., Oxford 1966–2010, Stowell Civil Law Fellow 1973–2007, Vice-Master 2001–10; Lecturer

in Law, Univ. of Oxford 1966–72, Rhodes Reader in the Laws of the Commonwealth and the United States 1972–89, Prof. of Law and Legal Philosophy 1989–2010, now Prof. Emer., mem. Philosophy Sub-Faculty 1984–2010, Chair. Bd of Faculty of Law 1987–89; Prof. and Head of Dept of Law, Univ. of Malawi 1976–78; Biolchini Family Prof. of Law, Univ. of Notre Dame, Ind., USA 1995–; Adjunct Prof. of Philosophy 1999–; barrister, Gray's Inn 1970–; Gov., Plater Coll., Oxford 1972–92; Consultor, Pontifical Commission Iustitia et Pax 1977–89, mem. 1990–95; Special Adviser, Foreign Affairs Cttee, House of Commons, on role of UK Parl. in Canadian Constitution 1980–82; mem. Catholic Bishops' Jt Cttee on Bioethical Issues 1981–89, Int. Theological Comm. (Vatican) 1986–92; Gov. Linacre Centre for Medical Ethics 1981–96, 1998– (Vice-Chair. 1987–96, 1998–2008); Huber Distinguished Visiting Prof., Boston Coll. Law School 1993–94; mem. Pontifical Acad. Pro Vita 2001–. *Publications include:* Halsbury's Laws of England (fourth edn) Vol. 6 (Commonwealth and Dependencies) 1974, 1990, 2003, (fifth edn) Vol. 13 (Commonwealth and Dependencies) 2009, Natural Law and Natural Rights 1980, Fundamentals of Ethics 1983, Nuclear Deterrence, Morality and Realism (with Joseph Boyle and Germain Grisez) 1987, Moral Absolutes 1991, Aquinas: Moral, Political and Legal Theory 1998; articles on constitutional law, legal philosophy, ethics, moral theology and late sixteenth-century history. *Address:* University College, Oxford, OX1 4BH, England (office); Notre Dame Law School, South Bend, IN 46556, USA (office). *Telephone:* (1865) 281948 (UK) (office); (574) 631-5989 (USA) (office); (1865) 558660 (UK) (home).

FINO, Bashkim Muhamet; Albanian economist and politician; b. 12 Oct. 1962, Gjirokaster; m.; two c.; ed Tirana Univ. and studies in USA; economist, Economic Data Inst., Gjirokaster Dist 1986–89, Dir 1989–92; Mayor of Gjirokaster (Socialist Party of Albania) 1992–96; Prime Minister of Albania March–July 1997; Deputy Prime Minister 1997–98; mem. Kuvendi Popullor (People's Ass.) for Berat 2005–. *Address:* Kuvendi Popullor (People's Assembly), Bulevardi Dëshmorët e Kombit 4, Tirana, Albania. *Telephone:* (4) 2264887. *Fax:* (4) 2221764. *E-mail:* marlind@parlament.al. *Website:* www.parlament.al.

FINSCHER, Ludwig, PhD; German musicologist, lexicographer and academic (retd); b. 14 March 1930, Kassel; ed Univ. of Göttingen; Asst Lecturer, Univ. of Kiel 1960–65, Univ. of Saarbrücken 1965–68; Ed. Die Musikforschung 1961–68, Co-Ed. 1968–74; Prof. of Musicology, Univ. of Frankfurt am Main 1968–81, Univ. of Heidelberg 1981–95; mem. Akad. der Wissenschaften, Heidelberg, Akad. der Wissenschaften und der Literatur, Mainz, Academia Europaea; Corresp. mem. American Musicological Soc.; Hon. mem. Int. Musicological Soc., Gesellschaft für Musikforschung; Hon. Foreign mem. Royal Musical Asscn, London 1978; Ordre pour le Mérite 1994, Grand Order of Merit (Germany) 1997; Dr hc (Athens) 2002, (Zürich) 2003, (Saarbrücken) 2009; Akad. der Wissenschaften Prize, Göttingen 1968, Balzan Prize 2006. *Publications:* Collected Works of Gaffurius (ed., two vols) 1955, 1960, Collected Works of Compère (ed., five vols) 1958–72, Loyset Compère (c. 1450–1518): Life and Works 1964, Geschichte der Evangelischen Kirchenmusik (co-ed., second edn) 1965, Studien zur Geschichte des Streichquartetts: I, Die Entstehung des klassischen Streichquartetts: Von den Vorformen zur Grundlegung durch Joseph Haydn 1974, Collected Works of Hindemith (co-ed. with K. von Fischer) 1976–, Renaissance-Studien: Helmuth Osthoff zum 80. Geburtstag (ed.) 1979, Quellenstudien zu Musik der Renaissance (ed., two vols) 1981, 1983, Ludwig van Beethoven (ed.) 1983, Claudio Monteverdi: Festschrift Reinhold Hammerstein zum 70. Geburtstag (ed.) 1986, Die Musik des 15. und 16. Jahrhunderts: Neues Handbuch der Musikwissenschaft (ed., Vol. 3/1–2) 1989–90, Die Mannheimer Hofkapelle im Zeitalter Carl Theodors (ed.) 1992, Die Musik in Geschichte und Gegenwart (ed., second edn, 26 vols) 1994–2007, Joseph Haydn 2000, Geschichte und Geschichten: Ausgewählte Aufsätze zur Musikhistorie 2003; contrib. editorially to the complete works of Mozart and Gluck, contrib. to scholarly books and journals. *Address:* Am Walde 1, 38302 Wolfenbüttel, Germany (home). *Telephone:* (5331) 32713 (home). *Fax:* (5331) 33276 (home).

FIONDA, Andrew, MA, M.Design; British fashion designer; b. 8 Feb. 1967, Middlesbrough, Cleveland, England; s. of Frederick Fionda and Sarah Park; ed Nottingham Trent Univ., Royal Coll. of Art, London; designer for fashion houses in UK and for John McIntyre, Hong Kong; Co-founder, with Reynold Pearce (q.v.), Owner and Designer, Pearce Fionda 1994–2013, Dir 2013–; first capsule collection for Spring/Summer 1995 shown in New Generation show during London Fashion Week; also designs PIIF collection for Designers at Debenhams range 1997–, duo now concentrate on eveningwear range and children's bridesmaid creations; teacher, Univ. of Brighton 1996–98; Fashion Ed. at Brighton Visitor 2009–13; exhbns include Design of the Times, RCA 1996, The Cutting Edge of British Fashion 1997; with Reynold Pearce received Newcomers Award for Export, British Knitwear Clothing Export Council and Fashion Weekly 1994, New Generation Award, Lloyds Bank British Fashion Awards 1995, World Young Designers Award, Int. Apparel Fed. 1996, Glamour Award, Lloyds Bank British Fashion Awards 1997. *Leisure interests:* cinema, gym, music, reading. *Telephone:* 7889-602317 (mobile). *E-mail:* andrewfionda@btinternet.com. *Website:* pearcefionda .com.

FIORASO, Geneviève, BA, MA, MA (Econ); French politician and fmr teacher; b. 10 Oct. 1954, Amiens (Somme); ed Univ. of Amiens; worked as an English teacher in Amiens; left teaching and moved to Grenoble 1978, served as Information Officer, then managing Documentation and Press for the City of Grenoble; became parl. attaché to Mayor Hubert Dubedout 1983; participated in cantonal electoral campaign 1985; mem. management team of Corys (startup of the CEA) 1989–95; Chief of Staff to Mayor of Grenoble, Michel Destot 1995; Dir Agence Régionale du Numérique (set up by the digital network of cities of Rhône-Alpes region) 1999–2001; Sr Marketing Man., France Telecom 2001–04; Deputy Asst for the Economy, Innovation, Trade and Craft, and First Vice-Pres. Metro-Agglomeration community of the Grenoble Alpes Métropole, in charge of econ. devt 2003–08, Deputy for the Economy, Universities and Research for the City Council of Grenoble 2008–; CEO S.E.M. Minatec Entreprises (public-pvt. venture, entrusted with the marketing of high-tech building of Minatec) 2007–; Chair. Institut d'Admin des Entreprises Grenoble; Deputy (Parti socialiste—PS) to Nat. Ass. for First Dist of Isère 2007–; Bd mem. Socialist, Radical, Citizen and other groups, mem. Cttee on Econ. Affairs, the Environment and Territory, mem. Parl. Office for Scientific and Technological Choices (OPECST); Minister of Higher Educ. and

Research 2012–14. *Address:* c/o Ministry of Higher Education and Research, 1 rue Descartes, 75231 Paris, Cedex 05, France (office). *Website:* genevieve-fioraso.fr.

FIORELLO, Rosario Tindario, (Fiorello); Italian singer and radio and television presenter; *Co-host, Viva Radio 2, Radiotelevisione Italiana SpA (RAI);* b. 16 May 1960, Catania; began career working in tourist villages, first as barman and then as singer, mimic and entertainer; spotted by talent scout Claudio Cecchetto late 1980s; began hosting show Viva Radio Deejay; host TV show Karaoke, went on to host various other shows, first on Mediaset networks, then with RAI on Stasera Pago Io 2001, 2002, 2004; Co-host, with Marco Baldini, Francesco Bozzi and Enrico Cremonesi, radio show Viva Radio 2 2002–. *Discography:* Veramente falso 1992, Nuovamente falso 1992, Spiagge e lune 1993, Karaoke 1993, Finalmente tu 1995, Sarò Fiorello 1996, Dai miei amici cantautori 1997, Batticuore (CD Bianco) 1998, Batticuore (CD Rosso) 1998, I miei amici cantautori 2000, Fiorello The Greatest 2002, Uno è famoso, l'altro no: Il meglio di Viva Radio 2 (CD and book) 2002, Viva Radio 2 (il meglio del 2003) 2003, A modo mio 2004, Viva Radio 2 (il meglio del 2005) 2005. *Address:* Viva Radio 2, Radiotelevisione Italiana SpA, Viale Mazzini 14, 00195 Rome, Italy (office). *Telephone:* (06) 38781 (office). *E-mail:* info@vivaradio2.it (office). *Website:* www.radio.rai.it/radio2/vivaradio2/index.cfm (office); www.rosariofiorello.it.

FIORENTINO, Linda; American actress and photographer; b. 9 March 1960, Philadelphia, Pa; ed Rosemont Coll., Circle in the Square Theatre School; mem. Circle in the Square Performing Workshops. *Films include:* Vision Quest 1985, Gotcha! 1985, After Hours 1985, The Moderns 1988, Queens Logic 1991, Shout 1991, Wildfire 1992, Chain of Desire 1993, The Desperate Trail 1994, The Last Seduction 1994, Bodily Harm 1995, Larger Than Life 1996, Jade 1995, Unforgettable 1997, The Split 1997, Men in Black 1997, Kicked in the Head 1997, Body Count 1998, Dogma 1999, Ordinary Decent Criminal 2000, Where the Money Is 2000, What Planet Are You From? 2000, Liberty Stands Still 2002, Once More with Feeling 2009. *Television include:* The Neon Empire 1989, The Last Game 1992, Acting on Impulse 1993, Beyond the Law 1994, The Desperate Trail 1995. *Website:* www.lindafiorentino.com.

FIORI, Publio; Italian politician and lawyer; *Leader, Rifondazione Democristiana;* b. 1938; elected Christian Democrat mem. Rome City Council 1971, Lazio Regional Council 1975; Christian Democrat Deputy 1979–94, Alleanza Nazionale Deputy 1994, Vice-Pres., Chamber of Deputies 2001; resgnd Alleanza Nazionale 2005, joined Democrazia Cristiana per le Autonomie but resgnd 2006; Founder and Leader Rifondazione Democristiana 2006–; fmr mem. Parl. Comm. on Finance, Under-Sec. for Posts and Telecommunications, for Health; Minister of Transport 1994–95. *Address:* Via Monte Zebio 32, 00195 Rome, Italy (office). *Telephone:* (06) 3227658 (office); (06) 3225931 (office). *Fax:* (06) 3612170 (office). *E-mail:* sedenazionale@rifondazionedc.it (office); ufficiostampa@rifondazionedc.it (office); studiolegalefiori@libero.it (office). *Website:* www.rifondazionedc.it (office); www.publiofiori.com (office).

FIORINA, Carleton (Carly) S., BA, MS, MBA; American computer industry executive and politician; *Chairman and CEO, Carly Fiorina Enterprises;* b. (Cara Carleton Sneed), 6 Sept. 1954, Austin, Tex.; d. of Joseph Tyree Sneed III and Madelon Montross (née Juergens); m. 1st Todd Bartlem 1977 (divorced 1984); m. 2nd Frank Fiorina 1985; two step-d.; ed attended secondary schools in Ghana, UK, N Carolina, and Calif., Charles E. Jordan High School, Durham, NC, Stanford Univ., Robert H. Smith School of Business at Univ. of Maryland, Sloan School of Man. at Massachusetts Inst. of Tech.; began career with entry-level job, Hewlett-Packard Shipping Dept; fmr English teacher in Italy and seller of telephone services to fed. agencies; spent nearly 20 years at AT&T Corpn and Lucent Technologies Inc., Exec. Vice-Pres. Computer Operations, oversaw formation and spin-off of Lucent Technologies from AT&T, served as Lucent's Pres. Global Service Provider Business and Pres. Consumer Products; Pres., CEO and Dir Hewlett-Packard Co. 1999–2000, Chair. and CEO 2000–05; Chair. and CEO Carly Fiorina Enterprises; mem. Bd of Dirs US-China Bd of Trade, PowerUp, Revolution Health Group 2005–, Cybertrust 2005–, Taiwan Semiconductor Manufacturing Co. Ltd 2006–; Gen. Business News Contrib., Fox Business Network 2007–; econ. adviser to Senator John McCain's campaign for US Pres. 2008; Republican nominee for US Senate representing Calif. June 2010; mem. Exec. Bd NY Stock Exchange; adviser, US Space Comm.; mem. Bd of Dirs Revolution Healthcare Group LLC, Taiwan Semiconductor Manufacturing; fmr mem. Bd of Dirs Cisco Systems, Kellogg Co., Merck & Co., Telecommunications Industry Asscn, USA-Repub. of China Econ. Council, Goldstar Information & Communications Inc., Seoul, S Korea, AT&T Taiwan Telecommunications, Taipei; Chair. Good360; Founder One Woman Initiative; Global Amb. for Opportunity International; Hon. Fellow, London Business School 2001; listed in Forbes' America's Most Powerful People, ranked by Fortune magazine amongst 50 Most Powerful Women in Business in the US (first) 1998–2003, (second) 2004, ranked by silicon.com amongst Top 50 Agenda Setters (22nd) 2002, (10th) 2003, Appeal of Conscience Award 2002, Concern Worldwide 'Seeds of Hope' Award 2003, Private Sector Council Leadership Award 2004, ranked by Forbes magazine amongst The World's 100 Most Powerful Women (tenth) 2004, (51st) 2010. *Publication:* Tough Choices: A Memoir 2006. *Leisure interests:* piano, gardening. *Address:* 3150 South Street NW, No. 3B, Washington, DC 20007, USA (home). *E-mail:* contact@carlyfiorina .com (office). *Website:* www.carlyfiorina.com; www.carlyforca.com.

FIORINI, Matteo; San Marino civil engineer and politician; *Secretary of State for Land and Environment, Agriculture, Telecommunications, Youth, Sport, Civil Defence and Relations with the Azienda Autonoma di Stato di Produzione;* b. 10 Feb. 1978, San Marino city; m. Marina Spadini 2011; ed Univ. of Bologna; Project Man. Gruppo SIT (packaging co.); mem. Consiglio Grande e Generale (Parl.) 2008–, mem. Foreign Affairs Standing Cttee; Captain-Regent (head of govt) 2011–12; currently Sec. of State for Land and Environment, Agric., Telecommunications, Youth, Sport, Civil Defence and Relations with the Azienda Autonoma di Stato di Produzione (AASP); mem. Alleanza Popolare. *Leisure interest:* hockey. *Address:* Secretariat of State for Land, Environment, Agriculture, Telecommunications, Youth, Sport, Civil Defence and Relations with the Azienda Autonoma di Stato per i Lavori Pubblici (AASLP), Contrada Omerelli 43, 47890 San Marino, San Marino (office). *Telephone:* 0549 882474 (office). *Fax:* 0549 885265 (office). *E-mail:* segreteria.territorio@gov.sm (office). *Website:* www.segreteriaterritorio .sm (office).

FIQI, Abdihakim Mohamed Haji; Somali diplomatist and politician; *Minister of Defence;* b. Bay Region, S Somalia; held diplomatic posting in Canada; Minister of Defence 2010–11, 2012–, also Deputy Prime Minister 2010–11. *Address:* Ministry of Defence, 2525 Mogadishu, Somalia (office). *Website:* www.mod.somaligov.net (office).

FIRE, Andrew Z., BA, PhD; American microbiologist and academic; *Professor of Pathology and Genetics, School of Medicine, Stanford University;* b. 1959, Santa Clara Co., Calif.; ed Univ. of California, Berkeley and Massachusetts Inst. of Tech.; Researcher, Univ. of Cambridge, UK 1983–86; mem. of staff, Dept of Embryology, Carnegie Inst. of Washington, Baltimore, Md 1986–2003, Carnegie Investigator 2003–; Prof. of Pathology and Genetics, Stanford Univ. School of Medicine 2003–; Adjunct Prof., Dept of Biology, Johns Hopkins Univ., Baltimore 2003–; Fellow, American Acad. of Arts and Sciences; mem. Inst. of Medicine, NAS; Genetics Soc. of America Medal, Maryland Distinguished Young Scientist Award 1997, NAS Award in Molecular Biology (jtly) 2003, Wiley Prize in the Biomedical Sciences, Mellon Lecturer, Univ. of Pittsburgh 2003, Bernard Cohen Memorial Lecturer, Univ. of Pennsylvania School of Medicine 2004, Dr H.P. Heineken Prize for Biochemistry and Piophysics 2004, Gairdner Foundation Int. Award 2005, Nobel Prize in Medicine (with Craig C. Mello) 2006. *Publications:* numerous publs in scientific journals. *Address:* Departments of Pathology and Genetics, Stanford University School of Medicine, 300 Pasteur Drive, L235, Stanford, CA 94305-5324, USA (office). *Telephone:* (650) 723-2885 (office). *Fax:* (650) 725-6902 (office). *E-mail:* afire@stanford.edu (office). *Website:* genome-www.stanford.edu/group/fire (office).

FIRTASH, Dmytro (Dmitrii); Ukrainian business executive; *Executive Chairman, Group DF;* b. 2 May 1965; m. Maria Firtash (divorced); expert in gas trading and distribution business in Eastern and Cen. Europe; secured gas deal with Turkmenistan Govt in exchange for supplies of fresh produce 1993; est. Highrock Holdings, partnership with gas trader Itera to oversee trade between Turkmenistan and Ukrainian state energy-provider Naftogaz 2001; f. Eural Trans Gas 2002 (replaced Highrock Holdings 2003); through his co. Centragas Holdings AG est. partnership with Russian energy corpn Gazprom to set up RosUkrEnergo (headquartered in Switzerland) 2004, which distributes gas from Cen. Asian states to Ukraine and EU; f. OSTCHEM Holding AG 2004, to consolidate his investments in titanium, soda ash, mineral fertilizers and other chemical products; f. Group DF in 2007 to bring together business interests in energy, chemicals and property with other cos including Hungarian gas trader Emfesz and Estonian fertilizer manufacturer Nitrofert, currently Exec. Chair.; took over Nadra Bank 2011; Chair. Fed. of Employers of Ukraine 2010–. *Address:* RosUkrEnergo, Bahnhofstrasse 7, 6300 Zug, Switzerland (office). *Telephone:* 415607530 (office). *Fax:* 415607535 (office). *E-mail:* info@groupdf.com (office). *Website:* www.groupdf.com (office); www.rosukrenergo.ch (office).

FIRTH, Colin Andrew, CBE; British actor; b. 10 Sept. 1960, Grayshott, Hants.; s. of David Firth and Shirley Firth; m. Livia Giuggioli 1997, two s.; one s. by Meg Tilly; ed Montgomery of Alamein School, Winchester and Drama Centre, London; Commdr, Order of the Star of Italian Solidarity 2005. *Theatre includes:* Another Country 1983, Doctor's Dilemma 1984, The Lonely Road 1985, Desire Under the Elms 1987, The Caretaker 1991, Chatsky 1993, Three Days of Rain 1999. *Films include:* Another Country 1983, Camille 1984, A Month in the Country 1986, Apartment Zero 1988, Valmont (title role) 1988, Wings of Fame 1989, Femme Fatale 1990, The Hour of the Pig 1992, Good Girls 1994, Circle of Friends 1995, The English Patient 1996, Fever Pitch 1996, Shakespeare in Love 1998, The Secret Laughter of Women 1999, My Life So Far 1999, Relative Values 1999, Londinium 2000, Bridget Jones's Diary 2000, The Importance of Being Earnest 2002, Hope Springs 2003, Love Actually 2003, Trauma 2004, Bridget Jones: The Edge of Reason 2004, Where the Truth Lies 2005, Nanny McPhee 2005, The Last Legion 2007, And When Did You Last See Your Father? 2007, St Trinian's 2007, In Prison My Whole Life 2007, Then She Found Me 2007, The Accidental Husband 2008, Mamma Mia! 2008, Genova 2008, Easy Virtue 2008, Dorian Gray 2009, A Single Man (Volpi Cup for Best Actor, 66th Venice Int Film Festival 2009, BAFTA Award for Leading Actor 2010) 2009, A Christmas Carol 2009, St Trinian's 2: The Legend of Fritton's Gold 2009, The King's Speech (Golden Globe Award for Best Actor 2011, BAFTA Award for Leading Actor 2011, Academy Award for Actor in a Leading Role 2011) 2010, Steve (short) 2010, Main Street 2010, Tinker, Tailor, Soldier, Spy 2011. *Radio:* Richard II in Two Planks and a Passion 1986, Rupert Brooke in The One Before The Last 1987. *Television appearances:* Dutch Girls 1984, Lost Empires (series) 1985–86, Robert Lawrence in Tumbledown (Radio Times Best Actor Award) 1987, Out of the Blue 1990, Hostages 1992, Master of the Moor 1993, The Deep Blue Sea 1994, Mr Darcy in Pride and Prejudice (Best Actor Award, Broadcasting Press Guild 1996) 1994, Nostromo 1997, The Turn of the Screw 1999, Donovan Quick 1999, Celebration 2006, Born Equal 2006. *Publication:* The Department of Nothing (appeared in 'Speaking with the Angel' short story collection) 2000. *Address:* c/o Independent, Oxford House, 76 Oxford Street, London, W1D 1BS, England (office). *Telephone:* (20) 7636-6565 (office). *Fax:* (20) 7323-0101 (office).

FIRTH, Peter; British actor; b. 27 Oct. 1953, Bradford; s. of Eric Firth and Mavis Firth; m. Lindsey Readman 1990; two s. one d.; has appeared with Nat. Theatre in Equus, Romeo and Juliet, Spring Awakening; Broadway appearances include role of Mozart in Amadeus; Acad. Award for Best Supporting Actor, Tony Award, Golden Globe for Best Supporting Actor (all for Equus) and numerous other awards. *Films include:* Fratello sole, sorella luna 1972, Daniele e Maria 1973, King Arthur, the Young Warlord 1975, Aces High 1976, Joseph Andrews 1977, Equus 1977, When You Comin' Back, Red Ryder? 1979, Tess 1979, Feuer und Schwert: Die Legende von Tristan und Isolde 1982, White Elephant 1983, Born of Fire 1983, Letter to Brezhnev 1985, Lifeforce 1985, A State of Emergency 1986, Prisoner of Rio 1988, Tree of Hands 1989, Trouble in Paradise 1989, The Laughter of God 1990, The Hunt for Red October 1990, Burndown 1990, The Rescuers Down Under (voice) 1990, The Pleasure Principle 1991, White Angel 1993, El Marido perfecto 1993, Shadowlands 1993, An Awfully Big Adventure 1995, Marco Polo: Haperek Ha'aharon 1996, Merisairas 1996, Gaston's War 1997, Amistad 1997, Woundings 1998, Mighty Joe Young 1998, Chill Factor 1999, Pearl Harbor 2001, The Greatest Game Ever Played 2005. *TV includes:* The Flaxton Boys (series) 1969, Here Come the Double Deckers (series) 1970, Her Majesty's Pleasure 1973, Diamonds on

Wheels 1974, The Picture of Dorian Gray 1976, The Lady of the Camellias 1976, The Flipside of Dominick Hide 1980, Another Flip for Dominick 1982, The Aerodrome 1983, Northanger Abbey 1986, Blood Royal: William the Conqueror 1990, The Incident 1990, Children Crossing 1990, Murder in Eden (miniseries) 1991, Prisoner of Honor 1991, Heartbeat (series) 1994, Resort to Murder (miniseries) 1995, The Witch's Daughter 1996, And the Beat Goes On (series) 1996, The Garden of Redemption 1997, The Broker's Man (series) 1997, Holding On (miniseries) 1997, That's Life (series) 2000, Spooks (series) 2002–09, Me & Mrs Jones 2002, Hawking 2004, The Battle for Rome (mini-series) 2006. *Leisure interests:* cookery, sailing. *Address:* Susan Smith Associates, 121 North San Vicente Boulevard, Beverly Hills, CA 90211, USA. *Telephone:* (213) 852-4777. *Fax:* (213) 658-7170.

FISCHER, Adam; Hungarian conductor; *Music Director, Austro-Hungarian Haydn Orchestra;* b. 9 Sept. 1949, Budapest, Hungary; m. Doris Fischer 1979; one s. one d.; ed Budapest School of Music; conducting and composition studies in Budapest and Vienna with Swarowsky; held posts at Graz Opera, Karlsruhe; Gen. Music Dir Freiburg; work with Bavarian State Opera; regular conductor with Vienna State Opera 1973–, and with Zurich Opera; major debuts Paris Opera 1984, La Scala 1986, Royal Opera House 1989, ENO 1991, San Francisco Opera 1991, Chicago Lyric Opera 1991, Metropolitan Opera, New York 1994; has conducted many world-class orchestras, particularly Helsinki Philharmonic, Boston and Chicago Symphony and LA Philharmonic and Vienna Chamber Orchestra; concert tours to Japan and USA; Music Dir Kassel Opera 1987–92, founder and Artistic Dir, first Gustav Mahler Festival, Kassel 1989; f. Austro-Hungarian Haydn Orchestra (AHHO) and Festival, Eisenstadt, Austria 1987, later Music Dir AHHO; Chief Conductor, Danish Nat Chamber Orchestra 1999–; Conductor, Bayreuth Festival (Ring Cycle) 2001; Music Dir, Orchestra of the Hungarian Radio 2004–; f. Wagner Days festival 2006; Music Dir, Hungarian State Opera 2007–10, Prin. Guest Conductor 2010–; first prize (jtly) Milan Cantelli Competition 1973. *Film:* BBC TV film of Bartok's Bluebird's Castle with London Philharmonic Orchestra (Italia Prize 1989 and Charles Heidsieck Prize). *Recordings include:* complete Haydn symphonies, Lucio Silla and Des Knabaen Wunderhorn with Danish Radio Sinfonietta. *Address:* c/o Angelika Csillag, Raab und Böhm Agentur, Plankengasse 7, 1010 Vienna, Austria (office). *Telephone:* (1) 5120501 (office). *Fax:* (1) 5127743 (office). *E-mail:* csillag@rbartists.at (office). *Website:* www.rbartists.at (office).

FISCHER, Andreas, PhD; Swiss professor of philology and university administrator; *President, University of Zurich;* b. 1947; ed Univ. of Basel, Durham Univ., UK; Prof. of English Philology, Univ. of Basel 1981; Visiting Prof., Univ. of Michigan, USA 1984–85; Prof. of English Philology, Univ. of Zurich 1985–, Deputy Dean, Faculty of Arts 2002–04, Dean 2004–06, Pres. (Rector) Univ. 2008–; Gen. Ed. Swiss Papers in English Language and Literature 1995–2007; mem. Advisory Bd Journal of Historical Pragmatics, Inst. for Historical Study of Language, Dept of English Language, Univ. of Glasgow; mem. Zurich James Joyce Foundation. *Publications:* Dialects in the South West of England, Engagement, Wedding and Marriage in Old England; co-ed.: Schweizer Anglistische Arbeiten/Swiss Studies in English, Englisch-deutsche Studienausgabe der Dramen Shakespeares. *Address:* Office of the President, University of Zurich, Künstlergasse 15, 8001 Zurich, Switzerland (office). *Telephone:* (44) 6342211 (office). *E-mail:* rektor@uzh.ch (office). *Website:* www.uzh.ch/about/management/unileitung_en.html (office).

FISCHER, August A.; Swiss fmr publishing executive; b. 7 Feb. 1939, Zürich; m. Gillian Ann Fischer 1961; one s. one d.; various positions E.I. Du Pont De Nemours & Co. 1962–78; Man. Dir European subsidiary of Napp Systems Inc. 1978–81, Exec. Vice-Pres., then Pres. and COO Napp Systems Inc., San Diego 1981–89; Gen. Man. Devt, News International PLC 1989–90, Man. Dir 1990–95, mem. Bd and COO News Corpn Ltd 1991–95, Chief Exec. News International PLC (UK subsidiary of News Corpn) 1993–95; mem. Supervisory Bd Ringier AG, Zürich, consultant 1995–97; Chair. Bd and CEO Axel Springer Verlag AG 1998–2001; mem. Advisory Bd, RocSearch; mem. American Man. Asscn, The Pres.'s Asscn; Trustee, St Katharine and Shadwell Trust. *Address:* c/o RocSearch Ltd, 36–40 Rupert Street, London, W1D 6DW, England.

FISCHER, Debra (Deb) Strobel, BS; American politician and rancher; *Senator from Nebraska;* b. 1 March 1951, Lincoln, Neb.; d. of Jerry Strobel; m. Bruce Fischer 1972; three s.; ed Univ. of Nebraska, Lincoln; mem. Nebraska Legislature from 43rd Dist 2005–13, Chair. Transportation and Telecommunications Cttee, mem. Exec. Bd and Revenue Cttee; Senator from Nebraska 2013–; with husband, runs the family ranch, Sunny Slope Ranch, nr Valentine, Neb.; Republican. *Address:* United States Senate, Washington, DC 20510, USA (office). *Telephone:* (202) 224-3121 (office). *Website:* www.senate.gov (office).

FISCHER, Edmond H., DèsSc; American biochemist and academic; *Professor Emeritus of Biochemistry, University of Washington;* b. April 1920, Shanghai, China; s. of Oscar Fischer and Renee C. Fischer (née Tapernoux); m. Beverley B. Bullock; two s.; ed Univ. of Geneva; Asst, Labs of Organic Chem., Univ. of Geneva 1946–47; Fellow, Swiss Nat. Foundation 1948–50; Research Fellow, Rockefeller Foundation 1950–53; Privat-dozent, Univ. of Geneva 1950; Research Assoc., Div. of Biology, Calif. Inst. of Tech., USA 1953; Asst Prof., Univ. of Washington, USA 1953–56, Assoc. Prof. 1956–61, Prof. of Biochemistry 1961–90, Prof. Emer. 1990–; mem. numerous cttees, professional orgs etc.; Gov. Basel Inst. for Immunology 1996–, Weizmann Inst. of Science, Rehovot, Israel 1997–; mem. NAS, AAAS, American Acad. of Arts and Sciences, Swiss Chem. Soc., British Biochemical Soc.; Dr hc (Montpellier) 1985, (Basel) 1988; shared Nobel Prize for Medicine 1992, several other awards and honours. *Leisure interests:* classical piano, flying (pvt. pilot). *Address:* Department of Biochemistry, University of Washington, 1959 NE Pacific Street, HSB J-405, Seattle, WA 98195-7350 (office); 5540 NE Windermere Road, Seattle, WA, USA (home). *Telephone:* (206) 523-7372 (home). *E-mail:* efischer@u.washington.edu (office). *Website:* depts.washington.edu/biowww (home).

FISCHER, Heinz, DIur; Austrian politician and head of state; *President;* b. 9 Oct. 1938, Graz; m. Margit Fischer; two c.; ed Univ. of Vienna; Assoc. Prof. of Political Science, Univ. of Innsbruck 1978–94, Prof. 1994–; Sec. Socialist Parl. Party 1963–75, Exec., Floor Leader 1975–83, 1987–90, Deputy Chair. Socialist Party 1979–2004; mem. Nationalrat (Parl.) for Vienna 1971–2004, Pres. Nationalrat

1990–2002, Second Pres. 2002–04; Fed. Minister for Science and Research 1983–87; Deputy Chair. European Socialist Party 1992–2004; Pres. of Austria 2004– (re-elected 2010); Co-Ed. Europäische Rundschau; fmr mem. Nat. Security Council and Foreign Affairs Council; Pres. Nat. Fund of the Repub. of Austria for Victims of Nat. Socialism 1995–2002, Austrian Friends of Nature –2005, Austrian Univ. Extension Asscn; Vice-Pres. Inst. for Advanced Studies –2004. *Publications:* Positions and Outlook 1977, The Kreisky Era 1993, Reflexionen 1999, Times of Change: An Austrian Interim Report 2003; numerous books and articles on law and political science. *Address:* Office of the Federal President, Hofburg, 1014 Vienna, Austria (office). *Telephone:* (1) 534-22-0 (office). *Fax:* (1) 535-65-12 (office). *Website:* www.hofburg.at (office).

FISCHER, Iván; Hungarian/Dutch conductor; *Music Director, Budapest Festival Orchestra;* b. 20 Jan. 1951, Budapest; s. of Sándor Fischer and Evelin Boschán; two s. two d.; ed B. Bartók Music Conservatory, Budapest and Wiener Hochschule für Musik under Hans Swarowsky, Mozarteum, Salzburg under Nikolaus Harnoncourt; Jt Music Dir Northern Sinfonia of England, Newcastle 1979–82; Music Dir and Artistic Dir, Kent Opera 1982–2000; Prin. Guest Conductor Cincinnati Symphony Orchestra 1989–96; Music Dir Lyon Opera House 2000–03; Prin. Conductor Nat. Symphony Orchestra, Washington, DC 2008–; Co-founder and Music Dir Budapest Festival Orchestra 1983–; debut in London with Royal Philharmonic Orchestra 1976; concerts with London Symphony Orchestra, Berlin Philharmonic Orchestra, Concertgebouw Orchestra etc.; main performances in USA: Los Angeles Philharmonic, Cleveland, Philadelphia, San Francisco Symphony and Chicago Symphony Orchestras; operas: Idomeneo, Don Giovanni, Julius Caesar, La Bohème, La Clemenza di Tito, Marriage of Figaro, Magic Flute in London, Paris, Vienna; Premio Firenze 1974, Rupert Foundation Award, BBC, London 1976, Gramophone Award for Best Orchestral Recording of the Year (for The Miraculous Mandarin) 1998, Golden Medal, Republic of Hungary 1998, Crystal Award, World Econ. Forum 1998, Kossuth Prize 2006, Gramophone Editor's Choice Award (for Mahler's Second Symphony) 2007, Royal Philharmonic Soc.'s Conductor Award 2011. *Address:* c/o Edward Yim, IMG Artists, Carnegie Hall Tower, 152 West 57th Street, 5th Floor, New York, NY 10019, USA (office); Budapest Festival Orchestra, Alkotás utca 39/c., 1123 Budapest, Hungary (office). *Telephone:* (212) 994-3500 (New York) (office); (1) 489-4330 (Budapest) (office). *Fax:* (212) 995-3550 (New York) (office); (1) 355-4049 (Budapest) (office). *E-mail:* artistsny@imgartists.com (office); bfofound@mail.datanet.hu (office). *Website:* www.imgartists.com (office); www.bfz.hu (office).

FISCHER, Jan; Czech economist, statistician and politician; b. 2 Jan. 1951, Prague; m.; two s. one d.; ed Univ. of Econs, Prague; researcher, Research Inst. of Socio-econ. Information (part of Fed. Statistical Office) 1974–82; with Fed. Statistical Office 1982–90, Vice-Pres. 1990–92; Vice-Pres. Czech Statistical Office 1993–2000, Pres. 2003–09; Production Dir, Taylor Nelson Sofres Factum Co. 2000–02; Prime Minister 2009–10 (resgnd); Deputy Prime Minister and Minister of Finance 2013–14; Pres. European Council 2009; mem. Czech Statistical Soc., Academic Council and Bd of Dirs Univ. of Econs, Prague, Academic Council J.E. Purkyne Univ., Usti nad Labem; mem. Int. Statistical Inst., Statistical Programme Cttee, UN Statistical Comm., UN Economic Comm. for Europe, Cttee on Statistics, and others. *Address:* c/o Office of the Government, náb. Edvarda Beneše 4, 118 01 Prague 1, Czech Republic. *E-mail:* posta@vlada.cz.

FISCHER, Joseph (Joschka); German academic and fmr politician; b. 12 April 1948, Gerabronn; m. 1st 1967 (divorced 1984); m. 2nd (divorced); m. 3rd Claudia Bohm 1987 (divorced 1999); m. 4th Nicola Leske 1999 (divorced 2003); m. 5th Minu Barati 2005; joined Green Party 1982, fmr Leader; mem. German Bundestag 1983–85; Minister of the Environment and Energy, Hesse 1985–87, of the Environment, Energy and Fed. Affairs 1991–94; Deputy Bundesrat 1985–87, Chair. Green Parl. Group, Hesse Parl. 1987–91; Deputy Minister-Pres. of Hesse 1991–98; Speaker Parl. Group Alliance 90/Greens, Bundestag 1994–98; Vice-Chancellor of Germany and Minister of Foreign Affairs 1998–2005; Sr Fellow, Liechtenstein Inst. on Self-Determination, Princeton Univ. 2006–07, also Frederick H. Schultz Class of 1951 Prof. of Int. Econ. Policy, Woodrow Wilson School of Public and Int. Affairs and Fellow, European Union Program; Sr Strategic Counsel, Albright Group LLC and Strategic Consultant to Albright Capital Management LLC, Washington, DC 2008–; consultant on strategic issues to Bayerische Motoren Werke AG (BMW), Siemens AG, RWE AG; adviser to planned Nabucco natural gas pipeline project 2009–; mem. Bd of Dirs International Crisis Group, European Council on Foreign Relations. *Publication:* The Red-Green Years: German Foreign Policy from Kosovo to Sept. 11 2007. *Address:* Joschka Fischer & Company GmbH, Brahmsstraße 16, 14193 Berlin, Germany (office).

FISCHER, Stanley, BSc (Econ), MSc (Econ), PhD; American/Israeli economist and central banker; *Governor, Bank of Israel;* b. 15 Oct. 1943, Lusaka, Northern Rhodesia (now Zambia); s. of Philip Fischer and Ann Kopelowitz; m. Rhoda Keet 1965; three s.; ed London School of Econs, UK, Massachusetts Inst. of Tech.; Postdoctoral Fellow, Univ. of Chicago 1969–70, Asst Prof. of Econs 1970–73; Assoc. Prof., MIT 1973–77, Prof. 1977–88, 1990, Killian Prof. 1992–94, Head of Dept 1993–94; Vice-Pres. and Chief Economist, IBRD (World Bank), Washington, DC 1988–90; Visiting Sr Lecturer, Hebrew Univ., Jerusalem 1972; Fellow, Inst. for Advanced Studies, Princeton, NJ 1976–77, Visiting Prof. 1984; Visiting Scholar, Hoover Inst., Stanford Univ. 1981–82; consultant on Israeli economy, US Dept of State 1984–87, 1991–94; First Deputy Man. Dir IMF 1994–2001; Vice-Chair. Citigroup 2002–05, Head of Public Sector Group 2004–05, Chair. Country Risk Cttee, Pres. Citigroup International 2002–05; Gov. Bank of Israel 2005–; Research Assoc., Nat. Bureau of Econ. Research (NBER); Ed. NBER Macroeconomics Annual 1986–94 (Co-Ed. with O. Blanchard 1989–93, with J. Rotemberg 1994); Assoc. Ed. Journal of Monetary Economics 1975–94 (mem. Advisory Bd 1995–; Assoc. Ed. of Economic Theory 1973–75, Journal of Money, Credit and Banking 1973–75, Econometrica 1975–84, Journal of Economic Literature 1982–84, Journal of Economic Perspectives 1986–88, Journal of Comparative Economics 1994–; mem. Editorial Advisory Bd The World Economy 1990–; mem. Editorial Bd Journal of Policy Reform 1994–; newspaper columnist, Il Messaggero (monthly), Rome, Italy 1990–93; mem. Council on Foreign Relations, Group of Thirty Consultative Group on Int. Econ. and Monetary Affairs, Inc. (G-30), Washington, DC, Trilateral Comm.; fmr mem. Bd Inst. for Int. Econs, Women's

World Banking, Int. Crisis Group; fmr mem. Int. Advisory Bd New Econ. School, Moscow; Guggenheim Fellow; Fellow, Econometric Soc., American Acad. of Arts and Sciences; Hon. Adviser, Inst. for Monetary and Econ. Studies, Bank of Japan 1987–94; Hon. Prof., Faculty of Econs, St Petersbug State Univ., Russian Fed. 2003, Acad. of Nat. Economy under Govt of Russian Fed. 2004; Hon. Fellow, LSE; Dr hc (Tbilisi State Univ.) 1996, (Ben Gurion Univ.) 1998, (Tel-Aviv Univ.) 2001, (LSE) 2002, (Univ. of Sofia, Bulgaria) 2004, (Hebrew Univ.) 2006; Cen. Bank Gov. of the Year, Euromoney magazine 2010. *Publications:* Rational Expectations and Economic Policy (ed.) 1980, Indexing, Inflation and Economic Policy 1986, Macroeconomics and Finance: Essays in Honor of Franco Modigliani (co-ed.) 1987, Inflation Stabilization (co-ed.) 1988, Economics (with Rudiger Dornbusch and Richard Schmalensee; 2nd edn) 1987, Lectures in Macroeconomics (with O. Blanchard) 1989, Lessons of Economic Stabilization and Its Aftermath (co-ed.) 1990, Economic Reform in Sub-Saharan Africa (co-ed.) 1991, Adjustment Lending Revisited (co-ed.) 1992, Monetary Theory and Thought: Essays in Honor of Don Patinkin (co-ed.) 1993, The Economics of Middle East Peace (co-ed.) 1993, Macroeconomics (with Rudiger Dornbusch) 1994 (ninth edn with R. Dornbusch and R. Startz 2004), Securing Peace in the Middle East: Project on Economic Transition (co-ed.) 1994, IMF Essays From a Time of Crisis: The International Financial System, Stabilization, and Development 2004, Living Standards and the Wealth of Nations (co-ed. with Leszek Balcerowicz) 2006; reports: World Bank: Responsibility for World Development Report 1988, 1989, 1990, Report on Adjustment Lending, I 1988, II 1990, Report on Trade Policy Reform 1989, participated in jt (IMF, IBRD, OECD, EBRD) study of the Soviet economy 1990; numerous publs on int. econ. and macroeconomic issues. *Address:* Bank of Israel, PO Box 780, Kiryat Ben-Gurion, Jerusalem 91007, Israel (office). *Telephone:* (2) 6552211 (office). *Fax:* (2) 6528805 (office). *E-mail:* webmaster@bankisrael.gov.il (office). *Website:* www.bankisrael.gov.il (office).

FISCHER, Thomas R., BEcons, PhD; German banker and business executive; b. 6 Oct. 1947, Berlin; ed Univ. of Freiburg, Breisgau; fmr amateur boxer, employed in family-owned business 1965–68, 1973–76; Research Asst, Univ. of Freiburg, Breisgau 1980–81; Head of Controlling, VARTA Batterie AG 1981–85; Deputy Dir Group Devt Dept, Deutsche Bank AG, Hanover 1985–91; Man. Dir Deutsche Immobilien Anlagegesellschaft mbH (subsidiary of Deutsche Bank) 1991–92, Global Head of Derivatives Deutsche Bank AG, Frankfurt 1992–95, Chair. Risk Man. Cttee, mem. Bd Man. 1999–2002; Vice-Chair. Landesgirokasse, Stuttgart 1995–96, Chair. 1996–98; Chair. WestLB AG 2004–07, CEO –2007; Pres. Asscn of German Public Sector Banks 2004–; Chair. Supervisory Bd RWE AG 2006–09; mem. Bd (non-exec.) RWE 2010. *Address:* RWE AG, Opernplatz 1, 45128 Essen, Germany (office). *Telephone:* (201) 1200 (office). *Website:* www.rwe.com (office).

FISCHER, Timothy Andrew, AC; Australian politician and diplomatist; *Ambassador to the Holy See;* b. 3 May 1946, Lockhart, NSW; s. of J. R. Fischer and Barbara Mary Fischer; m. Judy Brewer 1992; two s.; ed Boree Creek School, Xavier Coll., Melbourne; joined Army 1966, officer with First Bn, Royal Australian Regt, Australia and Viet Nam 1966–69; farmer, Boree Creek, NSW; mem. NSW Legis. Ass. 1970–84; MP for Farrer, NSW 1984–2002; Shadow Minister for Veterans' Affairs 1985–89 and Deputy Man. of Opposition Business 1989–90; Leader Nat. Party of Australia 1990–99; Shadow Minister for Energy and Resources 1990–93, for Trade 1993–96; Deputy Prime Minister and Minister for Trade 1996–99; Chair. Tourism Australia 2004–07; Nat. Chair. Flying Doctor Service 2007; Amb. to the Holy See, Vatican City, Rome 2009–; Royal Decoration for Service to the Kingdom of Thailand 1997 Hon. DLit (ANU) 2005. *Leisure interests:* chess, tennis, skiing, water skiing, bush-walking, mountaineering. *Address:* Embassy of Australia, Via Paola 24/10, 00186 Rome, Italy (office). *Telephone:* (06) 6877688 (office). *Fax:* (06) 6896255 (office). *E-mail:* holysee .embassy@dfat.gov.au (office). *Website:* www.holysee.embassy.gov.au (office).

FISCHER-APPELT, Peter, DrTheol; German university administrator and educator; b. 28 Oct. 1932, Berlin; s. of Hans Fischer-Appelt and Margret Fischer-Appelt; m. Hildegard Zeller 1959; two s. one d.; ed Schubart-Oberschule, Aalen and Univs of Tübingen, Heidelberg and Bonn; Scientific Asst, Protestant Theology Faculty, Univ. of Bonn 1961–70; Pastor, Cologne-Mülheim 1964–65; Co-founder and Chair. Bundesassistentenkonferenz, Bonn 1968–69; Pres. Univ. of Hamburg 1970–91, Pres. Emer. 1991–; teaching assignment in Systematic Theology 1972–; Pres. 'Cyril and Methodius' Int. Foundation, Sofia 1992–98, Hon. Pres. 2002; mem. Exec. Cttee Inter-Univ. Centre for Postgrad. Studies, Dubrovnik 1974–81, Chair. of Council 1981–98, Hon. mem. 1998; mem. Standing Conf. on Univ. Problems, Council of Europe 1987–94, Deputy Chair. 1987–88, Chair. 1989–90; Chair. Steering Group, Higher Educ. Legislation Reform Programme for Cen. and Eastern Europe 1992–98; mem. and Chair. Bd of Trustees UNESCO Inst. for Educ., Hamburg 1992–96; mem. German Comm. UNESCO 1991–2002, Hon. mem. 2002; mem. Bd of Trustees, Deutscher Akad. Austauschdienst 1972–2007 and various other comms, etc.; mem. European Acad. of Sciences and Arts, Salzburg; Horseman of Madara (First Class), Order of Cyril and Methodius (First Class), Bulgaria, Order of the Croatian Star with the Effigy of Rudjer Bošković; numerous hon. degrees including Hon. LHD (Temple Univ.), Hon. LittD (Purdue Univ.), Hon. LLD (Indiana Univ.), Dr hc (Technical Univ., Varna), (Technological Univ., Sofia), (Kliment Ohridski Univ., Sofia); Gold Medal, Bulgarian Acad. of Sciences, Pro Cultura Hungarica Medal, Medal of the Comm. of Nat. Educ., Poland 2000, Medal Pro Merito of the Council of Europe 2000. *Achievements:* annual Peter Fischer-Appelt Award for eminent achievements in acad. teaching, Univ. of Hamburg 1991, annual Prof. Dr Peter Fischer-Appelt Awards for best Bulgarian school teachers in Bulgarian, German, Spanish, Classic languages Cyril and Methodius Int. Foundation, Sofia 2004. *Publications:* Metaphysik im Horizont der Theologie Wilhelm Herrmanns 1965, Albrecht Ritschl und Wilhelm Herrmann 1968, Rechtfertigung 1968, Wissenschaft und Politik 1971, Zum Verständnis des Glaubens in der liberalen und dialektischen Theologie 1973, Zum Gedenken an Ernst Cassirer 1975, Integration of Young Scientists into the University 1975, Wilhelm Herrmann 1978, Hiob oder die Unveräusserlichkeit der Erde 1981, The Future of the University as a Research Institution 1982, Was darf ich hoffen? Erwartungen an das Musiktheater 1982, Die Oper als Denk- und Spielmodell 1983, Die Kunst der Fuge: Ein deutsches Forschungsnetz im Aufbau 1984, Dialogue and Co-operation for World Peace Today 1985, Die Universität zwischen Staatseinfluss und Autonomie 1986, The University in the 21st Century 1988, Die Ostpolitik der Universitäten 1992, Die Universität im Prozess der Humanisierung

der Gesellschaft 1994, Wer hat Angst vor den Wandlungen der Universität 1994, Die Erhellung des Mythos durch die Sprache der Musik 1995, The University: Past, Present and Future 1996, Concepts of the University 1997, Die Buchstaben und Europa 1997, One Europe to Tend 2000, Gottes Sein im Werden des Wissens 2000, Hochschulpolitik als Sozialpolitik 2001, Wissenschaft in der Kaufmannsre- publik 2002, Das Modell Byzanz und seine Einflüsse auf die Lebenswelt Osteuropas 2003, Felix Mendelssohn Bartholdy und Arnold Schönberg 2003, Hermann Cohen und Arnold Schönberg 2003, Die Göttlichen Stimmen in Schönberg's oper Moses und Aron 2003, Wie weit reicht Europa? 2004, The University of Reason 2004, Curt Kosswig, ein Wegbereiter der Türkei nach Europa 2004, Der Präsident in der Rolle des Mitmenschen und Übermenschen 2007, Die stille Erhebung Bulgariens 2010, Die neue Universität 2011, Die Aufhebung der Epoche aus dem verlorenen Gedanken der Einzigkeit Gottes 2011, Wilhelm Herrmann und Hermann Cohen 2012, Die Universität als Kunstwerk 2012, Albrecht Ritschl/Wilhelm Herrmann: Briefwechsel 1875–1889 (co-ed.) 2013. *Leisure interests:* chess, skiing, music, opera, theatre. *Address:* Waldweg 22, 25451 Quickborn-Heide, Germany. *Telephone:* (4106) 71212 (home). *Fax:* (4106) 78637 (home). *E-mail:* peter.fischerappelt@fischerappelt.de (home).

FISCHL, Eric, BFA; American artist; b. 9 March 1948, New York; ed Phoenix Junior Coll., Ariz., Ariz. State Univ., Tempe, Calif. Inst. of the Arts; moved to Chicago and worked as guard at Museum of Contemporary Art; taught painting at Nova Scotia Coll. of Art and Design, Halifax 1974–78; moved to New York 1978. *Address:* c/o Mary Boone Gallery, 745 Fifth Avenue, New York, NY 10151, USA. *Telephone:* (212) 941-1304. *Fax:* (212) 941-8674. *E-mail:* fischlstudio@gmail.com. *Website:* www.ericfischl.com.

FISCHLER, Franz, Dipl.Ing, PhD; Austrian fmr politician and consultant; *President, European Forum Alpbach;* b. 23 Sept. 1946, Absam, Tyrol; m. Heidi Fischler; two s. two d.; ed Franciscan secondary school, Tyrol, Agricultural Univ., Vienna; Asst, Dept of Agricultural Man., Univ. of Vienna 1973–79; Dept Head, Tyrolean Prov. Chamber of Agric. 1979, Sec. 1982, Dir 1985–89; Minister of Agric. and Forestry 1989–94; EU Commr for Agric. and Rural Devt 1995–99, for Agric., Rural Devt and Fisheries 1999–2004; consultancy work, Franz Fischler Consult GmbH 2005–; Pres. EcoSocial Forum Europe 2012, European Forum Alpbach 2012; ten hon. degrees; Mansholt Award. *Publications:* as co-author: Europa Der Staat, den keiner will 2006, Erinnerungen 2006. *Leisure interests:* skiing, mountaineering. *Address:* Franz Fischler Consult GmbH, Dörferstrasse 30B, 6067 Absam, Austria (office). *Telephone:* (5223) 57075 (office). *Fax:* (5223) 57076 (office). *E-mail:* ffc@franz-fischler-consult.co.at (office). *Website:* www.franz -fischler-consult.co.at (office).

FISCHLI, Peter; Swiss artist; b. 8 June 1952, Zurich; ed Accad. di Belle Arti, Urbino, Acad. di Belle Arti, Bologna, Italy; best known for collaboration with David Weiss 1979–; works held in many int. galleries including Tate Gallery, London, Solomon R. Guggenheim Museum, New York; Leopold-Hoesch-Museum Günther Peill Prize 2000 (with David Weiss). *Films:* Der rechte Weg (The Right Way) 1983, Der Lauf der Dinge (The Way Things Go) 1987, Kanalvideo (Sewage Video) 1992, Arbeiten im Dunkeln (Works in the Dark) 1995, Büsi (Kitty) 2001, Hunde (Dogs) 2003. *Address:* c/o Matthew Marks Gallery, 522 West 22nd Street, New York, NY 10011, USA (office). *Telephone:* (212) 243-0200 (office). *Website:* www .matthewmarks.com (office).

FISHBURNE, Laurence; American actor; b. 30 July 1961, Augusta, Georgia; s. of Laurence John Fishburne, Jr and Hattie Bell Crawford Fishburne; m. Hanja Moss 1985 (divorced); one s. one d. *Stage appearances include:* Short Eyes, Two Trains Running, Riff Raff (also writer and dir). *Television includes:* One Life to Live (series, debut aged 11), Pee-wee's Playhouse, Tribeca (Emmy Award 1993), A Rumour of War, I Take These Men, Father Clements Story, Decoration Day, The Tuskegee Airmen, Miss Ever's Boys, Always Outnumbered, CSI: Crime Scene Investigation (series) 2008–, Thurgood (film) 2011. *Films include:* Cornbread Earl and Me 1975, Fast Break, Apocalypse Now, Willie and Phil, Death Wish II, Rumble Fish, The Cotton Club, The Color Purple, Quicksilver, Band of the Hand, A Nightmare on Elm Street 3: Dream Warriors, Gardens of Stone, School Daze, Red Heat, King of New York, Cadence, Class Action, Boyz 'N the Hood, Deep Cover, What's Love Got to Do With It? Searching for Bobby Fischer, Higher Learning, Bad Company, Just Cause, Othello, Fled, Hoodlums (also exec. producer), Event Horizon, Welcome to Hollywood, The Matrix 1999, Michael Jordan to the Max 2000, Once in the Life (also writer) 2000, Osmosis Jones 2001, The Matrix Reloaded 2003, The Matrix Revolutions 2003, Mystic River 2003, Assault on Precinct 13 2005, Akeelah and the Bee 2005, Mission: Impossible III 2006, Five Fingers 2006, Bobby 2006, TMNT (voice) 2007, The Death and Life of Bobby Z 2007, Fantastic Four: Rise of the Silver Surfer (voice) 2007, 21 2008, Tortured 2008, Days of Wrath 2008, Black Water Transit 2009, Armored 2009, Predators 2010. *Address:* c/o Sam Gores, Paradigm, 10100 Santa Monica Boulevard, 25th Floor, Los Angeles, CA 90067, USA.

FISHER, Carrie; American actress and author; b. 21 Oct. 1956, Beverly Hills; d. of Eddie Fisher and Debbie Reynolds (q.v.); m. Paul Simon 1983 (divorced 1984); one d.; ed Beverly Hills High School and Cen. School of Speech and Drama, London; appeared with her mother in nightclub act aged 13; appeared in chorus of Broadway production of Irene, starring Debbie Reynolds, aged 15; Broadway stage appearances in Censored Scenes from King Kong, Agnes of God; several TV credits; film début in Shampoo (Photoplay Award as Best Newcomer of the Year) 1974. *Films include:* Shampoo 1974, Star Wars 1977, The Empire Strikes Back 1980, The Blues Brothers 1980, Return of the Jedi 1983, Under the Rainbow, Garbo Talks, The Man With One Red Shoe 1985, Hannah and Her Sisters 1986, Amazing Women on the Moon 1987, Appointment With Death 1988, The 'Burbs 1989, Loverboy 1989, She's Back 1989, When Harry Met Sally. . . 1989, The Time Guardian 1990, Sibling Rivalry 1990, Drop Dead Fred 1991, Soapdish 1991, This is My Life 1992, Austin Powers: International Man of Mystery 2000, Scream 3 2000, Famous 2000, Heartbreakers 2001, Jay and Silent Bob Strike Back 2001, A Midsummer Night's Rave 2002. *Publications include:* Postcards From the Edge (novel and screenplay, PEN Award for first novel 1987) 1987, Surrender the Pink 1990, Delusions of Grandma 1994 (novels), The Best Awful There Is 2003, Wishful Drinking (memoir) 2009, Shockaholic 2011; short stories. *Address:* c/o William Morris Agency, 1 William Morris Place, Beverly Hills, CA 90212, USA (office).

FISHER, Joel, BA; American sculptor and academic; *Head of Sculpture, Northumbria University;* b. 6 June 1947, Salem, Ohio; s. of James R. Fisher and Marye Fisher (née Giffin); m. 1st Pamela Robertson-Pearce 1977 (divorced); one s.; m. 2nd Gabrielle Wambaugh 2003; one d.; ed Kenyon Coll., Ohio; Artist in Residence, Univ. of Auckland 2000; currently Head of Sculpture, Northumbria Univ.; Kress Foundation Art History Award 1967, 1968, Gast der Berliner Kunstler Program des DAAD (German Academic Exchange Service) 1973–74, 1994, George A. and Eliza Gardner Howard Foundation Fellow 1987, Guggenheim Fellow 1993, Pollock-Krassner Foundation Award 1993, Henry Moore Fellowship (Newcastle upon Tyne) 2001–03. *Publications:* A Shadow of the Earth 1968, Double Camouflage 1970, Berliner Book 1974, Instances of Change 1975, False History 1978, Between Two and Three Dimensions – Drawings and Objects Since 1979 1984, Little Buttercup: Happiest Bear in the World (photos) 2004. *Address:* 29 Goldspink Lane, Newcastle upon Tyne, NE2 1NQ, England; P.O. Box 349, River Road, North, Troy, VT 05859, USA (home). *Telephone:* (191) 227-3140 (office); (191) 230-0370 (home); (802) 988-2870 (home). *E-mail:* joel.fisher@unn.ac.uk (office); jfisher@together.net (office).

FISHER, Kenneth (Ken) L., BA; American business executive and writer; *CEO and Chief Investment Officer, Fisher Investments Inc.;* b. 29 Nov. 1950, San Francisco; s. of Philip A. Fisher; m. Sherrilyn Fisher; three s.; ed Humboldt State Univ.; began career in father's investment firm; founder, CEO and Chief Investment Officer Fisher Investments Inc. 1978–, f. Fisher Investments Europe 2000, Gruner Fisher 2008; columnist, Forbes Magazine 1984–; est. Kenneth L. Fisher Chair in Redwood Forest Ecology, Humboldt State Univ. 2006; Bernstein Fabozzi/Jacobs Levy Award for outstanding published research article of the year 2000. *Publications include:* Super Stocks 1984, The Wall Street Waltz 1987, 100 Minds that Made the Market 1996, The Only Three Questions that Count 2006, The Ten Roads To Riches 2008, How to Smell a Rat: The Five Signs of Financial Fraud (with Lara Hoffmans) 2009; various research papers on investment and stocks. *Address:* Fisher Investments Inc., 13100 Skyline Boulevard, Woodside, CA 94062-4547, USA (office). *Telephone:* (800) 851-8845 (office). *Fax:* (650) 851-3514 (office). *E-mail:* webresponse@fi.com (office). *Website:* www.fi.com (office).

FISHER, Mark Andrew, BA, MBA; British banker; b. 29 April 1960; ed Warwick Business School; joined NatWest in 1981, joined Royal Bank of Scotland (RBS) (following its acquisition of NatWest in 2000), Chief Exec. RBS Manufacturing Div. 2000–07, mem. bd of Dirs RBS Group 2006–, Chair. Man. Bd and CEO ABN AMRO (bank partially owned by RBS) 2007–09; Fellow, Chartered Inst. of Bankers in Scotland. *Address:* c/o ABN AMRO Holding NV, Gustav Mahlerlaan 10, 1082 PP Amsterdam, Netherlands (office). *Telephone:* (20) 628-9393 (office). *Fax:* (20) 629-9111 (office). *E-mail:* info@abnamro.com (office). *Website:* www.abnamro.com (office).

FISHER, Michael Ellis, BSc, PhD, FRS; British theoretical scientist, university teacher and researcher and consultant; *Distinguished University Professor Emeritus and University System of Maryland Regents Professor, Institute for Physical Science and Technology, University of Maryland;* b. 3 Sept. 1931, Trinidad, West Indies; s. of Harold Wolf Fisher and Jeanne Marie Fisher (née Halter); m. Sorrel Castillejo 1954; three s. one d.; ed King's Coll., London; Lecturer in Math., RAF Tech. Coll. 1952–53; London Univ. Postgraduate Studentship 1953–56; Dept of Scientific and Industrial Research Sr Research Fellow 1956–58; Lecturer in Theoretical Physics, King's Coll., London 1958–62, Reader in Physics 1962–64, Prof. of Physics 1965–66, Fellow 1981; Prof. of Chem. and Math., Cornell Univ., USA 1966–73, Horace White Prof. of Chem., Physics and Math. 1973–89, Chair. Dept of Chem. 1975–78; Wilson H. Elkins Prof., Inst. for Science and Tech., Univ. of Md 1987–93, Distinguished Univ. Prof. and Univ. System of Md Regents Prof. 1993–2012, Prof. Emer. 2012–; Guest Investigator, Rockefeller Inst., New York 1963–64; Visiting Prof. of Applied Physics, Stanford Univ., USA 1970–71; Walter Ames Prof., Univ. of Wash. 1977; Visiting Prof. of Physics, MIT 1979; Sherman Fairchild Distinguished Scholar, Caltech 1984; Visiting Prof. of Theoretical Physics, Oxford 1985; Lorentz Prof., Univ. of Leiden 1993; Visiting Prof., Nat. Inst. of Standards and Tech., Gaithersburg, Md 1993; George Fisher Baker Lecturer, Cornell Univ. 1997; Distinguished Lecturer in Theoretical Physics, The Technion 2004; Oppenheimer Lecturer, Univ. of California, Berkeley 2006; Raman Lecturer, Indian Inst. of Science, Bangalore 2007; Bhabha Lecturer, Tata Inst., Mumbai 2007; Hudspeth Centenial Lecturer, Univ. of Texas, Austin 2007; Kac Memorial Lecturer, Los Alamos 2008; Sherman Memorial Lecturer, Indiana Univ. 2009; John Simon Guggenheim Memorial Fellow 1970–71, 1978–79; Fellow, American Acad. of Arts and Sciences; Foreign Assoc., NAS, American Philosophical Soc.; Foreign mem. Brazilian Acad. of Sciences, Royal Norwegian Soc. of Sciences and Letters; Hon. FRSE, Hon. Fellow, Indian Acad. of Sciences (Bangalore) 2000; Hon. DSc (Yale) 1987, Hon. DPhil (Tel-Aviv) 1992, (Weizmann Inst. of Science) 2009, (École Normale Supérieur de Lyon) 2012; Jr Collectors Silver Cup, British Philatelic Exhbn 1946, Irving Langmuir Prize in Chemical Physics, American Physical Soc. 1970, Award in Physical and Math. Sciences, New York Acad. of Sciences 1978, Guthrie Medal, Inst. of Physics 1980, Wolf Prize in Physics, Israel 1980, Michelson-Morely Award, Case-Western Reserve Univ. 1982, James Murray Luck Award, NAS 1983, Boltzmann Medal, IUPAP 1983, Festschrift and Conf. in honour of 60th Birthday: Current Problems in Statistical Mechanics 1991, Lars Onsager Medal, Norwegian Inst. of Tech. 1993, Joel H. Hildebrand Award for Chem. of Liquids 1995, Hirschfelder Prize in Theoretical Chem., Univ. of Wis. 1995, First Lars Onsager Memorial Prize, American Physical Soc. 1995, G. N. Lewis Memorial Lecture Award, Univ. of Calif. 1995, American Physical Soc. Centennial Speaker 1998, Royal Medal Royal Soc. of London 2005, Queen's Medal, Royal Soc., London 2005, BBVA Foundation, Madrid 2009, Frontiers of Knowledge Award in Basic Sciences 2010. *Achievements:* performer and teacher of the Flamenco guitar and writer about Flamenco. *Publications include:* Analogue Computing at Ultra-High Speed (with D. M. MacKay) 1962, The Nature of Critical Points 1964, also in Russian 1968; more than 410 contribs to scientific journals, proceedings and reviews. *Leisure interests:* Flamenco guitar, travel, art work. *Address:* Institute for Physical Science and Technology, University of Maryland, 2100 A, Bldg 085, College Park, MD 20742-8510, USA (office). *Telephone:* (301) 405-4819 (office). *Fax:* (301) 314-9404 (office). *E-mail:* xpectnil@umd.edu (office). *Website:* http://www.ipst.umd.edu/researchandfaculty/xpectnil.php (office).

FISHER, Robert (Bob) J.; American retail executive; b. 1955; s. of the late Donald G. Fisher and Doris F. Fisher; ed Phillips Exeter Acad., Princeton Univ., Stanford Univ. School of Business; Man. The Gap, Inc. 1980–85, Exec. Vice-Pres. of Merchandise, Banana Republic 1985–89, Pres. 1989–90, mem. Bd of Dirs The Gap Inc. 1990–99, Exec. Vice-Pres. 1992–99, COO 1992–93, 1995–97, CFO 1993–95, Pres. Gap Div. 1997–99 (resgnd), Chair. The Gap Inc. 2004–07, currently mem. Bd of Dirs, Interim CEO 2007–; mem. Bd of Dirs Sun Microsystems Inc.; mem. Bd of Trustees, Golden Gate Nat. Park Asscn, Natural Resources Defense Council. *Address:* The Gap Inc., 2 Folsom Street, San Francisco, CA 94105, USA (office). *Telephone:* (650) 952-4400 (office). *Fax:* (415) 427-2553 (office). *Website:* www.gap.com (office).

FISHLOW, Albert, PhD; American economist, academic and fmr government official; *Professor of International and Public Affairs, Director of the Columbia Institute of Latin American Studies, and Director of the Center for the Study of Brazil, Columbia University;* b. 21 Nov. 1935, Philadelphia; m. Harriet Fishlow 1957; one s. two d.; ed Univ. of Pennsylvania, Harvard Univ.; Acting Asst Prof., Assoc. Prof., then Prof., Univ. of Calif., Berkeley 1961–77, Prof. of Econs 1983, Chair. Dept of Econs 1973–75, 1985–89, Dean Int. and Area Studies 1990, Dir Int. House 1990, now Prof. Emer.; currently Prof. of Int. and Public Affairs, Dir of Columbia Inst. of Latin American Studies, and Dir of Center for Study of Brazil, Columbia Univ., New York; mem. Berkeley Foundation Trustees Int. Cttee 1990–; Prof. of Econs, Yale Univ. 1978–83; Visiting Fellow, All Souls Coll. Oxford, UK (Guggenheim Fellow) 1972–73; Co-Ed. Journal of Devt Econs 1986–; Dir-at-Large, Bd of Social Science Research Council 1990–; Deputy Asst Sec. of State for Inter-American Affairs 1975–76; mem. Council on Foreign Relations 1975–, Paul A. Volcker Sr Fellow for Int. Econ. –1999; Consultant to Rockefeller, Ford and other foundations, fmr Consultant to World Bank, IDB, UNDP; Nat. Order of the Southern Cross (Brazil) 1999; David Wells Prize, Harvard 1963, Arthur H. Cole Prize, Econ. History Asscn 1966, Joseph Schumpeter Prize, Harvard 1971, Outstanding Service Award, Dept of State 1976. *Publications include:* American Railroads and the Transformation of the Ante Bellum Economy 1965, International Trade, Investment, Macro Policies and History: Essays in Memory of Carlos F. Diaz-Alejandro (co-ed.) 1987; numerous articles. *Address:* 834 International Affairs Building, Columbia University, Mail Code 3323, New York, NY 10027, USA (office). *Telephone:* (212) 854-1555 (office). *Fax:* (212) 864-4847 (office). *E-mail:* af594@columbia.edu (office). *Website:* www.sipa.columbia.edu (office).

FISHMAN, Gerald (Jerry) Jay, BS, MS, PhD; American astrophysicist; *Chief Scientist, Marshall Space Flight Center;* b. 10 Feb. 1943, St Louis, Mo.; s. of Irwin Fishman and Minnie Fishman; m. Nancy Neyman 1967; two d.; ed Univ. of Missouri, Rice Univ.; fmr Research Asst/Research Assoc., Space Science Dept, Rice Univ.; began career as a Sr Scientist working on aerospace projects at Research Labs, Teledyne Brown Engineering, Huntsville, Ala; Research Scientist, NASA Marshall Space Flight Center, Huntsville 1974–78, Chief Scientist 1979–, Staff Scientist, Astrophysics Div., Office of Space Science, NASA HQ 1978–79, Prin. Investigator of Burst and Transient Source Experiment (BATSE), Compton Gamma Ray Observatory, currently a Co-Investigator of Gamma-ray Burst Monitor, Fermi Gamma-ray Space Telescope 2008–; Fellow, American Physical Soc. 1995; NASA Medal for Outstanding Scientific Achievement 1982, 1991, 1992, Alan Berman Research Publs Award, Naval Research Lab. 1992, Sigma Xi Research Scientist of the Year, Huntsville 1993, Distinguished Alumnus Award, Univ. of Missouri 1994, Bruno Rossi Prize, High Energy Astrophysics Div., AAS 1994, NASA Exceptional Service Medal 2011, Shaw Prize in Astronomy (co-recipient) 2012. *Publications:* more than 900 publs, including encyclopedia articles, published proceedings, published abstracts, reports and patents. *Address:* Marshall Space Flight Center, Building 4600, Rideout Road, Huntsville, AL 35812, USA (office). *Website:* www.nasa.gov/centers/marshall/home (office).

FISHMAN, Jay S., MA; American insurance executive; *Chairman and CEO, The Travelers Companies Inc.;* b. NJ; ed Wharton School, Univ. of Pennsylvania; fmr Dir of Mergers and Acquisitions, American Can Co.; Sr Vice-Pres. of Merchant Banking, Shearson Lehman Brothers –1989; Exec. Vice-Pres. and Chief Financial Officer, then Sr Vice- and Treasurer, Primerica Corpn 1989–93; Chief Financial Officer, Travelers Insurance Group 1993, various positions including Chief Financial Officer, Chief Admin. Officer, Pres. and COO Commercial Lines, Travelers Property Casualty 1996–98, Pres. and CEO Travelers Property Casualty Corpn 1998–2000, Chair. and CEO Travelers Insurance 2000, Chair., Pres. and CEO The St Paul Co. –2004, CEO The St Paul Travelers Cos Inc. (following merger of The St Paul Co. and Travelers Insurance Group 2004) 2004–, Chair. 2005– (renamed The Travelers Cos Inc. 2007); COO, Finance and Risk, Citigroup 2000–01; mem. Bd of Dirs Cttee Encouraging Corp. Philanthropy, The Philharmonic-Symphony Society of New York, Inc., Nat. Acad. Foundation, ExxonMobil Corpn 2010–; mem. Bd of Overseers Carlson School of Man. at Univ. of Minnesota; Trustee, Univ. of Pennsylvania, mem. Bd of Overseers for the School of Veterinary Medicine, mem. Industry Advisory Bd Financial Insts Center for the Wharton School, Chair. Advisory Bd Travelers/Wharton Partnership for Risk Man. and Leadership Fund 2010–. *Address:* The Travelers Companies Inc., 485 Lexington Avenue, New York, NY 10017-2630, USA (office). *Telephone:* (917) 778-6000 (office). *E-mail:* info@travelers.com (office). *Website:* www.travelers.com (office).

FISIAK, Jacek, OBE, PhD, DLitt; Polish philologist, linguist and academic; *Head, School of English, Warsaw Division, Academy of Management in Łódź;* b. 10 May 1936, Konstantynów Łódzki; s. of Czesław Fisiak and Jadwiga Fisiak; m. Liliana Sikorska; ed Warsaw Univ.; staff mem. Łódź Univ. 1959–67, Asst Prof. 1962–67; staff mem. Adam Mickiewicz Univ., Poznań 1965–, Head of English Dept 1965–69, Head of Dept of History of English, School of English 1969–, Extraordinary Prof. 1971–77, Prof. 1977–, Rector 1985–88; Head, School of English, Warsaw Div., Acad. of Man., Łódź 2007–; Chair. Comm. on Modern Languages and Literature, Ministry of Higher Educ. 1974–88; Minister of Nat. Educ. 1988–89; participant in Round Table debates 1989; Visiting Prof., UCLA 1963–64, Univ. of Kan. 1970, Univ. of Fla 1974, State Univ. of New York 1975, American Univ., Washington, DC 1979–80, 1991–92, Univ. of Kiel 1979–80, Vienna Univ. 1983, 1988–89, 1990–91, Univ of Zürich 1984, 1994, Univ. of Tromsø 1986, Univ. of Jyväskylä 1987, Univ. of Saarbrücken 1990, Univ. of Bamberg 1994; Ed. Studia Anglica Posnaniensia 1967–, Papers and Studies in Contrastive Linguistics 1972–, Ed.-in-Chief Folia Linguistica Historica 1978–; Pres. Int. Asscn of Univ.

Profs of English 1974–77, Societas Linguistica Europaea 1982–83, Int. Soc. for Historical Linguistics 1981–83; Chair. Neophilological Cttee, Polish Acad. of Sciences 1981–93; mem. Finnish Acad. of Sciences and Humanities 1990, Academia Europaea 1990, Finnish Acad. of Arts and Sciences, Norwegian Acad. of Sciences 1996, New York Acad. of Sciences 1996, Medieval Acad. of America 2001, Polish Acad. of Sciences 2004; Pres. Polish-British Friendship Soc. 1989–; mem. editorial bds of numerous foreign and int. philological journals, numerous scientific socs; consultant, Ford Foundation, IREX, Swedish Govt, Austrian Ministry of Higher Educ., Encyclopaedia Britannica (Chicago); Dr. hc (Jyväskylä) 1982, (Opole) 2005; Commdr.'s Cross of the Order Polonia Restituta with Star, Grand Cross of the Order Polonia Restituta, Officer's Cross of the Order of the British Empire (OBE), Nat. Educ. Comm. Medal, Commdr's Cross of Lion of Finland Order, Officier, Ordre des Palmes Académiques and numerous other decorations. *Publications:* 177 publs, 50 books including Morphemic Structure of Chaucer's English 1965, A Short Grammar of Middle English 1968, 1996, Recent Developments in Historical Phonology (ed.) 1978, Historical Syntax (ed.) 1983, A Bibliography of Writings for the History of English 1987, Historical Dialectology (ed.) 1990, An Outline History of English 1993, 2000, Medieval Dialectology 1995, Linguistic Change Under Contact Conditions 1995, Studies in Middle English Linguistics 1997, Typology and Linguistics Reconstruction 1997, East Anglia (co-author with P. Trudgill) 2001, The New Kościuszko Foundation Dictionary (English–Polish, Polish–English) 2003, Foreign Influences on Medieval English (co-ed. with M. Bator) 2011. *Leisure interests:* history, sport. *Address:* School of English, Warsaw Division, Academy of Management, Sienkiewicza 9, 90-050 Łódź (office); School of English, A Mickiewicz Univ., Al. Niepodleglosci 4, 61-874 Poznan, Poland (office). *Telephone:* (42) 6325023 (office); (61) 8293536 (office); (61) 8243153 (home); (61) 8293510 (office). *Fax:* (61) 8523103 (office); (61) 8243159 (home). *E-mail:* fisiak@amu.edu.pl (office); office@swspiz.pl (office). *Website:* www.swspiz .pl (office); www.amu.edu.pl (office).

FISICHELLA, Domenico; Italian politician and academic; b. 15 Sept. 1935, Messina, Sicily; m. Loredana Fisichella; two d.; Prof. of Political Science, Univ. of Florence, Università La Sapienza and Libera Università Internazionale degli Studi Sociali (LUISS), Rome; co-f. Alleanza Nazionale Party 1992, elected Senator 1994, Vice-Pres. of Senate 1996–2006; Minister of Culture 1994–95; Gold Medal for achievement in field of culture, education and art, Carlo Casalegno Journalism Prize 1985, Culture Prize for essays 1988, Guido and Roberto Cortese Prize for essays 1996. *Publications include:* Denaro e democrazia: Dall'antica Grecia all'economia globale (Money and Democracy: From Ancient Greece to Global Economy) 2000, Totalitarismo: Un regime del nostro tempo (Totalitarianism: A Regime of Our Times) 2002, Politica e mutamento sociale (Politics and Social Changes) 2002, La destra e l'Italia (The Right and Italy) 2003, Lineamenti di scienza politica: Concetti, problemi, teorie (Fundamentals of Political Science: Concepts, Problems, Theories) 2003, Contro il federalismo (Against Federalism) 2004, and numerous articles in nat. dailies. *Address:* Faculty of Political Science, Università degli Studi di Roma "La Sapienza", Piazzale Aldo Moro 5, 00185 Rome, Italy (office). *E-mail:* info@www.fisichella.it. *Website:* www.fisichella.it.

FISK, David John, CB, ScD, CEng, FREng, FInstP; British engineer and academic; *BP/Royal Academy Chair in Engineering for Sustainable Development, Imperial College London;* b. 9 Jan. 1947; s. of the late John Howard Fisk and of Rebecca Elizabeth Fisk (née Haynes); m. Anne Thoday 1972; one s. one d.; ed Stationers' Co. School, Hornsey, St John's Coll. Cambridge and Univ. of Manchester; joined Bldg Research Establishment, Sr Prin. Scientific Officer, Head, Mechanical and Electrical Eng Div. 1978–84; with Dept of Environment, then Dept of the Environment, Transport and the Regions, then Dept for Transport, Local Govt and the Regions, now Office of the Deputy Prime Minister 1984–2005, Asst Sec. Cen. Directorate of Environmental Protection 1984–87, Under-Sec. 1987, Deputy Chief Scientist 1987–88, Chief Scientific Adviser 1988– (Dir Air Climate and Toxic Substances Directorate 1990–95, Environment and Int. Directorate 1995–98, Cen. Strategy Directorate 1999–2002); Visiting Prof., Univ. of Liverpool 1988–2002; Dir Watford Palace Theatre 2000–; Royal Acad. of Eng Prof. of Eng for Sustainable Devt, Imperial Coll. of Science, London 2002, now BP/RA Eng Chair in Eng for Sustainable Devt, also Co-Dir BP Urban Energy Systems Project; mem. Gas and Electricity Markets Authority 2009–; Hon. Fellow, Chartered Inst. of Bldg Service Engineers, RIBA. *Publications:* Thermal Control of Buildings 1981; numerous papers on bldg science, systems theory and econs. *Leisure interests:* theatre, music. *Address:* Department of Civil and Environmental Engineering, Imperial College, London, SW7 2BU, England (office). *Telephone:* (20) 7594-6109. *Fax:* (20) 7594-6049. *E-mail:* d.fisk@imperial.ac.uk (office). *Website:* www.cv.ic.ac.uk (office).

FISMER, Christiaan (Chris) Loedolff; South African politician and government official; b. 1956, Pretoria; s. of William Fismer and Elizabeth Fismer; m. Linda Mills; twin d.; ed Univ. of Pretoria; served in mil. service; admitted to Pretoria Bar 1986; practised as advocate 1986–87; fmr Chair. Student Rep. Council, Univ. of Pretoria, Pres. Afrikaanse Studentebond (umbrella org. for univ. governing bodies); mem. Nat. Party; co-f. Nat. Party Youth Action; MP for Rissik 1987, Sr Transvaal Whip of Nat. Party 1989; apptd party rep. to Conf. for a Democratic S Africa working group on implementation of decisions 1991; Prov. Leader Nat. Party in Eastern Transvaal 1994; fmr Deputy Minister in Office of State Pres. F. W. de Klerk; Deputy Minister of Justice 1994–95; Minister of Gen. Services 1995–96, of Provincial and Constitutional Affairs March–May 1996; Chair. Nat. Gaming Board of SA 1998–2009 (retd); Univ. of Pretoria Gold Medal. *Address:* c/o National Gaming Board of South Africa, The dti Campus, Block G, Ground Floor, Mapungubwe Building, 77 Meintjies Street, Sunnyside, Pretoria, South Africa.

FISZEL, Roland Henri Léon; French engineer; b. 16 July 1948, Paris; s. of Jean Fiszel and Marie Eber; m. Nadine Kohn 1974; one s. two d.; ed Lycée Pasteur, Neuilly-sur-Seine, Ecole polytechnique, Massachusetts Inst. of Tech., USA; Head of Housing Dept, Ministry of Construction 1974–77; Head of Studies and Planning Group, Infrastructure Div., Hauts-de-Seine 1977–81; Deputy Sec.-Gen. Codis-Cidise, in charge of Treasury 1981–82; Tech. Adviser, Office of Minister of Social Affairs and Nat. Solidarity 1983–84, then of Minister of the Economy and Finance 1984–86; Dir Nat. Printing Office 1986–92; Adviser to Chair. of Euris 1996, mem. Bd of Dirs 2002–06; Pres. and Dir-Gen. Société francaise de production 1997–2001;

Ingénieur en chef des ponts et chaussées; Dir representing State, Agence Havas 1986–87; Dir Antenne 2 1988–92; fmr Sec.-Gen. Caisse nationale du Crédit agricole. *Leisure interests:* skiing, tennis. *Address:* 4 rue Jobbé Duval, 75015 Paris, France (home). *E-mail:* roland@fiszel.fr.

FITCH, Val Logsdon, BEng, PhD; American physicist and academic; *James S. McDonnel Distinguished University Professor of Physics, Princeton University;* b. 10 March 1923, USA; s. of Fred B. Fitch and Frances M. Fitch (née Logsdon); m. 1st Elise Cunningham 1949 (died 1972); two s. (one deceased); m. 2nd Daisy Harper Sharp 1976; ed McGill and Columbia Univs; US Army 1943–46; Instructor, Columbia Univ. 1953–54; Instructor, Princeton Univ. 1954, Prof. 1960–, Chair. Dept of Physics 1976, Cyrus Fogg Brackett Prof. of Physics 1976–84, James S. McDonnell Distinguished Univ. Prof. of Physics 1984–; Pres. American Physical Soc. 1987–88; Sloan Fellow 1960–64; mem. NAS, American Acad. of Arts and Sciences, President's Science Advisory Cttee 1970–73, American Philosophical Soc.; three hon. degrees; Research Corpn Award 1968, Ernest Orlando Laurence Award 1968, John Witherill Medal, Franklin Inst. 1976, Distinguished Alumnus Award, Columbia Univ., Nobel Prize for Physics (jtly with J. W. Cronin) for work on elementary particles 1980, Nat. Medal of Science 1993. *Publications:* major publs in area of elementary particles. *Leisure interest:* conservation. *Address:* PO Box 708, Princeton University, Department of Physics, Princeton, NJ 08544, USA (office). *Telephone:* (609) 258-4374 (office). *Fax:* (609) 258-6360 (office). *E-mail:* vfitch@princeton.edu (office). *Website:* www.princeton.edu (office).

FITERMAN, Charles; French politician; b. 28 Dec. 1933, St-Etienne; s. of Moszek Fiterman and Laja Rozenblum; m. Jeannine Poinas 1953; Departmental Sec. Jeunesse Communiste 1952; Sec. CGT, St-Etienne SFAC 1958–62; Dir Cen. School, Parti Communiste Français (PCF) 1963–65; elected to PCF Cen. Cttee 1972, to Political Bureau and Cen. Cttee Sec. 1976; Gen. Councillor, Head, Econ. Section and PCF Rep. to Liaison Cttee of Signatory Parties to Common Programme of the Left 1977; Deputy (Val-de-Marne) to Nat. Ass. 1978–81; Minister of State, Minister of Transport 1981–84; Deputy for Rhône 1986–88; Mayor of Tavernes 1989–; f. Refondations Movt 1990, Convention pour une alternative progressiste 1994; Pres. Forum Alternatives Européennes 1994–99; mem. Socialist Party 1998–, Conseil Economique et Socialde France; Chevalier Légion d'honneur. *Address:* BP 3218, 75122 Paris cedex 3, France (office). *E-mail:* charles.fiterman@wanadoo.fr (office).

FITIAL, Benígno Repeki, BBA; American politician, fmr state governor and business executive; b. 27 Nov. 1945, Saipan, Northern Mariana Islands (NMI); m. Josepina (Josie) Padiermos; six c.; ed Mt Carmel High School, Univ. of Guam; govt positions include News Dir, KJQR Radio Station; Budget Analyst, Trust Territory Govt; Budget Officer, 1st NMI Legislature; Chief Admin. Officer, 1st NMI Legislature, Minority Leader, 2nd and 4th NMI Legislature, Vice-Speaker, 5th NMI Legislature, Speaker of the House of Reps, 3rd, 12th and 14th NMI Legislature; business positions include Pres. Bank of Saipan, Century Insurance Corpn, Century Travel Corpn, Consolidated Transportation Services Inc., Pacific Oriental Inc., Home Improvement (MPI); Vice-Pres. Tan Holdings Corpn; Special Consultant, L&T Corpn; Founder CNMI Covenant Party; Chair. Northern Marianas Republican Party, Bush for President Cttee for the CNMI, CNMI Zoning Bd, NMI Trusteeship Termination Task Force, 1st CNMI Civil Service Comm., Saipan Municipal Scholarship Bd; mem. CNMI Tax Task Force, Republican Presidential Task Force (US); Del., 1st Northern Marianas Constitutional Convention; Chair. Constitutional Convention Cttee (s) on Tax, Public Debt, Educ. and Local Govt; Gov. of the Commonwealth of the Northern Mariana Islands (CNMI) 2006–13 (impeached 11 Feb. 2013, resgnd 20 Feb. 2013); Republican –2001, 2011–, Covenant Party 2001–11; Distinguished Alumni, Univ. of Guam. *Address:* c/o Office of the Governor, Juan A. Sablan Memorial Building, Capital Hill, Caller Box 10007, Saipan, MP 96950, Commonwealth of the Northern Mariana Islands (office).

FITOUSSI, Jean-Paul Samuel, DèsScEcon; French economist and academic; *President, Observatoire Français des Conjonctures Economiques (OFCE);* b. 19 Aug. 1942, La Goulette; s. of Joseph Fitoussi and Mathilde Cohen; m. Anne Krief 1964; one s. one d.; ed Acad. Commerciale, Paris and Univs of Paris and Strasbourg; Asst Lecturer 1968–71; Dir of Studies 1971–73; Maître de Conférence Agrégé 1974–75; Prof. 1975–78; Titular Prof. 1978–82; Dean, Faculty of Econ. Science and Dir Dept of Econ. Science, Strasbourg 1980–81; Prof. in charge of research programme on foundation of macroeconomic policy, Inst. Universitaire Européen, Florence 1979–83; Prof., Inst. d'Etudes Politiques, Paris 1982–; Dir Dept of Studies Observatoire Français des Conjonctures Economiques (OFCE) 1982–89, Pres. 1990–; Chair. Scientific Council of Inst. d'Etudes Politiques, Paris 1997–; Sec.-Gen. Int. Econ. Asscn 1984–; consultant to EC Comm. 1978–; mem. Bd Ecole Normale Supérieure, Paris 1998–; External Prof., Univ. Européenne, Florence 1984–93, mem. Research Council, Université Européen, Florence 2003–; mem. Econ. Comm. of the Nation 1996–, Council of Econ. Analysis of the Prime Minister 1997–; Expert, Comm. of the European Parl. 2000–; mem. UN Research Inst. for Social Devt 2001–, Exec. Cttee Aspen Inst. Italia 2001–, Comité nationale d'évaluation de la politique de la ville 2002–, Comité national d'initiative et de proposition pour la recherche 2004–, Scientific Bd Austrian Inst. of Economic Research 2004–, Bd of Dirs École Normale Supérieure 2004–, Advisory Bd Centre on Capitalism and Soc., Columbia Univ. 2004–, Cttee for Evaluation of Research 2005–; columnist for Le Monde and La Repubblica; Hon. Prof., Univ. of Trento, Italy; Officier Ordre nat. du Mérite, Chevalier, Légion d'honneur, Grand Officier de l'Ordre de l'Infant Henri (Portugal); Dr hc (Buenos Aires); Prix Asscn Française de Sciences Economiques, Prix Acad. des Sciences Morales et Politiques. *Publications:* Inflation, équilibre et chômage 1973, Le fondement macroéconomique de la théorie Keynesienne 1974, Modern Macroeconomic Theory 1983, Monetary Theory and Economic Institutions (with N. de Cecco) 1985, The Slump in Europe (with E. Phelps) 1988, Competitive Disinflation (with others) 1993, Pour l'emploi et la cohésion sociale 1994, Le débat interdit: monnaie, Europe, pauvreté 1995, Economic Growth, Capital and Labour Markets 1995, Le nouvel âge des inégalités (with Pierre Rosanvallon) 1996, Rapport sur l'état de l'Union européenne 1999, 2000, 2002, Réformes structurelles et politiques macroéconomique: les enseignements des modèles de pays (with O. Posset) 2000, contrib. to collected publs, L'enseignement supérieur de l'économie en question, Rapport au ministre de l'éducation nationale 2001, Rapport sur l'état de l'union européenne 2002; La

Règle et le choix 2002, How to Reform the European Central Bank (with J. Creel) 2002, Il dittatore benevolo 2003, Rapport sur l'état de l'union européene 2004, Les inégalités 2003, La démocratie et le marché 2004, L'ideologie du monde 2004, Ségrégation urbaine et intégration sociale (jtly) 2004, Macroeconomic Theory and Economic Policy 2004, La politique de l'impuissance 2005, Report on the State of the European Union 2005. *Leisure interests:* travel, cinema, guitar, scuba-diving. *Address:* Observatoire Français des Conjonctures Economiques, 69 quai d'Orsay, 75340 Paris Cedex 07 (office); 47 rue de boulainvilliers, 75016 Paris, France (home). *Telephone:* 1-44-18-54-01. *Fax:* 1-44-18-54-71. *E-mail:* presidence@ofce .sciences-po.fr (office). *Website:* www.ofce.sciences-po.fr (office).

FITRAT, Abdul Qadeer, BA, MA; Afghan banker; b. 1 May 1963, Badakhshan; ed secondary school, Kabul, Int. Islamic Univ., Islamabad, Pakistan, Wright State Univ., Dayton, Ohio, USA; fmr Asst Research Co-ordinator for USAID-supported project, ESSP, Peshawar, Pakistan; fmr Chair. Bank-Millie Afghan, Kabul early 1990s; Consultant Economist, IMF, Washington, DC, USA in late 1990s; First Deputy Gov. Da Afghanistan Bank (Cen. Bank of Afghanistan) 1995, Gov. 1996, Gov. and Chair. Supreme Council (Supervisory Bd) 2007–11; fled to the USA 2011, warrant for his arrest issued by Afghan Govt June 2011, ordered by Pres. Karzai to return to Afghanistan Oct. 2012; consumer banker to First Union Nat. Bank, northern Va 2000–01; Adviser to Exec. Dir, World Bank 2004–07. *Address:* c/o Da Afghanistan Bank, Ibne Sina Wat, Kabul, Afghanistan.

FITSCHEN, Jürgen, MBA; German business executive; *Co-Chairman of the Management Board and Co-CEO, Deutsche Bank AG;* b. 1948, Harsefeld; ed Univ. of Hamburg; worked at Citibank in various positions in Hamburg and Frankfurt am Main 1975–87, mem. Exec. Cttee Germany 1983–87; joined Deutsche Bank 1987, held executive positions in Thailand, Japan and Singapore before becoming mem. of the Global Corps and Insts Div. Bd, Frankfurt 1997–98, London 1998–2001, mem. Bd of Man. Dirs 2001–09, responsible for Corp. and Investment divs, mem. Group Exec. Cttee 2002–, Head of Regional Man. team world-wide, CEO Germany and Chair. Man. Cttee Germany, Frankfurt 2005–12, mem. Man. Bd Deutsche Bank AG 2009–, Co-Chair. Man. Bd 2012–, Co-CEO 2012–; mem. Bd of Dirs Kuehne + Nagel International AG; mem. Supervisory Bd METRO AG, Schott AG. *Address:* Deutsche Bank AG, Taunusanlage 12, 60262 Frankfurt am Main, Germany (office). *Telephone:* (69) 910-00 (office). *Fax:* (69) 910-34225 (office). *E-mail:* info@db.com (office). *Website:* www.db.com (office).

FITTIPALDI, Emerson; Brazilian fmr racing driver; b. 12 Dec. 1946, São Paulo; s. of Wilson Fittipaldi and Juze Fittipaldi; m. 1st Maria Helena Dowding 1970; one s. two d.; m. 2nd Teresa Hotte 1995; one s. one d.; m. 3rd Rossana Fanucchi 2001; one s. one d.; ed scientific studies; Brazilian champion Formula V and Go-Kart 1967; Formula 3 Lombard Championship 1969; Formula 1 World Champion 1972 (youngest ever), 1974; second in World Championship 1973, 1975; won Indianapolis 500 1989, 1993; retd (following injury) 1996 with 17 Indy Car victories; owns Fittipaldi Motoring Accessories, 500,000-acre orange plantation and exports orange concentrate; has Mercedes-Benz partnership in Brazil; Pnr, Hugo Boss fashion retailer; set up the Fittipaldi Foundation to help impoverished children in Brazil; runs Fittipaldi-Dingman Racing; mem. Bd Laureus World Sports Acad. *Leisure interests:* sport, music, water-skiing, flying. *Address:* Av. Rebouças, 3551, Jardim Paulistano, São Paulo, SP 05401-400, Brazil. *Telephone:* (11) 3215-6050; (11) 3215-6072 (office). *Fax:* (11) 3215-6051. *Website:* www.emersonfittipaldi.com.

FITZGERALD, Edmund Bacon, BSE; American business executive; *Managing Director, Woodmont Associates;* b. 5 Feb. 1926, Milwaukee, Wis.; s. of Edmund Fitzgerald and Elizabeth McKee Christensen Fitzgerald; m. Elisabeth McKee Christensen 1947; two s. two d.; ed Univ. of Michigan; fmr Chair. and CEO Cutler-Hammer Inc., Milwaukee; then Vice-Chair. and COO, Industrial Products, Eaton Corpn (following merger with Cutler-Hammer); Pres. Northern Telecom Inc., USA (subsidiary of Northern Telecom Ltd) 1980–82; CEO Northern Telecom Ltd 1984–89, Chair. 1985–90; Man. Dir Woodmont Assocs., Nashville 1990–; Adjunct Prof. of Strategy and Business Economics, Owen Graduate School of Man., Vanderbilt Univ. 1990–; Dir Ashland Oil Inc., Becton Dickinson and Co., GTI; mem. Pres. Reagan's Nat. Telecommunications Security Advisory Council; Trustee, Cttee for Econ. Devt, Washington, DC; fmr Pres. Nat. Electrical Mfrs Asscn; fmr Vice-Chair. Industry Advisory Council, Dept of Defense; mem. Korea-US Wisemen Council; Co-founder Milwaukee Brewers Major League Baseball team 1970, Chair. 1970–82; Order of the Rising Sun Gold and Silver Star (Japan) 1997. *Publications:* Globalizing Customer Solutions 2001, Edmund Fitzgerald: The Ship and the Man 2002, Lizzy's Curacao 2003. *Address:* Woodmont Associates, 3434 Woodmont Blvd., Nashville, TN 37215-1422, USA.

FITZGERALD, Frances; American writer; b. 21 Oct. 1940; d. of Desmond Fitzgerald and Marietta Peabody Fitzgerald Tree; m. James Paul Sterba 1990; ed Radcliffe Coll.; author of series of profiles for Herald Tribune magazine; freelance author of series of profiles, Vietnam 1966; frequent contrib. to The New Yorker; Vice-Pres. PEN International; mem. editorial bds The Nation, Foreign Policy; Overseas Press Club Award 1967, Nat. Inst. of Arts and Letters Award 1973, Sydney Hillman Award 1973, George Polk Award 1973, Bancroft Award for History 1973. *Publications include:* Fire in the Lake – The Vietnamese and the Americans in Vietnam (Pulitzer Prize 1973, Nat. Book Award 1973) 1972, America Revised – History Schoolbooks in the Twentieth Century 1979, Cities on a Hill – A Journey Through Contemporary American Cultures 1986, Way Out There in the Blue – Reagan, Star Wars and the End of the Cold War (New York Times Ed.'s Choice, New York Public Library Helen Bernstein Award) 2000, Vietnam: Spirits of the Earth 2002, Our Cat Cookie 2011; contribs to The New York Review of Books, The New York Times Magazine, Esquire, Architectural Digest, Islands, Rolling Stone. *Address:* 531 E 72nd Street, Apartment 3B, New York, NY 10021-4017, USA (home).

FITZGERALD, Mgr Michael Louis, BA, DTheol; British ecclesiastic and diplomatist (retd); b. 17 Aug. 1937, Walsall, West Midlands, England; s. of Dr Thomas Walter Fitzgerald and Dr Nora Josephine Fitzgerald (née Twomey); ed Pontifical Gregorian Univ., School of Oriental and African Studies, Univ. of London; ordained priest, Soc. of Missionaries of Africa (White Fathers) 1961; teacher, Makarere Univ., Kampala, Uganda and later Pontifical Inst. of Arabic and Islamic Studies, Rome; two years pastoral work, Sudan; mem. Gen. Council of Missionaries of Africa 1980–86; Sec. Secr. for Non Christians (now renamed

Pontifical Council for Inter-Religious Dialogue) 1987–2002, Pres. 2002–06; Apostolic Nuncio in Egypt and Del. to the Arab League 2006–12; Titular Bishop of Nepte 1991–2002, Titular Archbishop of Nepte 2002–; presented von Hügel Lecture on Christian-Muslim Relations, Cambridge 2002; Conventual Chaplain ad honorem of the Sovereign Mil. Order of Malta; Officier, Légion d'honneur 2005; Mohammed Nafi Tschelebi Medienpreis 2004, Pax Christi Award, St John's Abbey and Univ., Collegeville, Minn. 2007. *Publications include:* Signs of Dialogue: Christian Encounter with Muslims (co-author) 1992, Catalysts (co-author) (second edn) 1998, Dieu reve d'unité. Les catholiques et les religions: les leçons du dialogue. Entretiens avec Annie Laurent 2005, Interfaith Dialogue – A Catholic View (co-author) 2006; numerous specialist articles and lectures. *Address:* Missionari d'Africa (Padri Bianchi), Via Aurelia 269, 00165 Rome, Italy (office). *Telephone:* (06) 3936341 (office).

FITZGERALD, Niall, FRSA, BComm; Irish business executive; *Chairman, British Museum;* b. 13 Sept. 1945; m.; two s. two d.; ed Univ. Coll., Dublin; joined Unilever 1967, various man. roles including CEO, Unilever Food Div., S Africa, early 1980s, later Treasurer, Unilever, London, Dir Unilever PLC and Unilever NV 1987–2004, Financial Dir 1987–89, Co-ordinator, Edible Fats and Dairy 1989–90, mem. Foods Exec. 1989–91, Co-ordinator, Detergents 1991–95, Vice-Pres. Unilever PLC 1994–96, Chair. 1996–2004, also becoming Vice-Chair. Unilever NV 1996–2004; Dir Reuters Group 2003–08, Chair. 2004–08, Deputy Chair. Thomson Reuters (following acquisition of Reuters) 2008–11; Chair. British Museum 2006–; Pres. Advertising Asscn, S Africa Int. Investment Advisory Council, Shanghai Major's Int. Business Leaders' Council; Vice-Chair. The Conf. Bd; mem. World Econ. Forum, Int. Advisory Bd, Council on Foreign Relations, Trilateral Comm., EU–China Cttee, US Business Council; Gov. Nat. Inst. of Econ. and Social Research; Trustee, Leverhulme Trust; fmr Dir Merck, Ericsson, Bank of Ireland, Prudential Corpn; Hon. KBE. *Leisure interests:* jazz, opera, football, rugby, golf. *Address:* British Museum, Great Russell Street, London, WC1B 3DG, England. *Telephone:* (20) 7323-8000. *E-mail:* information@britishmuseum.org. *Website:* www.britishmuseum.org.

FITZGERALD, Peter Gosselin, AB, JD; American banker, lawyer and fmr politician; *Chairman, Chain Bridge Bancorp Inc.;* b. 20 Oct. 1960, Elgin, Ill.; s. of Gerald Francis Fitzgerald and Marjorie (née Gosselin) Fitzgerald; m. C. Nina Kerstiens 1987; one s.; ed Dartmouth Coll., Univ. of Michigan; called to Bar Ill. 1986; with US Dist Court Ill. 1986; Assoc. Isham, Lincoln & Beale 1986–88; Pnr, Riordan, Larson, Bruckert & Moore 1988–92; Counsel, Harris Bankmont Inc. 1992–96; mem. Ill. Senate 1993–98, Chair. State Govt Operations Cttee 1997–99, US Senator from Illinois 1999–2005 (retd), Chair. Senate Sub-Cttee on Consumer Affairs and Product Safety 2003–05, Sub-Cttee on Financial Man., the Budget and Int. Security 2003–05; Chair. Chain Bridge Bancorp Inc. 2006–; mem. various bds and asscns. *Address:* 1320 Old Chain Bridge Road, Suite 420, McLean, VA 22101, USA (office). *Telephone:* (703) 748-2005 (office). *Fax:* (703) 748-2007 (office). *E-mail:* dgumino@fitzgeraldpeter.com (office).

FITZGERALD, Stephen Arthur, AO, BA, PhD; Australian scholar and diplomatist; b. 18 Sept. 1938, Hobart, Tasmania; s. of F.G. FitzGerald; m. Helen Overton; one s. two d.; ed Tasmania Univ., Australian Nat. Univ.; Dept of Foreign Affairs 1961–66; Research Scholar, ANU 1966–69, Research Fellow 1969–71, Fellow 1972–73, Professorial Fellow 1977–, Head Dept of Far Eastern History 1977–79, Head Contemporary China Centre, Research School of Pacific Studies 1977–79; Amb. to People's Repub. of China (also accred to Democratic People's Repub. of Korea) 1973–76; Ed. Australian Journal of Chinese Affairs; Deputy Chair. Australia–China Council 1979–86; mem. Australian Acad. of Science Sub-Cttee on Relations with China; Trustee, Australian Cancer Foundation 1985–99; Chair. Asian Studies Council 1986–91; Chair. and Man. Dir Stephen Fitzgerald and Co. Ltd; Chair. Asia-Australia Inst., also Prof. Univ. of NSW 1990–; Co-Chair. Jt Policy Cttee on Relations between Northern Territory and Indonesia; currently adviser to Australian govt-funded China-Australia Governance Program; Fellow, Australian Inst. of Int. Affairs 2009; mem. council Musica Viva Australia; Dunlop Asia Medal 1999, Australia–China Council Award 1999. *Publications:* China and the Overseas Chinese 1972, Talking with China 1972, China and the World 1977, Immigration: A Commitment to Australia (jtly) 1988, A National Strategy for the Study of Asia in Australia (jtly) 1988, Asia in Australian Education (jtly) 1989, Australia's China (jtly) 1989, Ethical Dimension to Australia's Engagement with Asia 1993, Is Australia an Asian Country? 1997, East View-West View: Divining the Chinese Business Environment 1999. *Address:* Stephen Fitzgerald & Co., P.O. Box 620, Woollahra, NSW 2025, Australia. *Telephone:* (2) 9385-9111. *Fax:* (2) 9385-9221. *E-mail:* aai@unsw.edu.au (office). *Website:* www.aai@unsw.edu.au (office).

FITZGERALD, Tara; British actress; b. 18 Sept. 1969, Sussex; d. of the late Michael Callaby and of Sarah Geraldine Fitzgerald; stage debut in Our Song, London; appeared in London as Ophelia in Hamlet 1995, Antigone 1999. *Theatre:* Our Song, London, Hamlet (Drama Desk Award Best Supporting Actress 1995), New York, A Streetcar Named Desire 1999, The Doll's House 2003, And Then There Were None, Gielgud Theatre, London 2005, A Doll's House, Donmar Theatre, London 2009, The Misanthrope, The Comedy Theatre, London 2009–10. *Films:* Hear My Song 1991, Galleria 1993, Sirens 1994, A Man of No Importance 1994, The Englishman Who Went up a Hill but Came Down a Mountain 1995, Brassed Off 1996, Conquest 1998, The Snatching of Bookie Bob 1998, Childhood 1999, New World Disorder 1999, Rancid Aluminium 2000, Dark Blue World 2001, I Capture the Castle 2003, Five Children and It 2004, Secret Passage 2004, In a Dark Place 2006. *Television includes:* Six Characters in Search of an Author 1992, The Camomile Lawn (miniseries) 1992, Anglo Saxon Attitudes 1992, Fall from Grace 1994, The Vacillations of Poppy Carew 1995, The Tenant of Wildfell Hall 1996, The Woman in White 1997, The Student Prince 1997, Little White Lies 1998, Frenchman's Creek (Best Actress Award, Reims Int. TV Festival 1999) 1998, In the Name of Love 1999, Love Again 2003, Marple: The Body in the Library 2004, Like Father Like Son 2005, The Virgin Queen (miniseries) 2005, Jane Eyre (miniseries) 2006, Waking the Dead (series) 2007–11, U Be Dead 2008, The Body Farm 2011, Game of Thrones 2013. *Address:* c/o Lindy King, United Agents, 12–26 Lexington Street, London, W1F 0LE, England (office). *Telephone:* (20) 3214-0800 (office). *Fax:* (20) 3214-0801 (office). *E-mail:* info@unitedagents.co.uk (office). *Website:* www.unitedagents.co.uk (office).

FITZGIBBON, Joel; Australian politician; b. 16 Jan. 1962, Bellingen, NSW; m. Dianne Fitzgibbon; one s. two d.; ed Univ. of New England, NSW, Univ. of Newcastle; automotive electrician 1978–90; Dir Hunter-Manning Tourist Authority 1987–89; Deputy Mayor of Cessnock 1989–90; part-time Lecturer, Tech. and Further Educ. (TAFE); Del. Hunter Region Asscn of Councils 1994–95; MP (Australian Labor Party) for Hunter 1996–, various portfolios including Small Business, Tourism, Banking and Financial Services, Forestry, Mining and Energy, Asst Treas., Shadow Minister for Defence; Minister for Defence 2007–09 (resgnd), Minister for Agric., Fisheries and Forestry July–Sept. 2013, Shadow Minister for Agric. Oct. 2013–. *Address:* Parliament House, R1 48, Canberra, ACT 2600, Australia (office). *Telephone:* (2) 6277-4550 (office). *Fax:* (2) 6277-8422. *E-mail:* Joel .Fitzgibbon.MP@aph.gov.au (office). *Website:* www.joelfitzgibbon.com.

FITZPATRICK, Sean; New Zealand fmr rugby union player; b. 4 June 1963, Auckland; s. of Brian Fitzpatrick; ed Sacred Heart Coll., Auckland; hooker for New Zealand All Blacks 1986–97, capt. 1992–97; int. debut 28 June 1986; final appearance before retirement 29 Nov. 1997; rugby consultant to NZ Rugby Football Union 1999–; Man. Auckland Blues Super 12 Team 2001–03; second-most capped NZ player of all time, most consecutive int. rugby union appearances (63 in 1986–95), missed only two test matches during his career; totals: 128 All Blacks games, including 92 tests (55 test points, including 12 tries); f. www.whatwe-canbe.com (motivational speaking co.). *Publication:* Turning Point – The Making of a Captain. *E-mail:* sean@whatwecanbe.com. *Website:* www.whatwecanbe.com.

FITZWATER, Marlin, BA; American fmr government official; b. 24 Nov. 1942, Salina, Kan.; s. of Max Fitzwater and Phyllis Seaton; m.; two c.; ed Univ. of Kansas; served with USAF 1968–70; speechwriter, US Dept of Transportation, Washington, DC 1970–72; with press relations dept, US Environmental Protection Agency 1972–74, Dir Press Office 1974–81; Deputy Asst Sec. for Public Affairs, Dept of Treasury 1981–83; Deputy Press Sec. to Pres. 1983–85, Press Sec. to Vice-Pres. 1985–87, Prin. Deputy Press Sec. to Pres. 1987–89, Press Sec. to Pres. 1989–93; Advertising Pres. Fitzwater & Tutweiler, Inc. 1993; mem. Bd of Trustees Franklin Pierce Coll. 1999–, mem. Advisory Bd, Marlin Fitzwater Center for Communication; Presidential Merit Award 1982. *Publication:* Call the Briefing 1995. *Address:* c/o Marlin Fitzwater Center for Communication, Franklin Pierce College, 20 College Road, Rindge, NH 03461-0060, USA.

FIVE, Karin Cecilie (Kaci) Kullmann; Norwegian company director and fmr politician; b. 13 April 1951, Oslo; m.; two c.; ed Univ. of Oslo; mem. Baerum Municipal Council 1975–81; Chair. Young Conservatives 1977–79; Deputy mem. Storting (Parl.) 1977–81, mem. Storting 1981–97, mem. Finance and Foreign Affairs Cttee, Vice-Chair. Conservative Party Parl. Group 1985–89, Conservative Party Spokesperson for Foreign Affairs and EU 1994; Cabinet Minister of Trade, Shipping and European Affairs 1989–90; Deputy Chair. Conservative Party 1982–88, Chair. 1991–94; Deputy mem. Nat. Council on Youth Affairs 1979–81; Exec. Officer, Norwegian Employers' Fed. 1980–81; Sr Pnr, European Public Policy Advisers (EPPA) 1997–98; Sr Vice-Pres. Aker RGI 1998–2002, now adviser; mem. Bd of Dirs Asker og Baerums Budstikke ASA 1997–, Norsk Medisinaldepot AS 2001–, Bluewater Insurance ASA 2004–, Clavis Pharma ASA 2007–, AS J. Ludwig Mowinckels Rederi 2008–, Magda Müller Mowinckels Foundation 2002–, Statoil ASA 2002–07 (Deputy Chair. 2003–07); Chair. Norwegian Asscn of Foundations 2003–; Vice-Chair. Scheiblers Foundation 1998–; Chair. Norwegian Export Council 2000–02; mem. Norwegian Nobel Cttee 2003–. *Address:* Lille Toppenhaug 4, 1353 Baerums Verk, Norway. *Telephone:* 916-300-40. *Fax:* 67-56-17-11. *E-mail:* kaci@kaci.no. *Website:* www.kaci.no.

FIXMAN, Marshall, PhD; American chemist and academic; *Professor Emeritus, Colorado State University;* b. 21 Sept. 1930, St Louis, Mo.; s. of Benjamin Fixman and Dorothy Finkel; m. 1st Marian Beatman 1959 (died 1969); one s. two d.; m. 2nd Branka Ladanyi 1974; ed Univ. City High School, Mo., Washington Univ., Mo. and MIT; Postdoctoral Fellow, Yale Univ. 1953–54; served in US Army 1954–56; Instructor in Chem., Harvard Univ. 1956–59; Sr Fellow, Mellon Inst., Pa 1959–61; Dir Inst. of Theoretical Science, Univ. of Oregon 1961–64, Prof. of Chem. 1961–65; Sloan Visiting Prof. of Chem., Harvard Univ. 1965; Prof. of Chem., Yale Univ. 1965–79; Prof. of Chem. and Physics, Colorado State Univ. 1979–2000, Distinguished Prof. 1986–2000, Prof. Emer. 2000–; Assoc. Ed. Journal of Chemical Physics 1994–; mem. Editorial Bd Macromolecules, Journal of Physical Chemistry, Accounts of Chemical Research, Journal of Polymer Science; mem. NAS; Fellow, American Acad. of Arts and Sciences, American Physical Soc.; Alfred P. Sloan Fellowship 1962–64, ACS Award in Pure Chem. 1964, High Polymer Physics Prize, American Physical Soc. 1980, ACS Polymer Chem. Award 1991. *Leisure interests:* hiking and photography. *Address:* Department of Chemistry, Colorado State University, Fort Collins, CO 80523-0001, USA (office). *Telephone:* (970) 491-6037 (office). *Fax:* (970) 491-3361 (office). *Website:* www.chm.colostate.edu (office).

FJÆRVOLL, Dag Jostein; Norwegian politician; b. 20 Jan. 1947, Hadsel; s. of Edmund Fjærvoll; m.; two c.; fmr teacher; Head Teacher, Melbu School 1984; mem. Hadsel Municipal Council 1975, mem. Exec. Bd 1980, Mayor 1980–85; mem. Storting Nordland Co. 1985–97, mem. Standing Cttee on Local Govt and the Environment 1985–89, on Shipping and Fisheries 1989–93, on Scrutiny and the Constitution 1993–97; Vice-Pres. Lagting 1989–93, Odelsting 1993–97; Minister of Defence 1997–99, of Transport and Communications 1999–2000; mem. Kristelig Folkeparti (Christian Democratic Party). *Address:* c/o Kristelig Folkeparti (Christian Democratic Party), Øvre Slottsgt. 18–20, POB 478 Sentrum, 0105 Oslo, Norway.

FLACH, Christian; German business executive; *Chairman of the Executive Board and CEO, Marquard & Bahls AG;* joined Marquard & Bahls AG 1993, held several man. positions at Marquard & Bahls, Oiltanking and Mabanaft in Germany as well as abroad, Man. Dir Mabanaft GmbH & Co. KG 2006–11, mem. Bd of Dirs Marquard & Bahls AG 2008–, Chair. Exec. Bd and CEO 2011–; Chair. AFM+E (Außenhandelsverband für Mineralöl und Energie e.V.). *Address:* Marquard & Bahls AG, Admiralitaetstr. 55, 20459 Hamburg, Germany (office). *Telephone:* (40) 37004-0 (office). *Fax:* (40) 37004-332 (office). *E-mail:* office@ mbholding.de (office). *Website:* www.mbholding.com (office).

FLAHAUT, André, MA; Belgian politician; *President, Chambre des Représentants/Kamer van Volksvertegenwoordigers (Chamber of Representatives);* b. 18 Aug. 1955, Walhain; ed Université Libre de Bruxelles; Asst to Emile Vandervelde Inst. 1979, Man. 1989; Councillor of Walhain 1982–94; Chair. Parti Socialiste Fed. of Wallon Brabant 1983–95; Prov. Councillor of Brabant 1987–91; Chair. Office de la Naissance et de l'Enfance 1989–95; Vice-Chair. of Intercommunale des Oeuvres Sociales du Brabant Wallon 1993–95; Chair. Mutualité Socialiste du Brabant Wallon 1993; Parl. Rep. 1994; Minister for Civil Service 1995–99, for Defence 1999–2007; Pres. Chambre des Représentants (Chamber of Representatives) 2010–. *Address:* Office of the President, Chambre des Représentants/Kamer van Volksvertegenwoordigers (Chamber of Representatives), Palais de la Nation, 1008 Brussels, Belgium (office). *Telephone:* (2) 549-81-11 (office). *E-mail:* pri@lachambre .be (office). *Website:* www.lachambre.be (office).

FLAKE, Jeffry (Jeff) Lane; American foundation director and politician; *Senator from Arizona;* b. 31 Dec. 1962, Snowflake, Ariz.; s. of Dean Maeser Flake and Nerita Flake (née Hock); m. Cheryl Flake 1985; five c.; ed Brigham Young Univ.; served as Mormon missionary for The Church of Jesus Christ of Latter-day Saints in South Africa early 1980s, worked in public affairs sector after college and served as Exec. Dir Foundation for Democracy in Namibia and of Goldwater Inst. –2001; mem. US House of Reps for 1st Congressional Dist of Ariz. 2001–03, 6th Congressional Dist 2003–13, mem. Cttee on Appropriations; Senator from Arizona 2013–; Republican. *Address:* United States Senate, Washington, DC 20510, USA (office). *Telephone:* (202) 224-3121 (office). *Website:* www.senate.gov (office).

FLAMMARION, Charles-Henri, LèsL, LèsLet, MBA; French publishing executive; b. 27 July 1946, Boulogne-Billancourt; s. of the late Henri Flammarion and of Pierrette Chenelot; m. Marie-Françoise Mariani 1968; one s. two d.; ed Lycée de Sèvres, Sorbonne, Paris, Institut d'Etudes Politiques, Paris and Columbia Univ., USA; Asst Man., Editions Flammarion 1972–81, Gen. Man. 1981–85, Pres. Flammarion SA 1985–2003; Pres. Editions J'ai Lu 1982–2003, Audie-Fluide Glacial 1990–2003; mem. Bureau du Syndicat Nat. de l'Édition 1979–88, 1996–2003; Vice-Pres. Cercle de la Librairie 1988–94, Pres. 1994–2003; Pres. Casterman 1999–2003. *Leisure interests:* cooking, travel, skiing, walking. *Address:* 15 rue des Barres, 75004 Paris, France (home). *E-mail:* flammarionch@gmail.com (home).

FLANAGAN, Andrew Henry, CA; British media industry executive and charity executive; *CEO, National Society for the Prevention of Cruelty to Children (NSPCC);* b. 15 March 1956, Glasgow, Scotland; s. of Francis Desmond Flanagan and Martha Donaldson Flanagan; m. Virginia Walker 1972; one s. one d.; ed Univ. of Glasgow; chartered accountant with Touche Ross 1976–79, Price Waterhouse 1979–81; Financial Control Man. ITT 1981–86; Finance Dir PA Consulting Group 1986–91; Group Finance Dir and Chief Financial Officer BIS Ltd 1991–94; Finance Dir Scottish TV PLC 1994–96, Man. Dir 1996–97; Chief Exec. Scottish Media Group (later SMG PLC) 1997–2006; Dir ITV Network Ltd, Heart of Midlothian PLC, Scottish Rugby Union 2006; CEO Nat. Soc. for the Prevention of Cruelty to Children (NSPCC), London 2009–. *Leisure interests:* golf, cinema, reading, skiing.

FLANAGAN, Richard; Australian writer and film director; b. 1961, Tasmania; ed Univ. of Oxford, UK; fmr river guide; scriptwriter, journalist, novelist; Rhodes Scholar. *Film:* The Sound of One Hand Clapping (dir), Australia (co-writer). *Publications include:* non-fiction: A Terrible Beauty: A History of the Gordon River Country, Codename Iago: The Story of John Friedrich, Parish-Fed Bastards: A History of the Politics of the Unemployed in Britain 1884–1939 1994; novels: Death of a River Guide (Victorian Premier's Award for Fiction) 1995, The Sound of One Hand Clapping 1998, Gould's Book of Fish (Commonwealth Writer's Prize) 2002, The Unknown Terrorist 2007, Wanting 2008, The Narrow Road to the Deep North 2013. *Address:* c/o The Wylie Agency, 250 West 57th Street, Suite 2114, New York, NY 10107, USA (office). *Telephone:* (212) 246-0069 (office). *Fax:* (212) 586-8953 (office). *E-mail:* mail@wylieagency.com (office). *Website:* www.wylieagency.com (office).

FLANAGAN, William F., JD, DEA, LLM; Canadian professor of law; *Dean, Faculty of Law, Queen's University;* ed Univ. of Toronto, Columbia Univ., Univ. Paris I, France; began career as law clerk to Hon. Justice W. Z. Estey, Supreme Court of Canada, Ottawa 1986–87; joined Law Faculty, Queen's Univ., Kingston, Ont. 1991, Queen's Nat. Scholar 1996, becoming Prof. of Law, also Dir and Founder, Int. Law Spring Program, Queen's Univ. Int. Study Centre, Herstmonceux, UK 2001–05, Dean Faculty of Law 2005–, Co-Chair. Queen's Annual Business Law Symposium 1998–; Vice-Chair. Workplace Safety and Insurance Appeals Tribunal 1991–2003; Exec. Dir Canada AIDS Russia Project. *Publications:* several casebooks on property law, int. human rights, int. trade law and business law. *Address:* Office of the Dean, Faculty of Law, Queen's University, Kingston, ON K7L 3N6, Canada (office). *Telephone:* (613) 533-6000 (office). *Fax:* (613) 533-6509 (office). *E-mail:* w.flanagan@queensu.ca (office). *Website:* law .queensu.ca (office).

FLANDERS, Stephanie Hope, BA (Hons); British investment analyst and fmr broadcast journalist; *Chief Market Strategist for the UK and Europe, J.P. Morgan Asset Management;* b. 5 Aug. 1968; d. of the late Michael Flanders (actor and comic singer of Flanders and Swann duo) and Claudia Flanders (née Cockburn); granddaughter of Claud Cockburn; partner John Arlidge; one s. one d.; ed St Paul's Girls' School, Balliol Coll., Oxford, Harvard Univ., USA (Kennedy Scholar); began career as an economist at London Business School and Inst. for Fiscal Studies; leader writer and columnist, Financial Times 1994–97; speechwriter and adviser to US Treasury Sec. Lawrence H. Summers 1997–2001; with New York Times 2001–02; Econs Ed., BBC Newsnight 2002–08, Econs Ed., BBC 2008–13; Chief Market Strategist for the UK and Europe, J.P. Morgan Asset Management 2013–; Visiting Fellow, Nuffield Coll., Oxford 2008–; Bob Friend Memorial Lecturer, Pilkington Lecture Theatre, Univ. of Kent's Medway Campus, Chatham 2013. *Leisure interest:* cycling. *Address:* J.P. Morgan Asset Management, Finsbury Dials, 20 Finsbury Street, London, EC2Y 9AQ, England (office). *Telephone:* (20) 7742-6000 (office). *Website:* www.jpmorgan.com/pages/jpmorgan/am (office).

FLANNERY, Timothy (Tim), BSc, MSc, PhD; Australian mammalogist, palaeontologist and academic; *Professor, Macquarie University;* b. 28 Jan. 1956; ed La Trobe Univ., Monash Univ., Univ. of New South Wales; fmr Prof., Univ. of Adelaide; fmr Dir South Australian Museum, Adelaide; fmr Prin. Research Scientist, Australian Museum; fmr Chair in Australian Studies, Harvard Univ., USA; fmr adviser on environmental issues to Australian Fed. Parl.; currently mem. Climate Risk Concentration of Research Excellence and Prof., Macquarie

Univ. 2007–; Chair. Copenhagen Climate Council; mem. Wentworth Group of Concerned Scientists; surveyed mammals of Melanesia, discovered 16 new species 1990s; Greater Monkey-faced Bat (*Pteralopex flanneryi*) named after him 2005, named Australian of the Year 2007. *Publications:* Mammals of New Guinea 1990, The Future Eaters: An Ecological History of the Australasian Lands and People 1994, Mammals of the South-West Pacific & Moluccan Islands 1995, Throwim Way Leg: An Adventure 1998, The Eternal Frontier: An Ecological History of North America and Its Peoples 2001, A Gap in Nature (co-author) 2001, Astonishing Animals (co-author) 2004, Country: A Continent, a Scientist & a Kangaroo 2005, The Weather Makers: The History & Future Impact of Climate Change (Book of the Year, New South Wales Premier's Literary Awards 2006) 2006, Chasing Kangaroos: A Continent, a Scientist, and a Search for the World's Most Extraordinary Creature 2007, Now or Never: Why We Must Act Now to End Climate Change and Create a Sustainable Future 2009, Here on Earth 2010; Ed.: The Birth of Melbourne, The Birth of Sydney, The Explorers, Watkin Tench, 1788, Terra Australis – Matthew Flinders' Great Adventures in the Circumnavigation of Australia, John Morgan – The Life and Adventures of William Buckley, John Nicol – Life and Adventures: 1776–1801, Joshua Slocum – Sailing Alone Around the World; more than 90 scientific papers in professional journals. *Address:* E8B 321, Faculty of Science, Macquarie University, Sydney, NSW 2109, Australia (office). *Telephone:* (2) 9850-8418 (office). *E-mail:* tflanner@els.mq.edu.au (office); tim .flannery@mq.edu.au (office). *Website:* www.mq.edu.au (office).

FLAVELL, Richard Anthony, PhD, FRS; British professor of immunobiology; *Sterling Professor and Chairman, Department of Immunobiology, School of Medicine, Yale University;* b. 23 Aug. 1945, Chelmsford, Essex; s. of John Trevor Flavell and Iris Flavell (née Hancock); m. Madlyn Nathanson 1987; one d.; two s. from previous m.; ed Univ. of Hull, Univ. of Amsterdam and Univ. of Zurich, Wetenschappelijk Medewerker, Univ. of Amsterdam, The Netherlands; Head, Lab. of Gene Structure and Expression, Nat. Inst. for Medical Research, Mill Hill, London 1979–82; Pres. and Chief Scientific Officer, Biogen NV 1982–88; Sterling Prof. and Chair. of Immunobiology, Yale Univ. School of Medicine and Investigator, Howard Hughes Medical Inst., USA 1988–; Adjunct Prof., Scripps Research Inst., Fla 2009; mem. NAS 2002–, Inst. of Medicine 2006–, Henry Kunkel Soc. 2007, European Research Inst. for Integrated Cellular Pathology (ERI-ICP) 2009, Yale Comprehensive Cancer Center, Yale Univ. 2010; Fed. of European Biochemical Socs Anniversary Prize 1980, Colworth Medal 1980, Darwin Trust Prize 1995, Distinguished Service Award, Miami Nature Biotechnology Winter Symposia 2001, Rabbi Shai Shacknai Memorial Prize and Lectureship in Immunology and Cancer Research 2008, AAI-Invitrogen Meritorious Career Award 2008, Andrew Lazarovitz Award, Canadian Soc. of Transplantation, Quebec 2011, Cell Signaling Networks in Merida, Yucatan, Mexico 2011, Gold Medal and Certificate of Honour for "outstanding contributions to understanding of the immune system using reverse genetics in the mouse" 2011. *Publications:* approx. 650 scientific articles. *Leisure interests:* music, tennis, horticulture. *Address:* Department of Immunobiology, Yale University School of Medicine, TAC S-569, PO Box 208011, New Haven, CT 06520-8011, USA (office). *Telephone:* (203) 737-2216 (office). *Fax:* (203) 737-2958 (office). *E-mail:* richard.flavell@yale.edu (office). *Website:* medicine.yale .edu (office).

FLAY, Jennifer; New Zealand/French gallery director; *Director, Foire Internationale d'Art Contemporain (FIAC);* b. New Zealand; studied art history; worked in several contemporary art galleries, including with Catherine Issert at St-Paul-de-Vence 1982–91, then with Daniel Templon and Ghislaine Hussenot in Paris; operated own Paris gallery, Galerie Jennifer Flay 1991–2003; among the first to exhibit the work of Felix Gonzalez-Torres, Andrea Zittel, John Currin, Karen Kilimnik, Dominque Gonzalez-Foerster and Claude Closky; one of pioneer dealers to move to rue Louise-Weiss art dist, 13th arrondissement, now home to several leading art galleries; scholar of contemporary art and author of several publs and numerous articles on art history; Artistic Dir Foire Internationale d'Art Contemporain (FIAC—Int. Contemporary Art Fair), Paris 2004–; Dir 2010–; mem. jury, FILAF 2013; Officier des Arts et des Lettres. *Address:* Reed Expositions France, 52/54 quai de Dion-Bouton – CS 80001, 92806 Puteaux Cedex, France (office). *Telephone:* 1-47-56-64-20 (office). *Fax:* 1-47-56-64-29 (office). *E-mail:* jennifer.flay@reedexpo.fr (office); info@fiac.com (office). *Website:* www.fiac.com (office).

FLEISCHER, Ari; American public relations consultant and fmr government official; b. 13 Oct. 1960; m. Becki Davis 2002; two c.; ed Middlebury Coll.; Press Sec. for Senator Pete Domenici 1989–94; Deputy Communications Dir for Pres. George H. W. Bush's 1992 re-election campaign; fmr Communications Dir for Elizabeth Dole; White House Press Sec. for Pres. George W. Bush 2001–03; f. Ari Fleischer Sports Communications LLC 2008; sports marketing consultant with IMG 2004–; Spokesman Don't Take My Bat Away coalition; consultant for US Olympic Cttee 2009–. *Publications:* Taking Heat: The President, the Press and My Years in the White House 2005. *Address:* Ari Fleischer Sports Communications LLC, 767 Fifth Avenue, 44th Floor, New York, NY 10153, USA (office). *Telephone:* (212) 255-3000 (office). *Fax:* (646) 688-1607 (office). *E-mail:* info@fleischersports.com (office). *Website:* www.fleischersports.com (office).

FLEISCHMANN, Peter; German film director and producer; b. 26 July 1937, Zweibrücken; s. of Alexander Fleischmann and Pascal Fleischmann; two c.; ed Inst. de Hautes Etudes Cinématographiques, Paris; fmrly asst to dir of short feature films, documentaries and animations; Co-founder Hallelujah Film with Volker Schlondorff; now produces and directs feature and documentary films; consultant to Studio Babelsberg; Pres. Fédération Européene des Réalisateurs Audiovisuels; Chair. European Audiovisual Centre, Babelsberg; mem. EC Expert Council for reform of audiovisual politics. *Films include:* Alexander und das Auto ohne linken Scheinwerfer 1965 (animation), Herbst der Gammler 1967 (documentary), Jagdszenen aus Niederbayern (feature) 1968, Der Dritte Grad 1971 (feature), Hamburger Krankheit 1979 (feature), Frevel 1983 (feature), Al Capone von der Pfalz 1984 (documentary), Es ist nicht leicht ein Gott zu sein 1988 (feature), Deutschland, Deutschland 1991 (documentary), Mein Onkel, der Winzer 1993 (documentary), Mein Freund, der Mörder 2006. *Address:* Europäisches Filmzentrum Babelsberg, August-Bebel-Strasse 26-53, 14482 Potsdam, Germany. *Telephone:* (331) 7062700 (office). *Fax:* (331) 7062710 (office).

FLEMING, Graham Richard, PhD, FRS; British chemist and academic; *Professor of Chemistry, University of California, Berkeley;* b. 3 Dec. 1949, Barrow; s. of Maurice N. H. Fleming and Lovima E. Winter; m. Jean McKenzie 1977; one s.; ed Univs of London and Bristol; Research Fellow, Calif. Inst. of Tech., USA 1974–75; Univ. Research Fellow, Univ. of Melbourne, Australia 1975, ARGC (Australian Research Grants Cttee) Research Asst 1976; Leverhulme Fellow, Royal Inst. 1977–79; Asst Prof., Univ. of Chicago, USA 1979–83, Assoc. Prof. 1983–85, Prof. 1985–87, Arthur Holly Compton Distinguished Service Prof. 1987–97; Prof. of Chem., Univ. of Calif., Berkeley 1997–, Melvin Calvin Distinguished Prof. of Chem. 2002–, Dir Physical Biosciences Div., Lawrence Berkeley Nat. Lab. 1997–2004, Assoc. Lab. Dir for Physical Sciences, Deputy Lab. Dir 2004–07; Dir Calif. Inst. for Quantitative Biosciences Research 2001; Fellow, American Acad. of Arts and Sciences; A. P. Sloan Foundation Fellow, Guggenheim Fellowship; mem. NAS; Marlow Medal, Royal Soc. of Chem., Coblentz Award, Tilden Medal, ACS Nobel Laureate Signature Award for Grad. Educ. in Chem., ACS Peter Debye Award in Physical Chem., ACS Harrison Howe Award, Earle K. Pyler Prize, American Physical Soc. *Leisure interest:* climbing mountains. *Address:* Department of Chemistry, 221 Hildebrand, University of California, Berkeley, CA 94720, USA (office). *Telephone:* (510) 643-2735 (office). *Fax:* (510) 642-6340 (office). *E-mail:* fleming@cchem.berkeley.edu (office). *Website:* chemistry.berkeley.edu/ index.shtml (office).

FLEMING, Osbourne Berrington; Anguillan/British politician and business executive; b. 18 Feb. 1940, East End; ed Valley Secondary School; Customs Officer, Saint Kitts 1959–64; lived in St Thomas, US Virgin Islands 1964–68, Saint Kitts 1968–81; f. Fleming's Transport (transport and shipping co.), St Croix 1974; MP (People's Progressive Party), Minister of Tourism, Agric. and Fisheries 1981–85; MP (Anguilla Nat. Alliance—ANA), Minister of Finance 1985–89; ind. MP, Minister of Finance and Econ. Devt 1989–94; rejoined ANA, apptd Leader Opposition in House of Ass. 1994–2000; mem. ANA/Anguilla Democratic Party United Front; Chief Minister 2000–10, also Minister of Minister of Home Affairs, Tourism, Agric., Fisheries and Environment 2000–08, of Home Affairs, Natural Resources, Lands and Physical Planning 2008–10 (retd). *Leisure interests:* playing draughts, dominoes and cards. *Address:* Sea Feathers, East End, Anguilla (home). *Telephone:* 497-4783 (home).

FLEMING, Renée, MMus; American singer (soprano); b. 14 Feb. 1959, Indiana, PA; d. of Edwin Davis Fleming and Patricia (Seymour) Alexander; m. Richard Lee Ross 1989 (divorced 2000); two d.; ed Potsdam State Univ., Eastman School of Music of Univ. of Rochester, Juilliard School American Opera Center; debuts Houston Grand Opera in Marriage of Figaro 1988, Spoleto Festival, Charleston and Italy 1987–90, New York City Opera in La Bohème 1989, San Francisco Opera, Metropolitan Opera, Paris Opera at Bastille, Teatro Colón, Buenos Aires all in Marriage of Figaro 1991, Glyndebourne in Così fan tutte 1992, La Scala Milan in Don Giovanni 1993, Vienna State Opera in Marriage of Figaro 1993, Lyric Opera of Chicago in Susannah 1993, San Diego Opera in Eugene Onegin 1994, Paris Opera 1996, Massenet's Thaïs at Nice and Gounod's Marguerite at the Met 1997, Floyd's Susannah at the Met 1999, Louise at Barbican Hall, London and the Marschallin at Covent Garden 2000; premiered Previn's A Streetcar Named Desire 1998; recital tour with Jean-Yves Thibaudet 2001–02; London Proms 2002, Dvořák's Rusalka in concert at Covent Garden 2003, Bellini's Il Pirata at the Met 2003; Fulbright Scholar to Germany 1984–85; Hon. mem. RAM 2003; Chevalier, Légion d'honneur 2005; Hon. doctorate Juilliard School, New York 2003; Fulbright Scholar 1984–85, George London Prize 1988, Richard Tucker Award 1990, Solti Prize, Acad. du Disque Lyrique 1996, Prix Maria Callas Acad. du Disque Lyrique 1997, 2004, Musical America Vocalist of the Year 1997, Prize Acad. du Disque Lyrique 1998, Grammy Awards 1999, 2002, 2010, creation of the dessert 'La Diva Renée' by Master Chef Daniel Boulud 1999, Classical BRIT Awards for Top-selling Female Artist 2003, for Outstanding Contribution to Music 2004, LOTOS Medal of Merit 2005, Polar Music Prize 2008, Opera News Award 2008, Nat. Medal of Arts 2012. *Recordings include:* Sacred Songs 2005, R. Strauss's Daphne (with Cologne Radio Chorus and Symphony Orchestra) 2005, Love Sublime (with Brad Mehldau) 2006, Homage: The Age of the Diva 2006, Four Last Songs 2008, Verismo Arias 2009, Dark Hope 2010, Ravel/Messiaen, Dutilleux: Poèmes (ECHO Klassik Award for Female Singer of the Year) (Grammy Award for Best Classical Vocal Solo 2013) 2012. *Publication:* The Inner Voice: The Making of a Singer (autobiog.) 2005. *Address:* c/o Alec C. Treuhaft, IMG Artists, Carnegie Hall Tower, 152 West 57th Street, 5th Floor, New York, NY 10019, USA (office). *Telephone:* (212) 994-3500 (office). *Fax:* (212) 994-3550 (office). *E-mail:* atreuhaft@imgartists.com (office). *Website:* www.imgartists.com (office); www.renee-fleming.com.

FLEMING, Stephen Paul; New Zealand professional cricketer; b. 1 April 1973, Christchurch, Canterbury; s. of Pauline Fleming; m. Kelly Payne 2007; one s. one d.; ed Waltham Primary School, Cashmere High School, Christchurch Teachers' Coll.; left-handed batsmen; teams: Canterbury 1991–2000, New Zealand 1994–2008 (Capt. 1997–2007), Wellington 2000–, Middx 2001, Yorks. 2003, Notts. 2005–07 (Capt.), Chennai Super Kings 2008; First-class debut: 1991/92; Test debut: NZ v India, Hamilton 19–23 March 1994; ODI debut: NZ v India, Napier 25 March 1994; T20I debut: NZ v Australia, Auckland 17 Feb. 2005; played in 111 tests, scored 7,172 runs (average 40.06, highest score 274 not out against Sri Lanka 2003) with nine hundreds; ODIs: 280 matches, scored 8,037 runs (average 32.40, highest score 134 not out) with eight hundreds; scored 16,409 first-class runs (average 43.87) with 35 hundreds; youngest Capt. in NZ history; NZ's highest run-scorer in ODIs; holds NZ record for number of Test caps, Test runs and Test catches; retired from int. cricket 26 March 2008. *Publication:* Cricketing Safari (with Nathan Astle) 2000. *Leisure interests:* golf, computer games, reading. *Address:* c/o Cricket Wellington, The Brierley Pavilion, Allied Nationwide Finance Basin Reserve, Rugby Street, PO 578, Wellington, New Zealand. *Telephone:* (4) 384-3171. *Fax:* (4) 384-3498. *E-mail:* cricket@firebirds.co.nz. *Website:* www .cricketwellington.co.nz.

FLETCHER, Ernest (Ernie) Lee, BS, MD; American physician and fmr politician; b. 12 Nov. 1952, Mount Sterling, Ky; m. Glenna Foster; one s. one d.; ed Univ. of Kentucky Coll. of Eng and Coll. of Medicine; served in USAF as F-4E Aircraft Commdr and N American Aerospace Defense Command (NORAD) Alert Force Commdr 1980s; physician in family practice 1983–95; CEO St Joseph Medical Foundation 1997–99; mem. Ky State Legislature for 78th Congressional

Dist 1995–99, mem. Ky Comm. on Poverty, Task Force on Higher Educ.; mem. US House of Reps from 6th Congressional Dist 1999–2003, mem. House Cttee on Energy and Commerce, Chair. Policy Sub-Cttee on Health; Gov. of Kentucky 2003–07; Founder and CEO Alton Healthcare LLC, Cincinnati 2008–; fmr Chair. Southern States Energy Bd; mem. Bd of Dirs Achieve, Inc.; Republican. *Address:* Alton Healthcare LLC, 1065 Jodeco Road, Stockbridge, GA 30281, USA (office). *Telephone:* (513) 530-0340 (office). *Fax:* (513) 530-0160 (office). *Website:* www .altonhealthcare.com (office).

FLETCHER, Hugh Alasdair, BSc, MCom (Hons), MBA; New Zealand company director and fmr university administrator; *Chairman, Fletcher Brothers Ltd;* b. 28 Nov. 1947, Auckland; s. of Sir James Muir Cameron Fletcher and Margery V. Fletcher (née Gunthorp); m. Rt Hon. Dame Sian Seerpoohi Elias (Chief Justice of New Zealand) 1970; two s.; ed Auckland Univ. and Stanford Univ.; CEO Fletcher Holdings Ltd 1980, Man. Dir Fletcher Challenge Ltd 1981, CEO 1987–97, Dir Fletcher Building 2002–12, now Chair. Fletcher Brothers Ltd; Chair. Air NZ 1985–89; mem. Prime Minister's Enterprise Council 1992–98, Asia-Pacific Advisory Cttee, New York Stock Exchange 1995–2004; Chancellor Univ. of Auckland 2004–08; Chair. Ministerial Inquiry into Telecommunications 2000–01; mem. Council, Univ. of Auckland 1999–2011; mem. Bd of Dirs Rubicon 2002–, IAG New Zealand 2003–, Reserve Bank of New Zealand 2003–12, Vector 2007–, IAG 2008–, Dilworth Trust 2008–, L.E.K. Australasian Advisory Bd 2010–13; Harkness Fellowship 1970–72; Hon. LLD (Auckland) 2011; Distinguished Alumni Award, Univ. of Auckland 1996. *Leisure interests:* horse riding, hunting, breeding, racing. *Address:* PO Box 11468, Ellerslie, Auckland 1542, New Zealand (office). *Telephone:* (2) 1369016 (office); (9) 579-4226 (office); 21-369016 (mobile) (office). *E-mail:* hugh .fletcher@xtra.co.nz (office).

FLETCHER, John E.; Australian retail executive; b. 1952, Melbourne, Vic.; m. Nola Fletcher; three c.; accounting, operating and sr man. positions, Brambles Industries 1974–82, Gen. Man. Transport Div. 1982–84, Commercial Dir, Europe 1984–86, Man. Dir CHEP Australia 1986–88, Man. Dir Brambles Australia 1988–93, CEO Brambles Industries 1993–2001; CEO and Man. Dir Coles Myer Ltd (renamed Coles Group Ltd 2006) 2001–07; mem. Bd of Dirs Telstra Corpn 2001–06. *Leisure interests:* golf, tennis, skiing. *Address:* c/o Coles, 800 Toorak Road, Tooronga, Vic. 3146, Australia. *Telephone:* (3) 9829-5111.

FLETCHER, Neville Horner, AM, PhD, DSc, FAA, FTSE, FInstP, FAIP, FASA; Australian physicist and academic; *Visiting Fellow, Research School of Physics and Engineering, Australian National University;* b. 14 July 1930, Armidale, NSW; s. of Alleine Horner Fletcher and Florence Mabel Glass; m. Eunice M. Schiffer 1953; one s. two d.; ed Armidale High School, New England Univ. Coll., Univ. of Sydney, Harvard Univ.; part-time Research Engineer, Clevite Transistor Products, USA 1953–55; Researcher, CSIRO Radiophysics Lab. 1956–59; mem. staff, Univ. of New England, Australia 1960–83, Sr Lecturer in Physics 1960–63, Prof. of Physics (personal chair) 1963–83, Dean, Faculty of Science 1963–65, mem. Univ. Council 1968–72, Chair. Professorial Bd 1970–72, Pro Vice-Chancellor 1969–72, Prof. Emer. 1983–; Dir CSIRO Inst. of Physical Sciences 1983–88; Chief Research Scientist 1988–95; Adjunct Prof., ANU 1990–95, Visiting Fellow, Research School of Physics and Eng 1995–; Adjunct Prof., Univ. of NSW 1997–; Chair. Australian Antarctic Science Advisory Cttee 1990–96; mem. Australian Research Grants Cttee 1974–78, 1995–98; Sec. for Physical Sciences, Australian Acad. of Science 1980–84; mem. Govt Meteorology Policy Cttee 1981–84, Int. Comm. on Acoustics 1985–90; Fellow, Australian Acad. of Science 1976, Australian Acad. of Technological Sciences and Eng 1987, Australian Inst. of Physics (Pres. 1981–83), Australian Acoustical Soc., Acoustical Soc. of America; Univ. Medal, Univ. of Sydney 1951, Frank Knox Fellowship, Harvard Univ., USA 1952, Edgeworth David Medal, Royal Soc. of NSW 1963, Lyle Medal, Australian Acad. of Science 1993, Distinguished Alumni Award, Univ. of New England 1994, Silver Medal in Musical Acoustics, Acoustical Soc. of America 1998, Centenary Medal, Australia 2003. *Music includes:* played the organ at Armidale Methodist Church for 25 years and occasionally in other churches (though an atheist); played flute in Harvard-Radcliffe Orchestra and Sydney Univ. Orchestra; plays bassoon in Brindabella Orchestra, Canberra. *Publications includes:* The Physics of Rainclouds 1962, The Chemical Physics of Ice 1970, Physics and Music 1976, The Physics of Musical Instruments (with T. D. Rossing) 1990 (revised edn 1998), Acoustic Systems in Biology 1992, Principles of Vibration and Sound (with T. D. Rossing) 1995 (revised edn 2004), An Informal History of Physics at the University of New England 1938–2001 (with C. A. Sholl) 2002, Brief Candles (short stories) 2007, Philosophical Ramblings 2010; more than 200 papers in scientific journals. *Leisure interests:* music (flute, bassoon and organ, plays flute or bassoon in amateur orchestras), writing stories and books, held private pilot's aircraft licence for five years until heart attack in 1977. *Telephone:* (2) 6125-4406 (office); (2) 6169-3508 (home). *Fax:* (2) 6215-0511 (office). *E-mail:* neville.fletcher@anu.edu.au (office). *Website:* physics .anu.edu.au/eme/people/profile.php?ID=113 (office); www.phys.unsw.edu.au/ music/people/fletcher.html (office); www.science.org.au/scientists/interviews/f/nf .html (office).

FLETCHER, Philip John, CBE, MA; British public servant; *Chairman, Water Services Regulation Authority (Ofwat);* b. 2 May 1946, London; s. of the late Alan Philip Fletcher and Annette Grace Fletcher (née Wright); m. Margaret Anne Boys; two d. (one deceased); ed Marlborough Coll., Trinity Coll., Oxford; joined Civil Service 1968, Under-Sec. of Housing, Water and Cen. Finance, Dept of the Environment 1986–90; Planning and Devt Control 1990–93; Chief Exec. PSA Services 1993–94; Deputy Sec. Cities and Countryside Group 1994–95; Receiver for the Metropolitan Police Dist 1996–2000; Dir-Gen. of Water Services 2000–06, Chair. Water Services Regulation Authority (Ofwat) 2006–; Reader, Church of England; mem. Archbishops' Council for the Church of England; Dir (non-exec.) Ofqual Bd. *Leisure interest:* walking. *Address:* Ofwat, Centre City Tower, 7 Hill Street, Birmingham, B5 4UA, England (office). *Telephone:* (121) 644-7500 (office). *Fax:* (121) 644-7548 (office). *E-mail:* philip.fletcher@ofwat.gsi.gov.uk (office). *Website:* www.ofwat.gov.uk (office).

FLEURY, Gen. (retd) Jean André; French air force officer (retd) and aeronautics industry executive; b. 1 Dec. 1934, Brest; s. of René Fleury and Blanche-Marie Marsille; m. Madeleine Fleury; Commdt, Saint Dizier Air Base 1977–78; Head, Office of Supply, Air Force Gen. Staff 1978–81; Deputy Chief of Planning, Armed Forces Gen. Staff 1983–85; Commdt, Strategic Air Forces

1985–87; Chief of Staff to Pres. of Repub. 1987–89; Chief of Staff of Air Force 1989–91; mem. Supreme Council of Army and Air Forces 1989; Pres. Aéroports de Paris 1992–99; Chair. Airports Council Int. 1998–99; aeronautics consultant 2000–09; mem. Econ. and Social Regional Council of Britanny 2001–07; Grand Croix, Légion d'honneur, Commdr, Ordre nat. du Mérite, Croix de la Valeur militaire, Commdr, Legion of Merit (USA). *Publication:* Faire face: Memoires d'un chef d'état major 1996, Le Général qui pensait comme un civil 2004, Le mystère de la Chesnaie 2007, Les guerres du Golfe 2009, Le bourbier afghan 2011, Crise libyenne: la nouvelle donne géopolitique 2012, La France en guerre au Mali 2013. *Address:* Les Mirages, La Combe de Haut, 56140 Pleucadeuc, France (office). *Telephone:* (2) 97-26-96-85 (office). *E-mail:* fleurygeneral@wanadoo.fr (office).

FLIER, Jeffrey S., BS, MD; American endocrinologist and academic; *Dean, Faculty of Medicine, Harvard University;* b. 1948, New York; m. Dr Eleftheria Maratos-Flier; two c.; ed City Coll. of New York, Mount Sinai School of Medicine; intern, Mount Sinai Hosp., New York 1972–73, residency training in internal medicine 1973–74; Clinical Assoc., NIH, Bethesda, Md 1974–78; Asst Prof. of Medicine, Harvard Medical School 1978–82, Assoc. Prof. 1982–93, Prof. 1993–, George C. Reisman Prof. of Medicine 1999–, Chief of Endocrine Div. 1990, Chief Academic Officer, Beth Israel Deaconess Medical Center (BIDMC) 2002–07, also Carolyn Shields Walker Prof. of Medicine, Harvard Medical School, Dean, Faculty of Medicine 2007–; Chief of Diabetes Unit, Beth Israel Deaconess Medical Center 1998–2002; Visiting Scientist, Whitehead Inst., MIT 1985–86; Fellow, American Acad. of Arts and Sciences; mem. AAAS, NAS Inst. of Medicine (Pres. 2001); Hon. MD (Univ. of Athens) 1997; American Diabetes Assen Eli Lilly Award, American Physiological Soc. Berson Lecture, American Diabetes Assen Banting Medal 2005. *Publications:* over 200 scholarly papers and reviews. *Address:* Office of the Dean, Harvard Medical School, Gordon Hall, 25 Shattuck Street, Boston, MA 02115, USA (office). *Telephone:* (617) 432-1000 (office). *E-mail:* jflier@bidmc.harvard.edu (office). *Website:* hms.harvard.edu/hms (office).

FLIGHT, Baron (Life Peer), cr. 2011, of Worcester in the County of Worcestershire; **Howard Emerson Flight,** MA (Cantab.), MBA, FRSA; British politician and investment manager; b. 16 June 1948; m. Christabel Flight 1973; one s. three d.; ed Brentwood School, Magdalene Coll., Cambridge, Univ. of Michigan Ross School of Business, USA; worked as investment adviser and dir 1970–98; Jt Man. Dir Guinness Flight 1986–98 (acquired by Investec); MP (Conservative) for Arundel and South Downs 1997–2005; Shadow Econ. Sec. to the Treasury 1999–2001, Shadow Paymaster Gen. 2001–02, Shadow Chief Sec. to the Treasury 2002–04; Deputy Chair. Conservative Party 2004–05 (resgnd); mem. (Conservative) House of Lords 2011–; Chair. CIM Investment Management Ltd 2006, Downing Structured Opportunities VCT 1 PLC 2009, Aurora Investment Trust plc 2011, EIS Assen; Chair. Flight and Partners 2007–; mem. Bd of Dirs Investec Asset Management Ltd 1998, Marechale Capital 2006, Edge Performance VCT plc 2011; Sr Dir (non-exec.) Metrobank plc 2010; Commr Guernsey Financial Services Comm.; consultant, TISA (previously PIMA), Kinetic Partners; mem. Advisory Bd, Financial Services Forum; Gov., Brentwood School, Essex; Chair. Croome Court Nat. Trust Appeal Cttee; Vice-Pres. and Trustee, Elgar Foundation; Liveryman of the Carpenters' Co. *Publications:* All You Need to Know about Exchange Rates 1988, The City in Europe and the World 2005 (contrib.). *Leisure interests:* classical music/opera, skiing, gardening, India. *Address:* House of Lords, Westminster, London, SW1A 0PW, England (office). *Telephone:* (20) 7222-7559 (office). *Fax:* (20) 7976-7059 (office). *E-mail:* hflight@btinternet.com (office); flighth@parliament.uk (office). *Website:* www.howardflight.com.

FLIMM, Jürgen; German theatre director; *Artistic Director, Salzburg Festspiele;* b. 17 July 1941, Giessen; s. of Werner Flimm and Ellen Flimm; m. Susanne Ottersbach 1990; early work at the Munich Kammerspiele; Dir Nationaltheater, Mannheim 1972–73; Prin. of the Thalia Theater, Hamburg 1973–74; directed plays in Munich, Hamburg, Bochum, Frankfurt 1974–79 and in Zürich, Amsterdam, Salzburg, Vienna, Milan; Dir Cologne Theatre 1979–85, Thalia Theatre, Hamburg 1985–2000, Salome at the Met, New York 2004, Monteverdi's Poppea at Zürich Opera 2005; Pres. German Bühnenverein 1999–2003; Acting Dir Salzburg Festspiele 2001–06, Artistic Dir 2006–; Artistic Dir Festival Ruhrtriennale 2005–07; Gen. Man. Deutsche Staatsoper Unter den Linden, Berlin 2010–; Dr hc (Hildesheim) 2002; Bundesverdienstkreuz 1992, Konrad-Wolf-Preis, Berlin 1995. *Films:* Wer zu spät kommt – die letzten Tage des Politbüros 1990, Käthchens Traum 2004. *Publications:* Theatergänger 2004. *Address:* Salzburger Festspiele, Hofstallgasse 1, 5020 Salzburg, Austria (office). *Telephone:* (662) 8045-200 (office). *Fax:* (662) 8045-720 (office). *E-mail:* j.flimm@salzburgfestival.at (office). *Website:* www.salzburgfestival.at (office).

FLINT, Doug J., CBE; British business executive; *Group Chairman, HSBC Holdings;* fmr Partner, KPMG; joined HSBC as Exec. Dir 1995, Chief Financial Officer and Exec. Dir, Risk and Regulation Feb.–Dec. 2010, Group Chair. HSBC Holdings 2010–; Chair. Financial Reporting Council's review of the Turnbull Guidance on Internal Control 2004; Co-Chair. Counterparty Risk Man. Policy Group III 2008; mem. Standards Advisory Council of Int. Accounting Standards Bd 2001–04; fmr mem. Accounting Standards Bd, Large Business Forum on Tax and Competitiveness, Consultative Cttee of the Large Business Advisory Bd of HM Revenue and Customs; Dir (non-exec.) BP plc 2005–11; Dir, The Hong Kong Assen 2011–; Chair. (fmrly Vice-Chair. and Chair. Desig.) Inst. of Int. Finance 2012–; mem. Inst. of Chartered Accountants of Scotland, Assen of Corp. Treasurers; Fellow, Chartered Inst. of Man. Accountants. *Address:* HSBC Holdings, 8 Canada Square, London, E14 5HQ, England (office). *Telephone:* (20) 7991-8888 (office). *Fax:* (20) 7992-4880 (office). *E-mail:* pressoffice@hsbc.com (office). *Website:* www .hsbc.com (office).

FLINTOFF, Andrew (Freddie), MBE; British fmr professional cricketer; b. 6 Dec. 1977, Preston, Lancs.; s. of Colin Flintoff; m. Rachel Wools 2005; two s. one d.; ed Ribbleton Hall High School; all-rounder; right-hand batsman; right-arm fast bowler; played for Lancs. 1995–2010, England 1998–2009 (Capt. 2006, 2006–07), Int. Cricket Council (ICC) World XI 2006, Chennai Super Kings 2009; First-class debut: 1995; Test debut: England v S Africa, Nottingham 23–27 July 1998; One-Day Int. (ODI) debut: England v Pakistan, Sharjah 7 April 1999; T20I debut: England v Australia, Southampton 13 June 2005; has played in 79 Tests, taken 226 wickets and scored 3,845 runs (five centuries), highest score 167, average 31.77, best bowling (innings) 5/58, (match) 8/156; ODIs: 141 matches, scored 3,394 runs, average 32.01, highest score 123, took 169 wickets, average 24.38, best bowling 5/19; First-class: 183 matches, 9,027 runs, average 33.80, highest score 167, took 350 wickets, average 31.59, best bowling 5/24; retd from Test cricket at conclusion of Ashes series 2009; announced retirement from all cricket 16 Sept. 2010; holds the record for the most sixes (68) scored for England 2006; only the seventh player to have batted on all five days of a Test match 2006; Freedom of the City of Preston 2006; NBC Denis Compton Award 1997, Cricket Writers' Club Young Cricketer of the Year 1998, Walter Lawrence Trophy 1999, Wisden Cricketer of the Year 2004, Wisden Leading Cricketer in the World 2005, ICC One-Day Player of the Year 2004, PCA Player of the Year 2004, 2005, ICC World One-Day XI 2004, 2005, 2006, BBC Sports Personality of the Year (Third Place) 2004, Beard of the Year Award, Beard Liberation Front 2004 (jt winner) 2005, ICC Player of the Year 2005, Compton-Miller Medal 2005, Sir Garfield Sobers Trophy 2005, BBC Sports Personality of the Year 2005, MCC Spirit of Cricket Award 2005, ICC World Test XI 2006. *Television:* team capt., A League of Their Own (Sky1) 2010, guest commentator, PDC World Darts Championship 2010, Freddie Flintoff versus The World (ITV 4) 2011. *Publications:* Being Freddie, Freddie, Andrew Flintoff – My Life in Pictures, Ashes to Ashes 2009. *Leisure interests:* rugby (both codes), Manchester City Football Club. *Address:* c/o Lancashire County Cricket Club, Old Trafford Cricket Ground, Talbot Road, Manchester, M16 0PX, England. *Telephone:* (161) 282-4000. *Fax:* (161) 282-4151. *E-mail:* info@lccc.co.uk. *Website:* www.lccc.co.uk.

FLOCKHART, Calista; American actress; b. 11 Nov. 1964, Freeport, Ill.; d. of Ronald Flockhart and Kay Flockhart; m. Harrison Ford; one adopted s. *Films include:* Naked in New York 1993, Quiz Show 1994, Getting In 1994, Pictures of Baby Jane Doe 1995, Drunks 1995, The Birdcage 1996, Telling Lies in America 1997, Milk and Money 1997, A Midsummer Night's Dream 1999, Like a Hole in the Head 1999, Bash 2000, Things You Can Tell Just By Looking At Her 2000, The Last Shot 2004, Fragile 2005. *Plays on Broadway include:* The Glass Menagerie, The Three Sisters. *Television work includes:* The Guiding Light 1978, Darrow 1991, An American Story 1991, Life Stories: Families in Crisis 1992, Ally McBeal (Best Actress Award, Golden Globes 1998) 1997–2002, Bash: Latter-Day Plays 2000, Brothers and Sisters (series) 2006–11. *Address:* c/o Bill Butler, The Gersh Agency, 9465 Wilshere Blvd, 6th Floor, Beverly Hills, CA 90212, USA (office).

FLOOD, Philip James, AO, BEc (Hons); Australian diplomatist; b. 2 July 1935, Sydney, NSW; s. of Thomas C. Flood and Maxine S. Flood; m. 2nd Carole Henderson 1990; two s. one d. from previous m.; ed North Sydney Boys High School, Univ. of Sydney; mem. Mission to EEC and Embassy, Brussels 1959–62, Rep. to OECD Devt Assistance Cttee, Paris 1966–69, Asst Sec., Dept of Foreign Affairs 1971–73, High Commr to Bangladesh 1974–76, Minister, Embassy, Washington, DC 1976–77, CEO Dept Special Trade Representations 1977–80; First Asst Sec., Dept of Trade 1980–84, Deputy Sec., Dept of Foreign Affairs and Trade 1985–89, Amb. to Indonesia 1989–93, Dir-Gen. Australian Int. Devt Assistance Bureau (AusAID) 1993–95, Dir-Gen. Office of Nat. Assessments 1995–96, Sec., Dept of Foreign Affairs and Trade 1996–98; High Commr to UK 1998–2000; Head of Inquiry into Immigration Detention 2000–01; Chair. Australia-Indonesia Inst. 2001–04; Head of Inquiry into Australian Intelligence Agencies 2004; Chair., Inquiry into Plasma Fractionation 2006; Advisor, Nat. Human Rights Consultation 2009; mem. Bd Asialink 2004–09, CARE Australia 2003–11; Fellow, Royal Australian Inst. Public Admin.; Bintang Jasa Utama (Indonesian Order of Merit) 1993, Centenary Medal 2003. *Publications:* Odyssey by the Sea 2005, Dancing with Warriors – A Diplomatic Memoir 2011. *Leisure interests:* reading, music, walking, swimming.

FLOR, Claus Peter; German conductor; *Music Director, Malaysian Philharmonic Orchestra;* b. 16 March 1953, Leipzig; adopted s. of Richard Flor and Sigrid Langer; ed Music School, Weimar and High School of Music, Weimar/Leipzig; studied under Rolf Reuter, Rafael Kubelik and Kurt Sanderling; learnt violin and clarinet before commencing conducting studies; Chief Conductor, Music Dir Berliner Sinfonie Orchester 1984–92; Artistic Adviser, Zürich Tonhalle Orchestra 1991–96; Prin. Guest Conductor, Philharmonia Orchestra, London 1991–94, Dallas Symphony Orchestra 1999–2008, Orchestra Sinfonica di Milano Giuseppe Verdi 2003–08; Music Dir, Malaysian Philharmonic Orchestra 2008–; debut with Los Angeles Philharmonic 1985; debut with Berlin Philharmonic 1988; regular appearances with Vienna Symphony, Orchestre de Paris, Royal Concertgebouw, Rotterdam Philharmonic and major German orchestras; frequent guest engagements with leading orchestras in UK, USA, Canada etc.; conductor of opera at many German opera houses including Berlin Staatsoper and Deutsche Oper, Berlin. *Recordings include:* Mendelssohn, Cherubini, Dvořák, Mozart, Shostakovich. *Leisure interests:* collecting red wines, history and genealogy of European nobility. *Address:* c/o IMG Artists, The Light Box, 111 Power Road, London, W4 5PY, England (office). *Telephone:* (20) 7957-5800 (office). *Fax:* (20) 7957-5801 (office). *E-mail:* pmartin@imgartists.com (office). *Website:* www.imgartists.com (office).

FLORES ALEMÁN, (José) Armando; Salvadorean politician; *Minister of the Economy;* ed Universidad de El Salvador; Coordinator, Dept of Educ., Consumer Fed. of Cooperatives of El Salvador 1989–90; Co-founder Centro para la Defensa del Consumidor (Centre for Consumer Protection), Deputy Dir 1991–95, Exec. Dir 1997; Coordinator, Consumers Int. in Central America 1996; fmr Deputy Minister of Trade and Industry, Minister of the Economy 2012–. *Address:* Ministry of the Economy, Edif. C1–C2, Centro de Gobierno, Alameda Juan Pablo II y Calle Guadalupe, San Salvador, El Salvador (office). *Telephone:* 2231-5600 (office). *Fax:* 2221-5446 (office). *E-mail:* info@minec.gob.sv (office). *Website:* www.minec.gob.sv (office).

FLORES BERMÚDEZ, Roberto, LLB; Honduran politician and diplomatist; b. 15 Aug. 1949; m. Laura Flores; two c.; ed Univ. of Honduras; Dir-Gen. Diplomatic Protocol, Ministry of Foreign Affairs 1984–86, Dir-Gen. Foreign Politics 1986–87, Head of Cabinet 1988–89, Dir-Gen. Int. Orgs 1990, Amb. and Perm. Rep. to UN, New York 1990–92, Amb. to USA 1994–98, 2006–09, to UK 1998–99, Minister of Foreign Affairs 2000–06, 2009–10; fmr mem. Honduran Del. to Cen. American Parl.; fmr Head of Tech. Del., Cen. American Peace Negotiation Process. *Address:* c/o Ministry of Foreign Affairs, Centro Cívico Gubernamental, Antigua Casa Presidencial, Blvd Kuwait, Contiguo a la Corte Suprema de Justicia, Tegucigalpa,

Honduras. *Telephone:* 234-1962. *Fax:* 234-1484. *E-mail:* consultas.sre@gmail.com. *Website:* www.sre.hn.

FLORES FACUSSÉ, Carlos Roberto, BEng, MIntEcon, PhD; Honduran fmr head of state; b. 1 March 1950, Tegucigalpa; s. of Oscar A. Flores and Margarita Facussé de Flores; m. Mary Carol Flake; one s. one d.; ed American School, Tegucigalpa and Louisiana State Univ.; Rep. for Francisco Morazan to Liberal Convention, Pres. Departmental Liberal Council, Francisco Morazan; Finance Sec. Nat. Directorate Movimiento Liberal Rodista; Congressman Nat. Ass. for Francisco Morazan 1980–97; Presidential Sec. 1982–83; Gen. Co-ordinator Movimiento Liberal Florista; fmr Pres. Cen. Exec. Council Partido Liberal de Honduras; Pres. of Honduras 1998–2002; Co-owner, Man. and mem. Editorial Bd La Tribuna, Co-owner and Man. Lithopress Industrial; fmr Man. CONPACASA; fmr Prof., School of Business Admin, Nat. Univ. of Honduras; Cen. American Higher School of Banking; fmr mem. Bd of Dirs Honduran Inst. of Social Security, Cen. Bank of Honduras, Inst. Nacional de Formación Profesional; mem. Industrial Eng Asscn of Honduras, Nat. Asscn of Industries, Consejo Hondureño de la Empresa Privada (COHEP), Honduran Inst. of Inter-American Culture. *Publication:* Forjemos Unidos el Destino de Honduras. *Address:* c/o Partido Liberal, Col. Miramonte, Tegucigalpa, Honduras.

FLORES FLAKE, Mary Elizabeth, BA; Honduran lawyer, journalist, politician and diplomatist; *Permanent Representative, United Nations;* b. 6 Dec. 1973; d. of Carlos Roberto Flores (Pres. of Honduras 1998–2002) and Mary Flores; one s. one d.; ed Univ. of Loyola, New Orleans, USA, Nat. Autonomous Univ. of Honduras; became the youngest and first woman to hold position of First Vice-Pres. of Nat. Congress 2006–10, Pres. Ethics and Transparency Cttee; Amb. and Perm. Rep. to UN, New York 2010–, Vice-Pres. UN Gen. Ass. 2012–13; Vice-Pres. of Admin of Asscn of Newspapers and Magazines (PYRSA); participated in Fifth Language Congress sponsored by Royal Language Acad. (Spain), published paper on Intercultural Bilingual Educ. as a tool in devt of the indigenous groups in Latin America; presided over Support Cttee of Nat. Inst. of Thorax Hosp. for more than ten years; mem. Friedrich Naumann Foundation; chosen by World Econ. Forum to be part of the Young Global Leaders initiative 2007; mem. Rotary Club International of Nueva Tegucigalpa; Kappa Tae Alpha Award, Press Soc. of US for High Academic Standing 1997. *Address:* Permanent Mission of Honduras to the United Nations, 866 United Nations Plaza, Suite 417, New York, NY 10017, USA (office). *Telephone:* (212) 752-3370 (office). *Fax:* (212) 223-0498 (office). *E-mail:* honduras_un@hotmail.com (office). *Website:* www.un.int/honduras (office).

FLORES LOAISIGA, Mario José, MS; Nicaraguan economist and politician; ed Univ. of Louvaine, Belgium; Minister of Finance and Public Credit 2006–07; fmr mem. Bd of Govs IDB; fmr Vice-Pres. of Cen. Bank of Nicaragua. *Address:* c/o Ministry of Finance and Public Credit, Frente a la Asamblea Nacional, Apdo 2170, Managua, Nicaragua (office).

FLORES PEREZ, Francisco; Salvadorean fmr head of state; b. 17 Oct. 1959, Santa Ana; m. Lourdes Rodríguez de Flores; one s. one d.; ed Amherst Coll., USA, Trinity Coll., Univ. of Oxford, UK; fmr Prof. of Philosophy, Universidad Dr. José Matías Delgado; fmr Deputy and Pres. Legislative Ass.; fmr Vice-Minister of Planning, then Vice-Pres. and Adviser to Pres. Cristiani; Information Sec. to Pres. Armando Calderón Sol; Pres. of El Salvador 1999–2004; mem. Nat. Republican Alliance (ARENA). *Address:* c/o Alianza Republicana Nacionalista (ARENA), Prolongación Calle Arce 2423, entre 45 y 47 Avda Norte, San Salvador, El Salvador (office).

FLOSSE, Gaston; French Polynesian politician and head of state; *President;* b. 24 June 1931, Rikitea (Gambier archipelago); m. Marie-Jeanne Mao 1994; Pres. City Council Pirae 1963–65, Mayor 1965–2000; Govt Councillor in charge of Agric. 1965–67; mem. French Polynesian Territorial Ass. for Windward Islands 1967, Pres. 1972–77; Pres. Tahoeraa Huiraatira Party 1971; Vice-Pres. Govt Council 1982–84, Pres. Governing Council 1984–87, 1991–2004; Pres. of French Polynesia Feb.–June 2004, Oct. 2004–05, 2008; mem. Cen. Cttee Union des Democrates pour la République (UDR), France, then Founding mem. RPR; Deputy for French Polynesia, Nat. Ass., France 1978–97; Sec. of State in charge of S Pacific Affairs, France 1986–88; apptd Senator of French Repub. 1998; Pres. of French Polynesia 2013–; Chevalier, Légion d'honneur, Ordre nat. du Mérite, First 'Grand Maître', Order of Tahiti Nui; Dr hc (Kyung Hee Univ., Korea) 1985. *Address:* Office of the President of the Government, ave Pouvana'a A Opa, BP 2551, 98713 Papeete, French Polynesia (office). *Telephone:* 472000 (office). *Fax:* 472210 (office). *Website:* www.presidence.pf (office).

FO, Dario; Italian playwright, clown, actor and painter; b. 24 March 1926, San Giano; m. Franca Rame 1954; one c.; ed Acad. of Fine Arts, Milan; comedian, Teatro di Rivista; Co-founder theatre groups, Fo-Rame Co. 1957–68, Associazione Nuova Scena 1968–69, Collettivo Teatrale la Comune 1970–; cand. for Mayor of Milan 2006; Hon. DLitt (Westminster) 1997; Dr hc (Univ. La Sapienza, Rome) 2006; Univ. of Copenhagen Sonning Prize 1981, Associazione Torre Nat. Award Against Violence and the Camorra 1986, Obie Prize 1986, Campione d'Italia Agro Dolce Prize 1987, Nobel Prize for Literature 1997. *Film scripts:* Lo Svitato 1956, Musica per vecchi animali 1989. *Plays include:* Il dito nell'occhio (with Franco Parenti and Giustino Durano) 1953, I sani da legare (with Parenti and Durano) 1954, Ladri, manichini e donne nude 1957, Comica finale 1958, Gli arcangeli non giocano a flipper 1959, La storia vera di Piero d'Angera, che alla crociata non c'era 1960, Aveva due pistole con gli occhi bianchi e neri 1960, Chi ruba un piede è fortunato in amore 1961, Isabella, tre caravelle e un cacciaballe 1963, Settimo: ruba un po' meno 1964, La colpa è sempre del diavolo 1965, La signora è da buttare 1967, Grande pantomima per pupazzi piccoli, grandi e medi 1968, L'operaio conosce 300 parole, il padrone 1000, per questo lui è il padrone 1969, Legami pure, tanto spacco tutto lo stesso 1969, Il funerale del padrone 1969, Mistero buffo 1969, Morte accidentale di un anarchico 1970, Fedayin 1971, Basta con i fascisti 1973, Ci ragiono e canto N.3 1973, Guerra di popolo in Cile 1973, Non si paga, non si paga! 1974, Fanfani rapito 1975, La marijuana della mamma è la più bella 1975, Tutta casa, letto e chiesa 1977, La tragedia di Aldo Moro 1979, Storia della tigre e altre storie 1979, Una madre (with Franca Rame) 1981, Clacson, trombette e pernacchi 1981, L'Opera dello sghignazzo 1982, Il fabulazzo osceno 1982, Coppia aperta 1982, Patapunfete 1983, Quasi per caso una donna: Elisabetta 1983, Dio li fa poi li accoppa 1983, Lisistrata romana 1983, Hellequin, Harlekin, Arlecchino 1985,

Diario di Eva 1985, Parti femminili (with Franca Rame) 1986, Il ratto della Francesca 1986, La rava e la fava (aka La parte del leone) 1987, Lettera dalla Cina 1989, Il braccato 1989, Il papa e la strega 1989, Zitti! Stiamo precipitando! 1990, Johan Padan a la descoverta de le Americhe 1991, Parliamo di donne (two one-act pieces, L'Eroina and Grassa è bello) 1991, Settimo: ruba un po' meno! n. 2 1992, Dario Fo incontra Ruzzante 1993, Mamma! I sanculotti! 1993, Un palcoscenico per le donne 1994, Sesso? Grazie, tanto per gradire! 1994, Bibbia dei villani 1996, Il diavolo con le zinne 1996, Lu Santo Jullare Francesco 1999, My First Seven Years (Plus a Few More) (memoir) 2005, L'Anomalo Bicefalo (on the Premier Silvio Berlusconi) 2006, Francis the Holy Jester 2009, Ein Leben aus dem Stegreif 2010. *Radio:* Poer Nano 1950, Chicchirichì, Cocoricò, Ragazzi in Gamba, Non si vive di solo pane 1951. *Television:* Canzonissima 1962, Il teatro di Dario Fo 1976, Buona sera con Franca Rame 1980, Trasmissione forzata 1987. *Address:* C. So di Porta Romana 132, 20122 Milan, Italy (office). *Telephone:* (02) 58430506 (office). *E-mail:* francarame@iol.it (office). *Website:* www.dariofo.it (office).

FOALE, Marion Ann, RCA; British designer; b. 13 March 1939, London; d. of S. D. Foale; one s. one d.; ed South West Essex Tech and School of Art, RCA; career fashion designer; designed Queen's mantle for OBE dedication ceremony 1960; Founding pnr (with Sally Tuffin) Foale and Tuffin Ltd 1961–72; signed with Puritan Fashion Corps, NY 1965–70; designed clothes for films, including for Susannah York in Kaleidoscope 1966 and Audrey Hepburn in Two for the Road 1966; f. own label Marion Foale–Knitwear Designer 1982; exhibition at Fashion and Textile Museum, London 2009–10. *Leisure interests:* Marion Foale's Classic Knitwear 1987. *Leisure interests:* studying fine art, painting. *Address:* Foale Ltd, The Cottage, 133A Long Street, Atherstone, Warwicks., CV9 1AD, England (office). *Telephone:* (1827) 720333 (office). *Fax:* (1827) 720444 (office). *E-mail:* foale@talk21.com (office).

FODOR, Gen. (retd) Lajos; Hungarian army officer (retd) and diplomatist; b. 29 July 1947, Debrecen; m. Eva Kovács; one s. one d.; ed Lajos Kossuth Land Forces Mil. Acad., Szentendre, Frunze Mil. Acad., Moscow, Defence Language Inst., San Antonio, American Nat. Defence Univ.; infantry officer, 1970; platoon leader, 14th Mechanized Infantry Regt Nagykaniza 1971; Bn Commdr 63rd Mechanized Infantry Regt Nagyatád 1971–79, Deputy Commdr 1981–83, Regt Commdr 1983–85; Brig. 26th Mechanized Infantry Regt Lenti 1985–87; Deputy Chief and Chief of Mechanized Infantry and Armoured Service, Gen. Dir of Training 1989; Deputy Commdr 5th Army, Székesfehérvár; Deputy Commdr and Maj.-Gen. of Hungarian Army 1992; Dir of Mil. Intelligence Office 1993; Deputy Chief of Defence Staff 1996–99, Chief 1999–2003, also Under-Sec. for Policy, Ministry of Defence; Amb. to Australia 2003–07.

FOFANA, Mohamed Said; Guinean economist and politician; *Prime Minister;* b. 1952, Forécariah, Lower Guinea; ed Inst. Polytechnique Gamal Abdel Nasser, Conakry, Centre Demographique de l'ONU-Roumanie, Bucharest, WTO Graduate Inst., Geneva; Lecturer in Econs, Tabossi Coll., Fria 1976–77; Sec.-Gen. Chamber of Trade and Industry 1985, Nat. Dir for Trade and Competition 2003–08, Nat. Dir for Foreign Trade 2008–09, Dir for Co-ordination of Projects, Ministry of Trade and Industry 2009; participated in negotiations with several int. orgs including WTO, ICC, UNCTAD, EU; Prime Minister 2010–. *Address:* Office of the Prime Minister, BP 5141, Conakry, Guinea (office). *Telephone:* 30-41-51-19 (office). *Fax:* 30-41-52-82 (office).

FOGARTY, Thomas James, BS, MD; American thoracic surgeon and academic; *Clinical Professor of Surgery, Stanford University Medical Center;* b. 25 Feb. 1934, Cincinnati, OH; ed Xavier Univ., Univ. of Cincinnati; worked as scrub technician, Good Samaritan Hosp., Cincinnati; Peripheral Vascular Fellowship, Univ. of Cincinnati Coll. of Medicine 1962; Residency in Gen. Surgery, Univ. of Oregon Medical School 1965; Clinical Assoc. for NIH Surgery Br. 1967; Advanced Research Fellow in Cardiovascular Surgery, Stanford Univ. Medical Center 1969, Instructor of Surgery, Div. of Cardiovascular Surgery 1969–70, Asst Prof. of Surgery, Volunteer Clinical Faculty 1970–71, Asst Clinical Prof. of Surgery, Medical Center 1971–73, pvt. practice in Stanford Medical Center 1973–78, Pres. of Medical Staff 1977–79, Clinical Prof. of Surgery 1993–; Dir of Cardiovascular Surgery, Sequoia Hosp., Redwood City, Calif. 1980–93; Pres. Fogarty Eng Lab.; Co-founder Three Arch Pnrs (venture capital firm); f. Fogarty Medical Foundation 2000; est. Thomas Fogarty Winery and Vineyards, Santa Cruz, Calif. 1978; Co-Ed.-in-Chief Journal of Endovascular Therapy; mem. numerous professional socs including American Bd of Surgery, American Bd of Thoracic Surgery, American Coll. of Surgeons, American Medical Asscn, Calif. Medical Soc., San Francisco Surgical Soc., Soc. of Vascular Surgery; Hon. PhD (Xavier Univ.) 1987; San Francisco Patent and Trademark Asscn Inventor of the Year 1980, Lemelson-MIT Prize 2000. *Medical inventions include:* Fogarty® Embolectomy Balloon Catheter 1961, Medtronic/ AneuRx Endovascular Aortic Stent-Graft, Fogarty® Surgical Clips and Clamps, Hancock Tissue Heart Valve (with Warren Hancock); holds 63 US patents for medical devices; founder or co-founder of over 30 start-up cos mfg medical devices. *Publications:* chapters in numerous surgical textbooks, over 150 articles in professional journals in fields of cardiac, vascular and gen. surgery. *Leisure interests:* fishing, model-building, wine-making, inventing, design. *Address:* Stanford University School of Medicine, 300 Pasteur Drive, Stanford, CA 94305 (office); Thomas Fogarty Winery & Vineyards, 3270 Alpine Road, Portola Valley, CA 94028, USA (office). *Telephone:* (650) 723-4000 (office); (650) 854-1822 (office). *E-mail:* tjf@fogartybusiness.com (office); info@fogartywinery.com (office). *Website:* med.stanford.edu (office); www.ctsnet.org (office).

FOGELBERG, Graeme, MCom, MBA, PhD; New Zealand university administrator; b. 10 Dec. 1939, Wellington; s. of the late Frederick Edward Fogelberg and Evelyn Fogelberg (née Greenwell); m. (divorced); three s. two d.; ed Wellington Coll., Victoria Univ. of Wellington and Univ. of Western Ontario, Canada; Prof. of Business Admin., Victoria Univ. of Wellington 1970, Dean, Faculty of Commerce Admin. 1977–82, Deputy Vice-Chancellor 1986–92; professorial appointments at Univ. of Western Ont. 1975–76, 1986–87 and Pennsylvania State Univ., USA 1992–93; Vice-Chancellor Univ. of Otago, Dunedin 1994–2004; Chair. NZ Vice-Chancellors Cttee 1999–2000; Chair. and Trustee, New Zealand Univs' Superannuation Scheme –2008; fmr Chair. Asscn of Commonwealth Univs; Fellow, New Zealand Inst. of Dirs; Pres. Rotary Club of Wellington 1988–89; Companion, New Zealand Order of Merit 2004; Hon. LLD (Otago) 2004. *Publications include:*

several business study books and articles in accounting, business, man. and econs journals. *Leisure interests:* tennis, skiing, fine New Zealand wines, travel. *Address:* PO Box 2937, Wellington 6140, New Zealand (home). *Telephone:* (21) 320752 (home). *E-mail:* graemefogelberg@gmail.com (home).

FOGELHOLM, Markus, MA; Finnish banker and business executive; b. 11 March 1946, Helsinki; s. of Eila Fogelholm and Georg Fogelholm; m. Saara RI Suokas 1969; one s. one d.; ed Univ. of Helsinki; joined Bank of Finland 1972, Head of Foreign Financing Dept 1984–87, Market Operations Dept 1992–2001; Special Asst to Exec. Dir of UN Centre on Transnational Corpns 1978–81; Alt. Exec. Dir IMF 1987–89, Exec. Dir 1989–91; Man. Dir Finnish Bankers' Asscn 2001–06; mem. Bd of Dirs Julius Tallberg Real Estate Corpn 2008–; Hon. mem. Forex Finland. *Leisure interests:* wine, music, tennis, hiking, skating. *Address:* c/o Board of Directors, Julius Tallberg-Kiinteistöt Oyj, Suomalaistentie 7, 02270 Espoo, Finland.

FOGERTY, John; American singer, composer, songwriter and musician (guitar); b. 28 May 1945, Berkeley, Calif.; mem. Blue Velvets, renamed the Golliwogs 1959–67, then renamed Creedence Clearwater Revival 1967–71; solo artist 1972–. *Recordings include:* albums: with Creedence Clearwater Revival: Creedence Clearwater Revival 1968, Bayou Country 1969, Green River 1969, Willie and The Poor Boys 1969, Cosmo's Factory 1970, Pendulum 1970, Mardi Gras 1972, Live In Europe 1973, Live At The Royal Albert Hall 1980; solo: The Blue Ridge Rangers 1973, John Fogerty 1975, Centerfield 1985, Eye of a Zombie 1986, Premonition 1998, Blue Moon Swamp 2004, Deja Vu All Over Again 2004, The Long Road Home 2005, Revival 2007, The Blue Ridge Rangers Rides Again 2009, Wrote a Song For Everyone 2013. *Address:* c/o Verve Music Group Inc., 1755 Broadway, 3rd Floor, New York, NY 10019, USA. *Telephone:* (212) 331-2000. *Fax:* (212) 331-2064. *E-mail:* contact@vervemusicgroup.com. *Website:* www.vervemusicgroup.com; www.johnfogerty.com.

FOING, Bernard H., MS, PhD (Habil.); French space scientist, technologist, academic and explorer; *Chairman, ESTEC Staff Committee and Chief Scientist, SMART-1 Project, European Space Agency;* ed Lycee Louis-Le-Grand, Paris, Ecole Normale Superieure, ENSET, Observatoire de Paris-Meudon, Univ. of Paris, Laboratoire de Physique Stellair et Planetaire, CNRS France, Sac Peak, New Mexico, Boulder, Colo and Harvard Univ., USA; Chair. ESTEC Staff Cttee, Chief Scientist and Sr Research Coordinator, ESA, Exec. Dir Int. Lunar Exploration Working Group (ILEWG), Co-Investigator, Mars Express, Exomars, COROT, Int. Space Station, Head of Research Div., ESA Research and Scientific Support Dept, SMART-1 Lead Project Scientist; Convener EGS/EGU sessions 1997–, Cttee on Space Research (COSPAR) 1992–, ILEWG 2000–; numerous radio and TV interviews on space and lunar exploration; mem. Int. Acad. of Astronautics; Extraordinary Prof., Vrije Universiteit Amsterdam, Distinguished Research Prof., Florida Inst. of Tech.; Space Visionaries, ILEWG Tech. Award. *Films:* Black Sun Highlights, documentaries on space and lunar exploration. *Music:* plays viola (superior studies), guitar and piano accompaniment (classical/jazz), performer in int. amateur orchestras, quartet and chamber music groups. *Publications:* more than 585 publs, including more than 187 refereed papers on space science and tech., lunar and planetary exploration; main ed. 20 books on space science and exploration, including: Multi-Site Continuous Spectroscopy Workshops Proceedings (co-ed.) 1988, 1990, 1994, Helioseismology from Space (Advances in Space Research (ASR), Vol. 11, No. 4) 1991, Astronomy and Space Research, from the Moon (ASR Vol. 14, No. 6) 1994, Special Issue, Open Session on Solar & Heliospheric Physics, Journal of Physical Chemistry of Earth 1996, Missions to the Moon, Advances in Moon and Exploring the Cold Universe (ASR Vol. 18, No. 11) 1998, Solar Seismology and Variability (ASR Vol. 24, No. 2) 1999, The Moon and Mars (ASR Vol. 23, No. 11), Lunar Exploration 2000 (ASR Vol. 30, No. 8) in Special Issue on Lunar Exploration (Planetary and Space Science, Vol. 50, Issue 14–15) 2002, Earth-Like Planets and Moons 2002, ESA report to COSPAR 2002, The Next Steps in Exploring Deep Space 2003, The Moon and Near-Earth Objects (ASR Vol. 37, No. 1, co-ed.) 2006, 9th ILEWG ed. on Exploration and Utilisation of the Moon (abstracts) 2007, The Moon: Science, Exploration and Utilisation 2008; Organiser/ Ed. Forum ed. Française des Spécialistes in Astronomie (1987): ESA Horizon 2000. *Address:* ESTEC/SRE-S, Postbus 299, 2200 AG Noordwijk, Netherlands (office). *Telephone:* (71) 565-5647 (office). *Fax:* (71) 565-4697 (office). *E-mail:* bfoing@rssd.esa.int (office); bernard.foing@esa.int (office). *Website:* www.esa.int (office); sci.esa.int/smart-1 (office); sci.esa.int/ilewg (office).

FOK, Canning Kin-ning, BA, CA; Hong Kong telecommunications executive; *Group Managing Director and Executive Director, Hutchison Whampoa Ltd;* b. 1951; four c.; ed St John's Univ., Minn., USA, Univ. of New England, Australia; began career with Cheung Kong (real estate co.) 1979; joined Hutchison Whampoa Group 1984, Exec. Dir Hutchison Whampoa Ltd 1984–, Group Man.-Dir 1993–, also Chair. Hutchison Telecom Int., Hutchison Harbour Ring Ltd, Hutchison Telecommunications International Ltd, Hutchison Telecommunications (Australia) Ltd, Hutchison Global Communications Holdings Ltd, Partner Communications Co. Ltd, Hongkong Electric Holdings Ltd; Partner and Co-Chair. Husky Energy Inc. 2000–; Deputy Chair. Cheung Kong Infrastructure Holdings Ltd; Dir, Cheung Kong (Holdings) Ltd, Hutchison Whampoa Finance (CI) Ltd; mem. Australian Inst. of Chartered Accountants. *Address:* Hutchison Whampoa Ltd, 22nd Floor, Hutchison House, 10 Harcourt Road, Hong Kong Special Administrative Region, People's Republic of China (office). *Telephone:* 2128-1188 (office). *Fax:* 2128-1705 (office). *E-mail:* info@hutchison-whampoa.com (office). *Website:* www .hutchison-whampoa.com (office).

FOK, Ian, BS, MBA; Hong Kong business executive; *Managing Director, Yau Wing Company Ltd;* b. (Fok Chun-wan), s. of the late Henry Fok; ed Univ. of British Columbia, Canada; Man. Dir Yau Wing Co. Ltd; Deputy 11th Nat. People's Congress, People's Repub. of China; Vice-Chair. China Overseas Friendship Asscn, Guangdong Overseas Friendship Asscn, All China Fed. of Industry and Commerce; mem. Standing Cttee 10th Guangdong Prov. Cttee of CPPCC; Councillor, China Council for the Promotion of Peaceful Nat. Reunification; Supervisor Gen., Hongkong Asscn for the Promotion of Peaceful Reunification of China; mem. Standing Council, China Overseas Exchange Asscn; Man. Dir Fok Ying Tung Foundation Ltd; Pres. Hong Kong Wushu Union, Vice-Chair. Wushu Fed. of Asia, mem. Exec. Cttee and Chair. of Marketing and Devt Cttee Int. Wushu Fed.; fmr mem. Hong Kong Trade and Devt Council; Deputy Chair. Council and Exec. Cttee,

Hong Kong Man. Asscn; mem. Advisory Council, Boao Forum for Asia; mem. Court, Univ. of Hong Kong; mem. Council, Hong Kong Univ. of Science & Tech.; mem. Greater Pearl River Delta Business Council; Trustee, Chinese Univ. of Hong Kong United Coll. 1996–2005; Hon. Citizen of Panyu and Guangzhou, Hon. Univ. Fellow, Open Univ. of Hong Kong, Chinese Univ. of Hong Kong; Life Hon. Chair. Chinese Gen. Chamber of Commerce in Hong Kong; Silver Bauhinia Star 2005. *Address:* Yau Wing Co. Ltd, Units 1105–1112, West Tower Shun Tak Centre, 168–200 Connaught Road Central, Hong Kong Special Administrative Region, People's Republic of China (office). *Telephone:* 2522-7131 (office). *Fax:* 2526-9858 (office).

FOK, Timothy, JP; Hong Kong business executive; *Managing Director, Yau Wing Company Ltd;* b. (Fok Tsun-ting), 14 Feb. 1946, Hong Kong; s. of the late Henry Fok; m. Loletta Chu (divorced 2006); three s.; ed Millfield Coll., UK, Univ. of Southern California, USA; Man. Dir Yau Wing Co. Ltd, Chair. H.Y.T. Fok Group of Cos; mem. Legis. Council of Hong Kong, representing the Sports, Performing Arts, Culture and Publication functional constituency; mem. CPPCC; mem. IOC 2001–; Pres. Sports Fed. and Olympic Cttee of Hong Kong, Hong Kong Sports Writer Asscn, Hong Kong Football Asscn; Vice-Pres. Olympic Council of Asia, Organizing Cttee of 2008 Olympics and Paralympics Equestrian Events, Hong Kong East Asian Games Organizing Cttee; mem. 2008 Olympics Coordination Comm.; Gov. Fok Ying Tung Foundation; Grand Bauhinia Star. *Address:* Yau Wing Co. Ltd, Units 1105–1112, West Tower Shun Tak Centre, 168–200 Connaught Road Central, Hong Kong Special Administrative Region, People's Republic of China (office). *Telephone:* 2522-7131 (office). *Fax:* 2810-4580 (office).

FOKIN, Valery Vladimirovich; Russian theatre and film director; *Artistic Director, Alexandrinsky Theater;* b. 28 Feb. 1946, Moscow; m. Tatiana Krivenko; two s.; ed Moscow Shchukin Theatre School; Stage Dir Moscow Sovremennik Theatre 1971–85; Chief Stage Dir Yermolova Theatre 1985–90; Artistic Dir M. Yermolova Theatre Centre 1990–2000; Founder, Artistic Dir and Dir-Gen. Meyerhold Artistic Centre 1991–, Artistic Dir Russian State Pushkin Acad. Drama Theater (Alexandrinsky Theater) 2006–; Order of Service to the Fatherland, IV degree 2006; Theatre Prize, BITEF Prize, State's Prize, Honoured Art Worker of Poland, three Crystal Turandot awards including for Last Night of the Tsar, Hon. Badge of Service to St Petersburg for outstanding contribution to the devt of Russian theater, The Golden Mask (Russian Nat. Theater Award) 2008, Special Jury's Prize for the renaissance of the Alexandrinsky Theater 2009. *Film:* The Metamorphosis. *Theatre includes:* (Stage Dir) Valentin and Valentina, I'll Go and Go, Inspector, Provincial Anecdotes, Lorenzaccio, Who's Afraid of Virginia Woolf, In Spring I Shall Come Back to You, Transformation, (Chief Stage Dir) Speak Up, Second Year of Freedom, Sports Scenes of 1980, Invitation to Punishment (Artistic Dir), Hotel Room in Town N (Best Dir), (Dir) Artand and His Double, The Queen of Spades (opera). *Television:* over 25 films and performances. *Publications:* Hotel Room in Town N, The Metamorphosis; numerous articles and speeches. *Address:* Vsevolod Meyerhold Centre, Novoslobodskaya str. 23, Moscow (office); Triohprudniy pereulok 13/11, 5, Moscow, Russia (home). *Telephone:* (495) 363-10-46 (office); (495) 299-16-76 (home). *Fax:* (495) 363-1041 (office). *Website:* en.alexandrinsky.ru/articles/about/artistic_director (office).

FOKIN, Vitold Pavlovych; Ukrainian politician; b. 25 Oct. 1932, Novomikolaivka, Zaporozhye region; m.; one s. one d.; ed m. Dnepropetrovsk Mining Inst.; fmr mem. CP; mining engineer 1954–71; Deputy Chair. Council of Ministers of Ukraine 1987–90; Chair. State Cttee for Econs Aug.–Nov. 1990; Chair. Council of Ministers (Prime Minister) of Ukraine 1990–92; Sr Researcher Inst. of World Econ. and Int. Relations 1993–, Pres. Int. Fund for Humanitarian and Econ. Relations with Russian Fed. 1993–; mem. Higher Econ. Council of Pres. of Ukraine 1997–; People's Deputy 1998–; Prof. Nat. Acad. of Mines; Chair. Supervisory Bd DEWON Inc. 2000–; Miner's Glory Order 1st, 2nd, 3rd class 1961–1963, Decoration of Honour 1967, 2 Orders of Working Red Banner 1970, 1975, Order of St Prince Volodymyr 2002, Order of Yaroslav the Wise 2002, Order of Honour 2004; Laureate of State Prize of Ukraine 1983, Medal for Services 2004, seven medals. *Publications:* about 30 published works and articles in social, political and technical journals and books. *Leisure interests:* hunting, fishing, tennis, tourism. *Address:* International Fund for Humanitarian and Economic Relations with Russian Federation, 19 Panasa Myrnogo Street, 01011 Kyiv (office); Verkhovna Rada, M. Hrushevskoho rul 5, 252019 Kyiv; Flat 266, 13 Suvorova Street, 01010 Kyiv, Ukraine (home). *Telephone:* (44) 290-75-85 (office); (44) 290-52-55 (home). *Fax:* (44) 290-05-92 (office). *E-mail:* vitold.fokin@dewon.com.ua.

FOKIN, Yuri Yevgenyevich; Russian diplomatist; b. 2 Sept. 1936, Gorky (now Nizhny Novgorod); m.; one s. one d.; ed Moscow Inst. of Int. Relations; on staff, USSR Ministry of Foreign Affairs 1960–; with USSR Mission in UN 1960–65, Secr. of Minister of Foreign Affairs 1966–73, Sr Adviser, Dept of Planning of Int. Events 1973–76; Deputy Perm. Rep. of USSR to UN 1976–79; Deputy Dir-Gen. Ministry of Foreign Affairs 1979–80, Dir-Gen. 1980–86; Amb. to Cyprus 1986–90, to Norway 1995–97, to UK 1997–2000; Head, Second European Dept, Russian Ministry of Foreign Affairs 1990–92, Dir Second European Dept 1991–95; on staff, Ministry of Foreign Affairs 1995–, Rector, Diplomatic Acad. of Ministry of Foreign Affairs –2006; decorations from Russia, Austria, Norway. *Publications:* Diplomatic Yearbook 2000–12, State & Diaspora: A Record of Interaction, A Word of the President (A. A. Akaev). *Leisure interests:* reading, ballet, theatre. *Address:* c/o Diplomatic Academy of the Ministry of Foreign Affairs, 53/2 Ostozhenka, 119992 Moscow, Russia. *Telephone:* (499) 940-13-56; (499) 246-47-56; (499) 255-80-34. *E-mail:* yuri.fokine@dipacademy.ru.

FOLBRE, Nancy, MA, PhD; American economist and academic; *Professor of Economics, University of Massachusetts;* ed Univ. of Texas, Univ. of Massachusetts; consultant, Maine Comm. for Women 1981, Kenya Fuelwood Project 1981, Beijer Inst. 1981, 1983, Royal Swedish Acad. of Science 1981, 1983, Zimbabwe Energy Planning Project, 1983, Int. Center for Research on Women 1989–90, The Population Council 1989–94, ILO 1992, World Bank 1994–95; Asst Prof. of Econs, Bowdoin Coll. 1980–83; Assoc. Prof. of Econs, Univ. of Mass 1984–91, Prof. of Econs 1991–, Chair. Dept of Econs 2003–04; Visiting Assoc. Prof., American Univ. 1991; Visiting Lecturer, Eugene Havens Center, Univ. of Wisconsin 1991; Visiting Scholar, Women's Research and Resource Center, Univ. of California, Davis 1992, Gender Inst., LSE, UK 1995; Visiting Chair. in American Studies, Ecole des Hautes Etudes en Sciences Sociales, Paris, France 1995–96; Visiting Research

Fellow, ANU 2000, 2002, Adjunct Prof., Social and Political Theory Program 2003–; Phi Beta Kappa Visiting Scholar 2000–01; Visiting Fellow, Russell Sage Foundation 2005–06; Co-Founder and CEO The Dancing Monkey Project 1998–; Pres. Int. Asscn for Feminist Econs 2002–; Staff Economist, Center for Popular Econs 1979–; Consultant to UN Human Devt Office 2005; Assoc. Ed. Feminist Economics 1995–; mem. Bd Foundation of Child Devt; mem. NAS; French-American Foundation Fellow 1995–96, MacArthur Foundation Fellow 1998–2003; Olivia Schieffelin Nordberg Award 1999, Distinguished Visiting Scholar Award, Univ. of Massachusetts 2002. *Publications include:* A Field Guide to the US Economy 1988, Issues in Contemporary Economics, Vol. 4 (co-ed.) 1991, Who Pays for the Kids? Gender and the Structures of Constraint 1994, The New Field Guide to the US Economy 1995, War on the Poor: A Defense Manual 1996, The Economics of the Family (ed.) 1996, De la différence des sexes en économie politique 1997, The Ultimate Field Guide to the US Economy 2000, The Invisible Heart: Economics and Family Values 2001, Family Time (co-ed.) 2003, Greed, Lust and Gender 2009, Valuing Children: Rethinking the Economics of the Family 2010, Saving State U 2010; numerous articles in professional journals, chapters in books and newspaper articles. *Address:* Department of Economics, Thompson Hall, University of Massachusetts, Amherst, MA 01003, USA (office). *Telephone:* (413) 545-3283 (office). *Fax:* (413) 545-2921 (office). *E-mail:* folbre@econs.umass.edu (office). *Website:* people.umass.edu/~folbre/folbre (office).

FOLEY, Lt-Gen. John Paul, Kt, KCB, KStJ, CB, OBE, MC, DL; British business executive, fmr civil servant and fmr army officer; *Vice Lord-Lieutenant of Herefordshire;* b. 22 April 1939, London; s. of Henry Thomas Hamilton Foley and Helen Constance Margaret Foley (née Pearson); m. Ann Rosamond Humphries 1972; two d.; ed Bradfield Coll., Berks., Army Staff Coll., Camberley, Royal Coll. of Defence Studies, London; nat. service with Royal Green Jackets (RGJ) 1959–61, then Regimental Service 1962–70, attached to Staff Coll. 1971; Brig.-Maj. 1974–75; instructor, Staff Coll. 1976–78; CO 3 RGJ 1978–80, Commdt, Jr Div. Staff Coll. 1981–82, Dir SAS 1983–85, Royal Coll. of Defence Studies 1986; Chief, British Mission to Soviet Forces, E Germany 1987–89; Deputy Chief, Defence Intelligence 1989–91, Chief, Defence Intelligence 1994–97; Commdr British Forces Hong Kong 1992–94, retd 1997; Lt-Gov. of Guernsey 2000–05; High Sheriff of Herefords. and Worcs. 2006–07; Vice Lord-Lt of Herefords. 2010–; mem. Security Comm.; mem. Int. Advisory Bd, Group 4 1998–2000; Chair. British Greyhound Racing Bd 1999–2000; Dir AD Systems (UK) Ltd 2009–; US Legion of Merit (Officer). *Leisure interests:* gardening, reading, walking, tennis, bird watching, golf.

FOLEY, Thomas C., BA, MBA; American business executive and fmr diplomatist; *Chairman, NTC Group;* one s.; ed Harvard Univ., Harvard Business School; worked for McKinsey & Co., New York, later for Citicorp Venture Capital, New York; f. NTC Group (pvt. equity investment business) 1985, Chair. 2009–; Dir of Pvt. Sector Devt for Coalition Provisional Authority, Iraq 2003–04, Amb. to Ireland 2006–09; recently served as Trustee, Kennedy Center for the Performing Arts, Washington, DC and two Conn. State Comms involving educ. and children's rights; Dept of Defense Distinguished Public Service Award for service in Iraq 2004. *Leisure interest:* charity work. *Address:* NTC Group, 3 Pickwick Plaza, Greenwich, CT 06830-5538, USA (office). *Telephone:* (203) 862-2850 (office). *Fax:* (203) 622-6538 (office). *Website:* www.ntcgroupinc.com (office).

FØLLESDAL, Dagfinn, PhD; Norwegian academic; *Clarence Irving Lewis Professor of Philosophy, Stanford University;* b. 22 June 1932, Askim; s. of Trygve Føllesdal and Margit Teigen; m. Vera Heyerdahl 1957; five s. one d.; ed Univs of Oslo and Göttingen and Harvard Univ.; Research Asst in Ionospheric Physics, Norwegian Research Council 1955–57; Instructor and Asst Prof. of Philosophy, Harvard Univ. 1961–64; Prof. of Philosophy, Univ. of Oslo 1967–99; Prof. of Philosophy, Stanford Univ. 1968–76, Clarence Irving Lewis Prof. of Philosophy 1976–; Visiting Prof. Coll. de France 1977; Guggenheim Fellow 1978–79; Fellow, Center for Advanced Study in Behavioral Sciences 1981–82, American Council of Learned Socs 1983–84, Inst. for Advanced Study, Princeton 1985–86, Wissenschaftskolleg, Berlin 1989–90, Centre for Advanced Study, Oslo 1995–96, 2003–04; mem. American Acad. of Arts and Sciences, Academia Europaea and scientific acads in Norway, Denmark, Sweden and Finland; Pres. Norwegian Acad. of Science 1993, 1995, 1997; Univ. of Oslo Research Prize 1995, Alexander von Humboldt Research Award 1997, Lauener Prize 2006. *Publications:* Husserl and Frege 1958, Referential Opacity and Modal Logic 1966, Argumentasjonsteori språk og vitenskapsfilosofi (with L. Walløe and J. Elster) 1977; Ed. Journal of Symbolic Logic 1970–82, Philosophy of Quire, 5 vols 2000; numerous articles on philosophy of language, phenomenology, existentialism, action theory, educational and ethical issues. *Leisure interests:* skiing, running. *Address:* Department of Philosophy, Building 90, Stanford University, Stanford, CA 94305-2155, USA (office); Filosofisk institutt, Universitetet i Oslo, PB 1024, Blindern 0317, Oslo (office); Staverhagan 7, 1314 Slependen, Norway (home). *Telephone:* (650) 723-2587 (office); (47) 67-55-00-01 (home). *Fax:* (47) 67-55-00-02 (home). *E-mail:* dagfinn@csli.stanford.edu (office). *Website:* www-philosophy.stanford.edu (office); www.hf.uio.no/filosofi/organisasjon/ansatte/follesdal.html (office).

FOLLETT, Kenneth (Ken) Martin, BA; British writer; b. 5 June 1949, Cardiff, Wales; s. of Martin D. Follett and Veenie Evans; m. 1st Mary Elson 1968 (divorced 1985); one s. one d.; m. 2nd Barbara Broer 1985; one step-s. two step-d.; ed Univ. Coll. London; trainee reporter, South Wales Echo, Cardiff 1970–73; reporter, London Evening News 1973–74; Editorial Dir Everest Books, London 1974–76, Deputy Man. Dir 1976–77; full-time writer 1977–; Fellow, Univ. Coll. London 1994; Chair. Nat. Year of Reading 1998–99, Advisory Cttee, Reading is Fundamental UK 2003–07; Pres. Dyslexia Inst. 1998–2009; Vice-Pres. Stevenage Borough Football Club 2000–, Stevenage Community Trust 2002–; Chair. Govs, Roebuck Primary School and Nursery 2001–08; mem. Council, Nat. Literary Trust 1996–; Bd mem. Nat. Acad. of Writing 2003–10; Dir, Stevenage Leisure Ltd 1999–2004; Patron, Stevenage Home-Start 2000–. *Publications:* The Shakeout 1975, The Bear Raid 1976, The Modigliani Scandal 1976, The Power Twins and the Worm Puzzle 1976, The Secret of Kellerman's Studio 1976, Paper Money 1977, Eye of the Needle (MWA Edgar Award 1979) 1978, Triple 1979, The Key to Rebecca 1980, The Man from St Petersburg 1982, On Wings of Eagles 1983, Lie Down with Lions 1986, The Pillars of the Earth 1989, Night Over Water 1991, A Dangerous Fortune 1993, A Place Called Freedom 1995, The Third Twin 1996, The Hammer of

Eden 1998, Code to Zero 2000, Jackdaws (Corine Readers' Award, Germany 2003) 2001, Hornet Flight 2003, Whiteout 2004, World Without End 2007, Fall of Giants 2010, Winter of the World 2012; screenplays; contrib. to book reviews and essays. *Leisure interests:* left-wing politics, bass guitarist in blues band Damn Right I Got The Blues, Shakespeare. *Address:* Broadlands House, Primett Road, Stevenage, Herts., SG1 3EE, England (office). *Telephone:* (1438) 810400 (office). *Fax:* (1438) 810444 (office). *E-mail:* ken@ken-follett.com (office). *Website:* www.ken-follett .com.

FOLT, Carol L., BS, PhD; American environmental scientist, academic and university administrator; *Chancellor, University of North Carolina;* b. Akron, Ohio; m. Prof. David Peart; one s. one d.; ed Univ. of California, Santa Barbara, Univ. of California, Davis; postdoctoral work at W.K. Kellogg Biological Station, Michigan State Univ.; mem. Faculty, Dartmouth Coll. 1983, later Dartmouth Prof. of Biological Sciences, Ivy League Inst., Assoc. Dir Toxic Metals Research Program 1998–2000, Assoc. Dir Center for Environmental Health Sciences 2000–01, Dean of Grad. Studies and Assoc. Dean of Faculty for Interdisciplinary Programs 2001–04, Dean 2004–09, Acting Provost Dartmouth Coll. 2009–10, Provost 2010–12, Interim Pres. 2012–13; Chancellor Univ. of North Carolina, Chapel Hill 2013–; Fellow, AAAS. *Address:* Office of the Chancellor, 103 South Building, Campus Box 9100, Chapel Hill, NC 27599-9100, USA (office). *Telephone:* (919) 962-1365 (office). *Fax:* (919) 962-1647 (office). *E-mail:* chancellor@unc.edu (office). *Website:* chancellor.unc.edu (office).

FOMENKO, Anatoly Timofeevich; Russian mathematician and academic; *Professor, Department of Mathematics and Mechanics, Moscow State University;* b. 13 March 1945; m.; ed Moscow State Univ.; Asst, Sr Researcher, now Prof. Dept of Math. and Mechanics Moscow State Univ.; Corresp. mem. USSR (now Russian) Acad. of Sciences 1990, mem. 1994; research in theory of minimal surfaces, topology of multidimensional manifolds, simplectic geometry and theory of topological classifications of integrable differential equations; Chair. Moscow Math. Soc.; Award of Moscow Math. Soc. 1974, Award of Presidium of Russian Acad. of Sciences 1987, State Award of Russian Fed. 1996. *Publications include:* Simplectic Geometry: Methods and Applications 1988, The Plateau Problem 1990. *Leisure interests:* statistical analysis of historical texts, painting. *Address:* Department of Mathematics and Mechanics, Moscow State University, Vorobyevy gory, 119992 Moscow, Russia (office). *Telephone:* (495) 939-39-40 (office). *Website:* www.math.msu.su (office).

FONDA, Bridget; American actress; b. 27 Jan. 1964, Los Angeles; d. of Peter Fonda (q.v.) and Susan Fonda; m. Danny Elfman 2003; one s.; ed New York Univ. theater programme; studied acting at Lee Strasberg Inst. and with Harold Guskin; workshop stage performances include Confession and Pastels. *Films:* Aria (Tristan and Isolde sequence) (début) 1987, You Can't Hurry Love 1988, Shag 1988, Scandal 1989, Strapless 1989, Frankenstein Unbound 1990, The Godfather: Part III 1990, Doc Hollywood 1991, Out of the Rain 1991, Single White Female 1992, Singles 1992, Bodies Rest and Motion 1993, Point of No Return 1993, Little Buddha 1994, It Could Happen To You 1994, Camilla 1994, The Road to Welville 1994, Rough Magic 1995, Balto (voice) 1995, Grace of My Heart 1996, City Hall 1996, Drop Dead Fred, Light Years (voice), Iron Maze, Army of Darkness, Touch, Jackie Brown, Finding Graceland, The Break Up, South of Heaven West of Hell, Lake Placid 1999, Delivering Milo, Monkey Bone 2001, Kiss of the Dragon 2001, The Whole Shebang 2001. *Television includes:* Leather Jackets 1991, In the Gloaming 1997, After Amy 2001, The Chris Isaak Show 2002, Snow Queen 2002. *Address:* 114 Fremont Place, Los Angeles, CA 90005, USA.

FONDA, Jane; American actress and activist; b. 21 Dec. 1937, New York City; d. of the late Henry Fonda and of Frances Seymour; sister of Peter Fonda (q.v.); m. 1st Roger Vadim 1967 (divorced 1973, died 2000); one d.; m. 2nd Tom Hayden 1973 (divorced 1989); one s.; m. 3rd Ted Turner 1991 (divorced 2001); ed Emma Willard School, Troy, NY, Vassar Coll.; studied with Lee Strasberg and became mem. Actors Studio, New York; Founder and Chair. Georgia Campaign for Adolescent Pregnancy Prevention 1995–; est. Jane Fonda Center for Adolescent Reproductive Health, Emory Univ. School of Medicine 2002; produced 23 home exercise videos including Jane Fonda's Workout 1982 (top-grossing home video of all time); Acad. Award for Best Actress 1972, 1979, Golden Globe Award 1978, Great Medal of Paris 2010. *Films include:* Tall Story 1960, A Walk on the Wild Side 1962, Period of Adjustment 1962, Sunday in New York 1963, The Love Cage 1963, La Ronde 1964, Cat Ballou 1965, Histoires extraordinaires 1967, Barefoot in the Park 1967, Hurry Sundown 1967, Barbarella 1968, They Shoot Horses Don't They? 1969, Klute 1970, Steelyard Blues 1972, Tout va bien 1972, A Doll's House 1973, The Blue Bird 1975, Fun with Dick and Jane 1976, Julia 1977, Coming Home 1978, California Suite 1978, The Electric Horseman 1979, The China Syndrome 1979, Nine to Five 1980, On Golden Pond 1981, Roll-Over 1981, Agnes of God 1985, The Morning After 1986, The Old Gringo 1988, Stanley and Iris 1990, Monster-in-Law 2005, Georgia Rule 2007; producer Lakota Woman 1994. *Plays include:* There Was a Little Girl, Invitation to a March, The Fun Couple, Strange Interlude, 33 Variations (Broadway) 2009. *Television:* The Dollmaker (ABC-TV) 1984 (Emmy Award). *Publications:* Jane Fonda's Workout Book 1982, Women Coming of Age 1984, Jane Fonda's New Workout and Weight Loss Program 1986, Jane Fonda's New Pregnancy Workout and Total Birth Program 1989, Jane Fonda Workout Video, Jane Fonda Cooking for Healthy Living 1996, My Life So Far (autobiography) 2005. *Address:* c/o Kim Hodgert, Creative Artists Agency, 9830 Wilshire Boulevard, Beverly Hills, CA 90212-1825 (office); Georgia Campaign for Adolescent Pregnancy Prevention, 100 Auburn Avenue, Suite 200, Atlanta, GA 30303, USA (office). *Telephone:* (310) 288-4545 (office). *Fax:* (310) 288-4800 (office).

FONDA, Peter; American film actor, director and producer; b. 23 Feb. 1939, New York; s. of the late Henry Fonda and of Frances Seymour; brother of Jane Fonda (q.v.); m. Susan Brewer (divorced 1974); two c.; ed Univ. of Omaha. *Films include:* Tammy and the Doctor 1963, The Victors 1963, Lilith 1964, The Young Lovers 1964, The Wild Angels 1966, The Trip 1967, Easy Rider (also co-screenplay writer, co-producer) 1969, The Last Movie 1971, The Hired Hand (also dir) 1971, Two People (also dir) 1973, Idaho Transfer (dir) 1973, Dirty Mary, Crazy Larry 1974, Race with the Devil 1975, 92 in the Shade 1975, Killer Force 1975, Fighting Mad 1976, Futureworld 1976, Outlaw Blues 1977, High Ballin' 1978, Wanda Nevada (also dir) 1979, Open Season, Smokey and the Bandit II 1980, The Cannonball Run (cameo) 1981, Split Image 1982, Spasms 1983, Dance of the Dwarfs (also known as

Jungle Heat) 1983, Peppermint-Frieden 1983, Certain Fury 1985, Mercenary Fighters 1987, The Rose Garden 1989, Fatal Mission 1990, South Beach 1992, Deadfall 1993, Nadja 1994, Love and a 45 1994, Painted Hero 1996, Escape from LA 1996, Ulee's Gold 1997, Reckless, Diajobu My Friend, Family Spirit, Bodies Rest and Motion, Molly and Gina, The Limey 1999, South of Heaven, West of Hell 2000, Thomas and the Magic Railroad 2000, Second Skin 2000, Wooly Boys 2001, The Laramie Project 2002, The Heart Is Deceitful Above All Things 2004, Ghost Rider 2007, Wild Hogs 2007, 3:10 to Yuma 2007, Japan 2008, The Perfect Age of Rock 'n' Roll 2009, The Boondock Saints II: All Saints Day 2009, The Trouble with Bliss 2011. *Television films:* The Hostage Tower 1980, Don't Look Back 1996, A Reason to Live, A Time of Indifference, Sound, Certain Honorable Men, Montana, The Maldonado Miracle 2003, Capital City 2004, A Thief of Time 2004, Back When We Were Grownups 2004, Supernova (mini-series) 2005, The Gathering (mini-series) 2007, Journey to the Center of the Earth 2008. *Other work includes:* Grand Theft Auto: San Andreas (video game, voice) 2004. *Address:* IFA Talent Agency, 8730 West Sunset Boulevard, Suite 490, Los Angeles, CA 90069, USA (office).

FONSECA, Jorge Carlos, MA; Cape Verde lawyer, politician and head of state; *President;* b. (Jorge Carlos de Almeida Fonseca), 20 Oct. 1950, Mindelo; m.; three c.; ed Univ. of Lisbon; Dir-Gen. of Emigration 1975–77; Sec.-Gen., Ministry of Foreign Affairs 1977–79, Minister of Foreign Affairs 1991–93; Teaching Asst, Faculty of Law, Univ. of Lisbon 1982–90; Guest Prof. of Criminal Law, Inst. of Forensic Medicine, Lisbon 1987; Resident Dir and Guest Assoc. Prof., Law Course and Public Admin, Univ. da Asia Oriental, Macau 1989, 1990; unsuccessful cand. in presidential election 2001; Founder and Dir Direito e Cidadania (journal), Inst. of Legal and Social Science 2004–; Pres. of Cape Verde 2011–; mem. Editorial Bd Revista de Economia e Direito; Combatente da Liberdade da Pátria. *Publications:* several books and over 50 scientific and technical works in the field of law; two books of poetry. *Address:* Presidência da República, Palácio do Plateau, CP 100, Plateau, Praia, Santiago, Cape Verde. *Telephone:* 2616555 (office). *Fax:* 2614356 (office). *Website:* www.presidencia.cv (office).

FONSECA, Ralph H.; Belizean politician; b. 9 Aug. 1949; m.; three c.; ed St John's Coll.; fmr Asst Gen. Man. Texaco, Belize; fmr Area Gen. Man. Cardinal Distributors, Canada; fmr Research Engineer, Control Data; fmr Systems Analyst, Prescribe Data System; fmr gen. man. brewing co.; fmr Man. Dir Hillbank Agroindustry; fmr Chair. Belize Electricity Co.; fmr Chair. Belize Telecommuni-cations Authority Ltd; fmr Pres. Consolidated Electricity Services; mem. Parl. 1993–2008; Minister of Budget Man., Investment and Home Affairs 1999–2003, Minister of Finance and Home Affairs 2003–05; Minister of Home Affairs and Public Utilities 2005–08, of Housing 2007–08. *Address:* c/o People's United Party, 3 Queen St, Belize City, Belize. *Telephone:* 223-2428. *Fax:* 223-3476. *Website:* www .pupbelize.bz.

FONSECA, Rubem; Brazilian writer and screenwriter; b. 11 May 1925, Juiz de Fora, Minas Gerais; m. Théa Maud (deceased 1996); three c.; ed Escola de Policia, Rio de Janeiro, Fundação Getúlio Vargas, New York Univ.; started career as cop, apptd Police Commr São Cristóvão (RJ) 1952; Premio Camões 2003, Premio Juan Rulfo 2003. *Television:* Mandrake 1983, 2005, Agosto 1993. *Films:* Lúcia McCartney, Uma Garota de Programa 1971, Relatório de Um Homem Casado 1974, A Extorsão 1975, Stelinha 1990, A Grande Arte 1991, Bufo & Spallanzani 2001, The Man of the Year 2003, O Caso Morel 2006, El cobrador: In God We Trust 2006. *Publications:* Os prisioneiros 1963, A coleira do cão 1965, Lucía McCartney 1967, O caso Morel 1973, O homen de fevereiro ou março 1973, Feliz ano novo 1975, O cobrador (Prêmio Estácio de Sá) 1979, A grande arte (Prêmio Goethe, Prêmio Jabuti) 1983, Buffo & Spallanzani 1986, Vastas emoções e pensamentos imperfeitos (Prêmio Pedro Nava) 1988, Agosto 1990, Romance negro e outras histórias 1992, Contos reunidos 1994, O selvagem da ópera 1994, O buraco na parede (Prêmio Jabuti) 1995, Romance negro, Felis ano novo e outras histórias 1996, Histórias de amor 1997, E do meio do mundo prostitute só amores guardei ao meu charuto (Prêmio Machado de Assis) 1997, Confraria dos espadas (Prêmio Eça de Queiroz) 1998, O doente Molière (Prêmio de melhor romance do ano, Associação Paulista de Críticos de Arte) 2000, Secreções, excreções, desatinos 2001, Pequenas criaturas 2002, Diário de um fescenino 2003, 64 contos de Rubem Fonseca 2004, Ela e outras mulheres 2006, Los mejores relatos 2007, O Seminarista 2009, José 2011, Axilas e Outras Histórias Indecorosas 2011; contrib. to numerous antholo-gies. *Address:* Companhia das Letras, Rua Bandeira Paulista 702 cj. 32, 04532-002 São Paulo, SP, Brazil. *Telephone:* (11) 3707-3500. *Fax:* (11) 3707-3501. *Website:* www.ciadasletras.com.br.

FONSEKA, Gen. (retd) Sarath; Sri Lankan army officer (retd) and politician; b. 18 Dec. 1950; m. Anoma Indumathi Munasinghe; two c.; ed Dharmasoka Coll., Ambalangoda, Ananda Coll., Colombo; joined army 1970; has held numerous staff appointments, involved in operations Balawegaya and Jayasikuru that led to capture of Elephant Pass and Mankulam, wounded in Yaldewee operation 1993, as a Col, commanded 23 Brigade of Sri Lankan Army at Polonnaruwa 1993, led troops in Operation 'Midnight Express' to rescue besieged troops in Jaffna Fort 1993, as Deputy GOC, captured Jaffna from Tamil Tigers (LTTE) 1995, among other appointments held were Col, Gen. Staff Army HQ, Sri Lankan Army, Centre Commdt, Sri Lanka Sinha Regt, Brigade Commdr in Operation Ballavegaya, Deputy Commdt-5 Brigade Group, Mannar and Co-ordinating Officer for Gampaha Gum Gumaga, Sri Lanka Army, Chief of Staff of Sri Lankan Army, relinquished post to become Commdr of the Army, Chief of Defence Staff July–Nov. 2009 (resgnd); United National Party cand. for Pres. 2010; numerous decorations including Rana Wickrama Padakkama, Rana Sura Padakkama, Vishista Seva Vibhushanaya, Uttama Seva Padakkama, Desha Putra Sammanaya, Riviresa Campaign Services Medal, Poorna Bhoomi Padakkama, North and East Oper-ations Medal, Desha Putra Sammanaya, and several others. *Address:* c/o Ministry of Defence, 15/5 Baladaksha Mawatha, POB 572, Colombo 3, Sri Lanka.

FONTANA, Bernard, BEng; French business executive; *CEO, Holcim Ltd;* b. 1961; ed Ecole Polytechnique and the Ecole Nationale Supérieure des Techniques Avancées in Paris; began career with Groupe SNPE in France, Head of US operations 1998–2001, mem. Exec. Cttee 2001–04; joined ArcelorMittal 2004, given responsibility for HR, IT and Business Devt at Flat Carbon 2004–06, mem. Exec. Cttee ArcelorMittal with responsibility for Automotive Worldwide Business Unit 2006–07, mem. Group Man. Cttee responsible for HR and global alliance with Nippon Steel 2007–10; CEO Aperam (spun off from ArcelorMittal 2010) 2010–11;

CEO Holcim Ltd 2012–. *Address:* Holcim Group Support Ltd, Hagenholzstrasse 85, 8050 Zurich, Switzerland (office). *Telephone:* (58) 858-58-58 (office). *Fax:* (58) 858-58-59 (office). *E-mail:* info@holcim.com (office). *Website:* www.holcim.com (office).

FONTANA, Carlo; Italian opera house director and journalist; b. 15 March 1947, Milan; s. of Ciro Fontana; m. Roberta Cavallini; ed Univ. Statale di Milano; journalist 1968–77; responsible for youth activities, Piccolo Teatro di Milano 1968–71; Asst to Gen. Man. Teatro all Scala, Milan 1977–79, mem. Admin. Council 1980–84; Deputy Admin. Fonit Cetra 1979–84; Pres. Associazione Lirica Concertistica Italiana 1980–83; Dir Music Section, Venice Biennale 1983–86; Dir Ente Autonomo Teatro Comunale di Bologna 1984–90; Sovrintendente, Teatro alla Scala, Milan 1990–2005; Senator (cultural) 2006–08; Prof., Univ. of Pavia; Pres. Associazione Enti Lirici e Sinfonici 1986; mem. Commissione Centrale Musica, Consiglio Nazionale dello Spettacolo; Grande Ufficiale della Repubblica Italiana, Ambrogino d'Oro, Milan 1999. *Publication:* A scena aperta 2007. *Leisure interests:* sport, music. *Address:* c/o Mondadori Electa SpA, Via Trentacoste 7, 20134, Milan, Italy.

FONTANELLI, Paolo, MBA, PhD; Italian business executive; *CEO, Furla;* ed Classical Lyceum degree, Florence, Univ. of Florence (thesis work at Cornell Univ., USA), Bocconi Univ., Milan, Advanced Man. Program, Harvard Business School, USA; conducted research in astrophysics and achieved fellowships from Cornell Univ., Observatoire de Paris, Arecibo Observatory, Puerto-Rico and Nat. Radio Astronomy Observatory, Va, USA 1982–85; Payload Expert, Sax satellite project at Aeritalia SpA (Italian aerospace co.) 1986–88; Controller Eli Lilly Italia SpA 1988–89, Treasury Man. 1989–90; Chief Financial Officer, Industrie Puccioni SpA 1991–95; Asst to the CEO, Salvatore Ferragamo Italia SpA 1995–98, Group Chief Financial Officer 1998–99; Chief Financial Officer, Giorgio Armani Group 1999–2007, Pres. and CEO Giorgio Armani Hong Kong and Greater China 2000–07; CEO Furla 2007–. *Address:* Furla SpA, Via Bellaria 3/5, 40068 San Lazzaro di Savena, Bologna, Italy (office). *Telephone:* (051) 6202711 (office). *Fax:* (051) 450660 (office). *E-mail:* webmaster@furla.com (office). *Website:* www.furla .com (office).

FONTENEAU, Pascale; Belgian writer; b. 1963, Fougères, Ille-et-Vilaine; ed Université libre de Bruxelles; broadcast first story Chronique des polars on campus radio, Université libre de Bruxelles; works for Passa Porta (literary asscn); contrib. to Le Monde newspaper, Paris 2003–. *Publications include:* Confidences sur l'escalier 1992, Etats de lame 1993, Les Fils perdus de Sylvie Derijke 1995, Les Damnés de l'artère 1996, Otto 1997, La Puissance du désordre 1997, Curieux Sentiments 2000, La Vanité des pions 2000, Où est passé René (with Didier Lange) 2003, Trop c'est Trop 2003, TGV 2003, Crois-moi 2005, Jour de gloire 2006, Contretemps 2007, 1275 Ares 2008, Propriétés privées 2010, Hasbeen 2010. *Address:* c/o Les Éditions du Masque, 17 rue Jacob, 75006 Paris, France.

FONTES LIMA, Maria Cristina Lopes; Cape Verde lawyer and politician; b. 15 June 1958, Praia, Santiago; Minister of Local Admin 2001–02, Minister of Justice 2001–06, Minister of Interior 2002–04, Minister Adjunct to Prime Minister and Govt Spokesperson 2004–06, Minister of the Presidency of Council of Ministers 2006–08, Minister of State Reform and Nat. Defence 2006–11; fmr Chair. Network of African Women Ministerial and Parliamentarian Bureau. *Address:* c/o Ministry of State Reform and National Defence, Praia, Santiago, Cape Verde.

FOON, Momodou S.; Gambian economist, academic and government official; ed Haverford Coll., Pa, Univ. of Glasgow, Scotland; fmr Asst Lecturer, Dept of Econs, Univ. of The Gambia; fmr consultant to UNDP on macroeconomic issues; joined Cen. Bank of The Gambia 1979, becoming Prin. Economist and Head of Money and Credit Div., Economic Research Dept, later Special Asst to Gov., Cen. Bank of The Gambia; Sr Policy Adviser to Minister of Finance and Econ. Affairs 1993–95; joined West African Inst. for Financial and Econ. Man. (WAIFEM), Lagos, Nigeria 1999, becoming Dir, Macroeconomic Man. Dept, Acting Dir-Gen., WAIFEM Feb.–May 2009; Perm. Sec., Ministry of Econ. Planning and Industry – March 2010, Ministry of Finance and Econ. Affairs March–July 2010. *Address:* c/o Ministry of Finance and Economic Affairs, The Quadrangle, POB 9686, Banjul, Gambia (office).

FOOT, Michael David Kenneth Willoughby, CBE, MA, FCIB; British financial services industry executive and fmr financial regulator; *Non-Director Chairman, Promontory Financial Group (UK) Ltd;* b. 16 Dec. 1946; s. of Kenneth Willoughby Foot and Ruth Joan Foot (née Cornah); m. Michele Annette Cynthia Macdonald 1972; one s. two d.; ed Pembroke Coll., Cambridge and Yale Univ.; joined Bank of England 1969, Man. 1978, Sr Man. 1985; seconded to IMF, Washington, DC as UK Alt. Exec. Dir 1985–87; Head of Foreign Exchange Div., England 1988–90, European Div. 1990–93, Banking Supervision Div. 1993–94, Deputy Dir Supervision and Surveillance 1994–96, Exec. Dir 1996–98; Man. Dir Financial Services Authority 1998–2004; Inspector of Bank and Trust Cos, Cen. Bank of the Bahamas 2004–07; Non-Dir Chair. Promontory Financial Group (UK) Ltd, London 2007–; Hon. Pres. ACI (UK) 2002–04. *Publications:* essays on monetary econs in various books and professional journals. *Leisure interests:* choral singing, tennis. *Address:* Promontory Financial Group (UK) Ltd, 14 Devonshire Square, London, EC2M 4YT, England (office). *Telephone:* (20) 7377-2360 (office). *Fax:* (20) 7377-2361 (office). *Website:* www.promontory.com (office).

FOOTE, Huger, BA; American photographer and artist; b. 13 Nov. 1961, Memphis, Tenn.; s. of the late Shelby Foote and Gwyn Foote; ed Sarah Lawrence Coll., New York; began photography aged 12; photo assistant, Paris 1983–87; freelance photographer, New York 1987–93; began working as professional artist, Memphis 1993–98; moved to London 1998; has held exhbns across Europe and the USA. *Solo exhibitions include:* Ledbetter Lusk Gallery, Memphis 1996, Gallery of Contemporary Photography, Santa Monica 1997, Dorothy de Pauw Gallery, Brussels 2000, Patrick de Brock Gallery, Knokke. *Group exhibitions include:* Ledbetter Lusk Gallery 1995, Memphis Coll. of Art 1996, Artfair Seattle 1997, Memphis Arts Council 1997, The Armory, New York 1998, River Gallery, Chatanooga 1999, Belgian Art Fair 1999, Hamiltons Gallery, Brussels 2000, Sotheby's, London 2000, Contemporary Art Center of Virginia 2000, Houldsworth Fine Art, London 2000, Hamiltons Gallery, London 2005. *Publications:* Seasons 1997, Sleep (photo essay) 2000, My Friend From Memphis (monograph) 2000; contribs to Wall Street Journal, Vanity Fair, Vogue etc. *Leisure interests:* cycling,

travelling in Africa and Pakistan. *Address:* c/o Hamiltons Gallery, 3 Carlos Place, London, W1 2TU, England (office).

FORAU SOALAOI, Clay; Solomon Islands politician; *Minister for Foreign Affairs and Trade Relations;* b. 10 Oct. 1976; ed Solomon Islands Coll. of Higher Educ.; worked in educ. before entering politics; mem. Nat. Parl. for Temotu Vatud 2006–, Chair. Constitution Review Cttee 2008–, Leader of the Independent Mems 2010–11; Minister for Justice and Legal Affairs April–May 2006, for Health and Medical Services 2006–07, for Police, Nat. Security and Correctional Services April–Nov. 2011, for Foreign Affairs and Trade Relations 2012–; fmr mem. Social Credit Party; mem. People's Federation Party. *Address:* Ministry of Foreign Affairs and External Trade, POB G10, Honiara, Solomon Islands (office). *Telephone:* 28612 (office). *Fax:* 20351 (office). *E-mail:* psforeign@pmc.gov.sb (office).

FORBES, Adm. (retd) Sir Ian, Kt, KCB, CBE; British naval officer (retd) and business executive; *Senior Adviser, Booz & Company;* ed RAF Staff Coll., Bracknell, Royal Coll. of Defense Studies (RCDS); joined RN 1965, tours in HM Yacht Britannia and on American Exchange with USS WH Standley; qualified as Prin. Warfare Officer 1979; specialised as Anti Air Warfare Officer 1978; fmr Commdr HMS Kingfisher, HMS Diomede, HMS Chatham, HMS Invincible (involved in NATO bombing campaign over Bosnia 1995, Operation Desert Fox in Gulf 1999), HMS Illustrious; engaged in active operations off Iceland, the Falklands, the Gulf and Adriatic; Staff Officer Operations to Comas Wsrikfor 1986–88; participant in Standing Naval Force Atlantic; promoted Rear Adm. 1995; served as Mil. Adviser to High Rep. in Sarajevo and Chief of Staff, Office of the High Rep., Bosnia; Commdr UK maritime contribs to NATO operations in Kosovo 1999; Flag Officer Surface Flotilla, NATO 2000, Deputy Saclant 2001, Adm. Supreme Allied Command Atlantic 2002–04; retd from service 2004; Sr Adviser, Booz & Co. 2006–; Assoc. Fellow, Royal United Services Inst.; Mentor to Sr Mil. Command Courses; mem. Windsor Leadership Trust; Gov. Portsmouth High School for Girls; Chair. Council, Eastbourne Coll. 2005–; NATO Meritorious Service Medal, HRH Queen' Commendation for Valuable Service 1995. *Address:* Booz & Company, 7 Savoy Court, Strand, London, WC2R 0JP, England (office). *Telephone:* (20) 7393-3333 (office). *Fax:* (20) 7393-0025 (office). *Website:* www.booz .com (office).

FORBES, Malcolm Stevenson (Steve), Jr, LHD; American publishing executive; *President and CEO, Forbes Inc.;* b. 18 July 1947, Morristown, NJ; s. of Malcolm Forbes and Roberta Laidlaw; m. Sabina Beekman 1971; ed Princeton Univ. and Lycoming Coll. Jacksonville Univ.; with Forbes Inc., New York 1970–, Pres. and COO 1980–90, Pres. and CEO 1990–; Deputy Ed.-in-Chief, Forbes magazine 1982–90, Ed.-in-Chief 1990–, Chair. 2008–; Chair. Forbes Newspapers 1989–; mem. Bd for International Broadcasting 1983–93, Chair. 1985–93; mem. Advisory Council, Dept of Econs Princeton Univ. 1985–; mem. Bd of Dirs FreedomWorks 2006–; mem. Bd of Trustees, Heritage Foundation; several hon. degrees. *Films:* Some Call It Greed (scriptwriter) 1977. *Publication:* Fact and Comment (ed.) 1974, A New Birth of Freedom 1999, Flat Tax Revolution: Using a Postcard to Abolish the IRS 2005, How Capitalism Will Save Us: Why Free People and Free Markets Are the Best Answer in Today's Economy (with Elizabeth Ames) 2009, Power Ambition Glory: The Stunning Parallels between Great Leaders of the Ancient World and Today. . . and the Lessons You Can Learn (with John Prevas) 2009. *Address:* Forbes Inc., 60 Fifth Avenue, New York, NY 10011, USA (office). *Website:* www.forbesinc.com (office).

FORD, Anna, BA, FRGS; British company director and fmr broadcaster; b. 2 Oct. 1943; d. of John Ford and Jean Beattie Winstanley; m. 1st Alan Holland Bittles (divorced 1976); m. 2nd Charles Mark Edward Boxer (died 1988); two d.; ed Minehead Grammar School, White House Grammar School, Brampton and Univ. of Manchester; work for students' interests, Univ. of Manchester 1966–69; Lecturer, Rupert Stanley Coll. of Further Educ., Belfast 1970–72; staff tutor, Social Sciences, NI Region, Open Univ. 1972–74, 1974–78; presenter and reporter, Man Alive (Granada TV), Tomorrow's World (BBC); newscaster, ITN 1978–80; with TV-AM 1980–83; freelance broadcasting and writing 1983–86; BBC News and Current Affairs 1989–2006; mem. Bd of Dirs J Sainsbury plc 2006–12; Trustee, Royal Botanic Gardens, Kew 1995–; Chancellor, Univ. of Manchester 2001–04, Co-Chancellor 2004–08; Fellow, Royal Geographical Soc.; Hon. Fellow, Open Univ. 1998; Hon. Bencher Middle Temple 2002; Hon. BA (Cen. Lancs.) 1998; Hon. LLD (Manchester) 1998; Dr hc (Univ. of St Andrews) 2006. *Publication:* Men: A Documentary 1985. *Leisure interests:* talking, walking, drawing. *Address:* c/o June Ford-Crush, PO Box 57948, London, W4 2UJ, England.

FORD, Hon. Anthony David, LLB; New Zealand judge; *Chief Justice of Tonga;* b. 8 May 1942, Hokitika; s. of Tom Ford and Cath Ford; five d. two s.; ed Auckland Univ.; currently Chief Justice of Tonga; Grand Cross of the Order of Queen Salote. *Address:* PO Box 1309, Nuku'alofa, Tonga (home). *Telephone:* (676) 25-906 (home); (676) 24-771 (office). *Fax:* (676) 25-906 (office). *E-mail:* valda@kalianet.to (office).

FORD, Bruce; American singer (tenor); m. H. Ypma 1982; one s.; ed Texas Tech. Univ., Houston Opera Studio; sings in major opera houses in N America and Europe, specializing in Mozart and bel canto composers; Rossini's Otello (Covent Garden), Ermione (Glyndebourne), Zelmira, Ricciardo e Zoraide (Pesaro) revived for him; concert appearances include La Scala, Edinburgh Festival, Covent Garden, San Francisco Opera, Düsseldorf Symphonic, Chicago Lyric Opera and Amsterdam Concertgebouw; extensive recording career including many rare 19th century operas; Seal of Texas Tech. Univ. 1997. *Leisure interests:* scuba diving, sailing. *Address:* c/o Athole Still Opera Ltd, 25–27 Westow Street, London, SE19 3RY, England (office). *Telephone:* (20) 8771-5271 (office). *Fax:* (20) 8771-8172 (office). *Website:* www.atholestill.co.uk (office); www.bruce-ford.com. *E-mail:* tenorbruceford@gmail.com (office); hetty.ford@gmail.com (office).

FORD, David Frank, MA, PhD, STM; Irish professor of divinity; *Regius Professor of Divinity, University of Cambridge;* b. 23 Jan. 1948, Dublin; s. of George Ford and Phyllis Woodman; m. Deborah Hardy 1982; one s. two d. (one d. deceased); ed High School, Dublin, Trinity Coll., Dublin, St John's Coll., Cambridge, Yale Univ., USA, Univ. of Tübingen, Germany; Lecturer in Theology, Univ. of Birmingham 1976–90, Sr Lecturer 1990–91; Regius Prof. of Divinity, Univ. of Cambridge 1991–, Chair. Faculty Bd of Divinity 1993–95, Fellow, Selwyn Coll. Cambridge 1991–, Foundation mem. Trinity Coll. Cambridge 1991–, mem.

Syndicate Cambridge University Press 1993–, Chair. Man. Cttee Centre for Advanced Religious and Theological Studies, Univ. of Cambridge 1995–; Chair. Council Westcott House Theological Coll. 1991–2006; mem. Archbishop of Canterbury's Urban Theology Working Group 1991–96; Fellow, Center of Theological Inquiry, Princeton Univ. 1993–; Founding mem. and mem. Man. Cttee Soc. for Scriptural Reasoning 1996–; Pres. Soc. for the Study of Theology 1997–98; mem. Postgraduate Studies in Philosophy and Theology, Humanities Research Bd of The British Acad. 1997–99, Church of England Doctrine Comm. 1998–2003; Founding Dir Cambridge Inter-Faith Programme 2002–; Academic mem. World Econ. Forum Council of 100 Leaders for West-Islamic World Dialogue 2003–; mem. Arts and Humanities Research Council Peer Review Coll. 2005–; mem. Advisory Bd Centre for Christian Studies, Hong Kong 2006–; Advisory Bd of ResponsAbility 2007–; mem. Bd of Advisors, John Templeton Foundation 2008–; Trustee, Golden Web Foundation 2006–, Center of Theological Inquiry, Princeton 2007–, The Murray Cox Foundation 2007–; Lay Canon Theologian of Birmingham Cathedral 2006–; Hon. DD (Birmingham) 2000. Publications: Barth and God's Story 1981, Jubilate: Theology in Praise (with D. W. Hardy) 1984, Meaning and Truth in 2 Corinthians (with F. M. Young) 1987, The Modern Theologians 1997, The Shape of Living 1997, Self and Salvation: Being Transformed 1999, Theology: A Very Short Introduction 1999, Jesus (ed. with M. Higton) 2002, Reading Texts, Seeking Wisdom (co-ed. with Graham Stanton) 2003, Fields of Faith: Theology and Religious Studies for the Twenty-First Century (co-ed. with Ben Quash and Janet Martin Soskice 2005, The Promise of Scriptural Reasoning (co-ed. with C. C. Pecknold) 2006, Musics of Belonging: The Poetry of Micheal O'Siadhail (co-ed. with Marc Caball) 2006, Christian Wisdom: Desiring God and Learning in Love 2007, Shaping Theology: Engagements in a Religious and Secular World 2007. Leisure interests: literature, walking, ball games, kayaking, family and friends. Address: Faculty of Divinity, West Road, Cambridge, CB3 9BS, England (office). Telephone: (1223) 763031 (office). Fax: (1223) 763003 (office). E-mail: dff1000@cam.ac.uk (office). Website: www.divinity.cam.ac.uk (office).

FORD, Sir David Robert, KBE, LVO; British government official (retd) and business executive; b. 22 Feb. 1935; s. of William Ewart Ford and Edna Ford; m. 1st Elspeth Anne Muckart 1958 (divorced 1987); two s. two d.; m. 2nd Gillian Petersen (née Monsarrat) 1987; ed Tauntons School, Royal Coll. of Defence Studies; officer, RA 1955–72, retd from army, rank of Maj.; seconded to Hong Kong Govt 1967; Deputy Dir Hong Kong Govt Information Service 1972–74, Dir 1974–76; Deputy Sec. Hong Kong Govt Secr. 1976; Under-Sec. NI Office 1977–79; Sec. for Information, Hong Kong Govt 1979–80; Hong Kong Commr in London 1980–81, 1994–96; Royal Coll. of Defence Studies 1982; Dir of Housing, Hong Kong Govt 1983–84, Sec. for Housing 1985, for the Civil Service 1985–86; Chief Sec., Hong Kong 1986–93, Hong Kong Commr in London 1994–97; retd from public service June 1997; Chair. UK Broadband Ltd; mem. Bd of Dirs PCCW Limited; fmr Chair. Council for the Protection of Rural England. Leisure interests: rare breeds of cattle and sheep, fishing, tennis. Address: Culverwell Farm, Branscombe, Devon, EX12 3DA, England (home).

FORD, Harrison; American actor; b. 13 July 1942, Chicago; m. 1st Mary Ford; two s.; m. 2nd Melissa Ford (divorced 2004); one s. one d.; m. 3rd Calista Flockhart 2010; one s.; ed Ripon Coll.; numerous TV appearances; Cecil B. DeMille Award, Golden Globes 2002, American Film Inst. Lifetime Achievement Award 2000. Films include: Dead Heat on a Merry-Go-Round 1966, Luv 1967, A Time for Killing 1967, Journey to Shiloh 1968, The Long Ride Home 1967, Getting Straight 1970, Zabriskie Point 1970, The Conversation 1974, American Graffiti 1974, Star Wars 1977, Heroes 1977, Force 10 from Navarone 1978, Apocalypse Now 1979, Hanover Street 1979, Frisco Kid 1979, The Empire Strikes Back 1980, Raiders of the Lost Ark 1981, Blade Runner 1982, Return of the Jedi 1983, Indiana Jones and the Temple of Doom 1984, Witness 1985, The Mosquito Coast 1986, Working Girl 1988, Frantic 1988, Indiana Jones and the Last Crusade 1989, Presumed Innocent 1990, Regarding Henry 1991, The Fugitive 1992, Patriot Games 1992, Clear and Present Danger 1994, Sabrina 1995, The Devil's Own 1996, Air Force One 1996, Six Days and Seven Nights 1998, Random Hearts 1999, What Lies Beneath 2000, K-19: The Widowmaker (also exec. producer) 2002, Hollywood Homicide 2003, No True Glory: The Battle for Fallujah 2006, Firewall 2006, Indiana Jones and the Kingdom of the Crystal Skull 2008, Crossing Over 2009, Extraordinary Measures 2010, Morning Glory 2010, 42 2013. Address: c/o United Talent Agency, 9560 Wilshire Boulevard, Beverly Hills, CA 90212, USA (office).

FORD, Richard, BA, MFA; American writer and academic; Professor, Trinity College, Dublin; b. 16 Feb. 1944, Jackson, Miss.; m. Kristina Hensley Ford 1968; ed Michigan State Univ., Univ. of California, Irvine; Lecturer, Univ. of Michigan, Ann Arbor 1974–76; Asst Prof. of English, Williams Coll., Williamstown, Mass 1978–79; Lecturer, Princeton Univ. 1980–81; Prof., Trinity Coll., Dublin 2008–; Guggenheim Fellowship 1977–78; Nat. Endowment for the Arts Fellowships 1979–80, 1985–86; mem. American Acad. of Arts and Letters, PEN, Writers' Guild, American Acad. of Arts and Sciences; Dr hc (Rennes, France, Michigan); Miss. Acad. of Arts and Letters Literature Award 1987, American Acad. of Arts and Letters Award for Literature 1989, American Acad. of Arts and Letters Award in Merit for the Novel 1997, PEN-Malamud Award for Short Fiction 2001; Commdr, Ordre des Arts et des Lettres. Screenplays: American Tropical 1983, Bright Angel 1991. Publications: A Piece of My Heart (novel) 1976, The Ultimate Good Luck (novel) 1981, The Sportswriter (novel) 1986, Rock Springs (short stories) 1987, My Mother in Memory (ed.) 1988, The Best American Short Stories (ed.) 1990, Wildlife (novel) 1990, The Granta Book of the American Short Story (ed.) 1992, Independence Day (novel, Pulitzer Prize for Fiction 1996, PEN/Faulkner Award for Fiction 1996) 1995, Women with Men (short stories) 1997, The Granta Book of the American Long Story (ed.) 1999, A Multitude of Sins (short stories) 2002, The Lay of the Land (novel) 2006, The New Granta Book of the American Short Story (ed.) 2007, The Bascombe Novels 2009, Canada (novel) 2012. Address: International Creative Management, 825 Eighth Avenue, New York, NY 10019, USA (office). Telephone: (212) 556-5764 (office).

FORD, Robert (Rob); Canadian business executive and politician; Mayor of Toronto; b. 28 May 1969; s. of Doug Ford; m. Renata Ford; one s. one d.; mem. Toronto City Council for Etobicoke North 2000–10; Mayor of Toronto 2010–; Prin. Deco Labels & Tags (family printing business); f. Rob Ford Football Foundation. Address: Office of the Mayor, Toronto City Hall, 2nd Floor, 100 Queen St West,

Toronto, ON M5H 2N2, Canada (office). Telephone: (416) 397-3673 (office). E-mail: mayor_ford@toronto.ca (office). Website: www.toronto.ca/mayor_ford/index.htm (office).

FORD, Tom; American fashion designer and film maker; President and CEO, Tom Ford International; b. 1962, Texas; ed New York Univ., Parsons School of Design; fmrly acted in TV commercials, asst to designer Cathy Hardwick, with Perry Ellis Co.; joined Gucci Group 1990, Design Dir 1992–94, Creative Dir 1994–2004, Vice-Chair. Man. Bd 2002–04; Creative Dir, Yves St Laurent Rive Gauche and YSL Beauté 2000–04; est. Tom Ford Int. 2005, currently Pres. and CEO, launched menswear collection Spring 2007; involved in fund raising in US and Europe; four Council of Fashion Designers of America awards, five VH-1/Vogue Fashion awards, two Fashion Editor's Club of Japan awards, two US Accessory Council awards, Best Fashion Designer, Time Magazine 2001, GQ Designer of the Year 2001, Fashion Design Achievement Award, Cooper Hewitt Museum 2002, Andre Leon Talley Lifetime Achievement Award, Savannah Coll. of Art and Design 2005. Films: A Single Man (dir) 2009. Address: Tom Ford HQ, 845 Madison Avenue, New York, NY 10022, USA (office). Telephone: (212) 359-0300 (office). Fax: (212) 359-0301 (office). Website: www.tomford.com (office).

FORD, Wendell Hampton; American fmr politician; b. 8 Sept. 1924, Owensboro, Ky; s. of E. M. Ford and Irene Ford (née Schenk); m. Jean Neel 1943; one s. one d.; ed Daviess County High School, Univ. of Kentucky, Maryland School of Insurance; served in US Army, Ky 1944–46, Nat. Guard 1949–62; Chief Asst to Gov. of Kentucky 1959–61; mem. Ky Senate 1966–67; Lt-Gov. Kentucky 1967–71, Gov. 1971–74; Senator from Kentucky 1974–97, Asst Minority Leader 1995–97, fmr mem. Senate Energy and Natural Resources Cttee, Commerce, Science, Transportation Cttee (Chair. Consumer Sub-Cttee); mem. Democratic Steering Cttee, Chair. Democratic Nat. Campaign Cttee 1976, Head of Democratic Senatorial Campaign Cttee; Majority Whip 1991–97; Chair. Senate Rules Cttee, Jt Cttee on Printing; Chair. Nat. Democratic Govs 1973–74; Chair. Jt Congressional Cttee on Inaugural Ceremonies; fmr mem. Nat. Democratic Party Advisory Council; fmr Chair. Common Law Enforcement, Justice and Public Safety, Southern Govs Conf.; mem. US Chamber of Commerce, Pres. 1956–57; Int. Vice-Pres. Jaycees, Distinguished Fellow, Martin School of Public Policy and Admin., Univ. of Ky 1999–. Leisure interests: fishing, hunting. Address: 2017 Fieldcrest Drive, Owensboro, KY 42301, USA (home).

FORD, William Clay, Jr, MS; American automobile industry executive; Executive Chairman and Chairman of the Board of Directors, Ford Motor Company; b. 3 May 1957, Detroit, Mich.; s. of William Clay Ford and Martha Firestone; m. Lisa Ford; four c.; ed Princeton Univ., Massachusetts Inst. of Tech.; joined Ford Motor Co. as product-planning analyst 1979, then various positions in mfg, sales, marketing, product devt and finance; served on Ford's Nat. Bargaining Team in Ford–United Auto Workers talks 1982; Planning Man., Car Product Devt 1985–86; Dir, Comm. Vehicle Marketing, Ford of Europe 1986–87; Chair. and Man. Dir, Ford of Switzerland 1987–89; elected to Bd of Dirs Ford Motor Co. 1988, Chair. Bd Finance Cttee 1995–99, Bd's Environmental and Public Policy Cttee 1997, Bd's Nominating and Governance Cttee 1999, Chair. of Bd 1999–, Vice-Pres. Ford Motor Co. 1994, CEO 2001–06, Exec. Chair. 2006–; Exec. Dir Business Strategy, Ford Automotive Group 1991–92, Gen. Man., Climate Control Div. 1992–94, Head of Commercial Truck Vehicle Centre 1994–95; mem. World Econ. Forum's Global Leaders for Tomorrow; Chair. Detroit Econ. Club; Bd of Dirs, Business Leaders for Michigan; Trustee, Henry Ford Health System; Vice-Chair. Detroit Lions Inc. (professional football team); Co-Chair. Country Music Hall of Fame Capital Campaign 2011; mem. Bd of Dirs e-Bay, Princeton Varsity Club 2013; mem. Nat. Football League Broadcast Cttee; Hon. Chair. Southeast Mich. Consortium for Water Quality, Hon. mem. Golden Key Int. Honour Soc.; Dr hc (Koc Univ., Istanbul) 2006; Hon. DIur (Univ. of Michigan) 2011; Hon. DHumLitt (Bradley Univ.) 2012; Automotive Exec. of the Year 2006, Boneh Kehillah Award, Jewish Community Center of Detroit 2007, inducted into Irish America Hall of Fame 2011. Leisure interests: fly-fishing, Tae Kwon Do, ice hockey, tennis, cars. Address: Ford Motor Company, World Headquarters, One American Road, Dearborn, MI 48126-2798, USA (office). Telephone: (313) 322-3000 (office). Fax: (313) 845-6073 (office). Website: www.ford.com (office).

FORDE, Sir Henry de Boulay, Kt, PC, QC, LLM, KA; Barbadian politician and lawyer; b. 20 March 1933, Christ Church; adopted s. of the late Courtley Ifill and of Elise Ifill; m. Cheryl Wendy Forde; four s.; ed Harrison Coll., Barbados, Christ's Coll., Cambridge, Middle Temple, London; Research Asst, Dept of Criminology, Univ. of Cambridge 1958, Research Student, Int. Law, worked on British Digest of Int. Law, Univ. of Cambridge 1958–59, Supervisor and Tutor in Int. Law, Emmanuel Coll., Cambridge 1958–59; called to English Bar 1959, to Barbadian Bar 1959; Lecturer, Extra-Mural Programme, Univ. of West Indies 1961–68, Part-time Lecturer, Caribbean Studies 1964–69; mem. House of Ass. for Christ Church West 1971–2003; Minister of External Affairs and Attorney-Gen. 1976–81; Minister of State 1993; Leader of the Opposition 1986–89, 1991–93; mem. Privy Council 1976–92, 1996–; Chair. and Political Leader, Barbados Labour Party 1986–93; Chair. Commonwealth Observer Group to the Seychelles 1991, to Fiji Islands 2001; mem. Commonwealth Cttee on Vulnerability of Small States 1985, Commonwealth Parl. Asscn, Editorial Bds of The Round Table, Int. Comm. of Jurists 1987–92, Barbados Bar Asscn, Hon. Soc. of Middle Temple, Int. Tax Planning Asscn, Interparl. Human Rights Network, Barbados Nat. Trust, Int. Acad. of Estate and Trust Law, Int. Inst. for Democracy and Electoral Assistance, Inter-American Comm. on Human Rights; Kt of St Andrew, Order of Barbados. Leisure interests: reading, walking, gardening. Address: Juris Chambers, Parker House, Wildey Business Park, Wildey Road, St Michael, Barbados (office); Codrington Court, Society, St John, Barbados, West Indies (home). Telephone: 429-5320 (office); 429-2203 (office); 423-3881 (home). Fax: 429-2206 (office); 423-3949 (home). E-mail: shf@jurischambers.com (office).

FOREHAND, Joe W., BS, MSc; American business executive; Chairman, Aricent Inc.; m.; two s.; ed Auburn Univ., Purdue Univ.; joined Accenture, Atlanta 1972, made Pnr 1982, held various man. positions including Leader, Global Communications and High Tech. Group, CEO 1999–2004, Chair. 2001–06 (retd); Sr Advisor, Kohlberg Kravis & Roberts 2006–; mem. Bd of Dirs Aricent Inc. 2006–, Chair. 2008–; mem. Hands On Network Advisory Council; fmr mem. Business Roundtable; Carl S. Sloane Award for Excellence in Man. Consulting 2003, Morgan

Stanley Leadership Award 2003. *Address:* Aricent Inc., 700 Hansen Way, Palo Alto, CA 94304, USA (office). *Telephone:* (650) 391-1088 (office). *Fax:* (650) 391-1089 (office). *Website:* www.aricent.com (office).

FOREMAN, Amanda, BA, PhD, FRSL; British historian, writer and journalist; b. 30 June 1968, London, England; d. of Carl Foreman; m.; one s. four d.; ed Sarah Lawrence Coll., Bronxville, NY, Lady Margaret Hall, Oxford; Henrietta Jex Blake Sr Scholarship, Univ. of Oxford 1998; TV and radio presenter 1998–; Whitbread Prize 1999. *Publications:* Georgiana: Duchess of Devonshire (Whitbread Award for Biography of the Year) 1998, Georgiana's World 2001, A World on Fire: An Epic History of Two Nations Divided 2010. *Address:* c/o The Wylie Agency, 17 Bedford Square, London, WC1B 3JA, England (office). *E-mail:* mail@wylieagency.co.uk (office). *Website:* www.wylieagency.co.uk (office); www.amanda-foreman.com.

FOREMAN, George; American fmr professional boxer; b. 10 Jan. 1949, Marshall, Tex.; s. of J.D. Foreman and Nancy Foreman; m. five times; five s. five d.; Olympic heavyweight champion Mexico 1968; World heavyweight champion 1973–74, 1994–95; lost title to Muhammad Ali (q.v.) (knockout in 8th) in 1974; recaptured it on 5 Nov. 1994 at age 45 with a 10-round knockout of WBC/IBF champion Michael Moorer, becoming oldest man to win heavyweight crown; successfully defended title at age 46 against Axel Schulz; gave up IBF title after refusing rematch with Schulz; now an evangelical minister; f. a youth and community centre; has diverse business interests, has endorsed or sold numerous products such as hamburgers, hot dogs and grilling machines and rotisseries; AP Male Athlete of the Year 1994. *Publication:* By George (autobiog.), God's in My Corner (with Ken Abraham) 2007, Knockout Entrepeneur (with Ken Abraham) 2009. *Leisure interests:* raising livestock, breeding horses. *Address:* c/o The Church of Lord Jesus Christ, 2501 Lone Oak, Houston, TX 77093, USA. *E-mail:* george@biggeorge.com. *Website:* www .biggeorge.com (office).

FORGEARD, Noël, LèsScEcon; French mining engineer and business executive; b. 8 Dec. 1946, Ferté-Gaucher; s. of Henri Forgeard and Laurence Duprat; m. Marie-Cécile de Place 1972; one s. three d.; ed Lycée Louis-le-Grand, Ecole Polytechnique, Paris; qualified as mining engineer; entered mining industry in Clermont-Ferrand, industry rep. to Auvergne prefecture 1972–73; Asst Sec.-Gen. Dept of Mining, Ministry for Industry 1973–76, Sec.-Gen. 1976–78; Tech. Adviser to Minister of Transport 1978–80, of Defence 1980; Head of Industrial Affairs and Armaments, Ministry of Defence 1980–81; Deputy Pres., Asst Gen. Man. Compagnie française des aciers spéciaux (CFAS) 1982–84, Prés., Dir-Gen. 1984–86; Man. Dir then Pres., Dir-Gen. Ascometal 1985–86; Chair. Asfor Steel Products 1986–87; Tech Adviser and Head of Industrial Affairs, Office of the Prime Minister 1986–87; Man. Defence and Space Divs Matra 1987, Pres., Dir-Gen. Matra-défense espace finance co. (Sofimades), Matra Hautes technologies, Matra Bac Dynamics, mem. Exec. and Strategy Cttee and Gen. Man. Lagardère SCA 1993–98; Man. Dir Airbus Industrie 1998–2005, CEO 2000–05, Jt CEO European Aeronautic Defence and Space Co. EADS NV (main shareholder of Airbus) 2005–06; Dir Matra systèmes et information, Snecma, Matra-Marconi Space NV; Vice-Pres. Groupement des industries de l'aéronautique et de l'espace (Gifas); Officier, Légion d'honneur, Ordre nat. du Mérite; Public Enterprise Foundation Award 1971. *Leisure interests:* modern art, swimming. *Address:* Airbus, 1 rond-point Maurice Bellonte, 31707 Blagnac cedex; 85 av. de Wagram, 75017 Paris (home); Le Roc, 35800 St-Briac-sur-Mer, France (home).

FORIEL-DESTEZET, Philippe, MBA; French business executive; *Honorary President, Adecco SA;* b. 12 Sept. 1935; m.; ed Hautes Etudes Commerciales; Founder Ecco SA, Lyon 1964, Dir, Adecco Group 1996–2006, Co-Chair. 2004–05, Jt Chair. Adecco SA 1996–2002, Hon. Pres. 2006–; Chair. Akila Finance, Luxembourg; Chevalier, Légion d'honneur. *Address:* PFD Office, 16 rue Jean Pierre Brasseur, 1258 Luxembourg, Luxembourg (office). *Telephone:* 27-44-92-80 (office). *Fax:* 27-44-92-81 (office). *E-mail:* secretariat@pfd-office.lu (office). *Website:* www .adecco.com (office).

FORMAN, Miloš; American film director; b. 18 Feb. 1932, Čáslav, Czechoslovakia; m. Martina Forman; four s.; ed Film Faculty, Acad. of Music and Dramatic Art, Prague; Dir Film Presentations, Czechoslovak TV 1954–56; of Laterna Magika, Prague 1958–62; mem. Artistic Cttee, Šebor-Bor Film Producing Group; Legion d'Honneur; Klement Gottwald State Prize 1967, Lifetime Achievement Award for Distinguished Achievement in Motion Picture Direction, Directors Guild of America 2013. *Films include:* Talent Competition, Peter and Pavla 1963 (Czechoslovak Film Critics' Award 1963, Grand Prix 17th Int. Film Festival, Locarno 1964), The Knave of Spades, A Blonde in Love (Cidalc Prize, Venice Festival 1965, Grand Prize French Film Acad. 1966) 1965, Episode in Zruč, Like a House on Fire (A Fireman's Ball) 1968, Taking Off 1971, Visions of Eight (Co-Dir) 1973, One Flew Over the Cuckoo's Nest 1975 (Acad. Award for Best Dir 1976), Hair 1979, Ragtime 1980, Amadeus 1983 (Acad. Award for Best Picture, César Award 1985), Valmont 1988, The People vs. Larry Flynt (Golden Globe for Best Dir 1996) 1996, Man on the Moon (Silver Bear for Best Dir, Berlin Film Festival 2000) 1999, Goya's Ghosts 2006, Dobre placená procházka 2009; appeared in New Year's Day 1989, Keeping the Faith 2000. *Publication:* Turnaround: A Memoir (with Jan Novak) 1993. *Address:* 150 Central Park South, New York, NY 10019, USA.

FORMIGONI, Roberto, MA; Italian politician; b. 30 March 1947, Lecco; s. of the late Emilio Formigoni and Doralice Baroni; ed Catholic Univ. of Milan, Univ. of Sorbonne, Paris; co-f. Movimento Popolare (political arm of Catholic Movt Comunione e Liberazione), Nat. Pres. 1976–87; MEP (Christian Democratic Party) 1984–94, Vice-Chair. Presidential Office 1989–94; elected Deputy 1987, 1992, 1994 (Christian Democratic Party); Under-Sec., Ministry of Environment 1993–94; Pres. Lombardy Region 1995–2013; Laurea hc (Libera Univ. di Lingue e Comunicazione, Milan) 2004; award for devt cooperation of Lombardy Region. *Leisure interests:* yachting, jogging. *Address:* c/o Palazzo della Regione Lombardia, Via Fabio Filzi 22, 20124 Milan, Italy. *Website:* www.formigoni.it.

FORMUZAL, Mihail; Moldovan politician and government official; *Başkan (Governor), Autonomous Territory of Gagauz-Yeri;* b. 7 Nov. 1959, Beşghioz, Ciadir-Lunga dist.; m.; three c.; ed M.V. Frunze Mil. High School of Artillery, Odesa, Ukrainian SSR, Public Admin Acad., Chişinău; specialist, public admin; mil. service 1977–94, achieved rank of Maj.; Deputy Mayor of Ceadir-Lunga 1995–99, Mayor 1999–2007; Chair. People's Republican Party (Respublika Halk Partiyası) 2005–; Başkan (Gov.) Autonomous Territory of Gagauz-Yeri 2006–,

mem. Govt 2007–; numerous awards. *Address:* Office of the Başkan of the Autonomous Territory of Gagauz-Yeri, 3800 Comrat, Moldova (office). *Telephone:* (29) 82-46-36 (office). *Fax:* (29) 82-20-34 (office). *E-mail:* formuzal@mail.ru (office). *Website:* www.gagauzia.md (office); www.gov.md/pageview .php?l=en&idc=566&id=2951 (office).

FORNÉ MOLNÉ, Marc; Andorran lawyer and politician; b. 30 Dec. 1946, La Massana; m. Maria Lluïsa Gispert Boronat; one s.; ed Univ. of Barcelona; lawyer; fmr Ed. Andorra 7 magazine; mem., fmrly Leader, Partit Liberal d'Andorra; Head of Govt of Andorra 1994–2004; Commdr, Légion d'honneur 2003. *Address:* Partit Liberal d'Andorra (PLA), Carrer Babot Camp 13, 2°, Andorra la Vella, AD500, Andorrà (office). *Telephone:* 807715 (office). *Fax:* 869728 (office). *E-mail:* advocatsforne@andorra.ad (office). *Website:* www.partitliberal.ad (office).

FORNÉS, María Irene; Cuban/American playwright; b. 14 May 1930, Havana; Man. Dir New York Theatre Strategy 1973–79; fmr TCG (Theatre Communications Group)/Pew Artist-in-Residence, Women's Project and Productions; contrib. to Performing Arts Journal and numerous anthologies; nine Obie awards; NEA (National Endowment for the Arts) awards, including Distinguished Artists Award; Rockefeller Foundation grants; Guggenheim grant; American Acad. and Inst. of Arts and Letters Award; NY State Governor's Arts Award; PEN/Nabokov Award 2002. *Plays (many unpublished):* The Widow 1961, Tango Palace (aka There! You Died) 1963, The Office 1964, Promenade 1965, The Successful Life of 3 1965, The Annunciation 1967, A Vietnamese Wedding 1967, The Red Burning Light (aka Mission XQ3) 1968, Dr Kheal 1968, Molly's Dream 1968, Baboon!!! 1972, Aurora 1974, Cap-a-Pie 1975, Washing 1976, Fefu and Her Friends 1977, In Service 1978, Evelyn Brown 1979, Eyes on the Harem 1979, A Visit 1981, Sarita 1982, The Danube 1982, The Curse of the Langston House 1983, Mud 1983, Abingdon Square 1984, The Conduct of Life 1985, Drowning 1985, The Trial of Joan of Arc on a Matter of Faith 1986, Lovers and Keepers 1986, The Mothers 1986, Oscar and Bertha 1987, Hunger 1988, And What of the Night? 1989, Terra Incognita 1991, Springtime 1992, Enter the Night 1993, Ibsen and the Actress 1995, Manual for a Desperate Crossing 1996, The Summer in Gossensass 1997, The Audition 1998, Letters from Cuba 2000. *Address:* c/o Morgan Jenness, Abrams Artists Agency, 275 Seventh Avenue, 26th Floor, New York, NY 10001, USA (office). *Telephone:* (646) 486-4600 (office). *E-mail:* vincent.devito@abramsartny .com (office); morgan.jenness@abramsartny.com (office). *Website:* www .abramsartists.com (office).

FORREST, Andrew; Australian business executive; *Chairman, Fortescue Metals Group Ltd;* b. 1961; s. of Donald Forrest and Judith Forrest; m. Nicola Forrest; three c.; early career as investment banker; Founding CEO and Deputy Chair. Anaconda Nickel Ltd (now Minara Resources Ltd) 1994, also Chair. Murrin Murrin Jt Venture; fmr Chair. Moly Mines Ltd, Siberia Mining Corpn Ltd; Founder and CEO Fortescue Metals Group Ltd 2003–11, Chair. 2003–05, 2011–; Chair. Poseidon Nickel Ltd, Australian Children's Trust; Founder GenerationOne; fmr Chair. Athletics Australia; fmr Dir West Australian Chamber of Minerals and Energy; Fellow, Australian Inst. of Mining and Metallurgy. *Address:* Fortescue Metals Group Ltd, Level 2, 87 Adelaide Terrace, East Perth, WA 6004, Australia (office). *Telephone:* (8) 6218-8888 (office). *Fax:* (8) 6218-8880 (office). *E-mail:* fmgl@ fmgl.com.au (office). *Website:* www.fmgl.com.au (office).

FORREST, Sir (Andrew) Patrick McEwen, Kt, MD, ChM, FRCS, FRCPE, FRSE; British surgeon; b. 25 March 1923, Mount Vernon, Scotland; s. of Andrew J. Forrest and Isabella Pearson; m. 1st Margaret B. Hall 1955 (died 1961); m. 2nd Margaret A. Steward 1964; one s. two d.; ed Dundee High School and St Andrew's Univ.; Mayo Foundation Fellow, Rochester, Minn. 1952–53; Lecturer, then Sr Lecturer, Univ. of Glasgow 1954–62; Prof. of Surgery, Welsh Nat. School of Medicine 1962–71; Regius Prof. of Clinical Surgery, Univ. of Edinburgh 1970–88, Prof. Emer. 1989–; Hon. Fellow, Faculty of Medicine 1989–95; Visiting Scientist, NIH 1989–90; Assoc. Dean (Clinical Studies) Int. Medical Coll., Kuala Lumpur 1993–96; mem. MRC 1975–79; Chief Scientist, Scottish Home and Health Dept (part-time) 1981–87; mem. Advisory Bd for Research Councils 1982–85; Hon. FACS; Hon. FRACS; Hon. FRCS (Canada); Hon. FRCR; Hon. FFPH; Hon. DSc (Wales, Chinese Univ. of Hong Kong); Hon. LLD (Dundee); Gimbernat Prize, Catalonian Surgical Asscn 1996; European Inst. of Oncology Breast Cancer Award 2000; Lister Medal 1987, Gold Medal, Netherlands Surgical Asscn 1988. *Publications:* Prognostic Factors in Breast Cancer (jtly) 1968, Principles and Practice of Surgery (jtly) 1985, Breast Cancer: The Decision to Screen 1990; over 250 publs in scientific and medical journals. *Leisure interests:* golf, sailing. *Address:* 19 St Thomas Road, Edinburgh, EH9 2LR, Scotland (home). *Telephone:* (131) 667 3203 (home). *Fax:* (131) 662 1193 (home). *E-mail:* patforresthome@aol.com (home).

FORSEE, Gary D.; American university administrator and fmr telecommunications industry executive; *President, University of Missouri;* b. 10 April 1950, Kansas City; m. Sherry Forsee; two d.; ed Missouri Univ. of Science and Tech.; with Southwestern Bell Telephone 1972–80; with AT&T 1980–89; Vice-Pres. and Gen. Man. Govt System Div., Sprint Corpn 1989–91, Pres. Govt System Div., Business Services Group 1991–93, Sr Vice-Pres. of Staff Operations, Long Distance Div. 1993–95, Interim CEO Sprint PCS 1995, Pres. and COO Sprint Long Distance Div. 1995–98, Pres. and CEO Sprint Corpn (now Sprint Nextel Corpn) 2003–07 (resgnd), Pres. and CEO Global One (subsidiary co.), Brussels, Belgium 1998–2000; Chief Staff Officer and Exec. Vice-Pres. BellSouth Int. 1999–2000, Pres. 2000–01, Vice-Chair. Domestic Operations, BellSouth Corpn 2002–03; Chair. Cingular Wireless 2001–02; Pres. Univ. of Missouri 2007–; mem. Bd of Dirs Goodyear Tire & Rubber Co., Great Plains Energy Inc. 2008–. *Address:* Office of the President, University of Missouri, 321 University Hall, Columbia, MO 65211, USA (office). *Telephone:* (573) 882-2011 (office). *E-mail:* umpresident@umsystem .edu (office). *Website:* www.umsystem.edu/ums/president (office).

FORSÉN, K. Sture, MSc, DTech; Swedish chemist and academic; *Senior Scientific Adviser, Pufendorf Institute for Advanced Studies, Lund University;* b. 12 July 1932, Piteå; s. of Helmer Forsén and Signe Forsén; m. Dr Gunilla Isaksson 1973 (divorced 1986); ed Royal Inst. of Tech., Stockholm; Assoc. Prof. of Chemical Physics, Royal Inst. of Tech. 1963–67, Prof. of Physical Chem., Lund Univ. 1966, now Prof. Emer.; mem. Bd of Dirs Swedish Natural Science Research Council 1983–86, Perstorp AB 1986–, Swedish Nat. Chemicals Inspectorate 1989–; Fairchild Scholar, Calif. Inst. of Tech. 1986–87, Fogarty Scholar, NIH, USA

1987–94, Visiting Investigator, Scripps Research Inst., La Jolla 1990–; Man. Dir SWEGENE (postgenomic consortium) 2000–05; mem. Bd of Dirs Wallenberg Global Learning Network 2005–; Scientific Adviser to Rectrix Magnifica Boel Flodgrenthe, Lund Univ. 1998–2000, to Rector Magnificus Goran Bexell 2004–09, Sr Scientific Adviser, Pufendorf Inst. for Advanced Studies, Lund Univ. 2009–; mem. Scientific Advisory Council of Volvo Research Foundation 1987–92; mem. Royal Swedish Acad. of Sciences 1973–, Nobel Cttee for Chem. 1976–95; mem. Royal Swedish Acad. of Eng Sciences 1986–; Celsius Gold Medal, Royal Soc. of Uppsala 1979. *Publications include:* co-author of two books on NMR spectroscopy 1972, 1976; over 300 scientific articles, at present mainly concerning biophysical studies of calcium-binding proteins, in int. journals. *Leisure interests:* music from Frescobaldi to Keith Jarrett, renovating old farmhouses. *Address:* Pufendorf Institute, Lund University, PO Box 117, 221 00 Lund, Sweden (office). *Telephone:* (46) 222-62-01 (office). *E-mail:* sture.forsen@pi.lu.se (office). *Website:* www.pi.lu.se (office).

FORSTER, Carl-Peter, BSc; German automobile industry executive; b. 9 May 1954, London, England; m.; three c.; ed Bonn Univ., Munich Tech. Univ.; raised in London, Bonn and Athens; consultant, McKinsey and Co., Munich 1982–86; Head of Planning and Logistics, Tech. Devt Dept, BMW AG 1986–88, Systems and Project Man. 5-series 1988–90, Head of Dept for Test and Pilot Car Mfg, Tech. Devt Centre 1990–93, Head of 5-series 1993–96, Man. Dir BMW (SA) Pty Ltd 1996–99, mem. Man. Bd BMW AG 1999–2000; Chair. and Man. Dir Opel AG 2001–04, Chair. 2004–09, Chair. Supervisory Bd 2004–09; mem. Bd of Dirs Fiat-GM Motors Powertrain 2001–09; GM Vice-Pres. and Pres. General Motors Europe 2004–09, Chair. Saab 2005–09, GM Group Vice-Pres. 2006–09; Group CEO and Man. Dir Tata Motors Ltd 2010–11, Dir (non-exec.) 2011–. *Leisure interests:* skiing, regatta-sailing. *Address:* Tata Motors Ltd, Bombay House, 24 Homi Mody Street, Fort, Mumbai 400 001, India (office). *Telephone:* (22) 66658282 (office). *Website:* www.tatamotors.com (office).

FORSTER, Margaret, BA, FRSL; British writer; b. 25 May 1938, Carlisle; d. of Arthur Gordon Forster and Lilian Forster (née Hind); m. Edward Hunter Davies 1960; one s. two d.; ed Carlisle Co. High School and Somerville Coll., Oxford; chief non-fiction reviewer, London Evening Standard 1977–80; mem. Arts Council Literary Panel 1978–81; RSL Award 1988, Fawcet Soc. Prize 1993. *Publications include:* non-fiction: The Rash Adventurer: The Rise and Fall of Charles Edward Stuart 1973, William Makepeace Thackeray: Memoirs of a Victorian Gentleman 1978, Significant Sisters: Grassroots of Active Feminism 1839–1939 1984, Elizabeth Barrett Browning: A Biography 1988, Elizabeth Barrett Browning: Selected Poems (ed.) 1988, Daphne du Maurier: The Authorised Biography 1993, Hidden Lives: A Family Memoir 1995, Rich Desserts and Captains Thin: A Family and Their Times 1831–1931 1997, Precious Lives (memoir) 1997, Good Wives?: Mary, Fanny, Jennie and Me 1845–2001 2001; novels: Georgy Girl (filmscript with Peter Nichols 1966) 1965, Dame's Delight 1964, The Bogeyman 1965, The Travels of Maudie Tipstaff 1967, The Park 1968, Miss Owen-Owen is at Home 1969, Fenella Phizackerley 1970, Mr Bone's Retreat 1971, The Seduction of Mrs Pendlebury 1974, Mother, Can You Hear Me? 1979, The Bride of Lowther Fell 1980, Marital Rites 1981, Private Papers 1986, Have the Men had Enough? 1989, Lady's Maid 1990, The Battle for Christabel 1991, Mothers' Boys 1994, Shadow Baby 1996, The Memory Box 1999, Diary of an Ordinary Woman 1914–1995 2003, Is There Anything You Want? 2005, Keeping the World Away 2006, Over 2007, Isa and May 2010. *Leisure interests:* walking, reading contemporary fiction. *Address:* c/o The Sayle Literary Agency, 1 Petersfield, Cambridge, CB1 1BB, England (office); Grasmoor House, Loweswater, nr Cockermouth, Cumbria, CA13 0RU, England. *Telephone:* (1223) 303035 (office); (1900) 85303. *E-mail:* info@sayleliteraryagency.com (office). *Website:* www.sayleliteraryagency.com (office).

FORSTMOSER, Peter, LLM, DrIur; Swiss lawyer and business executive; *Partner, Niederer Kraft & Frey AG;* b. 22 Jan. 1943, Zurich; s. of Alois Forstmoser-Locher and Ida Forstmoser-Locher; two s.; ed Zurich Univ. Law School, Harvard Law School, USA; admitted to the Bar 1971; attorney 1971–, Partner, Niederer Kraft & Frey AG 1975–; Lecturer, Faculty of Law and Political Science, Univ. of Zürich 1971–74, Assoc. Prof., Univ. of Zürich Law School 1974–78, Full Prof. of Civil, Corp. and Capital Market Law 1978–2008, Prof. Emer. 2008–; mem. Bd of Dirs Swiss Reinsurance Co. (Swiss Re) 1990–2009, Chair. 2000–09; Chair. and mem. various corp. bds. *Publications:* Schweizer Aktienrecht 1996, Organisation und Organisationsreglement der Aktiengesellschaft 2011, Schweizer Gesellschaftsrecht 2012, Einführung in das Recht 2012 and numerous other publs on Swiss company and capital market law. *Leisure interests:* sports, modern art. *Address:* Niederer Kraft & Frey AG, Bahnhofstrasse 13, 8001 Zurich, Switzerland (office). *Telephone:* (58) 800-80-00 (office). *Fax:* (58) 800-80-80 (office). *E-mail:* peter.forstmoser@nkf.ch (office). *Website:* www.nkf.ch (office).

FORSYTH, Frederick, CBE; British writer; b. 25 Aug. 1938, Ashford, Kent; m. 1st Carole Cunningham 1973; two s.; m. 2nd Sandy Molloy; ed Tonbridge School, Univ. of Granada, Spain; with RAF 1956–58; reporter, Eastern Daily Press, Norfolk 1958–61; joined Reuters 1961, reporter, Paris 1962–63, Chief of Bureau, E Berlin 1963–64; radio and TV reporter, BBC 1965–66; Asst Diplomatic Corresp., BBC TV 1967–68; freelance journalist, Nigeria and Biafra 1968–69; MWA Edgar Allan Poe Award 1971, Diamond Dagger Award (for lifetime achievement), Crime Writers Asscn 2012. *Television appearances include:* Soldiers (narrator) 1985, Frederick Forsyth Presents 1989. *Film appearance:* I Have Never Forgotten You: The Life and Legacy of Simon Wiesenthal 2006. *Publications:* fiction: The Day of the Jackal 1971, The Odessa File 1972, The Dogs of War 1974, The Shepherd 1975, The Devil's Alternative 1979, No Comebacks (short stories) 1982, The Fourth Protocol 1984, The Negotiator 1988, The Deceiver 1991, Great Flying Stories (ed.) 1991, The Fist of God 1993, Icon 1996, The Phantom of Manhattan 1999, Quintet 2000, The Veteran and Other Stories 2001, Avenger 2003, The Afghan 2006, The Cobra 2010; non-fiction: The Biafra Story 1969 (revised edn as The Making of an African Legend: The Biafra Story 1977), Emeka 1982, I Remember: Reflections on Fishing in Childhood 1995. *Leisure interests:* sea angling, reading. *Address:* c/o Penguin Group (USA) Inc., c/o Putnam Publicity, 375 Hudson Street, New York, NY 10014, USA (office). *Website:* us.penguingroup.com (office).

FORSYTH OF DRUMLEAN, Baron (Life Peer), cr. 1999, of Drumlean in Stirling; **Rt Hon. Michael Bruce Forsyth,** Kt, PC, MA; British fmr politician and investment banker; *Deputy Chairman, JP Morgan (UK);* b. 16 Sept. 1954,

Montrose, Scotland; s. of John Forsyth and Mary Watson; m. Susan Jane Clough 1977; one s. two d.; ed Arbroath High School, St. Andrews Univ.; Minister of State for Health/Educ. (Scotland) 1981–92, Minister of State, Dept of Employment 1992–94, Home Office 1994–95, Sec. of State for Scotland and Lord Keeper of the Great Seal of Scotland 1995–97; Dir Flemings 1997–2000; Vice-Chair. Investment Banking (Europe), JP Morgan 2000–02, Deputy Chair. JP Morgan (UK) 2002–; Parliamentarian of the Year 1996. *Publications:* Reservicing Britain 1980, The Myths of Privatisation 1983. *Leisure interests:* mountaineering, astronomy, gardening, art, fly fishing, photography. *Address:* JP Morgan, 10 Aldermanbury, London, EC2V 7RF (office); c/o House of Lords, London, SW1A 0PN, England. *Telephone:* (20) 7325-6366 (office). *E-mail:* Michael.Forsyth@jpmorgan.com (office). *Website:* www.jpmorgan.com (office).

FORSYTH, William (Bill) David; British film director; b. 29 July 1946, Glasgow; one s. one d.; ed Nat. Film School, Beaconsfield; Hon. DLitt (Glasgow) 1984; Hon. DUniv (Stirling) 1989; BAFTA Award for Best Screenplay 1982, for Best Dir 1983. *Films include:* That Sinking Feeling 1979, Gregory's Girl 1980, Andrina (TV film) 1981, Local Hero 1982, Comfort and Joy 1984, Housekeeping 1987, Breaking In 1988, Being Human 1994, Gregory's Two Girls 1999. *Address:* c/o Anthony Jones, United Agents, 12–26 Lexington Street, London, W1F 0LE, England (office). *Telephone:* (20) 3214-0800 (office). *Fax:* (20) 3214-0801 (office). *E-mail:* info@unitedagents.co.uk (office). *Website:* unitedagents.co.uk (office).

FORSYTH-JOHNSON, Sir Bruce Joseph, (Bruce Forsyth), Kt, CBE, OBE; British television personality, entertainer, singer, songwriter and musician and dancer; b. 22 Feb. 1928, Edmonton, London Borough of Enfield; s. of John Thomas Forsyth-Johnson and Florence Ada Forsyth-Johnson (née Pocknell); m. 1st Penny Calvert 1953 (divorced 1973); three d.; m. 2nd Anthea Redfern 1973 (divorced 1979); two d.; m. 3rd Wilnelia Merced 1983; one s.; ed The Latymer School, Edmonton, North London; trained in dance in Tottenham and Brixton; began in show business with a song, dance and accordion act called Boy Bruce, the Mighty Atom aged 14; first appearance at Theatre Royal, Bilston; TV debut as a child, singing and dancing on BBC talent show 1939; appeared with comedian Dickie Henderson and received offer to compere Val Parnell's weekly TV variety show, Sunday Night at the London Palladium 1957–60, 1961; own co., Bruce Forsyth Enterprises Ltd; Variety Club Show Business Personality of the Year 1975, TV Times Male TV Personality of the Year 1975, 1976, 1977, 1978, The Great Bruce Forsyth Social Club est. 1987, BBC TV Personality of the Year 1991, A BAFTA Tribute to Bruce Forsyth screend by BBC to mark his 60 years in show business 2005, bronze bust of himself unveiled at London Palladium 2005, catchphrase 'Nice to see you, to see you, nice' voted the most popular UK catchphrase by the British public 2007, BAFTA Fellowship 2008, Theatre Performers Award, Carl Alan Awards hosted by Int. Dance Teachers' Asscn 2009, Lifetime Achievement Award, Royal Television Soc. 2009, Special Recognition Award, Nat. TV Awards 2011. *Albums:* Both Sides of Bruce (Live) 1977, Come Get It! 1979, Mr. Entertainment 2007. *Films include:* Star! 1968, Can Hieronymus Merkin Ever Forget Mercy Humppe and Find True Happiness? 1969, Red Peppers 1969, Bedknobs and Broomsticks 1971, The Magnificent Seven Deadly Sins 1971, Pavlova: A Woman for All Time 1983. *Television includes:* Sunday Night at the London Palladium 1957–61, Spectacular (series) 1958, New Look (series) 1958, Mystery and Imagination (series) – The Canterville Ghost 1966, The Bruce Forsyth Show 1966, Rolf Harris Show (series) 1971, The Generation Game (host) 1971–77, 1990–94, Frankie and Bruce 1975, The Muppet Show 1976, The Mating Season (film) 1976, Disco Bruce 1978–80, Bruce Forsyth's Big Night 1978, Bruce Forsyth's Play Your Cards Right (host) 1980–87, 1994–99, 2002–03, De Mike Burstyn show (series, performer: It's Best To Leave While I'm In Love, Top Hat, Tomorrow) 1981, Forsyth Follies (film) 1982, Hollywood Or Bust (host) 1984, Bruce Forsyth's Hot Streak (host, ABC) 1986, Magnum, P.I.: A Little Bit of Luck… A Little Bit of Grief (CBS) 1986, Slinger's Day (Thames Television, series) 1986–87, Bruce and Ronnie 1988, You Bet! 1988–90, Takeover Bid (host) 1990–91, Fiddley Foodle Bird (series, voice) 1991, Bruce's Guest Night (host) 1992–93, The Price is Right (host) 1995–2001, An Audience with Bruce Forsyth 1997, The Game 1998, Tonight at the London Palladium 2000, Have I Got News for You (host, BBC) 2003, 2010, Didn't They Do Well (host) 2004, Strictly Come Dancing (co-host and writer, BBC 1) 2004–13, Bruce Forsyth's Comedy Heroes (documentary, writer) 2005, The Generation Game: Then Again (host) 2007. *Publication:* Bruce Forsyth: The Autobiography 2001. *Leisure interests:* golf, Arsenal Football Club and Tottenham Hotspur Football Club. *Address:* Forsyth Enterprises, Straidarran, Wentworth Drive, Virginia Water, Surrey, GU25 4NY (office); c/o Artists' Mail, BBC Television Centre, Wood Lane, London, W12 7RJ, England; c/o IMWP Artist Management, 3 The Raven, 140 Westbridge Road, London, SW11 3PF, England (office). *Telephone:* (20) 7223-7112 (office). *Fax:* (20) 7223-7414 (office). *Website:* www.imwpuk.com (office).

FORSYTH MEJÍA, Harold Winston; Peruvian journalist, politician and diplomatist; *Ambassador to USA;* b. 27 May 1951, Lima; s. of Willy Forsyth Cauvi and Lucciola Mejía de Forsyth; m. María Verónica Sommer Mayer; two s. one d.; ed Pontifical Catholic Univ. of Peru, Diplomatic Acad. of Peru; Third Sec., Embassy in Santiago 1977–78, Second Sec. and Chargé d'affaires a.i., Embassy in Sofia 1978–79, Second Sec., Embassy in Caracas 1980–82, Chief of Cabinet of Perm. Sec., Sistema Económico Latinoamericano y del Caribe (SELA) 1982–84, First Sec., Chief of Evaluation and Control, Diplomatic Acad. of Peru 1984– 85, Under-Dir of Latin-American Cooperation, Ministry of Foreign Affairs (MFA) 1986, Counsellor, Embassy in Ottawa 1987–89, Minister-Counsellor, Embassy Berlin 1990–92, Amb. to Colombia 2001–04, to Italy 2004–06, Deputy Minister and Sec.-Gen. of Foreign Affairs 2006, MFA Adviser 2006–09, Amb. to People's Repub. of China 2009–11, to USA 2011–; mem. Congreso (Parl.) for Lima 1995–2000; numerous int. honours, including Grand Cross, Order of Bernardo O'Higgins (Chile) 2001, Peruvian Cross for Naval Merit 2003, Order Francisco de Miranda, First Class (Venezuela) 2003, Grand Cross, Simón Bolívar Order of Democracy 2004, Grand Cross, José Gregorio Paz Soldán Order 2006, Grand Cross, Peruvian Order of Merit for Distinguished Service 2006. *Publication:* Conversation with Javier Pérez de Cuéllar 2001. *Address:* Embassy of Peru, 1700 Massachusetts Avenue NW, Washington, DC 20036, USA (office). *Telephone:* (202) 833-9860 (office). (202) 261-0271 (office). *Fax:* (202) 659-8124 (office). *E-mail:* sbarboza@embassyofperu.us (office); webadmin@embassyofperu.us (office). *Website:* www.embassyofperu.org (office).

FORSYTHE, William; American choreographer; b. 1949, New York; ed Jacksonville Univ., Fla, Joffrey Ballet School, NY; joined Stuttgart Ballet 1973, dancer, then choreographer; choreographed works commissioned by cos including NY City Ballet, San Francisco Ballet, Nat. Ballet of Canada, Royal Ballet, Covent Garden and Nederlands Dans Theater; Founder and Dir Ballett Frankfurt 1984–2004, Ballett Frankfurt and TAT 1999–2004; f. The Forsythe Co. 2005; f. Forsythe Foundation; Chevalier des Arts et Métiers 1991, Commdr des Arts et Lettres 1999; Harlekin Preis, Frankfurt 1986, Bessie Award 1988, Deutscher Kritikerpreis 1988, Olivier Award 1992, Evening Standard Award 1999 and numerous other awards. *Ballets include:* Urlicht 1976, Gänge 1983, Artifact 1984, Impressing the Czar 1988, Limb's Theorem 1991, The Loss of Small Detail 1991, Eidos: Telos 1995, Endless House 1999, Kammer/Kammer 2000 (Paris 2002). *Films include:* Berg Ab 1984, Solo 1995, From a Classic Position 1997. *Address:* The Forsythe Company, Schmidtstrasse 12, 60326 Frankfurt, Germany (office). *E-mail:* info@theforsythecompany.de (office). *Website:* www.theforsythecompany.de (office).

FORT-BRESCIA, Bernardo, BA, MArch, FAIA; American (b. Peruvian) architect; b. 19 Nov. 1951, Lima, Peru; s. of Paul Fort and Rosa Brescia; m. Laurinda Spear 1976; five s. one d.; ed Princeton Univ., Harvard Univ.; co-f. (with Laurinda Spear) Arquitectonica Int. Corpn 1977–; projects in USA, Europe, S America, Cen. America, Asia and Caribbean; Prof. Univ. of Miami 1975–77; mem. Bd of Dirs New World Symphony, Wolfsonian-FIU Museum; numerous AIA Awards and Honors for Design Excellence; Founder's Award, Salvadori Center 2000. *Publications:* Arquitectonica 1991, numerous articles in specialist and non-specialist journals. *Address:* Arquitectonica International Corporation, 801 Brickell Avenue, Suite 1100, Miami, FL 33131-2517, USA (office). *Telephone:* (305) 372-1812 (office). *Fax:* (305) 372-1175 (office). *E-mail:* bfort@arquitectonica.com (office). *Website:* www.arquitectonica.com (office).

FORTE, Sir Rocco, Kt, MA, FCA; British hotel industry executive; *Chairman and CEO, The Rocco Forte Collection;* b. 18 Jan. 1945; s. of Lord Forte; m. Aliai Ricci 1986; one s. two d.; ed Downside and Pembroke Coll., Oxford; Dir of Personnel, Trusthouse Forte 1973–78, Deputy Chief Exec. 1978–82, Jt Chief Exec. 1982–83; Chief Exec. Trusthouse Forte PLC 1983–92; Chair. Forte PLC 1992–96; Chair. and CEO Rocco Forte Collection 1996–; mem. Chairs' Cttee Savoy Group 1994–96; Trustee, London Symphony Orchestra; Prin. Patron Hospitality Action; fmr Vice-Pres. Commonwealth Games Council for England; Cavaliere di Gran Croce al Merito della Republica 2005. *Achievements include:* represented Britain within his age group at World Triathlon Championships 2005, 2006, 2007, 2009. *Leisure interests:* shooting, golf. *Address:* The Rocco Forte Collection, 70 Jermyn Street, London, SW1Y 6NY, England (office). *Telephone:* (20) 7321-2626 (office). *Fax:* (20) 7321-2424 (office). *E-mail:* cwilliams@roccofortehotels.com (office). *Website:* www.roccofortehotels.com (office).

FORTEY, Richard Alan, PhD, ScD, FRS, FRSL; British palaeontologist and writer; *Research Associate, Natural History Museum, London;* b. 15 Feb. 1946, London, England; s. of Frank Allen Fortey and Margaret Fortey (née Wilshin); m. 1st Bridget Elizabeth Thomas (divorced); one s.; m. 2nd Jacqueline Francis 1977; one. s. two d.; ed Ealing Grammar School for Boys, King's Coll., Cambridge; Research Fellow, then Sr Scientific Officer, Natural History Museum, London 1970–77, Prin. Scientific Officer 1978–86, Sr Prin. Scientific Officer 1986–98, Merit Researcher 1998, currently Research Assoc.; Howley Visiting Prof., Memorial Univ. of Newfoundland, Canada 1977–78; Visiting Prof. of Palaeobiology, Univ. of Oxford 2000–; Collier Chair in Public Understanding of Science and Tech., Univ. of Bristol 2002–03; mem. Geological Soc. of London 1972– (Pres. 2007), British Mycological Soc. 1980–; Hon. Fellow, BAAS 2008; Dr hc (St Andrews) 2007, (Open Univ.) 2007, (Birmingham) 2010, (Leicester) 2012; Natural World Book of the Year Award 1994, Lyell Medal, Geological Soc. of London 1996, Frink Medal, Zoological Soc. of London 2001, Lewis Thomas Prize, Rockefeller Univ. 2003, Linnean Medal for Zoology 2006, Michael Faraday Prize, Royal Soc. 2006, T.N. George Medal, Glasgow Geological Soc. 2007, Linnean Legacy Lecturer, Univ. of Arizona 2009. *Publications:* The Roderick Masters Book of Money Making Schemes (as Roderick Masters) 1981, Fossils: The Key to the Past 1982, The Hidden Landscape 1993, Life: An Unauthorised Biography 1997, Trilobite! 2000, The Earth: An Intimate History 2004, Dry Store Room No. 1: The Secret Life of the Natural History Museum 2008, Horseshoe Crabs and Velvet Worms: The Story of the Animals and Plants That Time Has Left Behind 2012. *Leisure interests:* mycology, humorous writing, walking. *Address:* Department of Palaeontology, Natural History Museum, Cromwell Road, London, SW7 5BD, England (office). *Telephone:* (20) 7942-5493 (office). *Fax:* (20) 7942-5546 (office). *E-mail:* r.fortey@nhm.ac.uk (office). *Website:* www.nhm.ac.uk/palaeontology (office).

FORTIER, L. Yves, CC, QC, BCL, BLitt; Canadian lawyer, diplomatist and business executive; *Chairman, Alcan Inc.;* b. 11 Sept. 1935, Québec City; s. of François Fortier and Louise Fortier (née Turgeon); m. Cynthia Carol Eaton 1959; one s. two d.; ed Univ. of Montréal, McGill Univ. and Univ. of Oxford, UK; called to Bar of Québec 1960; Chair. and Sr Partner, Ogilvy, Renault (law firm), Montréal; Pres. Jr Bar Asscn Montreal 1965–66, Jr Bar Section, Canadian Bar Asscn 1966–67; mem. Gen. Council, Bar of Québec 1966–67; Councillor, Bar of Montréal 1966–67; Perm. Rep. to UN, New York 1988–91, Pres. UN Security Council 1989, Vice-Pres. UN Gen. Ass. 1990; Pres. London Court of Int. Arbitration 1998–2001; Dir Alcan Inc, Montréal 2002–, now Chair.; Chair. Hudson's Bay Co. –2006; Chair. Emer. and Sr Pnr, Ogilvy Renault LLP (law firm), Montréal; mem. Council, Canadian Section, 1st Comm. of Jurists 1967–87; mem. Canadian Bar Asscn (Pres. Québec br. 1975–76, Nat. Pres. 1982–83); Founding Dir Canadian Bar Asscn Law for the Future Fund; mem. Perm. Court of Arbitration, The Hague, American Arbitration Asscn Panel of Arbitrators and other arbitration insts; Fellow, American Coll. of Trial Lawyers (Regent 1992–96); Hon. mem. ABA; Dir Canadian Inst. of Advanced Legal Studies, Canadian Law Inst. of the Pacific Rim 1986–88; mem. Int. Trade Advisory Council Canada; Advisor to the UN Sec.-Gen. on territorial dispute between Gabon and Equatorial Guinea 2003; Gov. McGill Univ. 1970–85; Dir Canadian Asscn of Rhodes Scholars (Pres. 1975–77). *Leisure interests:* skiing, tennis, golf, reading. *Address:* Ogilvy Renault LLP, Suite 2500, 1 Place Ville Marie, Montréal, PQ H3B 1R1 (office); Alcan Inc., 1188 Sherbrooke Street West, Montréal, PQ H3A 3G2 (office); 19 Rosemount Avenue, Westmount, PQ H3Y 3G6, Canada (home). *Telephone:* (514) 848-8000 (Alcan) (office); (514) 847-

4740 (Ogilvy Renault) (office). *Fax:* (514) 848-8115 (Alcan) (office); (514) 286-5474 (office). *E-mail:* yfortier@ogilvyrenault.com (office). *Website:* www.ogilvyrenault.com (office); www.alcan.com (office).

FORTIER, Hon. Michael M., PC; Canadian financier, lawyer and politician; m. Michelle Setlakwe; six c.; joined Ogilvy Renault law firm, Montreal 1985–99, managed office in London, UK 1992–96; joined Credit Suisse First Boston 1999, Man. Dir and Sr Advisor and headed Montreal office –2004; Man. Dir (Quebec) TD Securities (subsidiary of TD Bank Financial Group) 2004–06; Pres. Progressive Conservative Party of Canada 1990s, cand. in leadership election 1998, cand. for party in gen. election 2000, mem. Conservative Party of Canada 2003–, Co-Chair. Stephen Harper's nat. leadership campaign 2004, Co-Chair. Conservative nat. elections campaign 2004, 2006; Minister of Public Works and Govt Services 2006–08, of Int. Trade 2008; mem. Senate 2006–. *Address:* Conservative Party of Canada, 130 Albert Street, Suite 1204, Ottawa, ON K1P 5G4, Canada (office). *Telephone:* (613) 755-2000 (office). *Fax:* (613) 755-2001 (office). *Website:* www.conservative.ca (office).

FORTIER, Suzanne, BSc, PhD; Canadian chemist, academic and university administrator; *Principal and Vice-Chancellor, McGill University;* b. St-Timothée, Québec; ed McGill Univ.; Postdoctoral Assoc., Medical Foundation of Buffalo, Inc. 1976–78, Research Scientist 1980–82; Research Assoc., Nat. Research Council of Canada 1978–79; Prof. of Chem. and of Computing and Information Science, Queen's Univ., Kingston, Ont. 1982–2013, Assoc. Dean of Grad. Studies and Research, Vice-Prin. (Research) 1995–2000, Vice-Prin. (Academic) 2000–05; Pres. Natural Sciences and Eng Research Council of Canada, Ottawa 2006–13; Prin. and Vice-Chancellor, McGill Univ. 2013–; fmr mem. Protein Eng Network of Centres of Excellence, Inst. for Robotics and Intelligent Systems, Communications and Information Tech. Ontario, Bd of Dirs Ontario Centres of Excellence Inc., Bd Govs Royal Mil. Coll. of Canada, Fed. Govt's Council of Science and Tech. Advisors; mem. Bd of Dirs Canada Foundation for Innovation, Strategic Cttee of Investissements d'Excellence Bordeaux, Steering Cttee of the Networks of Centres of Excellence, Ontario Task Force on Competitiveness, Productivity and Economic Econ.; Fellow, AAAS; Officier, Ordre nat. du Mérite; Hon. DLitt Thompson Rivers Univ., BC 2006; Entrance Scholarship and R.P.D. Graham Scholarship, McGill Univ., Clara Benson Award for distinguished contributions to chemistry by a woman 1997, Entrepreneurship Award, Communications and Information Tech. Ontario 1997, Queen's Univ. Distinguished Service Award 2005, Queen Elizabeth II Diamond Jubilee Medal 2012. *Publications:* more than 80 scientific publs on protein crystallography. *Address:* Office of the Principal and Vice-Chancellor, Room 506, James Administration Building, McGill University, 845 Sherbrooke Street West, Montreal, PQ H3A 0G4, Canada (office). *Telephone:* (514) 398-4180 (office). *Fax:* (514) 398-4768 (office). *E-mail:* suzanne.fortier@mcgill.ca (office). *Website:* www.mcgill.ca/principal (office).

FORTÍN, Mario; Honduran government official and diplomatist; b. 11 Jan. 1954; m. Rosario Duarte de Fortín; four c.; ed Univ. of Chicago, USA; Dir of External Affairs 1978; fmr Amb. to Germany, Perm. Rep. to UN; fmr Minister of Economy and Commerce; Minister of Foreign Affairs 2005–06, currently Adviviser to Foreign Ministry; est. Foundation for Investment and Devt of Exports; Hon. Pres. Consular Asscn; Commdr Order of Bernardo O'Higgins Riquelme, Grand Cross Order of Merit (Chile). *Address:* Ministry of Foreign Affairs, Centro Cívico Gubernamental, Antigua Casa Presidencial, Blvd Kuwait, Contiguo a la Corte Suprema de Justicia, Tegucigalpa, Honduras (office). *Telephone:* 234-1962 (office). *Fax:* 234-1484 (office). *Website:* www.sre.hn (office).

FORTOV, Vladimir Yevgenyevich; Russian physicist; *Head of Division of Energetics, Machinery, Mechanics and Control Systems, Russian Academy of Sciences;* b. 23 Jan. 1946, Noginsk, Moscow Region; m.; one d.; ed Moscow Inst. of Physics and Tech.; researcher, Head of Lab., Inst. of Chemical Physics USSR (now Russian) Acad. of Sciences 1971–86; Head of Div., Inst. of High Temperature Physics, USSR Acad. of Sciences 1986–92; Dir Inst. for High Energy Densities, Russian Acad. of Sciences 1992–; Chair. Russian Foundation for Basic Research 1993–97; Deputy Chair., then Chair. State Cttee on (now Ministry of) Science and Tech. of Russian Fed. 1996–98; Corresp. mem. USSR (now Russian) Acad. of Sciences 1987, mem. 1992, Vice-Pres. 1996–2001, Head, Div. for Energetics, Machinery, Mechanics and Control Systems, Russian Acad. of Sciences 2002–; Chair. Tech. Cttee of Judges for the prize 'Novaya generatsiya' (New Generation) 2004–; mem. Advisory Academic Panel Skolkovo Foundation 2010–; mem. Presidium Russian Nat. Prize Russkie sozidateli (Russian Creators) 2005–; Corresp. mem. Int. Asscn on Physics and Tech. of High-Pressures; Fellow, US Nat. Acad. of Eng; mem. American Physics Soc., European Acad. of Arts and Sciences, Int. Acad. of Astronautics, Max Plank Soc., Royal Acad. of Eng of GB, Royal Acad. of Eng, Sweden; State Award of Russian Fed., P. Bridgeman Prize for High Pressure Technology, Max Plank Award, A. Einstein Gold Medal UNESCO, Hannes Alfven Prize, EPS, Shock Compression Science Award, APS, Medal of the Pres. of Chechen Repub. for Personal Contrib. to Peace and Co-operation in the Caucasus 2004. *Publications:* numerous works on thermophysics of extremely high temperatures and pressures, physics of gas dynamics and physics of strong shock waves. *Leisure interests:* skiing, sailing. *Address:* Presidium of the Russian Academy of Sciences, Leninski prospekt 32A, 119991 Moscow (office); Institute for High Energy Densities, Izhorskaya str. 13/19, 127412 Moscow, Russia. *Telephone:* (495) 938-18-14 (Acad.) (office); (495) 485-79-88 (Inst.) (office); (495) 975-70-29 (Inst.) (office). *Fax:* (495) 938-52-34 (office). *E-mail:* fortov@ras.ru (office). *Website:* www.ihed.ras.ru.

FORTUÑO BURSET, Luis Guillermo, BSFS, JD; American lawyer, politician and fmr state official; b. 31 Oct. 1960, San Juan, Puerto Rico; s. of Luis Fortuño Moscoso and Shirley Joyce Burset de Mari; m. Lucé Vela-Gutierrez 1984; two s. one d. (triplets); ed Colegio Marista, Guaynabo, Georgetown Univ., Univ. of Virginia Law School; Pres. Puerto Rico Statehood Students Asscn 1980–81; Exec. Dir Puerto Rico Tourist Co. and Pres. Hotel Devt Corpn 1993–94; Sec., Puerto Rico Dept of Econ. Devt and Commerce 1994–96; Pnr, Correa, Collazo, Herrero, Jiménez and Fortuño (law firm) 1996–2005; Resident Commr of Puerto Rico 2005–09; mem. US House of Reps for Puerto Rico 2005–09, Vice-Chair. Congressional Hispanic Conf. 2005–07, Chair. 2007–09; Gov. of the Commonwealth of Puerto Rico 2008–13; mem. Partido Nuevo Progresista (PNP—New Progressive Party, affiliated to the Republican Party), currently Pres.; Pres. Southern

Governors Assen 2011–12, Council of State Govts 2012; mem. Republican Nat. Cttee; Orden de Isabel la Católica, Grand Cross with Collar (Spain) 2009. *Address:* c/o Puerto Rico Federal Affairs Administration, 1100 17th Street NW, Suite 800, Washington, DC 20036, USA. *E-mail:* info@prfaa.pr.gov.

FOSHEE, Douglas L., MBA; American oil industry executive; *President, CEO and Director, El Paso Corporation;* b. 1960; ed Southwest Texas State Univ., Jesse E. Jones Grad. School, Rice Univ., Southwestern Methodist Univ.; began career in commercial banking; various finance and business venture positions at ARCO Int. Oil and Gas Co. –1993; joined Torch Energy Advisers Inc. 1993, held positions successively as Vice-Pres. Special Projects, Exec. Vice-Pres. Acquisitions and Financial Analysis, Pres., COO, CEO 1993–97; Pres., CEO and Chair. Nuevo Energy Co. 1997–2001; Exec. Vice-Pres. and Chief Financial Officer, Halliburton Co. 2001–03, Exec. Vice-Pres. and COO 2003; Pres., CEO and Dir El Paso Corpn 2003–; mem. Bd of Dirs Cameron International Corpn, El Paso Pipeline Pnrs, LP, Goodwill Industries, Small Steps Nurturing Center; mem. Ind. Petroleum Assen of America, Nat. Petroleum Council; mem. Council of Overseers, Jesse E. Jones Grad. School, Rice Univ. *Address:* El Paso Corporation, 1001 Louisiana Street, Houston, TX 77002, USA (office). *Telephone:* (713) 420-2600 (office). *Fax:* (713) 420-4417 (office). *Website:* www.elpaso.com (office).

FOSS, Per-Kristian; Norwegian politician; b. 19 July 1950, Oslo; ed Univ. of Oslo; journalist 1971–73; mem. Høyre (Conservative Party), Chair. Høyre Municipal Council 1973–77, Chair. Unge Høyre (Young Conservatives) 1973–77, Chair. Høyre Cttee on Party Program 1981–85, Chair. Høyre Cttee on Cultural Objectives and Strategies 1983–85, Deputy Chair. Høyre Party Parl. Mems' Group 1993–2001, Leader of Høyre 2002; mem. Storting (Parl.) for Oslo 1977–, mem. Cttee on Energy and Industry 1981–89 (Second Vice-Chair. 1985–89), mem. Standing Cttee on Finance 1989–2001 (Chair. 1989–93, Vice-Chair. 1993–97), mem. Enlarged Foreign Affairs Cttee 1997–2001, Second Vice-Pres. 2009–; Minister of Finance 2001–2005; Ed. of Kontur (periodical) 1979–80; Consultant, Norges Rederforbund (Norwegian Shipowners' Assen) 1980–81; mem. Lillehammer Olympic Organizing Cttee 1994. *Address:* Storting, Karl Johansgt. 22, 0026 Oslo, Norway (office). *E-mail:* per-kristian.foss@stortinget.no. *Website:* www .stortinget.no.

FOSSE, Jon, Cand. Philol; Norwegian writer, dramatist and poet; b. 29 Sept. 1959, Haugesund; ed Univ. of Bergen; teacher of creative writing, Acad. of Writing, Bergen 1987–93; professional writer 1993–; Hon. mem. Norwegian Actors' Soc., Det Norske Samlaget, Norwegian Dramatists' Soc.; Chevalier, Ordre nat. du Mérite, Commdr, St Olavs Orden; Noregs Mållags Prize for Children's Books 1990, Andersson-Rysst Fondet 1992, Prize for Literature in New Norwegian 1993, 2003, Samlags Prize 1994, Ibsen Prize 1996, Sunnmoers Prize 1996, Melsom Prize 1997, Asshehoug Prize 1997, Dobloug Prize 1999, Gyldendal Prize 2000, Nordic Prize for Dramatists 2000, Nestroy Prize 2001, Scandinavian Nat. Theatre Prize 2002, Norwegian Council of Culture Prize of Honour 2003, Norwegian Theatre Prize of Honour (Hedda) 2003, UBU Prize for best foreign play, Italy 2004, Norwegian Prize for Literature of Honour (Brage) 2005, Anders Jahre Prize for Culture 2006, Nordic Prize, Swedish Acad. 2007, Deutscher Jugendliteraturpreis 2007, Bergen Prize for Artists 2009, Medal from Benedict XVI for participation in Meeting with the Artist in The Sistine Chapel 2009, Int. Ibsen Award 2010, given Grotten as hon. residence from Norwegian Govt 2011. *Plays:* Og aldri skal vi skiljast 1994, Namnet 1995, Nokon kjem til å komme 1996, Barnet 1996, Mor og barn 1997, Sonen 1997, Natta syng sine songar 1997, Ein sommars dag 1999, Gitarmannen 199, Draum om hausten 1999, Besoek 2000, Vinter 2000, Ettermiddag 2000, Vakkert 2001, Doedsvariasjonar 2002, Jenta i sofaen 2003, Suzannah 2004, Sa ka la, 2004, Varmt 2005, Svevn 2005, Rambuku 2006, Skuggar 2006, Eg er vinden 2007, Desse auga 2008, Jente i gul regnjakke 2009. *Publications:* fiction: Raudt, svart 1983, Stengd gitar 1985, Naustet 1989, Flaskesamlaren 1991, Bly og vatn 1992, Melancholia I 1995, Melancholia II 1996; shorter prose: Blod. Steinen er Forteljing 1987, To forteljingar 1993, Prosa frå ein oppvekst. Kortprosa 1994, Eldre kortare prosa 1997, Morgon og kveld 2000, Det er Ales 2004, Andvake 2007; poetry: Engel med vatn i augene 1986, Hundens bevegelsar 1990, Hund og engel 1992, Nye dikt 1997, Ange i vind 2003, Songar 2009; essays: Frå telling via showing til writing 1989, Gnostiske essays 1999; also books for children. *Address:* c/o Samlaget, Boks 4672, Sofienberg, 0506 Oslo, Norway (office); Colombine Teaterförlag, Gaffelgränd 1A, 111 30 Stockholm, Sweden (office).

FOSTER, Brendan, CBE, MBE, BSc; British sports commentator, business executive and fmr athlete; *Chairman, Nova International;* b. 12 Jan. 1948, Hebburn, Co. Durham, England; s. of Francis Foster and Margaret Foster; m. Susan Margaret Foster 1972; one s. one d.; ed Univ. of Sussex, Carnegie Coll., Leeds; competed at Olympic Games, Munich 1972, 5th in 1,500m; Montreal 1976, won bronze medal in 10,000m, 5th in 5,000m, Moscow 1980, 11th in 10,000m; competed Commonwealth Games, Edinburgh 1970, won bronze medal at 1,500m; Christchurch 1974, won silver medal at 5,000m; Edmonton 1978, won gold medal at 10,000m and bronze medal 5,000m; European Champion at 5,000m 1974 and bronze medallist at 1,500m 1971; has held world record at 3,000m and 2 miles, European record at 10,000m, Olympic record at 5,000m; Dir Recreation, Gateshead 1982; Man. Dir Nike International 1982–86, Vice-Pres. Marketing (Worldwide) and Vice-Pres. (Europe) 1986–87; Chair. Nova International; BBC TV commentator 1980–; Hon. Fellow, Sunderland Polytechnic; Hon. MEd (Newcastle); Hon. DLitt (Sussex) 1982; Hon. DArts (Leeds Metropolitan); Hon. DCL (Northumbria); BBC Sports Personality of the Year 1974. *Publications:* Brendan Foster (with Cliff Temple) 1978, Olympic Heroes 1896–1984 1984. *Leisure interests:* sport and running every day. *Address:* Nova International, Newcastle House, Albany Court, Monarch Road, Newcastle upon Tyne, NE4 7YB, England. *Telephone:* (191) 272-7033. *Website:* www.greatrun.org.

FOSTER, Brian, OBE, BSc, MA, DPhil, CPhys, FInstP, FRS; British physicist and academic; *Alexander von Humboldt Professor, University of Hamburg;* b. 4 Jan. 1954, Crook, Co. Durham; s. of John Foster and Annie Foster; m. Sabine Margot Foster 1983; two s.; ed Wolsingham Secondary School, Co. Durham, Queen Elizabeth Coll., Univ. of London, Univ. of Oxford; Research Assoc., Rutherford Appleton Lab., Chilton, Oxon. 1978–82; Research Assoc., Dept of Physics, Imperial Coll., London 1982–84; Lecturer, Dept of Physics, Univ. of Bristol 1984–92, Reader 1992–96, Particle Physics and Astronomy Research Council (PPARC) Advanced Fellow 1991–97, Head of Particle Physics Group 1992–2003, Lecturer Fellow

1999–2000, Prof. of Experimental Physics 1996–2003, Prof. Emer. 2003–; Prof. of Experimental Physics, Univ. of Oxford 2003–, also Head of Particle Physics Dept 2004–11 and Professorial Fellow, Balliol Coll.; Alexander von Humboldt Prof., Univ. of Hamburg and Leading Sr Scientist, Deutsches Elektronen Synchrotron (DESY), Hamburg, Germany 2011–; European Dir Global Design Effort for Int. Linear Collider 2005–13; European Dir Linear Collider Collaboration 2013–; guest lecturer at numerous int. univs; mem. Scientific Council, DESY 1999–2010 (Group Leader, Bristol group on TASSO 1984–90, Group Leader, Bristol group on ZEUS experiment 1985–2003); Chair. Inst. of Physics Nuclear and Particle Physics Div. 1989–93; mem. CERN Large Hadron Collider Cttee, Geneva, Switzerland 1996–99; Acting Dir John Adams Inst. for Accelerator Science 2004–05; mem. many expert cttees including European Cttee for Future Accelerators 1992–96 (Chair. 2002–05, ex officio CERN Council, CERN Scientific Policy Cttee), PPARC Council 2001–06 and many PPARC cttees including Science Cttee, Inst. of Physics Council 2009–13; Admin. Dir Oxford May Music; Consultant Ed. for particle physics, Inst. of Physics Publishing 1991–2005, Taylor & Francis Ltd 2005–; mem. Royal Inst. of GB 1979, BAAS (now the British Science Assen 1993; Special European Physical Soc. Prize in Particle Physics 1995, Alexander von Humboldt Foundation Research Prize 1999, Max Born Medal and Prize 2003, Alexander von Humboldt Professorship 2010. *Radio:* Einstein's Fiddle (BBC Radio 4) 2008, Private Passions (BBC Radio 3) 2008, Essential Classics (BBC Radio 3) 2012. *Publications include:* Topics in High Energy Physics 1988, 40 Years of Particle Physics 1988, Electron-Positron Annihilation Physics 1990. *Leisure interests:* sport, history and politics, music (violin), collecting first edns of books. *Address:* Gruppe FLA, Room 01E/O2.518, DESY, Notkestrasse 85, 22607 Hamburg, Germany (office); 2 Hillview Cottage, Blackford, nr Wedmore, Somerset, BS28 4NL, England (home). *Telephone:* (40) 8998-3201 (office); (1934) 712699 (home). *Fax:* (40) 8998-3282 (Hamburg) (office); (1865) 273417 (Oxford) (office). *E-mail:* b.foster1@physics.ox.ac.uk (office). *Website:* www.physics.ox.ac.uk/users/foster (office).

FOSTER, Sir Christopher David, Kt, MA; British economist; b. 30 Oct. 1930, London; s. of George Cecil Foster and Phyllis Joan Foster (née Mappin); m. Kay Sheridan Bullock 1958; two s. three d.; ed Merchant Taylors School and King's Coll., Cambridge; Fellow and Tutor, Jesus Coll., Cambridge 1964–66; Dir-Gen. of Econ. Planning, Ministry of Transport 1966–70; Head, Unit for Research in Urban Econs, LSE 1970–76, Prof. of Urban Studies and Econs 1976–78, Visiting Prof. 1978–86; Gov. Centre for Environmental Studies 1967–70, Dir 1976–78; Visiting Prof. of Econs MIT 1970; Head of Econ. and Public Policy Div. Coopers & Lybrand (fmrly Coopers & Lybrand Assocs., then Coopers & Lybrand Deloitte) 1978–84, Public Sector Practice Leader and Econ. Adviser 1984–86, Dir and Head Econs Practice Div. 1988–, Partner 1988–94, mem. Man. Cttee 1988–90, Adviser to Chair. 1990–92, 1994–99; Special Adviser to Sec. of Transport on Privatization of British Rail 1992–94; mem. Bd Railtrack 1994–2000; Commercial Adviser to Bd of British Telecommunications PLC 1986–88; Chair. RAC (Royal Automobile Club) Foundation 1999–2003; Hon. Fellow Jesus Coll., Cambridge 1992. *Publications:* The Transport Problem 1963, Politics, Finance and the Role of Economics: The Control of Public Enterprise (jtly) 1972, Local Government Finance 1980, Privatization, Public Ownership and the Regulation of Natural Monopoly 1992, The State Under Stress 1996; papers in various econ. and other journals. *Leisure interests:* theatre, reading. *Address:* c/o RAC Foundation for Motoring, 89–91 Pall Mall, London, SW1Y 5HS (office); 6 Holland Park Avenue, London, W11 3QU, England. *Telephone:* (20) 7727-4757. *Fax:* (20) 7229-6581 (home). *E-mail:* cd@ foster46.fsnet.co.uk (home).

FOSTER, David Manning, BSc, PhD; Australian writer; b. 15 May 1944, Katoomba, NSW; m. 1st Robin Bowers 1964; one s. two d.; m. 2nd Gerda Busch 1975; one s. two d.; ed Univ. of Sydney, Australian Nat. Univ., Univ. of Pennsylvania; professional fiction writer 1973–; The Age Award 1974, Australian Nat. Book Council Award 1981, NSW Premier's Fellowship 1986, Keating Fellowship 1991–94, James Joyce Foundation Award 1996, Miles Franklin Award 1997, Courier Mail Award 1999, Patrick White Award 2010. *Publications:* novels: The Pure Land 1974, The Empathy Experiment 1977, Moonlite 1981, Plumbum 1983, Dog Rock: A Postal Pastoral 1985, The Adventures of Christian Rosy Cross 1986, Testostero 1987, The Pale Blue Crochet Coathanger Cover 1988, Mates of Mars 1991, The Glade Within the Grove 1996, The Ballad of Erinungarah 1997, In the New Country 1999, The Land Where Stories End 2001, Sons of the Rumour 2009, Man of Letters 2012. *Leisure interests:* gardening, bush walking. *Address:* PO Box 57, Bundanoon, NSW 2578, Australia (office).

FOSTER, Ian T., PhD; American computer scientist and academic; *Arthur Holly Compton Distinguished Service Professor of Computer Science and Director, Computation Institute, University of Chicago;* Distinguished Fellow and Assoc. Div. Dir, Math. and Computer Science Div., Argonne Nat. Lab., Head of Distributed Systems Lab.; currently Arthur Holly Compton Distinguished Service Prof. of Computer Science, Univ. of Chicago; Dir Computation Inst. (jt project between Univ. of Chicago and Argonne Nat. Lab.) 2006–; co-f. Globus Project 1995; open source strategist, Open Grid Forum and Globus Alliance; co-f. Univa Corpn, Elmhurst, Ill. 2004 (merged with United Devices to form Univa UD 2007); mem. Advisory Bd for IOCOM Communications; Fellow, AAAS 2003, British Computer Soc.; Lovelace Medal, British Computer Soc., Gordon Bell Prize for high-performance computing 2001, named by Network World magazine as one of "the 50 most powerful people in networking" 2004. *Achievements include:* called "the father of the Grid"; research resulted in devt of techniques, tools and algorithms for high-performance distributed computing and parallel computing; led research and devt of software for I-WAY wide-area distributed computing experiment across N America 1995. *Publications:* numerous influential documents on Grid architecture and principles. *Address:* Computation Institute, University of Chicago, 5640 S Ellis Avenue, RI 405, Chicago, IL 60637 (office); Argonne National Laboratory, 9700 South Cass Avenue, Building 221-D156, Argonne, IL 60439, USA (office). *Telephone:* (773) 834-6812 (Chicago) (office); (630) 252-4619 (Argonne) (office). *Fax:* (773) 834-6818 (Chicago) (office). *E-mail:* foster@mcs.anl.gov (office). *Website:* www-fp.mcs.anl.gov/~foster (office); ianfoster.typepad.com.

FOSTER, Jodie (Alicia Christian), BA; American actress, film director and producer; b. 19 Nov. 1962, Los Angeles; d. of Lucius Foster and Evelyn Foster (née Almond); two s.; ed Yale Univ.; acting début in TV programme Mayberry R.F.D.

1968; owner and Chair. EGG Pictures Production Co. 1990–; Hon. DFA (Yale) 1997; Cecil B DeMille Award, Golden Globe Awards, Hollywood Foreign Press Association 2012. *Films include:* Napoleon and Samantha 1972, Kansas City Bomber 1972, One Little Indian 1973, Tom Sawyer 1973, Alice Doesn't Live Here Any More 1975, Taxi Driver 1976, Echoes of a Summer 1976, Bugsy Malone 1976, Freaky Friday 1976, The Little Girl Who Lives Down the Lane 1977, Candleshoe 1977, Foxes 1980, Carny 1980, Hotel New Hampshire 1984, The Blood of Others 1984, Siesta 1986, Five Corners 1986, The Accused (Acad. Award for Best Actress 1989) 1988, Stealing Home 1988, Catchfire 1990, The Silence of the Lambs (Acad. Award for Best Actress 1992) 1990, Little Man Tate (also dir) 1991, Shadows and Fog 1992, Sommersby 1993, Maverick 1994, Nell 1994, Home for the Holidays (dir, co-producer only) 1996, Contact 1997, The Baby Dance (exec. producer only) 1997, Waking the Dead (exec. producer only) 1998, Anna and the King 1999, Panic Room 2001, The Dangerous Lives of Altar Boys (also producer) 2002, Un long dimanche de fiançailles 2004, Flightplan 2005, Inside Man 2006, The Brave One (also producer) 2007, Nim's Island 2008, The Beaver (also dir) 2010, Carnage 2011. *Address:* EGG Pictures Production Co., Jerry Lewis Annex, 5555 Melrose Avenue, Los Angeles, CA 90038-3112, USA.

FOSTER, Kent B., BS, MS; American computer distribution industry executive (retd); b. 1944; ed North Carolina State Univ., Univ. of South Carolina; worked 29 years with GTE Corpn, becoming Dir 1992–99, Vice-Chair. 1993–99, Pres. 1995–99; CEO and Pres. Ingram Micro Inc. 2000–05, Chair. 2000–05, Chair. 2005–07 (retd); mem. Bd of Dirs Campbell Soup Co. Inc., J. C. Penney Co. Inc., New York Life Insurance Co. *Address:* c/o Ingram Micro Incorporated, 1600 East St Andrew Place, Santa Ana, CA 92705-4931, USA.

FOSTER, Lawrence Thomas; American conductor; *Music Director, Orchestre et Opéra National de Montpellier;* b. 23 Oct. 1941, Los Angeles, Calif.; m. Angela Foster 1972; one d.; studied with Fritz Zweig and Karl Böhm and at Bayreuth Festival and Tanglewood Master Classes; Music Dir, Young Musicians Foundation, Los Angeles 1960–64; Conductor, San Francisco Ballet 1960–64; Asst Conductor, LA Philharmonic Orchestra 1965–68; Chief Guest Conductor, Royal Philharmonic Orchestra, London 1969–74; Music Dir, Houston Symphony Orchestra 1971–78; Music Dir, Orchestre Philharmonique, Monte Carlo 1978–96; Music Dir, Duisburg Orchestra, FRG 1982–86; Music Dir, Chamber Orchestra of Lausanne 1985; conductor, Jerusalem Symphony Orchestra 1990; Music Dir, Aspen Music Festival and School 1990–96; Music Dir, Orquestra Ciutat de Barcelona 1995–2002, Prin. Guest Conductor 2002–; Artistic Dir, Georg Enescu Festival 1998–2001; Music Dir, Gulbenkian Orchestra, Lisbon 2002–13; Music Dir, Orchestre et Opéra Nat. de Montpellier 2009–, Orchestre Philharmonique et Opéra de Marseille 2012–; Pres.'s decoration for services to Romanian music 2003; Koussevitsky Memorial Conducting Prize, Tanglewood 1966. *Film appearance:* Belle toujours 2006. *Leisure interests:* reading history and biographies, films. *Address:* c/o Opus 3 Artists, Pariser Straße 62, 10719 Berlin, Germany (office). *Telephone:* (30) 88910150 (office). *Fax:* (30) 88910152 (office). *E-mail:* info.berlin@opus3artists.com (office). *Website:* www.opus3artists.com (office).

FOSTER, Maria das Graças Silva, MSc, MBA; Brazilian chemist and oil company executive; *President and CEO, Petróleo Brasileiro SA (Petrobras);* b. 26 Aug. 1953, Morro do Adeus, Rio de Janeiro; m.; two c.; ed Universidade Federal Fluminense, Universidade Federal do Rio de Janeiro, Fundação Getulio Vargas; joined Petróleo Brasileiro SA (Petrobras) as trainee 1978, Exec. Dir of Natural Gas and Energy 2007–12, Pres. and CEO 2012–; Sec. of Oil, Natural Gas and Renewable Fuels, Ministry of Mines and Energy 2003–05; CEO Petroquisa-Petrobras Quimica SA 2005–06; CEO and Chief Financial Officer, Petrobras Distribuidora SA 2006–07; Chair. of Bd Transportadora Associada de Gas SA; mem. Bd of Dirs, Transpetro-Petrobras Transporte SA, Petrobras Biocombustivel SA, Braskem SA; Commdr, Rio Branco Order, Ministry of External Affairs 2007; ranked by Forbes magazine amongst The World's 100 Most Powerful Women (20th) 2012, (18th) 2013, ranked by Fortune magazine amongst the 50 Most Powerful Women in Business outside the US (first) 2012, voted the best CEO in Latin America in Institutional Investor magazine's oil, gas and petrochemical industry ranking 2013. *Address:* Petrobras Brasil, Av. Republica do Chile #65, Centro, Rio de Janeiro, Brazil (office). *Telephone:* (21) 32244477 (office). *Fax:* (21) 32246055 (office). *E-mail:* petroinvest@petrobras.com.br (office). *Website:* www .petrobras.com.br (office).

FOSTER, Robert Fitzroy (Roy), FBA; Irish historian, writer and academic; *Carroll Professor of Irish History, Hertford College, University of Oxford;* b. 16 Jan. 1949, Waterford; ed Trinity Coll. Dublin; Prof. of Modern British History, Birkbeck College, London 1989-91; Carroll Prof. of Irish History and Fellow, Hertford Coll., Oxford 1991–; visiting fellowships include St. Anthony's Coll., Oxford, Inst. for Advanced Study, Princeton, New Jersey, Princeton Univ.; Hon. DLitt (Aberdeen) 1997, (Queen's, Belfast) 1998, (Trinity Coll. Dublin) 2003, (Nat. Univ. of Ireland) 2004; Hon. Fellow, Birkbeck Coll., Univ. of London 2005. *Publications include:* biographies of Charles Stewart Parnell 1976 and Lord Randolph Churchill 1981, Modern Ireland 1600–1972 1988, The Oxford Illustrated History of Ireland 1989, Paddy and Mr Punch 1997, W. B. Yeats: A Life, Vol. I: The Apprentice Mage 1865–1914 2001, The Irish Story: Telling Tales and Making it Up in Ireland 2001 (Christian Gauss Award from Phi Beta Kappa 2003), W. B. Yeats: A Life, Vol. II: The Arch-Poet 1915–1939 2003, Conquering England: the Irish in Victorian London (with Fintan Cullen) 2005, Luck and the Irish 2007, Words Alone: Yeats and His Inheritances 2011. *Address:* Hertford College, Catte Street, Oxford, OX1 3BW, England (office). *Telephone:* (1865) 279400 (office). *E-mail:* roy.foster@hertford.ox.ac.uk (office). *Website:* www.hertford.ox.ac.uk (office).

FOSTER OF THAMES BANK, Baron (Life Peer), cr. 1999 of Reddish in the County of Greater Manchester; **Norman Robert Foster,** Kt, OM, DipArch, MArch, RA, RWA, RIBA; British architect; *Chairman and Founder, Foster + Partners;* b. 1 June 1935, Manchester; s. of Robert Foster and the late Lilian Foster; m. 3rd Elena Ochoa 1996; ed Manchester Univ. School of Architecture and City Planning, Yale Univ. School of Architecture; Urban Renewal and City Planning Consultants work 1962–63; pvt. practice, as "Team 4 Architects" (with Wendy Cheesman, Georgie Wolton, Lord Rogers of Riverside) London 1963–67, Foster Associates (now Foster + Partners), offices Berlin, Singapore 1967–, Chair. Foster + Partners 1967–; collaboration with Buckminster Fuller 1968–83; Consultant Architect to Univ. of E Anglia 1978–87; fmr External Examiner

RIBA Visiting Bd of Educ.; fmr mem. Architectural Asscn Council (Vice-Pres. 1974); fmr teacher Univ. of Pa, Architectural Asscn, London, London Polytechnic, Bath Acad. of Arts; FCSD 1975; IBM Fellow, Aspen Design Conf. 1980; Council mem. RCA 1981–; mem. Int. Acad. of Architecture (IAA), European Acad. of Sciences and Arts, American Acad. of Arts and Sciences; mem. Order of French Architects, Akad. der Kunst, Royal Acad. of Fine Arts, Sweden; Hon. FAIA 1980; Royal West of England Academician; Hon. Fellow Royal Acad., Inst. of Structural Engineers, Royal Coll. of Eng, Kent Inst. of Art and Design; Hon. mem. Bund Deutscher Architekten (BDA); Royal Designer for Industry (RDI); Assoc. Acad. Royale de Belgique; Hon. LittD (Univ. of E Anglia) 1980; Hon. DSc (Bath) 1986, (Humberside) 1992, (Valencia) 1992, (Manchester) 1993; Dr hc (Royal Coll. of Art) 1991, (Tech. Univ. Eindhoven) 1996; Hon. DLitt. (Oxford) 1996, (London) 1997; numerous awards including Architectural Design Projects Awards 1964, 1965, 1966, 1969, Financial Times Industrial Architecture Awards 1967, 1974, 1984, RIBA Awards 1969, 1972, 1977, 1978, 1992, 1993, 1997, 1998, 1999; RSA Business and Industry Award 1976, 1991, Int. Design Awards (Brussels) 1976, 1980, R. S. Reynolds Int. Memorial Awards (USA) 1976, 1979, 1986, Structural Steel Awards 1972, 1978, 1984, 1986, 1992, 1999, 2000, Ambrose Congreve Award 1980, Royal Gold Medal for Architecture 1983, Civic Trust Award 1984, 1992, 1995, 1999, 2000, Constructa-European Award Program for Industrial Architecture 1986, Premio Compasso d'Oro Award 1987, Japan Design Foundation Award 1987, PA Innovations Award 1988, Annual Interiors Award (USA) 1988, 1992, 1993, 1994, Kunstpreis Award, Berlin 1989, British Construction Industry (BCI) Award 1989, 1991, 1992, 1993, 1997, 1998, Mies van der Rohe Award, Barcelona 1991, Gold Medal, Acad. Française 1991, Concrete Soc. Award 1992, 1993, 1999, American Inst. of Architects (AIA) Gold Medal 1994, Queen's Award for Export Achievement 1995, AIA Award 1995, 1997, 'Mipim' Man of the Year 1996, 'Building' Construction Personality of the Year 1997, Silver Medal of Chartered Soc. of Designers 1997, Pritzker Prize for Architecture 1999, Visual Arts Award 2000, Praemium Imperiale 2002, British-German Asscn Medal of Honour for Services to Anglo-German Relations 2006, China Friendship Award from Chinese State Admin of Foreign Experts Affairs 2008, Premio Príncipe de Asturias, Spain 2009; German Federal Order of Merit 1999, Officier, Ordre des Arts et des Lettres (France), Order of N Rhine-Westphalia. *Major works include:* Pilot Head Office for IBM, Hampshire 1970, Tech. Park for IBM, Greenford 1975, Willis, Faber and Dumas, Ipswich 1975, Sainsbury Centre for Visual Arts, Norwich 1977, Renault Centre UK 1983, Hong Kong Bank HQ 1986, Third London Airport Terminal Stansted 1991, Century Tower Tokyo 1991, Barcelona Telecommunications Tower 1992, Sackler Galleries, Royal Acad. 1991, Cranfield Univ. Library 1992, Arts Centre, Nîmes 1993, Lycée, Fréjus 1993, Microelectronics Park, Duisburg 1993, Bilbao Metro System 1995, Univ. of Cambridge Faculty of Law 1996, American Air Museum, Duxford 1997, Commerzbank HQ Frankfurt 1997, Chek Lap Kok Airport, Hong Kong 1998, new German Parl. (Reichstag), Berlin 1999, Great Court, British Museum 2000, Al Faisaliah Complex, Riyadh 2000, Research Facility, Stanford Univ. Calif. 2000, Greater London Authority Bldg, London, Millennium Bridge, London, Swiss Re Tower (RIBA Stirling Prize 2004) 2002–03, Wembley Stadium, London 2003–07, Torre Caja Madrid 2004–08, Millau Viaduct, France 2005, Supreme Court, Singapore 2005, Petronas Univ. Campus, Malaysia, Hearst Headquarters tower, New York 2006, Khan Shatyr Entertainment Center, Astana, Kazakhstan 2006–10, Museum of Fine Arts, Boston, Opera House, Dallas, Smithsonian Inst. Courtyard, Washington DC 2007, The Bow, Calgary, Canada 2007–10, SSE Hydro, Glasgow 2005–13, Dolder Grand Hotel, Zürich 2008, Beijing Int. Airport Terminal 3, China 2008, Ombrelle, Old Port, Marseille 2013, Tower 2 of planned reconstruction of World Trade Center, New York City (under construction); work exhibited in Moscow, Antwerp, Barcelona, Berlin, Bilbao, Bordeaux, London, Lyons, Madrid, Milan, Munich, New York, Paris, Tokyo, Valencia, Venice, and Zürich; work in perm. collection of Museum of Modern Art, New York and Centre Georges Pompidou, Paris. *Publications include:* Norman Foster: Buildings and Projects Vols 1, 2, 3, 4, On Foster . . . Foster On 2000 and numerous contribs to the architectural and tech. press. *Leisure interests:* flying, skiing, running. *Address:* Foster + Partners, Riverside Three, 22 Hester Road, London, SW11 4AN, England (home). *Telephone:* (20) 7738-0455 (home). *Fax:* (20) 7738-1107 (home). *E-mail:* enquiries@fosterandpartners.com (office). *Website:* www.fosterandpartners.com (office).

FOTIOU, Fotis, BBA; Cypriot accountant and politician; b. 1960, Larnaca; m. Maro Arestis; three s.; ed American Acad., Larnaca, Eastern Michigan Univ., USA; began career as chartered accountant, auditor and business consultant, worked for several int. auditing firms including PriceWaterhouseCoopers and Deloitte Haskins & Sells, and for Inland Revenue Dept of Ministry of Finance; Founder and Man. Partner, PKP Consultants; Minister of Agric., Natural Resources and Environment 2006–08, Minister of Defence 2013–14; mem. Dimokratiko Komma (DIKO—Democratic Party), Spokesman 2008–13; mem. Cyprus Inst. of Certified Accountants, Inst. of Financial Accountants; Dir Electricity Authority of Cyprus 1993–99, Cyprus Tourism Org. 2000–03 (Chair. 2003); mem. Chamber of Commerce and Industry of Larnaca; fmr Vice Pres. and Sec. to Bd AEK Larnaca (football club). *Address:* c/o Ministry of Defence, 4 Emmanuel Roides Ave, 1432 Nicosia, Cyprus (office). *Website:* www.mod.gov.cy (office).

FOTTRELL, Patrick, BSc, MSc, PhD, DSc, MRIA; Irish biochemist, academic, business executive and fmr university administrator; *Chairman, Westgate Biological Ltd;* b. 26 Sept. 1933, Youghal, Co. Cork; s. of Matthew Fottrell and Mary Fottrell (née O'Sullivan); m. Esther Kennedy 1963; two s. two d.; ed Christian Brothers School, Youghal and North Mon Schools, Univ. Coll., Cork, Univ. of Glasgow, UK, Univ. Coll., Galway; Sr Research Officer, Agric. Inst., Johnstown Castle, Wexford 1963–65; Lecturer, later Assoc. Prof., Prof. of Biochemistry, Univ. Coll., Galway 1965, Pres. Univ. Coll., Galway 1996–2000; currently Chair. Westgate Biological Ltd, Science Foundation Ireland 2003–; Visiting Prof., Harvard Univ., USA 1972, 1982; fmr Chair. Dublin Inst. of Tech.; fmr Chair. Irish Council of Bioethics; fmr Vice-Pres. Royal Irish Acad.; Beit Memorial Fellow; EEC Science Writers Award, Conway Medal, Royal Acad. of Medicine (Ireland). *Publications:* Perspectives on Coeliac Disease (co-author); more than 100 scientific publs in int. journals on biochemistry. *Leisure interests:* walking, music, soccer. *Address:* Westgate Biological Ltd, 56, Sir Rogerson's Quay, Dublin 2 (office). Bunowen, Taylorshill, Galway, Ireland (home). *Telephone:* (23) 54944 (office); (91) 21022 (home). *Website:* www.westgate.ie (office).

FOTYGA, Anna; Polish politician; b. 12 Jan. 1957, Lębrok; m.; two c.; ed Univ. of Gdańsk; worked in Int. Dept, Nat. Election Comm., NSZZ Trade Union (Solidarity) 1981, Dir 1989–91; mem. Man. Bd, Modem Co. 1987–89; worked at Przekaz publishing house 1992–94; involved in World Bank projects, GPEC Gdańsk 1994–96, Consultant 1996; Vice-Chair. Supreme Supervisory Bd, Social Insurance Inst. (ZUS) 1998–2002; European Integration Adviser to Pres. of Office of Health Insurance Oversight 1999–2001; Int. Affairs Adviser to Prime Minister 2000; Dir Dept of Int. Affairs, Chancellery of the Prime Minister 2001; mem. City Council of Gdańsk 2002, Council Vice-Pres. (Deputy Mayor) responsible for Econ. Affairs and European Integration 2002–04; mem. European Parl. 2004–05, coordinated Union for Europe of the Nations Group in Cttee on Foreign Affairs; Sec. of State, Ministry of Foreign Affairs 2005–06, Minister of Foreign Affairs 2006–07; Chief Office of the Pres. –2008. *Address:* Prawo i Sprawiedliwość, ul. Nowogrodzka 84/86, 02-018 Warszawa, Poland (office). *Telephone:* (22) 6215035 (office). *Fax:* (22) 6216767 (office). *E-mail:* biuro@pis.org.pl (office). *Website:* www.pis.org.pl (office).

FOU, Ts'ong; British (b. Chinese) pianist; b. 10 March 1934; s. of the late Fu Lei; m. 1st Zamira Menuhin 1960 (divorced 1970); one s.; m. 2nd Hijong Hyun 1973 (divorced 1978); m. 3rd Patsy Toh 1987; one s.; ed studied in China with Mario Paci, Warsaw Conservatory with Zbigniew Drzewiecki; debut with Shanghai Municipal Orchestra, playing Beethoven's Emperor Concerto 1951; gave 100 concerts in E. Europe while studying in Poland 1953–58; moved to UK 1958, London debut 1959; solo appearances in Europe, Scandinavia, the Far East, Australia and New Zealand, North and South America; currently Visiting Prof. Int. Foundation for Pianists, Como, Italy and Shanghai Conservatory, China; Dr hc (Hong Kong Univ.); third prize Bucharest Piano Competition 1953, Int. Chopin Competition, Warsaw 1955. *Solo piano CDs:* Bach, Chopin, Debussy, Handel, Mozart, Scarlatti, Schubert and Schumann. *Piano concerto CDs:* Chopin and Mozart. *Leisure interests:* bridge, sport, oriental art. *Address:* 62 Aberdeen Park, London, N5 2BL, England (home). *Telephone:* (20) 7226-9589 (home). *Fax:* (20) 7704-8896 (home). *E-mail:* foutoh@yahoo.co.uk (home).

FOUDA, Yosri; Egyptian journalist; b. 1964; ed American Univ. in Cairo; taught mass communication and various media courses, Cairo Univ. 1986–92; producer for Arabic-language TV Service, BBC, London, UK –1996; reporter, Al Jazeera London Bureau, UK 1996–2009, Bureau Chief –2009 (resgnd), also presenter, Top Secret TV programme; Ed. and Presenter, Last Word TV programme, ONTV 2009–; Pan-Arab Cairo Radio and TV Production Festival award 1998, AUC's Outstanding Professional Performance Award (2000). *Publication:* Masterminds of Terror: The Truth Behind the Most Devastating Attack The World Has Ever Seen (with Nick Fielding) 2003. *Website:* www.ontveg.com (office).

FOURCADE, Jean-Pierre; French politician; b. 18 Oct. 1929, Marmande; s. of Raymond Fourcade and Germaine Fourcade (née Raynal); m. Odile Mion 1958; one s. two d.; ed Coll. de Sorèze, Bordeaux Univ. Faculté de Droit, Inst. des Etudes politiques; student, Ecole Nat. d'Admin. 1952–54; Insp. des Finances 1954–73; Chargé de Mission to Sec. of State for Finance (later Minister of Finance) 1959–61, Conseiller technique 1962, Dir Adjoint du Cabinet 1964–66; Asst Head of Service, Inspection gén. des Finances 1962; Head of Trade Div., Directorate-Gen. of Internal Trade and Prices 1965, Dir-Gen. 1968–70; Asst Dir-Gen. Crédit industriel et commercial 1970, Dir-Gen. 1972–74, Admin. 1973–74; Admin., later Pres. and Dir-Gen. Soc. d'Epargne mobilière 1972–74; Admin. Banque transatlantique 1971–74, Soc. commerciale d'Affrètement et de Combustibles 1972–74; Minister of Econ. and Finance 1974–76, of Supply 1976–77, of Supply and Regional Devt 1977; Mayor of St-Cloud 1971–92, of Boulogne-Billancourt 1995–2007; Conseiller-Gén., canton of St-Cloud 1973–89; Conseiller Régional, Ile de France 1976, Vice-Pres. 1982–86, First Vice-Pres. 1986–95; Senator, Hauts de Seine 1977–2011; Pres. Comité des Finances Locales 1980–2004, Comm. des Affaires Sociales du Sénat 1983–99; Pres. Clubs Perspectives et Réalités 1975–82; mem. Union pour la Démocratie française (UDF) 1978–, Vice-Pres. 1978–86; mem. UMP Parl. group 2002–; mem. Admin. Council of RATP 1984–93, Epad 1985–95, SNCF 1993–98; Pres. Conseil de Surveillance de la Caisse Nat. des Allocations Familiales 2002–04; Vice-Pres. Asscn des Maires des Grandes Villes de France 2002–; Pres. Comm. Consultative d'Evaluation des Charges 2005–; Commdr, Ordre nat. du Mérite. *Publications:* Et si nous parlions de demain 1979, la Tentation social-démocrate 1985, Remèdes pour l'assurance maladie 1989. *Address:* 8 Parc de Béarn, 92210 St-Cloud, France (home). *E-mail:* jeanpierre.fourcade92@gmail.fr (home).

FOURNEYRON, Valérie; French physician and politician; b. (Valérie Absire), 4 Oct. 1959, Le Petit-Quevilly (Seine-Maritime); m.; four c.; sports doctor, CHU de Rouen 1981–89, Rouen ice-hockey team 1984–90; Regional Insp. for Youth and Sports 1989–90; Chief of Mission, Sport Medicine, Ministry for Youth and Sport 1989–91; Dir Regional Centre of Sports Medicine, Sotteville-le-Rouen and doctor to French volleyball team 1991–95; mem. interdepartmental group for sports medicine and doping and participant of working group on development of new legislation on doping 1998; doctor to Rouen professional basketball team 2002–05; Regional Councillor for Haute-Normandie 1998–2007; Gen. Councillor for Rouen 5 2004–08; Deputy (Parti socialiste) to Nat. Ass. for First Dist of Seine-Maritime 2007–12; Mayor of Rouen 2008–12; Minister for Sport, Youth, Popular Educ. and Community Life 2012–14; holds several other elected political offices. *Address:* c/o Ministry of Sport, Youth, Popular Education and Community Life, 95 avenue de France, 75650 Paris Cedex 13, France (office).

FOURNIER, Guy, OC; Canadian author, screenwriter, producer and broadcasting executive; *Administrator, Canada Medium Fund;* b. 23 July 1931, Waterloo, Quebec; m. Maryse Beauregard; has written TV drama as well as films, has also produced dramatic films and documentaries; mem. Bd of Dirs and Chair. CBC 2005–06 (resgnd); currently TV commentator and columnist, Le Journal de Montreal; mem. Bd of Dirs and Admin., Canada Media Fund 2009–; Gold Medal Cuisine (Canada), five Gemini Awards, Gérard Philippe Medal (France). *Plays:* C'est maintenant qu'il faut boire, L'amour ou la vie, Soleil, maudit soleil, Je t'aime clés en main (adaptation). *Film screenplays include:* Y'a toujours moyen de moyenner! (There's Always a Way to Find a Way) 1973, La mer mi-sel 1974, Maria Chapdelaine 1983, Mon amie Max 1994, Histoire de famille 2006. *Television screenplays include:* Les enquêtes Jobidon (series) 1962, Ti-Jean caribou (series) 1963, Bidule de Tarmacadam (series) 1969, Jo Gaillard (series) 1975, Jamais deux sans toi (series) 1977, Rue de l'anse (series) 1983, Manon (series) 1985, L'or et le papier (series) 1990, Coeur à prendre 1994, Jamais deux sans toi (series) 1996, Les

parfaits (series) 2001, Trudeau II: Maverick in the Making (mini-series) 2005. *Publications:* has published poems, humorous essays, novels, cookbooks and children's books. *Address:* 150 Berlioz, Verdun, PQ H3E 1K3, Canada (office); c/o Canadian Television Fund, 50 Wellington Street East, 4th Floor, Toronto, ON M5E 1C8, Canada. *Telephone:* (514) 762-1785 (office); (416) 214-4400. *E-mail:* gfmb@ videotron.ca (office); ctf@ctf-fct.ca. *Fax:* (416) 214-4420. *Website:* www .canadiantelevisionfund.ca.

FOURNIER, Jacques, LenD; French lawyer; b. 5 May 1929, Épinal; s. of Léon Fournier and Ida Rudmann; m. 1st Jacqueline Tazerout (deceased); three s.; m. 2nd Michèle Dubez 1980 (divorced); m. 3rd Noëlle Fréaud-Lenoir 1989 (divorced); ed Inst. for Political Studies, Paris and Nat. School of Admin; Civil Servant, French State Council 1953, Master of Petitions 1960, State Councillor 1978; Legal Adviser, Embassy in Morocco 1961–64; Head of Dept of Social Affairs, Gen. Planning Office 1969–72; Asst Sec.-Gen. to Pres. of France 1981–82; Sec.-Gen. of the Govt 1982–86; Pres. of Admin. Council of Gaz de France 1986–88; Pres. SNCF 1988–94, Centre européen des entreprises publiques 1988–94, Sceta 1989–94, Ciriec-France 1994; Chair. Carrefour 1992–98; fmr mem. Council of State, renewed mem. 1994–98; mem. Conseil supérieur de la magistrature 1998–2002; Chevalier, Ordre Nat. du Mérite; Commdr, Légion d'honneur. *Publications:* Politique de l'Education 1971, Traité du social, situations, luttes politiques, institutions 1976, Le Pouvoir du social 1979, Le travail gouvernemental 1987, le Train, l'Europe et le service public 1993. *Address:* 19 rue Presbourg, 75116 Paris, France (home). *E-mail:* jfrnier@ easynet.fr (home).

FOURTOU, Jean-René, MA; French business executive; *Chairman of the Supervisory Board, Vivendi;* b. 20 June 1939, Libourne; ed Ecole Polytechnique, Paris, Massachusetts Inst. of Tech., USA; Eng Consultant, Bossard & Michel 1963, mem. Bd of Dirs Bossard Consultants 1972, Chair. and CEO 1977; apptd Chair. and CEO Rhône-Poulenc SA 1986; Vice-Chair. Supervisory Bd AXA (ADR) 1990–2009, fmr mem. Supervisory Bd AXA Millésimes SAS; Vice-Chair. and CEO Aventis 1999–2002, Hon. Chair. and Vice-Chair. Supervisory Bd 2002–; Chair. and CEO Vivendi Universal (now Vivendi) 2002–05, Chair. Supervisory Bd 2005–; Co-Chair. Franco-Moroccan Impetus Group; fmr Chair. Supervisory Bd Canal+; Vice-Chair. ICC –2003, Chair. 2003–05, Hon. Chair. 2005–09; mem. Bd Dirs Sanofi, Nestlé (Switzerland) –2012; fmr Dir, Cap Gemini, NBC Universal (USA); mem. Supervisory Bd Maroc Telecom; mem. European Round Table of Industrialists (ERT); Co-founder Entreprise & Cité; Chair. Bordeaux Univ. Foundation; Officier, Légion d'honneur, Commdr, Ordre nat. du Mérite; Int. Leadership Award, US Council for Int. Business 2004. *Publications include:* La Passion d'Entreprendre 1985. *Address:* Vivendi, 42 avenue de Friedland, 75380 Paris Cedex 08, France (office). *Telephone:* 1-71-71-10-00 (office). *Fax:* 1-71-71-11-79 (office). *E-mail:* info@vivendi.com (office). *Website:* www.vivendi.com (office).

FOWKE, Philip Francis, FRAM; British concert pianist; b. 28 June 1950, Gerrards Cross, Bucks.; s. of Francis H.V. Fowke and Florence L. (née Clutton) Fowke; ed Downside Abbey School; began piano studies with Marjorie Withers 1957; awarded RAM Scholarship to study with Gordon Green 1967; Wigmore Hall debut 1974; UK concerto debut with Royal Liverpool Philharmonic 1975; Royal Festival Hall debut 1977; BBC Promenade Concert debut 1979; US debut 1982; debuts in Denmark, Bulgaria, France, Switzerland, Hong Kong, Belgium and Italy 1983; Austrian debut at Salzburg Mozart week 1984; German debut 1985; New Zealand debut 1994; now appears regularly with all the leading orchestras in UK and gives regular recitals and concerto performances for BBC Radio; Prof. RAM 1984–91, Welsh Coll. of Music and Drama 1994; Head of Keyboard Dept, Trinity Coll. of Music, London 1995–98, Sr Fellow 1998; recordings of Bliss, Chopin, Delius, Finzi, Rachmaninoff and Tchaikovsky piano concertos; Recitalist and Piano Tutor, Dartington Int. Summer School 1996, 1997, 2000; Concerto appearances with the Hallé Orchestra and in USA 1997; 50th Birthday Recital, Wigmore Hall, London 2000; soloist, BBC Proms 2001; mem. London Piano Quartet; Vice-Chair. European Piano Teachers' Asscn (UK) presenter and contrib. to music programmes on BBC Radio and to nat. press; Countess of Munster Musical Trust Award 1972, Nat. Fed. of Music Socs. Award 1973, BBC Piano Competition 1974, Winston Churchill Fellowship 1976 and numerous other awards and prizes. *Recordings include:* Hoddinott Piano Concerto, CD album of film scores 1998. *Publications:* reviews and obituaries in nat. press. *Leisure interests:* architecture, monasticism. *Address:* Patrick Garvey Management, 40 North Parade, York YO30 7AB, England (office). *Telephone:* (1904) 621222 (office). *Fax:* (1723) 330050 (office). *E-mail:* patrick@patrickgarvey.com (office). *Website:* www.patrickgarvey .com (office).

FOWLER, Sir (Edward) Michael Coulson, Kt, MArch, FNZIA, ARIBA; New Zealand architect; b. 19 Dec. 1929, Marton; s. of William Coulson Fowler and Faith Agnes Fowler (née Netherclift); m. Barbara Hamilton Hall 1953; two s. one d.; ed Christ's Coll., Christchurch, Auckland Univ.; with Ove Arup & Pnrs, London 1954–55; Pnr, Gray Young, Morton Calder & Fowler, Wellington 1959; Sr Pnr, Calder, Fowler & Styles 1960–89; travelled abroad to study cen. banking systems' security methods; work includes Overseas Terminal, Wellington, Reserve Bank, Wellington, Dalmuir House, Wellington Club, office bldgs, factories, houses, churches; mem. Wellington City Council 1968–74; Chair. NZIA Educ. Cttee 1967–73; Mayor of Wellington 1974–83; Chair. Queen Elizabeth II Arts Council of New Zealand 1983–86; Pres. New Zealand Youth Hostel Asscn 1983–86; architectural consultant 1983–; regular dealer at gallery exhbns and sales of paintings; Award of Honour, New Zealand Inst. of Architects 1983, Alfred O. Glasse Award, New Zealand Planning Inst. 1984. *Publications:* Country Houses of New Zealand 1972, Wellington Sketches: Folios I, II 1973, The Architecture and Planning of Moscow 1980, Eating Houses in Wellington 1980, Wellington-Wellington 1981, Eating Houses of Canterbury 1982, Wellington Celebration 1983, The New Zealand House 1983, Buildings of New Zealanders 1984, Michael Fowler's University of Auckland 1993. *Leisure interests:* sketching, writing, history, politics. *Address:* 1 May Street, Wellington (office); 30 Goring Street, Thorndon, Wellington, New Zealand (home). *Telephone:* (4) 499-9991 (office); (4) 473-0888 (home). *Fax:* (4) 471-0017 (office). *E-mail:* michael.fowler@xtra.co.nz (home). *Website:* www.sirmichaelfowler.com/paintings.php.

FOWLER, Baron (Life Peer), cr. 2001, of Sutton Coldfield in the Co. of West Midlands; **Rt Hon. (Peter) Norman,** Kt, PC, MA; British politician; b. 2 Feb. 1938; s. of the late N.F. Fowler and Katherine Fowler; m. 1st Linda Christmas

1968; m. 2nd Fiona Poole 1979; two d.; ed King Edward VI School, Chelmsford, Trinity Hall, Cambridge; Nat. Service Comm., Essex Regt 1956–58; joined The Times 1961, Special Corresp. 1962–66, Home Affairs Corresp. 1966–70; mem. Council, Bow Group 1967–69, Editorial Bd, Crossbow 1962–69; Vice-Chair. N Kensington Conservative Asscn 1967–68; Chair. E Midlands Area, Conservative Political Centre 1970–73; MP for Nottingham S 1970–74, for Sutton Coldfield 1974–2001, mem. Parl. Select Cttee on Race Relations and Immigration 1970–74; Jt Sec. Conservative Parl. Home Affairs Cttee 1971–72, Vice-Chair. 1974; Parl. Pvt. Sec. NI Office 1972–74; Opposition Spokesman on Home Affairs 1974–75; Chief Opposition Spokesman on Social Services 1975–76, on Transport 1976–79; Minister of Transport 1979–81, Sec. of State for Transport 1981, for Social Services 1981–87, for Employment 1987–90; Chair. Conservative Party 1992–94; Opposition Front Bench Spokesman on Environment, Transport and the Regions 1997–98, on Home Affairs 1998–99; mem. House of Lords 2001–, Chair. Select Cttee on Future of BBC 2005–06, Chair. Select Cttee on Communications 2005–10, Chair. Select Cttee on HIV/AIDS 2011–; mem. Lloyds 1989–98; Chair. Nat. House Bldg Council 1992–98, Midland Ind. Newspapers 1992–98, Regional Ind. Media (the Yorkshire Post Group) 1998–2002, Numark Ltd 1998–2005, Aggregate Industries 2000–06; mem. Bd Group 4 Security 1990–93; Dir NFC 1990–97; Dir (non-exec.) Holcim Ltd (Switzerland) 2006–09, ABTA the Travel Business 2000–, Aggregate Industries 2010–14; Dr hc (City of Birmingham) 2011. *Publications:* The Cost of Crime 1973, The Right Track 1977, After the Riots: The Police in Europe 1979, Ministers Decide: A Memoir of the Thatcher Years 1991, A Political Suicide: The Conservatives' Voyage into the Wilderness 2008. *Address:* House of Lords, Westminster, London, SW1A 0PN, England (office). *Telephone:* (20) 7219-3525 (office). *E-mail:* fowlern@parliament.uk (office). *Website:* www.parliament .uk/biographies/lords/lord-fowler/315 (office).

FOX, Edward, OBE; British actor; b. 13 April 1937; s. of Robin Fox and Angela Fox; brother of James Fox (q.v.); m. 1st Tracy Pelissier 1958 (divorced 1961); one d.; m. 2nd Joanna David; one s. one d.; ed Ashfold School, Harrow School and Royal Acad. of Dramatic Art; actor since 1957; started in provincial repertory theatre 1958 and has since worked widely in films, stage plays and TV; recipient of several awards for TV performance as Edward VIII in Edward and Mrs Simpson 1978. *Stage appearances include:* Knuckle 1973, The Family Reunion 1979, Anyone for Denis 1981, Quartermaine's Terms 1981, Hamlet 1982, The Dance of Death 1983, Interpreters 1986, The Admirable Crichton 1988, Another Love Story 1990, The Philanthropist 1991, My Fair Lady, Father 1995, A Letter of Resignation 1997, The Chiltern Hundreds 1999, The Browning Version 2000, The Twelve Pound Look 2000, An Evening with Anthony Trollope 2010. *Films include:* The Go-Between 1971, The Day of the Jackal 1973, A Doll's House 1973, Galileo 1976, A Bridge Too Far 1977, The Duellists 1977, The Cat and the Canary 1977, Force Ten from Navarone 1978, The Mirror Crack'd 1980, Gandhi 1982, Never Say Never Again 1983, Wild Geese 1984, The Bounty 1984, The Shooting Party 1989, Return from the River Kwai 1989, Prince of Thieves 1990, They Never Slept 1991, A Month by the Lake 1996, Prince Valiant 1997, Nicholas Nickleby 2002, The Republic of Love 2003, Stage Beauty 2004, Lassie 2005. *Television includes:* Circles of Deceit 1989, Daniel Deronda 2002, Oliver Twist 2007, Marple 2010. *Leisure interest:* playing the piano. *Address:* c/o CDA, 19 Sydney Mews, London, SW3 6HL, England.

FOX, James; Canadian diplomatist and government official; b. 1952; m. Nurys Estrella-Fox; joined Dept of Foreign Affairs 1976, assignments have included positions as Deputy Dir of Int. Relations and G8 Co-ordinator and postings to Zimbabwe, Cuba and Spain, Exec. Asst to Asst Under-Asst of External Affairs with special responsibilities for man. issues 1991–93, Amb. to Guatemala and El Salvador 1993–96, Dir APEC Div., Dept of Foreign Affairs 1996–98, Dir Japan Div. 1998–2002, Dir-Gen. for S and SE Asia and Sr Official for Canada's relations with ASEAN 2002–06, Asst Deputy Minister for Bilateral Relations, responsible for overseeing relations with all countries except USA, Mexico and Afghanistan 2006–08, Asst Deputy Minister for Europe, the Middle East and Maghreb 2008–09, Amb. to Italy (also accred to Albania and San Marino and as High Commr to Malta) 2008–13. *Address:* Department of Foreign Affairs, Trade and Development, Lester B. Pearson Building, 125 Sussex Dr., Ottawa, ON K1A 0G2, Canada (office). *Telephone:* (613) 944-4000 (office). *Fax:* (613) 996-9709 (office). *E-mail:* enqserv@ international.gc.ca (office). *Website:* www.international.gc.ca (office).

FOX, James; British actor; b. 19 May 1939, London; s. of Robin Fox and Angela Fox (née Worthington); brother of Edward Fox (q.v.) and Robert Fox; m. Mary Elizabeth Fox 1973; four s. one d.; ed Ashfold Prep. School and Harrow School. *Films include:* Mrs Miniver 1952, The Servant 1963, King Rat 1965, Those Magnificent Men in Their Flying Machines 1965, Thoroughly Modern Millie 1966, Isadora 1967, Performance 1969, A Passage to India 1984, Runners 1984, Farewell to the King 1987, Finding Mawbee (video film as the Mighty Quinn) 1988, She's Been Away 1989, The Russia House 1990, Afraid of the Dark 1991, Patriot Games 1991, As You Like It 1992, The Remains of the Day 1993, Elgar's Tenth Muse 1995, Anna Karenina 1997, Mickey Blue Eyes 1998, Jinnah 1998, Up at the Villa 1998, The Golden Bowl 1999, Sexy Beast 2000, The Mystic Masseur 2001, The Prince and Me 2004, The Freediver 2004, Charlie and the Chocolate Factory 2005, Goodbye Mr Snuggles 2006, Mister Lonely 2006, Sherlock Holmes 2009. *Plays include:* Uncle Vanya 1995. *Television includes:* A Question of Attribution 1991, Gulliver's Travels 1995, The Lost World 2001, The Falklands Play 2002, Cambridge Spies 2003, Colditz 2005, Celebration 2006. *Publications include:* Comeback: An Actor's Direction 1983. *Leisure interests:* Russian language and culture.

FOX, Kerry; New Zealand actress; b. 30 July 1966; m. Jaime Robertson; ed New Zealand Drama School; fmr lighting designer. *Television appearances include:* Mr Wroe's Virgins, A Village Affair, Saigon Baby, The Affair, 40, Footprints in the Snow 2005, Nostradamus 2006, The Shooting of Thomas Hurndall 2008, Cloudstreet (mini-series) 2011. *Films include:* The Affair 1973, The Decline of Western Civilization 2: The Metal Years 1988, An Angel at My Table (Elvira Notari Best Performance Award) 1991, The Last Days of Chez Nous 1992, Rainbow Warrior 1993, The Last Tattoo 1994, Friends 1994, Shallow Grave 1995, Country Life 1995, The Affair 1995, Saigon Baby 1995, Welcome to Sarajevo 1997, Hanging Garden 1997, Immortality 1998, The Sound of One Hand Clapping 1998, The Wisdom of Crocodiles 1998, The Darkest Light 1998, Fanny and Elvis 1999, To

Walk With Lions 1999, The Point Men 2001, Intimacy 2001, Black and White 2002, The Gathering 2002, So Close to Home 2003, Niceland 2004, Rag Tale 2005, The Ferryman 2007, Intervention 2007, He Said 2007, Inconceivable 2008, Storm 2009, Bright Star 2009, Burning Man 2011, Intruders 2011, Mental 2012, Trap for Cinderella 2013. *Address:* c/o Hamilton Hodell, Fifth Floor, 66–68 Margaret Street, London, W1W 8SR, England.

FOX, Rt Hon. Liam, MB, ChB; British physician and politician; b. 22 Sept. 1961; s. of William Fox and Catherine Young; m. Jesme Fox; ed St Bride's High School, E Kilbride, Univ. of Glasgow; civilian army medical officer, Royal Army Educ. Corps 1981–91; gen. practitioner, Beaconsfield 1987–91; Div. Surgeon, St John's Ambulance 1987–91; contested Roxburgh and Berwickshire 1987; MP for North Somerset (fmrly Woodspring) 1992–; Parl. Pvt. Sec. to Home Sec. Michael Howard 1993–94, Asst Govt Whip 1994–95, Lord Commr, HM Treasury (Sr Govt Whip) 1995–96, Parl. Under-Sec. of State, FCO 1996–97, Opposition Front Bench Spokesman on Constitutional Affairs 1997–98, Shadow Sec. for Constitutional Affairs 1998–99, Shadow Sec. of State for Health 1999–2003, Shadow Foreign Sec. 2005, Shadow Defence Sec. 2005–10; Sec. of State for Defence 2010–11 (resgnd); Co-Chair. Conservative Party 2003–05; mem. Scottish Select Cttee 1992–93; Sec., Conservative Backbench Health Cttee 1992–93; Pres. Glasgow Univ. Conservative Club 1982–83; Nat. Vice-Chair. Scottish Young Conservatives 1983–84; mem. Conservative Political Centre; Sec., Conservative West Country Mems Group 1992–93. *Publications include:* Making Unionism Positive 1988, Bearing the Standard (contrib.) 1991, contrib. to House of Commons Magazine. *Leisure interests:* tennis, swimming, cinema, theatre. *Address:* House of Commons, Westminster, London, SW1A 0AA (office); Constituency Office, 71 High Street, Nailsea, North Somerset, BS48 1AW, England (office). *Telephone:* (20) 7219-4198 (Westminster) (office); (1275) 790090 (Nailsea) (office). *Fax:* (1275) 790091 (Nailsea) (office). *E-mail:* douglasi@parliament.uk (office). *Website:* admin@ northsomersetconservatives.com (office); www.parliament.uk/biographies/ commons/dr-liam-fox/223 (office); www.liamfox.co.uk.

FOX, Marye Anne, BS, MS, PhD; American chemist and university chancellor; *Chancellor Emeritus and Distinguished Professor of Chemistry, University of California San Diego;* b. 9 Dec. 1947, Canton, Ohio; m. James K.Whitesell; three s. two step-s.; ed Notre Dame Coll., Cleveland State Univ., Dartmouth Coll.; Postdoctoral Fellow, Univ. of Maryland 1974-76; Asst Prof. of Organic Chem., Univ. of Texas 1976-81, Assoc. Prof. 1981–85, Prof. 1985–86, Rowland Pettit Centennial Prof. 1986–91, Dir Center for Fast Kinetics Research 1986–91, M. June and J. Virgil Waggoner Regents Chair in Chem. 1991–98, Vice-Pres. for Research, Univ. of Texas 1994–98; Chancellor and Distinguished Univ. Prof. of Chem., North Carolina State Univ. 1998–2004; Chancellor Univ. of California, San Diego 2004–12, currently Chancellor Emer. and Distinguished Prof. of Chem.; Visiting Scholar, Harvard Univ. 1989, Univ. of Iowa 1993; Professeur Invitée, Université Pierre et Marie Curie, Paris VI 1992; Visiting Prof., Chem. Research Promotion Center, Nat. Science Council, Taipei, Taiwan 1993; Morris S. Kharasch Visiting Prof., Univ. of Chicago 1997; consultant/contrib., McGraw-Hill Encyclopedia of Science and Technology 1992–94; mem. Bd of Dirs Asscn for Advancement of Tech. in Biomedical Sciences 1989–90, Boston Scientific, Inc. (Audit and Strategic Planning Cttee) 2001–, PPD, Inc. 2002–, Red Hat, Inc. 2002–, W.R. Grace, Inc.; mem. Camille and Henry Dreyfus Foundation Bd 1990–2002, Nat. Science Bd (Chair. Cttee on Programs and Plans 1993–96, mem. Exec. Cttee 1993–94) 1991–96, Associated Western Univs 1996–98, Council NAS (Exec. Cttee) 1996–99, Environmental Defense Fund (Texas Bd) 1996–98, Oak Ridge Associated Univs 1996–98, Oak Ridge Foundation Bd 1996–98, Nat. Research Council Governing Bd 1997–99, Kenan Inst. for Eng, Tech., and Science (Chair.) 1998–, Microelectronic Center of N Carolina (Chair. 2001) 1998–, Raleigh Cooperating Colls 1998–, Research Triangle Inst. Bd Govs 1998–2003, Robert A. Welch Foundation Scientific Advisory Bd 1998–, Univ. of Texas-Battelle Man. Bd of Oak Ridge Nat. Lab. (Chair. Science and Tech. Cttee) 1999–, Nat. Inst. for the Environment 2001–, Pres.'s Council of Advisors on Science and Tech. 2001–, Burroughs-Wellcome Fund 2002–, North Carolina Bd of Science and Tech. 2002–, Nat. Asscn of State Univs and Land Grant Colls 2003–; Assoc. Ed. Journal of the American Chemical Society 1986–95; Invited Expert Analyst, Chemtracts 1989–96; mem. Editorial Advisory Bd Journal of Organic Chemistry 1984–89, Molecular Structure and Energetics 1985–88, American Chemical Society Symposium Series and Advances in Chemistry 1986–89, CRC Critical Reviews in Surface Chemistry 1988, New Journal of Chemistry 1995–99, The Chemical Intelligencer 1997–2001, Organic Letters 1999; mem. Advisory Bd Heterogeneous Chemistry Reviews 1993–96, Chemical and Engineering News 1994–99, Chemical Reviews 1994–2002, Issues in Science and Technology 1996–2002; mem. Int. Advisory Bd Contemporary Concepts in Chemistry 1994–96; mem. numerous advisory and scientific bds and review cttees; mem. ACS, Inter-American Photochemical Soc., NAS 1994, American Philosophical Soc. 1996; Foreign Corresp. mem. Royal Acad. of Science and Arts, Barcelona 1996; Fellow, AAAS 1993, American Acad. of Arts and Sciences 1994, American Women in Science 2001, ACS 2010–; Trustee Univ. of Notre Dame 2002–; Hon. DSc (Notre Dame Coll.) 1994, (Cleveland State Univ.) 1998, Hon. JD (Sandhills Community Coll.) 2000, Hon. DUniv (Univ. of Ulster) 2002, Hon. DHumLitt (Texas A&M Univ.) 2002, Dr hc (Université Pierre et Marie Curie—Paris VI) 2001, (Universidad Nacional de Educacion a Distancia, Madrid) 2003; numerous awards including Honour Scholarship, Notre Dame Coll. 1965–69, Outstanding Freshman Chemist Award, Chemical Rubber Co. 1965, NSF Undergraduate Research Fellow, Illinois Inst. of Tech. 1968, Medal of Excellence, American Inst. of Chemists 1969, Dartmouth Fellow 1972–73, Goodyear Tire Fellow 1973–74, Postdoctoral Fellow (NSF and RANN), Univ. of Maryland 1974–76, Alfred P. Sloan Research Fellow 1980, Distinguished Alumna Award, Notre Dame Coll. 1981, Agnes Fay Morgan Research Award, Selection, Teaching Excellence Award, Univ. of Texas Coll. of Natural Sciences 1986, ACS Garvan Medal 1988, Döbereiner Medal, Friedrich Schiller Univ., Jena, GDR 1988, ACS Arthur C. Cope Scholar Award 1989, Medallion for Contribs to Photographic Sciences, Inst. of Chemical Physics, USSR Acad. of Sciences, Moscow 1990, Havinga Medal, Gorleaus Laboratoria der Rijksuniversiteit, Leiden 1991, ACS Research Award (Southwest Region) 1993, Paul Harris Fellowship, Raleigh Rotary Club 1999, Citation as Outstanding Woman in Science by the Women's History Cttee of New York Acad. of Science 1999, Distinguished Mem. Nat. Soc. of Collegiate Scholars 2001, Hall of Honor, Coll. of Natural Sciences Foundation

Advisory Council, Univ. of Texas at Austin 2001, Nat. Order of Omega 2001, Gov.'s Old North State Award (North Carolina) 2004, ACS Parsons Award for Public Service 2005, Nat. Medal of Science 2010. *Publications include:* Orbital Symmetry Concepts in Organic Chemistry 1987, Photoinduced Electron Transfer (four vols, co-ed.) 1988, Organic Chemistry (co-author) 1994, Supplemental Problems for Organic Chemistry (co-author) 1995, Instructor's Resource Manual of Tests and Additional Problems to Accompany Organic Chemistry (co-author) 1995, Organic Chemistry (co-author) 1997, Cultivating Academic Careers (co-author) 1998, Containing the Threat from Illegal Bombings (co-author) 1998, Transforming Undergraduate Education in Science, Mathematics, Engineering, and Technology 1999, Evaluating, Rewarding, and Improving Quality Teaching in Science, Mathematics, Engineering, and Technology (co-author) 2007; nearly 30 book chapters, 49 policy papers, three patents and more than 400 scientific papers, mostly on organic photochemistry and electrochemistry. *Address:* c/o Chancellor's Office, University of California San Diego, Department of Chemistry and Biochemistry, 2050 Urey Hall Addition, 9500 Gilman Drive, MC 0358, La Jolla, CA 92093-0332, USA. *Telephone:* (858) 534-5871 (office). *Fax:* (858) 534-0202 (office). *E-mail:* mafox@ucsd.edu (office). *Website:* www-chem.ucsd.edu (office).

FOX, Maurice Sanford, PhD, FAAS; American molecular biologist and academic; *Professor Emeritus of Molecular Biology, Massachusetts Institute of Technology;* b. 11 Oct. 1924, New York; s. of Albert Fox and Ray Fox; m. Sally Cherniavsky 1955 (died 2006); three s.; ed Stuyvesant High School, Queen's Coll., Univ. of Chicago; Instructor, Univ. of Chicago 1951–53; Asst, Rockefeller Univ. 1953–55, Asst Prof. 1955–58, Assoc. Prof. 1958–62; Nuffield Research Fellow 1957; Assoc. Prof., MIT 1962–66, Prof. 1966–79, Lester Wolfe Prof. of Molecular Biology 1979–96, Head, Dept of Biology 1985–89, now Prof. Emer.; mem. Bd Council for a Liveable World 1962–2006, Breast Cancer Task Force 1977–80; mem. NAS Inst. of Medicine, American Acad. of Arts and Sciences, Radiation Effects Research Foundation, Hiroshima 1994–99, Int. Bioethics Cttee, UNESCO 1994–2004; hon. degree (Univ. Paul Sabatier, Toulouse, France). *Publications include:* numerous learned papers. *Leisure interest:* ancient history. *Address:* Department of Biology, Massachusetts Institute of Technology, 77 Massachusetts Avenue, Cambridge, MA 02139 (office); 983 Memorial Drive, Cambridge, MA 02138, USA (home). *Telephone:* (617) 253-4728 (office). *E-mail:* msfox@mit.edu (office). *Website:* web.mit.edu/biology (office).

FOX, Michael J., OC; American actor; b. (Michael Andrew Fox), 9 June 1961, Edmonton, Alberta, Canada; s. of Bill Fox and Phyllis Fox; m. Tracy Pollan 1988; one s. two d.; ed Burnaby Cen. High School, Vancouver, BC, Canada. *TV appearances include:* Leo and Me 1976, Palmerstown USA 1980, Family Ties (series) 1982–89 (Emmy Awards 1987, 1988), Spin City (series) 1996–2000, Otherwise Engaged (exec. producer) 2002, Hench at Home (writer) 2003, Scrubs 2004, The Magic 7 (voice) 2009, The Good Wife 2010. *TV films include:* Letters from Frank 1979, Poison Ivy 1985, High School USA 1985. *Film appearances include:* Midnight Madness 1980, Class of '84 1981, Back to the Future 1985, Teen Wolf 1985, Light of Day 1986, The Secret of My Success 1987, Bright Lights, Big City 1988, Back to the Future II 1989, Back to the Future III 1990, The Hard Way 1991, Doc Hollywood 1991, The Concierge 1993, Give Me a Break 1994, Greedy 1994, The American President 1995, Mars Attacks! 1996, The Frighteners 1996, Stuart Little (voice) 1999, Atlantis: The Lost Empire (voice) 2001, Interstate 60 2002, Stuart Little 2 (voice) 2002, Stuart Little 3: Call of the Wild (voice) 2005. *Publications:* Lucky Man: A Memoir 2002, Always Looking Up: The Adventures of an Incurable Optimist 2009, A Funny Thing Happened on the Way to the Future: Twists and Turns and Lessons Learned 2010. *Address:* c/o Philpott, Bills, Stoll & Meeks, 16030 Ventura Blvd, #380, Encino, CA 91436, USA.

FOX, Sir Paul Leonard, Kt, CBE; British media executive; b. 27 Oct. 1925; m. Betty R. Nathan 1948; two s.; ed Bournemouth Grammar School; with Parachute Regt 1943; reporter, Kentish Times 1946, The People 1947; scriptwriter, Pathe News 1947; BBC TV scriptwriter 1950; Ed. Sportsview 1953, Panorama 1961; Head, BBC TV Public Affairs Dept 1963, Current Affairs Group 1965; Controller, BBC 1 1967–73; Dir of Programmes, Yorkshire TV 1973–84, Man. Dir Yorkshire TV 1977–89; Dir Independent Television News 1977–86, Chair. 1986–89; Man. Dir BBC TV 1988–91; Chair. BBC Enterprises 1988–91, Stepgrades Consultants 1991–2002; Chair. ITV Network Programme Cttee 1978–80, Council, Independent Television Cos Asscn Ltd 1982–84; mem. Royal Comm. on Criminal Procedure 1978–80; Pres. Royal TV Soc. 1985–92; Dir Channel Four 1985–88, World TV News 1986–88, Thames TV Ltd 1991–95; Chair. Racecourse Asscn Ltd 1993–97, Racecourse Tech. Services 1994–, Disasters Emergency Cttee 1996–99; Dir British Horse Racing Bd 1993–97, Horserace Betting Levy Bd 1993–97, Barnes TV Trust Ltd 1997–; consultant, Oflot 1994–; mem. Cttee Nat. Museum of Photography, Film and TV 1985–95, Cinema and TV Benevolent Fund 1986–92, Pres. 1992–95; Hon. LLD (Leeds) 1984; Hon. DLitt (Bradford) 1991. *Leisure interests:* television, attending race meetings.

FOX, Peter Kendrew, MA; British librarian (retd); *University Librarian Emeritus, University of Cambridge;* b. 23 March 1949, Beverley, Yorks., England; s. of Thomas Kendrew Fox and Dorothy Wildbore; m. Isobel McConnell 1983; two d.; ed Baines Grammar School, Poulton-le-Fylde, Lancs., King's Coll. London, Univ. of Sheffield; Asst Library Officer, Univ. of Cambridge Library 1973–77, Asst Under-Librarian 1977–78, Under-Librarian 1978–79, Univ. Librarian 1994–2009, now Univ. Librarian Emer.; Deputy Librarian, Trinity Coll., Dublin 1979–84, Librarian 1984–94; Fellow, Selwyn Coll., Cambridge 1994–; mem. British Library Project on Teaching and Learning Skills for Librarians 1978–79, Soc. of Coll., Nat. and Univ. Libraries (SCONUL) Advisory Cttee on Information Services 1979–91 (Chair. 1987–91), An Chomhairle Leabharlanna (Ireland) 1982–94, Cttee on Library Co-operation in Ireland 1983–94 (Chair. 1990–91), Nat. Preservation Advisory Cttee, British Library 1984–95 (mem. Man. Cttee 1996–2002, mem. Bd 2002–09, Chair. 2002–05), Brotherton Collection Advisory Cttee, Univ. of Leeds 1995–2002, 2009–12 (Chair. 1999–2002), Wellcome Trust Library Advisory Cttee 1996–2005, Chair. 2000–05, Consortium of Univ. Research Libraries (Chair. 1997–2000), Lord Chancellor's Advisory Council on Public Records 2001–06, Legal Deposit Advisory Panel (DCMS) 2005–08, External Advisory Bd Trinity Coll. Dublin Long Room Hub 2008–11; Assoc., King's Coll., London; Visiting Fellow, Trinity Coll. Dublin 2011. *Publications:* Reader Instruction Methods in Academic Libraries 1974, User Education in the Humanities in US Academic Libraries 1979,

Trinity College Library Dublin 1982, Trinity College Library Dublin: A History 2014; Ed.: Library User Education – Are New Approaches Needed? 1980, Second (and Third) Int. Conf. on Library User Educ. Proc. 1982 (and 1984), Treasures of the Library – Trinity College Dublin 1986, Commentary Volume: Book of Kells Facsimile 1990, Cambridge University Library: The Great Collections 1998; co-ed. An Leabharlann: The Irish Library 1982–87; contribs to books and journals. *Address:* Selwyn College, Grange Road, Cambridge, CB3 9DQ, England (office).

FOX QUESADA, Vicente; Mexican politician, business executive and fmr head of state; b. 2 July 1942, Mexico City; s. of the late José Luis Fox and of Mercedes Quesada; m. 1st (divorced); two s. two d.; m. 2nd Marta Sahagún 2001; ed Universidad Iberoamericana, Mexico City, Harvard Univ.; worked for Coca Cola Group, first as route supervisor, becoming Regional Pres. for Mexico and Latin America; also worked as farmer and shoemaker; joined Partido Acción Nacional (Nat. Action Party—PAN); Fed. Deputy 1988; Gov. of Guanajuato 1995–2000; Pres. of Mexico 2000–Dec. 2006; Co-Pres. Centrist Democratic International, Rome 2007–. *Publication:* Revolution of Hope: The Life, Faith and Dreams of a Mexican President 2007. *Address:* c/o Partido Acción Nacional, Avda Coyoacán 1546, Col. del Valle, Del. Benito Juárez, 03100 México, DF, Mexico (office). *Telephone:* (55) 5200-4000 (office). *E-mail:* correo@cen.pan.org.mx (office). *Website:* www.pan.org.mx (office).

FOXLEY RIOSECO, Alejandro, MSc, PhD; Chilean politician and economist; b. 26 May 1939, Viña del Mar; s. of Harold Foxley (Chapman) and Carmen Rioseco; m. Gisela Tapia 1963; two c.; ed Univ. of Wisconsin, Harvard Univ. and Catholic Univ., Valparaíso; Dir Global Planning Div., Nat. Planning Office, Govt of Chile 1967–70; Dir Center for Nat. Planning Studies, Catholic Univ. of Chile 1970–76; mem. Exec. Council, Latin-American Social Science Council (CLACSO) 1975–81; mem. Jt Cttee Latin-American Studies, Social Science Research Council, New York 1975–78; founder and Pres. Corpn for Latin-American Econ. Research (CIEPLAN), Santiago 1976–90; Minister of Finance 1990–94, also Gov. World Bank and Inter-American Devt Bank; Pres. Christian Democratic Party (PDC) 1994–96; Senator 1998–2006; Minister of Foreign Affairs 2006–09; Helen Kellogg Prof. of Econs (part-time) and Int. Devt, Univ. of Notre Dame 1982–; Assoc. Ed. Journal of Development Economics 1977–; Visiting Fellow, Univ. of Sussex 1973, Oxford 1975, MIT 1978; Ford Int. Fellow 1963–64, Daugherty Foundation Fellow 1965–66; Ford Foundation Fellow 1970; Co-Pres. Inter-American Dialogue, Wash. 1994–99, now mem. Exec. Cttee; mem. Int. Advisory Bd Journal Latin American Studies; Dr hc (Univ. of Notre Dame) 1991, (Univ. of Wis.) 1993; Orden al Mérito Civil, Rey de Espana 1991, Gran Cruz Orden Nacional Cruzeiro do Sul (Brazil) 1993, Gran Insignia de Honor (Austria) 1994. *Publications:* Income Distribution in Latin-America 1976, Redistributive Effects of Government Programmes 1979, Estrategia de Desarrollo y Modelos de Planificación, Legados del Monetarismo: Argentina y Chile, Para una Democracia Estable 1985, Chile y su futuro: Un país posible 1989, Chile puede más 1989, numerous articles and working papers. *Address:* c/o Ministry of Foreign Affairs Catedral 1158, Santiago (office); Golfo de Darién 10236, Santiago (Las Condes), Chile (home).

FOXX, Jamie; American actor, comedian and singer; b. (Eric Marlon Bishop), 13 Dec. 1967, Terrell, Tex.; s. of Darrell Bishop and Louise Annette Talley Dixon; adopted and raised by his mother's adoptive parents, Mark Talley and Esther Marie Talley (née Nelson); two d.; began playing the piano aged five; made TV debut in comedy series In Living Color 1991; writer, performer, dir and producer on The Jamie Foxx Show 1996–2001; writer, performer and producer, two songs on Any Given Sunday film soundtrack 1999; tours: The Unpredictable Tour 2006, The Blame It Tour 2009; Image Award for Best Musical Artist 2006, BET Award for Best Duet/Collaboration (for Gold Digger, with Kanye West) 2006, American Music Award for Favorite Male Soul/R&B Artist 2006, Grammy Award for Best R&B Performance by a Duo or Group with Vocals (for Blame It with T-Pain) 2010. *Films include:* Toys 1992, The Truth About Cats and Dogs 1996, The Great White Hype 1996, Booty Call 1997, The Players Club 1998, Held Up 1999, Any Given Sunday 1999, Bait 2000, Date from Hell 2001, Ali 2001, Shade 2003, Redemption: The Stan Tookie Williams Story 2004, Breakin' All the Rules 2004, Collateral (BET Award for Best Supporting Actor) 2004, Ray (Best Actor in a Musical or Comedy, Golden Globe Awards 2005, Best Actor, Screen Actors Guild Awards 2005, Best Actor in a Leading Role, BAFTA Awards 2005, Best Actor, Acad. Awards 2005) 2004, Stealth 2005, Jarhead 2005, Miami Vice 2006, Dreamgirls 2006, The Kingdom 2007, The Soloist 2009, Law Abiding Citizen 2009, Valentine's Day 2010, Malice N Wonderland (video short) 2010, Due Date 2010, I'm Still Here 2010, Rio (voice) 2011, Horrible Bosses 2011, Django Unchained 2012, White House Down 2013. *Television includes:* In Living Colour 1991–94, C-Bear and Jamal (voice) 1996, The Jamie Foxx Show 1996–2001, Jamie Foxx: I Might Need Security (HBO Comedy Special) 2002. *Recordings include:* Peep This 1994, Unpredictable (Soul Train Award for Best R&B/Soul Album by a Male Artist 2007) 2005, Intuition 2008, Best Night of My Life 2010. *Address:* Foxxhole Productions, Inc., 15821 Ventura Boulevard 525, Encino, CA 91436, USA (office). *Telephone:* (310) 205-2800 (office). *Website:* www.jamiefoxx.com.

FRACKOWIAK, Richard S. J., MA, MB, BChir, MD, DSc, FRCP, FMedSci; British neurologist, clinical neuroscientist and academic; *Professor of Neurology and Chairman, Department of Clinical Neuroscience, Université de Lausanne and Centre Hospitalier Universitaire Vaudois;* b. 26 March 1950, London, England; s. of Jozef Frackowiak and Wanda Frackowiak (née Majewska); m. 1st Christine Frackowiak (divorced 2003); one s. two d.; m. 2nd Laura Spinney; ed Latymer Upper School, Peterhouse, Cambridge, Middx Hosp. Medical School; MRC Clinical Scientist 1989–94; Asst Dir MRC Cyclotron Unit; Prof. of Cognitive Neurology, Univ. Coll., London 1994–2009, Dean, Inst. of Neurology 1998–2002; Dir Leopold Muller Functional Imaging Lab. 1994–2002; Chair. Wellcome Dept of Cognitive Neurology 1994–2002; Prin. Clinical Research Fellow and programme grant holder, Wellcome Trust 1994–2004; Vice-Provost Univ. Coll., London 2002–09; Prof. of Neurology and Chair., Dept of Clinical Neuroscience, Centre Hospitalier Universitaire Vaudois, Univ. of Lausanne, Switzerland 2009–; Dir Departement d'Etudes Cognitives, Ecole Normale Superieure, Paris 2005–09; Adjunct Prof., Cornell Univ. Medical School 1992–; Visiting Prof., Univ. Catholique de Louvain, Yale Medical School, Beth Israel & MGH Boston, La Sapienza, Rome; Hon. Dir Neuroimaging Unit, Fondazione Santa Lucia, Rome 2002–10; Scientific Adviser and Pres.-Dir-Gen. Institut Nat. de la Santé et Recherche Médicale, France 2005–;

fmr MRC Training Fellow; Hon. mem. American Neurological Asscn, Royal Belgian Acad. de Medicine, French Acad. de Médecine, Inst. of Medicine (USA), Academia Europaea, Acad. of Medicine (UK); Hon. MD (Liège); Ipsen Prize, Feldberg Prize, Zulch Prize. *Publications include:* Human Brain Function 1997, Brain Mapping: The Disorders 2000; numerous papers in scientific journals. *Leisure interests:* reading, travel, motorcycling. *Address:* Service de neurologie, Centre Hospitalier Universitaire Vaudois, Rue du Bugnon 46, 1011 Lausanne, Switzerland (office). *Telephone:* (21) 314-1220 (office); (21) 711-1005 (home). *E-mail:* richard.frackowiak@gmail.com (office). *Website:* www.unil.ch/lren/page77656_en.html (office).

FRADKOV, Mikhail Yefimovich; Russian politician; *Director, Federal Foreign Intelligence Service;* b. 1 Sept. 1950, Kuibyshev (now Samara) Oblast; m. Yelena Ludenko-Fradkova; two c.; ed Moscow Inst. of Machines and Tools, USSR Acad. of Foreign Trade; on staff, office of Counsellor on econ. affairs, USSR Embassy to India 1973–75; on staff, Foreign Trade Agency Tyazhpromeksport, USSR State Cttee on Econ. Relations 1975–84; Deputy, later First Deputy Dir of Dept, USSR State Cttee on Econ. Relations 1985–91; Deputy Perm. Rep. of Russian Fed. to GATT 1991–92; Sr Adviser, Perm. Mission of Russian Fed. to UN; Deputy, First Deputy Minister of External Econ. Relations 1993; Interim Acting Minister of External Econ. Relations 1997, Minister of External Econ. Relations and Trade 1997–98; Chair. Bd of Dirs Ingosstrakh 1998–99, Dir-Gen. 1999; Minister of Trade 1999–2000; First Deputy Sec., Security Council of Russia 2000–01; Head, Fed. Service of Tax Police 2001–03; Plenipotentiary Rep. to EU 2003–04; apptd Special Rep. of the Pres. of the Russian Fed. on the Devt of Relations with the EU June 2003; Chair. of the Govt (Prime Minister) of Russian Fed. 2004–07; Dir Fed. Foreign Intelligence Service (SVR) of Russian Fed. 2007–; Medal 'For Valiant Labour. To commemorate the 100th anniversary of Lenin's birth', Medal 'In Commemoration of the 850th Anniversary of Moscow', Order of Honour, Order of Merit for the Fatherland (Second Class) 2005, (First Class) 2007. *Address:* Federal Foreign Intelligence Service, 101000 Moscow, Glavpochtamt, PO Box 958, Russia (office). *Telephone:* (499) 245-33-68 (office). *Fax:* (499) 255-25-29 (office). *E-mail:* svr@gov.ru (office). *Website:* svr.gov.ru (office).

FRAGA NETO, Armínio, PhD; Brazilian economist and banker; *Member, International Council, JP Morgan Chase & Company;* b. 20 July 1957, Rio de Janeiro; m.; two c.; ed Pontificia Univ. Católica do Rio de Janeiro, Princeton Univ., USA; trainee, Atlantica-Companhia de Seguros Boavista 1976–77, Banco do Estado do Rio de Janeiro 1979–80, Int. Finance Div., Fed. Reserve Bd, Washington, DC 1984; Chief Economist and Operations Man. Banco de Investimentos Garantia 1985–88; Vice-Pres. Salomon Brothers, New York 1988–91; consultant IBRD 1988–89; Dir responsible for Int. Affairs, Banco Cen. do Brasil 1991–92, Gov. 1999–2002; Man. Dir Soros Fund Man., New York 1993–99; Founding Partner, Gavea Investimentos, Rio de Janeiro 2003–; mem. Int. Council, JP Morgan Chase & Co. 2004–; Prof., Grad. School in Econs, Fundação Getúlio Vargas 1985–88, 1999–; Visiting Asst Prof., Finance Dept, Wharton School, Pennsylvania Univ. 1988–89; Adjunct Prof. of Int. Affairs, Columbia Univ., New York 1993–99; mem. Bd Pro-Natura USA 1993–99; mem. Council on Foreign Relations, Princeton Univ. Center for Econ. Policy Studies 1993–, Group of Thirty Consultative Group on Int. Econ. and Monetary Affairs, Inc. (G-30), Washington, DC 2001–, Int. Advisory Council of Chinese sovereign wealth fund China Investment Corpn 2009–; Banco Boavista Award. *Publications:* numerous articles on banking and econs. *Address:* Fundação Getulio Vargas, Praia de Botafogo 190, 10° andar, 22250-900, Rio de Janeiro, RJ, Brazil (office). *Telephone:* (21) 3799-6000 (office). *Fax:* (21) 3799-5996 (office). *E-mail:* arminio@fgv.br (office); faleconosco@fgv.br (office). *Website:* gaveainvestimentos@virusbusters.com.br (office); www.fgv.br (office); www.gaveainvestimentos.com.br (office).

FRALEY, Robert T., PhD; American plant biotechnologist and business executive; *Executive Vice-President and Chief Technology Officer, Monsanto Company;* b. 1953, Wellington, Ill.; ed Univ. of Illinois, Univ. of California, San Francisco; successive positions at Monsanto include Sr Research Specialist, Monsanto Biological Sciences Program, Dir Plant Science Research Group, Vice-Pres. of Tech. for Crop Chemical and Plant Biotechnology R&D, Group Vice-Pres. and Gen. Man., New Products Div., Pres. Ceregen Business Unit (before merger with Pharmacia and Upjohn), Co-Pres. Agricultural Sector, currently Exec. Vice-Pres. and Chief Tech. Officer; fmr mem. Agric. Biotechnology Research Advisory Cttee, NIH Molecular Cytology Study Section; tech. adviser to numerous govt and public agencies, including US Dept of Agric., NSF, Office of Tech. Assessment, CAST, Agency for Int. Devt, NAS of Science, Int. Service for Acquisition of Agri-Biotech Applications; Fellow, AAAS; Monsanto Thomas and Hochwalt Award, Monsanto Edgar M. Queeny Award, Man. of the Year, Progressive Farming magazine 1995, Kenneth A. Spencer Award for Outstanding Achievement in Agricultural and Food Chem. 1995, Nat. Award for Agricultural Excellence in Science, Nat. Agri-Marketing Asscn 1995, Nat. Medal of Tech. 1999, World Food Prize (co-recipient) 2013. *Publications:* more than 100 publs and patent applications. *Address:* Monsanto Co., 800 North Lindbergh Blvd, St Louis, MO 63167, USA (office). *Telephone:* (314) 694-1000 (office). *E-mail:* info@monsanto.com (office). *Website:* www.monsanto.com/whoweare/pages/robert-fraley-bio.aspx (office).

FRAME, Ronald William Sutherland, MA, MLitt; British author; b. 23 May 1953, Glasgow, Scotland; s. of the late Alexander D. Frame and Isobel D. Frame (née Sutherland); ed The High School of Glasgow, Univ. of Glasgow, Jesus Coll. Oxford; full-time author 1981–; many recent Scottish-set short stories published in UK, N America and Australia; regular weekly 'Carnbeg' short story in The Herald (Scotland) 2008, 'Carnbeg Days' in The Scotsman (Scotland) 2008–09, regular contrib. Scottish Review of Books (Sunday Herald); Betty Trask Prize (jt first recipient) 1984, Samuel Beckett Prize 1986, TV Industries' Panel's Most Promising Writer New to TV Award 1986, Saltire Scottish Book of the Year 2000, American Library Asscn's Barbara Gittings Honor Prize for Fiction 2003. *Radio scripts include:* Winter Journey 1985, Twister 1986, Rendezvous 1987, Cara 1989, A Woman of Judah 1991, The Lantern Bearers 1997, The Hydro (serial) 1997–99, Havisham 1998, Maestro 1999, Pharos 2000, Don't Look Now (adaptation) 2001, Sunday at Sant' Agata 2001, Greyfriars 2002, The Servant (adaptation) 2005, The Razor's Edge (adaptation) 2005, A Tiger for Malguidi (adaptation) 2006, The Blue Room (adaptation) 2007, The Shell House 2008, Blue Wonder 2008, Monsieur

Monde Vanishes (adaptation) 2009, Pinkerton 2010, Sunday (adaptation) 2010, Striptease (adaptation) 2010, The Other Simenon 1 (three adaptations) 2011, The Dreamer 2012, The Other Simenon 2 (three adaptations) 2012, Before the Fact (adaptation) 2013, The Other Simenon 3 (three adaptations) 2014. *Television screenplays:* Paris 1985, Out of Time 1987, Ghost City 1994, A Modern Man 1996, M R James: Four Ghost Stories for Christmas (adaptation) 2000, Darien: Disaster in Paradise 2003, Cromwell 2003, The Two Loves of Anthony Trollope (script contrib.) 2004. *Publications include:* Winter Journey 1984, Watching Mrs. Gordon 1985, A Long Weekend with Marcel Proust 1986, Sandmouth People 1987, Paris (TV play) 1987, A Woman of Judah 1987, Penelope's Hat 1989, Bluette 1990, Underwood and After 1991, Walking My Mistress in Deauville 1992, The Sun on the Wall 1994, The Lantern Bearers 1999, Permanent Violet 2002, Time in Carnbeg 2004, Unwritten Secrets 2010, A Carnbeg Affair, Carnbeg Piccalilli, Mysteries of Carnbeg (Kindle) 2011, Havisham 2012. *Leisure interests:* swimming, film, walking in the wind. *Address:* (Literary): c/o Adrian Searle, Freight Design (Scotland) Ltd, Jacobean Building, 49–53 Virginia Street, Glasgow, G1 1TS, Scotland (office); (Media): c/o Sayle Screen Ltd, 11 Jubilee Place, London, SW3 3TD, England (office); c/o Faber & Faber Ltd, Bloomsbury House, 74–77 Great Russell Street, London, WC1B 3DA, England. *Telephone:* (141) 552-5303 (Glasgow) (office); (20) 7823-3883 (London) (office); (20) 7927-3800. *Fax:* (20) 7823-3363 (London) (office); (20) 7927-3801. *E-mail:* asearle@freightdesign.co.uk (office); info@saylescreen.com (office). *Website:* www.carnbeg.com.

FRAMLINGHAM, Baron (Life Peer), cr. 2011, of Eye in the County of Suffolk; **Michael Nicholson Framlingham,** Kt, MA; British politician and company director; b. 17 Oct. 1938, South Manchester; m. Jennifer Margaret Childs 1965; one s. one d.; ed William Hulme's Grammar School, Whalley Range, Manchester, Christ's Coll., Cambridge; Dir Power Line Maintenance Ltd 1966–68; f. Lords Tree Services Ltd 1968; Councillor, Bedford Borough Council (fmrly N Beds. Borough Council) 1974–77, Beds. Co. Council 1981–83; Parl. cand. for Manchester Gorton 1979; arboricultural consultant 1983–; MP (Conservative) for Suffolk Cen. 1983–97, for Cen. Suffolk and N Ipswich 1997–2010, Parl. Pvt. Sec. to John MacGregor 1984–87, Deputy Speaker of House of Commons 1997–2005, Second Deputy Chair. of Ways and Means 1997–2010; Fellow and Past Pres. Arboricultural Asscn; Cambridge Rugby Blue. *Address:* House of Lords, Westminster, London, SW1A 0PW, England (office). *Telephone:* (20) 7219-5353 (office). *Fax:* (20) 7219-5979 (office).

FRAMPTON, Kenneth, A.A.Dip., ARIBA,; British architect and academic; *Ware Professor of Architecture, Graduate School of Architecture, Planning and Preservation, Columbia University;* ed Architectural Asscn, London; Tech. Ed. Architectural Design (magazine) 1962–65; emigrated to USA 1964; Faculty mem., School of Architecture, Princeton Univ. 1964–72; Faculty mem., Dept of Architecture, Columbia Univ. 1972–, Chair. Div. of Architecture 1986–89, Dir Postgraduate Program in History and Theory of Architecture 1993–, also Ware Prof. of Architecture; Faculty mem., RCA, London 1974–77; Visiting Prof. at numerous schools of architecture including Berlage Inst., Amsterdam, ETH, Switzerland, Chinese Univ. of Hong Kong, Univ. della Svizzera Italiana, Mendrisio, Switzerland; mem. jury Alvar Aalto Medal Cttee 1988; Pres. EEC Jury, Mies van der Rohe Foundation, Barcelona; presented Raoul Wallenberg Lecture 1999; Fellow Graham Foundation 1969–72; Loeb Fellow Harvard Univ. Grad. School of Design 1972; Guggenheim Fellow 1975; Fellow Inst. for Architecture and Urban Studies, New York; Fellow Wissenschaftskolleg, Berlin 1986, American Acad. of Arts and Sciences 1993; Dr hc (Royal Inst. of Tech., Stockholm) 1991, (Univ. of Waterloo) 1995, (Calif. Coll. of Arts and Crafts) 1999; AIA Nat. Honors Award 1988, Acad. d'Architecture Gold Medal 1987, AIA New York Chapter Award of Merit 1988, ASCA Topaz Award 1990, President's Medal, Architectural League of New York 2007, Architectural Award, American Acad. of Arts and Letters 2008. *Design work includes:* Duplex apartment building, London 1962–65, Low-Rise High Density, Brownsville, Brooklyn USA 1972–75. *Publications include:* Modern Architecture: A Critical History 1980, 2008, Modern Architecture and the Critical Present 1993, American Masterworks 1995, Studies in Tectonic Culture 1995, Latin American Architecture: Six Voices (co-author) 2002, Le Corbusier 2002, Labor, Work and Architecture 2002, Evolution of 20th Century Architecture: A Synoptic Account 2007. *Address:* Graduate School of Architecture, Planning and Preservation, Columbia University, 1172 Amsterdam Avenue, New York, NY 10027, USA (office). *Telephone:* (212) 854-3414 (office). *E-mail:* Kf7@columbia.edu (office). *Website:* www.arch.columbia.edu (office).

FRANÇA, José-Augusto, DèsLitt et Sc Hum, DHist; Portuguese writer, art historian and academic; *Professor Jubilado, Department of Art History, University of Lisbon;* b. 16 Nov. 1922, Tomar; s. of José M. França and Carmen R. França; m. 2nd Marie-Thérèse Mandroux; one d. (by previous m.); ed Lisbon Univ., Ecole des Hautes Etudes and Univ. of Paris; travels in Africa, Europe, Americas and Asia 1945–; Ed. Lisbon literary review Unicornio 1951–56, Co-Ed. Cadernos de Poesia 1951–53; Founder-Dir Galeria de Marco, Lisbon 1952–54; art critic 1946–; film critic 1948–; lexicographical publr 1948–58; Ed. Pintura & Näo 1969–70, Colóquio Artes 1970–96; Prof., Cultural History and History of Art, Dir Dept of Art History, New Univ. of Lisbon 1992–, Prof. Jubilado 1994–, Dir elect Faculty of Social Sciences 1982; Dir Fondation C. Gulbenkian, Centre Culturel Portugais, Paris 1983–89; Visiting Prof., Univ. of Paris III 1985–89; Vice-Pres. Int. Asscn of Art Critics 1970–73, Pres. 1985–87, Hon. Pres. 1987–; Vice-Pres. Acad. Européenne de Sciences, Arts et Lettres Paris 1985–2000, Hon. Pres. 2000–; City Councillor, Lisbon 1974–75; mem. of City Ass. Lisbon 1990–93; Pres. Inst. Cultura Portuguesa 1976–80, World Heritage Cttee, UNESCO 1999–2005, J-A F's art collection Museu of Tomar 2004; mem. Int. Asscn of Art Critics, Int. Cttee of Art History, PEN Club, Soc. Européenne de Culture, Soc. de l'Histoire de l'Art français, Acad. Nacional de Belas Artes (Pres. 1977–80, Emer. 2012–), Acad. das Ciencias de Lisboa (Emer. 2012–), Acad. Européenne de Sciences, Arts et Lettres, World Acad. of Arts and Science, Acad. Nat. Sciences, Arts et Lettres de Bordeaux, Ateneo Veneto, Real Acad. Bellas Artes San Fernando (Spain); Hon. mem. Union Journalistes Cinéma 2008, Ordem dos Arquitectos 2009; Officier, Ordre nat. du Mérite, Chevalier, Ordre des Arts et des Lettres, Commdr, Ordem Rio Branco (Brazil), Grand Cross Order of Public Instruction, Grand Cross Ordem Infante Dom Henrique, Officer, Ordem Santiago; Medals of Honour (Lisbon, Tomar), Medal of Cultural Merit 2012. *Publications:* Natureza Morta (novel) 1949, Charles Chaplin—the Self-Made Myth 1952, Amadeo de Souza-Cardoso 1957, Azazel (play) 1957, Despedida Breve (short stories) 1958, Situação da Pintura Ocidental 1959, Da Pintura Portuguesa 1960, Dez Anos de Cinema 1960, Une ville des lumières: La Lisbonne de Pombal 1963, A Arte em Portugal no Século XIX 1967, Oito Ensaios sobre Arte Contemporânea 1967, Le romantisme au Portugal 1972, Almada, o Português sem Mestre 1972, A Arte na Sociedade Portuguesa no Século XX 1972, Antonio Carneiro 1973, A Arte em Portugal no século XX 1974, Zé Povinho 1975, Manolo Millares 1977, Lisboa: Urbanismo e Arquitectura, O Retrato na Arte Portuguesa, Rafael Bordalo Pinheiro, o Português tal e qual 1980, Malhoa & Columbano, Historia da Arte Occidental 1780–1980 1987, Os Anos 20 em Portugal 1992, Bosch ou le visionnaire intégral, Thomar revisited 1994, Lisboa 1898, (In) definições de Cultura 1997, Memorias para o Ano 2000 2000, Monte Olivete, minha aldeia 2001, Buridan (novel) 2002, Regra de Três (novel), Cem Cenas, quadros e contos (short stories) 2003, A Bela Angevina (novel), Historia da Arte em Portugal 1750–2000 2004, José e os outros (novel), Exercícios de Passamento (short stories) 2005, Ricardo Coração de Leão (novel) 2007, João sem Terra (novel) 2008, Lisboa: história física e moral 2008, Guerra e Paz (novel) 2009, Ano X – Lisboa 1936 (essay) 2010, Mina e as coincidencias (novel) 2011, Ano XX — Lisboa 1946 (essay) 2012, Memórias após o Ano 2000 2012, Memórias do Conselheiro Adalberto (essay) 2014. *Leisure interests:* travel and detective stories. *Address:* Av. Infante Santo, 17/8D, 1350-175 Lisbon, Portugal (home); 12 route de Beauvau, 49140 Jarzé, France (home). *Telephone:* (21) 3953512 (Lisbon) (home); 2-41-95-40-04 (Jarzé) (home). *Fax:* 2-41-95-40-04 (Jarzé) (home).

FRANCESCHI, Patrice, PhD; French writer, sailor and aviator; *Honorary President, Société des explorateurs français;* b. 18 Dec. 1954, Toulon; ed Sorbonne, Paris, Aix-Marseille Univ.; explorer and humanitarian activist; sponsored by UNESCO to promote dialogue between different cultures; journeys in Guyana 1974, Congo 1975, the Amazon 1976, Burundi, Tanzania, Uganda and Egypt 1978, Viet Nam 1979, New Guinea 1989, SE Asia 1999–2000; descended the Nile on foot 1978; first world tour in ultra-light motorized vessel 1984–97; world exploration tour with tall ship La Boudeuse 2004–07; Founding mem. and Pres. Solidarités aid agency, has engaged in numerous humanitarian missions in Thailand 1980, Romania 1989–90, Kurdistan 1991–92, Sarajevo 1992, Rwanda 1996, Afghanistan 1979–99, Bosnia-Herzegovina 1997; Coordinator French Governmental Aid in Somalia 1992–93; currently Hon. Pres. Soc. des explorateurs français; Chevalier, de la Légion d'honneur; Medal, Acad. de la Marine 1980, Lauréat de l'Acad. Française 1981, Gold Medal Acad. des sports 1987. *Television:* 18 documentary films about exploration of New Guinea, Amazon, Nagaland, Pacific, SE Asia etc. *Publications include:* Au Congo jusqu'au cou 1977, Terre farrouche 1977, L'exode vietnamien 1979, Ils ont choisi la liberté 1981, Guerre en Afghanistan 1984, Un capitane sans importance 1987, La folle équipée 1987, Qui a bu l'eau du Nil 1989, Raid papou 1990, Chasseurs d'horizons 1991, Quelque chose qui prend les hommes 1992, Tout l'or du fleuve 1995, De l'esprit d'aventure (with J-C Guilbert, G. Chaliand) 2003, La Boudeuse en Amazonie (illustrator N. Clérice) 2005, La Grande Aventure de La Boudeuse 2008, Le chemin de la mer 2009. *Leisure interests:* literature, philosophy, science, exploration. *Address:* Société des explorateurs français, 184 boulevard Saint-Germain, 75006 Paris, France (office). *Telephone:* 1-45-49-03-51 (office). *E-mail:* navire@la-boudeuse.org (office). *Website:* www.la-boudeuse.org (office).

FRANCHET, Yves Georges; French international public servant; b. 4 March 1939, Paris; m. Marie Bernard Robillard; two s.; ed Ecole polytechnique, Paris, Université Paris I, Ecole nationale de la statistique et de l'admin économique de Paris; Dir Statistics Office, UDEAC, Brazzaville, Congo 1964–68; mem. Govt econ. planning staff 1968–69; economist, World Bank, Washington, DC 1969–74; Head of Planning, Co-operation Div., Inst. Nat. de la Statistique et des Etudes Economiques (INSEE) 1974–77; Dir Ecole Nat. de la statistique et de l'admin économique (ENSAE) 1977–80; Deputy Dir European Office of World Bank, Paris 1980–83; Vice-Pres. IDB, Washington, DC 1983–87; Dir-Gen. Statistical Office of the European Communities (EUROSTAT) 1987–2003; Chevalier Légion d'honneur, Commdr Order of Merit (Niger); Dr hc (Bucharest). *Address:* 7 rue J. P. Brasseur, 1258 Luxembourg, Luxembourg (home).

FRANCIONI, Reto; Swiss business executive; *CEO, Deutsche Börse AG;* b. 18 Aug. 1955, Zürich; m.; two s.; ed Univ. of Zurich; with UBS 1981–85, Credit Suisse 1985–88; Deputy CEO of Man., Asscn Tripartite Bourses 1988–92; Dir, Corp. Finance Div., Hofmann-La Roche 1992–93; mem. Exec. Bd, Deutsche Börse AG 1993–2000, Deputy CEO 1999–2005, CEO 2005–; Co-CEO and Spokesman, Consors 2000–02; Pres. and Chair. SWX Swiss Exchange 2002–05. *Publications:* Equity Markets in Action (co-author) 2004, The Equity Trader Course (co-author) 2006. *Address:* Deutsche Börse AG, 60485 Frankfurt, Germany (office). *Telephone:* (69) 21112000 (office). *Fax:* (69) 21112001 (office). *E-mail:* reto.francioni@deutsche-boerse.com (office). *Website:* deutsche-boerse.com (office).

FRANCIS, Julian W., BSc, MBA; Bahamian financial services industry executive and fmr central banker; *Chairman, Providence Advisors Ltd;* m.; two s.; ed New York Univ., USA; Accounting Officer and Credit Officer, SFE Banking Corpn, Nassau 1969–72, Asst Vice-Pres. Credit Dept 1976–79; worked for Barclays Bank, Nassau and Eleuthera; with Banque de la Soc. Financière Européenne, Paris, France 1980–92, positions include Asst Man. for Business Devt in Latin America, Deputy Man. for Assets Man., Man. of Assets Trading Dept, Cen. Man. for Corp. Finance, Jt Gen. Man. and mem. Man. Cttee; Deputy Gov. and mem. Bd of Dirs Cen. Bank of the Bahamas 1993–97, Gov. 1997–2005; Co-Chair. and CEO Grand Bahama Port Authority 2005; currently Chair. Providence Advisors Ltd; mem. Bd of Dirs Butterfield Bank Group 2007–, Bahamas Cancer Centre; Vice-Chair. Securities Bd; Chair. The Bridge Authority; Bahamian jt negotiator on Competition Policy, Free Trade of the Americas negotiations 1997; fmr Vice-Chair. Securities Market Task Force. *Leisure interests:* reading, fishing, tennis. *Address:* Providence Advisors Ltd, Goodman's Bay Corporate Centre, PO Box AP 59223, Slot 409, West Bay Street, Nassau, Bahamas (office). *Telephone:* 328-7115 (office). *Fax:* 328-7129 (office). *E-mail:* info@providenceadvisors.net (office). *Website:* www.providenceadvisors.net (office).

FRANCIS I, His Holiness Pope (Jorge Mario Bergoglio), SJ; Argentine ecclesiastic; b. 17 Dec. 1936, Buenos Aires; ed San José Major Coll.; ordained priest of Soc. of Jesus 1969; at Prov. San José Major Coll. 1973–79, Rector 1980–86; Auxiliary Bishop of Buenos Aires 1992–97, Coadjutor Bishop of Buenos Aires 1997–98, Archbishop of Buenos Aires 1998–2013; Titular Bishop of Auca May-

June 1992; Vicar Gen. Archdiocese of Buenos Aires 1993; apptd Bishop of Argentina 1998; Ordinary of the Ordinariate for the Faithful of the Eastern Rites in Argentina 1998–2013; cr. Cardinal (Cardinal-Priest of S. Roberto Bellarmino) 2001; Pres. Argentine Episcopal Conf. 2005–08; participated in Papal Conclave March 2013, elected Pope and Bishop of Rome 2013– (first non-European in more than 1,200 years and first Jesuit priest ever to become Pope); Grand Chancellor, Universidad Católica Argentina; mem. Congregation for Divine Worship and Discipline of Sacraments, Congregation for the Congregation for the Clergy, Congregation for Insts of Consecrated Life and Socs of Apostolic Life, Pontifical Council for the Family, Episcopal Comm. for Latin America; ranked by Forbes magazine amongst The World's Most Powerful People (fourth) 2013. *Publications include:* Meditaciones para religiosos 1982, Reflexiones sobre la vida apostólica 1986, Reflexiones de esperanza 1992, Diálogos entre Juan Pablo II y Fidel Castro 1998, Educar: exigencia y pasión 2003, Ponerse la patria al hombro 2004, La nación por construir 2005, Corrupción y pecado 2006, Sobre la acusación de sí mismo 2006, El verdadero poder es el servicio 2007, Mente abierta, corazón creyente 2012. *Address:* Palazzo Apostolico Vaticano, 00120 Città del Vaticano, Rome, Italy (office). *Website:* www.vatican.va (office).

FRANCO, James Edward, MFA; American actor, director and screenwriter; b. 19 April 1978, Palo Alto, California; s. of Douglas Franco and Betsy-Lou Franco; ed Columbia Univ.; early acting experience in school plays; career breakthrough with leading role in TV series Freaks and Geeks 1999; f. own production co. Rabbit Bandini Productions. *Television includes:* Freaks and Geeks (series) 1999, James Dean (TV film) (Broadcast Film Critics Asscn Award for Best Actor in TV Film, Golden Globe Award for Best Actor - Miniseries or TV Film) 2001. *Films include:* At Any Cost 2000, Whatever It Takes 2000, Spider-Man 2002, City by the Sea 2002, Sonny 2002, The Company 2003, Spider-Man 2 2004, The Ape 2005, Annapolis 2006, Flyboys 2006, Good Time Max (writer and dir) 2007, Spider-Man 3 2007, Pineapple Express 2008, Milk 2008, Eat Pray Love 2010, 127 Hours (several awards including Dallas-Fort Worth Film Critics Asscn Award for Best Actor, Indiana Film Journalists Asscn Award for Best Actor, Las Vegas Film Critics Soc. Award for Best Actor, New York Film Critics Online Award for Best Actor, Santa Barbara Int. Film Festival Award for Outstanding Performance, Utah Film Critics Asscn Award for Best Actor) 2010, The Broken Tower (actor and dir) 2011, Oz the Great and Powerful 2013, This Is the End 2013, As I Lay Dying 2013, Spring Breakers (Best Supporting Actor, Nat. Soc. of Film Critics) 2013. *Address:* c/o James/Levy/Jacobson Management, Inc., 3500 West Olive Avenue, Suite 1470 Burbank, CA 91505, USA (office). *Telephone:* (818) 955-7070 (office). *Fax:* (818) 955-7073 (office).

FRANCO ESTADELLA, Antonio; Spanish journalist; *Editor, El Periódico de Catalunya;* b. 21 Jan. 1947, Barcelona; s. of Alfonso Franco and Lolita Estadella; m. Marie-Hélène Bigatá; one s. one d.; Ed. Sports Section Diario Barcelona 1970, Ed.-in-Chief 1973, Asst Dir 1975; Dir Siete Días (TV programme) 1977; f. El Periódico de Catalunya 1977, Ed.-in-Chief 1987–2006; Jt Ed. El País 1982; apptd Asst Ed., Grupo Zeta 2006, currently Adviser to Pres. of Zeta Group; apptd Ed. Espai Public (TV programme, BTV) 2007; Pres. Asscn of Friends, Universitat Autònoma de Barcelona 2010–; mem. International Inst. for the Defense of Press Freedom; Creu de Sant Jordi (Catalonian order) 2006; for journalism: Premio Ortega y Gasset, Premio Godó, Premio Luca de Tena, Premio Ciutat de Barcelona, Luca de Tena Journalism Award 2000, Antonio Asensio Prize 2007. *Publications:* Deporte y sociedad 1975. *Leisure interests:* literature, music, sports. *Address:* El Periódico de Catalunya, Consell de Cent 425–427, 08009 Barcelona, Spain (office). *Telephone:* (93) 2655353 (office). *Fax:* (93) 4846517 (office). *E-mail:* afranco@elperiodico.com (office); sac@elperiodico.com (office). *Website:* www.elperiodico.es (office).

FRANCO GOMEZ, Julio César, PhD; Paraguayan physician and politician; b. 1952; ed Nat. Univ. of Cordoba, Argentina, Asunción Univ.; Senator 1998; Pres. of the Comm. for Public Health, Social Security and Drug Control 1999; Vice-Pres. of Paraguay 2000–03; fmr Chair. Partido Liberal Radical Auténtico (PLRA), PLRA presidential cand. 2003. *Address:* c/o Partido Liberal Radical Auténtico, Iturbe 936, entre Manuel Domínguez y Teniente Fariña, Asunción, Paraguay (office).

FRANCO GÓMEZ, Luis Federico, DrMed; Paraguayan surgeon, politician and fmr head of state; b. 23 July 1962, Asunción; m. Emilia Alfaro Patricia de Franco; four c.; ed Nat. Univ. of Asunción; Head of Interns and Residents, 1CCM Univ. Hosp. de Clínicas, Asunción 1990–91, also Chief of Emergency, Instructor in Medicial Semiology 1991–92; Chief of Nat. Guard Hosp. MSP and BS, 1994–96, also Chief Resident of Internal Medicine and Chief of Cardiology; Town Councillor Fernando de la Mora 1991–96, also becoming Pres. of Legislation and Pres. of Health, Hygiene and Social Services, Mayor, Fernando de la Mora 1996–2001; mem. Partido Liberal Radical Auténtico, apptd Dir 2002; Gov. Cen. Prov. 2003–08; Vice-Pres. of Paraguay 2008–12, Pres. 2012–13; mem. Paraguayan Soc. of Internal Medicine. *Address:* c/o Office of the President, Palacio de los López, Asunción, Paraguay (office).

FRANCON, Nathalie; French business executive; *CEO, Azzaro;* fmr exec. with Chanel; COO Christian Lacroix –2007; CEO Azzaro 2007–. *Address:* Azzaro, 65 rue du faubourg, Saint-Honoré, 75008 Paris, France (office). *Telephone:* 1-42-66-92-06 (office). *Fax:* 1-42-66-08-02 (office). *E-mail:* info@azzaroparis.com (office). *Website:* www.azzaroparis.com (office); lorisazzaro.com (office).

FRANGIALLI, Francesco; French international organization official; b. 23 Jan. 1947, Paris; m. Leila Niiranen; two s. one d.; ed Université de Paris, Institut d'Études Politiques de Paris, École Nationale d'Admin; Lecturer, Institut d'Études Politiques de Paris 1972–89; extensive background in public admin; Dir Tourism Industry, Govt ministry responsible for tourism 1986–90; Perm. Rep. to World Tourism Org. 1986–89, Deputy Sec.-Gen. 1990–96, Sec.-Gen. a.i. 1996–97, Sec.-Gen. 1998–2009, led the org.'s conversion to a specialized agency of the UN 2003. *Publications:* La France dans le tourisme mondial 1991, Tourisme et loisirs – Une question sociale (co-author), published in Observations on International Tourism 1997–2000, and in International Tourism: The Great Turning Point 2001–2003; numerous articles, speeches and papers. *Address:* c/o World Tourism Organization, Capitán Haya 42, 28020 Madrid, Spain. *Telephone:* (91) 567-81-00. *E-mail:* omt@unwto.org.

FRANGOU, Angeliki, BEng, MEng; Greek business executive; *Chairman and CEO, Navios Maritime Holdings;* ed Fairleigh Dickinson Univ. and Columbia Univ., USA; analyst on trading floor of Republic National Bank of New York 1987–89; CEO Franser Shipping SA, Piraeus 1990–2001, CEO Maritime Enterprises Management SA, Piraeus 2001–05; Chair., Pres. and CEO International Shipping Enterprises Inc. (ISE) 2004–05, Chair. and CEO Navios Maritime Holdings (following acquisition of Navios Holdings by ISE) 2005–, Chair. and CEO Navios Maritime Partners LP (affiliate of Navios Holdings) 2007–, Navios Maritime Acquisition Corpn 2008–, Chair. Navios South American Logistics 2007–; Chair. Proton Bank, Athens 2006–08, IRF European Finance Investments Ltd; mem. Bd of Dirs Emporiki Bank of Greece 2004–05; mem. Bd The United Kingdom Mutual Steam Ship Assurance Asscn (Bermuda) Ltd; Vice-Chair. China Classification Soc. Mediterranean Cttee; mem. Hellenic and Black Sea Cttee of Bureau Veritas, Greek Cttee of Nippon Kaiji Kyokai; ranked by Fortune magazine amongst the 50 Most Powerful Women in Business outside the US (50th) 2011. *Address:* Navios Maritime Holdings, 85 Akti Miaouli Street, Piraeus 185 38, Greece (office); Navios Corporation, 825 Third Avenue, 34th Floor, New York, NY 10022, USA (office). *Telephone:* (210) 417-2050 (Piraeus) (office); (212) 223-7000 (New York) (office). *Fax:* (210) 417-2070 (Piraeus) (office); (212) 223-7650 (New York) (office). *E-mail:* info@navios.com (office). *Website:* www.navios.com (office).

FRÄNGSMYR, Tore, DPhil; Swedish historian and academic; *Professor of History of Science, Uppsala University;* b. 8 July 1938, Skellefteå; s. of Johan Frängsmyr and Linnea Frängsmyr (née Lindberg); m. Birgitta Thunholm 1970; two s. two d.; ed Uppsala Univ.; Assoc. Prof., Uppsala Univ. 1969, Prof. of History of Science 1982–; Prof. of Tech. and Social Change, Linköping Univ. 1981–82; Dir Center for History of Science, Royal Swedish Acad. of Sciences, Stockholm 1988–; Ed. Les Prix Nobel 1988–; Sec.-Gen. Int. Union of History of Science 1989–93; Fellow, Royal Swedish Acad. of Sciences, Royal Acad. of Eng Sciences, Academia Europaea, American Philosophical Soc. *Publications include:* Linnaeus, the Man and His Work 1984, Science in Sweden; The Royal Swedish Acad. of Sciences 1739–1989 1989, The Quantifying Spirit in the Eighteenth Century (co-ed.) 1990, Solomon's House Revisited: The Organization and Institutionalization of Science 1990, Enlightenment Science in the Romantic Era: The Chemistry of Berzelius and its Cultural Setting (co-ed.) 1992, A la recherche des lumières 1999. *Address:* Avd. för vetenskapshistoria, Uppsala University, Box 629, 751 26 Uppsala, Sweden (office). *Telephone:* (18) 471-15-79 (office). *E-mail:* Tore.Frangsmyr@idehist.uu.se (office). *Website:* www.vethist.idehist.uu.se (office).

FRANGULYAN, Georgy; Russian sculptor; b. 29 May 1945, Tbilisi, Georgia; m. Yelena Maximova; four c.; ed Moscow Stroganov Higher School of the Arts; Diploma of Russian Acad. of Fine Arts 1999; Grekov Medal 1979, Grand Prix Int. Competition of Plastic Arts, Hungary 1982, Grand Prix Int. Competition of Sculpture, Poznań, Poland 1987, Jury Prize at the Int. Competition of Sculpture, Ravenna, Italy 1988, Silver Medal of Russian Acad. of Fine Arts 1996, Gold Medal of Russian Acad. of Fine Arts 1996. *Address:* Moscow 119121, Zemledelchesky per. 9 bldg. 1, Russia (home). *Telephone:* (495) 248-24-67 (home).

FRANK, Charles Raphael, Jr, PhD; American banker, economist, government official and business executive; *Chief Financial Officer, Central European Media Enterprises Ltd;* b. 15 May 1937, Pittsburgh, Pa; s. of Charles Raphael Frank and Lucille Frank (née Briscoe); m. 1st Susan Patricia Buckman (divorced 1976; one s. one d.; m. 2nd Eleanor Sebastian 1976; two s.; one step s. one step d.; ed Rensselaer Polytechnic Inst. and Princeton Univ.; Sr Research Fellow, East African Inst. for Social Research, Makerere Univ. Coll., Kampala 1963–65; Asst Prof. of Econs, Yale Univ. 1965–67; Assoc. Prof. of Econs and Int. Affairs, Princeton Univ. 1967–70, Prof. 1970–74; Assoc. Dir Research Programme on Econ. Devt, Woodrow Wilson School 1967–70, Dir 1970–74; Sr Fellow, Brookings Inst. 1972–74; mem. Policy Planning staff and Chief Economist, US Dept of State 1974–77, Deputy Asst Sec. of State for Econ. and Social Affairs 1977–78; Vice-Pres. Salomon Bros, Inc. 1978–87; Pres. Frank & Co., Inc. 1987–88; Vice-Pres. and Man. Dir for Structured Finance GE Capital Corpn, Stamford, Conn. 1988–97; First Vice-Pres. EBRD 1997–2001; currently Adviser, Sabre Capital, RAO UES; Chair. Baneasa Investments, SA; mem. Bd of Dirs Central European Media Enterprises Ltd 2001–09, Chief Financial Officer 2009–; mem. Bd of Dirs Mittal Steel Galati, Romanian-American Enterprise Fund; mem. Investment Cttee Darby Converging Europe Mezzanine Fund; mem. Council on Foreign Relations. *Publications:* The Sugar Industry in East Africa 1965, Production Theory and Indivisible Commodities 1969, Economic Accounting and Development Planning (with Brian Van Arkadie) 1969, Debt and the Terms of Aid 1970, Statistics and Econometrics 1971, American Jobs and Trade with the Developing Countries 1973, Foreign Exchange Regimes and Economic Development: The Case of South Korea 1975, Foreign Trade and Domestic Adjustment 1976, Income Distribution and Economic Growth in the Less Developed Countries (jtly) 1977. *Address:* c/o Board of Directors, Central European Media Enterprises Ltd, 52 Charles Street, London, W1J 5EU (office); Flat 5, 70–72 Cadogan Square, London, SW1X 0EA, England (home). *Website:* www.cetv-net .com (office).

FRANK, Mary E., MD; American physician and academic; b. New Jersey; ed Fairleigh Dickinson Univ., Teaneck, NJ, Penn State Univ., Hershey, Pa; residency and teaching fellowship, Medical Univ. of S Carolina; joined a family practice, Charleston, Calif. 1977; in full-time practice 1977–; fmr Residency Program Dir, Sutter Hosp., Santa Rosa, Calif.; fmr Clinical Instructor of Family, Community and Preventive Medicine, Stanford Univ., Calif.; fmr Facility Medical Dir, Primary Care Assocs, Rohnert Park; currently Assoc. Clinical Prof. of Ambulatory and Community Medicine, Univ. of Calif., San Francisco; mem. American Acad. of Family Physicians (AAFP) 1973–, served as Chair. Comm. on Legislation and Govt Affairs, Cttee on Women, liaison to Carnegie Foundation Conf. on Healthy Youth for the 21st Century, American Coll. of Obstetricians and Gynaecologists Cttee on Adolescent Health, Rep. to Nat. Quality Forum, Nat. Conf. of State Legislatures, Pres. Calif. Acad. of Family Physicians, mem. Bd of Dirs AAFP 2000–03, Pres. (first woman) 2003–05, Chair. 2005–06; Fellow, American Acad. of Family Physicians; mem. Bd of Dirs Comm. on Office Lab. Accreditation (COLA); Vice-Chair. Council on Scientific Affairs, Calif. Medical Asscn; mem. Sonoma Co. Medical Asscn; volunteer, Special Olympics 1994–; regular speaker, Nat. Youth Leadership Forum; nominated Local Legend, American Medical Women's Asscn. *Leisure interests:* photography, reading mystery novels, hiking. *Address:* Ameri-

can Academy of Family Physicians, 11400 Tomahawk Creek Parkway, Leawood, KS 66211-2680 (office); American Academy of Family Physicians, PO Box 11210, Shawnee Mission, KS 66207-1210, USA (office). *Telephone:* (800) 274-2237 (office); (913) 906-6000 (office). *Fax:* (913) 906-6075 (office). *Website:* www.aafp.org (office).

FRANK, Sergey Ottovich; Russian politician; *General Director, Sovkomflot;* b. 13 Aug. 1960, Novosibirsk; m.; one s.; ed Far East Higher Marine School of Eng, Far East State Univ., Higher School of Commerce, Ministry of Foreign Econ. Relations of Russian Fed.; Sec., Comsomol Cttee, later Deputy Head, Far East Higher Marine School; on staff, Far East Marine Navigation Agency 1989–93, Deputy Dir-Gen. 1993–95; Deputy Head, Dept of Marine Transport, Ministry of Transport of Russian Fed. 1995–96; First Deputy Minister of Transport of Russian Fed. 1997–98, Minister 1998–2004, First Deputy Minister of Transport and Communications 2004; Chair. Aeroflot 1999–; Gen. Dir Sovkomflot 2004–. *Address:* Sovcomflot, 6 Gasheka str., 125047 Moscow, Russia (office). *Telephone:* (495) 626-1434 (office). *Fax:* (495) 626-1850 (office). *E-mail:* moscow@sovcomflot.ru (office). *Website:* www.sovcomflot.ru (office).

FRANKEL, Bethenny; American television personality, author, entrepreneur and natural foods chef; b. 4 Nov. 1970; d. of Robert J. Frankel and Bernadette Burke; m. 1st Peter Sussman 1996 (divorced); m. 2nd Jason Hoppy 2010; one d.; ed Pine Crest School, Fort Lauderdale, Fla, Nat. Gourmet Inst. for Healthy and Culinary Arts, New York, New York Univ., Boston Univ.; began career appearing in short film Soiree Sans Hors D'oeuvres 1993; an original cast mem. on series The Real Housewives of New York City; appeared on The Apprentice: Martha Stewart show 2005, one of two finalists; launched own co. Skinnygirl Cocktails 2009; starred in Bravo reality show Bethenny Getting Married? 2010; host of series Bethenny 2012–. *Films include:* actor: Hollywood Hills 90028 1994, Wish Me Luck 1995. *Publications:* Naturally Thin: Unleash Your SkinnyGirl and Free Yourself from a Lifetime of Dieting 2009, The Skinnygirl Dish: Easy Recipes for Your Naturally Thin Life 2009, Body by Bethenny: Body-sculpting Workouts to Unleash Your SkinnyGirl 2010, A Place of Yes: 10 Rules for Getting Everything You Want Out of Life 2011. *Website:* www.bethenny.com.

FRANKEL, Max, MA; American journalist; b. 3 April 1930, Gera, Germany; s. of Jacob A. Frankel and Mary Frankel (née Katz); m. 1st. Tobia Brown 1956 (died 1987); two s. one d.; m. 2nd Joyce Purnick 1988; ed Columbia Univ., New York; mem. staff, The New York Times 1952, Chief Washington Corresp. 1968–72, Sunday Ed. 1973–76, Editorial Pages Ed. 1977–86, Exec. Ed. 1986–94, 1994–95, also columnist, New York Times magazine 1995–2000; Pulitzer Prize for Int. Reporting 1973. *Publications include:* The Time of My Life and My Life with the Times 1999, High Noon in the Cold War: Kennedy, Khrushchev and the Cuban Missile Crisis 2004. *Address:* c/o The New York Times Co., 620 Eighth Avenue, New York, NY 10018, USA (office).

FRANKEN, Alan (Al) Stuart; American comedian, author and politician; *Senator from Minnesota;* b. 21 May 1951, New York, NY; m. Franni Franken; one s. one d.; ed Harvard Univ.; grew up in St Louis Park, Minn.; performed stand-up comedy and stage shows with pnr Tom Davis at Harvard Univ. in early 1970s; Franken and Davis signed by Lorne Michaels for TV show Saturday Night Live, New York 1975–80, 1985–95; wrote several unproduced screenplays; political satirist at Democratic Nat. Convention, Atlanta, Ga 1988; co-anchored Comedy Central's election coverage 1992, 1996; wrote and starred in Lateline (NBC) 1998–99; has given speeches to hundreds of corpns, univs and other orgs and has twice been keynote speaker at White House Correspondents' Dinner for Pres. Clinton, Nat. Press Club, USO tours, DNC dinners and commencement speaker at Harvard Univ. 2002; Host, The Al Franken Show (Air America Radio) 2004–07; Fellow, Harvard Univ. Kennedy School of Govt, Shorenstein Center on the Press, Politics and Public Policy; Senator from Minn. 2009–; mem. Democratic-Farmer-Labor Party; five Emmy Awards (four writing and one producing). *Films:* Tunnel Vision 1976, Trading Places 1983, One More Saturday Night (also writer) 1986, When a Man Loves a Woman (also writer and exec. producer) 1994, Stuart Saves His Family (also writer) 1995, The Definite Maybe 1997, Harvard Man (as himself) 2000. *Television:* writer: The Paul Simon Special 1977, Saturday Night Live (series) 1975–80, 1985–95, The Coneheads 1983, Franken and Davis at Stockton State 1984, Best of John Belushi 1985, Best of Dan Aykroyd 1986, Saturday Night Live Goes Commercial 1991, Politically Incorrect (series) 1996, The 67th Annual Academy Awards 1995, Lateline (series) 1998, Saturday Night Live: Presidential Bash 2000; producer: Saturday Night Live 1985–95, Saturday Night Live Goes Commercial 1991, Lateline (Exec. Producer series, NBC) 1998, Saturday Night Live: Presidential Bash (Consulting Producer, NBC) 2000. *Publications:* I'm Good Enough, I'm Smart Enough and Doggone It, People Like Me 1992, Rush Limbaugh is a Big Fat Idiot (Grammy Award for audio version) 1996, A Father and Son Learn From Newt's Mistakes 1997, Why Not Me? – The Making and Unmaking of the Al Franken Presidency 1999, Franken Sense 1999, Home-Fried Franken 2000, Block That Rush 2000, Is George W. Bush Dumb? 2000, Oh, The Things I Know: A Guide to Success, Or, Failing That, Happiness 2002, Norm and the Other 1 Percent 2003, Lies and the Lying Liars Who Tell Them: A Fair and Balanced Look at the Right (Grammy Award for audio version) 2003, The Truth (With Jokes) 2005; has contributed news commentary to Newsweek, The Nation Rolling Stone and other publications. *Address:* 309 Hart Senate Office Building, Washington, DC 20510, USA (office). *Telephone:* (202) 224-5641 (office). *E-mail:* info@franken.senate.gov (office). *Website:* franken.senate.gov (office); www.alfranken.com (office).

FRANKEN, Hendrik (Hans), PhD; Dutch lawyer and academic; b. 17 Sept. 1936, Haarlem; s. of Albert J. Franken and Catherine G. Weijland; m. 1st Boudewine D. M. Bonebakker 1966 (divorced 1993); two s. one d.; m. 2nd Ingrid L. E. Sanders 1995 (died 2008); ed Univ. of Leiden, Sorbonne, Paris, Univ. of Amsterdam; Sec., Mil. Tribunal 1960; Asst Prosecutor, Dist Court, Rotterdam 1964; mem. Rotterdam Bar 1967; judge 1969; Prof. of Jurisprudence, Erasmus Univ., Rotterdam 1974, of Jurisprudence, Univ. of Leiden 1977–, of Information Law 1987–; Prof. of Information Law, Univ. of Groningen 1989–95; mem. State Council 1982–87, Court of Appeal, The Hague 1977–2006; Chair. Nat. Cttee of Information Tech. and Law; mem. Social Econ. Council 1988–2004, Sec.-Gen. Royal Acad. of Arts and Sciences 1998–2001; mem. Senate (Eerste Kamer) 2004–; Kt of Netherlands Lion 1995; Modderman Prijs 1973, Wolffert van Borselenpenning 1982. *Publications:* Vervolgingsbeleid: The Policy of Public Prosecutors 1973, Maat en Regel 1975, Jurimetrics and the Rule of Law 1975, The New Law and Economics 1982, Models of Contracts in Information Law 1992, Introduction to the Law (10th edn) 2003, Trusted Third Parties 1996, Law and Computer (5th edn) 2004, Independence and Responsibility of the Judge 1997, Nemo Plus 2001. *Address:* Kamerlingh Onnes Gebouw, Steenschuur 25, 2311 ES Leiden (office); Weipoortseweg 95A, 2381 NJ Zoeterwoude, Netherlands (home). *Telephone:* (71) 5278838 (office); (71) 5804764 (home). *Fax:* (71) 5809794 (home). *E-mail:* h.franken@law.leidenuniv.nl (office); h.franken@xs4all.nl (home). *Website:* law.leiden.edu (office); www.eerstekamer.nl (office).

FRANKL, Peter; British pianist and academic; *Professor of Piano, School of Music, Yale University;* b. 2 Oct. 1935, Budapest, Hungary; s. of Tibor Frankl and Laura Frankl; m. Annie Feiner 1958; one s. one d.; ed Franz Liszt Acad. of Music, Budapest with Profs Hernadi, Kodály and Weiner; began career on int. circuit 1960s, London debut 1962, New York debut with Cleveland Orchestra 1967; has performed with numerous orchestras in USA (Chicago, Philadelphia, Boston, Washington, Los Angeles, San Francisco, Pittsburgh etc.), Berlin Philharmonic, Leipzig Gewandhaus, Amsterdam Concertgebouw, Orchestre de Paris, Israel Philharmonic, all London orchestras and many others in Europe and all parts of the world; has appeared with conductors including Abbado, Ashkenazy, Barbirolli, Blomstedt, Boulez, Chailly, Davis, Dorati, Fischer, Haitink, Kempe, Kertesz, Leinsdorf, Maazel, Masur, Muti, Sanderling, Solti, Szell, among others; numerous tours to Japan, Australia, NZ and South Africa, playing with orchestras, in recitals and in chamber music concerts; more than 20 appearances at BBC Promenade Concerts, London; regular participant at Edinburgh, Cheltenham, Aldeburgh, Verbier, Kuhmo, Naantali and Casals Festivals; highlights at Edinburgh Festival include Britten Concerto under baton of the composer and an opening televised concert with the Philharmonia Orchestra under Riccardo Muti; soloist at Enescu Festival, Bucharest with Budapest Festival Orchestra at one of the last concerts Yehudi Menuhin ever conducted; regular guest artist at summer festivals in Aspen, Chautauqua, Hollywood Bowl, Marlboro, Norfolk, Ravinia, Santa Fe and Yellow Barn, USA; toured with Frankl-Pauk-Kirshbaum Trio world-wide; frequent performances with string quartets including Amadeus, Bartók, Borodin, Fine Arts, Guarneri, Lindsay, Panocha, Takacs, Tokyo and Vermeer; masterclasses world-wide, including RAM and Royal Coll. of Music, London, Liszt Acad., Budapest, Van Cliburn Inst., Texas, in Berlin, Madrid, Beijing, Hong Kong and Seoul; mem. numerous jury panels at int. piano competitions, including Van Cliburn, Rubinstein, Leeds, Santander, Hilton Head, William Kappell, Hong Kong, Clara Haskil, Paderewski, Marguerite Long, Cleveland, Shanghai, Manchester and Brussels (Queen Elisabeth); Prof. (Piano), Yale Univ. School of Music 2013–; Hon. Prof., Franz Liszt Acad. of Music; Officer's Cross and Middle Cross (Hungary) 1972; won first prize in several int. competitions. *Recordings include:* complete Schumann and Debussy piano works (with Andras Schiff, the Schumann two-piano and four-hand repertoire); both Brahms Concerti and the Violin Sonatas (with Kyung Wha Chung) and Piano Trios; Piano Concerti, Violin Sonatas and four-hand works by Mozart; Bartók solo and violin pieces; Piano Quintets by Brahms, Schumann, Dvořák, Martinů and Dohnányi. *Leisure interests:* football, opera, theatre, tennis. *Address:* 5 Gresham Gardens, London, NW11 8NX, England (home). *Telephone:* (20) 8455-5228 (home). *Fax:* (20) 8455-2176 (home). *E-mail:* info@peterfrankl.co.uk. *Website:* www.peterfrankl.co.uk.

FRANKLIN, Aretha; American singer and songwriter; b. 25 March 1942, Memphis, Tenn.; d. of the late Rev. C. L. Franklin; m. 1st Ted White (divorced); m. 2nd Glynn Turman 1978 (divorced); began singing in choir at New Bethel Baptist Church, Detroit, where her father was pastor; numerous Grammy Awards 1967–, American Music Award 1984, NARAS Living Legend Award 1990, Rhythm and Blues Foundation Lifetime Achievement Award 1992, John F. Kennedy Center Award 1994; elected to Rock and Roll Hall of Fame (first woman) 1987, Lady of Soul Lena Horne Award for Outstanding Career Achievements 2005, Presidential Medal of Freedom 2005, Grammy Award for Best Traditional R&B Vocal Performance (for A House is Not a Home) 2006, United Negro Coll. Fund Award of Excellence 2006, inducted into Gospel Music Hall of Fame 2012. *Film appearances:* The Blues Brothers 1980, Blues Brothers 2000 1998. *Recordings include:* albums: The Great Aretha Franklin 1960, Aretha 1961, The Electrifying Aretha Franklin 1962, The Tender, the Moving, the Swinging Aretha Franklin 1962, Unforgettable: A Tribute to Dinah Washington 1964, The Gospel Sound Of Aretha Franklin 1964, Runnin' Out Of Fools 1965, Yeah!!! 1965, Soul Sister 1966, I Never Loved A Man (The Way I Loved You) 1967, Aretha Arrives 1967, Aretha: Lady Soul 1968, Aretha In Paris 1968, Aretha's Gold 1969, This Girl's in Love With You 1969, Spirit In The Dark 1970, Live At Fillmore West 1971, Young, Gifted And Black 1972, Amazing Grace 1972, Hey Now Hey (The Other Side Of The Sky) 1973, The First Twelve Sides 1973, Let Me In Your Life 1974, With Everything I Feel In Me 1974, You 1975, Sweet Passion 1977, Almighty Fire 1978, La Diva 1979, Aretha 1980, Love All The Hurt Away 1981, Jump To It 1982, Get It Right 1983, Who's Zoomin' Who? 1985, The First Lady Of Soul 1986, Aretha 1987, One Lord, One Faith, One Baptism 1988, Through The Storm 1989, What You See Is What You Sweat 1991, Jazz To Soul 1992, Queen Of Soul 1993, Aretha After Hours, Chain Of Fools 1993, Love Songs 1997, The Delta Meets Detroit 1998, A Rose Is Still A Rose 1998, You Grow Closer 1998, So Damn Happy 2003, Jewels in the Crown: All-Star Duets with the Queen 2007, Rare and Unreleased Recordings from the Golden Reign of the Queen of Soul 2007, A Woman Falling Out of Love 2008, This Christmas Aretha 2008, A Woman Falling Out of Love 2010. *Publication:* Aretha: From these Roots (with David Rib) 1999. *Address:* c/o Arista Records, 888 7th Avenue, New York, NY 10106, USA (office). *Telephone:* (212) 489-7400 (office). *Website:* www.jrecords.com (office).

FRANKLIN, Barbara Ann Hackman, BA, MBA; American business executive and fmr government official; *President and CEO, Barbara Franklin Enterprises;* b. (Barbara Ann Hackman), 19 March 1940, Lancaster, Pa; d. of Arthur A. Hackman and Mayme M. Hackman (née Haller); m. Wallace Barnes 1986; ed Pennsylvania State Univ., Harvard Business School; with Singer Co., New York 1964–68; Asst Vice-Pres. Citibank, New York 1969–71; White House Staff Asst to the Pres. for Recruiting Women to Govt, Washington, DC 1971–73; Commr and Vice-Chair. US Consumer Product Safety Comm., Washington, DC 1973–79; Sr Fellow and Dir Govt and Business Program, Wharton School, Univ. of Pa 1980–88; Pres. and CEO Franklin Assocs, Washington, DC 1984–92, Pres. and CEO Barbara Franklin Enterprises 1995–; US Sec. of Commerce, Dept of Commerce, Washington, DC 1992–93; mem. Pres.'s Advisory Cttee for Trade Policy and Negotiations 1982–86,

1989–92; mem. US Comptroller Gen.'s Consultant Panel 1984–92; mem. Bd of Dirs Aetna Inc. 1979–92, 1993–, Dow Chemical Co. 1980–92, 1993–2012; Chair. Emer. Bd of Trustees, Econ. Club of New York; mem. Bd of Dirs Nat. Asscn of Corp. Dirs (NACD), Chair. 2009–12; Vice-Chair. US-China Business Council; Chair. Asian Studies Advisory Council, Heritage Foundation; Dir or Trustee of three funds in American Funds Family of Mutual Funds; mem. Council on Foreign Relations, Int. Women's Forum (founding mem.), Nat. Cttee for US-China Relations; mem. Int. Advisory Bd Lafarge Inc.; mem. Advisory Council Public Co. Accounting Oversight Bd; several hon. degrees; numerous awards for professional achievement, including John J. McCloy Award, NACD Dir of the Year Award 2000, Bd Alert Outstanding Dir 2003, Woodrow Wilson Award for Public Service 2006, recognized by Directorship as one of the 100 most influential people in corp. governance 2007, CT Women's Hall of Fame Inductee 2013. *Television:* regular commentator, Nightly Business Report, Public Broadcasting Service 1997–. *Leisure interests:* exercise, hiking, reading, painting. *Address:* Barbara Franklin Enterprises, 2600 Virginia Avenue NW, Suite 506, Washington, DC 20037, USA (office). *Telephone:* (202) 337-9100 (office). *Fax:* (202) 337-9104 (office). *E-mail:* bhfranklin@bhfranklin.com (office). *Website:* www.bhfranklin.com (office).

FRANKLIN, Kirk; American singer, songwriter and record company executive; b. (Kirk Smith), 26 Jan. 1970, Fort Worth, Tex.; m.; one s.; Choir Dir Greater Stranglers Rest Baptist Church, Fort Worth 1988; worked with Dallas-Fort Worth Mass Choir on albums I Will Not Let Nothing Separate Me 1991, Another Chance 1993; f. choir group The Family; f. record company Fo Yo Soul; BET Award for Best Gospel Artist 2006, 2007, American Music Award for Favorite Contemporary Inspirational Artist 2006, Grammy Awards for Best Gospel Song (for Imagine Me) 2007, (for Help Me Believe) 2009, (for Hello Fear) 2012. *Film soundtrack contributions include:* My Life is in Your Hands (for Get on the Bus 1996), Joy (for The Preacher' Wife 1996). *Recordings include:* albums: with The Family: Kirk Franklin and The Family 1992, Christmas 1995, Watcha Lookin' 4 (Grammy Award for Best Contemporary Soul Gospel Album 1997) 1996; solo: God's Property from Kirk Franklin's Nu Nation (Grammy Award for Best Gospel Album by a choir or chorus 1998) 1997, The Nu Nation Project (Grammy Award for Best Contemporary Soul Gospel Album 1999) 1998, Kirk Franklin and the Family 2001, The Rebirth of Kirk Franklin 2002, Hero (Grammy Award for Best Contemporary R&B Gospel Album 2007) 2005, Songs from the Storm, Vol. 1 2006, The Fight of My Life (Grammy Award for Best Contemporary R&B Gospel Album 2009) 2007, Hello Fear (Grammy Award for Best Gospel Album 2012) 2011. *Publications include:* Church Boy: My Music and My Life (auto-biography) 1998, The Blueprint: A Plan for Living Above Life's Storms 2010. *Address:* William Morris Agency, 1325 Avenue of the Americas, New York, NY 10019, USA (office). *Telephone:* (212) 903-1100 (office). *Fax:* (212) 246-3583 (office). *Website:* www.wma.com (office); www.kirkfranklin.us.

FRANKLIN, Melissa Jeanette (Missy); American swimmer; b. 10 May 1995, Pasadena, Calif.; d. of Dick Franklin and D. A. Franklin; began swimming aged five; competed at Olympic Team Trials 2008 aged 13; competed in six individual events Nat. Championships 2010; won first int. medal at Fédération Internationale de Natation (FINA) World Championships, Dubai 2010; silver medal, 100m, 200m backstroke, 4×100m medley relay, Pan Pacific Swimming Championships 2010; gold medal, 200m freestyle, 200m backstroke, 4×100m medley relay, silver medal, 4×100m freestyle relay, bronze medal, 50m backstroke, World Aquatics Championships, Shanghai 2011; winner, 100m backstroke, 100m backstroke freestyle, US Nat. Championships 2011; winner 200m backstroke, FINA Swimming World Cup 2011; gold medal, 4×100m medley relay, Duel in the Pool, Atlanta 2011; gold medal, 100m backstroke, 200m backstroke, 4×200m freestyle relay, 4×100m medley realay, bronze medal, 4×100m freestyle relay, Olympic Games, London 2012; gold medal, 100m backstroke, 200m backstroke, 200m freestyle, 4×100m medley relay, 4×100m freestyle relay, 4×200m freestyle relay, FINA World Championships, Barcelona 2013; swims for Colorado Stars; Breakout Performer of the Year Award at Golden Goggle Awards 2010, Female Athlete of the Year and Race of the Year Award (200m backstroke) and Relay Performance of the Year (4×100m medley relay), Swimming's Annual Awards Night 2011, Best Female Swimmer, FINA Aquatics World Magazine 2011, FINA Swimmer of the Year 2011–12, World Swimmer of the Year 2012, American Swimmer of the Year 2012. *Leisure interests:* reading, dancing. *Website:* www.coloradostars.org.

FRANKLIN, Raoul Norman, CBE, DSc, FREng; British scientist, academic and university administrator; b. 3 June 1935, Hamilton, NZ; s. of N. G. Franklin and T. B. Franklin (née Davis); m. 1st Faith Ivens 1961 (died 2004); two s.; m. 2nd Christine Penfold 2005; ed Auckland Grammar School, Univ. of Auckland, Univ. of Oxford; Sr Research Fellow, Royal Mil. Coll. of Science 1961–63; Tutorial Fellow, Keble Coll., Oxford 1963–78; Univ. Lecturer, Eng Science, Oxford Univ. 1967–78; Consultant, UKAEA Culham Lab. 1968–; Vice-Chancellor, City Univ., London 1978–98, Prof. Plasma Physics and Tech. 1986–98; Visiting Prof., Open Univ. Oxford Research Unit 1998; Chair. City Tech. Ltd 1978–93; Chair. Assoc. Examining Bd 1994–98, Assessment and Qualifications Alliance (AQA) 1998–2003; Vice-Chair. Gen. Bd of the Faculties, Oxford Univ. 1971–74; mem. of Hebdomadal Council, Oxford Univ. 1971–74, 1976–78, of Science Bd, Science and Eng Research Council 1982–85, of London Pensions Fund Authority 1989–95, of Bd Arab-British Chamber of Commerce 1995–2002; mem. Council Gresham Coll. 1980–98; mem. Int. Cttee of ESCAMPIG (Europhysics Conf. on Atomic & Molecular Physics of Ionized Gases) 1993–96; Gov. Ashridge Man. Coll. 1986–99, Council City & Guilds 1996–2000, Council Univ. of Buckingham 2001–; Foundation Master, Guild of Educators 2001–02; Trustee, Trust Fund 2009; Master, Worshipful Co. of Curriers 2002–03; Hon. Fellow, Keble Coll., Coll. of Preceptors, Guildhall School of Music and Drama, Royal Inst. of Chartered Surveyors; Freeman, City of London; Distinguished Alumni Award, Univ. of Auckland 2004. *Publications:* Plasma Phenomena in Gas Discharges 1976, Physical Kinetics, Vol. XII 1981, Interaction of Intense Electromagnetic Fields with Plasmas (ed.) 1981. *Leisure interests:* walking, gardening. *Address:* 12 Moreton Road, Oxford, OX2 7AX, England (home). *Telephone:* (1865) 558311 (home). *E-mail:* raoulnf_1935@gmail.com (home).

FRANKS, Gen. (retd) Tommy Ray, KBE, MS; American army officer (retd); b. 17 June 1945, Wynnewood, Okla; m. Cathryn Carley 1969; one d.; ed Univ. of Texas, Shippensburg Univ., Pa, Armed Forces Staff Coll., US Army War Coll.;

commissioned 2nd Lt 1967; served with 9th Infantry Div., Viet-nam, 2nd Armored Cavalry Regt, FRG; Commdr 2nd Bn 78th Field Artillery, FRG 1981–84; Deputy Asst G3, III Corps, Fort Hood, Tex. 1985–87; Commdr Div. Artillery, 1st Cavalry Div. 1987–88; Chief of Staff 1st Cavalry Div. 1988–89; Asst Div. Commdr (Maneuver), 1st Cavalry Div., Operation Desert Shield/Desert Storm, Saudi Arabia, Iraq 1990–91; Asst Commdt Field Artillery School, Fort Sill, Okla 1991–92; Dir La. Maneuvers Task Force, Office Chief of Staff US Army, Fort Monroe, Va 1992–94; Asst Chief of Staff Combined Forces Command and US Forces Korea 1994; Commdr 2nd Infantry Div., Korea 1995–97, Commdr 3rd US Army, Fort McPherson, Ga 1997–2000; promoted Gen., C-in-C US Cen. Command, MacDill Air Force Base, Fla 2000–03; lead American and Coalition troops in Operation Enduring Freedom in Afghanistan 2001 and Operation Iraqi Freedom in Iraq 2004; f. Franks & Assocs LLC 2003; mem. Bd of Dirs Nat. Park Foundation, Intrepid Fallen Heroes; spokesperson Salute America's Heroes Foundation, Southeastern Guide Dogs Org.; Defense Distinguished Service Medal, Distinguished Service Medal (with oak leaf cluster), Legion of Merit (with three oak leaf clusters), Bronze Star Medal (with 'V' device and three oak leaf clusters), Purple Heart (with two oak leaf clusters), Air Medal (with 'V' device), Presidential Medal of Freedom 2004; Hon. Co-Chair. Flight 93 Nat. Memorial 2005. *Publications:* American Soldier 2004. *Leisure interests:* country music, Mexican food, antiques, golf. *Address:* 4 Star Ranch, 15273 North 2280 Road, Roosevelt, OK 73564, USA (office). *Website:* www.tommyfranks.com.

FRANTZ, Justus; German pianist; b. 18 May 1944, Hohensalza; ed under Prof. Eliza Hansen in Hamburg, Wilhelm Kempf in Positano and Wilhalm Brückner-Rückeberg in Hamburg; prizewinner, Int. Music Competition, Munich 1967; since 1969 has appeared at all major European concert venues and toured USA, Far East and Japan; US debut with Leonard Bernstein and the New York Philharmonic Orchestra 1975; has made many tours and recordings in piano duo with Christoph Eschenbach and received Edison Int. Award for their recording of Schubert marches 1983; Co-Founder and Dir Schleswig-Holstein Music Festival; Prof. Hamburg Musikhochschule 1985–; Founder Schleswig-Holstein Music Festival 1986, Dir 1986–94; performed complete cycle of Mozart concertos in several European cities 1987–88; f. Chief Conductor Philharmonia of the Nations 1995; concert with Philharmonia of the Nations for Pope John Paul II 2001; fmr Special Amb. for UNHCR; Grosse Bundesverdienstkreuz 1989. *Recordings include:* works by Scarlatti, Beethoven, Mozart and concertos for two, three and four pianos by J.S. Bach. *Address:* Gemeinnützige PN Orchester Verwalfunk GmbH, Tempelhofer Ufer 11, 10963 Berlin, Germany (office). *Telephone:* (30) 6416-730 (office). *Fax:* (30) 6416-7320 (office).

FRANZ, Christoph, Dr rer. pol; German business executive; *Chairman of the Executive Board and CEO, Deutsche Lufthansa AG;* b. 2 May 1960, Frankfurt am Main; ed studies in Germany, France and USA, Darmstadt Tech. Univ.; joined Deutsche Lufthansa AG 1990, initially involved in strategy, sales and controlling projects in Germany, France and Turkey, later mem. staff team of then-CEO Jürgen Weber 1992–94, mem. Exec. Bd Deutsche Lufthansa AG and CEO Lufthansa German Airlines 2009–10, served as Deputy to Exec. Bd Chair. and CEO, Chair. Exec. Bd and CEO Deutsche Lufthansa AG 2011–, mem. Supervisory Bd Lufthansa Technik and Swiss International Air Lines; with Deutsche Bahn AG 1994, held various exec. functions 1994–2003, mem. Exec. Bd and CEO Passenger Transport Div. 2004; CEO Swiss International Air Lines (SWISS) 2004–09; mem. Admin. Bd Roche. *Address:* Lufthansa Group, Von-Gablenz-Strasse 2–6, 50679 Cologne, Germany (office). *Telephone:* (69) 6960 (office). *Fax:* (69) 6966818 (office). *Website:* www.lufthansa.com (office).

FRANZ, Judy R., BA, MS, PhD; American physicist and academic; *Executive Officer Emeritus, American Physical Society;* b. 3 May 1938, Chicago, Ill.; m. Frank A. Franz; one s.; ed Cornell Univ., Univ. of Ill.; Research Scientist, IBM Research Labs, Switzerland 1965–67; Asst Prof. of Physics, Ind. Univ., Bloomington 1968–74, Assoc. Prof. 1974–79, Prof. 1979–87, Assoc. Dean, Coll. of Arts and Sciences 1980–82; Prof. of Physics, Univ. of W Va 1987–94; Prof. of Physics, Univ. of Ala 1994–; Visiting Prof., Cornell Univ. 1985–86, 1988, 1990; Councillor-at-Large, American Physical Soc. 1984–88, Exec. Officer 1994–, now Emer.; Councillor-at-Large, Asscn for Women in Science (AWIS) 1981–83; mem. Editorial Bd, American Journal of Physics 1985–88; mem. Exec. Bd Council of Scientific Soc. Presidents 1990; Pres. American Asscn of Physics Teachers 1990; mem. Council, AAAS 1995–98; Assoc. Sec.-Gen., IUPAP 1999–2002, Sec.-Gen. 2002–08; mem. Governing Bd, Exec. Cttee of American Inst. of Physics; Rep. to US Nat. Cttee to UNESCO 2004–08; mem. Bd, ASTRA; Fellow, American Physical Soc., AAAS, AWIS; Humboldt Research Fellowship, Munich, Germany 1978–79; Distinguished Teaching Award, Ind. Univ. 1978, Alumni Honor Award for Distinguished Service, Coll. of Eng, Univ. of Illinois, Urbana-Champaign 1997, Melba Newell Phillips Medal, American Asscn of Physics Teachers 2008. *Publications:* Physics in the 20th Century (co-ed.) 1999; numerous contribs to Physics Review, Journal of Physics and other professional journals. *Leisure interests:* hiking, reading, concerts. *Address:* 1177 22nd Street NW, #5K, Washington, DC 20037, USA (office). *Telephone:* (202) 296-3736 (office). *E-mail:* franz@aps.org (office).

FRANZEN, Jonathan, BA; American writer; b. 17 Aug. 1959, Western Springs, IL; ed Swarthmore Coll., Free Univ. of Berlin, Germany; fmrly worked part-time in seismology lab., Harvard Univ. Dept of Earth and Planetary Sciences; currently full-time novelist, essayist, and journalist affiliated with The New Yorker; Hon. DHumLitt (Swarthmore Coll.) 2005; Whiting Award 1988, Guggenheim Fellowship, American Acad. Berlin Prize 2000, Granta Best Young American Novelist. *Publications include:* The Twenty-Seventh City (Whiting Award) 1988, Strong Motion 1991, The Corrections (Nat. Book Award for Fiction, New York Times Ed.'s Choice, James Tait Black Memorial Prize for Fiction 2003) 2001, How to be Alone (essays) 2002, The Discomfort Zone: A Personal History 2006, Spring Awakening (new trans. of Frank Wedekind play) 2007, Freedom (International Author of the Year, Specsavers Nat. Book Awards) 2010, Farther Away (essays) 2012. *Address:* Steven Barclay Agency, 12 Western Avenue, Petaluma, CA 94952, USA (office). *Telephone:* (707) 773-0654 (office). *Fax:* (707) 778-1868 (office). *Website:* www .barclayagency.com (office); www.jonathanfranzen.com.

FRASER, Lady Antonia, DBE, CBE, MA, FRSL; British writer; b. (Antonia Margaret Caroline Pakenham), 27 Aug. 1932, London, England; d. of the late 7th Earl and Countess of Longford; m. 1st Hugh Fraser 1956 (divorced 1977, died

1984); three s. three d.; m. 2nd Harold Pinter 1980 (died 2008); one step-s.; ed Dragon School, Oxford, St Mary's Convent, Ascot and Lady Margaret Hall, Oxford; mem. Cttee English PEN 1979–88 (Pres. 1988–89, Vice-Pres. 1990–), Crimewriters Asscn 1980–86, Writers in Prison Cttee, Chair. 1985–88, 1990; Hon. DLitt (Hull) 1986, (Sussex) 1990, (Nottingham) 1993, (St Andrew's) 1994; Prix Caumont-La Force 1985, Norton Medlicott Medal, Historical Asscn 2000. *TV plays:* Charades 1977, Mister Clay 1985. *Publications:* King Arthur 1954, Robin Hood 1955, Dolls 1963, History of Toys 1966, Mary, Queen of Scots (James Tait Black Memorial Prize 1969) 1969, Cromwell: Our Chief of Men 1973, King James VI of Scotland and I of England 1974, Scottish Love Poems, A Personal Anthology 1974, Kings and Queens of England (ed.) 1975, Love Letters (anthology) 1976, King Charles II 1979, Heroes and Heroines (ed.) 1980, Oxford In Verse (ed.) 1982, The Weaker Vessel (Wolfson History Prize 1984) 1984, Boadicea's Chariot: The Warrior Queens 1988, The Six Wives of Henry VIII 1992, Charles II: His Life and Times 1993, The Gunpowder Plot (St Louis Literary Award 1996, CWA Non Fiction Gold Dagger 1996) 1996, The Lives of the Kings and Queens of England 1998, Marie Antoinette: The Journey (Enid McLeod Literary Prize, Franco-British Soc. 2001) 2001, Love and Louis XIV 2006, Must You Go? My Life with Harold Pinter 2010; Jemima Shore novels: Quiet as a Nun (TV adaptation 1978) 1977, The Wild Island 1978, A Splash of Red 1981, Cool Repentance 1982, Oxford Blood 1985, Jemima Shore's First Case 1986, Your Royal Hostage 1987, The Cavalier Case 1990, Jemima Shore at the Sunny Grave 1991, Political Death: A Jemima Shore Mystery 1994; anthologies (ed.): Scottish Love Poems 1975, Love Letters 1976; ed. The Pleasure of Reading 1992. *Leisure interests:* cats, grandchildren. *Address:* c/o Curtis Brown Group Ltd, Haymarket House, 28–29 Haymarket, London, SW1Y 4SP, England (office). *Telephone:* (20) 7396-6600 (office). *Fax:* (20) 7396-0110 (office).

FRASER, Bernard (Bernie) William, BA; Australian economist, bank governor and business executive; *Chairman, Members Equity Bank;* b. 26 Feb. 1941, Junee, NSW; s. of K. Fraser; m. Edna Gallogly 1965 (divorced); one s. two d.; ed Junee High School, NSW, Univ. of New England, Armidale, NSW, Australian Nat. Univ., ACT; joined Dept of Nat. Devt 1961; joined Dept of Treasury 1963, Treasury Rep., London, UK 1969–72, First Asst Sec. 1979, Sec. Dept 1984–89; with Dept of Finance 1976; mem. Bd of Dirs Nat. Energy Office 1981–83, Queensland Treasury Corpn; Chair. and Gov. Reserve Bank of Australia 1989–96; Chair. Govt Superannuation Office of Victoria, Members Equity; Trustee and Dir Construction and Bldg Unions Superannuation Trust (C+BUS) 1996–, Superannuation Trust of Australia 1996–, Australian Retirement Fund 1996–; currently Chair. Members Equity Bank (ME Bank). *Leisure interest:* farming. *Address:* Members Equity Bank, Level 16, 360 Collins Street, Melbourne, Vic. 3000 (office); Superannuation Trust of Australia (STA), Level 28, 2 Lonsdale Street, Melbourne, Vic. 3000; Construction and Building Unions Superannuation Trust, Level 12, 313 La Trobe Street, Melbourne, Vic. 3000, Australia. *Telephone:* (3) 9605-6000 (office). *Fax:* (3) 9605-6999 (office). *Website:* www.membersequitybank.com.au (office).

FRASER, Brendan; American actor; b. 3 Dec. 1968, Indianapolis; m. Afton Smith; two s.; ed Cornish Inst., Seattle. *Films include:* My Old School (TV) 1991, Dogfight 1991, Child of Darkness, Child of Light (TV) 1991, Guilty Until Proven Innocent (TV) 1991, Encino Man 1992, School Ties 1992, Twenty Bucks 1993, Younger and Younger 1993, With Honors 1994, Airheads 1994, The Scout 1994, The Passion of Darkly Noon 1995, Mrs Winterbourne 1996, Glory Daze 1996, George of the Jungle 1997, The Twilight of the Golds (TV) 1997, Still Breathing 1997, Gods and Monsters 1998, Blast from the Past 1999, The Mummy 1999, Dudley Do-Right 1999, Sinbad: Beyond the Veil of Mists (voice) 2000, Bedazzled 2000, Monkeybone 2001, The Mummy Returns 2001, The Quiet American 2002, Revenge of the Mummy: The Ride 2004, Crash 2004, Beach Bunny (voice) 2005, Journey to the End of the Night 2006, The Last Time 2006, The Air I Breathe 2007, Journey to the Center of the Earth 2007, The Mummy: Tomb of the Dragon Emperor 2008, Inkheart 2008. *Address:* c/o William Morris Agency Inc., 1 William Morris Place, Beverly Hills, CA 90212, USA (office). *Telephone:* (310) 859-4000 (office). *Fax:* (310) 859-4462 (office). *Website:* www.brendanfraser.com (office).

FRASER, Dawn, AO, MBE, JP; Australian fmr swimmer; b. 4 Sept. 1937, Balmain, near Sydney; d. of the late Kenneth Fraser and Rose Miranda Fraser; m. Gary Ware (divorced); one d.; first female swimmer to win gold medals in three consecutive Olympic Games 1956, 1960, 1964; broke women's 100m freestyle world record nine times 1956–64; first female to break 60 seconds in 100m freestyle; shares record for most Olympic medals won by a woman swimmer (four gold, four silver); set 39 world records; banned for 10 years after Tokyo Games for allegedly stealing an Olympic Flag from Japanese Imperial Hotel, forcing retirement; became involved in coaching, business ventures, politics; mem. NSW Parl. for Balmain 1988–91; attaché to Australian Olympic Team 2000; mem. Int. Swimming Hall of Fame Selection Cttee; dedicates most of her time to her sponsors; also guest speaking for a wide range of causes; Dir DF Prom., NRMA M&S, Wests Tigers NRL Football Club; Australian of the Year 1965, Int. Swimming Hall of Fame 1965, Olympic Order Award 1981, honoured as one of the greatest Olympians of all time at Atlanta Olympics 1996, named Nat. Living Treasure by Australian Govt, voted Athlete of the Century 1999. *Publication:* Below the Surface: Australian Title Gold Medal Girl (autobiog., with Harry Gordon) 1965, Dawn: One Hell of a Life (autobiog.) 2001. *Leisure interests:* spending time with grandson, jet skiing, cycling, walking the dogs. *Address:* PO Box 118, Balmain, NSW 2041, Australia (office). *Telephone:* (417) 900040 (office). *E-mail:* info@dawnfraser.com.au (office). *Website:* www.dawnfraser.com (office).

FRASER, Hon. John Allen, PC, OC, OBC, CD, QC; Canadian organization official and fmr politician; b. 15 Dec. 1931, Yokohama, Japan; m. Catherine Findlay; three d.; ed Univ. of BC; law practice, Vic., Powell River, Vancouver 1955–72; mem. House of Commons 1972–94; Minister of the Environment and Postmaster Gen. 1979–80; Minister of Fisheries and Oceans 1984–85 (resgnd), Speaker of the House of Commons 1986–94; Amb. for the Environment 1994–98; Chair. Pacific Fisheries Resource Conservation Council 1998–2005, now mem. Council; Chair. Nat. Defence Minister's Monitoring Cttee on Change 1996–2003; Chair. Parliamentary Precinct Oversight Advisory Cttee; Chair. BC Pacific Salmon Forum 2004–09; Hon. LLD (St Lawrence Univ.) 1999, (Simon Fraser Univ.) 1999, (Univ. of BC) 2004; Hon. Lt-Col Seaforth Highlanders of Canada 1994–, now Hon. Col.

FRASER, Rt Hon. (John) Malcolm, AC, CH, PC, MA; Australian politician; *Honorary Chairman, InterAction Council of Former Heads of Government;* b. 21 May 1930, Melbourne; s. of the late J. Neville Fraser and of Una Fraser; m. Tamara Beggs 1956; two s. two d.; ed Melbourne Grammar School and Oxford Univ.; MP for Wannon 1955–83; mem. Jt Parl. Cttee of Foreign Affairs 1962–66; Chair. Govt Mems' Defence Cttee; Sec. Wool Cttee; mem. Council of ANU, Canberra 1964–66; Minister for the Army 1966–68, for Educ. and Science 1968–69, for Defence 1969–71, for Educ. and Science 1971–72; Parl. Leader of Liberal Party 1975–83; Prime Minister 1975–83; Co-Chair. Commonwealth Eminent Persons Group 1985–86; Sr Adjunct Fellow, Center for Strategic and Int. Studies 1983; Fellow for Int. Council of Assocs at Claremont Univ. 1985; Chair. UN Cttee on African Commodity Problems 1989–90; mem. InterAction Council for Fmr Heads of Govt 1983– (Co-Chair. 1997–2006, Hon. Chair. 2006–), ANZ Int. Bd of Advice 1987–93; Chair. CARE Australia 1987–2001; Pres. CARE Int. 1990–95, Vice-Pres. 1995–99; Bd mem. Int. Crisis Group 1995–2000; Co-founder Australians All 2006; Hon. Fellow, Magdalen Coll., Oxford 1982; Hon. Vice-Pres. Oxford Soc. 1983, Hon. Professorial Fellow, Asia Pacific Centre for Mil. Law, Univ. of Melbourne 2007; Grand Cordon of the Order of the Rising Sun (Japan); Hon. LLD (S Carolina) 1981, (Univ. of NSW) 2002, (Univ. of Tech., Sydney), (Murdoch Univ., Perth), Hon. DLitt (Deakin Univ.) 1989; B'nai B'rith Gold Medal 1980, Australian Human Rights Medal 2000. *Publications:* Common Ground: Issues That Should Bind and Not Divide Us 2002. *Leisure interests:* fishing, photography, vintage cars, motorcycles, golf. *Address:* Level 32, 101 Collins Street, Melbourne, Vic. 3000, Australia (home). *Telephone:* (3) 9654-1822 (office). *Fax:* (3) 9654-1301 (office). *E-mail:* Malcolm .Fraser@aph.gov.au (office). *Website:* australiansall.com.au (office).

FRASER, Sir William Kerr, Kt, GCB, MA, LLD, FRSE; British civil servant and administrator; b. 18 March 1929, Glasgow, Scotland; s. of Alexander M. Fraser and Rachel Fraser; m. Marion Anne Forbes (Lady Marion Fraser) 1956; three s. one d.; ed Eastwood School, Clarkston and Univ. of Glasgow; Flying Officer, RAF 1952–55; joined Scottish Office, Edinburgh 1955, Perm. Under-Sec. of State 1978–88; Prin. and Vice-Chancellor, Univ. of Glasgow 1988–95, Chancellor 1996–2006; Chair., Royal Comm. on the Ancient and Historical Monuments of Scotland 1995–2000, Scottish Mutual Assurance PLC 1999; Hon. FRCP (Glas.) 1992, Hon. FRSAMD 1995; Hon. LLD (Glasgow) 1982, (Strathclyde) 1991, (Aberdeen) 1993, Dr hc (Edinburgh) 1995. *Leisure interests:* reading, meditating on democracy. *Address:* Broadwood, Edinburgh Road, Gifford, East Lothian, EH41 4JE, Scotland (home). *Telephone:* (1620) 810319 (home). *Fax:* (1620) 810319 (home). *E-mail:* wkfraser@tiscali.co.uk (home).

FRASER-PRYCE, Shelly-Ann, OD; Jamaican athlete; b. 27 Dec. 1986, Kingston; m. Jason Pryce 2011; ed Wolmer's High School For Girls, Univ. of Tech.; first Jamaican woman in history to win an Olympic gold medal, 100m, Beijing Olympics 2008 (personal best time of 10.78 seconds); gold medal, 100m, World Athletics Final, Stuttgart 2008, silver medal, Thessaloniki 2009; gold medal, 100m, 4×100m. relay, World Championships, Berlin 2009, silver medal, 4×100m. relay, World Championships, Daegu 2011, gold medal, 100m, 200m., 4×100m. relay, World Championships, Moscow 2013; gold medal, 100m, silver medal, 200m., 4×100m. relay, London Olympics 2012; coached by Stephen Francis; first UNICEF Nat. Goodwill Amb. for Jamaica 2010, Grace Goodwill Amb. for Peace 2010, Golden Cleats Award for Female Athlete of the Year 2010, 2013, Female Athlete of the Year 2013. *Address:* Jamaica Athletics Administrative Association Limited, PO Box 272, Kingston 5, Jamaica. *Telephone:* 978-7102. *Fax:* 946-0003. *E-mail:* athleticsja@cwjamaica.com.

FRASYNIUK, Władysław; Polish politician and trade union official; b. 25 Nov. 1954, Wrocław; s. of Stanisław Frasyniuk and Zofia Frasyniuk; m. 1978; one s. three d.; driver, mechanic Municipal Transport, Wrocław, organizer of strike in bus depot, Wrocław Aug. 1980; press spokesman Founding Cttee of Ind. Self-Governing Trade Union; Chair. Solidarity Trade Union, Lower Silesia 1981–90 (resgnd); mem. Nat. Consultative Comm. of Solidarity; active underground under martial law, Jt Founder Provisional Exec. Cttee of Solidarity; arrested 1982, amnestied 1984; arrested again Feb. 1985, sentenced to over 4 years, amnestied 1986; mem. Provisional National Council of Solidarity 1986–87, Nat. Exec. Comm. of Solidarity 1987–90; mem. Citizens' Cttee of Solidarity, Chair. 1988–90; took part in Round Table talks, Comm. for Trade Union Pluralism Feb.–April 1989; one of founders and leaders of Citizens' Movt for Democratic Action (ROAD) 1990–91; mem. Social-Liberal faction of Democratic Union 1991–94; Vice-Chair. Democratic Union 1991–94; mem. Freedom Union (now Democratic Party (Partia Demokratyczna), Chair. 2005–06; Deputy to Sejm (Parl.) 1991–2001. *Leisure interests:* dogs, individual sports, history of Russia. *Address:* c/o Democratic Party (Partia Demokratyczna), 00-581 Warsaw, ul. Marszałkowska 2/4, Poland.

FRATTINI, Franco, LLB; Italian lawyer and politician; b. 14 March 1957, Rome; s. of Alberto Frattini and Lea Frattini; ed La Sapienza Univ., Rome; State Attorney 1981, Attorney, State Attorney-Gen.'s Office 1984; Magistrate, Regional Admin. Tribunal, Piedmont 1984–86, Council of State Judge 1986–; Legal Adviser to Minister of the Treasury 1986, to Deputy Prime Minister 1990–91, to Prime Minister 1992; Deputy Sec.-Gen. Office of Prime Minister 1993, Sec.-Gen. 1994; Minister for Civil Service and Regional Affairs 1995–96; mem. Camera dei Deputati (Parl.) (Forza Italia) 1995–96, 2001–04; Pres. Parl. Cttee for Intelligence and Security Services and State Secrets 1996–2004; Minister for Civil Service and for Coordination of Intelligence and Security Services 2001–02, for Foreign Affairs 2002–04, 2008–11; Vice-Pres. European Comm., Commr for Justice, Freedom and Security 2004–08; City Councillor, Rome 1997–2000; mem. Exec. Cttee Forza Italia 1998–. *Publications include:* numerous specialist articles on law and public works. *Address:* c/o Ministry of Foreign Affairs, Piazzale della Farnesina 1, 00194 Rome, Italy (office).

FRAYLING, Sir Christopher John, Kt, MA, PhD; British historian, arts administrator, broadcaster and academic; *Professor Emeritus, Royal College of Art;* b. 26 Dec. 1946; m. Helen Anne Snowdon; ed Repton School, Churchill Coll., Cambridge; Lecturer, Univ. of Bath, Univ. of Exeter during 1970s; Prof. of Cultural History, RCA 1979–2009, Prof. Emer. 2009–, f. Dept of Cultural History, Rector 1996–2009; mem. Arts Council England 1987–2000, Chair. 2004–09; Chair. Design Council, Crafts Study Centre, Royal Mint Advisory Cttee; fmr Gov. BFI; mem. Arts & Humanities Research Bd; Trustee, Victoria & Albert Museum; Hon. FRSA 2004, Hon. FRIBA 2005; several hon. doctorates, including Dr hc (Sheffield

Hallam) 2010. *Television includes:* The Art of Persuasion (New York Film and Television Festival Gold Medal), The Face of Tutankhamun, Strange Landscape, Nightmare: The Birth of Horror 1996. *Radio includes:* The Rime of the Bounty (Sony Radio Award, Soc. of Authors Award). *Publications include:* Napoleon Wrote Fiction 1973, The Vampyre 1976, Spaghetti Westerns 1980, The Face of Tutankhamun 1992, Clint Eastwood: A Critical Biography 1993, Strange Landscape: A Journey through the Middle Ages 1995, Nightmare: The Birth of Horror 1996, Sergio Leone: Something to Do with Death 2000, Ken Adam: The Art of Production Design 2005, Mad, Bad and Dangerous? The Scientist and Cinema 2006. *Address:* Royal College of Art, 15-25 Howie Street, London, SW11 4AS, England (office). *Website:* www.rca.ac.uk (office).

FRAYN, Michael, BA, FRSL; British playwright and author; b. 8 Sept. 1933, London, England; s. of the late Thomas A. Frayn and Violet A. Lawson; m. 1st Gillian Palmer 1960 (divorced 1989); three d.; m. 2nd Claire Tomalin (q.v.) 1993; ed Kingston Grammar School and Emmanuel Coll., Cambridge; reporter, The Guardian 1957–59, columnist 1959–62; columnist, The Observer 1962–68; Cameron Mackintosh Prof. of Contemporary Theatre, Univ. of Oxford 2009–10; Hon. Fellow, Emmanuel Coll., Cambridge; Order of Merit (Germany) 2004; Hon. DLitt (Cambridge) 2001; Heywood Hill Literary Prize 2002, Golden PEN Award 2003, Saint Louis Literary Award 2006, McGovern Award 2006, Companion of Literature 2007, Writers' Guild Lifetime Achievement Award 2010. *Stage plays:* The Two of Us 1970, The Sandboy 1971, Alphabetical Order (Evening Standard Best Comedy of the Year 1975) 1975, Donkeys' Years (Laurence Olivier Award for Best Comedy 1976, Society of West End Theatre Comedy of the Year 1976) 1976, Clouds 1976, Balmoral 1978, Liberty Hall (new version of Balmoral) 1980, Make and Break 1980 (Evening Standard Best Comedy of the Year 1980), Noises Off (Evening Standard Best Comedy of the Year 1982, Laurence Olivier Award for Best Comedy 1982, Society of West End Theatre Comedy of the Year 1982) 1982, Benefactors (Laurence Olivier/BBC Award for Best New Play 1984) 1984, Look Look 1990, Here 1993, Now You Know 1995, Copenhagen (Evening Standard Award for Best Play of the Year 1998, West End Critics' Circle Best New Play Award 1998, Prix Molière Best New Play 1999, Tony Award for Best Play 2000) 1998, Alarms and Excursions 1998, Democracy (Evening Standard Theatre Award for Best Play, Critics' Circle Award for Best Play 2003) 2003, Afterlife 2007. *TV includes:* plays: Jamie, on a Flying Visit (BBC) 1968, Birthday (BBC) 1969; documentary series: Second City Reports (with John Bird, Granada) 1964, Beyond a Joke (with John Bird and Eleanor Bron) 1972, Making Faces 1975; documentaries: One Pair of Eyes 1968, Laurence Sterne Lived Here 1973, Imagine a City Called Berlin 1975, Vienna: The Mask of Gold 1977, Three Streets in the Country 1979, The Long Straight (Great Railway Journeys of the World) 1980, Jerusalem 1984, Magic Lantern, Prague 1993, Budapest: Written in Water 1996 (all BBC documentaries); films: First and Last 1989, A Landing on the Sun 1994. *Cinema:* Clockwise 1986, Remember Me? 1997. *Plays translated include:* The Cherry Orchard, Three Sisters, The Seagull, Uncle Vanya, Wild Honey, The Sneeze (Chekhov), The Fruits of Enlightenment (Tolstoy), Exchange (Trifonov), Number One (Anouilh). *Publications:* novels: The Tin Men (Somerset Maugham Award 1966) 1965, The Russian Interpreter (Hawthornden Prize 1967) 1966, Towards the End of the Morning 1967, A Very Private Life 1968, Sweet Dreams 1973, The Trick of It 1989, A Landing on the Sun (Sunday Express Book of the Year) 1991, Now You Know 1992, Headlong 1999, Spies (Whitbread Award for Best Novel) 2002, Skios 2012; non-fiction: Constructions (philosophy) 1974, Speak after the Beep 1995, Celia's Secret (with David Burke) 2000, The Human Touch: Our Part in the Creation of the Universe 2006, Stage Directions: Writing on Theatre 1970–2008 2008; Travels with a Typewriter 2009, My Father's Fortune: A Life 2010, Skios 2012; several vols of collections of columns, plays and trans. *Address:* c/o Greene & Heaton Ltd, 37A Goldhawk Road, London, W12 8QQ, England (office).

FRAZIER, Charles, PhD; American writer; b. 4 Nov. 1950, Asheville, NC; m. Catherine Frazier; one d.; ed Univ. of North Carolina, Appalachian State Univ., Univ. of South Carolina; fmr faculty mem., Univ. of Colo and North Carolina State Univ. *Publications:* Adventuring in the Andes: The Sierra Club Travel Guide to Ecuador, Peru, Bolivia, the Amazon Basin, and the Galapagos Islands (with Donald Secreast) 1985, Cold Mountain: Odyssey in North Carolina (novel, Nat. Book Award) 1997, Thirteen Moons (novel) 2006, Nightwoods 2012. *Address:* c/o Amanda Urban, International Creative Management, 825 Eighth Avenue, New York, NY 10019, USA (office). *Telephone:* (212) 556-5600 (office). *Website:* www .icmtalent.com (office).

FRAZIER, Kenneth C., BA, JD; American lawyer and business executive; *Chairman, President and CEO, Merck & Company, Inc.;* ed Pennsylvania State Univ., Harvard Law School; Pnr, Drinker Biddle & Reath (law firm), Philadelphia –1992; Vice-Pres., Gen. Counsel and Sec., Astra Merck Group 1992–94, Vice-Pres. of Public Affairs 1994–99, Asst Gen. Counsel, Corp. Staff 1997–99, Vice-Pres. and Deputy Gen. Counsel, Merck & Co., Inc. Jan.–Dec. 1999, Sr Vice-Pres. and Gen. Counsel 1999–2006, Exec. Vice-Pres. and Gen. Counsel 2006–07, Exec. Vice-Pres. and Pres. Global Human Health 2007–10, Pres. Merck & Co., Inc. 2010–, CEO Jan. 2011–, Chair. Dec. 2011–; mem. Bd of Dirs Exxon Mobil Corpn, Pennsylvania State Univ., Cornerstone Christian Acad., Philadelphia, Pa; mem. Council on Foreign Relations, Council of the American Law Inst., ABA. *Address:* Merck & Co. Inc., 1 Merck Drive, PO Box 100, Whitehouse Station, NJ 08889-0100, USA (office). *Telephone:* (908) 423-1000 (office). *Fax:* (908) 735-1253 (office). *E-mail:* info@merck .com (office). *Website:* www.merck.com (office).

FRCKOVSKY, Ljubomir; Macedonian lawyer, academic and fmr politician; *Professor of International Law and Theory of International Relations, SS Cyril and Methodius Skopje University;* b. 2 Dec. 1957; ed Skopje Univ., Ljubljana Univ.; Prof. of Int. Law and Theory of Int. Relations, SS Cyril and Methodius Skopje Univ. 1984–; co-author of new Constitution of Repub. of Macedonia 1991; Minister without Portfolio 1990–92; Minister of Interior 1992–96, of Foreign Affairs 1996–97; Exec. Dir Foundation for strategic analyses Kiro Gligorov 2000–01; adviser to Pres. Boris Trajkovski 2000–04; unsuccessful cand. (Social Democratic Alliance of Macedonia) in 2009 presidential election; Fellow, Schloss Leopoldskron, Salzburg, 21st Century Trust, London; mem. Inst. Francais des Relations Int., Paris, Int. Law Asscn Skopje, Forum for Human Rights Macedonia. *Address:* Slavejko Arsov, 38, 1000 Skopje; Faculty of Law, SS Cyril and Methodius University of Skopje, Bul. Krste Misirkov bb, 1000 Skopje, Macedonia (office).

Telephone: (91) 116323 (office). *E-mail:* frckoski@pf.ukim.edu.mk (office); frckoski@unet.com.mk. *Website:* www.pf.ukim.edu.mk (office).

FREARS, Stephen Arthur; British film director; b. 20 June 1941, Leicester; s. of Dr Russell E. Frears and Ruth M. Frears; m. Mary K. Wilmers 1968 (divorced 1974); two s.; pnr, Anne Rothenstein; one s. one d.; ed Gresham's School, Holt, Trinity Coll., Cambridge; Asst Dir Morgan, a Suitable Case for Treatment 1966, Charlie Bubbles 1967, If... 1968; worked in TV for 13 years, including several TV films and plays in collaboration with Alan Bennett; Chair. jury Cannes Film Festival 2007; Commdr, Ordre des Arts et des Lettres 2009; Hon. LittD (East Anglia, Norwich); Santa Fe Film Festival Lifetime Achievement Award 2003. *Films include:* Gumshoe 1971, Bloody Kids 1980, Going Gently 1981, Walter 1982, Saigon 1983, The Hit 1984, My Beautiful Laundrette 1985, Prick Up Your Ears 1986, Sammy and Rosie Get Laid 1987, Dangerous Liaisons 1989, The Grifters 1990, Hero 1992, The Snapper 1992, Mary Reilly 1996, The Van 1996, The Hi-Lo Country 1999, High Fidelity 2000, Liam 2000, Dirty Pretty Things (British Ind. Film Awards Best British Film, Best Dir, Best Screenplay) 2002, Mrs Henderson Presents 2005, The Queen (Best Film and co-winner Best Dir, Toronto Film Critics Asscn 2006, Goya Award for Best European Film 2007, Evening Standard Alexander Walker Special Award 2007, Attenborough Award for British Film of the Year 2007, Best British Dir, London Film Critics' Circle Awards 2007, BAFTA Award for Best Film 2007) 2006, Cheri 2009, Tamara Drewe 2010, Lay the Favourite 2011, Mohammed Ali's Greatest Fight 2012. *Television includes:* Fail Safe 2000, The Deal 2003. *Address:* c/o Casarotto Co. Ltd, National House, 60–66 Wardour Street, London, W1V 4ND, England. *Telephone:* (20) 7287-4450. *Fax:* (20) 7287-9128.

FRÉCHET, Jean M. J., BS, MS, PhD, PhD; French chemist and academic; *Professor Emeritus of Chemistry and of Chemical Engineering and Henry Rapoport Chair Emeritus of Organic Chemistry, University of California, Berkeley;* b. 19 Aug. 1944, Burgundy; ed Institut de Chimie et Physique Industrielles, Lyon, Coll. of Environmental Sciences and Forestry, State Univ. of NY and Syracuse Univ., USA; Asst/Assoc. Prof. of Chem., Univ. of Ottawa, Canada 1973–82, Prof. of Chem. 1982–87, Vice-Dean, School of Grad. Studies and Research 1983–87; Visiting Scientist, IBM Research Lab., San Jose, Calif. 1979, 1983; IBM Prof. of Chem., Cornell Univ., Ithaca, NY 1987–95, Peter J. Debye Chair of Chem. 1995–98; Faculty Sr Scientist, E.O. Lawrence Berkeley Nat. Lab., Berkeley, Calif. 2000–11, Scientific Dir The Molecular Foundry 2004–11; Prof. of Chem., Univ. of California, Berkeley 1996–2011, Prof. Emer. 2011–, Prof. of Chemical Eng 2003–11, Prof. Emer. 2011–, Henry Rapoport Chair of Organic Chem. 2003–11, Emer. 2011–; Vice-Pres. Research, King Abdullah Univ. of Science and Tech. (KAUST), Saudi Arabia 2010–; mem. NAS 2000–, Nat. Acad. of Eng 2000–, Academia Europaea 2009–; Fellow, ACS 2010, American Acad. of Art and Sciences 2000, AAAS 2000, PMSE Div. of ACS 2000; Hon. DSc (Université de Lyon I) 2002, (Univ. of Liverpool, UK) 2008; Hon. DUniv (Univ. of Ottawa) 2002; IUPAC Canadian Nat. Cttee Award 1983, Lecture Award, Polymer Soc. of Japan 1986, ACS Doolittle Award in Polymer Materials Science and Eng 1986, ACS Cooperative Research Award in Polymer Science 1994, ACS Award in Applied Polymer Science 1996, Kosar Memorial Award, Soc. of Imaging Science and Tech. 1999, ACS Award in Polymer Chem. 2000, ACS Cope Scholar Award 2001, ACS Salute to Excellence Award 2001, Chemical Communications 40th Anniversary Award 2005, Esselen Award for Chem. in the Service of the Public 2005, Macro Group UK Medal (jt RSC and Soc. of Chemical Industry award for outstanding achievement in the field of Macromolecular Chem.) 2006, ACS Arthur C. Cope Award for Outstanding Achievement in the Field of Organic Chem. 2007, Dickson Prize in Science, Carnegie Mellon Univ. 2007, Inst. of Industrial Science Medal (Japan) 2007, Arun Guthikonda Memorial Award, Columbia Univ. 2009, Carothers Award for "Outstanding contributions and advances in industrial applications of chemistry" 2009, ACS Herman Mark Award 2009, Remsen Award, Maryland Section of the ACS 2009, Nagoya Gold Medal 2009, Int. Award for the "Development of functional polymers from fundamentals to applications", Soc. of Polymer Science of Japan 2010, Erasmus Medal, Academia Europaea 2010, Grand Prix de la Maison de la Chimie, Paris 2010, Japan Prize 2013. *Achievements include:* with Donald A. Tomalia and Fritz Vögtle, invented and developed dendritic polymers. *Publications:* more than 900 publs and patents. *Address:* 718 Latimer Hall, Department of Chemistry, University of California, Berkeley, Berkeley, CA 94720-1460, USA (office). *Telephone:* (510) 643-3077 (office). *Fax:* (510) 643-3079 (office). *E-mail:* frechet@cchem.berkeley.edu (office); frechet@berkeley.edu (office). *Website:* chem.berkeley.edu/faculty/emeriti/frechet (office); www.kaust.edu.sa/academics/faculty/frechet.html (office); frechet.cchem.berkeley.edu (office).

FREDA, Fabrizio, BA, MBA; Italian/American business executive; *President and CEO, The Estée Lauder Companies Inc.;* m.; two c.; ed Univ. of Naples; directed marketing and strategic planning for Gucci SpA 1986–88; worked for Procter & Gamble 1988–2008, responsible for various operating, marketing and strategic efforts, including as Pres. Global Snacks; mem. Bd of Dirs, Pres. and COO, The Estée Lauder Companies Inc. 2008–09, Pres. and CEO 2009–. *Address:* The Estée Lauder Companies Inc., 767 Fifth Avenue, New York, NY 10153-0023, USA (office). *Telephone:* (212) 572-4200 (office). *Fax:* (212) 572-6633 (office). *Website:* www.elcompanies.com (office).

FREDERIK ANDRÉ HENRIK CHRISTIAN, HRH Crown Prince, MSc; b. 26 May 1968, Copenhagen; s. of HM Queen Margrethe II and HRH Prince Consort Henrik of Denmark; m. HRH Crown Princess Mary Elizabeth (née Donaldson) 2004; one s. one d.; ed Krebs' Skole, École des Roches, France, Øregaard Gymnasium, Univ. of Aarhus and Harvard Univ., USA; heir to the throne of Denmark; began mil. service with the Royal Life Guard 1986, apptd Lt Reserve Army 1988, Reconnaissance Platoon Commdr Royal Guard Hussars' Regt 1988, First Lt Reserve Army 1989, completed training with the Royal Danish Navy Frogman Corps 1995, First Lt Reserve Navy 1995, Capt., Reserve Army 1997, Lt Commdr, Reserve Navy 1997, Royal Danish Air Force Flying School 2000, Capt., Reserve Air Force 2000, Command and General Staff Course Royal Danish Defence Coll. 2001–02, Maj., Reserve Army and Air Force 2002, Commdr, Reserve Navy 2002, Staff Officer, Defence Command Denmark 2002–03, Sr Lecturer, Inst. of Strategy, Royal Danish Defence Coll. 2003–, Commdr Sr Grade in the Navy, Lt-Col in the Army and Air Force 2004–; served at the Danish UN Mission, New York

1994, First Sec. Embassy in Paris 1998–99; participated in expedition to Mongolia 1986, Expedition Sirius 2000 to Greenland 2000; Pres. The Royal Danish Geographical Soc.; patronages include Danish Red Cross, Deaf Asscn, Royal Acad. of Music, Aarhus, Save the Children Fund, Asscn of Fine Arts, Comm. for Scientific Research in Greenland, Dyslexia Org., Foreign Policy Soc., Georg Jensen Prize, Greenlandic Soc.; mem. Int. Sailing Fed. Events Cttee, Young Global Leaders; hon. memberships include Asscn of Cavalry Officers, Mongolian Soc., Naval Asscn, Ancient Guild of Christian IV, Aalborg, Guards' Asscn, Copenhagen, Royal Danish Yacht Club, Sailors' Soc. of 1856; Knight of the Order of the Elephant, Grand Commdr of the Order of Dannebrog, Silver Cross of the Order of Dannebrog, Commemorative Medal 50th Anniversary of HM Queen Ingrid's arrival in Denmark, Badge of Honour, Officers of the Reserve, Commemorative Medal of HM Queen Margrethe II and HRH Prince Consort Henrik's Silver Wedding, Silver Jubilee Medal of HM Queen Margrethe II, Danish Mil. Athletic Asscn Medal, King Frederik IX Centenary Medal, Royal Medal of Recompense with Crown, Commemorative Medal of Queen Ingrid, Greenland Home Rule Medal, Grand Cross of the Order of Honourable Service, Italy, Adolph of Nassau Civilian and Mil. Service Order, Grand Cross, Luxembourg, Orders of Ojaswi Rajanya, Grand Cross, Nepal, Seraphim, Sweden, Saint Olav Grand Cross, Norway, White Roses Grand Cross, Finland, Terra Mariana Grand Cross, Estonia, Three Stars Grand Cross, Latvia, Leopold Grand Cross, Belgium, Icelandic Falcon Grand Cross, Iceland, Jordanian Renaissance Grand Cross, Jordan, Chrysanthemum, Japan, Southern Cross, Brazil, Rio Branco Grand Cross, Brazil, Chula Chom Klao Grand Cross, Thailand, Stara Planina First Class, Bulgaria, Order of Service for the FRG, Grand Cross, Order of the Star of Romania, Grand Cross. *Address:* Court of TRH The Crown Prince and Crown Princess of Denmark, Christian VIII Palace, Amalienborg Slotsplads 7, 1257 Copenhagen K; POB 2143, 1015 Copenhagen K, Denmark. *Telephone:* 33-40-10-10. *Fax:* 33-40-11-15. *Website:* www.crownprincecouple.dk.

FREDERIKSEN, Claus Hjort, LLM; Danish politician; b. 4 Sept. 1947, Copenhagen; s. of Niels Frederiksen and Elna Frederiksen (née Hjort); ed Univ. of Copenhagen; Head of Div., Ministry of Food, Agric. and Fisheries 1977–79; Sec.-Gen. Asscn of Industrial Employers 1979–83; Admin Man., Liberal Party 1983–85, Sec.-Gen. 1985–2001; Minister for Employment 2001–09, of Finance 2009–11; mem. Folketing (Parl.) for Copenhagen Co. 2005–07, for North Zealand 2007–; mem. Parl. 2005–. *Address:* Gl Strandvej 40, 3050 Humlebaek, Denmark (office). *Telephone:* 33-37-45-67 (office); 33-37-45-80 (office). *E-mail:* claus.hjort .frederiksen@ft.dk (office); venstre@venstre.dk (office). *Website:* claushjort.venstre .dk; www.venstre.dk (office).

FREDRIKSEN, John; Cypriot (b. Norwegian) shipping industry executive; *Chairman, President and CEO, Frontline Ltd;* b. 1944, Oslo, Norway; m.; two c.; began as trainee in shipbrokering co.; owner of tanker fleet with more than 70 oil tankers, and major interests in oil rigs and fish farming; f. investment cos Hemen Holdings Ltd and Meisha; Chair. and CEO Old Frontline –1997, mem. Bd of Dirs, Chair., Pres. and CEO Frontline Ltd 1997–; Chair. Seadrill Ltd 2005–; mem. Bd of Dirs Seatankers Man. Co. Ltd, Golar LNG Ltd. *Leisure interest:* collecting classic Norwegian art. *Address:* Frontline Management AS, Bryggegata 3, PO Box 1327-VIKA, 0112 Oslo, Norway (office). *Telephone:* 23-11-40-00 (office). *Fax:* 23-11-40-40 (office). *E-mail:* Frontline@front.bm (office). *Website:* www.frontline.bm (office).

FREED, Karl Frederick, BS, AM, PhD; American chemist and academic; *Henry G. Gale Distinguished Service Professor Emeritus, James Franck Institute and Department of Chemistry, University of Chicago;* b. 25 Sept. 1942, Brooklyn, NY; m. Gina Freed; two d.; ed Columbia Univ., Harvard Univ.; Asst Prof., James Franck Inst., Univ. of Chicago 1968–73, Assoc. Prof. 1973–76, Prof. 1976–, Henry G. Gale Distinguished Service Prof. 2006–12, Prof. Emer. 2012–, Dir 1983–86; Visiting Scientist, Centre Nucléaires, Strasbourg, France 1977, Inst. of Physical and Chemical Research, Saitama, Japan 1979; Visiting Prof., Univ. of Minn. 1984, Univ. of Strasbourg 1991; Visiting Scientist, IBM Research Labs 1993; Chair. Gordon Conf. on Polymer Physics 1996; mem. Editorial Bd Journal of Statistical Physics 1976–78, Chemical Physics 1979–82, Journal of Chemical Physics 1982–85, Advances in Chemical Physics 1984–, International Journal of Quantum Chemistry 1995; Fellow, Alfred P. Sloan Foundation 1969–71, John S. Guggenheim Foundation 1972–73, American Physical Soc. 1983–, American Acad. of Arts and Sciences 2007–; Chemical Soc. Marlow Medal 1973, Award in Pure Chem. 1976, Case Centennial Scholar Medal 1980. *Publications:* Renormalization Group Theory of Macromolecules; more than 600 articles in scholarly journals. *Address:* James Franck Institute, University of Chicago, 929 East 57th Street, Chicago, IL 60637, USA (office). *Telephone:* (773) 702-7202 (office). *Fax:* (773) 702-5863 (office). *E-mail:* freed@uchicago.edu (office). *Website:* kff4.uchicago.edu/~freed (office).

FREEDBERG, Hugh; British business executive; *Chairman, NYSE Liffe;* b. 18 June 1945, Cape Town, South Africa; ed Univ. of Witwatersrand, Univ. of South Africa, Harvard Univ., Amos Tuck School of Business Admin, Dartmouth Coll., USA; Book Club Assocs, UK 1973–75; Marketing and Sales Dir for UK Card Div. American Express 1975–78, Gen. Man. 1978–86, Head of Divs in the Benelux countries, Southern Europe, the Middle East and Africa, the UK, Ireland, SE Asia; joined Salomon Inc. 1986, CEO The Mortgage Corpn –1990; joined TSB Group 1990, Exec. Dir, CEO Insurance and Investment Services Div., Deputy CEO 1992–96; CEO Hill Samuel Group (bought by TSB Group) 1991–96, then CEO Hill Samuel Bank Ltd (div. of Lloyds TSB Group PLC), Dir Macquarie Bank, Australia 1994–96; Man. Pnr, Financial Services Practice, Korn Ferry Int. 1996–98; CEO London Int. Financial Futures and Options Exchange (now NYSE Liffe) 1998–2009, Chair. 2009–, Group Exec. Vice-Pres. and Head of Global Derivatives 2007–09, mem. Supervisory Bd AtosEuronext SBF SA 2004–05, Atos Euronext Market Solutions Holding S.A.S. 2005–07. *Address:* NYSE Liffe, Cannon Bridge House, 1 Cousin Lane, London, EC4R 3XX, England (office). *Telephone:* (20) 7623-0444 (office). *Fax:* (20) 7588-3624 (office). *Website:* www.liffe.com (office).

FREEDMAN, Eugene M., MS; American business executive; *Chairman, Senior Advisory Board, Kaufman & Company LLC;* b. 1932; ed Wharton School, Univ. of Pennsylvania and Columbia Univ. Grad. School of Business; joined Coopers & Lybrand 1954, Deputy Chair., Vice-Chair. NE region, mem. Int. Exec. Comm., Chair. 1991–93, Chair. CEO Coopers and Lybrand Int., New York 1993; Sr Advisor Monitor Co. Group Ltd Partnership 1995–2003; Co-founder, Man. Dir and Pres. Monitor Clipper Pnrs (pvt. equity firm) 1997–99, Sr Advisor and Dir 1999–2002;

currently Chair. Sr Advisory Bd Kaufman & Co. LLC; mem. Bd or Dirs Outcome Services Inc. Epoch Holdings Corpn, Concord Coalition; mem. Advisory Bd Cross Country Group Inc. *Address:* Kaufman & Company LLC, 101 Federal Street, No 1310, Boston, MA 02110, USA (office). *Telephone:* (617) 426-0444 (office). *Fax:* (617) 542-6506 (office). *Website:* www.kcollc.com (office).

FREEDMAN, Sir Lawrence David, Kt, KCMG, CBE, DPhil, FRSA, FRHistS, FBA, FKC; British academic; *Professor of War Studies and Vice-Principal (Research), King's College London;* b. 7 Dec. 1948, Tynemouth; s. of the late Lt-Commdr Julius Freedman and Myra Robinson; m. Judith Hill 1974; one s. one d.; ed Whitley Bay Grammar School and Univs of Manchester, Oxford and York; Research Assoc., IISS 1975–76; Research Fellow, Royal Inst. of Int. Affairs 1976–78, Head of Policy Studies 1978–82; Fellow, Head Dept of War Studies, King's Coll. London 1978–, Prof. 1982–, Head School of Social Science and Public Policy 2001–, Vice-Principal (Research); mem. Council, IISS 1984–92, 1993–, School of Slavonic and E European Studies 1993–97; Chair. Cttee on Int. Peace and Security, Social Science Research Council (USA) 1993–98; occasional newspaper columnist; Trustee Imperial War Museum 2001–09; cttee mem., The Iraq Inquiry 2009–; Hon. Dir Centre for Defence Studies 1990–; Silver Medallist, Arthur Ross Prize, Council on Foreign Relations (USA) 2002, RUSI Chesney Gold Medal 2006, Lionel Gelber Prize 2009, Duke of Westminster Prize for Military History 2009. *Publications:* US Intelligence and Soviet Strategic Threat 1978, Britain and Nuclear Weapons 1980, The Evolution of Nuclear Strategy 1981, 1989, Nuclear War and Nuclear Peace (co-author) 1983, The Troubled Alliance (ed.) 1983, The Atlas of Global Strategy 1985, The Price of Peace 1986, Britain and the Falklands War 1988, US Nuclear Strategy (co-ed.) 1989, Signals of War (with V. Gamba) 1989, Europe Transformed (ed.) 1990, Military Power in Europe (essays, ed.) 1990, Britain in the World (co-ed.) 1991, Population Change and European Security (co-ed.) 1991, War, Strategy and International Politics (essays, co-ed.) 1992, The Gulf Conflict 1990–91, Diplomacy and War in the New World Order (with E. Karsh) 1993, War: A Reader 1994, Military Intervention in Europe (ed.) 1994, Strategic Coercion (ed.) 1998, The Revolution in Strategic Affairs 1998, The Politics of British Defence Policy 1979–1998 1999, Kennedy's Wars 2000, The Cold War 2001, Superterrorism (ed.) 2002, Deterrence 2004, The Official History of the Falklands Campaign 2005, A Choice of Enemies 2009; articles etc. *Leisure interests:* tennis, political cartoons. *Address:* King's College London, Office of the Principal, James Clerk Maxwell Building, 57 Waterloo Road, London, SE1 8WA, England (office). *Telephone:* (20) 7848-3984 (office); (20) 7848-3985 (office). *Fax:* (20) 7848-3668 (office). *E-mail:* lawrence.freedman@kcl.ac.uk (office); LFREED0712@aol.com (home).

FREEDMAN, Michael H., PhD; American mathematician and academic; *Director, Microsoft Station Q, University of California, Santa Barbara;* b. 21 April 1951, Los Angeles, Calif.; ed Univ. of California, Berkeley, Princeton Univ.; Lecturer in Math., Univ. of California, Berkeley 1973–75; mem. of staff, Inst. for Advanced Study, Princeton, NJ 1975–76, 1980–81; Asst Prof. of Math., Univ. of California, San Diego 1976–79, Assoc. Prof. 1979, Prof. 1982–2004, Charles Lee Powell Prof. of Math. 1985–2004; Sr Researcher and Dir Microsoft Station Q, Univ. of California, Santa Barbara 2004–; mem. NAS, American Acad. of Arts and Sciences, New York Acad. of Sciences 1984; Fellow, MacArthur Foundation 1984; Sloan Fellowship, California Scientist of the Year 1984, Fields Medal, Int. Congress of Mathematicians, Berkeley 1986, Veblen Prize, American Math. Soc. 1986, Nat. Medal of Science 1987, Humboldt Award 1988, Guggenheim Fellowship 1994. *Publications:* numerous publs in math. journals and physics journals. *Address:* Microsoft Station Q, CNSI Bldg, Office 2243, University of California, Santa Barbara, CA 93106-6105, USA (office). *Telephone:* (805) 893-8818 (office). *Fax:* (425) 708-1426 (office). *Website:* stationq.ucsb.edu (office).

FREEDMAN, Wendy L., BSc, MSc, PhD; American (b. Canadian) astronomer; *Director, Carnegie Observatories, Carnegie Institution of Science;* b. 17 July 1957, Toronto, Ont.; m.; one s. one d.; ed Univ. of Toronto; Postdoctoral Fellow, Carnegie Observatories, Pasadena, Calif. 1984, mem. Scientific Staff 1987, Crawford H. Greenewalt Chair, Dir 2003–, Chair. Bd of Dirs, Giant Magellan Telescope; mem. NAS 2003, American Astronomical Soc., American Physical Soc.; Fellow, American Acad. of Arts and Sciences 2000, American Philosophical Soc. 2007, American Physical Soc. 2011; Hon. DSc (Toronto) 2013; Marc Aaronson Prize 1994, Cosmos Club Award 2000, John P. McGovern Award 2000, American Philosophical Soc. Magellanic Prize 2002, Gruber Cosmology Prize 2009. *Address:* Carnegie Observatories, 813 Santa Barbara Street, Pasadena, CA 91101, USA (office). *Telephone:* (626) 304-0204 (office). *Fax:* (626) 304-0266 (office). *E-mail:* wendy@obs .carnegiescience.edu (office). *Website:* www.obs.carnegiescience.edu/users/wendy (office).

FREEH, Louis J., JD, LLM; American lawyer, judge, consultant and fmr government official; *Chairman and Treasurer, Freeh Group International Solutions LLC;* b. 6 Jan. 1950, Jersey City, New Jersey; m. Marilyn Freeh; six s.; ed Rutgers Coll., Rutgers Law School and New York Univ. Law School; special agent, FBI 1975–81, Dir 1993–2001; apptd Asst US Attorney, Attorney Gen.'s Office for Southern District of New York 1980, later Chief of the Organized Crime Unit, Assoc. US Attorney and Deputy US Attorney –1990; Judge, US Dist Court for Southern NY 1991–93; Gen. Counsel for MBNA America Bank 2001–06; Founder and Sr Man. Pnr, Freeh Group International Solutions LLC (consulting firm) 2006–, also Chair. and Treasurer; Founding Pnr, Freeh, Sporkin & Sullivan (law firm), Washington, DC; Chair. Governance and Nominating Cttee of Bd of Dirs, Bristol-Myers Squibb Co.; mem. bd of numerous public cos and non-profit organizations, including US Naval Acad. Foundation, Nat. Italian American Foundation, Int. Asscn of Chief of Police Foundation; John Marshall Award for Preparation of Litigation 1984, Attorney General's Award for Distinguished Service 1987, 1991, Fed. Law Enforcement Officers Asscn Award 1989. *Achievements:* lead prosecutor in the "Pizza Connection" case, one of the largest and most complex narcotics investigations ever undertaken by the Fed. Govt; investigations and prosecutions relating to racketeering, drugs, organized crime, fraud, white collar crime and terrorism. *Publications:* My FBI 2005. *Address:* Freeh Group International, 500 Delaware Avenue, Suite 600, Wilmington, DE 19801, USA (office). *Telephone:* (302) 824-7139 (office). *Fax:* (302) 824-7148 (office). *E-mail:* Bescript@FreehGroup.com (office). *Website:* www.freehgroup.com (office).

FREEMAN, Catherine (Cathy) Astrid; Australian fmr athlete; b. 16 Feb. 1973, Mackay; d. of Norman Freeman and Cecilia Barber; m. (Sandy) Alexander Bodecker; works as public relations adviser; winner Australian 200m 1990–91, 1994, 1996, Australian 100m 1996, Amateur Athletics Fed. 400m 1992, 200m 1993; Gold Medallist 4×100m Commonwealth Games 1990; Gold Medallist 200m, 400m, Silver Medallist 4×100m Commonwealth Games 1994; Silver Medallist 400m, Olympic Games, Atlanta 1996; winner World Championships 400m, Athens 1997 (first Aboriginal winner at World Championships); Gold Medallist 400m, Olympic Games, Sydney 2000; set 2 Australian 200m records, 5 Australian 400m records 1994–96; took break from athletics in 2001; returned to int. competition Commonwealth Games Manchester 2002, winning a gold medal in the 4×400m relay; retd from athletics 2003; f. Catherine Freeman Foundation; Media and Communications Officer, Australia Post; Hans Christian Andersen Amb. 2003–; numerous nat. awards including Young Australian of the Year 1990, Australian of the Year 1998 (only person to have been awarded both honours). *Leisure interests:* family, pets, children, movies. *Address:* c/o Jane Cowmeadow, Communications & Management, Bron Madigan, PO Box 5138, Ringwood, Vic. 3134, Australia. *Website:* www.cathyfreeman.com.au; www.cathyfreemanfoundation.org.au.

FREEMAN, Hon. Charles (Chas) Wellman, Jr, BA, JD; American fmr diplomatist and fmr government official; *Chairman, Projects International, Inc.;* b. 2 March 1943, Washington, DC; s. of Charles W. Freeman and Carla Park; m. 1st Patricia Trenery 1962 (divorced 1993); three s. (one deceased) one d.; m. 2nd Margaret Van Wagenen Carpenter 1993; ed Milton Acad., Milton, Mass., Nat. Autonomous Univ. of Mexico, México, Yale Univ., Harvard Law School, Harvard Univ., Foreign Service Inst. School of Chinese Language and Area Studies; entered US Foreign Service 1965, Vice-Consul, Madras, India 1966–68, Taiwan 1969–71, State Dept, China Desk 1971–74, Visiting Fellow, E Asian Legal Research, Harvard Univ. 1974–75, Deputy Dir, Maritime Affairs, US Dept of State 1975–76, Dir Public Programs, Dept of State 1976–77, Plans and Man. 1977–78, Dir US Information Agency programs 1978–79, Acting US Co-ordinator for Refugee Programs 1979, Dir, Chinese Affairs, Dept of State 1979–81, Minister, Embassy in Beijing 1981–84, Embassy in Bangkok 1984–86, Prin. Deputy Asst Sec. of State for African Affairs 1986–89, Amb. to Saudi Arabia 1989–92; Asst Sec. of Defense (Int. Security Affairs) 1993–94; Chair. Projects International, Inc. 1995–, Cttee for the Republic 2003–; Vice-Chair. Atlantic Council of USA 1996–2008; Co-Chair. US-China Policy Foundation 1996–2009; Pres. Middle East Policy Council 1997–2009; Distinguished Fellow, Inst. for Nat. Strategic Studies, Nat. Defense Univ. 1992–93; US Inst. of Peace, Washington, DC 1994–95; mem. American Acad. of Diplomacy 1995, mem. Bd 2001–10; mem. Bd Washington World Affairs Council 1998–2009, Pacific Pension Inst. 2001–06, Asscn for Diplomatic Studies and Training 2001–09, Inst. for Defense Analyses, Carnegie Endowment for Int. Peace 2009–; Overseer, Roger Williams Univ. 2006–09; Advisor, MIT Centre for Security Studies 2009–, Centre for Naval Analysis 2009–12; Order of King Abd Al-Aziz (First Class) 1992; Forrest Prize, Yale Univ., Superior Honor Awards 1978, 1982, Presidential Meritorious Service Awards 1984, 1987, 1989, Group Distinguished Honor Award 1988, Sec. of Defense Award for Meritorious Civilian Service 1991, Distinguished Honor Award 1991, Sec. of Defense Awards for Distinguished Public Service 1994. *Publications include:* Cooking Western in China 1987, The Diplomat's Dictionary (revised edn 2010), Arts of Power: Statecraft and Diplomacy 1997, America's Misadventures in the Middle East 2010, Interesting Times: China, America, and the Shifting Balance of Prestige 2013. *Leisure interests:* swimming, sailing, reading, computers, cookery. *Address:* Projects International, Inc., 888 17th Street, NW, Suite 1250, Washington, DC 20006, USA (office). *Telephone:* (202) 333-1277 (office). *Fax:* (202) 333-3128 (office). *E-mail:* CWFResidence@gmail.com; cfreeman@projectsinternational.com. *Website:* www.chasfreeman.net.

FREEMAN, Martin John C.; British actor; b. 8 Sept. 1971, Aldershot, Hants.; s. of the late Geoffrey Freeman and of Philomena Freeman; m. Amanda Abbington; one s. one d.; ed Central School of Speech and Drama, London; joined a youth theatre group aged 15, professional actor from the age of 17; has appeared in numerous TV series, theatre productions and several radio productions. *Films include:* I Just Want to Kiss You (short) 1998, The Low Down 2000, Fancy Dress (short) 2001, Ali G Indahouse 2002, Love Actually 2003, Call Register (short) 2004, Shaun of the Dead 2004, Blake's Junction 7 (short) 2005, The Hitchhiker's Guide to the Galaxy 2005, Round About Five (short) 2005, Long Hot Summer 2006, Confetti 2006, Breaking and Entering 2006, Dedication 2007, The Good Night 2007, Hot Fuzz 2007, Lonely Hearts (short) (voice) 2007, The All Together 2007, Rubbish (short) 2007, Nightwatching 2007, HIV: The Musical (short) 2009, Wild Target 2009, Nativity! 2009, The Girl Is Mime (short) 2010, The Voorman Problem (short) 2011, Swinging with the Finkels 2011, What's Your Number? 2011, The Pirates! In an Adventure with Scientists! (voice) 2012, Animals 2012, The Hobbit: An Unexpected Journey 2012, Svengali 2013, The Hobbit: The Desolation of Smaug 2013, The Hobbit: There and Back Again 2014. *Television includes:* The Bill (series) – Man Trap 1997, This Life (series) – Last Tango in Southwark 1997, Casualty (series) – She Loved the Rain 1998, Picking up the Pieces (series) 1998, Bruiser (series) 2000, Lock, Stock... (series) 2000, Black Books (series) – Cooking the Books 2000, Men Only (film) 2001, World of Pub (series) 2001, The Office (series) 2001–03, Helen West (series) 2002, Linda Green (series) – Easy Come, Easy Go 2002, Comic Relief 2003: The Big Hair Do (film) (Blankety Blank sketch) 2003, The Debt (film) 2003, Margery and Gladys (film) 2003, Charles II: The Power & the Passion (mini-series) 2003, Hardware (series) 2003–04, Pride (film) (voice) 2004, Not Tonight with John Sergeant 2005, The Robinsons (series) 2005, Comedy Showcase (series) – Other People 2007, The Old Curiosity Shop (film) 2007, Svengali (film) 2009, Boy Meets Girl (mini-series) 2009, Micro Men (film) 2009, Sherlock (series) (as Dr John Watson) (BAFTA Award for Best Supporting Actor 2011) 2010–. *Leisure interest:* Motown music. *Address:* c/o Creative Artists Management, 4th Floor, 111 Shoreditch High Street, London, E1 6JN, England (office). *Telephone:* (20) 7292-0600 (office). *E-mail:* reception@cam.co.uk (office). *Website:* www.cam.co.uk (office).

FREEMAN, Michael Alexander Reykers, BA, MB, BCh, MD, FRCS; British orthopaedic surgeon; b. 17 Nov. 1931, Surrey; s. of Donald G. Freeman and Florence J. Elms; m. 1st Elisabeth Jean Freeman 1951; one s. one d.; m. 2nd Janet Edith Freeman 1959; one s. one d.; m. 3rd Patricia Gill 1968; (one s. deceased) one d.; ed Corpus Christi Coll. Cambridge and London Hosp. Medical Coll.; Intern,

London Hosp.; Resident in Orthopaedic Surgery, Westminster Hosp. and Middx Hosp. 1962–68; Consultant, London Hosp. 1968–96; European Ed.-in-Chief Journal of Arthroplasty 1997–; Co-founder and Dir Biomechanics Unit, Imperial Coll. London 1956–75; fmr Visiting Prof., Dept of Biomechanical Eng, Univ. Coll. London; fmr mem. Bd MRC; Past-Pres. British Hip Soc., British Orthopaedic Soc., European Fed. of Nat. Asscns of Orthopaedics and Traumatology 1994–95; mem. numerous professional socs; Hon. Consultant, Royal Hosps NHS Trust 1996–; Robert Jones Medal, British Orthopaedic Asscn 1964 and numerous other awards. *Achievements include:* inventor of prostheses and surgical procedures for replacement of hip, knee, ankle and joints of the foot. *Publications:* The Scientific Basis of Joint Replacement 1977, Arthritis of the Knee 1980; Ed. Adult Articular Cartilage 1973–79; and 200 papers on hip and knee surgery. *Leisure interests:* gardening, reading. *Address:* 79 Albert Street, London, NW1 7LX, England (home). *Telephone:* (20) 7387-0817 (home). *Fax:* (20) 7388-5731 (home).

FREEMAN, Morgan; American actor and director; b. 1 June 1937, Memphis, Tenn.; s. of Grafton Freeman and Mayme Revere; m. 1st Jeanette Bradshaw 1967 (divorced 1979); two s. from previous relationships; m. 2nd Myrna Colley-Lee 1984 (divorced 2010); one adopted d. one c.; ed Los Angeles City Coll.; stage debut in Niggerlover 1967; other stage appearances include: Hello Dolly, Broadway 1967, Jungle of Cities 1969, The Recruiting Officer 1969, Purlie, ANTA Theatre, New York 1970, Black Visions 1972, Mighty Gents 1978 (Clarence Derwent Award, Drama Desk Award) 1978, White Pelicans 1978, Coriolanus, New York Shakespeare Festival 1979, Mother Courage and Her Children 1980, Othello Dallas Shakespeare Festival, 1982, Medea and the Doll 1984, The Gospel at Colonus (Obie Award), Driving Miss Daisy 1987, The Taming of the Shrew; Co-founder Revelations Entertainment (production co.) 1996, ClickStar (broadband entertainment co.) 2006; hon. degrees from Rhodes Coll. (Hon. Alumnus) 1997, (Brown Univ.) 2010; Crystal Globe Award for Outstanding Artistic Contrib. to World Cinema, Karlovy Vary Int. Film Festival 2003, Spencer Tracy Award, UCLA 2006, Guest of Honour, Cairo Int. Film Festival 2006, Lifetime Achievement Award (co-recipient with his wife), Mississippi Inst. of Arts and Letters 2007, Outstanding Contrib. To Film and TV Gong, Screen Nation Film and TV Awards 2007, Kennedy Center Honor 2008, Lifetime Achievement Award, American Film Inst. 2011, chosen as Favorite Movie Icon, People's Choice Awards 2012, Cecil B. DeMille Award, Golden Globe Awards 2012. *Films include:* Who Says I Can't Ride a Rainbow? 1971, Brubaker 1980, Eyewitness 1980, Harry and Son 1983, Teachers 1984, Street Smart 1987, Clean and Sober 1988, Lean On Me 1989, Johnny Handsome 1989, Driving Miss Daisy (Golden Globe Award) 1989, Glory 1989, Robin Hood 1991, Unforgiven 1992, The Power of Ore 1992, Chain Reaction 1993, The Shawshank Redemption 1994, Outbreak 1995, Se7en 1996, Moll Flanders, Amistad (NAACP Image Award) 1997, Kiss the Girls 1997, Hard Rain 1998, Deep Impact 1998, Water Damage 1999, Mutiny 1999, Under Suspicion 2000, Nurse Betty 2000, Along Came a Spider 2000, High Crimes 2002, The Sum of All Fears 2002, Levity 2003, Dreamcatcher 2003, Bruce Almighty 2003, Guilty by Association (video) 2003, The Big Bounce 2004, Million Dollar Baby (Best Supporting Actor, Screen Actors Guild Awards 2005, Acad. Awards 2005) 2004, A Remarkable Promise (short) (narrator) 2004, Unleashed 2005, Batman Begins 2005, War of the Worlds (voice) 2005, Danny the Dog 2005, An Unfinished Life 2005, Edison 2005, Magnificent Desolation: Walking on the Moon 3D (documentary short) 2005, Lucky Number Slevin 2006, 10 Items or Less 2006, The Contract 2006, Evan Almighty 2007, Gone Baby Gone 2007, Feast of Love 2007, The Bucket List 2007, Wanted 2008, The Dark Knight 2008, The Code 2009, The Maiden Heist 2009, Invictus (Nat. Bd of Review Award for Best Actor) 2009, Red 2010, Wish Wizard (short) 2011, Conan the Barbarian 2011, Dolphin Tale 2011, We the People 2011, The Dark Knight Rises 2012, The Summer of Monte Wildhorn 2012, Olympus Has Fallen 2013, Oblivion 2013; dir: Bopha! 1993. *Television includes:* American Masters (series documentary) 2000, Freedom: A History of Us (series documentary) 2003, Slavery and the Making of America (series) (narrator) 2005, A Raisin in the Sun (film) 2008, 30 for 30 (series) 2010. *Address:* Revelations Entertainment, 301 Arizona Avenue, Suite 303, Santa Monica, CA 90401; Clickstar Inc., 520 Broadway, #100, Santa Monica, CA 90401; c/o WME Entertainment, 9601 Wilshire Boulevard, Beverly Hills, CA 90210, USA (office). *Telephone:* (310) 394-3131 (Revelations); (310) 285-9000 (office). *Fax:* (310) 394-3133 (Revelations); (310) 883-6402 (Clickstar); (310) 285-9010 (office). *Website:* www.wma.com (office).

FREEMAN, Raymond (Ray), MA, DPhil, DSc, FRS; British chemist and academic; *Professor Emeritus, Department of Chemistry, University of Cambridge;* b. 6 Jan. 1932, Long Eaton, Derbyshire; s. of the late Albert Freeman and Hilda F. Freeman; m. Anne-Marie Périnet-Marquet 1958; two s. three d.; ed Nottingham High School and Lincoln Coll., Oxford; Engineer, French Atomic Energy Comm., Centre d'Etudes Nucléaires de Saclay 1957–59; Sr Scientific Officer, Nat. Physical Lab. 1959–63; Research Scientist, Instrument Div., Varian Assocs, Palo Alto, Calif. 1963–73; Univ. Lecturer in Physical Chem. and Fellow, Magdalen Coll., Oxford 1973–87, Aldrichian Praelector in Chem. 1982–87; John Humphrey Plummer Prof. of Magnetic Resonance, Univ. of Cambridge 1987–99, Prof. Emer. 1999–, Fellow, Jesus Coll., Cambridge 1987–99, Fellow Emer. 1999–; Hon. DSc (Durham) 1998; Leverhulme Medal, Royal Soc. 1990, RSC Longstaff Medal 1999, Queen's Medal, Royal Soc. 2002, Laukien Prize Experimental NMR Conf. 2005. *Publications:* A Handbook of Nuclear Magnetic Resonance 1987, Spin Choreography: Basic Steps in High Resolution NMR 1997, Magnetic Resonance in Chemistry and Medicine 2003; several scientific papers on nuclear magnetic resonance spectroscopy in various journals. *Leisure interests:* swimming, traditional jazz. *Address:* Jesus College, Cambridge, CB5 8BL (office); 29 Bentley Road, Cambridge, CB2 8AW, England (home). *Telephone:* (1223) 746543 (office); (1223) 323958 (home). *Fax:* (1223) 336362 (office). *E-mail:* rf110@hermes.cam.ac.uk (office). *Website:* www.ch.cam.ac.uk (office).

FREEMAN, Richard B., PhD; American economist and academic; *Ascherman Professor of Economics, Harvard University;* b. 29 June 1953, Newburgh, NY; m. Alida Castillo; one s. one d.; ed Dartmouth and Harvard Univs; fmr Program Dir, Science and Eng Workforce Project, Nat. Bureau of Econ. Research (NBER); fmr Faculty Co-Dir Labor and Worklife Program, Harvard Law School; fmr Sr Research Fellow, Centre for Econ. Performance, LSE, London, UK; fmr Fairchild Distinguished Research Prof., California Inst. of Tech.; fmr Asst Prof. of Econs, Yale Univ.; fmr Asst Prof. of Econs, Univ. of Chicago; fmr Assoc. Prof. of Econs, Harvard Univ., Ascherman Prof. of Econs 2009–; Frances Perkins

Fellow, American Acad. of Political and Social Science 2011–; has served on eight panels of the NAS, including Cttee on Assuring a Future US-based Nuclear Chem. Expertise, Cttee on Nat. Statistics Panel on Developing Science, Tech. and Innovation Indicators for the Future, Cttee on Capitalizing on the Diversity of the Science and Eng Workforce in Industry, Cttee on Nat. Needs for Biomedical and Behavioral Scientists, and jt NAS, Nat. Acad. of Eng and Inst. of Medicine Study on Policy Implications of Int. Grad. Students and Postdoctoral Scholars in the US, has also served on the Sub-cttee on Biomedical Research Workforce Modeling, an NIH Advisory Cttee to the Dir; mem. AAAS 2004 (Fellow 2007), American Acad. of Arts and Sciences; Hon. Professorial Fellow, Univ. of Melbourne 2013–14; Mincer Lifetime Achievement Prize, Soc. of Labor Econs 2006, IZA Prize in Labor Econs 2007. *Lectures:* Clarendon Lecturer, Univ. of Oxford 1994, Lionel Robins Lecturer, LSE 1999, Luigi Einaudi Lecturer, Cornell Univ. 2002, Okun Lecturer, Yale Univ. 2003, World Econ. Annual Lecturer, Univ. of Nottingham 2003, Dr Heinz Kienzl Lecturer, OeNB, Vienna 2003, Roco C. Siciliano Lecturer, Univ. of Utah 2004, W.J. Usery Lecturer, Georgia State Univ. 2005, Ernst Fraenkel Distinguished Lecturer, Freie Universität, Berlin 2006, Public Lecturer, LSE 2006, Public Lecturer, Inst. for Legal Research, Univ. of California, Berkeley 2007, Sawyer Lecturer, Stanford Univ. 2007, Jefferson Memorial Lecturer, Univ. of California, Berkeley 2007–08, Donald Wood Hon. Lecturer, Queen's Univ., Kingston, Canada 2008, Angelo Costa Lecturer, Universita LUISS Guido Carli, Rome 2008, Annual Kenneth M. Piper Lecturer, Chicago-Kent Law School 2009, Rupert Johnson Lecturer, Washington and Lee Univ., Va 2009, Ralph Milliband Public Lecturer, LSE 2012, V.V. Giri Memorial Lecturer, 53rd Annual Conf. of the Indian Soc. of Labour Economists, Mohanlal Sukhadia Univ., Udaipur, Rajasthan, India 2012. *Publications:* The Over-Educated American 1976, What Do Unions Do? 1984, Labor Markets in Action 1989, Working Under Different Rules 1994, What Workers Want 1999 (revised second edn with Joel Rogers 2007), Can Labor Standards Improve Under Globalization? (co-author) 2003, America Works: The Exceptional Labor Market 2007, What Workers Say: Employee Voice in the Anglo American World (co-author) 2007, International Differences in the Business Practices & Productivity of Firms (co-author) 2009, Science and Engineering Careers in the United States (co-author) 2009, Reforming the Welfare State: Recovery and Beyond in Sweden (co-author) 2010, Shared Capitalism at Work: Employee Ownership, Profit and Gain Sharing, and Broad-based Stock Options (co-author) 2010, The Citizen's Share: Putting Ownership Back into Democracy 2013. *Leisure interest:* professional wrestling. *Address:* National Bureau of Economic Research, 1050 Massachusetts Avenue, Cambridge, MA 02138, USA (office). *E-mail:* rbfreeman@gmail.com (office). *Website:* users.nber.org/~freeman (office).

FREETH, Peter, RA, RE; British artist and printmaker; b. 15 April 1938, Birmingham; s. of Alfred William Freeth and Olive Freeth (née Walker); m. Mariolina Meliadó 1967; two s.; ed King Edward's Grammar School, Aston, Birmingham, Slade School, London, British School, Rome; tutor, Etching Royal Acad. Schools 1966–; works on display in British Museum, Victoria & Albert Museum, Arts Council of England, Fitzwilliam Museum, Cambridge, Ashmolean Museum, Oxford, Nat. Gallery, Washington, DC, USA, Metropolitan Museum, New York, Hunterian Gallery, Glasgow; Prix de Rome (engraving) 1960, Best Print, Royal Acad. 1986, Drawing/Print Prize 2002, Hunting Art Prizes, Royal Coll. of Art 2004, 2005. *Publication:* Printmakers' Secrets (contrib.) 2009. *Leisure interests:* books, music, grandchildren. *Address:* 83 Muswell Hill Road, London, N10 3HT, England (home).

FREI RUIZ-TAGLE, Eduardo; Chilean civil engineer and fmr head of state; b. 24 June 1942, Santiago; s. of the late Eduardo Frei Montalva (fmr Pres. of Chile) and María Ruiz-Tagle; m. María Larraechea; ed Univ. of Chile; joined Christian Democrat (CD) Party 1958, fmr Pres.; CD presidential cand., Dec. 1993, Pres. of Chile 1994–2000; C-in-C of Armed Forces 1998–2000; elected to Senate 1989, Pres. 2006–08; Pres. Fundación Eduardo Frei Montalva 1992–93; unsuccessful CD presidential cand. 2010; Pnr, Sigdo Koppers SA (engineering co.). *Address:* c/o Partido Demócrata Cristiano, Almeda B. O'Higgins 1460, 2°, Santiago, Chile.

FREIJ, Gen. Fahd Jassem al-; Syrian army officer and politician; *Minister of Defence;* b. 1 Jan. 1950, Hama; m.; three c.; ed Syrian Mil. Acad.; attained rank of Lt 1971, Lt-Gen. 2001, Gen. 2009; Deputy Chief of Staff, Syrian Arab Army 2005, Chief of Staff 2011–12; commanded Syrian Army Special Forces in regions of Daraa, Idlib and Hama; Minister of Defence 2012–, also Deputy C-in-C of army and armed forces 2012–; several mil. decorations. *Address:* Ministry of Defence, place Omayad, Damascus, Syria (office). *Telephone:* (11) 7770700 (office). *Fax:* (11) 2237842 (office).

FREITAS DO AMARAL, Diogo de, PhD; Portuguese politician and academic; b. 21 July 1941, Póvoa de Varzim; s. of Duarte P. C. Freitas do Amaral and Maria Filomena Campos Trocado; m. Maria José Salgado Sarmento de Matos 1965; two s. two d.; Prof. of Admin. Law, Lisbon Univ. 1968, Head, Dept of Public Law and Prof., Portuguese Catholic Univ. 1978; mem. Council of State 1974–75; mem. Parl. 1975–82, 1992–93; Pres. Centre Democrat Party 1974–82, 1988–91; Pres. European Union of Christian Democrats 1981–82; Prime Minister of Portugal (interim) 1980–81, Minister of Foreign Affairs 1980–81, Deputy Prime Minister and Minister of Defence 1981–83, Minister of Foreign Affairs 2005–06; unsuccessful presidential cand. 1986; Pres. 50th Gen. Ass. of UN 1995–96; Minister of Foreign Affairs and Portuguese Communities Abroad 2005–06 (resgnd); Founder and Chair. School of Law, Universidade Nova de Lisboa 1996–2001, currently Prof.; Pres. Fundação Portugal Século XXI 1986–90, PETROCONTROL 1992–2000; Order of Christ, Order of Santiago, Order of Henry the Navigator; Calouste Gulbenkian Prize (twice), Henry the Navigator Prize. *Plays:* O Magnífico Reitor 2001, Viriato 2002. *Publications:* A Utilização do Domínio Público Pelos Particulares 1965, A Execução das Sentenças dos Tribunais Administrativos 1967, Conceito e natureza do recurso hierárquico 1981, Uma Solução para Portugal 1985, Curso de Direito Administrativo I, 1986, II 2001, O Antigo Regime e a Revolução (Memórias Políticas: 1941–76) 1995, História das Ideias Políticas, Vol. I 1998, D. Afonso Henriques. Biografia 2000, Estudios de Direito Público (two vols) 2004, Manual de Introdução ao direito (Vol. I) 2004. *Leisure interests:* music, horses, reading, theatre, writing, political philosophy. *Address:* Faculty of Law, Universidade Nova de Lisboa, Travessa Estevão Pinto, 1070 Lisbon, Portugal. *Telephone:* (21) 3870413. *Website:* www.unl.pt.

FRENCH, Dawn; British actress and comedienne; b. 11 Oct. 1957, Holyhead, Wales; m. 1st Lenny Henry (q.v.) 1984 (divorced 2010); one d. (adopted); m. 2nd Mark Bignell 2013; ed Manchester Univ., London Cen. School of Speech and Drama; stage shows and TV series with Jennifer Saunders (q.v.); co–founder and Man. Sixteen 47 Ltd (fashion business); Hon. Rose, Montreux 2002, Acad. Fellowship, BAFTA 2009. *Stage appearances include:* Silly Cow, When We are Married 1996, My Brilliant Divorce 2003, Smaller (Lyric Theatre, London and UK tour) 2006. *Radio:* guest appearances on numerous talk shows. *TV appearances include:* The Comic Strip (Strike, Consuela, Five Go Mad in Dorset, Supergrass, Ken, The Yob, Susie), French and Saunders 1987–2006, The Vicar of Dibley 1994–2007, Tender Loving Care 1993, Sex and Chocolate 1997, Jam & Jerusalem 2006–08, A Bucket o' French and Saunders 2007, Lark Rise to Candleford 2008, Psychoville 2009, Roger and Val Have Just Got In 2010–; presenter: Swank 1987, Scoff 1988 (UK Channel 4). *Films include:* The Supergrass 1985, Eat the Rich 1987, The Adventures of Pinocchio 1996, Maybe Baby 2000, Harry Potter and the Prisoner of Azkaban 2004, The Chronicles of Narnia: The Lion, the Witch and the Wardrobe (voice) 2005, Love and Other Disasters 2006, Coraline (voice) 2009. *Publication:* Dear Fatty (auto-biog.) 2008, A Tiny Bit Marvellous (novel) (Galaxy Nat. Book Award for Popular Fiction Book of the Year 2011) 2010. *Address:* c/o Maureen Vincent, United Agents, 12–26 Lexington Street, London, W1F 0LE, England (office). *Telephone:* (20) 3214-0800 (office). *Fax:* (20) 3214-0801 (office). *E-mail:* info@unitedagents.co.uk (office). *Website:* unitedagents.co.uk (office).

FRENCH, James (Jim), CBE; British airline industry executive; *Chairman and CEO, Flybe;* m.; three c.; began aviation career with Caledonian Airways 1970, then sr positions with Air UK; joined Jersey European Airways (now Flybe) 1990, CEO 2002–, Chair. 2005–, also part Owner. *Address:* Flybe, Jack Walker House, Exeter International Airport, Exeter, EX5 2HL, Devon, England (office). *Telephone:* (1392) 268529 (office); (845) 675-0681 (office). *Fax:* (1392) 672246 (office). *E-mail:* pressoffice@flybe.com (office). *Website:* www.flybe.com (office).

FRENDO, Michael, Dipl. Notary Public, LLM, LLD; Maltese lawyer, business executive and fmr politician; *Managing Partner, Scordis Papapetrou & Company LLC;* b. 29 July 1955; s. of the late Joseph Frendo and Josephine Frendo (née Felice); m. Irene Brincat 1984; one s. two d.; ed Univ. of Malta and Univ. of Exeter, UK; admitted to the Bar 1977; Sr Lecturer, Faculty of Law, Univ. of Malta 1987–; Dir Press and Media Relations and Editorial Dir (newspapers) of Partit Nazzjonalista (Christian Democrat) 1982–85; MP 1987–2013, Chair. Foreign and European Affairs Cttee, House of Reps 2008–10, Speaker (Pres.), House of Reps (Parl.) 2010–13; mem. of Parl. Ass. of Council of Europe 1987–92; mem. Malta Parl. Del. to European Parl. 1987–90, 1996–98 (Chair. 1990–92); Parl. Sec. for Youth, Culture and Consumer Protection 1990–92; Minister for Youth and the Arts 1992–94, for Transport, Communications and Tech. 1994–96; Minister of Foreign Affairs 2004–08; First Vice-Chair. Jt Parl. Cttee, European Parl. and Malta Parl. 1999–2004; Nationalist Party (Christian Democrat, European People's Party); mem. European Convention (EU) 2000–02; signatory to European Convention Draft Treaty establishing a Constitution for Europe 2002, to Treaty establishing a Constitution for Europe 2004, to Treaty of Lisbon 2007; Chair. Commonwealth Ministerial Action Group 2005–07, Commonwealth Connects Programme 2005–07, cand. for post of Sec. Gen. of Commonwealth 2007; consultant, Salamander (Consultancy) Ltd 2008–12; Prin., Frendo Advocates 2010–12; Man. Partner, Scordis Papapetrou & Co. LLC; Man. Dir Scordis Papapetrou & Co. Consultants Ltd 2012–; Chair. (non-exec.) Banif Bank (Malta) Plc 2013–; several decorations from Spain, Portugal, Italy, Tunisia, Austria, Cyprus, Latvia and other countries, including Grand Cross of the Order of Isabella la Católica (Spain) 2009; Parl. Ass. of the Mediterranean Award 2011. *Publications:* several books; articles in local and int. magazines and journals. *Leisure interests:* reading, listening to 'talking books'. *Address:* 41 St Christopher Street, Valletta VLT 1464, Malta (office). *Telephone:* 79-790790 (mobile) (office). *Fax:* (2123) 4444 (office). *E-mail:* m.frendo@scordispapapetrou.com (office); michaelfrendo@gmail.com (home). *Website:* www.scordispapapetrou.com (office).

FRENI, Mirella; Italian singer; b. (Mirella Fregni), 27 Feb. 1935, Modena; d. of Ennio Fregni and Gianna (née Arcelli) Fregni; m. 1st Leone Magiera 1955; one d.; m. 2nd Nicolai Ghiaurov (died 2004); debut 1955 as Micaëla in Carmen, debut at Glyndebourne Festival 1961, Royal Opera House, Covent Garden 1961, La Scala, Milan 1962, Metropolitan Opera, NY 1965; has sung at Vienna State Opera, Rome Opera, Barcelona Gran Teatro del Liceo, Boston Opera, La Scala and at Salzburg Festival and leading opera houses throughout the world; retd from the stage 2005; Midem Classical Award for Lifetime Achievement 2010, Opera News Award for invaluable contribution to opera 2012. *Recordings include:* Carmen, Falstaff, La Bohème, Madame Butterfly, Tosca, Verdi Requiem, Aïda, Don Giovanni. *Major roles include:* Nanetta in Falstaff, Mimi in La Bohème, Zerlina in Don Giovanni, Susanna, Adina in L'Elisir d'amore, Violetta in La Traviata, Desdemona in Otello. *Address:* c/o Jack Mastroianni, IMG Artists, Carnegie Hall Tower, 152 West 57th Street, 5th Floor, New York, NY 10019, USA (office). *Telephone:* (212) 994-3525 (office). *E-mail:* jmastroianni@imgartists.com (office). *Website:* www.imgartists .com (office).

FRENK, Alfons Hubert; German accountant and retail executive; b. 1950; m.; three c.; Man. Dir Edeka Minden-Hannover 1991–2002, also acted as spokesman for Minden-Hannover regional office, Man. Dir Edeka Zentrale AG & Co. KG 2002–03, CEO 2003–08, Chair. Supervisory Bd Edeka Group –2008. *Address:* c/o Edeka Zentrale AG & Co. KG, New-York-Ring 6, 22297 Hamburg, Germany. *Telephone:* (40) 63-77-0.

FRENK MORA, Julio José, MA, PhD, MD; Mexican physician, academic, public health administrator and fmr government official; *Dean of the Faculty, School of Public Health and T & G Angelopoulos Professor of Public Health and International Development, School of Public Health and Kennedy School, Harvard University;* b. 20 Dec. 1953, Mexico City; m. Dr Felicia Knaul; three c.; ed National Autonomous Univ. of Mexico, Univ. of Michigan, USA; Founding Dir Centre of Public Health Research, Ministry of Health 1984–87; Founding Dir Gen. Nat. Inst. of Public Health of Mexico 1987–92; Visiting Prof., Harvard Center for Population and Devt Studies 1992–93; Exec. Vice Pres. and Dir Centre for Health and Economy, Mexican Health Foundation 1995–98; Exec. Dir Evidence and Information for Policy, WHO, Geneva 1998–2000; Sec. of Health 2000–06; Pres. Carso Health Inst., Mexico City 2006–09; Sr Fellow in Global Health Program, Bill &

Melinda Gates Foundation 2006–09; Dean of Faculty and T & G Angelopoulos Prof. of Public Health and Int. Devt, Harvard School of Public Health 2009–; Chair. Inst. for Health Metrics and Evaluation, Univ. of Washington; Vice-Pres. for Latin America, American Public Health Asscn; fmr Pres. Mexican Soc. for Quality in Health Care; Nat. Researcher, Mexican Research System 1984–98; mem. Nat. Acad. of Medicine of Mexico, US Inst. of Medicine and numerous other professional orgs; mem. editorial bds of 10 journals; Int. Fellow in Health, W.K. Kellogg Foundation 1986–89; Fellow, Mich. Soc. of Fellows, Univ. of Mich. 1982–84; Cecilio A. Robelo Award for Scientific Research (State of Morelos) 1993, Clinton Global Citizen Award 2008. *Publications:* author of 28 books and monographs and 103 articles in cultural magazines and newspapers. *Address:* Office of the Dean, Harvard School of Public Health, Kresge Building, Room 1005, 677 Huntington Ave., Boston, MA 02115, USA (office). *Website:* www.hsph.harvard.edu (office).

FRENKEL, Jacob Aharon, BA, MA, PhD; Israeli economist, academic and business executive; *Chairman, JPMorgan Chase International;* b. 8 Feb. 1943, Tel-Aviv, British Mandate of Palestine; m. Niza Frenkel 1968; two d.; ed Univ. of Chicago, USA, Hebrew Univ. of Jerusalem; on staff, Univ. of Chicago 1973–87, held various positions including David Rockefeller Prof. of Int. Econs and Ed. Journal of Political Economy; Econ. Counsellor and Dir of Research, IMF 1987–91; joined Tel-Aviv Univ. 1991, Weisfeld Prof. of Econs of Peace and Int. Relations 1994–; Gov. Bank of Israel 1991–2000; Sr Vice-Pres. and Vice-Chair. Merrill Lynch International Inc. 2000–04, Chair. Sovereign Advisory Group and Global Financial Insts Group 2000–04; Vice-Chair. Global Econ. Strategies, American International Group (AIG) 2004–09; Chair. JPMorgan Chase International 2009–; Chair. and CEO Group of Thirty Consultative Group on Int. Econ. and Monetary Affairs, Inc., Washington, DC; Co-Chair. Israeli del. to multilateral peace talks on Regional Econ. Devts 1991; Chair. Bd of Govs Inter-American Devt Bank 1995–96; Vice-Chair. Bd of Govs EBRD, London 1999–2000; mem. Bd of Dirs Nat. Bureau of Econ. Research; mem. Int. Advisory Bd Council on Foreign Relations, Trilateral Comm., Bd of The Council for the United States and Italy, Investment Advisory Council of the Prime Minister of Turkey, Int. Advisory Council of the China Devt Bank; mem. Bd of Dirs Inst. for Int. Econs; mem. Int. Bd of Govs Peres Center for Peace, Israel; Distinguished mem. Advisory Cttee Inst. for Global Econs, Korea; Fellow, Econometric Soc.; Hon. Pres. Israel Asscn of Grads in the Social Sciences and Humanities; Foreign Hon. mem. American Acad. of Arts and Science, Japan Soc. of Monetary Econs; Gran Cruz, Orden de Mayo al Mérito (Argentina), Order of Merit (in the rank of Cavaliere di Gran Croce) (Italy); several hon. doctoral degrees; Karel Englis Prize in Econs (Czech Repub.), Hugo Ramniceanu Prize for Econs, Tel-Aviv Univ., Economic Policy Award, Emerging Markets 1993, Euromoney Cen. Banker of the Year Award 1997, Israel Prize 2002. *Publications:* numerous books and articles on int. econs and macro-econs. *Address:* JPMorgan Chase & Co., 270 Park Avenue, New York, NY 10017, USA (office). *Telephone:* (212) 270-6000 (office). *Fax:* (212) 270-1648 (office). *Website:* www.jpmorgan.com (office).

FRENZEL, Michael, Dr iur.; German business executive; *Chairman of the Executive Board, TUI AG;* b. 2 March 1947, Leipzig; ed Ruhr Univ., Bochum; joined Westdeutsche Landesbank (WestLB), Düsseldorf 1981, Man. Industrial Holdings Dept 1983–85, Man. Equity Holdings Div. 1985–88; mem. Bd of Dirs Preussag AG (renamed TUI AG 2002) 1988–, Vice-Chair. 1992–93, Chair. Exec. Bd 1994–, Chair. Hapag-Lloyd AG 1998–, also Chair. TUI Travel PLC 2007–; Chair. Creditanstalt AG, Vienna; mem. Supervisory Bd AWD Holding AG, AXA Konzern AG, Hapag-Lloyd AG (Chair.), TUIfly GmbH (Chair.), TUI Cruises GmbH, TUI Deutschland (Chair.), Volkswagen AG; mem. Bd TUI China Travel Co. Ltd, TUI Travel PLC (Chair.); Chair. Exec. Cttee, World Travel & Tourism Council 2012–. *Address:* TUI AG, Postfach 610209, 30602 Hanover (office); TUI AG, Karl-Wiechert-Allee 4, 30625 Hanover, Germany (office). *Telephone:* (511) 56600 (office). *Fax:* (511) 5661901 (office). *E-mail:* info@tui-group.com (office). *Website:* www.tui-group.com (office).

FRÈRE, Baron; **Albert Pol Oscar Ghislain;** Belgian business executive; *Chairman of the Board, Groupe Bruxelles Lambert;* b. 4 Feb. 1926, Fontaine-L'Evêque; s. of Oscar Frère and Madeleine Bourgeois; m. Christine Hennuy; three c.; ed Athénée Provincial du Centre, Morlanwelz; Chair. Frère Bourgeois SA 1970; Vice-Chair. Benelux Paribas Cobepa SA 1973–2000; Chair. Financière de la Sambre 1973–, Erbe SA 1975, Fingen SA 1999, Stichting Administratie Kantoor de Frère-Bourgeois (Pays-Bas) 1982; Vice-Chair., Man. Dir and mem. Exec. Cttee Pargesa Holding SA, Geneva, Switzerland 1981; Chair. Electrafina SA 1982–2001; Man. Dir Groupe Bruxelles Lambert SA 1982–, Chair. 1987–; Chair. PetroFina 1990–2003; Vice-Chair. and mem. Bd Dirs TotalFinaElf 1999–2001; mem. Bd Dirs LVMH (Louis Vuitton Moët Hennessy) (France) 1997, Raspail Investissements (France) 2006), Société Civile Du Château Cheval Blanc (France) 1998, Gruppo Banca Leonardo 2006–09; mem. Bd of Dirs Métropole Télévision M6 2000–, Chair. Supervisory Bd 2003–; Vice-Chair. Suez 2001–08, Vice-Chair. GDF SUEZ 2008–; mem. Int. Advisory Cttee Power Corpn, Montréal 1985–2005, Assicurazioni Generali SpA, Trieste 1992; Perm. Rep. of Belholding Belgium SA; mem. Bd Dirs Groupe Arnault SA (France); Perm. Rep. of Frère-Bourgeois SA; Man. GBL Verwaltung SARL (Luxembourg); Régent honoraire, Banque nat. de Belgique 1980; Grand Croix, Légion d'honneur, Grand Officier, Ordre de Léopold; Dr hc (Univ. of Laval). *Leisure interests:* golf, skiing, hunting. *Address:* Groupe Bruxelles Lambert, 24 avenue Marnix, 1000 Brussels, Belgium (office); 33 avenue Foch, 75008 Paris, France (home); La Peupleraie, allée des Peupliers 17, 6280 Gerpinnes, Belgium. *Telephone:* (71) 60-60-15 (office). *Fax:* (71) 60-60-16 (office). *E-mail:* adimillo@cnp.be (office). *Website:* www.gbl.be (office).

FRÈRE, Gérald; Belgian business executive; *Chairman, Compagnie Nationale à Portefeuille (CNP);* b. 17 May 1951, Charleroi; s. of Baron Albert Frère; joined Frère-Bourgeois Group (family co.) 1972, later Man. Dir; mem. Bd of Dirs Compagnie Nationale à Portefeuille (CNP) 1988–, currently Chair.; also Chair. Diane SA, Filux SA, Gesecalux SA, Loverfin SA, Stichting Administratie Kantoor Bierlaire, TVI SA; Vice-Chair. Pargesa Holding SA (Dir 1992–); Chair. and Man. Dir Haras de la Bierlaire SA, Groupe Bruxelles Lambert SA 1993– (Exec. Dir 1982–); Man. Dir Financière de la Sambre SA; Dir Power Financial Corpn 1990–; Compagnie Benelux Paribas SA, COBEPA SA (Belgium), Erbe SA, Fingen SA, Fonds Charles-Albert Frère asbl (fmrly Fondation Charles Albert Frère asbl), GBL Finance SA, Stichting Administratie Kantoor Frère-Bourgeois (NL), Suez-

Tractebel SA, Fomento de Construcciones y Contratas, GIB SA, Clt-Ufa SA, AXA Holding SA, AXA Royale Belge SA, Corporation Financière Power (CDN), Frabepar, Hexane, PetroFina SA, Taittinger SA, Suez-Tractebel SA (Belgium), Lafarge SA 2008–; Dir (non-exec.) RTL Group SA 2000–06; Man. Agriger SPRL; mem. Bd of Regency, Nationale Bank van België (Banque Nationale de Belgique SA); mem. Supervisory Bd, Financial Services Authority, Brussels; fmr Exec. Officer, Chrome Corpn Ltd (fmrly Preston Resources Ltd); fmr Dir Electrafina SA, Soc. Générale de Belgique SA; mem. Bd of Trustees Belgian Governance Inst.; Hon. Consul of France. *Address:* Compagnie Nationale à Portefeuille, Rue de la Blanche Borne 12, 6280 Gerpinnes (Loverval) (office); Groupe Bruxelles Lambert SA, Avenue Marnix 24, 1000 Brussels, Belgium (office). *Telephone:* (71) 60-60-60 (Gerpinnes) (office); (2) 547-23-52 (Brussels) (office). *Fax:* (71) 60-60-70 (Gerpinnes) (office); (2) 547-22-85 (Brussels) (office). *E-mail:* info@cnp.be (office); info@gbl.be (office). *Website:* www.cnp.be (office); www.gbl.be (office).

FRÉROT, Antoine, PhD; French business executive; *Chairman and CEO, Veolia Environnement;* b. 3 June 1958, Fontainebleau; ed Ecole Polytechnique, Ecole Nationale des Ponts et Chaussées (ENPC); began career as a research engineer at Bureau Cen. d'études pour l'Outre-Mer; Project Man., Centre d'Études et de Recherche de l'ENPC (Cergrene) 1983, Deputy Dir 1984–88; worked for the Crédit National 1988–90; Head of Mission, Compagnie Générale des Eaux 1990–95; CEO Compagnie Générale d'Entreprises Automobiles (CGEA) and CGEA Transport 1995–2000; mem. Bd of Dirs Vivendi Environnement (VE) and CEO CONNEX Transport Div., VE 2000–03, CEO Veolia Eau-Compagnie Générale des Eaux, mem. Exec. Cttee VE and Deputy Man. Dir Veolia Environment 2003–, CEO Veolia Transport 2005–09, CEO Veolia Environnement 2009–, Chair. 2010–, also Dir of Veolia Transport, Veolia Propreté, Veolia Environnement 2010–, SARP and Sade CGTH, and Chair. Compagnie des Eaux et de l'Ozone and Veolia Water Solutions & Technologies, also acts as a Veolia Rep. on Bd of Soc. des Eaux de Marseille. *Address:* Veolia Environnement, 36–38 Avenue Kléber, 75116 Paris, Cedex 8, France (office). *Telephone:* 1-71-75-00-00 (office). *Fax:* 1-71-71-15-45 (office). *E-mail:* info@veoliaenvironnement.com (office). *Website:* www.veoliaenvironnement.com (office).

FRESTON, Thomas (Tom) E., BA, MBA; American media executive; b. 22 Nov. 1945, New York; s. of Thomas E. Freston and Winifred Geng; m. Margaret Badali 1980; one s.; Dir of Marketing, MTV, MTV Networks, New York 1980–81; Dir of Marketing, The Movie Channel 1982–83; Vice-Pres. Marketing MTV, MTV Networks 1983–84, Vice-Pres. of Marketing 1984–85, Sr Vice-Pres. and Gen. Man. of Affiliate Sales, Marketing 1985, Sr Vice-Pres. and Gen. Man. MTV, VH-1 1985–86, Pres. Entertainment 1986–87, Pres. and CEO 1987–89, Chair. and CEO MTV Networks 1989–2004; Co-Pres. and Co-COO Viacom Inc. 2004–05, CEO Viacom (after split of Viacom Inc.) 2005–06; currently Prin. Firefly3 LLC (media consultancy); mem. Bd of Dirs Cable Advertising Bureau 1987–, Museum of Natural History, Rock and Roll Hall of Fame 1986–; mem. Smithsonian Comm. Music in America 1987–, Cable TV Admin. and Marketing Asscn, Nat. Acad. of Cable Programming; Gov.'s Award from Nat. Acad. of Cable Programming, Personality of the Year from MIPCOM, Pres. Award from Cable TV Public Affairs Asscn, Humanitarian of the Year Award from T.J. Martell Foundation; inducted into Cable TV Hall of Fame 2005. *Leisure interests:* photography, travel, antique rugs.

FRETTON, Anthony (Tony); British architect; *Professor of Architectural and Interior Design, Technical University of Delft;* b. 17 Jan. 1945, London; s. of Thomas C. Fretton and May Frances Diamond; m. Susan Pearce 1963 (divorced 1988); one s. one d.; ed Architectural Asscn School of Architecture; architect, Arup Assocs, then Neylan and Ungless 1972–81; f. own architectural practice Tony Fretton Architects 1982; Unit Master, AA School of Architecture 1989–91; Visiting Prof., Berlage Inst., Amsterdam, Netherlands, Ecole Polytechnique de Lausanne, Switzerland 1994–96; Prof. of Architectural and Interior Design, Tech. Univ. of Delft, Netherlands 1999–; Visiting Lecturer, Harvard Design School, USA 2005; Visiting Lecturer, ETH Zurich 2010; Corp. mem. RIBA; Dr hc (Oxford Brookes) 2006. *Major projects include:* Lisson Gallery, London 1992, Artsway Centre for Visual Arts, Sway, Hampshire 1996, Quay Arts Centre, Newport, Isle of Wight 1998, Two Apartments, Groningen, Netherlands 2001, The Red House, Chelsea, London (Stone Fed. of GB Natural Stone Award 2002, RIBA Award 2003, Chicago Athenaeum Int. Architecture Award 2004), Faith House, Holton Lee Centre for Disability in the Arts, Poole, Dorset (ACE/RIBA Awards for Religious Architecture 2003, Guardian Best British Building of the Year Award) 2002, Arts Council Sculpture Gallery, Yorkshire Sculpture Park 2003, Camden Arts Centre, London 2004, Constantijn Huygenstraat, Amsterdam 2004–11, House for Two Artists, Clerkenwell, London 2005, Stroud Valley Arts Space 2007, House for Anish Kapoor 2008, Vassall Road Housing, London 2008, Fuglsang Kunstmuseum, Lolland, Denmark (RIBA Award 2009) 2008, British Embassy, Warsaw, Poland (RIBA Award 2010) 2009, de Prinsendam, Amsterdam 2010, Tietgens Grund, Copenhagen 2010, Andreas Ensemble, Amsterdam 2010. *Publications:* Tony Fretton 1995, Tony Fretton Architects: Abstraction and Familiarity 2001, 10 x 10_2 100 Architects, 10 Critics, 2005, Designing the Warsaw Embassy: Tony Fretton Architects 2006, Two Minds: Artists and Architects in Collaboration 2006, 2G Tony Fretton Architects 2009; numerous exhbn catalogues. *Leisure interests:* travel, film, visual arts, poetry. *Address:* 109–123 Clifton Street, London, EC2A 4LD, England (office). *Telephone:* (20) 7729-2030 (office). *Fax:* (20) 7729-2050 (office). *E-mail:* mail@tonyfretton.com (office). *Website:* www.tonyfretton.com (office).

FRETWELL, Sir John Emsley, Kt, GCMG, MA; British diplomatist (retd); b. 15 June 1930, Chesterfield, Derbyshire, England; s. of Francis T. Fretwell and Dorothy Fretwell; m. Mary Ellen Eugenie Dubois 1959; one s. one d.; ed Chesterfield Grammar School, Lausanne Univ., King's Coll., Cambridge; Nat. Service, 2nd Lt, RA 1948–50; entered diplomatic service 1953, Third Sec., Hong Kong 1954–55, Second Sec., Embassy in Beijing 1955–57, Foreign Office 1957–59, 1962–67, First Sec., Moscow 1959–62, First Sec. (Commercial), Washington, DC 1967–70, Commercial Counsellor, Warsaw 1971–73, Head of European Integration Dept (Internal), FCO 1973–76, Asst Under-Sec. of State 1976–79, Minister, Washington, DC 1980–81; Amb. to France 1982–87; Political Dir and Deputy to Perm. Under-Sec. of State, FCO 1987–90; mem. Council of Lloyd's 1991–92; Specialist Adviser, House of Lords 1992–93; Chair. Franco-British Soc. 1995–2005,

mem. Council 2005–; currently freelance adviser in int. affairs; Commdr, Legion d'honneur; Grand Officier, Ordre nat. du Mérite. *Leisure interests:* walking, history, wine. *Address:* c/o Brooks's, St James's Street, London, SW1A 1LN, England. *E-mail:* chairman@passportsforpets.org (office).

FREUD, Anthony Peter, OBE, LLB; British opera administrator and barrister; *General Director, Lyric Opera of Chicago;* b. 30 Oct. 1957, London, England; s. of the late Joseph Freud and Katalin Freud (née Löwi); partner Colin Ure; ed King's Coll. School, Wimbledon, King's Coll., London; trained as barrister before becoming theatre manager at Sadler's Wells Theatre Co. 1980–84; Co. Sec., Welsh Nat. Opera 1984, Head of Planning 1989–92, Gen. Dir 1994–2005; Chair. Opera Europe 2001–05; Gen. Dir and CEO Houston Grand Opera, Tex., USA 2006–11; Gen. Dir Lyric Opera of Chicago 2011–; Exec. Producer, Opera, Philips Classics 1992–94; Chair. OPERA America 2008–12; Chair. Jury, BBC Cardiff Singer of the World Competition 1995–2005; Trustee, Nat. Endowment for Science, Tech. and the Arts 2004–05; Hon. Fellow, Univ. of Cardiff 2002, Royal Welsh Coll. of Music and Drama 2005. *Leisure interests:* music, theatre, cinema, visual arts, travel, cookery. *Address:* Lyric Opera of Chicago, 20 North Wacker Drive, Chicago, IL 60606, USA (office). *Telephone:* (312) 827-3550 (office). *Fax:* (312) 332-0503 (office). *E-mail:* afreud@lyricopera.org (office). *Website:* www.lyricopera.org (office).

FREUDENTHAL, David Duane (Dave), BA, JD; American lawyer, politician and fmr state governor; b. 12 Oct. 1950, Thermopolis, Wyo.; m. Nancy D. Freudenthal; two s. two d.; ed Amherst Coll., Mass, Univ. of Wyoming Coll. of Law; economist, Wyo. Dept of Econ. Planning and Devt 1973–75, apptd State Planning Co-ordinator 1975–80; f. law office, Cheyenne 1980; US Attorney, Wyo. 1994–2001; Gov. of Wyo. 2003–11; Chair. Wyoming State Democratic Cen. Cttee 1981–85; fmr Chair. Greater Cheyenne Chamber of Commerce; Founder-Dir Wyo. Student Loans Corpn; mem. Bd of Dirs Arch Coal, Inc. 2011–; mem. Wyoming Futures Project 1984–87, Wyo. State Econ. and Devt and Stabilization Bd 1985–89, Educ. Policy Implementation Council 1989–90, Bd Wyo. Community Foundation, Laramie Co. Community Action; Gov. Substance Abuse and Violent Crime Advisory Bd 1994–2001; Democrat. *Address:* Arch Coal, Inc., One CityPlace Drive, Suite 300, St Louis, MO 63141, USA (office). *Telephone:* (314) 994-2700 (office). *Fax:* (314) 994-2878 (office). *E-mail:* webmaster@archcoal.com (office). *Website:* www.archcoal.com (office).

FREY, Bruno S., FRSE; Swiss economist and academic; *Professor of Economics, University of Zürich;* b. 4 May 1941, Basel; s. of Leo Frey and Julie Frey (née Bach); ed Univs of Basel and Cambridge; Assoc. Prof., Univ. of Basel 1969–; Prof. of Econs, Univ. of Konstanz 1970–77, Univ. of Zürich 1977–; Visiting Fellow, All Souls Coll., Oxford 1983; Fellow, Coll. of Science, Berlin 1984–85; Visiting Research Prof., Univ. of Chicago, Ill. 1990; Visiting Prof., Univ. of Rome 1996–97, Antwerp Univ. 1999, Univs of Gothenburg, Stockholm, Linz, Klagenfurt, Siena, Kiel, Valencia, Groningen, Research School of Social Sciences, ANU, Queensland Univ. of Tech., ETH-Zürich 2007–; Research Dir Centre for Research in Econs, Man. and the Arts, Zürich 2000–; Fellow, Collegium Budapest 2002, European Econ. Asscn 2004, Public Choice Soc.; First Jelle Zijlstra Professorial Fellow, Inst. of Advanced Study, Wassenaar 2003; Distinguished Fellow, CESifo Research Network 2005; Man. Ed. Kyklos 1969–; Hon. DUniv (St Gallen) 1998, (Gothenburg) 1998; Vernon Prize, Asscn for Public Policy and Man., Stolper Prize of Verein für Socialpolitik. *Publications include:* Economics as a Science of Human Behaviour 1992, Not Just for the Money: An Economic Theory of Personal Motivation 1997, The New Democratic Federalism for Europe 1999, Arts and Economics: Analysis and Cultural Policy 2000, Managing Motivation: Wie Sie alte neue Motivationsforschung für Ihr Unternehmen nutzen können (co-author) 2000, Inspiring Economics: Human Motivation in Political Economy 2001, Successful Management by Motivation – Balancing Intrinsic and Extrinsic Incentives 2002, Happiness and Economics: How the Economy and Institutions Affect Human Well-Being 2002, Dealing with Terrorism: Stick or Carrot? 2004, Economics and Psychology 2007, Happiness: A Revolution in Economics 2008. *Leisure interest:* travel.

FREY JENSEN, Hugo, MEconSc; Danish economist and central banker; *Governor, Danmarks Nationalbank;* b. 11 Jan. 1958; m. Helle Frey Jensen 1984; ed Univ. of Århus; Asst Lecturer, Univ. of Århus 1980–84, Univ. of Copenhagen 1984–88, Copenhagen Business School 1989–92; Asst Admin. and Man. in various depts, Danmarks Nationalbank (central bank) 1984–93, Head of Monetary Policy Office and Econs Dept 1994–2000, later Head of Capital Markets Dept, Deputy Dir 2010, Gov. 2011–; Dir European Central Bank 1993–2001, 2008–10; mem. EU Econ. Policy Cttee 1997–2000, European Central Bank Supervision Cttee 2001–07, Banking Advisory Cttee 2001–03; Dir Fondsrådet (Danish Securities Council) 2003–07, 2010–11; mem. Bd of Dirs Bankernes Kontantservice (BKS) 2013–, Nets Holding 2013–; mem. Advisory Tech. Cttee, ESRB 2011; Chair. Danmarks Nationalbank's Pension Fund 2011–; Observer, Bankernes EDB Central (BEC) 2011–. *Address:* Board of Governors, Danmarks Nationalbank, Havnegade 5, 1093 Copenhagen K, Denmark (office). *Telephone:* 33-63-63-63 (office). *Fax:* 33-63-71-03 (office). *E-mail:* nationalbanken@nationalbanken.dk (office). *Website:* www.nationalbanken.dk (office).

FREYRE, Angela Mariana, BA, DEJG, LLM, JD; American (b. Cuban) lawyer and business executive; *Senior Vice-President and General Counsel, Export-Import Bank of the United States (Ex-Im Bank);* b. 18 Sept. 1954, Havana, Cuba; ed Wellesley Coll., Mass, Université de Droit d'Economie et des Sciences Sociales de Paris, Georgetown Univ., Washington, DC; admitted to NY Bar 1984; Assoc., Mudge, Rose, Guthrie, Alexander & Ferdon LLP, New York and Paris 1984–95; Pnr, Coudert Brothers LLP, New York (int. corp. finance firm) 1995–2005; Sr Vice-Pres. and Deputy Gen. Counsel for Legal and Strategic Affairs, The Nielsen Co. (global information services co.) 2005–11; Sr Vice-Pres. and Gen. Counsel, Export-Import Bank of the US (Ex-Im Bank), Washington, DC 2011–; mem. City of New York Conflicts of Interest Bd; Trustee, New York Studio School Drawing, Painting & Sculpture 1984–, LongHouse Reserve Ltd 2000–; mem. Bar Asscn, City of New York; Fulbright Scholar. *Address:* Export-Import Bank of the United States, 811 Vermont Avenue, NW, Washington, DC 20571, USA (office). *Telephone:* (202) 565-3946 (office). *Fax:* (202) 565-3380 (office). *E-mail:* info@exim.gov (office). *Website:* www.exim.gov (office).

FRICK, Aurelia, Lic.iur., DrIur; Liechtenstein lawyer and politician; *Minister of Foreign Affairs, Justice and Cultural Affairs;* b. 19 Sept. 1975; ed Univ. of Fribourg, Univ. of Basel; admitted to Zürich Bar 2004; attorney, Haymann & Baldi, Zürich 2004–05; Assoc., Bjørn Johansson Assocs AG, Zürich 2006–07; man. consultant 2008–09; Minister of Foreign Affairs, Justice and Cultural Affairs 2009–; mem. Progressive Citizens' Party. *Leisure interests:* music, sport, culture. *Address:* Regierungsgebäude, Postfach 684, 9490 Vaduz, Liechtenstein (office). *Telephone:* 2366111 (office). *Fax:* 2366022 (office). *E-mail:* office@liechtenstein.li (office). *Website:* www.liechtenstein.li (office).

FRICK, Mario, DrIur; Liechtenstein lawyer, politician and civil servant; *Partner, Seeger, Frick & Partner AG;* b. 8 May 1965, Balzers; s. of Kuno Frick-Kaufmann and Melita Frick-Kaufmann; m. Andrea Haberlander 1992; one s. one d.; ed Univ. of St Gallen, Switzerland; State Admin. Legal Service 1991–93; mem. Municipal Council of Balzers 1991–93; Deputy Head of Govt May–Dec. 1993, Head of Govt 1993–2001, also Minister of Finance and Construction; currently Pnr, Seeger, Frick & Pnr AG (law firm); Trustee, Univ. of St Gallen 2002–. *Leisure interests:* football, tennis, biking. *Address:* Seeger, Frick & Partner AG, Seeger-Haus, Kirchstrasse 6, 9494, Schaan, Liechtenstein (office). *Telephone:* 2652225 (office). *Fax:* 2652232 (office). *E-mail:* mario.frick@sfplex.li (office). *Website:* www.sfplex.li (office).

FRIDERICHS, Hans, Dr rer. pol; German politician and business executive; b. 16 Oct. 1931, Wittlich; s. of Dr Paul Friderichs and Klara Neuwinger; m. Erika Wilhelm; two d.; Man. Rhineland-Hesse Chamber of Industry and Trade 1959–63; Deputy Business Man. FDP 1963–64, Business Man. 1964–69; mem. Bundestag 1965–69, 1976–77; Sec. of State, Ministry of Agric., Viniculture and Protection of the Environment for Rhineland Palatinate 1969–72; Fed. Minister of Econs 1972–77; Deputy Chair. FDP 1974–77; Dir Dresdner Bank 1977–85, Chair. Bd Man. Dirs 1978–85 (resgnd); mem. Supervisory Bd AEG Telefunken 1979, Chair. 1980–84; Chair. Supervisory Bd allit AG Kunststofftechnik, Goldman Sachs Investment Management GmbH, Frankfurt, Germany, Leica Camera AG, Solms, Germany, Racke-Dujardin GmbH & Co. KG, Bingen, Germany, C.A. Kupferberg & Cie. KGaA, Mainz, Germany; Deputy Chair. Supervisory Bd adidas AG –2007, Chair. 2007–09; Deputy Chair. Supervisory Bd IIC The New German Länder Industrial Investment Council GmbH, Berlin, Germany; mem. Supervisory Bd Schneider Electric S.A., Paris, France –2005. *Leisure interests:* art, sport. *Address:* c/o Supervisory Board, adidas AG, Adi-Dassler-Straße 1, 91074 Herzogenaurach; Kappelhofgasse 2, 55116 Mainz, Germany.

FRIDJONSSON, Thordur, MA (Econs); Icelandic economist; *CEO, NASDAQ OMX Iceland;* b. 2 Jan. 1952, Reykjavík; s. of Fridjon Thordarson and Kristin Sigurdardottir; m. 1st Thrudur Haraldsdottir 1971 (divorced); two s. two d.; m. 2nd Ragnheidur Agnarsdottir; one d.; ed Univ. of Iceland and Queen's Univ., Ont., Canada; Chief Economist, Fed. of Icelandic Industries 1978–80; Econ. Adviser to Prime Minister of Iceland 1980–86; part-time lecturer, Dept of Econs, Univ. of Iceland 1979–87; Man. Dir Nat. Econ. Inst. 1987–2002; Sec.-Gen. Ministry of Industry and Commerce 1998–99; Pres. and CEO Iceland Stock Exchange 2002–06, CEO NASDAQ OMX Iceland 2006–; mem. Bd of Dirs Nordic Project Fund 1982–96; Chair. Asscn of Icelandic Economists 1982–85, Icelandic Man. Asscn 1986–87, Econ. Research. Inst. for Agric. 1991–2002, Co-ordinating Cttee Iceland-Norsk Hydro 1998–2001; Alt. Gov. EBRD 1998–99, IMF 1998–99; Rep. for Iceland, EDRC and OECD 1987–2002; mem. Econ. Policy Cttee, OECD 1987–2002; mem. Bd of Dirs NOREX Alliance 2002–06, OMX Nordic Exchanges; John Hicks Fellowship, Queen's Univ. 1978. *Publications:* Icelandic Economy 1984; numerous articles in journals and books. *Leisure interests:* outdoor activities and sport. *Address:* NASDAQ OMX Iceland, Laugavegur 182, 105 Reykjavík (office); Kolbeinsmyri 11, 170 Seltjarnarnes, Iceland (home). *Telephone:* 5252800 (office); 5626854 (home). *Fax:* 5252888 (office). *E-mail:* thuridur.gudmundsdottir@nasdaqomx.com (office); thordur.fridjonsson@nasdaqomx.com (home). *Website:* www.nasdaqomx.com (office).

FRIDMAN, Mikhail Maratovich; Russian business executive; *Chairman, Supervisory Board, Alfa-Group Consortium;* b. 21 April 1964, Lvov, Ukraine; m.; two c.; ed Moscow Inst. of Steel and Alloys; with Electrostal, Moscow region 1986–88; Founder Alfa-Foto, Alfa-Eco, Alfa-Capital 1988, Chair. Alfa-Bank (later Alfa-Group) from 1991, Alfa-Consortium from 1996, Alfa Commercial Bank from 1998, now Chair. Supervisory Bd Alfa-Group Consortium, Interim CEO TNK-BP (joint venture between BP and Alfa-Access-Renova) 2009–11, Exec. Chair. 2011–13 (co. acquired by Rosneft); mem. Bd of Dirs Russian Public TV (ORTV) 1995–98, Oil Co. SIDANKO 1996–2000, Perekrestok Trade House 1998–, VimpelCom; mem. Supervisory Bd X5 Retail Group NV; Founder, Vice-Pres. Russian Jewish Congress 1996–, Head of Cttee on Culture 1996–; mem. Council on Banking Activity, Fed. Govt 1996–, Council on Business, Council of Ministers 2001–; mem. Bureau of Man. Bd Russian Council of Industrialists and Entrepreneurs; elected to Russia's Public Chamber 2005; Founder and Chair. Genesis Philanthropy Group; mem. Int. Advisory Bd Council of Foreign Relations; Golden Plate Award, topped list of 1,000 most professional Russian managers, compiled by Managers Asscn and Kommersant publishing house 2001, recognized by Vedomosti newspaper as the entrepreneur for most effective business management 2001, topped list of inter-industry group managers in list of Russia's 1,000 most professional managers, Managers Asscn and Kommersant 2002, Golden Plate Award, Int. Acad. of Achievement, Washington, DC 2003, named by Business Week magazine as one of the outstanding businessmen of the year 2003, Businessman of the Year, Vedomosti newspaper 2003, included in Financial Times Leaders of the New Europe list 2004. *Address:* Alfa-Bank, 107078 Moscow, Kalanchevskaya str. 27, Russia (office). *Telephone:* (495) 929-91-91 (office). *Fax:* (495) 788-69-81 (office). *E-mail:* mail@alfabank.ru (office). *Website:* alfabank.com (office).

FRIDRIKSSON, Fridrik Thor; Icelandic film director; b. 12 May 1954; s. of Fridrik Gudmundson and Gudridur Hjaltested; m. (divorced); one s. one d.; founder Reykjavik Film Festival; est. Icelandic Film Corp. (production co.) 1984. *Films:* Eldsmiðurinn (The Blacksmith) 1981, Rokk í Reykjavik (Rock in Reykjavik) 1982, Kúreakr norðursins (Icelandic Cowboys) 1984, Hringurinn (The Circle) 1985, Skytturnar (White Whales) 1987, Flugprá (Sky Without Limit) 1989, Englakroppar (Pretty Angels) 1990, Börn náttúrunnar (Children of Nature) 1991, Bíódagar (Movie Days) 1994, Á köldum klaka (Cold Fever) 1995, Djöflaeyjan

(Devil's Island) 1996, Englar alheimsins (Angels of the Universe) 2000, Fálkar 2002, Næsland 2004, The Boss of It All 2006. *Address:* Icelandic Film Corporation, Hverfisgata 46, 101 Reykjavik (office); Bjarkargata 8, 101 Reykjavik, Iceland (home). *Telephone:* 5512260 (office); 5528566 (home). *Fax:* 5525154 (office). *E-mail:* icecorp@vortex.is (office); f.thor@vortex.is (home). *Website:* www.icecorp.is.

FRIED, Charles, LLB, MA; American lawyer and academic; *Beneficial Professor of Law, Harvard Law School;* b. (Karel Fried), 15 April 1935, Prague, Czechoslovakia; s. of Anthony Fried and Marta Fried (née Wintersteinova); m. Anne Sumerscale 1959; one s. one d.; ed Princeton and Columbia Univs, Univ. of Oxford, UK; law clerk to Assoc. Justice John M. Harlan, US Supreme Court 1960; mem. Faculty, Harvard Law School 1961–, Prof. of Law 1965–85, Carter Prof. of Gen. Jurisprudence 1981–85, 1989–95, Prof. Emer., Distinguished Lecturer 1995–, Beneficial Prof. of Law 1999–; Deputy Solicitor-Gen. and Counsellor to Solicitor-Gen. 1985, Solicitor-Gen. of USA 1985–89; Assoc. Justice Supreme Judiciary Court of Mass, Boston 1995–99; Fellow, American Acad. of Arts and Sciences. *Publications:* An Anatomy of Values 1970, Medical Experimentation: Personal Integrity and Social Policy 1974, Right and Wrong 1978, Contract as Promise: A Theory of Contractual Obligation 1981, Order and Law: Arguing the Reagan Revolution 1991, Making Tort Law (with David Rosenberg) 2003, Saying What the Law Is: The Constitution in the Supreme Court 2004, Modern Liberty 2006, Because it is Wrong: Torture, Privacy and Presidential Power in the Age of Terror (with Gregory Fried) 2010; contribs to legal and philosophical journals. *Address:* Harvard Law School, 1563 Massachusetts Avenue, Cambridge, MA 02138, USA (office). *Telephone:* (617) 495-4636 (home). *Fax:* (617) 496-4865 (office). *E-mail:* fried@law.harvard.edu (office). *Website:* www.law.harvard.edu (office).

FRIED, Jonathan T., BA, LLB, LLM; Canadian diplomatist and international organization official; *Ambassador to Japan;* b. 19 Aug. 1953, Edmonton, Alberta; m. Paula Vaillancourt; ed Univ. of Toronto, Columbia Univ., New York, Parker School of Foreign and Comparative Law (Program in Int. Business Law); articles of clerkship and pvt. practice with Field, Owen, Barristers and Solicitors, Edmonton, Alberta 1977–78; UN Sixth Cttee (Legal) 1980; Asst Sec. to Canadian Del. to Ottawa Summit 1981; Second Sec. and Vice-Consul, Embassy in Brasilia 1981–83; Counsel, Econ. Law and Treaty Div., Legal Affairs Bureau, Foreign Affairs and Int. Trade Canada 1983–86, Asst Gen. Counsel, Trade Negotiations Office 1986–87; Counsellor for Congressional and Legal Affairs, Embassy in Washington, DC 1987–91; Prin. Legal Counsel, N American Free Trade Agreement (NAFTA) Bureau, Foreign Affairs and Int. Trade Canada 1991–93, Dir Gen., Trade Policy Bureau and Co-ordinator for NAFTA 1995–97, Asst Deputy Minister, Trade, Econ. and Environmental Policy 1997–2000, Sr Asst Deputy Minister and G7 Deputy for Canada, Finance Canada 2000–03, Assoc. Deputy Minister, Foreign Affairs and Int. Trade Canada 2003; Sr Foreign Policy Advisor and Head, Canada-US Secr. to the Prime Minister of Canada, Privy Council Office 2003–06; Exec. for Canada, Ireland and the Caribbean, IMF 2006–08; Amb. to Japan 2008–; mem. Law Soc. of Alberta. *Address:* Embassy of Canada, 7-3-38, Akasaka, Minato-ku, Tokyo 107-8503, Japan (office). *Telephone:* (3) 5412-6200 (office). *Fax:* (3) 5412-6247 (office). *E-mail:* tokyo@international.gc.ca (office). *Website:* www.canadainternational.gc.ca/japan-japon (office).

FRIED, Linda Phyllis, BA, MD, MPh; American physician, academic and university administrator; *DeLamar Professor of Public Health and Dean, Mailman School of Public Health, Columbia University;* b. 1949, New York City; ed Hunter Coll. High School, New York, Rush Medical Coll., Chicago, Johns Hopkins Univ., Colgate Univ.; intern, Rush Presbyterian St Luke's Medical Center, Chicago 1979–80, resident in internal medicine 1980–82; Fellow in Gen. Internal Medicine, Johns Hopkins Medical Inst., Baltimore 1982–85, Fellow in Epidemiology 1983–85, Fellow in Geriatrics 1985–86, Prof. of Medicine, Epidemiology and Health Policy 2003–08, Mason F. Lord Prof. of Geriatric Medicine 2003–08, Dir Div. of Geriatric Medicine and Gerontology 2003–08, Medical Insts' Center of Excellence for Aging Research –2008, Center on Aging and Health –2008, Dir Program Epidemiology of Aging, Bloomberg School of Public Health –2008; Dean, Mailman School of Public Health, Columbia Univ. 2008–, DeLamar Prof. of Public Health 2008–, Prof. of Epidemiology 2008–, Sr Vice-Pres. Columbia Univ. Medical Center 2008–; Co-founder Experience Corps, Baltimore 2002; mem. Nat. Advisory Council on Aging 2003–; mem. Inst. of Medicine, NAS; mem. World Econ. Forum Council on Challenges of Gerontology; Herbert DeVries Distinguished Research Award, Council on Aging and Adult Devt 2000, Mary Betty Stevens Award, ACP 2007, Archstone Award, American Public Health Asscn, Maxwell Pollack Award, Gerontological Soc. of America, American Geriatrics Soc.'s Henderson Award, Merit Award from Nat. Inst. on Aging. *Address:* Office of the Dean, Mailman School of Public Health, Columbia Univ., 722 West 168th Street, R1408, New York, NY 10032, USA (office). *Telephone:* (212) 305-9300 (office). *Fax:* (212) 305-9342 (office). *E-mail:* lpfried@columbia.edu (office). *Website:* www.mailmanschool.org (office).

FRIEDBERG, Aaron L., AB, AM, PhD; American academic; *Professor of Politics and International Affairs, Woodrow Wilson School, Princeton University;* b. 1956, Pittsburgh; ed Harvard Univ.; joined Woodrow Wilson School, Princeton Univ. 1987, currently Prof. of Politics and Int. Affairs; Henry A. Kissinger Chair in Foreign Policy and Int. Relations, John W. Kluge Center, Library of Congress 2001–02; fmr Fellow, Woodrow Wilson Int. Center for Scholars, Smithsonian Inst., Norwegian Nobel Inst. 1998, Harvard Univ. Center for Int. Affairs; Deputy Asst for Nat. Security Affairs, Office of the Vice-Pres., Washington, DC 2003–05; Chair. Bd of Counselors, Kenneth B. and Anne H.H. Pyle Center for Northeast Asian Studies, Nat. Bureau of Asian Research; 1986. *Publications include:* The Weary Titan: Britain and the Experience of Relative Decline 1895–1905 (Edgar Furniss Nat. Security Book Award 1988), In the Shadow of the Garrison State: America's Anti-Statism and Its Cold War Grand Strategy 2000, Strategic Asia 2001–02: Power and Purpose (co-ed.) 2001, A Contest for Supremacy: China, America, and the Struggle for Mastery in Asia 2011. *Address:* Woodrow Wilson School, Bendheim 013, Princeton University, Princeton, NJ 08544-1013, USA (office). *Telephone:* (609) 258-9891 (office). *E-mail:* alf@princeton.edu (office). *Website:* www.princeton.edu (office).

FRIEDEL, Jacques, PhD, DèsSc; French fmr physicist; b. 11 Feb. 1921, Paris; s. of Edmond Friedel and Jeanne Friedel (née Bersier); m. Mary Winifred Horder 1952; two s.; ed Ecole Polytechnique, Ecole des Mines de Paris, Univ. of Bristol,

Paris Univ.; mining engineer, Ecole des Mines de Paris 1948–56; Maître de Conférences, Univ. de Paris 1956–59; Prof. of Solid State Physics, Univ. de Paris (later Paris Sud) 1959–89; Pres. Section 21, Consultative Cttee on Univs 1975–80; Pres. Consultative Comm. of Scientific and Tech. Research 1978–80; mem. Acad. of Sciences 1977–, Vice-Pres. 1991–92, Pres. 1992–94; Pres. Observatoire nat. de la lecture 1994–2001; Hon. mem. Royal Soc., London, NAS, American Acad. of Sciences and Letters, Swedish Acad. of Sciences, Leopoldina, Belgian Royal Acad. of Sciences, Brazilian Acad. of Sciences, American Physical Soc., Inst. of Physics, Max Planck Gesellschaft; Grand Officier, Légion d'honneur, Commdr Ordre nat. du Mérite, Commdr Order of Scientific Merit (Brazil); Hon. DSc (Bristol) 1977, (Lausanne) 1979, (Geneva) 1992, (Cambridge) 1995, (Zagreb) 1995; Gold Medal, Conseil Nat. de la Recherche Scientifique, Soc. Française de Metallurgie, Acta Metallurgica (USA); several int. scientific awards and prizes. *Publications:* Dislocations 1956, Graine de Mandarin 1994; 250 publs in scientific journals. *Leisure interest:* gardening. *Address:* 2 rue Jean-François Gerbillon, 75006 Paris, France (home). *Telephone:* 1-42-22-25-85 (home).

FRIEDEN, Luc; Luxembourg politician; b. 16 Sept. 1963, Esch-sur-Alzette; m.; two c.; ed Lycée de garçons, Esch-sur-Alzette, Athénée de Luxembourg, Centre universitaire de Luxembourg, Université de Paris I (Panthéon Sorbonne), France, Univ. of Cambridge, UK, Harvard Law School, USA; commentator RTL, Luxembourg Radio 1981–94; attorney-at-law 1989–98; fmr teacher Centre Universitaire de Luxembourg; mem. Parl. 1994–, Chair. Finance and Budget Cttee, Cttee on Constitutional Affairs 1994–98; Minister of Justice, of the Budget and for Relations with Parl. 1998–99; Minister of Justice and of the Treasury and Budget 1999, also Minister of Defence 2004–05, Minister of Finance 2009–13; Gov. World Bank 1998, Asian Devt Bank 2003–04; mem. moral sciences and politics section, Institut Grand-Ducal. *Address:* c/o Ministry of Finance, 3 rue de la Congrégation, 1352, Luxembourg (office).

FRIEDEN, Thomas R., BA, MD, MPH; American physician and public health official; *Director, Centers for Disease Control and Prevention;* ed Oberlin Coll., Columbia Univ., Yale Univ.; began career as Epidemic Intelligence Service Officer, New York City Health Dept 1990–92; Head of New York City tuberculosis control programme 1992–96; worked on tuberculosis control programme for WHO, India 1996–2002; Commr, New York City Health Dept 2002–09; Dir Centers for Disease Control and Prevention and Admin., Agency for Toxic Substances and Disease Registry 2009–; fmr adviser on health to New York City Mayor Michael Bloomberg; numerous awards and honours. *Publications:* more than 200 scientific articles. *Address:* Office of the Director, Centers for Disease Control and Prevention, 1600 Clifton Rd, Atlanta, GA 3033, USA (office). *E-mail:* cdcinfo@cdc.gov (office). *Website:* www.cdc.gov (office).

FRIEDERICI, Gonthier Jean-Claude; French government official; *Prefect of Finistère;* b. 23 Aug. 1945, Lille; ed Lycée de Pontoise, Lycée Clémenceau, Reims, Lycée Lakanl, Sceaux, Univ. de Paris VIII; teacher 1970–77; numerous positions in departmental prefectures 1977–84; Deputy Chief of Staff to Prime Minister Laurent Fabius 1984–86; Chief of Mission to Sec.-Gen. of Centre nat. d'études spatiales 1986–88; Sub-Prefect, Alès 1989–90; Sec.-Gen. of Prefecture, Saône-et-Loire 1991–92; Sub-Prefect Saint-Germain-en-Laye Dist 1993–97; Prefect Belfort Territory 1997–2000, Pyrénées-Orientales 2000–01, region and Dept of Réunion 2001–04, Finistère 2004–; Chevalier Légion d'Honneur, Ordre du Mérite Maritime, Ordre nat. du Mérite, Ordre du Mérite agricole. *Address:* Préfecture du Finistère, 42 boulevard Dupleix, 29320 Quimper Cedex, France (office). *Telephone:* 2-98-76-29-29 (office). *Fax:* 2-98-52-09-47 (office). *E-mail:* courrier@finistere.pref.gouv.fr (office). *Website:* www.finistere.pref.gouv.fr (office).

FRIEDKIN, William; American film director; b. 29 Aug. 1939, Chicago; s. of Louis Friedkin and Rae Green; m. 1st Lesley-Anne Down (divorced); one s.; m. 2nd Sherry Lansing (q.v.). *Films directed include:* Good Times 1967, The Night They Raided Minsky's 1968, The Birthday Party 1968, The Boys in the Band 1970, The French Connection 1971 (Acad. Award for Best Picture, 1971), The Exorcist 1973, Sorcerer 1977, The Brinks Job 1979, Cruising 1980, Deal of the Century 1983, To Live and Die in LA 1985, C.A.T. Squad 1986, The Guardian 1990, Rampage 1992, Blue Chip 1993, Jade 1995, Twelve Angry Men 1997, Rules of Engagement 2000, Night Train 2000, The Hunted 2003, Bug 2006; several TV films. *Address:* c/o ICM, 8942 Wilshire Boulevard, Los Angeles, CA 90211-1934, USA (office). *Telephone:* (310) 550-4000 (office).

FRIEDMAN, Jack; American business executive; *CEO, Innovative Ag Services;* Dir, FCStone from 1996, fmr Vice-Chair., Dir of International Assets following merger with International Assets Holding Corpn 2009–, Chair. INTL FCStone Inc. 2009–12; Partner, Innovative Ag Services, Monticello, Ia (or with its predecessor) for 21 years, currently CEO; Man. Swiss Valley Ag Center, Monticello 1995–; mem. Bd of Dirs Western Dubuque Biodiesel LLC. *Address:* INTL FCStone Inc., 708 Third Avenue, 15th Floor, New York, NY 10017, USA (office). *Telephone:* (212) 485-3500 (office). *Fax:* (212) 485-3505 (office). *E-mail:* info@intlfcstone.com (office). *Website:* www.intlfcstone.com (office).

FRIEDMAN, Jane, BA; American publishing executive; *CEO, Open Road Integrated Media;* b. Sept. 1945, Brooklyn, New York; ed New York Univ.; dictaphone typist, publicity dept Alfred A. Knopf, subsidiary co. of Random House 1968, later Assoc. Publr Alfred A. Knopf; Pres. Random House Audio 1985; Publr Vintage Books 1990; Exec. Vice-Pres. Knopf Publishing Group, Random House Inc. 1992; fmr mem. Random House Exec. Cttee; Pres., HarperCollins Worldwide 1997–2007, CEO 1997–2008 (resgnd); Co-founder and CEO Open Road Integrated Media (digital publishing co.) 2009–. *Address:* Open Road Integrated Media, 345 Hudson Street, Suite 6C, New York, NY 10014, USA (office). *Telephone:* (212) 691-0900 (office). *Fax:* (212) 937-3719 (office). *E-mail:* inquiries@openroadmedia.com (office). *Website:* www.openroadmedia.com; www.janefriedman.com (office).

FRIEDMAN, Jeffrey M., MD, PhD; American molecular geneticist and academic; *Head, Laboratory of Molecular Genetics, The Rockefeller University;* b. 20 July 1954, Orlando, Fla; m.; two d.; ed Hewlett High School, Rensselaer Polytechnic Inst., Albany Medical Coll. of Union Univ., Cornell Univ., The Rockefeller Univ.; completed two residencies at Albany Medical Center Hosp.; Assoc. Physician and Postgraduate Fellow, The Rockefeller Univ. 1980, Asst Prof. 1986–95, Head of Lab. of Molecular Genetics 1991–, Prof. 1995–, Marilyn M. Simpson Prof. 1999–, also Dir Starr Center for Human Genetics; Investigator,

Howard Hughes Medical Inst. 1986–; mem. Inst. of Medicine, NAS 2001, American Acad. of Arts and Sciences 2013; Foreign mem. Royal Swedish Acad. of Sciences 2005; Bristol-Myers Squibb Award 2001, Gairdner Foundation Int. Award 2004, Passano Foundation Award 2004, Danone Int. Prize for Nutrition 2007, Jessie Stevenson Kovalenko Medal 2007, Keio Medical Science Prize, Shaw Prize (co-recipient) 2009, Albert Lasker Basic Medical Research Award 2010, named Thomson Reuters Citation Laureate in Medicine 2010, Robert J. and Claire Passano Foundation Award 2010, Fondation IPSEN 11th Endocrine Regulation Prize 2012, UCL Prize Lecture in Clinical Science 2012, Sanofi-Institut Pasteur Award 2012, Frontiers of Knowledge Award in Biomedicine, BBVA Foundation (Spain) (co-recipient) 2013, King Faisal Int. Prize in Medicine (co-recipient) 2013. *Achievements include:* with Douglas Coleman, discovered leptin, a hormone that regulates appetite and metabolism. *Address:* The Rockefeller University, Laboratory of Molecular Genetics, 1230 York Avenue, New York, NY 10065, USA (office). *Telephone:* (212) 327-8000 (office). *Fax:* (212) 327-7974 (office). *E-mail:* jeffrey.friedman@rockefeller.edu (office). *Website:* www.rockefeller.edu/research/faculty/labheads/JeffreyFriedman (office).

FRIEDMAN, Jerome Isaac, PhD; American physicist and academic; *Institute Professor Emeritus, Massachusetts Institute of Technology;* b. 28 March 1930, Chicago; s. of Selig Friedman and Lillian Warsaw; m. 1st 1956; two s. two d.; m. 2nd Tania Baranovsky 1972; ed Univ. of Chicago; Research Assoc. Univ. of Chicago 1956–57, Stanford Univ. 1957–60; Asst Prof. then Assoc. Prof., Mass. Inst. of Tech. 1960–67, Prof. of Physics 1967, Dir Lab. of Nuclear Science 1980–83, Head, Dept Physics 1983–88, William A. Coolidge Prof. 1988–90, Inst. Prof. 1990, now Inst. Prof. Emer.; mem. NAS; Fellow, American Acad. of Arts and Sciences, American Physical Soc.; Hon. DSc (Trinity Coll.); W. K. H. Panofsky Prize (American Physical Soc.) (jt recipient) 1989, Nobel Prize in Physics (jt recipient) 1990. *Leisure interests:* painting, Asian ceramics, African Art. *Address:* Department of Physics, Room 24-512, Massachusetts Institute of Technology, Cambridge, MA 02139-4307 (office); 75 Greenough Street, Brookline, MA 02146, USA (home). *Telephone:* (617) 253-7585 (office). *Fax:* (617) 253-1755 (office). *E-mail:* jif@mit.edu (office). *Website:* web.mit.edu/physics (office).

FRIEDMAN, Stephen, BA, LLB; American lawyer, financial services industry executive and fmr government official; *Chairman, Stone Point Capital LLC;* b. 21 Dec. 1937; m. Barbara Benioff Friedman; one s. two d.; ed Cornell Univ., Columbia Univ. Law School, New York; fmr law clerk to Fed. Dist Court judge; attorney, New York City 1963–66; joined Goldman Sachs & Co. 1966, Pnr 1973–92, Vice-Chair. and Co-COO 1987–90, Co-Chair. 1990–92, Chair. and Sr Pnr 1992–94, Dir 2002, 2005–; Sr Prin., Marsh & McLennan Capital Inc. 1998–2002; Sr Advisor, Stone Point Capital LLC 1998–2002, Chair. 2004–; Asst to Pres. for Econ. Policy and Dir Nat. Econ. Council, White House, Washington, DC 2002–04; Chair. Harbor Point Ltd 2005–; fmr mem. Bd of Dirs Fannie Mae, Wal-Mart Stores; mem. Pres.'s Foreign Intelligence Advisory Bd 1993–95, Chair. 2005–; Trustee, Council on Foreign Relations, Aspen Inst. 2006–, Memorial Sloan-Kettering Cancer Center; Chair. Emer. Bd of Trustees, Columbia Univ., Exec. Cttee, The Brookings Inst.; fmr Chair. Fed. Reserve Bank of New York; Eastern Collegiate Wrestling Champion 1959, AAU Nat. Wrestling Champion 1961, Maccabiah Games Gold Medal 1961, NCAA Silver Anniversary Medal for outstanding athletic and career achievements 1984. *Address:* Stone Point Capital LLC, 919 Third Avenue, Suite 38N62, New York, NY 10022, USA (office). *Telephone:* (203) 862-2900 (office). *Fax:* (203) 625-8357 (office). *Website:* www.stonepointcapital.com (office).

FRIEDMAN, Thomas Lauren, OBE, BA, MPhil; American journalist and writer; *Foreign Affairs Columnist, New York Times;* b. 20 July 1953, St Louis Park, Minneapolis, Minn.; m. Ann Bucksbaum; two d.; ed St Louis Park High School, Brandeis Univ., St Antony's Coll. Oxford, UK; joined London bureau of United Press International, dispatched a year later to Beirut –1981; joined The New York Times 1981, Beirut Bureau Chief 1982–84, Israel Bureau Chief 1984–88, Washington Chief Diplomatic Corresp., Chief White House Corresp., Chief Econs Corresp., Foreign Affairs Columnist 1995–; fmr Visiting Prof., Harvard Univ.; hon. degrees from several US univs; Pulitzer Prize for Int. Reporting 1983, 1988, for Distinguished Commentary 2002, Overseas Press Club Award for Lifetime Achievement 2004. *Television:* documentaries: The Roots of 9/11 (New York Times TV), Straddling the Fence (Discovery Channel). *Publications include:* From Beirut to Jerusalem (Nat. Book Award for Non-Fiction, Overseas Press Club Award) 1989 (revised edn 1990), The Lexus and the Olive Tree: Understanding Globalization (Overseas Press Club Award for Best Non-Fiction Book on Foreign Policy 2000) 1999 (revised edn 2000), Longitudes and Latitudes: Exploring the World After September 11 2002 (reprinted as Longitudes and Attitudes: The World in the Age of Terrorism 2003), The World is Flat: A Brief History of the Twenty-first Century (Financial Times/Goldman Sachs Business Book Award) 2005 (expanded edn 2006, revised edn 2007), Hot, Flat and Crowded: Why We Need a Green Revolution – And How It Can Renew America 2008, That Used To Be Us (with Michael Mandelbaum) 2011. *Address:* The New York Times, 1627 Eye Street, NW, Suite 700, Washington, DC 20006, USA (office). *Telephone:* (202) 862-0300 (office). *Fax:* (202) 862-0340 (office). *E-mail:* fsg.publicity@fsgbooks.com. *Website:* www.nytimes.com (office); www.thomaslfriedman.com.

FRIEDRICH, Hans-Peter, PhD; German lawyer and politician; *Federal Minister of Food and Agriculture;* b. 10 March 1957, Naila, Bavaria; m.; three c.; ed Univ. of Augsburg; Higher Exec. Officer, Industrial Policy Directorate-Gen., Fed. Ministry of Econs 1988–90; seconded to Econs and Science Dept, Embassy in Washington, DC 1990–91; worked for CDU/CSU Parl. Group 1991–93, Pvt. Sec. to Chair. of CSU Parl. Group 1993–98; mem. Bundestag (Parl.) 1998–, Chair. Bundestag electoral district ass., Hof/Wunsiedel 1998–, Deputy Chair., CDU/CSU Parl. Group in Bundestag 2005–09; Deputy Chair., CSU in Upper Franconia 1999–; Fed. Minister of the Interior 2011–13, Acting Fed. Minister of Food, Agric. and Consumer Protection Sept.–Dec. 2013, Fed. Minister of Food and Agric. 2013–; mem. Christlich-Soziale Union. *Address:* Federal Ministry of Food and Agriculture, Wilhelmstrasse 54, 11055 Berlin, Germany (office). *Telephone:* (30) 185290 (office). *Fax:* (30) 185294262 (office). *E-mail:* poststelle@bmelv.bund.de (office). *Website:* www.bmelv.de (office).

FRIEL, Brian, FRSL; Irish writer; b. 9 Jan. 1929, Omagh, Co. Tyrone; s. of Patrick Friel and Christina MacLoone; m. Anne Morrison 1954; one s. four d.; ed St Columb's Coll., Derry, St Patrick's Coll., Maynooth, St Joseph's Training Coll.,

Belfast; taught in various schools 1950–60; full-time writer 1960–; mem. Irish Acad. of Letters, Aosdána 1983–, American Acad. of Arts and Letters, RSL; Hon. Fellow, Univ. Coll. Dublin; Hon. DLitt (Nat. Univ. of Ireland) 1983, (Queen's Univ., Belfast) 1992, (Georgetown Univ., Washington, DC, Dominican Coll., Chicago), (Trinity Coll., Dublin) 2004, (Glasgow); Ulysses Medal, Univ. Coll. Dublin; honoured with Brian Friel Theatre and Brian Friel Centre for Theatre Research, Queen's Univ., Belfast. *Plays:* Philadelphia, Here I Come! 1965, The Loves of Cass McGuire 1967, Lovers 1968, The Mundy Scheme 1969, Crystal and Fox 1970, The Gentle Island 1971, The Freedom of the City 1973, Volunteers 1975, Living Quarters 1976, Aristocrats 1979, Faith Healer 1979, Translations (Ewart-Biggs Memorial Prize, British Theatre Asscn Award) 1981, Three Sisters (trans.) 1981, The Communication Cord 1983, Fathers and Sons 1987, Making History (Best Foreign Play, New York Drama Critics Circle 1989) 1988, A Month in the Country 1990, Dancing at Lughnasa (Tony Award for Best Play 1992) 1990, The London Vertigo 1991, Wonderful Tennessee 1993, Selected Stories 1994, Molly Sweeney 1995, Give Me Your Answer, Do! 1997, Uncle Vanya (after Chekhov) 1998, The Yalta Game 2001, The Bear (trans.) 2002, Afterplay 2002, Performances 2003, The Home Place (Evening Standard Award for Best Play 2005) 2005, Hedda Gabler (trans.) 2008. *Publications:* The Last of the Name (ed.) 1988; collected stories: The Saucer of Larks 1962, The Gold in the Sea 1966. *Address:* Drumaweir House, Greencastle, Co. Donegal, Ireland (home). *Telephone:* (74) 9381119 (home). *Fax:* (74) 9381408 (home).

FRIEND, Cynthia M., BS, PhD; American chemist and academic; *Theodore William Richards Professor of Chemistry and Professor of Materials Science, Harvard University;* ed Univ. of California, Davis, Univ. of California, Berkeley, Stanford Univ.; Post-Doctoral Research Fellow, Stanford Univ. 1981–82; Asst Prof., Harvard Univ. 1982–86, Assoc. Prof. 1986–88, Morris Kahn Assoc. Prof. 1988–89, Prof. of Chem. 1989–98, Theodore William Richards Prof. of Chem. 1998–, Prof. of Materials Science 2002–, Assoc. Dir, Harvard Materials Research Science and Eng Center 2001–, Assoc. Dean, Faculty of Arts and Sciences 2002–05, Chair., Dept of Chem. and Chemical Biology 2004–; Visiting Prof. in Chemical Eng, Stanford Univ. 2001; Trustee, Radcliffe Coll. 1990–93; mem. numerous professional cttees, panels and bds including NATO Advisory Panel on Organic Chemistry 1987, NSF Chem. Advisory Panel 1989–92, Advanced Light Source Users' Exec. Cttee 1990–93, Bd on Chemical Science and Tech., Nat. Research Council 1992, 56th Annual Conf. on Physical Electronics Cttee 1995–96, Chemical and Eng (C&EN) Advisory Bd 2001–02, Claire Booth Luce Fellowship Selection Bd 2000–, Council of Gordon Research Confs 2002–05, US Dept of Energy Cttee of Visitors, Office of Basic Energy Sciences 2005; Gen. and Program Chair., Biennial Inorganic Chem. Symposium, Molecular Deisgn of Materials 1987, Program Chair., New England Catalysis Soc. 1987–89, Chair., Richards Medal Award Cttee 1994–96; Chair., Canvassing Cttee, ACS Award for Creative Research in Catalysis 1999–2000; US rep., Int. Union of Pure and Applied Chem. 2000–03; Co-Chair., Opportunities in Nanocatalysis Workshop 2005; chair. of numerous academic bds including Harvard Faculty of Arts and Sciences Standing Cttee on Women 1991–94, Elected Docket Cttee, Harvard Univ. 1998–2000; consultant to Lord Corpn, Cary, NC 1987–90, Advanced Tech. Materials, Danbury, Conn. 1988–92, Texaco Lubricants Div. 1995–98, Ryoka Systems, Tokyo, Japan 1995–2003, Kaelow and Assocs LLP 1998–99, Pennie and Edmonds LLP 2002–03, Paul Hastings LLP 2004, Mitsubishi Chemical Co. 2005–07; mem. ACS, American Vacuum Soc., AAAS, American Physical Soc., Iota Sigma Pi; mem. of several editorial bds including Journal of Cluster Science 1990–94, Langmuir 1991–2001, The Chemical Intelligencer 1997–, Surface Science 2000–, Chemical Eng News 1999–2001, e-Journal of Surface Science and Nano tech. (EJSSNT) 2005–; IBM Faculty Devt Award 1983–85, Presidential Young Investigator Award 1985–90, Union Carbide Innovation Recognition Program 1988-89, Distinguished Young Alumni Award, Univ. of Calif.-Davis 1990, Garvan Medal of ACS 1991, Iota Sigma Pi Agnes Fay Morgan Research Award 1991, Smithsonian Inst. Chosen Scientist for Perm. Exhibit "Science and American Life" 1992–. *Publications:* numerous articles in professional journals. *Address:* Harvard University Department of Chemistry and Chemical Biology, 12 Oxford Street, Office M018, Cambridge, MA 02138, USA (office). *Telephone:* (617) 495-4198 (office). *Fax:* (617) 496-8410 (office). *E-mail:* cfriend@seas.harvard.edu (office). *Website:* (office); www.seas.harvard .edu/friend.

FRIEND, Lionel; British conductor; b. 13 March 1945, London; s. of Norman A. C. Friend and Moya L. Dicks; m. Jane Hyland 1969; one s. two d.; ed Royal Grammar School, High Wycombe, Royal Coll. of Music, London, London Opera Centre; with Welsh Nat. Opera 1969–72, Glyndebourne Festival/Touring Opera 1969–72; Second Kapellmeister, Staatstheater, Kassel, West Germany 1972–75; Conductor ENO 1976–89; Musical Dir New Sussex Opera 1989–96; Conductor-in-Residence, Birmingham Conservatoire 2003–10; Guest Conductor BBC Symphony, Philharmonia, Royal Philharmonic, Nash Ensemble, Scottish Chamber, Royal Ballet etc. and in Australia, Belgium, Brazil, Denmark, France, Germany, Hungary, the Netherlands, NZ, Norway, Spain, Sweden, USA; Hon. Fellow, Birmingham Conservatoire. *Leisure interests:* reading, theatre. *Address:* c/o Robert Gilder & Co., 91 Great Russell Street, London, WC1B 3PS, England (office); 136 Rosendale Road, London, SE21 8LG, England (home). *Telephone:* (20) 7580-7758 (office); (20) 8761-7845 (home). *Fax:* (20) 7580-7739 (office). *E-mail:* rgilder@robert-gilder.com (office); lionelfriend@hotmail.com. *Website:* www.robert-gilder.com (office); lionelfriend.com.

FRIEND, Sir Richard Henry, Kt, PhD, FRS, FREng; British physicist and academic; *Cavendish Professor of Physics, University of Cambridge;* b. 18 Jan. 1953; ed Trinity Coll., St John's Coll., Cavendish Lab., Univ. of Cambridge; Research Assoc., Laboratoire de Physique des Solides, Université Paris-Sud 1977–78; Research Fellow, St John's Coll., Cambridge 1977–80, Demonstrator in Physics 1980–85, Dir of Studies in Physics 1984–86, Lecturer in Physics 1985–93, Tutor in Physics 1987–91, Reader in Experimental Physics 1993–95, Cavendish Prof. of Physics 1995–; Tan Chin Tuan Centennial Prof., Nat. Univ. of Singapore; Visiting Prof., Univ. of California, Santa Barbara 1986–87; Assoc. Chair, Centre de Recherche sur les Très Basses Temperatures, CNRS 1987; Chief Scientist, Cambridge Display Technology Ltd 1996–; Consultant, Epson Cambridge Lab. 1998–; Chief Scientist and Dir Plastic Logic Ltd 2000–; Mary Shepard B. Upson Visiting Prof., Cornell Univ. 2003; mem. Tech. Advisory Council, British Petroleum PLC 1998–2003; Nuffield Foundation Science Research Fellowship 1992–93;

Hon. FRSC 2004; Dr hc (Linkoping, Sweden) 2000, (Mons-Hainault, Belgium) 2002; Charles Vernon Boys Prize, Inst. of Physics 1988, RSC Interdisciplinary Award 1991, Hewlett-Packard Prize, European Physical Soc. 1996, Rumford Medal, Royal Soc. of London 1998, Italgas Prize 2001, Silver Medal, Royal Acad. of Eng 2002, McRobert Prize, Royal Acad. of Eng 2002, IEE Faraday Medal 2003, Gold Medal, European Materials Research Soc. 2003, EC Descartes Prize 2003, King Faisal Int. Prize for Science (co-recipient) 2009, Millennium Tech. Prize for the devt of plastic electronics 2010, Harvey Prize, Technion, Israel 2011. *Publications:* more than 600 papers in scientific journals. *Address:* Room K32, Kapitza Building, Cavendish Laboratory, University of Cambridge, Madingley Road, Cambridge, CB3 0HE, England (office). *Telephone:* (1223) 337218 (office). *Fax:* (1223) 764515 (office). *E-mail:* rhf10@cam.ac.uk (office). *Website:* www.phy .cam.ac.uk/people/friendr.php (office); www.oe.phy.cam.ac.uk/people/oestaff/rhf10 .htm (office).

FRIESEN, Dawna; Canadian broadcast journalist; *Anchor and Executive Editor, Global National with Dawna Friesen;* b. 8 Oct. 1964, Winnipeg; m. Tom Kennedy; one s.; ed Red River Coll.; fmr newspaper journalist, Portage Daily Graphic and news reporter at several radio and TV stations in western Canada, including Brandon, Saskatoon and Winnipeg; fmr Nat. News Corresp. and Anchor, CTV, Ottawa 1997–99 and CBC, Vancouver; London-based Foreign Corresp., NBC News, Today Show and MSNBC 1999–2010; Anchor and Exec. Ed. Global National with Dawna Friesen, Global Television 2010–; Univ. of Toronto Southam Fellowship for Journalists 1993, Emmy Award (for team coverage of US presidential campaign of Barack Obama) 2009. *Address:* Global National, 7850 Enterprise Street, Burnaby, BC V5A 1V7, Canada (office). *E-mail:* viewers@ globalnational.com (office). *Website:* www.globalnational.com (office).

FRIGGIERI, Oliver, BA, MA, PhD; Maltese academic, writer, poet and literary critic; *Professor of Maltese Literature, University of Malta;* b. 27 March 1947, Furjana, Malta; s. of Charles Friggieri and Mary Galea; m. Eileen Cassar; one d.; ed Univ. of Malta, Catholic Univ. of Milan; Prof. of Maltese Literature, Univ. of Malta 1987–, Head of Dept of Maltese 1987–2004; Founder-mem. Academia Internationale Mihai Eminescu, Craiova 1995; mem. Asscn Int. des Critiques Littéraires, Paris; participant and guest speaker at 70 int. congresses throughout Europe; guest poet at numerous poetry recitals in major European cities; Co-founder Saghtar (nat. student magazine) 1971; Literary Ed. In-Nazzjon 1971–82; Nat. Order of Merit 1999; First Prize for Literary Criticism XIV Concorso Silarus 1982, Premio Internazionale Mediterraneo, Palermo 1988, Malta Govt Literary Award 1988, 1996, 1997, 1999, Premio Sampieri per la Poesia 1995, Premio Internazionale Trieste Poesia 2002, Gold Medal Award Malta Soc. of Arts, Manufactures and Commerce 2003, Premio Faber (Italy) 2004. *Achievements:* author of first oratorio in Maltese: Pawlu ta' Malta 1985, first poetry album recording in Maltese 1997, various cantatas and religious hymns. *Radio:* weekly cultural programme presenter (Radio Malta). *Television:* regular appearances on Maltese and other networks. *Publications:* novels: Il-Gidba 1977, L-Istramb 1980, Fil-Parlament ma Jikbrux Fjuri 1986, Gizimin li Qatt ma Jiftah 1998, It-Tfal Jigu bil-Vapuri 2000, The Lie 2007; short stories: Stejjer ghal Qabel Jidlam Vol. I 1979, Vol. II 1983 (combined, enhanced edn) 1986, Fil-Gzira Taparsi jikbru I-Fjuri 1991, Koranta and Other Short Stories from Malta 1994, A Malte, histoires du crépuscule 2004; poetry: Mal-Fanal Hemm Harstek Tixghel 1988, Rewwixta (play-poem) 1990, Poeziji 1998, Il-Kliem li Tghidlek Qalbek 2001, Il-Poeziji Migbura 2002, A Poet's Creed 2006; literary criticism: Kittieba ta' Zmienna 1970, Ir-Ruh fil-Kelma 1973, Il-Kultura Taljana f'Dun Karm 1976, Fl-Gharbiel 1976, Storja tal-Letteratura Maltija 1979, Saggi Kritici 1979, Ellul Mercer f'Leli ta' Haz-Zghir Mir-Realta' ghall-Kuxjenza 1983, Gwann Mamo Il'Kittieb tar-Riforma Socjali 1984, Dizzjunarju ta' Termini Letterarji 1986, L'Idea tal'Letteratura 1986, Mekkanizmi Metaforici f'Dun Karm 1988, Dun Karm 'Il-Jien u Lil hinn Minnu' 1988, Il-Kuxjenza Nazzjonali Maltija 1995, L-Istudji Kritici Migbura 1995, L'Istorja tal-Poezija Maltija 2001; numerous works translated into various languages, poems in anthologies and articles in academic journals and newspapers. *Leisure interest:* gardening. *Address:* Faculty of Arts, University of Malta, Msida, Malta (office).

FRIIS, Lotte; Danish swimmer; b. 9 Feb. 1988, Blovstrød; ed Marie Kruses gymnasium, Farum; European Championships (short course), Vienna 2004: silver medal, 800m freestyle, Debrecen 2007: gold medal, 800m freestyle, Rijeka 2008: bronze medal, 800m freestyle, Istanbul 2009: gold medal, 800m freestyle, silver medal, 400m freestyle, Szczecin 2011: gold medal, 800m freestyle, silver medal, 400m freestyle; European Championships (long course), Eindhoven 2008: bronze medal, 1,500m freestyle, Budapest 2010: gold medal, 800m freestyle, 1,500m freestyle, bronze medal, 400m freestyle; Olympic Games, Beijing 2008: bronze medal, 800m freestyle; World Championships (long course), Rome 2009: gold medal, 800m freestyle, silver medal, 1,500m freestyle, Shanghai 2011: gold medal, 1,500m freestyle, silver medal, 800m freestyle, Barcelona 2013: silver medal, 800m freestyle, 1,500m freestyle; swims for Herlev club; coach: Paulus Wildeboer. *Address:* c/o f. reklame AS, Klosterstræde 23, 1157 Copenhagen K, Denmark. *Telephone:* 33-12-72-44. *E-mail:* info@f-reklame.dk. *Website:* www.lottefriis.net.

FRISELL, Bill; American jazz musician (guitar) and composer; b. 18 March 1951, Baltimore, Md; one d.; ed Univ. of Northern Colorado, Berklee Coll. of Music; played with numerous artists, including Eberhard Weber, Mike Gibbs, Jan Garbarek, Charlie Haden, Carla Bley, John Scofield; David Sylvian, Bono, Marianne Faithfull, Robin Holcomb, Gavin Bryars, Brian Eno, Daniel Lanois, Paul Simon, Van Dyke Parks, Vic Chesnutt, Elvis Costello, Suzanne Vega, Loudon Wainwright III, Ron Carter, Dave Douglas, Rinde Eckart, Wayne Horvitz, Ginger Baker, Rickie Lee Jones, Laurie Anderson, Vernon Reid, Ron Sexsmith, Caetano Veloso, Vinicius Cantuaria, Mark Ribot, Ron Carter, T-Bone Burnett, The Campbell Brothers, Chip Taylor & Carrie Rodriquez, Buddy Miller and Renée Fleming; fmr mem., Power Tools, John Zorn's Naked City, The Paul Bley Quintet, Paul Motian Trio; Music Dir, Century of Song Ruhr Triennale Arts Festival 2003–05; Harris Stanton Guitar Award, Downbeat Critics' Poll Guitarist of the Year 1998, Deutsche Schallplatten Preis 1998, 2005, Critics' Award for Best Guitarist, Industry Award for Best Guitarist 1998, Jazz Journalists' Asscn Award for Guitarist of the Year 2013. *Compositions include:* Tales from the Far Side (music to TV series). *Recordings include:* albums: In Line 1983, Theoretically (with Tim Berne) 1984, Rambler 1985, News For Lulu (with John Zorn, George Lewis)

1987, Strange Meeting (with Power Tools) 1987, Lookout For Hope 1988, Before We Were Born 1989, Is This You? 1990, Where In The World? 1991, More News For Lulu (with John Zorn, George Lewis) 1992, Grace Under Pressure (with John Scofield) 1992, Have A Little Faith 1993, Music From The Films of Buster Keaton 1995, Going Home Again (with Ginger Baker Trio) 1995, Deep Dead Blue: Live At Meltdown (with Elvis Costello) 1995, Quartet 1996, Nashville 1997, Gone, Just Like a Train 1998, Songs We Know 1998, The Sweetest Punch (with Elvis Costello) 1999, Good Dog, Happy Man 1999, Ghost Town 2000, Blues Dream 2001, Bill Frisell With Dave Holland and Elvin Jones 2001, Selected Recordings 2002, The Willies 2002, The Intercontinentals 2003, Unspeakable 2004, Petra Haden's Bill 2004, Richter 858 2005, East/West 2005, Bill Frisell, Ron Carter, Paul Motian 2005, Floratone 2007, History, Mystery 2007, All Hat 2008, Hemispheres (with Jim Hall) 2008, Disfarmer 2009, Beautiful Dreamers 2010, Lágrimas Mexicanas (with Vinicius Cantuária) 2011, Sign of Life: Music for 858 Quartet 2011, All We Are Saying... 2011, The Kentucky Derby Is Decadent and Depraved 2012, Window & Door 2012, Enfants Terribles: Live at the Blue Note 2012, Quiver 2012, Silent Comedy 2013, John Zorn: The Mysteries 2013, Big Sur 2013. *Publication:* Bill Frisell: An Anthology. *Address:* c/o Phyllis Oyama, Songline/Tone Field Productions, 1649 Hopkins Street, Berkeley, CA 94707, USA (office). *Telephone:* (510) 528-1191 (office). *Fax:* (510) 528-1193 (office). *E-mail:* staff@songtone.com (office). *Website:* www.songtone.com (office); www.billfrisell.com.

FRIST, William (Bill) Harrison, MD; American transplant surgeon, business executive and fmr politician; *Frederick H. Schultz Class of 1951 Professor of International Economic Policy, Princeton University;* b. 22 Feb. 1952, Nashville, Tenn.; m. Karyn McLaughlin; three s.; ed Montgomery Bell Acad., Nashville, Princeton Univ., Harvard Medical School; worked in Powell lab., Mass Gen. Hosp. 1977–78, Resident in Surgery 1978–83, Chief Resident and Fellow in Cardiothoracic Surgery 1984–85; worked at Southampton Gen. Hosp., Southampton, England 1983; Sr Fellow and Chief Resident in Cardiac Transplant Service and Cardiothoracic Surgery, Stanford Univ. School of Medicine 1985–86; mem. Faculty, Vanderbilt Univ. Medical Center 1986–89, est. center for new therapies of heart and lung transplantation, also served as Staff Surgeon, Nashville Veterans Admin Hospital; f. Vanderbilt Transplant Center 1989; Senator from Tennessee 1995–2007 (retd), Senate Majority Leader 2002–2007, fmr Chair. Nat. Representative Senatorial Cttee; Frederick H. Schultz Class of 1951 Prof. of Int. Econ. Policy, Princeton Univ. 2007–; Chair. Volunteer Political Action Cttee (VOLPAC) 2007–; Republican. *Publications:* Tennessee Senators, 1911-2001: Portraits of Leadership in a Century of Change 1999, When Every Moment Counts: What You Need To Know About Bioterrorism From the Senate's Only Doctor 2002, Good People Beget Good People: A Genealogy of the Frist Family (coauthor) 2003. *Address:* Woodrow Wilson School of Public and International Affairs, Princeton University, Robertson Hall, Princeton, NJ 08544-1013, USA (office). *Telephone:* (609) 258-2943 (office). *E-mail:* whfrist@princeton.edu (office). *Website:* www.wws.princeton.edu (office).

FRITZ, Johann P.; Austrian journalist and broadcasting executive; *Director Emeritus, International Press Institute;* b. 15 April 1940, Ober-Eggendorf; s. of Johann Fritz and Amalia Piringer; m. Brigitte Weick 1964; one d.; ed Univ. of Vienna, Case Western Reserve Univ., Cleveland, Ohio and Hochschule für Welthandel, Vienna; Sec.-Gen. Österreichische Jungarbeiterbewegung 1964–67, Exec. Vice-Pres. 1967–70; Ed. Der Jungarbeiter 1964–70, MC Report 1970–75; Deputy Sec.-Gen. Österreichischer Wirtschaftsbund 1970–75; Man. Dir Die Presse 1975–91; Man. Dir Kabel TV Wien 1975–83; Founder and Co-Man. Radio Adria 1977–84, Consultant 1984–90; Co-founder, Sec. Gen. and Report Ed. Man.-Club 1970–75; Founder and Chair. Cable TV Asscn, Austrian Chamber of Commerce 1980–90; mem. Supervisory Bd Telekabel Wien GmbH 1983–98; mem. Bd Austrian Press Agency 1982–91; Dir Int. Press Inst. (IPI) 1992–2007, now Dir Emer. Austrian Chapter of IPI, Vienna; Publr Jazz Information (monthly) 1967–70, Cable TV: Project Study for Austria 1975, iPi Report 1992–97; life-time title 'Senator' conferred by Int. Asscn for Newspaper and Media Tech. 1980; lifetime title Prof. conferred by Austrian Fed. Ministry of Science and Research 2000; Kommerzialrat Award 1991, Gold Medal for Meritorious Service to Province of Vienna 2003, Special Award, Austrian Press Club Concordia 2003. *Television:* scripts for jazz productions 1968–73. *Publication:* Little Jazzbook of Vienna. *Leisure interests:* skiing, ice-skating, jazz, art deco, jugendstil. *Address:* c/o International Press Institute, Speigelgasse 2, 1010 Vienna (office); Hasenauerstrasse 37, 1180 Vienna, Austria.

FRODSHAM, John David, MA, PhD, FAHA; British/Australian academic and consultant; *Foundation Professor of English and Comparative Literature, Murdoch University;* b. 5 Jan. 1930, Cheshire, England; s. of J. K. Frodsham and W. E. Frodsham; m. Tan Beng-choo 1964; three s. two d.; ed Emmanuel Coll., Cambridge, Australian Nat. Univ.; Lecturer in English, Univ. of Baghdad 1956–58, in Oriental Studies, Univ. of Sydney 1960–61, in Far Eastern History, Univ. of Malaya 1961–65, Sr Lecturer in Far Eastern History, Univ. of Adelaide 1965–67; Reader in Chinese, ANU 1967–71; Prof. of Comparative Literature, Univ. of Dar es Salaam,Tanzania 1971–73, Foundation Prof. English and Comparative Literature, Murdoch Univ. 1972–, Foundation Dean of School of Human Communication 1973–76; Visiting Prof., Cornell Univ. 1965, Univ. of Hawaii 1968, American Coll. of Greece 1985, Tamkang Univ. of Taiwan 1985; Visiting Fellow, Inst. of E Asian Philosophies, Univ. of Singapore 1989; Sr Teaching Fellow, NTU, Singapore 1990–92; Consultant, Ausean Int. Ltd 1987–89; Fellow and Pres. Profs' World Peace Acad. 1983; Pres. Australasian Soc. of Psychical Research 1979–; mem. Australia–China Council 1979–83; Current Affairs Commentator for ABC 1958–; Centenary Medal 2001. *Publications:* An Anthology of Chinese Verse, Vol. 1 1967, The Murmuring Stream (two vols) 1967, The Poems of Li Ho 1970, New Perspectives in Chinese Literature 1971, The First Chinese Embassy to the West 1973, Foundations of Modernism: Modern Poetry 1980, Goddesses, Ghosts and Demons: The Collected Poems of Li He 1983, Classicism and Romanticism: A Comparative Period Study (four vols) 1986, Turning Point 1988, Education for What? 1990, The Crisis of the Modern World and Traditional Wisdom 1990, The Decline of Sensate Culture 1990, Structure, Thought and Reality: A Reader (2 vols) 2000. *Leisure interests:* psychical research, sailing, swimming. *Address:* School of Social Sciences and Humanities, Room E/H 4.045, Murdoch University, Murdoch, WA 6150 (office); 24 Riversea View, Buckland Hill, Mosman Park, WA 6107, Australia (home). *Telephone:* (8) 9360-6203 (office); (8) 9284-3451 (home). *Fax:* (8)

9284-3451 (home). *E-mail:* J.Frodsham@murdoch.edu.au (office). *Website:* www .ssh.murdoch.edu.au (office).

FROGIER, Pierre Edouard Nahéa; New Caledonian politician; b. 16 Nov. 1950, Nouméa; m. Annick Morault; three c.; ed Lycée Lapérouse, Nouméa and Faculty of Law, Dijon, France; elected mem. Ass. Territoriale 1977–, Congress 1977–; Mayor of Mont-Dore 1987–2001; Sec.-Gen. Rassemblement pour la Calédonie dans la République (RPCR) 1989–; Territorial Sec., Rassemblement pour la République (RPR) 1995–; Deputy for New Caledonia in French Nat. Ass. 1993–97, 2002–; Pres. of New Caledonia 2001–04; Chevalier, Ordre nat. du Mérite. *Address:* BP 732, 98849 Nouméa Cédex, New Caledonia (office); Assemblée nationale, 126 rue de l'Université, 75355 Paris 07 SP, France. *E-mail:* pfrogier@assemblee-nationale.fr.

FRÖHLICH, Fritz W.; German business executive; *Chairman of the Supervisory Board, Randstad Holding NV;* b. 1942; fmr Chief Financial Officer and Vice-Chair. of Exec. Bd AkzoNobel NV; mem. Supervisory Bd Randstad Holding NV 2003–, currently Chair., also mem. Audit Cttee and Chair. Remuneration and Nomination Cttee; Chair. Supervisory Bd Altana AG, Draka Holding NV; mem. Supervisory Bd ASML Holding NV 2004–, Rexel SA, Allianz Nederland Groep NV, Aon Jauch & Hübener GmbH; mem. Investment Cttee ABP Vermogensbeheer. *Address:* Randstad Holding NV, PO Box 12600, 1100 AP Amsterdam z.o. (office); Randstad Holding NV, Diemermere 25, 1112 TC Diemen, Netherlands (office). *Telephone:* (20) 569-59-11 (office). *Fax:* (20) 569-55-20 (office). *E-mail:* info@randstad.com (office). *Website:* www.randstad.com (office).

FROHNMAYER, John Edward, MA, JD; American lawyer, civil servant and author; b. 1 June 1942, Medford, Ore.; s. of Otto Frohnmayer and Marabel Frohnmayer; m. Leah Thorpe 1967; two s.; ed Stanford Univ., Univs of Chicago and Oregon; Assoc. Johnson, Harrang & Mercer, Eugene, Ore. 1972–75; Pnr, Tonkon, Torp, Galen, Marmaduke & Booth, Portland 1975–89; Chair. Ore. Arts Comm. 1980–84; Chair. Nat. Endowment for the Arts, Washington, DC 1989–92; Visiting Professional Scholar, The Freedom Forum, 1st Amendment Center, Vanderbilt Univ. 1993; mem. Bd of Dirs Oregon Council for the Humanities 2007–, currently Vice-Chair.; fmr mem. Art Selection Cttee, Ore. State Capitol Bldg; currently Affiliate Prof. of Liberal Arts, Oregon State Univ.; trial lawyer in pvt. practice, Bozeman, Mont. 1995–; Republican; People for the American Way, 1st Amendment Award 1992, Oregon Gov.'s Award for the Arts 1993; Intellectual Freedom Award, Montana Library Asscn 1998. *Publication:* Leaving Town Alive 1993, Out of Tune: Listening to the First Amendment 1994. *Leisure interests:* skiing, rowing, reading, music. *Address:* 14080 Lone Bear Road, Bozeman, MT 59715, USA. *Telephone:* (406) 585-5918. *Fax:* (406) 582-4997. *E-mail:* frohn@wtp .net (office).

FROLOV, Alexander V., PhD; Russian physicist and business executive; *CEO, Evraz Group;* b. 1964; m.; one c.; ed Moscow Inst. of Physics and Tech.; worked as Research Fellow at I.V. Kurchatov Inst. of Atomic Energy, Moscow; Chair. Evraz Group 2006–08, CEO 2007–. *Address:* Evraz Group SA, 1 Allée Scheffer, 2520 Luxembourg, R.C.S. LuxembourgB 105615 (office); EvrazHolding OOO, 127006 Moscow, ul. Dolgorukovskaya 15, Bldgs 4 and 5, Russia (office). *Telephone:* (495) 234-46-31 (Moscow) (office). *Fax:* (495) 232-13-59 (Moscow) (office). *E-mail:* info@ evraz.com (office). *Website:* www.evraz.com (office).

FROMANTIN, Jean-Christophe; French politician and business executive; *Mayor of Neuilly-sur-Seine;* b. 30 Aug. 1962, Nantes (Loire-Atlantique); m.; four c.; ed secondary schools in Saintes, Dunkerque and Strasbourg, Ecole supérieure libre des sciences commerciales appliquées, Paris; nat. service in Lisbon 1987–88; f. Eurochallenge (service and advice for import/export) 1989–94, Head of newly created company, Export Entreprises, following merged with Interex 1994–, participated in launch of Globaltrade.net 2009 (public-pvt. partnership between US Dept of Commerce and Fed. of Int. Trade Asscns); Mayor of Neuilly-sur-Seine 2008–; elected mem. Paris Métropole jt asscn 2009–, co-host Comm. 'Economic Development and Solidarity', Vice-Pres. Paris Métropole 2010–; Gen. Councillor, Hauts-de-Seine, canton of Neuilly-sur-Seine-Nord 2011–; launched political party Territoires en mouvement 2011–; Deputy to Assemblée nationale (Parl.) 2012–. *Publications:* Mon village dans un monde global: la place de la France dans la mondialisation 2011, Le temps des Territoires 2012. *Leisure interests:* won the sailing Tour de France with the crew of the Dunkirk belonging to Damien Savatier 1980, marathon runner, regularly participates in Paris Marathon, 100 km Millau or the Transbaie (crossing Bay of Somme on bitumen, water, sand and mud). *Address:* Hôtel de Ville, 96 avenue Achille Peretti, 92522 Neuilly-sur-Seine Cedex, France (office). *Telephone:* 1-40-88-88-88 (office). *E-mail:* mr.lemaire@ville -neuillysurseine.fr (office). *Website:* www.ville-neuillysurseine.fr (office); www .territoiresenmouvement.com; www.fromantin.com.

FROMENT-MEURICE, Henri, LèsL; French diplomatist; b. 5 June 1923, Paris; m. Gabrielle Drouilh 1948 (deceased); three s. one d.; ed Ecole libre des Sciences Politiques, Ecole Nat. d'Admin; Sec., Ministry of Foreign Affairs 1950–52, Sec. for Far East, Tokyo 1952–53, Chief of Diplomatic Staff, Commissariat Gén. de France en Indochine 1953–54, Asst Pvt. Sec. to Sec. of State for Foreign Affairs 1954–56, First Sec. Embassy, Moscow 1956–59, with Cen. Admin. (Europe) 1959–63, Chargé d'Affaires, Embassy, United Arab Repub. (now Egypt) 1963–64, First Counsellor, Cairo Embassy 1964–65, Chief of Cultural Exchange Service, Cen. Admin. 1965–68, Minister Plenipotentiary 1968, Advisory Minister, Moscow 1968–69, Dir Cen. Admin., Asia and Pacific Ocean 1969–75, Econ. Affairs 1975–79, Amb. to USSR 1979–81, to FRG 1982–83; Ambassadeur de France 1984; Adviser to Chair. Banque Paribas 1985–91; Adviser Jeantet et Associés 1991–98; Admin. Phillips France 1984–96, Robert Bosch (France) 1984–97; Chair. Asscn France-Egypte 1984–2009, Hon. Chair. 2009–; Pres. (France) Action Cttee for EU 1995–2007, Association pour la Concorde Civile et la Fraternité dans les Balkans 2004–07; Pres. du Beirat, Inst. Michel-Brandebourg 1997–2004; Vice-Pres. Forum du Futur; founder Musée Mathurin Méheut, Lamballe, Brittany 1972; Commdr, Légion d'honneur, Officier, Ordre nat. du Mérite. *Publications:* Une puissance nommée Europe (Adolphe Bentinck Prize) 1984, Une éducation politique 1987, Europe 1992 1988, Vu du quai: Mémories 1945–83 1998, Journal d'Asie 1969–75 2005, Les femmes et Jésus, La mort dans le Café 2007, Journal de Moscou 1956–59, 1968–69, 1979–81, Journal de Bonn 1982–83; several articles in Preuves, Commentaire and Revue des Deux Mondes, Le Monde, Le Figaro, Ouest France. *Leisure interests:*

music, piano. *Address:* 23 rue de Civry, 75016 Paris, France (home). *Telephone:* 1-47-43-96-41 (home). *E-mail:* henri.froment_meurice@wanadoo.fr (home).

FROMHERZ, Peter, Dr rer. nat; German biophysicist; *Director, Max Planck Institute for Biochemistry;* b. 1942, Ludwigshafen; ed Technische Hochschule, Karlsruhe, Univ. Marburg; Postdoctoral Fellow, Max Planck Inst. for Biophysical Chem., Göttingen 1970–81; Chair. of Experimental Physics, Univ. of Ulm 1978–94, Full Prof. of Experimental Physics 1981–; Scientific Mem., Max Planck Soc. 1994–, Dir Max Planck Inst. for Biochemistry, Martinsried 1994–; Hon. Prof. of Physics, Technische Universität Munich 1994–; Pres. German Biophysical Soc.; mem. Heidelberg Acad. of Sciences 1992–; Julius Springer Prize for Applied Physics 1998, Philip Morris Research Award 2004. *Publications:* 150 research papers. *Address:* Max-Planck-Institut für Biochemie, Abteilung Membran- und Neurophysik, Am Klopferspitz 18a, 82152 Martinsried, Germany (office). *Telephone:* (89) 8578-2820 (office). *Fax:* (89) 8578-2822 (office). *E-mail:* fromherz@biochem.mpg.de (office). *Website:* www.biochem.mpg.de/mnphys (office).

FROST, David George Hamilton, CMG; British diplomatist (retd) and business executive; *Chief Executive, Scotch Whisky Association;* b. 21 Feb. 1965, Derby, England; m. Jacqueline Elizabeth Dias; one s. one d.; ed Nottingham High School, St John's Coll., Oxford; joined FCO 1987, Desk Officer for Afghanistan, S Asia Dept 1987–88, Third Sec. (Political), Nicosia 1988–90, Desk Officer for NATO and WEU, Security Policy Dept 1992–93, First Sec. (Econ.), UK Representation to EU 1993–96, First Sec. (Third Cttee), UK Mission to UN, New York 1996–98, Pvt. Sec. to Perm. Under-Sec., FCO 1998–99, Deputy Head of EU (External) Dept 1999–2001, Econ. and EU Counsellor, Paris 2001–03, Head of EU (Internal) Dept, FCO 2003–04, Dir EU (Internal) 2004–06, Amb. to Denmark 2006–08, Dir Directorate of Strategy, Policy Planning and Analysis, FCO 2008–10, on loan to Dept for Business, Innovation and Skills as Dir for Europe, Trade and Int. Affairs 2010–13; tax consultant, KPMG, London 1990–92; Chief Exec. Scotch Whisky Asscn 2014–; mem. Programme Cttee, The Ditchley Foundation. *Leisure interests:* languages and linguistics, medieval history, modern politics and economics, detective fiction and ghost stories, Richard Wagner and football. *Address:* The Scotch Whisky Association, 20 Atholl Crescent, Edinburgh, EH3 8HF, Scotland (office). *Telephone:* (131) 222-9201 (office). *Fax:* (131) 222-9200 (office). *E-mail:* chiefexecutive@swa.org.uk (office). *Website:* www.scotch-whisky.org.uk (office).

FROTSCHER, Michael, MD; German neuroscientist and academic; *Professor and Head, Institute for Structural Neurobiology, Centre for Molecular Neurobiology Hamburg (ZMNH), University Medical Centre Hamburg-Eppendorf;* b. 3 July 1947, Dresden; ed East-Berlin Humboldt Univ.; started scientific career at Inst. of Anatomy, East-Berlin Humboldt Univ., GDR; fled to FRG 1979, started new career at Max Planck Inst. of Brain Research, Frankfurt; fmr Prof. and Head of Dept, Inst. of Anatomy and Cell Biology, Albert-Ludwigs-Universität, Freiburg; currently Prof. and Head, Inst. for Structural Neurobiology, Centre for Molecular Neurobiology Hamburg (ZMNH), Univ. Medical Centre Hamburg-Eppendorf; hon. doctorate; German Research Foundation Leibniz Prize 1993, Max Planck Research Award for International Cooperation 2000, Ernst Jung Prize for Medicine 2002, Jacob Henle Medal 2013. *Publications:* numerous publs in medical and scientific journals. *Address:* Institute for Structural Neurobiology, Centre for Molecular Neurobiology Hamburg (ZMNH), University Medical Centre Hamburg-Eppendorf, Martinistr. 52, 20246 Hamburg, Germany (office). *Telephone:* (40) 741055028 (office). *Fax:* (40) 741040213 (office). *E-mail:* michael.frotscher@zmnh.uni-hamburg.de (office). *Website:* www.zmnh.uni-hamburg.de (office).

FROWEIN, Jochen Abraham, DJur, MCL; German professor of law; *Director Emeritus, Max-Planck-Institut für ausländisches öffentliches Recht und Völkerrecht;* b. 8 June 1934, Berlin; s. of Dr Abraham Frowein and Hilde Frowein (née Matthis); m. Lore Flume 1962; one s. two d.; ed Univs of Kiel, Berlin, Bonn and Univ. of Michigan Law School, Ann Arbor, USA; Research Fellow, Max-Planck-Inst. for Comparative Public and Int. Law 1962–66; Prof., Ruhr-Univ., Bochum 1967–69, Univ. of Bielefeld 1969–81; Dir Max-Planck-Inst. and Prof., Univ. of Heidelberg 1981–2002, now Dir Emer.; Visiting Prof., Univ. of Michigan Law School 1978, Georgetown Law Faculty, Washington, DC 2003; Expert of European Parl. for Beneš-Decrees 2002; mem. European Comm. on Human Rights 1973–93 (Vice-Pres. 1981–93), Arbitration Tribunal for BIS 2001; Vice-Pres. German Research Foundation 1977–80; Pres. Vereinigung Deutscher Staatsrechtslehrer (German Public Law Teachers Asscn) 1999–2001; Vice-Pres. Max Planck Soc. 1999–2002; Commr, Int. Comm. of Jurists, Geneva 1998–, mem. Exec. Cttee 2002–06, Vice-Pres. 2006–; Grosses Bundesverdienstkreuz 1994; Dr hc (Seville) 1984, (Louvain) 1997, (Szeged) 1998, (Bielefeld) 1999, (Univ. Panthéon-Assas Paris II) 2000. *Publications:* Das de facto-Regime im Völkerrecht 1968, EMRK-Kommentar (with W. Peukert) 1985; and many articles and contribs. *Address:* Max-Planck-Institut für ausländisches öffentliches Recht und Völkerrecht, Im Neuenheimer Feld 535, 69120 Heidelberg, Germany (office). *Telephone:* (6221) 482258 (office). *Fax:* (6221) 482677 (office). *E-mail:* sekrefro@mpil.de (office). *Website:* www.mpil.de (office).

FRÜHBECK DE BURGOS, Rafael; Spanish conductor; *Principal Conductor, Danish National Symphony Orchestra;* b. 15 Sept. 1933, Burgos; s. of Wilhelm Frühbeck and Stephanie Frühbeck (née Ochs); m. María Carmen Martínez 1959; one s. one d.; ed music acads in Bilbao and Madrid, Hochschule für Musik, Germany, Univ. of Madrid; Chief Conductor, Municipal Orchestra, Bilbao 1958–62; Music Dir and Chief Conductor, Spanish Nat. Orchestra, Madrid 1962–78, Hon. Conductor 1998–; Music Dir of Düsseldorf and Chief Conductor Düsseldorf Symphoniker 1966–71; Music Dir Montreal Symphony Orchestra 1974–76; Prin. Guest Conductor Yomiuri Nippon Symphony Orchestra 1980–90, Hon. Conductor 1991; Prin. Guest Conductor Nat. Symphony Orchestra, Washington, DC 1980–90; Music Dir Vienna Symphony Orchestra 1991–96; Gen. Music Dir Deutsche Oper Berlin 1992–97; Gen. Musik Dir Rundfunk Symphony Orchestra, Berlin 1994–2000; Prin. Conductor RAI Nat. Symphony Orchestra, Turin 2001–07; Prin. Guest Conductor, Dresden Philharmonic Orchestra 2003–04; Prin. Conductor and Artistic Dir 2004–11; Prin. Conductor, Danish Nat. Symphony Orchestra 2012–; has worked with Philharmonia Orchestra, London, London Symphony Orchestra, Nat. Orchestra (Madrid), Swedish Radio Orchestra, Spanish Nat. Orchestra; mem. Real Academia de Bellas Artes, Madrid 1975; Hon. mem. Israel Philharmonic Orchestra 1999; Gran Cruz al Mérito Civil Orden de Alfonso X 1966, Orden de Isabel la Católica 1966, Grand Cross of Civil

Merit (Germany) 2001, Gold Medal Labour Merit (Spain) 2004, Bundesverdienstkreuz (Austria); Dr hc (Univ. of Navarra) 1994, (Univ. of Burgos) 1998; Richard Strauss Prize, Hochschule für Musik, Prize for Musical Interpretation, Larios Foundation, Confed. Española de Orgs Empresariales, Madrid 1992, Fundación Guerrero Prize for Spanish Music, Madrid 1996, Gold Medal City of Vienna 1995, Medal of Civil Merit (Austria) 1996, Gold Medal, Int. Gustav Mahler Soc., Vienna 1996, Jacinto Guerrero Prize 1997, Gold Medal State of Vienna 2000, Conductor of the Year, Musical America 2011. *Orchestrations:* Suite Española (Albéniz) 1965, Tema y Variaciones (Turina) 1985. *Recordings include:* Mendelssohn's Elijah and St Paul, Mozart's Requiem, Orff's Carmina Burana, Bizet's Carmen, complete works of Manual de Falla. *Address:* c/o Columbia Artists Management Inc., 1790 Broadway, New York, USA (office); Danish National Symphony Orchestra, Concert Hall, Emil Holms Kanal 20, 0999 Copenhagen, Denmark (office); Avenida del Mediterráneo 21, Madrid 28007, Spain (home). *Telephone:* (212) 841-9500 (office); (341) 5016933 (home). *Fax:* (212) 841-9744 (office); (341) 5016933 (home). *E-mail:* info@cami.com (office). *Website:* www .cami.com (office); www.dr.dk/Koncerthuset (office).

FRUNZĂVERDE, Sorin, PhD; Romanian engineer and politician; b. 23 Sept. 1962, Bocsa, Caras-Severin Co.; m.; one c.; ed Faculty of Metallurgy, Polytechnic Inst., Bucharest, Western Univ., Timișoara, Nat. Defence Univ., Bucharest; Chief of Workshop, Resita Siderurgical Works 1985–88, Head Dept for Quality Control-Labs 1988–90; Pres. and Gen. Man. Chamber for Trade and Industry of Caras-Severin 1991–96; County Counsellor, Sec., Comm. for Budget and Finances Cttee 1992–96; Chair. Caras-Severin Co. Council 1996–97, 2004–06; Minister of Environment, Waters Man. and Forests 1997–98, of Tourism 1998; Chair. Nat. Authority for Tourism 1999–2000; Minister of Nat. Defence 2000, 2006–07; mem. Chamber of Deputies for Caras-Severin Electoral Ward 2000–04; mem. Partidul Democrat (PD), currently Vice-Pres. *Address:* c/o Ministry of National Defence, 050561 Bucharest 5, Str. Izvor 13–15, Sector 5, Romania (office).

FRY, Sir Graham Holbrook, Kt, KCMG; British diplomatist (retd); b. 20 Dec. 1949, Shrewsbury, Shropshire, England; m. Toyoko Fry; two s.; ed Brasenose Coll., Oxford; joined FCO 1972, with Rhodesia Dept 1972–73, full-time language training, UK 1973–74, Kamakura 1974–75, Second Sec., Information, Embassy in Tokyo 1975–76, Second Sec., Commercial, Embassy in Tokyo 1976–79; with Invest in Britain Bureau, Dept of Trade and Industry 1979–81, EC Dept (Internal), FCO 1981–83; First Sec., (Political), Embassy in Paris 1983–87; with Western European Dept, FCO 1987–89; Political Counsellor, Embassy in Tokyo 1989–93; Head of Far Eastern and Pacific Dept, FCO 1993–95, Dir Northern Asia and Pacific 1995–98; High Commr to Malaysia 1998–2001; Dir-Gen. (Econ.), FCO 2001–04; Amb. to Japan 2004–08 (retd); fmr Pres. Cambridge and Oxford Soc.; mem. Governing Body, SOAS, Univ. of London; Council mem. Wildfowl and Wetlands Trust 2010–12. *Address:* c/o Governing Body, School of Oriental and African Studies, University of London, Thornhaugh Street, Russell Square, London, WC1H 0XG, England (office).

FRY, Hedy, PC; Canadian physician and politician; b. 6 Aug. 1941, Trinidad; three s.; ed Coll. of Physicians and Surgeons, Dublin, Ireland; fmr family physician, Vancouver Centre, BC; MP for Vancouver Centre 1993–; Parl. Sec. to Minister of Health 1993–96; Sec. of State (Multiculturalism, Status of Women) 1996–2002; Parl. Sec. to Minister of Citizenship and Immigration with special emphasis on Foreign Credentials 2003–04; Parl. Sec. to Minister of Citizenship and Immigration and Minister of Human Resources and Skills Devt with special emphasis on the Internationally Trained Workers Initiative 2004–06; Critic for Sport Canada in Liberal shadow cabinet 2006–; Vice-Chair. Task Force on Canada–US Relations 2002; Chair. BC Caucus 2002–, Standing Cttee on Health 2002–03, Special Cttee on non-medical use of drugs 2002; fmr Pres. BC Medical Asscn. *Leisure interests:* drama, racquetball, reading, swimming. *Address:* House of Commons, Ottawa, ON K1A 0A9; Confederation Building, Room 583, House of Commons, Ottawa, ON K1A 0A6, Canada (office). *Telephone:* (613) 992-3213 (office). *Fax:* (613) 995-0056 (office). *E-mail:* contact@hedyfry.com; fryh0@parl.gc .ca (office). *Website:* www.hedyfry.com (office).

FRY, Jonathan Michael, MA; British business executive (retd); b. 9 Aug. 1937, Jerusalem; s. of the late Stephen Fry and of Gladys Yvonne Blunt; m. Caroline Mary Dunkerly 1970 (divorced 1997); four d.; m. 2nd Marilyn Russell 1999; ed Repton School, Trinity Coll., Univ. of Oxford; Account Exec., Pritchard Wood Ltd 1961–65; Account Supervisor, Norman Craig & Kummel Inc. 1965–66; Consultant, McKinsey & Co. 1966–73; Devt/Marketing Dir Unigate Foods Div. 1973, Man. Dir 1973, Chair. 1976–78; Group Planning Dir Burmah Oil Trading Ltd 1978–81, Chief Exec. Burmah Speciality Chemicals Ltd 1981–87, Chair. Burmah Castrol PLC 1998–2000 (Man. Dir 1990–93, Chief Exec. 1993–98), Chief Exec. Burmah Castrol Trading Ltd 1993–98, Chair. 1998–2000 (Man. Dir 1990–93), Chair. Castrol Int. (fmrly Castrol Ltd) 1993–96 (Chief Exec. 1987–93); Deputy Chair. Northern Foods PLC 1996–2002, Dir (non-exec.) 1991–2002; Chair. Christian Salvesen PLC 1997–2003, Dir (non-exec.) 1995–2003; Chair. Elementis PLC (fmrly Harrisons & Crosfield PLC) 1997–2004; Chair. Control Risks Group Holdings Ltd 2000–07. *Leisure interests:* cricket, skiing, archaeology. *Address:* Beechingstoke Manor, Pewsey, Wilts., SN9 6HQ, England (home). *Telephone:* (167285) 1669 (home).

FRY, Stephen John, MA; British actor, comedian, writer, journalist and television and radio presenter and director; b. 24 Aug. 1957, Hampstead, London, England; s. of Alan John Fry and Marianne Eve Fry (née Newman); ed Uppingham School, Queens' Coll. Cambridge; columnist, The Listener 1988–89, Daily Telegraph 1990–; wrote first play Latin, performed at Edinburgh Festival 1980 and at Lyric Theatre, Hammersmith 1983; appeared with Cambridge Footlights in revue The Cellar Tapes, Edinburgh Festival 1981; re-wrote script Me and My Girl, London, Broadway, Sydney 1984; Chair. Criterion Theatre Trust 2010–; Pres. Friends for Life Terrence Higgins Trust; mem. Amnesty International, Comic Relief; co-f. SamFry Ltd 2008; Co-owner, with Gina Carter and Sandi Toksvig, Sprout Pictures (incl. film and TV co.); mem. Bd Norwich City Football Club 2010–; Distinguished Supporter, British Humanist Asscn 2010–; Freedom of the City of London 2013; Hon. LLD (Dundee) 1995, (East Anglia) 1999, Hon. DLitt, Dr hc (Anglia Ruskin) 2005; Lifetime Achievement Award in Cultural Humanism, Humanist Chaplaincy at Harvard Univ. 2011. *Plays:* Forty Years On, Chichester Festival and London 1984, The Common Pursuit, London 1988 (TV 1992), three one-man shows in Australia 2010, stand-up performance, Royal Albert Hall, London 2010, Twelfth Night, Shakepeare's Globe 2012 (transferred to the West End). *Films include:* The Good Father, A Fish Called Wanda, A Handful of Dust, Peter's Friends 1992, IQ 1995, Wind in the Willows, Wilde 1997, Cold Comfort Farm 1997, A Civil Action 1997, Whatever Happened to Harold Smith? 2000, Relative Values 2000, Discovery of Heaven 2001, Gosford Park 2002, Bright Young Things (writer, dir, exec. producer) 2003, Mirrormask 2004, A Cock and Bull Story 2005, V for Vendetta 2005, Stormbreaker 2006, Little Claus and Big Claus 2006, Eichmann 2007, St Trinian's 2007, House of Boys 2009, Alice in Wonderland (voice) 2010, Animals United (voice) 2010, Sherlock Holmes: A Game of Shadows 2011, Wagner & Me 2012, Cicada Princess (short) 2012, The Look of Love 2013, The Hobbit: The Desolation of Smaug 2013. *Radio:* Loose Ends 1986–87, Whose Line Is It Anyway? 1987, Saturday Night Fry 1987, 1998. *Television includes:* series: There's Nothing to Worry About 1982, Alfresco 1983–84, The Young Ones 1984, Happy Families 1985, Blackadder II 1985, Saturday Live 1986–87, A Bit of Fry and Laurie 1987–95, Blackadder's Christmas Carol 1988, Blackadder Goes Forth 1989, Jeeves and Wooster 1990–93, Stalag Luft 1993, Laughter and Loathing 1995, Gormenghast 2000, Absolute Power 2003, QI (presenter) 2003–, Kingdom 2007–09, Bones 2007–09, Stephen Fry in America 2008, Last Chance to See 2009, Fry's Planet Word 2011, Playhouse Presents – The Man 2012; other: Doors Open (film) 2012. *Publications:* Paperweight (collected essays) 1992, Stephen Fry Mixed Shrinkwrap 1993, X10 Hippopotamus Shrinkwrap 1993, The Liar (novel) 1993, The Hippopotamus 1994, A Bit of Fry and Laurie (with Hugh Laurie) 1994, 3 Bits of Fry and Laurie (with Hugh Laurie) 1994, Fry and Laurie 4 (with Hugh Laurie) 1994, Paperweight Vol. II (collected essays) 1995, Making History 1996, Moab is My Washpot (autobiog.) 1997, The Stars' Tennis Balls (novel) 2000, The Salmon of Doubt by Douglas Adams (ed.) 2002, Revenge (novel) 2002, Rescuing the Spectacled Bear (novel) 2002, Incomplete & Utter History of Classical Music (with Tim Lihoreau) 2005, The Ode Less Travelled: Unlocking the Poet Within 2005, Stephen Fry in America 2008, The Fry Chronicles: An Autobiography (Galaxy Nat. Book Awards Biography of the Year) 2010. *Leisure interests:* smoking, drinking, swearing, pressing wild flowers. *Address:* c/o Hamilton Hodell Ltd, Fifth Floor, 66–68 Margaret Street, London, W1W 8SR, England (office); c/o Toni Howard, ICM, 8942 Wilshire Blvd, Beverly Hills, CA 90211-1908, USA (office). *Telephone:* (20) 7636-1221 (London) (office); (212) 556-5673 (Beverly Hills) (office). *Fax:* (20) 7636-1226 (London) (office). *Website:* www .stephenfry.com.

FRYER, Geoffrey, PhD, DSc, FRS; British biologist and academic; b. 6 Aug. 1927, Huddersfield; s. of W. Fryer and M. Fryer; m. Vivien G. Hodgson 1953; one s. one d.; ed Huddersfield Coll. and Univ. of London (External); served in Royal Navy 1946–48; colonial research student 1952–53; HM Overseas Research Service, Malawi 1953–55, Zambia 1955–57, Uganda 1957–60; Sr, then Prin., then Sr Prin. Scientific Officer, Freshwater Biological Asscn 1960–81; Deputy Chief Scientific Officer, Windermere Lab., Freshwater Biological Asscn 1981–88; H. R. Macmillan Lecturer, Univ. of BC 1963; Distinguished Visiting Scholar, Univ. of Adelaide 1985; Distinguished Lecturer, Dept of Fisheries and Oceans, Canada 1987; Frink Medal, Zoological Soc. of London 1983, Linnean Medal for Zoology, Linnean Soc. of London 1987, Elsdon-Dew Medal, Parasitological Soc. of Southern Africa 1998; Hon. Prof., Univ. of Lancaster 1988–2008. *Publications:* The Cichlid Fishes of the Great Lakes of Africa: Their Biology and Evolution (with T. D. Iles) 1972, A Natural History of the Lakes, Tarns and Streams of the English Lake District 1991, The Freshwater Crustacea of Yorkshire: A Faunistic and Ecological Survey 1993; numerous articles in scientific journals. *Leisure interests:* natural history, walking, church architecture, photography. *Address:* Greystones, Church Lane, Stonehouse, Gloucestershire, GL10 2BG, England.

FU, Chengyu, BSc, MSc; Chinese oil industry executive; *Chairman, China Petrochemical Corporation (Sinopec Group);* b. 1951; ed Northeast Petroleum Inst., Univ. of Southern California, USA; fmr oil engineer, worked in Daqing, Liaohe and Huabei oilfields; joined China Nat. Offshore Oil Corpn (CNOOC) 1982, chair. several jt ventures, Vice-Pres. CNOOC Nanhai East Corpn 1994–95; Vice-Pres. Phillips China Inc. 1995; Gen. Man. Xijiang Devt Project 1995; Pres. CNOOC Nanhai East Corpn 1999, Exec. Dir, Exec. Vice-Pres. and COO CNOOC Ltd 1999, Vice-Pres. CNOOC 2000–02, Pres. CNOOC Ltd 2002–03, Chair. and CEO China Oilfield Services Ltd (subsidiary) 2002–11, Chair. and CEO CNOOC Ltd 2003–10, Chair. 2003–11, Pres. and Party Leadership Group Sec. CNOOC Ltd 2003–11; Chair. China Petrochemical Corpn (Sinopec Group) 2011–, Sec. Party Cttee; mem. 17th CCP Cen. Cttee Cen. Comm. for Discipline Inspection 2007–. *Address:* China Petrochemical Corporation (Sinopec Group), 22 Chaoyangmen North Street, Chaoyang District, Beijing 100728, People's Republic of China (office). *Telephone:* (10) 59960114 (office). *Fax:* (10) 59760111 (office). *E-mail:* master@sinopec.com.cn (office). *Website:* www.sinopecgroup.com (office); www.sinopec.com (office).

FU, Jianhua, MA; Chinese banking executive; *Vice-Chairman and President, Shanghai Pudong Development Bank Company Limited;* ed Dongbei Univ. of Finance and Econs; Chair. Bank of Shanghai –2006; Vice-Chair., Pres. and Deputy Party Sec., Shanghai Pudong Development Bank Co. Ltd 2006–; Dir (non-exec.), Shanghai Commercial Bank Ltd 2004–09. *Address:* Shanghai Pudong Development Bank Company Ltd, 12 Zhongshan Dong Yi Road, Shanghai 200002, People's Republic of China (office). *Telephone:* (21) 6161-8888 (office). *E-mail:* webmaster@ spdb.com.cn (office). *Website:* www.spdb.com.cn (office).

FU, Lt-Gen. Kuiqing; Chinese army officer; b. 1920, Yingshan Co., Anhui Prov.; Sec. CCP Prov. Cttee, Heilongjiang 1971–74; Vice-Gov., Heilongjiang 1972–74; Deputy Political Commissar, Shenyang Mil. Region, PLA 1977; Political Commissar, Fuzhou Mil. Region, PLA 1981–85; mem. 12th CCP Cen. Cttee 1982–87; Political Commissar Nanjing Mil. Region, PLA 1985–90, rank of Lt-Gen. PLA 1988; mem. Standing Cttee of 7th NPC; 3rd Class Order of Independence and Freedom, 2nd Class Order of Liberation. *Address:* Nanjing Military Region Headquarters, Nanjing, Jiangsu, People's Republic of China.

FU, Mingxia; Chinese diver; b. Aug. 1978, Wuhan, Hubei Prov.; m. Antony Leung 2002; two s. one d.; ed Qinghua Univ., Beijing; youngest ever 10m platform diving world champion at the age of 12; first woman to win five Olympic diving medals; 10m platform diving gold medallist World Championships, Perth 1991, Rome 1994; 10m platform diving gold medallist at Olympics, Barcelona 1992, Olympics, Atlanta 1996 (also won 3m platform gold medal), 3m springboard gold medallist at

Sydney Olympics 2000; 3m springboard silver medallist Asian Games, Hiroshima 1994, 10m platform diving bronze medallist, Asian Games, Beijing 1990; Nation's Best 10 Athletes Award. *Address:* c/o State General Bureau for Physical Culture and Sports, 9 Tiyuguan Road, Chongwen District, Beijing, People's Republic of China.

FU, Qifeng; Chinese writer and former acrobat; b. 15 March 1941, Chengdu, Sichuan; d. of Fu Tianzheng and Ceng Qingpu; m. Xu Zhuang 1961; one s. one d.; performer, acrobatics troupe, Beijing 1960–70; Founder and Deputy Chief Ed. Acrobatics and Magic (journal); mem. Research Dept, Asscn of Chinese Acrobats 1987–, Council mem. 1991–; mem. Editorial Cttee Acrobatics, in series Contemporary China 1991–; mem. China Magic Cttee 1993–. *Publications include:* Chinese Acrobatics Through the Ages 1986, The Art of Chinese Acrobatics 1988; (with brother) Acrobatics in China 1983, History of Chinese Acrobatics 1989, History of Chinese Artistic Skills (in Japanese) 1993; (co-author) Literature and Art Volume of China Concise Encyclopedia 1994, Secret of Spiritualist Activities 1995, Illusions and Superstitions 1997, A Primer of Chinese Acrobatics 2003. *Address:* Chinese Acrobats Association, No.10, Nanli, Nongzhanguan (AgriCultural Exhibition Hall), Beijing 100026 (office); 5-2-501 Hongmiao Beili, Jintai Road, Beijing 100025, People's Republic of China. *Telephone:* 65005662 (office); 65002547.

FU, Gen. Quanyou; Chinese army officer; b. 1930, Yuanping Co., Shanxi Prov.; ed Mil. Acad. of the Chinese PLA; joined PLA 1946, took part in Yanqing Campaign; joined CCP 1947; Deputy Co. Commdr Northwest Field Army, PLA Services and Arms 1948–50, Co. Commdr and Bn Chief-of-Staff 1950–52; soldier, Korean War 1953, Bn Commdr Chinese People's Volunteers 1953–58; Regt Chief-of-Staff, Chengdu Mil. Region, PLA 1961–64, Div. Chief-of-Staff 1968–69, Div. Commdr 1978–80, Army Chief-of-Staff 1981–83, Army Commdr 1983–85, Commdr 1985–88, Lt-Gen. 1988–93, Commdr Lanzhou Mil. Region 1990–92, Dir Gen. Logistics Dept 1992–95, Gen. 1993–, Chief of Gen. Staff 1995–99; Vice-Chair. Nat. Afforestation Cttee; Deputy Dir Nat. Cttee for the Patriotic Public Health Campaign 1994–98; mem. 12th CCP Cen. Cttee 1983–87, 13th CCP Cen. Cttee 1987–92, 14th CCP Cen. Cttee (mem. Cen. Mil. Comm.) 1992–97, 15th CCP Cen. Cttee 1997–2002; mem. Cen. Mil. Comm. of People's Repub. of China 1993–2003. *Address:* c/o Chinese Communist Party Central Committee, Zhongnanhai, Beijing, People's Republic of China.

FU, Tianlin; Chinese poet; b. 24 Jan. 1946, Zizhong Co., Sichuan Prov.; ed Chongqing Electronic Tech. High School; worked in orchard Chongqing 1962–79; clerk, Beibei Cultural Centre 1980–82; Ed. Chongqing Publishing House 1982–; Vice-Pres. Poetry Inst. of China (PIC), Pres. PIC Chongqing; First Prize of Chinese Poetry 1983, voted as one of China's Ten Outstanding Poets by Poetry 1983 periodical 2008. *Publications include:* The Sweat (Nat. Outstanding Young Poet Award 1981), Green Musical Notes (First Chinese Nat. Poetry Works Award 1983) 1981, Between Children and the World 1983, Island of Music 1985, Red Strawberry 1986, Selected Poems of Seven Chinese Poets 1993, Futianlin Selected Works (Second Chinese Female Literature Award 2003) 2002, Lemon Leaves (Lu Xun Literature Award 2010) 2009. *E-mail:* futianlin023@163.com.

FU, Xishou; Chinese government official and engineer; b. 1931, Beijing; ed Tsinghua Univ.; joined CCP 1959; Chief Designer, Panzhihua Iron and Steel Project, Sichuan Prov. 1959; Deputy Chief Engineer, Chongqing Iron and Steel Designing Inst. 1966–78, Deputy Dir 1978–82; Dir Ma'anshan Iron and Steel Design and Research Inst., Anhui Prov. 1982–84; Man. Ma'anshan Iron and Steel Group Co. Ltd 1984–87 (Sec. CCP Party Cttee 1984–87); Deputy Sec. CCP Ma'anshan City Cttee 1984–87; Deputy Sec. Anhui Prov. CCP Cttee 1987–88; Deputy Gov. of Anhui Prov. 1988–89, Gov. 1989–94; Alt. mem. 14th CCP Cen. Cttee 1987–92, mem. 14th CCP Cen. Cttee 1992–97; mem. Standing Cttee 8th CPPCC Nat. Cttee 1993–98, 9th CPPCC Nat. Cttee 1998–2003; NPC Deputy to Anhui Prov.; Deputy Sec. CCP 5th Anhui Prov. Cttee 1988; Gov. Anhui Prov. People's Govt 1989–94; Chair. Anhui Prov. Disabled Persons' Fed. *Address:* c/o Office of Provincial Governor, Hefei City, Anhui Province, People's Republic of China.

FU, Ying; Chinese diplomatist; *Vice-Minister of Foreign Affairs;* b. Jan. 1953, Hohhot, Inner Mongolian Autonomous Region; m.; one d.; ed Foreign Languages Inst., Beijing, Univ. of Kent, UK; Attaché, Embassy in Romania 1978–82; Attaché, Dept of Translation and Interpretation, Ministry of Foreign Affairs 1982–85; Deputy Dir 1986–90, Deputy Dir, Dept of Asian Affairs 1990–92, Dir and Counsellor 1993–97, Dir-Gen. 2000–04; staff mem. UN Transitional Authority, Cambodia 1992–93; Minister Counsellor, Embassy in Jakarta 1997–98, Amb. to the Philippines 1998–2000, to Australia 2004–07, to UK 2007–09; Vice-Minister of Foreign Affairs 2009–. *Address:* Ministry of Foreign Affairs, 2 Chaoyangmen, Nan Dajie, Chao Yang Qu, Beijing 100701, People's Republic of China (office). *Telephone:* (10) 65961114 (office). *Fax:* (10) 65962146 (office). *E-mail:* webmaster@mfa.gov.cn (office). *Website:* www.fmprc.gov.cn (office).

FU, Yuning, PhD; Chinese business executive; *Chairman, China Merchants Group Limited;* b. March 1957; ed Brunel Univ., UK; fmr Asst Man. Dir Shenzhen Chiwan Petroleum Supply Base Co. Ltd, fmr Chair. Shenzhen Chiwan Wharf Holdings Ltd; fmr Chair. Union Bank of Hong Kong Ltd; fmr Gen. Man. China Nanshan Devt Group Inc., currently Chair.; fmr Vice-Pres. and Pres. China Merchants Group Ltd, currently Chair., Dir (non-exec.) China Merchants Bank Co. Ltd 1999–, Chair. 2010–, also Chair. China Merchants Holdings (International) Co. Ltd; Ind. Dir (non-exec.) Li & Fung Ltd; Exec. mem. Hong Kong Gen. Chamber of Commerce; mem. 12th Nat. Cttee of the CPPCC. *Address:* China Merchants Group Ltd, 40th Floor, China Merchants Building, 168–200 Conaught Road, Central, Hong Kong Special Administrative Region (office); China Merchants Bank Co. Ltd, 7088 Shen Nan Road, Futian District, Shenzhen 518040, Guangdong, People's Republic of China (office). *Telephone:* 25428288 (Hong Kong) (office); (755) 83198888 (Shenzhen) (office). *Fax:* 25448851 (Hong Kong) (office); (755) 83195109 (Shenzhen) (office). *E-mail:* cmhk@cmhk.com (office). *Website:* www.cmhk.com (office); www.cmbchina.com (office).

FU, Zhihuan; Chinese engineer and politician; b. March 1938, Haicheng Co., Liaoning Prov.; ed Moscow Railways Inst., USSR; technician, later Deputy Chief, later Chief, later Deputy Dir Zhuzhou Electric Eng Research Inst., Ministry of Railways 1961; joined CCP 1966; Chief Engineer, Science and Tech. Bureau,

Ministry of Railways 1983, Dir 1985; Dir Harbin Railway Bureau 1989; Vice-Minister of Railways 1990–97, Minister 2002–03; Chair. Financial and Econ. Cttee, NPC 2003–; mem. CCP Cen. Comm. for Discipline Inspection 1997–2002; mem. 15th CCP Cen. Cttee 1997–2002; Academician, Chinese Acad. of Engineering. *Address:* Chinese Academy of Engineering, 2 Bingjiaokou Hutong, Xicheng District, Beijing 100088, People's Republic of China. *Website:* www.cae.cn.

FUCHS, Alain, PhD, FRSC; French chemical engineer, academic and national organization official; *President, Centre National de la Recherche Scientifique;* b. 10 April 1953, Lausanne; ed École polytechnique fédérale de Lausanne, Univ. of Paris-Sud, Orsay, France; Sr Prof. of Chem., Univ. of Paris-Sud 1995, Dir Chimie physique des matériaux amorphes (Physical Chem. of Amorphous Materials) lab. 1997–2000, Founder-Dir Orsay Laboratoire de chimie physique (Lab. of Physical Chem.) 2000–06; Dir Ecole Nationale Supérieure de Chimie de Paris (Chimie ParisTech) 2006–10; Visiting Prof., Univ. of California, USA 1999; several industrial collaborations; Pres. Section 13 (Physical Chem.—Molecules, Environments), Nat. Cttee of Scientific Research, based at CNRS 2004–07, mem. Scientific Cttee of CNRS's Science and Citizens programme 1997–99, Sr Adviser on calculation to CNRS Chem. Dept 1997–2003, Pres. CNRS 2010–; Pres. Physical Chem. Div., Soc. française de chimie 2002–05, Soc. française de physique 2002–05; mem. Bd of Dirs Int. Adsorption Soc.; mem. CDEFI permanent (Conférence des directeurs des écoles françaises d'ingénieurs) 2007–, Educational Bd Institut nat. des sciences et techniques nucléaires (affiliated with French Atomic Energy Comm.), Comité de coordination des formations en sciences et technologies du nucléaire 2009–, Scientific Bd CECAM Lyon (Centre européen de calcul atomique et moléculaire) 1999–2008; Chevalier des Palmes académiques 1996, Chevalier légion d'honneur; Dr hc, Univ. of Quebec in Montreal. *Publications include:* numerous papers in professional journals on the modelization and molecular simulation of the behaviour of confined fluids. *Address:* CNRS, Campus Gérard-Mégie, 3 rue Michel-Ange, 75794 Paris Cedex 16, France (office). *Telephone:* 1-44-96-48-23 (office). *Fax:* 1-44-96-49-13 (office). *E-mail:* presidence.secretariat@cnrs-dir.fr (office). *Website:* www.cnrs.fr (office).

FUCHS, Elaine, BS, PhD; American cell biologist and academic; *Rebecca C. Lancefield Professor, Laboratory of Mammalian Cell Biology and Development, The Rockefeller University;* b. 1950, Chicago, Ill.; m. Dr David Hansen; ed Univ. of Illinois, Princeton Univ.; Postdoctoral Researcher, MIT 1977–80; Amgen Prof. of Basic Sciences, Univ. of Chicago 1980–2002; Rebecca C. Lancefield Prof., Lab. of Mammalian Cell Biology and Devt, The Rockefeller Univ. 2002–; Investigator, Howard Hughes Medical Inst. 1988–; mem. Bd Damon Runyon Cancer Research Foundation; Pres. American Soc. for Cell Biology 2001; mem. NAS Inst. of Medicine 1994, NAS 1996, American Acad. of Arts and Sciences 1994, American Acad. of Microbiology 1997, German Soc. of Dermatology 2001, New York Acad. of Sciences 2004, American Philosophical Soc. 2005; Foreign mem. European Molecular Biology Org. 2010; Fellow, Harvey Soc. 2004, AAAS 2008, Acad. of American Asscn for Cancer Research 2013; Dr hc (Mount Sinai School of Medicine, New York Univ.) 2003, (Univ. of Illinois) 2006; Sr Women's Career Achievement Award, Women in Cell Biology 1997, Cartwright Award, Columbia Univ. 2002, Novartis/Drew Award in Biomedical Research 2002, Dickson Prize in Medicine 2004, Award for Scientific Excellence, Fed. of American Socs for Experimental Biology 2006, Nat. Medal of Science 2009, Bering Award 2006, Laureate for North America, L'Oréal-UNESCO Awards for Women in Science 2010, Charlotte Friend Award 2010, Madison Medal 2011, Passano Prize 2011, Prize in Medicine and Biomedical Research, Albany Medical Center 2011, Biomedical Research Award, New York Acad. of Medicine 2012, March of Dimes Prize in Developmental Biology 2012, Lifetime Achievement Award, American Skin Asscn 2013, Pasarow Award in Cancer Research 2013. *Publications:* numerous papers in professional journals. *Address:* Laboratory of Mammalian Cell Biology and Development, The Rockefeller University, 1230 York Avenue, Box #300, New York, NY 10065, USA (office). *Telephone:* (212) 327-7953 (office). *Fax:* (212) 327-7954 (office). *E-mail:* elaine.fuchs@rockefeller.edu (office). *Website:* www.rockefeller.edu/research/faculty/labheads/ElaineFuchs (office).

FUCHS, Victor Robert, MA, PhD; American economist and academic; *Henry J. Kaiser, Jr Professor Emeritus of Economics, Stanford University;* b. 31 Jan. 1924, New York; s. of Alfred Fuchs and Frances S. Fuchs (née Scheiber); m. Beverly Beck 1948; two s. two d.; ed New York and Columbia Univs; Assoc. Prof. of Econs, New York Univ. 1959–60; Program Assoc. Econs Ford Foundation 1960–62; Research Assoc., Nat. Bureau of Econ. Research 1962–; Prof. of Community Medicine, Mount Sinai School of Medicine 1968–74; Prof. of Econs, CUNY Grad. Center 1968–74; Prof. of Econs (in Depts of Econs and Health Research and Policy), Stanford Univ. 1974–95, Henry J. Kaiser, Jr Prof. 1988–95, Prof. Emer. 1995–; Pres. American Econ. Asscn 1995; mem. Inst. of Medicine, American Philosophical Soc.; Fellow, American Acad. of Arts and Sciences; Distinguished Fellow, American Econ. Asscn 1990; Madden Memorial Award 1982, John R. Commons Award 2002 and other awards. *Publications:* The Economics of the Fur Industry 1957, Changes in the Location of Manufacturing in the US since 1929 1962, The Service Economy 1968, Production and Productivity in the Service Industries 1969, Who Shall Live? Health, Economics and Social Choice 1974 (expanded edn 1998), Economic Aspects of Health (ed.) 1982, How We Live 1983, The Health Economy 1986, Women's Quest for Economic Equality 1988, The Future of Health Policy 1993, Individual and Social Responsibility: Child Care, Education, Medical Care and Long Term Care in America (ed.) 1996. *Address:* National Bureau of Economic Research, 30 Alta Road, Stanford, CA 94305 (office); 796 Cedro Way, Stanford, CA 94305, USA (home). *Telephone:* (650) 326-7639 (office); (650) 858-1527 (home). *Fax:* (650) 328-4163 (office); (650) 858-0411 (home). *E-mail:* vfuchs@stanford.edu (office). *Website:* www-econ.stanford.edu (office).

FUDGE, Ann Marie, BA, MBA; American advertising executive (retd); b. 23 April 1951, Washington, DC; m. Richard E. Fudge 1971; two s.; ed Simmons Coll. and Harvard Univ. Grad. School of Business; began career as marketing asst with General Mills, Inc., later Marketing Dir; Pres. Beverage, Desserts and Post Div., Kraft Foods —2003; Chair. and CEO Young & Rubicam Brands and Y&R Advertising 2003–05, Chair. and CEO Y&R Brands 2003–06; Chair. US Programs Advisory Panel, Bill and Melinda Gates Foundation; mem. Bd of Dirs General Electric 1999–, Novartis 2008–, Buzzient, Inc. 2009–, Unilever 2009–, Infosys 2011–; Hon. Dir Catalyst; mem. Bd of Govs Boys and Girls Club of America; fmr

mem. Bd of Dirs Marriott International, The Advertising Council, Advertising Educational Foundation; mem. Harvard Bd of Overseers, Committee of 200, Council on Foreign Relations; mem. Nat. Comm. on Fiscal Responsibility and Reform 2010; Trustee, Brookings Inst., Rockefeller Foundation, Morehouse Coll.; Matrix Award for Advertising, New York Women in Communication, Leadership Awards, Minneapolis and New York City YWCA, Alumni Achievement Award, Harvard Business School 1998, Achievement Award, Executive Leadership Council 2000, Candace Award from Nat Coalition of 100 Black Women, named by Fortune magazine for several years as one of 50 Most Powerful Women in Business in the US, ranked 89th by Forbes magazine amongst 100 Most Powerful Women 2004, named as one of Time Magazine's Global Business Influentials 2004. *Address:* 2400 Beacon Street, PH1, Chestnut Hill, MA 02467, USA.

FUENTES KNIGHT, Juan Alberto, MA, PhD; Guatemalan economist and politician; ed McGill Univ. and Univ. of Toronto, Canada, Univ. of Geneva, Switzerland, Univ. of Sussex, UK; served for 20 years as economist with UN, becoming Co-ordinator Guatemalan Human Devt Report, UNDP; Exec. Dir and Research Co-ordinator Instituto Centroamericano de Estudios Fiscales (Cen. American Inst. for Fiscal Studies) —2007; Minister of Public Finance 2007–10. *Publications:* numerous articles in econ. journals. *Address:* c/o Ministry of Public Finance, Centro Cívico, 8a Avda y 21 Calle, Zona 1, Guatemala City, Guatemala (office).

FUGARD, Athol; South African actor, playwright and academic; b. 11 June 1932, Middelburg; s. of Harold David Fugard and Elizabeth Magdelene Potgieter; m. Sheila Fugard 1956; one d.; leading role in Meetings with Remarkable Men (film) 1977, The Guest (BBC production) 1977; acted in and wrote script for Marigolds in August (film); currently Adjunct Prof. of Playwriting, Acting and Directing, Univ. of California, San Diego; Hon. DLit (Natal and Rhodes); Dr hc (Univ. of Cape Town, Georgetown Univ., New York Univ., Univ. of Pennsylvania, CUNY); Hon. DFA (Yale Univ.) 1973; winner Silver Bear Award, Berlin Film Festival 1980, Commonwealth Award for Contrib. to American Theatre 1984. *Plays:* The Blood Knot, Hello and Goodbye, People are Living Here, Boesman and Lena 1970, Sizwe Banzi is Dead 1973, The Island 1973, Statements After an Arrest Under the Immorality Act 1974, No Good Friday 1974, Nongogo 1974, Dimetos 1976, The Road to Mecca 1984, My Children, My Africa, The Guest (film script) 1977, A Lesson from Aloes (author and dir Broadway production 1980) (New York Critics Award 1981) 1979, Master Harold and the Boys 1981 (London Evening Standard Award 1983), A Place with the Pigs (actor and dir) 1988, Playland 1992, Sign of Hope 1992, Valley Song (actor and dir) 1996, The Captain's Tiger 1999, Sorrows and Rejoicings 2001, Exits and Entrances 2004, Victory 2007, Coming Home 2009, The Train Driver 2010. *Films include:* Marigolds in August 1981, The Guest 1984; acted in films Gandhi 1982, Road to Mecca 1991 (also co-dir). *Publications:* Notebooks 1960–77, Playland 1992; novel: Tsotsi 1980; plays: Road to Mecca 1985, A Place with the Pigs 1988, Cousins: A Memoir 1994. *Address:* c/o Department of Theatre and Dance, University of California, San Diego, 9500 Gilman Drive, La Jolla, CA 92093, USA (office). *Website:* theatre.ucsd.edu (office).

FUJIMORI, Alberto Kenyo; Peruvian/Japanese fmr head of state and academic; b. 28 July 1939, Lima; s. of the late Nagochi Minami and Matsue Inomoto; m. 1st Susana Higushi (divorced 1996); two s. two d.; m. 2nd Satomi Kataoka 2006; ed Nat. School of Agric., Univ. of Wisconsin; fmr Rector, Nat. Agrarian Univ.; Pres. Nat. Ass. of Rectors 1984–89; Founder-mem. Cambio '90 (political party); Pres. of Peru 1990–2000; in exile in Japan Nov. 2000–05; arrested and charged in connection with state-sponsored murders, torture of a journalist, and embezzlement of public funds and dereliction of duty Sept. 2001, Peruvian Govt submitted 700-page document to back its charges 2003, Japanese Govt seeking further evidence in connection with Peruvian Govt's extradition request 2004; returned to Chile and arrested Nov. 2005; sentenced to six years in prison for abuse of power Dec. 2007; sentenced to 25 years in prison for ordering crimes against humanity during his presidency April 2009; Dr hc (Glebloux, Belgium, San Martín de Porres, Lima).

FUJIMORI, Fumio; Japanese business executive; *President, Aisin Seiki Company Ltd;* joined Aisin Seiki Co. Ltd 1971, Exec. Vice-Pres. and Dir of First Devt 2005–09, Pres. and Rep. Dir 2009–; Dir, Exedy Corpn, ADVICS Co. Ltd, Aisin AW Co. Ltd, Aisin Chemical Co. Ltd. *Address:* Aisin Seiki Company Ltd, 2-1 Asahi-machi, Kariya, Aichi 448-8650, Japan (office). *Telephone:* (5) 6624-8411 (office). *Fax:* (5) 6624-8003 (office). *E-mail:* info@aisin.com (office). *Website:* www.aisin.com (office).

FUJIMORI, Keiko Sofia Higuchi; Peruvian lawyer and politician; b. 25 May 1975; d. of Alberto Fujimori (fmr Pres. of Peru) and Susana Higuchi; m. Mark Villanella 2004; ed Columbia Business School, New York, Boston Univ. School of Man., USA; acted as First Lady of Peru during presidency of her father 1994–98; mem. Congress for Lima constituency 2006–; Leader, Alianza por el Futuro; unsuccessful cand. in 2011 presidential election. *Address:* Congreso de la República, Plaza Bolívar, Av. Abancay s/n, Lima, Peru (office). *E-mail:* kfujimori@congreso.gob.pe (office). *Website:* www.congreso.gob.pe/congresista/2006/kfujimori (office).

FUJISHIMA, Akira, PhD; Japanese chemist and academic; *Chairman, Kanagawa Academy of Science and Technology;* b. 10 March 1942; ed Yokohama Nat. Univ., Univ. of Tokyo; Lecturer, Kanagawa Univ. 1971, Asst Prof. 1973; Lecturer, Univ. of Tokyo 1975; Postdoctoral Fellow, Univ. of Texas 1976–77; Assoc. Prof., Univ. of Tokyo 1978, Prof. Grad. School 1994–2003, Prof. Emer. 2003–; Chair. Kanagawa Acad. of Science and Tech. 2003–; Pres. Electrochemical Soc. of Japan; advisory mem. Japanese Photochemistry Asscn; Pres. Chemical Soc. of Japan; Asahi Prize 1983, Inoue Harunari Prize 1998, Chemical Soc. of Japan Prize 2000, Japan Prize (jtly) 2004, The Japan Academy Prize 2004. *Address:* KSP West 614, 3-2-1 Sakado, Takatsu-ku, Kawasaki-shi, Kanagawa 213-0012, Japan. *Telephone:* (44) 819-2020. *Fax:* (44) 819-2038.

FUJITA, Hiroyuki, PhD; Japanese scientist and academic; *Professor, Fujita Laboratory, Institute of Industrial Science, University of Tokyo;* b. 13 Dec. 1952, Tokyo; s. of Shigeru Fujita and Tokiko Fujita; m. Yumiko Kato 1982; ed Univ. of Tokyo; Lecturer, Inst. of Industrial Science, Univ. of Tokyo 1980–81, Assoc. Prof. 1981–93, Prof., Fujita Lab. 1993–; Visiting Scientist, Francis Bitter Nat. Magnet Lab., MIT, USA 1983–85; M. Hetényi Award for Experimental Mechanics 1987.

Publications: contribs to books and numerous scientific papers in professional journals. *Leisure interests:* reading, skiing, tennis. *Address:* Fujita Laboratory, Room No. Ew304, 4-6-1 Komaba, Meguro-ku, Tokyo 153-8505 (office); Institute of Industrial Science, 7-22-1 Roppongi, Minato-ku, Tokyo 106 (office); 1-9-14 Senkawa, Toshima-ku, Tokyo 171, Japan (home). *Telephone:* (3) 5452-6248 (office); (3) 3402-6231 ext. 2353 (office). *E-mail:* fujita@iis.u-tokyo.ac.jp (office). *Website:* www.fujita3.iis.u-tokyo.ac.jp (office).

FUJITA, Yuzuru; Japanese insurance industry executive; *Chairman, Asahi Mutual Life Insurance Company;* b. 24 Nov. 1941; joined Asahi Mutual Life Insurance Company 1964, named Dir 1992, Man. Dir 1994–96, Pres. and Rep. Dir 1996–2008, Chair. 2008–; mem. Bd of Dirs and Auditor Furukawa Electric Co., Ltd; outside statutory auditor, Yokohama Rubber Co., Ltd 2000–; Chair. Japan Nat. Cttee for UWCs. *Address:* Asahi Mutual Life Insurance Company, 1-7-3 Nishi-Shinjuku, Shinjuku-ku, Tokyo 163-8611, Japan (office). *Telephone:* (3) 3342-3111 (office). *Fax:* (3) 3346-9397 (office). *Website:* www.asahi-life.co.jp (office).

FUKAYA, Koichi; Japanese automotive parts executive; joined DENSO Corpn 1966, becoming Gen. Man., Production Eng and Research and Devt Depts, later Pres. DENSO Manufacturing Michigan Inc., Man. Dir Thermal Systems Product Group, Dir DENSO Corpn 1995–, Sr Man. Dir, Production Promotion Centre 2002–03, Pres. and CEO DENSO Corpn 2003–08, Vice-Chair. 2008–09, Chair. 2009–13. *Address:* c/o DENSO Corpn, 1-1 Showa-cho, Kariya, Aichi 448-8661, Japan. *E-mail:* info@globaldenso.com.

FUKSAS, Massimiliano; Italian architect; b. 9 Jan. 1944, Rome; ed Univ. 'La Sapienza', Rome; teaching and research activities, Inst. of History of Architecture, Faculty of Architecture, Univ. 'La Sapienza', Rome; est. architecture practice, Rome 1967, Paris, France 1989, Vienna, Austria 1993; Consultant Architect, Town Planning Advisory Council, Berlin, Germany 1994–97, Planning Council, Salzburg, Austria 1994–97; Adviser, Admin Bd, Institut Français d'Architecture 1997–; writes architecture column of weekly publ. L'Espresso 2000–; Visiting Prof., Staatliche Akad. der Bildenden Kunste, Stuttgart, Germany 1988, Ecole Spéciale d'Architecture, Paris 1990, Columbia Univ., New York, USA 1990–91, Institut für Entwerten und Architektur, Hanover, Germany 1993, Akad. der Bildenden Kunste, Vienna 1995–97; mem. Accademico Nazionale di San Luca 2000; Hon. Fellow, American Inst. of Architects 2002; Hon. mem. RIBA 2006; Commandeur, Ordre des Arts et Lettres (France) 2000; numerous awards including Vitruvio a la Trayectoria, Buenos Aires 1998, Grand Prix d'Architecture Française 1999, Golden Cube Architecture Prize, Naples 2007. *Projects include:* Chamber of Commerce and Industry of Nîmes-Uzès-Le Vigan, Nîmes, France 1991, redevt of areas along bank of Seine, Clichy-la-Garenne, France 1991, renovation of Luth area, Gennevilliers, France 1991, Ecole Nat. Superieure de Mecanique et Aeronautique Futuroscope, Poitiers, France 1991, renovation of Allones town centre, France 1991, urban renovation, Port-de-Bouc, Marseille, France 1991, A tower on 11 towers, Frankfurt, Germany 1991, Ecole Nat. d'Ingenieurs and Institut Scientifique, Brest, France 1991–92, Saint-Exupéry Coll., Noisy-le-Grand, France 1991–93, renovation of old harbour area, Nagasaki, Japan 1993, European Inst. of Interior Design and Architecture, students' housing, Rouen, France 1991–93, Lu Jiazui, Int. Trade Centre, Pudong, China 1991, RIVP devt, Paris 1991–96, Faculty of Law and Econs, Limoges, France 1991–96, restoration and extension of Hotel Dieu, Chartres, France 1991–96, redevt of Domaine Bâti du Petit Arbois, Europole Méditerranéenne Programme, Aix-Les-Milles, France 1992, ZAC Berges-de-Seine, new quarter 'Cables de Lyon', Clichy, France 1992, renovation of Town Hall area, Limoges 1992, Centre Ville Univ., Brest 1992–94, renovation of Cité des Aigues Douces, Marseille 1992–95, residential complex, Clichy-la-Garenne 1992–96, Maison des Arts, exhbn centre, Bordeaux Univ., France 1992–95, masterplan of Tremblay in airport section of Roissy-Charles de Gaulle, Paris 1993–2001, Europark shopping centre, Salzburg 1994–97, Place des Nations, Geneva, Switzerland 1995, Maximilien Perret Coll., Alfortville, Paris 1995–98, Twin Tower, HQ for Wienerberger, Vienna 1995–2001, students and professors' housing, Alfortville, Paris (jtly with D. Mandrelli) 1997–98, Ilot Cantagrel, Paris XIII 1997–2000, harbour and urban rearrangement, Castellammare di Stabia, Italy 1998, Tuscolo Museum, Frascati, Rome 1998–2000, office bldg Hanse-Forum, Axel Springer Platz, Hamburg, Germany 1998–2002, residential and office complex, Alsterfleet, Hamburg 1998–2002, new commercial pavilion, Porta Palazzo, Turin 1998–2004, Peres Peace Centre, Jaffa, Israel 1998–2004, Piazza Mall complex, Eindhoven, Netherlands 1999–2004, Italia Congress and exhbn centre, Roma-Eur, Rome 1999–2003, residential centre, Brachmule, Vienna 2000, houses and commercial area, Rimini 2000–02, HQ Italian Space Agency (ASI), Rome 2000–07, devt of integrated cultural dist at West Kowloon Reclamation, Hong Kong 2001, Queensland Gallery of Modern Art, Brisbane, Australia 2001, devt of Water Front, Hong Kong West 2001, new HQ for Piedmont Region, Turin 2001–05, Emporio Armani Showroom, Hong Kong 2001–02, Europark Insein, Salzburg 2001–05, new HQ for Ferrari SpA, Maranello, Italy 2001–04, new Trade Fair Centre, Pero-Rho Milan 2002–05, inner city devt, Prague, Czech Repub. 2002, Canal+, Louveciennes, Paris 2002, new HQ for Bortolo Nardini Co., Bassano del Grappa, Vicenza, Italy 2002–04, MAB Zeil, Frankfurt, Germany 2002–06, exhbn centre, Rho-Pero, Milan 2002–05, new HQ for Miroglio-Vestebene, Alba, Italy 2003, Concert Hall Zenith, Amiens, France 2003–05, concept store for Palmers, Austria 2003, opera house, Astana, Kazakhstan 2003, Emporio Armani Showroom, Shanghai, China 2004, Sankei Bldg, Osaka, Japan 2004, exhbn complex for new capital of Kazakhstan, Astana 2004–06, tourist port, Marina di Stabia 2004, new HQ for FATER SpA, Pescara, Italy 2004, regeneration of Salford, UK 2005, tourist port at Margonara, Albissola, Savona, Italy 2005, African Inst. of Science and Tech., Abuja, Nigeria 2006, Montecatini Thermal Spa Devt, Italy 2007, Fujeirah Islands Masterplan, UAE 2007, New Silk Road Park, Xi'an, China 2007, Shenzhen Int. Airport, China 2008. *Address:* Massimiliano Fuksas architetto, Piazza del Monte di Pietà 30, 00186 Rome, Italy (office). *Telephone:* 68807871 (office). *Fax:* 68807872 (office). *E-mail:* office@fuksas.it (office). *Website:* www.fuksas.it (office).

FUKUDA, Yasuo; Japanese politician; b. 16 July 1936, Tokyo; s. of the late Takeo Fukuda (fmr Prime Minister of Japan); m. Kiyoko Fukuda; two s. one d.; ed Waseda Univ.; with Maruzen Oil (now Cosmo Oil) petroleum refining and marketing co. 1959–76; Chief Sec. to Prime Minister Takeo Fukuda (father) 1977–78, Pvt. Sec. 1979–89; Dir Kinzai Inst. for Financial Affairs 1978–89; mem.

Liberal-Democratic Party (LDP), Pres. 2007–; mem. House of Reps for Gunma 4th Dist 1990–; Parl. Vice-Minister of Foreign Affairs 1995–96; Minister of State, Chief Cabinet Sec., Dir-Gen. Okinawa Devt Agency 2000–01; Chief Cabinet Sec. (Gender Equality) and Minister of State 2001–04 (resgnd); Deputy Sec.-Gen. LDP 1997–98, Chair. Finance Cttee 1998, Dir-Gen. Treasury Bureau 1999–2000, Deputy Chair. Policy Research Council 2000–, Prime Minister 2007–08 (resgnd). *Address:* Liberal-Democratic Party—LDP (Jiyu-Minshuto), 1-11-23, Nagata-cho, Chiyoda-ku, Tokyo 100-8910, Japan (office). *Telephone:* (3) 3581-6211 (office). *Fax:* (3) 3581-1910 (office). *E-mail:* koho@ldp.jimin.or.jp (office). *Website:* www.jimin.jp (office).

FUKUDA, Yoshitaka; Japanese business executive; *President, CEO and Representative Director, Aiful Corporation;* b. 1948; m.; three c.; est. sole proprietorship as consumer finance co. 1967; est. Marutaka Inc. 1978, absorbed three related cos and changed name to Aiful Corpn 1982, currently Pres., CEO and Rep. Dir. *Address:* Aiful Corporation, 381-1 Takasago-cho, Gojo-agaru, Karasuma-Dori, Shimogyo-kyu, Kyoto 600-8420, Japan (office). *Telephone:* (75) 201-2000 (office).

FUKUI, Takeo, BS; Japanese automotive industry executive; *Adviser, Honda Motor Company;* b. 1945, Tokyo; ed Waseda Univ.; joined Honda Motor Co. 1969, engineer 1969–79, Dir 1988–90, Gen. Man. Motorcycle Devt 1991–92, Gen. Man. Motorcycle Operations, Hamamatsu Factory 1992–94, Man. Dir 1996–98, Sr Man. and Rep. Dir 1999–2003, Pres. and CEO 2003–09, Adviser 2009–, Chief Engineer, Honda R&D Co. 1979–82, Man. Dir 1987–88, Sr Man. Dir 1990–91, Pres. 1998–2003, Chief Engineer, Honda Racing Corpn 1982–83, Dir 1983–85, Exec. Vice-Pres. 1985–87, Pres. 1987–88, Exec. Vice-Pres. and Dir Honda of America Manufacturing Inc., OH, USA 1994–96, Pres. and Dir 1996–98. *Address:* Honda Motor Company, 2-1-1 Minami-Aoyama, Minato-ku, Tokyo 107-8556, Japan (office). *Telephone:* (3) 3423-1111 (office). *Fax:* (3) 5412-1515 (office). *E-mail:* info@honda.com (office). *Website:* www.honda.co.jp (office); world.honda.com (office).

FUKUI, Toshihiko; Japanese central banker (retd); b. 7 Sept. 1935; ed Univ. of Tokyo; joined Bank of Japan 1958, Rep. in Paris 1970–77, Dir, Head of Planning Div., Coordination and Planning Dept 1977–80, Gen. Man. Takamatsu Br. 1980–81, Deputy Gen. Man. Osaka Br. 1981–83, First Deputy Dir-Gen. Personnel Dept 1984–85, Dir-Gen. Research and Statistics Dept 1985–86, Dir-Gen. Banking Dept 1986–89, Dir-Gen. Policy Planning Dept 1989, Exec. Dir 1989–94, Deputy Gov. 1994–98, Gov. 2003–08 (retd); Chair. Fujitso Research Inst. 1998–2002; Vice-Chair. Japan Asscn of Corp. Execs (Keizai Doyukai) 2001–03. *Address:* c/o Nippon Ginko (Bank of Japan), 2-1-1, Hongoku-cho, Nihonbashi, Chuo-ku, Tokyo 100-8630, Japan (office).

FUKUJIN, Kunio; Japanese business executive; *Honorary Chairman, Alfresa Corporation;* Rep. Dir, Chair. and Pres. Alfresa Corpn –2009, Rep. Dir and Chair 2009–, fmr Rep. Dir, Pres. and CEO Alfresa Holdings Corpn, later Chair., now Dir and Hon. Chair. *Address:* Alfresa Holdings Corporation, 1-1-3 Otemachi, Chiyoda-ku, Tokyo 100-0004, Japan (office). *Telephone:* (3) 5219-5102 (office). *Fax:* (3) 5219-5103 (office). *E-mail:* info@alfresa.com (office). *Website:* www.alfresa.com (office).

FUKUKAWA, Shinji; Japanese business executive; b. 8 March 1932, Tokyo; s. of Tokushiro Fukukawa and Maki Fukukawa; m. Yoriko Kawada 1961; two d.; ed Univ. of Tokyo; served at Ministry of Int. Trade and Industry (MITI) 1955–88, Deputy Vice-Minister 1983–84, Dir-Gen. Industrial Policy Bureau 1984–86, Vice-Minister 1986–88; Pvt. Sec. to fmr Prime Minister Ohira 1978–80; Sr Adviser to MITI 1988–90, to Japan Industrial Policy Research Inst. 1988–90, to Global Industrial and Social Progress Research Inst. 1988–, to Nomura Research Inst. 1989–90; Exec. Vice-Pres. Kobe Steel Ltd 1990–94; CEO Dentsu Inst. for Human Studies 1994–2002, Exec. Adviser, Dentsu Inc. 2002–04; Chair. TEPIA (Machine Industry Memorial Foundation). *Publications:* Japan's Role in the 21st Century: Three Newisms 1990, Industrial Policy 1998, The Thinking of Successful Businessmen in the IT Age 2000, A Warning to Japan 2003. *Leisure interests:* tennis, golf, classical music, reading. *Address:* TEPIA, Machine Industry Memorial Foundation, 2-8-44 Kita-Aoyama, Minato-ku, Tokyo 107-0061 (office); 7-11, Okusawa 8-chome, Setagaya-ku, Tokyo 158-0083, Japan (home). *Telephone:* (3) 5474-6110 (office); (3) 3701-4956 (home). *Fax:* (3) 5474-6114 (office); (3) 3701-4956 (home). *E-mail:* fukukawa@tepia.jp (office). *Website:* www.tepia.jp (office).

FUKUSHIMA, Mizuho, LLB; Japanese lawyer and politician; *Chairman, Social Democratic Party of Japan;* b. 24 Dec. 1955, Nobeoka, Miyazaki Pref.; one d.; ed Univ. of Tokyo; called to the Bar 1987; fmr commentator on weekly TV show; entered politics 1998, mem. House of Councillors 1998–, mem. Cttee on Health, Welfare and Labour, Cttee on the Budget, Comm. on the Constitution, Research Cttee on Society of Cooperative Way of Life and Regional Vitalization; mem. Social Democratic Party, Sec.-Gen. 2001–03, Chair. 2003–; Minister of State for Consumer Affairs and Food Safety, Social Affairs and Gender Equality 2009–10. *Address:* Social Democratic Party of Japan, 2-4-3-7F, Nagata-cho, Chiyoda-ku, Tokyo 100-0014 (office); Member's Office Building, House of Councillors, 2-1-1, Nagata-cho, Chiyoda-ku, Tokyo 100-8962, Japan (office). *Telephone:* (3) 5253-2111 (office). *E-mail:* kokusai@sdp.or.jp (office). *Website:* www.cao.go.jp (office); www .mizuhoto.org (office); www.sdp.or.jp (office).

FUKUYAMA, Francis, PhD; American political scientist, writer and academic; *Olivier Nomellini Senior Fellow, Freeman Spogli Institute for International Studies, Stanford University;* b. 27 Oct. 1952, Chicago, Ill.; s. of Yoshio Fukuyama and Toshiko Fukuyama (née Kawata); m. Laura Holmgren; three c.; ed Cornell and Harvard Univs; fmrly Sr Social Scientist, RAND Corpn, Washington, DC 1979–80, 1983–89, 1995–96; Deputy Dir US State Dept's Policy Planning Staff 1981–82, 1989; Hirst Prof. of Public Policy, George Mason Univ., Fairfax 1996–2000; Dean of Faculty, Paul H. Nitze School of Advanced Int. Studies, Johns Hopkins Univ. 2002–04, then Bernard L. Schwartz Prof. of Int. Political Economy–2010; Olivier Nomellini Sr Fellow, Freeman Spogli Inst. for Int. Studies, Stanford Univ. 2010–, also resident Center on Democracy, Development, and the Rule of Law; Chair. Editorial Bd The American Interest (magazine); Trustee, RAND Corpn; mem. Bd of Govs Pardee Rand Graduate School; mem. Pres.'s Council on Bioethics 2001–04; mem. advisory Bd Journal of Democracy, Inter-American Dialogue, New America Foundation; mem. American Political Science Asscn, Council on Foreign Relations; mem. US del. to Egyptian-Israeli talks on Palestinian autonomy 1981–82; Dr hc (Connecticut Coll.), (Doane Coll.), (Doshisha Univ., Japan), (Kansai Univ., Japan), (Århus Univ., Denmark), (Rand Grad.

School). *Publications:* The End of History and the Last Man 1992, Trust: The Social Virtues and the Creation of Prosperity 1996, The Great Disruption: Human Nature and the Reconstitution of the Social Order 1999, Our Posthuman Future 2002, State-Building: Governance and World Order in the 21st Century 2004, Nation-Building: Beyond Afghanistan and Iraq (ed.) 2005, After the Neocons 2006, America at the Crossroads: Democracy, Power, and the Neoconservative Legacy 2006, Falling Behind: Explaining the Development Gap between Latin American and the US 2008, The Origins of Political Order 2011. *Address:* Freeman Spogli Institute for International Studies, Encina Hall, 616 Serra Street, Stanford, CA 94305, USA (office). *Telephone:* (650) 723-3214 (office). *Fax:* (650) 725-2592 (office). *E-mail:* f.fukuyama@stanford.edu (office). *Website:* fsi.stanford.edu (office); www .francisfukuyama.com.

FULD, Richard (Dick) S., Jr, BA, MBA; American investment banking executive; b. 1946; ed Univ. of Colorado, New York Univ. Stern School of Business; joined Lehman Brothers 1969, various man. positions, including Dir Lehman Brothers Inc. 1984–2008, Vice-Chair. Shearson Lehman Brothers Inc. 1984–90, Pres. and Co-CEO 1990–93, Dir Lehman Brothers Holdings Inc. 1990–2008 (after Chapter 11 filing by Lehman Brothers and acquisition by Barclays Capital); Pres. and COO 1993–94, CEO 1993–2008, Chair. 1994–2008, also Chair. Lehman Brothers Inc. 1994–2008; fmr mem. The Business Council, Exec. Cttee NY City Partnership, Univ. of Colorado Business Advisory Council; Trustee, Middlebury Coll., New York-Presbyterian Hosp. *Address:* c/o Lehman Brothers Holdings Inc., 745 Seventh Avenue, New York, NY 10019, USA (office).

FÜLE, Štefan; Czech diplomatist, politician and international organization official; *Commissioner for Enlargement and European Neighbourhood Policy, European Commission;* b. 24 May 1962, Sokolov; m. Hana Füleová; one s. two d.; ed Charles Univ., Prague, Moscow State Inst. of Int. Relations, USSR, UN disarmament study programme; Desk Officer, UN Dept, Fed. Ministry of Foreign Affairs, Czechoslovakia 1987–90; First Sec., Mission of Czech Repub. to UN, New York 1990–95, mem. Del./Alt. Rep. to Security Council 1994–95; Dir UN Dept, Ministry of Foreign Affairs 1995–96, Security Policy Dept 1996–98; Amb. to Lithuania 1998–2001, NATO Point of Contact Amb. to Lithuania 2000–01; First Deputy Minister, Ministry of Defence 2001–02; Amb. to UK 2003–05; Amb. and Perm. Rep. to NATO and WEU, Brussels 2005–09; Minister for European Affairs May–Nov. 2009; Commr for Enlargement and European Neighbourhood Policy, EC, Brussels 2010–; UN Disarmament Fellow 1988; Cross of Merit of Minister of Defence, Grade I 2001, Order of Grand Duke Gediminas, Third Class (Lithuania) 2002, Medal of Golden Lime Tree, Minister of Defence 2008. *Address:* European Commissioner for Enlargement and Neighbourhood Policy, 200 Rue de la Loi, 1049 Brussels, Belgium (office). *Telephone:* (2) 298-49-70 (office). *Fax:* (2) 295-01-38 (office). *E-mail:* stefan.fule@ec.europa.eu (office). *Website:* ec.europa.eu/commission_2010 -2014/fule (office).

FULFORD, Sir Adrian Bruce, QC; British barrister and judge; *Judge, Trial Division, International Criminal Court;* b. 8 Jan. 1948; ed Elizabeth Coll., Guernsey, Univ. of Southampton; called to the Bar, Middle Temple, London 1978; apptd QC 1994; Recorder (Judge in Crown Court) 2001–; Judge, Queen's Bench Div. of High Court of England and Wales 2002–; Judge, Trial Div., Int. Criminal Court 2003–; Lecturer in Advocacy, Middle Temple 1994–; Lecturer to the Bar and Judiciary 1999–2001; mem. Cttee of Criminal Bar Asscn 1997–99, 2001–; Chair. Disciplinary Procedures for Bar Council 1997–; Housing Adviser, Shelter Housing Aid Centre 1975–77; Legal Adviser, N Lambeth Law Centre 1979–80; fmr Contrib. Ed., Archbold Criminal Pleading, Practice and Evidence, Atkins Court Forms. *Publications:* A Criminal Practitioner's Guide to Judicial Review and Case Stated (co-author) 1999, United Kingdom Human Rights Reports (co-ed.) 2000–, Judicial Review: A Practical Guide (co-author) 2004; articles in professional journals and papers for Criminal Bar Asscn. *Address:* International Criminal Court, PO Box 19519, 2500 CM The Hague, The Netherlands (office); 14 Tooks Court, London, EC4A 1LB, England. *Telephone:* (70) 515-8515 (office); (20) 7405-8828 (London). *Fax:* (70) 515-8555 (office). *E-mail:* pio@icc-cpi.int (office). *Website:* www.icc-cpi.int (office).

FULLANI, Ardian; Albanian central banker; *Governor, Bank of Albania;* b. 15 Jan. 1955, Tirana; ed Univ. of Tirana; began career at State Bank of Albania 1985, Deputy Dir Foreign Dept 1987–90; Head of Foreign Relations Dept, Albanian Commercial Bank 1990–92; Deputy Gov. Bank of Albania (Banka e Shqipërisë) 1992–93, Head of Foreign Relations Dept 1993–96, Gov. and Chair. Supervisory Council 2004–; focused on consultancy in nat. and int. devt projects 1996–97; Deputy Gen. Man. and Head of Financial Dept, Italian-Albanian Bank 1997–2000, Gen. Man. 2000–04; also held positions including Pres. Albanian Asscn of Banks, Chair. Inst. of Banking Studies and Assistance, Commr Albanian Securities Comm.; Commendatore dell'Ordine della Stella della solidarietà italiana 2007. *Publications:* Growth in Albania and South East Europe: The Way Ahead 2013; numerous articles and scientific papers on economic and financial issues. *Address:* Office of the Governor, Bank of Albania (Banka e Shqipërisë), Sheshi Skënderbej 1, Tirana, Albania (office). *Telephone:* (4) 2222152 (office). *Fax:* (4) 2223558 (office). *E-mail:* public@bankofalbania.org (office). *Website:* www.bankofalbania.org (office).

FULLER, H. Laurence (Larry), BS, JD; American lawyer and business executive (retd); b. 8 Nov. 1938, Moline, Ill.; m. Nancy Fuller 1961; one s. two d.; ed Cornell Univ., DePaul Univ.; Dir Amoco Corpn 1981–2000, Chair. and CEO 1991–2000, Co-Chair. BP Amoco 2000 (retd); mem. Bd of Dirs Cabot Microelectronics Corpn 2002–, Abbott Labs.; fmr mem. Bd of Dirs JPMorgan Chase & Co., Motorola Inc., Catalyst, American Petroleum Inst., Rehabilitation Inst. of Chicago; Trustee, Orchestral Asscn. *Address:* c/o Board of Directors, Cabot Microelectronics Corporation, 870 North Commons Drive, Aurora, IL 60504, USA (office).

FULLER, Kathryn S., BA, MS, JD; American attorney, international organization executive and environmentalist; *Chairman, Board of Directors, Ford Foundation;* b. 8 July 1946, New York, NY; m. Stephen Paul Doyle 1977; two s. one d.; ed Brown Univ., Univs of Maryland and Texas; law clerk, New York, Houston and Austin, Tex. 1974–76, to Chief Justice John V. Singleton, Jr, US Dist Court, Southern Dist of Tex. 1976–77; called to Bar, DC and Tex.; attorney and adviser, Office of Legal Counsel, Dept of Justice, Washington, DC 1977–79, attorney, Wildlife and Marine Resources Section 1979–80, Chief Wildlife and Marine

Resources Section 1981–82; Exec. Vice-Pres. and Dir TRAFFIC USA 1982–89; Pres. and CEO World Wildlife Fund US 1989–2005, now mem. Advisory Council; Chair. Ford Foundation 2004–10; currently Man. Partner, Doyle Property Partners LLC, Washington, DC; Chair. Advisory Bd National Museum of Natural History, Smithsonian Inst., Washington, DC; Public Policy Scholar, Woodrow Wilson Int. Center for Scholars 2005–06; mem. Bd of Dirs Alcoa Inc. (Compensation and Benefits Cttee, Governance and Nominating Cttee, Public Issues Cttee) 2002–, Robert Wood Johnson Foundation 2011–; mem. Council on Foreign Relations, Int. Council of Environmental Law, Overseas Devt Council; Trustee, Summit Foundation, Greater Himalayas Foundation; fmr Trustee, Brown Univ. Corpn; Hon. DSc (Wheaton Coll.) 1990; Hon. LLD (Knox Coll.) 1992; Hon. DHumLitt (Brown Univ.) 1992; William Rogers Outstanding Grad. Award, Brown Univ. 1990, UNEP Global 500 Award 1990. *Publications include:* numerous articles in journals. *Address:* Doyle Property Partners LLC, 3718 Morrison Street, NW, Washington, DC 20015-1734, USA (office). *Website:* www.mnh.si.edu.

FULLER, Lawrence Robert, BJ; American newspaper publisher; b. 9 Sept. 1941, Toledo, Ohio; s. of Kenneth Fuller and Marjory Rairdon; m. Suzanne Hovik 1967; one s. one d.; ed Univ. of Missouri; reporter, Globe Gazette, Mason City, Ia 1963–67; reporter, later City Ed. Minneapolis Star 1967–75; Exec. Ed. Messenger-Inquirer, Owensborough, Ky 1975–77; Exec. Ed. Argus Leader, Sioux Falls, South Dakota 1977–78, Pres., Publr 1974–84, 1986–99; Pres. Gannett News Media, Washington, DC 1984–85; Dir Corp. Communications, Gannett Co. Inc. Washington 1985–86; Vice-Pres. Gannett/West Regional Newspaper Group 1986–97, The Honolulu Advertisers 1986–97; mem. American Newspaper Publishers' Asscn, American Soc. of Newspaper Eds etc..

FULLER, Simon; British music promoter, business executive and artist manager; m. Natalie Swanston 2008; Founder and Dir 19 Group 1985–2005 (comprising 19 Brands, 19 Entertainment, 19 International Sports Management, 19 Management, 19 Merchandising, 19 Productions, 19 Recordings, 19 Songs, 19 Touring, 19 TV, Brilliant 19), sold to CFX 2005 (mem. Bd of Dirs 2005–); current or fmr man. of numerous artists, including Annie Lennox, Emma Bunton, Will Young, Gareth Gates, Kelly Clarkson, Paul Hardcastle (1985), Madonna, Cathy Dennis, Spice Girls (–1997), 21st Century Girls and S Club 7 (later S Club, including TV series and S Club Juniors); dir of numerous other cos. *Television includes:* creator of Popstars (ITV 1), Pop Idol (ITV 1), American Idol – The Search for a Superstar (Fox TV), Popstars – The Rivals (ITV 1). *Address:* 19 Management, Unit 32, Ransomes Dock, 35–37 Parkgate Road, London, SW11 4NP, England (office). *Website:* www.19.co.uk (office); xixentertainment.com.

FULLERTON, William Hugh, CMG, MA; British diplomatist and consultant; b. 11 Feb. 1939, Wolverhampton; s. of the late Maj. A. H. T. F. Fullerton and of M. Fullerton (née Parker); m. Arlene Jacobowitz 1968; one d.; ed Cheltenham Coll. and Queens' Coll., Cambridge; with Shell Int. Petroleum Co., Uganda 1963–65; joined Foreign Office 1965; with MECAS, Shemlan, Lebanon 1965–66; Information Officer, Jeddah 1966–67; at Perm. Mission to UN, New York 1967; with FCO 1968–70; Head of Chancery, High Comm., Jamaica (also accred to Haiti) 1970–73, Head of Chancery, Embassy in Ankara 1973–77; at FCO 1977–80; Counsellor, Embassy in Islamabad 1980–83, Consul Gen. 1981–83; Amb. to Somalia 1983–87; on loan to Ministry of Defence 1987–88; Gov. Falkland Islands, Commr for South Georgia and South Sandwich Islands 1988–92, concurrently High Commr, British Antarctic Territory 1988–89; Amb. to Kuwait 1992–96, to Morocco and Mauritania 1996–99; mem. advisory bd Intrinsic Value Investors (IVI) LLP; Trustee, Arab-British Centre, London 2002–12, Soc. for the Protection of Animals Abroad, Lord Caradon Lecture Trust; mem. Nat. Trust, Campaign for the Protection of Rural England, World Wildlife Fund; Kuwait Medallion (First Class) 1995, Alaouite Decoration (Morocco) 1999. *Leisure interests:* travelling in remote places, reading, sailing, music, the environment. *Address:* c/o Travellers' Club, 106 Pall Mall, London, SW1Y 5EP, England. *Telephone:* (20) 7832-1310 (office).

FULTON, Daniel S., BA, MBA; American business executive; *President and CEO, Weyerhaeuser Company;* b. 1948; ed Miami Univ., Univ. of Washington, Stanford Univ.; fmr Officer, USN Supply Corps; mem. Investment Evaluation Dept, Weyerhaeuser Co. 1976–78, Planning Man. Weyerhaeuser Real Estate Co. 1978–79, Investment Man. Weyerhaeuser Venture Co. 1978–87, Chief Investment Officer Weyerhaeuser Realty Investors Inc. 1994–95, COO 1996–97, Pres. and CEO 1998–2000, Weyerhaeuser Real Estate Co. 2001–08, Pres. Weyerhaeuser Co. Jan. 2008–, mem. Bd Dirs and CEO April 2008–; mem. Bd of Dirs United Way of King Co.; mem. Advisory Bd Univ. of Washington Business School, Policy Advisory Bd Jt Center of Housing with Harvard Univ.; mem. Bd of Govs. Lambda Alpha Int. Land Econs Soc., Nat. Asscn of Homebuilders. *Address:* Weyerhaeuser Company, 33663 Weyerhaeuser Way South, Federal Way, WA 98063-9777, USA (office). *Telephone:* (253) 924-2345 (office). *Fax:* (253) 924-2685 (office). *E-mail:* info@ weyerhaeuser.com (office). *Website:* www.weyerhaeuser.com (office).

FULTON, Lt-Gen. Sir Robert, KBE; British Royal Marines officer and diplomatist; *CEO, Global Leadership Foundation;* b. 1948, London, England; m.; two s.; ed Eton Coll. and Univ. of East Anglia; joined Royal Marines 1972, has occupied several sr positions within the force, including Commdt-Gen. 1998–2001; moved to Ministry of Defence 2001, promoted to Lt-Gen. on appointment as Deputy Chief of Defence Staff (for Equipment Capability) 2003–06; Gov. and C-in-C of Gibraltar 2006–09; CEO Global Leadership Foundation 2010–. *Leisure interests:* sailing, cricket, rugby, golf, military history, theatre, music. *Address:* Global Leadership Foundation, 25 Knightsbridge, London, SW1X 7LY, England (office). *Telephone:* (20) 7838-7050 (office). *Fax:* (20) 7681-2263 (office). *E-mail:* secretariat@g-l-f.org. *Website:* www.g-l-f.org (office).

FUMAROLI, Marc, DèsL; French historian; *Honorary Chairman, Rhetoric and European Society of the 16th and 17th Centuries, Collège de France;* b. 10 June 1932, Marseille; ed Lycée Thiers Marseille, Univ. Aix-en-Provence, Univ. Sorbonne; Prof. Sorbonne, Paris 1976; Titular Prof., Chair of Rhetoric and European Soc. of 16th and 17th Centuries, Collège de France 1986–2002, now Hon. Chair.; Prof., Univ. of Chicago 1996–2006; Chair. Institut européen d'histoire de la Republique de Lettres, Société d'Histoire litterature de la France 2001–; Dir XVIIe siècle (journal) 1981–88; mem. Advisory Council, Bibliothèque Nationale 1988–92; fmr Pres. Soc. Int. d'Histoire de la Rhétorique; Pres. Soc. of Friends of the Louvre 1996–; mem. Acad. Française 1995–, High Cttee of Nat. Celebrations 1998–;

Corresp. mem. British Acad., mem. US Acad. of Sciences, Letters and Arts, Accad. dei Lincei; Officier, Légion d'honneur, Commdr, Ordre des Palmes académiques, Ordre nat. du Mérite, Cmmdr des Arts et des Lettres; Dr hc (Naples 1996, Bologna 1999, Madrid 2004); numerous other academic prizes; Balzan Prize 1995. *Publications include:* L'Age de l'éloquence 1980, Héros et Orateurs 1990, L'Etat Culturel: Une Religion Moderne 1991, La Diplomatie de l'esprit 1994, L'école du silence 1994, Trois institutions littéraires 1994, la Période 1600–1630 1994, Fables de Jean de la Fontaine (ed., Vol. I 1985, Vol. II 1995), Le Poète et le roi, Jean de La Fontaine et son siècle 1997, Poussin: Sainte Françoise Romaine 2001, Quand l'Europe parlait français 2001, Chateaubriand: Poésie et Terreur 2003, Exercises de lecture: De Rabelais à Valery 2006, De Rome à Paris : peinture et pouvoir aux XVIIe et XVIIIe siècles 2007, Paris-New York et retour. Voyage dans les arts et les images 2009, Le livre des métaphores 2012; numerous articles in professional journals; numerous pamphlets, essays and articles. *Leisure interest:* travel. *Address:* Collège de France, 11 place Marcelin Berthelot, 75231 Paris cedex 05 (office); 11 rue de l'Université, 75007 Paris, France (home). *Telephone:* 1-44-27-10-17 (office). *Fax:* 1-44-27-13-29 (office). *E-mail:* catherine.fabre@college-de-france.fr (office). *Website:* www.college-de-france.fr (office).

FUNADA, Hajime; Japanese politician; b. 22 Nov. 1953, Utsunomiya City, Tochigi Pref.; s. of Yuzuru Funada and Masako Funada; m. Rumi Funada 1978; one s. two d.; ed Keio Univ.; mem. House of Reps from Tochigi 1979–; Head, Youth Section of Nat. Organizing Cttee, LDP 1985–86; State Sec. for Man. and Co-ordination Agency 1986–87, for Ministry of Educ. 1987–88; Dir Educ. Div. of Policy Research Council, LDP 1988–89; Dir Foreign Affairs Div. 1990–92; Chair. Sub-Cttee of Counselling Japan Overseas Co-operation Volunteers 1989–90; Minister of State for Econ. Planning 1992–93; Co-Founder of Japan Renewal Party (Shinseito) 1993, Deputy Sec. Gen. for Organizational Affairs 1993–94, Deputy Sec. Gen. for Political Affairs 1994; Vice-Chair. Diet Man. Cttee, 'Reform' In-House Grouping (Kaikaku) 1994; Co-Founder New Frontier Party (Shinshinto) 1994, Vice-Chair. Org. Cttee 1994–95, Deputy Sec. Gen. 1995, Assoc. Chair. Gen. Council 1995–96, resgnd from Party 1996; Head of '21st Century' In-House Grouping (21seiki) 1996; rejoined Liberal Democratic Party 1997, Chair. Sub-Cttee on Asia and the Pacific, mem. Policy Deliberation Comm., mem. Gen. Council 1997–; mem. Ruling Parties Consultative Cttee on Guidelines for Japan–US Defence Co-operation 1997–; Dir Cttee on Health and Welfare, House of Reps 1998–. *Leisure interests:* astronomy, driving. *Address:* Shugiin Daini Giinkaikan, Room 412, 2-1-2 Nagata-cho, Chiyoda-ku, Tokyo 100, Japan. *Telephone:* (3) 3508-7412. *Fax:* (3) 3500-5612.

FUNAI, Tetsuro; Japanese electronics industry executive; *Chairman, Funai Electric Company Limited;* b. 24 Jan. 1927, Kobe, Hyogo; ed Murano Technical High School; est. Funai Mishin Shokai 1951 (co. name changed to Funai Keiki Kogyo 1959); est. Funai Electric Co. Ltd 1961, Pres. and CEO 1961–2008, Chair. 2008–. *Address:* Funai Electric Company Limited, 7-7-1 Nakagaito, Daito City, Osaka 574-0013, Japan (office). *Telephone:* (72) 870-4303 (office). *Fax:* (72) 871-1112 (office). *Website:* www.funai.jp (office).

FUNAR, Gheorghe, PhD; Romanian politician; *Secretary-General, Greater Romanian Party;* b. 29 Sept. 1949; m. Sabina Funar; one s.; ed Faculty of Econ. Science, Univ. of Cluj-Napoca; began career as agronomist, specialising in collective arm system; joined Party of Romanian Nat. Unity (PRNU) 1990, Leader 1992–97; Mayor of Cluj-Napoca 1992–2004; cand. in presidential elections 1992; Sec.-Gen. Greater Romanian Party (PRM–Partidul România Mare) 2000–. *Address:* Greater Romanian Party (Partidul România Mare), 70101 Bucharest, Str. G. Clemenceau 8–10, Romania (office). *Telephone:* (21) 6130967 (office). *Fax:* (21) 3126182 (office). *E-mail:* prm@prm.org.ro (office). *Website:* www.prm.org.ro (office).

FUNDANGA, Caleb M., BA, MA, PhD; Zambian economist, international organization official and central banker; *President, Institute for Finance and Economics;* b. 28 Feb. 1953, Mufulira; s. of James Mailoni Fundanga and Alita Mutaya Fundanga; m. Rosario Chailunga Fundanga; one s. two d.; ed Univ. of Zambia, Univ. of Manchester, UK, Konstanz Univ., Germany; Lecturer in Econs, Univ. of Zambia 1985–87; served as Perm. Sec. wth Zambian Ministry of Econs and Finance; Exec. Dir ADB, Abidjan, Côte d'Ivoire, representing Lesotho, Malawi, Mauritius, South Africa, Swaziland and Zambia 1995–98, Sr Adviser to Pres. of ADB 1998–2002; Gov. and Chair. Bank of Zambia 2002–11, Alt. Gov., IMF 2002–11 (retd); Pres. Inst. for Finance and Econs 2011–; mem. Bd of Dirs Zambia Revenue Authority, Afreximbank; fmr Chair. COMESA Cttee of Cen. Bank Govs; fmr mem. Advisory Comm., African Econ. Research Consortium 2002, Chair. Programme Cttee 2005–; fmr Pres. World Univ. Service International; Cen. Banker of the Year (Global and Africa), The Banker magazine 2007, Cen. Banker of the Year (Africa), Emerging Markets Magazine 2007, Cen. Banker of the Year (Africa), Annual Meetings Daily 2008. *Publications:* as contrib.: The IMF, the World Bank and the African Debt: The Economic Impact 1979, Planners and History: Negotiating Development in Rural Zambia 1994, Economic Development and Democracy: Critical Issues in the Third Republic 1994, Domination or Dialogue?: Experiences and Prospects for African Development Cooperation 1996; articles for Southern Africa, Southern Review, Issues on the Zambian Economy. *Address:* Institute for Finance and Economics, PO Box 32569, 32569 Lusaka, Zambia (office). *Telephone:* (211) 267282 (office). *Fax:* (211) 267282 (office). *E-mail:* cfundanga@gmail.com (office). *Website:* www.ifezambia.org (office).

FUNES CARTAGENA, Carlos Mauricio; Salvadorean broadcast journalist, politician and head of state; *President;* b. 18 Oct. 1959, San Salvador; s. of Roberto and María Mirna Funes; m. Vanda Pignato; one s.; ed Colegio Externado San José, Universidad Centroamericana José Simeón Cañas; began career as TV reporter, Canal 10 1986; Dir of News, Canal 12 1987; 15 years as Corresp., CNN Español; selected as Frente Farabundo Martí para la Liberación Nacional (FMLN) presidential cand. 2007, Pres. of El Salvador 2009–(14). *Address:* Office of the President, Avda Cuba, Calle Darío González 806, Barrio San Jacinto, San Salvador, El Salvador (office). *Telephone:* 2248-9000 (office). *Fax:* 2248-9370 (office). *E-mail:* casapres@casapres.gob.sv (office). *Website:* www.casapres.gob.sv (office).

FUNG, Victor K(wok-king), CBE, BS, MS, PhD; American (b. Chinese) business executive and fmr international organisation official; *Group Chairman, Fung Group;* b. 1945, Hong Kong; brother of William Fung; m. Julia Fung; three c.; ed Massachusetts Inst. of Tech., Harvard Business School, Harvard Univ., USA; Prof. of Finance, Harvard Business School 1972–76; joined Li & Fung 1973, Man. Dir 1981–89, Chair. 1989, currently Group Chair. Fung Group; Chair. Asia Advisory Bd Prudential Financial, Inc., Hong Kong Trade Devt Council 1991–2000, Hong Kong Airport Authority 1999–2008, Greater Pearl River Delta Business Council 2004–13, Hong Kong Univ. Council 2001–09, Airport Authority Hong Kong 1999–2008, Hong Kong-Japan Business Co-operation Cttee; Co-Chair. China Centre for Int. Econ. Exchanges; Vice-Chair. ICC 2007–08, Chair. 2008–10; mem. Bd of Dirs China Petrochemical Corpn, Bank of China Ltd, Chow Tai Fook Jewellery Group Ltd, Koc Holding AS; mem. Bd of Dirs Baosteel Group Corpn 2005–13; mem. Int. Business Leaders Advisory Council for Mayor of Beijing, Hong Kong Judicial Officers Recommendation Cttee –2006, Asian Business Advisory Council, CPPCC, Exec. Cttee of Hong Kong Govt Comm. on Strategic Devt of Hong Kong Special Admin. Region Govt, Advisory Bd of School of Econs and Man., Tsinghua Univ., WTO Panel on Defining the Future of Trade 2012–13; Hong Kong Rep. on APEC Business Advisory Council 1996–2003, Task Force on Econ. Challenges 2008–; Econ. Advisor to People's Government of Nanjing; Hon. Trustee Peking Univ., Hon. Prof., Renmin Univ.; Hong Kong Businessman of the Year 1995, Top 25 Managers in BusinessWeek magazine 1995, Harvard Medal 2001, Gold Bauhinia Star 2003, Businessman of the Year, Forbes Asia magazine 2005, Grand Bauhinia Medal 2010, MIT Sloan Dean's Award for Excellence in Leadership 2011. *Address:* Li & Fung Group, Li Fung Tower, 888 Cheung Sha Wan Road, Kowloon, Hong Kong Special Administrative Region, People's Republic of China (office). *Website:* www.lifunggroup.com (office).

FUNKE, Cornelia Caroline; German children's writer; b. 1958, Dorsten, Westphalia; m. Rolf Funke (died 2006); one s. one d.; ed Hamburg Univ., Hamburg State Coll. of Design; worked as designer of board games, illustrator of children's books; began writing/illustrating full-time aged 28; also works for ZDF state TV channel; numerous awards including Wildweibchenpreis for collected works 2000, Roswitha Prize 2008. *Publications:* Monstergeschichten 1993, Die Wilden Hühner 1993, Rittergeschichten 1994, Zwei wilde kleine Hexen 1994, Kein Keks für Kobolde 1994, Greta und Eule, Hundesitter 1995, Der Mondscheindrache 1996, Die Gespensterjäger auf eisiger Spur 1996, Die Wilden Hühner auf Klassenfahrt 1996, Hände weg von Mississippi 1997, Drachenreiter (trans. as Dragon Rider) (Sakura Medal 2006) 1997, Prinzessin Isabella (trans. as The Princess Knight) 1997, Tiergeschichten 1997, Das verzauberte Klassenzimmer 1997, Die Wilden Hühner Fuchsalarm 1998, Dachbodengeschichten 1998, Potilla und der Mützen-dieb 1998, Dicke Freundinnen 1998, Igraine Ohnefurcht (trans. as Igraine the Brave) 1998, Strandgeschichten 1999, Das Piratenschwein (trans. as Pirate Girl) 1999, Herr der Diebe (trans. as The Thief Lord) (Swiss Youth Literature Award, Zurich Children's Book Award, Venice House of Literature Book Award, Mildred L. Batchelder Award for the best trans. children's book of the year) 2000, Lilli und Flosse 2000, Mick und Mo im Wilden Westen (trans. as Mick and Mo in the Wild West) 2000, Die Wilden Hühner und das Glück der Erde 2000, Kleiner Werwolf 2001, Als der Weihnachtsmann vom Himmel fiel 2001, Dicke Freundinnen und der Pferdedieb 2001, Die Gespensterjäger im Feuerspuk 2001, Die Gespensterjäger in der Gruselburg 2001, Die Gespensterjäger in grosser Gefahr 2001, Der geheimnisvolle Ritter Namenlos 2001, Die Wilden Hühner Bandenbuch 2001, Emma und der blaue Dschinn 2002, Die schönsten Erstlesegeschichten 2002, Die Glücksfee 2003, Hinter verzauberten Fenstern 2003, Käpten Knitterbart 2003, Tintenherz (trans. as Inkheart) 2003, Kribbel Krabbel Käferwetter 2003, Der wildeste Bruder der Welt 2003, Der verlorene Wackelzahn 2003, Die Wilden Hühner und die Liebe 2003, Die Wilden Hühner Tagebuch 2004, Tintenblut (trans. as Inkspell) 2005, When Santa Fell to Earth 2006, Tintentod (trans. as Inkdeath) 2008, Reckless 2010, Saving Mississippi 2010, Reckless 2 2012. *Address:* c/o Oliver Latsch Literary Agency & Translations, Dudelsackstraße 36, 67227 Frankenthal, Rheinland-Pfalz, Germany (office). *Telephone:* (6233) 549419 (office). *Fax:* (6233) 62518 (office). *E-mail:* info@oliverlatsch.com (office). *Website:* www.oliverlatsch.com (office). *E-mail:* info@oliverlatsch.com (office). *Website:* www.oliverlatsch.com (office).

FURCHTGOTT-ROTH, Harold W., PhD; American economist and fmr government official; *President, Furchtgott-Roth Economic Enterprises;* b. 13 Dec. 1956, Knoxville, Tenn.; s. of Ernest Furchtgott and Mary A. Wilkes Furchtgott; m. Diana E. Roth; five s. one d.; ed Massachusetts Inst. of Tech., Stanford Univ.; Research Analyst, Center for Naval Analyses, Alexandria, Va 1984–88; Sr Economist, Economists Inc., Washington, DC 1988–95; Chief Economist, US House Cttee on Commerce 1995–97; Commr Fed. Communications Comm. 1997–2001; Visiting Fellow, American Enterprise Inst. 2001–03; Founder and Pres. Furchtgott-Roth Economic Enterprises 2003–. *Publications:* International Trade in Computer Software (co-author) 1993, Economics of a Disaster: The Exxon Valdez Oil Spill (co-author) 1995, Cable TV: Regulations or Competition (co-author) 1996, A Tough Act to Follow 2003, Telecommunications Act of 1996 2006. *Address:* Furchtgott-Roth Economic Enterprises, 1200 New Hampshire Avenue, NW, Suite 800, Washington, DC 20036 (office); 2705 Daniel Road, Chevy Chase, MD 20815, USA (home). *Telephone:* (202) 776-2032 (office); (301) 229-3593 (home). *E-mail:* hfr@furchtgott-roth.com (office). *Website:* www.furchtgott-roth.com (office).

FURLAN, Luiz Fernando, BEng; Brazilian business executive and government official; b. 1945; m. Ana Maria Gonçalves Furlan 1973; one s. one d.; ed São Paulo Univ., Univ. of Santana, INSEAD, France, Georgetown Univ., USA; joined Sadia SA (now Brasil Foods after merger with Perdigao 2009) 1976, mem. Bd 1978–2002, Exec. Vice-Pres. and Dir Investor Relations 1978–83, Chair. 1993–2002, 2008–09; Minister of Devt, Industry and Trade 2003–07; Chair. BRF Brasil Foods SA 2009–11; Co-Chair. BNDES 2003–07; Chair. Fundacao Amazonas Sustentavel FAS 2008–; Pres. Entrepreneurial Leaders Forum 2000–02; Pres. Brazilian Asscn of Open Cos 1991–94, Brazilian Asscn of Producers and Exporters of Chicken 1997–2001; fmr Pres. Mercosul European Business Forum; fmr Vice-Pres. Brazilian Foreign Trade Asscn; mem. Bd of Dirs Telefonica Brasil SA, Telefonica SA, AGCO Corpn; mem. Advisory Bd Panasonic, Walmart, McLarty & Associates, ABERTIS Infraestructuras SA, Brasmotor SA, ABN-Amro Bank Brazil, Global Ocean Comm.; mem. Global Corp. Governance Forum, Nat. Council of Human Rights, Int. Council INSEAD, France; fmr mem. Brazil-USA Business Devt Council. *Address:* Fundacao Amazonas Sustentavel, Rua Alvaro Braga, 351, Park Ten November, Manaus AM 69055-660, Brazil. *Website:* fas-amazonas.org.

FURNO, HE Cardinal Carlo, PhD, DIurUtr; Italian ecclesiastic; b. 2 Dec. 1921, Bairo Canavese; ed Diocesan Seminary, Ivrea, Pontifical Lateran Univ.; Sec. to Nunciature to Colombia 1953–57, to Ecuador 1957–60; Sec. Apostolic Del. to Jerusalem 1960–62; Sec. of State 1962–73; Apostolic Nuncio to Peru 1973–78, to Lebanon 1978–82, to Brazil 1982–92, to Italy 1992–94; Cardinal-Deacon of S. Cuore di Cristo Re (elevated to Cardinal) 1994, Cardinal-Priest of S. Cuore di Cristo Re 2005, de St Onofrio 2006; Archpriest St Mary Major Basilica 1997–2004; now Emer.; fmr mem. Pontifical Comm. for Vatican City State; Grand Master Equestrian Order of the Holy Sepulchre of Jerusalem 1995–2007 (retd); fmr Pres. Admin. Council, Lumsa Univ. *Address:* Piazza Città Leonina, 00193 Rome, Italy.

FURSE, Dame Clara Hedwig Frances, DBE, BSc, CIMgt; British/Canadian business executive; b. 16 Sept. 1957, Jonquière, Quebec, Canada; m. Richard Furse 1981; two s. one d.; ed schools in Colombia, Denmark and St James's School, West Malvern, London School of Econs; began career as broker, Heinold Commodities Ltd 1979; commodity broker, Philips & Drew 1983, Dir 1988, Exec. Dir 1992, Man. Dir UBS Philips & Drew (formed from merger with Union Bank of Switzerland; named changed to UBS following merger with Swiss Bank 1998) 1995–98, Global Head of Futures 1996–98; Deputy Chair. London Int. Financial Futures and Options Exchange (LIFFE) 1992–99 (mem. Bd 1992–99, Chair. Strategy Working Group 1994–95, Membership and Rules Cttee 1995–97, Finance Cttee 1998–99); Group Chief Exec. Crédit Lyonnais Rouse 1998–2000; Chief Exec. London Stock Exchange PLC 2001–09; mem. Bd of Dirs LCH.Clearnet SA, 2005–09; Euroclear PLC 2006–09, Fortis 2006–09, Legal & General Group PLC 2009–13, Nomura Holdings Inc. 2009–, Amadeus IT Holdings SA 2010–, Dept for Work and Pensions, UK 2011–; mem. Financial Policy Cttee, HM Treasury 2013–; mem. Panel of Sr Advisors, Chatham House 2012–; mem. Shanghai Int. Financial Advisory Council 2006–09; mem. Advisory Council Prince's Trust; Trustee, RICS Foundation 2002–05; ranked by Fortune magazine amongst 50 Most Powerful Women in Business outside the US (34th) 2003, (17th) 2004, (19th) 2005, (26th) 2006, (17th) 2007, (20th) 2008, ranked sixth in survey of Europe's most successful female execs 2003, ranked by Forbes magazine amongst 100 Most Powerful Women (97th) 2004, (50th) 2006, (54th) 2007, (85th) 2008, ranked by the Financial Times amongst Top 25 Businesswomen in Europe (tenth) 2005, (sixth) 2006, (fifth) 2007. *Address:* c/o Financial Policy Committee, HM Treasury, 1 Horse Guards Road, London, SW1A 2HQ, England (office).

FURSENKO, Andrei Aleksandrovich, DrPhys; Russian scientist and politician; *Minister of Education and Science;* b. 17 July 1949, Leningrad; ed Leningrad State Univ.; Head of Lab., Deputy Dir for Scientific Research, Chief Scientific Researcher Moscow Ioffe Physico-Tech. Inst. 1971–91; Vice-Pres. Centre of Prospective Techs and Elaborations, St Petersburg 1991–93; Gen. Dir Regional Fund for Scientific Tech. Devt 1994–2001; Deputy Minister of Science, Industry and Technology 2001, First Deputy Minister 2002, Acting Minister 2003; Minister of Educ. and Science 2004–. *Address:* Ministry of Education and Science, 125993 Moscow, ul. Tverskaya 11, Russia (office). *Telephone:* (495) 629-70-62 (office). *Fax:* (495) 629-08-91 (office). *Website:* www.mon.gov.ru (office).

FURSTENBERG, Hillel (Harry), BA, MSc, PhD; Israeli mathematician and academic; *Professor of Mathematics, Hebrew University of Jerusalem;* b. 29 Sept. 1935, Berlin, Germany; s. of Sally Furstenberg and Berta Grzyb; m. Rochelle Furstenberg; three s. two d.; ed Yeshiva and Princeton univs, USA; emigrated to USA as a child; began academic career at Univ. of Minnesota; moved to Israel 1965; Prof. of Math., Hebrew Univ. of Jerusalem 1965–; mem. Israel Acad. of Sciences and Humanities, NAS; Rothschild Prize 1978, Technion Harvey Prize 1993, Israel Prize 1993, Wolf Foundation Prize in Math. 2007. *Publications include:* Stationary Processes and Prediction Theory, Recurrence in Ergodic Theory and Combinatorial Number Theory. *Address:* Einstein Institute of Mathematics, Edmond J. Safra Campus, Givat Ram, The Hebrew University of Jerusalem, Jerusalem 91904 (office); 7 Alfasi Street, Jerusalem 92302, Israel (home). *Telephone:* 2-6584142 (office); 2-5617641 (home). *Fax:* 2-5630702 (office). *E-mail:* harry@math.huji.ac.il (office). *Website:* www.ma.huji.ac.il (office).

FURTH, Warren Wolfgang, AB, JD; American lawyer, consultant and international official (retd); b. 1 Aug. 1928, Vienna, Austria; s. of John W. Furth and Hedwig von Ferstel; m. Margaretha F. de la Court 1959; one s. one d.; ed Harvard Coll., Harvard Law School and Sloan School of Management, Massachusetts Inst. of Tech.; law clerk, Palmer, Dodge, Gardner, Bickford & Bradford, Boston, Mass 1951; admitted to New York Bar 1952; law clerk to Hon. H. M. Stephens, Chief Judge, US Court of Appeals, DC Circuit 1952–53; served in US Army 1953–57; Assoc. Cravath, Swaine & Moore (law firm) 1957–58; with ILO, Geneva 1959–70, Exec. Asst to Dir-Gen. 1964–66, Chief of Tech. Co-operation Branch and Deputy Chief, Field Dept 1966–68, Deputy Chief, later Chief, Personnel and Admin. Services Dept 1968–70; Asst Dir-Gen. WHO (Admin. Services; Co-ordinator, Special Programme for Research and Training in Tropical Diseases and responsibility for Special Programme for Research, Devt and Research Training in Human Reproduction) 1971–89; int. health consultant to US Govt, World Bank and pharmaceutical industry 1989–94; Assoc. Exec. Dir American Citizens Abroad 1994–2000; Chair. American Democrats Abroad, Switzerland 2001–03. *Address:* 13 route de Presinge, 1241 Puplinge (Geneva), Switzerland (home). *Telephone:* (22) 3497267 (home). *Fax:* (22) 3493826 (home). *E-mail:* wfurth@bluewin.ch (home).

FURUKAWA, Masaaki; Japanese business executive; *Chairman and Representative Director, Toyota Tsusho Corporation;* b. 3 March 1940; joined Toyota Tsusho Corpn 1962, apptd Dir 1987, Man. Dir 1993–97, Sr Man. Dir 1997–99, Exec. Vice-Pres. 1999–2001, Pres. 2001–05, Chair. and Rep. Dir 2005–. *Address:* Toyota Tsusho Corporation, 9-8 Meieki 4-chome, Nakamura-ku, Nagoya 450-8575, Japan (office). *Telephone:* (52) 584-5000 (office). *Fax:* (52) 584-5636 (office). *Website:* www.toyotsu.co.jp (office).

FUTA, Pierre André; Democratic Republic of the Congo economist and government official; ed Univ. of Florida, USA; fmr Prof., Oklahoma State Univ.; fmr Gov. IMF, African Devt Bank, World Bank; Minister of Industry, Small and Medium Size Cos 2003, Minister of Finance 2004–07. *Address:* c/o Ministry of Finance, blvd du 30 juin, BP 12998 KIN 1, Kinshasa-Gombe, Democratic Republic of the Congo (office).

FUTAMIYA, Masaya; Japanese business executive; *Representative Director, Chairman and Executive Officer, NKSJ Holdings, Inc.;* b. 25 Feb. 1952; joined Nippon Fire & Marine Insurance Co. Ltd (Nipponkoa Insurance Co. Ltd (Nipponkoa)) 1974, Gen. Man. Secr. Office 1998–2001, Gen. Man. Secr. Office of Nipponkoa 2001–02, Gen. Man. Chief Exec. Office and IR Office 2002–03, Exec. Officer and Gen. Man. Chief Exec. Office and IR Office 2003–04, Exec. Officer and Gen. Man. Chief Exec. Office and Customer Relationship Planning Dept April–June 2004, Man. Exec. Officer 2004–05, Dir and Man. Exec. 2005–09, Rep. Dir and Sr Man. Exec. Officer 2009–11, Rep. Dir, Pres. and CEO NKSJ Holdings, Inc. (following establishment of jt holding co. by Sompo Japan Insurance Inc. and Nipponkoa Insurance Co. Ltd 2010) 2011–12, Rep. Dir, Chair. and Exec. Officer 2012–. *Address:* NKSJ Holdings, Inc., 26-1, Nishi-Shinjuku 1-chome, Shinjuku-ku, Tokyo 160-8338, Japan (office). *Telephone:* (3) 3349-3111 (office). *Fax:* (3) 3349-4697 (office). *E-mail:* info@nksj-hd.com (office). *Website:* www.nksj-hd.com (office).

FUWA, Tetsuzo; Japanese politician; *President, Social Sciences Institute, Japanese Communist Party;* b. 26 Jan. 1930, Tokyo; ed Tokyo Univ.; mem. Secr. Fed. of Iron and Steel Workers' Union 1953; mem. Cen. Cttee, Japanese Community Party 1966–, Secr. Head 1970, Chair. Exec. Cttee 1982, Chair. Cen. Cttee 2000–06, Pres. Social Sciences Inst. *Publications:* Stalin and the Great Power Chauvinism 1994, Interference and Betrayal 1994, Remaking Japan 1998, Nuclear Deception: Japan–USA Secret Agreements 2000, On Marx's Scientific View 2001, Re-reading Critique of the Gotha Programme: Marx and Engel's View of a Future Society 2003, Lenin's State and Revolution: A Critical Approach 2003, Asia, Africa and Latin America in the Present-Day World 2005, Seven Days in Tunisia 2005, Breaking Japan's Diplomatic Stalemate 2005, The 21st Century World and Socialism 2006, Japan's War: History of Expansionism 2006, Engels and The Capital 1997, Lenin and The Capital 1998, Five Days in Beijing —JCP-CPC Theoretical Discussion 2002, Marx and The Capital 2003, Invitation to Marx and Engels's Works 2008, Study on Theory of Revolution by Marx and Engels 2010. *Address:* Central Committee of the Japanese Communist Party, 4-36-7 Sendagaya, Shibuya-ku, Tokyo 151-8586, Japan (office). *Telephone:* (3) 3403-6111 (office). *E-mail:* info@jcp.or.jp (office). *Website:* www.jcp.or.jp (office).

FYFE, William Sefton, CC, PhD, FRS, FRSC, FRSNZ; Canadian chemist and academic; *Professor Emeritus, Department of Earth Sciences, University of Western Ontario;* b. 4 June 1927, New Zealand; s. of Colin Fyfe and Isabella Fyfe; m. Patricia Walker 1981; two s. one d.; ed Univ. of Otago, New Zealand; Lecturer in Chem., Univ. of Otago 1955–58; Prof. of Geology, Univ. of Calif., Berkeley 1958–66; Royal Soc. Prof., Univ. of Manchester 1966–72; Chair. Dept of Geology, Univ. of Western Ont. 1972–84, Prof. of Geology 1984–92, Prof. Emer. 1992–, Dean Faculty of Science 1986–90; Pres. Int. Union of Geological Sciences 1992–96; Hon. mem. Brazilian, Russian and Indian Acad. of Sciences; Hon. DSc (Memorial Univ.) 1989, (Lisbon) 1990, (Lakehead) 1990, (Guelph) 1992, (St Mary's) 1994, (Otago) 1995, (Univ. of Western Ont.) 1995; awards include Guggenheim Fellowships, Logan Medal, Holmes Medal, European Union of Geosciences 1989, Day Medal, Geological Soc. of America 1990, NZ Commemorative Medal 1991, Canada Gold Medal 1992, Roebling Medal 1995, Nat. Order of Scientific Merit (Brazil) 1996, Wollaston Medal, Geological Soc., London 2000. *Publications:* five books, 800 scientific papers. *Leisure interests:* wildlife, swimming, travel. *Address:* Department of Earth Sciences, BGS 1018, University of Western Ontario, London, ON N6A 5B7 (office); 1197 Richmond Street, London, ON N6A 3L3, Canada (home). *Telephone:* (519) 661-3180 (office). *Fax:* (519) 661-3198 (office). *E-mail:* wsfyfe@uwo.ca (office). *Website:* www.uwo.ca/earth (office).

FYODOROV, Nikolai Vasilievich, DrSci; Russian/Chuvash lawyer and politician; *President of Chuvash Republic;* b. 9 May 1958, Chuvash Repub.; m. Svetlana Fyodorova; one s. one d.; ed Kazan State Univ., Inst. of State and Law, USSR Acad. of Sciences; worked in legal bodies since 1983; teacher, Chuvash State Univ. 1980–82, 1985–89; USSR People's Deputy 1989–91; Deputy Chair. Legis. Comm. Supreme Soviet 1989–90; Minister of Justice of RSFSR (later Russia) 1990–93; Pres. Chuvash Repub. 1994–; mem. Council of Fed. 1996–2002; Order for Merits to Fatherland 1998, 2003; State Prize of Russia 1999. *Publications:* more than 100 articles and several books on problems of democratic and federative structure of the state, freedom of mass media, independent judicial power and economic policy. *Leisure interests:* karate, swimming, skiing, water-skiing, chess. *Address:* 1, Ploshad Respubliki, Cheboksary, Chuvash Republic 428004, Russia (office). *Telephone:* (8352) 62-46-87 (office). *Fax:* (8352) 62-17-99 (office). *E-mail:* president@cap.ru (office). *Website:* www.cap.ru (office).

GABAGLIO, Emilio, BA (Econs); Italian trade union official; *Chairman, National Labour Forum, Partito Democratico;* b. 1 July 1937, Como; m.; two d.; ed Catholic Univ., Milan; fmr high school teacher; mem. Italian Workers Christian Asscn, Nat. Pres. 1969–72; Officer, Italian Workers Unions Confed. (CISL) 1974–, elected to Nat. Secr. 1983–, represented CISL in ILO and in Exec. Cttees of European Trade Union Confed. (ETUC) and ICFTU; Gen. Sec. ETUC 1991–2003; mem. European Convention 2002–03; Int. Dir Culture of Work' Section, World Forum of Cultures, Barcelona 2004; Chair. EU Employment Cttee 2007–09; mem. Notre Europe Steering Cttee 2006–; Chair. Nat. Labour Forum, Partito Democratico 2010–; Order of Merit (Poland) 1997, Légion d'honneur 2000. *Address:* Partito Democratico, via del Tritone 87, 00187 Rome, Italy (office). *Telephone:* (06) 91712424 (office); 331-1713379 (mobile). *E-mail:* emilio.gabaglio@partitodemocratico.it (office).

GABAIX, Xavier, MA, PhD; French economist and academic; *Martin J. Gruber Professor of Finance, Stern School of Business, New York University;* b. Aug. 1971; s. of Julien Gabaix and Pierrette Gabaix; ed École Normale Supérieure, Paris, Harvard Univ., USA; Asst Prof. of Econs 1999–2003, Rudi Dornbusch Career Devt Asst, then Assoc. Prof. of Econs 2004–07; Assoc. Prof. of Finance, Stern School of Business, New York Univ., USA 2007–09, Prof. of Finance 2009–10, Martin J. Gruber Prof. of Finance 2010–; mem. Conseil d'Analyse Economique 2010–12; Fellow, Econometric Soc. 2011; David A. Wells Prize for outstanding doctoral dissertation, Harvard Univ. 1999, Young Scientist Award for Socio- and Econophysics 2006, listed by The Economist amongst the top eight young economists in the world 2008, Bernacer Prize for the best European economist under 40 working in macro-finance 2010, TIAA-CREF Paul A. Samuelson Award; Certificate of Excellence 2011, Prix du meilleur jeune économiste de France, Le Cercle des Economistes/Le Monde 2011, Prize for Best Financial Economist under 40 2011, Fischer Black Prize, American Finance Asscn 2011. *Publications:* numerous papers in professional journals on asset pricing, behavioural economics, executive compensation, macroeconomics and the origins and consequences of scaling behaviour. *Address:* Room KMC 9-77, Department of Finance, Stern School of Business, New York University, 44 West Fourth Street, Suite 9-190, New York, NY 10012-1126, USA (office). *E-mail:* xgabaix@stern.nyu.edu (office). *Website:* pages.stern.nyu.edu/~xgabaix (office).

GABALLA, Ali Gaballa, PhD; Egyptian archaeologist and academic; *Honorary Professor, Department of Archaeology, Cairo University;* b. (El Menoufiah), Kufour Al- Raml; m. Jenny Gaballa; three c.; ed Cairo Univ., Univ. of Liverpool; Asst Lecturer, Cairo Univ. 1962–63, Lecturer –1974, Assoc. Prof. of Egyptology –1979, Chair. of Dept then Vice-Dean of Faculty of Archaeology, then Dean, now Hon. Prof.; f. Archaeology Section, Faculty of Arts, Kuwait Univ.; fmr Visiting Prof., Mohamed V Univ., Morocco; Sec.-Gen. Supreme Council of Antiquities –2002; mem. Save the Heritage of Hassan Fathy; Order of Merit for Sciences and Arts; State Award for History and Archaeology 1979. *Publications:* Glimpses of Ancient Egypt 1979, The Third Intermediate Period in Egypt 1996, The History and Culture of Nubia 1997, Encyclopaedia of the Egyptian Civilization (co-ed.) and numerous other books. *Address:* Department of Archaeology, Cairo University, BP 12611, Orman, Giza, Cairo, Egypt. *Website:* fa-arch.cu.edu.eg.

GABARRÓ SERRA, Salvador, PhD; Spanish engineer and business executive; *Chairman, Gas Natural Fenosa;* b. 1935, Sant Guim de Freixenet (Lleida); ed Tech. Univ. of Catalonia (UPC), IESE Business School; worked for a year in Perfumería Parera SA; joined Compañía Roca Radiadores, SA, held various posts there, Dir-Gen. Production 1969–74, Man. Dir 1974–2000, Advisor to Chair. Corporación Roca; mem. Bd of Dirs Gas Natural SDG SA (renamed Gas Natural Fenosa following acquisition of Unión Fenosa 2008) 2003–, Chair. 2004–; mem. Bd of Dirs and Deputy Chair. Criteria CaixaCorp 2003–, First Vice-Pres. La Caixa; mem. Bd of Dirs Caixabank Francia, Enagás –2009; Chair. Unión Fenosa 2009–; Chair. Círculo de Economía 1999–2002; mem. Bd Indra Sistemas, Plenary Session of Barcelona Chamber of Commerce, Barcelona Circle of Economists. *Address:* Gas Natural Fenosa, Plaça del Gas 1, 08003 Barcelona, Spain (office). *Telephone:* (902) 199-199 (office); (93) 402-58-97 (office). *Fax:* (93) 402-58-96 (office). *E-mail:* info@gasnaturalfenosa.com (office). *Website:* www.gasnaturalfenosa.com (office).

GABBANA, Stefano; Italian fashion designer; *President, Dolce & Gabbana;* b. 14 Nov. 1962, Milan; early career as asst in Milan atelier; with Domenico Dolce opened fashion consulting studio 1982, selected to take part in Milano Collezioni new talents show 1985; Co-f. Dolce & Gabbana 1985, launched first maj. women's collection 1985, knitwear 1987, beachwear, underwear 1989, men's wear 1990, women's fragrance 1992, men's fragrance 1994, eyewear 1995; est. Dolce & Gabbana Industria production units 1999–2000; acquired and renovated Cinema Metropol in Milan for fashion shows and exhibitions 2005; opened boutiques in major cities in Europe, America and Asia; with Domenico Dolce, Woolmark Award 1991, Perfume Acad. Int. Prize for Best Feminine Fragrance of Year 1993, Best Masculine Fragrance of Year 1995, French "Oscar des Parfums", FHM magazine Designers of the Year 1996, Footwear News Designers of the Year 1997, Harper's Bizarre Russia Style Award 1999, T de Telva Award for Best Designers of the Year, GQ magazine (US) Best Designers of the Year 2003, Elle Magazine (UK) Best Int. Designers 2004, Premio Risultati 2004, GQ magazine (Russia) Best Int. Designers 2005. *Publications:* with Domenico Dolce, 10 Years Dolce and Gabbana 1996, Wildness 1997, Dolce and Gabbana Mémoires de la Mode 1998, Hollywood 2003, Calcio 2004, Music 2004, 20 Years Dolce & Gabbana 2005. *Leisure interests:* boxing, gym, taking vacations. *Address:* Dolce & Gabbana, Via San Damiano 7, 20122 Milan, Italy (office). *Telephone:* (02) 774271 (office). *Fax:* (02) 76020600 (office). *Website:* www.dolcegabbana.it (office).

GABR, Shafik, BA, MA; Egyptian business executive; *Chairman and Managing Director, Artoc Group for Investment and Development;* b. 5 Nov. 1952, Cairo; m.; one d.; ed American Univ. in Cairo, Univ. of London, UK; Grad. Asst, Econs Dept, American Univ. in Cairo 1972–73; with Manufacturers Hanover Trust Bank, UK 1973–74; Chair. and Man. Dir Artoc Group for Investment and Devt 1976–; Chair. Int. Econ. Forum, Cairo, Arab Business Council, COMESA (Common Market for East and South Africa) Business Council; mem. Bd Egypt–US Business Council, World Econ. Forum Council, Geneva, Holding Co. for Metallurgical Industries, Egyptian Center for Econ. Studies, World Bank Council of Advisers for the MENA Region; mem. Advisory Bd Int. Org. for Migration 2005–; mem. Exec. Bd Int. Chamber of Commerce, Paris; mem. Zurich Financial Services Advisory Bd 2007–; mem. Egyptian Businessmen's Asscn (Dir 1996–98); Founding mem. American Chamber of Commerce in Egypt (Pres. 1995–97); mem. Initiative for Peace and Co-operation in the Middle East, Council Faith Community; Chair. Mohamed Shafik Gabr Foundation for Social Devt. *Address:* Artoc Group, 7 Hassan Al-Akbar Street, Mokattam, Cairo 11571, Egypt (office). *Telephone:* (2) 5055777 (office). *Fax:* (2) 5053222 (office). *E-mail:* chairman@artoc.com (office). *Website:* www.artoc.com (office).

GABRIADZE, Revaz (Rezo) Levanovich; Georgian scriptwriter, film director, sculptor and artist; b. 29 June 1936, Kutaisi; m. 2nd Yelena Zakharyevna Dzhaparidze; one s. one d.; ed Tbilisi State Univ., Higher Courses of Scriptwriters and Film Directors in Moscow; worked as corresp. for Molodezh Gruzii; with Gruzia Film Studio 1970–; wrote scripts for over 35 films including Do Not Grieve 1969, Serenade (after M. Zoshchenko) 1969, Jug (after L. Pirandello) 1970, Unusual Show 1970, White Stone 1973, Cranks 1974, Road, Mimino 1978, Kin-dza-dza; Founder and Artistic Dir Tbilisi Puppet Theatre 1981, wrote and produced plays Traviata, Diamond of Marshal Fantier, Fall of Our Spring (USSR State Prize), Daughter of the Emperor of Trapezund; puppet productions in Switzerland and France 1991–94 including Ree Triste la Fin de l'Allee (Lausanne), Kutaisi (Rennes); Artistic Dir Cen. Puppet Theatre, Moscow 1994–95; Dir St Petersburg Satire Theatre 1996; productions include Song of the Volga 1996, Battle of Stalingrad, Forbidden Christmas or The Doctor and the Patient; numerous monumental and miniature sculptures including Chizhik-Pyzhik, Nose (after N. Gogol) ceramics exhibited in St Petersburg, Rabinovich (Odessa); graphic and painting shows in Moscow, St Petersburg, Paris, Rennes, Berlin, Lausanne; in Dijon and St Petersburg; illustrated works of A. Pushkin. *Address:* Rezo Gabriadze Theatre, Tbilisi, 13 Shavteli St., Georgia. *Telephone:* (32) 98-65-93 (home). *Fax:* (32) 98-65-89. *E-mail:* gabriadzetheater@yahoo.com. *Website:* www.gabriadze.com.

GABRIEL, Edward M., BS; American business executive and fmr diplomatist; *President and CEO, Gabriel Company LLC;* m. Kathleen Linehan; ed Gannon Univ., Pa; fmr Owner and Pres. Gabriel Group; fmr Sr Vice-Pres. in charge of Corp. Public Affairs, CONCORD Corpn; fmr Pres. and CEO Madison Public Affairs Group; Amb. to Morocco 1997–2001; Pres. and CEO Gabriel Company, LLC, Washington, DC 2002–; Advisor on Middle East policy for General Wesley Clark's presidential campaign 2004; currently Visiting Fellow, Middle East Program, Center for Strategic and Int. Studies; Sr Counsellor, Middle Eastern and Russian Issues, Center for Democracy; Founding mem. Exec. Cttee and Bd of Dirs, American Task Force on Lebanon; Dir Keystone Center; mem. Advisory Bd Guggenheim Partners; mem. Bd of Dirs Tri-Valley Corpn, American School of Tangier, Casablanca American School; mem. Global Advisory Bd George Washington Univ. *Address:* 4801 Foxhall Crescent, NW, Washington, DC 20007, USA (office).

GABRIEL, Michal; Czech sculptor; b. 25 Feb. 1960, Prague; s. of František Gabriel and Jarmila Gabrielová; m. Milada Dočekalová 1987; two s. one d.; ed Secondary School of Applied Arts, Acad. of Fine Arts, Prague; apprenticed in timber industry; worked as skilled joiner 1975–78; graduated as woodcarver 1982, as sculptor 1987; Founding mem. creative group Tvrdohlaví ('The Stubborn' group) 1987; First Prize for statue Pegasus, Prague 1988, for gates for Nat. Gallery Bldg 1989 (completed 1992); Angel Sculpture (bronze), Bank in Opava 1995, 'The Winged Leopard', gilded bronze sculpture, entrance Pres.'s Office, Prague Castle 1996; City Hall windows, České Budějovice 2000; Fountain (metal), Hradec Králové 2001; 'Trunk' sculpture, Philosophy Faculty Brno 2002; Indonesian sculpture, Prague Zoo 2003; lecturer, Faculty of Performing Arts, Czech Univ. of Tech., Brno 1999–; Co-f. new exhbn hall, Palace Lucerne, Prague 2000; Jindřich Chalupecký Prize 1994. *Publication:* Tvrdohlaví 2000. *Address:* Dlouhá 32, 110 00 Prague 1, Czech Republic (home). *Telephone:* (2) 22314644 (home). *Fax:* (2) 22314644 (home). *E-mail:* michalgabriel@hotmail.com. *Website:* www.michal-gabriel.cz; www.ffa.vutbr.cz/gabriel

GABRIEL, Peter; British rock singer and songwriter; b. 13 Feb. 1950, Woking, Surrey; m. 1st Jill Gabriel; two d.; m. 2nd Meabh Flynn 2002; two s.; ed Charterhouse School; Founde-mem., rock band Genesis 1966–75; solo artist 1975–; f. World of Music, Arts and Dance (WOMAD) featuring music from around the world 1982; f. Real World Group to develop interactive projects in arts and tech. 1985, Real World Studios 1986, Real World Records (world music record label) 1989, Real World Multimedia 1994; launched 'Witness' Human Rights Programme 1992; co-f. Europe digital music wholesaler OD2; co-f., with Brian Eno, the Magnificent Union of Digitally Downloading Artists (MUDDA) 2004; co-f., with Richard Branson, the Elders. org. 2000, launched by Nelson Mandela 2007; Dr hc (City Univ.) 1991; Hon. MA (Univ. Coll., Salford) 1994; Hon. DMus (Bath) 1996; Ivor Novello Award for Outstanding Contribution to British Music 1983, Ivor Novello Award for Best Song (for Sledgehammer) 1987, BRIT Award for Best British Music Video (for Sledgehammer) 1987, for Best British Male Artist 1987, for Best Producer 1993, Grammy Awards for Best New Age Performance 1990, Best Short Form Video 1993, for Best Song Written for Motion Picture (for Down to Earth from Wall-E) 2009, for Best Instrumental Arrangement (for Define Dancing from Wall-E) 2009, Q Award for Lifetime Achievement 2006, Ivor Novello Lifetime Achievement Award 2007, BMI Icon 2007, Amb. of Conscience, Amnesty International 2008, Quadriga Award 2008, Time 100 Most Influential People Award 2008, Polar Music Prize 2009. *Film scores:* Birdy 1985, Last Temptation of Christ 1989, Long Walk Home (from Rabbit-Proof Fence) 2002, Wall-E (two Grammy Awards) 2009) 2008, A Year Ago in Winter 2008, Inside Job 2010, The Reluctant Fundamentalist 2012. *Recordings include:* albums: with Genesis: From Genesis To Revelation 1969, Foxtrot 1972, Genesis Live 1973, Selling England By The Pound 1973, Nursery Crime 1974, The Lamb Lies Down On Broadway 1974; solo: Peter Gabriel I 1977, II 1979, III 1980, IV 1982, Peter Gabriel Plays Live 1983, So 1986,

Passion 1989, Shaking The Tree 1990, Us 1992, Revisited 1992, Secret World 1995, Come Home to Me Snow 1998, Ovo 2000, Up 2002, Hit 2003, Big Blue Ball 2008, Scratch My Back 2010, New Blood 2011, Live Blood 2012, Scratch My Back/And I'll Scratch Yours 2013, Courage 2013. *Publication:* Genesis: Chapter and Verse (with other band mems) 2007. *Address:* Real World Holdings Ltd, Box Mill, Mill Lane, Box, Wiltshire, SN13 8PL, England (office). *Telephone:* (1225) 740600 (office). *Website:* www.petergabriel.com; www.realworld.co.uk; www.realworldrecords .com; www.realworldmultimedia.com.

GABRIEL, Sigmar; German politician; *Federal Vice-Chancellor and Federal Minister of Economics and Energy;* b. 12 Sept. 1959, Goslar; m. 1st (divorced), one d.; m. 2nd Anke Stadler 2012, one d.; ed Göttingen Univ.; children and youth work in Sozialistische Jugend Deutschlands – die Falken 1976–89; joined SPD 1977; adult educ. lecturer 1983–88; teacher, Saxony Adult Educ. Inst. 1989–90; Dist Councillor for Goslar 1987–98, City Councillor 1991–99, Chair. Environmental Cttee 1991–96, Econ. Affairs and Tourism Cttee 1996; mem. Lower Saxony Parl. 1990–2005, mem. Environment Cttee 1990–94, Deputy Chair. SPD Parl. Group 1997–98, Chair. 1998–99, 2003–05; SPD Speaker for Home Affairs 1994–97; mem. Exec. Cttee SPD 1999–2005, Chair. SPD 2009–; Minister-Pres. of Lower Saxony 1999–2003; mem. Bundestag for constituency 49 (Salzgitter-Wolfenbüttel) 2005–; Fed. Minister of the Environment, Nature Conservation and Nuclear Safety 2005–09, Fed. Vice-Chancellor and Fed. Minister of Econs and Energy 2013–. *Leisure interests:* cycling, sailing. *Address:* Federal Chancellery, Bundeskanzler-Amt, Willy-Brandt Str. 1, 10557 Berlin, Germany (office). *Telephone:* (30) 40000 (office). *Fax:* (30) 40002357 (office). *E-mail:* sigmar.gabriel@wk.bundestag.de (office). *Website:* www.spd.de (office); www.sigmargabriel.de (office).

GABRIELLI DE AZEVEDO, José Sergio, PhD; Brazilian economist, academic and business executive; b. 3 Oct. 1949, Salvador, Bahia; ed Fed. Univ. of Bahia, Boston Univ., USA; fmr Deputy Dir of Research and Postgraduate Studies, Fed. Univ. of Bahia, currently Prof. on leave; fmr Supt Foundation for Research and Extension Support; Visiting Research Scholar, LSE, UK 2000–01; Chief Financial Officer and Investor Relations, Dir Petróleo Brasileiro SA (Petrobras) 2003–05, Pres. and CEO 2005–12, mem. Bd of Dirs Petrobras Participaciones SA (PEPSA), Petrobras Energia SA (PESA); Brazilian Inst. of Finance Execs Equilibrist Award 2004, Nat. Assen of Execs in Finance, Admin and Accounting Professional of the Year 2004, Int. Stevie Business Awards Best Finance Exec. in Latin America 2005, named by Revista Época as one of the 100 most influential Brazilians of 2009, Global Energy Award, World Energy Council 2010, Petroleum Executive of the Year, Energy Intelligence 2011, Executive Entrepreneur of the Year, Ernst & Young 2011, most outstanding executive in trade relations between Brazil-Japan, Chamber of Commerce Brazil-Japan 2012. *Publications:* numerous books and articles on productive restructuring, the labour market, macroeconomics and regional development. *Address:* Universidade Federal da Bahia, Rua Augusto Viana, 1 - Canela, Salvador BA 40110-060, Brazil (office). *Telephone:* (71) 3283-7129 (office). *Website:* www.ufba.br (office).

GABRIELSE, Gerald, MS, PhD; American physicist and academic; *George Vasmer Leverett Professor of Physics, Harvard University;* ed Calvin Coll., Grand Rapids, Mich., Univ. of Chicago; teaching asst, Calvin Coll., Grand Rapids, Mich. 1971–72, research asst 1972–73; grad. student, Univ. of Chicago 1973–78; Research Assoc., Univ. of Washington, Seattle 1978–82, Research Asst Prof. 1985–86, Assoc. Prof. 1986–87; George Vasmer Leverett Prof. of Physics, Harvard Univ. 1987– (Chair. Physics Dept 2000–03); Physicist, CERN, leader of ATRAP antimatter physics research project, Geneva, Switzerland; Consultant, Intermagnetics General Corpn 1995, PolyChip Inc. 1999; Scientist in Residence, Lexington Christian Acad. 1995–96; mem. NAS 2007–; Levenson Prize, Harvard Univ. 2000, Davisson-Germer Prize, American Physical Soc. 2002. *Lectures include:* around 200 lectures at scientific confs and univs. *Publications include:* more than 100 scientific publs. *Address:* Department of Physics, Harvard University, 17 Oxford Street, Cambridge, MA 02138, USA (office). *Telephone:* (617) 495-4381 (office). *E-mail:* gabrielse@physics.harvard.edu (office). *Website:* physics.harvard.edu/ gabrielse.htm (office); hussle.harvard.edu/~gabrielse (office); hussle.harvard.edu/ ~atrap (office).

GACHCHHADAR, Bijay Kumar; Nepalese politician; *Leader, Madhesi Jana Adhikar Forum Nepal—Loktantrik (MPRFN—Democratic);* elected mem. Nepalese Constituent Ass. 2008; mem. Madhesi Jana Adhikar Forum –2009 (expelled); Founder and Chair. Madhesi Jana Adhikar Forum Nepal—Loktantrik (MPRFN—Democratic) 2009–; Deputy Prime Minister and Minister for Physical Planning and Works 2009–11, Deputy Prime Minister and Minister of Home Affairs 2011–13. *Address:* c/o Ministry of Home Affairs, Singha Durbar, Kathmandu, Nepal.

GACIYUBWENGE, Maj.-Gen. Pontien; Burundian army officer and politician; *Minister of National Defence and War Veterans;* b. Mwaro Prov.; spent long career in Forces de défense nationales (FDN), positions included Commdr, Army Bn, Bujumbura, Commdr, Southern Mil. Region 2003, Commdr, Fifth Mil. Region 2005, later Chief of Staff in charge of training; Minister of Nat. Defence and War Veterans 2010–. *Address:* Ministry of National Defence and War Veterans, Bujumbura, Burundi (office).

GADDAFI, Seif al-Islam, BSc; Libyan foundation executive; b. 25 June 1972, Tripoli; s. of Col Mu'ammar Muhammad al-Gaddafi by his second wife; ed Al-Fateh Univ., Tripoli, IMADEC Univ., Vienna, Austria, London School of Econs, UK; Co-owner Nat. Eng Service and Supplies Co.; Chair. Gaddafi Int. Charity and Devt Foundation (paid $2.7 billion compensation to families of the 270 victims of Lockerbie bombing); fmr Pres. Libyan Nat. Assen for Drugs and Narcotics Control; warrant issued for his arrest by Int. Criminal Court, The Hague on charges of crimes against humanity following popular uprising in Libya June 2011; arrested in southern Libya Nov. 2011, held in detention in Zintan. *Achievements include:* involved in assisting Muslims in Mindanao, southern Philippines 1999, later helped negotiate release of western hostages held by Islamic rebels there; mediated with US and British intelligence in negotiations that led to Libya's abandonment of its weapons programmes 2004.

GADDIS, John Lewis, PhD; American historian and academic; *Robert A. Lovett Professor of History, Yale University;* b. 1942; m. (divorced); two s.; m. 2nd Toni

Dorfman 1997; ed Univ. of Texas, Austin; Lecturer and later Prof., Dept of History, Ohio Univ. 1969–94, f. Contemporary History Inst., Ohio 1987; Sr Fellow, Hoover Inst. 2000–02; Robert A. Lovett Prof. of History, Yale Univ. 1997–; fmr Lecturer, US Naval War Coll., Univ. of Helsinki, Finland, Princeton Univ., Univ. of Oxford, UK; George Eastman Visiting Prof., Balliol Coll., Oxford 2000–01; mem. Editorial Bd Foreign Affairs; mem. Advisory Bd Cold War Int. History Project; Fellow, American Acad. of Arts and Sciences 1995; Nat. Humanities Medal 2005. *Publications include:* The United States and the Origins of the Cold War 1941–47 1972, Russia, The Soviet Union and the United States: An Interpretive History 1978, Strategies of Containment: A Critical Appraisal of Postwar American National Security Policy 1982, The Long Peace: Inquiries into the History of the Cold War 1987, The United States and the End of the Cold War: Reconsiderations, Implications, Provocations 1992, We Now Know: Rethinking Cold War History 1997, The Landscape of History: How Historians Map the Past 2002, Surprise, Security, and the American Experience 2004, The Cold War 2006, George F. Kennan: An American Life (Pulitzer Prize for Biography 2012) 2011. *Address:* Department of History, Yale University, PO Box 208324, New Haven, CT 06520-8353, USA (office). *Telephone:* (203) 432-1374 (office). *Fax:* (203) 432-6520 (office). *E-mail:* john.gaddis@yale.edu (office). *Website:* www.yale.edu/history/ faculty/gaddis.html (office).

GADE JENSEN, Søren, MSc, CandEcon; Danish politician; b. 27 Jan. 1963, Holstebro; s. of Poul Jørgensen and Anna Gade Jørgensen; ed Århus Univ.; served as Officer, Jutland Regiment of Dragoons 1983–85, Reserve Officer, rank of Maj. 1985–; UN Observer in Middle East, UNTSO 1990–01; Int. Market Analyst, Cheminova Agro A/S 1991–93; Man., Bilka 1993–95; teacher, Holstebro Business Coll. 1997–98; Chief Operating Finance Officer, Færch Plast A/S 1995–2001; Head of Centre, RAR Regnskabscenter 2001–03; cand. for Holstebro Constituency (Liberal Party) 1995; mem. (temp.) Folketing for Ringkøbing County Constituency Oct.–Nov. 1999, mem. 2001–, Deputy Chair. Defence Cttee 2001; Minister of Defence 2004–10 (resgnd); Commdr of the Order of Danneborg. *Address:* c/o Ministry of Defence, Holmens Kanal 42, 1060 Copenhagen K, Denmark (office).

GADGIL, Madhav, MSc, PhD; Indian ecologist, conservationist and academic; b. 1942; ed Univ. of Poona, Bombay Univ., Harvard Univ., USA; main contrib. to establishment of India's first biosphere reserve in the Western Ghats; worked at Indian Nat. Science Acad. from 1973; fmr IBM Fellow and Lecturer in Biology, Harvard Univ.; Visiting Prof., Stanford Univ., USA; fmr Distinguished Lecturer, Univ. of California, Berkeley, USA; Founder and Prof., Centre for Ecological Sciences, Bangalore, Indian Inst. of Science 1973–2004; mem. Science Advisory Council to Prime Minister 1986–90, Karnataka State Planning Bd; Vice-Pres. Scientific Advisory Bd to Convention on Biological Diversity 1995; Chair. Scientific and Tech. Advisory Panel of Global Environment Facility; represents Govt of India on Subsidiary Body on Scientific, Tech. and Technological Advice to Int. Convention on Biological Diversity; currently Chair. Cttee Environmental School Educ. Curriculum; fmr Chair. Fuel and Fodder Study Group of Planning Comm., Biodiversity Task Force of Dept of Biotechnology, Expert Group on Eastern and Western Ghats, Ministry of Environment and Forests; fmr mem. Steering Cttee Project Tiger, Steering Cttee Indian Bd for Wild Life, Silent Valley Cttee, Bastar Pine Plantation Cttee; Fellow, Indian Acad. of Sciences, Indian Nat. Science Acad., Third World Acad. of Sciences; Foreign Assoc., NAS; Hon. mem. British Ecological Soc., Ecological Soc. of America; Padma Shri 1981, Shanti Swarup Bhatnagar Award, Vikram Sarabhai Award, Iswarchandra Vidyasagar Award, Rajyotsava Award 1983, Centennial Medal, Harvard Univ. 2002, Govt of Karnataka, Volvo Environment Prize 2003, Padma Bhushan 2006, Firodia Award 2007. *Publications:* This Fissured Land, Ecology and Equity, Diversity: The Cornerstone of Life, Nurturing Biodiversity: An Indian Agenda, Ecological Journeys, People's Biodiversity Registers: A Methodology Manual; more than 215 research papers (two of them recognized as Citation Classics) on population biology, conservation biology, human ecology and ecological history; writes regularly for popular media in English and Indian languages. *Address:* c/o Centre for Ecological Sciences, Indian Institute of Science, Bangalore 560 012, India (office). *Telephone:* (80) 23600985 (office). *Fax:* (80) 23601428 (office). *E-mail:* madhav@ces.iisc.ernet.in (office); madhav.gadgil@gmail.com. *Website:* ces.iisc.ernet.in (office); ces.iisc.ernet .in/hpg/cesmg (office).

GADIESH, Orit, MBA; Israeli business executive; *Chairperson, Bain & Company;* ed Hebrew Univ., Jerusalem, Harvard Business School, USA; joined Israeli army age 17, worked as Aide to Deputy Chief of Staff Ezer Weizman; taught at Hebrew Univ., Jerusalem Inst. of Man.; joined Bain & Co. (consultancy firm), Boston 1977, worked in steel industry and automotive industry sectors, Chair. 1993–; mem. Bd Harvard Business School, Haute Ecole Commerciale, Paris, Peres Inst. for Peace, Fed. Reserve Bank of New England, WPP Group; mem. Harvard Medical School Advisory Council for Cell Biology and Pathology, Harvard Business School Visiting Cttee, Metropolitan Museum of Art Cttee, New York; mem. Bd of Trustees Eisenhower Fellowships; mem. Foundation Bd World Economic Forum (WEF), also mem. WEF International Business Council; Baker Scholar, Harvard Business School; Brown Award for Outstanding Marketing Student, Harvard Business School 1977, Harvard Business School Alumni Achievement Award 2000, IDC Univ. Distinguished Leadership Award 2000, 25th Annual Golden Door Award, Int. Inst. of Boston 2002, Lifetime Achievement Award from Consulting magazine 2007; ranked by Forbes magazine amongst 100 Most Powerful Women (91st) 2004, (95th) 2005, (99th) 2006, (98th) 2007. *Publications:* series of articles for Harvard Business Review. *Leisure interests:* reading. *Address:* Bain & Company Inc., 131 Dartmouth Street, Boston, MA 02116, USA (office). *Telephone:* (617) 572-2000 (office). *Fax:* (617) 572-2427 (office). *Website:* www.bain.com (office).

GADIO, Cheikh Tidiane, BA, PhD; Senegalese international organization official and government official; b. 16 Sept. 1956, Saint-Louis; ed Ohio State Univ., USA, Univ. of Montréal, Canada, Univ. of Paris, France; Ed.-in-Chief, Tribune Africaine, Paris 1980–84; Head of Audiovisual section, Festival Panafricain des Arts et de la Culture (FESPAC) 1987–88; various econ. and telecommunications devt advisory posts, World Bank Inst.; Adviser, UN Office for Project Services 1998–; Regional Dir for Africa, School for International Training, Vt, USA 1998–99; Co-ordinator for Africa, World Bank Inst. Jan.–April 2000; Minister of State, of Foreign Affairs, African Unity and Senegalese Abroad 2000–09; Founder and Pres. Mouvement politique citoyen (political party), unsuccessful cand. for Pres. of Senegal 2012.

GADJIYEV, Gadis Abdullayevich, DJur; Russian/Dagestan lawyer and judge; *Justice, Constitutional Court of Russian Federation;* b. 27 Aug. 1957, Shovkra; m.; four s.; ed Moscow State Univ. 1975; teacher Dagestan State Univ. 1975–79; legal consultant Supreme Soviet Dagestan ASSR 1979–80, Head Legal Dept Admin. 1980–90, Chair. Comm. on Law and Local Self-Man. 1990–91; Justice Constitutional Court of Russian Fed. 1991–. *Publications:* over 80 scientific publs including 4 monographs on constitutional law. *Leisure interest:* pigeon raising. *Address:* Constitutional Court of Russian Federation, Ilyinka 21, 103132 Moscow, Russia (office). *Telephone:* (095) 206-17-62 (office). *Fax:* (095) 206-19-78 (office).

GADKARI, Nitin, MCom, LLB; Indian politician, lawyer, business executive and agriculturalist; b. 27 May 1957, Nagpur; m. Kanchan Gadkari; two s. one d.; ed studies in Maharashtra; as a teenager, worked for Bharatiya Janata Yuva Morcha and student union Akhil Bharatiya Vidyarthi Parishad (ABVP) 1976–77; Co-ordinator for Purogami Lokashahi Aghdadi's Vidarbha region after Emergency was lifted 1977; elected as Vidarbha Region Sec. of ABVP 1979 (re-elected 1980); Pres. Bharatiya Janata Yuva Morcha, Nagpur City Unit 1981, Sec. Bharatiya Janata Party, Nagpur City Unit 1985–86, Gen. Sec. 1988–89; elected to Maharashtra Govt Legis. Council from graduates constituency, Nagpur Region 1989 (re-elected 1990, 1996, elected unopposed 2002); Minister of Public Works Dept, Govt of Maharashtra 1995–99, est. Maharashtra State Road Devt Corpn (govt-owned co.) to undertake construction work; Guardian Minister for Nagpur Dist, Govt of Maharashtra 1995–99; mem. High Power Cttee for Privatization, Govt of Maharashtra 1995–99; Founder and Chair. Maharashtra State Road Devt Corpn 1995–99; Chair. Mining Policy Implementation Cttee, Govt of Maharashtra 1995–99, Metropolis Beautification Cttee, Govt of Maharashtra 1995–99, Nat. Rural Road Devt Cttee; Chair. Nat. Rural Road Devt Cttee, Govt of India 1995–99, Review Cttee of CPWD, Govt of India 1995–99; Leader of Opposition, Maharashtra Legis. Council 1999–2004; Gen. Sec. Bharatiya Janata Party (BJP), Maharashtra 1992–94, State Pres. BJP, Maharashtra 2004–09, Pres. Bharatiya Janata Party (elected unanimously) 2009–13; Chair. Purti Group of Cos; Founder and Chair. Poly Sack Industrial Soc. Ltd; Promoter and Dir Nikhil Furniture and Appliances Pvt. Ltd; Founder and Chair. Empress Employees Co-operative Paper Mills Ltd; Founder and mem. Atyodaya Trust; exports fruits to various countries under the banner Ketaki Overseas Trading Co.; Mumbai Bhushan Award. *Achievements include:* constructed series of roads, highways and flyovers across the state, including Mumbai–Pune Expressway and Bandra–Worli Sea Link. *Address:* Bharatiya Janata Party (BJP), 11 Ashoka Road, New Delhi 110 001, India (office). *Telephone:* (11) 23005700 (office). *Fax:* (11) 23005787 (office). *E-mail:* webmaster@bjp.org (office). *Website:* www.bjp.org (office); nitingadkari.in.

GADONNEIX, Pierre, DEcon; French energy industry executive; *Chairman, World Energy Council;* b. 1943, New York, NY, USA; m.; three c.; ed École Polytechnique, Paris, Ecole Nationale Supérieure du Pétrole et des Moteurs, Harvard Business School, USA; began career as engineer, Groupe Elf Aquitaine 1966–69; f. SEFI 1969, Dir 1970–72; Dir Inst. de Développement Industriel (IDI) 1972–76; Tech. Adviser, Ministry of Industry 1976–78, Dir Mechanical and Metallurgical Industries Div. 1978–87; Pres. and Man. Dir Groupe Gaz de France 1987–96, Chair. and CEO 1996–2004; Chair. and CEO Électricité de France (EDF) 2004–09, Hon. Chair. 2009–; Chair. World Energy Council 2007–; mem. Bd Dirs Elf-Erap 1988–95, Renault 1978–86, SNCF 1983–87, France Télécom 1998–; Pres. Eurogas (trade asscn) 2000–, Fondation Gaz de France, Conseil Français de l'Energie 1993–99 (later Vice-Pres.); Lecturer, École Polytechnique 1983–92; mem. Conseil Economique et Social, Bd of Fondation Nationale des Sciences Politiques; Commdr, Légion d'honneur, Ordre nat. du Mérite, Ordre des Arts et des Lettres. *Address:* World Energy Council, 5th Floor, Regency House, 1–4 Warwick Street, London, W1B 5LT, England (office); EDF Group, 22–30 avenue de Wagram, 75382 Paris Cedex 8, France (office). *Telephone:* (20) 7734-5996 (London) (office); 1-40-42-22-22 (Paris) (office). *Fax:* (20) 7734-5926 (office). *E-mail:* info@worldenergy.org (office), info@edf.fr (office). *Website:* www.worldenergy.org (office); www.edf.fr (office).

GAEHTGENS, Thomas Wolfgang, DPhil; German art historian and academic; *Director, The Getty Research Institute;* b. 24 June 1940, Leipzig; m. Barbara Feiler 1969; two s.; ed Univs of Bonn and Freiburg and Univ. of Paris, France; teacher, Univ. of Göttingen 1973, Prof. of Art History 1974–79, Technische Hochschule, Aachen 1979, Freie Univ. Berlin 1979–2007; Founder and Dir German Centre for the History of Art, Paris 1997–2007; Visiting Scholar, Inst. for Advanced Study, Princeton 1979–80; Visiting Scholar, The Getty Research Inst., Los Angeles, 1985–86, Dir 2007–; Pres. Comité International d'histoire de l'art 1992–96; mem. Akad. der Wissenschaften, Göttingen; Chevalier, Légion d'honneur; Dr hc (Courtauld Inst. of Art) 2004; Grand Prix de la Francophonie 2009. *Publications include:* Napoleon's Arc de Triomphe 1974, Versailles als Nationaldenkmal 1984, Joseph-Marie Vien 1988, Anton von Werner 1990, Die Berliner Museuminsel im Deutschen Kaiserreich 1992. *Leisure interests:* art, history. *Address:* The Getty Research Institute, 1200 Getty Center Drive, Suite 1100, Los Angeles, CA 90049-1688, USA (office). *Telephone:* (310) 440-7335 (office). *E-mail:* griweb@getty.edu (office). *Website:* www.getty.edu/research (office).

GAFT, Valentin Iosifovich, Russian actor; b. 2 Sept. 1935, Moscow; m. Olga Mikhailovna Ostroumova; ed Studio-School of Moscow Art Theatre; worked in Mossoviet Theatre, Na Maloy Bronnoy, Lenkom, Satire Theatre 1959–69; leading actor Sovremennik Theatre 1969–; dozens of roles in classical and contemporary plays; in cinema since 1956; People's Artist of Russia 1984, Order of Friendship 1995, Laureate, Theatrical Prize I. Smoktunovskii 1995. *Theatre roles include:* Glumov (Balalaikin and Co.), Lopatin (From the Notes of Lopatin), George (Who's Afraid of Virginia Woolf?), Governor (Inspector), Vershinin (Three Sisters), Bridegroom (Something Like a Comedy), Husband, Wife and Lover (Trusotsii), The Government Inspector (Gorodnichii). *Film roles include:* Murder on Dante Street 1956, First Courier 1968, Crazy Gold 1977, Centaurs 1979, Parade 1980, Fuette 1986, Thieves by Law 1988, Blessed Heavens 1991, Khochu v Ameriku 1993, Tayna Marchello 1997, Nebo v almazakh 1999, Staryye klyachi 2000, Nezhnyy vozrast 2001, roles in TV productions and TV films including Buddenbrooks, The Mystery of Edwin Drood, Archipelago Lenoire, Kings and Cabbage, Po tu storonu volkov (miniseries) 2002, Master i Margarita (miniseries)

2005, 12 2007. *Publications:* Poetry and Epigrams 1989, Life is Theatre (with Leonid Alekseevich Filatov) 1998, Garden of Forgotten Memories 1999, Poems. Epigrams 2003. *Leisure interests:* writing verses and epigrams. *Address:* T. Shchevchenko nab. 1/2, Apt 62, 121059 Moscow, Russia (home). *Telephone:* (495) 243-76-67 (home).

GAGE, Fred H., BS, PhD; American geneticist and academic; *Professor and Vi and John Adler Chair for Research on Age-Related Neurodegenerative Diseases, Salk Institute for Biological Studies;* ed Univ. of Florida, Johns Hopkins Univ.; Nat. Inst. of Mental Health Predoctoral Fellow, Johns Hopkins Univ., Baltimore 1974–76; Asst, later Assoc. Prof., Texas Christian Univ. 1976–80; Assoc. Prof., Dept of Histology, Univ. of Lund, Sweden 1981–85; Assoc. Prof., Dept of Neurosciences, Univ. of California, San Diego 1985–88, Prof. 1988–; Prof. and Vi and John Adler Chair for Research on Age-Related Neurodegenerative Diseases, Lab. of Genetics, Salk Inst. for Biological Studies 1995–; co-f. StemCells Inc. 1988; Fellow, NAS, Inst. of Medicine, American Acad. of Arts and Sciences; mem. Soc. for Neuroscience (Pres. 2001); mem. Science Advisory Bd, Genetics Policy Inst.; numerous awards including Bristol-Myers Squibb Neuroscience Research Award 1987, IPSEN Prize in Neuronal Plasticity 1990, Christopher Reeve Research Medal 1997, Max Planck Research Prize 1999, MetLife Award for Medical Research 2002, Max Planck Soc. Klaus Joachim Zulch-Preis 2003, Keio Medical Science Prize 2008. *Address:* Salk Institute for Biological Studies, 10010 North Torrey Pines Road, La Jolla, CA 92037, USA (office). *Telephone:* (858) 453-4100 (office). *E-mail:* gage@salk.edu (office). *Website:* www.salk.edu (office).

GAGNÈRE, Olivier; French designer; b. 1952, Boulogne; began career working with Ettore Sottsass and Memphis design group, Milan 1980; worked in Murano, Italy 1989, Arita, Japan 1989–92; collaborated with Bernardaud Porcelain 1992, Cristalleries St Louis 1995; decorated Cafe Marly at Louvre Museum, Paris 1994; designed reception areas of Hotel Marignan Champs-Elysées; designs include lighting, furniture, china, glassware, accessories; works are included in collections of major museums including MOMA, New York, Museum of Decorative Arts, Paris, Nat. Center of Art and Culture Georges Pompidou, FNAC (Fonds Nat. d'Art Contemporain), Museum of Modern Art, San Francisco; Maison & Objet Designer of the Year 1998. *Exhibitions include:* retrospective exhibition, Nat. Museum of Fine Arts, Beijing and Museum of Modern Art, Shanghai 2006. *Address:* 47, Boulevard St Jacques, 75014 Paris, France (office). *Telephone:* 1-45-80-79-67 (office). *Fax:* 1-45-80-79-67 (office). *E-mail:* olivier@gagnere.net (office). *Website:* www.gagnere.net (office).

GAGNON, Jean-Marie, MBA, PhD, FRSC; Canadian academic; *Professor Emeritus of Finance, Laval University;* b. 16 July 1933, Fabre; s. of Pierre Gagnon and Yvette Langlois; m. Rachel Bonin 1959; three s.; ed Univ. of Chicago and Laval Univ.; chartered accountant, Clarkson, Gordon, Cie 1957–59; Prof. of Finance, Laval Univ. 1959–2000, Prof. Emer. 2004–; Visiting Prof., Faculté Universitaire Catholique, Mons, Belgium 1972–74, Univ. of Nankai, People's Repub. of China 1985; Médaille Alfred Houle, Prix Hermès de la recherche. *Publications:* Income Smoothing Hypothesis 1970, Belgian Experience with Mergers 1982, Taux de rendement et risque 1982, Traité de gestion financière (with N. Khoury) 1987, Taxes and Financial Decisions 1988, Taxes and Dividends 1991, Corporate Governance Mechanisms and Board Composition 1995, Distribution of Voting Rights and Takeover Resistance 1995, Tax Benefits of Hedging for Small and Medium Size Businesses (with S. Landry and N. Khoury) 2010. *Address:* Département de finance et assurance, Faculté des sciences de l'administration, Pavillon Palasis-Prince, bureau 3690, Université Laval, Québec, QC G1V 0A6 (office); 1340 Corrigan, Ste-Foy, QC G1W 3E9, Canada (home). *Telephone:* (418) 656-5535 (office). *Fax:* (418) 656-2164 (office). *E-mail:* jean-marie.gagnon@fas.ulaval.ca (office). *Website:* www4.fsa.ulaval.ca/cms/accueil/faculte/departementecole/fai/personnelenseignantfinanceassurance/jeanmariegagnon (office).

GAGOSIAN, Lawrence (Larry) Gilbert; American gallery owner and art dealer; b. 19 April 1945, Los Angeles, Calif.; s. of Ara Gagosian and Ann Louise Tonkin; ed Univ. of California, Los Angeles; fmr literary agent with William Morris Agency; began career in art by selling posters in Santa Monica 1970s; Founder and Owner Gagosian Galleries in New York, Beverly Hills, Calif., London, Paris, Rome, Athens, Geneva and Hong Kong; represents the estate of Andy Warhol. *Address:* Gagosian Gallery, 980 Madison Avenue, New York, NY 10075, USA (office); Gagosian Gallery, 6–24 Britannia Street, London, WC1X 9JD, England (office). *Telephone:* (212) 744-2313 (New York) (office); (20) 7841-9960 (London) (office). *Fax:* (212) 722-7962 (New York) (office); (20) 7841-9961 (London) (office). *E-mail:* newyork@gagosian.com (office); london@gagosian.com (office). *Website:* www.gagosian.com (office).

GAHMBERG, Carl G., MD, DMedSc; Finnish biochemist and academic; *Professor Emeritus of Biochemistry, University of Helsinki;* b. 1 Dec. 1942, Helsinki; s. of Gustaf-Adolf Gahmberg and Marie-Louise Gahmberg; m. Marianne Gripenberg-Gahmberg; one s. one d.; ed Univ. of Helsinki; Post-doctoral Fellow, Univ. of Washington 1972–74; Docent of Cell Biology, Univ. of Helsinki 1974; Prof. of Biochemistry, Åbo Akad. 1979–81, Univ. of Helsinki 1981–2012, Prof. Emer. 2012–; Research Prof., Acad. of Finland 1986–91; Visiting Prof., La Jolla Cancer Research Foundation 1988–89; Vice-Chair. Finnish Medical Asscn 1998–99, Chair. 2000–01; Exec. Ed. Biochimica et Biophysica Acta 2000–08; mem. Finnish Acad. of Science, Finnish Soc. of Sciences and Letters (Perm. Sec.), European Molecular Biology Org., Academia Europaea, World Cultural Council; foreign mem. Royal Swedish Acad. of Science, Royal Soc. of Arts and Sciences, Göteborg; Kt of the Finnish White Rose (First Class), Commdr; Order of the Finnish Lion; Chevalier, Ordre des Palmes académiques, Order of the White Rose of Finland; Komppa Prize 1971, Scandinavian Jahre Prize 1981, 150th Anniversary Prize, Finnish Medical Asscn 1985, Prof. of the Year in Finland 1995, Finnish Äyräpää Prize for Medicine 1997, J.W. Runeberg Prize for Medicine 2010. *Publications include:* 270 int. publs on cell membrane, glycoproteins, cell adhesion, cancer research. *Leisure interests:* nature, classical music, gardening. *Address:* University of Helsinki, Department of Biosciences, Division of Biochemistry, PO Box 56, Viikinkaari 5, 00014 Helsinki, Finland (office). *Telephone:* (9) 1915-9028 (office). *Fax:* (9) 1915-9068 (office). *E-mail:* carl.gahmberg@helsinki.fi (office).

GAI, Pratibha L., MSc, PhD, CEng, CPhys, FInstP, FRSC; British physicist and academic; *JEOL Professor, Yorkshire Forward Chair of Electron Microscopy and Co-Director, York JEOL Nanocentre, University of York;* b. India; ed Univ. of Cambridge; began career as Postdoctoral Researcher, Univ. of Oxford; worked at DuPont and Univ. of Delaware, USA for 18 years; currently JEOL Prof., Yorkshire Forward Chair of Electron Microscopy and Co-Dir York JEOL Nanocentre, Univ. of York; Gabor Medal and Prize, Inst. of Physics 2010, Laureate for Europe, L'Oréal-UNESCO Awards For Women in Science 2013. *Publications:* nine co-authored books and more than 250 papers in professional journals. *Address:* Department of Chemistry, University of York, Heslington, York, YO10 5DD (office); York JEOL Nanocentre, Helix House, University of York, Heslington, York, YO10 5DD, England (office). *Telephone:* (1904) 328403 (office). *Fax:* (1904) 322516 (office); (1904) 328485 (office). *E-mail:* pratibha.gai@york.ac.uk (office). *Website:* www.york.ac.uk/physics/people/gai (office); www.york.ac.uk/chemistry/staff/academic/d-g/pgai (office).

GAICIUC, Brig.-Gen. Victor, DrHistSc; Moldovan army officer, government official and diplomatist; b. 12 March 1957, Melons, Singerei dist; m.; two c.; ed Kharkov Aviation School, Moscow Acad. of Mil.-Political Dept (Air Force), NATO Coll., Rome, Italy; pilot, main pilot, patrol commdr, deputy commdr regimental aviation squadron in mil. dists Zabaikalie and Belarus 1978–86; Head of Deputy Commdr Aviation Regt, responsible for staff training in mil. dist of Belarusian Soviet Army 1989–93, returned to Moldova and apptd Chief Specialist, Head of Dept for Humanitarian Training, Training Directorate, Ministry of Defence 1993–97; Deputy Minister of Defence 1997–99 (removed from position), Commr in Dept of Mil. Admin, Ministry of Defence 1999–2000, Deputy Minister of Defence 2000–01, Minister of Defence 2001–04 (dismissed); promoted to rank of Brig.-Gen. 2002; Amb. to Belgium and Perm. Rep. NATO (also accred as Amb. to the Netherlands) 2005–10; mil. decorations from Moldova, Russia, Kazakhstan and Ukraine, Order of Fatherland, Service Class III 2007. *Publications:* Constituirea Armatei Naționale (cronica evenimentelor 1989–1992) (ed.) 1999; several articles. *Address:* c/o Ministry of Foreign Affairs and European Integration, 2012 Chișinău, str. 31 August 80, Moldova (office). *Telephone:* (22) 57-82-07 (office). *Fax:* (22) 23-23-02 (office). *E-mail:* secdep@mfa.md (office). *Website:* www.mfa.gov.md (office).

GAILANI, Fatima, BA, MA; Afghan politician and international organization official; *President, Afghan Red Crescent Society;* b. 1954, Kabul; d. of Pir Sayed Ahmed Gailani (leader of Nat. Islamic Front of Afghanistan during 1980s); m. 1st Hamid Nasser-Zia (divorced); m. 2nd Awar ul Haq Ahadi; one d.; ed Malalai High School, Kabul, Nat. Univ. of Iran, Muslim Coll., London, England; lived in exile during Soviet invasion of Afghanistan and acted as spokesperson in London for Afghan Mujahideen; attended Bonn Conf. on Afghanistan 2001; returned to Afghanistan, chosen as del. to Emergency Loya Jirga (Grand Council) 2002, apptd as constitution drafting and ratifying commr; Pres. Afghan Red Crescent Soc. 2004–. *Publications:* Mosques of London, A Biography of Mohammed Mosa Shafi. *Address:* Afghan Red Crescent Society, Afshar-e Silo, PO Box 3066, Shar Naw, Kabul, Afghanistan (office). *Telephone:* (75) 2014446 (office); 79-9385533 (mobile) (office). *Fax:* (75) 2023476 (office). *E-mail:* int.relation.arcs@gmail.com (office). *Website:* arcs.org.af/en/page/706 (office).

GAINES, Ernest James, BA; American writer and academic; b. 15 Jan. 1933, River Lake Plantation, Pointe Coupee Parish, La; m. Dianne Saulney; ed San Francisco State Univ., Stanford Univ.; Writer-in-Residence, Denison Univ. 1971, Stanford Univ. 1981; Visiting Prof., Whittier Coll. 1983, Writer-in-Residence 1986; Prof. of English and Writer-in-Residence, Univ. of Louisiana, Lafayette (fmrly Univ. of Southwestern Louisiana) 1983, now Writer-in-Residence Emer.; Fellow, American Acad. of Arts and Letters, Stanford Univ. (Creative Writing Program) 1958; Chevalier, Ordre des Arts et des Lettres 1996; Dr hc (Bard Coll.), (Brown Univ.), (Denison Univ.), (Louisiana State Univ.), (Loyola Univ.), (Savannah Coll. of Art and Design), (Tulane Univ.), (Univ. of Miami), (Univ. of the South, Sewanee), (Whittier Coll.); Black Acad. of Arts and Letters Award 1972, Commonwealth Club of Calif. Fiction gold medals 1972, 1984, American Acad. and Inst. of Arts and Letters Award 1987, La Humanist of the Year 1989, Louisiana Center for the Book Award 2000, Nat. Govs' Asscn Award for Distinguished Service in the Arts 2000, La Govs' Award for Lifetime Achievement 2000, Louisiana Writers' Award 2000, Nat. Humanities Medal 2000, Academy of Achievement Golden Plate Award 2001, Sidney Lanier Prize for Southern Literature 2012, Nat. Medal of Arts 2012. *Publications include:* Catherine Carmier 1964, Of Love and Dust 1967, Bloodline (short stories) 1968, The Autobiography of Miss Jane Pittman 1971, A Long Day in November 1971, In My Father's House 1978, A Gathering of Old Men 1983, A Lesson Before Dying (Nat. Book Critics Circle Award 1994, Southern Writers Conference Award 1994, La Library Asscn Award 1994) 1993, Mozart and Leadbelly 2005. *Address:* c/o Tanya Bickley Enterprises Inc., PO Box 1656, New Canaan, CT 06840, USA (office); c/o Department of English, University of Louisiana Lafayette, Griffin Hall, Room 221, Lafayette, LA 70504, USA (office). *Telephone:* (203) 966-5216 (office). *Fax:* (203) 966-6340 (office). *E-mail:* tbickley@optonline.net (office).

GAINUTDIN, Ravil Ibn Ismail, PhD; Russian (Tartar) religious leader; *Chairman, Council of Muftis of Russia;* b. 25 Aug. 1959, Tatarstan; m.; two d.; ed Islam Medrese Mir-Arab Bukhara, Russian Acad. of State Service, Moscow; First Imam-Khatyb Kazan Mosque Nur Islam; Exec. Sec. Ecclesiastical Dept of Moslems, European Section of USSR and Siberia, Ufa 1985–87; Imam-Khatyb Moscow Mosque 1987–88; Chief Imam-Khatyb 1988–; Pres. Islam Cen. of Moscow and Moscow Region 1991–; Chair. Council of Muftis of Russia; Chair. Religious Bd of Muslims of European Part of Russia; Prof., Moscow Higher Islam Coll.; mem. Public Chamber, Russian Fed.; mem. Int. Acad. of Sciences of Eurasia, Int. Slavic Acad., Int. Acad. of Information; mem. Council on Co-operation with Religious Unions, Russian Presidency, Public Chamber of the Russian Fed.; Order of Friendship 1987, 1997, Order of Honour 2004, Public Recognition 2006. *Publications include:* Islam in Russia, Elections in Russia: The Muslims' Choice; books on Moslem dogma and rituals. *Address:* Religious Board of European Region of Russia, Council of Mufties of Russia, Vypolzov per. 7, 129090 Moscow, Russia (office). *Telephone:* (495) 681-49-04 (office); (495) 207-53-07 (home). *Fax:* (495) 681-49-04 (office). *E-mail:* info@muslim.ru (office). *Website:* www.muslim.ru (office).

GÁL, Zoltán, DJur; Hungarian lawyer and politician; m. Krisztina Pölz; one s.; ed Eötvös Loránd Univ.; with Trade Union HQ 1964–74; worked at Exec. and Admin. Dept of Cen. Cttee of HSWP 1974–86; Lecturer, Political Coll. 1987–89; Deputy Minister of Interior, then State Sec. and Minister of Interior 1987–90; mem. Parl. 1990–, mem. Cttee on Constitution, Legislation and Justice 1990–94, Chair. Cttee for Constitutional Reform 1994–, Speaker of Nat. Ass. 1994–98, Vice-Chair. Cttee on Constitution, Legislation and Justice 1998–, Chair. Cttee on Law Enforcement; Govt Spokesman 2002–; Leader, faction of Hungarian Socialist Party 1990–94. *Leisure interests:* tennis, swimming and reading. *Address:* Országgyülés (National Assembly), 1055 Budapest, Kossuth Lajos tér 1–3, Hungary. *Telephone:* (1) 441-4000 (office); (1) 200-6735 (home). *Fax:* (1) 441-5000 (office). *E-mail:* zoltan.gal@parlament.hu (office); gal.zoltan@nextraimail.hu (home). *Website:* www.mkogy.hu (office).

GALA, Antonio, LicenDer; Spanish writer; b. 2 Oct. 1930, Brazatortas, Ciudad Real; s. of Luis Gala and Adoración Velasco; ed Univs of Seville and Madrid; Founder-Pres., Fundación Antonio Gala; Dr hc (Univ. of Córdoba); Nat. Prize for Literature, Hidalgo Prize, Planeta Prize; many other literary and theatre awards. *Publications include:* plays: Los Verdes Campos del Edén, El caracol en el espejo 1964, El sol en el hormiguero 1966, Noviembre y un poco de hierba 1967, Canatr del Santiago para todos 1971, Los buenos días perdidos 1972, Suerte, campeón 1973, Anillos para una Dama 1973, Las cítaras colgadas de los árboles 1974, Por qué corres Ulises? 1975, Petra regalada 1980, La vieja señorita del paraíso 1980, El Cementerio de los Pájaros 1982, Trilogía de la libertad 1983, Samarkanda 1985, El hotelito 1985, Séneca o el beneficio de la duda 1987, Carmen Carmen 1988, La Truhana 1992, Los Bellos Durmientes 1994, Café Cantante 1997, Las manzanas del viernes 2000; novels: El Manuscrito Carmesí (Planeta Prize) 1990, La Pasión Turca 1993, Más Allá del Jardín 1995, La Regla de Tres 1996, El Corazón Tardío 1998, Las Afuneras de Dios 1999, El imposible olvido 2001, Los invitados al jardin 2002, El dueño de la herida 2003, El pedestal de las estatuas 2007, Los papeles de agua 2008, Cosas nuestras 2008; poetry: Enemigo Intimo 1959, 11 Sonetos de la Zubia 1981, Poemas Cordobeses 1994, Testamento andaluz 1994, Poemas de amor 1997, El poema de Tobías desangelado 2005; essays: Charlas con Troylo, En Propia Mano, Cuaderno de la Dama de Otoño, Dedicado a Tobias. *Address:* Fundación Antonio Gala, Calle Ambrosio de Morales, 20, 14003 Córdoba, Spain (office). *Telephone:* (957) 487395 (office). *Fax:* (957) 487423 (office). *E-mail:* info@fundacionantoniogala.org (office). *Website:* www.fundacionantoniogala.org (office); www.antoniogala.es.

GALADARI, Rashid Abdul Wahab; United Arab Emirates real estate industry executive; *Chairman, Galadari Investment Office (GIO);* b. 1976; s. of the late Abdul Wahab Galadari; f. Galvest (holding group for large family-owned business) 2005, Chair. Galadari Investment Office (GIO) (real estate and property devt co.) 2005–. *Address:* GIO Investments, PO Box 214472, 2nd Floor, Building 4, Emaar Business Park, Dubai, United Arab Emirates (office). *Telephone:* (4) 3689991 (office). *E-mail:* info@gio.ae (office). *Website:* www.gio.ae (office).

GALAL, Ahmed, BCom, MEconSc, PhD; Egyptian economist and politician; ed Cairo Univ., Ain Shams Univ., Boston Univ., USA; served for 18 years with World Bank, becoming Sr Economist, Vice-Pres. and Adviser on Middle East and N Africa 2006–07; Exec. Dir and Dir of Research, Egyptian Centre for Econ. Studies 1996–97, 2000–06; Man. Dir Econ. Research Forum, Cairo 2007–; Minister of Finance and the Budget 2013–14; mem. Int. Bd of Govs Int. Devt Research Centre, Canada 2007–; Founding Co-Chair. MENA Health Policy Forum, Jordan; Founding Bd mem. Zewail City for Science and Tech. 2011; mem. Forum Euroméditerranéen des Instituts de Sciences Économiques, France; Econ. and Social Sciences Prize, Kuwait Foundation for Advancement of Sciences 2004. *Publications include:* The Road Not Traveled: Education Reform in the Middle East and North Africa (co-author) 2007, Rethinking the Role of the State: Industrial Policy in the Middle East and North Africa (ed.) 2008, Do Governments Pick Winners or Losers? An Assessment of Industrial Policy in Egypt (co-author) 2008. *Address:* c/o Ministry of Finance, Ministry of Finance Towers, Cairo, (Nasr City), Egypt (office).

GALAL, Mohamed Noman, BA, MA, PhD; Egyptian diplomatist and academic; *Political Adviser, Ministry of Foreign Affairs, Bahrain* and *Secretary General of the Gulf Cooperation Council;* b. 10 April 1943, Assiut; m. Kawther Elsherif 1969; two s.; ed Univ. of Cairo; joined Egyptian Ministry of Foreign Affairs 1965; Third Sec., Embassy in Amman 1969–72; Vice-Consul, Kuwait 1972; Consul, Abu Dhabi 1972–73; Second Sec. Oslo 1975–79; Lecturer, Diplomatic Inst. 1979–80; First Sec., New Delhi 1980, Counsellor 1981–85; Counsellor, Cabinet of Deputy Prime Minister and Minister of Foreign Affairs 1985–87; Counsellor, Egyptian Mission at UN 1987–90, Minister and Deputy Perm. Rep. 1990–92; Perm. Rep. to League of Arab States, Cairo 1992–95; Amb. to Pakistan 1995–98, to People's Repub. of China 1998–2001; Visiting Lecturer, Farleigh Dickinson Univ., NJ, USA 1989–91, Univ. of Cairo 1994–95; fmr Deputy Dir Centre for Int. Studies, Univ. of Bahrain; Adviser for Strategic Int. Studies and Dialogue of Civilizations, Bahrain Centre for Studies and Research 2003–10; Advisor, Sec.-Gen. of the Gulf Cooperation Council; Political Adviser, Ministry of Foreign Affairs, Bahrain 2010–; mem. Nat. Council on Human Rights, Egypt 2004–10; expert on Chinese Affairs; mem. World Cultural Forum, Beijing, Chinese Studies Forum, Shanghai Acad. for Social Sciences; St Olav Medal (Norway) 1972, Nat. Medal for Merit (Egypt) 1982. *Publications:* more than 45 publs in Arabic and English on Arab and int. affairs, foreign policy, human rights, Egypt, Middle East, Pakistan, China, non-alignment, Islam in a changing world, human rights and Islam, Egyptian revolution of 25 Jan. 2011 etc.; contrib. to several Egyptian, Bahraini and Chinese newspapers. *Leisure interests:* travelling, swimming, Asian, Europe, US and Arab regions. *Address:* PO Box 547, Manama, Bahrain (office). *Telephone:* (17) 200858 (office); (17) 625072 (home). *Fax:* (17) 226862 (office); (17) 208531 (office); (17) 623492 (home). *E-mail:* mjalal@mofa.gov.bh (office); galal_m@hotmail.com (home). *Website:* www.mofa.gov.bh (office); mohamed-n-galal.com.

GALANOS, James; American fashion designer (retd) and photographer; b. 20 Sept. 1924, Philadelphia, Pa; s. of Gregory Galanos and Helen Galanos (née Gorgoliatos); ed Traphagen School of Fashion, New York 1943; began career selling sketches to New York clothing mfrs; worked for Hattie Carnegie 1944; asst to Jean Louis, head designer, Columbia Studios, Hollywood 1946–47; apprentice, Robert Piguet, Paris 1947–48; designer, Davidow, New York 1949–50; est. own business, Galanos Originals, Beverly Hills, Calif. 1951–63, LA 1963–; produced collection of couture-quality furs in collaboration with Neustadter Furs 1968; designed costumes for Rosalind Russell in films Never Wave at a WAC, 1952 and

Oh Dad, Poor Dad, Mama's Hung You in the Closet and I'm Feeling So Sad 1967; retrospective exhbns LA Co. Museum of Art 1974, 1997, Inst. of Tech., New York 1976, Western Reserve Historical Soc. 1996, LA Co. Museum of Art 1997; designed Inaugural Gown worn by Nancy Reagan 1981; work represented in perm. collections including Metropolitan Museum of Art, New York, Smithsonian Inst. Washington and Art Inst. of Chicago; took up art photography 2006; Council of Fashion Designers of America Lifetime Achievement Award 1985 and numerous fashion awards. *Leisure interests:* collecting art books, music, reading, architecture. *Address:* 1316 Sunset Plaza Drive, Los Angeles, CA 90069-1235 (office); 2254 South Sepulveda Blvd., Los Angeles, CA 90064, USA. *Telephone:* (213) 272-1445. *Fax:* (310) 473-6725.

GALANTE, Edward G., BSc; American oil industy executive; b. Inwood, NY; ed Northeastern Univ.; joined Exxon Co. 1972, Man. Baton Rouge Refinery, LA 1988, CEO and Gen. Man. Esso Caribbean and Central America 1992, Exec. Asst to Chair. Exxon Corpn 1995, Chair. and Man. Dir Esso (Thailand) Public Co. Ltd, Bangkok 1997, Exec. Vice-Pres. Exxon Mobil Chemical Co., Houston, Tex. 1999, Sr Vice-Pres. Exxon Mobil Corpn 2001–06 (retd); Vice-Chair. US Council for Int. Business 2004; mem. Bd of Dirs Foster Wheeler AG 2008–; fmr Dir Nat. Council, Northeastern Univ., Council for the US and Italy, Council of the Americas, Jr Achievement Int., US–China Business Council. *Address:* 6414 Waggoner Drive, Dallas, TX 75230, USA.

GALASSI, Jonathan White, MA; American publishing executive; *President, Farrar, Straus & Giroux Inc.;* b. 4 Nov. 1949, Seattle, Wash.; s. of Gerard Goodwin Galassi and Dorothea Johnston Galassi (née White); m. Susan Grace Galassi 1975; two d.; ed Harvard Univ., Univ. of Cambridge, UK; Ed. Houghton Mifflin Co., Boston, New York 1973–81; Sr Ed. Random House, Inc., New York 1981–86; Exec. Ed. and Vice-Pres. Farrar, Straus & Giroux Inc., New York 1986–87, Ed.-in-Chief and Sr Vice-Pres. 1988–93, Exec. Vice-Pres. 1993–99, Publr 1999–, Pres. 2002–; Poetry Ed. Paris Review 1978–88; Guggenheim Fellow 1989; mem. Acad. of American Poets (Dir 1990–2002, Pres. 1994–99, Chair. 1999–2002, Hon. Chair. 2002–); Fellow, American Acad. of Arts and Sciences 2002; Roger Klein Award for Editing, PEN 1984, Award in Literature, American Acad. of Arts and Letters 2000. *Publications:* Morning Run (poetry) 1988, The Second Life of Art: Selected Essays of Eugenio Montale (ed., trans.) 1982, Otherwise: Last and First Poems of Eugenio Montale (ed., trans.) 1986, Eugenio Montale, Collected Poems 1916–56 (ed., trans.) 1998 (revised edn 2012), North Street (poetry) 2000, Eugenio Montale, Posthumous Diary 2001, Giacomo Leopardi, Canti (ed, trans.) 2010, Left-handed (poetry) 2012. *Address:* Farrar, Straus & Giroux Inc., 18 W 18th Street, New York, NY 10011, USA (office). *Telephone:* (212) 741-6900 (office). *Website:* www.fsgbooks.com (office).

GALATERI DI GENOLA, Count Gabriele, DIur, MBA; Italian business executive; *Chairman, Assicurazioni Generali SpA;* b. 11 Jan. 1947, Rome; s. of Gen. Angelo Galateri di Genola and Carla Fontana; m. Evelina Christillin; one d.; ed Liceo Ennio Quirino Visconti, Rome, Univ. of Rome, Columbia Univ., New York; Asst Lecturer in Econ. Science, Univ. of Rome 1969–70; Head Financial Analysis Dept, later Int. Financing Dept, Banco di Roma 1971–74; Financial Dir Saint Gobain, Italy, then Asst to Financial Group Dir, Paris 1974–77; Head of Foreign Finance Div., Fiat SpA 1977–83, Financial Dir 1983–86, CEO 2002–03; CEO Ifil SpA 1986–93; CEO and Gen. Man. IFI 1993–2002; Chair. Mediobanca SpA 2003–07; Chair. Telecom Italia SpA 2007–11, currently mem. Bd of Dirs; Vice-Chair. Assicurazioni Generali SpA 2003–10, Chair. 2011–; Chair. TIM Brasil Serviços e Parícipações SA; Vice-Chair. RCS MediaGroup SpA; Dir (non-exec.) TIM Participações SA, Banca CRS SpA, Banca CARIGE, Italmobiliare SpA, Azimut-Benetti SpA, Fiera di Genova SpA, Accad. Nazionale di Santa Cecilia – Foundation, Edenred SA; Chair. Italian Inst. of Tech.; mem. Int. Advisory Bd of Columbia Business School; Cavaliere del Lavoro. *Leisure interests:* arts, music, tennis, skiing, gym. *Address:* Assicurazioni Generali SpA, Piazza Duca degli Abruzzi 2, 34132 Trieste, Italy (office). *Telephone:* (040) 6711 (office). *Fax:* (040) 671600 (office). *E-mail:* info@generali.com (office). *Website:* www.generali.com (office).

GALAYR, Ali Khalif, BA, MA, PhD; Somali politician and academic; b. 15 Oct. 1941, Las Anod; ed Boston Univ., Syracuse Univ., USA; Political Officer, Ministry of Interior 1965–67; Training and Research Officer, Somali Inst. of Public Admin 1970–73, Dir Gen. 1973–74; Dir Gen. Jowhar Sugar Enterprise 1974–76; Exec. Chair. Juba Sugar Project 1976–80; Minister of Industry 1980–82; Fellow, Center for Int. Affairs, Harvard Univ., USA 1982–84, Fellow, Center for Middle Eastern Studies 1984–86; consultant on devt issues 1986–89; Asst Prof., Dept of Public Admin, Maxwell School, Syracuse Univ. 1989–91, Assoc. Prof. 1991–94, Prof. of Public Admin and Int. Relations 1994–96; Chair. and CEO SOMTEL, Sharjah, UAE 1996–2000; Prime Minister of Somalia 2000–01; Visiting Prof., Humphrey Inst., Univ. of Minnesota 2002–06; unsuccessful presidential cand. 2009.

GALE, Gwendoline Fay, AO, PhD, DUniv; Australian geographer and fmr university vice-chancellor; b. (Gwendoline Fay Gilding), 13 June 1932, Balaklava, S Australia; d. of George Jasper Gilding and Kathleen Gertrude Pengelley; one s. one d.; ed Methodist Ladies' Coll., Univ. of Adelaide, S Australia; Lecturer, then Sr Lecturer, Univ. of Adelaide 1966–74, Reader 1975–77, Prof. of Geography 1978–89, Pro-Vice-Chancellor 1988–89, Prof. Emer. 1989–; Australian Heritage Commr 1989–95; Vice-Chancellor Univ. of Western Australia 1990–97; Pres. Inst. of Australian Geographers 1989–90; Chair. Social Justice Advisory Cttee 1989; Chair. Festival of Perth 1992–97; Chair. West Australian Symphony Orchestra 1995–97; Pres. Australian Vice-Chancellors Cttee 1996–97; Fellow, Acad. of Social Sciences in Australia 1978, Pres. 1998–2000, Hon. Fellow 2001; Pres. Asscn Asian Social Science Councils 2001–03; Elin Wagner Fellowship 1971, Catherine Helen Spence Fellowship 1972; mem. Nat. Comm. of UNESCO, Australia 1999–, Australian Research Council 1999–2001; Hon. Life mem. Inst. of Australian Geographers 1994, Hon. Fellow, Asscn for Tertiary Educ. Man. 2003; Hon. DLitt (Western Australia) 1998; British Council Award 1972, John Lewis Gold Medal 2000, Griffith Taylor Medal 2001. *Publications:* Women's Role in Aboriginal Society (ed.) 1970, Urban Aborigines 1972, Race Relations in Australia: the Aboriginal Situation 1975, Poverty Among Aboriginal Families in Adelaide 1975, We are Bosses Ourselves: the Status and Role of Aboriginal Women Today (ed.) 1983, Tourists and the National Estate: Procedures to protect Australia's Heritage 1987, Aboriginal Youth and the Criminal Justice System: the Injustice of Justice

1990, Inventing Places: Studies in Cultural Geography 1991, Changing Australia 1991, Boyer Lectures 1991, Juvenile Justice: Debating the Issues 1993, Tourism and the Protection of Aboriginal Sites 1994, Cultural Geographies 1999, Making Space: Women and Education at St Aloysius College Adelaide 1880–2000 (ed.) 2000, Youth in Transition: The Challenges of Generational Change in Asia (ed.) 2005. *Leisure interests:* music, theatre, reading. *Address:* c/o Office of the Vice-Chancellor, The University of Adelaide, Adelaide, S Australia 5005, Australia.

GALEA, Censu; Maltese architect and politician; b. 28 Aug. 1956; s. of Joseph Galea; m. Grace Sammut; two s. two d.; ed Lyceum and Univ. of Malta; practising architect 1982; Sec.-Gen. then Pres. of Nationalist Party Youth Section 1978–81; MP (Nationalist Party) 1987–; Parl. Sec., Ministry for Social Security 1992–94; Minister for Food, Agric. and Fisheries 1994–96, for Transport and Communications 1998–2004, for Competitiveness and Communications 2004–08; Shadow Minister and Opposition Spokesman for Transport and Ports 1996–98; Sec. and Whip Nationalist Party Parl. Group 1997–98. *Address:* House of Representatives, The Palace, Valletta VLT 1115, Malta (office). *Telephone:* 25596000 (office). *Fax:* 25596314 (office). *E-mail:* parlinfo@parlament.mt (office). *Website:* parlament.mt (office).

GALEA, Louis, BA, LLD; Maltese lawyer and politician; *Auditor, European Court of Auditors;* b. 2 Jan. 1948, Mqabba; s. of Joseph Galea and Joan Galea (née Farrugia); m. Vincienne Zammit 1977; one s. three d.; mem. Gen. Council and Exec. Cttee Nationalist Party 1972–, Gen. Sec. 1977–87; mem. Parl. 1976–2008; Minister for Social Policy including Health 1987–92, for Home Affairs and Social Devt including Health 1992–95, Minister for Social Devt 1995–96; Shadow Minister for Educ. 1996–98; Minister of Educ. 1998–2008; Speaker, House of Reps 2008–10; Auditor, European Court of Auditors 2010–. *Leisure interests:* reading, music, tennis. *Address:* European Court of Auditors, 12, rue Alcide De Gasperi, 1615 Luxembourg, Luxembourg (office). *Telephone:* 4398-1 (office). *Fax:* 439342 (office). *E-mail:* eca-info@eca.europa.eu (office). *Website:* www.eca.europa.eu (office).

GALEYEV, Albert Abubakirovich, Dr PhysMathSC; Russian/Bashkir physicist; *Director, Institute of Space Research, Russian Academcy of Sciences;* b. 19 Oct. 1940, Ufa; m.; two c.; ed Univ. of Novosibirsk; worked at USSR Acad. of Sciences Inst. of Nuclear Physics 1961–70; Sr researcher at Acad. of Sciences Inst. of High Temperatures 1970–73; mem. CPSU 1976–91; Corresp. mem. USSR (now Russian) Acad. of Sciences 1987–92, mem. 1992; Head of Section at Acad. of Sciences Inst. of Space Research 1973–88, Dir 1988–; Ed.-in-Chief Earth Research from Space; Lenin Prize 1984, Order the Badge of Honour 2002. *Publications:* works on physics of plasma and cosmic physics. *Address:* Institute of Space Research, 117810 Moscow, Profsoyuznaya 84/32, Russia (office). *Telephone:* (495) 333-25-88 (office); (495) 135-10-94 (home). *Fax:* (495) 333-33-11 (office). *E-mail:* agaleyev@iki.rssi.ru (office).

GALGUT, Damon; South African playwright and novelist; b. 1963, Pretoria; ed Univ. of Cape Town; CNA Award 1992, Univ. of Johannesburg Prize 2008. *Plays:* Echoes of Anger, Party for Mother, Alive and Kicking, The Green's Keeper. *Publications include:* A Sinless Season 1984, Small Circle of Beings 1988, The Beautiful Screaming of Pigs 1991, The Quarry 1995, The Good Doctor (Commonwealth Writers Prize for Best Book, Africa Region 2004) 2003, The Impostor 2008, In a Strange Room 2010. *Address:* Peake Associates, 14 Grafton Crescent, London, NW1 8SL, England (office). *E-mail:* tony@tonypeake.com (office). *Fax:* (020) 7482-0609 (office). *Website:* www.tonypeake.com (office).

GALIBIN, Aleksander Vladimirovich; Russian actor and theatre director; b. 28 Sept. 1955, Leningrad; m.; three d.; ed Leningrad State Inst. of Theatre, Music and Cinematography, A. Vasilyev Drama School, Moscow; actor, Komissarzhevskaya Drama Theatre 1977–79; Stage Dir Aleksandrinsky Theatre 1995–; worked as stage dir in various St Petersburg theatres 1990–; Meritorious Artist of the RSFSR 1991. *Films include:* acted in more than 35 films 1976–, including Pyatnitskaya Street, Courage, Silver Strings, Letters from the Front, Red Crown, Ragin 2004, Master and Margarita 2005, The First Rule of the Queen 2005, Him, Her and Me 2007, Revenge 2007, 40 2007. *Theatre includes:* (stage dir) Three Sisters, Harp of Greeting, City Romance, Pupil, Tsar Piotr and His Dead Son Aleksey. *Address:* Griboyedova Canal 115, Apt 9, 190088 St Petersburg, Russia. *Telephone:* (812) 114-16-80.

GALIL, Zvi, BSc, MSc, PhD; Israeli computer scientist, academic and university administrator; b. 26 June 1947, Tel-Aviv; m. Bella Gorenstein Galil; one s.; ed Tel-Aviv Univ., Cornell Univ., USA; conducted postdoctoral research at IBM Thomas J. Watson Research Center, Yorktown Heights, NY 1975; Faculty mem. Computer Science Dept, Tel-Aviv Univ. 1976–81, Full Prof. 1981–95, Dept Chair. 1979–82; Prof., Dept of Computer Science, Columbia Univ., New York City 1982–2006, Chair. Dept of Computer Science 1989–94, Julian Clarence Levi Prof. of Math. Methods and Computer Science, School of Eng and Applied Sciences 1987–2006, Dean, Fu Foundation School of Eng and Applied Sciences, Columbia Univ. 1995–2006; Pres. Tel-Aviv Univ. 2007–09 (resgnd); Area Ed. Journal of the ACM (Asscn for Computing Machinery) 1984–2004; Ed. in Chief Journal of Algorithms 1988–2004; Man. Ed. SIAM (Soc. for Industrial and Applied Math.) Journal on Computing 1991–97; Chief Computer Science Adviser in the US to Oxford University Press 1992–2003; mem. Nat. Acad. of Eng 2004–; Fellow, American Acad. of Arts and Sciences 2005–, Asscn for Computing Machinery 1995; Dir Guglielmo Marconi Int. Fellowship Foundation 1997–; Guarantor, Italian Acad. for Advance Studies in America 1997–; Pupin Medal 2005. *Publications:* Combinatorial Algorithms on Words (co-ed.) 1985, SIAM Journal of Computing Special Issue on Cryptography (ed.) 1988, Theory of Computing and Systems, Lecture Notes in Computer Science 601 (co-ed.) 1992, Combinatorial Pattern Matching III, Lecture Notes in Computer Science 644 (co-ed.) 1992, Pattern Matching Algorithms (co-ed.) 1997; has written more than 200 scientific papers. *Address:* c/o Electrical Engineering Departmental Office, Columbia University, 1300 S.W. Mudd, 500 West 120th Street, New York, NY 10027, USA.

GALIMOV, Erik Mikhailovich, PhD, DSc; Russian geochemist; *Director, V.I. Vernadsky Institute of Geochemistry and Analytical Chemistry, Russian Academy of Sciences;* b. 29 July 1936, Vladivostok; s. of Mikhail Piskunov and Zeya Galimova; m. 1st; one d.; m. 2nd Galina Andriukhina; two d.; ed Moscow Inst. of Oil and Gas; operational engineer 1959–60; head of geophysics expeditions 1960–63; sr researcher 1965–73; Dir V. I. Vernadsky Inst. of Geochemistry and Analytical Chem. 1992– (Head of Lab. 1973–92); Prof., Moscow State Univ.; Chair. Geochemistry Council of Russian Acad. of Sciences, Int. Lunar Exploration Working Group; Vice-Pres. Int. Asscn of Geochemical Cosmochemistry 1996–2000, Pres. 2000–04; Ed.-in-Chief International Geochemistry; mem. Editorial Bd Chemical Geology, Astrobiology; Corresp. mem. USSR (now Russian) Acad. of Sciences 1991, mem. 1994–, mem. Presidium 2002–, Chair. Meteorite Cttee; Foreign mem. German Acad. of Sciences and Literature 1998; Geochemical Fellow 1998; research in geochemistry of stable isotopes, organic geochemistry and oil and gas geology, lunar and planetary research, origin of life; Order of Honour 1988, 1996; Vernadsky Prize 1984, Alfred Treibs Medal 2004. *Achievement:* developed theory of ordered isotope distribution in biological systems, devt of isotope thermodynamics, cavitational synthesis of diamond, isotope identification of oil and gas sources, new concept of sustaining ordering as a mechanism of life emerging and evolution, new model of Earth and the Moon formation as a twin system. *Publications:* more than 400 scientific works including Geochemistry of Stable Carbon Isotopes 1968, Carbon Isotopes in Oil and Gas Geology 1973, Biological Isotope Fractionation 1985, Sources and Mechanism of Formation of Natural Gases 1988, Kimberlite Magmatism and Diamond Formation 1991, Evolution of the Biosphere 1995, Origin of the Moon 1996, Origin of the Moon — New Concept: Geochemistry and Dynamics (co-author) 2012. *Address:* V.I. Vernadsky Institute of Geochemistry and Analytical Chemistry, Kosygin Street 19, 119991 Moscow (office); Nikitski Blvd 5–5, 119019 Moscow, Russia (home). *Telephone:* (495) 137-41-27 (office); (495) 291-48-60 (home). *Fax:* (495) 938-20-54 (home). *E-mail:* galimov@geokhi.ru (office). *Website:* www.geokhi.ru/eng (office).

GALIN, Alexander; Russian playwright, actor and film and theatre director; b. (Aleksandr Mikhailovich Pourer), 10 Sept. 1947, Rostovskaja oblast, USSR; s. of Mikhail Pourer and Lubov Pourer; m. Galina Alekseyevna Pourer 1950; one s.; ed Inst. of Culture, Leningrad; factory worker, later actor in puppet theatre; freelance writer 1978–; Amb. of the Arts, Fla 1989. *Plays include:* The Wall 1971, Here Fly the Birds 1974, The Hole 1975, The Roof 1976, Retro 1979, The Eastern Tribune 1980, Stars in the Morning Sky 1982, The Toastmaster 1983, Jeanne 1986, The Librarian 1987, Sorry 1990, The Title 1991, The Czech Photo 1993, The Clown and the Bandit 1996, The Anomaly 1996, Sirena and Victoria 1997, The Competition 1998; plays translated into several languages include Stars in the Morning Sky (selected plays translated into English) 1989, The Group 1995, Rendez-Vous in the Sea of Rain 2002, New Logic 2005, Dream of the Heroine 2005, The Companions 2008, Dzinrikisya 2009, The Face 2010, Golden Time, or Reading 'Candide' 2011, The Face 2012. *Films include:* Casanova's Coat (The Delegation) (scriptwriter and dir) 1993, Photo (scriptwriter, actor and dir) 2003, My Last Will (screenplay) 2004, The Heathen (screenplay) 2005, The Casualty (scriptwriter and dir) 2009. *Publications include:* Selected Plays 1989, Do-re-mi-do-re-do Novel 2013. *Address:* Gorohovsky pereulok 15, Apt 11, 103064 Moscow, Russia (home). *Telephone:* (499) 267-70-21 (home). *Fax:* (499) 267-70-21 (home). *E-mail:* galinalexander@gmail.com. *Website:* www.a-galin.ru.

GALJAARD, Hans, MD, PhD; Dutch professor of cell biology (retd); b. 8 April 1935, Leiden; m. Henriette H. van Boven 1960; two s. one d.; ed State Univ. Leiden; radiobiology training at Medical Biology Lab. Nat. Defence Org. Rijswijk 1962–65 and Atomic Energy Research Establishment, Harwell, England 1965; Prof. of Cell Biology, Erasmus Univ. Rotterdam 1966; Chair. Dept of Clinical Genetics, Univ. Hosp. 1980; Dir Rotterdam Foundation of Clinical Genetics 1980; mem. Nat. Health Council, Nat. Council for Science Policy, Advisory Council on Tech.; consultant for WHO and UNFPA; mem. Royal Dutch Acad. of Sciences 1984–, Acad. Europaea; Hon. mem. Dutch Soc. for Human Genetics, Indian Soc. for Prenatal Diagnosis and Therapy; Carter Memorial Medal, British Clincial Genetics Soc., Van Walree Prijs 1997. *Publications:* The Life of the Dutch 1981, Alle mensen zijn ongelijk 1994; approximately 400 articles in scientific journals, book chapters and monographs. *Leisure interests:* writing, filming, sailing. *Address:* c/o Department of Cell Biology, Erasmus University, Faculty Building, Dr. Molewaterplein 50, 3015 GE Rotterdam, Netherlands.

GALKO, Ľubomír; Slovak software engineer and politician; b. 14 Feb. 1968, Kliestina; m.; two c.; ed Technical High School of Mechanical Eng, Comenius Univ., Bratislava; Computer Programmer, Computer Tech. Enterprise, Bratislava 1991–92; Programmer-Analyst, CK Arrangement and Consulting Ltd, Bratislava 1992–93; man. with chain of retail and wholesale stores, responsible for software applications devt, Bratislava 1993–2001; Dir Kaufland Hypermarket, Bratislava 2001–03; Deputy Dir Interfruct Slovakia Co., Bratislava 2003–04; Dir DONA DN Co. (jt stock co.), Bratislava 2004–10; Minister of Defence 2010–11 (dismissed); mem. Freedom and Solidarity party 2009–; Deputy, Nat. Council of the Slovak Repub.. *E-mail:* lubomir_galko@nrsr.sk (office). *Website:* www.lubomirgalko.sk.

GALL, Hugues R.; French opera house director; b. 18 March 1940, Honfleur; s. of Max Gall and Geneviève Carel; ed Inst. des Sciences Politiques, Sorbonne; fmr official, Ministries of Agric., Educ. and Culture; Sec.-Gen. Réunion des Théâtres Lyriques 1969–73; Deputy Dir-Gen. Paris Opéra 1973–80; Dir-Gen. Grand Théatre, Geneva 1980–94; Dir-Gen. Paris Opéra 1995–2004; Chair. Bd of Dirs Institut pour le Financement du Cinéma et des Industries Culturelles 2004–; Conseiller d'État 2004–; Dir École du Louvre 2004–, Fondation Noureev 2004–, Fondation d'entreprise Veolia Environnement 2004–, Théâtre de l'Opéra-Comique 2004–; Pres. Orchestre Français des Jeunes 2007–; elected mem. Acad. des Beaux-Arts, Inst. de France 2002; Officier des Palmes académiques, Chevalier du Mérite agricole, Commdr des Arts et des Lettres, Légion d'honneur, Ordre nat. du Mérite, Bourgeois d'honneur de Genève, Switzerland; Prix Montaigne 1996, Prix Grand Siècle-Laurent Perrier 1999, Médaille Beaumarchais de la SACD 2004.

GALL, Joseph Grafton, BS, PhD; American biologist and academic; *American Cancer Society Professor of Developmental Genetics, Department of Embryology, Carnegie Institution;* b. 14 April 1928, Washington, DC; s. of the late John C. Gall and Elsie Gall (née Rosenberger); m. 1st Dolores M. Hogge 1955; one s. one d.; m. 2nd Diane M. Dwyer 1982; ed Yale Univ.; Instructor, Asst Prof., Assoc. Prof., Prof., Dept of Zoology, Univ. of Minnesota 1952–64; Prof. of Biology and Molecular Biophysics and Biochemistry, Yale Univ. 1964–83; mem. staff Dept of Embryology, Carnegie Inst. 1983–; American Cancer Soc. Prof. of Developmental Genetics 1984 (lifetime appointment); mem. Cell Biology Study Section, NIH 1963–67, Chair.

1972–74; Pres. American Soc. for Cell Biology 1968, Soc. for Developmental Biology 1984–85; mem. Bd of Scientific Counsellors, Nat. Inst. of Child Health and Human Devt, NIH 1986–90; mem. Bd of Scientific Advisers, Jane Coffin Childs Memorial Fund for Medical Research 1986–94; Visiting Prof., St Andrews Univ., UK 1960, 1968, Univ. of Leicester 1971; Visiting Scientist, Max Planck Inst., Tübingen, Germany 1960; mem. NAS, AAAS, American Acad. of Arts and Sciences, American Philosophical Soc., Accad. Naz. dei Lincei (Rome) 1988; Fellow, Yale Corpn 1989–95; Hon. DrMed (Charles Univ., Prague) 2002; E.B. Wilson Medal, American Soc. for Cell Biology 1983, Wilbur Cross Medal of Yale Univ. 1988, AAAS Mentor Award for Lifetime Achievement 1996, Jan E. Purkyne Medal, Czech Acad. of Science 1999, Lifetime Achievement Award, Soc. for Developmental Biology 2004, Albert Lasker Special Achievement in Medical Science Award 2006, Louisa Gross Horwitz Prize (co-recipient) 2007. *Publications:* scientific articles on chromosome structure, nucleic acid biochemistry, cell fine structure, organelles of the cell. *Leisure interest:* collecting books on the history of biology. *Address:* Department of Embryology, Carnegie Institution, 3520 San Martin Drive, Baltimore, MD 21218 (office); 107 Bellemore Road, Baltimore, MD 21210, USA (home). *Telephone:* (410) 246-3017 (office). *Fax:* (410) 243-6311 (office). *E-mail:* gall@ciwemb.edu (office). *Website:* www.ciwemb.edu (office).

GALLAGHER, Conrad; Irish chef and restaurateur; b. Letterkenny, Donegal; m. Domini Kemp (divorced); one c.; began career working in Great Northern Hotel, Bundoran and Renvale House, Connemara; moved to New York aged 17, chef at Queen's Restaurant, Blue Street, then the Plaza Hotel, then Waldorf Astoria Hotel; chef at Hotel de Paris, Monte Carlo; Founder and fmr owner Peacock Alley restaurant and Lloyd's Brasserie, Dublin, Conrad Gallagher, London; Group Exec. Consultant Chef and Dir of Food and Beverage (consulting), Sun Int. Group 2004–; with South African Airways 2005–06; Founder Conrad Gallagher Consulting Pty. Ltd 2005–; Best Irish Chef 1994, Michelin Star 1998. *Television:* Conrad's Kitchen, BBC Food Channel. *Publications:* New Irish Cooking, One Pot Wonders, Take 6 Ingredients: Simple Ideas Make Delicious Meals 2003. *Address:* Salon des Saveurs, 16 Aungier Street, Dublin 2, Ireland.

GALLAGHER, Katy, BA; Australian social worker, trade union organizer and politician; *Chief Minister of the Australian Capital Territory;* b. 17 March 1970, Weston Creek, Canberra, ACT; pnr Dave Skinner; one s. one d. and one d. with fiancé Brett Seaman (died 1997); ed Melrose High School, Stirling Coll., Australian Nat. Univ.; started career as social worker; worked as an advocate for People First ACT 1994–97; joined Community and Public Sector Union 1997, initially working as a case manager and then as a nat. organizer; mem. ACT Legis. Ass. (Australian Labor Party) for Molonglo constituency 2001–; Deputy Chief Minister of ACT with responsibilities including Disability and Community Services, and Women 2006–11, for Children and Young People 2007–11; ACT Minister for Health 2006–; Treas. of ACT 2008–; Minister for Industrial Relations 2009–; Chief Minister of ACT 2011–. *Address:* ACT Legislative Assembly, GPO Box 1020, Canberra, ACT 2601, Australia (office). *Telephone:* (2) 6205-0840 (office). *Fax:* (2) 6205-3030 (office). *E-mail:* gallagher@act.gov.au (office). *Website:* www.chiefminister.act.gov.au (office); www.act.gov.au (office).

GALLAGHER, Liam (William John Paul); British singer, musician (guitar, keyboards) and producer; b. 21 Sept. 1972, Burnage, Manchester; s. of Peggy Gallagher; brother of Noel Gallagher (q.v.); m. 1st Patsy Kensit 1997 (divorced 2000); one s.; one d. (with Lisa Moorish); m. 2nd Nicole Appleton; one s.; ed St Mark's High School, Didsbury, Manchester; founder mem., Oasis 1991–2009; f. and recorded for Big Brother Records 2000–; founder mem., Beady Eye 2009–; numerous concert and festival appearances; regular tours UK, Europe and USA; Q Awards for Best New Act 1994, Best Live Act 1995, BRIT Awards for Best Newcomers 1995, Best Single, Best Video, Best British Group 1996, NME Awards for Best UK Band, Artist of the Year 2003, Q Award for Best Act in the World Today 2006, BRIT Award for Outstanding Contribution to Music 2007. *Recordings include:* albums: with Oasis: Definitely Maybe 1994, (What's The Story) Morning Glory? (BRIT Award for Best Album 1996) 1995, Be Here Now 1997, The Masterplan 1998, Standing On The Shoulder of Giants 2000, Familiar To Millions (live) 2001, Heathen Chemistry 2002, Don't Believe The Truth (Q Award for Best Album) 2005, Stop the Clocks 2006, Dig Out Your Soul 2008; with Beady Eye: Different Gear, Still Speeding 2011, BE 2013. *Address:* Ignition Management, 54 Linhope Street, London, NW1 6HL, England (office). *Telephone:* (20) 7298-6000 (office). *Fax:* (20) 7258-0962 (office). *E-mail:* mail@ignition-man.co.uk (office). *Website:* www.oasisinet.com.

GALLAGHER, Noel David Thomas; British singer, songwriter and musician (guitar); b. 29 May 1967, Burnage, Manchester; s. of Peggy Gallagher; brother of Liam Gallagher (q.v.); m. Meg Matthews 1997 (divorced 2001); one d.; pnr Sara MacDonald; one s.; fmrly worked as guitar technician for Inspiral Carpets 1990–93; mem., Oasis 1991–2009; f. and recorded for Big Brother Records 2000–; numerous concert and festival appearances; regular tours UK, Europe and USA; founder Sour Mash Records 2001–; mem. Tailgunner; Q Awards for Best New Act 1994, Best Live Act 1995, BRIT Awards for Best Newcomers 1995, Best Single, Best Video, Best British Group 1996, Ivor Novello Award 1995, Music Week Award for Top Songwriter 1996, Grammy Award for Best Song (Wonderwall) 1997, NME Awards for Best UK Band, Artist of the Year 2003, Q Award for Best Act in the World Today 2006, BRIT Award for Outstanding Contribution to Music 2007. *Recordings include:* albums: Definitely Maybe 1994, (What's The Story) Morning Glory? (BRIT Award for Best Album 1996) 1995, Be Here Now 1997, The Masterplan 1998, Standing On The Shoulder of Giants 2000, Familiar To Millions (live) 2001, Heathen Chemistry 2002, Don't Believe The Truth (Q Award for Best Album) 2005, Stop the Clocks 2006, Dig Out Your Soul 2008, High Flying Birds 2011. *Leisure interest:* supporting Manchester City football club. *Address:* Ignition Management, 54 Linhope Street, London, NW1 6HL, England (office). *Telephone:* (20) 7298-6000 (office). *Fax:* (20) 7258-0962 (office). *E-mail:* mail@ignition-man.co.uk (office). *Website:* www.oasisinet.com.

GALLAND, Yves; French politician and business executive; *President, Boeing France;* b. 8 March 1941; s. of Jean Galland and Suzanne Vershave; m. Anne Marie Chauvin 1967; one s. two d.; pres. of publishing and publicity cos 1969; mem. European Parl. 1979–, Vice-Pres. 1989–91; Deputy Mayor of Paris in charge of housing 1983–95, of architecture 1995–1998; Minister of Local Affairs and Decentralization 1986–88, of Industry 1995, of Finance and Foreign Trade

1995–97; Pres. Valoise Radical Party 1988–94; mem. Nat. Council Union pour la démocratie française (UDF), del. to Paris 1979, mem. Nat. Political Bureau 1984–, Pres. Liberal Group, European Parl. 1991–94; Pres. UDF Group 1998–; Chair. European Assistance Group 2000–03; Vice-Pres. Int. Relations, Boeing Corpn 2003–, Pres. Boeing France 2003–. *Address:* Boeing, 75 rue du Faubourg Saint-Honoré, 75008 Paris (office); 6 rue des Haudriettes, 75003 Paris, France. *Telephone:* 1-70-37-07-47 (office). *E-mail:* BoeingFranceCommunication@boeing .com (office). *Website:* www.boeing.fr (office).

GALLEGOS, Carlos M., BS (Econs), MA; Peruvian economist and international organization executive; *Executive Secretary, Inter-American Committee on Ports (Comisión Interamericana de Puertos—CIP);* m.; two c.; ed Universidad La Molina, Lima, Univ. of East Anglia, UK; was involved with Peru's regional econ. integration process, served in govt agencies as Country Economist, Dir of Econ. Studies, Trade Sr Advisor and Financial Advisor to Andean Financial Corpn (CAF), among others; joined OAS in 1980, has served in high-level positions in int. trade, customs and other trade facilitation areas, Exec. Sec. Inter-American Cttee on Ports (Comisión Interamericana de Puertos—CIP), OAS, Washington, DC 1993–, OAS Rep. to IMO, Int. Asscn of Ports and Harbors, American Asscn of Port Authorities and other int. maritime port orgs; lectures at univs and grad. academic centres in Latin America and Spain. *Publications:* numerous papers, studies and articles in professional journals. *Address:* Inter-American Committee on Ports, 1889 F Street, NW, Suite 695, Washington, DC 20006, USA (office). *Telephone:* (202) 458-3871 (office). *Fax:* (202) 458-3517 (office). *E-mail:* cgallegos@oas.org (office). *Website:* www.oas.org/cip (office).

GALLIANO, John, CBE; British fashion designer; b. (Juan Carlos Antonio Galliano Guillén), 28 Nov. 1960, Gibraltar; s. of John J. Galliano and Anita Guillén; ed Wilson's Grammar School, Wallington, Central St Martin's Coll. of Art and Design, London; moved to Streatham, southwest London 1966, and later to Brockley; designer collections 1985–; worked on Courtelle project 1985; first British designer ever to show collection in Paris at the Louvre during Paris Fashion Week 1990; moved to Paris and introduced Galliano's Girl 1991; designer of costumes for Ballet Rambert 1990, Kylie Minogue's Let's Get to It UK tour 1991; Chief Designer Givenchy 1995–96, Christian Dior 1996–2011, launched 'galliano' womenswear collection 2007; recreated some of Dior's period clothing for Madonna in the film Evita; other clients have included Charlize Theron, Riley Keough (granddaughter of Elvis Presley), Kate Moss, Cate Blanchett, Nicole Kidman, Daphne Guinness and the late Princess Diana; found guilty by a French court of racial insults and fined Sept. 2011; British Designer of Year Award, British Council 1987, 1994, 1995, 1997 (co-recipient), Dress of the Year, Fashion Museum, Bath 1988, Int. Womenswear Designer of the Year, CFDA 1997, VH1 Womenswear Designer of the Year 1997, Int. Designer Award, Council of Fashion Designers of America 1998, Royal Designer for Industry 2002, appeared on The Independent on Sunday's 'pink list' for being one of "the most influential gay people in Britain" 2007 and other awards. *Address:* John Galliano, 384–386 rue St Honoré, 75001 Paris; 60 rue d'Avron, 75020 Paris, France. *Telephone:* 1-55-35-40-40. *Website:* www.johngalliano.com.

GALLIENNE, Guillaume; French actor and film director; b. 8 Feb. 1972, Neuilly-sur-Seine (Hauts-de-Seine); ed Conservatoire national; mem. Comédie-Française co. 1998–, Sociétaire 2005–; collaborated on writing of ballet Le Riche for paris Opera 2005; staged Huis Clos by Jean-Paul Sartre at Tessenkaï Noh Theatre, Tokyo 2006, Sur la Grand-rout by Anton Chekhov at Studio-Théâtre, Comédie-Française 2007; cr. Les Garçons et Guillaume, à table! (Molière de la Révélation Théâtrale Masculine 2010, Prix Nouveau Talent Humour/One Man Show, SACD 2010, Prix du Jeune Théâtre Béatrix, Dussane-André Roussin 2010) 2008; Chevalier, Ordre nat. du Mérite; Officier des Arts et des Lettres. *Theatre includes:* numerous plays including Fantasio (Alfred de Musset) 2008, Les trois soeurs (Chekhov) 2010–11, Un fil a la patte (Georges Feydeau) 2013. *Films include:* List of Merite 1992, Sabrina 1995, Un samedi sur la terre 1996, Jeunesse 1997, The Tango Lesson 1997, Monsieur Naphtali 1999, Une pour toutes 1999, Mon plus beau mariage (short) 1999, The Dancer 2000, Jet Set 2000, Fils de personne 2000, Le coeur sur la main (short) 2001, En scène! (short) 2001, Fanfan la tulipe 2003, Monsieur Ibrahim 2003, The Secret Adventures of Gustave Klopp 2004, Tu vas rire, mais je te quitte 2005, Orchestra Seats 2006, Marie Antoinette 2006, U (voice) 2006, The Jungle 2006, The Colonel 2006, Le dernier épisode de Dallas (short) 2006, The Candidate 2007, National Treasure: Book of Secrets (uncredited) 2007, Sagan 2008, Musée haut, musée bas 2008, The Concert 2009, Ensemble, nous allons vivre une très, très grande histoire d'amour… 2010, L'Italien 2010, De la table à la scène (documentary) (producer) 2011, Confession of a Child of the Century 2012, Astérix and Obélix: God Save Britannia 2012, Me, Myself and Mum (also writer, dir and producer) (Art Cinema Award, Cannes Film Festival) 2013, Yves Saint Laurent 2014. *Television includes:* Elles et moi (mini-series) 2008, Les Bonus de Guillaume (series) (also writer) 2008, Farewell De Gaulle, Farewell (film) 2009, The Little Prince (series) 2010–11, Hard (series) 2011. *Address:* c/o Cécile Felsenberg, UBBA, 6 rue de Braque, 75003 Paris, France (office). *Telephone:* 1-44-54-26-40 (office). *Fax:* 1-44-54-08-44 (office). *E-mail:* info@ubba.eu (office). *Website:* www.ubba.eu (office).

GALLINGER, Yuri Yiosifovich, DrMed; German surgeon; *Head, Department of Endoscopic Surgery, B. V. Petrovsky National Research Center for Surgery;* b. 3 Sept. 1939, Krasnaarmejsk, Saratov Region, Russian Federation; s. of Joseph Gallinger and Yekaterina Roor; m.; one s.; ed Kishinev Inst. of Medicine; gen. practitioner in polyclinics, then in 59th Clinic Hosp., Moscow 1962–67; researcher Moscow Medical Univ., Head Dept of Endoscopic Surgery, B. V. Petrovsky Nat. Research Center for Surgery 1986–; Pres. Russian Scientific Soc. of Endoscopic Surgery; mem. European Asscn of Endoscopic Surgery, Pirogov Asscn of Surgeons, New York Acad. of Sciences; State Prize of Russian Fed. 1990. *Publications:* over 200 scientific publs. *Leisure interests:* detective films and literature. *Address:* National Research Center of Surgery, Abrikosovski per. 2, 1199924 Moscow, Russia (office). *Telephone:* (495) 248-13-75 (office). *Fax:* (495) 246-89-88 (office).

GALLO, Max Louis, DenH, DèsSc; French politician, writer, historian and university teacher; b. 7 Jan. 1932, Nice; s. of Joseph Gallo and Mafalda Galeotti; ed Univ. de Paris and Inst. d'Etudes Politiques; early career in journalism; mem. CP –1956; teacher, Lycée de Nice 1960–65; Sr Lecturer, Univ. of Nice 1965–70; Gen. Ed. book series Ce Jour-là, l'Histoire que nous vivons, la Vie selon…, le Temps des

révélations; contrib. to various newspapers; devised TV programme Destins du Siècle 1973; Deputy (Socialist) for Alpes-Maritimes 1981–83; jr minister and Govt spokesman 1983–84; Ed. Matin de Paris newspaper 1985–86; mem. European Parl. 1984–94; mem. Parti Socialiste 1974–, Nat. Sec. (Culture) Parti Socialiste 1988–90; mem. Acad. française (Seat 24) 2007. *Publications:* L'Italie de Mussolini 1964, La Grande Peur de 1989 (as Max Laugham) 1966, L'Affaire d'Ethiopie 1967, Maximilien Robespierre, Histoire d'une solitude 1968, Gauchisme, réformisme et révolution 1968, Histoire de l'Espagne franquiste 1969, Cinquième Colonne 1930–1940 1970, La Nuit des longs couteaux 1970, Tombeau pour la Commune, Histoire de l'Espagne franquiste 1971, Le Cortège des vainqueurs 1972, La Mafia, un pas vers la mer 1973, L'Affiche, miroir de l'Histoire (illustrated) 1973, L'Oiseau des origines 1974: La Baie des anges (Vol. I) 1975, Le Palais des fêtes (Vol. II) 1976, La Promenade des Anglais (Vol. III) 1976, Le Pouvoir à vif, Despotisme, démocratie et révolution, Que sont les siècles pour la mer 1977, Les hommes naissent tous le même jour: Aurore (Vol. I) 1978, Crépuscule (Vol. II) 1979, Une affaire intime 1979, L'Homme Robespierre: histoire d'une solitude 1978, Un crime très ordinaire 1982, Garibaldi 1982, La Demeure des puissants 1983, La Troisième alliance, pour un nouvel individualisme, Le Grand Jaurès 1984, Le Beau Rivage 1985, Lettre ouverte à Maximilien Robespierre sur les nouveaux Muscadins, Belle Epoque 1986, Que passe la justice du roi, la Route Napoléon 1987, Jules Vallès 1988, Une Affaire publique 1989, Les Clés de l'histoire contemporaine 1989, Manifeste pour une fin de siècle obscure 1989, La Gauche est morte, vive la gauche! 1990, Le Regard des femmes 1991, La Fontaine des innocents (Prix Carlton 1992), Une femme rebelle: Vie et mort de Rosa Luxembourg 1992, L'Amour au temps des solitudes 1993, Les Rois sans visage 1994, Le Condottiere 1994, Le Fils de Klara H. 1995, L'Ambitieuse 1995, La Part de Dieu 1996, Le Faiseur d'or 1996, La Femme derrière le miroir, Napoléon, Le chant du départ (biog., Vol. I) 1997, L'Immortel de Saint-Hélène (Vol. IV) 1997, De Gaulle: L'Appel du destin (Vol. I) 1998, La Solitude du combattant (Vol. II) 1998, Le Premier des Français (Vol. III) 1998, La Statue du Commandeur (Vol. IV) 1998, L'Amour de la France expliqué a mon fils, le Jardin des oliviers 1999, Bleu, blanc, rouge (three vols) 2000, Les Patriotes (four vols) 2000–01, Victor Hugo: Je suis une force qui va (Vol. I) 2001, Je serai celui-là (Vol. II) 2001, Les Chrétiens (three vols) 2002, Morts pour la France (three vols) 2003, César Imperator 2003, L'Empire (three vols) 2004, Les Fanatiques 2006, Fier d'être Français 2006, La croix de l'Occident (two vols) 2005, Les Romains (five vols) 2006, Louis XIV: Le Roi-Soleil (Vol. I) 2007, L'Hiver du grand roi (Vol. II) 2007, Révolution française: Le Peuple et le Roi (Vol. I) 2009, Aux armes, citoyens! (Vol. II) 2009. *Address:* c/o XO Editions, 33 avenue du Maine, BP 142, 75755 Paris, France. *E-mail:* vtaillefer@xoeditions.com (office). *Website:* www.maxgallo.com.

GALLO, Robert C., MD; American biomedical scientist and academic; *Professor and Director, Institute of Human Virology, University of Maryland;* b. 23 March 1937, Waterbury, Conn.; m. Mary Jane Hayes 1961; two s. one d.; ed Providence Coll., Jefferson Medical Univ., Philadelphia, Yale Univ., Univ. of Chicago; Intern and Resident in Medicine, Univ. of Chicago 1963–65; Clinical Assoc. Nat. Cancer Inst. Bethesda, Md 1965–68, Sr Investigator 1968–69, Head, Section on Cellular Control Mechanisms 1969–72, Chief, Lab. of Tumor Cell Biology, Div. of Cancer Etiology 1972–93; Prof. and Dir Inst. of Human Virology, Univ. of Md, Baltimore 1993–; Rep. World Conf. Int. Comparative Leukemia and Lymphoma Asscn 1981–; mem. Bd of Govs Franco-American AIDS Foundation, World AIDS Foundation 1987; Co-founder Global Virus Network 2011; mem. NAS 1988, US Inst. of Medicine 1989; Hon. Prof., Johns Hopkins Univ. 1985–, Karolinska Inst., Stockholm 1998–; 30 hon. doctorates from 13 countries; numerous honours and awards including First Dameshek Award, American Soc. of Hematology 1974, Lasker Award for Basic Medical Research 1982, Otto Herz Cancer Prize, Tel Aviv Univ. 1982, Rabbi Shacknai Immunology Award, Hebrew Univ., Israel 1985, Gen. Motors Cancer Research Award 1984, Armand Hammer Cancer Research Award 1985, Lasker Award for Clinical Medical Research 1986, Gairdner Foundation Int. Award 1987 and other awards for cancer research, Japan Prize for Science and Technology 1988, 1st Dale McFarlin Award for Research, Int. Retrovirology Asscn 1994, Promesa Award 1997, Nomura Prize for AIDS and Cancer Research (Japan) 1998, Warren Alpert Prize, Harvard Univ. 1998, Paul Erlich Award (Germany) 1999, Príncipe de Asturias Award (Spain) 2000, Frank Annunzio Award in Science 2000, World Health Award 2001, Dan David Prize, Tel Aviv Univ. 2009, Award for Distinguished Research in the Biomedical Sciences, Asscn of American Medical Colls 2009, Most Cited Scientist in the World, Inst. of Scientific Information 1980–90. *Achievements include:* co-discoverer of HIV virus and first human retroviruses; discoverer of one of the first known cytokimes IL-2 (with co-workers); discoverer of Human Herpes Virus-6 (HHV-6) (with co-workers). *Publications:* over 1,200 scientific publs. *Leisure interests:* swimming, reading historical novels, tennis, theatre, biking. *Address:* Office of the Director, Institute of Human Virology, 725 West Lombard Street, Suite S307, Baltimore, MD 21201, USA (office). *Telephone:* (410) 706-8614 (office). *Fax:* (410) 706-1952 (office). *E-mail:* rgallo@ihv.umd.edu (office). *Website:* www.ihv.org (office).

GALLOGLY, James (Jim) L., BA, LLB; Canadian business executive; *CEO, LyondellBasell Industries;* b. St John's, Newfoundland; ed Univ. of Colorado, Univ. of Oklahoma, Advanced Exec. Program, J.L. Kellogg Grad. School of Man., Northwestern Univ.; began career with Phillips Petroleum Co. 1980, served in a variety of legal, financial and operational roles, including Man. of Business Services of N America Exploration and Production and Finance Man. 1990–93, Man. Ekofisk II, Norway 1993–95, Vice-Pres. of N America 1995–97, Vice-Pres. of Plastics 1997–98, of Olefins and Polyolefins 1998–99, Sr Vice-Pres. of Chemicals, ConocoPhillips 1999–2000, Exec. Vice-Pres. of Refining, Marketing and Transportation 2006–08, of Exploration and Production 2008–09, mem. Bd of Dirs and Pres. and CEO Chevron Phillips Chemical Co. 2000–06; CEO LyondellBasell Industries 2009–; mem. Bd of Dirs American Petroleum Inst.; fnr mem. Bd of Dirs American Chemical Council, American Plastics Council, Nat. Petrochemical and Refiners' Asscn; mem. Colorado, Oklahoma and Texas Bar Asscns; mem. Univ. of Colorado Dept of Chemical and Biological Eng Advisory Cttee. *Address:* LyondellBasell Industries, PO Box 2416, 3000 CK Rotterdam (office); LyondellBasell Industries, Weena 737, 3013 Rotterdam, The Netherlands (office). *Telephone:* (10) 275-55-00 (office). *E-mail:* info@lyondellbasell.com (office). *Website:* www .lyondellbasell.com (office).

GALLOIS, Louis; French business executive and fmr government official; *President, Fondation Villette-Entreprises;* b. 26 Jan. 1944, Montauban, Tarn-et-

Garonne; s. of Jean Gallois and Marie Prax; m. Marie-Edmée Amaudric du Chaffaut 1974; one s. two d.; ed École des Hautes Études Commerciales, Paris, École Nat. d'Admin, Strasbourg; Head of Bureau, Treasury 1972; Dir of Cabinet of Jean-Pierre Chevènement (Minister of Research and Tech. 1981–82, Minister of Research and Industry 1982); Dir-Gen. for Industry, Ministry of Research and Industry 1983; Civil Admin., Ministry of Econ. and Finance 1986; Dir of Civil and Mil. Cabinet, Minister of Defence 1988–89; Pres.-Dir-Gen. Soc. Nationale d'Etude et de Construction de Moteurs d'Aviation (SNECMA) 1989–92; Pres. (Econ. Interest Group) Avion de Combat européen-Rafale 1989; Pres., Dir-Gen. Aérospatiale 1992–96; Chair. Soc. Nationale des Chemins de Fer Français (SNCF) 1996–2006; Co-CEO European Aeronautic Defence and Space Co. (EADS) NV 2006–07, CEO 2007–12, CEO Airbus SAS 2006–07; Pres. Société Gestion de Participations Aéronautiques (SOGEPA) 1993–96; Vice-Pres. Supervisory Council Airbus-Industrie 1992–96; Pres. Communauté des chemins de fer européens 1999–, Fondation Villette-Entreprises; mem. Dassault aviation 1992–; Chevalier, Ordre nat. du Mérite, Commdr, Légion d'honneur. *Address:* Fondation Villette-Entreprises, Cité des sciences et de l'industrie, 30 avenue Corentin Cariou, 75019 Paris, France (office). *E-mail:* fve@universcience.fr (office). *Website:* www.cite-sciences.fr/english/fondation-villette-entreprises (office).

GALLOWAY, David A., BA, MBA; Canadian financial services industry executive; *Chairman, Bank of Montreal (BMO) Financial Group;* m.; two c.; ed Univ. of Toronto, Harvard Business School, USA; founding pnr Canada Consulting Group; joined Torstar Corpn 1981, Pres. and CEO Harlequin Worldwide 1982, Group Pres. and CEO 1988–2002; mem. Bd of Dirs Bank of Montreal (BMO) Financial Group 1998–, mem. Risk Oversight Cttee, Man. Compensation Cttee, Chair. BMO Financial Group 2004–; mem. Bd of Dirs Corel Corpn 2001–03, E.W. Scripps Co. 2002–, Toromont Industries Ltd 2002–, Hudson's Bay Co. 2003–06, Abitibi Consolidated Inc. 2006–07, Shell Canada Ltd 2006–07, Cognos Inc. 2007–; fmr Dir Clearnet Communications Inc., Visible Genetics, Westburne Inc., Harris Bankmont; Chair. Bd of Trustees, Hosp. for Sick Children, Toronto. *Address:* Bank of Montreal, 1 First Canadian Place, 100 King Street, West Toronto, ON M5X 1A1, Canada (office). *Telephone:* (416) 867-5000 (office). *Fax:* (416) 867-6793 (office). *E-mail:* info@bmo.com (office). *Website:* www.bmo.com (office).

GALLOWAY, James N., BS, PhD; American chemist, environmental scientist and academic; *Sidman P. Poole Professor in Environmental Science and Professor, Department of Environmental Sciences, University of Virginia;* ed Whittier Coll., Calif., Univ. of California, San Diego; Postdoctoral appointment, Cornell Univ.; apptd Asst Prof., Univ. of Virginia, Charlottesville 1976, currently Sidman P. Poole Prof. in Environmental Science and Prof., Dept of Environmental Sciences, Pres. Bermuda Biological Station for Research 1988–95, Chair. Dept of Environmental Sciences 1996–2001; currently Chair. Int. Nitrogen Initiative (sponsored by Scientific Cttee on Problems of the Environment and the Int. Geosphere-Biosphere Programme); mem. US Environmental Protection Agency's Science Advisory Bd; currently researching acidification of streams in Shenandoah Nat. Park, Va, composition of precipitation in remote regions, air-sea interactions and Asia's impact on global biogeochemistry; Fellow, AAAS 2002, American Geophysical Union 2008; Tyler Prize for Environmental Achievement (co-recipient) 2008, Alumnus Achievement Award, Whittier Coll. 2011. *Publications:* Asian Change in the Context of Global Climate Change: Impact of Natural and Anthropogenic Changes in Asia on Global Biogeochemical Cycles (co-ed.) 1998, Biogeochemical Cycling of Sulfur and Nitrogen in the Remote Atmosphere (co-ed.) 2002; numerous scientific papers in professional journals on biogeochemistry and chem. of natural waters at the watershed, regional and global scales, effects of nitrogen in the environment. *Address:* PO Box 400123, Clark Hall 210, Department of Environmental Sciences, University of Virginia, Charlottesville, VA 22903, USA (office). *Telephone:* (434) 924-1303 (office), (434) 924-0569 (office). *Fax:* (434) 982-2137 (office), (434) 982-2300 (office). *E-mail:* jng@virginia.edu (office). *Website:* www.evsc.virginia.edu/2008/11/galloway-james-n (office).

GALMOT, Yves, French judge (retd); b. 5 Jan. 1931, Paris; s. of Jean-Jacques Galmot and Marie Germaine Lengauer; m. Katrine-Marie Nicholson 1958; two s.; ed Lycée Louis le Grand, Paris, Inst. d'Etudes Politiques de Paris, Faculté de Droit de Paris, Ecole Nat. d'Admin; auditor, Council of State 1956; Tech. Adviser, Office of High Commr for Youth and Sport 1958; Maître des Requêtes, Council of State 1962–; Govt Commr Legal Section, Council of State 1964–68; Sec.-Gen., Entreprise Minière et Chimique 1970–74; Councillor of State 1981–94; Judge, Court of Justice of European Communities 1982–88; Chair. Financial Section, Council of State 1994–96; mem. Court of Budget and Finance 1996–99; Chair. Comm. Interministérielle des Installations Nucléaires de Base 1996–2006, Comm. of Appeal, Agence Intergouvernmentale de la Francophonie 1999–2009. *Leisure interest:* golf. *Address:* Conseil d'Etat, 75100 Paris (office); 95 rue de la Santé, 75013 Paris, France (home).

GALSWORTHY, Sir Anthony Charles, Kt, KCMG, MA; British organization official and fmr diplomatist; b. 20 Dec. 1944, London, England; s. of Sir Arthur Galsworthy and Lady Galsworthy; m. Jan Dawson-Grove 1970; one s. one d.; ed St Paul's School, London, Corpus Christi Coll., Cambridge; Foreign Office, London 1966, Third Sec., Hong Kong 1967, Third, later Second Sec., Beijing 1970, Second, later First Sec., FCO, London 1972, First Sec., Rome 1977, First Sec., later Counsellor, Beijing 1981, Counsellor and Head Hong Kong Dept, FCO 1984, Prin. Pvt. Sec. to Sec. of State for Foreign and Commonwealth Affairs 1986, with Royal Inst. of International Affairs, London 1988, British Sr Rep., Jt Liaison Group, Hong Kong 1989, Cabinet Office 1993, Deputy Under-Sec. of State, FCO 1995, Amb. to People's Repub. of China 1997–2002; Adviser on China, Standard Chartered Bank 2002–; Dir Earthwatch, Europe 2002–06; Dir Bekaert SA 2004–, WWT (Consulting) Ltd 2009–; Scientific Assoc. Nat. History Museum, London 2001–; Trustee, Wildfowl and Wetland Trust 2002–09, British Trust for Ornithology 2002–06; Hon. Fellow, Royal Botanic Gardens, Edin. 2002; Linnean Soc. Medal for Taxonomy 2000. *Leisure interests:* wildlife, entomology. *Address:* c/o Standard Chartered Bank, 1 Aldermanbury Square, London, EC2V 7SB, England (office).

GALTUNG, Johan Vincent, PhD (Math.), PhD (Sociology); Norwegian professor of peace studies and mediator; *Peace Mediator and Professor of Peace Studies, Transcend;* b. 24 Oct. 1930, Oslo; s. of August Galtung and Helga Holmboe; m. 1st Ingrid Eide 1956 (divorced 1968); two s.; m. 2nd Fumiko Nishimura 1969; one s. one d.; ed Univ. of Oslo; Prof. of Sociology, Columbia Univ., New York, USA

1957–60; Founder and Dir Int. Peace Research Inst., Oslo 1959–69; Prof. of Peace Research, Univ. of Oslo 1969–77; Prof., Princeton Univ., USA 1985–89; Prof. of Peace Studies, Univ. of Hawaii 1985–2004; Prof. of Peace and Co-operation Studies, Univ. of Witten-Herdecke, Germany; Olof Palme Prof. of Peace, Stockholm, Sweden 1990–91; Prof. of Peace Studies, Univ. of Alicante, Spain 2005–; Founder and Dir Transcend (peace devt network) 1993–, Rector Transcend Peace Univ., also Prof. of Peace Studies; mediator in more than 100 conflicts world-wide; Hon. Prof., Berlin, Alicante, Sichuan, Witten/Herdecke; Dr hc (Finland, Romania, Uppsala, Tokyo, Hagen, Alicante, Osnabrück, Turin, Puebla); Alternative Nobel Peace Prize (Right Livelihood Award), Bajaj Int. Gandhi Prize, Korean DMZ Peace Prize, Abdul Ghaffar Khan Int. Peace-Builder Prize. *Play:* Globalizing God 2011. *Publications:* Theory and Methods of Social Research (four vols) 1967, 1977, 1980, 1988, There are Alternatives 1983, Hitlerism, Stalinism, Reaganism 1984; Essays in Peace Research Vols I–VI 1974–88, Human Rights in Another Key, Peace by Peaceful Means: Peace, Conflict, Development, Civilization, Conflict Transformation by Peaceful Means 2000, Johan uten land: På fredsveien gjennom verden (Norwegian Brage Literary Prize) 2000, 50 Years: 100 Peace & Conflict Perspectives 2008, 50 Years: 2 Intellectual Landscapes Explored 2008, The Fall of the US Empire – And Then What? 2009, Globalizing God (with Graeme MacQueen) 2009, A Theory of Conflict 2010, A Theory of Development 2010, Reconciliation (with Joanna Santa Barbara and Diane Perlman) 2012, Peace Mathematics (with Dietrich Fischer) 2012, Peace Economics 2012. *Leisure interests:* travel, writing. *Address:* Casa 227, Urb. Escandinavia, ALFAZ Del Pi, Alicante, Spain (home); 11009 Kinship Court, Apt 302, Manassas, VA 20109, USA (home); Garden Court, Apt 912, Kawaramachi/Shomen, Kyoto 600, Japan (home); 7 Cret de neige, 01210 Versonnex, France (home). *Telephone:* (4) 50-42-73-06 (Versonnex) (home); (96) 5889919 (Alicante) (home). *Fax:* (4) 50-42-73-06 (Versonnex) (home); (96) 5889919 (Alicante) (home). *E-mail:* galtung@transcend.org (office). *Website:* www.transcend.org (office).

GALUN, (Amiel) Esra, PhD; Israeli biologist and academic; *Professor Emeritus of Biology, Department of Plant Sciences, Weizmann Institute of Science;* b. 7 April 1927, Leipzig, Germany; s. of David Mendel Galun and Erna Esther Markus; m. Margalith Katz 1953; two s.; ed Hebrew Univ. Jerusalem, California Inst. of Tech., USA; Sr Scientist, Plant Genetics, Weizmann Inst. of Science 1963–67, Assoc. Prof. of Plant Genetics 1968–72, Head, Dept of Plant Genetics 1970–88, Prof. of Biology 1972–, now Prof. Emer., Dean Feinberg Grad. School 1974–75, Dean, Faculty of Biology 1988–91; Maria Moors Cabot Research Fellow, Biological Labs, Harvard Univ., USA 1967–68; Chair. Israeli Nat. Council for Research and Devt 1982–84; Distinguished Visiting Scientist, The Roche Inst. of Molecular Biology, Nutley, NY 1985; Armando Kaminitz Award for Achievements in Agric. Research. *Publications:* Pollination Mechanisms, Reproduction and Plant Breeding (co-author) 1977, Transgenic Plants (with Adina Breiman) 1997, Manufacture of Medical and Health Products by Transgenic Plants (with Eithan Galun) 2001, Transposable Elements 2003, RNA Silencing 2005; more than 180 publs in learned journals. *Leisure interests:* music, archaeology, philosophy. *Address:* Department of Plant Sciences, The Weizmann Institute of Science, Rehovot 76100 (office); 54 Hanassi, Harishon Street, Rehovot 76302, Israel (home). *Telephone:* (8) 9342637 (office); (8) 9468103 (home). *Fax:* (8) 9344181 (office); (8) 9464016 (home). *E-mail:* esra.galun@weizmann.ac.il (office). *Website:* www.weizmann.ac.il/Plant_Sciences (office).

GALUŠKA, Vladimír, JD; Czech diplomatist and lawyer; *Deputy Minister of Foreign Affairs;* b. 2 Oct. 1952, Prague; s. of Miroslav Galuška and Milena Galušková (née Králová); m. Marcela Wintrová 1975; two s.; ed Charles Univ., Prague; corp. lawyer, Skoda Co., Prague 1975–90; Consul, Deputy Chief of Mission, Czech Embassy, Washington, DC 1990–94; Dir Personnel Dept, Ministry of Foreign Affairs 1994–97, Head of Int. Relations 2002–04; Perm. Rep. of Czech Repub. to UN 1997–2001; Amb. to Slovakia 2004–09, currently Deputy Minister, Ministry of Foreign Affairs; Pres. ECOSOC 1997, Exec. Bd UNDP/UNFPA 2000; Chair. 3rd Cttee 54th UN Gen. Ass. 1999. *Address:* Ministry of Foreign Affairs, Loretánské nám. 101/5, 118 00 Prague 1, Czech Republic (office). *Telephone:* 224181111 (office). *Fax:* 224182031 (office). *E-mail:* podatelna@mzv.cz (office). *Website:* www.mzv.cz (office).

GALVÁN GALVÁN, Gen. Guillermo; Mexican military officer and government official; b. 19 Jan. 1943, Mexico City; ed Colegio Militar, Colegio de Defensa; has been Commdr in numerous mil. zones; fmr Mil. Attaché Embassy in Madrid; fmr Rector Universidad del Ejército y Fuerza Aérea Mexicanos; Under-Sec. of Nat. Defence 2004–06, Sec. of Nat. Defence 2006–12. *Address:* c/o Secretariat of State for National Defence, Blvd Manuel Avila Camacho, esq. Avda Industria Militar, 3°, Col. Lomas de Sotelo, Del. Miguel Hidalgo, 11640 México, DF, Mexico.

GALVIN, Gen. John Rogers; American army officer (retd) and academic; *Dean Emeritus, Fletcher School of Law and Diplomacy, Tufts University;* b. 13 May 1929, Wakefield, Mass; s. of John James Galvin and Mary Josephine Rogers; m. Virginia Lee Brennan 1961; four d.; ed US Mil. Acad., West Point, Columbia Univ., Univ. of Pennsylvania, Command and Gen. Staff Coll. and Fletcher School of Law and Diplomacy, US Army War Coll., Carlisle, Pa; commissioned 2nd Lt, US Army 1954; Military Asst and ADC to Sec. of US Army 1968–69; Commdr, 1st Bn 8th Cavalry 1970; Mil. Asst to Supreme Allied Commdr, Europe (SACEUR) 1974–75; Commdr, Div. Support Command 3rd Infantry Div. 1975–77, Chief of Staff 1977–78; Commanding Gen., 24th Infantry Div. 1981–83; VII (US) Corps 1983–85; C-in-C, US Southern Command 1985–87; Supreme Allied Commdr Europe and C-in-C US European Command 1987–92; Olin Distinguished Prof. of Nat. Security, US Mil. Acad., West Point 1992–93; Distinguished Visiting Policy Analyst, Mershon Center, Ohio State Univ. 1994–95; Dean, Fletcher School of Law and Diplomacy, Tufts Univ., Boston 1995–2000, Dean Emer. 2000–; mem. Bd of Dirs J. & W. Seligman & Co. Inc.; fmr Dir Raytheon Co., US Life; 20 foreign decorations; Defense Distinguished Service Medal, Army, Navy and Air Force Distinguished Service Medal, Silver Star, Legion of Merit (with 2 oak leaf clusters), Soldier's Medal, Bronze Star with 2 oak leaf clusters, Air Medal (Valor), Combat Infantryman Badge, Ranger Tab. *Publications:* The Minute Men 1967, Air Assault 1969, Three Men of Boston 1974 and 80 articles on leadership, tactics and training. *Leisure interests:* reading, writing and walking. *Address:* 2714 Lake Jodeco Circle, Jonesboro, GA 30236, USA (home). *Telephone:* (770) 210-4110 (home). *Fax:* (770) 210-9488 (home). *E-mail:* johngalvin@comcast.net (home).

GALWAY, Sir James, Kt, KBE, FRCM, FRCO, FGSM; British flautist and conductor; b. 8 Dec. 1939, Belfast; s. of James Galway and Ethel Stewart Galway (née Clarke); m. 1st 1965; one s.; m. 2nd 1972; one s. two d. (twins); m. 3rd Jeanne Cinnante 1984; ed Mountcollyer Secondary School, Royal Coll. of Music, Guildhall School of Music, Conservatoire National Supérieur de Musique, Paris; first post in Wind Band of Royal Shakespeare Theatre, Stratford-on-Avon; later worked with Sadler's Wells Orchestra, Royal Opera House Orchestra, BBC Symphony Orchestra; Prin. Flute, London Symphony Orchestra and Royal Philharmonic Orchestra; Prin. Solo Flute, Berlin Philharmonic Orchestra 1969–75; int. soloist 1975–; soloist/conductor 1984–; Prin. Guest Conductor, London Mozart Players 1997–; performances worldwide include appearances in The Wall, Berlin, and at the Nobel Peace Prize Ceremony, 1998; as conductor, toured Germany with Wurttembergisches Kammerorchester and Asia with Polish Chamber Orchestra, 2000–01; has premiered many contemporary flute works commissioned by and for him; numerous recordings; James Galway Rose named after him by David Austin; Hon. MA (Open Univ.) 1979, Hon. DMus (Queen's Univ., Belfast) 1979, (New England Conservatory of Music) 1980, (St Andrew's Univ.); Officier, Ordre des Arts et des Lettres 1987; Grand Prix du Disque 1976, 1989, Nat. Acad. Recording, Arts & Sciences Pres. Merit Award 2004, Classical BRIT Award for Outstanding Contribution to Music 2005. *Recordings include:* Vivaldi The Four Seasons, Sometimes When We Touch, Mozart Concerto No. 1, Andante and Concerto for Flute and Harp, Song Of The Seashore 1979, Annie's Song 1981, Man With The Golden Flute 1982, The Wayward Wind 1982, Nocturne 1983, James Galway Plays Mozart 1984, In The Pink 1984, In Ireland 1986, Christmas Carol 1986, J.S. Bach Suite No. 2 Concerto - Trio Sonatas 1987, Mercadante Concertos 1987, James Galway Plays Beethoven 1988, The Enchanted Forest 1988, James Galway Plays Giuliani 1988, Quantz 4 Concertos 1989, C.P.E. Bach 3 Concertos 1989, The Concerto Collection 1990, Over The Sea To Skye 1990, J.S. Bach Suite No. 2 Concerto for Flute, Violin and Harpsichord 1991, Italian Flute Concertos 1991, In Dulci Jubilo 1991, The Wind Beneath My Wings 1991, Mozart Flute Quartets 1991, Mozart Concerto for Flute and Harp and Sonatas for Flute and Piano 1992, At The Movies 1992, The Magic Flute 1992, Danzi 1993, Dances For Flute 1993, Seasons 1993, The Classical James Galway 1993, Bach Sonatas 1993, Pachelbel Canon 1994, Wind Of Change 1994, The Lark In The Clear Air 1994, The French Recital 1994, Mozart Concerto for Flute and Harp, Concerto No. 1 and Concerto No. 2 1995, Bach Vol. 2 Trio Sonatas 1995, The Celtic Minstrel 1996, James Galway plays the music of Sir Malcolm Arnold 1996, Music for my Friends 1997, James Galway plays Lowell Liebermann 1997, Legends 1997, Flute Sonatas 1997, Meditations 1998, Serenade 1998, Tango del Fuego 1998, Winter's Crossing 1998, Unbreak My Heart 1999, Sixty Years-Sixty Flute Masterpieces Collection 1999, Love Song 2001, Hommage à Rampal 2001, A Song of Home: An American Musical Journey 2002, The Very Best of James Galway 2002, Music for my Little Friends 2002, Wings of Song 2004, My Magic Flute 2006, Ich war ein Berliner 2006, The Essential James Galway 2006, Celebrating 70: A Collection of Personal Favourites 2009, James Galway Plays Flute Concertos (12 cd set) 2011. *Film music:* flute soloist, soundtrack of Lord of the Rings – Return of the King. *Publications:* James Galway: An Autobiography 1978, Flute (Menuhin Music Guide) 1982, James Galway's Music in Time 1983, Flute Studies – Boehm 12 Grand Studies 2003. *Leisure interests:* music, walking, swimming, films, theatre, TV, computing, chess, backgammon, talking to people. *Address:* c/o Elizabeth Sobol Gomez, IMG Artists, Carnegie Hall Tower, 152 West 57th Street, 5th Floor, New York, NY 10019, USA (office). *Telephone:* (212) 994-3541 (office). *Fax:* (212) 994-3550 (office). *E-mail:* esobol-gomez@imgartists.com (office). *Website:* www.imgartists.com (office); www .thegalwaynetwork.com.

GAMA, Jaime José Matos Da; Portuguese politician; *President, Assembleia da República;* b. 8 June 1947, Azores; Founding mem. Partido Socialista 1977, unsuccessful cand. for leadership 1986, 1988; Pres. Parl. Comm. for Int. Business 1976–78, of Parl. Comm. for Nat. Defence 1985–91, of Parl. Comm. for European Affairs and Foreign Politics 2002–05; Minister of Home Affairs 1978, Minister of Foreign Affairs 1983–85, 1995–2002; Minister of Nat. Defence 1999; Minister of State 1999–2002; Pres. Assembleia da República (Parl.) 2005–. *Address:* Assembleia da República, Palácio de San Bento, 1249-068 Lisbon, Portugal (office). *Telephone:* (21) 3919244 (office). *Fax:* (21) 3917434 (office). *E-mail:* gabpar@ar.parlamento.pt (office). *Website:* www.parlamento.pt (office).

GAMATIÉ, Ali Badjo; Niger economist and politician; Head of Nat. Accounts Div. 1982–84, Dir-Gen. Institut nat. de la Statistique 1986–89; with Tech. Dept, World Bank, Washington, DC, USA 1989; with Centre Européen de Coopération Statistique, Luxembourg 1990–94, Bureau Régional de Coopération Statistique pour l'Afrique de l'Ouest et du Centre, Abidjan, Côte d'Ivoire and Ouagadougou, Burkina Faso 1995–99; Minister of the Economy and Finance 2000–03; Vice-Gov. Banque centrale des Etats de l'Afrique de l'Ouest (BCEAO) 2003–09; Special Adviser on Mineral Affairs to Pres. 2008; Prime Minister 2009–10 (ousted following coup d'état Feb. 2010); mem. Mouvement nat. pour la société de développement; Grand Officier, Légion d'honneur, Grand Officier, Ordre du mérite du Niger, Commdr, Ordre du mérite de l'enseignement supérieur de Côte d'Ivoire 2005; Robert Schuman Medal. *Address:* c/o Office of the Prime Minister, BP 893, Niamey, Niger (office).

GAMBARI, Ibrahim Agboola, CFR, BSc, MA, PhD; Nigerian diplomatist, academic and UN official; *Chancellor, Kwara State University;* b. 24 Nov. 1944, Ilorin, Kwara State; m. Fatima Oniyangi 1969; two s. one d.; ed Kings Coll., Lagos, London School of Econs, UK, Columbia Univ., New York, USA; Lecturer, Queen's Coll., CUNY 1969–74; Asst Prof., State Univ. of New York (Albany) 1974–77; Sr Lecturer, Ahmadu Bello Univ., Zaria 1977–80, Assoc. Prof. 1980–83, Prof. 1983–89, fmr Chair. Dept of Political Science and Founder, Undergraduate Programme in Int. Studies (first in Nigeria); Dir-Gen. Nigerian Inst. of Int. Affairs 1983–84; Minister for Foreign Affairs 1984–85; Visiting Prof., Johns Hopkins Univ. School of Advanced Int. Studies, Howard Univ., Georgetown Univ. and Brookings Inst. 1986–89; Resident Scholar, Rockefeller Foundation Bellagio Study and Conf. Centre, Italy Nov.–Dec. 1989; Perm. Rep. to UN, New York 1990–99, Chair. Special Cttee against Apartheid; UN Under-Sec.-Gen. and Special Adviser on Africa 1999–2005, Special Rep. of the Sec.-Gen. and Head of UN Mission to Angola 2002–03, Under-Sec.-Gen. for Political Affairs 2005–07, Special Adviser to the Sec.-Gen. on the Int. Compact with Iraq and Other Political Issues 2007–09, Special Envoy to Myanmar 2007–09, Jt Special Rep. to African Union/UN Hybrid

Operation in Darfur (UNAMID) 2010–13; Chancellor, Kwara State Univ. 2013–; Founder Savannah Centre for Diplomacy, Democracy and Devt (think-tank), Abuja, Nigeria; fmr Guest Scholar, Wilson Centre for Int. Scholars, Smithsonian Inst., USA; Chair. Nat. Seminar to Commemorate 25th Anniversary of OAU, Lagos 1988; mem. Soc. of Scholars, Johns Hopkins Univ. 2002–; Hon. Prof., Chugsan Univ., Guangzhou, People's Repub. of China 1985; Commdr, Fed. Repub. of Nigeria 2002; Hon. DHumLitt (Univ. of Bridgeport) 2002, (Fairleigh Dickinson Univ.) 2006, Dr hc (Chatham Univ.) 2008; Special Recognition for Int. Devt and Diplomacy award, Africa-America Inst. 2007, Distinguished Service Award 2008, Harry Edmonds Award for Lifetime Achievement 2009. *Publications include:* Party Politics and Foreign Policy in Nigeria During the First Republic 1981, Theory and Reality in Foreign Policy Making: Nigeria After the Second Republic 1989, Political and Comparative Dimensions of Regional Integration: The Case of ECOWAS 1991, Report of the Security Council Mission to Rwanda 1995, United Nations 21: Better Service, Better Value, Better Management, Progress Report of the Efficiency Board to the Secretary-General (co-author) 1996. *Address:* Kwara State University, PMB 1530, Malete 00234, Kwara State, Nigeria (office).

GAMBHIR, Gautam; Indian professional cricketer; b. 14 Oct. 1981, Delhi; s. of Deepak Gambhir; ed Modern School, New Delhi, Nat. Cricket Acad., Bangalore; opening batsman; left-handed batsman; right-arm leg-break bowler; plays for Delhi 1999–, India 2003–, Delhi Daredevils 2008–10, Kolkata Knight Riders 2011–, India Red, Indian Bd Pres.'s XI, Rajasthan Cricket Asscn Pres.'s XI; First-class debut: 1999/2000; Test debut: India v Australia, Mumbai 3–5 Nov. 2004; One-Day Int. (ODI) debut: Bangladesh v India, Dhaka 11 April 2003; T20I debut: India v Scotland, Durban 13 Sept. 2007; has played in 54 Tests and scored 4,021 runs (9 centuries, 21 fifties), highest score 206, average 44.18; ODIs: 147 matches, scored 5,238 runs, highest score 150 not out, average 39.68; First-class: 155 matches, 12,225 runs, highest score 233 not out, took seven wickets, best bowling 3/12; mem. Indian team, ICC (Int. Cricket Council) World Twenty20 2007, winning Indian team, ICC Cricket World Cup 2011; only fourth Indian batsman to score a double century in a tour game at home; only Indian batsman to score more than 300 runs in four consecutive Test series; only Indian, and one of only four int. cricketers, to have scored five hundreds in five consecutive test matches; No. 1 ranked batsman in ICC Test rankings for ten days July 2009; Best Asian Batsman T20 Castrol Asian Cricket Award 2008, ICC Test Player of the Year 2009. *Address:* c/o Delhi & District Cricket Association, Ferozeshah Kotla Grounds, New Delhi 110 002, India. *Telephone:* (11) 23319323; (11) 23312721; (11) 23752667. *Fax:* (11) 23722097. *E-mail:* info@delhicricket.org. *Website:* www.delhicricket.org; www .gautamgambhir.net.

GAMBI, Gen. Antoine; Central African Republic army officer and government official; Chief of Gen. Staff, Armed Forces 2002–06; Coordinator, Nat. Comm. Against the Proliferation of Small Arms and Light Weapons to the Disarmament and Reintegration (CNPDR) 2006–09; Pres. Nat. SSR Cttee (security reform preparatory group) 2007–08; Minister of Foreign and Francophone Affairs and Regional Integration 2009–13, Minister-Del. to Minister of Nat. Defence, in charge of Restructuring of the Armed Forces and the Programme of Disarmament, Demobilization and Reintegration 2013–14. *Address:* c/o Ministry of National Defence, War Veterans, War Victims and the Restructuring of the Armed Forces, Bangui, Central African Republic (office).

GAMBIER, Dominique, DèsSc Econ; French academic; b. 14 Aug. 1947, Rouen; s. of Michel Morel and Yvette Morel; two d.; ed Lycée Corneille, Rouen and Ecole Centrale de Paris; Asst Univ. of Rouen 1972–81; Prof. Ecole Centrale de Paris 1981–83; special assignment, Commissariat Général au Plan 1983–84; Maître de conférences and Dir Inst. of Research and Documentation in Social Sciences (IRED), Univ. of Rouen 1984–87; expert adviser, EEC, Brussels 1980–81; scientific adviser, Observatoire français des conjonctures économiques (OFCE) 1981–83; Regional Councillor, Haute-Normandie 1986–, Vice-Pres. of Regional Council 1998–; Pres. Univ. of Rouen 1987–88; Deputy for Seine Maritime 1988–93; Mayor of Déville-les-Rouen 1995–; Officier des Palmes académiques. *Publications:* Analyse conjoncturelle du chômage, Théorie de la politique économique en situation d'incertitude 1980, Le marché du travail 1991, L'emploi en France 1997; numerous articles on economy of work and labour etc. *Leisure interests:* football, tennis, skiing. *Address:* Mairie de Déville, 1 Place François Mitterrand, 76250 Déville; 5 allée du Houssel, 76130 Mont-St-Aignan, France (home). *Telephone:* 35-76-88-18. *Fax:* 35-74-30-73. *E-mail:* dominiquegambin@free.fr (home).

GAMBLE, Christine Elizabeth, PhD; British consultant on culture and sport and fmr equality and human rights diplomatist and researcher; b. 1 March 1950, Rotherham; d. of the late Albert Edward Gamble and of the late Kathleen Laura Wallis; m. Edward Barry Antony Craxton; ed Royal Holloway Coll., Univ. of London; worked in Anglo-French cultural org. 1974–75; Office of the Cultural Attaché, British Embassy, Moscow 1975–76; joined British Council, New Delhi 1977, UK 1979, Harare 1980–82, Regional Officer for the Soviet Union and Mongolia 1982–85, Deputy Dir Athens 1985–87, Corp. Planning Dept 1988–90, Head, Project Pursuit Dept and Dir Chancellor's Financial Sector Scheme 1990–92, Dir Visitor's Dept 1992–93, Gen. Man. Country Services Group and Head European Services 1993–96; Cultural Councillor, British Embassy, Paris and Dir British Council, France 1996–98; Dir Royal Inst. of Int. Affairs, London 1998–2002; Co. Sec., Ind. Football Comm. 2002–05; Consultant to Comm. for Racial Equality 2005–10; Order of Rio Branco, Brazil 2000. *Leisure interests:* literature, art, music, theatre, sport. *Address:* Syke Fold House, Dent, Sedbergh, LA10 5RE, England (home). *Telephone:* (1539) 625518 (home). *Fax:* (1539) 625518 (home). *E-mail:* cgamble@gmdsolutions.co.uk (office). *Website:* www.gmdsolutions .co.uk (office); www.phoenixhospitality.co.uk (office).

GAMBLIN, Jacques; French actor; b. 16 Nov. 1957, Granville, Manche; ed Centre dramatique de Caen; wrote the theatre play Quincaillerie. *Films:* Train d'enfer (Hell Train, USA) 1985, Périgord noir 1988, Il y a des jours... et des lunes (There Were Days... and Moons) 1990, Pont et soupirs 1992, La belle histoire (The Beautiful Story) 1992, Adeus Princesa (Goodbye Princess) 1992, Tout ça... pour ça! (All That... for This?!) 1993, La femme à abattre 1993, Fausto (aka À la mode (USA), aka In Fashion) 1993, Naissances 1994, Les braqueuses (Girls with Guns) 1994, Sans souci 1995, Les misérables (aka Les misérables du vingtième siècle) 1995, À la vie, à la mort! (Til Death Do Us Part) 1995, Au petit Marguery 1995, Mon homme (My Man) 1996, Pédale douce 1996, Une histoire d'amour à la con 1996, Tenue correcte exigée 1997, Mauvais genre 1997, Kanzo sensei (Dr. Akagi, USA) 1998, Au coeur du mensonge (The Color of Lies, USA) 1999, Les enfants du marais (The Children of the Marshland) (Best Actor Award, Cabourg Romantic Film Festival 1999) 1999, Mademoiselle 2001, Bella ciao 2001, Laissez-passer (Safe Conduct) (Silver Berlin Bear for Best Actor, Berlin Int. Film Festival 2002) 2002, Carnages (Carnage) 2002, À la petite semaine (Nickel and Dime) 2003, Dissonances 2003, 25 degrés en hiver (25 Degrees in Winter) 2004, Holy Lola 2004, L'enfer (Hell) 2005, Les brigades du Tigre (The Tiger Brigades) 2006, Sercko 2006, Les irréductibles 2006, Fragile(s) 2007, Nos retrouvailles (aka In Your Wake) 2007, Enfin veuve (A Widow at Last) 2008. *Television:* La double inconstance 1984, L'Été 36 1986, Le vagabond des mers (mini-series) 1990, Années de plumes, années de plomb 1991, C'est mon histoire: Présumé coupable 1992, Un cercueil pour deux 1993, Les brouches 1994, Coucheties express 1994, La bougeotte 1996, Les clients d'Avrenos 1996, Le voyageur sans bagage 2004, Les oubliées (mini-series) 2007.

GAMBLING, William Alexander, BSc, PhD, DSc, FRS, FREng; British electrical engineer and industrial consultant; b. 11 Oct. 1926, Port Talbot, Glamorgan, Wales; s. of George Alexander Gambling and Muriel Clara Gambling; m. 1st Margaret Pooley 1952 (separated 1987); one s. two d.; m. 2nd Barbara Colleen O'Neil 1994; ed Univs of Bristol and Liverpool; Lecturer in Electric Power Eng, Univ. of Liverpool 1950–55; Fellow, Nat. Research Council, Univ. of BC 1955–57; Lecturer, Sr Lecturer and Reader, Univ. of Southampton 1957–64, Prof. of Electronics 1964–80, Dean of Eng and Applied Science 1972–75, Head of Dept 1974–79, British Telecom Prof. of Optical Communication 1980–95, Dir UK Nat. Optoelectronics Research Centre 1989–95; Royal Soc. Visiting Prof. and Dir, Optoelectronics Research Centre, City Univ. of Hong Kong 1996–2001; Dir of Optoelectronics Research and Devt, LTK Industries Ltd 2002–05, Consultant 2005–07; Consultant in Optoelectronics, COTCO Holdings Ltd; Visiting Prof., Univ. of Colo 1966–67, Bhabha Atomic Research Centre, India 1970, Osaka Univ., Japan 1977; Pres. I.E.R.E. 1977–78; Chair. Comm.D, Int. Union of Radio Science 1981–84, Eng Council 1988; mem. Bd, Council of Eng Insts 1974–79, Electronics Research Council 1977–80, Nat. Electronics Council 1977–78 and 1984–89; Dir York Ltd 1980–97; mem. British Nat. Cttee for Radio Science 1978–87, Educational Advisory Council, IBA 1980–82, Eng Industries Training Bd 1985–88; mem. Council, Royal Acad. of Eng 1989–92; Selby Fellow, Australian Acad. of Science 1982; Foreign mem. Polish Acad. of Sciences 1985; Liveryman, Worshipful Co. of Engineers 1988; Fellow Hong Kong Acad. of Eng Sciences (Vice-Pres. 2004–); Hon. FIEE; Hon. Prof., Huazhong Univ. of Science and Tech., Wuhan, 1986–, Beijing Univ. of Posts and Telecommunications, Shanghai Univ. 1991–, Shandong Univ. 1999–; Hon. Dir Beijing Optical Fibres Lab., People's Repub. of China 1987–; Freeman, City of London 1988; Dr hc (Madrid) 1994, (Aston) 1995, (Bristol) 1999, (Southampton) 2005; Academic Enterprise Award 1982, IEE J. J. Thomson Medal 1982, IEE Faraday Medal 1983, Churchill Medal, Soc. of Engineers 1985, Simms Medal, Soc. of Engineers 1988, Micro-optics Award (Japan) 1989, Dennis Gabor Award (USA) 1990, Rank Prize for Optoelectronics 1991, C & C Medal (Japan) 1993, Mountbatten Medal 1993, Royal Soc./Inst. of Civil Engineers James Alfred Ewing Medal 2002; six awards for fundamental research publs, 11 int. prizes and medals for research in optical fibre communications tech. *Publications:* some 400 research papers on electrical discharges, microwave devices, quantum electronics, optical fibre communication and education. *Leisure interests:* reading, music, the Bible, Christian literature. *Address:* LTK Industries, 6/F Photonics Centre, Hong Kong Science Park, Sha Tin, Hong Kong Special Administrative Region, People's Republic of China (office). *Telephone:* 2410-3009 (office). *Fax:* 2943-1709 (office). *E-mail:* wag@ltkcable.com (office); wagconl@yahoo.com (office). *Website:* www.ltkcable.com (office).

GAMBON, Sir Michael John, Kt, CBE; British actor; b. 19 Oct. 1940, Dublin, Ireland; s. of Edward Gambon and Mary Gambon; m. Anne Miller 1962; one s.; ed St Aloysius School for Boys, London; fmr mechanical engineer; Trustee Royal Armouries 1995–98; Hon. DLitt 2003. *Theatre includes:* first stage appearance with Edwards/Mácliammoir Co., Dublin 1962; Nat. Theatre, Old Vic 1963–67; Birmingham Repertory and other provincial theatres 1967–69, title roles including Othello, Macbeth, Coriolanus; RSC Aldwych 1970–71; The Norman Conquests 1974, Otherwise Engaged 1976, Just Between Ourselves 1977, Alice's Boys 1978, The Caretaker 2000; with Nat. Theatre 1980, appearing in Galileo (London Theatre Critics' Award for Best Actor), Betrayal, Tales from Hollywood; with RSC, Stratford and London 1982–83, title roles in King Lear, Antony and Cleopatra, Old Times 1985, A Chorus of Disapproval, Nat. Theatre 1985 (Olivier Award for Best Comedy Performance), A Small Family Business 1987, Uncle Vanya 1988, Mountain Language 1988, Othello 1990, Taking Steps 1990, Skylight (play) 1995, Volpone (Evening Standard Drama Award) 1995, Tom and Clem 1997, The Unexpected Man 1998, Cressida 2000 (Variety Club Award for Best Actor), A Number, Jerwood Theatre, Royal Court, London 2002, End Game 2004, Henry IV parts I and II, Nat. Theatre 2005, Eh Joe 2006, No Man's Land 2008–09, Krapp's Last Tape 2010. *Films include:* The Beast Must Die 1975, Turtle Diary 1985, Paris by Night 1988, The Cook, The Thief, His Wife and Her Lover 1989, A Dry White Season 1989, The Rachel Papers 1989, State of Grace 1989, Mobsters 1992, Toys 1992, Clean Slate 1993, Indian Warrior 1993, The Browning Version 1993, Mary Reilly 1994, Midnight in Moscow 1994, A Man of No Importance 1995, The Innocent Sleep 1995, All Our Fault 1995, Two Deaths 1996, Nothing Personal 1996, The Gambler 1996, Dancing at Lughnasa 1997, Plunket and McClean 1997, The Last September 1998, Sleepy Hollow 1999, Dead On Time 1999, The Insider, End Game 1999, High Heels and Low Lifes 2001, Gosford Park 2001, Charlotte Gray 2001, Ali G Indahouse 2001, Path to War 2001, Christmas Carol: The Movie (voice) 2001, The Actors 2003, Open Range 2003, Sylvia 2003, Standing Room Only 2004, Harry Potter and the Prisoner of Azkaban 2004, Being Julia 2004, Sky Captain and the World of Tomorrow 2004, Layer Cake 2004, The Life Aquatic with Steve Zissou 2004, Harry Potter and the Goblet of Fire 2005, My Boy 2005, Elizabeth Rex 2005, The Good Sheperd 2006, Amazing Grace 2006, John Duffy's Brother 2006, The Good Night 2007, The Baker 2007, The Alps (voice) 2007, Harry Potter and the Order of the Phoenix 2007, Brideshead Revisited 2008, Harry Potter and the Half-Blood Prince 2009, Fantastic Mr Fox (voice) 2009, Harry Potter and the Deathly Hallows: Part 1 2010, The King's Speech 2010, Harry Potter and the Deathly Hallows: Part 2 2011, Quartet 2012. *Television includes:* Ghosts, Oscar Wilde, The Holy Experiment, Absurd Person Singular, The

Borderers, The Singing Detective (BAFTA for Best Actor 1987), The Heat of the Day, Maigret 1992, The Entertainer, Truth, Wives and Daughters (BAFTA for Best Actor 2000), Longitude 2000 (BAFTA for Best Actor 2001), Perfect Strangers (BAFTA Best Actor 2002), Cranford 2007, Emma 2009, Doctor Who (series) 2010, Comic Relief: Uptown Downstairs Abbey (film) (narrator, uncredited) 2011, Page Eight (film) 2011, Luck (series) 2012, Restless (film) 2012, National Theatre Live (series) – 50 Years on Stage 2013, Lucan (film) 2013, Fortitude (series) 2014, Quirke (mini-series) 2014, Common (film) 2014. *Leisure interests:* flying, gun collecting, clock making. *Address:* c/o ICM, Oxford House, 76 Oxford Street, London, W1N 0AX, England (office).

GAMEDZE, Chief Mgwagwa; Swazi government official; *Minister of Foreign Affairs;* Minister of Home Affairs 2008–11, of Justice and Constitutional Affairs 2011–13, of Foreign Affairs 2013–. *Address:* Ministry of Foreign Affairs, POB 518, Mbabane, Swaziland (office). *Telephone:* 24042661 (office). *Fax:* 24042669 (office). *E-mail:* ps_foreignaffairs@gov.sz (office).

GAMES, David Edgar, PhD, DSc, CChem, FRSC; British scientist and academic; *Professor Emeritus, Mass Spectrometry Research Unit, University of Wales, Swansea;* b. 7 April 1938, Ynysddu; s. of Alfred William Games and Frances Elizabeth Bell Games (née Evans); m. Marguerite Patricia Lee 1961; two s.; ed Lewis School, Pengam, King's Coll., Univ. of London; Lecturer, Sr Lecturer, Reader and Personal Chair., Univ. Coll., Cardiff 1965–89; Prof. of Mass Spectrometry and Dir of Mass Spectrometry Research Unit, Univ. of Wales at Swansea 1989–2003, now Prof. Emer., Head Dept of Chem. 1996–2001; fmr Chair. British Mass Spectrometry Soc.; Royal Soc. of Chem. Award in Analytical Separation Methods 1987, The Chromatographic Soc. Martin Medal 1991, Royal Soc. of Chem. SAC Gold Medal 1993, J. J. Thomson Gold Medal, Int. Mass Spectrometry Cttee 1997, Aston Medal, British Mass Spectrometry Soc. 1999. *Leisure interests:* swimming, walking. *Address:* 9 Heneage Drive, West Cross, Swansea, SA3 5BR, Wales, UK (home). *Telephone:* (1792) 405192 (home).

GAMKRELIDZE, Thomas V.; Georgian linguist and cultural historian; *President, Georgian National Academy of Sciences;* b. 23 Oct. 1929, Kutaisi, Georgia; s. of Valerian Gamkrelidze and Olimpiada Gamkrelidze; m. Nino Djavakhishvili 1968; one s. one d.; ed Tbilisi Univ.; post-grad. work 1952–55; Lecturer, Georgian Acad. of Sciences, Inst. of Linguistics 1956–60, Head of Dept 1960–73, Dir The Oriental Inst. 1973–; Head of Dept, Tbilisi State Univ. 1966–72; main work in area of theoretical linguistics, Kartvelian, Semitic and Indo-European linguistics and semiology; People's Deputy of the USSR 1989–91; mem. Parl., Repub. of Georgia 1992–; Ed.-in-Chief Voprosy Jazykoznanija (Russian Acad. of Sciences) 1988–94; mem. Georgian Nat. Acad. of Sciences 1974, Pres. 2005–; mem. USSR (now Russian) Acad. of Sciences 1984, Austrian Acad. of Sciences, Academia Europaea 2006, World Acad. of Art and Science 2007, Academia Scientiarum et Artium Europaea 2009; Corresp. FBA; Foreign Assoc., NAS 2006; Foreign mem. Sächsische Akad. der Wissenschaften, Latvian Acad. of Sciences 2007; Foreign Hon. mem. American Acad. of Arts and Sciences; Hon. mem. Indogermanische Gesellschaft, Linguistic Soc. of America, Societas Linguistica Europaea (Pres. 1986), Hungarian Acad. of Sciences 2007, Académie Internationale de Philosophie des Sciences 2009; Dr hc (Bonn, Chicago); Lenin Prize 1988, Humboldt Prize (FRG) 1989, Djavakhishvili Prize, Tbilisi Univ. 1992. *Publications:* Indo-European and the Indo-Europeans (two vols) (with V. V. Ivanov) 1984, Alphabetic Writing and the Old Georgian Script – Typology and Provenance of Alphabetic Writing Systems 1989. *Leisure interests:* music, tennis. *Address:* Georgian National Academy of Sciences, Rustaveli Avenue 52, Tbilisi 0108 (office); Jac. Nikoladze Street 6, 380009 Tbilisi, Georgia (home). *Telephone:* (32) 99-88-91 (office); (32) 22-64-92 (home). *Fax:* (32) 99-88-23 (office). *E-mail:* t.gamkrelidze@science.org.ge (office). *Website:* www.science.org.ge (office).

GAMLIN, Jarbom; Indian lawyer and politician; b. 16 April 1961, Along, Arunachal Pradesh; s. of Sokjar Gamlin and Gamde Ete Gamlin; m. 1st Shakuntala Doley Gamlin; m. 2nd Moter Jini Gamlin; one s. two d.; ed Sainik School, Assam, Univ. of Delhi; Pres. All Arunachal Pradesh Students Union 1981–83; mem. Lok Sabha (lower house of parl.) 1999–2004, mem. Cttee on Defence 1999–2000, Cttee on the Welfare of Scheduled Castes and Scheduled Tribes 1999–2000, 2000–01, Library Cttee 2000–01; mem. Arunachal Pradesh Congress Cttee; mem. Arunachal Pradesh Legis. Ass. 2004–; Home Minister of Arunachal Pradesh, then fmr Power Minister 2009–11, Chief Minister May–Oct. 2011; Pres. Arunachal Pradesh Bar Assn 1992–2001. *Address:* Arunachal Pradesh Congress Committee, Rajiv Gandhi Bhawan, F-Sector, Papum Pare District, Itanagar 791 113, India (office). *Telephone:* (360) 2217273 (office). *Fax:* (360) 2214859 (office). *Website:* www.apcc.in (office).

GAN, Ziyu; Chinese government official and engineer; b. 15 Oct. 1929, Xinyi, Guangdong Prov.; two s.; ed Zhongshan Univ.; engineer and Div. Chief, First Ministry of Machine-Building Industry 1952–56, Ministry of Heavy Industry 1952–56; joined CCP 1953; Sec. Chair.'s Office, State Science and Tech. Comm. 1956–58; apptd Deputy Chief of Planning Group, State Devt and Reform Comm. 1975, Vice-Minister 1978; Deputy Dir State Planning Comm. 1978–, State Admin. Comm. on Import and Export Affairs 1981–82, State Foreign Investment Comm. 1981–82; Vice-Chair. Drafting Cttee for Nat. Defence Law of People's Repub. of China 1993–; Deputy Chair. Nat. Leading Group for Work Concerning Foreign Capital 1994–; mem. Cen. Comm. for Discipline Inspection, CCP Cen. Committee 1992; mem. Preliminary Working Cttee of the Preparatory Cttee of the Hong Kong Special Admin. Region 1993–97, Chinese Govt Del., Hong Kong Handover Ceremony 1997; Chair. Overseas Chinese Affairs Cttee, 9th NPC 1998–2003; mem. Standing Cttee, 9th NPC 1998–2003; Pres. China Asscn for the Peaceful Use of Mil. Industrial Tech.; Prof., Man. Science Centre, Beijing Univ. *Address:* c/o Standing Committee of the National People's Congress, Beijing, People's Republic of China.

GANBAATAR, Adiya; Mongolian politician and academic; b. 8 Feb. 1959, Ulan Bator; s. of Adiya Ganbaatar and Ichinkhorlo Ganbaatar; m.; three d.; ed Łódź Univ., Poland; Lecturer, Mongolian State Univ. 1983–90; Chair. Democratic Socialist Movt 1990; mem. State Great Hural (Parl.) 1992–2000, Chair. Standing Cttee on the Budget 1997; fmr Ed-in-Chief UG (journal); Vice-Chair. Cen. Asia Devt Foundation 1992–; Pres. Mongolian Tennis Asscn 1997–; Distinguished

Officer, Banking and Finance 1999, Distinguished Officer, Educ. 2000. *Publications include:* three books on mathematics. *Leisure interests:* chess, tennis.

GANBOLD, Davaadorjiin, MSc (Econs), PhD; Mongolian politician; *National Security Adviser to the President;* b. 26 June 1957, Ulan Bator; s. of Tsedevsuren Davaadorj and Lodongiin Oyun; m. M. Tserengav Oyun; two d.; ed Moscow State Univ., USSR; Asst to Prof. of Political Econ., Mongolian State Univ. 1979–84; Prof. of Political Econ., State and Social Studies Acad. 1988–90; Founder-mem. Nat. Progress Party, Chair. Party Council; First Deputy Prime Minister 1990; mem. Great Hural (legislature) 1992–2000; Chair. Standing Cttee on Budget, Finance and Econs; Chair. Mongolian Nat. Democratic Party (merger of four opposition parties) 1992–96, Deputy Leader 1998; fmr Economic Policy Adviser to Prime Minister, currently Nat. Security Adviser to the Pres. and mem. Nat. Security Council; Chair. Railway Authority of Mongolia. *Leisure interests:* fishing, cycling, collecting stamps and model cars. *Address:* Room 258, Government House, Ulan Bator, Mongolia (office). *Telephone:* 942860 (office); 354045 (home). *Fax:* 942864 (office); 354060 (home).

GANDEL, John, AO; Australian business executive; *Chairman, Gandel Group of Companies;* b. 1935; m. Pauline Gandel; four c.; ed Univ. of Melbourne; inherited retailer Sussan from parents, sold co. to brother-in-law 1985, used proceeds to build business in shopping malls, currently Chair. Gandel Group Pty Ltd, fmr Chair. Gandel Retail Trust, Gandel Retail Management; f. Gandel Charitable Trust 1978; Chair. Jewish Museum of Australia 1983–93, currently Chair. Bd of Govs; fmr mem. Bd of Dirs Australian CSIRO; Fellow, Australian Inst. of Man., Australian Inst. of Co. Dirs; Patron Gandel Inst. for Adult Jewish Learning, Hebrew Univ. of Jerusalem; Dr hc (Tel-Aviv Univ.) 2006; Nat. Defense Medal 1994, Nat. Service Commemorative Medal 2002, Centenary Medal 2003. *Address:* Gandel Group Pty Limited, Level 3, 1341 Dandenong Road, Chadstone Shopping Centre, Melbourne, Vic. 3148, Australia (office).

GANDHI, Maneka; Indian politician; *Chairperson, People For Animals Trust;* b. 26 Aug. 1956, New Delhi; d. of the late Col T.S. Anand and of Amteshwar Anand; m. Sanjay Gandhi 1974 (died 1980); one s.; ed Lady Shri Ram Coll. for Women; Ed. Surya (Sun) magazine 1977–80; Founder and Leader of political party Rashtriya Sanjay Manch (merged with Janata Party 1988) 1983; Minister of State for the Environment and Forests 1989–91; mem. Lok Sabha (lower house of Parl.) for Pilibhit 1989–2008, for Aonla 2008–; Minister for Social Justice and Empowerment 1999–2001; Minister of State for Statistics and Programme Implementation 2002–04; Chair. People for Animals Trust, Cttee on Control and Supervision of Experiments on Animals, Soc. for Prevention of Cruelty to Animals; Founder Greenline Trees; Special Adviser to Voice (consumer action forum); cr. environmental film series New Horizons; writer and anchorwoman nat. TV programmes on animals, Heads and Tails, Maneka's Ark, Jeene ki Raah; Pres. Ruth Cowell Trust, Sanjay Gandhi Animal Care Centre; Patron Worldwide Fund for Nature; Chair. RUGMARK; Lord Erskine Award, Royal Soc. for the Prevention of Cruelty to Animals 1991, Vegetarian of the Year Award, Vegetarian Soc. 1995, Prani Mitra Award, Nat. Animal Welfare Bd 1997, Marchig Prize, Marchig Animal Welfare Trust (GB) 1997, Venu Menon Lifetime Achievement Award 1999, Bhagwan Mahavir Award 1999, Diwaliben Charitable Trust Award 1999, Dinanath Mangeshkar Aadishakti Puruskar 2001, Woman of the Year, Int. Women's Asscn 2001. *Publications include:* Sanjay Gandhi 1980, Mythology of Indian Plants, Animal Quiz, Penguin Book of Hindu Names, The Complete Book of Muslim and Parsi Names, First Aid for Animals, Animal Laws of India, Rainbow and Other Stories, Natural Health for Your Dog, Heads and Tails, Wise and Wonderful Animal Alphabet Quiz Book, Definitive Etymological Works, Animal Activism and Laws. *Leisure interests:* reading, writing, animal welfare, environmental protection, gardening, charity. *Address:* People For Animals Trust, 14, Ashoka Road, New Delhi 110 001 (office); A-4, Maharani Bagh, New Delhi 110 005, India (home). *Telephone:* (11) 23357088 (office). *Fax:* (11) 23354321 (office). *E-mail:* gandhim@nic .in. *Website:* www.peopleforanimalsindia.org (office).

GANDHI, Rahul, BA; Indian politician; *Vice-President, Indian National Congress;* b. 19 June 1970, New Delhi; s. of the late Rajiv Gandhi and of Sonia Gandhi; brother of Priyanka Gandhi-Vadra; ed St Stephen's Coll., New Delhi, Harvard Univ., Rollins Coll., USA, Trinity Coll., Cambridge, UK; descendant of Nehru-Gandhi political dynasty; worked in London with strategy consultancy firm Monitor Group; returned to India in 2002 to start software co.; canvassed for Congress Party on behalf of his mother in Amethi constituency, UP 1999; election campaign in parl. elections supervised by his sister Priyanka Gandhi 2004; MP (Lok Sabha) for Amethi constituency 2004–; mem. Indian Nat. Congress, Gen.-Sec. 2007–, mem. Congress Working Cttee 2007–, Vice-Pres. 2013–, also Chair. Indian Youth Congress and Nat. Students Union of India; Videocon India Youth Icon Award 2009, CNN-IBN Indian of the Year Award 2009. *Address:* Indian National Congress, 24 Akbar Road, New Delhi 110 011 (office); 10, Janpath, New Delhi 110 011, India. *Telephone:* (11) 23019080 (office); (11) 23012686 (home). *Fax:* (11) 23017047 (office); (11) 23018550 (home). *Website:* www.congress.org.in (office); rahulgandhi.co.in.

GANDHI, Sonia; Indian (b. Italian) politician; *President, Indian National Congress;* b. (Edvige Antonia Albina Maino), 9 Dec. 1946, Lusiana, nr Vicenza, Veneto, Italy; d. of Stefano Maino and Paola Maino; m. Rajiv Gandhi 1968 (fmr Prime Minister of India) (died 1991); one s. one d.; ed Univ. of Cambridge, UK, Nat. Gallery of Modern Art, Delhi; Pres. Rajiv Gandhi Foundation; mem. Indian Nat. Congress Cttee, Pres. 1998–2006 (resgnd), reappointed 2007–; Chair. Nat. Advisory Council 2004–06 (resgnd); elected MP (Lok Sabha) for Bellary constituency 1999, for Rae Bareli constituency 2004, 2009, Leader of Opposition –2004; Chair. United Progressive Alliance, Rajiv Gandhi Foundation, Indira Gandhi Memorial Trust, Jawaharlal Nehru Memorial Fund; Pres. Swaraj Bhavan Trust, Kamla Nehru Memorial Hosp. Soc.; Trustee, Jalianwala Bagh Nat. Memorial Trust; mem. Nehru Memorial Museum and Library; ranked by Forbes magazine amongst The World's 100 Most Powerful Women (third) 2004, (13th) 2006, (sixth) 2007, (21st) 2008, (13th) 2009, (seventh) 2011, (sixth) 2012, (ninth) 2013, ranked by Time magazine amongst the 100 Most Influential People in the World 2007, 2008, ranked by New Statesman magazine amongst The World's 50 Most Influential Figures (29th) 2010, ranked by Forbes magazine amongst The World's Most Powerful People (ninth) 2010, (11th) 2011, (12th) 2012, (21st) 2013. *Publications:* Rajiv 1992, Rajiv's World 1994. *Leisure interests:* reading, gardening.

Address: Indian National Congress, 24 Akbar Road, New Delhi 110 011 (office); Rajiv Gandhi Foundation, Jawahar Bhawan, Dr Rajendra Prasad Road, New Delhi 110 001; 10 Janpath, New Delhi 110 011, India (home). *Telephone:* (11) 23019080 (office); (11) 23014161 (home); (11) 23755117. *Fax:* (11) 23017047 (office). *E-mail:* aicc@congress.org.in (office); soniagandhi@sansad.nic.in (office). *Website:* www.congress.org.in (office); www.soniagandhi.org (home).

GANDOIS, Jean Guy Alphonse; French business executive; b. 7 May 1930, Nieul; s. of Eugène and Marguerite Gandois (née Teillet); m. Monique Testard 1953; two s.; ed École Polytechnique, Paris; Civil Engineer, Ministry of Public Works, French Guinea 1954–58; mem. of tech. co-operation missions to Brazil and Peru 1959–60; Asst to Commercial Dir Wendel & Cie 1961, Econ. Dir 1966; Econ. and Commercial Dir Wendel-Sidelor 1968; Gen. Man. Sacilor 1973; Pres., Dir-Gen. Sollac 1975; Dir-Gen. Rhône-Poulenc SA 1976, Vice-Pres. 1977–79, Chair. and CEO 1979–82 (resgnd); Chair. and CEO Pechiney 1986–94; Chair. Cockerill-Sambre (Belgium) 1987–99; Pres. CNPF (Nat. Council of French Employers) 1994, Hon. Pres. 2000–01; Chair. Supervisory Bd Suez-Lyonnaise des Eaux 2000–01, Vice-Chair. 2001–05; mem. Bd of Dirs, Eurazéo (fmrly Eurafrance); Hon. mem. Order of Australia, Commdr, Légion d'honneur, Grand Cordon, Ordre de Léopold, Grand Croix, Ordre de la Couronne (Belgium), Grand Officier, Couronne du Chêne (Luxembourg); Dr hc (Liège, Louvain). *Address:* c/o Board of Directors, Eurazéo, 32 rue de Monceau, 75008 Paris (office); 55 quai des Grands Augustins, 75006 Paris, France (home). *Telephone:* 1-42-96-29-85 (home). *E-mail:* jeangandois@aol.com (home).

GANELLIN, Charon Robin, PhD, DSc, FRS, FRSC; British scientist and academic; *Smith Kline & French Professor Emeritus of Medicinal Chemistry, University College London;* b. 25 Jan. 1934, London, England; s. of Leon Ganellin and Beila Cluer; m. 1st Tamara Greene 1956 (died 1997); one s. one d.; m. 2nd Dr Monique Garbarg 2003; ed Harrow County Grammar School for Boys and Queen Mary Coll., Univ. of London; Research Assoc., MIT, USA 1960; Research Chemist in Medicinal Chem., Smith Kline & French Labs Ltd (UK) 1958–59, Head of Dept 1961–75, Dir of Histamine Research, Smith Kline & French Research Ltd 1975–80, Vice-Pres. Research 1980–84, Vice-Pres. Chemical Research 1984–86; Advisory Tutor in Chem., Polytechnic of North London 1979–83; Hon. Lecturer, Dept of Pharmacology, Univ. Coll., London 1975–86, Hon. Research Fellow, Chem. 1985–86, Hon. Research Fellow, Pharmacology 1986–87, Smith Kline & French Prof. of Medicinal Chem. 1986–2003, Prof. Emer. 2003–; Fellow, Queen Mary and Westfield Coll., Univ. of London 1992; Pres. IUPAC Medicinal Chem. Section 2000–01, Chair. IUPAC Subcommittee Medicinal Chem. Drug Devt 2002–12, UK Govt Home Office Advisory Council on Misuse of Drugs 2002–07; Corresp. Academician, Académia Nacional Farmacia España 2006; Hon. Prof. of Medicinal Chem., Univ. of Kent 1979–89; Hon. mem. Sociedad Española de Química Terapéutica 1982, European Histamine Research Soc. 2007; Hon. DSc (Aston) 1995; UK Chemical Soc. Medallion in Medicinal Chem. 1977, Prix Charles Mentzer, Soc. de Chimie Thérapeutique (France) 1978, ACS (Div. of Medicinal Chem.) Award 1980, Royal Soc. of Chem. Tilden Medal 1982, Soc. for Chemical Industry Messel Medal 1988, Soc. for Drug Research Award 1989, Nat. Inventors Hall of Fame (USA) 1990, Royal Soc. of Chem. Adrien Albert Medal 1999, European Fed. for Medicinal Chem. Nauta Award in Pharmacochemistry 2004, Società Chimica Italiana Pratesi Gold Medal 2006, ACS (Div. of Medicinal Chem.) Hall of Fame 2007. *Achievements include:* co-inventor of Cimetidine (Tagamet™) 1970s, co-inventor of Tiprolisant 2000s. *Publications include:* Pharmacology of Histamine Receptors 1982, Frontiers in Histamine Research 1985, Dictionary of Drugs 1990, Medicinal Chemistry 1993, Dictionary of Pharmacological Agents 1997, Analogue-based Drug Discovery Vol. I 2006, Vol. II 2010, Vol. III 2013, Practical Studies for Medicinal Chemistry (Web edn) 2007, Introduction to Biological and Small Molecule Drug Research and Development 2013; research papers and reviews in various journals. *Address:* Department of Chemistry, University College London, 20 Gordon Street, London, WC1H 0AJ, England (office). *Telephone:* (20) 7679-4624 (office). *Fax:* (20) 7679-7463 (office). *E-mail:* c.r .ganellin@ucl.ac.uk (office). *Website:* www.ucl.ac.uk/silva/chemistry/staff/ emeritus/robin_ganellin (office).

GANGULY, Ashok S., MS, PhD, FRSC; Indian business executive and politician; *Chairman, ABP Private Limited;* b. 28 July 1935, Patna, Bihar; s. of the late Sekhar Nath Ganguly and Binapani Ganguly; m. Rooma Ganguly; two d.; ed Jaihind Coll., Mumbai Univ., Univ. of Illinois, USA; fmr Chair. Hindustan Lever Ltd 1980–90; fmr Chief Tech. Officer and Dir Unilever; Chair. ICI India Ltd 1996–2003; Chair. ICICI OneSource Ltd (I-OneSource, later Firstsource Solutions Ltd) –2010; currently Chair. ABP Pvt. Ltd (Ananda Bazar Patrika Group); Dir Cen. Bd Reserve Bank of India 2000–09; mem. (nominated) Rajya Sabha (Parl.) 2009–; Dir (non-exec.) British Airways plc 1996–2005, ICICI Knowledge Park Ltd, Mahindra & Mahindra Ltd, Tata AIG Life Insurance Co. Ltd; Ind. Dir Wipro Corpn 1999–; mem. Governing Council Centre for Advanced Financial Research and Learning; mem. Science Advisory Council to Prime Minister of India 1985–89, UK Advisory Bd of Research Councils 1991–94, Advisory Bd Microsoft Corpn (I) Pvt. Ltd, Hemogenomics Pvt. Ltd, Prime Minister's Council on Trade and Industry, Investment Comm., Nat. Knowledge Comm., India-USA CEO Council, Rajiv Gandhi Foundation; Trustee, Lever Hulme Trust UK; Hon. Prof., Chinese Acad. of Science, Shanghai 1996; Hon. CBE, UK 2006; Padma Bhushan 1987, Business Man of the Year, India 1996, Madhuri and Jagdish N. Sheth Int. Alumni Award for Exceptional Achievement 2003, Economic Times Lifetime Achievement Award 2008, Padma Vibhushan 2009, Outstanding Alumnus, Coll. of Food and Nutrition, Univ. of Illinois 1997, Int. Alumni Award, Univ. of Illinois 2003–04. *Publications include:* Industry and Liberalisation 1994, Strategic Manufacturing for Competitive Advantage 1998, Business Driven R&D: Managing Knowledge to Create Wealth 1999. *Leisure interests:* classical music, reading, golf. *Address:* ABP Private Ltd, Gandhi Mansion, 4th Floor, 20 Altamount Road, Mumbai 400 026 (office); N-6, Pemino Altamount Road, Mumbai 400 026, India (home). *Telephone:* (22) 23532331 (office); (22) 23538471 (home). *Fax:* (22) 23532333 (office). *E-mail:* ashok.ganguly01@gmail.com (office); ganguly.a@sansad.nic.in (office).

GANGULY, Sourav Chandidas, MBA; Indian professional cricketer; b. 8 July 1972, Calcutta (now Kolkata), Bengal; s. of late Chandidas Ganguly and of Nirupa Ganguly; m. Dona Roy; one d.; ed St. Xavier's, Calcutta; left-handed middle-order batsman, right-arm medium-pace bowler; played for Bengal 1989–2007, India

1992– (Capt. 2000–06), Lancs. 2000, Glamorgan 2005, Northants. 2006, Kolkata Knight Riders 2008–; First-class debut 1989/90; Test debut: England v India, Lord's 20–24 June 1996; ODI debut: India v West Indies, Brisbane 11 Jan. 1992; has played in 113 tests (49 as Capt.), scored 7,212 runs (average 42.17, highest score 239) with 16 hundreds and took 32 wickets; scored 15,025 First-class runs (average 43.93, highest score 239) with 31 hundreds and took 164 wickets (best bowling 6/46); 311 ODIs, scored 11,363 runs (average 41.02, highest score 183 v Sri Lanka at Taunton, England) with 22 hundreds and took 100 wickets; led India to second place at World Cup 2003; Arjuna Award 1997, Padma Shri 2004. *Address:* 2/6 Biren Roy Road, Behala, Kolkata 700 008, India (home). *Website:* www .souravganguly.net.

GANIĆ, Ejup, DSc; Bosnia and Herzegovina engineer, academic and politician; *President, Sarajevo School of Science and Technology;* b. 3 March 1946, Novi Pazar; m. Fahrija Ganić; one s. one d.; ed Univ. of Belgrade, Massachusetts Inst. of Tech.; researcher, consultant, Prof. of Mechanical Eng, Univ. of Illinois, Chicago 1975–82; returned to Bosnia and Herzegovina 1982; Prof., Univ. of Sarajevo 1982–; worked as Exec. Dir UNIS Co.; mem. Presidency of Bosnia and Herzegovina 1990–96, Vice-Pres. 1992–96; Vice-Pres. Fed. of Bosnia and Herzegovina 1994–96, Co-Pres. 1996–2002; Founder and Pres. Sarajevo School of Science and Tech. 2004–; Pres. MET Foundation. *Publications:* Handbook of Heat Transfer Applications 1985, Handbook of Heat Transfer Fundamentals 1985, Handbook of Essential Engineering Information and Data 1991, Engineering Companion 2003; more than 100 scientific papers. *Address:* Office of the President, Sarajevo School of Science and Technology, Bistrik 7, 71000 Sarajevo (office); Faculty of Mechanical Engineering, Chair for Process Technique, University of Sarajevo, West Building, Floor IV, Room 407, Vilsonovo šetalište 9, 71000 Sarajevo, Bosnia and Herzegovina (office). *Telephone:* (33) 617205 (office). *Fax:* (33) 617205 (office). *E-mail:* ejup_ganic@hotmail.com; ganic@mef.unsa.ba. *Website:* ssst.edu.ba (office).

GANIEV, Rivner Fazilovich; Russian mechanical engineer; *Director, Non-linear Wave Mechanics and Technology Centre, Russian Academy of Sciences;* b. 1 April 1937, Bashkiriya; m. Galina Mikhailovna Antonovskaya; two s.; ed Ufa Aviation Inst.; engineer constructor, jr, sr researcher, Head of Dept, Inst. of Mechanics Ukrainian Acad. of Sciences 1959–78; Head of Lab., Research Inst. of Machine Devt 1978–89, Deputy Dir 1989–95; Dir of Non-linear Wave Mechanics and Tech. Centre, Russian Acad. of Sciences 1995–; Head, Applied Physics Faculty, Moscow Aviation Inst.; Chair. Council of Dirs, United Inst. of Automobile Mechanics and Tech. in Oil Extraction of the Russian Acad. of Sciences and the Acad. of Sciences of the Repub. of Bashkortostan; mem. Scientific Council on Problem Reliability of Machines; Corresp. mem. USSR (now Russian) Acad. of Sciences 1987, mem. 1994; specialist in applied math., theoretical and applied mechanics, mechanical eng; more than 100 inventions and patents; research in theory of resonance phenomena at nonlinear spatial oscillations of solid and deformable matter, theory of nonlinear oscillations of multiphase systems, vibration and wave processes and tech. *Publications include:* Dynamics of Particles under Influence of Vibrations 1975, Solid Matter Oscillations 1976, Oscillatory Phenomena in Multiphase Media and their Applications to Technology 1980; more than 300 other published works, including 15 monographs and numerous articles in scientific journals. *Leisure interests:* sport, skiing. *Address:* Non-linear Wave Mechanics and Technology Centre, Russian Academy of Sciences, 4 Bardin Street, 117334 Moscow, Russia (office). *Telephone:* (495) 135-55-93 (office). *Fax:* (495) 135-61-26 (office). *E-mail:* wavete@ccas.ru (office). *Website:* www.nwmtc.ac.ru (office).

G'ANIYEV, Elyor Majidovich; Uzbekistani politician; *Minister of Foreign Economic Relations, Investment and Trade;* b. 1 Jan. 1960, Syrdarya Prov.; m.; five c.; ed Tashkent Polytechnic Inst.; Asst, Tashkent Polytechnic Inst. 1981–85; service in the Armed Forces 1985–90; Sr Adviser, State Cttee for Foreign Econ. and Trade Relations 1990–92; Head of Dept, Ministry of Foreign Econ. Relations 1992–93; Head of Div., Inst. for Strategic and Regional Studies under Pres. of Uzbekistan 1993–94; Deputy Minister of Foreign Econ. Relations 1994–95, First Deputy Minister 1995–97, Minister of Foreign Econ. Relations 1997–2002; Deputy Prime Minister and Chair. Agency for Foreign Econ. Relations 2002–05; Deputy Prime Minister and Minister of Foreign Affairs 2005–06; Minister of Foreign Econ. Relations, Investment and Trade 2006–09, 2012–; Deputy Prime Minister and Minister of Foreign Econ. Relations 2009–10; Deputy Prime Minister, Minister of Foreign Affairs, responsible for Foreign Econ. Activities, the Attraction of Foreign Investment and the Localization of Production 2010–12; Pres. Volleyball Fed. of Uzbekistan. *Address:* Ministry of Foreign Economic Relations, Investment and Trade, 100029 Tashkent, Shevchenko ko'ch. 1, Uzbekistan (office). *Telephone:* (71) 238-51-00 (office). *Fax:* (71) 238-51-00 (office). *E-mail:* secretary@mfer.uz (office). *Website:* www.mfer.uz (office).

GANNUSHKINA, Svetlana; Russian mathematician; b. 6 March 1942, Moscow; m.; one s. one d.; ed Moscow State Univ.; Lecturer, later Assoc. Prof. of Math., Historical and Archive Inst., Moscow (now Russian State Humanities Univ.) 1970–2000; involved in human rights work since late 1980s, including with UNHCR and Secours Catholique (French charity); Co-founder Grazhdanskoe Sodeistvie (Citizen's Assistance) 1990; Founding mem. Human Rights Centre Memorial 1993, Migration Rights Network 1996; went to Chechnya and Ingushetia to provide humanitarian aid and help establish legal advice centres; mem. Expert Council under the Commr Human Rights in Russia; mem. Civil Soc. Insts and Human Rights Council 2002–; UNHCR Nansen Award for Refugees 2004, Homo Homini Award 2006; For Faith and Service of Russia Order 2010. *Address:* Civil Society Institutions and Human Rights Council, 103132 Moscow, 4, Staraya Square, Russia (office). *Telephone:* (495) 606-49-14 (office).

GANSER, Gérard Roger Gaston; French civil servant; b. 6 Jan. 1949, Montreuil-Sous-Bois; s. of Pierre Ganser and Simone Braillon; m. Aimée Fontaine (divorced); one s.; ed Lycées Paul Valéry and Louis le Grand, Ecole polytechnique, Ecole nat. d'admin; auditor, Court of Revenue 1976–80, public auditor 1980, chief adviser 1993–98, Sec.-Gen. 1998–; with Interministerial Mission of the Sea 1979–80; commercial adviser in Mexico 1981–82; with Ministry of Agric. 1983, Jt Dir Ministry of Trade and Tourism 1983–84, with Ministry of Industrial Redeployment and Trade 1984, Ministry for Communications 1988, Dir 1989–91; Jt Dir-Gen. Commercial Affairs Télédiffusion de France 1984–86; reporter to Constitutional Council 1987–88; Pres., Chair. Soc. financière de radiodiffusion

(Sofirad) 1991–94; Vice-Pres. Radio Monte Carlo 1991–94; auditor, European Examinations Office 1995; auditor, Inst. des hautes études de la défense nat. 1996; Sec.-Gen. Cour des comptes 1998–99 (Chief Adviser 1993–); Chevalier Ordre nat. du Mérite. *Address:* Cour des Comptes, 13 rue Cambon, 75001 Paris (office); 11 rue de Verneuil, 75007 Paris, France (home). *Telephone:* 1-42-97-59-66 (home). *E-mail:* gganser@ccomptes.fr (office).

GANTAR, Pavel, MA, PhD; Slovenian sociologist and politician; *President, For Real—New Politics (Zares);* b. 26 Oct. 1949, Gorenja vas, Škofja Loka, Upper Carniola, Yugoslavia (now Slovenia); ed professional school for carpentry, Faculty of Political Sciences, Univ. of Ljubljana, Univ. of Essex, UK, Univ. of Zagreb, Croatia; as student, Co-founder student group 'November 13th' 1971; Asst Prof., Faculty of Social Sciences, Univ. of Ljubljana 1974–94; mem. Urban Planning Council of Ljubljana 1970s; mem. Editorial Bd Journal for the Critique of Science (Časopis za kritiko znanosti, ČKZ) 1976; columnist, Mladina magazine 1980s; Pres. SKUC-Forum (org. for alternative culture) 1980s; studied in UK 1984; apptd Chair. CP cell, Faculty of Social Sciences, Univ. of Ljubljana 1984, expelled from CP of Slovenia for using his position to defend essayist Spomenka Hribar accused of denigration of Yugoslav People's Liberation War 1985; among first scholars of contemporary underground social movts in Slovenia and Yugoslavia late 1980s, actively involved in 'Slovenian Spring'; Founding mem. Cttee for the Protection of Human Rights 1988–90; joined Liberal Democratic Party 1990; elected to Državni zbor (Nat. Ass.) 1990 (re-elected 2004, 2008), Chair. 2008–11; Minister of the Environment and Spatial Planning 1994–2000, of Information Society 2001–04; Founding mem. For Real—New Politics (Zares) 2007–, Pres. 2012–. *Publications include:* several articles on civil society under the socialist regime, theories of social planning, spatial planning, information society. *Address:* For Real—New Politics (Zares), 1000 Ljubljana, Zupančičeva 8, Slovenia (office). *Telephone:* (1) 2428750 (office). *Fax:* (1) 2428753 (office). *E-mail:* info@zares.si (office). *Website:* www.zares.si (office).

GANTNER, Carrillo Baillieu, AO, MFA; Australian theatre manager, director, actor and business executive; *Chairman, Victorian Art Centre;* b. 17 June 1944, San Francisco, Calif.; s. of Vallejo Gantner and Neilma Gantner; m. 1st Nancy Black 1971 (divorced 1982); two s. one d. (deceased); m. 2nd Dr Jennifer Webb; two s.; ed Melbourne Grammar School and Melbourne, Stanford and Harvard Univs; Fellow, Stanford Univ. 1968–69; Asst, Adelaide Festival of Arts 1969–70; Drama Officer, Australian Council for the Arts 1970–73; Gen. Man. Melbourne Theatre Co. 1973–75; Exec. Dir Playbox Theatre Co. Ltd 1976–84, The CUB Malthouse; Cultural Counsellor, Australian Embassy, Beijing 1985–87; Artistic Dir Playbox Theatre Centre 1988–93, Chair. Playbox Malthouse Ltd 1994–96; Councillor, City of Melbourne 1996–99 (Chair. Planning and Devt Cttee 1996–98, Docklands Cttee 1998–99, Deputy Chair. Finance and Service Cttee and Audit Cttee 1998–99); Chair. Performing Arts Bd Australia Council 1990–93, Nat. Circus Summit 1990, Nat. Dance Summit 1991, Nat. Advisory Council, Musica Viva 1993–, Melbourne Int. Comedy Festival 1995–, Victorian Art Centre; Pres. Melbourne Chapter of URASENKE 1995–; Dir Myer Foundation 1984–92 (Vice-Pres. 1992–), Asialink 1990–92 (Chair. 1992–), Mayfair Hanoi Ltd (Hong Kong) 1996–98, Deputy Chair. 1999–; mem. Australia–China Council 1989–94, Australia Abroad Council 1991–95, Exec. Cttee Asia Pacific Philanthropy Consortium 1994–, Nat. Advisory Council, Adelaide Festival 1996–; Corresp. mem. The Hague Club 1994–; Trustee, Sidney Myer Fund 1991–; Gov. Fed. for Asian Cultural Promotion 1994–; Japan Foundation Visitors Program 1991; mem. Working Group to establish an Asian Business Council for the Arts 1997–98; Chair. Arts Man. Course Advisory Cttee, Victorian Coll. of the Arts 1996–98; Chair. Barclay Investment Pty Ltd, Myer Investment Pty Ltd 1998–; Victorian of the Year 2007. *Publications:* articles in professional journals. *Leisure interests:* viticulture, tennis. *Address:* The Myer Foundation, Level 18, 8 Exhibition Street, Melbourne, Vic. 3000, Australia (office). *Telephone:* (3) 9207-3040 (office). *Fax:* (3) 9207-3070 (office). *E-mail:* enquiries@myerfoundation.org.au (office). *Website:* www .myerfoundation.org.au (office); www.theartscentre.com.au (office).

GANZ, Bruno; Swiss film actor; b. 22 March 1941, Zürich-Seebach; unsuccessful film debut 1960; theatre debut 1961; Co-founder, with Peter Stein, Schaubühne theatre co., Berlin 1970; leading man of the New German Wave of films. *Films include:* Der Herr mit der schwarzen Melone (The Man in the Black Derby) 1960, Es dach überem Chopf (A Roof Over Your Head) 1961, Chikita 1961, Der Sanfte Lauf 1967, Sommergäste (Summer Guests) 1976, Lumière 1976, Die Marquise von O. . . 1976, Die Wildente (The Wild Duck) 1976, Der amerikanische Freund (The American Friend) 1977, Messer im Kopf (Knife in the Head) 1978, Die Linkshandige Frau (The Left-Handed Woman) 1978, The Boys from Brazil 1978, Nosferatu: Phantom der Nacht 1979, Retour à la bien-aimée (Return to the Beloved) 1979, Oggetti smarriti (aka Lost and Found) 1980, Der Erfinder (The Inventor) 1980, 5% de risques 1980, La dame aux camelias (Lady of the Camelias) 1980, Rece do góry (aka Hands Up!) 1981, La provinciale (aka The Girl from Lorraine) 1981, Die Falschung (False Witness) 1981, Logik des Gefühls 1982, Polenta 1982, System ohne Schatten (aka Closed Circuit, USA) 1983, Killer aus Forida 1983, Dans la ville blanche (In the White City) 1983, De IJssalon (aka Private Resistance, USA) 1985, Der Pendler 1986, El Río de oro 1986, Der Himmel über Berlin (The Sky Over Berlin) 1987, The Legendary Life of Ernest Hemingway 1988, Un amore di donna (Love of a Woman) 1988, Nosferatu a Venezia 1988, Bankomatt 1989, Strapless 1989, Schrödingers kat 1990, Erfolg (Success) 1991, Börn náttúrunnar (Children of Nature) 1991, La domenica specialmente (Especially on Sunday) 1992, Prague 1992, The Last Days of Chez Nous 1992, Le quator des possibles (The Quartet of the Possibles) (voice) 1993, L'absence 1993, In weiter Ferne, so nah! (Faraway, So Close!) 1993, Brandnacht (Night on Fire) 1993, Heller Tag 1994, You Can't Go Home Again (voice) 1998, Mia aioniotita kai mia mera (Eternity and a Day) 1998, Pane e tulipani (aka Bread and Tulips) 2000, WerAngstWolf (WhoAfraidWolf) 2000, Epsteins Nacht (Epstein's Night) 2002, La Forza del passato (The Power of the Past) 2002, Luther 2003, The Manchurian Candidate 2004, Der Untergang 2004 (The Downfall: Hitler and the End of the Third Reich) 2004, Vitus 2006, Baruto no gakuen 2006, Youth Without Youth 2007, Stairway to Nowhere 2008, Der Baader Meinhof Komplex 2008, I skoni tou hronou 2008, The Reader 2008. *Television includes:* Der Spaßvogel 1964, Frühlings Erwachen 1966, Die Unberatenen 1966, Die Schlacht bei Lobositz 1968, Maß für Maß 1968, Im Dickicht der Städte 1968, Torquato Tasso 1969, Eine Große Familie 1970, Die Mutter 1971, Peer Gynt (mini-series) 1971, Der Ignorant und der Wahnsinnige 1972, Prinz Friedrich von Homburg 1973, Die Bakchen 1974, Geschichte einer Liebe 1978, Schwarz und weiß wie Tage und Nächte (Black and White Like Day and Night) 1978, Fermata Etna 1981, Der Park 1985, Väter und Söhne – Eine deutsche Tragödie" (Fathers and Sons) (mini-series) 1986, Die Wette (Journey's End) 1990, Tassilo – Ein Fall für sich (series) 1991, Il grande Fausto (aka The Price of Victory) (mini-series) 1995, Diario senza date 1995, Todliches Schweigen 1996, Anwalt Abel – Ein Richter in Angst 1996, Tatort – Schattenwelt 1996, Gegen Ende der Nacht (Daybreak) 1998, Johann Wolfgang von Goethe: Faust 2001, Have No Fear: The Life of Pope John Paul II 2005, Copacabana 2007, Ein starker Abgang 2008.

GAO, Bo; Chinese architect and photographer; b. 1954, Chongqing, Sichuan Prov.; m. Delphine Gao; ed Sichuan Fine Arts Inst., Central Acad. of Art and Design, Beijing, Catholic Inst. of Paris, France; architect, Beijing 1996–; Dir Beijing Boart Culture Devt Co. Ltd; f. China Heritage Soc.; worked as photographer for Agence VU (photographic agency), Paris 1989–95; mem. Chinese Photographers' Inst.; Winner, People's Daily Photography Competition 1986. *Works include:* Portraits and Masks Duality Series 1964, Faint Memory 2006, Unlimited Scenery 2007, Searching 2007. *Exhibitions include:* Int. Festival of Photography, Pingyao, Sichuan 2002, Arles Festival, France 2003, Museum of New Art, Pontiac, Michigan 2004, Three Shadows Photography Art Center, Beijing 2007, 2008. *Publications include:* volumes of photographs on rural China, Tibet and Tiananmen Square. *Address:* c/o Agence Vu, 17 boulevard Henri IV, 75004 Paris, France (office).

GAO, Changli; Chinese politician; b. July 1937, Yutai, Shandong Prov.; ed Chinese People's Univ.; joined CCP 1956; cadre Yutai Co. People's Govt, cadre Office of CCP Jining Pref. Cttee; Vice-Sec. CCP Yishui Co. Cttee, Sec. CCP Rizhao Co. Cttee, Vice-Chief Sec. then Chief Sec. CCP Shandong Prov. Cttee 1976–87; Vice-Gov. Shandong Prov. and Sec. Political and Legal Cttee of CCP Shandong Prov. Cttee; mem. Trial Cttee of Supreme People's Court; Vice-Chair. Supreme People's Court 1993–98; Minister of Justice 1998–2000; Alt. mem. 14th CCP Cen. Cttee 1992–97, 15th CCP Cen. Cttee 1997–2002. *Address:* c/o Ministry of Justice, 11 Xiaguangli, Sanyuanqiao, Chao Yang Qu, Beijing 100016, People's Republic of China.

GAO, Dezhan; Chinese state official and engineer; b. 6 Aug. 1932, Qixia, Shandong Prov.; ed Dalian Eng Inst., Liaoning Prov.; joined CCP 1950; engineer and Dir China Sugar Refinery, Jilin Prov. 1954–58; Deputy Chief Engineer and Deputy Dir Petrochemical Bureau, Jilin Prov. 1961–76; Dir Jilin Prov. Econ. Comm. 1980–81; Vice-Gov. Jilin Prov. 1983–85, Gov. 1985–87; Deputy Sec. CCP Jilin Prov. Cttee 1985–87; Minister of Forestry 1987–93; Vice-Chair. All-China Greening Cttee 1988–93, Deputy Head Cen. Forest Fire Prevention 1988–93; Deputy Head State Leading Group for Comprehensive Agricultural Devt 1990–; Deputy Head Cen. Forest Fire Prevention 1988–93; Alt. mem. 12th CCP Cen. Cttee 1982–87, 13th CCP Cen. Cttee 1987–92, mem. 14th CCP Cen. Cttee 1992–97; Sec. Tianjin City CCP Cttee 1993–97; Deputy, 8th NPC 1993–98, mem. 9th Standing Cttee of NPC 1998–2003, Chair. Agric. and Rural Affairs Cttee of NPC 1998–2003; Special Gold Prize for Chinese Greening Science and Tech. 1993. *Address:* c/o Standing Committee of the National People's Congress, Beijing, People's Republic of China.

GAO, Guofu, PhD; Chinese business executive; *Chairman, China Pacific Insurance (Group) Company Ltd;* ed Shanghai Jiao Tong Univ.; fmr Gen. Man. Shanghai Urban Construction Investment and Devt Corpn; fmr Gen. Man. Shanghai Waigaoqiao Free Trade Zone Devt Co.; fmr Acting Pres. Shanghai Wanguo Securities Ltd; fmr Sec. China Pacific Insurance (Group) Co. Ltd, Exec. Dir and Chair. 2006–, Sec. CCP China Pacific Insurance Group Cttee. *Address:* China Pacific Insurance (Group) Co. Ltd, 190 Yincheng Zhong Road, Shanghai 200120, Shanghai Province, People's Republic of China (office). *Telephone:* (21) 58776688 (office). *Fax:* (21) 68870922 (office). *E-mail:* info@cpic.com.cn (office). *Website:* www.cpic.com.cn (office).

GAO, Hongbo, (Xiang Chuan); Chinese poet; *Vice-President and Secretary of the Secretariat, Chinese Writers Association;* b. 1951, Kailu, Nei Monggol; ed Peking Univ.; joined the PLA 1969; Vice-Chief News Section, Literature and Art Gazette; Vice-Dir Gen. Office of Chinese Writers' Asscn, later Assoc. Ed., Ed. Journal of Poetry, currently Vice-Pres. and Sec. Secr. of Chinese Writers' Asscn. *Publications:* Elephant Judge, Geese, Geese, Geese, The Crocodile that Eats Stones, The Secret of the Shouting Spring, I Love You, Fox, The Fox that Grows Grapes, The Maid and the Bubble Gum, Flying Dragon and Magic Pigeon, I Wonder, Whisper (Nat. Award for Best Children's Literature). *Address:* Chinese Writers' Association, No.25, East Tucheng Road, Chaoyang District, Beijing 100013, People's Republic of China (office). *Telephone:* (10) 64221865 (office). *Fax:* (10)64222240 (office).

GAO, Hucheng, DSc; Chinese government official; *Minister of Commerce;* b. 1951, Shuozhou, Shanxi Prov.; ed Beijing Second Foreign Languages Inst., Nat. Univ. of Zaire (now Univ. of Kinshasa), Democratic Repub. of Congo, Univ. Paris VII, France; Commercial Officer, Embassy in Kinshasa, Zaire (now Democratic Repub. of Congo) 1977–80; Sec., China Nat. Machinery and Equipment Import and Export Corpn (CMEC) 1980–82, Operations Man. and Deputy Gen. Man., CMEC French Office, Paris 1982–87, Deputy Chief, Financial Dept, CMEC 1987–89, Chief 1989–90; Deputy Gen. Man. China Nat. Resources Corpn 1992–94, also Sec., CCP Party Cttee; Head, Planning and Finance Dept, Ministry of Foreign Trade and Econ. Cooperation 1994–97, Asst to Minister 1997–2002, also mem. CCP Leading Party Group 1997–2002; Vice-Chair., People's Govt, Guangxi Zhuang Autonomous Region 2002–03; Vice-Minister of Commerce 2003–13, Minister 2013–, mem. Ministry of Commerce CCP Leading Party Group 2003–09; Alt. mem. 18th CCP Cen. Cttee 2012–. *Address:* Ministry of Commerce, 2 Dongchangan Dajie, Dongcheng Qu, Beijing 100731, People's Republic of China. *Telephone:* (10) 65284671 (office). *Fax:* (10) 65599340 (office). *E-mail:* webmaster@mofcom.gov .cn (office). *Website:* www.mofcom.gov.cn (office).

GAO, Jianping, BA; Chinese economist and business executive; *Chairman, Industrial Bank Company Limited;* served as Deputy Gen. Man. Gen. Office of Industrial Bank, Dir of Industrial Bank's Office in Fuzhou Econ. and Technological Devt Zone, Gen. Man. Office of Industrial Bank, Head of Industrial Bank's Shanghai Br. Preparatory Team, Vice-Pres. of Industrial Bank and Pres. of Industrial Bank's Shanghai Br., Vice-Pres. of Industrial Bank (in charge of overall

management), Sec. of CP Cttee, mem. Bd of Dirs Industrial Bank Co. Ltd 2007–, currently also Chair. *Address:* Industrial Bank Co. Ltd, 154 Hudong Road, Fuzhou 350003, People's Republic of China (office). *Telephone:* (591) 87839338 (office). *Fax:* (591) 87841932 (office). *E-mail:* webmaster@cib.com.cn (office). *Website:* www.cib .com.cn (office).

GAO, Shangquan; Chinese government official and professor of economics; b. 1929, Jia Ding Co., Shanghai; s. of Gao Ruyu and Xiang Shi; m. Cha Peijun 1958; one s.; ed St John's Univ., Shanghai; worked as researcher, Deputy Div. Chief, Div. Chief, Bureau for Machine-Bldg Industry of Ministry of Industry of local North-Eastern People's Govt; Policy Research Dept, First Ministry of Machine-Bldg Industry; Research Dept, Ministry of Agricultural Machine-Bldg Industry; Office of Agricultural Mechanization, State Council; Policy Research Dept, State Comm. of Machine-Bldg Industry; Research Fellow, Research Centre for Agricultural Devt and Sr Economist, State Comm. of Machine-Bldg Industry; State Comm. for Restructuring Econ. System 1982, then Deputy Dir and Head, Research Inst. of Restructuring the Econ. System 1985–93; Vice-Minister in charge of State Comm. for Restructuring the Econ. System 1985–93; mem. preliminary working Cttee of preparatory Cttee of the Hong Kong Special Admin. Region and Head of Econ. Panel 1993–97, 9th Nat. Cttee of CPPCC 1998–2003; mem. Sino-Japanese Econ. Exchange Comm.; Vice-Group-Leader, Leading Group for Restructuring Housing System, under State Council; Pres. China Research Soc. for Restructuring the Econ. Systems, China Soc. of Enterprise Reform and Devt, China Inst. for Reform & Devt, China Reform Foundation, China Soc. of Urban Housing System Reform, Asscn of Future Market of China; Vice-Pres. Asscn of China's Urban Economy, Asscn of China's Industrial Economy, Asscn for Study of China's Specific Condition, Asscn of Social and Economics Publs; Chair. Research Group for Rural and Urban Housing Reform 1995–; mem. UN Cttee for Devt Policy; Doctorate Supervisor, Prof., Beijing Univ. and Shanghai Jiaotong Univ.; Dean Man. School, Zhejiang Univ.; Prof. Nankai Univ., Chinese People's Univ., Shanghai Univ. of Finance and Econs; MBA programme adviser of Nat. Univ. of Australia; Outstanding Scholar Award Hong Kong Polytechnic. *Publications:* Enterprises Should Enjoy Certain Autonomy 1956, Follow A Road of Our Own in Agricultural Modernization 1982, Nine Years of Reform in China's Economic System 1987, A Road To Success 1987, Selected Works of Gao Shangquan 1989, China: A Decade of Economic Reform 1989, The Reform of China's Economic System 1991, Lead to a Powerful Country 1991, On Planning and Market in China 1992, From Planned Economy to the Socialist Market Economy 1993, An Introduction to Socialist Market Economy 1994, China: The Second Revolution 1995, China's Economic Reform 1996, Extensive Talk About China's Market Economy 1998, The Second Revolution 1998, Market Economy and China's Reform 1999, Two Decades of Reform in China 1999; also ed. of numerous publications. *Address:* State Commission for Restructuring the Economic System, 22 Xianmen Street, Beijing 100017, People's Republic of China. *Telephone:* (10) 63096649. *Fax:* (10) 66014562. *E-mail:* sqgao@bj.col.com.cn (office).

GAO, Xingjian, BA; French (b. Chinese) writer and dramatist; b. 4 Jan. 1940, Ganzhou, Jiangxi Prov., People's Republic of China; ed Dept of Foreign Languages, Beijing; translator, China Reconstructs (magazine), later for Chinese Writers Asscn; spent five years in re-education during Cultural Revolution; Artistic Dir People's Art Theatre, Beijing 1981; left China 1987 after work banned in 1985, living in Paris 1988–, became French citizen 1998; Chevalier des Arts et des Lettres 1992, Légion d'honneur 2000; Prix Communauté française de Belgium 1994, Prix du Nouvel An Chinois 1997, Nobel Prize for Literature 2000. *Publications include:* plays: Absolute Signal 1982, Bus Stop 1983, Wild Man 1990, The Other Shore 1999, Fugitives 1993, Tales of Mountains and Seas 1993, The Man Who Questions Death 2003; novels: Soul Mountain 1999, Return to Painting 2001, One Man's Bible 2002; other: Snow in August (opera) 2002, Buying a Fishing Rod for my Grandfather (short stories) 2004. *Address:* c/o HarperCollins, 77-85 Fulham Palace Road, London, W6 8JB, England (office).

GAO, Xiqing, BA, LLM, JD; Chinese lawyer and banking executive; *Vice-Chairman and President, China Investment Corporation;* b. Sept. 1953; ed Univ. of Int. Business and Econs, Beijing, Duke Univ. School of Law, USA; worked as Assoc. at Mudge Rose Guthrie Alexander & Ferdon (law firm), Wall Street, New York; returned to China 1988; Deputy Chair. and CEO Bank of China International (Holdings) Ltd 1990s; Gen. Counsel and Dir Gen. Public Offering Supervision Dept, China Securities Regulatory Comm. (CSRC) 1992–95, later Vice-Chair.; Deputy Chief Exec. Hong Kong-Macao Regional Office, Bank of China 1997–99; later Vice-Chair. Nat. Council for the Social Security Fund; currently Vice-Chair. and Pres. China Investment Corpn; mem. Bd of Trustees Duke Univ. 2008–. *Achievements include:* first Chinese citizen to pass NY State Bar exam. *Address:* China Investment Corporation, New Poly Plaza, 1 Chaoyangmen Beidajie, Dongcheng District, Beijing 100010, People's Republic of China (office). *Telephone:* (10) 6408-6277 (office). *Fax:* (10) 6408-6908 (office). *E-mail:* pr@china -inv.cn (office). *Website:* www.china-inv.cn (office).

GAO, Yan; Chinese government official and engineer; b. 1942, Yushu Co., Jilin Prov.; joined CCP 1965; Deputy Dir Jilin Thermal Power Plant 1965–74 (also Sec. CCP and Communist Youth League); Sr Engineer and Deputy Dir, later Dir Electricity Bureau 1975; Head Org. Dept, CCP Jilin Prov. Cttee 1988–95, Deputy Sec. Jilin CCP Jilin Prov. Cttee 1988–95; Vice-Gov. of Jilin Prov. 1988–92, Gov. 1992–95; Sec. CCP Cttee, Yunan Prov. 1995–97; Dir Political Dept, Chinese People's Armed Police Force; Sec. CCP 6th Yunnan Prov. Cttee; mem. 14th CCP Cen. Cttee 1992–97, 15th CCP Cen. Cttee 1997–2002; Deputy Gen. Man. State Electrical Power Corpn 1997–98, Gen. Man. 1998–2002; Vice Minister of Power Industry 1997–98. *Address:* c/o State Council, Beijing, People's Republic of China.

GAO, Yaojie, MD; Chinese physician and activist; b. 1927, cen. Henan Prov.; m.; several c.; ed Henan Univ.; retd gynaecologist from Henan Coll. of Traditional Chinese Medicine who discovered wide-scale HIV infection amongst citizens of Henan Prov. in early 1990s, alerted Govt authorities 1996 but no action taken; spent much of her pension printing pamphlets to educate rural residents and to buy medicine for the sick; currently active in giving AIDS educ. lectures; placed under house arrest 2007; Jonathan Mann Award for Global Health and Human Rights, Global Health Council 2001, Ramon Magsaysay Award for Public Service 2003, named one of 10 People Who Moved China in 2003, Touching China Award from China Central TV 2004, Vital Voices Global Partnership Global Leadership

Award, Women Changing Our World 2007, New York Acad. of Sciences Heinz R. Pagels Human Rights of Scientists Award 2007. *Publications:* Ten Thousand Letters (First Chinese Publications and Media Award 2005) 2004, The Soul of Gao Yaojie 2008. *Address:* China AIDS Orphan Fund, The Minneapolis Foundation, 800 IDS Center, 80 South Eighth Street, Minneapolis, MN 55402, USA (office). *Website:* www.chinaaidsorphanfund.org (office).

GAO, Ying; Chinese author and poet; b. 25 Dec. 1929, Jiaozuo, Henan; s. of Gao Weiya and Sha Peifen; m. Duan Chuanchen 1954; one s. two d.; Vice-Chair. Sichuan Br. and mem. Council, Chinese Writers Asscn; Deputy Dir Ed. Bd, Sichuan Prov. Broadcasting Station 1983–; mem. Sichuan Political Consultative Conf. *Publications include:* The Song of Ding Youjun, Lamplights around the Three Gorges, High Mountains and Distant Rivers, Cloudy Cliff (novel), Da Ji and her Fathers (novel and film script), The Orchid (novel), Loving-Kindness of the Bamboo Storey (collection of prose), Mother in my Heart (autobiographical novel), Songs of Da Liang Mountains (poems), Frozen Snowflakes (poems), Reminiscences, Xue Ma (novel), Gao Ying (short stories). *Leisure interests:* painting, music. *Address:* c/o Sichuan Branch of Chinese Association of Literary and Art Workers, Bu-hou-jie Street, Chengdu, Sichuan, People's Republic of China (office). *Telephone:* 66782836 (office).

GAO, Youxi; Chinese physicist; *Director, Plateau Atmospheric Physics Institute;* b. 1920; ed Nat. Central Univ.; Dir Plateau Atmospheric Physics Inst., Lanzhou 1981–; mem. Dept of Earth Sciences, Academia Sinica, 1985–; Nat. Science Award 1989. *Address:* c/o Institute of Atmospheric Physics, Chinese Academy of Sciences, Beijing 100029, People's Republic of China.

GAO, Zhanxiang; Chinese party official; b. 1935, Tongxian Co., Hebei Prov.; joined CCP 1953; mem. Communist Youth League Cen. Cttee 1964, Sec. 1978–83; Vice-Chair. All-China Youth Fed. 1978–83; Deputy Sec. CCP Cttee, Hebei Prov. 1983–86; Dir State Ethnic Affairs Comm. 1986–89; Vice-Minister of Culture 1986–96; Sec. Secr. China Fed. of Literary and Art Circles 1990–, Vice-Chair. 1990–; Pres. Soc. of Mass Culture 1990–93; Vice-Chair. Chinese Asscn for Promotion of Popular Culture 1993–; Adviser, China Int. Tea Cultures Soc. 1993–; Chair. Soc. of Photographic Arts 1994; Vice-Chair. China Soc. of Tourism Culture 1994–; Dir, Ed.-in-Chief Chinese Arts 1994–; Alt. mem. 12th CCP Cen. Cttee 1982–87; Del., 13th CCP Nat. Congress 1987–92, 14th CCP Nat. Congress 1992–97, 15th CCP Nat. Congress 1997–2002; mem. 7th CPPCC Nat. Cttee 1988–93, Standing Cttee of 8th CPPCC Nat. Cttee 1993–98 (mem. Educ. and Culture Sub-cttee), Standing Cttee of 9th CPPCC Nat. Cttee 1998–2003; Hon. Chair. Soc. for the Promotion of Chinese Culture 1996–. *Publications:* author of several literary anthologies. *Address:* c/o Ministry of Culture, A83 Beiheyan, Dongamen, Beijing 100722, People's Republic of China.

GAOMBALET, Célestin-Leroy; Central African Republic politician; b. 1942; worked for Customs and Economic Union of Central Africa (UDEAC) 1970s; Dir-Gen Union Bank in Central Africa, Bangui –1981; Prime Minister of Central African Repub. 2003–05; mem. Assemblée nationale (Nat. Ass.) for Bambari constituency 2005–13, Speaker 2005–13. *Address:* c/o Assemblée nationale, Bangui, Central African Republic (office).

GAPONOV-GREKHOV, Andrey Viktorovich; Russian physicist and academic; *Scientific Chief Supervisor, Institute of Applied Physics, Russian Academy of Sciences;* b. 7 June 1926, Moscow; m.; one d.; ed Gorky State Univ.; Instructor, Gorky Polytech. Inst. 1952–55; Sr Scientific Assoc., Gorky (now Nizhny Novgorod) State Univ. 1955–, Head of Dept of Radio Physics, Inst. of Applied Physics 1977–2003, Scientific Chief Supervisor 2003–; Corresp. mem. USSR (now Russian) Acad. of Sciences 1964–68, mem. 1968–; USSR People's Deputy 1989–91; Hero of Socialist Labour 1986; State Prize 1967, 1983, 2003. *Publications:* numerous theoretical and experimental works in the field of electrodynamics and electronics of inducted cyclotronic radiation, which led to development of a new class of electronic instruments – masers with cyclotronic resonance. *Address:* Institute of Applied Physics, Ulyanova str. 46, Nizhny Novgorod 603950, Russia (office). *Telephone:* (831) 436-66-69 (office); (831) 436-36-67 (home). *Fax:* (831) 436-20-61 (office). *E-mail:* gapgr@appl.sci-nnov.ru (office). *Website:* www.ipfran.ru (office).

GARAIKOETXEA URRIZA, Carlos, LicenDer; Spanish (Basque) lawyer, economist and fmr politician; b. 2 June 1939, Pamplona; s. of Juan Garaikoetxea and Dolores Urriza; m. Sagrario Mina Apat 1966; three s.; mem. Inst. Príncipe de Viana, org. to protect and promote Basque culture, Navarra Dist Council 1971; Chair. Navarra Chamber of Commerce and Industry 1971; Chair. Nat. Council PNV 1977, re-elected 1978; mem. Navarra Dist Parl. 1979; Pres. Gen. Council of the Basque Country 1979; elected to Basque Parl. as PNV cand. for Guipúzcoa March 1980; Pres. of Basque Govt 1980–86; European Deputy 1987; Pres. Eusko Alkartaruna Party 1987–99. *Publications:* Euskadi: la transición inacabada, Memorias Políticas. *Leisure interests:* music (especially classical), skiing, Basque pelota, reading (especially political essays and history). *Address:* Nafarroa Behereko 43, 31002 Pamplona/Iruña, Spain. *Telephone:* (948) 203656.

GARAS, Klára, PhD; Hungarian art historian; b. 19 June 1919, Rákosszentmihály; d. of Pál Garas and Irén Strasser; ed Budapest Univ. of Sciences; joined staff Budapest Museum of Fine Arts 1945, Gen. Dir 1964–84; Ordinary mem. Hungarian Acad. of Sciences 1972, mem. 1985–; Labour Order of Merit (golden degree) 1974, 1979. *Publications:* Magyarországi festészet a XVII. században (Hungarian Painting in the 17th century) 1953, Magyarországi festészet a XVIII. században (Hungarian Painting in the 18th century) 1955, Franz Anton Maulbertsch 1724–1796, with preface by Oskar Kokoschka 1960, Olasz reneszánsz portrék a Szépművészeti Muzeumban (Italian Renaissance Portraits in the Museum of Fine Arts) 1965, 1973, Carlo Innocenzo Carloni (co-author) Milano 1966, Franz Anton Maulbertsch. Leben und Werk 1974, A velencei settecento festészete (Venetian Paintings of the 18th Century) 1977, A 17. század német és osztrák rajzművészete (Deutsche und Österreichische Zeichnungen des 18. Jahrhunderts) 1980; several publs on the Budapest Museum of Fine Arts, including Treasures of Venice: Paintings from the Museum of Fine Arts, Budapest (co-author) 1995. *Leisure interests:* 15th- to 18th-century European and Hungarian painting. *Address:* Kiss János altábornagy utca 48/c, 1126 Budapest, Hungary (home).

GARAVANI, Valentino; Italian fashion designer; b. 11 May 1932, Voghera, nr Milan; pnr Giancarlo Giammetti; ed Ecole des Beaux-Arts, Paris, Ecole de la Chambre Syndicale de la Couture, Paris; asst designer at Paris fashion houses of Jean Dessès 1950–55, Guy Laroche 1956–58; est. Valentino fashion house with Giancarlo Giammetti in Rome 1960, debut collection 1962, opened boutiques in Rome, Milan, Paris, New York, Tokyo and other cities; launched first Valentino perfume 1978; designed kit for Italian Olympic team 1984; designed costumes for opera The Dream of Valentino, J. F. Kennedy Center, USA 1994; sold Valentino fashion house to HdP 1998; announced decision to retire 2008; f. Valentino Acad. 1990; f. L.I.F.E for AIDS research and assistance to victims of the disease 1990; retrospective exhbn of creations in Rome 1991, at Columbus Festivities, New York 1992; Grande Ufficiale dell'Ordine al Merito della Repubblica Italiana 1985, Cavaliere del Lavoro 1996, Légion d'honneur, France 2005; Neiman Marcus Prize 1967, Premio speciale dell'arte nella moda, Florence 1995, CFDA Lifetime Achievement Award 2000, Medaille de Vermeil 2008. *Address:* c/o Li.ter Ltd, 26 Upper Brook Street, London W1K 7QE, England (office). *Telephone:* (20) 7409-1606 (office). *Fax:* (20) 7409-3110 (office). *E-mail:* ronaldfeijen@btconnect.com. *Website:* www.valentino.com.

GARAYEV, Tamerlan; Azerbaijani politician and fmr diplomatist; b. 1952, Gasimly, Agdam Region; s. of Yelmar Garayev and Khalida Garayeva; m. Farida Garayeva 1976; two s.; ed Azerbaijan Univ.; public prosecutor 1973–78; Lecturer, Azerbaijan Univ. 1978–91; became involved in opposition politics late 1980s; leader, moderate wing Popular Front, elected Deputy to Supreme Soviet 1990, Deputy Chair., First Deputy Chair. 1991–93; Amb. to China 1993–2000; mem. Org. for the Liberation of Karabakh. *Leisure interest:* golf. *E-mail:* safirprc@public.fhnet.cn.net.

GARCÉS CÓRDOBA, Mariana, LLB; Colombian lawyer and politician; *Minister of Culture;* b. Cali, Valle del Cauca; ed Universidad de los Andes, Universidad Icesi, Cali; Co-founder and fmr Gen. Man. Telepacífico (regional TV channel); Sec. of Culture and Tourism, City of Cali 2005–07; Minister of Culture 2010–; fmr Dir Cali Int. Art Festival; Exec. Dir Asscn for the Advancement of the Arts (Proartes), Cali, Orchestre Philharmonique de Cali 2002–; fmr mem. Nat. TV Comm. *Address:* Ministry of Culture, Carrera 8, No 8-43, Bogotá DC, Colombia (office). *Telephone:* (1) 342-4100 (office); (1) 342-1721 (office). *E-mail:* servicioalcliente@mincultura.gov.co (office). *Website:* www.mincultura.gov.co (office).

GARCETTI, Eric Michael; American politician; *Mayor of Los Angeles;* b. 4 Feb. 1971, Los Angeles; s. of Gil Garcetti and Sukey Roth; m. Amy Wakeland; one d.; ed Columbia Univ., London School of Econs, Queen's Coll., Oxford, UK; fmr Visiting Instructor, Dept of Int. Affairs, Univ. of Southern California; fmr Asst Prof., Occidental Coll., LA; mem. Council for Dist 13, Los Angeles City Council 2001–13, Pres. 2006–12; Mayor, City of Los Angeles 2013–. *Address:* Office of the Mayor, 200 North Spring Street, Los Angeles, CA 90012, USA (office). *Telephone:* (213) 978-0600 (office). *E-mail:* mayor.garcetti@lacity.org (office). *Website:* www.lamayor.org (office).

GARCIA, Andy; Cuban-American actor, producer and director; b. (Andres Arturo Garcia Menendez), 12 April 1956, Havana; s. of Rene Garcia and Amelie Garcia; m. Marivi Lorido Garcia; one s., three d.; ed Florida Int. Univ.; moved to USA 1961; several years acting with regional theatres Fla; Hon. DFA (St John's Univ. NY) 2000; numerous awards including Harvard Univ. Foundation Award 1994, Lifetime Achievement Award, American Cancer Soc. 1996, Spirit of Hope Award 2001, Desert Palm Award, Palm Springs Film Festival 2002, Imagen Foundation Creative Achievement Award 2002. *Films include:* The Mean Season 1985, 8 Million Ways to Die 1986, The Untouchables 1987, Stand and Deliver 1987, American Roulette 1988, Black Rain 1989, Internal Affairs 1990, The Godfather III 1990, Dead Again 1991, Jennifer Eight 1992, When A Man Loves A Woman 1994, Steal Big Steal Little (also producer) 1995, Things to Do in Denver When You're Dead 1995, Night Falls on Manhattan 1997, The Disappearance of García Lorca 1997, Hoodlum 1997, Desperate Measures 1998, Just the Ticket (also producer) 1999, The Unsaid (also producer) 2000, The Man from Elysian Fields (also producer) 2000, Oceans Eleven 2001, Confidence 2003, Blackout 2003, Twisted 2004, The Lazarus Child 2004, Ocean's Twelve 2004, The Lost City 2005, Smokin' Aces 2006, The Air I Breathe 2007, Ocean's Thirteen 2007, Beverly Hills Chihuahua (voice) 2008, New York, I Love You 2009, La linea 2009, City Island 2009, The Pink Panther 2 2009; dir: Cachao, Like His Rhythm There Is No Other 1993. *Albums produced include:* Cachao Master Sessions, Vol. I 1993 (Grammy Award 1994), Vol. II 1994 (Down Beat Critics Poll Winner 1996), Just the Ticket (soundtrack) 1999, Cachao-Cuba Linda 2000, For Love Or Country: The Arturo Sandoval Story (soundtrack) 2000, Score (Emmy Award) 2001. *Television appearances include:* Hill Street Blues, Brothers, Foley Square, Clinton and Nadine, Swing Vote (also producer) 1999, For Love Or Country: The Arturo Sandoval Story (also producer) 2000. *Leisure interests:* golf, fishing. *Address:* Paradigm, c/o Clifford Stevens, 200 West 57th Street, New York, NY 10019, USA. *Telephone:* (212) 246-1030 (office). *Fax:* (212) 246-1521 (office). *E-mail:* cineson@cineson.com (office). *Website:* www.cineson.com (office).

GARCIA, Marco Aurelio; Brazilian politician; b. Porto Alegre, Rio Grande do Sul; ed Fed. Univ. of Rio Grande do Sul, École des Hautes Etudes en Sciences Sociales, Paris; elected town councillor, Porto Alegre 1967; exiled in France and Chile, teacher Univs of Chile, Paris VIII, Paris X 1968–79; Int. Affairs Sec. and mem. Nat. Exec. Cttee Partido dos Trabalhadores (Workers' Party) 1980–; Municipal Sec. of Culture, Campinas 1989–90; co-f. Foro de São Paulo, pan-Latin American think-tank 1990; Municipal Sec. of Culture, São Paulo 2001–02; Pres.'s Special Adviser for Int. Affairs 2006; Pres., Partido dos Trabalhadores 2006–07. *Address:* Partido dos Trabalhadores (PT) Rua Silveira Martins 132, Centro, 01019-000 São Paulo SP, Brazil (office). *Telephone:* (11) 3243-1313 (office). *Fax:* (11) 3243-1345 (office). *Website:* www.pt.org.br (office).

GARCÍA BERNAL, Gael; Mexican actor; b. 30 Nov. 1978, Guadalajara, Jalisco; s. of José Angel García; one s.; ed Cen. School of Speech and Drama, London; founding mem. Canana production Co. *Films:* De tripas, corazón 1996, Cerebro 2000, Amores perros (Best Actor, Ariel Awards, Best Actor, Chicago Int. Film Festival) 2000, Y tu mamá también (Marcello Mastroianni Award, Venice Int. Film Festival) 2001, El Ojo en la nuca 2001, Vidas privadas 2001, Sin noticas de Dios 2001, The Last Post 2001, El Crimen del padre Amaro (The Crime of Father

Amaro) 2002, I'm With Lucy 2002, Dot the I 2003, Dreaming of Julia 2003, Diarios de motocicleta (The Motorcycle Diaries) 2004, La Mala educación (Bad Education) 2004, Babel 2006, La Science des Rêves (The Science of Sleep) 2006, Déficit (also Dir) 2007, El pasado 2007, Blindness 2008, Rudo y Cursi 2008, Mammoth 2009, The Limits of Control 2009. *Television includes:* Teresa 1989, El Abuelo y yo 1992, Fidel 2002. *Plays:* Blood Wedding (Almeida Theatre, London) 2005. *Address:* c/o Endeavor, 9701 Wilshire Blvd, 10th Floor, Beverly Hills, CA 90212, USA.

GARCÍA CARNEIRO, Gen. Jorge Luis; Venezuelan politician and army officer (retd); *Governor of Estado Vargas;* b. 8 Feb. 1952; m. María del Valle de García; three s.; two d.; ed Mil. Acad. Venezuela; fmr Commdt Pelotón, Batallion; Commdt and teacher, Mil. Acad. Venezuela; Commdt and teacher, Army Tech. Coll.; Commdt First Co. Ricaurte Infantry Battalion; Second in Command, Carabobo Battalion Edo. Táchira; First Commdt GB José Ignacio Pulido, San Juan de Colon, Edo. Táchira; Commdt Barinas, Mérida, Caracas and Táchira garrisons; Chief of Staff, Acquisition of War Materials USA; First Commdt, Ministry of Defence HQ; Dir, Mil. Acad. Venezuela; Minister of Nat. Defence –2005; Gov. of Estado Vargas 2008–; numerous decorations including Order Francisco de Miranda, Order Rafael Urdaneta, Order Nat. Defence, Order Estrella de Carabobo, Order of Merit Army, Civil Defence, Order José de Cruz Carrillo, Order Tulio Febres Cordero, Order García d'Hevia, Order Bicentenaria de la Ilustre Universidad de Los Andes, Order Rómulo Gallegos. *Address:* Office of the Governor, La Guaira, Estado Vargas, Venezuela (office). *Website:* estadovargas.gob.ve.

GARCÍA COCHAGNE, Manuela Esperanza; Peruvian lawyer and politician; b. 12 Dec. 1961; ed Universidad de San Martín de Porres, Lima; worked for 28 years in Ministry of Labour, Minister of Labour and Employment 2009–11. *Address:* c/o Ministry of Labour and Employment, Avda Salaverry 655, cuadra 8, Jesús María, Lima 11, Peru (office).

GARCÍA DE ALBA ZEPEDA, Sergio Alejandro, BA, MA; Mexican business executive, government official and academic; ed Instituto Tecnológico y de Estudios Superiores de Occidente, Guadalajara, IPADE, Mexico City; Prof. of Finance, Instituto Tecnológico y de Estudios Superiores de Occidente 1980–84; Pres. Regional Chamber of Manufacturing Industry of Jalisco 1993–94; Vice-Pres. Confed. of Industrial Chambers of Mexico 1993–95; Founding mem. and Dir-Gen. Fibrart –1995; Sec. of Econ. Promotion, Jalisco state 1995–2001; Regional Vice-Pres. Axtel 2001; Under-Sec. for Small and Medium-Sized Businesses, Secr. of the Economy 2003–05, Sec. of the Economy 2005–06; Pres. Instituto para la Innovación, Competitividad y Desarrollo Empresarial, Tecnológico de Monterrey 2007–09; CEO American Industries Guadalajara 2011–; Econ. Policy Advisor, Govt of Jalisco 2012–; CAREINTRA Outstanding Businessman Award 1989, Asscn of Sales and Marketing Execs of Guadalajara Exec. of 1993, Ocho Columnas newspaper Columna de Oro 1999, COPARMEX Jalisco Efraín González Luna Prize for Political Merit 2005. *Website:* www.americanindustriesgroup.com/ guadalajara.html.

GARCÍA DE ARNOLD, María Liz; Paraguayan academic, human rights lawyer and politician; b. 22 Nov. 1955, Asunción; d. of Antonio García Gómez and Teresa Ramona Frasquerí de García; m. Don Aníbal Arnold del Puerto; one s. two d.; ed Universidad Paranaense, Umuarama, Brazil, Universidad Tecnológica Intercontinental, Asunción, Instituto de Altos Estudios Estratégicos; worked for 20 years at Colegio Americano de Asunción; Rector, Universidad Metropolitana de Asunción –2012; Minister of Nat. Defence 2012–13; Vice-Pres. Paraguayan Asscn of Private Univs; Founder and Dir Metropolitan Inst. of Languages, Asscn of Metropolitan Studies and Research; mem. Paraguayan Nat. Human Rights Comm., Never Again to State Terrorism, Nat. Comm. for UNESCO, Org. of Women Politicians for Democracy and Power; Peace Amb., El Mensajero de la Paz. *Address:* c/o Ministry of National Defence, Avda Mariscal López, esq. Vicepresidente Sánchez y 22 de Septiembre, Asunción, Paraguay.

GARCÍA FRANCO, Marco Tulio; Guatemalan politician; Minister of Nat. Defence Jan.–Dec. 2008. *Address:* c/o Ministry of National Defence, Antigua Escuela Politécnica, Avda La Reforma 1–45, Zona 10, Guatemala City, Guatemala (office).

GARCÍA-GASCO Y VICENTE, HE Cardinal Agustín; Spanish ecclesiastic; *Archbishop of Valencia;* b. 12 Feb. 1931, Corral de Almaguer; ordained priest 1956; Auxiliary Bishop of Madrid and Titular Bishop of Nona 1985–92; Archbishop of Valencia 1992–; cr. Cardinal (Cardinal-Priest of S. Marcello) 2007; served as Sec.-Gen. Spanish Bishops' Conf. and Bishop-Del. of Caritas (Catholic Church's aid org.); f. distance-learning inst. of theology. *Address:* Archdiocese of Valencia, Palau 2, 46003 Valencia, Spain (office). *Telephone:* (963) 829700 (office). *Fax:* (963) 918120 (office). *E-mail:* info@archivalencia.org (office). *Website:* www .archivalencia.org (office).

GARCÍA-HERRERA, Trinidad Jiménez, LLB; Spanish politician; b. 4 June 1962, Málaga; m. (divorced 1995); ed Universidad Autonoma de Madrid; Co-founder Socialist Students Asscn 1983, joined Partido Socialista Obrero Español (PSOE) 1984, Sec. Int. Policy of Exec. Cttee PSOE Federal 2000, re-elected 2004; Rep. to North American NATO Youth Exchange Program 1989, also headed New Programs and Devt Dept, Spanish Del. of American Field Service; Officer in Charge of Political Relations with America, PSOE Int. Relations Secr. 1996–2000; chosen as PSOE cand. for Mayor of Madrid 2003; Sec. of State for Latin America 2006; Minister of Health and Social Policy 2009–10, of Foreign Affairs and Cooperation 2010–11; fmr Prof. of Political Law, Universidad Nacional de Educación a Distancia, Spanish school in Bata. *Address:* c/o Ministry of Foreign Affairs and Co-operation, Plaza de la Provincia 1, 28012 Madrid, Spain.

GARCÍA LINERA, Álvaro Marcelo; Bolivian politician, mathematician and sociologist; *Vice-President;* b. 19 Oct. 1962, Cochabamba; ed Colegio San Agustin, Nat. Autonomous Univ. of Mexico; fmr Prof. of Sociology, Universidad Mayor de San Andrés, La Paz; mem. Tupaj Katari guerilla group, served five years in prison 1992–97; fmr political commentator; mem. Movt Toward Socialism party; Vice-Pres. of Bolivia 2006–. *Publications:* several books and articles. *Address:* Ministry of the Presidency, Palacio de Gobierno, Plaza Murillo, La Paz, Bolivia (office). *Telephone:* (2) 237-1082 (office). *Fax:* (2) 237-1388 (office). *E-mail:* webmaster@ presidencia.gov.bo (office). *Website:* www.presidencia.gov.bo (office).

GARCÍA LUNA, Genaro, BSc; Mexican police officer and politician; *Secretary of Public Security;* b. 10 July 1968, Mexico City; ed Autonomous Metropolitan Univ.; researcher, Sub-Dept of Foreign Affairs, Center for Research and Nat. Security (CISEN) 1988–98; Gen. Intelligence Coordinator for Prevention, Fed. Preventive Police Force 1998–2000; Dir-Gen. of Planning and Operations, Fed. Judicial Police (now Fed. Investigations Agency) 2000–03, Co-ordinator Tech. Cttee 2003–04; Chair. Strategic Information Sub-cttee, Interpol 2004–05; Sec. of Public Security 2006–. *Address:* Secretariat of State for Public Security, Londres 102, 7°, Col. Juaréz, 06600 México DF, Mexico (office). *E-mail:* enlace@ssp.gob.mx (office). *Website:* www.ssp.gob.mx (office).

GARCÍA-MARGALLO Y MARFIL, José Manuel, LLB, LLM, LLD; Spanish lawyer and politician; *Minister of Foreign Affairs and Co-operation;* b. 13 Aug. 1944, Madrid; ed Univ. of Deusto, Bilbao, Univ. Miguel Hernández, Alicante, Harvard Univ.; joined Inspectorate of Finance 1968, becoming Head of Research and Programming, Technical Secr., Ministry of Finance 1974; Dir-Gen. of Community Devt, Ministry of Culture 1977–79; mem. Congreso de los Diputados (Parl.) 1977–82, 1986–94, Chair. Cttee on Petitions 1979–82, Spokesperson for Economy and Finance 1986–89, 1989–93, 1993–94; practising attorney 1990–; mem. European Parl., Brussels 1994–2011, Vice-Chair. Sub-Cttee on Monetary Affairs 1994–99, Cttee on Econ. and Monetary Affairs 1999–2004, Chief Observer for EU Election Observation Mission in Togo 2010, mem. parl. dels to China, India, Japan, New Zealand, Egypt, Namibia, Argentina, Brazil and Uruguay; Minister of Foreign Affairs and Co-operation 2011–; fmr Lecturer, Faculty of Law, Univ. of Deusto, San Sebastian; mem. Partido Popular; Gran Cruz del Mérito Civil 1982, Orden del Mérito Constitucional 1983. *Address:* Ministry of Foreign Affairs and Co-operation, Plaza de la Provincia 1, 28012 Madrid, Spain (office). *Telephone:* (91) 3799700 (office). *E-mail:* informaec@maec.es (office). *Website:* www.maec.es (office).

GARCÍA PADILLA, Alejandro Javier; Puerto Rican lawyer, politician and state governor; *Governor of Puerto Rico;* b. 3 Aug. 1971, Coamo, Puerto Rico; m. Wilma Pastrana 2001; one s. two d.; ed Univ. of Puerto Rico, Río Piedras, Interamerican Univ., San Germán; began career as law clerk at Court of Appeals, then worked as attorney, specializing in property, estates, contracts and admin. law; also Prof. of Law, Interamerican Univ.; later served as legis. aide for Cttees on Internal Affairs, Women's Affairs and on Agric., amongst others; Sec. Puerto Rico Dept of Consumer Affairs 2005–07 (resgnd); Senator-at-Large 2008–13; Gov. of the Commonwealth of Puerto Rico 2013–; fmr mem. Bd Puerto Rico Bar Asscn. *Address:* Office of the Governor, La Fortaleza, PO Box 9020082, San Juan 00902-0082, Puerto Rico (office); Puerto Rico Federal Affairs Administration, 1100 17th Street NW, Suite 800, Washington, DC 20036, USA (office). *Telephone:* (787) 721-7000 (San Juan) (office); (202) 778-0710 (DC) (office). *Fax:* (787) 724-1472 (San Juan) (office); (202) 778-0721 (DC) (office). *E-mail:* secretariomail@fortaleza .gobierno.pr (office). *Website:* prfaa.pr.gov (office); www.fortaleza.gobierno.pr (office); www.alejandrogarciapadilla.com.

GARCÍA PÉREZ, Alan Gabriel Ludwig; Peruvian politician and fmr head of state; b. 23 May 1949, Lima; s. of Carlos García Ronceros and Nyta Pérez de García; m. Pilar Nores; four d.; ed José María Eguren Nat. Coll., Universidad Católica, Lima, Universidad Nacional Mayor de San Marcos (graduated as lawyer), Universidad Complutense, Madrid, Spain, Sorbonne and Inst. of Higher Latin American Studies, Paris, France; mem. of Partido Aprista Peruano since his teens; returned to Peru and elected mem. of Constituent Ass. 1978; subsequently apptd Org. Sec. and Chair. Ideology of Aprista Party (now Alianza Popular Revolucionaria Americana), Parl. Deputy 1980–85, Sec.-Gen. of Party 1982, later Pres.; Senator for Life 1990–; nominated Presidential cand. 1984, obtained largest number of votes, nat. presidential elections April 1985; on withdrawal of Izquierda Unida cand., Alfonso Barrantes Lingán, proclaimed Pres.-elect June 1985, assuming powers 1985–89; granted political asylum in Colombia June 1992; returned from exile Jan. 2001; Pres. of Peru 2006–11. *Address:* c/o Alianza Popular Revolucionaria Americana, Avda Alfonso Ugarte 1012, Lima 5, Peru.

GARCÍA RAMÍREZ, Sergio, PhD; Mexican politician, lawyer and judge; b. 1 Feb. 1938, Guadalajara; ed Nat. Univ. of Mexico; Research Fellow and teacher of penal law, Inst. of Juridical Research, Nat. Univ. of Mexico 1966–76; Dir Correction Centre, State of Mexico and Judge, Juvenile Courts; Asst Dir of Govt Ministry of Interior; Attorney-Gen. of Fed. Dist; Under-Sec. Ministries of Nat. Resources, Interior, Educ., Industrial Devt; Dir Prevention Centre of Mexico City; fmr Minister of Labour; Attorney-Gen. 1982–88; Pres. Inter-American Court of Human Rights (IACHR) (Corte Interamericana de Derechos Humanos), OAS, San José, Costa Rica 2004–07; mem. Mexican Acad. of Penal Sciences, Mexican Inst. of Penal Law, Nat. Inst. of Public Admin., Ibero-American Inst. of Penal Law etc. *Publications:* Teseo Alucinado 1966, Asistencia a Reos Liberados 1966, El Artículo 18 Constitucional 1967, La Imputabilidad en el Derecho Penal Mexicano, El Código Tutelar para Menores del Estado Michoacán 1969, La Ciudadanía de la Juventud 1970, La Prisión 1975, Los Derechos Humanos y el Derecho Penal 1976, Legislación Penitenciaria y Correccional Comentada 1978, Otros Minotauros 1979, Cuestiones Criminológicas y Penales Contemporáneas 1981, Justicia Penal 1982. *Address:* Circuito Maestro Mario de la Cueva s/n, Cd. Universitaria, CP 04510, Mexico City, Mexico (office). *Telephone:* (55) 5622-7474 (office). *Fax:* (55) 5665-2193 (office). *E-mail:* sgr@servidor.unam.mx (office). *Website:* www.juridicas.unam.mx (office).

GARCÍA RODRÍGUEZ, Enrique, BEcons, MEcons; Bolivian economist and banking executive; *Executive President and CEO, Development Bank of Latin America;* ed St Louis Univ., American Univ.; fmr Operations Man., Banco Industrial SA; mem. Bd several industrial and financial cos; served as an officer of IDB for 17 years, including as Treas.; fmr Gov. for Bolivia in World Bank Group, IDB and Financial Fund for the River Plate Basin; Deputy Minister of Planning and Coordination and mem. Bd Bolivian Cen. Bank 1970s; Minister of Planning and Coordination and Head of Econ. and Social Cabinet 1989–91; Exec. Pres. and CEO CAF (Corporación Andina de Fomento—Devt Bank of Latin America) 1991–; fmr mem. Devt Cttee of IBRD and IMF representing Bolivia, Chile, Argentina, Peru, Uruguay and Paraguay; Vice-Pres. Canning House; mem. Bd Inter-American Dialogue, Advisory Council of the Center for Latin American Studies at Georgetown Univ., Policy Council of George Washington Univ.; mem. Center for Latin America and the Caribbean, Florida Int. Univ., Advisory Council of the Latin

American Program at the Woodrow Wilson Center, Dean's Council at the Kennedy School, Harvard Univ.; Trustee, Doña Maria de las Mercedes Foundation (Spain); fmr Prof., Universidad Mayor de San Andrés, La Paz, Catholic Univ., La Paz; mem. Bolivian Acad. of Econs, Council of Science and Tech. of the Bolivian Acad. of Sciences; Sovereign Order of Malta; decorations from Govts of Argentina, Bolivia, Brazil, Colombia, Ecuador, Peru, Venezuela; hon. doctorates and degrees from several univs; numerous awards, including being selected as Person of the Year by Ultima Hora newspaper 1990, Award for Latin American Integration, Business Council of Latin America – CEAL 2001, Award for Excellence in Regional Integration, América Economía magazine 2004, chosen as Man of the Year by Latin Finance magazine 2005, selected as Person of the Year by La Razón newspaper, ATB TV network and El Nuevo Día newspaper, Bolivia 2006, Americas Award for Excellence in Public Service, CIFAL Atlanta 2010. *Address:* CAF, Avenida Luis Roche, Torre CAF, Altamira, Caracas, Venezuela (office). *Telephone:* (212) 209-2111 (office). *Fax:* (212) 209-2444 (office). *E-mail:* Infocaf@caf.com (office). *Website:* www.caf.com (office).

GARCÍA-SAYÁN LARRABURE, Diego, LLB; Peruvian lawyer, judge, academic and government official; b. (Diego García-Sayán), 2 Aug. 1950, New York, NY, USA; three s.; ed Pontificia Universidad Catolica del Peru, Lima, Univ. of Texas, USA; Exec. Dir Andean Comm. of Jurists 1982–92, 1994–2000, Dir Gen. 2003–; Prof. of Law, Pontificia Universidad Catolica del Peru, Lima 1987–2004; with UN in Guatemala 1991–92; Dir of Human Rights Div., UN Observer Mission in El Salvador 1992–94; Prof., Peruvian Univ. of Applied Sciences 1998–2000; Minister of Justice 2000–01, of Foreign Affairs 2001–02; Judge, Inter-American Court of Human Rights, San José, Costa Rica 2004–09, Vice-Pres. 2008–09, Pres. 2010–13; Chair. UN Working Group on Enforced or Involuntary Disappearances 1988–; mem. Bd of Dirs American Inst. of Human Rights, San José, Costa Rica 1994–; fmr Visiting Prof., Univ. of Richmond, American Univ., Instituto de Altos Estudios de América Latina, Univ. of Paris (Sorbonne); Founding mem. Peruvian Centre for Int. Studies (CEPEI); mem. Exec. Cttee Int. Comm. of Jurists, Geneva 1996–2000; mem. Lima Bar Asscn (mem. Bd of Dirs 1985–86), Peruvian Soc. of Int. Law. *Address:* Los Sauces 285, Lima 27, Peru (office). *Telephone:* (1) 4215675 (office). *Fax:* (1) 2027199 (office). *E-mail:* dgs@rocketmail.com (home).

GARCÍA-VALDECASAS Y FERNÁNDEZ, Rafael, DJur; Spanish lawyer and judge; b. 9 Jan. 1946, Granada; m. Rosario Castaño Parraga 1975; ed Univ. of Granada; lawyer, Office of Attorney-Gen. 1976; mem. Office of Attorney-Gen. Tax and Judicial Affairs Office, Jaén 1976–85; mem. Office of Attorney-Gen. Econ. and Admin. Court of Jaén 1979–85; mem. Jaén Bar 1979–89, Granada Bar 1981–89; mem. Office of Attorney-Gen. Econ. and Admin. Court of Córdoba 1983–85, Tax and Judicial Affairs Office of Granada 1986–87; Head, Spanish State Legal Service for cases before EC Court of Justice (Ministry of Foreign Affairs) 1987–89; Judge, Court of First Instance of the European Communities (now Gen. Court) 1989–2007; currently govt lawyer; Encomienda de la Orden Civil del Mérito Agrícola 1982, Encomienda de la Orden de Isabel la Católica 1990, Gran Cruz de la Orden del Mérito Civil 1999. *Publications:* Comentarios al Tratado de Adhesión de España a la C.E.: La Agricultura 1985, El 'acquis' comunitario 1986, El medio ambiente: conservación de espacios protegidos en la legislación de la CE 1992, La Jurisprudencia del Tribunal de Justicia CE sobre la libertad de establecimiento y libre prestación de servicios por los abogados 1993, El Tribunal de Primera Instancia de las Comunidades Europeas 1993, El respeto del derecho de defensa en materia de competencia 1997, El desarollo normativo de los reglamentos comunitarios 1999; also papers in books and learned journals. *Leisure interests:* swimming, cycling, fishing. *Address:* c/o Ministry of Justice, San Bernardo 45, 28015 Madrid, Spain. *Telephone:* (91) 3904500. *Website:* www.mjusticia.es.

GARDAM, Jane Mary, OBE, BA, FRSL; British novelist; b. 11 July 1928, Coatham; d. of William Pearson and Kathleen Pearson (née Helm); m. David Hill Gardam 1954; two s. one d.; ed Saltburn High School for Girls, Bedford Coll. for Women, Univ. of London; co-ordinator UK Hosp. Libraries British Red Cross 1951–53; Literary Ed. Time and Tide 1952–54; mem. PEN; Hon. DLitt. *Radio play:* The Tribute. *Publications:* juvenile fiction: A Long Way from Verona 1971, A Few Fair Days 1971, The Summer After the Funeral 1973, Bilgewater 1977; novels: God on the Rocks (Prix Baudelaire) 1978, The Hollow Land (Whitbread Literary Award 1983) 1981, Bridget and William 1981, Horse 1982, Kit 1983, Crusoe's Daughter 1985, Kit in Boots 1986, Swan 1987, Through the Doll's House Door 1987, The Queen of the Tambourine (Whitbread Novel Award) 1991, Faith Fox 1996, Tufty Bear 1996, The Green Man 1998, The Flight of the Maidens 2000, Old Filth 2004, The People of Privilege Hill 2007, The Man in the Wooden Hat 2009, Last Friends 2013; short stories: Black Faces, White Faces (David Higham Award 1978, Winifred Holtby Award 1978) 1975, The Sidmouth Letters 1980, The Pangs of Love (Katherine Mansfield Award 1984) 1983, Showing the Flag 1989, Going into a Dark House 1994, Missing the Midnight 1997; non-fiction: The Iron Coast 1994. *Leisure interests:* agriculture. *Address:* Haven House, Sandwich, Kent, CT13 9ES (home); Throstlenest Farm, Crackpot, N Yorks; 34 Denmark Road, London, SW19 4PQ, England. *Telephone:* (1304) 612680 (home).

GARDE DUE, Ulrik; Danish business executive; *President and CEO, Georg Jensen;* b. 14 Jan. 1963, Copenhagen; ed Koebmandskolen, Copenhagen, Schiller Int. Univ., Paris/London, CEDSIP (CPA), Paris, Corp. Finance Programme, London Business School; Commercial Asst and Ship Broker, Holm & Wonsild ApS (EAC), Copenhagen 1981–83; Oil Broker, Fretoil (Hunting Group), Paris and London 1984–86; Commercial Counsellor and Export Consultant for the Danish Ministry of Foreign Affairs, Danish Embassy, Paris 1986–89; Commercial Officer in charge of launch/real-estate promotion of the WTC, CNIT (SARI), La Défense, Paris 1989–90; Commercial Officer, Europe Distribution, Wholesale, Licensees and DFS, Celine SA (LVMH), Paris 1990; Commercial Dir of SE Asia, Celine SA (LVMH), Tokyo, Vice-Pres. Celine Inc. (LVMH) N America, New York 1993–97; Int. Dir of Marketing and Sales, Cerruti 1881 GmbH (Escada Group), Paris, global responsibility for Marketing and Sales in SE Asia, the Middle East and USA 1997–98; Sr Vice-Pres., Int. Sales, Burberry Ltd, London 1998–2007, Gen. Man. role in brand turn-around; Dir (non-exec.) Royal Copenhagen (Axcel), Copenhagen 2004–; Pres. and CEO Georg Jensen 2007–. *Address:* Georg Jensen A/S, 7 Soendre Fasanvej, 2000 Frederiksberg, Denmark (office). *Telephone:* 38-14-98-98 (office). *Fax:* 38-14-99-70 (office). *E-mail:* info@georgjensen.com (office). *Website:* www .georgjensen.com (office).

GARDEL, Louis; French publishing editor, novelist and screenwriter; b. 8 Sept. 1939, Algiers, Algeria; s. of Jacques Gardel and Janine Blasselle; m. 1st Béatrice Herr (deceased) 1963; m. 2nd Hélène Millerand 1990; two s. two d.; ed Lycée Bugeaud, Algiers, Lycée Louis-le-Grand, Paris and Institut d'Etudes Politiques, Paris; Head of Dept Inst. des Hautes Etudes d'Outre-Mer 1962–64; Man. Soc. Rhône-Progil 1964–74; Head of Dept Conseil Nat. du Patronat 1974–80; Literary Consultant, Editions du Seuil 1980, Literary Ed. 1980–; mem. juries Prix Renaudot, Conseil Supérieur de la Langue Française; Chevalier, Légion d'honneur. *Film screenplays:* Fort Saganne, Nocturne Indien, Indochine, La Marche de Radetzky 1996, Est.Ouest, Himalaya 1999, Princesse Marie 2005, Gaspard le bandit 2006, Le temps des secrets 2007, Le temps des amours 2007, La baie d'Alger 2012, La chartreuse de Parme 2012. *Publications include:* L'Eté Fracassé 1973, Couteau de chaleur 1976, Fort Saganne 1980 (Grand Prix du Roman de l'Acad. française), Notre Homme 1986, Le Beau Rôle 1989, Darbaroud 1993. L'Aurore des Bien-Aimés 1997, Grand-Seigneur 1999, La Baie d'Alger 2007, Le scénariste 2012. *Leisure interest:* horses. *Address:* Editions du Seuil, 27 rue Jacob, 75006 Paris (office); 25 rue de la Cerisaie, 75004, Paris, France (home). *Telephone:* 1-40-46-50-50 (office). *E-mail:* froumens@seuil.com (office).

GÄRDENFORS, Peter, PhD; Swedish philosopher and academic; *Professor of Cognitive Science, Lund University;* b. 21 Sept. 1949, Degeberga; s. of Torsten Gärdenfors and Ingemor Gärdenfors (née Jonsson); m. Annette Wald 1975 (divorced 2002); three s. one d.; ed Lund Univ., Princeton Univ., USA; Lecturer in Philosophy, Lund Univ. 1974–80, Reader in Philosophy of Science 1975–77, Reader in Philosophy 1980–88, Prof. of Cognitive Science 1988–; Visiting Fellow, Princeton Univ., USA 1973–74, ANU, Australia 1986–87; Visiting Scholar, Stanford Univ., USA 1983–84; Visiting Prof., Univ. of Buenos Aires 1990; Ed. Theoria 1978–86, Journal of Logic, Language and Information 1991–96; mem. Royal Swedish Acad. of Letters, Academia Europaea, Deutsche Akad. für Naturforscher Leopoldina, Royal Swedish Acad. of Science; Rausing Prize 1986. *Publications:* Generalized Quantifiers (ed.) 1986, Knowledge in Flux 1988, Decision, Probability and Utility (with N.-E. Sahlin) 1988, Belief Revision (ed.) 1992, Blotta Tanken 1992, Fangslande Information 1996, Cognitive Semantics (with J. Allwood) 1998, Conceptual Spaces 2000, How Homo Became Sapiens 2003, The Dynamics of Thought 2005. *Leisure interests:* botany, walking, judo, climbing. *Address:* Department of Philosophy, Lund University, Kungshuset, Lundagard, 222 22 Lund, Sweden (office). *Telephone:* (6) 222-48-17 (office). *Fax:* (6) 222-44-24 (office). *E-mail:* peter.gardenfors@lucs.lu.se (office). *Website:* www.lucs.lu.se/Peter .Gardenfors (office).

GARDINER, Sir John Eliot, Kt, CBE, MA, FRSA; British conductor and music director; b. 20 April 1943, Fontmell Magna, Dorset; s. of the late Rolf Gardiner and of Marabel Gardiner (née Hodgkin); m. 1st Cherryl Anne Ffoulkes 1971 (divorced 1981); m. 2nd Elizabeth Suzanne Wilcock 1981 (divorced 1997); three d.; m. 3rd Isabella de Sabata 2001; ed Bryanston School, King's Coll., Cambridge, King's Coll., London, and in Paris and Fontainebleau with Nadia Boulanger; Founder and Artistic Dir Monteverdi Choir, 1964, Monteverdi Orchestra 1968, the English Baroque Soloists 1978, Orchestre Révolutionnaire et Romantique 1990; concert debut Wigmore Hall, London 1966; youngest conductor at Henry Wood Promenade Concerts, Royal Albert Hall 1968; operatic debut Sadler's Wells Opera, London Coliseum 1969; Prin. Conductor CBC Vancouver Orchestra 1980–83; Musical Dir Lyon Opera 1982–88, Chef fondateur 1988–; Artistic Dir Göttingen Handel Festival 1981–90, Veneto Music Festival 1986; Prin. Conductor, NDR Symphony Orchestra, Hamburg 1991–94; residency at the Théâtre du Châtelet, Paris 1999–2003; Bach Cantata Pilgrimage, with performances throughout Europe 2000; Guest Conductor at the Royal Opera House, Covent Garden: Iphigénie en Tauride 1982, Chérubin 1994, The Cunning Little Vixen 2003, La Finta Giardiniera 2006, Simon Boccanegra 2008; regular guest conductor with the London Symphony Orchestra, the Czech Philharmonic and other major orchestras in Amsterdam, Paris, Dresden, Vienna, Berlin, Chicago; Domaine privé, Cité de la musique, Paris 2007; appearances at European music festivals, including Aix-en-Provence, Aldeburgh, Bath, Berlin, Edinburgh, Flanders, Netherlands, London, Salzburg, BBC Proms; Visiting Fellow, Peterhouse Coll., Cambridge 2007–08; Hon. Fellow, King's Coll., London 1992, Royal Acad. of Music 1992; Commdr, Ordre des Arts et des Lettres 1997, Officer's Cross of the Order of Merit (Germany) 2005, Chevalier, Légion d'honneur 2011; Dr hc (Univ. Lumière de Lyon) 1987, (Complutense Univ. of Madrid) 2001, (New England Conservatoire) 2005, (Cremona) 2006; 17 Gramophone awards, including Record of the Year 1991, 2005, Artist of the Year 1994, eight Edison Awards, four Grands Prix du Disque, three Prix Caecilia, two Arturo Toscanini Music Critics' awards, three Deutscher Schallplattenpreis, Buxtehude Prize Lübeck 1994, Robert Schumann Preis Zwickau 2001, Halle Handel Prize 2001, Classic FM Gramophone Award 2005, Léonie Sonning Music Prize 2005, City of Leipzig and Bach Archiv Bach Medal for lifetime achievement in the performance of music by J. S. Bach 2005, Royal Acad. of Music/Kohn Foundation Bach Prize 2008, Diapason d'Or de l'année 2011. *Recordings:* over 250 albums including Bach Cantatas (Gramophone Award for Specialist Achievement 2011, J. C. Bach: Welt, gute Nacht (ECHO Klassik Award for Choral Recording of the Year – 16th/17th Century 2012) 2011, Bach Motets (Gramophone Award for Baroque Vocal 2013). *Leisure interests:* forestry, organic farming. *Address:* Askonas Holt Ltd, Lincoln House, 300 High Holborn, London, WC1V 7JH, England (office). *Website:* www.askonasholt.com (office).

GARDNER, David Pierpont, BSc, MA, PhD; American university president, professor of education and foundation executive; *President Emeritus, University of California;* b. 24 March 1933, Berkeley, Calif.; s. of Reed S. Gardner and Margaret Pierpont Gardner; m. 1st Elizabeth Fuhriman 1958 (died 1991); four d.; m. 2nd Sheila Sprague Gardner 1995; ed Brigham Young Univ., Univ. of Calif., Berkeley; Admin. Asst, Personnel Man. and Prin. Asst to Chief Admin. Officer, Calif. Farm Bureau Fed., Berkeley 1958–60; Field and Scholarship Dir Calif. Alumni Asscn, Univ. of Calif., Berkeley 1960–62, Dir Calif. Alumni Foundation 1962–64; Asst to Chancellor Univ. of Calif., Santa Barbara 1964–67, Asst Chancellor and Asst Prof. of Higher Educ. 1967–69, Vice-Chancellor, Exec. Asst and Assoc. Prof. of Higher Educ. 1969–70; Vice-Pres. Univ. of Calif. and Prof. of Higher Educ. (on leave from Univ. of Calif., Santa Barbara) 1971–73; Pres. Univ. of Utah and Prof. of Higher Educ. 1973–83, Pres. Emer. 1985; Pres. Univ. of Calif. 1983–92 (Pres. Emer. 1992–), Prof. of Higher Educ., Univ. of Calif., Berkeley 1983–92, Chair. Nat. Comm. on Excellence in Educ. 1981–83; Pres. William and Flora Hewlett

Foundation, Menlo Park Calif. 1993–99; Chair. Bd of Trustees, J. Paul Getty Trust, LA 2000–2004; Visiting Fellow, Clare Hall, Cambridge Univ. 1979, Life Mem. 1979–, Hon. Fellow 2002; numerous professional appointments, directorships, trusteeships etc.; Fellow, American Acad. of Arts and Sciences, Nat. Acad. of Public Admin.; mem. Nat. Acad. of Educ., American Philosophical Soc.; Fulbright Fellow, Japan 1987; Chevalier Légion d'honneur 1985, Kt Commdr's Cross Order of Merit (Germany) 1992; 12 hon. degrees; numerous awards and distinctions including James Bryant Conant Award, Educ. Comm. of USA 1985. *Publications:* The California Oath Controversy 1967, Earning My Degree: Memoirs of an American University President 2005; numerous articles in professional journals. *Leisure interests:* fly fishing, travel. *Address:* c/o Center for Studies in Higher Education, Evans Hall, University of California, Berkeley, CA 94720, USA (office). *Telephone:* (510) 642-5040 (office).

GARDNER, Edward, OBE; British conductor; *Music Director, English National Opera;* b. Gloucester; ed King's Coll., Cambridge and Royal Acad. of Music, London; fmr Asst Conductor Hallé Orchestra; Music Dir Glyndebourne Touring Opera 2004–06, with productions including La Bohème 2004, La Cenerentola 2005, The Turn of the Screw 2006, Fidelio 2006; has conducted Camerata Salzburg, London Philharmonic, Melbourne Symphony, Belgrade Philharmonic, Royal Scottish Nat. Orchestra, BBC Symphony Orchestra, Philharmonia, Alabama Symphony, Orchestre de Bretagne; season 2005–06 appearances included BBC Scottish Symphony Orchestra, BBC Nat. Orchestra of Wales, Vancouver Symphony, Orquestra Nacional do Porto, MDR Leipzig, Orchestre Philharmonique de Liège; opera highlights include Tchaikovsky's Eugene Onegin with Glyndebourne Touring Opera 2002, Meyerbeer's L'Africaine with Strasbourg Opera 2004, Mozart's Così fan tutte with ENO 2005, Adams' The Death of Klinghoffer with Scottish Opera 2005, Weill's Seven Deadly Sins with Paris Opéra 2005, Royal Opera debut Il re pastore 2006, Donizetti's L'Elisir d'amore, Paris Opéra 2006, Stravinsky's The Rake's Progress, Paris 2007–08; Music Dir, ENO 2006–; Prin. Guest Conductor, City of Birmingham Symphony Orchestra 2011–; Guest Conductor, Bergen Philharmonic Orchestra, Chief Conductor (2015–); co-f. (with tenor Toby Spence) song recital series Wardsbrook Concerts 2013; Royal Philharmonic Soc. Award for Best Young Artist 2005, for Best Conductor 2008, Olivier Award for Outstanding Achievement in Opera 2009. *Website:* www .askonasholt.co.uk (office).

GARDNER, Sir Richard Lavenham, Kt, PhD, FRS; British scientist and academic; *Royal Society Edward Penley Abraham Research Professor, Department of Zoology, University of Oxford;* b. 10 June 1943, Dorking; s. of the late Allan Constant and Eileen May Gardner; m. Wendy Joy Cresswell 1968; one s.; ed St John's School, Leatherhead, NE Surrey Coll. of Tech., St Catharine's Coll. Cambridge; Research Asst, Physiological Lab., Cambridge 1970–73; Lecturer in Devt and Reproductive Biology, Dept of Zoology, Oxford 1973–77, Research Student Christ Church 1974–77, Ordinary Students 1978–, Royal Soc. Henry Dale Research Prof. 1978–, Royal Soc. Edward Penley Abraham Research Prof. 2003–; Hon. Dir Imperial Cancer Research Fund Developmental Biology Unit 1986–96; ind. mem. Advisory Bd for the Research Councils 1990–93; Pres. Inst. of Biology 2006–08; Scientific Medal, Zoological Soc. 1977, March of Dimes Prize in Developmental Biology 1999, Royal Medal, Royal Soc. 2001, Albert Brachet Prize, Belgian Royal Acad. of Sciences, Letters and Fine Arts. *Publications:* various scientific papers. *Leisure interests:* ornithology, music, sailing, gardening, painting. *Address:* Christ Church, Oxford, OX1 1DP, England (office). *Telephone:* (1865) 281319 (office). *Fax:* (1865) 281310 (office). *E-mail:* richard.gardner@zoo.ox.ac.uk (office). *Website:* www.zoo.ox.ac.uk (office).

GARDNER, Richard Newton, DPhil; American lawyer, diplomatist and academic; *Professor of Law and International Organization, Columbia University;* b. 9 July 1927, New York, NY; s. of Samuel I. Gardner and Ethel E. Gardner; m. Danielle Almeida Luzzatto 1956 (died 2008); one s. one d.; ed Harvard Univ., Yale Law School, Univ. of Oxford, UK; Rhodes Scholar to Oxford Univ. 1951–54; Prof. of Law and Int. Org., Columbia Univ. 1957–61, 1965–76, 1981–; Deputy Asst Sec. of State for Int. Org. Affairs, US State Dept 1961–65; Amb. to Italy 1977–81; lawyer, Coudert Brothers 1981–93; Consultant to Sec.-Gen., UN Conf. on Environment and Devt 1992; Amb. to Spain 1993–97; Sr Counsel, Morgan, Lewis and Bockius LLP, New York 1997–; mem. US Advisory Cttee on Law of the Sea 1971–76, Pres.'s Advisory Cttee on Trade Policy and Negotiations 1998–2002; Del. to UN Gen. Ass. 2000; mem. Trilateral Comm., Council on Foreign Relations; mem. American Philosophical Soc.; Arthur S. Flemming Award 1963, Thomas Jefferson Award 1998. *Publications:* Sterling-Dollar Diplomacy 1956, In Pursuit of World Order 1964, Blueprint for Peace 1966, The Global Partnership: International Agencies and Economic Development 1968, Negotiating Survival: Four Priorities after Rio 1992, Mission Italy: On the Frontlines of the Cold War 2005. *Leisure interests:* tennis, classical music, reading. *Address:* Columbia University School of Law, 435 West 116th Street, New York, NY 10027, USA (office). *Telephone:* (212) 854-4635 (office). *Fax:* (212) 854-7946 (office). *E-mail:* rgardn@law.columbia.edu (office). *Website:* www.law.columbia.edu (office).

GARDNER, Sir Roy Alan, Kt, FCCA, FRAeS, FRSA; British business executive; *Chairman, Compass Group PLC;* b. 20 Aug. 1945, Chiswick, London, England; s. of Thomas Gardner and Iris Gardner; m. Carol Gardner 1969; one s. two d.; ed Strodes School, Egham; Finance Dir, Marconi Space and Defence Systems 1975–84, Marconi 1984–85; Finance Dir STC PLC, Man. Dir STC Communications Ltd 1986–91, mem. Bd Dirs STC PLC 1986–91; COO Northern Telecom Europe Ltd 1991–92; Man. Dir GEC-Marconi Ltd 1992–94; Dir GEC PLC 1994; Finance Dir British Gas PLC 1994–95, Exec. Dir 1995–96; CEO Centrica 1997–2005; Sr Ind. Dir (non-exec.) Compass Group 2005–06, Chair. 2006–, Chair. Nomination Cttee, mem. Corp. Responsibility Cttee; Chair. (non-exec.) Connaught plc –2010; Chair. Plymouth Argyle Football Club –2010; Chair. Spice Ltd 2010–; Dir (non-exec.) Manchester United PLC (Chair. (non-exec.) 2002–05); Willis Group Holdings Ltd, Mainstream Renewable Power Ltd (Chair. 2011–); fmr Dir (non-exec.) Laporte plc; Sr Advisor, Credit Suisse; Pres. Energy Inst., Carers UK; Chair. Advisory Bd of Energy Futures Lab., Imperial Coll. London; Chair. Apprenticeship Ambassadors Network, EnServe Group Ltd; mem. Int. Advisory Bd IESE Business School at Univ. of Navarra –2011. *Leisure interests:* golf, running family. *Address:* Compass Group PLC, Compass House, Guildford Street, Chertsey, Surrey KT16 9BQ, England (office). *Telephone:* (1932) 573000 (office). *Fax:* (1932) 573184

(office). *E-mail:* info@compass-group.com (office). *Website:* www.compass-group .com (office).

GARDNER, Susan (Sue) P., BA; Canadian journalist and media executive; *Executive Director, WikiMedia Foundation;* b. 11 May 1967, Bridgetown, Barbados; m.; ed Ryerson Polytechnic Inst.; began career as producer with CBC's As It Happens news and current events radio programme 1990, worked for more than a decade as a producer, reporter and documentary-maker for CBC Radio current-affairs and for Newsworld International, focusing on pop culture and social issues, Sr Dir of CBC.ca website 2006–07; began consulting for WikiMedia Foundation (non-profit org.) as special adviser on operations and governance May 2007, Exec. Dir WikiMedia Foundation Dec. 2007–; mem. Bd The Ada Initiative 2011–; ranked by Forbes magazine amongst The World's 100 Most Powerful Women (70th) 2012. *Address:* WikiMedia Foundation, 149 New Montgomery Street, Third Floor, San Francisco, CA 94105, USA (office). *Telephone:* (415) 839-6885 (office). *E-mail:* sue@wikimedia.org (office). *Website:* www.wikimedia.org (office); suegardner.org.

GARDOCKI, Lech; Polish judge and professor of law; *First President, Supreme Court;* b. 13 April 1944, Rydzewo; s. of Józef Gardocki and Filomena Gardocki; one s. two d.; ed Univ. of Warsaw; Deputy Head, Inst. of Criminal Law, Warsaw Univ. 1977–81, 1981–84, Asst Prof. of Law 1980–91, held Chair, Dept of Comparative Studies in Criminal Law 1985–95, Prof. Extraordinary 1991–, Prof. in Legal Art 1992–, holds Chair, Dept of Material Criminal Law 1996–; Justice of the Supreme Court 1996–, First Pres. 1998–; mem. Int. Advisory Cttee on Zeitschrift für die gesamte Strafrechtswissenschaft magazine; First Degree Award in competition organized by State and Law magazine 1979. *Publications:* more than 80 publs including An Outline of International Criminal Law (Second Degree Award of Ministry of Educ.) 1985, Problems of Theory of Criminalization 1990, Criminal Law (Award of Minister of Educ.) 1994. *Leisure interest:* film. *Address:* Office of the First President, Supreme Court, 00-951 Warsaw, pl. Krasińskich 2/4/6, Poland (office). *Telephone:* (22) 5308203 (office). *Fax:* (22) 5309100 (office). *E-mail:* pp@sn .pl (office). *Website:* www.sn.pl (office).

GAREYEV, Gen. Makhmud Akhmedovich; Russian army officer and historian; *President, Russian Academy of Military Science;* b. 23 July 1923; m.; two c.; ed Tashkent Infantry School, M. Frunze Mil. Acad., Gen. Staff Acad.; involved in mil. operations on Western Front, officer Operative Div., Gen. Staff of Far E Army at end of Second World War; Commdr of Regt, Tank Div. Belarus Mil. Command, Head of Gen. Staff Urals Mil. Command, then officer Gen. Staff; Head Mil. Scientific Dept, then Deputy Head of Chief Operative Dept, apptd Deputy Head of Gen. Staff 1974; Chief Mil. Counsellor, Afghanistan, then Commdr 1989–; mem. Russian Acad. of Mil. Sciences (later Pres.), Council on Interaction with Orgs of War Veterans; Order of Lenin and numerous other decorations and medals. *Publications:* Frunze – Military Theoretician, General Army Exercises, Marshal G. Zhukov and more than 60 scientific works. *Leisure interest:* athletics. *Address:* Academy of Military Sciences, Myasnitskaya str. 37, 103175 Moscow, Russia (office). *Telephone:* (495) 293-33-55 (office).

GARFUNKEL, Arthur (Art), MA; American singer and actor; b. 5 Nov. 1941, Forest Hills, NY; m. 1st Linda Marie Grossman 1972 (divorced 1975); m. 2nd Kim Cermak 1988; one s.; ed Columbia Univ.; mem. singing duo Simon & Garfunkel (with Paul Simon) 1964–71; solo artist 1972–; Britannia Award for Best International Pop LP and Single 1977, six Grammy Awards, inducted into Rock and Roll Hall of Fame (with Paul Simon) 1990. *Films include:* Catch 22 1970, Carnal Knowledge 1971, Bad Timing 1980, Good To Go 1986, Boxing Helena 1993, 54 1998, The Rebound 2009. *Recordings include:* albums: as Simon & Garfunkel: Wednesday Morning 3am 1964, Sounds of Silence 1966, Parsley, Sage, Rosemary and Thyme 1966, The Graduate (film soundtrack) (two Grammy Awards) 1968, Bookends 1968, Bridge Over Troubled Water (six Grammy Awards 1971) 1970, Concert in Central Park (live) 1982, Early Simon & Garfunkel 1993, Old Friends 1997; solo: Angel Clare 1973, Breakaway 1975, Watermark 1977, Fate for Breakfast (Doubt for Dessert) 1979, Art Garfunkel 1979, Scissors Cut 1981, The Animals' Christmas 1986, Lefty 1988, Garfunkel 1989, Up Till Now 1993, Across America 1997, Songs from a Parent to a Child 1997, Everything Waits to be Noticed 2002, Some Enchanted Evening 2007. *Publication:* Still Water 1989. *Address:* Metropolitan Talent, Inc., 100 Fifth Avenue, 11th Floor, New York, NY 10011, USA (office). *E-mail:* contact@artgarfunkel.com. *Website:* www .artgarfunkel.com.

GARGANAS, Nikolaos C., MSc (Econ), PhD; Greek economist; *Honorary Governor, Bank of Greece;* b. 20 Jan. 1937, Soufli; m. Maria L. Kokka; one d.; ed Athens School of Econs and Business Studies, London School of Econs and Univ. Coll., London, UK; Head, Research Unit, Agricultural Bank of Greece 1964–66; Research Officer, Nat. Inst. of Econ. and Social Research, London 1968–75; Lecturer, Brunel Univ., Uxbridge, UK 1970–71; Sr Economist, Bank of Greece 1975–84, Dir/Adviser, Econ. Research Dept 1984–93, Econ. Counsellor (Chief Economist) 1993–96, Deputy Gov. Bank of Greece 1996–2002, mem. Monetary Policy Council 1998–2008, Gov. 2002–08, currently Hon. Gov.; Chief Econ. Adviser, Ministry of Nat. Economy and mem. Council of Econ. Experts 1985–87; mem. Governing Bd Centre of Econ. Planning and Research (KEPE) 1985–87; mem. *ad hoc* Prime Minister's Cttee for the Examination of Long Term Econ. Policy 1996–97; Chair. Deposit Guarantee Fund in Greece 1996–2002; Greek Rep. to OECD Econ. Policy Cttee of the European Communities 1975–88, Econ. Policy Cttee of the European Communities 1982–85, European Communities Monetary Cttee 1985–87, 1994–98, EU Econ. and Financial Cttee 1998–2002; mem. European Cen. Banks' Governing Council and Gen. Council 2002–08; Hon. Fellow, LSE. *Publications:* Greece's Economic Performance and Prospects (co-ed. and contrib.) 2001; books and articles on macro-economics, economic modelling, European economic and monetary union, monetary policy. *Address:* Bank of Greece, Leoforos E. Venizelos 21, 102 50 Athens, Greece (office). *Telephone:* (210) 3203680 (office). *Fax:* (210) 3222784 (office). *E-mail:* ngarganas@bankofgreece.gr (office).

GARGAWI, HH Mohammed bin Abdullah al-; United Arab Emirates business executive and politician; *Minister of Cabinet Affairs;* b. 1963, Dubai; m.; three c.; ed Univ. of Mich., USA; CEO Dubai Holding (which manages cos, including Dubai Properties, Dubai International Properties, Jumeirah International, Dubai International Capital, Dubai Internet City, Dubai Media City, Dubai Knowledge Village, Dubai Industrial City, Dubai Humanitarian City) 2004–; Minister of State for Cabinet Affairs, UAE Council of Ministers 2006–; fmr Sec.-Gen. Govt of Dubai Exec. Council; fmr Chair. Dubai Devt & Investment Authority (DDIA); CEO Exec. Office of HH Sheikh Muhammad bin Rashid al-Maktoum, ruler of Dubai; Chair. Arab Strategy Forum; Chair. Young Arab Leaders; mem. Bd Dubai Media Inc.; Founder Dubai Autism Centre, UAE Disabled Sports Fed.; Vice-Chair. Handicapped Club; Royal Order of Merit (Morocco); American Business Council Award. *Address:* Ministry of Cabinet Affairs, POB 2350, Abu Dhabi (office); Dubai Holding, PO Box 66000, Dubai, United Arab Emirates (office). *Telephone:* (2) 6268100 (Ministry) (office); (4) 3300300 (office). *Fax:* (2) 6268033 (Ministry) (office); (4) 3300303 (office). *E-mail:* info@moca.gov.ae (office). *Website:* www.moca.gov.ae (office); www.dubaiholding.com (office).

GARIBASHVILI, Irakli; Georgian business executive and politician; *Prime Minister;* b. 28 June 1982, Tbilisi; m. Nunu Tamazashvili; two s.; ed Tbilisi State Univ., Univ. Pantheon-Sorbonne, France; Probationer, Foreign Affairs Cttee, Sakartvelos Parlamenti (Parl. of Georgia) 2001–02; Man., External Purchase Office of Logistics Dept, Burji Ltd (Cartu Group) 2004–05, Asst to Pres., JSC Cartu Group 2005–08, Head, Bd of Admin. and Gen. Dir, Cartu Int. Charity Fund 2005–12; mem. Supervisory Bd JSC Cartu Bank 2007–12; Dir Georgian Dream Ltd (record label) 2009–12; Founder-mem. Georgian Dream-Democratic Georgia party, also Head of Review Cttee 2012; Minister of Internal Affairs 2012–13; Prime Minister 2013–. *Address:* Chancellery of the Government, 0134 Tbilisi, P. Ingorovka 7, Georgia (office). *Telephone:* (32) 299-09-00 (office). *Fax:* (32) 292-10-69 (office). *E-mail:* primeminister@geo.gov.ge (office). *Website:* www.government .gov.ge (office).

GARLAND, Greg C., BS (ChemEng); American chemical engineer and business executive; *Chairman and CEO, Phillips 66;* ed Texas A&M Univ.; began career with Phillips as project engineer for Plastics Technical Center 1980, later worked as sales engineer for Phillips' plastics resins, Business Service Man. for Advanced Materials, Business Devt Dir, and Olefins Man. for Chemicals, Man. of K-Resin® Business Unit 1992–94, Man. of Planning and Devt in Planning and Tech. 1994–95, Gen. Man. of Natural Gas Liquids 1995–97, apptd Gen. Man. Qatar/Middle East 1997; Sr Vice-Pres., Planning and Specialty Chemicals, Chevron Phillips Chemical Co. (now a jt venture between Phillips 66 and Chevron), Pres. and CEO –2010; Sr Vice-Pres., Exploration and Production, Americas for ConocoPhillips 2010–13, Chair. and CEO Phillips 66 (refining arm of ConocoPhillips) 2013–; mem. Bd of Dirs DCP Midstream; mem. Bd and Exec. Cttee American Petroleum Inst., Junior Achievement for Southeast Texas; mem. Bd Greater Houston Partnership; mem. Eng Advisory Bd Texas A&M Univ. *Address:* ConocoPhillips Company, Conoco Center, 600 North Dairy Ashford, Houston, TX 77079-1175, USA (office). *Telephone:* (281) 293-1000 (office). *Fax:* (281) 293-1440 (office). *E-mail:* info@conocophillips.com (office). *Website:* www.conocophillips.com (office).

GARN, Edwin Jacob (Jake), BS; American business executive and fmr politician; b. 12 Oct. 1932, Richfield, Utah; s. of Jacob E. Garn and Fern Christensen; m. 1st Hazel R. Thompson 1957 (died 1976); two s. two d.; m. 2nd Kathleen Brewerton 1977; two s. one d.; ed Univ. of Utah; private pilot then USN pilot on active duty for four years; USAF pilot for 20 years; Special Agent, John Hancock Mutual Life Insurance Co., Salt Lake City 1960–61; Asst Man. Home Life Insurance Co. New York, Salt Lake City 1961–66; Gen. Agent, Mutual Trust Life Insurance Co., Salt Lake City 1966–68; City Commr Salt Lake City 1968–72, Mayor 1972–74; Dir Metropolitan Water Dist 1968–72; Senator from Utah 1974–93; Congressional observer and payload specialist space shuttle Discovery Mission STS-51-D 1985; Vice-Chair. Huntsman Chemical Corpn, Salt Lake City 1993–99; Man. Dir Summit Ventures LLC, Salt Lake City 2000–04; currently self-employed consultant; Chair. Primary Children's Medical Center Foundation; mem. Bd of Dirs United Space Alliance, Franklin Covey Co., Headwaters, Inc., Nu Skin Enterprises, Inc.; Republican; six hon. doctorate degrees; Wright Brothers Memorial Trophy. *Publication:* Night Launch 1989. *Address:* 1267 Chandler Circle, Salt Lake City, UT 64103, USA.

GARNAUT, Ross Gregory, AO, BA, PhD; Australian economist and fmr diplomatist; *Vice-Chancellor's Fellow, University of Melbourne;* b. 28 July 1946, Perth, WA; s. of the late L. Garnaut and P. W. Garnaut; m. Jayne Potter 1974; two s.; ed Perth Modern School, WA and Australian Nat. Univ. (ANU), Canberra; Research Fellow, Sr Research Fellow and Sr Fellow, Econs Dept, Research School of Pacific Studies, ANU 1972–75, 1977–83; First Asst Sec.-Gen., Financial and Econ. Policy, Papua New Guinea Dept of Finance 1975, 1976; Research Dir ASEAN-Australia Econ. Relations Research Project 1980–83; Sr Econ. Adviser to Prime Minister Bob Hawke 1983–85; Amb. to People's Repub. of China 1985–88; Prof. of Econs, Head of Dept, Research School of Pacific Studies, ANU 1989–, Dir Asia Pacific School of Econs and Man. 1998–; Vice-Chancellor's Fellow, Univ. of Melbourne 2008–; econs adviser to Prime Minister Kevin Rudd 2007–10; Chair. Aluminium Smelters of Victoria 1988–89, Rural and Industries Bank of Western Australia 1988–95, Primary Industry Bank of Australia 1988–94, Lihir Gold 1995–, Australian Centre for Int. Agric. Research 1994–; Hon. DLit (ANU). *Publications:* Irian Jaya: The Transformation of a Melanesian Economy 1974, ASEAN in a Changing Pacific and World Economy 1980, Indonesia: Australian Perspectives 1980, Taxation and Mineral Rents 1983, Exchange Range and Macro-Economic Policy in Independent Papua New Guinea 1984, The Political Economy of Manufacturing Protection: Experiences of ASEAN and Australia 1986, Australian Protectionism: Extent, Causes and Effects 1987, Australia and the Northeast Asian Ascendancy (report to Prime Minister) 1989, Economic Reform and Internationalization 1992, Grain in China 1992, Structuring for Global Realities (report on Wool Industry to Commonwealth Governments) 1993, The Third Revolution in the Chinese Countryside 1996, Open Regionalism: An Asian Pacific Contribution to the World Trading System 1996, East Asia in Crisis 1998, Private Enterprise in China (co-author) 2001, Social Democracy in Australia's Asian Future (co-author) 2001, Resource Management in Asia Pacific Developing Countries (ed.) 2002, China 2002: WTO Entry and World Recession (co-ed.) 2002, China: New Engine of World Growth (co-ed.) 2003, China: Is Rapid Growth Sustainable? (co-ed.) 2004, China's Third Economic Transformation (co-ed.) 2004, China's Ownership Transformation (co-author) 2005, The China Boom and its

Discontents (co-ed.) 2005, The Turning Point in China's Economic Development (co-ed.) 2006, China: Linking Markets for Growth (co-ed.) 2007, The Garnaut Climate Change Review 2008, The Great Crash of 2008 2009. *Leisure interests:* cricket, tennis, Australian football, the history of humanity. *E-mail:* Ross .Garnaut@unimelb.edu.au (office). *Website:* www.rossgarnaut.com.au.

GARNEAU, Marc, OC, BSc, DEng; Canadian astronaut, politician and fmr naval engineer; b. Feb. 1949, Quebec City; ed Royal Mil. Coll., Kingston, Imperial Coll. of Science and Tech., London, UK, Canadian Forces Command and Staff Coll., Toronto; Combat Systems Engineer, HMCS Algonquin 1974–76; Instructor in Naval Weapon Systems, Canadian Forces Fleet School, Halifax 1976–77, with Naval Eng Unit 1980–82; Project Engineer in Naval Weapon Systems, Ottawa 1977–80; promoted Commdr 1982; Design Authority for Naval Communications and Electronic Warfare Equipment and Systems, Ottawa 1983–86; promoted Capt. 1986; retd from Navy 1989; selected to be astronaut 1983; seconded to Canadian Astronaut Program from Dept of Nat. Defence 1984; first Canadian to fly in space as Payload Specialist on Shuttle Mission 41-G, Oct. 1984; Deputy Dir Canadian Astronaut Program 1989; selected to be Mission Specialist 1992; trained at NASA's Johnson Space Center 1992–93, worked on tech. issues, Astronaut Office Robotics Integration Team, Capsule Communicator (CAPCOM) in Mission Control during Shuttle flights; served as Mission Specialist on flight STS-41G 1984, STS-77 1996 and STS-97 2000; has logged 677 hours in space; Exec. Vice-Pres., then Pres. Canadian Space Agency 2001–06; MP for Westmount—Ville-Marie, Ottawa 2008–; Chancellor Carleton Univ. 2003–; Pres. Bd McGill Univ. Chamber Orchestra; mem. Asscn of Professional Engineers of Nova Scotia, Navy League of Canada, Int. Acad. of Astronauts 2002; Hon. Fellow, Canadian Aeronautics and Space Inst., Nat. Hon. Patron of Hope Air and Project N Star, Hon. mem. Canadian Soc. of Aviation Medicine 1998; Canadian Mil. Decoration 1980; Hon. PhD (Univ. of Laval, Tech. Univ. of Nova Scotia, Royal Mil. Coll. of Kingston) 1985, (Royal Mil. Coll. of St-Jean) 1990, (Univ. of Ottawa) 1997, Hon. DSci (Univ. of Lethbridge) 2001, (York Univ.) 2002; Athlone Fellowship 1970, NASA Space Flight Medals 1984, 1996, 2000, F.W. Baldwin Award, Canadian Aeronautics and Space Journal 1985, NASA Exceptional Service Medal 1997, Queen's Golden Jubilee Medal 2002, Prix Montfort en sciences 2003. *Achievements include:* first Canadian to fly on a NASA mission to space 1984. *Address:* House of Commons, Ottawa, ON K1A 0A6, Canada (office). *Telephone:* (613) 996-7267 (office). *Fax:* (613) 995-8632 (office). *E-mail:* GarneM@parl.gc.ca (office). *Website:* www.marcgarneau.ca.

GARNER, Alan, OBE; British writer; b. 17 Oct. 1934, Cheshire, England; s. of Colin Garner and Marjorie Garner (née Greenwood Stuart); m. 1st Ann Cook 1956 (divorced); one s. two d.; m. 2nd Griselda Greaves 1972; one s. one d.; ed Manchester Grammar School, Magdalen Coll., Oxford; mil. service with rank of Lt, RA; mem. Editorial Bd Detskaya Literatura Publrs, Moscow; Visiting Prof., School of Applied Sciences, Univ. of Huddersfield; Hon. DLitt (Warwick), (Salford), (Manchester Metropolitan); Hon. DUniv (Huddersfield); Carnegie Medal 1968, Guardian Award 1968, Lewis Carroll Shelf Award, USA 1970, Chicago Int. Film Festival Gold Plaque 1981, Phoenix Award, Children's Literature Asscn of America 1996, Karl Edward Wagner Award 2003, World Fantasy Lifetime Achievement Award 2012. *Plays:* Holly from the Bongs 1965, Lamaload 1978, Lurga Lom 1980, To Kill a King 1980, Sally Water 1982, The Keeper 1983, Pentecost 1997, The Echoing Waters 2000. *Dance drama:* The Green Mist 1970. *Libretti:* The Bellybag 1971, Potter Thompson 1972, Lord Flame 1996. *Screenplays:* The Owl Service 1969, Red Shift 1978, Places and Things 1978, Images 1981 (First Prize, Chicago Int. Film Festival), Strandloper 1992. *Publications:* The Weirdstone of Brisingamen 1960, The Moon of Gomrath 1963, Elidor 1965, Holly from the Bongs 1966, The Old Man of Mow 1967, The Owl Service (Library Asscn Carnegie Medal 1967, Guardian Award 1968) 1967, The Book of Goblins (ed.) 1969, Red Shift 1973, The Breadhorse 1975, The Guizer 1975, The Stone Book Quartet (Children's Book Asscn of USA Phoenix Award 1996) 1976–78, Tom Fobble's Day 1977, Granny Reardun 1977, The Aimer Gate 1978, Fairy Tales of Gold 1979, The Lad of the Gad 1980, A Book of British Fairy Tales (ed.) 1984, A Bag of Moonshine 1986, Jack and the Beanstalk 1992, Once Upon a Time 1993, Strandloper 1996, The Little Red Hen 1997, The Voice That Thunders 1997, The Well of the Wind 1998, Thursbitch 2003, Collected Folk Tales 2011, Boneland 2012. *Leisure interest:* work. *Address:* c/o Curtis Brown Ltd, 28–29 Haymarket, London, SW1Y 4SP, England (office). *Telephone:* (20) 7393-4400 (office). *Fax:* (20) 7393-4401 (office). *E-mail:* info@curtisbrown.co.uk (office). *Website:* www.curtisbrown.co.uk (office); alangarner.atspace.org.

GARNER, James; American actor; b. (James Baumgardner), 7 April 1928, Norman, Okla; m. Lois Clarke 1956; one s. two d.; ed New York Berghof School; worked as travelling salesman, oil field worker, carpet layer, bathing suit model; Purple Heart; Emmy Award, Life Achievement Award, Screen Actors Guild Awards 2005. *Television appearances include:* Cheyenne, Maverick 1957–62, Nichols 1971–72, The Rockford Files 1974–79, Space 1985, The New Maverick, The Long Summer of George Adams, The Glitter Dome, Heartsounds, Promise (also exec. producer) 1986, My Name is Bill W. (also exec. producer), 1989, Decoration Day 1990, Barbarians at the Gate 1993, God, the Devil and Bob (voice) 2000, First Monday (series) 2002, Roughing It 2002, 8 Simple Rules for Dating My Teenage Daughter (series) 2003–05. *Films include:* Toward the Unknown 1956, Shoot-out at Medicine Bend 1957, Darby's Rangers 1958, Sayonara, Up Periscope 1959, Cash McCall 1960, The Great Escape 1963, The Americanization of Emily 1964, 36 Hours 1964, The Art of Love 1965, A Man Could Get Killed 1966, Duel at Diablo 1966, Mister Buddwing 1966, Grand Prix 1966, Hour of the Gun 1967, Marlowe 1969, Support Your Local Sheriff 1971, Support Your Local Gunfighter 1971, Skin Game 1971, They Only Kill Their Masters 1972, One Little Indian 1973, Health 1979, The Fan 1980, Victor/Victoria 1982, Murphy's Romance 1985, Sunset 1987, Fire in the Sky 1993, My Fellow Americans 1996, Twilight 1998, Space Cowboys 2000, Atlantis: The Lost Empire 2001, Divine Secrets of the Ya-Ya Sisterhood 2002, The Notebook 2004, Al Roach: Private Insectigator 2004, The Ultimate Gift 2006, Terra (voice) 2007, First Night 2007. *Publication:* The Garner Files: A Memoir 2011. *Address:* 33 Oakmont Lane, Suite 590, Los Angeles, CA 90049, USA.

GARNETT, Tony; British television producer; b. 3 April 1936, Birmingham; ed Central Grammar School, Univ. Coll., London; began career as TV actor; producer of numerous TV programmes and films; worked in USA 1980–90; Co-founder and Chair. World Productions 1990–2012; Visiting Prof. of Media Arts, Royal Holloway

Coll., Univ. of London 2000–. *TV appearances include:* Dixon of Dock Green 1960s. *TV productions include:* Up the Junction 1965, Cathy Come Home 1966, The Resistable Rise of Arturo Ui 1972, Hard Labour 1973, The Enemy Within 1974, Days of Hope 1975, Law and Order 1978, Between the Lines 1992, Cardiac Arrest 1994, Ballykissangel 1996, This Life 1996–97, The Cops 1998, Attachments 2000. *Films produced include:* Kes 1969, Handgun 1983, Earth Girls are Easy 1989, Shadow Makers 1989. *Address:* Flat 60, Arlington House, Arlington Street, London, SW1A 1RL, England.

GARNIER, Sir Edward Henry, Kt, QC, BA, MA; British barrister and politician; b. 26 Oct. 1952, Germany; m. Anna Caroline Mellows 1982; two s. one d.; ed Wellington Coll., Berks., Jesus Coll., Oxford, Coll. of Law, London; called to the Bar, Middle Temple 1976, QC 1995, Bencher 2001; practising barrister specializing in libel and media law; Crown Court Asst Recorder 1998, Recorder (part-time Circuit Judge) 2000; fmr lawyer for The Guardian newspaper; contested Hemsworth constituency 1987; MP for Harborough 1992–2010, for Harborough (revised boundary) 2010–, Sec. Conservative House of Commons Foreign Affairs Cttee 1992–94, mem. Home Affairs Select Cttee 1992–95; Parl. Pvt. Sec. to Alastair Goodlad and David Davis as Ministers of State, FCO 1994–95, to Sir Nicholas Lyell as Attorney Gen. and to Sir Derek Spencer as Solicitor Gen. 1995–97, to Roger Freeman as Chancellor of the Duchy of Lancaster 1996–97; Shadow Minister, Lord Chancellor's Dept 1997–99; Shadow Attorney Gen. 1999–2001, 2009–10; Shadow Minister for Home Affairs 2005–07, for Justice 2007–09; Solicitor Gen. for England and Wales 2010–12; Hon. Sec. Foreign Affairs Forum 1988–92, Vice-Chair. 1992–; Treas. Macleod Group of Conservative MPs 1995–97; mem. Exec. 1922 Committee 2002–05; Chair. Exec. Cttee Soc. of Conservative Lawyers 2003–09; Dir, GB-China Centre 1998–2010; Visiting Parl. Fellow, St Anthony's Coll., Oxford 1996–97; Conservative. *Publications:* Facing the Future 1993; contribs to Halsbury's Laws of England 1985, Bearing the Standard: Themes for a Fourth Term 1991. *Leisure interests:* cricket, history, music, shooting. *Address:* House of Commons, Westminster, London, SW1A 0AA (office); Constituency Office, 24 Nelson Street, Market Harborough, Leics., LE16 9AY, England. *Telephone:* (20) 7219-4034 (office); (1858) 464146. *Fax:* (1858) 410013. *E-mail:* edward.garnier.mp@parliament.uk (office); office@harboroughconservatives.com (office). *Website:* www.parliament.uk/biographies/commons/edward-garnier/25652; www.harboroughconservatives.com; www.edwardgarnier.co.uk.

GARNIER, Jean-Pierre (JP), PhD, MBA; French business executive; b. 31 Oct. 1947, Le Mans; m.; three d.; ed Univ. of Louis Pasteur, Stanford Univ., USA; joined Schering-Plough 1975, numerous man. positions including Gen. Man. of numerous overseas subsidiaries, then Vice-Pres. of Marketing, US Pharmaceutical Products Div. 1983, then Sr Vice-Pres. and Gen. Man. with responsibility for sales and marketing for US prescription business, then Pres. US business; Pres. pharmaceutical business in N America, SmithKline Beecham 1990, mem. Bd Dirs 1992, Chair. Pharmaceuticals 1994–95, COO 1995–2000, CEO GlaxoSmithKline plc 2000–08; mem. Bd Dirs United Technologies Corpn, Eisenhower Exchange Fellowships Inc., INSEAD, Global Business Coalition on HIV/AIDS, John Hopkins Univ., Hole in the Wall Foundation, Cttee to Encourage Corp. Philanthropy; mem. Quaker BioVentures Int. Business Advisory Council for UK; Chevalier, Légion d'honneur, Officier 2007; Oliver R. Grace Award for distinguished service in advancing cancer research 1997, named a Star of Europe, Business Week 2001, Marco Polo Award 2001, Corporate Citizenship Award, Henry H. Kessler Foundation, Sabin Vaccine Inst. Humanitarian Award 2002, CNBC Leadership Award 2007. *Leisure interests:* competitive tennis and paddle playing, squash, golf, windsurfing. *Address:* c/o GlaxoSmithKline plc, 980 Great West Road, Brentford, London, TW8 9GS, England (office).

GAROFANO, Giuseppe, MBA; Italian engineer and business executive; *Vice-Chairman, Alerion Cleanpower SpA;* b. 25 Jan. 1944, Nereto, Teramo; ed Milan Polytechnic Inst., Bocconi Univ. Business School; Man. Dir Cotonificio Cantoni 1981–84; Vice-Chair. and Man. Dir Iniziativa META SpA 1984–88, Chair. and CEO 1988; Man. Dir Ferruzzi Finanziaria SpA 1988–92, Vice-Chair. 1989; Vice-Chair. Milano Assicurazioni SpA 1987, Fondiaria SpA 1989, La Previdente Assicurazioni SpA 1991; Vice-Chair. Montedison SpA 1989–90, Chair. 1990–92; Chair. Reno de Medici SpA 2003–09; Founder and Vice-Chair. Alerion Cleanpower SpA 2002–; mem. Bd of Dirs Realty Vailog SpA, RCR Cristalleria Italiana SpA, Efibanca SpA Autostrada Torino—Milano SpA. *Address:* Alerion Cleanpower SpA, via Durini 16/18, 20122 Milan, Italy (office). *Website:* www.alerion.it (office).

GAROUSTE, Gérard; French painter and sculptor; b. 10 March 1946, Paris; s. of Henri Garouste and Edmée Sauvagnac; m. Elizabeth Rochline 1970; two s.; ed Acad. Charpentier, Beaux-Arts de Paris; cr. nine sculpted bronze doors, 23 rue de l'université, Paris; Chevalier, Ordre des Arts et Lettres, Légion d'honneur, Officier, Ordre Nat. du Mérite, Commdr Ordre des Arts et Lettres. *Theatre includes:* Le classique et l'indien (Théâtre du rondpoint, Paris) 2010. *Publication includes:* L'Intranquille (co-author) 2009. *Address:* La Mésangère, 27810 Marcilly-sur-Eure, France (home). *Telephone:* (2) 37-48-47-18 (home).

GARRÉ, Nilda, BA; Argentine lawyer and politician; b. 3 Nov. 1945, Buenos Aires; m. Juan Manuel (divorced); three c.; ed Universidad del Salvador; active in Juventud Peronista in 1970s; elected to prov. ass. Buenos Aires as rep. of Frente Justicialista de Liberación 1973–76; lawyer and human rights activist 1976–82; participated in Renovación Peronista of Partido Justicialista 1983; joined Frente del País Solidario; elected to Cámara de Diputados 1995–2000; Deputy Interior Minister 2000–01; elected to Senado 2001–05; Amb. to Venezuela June 2005; Minister of Defence 2005–10, of Security 2010–13; Rep. of Nat. Chamber of Deputies to UN on Penal Legislation 1997; Vice-Pres. Fundación Carlos Auyero 1997–2002, Pres. 2004–05; mem. Advisory Cttee on Penal Reform 2003–04; Gen. Coordinator Centre for Research and Public Policy Advice (CEAPP). *Address:* c/o Ministry of Security, 1328 Buenos Aires, Argentina.

GARRETT, Lesley, CBE, FRAM; British singer (soprano); b. 10 April 1955; d. of Derek Arthur Garrett and Margaret Wall; m. 1991; one s. one d.; ed Thorne Grammar School, Royal Acad. of Music, Nat. Opera Studio; performed with Welsh Nat. Opera, Opera North, at Wexford and Buxton Festivals and at Glyndebourne; joined ENO (Prin. Soprano) 1984; Hon. DArts (Plymouth) 1995; winner Kathleen Ferrier Memorial Competition 1979, Gramophone Award for Best Selling Classical Artist 1996. *Television:* appeared in BBC TV series Lesley Garrett... Tonight, The

Lesley Garrett Show. *Major roles include:* Susanna in The Marriage of Figaro, Despina in Così Fan Tutte, Musetta in La Bohème, Jenny in The Rise and Fall of The City of Mahagonny, Atalanta in Xerxes, Zerlinda in Don Giovanni, Yum-Yum in The Mikado, Adèle in Die Fledermaus, Oscar in A Masked Ball, Dalinda in Ariodante, Rose in Street Scene, Bella in A Midsummer Marriage, Eurydice in Orpheus and Eurydice and title roles in The Cunning Little Vixen and La Belle Vivette; numerous concert hall performances in UK and abroad (including Last Night of the Proms); TV and radio appearances. *Recordings:* albums: Diva! A Soprano at the Movies 1991, Prima Donna 1992, Simple Gifts 1994, Soprano in Red 1995, Soprano in Hollywood 1996, A Soprano Inspired 1997, Lesley Garrett 1998, I Will Wait for You 2000, Travelling Light 2001, The Singer 2002, So Deep is the Night 2003, When I Fall in Love 2007, Amazing Grace 2008, You'll Never Walk Alone: The Collection 2010. *Publication:* Notes From a Small Soprano (autobiog.) 2001. *Leisure interest:* watching cricket. *Address:* The Music Partnership Ltd, New Broad Street House, New Broad Street, London, EC2M 1NH, England. *Telephone:* (20) 7840-9592. *Website:* www.musicpartnership.co.uk; www.lesleygarrett.co.uk.

GARRETT, Malcolm, BA (Hons), FISTD, FRSA; British graphic designer; *Creative Director, Applied Information Group;* b. 2 June 1956, Northwich, Cheshire; ed Univ., of Reading, Manchester Polytechnic; f. Assorted Images Design Co. 1978, renamed Assorted Images Ltd 1983, Design Dir 1978–94; designed for artists such as Buzzcocks, Duran Duran, Culture Club and Simple Minds, and pioneered digital and interactive work with Peter Gabriel; f. AMX Digital Ltd 1994, joined Havas Advertising (re-named AMX Studios, then AMX) 1998, Chair. 1999–2001; Visiting Prof. Univ. of the Arts, London (fmrly London Inst.); Visiting Prof. in Interactive Communication, RCA 2001–04; currently Creative Dir Applied Information Group; mem. RDI Exec. Cttee 2006–, Eye Magazine Editorial Bd 2007–, FontShop Type Bd 2007–08; External Examiner, Manchester Metropolitan Univ. 2008–; Hon. MA (Salford Univ.) 1999, Hon. Dr of Design (Robert Gordon Univ.) 2005. *Publications:* Duran Duran: Their Story (with Kasper de Graaf) 1982, When Cameras go Crazy: Culture Club (with Kasper de Graaf) 1983, Duran Duran Unseen: Photographs by Paul Edmond (with Kasper de Graaf) 2005. *Address:* Applied Information Group, 26–27 Great Sutton Street, London, EC1V 0DS, England (office). *Telephone:* (20) 7017-8488 (office). *Fax:* (20) 7017-8489 (office). *E-mail:* mx@aiglondon.com (office). *Website:* www.aiglondon.com (office).

GARRETT, Peter Robert, AM, BA, LLB; Australian environmentalist, musician and politician; *Minister for School Education, Early Childhood and Youth;* b. 16 April 1953, Wahroonga, NSW; s. of the late Peter Maxwell Garrett and Betty Garrett; m.; three d.; ed Barker Coll., Hornsby, Australian Nat. Univ., Univ. of New South Wales; mem. Rock Island Line; lead singer, Midnight Oil –2002; benefit concerts for Aboriginal Rights Asscn, Tibet Council, Rainforest Action Network, other orgs; Exxon Valdez oil spill protest concert 1990; ran for Australian Senate, Nuclear Disarmament Party 1984; Pres. Australian Conservation Foundation 1989–91, 1998–2004; mem. Bd Greenpeace International 1991–93; mem. Australian Labor Party 2004–; MP for Kingsford Smith 2004–; Minister for the Environment, Heritage and the Arts 2007–10, for School Educ., Early Childhood and Youth 2010–; Officier des Arts et des Lettres 2009; Hon. DLitt (Univ. of NSW); four Australian Record Industry Asscn Awards 1991, Sony Music Crystal Globe Award 1991, Australia's Living Treasures Award, Nat. Trust of Australia 1999, Australian Humanitarian Foundation Award (Environment category) 2000, Leaders for a Living Planet Award, WWF Australia and International 2010. *Recordings:* albums with Midnight Oil: Midnight Oil 1978, Head Injuries 1979, Bird Noises 1980, Place Without A Postcard 1981, Red Sails In The Sunset 1982, 10 9 8 7 6 5 4 3 2 1 1983, Diesel and Dust 1987, Blue Sky Mining 1990, Scream In Blue – Live 1992, Earth, Sun and Moon 1993, Breathe 1996, 20,000 Watt RSL – The Midnight Oil Collection 1997, Redneck Wonderland 1998, The Real Thing (live) 2000, Capricornia 2002, Best of Both Worlds 2004, Essential Oils 2012. *Publication:* Political Blues 1987. *Leisure interests:* surfing, Australian literature. *Address:* Electorate Office, PO Box 249, Maroubra, NSW 2035 (office). *Website:* www.petergarrett.com.au.

GARRICK, Sir Ronald (Ron), Kt, CBE; British business executive; b. 1940, Springburn, Glasgow, Scotland; ed Albert Secondary School; chartered engineer; joined Weir Group as grad. trainee 1962, CEO 1982–99, Chair. 1999–2002; Deputy Chair. Scottish Enterprise 1992–96; Dir (non-exec.) Bank of Scotland plc 2000–09, Chair. 2005–06, Dir (non-exec.) HBOS plc 2001–09, Deputy Chair. 2003–09, Chair. Irish Unit of HBOS plc 2005–09; Sr Ind. Dir (non-exec.) 2004–09, Chair. Nomination Cttee, Dir, Halifax Group Ltd, Dir (non-exec.) Bank of Scotland (Ireland) Ltd; fmr mem. Bd of Dirs Shell UK, Scottish Power plc; Fellow, Royal Acad. of Eng 1984. *Address:* Halifax Group Ltd, Trinity Road, Halifax, W Yorks., HX1 2RG, England (office). *Telephone:* (1422) 333333 (office). *Fax:* (1422) 333000 (office). *Website:* www.halifax.co.uk (office).

GARTON ASH, Timothy John, CMG, MA, FRSA, FRHistS, FRSL; British writer and academic; *Professor of European Studies, University of Oxford;* b. 12 July 1955, London; m. Danuta Maria 1982; two s.; ed Exeter Coll., Oxford, St Antony's Coll., Oxford; editorial writer The Times 1984–86; Foreign Ed. The Spectator 1984–90; Fellow Woodrow Wilson Int. Center for Scholars, Washington, DC 1986–87; Sr Assoc. mem., St Antony's Coll., Oxford 1987–89, Fellow and Sr Research Fellow in Contemporary European History 1990–, currently Prof. of European Studies, Isaiah Berlin Professorial Fellow, Univ. of Oxford; columnist The Independent 1988–90, The Guardian 2002–; Sr Fellow Hoover Inst., Stanford Univ. 2000–; Fellow Acad. of Sciences, Berlin-Brandenburg, European Acad. of Arts and Sciences; Corresp. Fellow Inst. for Human Sciences, Vienna; mem. PEN, Soc. of Authors; Golden Insignia of the Order of Merit, Poland 1992, Kt's Cross of the Order of Merit, Germany 1995, Order of Merit, Czech Repub. 2000; Hon. DLitt (St Andrew's) 2004; Soc. of Authors Somerset Maugham Award 1984, Veillon Foundation Prix Européen de l'Essai 1989, David Watt Memorial Prize 1989, Granada Award for Commentator of the Year 1989, Friedrich Ebert Stiftung Prize 1991, Imre Nagy Memorial Plaque, Hungary 1995, Premio Napoli 1995, Orwell Prize for Journalism 2006, Ischia Prize for Int. Journalism 2008. *Publications:* 'Und willst du nicht mein Bruder sein...': Die DDR heute 1981, The Polish Revolution: Solidarity 1983, The Uses of Adversity: Essays on the Fate of Central Europe 1989, We the People: The Revolution of '89 Witnessed in Warsaw, Budapest, Berlin and Prague 1990, In Europe's Name: Germany and the Divided

Continent 1993, Freedom for Publishing for Freedom: The Central and East European Publishing Project (ed.) 1995, The File: A Personal History 1997, History of the Present 1999, Free World 2004, Facts are Subversive: Political Writing from a Decade Without a Name 2009; contribs to books, newspapers and magazines. *Address:* St Antony's College, Oxford, OX2 6JF, England (office). *Telephone:* (1865) 274470 (office). *Fax:* (1865) 274478 (office). *E-mail:* european.studies@sant.ox.ac.uk (office). *Website:* www.sant.ox.ac.uk (office); www.timothygartonash.com.

GARWIN, Richard L., MS, PhD; American physicist; b. 19 April 1928, Cleveland, Ohio; s. of Robert Garwin and Leona S. Garwin; m. Lois E. Levy 1947; two s. one d.; ed Case Western Reserve Univ. and Univ. of Chicago; Instructor and Asst Prof. of Physics, Univ. of Chicago 1949–52; mem. staff, IBM Watson Lab., Columbia Univ. 1952–65, Dir of Applied Research 1965–66, Lab. Dir 1966–67, Fellow 1967–93, Fellow Emer. 1993–; Adjunct Prof. of Physics, Columbia Univ. 1957–; Phillip D. Reed Sr Fellow for Science and Tech., Council on Foreign Relations 1994–2004; mem. Defense Science Bd 1966–69; mem. President's Science Advisory Cttee 1962–66, 1969–72; mem. IBM Corporate Tech. Cttee 1970–71; Adjunct Prof., Columbia Univ. 1957; Prof. of Public Policy, Kennedy School of Govt, Harvard Univ. 1979–81, Adjunct Research Fellow 1982–; Andrew D. White Prof.-at-Large, Cornell Univ. 1982–87; mem. NAS 1966–, Inst. of Medicine 1975–81, Nat. Acad. of Eng 1978–, American Philosophical Soc. 1979–, Council on Foreign Relations; Consultant to Los Alamos 1950–93, to Sandia Nat. Lab. 1994–; Fellow, American Physical Soc. American Acad. of Arts and Sciences; Ford Foundation Fellow, CERN, Geneva 1959–60; Dr hc (Case Western Reserve Univ.) 1966, (Rensselaer Polytechnic Inst.), (State Univ. of New York); R. V. Jones Intelligence Award (Nat. Foreign Intelligence Community) 1996, Enrico Fermi Award 1997, Nat. Medal of Science 2002. *Publications:* Nuclear Power Issues and Choices (co-author) 1977, Nuclear Weapons and World Politics 1977, Energy, the Next Twenty Years (co-author) 1979, The Dangers of Nuclear Wars 1979, Unresolved Issues in Arms Control 1988, A Nuclear-Weapon-Free World: Desirable? Feasible? 1993, Managing the Plutonium Surplus: Applications and Technical Options 1994, U.S. Intervention Policy for the Post-Cold War World: New Challenges and New Responses 1994, Feux Follets et Champignons Nucléaires (with G. Charpak) 1997; about 200 published papers and 42 US patents. *Leisure interests:* skiing, military technology, arms control, social use of technology.

GARZA, Antonio O., Jr, BBA, JD; American lawyer, diplomatist, politician and business executive; *Partner, ViaNovo LP;* m. 1st María Aramburuzabala Larregui 2005 (divorced 2010); m. 2nd Liz Beightler 2012; ed Univ. of Texas, Southern Methodist Univ. School of Law; elected to US House of Reps for S Texas 1988; apptd Tex. Sec. of State and Sr Adviser to Tex. Gov. George W. Bush 1994, later Chief Elections Officer; served on Presidential dels to observe elections in Nicaragua and El Salvador; Cameron Co. Judge –1995; Pnr, Bracewell & Patterson LLP (law firm), Austin –1998; Tex. Railroad Commr 1998–2002; Amb. to Mexico 2002–09; Pnr, ViaNovo LP (man. and communications consultancy) 2009–, also Chair. ViaNovo Ventures (cross-border business devt unit); serves as Counsel, White & Case (law firm), Mexico City; mem. Bd of Dirs Basic Energy Services; Trustee, Southern Methodist Univ.; mem. Advisory Bd Bush School of Govt and Public Service, Texas A&M Univ., FameCast, Maguire Energy Inst.; SMU Distinguished Alumnus Award 2001, named amongst Top 100 Most Influential Hispanics by Hispanic Business Magazine, Azteca Aguila Award (Mexico) 2009. *Address:* ViaNovo LP, 327 Congress, Suite 450, Austin, TX 78701 (office); PO Box 685284, Austin, TX 78768, USA; White & Case, S.C., Torre del Bosque - PH, Blvd. Manuel Avila Camacho #24, Col. Lomas de Chapultepec, 11000 México, DF, Mexico (office). *Telephone:* (512) 744-0044 (ViaNovo LP) (office). *E-mail:* agarza@vianovo.com (office); antonio.garza@whitecase.com (office); aog@tonygarza.com. *Website:* www.tonygarza.com.

GARZÓN, Angelino; Colombian politician and fmr trade unionist; *Vice-President;* b. 29 Oct. 1946, Buga, Valle del Cauca; m. Monserrat Muñoz; ed Univ. Jorge Tadeo Lozano, Bogotá, Univ. de Salamanca, Spain, Int. Labour Org. Training Centre, Turin, Italy; fmr mem. Exec. Cttee, Partido Comunista Colombiano; fmr Vice-Pres. Unión Patriótica; fmr Sec.-Gen. of various trade unions including Federación Nacional de Trabajadores al Servicio del Estado (Fenaltrase), Confederación Sindical de Trabajadores de Colombia (CSTC), Central Unitaria de Trabajadores (CUT); fmr Rep. of Colombia to UN, Geneva; mem. Asamblea Nacional Constituyente (responsible for writing new constitution of Colombia) 1991; Minister of Work and Social Security 2000–02; Gov. Valle del Cauca Dept 2004–07; Vice-Pres. of Colombia 2010–. *Address:* Office of the Vice-President, Palacio de Nariño, Carrera 8, No 7-26, Bogotá DC, Colombia (office). *Telephone:* (1) 562-9300 (office). *Fax:* (1) 286-8063 (office). *Website:* www.presidencia.gov.co (office); www.angelinogarzon.com.

GARZÓN, Baltasar; Spanish judge; *Investigating Judge, Audiencia Nacional;* b. 1955, Villa de Torres (Jaen); m. Jaen; three c.; prov. judge 1978-87, Audiencia Nacional (Nat. Court) 1987–; mem. Parl. 1993–94; has investigated numerous high profile cases involving drug trafficking, Basque terrorism, govt corruption, Spain's security forces and human rights abuses and Islamic fundamentalism; issued arrest warrant for Gen. Augusto Pinochet Ugarte to face charges of genocide, terrorism and torture 1998; banned Basque politicial party Batasuna Aug. 2002; Hon. DJur (New York Univ.) 2007. *Address:* Audiencia Nacional, García Gutiérrez 1, 28004 Madrid, Spain (office). *Telephone:* (91) 3973339 (office). *Fax:* (91) 3973306 (office). *Website:* www.audiencianacional.es (office).

GARZÓN, Luis Eduardo (Lucho); Colombian politician and fmr trade union official; b. 15 Feb. 1951, Bogota; s. of Eloísa Garzón; ed Universidad Libre; early work experience as caddie, carpenter and street trader; fmr messenger, Public Relations Div., Ecopetrol; fmr leader Unión Sindical Obrera (USO), later Vice-Pres.; fmr leader Central Unitaria de Trabajadores (CUT); fmr presidential cand., coalición Polo Democrático; fmr mem. Comité Central del Partido Comunista Colombiano; mem. Polo Democrático Independiente (PDI); Mayor of Bogota 2004–07; mem. several official cttees including Consejo Nacional de Paz, Comisión de Conciliación Nacional, Comité de Búsqueda de la Paz, Comisión Facilitadora par los diálogos con el Eln; AFL-CIO George Meany-Lane Kirkland Prize 2001. *Address:* c/o Office of the Mayor, Bogota, Colombia (office). *E-mail:* info@luchogarzon.com (office). *Website:* www.luchogarzon.com (office).

GASCOIGNE, Paul John, (Gazza); British fmr professional footballer; b. 27 May 1967, Dunston, Gateshead, Tyne and Wear; s. of John Gascoigne and Carol Gascoigne (née Harold); m. Sheryl Failes 1996 (divorced 1998); one s. and two step-c.; ed Heathfield Sr School; midfielder; youth player with Newcastle United 1980–85 (won FA Youth Cup 1985), sr player 1985–88 (won FA Cup 1991); played for Tottenham Hotspur 1988–92 (FA Cup Winners' Medal 1991), Lazio, Italy 1992–95, Rangers 1995–98 (won Scottish League Championship 1995/96, 1996/97, Scottish Cup 1996, Scottish League Cup 1996), Middlesbrough 1998–2000, Everton 2000–02, Burnley 2002; signed as player-coach for Gansu Tianma (Gansu Sky Horses), Chinese B-League 2003; Wolverhampton Wanderers reserves 2003; player-coach, Boston United 2004; played for England, 13 Under-21 caps and five goals 1987–88, four England B caps and one goal 1989, 57 full caps and ten goals 1988–98 (won Rous Cup 1989, Tournoi de France 1997, FIFA World Cup (Fourth Place)/FIFA Fair Play Award 1990); Man. Kettering Town 2005; Professional Footballers' Asscn Young Player of the Year 1988, BBC Sports Personality of the Year 1990, World Cup All-Star Team Player 1990, Scottish Players' Player of the Year 1996, Scottish Football Writers' Player of the Year 1996, inducted into English Football Hall of Fame 2002. *Publications:* Paul Gascoigne (autobiography with Paul Simpson) 2001, Gazza: My Story (with Hunter Davies) (British Book Award for Sports Book of the Year 2005) 2004. *Leisure interests:* football, fishing, tennis, swimming. *Address:* c/o Robertson Craig & Co., Clairmont Gardens, Glasgow, G3 7LW, Scotland. *Telephone:* (141) 332-1205. *Fax:* (141) 332-8035.

GASKILL, William; British theatre and opera director; b. 24 June 1930; s. of Joseph Linnaeus Gaskill and Maggie Simpson; ed Salt High School, Shipley and Hertford Coll., Oxford; Dir, Granada Television 1956–57; Asst Artistic Dir Royal Court Theatre, London 1958–60; Dir Royal Shakespeare Co. 1961–62; Assoc. Dir Nat. Theatre, London 1963–65, 1979; Artistic Dir English Stage Co., Royal Court Theatre 1965–72; Dir Jt Stock Theatre Group 1974–83; returned to direct at Arcola Theatre 2005. *Stage productions include:* (Royal Court Theatre) Epitaph for George Dillon, One Way Pendulum, Saved, Early Morning, Man is Man, Lear, Big Wolf, The Sea, The Gorky Brigade; (Nat. Theatre) The Recruiting Officer, Mother Courage, Philoctetes, Armstrong's Last Goodnight, The Beaux Stratagem, The Madras House, A Fair Quarrel, Man, Beast and Virtue, Black Snow; (Royal Shakespeare Co.) The Caucasian Chalk Circle, Richard III, Cymbeline; (Joint Stock) The Speakers, Fanshen, Yesterday's News, A Mad World, My Masters, The Ragged Trousered Philanthropists; other productions include The Way of the World; opera productions include: The Barber of Seville, La Bohème and Lucia di Lammermoor (Welsh Nat. Opera), Carver. *Publication:* A Sense of Direction: life at the Royal Court (autobiog.) 1988. *Address:* 124A Leighton Road, London, NW5 2RG, England.

GASKÓ, István; Hungarian trade union official; *President, Democratic League of Independent Trade Unions (LIGA)* and *Free Trade Union of Railway Workers (VDSZSZ);* b. 21 July 1954, Sajószentpèter; m.; one s.; ed Econ. Univ., Budapest; mem. Democratic Trade Union of Scientific Workers 1988; f. Social Democratic Party 1989; f. Free Trade Union of Railway Workers (VDSZSZ) 1989, Pres. 1991–; Pres. Democratic League of Ind. Trade Unions (LIGA) 1996–. *Leisure interests:* reading, music, film, theatre, travelling. *Address:* LIGA and VDSZSZ, Ajtósi Dürer sor 27/A, 1146 Budapest, Hungary (office). *Telephone:* (1) 321-5262 (office). *Fax:* (1) 321-5405 (office). *E-mail:* info@liganet.hu (office). *Website:* www.liganet.hu (office).

GASPAR, Vítor Louçã Rabaça, DEcon; Portuguese economist and politician; b. 9 Nov. 1960; s. of Vítor Manuel Rabaça Gaspar and Maria Laura Seixas Louçã; m. Sílvia Luz; three d.; ed Univ. Católica Portuguesa, Univ. Nova de Lisboa; Dir of Econ. Studies, Ministry of Finance 1989–92; Adviser to the Bd and Dir Research and Statistics Dept, Banco de Portugal 1993–98, Adviser, Banco de Portugal 2005–06, Special Adviser 2010–11; Dir-Gen. of Research, European Central Bank 1998–2004; Head, Bureau of European Policy Advisers 2007–10; Minister of State and Finance 2011–13; Ind. *Publications:* several books and articles in econ. journals. *Address:* c/o Ministry of State and Finance, Av. Infante D. Henrique 1, 1149-009 Lisbon, Portugal.

GASPARI, Mitja, BSc; Slovenian economist, fmr central banker and politician; b. 25 Nov. 1951, Ljubljana; ed Univ. of Ljubljana, Univ. of Belgrade; Research Economist, Nat. Bank of Slovenia 1975–81, Head of Research 1981–87, Deputy Gov. 1987–88; Deputy Gov., Nat. Bank of Yugoslavia 1988–91; Sr Financial Economist, Trade and Finance Div., Tech. Dept Europe and USSR, The World Bank 1991–92; Minister of Finance 1992–2000; mem. Parl. 2000–01; Gov. Bank of Slovenia 2001–07; Minister without Portfolio, responsible for Devt and European Affairs 2008–12. *Publications:* numerous articles on fiscal studies. *Address:* c/o Government Office for Development and European Affairs, 1000 Ljubljana, Gregorčičeva 25, Slovenia (office).

GASPARINI, Massimo; Italian business executive; *CEO, Missoni SpA;* has over 20 years of experience working for Italian and multinational cos; has worked in fashion since 2001, overseeing Gucci's watch and jewellery div. –2006; CEO Missoni SpA, Milan 2007–. *Address:* Missoni SpA, Via Salvini 1/A, Milan, Italy (office). *Telephone:* (02) 7600-1479 (office). *E-mail:* press.info@missoni.it (office). *Website:* www.missoni.it (office).

GAŠPAROVIČ, Ivan, JUDr, CSc; Slovak politician, lawyer and fmr head of state; b. 27 March 1941, Poltár, Lučenec Dist; s. of Vladimír Gašparovič and Elena Gašparovič; m. Silvia Beníková 1964; one s. one d.; ed Comenius Univ., Bratislava; clerk, Prosecutor's Office, Martin Trenčín 1965–66; Municipal Public Prosecutor, Bratislava 1966–68; teacher, Faculty of Law, Comenius Univ., Bratislava 1968–90, Vice-Rector 1990–; Gen. Prosecutor of CSFR 1990–92; mem. Movt for Democratic Slovakia 1992–2002 (movt became a political party 2000); Deputy to Slovak Nat. Council 1992–2002, mem. of Presidium; Chair. of Slovak Nat. Council 1992–98; Chair. Special Body of Nat. Council of Slovakia for Control of Slovak Intelligence Services 1993–98; Acting Pres. of Slovakia (served alongside Vladimír Mečiar) March–Oct. 1998; Founder and Leader Movt for Democracy 2002–; Pres. of Slovakia 2004–14; a leader of the ice hockey club Slovan ChZJD (later called HC Slovan Bratislava); fmr Vice-Pres. Int. Comm. of the Czechoslovak Ice Hockey Union, hockey team of the sports unit ŠK Slovan Bratislava; Order of the White Double Cross, Order of Ľudovít Štúr, Pribina Cross, Cross of Milan Rastislav Štefánik, Order of Andrej Hlinka; Grand Cross of the Order of Vytautas the Great (Lithuania) 2005, Kt Grand Cross with Grand Cordon, Order of Merit of the Italian

Repub. 2007, Order of the Netherlands Lion 2007, Order of Isabella the Catholic (Spain) 2007, Kt Grand Cross, Grand Order of King Tomislav (Croatia) 2008, Order Orła Białego (Poland) 2009, Order of St Olav (Norway) 2010, Collar of the Order of the Cross of Terra Mariana (Estonia) 2011, Kt of the Order of the Elephant (Denmark) 2012, Order of the Repub. of Serbia 2013, Order of the White Lion (Czech Repub.) 2013. *Publications:* author and co-author of many univ. textbooks, numerous articles and reviews on criminal law. *Leisure interests:* American basketball, Korean cars, tennis, ice hockey, motoring. *Address:* c/o Office of the President, Hodžovo nám. 1, PO Box 128, 810 00 Bratislava, Slovakia. *E-mail:* informacie@prezident.sk.

GASPIN, Jeff, BA, MBA; American media executive; *Chairman, NBC Universal Television Entertainment;* b. 29 Dec. 1960, Bayside, Long Island; m. Karen Gaspin; two s. one d.; ed State Univ. of New York, New York Univ. Grad. School of Business Admin; Dir of Financial Planning, NBC News 1988–89, Vice-Pres. of Programming and Devt 1989–94; Sr Vice-Pres. Programming, QVC 1994–96; Sr Vice-Pres. Programming and Production, VH1 1996–98, Exec. Vice-Pres. 1998–2001; Exec. Vice-Pres. Alternative Series, Longform, Specials and Program Strategy, NBC Entertainment 2001–02; Pres. Bravo 2002–04; Pres. Cable Entertainment, NBC Universal 2004–07, Pres. Cable and Digital Content 2007, Pres. and COO NBC Universal TV Group 2007–09, Chair. NBC Universal TV Entertainment 2009–. *Address:* NBC Universal Television Entertainment, 100 Universal City Plaza, Universal City, CA 91608, USA (office). *Telephone:* (818) 777-4317 (office). *Website:* www.nbcuni.com (office).

GASS, Michelle, BS, MBA; American business executive; *President, Europe, Middle East and Africa, Starbucks Corporation;* m.; two c.; ed Worcester Polytechnic Inst., Univ. of Washington; worked with Procter & Gamble in marketing and new product devt –1996; joined Starbucks as Marketing Man. for Frappuccino blended beverages 1996, various man. positions 1996–2004, Sr Vice-Pres. and US Category Man. 2004–07, Sr Vice-Pres. Global Product and Brand 2007–08, served a special assignment in Office of the CEO leading the Global Strategy function Jan.–July 2008, Sr Vice-Pres., Marketing and Category July–Nov. 2008, Exec. Vice-Pres. 2008–09, Pres. Seattle's Best Coffee 2009–11, Pres. Europe, Middle East and Africa, Starbucks 2011–; mem. Bd of Dirs Ann, Inc.; ranked by Fortune magazine amongst the 50 Most Powerful Women in Business outside the US (38th) 2012. *Address:* Starbucks Coffee Co. (UK) Ltd, Building 4, Chiswick Park, 566 Chiswick High Road, London, W4 5YE, England (office). *Telephone:* (20) 8834-5050 (office); (20) 8834-5000 (office). *E-mail:* ukinfo@ starbucks.co.uk (office). *Website:* www.starbucks.co.uk (office).

GASSIEV, Nikolai Tengizovich; Russian singer (tenor); b. 2 Feb. 1952, Tskhinvali, Georgia; ed Leningrad State Conservatory; soloist, Mariinsky Opera and Ballet Theatre 1990–; debut in Metropolitan Opera as Yurodivy (Boris Godunov) and Agrippina (Fairy Angel) 1992, Dresdner Staatsoper 1993, Brooklyn School of Music 1995, Edinburgh Festival 1995, Albert Hall 1995, La Scala 1996; Prize of Union of Theatre Workers Best Actor of the Year 1994. *Address:* Mariinsky Theatre, Teatralnaya pl. 1, St Petersburg, Russia. *Telephone:* (812) 315-57-24. *Website:* www.mariinsky.ru.

GAT, Joel R., MSc, PhD; Israeli professor of isotope research; *Professor Emeritus, Weizmann Institute of Science;* b. (Joel R. Gutmann), 17 Feb. 1926, Munich, Germany; m.; two c.; ed Hebrew Univ., Jerusalem; emigrated to Israel 1936; Asst, Dept of Physical Chem., Hebrew Univ. 1949–50; Research Officer, Ministry of Defence Labs, Jerusalem 1950–52; Israel Atomic Energy Comm., Rehovot 1952–59; at Isotope Dept (renamed Dept of Environmental Sciences and Energy Research 1990), Weizmann Inst. of Science, Rehovot 1959–, Acting Prof. 1967–71, Prof. 1971–92, Prof. Emer. 1992–, Head of Dept 1975–86, Dean, Faculty of Chem. 1986–89; Dir Centre for Water Science and Tech., Ben Gurion Univ. of the Negev 1997–2003; Visiting Scientist, Enrico Fermi Inst. for Nuclear Science, Univ. of Chicago 1955–56, Scripps Inst. of Oceanography, Univ. of California 1964–65, Nat. Centre for Atmospheric Research, Boulder, Colo 1972–73, Univ. of Wisconsin 1988–89; mem. Editorial Bd Isotope Geosciences, Earth and Planetary Science Letters; undertook IAEA-sponsored projects in Brazil, Iran, Mexico and Turkey. *Publications:* Physics and Chemistry of Lakes (co-ed.) 1995, The Dead Sea: The Lake and its Setting. Oxford Monograph on Geology and Geophysics (co-ed.) 1997, Environmental Isotopes in The Hydrological Cycle: Vol. II, Atmospheric Waters 2001. *Address:* Department of Environmental Sciences and Energy Research, The Weizmann Institute of Science, Sussman Building, Room 307, PO Box 26, Rehovot, Israel (office). *Telephone:* (8) 9342545 (office). *E-mail:* joel.gat@weizmann.ac.il (office). *Website:* www.weizmann.ac.il/ESER (office).

GATES, Bill; American software industry executive and foundation executive; *Founder and Technology Advisor, Microsoft Corporation;* b. (William Henry Gates, III), 28 Oct. 1955, Seattle, Wash.; s. of William H. Gates II and the late Mary M. Gates (née Maxwell); m. Melinda Gates 1994; one s. two d.; ed Lakeside School, Seattle, Harvard Univ.; while at Harvard developed version of BASIC programming language for MITS 1975; programmer for Honeywell 1975; Co-founder, with Paul Allen, Microsoft Corpn 1975, Gen. Partner 1975–77, Pres. 1977–82, Chair. 1981–2014 (part-time, non-exec. Chair. 27 June 2008–14), Chief Software Architect 1999–2006, CEO –2000, Technology Advisor 2014–; f. Corbis (digital archive of art and photography) 1989; co-f. Bill and Melinda Gates Foundation 1994, currently Co-Chair. and Trustee; f. Gates Library Foundation 1997, name changed to Gates Learning Foundation 1999, merged with Bill and Melinda Gates Foundation 2000; mem. Bd of Dirs ICOS (biotechnology co.) 1990–, Berkshire Hathaway Inc. 2004–; Hon. KBE (UK) 2005; Hon. DJur (Harvard) 2007; Howard Vollum Award, Reed Coll. Portland, Ore. 1984, Nat. Medal for Tech. from US Commerce Dept 1992, CEO of the Year, Chief Executive Magazine 1994, named by Time magazine amongst Persons of the Year 2005, Prince of Asturias Award for Int. Cooperation (co-recipient with wife) 2006, voted by New Statesman magazine eighth in list of Heroes of Our Time 2006, ranked by Forbes magazine amongst The World's Most Powerful People (tenth) 2009–10, (fifth) 2011, (fourth) 2012, (sixth) 2013, ranked by Forbes magazine amongst The World's Richest people (first) 2000–07, (third) 2008, (first) 2009, (second) 2010–13, (first) 2014, Bower Award for Business Leadership, The Franklin Inst. 2010, Buffalo Award, Boy Scouts of America 2010, numerous other awards. *Publications include:* The Future 1994, The Road Ahead 1995, Business @ the Speed of Thought 1999. *Leisure interests:* reading, golf, tennis, bridge. *Address:* Microsoft Corporation, 1 Microsoft Way,

Redmond, WA 98052-6399 (office); Bill and Melinda Gates Foundation, 500 Fifth Avenue North, Seattle, WA 98109, USA. *Telephone:* (425) 882-8080 (office). *Fax:* (425) 936-7329 (office). *E-mail:* info@gatesfoundation.org. *Website:* www.microsoft .com/en-us/news/exec/billg/ (office); www.gatesfoundation.org.

GATES, Henry Louis, Jr, BA, MA, PhD; American academic, author and editor; *Alphonse Fletcher University Professor and Director, W. E. B. DuBois Institute for African and African-American Research, Harvard University;* b. 16 Sept. 1950, Piedmont, W Va; s. of Henry-Louis Gates and Pauline Augusta Gates (née Coleman); m. Sharon Lynn Adams 1979; two d.; ed Yale Univ. and Clare Coll., Cambridge; fmr European corresp. for Time magazine; Lecturer in English, Yale Univ. 1976–79, Asst Prof. English and Afro-American Studies 1979–84, Assoc. Prof. 1984–85; Prof. of English, Comparative Literature and Africana Studies, Cornell Univ. 1985–90; John Spencer Bassett Prof. of English, Duke Univ. 1990–91; W. E. B. DuBois Prof. of the Humanities and Chair. Dept of African and African-American Studies, Harvard Univ. 1991–2006, Alphonse Fletcher Univ. Prof. 2006–, also Dir W. E. B. DuBois Inst. for African and African-American Research, Walter Channing Cabot Fellow 2011; Pres. Afro-American Acad. 1984–; Ed.-in-Chief, Oxford African American Studies Center 2006–, TheRoot.com 2008–; Co-founder and Co-owner, AfricanDNA.com 2008–; contrib. New Yorker, New York Times; MacArthur Fellowship 1981–86; mem. American Acad. of Arts and Letters 1999–, Pulitzer Prize Bd; Hon. Citizenship of Benin 2001; numerous hon. degrees; numerous awards, including Zora Neale Hurston Soc. Award for Cultural Scholarship 1986, Candle Award, Morehouse Coll. 1989, Norman Rabb Award, American Jewish Cttee 1994, Tikkun Nat. Ethics Award 1996, Roger Joseph Prize, Hebrew Union Coll. 1997, Nat. Humanities Medal 1998, Henry James Award, Edith Wharton Soc. 2004, Carl Sandburg Literary Award 2004, Jay B. Hubbell Award for Lifetime Achievement in American Literary Studies, Modern Language Asscn 2006, National Arts Club, Lifetime Achievement Award 2007, Gondobay Manga Foundation Sankofa Award 2009, Ralph Lowell Award 2009, Leon H. Sullivan Honors Award 2009, Madison Freedom Award 2009, Lifetime Achievement Award in Genealogy and Genetics, New England Historical and Genealogical Soc. 2010, Media Bridge-Builder Award, Tanenbaum Center, 2011, Public Interest Law Asscn Award, CUNY 2012. *Television includes:* American Lives 2006, African American Lives 2 2008, Faces of America 2010, Finding Your Roots 2012. *Publications include:* Figures in Black (literary criticism) 1987, The Signifying Monkey (American Book Award 1989) 1988, Loose Canons (literary criticism) 1992, Colored People (short stories) 1994, The Future of the Race (with Cornel West) 1996, Thirteen Ways of Looking at a Black Man 1998, Africana (jtly) (TV documentary) 1999, Wonders of the African World 1999, The Curitas Anthology of African – American Slave Narratives, The African-American Century 2000; Encarta Africana Encycloaedia (co-ed.) 1999; as ed. The Bondswoman's Narrative 2002, America Behind the Color Line 2004, In Search of Our Roots: How Nineteen Extraordinary African Americans Reclaimed Their Past 2009, Tradition and the Black Atlantic: Critical Theory in the African Diaspora 2010, Black in Latin America 2011, Life Upon These Shores 2011, Dictionary of African Biography (co-ed.) 2011. *Address:* W.E.B. Du Bois Institute, 104 Mount Auburn Street, Room 3R, Cambridge, MA 02138, USA (office). *Telephone:* (617) 496-5468 (office). *Fax:* (617) 495-9490 (office). *E-mail:* gates@harvard.edu (office). *Website:* www.aaas.fas .harvard.edu (office).

GATES, Holly G.; American computer engineer; *Senior Hardware Engineer, E Ink Corporation;* ed Weihai Br. of Shandong Univ., China, Massachusetts Inst. of Tech., Massachusetts Coll. of Art, Harvard Univ.; worked for Brown Innovations Inc., Boston Mass 1995–96; Lecturer, MIT Edgerton Center, Cambridge, Mass 1996–97; worked for Zond Systems Inc., Searsburg, Vt June–Aug. 1997; worked for MIT Media Lab., Cambridge, Mass 1996–98; Hardware Engineer, E Ink Corpn, Cambridge, Mass 1998–2002, Sr Hardware Engineer 2002–; First Prize for robot called 'dog' (built with Leila Hasan), 6.270 LEGO Robotics Competition 1998, Rudenberg Memorial Fund 1998, World Tech. Award in Information Tech. (Hardware), The World Tech. Network 2005. *Publications:* papers in professional journals and several patents. *Leisure interests:* welding, renovating, dancing, mountaineering, electronics, sculpture, clothing design, fashion devices. *Address:* E Ink Corporation, 733 Concord Avenue, Cambridge, MA 02138 (office); 189 Summer Street, Apartment 2, Somerville, MA 02145, USA (home). *Telephone:* (617) 499-6000 (office). *Fax:* (617) 499-6200 (office). *E-mail:* info@eink.com (office). *Website:* www.eink.com (office); www.positron.org/people/hgates (office).

GATES, Melinda, BSc, BEcons, MBA; American foundation executive; *Co-Director, Bill and Melinda Gates Foundation;* b. (Melinda Ann French), 15 Aug. 1964, Dallas, Tex.; m. William (Bill) Henry Gates III 1994; one s. two d.; ed Ursuline Acad., Dallas, Duke Univ. and Duke Univ. Fuqua School of Business; several positions at Microsoft Corpn 1987–96, including Product Unit Man. Microsoft Publisher, Microsoft Bob, Microsoft Encarta and Microsoft Expedia; co-f. Bill and Melinda Gates Foundation 1994; mem. Bd of Dirs Drugstore.com –2006, The Washington Post –2010; attends the Bilderberg Group; Trustee, Duke Univ. 1996–2003; named by TIME magazine amongst Persons of the Year 2005, ranked by Forbes magazine amongst The World's 100 Most Powerful Women (10th) 2005, (12th) 2006, (24th) 2007, (40th) 2008, (34th) 2009, (27th) 2010, (sixth) 2011, (fourth) 2012, (third) 2013, Prince of Asturias Award for Int. Co-operation (co-recipient with husband) 2006. *Address:* Bill and Melinda Gates Foundation, PO Box 23350, Seattle, WA 98102, USA (office). *Telephone:* (206) 709-3100 (office). *E-mail:* info@gatesfoundation.org (office). *Website:* www.gatesfoundation.org (office).

GATES, Robert M., PhD; American government official and fmr academic administrator; b. 25 Sept. 1943, Wichita, Kan.; m. Becky Gates; two c.; ed Coll. of William and Mary, Indiana Univ., Georgetown Univ.; service with USAF 1966–68; career training program CIA 1968, intelligence analyst 1969–72, staff of Special Asst to the Dir of Central Intelligence for Strategic Arms Limitations 1972–73, Asst Nat. Intelligence Officer for Strategic Programs 1973–74, staff Nat. Security Council The White House 1974–76, staff Center for Policy Support 1976–77, Special Asst to Pres. for Nat. Security Affairs 1977–79, Dir Strategic Evaluation Center 1979–80, Exec. Asst to Dir of Cen. Intelligence and Dir of the Exec. Staff, Dir of Office of Policy and Planning and Nat. Intelligence Officer for the Soviet Union and Eastern Europe 1980–81, Deputy Dir for Intelligence 1982–86, Chair. Nat. Intelligence Council 1982–86, Acting Dir of Central Intelligence 1986–87,

Deputy Dir of Central Intelligence 1986–89, Asst to the Pres. and Deputy for Nat. Security Affairs The White House 1989–91, Dir CIA 1991–93; Interim Dean, George Bush School of Govt and Public Service, 1999-2001, Pres. Texas A&M Univ. 2002–06; US Sec. of Defense 2006–11; fmr mem. Bd of Dirs NACCO Industries Inc., Brinker International Inc., Parker Drilling Co. Inc.; fmr mem. Bd of Trustees The Fidelity Funds; mem. Iraq Study Group, US Inst. for Peace 2006; Fellow, American Acad. of Arts and Sciences 2009–; Nat. Intelligence Distinguished Service Medal, Distinguished Intelligence Medal (twice), Intelligence Medal of Merit, Arthur S. Fleming Award, Nat. Security Medal, Presidential Citizen's Medal. *Publication:* From the Shadows: The Ultimate Insider's Story of Five Presidents and How They Won the Cold War 1996. *Address:* c/o Department of Defense, 1000 Defense Pentagon, Washington, DC 20301, USA (office).

GATES, Theaster, BS, MA, MS; American artist and curator; b. 1973, Chicago, Ill.; ed Iowa State Univ., Univ. of Cape Town, S Africa; Transit Arts Planner and Special Projects Manager, Chicago Transit Authority 2000; Dir of Educ. and Outreach, Little Black Pearl 2005; Co-ordinator of Arts Programming, Humanities Div., Univ. of Chicago 2007, Lecturer, Dept of Visual Arts 2008, Dir of Arts Program Devt, Office of the Provost, and Artist-in-Residence, Dept of Visual Arts 2009, Dir and Project Leader, Arts and Public Life Initiative 2011; Loeb Fellowship, Harvard Grad. School of Design, Int. Studio and Curatorial Program, New York Arts/Industry Residency Program, John Michael Kohler Arts Center, Sheboygan, Wis., Gestures of Resistance, Museum of Contemporary Craft, Portland 2010; Global Residency, Creative Time, New York 2013; mem. Bd Hyde Park Alliance for the Arts, Chicago, Univ. of Chicago Arts Council, Experimental Station, Chicago, South Side Community Art Center, Chicago; mem. Artspeaks, Chicago; artistic practice includes space development, object making and performance; Joyce Award, The Joyce Foundation, Chicago 2009, Artadi a Award, Artadia: The Fund for Art and Dialogue, New York 2009, Artist Grant, Graham Foundation, Chicago 2009, 2011, Harpo Foundation Grant, Bemis Center for Contemporary Arts, Omaha, Nebraska 2010, USA Kippy Fellow – Visual Arts, USA Projects, Los Angeles 2012, Innovator of the Year – Art Award, Wall Street Journal 2012, Vera List Center Prize, The New School, New York 2012, Creative Capital Visual Arts Grant 2012, Armory Show Artist Commission 2012, Prize for Arts and Politics, Vera List Center, Parsons The New School for Design, New York 2013. *Address:* University of Chicago, 5801 South Ellis Avenue, ADM 510, Chicago, IL 60637 (office); 6918 South Dorchester Avenue, Chicago, IL 60637, USA (home). *Website:* theastergates.com; www.kavigupta.com/artist/theastergates; whitecube.com/artists/theaster_gates.

GATETE, Claver; Rwandan economist, diplomatist and central banker; *Minister of Finance and Economic Planning;* m. Jeanne Gatete; worked in Canada as an economist 1991–97, Agric. and Agri-food Canada (Statistics), Univ. of British Columbia and Algonquin Coll.; Nat. Economist, UNDP– Kigali-Rwanda 1997–2000; fmr Sr Adviser and Personal Rep. of Pres. Paul Kagame to NEPAD (New Partnership for Africa's Devt) Steering Cttee; Dir-Gen. for Social and Econ. Affairs and mem. Presidential Advisory Council, Office of the Pres. 2000–03; Sec.-Gen. Ministry of Finance and Econ. Planning and Sec. to the Treasury 2003–05; Amb. to UK (also accred to Ireland, Denmark, Norway and Sweden) 2005–09; mem. Bd of Dirs Nat. Bank of Rwanda 2003–05, Deputy Gov. 2009–11, Gov. 2011–13; Minister of Finance and Econ. Planning 2013–; Chair. Rwanda Revenue Authority 2001–03, School of Finance and Banking 2003–05, Nat. Privatization Tech. Cttee (Chair. 2003–05, Nat. Treasury Man. Cttee 2003–05; Vice-Chair. Community Devt Fund 2003–05; Co-Chair. Development Partners Coordination Group 2004–05. *Publications include:* Canadian Agri-food Medium Term Policy Baseline (with Merritt Cluff, Hsin Huang, Rebecca Ewing and Mitch Wensley 1997, Pacific Food Outlook (with Brad Gilmour and Lars Brink) 1997; several papers in professional journals. *Address:* Ministry of Finance and Economic Planning, blvd de la Révolution, opp. Kigali City Council, BP 158, Kigali, Rwanda (office). *Telephone:* 250576701 (office). *Fax:* 250577581 (office). *E-mail:* mfin@minecofin.gov.rw (office). *Website:* www.minecofin.gov.rw (office).

GATLAND, Warren David; New Zealand rugby union coach and fmr rugby union player; *Head Coach, Wales National Rugby Union Team;* b. 17 Sept. 1963, Hamilton; ed Hamilton Boys' High School, Waikato Univ.; hooker; played for Waikato 1986–94, record-holder for most games for Waikato near end of 1994 season, finished with 140 games in total and announced retirement before start of 1995 season; played 17 non-int. matches for NZ; Coach, Galwegians RFC 1989–94, Thames Valley 1994–96, Connacht Rugby 1996–98, Ireland 1998–2001, London Wasps 2002–05, Waikato 2005–07, Wales 2007– (won RBS Six Nations Grand Slam 2008, 2012), British and Irish Lions 2013 (won series against Australia 2–1); UK Coach of the Year, UK Coaching Awards 2013. *Address:* Welsh Rugby Union, Millennium Stadium, Westgate Street, Cardiff, CF10 1NS, Wales (office). *E-mail:* info@wru.co.uk (office). *Website:* www.wru.co.uk (office).

GATLIN, Justin; American sprinter; b. 10 Feb. 1982, Brooklyn, New York; ed Woodham High School, Fla, Univ. of Tennessee; first athlete since 1957 to win consecutive Nat. Collegiate Athletic Asscn (NCAA) titles in both 100m and 200m; five NCAA titles in total; US Jr Champion on three occasions; finished second in 60m (beating Maurice Greene) on professional debut at Verizon Millrose Games 2003; secured US $500,000 by winning Moscow Challenge 100m 2003; World Indoor Champion and US Champion 60m 2003; gold medal, 100m (in a personal-best time of 9.85 seconds), bronze medal 200m Olympic Games, Athens 2004; received four-year ban from athletics for positive doping test 2006; silver medal, 4×100m relay, bronze medal, 100m, Olympic Games, London 2012; USA Track and Field Jesse Owens Award 2004. *Website:* justingatlinusa.com.

GATSINZI, Gen. Marcel, BSc; Rwandan army officer and politician; b. 9 Jan. 1948, Kigali; s. of Phocas Mpagazehe and Anastasie Nyirabagahe; m. Irene Mukanaho; six c.; ed Ecole de Guerre, Brussels, Belgium, Inst. of World Politics, Washington, DC, USA; served in Rwandan Armed Forces, rank of Gen.; fmr Deputy Chief of Staff, then Chief of Staff, Nat. Gendarmerie; mem. Neutral Mil. Observer Group of fmr OAU (now the African Union) 1992–93; Sec.-Gen., Nat. Security Council 2002; Minister of Defence 2002–10, of Disaster Man. and Refugee Affairs 2010–13; rep. to numerous int. negotiations and meetings including African Union, Easbrig, Golden Spear, East African Community, UN Consultative Cttee on Security Matters in Cen. Africa.

GATT, Austin, LLD; Maltese politician and lawyer; b. 29 July 1953; m. Marisa Zammit Maempel; two s.; ed Lyceum and Univ. of Malta; practised law 1975–82; Nationalist Party org. 1980; Chair. Man. Bd Independence Print Co. Ltd 1982–87; Head, Legal Office of Nationalist Party 1982–87, Sec. Gen. 1988–98; Chair. Euro Tours Co. Ltd; MP 1996–, Opposition Spokesman for Justice, Local Councils and Housing 1996–98; Parl. Sec. Office of Prime Minister 1998–99; Minister for Justice and Local Govt 1999–2003, for Information Technology and Investment 2004–08, for Infrastructure, Transport and Communications 2008–13. *Address:* Nationalist Party, Herbert Ganado Street, Pietà PTA 1541, Malta (office). *Telephone:* 21243641 (office). *Fax:* 21243640 (office). *E-mail:* admin@pn.org.mt (office). *Website:* www.pn.org.mt (office).

GATTI, Daniele; Italian conductor; *Music Director, Orchestre Nationale de France;* b. 6 Nov. 1961, Milan; ed Giuseppe Verdi Conservatory, Milan; debut at La Scala, Milan with Rossini's L'occasione fa il Ladro 1987–88 season; US debut with American Symphony Orchestra, Carnegie Hall, New York 1990; Covent Garden debut with I Puritani 1992; Music Dir Accad. di Santa Cecilia, Rome 1992–97; Prin. Guest Conductor, Royal Opera House, Covent Garden 1994–97; debut at Metropolitan Opera, New York with Madama Butterfly 1994–95 season; debut with Royal Philharmonic Orchestra 1994, Music Dir 1995–2009; debut with New York Philharmonic 1995; Music Dir Teatro Communale, Bologna 1997–2007; Music Dir, Orchestre Nat. de France 2008–; Music Dir, Opernhaus Zürich 2009–; has led many orchestras in Europe and USA, including Vienna Philharmonic, Concertgebouw Amsterdam, Staatskapelle Dresden, Bavarian Radio Symphony, Munich Philharmonic, London Philharmonic, New York Philharmonic, Boston and Chicago Symphonies, Filarmonica della Scala, Milan and Accademia Santa Cecilia, Rome; has conducted at many leading opera houses; conducting new production of Parsifal, Bayreuth 2008–10. *Recordings:* Tschaikovsky's Fourth and Fifth Symphonies, Pathétique Symphony No. 6 2005. *Address:* Orchestre Nationale de France, c/o Radio France, 116 Président Kennedy, 75786 Paris, France (office). *Telephone:* 1-56-40-29-07 (office). *Fax:* 1-56-40-43-33 (office). *E-mail:* elisa.patria@radiofrance.com (office). *Website:* radiofrance.fr/chaines/orchestres/national (office).

GATTI, Gabriele, MA; San Marino politician; b. 1943, Domagnano; m. Gina Fiorini; two d.; mem. Parl. 1978–; Deputy Sec. Christian Democratic Party 1979–85, Sec.-Gen. 1985–87; apptd Sec. of State for Foreign Relations and Political Affairs 1986; Pres. Ministerial Chief, Council of Europe; mem. Gen. Comm. of the Inst. for Social Security, Urban Comm.; Sec. of State for Finance, the Budget, Post and Relations with the Azienda Autonoma di Stato Filatelica e Numismatica 2008–11; Captain Regent (Jt head of state) 2011–12. *Address:* c/o Office of the Captains Regenti, 47890 San Marino (office).

GATTING, Michael (Mike) William, OBE; British professional cricket coach and fmr professional cricketer; b. 6 June 1957, Kingsbury, Middx; m. Elaine Mabbott 1980; two s.; ed John Kelly High School; right-hand batsman and right-arm medium bowler; played for Middx 1975–99 (Capt. 1983–97), MCC 1978–87; 79 Tests for England 1977–95 (23 as Capt. 1986–88), scoring 4,409 runs (average 35.55, highest score 207) including 10 hundreds, took four wickets; 92 One-Day Ints (37 as Capt.), scoring 2,095 runs (average 29.50, highest score 115 not out) including one hundred; scored 36,549 first-class runs (94 hundreds), average 49.52, highest score 258; toured Australia 1986–87 (Capt.), 1987–95; Capt. rebel cricket tour to SA 1989–90; mem. England Selection Cttee 1997–99; Dir of Coaching, Middx Cricket Club 1999–2000; Dir Ashwell Leisure 2001–; Pres. Lord's Taverners 2005–06; mem. MCC Cttee; Grand Cru Travel Consultant; Wisden Cricketer of The Year 1984. *Radio:* analyst on Test Match Special. *Publications:* Limited Overs 1986, Triumph in Australia 1987, Leading from the Front (autobiog.) 1988. *Leisure interests:* golf, soccer and sport in general. *Address:* c/o Middlesex County Cricket Club, Lord's Cricket Ground, St John's Wood Road, London, NW8 8QN; 8A Villlage Road, Enfield, Middlesex, EN1 2DH, England (home). *Telephone:* (20) 7289-1300; 7768-541693 (mobile) (home). *Website:* www .middlesexccc.com.

GATTUNG, Theresa, BA, LLB; New Zealand business executive; b. 11 April 1962; ed Univ. of Waikato, Victoria Univ. of Wellington; fmr Chief Man. of Marketing, Nat. Mutual; Chief Man. of Marketing, Bank of New Zealand –1994; Gen. Man. Marketing, Telecom Corpn Ltd (largest co. in New Zealand) 1994–96, Group Gen. Man. Services 1996–99, Chief Exec. and Man. Dir Telecom Corpn of New Zealand Ltd 1999–2007; mem. Bd of Dirs AIA Australia (insurance co.) 2009–, Chair. 2010–; Chair. Wool Partners Int. 2008–11, Co-founder My Food Bag Ltd; ranked by Fortune magazine amongst 50 Most Powerful Women in Business outside the US (37th) 2003, (32nd) 2004, (29th) 2005, (23rd) 2006, ranked by Forbes magazine amongst 100 Most Powerful Women (49th) 2006. *Publication:* Bird On a Wire 2010. *Address:* Office of the Chairman, AIA Australia Ltd, 553 St Kilda Road, Melbourne, VIC 3000, Australia (office). *Telephone:* (3) 9009-4000 (office). *E-mail:* chris@theresagattung.com. *Website:* www.aia.com.au (office). www.theresagattung.com.

GATZOULIS, Michael Athanasios, MD, PhD, FESC, FACC; Greek cardiologist; *Academic Head, Adult Congenital Heart Centre and Centre for Pulmonary Hypertension, Royal Brompton Hospital; Professor of Cardiology and Congenital Heart Disease, National Heart and Lung Institute;* b. Drama; s. of Dr Athanasios K. Gatzoulis; m. Julie Kohls-Gatzoulis; two s.; ed Aristotelian Univ., Thessaloniki, Greece, MRCPCH, London, Univ. of London, UK; fmr Staff Cardiologist and Asst Prof., Univ. of Toronto Congenital Cardiac Centre for Adults; currently Prof. of Cardiology, Congenital Heart Disease and Consultant Cardiologist and Academic Head, Adult Congenital Heart Centre and Centre for Pulmonary Hypertension, Royal Brompton Hosp.; Prin. Investigator, Adult Congenital Heart Programme, Nat. Heart and Lung Inst., Imperial Coll. School of Medicine, also Prof. of Cardiology and Congenital Heart Disease 2005–; Visiting Prof., Vanderbilt Univ. 2006, Stanford Univ. 2006, Harvard Univ. 2007, Erasmus Univ. and Thorax Centre, Rotterdam, Netherlands, Japan Heart Inst. and Univ. of Tokyo, King Faisal Specialist Hosp. and Research Center, Jeddah, Leiden Univ., Netherlands, Idriss Distinguished Prof., Northwestern Univ., Chicago, USA; Assoc. Ed., Int. Journal of Cardiology 2003–; mem. Int. Editorial Bd and Guest Ed., European Heart Journal; Section Ed., Congenital Heart Disease, Hellenic Journal of Cardiology 2002–; Journal Reviewer, Heart 1994–, Circulation 1997–, Clinical Science 1998–, European Heart Journal 1999–, Arch Dis Child 2001–, Europace

2002–, Lancet, 2003–, American Heart Journal 2003–, Journal of the American College of Cardiology 1997–, Int. Journal of Cardiology 1999–, Drugs 2000–; Sec. Gen. Int. Soc. of Adult Congenital Cardiac Disease 2000–01, Pres. 2004–05; ESC Nucleus and UK Rep. EuroHeart Survey for Adult Congenital Heart Disease 2001–03. *Publications include:* The Adult with Tetralogy of Fallot 2001, Diagnosis and Management of Adult Congenital Heart Disease 2003, Adult Congenital Heart Disease: A Practical Guide 2004, Heart Disease and Pregnancy 2006; co-ed. 40th Edn of Gray's Anatomy; author of more than 150 peer-reviewed scientific papers, including articles in Nature, New England Journal of Medicine, The Lancet, and Circulation. *Leisure interests:* tennis, skiing, model rail (Marklin). *Address:* Royal Brompton Hospital, Sydney Street, London, SW3 6NP, England (office). *Telephone:* (20) 7352-8602 (PA Mrs Rachel Collumbell) (office); (20) 7351-8227 (direct line) (office). *Fax:* (20) 7351-8629 (office). *E-mail:* m.gatzoulis@imperial.ac.uk (office); m.gatzoulis@rbh.nthames .nhs.uk (office). *Website:* www.rbh.nthames.nhs.uk (office).

GAUCK, Joachim; German politician, Lutheran pastor and head of state; *President;* b. 24 Jan. 1940, Rostock; family suffered discrimination under communist regime of East Germany; became Lutheran pastor and anti-communist human rights activist under the communist state; Co-founder New Forum opposition movement in East Germany 1989, contributed to the downfall of the Soviet-backed dictatorship of the Socialist Unity Party of Germany (SED); mem. only freely elected People's Chamber (Volkskammer) for the Alliance 90 March–Oct. 1990; mem. Bundestag following reunification 3–4 Oct. 1990 (stepped down following appointment as Special Rep. of Fed. Govt); first Fed. Commr for Stasi Archives 1990–2000, earned recognition for exposing crimes of the fmr communist political police; founding signatory of Prague Declaration on European Conscience and Communism, together with Václav Havel and other statesmen, and Declaration on Crimes of Communism; unsuccessful cand. of SPD and the Greens for Pres. of Germany in 2010 election; selected as nonpartisan consensus cand. for Pres. of Germany in 2012 election by the Govt parties CDU, Christian Social Union in Bavaria (CSU) and Free Democratic Party, and opposition SPD and the Alliance '90/The Greens Feb.–March 2012, Pres. of Germany March 2012–; Chair. Gegen Vergessen – Für Demokratie 2003–; mem. Man. Bd, European Monitoring Centre on Racism and Xenophobia 2001–04; Fed. Cross of Merit 1995; Dr hc (Rostock) 1999, (Augsburg) 2005; Theodor Heuss Medal 1991, Hermann Ehlers Prize 1996, Hannah Arendt Prize 1997, Imre Nagy Prize (Hungary) 1999, Dolf Sternberger Prize 2000, Erich Kästner Prize 2001, 'Goldenes Lot' des Verbandes Deutscher Vermessungsingenieure 2002, Courage Prize 2003, Thomas Dehler Prize 2008, Das Glas der Vernunft 2009, Geschwister-Scholl Prize 2010. *Publications include:* Die Stasi-Akten. Das unheimliche Erbe der DDR 1991, Von der Würde der Unterdrückten (contrib.) 1992, Verlust und Übermut. Ein Kapitel über den Untertan als Bewohner der Moderne (contrib.) 1993, Das Schwarzbuch des Kommunismus – Unterdrückung, Verbrechen und Terror (contrib. of the chapter 'Vom schwierigen Umgang mit der Wahrnehmung', on political oppression in East Germany) 1998, Reite Schritt, Schnitter Tod! Leben und Sterben im Speziallager Nr. 1 des NKWD Mühlberg/Elbe (contrib.) 2007, Winter im Sommer – Frühling im Herbst: Erinnerungen 2009, Freiheit: Ein Plädoyer 2012. *Address:* Office of the Federal President, 11010 Berlin, Bundespräsidialamt, Spreeweg 1, 10557 Berlin, Germany (office). *Telephone:* (30) 20000 (office). *Fax:* (30) 20001999 (office). *E-mail:* poststelle@bpra.bund.de (office). *Website:* www.bundespraesident .de (office).

GAUDÉ, Laurent; French novelist and playwright; b. 6 July 1972, Paris. *Plays include:* Combats de possédés 1999, Onysos le furieux 2000, Cendres sur les mains 2001, Pluie de cendres 2001, Le Tigre bleu de l'Euphrate 2002, Médée Kali 2003, Salina 2003, Les Sacrifiées 2004, Sofia Douleur 2008, Sodome, ma douce 2009. *Publications include:* novels: Cris 2001, La Mort du roi Tsongor (Prix Goncourt, Prix des Libraires 2003) 2002, Le Soleil des Scorta (Prix Goncourt) 2004, Eldorado 2006, Dans la nuit Mozambique 2007, La Porte des Enfers 2008, Ouragan 2010, Les oliviers du Négus 2011, Pour seul cortège 2012. *Address:* c/o Actes Sud, BP 38, 13633 Arles Cédex, France (office). *E-mail:* n.giquel@actes-sud.fr. *Website:* www .actes-sud.fr (office); www.laurent-gaude.com.

GAUDET, Tracy W., BA, MD; American obstetrician, gynaecologist, academic and author; *Director of Office of Patient Centered Care and Cultural Transformation, Department of Veterans Affairs;* one s.; ed Univ. of Texas Medical School, San Antonio; practised and taught at Univ. of Texas, San Antonio –1996; Founding Exec. Dir Univ. of Arizona Program in Integrative Medicine 1996–2000; joined faculty of Duke Univ. 2000, Exec. Dir Duke Integrative Medicine, Duke Univ. Medical Center 2001–11, Asst Prof. of Obstetrics and Gynaecology, Duke Univ. Medical Center; Dir Office of Patient Centered Care and Cultural Transformation, US Dept of Veterans Affairs, Washington, DC 2011–; Co-founder Consortium of Academic Health Centers for Integrative Medicine, Chair. Membership Cttee 2002–04, mem. Steering, Exec., Educ. and Policy Cttees; mem. of Editorial Bds, Clinical Acupuncture and Oriental Medicine, Integrative Medicine Journal, Seminars in Integrative Medicine; columnist, Body + Soul magazine. *Publications include:* Consciously Female 2004, Body, Soul and Baby 2007. *Address:* US Department of Veterans Affairs, 810 Vermont Avenue, NW, Washington, DC 20420 (office); Duke Integrative Medicine, Duke Center for Living Campus, 3475 Erwin Road, Durham, NC 27705, USA (office). *Telephone:* (866) 313-0959 (Durham) (office); (919) 660-6826 (Durham) (office). *Website:* www.va.gov (office); www.dukeintegrativemedicine.org (office).

GAUDIN, Christian; French government official; b. 13 Jan. 1959; fmr teacher; fmr Mayor of Le Fuilet; fmr Councillor Gen., Montrevault canton, Maine-et-Loire; mem. Senate for Maine-et-Loire département 2001–10; Admin.-Superior, French S and Antarctic Territories 2010–12; mem. Groupe Union centriste. *Address:* c/o Office of the Administrator-Superior, rue Gabriel Dejean, 97410 Saint Pierre, Réunion (office).

GAULTIER, Jean-Paul; French fashion designer; b. 24 April 1952, Arcueil, Paris; s. of Paul Gaultier; first show in 1976; launched first commercial collection with his Japanese pnr 1978; since then known on int. scale for his women's and men's collections as well as haute couture from 1997; first jr collection 1988; costume designs for film The Cook, The Thief, His Wife and Her Lover 1989, for ballet Le Défilé de Régine Chopinot 1985, Madonna's World Tour 1990; released record How to Do That (in collaboration with Tony Mansfield) 1989; designed

costumes for Victoria Abril (q.v.) in Pedro Almodóvar (q.v.) 's film Kika 1994, film La Cité des Enfants Perdus 1995, The Fifth Element 1996; two more collaborations with Almodóvar with Bad Education 2005 and The Skin I Live In 2011; launched perfume brands Jean-Paul Gaultier 1993, Le Mâle 1995, Fragile 1999, Madame 2008, Kokorico 2011; women's wear Design Dir, Hermès 2004–11; exhbn spanning 35 years of his career opened in Montreal 2011, Dallas and San Francisco 2012; Chevalier, Légion d'honneur; Fashion Oscar 1987, Progetto Leonardo Award for How to Do That 1989. *Leisure interests:* film, theatre, ballet. *Address:* 325 rue Saint-Martin, 75003 Paris, France. *Telephone:* 1-72-75-83-00 (office). *Website:* www.jeanpaulgaultier.com.

GAUR, Varsh Shri Babulal, BA, LLB; Indian politician; b. 2 June 1930, UP; s. of the late Shri Ramprasad; fmr trade union activist; elected mem. MP Legis. Ass. 1974–, Leader of Opposition 2002–03; fmr MP State Minister of Local Admin, Legal Affairs, Legis. Affairs, Bhopal Gas Tragedy Relief, Public Relations, Urban Admin and Devt 2003; Chief Minister MP 2004–05; currently MP Minister of Urban Admin and Devt; Founder mem. Bhartiya Majdoor Sangh; Sec. Bhartiya Jansangh; mem. Bharatiya Janata Party; Swatantrata Sangram Senani Samman 1974. *Address:* Urban Administration and Development Department, Palika Bhawan, Shivaji Nagar, Bhopal, Madhya Pradesh, India (office). *Telephone:* (755) 2552396 (office). *Website:* www.mpurban.gov.in (office).

GAUTAM, Bamdev; Nepalese politician; *Deputy Prime Minister and Minister of Home Affairs;* b. 14 June 1948, Puthan; m.; joined Communist Party of Nepal (CPN) 1964, Dist Sec. Rupandehi CPN 1972–79, became W Cttee Sec. 1979–80, mem. CPN Cen. Cttee 1980–97, fmr Deputy Sec.-Gen. CPN, Gen. Sec. Communist Party of Nepal–Unified Marxist Leninist (CPN- UML) 1991–; mem. Parl. for Bardiya Constituency 1991–; Deputy Prime Minister and Minister of Home Affairs 1997–99, 2008–11, 2014–. *Address:* Ministry of Home Affairs, Singha Durbar, Kathmandu, Nepal (office). *E-mail:* info@moha.gov.np (office). *Website:* www.moha .gov.np (office).

GAUTRAND, Manuelle; French architect; *Partner and Principal Architect, Manuelle Gautrand Architecture;* b. 14 July 1961, Marseille; d. of the late Alain Gautrand and Janine Gautrand; m. Marc Blaising; two s.; ed Ecole Nationale Supérieure d'Architecture, Montpellier; qualified as architect 1985; set up practice in Paris 1991; numerous projects, ranging from housing and offices to cultural bldgs, business premises and leisure facilities; clients include public contracting authorities as well as private firms, in France and abroad; earned int. recognition for C42 Citroën Flagship Showroom bldg, Champs-Elysée, Paris; Chevalier des Arts et des Lettres 2007, de la Légion d'honneur 2010; Albums de la Jeune Architecture Award, Ministry of Culture 1992, Silver Medal, Acad. d'Architecture 2002, Trophée de la Construction, Asscn des Journalistes de la Construction 2003. *Major works include:* footbridge, Lyon 1993, Le Fellini four-screen cinema, Villefontaine 1994, Univ. Inst. of Professional Educ., Annecy-le-Vieux 1996, restructuring of admin. unit of Georges Pompidou Centre, Paris 1996, restructuring of two-screen cinema, Saint-Priest 1996, Laurent-Mourguet School, Ecully 1997, toll plazas on A16 motorway 1998, airport catering bldg, Nantes (Architecture and Work Places, Architecture et Maîtrise d'Ouvrage Asscn and Ministry of Culture 2000) 1998, Nat. Drama Theatre, Béthune 1998, Univ. Inst. of Professional Educ., Lieusaint 1999, La Coupole cultural centre, Saint-Louis 2000, two metro stations for the Val line, Rennes 2002, complex of 104 ecological apartments, Rennes 2006, Citroën showroom, Champs-Elysées, Paris (MIPIM Architectural Review Future Project Award 2005, Third Prize for int. Interior Design Competition, Int. Interior Design Asscn (USA) 2008, Int. Interior Design Asscn Interior Design Award 2008, AIT Magazine (Germany) Int. Contract World Award 2009, World Architecture News Architecture Award (commercial category) 2009, European Contractworld Award, AIT Magazine 2009) 2007, block of 35 apartments, Boulogne-Billancourt 2007, began studies for the AVA Tower in La Défense, shopping mall, Bangkok (first building abroad) 2009, Lille Museum of Modern, Contemporary and Outsider Art 2010, Origami office bldg, Paris 2010, Business Centre in Saint-Etienne (The Chicago Athenaem Award 2011, "des plus beaux ouvrages de construction métallique" Award 2011) 2010, Le Monolith office bldg in Lyon 2010, housing block in Aciqné, estructuring and reconversion of the old theatre Gaîté Lyrique into an interactive platform for 21st century music and arts 2011. *Exhibitions include:* perm. exhbn, Cité de l'Architecture et du Patrimoine, Paris 2007, Nouvelle Vague, Galerie Taisei, Tokyo 1998, Rushes, Institut Français, Madrid 1999, Les maisons du bonheur, Institut Français de l'Architecture 2001, Hybrid Landscapes, Rotterdam 2001, Extension M.A.M. Lille, Lille Museum of Modern Art 2002, Hybrid Landscapes, Spain 2002, collective exhbn featuring Cultural Platform in Paris, De Singel Int. Arts Centre, Antwerp 2002, Hybrid Landscapes, Berlin 2002, Inaccoutumance solo exhbn, Galerie de l'Architecture, Paris 2003, Mini-Maousse IFA exhbn, Jardin du Luxembourg 2003, Post-Modernism Revisited, Deutsches Architektur Museum, Frankfurt 2004, Gaite-Lyrique competition and perm. exhbn, Pavillon de l'Arsenal, Paris 2004, London Architecture Biennale 2006, Exo-Architectural, Pavillon de l'Arsenal, Paris 2007, Generocité, Cité de l'Architecture et du Patrimoine, Paris 2008, Venice Architecture Biennale 2008, Re-sampling Ornament, Swiss Architecture Museum, Basel 2008, Rives créatives, Cité de l'Architecture et du Patrimoine, Paris 2008, Projets construits, Pavillon de l'Arsenal, Paris 2009, São Paulo Architecture Biennale 2009, Dentelles d'architecture, Maison de l'Architecture, Lille 2009, Tour Europenne scenography exhbn, Pavillon de l'Arsenal, Paris 2009, Re-sampling Ornament, Arkitectur Museet, Stockholm 2009, Elles@Centrepompidou, Centre Georges Pompidou, Paris 2009, Cut_Out solo exhbn, ZeZeZe Architecture Gallery, Tel-Aviv 2009, Munch Museum Competition, Nat. Art Museum, Oslo 2009, Habiter, Pavillon de l'Arsenal, Paris 2010, Chef d'œuvres?, Centre Pompidou, Metz 2010, Nouvelles acquisitions: le LaM, Cité de l'Architecture et du Patrimoine, Paris 2011, Permis de construire, Galerie Marquart, Paris 2011, Architectures et espace public, Maison de l'Architecture, Paris 2011. *Films:* L'Art et la Manière 2008, Chic 2008. *Publications:* La coupole a Saint-Louis 2003, Unaccustomed – Manuelle Gautrand 2004, Manuelle Gautrand Architectures 2005, Manuelle Gautrand Architect 2006, Manuelle Gautrand 2007, Monograph Manuelle Gautrand Architect 2008, Ré-enchanter la Ville 2008, LaM, le Musée d'Art Moderne de Lille Métropole 2010, Ceux que j'ai (déjà) construits – Those I Have (Already) Built 2011, La Gaîté du Lyrique au Numérique 2011. *Address:* Manuelle Gautrand Architecture, 36 boulevard de la Bastille, 75012 Paris, France (office).

Telephone: 1-56-95-06-46 (office). *Fax:* 1-56-95-06-47 (office). *E-mail:* contact-com@manuelle-gautrand.com (office). *Website:* www.manuelle-gautrand.com (office).

GAVAI, Ramkrishnan Suryabhan, BA; Indian agriculturist, social activist and government official; b. 30 Oct. 1929, Darapur village, Amravati Dist, Maharashtra; s. of Suryabhanji Gavai; m. Kamaltai Gavai 1959; two s. one d.; ed Nagpur Univ., Amravati; mem. Maharashtra Legis. Council 1964–94, Deputy Chair. 1968–78, Chair. 1978–84, Leader of Opposition 1986–88; mem. Lok Sabha 1998–, mem. Cttee on Urban and Rural Devt, Consultative Cttee (Ministry of Agric.) 1998–99; elected to Rajya Sabha (Parl.) 2002; Gov. of Bihar 2006–08, of Kerala 2008–11; mem. 15th and 20th Commonwealth Parl. Conf., Trinidad and Tobago 1969, Colombo 1974, Lusaka 1978, Asian Conf. on Family Planning and Women, Child Welfare, Beijing 1980, 13th to 19th Gen. Confs of World Fellowship of Buddhists, Thailand, Sri Lanka, Nepal, USA, S Korea, Taiwan, Thailand, 20th Conf. of World Fellowship of Buddhists, Sydney 1998; Pres. Dr Babasaheb Ambedkar Smarak Samiti, Deeksha Bhoomi, Nagpur, Dr Babasaheb Ambedkar Shiksha Prasarak Mandal, Amravati; Pres. Parl. Forum for Scheduled Castes and Scheduled Tribes; Vice-Pres. and mem. Exec. Cttee World Fellowship of Buddhists, Maharashtra Br. of Commonwealth Parl. Asscn; mem. Western India Football Asscn, Mumbai; Nat. Integration Award, Kusta Mitra Award. *Publications include:* 5-Year Plan in Relation to the Scheduled Castes and Schedule Tribes, Scheduled Castes and Scheduled Tribes – Their Service Privileges, The Caste War Over Reservation – A Case Before the People's Bar, Facilities to Buddhists Converted from Scheduled Castes, Dr. Babasaheb Ambedkar – Deserved the Thanks of the Country, Dr Babasaheb Ambedkar Marathwada Vidyapeeth – Petition Before the People of Marathwada, Report for Eradication of Leprosy, Reports on Employment Guarantee Scheme. *Leisure interests:* wrestling, swimming, running, reading. *Address:* 44, Kamalpushpa, Congress Nagar, Amravati 444 601 (home); 151 MP Flats, North Avenue, New Delhi 110 001, India (home). *Telephone:* (11) 23094315 (home); (11) 23094409 (home).

GAVASKAR, Sunil ('Sunny') Manohar, BA; Indian business executive, sports administrator and fmr professional cricketer; b. 10 July 1949, Bombay (now Mumbai), Maharashtra; s. of Manohar Keshav Gavaskar and Meenal Manohar Gavaskar; m. Marshniel Mehrotra 1974; one s.; ed St Xavier's High School, Bombay, St Xavier's Coll., Bombay Univ.; right-hand opening batsman; played for Mumbai 1967–87, Somerset 1980; 125 Tests for India 1970–97 (47 as Capt.), scoring 10,122 runs (average 51.12, highest score 236 not out) with 34 hundreds and holding 108 catches; toured England 1971, 1974, 1975 (World Cup) 1979, 1982, 1983 (World Cup); One-Day Ints: 108 matches, scored 3,092 runs, average 35.13, highest score 103 not out; scored 25,834 First-class runs with 81 hundreds, average 51.46, highest score 340; first player to score more than 10,000 Test runs 1987; first player to score over 2,000 runs against three countries 1987; only man to play in a hundred successive Tests; nominated to Rajya Sabha 1992; Match Referee Int. Cricket Council (ICC) 1993–94; f. Sunil Gavaskar Foundation for Cricket in Bengal 1996; Chair. ICC Cricket Cttee –2008, Indian Nat. Cricket Acad. 2001–05; Sheriff of Mumbai 1994; Dr hc (D.Y. Patil Univ.) 2009; India's Best Schoolboy Cricketer of the Year 1966, Arjuna Award 1975, Padma Bhushan 1980, Wisden Cricketer of The Year 1980. *Films include:* Premachi Saavli, Maalamal. *Publications include:* Sunny Days – An Autobiography 1976, Idols (autobiog.) 1982, Runs 'n' Ruins 1984, One-day Wonders. *Address:* Nirlon Synthetic Fibres and Chemicals Ltd, Nirlon House, 254-B, Dr Annie Besant Road, Worli, Mumbai 18, India (office).

GAVIDIA, Yolanda Mayora de; Salvadorean economist, civil servant and international organization official; m.; ed Cen. American Inst. of Business Admin, INCAE; worked with various nat. devt orgs; mem. Panel of Econ. Advisers, Ministry of Social Planning 1990–92; Tech. Sec.-Gen. for Econ. and Social Policy, Ministry of Planning 1993–95; Program Coordinator for Improvement of Competitiveness, Presidential Comm. for Modernization of the Public Sector 1995–97; joined Ministry of the Economy 1996, Minister of the Economy 2004–08; Sec.-Gen. Secretaría de Integración Económica Centroamericana (SIECA), Guatemala City, Guatemala 2009–11 (resgnd). *Address:* c/o Secretaría de Integración Económica Centroamericana (SIECA), 4a Avda 10–25, Zona 14, Apdo 1237, 01901 Guatemala City, Guatemala.

GAVIN, John, BA; American actor and diplomatist; *Partner, Gavin, Dailey & Co.;* b. 8 April 1932, Los Angeles; s. of Herald Ray Gavin and Delia Diana Pablos; m. Constance Mary Towers; one s. three d.; ed Stanford Univ.; actor in feature films 1956–80; Special Adviser to Sec.-Gen. OAS 1961–74; Vice-Pres. Atlantic Richfield Co. (to head Fed. & Int. Relations Unit) 1986–87; Pres. Univisa Satellite Communications 1987–90; Pres. Gamma Services Corpn 1968–; spokesman Bank of America 1973–80; Amb. to Mexico 1981–86; Chair. the Century Council 1990–; Pnr, Gavin, Dailey & Co., LA 1990–; fmr consultant to Dept of State; mem. Screen Actors' Guild (Pres. 1971–73). *Films include:* A Time to Live, A Time to Die 1958, Imitation of Life 1959, Psycho 1960, Midnight Lace 1960, Spartacus 1960, A Breath of Scandal 1960, Backstreet 1961, Romanoff and Juliet 1961, Tammy Tell Me True 1961, Thoroughly Modern Millie 1967, Mad Woman of Chaillot 1969, Pussycat Pussycat I Love You 1970, Jennifer 1978, The P.A.C.K. (1997). *Television includes:* Destry (series) 1964, Convoy (series) 1965, Cutter's Trail 1970, The Lives of Jenny Dolan 1975, Doctors' Private Lives 1978, The New Adventures of Heidi 1978, Sophia Loren: Her Own Story 1980. *Address:* 2100 Century Park West, #10263, Los Angeles, CA 90067-6900, USA.

GAVIRIA DÍAZ, Carlos, PhD; Colombian lawyer, magistrate and politician; b. 8 May 1937, Sopetrán, Antioquia; ed Univ. of Antioquia, Medellín, Harvard Univ. Law School, USA; Dean Law Faculty, Univ. of Antioquia 1967–69, Dir Dept of Public Law 1974–80, Dir Inst. of Political Sciences 1988, Vice-Rector Univ. of Antioquia 1989–92; Magistrate, Constitutional Court, Bogotá 1993–2001, Pres. Constitutional Court 1996; elected Senator for Frente Social y Politico 2002–06; cand. for Polo Democratico Alternativo (Alternative Democratic Pole—PDA) in presidential election March 2006; Pres. PDA 2006–10. *Address:* Polo Democratico Alternativo, Carrera 17A 37-27, Bogotá, Colombia (office). *Telephone:* (1) 2886188 (office). *Website:* www.polodemocratico.net (office).

GAVIRIA TRUJILLO, César; Colombian economist, politician and fmr international organization official; *President, Partido Liberal Colombiano;* b. 31 March 1947, Pereira; m. Ana Milena Muñoz de Gaviria; ed Univ. of the Andes; mem. town council of Pereira, later Mayor; mem. Chamber of Deputies (Partido Liberal Colombiano) and Dir Comm. for Econ. Affairs 1974; Vice-Minister for Econ. Devt 1978; Speaker of Parl. 1983; journalist in early 1980s; Minister of Finance and Public Credit 1986–87, of the Interior 1987–89; Pres. of Colombia 1990–94; Sec.-Gen. OAS 1994–2004; Pres. Partido Liberal Colombiano 2005–; mem. Inter-American Dialogue, Club de Madrid, La Conférence de Montréal; est. Nueveochenta (art gallery), Bogotá; Hon. Prof., Universidad ICESI, Colombia, Univ. of Miami, USA, Universidad Libre Colombia 1990, Universidade Estácio de Sá, Rio de Janeiro 1991, Northeastern Univ., USA 2002; Hon. LLB (Univ. Libre de Colombia); Hon. DCL (Northeastern Univ.) 2002; W. Averell Harriman Democracy Award 2002, Nat. Democratic Inst. Democracy Award 2002, Washington Times Int. Courage in Leadership Award 2002. *Publications include:* La Deuda Latinoamericana 1982, Reflexiones para una nueva Constitución 1990, La Revolución Pacífica 1990, Las Bases de la Nueva Colombia: El Revolcón Institucional 1990–1994 1994, Reformas Económicas 1990–1994 1994, Plan de Desarrollo Económico y Social 1990–1994 1994, A New Vision of the OAS 1995, Toward the New Millennium: The Road Travelled 1994–1999 1999; book chapters and articles in journals. *Address:* Partido Liberal Colombiano, Avda Caracas, No 36-01, Bogotá, DC, Colombia (office). *Telephone:* (1) 593-4500 (office). *Fax:* (1) 288-1138 (office). *E-mail:* direcciondecomunicaciones@partidoliberal.org.co (office). *Website:* www.partidoliberal.org.co (office); www.nueveochenta.com (office).

GAVRIISKI, Svetoslav; Bulgarian government official and banker; *Chief Executive Director, Allianz Bank Bulgaria;* b. 18 Dec. 1948, Svishtov; ed Karl Marx Higher Inst. of Econs, Sofia; economist, Ministry of Finance 1972; Sr Expert, Nat. Balance Sheets Directorate, Ministry of the Economy and Planning 1988; Sr Expert in Int. Financial Relations, Ministry of Finance 1990, Head of Int. Finance Dept 1991–92; Deputy Minister of Finance 1992–97, Minister Feb.–May 1997; Gov. of Bulgaria to IMF 1992–96, 1997, to IBRD, EBRD and European Investment Bank 1997, to Black Sea Trade and Devt Bank 1998; Leader Group Negotiations on Bulgaria's External Debt 1991–94; mem. Man. Bd Bulbank 1991–97; Gov. Bulgarian Nat. Bank 1997–2003; currently Chief Exec. Dir Allianz Bank Bulgaria; Man. mem. Int. Bank for Econ. Co-operation, Moscow 1992, Int. Investment Bank, Moscow 1992; mem. Bd of Dirs Bank Consolidation Co. 2001–; mem. Supervisory Bd Municipal Bank 2005–; nominee for mayoral elections in Sofia 2005. *Address:* Allianz Bank Bulgaria, 1202 Sofia, 79, Maria Louisa Blvd, Bulgaria (office). *Telephone:* (2) 921-54-04 (office). *Fax:* (2) 981-93-07 (office). *E-mail:* admin@bank .allianz.bg (office). *Website:* bank.allianz.bg (office).

GAVRILOV, Andrei Vladimirovich; Russian pianist; b. 21 Sept. 1955, Moscow; ed Moscow Conservatory; performs regularly throughout Europe, America and Japan, including recitals at Salzburg, Roque d'Antheron, Schleswig-Holstein, Istanbul and Chichester Festivals; has performed in UK with Philharmonia, London Philharmonic, Royal Philharmonic, BBC Symphony and London Symphony Orchestras, in USA with Baltimore Symphony, Detroit Symphony, New York Philharmonic and Philadelphia Orchestras; recorded works with Sviatoslav Teofilovich Richter; lives in Switzerland; winner of the Tchaikovsky Competition in Moscow 1974; disc awards include French suites of J. S. Bach and Etudes of Chopin; several int. prizes. *Address:* c/o Konzertdirektion Schlote, Danreitergasse 4, 5020 Salzburg, Austria (office).

GAVRIN, Alexander Sergeyevich; Russian engineer and politician; b. 22 July 1953, Orlovo, Zaporozhye Region, Ukraine; ed Tumen Industrial Inst., Tumen State Inst. of Oil and Gas; army service 1972–74; controller, master Zaporozhye plant Radiopribor 1974–79; controlling master, Manuylsky Research Inst., Kiev 1979–80; engineer constructor, Kiev plant generator 1980–81; technician, Kiev production co. 1981–83; electrician, Povkhneft Kogalym, Tumen Region 1983–88; engineer and head of group, Kogalymneftegas Co., Tumen Region 1988–89; Chair. Trade Union LUKOil-Kogalymneftegas 1989–93; Head of Admin. Kogalym., Tumen Region 1993–96; Mayor of Kogalym 1996–2000; Minister of Energy of Russian Fed. 2000–01; currently Senator of the Russian Fed.; mem. Bd of Dirs Bankhaus Erbe; fmr Rep. of Tumen Region to Council of Fed., Russian Fed. Ass. *Address:* c/o Board of Directors, Bankhaus Erbe, 123056, Moscow, ul. Zoologicheskaya h. 26, p. 1, Russia.

GAY, Peter, PhD; American historian and academic; *Sterling Professor Emeritus of History, Yale University;* b. 20 June 1923, Berlin, Germany; s. of Morris Fröhlich and Helga Fröhlich; m. Ruth Slotkin 1959; three step-d.; ed Univ. of Denver and Columbia Univ.; left Germany 1939; Dept of Public Law and Govt, Columbia Univ. 1947–56, Dept of History 1956–69, Prof. of History 1962–69, William R. Shepherd Prof. 1967–69; Prof. of Comparative European Intellectual History, Yale Univ. 1969–, Durfee Prof. of History 1970–84, Sterling Prof. of History 1984–93, Sterling Prof. Emer. 1993–; Guggenheim Fellow 1967–68; Overseas Fellow, Churchill Coll., Cambridge, UK 1970–71; Visiting Fellow, Inst. for Advanced Study, Berlin 1984; Dir Center for Scholars and Writers, New York Public Library 1997–; mem. American Historical Asscn, French Historical Soc.; Hon. DHumLitt (Denver) 1970, (Maryland) 1979, (Hebrew Univ. Coll., Cincinnati) 1983, (Clark Univ., Worcester) 1985; Nat. Book Award 1967, Melcher Book Award 1967, Gold Medal for Historical Science, Amsterdam 1990, Geschwister Scholl Prize 1999. *Publications include:* The Dilemma of Democratic Socialism: Eduard Bernstein's Challenge to Marx 1951, Voltaire's Politics: The Poet as Realist 1959, Philosophical Dictionary 1962, The Party of Humanity: Essays in the French Enlightenment 1964, The Loss of Mastery: Puritan Historians in Colonial America 1966, The Enlightenment: An Interpretation, Vols I, II 1966, 1969, Weimar Culture: The Outsider as Insider 1969, The Bridge of Criticism: Dialogues on the Enlightenment 1970, Modern Europe (with R. K. Webb) 1973, The Question of Jean-Jacques Rousseau 1974, Style in History 1974, Art and Act: On Causes in History – Manet, Gropius, Mondrian 1976, Freud, Jews and Other Germans: Masters and Victims in Modernist Culture 1978, The Bourgeois Experience: Victoria to Freud, Vols I, II, III 1984, 1986, 1993, Freud for Historians 1985, Freud: A Life for Our Time 1988, A Freud Reader 1989, Reading Freud: Explorations and Entertainments 1990, The Cultivation of Hatred 1993, The Naked Heart 1995, Pleasure Wars 1998, My German Question: Growing Up in Nazi Berlin 1998, Mozart 1999, Schnitzler's Century 2001, Savage Reprisals 2002, Modernism 2007; also trans and anthologies. *Leisure interests:* reading, listening to music. *Address:* Department of History, Yale University, 320 York Street, PO Box 208324, New Haven, CT 06520-8324, USA (office); 270 Riverside Drive, Apt 8CA, New York, NY 10025, USA (home). *Telephone:* (212) 930-9257 (office); (212) 865-3968 (home). *Fax:* (212) 930-0040 (office). *E-mail:* peter.gay@yale.edu; pgay@nypl.org (office); petergay@verizon.net (home).

GAYAN, Anil Kumarsingh, LLM; Mauritian lawyer and politician; *Leader, Front National Mauricien;* b. 22 Oct. 1948; m. Sooryakanti Nirsimloo; three c.; ed Royal Coll., Port Louis, London School of Econs, UK; called to the Bar, Inner Temple, London 1972; mem. Mauritius Bar and Seychelles Bar 1972–73, pvt. practice 1973–74, 1982, 1986–90, 1995–2000; Chair. Bar Council 1989–90; joined Chambers of Mauritius Attorney Gen. as Crown Counsel 1974, Sr Counsel 1995; Del. to UN Conf. on the Law of the Sea 1974–82; mem. Parl. 1982–86, Minister of External Affairs, Tourism and Emigration 1983–86, Foreign Affairs and Regional Co-operation 2000–03; Founder and Leader Front National Mauricien (FNM) party 2009–; Chair. Council of Univ. of Mauritius 1983; Consultant for Geneva-based Centre for Human Rights, consultancy work in Bhutan, Mongolia, Armenia and Togo 1991; Hon. Minister. *Address:* Front National Mauricien, Port Louis, Mauritius (office).

GAYDAMAK, Arcadi Alexandrovich; Russian/Israeli business executive; b. 1952, Moscow; moved from USSR to Israel aged 20, moved to France 1973, to Israel 2000; f. Gaydamak Translations, Paris; Owner, Moskovskie Novosti newspaper 2005–08, Beitar Jerusalem FC football team 2005–09, Tiv Taam supermarkets 2007–; Pres. Hapoel Jerusalem professional basketball team; organized and paid for emergency accommodation for civilians in northern Israel affected by conflict with Lebanon 2006; Founder and Leader Social Justice (Tzedek Hevrati—Za'am) political party 2007–; unsuccessful cand. for Mayor of Jerusalem 2008; Pres. Congress of Jewish Religious Communities and Orgs of Russia; warrant issued for his arrest by French authorities in connection with alleged arms dealing with Angola 2000, acquitted by Court of Appeal 2011; Hon. Pres. World Betar.

GAYE, Lt-Gen. Babacar; Senegalese army officer, diplomatist and UN official; *Secretary-General's Representative to Central African Republic, United Nations;* b. 31 Jan. 1951, Saint Louis; s. of Amadou Karim Gaye; m.; two c.; ed École Spéciale Militaire de Saint-Cyr, École Supérieure de Guerre, France; served with UN Emergency Force 1974–75, Commdr, Senegalese contingent, UN Interim Force in Lebanon 1979–80; several posts working for Govt of Senegal, including Dir of Information and Public Relations 1993–94, Dir of Documentation and External Security 1994–97, Commdr, Mil. Zone 6 1997–2000, Chief of Defence Staff 2000–03; Amb. to Germany 2004–05; Commdr UNO Mission in the Democratic Repub. of the Congo 2005–10, UN Mil. Adviser for Peacekeeping Operations 2010–13, UN Sec.-Gen.'s Rep. to Central African Repub. 2013–; attained rank of Lt 1979, Capt. 1981, Commdr 1984, Lt-Col 1988, Col 1991, Brig-Gen. 2000, Div.-Gen. 2002, currently Lt-Gen.; numerous awards including Grand officier, ordre nat. du Lion, Croix de la Valeur Militaire, Officier, Légion d'honneur, Officier, Ordre du Mérite (Gabon), several UN medals. *Address:* Bureau intégré des Nations Unies pour la Consolidation de la paix en République centrafricaine (BINUCA), Bangui, Central African Republic. *Telephone:* 75-49-53-83 (office). *E-mail:* ikavi@un.org (office). *Website:* binuca.unmissions.org (office).

GAYER, Yevdokiya Alexandrovna, CandHistSc; Russian/Nanai ethnographer and public servant; *Secretary-General, International League of Small Nations and Ethnic Groups;* b. 8 March 1934, Podali, Khabarovsk Territory; m. (deceased); two s.; ed in Vladivostok; researcher Inst. of History, Archaeology and Ethnography Far E br. of USSR Acad. of Sciences in Vladivostok 1969–89; USSR People's Deputy, mem. Soviet of Nationalities, mem. Comm. on Problems of Int. Relations and Nat. Policy 1989–92; adviser to Pres. 1992–; Deputy Chair. State Cttee on Social-Econ. Devt of the North 1993–; mem. Council of Fed. of Russia 1993–96; Deputy Chair. Comm. of the North and Indigenous Peoples 1996–2000; Sec.-Gen. Int. League of Small Nations and Ethnic Groups 1996–; Chief Adviser State Cttee on Problems of Devt of North Territories (later Cttee on Northern, Siberian and Far Eastern Affairs, Council of Fed.) 1997–98; Prof., Int. Acad. of Marketing and Man. (Mamarmen); mem. Presidium Russian Acad. of Natural Sciences, Acad. of Information Science, Acad. of Polar Medicine. *Address:* Rublyovskoye Sh. 3, korp. 2, Apt 388, 121609 Moscow, Russia. *Telephone:* (495) 413-76-95.

GAYLARD, Max; Australian UN official; *Deputy Special Coordinator for the Middle East Peace Process and UN Coordinator for Humanitarian and Development Activities in the Occupied Palestinian Territory, United Nations;* b. 1946, Nambour, Queensland; ed Univ. of Queensland, Australian Nat. Univ.; served with Australian mil. forces 1968–70; several postings with Australian Dept of Foreign Affairs and Commonwealth Secretariat before joining UN; worked as a sr UN humanitarian and coordination official in Somalia, Sudan and N Iraq, Dir UN Mine Action Service –2007, Deputy Special Coordinator for Middle East Peace Process and UN Coordinator for Humanitarian and Devt Activities in the Occupied Palestinian Territory 2008–. *Address:* Office of the Secretary-General, UN Headquarters, First Avenue at 46th Street, New York, NY 10017, USA (office). *Website:* www.un.org (office).

GAYLE, Christopher Henry (Chris); Jamaican professional cricketer; b. 21 Sept. 1979, Kingston; all-rounder; left-handed opening batsman; right-arm off-break bowler; plays for Jamaica (domestic) 1998–2008, 2010–, West Indies 1999– (Capt. 2007–08, 2009–10), Worcestershire 2005, Kolkata Knight Riders 2008–10, Western Warriors 2009–11, Royal Challengers Bangalore 2011–, Sydney Thunder 2011–, Barisal Burners 2012–, ICC (Int. Cricket Council) World XI, Stanford Superstars; First-class debut: 1998/99; Test debut: West Indies v Zimbabwe, Port of Spain 16–20 March 2000; One-Day Int. (ODI) debut: India v West Indies, Toronto 11 Sept. 1999; T20I debut: NZ v West Indies, Auckland 16 Feb. 2006; mem. of the victorious West Indies team that won ICC World Twenty20 Championship in Sri Lanka 2012; named Player of the Champions Trophy 2006. *Achievements include:* one of only five players in ODI to have three or more scores of 150; first batsman to score a century in a Twenty20 Int., scoring 117 against S Africa in first match of ICC World Twenty20, South Africa 2007; became first int. player to 'carry his bat' (not out) through entire innings in this format of the game in semi-final match against Sri Lanka in World Twenty20 Tournament 2009; made jt 12th highest Test score of 333 v Sri Lanka, Galle 16 Nov. 2010, one of only four players to have scored two triple centuries at Test level (including 317 against South Africa 2005); first ever batsman to hit a six off the opening ball of a Test match, against Bangladesh off-spinner Sohag Gazi in Dhaka 14 Nov. 2012; set a new record for the

fastest century in professional cricket by reaching 100 off 30 balls when his team the Royal Challengers Bangalore hit a T20 record 263 for 5 and beat Pune Warriors in the Indian Premier League 23 April 2013, went on to record the highest Twenty20 score of 175 not out (17 sixes and 13 fours off 66 balls). *Address:* c/o West Indies Cricket Board Inc., PO Box 616 W, St John's, Antigua. *Telephone:* 481-2450. *Fax:* 481-2498. *E-mail:* wicb@windiescricket.com. *Website:* www.windiescricket.com.

GAYMARD, Clara; French business executive and author; *President and CEO, General Electric France;* b. 27 Jan. 1960, Paris; d. of Jérôme Lejeune; m. Hervé Gaymard; nine c.; ed Institut d'Études Politiques, Ecole Nationale d'Admin, Paris; Admin. attaché, Office of Mayor of Paris 1982–84; served as auditor and counsellor, State Audit Office 1986–90; Commercial Counsel, Econ. and Commercial Section, embassy in Cairo 1991–93; Head of Europe Bureau 1993–95; Dir Office of Minister for Solidarity between Generations Colette Codaccioni 1995–96; Sub-Dir for Regional Action, PME 1996–99, Head of PME 1999–2003; Chair. Invest in France Agency 2003–06; Pres. and CEO General Electric (GE) France 2006–, Pres. Northwest Europe Region 2008–, Vice-Pres. GE International 2009–, Vice-Pres. in charge of Govt and Cities 2010–; lecturer in public law and general culture; Auditor of 53rd session of IHEDN; Founding mem. Fondation Jérôme Lejeune; ranked by Fortune magazine amongst the 50 Most Powerful Women in Business outside the US (47th) 2007, (36th) 2008, (34th) 2009–10, (30th) 2011, (33rd) 2012. *Publications:* (as Clara Lejeune): La vie est un bonheur, Jérôme Lejeune, mon père 1997, Histoires de femme autres simples bonheurs 1999, S'il suffisait d'aimer 2003. *Address:* General Electric France, 2 rue Pillet Will, 75009 France (office). *Telephone:* 1-43-12-16-16 (office); 1-43-12-78-27 (office). *Fax:* 1-43-12-78-40 (office); 1-47-65-76-90 (office). *E-mail:* alexandra.panseri@ge.com (office). *Website:* www.ge.com/fr (office).

GAYMARD, Hervé, LenD; French politician; *Chairman, Savoie General Council;* b. 31 May 1960, Bourg-Saint-Maurice (Savoie); m.; eight c.; ed Ecole Nationale d'Admin and Institut d'Etudes Politiques, Paris; worked at Budget Ministry 1986–90; Financial Attaché, Cairo Embassy 1990–92; Deputy for Savoie to Nat. Ass. 1993– (from UMP 2002–), mem. Finance Cttee, Vice-Chair. RPR Group; Minister of State for Finance May–Nov. 1995; Minister of State with responsibility for Health and Social Security 1995–97; Minister for Agric., Food, Fisheries and Rural Affairs 2002–04; Minister of the Economy, Finance and Industry 2004–05 (resgnd); Chair. Savoie Gen. Council 1999–2002, 2008–, Vice-Chair. 2002–08; mem. Cttee RPR 1995–98, Political Bureau 1995–2002 (then UMP 2002–05); regional counsellor Rhône Alpes 2004–07; Pres. Assemblée du Pays de Tarentaise Vanoise 2005–; mem. Bd Centre Georges Pompidou. *Publications:* Pour Malraux 1996, La route des Chapieux 2004, Un nouvel usage du monde – Mille et une nuits 2007, Nation et engagements 2010. *Address:* Secrétariat Parlementaire, BP 78 - 5, Place Ferdinand Million, 73203 Albertville Cedex (office); Assemblee Nationale, 126 rue de l'Université, 75355 Paris Cedex 07, France (office). *Telephone:* 4-79-32-03-68 (office); 1-40-63-60-00 (office). *Fax:* 4-79-37-82-74 (office); 1-45-55-75-23 (office). *E-mail:* infos@assemblee-nat.fr (office); hervegaymard.savoie@cg73.fr (office). *Website:* www.gaymard-rolland-savoie.com; www.assemblee-nationale.fr (office).

GAYOOM, Maumoon Abdul, MA; Maldivian politician, diplomatist and fmr head of state; *Founder and Chairman, Progressive Party of Maldives (PPM);* b. 29 Dec. 1937, Malé; m. Nasreena Ibrahim 1969; two s. two d.; ed Al-Azhar Univ., Cairo, Egypt; Research Asst in Islamic History, American Univ. of Cairo 1967–69; Lecturer in Islamic Studies and Philosophy, Abdullahi Bayero Coll., Ahmadu Bello Univ., Nigeria 1969–71; teacher, Aminiya School 1971–72; Man. Govt Shipping Dept 1972–73; writer and trans., Press Office 1972–73, 1974; Under-Sec. Telecommunications Dept 1974; Dir Telephone Dept 1974; Special Under-Sec. Office of the Prime Minister 1974–75; Deputy Amb. to Sri Lanka 1975–76; Under-Sec. Dept of External Affairs 1976; Perm. Rep. to UN 1976–77; Deputy Minister of Transport 1976, Minister 1977–78; Pres. of Repub. of Maldives and C-in-C of the Armed Forces and of the Police 1978–2008; Gov. Maldives Monetary Authority 1981–2004; Minister of Defence and Nat. Security 1982–2004, of Finance 1989–93, of Finance and Treasury 1993–2004; Hon. Leader, Dhivehi Rayyithunge Party (DRP—Maldivian People's Party); Founder and Interim Chair. Progressive Party of Maldives (PPM) 2011–13, Chair. 2013–; mem. Constituent Council of Rabitat Al-Alam Al-Islami; Grand Order of Mugunghawa 1984, Hon. GCMG 1997; Hon. DLitt (Aligarh Muslim Univ. of India) 1983, Hon. Dr.Lit (Jamia Millia Islamia Univ., India) 1990, Hon. DLit (Pondicherry Univ.) 1994; UNEP Global 500 Honour Roll 1988, Man of the Sea Award, Lega Navale Italiana 1991, WHO Health-for-All Gold Medal 1998, DRV Int. Environment Award 1998, Al-Azhar Univ. Shield 2002. *Publication:* The Maldives: A Nation in Peril. *Leisure interests:* astronomy, calligraphy, photography, badminton, cricket. *Address:* Progressive Party of Maldives (PPM), Office B, 8th Floor, Sakeenaa Manzil, Medhuziyaaraiyy Magu, Malé 20127, The Maldives (office). *Telephone:* 3303838 (office). *E-mail:* ppm.head.office@gmail.com (office). *Website:* www.ppm.mv (office).

GAYSSOT, Jean-Claude; French politician and trade union official; b. 6 Sept. 1944, Béziers (Hérault); m. Jacqueline Guiter 1963; three c.; ed Lycée Technique, Béziers; worked as technician, SNCF (French state railways); official in Rail-workers' Union, then in Conféd. générale du travail (CGT) 1976–79; mem. Parti Communiste Français 1963–, mem. Nat. Secr. 1985–, head dept for relations with other political parties and trade union and community movt 1994–; elected municipal councillor, Bobigny (Seine-Saint-Denis) 1977; Nat. Ass. Deputy for 5th Seine-Saint-Denis Constituency 1986–97; Minister for Public Works, Transport and Housing 1997–2002; Mayor of Drancy 1997–2002; Trombinoscope Prize for Minister of the Year 2000. *Publications:* Le Parti communiste français 1989, Sur ma route 2000. *Address:* Parti Communiste Français, 2 place du Colonel Fabien, 75940 Paris, France.

GAZALI, Lihadh al-, MB, ChB, DCH, MSc, MRCP, FRCP (I), FRCPCH; United Arab Emirates geneticist and academic; *Professor in Clinical Genetics and Paediatrics, UAE University;* ed Baghdad Medical Coll., Baghdad Univ., Iraq, Royal Coll. of Physicians and Univ. of Edinburgh, UK, Royal Coll. of Physicians, Ireland; Clinical Research Fellow in Clinical Genetics, Univ. of Leeds, UK 1986–90; Asst Prof. in Clinical Genetics, FMHS, UAE Univ. 1990–97, Assoc. Prof. in Clinical Genetics 1997–2003, Prof. in Clinical Genetics and Paediatrics 2003–; Fellow, Royal Coll. of Physicians (Ireland) 1993, Royal Coll. of Paediatrics and

Child Health (UK) 1997; Distinguished Performance Award in Research and Clinical Services, UAE Univ. 2003, Laureate for Africa and the Arab States, L'Oréal-UNESCO Awards for Women in Science 2008. *Publications:* more than 130 papers in professional journals. *Address:* College of Medicine and Health Sciences, UAE University, PO Box 17666, Al-Ain, United Arab Emirates (office). *Telephone:* (3) 7137415 (office). *Fax:* (3) 7672022 (office). *E-mail:* l.algazali@uaeu.ac.ae (office). *Website:* www.cmhs.uaeu.ac.ae/home.asp?l.algazali (office).

GAZIT, Maj.-Gen. (retd) Shlomo, MA; Israeli army officer (retd) and university administrator; *Chairman, Galili Centre for Defence-Hagana Studies;* b. 1926, Turkey; s. of Efrayim Gazit and Zippora Gazit; m. Avigayil-Gala Gazit; one s. two d.; ed Tel-Aviv Univ.; joined Palmach 1944, Co. Commdr Harel Brigade 1948; Dir Office of Chief of Staff 1953; Liaison Officer with French Army Del., Sinai Campaign 1956; Instructor, Israel Defence Forces (IDF) Staff and Command Coll. 1958–59; Gen. Staff 1960–61; Deputy Commdr Golani Brigade 1961–62; Instructor, Nat. Defence Coll. 1962–64; Head of IDF Intelligence assessment div. 1964–67; Co-ordinator of Govt Activities in Administered Territories, Ministry of Defence 1967–74; attained rank of Maj.-Gen. 1973; Head of Mil. Intelligence 1974–79; Fellow, Center for Int. Affairs, Harvard Univ. 1979–80; Pres. Ben Gurion Univ. of the Negev 1981–85; Dir-Gen. Jewish Agency, Jerusalem 1985–88; Sr Research Fellow, Jaffee Centre for Strategic Studies, Tel-Aviv Univ. 1988–94; Fellow, Woodrow Wilson Center, Washington, DC 1989–90; Distinguished Fellow, US Inst. of Peace, Washington, DC 1994–95; Adviser to Israeli Prime Minister on Palestinian Peace Process 1995–96; Chair. Galili Centre for Defence-Hagana Studies 1996–; Ben-Gurion Award 1972. *Publications:* Estimates and Fortune-Telling in Intelligence Work 1980, Early Attempts at Establishing West Bank Autonomy 1980, Insurgency, Terrorism and Intelligence 1980, On Hostages' Rescue Operations 1981, The Carrot and the Stick – Israel's Military Govt in Judea and Samaria 1985, The Third Way – The Way of No Solution 1987, Policies in the Administered Territories 1988, Intelligence Estimates and the Decision Maker 1988, (ed.) The Middle East Military Balance 1988–89, 1990–91, 1993–94, Trapped Fools: 30 Years of Israeli Policy in Judea, Samaria and Gaza Strip, 2003, The Arab-Israeli Wars: War and Peace in the Middle East 1948–2005 2005. *Address:* 58 Enzo Sireni Street, Kfar-Saba 44285 (home); 40 Levanon Street, Tel-Aviv, Israel (office). *Telephone:* (3) 6400400 (ext. 478) (office); (9) 7466554 (home). *Fax:* (3) 7447589 (office); (9) 7416815 (home). *E-mail:* shagaz@inss.org.il (office). *Website:* www.galili.org.il (office).

GAZIZULLIN, Farit Rafikovich, CPhilSc, DSc; Russian/Tatar engineer and politician; b. 20 Sept. 1946, Zelenodolsk, Tatar ASSR; m.; one s.; ed Gorky (now Nizhny Novgorod) Inst. of Water Transport Eng; engineer, Zelenodolsk 1965–67; Comsomol and CP work 1967–87; Head of Dept, First Deputy Chair., State Planning Cttee Tatar Autonomous Repub. 1987–95; Vice-Prime Minister of Tatarstan, Chair. State Cttee on Property 1995–96; First Deputy Chair. Cttee on State Property of Russian Fed. 1996–97; Deputy Chair. Govt of Russian Fed. 1997–98; Minister of State Property (temporarily Ministry of Property Relations) 1997–2004; Prof. 2004–; Chair. OAO Gazprom 1998–. *Address:* c/o Board of Directors, OAO Gazprom, 117997 Moscow, 16 Nametkina str., Russia.

GAZMIN, Lt-Gen. (retd) Voltaire Tuvera; Philippine diplomatist, government official and fmr army officer; *Secretary of National Defense;* b. Moncada; s. of Segundo L. Gazmin and Petra T. Gazmin; m. Rhodora Hernandez 1969; ed Univ. of the Philippines, Philippine Mil. Acad.; served 32 years in various positions in Philippine Army, including Commdr of three Battalions in Mindanao (45th Infantry Bn, 4th Infantry Div. 1979, 26th Infantry Bn, 4th Infantry Div. 1980, 2nd Scout Ranger Bn, First Scout Ranger Regt), Commdr, Presidential Security Group (PSG) 1986–92, Commanding Gen., Philippine Army 1999–2000, retd with rank of Lt-Gen. 2000; fmr Defense and Armed Forces Attaché, Embassy in Washington, DC; Amb. to Cambodia 2002–04; Sec. of Nat. Defense 2010–; numerous mil. hons including Philippine Legion of Honor. *Address:* Department of National Defense, DND Bldg, 3rd Floor, Camp Aguinaldo, Quezon City, 1110 Metro Manila, Philippines (office). *Telephone:* (2) 9116402 (office). *Fax:* (2) 9111651 (office). *E-mail:* webmaster@dnd.gov.ph (office). *Website:* www.dnd.gov.ph (office).

GBAGBO, Laurent, MA, PhD; Côte d'Ivoirian fmr head of state; b. 31 May 1945, Central-Western Prov.; m.; four c.; ed Univ. of Abidjan, Univ. of Lyon, Sorbonne, Paris VII Univ.; taught history and geography at Lycée Classique d'Abidjan 1970–71; imprisoned for unauthorized political activities 1971–73; worked in Dept of Educ. 1973–79; exile in France 1982–88; f. Front populaire Ivoirien (FPI) in secret 1982, FPI Sec.-Gen. 1988–96; mem. Parl. for Ouragahio 1990–2000; arrested Feb. 1992, sentenced to three years' imprisonment under anti-riot law, granted presidential pardon Aug. 1992; Pres. of Côte d'Ivoire Oct. 2000–11 (re-elected Dec. 2010 but election disputed by int. observers including UN Security Council); arrested April 2011. *Address:* c/o Office of the President, 01 BP 1354 Abidjan 01, Côte d'Ivoire (office).

GBEHO, James Victor; Ghanaian international organization official and fmr diplomatist; s. of Philip Gbeho; worked in Ghana Foreign and Commonwealth Service and later in Ministry of Foreign Affairs and served in various capacities at diplomatic missions abroad as well as in Accra, postings to Missions in China, India, Nigeria, New York (UN), Germany, UK and Geneva (UN), Deputy High Commr to UK 1972–76, Amb. and Perm. Rep. to UN, Geneva, also accred to UNIDO, Vienna 1978–80, IAEA, Vienna, held several posts, including Chair. UNCTAD IV's Cttee on Econ. Cooperation Among Developing Countries (ECDC) held in Manila, Philippines 1979, Chair. Geneva-based UNCTAD Preparatory Cttee for the establishment of the Common Fund for Commodities 1980–82; Perm. Rep. to UN, New York 1980–90, also accred to Cuba, Jamaica and Trinidad and Tobago, held several positions at UN, including Chair. First Cttee (Political and Security), Chair. Fourth Cttee (Decolonisation), Chair. Disarmament Cttee, mem. Anti-Apartheid Cttee and Chair. Sub-cttee on the Implementation of Sanctions against Apartheid South Africa, Chair. Exec. Council of the Int. Convention against Apartheid in Sports, elected to UN Security Council 1986–87, served twice as Pres. of the Council; also served on or led dels of Ghana to Sessions of UN Gen. Ass., Summit Meetings of the Commonwealth Heads of Govt, Commonwealth Ministerial Action Group, Non-Aligned Summit and Ministerial Meetings; has attended several Ministerial and Summit Meetings of OAU, African Union, Econ. Community of West African States (ECOWAS); Dir Non-Aligned Movement Secr., Ministry of Foreign Affairs from 1990, also Dir of State Protocol and also Acting

Chief Dir of the Ministry; Special Rep. of UN Sec.-Gen. in Somalia 1994–95; Special Rep. of the Chair. of Econ. Community of West African States (ECOWAS) in Liberia 1995–96, led ECOWAS Team that negotiated the Status of Forces Agreement with govt of Charles Taylor 1996; Deputy Minister of Foreign Affairs 1996–97, Minister of Foreign Affairs 1997–2001; mem. Parl. for Anlo Constituency 2001–04; worked in offices of Flight-Lt Jerry John Rawlings as the fmr Pres.'s Special Asst 2005–08; Adviser on Foreign Affairs to Pres. of Ghana 2008–10; Pres. ECOWAS Comm. 2010–12. *Address:* c/o Ministry of Foreign Affairs and Regional Integration, Treasury Road, POB M53, Accra, Ghana.

GBEZERA-BRIA, Michel, BL; Central African Republic politician, diplomatist and banker; b. 1946, Bossongoa; m.; five c.; ed Brazzaville School of Law, Caen School of Econs and Int. Inst. of Public Admin.; with civil service 1973–, Vice-Minister Sec.-in-charge of diplomatic missions 1975; Deputy Minister of Foreign Affairs 1976; Minister of Public Works, Labour and Social Security 1976–77, of Foreign Affairs 1977–78, of Public Works and Social Security 1978–79; State Comptroller 1979–80, Perm. Rep. to UN, Geneva 1980–83, New York 1983–89; Minister of Justice 1987–88, of Foreign Affairs 1988–90; Prime Minister of Cen. African Repub. 1997–99; Cabinet Dir of the Presidential Palace and Minister of State 2008; fmr Chair. Ecobank Centrafrique; Dir Econ. Man. Project 1991. *Address:* c/o Ecobank Centrafrique, Place de la République, PO Box: BP 910, Bangui, Central African Republic (office).

GBIAN, Jonas Aliou; Benin economist and politician; *Minister of Finance;* b. 29 March 1965, Ina, Borgou; m.; three c.; ed Centre Ouest africain de Formation et d'Etudes Bancaires, Dakar, Université Nationale du Bénin; 15 years with Banque Centrale des Etats de l'Afrique de l'Ouest; fmr adviser on econ. affairs to Pres.; Minister of Energy, Mining and Petroleum Research, Water and the Devt of Renewable Energy Sources 2011–12, of Economy and Finance 2012–. *Address:* Ministry of the Economy and Finance, BP 302, Cotonou, Benin (office). *Telephone:* 21-30-02-81 (office). *Fax:* 21-31-18-51 (office). *E-mail:* sgm@finance.gouv.bj (office). *Website:* www.finances.bj (office).

GBOWEE, Leymah Roberta, AA, MA; Liberian social worker, peace activist and women's rights advocate; *President, Gbowee Peace Foundation Africa;* b. 1 Feb. 1972, Monrovia; d. of Joseph Gbowee and Rachel Gbowee; six c.; ed Mother Patern Coll. of Health Sciences, Monrovia, Eastern Mennonite Univ., Harrisonburg, Va, USA, certifications: Conflict Prevention and Peacebuilding Training at UNITAR, the Healing Victims of War Trauma Centre in Cameroon, Non-Violent Peace Educ. in Liberia; Co-founder and Exec. Dir Women Peace and Security Network Africa (WIPSEN-A); Founding mem. and fmr Liberia Coordinator of Women in Peace-building Network/West Africa Network for Peacebuilding (WIPNET/WANEP); Founder and Pres. Gbowee Peace Foundation Africa; her leadership of Women of Liberia Mass Action for Peace brought together Christian and Muslim women in a nonviolent movement that played a pivotal role in ending Liberia's civil war 2003; Commr-designate for the Liberia Truth and Reconciliation Comm. 2004–05; selected by Pres. Johnson Sirleaf to serve as Head of the Liberia Reconciliation Initiative; Africa columnist, Newsweek Daily Beast; mem. Bd of Dirs Nobel Women's Initiative, PeaceJam Foundation; mem. African Women Leaders Network for Reproductive Health and Family Planning; Hon. LLD (Rhodes Univ., SA), (Univ. of Alberta, Canada); Blue Ribbon for Peace, John F. Kennedy School of Govt, Harvard Univ. 2007, Women's eNews Leaders for the 21st Century Award 2008, Gruber Prize for Women's Rights 2009, John F. Kennedy Profile in Courage Award 2009, John Jay Medal for Justice, John Jay Coll. of Criminal Justice 2010, Living Legends Award for Service to Humanity 2010, Joli Humanitarian Award, Riverdale Country School 2010, Villanova Peace Award, Villanova Univ. 2010, Nobel Peace Prize (jtly) for "non-violent struggle for the safety of women and for women's rights to full participation in peace-building work" 2011, honoured as a flag-bearer for the Olympic Games Opening Ceremony, London 2012. *Film:* central character in documentary film Pray the Devil Back to Hell (shown at Tribeca Film Festival, New York) 2008. *Publication:* Mighty Be Our Powers: How Sisterhood, Prayer and Sex Changed a Nation at War (autobiog.). *Address:* Gbowee Peace Foundation Africa, Sophie Ice Cream Road, Congo Town, Monrovia, Liberia. *Telephone:* 776-976584 (mobile) (office). *E-mail:* info@gboweepeaceafrica.org (office).

GE, Wujue; Chinese writer; b. 12 Sept. 1937, Wenzhou, Zhejiang; s. of Ge Luyan and Zhang Wencang; m. Zhao Baoqing 1962 (divorced); one s.; ed Beijing Univ.; worked as journalist for over 20 years; published first book 1961; in political disgrace 1963–77; some works translated into English, French and Japanese; Vice-Chair. Fed. of Art and Literature, Ningxia and Ningxia Branch of Union of Chinese Writers. *Publications:* The Wedding, A Journalist and Her Story, An Experience in the Summer, She and her Girl Friend, The Golden Deer, A View of an Ancient Ferry (short stories), Meditate on the Past (novel), Years and Man (novel), Going to the Ancient Ferry on Today (TV Drama), Four Days in All of Life 1988 (short stories), The Earth. The Moon (novel), The Passport on the Earth, Zhang Daqian in Dunhuan (TV drama) 1991, Quality of Life (reportage) 1995, Tango Rumba (screenplay) 1996. *Leisure interests:* sports, music, drawing, calligraphy. *Address:* 268-9 Bailidong Road, Wenzhou, Zhejiang, People's Republic of China. *Telephone:* (577) 8282374 (office); (577) 8525866 (home).

GE, You; Chinese actor; b. 19 April 1957; joined All-China Fed. of Trade Unions Art Troupe 1979. *Films include:* Farewell My Concubine 1993, To Live 1994 (Cannes Film Festival for Best Actor 1994), The Emperor's Shadow 1996, A World without Thieves 2004, Suffocation 2005, Shanghai Red 2006, The Banquet 2006, Crossed Lines 2007, Let the Bullets Fly 2010. *Address:* All-China Federation of Trade Unions Art Troupe, Beijing, People's Republic of China.

GEBREAB, Newaye-Kirstos; Ethiopian central banker; *Chairman, National Bank of Ethiopia;* b. Adwa, Tigray; ed Addis Ababa Univ. Coll., Sidist Kilo; fmr econ. adviser to Prime Minister Meles Zenawi; currently Chair. Nat. Bank of Ethiopia. *Address:* Office of the Chairman, National Bank of Ethiopia, Sudan Avenue, POB 5558, Addis Ababa, Ethiopia (office). *Telephone:* (11) 5517438 (office). *Fax:* (11) 5514588 (office). *E-mail:* nbe.gov@ethionet.et (office). *Website:* www.nbe.gov.et (office).

GEBRSELASSIE, Haile; Ethiopian professional athlete; b. 18 April 1973, Arssi; m. 1996; two c.; set 21 world records or best times indoors and outdoors 1994–98, including world 5,000m and 10,000m records 1997, 1998; silver medal World Jr

Cross Country Championships 1992; gold medals World Jr Championships 5,000m and 10,000m 1992; silver medal World Championships 5,000m 1993; gold medal World Championships 10,000m 1995, 1997; gold medal World Indoor Championships 3,000m 1995, 1999, 2003; gold medal Olympic Games 10,000m 1996, 2000, silver medal 2004; winner IAAF World Half-Marathon Championship, England 2001; bronze medal World Championships 10,000m 2001; silver medal World Championships 10,000m 2003; winner Berlin Marathon 2006, 2007, 2008, 2009; 5,000m (indoor and outdoor), 10,000m, 10km road race world record holder, one-hour running event world record holder 2007; indoor record holder for two miles; previous world record holder marathon. 2.03.59; IAAF Athlete of the Year 1998. *Leisure interests:* boxing, soccer. *Address:* c/o Jos Hermens, Global Sports Communication, Snelliusstraat 10, 6533 TD Nijmegen, Netherlands (office). *E-mail:* gsc@global-sports-comm.nl (office). *Website:* www .globalsportscommunication.nl (office).

GEDDES, John M., MA; American newspaper editor; b. 1952; ed Univs. of RI and Wis.; reporter Ansonia Evening Sentinel, Ansonia, Conn. 1976; reporter Associated Press-Dow Jones News Service, NY 1976–78, Bonn, Germany 1978–79; econs corresp. The Times, Bonn 1979–80; joined Wall Street Journal 1980, various positions including Bureau Chief, Bonn, Deputy Man. Ed. then Man. Ed. European Edn, News Ed., Asst Man. Ed., Sr Ed. and Nat. News Ed. –1993; fmr Prin. Friday Holdings; CEO BIS Strategic Decisions (market research co.) 1993–94; Business and Financial Ed. New York Times 1994–97, Deputy Man. Ed. 1997–2003, Man. Ed. for News Operations 2003–13. *Address:* c/o The New York Times, 620 Eighth Avenue, New York, NY 10018, USA.

GEDVILAS, Vydas, PhD; Lithuanian basketball coach, medical scientist and politician; b. 17 May 1959, Užgiriuose, Kelme dist; m. Elena Gevilienė; one s. one d.; ed Lithuanian State Inst. of Physical Educ.; teacher, Lithuanian Acad. of Physical Educ. (LVKKI) from 1981, Asst Coach, LVKKI men's basketball team 'Atletas' (three times Lithuanian champions) 1988–93, Chief Coach, LKKA women's basketball team 'Viktorija' (Lithuanian and Baltic women's basketball champions) 1993–2004, Vice-Rector LVKKI 2001–04; Head Coach, Lithuanian women's basketball team (European champions) 1996–2002; mem. Labour Party (Darbo Partija) 2004–; mem. Seimas (Parl.) 2004–, Chair. (Speaker) 2012–13, First Deputy Speaker 2013–, mem. Conf. of Chairs 2012–13, Chair. Seimas Del. to the Ass. of Mems of the Seimas of the Repub. of Lithuania, the Sejm and Senate of the Repub. of Poland and the Verkhovna Rada of Ukraine 2012–13; mem. Kaunas City Council 2011–12; mem. Lithuanian Basketball Coaches Asscn; Hon. Pres. Exec. Cttee, Lithuanian Basketball Fed.; Hon. Coach of Lithuania; Order of Grand Duke Gediminas, Third Class. *Publications:* research papers on methodological tools for students and at numerous int. scientific confs. *Address:* Seimas (Parliament), Gedimino pr. 53, Vilnius 01109 (office). *Telephone:* (5) 239-6341 (office). *Fax:* (5) 239-6289 (office). *E-mail:* vydas.gedvilas@lrs.lt (office). *Website:* www.lrs.lt (office).

GEE, E. Gordon; American lawyer and university administrator; b. 2 Feb. 1944; m. 1st Elizabeth D. Gee; one d.; m. 2nd Constance Gee (divorced); ed Columbia Univ.; completed a fed. judicial clerkship; served as Asst Dean for Univ. of Utah Coll. of Law; fmr Judicial Fellow and Sr Staff Asst for US Supreme Court Chief Justice Warren Burger; fmr Assoc. Dean and Prof., J. Reuben Clark Law School, Brigham Young Univ.; Dean Law School, West Virginia Univ. 1979, Pres. West Virginia Univ. 1981–85; Pres. Univ. Colorado at Boulder 1985–90; Pres. Ohio State Univ. 1990–97, 2007–13; Pres. Brown Univ. 1997–2000; Chancellor Vanderbilt Univ. 2000–07; mem. Bd of Dirs Freedom Forum Diversity Inst., Inc., Montgomery Bell Acad., Tennessee Coll. Asscn; mem. Advisory Cttee Nashville Alliance for Public Educ., Pres.'s Council for Imagining America: Artists and Scholars in Public Life, Bd Christopher Isherwood Foundation, Business-Higher Educ. Forum, Nat. Cttee to Unite a Divided America; has carried out research on behalf of Ford Foundation, Guy Anderson Foundation, American Bar Foundation, and others; mem. Circle of Hope; currently Dir or Trustee The Jason Foundation, Nat. Hospice Foundation, Historic Black Coll. and Univ. Advisory Cttee Kresge Foundation, Hasbro, The Limited, Dollar General Corpn, Massey Energy Corpn, Gaylord Entertainment Co.; Trustee Harry S. Truman Scholarship Foundation 1995–; Mellon Fellow, Aspen Inst. for Humanistic Studies, W. K. Kellogg Fellow, Distinguished Alumnus Award, Univ. of Utah 1994, Distinguished Alumnus Award, Teachers' Coll., Columbia Univ. 1994, Outstanding Promotion of Diversity Award, Nashville Br., Nat. Asscn for the Advancement of Colored People, Nashville Women's Political Caucus' Good Guy Award 2004, Apollo Award for Communications Leadership, Public Relations Soc. of America (Nashville chapter) 2004. *Publications:* co-author of six books; numerous papers and articles in fields relating to both law and education. *Address:* c/o Office of the President, Ohio State University, 205 Bricker Hall, 190 North Oval Mall, Columbus, OH 43210-1357, USA.

GEE, Maurice Gough, MA; New Zealand novelist; b. 22 Aug. 1931, Whakatane; m. Margaretha Garden 1970; one s. two d.; ed Avondale Coll., Auckland, Auckland Univ.; school teacher, librarian, other casual employment 1954–75; Robert Burns Fellow, Univ. of Otago 1964; Writing Fellow, Vic. Univ. of Wellington 1989; Katherine Mansfield Memorial Fellow, Menton, France 1992; Hon. DLitt (Victoria) 1987, (Auckland) 2004; NZ Fiction Award 1976, 1979, 1982, 1991, 1993, NZ Book of the Year Award (Wattle Award) 1979, 1993, James Tait Black Memorial Prize 1979, NZ Children's Book of the Year Award 1986, 1995, Prime Minister's Prize 2004. *Publications include:* Plumb 1978, Meg 1981, Sole Survivor 1983, Collected Stories 1986, Prowlers 1987, The Burning Boy 1990, Going West 1992, Crime Story 1994, Loving Ways 1996, Live Bodies 1998, Ellie and the Shadow Man 2001, The Scornful Moon 2004, Blindsight (Deutz Medal for Fiction 2006, Montana New Zealand Book Award for Fiction 2006) 2005; juvenile fiction includes: Under the Mountain 1979, The O Trilogy 1982–85, The Fat Man 1994; also scripts for film and TV. *Address:* 56 Nile Street, 7010 Nelson, New Zealand (home).

GEENS, Koenraad (Koen) Frans Julia, PhD; Belgian lawyer and politician; *Minister of Finance and of Sustainable Development, in charge of Civil Service;* b. 22 Jan. 1958, Brasschaat; ed Katholieke Universiteit (KU) Leuven, Harvard Univ., USA; Prof. of Corp. Law, KU Leuven, also Chair., Research Unit on Econ. Law and Dir Jan Ronse Inst. for Company Law; Chair. Bd of Govs. Thomas More Univ. Coll.; Co-founder Eubelius (law firm); Chief of Staff for Flemish Minister-Pres. Kris Peeters 2007–09; Minister of Finance and of Sustainable Devt, in charge of Civil Service 2013–; Chair. Bd of Elders, Flanders in Action - 2020 Pact; mem.

Royal Flemish Acad. of Belgium, Academia Europaea; mem. Christen-Democratisch en Vlaams (CD&V). *Address:* Federal Public Service of Finance, 33 blvd du Roi Albert II, BP 70, 1030 Brussels, Belgium (office). *Telephone:* (92) 572-57-57 (office). *E-mail:* info.tax@minfin.fed.be (office). *Website:* www.minfin .fgov.be (office). www.koengeens.be.

GEFFEN, David Lawrence; American film, recording and theatre executive; b. 21 Feb. 1943, Brooklyn, New York; s. of Abraham Geffen and Batya Geffen (née Volovskaya); ed New Utrecht High School, Brooklyn, Univ. of Texas, Brooklyn Coll.; joined William Morris talent agency as mail clerk 1964, promoted to jr agent; launched new film studio with Steven Spielberg (q.v.) and Jeffrey Katzenberg (q.v.); f. music publishing co. Tunafish Music, with Laura Nyro; joined Ashley Famous Agency, then apptd Exec. Vice-Pres. Creative Man. (now Int. Creative Man.) 1968; f. Asylum Records and Geffen-Roberts Man. Co. with Elliot Roberts 1970, sold Asylum to Warner Communications, but remained Pres. 1971, merged it with Elektra, signed Bob Dylan and Joni Mitchell, Vice-Chair. Warner Brothers Pictures 1975–76; taught business studies at Yale Univ.; f. Geffen Records, Pres. 1980, signed Elton John, John Lennon and Yoko Ono and many others, sold label to Music Corpn of America Inc. 1990; f. Geffen Film Co.; Co-Producer musical Dreamgirls 1981–85, Cats 1982, M. Butterfly 1986, Social Security, Chess 1990, Miss Saigon; f. DGC record label 1995; Co-founder and Prin. Dreamworks SKG 1995–2005; Ahmet Ertegun Award, inducted into Rock and Roll Hall of Fame 2010, President's Merit Award for Indelible Contrib. to the Music Industry, Nat. Acad. of Recording Arts and Sciences 2011.

GEHLOT, Ashok, BSc, LLB, MA; Indian politician; b. 3 May 1951, Mahamandir, Jodhpur, Rajasthan; s. of the late Shri Lachman Singh Gehlot; m. Smt. Sunita Gehlot 1977; one s. one d.; worked in refugee camps at Bangaon and 24 Parganas dists (West Bengal) during liberation war of Bangladesh 1971; Pres. Rajasthan Nat. Students' Union of India 1974–79; City District Congress Cttee 1979–82; mem. Indian Nat. Congress party; mem. Lok Sabha (Parl.) 1980–89, 1991–99, Public Accounts Cttee 1980–82, Consultative Cttee on Communication 1991–96, Standing Cttee on Railways 1991–98, Consultative Cttee on External Affairs 1996–98; mem. Rajasthan Legis. Ass. 1999–; Union Deputy Minister, Dept of Tourism 1982–83, of Tourism and Civil Aviation 1983–84, 1984–85, of Sports 1984; Minister Dept of Home and Public Health Eng, Govt of Rajasthan 1989; Union Minister of State, Dept of Textiles 1989; Chief Minister of Rajasthan 1998–2003, 2008–13; Gen. Sec. Rajasthan Pradesh Congress Cttee (Pres. 1997–99); mem. various Indian dels abroad, including to China as mem. All India Congress Cttee del. 1994, Leader Indian del. to Commonwealth Youth Affairs to Cyprus, Indian del. to Bulgaria, visited various countries, including Bangkok, Ireland, Frankfurt, USA (as mem. Indian del. to UN and for RIC convention), Canada, Hong Kong, UK, Italy, Dubai, France; Founder-Pres. Bharat Seva Sansthan; Chair. Rajiv Gandhi Study Circle, New Delhi. *Address:* Rajasthan Pradesh Congress Committee Jaipur, Indira Gandhi Bhavan, Station Road, Jaipur, Rajasthan, India (office). *Telephone:* (141) 2361355 (office). *Fax:* (141) 2361369 (office). *E-mail:* Office@ rajasthanpcclcom. *Website:* rajasthanpcc.com.

GEHRIG, Bruno, Dr rer. pol; Swiss economist, academic and insurance industry executive; *Chairman, Swiss Life Holding;* b. 26 Dec. 1946; ed Univ. of Berne, Univ. of Rochester, NY, USA; Asst, then Lecturer on Econs, Univ. of Berne 1970–78, Asst Prof. 1978–80; Head of Econs Section, Union Bank of Switzerland (UBS) 1981–84, with Stock Markets and Securities Sales Div., UBS Group 1986–88, Head of Div. 1988–89; Chair. Exec. Bd, Bank Cantrade, Zürich 1989–91; Prof. of Business Admin and Head of Swiss Inst., Univ. of St Gallen 1992–96; apptd mem. Governing Bd, Swiss Nat. Bank 1996, Head of Dept III 1996–2001, Vice-Chair. Governing Bd 2001–03; Chair. Swiss Life Holding 2003–; Dir Roche Holding AG, Basel (Vice-Chair. 2004–, Ind. Lead Dir –2008); Chair. Econ. Policy Study Group, Swiss Christian Democratic Party (CVP) 1984–91; Chair. Bd of Trustees Swiss Air Transport Foundation; mem. Swiss Fed. Banking Comm. 1992–96; Hon. LLD (Univ. of Rochester, NY) 2006. *Address:* Swiss Life Holding, General Guisan-Quai 40, 8022 Zürich, Switzerland (office). *Telephone:* (4) 32843253 (office). *Fax:* (4) 33383253 (office). *E-mail:* bruno.gehrig@swisslife.ch (office). *Website:* www .swisslife.com (office).

GEHRING, Gillian Anne, OBE, MA, DPhil, FInstP; British physicist and academic; *Professor Emeritus of Physics, University of Sheffield;* b. 19 May 1941, Nottingham, England; d. of H. L. (Max) Murray and F. Joan Murray; m. Karl A. Gehring 1968; two d.; ed Univs of Manchester and Oxford; Leverhulme Postdoctoral Research Fellowship, St Hugh's Coll., Oxford 1965–67; NATO Fellowship, Univ. of California, Berkeley, USA 1967–68; Fellow and Tutor in Physics, St Hugh's Coll., Oxford 1968–70; CUF Lecturer in Theoretical Physics, Univ. of Oxford 1970–89; Prof. of Physics, Univ. of Sheffield 1989–2007, Prof. Emer. 2007–; Leverhulme Emer. Fellow 2007–09, 2012–14; Hon. mem. European Physical Soc. 2010; Hon. Fellow, St Hugh's Coll., Oxford; Hon. Fellow, Inst. of Physics; Hon. DSc (Salford) 1994, (Sheffield) 2012, (Hull) 2013. *Publications:* research papers on theoretical condensed matter physics. *Leisure interest:* family activities. *Address:* Department of Physics and Astronomy, University of Sheffield, Hicks Building, Hounsfield Road, Sheffield, S3 7RH (office); Flat 3, West Royd, 119 Manchester Road, Sheffield, S10 5DN, England (home). *Telephone:* (114) 222-4299 (office). *E-mail:* g.gehring@sheffield.ac.uk (office). *Website:* www.shef.ac.uk/ physics/people/ggehring (office).

GEHRING, Walter Jakob, PhD; Swiss geneticist, biologist and academic; *Professor Emeritus of Genetics and Developmental Biology, University of Basel;* b. 20 March 1939, Zurich; s. of the late Jakob Gehring and of Marcelle Gehring-Rebmann; m. Elisabeth Lott 1964; two s. d.; ed Realgymnasium, Zürich, Univ. of Zurich and Yale Univ., USA; Assoc. Prof., Depts of Anatomy and Molecular Biophysics, Yale Univ. 1969–72; Prof. of Genetics and Developmental Biology, Dept of Cell Biology, Univ. of Basel 1972–2009, Prof. Emer. 2009–; mem. European Molecular Biology Org., European Developmental Biology Org., AAAS, Genetics Soc. of America, Int. Soc. of Developmental Biologists, Swiss Soc. for Cell Biology, Molecular Biology and Genetics, American Soc. for Developmental Biology, Human Genome Org.; Foreign mem. Royal Soc. 1997; Ehrenmitgliedschaft Naturforschende Gesellschaft, Basel 2007, Bundesverdienstkreuz 2010; Hon. Dr med (Univ. of Turin, Italy) 2003, (Universität Nuevo Léon, Mexico) 2003; Dr hc (Université Pierre et Marie Curie (UPMC) in Sorbonne) 2007, (Univ. of Salento, Italy) 2008, (Univ. of Barcelona) 2009; Otto Naegeli Prize 1982, Warren Triennial

Prize, Harvard Medical School 1986, Dr Albert Wander Preis, Wander AG 1986, Prix Charles-Léopold Mayer, Institut de France 1986, Prix Louis Jeantet de Médecine, Fondation Jeantet Genève 1987, Gairdner Foundation Int. Award (Canada) 1987, Prix d'Honneur Science pour l'Art, Moët Hennessy-Louis Vuitton 1993, Runnström Medal 1995, 1994-95 AAAS Newcomb Cleveland Prize for outstanding research article in Science 1996, Otto Warburg-Medaille 1996, Prix Paul Wintrebert 1997, Mendel-Medal, Deutsche Akademie der Naturforscher Leopoldina 1997, March of Dimes Prize in Developmental Biology 1997, Karl Ritter Von Frisch-Medaille, Deutsche Zoologische Gesellschaft, Bonn 2000, Kyoto Prize, The Inamori Foundation, Japan 2000, Preis der Alfred Vogt Stiftung zur Förderung der Augenheilkunde, Zürich 2001, Premio Balzan, Fondazione Internazionale Premio E. Balzan for Developmental Biology 2002, Alexander Kowalevsky Medal, St Petersburg Soc. of Naturalists 2004. *Publications:* Zoologie (with R. Wehner) 1990, Master Control Genes in Development and Evolution: The Homeobox Story; more than 260 publs. *Leisure interests:* bird watching, photography. *Address:* Hochfeldweg 32, 4106 Therwil (home); Department of Cell Biology, Biozentrum, University of Basel, Klingelbergstrasse 50/70, 4056 Basel, Switzerland (office). *Telephone:* (61) 2672050 (office); (61) 7213593 (home). *Fax:* (61) 2671613 (office). *E-mail:* walter.gehring@unibas.ch. *Website:* www .biozentrum.unibas.ch (office).

GEHRY, Frank Owen, CC, BArch, FAIA; Canadian/American architect; b. (Ephraim Owen Goldberg), 28 Feb. 1929, Toronto, Canada; s. of Irving Gehry and Thelma Caplan; m. 1st Anita Snyder (divorced); two d.; m. 2nd Berta Aguilera 1975; two s.; ed Univ. of Southern California and Harvard Univ. Grad. School of Design; designer, Victor Gruen Assocs, LA 1953–54, Planning, Design and Project Dir 1958–61; Project Designer and Planner, Pereira & Luckman, LA 1957–58; Design Prin. Frank O. Gehry & Assocs, Santa Monica, Calif. 1962–; f. Gehry Partnership LLP 2002; f. Gehry Technologies Inc. (building industry tech. co.); architect for Temporary Contemporary Museum 1983, Calif. Aerospace Museum 1984, Loyola Law School 1981–84, Frances Howard Goldwyn Regional Br. Library 1986, Information and Computer Science Eng Research Facility, Univ. of Calif. Irvine 1986, Vitra Furniture Mfg Facility and Design Museum, Germany 1989, Chiat/Day HQ, Venice, Calif. 1991, American Center, Paris 1992–94, Weisman Art Museum, Minneapolis 1993, Disney Ice, Anaheim 1995, EMR Communication & Tech. Centre, Bad Oeynhausen, Germany 1995, Team Disneyland Admin., Anaheim 1996, ING Office Bldg, Prague 1996, Guggenheim Museum, Bilbao 1997, Experience Music Project, Seattle 2000, Walt Disney Concert Hall, LA 2003, Maggie's Cancer Care Centre, Dundee 2003, bandshell, Millennium Park, Chicago 2004, IAC HQ 2006; Fellow, American Inst. of Architects, American Acad. of Arts and Letters, American Acad. of Arts and Sciences; Charlotte Davenport Chair. Yale Univ. 1982, 1989; Eliot Noyes Design Chair. Harvard 1984; currently Distinguished Prof., Grad. School of Architecture, Planning and Preservation, Columbia Univ.; Dr hc (Calif. Coll. of Arts and Crafts) 1987, (Rhode Island School of Design) 1987, (Tech. Univ. of Nova Scotia) 1989, (Calif. Inst. of Arts), (Otis Art Inst., Parsons School of Design) 1989, (Occidental Coll.) 1993, (Whittier Coll.) 1995, (Southern Calif. Inst. of Architecture) 1997, (Univ. of Toronto) 1998, (Univ. of Edinburgh) 2000, (Univ. of Southern Calif.) 2000, (Yale Univ.) 2000, (Harvard Univ.) 2000, (School of The Art Inst. of Chicago) 2004; Arnold W. Brunner Memorial Architecture Prize 1983, Pritzker Architecture Prize 1989, shared Wolf Prize 1992, Imperial Prize (Japan) 1992, Lillian Gish Award 1994, National Medal of Arts 1998, Kiesler Prize for Architecture and the Arts 1998, Gold Medal of Inst. of Architects 1999, Gold Medal for Architecture, American Acad. of Arts and Letters 2002, Royal Fine Art Comm. Trust Building of the Year Award 2004, Woodrow Wilson Award for Public Service 2004. *Film appearance:* The Cool School 2007. *Publications:* Individual Imagination and Cultural Conservatism 1995, Gehry Draws 2005. *Address:* Gehry Partners LLP, 12541 Beatrice Street, Los Angeles, CA 90066 (office); Frank O. Gehry & Associates, 1520-B Cloverfield Boulevard, Santa Monica, CA 90404 (office). *Telephone:* (310) 482-3000 (office). *Fax:* (310) 482-3006 (office). *Website:* www.gehrypartners.com (office).

GEIDUSCHEK, E(rnest) Peter, PhD; American biologist and academic; *Professor Emeritus, Division of Biological Sciences, University of California, San Diego;* b. 11 April 1928, Vienna, Austria; s. of Sigmund Geiduschek and Frieda Tauber; m. Joyce B. Brous 1955; two s.; ed Columbia and Harvard Univs; Instructor in Chem., Yale Univ. 1952–53, 1955–57; Asst Prof. of Chem., Univ. of Mich. 1957–59; Asst Prof. of Biophysics and Research Assoc. in Biochemistry, Univ. of Chicago 1959–62, Assoc. Prof. of Biophysics and Research Assoc. in Biochemistry 1962–64, Prof. of Biophysics and Research Assoc. in Biochemistry 1964–70; Prof. of Biology, Univ. of Calif., San Diego 1970–94, Chair. 1981–83, Acting Chair. 1994, Research Prof., Dept of Biological Sciences 1994–2013, Prof. Emer. 2013–; mem. Bd of Scientific Counselors, Nat. Cancer Inst., NIH 1998–2003; European Molecular Biology Org. (EMBO) Lecturer 1977, Hilleman Lecturer, Univ. of Chicago 1978, Paul Doty Lecturer, Harvard Univ. 1993, Adriano Buzzati-Traverso Lecture, Rome 1996; Jean Weigle Lecture, Geneva 2001; Lalor Foundation Faculty Fellow, Yale 1957, Guggenheim Fellow, Inst. de Biologie Moléculaire, Geneva 1964–65; mem. NAS, American Acad. of Arts and Sciences; Fellow, AAAS, Acad. of Microbiology (USA); Grande Ufficiale, Ordine al Merito della Repubblica Italiana 1997; Gregor Mendel Medal, Acad. of Sciences of the Czech Repub. 2004. *Publications:* numerous articles on molecular biology, biochemistry and virology. *Address:* University of California, San Diego, Division of Biological Sciences, Section of Molecular Biology, 9500 Gilman Drive, La Jolla, CA 92093-0377, USA (office). *Telephone:* (858) 534-3029 (office). *Fax:* (858) 534-0780 (office). *E-mail:* epg@ucsd.edu (office). *Website:* www.biology.ucsd.edu (office).

GEIGER, Helmut; German banker and lawyer; b. 12 June 1928, Nuremberg; m.; one s. one d.; ed Univs of Erlangen and Berlin; legal asst, Deutsche Bundestag and asst lawyer, Bonn 1957–59; lawyer in Bonn and man. of office of Öffentliche Bausparkassen 1959–66; Man. Dir Deutsche Sparkassen-und Giroverband 1966–72, Pres. 1972–93; Pres. Int. Inst. der Sparkassen (Int. Savings Bank Inst.), Geneva 1978–84; Pres. EEC Savings Bank Group, Brussels 1985–88; Chair. Sparkassenstiftung für Int. Kooperation 1992–98; mem. Bundestag 1965; Chair. and mem. of various charitable and professional bodies; Grand Fed. Cross of Merit; Dr hc (Cologne). *Publications include:* Herausforderungen für Stabilität und Fortschritt 1974, Bankpolitik 1975, Gespräche über Geld 1986, Die deutsche Sparkassenorganisation 1992 and numerous publs on banking matters. *Address:* Simrockstr. 4, 53113 Bonn, Germany. *Telephone:* (228) 9703610.

GEIM, Sir Andre Konstantinovich, Kt, MSc, PhD, FRS; British/Dutch (b. Russian) physicist and academic; *Royal Society 2010 Anniversary Research Professor and Regius Professor of Physics, University of Manchester;* b. 21 Oct. 1958, Sochi, Russian SFSR, USSR; s. of the late Konstantin Alekseyevich Geim (Heim) and of Nina Nikolayevna Bayer; m. Irina V. Grigorieva; ed Moscow Inst. of Physics and Tech., Inst. of Solid State Physics, USSR (now Russian) Acad. of Sciences, Chernogolovka; worked as research scientist at Inst. for Microelectronics Tech., Russian Acad. of Sciences, Chernogolovka 1987–90, then as post-doctoral fellow at Univs of Nottingham and Bath, UK and at Univ. of Copenhagen, Denmark 1990–94; Assoc. Prof., Radboud Univ., Nijmegen 1994–2001, Prof. of Innovative Materials and Nanoscience 2010–; Prof. of Physics, Univ. of Manchester, UK 2001–07, Langworthy Research Prof. of Physics 2007–13, Royal Society 2010 Anniversary Research Prof. 2010–, Regius Prof. of Physics 2013–, Dir Manchester Centre for Mesoscience and Nanotechnology 2002–; EPSRC Sr Research Fellow 2007–; Prof. of Innovative Materials and Nanoscience, Radboud Univ. Nijmegen 2010–; Foreign Assoc. NAS 2012; Corresponding mem. Royal Netherlands Acad. of Arts and Sciences; Hon. Prof., Nat. Univ. of Singapore, Moscow Phys-Tech, Univ. of Nijmegen; Einstein Prof., Chinese Acad. of Sciences; Hon. FInstP; Hon. FRSC; Hon. Fellow, Singapore Inst. of Physics; Kt Commdr, Order of the Netherlands Lion 2010; Dr hc (Delft Univ. of Tech., ETH Zurich, Univ. of Antwerp, Univ. of Manchester); Ig Nobel Prize (jtly) 2000, Mott Prize, Inst. of Physics 2007, Europhysics Prize (jtly) 2008, Körber European Science Award 2009, named by Thomson-Reuters amongst the top 10 most active, "hottest" researchers 2009–11, NAS John J. Carty Award for the Advancement of Science 2010, Hughes Medal 2010, Royal Soc. 2010 Anniversary Research Professorship 2010, Nobel Prize in Physics (with Konstantin Novoselov) 2010, Niels Bohr Medal 2011, Copley Medal, Royal Soc. 2013. *Achievements include:* best known for his discovery, with Konstantin Novoselov, of two-dimensional crystals made of carbon atoms – and most notably graphene – in 2004 at Univ. of Manchester; original jt paper on graphene in Science in 2004 acknowledged by ISI citation index as "one of the most cited recent papers in the field of physics"; earlier experiments on diamagnetic levitation publicized by worldwide media and featured in textbooks, famously levitated a frog; also well known for demonstrating a new microfabricated adhesive based on the same physics mechanism underlying the climbing ability of geckos. *Publications:* more than 150 peer-refereed research papers, including many in Nature and Science, on condensed matter physics. *Address:* Room 2.14, Schuster Building, The School of Physics and Astronomy, University of Manchester, Manchester, M13 9PL, England (office). *Telephone:* (161) 275-4120 (office). *E-mail:* andre.k.geim@manchester.ac.uk (office). *Website:* www.manchester.ac.uk/research/Andre.k.geim (office); www.condmat.physics.manchester.ac.uk/people/academic/geim (office).

GEIMAN, Leonid Mikhailovich, DrTechSci; Russian scientific publisher; b. 12 Aug. 1934, Moscow; ed Moscow Ore Inst.; researcher, ore industry research orgs; Head of Div. Publrs' Sovietskaya Encyclopaedia 1963–88; Prof., Moscow Ore Inst.; researcher, All-Union Inst. of Foreign Geology; f. Ind. Encyclopaedic Ed. House (ETA); Pres. Encyclopaedic Creative Asscn; mem. Russian Acad. of Natural Sciences 1992, Academician-Sec. Dept of Encyclopaedia. *Publications:* Russian Encyclopaedia of Banks 1995, Russian National Electronic Encyclopaedia 1995, Encyclopaedia of Moscow Streets 1996, Encyclopaedia America 1997. *Address:* c/o Russian Academy of Natural Sciences, Varshavskoye shosse 8, 113105 Moscow, Russia.

GEINGOB, Hage Gottfried, MA; Namibian politician; *Prime Minister;* b. 3 Aug. 1941, Grootfontein Dist; m. Loine Kandume 1993; one s. three d. from previous marriage; ed Augustineum Coll. Okahandja and studies in int. relations in USA; joined SWAPO 1962; teacher, Tsumeb 1962; exiled for political activities Dec. 1962; became SWAPO Asst Rep. Botswana 1963–64; subsequently moved to USA, studied at Fordham Univ. and New School for Social Research, New York and became SWAPO Rep. at UN –1971; mem. SWAPO Politburo 1975, Vice-Pres. SWAPO 2007–; Dir UN Inst. for Namibia, Lusaka, Zambia 1975–89; returned to Namibia as Election Dir 1989; Chair. Constituent Ass. and Namibia Independence Celebrations Cttee 1989; Prime Minister of Namibia 1990–2003, 2012–; Exec. Sec., Global Coalition for Africa, Washington, DC 2003–04; mem. Parl. 2004–; Minister of Trade and Industry 2008–12; Officier, Palmes académiques 1980, Ongulumbashe Medal for bravery and long service 1987; Hon. LLD (Colby Coll., Chicago) 1994. *Leisure interests:* playing tennis, reading, watching soccer and rugby. *Address:* Office of the Prime Minister, Robert Mugabe Avenue, PMB 13338, Windhoek, Namibia (office). *Telephone:* (61) 2879111 (office). *Fax:* (61) 226189 (office). *Website:* www.opm.gov.na (office).

GEISS, Johannes, Dr rer. nat; Swiss physicist and academic; *Honorary Director, International Space Science Institute;* b. 4 Sept. 1926, Stolp, Pomerania, Poland; s. of Hans Geiss and Irene Wilke; m. Carmen Bach 1955; one d.; ed Univ. of Göttingen, Germany; Research Assoc., Enrico Fermi Inst., Univ. of Chicago, USA 1955–56; Assoc. Prof., Marine Lab., Univ. of Miami, USA 1958–59; Assoc. Prof., Univ. of Berne 1960, Prof. of Physics 1964–91, Dir Inst. of Physics 1966–90; Visiting Scientist, NASA Goddard Inst. for Space Studies, New York 1965, NASA Manned Spacecraft Center, Houston 1968–69; Chair. Launching Programme Advisory Cttee, ESA, Paris 1970–72; Visiting Prof., Univ. of Toulouse 1975; Chair. Space Science Cttee, European Science Foundation 1979–86; Exec. Dir Int. Space Science Inst. 1995–2002, Hon. Dir 2003–; Adjunct Prof., Univ. of Michigan; Rector, Univ. of Berne 1982–83; Fellow, American Geophysical Union; Foreign mem. American Acad. of Arts and Sciences, NAS, Max-Planck-Inst. für Aeronomie, Int. Acad. of Astronautics, Max-Planck-Inst. für Kernphysik, Austrian Acad. of Sciences, Academia Europaea; Dr hc (Univ. of Chicago); NASA Medal for Exceptional Scientific Achievement, Leonard Medal 1983, Allan D. Emil Memorial Award 1989, Sir Harry Massey Medal 1992, Albert Einstein Medal 2001, William Bowie Medal 2004. *Publications:* over 300 publs on nucleosynthesis, cosmology, the origin of the solar system, geochronology, climatic history of the earth, the age of meteorites and lunar rocks, comets, solar wind, solar terrestrial relations. *Address:* International Space Science Institute, Hallerstr. 6, 3012 Berne, Switzerland (office). *Telephone:* (31) 6313253 (office). *Fax:* (31) 6314897 (office). *E-mail:* Geiss@issibern.ch (office). *Website:* www.issibern.ch (office).

GEISSLER, Heiner, DJur; German politician; b. 3 March 1930, Oberndorff; s. of Heinrich Geissler and Maria Buck; m. Susanne Thunack 1962; three s.; ed Univs of

Tübingen and Munich; Dir Office of Minister of Labour and Social Welfare, Baden-Wurttemberg; mem. Bundestag 1965–67, 1980–2002; Minister for Social Welfare, Health and Sport, Rheinland-Pfalz 1967–77; mem. Parl. of Rheinland-Pfalz 1971–79; Gen. Sec. CDU 1977–89, Deputy Chair. 1989–90, mem. Presiding Bd 1990; Deputy Chair. CDU/CSU Parl. group 1991–98; mem. CDU Parl. Cttee 1994; mem. TV Council, Second German TV 1970–82, 1987–92; Fed. Minister for Youth, Family and Health 1982–85; Chair. Kuratoriums Sport und Natur 1992–; Chair. AktionCourage 2002–; Dir Evangelischen Akademie Tutzing 2003–; Bundesverdienstkreuz 1970, Bergverlagspreis Deutsches Alpenverein 1983. *Publications:* Die neue soziale Frage 1976, Der Weg in die Gewalt 1978, Sicherheit für unsere Freiheit 1978, Verwaltete Bürger-Gesellschaft in Fesseln 1978, Grundwerte in der Politik 1979, Zukunftschancen der Jugend 1979, Sport – Geschäft ohne Illusionen? 1980, Mut zur Alternative 1981, Zugluft-Politik in stürmischer Zeit 1990, Heiner Geissler im Gespräch mit Gunter Hofmann und Werner A. Perger 1993, Gefährlicher Sieg 1995, Der Irrweg der Nationalismus 1995, Bergsteigen 1997, Das nicht gehaltene Versprechen 1997, Zeit, das Visier zu öffnen 1998, Where is God? Discussions with the Next Generation 2000, Intolerance: The Misfortune of Our Time 2002, What Say Jesus Today? The Political Message of the Gospel 2003. *Leisure interest:* mountaineering. *Address:* POB 1167, 66990 Dahn, Germany. *Telephone:* (6391) 924949. *Fax:* (6391) 924950. *E-mail:* heiner_geissler@t-online .de. *Website:* www.heiner-geissler.de.

GEITHNER, Timothy Franz, AB, MA; American banking executive, economist and fmr government official; *President and Managing Director, Warburg Pincus LLC;* b. 18 Aug. 1961, Brooklyn, New York; m. Carole M. Sonnenfeld; one s. one d.; ed Dartmouth Coll., Johns Hopkins School of Advanced Int. Studies; worked for Kissinger Assocs, Inc., Washington, DC 1985–88; joined US Treasury Dept 1988, served in several positions in Int. Affairs Div. including Under-Sec. of Treasury for Int. Affairs 1999–2001; Sr Fellow in Int. Econs, Council on Foreign Relations, Washington, DC Feb.–Aug. 2001; Dir Policy Devt and Review Dept, IMF, Washington, DC 2001–03; Pres. and CEO Fed. Reserve Bank of New York 2003–09, Vice-Chair. and Perm. mem. Fed. Open Market Cttee 2003–09; US Sec. of the Treasury, Washington, DC 2009–13; Pres. and Man. Dir Warburg Pincus LLC (pvt. equity firm) 2014–, also mem. Exec. Man. Group; mem. Council on Foreign Relations, Distinguished Fellow 2013–; mem. Bd of Dirs Center for Global Devt, Washington, DC, Nat. Acad. Foundation 2007–; mem. Bd of Trustees RAND Corpn 2006–08; Trustee, Econ. Club of New York; ranked by Forbes magazine amongst The World's Most Powerful People (21st) 2009, (28th) 2010, (18th) 2011. *Address:* Warburg Pincus LLC, 450 Lexington Avenue, New York, NY 10017, USA (office). *Telephone:* (212) 878-0600 (office). *Fax:* (212) 878-9351 (office). *Website:* www .warburgpincus.com (office).

GELB, Bruce S.; American business executive and administrator; fmr Vice-Chair. Bristol-Myers Co., now Sr Consultant; Dir US Information Agency 1989–91; Amb. to Belgium 1991–93; fmr Commr for the UN, Consular Service and Int. Business, New York; fmr Pres. Wilson Council (pvt. sector advisory group for Woodrow Wilson Int. Center for Scholars), also mem. Wilson Center Bd of Trustees; fmr mem. Pres. Bush's Arts and Humanities Cttee; fmr mem. Bd of Trustees John F. Kennedy Center for the Performing Arts; fmr Trustee Howard Univ.; Vice-Chair. Exec. Cttee Madison Square Boys' and Girls' Club; Life Trustee Choate Rosemary Hall School, CT; mem. Bd of Dirs UN Devt Corpn for New York City. *Address:* Wilson Council, Woodrow Wilson International Center for Scholars, Ronald Reagan Building and International Trade Center, One Woodrow Wilson Plaza, 1300 Pennsylvania Avenue, NW, Washington, DC 20004-3027, USA (office). *Telephone:* (202) 691-4000 (office). *Fax:* (202) 691-4001 (office). *Website:* www .wilsoncenter.org (office).

GELB, Peter; American business executive, film and television producer and arts administrator; *General Manager, Metropolitan Opera;* b. 1959; s. of Arthur Gelb and Barbara Gelb; m. Keri-Lynn Wilson; two s. (from a previous m.); fmr Man., Vladimir Horowitz; Pres. Sony Classical USA 1993–95, Pres. Sony Classical Int. Operations 1995–2005; Gen. Man. Metropolitan Opera, New York 2006–; Officer, Ordre des Arts et des Lettres 2010, Chevalier, Légion d'honneur 2013; Dr hc (Macaulay Honors Coll., CUNY) 2008; Emmy Award for Outstanding Classical Program in the Performing Arts 1987, 1990, 1991, Emmy Award for Outstanding Individual Achievement in Int. Programming 1991, Int. Documentary Asscn Award 1991, Grammy Award 2002, Diplomacy Award, Foreign Policy Asscn 2012. *Address:* The Metropolitan Opera, Lincoln Center, New York, NY 10023, USA (office). *Telephone:* (212) 799-3100 (office). *Website:* www.metoperafamily.org (office).

GELBER, (J.) David; American television news producer; b. 1941, New York; s. of the late Isaac Gelber and Florence Gelber; m. Kyoko Inouye 2001; ed Swarthmore Coll.; worked several years with Pacifica Radio in 1970s; fmr TV reporter and producer, Boston, Chicago and New York; fmr Exec. Producer, Peter Jennings Reporting, ABC News; consultant, Soros Foundation 1996; joined CBS News 1976, Exec. Producer, Ed Bradley on Assignment and 60 Minutes; mem. Bd of Mans Swarthmore Coll.; Peabody Award 2000. *Award-winning TV Productions include:* While America Watched: The Bosnia Tragedy (Emmy, DuPont Award), The Peacekeepers: How the UN Failed in Bosnia (Emmy, DuPont Award), Ed Bradley on Assignment: Town Under Siege 1997 (named by Time Magazine Award as one of 10 Best TV shows of the year), CBS News 60 Minutes II: The Church on Trial 2003 (Emmy Award for Outstanding Coverage of a Feature News Story in a News Magazine). *Address:* CBS News, 555 West 57th Street, New York, NY 10019, USA (office). *Telephone:* (212) 975-4114 (office). *Website:* www.cbsnews.com (office).

GELDOF, Bob; Irish rock singer and songwriter; b. 5 Oct. 1954, Dublin; m. Paula Yates 1986 (divorced 1996, died 2000); three d. (one deceased); ed Blackrock Coll.; worked in several casual jobs, including lorry driving, busking, teaching English, working in factory, etc., then journalist on pop music paper, Georgia Strait, Vancouver, Canada; later journalist for New Musical Express, Melody Maker; returned to Dublin and f. rock group, Boomtown Rats 1975–84; solo artist 1986–; organized recording of Do They Know It's Christmas? by Band Aid, raising money for African famine relief Nov. 1984, f. Band-Aid Trust (incorporating Live Aid, Band Aid, Sport Aid) to distribute proceeds 1984, Chair.; organized Live Aid concerts in Wembley Stadium, London and JFK Stadium, Philadelphia, USA with int. TV link-up by satellite 13 July 1985, raised £40 million for famine relief in

Africa; f. Live Aid Foundation, USA; organized publ. of Live Aid book The Greatest Show on Earth 1985; Owner, Planet 24 (TV production co.) 1990–99; Co-founder and Dir (non-exec.) Ten Alps plc 2001–; mem. Africa Comm. 2004–; organized re-recording of Do They Know It's Christmas?, raising money for African famine relief Nov. 2004; organized Live 8 concerts in London, Philadelphia, Paris, Rome and Berlin, with int. TV link-up by satellite, to highlight ongoing problem of global poverty and debt 2 July 2005, The Long Walk to Justice, Edinburgh, Scotland, to present leaders of G8 Summit at Gleneagles with plan to double aid, drop debt and make trade laws fair 6 July 2005; Patron, Exeter Entrepreneurs Society, Univ. of Exeter; Freeman of Ypres 1986; Hon. KBE 1986, Elder of the Repub. of Tanzania; Dr hc (Ghent) 1986, (Univ. Coll. Dublin) 2005; Hon. DLit (London) 1987; Hon. DCL (Newcastle) 2007; Hon. MA (Univ. for the Creative Arts) 2010; Hon. DPhil (Ben-Gurion Univ. of the Negev) 2011; Order of Two Niles (Sudan), Order of Leopold II (Belgium), Irish Peace Prize, UN World Hunger Award, EEC Gold Medal, four Ivor Novello Awards, MTV Video Awards Special Recognition Trophy 1985, American Music Awards Special Award of Appreciation 1986, Third World Prize 1986, BRIT Award for Outstanding Contrib. to Music 2005, Golden Rose Charity Award (Switzerland) 2005, MTV Europe Free Your Mind Award 2005, Man of Peace Award 2005, Nichols-Chancellor's Medal, Vanderbilt Univ. 2008. *Film appear-ances include:* Pink Floyd – The Wall 1982, Number One 1985, Sketches of Frank Gehry 2006, Oh My God 2009. *Recordings include:* albums: with Boomtown Rats: The Boomtown Rats 1977, A Tonic For The Troops 1978, The Fine Art Of Surfacing 1979, Mondo Bongo 1981, V Deep 1982, In the Long Grass 1984; solo: Deep In The Heart Of Nowhere 1986, The Vegetarians Of Love 1990, The Happy Club 1993, Sex Age And Death 2001, How to Compose Popular Songs That Will Sell 2011. *Publications include:* Is That It? (autobiog.) 1986, Geldof in Africa 2005. *Address:* c/o Amanda Hon, PO Box 13995, London, W9 2FL, England (office); Ten Alps plc, 9 Savoy Street, London, WC2E 7HR, England. *Telephone:* (20) 7289-7331 (office); (20) 7878-2484. *E-mail:* amanda.hon@dsl.pipex.com (office). *Website:* www .bobgeldof.com.

GELDYMYRADOV, Khojamyrat; Turkmenistani politician; Deputy Minister of Economy and Finance 2005–07, Co-ordinator of Int. Tech. Aid to Turkmenistan 2005–07, Deputy Prime Minister responsible for Econ. Affairs 2007–09. *Address:* c/o Ministry of Finance, 744000 Aşgabat, ul. 2008 4, Turkmenistan.

GELL-MANN, Murray, PhD; American physicist and academic; *Professor and Distinguished Fellow, Sante Fe Institute;* b. 15 Sept. 1929, New York City; s. of the late Arthur Gell-Mann and Pauline (Reichstein) Gell-Mann; m. 1st J. Margaret Dow 1955 (died 1981); one s. one d.; m. 2nd Marcia Southwick 1992 (divorced 2005); one step-s.; ed Yale Univ., Massachusetts Inst. of Tech.; mem. Inst. for Advanced Study, Princeton 1951, 1955, 1967–68; Instructor, Asst Prof. and Assoc. Prof., Univ. of Chicago 1952–55; Assoc. Prof., Calif. Inst. of Tech. 1955–56, Prof. 1956–66, R. A. Millikan Prof. of Theoretical Physics 1967–93, R. A. Millikan Prof. Emer. 1993–; Research Assoc. Univ. of Illinois 1951, 1953; Visiting Assoc. Prof. Columbia Univ. 1954; Visiting Prof. Collège de France and Univ. of Paris 1959–60, Mass. Inst. of Tech. 1963, European Council for Nuclear Research 1971–72, 1979–80, Univ. of NM 1995–; Consultant, Inst. for Defense Analyses, Arlington, Va 1961–70, RAND Corpn, Santa Monica, Calif. 1956; Overseas Fellow, Churchill Col, Cambridge, England 1966; mem. NASA Physics Panel 1964, President's Science Advisory Cttee 1969–72, Council on Foreign Relations 1975–, President's Council of Advisors on Science and Tech. 1994–2001; Consultant to Los Alamos Scientific Laboratory, Los Alamos, NM 1956–, Laboratory Fellow 1982–; Citizen Regent, Smithsonian Inst. 1974–88; Chair. Western Center, American Acad. of Arts and Sciences 1970–76; Chair. of Bd Aspen Center for Physics 1973–79; Founding Trustee Santa Fe Inst. 1982, Chair. Bd of Trustees 1982–85, Co-Chair. Science Bd 1985–2000, Prof. and Distinguished Fellow 1993–; mem. Bd Calif. Nature Conservancy 1984–93, J. D. and C. T. MacArthur Foundation 1979– (Chair. World Environment and Resource Cttee 1982–97), Lovelace Insts 1993–95; mem. Science and Grants Cttee, Leakey Foundation 1977–88, NAS, American Physical Soc. 1960–, American Acad. of Arts and Sciences 1964–, American Philosophical Soc. 1993–, Science Advisory Cttee, Conservation Inst. 1993, AAAS 1994–, Advisory Bd Network Physics 1999–; Hon. mem. French Physical Soc. 1970; Foreign mem. Royal Soc. 1978–, Pakistan Acad. of Sciences 1985–, Indian Acad. of Sciences 1985–, Russian Acad. of Sciences 1993–; Hon. ScD (Yale) 1959, (Chicago) 1967, (Illinois) 1968, (Wesleyan) 1968, (Utah) 1970, (Columbia) 1977, (Cambridge Univ.) 1980, (Oxford Univ.) 1992, (Southern Illinois Univ.) 1993, (Univ. of Florida) 1994, (Southern Methodist Univ.) 1999; Dr hc (Turin, Italy) 1969; Dannie Heineman Prize, American Physical Soc. 1959, Ernest O. Lawrence Award 1966, Franklin Medal 1967, John J. Carty Medal, NAS 1968, Nobel Prize in Physics 1969, Research Corpn Award 1969, UNEP Roll of Honor for Environmental Achievement 1988, Erice Prize 1990, Sigma Xi Procter Prize for Scientific Achievement 2004, Ellis Island Family Heritage Award 2005, Albert Einstein Medal 2005. *Achievements include;* developed strangeness theory, theory of neutral K mesons, eightfold way theory of approximate symmetry; current algebra, quark scheme; contributed to theory of dispersion relations, theory of weak interaction and formulation of quantum chromodynamics. *Publications:* (with Yuval Ne'eman) The Eightfold Way 1964, The Quark and the Jaguar 1994. *Leisure interests:* historical linguistics, wilderness trips, ornithology, numismatics. *Address:* c/o Santa Fe Institute, 1399 Hyde Park Road, Santa Fe, NM 87501, USA (office). *Telephone:* (505) 984-8800. *Fax:* (505) 982-0565. *E-mail:* mgm@santafe.edu (office). *Website:* www.santafe.edu/sfi/people/mgm (office).

GELLEH, Ismael Omar; Djibouti head of state; *President and Commander-in-Chief of the Armed Forces;* b. 1947, Dire Dawa, Ethiopia; m. Kadra Mahamoud Haïd; joined gen. security dept, French police force 1968, rank of Police Insp. 1970; fmr Chief of Staff of Pres. Hassan Gouled Aptidon; mem. Rassemblement populaire pour le progrès (RPP), currently Pres.; Pres. of Djibouti and Commdr-in-Chief of the Armed Forces May 1999–. *Address:* Office of the President, Djibouti, Republic of Djibouti (office). *E-mail:* sggpr@intnet.dj (office). *Website:* www .presidence.dj (home).

GELLERT, Jay M., BA; American healthcare industry executive; *President and CEO, Health Net Inc.;* b. 13 March 1954; ed Stanford Univ.; Sr Vice-Pres. and COO California Healthcare System 1985–88; Pres. and CEO Bay Pacific Health Corpn (HMO) 1988–91; Advisor, Shattuck Hammond Pnrs –1996; Pres. and COO Health Systems Int. Inc. (HIS, later Health Net Inc.) 1996–97, Dir 1996–97, Exec. Vice-

Pres. and COO Health Net Inc. April–May 1997, Pres. and CEO 1998–, also COO May–Aug. 1998, Dir Feb. 1999–; mem. Bd of Dirs Ventas 2001–, America's Health Insurance Plans (Chair. 2008–), Council for Affordable Quality Healthcare. *Address:* Health Net Incorporated, 21650 Oxnard Street, Woodland Hills, CA 91367, USA (office). *Telephone:* (818) 676-6000 (office). *Fax:* (818) 676-8591 (office). *E-mail:* jay.m.gellert@health.net (office). *Website:* www.healthnet.com (office).

GELMAN, Aleksandr Isaakovich; Russian playwright and scriptwriter; b. 25 Oct. 1933, Moldavia; m. Tatyana Pavlovna Kaletskaya; two s.; ed Kishinev Univ.; mem. CPSU 1956–90; worked in factories 1956–67; corresp. for daily papers 1967–71; wrote scripts for series of documentary films 1971–74; worked with Moscow Art Theatre; People's Deputy of the USSR 1989–91; USSR State Prize 1976. *Film scripts include:* Night Shift 1971, Consider me Grown Up 1974, Xenia, Fyodor's Favourite Wife 1974 (all with T. Kaletskaya), Prize 1975, Feedback (Best Script Writer, All-Union Film Festival 1978) 1977, Clumsy Man 1979, We, The Undersigned 1981, Zinulya 1984, We Met in a Strange Way 1990, Gorbachev: After the Empire 2001, Arie (with Roman Kachanov) 2004. *Theatre work includes:* Feedback 1976, We, the Undersigned 1979, The Bench 1983, Zinulya 1984, Misha's Party (co-author), Pretender 1999, The Most Recent Future 2010, Back, Connection,A Man with Connections, The Bonus. *Television documentary:* Gorbachev: After Empire 2001. *Publication:* Book of Plays 1985. *Address:* Tverskoy, Blvd 3, Apartment 12, 103104 Moscow, Russia (home). *Telephone:* (495) 202-68-59 (home). *E-mail:* idcg@cityline.ru.

GEMAYEL, Amin; Lebanese politician; *President, Al-Kataeb (Lebanese Social Democratic Party);* b. 10 Nov. 1942, Bikfayya; s. of the late Pierre Gemayel; brother of the late Bashir Gemayel; ed St Joseph Univ., Beirut; mem. Parl. 1970–82; Pres. of Lebanon 1982–88; moved to USA 1988, to France 1989, back to Lebanon 2000; The House of the Future, The Amin Gemayel Educational Foundation, Le Reveil newspaper; Pres. Al-Kataeb (Lebanese Social Democratic Party). *Address:* Al-Kataeb, POB 992, place Charles Hélou, Beirut, Lebanon (office). *Telephone:* (1) 584107 (office). *Website:* www.kataeb.org (office).

GEMEDA, Gen. Abedula; Ethiopian army officer and politician; *President, Oromia Regional Government;* career in Ethiopian Armed Forces, fmr Head of Operation and Information Dept, fmr Head of Defence Intelligence Unit –2001 (resgnd); fmr Minister of Defence; Chair. Oromo People's Democratic Org.; Pres. Oromia Regional Govt 2008–. *Address:* Office of the President, Oromia Regional Government, Addis Ababa, Ethiopia (office). *Telephone:* (11) 5510455 (office).

GEMKOW, Stephan; German business executive; *Chairman of the Managing Board, Franz Haniel & Cie. GmbH;* b. 1960; began career as man. consultant for BDO Deutsche Warentreuhand AG; held various management positions at Lufthansa Group from 1990, mem. Man. Bd responsible for Finances 2006–12, for Aviation Services 2009–12; Chair. Man. Bd and Group Human Resources Man. Franz Haniel & Cie. GmbH 2012–; mem. Supervisory Bd Evonik Industries AG; mem. Bd of Dirs Amadeus IT Group, JetBlue Airways Corpn; mem. Comm. of Exchange Experts. *Address:* Franz Haniel & Cie. GmbH, Franz-Haniel-Platz 1, 47119 Duisberg, Germany (office). *Telephone:* (203) 806-0 (office). *Fax:* (203) 806-622 (office). *E-mail:* info@haniel.de (office). *Website:* www.haniel.de (office).

GENACHOWSKI, Julius, BA, JD; American lawyer, business executive and fmr government official; b. 19 Aug. 1962; m. Rachel Goslins; ed Columbia Coll., Columbia Univ., Harvard Law School; Law Clerk to Chief Judge Abner Mikva, US Court of Appeals for DC Circuit 1991–92, to US Supreme Court Justice William J. Brennan Jr 1992, to US Supreme Court Justice David Souter 1993–94; Chief Counsel to Chair. Fed. Communications Comm. (FCC) 1994–97, fmr Sr Official, Chair. FCC 2009–13 (resgnd); worked with mems of US Congress 1995–98, including as mem. Congressional Cttee investigating Iran-Contra Affair; Gen. Counsel and Sr Vice-Pres. of Business Devt, USA Broadcasting 1997–2000; Vice-Pres. of Corp. Devt Ticketmaster Online-Citysearch, Inc. 2000; Sr Vice-Pres. and Gen. Counsel USA Networks Inc, InterActiveCorp 2000–02, Exec. Vice-Pres. and Gen. Counsel 2002, Chief of Business Operations and mem. Office of the Chair. IAC/InterActive Corpn 2003–06; Special Adviser, General Atlantic LLC, Greenwich, Conn. 2006–09; mem. Bd of Dirs The Motley Fool, Web.com, Mark Ecko Enterprises, Beliefnet, Common Sense Media; fmr mem. Bd of Dirs Expedia, Hotels.com, Ticketmaster, Truveo, Rapt; mem. of Advisory Bd Environmental Entrepreneurs (E2). *Address:* c/o Federal Communications Commission, 445 12th Street, SW, Washington, DC 20554, USA.

GENBA, Koichiro; Japanese politician; b. 20 May 1964, Tamura, Fukushima Pref.; ed Sophia Univ., Matsushita Inst. of Govt and Man.; mem. Fukushima Prefectural Ass. 1991–93; mem. House of Reps for Fukushima No 2 Dist (New Party Sakigake) 1993–96, for Tōhoku (Democratic Party of Japan—DPJ) 1996–2000, for Fukushima No 3 Dist 2000–; mem. New Party Sakigake 1993–96; Founder mem. DPJ 1996–, fmr Deputy Sec.-Gen., Chair. Election Campaign Cttee, Policy Research Council 2010–11; Minister of State for Civil Service Reform 2010, for Social Affairs and Gender Equality 2010, for Nat. Policy 2010–11, for Space Policy and Science and Tech. Policy 2011, Minister of Foreign Affairs 2011–12. *Leisure interests:* watching films, reading, sports. *Address:* Democratic Party of Japan, 1-11-1, Nagata-cho, Chiyoda-ku, Tokyo 100-0014, Japan (office). *Telephone:* (3) 3595-9988 (office). *Fax:* (3) 3595-9961 (office). *E-mail:* dpjenews@dpj.or.jp (office). *Website:* www.dpj.or.jp (office).

GENDREAU-MASSALOUX, Michèle; French public servant and organization official; *Rector, Agence Universitaire de la francophonie (AUF);* b. 28 July 1944, Limoges; d. of François Massaloux and Marie-Adrienne Delalais; m. Pascal Gendreau 1970; ed École Normale Supérieure de Jeunes Filles, Sèvres, Inst. d'Etudes Politiques, Paris; univ. teacher, Sorbonne, Villetaneuse (Paris XIII), then Univ. of Limoges (fmr Vice-Pres.); Rector Acad. d'Orléans-Tours 1981–84; Tech. Adviser to Secr.-Gen. for Nat. Educ. and Univs., Presidency of the Repub., then to Secr.-Gen. for Admin. Reform and Improvement of Relations between Public Services and their Users, Deputy Sec.-Gen. 1985–88, Spokesperson 1986–88, Head of Mission May 1988; Rector, Acad. de Paris 1989–98; Conseiller d'Etat 1998; mem. Comm. Nat. de la Communication et des Libertés 1988–89, French Comm. for UNESCO 1991, Conseil orientation Ecole du Louvre 1991, Council, Coll. Univ. Français de Moscou 1991, Council, Coll. Univ. Français de Saint-Petersbourg 1992, Conseil Scientifique de la Cinquième 1996; mem. Comm. de contrôle des sondages 1999; Rector, Agence Universitaire de la francophonie (AUF), Paris

1999–; Prof. Univ. Paris VIII–Vincennes St-Denis 1999–; Dr hc (Univ. of Aberdeen, Univ. of Chile, Laval Univ., Univ. of Moldova, New York Univ., Univ. of Toronto, Univ. of Sofia, Univ. of Bucharest, Univ. of Moncton, Univ. of Ouagadougou); Chevalier, Légion d'honneur, Officier, Ordre Nat. du Mérite, Chevalier, Ordre des Palmes Académiques. *Publication:* Recherche sur l'Humanisme de Francisco de Quevedo 1977, works and translations concerning the Spanish Golden Age. *Leisure interest:* music. *Address:* Agence Universitaire de la francophonie (AUF), 4, place de la Sorbonne, 75005, Paris (office); Conseil d'Etat, 75100 Paris 01 SP (office); 34 rue de Penthièvre, 75008 Paris, France (home). *Telephone:* 1-44-41-18-18 (office). *Fax:* 1-44-41-18-19 (office). *E-mail:* recteur@auf.org (office). *Website:* www.auf.org (office).

GENERALOV, Sergey Vladimirovich; Russian politician and business executive; *Chairman, Russian Biotechnologies;* b. 7 Sept. 1963, Simferopol; ed Moscow Inst. of Energy, Higher School of Man. at State Acad. of Man.; Commercial Dir TET 1991–92; Deputy Chair. NIPEBANK 1992–93; Head of Div., Head of Dept, Promradtechbank 1993; Vice-Pres. YUKOS Oil Co., 1993–97, ROSPROM-YUKOS 1997; Deputy Chair. MENATEP 1997–98; Minister of Fuel and Power Eng of Russian Fed. 1998–99; Dir Fuel and Energy Complex Investments Agency 1999–2000; mem. State Duma 1999–, faction Right-Wing Forces; Head State Duma Comm. for Protection of Investors' Rights –2002; Chair. Russian Biotechnologies Co., Investor Protection Asscn 2002–, Industrial Investors. *Address:* CJSC Russian Biotechnologies, 40/4 Bolshaya Ordynka str., 119017 Moscow, Russia (office). *Telephone:* (495) 981-29-22 (home). *Fax:* (495) 981-29-22 (office). *E-mail:* enp@rusbio.com (office). *Website:* www.rusbio.com (office).

GENG, Huichang; Chinese politician; *Minister of State Security;* b. 1951, Hebei Prov.; Deputy Dir Univ. of Int. Relations, American Research Dept, Beijing Municipality 1985–90, Dir 1990–92; Head, China Inst. of Contemporary Int. Relations 1992–98; Vice-Minister of State Security 1998–2007, Minister of State Security 2007–; mem. Nat. Energy Comm. 2010–; mem. 17th CCP Cen. Cttee 2007–12, 18th CCP Cen. Cttee 2012–. *Address:* Ministry of State Security, 14 Dongchangan Jie, Dongcheng Qu, Beijing 100741, People's Republic of China (office). *Telephone:* (10) 65244702 (office).

GENIEVA, Yekaterina Yuryevna, DLitt, DPhil; Russian librarian and literary scholar; *Director-General, All-Russia State Library of Foreign Literature (VGBIL);* b. 1 April 1946, Moscow; m. Yuri S. Belenky; one d.; ed Moscow State Univ.; nurse, Moscow hosp. 1962–63; Sr Deputy Dir All-Russia State Library of Foreign Literature (VGBIL) 1971–92, Dir-Gen. 1992–; Pres. Inst. Open Soc. (Soros Foundation) 1995–2003, The English-Speaking Union; Vice-Pres. Russian Library Asscn 1994–; mem. Council on Culture, Russian Presidency 1996–2000; mem. Bd First Vice-Pres. Int. Fed. of Library Asscns 1990–99; mem. Editorial Bds journals Biblioteka, Libri, Inostrannaya Literatura, Znamya; Order of Friendship 1999, Order of Gabriela Mistral (Chile) 2002, Cross of Recognition (Latvia) 2005, Order of Merit (Lithuania) 2006, Cross of Merit for Service, First Class (Germany) 2007, Hon. OBE (UK) 2007, Cross Maaryamaa (Estonia) 2008; Hon. DLitt (Univ. of Ill. at Urbana-Champaign) 2001. *Publications include:* monographs, trans. of English authors, numerous articles. *Leisure interests:* books, travelling, Irish culture. *Address:* Office of the Director-General, VGBIL, Nikoloyamskaya str. 1, 109189 Moscow, Russia (office). *Telephone:* (495) 915-36-21 (office). *Fax:* (495) 915-36-37 (office). *E-mail:* genieva@libfl.ru (office). *Website:* www.libfl.ru (office).

GENISARETSKY, Oleg Igorevich; Russian sociologist and organization executive; *Deputy Director, Institute of Management, Russian Academy of Sciences;* b. 28 Feb. 1942, Kovrov, Vladimir region; ed Moscow Inst. of Physics and Eng, Moscow State Univ.; researcher, All-Union Inst. of Tech. Aesthetics 1965–93; Deputy Dir Inst. of Man., Russian Acad. of Sciences 1993–; Pres. Open Museum Asscn, Russian Asscn of Visual Anthropology; CEO Inst. of Synergetic Anthropology; Prof., Inst. of Corp. Entrepreneurship, Higher School of Econs; Triumph Prize. *Publications:* numerous publs on theory and methods of system and artistic design, ecology of culture, aesthetic educ., theoretical sociology of culture and psychology of creativity. *Address:* Institute of Management, Russian Academy of Sciences, Volkhonka str. 14, 119842 Moscow (office); Institute of Synergetic Anthropology, 31-120 Festivalnaya str., 125195 Moscow; Open Museum Association, krasnoyarsk p/b 25221, 660049 Moscow, Russia. *Telephone:* (495) 203-01-09 (office). *Fax:* (495) 203-91-69 (office). *E-mail:* olegen@msses.ru. *Website:* www.im.mesi.ru (office); www.aom.ru; www.synergia-isa.ru.

GENOVÉS, Juan; Spanish artist; b. 31 May 1930, Valencia; ed Escuela Superior de Bellas Artes, Valencia; has taken part in numerous group exhbns; solo exhbns in Spain, Portugal, USA, Italy, Germany, Netherlands, Japan, UK, Cuba, Puerto Rico, Canada, Switzerland, France and S America 1957–; took part in Paris Biennale 1961, Venice Biennale 1962, 1966, São Paulo Biennale 1965; works in collections and museums in Germany, SA, Guinea, Australia, Austria, Belgium, Brazil, Canada, Colombia, Cuba, Spain, Finland, France, Netherlands, England, Israel, Italy, Japan, Mexico, Nicaragua, Poland, Switzerland, USA and Venezuela; Gold Medal, San Marino Biennale 1967, Premio Marzotto Internazionale 1968, Premio Nacional de Artes Plásticas 1984. *Address:* c/o Galería Marlborough, Madrid Orfila 5, 28010 Madrid; Arandilla 17, 28023 Aravaca, Madrid, Spain (home). *Website:* www.juangenoves.com/en.

GENSCHER, Hans-Dietrich; German politician; b. 21 March 1927, Reideburg, Saalkreis; s. of Kurt Genscher and the late Hilda Kreime; m. 1st Luise Schweitzer 1958; m. 2nd Barbara Schmidt 1969; one d.; ed Leipzig and Hamburg Univs; Scientific Asst, Parl. Free Democratic Party (FDP) 1956, later Sec., Hon. Chair. 1992–; Fed. Party Man. 1962–64, Vice-Chair. 1968–74, Chair. 1974–85; Deputy in Bundestag 1965–98; Fed. Minister of the Interior 1969–74; Vice-Chancellor, Minister of Foreign Affairs 1974–92; Chair. WMP Eurocom AG, Berlin 1998–; Counsel Büsing, Müffelmann & Theye, Berlin 1999–; Man. Partner, Hans-Dietrich Genscher Consult GmbH 2000–; Pres. German Council on Foreign Relations 2001–03; Asscn Friends and Patrons State Opera, Berlin; Hon. Prof., Free Univ. of Berlin 1994, Peking 1999; Hon. Citizen of Costa Rica 1988; Freeman of Halle 1993, of Berlin 1997; Bundesverdienstkreuz 1973 and other medals; numerous hon. doctorates 1977–2002; Onassis Foundation Award 1991. *Publications include:* Bundestagsreden 1972, Deutsche Aussenpolitik, Reden und Aufsätze aus 10 Jahren, 1974–84, Nach vorn gedacht... Perspektiven deutscher Aussenpolitik 1986, Erinnerungen (memoirs) 1995. *Leisure interest:* reading. *Address:* Hans-

Dietrich Genscher's Personal Office, Postfach 200 655, 53136 Bonn, Germany (office). *Fax:* (228) 264652 (office). *E-mail:* buero@genscher.de (office). *Website:* www.genscher.de (office).

GENSLER, Gary, BS, MBA; American government official; *Chairman, Commodity Futures Trading Commission;* b. Baltimore, Md; m. Francesca Danieli (died 2006); three d.; ed Wharton School, Univ. of Pennsylvania; joined The Goldman Sachs Group, LP (int. investment banking firm) in 1979, worked in Mergers and Acquisition Dept 1979–84, assumed responsibility for firm's efforts advising media cos 1984–88, Pnr 1988–97, joined Fixed Income Div. and directed Goldman's Fixed Income and Currency trading efforts in Tokyo –1995, Co-head of Finance for Goldman Sachs world-wide 1995–97; Asst US Sec. of the Treasury for Financial Markets, Washington, DC 1997–99, also served as a sr mem. Treasury Financing Group and Working Group on Financial Markets, Under-Sec. of the Treasury for Domestic Finance 1999–2001; fmr Sr Adviser to US Senator Paul Sarbanes (one of authors of legislation that eventually became Sarbanes-Oxley Act); sr adviser to Senator Hillary Clinton's presidential campaign and, after Democratic Primary, to Barack Obama presidential campaign 2008; Chair. US Commodity Futures Trading Comm., Washington, DC 2009–. *Publication:* The Great Mutual Fund Trap – An Investment Recovery Plan (with Gregory Arthur Baer) 2002. *Address:* Commodity Futures Trading Commission, Three Lafayette Centre, 1155 21st Street, NW, Washington, DC 20581, USA (office). *Telephone:* (202) 418-5000 (office). *Fax:* (202) 418-5521 (office). *E-mail:* Questions@cftc.gov (office). *Website:* www.cftc.gov (office).

GENTIL DA SILVA MARTINS, António (Tony), MD; Portuguese paediatric and plastic surgeon and paediatric oncologist; *Consultant in Surgical Pediatric Oncology, Instituto Português de Oncologia Lisboa Francisco Gentil;* b. 10 July 1930, Lisbon; s. of António Augusto da Silva Martins and Maria Madalena Gentil da Silva Martins; m. Maria Guilhermina Ivens Ferraz Jardim 1963; three s. five d.; ed Univ. of Lisbon; Medical Faculty 1953, Univ. of Lisbon, Course of Pedagogical Sciences 1954; intern, Hospitais Civis, Lisbon; fmr Registrar, Alder Hey Children's Hosp., Liverpool, UK; Founder and Head, Paediatric multidisciplinary Dept, Instituto Português de Oncologia de Lisboa Francisco Gentil 1960–87, Consultant in Surgical Pediatric Oncology 1987–; paediatric surgeon, Hosp. D. Estefânia (Children's Hosp.), Lisbon 1965, Dir of Paediatric Surgery 1987–2000; Assoc. Prof. of Paediatric Surgery, Faculty of Medical Sciences, Lisbon 1984–2000; Temporary Consultant, Paediatric Cancer, WHO 1977, EEC 1991; Pres. Portuguese Soc. of Plastic and Reconstructive Surgery 1968–74, Ordem dos Médicos (Portuguese Medical Asscn) 1978–86, Portuguese Asscn of Paediatric Surgeons 1975–84, 1991–94, World Medical Asscn 1981–83, Southern Br. Portuguese League Against Cancer 1988–94, Portuguese League Against Cancer 1995–97; Founder-Acreditar Int. Confed. of Children's Cancer Parents Orgs; Founder and mem. Int. Soc. of Pediatric Oncology (SIOP), Int. Soc. of Pediatric Surgical Oncology (IPSO); Hon. mem. and Vice-Pres. Gen. Ass., Nat. Confed. of Portuguese Family Asscns 2004–08; Founder and Hon. mem. Portuguese Fed. of Badminton 1956, Int. Coll. of Surgeons 1965, Vice-Pres. 2004–06 (Founder and Pres. Portuguese Section 2005–07); mem. Exec. Council World Fed. of Asscns of Paediatric Surgeons 1983–89, Council Int. Conf. of Childhood Cancer Parent Orgs 1994–95; Founder and Pres. Portuguese Olympic Athletes Asscn 2003–12, CAVITOP (Center for Support of Victims of Torture Portugal) 2002–; Accreditar (Children with Cancer), Rarissimas (Rare Diseases), Ethics in Sports; mem. Emer. Portugal Acad. of Medicine; mem. numerous other professional socs; Hon. mem. Portuguese League against Cancer, AMI (Int. Medical Assistance), Portuguese Cancer League; Grande Oficial da Ordem do Infante D. Henrique 1980, Great Cross 2009, Order of Henry the Navigator; Silva Pereia Award 1972, awarded Silver Plate for film on separation of conjoined twins 1980, Keys of Miami and Dale County 1983, Diploma of Honour, Cuban Medical Asscn in Exile 1983, Gold Medal Ministry of Health 2001, Medal of Honour, Portuguese Medical Asscn 2002, Ordem dos Médicos, Medal of Our Lady of Vila Viçosa 2007; Merit Prize for prevention in oncology, Prize for Ethics in Sports and numerous other awards. *Achievements include:* separation of six pairs of conjoined twins with nine survivors. *Films:* Separation of Siamese Twins, Vagimoplasty with Labia Minora, Partial Nephrectomy for Unilatral Wilms Tumours, A So-called Inoperable Neuroblastoma, and others. *Publications include:* textbook on Plastic Surgery of the Ibero-Latin-American Foundation of Plastic Surgery (co-author) 1986 (revised edn 2008), Le Médecin et les droits de l'homme (co-author) 1982, Head and Neck Cancer in Children, Elementos de Psiquiatria da Criança e do Adolescente, O Médico e a Eutanásia, Atlas of Paediatric Surgery (co-author), Psychosocial Issues in Pediatric Cancer (co-author), Educação pelo Desporto; paediatric chapter in Textbook of Surgery 2006, Atlas of Pediatric Surgery (co-author), Medical Associations and Human Rights, Pediatric Urology (co-author). *Leisure interests:* target-shooting (pistol, Olympics, Rome 1960, Portuguese rifle champion and record holder), volleyball (Portuguese champion), lawn tennis (Portuguese Jr Champion, men's doubles), table tennis, badminton, collecting stamps and coins, music, photography. *Address:* Rua de Campolide 166G, 1070-037 Lisbon (office); Av. Almirante Reis 242, 000-057 Lisbon, Portugal (home). *Telephone:* (21) 384-1860 (office); (21) 848-9540 (home); 93-9555162 (mobile). *E-mail:* agentilmartins@gmail.com (home).

GENTZ, Manfred, LLB, LLD; German business executive; *Chairman, Commission for German Corporate Governance;* b. 22 Jan. 1942, Riga, Latvia; ed Univ. of Berlin, Univ. of Lausanne, Switzerland, Berlin Free Univ.; joined Daimler-Benz AG 1970, mem. Man. Bd 1983–90, CEO Daimler-Benz Interservices 1990–95, Chief Financial Officer Daimler-Benz AG 1995–98, mem. Man. Bd Daimler Chrysler AG (after merger of Daimler-Benz and Chrysler Corpn) 1998–2004; Chair. Zurich Financial Services Ltd and Zurich Insurance Co. Ltd 2005–12; Chair. Supervisory Bd Eurohypo AG 2005–06, Deutsche Börse AG 2008–; mem. Bd of Supervisors Hannoversche Lebensversicherung AG 1985–2005 (Proxy Chair. 1990–2005), Agrippina Versicherung AG 1987–95, DWS Investment GmbH 1995–2009, Zurich Beteiligungs-Aktiengesellschaft (Deutschland) 1996–2005, Deutsche Börse AG 2003–12 (Chair. 2008–12), Adidas AG 2004–09; mem. Exec. Bd ICC, Chair. German Nat. Cttee 2014; Chair. Curatorship of Technische Universität Berlin 2007–10; mem. Comm. for German Corporate Governance 2006– (Chair. 2013–) mem. several scientific and cultural insts. *Address:* Alte Potsdamer Straße 5, 10785 Berlin, Germany (office). *Telephone:* (30) 25941500 (office); (30) 25941505 (office). *E-mail:* manfred.gentz@mg-office-berlin.com (office).

GENZEL, Reinhard, PhD; German astrophysicist and academic; *Director and Scientific Member, Max Planck Institute for Extraterrestrial Physics;* b. 24 March 1952, Bad Homburg vor der Höhe; ed Univs of Freiburg and Bonn, Max Planck Inst. for Radio Astronomy; Postdoctoral Fellow, Harvard-Smithsonian Center for Astrophysics, Cambridge, Mass, USA 1978–80, Miller Fellow 1980–82; Assoc. Prof. of Physics and Assoc. Research Astronomer, Space Sciences Lab., Univ. of California, Berkeley 1981–85, Prof. of Physics 1985–86, 1999–; Dir and Scientific mem., Max Planck Inst. for Extraterrestrial Physics, Garching 1986–; lectured at Ludwig Maximilians Univ., Munich; mem. US and German Astronomical and Physical Socs; Foreign mem. NAS 2000, Acad. des sciences (Institut de France) 1998, Royal Spanish Acad. of Sciences 2011, Royal Soc.; mem. Deutsche Akad. der Naturforscher Leopoldina 2002, European Acad. of Sciences 2002; Sr mem. Bayerische Akad. der Wissenschaften 2003; Fellow, American Physical Soc. 1985; Hon. Prof., Univ. of Munich 1988; Dr hc (Leiden); Otto Hahn Medal, Max Planck Gesellschaft 1980, NSF Presidential Young Investigator Award 1984, Newton Lacy Pierce Prize, American Astronomical Soc. 1986, Gottfried Wilhelm Leibniz Prize, Deutsche Forschungsgemeinschaft 1990, De Vaucouleurs Medal, Univ. of Texas 2000, Prix Jules Janssen, French Astronomical Soc. 2000, Stern Gerlach Medal for experimental physics, Deutsche Physikalische Gesellschaft 2003, Balzan Prize for Infrared Astronomy 2003, Petrie Prize, Canadian Astronomical Soc. 2005, Albert Einstein Medal 2007, Shaw Prize (co-recipient) 2008, 'Galileo 2000' Prize 2009, Karl Schwarzschild Medal, Deutsche Astronomische Gesellschaft 2011, Crafoord Prize, Royal Swedish Acad. of Sciences (co-recipient) 2012. *Publications:* numerous papers in professional journals. *Address:* Max-Planck-Institut für extraterrestrische Physik, PO Box 1312, 85741 Garching, Germany (office). *Telephone:* (89) 30000-3280 (office). *Fax:* (89) 30000-3601 (office). *E-mail:* genzel@mpe.mpg.de (office); genzel@socrates.berkeley.edu (office). *Website:* www.mpg.de/463069/extraterrestrische_physik_wissM1 (office); www .physics.berkeley.edu/research/faculty/genzel.html (office).

GEOANĂ, Mircea Dan, LLB; Romanian politician and international organization official; b. 14 July 1958, Bucharest; m. Mihaela Geoană; one s. one d.; ed Bucharest Polytechnic Inst., Univ. of Bucharest, Ecole Nat. d'Admin, Paris, France, Harvard Univ., USA, Acad. for Econ. Studies, Bucharest; joined Ministry of Foreign Affairs 1990, Dir European Affairs Dept, Head of Romanian Del. to CSCE Cttee of Sr Officials 1991, Ministry Spokesperson 1993–95, Dir-Gen. for Asia, Latin America, Middle East and Africa 1994, Dir-Gen. for Europe, N America, Asia, Latin America, Middle East and Africa 1995; Amb. to USA 1996–2000; Minister of Foreign Affairs 2000–05; Chair.-in-Office OSCE 2001–; cand. for Mayor of Bucharest 2004; mem. Senate (Partidul Social Democrat (PSD—Social Democratic Party) 2004–11, Ind. 2011–) 2004–, Pres. 2008–11; Pres. PSD 2005–10, dismissed from party for refusing to stand down as Pres. of the Senate Nov. 2011; unsuccessful presidential cand. 2009; Prof., Nat. School for Political and Admin Sciences, Nicolae Titulescu Univ., Bucharest; NATO Fellow on Democratic Insts 1994; Commdr of Nat. Order Star of Romania 2000. *Publications:* numerous articles on Euro-Atlantic integration. *Address:* Senatul (The Senate), 050711 Bucharest 5, Calea 13 Septembrie 1–3, Romania (office). *Telephone:* (21) 3113532 (office). *Fax:* (21) 2223272 (home). *E-mail:* geoana .mircea@senat.ro (office). *Website:* www.senat.ro (office); www.mirceageoana.ro.

GEOGHEGAN, Michael F., CBE; British banking executive; b. 4 Oct. 1953, Windsor; m.; two s.; joined HSBC (Hong Kong and Shanghai Banking Corpn) Group 1973, spent 12 years in N and S America, eight years in Asia, seven years in Middle East, Pres. HSBC Bank Brasil SA/Banco Múltiplo 1997–2003, responsible for all of HSBC's business throughout S America 2000–03, Chief Exec. HSBC PLC 2004–06, Exec. Dir HSBC Holdings 2004–10, Group Chief Exec. 2006–10 (resgnd), Chair. Group Man. Bd, Chair. The Hongkong and Shanghai Banking Corpn Ltd 2010, Chair. HSBC Bank USA, N.A. –2009, HSBC USA Inc. –2009, HSBC Bank Canada, Deputy Chair. HSBC Bank plc, a Dir of HSBC France, HSBC North America Holdings Inc., HSBC Nat. Bank USA, HSBC Latin America Holdings (UK) Ltd (Chair. –2009); Dir (non-exec.) and Chair. Young Enterprise UK. *Address:* c/o HSBC Holdings, 8 Canada Square, London, E14 5HQ, England. *Telephone:* (20) 7991-8888. *E-mail:* pressoffice@hsbc.com. *Website:* www.hsbc.com.

GEOGHEGAN-QUINN, Máire; Irish EU official, politician, international organization official and fmr business consultant; *Commissioner for Research, Innovation and Science, European Commission;* b. 5 Sept. 1950, Carna, Co. Galway; d. of the late John Geoghegan and of Barbara Folan; m. John V. Quinn 1973; two s.; ed Carysfort Teacher Training Coll. Blackrock, Co. Dublin; fmr primary school teacher; mem. Galway City Council 1985–92; mem. Dáil (Parl.) 1975–97; Parl. Sec. to Minister of Industry, Commerce and Energy 1977–78; Minister of State with responsibility for Consumer Affairs, Ministry of Industry, Commerce and Energy 1977–78; Minister for the Gaeltacht 1979–81; Minister of State with responsibility for Youth and Sport, Dept of Educ. March–Dec. 1982; Minister of State for European Affairs 1987, 1991; Minister for Tourism, Transport and Communications 1992, of Justice 1993; columnist, Irish Times 1997–2000; mem. Audit Devt and Reports Group, Court of Auditors of the EC 2000–10; Commr for Research, Innovation and Science, EC 2010–; consultant to several cos; fmr Chair. The Saffron Initiative; fmr Vice-Pres. Fianna Fáil; fmr Dir (non-exec.) The Ryan Hotel Group, Aer Lingus; fmr TV broadcaster. *Publication:* The Green Diamond (novel) 1996. *Leisure interests:* reading, writing and travel. *Address:* European Commission, rue de la Loi 200, 1049 Brussels, Belgium (office). *Telephone:* (2) 299-11-11 (office). *Fax:* (2) 295-01-38 (office). *Website:* ec.europa.eu (office).

GEORGE; British artist; b. (George Passmore), 1942, Devon; ed Dartington Hall Adult Educ. Centre, Dartington Hall Coll. of Art, Oxford Art School, St Martin's School of Art, London; began working with Gilbert (Proesch) in 1967 as Gilbert & George; est. reputation as performance artists, presenting themselves, identically dressed, as living sculptures; later work includes large composite drawings and vividly coloured photo-pieces often featuring likenesses of the artists; work underpinned by 'Art for all' philosophy; works address social issues, taboos and artistic conventions; work held in public collections in UK and abroad; Dr hc (London Metropolitan Univ.) 2008; Turner Prize 1986. *Publications include:* Manifesto: What Our Art Means, Gilbert and George: The Complete Pictures 2007. *Address:* White Cube, 48 Hoxton Square, London, N1 6PB, England (office).

Telephone: (20) 7930-5373 (office). *Fax:* (20) 7749-7480 (office). *E-mail:* g-and-g@dircon.co.uk (office). *Website:* www.whitecube.com (office).

GEORGE, HE Cardinal Francis Eugene, OMI, PhD, STD; American ecclesiastic; *Archbishop of Chicago;* b. 16 Jan. 1937, Chicago, Ill.; ed Univ. of Ottawa, Canada, Catholic Univ. of America, Tulane Univ., Pontifical Urban Univ., Rome; ordained Priest of Oblates of Mary Immaculate 1963; Bishop of Yakima 1990–96; Archbishop of Portland, Ore. 1996–97; Archbishop of Chicago 1997–; cr. Cardinal (Cardinal-Priest of San Bartolomeo all'Isola) 1998; participated in Papal Conclave 2005, 2013; Vice-Pres. US Conf. of Catholic Bishops 2004–07, Pres. 2007–10; mem. Congregation for Evangelization of Peoples 1999–, Congregation for Insts of Consecrated Life and for Socs of Apostolic Life 1998–, Congregation for Oriental Churches 2001–, Pontifical Comm. for the Cultural Heritage of the Church 1999–, Pontifical Council Cor Unum 1998–, Pontifical Council for Culture 2004–, Council for World Synod of Bishops 2001–; Chancellor Catholic Church Extension Soc., Chicago 1997–, Univ. of St Mary of the Lake, Mundelein, Ill. 1997–; Publr Catholic New World and Chicago Catolico 1997–; Papal Appointee to Synod on Consecrated Life 1994; Trustee, Basilica of Nat. Shrine of Immaculate Conception 1997–, Catholic Univ. of America 1993–, Papal Foundation 1997–; mem. Bd of Dirs Nat. Catholic Bio-ethics Center, Boston 1994–; Kt of Malta; Dr hc (Univ. of Portland) 1997, (John Marshall Law School) 1998, (Loyola Univ. of Chicago) 1998, (Franciscan Univ. of Steubenville) 2000, (Barat Coll.) 2000, (Creighton Univ.) 2001, (St Xavier Univ.) 2004; Outstanding Educator of America 1972, 1973. *Publications:* Inculturation and Ecclesi Communion 1990, The Difference God Makes: A Catholic Vision of Faith, Communion, and Culture 2009. *Address:* Archdiocese of Chicago, PO Box 1979, Chicago, IL 60690-1979 (office); Archdiocese of Chicago, 835 North Rush Street, Chicago, IL 60611, USA (office). *Telephone:* (312) 751-8230 (office). *Fax:* (312) 534-6379 (office). *E-mail:* archbishop@archchicago.org (office). *Website:* www.archdiocese-chgo.org (office).

GEORGE, Jennie, BA; Australian trade union official and politician; b. 20 Aug. 1947, Italy; ed Burwood Girls High School, Univ. of Sydney; Gen. Sec. NSW Teachers Fed. 1980–82, Pres. 1986–89, Life mem.; mem. Exec. Australian Council of Trade Unions 1983, Vice-Pres. 1987, Asst Sec. 1991–95, Pres. 1996–2000; Asst Nat. Dir Trade Union Training Authority 1989–91; Fed. MP for Throsby 2001–10; currently Alumnus, Faculty of Educ. and Social Work. *Address:* The University of Sydney, Sydney, 2600 NSW, Australia (office). *Telephone:* (2) 9036-9222 (office). *Website:* sydney.edu.au/education_social_work (office).

GEORGE, Marcus, MEng, PhD; Iraqi/Canadian civil engineer and business executive; *CEO, EC Consulting Engineers;* ed Baghdad Univ., Univ. of Glamorgan, UK; early career working in Kuwait and Canada; worked several years in Iraqi public sector, worked with numerous int. construction cos including Skidmore Owings Merrill Architects; moved to Dubai 1992; f Engineering Consortium (EC) Consulting Engineers 1997, currently CEO. *Address:* EC Consulting Engineers, Dubai, United Arab Emirates (office). *Fax:* (4) 2830771 (office). *Website:* www.ec-uae.com (office).

GEORGE, Peter J., CM, BA, MA, PhD; Canadian economist, academic and university administrator; *President and Vice-Chancellor, McMaster University;* b. 12 Sept. 1941, Toronto, Ont.; m. Allison Barrett; one s. two d.; ed Univ. of Toronto; Lecturer, McMaster Univ. 1965–67, Asst Prof. 1967–71, Assoc. Prof. 1971–80, Prof. of Econs 1980–, Assoc. Dean of Grad. Studies 1974–79, Dean Faculty of Social Sciences 1980–89, Pres. and Vice-Chancellor, McMaster Univ. 1995–; Pres. Council of Ont. Univs 1991–95; fmr Chair. Council of Deans of Arts and Science of Ont.; fmr mem. Ont. Council on Univ. Affairs; mem. Bd of Dirs C. D. Howe Inst., Golden Key Int. Honour Soc., Foundation for Educ. Exchange between Canada and USA, Ont. Inst. for Cancer Research; Trustee, Univ. Sharjah, UAE; Hon. DUniv, Hon. DLitt, Hon. LLD. *Publications:* Government Subsidies and the Construction of the Canadian Pacific Railway 1981, The Emergence of Industrial America: Strategic Factors in American Economic Growth Since 1870 1982. *Leisure interests:* fishing, golf. *Address:* Office of the President, McMaster University, 1280 Main Street West, Hamilton, ON L8S 4L8, Canada (office). *Telephone:* (905) 525-9140 (office). *E-mail:* preswww@mcmaster.ca (office). *Website:* www.mcmaster.ca/pres (office).

GEORGE, Richard (Rick) Lee, OC, BS, JD; Canadian (b. American) energy industry executive; b. 16 May 1950, Bush, Colo; s. of Albert H. George and Betty Lou McDill; m. Julie G. White 1972; two s. one d.; ed Colorado State Univ., Univ. of Houston, Harvard Business School; Deputy Man. Dir Sun Oil Britain, London, UK 1982–86, District Man., Aberdeen, UK 1986–87; Vice-Pres. Sun Exploration and Production, Dallas, Texas 1987–88; Man. Dir Sun Int. Exploration and Production, London 1988–91, Pres. and COO Suncor Energy Inc., Ont. Feb.–Oct. 1991, Pres. and CEO 1991–2011 (merged with Petro-Canada 2009), CEO 2011–12; mem. Bd of Dirs Enbridge Inc., Dofasco Inc., GlobalSantaFe Corpn, Transocean Offshore Deepwater Drilling Inc., Canadian Pacific Railway 2011–, Royal Bank of Canada 2012–; Chair. Canadian Council of Chief Execs 2003–06 (mem. Bd of Dirs), Gov. Gen.'s Canadian Leadership Conf. 2008; mem. North American Competitiveness Council 2006– (Chair. Canadian contingent 2008), Calgary Cttee to End Homelessness 2007; Outstanding CEO of the Year 1999, Canadian Business Leader Award 2001, Alberta Business Person of the Year 2001, inducted into Petroleum Hall of Fame 2008. *Leisure interests:* skiing, golf, fitness. *Address:* Office of the Board, Royal Bank of Canada, 200 Bay Street, South Tower, Toronto, ON M5J 2J5, Canada (office). *E-mail:* info@rbc.com (office). *Website:* www.rbc.com (office).

GEORGE, Susan; British actress, producer, photographer, author and horse breeder; b. (Susan Melody George), 26 July 1950, London, England; d. of Norman Alfred George and Eileen Percival; m. Simon MacCorkindale 1984 (died 2010); began acting career 1954; Owner Georgian Arabians, Somerset, Amy Int. Productions, London; Dir SG Naturally Ltd, Susan George Photography Ltd. *Theatre:* The Sound of Music 1962, The Country Girl 1984, Rough Crossing 1987. *Films include:* Cup Fever, Davey Jones' Locker, Billion Dollar Brain, Twinky 1969, Spring and Port Wine 1970, Eyewitness 1970, Straw Dogs 1971, Dirty Mary and Crazy Larry 1974, Mandingo 1975, Out of Season 1975, A Small Town in Texas 1977, Tomorrow Never Comes 1978, Venom 1980, A Texas Legend 1981, The House Where Evil Dwells 1982, The Jigsaw Man 1984, Czechmate 1985, Lightning, The White Stallion 1986, Stealing Heaven (producer) 1987, That Summer of White Roses (also producer) 1988, The House That Mary Bought (also

producer) 1994, Diana and Me 1997, In Your Dreams 2008, City of Life 2009, The Silence (short) 2010. *Television appearances include:* Swallows and Amazons, Human Jungle, The Right Attitude 1968, Dr Jekyll and Mr Hyde 1973, Lamb to the Slaughter 1979, Royal Jelly 1979, The Bob Hope Special 1979, Pajama Tops 1982, Masquerade 1983, Hotel 1985, Blacke's Magic 1986, Jack the Ripper 1988, The Castle of Adventure 1990, Counterstrike 1990, Cluedo 1992, Stay Lucky 1992, Tales of Mystery and Imagination – The Black Cat 1995, EastEnders 2001. *Publication:* illustrated book of poetry 1987. *Leisure interests:* singing, riding, homœopathy, travel. *Address:* c/o Chatto & Linnit Ltd, 123 King's Road, Chelsea, London, SW3 4PL, England (office); Georgian Arabians, PO Box 55, Minehead, Somerset, TA24 7WA, England (office). *Telephone:* (20) 7352-7722 (office); (1398) 371187 (office). *Fax:* (20) 7636-2888 (office). *E-mail:* info@georgianarabians.com. *Website:* www.georgianarabians.com (office); www.susangeorgeofficialwebiste.co.uk; www.sgnaturally.com.

GEORGE-WOUT, Lucille Andrea; Curaçao politician; *Governor of Curaçao;* b. 26 Feb. 1950; m. Herman George; began career as youth social worker 1971–80; Sec., Partido MAN (Movementu Antia Nobo) 1979; mem. Island Council of Curaçao (Parl.) 1980–84, 1986–90; Co-founder Partido Alternativo Real (PAR) (Real Alternative Party) 1993; Speaker, States (Parl.) of Netherlands Antilles 1994–98; fmr Commr of Finance, Island Territory of Curaçao; Minister for Work and Social Affairs, Netherlands Antilles 1999–2001; Gov. of Curaçao (first female) 2013–. *Address:* Office of the Governor, Fort Amsterdam 2, Willemstad, Curaçao (office). *Telephone:* (9) 461-2148 (office). *Fax:* (9) 461-2045 (office). *E-mail:* adjudant@kgcur.org (office). *Website:* www.gouverneurvancuracao.org (office).

GEORGEL, Pierre, DEnLett; French museum director; *Director, Musée de l'Orangerie;* b. 14 Jan. 1943, Safi, Morocco; s. of Lucien Georgel and Santia Maria Georgel (née Santini); m. Chantal Martinet 1985; ed Univs of Montpellier, Paris and Lille, Ecole du Louvre, Paris; Asst, Musée du Louvre 1966–70; seconded to CNRS, Paris 1970–74; Curator of Graphic Art, Musée Nat. d'Art Moderne 1974–79; Dir Musée des Beaux-Arts, Dijon 1980–86; Dir Musée Picasso, Paris 1986–89; Chief Curator of French Museums (based at Musée Picasso) 1989–93; Dir Musée nat. de l'Orangerie des Tuileries 1993–; Prof., Ecole du Louvre 1980–85, 1995–96; Conservateur-général du Patrimoine 2000. *Publications:* Dessins de Victor Hugo 1971, La Gloire de Victor Hugo 1985, La Peinture dans la peinture 1987, Courbet: le Poème de la nature 1995, Monet: le Cycle Nymphéas 1999. *Address:* Musée de l'Orangerie, Jardin des Tuileries, 75041 Paris, Cedex 01 (office); 41 Boulevard Saint-Germain, 75005 Paris, France (home). *Telephone:* 1-44-77-80-07 (office). *Website:* www.musee-orangerie.fr (office).

GEORGELIN, Gen. Jean-Louis; French military officer; *Grand Chancellor, Ordre National de la Légion d'honneur;* b. 30 Aug. 1948, Aspet (Haute-Garonne); ed Prytanée Nat. Militaire, Mil. Acad. of St Cyr, Command and Gen. Staff Coll., Fort Leavenworth, Kan., USA, Centre for Advanced Mil. Studies, Paris; First Lt, Platoon Leader, 9th Airborne Infantry Bn 1970–73; Instructor, Infantry School, Montpellier 1973–76; Capt. Co. Cadre, 153rd Infantry Bn 1976–79; Dept of Mil. Intelligence 1979–80; ADC to Army Chief of Staff 1980–82; promoted to Maj. 1982, to Lt Col 1985, to Col 1988; Chief of Financial Planning Office, Army Staff 1988–91; Commdr 153rd Infantry Bn 1991–93; Army Asst to Chief of Mil. Cabinet of the Prime Minister 1994–97; promoted to Brig. Gen. 1997; Second-in-Command 11th Airborne Div., then Chief J5, Stabilization Force (SFOR) in fmr Yugoslavia 1997–98; Chief of Plans and Programmes Div., Jt Defence HQ 1998–2001; promoted to Maj. Gen. 2000, to Lt Gen. 2002; Chief of Mil. Staff 2002–06; promoted to Army Gen. (France) 2003; Chief of Defence Staff 2006–10; Grand Chancellor, Ordre nat. de la Légion d'honneur and Chancellor, Ordre nat. du Mérite 2010–; Grand' Croix, Légion d'honneur, Ordre nat. du Mérite; numerous other foreign decorations. *Address:* Grande chancellerie de la Légion d'honneur, 1 rue de Solférino, 75700 Paris 07 SP, France (office). *Telephone:* 1-40-62-83-13 (office). *Fax:* 1-45-56-02-98 (office). *Website:* www.legiondhonneur.fr (office).

GEORGES, Michel A. J., MSc; Belgian geneticist and academic; *Professor of Genetics, Faculty of Veterinary Medicine, University of Liège;* b. 1959, Schoten; ed Univ. of Liège, Univ. of Brussels; Asst Prof., Univ. of Liège 1983–88, Prof. of Genetics, Faculty of Veterinary Medicine 1994–; specializes in animal genetics and genomics; Assoc. Prof., Dept of Human Genetics, Univ. of Utah, USA 1991–93; mem. Belgian Royal Acad. of Medicine; Wolf Foundation Prize in Agric. 2007, Francqui Prize 2008. *Address:* Université de Liège, Faculty of Veterinary Medicine, 9 place du 20 Août, Liège 4000, Belgium (office). *Telephone:* (4) 366-21-11 (office). *E-mail:* michel.georges@ulg.ac.be (office). *Website:* www.ulg.ac.be/fmv (home).

GEORGESCU, Florin, PhD; Romanian economist, politician and central banker; b. 25 Nov. 1953, Bucharest; ed Acad. of Econ. Studies, Bucharest; Fulbright Scholar, Kansas City Univ., USA 1991–92; Assoc. Prof., Acad. of Econ. Studies; Sec. of State, Ministry of Finance 1992, Minister of State 1992–96; mem. Chamber of Deputies (Social Democratic Party) for Olt Electoral Constituency 1996–2004, Pres. Chamber of Deputies Comm. for Budget, Finance and Banks 2000–04, mem. Del. to Parl. Ass. of Black Sea Econ. Cooperation, Parl. Group of Friendship with Repub. of Slovenia 2000–, Pres. Parl. Group of Friendship with Repub. of Bulgaria 2000; First Deputy Gov. and Vice-Chair. Nat. Bank of Romania (Banca Naţională a României) 2004–12; Deputy Prime Minister and Minister of Public Finance May–Dec. 2012; Prof., Bucharest Univ. of Econ. Studies; Kt, Order of the Star of Romania 2002, Order of Industrial and Commercial Merit 2007, Grand Officer, Order of the Star of Romania 2010. *Publications include:* more than 200 studies and papers. *Address:* Faculty of Economics, Bucharest University of Economic Studies, 71131 Bucharest, 15–17 Dorobanti Avenue, District 1, Romania (office). *Telephone:* (21) 3191900 (office). *Fax:* (21) 3129549 (office). *E-mail:* international@ase.ro (office). *Website:* www.ase.ro (office).

GEORGESCU, Peter Andrew, MBA; American advertising executive (retd); *Chairman Emeritus, Young & Rubicam Inc.;* b. 9 March 1939, Bucharest, Romania; s. of V. C. Georgescu and Lygia Bocu; m. Barbara A. Armstrong 1965; one s.; ed Princeton and Stanford Univs; joined Young & Rubicam Inc., New York 1963, Dir of Marketing 1977–79, Exec. Vice-Pres. and Dir Cen. Region, Young & Rubicam Inc., Chicago 1979–82, Pres. Young & Rubicam Int., New York 1982–86, Young & Rubicam Advertising, New York 1986–99, Pres. Young & Rubicam Inc. 1994–2000, Chair. and CEO 1994–99, Chair. Emer. 2000–; mem. Bd of Dirs Briggs

& Stratton Inc.; mem. Council on Foreign Relations. *Address:* 435 East 52nd Street, New York, NY 10022, USA.

GEORGIADES, Haris, BA, MA; Cypriot politician; *Minister of Finance;* b. 9 April 1972, Nicosia; m. Eva Yiangou Georgiades; one d.; ed English School, Nicosia, Univ. of Reading, UK; postgraduate researcher, Inst. of European and Int. Studies, Univ. of Reading, UK 1996–98; Gen. Sec. NEDISY (DISY—Democratic Rally Youth Org.) 2001–03, Dir, DISY Pres.'s Office 2006–11, DISY Press Spokesman 2009–13, also Deputy Head, DISY Econ. Policy Div.; mem. House of Reps (Parl.) (DISY—Democratic Rally) for Nicosia constituency 2011–, mem. Financial and Budgetary Affairs Cttee, Watchdog Cttee, Communications and Public Works Cttee; Minister of Labour and Social Insurance March–April 2013, of Finance April 2013–; mem. DISY Exec. Council and Political Bureau. *Address:* Ministry of Finance, Cnr Michalakis Karaolis Street and Gregoriou Afxentiou Street, 1439 Nicosia, Cyprus (office). *Telephone:* 22601104 (office). *Fax:* 22602741 (office). *E-mail:* registry@mof.gov.cy (office). *Website:* ww.mof.gov.cy (office).

GEORGIEV, Georgii Pavlovich; Russian molecular biologist; *Advisor and Scientific Director, Institute of Gene Biology, Russian Academy of Sciences;* b. 4 Feb. 1933, Leningrad (now St Petersburg); s. of Pavel K. Georgiev and Anastasia Georgieva; m. Nekrasova Anastasia Georgieva; one s. one d.; ed First Moscow Medical Inst.; qualified as medical doctor; researcher, A. Severtsev Inst. of Morphology of Animals, USSR (now Russian) Acad. of Sciences 1956–63, Head of Lab., V. Engelhart Inst. of Molecular Biology 1963–88, Founder and Dir Inst. of Gene Biology 1990–, currently Advisor and Scientific Dir; Corresp. mem. USSR (now Russian) Acad. of Sciences 1970, mem. 1987; mem. Academia Europaea, Royal Acad. of Spain, German Acad. Leopoldina, Scientific Acad. of Norway, European Molecular Biology Org.; research in molecular biology and genetics; author of discoveries of pro-m RNA and study of nuclear RNP particles containing pro-m RNA and investigation of a new type of nucleoprotein complex structure; first description of nuclear skeleton components; discovery of mobile elements in animals; studies of chromosome structure and transcription-active chromatin, tumour metastasis genes and cancer gene therapy; Lenin Prize 1976, USSR State Prize 1983, Russian State Prize 1996. *Publications include:* Genes of Higher Organisms and their Expression 1989; more than 400 scientific articles. *Leisure interest:* mountain climbing. *Address:* Institute of Gene Biology, Russian Academy of Sciences, Vavilov str. 34/5, 117334 Moscow (office); App. 75, home 7, Gubkin str., 117334 Moscow, Russia (home). *Telephone:* (495) 135-60-89 (office); (495) 125-74-54 (home). *Fax:* (495) 135-41-05 (office). *E-mail:* georgiev@igb.ac.ru (office). *Website:* www.igb.ac.ru (office).

GEORGIEVA, Kristalina Ivanova, MA, PhD; Bulgarian economist, international organization official and politician; *Commissioner for International Co-operation, Humanitarian Aid and Crisis Response, European Commission;* b. 13 Aug. 1953, Sofia; m.; one c.; ed Karl Marx Higher Inst. of Econs (now Univ. of Nat. and World Economy), Sofia, Harvard Business School and Massachusetts Inst. of Tech., USA; Assoc. Prof. of Econs, Univ. of Nat. and World Economy, Sofia 1977–93; Research Fellow, Dept of Econs, LSE, UK 1987–88; Consultant, Environmental Policy Services for Central and Eastern Europe, Environomics and Merser Management Consulting, Inc. 1992; Environmental Economist/Sr Environmental Economist, Environment Div., Europe and Cen. Asia, The World Bank Group 1993–97, Sector Man., Environment, East Asia and Pacific Region, responsible for regional environmental programmes, environmental projects (investments and tech. assistance) 1997–98, Sector Dir, Environment and Social Devt, East Asia and Pacific Region, responsible for social devt operations, including extensive work on social safety nets, community devt and women's empowerment, global environment projects, and regional initiatives in areas of social devt and environment 1998–99, Dir Environment Dept, in charge of World Bank environmental strategy, policies and lending 2000–04, Dir and Resident Rep., Russian Fed., based in Moscow, responsible for World Bank projects in more than 40 regions of the Fed. 2004–07, Dir, Strategy and Operations, Sustainable Devt, in charge of overall directions and delivery of World Bank policy and lending operations in infrastructure, urban devt, agriculture, environment and social devt, including co-ordination of World Bank support to fragile and conflict-affected countries 2007–08, Vice-Pres. and Corp. Sec., World Bank Group 2008–10; Commr for Int. Co-operation, Humanitarian Aid and Crisis Response, EC 2010–; Visiting Prof., at numerous insts, including ANU 1991, Yale Univ., Harvard Univ., MIT, Tsinghua Univ., Univ. of the South Pacific, Fiji 1991; mem. Bd of Trustees, Inst. for Sustainable Communities 2003–05, LEAD International 2003–09, Univ. of Nat. and World Economy 2009–; European Voice Commr of the Year 2010, European of the Year 2010. *Publications:* textbook on microeconomics; more than 100 publs on environmental policy and sustainable devt. *Address:* Commissioner for International Co-operation, Humanitarian Aid and Crisis Response, 200 Rue de la Loi, 1049 Brussels, Belgium (office). *Telephone:* (2) 298-71-37 (office); (2) 299-11-11 (switchboard) (office). *Fax:* (2) 295-01-38 (office). *Website:* ec.europa.eu/commission_2010-2014/georgieva (office); blogs.ec.europa.eu/georgieva (home).

GEORGIEVSKI, Ljubiša; Macedonian diplomatist, politician, writer and director; b. 30 May 1937, Bitola; ed Acad. of Theatre, Film, Radio and Television, Belgrade; fmr Visiting Prof. of Theatre Ontology and Phenomenology, Univ. of Southern California and Univ. of Texas, USA; Dir of more than 120 plays performed throughout fmr Yugoslavia, Poland, Italy, Romania, Bulgaria and USA; active in movt for autonomous and independent Macedonia 1990–; Amb. to Bulgaria (also accred to Moldova) 2000–04; Pres. Sobranie (Parl. Ass.) 2006–09; Amb. to Serbia 2009–13; unsuccessful cand. in presidential elections 1994; two Jovan Sterija Popovich Awards, six Golden Wreath Awards, 11 October Award. *Plays directed include:* Joan of Arc, Drama Theatre Co., Kurshumli 2000. *Films directed include:* The Mountain of Anger, Under the Same Sky, Republic in Flames, The Price of the City. *Publications:* Apocalypse 1988, City 1991, Direct Investments and Short Stories (essays) 1994, Holy Dream, Exercises in Acting Mastery, Ontology of the Theatre, The Political Future of Macedonia; more than 200 articles in Dnevnik newspaper. *Address:* c/o Ministry of Foreign Affairs, 1000 Skopje, Filip II Makedonski 7, The former Yugoslav Republic of Macedonia.

GEPHARDT, Richard (Dick) Andrew, BS, JD; American lawyer and fmr politician; *Senior Counsel, DLA Piper Rudnick Gray Cary US LLP;* b. 31 Jan. 1941, St Louis, Mo.; s. of Louis Andrew Gephardt and Loreen Estelle Cassell; m. Jane Ann Byrnes 1966; one s. two d.; ed Northwestern Univ. and Univ. of Michigan Law School; mem. Mo. Bar 1965; Pnr, Thompson and Mitchell (law firm), St Louis 1965–76; Alderman 14th Ward, St Louis 1971–76, Democratic Committeeman 1968–71; mem. 95th to 105th Congress from Third Mo. Dist 1979–2005, Democratic Leader 1989–2002; mem. Labor Advisory Bd, American Income Life Insurance Co. 2005–; Sr Counsel, DLA Piper Rudnick Gray Cary US LLP, Washington, DC 2005–; cand. for Democratic nomination to US Presidency 1988, 2004; Pres. Children's Hematology Research Asscn, St Louis Children's Hosp. 1973–76; Advisory Bd Chair. Richard A. Gephardt Inst. for Public Service, Washington Univ. in St. Louis; mem. Bar Asscn, St Louis, American Legion, Young Lawyers' Soc. (Chair. 1972–73). *Address:* DLA Piper Rudnick Gray Cary US LLP, 500 Eighth Street, NW, Washington, DC 20004, USA (office). *Telephone:* (202) 799-4317 (office). *Fax:* (202) 799-5317 (office). *E-mail:* info@dlapiper.com (office). *Website:* www.dlapiper.com (office).

GERASHCHENKO, Victor Vladimirovich; Russian banker (retd) and fmr politician; b. 21 Dec. 1937, Leningrad (now St. Petersburg); s. of Vladimir Gerashchenko and Anastasia Klinova; m. Nina Drozdkova 1960; one s. one d.; ed Moscow Financial Inst.; Man. Div. of Foreign Exchange Dept, USSR Bank for Foreign Trade (BFT) 1960–65, Man. Dir of Dept 1972–74, Man. Dir Foreign Exchange Dept 1982–83, Deputy Chair. 1983–89; Dir Moscow Narodny Bank Ltd, London 1965–67, Deputy Gen. Man., then Gen. Man. Beirut 1967–71, Gen. Man. Singapore 1977–82; Chair. Bd Ost-West Handelsbank, Frankfurt am Main 1974–77; Chair. Bd State Bank of USSR 1989–91, Head of Dept Fund Reforma 1991–92; Chair. Cen. Bank of Russian Fed. 1992–94, 1998–2002 (resgnd), Adviser 1994–96; Chair. Bd Moscow Int. Bank (MIB) 1996–98; Chair. Supervisory Bd Vneshtorgbank 1998–2003; mem. State Duma (Parl.) 2003–04; co-Chair. Party of the Russian Regions (Partiya Rossiiskikh Regionov–PRR), now Motherland (Rodina) 2004; mem. Bd of Dirs Yukos 2004; now retd; Order of Banner of Labour (twice), Order of Merit for the Fatherland 2000. *Leisure interest:* literature. *Address:* c/o Motherland (Rodina), 107031 Moscow, ul. B. Dmitrovka 32/1, Russia (home).

GERASIMOV, Gen. Valerii Vasilevich; Russian army officer and government official; *Chief of the General Staff;* b. 8 Sept. 1955, Kazan, Tatar Autonomous SSR, Russian SFSR, USSR; m.; one s.; ed Kazan Suvorov Mil. School, Kazan Higher Tank Command School, Malinovsky Mil. Acad. of Armoured Forces, Mil. Acad. of the Gen. Staff of the Armed Forces of Russia; following graduation, became commdr of a platoon, co. and bn of the Eastern Mil. Dist; later a chief of staff of a tank regt, then of a motorized rifle div. in Baltic Mil. Dist; commdr of a motorized infantry div. in North Western Force 1993–95; First Deputy Army Commdr in Moscow Mil. Dist and Commdr of 58th Army in North Caucasus Mil. Dist during Second Chechen War; Commdr Leningrad Mil. Dist 2006–09, Moscow Mil. Dist 2009–12, Cen. Mil. Dist 2012; ran Victory Day parades in Moscow 2009–12; Deputy Chief of Gen. Staff 2010–12, First Deputy Defence Minister and Chief of Gen. Staff 2012–; Merit for Motherland in USSR Armed Forces (Third Grade), Merit for Motherland (Fourth Grade), Order of Mil. Merit. *Address:* Ministry of Defence, 119169 Moscow, ul. Znamenka 19, Russia (office). *Telephone:* (495) 696-71-71 (office); (495) 696-86-73 (office). *Website:* mil.ru (office).

GERBERDING, Julie Louise, BA, MD, MPH; American professor of medicine (infectious diseases); *Associate Adjunct Professor of Medicine (Infectious Diseases), University of California, San Francisco;* b. 22 Aug. 1955, Estelline, SDak; m. David Rose; one step-d.; ed Case Western Reserve Univ., Cleveland, Ohio; internship and residency in internal medicine, Univ. of California, San Francisco (UCSF); Fellowship in Clinical Pharmacology and Infectious Diseases, UCSF; Faculty mem. and Dir of Prevention Epicentre, UCSF –1998; Dir Healthcare Quality Promotion Div., Nat. Center for Infectious Diseases (NCID) 1998–2001, Acting Deputy Dir NCID 2001–02; Dir Centers for Disease Control and Prevention (CDC) and Admin. Agency for Toxic Substances and Disease Registry 2002–09; currently Assoc. Adjunct Prof. of Medicine (Infectious Diseases), UCSF and Assoc. Clinical Prof. of Medicine (Infectious Diseases), Emory Univ.; Scientific Advisor, Edelman 2009–10; Pres., Merck Vaccines, Merck & Co., Inc. 2010–; Dir, MSD Wellcome Trust Hilleman Laboratories Pvt. Sec. Ltd (jt initiative between Merck and The Wellcome Trust); Assoc. Ed. American Journal of Medicine; mem. Editorial Bd Annals of Internal Medicine; fmr mem. Bd of Scientific Counselors, Nat. Center for Infectious Diseases, CDC HIV Advisory Cttee, Scientific Program Cttee, Nat. Conf. on Human Retroviruses; mem. American Soc. for Clinical Investigation, American Coll. of Physicians, Soc. for Healthcare Epidemiology of America, American Epidemiology Soc., Phi Beta Kappa, Alpha Omega Alpha; Fellow, Infectious Diseases Soc. of America, also Chair. Cttee on Professional Devt and Diversity and mem. Nominations Cttee; consultant to Nat. Insts of Health, American Medical Asscn, Occupational Safety and Health Admin, Nat. AIDS Comm., Congressional Office of Tech. Assessment, WHO; Alice Paige Cleveland Award 1981, ranked by Forbes magazine amongst 100 Most Powerful Women (12th) 2005, (23rd) 2006, (32nd) 2007, (24th) 2008, Surgeon Gen.'s Medallion 2007, Global Health Leadership Award 2008. *Publications:* more than 140 peer-reviewed publs and textbook chapters. *Leisure interests:* scuba diving, reading on the beach, gardening. *Address:* Box 0811, University of California – San Francisco, San Francisco, CA 94143-0811 (office); Merck Corporate Headquarters, One Merck Drive, PO Box 100, Whitehouse Station, NJ 08889-0100, USA (office). *Telephone:* (908) 423-1000 (Whitehouse Station) (office). *Website:* www.ucsf.edu (office); www.merck.com/product/vaccines (office).

GERDAU JOHANNPETER, André; Brazilian business executive; *CEO, Metalúrgica Gerdau;* b. 1963; s. of Jorge Gerdau Johannpeter and Erica Johannpeter (neé Bier); s. of Jorge Gerdau Johannpeter; m.; three c.; ed Catholic Univ. of Rio Grande do Sul, Univ. of Toronto, Canada, Univ. of Pennsylvania, USA; joined Metalúrgica Gerdau 1981, Asst to Exec. Pres., Gerdau Ameristeel (US operation), Cambridge, Mass 1992–94, Business Devt Dir 2001–02, COO Canada operations 2002–03, COO 2002–03, Vice-Pres. Gerdau Ameristeel 2003–04, Exec. Vice-Pres. Metalúrgica Gerdau 2002–07, Dir of Marketing and Sales, Raw Materials, Procurement, Logistics, Human Resources, and Organizational Devt 2004–07, CEO 2007–, also Pres. Gerdau Exec. Cttee; mem. Brazilian Olympic Equestrian Team 1996–2000. *Sporting achievements:* won Olympic Bronze Medal for Equestrianism 1996, 2000. *Leisure interest:* riding horses. *Address:* Gerdau Grupo, Avenida Farrapos 1811, Floresta, 90220-005 Porto Alegre, Rio Grande do Sul, Brazil (office). *Website:* www.gerdau.com.br (office).

GERDAU JOHANNPETER, Jorge; Brazilian business executive; *Chairman Gerdau Group;* b. 8 Dec. 1936, Rio de Janeiro; s. of Curt Johannpeter and Helda Gerdau; m. 1st Erica Bier; five s. including Andre Gerdau Johannpeter; m. 2nd Cristina Harbich; m. 3rd Maria Helena; ed Fed. Univ. of Rio Grande do Sul; began career at Metalúrgica Gerdau (now Gerdau Group) as steelworker 1950, Dir 1973–, CEO 1983–2006, Chair. 1983–; Pres. Quality and Productivity Programme, Rio Grande do Sul; Pres. Council for Competitive Brazilian Devt 2001–; Coordinator, Brazilian Business Action; mem. Bd of Dirs and Human Resources Cttee, Petrobras; mem. Exec. Cttee Int. Iron and Steel Inst.; mem. Council on Econ. and Social Devt; Grand Cross, Nat. Scientific Order of Merit 2002; Willy Korf Steel Vision Award 2001. *Leisure interests:* race horse training, surfing. *Address:* Presidência Grupo Gerdau, Avenida Farrapos 1811, Floresta, 90220-005 Porto Alegre, Rio Grande do Sul, Brazil (office). *E-mail:* jorge.gerdau@gerdau.com.br (office). *Website:* www.gerdau.com.br (office).

GERE, Richard; American actor and activist; b. 31 Aug. 1949, Phila; m. 1st Cindy Crawford (q.v.) 1991 (divorced 1995); m. 2nd Carey Lowell 2002; one s. one step-d.; ed Univ. of Massachusetts; fmrly played trumpet, piano, guitar and bass and composed music with various groups; stage performances with Provincetown Playhouse and off-Broadway; appeared in London and Broadway productions of The Taming of the Shrew, A Midsummer Night's Dream and Broadway productions of Habeas Corpus and Bent; film debut 1975; Founding Chair. and Pres. Tibet House, New York 1987–91; f. Gere Foundation 1991; mem. Bd of Dirs Int. Campaign for Tibet 1992–, Chair. 1995–; Founder and Dir Healing the Divide Foundation 2001–; Hon. DLit (Leicester) 1992; Eleanor Roosevelt Humanitarian Award 2000, Marian Anderson Award 2007. *Films include:* Report to the Commissioner 1975, Baby Blue Marine 1976, Looking for Mr Goodbar 1977, Days of Heaven 1978, Blood Brothers 1978, Yanks 1979, American Gigolo 1980, An Officer and a Gentleman 1982, Breathless 1983, Beyond the Limit 1983, The Cotton Club 1984, King David 1985, Power 1986, No Mercy 1986, Miles From Home 1989, 3000 1989, Internal Affairs 1990, Pretty Woman 1990, Rhapsody in August 1991, Final Analysis 1991, Sommersby (co-exec. producer) 1993, Mr Jones (co-exec. producer) 1994, Intersection 1994, First Knight 1995, Primal Fear 1996, Red Corner 1997, Burn Hollywood Burn 1998, Runaway Bride 1999, Dr T. and the Women 2000, Autumn in New York 2000, The Mothman Prophecies 2002, Unfaithful 2002, Chicago (Golden Globe for Best Actor in a Musical 2003) 2002, Shall We Dance? 2004, Bee Season 2005, The Hoax 2006, The Flock 2007, The Hunting Party 2007, I'm Not There 2007, Nights in Rodanthe 2008, Amelia 2009, Brooklyn's Finest 2010. *Publication:* Pilgrim Photo Collection 1998. *Address:* c/o Andrea Jaffe Inc., 9229 Sunset Boulevard, Suite 414, Los Angeles, CA 90069; c/o Healing the Divide, 341 Lafayette Street, #4416, New York, NY 10012, USA. *Website:* www.healingthedivide.org; www.gerefoundation.org.

GERGEN, David Richmond, BA, LLB, JD; American fmr govt official; *Professor of Public Service and Director, Center for Public Leadership, John F. Kennedy School of Government, Harvard University;* b. 9 May 1942, Durham, NC; s. of Dr John Gergen; m. Anne Gergen; one s. one d.; ed Yale and Harvard Univs; staff asst, Nixon Admin, Washington, DC 1971–72; Special Asst to Pres. and Chief, White House writing/research team 1973–74; Special Counsel to Pres. Ford and Dir White House Office Communications 1975–77; Research Fellow, American Enterprise Inst.; Man. Ed. American Enterprise Inst. Public Opinion magazine 1977–81; Asst to Pres. Reagan, Staff Dir White House 1981; Asst to Pres. Reagan for Communications 1981–83; Research Fellow, Inst. of Politics, John F. Kennedy School of Govt, Harvard Univ. 1983–85, Prof. of Public Service 1999–, Dir Center for Public Leadership 2000–; Man. Ed. US News & World Report, Washington, DC 1985–86, Ed.-at-Large 1986–; Commentator, ABC News Nightline 2000–, Marketplace 2002–; Moderator World @ Large PBS discussion series 2000–02; Adviser to Pres. Clinton 1993–2001, for Foreign Policy 1994–95, to Sec. of State 1994; Visiting Prof., Duke Univ., N Carolina 1995–98; currently Sr Political Analyst CNN; Sr Fellow, Aspen Inst.; mem. Bd of Dir American Assembly, Nat. Council Against Teenage Pregnancy, Center for Study of Presidency, Duke Univ., City Year, Kenan Inst. for Ethics; mem. Advisory Bd Intel Corpn, Leadership Center at Morehouse Coll.; mem. DC Bar, Council on Foreign Relations, Trilateral Comm.; several honorary degrees. *Publications include:* Eyewitness to Power: The Essence of Leadership – Nixon to Clinton 2000. *Address:* J.F. Kennedy School of Government, Harvard University, 79 J.F. Kennedy Street, Cambridge, MA 02138 (office); 31 Ash Street, Cambridge, MA 02138, USA (home). *E-mail:* David_Gergen@harvard.edu (office). *Website:* www.ksg.harvard.edu/leadership (office); www.usnews.com/usnews/opinion/dgergen.htm (office); www.davidgergen.com.

GERGIEV, Valery Abesalovich; Russian conductor; *Principal Conductor, London Symphony Orchestra; General Director and Artistic Director, Mariinsky Theatre;* b. 2 May 1953, Moscow; m. Natalia Gergieva; two s. one d.; ed Leningrad Conservatory; prize winner at All-Union Conductors' Competition, Moscow (while still a student) and at Karajan Competition, Berlin; Chief Conductor Armenian State Orchestra 1981–84; Asst Conductor (to Yuriy Temirkanov) Kirov Opera, Leningrad; Music Dir Kirov (now Mariinsky) Opera Theatre Orchestra 1988–, also Artistic and Gen. Dir 1996–; Prin. Guest Conductor Rotterdam Philharmonic 1989–92, Prin. Conductor 1992–2008, Music Dir 1995–2008; Prin. Guest Conductor New York Metropolitan Opera 1998–2008; Prin. Conductor London Symphony Orchestra 2007–; Artistic Dir St Petersburg Stars of the White Nights Festival, Moscow Easter Festival, Gergiev Festival Rotterdam, Mikkeli Int. Festival, Finland; tours extensively in Europe and the USA; has guest-conducted Berlin Philharmonic, Dresden Philharmonic, Bayerischer Rundfunk, Royal Concertgebouw, London Philharmonic, City of Birmingham Symphony, Royal Philharmonic, London Symphony, Orchestra of Santa Cecilia, Japan Philharmonic; orchestras of Boston, Chicago, Cleveland, New York, San Francisco and Toronto; operas at Covent Garden, Metropolitan and San Francisco; State Prize of Russia 1994, 1999, Musical Life Magazine Musician of the Year 1992, 1993, Classical Music Award 1994, Musical America Yearbook Conductor of the Year 1996, People's Artist of Russia 1996, Triumph Prize 1999, Order of Friendship, Russia 2000, Order of St Mesrop Mashtots, Armenia 2000, Russian Presidential Prize 2002, UNESCO Artist of the World 2003, Nat. Pride of Russia Award 2003, For Work and the Fatherland Award 2003, World Econ. Forum Crystal Prize 2004, People's Artist of Ukraine 2004, Royal Swedish Acad. of Music Polar Music Prize 2005, Royal Philharmonic Soc. Award for Best Conductor 2009. *Recordings:* numerous recordings of operas and ballets including Shostakovich War Symphon-

ies (No 4-9) 2005, Prokofiev Complete Symphonies (Gramophone Award for Best Orchestral Recording 2007) 2006, Tchaikovsky Swan Lake 2007, Shostakovich The Nose 2009, Wagner Parsifal 2010. *Address:* Columbia Artists Management, 1790 Broadway, New York, NY 10019-1412, USA (office); London Symphony Orchestra Administration, 6th Floor, Barbican Centre, Silk Street, London, EC2Y 8DS, England; Mariinsky Theatre, Teatralnaya pl. 1, St Petersburg, 190000, Russia. *Telephone:* (212) 841-9500 (office); (20) 7588-1116 (London); (812) 326-41-41. *Fax:* (212) 841-9744 (office); (20) 7374-0127 (London); (812) 314-17-44. *E-mail:* info@cami.com (office); admin@lso.co.uk; post@mariinsky.ru. *Website:* www.cami.com (office); lso.co.uk; www.mariinsky.ru/en.

GËRGURI, Gani, MBA; Kosovo economist and central banker; *Governor, Central Bank of the Republic of Kosovo;* b. 1960, Istog; m. Muzafere Gërguri; two s.; ed Univ. of Prishtina, Univ. of Zagreb, Croatia, Univ. of Sheffield, UK; started career in Statistics and Analysis Dept, Nat. Bank of Kosovo 1983; Head of Research and Statistics Dept, Central Bank of the Repub. of Kosovo 2000–04, Chief Operations Officer 2004–06, Deputy Man. Dir 2006–08, Deputy Gov. 2008–10, Acting Gov. 2010–11, Gov. 2011–; Co-Chair. Nat. Payments Council; mem. Bd Financial Intelligence Unit of Kosovo (ind. nat. inst. within Ministry of Finance and Economy). *Address:* Office of the Governor, Central Bank of the Republic of Kosovo, 10000 Prishtina, Rruga Garibaldi 33, Kosovo (office). *Telephone:* (38) 222055 (office). *Fax:* (38) 243763 (office). *E-mail:* publicrelations@cbak-kos.org (office). *Website:* www.bqk-kos.org (office).

GERHARDS, Kaspars; Latvian economist and politician; b. 7 Feb. 1969, Jelgava; ed Univ. of Latvia, Goethe Inst. and Westfälische Wilhelms-Universität, Germany; CEO Selga 1991–93; Asst Minister, Ministry of the Economy 1993–95; Programme Ed. Economists Asscn May–Sept. 1995; Project Man. Norway–Latvia Business Devt Fund 1995–96; adviser to the Pres. of Latvia on econ. affairs 1996–99; State Sec., Ministry of the Economy 1999–2007, Minister of the Economy 2007–09, of Transport 2009–10; mem. For Fatherland and Freedom Union/Latvian Nat. Independence Movt Party; mem. Bd of Dirs Naukšēni 1995–96, Lords 1995–96, Libanons 1995–96. *Address:* c/o For Fatherland and Freedom Union, Jēkaba iela 20/22–9, Rīga 1050, Latvia (office).

GERHARDT, Wolfgang, PhD; German politician; *President, Friedrich-Naumann-Foundation;* b. 31 Dec. 1943, Ulrichstein-Helpershain; two c.; ed Univ. of Marburg; mem. State Parl., Hesse 1983–94, Hessian Minister for Science and Art and Deputy Prime Minister 1987–91, Party Whip FDP; mem. Bundestag (Parl.) 1994–; Nat. Chair. FDP 1995–2001, Chair. FDP Parl. Group in Bundestag 1998–2006; Vice-Pres. Liberal Int. 2002–; Pres. Friedrich Naumann Foundation for Liberty 2006–; Chair. Bd of Trustees Theodor-Heuss-Haus-Stiftung Foundation 2006–. *Publication:* Es geht – wir haben alle Chancen 1997. *Address:* Bundestag, Platz der Republik 1, 11011 Berlin, Germany (office). *Telephone:* (30) 22773688 (office). *Fax:* (30) 22776688 (office). *E-mail:* wolfgang.gerhardt@bundestag.de (office). *Website:* www.wolfgang-gerhardt.de.

GERINGER, James E. (Jim), BS; American business executive and fmr politician; *Director of Policy, Environmental Systems Research Institute (ESRI);* b. 24 April 1944, Wheatland, Wyo.; m. Sherri Geringer; five c.; ed Kansas State Univ.; fmr farmer and substitute teacher; officer USAF, Space Devt Programs; fmr Wyo. State Rep. Platte Co.; mem. Wyo. State Senate for Platte Co., Dist 3 until 1995; Gov. of Wyoming 1994–2003; Dir Policy, Environmental Systems Research Institute (ESRI) (software firm) 2003–; fmr Chair. Western Govs Asscn, Educ. Comm. of States; Co-Chair. Nat. Policy Consensus Center 2009; mem. Bd of Dirs Dakota Gasification Co. 2012–; mem. Bd of Trustees, Western Govs Univ., Chair. 2005–. *Address:* ESRI, 380 New York Street, Redlands, CA 92373-8100, USA. *Telephone:* (909) 793-2853. *Website:* www.esri.com (office).

GERMAIN, Sylvie, PhD; French writer; b. 1948, Châteauroux; ed Univ. of Paris (Sorbonne), Univ. of Paris X – Nanterre; civil servant, attached to Ministry of Culture 1981–86, taught at L'École française, Prague 1986–93, full-time novelist 1994–. *Publications:* novels: Le Livre des nuits 1985, Nuit d'Ambre 1987, Jours de colère (Prix Femina) 1989, Opéra muet 1989, L'Enfant Méduse 1991, La Pleurante des rues de Prague 1992, Immensités 1993, Eclats de sel 1996, L'Encre du poulpe 1998, Tobie des marais 1998, La Chanson des mal-aimants 2002, Ateliers de lumière 2004, Magnus (Prix Goncourt des Lycéens) 2005, Frères 2006, L'inaperçu 2008, Hors Champ 2009; essays: Les Echos du silence 1996, Céphalophores 1996, Patience et songe de lumière: Vermeer 1996, Bohuslav Reyneck à Petrov: un nomade en sa demeure 1998, Etty Hillesum 1999, Mourir un peu 2000, La Grande nuit de Toussaint, Le Temps qu'il fait 2000, Cracovie à vol d'oiseau 2000, Célébration de la Paternité 2001, J'ai envie de rompre le silence (with René Vouland and Gérard Vouland) 2001, Songes du temps 2003, Les Personnages 2004, Les Echos du Silence 2006. *Address:* c/o Albin Michel, 22 rue Huyghens, 75014 Paris, France (office). *Website:* www.albin-michel.fr (office).

GERMÁN, Alejandrina; Dominican Republic academic and politician; *Secretary of State for Women;* b. Duarte Prov.; d. of Tomás Germán García and Teodora Mejía de Germán; m. José María Sosa Vásquez; two s.; ed Universidad Autónoma de Santo Domingo; Prof., Dept of Pedagogy, Universidad Autónoma de Santo Domingo (UASD) 1976–; fmr Pres. Asscn of UASD Humanities Profs; Pres. Nat. Council of Higher Educ., with rank of Sec. of State 1996–99; Sec. of State for the Presidency 1999–2000, for Educ. 2004–08, for Women 2008–; Adviser, UNDP Education Programme 1990–96; Consultant, Universidad Iberoamericana; mem. Partido de la Liberación Dominicana 1974–, mem. Cen. Cttee 1990, mem. Political Cttee 1994–. *Address:* Secretariat of State for Women, Edif. de Ofs. Gubernamentales, Bloque D, 2°, Avda México, esq. 30 de Marzo, Santo Domingo DN, Dominican Republic (office). *Telephone:* 685-3755 (office). *Fax:* 686-0911 (office). *E-mail:* info@mujer.gob.do (office). *Website:* www.mujer.gob.do (office).

GERNANDT LUNDIUS, Marianne; Swedish lawyer and judge; *President, Supreme Court;* b. (Marianne Lundius); 28 April 1949, Malmö; court clerk 1976–78; Pnr, Lagerlof & Leman Attorneys 1978–98; mem. Supreme Court of Sweden 1998–, Pres. (first woman) 2010–; Vice-Chair. Fideikommiss; replacement of Chair. of Oil Crisis Bd, Examination Bd for support to financial Insts; Vice-Chair. Bd of Nomination of Judges; Vice-Pres. Disciplinary Cttee, Stockholm Stock Exchange, OMX Nasdaq, Disciplinary Cttee, Swedsec AB; Vice-Chair. Securities Council; Vice-Chair. Heijne Foundation; Prin. Stockholm Nursing Home Foundation; Head of Heart-Lung Foundation, Swedish Nat. Asscn against Heart and

Lung Diseases, King Oscar II Jubilee Foundation; Chair. Sven and Lilly Lawskis Fund for Scientific Research; mem. Royal Physiographic Soc. in Lund; Hon. LLD. *Address:* Högsta domstolen (Supreme Court), Box 2066, 103 12 Stockholm (office); Högsta domstolen, Riddarhustorget 8, 111 28 Stockholm, Sweden (office). *Telephone:* (8) 561-666-00 (office). *Fax:* (8) 561-666-86 (office). *E-mail:* hogsta .domstolen@dom.se (office). *Website:* www.hogstadomstolen.se (office).

GERONZI, Cesare; Italian banking executive; b. 15 Feb. 1935, Marino, Rome; m. Giuliana Iozzi; two d.; hired by Bank of Italy following a competitive examination in 1960, continued to work there until 1980; moved to Banco di Napoli 1980, arranged first bank merger in Italy, between Cassa di Risparmio di Roma, Banco di Santo Spirito and Banco di Roma, whose subsequent merger with Mediocredito Centrale, Banco di Sicilia and Bipop-Carire gave rise to the Capitalia banking group, directed takeover of Capitalia by the Unicredit Group 2007; Vice-Chair. UniCredit SpA (fmrly Unicredito Italiano SpA) 2007–; Deputy Chair. Mediobanca SpA 2001–06, Deputy Chair. Supervisory Bd Jan.–June 2007, Chair. Mediobanca SpA 2007–10; Chair. Assicurazioni Generali SpA 2010–11 (resgnd); mem. Bd of Dirs Telecom Italia SpA (fmrly Olivetti SpA and Stet-Società Finanziaria Telefonica p.A.) 2001–, RCS Mediagroup SpA 2004–, Capitalia SpA 2007–, RCS Quotidiani, Italian Bankers Asscn, CASPIE; mem. governing bodies of various pvt. law orgs and insts, including Istituto della Enciclopedia Italiana Treccani, Assonime, Associazione 'Guido Carli', Aspen Inst. Italia, Fondazione di Diritto Vaticano dell'Ospedale Bambino Gesù; Hon. Fellow, Tel-Aviv Museum of Art; numerous honours, including High Official of Order of Merit of the Repub. of Italy, Commdr, Holy Order of St Gregory the Great, Commdr's Cross of Maltese Order of Merit of Sovereign Mil. Hospitaller Order of St John of Jerusalem of Rhodes and of Malta; hon. degree in Econs and Business Studies from Bari Univ. *Address:* c/o Assicurazioni Generali SpA, Piazza Duca degli Abruzzi 2, 34132 Trieste, Italy. *E-mail:* info@cesaregeronzi.it. *Website:* www.cesaregeronzi.it.

GERSHON, Sir Peter, Kt, KBE, CBE, FREng, FRAeS; British business executive and fmr civil servant; *Chairman, National Grid;* m.; three c.; ed Univ. of Cambridge; joined Int. Computers Ltd and worked in the computer industry 1969–86; held sr line managerial positions in the telecommunications industry 1987–94; apptd Main Bd Dir of GEC plc 1994–2000; Chief Exec. of the Office of Govt Commerce 2000–04; Chair. Premier Farnell plc 2004–, Symbian Ltd; fmr Man. Dir Marconi Electronic Systems; fmr Chair. Tate & Lyle plc; fmr mem. UK Defence Acad. Advisory Bd, HM Govt Efficiency Bd; mem. Bd of Dirs and Deputy Chair. National Grid Aug.–Dec. 2011, Chair. 2012–; Dir (non-exec.) HM Treasury; mem. Council Royal Acad. of Eng, Imperial Coll. London; served as adviser to the Conservative Party at the time of the 2010 Gen. Election; Fellow, British Computer Soc., Chartered Inst. of Purchasing and Supply; Companion, Chartered Man. Inst.; Hon. FIEE; Hon. Fellow, Asscn for Project Man.; Liveryman, Worshipful Co. of Information Technologists; Hon. DTech (Kingston Univ.). *Achievements include:* known for conducting the Gershon Review which recommended savings across the UK's public services 2004–05. *Leisure interests:* skiing, swimming, reading, travel, the theatre. *Address:* National Grid PLC, 1–3 The Strand, London, WC2N 5EH, England (office). *Telephone:* (20) 7004-3000 (office). *Fax:* (20) 7004-3004 (office). *E-mail:* info@nationalgrid.com (office). *Website:* www .nationalgrid.com (office).

GERSON, Allan, MA, JD, LLM, JSD; American lawyer and academic; *Chairman, Gerson International Law Group;* ed New York Univ. Law School, Hebrew Univ. of Jerusalem, Israel, Yale Univ.; joined US Dept of Justice 1977, joined Office of Special Investigations (OSI) to prosecute Nazi collaborators 1979; apptd Counsel to US Ambs to UN Jeane Kirkpatrick and Gen. Vernon Walters 1981; fmr Deputy Asst Attorney Gen. for Legal Counsel and Counsellor for Int. Affairs, US Dept of Justice; brought first lawsuit against Libya on behalf of families of victims of 1988 Pan Am Lockerbie bombing, led lawsuit against Saudi Royal family and Govt of Sudan on behalf of families of victims of World Trade Center bombing 2001; Sr Fellow, American Enterprise Inst. 1986–89; Distinguished Prof. of Int. Law and Transactions, George Mason Univ. 1989–95; currently Chair. Gerson Int. Law Group PLLC, Washington, DC; fmr Research Prof. of Int. Relations, George Washington Univ. and Co-Dir Inst. for Peacebuilding and Devt, Elliott School of Int. Affairs; fmr Exec. Dir Morocco-US Council on Trade and Investment; Sr Fellow for Int. Law and Orgs, Council on Foreign Relations 1998–2000; fmr Resident Scholar, American Enterprise Inst. *Publications:* Israel, the West Bank and International Law 1978, Lawyers' Ethics: Contemporary Dilemmas 1980, The Kirkpatrick Mission: Diplomacy without Apology 1991, The Price of Terror: One Bomb. One Plane. 270 Lives. The History-Making Struggle for Justice After Pan Am 103 (co-author) 2001, Privatizing Peace: From Conflict to Security 2002; articles in professional and popular publs. *Address:* Gerson International Law Group, 2131 S Street NW, Washington, DC 20008, USA (office). *Telephone:* (202) 234-9717 (office).

GERSON, Mark; British photographer; b. 3 Oct. 1921, London; s. of Bernard Gerson and Esther Gerson; m. Renée Cohen 1949; two d.; ed Cen. Foundation School for Boys, London and Regent Polytechnic, London; served in RAF 1941–46; taught photography under EVT scheme while serving in RAF in Paris 1946; specialist portrait photographer concentrating on literary personalities and industrialists; ran photographic studio 1947–87; now freelance photographer; major exhbns Fox Talbot Museum, Lacock, Wilts. 1981, Shaw Theatre, London 1983, Writers Observed, Nat. Theatre, London 1984, The Poetry Library, Royal Festival Hall 1991, Literati, Nat. Portrait Gallery, London 1996; Fellow, British Inst. of Professional Photography. *Leisure interests:* cinema, theatre. *Address:* 3 Regal Lane, Regent's Park, London, NW1 7TH, England. *Telephone:* (20) 7485-6437 (home). *E-mail:* mark@reneegerson.plus.com (home). *Website:* www .markgersonphotography.com (home).

GERSTNER, Louis Vincent, Jr, BA, MBA; American business executive; *Senior Advisor, Carlyle Group;* b. 1 March 1942, New York; s. of Louis Vincent Gerstner and Marjorie Rutan Gerstner; m. Elizabeth Robins Link 1968; one s. one d.; ed Dartmouth Coll. and Harvard Univ.; Dir McKinsey & Co., New York 1965–78; Exec. Vice-Pres. American Express Co., New York 1978–81, Vice-Chair. 1981–83, Chair. Exec. Cttee 1983–85, Pres. 1985–89, Chair., CEO RJR Nabisco 1989–93; Chair., CEO IBM 1993–2002; Vice-Chair. New American Schools Devt Corpn Bd 1991–98; Dir The New York Times Co. 1986–97, Bristol-Myers Squibb Co.; mem. Exec. Cttee, Bd of Trustees Jt Council on Econ. Educ. 1975–87, Chair. 1983–85;

mem. Bd of Dirs Memorial Sloan Kettering Hosp. 1978–89, 1998–, Vice-Chair. 2000–; Chair. Computer Systems Policy Project 1999–2001; Advisory Bd DaimlerChrysler 2001–, Sony Corpn 2002–; Chair. Carlyle Group 2002–08, currently Sr Advisor; mem. Policy Cttee, Business Roundtable 1991–98; mem. Bd of Overseers Annenberg Inst. for School Reform, Brown Univ.; mem. Business Council, American China Soc., Council on Foreign Relations, Nat. Security Telecommunications Advisory Cttee 1994–97, Advisory Cttee for Trade Policy and Negotiations 1995–, Nat. Acad. of Eng; Trustee NY Public Library 1991–96, American Museum of Natural History 2004–; Co-Chair. of Achieve 1996–2002; founder and Chair. The Teaching Commission 2003–; Fellow, American Acad. of Arts and Sciences; Hon. KBE 2001; Hon. DBA (Boston Coll.) 1994; Hon. LLD (Wake Forest, Brown) 1997; Hon. DEng (Rensselaer Polytechnic Inst.) 1999; Washington Univ. Acad. for Excellence in Business, Eng and Technology 1999; numerous awards for work in educ. *Publication:* Reinventing Education (co-author) 1994; Who Says Elephants Can't Dance: Inside IBM's Historic Turnaround 2002. *Address:* The Carlyle Group, 1001 Pennsylvania Avenue, NW, Suite 220 South, Washington, DC 20004-2505 (office); The Teaching Commission, 365 Fifth Avenue, Suite 6200, New York, NY 10016, USA. *Telephone:* (202) 347-2626 (office). *Fax:* (202) 347-1818 (office). *Website:* www.thecarlylegroup.com (office); www .theteachingcommission.org.

GERTH, Donald R., BA, MA, PhD; American academic and university administrator; *President Emeritus, California State University, Sacramento;* b. 4 Dec. 1928, Chicago, Ill.; s. of George C. Gerth and Madeleine A. Canavan; m. Beverly J. Hollman 1955; two d.; ed Georgetown Univ., Univ. of Chicago; Field Rep. for Southeast Asia, World Univ. Service 1950; served in USAF 1952–56; Lecturer in History, Univ. of the Philippines 1953–54; Admissions Counsellor, Univ. of Chicago 1956–58; Assoc. Dean of Students, Admissions and Records and mem. Dept of Govt, San Francisco State Univ. 1958–63; Assoc. Dean of Institutional Relations and Student Affairs, California State Univ. system 1963–64; Dean of Students, California State Univ., Chico 1964–68, Prof. of Political Science 1964–76, Co-Dir Danforth Foundation Research Project 1968–69, Coordinator, Inst. for Local Govt and Public Service and of Public Admin. 1968–70, Assoc. Vice-Pres. for Acad. Affairs and Dir Int. Programs (Dir of Center at Univ. of Skopje, Yugoslavia) 1969–70, Vice-Pres. for Acad. Affairs 1970–76, Pres. and Prof. of Political Science and Public Admin., California State Univ., Dominguez Hills 1976–84, Pres. and Prof. of Public Policy and Admin., California State Univ., Sacramento 1984–2003, Prof. Emer. 2003–; Pres. Int. Asscn of Univ. Presidents 1996–99; numerous other appointments; Hon. Prof.; numerous hon. doctorates. *Publications:* The Invisible Giant 1971, The People's University: A History of the California State University 2010; numerous articles. *Leisure interest:* international affairs. *Address:* 7132 Secret Garden Loop, Roseville, CA 95747-8041, USA (home). *Telephone:* (916) 771-3412 (home). *Fax:* (916) 771-3413 (home). *E-mail:* dongerth@csus.edu (home). *Website:* www.calstate.edu (office).

GERTLER, Meric, PhD, FRSC, AcSS, MCIP; Canadian professor of geography, academic and university administrator; *President, University of Toronto;* ed Harvard Univ., USA; Vice-Dean, Grad. Educ. and Research, Faculty of Arts & Science, Univ. of Toronto –2008, Dean 2008–13, Pres. Univ. of Toronto 2013–, Founding Co-Dir Program on Globalization and Regional Innovation Systems (PROGRIS), Munk School of Global Affairs, served as Dir Dept of Geography's Program in Planning, holds the Goldring Chair in Canadian Studies; visiting appointments at Univ. of Oxford, UK, Univ. Coll., London, UCLA and Univ. of Oslo; has served as adviser to local, regional and nat. govt in Canada, USA and Europe, and to OECD and EU; mem. Expert Panel on Business Innovation established by Council of Canadian Acads 2009; Academician, Acad. of Social Sciences (UK) 2012; mem. Canadian Inst. of Planners; Hon. PhD (Lund Univ., Sweden) 2012; Award for Scholarly Distinction, Canadian Asscn of Geographers 2007. *Publications:* six books, including Manufacturing Culture: The Institutional Geography of Industrial Practice, Innovation and Social Learning (co-ed.), Oxford Handbook of Economic Geography (co-ed.) (Outstanding Academic Book Award, Choice Magazine); more than 80 journal articles and book chapters on the geography of innovative activity and the economies of city regions. *Address:* Office of the President, University of Toronto, 27 King's College Circle, Room 206, Toronto, ON M5S 1A1, Canada (office). *Telephone:* (416) 978-4163 (office). *E-mail:* president@utoronto.ca (office). *Website:* www.president.utoronto.ca (office).

GERVASI, (Alexander) Sacha Simon; British film director, journalist and screenwriter; b. 1966, London; s. of Sean Gervasi and Milli Kasoy; m. Jessica de Rothschild 2010; ed Westminster School, King's Coll., London, Univ. of California, Los Angles Film School; befriended Canadian metal band Anvil 1981, toured London and became a roadie for the band on three tours, left band 1986; original mem. of alternative rock group Bush; worked for the Poet Laureate of England, Ted Hughes at Arvon Writing Foundation; subsequently worked for John Calder of the Samuel Beckett archive; moved to Los Angeles to attend grad. screen-writing programme at UCLA Film School 1995; worked as journalist, writing for newspapers and magazines, including The Sunday Times, The Observer and Punch; the voice of Jaguar cars on US radio and TV 1999–2000; began writing for film as co-writer with Craig Ferguson for The Big Tease 1999; twice won the BAFTA/LA scholarship, Ind. Spirit Award, Emmy Award. *Films directed:* Anvil: The Story of Anvil (documentary) (also exec. producer) 2008, Hitchcock 2012. *Screenplays:* The Big Tease (also exec. producer) 1999, The Terminal 2004, Henry's Crime (also exec. producer) 2010, My Dinner with Herve 2013.

GESANG, Doje; Chinese party official; b. Feb. 1936, Qinghai Prov.; s. of Giamucuo and Sangdang Shiji; m. Zenen Namu 1956; one s. three d.; ed Nat. Middle School, Sining, Qinghai and in Beijing; returned to Sining as a corresp. 1955; Vice-Chair. Qinghai Provincial People's Congress Standing Cttee 1991–; started writing poetry 1956. *Publications:* Legend of Hot Spring, The Childbirth of a New Town at Daybreak, The Name of Maji Snow Mountain, You are an Infant of Daylight, Raindrops from the Clouds 1992. *Leisure interests:* riding, hunting, painting.

GESCHKE, Charles M. (Chuck), AB, MS, PhD; American computer industry executive; *Co-Chairman, Adobe Systems Inc.;* b. 11 Sept. 1939, Cleveland, Ohio; m. Nan Geschke 1964; several c.; ed Saint Ignatius High School, Xavier Univ., Carnegie-Mellon Univ.; fmr Prin. Scientist and Researcher, Xerox Palo Alto Research Center (PARC), f. PARC Imaging Sciences Lab. 1980; Co-founder, with

John Warnock, Adobe Systems Inc. 1982, COO 1986–94, Pres. 1989–2000, Co-Chair. 1997–; Dir Rambus, Inc.; mem. Nat. Acad. of Eng, Govt-Univ. Industry Research Roundtable, Nat. Acad. of Sciences; mem. Bd of Govs San Francisco Symphony, Commonwealth Club of Calif., Egan Maritime Foundation, Nat. Leadership Roundtable on Church Man., Nantucket Boys and Girls Club, Tableau Software; mem. Advisory Bd Carnegie-Mellon Univ., Princeton Univ.; mem. Bd of Trustees Univ. of San Francisco (Chair. –2010); mem. Nat. Acad. of Eng 1995, American Acad. of Arts and Sciences 2008; Fellow, Asscn for Computing Machinery (ACM) 1999, Computer History Museum 2002; Hon. DHumLitt (John Carroll Univ.) 2012; honoured by several orgs, including ACM, Nat. Computer Graphics Asscn, Rochester Inst. of Tech., John W. Gardner Leadership Award, Entrepreneur of the Year Award, Medal of Achievement, American Electronics Asscn (with John Warnock) 2006, Computer Entrepreneur Award, IEEE Computer Soc. (with John Warnock) 2008, Nat. Medal of Tech. and Innovation (with John Warnock) 2008, Marconi Prize (with John Warnock) 2010. *Address:* Adobe Systems Inc., 345 Park Avenue, San Jose, CA 95110-2704, USA (office). *Telephone:* (408) 536-6000 (office). *Fax:* (408) 537-6000 (home). *Website:* www.adobe.com (office).

GETTU, Tegegnework; Ethiopian economist and UN official; *Under-Secretary-General for General Assembly and Conference Management, United Nations;* b. 1952; m.; two c.; fmr Country Dir for Southern Africa and Indian Ocean countries, Acting Resident Rep. in Liberia and Sierra Leone –2003, UN Resident Coordinator and UNDP Resident Rep. in Nigeria 2003–06, Chief of Staff and Dir, Exec. Office, UNDP 2006–09, Asst Sec.-Gen. and Regional Bureau Dir for Africa, UNDP 2009–13, Under-Sec.-Gen. for Gen. Ass. and Conf. Man., UN 2013–; fmr Asst Prof. and Lecturer, Univ. of Rochester, Hunter Coll., Addis Ababa Univ.; also served as Sr Econ. and Political Adviser, UNDP Africa Bureau, New York, Sr Adviser, Ministry of Planning and Econ. Devt. *Address:* Department for General Assembly and Conference Management, United Nations, New York, NY 10017, USA (office). *Telephone:* (212) 963-1234 (office). *Fax:* (212) 963-4879 (office). *Website:* www.un .org/Depts/DGACM (office).

GETTY, Donald, OC, BA, MBA; Canadian business executive and fmr politician; b. 30 Aug. 1933, Westmount, Québec; s. of Charles Ross Getty and Beatrice Lillian Getty; m. Margaret Mitchell 1955; four s.; ed Univ. of Western Ont.; joined Imperial Oil Ltd Edmonton 1955; Lands and Contracts Man. Midwestern Industrial Gas Ltd 1961; Pres. and Man. Dir Baldonnel Oil and Gas Ltd 1964–67; Partner, Doherty, Roadhouse & McCuaig Ltd (investment firm) 1967; mem. Alberta Legis. 1967–79, 1985–92; Minister of Fed. and Intergovernmental Affairs, Prov. of Alberta 1971–75, of Energy and Natural Resources 1975–79; Pres. D. Getty Investments Ltd 1979; Chair. of Bd Ipsco 1981–85; Pres., CEO Sunnybank Investments Ltd 1993–94; Leader Progressive Conservative Party, Alberta 1985–93; Premier of Alberta 1985–92; fmr mem. Bd of Dirs Alberta Gas and Ethylene Co. Ltd, Brinco Ltd, Celanese Canada Inc., D. Getty Investments Ltd, Interprovincial Steel and Pipe Corpn, Nortek Energy Corpn, Nova Corpn, Northern Life Assurance Co., Novacor Chemicals Ltd, Pacific Copper Mines Ltd, Placer Devt Ltd, Pacific Trans-Ocean Resources Ltd, Royal Bank of Canada, Edmonton Eskimos Football Club, Derrick Golf and Winter Club; mem. Bd of Govs Resources of Canada Fund, Edmonton Petroleum Club; Hon. Chief, Whitefish Lake Band; Claude Brown Trophy 1955. *Leisure interests:* football, golf, horse-racing, hunting. *Address:* Box 300, Erskine, AB T0C 1G0, Canada.

GETTY, Mark; American business executive; *Chairman, Getty Images, Inc.;* b. 9 July 1960, Oxfordshire, UK; s. of Sir Paul Getty; m. Domitilla Harding; two s. one d.; fmr investment banker, Kidder Peabody, New York then Hambros Bank Ltd, London 1991; co-founded Getty Investments LLC 1993; Co-founded Getty Images Inc. 1995, Chair. 1995–; Trustee, Nat. Gallery, London. *Address:* Getty Images Inc., 601 North 34th Street, Seattle, WA 98103, USA (office). *Telephone:* (206) 925-5000 (office). *Fax:* (206) 925-5001 (office). *Website:* www.gettyimages.com (office).

GEVORGIAN, Armen, MA; Armenian politician; *Deputy Prime Minister and Minister of Territorial Administration;* b. 8 July 1973, Yerevan; m.; two s. one d.; ed School No. 28, Yerevan, Orenburg State Pedagogical Inst., Russia, St Petersburg Inst. of Public Service, Russia, Twente Univ., Netherlands, St Petersburg Gertsen Russian Pedagogical Inst., Russia; Asst to the Prime Minister 1997–98; Asst to the Pres. of Armenia and First Deputy Head of Admin 1998–2000, First Asst to the Pres. 2000–06; Chief of Staff to the Pres. 2006–08; Sec. Nat. Security Council, Pres.'s Office 2007–08; Deputy Prime Minister and Minister of Territorial Admin 2008–; mem. CIS Econ. Council 2008–. *Address:* Ministry of Territorial Administration, 0010 Yerevan, Republic Square, Government House 2, Armenia (office). *Telephone:* (10) 51-13-02 (office). *Fax:* (10) 51-13-32 (home). *E-mail:* mta@mta.gov.am (office). *Website:* www.mta.gov.am (office).

GHADHBAN, Thamir Abbas al-, BSc, MSc; Iraqi petroleum engineer; b. 1945, Babil; ed Univ. Coll. London, Imperial Coll., London Univ., UK; worked for Ministry of Oil 1973–2003, first as reservoir engineer, then Head of Petroleum and Reservoir Eng –1989, Dir Gen. of Reservoir and Field Devt 1989–90, Dir Gen. of Studies and Planning 1991–92, Tech. Advisor to Oil Ministry 1993–2001, Dir Gen. of Planning 2002–03; Chief Geologist and CEO 2003–04; Interim Minister of Oil 2004–05; Acting Chair. Nat. Investment Comm. 2009; currently Chair. Advisory Cttee to Prime Minister; OAPEC Distinguished Science Award 2000. *Address:* c/o Ministry of Oil, POB 19244, Zayouna, Baghdad, Iraq (office).

GHADIRIAN, Shadi, BA; Iranian photographer; b. 1974, Tehran; m. Peyman Hooshmand-zadeh; ed Islamic Azad Univ., Tehran; Man. www.fanoosphoto.com (first Iranian specialized photography website); Photo Ed. Women in Iran website (www.womeniniran.com); collaborates with Akskhaneh Shahr (Museum of Photography), Tehran; works held in several int. public collections including Museum of Contemporary Art, Tehran, British Museum, Victoria and Albert Museum and Satchi Gallery, London, Musée des Arts Contemporains, Centre Georges Pompidou, Paris, Museum Moderner Kunst Stiftung Ludwig, Vienna, Los Angeles County Museum of Art, Sackler Gallery, Smithsonian Inst., Washington DC, Devi Art Foundation, Delhi. *Address:* c/o Silk Road Art Gallery, 103 Lavasani Avenue, 19368-39631 Tehran, Iran (office). *Website:* shadighadirian.com (office).

GHAFARI, Yousif Boutrous, BA, MA, MS, MBA; American engineer, business executive and fmr diplomatist; *Chairman, GHAFARI Inc.;* b. 27 Sept. 1952, southern Lebanon; m. Dr Mara Kalnins-Ghafari; three c.; ed Wayne State Univ.,

Detroit, Michigan State Univ. Advanced Man. Program; emigrated to USA early 1970s, US citizen 1978; licensed professional engineer 1984; Founder and Chair. GHAFARI Inc. (firm of architects, engineers, consultants and staffing specialists) 1982–; Public Del. Designate, US Mission to UN for 59th UN Gen. Ass. 2004–05; apptd by Pres. George W. Bush to J. William Fulbright Foreign Scholarship Bd 2005; Founding mem. 'Partnership for Lebanon'; Amb. to Slovenia 2008–10; Hon. DrIur (Wayne State Univ.) 2008; Corp. Leadership Award 1994, named as one of the Top 100 Exec. Heroes in Southeastern Michigan 1995, mem. Int. Inst. of Metropolitan Detroit's Hall of Fame, residence bldg renamed Yousif B. Ghafari Hall by Wayne State Univ. 2005. *Leisure interests:* enthusiastic athlete (ran the Boston Marathon and Detroit Free Press International Marathon), philanthropic works. *Address:* GHAFARI Inc., 17101 Michigan Ave., Dearborn, MI 48126-2736, USA (office). *Telephone:* (313) 441-3000 (office). *Fax:* (313) 441-1545 (office). *E-mail:* dearborn@ghafari.com (office). *Website:* www.ghafari.com (office).

GHAFERI, Amal Al, BSc, PhD; United Arab Emirates physicist and academic; *Assistant Professor, Materials Science and Engineering, Masdar Institute of Science and Technology;* ed UAE Univ., Univ. of Pittsburgh, USA; Asst Prof., Physics Dept, UAE Univ., Al Ain 2007–10; Asst Prof., Materials Science and Eng, Masdar Inst. of Science and Tech. 2010–; Visiting Scholar, MIT, USA 2010–; Sheikh Rashid Scientific Distinction Award 2000, 2007, UK Prime Minister's Initiative Award – PMI2 2009, Women in Science and Tech. Fellowship (USA) 2009. *Publications:* numerous papers in professional journals on implementing nanotechnology in renewable energy. *Address:* Masdar Institute of Science and Technology, Masdar City, Adu Dhabi, United Arab Emirates (office). *Telephone:* (2) 810-9103 (office). *Fax:* (2) 810-9901 (office). *E-mail:* aalghaferi@masdar.ac.ae (office). *Website:* www.masdar.ac.ae (office).

GHAFOOR, Ahmed Adheeb Abdul; Maldivian politician; *Minister of Tourism, Arts and Culture;* Pres. Maldives Nat. Chamber of Commerce and Industry –2012; Acting Minister of Fisheries and Agriculture Feb.–March 2012; Minister of Tourism, Arts and Culture 2012–. *Address:* Ministry of Tourism, Arts and Culture, Velanaage, 5th Floor, Ameer Ahmed Magu, Malé 20-096, Maldives (office). *Telephone:* 3323224 (office). *Fax:* 3322512 (office). *E-mail:* info@tourism.gov.mv (office). *Website:* www.tourism.gov.mv (office).

GHAFOOR MOHAMED, Abdul, BA, MA; Maldivian diplomatist and international organization official; b. 20 Nov. 1959, Malé; m.; one s. one d.; ed Univ. of Tasmania, Australia, The Fletcher School of Law and Diplomacy, Tufts Univ., USA; career diplomat; Programme Officer, Ministry of Foreign Affairs 1983, Asst Undersecretary 1985, Asst Dir (Political Affairs) 1989, Deputy Dir (Foreign Relations) 1992, Dir (Foreign Relations) 1994; Dir (Maldives), South Asian Asscn for Regional Cooperation Secr., Kathmandu, Nepal 1997–2000; Dir-Gen. (Foreign Relations), Ministry of Foreign Affairs 2000; Counsellor, Embassy in Colombo 2003; Asst Exec. Dir, Ministry of Foreign Affairs 2005; Deputy High Commr to Sri Lanka 2005, to Malaysia 2006; Exec. Dir, Ministry of Foreign Affairs 2007; Perm. Rep. to UN, Geneva 2007–09; Perm. Rep. to WTO 2008–09; Amb.-at-Large, Ministry of Foreign Affairs, seconded to Office of the Pres. 2009–10; Perm. Rep. to UN, New York (also accred as Amb. to USA) 2010–12 (resgnd). *Address:* Ministry of Foreign Affairs, Boduthakurufaanu Magu, Malé 20-077, Maldives (office). *Telephone:* 3323400 (office). *Fax:* 3323841 (office). *E-mail:* admin@foreign.gov.mv (office). *Website:* www.foreign.gov.mv (office).

GHAI, Dharam Pal, PhD; Kenyan international civil servant and economist; b. 29 June 1936, Nairobi; s. of Basti Ghai and Widya Wati; m. Neela Korde 1963; one s. two d.; ed Queen's Coll., Oxford, UK and Yale Univ., USA; Lecturer in Econs, Makerere Univ., Uganda 1961–65; Visiting Fellow, Econ. Growth Center, Yale Univ. 1966–67; Research Prof. and Dir of Econs Research, Inst. of Devt Studies, Univ. of Nairobi 1967–71, Dir Inst. of Devt Studies 1971–74; Sr Economist, Comm. on Int. Devt (Pearson Comm.), Washington, DC 1968–69; Chief, World Employment Programme Research Br., Employment and Devt Dept, ILO, Geneva 1973–74, Chief, Tech. Secr., World Employment Conf. 1975–76, Chief, Rural Employment Policies Br., Employment and Devt Dept 1977–87; Dir UN Research Inst. for Social Devt 1987–97; Coordinator ILO Transition Team 1998–99; Adviser, Int. Inst. of Labour Studies; Fellow, African Acad. of Sciences. *Publications:* Collective Agriculture and Rural Development in Soviet Central Asia (with A. R. Khan) 1979, Planning for Basic Needs in Kenya (co-author) 1979, Agricultural Prices, Policy and Equity in Sub-Saharan Africa (with Lawrence Smith) 1987, Labour and Development in Rural Cuba (co-author) 1987, Social Development and Public Policy (ed.), Renewing Social and Economic Progress in Africa (ed.); contrib. to UN Intellectual History Project; co-ed. and contrib. to several other books. *Leisure interests:* photography, gardening, swimming. *Address:* 32 chemin des Voirons, 1296 Coppet, Vaud, Switzerland (home). *Telephone:* (22) 7765281 (home). *Fax:* (22) 7765282 (home). *E-mail:* ghai@bluewin.ch (home).

GHAI, Yash P., BA, LLM, DCL; Kenyan constitutional lawyer, legal scholar and UN official; b. 1938; ed Univ. of Oxford, UK, Harvard Univ., USA; barrister, Middle Temple, London, UK 1962; Lecturer, Univ. of Dar-es-Salaam 1963–66, Sr Lecturer 1966–69, Prof. and Dean 1969–70; Sr Fellow and Lecturer, Yale Univ., USA 1971–73; Prof., Univ. of Warwick, UK 1974–89; Sir Y. K. Pau Prof. of Public Law, Univ. of Hong Kong 1989–95, Prof. Emer. 1995–; involved in drafting constitutions for Papua New Guinea, Fiji, Solomon Islands and others; Chair. Constitution of Kenya Review Comm. 2000–03; UN Sec.-Gen.'s Special Rep. for Human Rights in Cambodia 2005–08 (resgnd); Distinguished Researcher Award, Univ. of Hong Kong 2001. *Publications include:* Hong Kong's New Constitutional Order: The Resumption of Chinese Sovereignty and Basic Law 1997, Hong Kong's Constitutional Debate: Conflict over Interpretation (co-author) 1999, Autonomy and Ethnicity: Negotiating Competing Claims in Multi-Ethnic States (ed. and contrib.) 2000, Public Participation and Minorities 2001. *Address:* c/o Department of Law, University of Hong Kong, Pokfulam Road, Hong Kong Special Administrative Region, People's Republic of China.

GHALIB, Omar Arteh; Somali politician; b. 1930, Hargeisa; s. of the late Arteh Ghalib and Sahra Sheikh Hassan; m. Shakri Jirdeh Hussein 1954; six s. six d.; ed St Paul's Coll., Cheltenham, UK and Univ. of Bristol; teacher 1946–49; Headmaster of various elementary schools 1949–54; Vice-Prin. Intermediate School, Sheikh, Somalia 1954–56; Prin. Intermediate School, Gabileh 1958; Officer in charge of Adult Educ. 1959; District Commr in Public Admin 1960–61; First Sec.

Somali Embassy, Moscow 1961–62; Rapporteur, Special Cttee on SW Africa, UN 1962–63; Counsellor, Perm. Mission of Somalia at UN, New York 1964; Amb. to Ethiopia 1965–68; mem. Somali Nat. Ass. 1969; Sec. of State for Foreign Affairs 1969–76; Minister of Culture and Higher Educ. 1976–78, in the President's Office 1978–80; mem. Cttee for Social and Political Thought 1976; Speaker, People's Ass. 1982–91; Prime Minister of Somalia 1991–93; numerous awards and decorations. *Publications include:* Back from the Lion of Judah. *Leisure interests:* reciting the Koran, writing, poetry, horse riding, social welfare activities. *Address:* c/o Office of the President, People's Palace, Mogadishu, Somalia.

GHALIBAF, Mohammad Baqer, PhD; Iranian politician; *Mayor of Tehran;* b. 23 Sept. 1961, Mashhad; m.; two s. one d.; ed Tarbiat Modares Univ., Tehran; Chief of IRI (Islamic Repub. of Iran) Police Forces 2000–05 (resgnd); unsuccessful cand. in presidential election 2005; Mayor of Tehran 2005–. *Publication:* Local Government in Iran. *Leisure interests:* reading (novels, history, politics), horse-riding, tennis, swimming. *Address:* Municipality of Tehran, Tehran, Iran (office). *Telephone:* (21) 55630144 (office). *Fax:* (21) 55811985 (office). *E-mail:* ghalibaf@tehran.ir (office). *Website:* www.tehran.ir (office); www.ghalibaf.ir.

GHANDOUR, Fadi, BA; Jordanian business executive; *Co-founder and Vice-Chairman, Aramex International Ltd;* b. 1959; s. of Ali Ghandour; m. Rula Atalla; two s.; ed George Washington Univ., Washington, DC, USA; Co-founder Aramex International Ltd 1982, CEO 1982–2012, Vice-Chair. 2012–; Founding Pnr, Maktoob.com; Middle East and North Africa Area Chair. Young Presidents' Org. 2003–05; fmr Vice-Chair. Bd of Trustees, Jordan River Foundation; fmr Chair. Nat. Microfinance Bank, Jordan; Founder Ruwwad Devt; mem. Bd of Dirs Abraaj Capital; Founding Bd mem. Endeavor Jordan; mem. Advisory Bd Suliman S. Olayan School of Business, American Univ. of Beirut; ranked by Arabian Business amongst the Power 500: The World's Most Influential Arabs (ninth) 2010, (45th) 2012, (41st) 2013. *Address:* Aramex International Ltd, PO Box 960913, Amman 11196, Jordan (office). *Telephone:* (6) 5522192 (office). *Fax:* (6) 5527461 (office). *Website:* www.aramex.com (office); www.fadighandour.com.

GHANI, Ashraf, MPh, PhD; Afghan anthropologist, academic, government official and fmr university administrator; *Chairman, Institute for State Effectiveness;* has taught at Arhus Univ., Denmark and Univ. of Calif., Berkeley, USA; fmr Adjunct Prof. of Anthropology, Johns Hopkins Univ., USA; broadcasts on BBC and Voice of America Persian and Pashto services 1982–; anthropologist at World Bank 1991–2001; Special Adviser to UN Sec.-Gen.'s Special Rep. for Afghanistan 2001 (adviser during the Bonn process and the establishment of the first post-Taliban admin. in Afghanistan); Minister of Finance, Transitional Authority 2002–04; Chancellor, Kabul Univ. 2004; Co-founder and Chair. Inst. for State Effectiveness 2005–; mem. Comm. on Legal Empowerment of the Poor (UNDP initiative); Chair. Global Agenda Council on Fragile States, World Econ. Forum; cand. in presidential elections 2009, 2014; apptd Chair. of govt comm. on transition 2010. *Publication:* Fixing Failed States: A Framework for Rebuilding a Fractured World (co-author) 2008. *Address:* Institute for State Effectiveness, Kabul, Afghanistan (office). *E-mail:* info@effectivestates.org (office). *Website:* www.effectivestates.org (office).

GHANI, Nasimul; Bangladeshi television industry executive; fmr Dir-Gen. Prime Minister's Office; Dir-Gen. Bangladesh TV (govt controlled) 2006–08; mem. Advisory Council Citigroup Microentrepreneurship Awards 2006. *Address:* c/o Bangladesh Television Bhaban, Rampura, Dhaka 1219, Bangladesh. *Telephone:* (2) 9330131. *E-mail:* info@btv.gov.bd. *Website:* www.btv.gov.bd.

GHANI, Owais Ahmed; Pakistani engineer and government official; m. Ghazala Owais Ghani; Kakar Pushtun by tribe; fmr Fed. Minister for Labour in Musharraf-led mil. govt and later Minister for Industries in North West Frontier Prov. –2003; Gov. of Balochistan 2003–08, of North West Frontier Prov. (renamed Khyber Pakhtoonkhwa April 2010) 2008–11; Pres. Pakistan Red Crescent Soc. Balochistan Br.; Chancellor Balochistan Univ. of Information Tech. and Man. Sciences. *Address:* c/o Office of the Governor, Peshwar, Khyber Pakhtoonkhwa, Pakistan.

GHANNOUCHI, Muhammad; Tunisian politician; b. 18 Aug. 1941, Sousse, French Tunisia; ed Tunis Univ.; Minister of Finance and the Economy 1989–92, of Int. Co-operation and Foreign Investment 1992–99; Prime Minister 1999–2011 (resgnd); Acting Pres. of Tunisia following the fall of Pres. Zine El Abidine Ben Ali in the wake of popular protests 14–15 Jan. 2011; mem. Constitutional Democratic Rally party. *Address:* c/o Bureau du Premier Ministre, La Kasbah, 1008 Tunis, Tunisia.

GHARBI, El Mostafa, LLB; Moroccan international postal official; b. 9 Feb. 1935, El Jadida; m. Lalla Hafida Regragui 1962; three d.; ed Ecole Nat. Supérieure des Postes, Télégraphes et Téléphones, Paris; various positions, Ministry of Posts, Telegraphs and Telephones, Rabat 1956–65, Dir of Postal and Financial Services 1965–71; Counsellor, Universal Postal Union (UPU), Berne 1971–78, Sr Counsellor 1978–81, Asst Dir-Gen. in charge of postal services and studies 1981–90, in charge of legal and admin. questions 1990–, later Asst Dir-Gen., Int. Bureau; Médaille de Chevalier. *Publications include:* The UPU: Present Situation – Main Policies 1990; other books on postal services and strategies. *Leisure interests:* reading, sport. *Address:* c/o International Bureau Universal Postal Union, CP 3000, Berne 15, Switzerland.

GHARIANI, Muhammad; Tunisian diplomatist; m. Olfa Ghariani; activist in youth wing of Democratic Constitutional Rally (RCD) 1980s, Sec.-Gen. RCD Students' party 1987, Deputy Sec.-Gen. for Youth, Educ. and Culture 1995–96; mem. Econ. and Social Council 1992–96; Gov. southern Tunisian prov. of Sidi Bouzid 1996–2001; Deputy Sec.-Gen. for Relations with Orgs and Asscns 2001–05; Amb. to UK (also accred to Ireland) 2005–07; Sec.-Gen. Rassemblement constitutionnel démocratique (political party) 2008–11; arrested on charges of embezzlement 2011. *Leisure interest:* literature.

GHASEMI, Brig.-Gen. (retd) Rostam; Iranian military officer and government official; b. 22 May 1964, Shiraz, Fars Prov.; ed Aryamehr Univ. of Tech.; joined Army of the Guardians of the Islamic Revolution 1981, participated in Iran–Iraq War 1980s; later joined Khatam Anbia Troops (Guards' eng and construction co.), Deputy Commdr 2001–07, Chief Commdr Iranian Revolutionary Guard 2007–11 (retd); elected mem. Parl. 1988, re-elected 1992, 1996; Minister of Petroleum 2011–13; Adviser to Minister of Defence 2013–; Chair. Iranian Marine Industrial

Co. (SADRA), Khalij Fars Shipbuilding Complex (ISOICO); Man. Iran Sepah Marine Eng Div.; Man. Dir Khatam-Ul-Anbia Construction HQR (upstream and downstream oil, gas and petrochemical projects) 2006–11; Pres. of the Conf., OPEC; mem. Iran Chamber of Commerce, Industries and Mines, Bd of Dirs Industrial Devt and Renovation Org. of Iran; ranked by Forbes magazine amongst The World's Most Powerful People (32nd) 2011, (57th) 2012. *Address:* Ministry of Defence and Armed Forces Logistics, Shahid Yousuf Kaboli St, Sayed Khandan Area, Tehran, Iran (office). *Telephone:* (21) 26126988 (office). *E-mail:* info@mod.ir (office). *Website:* www.mod.ir (office).

GHAZAL, Mohammed Iyad, BEng; Syrian government official; *Governor, Homs Governorate;* b. Aleppo; ed Univ. of Aleppo; Pres. and Gen. Dir Syrian Railways 1999–2005; Gov. Homs Governorate 2005–. *Address:* Office of the Governor, Homs, Syria (office). *Website:* www.homs-city.gov.sy (office).

GHAZANFAR, Hosna Banu, BA, MA, PhD; Afghan politician, academic and poet; b. 1 Feb. 1957, Balkh; d. of Abdul Ghafar; ed Sultan Razia High School, Mazar-e-Sharif, Stawarpool Qafqaaz Univ., St Petersburg Univ., Russia; fmr Lecturer in Literature, Kabul Univ. for two years, fmr Dean of Faculty of Literature and Language; Minister of Women's Affairs (first female minister in cabinet) 2006–10; mem. High Council of Ministry of Higher Educ., Speranto Int. Asscn of Women, Int. Asscn of Turk Zabanan, Bd of Dirs Hakim Naser Khesro Balkhi Asscn. *Publications include:* The Human Fate, Predations in the 21st Century, The Secrets of Beauty and Attraction, Self Realization (trans.); scientific articles and essays published in nat. and int. newspapers. *Address:* c/o Ministry of Women's Affairs, beside Cinema Zainab, Shar-i-Nau, Kabul, Afghanistan.

GHAZZALI, Dato' Sheikh Abdul Khalid, BEcons; Malaysian diplomatist and consultant; *Senior Advisor, Malaysia, Bower Group Asia;* b. 20 March 1946; m. Datin Faridah Ghazzali; ed Univ. of La Trobe, Australia; fmr Deputy Perm. Rep. to UN and Security Council, New York, fmr Deputy High Commr to UK, fmr High Commr to Zimbabwe, fmr Dir-Gen. Inst. of Diplomacy and Foreign Relations, Malaysia, fmr Deputy Sec.-Gen., Ministry of Foreign Affairs, Amb. to USA 1999–2006, Amb.-at-Large, Ministry of Foreign Affairs 2006–10; currently Sr Advisor, Malaysia, Bower Group Asia; ASEAN-USA Eminent Person for Malaysia; mem. Bd of Trustees Axiata Foundation. *Leisure interests:* reading, walking. *Address:* Bower Group Asia, 11350 Random Hills Road, Suite 400, Fairfax, VA 22030, USA. *E-mail:* tansrighazzali@bowergroupasia.com (office). *Website:* bowergroupasia.com (office).

GHEDI, Ali Mohamed; Somali politician and academic; b. Mogadishu; m.; ed Somali Nat. Univ., Univ. of Pisa, Italy; qualified veterinary physician; Lecturer and researcher, Somali Nat. Univ. –1991; fmr special adviser and consultant to regional livestock orgs; served with UN, Nairobi, animal disease programme for Somalia; Founding mem. and Pres. Somalia NGO Consortium; Prime Minister of Somalia 2004–07 (resgnd). *Address:* c/o Office of the Prime Minister, PO Box 623, Sarit, 00606, Somalia (office).

GHEORGHE, Mariana; Romanian business executive; *President of the Executive Board and CEO, OMV Petrom SA;* ed Acad. of Econ. Studies, Univ. of Bucharest Law School, London Business School, UK; worked for Ministry of Finance 1991–93, held position of Deputy Gen. Dir, Int. Finance Dept; apptd Assoc. Banker, EBRD, London 1993, currently Sr Banker, South-Eastern Europe and the Caucasus Group, Banking; currently Pres. Exec. Bd and CEO OMV Petrom SA, Dir, Snp Petrom SA; ranked by Fortune magazine amongst the 50 Most Powerful Women in Business outside the US (32nd) 2012. *Address:* OMV Petrom SA, 239 Calea Dorobantilor Sector 1, 010567 Bucharest, Romania (office). *Telephone:* (21) 2125001 (office). *Fax:* (21) 3155166 (office). *E-mail:* info@petrom.com (office). *Website:* www.petrom.com (office); www.omv.com/portal/01/com/omv/OMV_Group/Business_Segments/OMV_Gas_and_Power/Subsidiaries/OMV_Petrom_SA (office).

GHEORGHIU, Angela; Romanian singer (soprano); b. 7 Sept. 1965, Adjud; m. 1st Andrei Gheorghiu 1988; m. 2nd Roberto Alagna (q.v.) 1996; ed Bucharest Acad.; debut at Bucharest as Solveig in Grieg's Peer Gynt 1983; appearances at Covent Garden from 1992, Met debut 1993, and in Washington, Vienna, Monte Carlo, Berlin, Nat. Opera Cluj; repertoire includes Zerlina, Mimi, Nina (all in Cherubin), Suzel (L'Amico Fritz), Juliette (Roméo et Juliette), Magda (La Rondine), Nedda (Pagliacci), Tosca, Manon, and roles in Don Giovanni, La Bohème, Turandot, Carmen, La Traviata (Violetta), L'Elisir d'Amore, Falstaff; Belvedere Prize, Vienna, Schatzgraber-Preis, Hamburg State Opera, Gulbenkian Prize. *Recordings include:* La Traviata (as Violetta) 1994, Casta Diva 2001, Tosca (solo) 2001, Diva 2004, Manon 2007, Live From La Scala 2007, My Puccini 2008, Madama Butterfly 2009, Puccini Opera Arias 2010, Tosca 2011, Fedora 2011, Homage to Maria Callas 2011. *Address:* IMG Artists, Carnegie Hall Tower, 152 West 57th Street, 5th Floor, New York, NY 10019, USA (office). *Telephone:* (212) 994-3500 (office). *Fax:* (212) 994-3550 (office). *E-mail:* jmastroianni@imgartists.com (office); agerdanovits@gmx.net. *Website:* www.imgartists.com (office); www.angelagheorghiu.com.

GHERMAN, Natalia, MA; Moldovan diplomatist and government official; *Deputy Prime Minister and Minister of Foreign Affairs and European Integration;* b. 20 March 1969, Chişinău; d. of Mircea Snegur (fmr Pres. of Moldova) and Georgette Snegur; m. Artur Gherman; one c.; ed Moldova State Univ., Nat. School of Political and Admin. Studies, Romania, King's Coll., London, UK; Second Sec., Dept of Int. Orgs, Ministry of Foreign Affairs (MFA) 1991–92, First Sec., Dept of European Orgs 1992–94, Counsellor and Deputy Head of Perm. Del. of Moldova to OSCE and other Int. Orgs in Vienna 1994–97, Deputy Head, Dept of European Security and Political-Military Affairs, MFA 1997–2001, Minister-Counsellor, Embassy in Brussels and Deputy Head, Mission of Moldova to NATO 2001–02, Amb. to Austria, also Perm. Rep. to OSCE and other Int. Orgs in Vienna 2002–06, Amb. to Sweden (also accred to Norway and Finland) 2006–09, Deputy Minister of Foreign Affairs and European Integration 2009–13, Deputy Prime Minister and Minister of Foreign Affairs and European Integration 2013–. mem. Liberal Democratic Party of Moldova. *Address:* Ministry of Foreign Affairs and European Integration, 2012 Chişinău, str. 31 August 1989 80, Moldova (office). *Telephone:* (22) 57-82-07 (office). *Fax:* (22) 23-23-02 (office). *E-mail:* secdep@mfa.md (office). *Website:* www.mfa.gov.md (office).

GHESQUIÈRE, Nicolas; French fashion designer; *Creative Director, Louis Vuitton;* b. 9 May 1971, Comines, Nord Département; internship with agnès b. (Paris-based fashion designer) 1986; Asst to designer Jean-Paul Gaultier 1990–92; fmr stylist with designers Thierry Mugler and Trussardi; fmr designer, Pôles (Parisian knitwear manufacturer); joined fashion house Balenciaga as licensed product designer 1995, becoming Artistic Dir 'Le Dix' womenswear collection 1997, Creative Dir, Balenciaga 1997–2012; joined Louis Vuitton 2013, becoming Creative Dir (women's collections) 2013–; Chevalier, Ordre des Arts et des Lettres 2007; Avant-Garde Designer of the Year, VH1/Vogue Fashion Awards 2000, Womenswear Designer of the Year, Council of Fashion Designers of America 2001. *Address:* Louis Vuitton, 22 avenue Montaigne, 75008 Paris, France (office). *Telephone:* (1) 44-13-22-22 (office). *Fax:* (1) 44-13-21-19 (office). *Website:* www .louisvuitton.com (office).

GHEZ, Andrea Mia, BS, PhD; American physicist, astronomer and academic; *Professor of Physics and Astronomy and Lauren B. Leichtman & Arthur E. Levine Chair in Astrophysics, University of California, Los Angeles;* b. 16 June 1965, New York, NY; ed Massachusetts Inst. of Tech., California Inst. of Tech.; Hubble Postdoctoral Research Fellow, Steward Observatory, Univ. of Arizona 1992–93; Asst Prof. of Physics and Astronomy, UCLA 1994–97, Assoc. Prof. 1997–2000, Prof. 2000–; mem. American Acad. of Arts and Sciences 2004, NAS 2004; Packard Fellowship 1996, UCLA Physics Dept Teaching Award 1997, 1998, 2005, Newton Lacy Pierce Prize, American Astronomical Soc. 1998, Maria Goeppert-Mayer Award, American Physical Soc. 1999, Sackler Prize 2004, Aaronson Award 2006, MacArthur Fellowship 2008, Crafoord Prize, Royal Swedish Acad. of Sciences (co-recipient) 2012. *Publications:* more than 160 papers in professional journals. *Address:* Department of Physics and Astronomy, 430 Portola Plaza, University of California, Los Angeles, CA 90095-1547, USA (office). *Telephone:* (310) 206-0420 (office). *E-mail:* ghez@astro.ucla.edu (office). *Website:* www.astro.ucla.edu/~ghez (office).

GHEZALI, Salima; Algerian newspaper editor; *Editor-in-Chief, La Nation;* b. 1958, Bouira; m. (divorced); two c.; fmr schoolteacher, Mitidja Hills; Ed.-in-Chief La Nation weekly newspaper 1994–96, 2001–, newspaper suspended by Algerian authorities 1996–2001; f. Women of Europe and North Africa Asscn, Asscn for Women's Emancipation 1989; f. Nyssa magazine; Int. Press Club Award 1996, Sakharov Human Rights Prize 1997, Olof Palme Prize 1997. *Publications:* Le Reve Algérien 1999, Los amantes de Sherezade 2000. *Address:* La Nation, 33 rue Larbi Ben M'hidi, Algiers, Algeria (office). *Telephone:* (21) 43-21-76 (office).

GHIGO, Enzo; Italian politician; b. 1953, Turin; m. Anna Casale; one s.; fmr Scientific Ed., UTET (publishing co.), Turin; self-employed in tech. components industry –1982; joined Pubblitalia '80 (advertising co.) 1982, Man. 1986–90, Area Man. for Veneto and Marche 1990; Regional Co-ordinator, Forza Italia 1993; mem. Parl. for Piedmont 2 1994, Pres. Piedmont 1995–2005, Vice-Pres. Regional Presidential Congress 1997; Pres. Conf. of Presidents of Italian Regions 2000–05; Vice-Pres. Foundation Italia in Japan 2001; Senator 12th Standing Cttee 2008; Co-ordinator Piedmont Blue 2008–; Grand'Ufficiale al merito della Repubblica Italiana 1999, Cavaliere di Gran Croce 2002. *Leisure interests:* cinema, reading, cycling.

GHIMIRE, Madhav Prasad, MSc, MBA; Nepalese civil servant, diplomatist and politician; *Minister for Home Affairs and Minister for Foreign Affairs;* b. 7 Feb. 1961, Tansen Municipality-12, Palpa; ed Tribhuvan Univ., Asian Inst. of Tech., Thailand; joined civil service as Planning Officer at Nat. Planning Comm. 1985–92, Under-Sec. 1992–98, Jt Sec. 1998–2004, responsible for overall human resource management at Ministry of Water Resources, also served as Chief Admin. Officer at Dept of Irrigation, introducing and institutionalizing VAT system in Nepal, headed Foreign Aid Co-ordination Div. of Ministry of Finance 1998–2003, architect of Nepal Devt Forum, Paris 2000, Kathmandu 2002, Consul Gen. to Hong Kong and Macao Special Admin. Regions of People's Repub. of China 2003, Sec. to Ministry of Gen. Admin 2004–06, to Ministry of Culture, Tourism and Civil Aviation 2006–09, to Ministry of Peace and Reconstruction 2008–09, Chief Sec. of the Govt 2009–12; Minister for Home Affairs and Minister for Foreign Affairs 2013–; Suprabal Gorkha Daxinbahu, Fourth Medal, and Suprabal Gorkha Daxinbahu, Third Medal from the then King of Nepal, Rastra Deep (Light of the Nation) from Pres. Dr Ram Baran Yadav; Best Youth of the Year, Nepal Jaycees 1999, Best Civil Service Employee of the Year, Govt of Nepal 2001, Best Alumnus, Asian Inst. of Tech. Alumni Asscn Annual Meeting, Indonesia 2005. *Publications:* Bibliography on Environmental Studies (co-ed.) 1993; several articles in journals, mostly on economic reforms, governance, foreign aid management and peace building. *Address:* Ministry of Foreign Affairs, Narayanhiti, Kathmandu, Nepal (office). *Telephone:* (1) 4416001 (office); (1) 4416011 (office). *Fax:* (1) 4416016 (office). *E-mail:* fmo@mofa.gov.np (office). *Website:* www.mofa.gov.np (office).

GHIMPU, Mihai; Moldovan lawyer and politician; *Chairman, Liberal Party;* b. 19 Nov. 1951, Colonița; s. of Toader Ghimpu and Irina Ursu; m. Dina Ghimpu; ed Moldova State Univ.; served in Soviet army –1972; began career as legal counsel, becoming head of legal dept of several state enterprises; Judge, Sectorul Rîșcani, Chișinău 1978–90; Founder mem. Popular Front of Moldova 1988–93; mem. Parl. (Popular Front) 1990–94, (Bloc of the Intellectuals) 1994–98, Vice-Chair. Parl. Legal Cttee, Chair. (Speaker) 2009–10; mem. Party of Reform 1993–, Chair. 1998– (renamed Liberal Party of Moldova 2005); Alderman, Chișinău Municipal Council 2007–09, Chair. 2007–08; Acting Pres. of Moldova 2009–10. *Address:* Liberal Party (Partidul Liberal), 2012 Chișinău, str. București 87A, Moldova (office). *Telephone:* (22) 23-26-89 (office); (22) 22-80-97 (office). *E-mail:* liberal@pl.md (office). *Website:* www.pl.md (office).

GHIUSELEV, Nicola; Bulgarian singer (bass) and opera teacher; b. 17 Aug. 1936, Pavlikeni; s. of Nicolai Ghiuselev and Elisaveta Ghiuseleva; m. 1st Roumiana Ghiuseleva 1960; m. 2nd Anna Maria Petrova-Ghiuseleva 1984; two s. one d.; ed Acad. of Fine Arts, Sofia and singing studies under Christo Brumbarov; won vocal competitions in Sofia 1959, Prague 1960, Helsinki 1962; joined State Opera Co., Sofia; debut as Timur in Puccini's Turandot, State Opera, Sofia 1961; has since appeared at most of the major opera houses of the world; major roles include Philip II, Boris Godounov, Don Giovanni, Attila, Wotan and the Mefistofele roles of Gounod, Berlioz and Boito; noted for Russian roles such as Dositheus, Prince Igor, Ivan the Terrible and the bass repertoire of Verdi, Rossini,

Bellini, Donizetti, Mozart, Berlioz, Cherubini, Ponchielli, etc.; Commendatore della Repubblica Italiana; Dr hc (Bulgarian Acad. of Sciences); Golden Verdi-Parma; many awards from Bulgaria and Italy. *Recordings include:* Turandot 1961, Les Huguenots 1969, Offenbach: Les Contes d'Hoffmann, Mefistofele 1983, Orthodox Chants 1997, Opera Arias 1997. *Address:* ul. Vassil Chekalarov 11, 1616 Sofia, Bulgaria; Largo Don G., Morosini 1, 00195 Rome, Italy. *Telephone:* (2) 8562929 (Sofia); (06) 37513321 (Rome). *Fax:* (2) 8562929 (Sofia); (06) 37513321 (Rome). *E-mail:* adriafilm@libero.it (office); petrova@annamaria@gmail.com (home). *Website:* www.ghiuselev-opera.com.

GHIZ, Robert, BA; Canadian politician; *Premier, Prince Edward Island;* b. 21 Jan. 1974, Charlottetown; s. of the late fmr Premier of PEI Joseph Ghiz; m. Dr Kate Ellis; one d.; ed Bishop's Univ.; Special Asst to Minister of Canadian Heritage 1997–98; lobbyist for Bank of Nova Scotia, Ottawa 1998–2001; Atlantic Canada Advisor, Office of the Prime Minister, Ottawa 2001–03; Leader PEI Liberal Party 2003–; MLA for Charlottetown-Rochford Square 2003–07, for Charlottetown-Brighton 2007–, Leader of the Opposition 2003–07; Premier of PEI 2007–. *Address:* Office of the Premier, Shaw Building, 5th Floor South, 95 Rochford Street, PO Box 2000, Charlottetown, PE C1A 7N8, Canada (office). *Telephone:* (902) 368-4400 (office). *Fax:* (902) 368-4416 (office). *E-mail:* premier@gov.pe.ca (office). *Website:* www.gov.pe.ca/premier (office).

GHIZZONI, Federico; Italian business executive; *CEO, UniCredit Group;* b. 14 Oct. 1955, Piacenza; ed Univ. of Law, Parma; began career as Customer Relations Man. at Credito Italiano's Piacenza Br. 1980, worked as Head of Credit and Marketing Dept, later Br. Dir, Trieste 1988–89, Dir Seriate Br. 1990–92, Deputy Gen. Man. Credito Italiano's London Office 1992–95, Gen. Man. Singapore Office 1995–2000, Exec. Dir responsible for Corp. and Int. Banking, Bank Pekao SA (affiliate of UniCredit Group) 2000–02, worked at Koç Financial Services (joint venture with UniCredit Group) 2003, COO and Exec. Bd mem. Koç Financial Services and COO & Vice-Chair. Yapi ve Kredi Bankasi (following acquisition by Koç Financial Services), Head of Poland's Markets Div. at UniCredit, Head of CEE Banking Operations and Bd mem. responsible for CEE Banking Div., Bank Austria AG 2007–10, Deputy CEO and Deputy Gen. Man. UniCredit Aug.–Sept. 2010, CEO UniCredit 2010–, mem. Perm. Strategic Cttee, Corp. Governance, HR and Nomination Cttee, Chair. Supervisory Bd UniCredit Bank AG, Munich 2011–; Chair. Orchestra Filarmonica della Scala Asscn, Milan; mem. Int. Monetary Conf., Washington, DC, Institut Int. d'Etudes Bancaires, Brussels. *Address:* UniCredit Group, Piazza Cordusia, 20123 Milan, Italy (office). *Telephone:* (02) 88621 (office). *Fax:* (02) 88628503 (office). *E-mail:* info@unicreditgroup.eu (office). *Website:* www .unicreditgroup.eu (office).

GHONDA MANGALIBI, Antoine; Democratic Republic of the Congo politician; b. 19 Feb. 1965, Leuven, Belgium; Minister of Foreign Affairs and Int. Co-operation 2003–04; Amb. to Pres. Kabila 2005; mem. Nat. Ass. 2006–. *Address:* c/o National Assembly, Brazzaville, Democratic Republic of the Congo (office). *Website:* www.assemblee-nationale.cg/ (office).

GHOSE, Gautam; Indian film director and actor; b. 24 July 1950, Calcutta; s. of Prof. Himangshu Ghosh and Santana Ghosh; m. Neelanjana Ghosh 1978; one s. one d.; ed Cathedral Mission School, Calcutta, City Coll., Calcutta and Calcutta Univ.; mem. Int. Jury (Oberhausen) 1979; official del., Cannes and London Film Festivals 1982, Venice and Tokyo Film Festivals 1984; mem. Nat. Jury 1985; Exec. Dir Nat. Film Inst. 1987; Dir Nat. Film Devt Corpn, West Bengal Film Devt Corpn; Knighthood of the Star of the Italian Solidarity 2006; Pres. Award (five times), Human Rights Award (France), Silver Medal and UNESCO Award, Grand Prix Award (USSR), Vittori Di Sica Award, several Nat. and Int. awards. *Films include:* Hungry Autumn 1974, Maabhoomi 1980, Dakhal 1981, Paar 1984, Antarjali Yatra 1987, Padma Nadir Majhi 1992, Patang 1993, Gudiya 1997, Dekha 2001, Abar Aranye 2003, Yatra 2006, Kaalbela 2009. *Publications include:* numerous articles on the cinema. *Leisure interests:* music, reading, travel. *Address:* Block 5, Flat 50, 28/1A Gariahat Road, Kolkata 700 029, India. *Telephone:* (33) 4405630 (home). *Fax:* (33) 4640315 (home).

GHOSH, Amitav, BA, MA, DPhil; Indian writer and academic; b. 11 July 1956, Kolkata; m. Deborah Baker; two c.; ed St Stephen's Coll., Univ. of Delhi, Institut Bourguiba des Langues Vivantes, Tunis and Univ. of Oxford, UK; Visiting Fellow, Centre for Social Sciences, Trivandrum, Kerala 1982–83; Research Assoc., Dept of Sociology, Univ. of Delhi 1983–87, Lecturer, Dept of Sociology 1987; Visiting Prof., Depts of Literature and Anthropology, Univ. of Virginia, Charlottesville 1988, South Asia Centre, Columbia Univ. 1989, Dept of Anthropology, Univ. of Pennsylvania 1989; Fellow, Centre for Studies in Social Science, Kolkata 1990–92; Adjunct Prof., Dept of Anthropology, Columbia Univ. 1993, Visiting Prof. 1994–97; Distinguished Visiting Prof., American Univ. in Cairo 1994; fiction workshop, Sarah Lawrence Coll., New York 1996; Distinguished Prof., Dept of Comparative Literature, Queens Coll., CUNY 1999–2003; Visiting Prof., Dept of English and American Literature and Language, Harvard Univ. 2004; Best American Essays Award 1995, Padma Shri 2007, Pushcart Prize 1999, Grinzane Cavour Prize 2007, Dan David Prize 2010. *Publications include:* The Circle of Reason (New York Times Notable Book 1987, Prix Médicis Étranger 1990) 1986, The Shadow Lines (Sahitya Akademi Award, Ananda Puraskar 1990) 1988, In an Antique Land (non-fiction) (New York Times Notable Book of 1993) 1992, The Calcutta Chromosome (Arthur C. Clark Award 1997) 1996, Dancing in Cambodia and At Large in Burma (essays) 1998, Countdown 1999, The Glass Palace (Frankfurt International e-Book Awards Grand Prize for Fiction, New York Times Notable Book, Los Angeles Times Notable Book, Chicago Tribune Favourite Book 2001) 2000, The Imam and the Indian (essays) 2002, The Hungry Tide (Hutch Crossword Book Prize 2006) 2004, Sea of Poppies (Indiaplaza Golden Quill Awards for Best Book, Readers' Choice Award for Fiction, Vodafone Crossword Book Award 2009) 2008, River of Smoke 2011; contrib. to articles in Ethnology, Granta, The New Republic, New York Times, Public Culture, Subaltern Studies, Letra Internacional, Cultural Anthropology, Observer Magazine, Wilson Quarterly, The New Yorker, Civil Lines, American Journal of Archaeology, Kenyon Review, Desh. *E-mail:* amitav@amitavghosh.com (office). *Website:* www.penguinbooksindia.com/ amitavghosh; www.amitavghosh.com.

GHOSH, Asim; Canadian business executive; *President and CEO, Husky Energy;* began career with Procter & Gamble in Canada; then Sr Vice-Pres., Carling

O'Keefe; later became Founding CEO Pepsi Foods' start-up operations in India; subsequently served in sr exec. positions and as CEO of AS Watson consumer packaged goods subsidiary of Hutchison Whampoa, managed a group of 13 business units 1991–98, expanded group's operations from Hong Kong to China and Europe; fmr Man. Dir and CEO Vodafone Essar Ltd; mem. Bd of Dirs Husky Energy 2009–, Pres. and CEO 2010–; mem. Bd of Dirs Kotak Mahindra Bank Ltd; Dir, Li Ka Shing (Canada) Foundation. *Address:* Husky Energy, 707 Eighth Avenue SW, Box 6525, Station 'D', Calgary, Alberta, T2P 3G7, Canada (office). *Telephone:* (403) 298-6111 (office). *Fax:* (403) 298-7464 (office). *E-mail:* info@huskyenergy.com (office). *Website:* www.huskyenergy.com (office).

GHOSN, Carlos, BEng; Brazilian/French/Lebanese automotive industry executive; *Chairman and CEO, Renault SA; Chairman, President and CEO, Nissan Motor Co. Ltd;* b. 9 March 1954, Porto-Velho, Brazil; m. Rita Ghosn; one s. three d.; ed Collège Notre-Dame de Jamhour, Beirut, Ecole Polytechnique, Ecole des Mines, Paris; moved to Beirut, Lebanon with his mother 1960; trained as mining eng; Man. Dir Michelin Le Puy factory 1981, CEO Michelin Brazil 1985, Michelin North America 1989; Asst Dir-Gen. Renault Group 1996, Dir (non-exec.) 2001–, Pres. and CEO Renault SA 2005–, Chair. 2008–; COO Nissan Motor Co. Ltd 1999–2001, Dir 1999–, Pres. 2000–, CEO 2001–, Co-Chair. 2003–08, Chair. 2008–, Pres. and CEO Nissan N America –2007; Chair. Alliance Bd Renault-Nissan b.v.; mem. Bd of Dirs Alcoa Inc. 2002–11, Alcoa of Australia Ltd 2002–, Alcoa Automotive Inc. 2002–, Closure Systems International Inc. 2002–, Sony Corpn 2003–, IBM Corpn 2004–05, Mirant Corpn, Public Jt Stock Co. AVTOVAZ, Public Jt Stock Co. AVTOVAZ; mem. Int. Advisory Bd Itaú Unibanco Holding SA; Hon. KBE 2006; voted Man of the Year by Fortune magazine's Asian edn 2003, Japan Automotive Hall of Fame 2004, named by CEO Quarterly Magazine as one of the Most Respected CEOs 2010, named by Forbes as one of the Seven Most Powerful South Americans 2010, ranked by Arabian Business amongst the Power 500: The World's Most Influential Arabs (14th) 2011, (86th) 2012. *Publications:* Renaissance 2001, Shift: Inside Nissan's Historic Revival 2005. *Address:* Renault SA, 13–15 quai Le Gallo, 92513 Boulogne-Billancourt Cedex, France (office); Nissan Motor Co. Ltd, 1-1, Takashima 1-chome, Nishi-ku, Yokohama-shi, Kanagawa 220-8686, Japan (office). *Telephone:* 1-76-84-50-50 (Paris) (office); (45) 523-5523 (Kanagawa) (office). *Fax:* 1-41-04-51-49 (Paris) (office). *Website:* www.renault.com (office); www.nissan-global.com (office).

GHOSN, Fayiz, BA, MA; Lebanese politician; b. 1950, Kousba; m.; two d.; ed Lebanese Univ., St Joseph Univ., Beirut; mem. Majlis al-Nuab (Nat. Ass.) for Koura 1992–2005, mem. Lebanese–French Parl. Cttee; Minister of Nat. Defence 2011–14; mem. El-Marada Movt, currently Vice-Pres. *Address:* c/o Ministry of National Defence, Yarze, Beirut, Lebanon (office).

GHOSSOUB, Joseph; Lebanese marketing executive; *Chairman and CEO, MENA Communications Group (MENACOM);* b. Beirut; m. Daad Rahme 1977; three c.; f. Low One (night club), Reyfoun 1974; opened restaurant, Kaslik 1976; worked in Saudi Arabia 1980–83; worked in advertising in Lebanon 1983–85; moved to Dubai 1985; f. Team Advertising 1994, CEO 1993, affiliated with Young and Rubicam 1997, consolidated all businesses under The Holding Group (THG) 2000, renamed MENA Communications Group (MENACOM) 2009, currently Chair. and CEO; Chair. and World Pres. Int. Advertising Asscn 2004–08; fmr Pres. Lebanese Business Council in the UAE; mem. Bd Arab Forum for Environment and Devt; Dir Dubai Media Inc. 2003, 2007–; fmr Dir American Univ. in Dubai; Kt, Nat. Order of the Cedar 2004, Presidency Shield of the Repub. of Lebanon 2006, Pontifical Equestrian Order of St Gregory the Great (Vatican) 2009; Campaign Middle East's Man of the Year Award 2006, Dubai Lynx Advertising Personality of the Year 2008, Arabian Business Achievement Award for Business Leadership 2008, Arab Ad Man of the Year 2012, ranked by Arabian Business amongst the Power 500: The World's Most Influential Arabs (19th) 2010, (55th) 2012, (25th) 2013. *Leisure interest:* golf. *Address:* MENA Communications Group, 2nd Floor, Arjaan Office Tower, Office No. 201, Dubai, United Arab Emirates (office). *Telephone:* (4) 4354211 (office). *Fax:* (4) 4341739 (office). *Website:* www.wpp.com (office); josephghossoub.com.

GHOZALI, Sid Ahmed; Algerian politician and diplomatist; b. 31 March 1937, Marnia; ed Ecole des Ponts et Chaussées, Paris; fmr Dir of Energy, Ministry of Industry and Energy; Adviser, Ministry of the Economy 1964; Under-Sec., Ministry of Public Works 1964–65; Pres., Dir-Gen. Soc. nationale pour la recherche, la production, le transport, la transformation et la commercialisation des hydrocarbures (SONATRACH) 1966–84, Chair., Man. Dir; Minister of Hydraulics March–Oct. 1979, of Foreign Affairs 1989–91; Prime Minister of Algeria 1991–92; Amb. to Belgium 1987–89, to France 1992–93; mem. Cen. Cttee Front de Libération Nat.; Chair. Front Démocratique 2000–; mem. Org. technique de mise en valeur des richesses du sous-sol saharien 1962; unsuccessful cand. cand. in presidential elections 1999, 2004. *Address:* Front Démocratique, Algiers, Algeria (office).

GHUKASSIAN, Arkady Arshavirovich, MA; Armenian politician, diplomatist and fmr journalist; *Special Envoy of the President of Armenia;* b. 21 June 1957, Stepanakert, Azerbaijan; m.; two c.; ed Yerevan State Univ., Armenia; reporter, Sovetskii Karabakh newspaper (Russian edn) 1979–81, First Deputy Ed. 1981–88; sr mem. Karabakh Movt 1988; elected Deputy to Supreme Soviet (Supreme Council) of Nagornyi Karabakh 1992; Minister of Foreign Affairs of 'Repub. of Nagornyi Karabakh' 1993–98; Pres. of 'Repub. of Nagornyi Karabakh' 1997–2007 (sustained serious injuries as result of assassination attempt 2000); currently Special Envoy of the Pres. of Armenia; Vice-Chair. Bd of Trustees All-Armenian Hayastan Fund 2009–; Hon. mem. Acad. of Sciences on Security, Defence and Law and Order, Acad. of Sciences on Int. Relations, Acad. of Sciences on Nature and Society, Acad. of Sciences on Nat. Security Problems, Acad. of Spiritual Unity of Nations; Golden Eagle Order of the Hero of Artsakh. *Address:* All-Armenian Hayastan Fund, Government Building #3, 0010 Yerevan, Armenia (office). *Telephone:* (10) 521505 (office). *Fax:* (10) 523795 (office). *E-mail:* a.ghukasyan@president.am (office). *Website:* www.president.am/en/staff/ (office).

GHULAM ALI, Anita; Pakistani academic; *Managing Director, Sindh Education Foundation;* Lecturer in Microbiology, Sindh Muslim Science Coll., Karachi 1961–; Man. Dir Sindh Educ. Foundation 1992–; Minister for Educ., Culture, Science, Tech., Youth and Sports 1996, 1999; has represented Prov. of Sindh and Pakistan at various nat. and int. forums on educ. and devt including World UN Conf., Copenhagen, Nat. Muslim Women's Conf., Islamabad, SAARC Conf. on Educ. in the Underserved Areas, Bhutan, World Educ. Conf., Dakar, Senegal, World Conf. on Educ. For All at Jomtien, Thailand; Sitara-e-Imtiaz Award. *Address:* Sindh Education Foundation, Head Office, Plot 9, Block 7, Kehkashan Clifton 5, Karachi, Pakistan (office). *Telephone:* (21) 111424111 (office). *Fax:* (21) 99251652 (office); (21) 9251671 (office). *E-mail:* info@sef.org.pk (office). *Website:* www.sef.org.pk (office).

GHUNAIM, Maha K. al-, BSc; Kuwaiti business executive; *Chairperson and Managing Director, Global Investment House;* m.; four c.; ed San Francisco State Univ., USA; began career with Kuwait Foreign Trading Contracting & Investment Co. 1982–98; Founder, Vice-Chair. and Man. Dir Global Investment House, Kuwait 1998–2006, Chair. and Man. Dir 2006–; Pres. Kuwait Chapter, Young Arab Leaders Org.; mem. Bd of Dirs Nat. Industries Group, BankMuscat International (Bahrain); Chair. Global Bahrain; Vice-Chair. Al-Soor Finance Co., Shurooq Investment Services Co. (Oman); mem. DEPA United Group, UAE; mem. Practitioner Cttee Dubai Int. Financial Exchange; Gulf Excellence Award 2005, Arabian Business magazine Business Women of the Year Award 2005, named by Forbes Arabia Magazine as one of Top 50 Leading Arab Women, named by Forbes International amongst Women to Watch in the Middle East 2005, named by Newsweek Arabia amongst the 43 Most Influential Personalities in the Middle East 2005, ranked by Forbes magazine amongst The World's 100 Most Powerful Women (91st) 2006, (72nd) 2007, (89th) 2008, (94th) 2010. *Address:* Global Investment House, Souk Al-Safat Bldg, 2nd Floor, PO Box 28807, Safat 13149, Kuwait (office). *Telephone:* 804242 (office). *Fax:* 2400661 (office). *E-mail:* maha@global.com.kw (office). *Website:* www.globalinv.net (office).

GHURAIR, Abd al-Aziz Abdullah al-, BEng; United Arab Emirates banking executive; *CEO, Mashreq Bank;* b. 12 Nov. 1954; s. of Abdullah al-Ghurair; m.; three s.; ed California Polytechnic State Univ., USA; joined Mashreq Bank 1977, Exec. Dir 1989–, CEO 1990–; Dir Al Ghurair Group, Masafi Mineral Water, Dubai Int. Financial Centre, Emirates Foundation, Dubai Econ. Council; Chair. Arab Business Angels Network 2006–; Speaker of the House, UAE Fed. Nat. Council (Parl.); fmr mem. Bd of Dirs Emaar, Dubai Investments, Visa International, MasterCard, Dubai Chamber of Commerce and Industry; Lifetime Achievement Award, CEO Middle East Awards, Achievement Award, Arab Bankers Asscn of N America 2008, ranked by Arabian Business amongst the Power 500: The World's Most Influential Arabs (41st) 2012. *Address:* Mashreq Bank Building, Omar Bin Al Khatab Street, Dubai, United Arab Emirates (office). *Telephone:* (4) 2223333 (office). *Fax:* (4) 2226061 (office). *E-mail:* info@mashreqbank.com (office). *Website:* www.mashreqbank.com (office).

GIACCONI, Riccardo, PhD; American astrophysicist and academic; *Research Professor, Department of Physics and Astronomy, Johns Hopkins University;* b. 6 Oct. 1931, Genoa, Italy; s. of Antonio Giacconi and Elsa Giacconi (Canni); m. Mirella Manaira 1957; one s. two d.; ed Univ. of Milan; Asst Prof. of Physics, Univ. of Milan 1954–56; Research Assoc. Indiana Univ. 1956–58, Princeton Univ., 1958–59; joined American Science & Eng Inc. 1959–73, mem. Bd of Dirs. 1966–73 Exec. Vice-Pres. 1969–73; Assoc. Harvard Coll. Observatory 1970–72; Assoc. Dir Harvard-Smithsonian Center for Astrophysics 1973–81; Prof. of Astrophysics, Harvard Univ. 1973–82; Prof. of Astrophysics, Johns Hopkins Univ. 1981–99, Research Prof. 1999–; Dir Space Telescope Science Inst., Baltimore 1981–92; Prof. of Astrophysics, Milan Univ., Italy 1991–99; Dir-Gen. European Southern Observatory, Garching, Germany 1993–99; Pres. Associated Universities, Inc. (operates Nat. Radio Astronomy Observatory 1999–2004; Chair. Task Group on Directions in Space Science 1995; mem. NASA Space Science Advisory Cttee 1978–79, NASA Advisory Council's Informal Ad Hoc Advisory Sub-Cttee for the Innovation Study 1979; mem. NAS (mem. Space Science Bd and High Energy Astrophysics Panel of the Astronomy Survey Cttee 1979), American Acad. of Arts and Sciences, AAAS, American Astronomical Soc., American Physical Soc. (Fellow 1976), Italian Physical Soc., Int. Astronomical Union; Vice-Chair. COSPAR, I.S.C.E.-1 1980; Astronomy Rep. to Int. Astronomical Union 1979–81; mem. High Energy Astrophysics Div., American Astronomical Soc., Chair. 1976–77, mem. Fachbeirat, Max-Planck Institut für Physik and Astrophysik, Comitato Scientifico del Centro Internazionale di Storia dello Spazio e del Tempo; Foreign mem. Accademia Nazionale dei Lincei; External mem. Max-Planck Soc.; Fulbright Fellow 1956–58; Laurea hc in Astronomy (Univ. of Padua) 1984, Laurea hc in Physics (Rome) 1998; Hon. DSc (Chicago) 1983, (Warsaw) 1996; Hon. DTech and Science (Uppsala) 2000; Richtmeyer Memorial Award 1975, Space Science Award, AIAA 1976, Elliot Cresson Medal 1980, NASA Medal for Exceptional Scientific Achievement 1980, Bruce Medal 1981, Gold Medal, Royal Astronomical Soc. 1982, Dannie Heineman Prize for Astrophysics 1981, A. Cressy Morrison Award in Natural Sciences, New York Acad. of Sciences 1982, Wolf Prize 1987, Marcel Grossmann Award 2000, Nobel Prize in Physics (jtly) 2002, Nat. Medal of Science 2003, Karl Schwarzschild Medal 2004 and numerous other awards. *Publications:* X-ray Astronomy (co-ed) 1974, Physics and Astrophysics of Neutron Stars and Black Holes (co-ed) 1978, A Face of Extremes: The X-ray Universe (co-ed.) 1985, also numerous articles in professional journals. *Leisure interest:* painting, climbing, hiking, skiing. *Address:* Department of Physics and Astronomy, Johns Hopkins University, Bloomberg 501, 3400 North Charles Street, Baltimore, MD 21218-2686 (office); 5630 Wisconsin Avenue, Apt 604, Chevy Chase, MD 20815, USA (home). *Telephone:* (410) 516-0621 (office); (301) 941-0464 (home). *Fax:* (410) 516-7239 (office). *E-mail:* giacconi@pha.jhu.edu (office). *Website:* www.aui.edu (office); www.pha.jhu.edu (office).

GIACOMELLI, Giorgio, MA; Italian international civil servant and diplomatist; *Chairman, Hydroaid;* b. 25 Jan. 1930, Milan; s. of Gino Giacomelli and Maria Van der Kellen; m. Elisabetta Belloni; one s. one d.; ed Padua Univ., Univ. of Cambridge, UK and Geneva Inst. of Higher Int. Studies, Switzerland; joined diplomatic service 1956, Second Sec., Madrid 1958, Second Sec., NATO Del. 1961, First Sec. 1962, Chargé d'affaires, Léopoldville (now Kinshasa) 1964, Counsellor, New Delhi 1966, Ministry of Foreign Affairs, Rome: Personnel 1969, Cultural Dept 1971, Head of Service for Tech. Co-operation 1972, Amb. to Somalia 1973–76, to Syria 1976–80; Deputy Dir-Gen., Emigration Dept, with Ministry of Foreign Affairs, Rome 1980, Dir-Gen. 1981, Dir-Gen. Devt Co-operation Dept 1981; Commr-Gen. UNRWA 1985–90; Under-Sec. Gen. UN Vienna Office 1992–97; Exec.

Dir UN Int. Drug Control Program; Dir Gen. UN Office, Vienna; Chair. Hydroaid (NGO for water resource man.) 2002–; mem. UN Advisory Bd on Water and Sanitation 2006–; Chevalier de la Légion d'honneur, Kt Order of Merit (Italy), Silver Medal for Civil Bravery (Italy). *Leisure interests:* music, literature, mountaineering, hunting and riding. *Address:* Hydroaid, Via Pomba 29, 10123 Turin, Italy (office). *Telephone:* (11) 5694336 (office). *Fax:* (11) 5693690 (office). *E-mail:* hydroaid@hydroaid.it (office). *Website:* www.hydroaid.it (office).

GIAEVER, Ivar, PhD; American physicist and academic; *CEO, Applied BioPhysics, Inc.;* b. 5 April 1929, Bergen, Norway; s. of John A. Giaever and Gudrun M. Skaarud; m. Inger Skramstad 1952; one s. three d.; ed Norwegian Inst. of Tech., Rensselaer Polytechnical Inst., NY; Norwegian Army 1952–53; Patent Examiner, Norwegian Patent Office 1953–54; Mechanical Engineer, Canadian Gen. Electric Co. 1954–56; Applied Mathematician, Gen. Electric Co. 1956–58; Physicist, Gen. Electric Research and Devt Center 1958–88; Inst. Prof., Physics Dept, Rensselaer Polytechnic, NY 1988–; Prof., Univ. of Oslo 1988–; co-f. Applied Biophysics Inc. 1991, currently CEO; mem. NAS 1974–; eight Hon. PhD degrees; Oliver E. Buckley Prize 1965, Nobel Prize for Physics 1973, Zworkin Award 1974. *Publications in Physics Review Letters:* Energy Gap in Superconductors Measured by Electron Tunneling 1960, Study of Superconductors by Electron Tunneling 1961, Detection of the AC Josephson Effect 1965, Magnetic Coupling Between Two Adjacent Superconductors 1965, The Antibody-Antigen Reaction: A Visual Observation 1973, A Morphological Biosensor for Mammalian Cells 1993, Cell Adhesion Force Microscopy 1999. *Leisure interests:* skiing, sailing, tennis, hiking, camping, playing Go. *Address:* Applied BioPhysics, Inc., 175 Jordan Road, Troy, NY 12180 (office); 2080 Van Antwerp Road, Schenectady, NY 12309, USA (home). *Telephone:* (518) 880-6860 (office). *Fax:* (518) 880-6865 (office). *E-mail:* giaever@biophysics.com (office). *Website:* www.biophysics.com (office).

GIAMATTI, Paul, MFA; American actor; b. (Paul Edward Valentine Giamatti), 6 June 1967, New Haven, Conn.; s. of the late A. Bartlett Giamatti and of Toni Smith; m. Elizabeth Giamatti 1997; one s.; ed Choate Rosemary Hall prep school, Yale Univ.; began career in regional theatre before developing a successful film career. *Films include:* Singles 1992, Past Midnight 1992, Mighty Aphrodite 1995, Sabrina 1995, Breathing Room 1996, Ripper 1996, Donnie Brasco 1997, Private Parts 1997, My Best Friend's Wedding 1997, Deconstructing Harry 1997, A Further Gesture 1997, Arresting Gena 1997, The Truman Show 1998, Doctor Dolittle 1998, Saving Private Ryan 1998, The Negotiator 1998, Safe Men 1998, Cradle Will Rock 1999, Man on the Moon 1999, Big Momma's House 2000, Duets 2000, Storytelling 2001, Planet of the Apes 2001, Big Fat Liar 2002, Thunderpants 2002, Confidence 2003, American Splendor 2003, Paycheck 2003, Sideways (Best Male Lead, Ind. Spirit Awards 2005) 2004, The Cinderella Man (Critics' Choice Award for Best Supporting Actor 2006, Screen Actors Guild Award for Best Supporting Actor 2006) 2005, Robots (voice) 2005, The Fan and the Flower (voice) 2005, The Hawk Is Dying 2006, Asterix and the Vikings (voice) 2006, The Illusionist 2006, Lady in the Water 2006, The Ant Bully (voice) 2006, The Nanny Diaries 2007, Shoot 'Em Up 2007, Fred Claus 2007, Pretty Bird 2008, Cold Souls 2009, The Haunted World of El Superbeasto (voice) 2009, Duplicity 2009, The Last Station 2009, Barney's Version (Golden Globe Award for Best Actor in a Comedy or Musical 2011) 2010, Ironclad 2011, Win Win 2011. *Television includes:* Tourist Trap 1998, Winchell 1998, If These Walls Could Talk 2 2000, The Pentagon Papers 2003, The Amazing Screw-On Head (voice) 2006, John Adams (series, HBO) (Golden Globe Award for Best Actor in a Mini-Series 2009) 2008–, 30 Rock (series) 2010. *Address:* c/o WME Entertainment, 9601 Wilshire Boulevard, Beverly Hills, CA 90210, USA (office). *Telephone:* (310) 285-9000 (office). *Fax:* (310) 285-9010 (office). *Website:* www.wma.com (office).

GIAMBASTIANI, Adm. (retd) Edmund P., Jr; American naval officer (retd) and business executive; *Chairman, Alenia North America Inc.;* b. Canastota, NY; ed US Naval Acad.; assignments included Program Man. Navy Recruiting Command HQ, Washington, DC, Special Asst to Deputy Dir of Intelligence, CIA, Deputy Chief of Staff for Resources, Warfare Requirements and Assessments, US Pacific Fleet, Dir Submarine Warfare Div., Naval Operations, Deputy Chief of Naval Operations for Resources, Requirements and Assessments; fmr Commdr Submarine NR-1 (nuclear-powered deep diving submarine), USS Richard B. Russell (nuclear-powered attack submarine); fmr Leader Submarine Devt Squadron Twelve; fmr First Dir Strategy and Concepts, Naval Doctrine Command; fmr Commdr Atlantic Fleet Submarine Force, Anti-Submarine and Reconnaissance Forces Atlantic; Sr Mil. Asst to Sec. of Defense Donald Rumsfeld –2003; Commdr US Jt Forces Command and Supreme Allied Commdr Transformation (SACT), NATO 2003–05; Vice-Chair. Jt Chiefs of Staff, Washington, DC 2005–07, also served as Chair. Jt Requirements Oversight Council, Vice-Chair. Defense Acquisition Bd, mem. Nat. Security Council Deputies Cttee, Nuclear Weapons Council; Chair. Alenia North America Inc. 2008–; mem. Bd of Dirs Boeing Co. 2009–; mem. Guiding Coalition, Project on Nat. Security Reform; Trustee, Mitre Corpn 2008–; currently consultant to SRA International, Inc., Monster Worldwide, Inc., QinetiQ Group plc; numerous awards including Defense Distinguished Service Medal, Jt Meritorious Unit Award, eight Battle Efficiency E's, five Navy Unit Commendations, five Navy Meritorious Unit Commendations. *Address:* Alenia North America Inc., 1625 Eye Street, NW, Washington, DC 20006-4073, USA (office). *Telephone:* (202) 293-3433 (office). *Website:* www.aleniana.com (office).

GIAMPIETRI ROJAS, Adm. (retd) Luis; Peruvian naval officer (retd) and politician; b. 31 Dec. 1940, Bellavista; s. of Luis Giampietri Berenice and Rosa Rojas Lapoint; m. Lida Marcela Ramos Seminario; four c.; ed Peruvian Naval School; joined Peruvian Navy as ensign in 1960, positions included Commdr Gen. Naval Zones, Commdr Gen. Defence Coast, Dir Peruvian Naval School; fmr Deputy Rep. of Perm. Del. to OAS; fmr del. to Inter-American Defence Council, Washington, DC; Chair. Bd of Dirs Peruvian Sea Inst. 1996–2000, Chair. Multi-Sector Cttee in charge of Nat. Study of "El Niño" (ENFEN), mem. Nat. Environment Comm., Perm. Comm. for the Pacific SE, Nat. Comm. for Antarctic Affairs; Councillor for Lima 1998–2002; First Vice-Pres. of Peru 2007–11; mem. Mexican Acad. of Sciences, Inst. of Maritime History, Peruvian Centre of Mil. Maritime History. *Address:* c/o Office of the President of the Council of Ministers, Avda 28 de Julio 878, Miraflores, Lima, Peru (office).

GIANNITSIS, Anastasios; Greek economist, academic, business executive and government minister; b. 1944; Prof. of Devt and Int. Econs, Univ. of Athens; Chief Econ. Advisor to the Prime Minister, Minister of Labor 2000–01; Alt. Foreign Minister 2001–04; Minister of the Interior 2011–12; mem. Panhellenic Socialist Movt (PASOK); Chair. Hellenic Petroleum SA 2009–; mem. Bd of Dirs Lambrakis Press SA. *Publications:* numerous publs on industrial issues, int. integration, specialization and competitiveness, foreign investment, social policy, technology-innovation and technology policy and on Greek econ. policy issues. *Address:* c/o Ministry of the Interior, Odos Stadiou 27, 101 83 Athens. *E-mail:* info@ypes.gr.

GIANOTTI, Fabiola, PhD; Italian physicist; *Head, ATLAS Experiment, Large Hadron Collider, European Organization for Nuclear Research (CERN);* b. 29 Oct. 1962; ed Univ. of Milan, CERN, Switzerland; originally trained as pianist at Milan Conservatory; joined CERN 1987, worked on various experiments including UA2 experiment and ALEPH on the Large Electron Positron Collider (precursor to Large Hadron Collider), ATLAS experiment physics coordinator 1999–2003, Head of ATLAS 2009–; mem. Physics Advisory Cttee Fermilab (particle physics lab.), Batavia, Ill., USA; mem. Accad. dei Lincei; Commendatore della Repubblica Italiana 2009, City of Milan Ambrogino d'oro 2012, Special Fundamental Physics Prize 2012, Premio Nonino 2013, ranked by Forbes magazine amongst The World's 100 Most Powerful Women (78th) 2013. *Leisure interests:* jogging, playing the piano. *Address:* European Organization for Nuclear Research (CERN), Geneva 23, Switzerland (office). *Telephone:* 22-76-761-11 (office). *Fax:* 22-76-765-55 (office). *E-mail:* fabiola.gianotti@cern.ch (office). *Website:* consult.cern.ch (office); atlas.ch (office).

GIANVITI, François Paul Frédéric, DenD; French lawyer, academic and international organization official; b. 2 Aug. 1938, Paris; s. of Dominique Gianviti and Suzanne Fournier; m. Barbara Zawadsky 1965; one s. two d.; ed Lycées Henri IV and Louis-le-Grand, Paris, Facultés des Lettres et de Droit, Paris and New York Univ. School of Law; Asst Faculté de Droit, Paris 1963–67; Lecturer, Faculté de Droit, Nancy 1967–68, Caen 1968–69; Maître de conférences, Faculté de Droit, Besançon, on secondment to IMF 1970–74; Maître de conférences, Univ. of Paris XII 1974–75, Prof. of Law 1975, Dean 1979–85; Dir of Legal Dept, IMF 1986–2004, Gen. Counsel 1987–2004 (retd); mem. Monetary Cttee, Int. Law Asscn; mem. Qatar Financial Centre Regulatory Tribunal, Doha 2007–; Chevalier, Ordre Nat. du Mérite, Chevalier des Palmes académiques. *Publication:* Les Biens 1984; numerous book chapters and journal articles. *Address:* Qatar Financial Centre Regulatory Tribunal, QFC Tower 2, Al Wahda Street, West Bay, PO Box 13667, Doha, Qatar (office). *Telephone:* 44968359 (office) *Fax:* 44968362 (office). *E-mail:* registry@qfcj.org.qa (office). *Website:* www.qfctribunal.com (office).

GIBARA, Samir G., BBA, MBA; French business executive (retd); b. 23 April 1939, Cairo, Egypt; s. of the late Selim Gibara and Renée Bokhazi; m. Salma Tagher 1968; ed Cairo Univ., Harvard Business School, USA; Adviser, Inst. for Int. Trade, Paris 1967–70; Pres. and Man. Dir Goodyear France 1983; Pres. and CEO Goodyear Canada 1989; Vice-Pres. and Gen. Man. Goodyear Europe 1990; Vice-Pres. Strategic Planning and Acting Chief Financial Officer, Goodyear Tire & Rubber Co. 1992, Exec. Vice-Pres. N American Operations 1994, Pres. and COO 1995–96, Chair., Pres. and CEO Jan. 1996, Chair. and CEO July 1996–2003 (retd); mem. Bd of Dirs Int. Paper Co. 1999–, Sumitomo Rubber Industries 1999–2002, Dana Corpn 2004–08, W & T Offshore, Inc. 2008–; mem. Bd of Dean's Advisors, Harvard Business School; mem. Advisory Bd Proudfoot Consultants; Trustee, Univ. of Akron Foundation; Chevalier, Ordre nat. du Mérite; Chevalier du Tastevin. *Publications:* articles in Le Monde and business journals. *Leisure interests:* theatre, music, reading, tennis, swimming. *Address:* c/o Board of Directors, International Paper Company, 400 Atlantic Street, Stamford, CT 06921, USA.

GIBB, Barry, CBE; British/American singer, songwriter and record producer; b. 1 Sept. 1946, Isle of Man; s. of Hughie Gibb and Barbara Gibb; m. Linda Gray; five c.; emigrated to Australia 1958, returned to UK 1967; formed The Bee Gees (with brothers Robin, Maurice and Andy) 1958; started singing in nightclubs, Australia; numerous performances at major venues around the world; Hon. degree (Univ. of Manchester) 2004; seven Grammy awards, American Music Award for Int. Achievement 1997, BRIT Award for Outstanding Contribution to Music 1997, World Music Award for Lifetime Achievement 1997, Q Lifetime Achievement Award 2005, Ivor Novello Acad. Fellowship 2006, BMI Icon Award 2007, Freeman of the Borough of Douglas (Isle of Man) 2009. *Compositions include:* writer or co-writer, producer or co-producer of numerous songs for other artists including: Elvis Presley (Words), Cliff Richard (I Cannot Give You My Love), Sarah Vaughan (Run To Me), Al Green, Janis Joplin, Barbra Streisand (Guilty album), Diana Ross (Chain Reaction), Dionne Warwick (Heartbreaker), Dolly Parton and Kenny Rogers (Islands In The Stream), Ntrance (Staying Alive), Take That (How Deep Is Your Love), Boyzone (Words), Yvonne Elliman (If I Can't Have You). *Recordings include:* albums: with The Bee Gees: Bee Gees Sing and Play 14 Barry Gibb Songs 1965, Monday's Rain 1966, Bee Gees 1st 1967, Horizontal 1968, Idea 1968, Odessa 1969, Cucumber Castle 1970, Marley Purt Drive 1970, Sound of Love 1970, Two Years On 1971, Melody (OST) 1971, Trafalgar 1971, To Whom It May Concern 1972, Life in a Tin Can 1973, Mr Natural 1974, Main Course 1975, Children of the World 1976, Here at Last... Bee Gees Live 1977, Saturday Night Fever (OST) 1977, Spirits Having Flown 1979, SWALK 1979, Living Eyes 1981, Staying Alive (OST) 1983, E.S.P. 1987, One 1989, High Civilization 1991, Size Isn't Everything 1993, Still Waters 1997, One Night Only 1998, This Is Where I Came In 2001, Harmonies Down Under 2002, Alone 2002, In the Beginning 2003, Merchants of Dream 2003, Bee Gees Number Ones 2004; solo: Now Voyager 1984, Hawks 1988. *Address:* c/o Crompton Songs, 5820 North Bay Road, Miami Beach, FL 33140, USA. *Telephone:* (305) 672-2390. *Fax:* (305) 531-8041. *E-mail:* middleear@earthlink.het. *Website:* www.barrygibb.com.

GIBBARD, Allan Fletcher, PhD; American academic; *Richard B. Brandt Distinguished University Professor of Philosophy, University of Michigan;* b. 7 April 1942, Providence, RI; s. of Harold A. Gibbard and Eleanor Reid Gibbard; m. 1st Mary Craig 1972 (died 1990); m. 2nd Beth Genné 1991; two s.; ed Swarthmore Coll., Harvard Univ.; teacher of math. and physics with US Peace Corps, Achimota School, Ghana 1963–65; Asst Prof. then Assoc. Prof. of Philosophy, Univ. of Chicago 1969–74; Assoc. Prof. of Philosophy, Univ. of Pittsburgh 1974–77; Prof. of Philosophy, Univ. of Michigan, Ann Arbor 1977–, Richard B. Brandt Univ. Prof.

1992–; Fellow Econometric Soc. 1984, American Acad. of Arts and Sciences 1990. *Publications:* Wise Choices, Apt Feelings: A Theory of Normative Judgement 1990, Thinking How to Live 2003; articles in journals. *Address:* Department of Philosophy, University of Michigan, Angell Hall, 435 South State Street, Ann Arbor, MI 48109-1003, USA (office). *Telephone:* (313) 764-6285 (office); (313) 769-2628 (home). *Fax:* (313) 763-8071 (office). *E-mail:* gibbard@umich.edu (office). *Website:* www-personal.umich.edu/~gibbard (office).

GIBBON, Gary, BA; British journalist; *Political Editor, Channel 4 News;* b. 15 March 1965; s. of Robert Gibbon and Elizabeth Gibbon; m. Laura Pulay 1993; two s.; ed Balliol Coll., Oxford; fmr journalist, BBC; joined Channel 4 News 1990, Political Producer 1992–94, Political Corresp. 1994–2005, Political Ed. 2005–; RTS Home News Award 2006, Political Studies Asscn Political Broadcaster of the Year Award 2008. *Address:* Channel 4 News, 200 Gray's Inn Road, London, WC1X 8XZ, England (office). *Telephone:* (20) 7430-4996 (office). *E-mail:* gary.gibbon@itn.co.uk (office). *Website:* www.channel4.com/news (office).

GIBBONS, Gary William, PhD, FRS; British theoretical physicist and academic; *Professor of Theoretical Physics, University of Cambridge;* b. 1 July 1946, Coulsdon, Surrey; m.; two c.; ed Purley Co. Grammar School, Old Coulsdon, Surrey, St Catharine's Coll., Cambridge, Univ. of Cambridge; elected Denman-Baynes Student, Clare Coll., Cambridge 1971–75; SRC Research Asst, Dept of Applied Math. and Theoretical Physics, Univ. of Cambridge 1975–76, 1977–78, SRC Advanced Fellow 1978–80, Univ. Lecturer 1980–90, Reader in Theoretical Physics 1990–97, Prof. of Theoretical Physics 1997–, Fellow, Trinity Coll. Cambridge 2002–; Max Planck Institut für Physik and Astrophysik, Munich, FRG 1976–77; mem. Inst. of Theoretical Physics, Univ. of California, Santa Barbara, USA Jan.–April 1980; sabbatical leave at Observatoire de Meudon and Ecole Normale Superieure, Paris, France 1986–87, at IHES, Bures-sur-Yvette, France Jan.–April 1990, as Kramers Prof. at Inst. for Theoretical Physics, Univ. of Utrecht, Netherlands April–June 1992, at Laboratoire de Physique Théorique, Ecole Normale Superieure, Paris Oct.–Dec. 1999, as Yukawa Prof. at Yukawa Inst. for Theoretical Physics, Kyoto Univ., Japan Jan.–April 2000; Visiting Prof., Center for Theoretical Physics, MIT, USA Sept.–Dec. 2003. *Publications include:* Euclidean Quantum Gravity 1993; numerous articles in professional journals on supergravity, p-branes and M-theory. *Address:* Pavilion B, Room B1.24, Department of Applied Mathematics and Theoretical Physics, Centre for Mathematical Sciences, Wilberforce Road, Cambridge, CB3 0WA, England (office). *Telephone:* (1223) 337899 (office). *Fax:* (1223) 764984 (office). *E-mail:* G.W.Gibbons@damtp.cam.ac.uk (office). *Website:* www.damtp.cam.ac.uk (office).

GIBBONS, Ian Read, PhD, FRS; British biophysicist and academic; *Research Cell Biologist, University of California, Berkeley;* b. 30 Oct. 1931, Hastings, Sussex, England; s. of Arthur A. Gibbons and Hilda R. Cake; m. Barbara R. Hollingworth 1961; one s. one d.; ed Faversham Grammar School and King's Coll., Cambridge; Research Fellow, Univ. of Pa 1957, Harvard Univ. 1958; Asst Prof. of Biology, Harvard Univ. 1963; Assoc. Prof. of Biophysics, Univ. of Hawaii 1967, Prof. 1969–97; Research Cell Biologist, Univ. of Calif. at Berkeley 1997–; Visiting Prof., Univ. of Siena 1981–82; Guggenheim Fellowship 1973; Excellence in Research Prize, Univ. of Hawaii 1984, Lizeonii Lincei, Academia dei lincei 1988, E. B. Wilson Medal, American Soc. for Cell Biology 1994, Int. Prize for Biology (Japan) 1995. *Publications:* numerous articles in learned journals related to cell motility, especially that of cilia, flagella and other microtubule organelles. *Leisure interests:* gardening, music, computer programming. *Address:* 79 Estates Drive, Orinda, CA 94563, USA (office). *Telephone:* (510) 642-2439 (office). *Fax:* (510) 643-6791 (office). *E-mail:* igibbons@socrates.berkeley.edu (office). *Website:* mcb.berkeley.edu (office).

GIBBONS, James Arthur (Jim), BS, MS, JD; American geologist, lawyer, politician and fmr state governor; b. 16 Dec. 1944, Sparks, Nev.; s. of Leonard A. Gibbons and Matilda Gibbons (née Hancock); m. 1st; one s. one d.; m. 2nd Dawn Gibbons 1986 (divorced 2010); one s.; ed Univ. of Nevada, Reno, Southwestern Law School, Los Angeles, Univ. of Southern California, graduate of USAF Air Command and Staff Coll. and Air War Coll.; Hydrologist, Office of Fed. Watermaster, Reno 1963–67; served in USAF during Viet Nam War 1967–71, rank of Col, Col, Nev. Air Nat. Guard 1975–96, Vice-Commdr 1990–96, participated in first Gulf War, Col, USAF Reserve 1996–98; mining geologist, Union Carbide Co. 1971–73; commercial pilot, Western Airlines, LA 1979–87, Delta Airlines, Salt Lake City 1987–97; admitted to Nevada Bar 1982, US Dist Court, Nev. 1982; Sr Land Man. and Attorney, Homestake Mining Co. 1980–82; lawyer, Haase, Harris & Morrison 1982–84; attorney, pvt. practice 1984–86; mem. Nev. State Ass. 1989–93, called to active service in Gulf War as RF-4C Flight Leader; cand. for Gov. of Nev. 1994; mem. US House of Reps for 2nd Congressional Dist of Nev. 1997–2006, Vice-Chair. House Resources Cttee, mem. Armed Services Cttee, Homeland Security Cttee, Permanent Select Cttee on Intelligence; Gov. of Nev. 2007–11; fmr Co-Chair. Congressional Mining Caucus, House Gaming Caucus; mem. Bd of Dirs Nevada Council on Econ. Educ. 1984–87; mem. Nevada Landman's Asscn (Chair. 1981–82), Commercial Law League of America, Nevada Trial Lawyers Asscn (consulting attorney 1982–83), Asscn of Trial Lawyers of America, American Inst. of Mining Engineers, Rocky Mount Mineral Law Foundation; Republican; earned 19 service medals, including the Legion of Merit, Distinguished Flying Cross, Air Medal with Two Oak Leaf Clusters, Aerial Achievement Medal and Air Force Commendation Medal with One Oak Leaf Cluster; Mackay School of Mines Alumnus of the Year 1999. *Publications:* contrib. of articles to professional journals. *Leisure interest:* flying. *Address:* c/o Office of the Governor, State Capitol, 101 North Carson Street, Carson City, NV 89701, USA.

GIBBONS, John Howard (Jack), BS, PhD; American physicist and fmr government official; b. 15 Jan. 1929, Harrisonburg, Virginia; s. of Howard Kemper Gibbons and Jessie Conrad; m. Mary Ann Hobart 1955; three d.; ed Randolph-Macon Coll., Ashville, Va, Duke Univ., Durham, NC; Group leader (nuclear geophysics), Oak Ridge Nat. Lab. 1954–69, Environmental Programme Dir 1969–73; Dir of Energy, Environmental and Resources Center and Prof. of Physics, Univ. of Tennessee 1973–79; Dir Office of Energy Conservation, Fed. Energy Admin. 1974; Dir Congressional Office of Tech. Assessment 1979–92; Asst to Pres. Clinton for Science and Tech. and Dir Office of Science and Tech. Policy 1993–98; Compton Lecturer, MIT 1998–99; Pres. Resource Strategies Inc. 1998–2005; Sr Advisor, US Dept of State 1999–2001; Pres. Sigma Xi 2000–01, Virginia Gov.'s Comm. on Climate Change 2008, S&T Cttee, Idaho Nat. Lab.

2002–11, Population Action Int. Bd 2003–12, (Chair 2003–06); Sr Fellow, Nat. Acad. of Eng 1999–2000; mem. Bd of Environmental and Energy Study Inst. 2008–13; Fellow, AAAS, American Physical Soc., American Philosophical Soc., Nat. Acad. of Eng; numerous professional appointments and affiliations; Commdr Ordre des Palmes Académiques (France), Officer's Cross of the Order of Merit (Germany); Hon. PhD (Illinois Inst. of Tech.) 1994, (Mount Sinai Medical School) 1995, (Univ. of Delaware) 1996, (Univ. of Maryland) 1997, Hon. ScD (Duke Univ.) 1997; Fed. of American Scientists Public Service Award 1990, Leo Szilard Award, American Physical Soc. 1991, Distinguished Service Award, James Madison Univ. 1993, State of Tennessee Gov.'s Outstanding Tennessean Award 1997, NASA Distinguished Service Medal 1998, Art Beuche Prize, Nat. Acad. of Eng 1998, Abelson Prize, AAAS 1998, Seymour Cray Award 1998; numerous other awards and distinctions. *Publications include:* Energy: The Conservation Revolution 1981, This Gifted Age: Science and Technology at the Millennium 1997; numerous journal articles in the areas of energy and environmental policy, etc. *Leisure interests:* farming, hiking. *Address:* c/o S. Bachtel, 4505 15th Street North, Arlington, VA 22207, USA (office); PO Box 497, The Plains, VA 20198, USA. *Telephone:* (703) 812-9559 (office); (540) 253-5409 (home). *E-mail:* susiebachtel@aol.com (office); jackgibbons02@gmail.com. *Website:* www.johnhgibbons.org.

GIBBONS, Michael Gordon, MBE, BSc, BEng, MSc, PhD; Canadian academic; *Honorary Professor, Science and Technology Policy Research, University of Sussex;* b. 15 April 1939, Montreal; s. of Albert Gordon Gibbons and Dorothy Mildred Gibbons; m. Gillian Monks 1968; one s. one d.; ed Concordia Univ., Montreal, McGill Univ., Montreal, Queens Univ., Ont., Univ. of Manchester, UK; Lecturer, Univ. of Manchester 1967–72, Sr Lecturer 1972–75, Prof. 1975–92, Head of Dept 1975–92; Dir Univ. of Manchester Inst. of Science and Tech. (UMIST) Pollution Research Unit, UK 1979–86, Chair. and Founding Dir Policy Research in Eng, Science and Tech. 1979–92, Dir Research Exploitation and Devt, Vice-Chancellor's Office 1984–92; Dean Grad. School and Dir Science Policy Research Unit (now Science and Tech. Policy Research), Univ. of Sussex 1992–96, Dir 2004, now Hon. Prof.; Sec.-Gen. Asscn of Commonwealth Univs 1996–2004; Visiting Prof., Univ. of Montreal 1976–81, Univ. of Calif., Berkeley 1992; Special Advisor to House of Commons Science and Tech. Cttee 1993; mem. Council, ESRC 1997; mem. Research Priorities Bd 1994, Chair. 1997; Consultant, Cttee of Science and Tech. Policy, OECD, Paris; Fellow, Royal Swedish Acad. of Eng Sciences 2000; Hon. LLD (Univ. of Ghana, Legon) 1999, (Concordia Univ., Montreal) 2004; Hon. DUniv (Univ. of Surrey) 2005; Lt-Gov.'s Silver Medal 1959, Govt of Canada Commemorative Medal 2002. *Publications:* Wealth from Knowledge (jtly.) 1972, Science as a Commodity 1984, Post-Innovation Performance: Technical Development and Competition 1986, The Evaluation of Research: A Synthesis of Current Practice 1987, The New Production of Knowledge 1994, Re-thinking Science 2000. *Leisure interests:* classical music, American football. *Address:* SPRU, Freeman Centre, Falmer, University of Sussex, Brighton, BN1 9QE (office); 24 Fletsand Road, Wilmslow, Cheshire, SK9 2AB, England (home). *Telephone:* (1273) 678175 (office); (1625) 527924 (home). *E-mail:* michael_gibbons@onetel.net. *Website:* www.sussex.ac.uk/spru (office).

GIBBS, Anthony Matthews, BA, BLitt, MA, FAHA; Australian academic; *Professor Emeritus of English, Macquarie University;* b. 21 Jan. 1933, Vic.; s. of J. F. L. Gibbs and S. T. Gibbs; m. 1st Jillian Irving Holden 1960; m. 2nd Donna Patricia Lucy 1983; two s. one step d.; ed Ballarat Church of England Grammar School, Trinity Coll., Univ. of Melbourne, and Magdalen Coll., Oxford; Lecturer in English, Univ. of Adelaide 1960–66, Univ. of Leeds 1966–69; Prof. of English, Univ. of Newcastle, NSW 1969–75; Prof. of English, Macquarie Univ. 1975–98, Prof. Emer. 1999–; mem. Exec. Cttee Int. Asscn for the Study of Anglo-Irish Literature 1973–78, Exec. Cttee English Asscn (Sydney Br.) 1975–91, Founding Council Int. Shaw Soc. 2004; Vice-Pres. Australian Acad. of Humanities 1988–89; Ed. 1989–93; Rhodes Scholarship 1956, Centenary Medal 2003. *Publications includes:* Shaw 1969, Sir William Davenant 1972, The Art and Mind of Shaw 1983, Shaw: Interviews and Recollections 1990, Bernard Shaw: Man and Superman and Saint Joan 1992, Heartbreak House: Preludes of Apocalypse 1994, A Bernard Shaw Chronology 2001, Bernard Shaw: A Life 2005. *Leisure interests:* theatre, cooking. *Address:* 4 Acacia Close, Turramurra, NSW 2074, Australia (home). *Telephone:* (2) 9449-2668 (office). *E-mail:* gibbston@gmail.com (home). *Website:* www.engl.mq.edu.au/staff/tonygibbs.html (office).

GIBBS, Herschelle Herman; South African professional cricketer; b. 23 Feb. 1974, Green Point, Cape Town, Cape Prov.; m. Tennielle Povey 2007 (divorced 2007); ed St Joseph's Marist Coll., Diocesan Coll., Rondebosch; right-handed top order batsman; right-arm bowler; Jr Rep. Cricket: WP Nuff 1989–92, SA Schools 1991–92; played for Western Prov. 1990–2004, S Africa 1996–, Cape Cobras 2004–06, Deccan Chargers 2008–10, Glamorgan 2008, Yorkshire 2010–, Northern Districts 2010–, Perth Scorchers 2011–12, Mumbai Indians 2012–, Durham Dynamos 2012–; First-class debut: 1990/91; Test debut: India v S Africa, Kolkata 27 Nov.–1 Dec. 1996; One-Day Int. (ODI) debut: Kenya v S Africa, Nairobi (Gym) 3 Oct. 1996; T20I debut: S Africa v NZ, Johannesburg 21 Oct. 2005; has played in 90 Tests and scored 6,167 runs (14 centuries, 26 half-centuries), highest score 228, average 41.95; ODIs: 248 matches, scored 8,094 runs, highest score 175, average 36.12; T20Is: 23 matches, scored 400 runs, highest score 90 not out, average 18.18; awarded citizenship of Saint Kitts and Nevis 2007. *Achievements include;* first player to hit six sixes in one over in ODI cricket, doing so against the Netherlands off bowling of Daan van Bunge in Cricket World Cup 2007; with Graeme Smith, only pair in Test history to break 300 on three occasions; also holds S African second wicket record, a partnership of 315 not out with Jacques Kallis; one of only three batsmen in ODI history to score hundreds in three consecutive innings. *Address:* c/o Western Province Cricket Club, 146 Campground Road, Newlands, Cape Town 7700, South Africa. *Telephone:* (21) 657-3300. *Fax:* (21) 683-2322. *E-mail:* members@wpcc.co.za. *Website:* www.wpcc.co.za.

GIBBS, Lancelot (Lance) Richard; Guyanese sports organizer and fmr professional cricketer; b. 29 Sept. 1934, Georgetown, British Guiana (now Guyana); s. of Ebenezer Gibbs and Marjorie Gretna Gibbs (née Archer); cousin of cricketer Clive Lloyd; m. Joy Roslyn Margarete Rogers 1963; one s. one d.; ed St Ambrose Anglican Primary School and Day Commercial Standard High School; right-arm off-spin bowler; played for British Guiana/Guyana 1953/54–74/75, Warwickshire 1967–73, S Australia 1969–70; played in 79 Tests for West Indies

1957/58–75/76, taking then world record 309 wickets (average 29.09), best bowling (innings) 8/38, (match) 11/157; only bowler to take 100 or more wickets against both England and Australia; toured England 1963, 1966, 1969, 1973, 1975 (World Cup); took 1,024 First-class wickets, average 27.22, best bowling (innings) 8/37; Man. 1991 West Indies tour of England; now a sports organizer based in USA, which he represented against Canada 1983; Chair. of Lauderhill, Fla bid to host Cricket World Cup in 2007; man. posts in transportation business including Booker Shipping, Guyana and Kent Line, Canada; Indian Cricket Cricketer of the Year 1967, Professional Cricketers' Asscn Player of the Year 1971, Wisden Cricketer of The Year 1972. *Leisure interests:* reading, all sports. *Address:* USA/Broward/Lauderhill World Cup Host Committee 2007, 2100 NW 55 Avenue, Lauderhill, FL 33313, USA (office); 276 Republic Park, Peter's Hall, E.B.D., Guyana. *Telephone:* (954) 730-3008 (office).

GIBBS, Nancy, MA; American author, journalist and publishing executive; *Managing Editor, Time magazine;* b. 1960; m.; two c.; ed Yale Univ., New Coll., Oxford, UK; began career as fact checker in int. section, TIME, Inc. 1985–88, becoming Feature writer 1988–91, Sr Ed. 1991–96, Chief political writer 1996–2002, Ed.-at-Large 2002, Exec. Ed., Deputy Man. Ed. 2011–13, Man. Ed. 2013–; Ferris Prof., Princeton Univ. 1993, 2006. *Publications include:* The Preacher and the Presidents: Billy Graham in the White House (with Michael Duffy) 2007, The Presidents Club: Inside the World's Most Exclusive Fraternity (with Michael Duffy) 2012. *Address:* TIME, Inc, 1271 Avenue of the Americas, New York, NY 10020, USA (office). *Website:* www.time.com/time (office).

GIBBS, Robert L., BA; American political consultant and government official; *White House Press Secretary;* b. 29 March 1971, Auburn, Ala; s. of Robert Gibbs and Nancy Gibbs; m.; one s.; ed North Carolina State Univ.; Press Sec. for US Congressman Bob Etheridge 1997; spokesman for Fritz Hollings' senatorial campaign 1998; Press Sec. for John Kerry's presidential campaign 2004; Communications Dir Democratic Senatorial Campaign Cttee and Barack Obama's senatorial campaign 2004; Communications Dir for Senator Barack Obama, Washington, DC 2004–08; Communications Dir Senator Barack Obama's presidential campaign 2007–08; White House Press Sec. 2009–. *Address:* Office of the Press Secretary, The White House, 1600 Pennsylvania Avenue, NW, Washington, DC 20500, USA (office). *Telephone:* (202) 456-1414 (office). *Fax:* (202) 456-2461 (office). *Website:* www.whitehouse.gov/news/briefings (office).

GIBBS, Sir Roger Geoffrey, Kt; British business executive and administrator; b. 13 Oct. 1934, Herts.; s. of Sir Geoffrey Gibbs, KCMG and Lady Gibbs; m. Jane Lee Gibbs; ed Eton Coll. and Millfield School; with Jessel Toynbee & Co. Ltd 1954–64, Dir 1960, de Zoete & Gorton (later de Zoete & Bevan) stockbrokers 1964–71; Gov. The Wellcome Trust 1983–99 (Chair. 1989–99); Chair. London Discount Market Asscn 1984–86; Dir (non-exec.) Arsenal Football Club 1980–2005; mem. Bd of Dirs Gerrard & Nat. Holdings PLC 1989–94 (Chair. 1975–89), Howard De Walden Estates Ltd 1989–2001 (Chair. 1993–98), The Colville Estate Ltd 1989–; Chair. Arundel Castle Cricket Foundation 1986–95, Council for Royal Nat. Pension Fund for Nurses 1975–2000; Court of Advisers, St Paul's Cathedral 1989–2000, Fleming Family & Partners, Court of Advisers 2000; mem. Cttee Marylebone Cricket Club 1991–94, St Paul's Cathedral Foundation (Chair. 2000); Trustee, Winston Churchill Memorial Trust 2001; Liveryman, Merchant Taylor's Co.; Freeman, City of London, Hon. Fellow, Acad. of Medical Sciences. *Leisure interests:* sport, travel. *Address:* 23 Tregunter Road, London, SW10 9LS, England. *Telephone:* (20) 7370-3465 (home). *Fax:* (20) 7373-5263.

GIBSON, Charles DeWolf, AB; American newscaster; *Anchor, World News Tonight with Charles Gibson, ABC Television;* s. of Burdett Gibson and Georgiana Gibson (née Law); m. Arlene Joy Gibson 1968; two d.; ed Princeton Univ.; Washington Producer, RKO Network, Washington, DC 1966; News Dir Station-WLVA-TV, Lynchburg, Va 1967–69; anchorman, reporter Station-WMAL-TV (now WJLA-TV), Washington, DC 1970–73; corresp., TVN, Inc. (TV News, Inc.) 1974–75; joined ABC News 1975, White House Corresp., Washington, DC 1976–77, Corresp., gen. assignment 1977–81, Capitol Hill Corresp. 1981–87; Co-host Good Morning America, ABC TV, New York City 1987–98, 1999–2006, Anchor, World News Tonight with Charles Gibson 2006–09; mem. Bd of Dirs Knight-Wallace Fellows at Mich. 1988; Trustee Princeton Univ. 2006–; Nat. Journalism Fellow, Nat. Endowment of the Humanities, Univ. of Mich. 1973–74, John Maclean Fellowship, Princeton Univ. 1992. *Address:* ABC World News with Charles Gibson, 77 West 66th Street, New York, NY 10023, USA (office). *Telephone:* (212) 456-4040 (office). *Fax:* (212) 456-3720 (office). *Website:* abcnews.go.com/WNT (office).

GIBSON, Sir Ian, Kt, BSc, CBE; British business executive; *Chairman, William Morrison Supermarkets PLC;* m. 1st Joy Musker (divorced); two d.; m. 2nd Sue Wilson (divorced); one s.; ed Univ. of Manchester; joined Ford Motor Co., 1968, served several exec. positions in UK and Germany –1984; joined Nissan Motor Manufacturing (UK) Ltd as purchasing and production control dir 1984, Man. Dir and CEO 1989–98, Chair. 1998, Pres. Nissan Europe and Sr Vice-Pres. Nissan Motor Co. Ltd 1999–2001; Deputy Chair. (non-exec.) William Morrison Supermarkets PLC 2007–08, Chair. 2008–; Chair. (non-exec.) Trinity Mirror PLC 2006–; fmr Chair. BPB PLC; fmr Deputy Chair. Asda Group PLC; fmr mem. Bd of Dirs Chelys Ltd; fmr Sr Dir (non-exec.) Northern Rock plc; fmr Dir (non-exec.) GKN plc, Greggs plc; fmr mem. Court of the Bank of England. *Address:* William Morrison Supermarkets PLC, Hilmore House, Gain Lane, Bradford, BD3 7DL (office); Trinity Mirror PLC, One Canada Square, Canary Wharf, London, E14 5AP, England (office). *Telephone:* (845) 611-5000 (Morrisons) (office); (20) 7293-3000 (Trinity Mirror) (office). *Fax:* (20) 7510-3000 (Trinity Mirror) (office). *E-mail:* info@morrisons.co.uk (office); info@trinitymirror.com (office). *Website:* www.morrisons.co.uk (office); www.trinitymirror.com (office).

GIBSON, Mel; Australian actor, director and producer; b. 3 Jan. 1956, Peekskill, NY, USA; s. of Hutton Gibson and Anne Gibson; m. Robyn Moore (divorced); six s. two d.; ed Nat. Inst. for Dramatic Art, Sydney; f. ICONS Productions; Commdr Ordre des Arts et des Lettres. *Films include:* Summer City, Mad Max 1979, Tim 1979, Attack Force Z, Gallipoli 1981, The Road Warrior (Mad Max II) 1982, The Year of Living Dangerously 1983, The Bounty 1984, The River 1984, Mrs. Soffel 1984, Mad Max Beyond Thunderdome 1985, Lethal Weapon, Tequila Sunrise, Lethal Weapon II, Bird on a Wire 1989, Hamlet 1990, Air America

1990, Lethal Weapon III 1991, Man Without a Face (also dir) 1992, Maverick 1994, Braveheart (also Dir, co-producer, Acad. Award for Best Picture 1996) 1995, Ransom 1996, Conspiracy Theory 1997, Lethal Weapon IV 1998, Payback 1997, The Million Dollar Hotel 1999, The Patriot 2000, What Women Want 2000, We Were Soldiers 2002, Signs 2002, The Singing Detective 2003, The Passion of the Christ (dir, producer; US People's Choice Award for Best Drama 2005) 2004, Apocalypto (dir) 2006, Edge of Darkness 2010, The Beaver 2011. *Plays include:* Romeo and Juliet, Waiting for Godot, No Names No Pack Drill, Death of a Salesman. *Address:* c/o ICONS Productions, 4000 Warner Boulevard, Room 17, Burbank, CA 91522, USA; c/o Shanahan Management, P.O. Box 478, King's Cross, NSW 2011, Australia.

GIBSON, Rt Hon. Sir Peter (Leslie), Kt; British judge; *Chairman, Detainee Inquiry;* b. 10 June 1934; s. of Harold Leslie Gibson and Martha Lucy Gibson (née Diercking); m. Dr Katharine Mary Beatrice Hadow 1968 (died 2002); two s. one d.; ed Malvern Coll., Worcester Coll., Oxford; Nat. Service 2nd Lt RA 1953–55; called to Bar, Inner Temple 1960; Bencher, Lincoln's Inn 1975; Second Jr Counsel to Inland Revenue (Chancery) 1970–72; Jr Counsel to the Treasury (Chancery) 1972–81; Judge of the High Court of Justice, Chancery Div. 1981–93; Chair. Law Comm. for England and Wales 1990–92; a Judge of the Employment Appeal Tribunal 1984–86; Lord Justice of Appeal 1993–2005; Intelligence Services Commr 2006–10; Chair. Detainee Inquiry 2010–; conducted Omagh bombing intelligence review 2008; Judge, Qatar Financial Centre Civil and Commercial Court 2007–; Chair. Trust Law Cttee 2005–; Treas., Lincoln's Inn 1996; Hon. Fellow, Worcester Coll., Oxford 1993. *Address:* Royal Courts of Justice, Strand, London, WC2A 2LL, England (office).

GIBSON, Robert Dennis, AO, MSc, PhD, DSc, FTS, FAIM; Australian university chancellor; *Chancellor, RMIT University;* b. 13 April 1942, Newcastle, UK; s. of Edward Gibson and Euphemia Gibson; m. 1st. Eileen Hancox 1964; one s. two d.; m. 2nd Catherine Bull 1994; ed Univs of Hull and Newcastle, UK; Prof. and Head, School of Math. and Computing, Newcastle Polytechnic 1977–82; Deputy Dir Queensland Inst. of Tech. 1982–83, Dir 1983–88; Vice-Chancellor Queensland Univ. of Tech. (QUT) 1989–2003; mem. Australian Research Council 1988–93; Chair. Grad. Careers Council of Australia 1999–2005, M&MD Ltd 2003–; Premier of Queensland SMART Awards Panel 2003–; Chancellor RMIT (fmrly Royal Melbourne Inst. of Tech.) 2003–; Fellow, Australian Inst. of Co. Dirs; Hon. DSc (CNAA) 1984, Hon. DUniv (USC) 2000, (QUT) 2003). *Publications:* over 80 publs in mathematical modelling. *Leisure interests:* cricket, running. *Address:* GPO Box 2434, Brisbane 4001 (office); RMIT University, PO Box 2476V, Melbourne 3001, Victoria; 173/350 St Kilda Road, Melbourne 3004, Victoria, Australia (home). *Telephone:* (3) 9925-3635 (office); (3) 9690-5222 (home). *Fax:* (3) 9925-3939 (office). *E-mail:* d.gibson@rmit.edu.au (office). *Website:* www.rmit.edu.au (office).

GIBSON, Toby J., PhD; British biologist/biochemist; *Team Leader, European Molecular Biology Laboratory;* ed Univ. of Cambridge; on staff, Lab. of Molecular Biology, Cambridge 1981–86; Team Leader, Gibson Team, Structural and Computational Biology Unit, European Molecular Biology Lab., Heidelberg, Germany 1986–. *Publications:* numerous publs in scientific journals. *Address:* European Molecular Biology Laboratory, Meyerhofstraße 1, 69117 Heidelberg, Germany (office). *Telephone:* (6221) 387-8398 (office). *Fax:* (6221) 387517 (office). *E-mail:* toby.gibson@embl.de (office). *Website:* www.embl.org/aboutus (office).

GIBSON-SMITH, Christopher (Chris) Shaw, CBE, BSc, MS, PhD; British business executive; *Chairman, London Stock Exchange;* m. Marjorie Gibson-Smith; two c.; ed Univs of Durham and Newcastle and Stanford Business School, USA; with British Petroleum (BP) 1970–2001, positions include COO BP Chemicals, CEO BP Exploration Europe, Group Man. Dir 1997–2001; Chair. Nat. Air Traffic Services 2001–03; Chair. London Stock Exchange 2003–; mem. Bd of Dirs (non-exec.) Lloyds TSB Group PLC 1999–2005, Powergen UK PLC 2001–02, Qatar Financial Centre Authority, British Land Co. PLC 2003–07 (Chair. 2007–); fmr Chair. Calif. Marine Mammal Centre; Gov. London Business School; fmr Trustee, Arts and Business, Inst. of Public Policy Research; Sloan Fellow, Stanford Business School 1984–85; fmr mem. Advisory Bd Stanford Business School; fmr mem. Council CBI Scotland, Sustainability Comm. *Leisure interests:* skiing, golf, music, the arts. *Address:* London Stock Exchange, 10 Paternoster Square, London, EC4M 7LS, England (office). *Telephone:* (20) 7797-1318 (office). *E-mail:* enquiries@londonstockexchange.com (office). *Website:* www.londonstockexchange.com (office).

GIDADA, Negaso, BA, MA, PhD; Ethiopian politician and fmr head of state; *Chairman, Unity for Democracy and Justice Party;* b. 8 Sept. 1943, Dembi Dollo, Wollega; m. Regina Abelt; one s. two d.; ed Addis Ababa Univ., Johann Wolfgang Goethe Univ., Frankfurt-am-Main, Germany; teacher and School Dir, Mekane Yesus Church, Lalo Aira School 1971–74; mem. Union of Oromo Students and Oromo Liberation 1975–81, Union of Oroms in Europe 1987–91; Librarian, Inst. of Anthropology and teacher of Oromo Language, Inst. of African Languages, Johann Wolfgang Goethe Univ. 1985–87; Dir Dritte Welt Hause, Frankfurt-am-Main 1986–91; mem. OPDO/EPRDF 1991–2001; Minister of Labour and Social Affairs 1991–92, of Information 1992–95; Peoples' Rep. of the Transitional Govt of Ethiopia 1991–95; Chair. Constitution Ass. Nov.–Dec. 1994; Pres. of Ethiopia 1995–2001; mem. House of Reps (Parl.) 2005–10; mem. Unity for Democracy and Justice Party 2009–, currently Chair.; Deputy Chair. Ethiopian Forum (Front) for Fed. Democratic Unity (Medrek); Guest Prof., Frobenius Inst. and Excellence 'Normative Orders', Johann Wolfgang Goethe Univ., Frankfurt May–June 2012; Interreligious and Int. Fed. for World Peace Amb. for Peace, Int. Lions Club Melvin Jones Fellow. *Publications include:* History of the Sayo Oromo of Southwestern Wollega, Ethiopia 2001. *Leisure interests:* reading, walking. *Address:* Woreda 23, House Number 1031, Nefas Silk-Lafto Kifle Ketema, Addis Ababa (office); PO Box 26749, C-1000, Addis Ababa, Ethiopia (office). *Telephone:* (912) 096650 (office); (11) 3205612 (home). *E-mail:* nereta2003@yahoo.com (home).

GIDDENS, Baron (Life Peer), cr. 2004, of Southgate in the London Borough of Enfield; **Anthony Giddens,** PhD; British sociologist; *Chairman and Director, Polity Press Ltd;* b. 18 Jan. 1938, Edmonton; m. Jane Ellwood 1963; two d.; ed Minchenden School, Southgate, Univ. of Hull, London School of Economics, Univ. of Cambridge; Lecturer in Sociology, Univ. of Leicester 1961–70; Visiting Asst Prof., Simon Fraser Univ., Vancouver 1967–68, Univ. of California, Los Angeles

1968–69; Lecturer in Sociology and Fellow, King's Coll., Cambridge 1970–84, Reader in Sociology 1984–86, Prof. of Sociology 1986–96; Dir LSE 1997–2003, Prof. Emer. 2004–; Chair. and Dir Polity Press Ltd 1985–; apptd Dir Blackwell-Polity Ltd 1985; Chair. and Dir Centre for Social Research 1989–; BBC Reith Lecturer 1999; numerous visiting professorships; Founder of 'The Third Way'; mem. Russian Acad. of Sciences, American Acad. of Science; Hon. Fellow, LSE 2004, Chilean Acad., Chinese Acad. of Social Sciences; Nat. Order of the Southern Cross (Brazil), Grand Cross, Order of the Infante Dom Henrique (Portugal); Hon. DLitt (Univ. of Anglia), (Open Univ.), (Univ. of Salford), (South Bank Univ.), (Univ. of Hull), (Univ. of Leicester), Hon. DScS (Univ. of Helsinki), Dr hc (Vesalius Coll., Vrije Univ. Brussels), (Univ. of Buenos Aires, Argentina), (Univ. of Twente, Netherlands); German British Forum Award 1999, Prince of Asturias Award (Spain) 2002, Gold Medal, Norwegian Acad. *Publications:* Capitalism and Modern Social Theory 1971, Politics and Sociology in the Thought of Max Weber 1972, Emile Durkheim: selected writings (ed. and trans.) 1972, The Class Structure of the Advanced Societies 1973, New Rules of Sociological Method 1976, Positivism and Sociology (ed.) 1973, Elites and Power in British Society (with P. H. Stanworth) 1974, Studies in Social and Political Theory 1977, Emile Durkheim 1978, Central Problems in Social Theory 1979, A Contemporary Critique of Historical Materialism 1981, Sociology: A Brief but Critical Introduction 1982, Classes, Conflict and Power (with D. Held) 1982, Classes and the Division of Labour (with G. G. N. Mackenzie) 1982, Profiles and Critiques in Social Theory 1983, The Constitution of Society: Outline of the Theory of Structuration 1984, The Nation-State and Violence 1985, Durkheim on Politics and the State 1986, Social Theory and Modern Sociology 1987, Social Theory Today (with Jon Turner) 1988, Sociology 1988, The Consequences of Modernity 1990, Modernity and Self-Identity 1991, Human Societies 1992, The Transformation of Intimacy 1992, Beyond Left and Right 1994, Reflexive Modernisation (with Ulrich Beck and Scott Lash) 1994, Politics, Sociology and Social Theory 1995, In Defence of Sociology 1996, Conversations with Anthony Giddens: Making Sense of Modernity (with Christopher Pierson) 1998, The Third Way: The Renewal of Social Democracy 1998, Runaway World: How Globalisation is Reshaping Our Lives 1999, The Third Way and its Critics 2000, On the Edge: Living with Global Capitalism (ed with Will Hutton) 2000, The Global Third Way Debate 2001, The Progressive Manifesto 2003, Essentials of Sociology 2006, Europe In The Global Age 2007, Over to You, Mr Brown - How Labour Can Win Again 2007, The Politics of Climate Change 2009; contrib. of articles, review articles and book reviews to professional journals and newspapers. *Leisure interests:* theatre, tennis, cinema. *Address:* Polity Press, 65 Bridge Street, Cambridge, CB2 1UR, England (office). *Telephone:* (1223) 324315 (office). *Fax:* (1223) 461385 (office). *E-mail:* editorial@politybooks.com (office). *Website:* www.polity.co.uk (office).

GIDDINGS, Hon. Larissa Tahireh (Lara), BA, LLB; Australian politician; *Premier of Tasmania;* b. 14 Nov. 1972, Goroka, Papua New Guinea; ed Univ. of Tasmania; worked in Australian Senate as Whip's Clerk, then as an electorate officer with Senator Sue Mackay; travelled to UK to carry out temporary admin. work in London, later worked as a parl. research officer for Helen Eadie MSP, Edinburgh; mem. Tasmanian House of Ass. (Australian Labor Party) for Lyons 1996–98, for Franklin 2002–, worked for Tasmanian Premier as speech writer and media asst; Minister for Econ. Devt and the Arts 2004–06, for Health and Human Services 2006–10, for Infrastructure and Econ. Devt April–Nov. 2010; Deputy Premier of Tasmania, Attorney Gen. and Minister for Justice 2008–11, Treas. of Tasmania and Minister for the Arts 2010–, also Premier (first woman) 2011–. *Address:* Office of the Premier, GPO Box 123, Hobart, Tas 7001 (office); Office of the Premier, Executive Building Level 11, 15 Murray Street, Hobart, Tas 7000, Australia (office). *Telephone:* (3) 6233-3464 (office). *Fax:* (3) 6234-1572 (office). *E-mail:* lara.giddings@dpac.tas.gov.au (office); premier@dpac.tas.gov.au (office). *Website:* www.premier.tas.gov.au (office); www.laragiddings.com.

GIELEN, Michael Andreas; Austrian conductor and composer; b. 20 July 1927, Dresden, Germany; m. Helga Augsten 1957; one s. one d.; ed Univ. of Buenos Aires; studied composition under E. Leuchter and J. Polnauer; pianist in Buenos Aires; on music staff, Teatro Colón 1947–50; with Vienna State Opera 1951–60, Perm. Conductor, 1954–60; First Conductor, Royal Swedish Opera, Stockholm 1960–65; conductor and composer in Cologne 1965–69; Musical Dir Nat. Orchestra of Belgium 1969–73; Chief Conductor, Netherlands Opera 1973–75; Music Dir and Gen. Man. Frankfurt Opera House 1977–87; Music Dir Cincinnati Symphony 1980–86; Prin. Conductor, SWF Radio Orchestra, Baden-Baden 1986–99, Hon. Conductor 2002–; Prof. of Conducting, Mozarteum, Salzburg 1987–95, Emer. 1995–; Chief Guest Conductor, BBC Symphony Orchestra 1979–82; Perm. Guest Conductor, Berlin State Opera 1998–, Berlin Symphony Orchestra 1998–; Dr hc (Berlin Hochschule der Künste) 2000; State Prize, Hessen 1985, Adorno Prize, Frankfurt 1986, Vienna Music Prize 1997, Frankfurt Music Prize 1999, MIDEM Prize for Lifetime Achievement 2005, Der Faust Prize for Lifetime Achievement 2007, ECHO Klassik Prize 2008, Ernst von Siemens Music Foundation Music Award 2010. *Compositions:* Au vieux souvenirs (string quartet) 1983. *Recordings:* as conductor: Schöenberg, Moses und Aron, Gurre-Lieden, complete Beethoven symphonies, complete Mahler symphonies. *Publications:* Mahler im Gesprach 2002, Unbedingt Musik (autobiog.) 2005. *Address:* Niedersee 49, 5311, Innerschwand am Mondsee, Austria (home). *Telephone:* (6232) 2082 (home).

GIELGUD, Maina Julia Gordon, AO, BEPC; British ballet director and teacher; b. 14 Jan. 1945, London, England; d. of the late Lewis Gielgud and of Elisabeth Grussner; with Cuevas Co. and Roland Petit Co. –1963; Grand Ballet Classique de France 1963–67; Béjart Co. 1967–71; Berlin 1971; London Festival Ballet 1972–76; ballerina, Sadler's Wells Royal Ballet 1976–78; freelance ballerina and guest artist 1978–82; Rehearsal Dir London City Ballet 1982; Artistic Dir The Australian Ballet 1983–96; Ballet Dir Royal Danish Ballet 1997–99; Artistic Assoc., Houston Ballet 2003–05; freelance dir, regular guest repetiteur and teacher, English Nat. Ballet 2006–12, Boston Ballet, Nat. Ballet of Canada, La Scala, Milan, The Australian Ballet, Rome Opera and other ballet cos and schools world-wide; freelance stager, guest teacher, coach and stager; Hon. AO 1991. *Plays:* L'Heure Exquise (Maurice Bejart, after Happy Days by Samuel Beckett). *Film:* L'Age en Fleurs. *Ballets produced:* Steps Notes and Squeaks 1968; for The Australian Ballet: The Sleeping Beauty 1985, Giselle 1987; for Boston Ballet: Giselle 2002, 2007; for Ballet du Rhin: Giselle 2003; for Houston Ballet: Giselle 2005. *Ballets performed:* L'Heure Exquise. *Address:* 1/9 Stirling Court, 3 Marshall Street,

London, W1F 9BD, England. *Telephone:* (20) 7734-6612. *E-mail:* mainagielgud@gmail.com. *Website:* www.mainagielgud.com.

GIENOW, Herbert Hans Walter, DIur; German business executive; b. 13 March 1926, Hamburg; s. of Günther and Margarethe Gienow; m. Imina Brons 1954; one s. one d.; ed Hamburg Univ.; Head Clerk Deutsche Warentreuhand AG, mem. Man. Bd 1959; mem. Hamburg Bar; chartered accountant 1961; mem. Man. Bd, Klöckner-Werke AG 1962, Chair. Exec. Bd 1974–91; Pres. ALSTOM Germany 1991–98; Sr Adviser, Gen. Capital Group, Munich; Chair. Supervisory Bd ALSTOM GmbH 1994–99, SteelDex AG; fmr Chair. Consultative Cttee Deutsche Bank AG, Essen; Hon. mem. World Steel Inst., Brussels 1992, Hon. Pres. Academia Baltica 2008; Commdr, Confrèrie des Chevaliers du Tastevin, Dijon 1982, Chevalier, Légion d'honneur 1998. *Leisure interests:* books, shooting, model soldiers. *Address:* An der Pont 51, 40885 Ratingen (office); Am Adels 7, 40883 Ratingen, Germany (home). *Telephone:* (2102) 126903 (office); (2102) 60692 (home). *Fax:* (2102) 126909 (office). *E-mail:* woneigoffice@t-online.de (office).

GIEROWSKI, Stefan; Polish painter; b. 21 May 1925, Częstochowa; s. of Józef Gierowski and Stefania Gierowska (née Wasilewska); m. Anna Golka 1951; one s. one d.; ed Acad. of Fine Arts, Kraków, Jagiellonian Univ.; worked with Gallery Krzywe 1956–61; Docent, Acad. of Fine Arts, Warsaw, Dean of Painting Dept 1975–80, Extraordinary Prof. 1976–96; mem. Union of Polish Artists and Designers, Sec.-Gen. 1957–59, Pres. of Painting Section 1959–61, 1963–66; mem. Organizing Cttee, Congress of Polish Culture 1981; Kt's and Officer's Cross of Order of Polonia Restituta; Silver Medal, Third Festival of Fine Arts, Warsaw 1978, Prize of Chair. Council of Ministers (1st class) 1979, Jan Cybis Prize 1980. *Address:* ul. Gagarina 15 m. 97, 00-753 Warsaw, Poland. *Telephone:* (22) 8411633.

GIERTYCH, Roman, MA, LLM; Polish politician and lawyer; b. 27 Feb. 1971, Srem; s. of Maciej Giertych and Antonina Giertych; m. Barbara Giertych; two c.; ed Adam Mickiewicz Univ., Poznań; owner of a legal practice, Warsaw; reactivated All-Polish Youth (Młodzież Wszechpolska), Chair. 1989 (now Hon. Chair.); mem. Nat. Democratic Party (Stronnictwo Narodowo-Demokratyczne) and Nat. Party (Stronnictwo Narodowe), Vice-Pres. Bd Nat. Party 1994–, both parties merged with several others orgs to form League of Polish Families 2001, Pres. Congress of League of Polish Families (Liga Polskich Rodzin) 2002–; Deputy to Sejm (Parl.) 2001–; Deputy Prime Minister and Minister for Nat. Educ. 2006–07; mem. Polish Academic Union 1988–; mem. and Vice-Chair. PKN Orlen Investigation Comm. (to investigate biggest corruption scandal in modern Polish political history) 2004–. *Publications include:* Kontrrewolucja mlodych (Counter-Revolution of the Young) 1994, Pod walcem historii. Polityka zagraniczna ruchu narodowego 1938–1945 (Under History's Roller. Foreign Policy of the National Movement 1938–1945) 1995, Lot orla (Flight of the Eagle) 2000, Możemy wygrać Polskę (We Can Win Poland) 2001; numerous articles, including several publs in Nasz Dziennik, Mysl Polska, Rodzina Radia Maryja, Wszechpolak. *Leisure interests:* historical books, chess (Vice-Champion of Poznań Voivodship), tennis. *Address:* League of Polish Families (Liga Polskich Rodzin), 00-528 Warsaw, ul. Hoża 9, Poland (office). *Telephone:* (22) 6223648 (office). *Fax:* (22) 6223138 (office). *E-mail:* roman .giertych@sejm.pl (office). *Website:* www.sejm.gov.pl (office).

GIESBERT, Franz-Olivier; French journalist and writer; *Editor, Le Point;* b. 18 Jan. 1949, Wilmington, Del., USA; s. of Frederick Giesbert and Marie Allain; m. 1st Christine Fontaine (divorced); two s. one d.; m. 2nd Natalie Freund 2000; one s., one d.; ed Centre de Formation des Journalistes; journalist at Le Nouvel Observateur 1971, Sr Corresp. in Washington, DC 1980, Political Ed. 1981, Ed.-in-Chief 1985–88; Ed.-in-Chief Le Figaro 1988–2000, Figaro Magazine 1997–2000, mem. Editorial Bd 1993–2000, Figaro Magazine 1997–2000; Ed. Le Point 2000–; Dir/presenter 'le Gai savoir' TV programme, Paris Première cable channel 1997–2001, Dir Culture et Dépendances France 3 TV channel 2001–; mem. jury Prix Théophraste Renaudot 1998–, Prix Louis Hachette, Prix Aujourd'hui; mem. Conseil Admin Musée du Louvre Paris 2000; Aujourd'hui Best Essay Prize 1975, Prix Gutenberg 1987, Grand Prix du roman de l'Académie française 1992, Prix Interallié 1995, Prix Pierre de Monaco 1997, Prix Richelieu 1999, Prix Itheme for Best Talk Show 1999. *Publications:* François Mitterrand ou la tentation de l'Histoire (essay) 1977, Monsieur Adrien (novel) 1982, Jacques Chirac (biog.) 1987, Le Président 1990, L'Affreux (Grand Prix du Roman de l'Acad. Française) 1992, La Fin d'une Époque 1993, La Souille (William the Conqueror and Interallie Prize), Le Vieil homme et la Mort 1996, François Mitterrand, une vie 1996, Le Sieur Dieu (Prix Jean d'Heurs de Nice Baie des Anges) 1998, Mort d'un berger 2002, L'Abatteur 2003, L'Américain 2004, L'Immortel 2007, La Tragédie du président: scènes de la vie politique 2006, Le Huitième Prophète 2008, Le lessiveur 2009, Un très grand amour 2010, Dieu, ma mère et moi 2012. *Address:* Le Point, 74 avenue du Maine, 75014 Paris Cedex, France (office). *Telephone:* 1-44-10-10-10 (office). *Fax:* 1-44-10-12-49 (office). *E-mail:* fogiesbert@lepoint.tm.fr (office). *Website:* www .lepoint.fr (office).

GIEVE, Sir John, Kt, CB, MPhil; British civil servant and financial executive; *Senior Advisor, GLG Partners LP;* b. 20 Feb. 1950; m.; two c.; ed New Coll., Oxford; several positions at HM Treasury 1978–2001, including working in Dept of Employment, Pvt. Sec. to the Chief Sec., Treasury Press Sec., Prin. Pvt. Sec. to the Chancellor; Perm. Sec. Home Office 2001–05; Deputy Gov. and mem. Monetary Policy Cttee, Bank of England 2006–09, with responsibility for Bank's Financial Stability work; Sr Advisor, GLG Partners LP 2010–; mem. Bd Financial Services Authority; Gov. Islington Primary School. *Address:* GLG Partners LP, One Curzon Street, London, W1J 5HB, England (office). *Telephone:* (20) 7016-7000 (office). *E-mail:* info@glgpartners.com (office). *Website:* www.glgpartners.com.

GIFFEN, John A., BSc, MBA; Canadian business executive; b. 17 Dec. 1938, Ingersoll, Ont.; s. of John Giffen and Kathleen Marion Giffen (née McQuinn); m. Joan E. Rothwell 1962; one s. two d.; ed Univ. of Windsor; plant foreman, Hiram Walker 1962, Project Engineer 1965, Div. Supt 1972, Inventory Man. 1973, N American Distribution Man. 1977, Asst to Pres. 1979, Vice Pres. Worldwide Production 1980–87, Pres. Hiram Walker & Sons Ltd 1987–88, Chair., CEO Hiram Walker-Allied Vintners (Canada) Ltd 1988–89, Allied-Lyons PLC 1988–93, Man. Dir Hiram Walker-Allied Vintners 1989–91, Chair., CEO The Hiram Walker Group 1991–92, Chair. Corby Distilleries Ltd 1992–2003 (Dir 1980–2003); Regional Chair. The Americas, Allied-Lyons 1992–93; Pres. HW-G & W Ltd 1989–92; Deputy Chair. 1992–93; Dir Hallmark Technologies Inc. 1995–2001;

mem. of Windsor Advisory Bd Royal Trustco, of Canadian-UK Cttee, Canadian Chamber of Commerce 1983–91; Dir and Vice-Pres., Windsor Chamber of Commerce 1979–83; Gov. Metropolitan Gen. Hosp., Windsor 1979–85; Dir Inst. of Canadian-American Studies 1983–86. *Leisure interests:* golf, curling. *Address:* PO Box 2518, Walkerville, Windsor, ON N8Y 4S5, Canada.

GIFFORD, Charles (Chad) K., BA; American banking executive; b. 8 Nov. 1942, Rhode Island; s. of Clarence H. Gifford and Priscilla Kivert Gifford; m. Anne Dewing; four c.; ed Princeton Univ.; Chair., Pres. and CEO BankBoston 1995–96, CEO 1996–97, Chair. and CEO 1997–99; Pres. and COO FleetBoston Financial Corpn 1999–2001, Pres. and CEO 2001–02, Chair. and CEO 2002–04; Chair. Bank of America Corpn (following acquisition of FleetBoston) 2004–05 (retd), now Chair. Emer. and mem. Bd of Dirs; mem. Bd of Dirs Mass Mutual Life Insurance Co., CBS Corpn; Trustee, NSTAR, Dana-Farber Cancer Inst. *Address:* c/o Board of Directors, Bank of America Corporation, Bank of America Corporate Center, 100 North Tryon Street, Charlotte, NC 28255, USA (office).

GIL, Gilberto; Brazilian politician, musician (guitar, accordion) and singer; b. (Gilberto Passos Gil Moreira), 26 June 1942, Salvador, Bahia State; s. of José Gil Moreira and Claudina Passos Gil Moreira; ed Fed. Univ., Bahia; began playing accordion aged eight; composed songs for TV advertisements in early 1960's; appeared in Nós Por Exemplo (show directed by Caetano Veloso) 1964; moved to São Paulo 1965; had first hit when Elis Regina recorded Louvação; participated in Tropicalia movt, sang protest songs that proved controversial with mil. dictatorship; imprisoned 1968; forced to leave Brazil on release and moved to UK; worked with groups such as Pink Floyd, Yes, Incredible String Band and Rod Stewart's band in London clubs; returned to Brazil in 1972; toured with Caetano Veloso, Gal Costa and Maria Bethânia; recorded album Nightingale in USA 1978; appearances at Montreux Jazz Festival; Pres. Fundação Gregorio de Matos, Salvador 1987; mem. Council of City Hall of Salvador 1988–92, Pres. Environmental Defence Cttee 1989; mem. Advisory Council Fundação Mata Virgem and Fundação Alerta Brasil Pantanal; Pres. Negro-Mestizo Reference Centre (CERNE); mem. Green Party 1989, later mem. Nat. Exec. Cttee; mem. Parl. for Salvador; Minister of Culture 2003–08 (resgnd); fmr Pres. Fundação Onda Azul (Blue Wave Foundation); Cruz da Ordem de Rio Branco, Chevalier, Ordre des Arts et des Lettres, Grand Officier, Légion d'honneur 2005; Shell and Sharp Prize 1990, UNESCO Artist for Peace 1999, Polar Music Prize 2004, 2005. *Recordings include:* albums: Louvação 1967, Gilberto Gil 1968, Tropicália ou Panis et Circensis 1968, Gilberto Gil 1969, Expresso 2222 1972, Barra 69 1972, Temporada de Verão 1974, Gilberto Gil ao Vivo 1974, Gil Jorge Ogum Zangô 1975, Refazenda 1975, Doces Bárbaros 1976, Refavela 1977, Refestança 1978, Antologia do Samba-Choro: Gilberto Gil e Germano Mathias 1978, Gilberto Gil ao Vivo em Montreux 1978, Nightingale 1978, Realce 1979, A Gente Precisa Ver o Luar 1981, Brasil: João Gilberto Gil, Caetano e Bethânia 1981, Um Banda Um 1982, Extra 1983, Quilombo 1984, Vamos Fugir (with The Wailers) 1984, Raça Humana 1984, Dia Dorim Noite Neon 1985, Gilberto Gil em Concerto 1987, Ao Vivo Em Tóquio 1987, Soy Loco por Ti, América 1987, O Eterno Deus Mu Dança 1989, Parabolicamará 1992, Tropicália 2 1993, Gilberto Gil Unplugged 1994, Quanta 1997, O sol de Oslo 1998, Ensaio Geral 1999, Cidade do Salvador 1999, O Viramundo 1999, Gilberto Gil – Satisfação 1999, Gil & Milton 2000, São João Vivo 2001, Kaya N'Gan Daya 2002, Eletracústico (Grammy Award for Best Contemporary World Music Album 2006) 2005, Gil Luminoso 2006, Banda Larga de Cordel 2008, BandaDois (Latin Grammy Award for Best Música Popular Brasileira Album 2010) 2009, Fé na Festa (Latin Grammy Award for Best Native Brazilian Roots Album) 2010, Concerto de cordas & máquinas de ritmo. *Address:* Gege Produções, Estrada de Gávea 135, 22451-260 Rio de Janeiro, RJ, Brazil (office). *Telephone:* (21) 3323-1600 (office). *Fax:* (21) 2239-9727 (office). *E-mail:* atendimento@gege.com.br (office). *Website:* www.gege.com.br (office); www.gilbertogil.com.br.

GILAD, Nir, BA, MA; Israeli business executive and fmr government official; *President and CEO, Israel Corporation;* ed Hebrew Univ., Jerusalem, Bar Ilan Univ.; fmr Chief Financial Officer Israel Aircraft Industries; fmr Accountant Gen. and Deputy Head of Budget Div., Ministry of Finance; Sr Vice-Pres., Migdal Insurance Co., CEO Migdal Investment Man. Ltd and Chair. Migdal Capital Markets Ltd; Sr Vice-Pres. for Business Devt and Strategy, Israel Corpn –2006, Pres. and CEO 2006–; Chair. ICL, IC Green Energy Ltd; mem. Bd of Dirs Zim Integrated Shipping Services Ltd, Tower Semiconductors Ltd, Chery Quantum Ltd, and several ICL subsidiaries; mem. Yedidei Atidim Asscn; holds rank of Lt Col in Israel Defense Force reserves. *Address:* Israel Corporation, Millennium Tower, 23 Aranha Street, PO Box 20456, Tel-Aviv 61204, Israel (office). *Telephone:* (3) 684-4500 (office). *Fax:* (3) 684-4570 (office). *E-mail:* info@israelcorp.com (office). *Website:* www.israelcorp.com (office).

GILANI, Makhdoom Syed Yousaf Raza, BA, MA; Pakistani politician; *Vice-Chairman, Pakistan Peoples's Party;* b. 9 June 1952, Karachi; s. of Alamdar Hussain Gilani; m. Elahi Gilani; four s. one d.; ed Univ. of the Punjab, Lahore; mem. Pakistan People's Party 1988–, Vice-Chair. Cen. Exec. Cttee 1998–; mem. Cen. Leadership Muslim League, Pakistan 1978; cabinet mem. in three-year govt of Prime Minister Muhammad Khan Junejo, Minister of Housing and Works 1985–86, of Railways Jan.–Dec. 1986; Chair. Dist Council, Multan; mem. Nat. Ass. from Multan 1985–, Speaker 1993–97; served in cabinet of fmr Prime Minister, the late Benazir Bhutto, as Minister of Tourism 1989–90, of Housing and Works Jan.–Aug. 1990; tried on charges of abusing his authority by govt anti-corruption agency 1997, accused of putting more than 500 unqualified people from his constituency on govt payroll when he was House Speaker, imprisoned 2001–06; Prime Minister of Pakistan 2008–12 (indicted by Pakistan Supreme Court for contempt for failing to pursue corruption charges against Pres. Asif Ali Zardari April 2012, disqualified from holding office and from parliament June 2012); ranked 38th by Forbes magazine amongst The World's Most Powerful People 2009. *Publication:* Reflections of Yusuf's Well. *Address:* Pakistan Peoples Party (PPP), 8 Street 19, F-8/2, Islamabad (office); Gilani House, Ghaus-al-Azam Road, Multan, 155-B, Phase-I, Defence, Lahore, Pakistan. *Telephone:* (51) 2255264 (office); (61) 542424; 300-8730662 (mobile); (42) 5723234; 300-8448141. *Fax:* (51) 2282741 (office). *E-mail:* makhdoomyrgillani@hotmail.com (home); chairman@ppp.org.pk (office); ppp@comsats.net.pk (office). *Website:* www.ppp.org.pk (office).

GILAURI, Nikoloz (Nika) Zurabis, BA, MA; Georgian economist and politician; b. 14 Feb. 1975, Tbilisi; m. Marine Shamugia 2010; one d.; ed Ivane Javakhishvili

Tbilisi State Univ., Bournemouth Coll., UK, Limerick Univ., Ireland, Temple Univ., Philadelphia, USA, Univs of Paris and Tokyo; worked at Dublin Int. Finance Centre as an Admin./Man. Invesco assets man. corpn 1999; financial consultant for energy conservation projects at Philadelphia Small Business Devt Center 2000; financial consultant, Georgia Telecom 2001; financial consultant, Spanish corpn Iberdrola (Georgian energy market man. contractor) 2002; worked for SBE (Ireland) as man. contractor and financial controller of Georgian state electricity 2003–04; Minister of Energy 2004–07, of Finance 2007–09; First Deputy Prime Minister 2008–09, Prime Minister 2009–12; Head of JSC Partnership Fund (state-owned stock fund) 2012–. *Address:* JSC Partnership Fund, 0108 Tbilisi, 8 Rustaveli Avenue (Old Parliament Building), Georgia (office). *Telephone:* (322) 99-04-48 (office). *E-mail:* info@fund.ge (office). *Website:* www.fund.ge (office).

GILBERT; British artist; b. (Gilbert Proesch), 1943, Dolomites, Italy; ed Wolkenstein School of Art, Hallein School of Art, Munich Acad. of Art, St Martin's School of Art, London; began working with George (Passmore) in 1967 as Gilbert & George; est. reputation as performance artists, presenting themselves, identically dressed, as living sculptures; later work includes large composite drawings and vividly coloured photo-pieces often featuring likenesses of the artists; work underpinned by 'Art for all' philosophy; works address social issues, taboos and artistic conventions; work held in public collections in UK and abroad; Dr hc (London Metropolitan Univ.) 2008; Turner Prize 1986. *Publications include:* What Our Art Means, Gilbert and George: The Complete Pictures 2007. *Address:* White Cube, 48 Hoxton Square, London, N1 6PB, England (office). *Telephone:* (20) 7930-5373 (office). *Fax:* (20) 7749-7480 (office). *E-mail:* g-and-g@dircon.co.uk (office). *Website:* www.whitecube.com (office).

GILBERT, Kenneth Albert, OC, DMus, FRCM, FRSC; Canadian/Austrian harpsichordist and organist; *Adjunct Professor of Harpsichord and Organ, Faculty of Music, McGill University;* b. 16 Dec. 1931, Montreal; s. of Albert George Gilbert and Reta Mabel (née Welch); ed Conservatoire de Musique, Montréal and Conservatoire Nat. Supérieur de Musique, Paris; Prof., Conservatoire de Musique, Montreal 1965–72; Assoc. Prof., Laval Univ., Québec 1970–76; Guest Prof., Royal Antwerp Conservatory, Belgium 1971–73; Dir Early Music Dept Conservatoire de Strasbourg, France 1981–85; Prof., Staatliche Hochschule für Musik, Stuttgart, Germany 1981–89, Paris Conservatoire 1988–96; Prof., Hochschule Mozarteum, Salzburg, Austria 1984–2000, Prof. Emer. 2000–; Adjunct Prof. of Harpsichord and Organ, McGill Univ., Montreal 1998–; Visiting Prof., RAM and Royal Coll. of Music, London; instructor at other music acads, summer schools etc.; Pres. Editions de l'Oiseau-Lyre, Monaco 2001–12; Hon. RAM; Hon. FRCO; Officier des Arts et des Lettres, Cross of Honour 1st Class (Austria); Hon. DMus (McGill), (Melbourne), (Laval); Fellowships from Canada Council 1968, 1974, and Calouste Gulbenkian Foundation 1971, Prix Opus Québec 2006. *Recordings:* complete harpsichord works of F. Couperin, Scarlatti and Rameau, Suites and Partitas of J.S. Bach, Well-Tempered Clavier and Concertos for 2, 3 and 4 Harpsichords by Bach. *Publications:* editions of complete harpsichord works of Couperin, Scarlatti and Rameau, Bach's Goldberg Variations, Frescobaldi Toccatas, Kapsberger's lute works transcribed for harpsichord. *Address:* Strathcona Music Building, 555 West Sherbrooke Street, Montreal, PQ H3A 1E3, Canada (office). *E-mail:* kenneth .gilbert@mcgill.ca (office). *Website:* www.mcgill.ca/music (office).

GILBERT, Lewis, CBE; British film director; b. 6 March 1920, London; m. Hylda Henrietta Tafler; two s.; entered films as child actor; joined RAF and became Asst Dir to William Keighley on Target for Today 1939; joined GB Instructional (GBI) 1944, for whom he wrote and directed The Ten Year Plan, Sailors Do Care, Arctic Harvest, etc. 1946–47; wrote and directed The Little Ballerina 1947–48, worked on series of documentaries for GBI; Producer/Dir Int. Realist 1948; numerous awards including Special Evening Standard Film Award 1996, Fellowship, British Film Inst. 2001. *Films include:* The Little Ballerina 1947, Once a Sinner 1950, Scarlet Thread 1951, There is Another Sun 1951, Time Gentlemen Please 1952, Emergency Call 1952, Cosh Boy, Johnny on the Run 1953, Albert RN 1953, The Good Die Young 1954, The Sea Shall Not Have Them 1954, Cast a Dark Shadow 1955, Reach for the Sky (BAFTA Award) 1956, The Admirable Crichton 1957, Carve Her Name With Pride 1957, A Cry From the Streets 1958, Ferry to Hong Kong 1959, Sink the Bismarck 1960, Light Up The Sky 1960, The Greengage Summer 1961, HMS Defiant 1962, The Seventh Dawn 1964, Alfie 1966, You Only Live Twice 1967, Paul and Michelle (also producer) 1973, Seven Men at Daybreak 1975, Seven Nights in Japan 1976, The Spy Who Loved Me 1977, Moonraker 1978, Dubai (also producer), Educating Rita (BAFTA Award) 1982, Shirley Valentine (also producer) 1989, Stepping Out 1991, Haunted 1995, Before You Go 2002; co-produced Spare The Rod 1959–60. *Television includes:* A Bob Hope Comedy Special 1966, The Golden Gong 1985, Michael Caine: Breaking The Mold 1991, Inside The Spy Who Loved Me 2000, Edmund North: The Man Who Made the Earth Stand Still 2008. *Publications include:* All My Flashbacks (autobiography) 2010. *Address:* 19 blvd de Suisse, Monaco.

GILBERT, The Rt Hon Sir Martin John, Kt, CBE, MA, DLitt, FRSL; British historian and academic; *Fellow, Merton College, Oxford;* b. 25 Oct. 1936; s. of Peter Gilbert and Miriam Gilbert; m. 1st Helen Robinson 1963; one d.; m. 2nd Susan Sacher; two s.; m. 3rd Esther Poznansky; ed Highgate School and Magdalen Coll., Oxford; Sr Research Fellow, St Antony's Coll., Oxford 1960–62, Fellow, Merton Coll., Oxford 1962–; Visiting Prof., Univ. of S Carolina 1965, Tel-Aviv Univ. 1979, Hebrew Univ. of Jerusalem 1980–; official biographer of Sir Winston Churchill 1968–; Gov. Hebrew Univ. of Jerusalem 1978–; Non-Governmental Rep., UN Comm. on Human Rights, Geneva 1987, 1988; mem. Prime Minister's del. to Israel, Gaza and Jordan 1995, to USA 1995, to Israel 2008; Cttee mem., The Iraq Inquiry 2009–11; Privy Councillor 2009; adviser to BBC and ITV for various documentaries; script designer and co-author, Genocide (Acad. Award for best documentary feature film) 1981; presenter, History Channel 1996–; Recent History Corresp. Sunday Times 1967; Hon. Fellow, Univ. of Wales, Lampeter 1997; Hon. DLitt (Westminster Coll., Fulton, Mo.) 1981, (Univ. of Buckingham) 1992, (Univ. of Leicester) 2004. *Publications:* The Appeasers (with R. Gott) 1963, Britain and Germany between the Wars 1964, The European Powers 1900–1945 1965, Plough My Own Furrow: The Life of Lord Allen of Hurtwood 1965, Servant of India: A Study of Imperial Rule 1905–1910 1966, The Roots of Appeasement 1966, Recent History Atlas 1860–1960 1966, Winston Churchill 1966, British History Atlas 1968, American History Atlas 1968, Jewish History Atlas 1969, First World

War Atlas 1970, Winston S. Churchill, Vol. III, 1914–16 1971, companion vol. 1973, Russian History Atlas 1972, Sir Horace Rumbold: Portrait of a Diplomat 1973, Churchill: A Photographic Portrait 1974, The Arab-Israeli Conflict: its history in maps 1974, Winston S. Churchill, Vol. IV, 1917–22 1975, companion vol. 1977, The Jews in Arab Lands: Their History in Maps 1975, Winston S. Churchill, Vol. V, 1922–39, 1976, companion Vols 1980, 1981, 1982, The Jews of Russia: Illustrated History Atlas 1976, Jerusalem Illustrated History Atlas 1977, Exile and Return: The Emergence of Jewish Statehood 1978, Children's Illustrated Bible Atlas 1979, Final Journey: The Fate of the Jews of Nazi Europe 1979, Auschwitz and the Allies 1981, Atlas of the Holocaust 1982, Winston S. Churchill, Vol. VI, 1939–41 1983, The Jews of Hope: A Study of the Crisis of Soviet Jewry 1984, Jerusalem: Rebirth of a City 1985, Shcharansky: Hero of our Time 1986, Winston S. Churchill, Vol. VII, 1941–45 1986, The Holocaust, The Jewish Tragedy 1986, Winston Churchill, Vol. VIII 1945–65 1988, Second World War 1989, Churchill, A Life 1991, The Churchill War Papers: At the Admiralty (ed.), Atlas of British Charities 1993, In Search of Churchill: A Historian's Journey 1994, The First World War: A Complete History 1994, The Churchill War Papers: Never Surrender (ed.) 1995, The Day the War Ended 1995, Jerusalem in the 20th Century 1996, The Boys, Triumph over Adversity 1996, A History of the World in the Twentieth Century (Vol. I 1900–1933) 1997, (Vol. II 1933–1951) 1998, (Vol. III 1952–1999) 1999, Holocaust Journey: Travelling in Search of the Past 1997, Israel, A History 1998, Winston Churchill and Emery Reeves: Correspondence 1998, Never Again: A History of the Holocaust 1999, The Jewish Century 2001, History of the Twentieth Century 2001, The Churchill War Papers: '1941, the Ever-Widening War' (ed.) 2001, Letters to Auntie Fori: 5,000 Years of Jewish History and Faith 2002, The Righteous: the Unsung Heroes of the Holocaust 2002, D-Day 2004, Churchill at War: His "Finest Hour" in Photographs, Churchill and America 2005, Kristallnacht: Prelude to Destruction 2006, Somme: The Heroism and Horror of War 2006, Will of the People: Churchill and Parliamentary Democracy 2006, Churchill and the Jews 2007, Routledge Atlas of the Second World War 2008, In Ishmael's House: A History of Jews in Muslim Lands 2010. *Leisure interest:* travel. *Address:* Merton College, Oxford OX1 4JD, England (office). *Website:* www.martingilbert.com.

GILBERT, Walter, AB, MA, PhD; American molecular biologist, investment company executive and artist; *Managing Director, BioVentures Investors;* b. 21 March 1932, Boston, Mass; s. of Richard V. Gilbert and Emma Gilbert (née Cohen); m. Celia Stone 1953; one s. one d.; ed Harvard Univ., Univ. of Cambridge, UK; NSF Postdoctoral Fellow, Harvard Univ. 1957–58, Lecturer in Physics 1958–59, Asst Prof. of Physics 1959–64, Assoc. Prof. of Biophysics 1964–68, Prof. of Biochemistry 1968–72; American Cancer Soc. Prof. of Molecular Biology 1972–81, Prof. of Biology 1985–86; H. H. Timken Prof. of Science 1986–87; Carl M. Loeb Univ. Prof. 1987–2002, Prof. Emer. 2002–, Chair. Dept of Cellular and Developmental Biology 1987–93; Chair. Scientific Bd, Biogen NV 1978–83, Co-Chair. Supervisory Bd 1979–81, Chair. Supervisory Bd and CEO 1981–84; Vice-Chair. Myriad Genetics, Inc. 1992–; Chair. Paratek Pharmaceuticals, Inc. 1996–2012, mem. Bd of Dirs 2012–; Man. Dir BioVentures Investors, Cambridge, Mass 2002–; mem. NAS, American Physical Soc., American Soc. of Biological Chemists, American Acad. of Arts and Sciences; Foreign mem. Royal Soc.; V.D. Mattia Lectureship, Roche Inst. of Molecular Biology 1976; Smith, Kline and French Lecturer, Univ. of California, Berkeley 1977; Hon. Fellow, Trinity Coll. Cambridge, UK 1991; Hon. DSc (Univ. of Chicago, Columbia Univ.) 1978, (Univ. of Rochester) 1979, (Yeshiva Univ.) 1981, (Tulane Univ.) 2011; Guggenheim Fellowship, Paris 1968–69, US Steel Foundation Award in Molecular Biology, NAS 1968, Ledlie Prize, Harvard Univ. (with M. Ptashne) 1969, Warren Triennial Prize, Massachusetts Gen. Hosp. (with S. Benzer) 1977, Louis and Bert Freedman Award, New York Acad. of Sciences 1977, Prix Charles-Léopold Mayer, Acad. des Sciences, Inst. de France (with M. Ptashne and E. Witkin) 1977, Harrison Howe Award of the Rochester br. of ACS 1978, Louisa Gross Horwitz Prize, Columbia Univ. (with F. Sanger) 1979, Gairdner Foundation Annual Award 1979, Albert Lasker Basic Medical Research Award (with F. Sanger 1979), Prize for Biochemical Analysis, German Soc. for Clinical Chem. (with A. M. Maxam, F. Sanger and A. R. Coulsen) 1980, Sober Award, American Soc. of Biological Chemists 1980, Nobel Prize for Chem. (with F. Sanger and P. Berg) for work on deoxyribonucleic acid (DNA) 1980, New England Entrepreneur of the Year Award 1991, Ninth Nat. Biotechnology Ventures Award 1997. *Address:* BioVentures Investors, 70 Walnut Street, Suite 302, Wellesley, MA 02481, USA (office). *Telephone:* (617) 252-3443 (office). *Fax:* (617) 621-7993 (office). *E-mail:* wgilbert@bioventureinvestors.com (office). *Website:* www .bioventuresinvestors.com (office); wallygilbert.artspan.com (home); wallygilbert .30art.com (home).

GILCHRIST, Adam Craig, AM; Australian fmr professional cricketer; b. 14 Nov. 1971, Bellingen, NSW; m. Melanie Gilchrist; one s. one d.; left-handed batsman and wicketkeeper; teams played for include NSW 1992–94, Western Australia 1994–2008 (Capt. since 2001), Australia 1996–2008 (retd), Deccan Chargers 2008–10, Kings XI Punjab 2011–13; test debut versus Pakistan at Brisbane 5–9 Nov. 1999; One-Day Int. (ODI) debut: Australia v S Africa, Faridabad, Pakistan 25 Oct. 1996; T20I debut: NZ v Australia, Auckland 17 Feb. 2005; scored 5,570 runs in 96 tests (average 47.60) with 17 hundreds and 26 fifties, highest score 204 not out; 9,619 runs in 287 ODIs (average 35.89) with 16 hundreds and 55 fifties; 10,334 runs in 190 First-class matches; holds record for most wicketkeeping dismissals in ODIs; fastest strike-rate in test-cricket history for a batsman scoring over 2,000 runs; captained Australia to first test-series victory in India for 34 years; mem. Australia's World Cup winning side 2003; retd from int. cricket March 2008; Wisden Cricketer of the Year 2002, Allan Border Medal 2003, One-Day Int. Player of the Year 2003, 2004, Wisden Australia Cricketer of the Year 2003, awarded a record total of six Carlton & United Beverages Gold Cups as Western Australia's best player; selected in Richie Benaud's Greatest XI, inducted into Sport Australia Hall of Fame 2012, ICC Hall of Fame 2013. *Publications:* One-Day Cricket: Playing the One-Day Game 2000, Walking to Victory 2003; newspaper columns for Sydney Morning Herald, Melbourne Age and West Australian. *Address:* c/o Western Australian Cricket Association, WACA Ground, PO Box 6045, East Perth, WA 6892, Australia. *Telephone:* (8) 9265-7222. *Fax:* (8) 9221-1823. *E-mail:* info@waca .com.au. *Website:* www.waca.com.au; www.adamgilchrist.info.

GILES, Alan James, MA, MS; British business executive; b. 4 June 1954, Dorchester, Dorset, England; m. Gillian Rosser 1978; two d.; ed Blandford School, Dorset, Merton Coll. Oxford, Stanford Univ., USA; buyer, Boots the Chemists 1975–78, Promotions Man. 1978–80, Asst Merchandise Controller 1980–82; Retail Devt Man., WHSmith 1982–85, Merchandise Controller (Books) 1985–88, Operations & Devt Dir, Do It All 1988–92; Man. Dir Waterstone's Booksellers 1992–99; CEO HMV Group PLC 1998–2006; Chair. (non-exec.) Fat Face 2006–13, Dir (non-exec.) 2013–; mem. Bd of Dirs Somerfield PLC 1993–2004, Wilson Bowden PLC 2004–07, Rentokil Initial PLC 2006–, Book Tokens Ltd 2007–13, The Office of Fair Trading 2007–, The Competition & Markets Authority 2013–; Assoc. Fellow, Said Business School, Univ. of Oxford; Hon. Visiting Prof., Cass Business School. *Leisure interests:* watching football, cycling, walking.

GILIOMEE, Hermann Buhr, MA, DPhil; South African historian, academic and political columnist; *Extraordinary Professor of History, University of Stellenbosch;* b. 4 April 1938, Sterkstroom; s. of Gerhardus Adriaan Giliomee and Catherine Geza Giliomee; m. Annette van Coller 1965; two d.; ed Porterville High School and Univ. of Stellenbosch; diplomatic service 1963–64; Lecturer in History, Univ. of Stellenbosch 1967–83, Extraordinary Prof. of History 2002–; Prof. of Political Studies, Univ. of Cape Town 1983–2002; recipient of Fellowships to Yale Univ., USA 1977–78, Univ. of Cambridge, UK 1982–83, Woodrow Wilson Center for Int. Scholars, Washington, DC 1992–93; Pres. South African Inst. of Race Relations 1995–97; f. Die Suid-Afrikaan journal 1984; political columnist for Cape Times, Rand Daily Mail, and other periodicals 1980–97, presently writing political column for Die Burger, Beeld and Volksblad morning newspapers; Stals Prize for Political Sciences 2001, Stals Prize for History 2004. *Publications:* The Shaping of South African Society 1652–1820 1979, Ethnic Power Mobilized: Can South Africa Change? 1979, Afrikaner Political Thought 1750–1850 1983, Up Against the Fences: Poverty, Passes and Privilege 1985, From Apartheid to Nation-building 1990, The Bold Experiment: South Africa's New Democracy 1994, Liberal and Populist Democracy in South Africa 1996, Surrender Without Defeat 1997, The Awkward Embrace: Dominant-Party Rule and Democracy in Semi-Industrialized Countries 1999, Kruispad 2001, The Afrikaners – Biography of a People 2003, Die Afrikaners: in Biografie 2004. *Leisure interest:* tennis. *Address:* 5 Dennerandweg, Stellenbosch 7600, South Africa (home). *Telephone:* (21) 8832964 (home). *Fax:* (21) 8878026 (home). *E-mail:* hgiliome@mweb.co.za (home).

GILL, Sir Anthony (Keith), Kt, BSc (Eng), FREng, FCGI, FIMechE; British business executive (retd); b. 1 April 1930, Colchester, Essex; s. of Frederick W. Gill and Ellen Gill; m. Phyllis Cook 1953; one s. two d.; ed Colchester High School and Imperial Coll., London; Nat. Service, REME 1954–56; Production Engineer, Bryce Berger Ltd 1956, Dir 1960, Gen. Man. 1965; Dir Lucas CAV Ltd 1967; Gen. Man. Fuel Injection Equipment 1972–74; Dir Joseph Lucas Ltd 1974, Div. Man. Dir 1978; Dir Lucas Industries PLC 1978, Jt Group Man. Dir 1980, Group Man. Dir 1984–87, Deputy Chair. 1986–87, Chair. and CEO 1987–94; Pres. Inst. of Production Eng 1985–86; Chair. London Docklands Light Railway 1994–99; mem. Council IMechE 1986–91, Advisory Council on Science and Tech. 1985–91; Chair. Educ. and Training Comm. 1988–91, Tarmac PLC 1992–2000; Dir (non-Exec.) Post Office 1989–91, Nat. Power PLC 1990–98; mem. Eng Council (Deputy Chair. 1994–96); Chair. Teaching Co. Scheme 1990–96; Pro-Chancellor Cranfield Univ. 1991–2001; mem. Nat. Training Task Force 1991–94; Chair. Council, British Inst. of Man. 1996–99, Pres. 1998–99; Hon. Fellow, Inst. of Eng and Tech.; Hon. DEng (Univ. of Birmingham) 1990, Hon. DSc (Cranfield Univ.) 1991, (Southampton Univ.) 1992, (Warwick Univ.) 1992, Hon. DTech (Coventry Univ.) 1992, Dr hc (Sheffield Hallam Univ.) 1993. *Leisure interests:* music, boating. *Address:* The Point House, Astra Court, Hythe Marina Village, Hythe, Hants., SO45 6DZ, England (home). *Telephone:* (23) 8084-0165 (home). *E-mail:* anthony.gill@ btinternet.com (home).

GILL, Michael; Australian editor and media executive; *CEO, Fairfax Business Media;* presenter, Business Sunday (TV) 1988–90; sr writer, The Australian Financial Review 1990–93, Deputy Ed. 1993–96, Gen. Man. Business Devt, John Fairfax Holdings Ltd 1996–98, Publr and Ed.-in-Chief; Publr and Ed.-in-Chief Fairfax Business Media 1998–2007, CEO 2007–, responsible for business man. and editorial direction of The Australian Financial Review, AFR Access, AFR Magazine, BOSS, afr.com, BRW, The Australian Financial Review Smart Investor, CFO, MIS (Australia, NZ, Asia and UK) and Fairfax Business Research; Chair. Australian Associated Press, Nat. Inst. of Econ. and Industry Research; mem. Bd of Dirs UNICEF Australia; fmr Dir The Ian Potter Museum of Art, Victorian Community Foundation, Blue Mountains Festival, Circus Oz. *Address:* John Fairfax Holdings Ltd, PO Box 506, Sydney, NSW 2001, Australia (office); Fairfax Business Media, PO Box 6813, Wellesley Street, Auckland, New Zealand (office). *Telephone:* (2) 9282-2833 (Sydney) (office); (9) 377-9902 (Auckland) (office). *Fax:* (2) 9282-3133 (Sydney) (office); (9) 377-4604 (Auckland) (office). *E-mail:* rvictor@mail .fairfax.com.au (office). *Website:* www.fxj.com.au (office); fairfaxbm.com.nz (office).

GILL, (Robert) Bates, PhD; American political scientist and research institute director; *CEO, United States Studies Centre, University of Sydney;* m. Dr Sarah Palmer; ed Woodrow Wilson Dept of Government and Foreign Affairs, Univ. of Virginia; assignments have included directing the East Asia programmes at the Center for Nonproliferation Studies, Monterey Inst. of Int. Studies, Monterey, Calif.; also held Fei Yiming Chair in Comparative Politics, Johns Hopkins Univ. Center for Chinese and American Studies, Nanjing Univ., People's Repub. of China; fmr Sr Fellow in Foreign Policy Studies and inaugural Dir Center for Northeast Asian Policy Studies, Brookings Inst., Washington, DC; Freeman Chair in China Studies, Center for Strategic and Int. Studies, Washington, DC 2002–07; Dir Stockholm Int. Peace Research Inst. (first American) 2007–12, initiated and led the East Asia Arms Control and Security Project 1993–97; CEO US Studies Centre, Univ. of Sydney 2012–; mem. Council on Foreign Relations, IISS; has consulted for several multinational corpns and govt agencies; Commdr, Royal Order of the Polar Star (Sweden). *Publications include:* author: Chinese Arms Transfers 1992, Contrasting Visions: U.S., China, and World Order 2006, Rising Star: China's New Security Diplomacy 2007 (revised edn 2010); co-author: China's Arms Acquisitions from Abroad: A Quest for "Superb and Secret Weapons" 1995, Chinese Arms Exports: Policy, Players, and Process 2004, China: The Balance Sheet – What the World Needs to Know Now About the Emerging Superpower 2006, Asia's New Multilateralism: Cooperation, Competition, and the Search for Community 2009; co-ed.: Weathering the Storm: Taiwan, Its Neighbours, and the Asian Financial 2000; more than 120 other publs, including monographs, book chapters, journal articles, essays, magazine columns and opinion pieces. *Address:*

United States Studies Centre, University of Sydney, Institute Building H03, City Road, NSW 2006, Australia (office). *Website:* www.ussc.edu.au (office).

GILLAM, Sir Patrick, Kt, BA; British business executive; b. 15 April 1933, London; s. of the late Cyril B. Gillam and of Mary J. Gillam; m. Diana Echlin 1963; one s. one d.; ed London School of Econs; Foreign Office 1956–57; joined British Petroleum (BP) 1957, Vice-Pres. BP North America Inc. 1971–74, Gen. Man. Supply Dept 1974–78, Dir BP Int. Ltd 1978–82, Chair. BP Shipping Ltd 1981–88, BP Minerals Int. Ltd 1981–88, Man. Dir BP Co. 1981–91, Chair. BP Africa Ltd 1982–88, BP Coal Inc. 1988–90, BP Nutrition 1989–91, BP America 1989–91, BP Oil 1990–91; Chair. Booker Tate Ltd 1991–93, Asda Group PLC 1991–96, Royal and Sun Alliance 1997–2003; Deputy Chair. Standard Chartered Bank Africa PLC 1988–89, Standard Chartered Overseas Holdings Ltd 1988–89, Standard Chartered Bank Aug.–Nov. 1988, Chair. 1993–2003, Standard Chartered PLC 1991–92, Chair. 1993–2003 (Dir 1988–2002); Chair. Asia House 2003–05; Consultant, CMi; Dir Commercial Union PLC 1991–96; Chair. ICC (UK) 1989–98; apptd mem. of Court of Govs, LSE 1989, Hon. Fellow 2000. *Leisure interest:* gardening. *Address:* 3 St Leonards Terrace, London, SW3 4QA, England.

GILLAN, Rt Hon. Cheryl Elise Kendall, PC, FCIM; British politician and marketing consultant; b. 21 April 1952, Llandaff, Cardiff, Glamorgan, Wales; m. John Coates (Jack) Leeming 1985; ed Cheltenham Ladies Coll., The Coll. of Law; marketing exec. for International Management Group 1977–84; Dir, British Film Year 1984–86; Sr Marketing Consultant, Ernst & Young 1986–91; Marketing Dir, Kidsons Impey 1991–93; Chair. Bow Group 1987–88; contested Greater Manchester Cen. in European Parl. Elections 1989; MP for Chesham and Amersham, Bucks. 1992–2010, for Chesham and Amersham (revised boundary) 2010–, mem. (Select Cttees), Science and Tech. 1992–95, Procedure 1994–95, Public Accounts 2003–04; Parl. Pvt. Sec. to Viscount Cranborne as Leader of House of Lords and Lord Privy Seal 1994–95; Parl. Under-Sec. of State, Dept of Educ. and Employment 1995–97; Shadow Minister for Trade and Industry 1997–98, for Foreign and Commonwealth Affairs 1998–2001, for Int. Devt 1998–2001; Opposition Whip 2001–03; Shadow Minister for Home Affairs 2003–05; Shadow Sec. of State for Wales 2005–10; Sec. of State for Wales 2010–12; mem. Exec. Cttee UK Br., Commonwealth Parl. Asscn 1998–, UK Rep. British Islands and Mediterranean region 1999–2004, Int. Treas. 2004–06; mem. NATO Parl. Ass. 2003–05; Fellow, Chartered Inst. of Marketing; Conservative; Freeman of the City of London 1991; mem. Worshipful Co. of Marketors. *Leisure interests:* singing (mem. Parliamentary Choir), gardening, golf, keeping chickens. *Address:* House of Commons, Westminster, London, SW1A 0AA (office); Constituency Office, 7A Hill Avenue, Amersham, Bucks., HP6 5BD, England (office). *Telephone:* (20) 7219-4061 (London); (1494) 721577 (Amersham). *Fax:* (20) 7219-2762 (London); (1494) 722107 (Amersham). *E-mail:* cheryl.gillan.mp@parliament.uk (office); shawmj@parliament.uk (office). *Website:* www.parliament.uk/biographies/commons/cheryl -gillan/25627 (office); www.cherylgillan.co.uk.

GILLAN, Michael J., DPhil; British physicist and academic; *Professor of Condensed Matter and Materials Physics, University College London;* ed Univ. of Oxford, Univ. of Minnesota, USA; early position as post-doctoral researcher, Univ. of Minn.; mem. staff, Harwell 1970–88; Prof. of Theoretical Physics, Univ. of Keele 1988–98; Prof. of Condensed Matter and Materials Physics, Physics and Astronomy Dept, Univ. Coll. London 1998–; mem. Peer Review Coll. of UK Eng and Physical Sciences Research Council; Dirac Prize and Medal, Inst. of Physics 2006. *Publications:* numerous scientific papers in professional journals on theory of condensed matter, with a strong emphasis on computer simulation. *Address:* London Centre for Nanotechnology, Room 3.C1, University College London, 17-19 Gordon Street, London, WC1H 0AH, England (office). *Telephone:* (20) 7679-7049 (office). *Fax:* (20) 7679-7145 (office). *E-mail:* m.gillan@ucl.ac.uk (office). *Website:* www.london-nano.com (office).

GILLARD, Julia Eileen, BA, LLB; Australian lawyer and politician; b. 29 Sept. 1961, Barry, Wales, UK; d. of the late John Gillard and of Moira Gillard; ed Univ. of Adelaide, Univ. of Melbourne; solicitor, Slater & Gordon, Werribee 1987–95, Partner 1990–95; Del. Australian Labor Party (ALP) State Conf. (Victoria) 1982–, Pres. ALP Carlton Br. 1985–89, Co-Convenor, Affirmative Action Working Party 1993–94, mem. Cttee 1993–97, Deputy Leader Fed. ALP 2006–07; Chief of Staff to Vic. Leader of Opposition J. Brumby 1995–98; MP (Australian Labor Party) for Lalor, Vic. 1998–; Shadow Minister for Population and Immigration 2001–03, for Reconciliation and Indigenous Affairs 2003, for Health 2003–06, for Employment, Industrial Relations and Social Inclusion 2006–07, Deputy Leader of Opposition 2006–07; Deputy Leader of the Labor Party 2006–10, Leader 2010–13; Deputy Prime Minister and Minister for Educ., Employment and Workplace Relations, and Social Inclusion 2007–10; Prime Minister 2010–13; Hon. Visiting Prof., Univ. of Adelaide 2013–; ranked by Forbes magazine amongst The World's 100 Most Powerful Women (58th) 2010, (23rd) 2011, (27th) 2012, (28th) 2013. *Address:* c/o Australian Labor Party, PO Box 6222, Kingston, ACT 2604, Australia.

GILLES, Herbert Michael Joseph, CMG, KStJ, DMedSc, DSc, MD, FRCP, FFPH, DTM&H; British professor of tropical medicine; *Professor Emeritus, University of Liverpool;* b. 10 Sept. 1921, Port Said, Egypt; s. of Joseph Gilles; m. 1st Wilhelmina Caruana 1955 (died 1972); three s. one d.; m. 2nd Mejra Kacic-Dimitri 1979; ed St Edward's Coll., Malta, Royal Univ. of Malta, Univ. of Oxford; mem. Scientific Staff MRC 1954–58; Sr Lecturer in Tropical Medicine, Univ. of Ibadan, Nigeria 1959–61, Prof. 1962–65; Sr Lecturer in Tropical Medicine, Univ. of Liverpool, England 1965–70, Prof. 1970–86, Prof. Emer. 1986–; Dean Liverpool School of Tropical Medicine 1978–83, Vice-Pres. 1991–; Visiting Prof. of Public Health, Univ. of Malta 1989–; Visiting Prof. of Int. Health, Royal Coll. of Surgeons in Ireland 1994–, of Tropical Medicine, Mahidol Univ. Bangkok 1994–; Pres. Royal Soc. of Tropical Medicine and Hygiene (RSTMH) 1985–87; Hon. Pres. Malta Asscn of Public Health; Consultant in Malariology, British Army 1972–86, in Tropical Medicine, RAF and DHSS 1972–86; Hon. Mem. Swedish Soc. of Tropical Medicine 1999; Officer, Nat. Order of Merit of Malta 2003; Companion, Exalted Order of the White Elephant (Kingdom of Thailand) 2008; Rhodes Scholar (Malta) 1943; WHO Darling Foundation Medal and Prize 1989, Mary Kingsley Medal 1995, BMA Medical Book Competition, First Prize, Medicine Section 1996, BMA Medical Book Competition, Highly Commended, Public Health Section 2002, RSTMH Manson Medal 2007. *Publications:* Management and Treatment of Tropical Diseases 1971, Pathology in the Tropics 1976, Tropical Medicine for Nurses 1979, Recent

Advances in Tropical Medicine 1984, Human Antiparasitic Drugs 1985, Epidemiology and Control of Tropical Diseases 1986, Hookworm Infections 1991, Management of Severe and Complicated Malaria 1991, Atlas of Tropical Medicine and Parasitology 1994, Protozoal Diseases 1999, Essential Malariology 2002, Preventive Medicine for the Tropics 2003, Tropical Medicine: A Clinical Text 2006. *Leisure interests:* swimming, music. *Address:* 3 Conyers Avenue, Birkdale, Southport, PR8 4SZ, Merseyside, England (home). *Telephone:* (1704) 566664 (home).

GILLESPIE, Norman, BA (hons), PhD; British arts administrator and business executive; *CEO, UNICEF Australia;* b. 1957, Lurgan, NI; m. Nicole Gillespie; one d.; ed Queen's Univ. Belfast, Univ. of London, Harvard Business School, USA, Chinghua Univ., Beijing, China; grad. trainee UK civil service; joined BP (British Petroleum) 1987, various positions including Tax Controller for North Sea Operations, Glasgow, mem. Group Strategy Team, London, Head of Pvt. Office of CEO and Chair. 1990–91, US Man. of Planning and Reporting, Houston, Tex. 1992–94; Dir of Group Planning and Financial Control, Cable & Wireless, London 1994–97, Head of Group Strategy 1995–97; Chief Financial Officer Cable & Wireless Optus (following merger of Cable & Wireless and Optus 1997), Sydney, Australia 1997–2002, Deputy CEO 1997–2002; Deputy Chair. Australian Brandenburg Orchestra 1999–2012; Deputy Chair. NSW Div., Australian Business Arts Foundation 2001–07, mem. Bd of Dirs 2003–07; CEO UNICEF Australia 2010–, Sydney Opera House 2002–07, Australian Jockey Club 2007–09; mem. Bd of Dirs Sydney Convention and Visitors Bureau 2002–05; Bd mem. Pinchgut Opera 2013; mem. Editorial Advisory Cttee The Global Mail 2012–14. *Leisure interests:* early music, opera, contemporary dance, mountain trekking. *Address:* UNICEF Australia, Level 4, 280 Pitt Street, Sydney, NSW 2000, Australia (office). *Telephone:* (2) 9261-2811 (office). *Fax:* (2) 9261-2844 (office). *E-mail:* unicef@unicef.org.au (office). *Website:* www.unicef.org.au (office).

GILLESPIE, Ronald James, PhD, DSc, FRS, FRSC, FRSC (UK), FCIC, CM; Canadian/British chemist and academic; *Professor Emeritus of Chemistry, McMaster University;* b. 21 Aug. 1924, London, England; s. of James A. Gillespie and Miriam Gillespie (née Kirk); m. 1st Madge Ena Garner 1950 (died 2008); two d.; m. 2nd Marcelle Roy 2011; ed Univ. Coll., London; Asst Lecturer, Dept of Chem., Univ. Coll., London 1948–50, Lecturer 1950–58; Commonwealth Fund Fellow, Brown Univ., RI, USA 1953–54; Assoc. Prof., Dept of Chem., McMaster Univ., Hamilton, Ont., Canada 1958–60, Prof. 1960–88, Prof. Emer. 1988–, Chair. Dept of Chem. 1962–65; Assoc. Prof., Univ. des Sciences et Techniques de Languedoc, Montpellier, France 1972–73; Visiting Prof., Univ. of Geneva, Switzerland 1976, of Göttingen, FRG 1978; mem. The Chemical Soc., ACS; Hon. LLD (Concordia) 1988, (Dalhousie) 1988; Dr hc (Montpellier) 1991; Hon. DSc (McMaster Univ.) 1993, (Lethbridge) 2007; numerous medals and awards. *Publications:* Molecular Geometry 1972, Chemistry (co-author) 1986, 1989, The VSEPR Model of Molecular Geometry (with I. Hargittai) 1991, Atoms, Molecules and Reactions: An Introduction to Chemistry (co-author) 1994, Chemical Bonding and Molecular Geometry: From Lewis to Electron Densities (co-author) 2001; papers in scientific journals. *Leisure interests:* chess, travel. *Address:* Department of Chemistry, McMaster University, Hamilton, ON L8S 4M1 (office); 50 Hatt Street, Dundas, ON L9H 0A1, Canada (home). *Telephone:* (905) 628-1502 (office); (905) 628-1502 (home). *Fax:* (905) 522-2509 (office). *E-mail:* ronald.gillespie@sympatico.ca (home).

GILLIAM, Terry Vance, BA; British (b. American) film director, animator, actor, illustrator and writer; b. 22 Nov. 1940, Minn.; s. of James Hall Gilliam and Beatrice Gilliam (née Vance); m. Margaret Weston 1973; one s. two d.; ed Occidental Coll., Calif.; Assoc. Ed. HELP! magazine 1962–64; freelance illustrator 1964–65, advertising copywriter/art dir 1966–67; Hon. Dr of Arts (Occidental Coll.), (Wimbledon Coll. of Art, London) 2000; Hon. DFA (Royal Coll. of Art, London) 1989; BAFTA Fellowship 2009. *Television:* Do Not Adjust Your Set (series writer) 1967, Marty (series writer) 1968, Broaden Your Mind (series writer) 1968, Monty Python's Flying Circus (series writer, actor) 1969–74, presenter The Last Machine (series) 1995. *Films:* Storytime (dir) 1968, Monty Python's And Now for Something Completely Different (writer, actor, animator) 1971, The Miracle of Flight (dir) 1974, Monty Python and the Holy Grail (writer, actor, dir) 1975, Jabberwocky (screenplay, actor, dir) 1977, Monty Python's Life of Brian (writer, actor, animator) 1979, Time Bandits (writer, dir) 1981, Monty Python Live at the Hollywood Bowl (writer, actor) 1982, Monty Python's The Meaning of Life (writer, actor, dir) 1983, The Crimson Permanent Assurance (writer, actor, dir) 1983, Brazil (screenplay, actor, dir) 1985, Spies Like Us (actor) 1985, The Adventures of Baron Munchausen (screenplay, actor, dir) 1988, The Fisher King (dir) 1991, Twelve Monkeys (dir) 1995, Fear and Loathing in Las Vegas (screenplay, dir) 1998, Lost in La Mancha (appeared in documentary about film project The Man Who Killed Don Quixote) 2002, Tideland (writer, dir) 2005, The Brothers Grimm (dir) 2005, Enfermés dehors (actor) 2006, The Imaginarium of Doctor Parnassus (co-writer, dir, producer) 2009, The Legend of Hallowdega (short) 2010. *Publications:* Monty Python's Big Red Book, Monty Python's Paperbok 1977, Monty Python's Scrapbook 1979, Animations of Mortality 1979, Monty Python's The Meaning of Life, Monty Python's Flying Circus – Just the Words (co-ed.) 1989, The Adventures of Baron Munchhausen 1989, Not the Screenplay of Fear and Loathing in Las Vegas 1998, Gilliam on Gilliam 1999, Dark Nights and Holly Fools 1999, The Pythons Autobiography (co-author) 2003. *Address:* c/o Jenne Casarotto, National House, 60–66 Wardour Street, London, W1V 4ND, England (office). *Telephone:* (20) 7287-4450 (office). *Fax:* (20) 7287-9128 (office). *E-mail:* jenne@casarotto.co.uk (office). *Website:* www.casarotto.co.uk (office).

GILLIBRAND, Kirsten Elizabeth Rutnik, AB, JD; American attorney and politician; *Senator from New York;* b. 9 Dec. 1966, Albany, NY; d. of Douglas P. Rutnik and Polly Noonan Rutnik; m. Jonathan Gillibrand; two s.; ed Acad. of Holy Names, Emma Willard School, Troy, Dartmouth Coll., Univ. of California, Los Angeles School of Law; fmr intern for Senator Alfonse D'Amato; fmr law clerk for Judge Roger Miner, US Court of Appeals for the Second Circuit 1992–93; Sr Assoc. Davis, Polk & Wardell; fmr Special Counsel, US Sec. of Housing and Urban Devt, Washington, DC 2000–01; Pnr, Boies, Schiller & Flexner LLP, Albany 2001–07; mem. US House of Reps 2007–09, mem. Cttees on House Armed Services, on Agric., Nutrition and Forestry, on Environment and Public Works, Special Cttee on Aging; Senator from NY (apptd) 2009–11, won re-election 2010–. *Address:* 478

Russell Senate Office Building, Washington, DC 20510, USA (office). *Telephone:* (202) 224-4451 (office). *Fax:* (202) 228-0282 (office). *Website:* gillibrand.senate.gov (office).

GILLICK, Liam, BA; British artist; b. 1964, Aylesbury, Bucks., England; ed Univ. of London, Goldsmiths Coll., London; staged first solo exhbn, 84 Diagrams, Karsten Schubert, London 1989; has exhibited in galleries and insts in Europe and USA, including collaborative projects with other artists, architects, designers and writers; selected to produce artworks for the canopy, glass facade, kiosks, entrance ikon and vitrines of Home Office bldg, Marsham Street, London 2002; represented Germany at Venice Biennale 2009; mem. Grad. Cttee Center for Curatorial Studies and Art in Contemporary Culture, Bard Coll., Annandale-on-Hudson, NY, USA; mem. Faculty, School of the Arts, Columbia Univ., New York 1997–; lives and works in New York; Paul Cassirer Kunstpreis, Berlin 1998. *Film:* Exhibition (dir Joanna Hogg) 2014. *Publications include:* Proxemics (Selected Writing 1988–2006), 2007, Factories in the Snow by Lilian Haberer (monograph) 2007, Meaning Liam Gillick (critical reader) 2009, Allbooks (anthology of his artistic writing) 2009, Why Work? 2010, Memoirs of the Twentieth Century/Prevision: Should the Future Help the Past 2010; contrib. to numerous art magazines and journals, including Parkett, Frieze, Art Monthly, October and Art Forum. *Address:* c/o Maureen Paley, 21 Herald Street, London, E2 6JT, England (office); c/o Casey Kaplan, 525 West 21st Street, New York, NY 10011, USA (office). *Telephone:* (20) 7729-4112 (office); (212) 645-7335 (office). *Fax:* (20) 7729-4113 (office); (212) 645-7835 (office). *E-mail:* info@maureenpaley.com (office); info@caseykaplangallery .com (office). *Website:* www.maureenpaley.com (office); www.caseykaplangallery .com (office); www.liamgillick.info.

GILLIES, Pamela Ann, CBE, BSc, PGCE, MEd, MMedSci PhD, FRSA, FFPH, AcSS; British public health scientist, academic and university administrator; *Principal and Vice-Chancellor, Glasgow Caledonian University;* b. 13 Feb. 1953, Scotland; ed Univs of Aberdeen and Nottingham; Lecturer in Public Health Medicine, Univ. of Nottingham 1980s, later Pro-Vice-Chancellor 2001–06; Abbott Fellowship for AIDS Research, San Francisco 1988; mem. WHO Global Programme on AIDS, Geneva 1989–90; Harkness Fellow, Commonwealth Fund of New York and Visiting Prof. in Health and Human Rights, Harvard Univ., USA 1992–93; seconded as first Exec. Dir of Research, Health Educ. Authority for England, London 1996–99; Prin. and Vice-Chancellor Glasgow Caledonian Univ. (GCU) 2006–, mem. Bd INTO GCU, the Foundation Coll. for the Univ., Pres. New York Campus; mem. Bd of Trustees, British Council 2008–; Founding Trustee, Grameen Scotland Foundation; Founding Bd mem. Grameen Caledonian Coll. of Nursing, Dhaka, Bangladesh (partnership with Grameen Healthcare Trust) 2010–; mem. London Higher Group of Univs; Founding Patron of a school for children of sex workers in Domjur, Kolkata; Academician, Acad. for the Social Sciences 2005; Fellow, Faculty of Public Health of the Royal Coll. of Physicians of London 2002; Hon. Fellow, Royal Coll. of Physicians and Surgeons (Glasgow) 2007. *Publications include:* numerous articles on HIV/AIDS, health development, and inequalities in health focusing on the potential of social action for health. *Leisure interests:* tennis, gardening. *Address:* Office of the Principal, Glasgow Caledonian University, Britannia Building, City Campus, Cowcaddens Road, Glasgow, G4 0BA, Scotland (office). *Telephone:* (141) 331-3113 (office). *Fax:* (141) 331-3174 (office). *E-mail:* pamela.gillies@gcu.ac.uk (office). *Website:* www.gcu.ac.uk (office).

GILLIES, Rowan, MBBS; Australian physician and international organization official; *President, Médecins Sans Frontières;* b. 1971, Longueville; fmr Surgical Registrar, Mona Vale Hosp., Sydney; with Médecins Sans Frontières 1998–, postings included Liberia, Sudan, Sierra Leone, Afghanistan, Pres. Feb. 2004–. *Address:* Médecins Sans Frontières, Rue de Lausanne 78, CP 116, 1211 Geneva 21, Switzerland (office). *Telephone:* (22) 8498400 (office). *Fax:* (22) 8498404 (office). *Website:* www.msf.org (office).

GILLINSON, Sir Clive Daniel, Kt, CBE, ARAM, FRAM, FRNCM; British cellist and arts administrator; *Executive and Artistic Director, Carnegie Hall;* b. 7 March 1946, Bangalore, India; m. Penny Gillinson; one s. two d.; ed Frensham Heights School, Queen Mary Coll., Univ. of London, Royal Acad. of Music, London; played in Nat. Youth Orchestra of GB 1963–65, Philharmonia Orchestra –1970, London Symphony Orchestra 1970–84; elected to Bd of Dirs London Symphony Orchestra 1976–79, 1983–, Finance Dir 1979, Man. Dir 1984–2005; Exec. and Artistic Dir Carnegie Hall, New York 2005–; owned an antique shop, Hampstead, London 1978–86; Chair. Asscn of British Orchestras 1992–95; Gov. and mem. of Exec. Cttee Nat. Youth Orchestra 1995–2004; Founding Partner, Masterprize 1997–; Founding Trustee, Nat. Endowment for Science, Tech. and the Arts 1998–2004; mem. Int. Music Council of the Children's Hearing Inst., New York 1998–, Brubeck Inst. Hon. Bd 2007–, Curtis Inst. Bd of Overseers 2007–08; Hon. GSMD 1992, Freeman of the City of London 1993; Dr hc (City Univ.) 1995, (Curtis Inst.) 2007; Hon. DHumLitt (Skidmore Coll.) 2010; RAM May Mukle Cello Prize, ABSA Garrett Award 1992, Luminary Award, Eastman School of Music 2010, Int. Citation of Merit, Int. Soc. for the Performing Arts 2012. *Leisure interests:* reading, theatre, cinema, sport. *Address:* Carnegie Hall, 881 Seventh Avenue, New York, NY 10019-3210, USA (office). *Telephone:* (212) 903-9820 (office). *Fax:* (212) 903-0820 (office). *E-mail:* cgillinson@carnegiehall.org (office). *Website:* www .carnegiehall.org (office).

GILMAN, Alfred Goodman, MD, PhD; American pharmacologist and academic; *Chief Scientific Officer, Cancer Prevention and Research Institute of Texas;* b. 1 July 1941, New Haven, Conn.; s. of Alfred Gilman and Mabel Schmidt; m. Kathryn Hedlund 1963; one s. two d.; ed Yale and Case Western Reserve Univs; Research Assoc. NIH, Bethesda, Md 1969–71; Asst Prof., Assoc. Prof. of Pharmacology, Univ. of Virginia, Charlottesville 1971–77, Prof. 1977–81; Prof. of Pharmacology and Chair. Dept of Pharmacology, Univ. of Texas (UT) Southwestern Medical Center, Dallas 1981–2009, Raymond and Ellen Willie Distinguished Chair. of Molecular Neuropharmacology 1987–2009, Regental Prof. of Pharmacology 1994–2009, Emer. 2009–, also Exec. Vice Pres. for Academic Affairs, Provost and Dean, UT Southwestern Medical School; Dir Regeneron Pharmaceuticals 1989, Eli Lilly and Co. 1995; Chief Scientific Officer, Cancer Prevention and Research Inst. of Texas 2009–; mem. numerous scientific advisory socs; mem. NAS, Inst. of Medicine of NAS, American Soc. of Biological Chemists etc.; Fellow, American Acad. of Arts and Sciences; Hon. DSc (Chicago) 1991, (Case Western Reserve) 1995, (Miami) 1999, Hon. DMedSc (Yale) 1997; Gairdner Foundation Int. Award 1984; Albert

Lasker Basic Medical Research Award 1989, Nobel Prize in Physiology or Medicine (with Martin Rodbell) 1994, many other awards and distinctions. *Publications:* over 220 peer-reviewed scientific journal articles, numerous invited book chapters and reviews; Ed.-in-Chief, Goodman & Gilman's The Pharmacological Basis of Therapeutics, 6th, 7th and 8th edns. *Leisure interests:* reading, golf. *Address:* Cancer Prevention and Research Institute of Texas, 211 East 7th Street, Suite 300, Austin, TX 78701 (office); 5323 Harry Hines Boulevard, Dallas, TX 75390-8520, USA (office). *Telephone:* (512) 463-3190 (office). *Fax:* (512) 475-2563 (office). *E-mail:* agilman@cprit.state.tx.us (office). *Website:* www.cprit.state.tx.us (office).

GILMARTIN, Raymond V., MBA; American business executive and academic; b. 6 March 1941, Washington, DC; m. Gladys Higham 1965; one s. two d.; ed Union Coll. and Harvard Univ.; Devt Engineer, Eastman Kodak 1963–67; various exec. positions at Becton Dickinson & Co. 1976–92, Chair., Pres. and CEO 1992–94; Chair., Pres. and CEO Merck & Co. Inc. 1994–2005 (resgnd); Adjunct Prof., Harvard Business School 2006–, also fmr mem. Bd of Dean's Advisors; fmr Chair. Healthcare Leadership Council, Pharmaceutical Research and Mfrs of America, Council on Competitiveness, United Negro College Fund; fmr Pres. Int. Fed. of Pharmaceutical Mfrs; mem. Bd of Dirs General Mills Inc. 1991– (currently presiding Dir), Microsoft 2001–12, National Association of Corporate Directors 2013–; mem. Transatlantic Business Dialogue, Trade and Poverty Forum, German Marshall Fund.

GILMORE, Éamon; Irish politician and fmr trade unionist; *Tánaiste (Deputy Prime Minister) and Minister for Foreign Affairs and Trade;* b. 24 April 1955; m. Carol Gilmore; two s. one d.; ed St Joseph's Coll., Garbally, Co. Galway, Univ. Coll. Galway; Pres. Union of Students in Ireland 1976–78; joined Irish Transport & General Workers' Union (now SIPTU) 1978, Acting Sec., Galway Br. 1978–79, Sec., Tralee Br. 1979–81, Sec., Professional and Managerial Staffs Br. 1981–89; mem. Dáil Éireann for Dun Laoghaire 1989–; Minister of State at Dept of the Marine 1994–97; Tánaiste (Deputy Prime Minister) and Minister for Foreign Affairs and Trade 2011–; fmr mem. Workers' Party; co-f. Democratic Left 1992 (merged with Labour Party 1999); mem. Labour Party, Labour Party Spokesperson on Environment, Housing and Local Govt 2002–07, Labour Party Leader 2007–; mem. Parl. Ass. of Council of Europe 2005–07. *Publications:* Leading Lights: People Who've Inspired Me 2010. *Address:* Department of Foreign Affairs and Trade, 80 St Stephen's Green, Dublin 2, Ireland (office). *Telephone:* (1) 4780822 (office). *Fax:* (1) 4082400 (office). *Website:* www.dfa.ie (office).

GILMORE, James Stuart, III, BA, LLB, JD; American fmr politician and lawyer; *Partner, Kelley Drye and Warren LLP;* b. 6 Oct. 1949, Richmond, Va; s. of James Stuart Gilmore, Jr and Margaret Kandle Gilmore; m. Roxane Gatling Gilmore; two s.; ed Univ. of Virginia; served in US Army 1971–74; Pnr, Benedetti, Gilmore, Warthen and Dalton (law firm) 1977–80, 1984–87; fmrly Commonwealth's Attorney, Henrico Co., Va; fmr Attorney Gen. State of Va; Gov. of Virginia 1997–2001; Alt. Del. Repub. Nat. Convention 1976; Chair. Henrico Co. Repub. Cttee 1982–85, now Vice-Chair.; Chair. Repub. Nat. Cttee 2001–02; Chair. Congressional Advisory Panel to Assess Domestic Response Capabilities for Terrorism Involving Weapons of Mass Destruction 1999–2003; Bd of Visitors Air Force Acad. 2003, Chair. 2003–; currently Pnr, Kelley Drye and Warren (law firm) and Chair. Homeland Security Practice Group; Pres. Free Congress Foundation, Nat. Council on Readiness and Preparedness; Ind. Dir Everquest Financial Ltd, CACI Int. Inc. 2009–; mem. Bd of Dirs Barr Pharmaceuticals Inc. 2002–, Xybernaut Corpn 2002–, Atlas Air Worldwide Holdings 2004–, Nat. Rifle Asscn, Cypress Communications; mem. Bd of Advisors Lucent Technologies Inc., Unisys, Abraxas Corpn; commentator for Fox News. *Address:* Kelley Drye and Warren LLP, 1200 19th Street, NW, Suite 500, Washington, DC 20036, USA (office). *Telephone:* (202) 955-9660 (office). *Fax:* (202) 955-9792 (office). *E-mail:* jgilmore@ kelleydrye.com (office). *Website:* www.kelleydrye.com (office).

GILMORE, Rosalind E. J., CB, MA, FRSA; British fmr business executive and civil servant; *Member of the Court and Advisory Board, Cranfield University;* b. 23 March 1937, London; d. of Sir Robert Fraser and Lady (Betty) Fraser; m. Brian Terence Gilmore 1962; ed King Alfred School, N London, Univ. Coll., London and Newnham Coll., Cambridge; entered HM Treasury 1960; Exec. Asst to Econs Dir IBRD 1966–67, HM Treasury 1968–74, Cabinet Office 1974; Asst Sec. HM Treasury 1975, Head Financial Insts. Div. 1977–80; Press Sec. to Chancellor of Exchequer 1980–82; Gen. Man. Corp. Planning, Dunlop Ltd 1982–83; Dir of Marketing, Nat. Girobank 1983–86; Directing Fellow, St George's House, Windsor Castle 1986–89; Dir Mercantile Group PLC 1986–89, Mercantile Credit Co. Ltd 1986–89, London and Manchester Group PLC 1986–89; Marketing Consultant, FI Group PLC (Software) 1986–89; mem. Financial Services Act Tribunal 1986–89; Deputy Chair. and Commr Bldg Socs Comm. 1989–91, Chair. and First Commr; Chief Registrar of Friendly Socs and Industrial Insurance Commr 1991–94; Chair. Homeowners Friendly Society Ltd 1996–98, CLT Broadcasting subsidiaries 1989–98; Dir Moorfields Eye Hosp. Trust 1994–2000, BAT Industries PLC 1996–98, Zurich Financial Services AG (Zurich) 1998–2007; mem. Securities and Investment Bd 1993–96; Dir Leadership Foundation 1997–2009 (Pres. 2005–07), Trades Union Fund Mans 2000–06, Int. Women's Forum 2005–07; mem. Court, Cranfield Univ. 1992–, mem. Advisory Bd and mem. Advisory Bd, Cranfield School of Man.; mem. Bd Opera North 1993–96; mem. Lloyd's Regulatory Bd 1994–98 (Dir Regulatory Services, Lloyds 1994–95); mem. Council Royal Coll. of Music 1997–2007; mem. Winton Centre for Financial History, Univ. of Cambridge; Hon. Fellow, Univ. Coll., London 1988, Newnham Coll. Cambridge 1993; Hon. mem. Royal Coll. of Music 2008. *Achievements include:* mem. Cambridge Univ. Swimming Team (blue 1960), Cambridge Univ. Squash Team. *Publication:* Mutuality for the Twenty-first Century 1998. *Leisure interests:* music, reading, house in Greece, languages (Greek, French and Spanish). *Address:* 3 Clarendon Mews, London, W2 2NR, England. *Telephone:* (20) 7402-8554. *Fax:* (20) 7402-8554. *E-mail:* rosalindgilmore@btinternet.com.

GILMOUR, David, CBE; British singer, musician (guitar) and composer; b. 6 March 1946, Cambridge; m. Polly Samson 1994; eight c.; mem. Pink Floyd 1968–; numerous live performances, festival appearances; Exec. Producer for Kate Bush's album, The Kick Inside; solo artist; Nordoff-Robbins Music Therapy Silver Clef Award 1980, MTV Music Video Award 1988, Ivor Novello Award for Outstanding Contribution to British Music 1992, Q Award for Best Live Act 1994, Grammy Award for Producer in Best Instrumental Performance (for Marooned), Polar

Music Prize 2008. *Recordings include:* albums: with Pink Floyd: A Saucerful Of Secrets 1968, More (film soundtrack) 1969, Ummagumma 1969, Atom Heart Mother 1970, Relics 1971, Meddle 1971, Obscured By Clouds 1972, The Dark Side Of The Moon 1973, Wish You Were Here 1975, Animals 1977, The Wall 1979, The Final Cut 1983, A Momentary Lapse Of Reason 1987, The Delicate Sound Of Thunder 1988, Shine On (box set) 1992, The Division Bell 1994, Pulse 1995, Echoes: The Very Best Of Pink Floyd 2001; solo: David Gilmour 1978, About Face 1984, Live In Concert 2002, On An Island 2006, Metallic Spheres (with The Orb) 2010. *Address:* Steve O'Rourke, EMKA Productions Ltd, 43 Portland Road, Holland Park, London, W11 4LJ, England (office). *Website:* www.davidgilmour .com; www.davidgilmourblog.com.

GILOWSKA, Zyta, PhD; Polish academic and politician; *Professor, Katolicki Uniwersytet Lubelski Jana Pawła II (John Paul II Catholic University of Lublin);* b. 7 July 1949, Nowe Miasto Lubawskie; ed Inst. of Econ. Sciences, Warsaw Univ., Maria Curie-Skłodowska Univ., Lublin; Asst Prof., Maria Curie-Skłodowska Univ. 1972–85, Adjunct Prof. 1985–94, Assoc. Prof. 1995–99; Polish Del. to Council of Congress of Local and Regional Authorities of Europe 1992–98; Deputy Chair. Polish Pres.'s Council for Territorial Self-Govt 1992–95; mem. Joint Govt and Territorial Self-Govt Comm. 1993–95; mem. Nat. Council of Freedom Union 1994–96; Prof., Catholic Univ. of Lublin (now John Paul II Catholic Univ. of Lublin) 2001–; mem. leadership of Civic Platform –2005; Deputy Prime Minister and Minister of Finance Jan.–June 2006, Sept. 2006–07. *Publications:* 20 books and over 200 academic publications on public finance, coauthored drafts of Chapter seven of the Polish constitution, and the law on provincial self-government. *Address:* Department of Economics, Katolicki Uniwersytet Lubelski Jana Pawła II, Al. Racławickie 14, 20-950 Lublin, Poland (office). *Telephone:* (81) 445-41-05 (office). *Fax:* (81) 445-41-91 (office). *E-mail:* dwz@kul.lublin.pl (office). *Website:* (office).

GIMBRONE, Michael A., Jr, AB, MD, FAAS; American pathologist and academic; *Ramzi S. Cotran Professor of Pathology, Harvard Medical School; Chairman, Department of Pathology, Brigham and Women's Hospital;* b. 6 Nov. 1943, Buffalo, NY; ed Cornell Univ., Ithaca, NY and Harvard Medical School, Boston, Mass; NSF Summer Fellow, Roswell Park Memorial Inst., Buffalo 1960–63; Summer Research Fellow, Dept of Physiology, New York Univ. Medical School 1964, Depts of Anatomy, Biochemistry and Surgery, Harvard Medical School 1965–67 (ind. study and research 1968–69); Intern in Surgery, Massachusetts Gen. Hosp., Boston 1970–71; Research Fellow, Dept of Surgery, Children's Hosp. Medical Center, Boston 1971–72; Commissioned Officer, NIH US Public Health Service, Bethesda, Md 1972–74, Staff Assoc., Lab. of Pathophysiology, Nat. Cancer Inst., NIH 1972–74; Resident in Pathology, Peter Bent Brigham Hosp., Boston 1974–76; Instructor, Dept of Pathology, Harvard Medical School 1975–76, Asst Prof. 1976–79, Assoc. Prof. 1979–85, Prof. 1985, Elsie T. Friedman Prof. of Pathology 1987, currently Ramzi S. Cotran Prof. of Pathology; Adjunct Faculty, W. Alton Jones Cell Science Center, Lake Placid, NY 1976–78; Assoc. in Pathology, Brigham and Women's Hosp., Boston 1976–79, Head, Vascular Pathophysiology Research Lab. 1976–85, Assoc. Pathologist 1979–80, Pathologist 1980, Dir Vascular Research Div. 1985, Dir Center for Excellence in Vascular Biology 1998, mem. Bd of Dirs Brigham and Women's Hosp. Pathology Foundation, Inc. 1998, Vice-Chair. for Research and Academic Affairs, Dept of Pathology 2000–01, Chair. Dept of Pathology 2002–; Special Consultant, Hypertension Task Force, Nat. Heart, Lung and Blood Inst., Bethesda 1977, Consultant, Arteriosclerosis Task Force 1979; Visiting Prof., Cardiovascular Research Div., Cleveland Clinic Foundation 1980, Johns Hopkins Univ. School of Medicine, Baltimore, Md 1988–90, Washington Univ. School of Medicine, St Louis, Mo. 1988–90, 1994, Univ. of Pennsylvania School of Medicine, Philadelphia 1988–90, Univ. of S Carolina School of Medicine, Columbia 1988–90, Medical Coll. of Wisconsin, Milwaukee 1996, Bowman Gray School of Medicine, Wake Forest Univ., Winston-Salem, NC 1998; Johanaoff Visiting Prof., Mario Negri Inst. of Pharmacological Research, Milan, Italy 1982; Visiting Scholar in Pulmonary Medicine, Duke Univ. Medical Center and Univ. of N Carolina School of Medicine Research, Triangle Park, Nat. Inst. of Environmental Health Sciences, NC 1988; Pfizer Visiting Professorship in Cardiovascular Medicine, Univ. of Minnesota-Duluth School of Medicine 1991; First Annual Vascular Visiting Prof., Cornell Univ. Medical Coll., New York Hosp. 1992; Distinguished Visiting Prof., Johns Hopkins Univ. School of Medicine 1993, Nat. Cardiovascular Research Inst., Osaka, Japan 1996, Kyoto Univ., Japan 1996, Yamanashi Medical Univ., Japan 1996, Tokyo Medical and Dental Univ., Japan 1996; Woznicki Lecturer and Visiting Prof. in Pathology, Baylor Coll. of Medicine Houston, Tex. 1994; Hans Selye Visiting Prof., Univ. of California, Irvine Medical School 1996; Co-Founder N American Vascular Biology Org. 1994, Pres. 1994–95, Past Pres. 1995–96; mem. Editorial Bd numerous journals; mem. American Heart Asscn 1975 (Fellow 2001), NAS (mem. Inst. of Medicine 1999), American Acad. of Arts and Sciences, American Soc. for Investigative Pathology 1975 (Vice-Pres. 1991–92, Pres. 1992–93), Tissue Culture Asscn 1976, American Soc. for Cell Biology 1976, Massachusetts Medical Soc. 1978, New York Acad. of Sciences 1979, Int. Soc. on Thrombosis and Haemostasis 1979, American Soc. of Haematology 1980, American Fed. for Clinical Research 1981, American Soc. for Clinical Investigation 1986, Int. Acad. of Pathology 1987, European Vascular Biology Asscn 1991, Asscn of American Physicians 1992–, Microcirculatory Soc. 1996, New England Soc. of Pathologists, Inc. 2002; mem. Cttee of Profs, Harvard Medical School 1985; Trustee, Karin Grunebaum Cancer Research Foundation 1990; Harvard Medical School awards: Karin Grunebaum Research Award 1968–69, Soma Weiss Research Prize 1969, Leon Reznick Research Prize 1970, Mellon Faculty Award 1975–77; other awards include: Herbert I. Horowitz Memorial Lecturer, New York Univ. Medical Center 1977, Established Investigator Award, American Heart Asscn 1977–82, Warner-Lambert/Parke-Davis Award in Experimental Pathology, American Asscn of Pathologists 1982, Erst Roche Distinguished Lecturer, Hoffman-La Roche Co. 1986, Rufus Cole Lecturer in Medicine, Rockefeller Univ. 1990, Dutkevich Memorial Lecturer, Toronto Acad. of Medicine and Univ. of Toronto 1993, Basic Research Prize, American Heart Asscn 1993, MERIT Award, Nat. Heart, Lung and Blood Inst. 1994, Cardiovascular Research Award, Bristol-Myers Squibb Research Inst. 1994, Remold Memorial Lecturer, European Soc. for Clinical Investigation 1995, Simon Dack Plenary Lecturer, American Coll. of Cardiology 1995, Pasarow Foundation Award in Cardiovascular Disease 1996, J. Allyn Taylor Int. Prize in

Medicine (jtly) 1999, Bristol-Myers Squibb Award for Distinguished Achievement in Cardiovascular Research 2001. *Publications:* more than 450 publs in medical journals. *Address:* Department of Pathology, Brigham and Women's Hospital, 221 Longwood Avenue, LMRC-401, Boston, MA 02115-5817, USA (office). *Telephone:* (617) 732-5901 (office). *Fax:* (617) 732-5933 (office). *E-mail:* mgimbrone@rics.bwh .harvard.edu (office). *Website:* vrd.bwh.harvard.edu/pis/gimbrone (office).

GIMFERRER, Pere; Spanish writer and literary manager; b. 22 June 1945, Barcelona; s. of the late Pere Gimferrer and Carmen Torrens; m. 1st María Rosa Caminals 1971 (died 2003); m. 2nd Cuca de Cominges 2006; ed Univ. at Barcelona; Head of Literary Dept, Editorial Seix Barral 1970, Literary Consultant 1973, Literary Man. 1981–; Academician, Real Acad. Española 1985–, Acad. Européenne de Poésie, Luxembourg, World Acad. of Poetry, Verona; Nat. Prize for Poetry 1966, 1989, Critic's Prize 1983, 1989, Premio Nacional de las Letras Españolas 1998, Queen Sofia Prize for Iberoamerican Poetry 2000, Int. Octavio Paz Prize for Poetry and Essay 2006, Prize for Bullfighting 2010. *Publications:* Arde el Mar 1966, L'Espai Desert 1977, Dietari 1981, Fortuny 1983, El Vendaval 1988, La Llum 1991, The Roots of Miró 1993, Complete Catalan Work, Vol. I 1995, Vol. II 1995, Vol. III 1996, Vol. IV 1996, Vol. V 1997, Masquerade (poem) 1996, L'Agent Provocador 1998, Marea Solar, Marea Lunar 2000, El Diamant dins l'Aigua 2001, Interludio azul 2006, Amor en vilo 2006, Tornado 2008, Rapsodia (poem) 2011, Alma Venus (poem) 2013, El Castell de la Puresa 2014. *Leisure interests:* cinema, travel. *Address:* Editorial Seix Barral, Diagonal 662, Barcelona 08034 (office); Rambla de Catalunya 113, Barcelona 08008, Spain (home). *Telephone:* (93) 4967003 (office); (93) 2150242 (home). *Fax:* (93) 4967004 (office).

GINER DE SAN JULIAN, Salvador, MA, PhD; Spanish sociologist and academic; *Professor Emeritus of Sociology, University of Barcelona;* b. 10 Feb. 1934, Barcelona; m. Montserrat Sariola 1966; one s. one d.; ed Int. School Barcelona, Univs of Barcelona, Cologne, Germany and Chicago, USA; Visiting Prof., Univ. of Puerto Rico 1962–63; Lecturer, Univ. of Reading, UK 1965–70; Sr Lecturer, Univ. of Lancaster, UK 1970–76; Reader, then Prof. and Head Dept of Sociology and Social Anthropology, Brunel Univ., West London, UK 1976–87; Prof. and Head, Dept of Sociology, Univ. of Barcelona 1987–90, Prof. Emer. 2005–; Dir Inst. of Advanced Social Studies, Higher Council for Scientific Research 1988–97, Barcelona Metropolitan Region Sociological Survey 2001–02; Pres. Spanish Sociological Asscn 1986–91; Vice-Pres. Inst. of Catalan Studies, Barcelona 2000–05, Pres. 2005–; Ed. Revista Internacional de Sociología 1992–; Asst Ed. European Journal of Social Theory 1988–; mem. Scientific Cttee European Prize for Social Science (Amalfi Prize) 1989–; Pres. Acad. of Sciences and Humanities of Catalonia, Barcelona; Order of Civil Merit (Spain) 1987, St George's Cross, Catalonia 1998. *Publications:* Contemporary Europe (Vol. I) 1971, (Vol. II) 1978, Mass Society 1976, Ensayos Civiles 1985, El Destino de la Libertad 1988, España: Sociedad y Política 1990, La Gobernabilidad 1992, Religión y Sociedad en España 1994, Carta sobre la Democracia 1996, Buen Gobierno y Política Social 1997, La Societat Catalana (Coll. of Economists Prize 1999) 1998, Diccionario de Sociología (ed.) 1998, Sociology (revised edn) 2001, Historia del Pensamiento Social (revised edn) 2002, Teoría Sociológica Clásica 2001, 2006, Carisma y Razón 2003, Teoría Sociológica Moderna 2004. *Address:* Department of Sociology, University of Barcelona, Diagonal 690, 08034 Barcelona, Spain (office). *Telephone:* (93) 2110686 (home); (93) 4035553 (office). *Fax:* (93) 4021894 (office). *E-mail:* sginer@ ub.edu (office); sginer@iec.cat (office); sginer@diginter.com (home). *Website:* www .ub.edu/sociologia (office); directori.ub.edu/dir (office); www.iec.cat (office).

GINGRICH, Newton (Newt) Leroy, BA, MA, PhD; American politician; b. 17 June 1943, Harrisburg, Pa; s. of Newton Searles McPherson and the late Kathleen (Kit) Daugherty (later Gingrich), adopted s. of the late Robert Bruce Gingrich; m. 1st Jackie Battley 1962 (divorced 1980); two d.; m. 2nd Marianne Ginther 1981 (divorced 2000); m. 3rd Callista Bisek 2000; ed Baker High School, Columbus, Ga, Emory Univ., Atlanta, Tulane Univ., New Orleans; mem. faculty, West Georgia Coll., Carrollton 1970–78, Prof. of History –1978; mem. US House of Reps from 6th Dist of Ga, Washington, DC 1979–92, House Republican Whip 1989, Speaker of House 1994–98, co-f. Congressional Mil. Reform Caucus, Congressional Space Caucus; Chair. GOPAC, now Chair. Emer.; cand. for Republican US presidential nomination 2012; mem. US Comm. on Nat. Security in 21st Century 1999; Founder and CEO Gringrich Group LLC (communications and consulting firm) 1999–; Founder and Chair. American Solutions for Winning the Future 2007–11 (org. disbanded); Adjunct Prof., Reinhardt Coll., Waleska, Ga 1994–95; Co-Chair. Nat. Comm. for Quality Long Term Care; mem. AAAS; mem. Advisory Bd Agency for Healthcare Quality and Research; mem. Bd of Regents, Nat. Library of Medicine; fmr Sr Fellow, American Enterprise Inst., Distinguished Visiting Fellow, Hoover Inst.; March of Dimes Georgian of the Year 1995, Georgia Breast Cancer Coalition Honoree 1996, Mental Health Asscn Advocacy Award 1996, Juvenile Diabetes Foundation Advocate of the Year 1997, American Asscn of Endocrinologists Patients Advocate of the Year 1998, American Diabetes Asscn Charles Best Medal 1998, Nat. Asscn of Community Health Centers Diabetes Healthcare Advocate of the Year 1998, named by Modern Healthcare as one of its 100 Most Powerful People in Healthcare 2003–11, Health Quality Award, Nat. Cttee for Quality Assurance 2005, Louis Sullivan Award, Workgroup for Electronic Data Interchange 2005, HIMSS Advocacy Award 2005, Nat. Hispanic Youth Initiative Award for Leadership 2006, Indispensible Person of the Year Award, Alliance on Aging 2008. *Film:* Nine Days that Changed the World 2010. *Publications:* Window of Opportunity, 1945 1995, To Renew America 1995, Winning the Future: A 21st Century Contract with America 2005, Pearl Harbor: A Novel of December 8th (with William R. Forstchen) 2007, A Contract with the Earth (co-author) 2007, Rediscovering God in America 2007, Real Change: From the World That Fails to the World That Works 2008, To Try Men's Souls (co-author) 2009, To Save America (co-author) 2010, Valley Forge (co-author) 2010. *Address:* Gringrich Group LLC, 1425 K Street, NW, Suite 450, Washington, DC 20005, USA (office). *Telephone:* (202) 375-2001 (office). *Fax:* (202) 375-2036 (office). *E-mail:* info@healthtransformation.net (office). *Website:* www.gingrichgroup.com (office).

GINKAS, Kama Mironovich; Russian theatre director; *Professor, Swedish Theatre Academy, Helsinki;* b. 7 May 1941, Kaunas, Lithuania; m. Yanovskaya Henrietta Yanovna; one s.; ed Leningrad Inst. of Theatre, Music and Cinema; worked in Krasnoyarsk Theatre of Young Spectators 1971–73; accused of aestheticism and barred from working in theatres; currently Prof., Swedish Theatre Acad., Helsinki; teaches directing at Moscow Art Theatre School. *Theatre includes:* Little Car, Moscow Art Theatre 1981, Hedda Gabler, Moscow Mossoviet Theatre 1984, Performing Crime, Moscow Theatre of Young Spectators 1991, Love is Wonderful, Finland, K.I. from Crime, Moscow Theatre of Young Spectators, Idiot (opera), Germany, Lady with a Lapdog 1995, Macbeth, Finland. *Publications:* Provoking Theater (with John Freedman) 2003. *Address:* Moscow Art Theatre School, Tverskaya str., 6, Bldg 7, 125009 Moscow (office); Tishinsky per. 24, Apt 7, Moscow, Russia (home). *Telephone:* (495) 299-53-60 (office); (495) 253-43-15 (home). *Website:* mhatschool.theatre.ru (office).

GINÓBILI, Emanuel (Manu) David; Argentine professional basketball player; b. 28 July 1977, Bahía Blanca; professional debut with Andino 1995–96; with Estudiantes Bahía Blanca 1996–98, Basket Viola Reggio Calabria 1998–2000, Virtus Bologna 2000–02; titles: Italian League Championship 2001, Italian Cup 2001, 2002, Euroleague 2001, Americas Championship 2001; joined Nat. Basketball Assen (NBA) San Antonio Spurs 2002–; mem. Gold Medal-winning Nat. Team, FIBA Americas Championships, Neuquén 2001, Silver Medal-winning team, San Juan 2003; mem. Silver Medal-winning All-Tournament Team, World Championships 2002; NBA Championship 2003, 2005, 2007; mem. Argentine Nat. Team 1998–, Gold Medal, Olympic Games, Athens 2004, Bronze Medal, Olympic Games, Beijing 2008; UNICEF Goodwill Amb. 2007–; Italian League All-Star 1999, 2000, 2001, Italian League Most Improved Player 2000, 2001, 2002, Euroleague Finals Most Valuable Player 2001, Italian Cup Most Valuable Player 2002, NBA All-Star 2005, All-Tournament Team, FIBA World Championship 2002, 2006, Ideal Olympics Team 2004, Summer Olympic Games Most Valuable Player 2004, Olimpia de Oro 2003, 2004 (shared with Carlos Tévez), 50 Greatest Euroleague Contributors 2008, NBA Sixth Man of the Year Award 2008, All-NBA Third Team 2008. *Address:* San Antonio Spurs, One SBC Center, San Antonio, TX 78219, USA (office). *Telephone:* (210) 444-5000 (office). *Website:* aol.nba.com/spurs (office); www .manuginobili.com.

GINOLA, David; French fmr professional footballer, actor and model; b. 25 Jan. 1967, Gassin, Var; s. of René Ginola and Mireille Collet; m. Coraline Delphin 1990; two d.; ed Lycée du Parc Impérial, Nice; winger; played for first div. Toulon clubs 1985–88, Racing Club Paris 1988–90, Brest 1990–92, Paris Saint-Germain 1992–95 (French nat. champions 1993/94, winners Coupe de France 1993, 1995, Coupe de la ligue 1995), Newcastle United, England 1995–97, Tottenham Hotspur 1997–2000 (winners Football League Cup 1999), Aston Villa 2000–02, Everton 2002; 17 caps for France, scored three goals 1990–95; anti-landmine campaigner for Red Cross 1998–; f. The Centre (retreat) 2004; starred in commercial for L'Oréal hair products; featured in ITV commercial for Renault Laguna motor car 1996; Club Player of Year 1998, Professional Football Assen Player of the Year 1999, Football Writers' Assen Player of the Year 1999. *Films include:* Rosbeef 2004, Mr Firecul 2004, The Last Drop 2005, Soccer Aid (TV) 2006. *Television includes:* cameo appearance in first episode of ITV drama series At Home with the Braithwaites, playing himself and announcing results of first ever Euro Lottery 2000; also appeared in episode 22 of Channel 4's Coach Trip (acted as tour guide of Ste Maxime); cameo appearance as Daveed Ginjola in Beezly'n'Cool comic Sept. 2009. *Publication:* David Ginola: The Autobiography (with Neil Silver) 2000. *Leisure interests:* golf, tennis, skiing, car racing. *Website:* www.ginola14.com (office).

GINSBURG, Ruth Joan Bader, BA, LLB; American lawyer, academic and judge; *Associate Justice, United States Supreme Court;* b. 15 March 1933, Brooklyn, New York; d. of Nathan Bader and Celia Bader (née Amster); m. Martin D. Ginsburg 1954 (died 2010); one s. one d.; ed Cornell Univ. and Harvard and Columbia Law Schools; admitted New York Bar 1959, DC Bar 1975, US Supreme Court Bar 1967; Law Sec. to Judge, US Dist Court (southern Dist), New York 1959–61; Research Assoc., Columbia Law School, New York 1961–62, Assoc. Dir project on int. procedure 1962–63; Asst Prof., Rutgers Univ. Law School, Newark 1963–66, Assoc. Prof. 1966–69, Prof. 1969–72; Prof. Columbia Univ., School of Law, New York 1972–80; Fellow, Center for Advanced Study in Behavioral Sciences, Stanford, Calif. 1977–78; Gen. Counsel, American Civil Liberties Union 1973–80; US Circuit Judge, US Court of Appeals, DC Circuit, Washington, DC 1980–93; Assoc. Justice, US Supreme Court 1993–; mem. ABA, AAAS, American Law Inst., Council on Foreign Relations; numerous hon. degrees; ranked by Forbes magazine amongst The World's 100 Most Powerful Women (seventh) 2004, (23rd) 2005, (32nd) 2006, (20th) 2007, (72nd) 2008, (48th) 2009, (31st) 2010. *Publications:* Civil Procedure in Sweden (with A. Bruzelius) 1965, Swedish Code of Judicial Procedure 1968, Sex-Based Discrimination (with others); articles in legal journals. *Address:* United States Supreme Court, One First Street, NE, Washington, DC 20543, USA (office). *Telephone:* (202) 479-3000 (office). *E-mail:* info@supremecourt.gov (office). *Website:* www.supremecourt.gov (office).

GINWALA, Frene Noshir, LLB, DPhil; South African journalist and politician; b. 25 April 1932, Johannesburg; ed Univs of Oxford and London, UK; left SA in 1960 to establish external mission of the African National Congress (ANC), fmr ANC Spokeswoman, UK; contrib. to The Guardian, The Economist and the BBC, UK; Ed. Tanzania Standard and Sunday News, Tanzania; returned to SA 1991; mem. Secr., Office of Pres. of ANC, Head of ANC Research Dept 1991–94; Speaker, Nat. Ass. 1994–2004; Chancellor, Univ. of KwaZulu-Natal 2005–; Chair. (SA), Commonwealth Parliamentary Assen, Southern African Devt Community Parliamentary Forum, International Parliamentary Union (SA), ANC Archives Cttee; Co-Chair. Global Coalition for Africa (GCA); apptd to head enquiry into Nat. Dir of Public Prosecutions Vusi Pikoli's fitness to hold office 2007–08; Pres. South African Speakers Forum; Chair. Presidential Award for Youth Empowerment; Hon. Fellow, Linacre Coll. Oxford, UK; Grand Officier, Ordre nat. (Côte d'Ivoire) 1998, Grand Cordon of the Order of the Rising Sun (Japan) 2008; Dr hc (Rhodes) 1996, (Natal) 1996, (Cape Town) 1997, (Connecticut, USA) 2002, (Nelson Mandela Metropolitan Univ.) 2003; Global Award for Outstanding Contrib. to the Promotion of Human Rights and Democracy, Priyadarshini Acad., India 2000, Black Man. Forum Leadership Award 2000, Woman of the Year Award (Univ. of Pretoria Law Faculty) 2000. *Publications include:* Sanctions in South Africa in Question, Gender and Economic Policy in a Democratic South Africa, Women and the Elephant: Putting Women on the Agenda. *Leisure interest:* reading. *Address:* c/o

African National Congress of South Africa, POB 61884, Marshalltown 2107, South Africa (office).

GIOIA, (Michael) Dana, MA, MBA; American writer and poet; *Judge Widney Professor of Poetry and Public Culture, University of Southern California;* b. 24 Dec. 1950, Los Angeles, Calif.; s. of Michael Gioia and Dorothy Gioia (née Ortiz); m. Mary Hiecke 1980; three s. (one deceased); ed Stanford and Harvard Univs; fmr Visiting Writer, Colorado Coll., Johns Hopkins Univ., Wesleyan Univ.; Chair. Nat. Endowment for the Arts 2003–09; Dir Harman-Eisner Program in the Arts, Aspen Inst. 2009–11, Harman-Eisner Sr Fellow in the Arts 2011–; Judge Widney Prof. of Poetry and Public Culture, Univ. of Southern California 2011–; mem. Bd and Vice-Pres. Poetry Soc. of America; mem. Wesleyan Univ. Writers' Conf., Citizens' Stamp Advisory Cttee (USA) 2009–12; mem. US Del. to UNESCO 2003–09; 11 hon. doctorates; Esquire Best of New Generation Award 1984, Frederick Bock Prize for Poetry 1985, American Book Award 2001, Smithsonian Latino Legacy Award 2007, Nat. Civilian's Medal 2009, Laetare Medal 2010, John Carroll Medal 2011, Aiken-Taylor Poetry Award 2014. *Dance:* Counting the Children 1994. *Operas:* Nosferatu 2001, Tony Caruso's Final Broadcast 2008. *Song cycles:* Becoming a Redwood 2004, Prayer 2012. *Radio:* Nat. Endowment for the Arts Big Read radio shows (32 episodes), contrib./writer, BBC 1992–2012. *Publications include:* The Ceremony and Other Stories 1984, Daily Horoscope 1986, Mottetti: Poems of Love (trans.) 1990, The Gods of Winter 1991, Can Poetry Matter? 1992, An Introduction to Poetry 1994, The Madness of Hercules (trans.) 1995, Interrogations at Noon (American Book Award 2002) 2001, Nosferatu (opera libretto with Alva Henderson) 2001, The Barrier of a Common Language (essays) 2003, Twentieth-century American Poetry 2004, Twentieth-century American Poetics 2004, 100 Great Poets of the English Language 2005, Literature for Life 2012, Pity the Beautiful 2012; also ed. of several works of literary criticism; regular contrib. to various journals, reviews and periodicals, including San Francisco magazine (classical music critic). *Leisure interests:* opera, jazz, book collecting. *Address:* Taper Hall 355-K, University of Southern California, 3501 Trousdale Parkway, Los Angeles, CA 90089-0354 (office); 7190 Faught Road, Santa Rosa, CA 95403, USA (home). *Telephone:* (213) 740-2797 (office). *E-mail:* gioia@usc.edu (office). *Website:* www.danagioia.net.

GIOJA, José Luis; Argentine politician and lawyer; *Governor of the Province of San Juan;* b. 4 Dec. 1949, San Juan Prov.; m. Rosa Palacio; four c.; ed Escuela Normal de Jáchal, San Juan and Nat. Univ. of Cuyo; Pres. Agrupación Nacional de Estudiantes Universitarios 1972–73; Pvt. Sec. to Gov. Eloy Camus 1973; Sec.-Gen. Juventud Peronista, Partido Justicialista de San Juan 1975, Congresal Prov. 1975–76; Interventor Instituto Prov. de la Vivienda 1974–75; Pres. Unidad Básica del Barrio Edilco 1983; Cand., Departamento de Rawson 1983; Pres. Junta Departamental de Rawson 1984–85; mem. Consejo Nacional Justicialista 1987–93, Consejo Prov. Justicialista 1987–93; Prov. Deputy and Vice-Pres. Justicialista Bloc, Chamber of Deputies, San Juan Prov. 1987–91, Pres. Comisión de Minería, Obras Públicas y Recursos Hídricos; Deputy in Nat. Ass. 1991–99, Pres. Jt Party Comm. Argentina–Chile 1993; Senator 1995–2002, Pres. Comisión Bicameral de Minería y de Coparticipación Fed. de Impuestos, Pres. Senate Justicialistas Bloc 2000–02, Pres. (provisional) of Senate 2002; Gov. of Province of San Juan 2003–. *Address:* Office of the Governor, San Juan 5400, Argentina (office). *Website:* www .sanjuan.gov.ar (office).

GIONI, Massimiliano; Italian curator and art critic; *Artistic Director, Fondazione Nicola Trussardi;* b. 1973, Milan; m. Cecilia Alemani; US Ed. Flash Art (magazine) 2000–02; Co-Dir The Wrong Gallery, New York 2002–05; Artistic Dir Fondazione Nicola Trussardi, Milan 2003–; Assoc. Dir of Exhbns, New Museum of Contemporary Art, New York 2007–; Founder Family Business, New York 2012–; Artistic Dir 55th Venice Biennale 2013; Ed. Charley and Wrong Times (visual magazines); columnist, Domus magazine, Wired Italy, Rolling Stone Italy; contrib., Flash Art magazine, Artforum, Frieze, Parkett, ArtPress. *Exhibitions curated include:* Uniform. Order and Disorder, PS1, New York 2001, The Fourth Sex. Adolescent Extremes, Pitti Discovery, Florence 2002, Yesterday Begins Tomorrow, Deste Foundation, Athens 2003, Short Cut (Elmgreen and Dragset), Milan 2003, The Zone, 50th Venice Biennale 2003, If I Had You (Darren Almond), Milan 2003, Untitled (Maurizio Cattelan), Milan 2004, Manifesta 5, San Sebastian, Spain (co-curator) 2004, Monument to Now, Athens 2004, Meechfieber (John Bock), Milan 2004, Jet Set Lady (Urs Fisher), Milan 2005, Long Sorrow (Anri Sala), Milan 2005, Of Mice and Men, Berlin Biennial (co-curator) 2006, I Like Things (Martin Creed), Milan 2006, My Religion Is Kindness (Paola Pivi), Milan 2006, One of Many (Pawel Althamer), Milan 2007, The Fractured Figure, Athens 2007, Altri fiori e altre domande (Fishli and Weiss), Milan 2008, After Nature, New York 2008, Tino Sehgal, Milan 2008, The Generational: Younger Than Jesus, New York 2009, Urs Fischer: Marguerite de Ponty, New York 2009, Still Life (Tacita Dean), Milan 2009, Pig Island (Paul McCarthy), Milan 2010, 10,000 Lives, 8th Gwangju Biennale 2010, Alighiero e Boetti Day, Turin 2011, Lynda Benglis, New York 2011, Gustav Metzger, New York 2011, Apichatpong Weerasethakul, New York 2011, Ostalgia, New York 2011, Parasimpatico (Pipilotti Rist), Milan 2011, Carsten Höller, New York 2012, Ego (Takashi Murakami), Doha, Qatar 2012, Tacita Dean, New York 2012, Klara Liden, New York 2012, Rosemarie Trockel, New York 2012, Ghosts in the Machine, New York 2012, Rubble and Revelation (Cyprien Gaillard), Milan 2012, NYC 1993. Experimental Jet Set, Trash and No Star, New York 2013, The Encyclopedic Palace, 55th Venice Biennale 2013, Fault Lines (Allora & Calzadilla), Milan 2013. *Publications:* numerous articles and books on contemporary art, several monographs. *Address:* Fondazione Nicola Trussardi, Piazza della Scala 5, 20121 Milan, Italy (office). *Telephone:* (02) 8068821 (office). *Fax:* (02) 80688281 (office). *E-mail:* info@fondazionenicolatrussardi.com (office). *Website:* www.fondazionenicolatrussardi.com (office).

GIORDANA, Marco Tullio; Italian film director and screenwriter; b. 1 Oct. 1950, Milan. *Films include:* Forza Italia! (screenwriter) 1978, Maledetti vi amerò (To Love the Damned) (also screenwriter) 1980, Car Crash (screenwriter) 1980, La caduta degli angeli ribelli (also screenwriter) 1981, Notti e nebbie (TV) (also screenwriter) 1984, Appuntamento a Liverpool (also screenwriter) 1988, La domenica specialmente (Especially on Sunday, USA) 1991, L'unico paese al mondo 1994, Pasolini, un delitto italiano (Pasolini, an Italian Crime) (also screenwriter) 1995, I cento passi (The Hundred Steps) (also screenwriter) 2000, Un altro mondo è possibile (Another World Is Possible, USA) 2001, Il cineasta e il labirinto (as himself) 2002, La meglio gioventù (The Best of Youth) (Un certain Regard, Cannes Film Festival 2003) 2003, Quando sei nato non puoi più nasconderti (Once You're Born You Can No Longer Hide, UK) 2004, Wild Blood 2008.

GIORDANI, Jorge A.; Venezuelan economist, academic and politician; *Minister of Planning;* b. 1940, San Pedro de Macoris, Dominican Republic; ed Univ. of Bologna, Italy, Univ. of Sussex, UK; fmr Prof., Universidad Central de Venezuela, also Dir of Grad. Studies, Ciencias Económicas y Sociales; fmr Dir Cordiplan (Cen. Office of Co-ordination and Planning); Minister of Planning and Devt –2010, of Planning and Finance 2010–13, of Planning 2013–. *Publications:* Human Development in Venezuela 2004. *Address:* Ministry of Planning and Finance, Edif. Ministerio de Finanzas, esq. Carmelitas, Avda Urdaneta, Caracas 1010, Venezuela (office). *Telephone:* (212) 802-1000 (office). *Website:* www.mppef.gob.ve (office).

GIORDANO, HE Cardinal Michele; Italian ecclesiastic; *Archbishop Emeritus of Naples;* b. 26 Sept. 1930, S. Arcangelo (Pz); ordained 1953, Pastor Scanzano 1953–59, Dir Catechetics Centre, Diocesan Centre of Social Studies 1959–68, Vicar Gen. 1971, elected to the titular Church of Lari Castello 1971, consecrated bishop 1972, Archbishop of Matera 1974–77, Archbishop of Matera e Irsina 1977–87, Archbishop of Naples 1987–2006, Archbishop Emer. 2006–, cr. Cardinal Priest of S. Gioacchino ai Prati di Castello 1988. *Address:* Arcivescovado di Napoli, Largo Donnaregina 22, 80138 Naples, Italy. *Telephone:* (081) 449118. *Fax:* (081) 292487.

GIORDANO, Richard Vincent, BA, LLB, PhD; American business executive; b. 24 March 1934, New York; s. of Vincent Giordano and Cynthia Giordano (née Cardetta); m. Barbara Claire Beckett 1956 (divorced); one s. two d.; ed Stuyvesant School, New York, Harvard Univ. and Columbia Univ. Law School; admitted New York Bar 1961; Assoc. Shearman and Sterling (law firm), New York 1959–63; Asst Sec. Air Reduction Co. Inc., New York 1963–64, Vice-Pres. Distribution of Products Div. 1964–65, Exec. Vice-Pres. 1965–67, Group Vice-Pres. 1967–71, Pres. and COO 1971–74, CEO 1977–79; Dir BOCI 1974; Man. Dir and CEO BOC Group 1979–84, Chair. 1985–92, CEO 1985–91, Chair. (non-exec.) 1994–96; Dir (non-exec.) Reuters 1991–94; Chair. (non-exec.) British Gas PLC (renamed BG PLC 1997, BG Group PLC 1999) 1994–2003; mem. Bd of Dirs (non-exec.) Cen. Electricity Generating Bd 1982–89, Georgia Pacific Corpn 1984–2006, Grand Metropolitan 1985–97 (Deputy Chair. (non-exec.) 1991–97), RTZ (renamed Rio Tinto PLC), Deputy Chair. (non-exec.) 1992–, Lucas Industries (non-exec.) 1993–94; Hon. Fellow, Royal Coll. of Anaesthetists, London Business School; Hon. KBE; Hon. DCS (St John's Univ., USA); Hon. LLB (Bath) 1998. *Leisure interests:* sailing, opera. *Address:* c/o 20 Villet Drive, East Setauket, NY 11733, USA (office). *Telephone:* (631) 689-8523 (office). *Fax:* (631) 675-6182 (office). *E-mail:* kastwood54@optonline.net (office).

GIOVANNI, Nikki, BA; American poet and academic; *University Distinguished Professor, Virginia Polytechnic Institute and State University;* b. (Yolande Cornelia Giovanni), 7 June 1943, Knoxville, Tenn.; d. of Jones Giovanni and Yolande Watson; one s.; ed Fisk Univ., Univ. of Cincinnati and Univ. of Pennsylvania; Asst Prof. of Black Studies, City Coll. of New York 1968; Assoc. Prof. of English, Rutgers Univ. 1968–72; Prof. of Creative Writing, Coll. Mt St Joseph on the Ohio 1985; Prof. of English, Va Polytechnic Inst. and State Univ. 1987–, Gloria D. Smith Prof. of Black Studies 1997–99, Univ. Distinguished Prof. 1999–; Founder, Nixtom Ltd 1970; Visiting Prof., Ohio State Univ. 1984; recipient of numerous awards and hon. degrees. *Publications include:* Black Feeling, Black Talk 1968, Black Judgement 1968, Re: Creation 1970, Poem of Angela Yvonne Davis 1970, Spin A Soft Black Song 1971, Gemini 1971, My House 1972, A Dialogue: James Baldwin and Nikki Giovanni 1973, Ego Tripping and Other Poems for Young Readers 1973, A Poetic Equation: Conversations Between Nikki Giovanni and Margaret Walker 1974, The Women and the Men 1975, Cotton Candy on a Rainy Day 1978, Vacationtime 1980, Those Who Ride the Night Winds 1983, Sacred Cows . . . and other Edibles 1988, Conversations with Nikki Giovanni 1992, Racism 101 1994, Grand Mothers 1994, Selected Poems of Nikki Giovanni 1996, Shimmy Shimmy Shimmy Like My Sister Kate 1996, Nikki in Philadelphia 1997, Love Poems 1997, Blues: For All the Changes 1999, Grand Fathers 1999, Quilting the Black-Eyed Pea: Poems and Not-Quite Poems 2002, The Collected Poetry of Nikki Giovanni 2003, The Prosaic Soul of Nikki Giovanni 2003, The Girls in the Circle 2004, Rosa 2005, Acolytes 2007, On My Journey Now 2007, The Grasshopper's Song 2008, Lincoln and Douglass: An American Friendship 2008, Hip Hop Speaks to Children 2008, Bicycles: Love Poems 2009, Best African American Fiction 2010 (co-ed.) 2009. *Address:* Department of English, Virginia Polytechnic Institute and State University, 323 Shanks Hall, Blacksburg, VA 24061, USA (office). *Telephone:* (540) 231-9453 (office). *E-mail:* info@nikki-giovanni.com (office). *Website:* www.english.vt.edu (office); www.nikki-giovanni.com.

GIRALDO, Luis Guillermo, LLB; Colombian economist, politician and fmr diplomatist; b. Manizales; ed Pontificia Universidad Javeriana, Bogota; Sec.-Gen. of Treasury, Manizales 1967; mem. House of Reps 1970–78; Mayor of Manizales 1978; Senator of the Repub. 1978–98; Pres. of Senate 1989; Amb. to Germany 1990–91, to Venezuela 1998–99; Chief of Presidential Campaign of Alvaro Uribe, then mem. team preparing Govt Plan of Action –2003; Perm. Rep. to UN, New York 2003; Amb. to Mexico 2003–05; Sec.-Gen. Partido Social de la Unidad Nacional (Partido de la U) 2005–08; mem. Peace Negotiations 1999. *Publications:* Contrapuntos del Poder y la Fama, Algunas Palabras, De Relojes y de Nostalgias, El Antiheroe. *Address:* Partido Social de la Unidad Nacional (Partido de la U) 32-16 Carrera 7, 21°, Bogotá, DC, Colombia (office). *Telephone:* (1) 340-1394 (office). *Website:* www.partidodelau.com (office).

GIRARD, Jean-François, MD, MSc; French fmr civil servant and professor emeritus of medicine; *Adviser to the President, SATT IdFInnov;* b. 20 Nov. 1944, Luçon (Vendée); one s. two d.; ed Univ. of Paris; Prof. of Medicine 1979–97, Prof. Emer. 1997–; Dir-Gen. Ministry of Health 1986–97; Chair. Exec. Council WHO 1992, 1993; Conseiller d'Etat 1997–2013; Pres. Inst. de recherche pour le développement 2001–09; Pres. Pôle de recherche et d'enseignement supérieur, Sorbonne Paris Cité 2010–13; Adviser to the Pres. of SATT Ile-de-France Innov (IdFInnov—pvt. tech. transfer org.) 2013–; Officier, Légion d'honneur; Commdr, Ordre nat. du Mérite. *Publications:* Quand la santé devient publique 1998, La maladie d'Alzheimer 2000. *Leisure interest:* sailing. *Address:* PRES Sorbonne Paris Cité, 190 avenue de France, 75013 Paris, France (office). *Telephone:* 1-49-54-83-41 (office). *E-mail:* jean-francois.girard@sorbonne-paris-cite.fr (office).

GIRARD, René Noël, PhD; French/American academic and writer; *Professor Emeritus, Stanford University;* b. 25 Dec. 1923, Avignon; s. of Joseph Girard and Thérèse Fabre; m. Martha Virginia McCullough 1951; two s. one d.; ed Lycée d'Avignon, Ecole des Chartes and Indiana Univ.; Instructor of French, Indiana Univ. 1947–51, Duke Univ. 1952–53; Asst Prof., Bryn Mawr Coll. 1953–57; Assoc. Prof., Johns Hopkins Univ 1957–61, Prof. 1961–68, Chair. Romance Languages 1965–68, James M. Beall Prof. of French and Humanities 1976–80; Prof. Inst. d'études françaises Bryn Mawr, Avignon 1961–68, Dir 1969; Distinguished Faculty Prof. of Arts and Letters, State Univ. of New York at Buffalo 1971–76; Andrew B. Hammond Prof. of French Language, Literature and Civilization, Stanford Univ. 1981–95, Courtesy Prof. of Religious Studies and Comparative Literature 1986–95, Dir Program of Interdisciplinary Research, Dept of French and Italian 1987–95, Prof. Emer. 1995–; mem. Center for Int. Security and Arms Control, 1990–95; Fellow, American Acad. of Arts and Sciences 1979, Guggenheim Fellow 1960, 1967; elected mem. Acad. Française 2005; Hon. DLit (Vrije Univ.) 1985, Hon. DTheol (Innsbruck) 1988, (St Mary's Seminary, Baltimore) 2003, (Montreal) 2004, (London) 2005, Hon. DLit (Padua) 2001, Dr hc (Univ. of Antwerp) 1995, (Montreal) 2004, (St Andrews) 2008; Chevalier, Ordre Nat. de la Légion d'honneur 1984, Officier, Ordre des Arts et Lettres 1984; Acad. Française Prize 1973, Grand Prix de Philosophie 1996; Prix Médicis-Essai 1990, Premio Nonino (Percoto, Udine, Italy) 1998, Dr Leopold Lucas Prize, Tübingen 2006, Lifetime Achievement Award, Modern Language Asscn 2008. *Publications include:* Mensonge romantique et vérité romanesque 1961, Dostoïevski: du double à l'unité 1963, La violence et le sacré 1972, Des choses cachées depuis la fondation du monde 1978, Le bouc émissaire 1982, La route antique des hommes pervers 1985, Shakespeare: Les feux de l'envie 1990, A Theatre of Envy. William Shakespeare 1991, Quand ces choses commenceront 1994, The Girard Reader 1996, Je vois Satan tomber comme l'éclair 1999, (in English) 2001, Celui par qui le scandale arrive 2001, La voix méconnue du réel 2002, Les Origines de la Culture 2004, Achever Clausewitz 2007, Battling to the End 2009.

GIRARD-diCARLO, David F., BA, JD; American lawyer and fmr diplomatist; *Partner, Cozen O'Connor;* b. 1942, Philadelphia, Pa; ed St Joseph's Univ., Villanova Univ. School of Law; began career as an Assoc. with Wolf Block LLP before moving on to Dilworth Paxon LLP, later Partner; Chair. South Eastern Pennsylvania Transportation Authority —1981; returned to law firm 1981; began work for Blank Rome LLP, served for 16 years as Man. Partner and CEO, later Chair. for six years; appointed Man. Dir Blank Rome Govt Relations LLC (subsidiary and lobbying br. of law firm), Washington, DC; Chair. Bush-Cheney election campaign 2000; Co-Chair. Republican Convention in Philadelphia 2000; Pennsylvania Chair. Bush-Cheney campaign 2004; Amb. to Austria 2008–09; currently Pnr, Cozen O'Connor (law firm), Philadelphia; Pres. The Pennsylvania Soc.; Trustee, Saint Joseph's Univ.; mem. Bd of Consultors, Villanova Univ. School of Law; mem. Philadelphia School Reform Comm. 2009–11; mem. Council of American Ambs, Diplomatic Council on Energy Security; fmr Chair. Bd and Chair. Exec. Cttee Greater Philadelphia Chamber of Commerce; Kt of St Gregory the Great from Pope John Paul 2003; named to PoliticsPA list of 'Sy Snyder's Power 50' list of politically influential individuals 2003, 2004. *Address:* Cozen O'Connor, 1900 Market Street, Philadelphia, PA 19103, USA (office). *Telephone:* (215) 665-5550 (office). *Fax:* (215) 701-2291 (office). *E-mail:* dgirarddicarlo@cozen.com (office). *Website:* www.cozen.com (office).

GIRARDET, Herbert, BSc (Econ); German ecologist, consultant, writer and television producer; *Co-founder, Honorary Member and Senior Consultant, World Future Council;* b. 28 May 1943, Essen; s. of Herbert Girardet and Ingrid Girardet; m. Barbara Hallifax 1967; two s.; ed Tübingen and Berlin Univs, London School of Econs, UK; consultant to Town and Country Planning Asscn, London 1976–86, Environment consultant Channel 4 TV, London 1987–89, Consultant to UN Habitat II Conf., Istanbul 1995–96; Visiting Prof. of Environmental Planning, Middlesex Univ. 1995–2003; Visiting Prof. of Sustainable Urban Devt, Univ. of Northumbria 2003–06; Visiting Prof. of Cities and the Environment, Univ. of the West of England 2004–; Thinker-in-Residence, Adelaide 2003; Dir Under the Sky Urban Regeneration Co., Bristol 2004–; Co-founder and Dir of Programmes, World Future Council 2004–11, Hon. mem. and Sr Consultant 2011–; Chief Consultant to Shanghai City Govt on design of Dongtan Eco-City on Chongming Island; mem. Balaton Group of int. environment experts 1993–; Sr Consultant, Saudi Sustainability Initiative 2009; Chair. The Schumacher Soc., UK 1994–2006; Trustee, The Sustainable London Trust 1996–2004; Patron The Soil Asscn, UK 1990–; Hon. FRIBA 2000; UN Global 500 Award for Outstanding Environmental Achievements, prizes for TV documentaries. *Television:* initiator and researcher: Far from Paradise (series) 1983–86; writer and producer: Jungle Pharmacy 1988, Halting the Fires 1989, Metropolis 1994, Urban Best Practices 1996, UN Habitat 1996, Deadline 2000 (28 three-minute films) 1997–99; series consultant: The People's Planet 1999–2000. *Publications:* Far From Paradise: The Story of Human Impact on the Environment (co-author) 1986, Blueprint for a Green Planet (co-author) 1987, Earthrise 1992, The Gaia Atlas of Cities 1992, Making Cities Work (co-author) 1996, Getting London in Shape for 2000 1997, Creating a Sustainable London (co-author) 1998, Creating Sustainable Cities 1999, Tall Buildings and Sustainable Development (co-author) 2001, Creating a Sustainable Adelaide 2003, Cities, People, Planet 2004, Shanghai Dongtan: An Ecocity (co-author) 2006, Surviving the Century (ed.) 2007, A Renewable World, Energy, Ecology, Equality 2009 (co-author), Regenerative Cities 2010. *Leisure interests:* gardening, country walking. *Address:* World Future Council, Trafalgar House, 100 Pall Mall, London, SW1Y 4AU, England (office); Forest Cottage, Trelleck Road, Tintern, Chepstow, Monmouthshire, NP16 6SN, Wales (home). *Telephone:* (20) 7321-3810 (office); (1291) 689392 (home). *Fax:* (20) 7321-3738 (office); (1291) 689392 (home). *E-mail:* herbie@worldfuturecouncil.org (office). *Website:* www.worldfuturecouncil.org (office).

GIRI, Rt Hon. Kedar Prasad; Nepalese judge; experience with various judicial and quasi-judicial bodies, including Royal Law Reform Comm., Chair. Land Limitation Execution Cttee, Land Reform Ministry and all levels of courts in Nepal, Acting Chief Justice of Nepal Sept.–Oct. 2007, Chief Justice of Nepal 2007–09 (retd). *Address:* c/o Supreme Court of Nepal, Ramashah Path, Kathmandu, Nepal. *E-mail:* info@supremecourt.gov.np.

GIRI, Tulsi; Nepalese politician; b. Sept. 1926; Deputy Minister of Foreign Affairs 1959; Minister of Village Devt 1960; Minister without Portfolio 1960; Minister of Foreign Affairs, the Interior, Public Works and Communications 1961; Vice-Chair. Council of Ministers and Minister of Palace Affairs 1962; Chair. Council of Ministers and Minister of Foreign Affairs 1962–65; mem. Royal Advisory Cttee 1969–74; apptd Adviser to the King 1974; Prime Minister, Minister of Palace Affairs and Defence 1975–77; Vice-Chair. Council of Ministers and Minister of Land Reform and Man. and of Water Resources 2005. *Address:* c/o Ministry of Land Reform and Management, Singha Durbar, Kathmandu, Nepal.

GIROLAMI, Sir Paul, Kt, BCom, FCA; British/Italian company chairman (retd) and chartered accountant; b. (Paolo Girolami), 25 Jan. 1926, Fanna, Italy; s. of Pietro Girolami and Assunta Bertossi; m. Christabel Mary Gwynne Lewis 1952; two s. one d.; ed London School of Econs; with Chantrey and Button (Chartered Accountants) 1950–54, Cooper Brothers 1954–65; mem. Bd Glaxo 1965–94, Finance Dir 1965–80, Chief Exec. 1980–86, Exec. Chair. 1985–94; Pres. Glaxo Finanziaria SpA Italy; mem. Bd of Dirs Nippon Glaxo Ltd, Japan 1975–94, Glaxo-Sankyo Ltd 1984–94, Credito Italiano Int. 1990–93, Forte PLC 1992–96, UIS France 1994–2000; mem. CBI Council 1986–93; Chair. Senate for Chartered Accountants in Business 1990–; Chair. Council Goldsmith's Coll., Univ. of London 1994–2002; Dir American Chamber of Commerce (UK) 1983; mem. Appeal Cttee of Inst. of Chartered Accountants 1987, Stock Exchange Listed Cos Advisory Cttee 1987–92, Open Univ. Visiting Cttee 1987–89; mem. Worshipful Co. of Apothecaries, Worshipful Co. of Chartered Accountants, Court of Assts of The Worshipful Co. of Goldsmiths (Prime Warden) 1986; Pres. British-Italian Soc.; Freeman, City of London Liveryman 1980, Hon. Fellow, LSE 1989, Goldsmiths Coll., Emmanuel Coll., Cambridge 1994; Grande Ufficiale, Ordine al Merito della Repubblica Italiana 1987, Insignia of the Order of the Rising Sun (Japan), Cavaliere del Lavoro (Italy) 1991, Grand Cross, Order of the Holy Sepulchre; Dr hc (Trieste) 1991; Hon. DSc (Aston) 1991, (Sunderland) 1991, (Bradford) 1993; Hon. LLD (Singapore) 1993, (Warwick) 1996; City and Guilds Insignia Award in Tech. (hc) 1988, Public Service Star, Singapore 2000. *Leisure interests:* reading, music. *Address:* Piazza Conte Nicolo' di Maniago 16, Maniago (PN), Italy (office). *Telephone:* (0427) 709005 (office). *E-mail:* pgirol@aol.com (home); paolo .girolami@alice.it (home).

GISCARD D'ESTAING, Valéry Marie René George; French politician, civil servant and fmr head of state; b. 2 Feb. 1926, Koblenz, Germany; s. of Edmond Giscard d'Estaing and May Bardoux; m. Anne-Aymone de Brantes 1952; two s. two d.; ed Ecole Polytechnique, Ecole Nat. d'Admin; Official, Inspection des Finances 1952, Insp. 1954; Deputy Dir du Cabinet of Prés. du Conseil June–Dec. 1954; Deputy for Puy de Dôme 1956–58, re-elected for Clermont 1958, for Puy de Dôme 1962, 1967, 1984, 1986, 1988, resgnd 1989; Sec. of State for Finance 1959, Minister for Finance and Econ. Affairs 1962–66, 1969–74; Pres. Comm. des Finances, de l'Economie général et du plan 1967–68; Pres. Cttee des Affaires Etrangères 1987–89; Pres. of the French Repub. 1974–81; Founder-Pres. Fed. Nat. des Républicains Indépendants (from May 1977 Parti Républicain) 1965; Del. to UN Gen. Ass. 1956, 1957, 1958; Chair. OECD Ministerial Council 1960; mem. (ex officio) Conseil Constitutionnel 1981–; Conseiller gen., Puy-de-Dôme 1982–88; Pres. Regional Council of Auvergne 1986–2004; Pres. Union pour la democratie française (UDF) 1988–96; Deputy to European Parl. 1989–93; Pres. European Movt Int. 1989–97; Pres. Council of European Municipalities and Regions 1997–2004; Deputy for Puy-de-Dôme 1993–2002; Pres. Comm. of Foreign Affairs, Nat. Ass. 1993–97; Chair. EU Convention on the Future of Europe 2002–03; mem. Royal Acad. of Econ. Science and Finance (Spain) 1995–, Acad. française 2003–; Grand Croix, Ordre de la Légion d'honneur, Grand Croix, Ordre nat. du Mérite, Croix de guerre, Kt Grand Cross, Order of St Olav (Norway) 1962, Kt Grand Cross, Order of Merit of the Italian Repub. 1973, Grand Collar, Order of St James of the Sword (Portugal) 1975, Gran Cruce, Ordén de Isabel la Católica 1976, Kt, Order of the Elephant (Denmark) 1978, Grand Collar, Order of Prince Henry (Portugal) 1978, Kt, Order of the Seraphim (Sweden) 1980, Baillif Grand Cross of Honour and Devotion of the Sovereign Mil. Order of Malta, Hon. Kt, Grand Cross of the Order of the Bath (England); Nansen Medal 1979, Onassis Foundation Prize 2000, Trombinoscope Prize for Political Personality of the Year 2000, Jean Monnet Foundation Medal 2001, Trombinoscope European of the Year 2002, Charlemagne Prize 2002. *Publications include:* Démocratie française 1976, Deux français sur trois 1984, Le Pouvoir et la vie, Vol. I 1988, Vol. II: L'Affrontement 1991, Vol. III: Choisir 2006, Le Passage 1994, Dans cinq ans, l'an 2000 (essay) 1995, Les Français 2000, La Princesse et le Président 2009, La victoire de la Grande Armée 2010, Matilda 2011. *Leisure interests:* shooting, skiing. *Address:* 199 blvd Saint-Germain, 75007 Paris, France (office). *Telephone:* 1-45-44-30-30 (office). *Fax:* 1-45-49-11-16 (office). *E-mail:* secretariat@cab-vge.fr (office); international@cab-vge .fr (office).

GISKE, Trond; Norwegian politician; b. 7 Nov. 1966; ed Univ. of Oslo, Norwegian Univ. of Science and Tech.; Leader, Labour Youth League, Sør-Trøndelag Co. 1989–90, mem. Cen. Exec. Cttee 1990–96, Leader, Labour Youth League 1992–96, mem. Labour Party Cen. Exec. Cttee 1992–96, mem. Parl. Election Cttee 1997–2001; mem. Storting (Parl.) for Sør-Trøndelag Co. 1997–2005, mem. Standing Cttee on Finance and Econ. Affairs 1997–2001, Standing Cttee on Family, Cultural Affairs and Govt Admin 2001–05, Labour Party Parl. Group 2001–05; Minister of Educ., Research and Church Affairs 2000–01, of Culture and Church Affairs 2005–09, of Trade and Industry 2009–13; del. to UN Gen. Ass. 1999. *Address:* c/o Ministry of Trade and Industry, Einar Gerhardsens plass 1, PO Box 8014 Dep, 0030 Oslo, Norway (office).

GÍSLADÓTTIR, Ingibjörg Sólrún, BA; Icelandic politician; b. 31 Dec. 1954, Reykjavík; m. Hjörleifur Sveinbjörnsson; two s.; ed Univ. of Iceland, Univ. of Copenhagen, Denmark; began political career in Samtök um kvennalista (Women's Alliance), which she represented in Reykjavík's City Council 1982–88; mem. Althing (Parl.) for Reykjavík 1991–94, for Reykjavík N 2005–, mem. Cttee on Foreign Affairs 1991–93, Cttee on Health and Social Security 1991–94, Cttee on Social Affairs 1991–94 (Vice-Chair. 1993–94), Cttee on Economy and Trade 2005–06, Icelandic Del. to EFTA and European Econ. Area Parl. Cttees 2005–; Founding mem. Samfylkingin (Social Democratic Alliance) 2000, Deputy Leader 1994–2003, Leader 2003–05, Chair. 2005–09; Mayor of Reykjavík 1994–2003 (resgnd); Minister for Foreign Affairs and External Trade 2007–09 (resgnd); fmr

Ed. Vera (feminist journal); mem. Exec. Bd Cen. Bank of Iceland 2003–05. *Publication:* Þegar sálin fer á kreik. *Address:* c/o Samfylkingin, Hallveigarstíg 1, 101 Reykjavík, Iceland.

GITHAE, Robinson Njeru, LLB; Kenyan lawyer and politician; b. 1957, Central Prov.; ed Univ. of Nairobi, Kenya School of Law; mem. Nat. Ass. (Parl.) for Ndia constituency 2002–; fmr Asst Minister for Local Govt, fmr Minister of Nairobi Metropolitan Devt, Minister of Finance 2012–13; mem. Party of National Unity (PNU). *Address:* c/o Ministry of Finance, Treasury Bldg, Harambee Ave, POB 30007, Nairobi, Kenya (office).

GITONAS, Constantinos I.; Greek politician; b. Lagadia, Arcadia; m.; two d.; ed Nat. Tech. Univ. of Athens; Gen. Sec. Ministry of Public Works 1981–85; Deputy Minister of Environment, Land Use and Public Works 1985–86, Alt. Gen. Dir Pvt. Political Office of Prime Minister 1986–89; mem. Parl. for Athens B 1989–, First Vice-Pres. of Parl. 2000–04; Deputy Minister of Public Order 1993–94, Alt. Minister of Environment, Land Use and Public Works 1994–96, Minister of Public Order 1996, Minister of Health and Welfare 1996–98, Minister of State (attached to Prime Minister) 1998–2000; mem. Cen. Cttee PASOK (Panhellenic Socialist Movt). *Address:* Patision 14, 106 77 Athens, Greece (office). *Telephone:* (210) 3847530 (office). *Fax:* (210) 3818144 (office). *E-mail:* gitonas@parliament.gr (office); info@gitonas.gr. *Website:* www.gitonas.gr.

GIULIANI, Rudolph (Rudy) W., KBE, BA, JD; American lawyer, business executive and fmr politician; *Senior Partner, Bracewell & Giuliani LLP;* b. 28 May 1944, Brooklyn, NY; s. of the late Harold Giuliani and Helen Giuliani; m. 1st Regina Peruggi (divorced); m. 2nd Donna Hanover (divorced 2002); one s. one d.; m. 3rd Judith Nathan 2003; ed Manhattan Coll., New York Univ. School of Law; law clerk; judge; US Dist Court, New York City 1968–70; Asst US Attorney Southern Dist, New York; US Attorney 1983–89; with Patterson, Belknap, Webb and Tyler 1977–81; with White & Case 1989–90; with Anderson Kill Olick & Oshinsky 1990–93; Mayor of New York 1994–2001; f. Giuliani Partners LLC (with Ernst & Young) 2002, Chair. and CEO 2002–, f. Giuliani Advisors LLC (investment advisory firm) 2004 (acquired by Macquarie Group 2007); Chair. Bd of Advisors Leeds Weld and Co. 2002–; Sr Pnr, Bracewell & Giuliani LLP (law firm), New York 2005–; unsuccessful cand. for Republican nominiation for Pres. of US 2007–08; Time Magazine Person of the Year 2001. *Publications:* Leadership 2002. *Address:* Bracewell & Giuliani LLP, 1177 Avenue of the Americas, 19th Floor, New York, NY 10036-2714, USA (office). *Telephone:* (212) 508-6102 (office). *Fax:* (212) 938-3802 (office). *E-mail:* rudy.giuliani@bgllp.com (office). *Website:* www.bracewellgiuliani.com (office).

GIULIANO, Louis J., BA, MBA; American business executive; *Chairman of the Board of Governors, United States Postal Service;* ed Syracuse Univ.; served in numerous positions with Allied-Signal, including as Pres. Avionics Systems Group; joined ITT Corpn as Vice-Pres. of Corpn and Vice-Pres. of Defense Operations at ITT Defense 1988, later Pres. and CEO ITT Corpn; mem. Bd of Govs US Postal Service 2005–, Vice-Chair. 2009–10, Chair. 2010–, Chair. Operations Subcommittee, mem. Compensation and Man. Resources Cttee; mem. Bd of Dirs John Maneely Co.; Sr Advisor to The Carlyle Group; mem. CEO Forum, Advisory Bd Princeton Univ. Faith and Work Initiative. *Address:* United States Postal Service, 475 L'Enfant Plaza SW, Washington, DC 20260-0010, USA (office). *Telephone:* (202) 268-2500 (office). *Fax:* (202) 268-4860 (office). *E-mail:* pmgceo@ usps.gov (office). *Website:* www.usps.com (office).

GIURANNA, Bruno; Italian violist and conductor; *Viola Professor, Fondazione Stauffer, Cremona;* b. 6 April 1933, Milan; ed Coll. S. Giuseppe and Conservatorio di Musica Santa Cecilia, Rome and Conservatorio di Musica S. Pietro a Maiella, Naples; Founder-mem. I Musici 1951–61; Prof., Conservatorio G. Verdi, Milan 1961–65, Conservatorio S. Cecilia, Rome 1965–78, Accad. Chigiana, Siena 1966–83, Nordwest-deutsche Musikakademie, Detmold, Germany 1969–83, Hochschule der Künste, Berlin 1981–98, Fondazione Stauffer, Cremona 1985–, RAM, London 1994–96, Accad. S. Cecilia, Rome 1995–97; mem. Int. Music Competition jury, Munich 1961–62, 1967, 1969, Geneva 1968, Budapest 1975; soloist at concerts in festivals including Edinburgh and Holland Festivals, and with orchestras including Berlin Philharmonic, Amsterdam Concertgebouw and Teatro alla Scala, Milan; Artistic Dir Orchestra da Camera di Padova 1983–92; Academician of Santa Cecilia 1974; Pres. European String Teachers Asscn 2011; Cavaliere, Gran Croce della Repubblica Italiana 1987; Hon. DLit (Univ. of Limerick) 2003. *Address:* Via Bembo 96, 31011 Asolo, Treviso, Italy. *Telephone:* (0423) 55734. *Fax:* (0423) 529913. *E-mail:* brgiuranna@gmail.com. *Website:* www .giuranna.com.

GIURESCU, Dinu C., PhD; American historian, academic and museum curator; b. 15 Feb. 1927, Bucharest, Romania; s. of Constantin C. Giurescu and Maria S. Giurescu; m. Anca Elena Dinu 1960; two d.; ed Univ. of Bucharest; curator Bucharest Art Museum 1956–64; with Ministry of Foreign Affairs 1964–68; Prof. of European Civilization, Acad. of Fine Arts, Bucharest 1968–87; has lectured in Switzerland, France, Bulgaria, Hungary, FRG, Dallas (USA) 1977, Washington, DC 1980, Columbia Univ., Ind. Univ., Univ. of Ill., Univ. of Ariz., Univ. of Calif., Berkeley, Univ. of Kan., Univ. of Colo, Univ. of Ore., Univ. of Neb., Ohio Univ., Univ. of Rochester and Huntington Coll. 1982–85; Prof., Faculty of History, Univ. of Bucharest 1990–97 and currently; Pres. Nat. Comm. of Museums and Collections, Bucharest 1991–92, 1996–2000; Gen. Dir Museum of the Romanian Peasant 2001–05; Visiting Prof., William Paterson Coll., NJ 1988–89, Texas A&M Univ., USA 1989–90, Cen. European Univ., Hungary 1993; mem. Romanian Acad. 1990–; Prize of the Romanian Acad. 1973. *Publications:* Ion Vodă cel Viteaz 1966, History of the Romanians from Ancient Times Until Today (in Romanian) 1971 (with C. C. Giurescu), Wallachia in the 14th–15th Centuries (in Romanian) 1971, Istoria Românilor I-II, Din cele mai vechi timpuri pînă la finele sec. XVI (History of the Romanians I–II. From Ancient Times to the end of the XVI century) 1974–76 (with C. C. Giurescu), Illustrated History of the Romanian People (in Romanian, English, French, German, Russian, Spanish) 1981–82, The Razing of Romania's Past 1989, The Communist Takeover in Romania, I 1994, The Radescu Government (in Romanian) 1996, The Fall of the Iron Curtain: Romania (in Romanian) 1997, Romania in World War II (in Romanian) 1999 (in English) 2000, The Impossible Attempt. The Royal Strike (1945) (in Romanian) 1999, The "Elections" of November 1946 (in Romanian) 2001. *Leisure interests:* walking, visiting sites and museums, jazz music. *Address:* Department of History, University of Bucharest, Bdul Regina Elisabeta 4-12, Sector 5, 030018 Bucharest, Romania (office). *Telephone:* (21) 314-53-89 (office). *Fax:* (21) 310-06-80 (office). *Website:* www.unibuc.ro/n/facultati/istorie (office).

GIURGIU, Tudor, (Todor Giurgiu); Romanian film director and broadcasting executive; b. 1972, Cluj-Napoca; fmr Dir Transylvania Film Festival; Pres. and Dir-Gen. Televiziunea Română (TVR) 2005–07. *Films:* Vecini (Neighbours) (dir) 1993, E pericoloso sporgersi (aka Don't Lean Out the Window) (asst set designer) 1994, Prea târziu (aka Too Late (USA)) (first asst dir) 1996, The Midas Touch (first asst dir) 1997, The Shrunken City (video) (first asst dir) 1998, Train de vie (Train of Life) (casting: Romania) 1998, Clockmaker (video) (uncredited casting dir) 1998, Phantom Town (video) (casting: Romania) 1999, Tuvalu (casting: Bucharest; as Todor Giurgiu) 1999, Popcorn Story (dir and producer) 2001, Marele jaf comunist (aka Great Communist Bank Robbery) (producer) 2004, Legaturi bolnavicioase (aka Love Sick) (dir and producer) 2006, Agentul VIP (as himself, Episode 1.46) 2007. *Address:* c/o Televiziunea Română (TVR), PO Box 63-1200, Calea Dorobanților 191, 015089 Bucharest, Romania. *Telephone:* (21) 2312704.

GIVENCHY, Hubert de; French fashion designer; b. 21 Feb. 1927, Beauvais; s. of Lucien Taffin de Givenchy and Béatrice Badin; ed Coll. Félix-Faure, Beauvais, Ecole Nat. Supérieure des Beaux-Arts, Paris and Faculté de Droit, Univ. de Paris; apprentice, Paris fashion houses of Lucien Lelong 1945–46, Robert Piguet 1946–48, Jacques Fath 1948–49, Elsa Schiaparelli 1949–51; est. own fashion house in Parc Monceau, Paris 1952–56, in Avenue George V 1956–1988, sold business to Moet Hennessy-Louis Vuitton 1988; retd 1995; Pres.-Dir-Gen. Soc. Givenchy-Couture and Soc. des Parfums Givenchy, Paris 1954; Hon. Pres. Admin. Council Givenchy SA 1988–; Pres. Christie's France 1997–2000; mem. Int. Advisory Cttee Mona Bismarck Foundation; work included in Fashion: An Anthology, Victoria and Albert Museum, London 1971; costume designer for films Breakfast at Tiffany's 1961, Charade 1963, The VIPs 1963, Paris When It Sizzles 1964, How to Steal a Million 1966; Chevalier, Légion d'honneur; Designer of the Year Award, British Fashion Council 1987. *Leisure interests:* tennis, riding, skiing. *Address:* 3 Avenue George V, 75008 Paris, France (office). *Telephone:* 1-44-31-50-00 (office). *Fax:* 1-49-52-03-62 (office). *Website:* www.givenchy.com.

GIZENGA, Antoine, (Fundji); Democratic Republic of the Congo politician; *Secretary-General, Parti Lumumbiste Unifié (PALU);* b. 5 Oct. 1925, Mushiko, Bandundu; m.; one d.; Deputy Prime Minister 1960, 1961–62, Prime Minister 1960–61, 2006–08 (resgnd); Pres. and Head of State, in rebellion, at Stanleyville after death of Patrice Lumumba March–Aug. 1961; imprisoned 1962–64, Oct. 1964–65; exiled in fmr USSR, France, Angola, Congo-Brazzaville (now Repub. of the Congo) 1965–92; Sec.-Gen. Parti Lumumbiste Unifié (PALU) 1992–; unsuccessful cand. in presidential elections 2006; Order of the National Heroes 2009. *Publication:* Mon témoignage – Ma vie et mes luttes. *Leisure interests:* music, football, reading. *Address:* Parti Lumumbiste Unifié (PALU), 9 rue Cannas, C/ Limete, Kinshasa, Democratic Republic of the Congo (office).

GJEDREM, Svein, MA; Norwegian fmr central banker; b. 25 Jan. 1950; ed Univ. of Oslo; Exec. Officer, Norges Bank (Cen. Bank of Norway) 1975–79, Gov. 1999–2010; Head, Div. for Banking and Monetary Affairs, Ministry of Finance and Customs 1979–82, Deputy Dir 1982–86, Dir.-Gen. Head of Econ. Policy Dept 1986–95, Sec.-Gen. 1996–98; Administrative Leader, Ministry of Finance 2011–; visiting engagement, EU Comm., Brussels 1994–95; currently lecturer, Norwegian School of Econs and Business Admin. *Address:* Ministry of Finance, PO Box 8008, Dep, 0030, Oslo, Norway (office). *Telephone:* 22-24-41-08 (office). *Fax:* 22-24-95-14 (office). *E-mail:* Svein.Gjedrem@fin.dep.no (office). *Website:* www.regjeringen.no (office).

GJINUSHI, Skënder; Albanian politician; *Chairman, Social Democratic Party of Albania;* b. 24 Dec. 1949, Vlorë; ed Univ. of Tirana; fmr univ. lecturer in science; mem. Kuvendi Popullor (People's Ass.) 1992–; fmr Minister of Educ.; Speaker of Parl. 1997–2001; apptd Deputy Prime Minister and Minister of Labour and Social Affairs 2002; Chair. Social Democratic Party of Albania. *Address:* Social Democratic Party of Albania, Rruga Asim Vokshi 26, Tirana, Albania (office). *Telephone:* (4) 226540 (office). *Fax:* (4) 227485 (office). *E-mail:* info@psd-al.org (home). *Website:* www.psd-al.org (office).

GJOSHA, Klajda, BA, MA; Albanian politician; *Minister of European Integration;* b. 28 July 1983, Tirana; m. Ardian Gjoni; ed Strode Coll. and Univ. of Reading, UK; held various offices in insts including Tirana Municipality, Tirana Regional Employment Directorate and Nat. Tourism Agency; Deputy Chair. Socialist Movt Integration (SMI) and mem. Chairmanship 2012–, also Chair. SMI Women Forum; has attended training courses and internships in various orgs, including Japanese Int. Co-operation Agency, European Parl. at office of Ms Doris Pack, Brussels; Deputy Minister of Labour, Social Affairs and Equal Opportunities 2012–13; Minister of European Integration 2013–. *Address:* Ministry of European Integration, Rruga Papa Gjon Pali II 3, PO Box 832, Tirana, Albania (office). *Telephone:* (4) 2228358 (office). *Fax:* (4) 2256267 (office). *E-mail:* klajda.gjosha@mie.gov.al (office). *Website:* www.integrimi.gov.al (office).

GLADDEN, Lynn Faith, CBE, OBE, BSc, PhD, FRS, FREng; British chemical engineer and academic; *Shell Professor of Chemical Engineering Science and Head of Department of Chemical Engineering and Biotechnology, University of Cambridge;* ed Univs of Bristol and Cambridge; currently Shell Prof. of Chemical Eng and Head of Dept of Chemical Eng and Biotechnology, Univ. of Cambridge, Lead Researcher at Magnetic Resonance Research Centre, Fellow, Trinity Coll. 1999–; Miller Visiting Prof., Univ. of California, Berkeley, USA 1996; Beilby Medal, Univ. of Cambridge 1995, Tilden Lectureship and Silver Medal, Royal Soc. of Chem. 2000. *Publications:* numerous papers in professional journals on multi-component adsorption, diffusion and flow processes. *Address:* Department of Chemical Engineering and Biotechnology, University of Cambridge, New Museums Site, Pembroke Street, Cambridge, CB2 3RA, England (office). *Telephone:* (1223) 334762 (office). *E-mail:* lfg1@cam.ac.uk (office). *Website:* www.cheng.cam.ac.uk/people/gladden.html (office).

GLADILIN, Anatoliy Tikhonovich; Russian writer; b. 21 Aug. 1935, Moscow; s. of Tikhon Illarionovich Gladilin and Polina Moïseevna Dreizer; m. Maria Gladilina 1955; two d.; ed Gorky Literary Inst., Moscow; literary activity started 1956; one of

main contribs (with V. Aksyonov, to Katayev's journal Youth 1956–65; one of founders of 'Youth Prose' movt in early 1960s; signed letter of 80 writers in support of Solzhenitsyn's letter on abolition of censorship 1967; left USSR, expelled from Union of Writers 1976 (readmitted 1998); settled in France. *Publications include:* Chronicle of the Times of Viktor Podgursky 1956, The Gospel from Robespierre 1970, Prognosis for Tomorrow 1972, The Dreams of Shlisselburg Fortress 1974, The Making and Unmaking of a Soviet Writer 1979, The Paris Fair 1980, A Big Race Day 1983, F.S.S.R. The French Soviet Socialist Republic Story 1985, As I Was Then: Tales 1986, The Beast Pell Killed Me 1991, 2001, A Rider's Shadow 2000, The Big Racing Day: Novels 2001. *Address:* 11 Château Gaillard, Maisons Alfort, 94700 Paris, France (home). *Telephone:* 1-43-96-21-99 (home).

GLADSTONE, Barbara; American gallery owner, art dealer and film producer; *Owner and Director, Gladstone Gallery;* b. (Barbara Levitt), m. Elliot B. Regen (deceased); three s. (one deceased); first opened in SoHo, New York in 1979, Owner and Dir Gladstone Gallery, represents many contemporary artists, including filmmaker Shirin Neshat, photographer and installation artist Sarah Lucas and sculptor and filmmaker Matthew Barney, also Allora & Calzadilla, Ahmed Alsoudani, Kai Althoff, Miroslaw Balka, Robert Bechtle, Alighiero Boetti, Jan Dibbets, Carroll Dunham, Cecilia Edefalk, Roe Ethridge, Cyprien Gaillard, Keith Haring, Gary Hill, Thomas Hirschhorn, Jim Hodges, Huang Yong Ping, Cameron Jamie, Anish Kapoor, Sol Lewitt, Sharon Lockhart, Andrew Lord, Victor Man, Fausto Melotti, Mario Merz, Marisa Merz, Dave Muller, Wangechi Mutu, Jean-Luc Mylayne, Shirin Neshat, Damián Ortega, Elizabeth Peyton, Walter Pichler, Lari Pittman, Magnus Plessen, R. H. Quaytman, Ugo Rondinone, Gedi Sibony, Jack Smith Archive, Rosemarie Trockel, Paloma Varga Weisz, Andro Wekua. *Films include:* producer; Cremaster 1 1996, Cremaster 5 1997, Cremaster 2 1999, Cremaster 3 2002, Drawing Restraint 9 (exec. producer) 2005, De Lama Lamina 2007, Women Without Men (exec. producer) 2009; appears in Drawing Restraint 13, a later film by Barney. *Address:* Gladstone Gallery, 515 West 24th Street, New York, NY 10011, USA (office). *Telephone:* (212) 206-9300 (office). *Fax:* (212) 206-9301 (office). *E-mail:* info@gladstonegallery.com (office). *Website:* www .gladstonegallery.com (office).

GLADYSZ, John A., BS, PhD, FRSC; American chemist and academic; *Distinguished Professor of Chemistry and Dow Chair in Chemical Invention, Texas A&M University;* b. 13 Aug. 1952, Kalamazoo, Mich.; s. of Edward Matthew and Margean Alice Gladysz (née Worst); m. Janet Bluemel 1997; ed Western Michigan Univ., Univ. of Michigan, Stanford Univ., Calif.; Asst Prof., UCLA 1974–82; Assoc. Prof., Univ. of Utah 1982–85, Prof. 1985–88, Adjunct Prof. of Chem. 1999–; Prof. Ordinarius and Chair., Organic Chem., Friedrich-Alexander-Universität Erlangen-Nurnberg, Germany 1998–; Distinguished Prof. of Chem. and Dow Chair. in Chemical Invention, Texas A&M Univ. 2008–; Visiting Assoc. in Chem., California Inst. of Tech. 1989; consultant or fmr consultant to several cos and corpns, including Gas Research Inst., Chicago, G.D. Searle & Co., Chicago, Procter & Gamble Co., Monsanto Corpn, Union Camp Corpn, Exxon Research and Eng, Kimberly Clark Corpn, 3M Corpn, Rhodia (Rhône-Poulenc) Corpn, Lyons, France, Total/Fina/Elf, Paris, France; mem. Editorial Bd Organometallics 1990–92, Ed.-in-Chief 2010–; mem. Editorial Bd Organometallics 1990–92 (Ed. in Chief 2010–), New Journal of Chemistry 2000–; Assoc. Ed. Chemical Reviews 1984–2010; mem. ACS 1970, The Chemical Soc. 1974, AAAS 1975 (Fellow 2004), German Chemical Soc. 1997–; Alfred P. Sloan Foundation Fellow 1980–84, Camille and Henry Dreyfus Scholar and Grantee 1980–85, Arthur C. Cope Scholar 1988, Univ. of Utah Distinguished Research Award 1992, Humboldt Award 1994, ACS Award in Organometallic Chemistry 1994, Int. Fluorous Technologies Award 2007, Texas A&M Distinguished Achievement Award in Research 2013, RSC Award in Organometallic Chemistry 2013. *Address:* Department of Chemistry, Texas A&M University, 318 Reed McDonald Building, 580 Ross Street, College Station, TX 77843, USA (office). *Telephone:* (979) 845-1399 (office). *Fax:* (979) 845-5629 (office). *E-mail:* gladys2@mail.chem.tamu.edu (office). *Website:* www.chem.tamu .edu/rgroup/gladysz (office).

GLAMANN, Kristof, DrPhil; Danish business executive, historian, professor of history and writer; b. 26 Aug. 1923, Kerteminde; s. of Kai Kristof Glamann and Ebba H. K. Glamann (née Madsen); m. Kirsten Jantzen 1954; two s.; ed Univ. of Copenhagen; Assoc. Prof. of History, Univ. of Copenhagen 1948–60, Prof. of Econ. History 1961–80; Visiting Prof., Univ. of Pennsylvania 1960, Univ. of Wisconsin 1961, Visiting Northern Scholar, LSE 1966, Visiting Overseas Fellow, Churchill Coll., Univ. of Cambridge 1971–72, 1994, Visiting Fellow, Toho Gakkai, Tokyo 1977; Master, 4th May and Hassager Coll., Copenhagen; mem. and Chair. Danish Research Council on Humanities 1968–70; Ed.-in-Chief Scandinavian Econ. History Review 1961–80; mem. Bd of Dirs Carlsberg Foundation 1969–93 (Pres. 1976–93), Carlsberg Ltd 1970–94 (Deputy Chair. 1975–77, Chair. 1977–93), Carlsberg Brewery Ltd 1978–94, Royal Copenhagen Ltd 1978–93, Fredericia Brewery 1979–94, Politiken Foundation 1990; Chair. Council, Investor and Reinvest Ltd; Deputy Chair. The Scandinavia-Japan Sasakawa Foundation 1985–2005; mem. Royal Danish Acad. of Science and Letters 1969, Royal Danish History Soc. 1961, Swedish Acad., Lund 1963, History Soc. of Calcutta 1962; Corresp. mem. Royal History Soc. 1972; Corresp. Fellow, Royal Belgian Acad. 1989; Hon. Pres. Int. Econ. History Asscn 1974, Hon. FBA 1985; Commdr, Order of Dannebrog (First Class), Commdr, Falcon of Iceland 1987, Das Grosse Verdienstkreuz (Germany) 1989, Order of Gorkha Dakshina Bahu (3rd Class) (Nepal) 1989, Hon. OBE; Hon. DScS (Gothenburg) 1974; Erasmus Medal, Academia Europaea 2000. *Publications include:* History of Tobacco Industry in Denmark 1875–1950 1950, Prices and Wages 1500–1800 1958, Dutch-Asiatic Trade 1620–1740 1958, Beer and Brewing 1962, 2005, European Trade 1500–1750 1971, Carlsberg Foundation (in Danish) 1976, contributed to the Cambridge Economic History of Europe (Vol. V) 1977, Mercantilism 1982, Festschrift 1983, 1993, J. C. Jacobsen of Carlsberg: A Biography 1990, Beer and Marble: A Biography of Carl Jacobsen 1995, The Carlsberg Group Since 1970 1997, Time-Out 1998, Memoirs 2002, The Carlsberg Foundation 1876–1976 2003, The Scandinavian Pasteür 2004. *Leisure interests:* walking and drawing. *Address:* Hoeghsmindeparken 10, 2900 Hellerup, Denmark (home). *Telephone:* 39-40-39-77 (home). *E-mail:* k.glamann@mail.dk.

GLANVILLE, Brian Lester; British writer and journalist; b. 24 Sept. 1931, London; s. of James A. Glanville and Florence Manches; m. Elizabeth De Boer

1959; two s. two d.; ed Charterhouse School; first sports columnist and football corresp., Sunday Times 1958–92; sports columnist, The People 1992–96, football writer, The Times 1996–98, Sunday Times 1998–; literary adviser, Bodley Head 1958–62. *Plays for radio:* The Rise of Gerry Logan, The Diary, I Could Have Been King, A Visit to the Villa. *Television:* original writer of That Was The Week That Was 1962; wrote BBC documentary European Centre Forward (winner Silver Bear Award, Berlin Film Festival) 1963. *Publications:* novels: Along the Arno 1956, The Bankrupts 1958, Diamond 1962, The Rise of Gerry Logan 1963, A Second Home 1965, A Roman Marriage 1966, The Artist Type 1967, The Olympian 1969, A Cry of Crickets 1970, The Comic 1974, The Dying of the Light 1976, The Catacomb 1988, Dictators 2001; sport: Soccer Nemesis 1955, Champions of Europe 1991, Story of the World Cup 1993, The Arsenal Stadium History 2006, England Managers: The Toughest Job in Football 2007, For Club and Country (Obits) 2008, The Real Arsenal 2009; short stories: A Bad Streak 1961, The Director's Wife 1963, The King of Hackney Marshes 1965, The Thing He Loves 1985, Love Is Not Love; plays: A Visit to the Villa 1981, Underneath the Arches (musical, co-author) 1982, The Diary (radio play) 1986; other: Football Memories (autobiog.) 1999. *Address:* 160 Holland Park Avenue, London, W11 4UH, England (home). *Telephone:* (20) 7603-6908 (home). *E-mail:* grandpam21@aol.com (home).

GLASENBERG, Ivan, BAcc, MBA; South African chartered accountant and business executive; *CEO, Glencore Xstrata plc;* ed Univ. of the Witwatersrand, Univ. of Southern California, USA; worked at Levitt Kirson Chartered Accountants 1979–84; joined Glencore International plc 1984, worked in coal/coke commodity dept in SA as a marketer 1984–87, head of Asian coal/coke commodity div., Australia 1987–88, Man. and Head of Glencore's Hong Kong and Beijing offices and Head of Coal Marketing in Asia 1988–89, Head of worldwide coal business for both marketing and industrial assets 1990–2002, CEO Glencore International plc (merged with Xstrata plc to form Glencore Xstrata plc May 2013) 2002–; mem. Bd of Dirs United Co. Rusal plc, JSC Zarubezhneft. *Address:* Glencore Xstrata plc, Baarermattstrasse 3, 6340 Baar, Switzerland (office). *Telephone:* (41) 7092000 (office). *Fax:* (41) 7093000 (office). *E-mail:* info@glencorexstrata.com (office). *Website:* www.glencorexstrata.com (office).

GLASER, Robert (Rob) Denis, BA, BS; American software industry executive; *Founding Chairman and CEO, RealNetworks Inc.;* b. 16 Jan. 1962, New York City; ed Yale Univ.; joined Microsoft Corpn 1983, head of multimedia tech. and consumer digital appliances, Vice-Pres. Multimedia and Consumer Systems, –1994; Founding Chair. and CEO RealNetworks Inc. (internet software co.) 1994–, cr. RealAudio 1995, RealVideo and RealPlayer; co-owner Seattle Mariners professional baseball team; Founding Chair. Atrium Group, US Library of Congress; apptd to Advisory Cttee on Public Interest Obligations of Digital TV Broadcaster by Pres. Bill Clinton; mem. Bd of Dirs Electronic Frontier Foundation, Wash. Public Affairs Network, Foundation for Nat. Congress, Target Margin Theater Co. of NY, Dwight Hall (Yale Univ. Student Community Service), TVW 1994–. *Address:* RealNetworks Inc., 2601 Elliott Avenue, Suite 1000, Seattle, WA 98121, USA (office). *Telephone:* (206) 674-2700 (office). *Fax:* (206) 674-2699 (office). *Website:* www.realnetworks.com (office).

GLASHOW, Sheldon Lee, PhD, FAAS; American physicist and academic; *Arthur G. B. Metcalf Professor, Physics Department, Boston University;* b. 5 Dec. 1932, New York; s. of Lewis Glashow and Bella Rubin; m. Joan Shirley Alexander 1972; three s. one d.; ed Bronx High School of Science, Cornell and Harvard Univs; NSF Post-Doctoral Fellow, Univ. of Copenhagen 1958–60; Research Fellow, Calif. Inst. of Tech. 1960–61; Asst Prof., Stanford Univ. 1961–62; Assoc. Prof., Univ. of Calif., Berkeley 1962–66; Prof. of Physics, Harvard Univ. 1967–84, Higgins Prof. 1979–2000, Mellon Prof. of Sciences 1988–93, Prof. Emer. 2000–; Visiting Prof., Boston Univ. 1983–84, Distinguished Visiting Scientist 1984–2000, Arthur G. B. Metcalf Prof. 2000–; Alfred P. Sloan Foundation Fellowship 1962–66; Visiting Scientist, CERN 1968; Visiting Prof., Univ. of Marseille 1970, MIT 1974, 1980–81; Consultant, Brookhaven Lab. 1966–73, 1975–; Affiliated Sr Scientist, Univ. of Houston 1983–96; Univ. Scholar, Texas A&M Univ. 1983–86, Einstein Prof., Chinese Acad. of Science 2003–; Fellow, American Physical Soc.; Pres. Int. Sakharov Cttee 1980–85; mem. American Acad. of Arts and Sciences, NAS, American Philosophical Soc.; Sponsor, Fed. of American Scientists (FAS) and Bulletin of the Atomic Scientists; mem. Advisory Council American Acad. of Achievement 1979–, Science Policy Cttee, CERN 1979–84; Founding Ed. Quantum (magazine) 1989–2000; Hon. Prof., Univ. of Nanjing 1998–; Dr hc (Univ. of Aix-Marseille) 1982; Hon. DSc (Yeshiva Univ.) 1978, (Bar Ilan Univ., Gustavus Adolphus Coll., Adelphi Univ.) 1989, (Case Western Reserve Univ.) 1995, (Bologna) 2005; Oppenheimer Memorial Medal 1977, George Ledlie Award 1978; shared Nobel Prize for Physics with Abdus Salam and Steven Weinberg (q.v.) for work on elementary particles 1979. *Publications:* Interactions (with Ben Bova) 1989, Charm of Physics 1990, From Alchemy to Quarks 1994; over 200 articles on elementary particle physics. *Address:* Department of Physics, Boston University, 590 Commonwealth Avenue, Boston, MA 02215 (office); 30 Prescott Street, Brookline, MA 02446, USA (home). *Telephone:* (617) 353-9099 (office). *E-mail:* slg@bu.edu (office). *Website:* buphy.bu.edu (office).

GLASMAN, Baron (Life Peer), cr. 2011, of Stoke Newington and of Stamford Hill in the London Borough of Hackney; **Maurice Glasman,** MA, PhD; British political scientist and academic; *Senior Lecturer in Political Theory, London Metropolitan University;* b. Walthamstow, London; ed JFS Comprehensive School, Univs of Cambridge and York, European Univ. Inst., Florence, Italy; Dir Faith and Citizenship Programme and Sr Lecturer in Political Theory, London Metropolitan Univ.; has worked with London Citizens; three-year Arts and Humanities Research Council Grant to study religion and politics in London (in partnership with Dr Luke Bretherton, King's Coll. London). *Publications include:* Unnecessary Suffering 1996. *Address:* Room CS3-13, Department of Governance and International Relations, London Metropolitan University, 16 Goulston Street, London, E1 7TP (office); House of Lords, Westminster, London, SW1A 0PW, England. *Telephone:* (20) 7320-2203 (office); (20) 7219-5353. *Fax:* (20) 7320-1157 (office); (20) 7219-5979. *E-mail:* m.glasman@londonmet.ac.uk (office). *Website:* www.londonmet.ac.uk/depts/lgir/gir (office).

GLASS, David D., BA; American retail executive; b. 1935, Liberty, Mo.; s. of Marvin Glass and Myrtle Van Winkle; m. Ruth Glass; three c.; ed SW Missouri State Univ.; Gen. Man. Crank Drug Co. 1957–67; Vice-Pres. Consumers Markets

Inc. 1967–76; Exec. Vice-Pres. Wal-Mart Stores Inc. –1976, Chief Financial Officer 1976–84, Pres. 1984–2000, COO 1984–88, CEO 1988–2000, Chair. Exec. Comm. 2000–06, also Dir; CEO and Chair. Kansas City Royals professional baseball team 1993–; mem. Bd of Dirs Nat. Baseball Hall of Fame and Museum 2000–. *Address:* Kansas City Royals, PO Box 419969, Kansas City, MO 64141, USA (office). *Website:* www.kcroyals.com (office).

GLASS, Philip; American composer; b. 31 Jan. 1937, Baltimore, Md; s. of Benjamin Glass and Ida Glass (née Gouline); m. 1st JoAnne Akalaitis (divorced); m. 2nd Luba Burtyk (divorced); one s. one d.; m. 3rd Candy Jernigan (died 1991); m. 4th Holly Critchlow 2001; two s. one d.; ed Peabody Conservatory, Baltimore, Univ. of Chicago and Juilliard School of Music; Composer-in-Residence, Pittsburgh Public Schools 1962–64; studied with Nadia Boulanger, Paris 1964–66; f. Philip Glass Ensemble 1968–, concert tours USA and Europe; f. record co. Chatham Square Productions, New York 1972, Dunvagen Music Publrs, Orange Mountain Music record co. 2002; mem. ASCAP; BMI Award 1960, Lado Prize 1961, Benjamin Award 1961, 1962, Ford Foundation Young Composer's Award 1964–66, Fulbright Award 1966–67, Musical America Magazine Musician of the Year 1985, New York Dance and Performance Award 1995, Nat. Endowment for the Arts Opera Honor 2010. *Film scores include:* North Star 1977, Koyaanisqatsi 1983, Mishima 1985, Powaqqatsi 1987, The Thin Blue Line 1988, Hamburger Hill 1989, Mindwalk 1990, A Brief History of Time 1991, Anima Mundi 1991, Candyman 1992, The Voyage 1992, Orphée 1993, Candyman II: Farewell to the Flesh 1994, Monsters of Grace 1998, Bent 1998, Kundun 1998, The Hours (BAFTA Anthony Asquith Award 2003, Classical BRIT Award for Contemporary Music 2004) 2002, Cassandra's Dream 2007, Mr Nice 2010, They Were There 2011. *Compositions include:* String Quartets (1–4), Violin Concerto, Low Symphony, The Palace of the Arabian Nights, Einstein on the Beach 1976, Madrigal Opera: The Panther 1980, Satyagraha 1980, The Photographer 1982, The Civil Wars: A Tree Is Best Measured When It Is Down 1983, Akhnaten 1983, The Juniper Tree 1985, A Descent Into The Maelstrom 1986, In The Upper Room 1986, Violin Concerto 1987, The Light for Orchestra 1987, The Making of the Representative for Planet 8 1988, The Fall of The House Of Usher 1988, 1,000 Airplanes on the Roof (with David Henry Hwang) 1988, Mattogrosso 1989, Hydrogen Jukebox (with Allen Ginsberg) 1989, The White Raven 1991, Orphée, chamber opera after Cocteau 1993, La belle et la bête, after Cocteau 1994, Witches of Venice (ballet) 1995, Les enfants terrible (dance opera) 1996, The Marriages Between Zones Three, Four and Five 1997, Symphony No. 5 1999, Symphony No. 6 (Plutonian Ode) 2000, In the Penal Colony (theatre) 2000, Tirol Concerto, piano and orchestra 2000, Concerto Fantasy for two timpanists and orchestra 2000, Voices for Organ, Didgeridoo and Narrator 2001, Concerto for Cello and Orchestra 2001, Danassimo 2001, The Man in the Bath 2001, Passage 2001, Diaspora 2001, Notes 2001, Galileo Galilei (opera) 2002, Waiting for the Barbarians (opera) 2005, Appomattox (opera) 2007, The American Four Seasons 2010. *Publications:* Music by Philip Glass 1987, Opera on the Beach 1988. *Address:* Dunvagen Music, 632 Broadway, Suite 902, New York, NY 10012, USA (office). *Telephone:* (212) 979-2080 (office). *Fax:* (212) 473-2842 (office). *E-mail:* info@dunvagen.com (office). *Website:* www.philipglass.com (office).

GLASSCOCK, Larry Claborn, BA; American insurance executive; b. 4 April 1948, Cullman, Ala; m. Lee Ann Roden 1969; one s. one d.; ed Cleveland State Univ., Commercial Bank Man. Program, Columbia Univ., New York, School of Int. Banking, participated in American Bankers Asscn Conf. of Exec. Officers; served in US Marine Corps 1970–76; Vice-Pres. of Personnel, AmeriTrust Corpn, Cleveland, OH 1974–75, Vice-Pres. Nat. Div. 1976–78, Vice-Pres. and Man. Credit Card Center 1978–79, Sr Vice-Pres. Consumer Finance 1980–81, Sr Vice-Pres. Nat. Div. 1981–83, Exec. Vice-Pres. Corp. Banking Admin 1983–87, Group Exec. Vice-Pres. AmeriTrust Corpn and AmeriTrust Co. 1987–92; fmr Pres. and CEO Essex Holdings, Inc.; fmr Pres. and COO First American Bank; Pres. and CEO Blue Cross and Blue Shield, Nat. Capital Area 1993–98; COO CareFirst, Inc. Jan.–April 1998; Sr Exec. Vice-Pres. and COO Anthem Insurance (renamed Wellpoint, Inc. following merger with WellPoint Health Networks 2004) 1998–99, Pres. and CEO 1999–2007, Chair. 2005–10; mem. Bd Dirs Sprint Corpn (fmrly Sprint Nextel Corpn) 2007–13, Zimmer Holdings, Inc., BCS Financial Services Corpn, Blue Cross and Blue Shield Asscn, Council for Affordable Quality Healthcare (Chair. 2002–03), Nat. Inst. for Health Care Man., Cen. Indiana Corp. Partnership, United Way of Cen. Indiana, Greater Indianapolis Progress Cttee; fmr Pres. Cleveland State Univ. Alumni Asscn; Indiana Ernst & Young Entrepreneur of the Year Award (jtly) 2003. *Address:* c/o Wellpoint, Inc., 120 Monument Circle, Indianapolis, IN 46204, USA. *E-mail:* info@wellpoint.com.

GLATZ, Ferenc, PhD; Hungarian historian; *Director, Institute of History, Hungarian Academy of Sciences;* b. 2 April 1941, Csepel; m. Katalin; one s., one d.; ed Eötvös Loránd Univ.; Research Fellow, Inst. of History of Hungarian Acad. of Sciences 1968–, Scientific Deputy Dir 1986–88, Dir of Inst. 1988–; Corresp. mem. Hungarian Acad. of Sciences 1993, full mem. 2000, Pres. 1996–2002; Pres. Scientific Council, Teleki László Foundation 1990–98; Prof., Eötvös Loránd Univ., Budapest 1974–; Minister for Culture and Educ. 1989–90; Organizer and Dir Europa Inst., Budapest 1990–; mem. Bd of Dirs Holy Crown 1999–2002; Grand Cross of Honour 2003 (Germany), Grand Cross of Honour (Hungary) 2004; Szèchenyi Prize 1995, Herder Prize 1997, Presidential Silver Medal (Italy) 2003. *Publications:* numerous studies and books on 19th- and 20th-century history of Hungarian and European culture and historiography, including Hungarians and Their Neighbors in Modern Times 1867–1950 (ed.) 1995. *Leisure interests:* tennis, gardening. *Address:* Institute of History, Hungarian Academy of Sciences, Uri Utca 53, 1014 Budapest (office); Magyar Tudományos Akadémia, 1051 Budapest, Roosevelt tér. 9, Hungary. *Telephone:* (1) 2246750 (office). *Fax:* (1) 2246756 (office). *E-mail:* titkarsag@tti.hu (office). *Website:* www.tti.hu (office).

GLAUBER, Robert R., BA, PhD; American economist, academic, business executive and fmr government official; *Senior Advisor, Peter J. Solomon Company;* b. 22 March 1939, New York City; m.; two c.; ed Harvard Univ.; Lecturer, Harvard Business School 1964–65, Asst Prof. of Finance 1965–68, Assoc. Prof. of Finance 1968–72, Prof. of Finance 1972–2000, Lecturer, John F. Kennedy School of Govt 1992–2000; Under-Sec. for Finance, US Treasury Dept, Washington, DC 1989–92; Exec. Dir Pres. Reagan's Task Force on Market Mechanisms ('Brady Commission') 1987–88, consultant to Bush Admin. 1989; Prof., Nat. Asscn of Securities Dealers 2000–01, CEO 2000–06, Chair. 2001–06; Sr Advisor, Peter J. Solomon (investment bank), New York 2006–; Chair. XL Group PLC 1998–; mem. Bd of Dirs Moody's Corpn 1998–, XL Capital Ltd, Freddie Mac 2006–11 (interim Chair. 2009–11), Fed. Reserve Bank of Boston, Investment Co. Inst., Dreyfus Municipal Income Inc. 1988–2000, 2006–, Ocean Reinsurance Ltd, Circuit City Stores, Inc., Quadra Realty Trust Inc. 2007–; mem. Council on Foreign Relations, Boston Cttee on Foreign Relations, Cttee on Capital Markets Regulation, Int. Advisory Bd Korean Financial Supervisory Service; fmr Pres. Boston Econ. Club; Trustee, Int. Accounting Standards Cttee Foundation. *Address:* Peter J. Solomon Company, 520 Madison Avenue, New York, NY 10022, USA; XL Group PLC, 1 Hatch Street Upper, Dublin 2, Ireland (office). *Telephone:* (212) 508-1600 (New York). *Fax:* (212) 508-1633 (New York). *E-mail:* rglauber@pjsolomon.com. *Website:* www.pjsolomon.com; www.xlgroup.com (office).

GLAUBER, Roy J., BS, MA, PhD; American physicist and academic; *Mallinckrodt Professor of Physics, Harvard University;* b. 1 Sept. 1925, New York City; s. of Emanuel Glauber and Felicia Fox; ed Bronx High School of Science, Harvard Univ.; research areas include quantum optics; fmr mem. staff Manhattan Project; Mallinckrodt Prof. of Physics, Harvard Univ. 1976–; Adjunct Prof. of Optical Sciences, Univ. of Ariz.; fmr Visiting Scientist, Visiting Prof., CERN, Univ. of Leiden, NORDITA Copenhagen, Collège de France; mem. Advisory Bd Program for Science and Tech. for Int. Security, MIT; hon. degrees (Essen, Erlangen, Arizona); Franklin Inst. A.A. Michelson Medal 1985, American Optical Soc. Max Born Award 1985, A. von Humboldt Research Award 1989, American Physical Soc. Dannie Heineman Prize 1996, Nobel Prize in Physics (co-recipient) 2005, W.E. Lamb Medal 2006. *Publications:* numerous articles and book chapters. *Leisure interest:* gardening. *Address:* Lyman 331, 17 Oxford Street, Cambridge, MA 02138, USA (office). *Telephone:* (617) 495-2869 (office). *Fax:* (617) 495-0416 (office). *E-mail:* glauber@physics.harvard.edu (office). *Website:* www.physics.harvard.edu/people/facpages/glauber.html (office).

GLAVIN, William F., BA, MBA; American business executive and academic administrator; *President Emeritus, Babson College;* b. 29 March 1932, Albany, NY; s. of John Glavin; m. Cecily McClatchy 1955; three s. four d.; ed Coll. of the Holy Cross, Worcester and Wharton Graduate School Univ. of Pennsylvania; fmr Exec. Int. Business Machines and Vice-Pres. Operations, Service Bureau Corpn (an IBM subsidiary); Exec. Vice-Pres. Xerox Data Systems 1970, Group Vice-Pres. 1972, Man. Dir and COO 1974, Exec. Vice-Pres. Xerox 1980, Exec. Vice-Pres. for Reprographics and Operations 1982, Pres. Business Equipment Group 1983–89, Vice-Chair. Xerox Corpn 1985–89; Pres. Babson Coll., Wellesley, Mass. 1989–97, now Pres. Emer.; mem. Bd of Dirs Gould Inc., State Street Boston Corpn, Norton Co.; mem. Bd of Trustees and Pres.'s Council Coll. of the Holy Cross; Trustee Emer., Franklin W. Olin Coll. of Engineering; Dr hc (College of the Holy Cross), (Babson College); Distinguished Alumni Award, Univ. of Pennsylvania. *Leisure interests:* golf, reading, art, music.

GLAZER, Malcolm; American business executive; *President and CEO, First Allied Corporation;* b. 25 May 1928, Rochester, NY; m. Linda Glazer; six c.; head of family watch parts co. 1943; business interests include real estate, broadcasting, food services equipment, health care and banking; Pres. and CEO First Allied Corpn 1984–; Dir Specialty Equipment Cos Inc., Omega Protein Corpn; Dir Zapata 1993, Chair. Pres. and CEO 1994–95; Owner, Tampa Bay Buccaneers (Nat. Football League American football team) 1995–; Manchester United football team 2005–; Founder and Pres. Glazer Family Foundation 1999–. *Address:* First Allied Corporation, 270 Commerce Drive, Rochester, NY 14623-3506 (office); Tampa Bay Buccaneers, One Buccaneer Place, Tampa, FL 33607, USA (office); Manchester United PLC, Sir Matt Busby Way, Old Trafford, Manchester M16 0RA, England (office). *Website:* www.buccaneers.com; www.glazerfamilyfoundation.com (office); www.manutd.com (office).

GLAZER, Nathan, PhD; American academic; *Professor Emeritus, Graduate School of Education, Harvard University;* b. 25 Feb. 1923, New York; s. of Louis Glazer and Tillie Glazer (née Zacharevich); m. 1st Ruth Slotkin 1943 (divorced 1958); three d.; m. 2nd Sulochana Raghavan 1962; ed City Coll. of New York, Univ. of Pennsylvania and Columbia Univ; mem. of staff, Commentary Magazine 1944–53; Ed. and Editorial Adviser, Doubleday Anchor Books 1954–57; Visiting Lecturer, Univ. of Calif., Berkeley 1957–58; Instructor, Bennington Coll., Vermont 1958–59; Visiting Lecturer, Smith Coll. 1959–60; lived and studied Japan 1961–62; Prof. of Sociology, Univ. of Calif., Berkeley 1963–69; Prof. of Educ. and Sociology, Harvard Univ. 1969–93, now Prof. Emer.; Fellow, Center for Advanced Study in the Behavioural Sciences, Stanford, Calif. 1971–72; Co-Ed. The Public Interest Magazine 1973–2002, now Sr Editorial Assoc.; Contributing Ed. The New Republic; mem. American Acad. of Arts and Sciences, Library of Congress Council of Scholars; Guggenheim Fellow 1954, 1966; Hon. LLD (Franklin and Marshall Coll.) 1971, (Colby Coll.) 1972; Hon. DHL (Long Island Univ.) 1978, (Hebrew Union Coll.) 1986. *Publications:* American Judaism 1957, 1972, The Social Basis of American Communism 1961, Remembering the Answers 1970, Affirmative Discrimination 1976, Ethnic Dilemmas 1964–1982 1983, The Limits of Social Policy 1989, From as Cause to a Style: Modernist Architecture's Encounter with the American City 2007; co-author: The Lonely Crowd 1950, Faces in the Crowd 1952, Studies in Housing and Minority Groups 1960, Beyond the Melting Pot 1963, Conflicting Images, India and the United States 1990, We Are All Multiculturalists Now 1997, Sovereignty under Challenge: How Governments Respond (co-ed.) 2002. *Address:* Graduate School of Education, Harvard University, Appian Way, Cambridge, MA 02138, USA (office). *Telephone:* (617) 495-4671 (office). *E-mail:* nglazer@fas.harvard.edu (office).

GLAZ'IEV, Sergey Yurievich, DrEcSc; Russian economist and politician; b. 1 Jan. 1961, Zaporozhye; m.; three c.; ed Moscow State Univ.; Head of Lab., Cen. Econ. Math. Inst. 1986–91; First Deputy Chair. Cttee on External Econ. Relations Ministry of Foreign Affairs 1991–92; First Deputy Minister of External Econ. Relations of Russia 1992, Minister 1992–93; mem. State Duma (Parl.) 1993–95 (CP of Russian Fed. faction) 1999–; Chair. Cttee for Econ. Policy of State Duma 1994–95, 2000–; Chair. Nat. Cttee of Democratic Party of Russia 1994–97; Head of Econ. Dept, Security Council 1996; Head, Information-Analytical Bd, Council of Fed. (Parl.) 1996–; Co-Chair. Party of the Russian Regions (Partiya Rossiiskikh Regionov—PRR) –2004; Head of Motherland election bloc, then For a Worthy Life Org.; author of econ. programme for CP of Russian Fed. for Parl. Elections 1999; Corresp. mem. Russian Acad. of Sciences 2000. *Publications include:* Economic

Theory of Technical Development 1993, Economy and Politics 1994, One and a Half Years in the Duma 1995, Under the Critical Level 1996, Genocide 1997 1998, I'm Just Paying My Debt 2007.

GLAZUNOV, Ilya Sergeyevich; Russian painter; *Rector, Russian Academy of Painting, Sculpture and Architecture;* b. 10 June 1930, Leningrad; s. of S. F. Glazunov and O. K. Glazunova (née Flug); m. M. Vinogradova-Benua (deceased); one s. one d.; ed Repin Arts Inst. (pupil of B. Ioganson); first solo exhbn, Moscow 1957; teacher of drawing in Izhevsk, then Ivanovo; moved to Moscow 1960; Prof., Surikov Inst., Moscow 1978–; exhibited in art exhbns in Moscow 1959–99, Warsaw, Rome, Copenhagen, Viet Nam, Laos, Paris, Leningrad, Santiago, Stockholm, Berlin (East and West), Leipzig, FRG 1960–77, London (Barbican) 1987; Founder and Rector Russian Acad. of Painting, Sculpture and Architecture 1991–; projects include designs for the decoration of the interior of the Kremlin, Moscow and the Russian Embassy, Madrid; gallery of works est. in Moscow 1999; Corresp. mem. Russian Acad. of Arts 1997; Hon. mem. Royal Acads of Art, Madrid, Barcelona 1979; Order (First Class) for Services to the Motherland 1996; Order of Sergei Radonezsky 1998; First Prize Int. Art Exhbn, Prague 1956, People's Artist of the USSR 1980, Russian State Prize 1997, Pablo Picasso Gold Medal, UNESCO 1999, Jawaharlal Nehru Award. *Publications:* The Road to You 1965, Russia Crucified 1996. *Leisure interests:* philosophy, history, classical music. *Address:* Russian Academy of Painting, Sculpture and Architecture, Myasnitskaya str. 21, 101000 Moscow (office); Ilya Glazunov Art Gallery, 13 Volkhonka str., Moscow; Kamergerski pr. 2, 103009, Moscow, Russia. *Telephone:* (495) 292-33-74 (office). *E-mail:* ilya-glazunov@ya.ru. *Website:* glazunov.ru.

GLEAN, Sir Carlyle Arnold, GCMG, BEd, MA; Grenadian educator and government official; b. 11 Feb. 1932; s. of George Glean and Olive McBurnie; m. Norma Glean (née DeCoteau) 1955; one s. five d. (one deceased); ed Univ. of Calgary, Canada; began career as teacher, St John's RC School 1950; Principal, Happy Hill RC School 1964–65, 1967; tutor, Grenada Teachers Coll. 1970–72; fmr Prin. Grenada Teachers Coll.; fmr Lecturer, Univ. of the West Indies, Barbados; fmr Asst Chief Examiner, Caribbean Examinations Council; Minister of Educ. 1990–95 (retd); Gov.-Gen. 2008–13. *Publications include:* Heinemann Social Studies for Lower Secondary (three vols, jtly): The Caribbean: Our Land and People, The Caribbean: Our Changing Environment, The Caribbean and the Wider World; for infants: Our Family, Home and School, Our Neighbourhood.

GLEESON, Hon. (Murray) Anthony Murray, AO; Australian lawyer and judge; *Non-Permanent Judge, Court of Final Appeal, Hong Kong Special Administrative Region;* b. 30 Aug. 1938, Wingham, NSW; s. of L. J. Gleeson; m. Robyn Gleeson 1965; one s. three d.; ed Univ. of Sydney; barrister 1963; tutor in law, St Paul's Coll., Univ. of Sydney 1963–65, Lecturer in Co. Law 1965–74; appointed QC 1974; mem. Council NSW Bar Asscn 1979–86, Pres. 1984–86; Chief Justice Supreme Court NSW 1988–98; Pres. Judicial Comm. NSW 1988–98; Lt-Gov. NSW 1989–98; Chief Justice, High Court of Australia 1998–2008; Non-Perm. Judge, Court of Final Appeal, Hong Kong Special Admin. Region 2008–; mem. Perm. Court of Arbitration 1999; Hon. Bencher Middle Temple 1989; Dr hc (Univ. of Sydney) 1999; Centenary Medal 2001. *Publications:* The Rule of Law and the Constitution. *Leisure interests:* tennis, skiing. *Address:* Court of Final Appeal, 1 Battery Path, Central, Hong Kong Special Administrative Region, People's Republic of China (office). *Telephone:* 21230123 (office). *Fax:* 21210300 (office). *Website:* www.judiciary.gov.hk (office).

GLENDENING, Parris Nelson, MA, PhD; American fmr state governor; *President, Leadership Institute, Smart Growth America;* b. 11 June 1942, Bronx, NY; m. 1st Frances A. Hughes 1976; one s.; m. 2nd Jennifer E. Crawford; one d.; ed Florida State Univ. Fort Lauderdale and Tallahassee; Asst Prof., Univ. of Maryland, College Park 1967–72, Assoc. Prof. 1972–95; Co. Exec. Prince George's Co. Council, Upper Marlboro, Md 1982–94; various public appointments at co. level; Dir World Trade Center 1990–97; Gov. of Maryland 1995–2003; Pres. Smart Growth Leadership Inst., Washington DC 2003–; Chair. Bd Dirs Smart Growth Investments 2003–; Chair. Nat. Govs' Asscn 2001–03; mem. AAAS, American Political Science Asscn; Democrat; Hon. LLD (Bowie State) 1995, (Baltimore) 1996, (Maryland at Baltimore) 1998; Hon. Dr of Public Service (Washington Coll.) 1995, (Carroll Community Coll.) 1997, (Maryland Univ. Coll.) 2000, (Bridgewater State Coll.) 2003; Hon. DHumLitt (Towson) 2000; numerous awards including Public Official of the Year Award Governing magazine 1990, 2000, Donald C. Stone Award American Soc. for Public Admin 1995, American Soc. of Landscape Architects' Olmstead Award, Harward Innovations in American Govt Award 2000, Hubert H. Humphrey Award 2002, Morris H. Blum Humanitarian Award 2006. *Publications:* Controversies of State and Local Political Systems (with M. M. Reeves) 1972, Pragmatic Federalism 1977; articles in professional publs. *Address:* Leadership Institute, Smart Growth America, 1707 L Street NW, Suite 250, Washington, DC 20036, USA (office). *Telephone:* (202) 207-3355 (office). *E-mail:* info@smartgrowthamerica.org (office). *Website:* www.smartgrowthamerica.org (office).

GLENDON, Mary Ann, BA, MCompL, JD; American academic, lawyer, writer and fmr diplomatist; *Learned Hand Professor of Law, Harvard University;* b. 7 Oct. 1938, Pittsfield, Mass; m. Edward R. Lev; three d.; ed Univ. of Chicago, Université Libre, Belgium; early career included period as volunteer civil rights attorney; practised law with Mayer, Brown and Platt, Chicago 1963–68; Prof. of Law, Boston Coll. Law School 1968–86; Prof. of Law, Harvard Law School 1986–93, Learned Hand Prof. of Law 1993–; Amb. to the Holy See (Vatican) 2008–09; fmr Visiting Prof., Univ. of Chicago Law School 1974, Gregorian Univ., Rome; fmr Pres. UNESCO-sponsored Int. Asscn of Legal Science 1991; mem. Pontifical Acad. of Social Sciences 1994–, Pres. 2004–; Head of Del. of Holy See to UN Women's Conf., Beijing 1995; hon. doctorates from Univ. of Chicago, Univ. of Louvain and others; Nat. Humanities Medal, Order of the Coif Triennial Book Award, Capalbio, Premio Capri-San Michele. *Publications:* as author: The New Family and the New Property 1981, Abortion and Divorce in Western Law 1987, The Transformation of Family Law 1989, Rights Talk: The Impoverishment of Political Discourse 1991, Law of Decedent's Estates (co-author) 1991, A Nation Under Lawyers 1994, Seedbeds of Virtue (co-author) 1995, Comparative Legal Traditions (co-author) 1999, A World Made New: Eleanor Roosevelt and the Universal Declaration of Human Rights 2001, Traditions in Turmoil 2006. *Address:* Hauser Hall 504, Harvard Law School, 1575 Massachusetts Avenue, Cambridge, MA 02138, USA (office). *Telephone:* (617) 495-4769 (office). *E-mail:* glendon@law.harvard.edu (office). *Website:* www.law.harvard.edu (office).

GLENDONBROOK, Baron (Life Peer), cr. 2011, of Bowdon in the County of Cheshire; **Michael David Bishop,** Kt, CBE; British business executive and foundation administrator; *Chairman, The Michael Bishop Foundation;* b. 10 Feb. 1942, Bowdon, Cheshire; s. of Clive Leonard Bishop; ed Mill Hill School, North London; first job as a baggage handler at Manchester Airport; joined Mercury Airlines, Manchester 1963, British Midland Airways Ltd 1964–; Chair. British Midland PLC 1978–2009 (sold stake in renamed bmi, British Midland International to Lufthansa); Chair. Manx Airlines 1982–2001, British Regional Airlines Group PLC 1982–2001; Deputy Chair. Channel 4 TV Corpn 1991–93, Chair. 1993–97; Chair. D'Oyly Carte Opera Trust Ltd 1989–; Deputy Chair. Airtours PLC 1996– (Dir 1987–2001); Dir Williams PLC 1993–2000, Kidde PLC 2000–02; Founder and Chair. The Michael Bishop Foundation 1989–; mem. (Conservative) House of Lords 2011–; Hon. DTech (Loughborough Univ. of Tech.) 1989, Hon. DLitt (Salford) 1991, Hon. LLD (Nottingham) 1993, Hon. DUniv (Cent. England) 1993, Hon. DLitt (Coventry) 1994, Hon. LLD (Univ. of Leicester) 2007; ranked by The Independent newspaper amongst the UK's most influential gay men and women (fifth) 2005, (sixth) 2006. *Leisure interests:* music, reading. *Address:* c/o bmi, Donington Hall, Castle Donington, nr Derby, DE74 2SB; House of Lords, Westminster, London, SW1A 0PW, England. *Telephone:* (20) 7219-5353 (House of Lords). *Website:* www.parliament.uk/biographies/lords/michael-bishop/90414.

GLENN, Lt-Col (retd) John Herschel, Jr; American astronaut, politician and aviator; *Chairman, John Glenn Institute of Public Service and Public Policy, Ohio State University;* b. 18 July 1921, Cambridge, Ohio; s. of John H. Glenn and Clare Sproat; m. Anna Margaret Castor 1943; one s. one d.; ed Muskingum Coll., Univ. of Maryland; naval aviation cadet 1942; commissioned Marine Corps 1943; Marine Fighter Squadron 155 in Marshall Islands 1944 (59 combat missions); mem. Fighter Squadron 218 North China Patrol; Instructor Corpus Christi, Texas 1948–50; Marine Fighter Squadron Korea (63 missions); Fighter Design Branch, Navy Bureau of Aeronautics, Washington 1956; speed record Los Angeles–New York (3 hr 23 min) 1957; training for space flight 1960–61; completed 3 orbits of the Earth in Spaceship Friendship VII, 20 Feb. 1962; resgnd from US Marine Corps 1965; Dir Royal Crown Cola Co. 1965–74; Consultant to NASA; US Senator from Ohio 1975–99; Chair. Bd of Dirs, John Glenn Inst. of Public Service and Public Policy, Ohio State Univ. 1999–, currently Adjunct Prof., John Glenn School of Public Affairs, Ohio State Univ.; Chair. Cttee on Governmental Affairs; announced return as astronaut Oct. 1997, on board Discovery shuttle 1998; Trustee, Muskingum Coll.; mem.-at-large Ohio State Democratic Cttee 1999–; Dr hc (Ohio Northern Univ.) 2010; DFC (eight times) and Air Medal with 18 clusters, NASA Distinguished Service Medal 1962, US Nat. Space Hall of Fame Award 1969, Centennial Award, Nat. Geographic Soc. 1988, Nat. Air and Space Museum Trophy 2000, Presidential Medal of Freedom 2012. *Publications:* (co-author) We Seven 1962, P.S., I Listened to Your Heart Beat. *Address:* John Glenn Institute, Ohio State University, 350 Page Hall, 1810 College Road, Columbus, OH 43210, USA (office). *Telephone:* (614) 292-4545. *Fax:* (614) 292-4868. *Website:* www.glenninstitute.org.

GLENNIE, Dame Evelyn Elizabeth Ann, DBE, GRSM, FRAM, FRCM, FRNCM; British percussionist, composer, consultant, motivational speaker and jewellery designer; b. 19 July 1965, Aberdeen, Scotland; d. of Isobel Glennie and Herbert Arthur Glennie; ed Ellon Acad., Aberdeenshire, Royal Acad. of Music, London; solo debut at Wigmore Hall, London, 1986; concerto, chamber and solo percussion performances worldwide; gave Promenade concerts' first-ever percussion recital 1989; numerous TV appearances, three documentaries on her life including Touch the Sound 2004 (BAFTA Award); composer of music for TV and radio; many works written for her by composers, including Bennett, Rouse, Heath, Macmillan, McLeod, Muldowney, Daugherty, Turnage and Musgrave; Munster Trust Scholarship 1986; professional jewellery designer; Hon. DMus (Aberdeen) 1991, (Bristol, Portsmouth) 1995, (Leicester, Surrey) 1997, (Queen's, Belfast) 1998, (Southampton) 2000, (Williams Coll., USA) 2005, (Binghampton) 2007, (Edinburgh Napier Univ.) 2009, (Cambridge) 2010, Hon. DLitt (Warwick) 1993, (Loughborough) 1995, (Salford) 1999, Hon. LLD (Dundee) 1996, Hon. DUniv (Essex, Durham) 1998, (Open Univ.) 2007, (Queen Margaret Univ., Edinburgh) 2008; many int. prizes and awards, including Shell/LSO Music Gold Medal 1984, Queen's Commendation Prize at RAM 1985, Grammy Award 1988, Scotswoman of the Decade 1990, Charles Heidsieck Soloist of the Year, Royal Philharmonic Soc. 1991, Personality of the Year, Int. Classical Music Awards 1993, Young Deaf Achievers Special Award 1993, Best Studio Percussionist, Rhythm Magazine 1998, 2000, 2002, 2003, 2004, Best Live Percussionist, Rhythm Magazine 2000, Classic FM Outstanding Contribution to Classical Music 2002, Walpole Medal of Excellence 2002, Musical America 2003, Tartan Clef Award 2005, Scotland with Style Classical Award 2005, Best Orchestral Percussionist, Drummies Readers' Poll Awards 2005, Incorporated Soc. of Musicians Distinguished Musician Award 2006, Sabian Lifetime Achievement Award 2006, inducted into PASIC Hall of Fame 2008, Drummies Readers Poll Awards, Orchestral Percussionist 2009, Percuaction Lifetime Achievement Award 2014, Grammy Award 2014. *Films:* wrote and played music for The Trench, Touch the Sound (Critics' Prize, Locarno Int. Film Festival), Golf in the Kingdom. *Play:* Playing from the Heart. *Recordings include:* Rhythm Song, Dancin', Light in Darkness, Rebounds, Veni Veni Emmanuel, Wind in the Bamboo Grove, Drumming, Her Greatest Hits, The Music of Joseph Schwantner, Sonata for Two Pianos and Percussion (Bartók), Last Night of the Proms – 100th Season, Street Songs, Reflected in Brass, Shadow Behind the Iron Sun, African Sunrise, Manhattan Rave, UFO: The Music of Michael Daugherty, Bela Fleck-Perpetual Motion, Oriental Landscapes, Fractured Lines, Michael Daugherty: Philadelphia Stories/UFO, Philip Glass: The Concerto Project 2004, Christopher Rouse 2004, Touch the Sound soundtrack 2004, Margaret Brouwer: Auroluncet Circles 2006. *Television includes:* music for Trial and Retribution 1–5 (Yorkshire TV), music for Mazda commercial Blind Ambition, Survival Special (Anglia) and others. *Publications:* Good Vibrations (autobiography) 1990, Great Journeys of the World, Beat It!, African Dances, Marimba Encores, 3 Chorales for Marimba. *Leisure interests:* reading, walking, cycling, antiques, collecting musical instruments, psychology, designing jewellery, pets. *Address:* Evelyn Glennie Office, Unit 6, Ramsay Court, Hinchingbrooke Business Park, Huntingdon, Cambs., PE29 6FY, England (office). *Telephone:*

(1480) 459279 (office). *Fax:* (1480) 451610 (office). *E-mail:* admin@evelyn.co.uk (office); brenda@evelyn.co.uk (office). *Website:* www.evelyn.co.uk (office).

GLICKMAN, Daniel Robert, BA, JD; American lawyer, association executive and fmr politician; *Executive Director, Congressional Program, Aspen Institute;* b. 24 Nov. 1944, Wichita, Kan.; s. of Milton Glickman and Gladys A. Kopelman; m. Rhoda J. Yura 1966; one s. one d.; ed Univ. of Michigan and George Washington Univ.; mem. Kan. Bar 1969, Mich. Bar 1970; trial attorney, Securities & Exchange Comm. 1969–70; Assoc. then Partner, Sargent, Klenda & Glickman, Wichita 1971–76; mem. 95th–103rd Congresses from 4th Kansas Dist 1977–95; Sec. of Agric. 1995–2001; Partner Akin, Gump, Strauss, Hauer & Feld LLP 2001–04, Advisor 2008; Dir Inst. of Politics, John F. Kennedy School of Govt, Harvard Univ. 2002–04; Pres. and CEO Motion Picture Asscn of America 2004–11 (retd); Exec. Dir Congressional Program, Aspen Inst., Washington, DC 2011–; Sr Fellow, Bipartisan Policy Center; mem. Bd of Dirs Chicago Mercantile Exchange 2001–, Hain-Celestial Corpn, Ready Pac Produce Corpn, Communities in Schools, America's Second Harvest, Food Research and Action Center, RFK Memorial Foundation; mem. Int. Advisory Bd of The Coca-Cola Co.; co-Chair. US Consensus Council, The Pew Initiative on Food and Biotechnology. *Address:* Aspen Institute, One Dupont Circle, NW, Suite 700, Washington, DC 20036-1133, USA (office). *Telephone:* (202) 736-5800 (office). *Fax:* (202) 467-0790 (office). *Website:* www.aspeninstitute.org (office).

GLIDEWELL, Rt Hon. Sir Iain (Derek Laing), Kt, PC; British judge; b. 8 June 1924; s. of Charles Norman Glidewell and Nora Glidewell; m. Hilary Winant 1950; one s. two d.; ed Bromsgrove School, Worcester Coll., Oxford; served RAFVR (pilot) 1942–46; called to Bar, Gray's Inn 1949, Bencher 1977, Treas. 1995; QC 1969; a Recorder of the Crown Court 1976–80; a Judge of Appeal, Isle of Man 1979–80; a Judge of the High Court of Justice, Queen's Bench Div. 1980–85; Presiding Judge, NE Circuit 1982–85; a Lord Justice of Appeal 1985–95; conducted review of Crown Prosecution Service 1997–98; a Judge of Court of Appeal, Gibraltar 1998–2003, Pres. 2003–04; mem. Senate of Inns of Court and the Bar 1976–79; mem., Supreme Court Rule Cttee 1980–84; Chair. Judicial Studies Bd 1989–92, Panels for Examination of Structure Plans: Worcs. 1974, W Midlands 1975; conducted Heathrow Fourth Terminal Inquiry 1978; Hon. Fellow, Worcester Coll. Oxford 1986. *Leisure interests:* walking, theatre. *Address:* Rough Heys Farm, Macclesfield, Cheshire, SK11 9PF, England (home).

GLIMCHER, Marc; American art gallery executive; *President, Pace Gallery;* b. 1963; s. of Arnold Glimcher and Milly Glimcher; m. Andrea Budonis; ed Harvard Univ.; Exec. Producer The Paint Job 1992; Assoc. Dir Pace Gallery (fmrly PaceWildenstein Gallery) 1985, Pres. 1993–, past exhbns include Keith Tyson, Chuck Close, Donald Judd, Bridget Riley, Mark Rothko, Julian Schnabel; f. Artifex Press LLC 2008; Creative Time Art Gala Award 2010. *Address:* Pace Gallery, 32 East 57th Street, 2nd Floor, New York, NY 10022, USA (office). *Telephone:* (212) 421-3292 (office). *Fax:* (212) 421-0835 (office). *Website:* www.pacegallery.com (office).

GLOAG, Ann Heron, OBE; British business executive; b. 10 Dec. 1942; d. of Iain Souter and Catherine Souter; m. 1st Robin N. Gloag 1965 (deceased); one s. (deceased) one d.; m. 2nd David McCleary 1990; ed Perth High School; trainee nurse, Bridge of Earn Hosp., Perth 1960–65, Theatre Sister 1969–80; ward sister, Devonshire Royal Hosp., Buxton 1965–69; Founding Partner, Gloagtrotter (renamed Stagecoach Express Services) 1980–83, Co-Dir Stagecoach Ltd 1983–86, Dir Stagecoach Holdings PLC 1986–, Exec. Dir 1986–2000, Man. Dir 1986–94; Trustee Princess Royal Trust for Carers; mem. Int. Bd Mercy Ships; Dir (non-exec.) OPTOS, The Balcraig Foundation, The Gloag Foundation, The Freedom From Fistula Foundation; Scottish Marketing Woman of the Year, Scottish Univs 1989, UK Businesswoman of the Year, Veuve Clicquot and Inst. of Dirs 1989–90, Susan B Anthony Award, Nat. Council of Women of the United States 2009. *Leisure interests:* family, travel, charity support. *Address:* Stagecoach Group plc, 10 Dunkeld Road, Perth, PH1 5TW, Scotland (office). *Website:* www.stagecoachgroup.com.

GLOBUS, Yoram; Israeli film producer; b. 7 Sept. 1943; f. Noah Films with Menahem Golan (q.v.) 1963; bought Cannon Films (USA) with Menahem Golan 1979 and has since produced over 100 motion pictures; Chair., CEO Cannon Entertainments 1989; Officer Cannon Group Inc. 1989; Co-Pres. Pathé Communications Corpn, Chair., CEO Pathé Int. until 1991; fmr mem. Bd of Dirs MGM Studios; f. Melrose Entertainment. *Films produced include:* Over the Top, Barfly, Dancers, Missing in Action I, II & III, Death Wish IV, The Assault (winner of 1986 Acad. Award for Best Foreign Language Film), Surrender, Runaway Train, Hanna's War, Masters of the Universe, King Lear, Tough Guys Don't Dance, Shy People, A Cry In The Dark, Lelakek Tatut, Tipat Mazal, Mashehu Matok, Rak Klavim Ratzim Hofshi.

GLOCER, Thomas (Tom) Henry, BA, JD; American lawyer and business executive; b. 8 Oct. 1959, NY; s. of Walter Glocer and Ursula Glocer (née Goodman); m. Maarit Leso 1988; one s. one d.; ed Columbia Univ., Yale Univ. Law School; mergers and acquisitions lawyer, Davis Polk and Wardwell, New York, Paris and Tokyo 1985–93; joined Reuters 1993, mem. Legal Dept Gen. Counsel, Reuters America Inc., New York 1993–96, Exec. Vice-Pres., Reuters America Inc. and CEO Reuters Latin America 1996–98, CEO Reuters business in the Americas 1998–2001, Reuters Inc. 2000–01, CEO Reuters Group PLC (Thomson-Reuters following merger with Thomson 2007) 2001–12; mem. Bd of Dirs Merck & Co. Inc. 2007–, New York City Investment Fund 1999–2003, Instinet Corpn 2000; mem. International Business Council of World Econ. Forum, International Advisory Bd of British American Business Inc., Columbia College Bd of Visitors, President's Council on International Activities at Yale Univ., Advisory Bd of Judge Inst. of Management, Univ. of Cambridge, European Business Leaders Council, Corp. Advisory Bd, Tate Britain, Madison Council of US Library of Congress; mem. Council on Foreign Relations; New York Hall of Science Award 2000, John Jay Alumni Award 2001. *Publications include:* author of computer software, including Coney Island: A Game of Discovery (co-author) 1983. *Website:* www.tomglocer.com (home).

GLOS, Michael; German politician and banking executive; b. 14 Dec. 1944, Brünnau; m.; three c. (one died 1997); served apprenticeship as miller and passed professional examination 1967; managed family flour mill, Prichsenstadt 1968–70;

mem. CSU (Christlich-Soziale Union in Bayern) 1970–, first Chair. CSU-chapter, Prichsenstadt 1972–75, Chair. CSU-Dist of Kitzingen 1975–93, mem. Exec. Bd CSU Lower Franconia 1976–, mem. Presidency of CSU Bavaria 1976–, Chair. CSU Bavaria and Asst Chair. CDU/CSU Parl. Group 1993–; mem. Dist Council of Prichsenstadt 1972–78; mem. Council of Dist (Kreistag) of Kitzingen 1975–93; mem. Bundestag (Parl.) 1976–; Fed. Minister for Econs and Tech. 2005–09 (resgnd); Chair. Bd of Supervisory Dirs and Chair. Exec. Cttee KfW Bankengruppe 2008–09. *E-mail:* info@glos.de. *Website:* www.glos.de.

GLOUCESTER, HRH The Duke of Richard Alexander Walter George, Earl of Ulster and the Baron Culloden, KG, GCVO; b. 26 Aug. 1944, Northampton, England; s. of the late Duke of Gloucester (third s. of HM King George V) and the late Lady Alice Montagu-Douglas-Scott (d. of the 7th Duke of Buccleuch); m. Birgitte van Deurs 1972; one s. (Alexander, Earl of Ulster) two d. (the Lady Davina Windsor and the Lady Rose Windsor); ed Wellesley House, Broadstairs, Eton Coll. and Magdalene Coll., Cambridge; Corp. mem. RIBA 1972; Commdr-in-Chief St John Ambulance Brigade 1972–74; Col-in-Chief Glos. Regt 1974–94, Deputy Col-in-Chief Royal Glos., Berks. and Wilts. Regt 1994; Royal Col The Rifles 1993; Deputy Col-in-Chief The Royal Logistic Corps 1993; Col in Chief Royal Army Medical Corps 2003, NZ Army Medical Corps 2008, The Royal Anglian Regt 2006; Hon. Col Royal Monmouthshire Royal Engineers (Militia) 1977; Hon. Air Cdre RAF Odiham 1993; Grand Prior Order of St John 1975; Pres. The London Soc., Cancer Research Campaign 1973, Nat. Asscn of Clubs for Young People (now Ambition) 1974, Christ's Hosp. 1975, St Bartholomew's Hosp. 1975, Royal Smithfield 1975, British Consultants and Construction Bureau (now British Expertise) 1978, Cambridge House 1983, Britain Nepal Soc. 1989, Public Monuments and Sculpture Assen 1998, Royal Agricultural Benevolent Inst. 2010, Crown Agents 2011; Jt Pres. Cancer Research UK 2002; Vice-Pres. LEPRA 1971; Commr Historic Buildings and Monuments Comm. for England 1983–2001; Royal Bencher, Gray's Inn 2000; Chancellor Univ. of Worcester 2008; Royal Trustee, British Museum 1973–2003; Royal Patron Peace and Prosperity Trust 2010, Global Heritage Fund 2012; Patron in Chief Scottish Veterans Residences 2005; Patron Action on Smoking and Health (ASH) 1971, Pestalozzi Int. Village Trust 1973, London Playing Fields Foundation 1975, Nuffield Farming Scholarships Trust 1975, Richard III Soc. 1980, Kensington Soc. 1981, Heritage of London Trust 1982, Int. Council on Monuments and Sites (ICOMOS) 1983, Fortress Study Group 1985, Normandy Veterans Assen 1986, Construction Youth Trust 1987, London Chorus 1991, Building Centre Trust 1992, Japan Soc. 1994, Habitat for Humanity 1997, Severn Valley Railway 1997, St George's Soc. of New York 2000, British Limbless Ex-Service Men's Assen (BLESMA) 2005, Architects Benevolent Soc. 2011; Co-Patron Abbotsford Trust 2009; Vice-Patron Nat. Churches Trust 2007; Sr Fellow, RCA 1984; Hon. Pres. Somme Assen 2005, 20-Ghost Club 2012. *Publication:* On Public View, The Face of London, Oxford and Cambridge. *Address:* Kensington Palace, London, W8 4PU, England. *Telephone:* (20) 7368-1000 (office). *Fax:* (20) 7368-1019 (office). *Website:* www.royal.gov.uk.

GLOVER, Danny; American actor; b. 22 July 1946, San Francisco, Calif.; m. Asake Bomani; one d.; ed San Francisco State Univ.; researcher, Office of Mayor, San Francisco 1971–75; Head TransAfrica (African-American Lobby) 2002–; mem. American Conservatory Theater's Black Actor Workshop; Broadway debut, Master Harold . . . and the Boys 1982; other stage appearances include: The Blood Knot 1982, The Island, Sizwe Banzi is Dead, Macbeth, Suicide in B Flat, Nevis Mountain Dew, Jukebox; appearances in TV movies and series; f. Carrie Productions (film production co.); with his wife f. Bomani Gallery, San Francisco; Chair.'s Award, Nat. Assen for the Advancement of Colored People (NAACP) 2003. *Films:* Escape from Alcatraz 1979, Chu Chu and the Philly Flash 1981, Out 1982, Iceman 1984, Places in the Heart 1984, Birdy 1984, The Color Purple 1984, Silverado 1985, Witness 1985, Lethal Weapon 1987, Bat 21 1988, Lethal Weapon II 1989, To Sleep with Anger 1990, Predator 2 1990, Flight of the Intruder 1991, A Rage in Harlem 1991, Pure Luck 1991, Grand Canyon 1992, Lethal Weapon III 1992, The Saint of Fort Washington 1993, Bopha 1993, Angels in the Outfield 1994, Operation Dumbo Drop 1995, America's Dream 1996, The Rainmaker 1997, Wings Against the Wind 1998, Beloved 1998, Lethal Weapon IV 1998, Prince of Egypt (voice) 1998, Antz (voice) 1998, The Monster 1999, Battu 2000, Boseman and Lena 2000, Wings Against the Wind 2000, Freedom Song 2000, 3 A.M. 2001, The Royal Tenenbaums 2001, Saw 2004, The Cookout 2004, Missing in America 2005, Manderlay 2005, The Shaggy Dog 2006, The Adventures of Brer Rabbit (voice) 2006, Bamako 2006, Dreamgirls 2006, Barnyard (voice) 2006, Shooter 2007, Honeydripper 2007, Be Kind Rewind 2007, Blindness 2008. *Television includes:* The Henry Lee Project 2003, Legend of Earthsea 2004, The Exonerated 2005. *Address:* Carrie Productions, 4444 Riverside Drive, Suite 110, Burbank, CA 91505, USA. *Telephone:* (818) 567-3292.

GLOVER, Jane Alison, CBE, MA, DPhil, FRCM; British conductor; *Director of Opera, Royal Academy of Music;* b. 13 May 1949; d. of the late Robert Finlay Glover and Jean Muir; ed Monmouth School for Girls and St Hugh's Coll., Oxford; Jr Research Fellow, St Hugh's Coll. 1973–75, Lecturer in Music 1976–84, Sr Research Fellow 1982–84; Lecturer, St Anne's Coll., Oxford 1976–80, Pembroke Coll. 1979–84; mem. Univ. of Oxford Faculty of Music 1979–; professional conducting debut at Wexford Festival 1975; operas and concerts for BBC, Glyndebourne 1982–, Royal Opera House 1988–, Covent Garden, ENO 1989–, London Symphony Orchestra, London Philharmonic Orchestra, Royal Philharmonic Orchestra, Philharmonia, Royal Scottish Orchestra, English Chamber Orchestra, Royal Danish Opera, Glimmerglass Opera, New York 1994–, Australian Opera 1996– and many orchestras in Europe and USA; Prin. Conductor London Choral Soc. 1983–2000; Artistic Dir London Mozart Players 1984–91; Prin. Conductor Huddersfield Choral Soc. 1989–96; Music Dir Music of the Baroque, Chicago, USA 2002–; Dir of Opera, RAM 2009–; mem. BBC Cen. Music Advisory Cttee 1981–85, Music Advisory Cttee, Arts Council 1986–88; Gov. RAM 1985–90, BBC 1990–95; Hon. DMus (Exeter) 1986, (CNAA) 1991, (London) 1992, (City Univ.) 1995, (Glasgow) 1996; Hon. DLitt (Loughborough) 1988, (Bradford) 1992; Dr hc (Open Univ.) 1988, (Brunel) 1997. *Television:* documentaries and series and presentation, especially Orchestra 1983, Mozart 1985. *Radio:* talks and series including Opera House 1995, Musical Dynasties 2000. *Publications:* Cavalli 1978, Mozart's Women: His Family, His Friends, His Music 2005; contribs to The New Monteverdi Companion 1986, Monteverdi 'Orfeo' Handbook 1986; articles in numerous journals. *Leisure interests:* The Times crossword puzzle, theatre, skiing,

walking. *Address:* Royal Academy of Music, Marylebone Road, London, NW1 5HT, England (office). *Telephone:* (20) 7873-7373 (office). *E-mail:* j.glover@ram.ac.uk (office). *Website:* www.ram.ac.uk (office); www.janeglover.co.uk; www.baroque .org.

GŁOWACKI, Janusz; Polish writer, playwright and screenwriter; b. 13 Sept. 1938, Poznań; m.; one d.; ed Warsaw Univ.; columnist in Kultura weekly 1964–81; lecturer in many colls and univs in USA including Bennington, Yale, Cornell, Columbia; Playwright-in-Residence, New York Shakespeare Festival 1984 and Mark Taper Forum, Los Angeles 1989; Fellow in Writing, Univ. of Iowa 1977, 1982; Hon. mem. Univ. of Iowa 1977, 1982; mem. American and Polish PEN Club 1984–, Polish Film Union; Joseph Kesserling Award 1987, Drama League of New York Playwrighting Award 1987, Guggenheim Award 1988, Alfred Jurzykowski Foundation Award 1997. *Publications:* short stories: Nowy taniec la-ba-da 1970, Paradis 1973, Polowanie na muchy 1974, My Sweet Raskolnikov 1977, Opowiadania wybrane 1978, Skrzek. Coraz trudniej kochać 1980, Rose Café 1997; novels: Moc truchleje 1981, Ostani cieć 2001; screenplays: Rejs 1970, Psychodrama (with Marek Piwowski) 1971, Polowanie na muchy 1971, Trzeba zabić tę miłość 1974, No Smoking Section (co-author) 1987, Hairdo (Tony Cox Screenwriting Award, Nantucket Film Festival, USA 1999) 1999; plays: Cudzołóstwo ukarane 1971, Mecz 1977, Obciach 1977, Kopciuch (Cinders) (Premio Molière, Argentina 1986) 1981, Fortinbras Gets Drunk 1986, Hunting Cockroaches (First Prize, American Theatre Critics Assen 1986, Joseph Kesselring Award 1987, Hollywood Drama League Critics' Award 1987) 1986, Antigone in New York (Le Balladine Award for the Best Play of 1997) 1993, Scieki, Skrzeki, karaluchy (selected works) 1996, Czwarta siostra (Grand Prize, Int. Theatre Festival, Dubrovnik 2001) 2000. *Address:* ul. Bednarska 7 m. 4, 00-310 Warsaw, Poland; 845 West End Avenue, Apartment 4B, New York, NY 10025, USA. *Website:* www.januszglowacki.com.

GLÜCK, Louise Elisabeth; American poet, writer and academic; *Rosenkranz Writer-in-Residence, Yale University;* b. 22 April 1943, New York City; d. of Daniel Glück and Beatrice Glück (née Grosby); m. 1st Charles Hertz (divorced); one s.; m. 2nd John Dranow 1977 (divorced 1996); ed Sarah Lawrence Coll., Bronxville, New York and Columbia Univ.; Artist-in-Residence, Goddard Coll., Plainfield, Vt 1971–72, Faculty mem. 1973–74; Poet-in-Residence, Univ. of North Carolina at Greensboro 1973; Visiting Prof., Univ. of Iowa 1976–77; Elliston Prof. of Poetry, Univ. of Cincinnati 1978; Visiting Prof., Columbia Univ. 1979; Holloway Lecturer, Univ. of California, Berkeley 1982; Faculty mem. and Bd mem. MFA Writing Program at Warren Wilson Coll., Swannoa, NC 1980–84; Visiting Prof., Univ. of California, Davis 1983; Scott Prof. of Poetry, Williams Coll., Mass 1983, part-time Sr Lecturer in English 1984–97, Parish Sr Lecturer in English 1997–; Regents Prof. of Poetry, UCLA 1985–88; Baccalaureate Speaker, Williams Coll. 1993; Poet Laureate of Vt 1994; Visiting Mem. of Faculty, Harvard Univ. 1995; Hurst Prof., Brandeis Univ. 1996; Special Consultant in Poetry at Library of Congress, Washington, DC 1999–2000; Poet Laureate of USA 2003–04; currently Rosenkranz Writer-in-Residence, Yale Univ.; Fellow, American Acad. of Arts and Sciences; mem. PEN, American Acad. and Inst. of Arts and Letters, Acad. of American Poets (mem. Bd of Chancellors 1999–2006); Hon. LLD (Williams Coll.) 1993, (Skidmore Coll.) 1995, (Middlebury Coll.) 1996; Acad. of American Poets Prize 1967, Rockefeller Foundation Grant 1968–69, Nat. Educ. Assen grants 1969–70, 1979–80, 1988–89, Nat. Endowment for the Arts Fellowships 1969–70, 1979–80, 1988–89, Vt Council for the Arts Grant 1978–79, Lannan Foundation Grant, Eunice Tietjens Memorial Prize 1971, Guggenheim Foundation Grant 1975–76, 1987–88, American Acad. and Inst. of Arts and Letters Literary Award 1981, Nat. Book Critics' Circle Award for poetry 1985, Poetry Soc. of America Melville Cane Award 1986, Wellesley Coll. Sara Teasdale Memorial Prize 1986, Bobbitt Natil Prize, Library of Congress 1992, William Carlos Williams Award 1993, PEN/Martha Albrand Award 1995, New Yorker Magazine Award in Poetry 1999, English Speaking Union Amb. Award 1999, 2001, Bollingen Prize 2001, Wallace Stevens Award 2008. *Publications:* poetry: Firstborn 1968, The House on the Marshland 1975, The Garden 1976, Descending Figure 1980, The Triumph of Achilles 1985, Ararat 1990, The Wild Iris (Pulitzer Prize for Poetry 1993) 1992, Proofs and Theories: Essays on Poetry 1994, The First Four Books of Poems 1995, Meadowlands 1996, Vita Nova 1999, The Seven Ages 2001, October 2004, Averno 2007, A Village Life 2009, Poems 1962-2012 2012; contrib. to many anthologies and periodicals. *Address:* Steven Barclay Agency, 12 Western Avenue, Petaluma, CA 94952, USA (office); 14 Ellsworth Park, Cambridge, MA 02139, USA (home). *Telephone:* (707) 773-0654 (office). *Fax:* (707) 778-1868 (office). *Website:* www .barclayagency.com (office).

GLUSHCHENKO, Fedor Ivanovich; Russian conductor; *Principal Guest Conductor, National Symphony Orchestra of Ukraine;* b. 29 March 1944, Rostov Region; m. 1st; one s. one d.; m. 2nd Galina Baryshnikova; one d.; ed Moscow and Leningrad State Conservatories, Vienna Acad. of Music; studied under Herbert von Karajan; Chief Conductor, Karelian Radio and TV Symphony Orchestra, Petrozavodsk 1971–73; Chief Conductor and Artistic Dir, Ukrainian State Symphony Orchestra, Kiev 1973–87; British debut in 1989 with BBC Scottish Symphony, also appeared with Royal Liverpool Philharmonic and Scottish Chamber Orchestra; Conductor, Istanbul Opera 1990–91; Principal Guest Conductor, Nat. Symphony Orchestra of Ukraine 2010–; fmr Chief Conductor and Artistic Dir J.S. Bach Chamber Orchestra, Yekaterinburg; Guest Conductor, Moscow Philharmonic Orchestra, Russian State Symphony Orchestra, Moscow Symphony, Ministry of Culture Orchestra and orchestras in Riga, Vilnius, Leningrad (now St Petersburg), Sverdlovsky, Tbilisi and Tashkent; tours in UK, Sweden, Italy, Denmark, China, Germany, France, Spain, Netherlands, Greece, Turkey, Portugal, Slovenia, Ireland, Poland; Artist of Ukraine 1979, People's Artist of Ukraine 1982. *Address:* 1st Pryadilnaya str. 11, Apartment 5, 105037 Moscow, Russia. *Telephone:* (499) 165-49-46; 903-1142086 (mobile). *E-mail:* f.glushchenko@mail.ru.

GLUSHENKO, Yevgeniya Konstantinovna; Russian actress; b. 4 Sept. 1952, Rostov-on-Don; m. Aleksandr Kalyagin; one s. one d.; ed Shchepkin Theatre School; worked with Maly Theatre 1974–97, 2000–, Russian Army Theatre 1997–2000; Order of Friendship 2004; State Prize of Russia 2001. *Films include:* Unfinished Play for Mechanical Piano 1977, Profile and Front-View 1979, Oblomov 1980, First-Time Married 1980, In Love of One's Own Accord (Moscow and West Berlin Film Festival Prizes 1983) 1982, Unikum 1983, Zina-Zinulya 1986,

Politseiskiye i vory 1997, Proshchaniye v iyune 2003, Live and Remember 2008. *Stage roles:* Liza in Misfortune from Sense 1975, Cordelia in King Lear 1979, Masha in The Savage 1990, Yefrosinya in Infanticide 1991, Matrena in The Hot Heart 1992, Susanna in A Criminal Mother or the Second Tartuffe 1993, Glafira in The Feast of Victors 1995, Vera in The Heart is not a Stone 1997, Vasilisa in The Lower Depths 1998, Emilia in Othello 1999, Kupavina in Sheep and Wolves 2000, Josephine in The Corsican Fury 2001, Zinaida Savishna in Ivanov 2002, Mavra Tarasovna in Truth is Dear, but Happiness is Yet Dearer 2003, Belina in The Imaginary Invalid 2005, Melanya in Children of the Sun 2008. *Television includes:* Zhizn Klima Samgina (series) 1986, Zhenshchiny, kotorym povezlo (miniseries) 1989, Koroleva Margo (series) 1996, Zal ozhidaniya (series) 1998, S novym schastiem! (series) 1999. *Address:* Apt 95, Building 17-2, Lavrushinsky Alley, Moscow, Russia (home). *Telephone:* (495) 959-07-52 (home). *E-mail:* dkaliaguin@hotmail.com (home).

GLVÁČ, Martin, JUDr; Slovak lawyer, business executive and politician; *Minister of Defence;* b. 20 Nov. 1967, Bratislava; two c.; ed Comenius Univ., Bratislava; Asst Head of Inventory Dept, Otex sp. 1986–87; lawyer, Davao sro 1992–94; Exhbn Man., UAE 1994–97; Business Man., DONAR as 1997–98; Man., VOSS Slovakia sro 1998–2001; pvt. practice as lawyer 2001–06; Sec. of State, Ministry of Construction and Regional Devt 2006–10; mem. Slovak Nat. Council (Parl.) 2010–12; Minister of Defence 2012–. *Leisure interests:* basketball, tennis, skiing, cinema. *Address:* Ministry of Defence, Kutuzovova 8, 832 47 Bratislava, Slovakia (office). *Telephone:* (960) 312740 (office); (960) 312958 (office). *Fax:* (2) 44258904 (office); (2) 44253242 (office). *E-mail:* minister@mod.gov.sk (office). *Website:* www.mosr.sk (office).

GLYNN, Ian Michael, MD, PhD, FRS, FRCP; British scientist and academic; *Professor Emeritus of Physiology, University of Cambridge;* b. 3 June 1928, London, England; s. of Hyman Glynn and Charlotte Glynn; m. Jenifer Muriel Franklin 1958; one s. two d.; ed City of London School, Trinity Coll. Cambridge, Univ. Coll. Hosp. London; House Physician, Cen. Middlesex Hosp. 1952–53; Nat. Service, RAF Medical Br. 1956–57; MRC Scholar, Physiological Lab., Cambridge 1956, Fellow, Trinity Coll. 1955–, Demonstrator in Physiology 1958–63, Lecturer 1963–70, Reader 1970–75, Prof. of Membrane Physiology 1975–86, Prof. of Physiology 1986–95, Prof. Emer. 1995–, Vice-Master Trinity Coll. 1980–86; Visiting Prof., Yale Univ. 1969; mem. British MRC 1976–80, Council of Royal Soc. 1979–81, 1991–92, Agric. Research Council 1981–86; Chair. Editorial Bd Journal of Physiology 1968–70; Hon. Foreign mem. American Acad. of Arts and Sciences 1984, American Physiological Soc.; Hon. MD (Arhus) 1988. *Publications:* The Sodium Pump (with J. C. Ellory) 1985; An Anatomy of Thought: the Origin and Machinery of the Mind 1999; The Life and Death of Smallpox (with Jenifer Glynn) 2004; papers in scientific journals. *Address:* Trinity College, Cambridge, CB2 1TQ, England (office). *Telephone:* (1223) 353079 (office). *E-mail:* img10@cam.ac.uk (office). *Website:* www.trin.cam.ac.uk (office).

GLYNN, Robert (Bob) D., Jr, BS, MS; American energy industry executive; b. 1942, Orange, NJ; s. of the late Robert D. Glynn and Helen Josephine Glynn; m.; ed Manhattan Coll., Long Island Univ.; early career with Long Island Lighting Co. and Woodward-Clyde Consultants; joined Pacific Gas & Electric Co. 1984, Pres. and COO 1995–97, Pres. and CEO Pacific Gas & Electric Corpn 1997–2004, Chair. 1998–2005; mem. Bd of Govs San Francisco Symphony; mem. Business Council, Calif. Comm. for Jobs and Econ. Growth, Calif. Business Roundtable. *Address:* c/o Pacific Gas & Electric Corporation, 1 Market Square, Suite 2400, San Francisco, CA 94105, USA.

GNAEDINGER, Angelo; Swiss lawyer and international organization official; *Director-General, International Committee of the Red Cross;* b. 1951; m.; two c.; trained as lawyer; examining magistrate, Schaffhausen –1984; joined ICRC 1984, followed field assignments in Middle East and Africa, held various positions in Dept of Operations, Geneva, Head of Detention Div. 1992–94, Del.-Gen. for W Cen. Europe and the Balkans 1994–98, Del.-Gen. for Europe, the Middle East and N Africa 1998–2002, Dir-Gen. ICRC 2002–. *Address:* International Committee of the Red Cross, 19 avenue de la Paix, 1202 Geneva, Switzerland (office). *Telephone:* (22) 7346001 (office). *Fax:* (22) 7332057 (office). *E-mail:* press.gva@icrc.org (office). *Website:* www.icrc.org (office).

GNANAM, Arumugham, PhD; Indian scientist; b. 5 Oct. 1932, Veeracholagan, Tamil Nadu; s. of Arumugham Pillai; m. Saratham Gnanam 1953; one s. three d.; ed Cornell Univ., USA; Asst Prof. of Plant Sciences, Cornell Univ. 1967–68; Lecturer, Annamalai Univ. 1968–69; Reader, Madurai Kamaraj Univ. 1969–73, Prof. 1973–85, Dir Centre for Plant Molecular Biology 1990–91; Vice-Chancellor, Pondicherry Univ. 1991–99; Vice-Chancellor, Bharathidasan Univ., Trichy 1985–88, Univ. of Madras 1988–90; elected Founder Fellow, Tamil Nadu Acad. of Sciences 1976; Nat. Fellow Univ. Grants Comm. 1978, Nat. Lecturer in Botany 1980; Fellow, Indian Nat. Science Acad., New Delhi 1984, Nat. Acad. of Sciences, Allahabad 1985, fmr Chair. Nat. Assessment and Accreditation Council; Rafi Ahmed Kidwai Award, Best Teacher Award, Govt of Tamil Nadu. *Publications include:* numerous scientific papers. *Leisure interests:* photography, music, pets. *Address:* c/o Office of the Vice-Chancellor, University of Pondicherry, R. Venkataraman Nagar, Kalapet, Pondicherry 605014, India.

GNASSINGBÉ, Faure Essozimna, MBA; Togolese politician and head of state; *President;* b. 1966; s. of the late Gnassingbe Eyadéma, fmr Pres. of Togo; ed Paris-Dauphine, France, Georgetown Univ., USA; fmr Deputy, Nat. Ass.; Minister of Public Works, Mines and Telecommunications 2003–05; Pres. of Togo 2005–. *Address:* Office of the President, Palais Présidentiel, ave de la Marina, Lomé, Togo (office). *Telephone:* 221-27-01 (office). *Fax:* 221-18-97 (office). *E-mail:* presidence@republicoftogo.com (office). *Website:* www.republicoftogo.com (office).

GNASSINGBÉ, Kpatcha; Togolese government official; s. of the late Gnassingbé Eyadéma; brother of Faure Essozimna Gnassingbé, Pres. of Togo; fmr Dir-Gen. Togo Free Zone Authority (SAZOF); Minister-del. at the Presidency of the Repub., responsible for Defence and Veterans 2005–07; mem. Nat. Ass. 2008–; arrested on suspicion on plotting to overthrow brother April 2009. *Address:* c/o Ministry of Defence and Veterans, Lomé, Togo (office).

GNEDOVSKY, Yuri Petrovich, PhD; Russian architect; b. 3 July 1930, Sverdlovsk (Ekaterinburg); m. Elena Andreyevna Borisova; one s. one d.; ed Moscow Inst. of Architecture, Acad. of Architecture; Sr Researcher Research Inst. of Public Bldgs Acad. of Architecture 1957–63; Head of div., Deputy Dir Cen. Research Inst. of Public Bldg Design 1964–82; Sec. Bd USSR Union of Architects 1982–91; Pres. Russian Union of Architects 1992–2008; fmr Pres. Theatre Architects Partnership; mem. Council of Int. Union of Architects 1996–2002, fmr Vice-Pres.; mem. Presidium; Fellow, Russian Acad. of Architecture and Construction Sciences, Int. Acad. of Architecture Sofia; author of projects of numerous . bldgs including Taganka Theatre, Meyerhold Cen., Russian Cultural Cen. Red Hills in Moscow, Moscow Int. Music House; Pres.'s Prize for Arts and Literature 1999, People's Architect of Russia 2002. *Publications include:* Architecture of Soviet Theatre, Architecture of Public Buildings, World Architecture: A Critical Mosaic 1900–2000 (Vol. 7) 2000, over 60 articles. *Address:* c/o Union of Architects of Russia, 123001 Moscow, Granatny per. 22, Russia.

GNEHM, Edward William, Jr, (Skip), MA; American diplomatist and academic; *Kuwait Professor of Gulf and Arabian Peninsula Affairs, Elliott School of International Affairs, George Washington University;* b. 10 Nov. 1944, Ga; s. of Edward W. Gnehm, Sr and Beverly Thomasson; m. Margaret Scott 1970; one s. one d.; ed George Washington Univ. and American Univ. Cairo; Head, Liaison Office, Riyadh 1976–78; Deputy Chief of Mission, Embassy, Sanaa 1978–81; Dir Jr Officer Div. Personnel, Washington, DC 1982–83, Dir Secr. Staff 1983–84; Deputy Chief of Mission, Amman 1984–87; Deputy Asst Sec. of Defense for Near East and S Asia 1987–89; Deputy Asst Sec. of State, Bureau of Near East and S Asian Affairs 1989–90; Amb. to Kuwait 1990–94, to Australia 2000–01, to Jordan 2001–04; J.B. and Maurice C. Shapiro Visiting Prof. of Int. Affairs, Co-Dir Undergraduate Program in Int. Affairs, Dir ME Policy Forum and Kuwait Chair for Gulf and Arabian and Peninsula Affairs, Elliott School of Int. Affairs, George Washington Univ., Washington, DC 2004–06, Kuwait Prof. of Gulf and Arabian Peninsula Affairs 2006–; Deputy Perm. Rep. to UN, New York 1994–97; Dir-Gen. of Foreign Service, Dir of Personnel, US Dept of State, Washington, DC 1997–2000; mem. Middle East Inst., American Philatelic Soc., American Foreign Service Asscn, American Acad. of Diplomacy, Diplomatic and Consular Officers Retired; Order of Independence, First Class (Jordan), Decoration of Medallion, Special Class (Kuwait); Presidential Distinguished Service Award 2000, Dept of Defense Meritorious Service Award 1989 and 1994, Dept of State Superior Honor Award 1991, Sec. of State Distinguished Service Award 2004. *Leisure interests:* history, foreign policy, cycling, stamps. *Address:* Elliott School of International Affairs, George Washington University, 1957 East Street NW, Suite 512, Washington, DC 20052, USA (office). *Telephone:* (202) 994-0155 (office). *Fax:* (202) 994-4055 (office). *E-mail:* ambgnehm@gwu.edu (office).

GNEUSS, Helmut Walter Georg, DPhil; German academic; *Professor Emeritus of English, University of Munich;* b. 29 Oct. 1927, Berlin; s. of Kurt Gneuss and Margarete Gneuss (née Grimm); m. Mechthild Gretsch 1974; ed Freie Universität Berlin, St John's Coll., Cambridge; Lecturer, German Dept, Univ. of Durham 1955–56, Dept of English, Freie Univ., Berlin 1956–62, Heidelberg Univ. 1962–65; Prof. of English, Univ. of Munich 1965–, now Prof. Emer.; Visiting Professorial Fellow, Emmanuel Coll., Cambridge 1970; Visiting Prof., Univ. of N Carolina, Chapel Hill 1974; mem. Bayerische Akad. der Wissenschaften, British Acad., Österreichische Akad. der Wissenschaften, Medieval Acad. of America; Vice-Pres. Henry Bradshaw Soc. *Publications:* Lehnbildungen und Lehnbedeutungen im Altenglischen 1955, Hymnar und Hymnen im englischen Mittelalter 1968, English Language Scholarship 1996, Language and History in Early England 1996, Books and Libraries in Early England 1996; Handlist of Anglo-Saxon Manuscripts 2001, Ælfric of Eynsham 2009. *Address:* Institut für Englische Philologie, Universität Munich, Schellingstrasse 3, 80799 Munich, Germany (office). *Telephone:* (89) 21803388 (office). *Fax:* (89) 2180 3399 (office). *E-mail:* department3@anglistik.uni-muenchen.de (office). *Website:* www.anglistik.uni-muenchen.de (office).

GNININVI, Léopold Messan Kokou, DSc; Togolese physicist and politician; *Secretary-General, Convention Démocratique des Peuples Africains;* b. 19 Dec. 1942, Aného; ed Univ. of Dijon, France; Head of Solar Energy Lab., Univ. of Lomé 1978–93, Prof. 1981–97; Dir Nat. Inst. of Educational Science 1979–88, Nat. Dir of Scientific Research 1987–93; three years in exile 1995–98; Sec.-Gen. Convention Démocratique des Peuples Africains, unsuccessful cand. in 1998 presidential election; Minister of State for Mines and Energy 2006–07, for Foreign Affairs and Regional Integration 2007–08, for Industry, Crafts, and Technological Innovations 2008–09. *Address:* Convention démocratique des peuples africains, 5 rue Djidjollé, BP 13963, Lomé, Togo (office). *E-mail:* cdpa-bt.cdpa-bt@orange.fr (office). *Website:* www.cdpa-bt.net (office).

GNUDI, Piero, BEcons; Italian business executive; b. 17 May 1938, Bologna; m. Francesca Pagnini; ed Univ. of Bologna; mem. Bd Credito Italiano 1980–83, STET 1984–94, EniChem 1992–93; mem. Bd Istituto per la Ricostruzione Industriale (IRI) (state holding co.) 1994–99, Resp. for Privatization 1997–99, Chair. and CEO 1999–2000, Chair. Bd of Liquidators 2000–, Chair. IRI Foundation 2000–; Chair. Enel SpA (electricity co.) 2002–11; Minister of Regional Affairs, Tourism and Sport 2011–13; mem. Bd ENI (state energy co.) 1995–96; Econ. Counsellor to Ministry of Industry 1995–96; Deputy Chair. Rolo Banca 1473 SpA, Bologna 1994–; Chair. Locat SpA 1995–99, Profingest School of Man. 1995–99; Chair. Bd of Auditors, Marino Golinelli & C. Sapa; Vice-Chair. Consorzio Alma; mem. Econ. Policy Comm., Consiglio Nazionale dell'Economia e del Lavoro (CNEL) 2000–; mem. Bd Dirs Unicredito Italiano, Il Sole 24 Ore SpA, Alfa Wassermann SpA, D & C Compagnia di Importazione prodotti Alimentari, Dolciari, Vini e Liquori SpA, Galotti SpA, ACB Group SpA, Ferrero, Gnudi, Guatri, Uckmar; mem. Exec. Cttee Confindustria, Steering Cttee Assonime (asscn of Italian corpns), Cttee in charge of strategic devt of the Italian Financial Markets, Exec. Cttee of Aspen Inst., Cttee on corp. governance of listed cos reconstituted on initiative of Borsa Italiana; Pres. Mediterranean Energy Observatory, 'e8' (org. of chairmen of major electricity production cos in the world); Chair. Emittenti Titoli; Cavaliere, gran croce dell'Ordine al merito della Repubblica italiana 2002. *Address:* UniCredit SpA, Piazza Cordusio, 20123 Milan, Italy (office). *Telephone:* (02) 88621 (office). *Fax:* (02) 8862-8652 (office). *E-mail:* info@unicredit.eu (office); azionisti@unicredit.eu (office). *Website:* www.unicreditgroup.eu (office).

GOBA, John; Sierra Leonean artist; b. 1944, Mattru Jong; sculptor, based in Freetown. *Website:* caacart.com/goba/goba_frameset.html.

GOBER, Robert; American sculptor; b. 12 Sept. 1954, Wallingford, Conn.; ed Middlebury Coll., Vt, Rome campus of Tyler School of Art (div. of Temple Univ.); arrived in New York 1976, worked as carpenter and handyman; also worked as asst to painter Elizabeth Murray; first solo exhbn at Paula Cooper Gallery, New York, consisting of single work titled Slides of a Changing Painting (1982–83) 1984; began creating three-dimensional works 1980s–90s; in recent years sculptures have become more conceptual, with photography in installations; represented USA at Venice Biennale 2001; Larry Aldrich Foundation Award 1996, Skowhegan Medal for Sculpture 1999, Artist's Space Honoree, Spring Benefit 2002, AICA Award 2005. *Address:* c/o Marianne Boesky Fine Art, 535 West 22nd Street, New York, NY 10011, USA.

GOCHIYEV, Annamuhammet; Turkmenistani politician; *Deputy Chairman of the Government, responsible for Economic Affairs;* b. 1973, Bendesen, Balkan Velayat; ed Turkmen State Inst. of Nat. Economy; Deputy Chair. Aşgabat Bakery Products 'Kuvvat' Co.; accountant and economist at 'Arvana' Co. specializing in agricultural statistical analysis; Chief Financial Insp. and Deputy Chair. 'Turkmenillinasabat' Nat. Inst. of Statistics and Forecasting 1997–2001; Head of Dept of Finance and Econs, Land Resources Service, Ministry of Agric., Chief Controller/Insp. in Control and Revision section, Ministry of Economy and Finance, then Head of Law Enforcement, Mil. and State Structures, Ministry of Economy and Finance 2001–07; Deputy Minister of Finance 2007–08, Minister of Finance 2008–11; Deputy Chair. of the Govt, responsible for Econ. Affairs 2011–. *Address:* Office of the President and the Council of Ministers, 744000 Aşgabat, Galkynyş köç. 20, Turkmenistan (office). *Telephone:* (12) 35-45-34 (office). *Fax:* (12) 35-51-12 (office). *E-mail:* nt@online.tm (office). *Website:* www.turkmenistan.gov .tm (office).

GOCKLEY, (Richard) David, BA, MBA; American opera director; *General Director, San Francisco Opera;* b. 13 July 1943, Philadelphia, PA; s. of Warren Gockley and Elizabeth Gockley; m. Adair Lewis; one s. two d.; ed Brown Univ., Columbia Univ., New England Conservatory, Boston; Dir of Music, Newark Acad. 1965–67; Dir of Drama, Buckley School, New York 1967–69; Box Office Man., Santa Fe Opera 1969–70; Asst Man.-Dir Lincoln Center, New York 1970; Business Man., Houston Grand Opera 1970–71, Assoc. Dir 1971–72, Gen. Dir 1972–2006; co-founder Houston Opera Studio 1977; Gen. Dir San Francisco Opera 2006–; mem. Bd of Dirs Texas Inst. of Arts in Educ.; mem. Opera America (pres. 1985–); fmr Chair. Houston Theater Dist; Hon. DHL (Univ. of Houston) 1992, Hon. DFA (Brown Univ.) 1993; League of New York Theaters and Producers Tony Award 1977, Columbia Business School Dean's Award 1982, Nat. Inst. of Music Theater Award 1985, Brown Univ. William Rogers Award 1995. *Operas produced include:* Pasatieri's The Seagull 1974, Porgy and Bess (Grammy Award 1977) 1976, Floyd's Bilby's Doll 1976, Willie Stark 1981, Harvey Milk (by Stewart Wallace and Michael Korie), Philip Glass's Akhnaten 1984, John Adams' Nixon in China (Emmy Award 1988) 1987, Tippett's New Year 1989, The Passion of Jonathan Wade 1991, Meredith Monk's Atlas 1991, Robert Moran's Desert of Roses 1992, Florencia en el Amazonas, Treemonisha, A Quiet Place, Resurrection, Carmen. *Leisure interest:* tennis. *Address:* San Francisco Opera, 301 Van Ness Avenue, San Francisco, CA 94102, USA (office). *Website:* www.sfopera.com (office).

GODAHEWA, Nalaka, BSc, MBA, PhD; Sri Lankan academic and business executive; *Chairman, Securities Exchange Commission;* ed Univs of Moratuwa, Sri Jayawardenapura, South Australia; started career at Unilever, held various positions including Head of Business Devt; fmr Marketing Dir Suntel, Gen. Man. MAS Shadowline, CEO MAS Holdings; Man. Dir Sri Lanka Insurance Corpn 2009–10; Chair. Sri Lanka Tourism Devt Authority 2010–12, Sri Lanka Tourism Promotions Bureau 2010–12, Sri Lanka Inst. of Tourism and Hotel Man. 2010–12, Sri Lanka Convention Bureau 2010–12, Securities Exchange Comm. 2012–, Asia Commerce Pvt. Ltd, Asscn of Licensed Banker Operations of Sri Lanka; Pres. Sri Lanka Br., Inst. of Certified Man. Accountants of Australia; mem. Certified Man. Accountants, Australia; Visiting Lecturer, Univ. of Colombo, Univ. of Keleniya, Univ. of Sri Jayewardenepura; mem. Bd of Dirs Seylan Bank PLC 2009–10, Urban Devt Authority, Colombo Land Pvt. Ltd, Sri Lanka Handicrafts Bd, Lanka Hospitals Pvt. Ltd, Sri Lankan Catering Pvt. Ltd; Fellow, Chartered Inst. of Marketing, UK, Inst. of Chartered Man. Accountants, UK; mem. Industry Consultative Cttee, Faculty of Eng, Univ. of Moratuwa; fmr Chair. Imperial Coll. of Business Studies; Hon. Pres. Global Marketing Network in Sri Lanka. *Address:* Securities and Exchange Commission of Sri Lanka, Level 28 and 29, East Tower, World Trade Centre, Echelon Square, Colombo 01 (office); 12-1, Park Tower, Havelock City, 324 Havelock Road, Colombo 05, Sri Lanka (home). *Telephone:* (11) 2331013 (office). *Fax:* (11) 2439149 (office). *E-mail:* mail@sec.gov.lk (office). *Website:* www.sec.gov.lk (office).

GODAL, Bjørn Tore; Norwegian diplomatist and politician; b. 20 Jan. 1945, Skien; s. of Kari Godal and Aksel Godal; m. Gro Balas 1988; one c.; ed Oslo Univ.; office clerk, Skien 1964–65; Pres. Labour League of Youth 1971–73 (Sec. for org. 1970–71), Fritt Forum (Labour Party's Student Org.) 1967–68; research officer, Labour Party 1973–80, Sec.-Gen. Oslo Labour Party 1980–82, Leader 1982–90 (mem. Cen. Cttee Labour Party 1983–90); Pres. Council of European Nat. Youth Cttees 1973–75; Head of Secr. Labour Party Group of the Oslo Municipal Council 1986; Deputy Rep. Storting (Parl.), then elected Rep.; Minister of Trade and Shipping 1991–94, of Foreign Affairs 1994–97, of Defence 2000–01; Amb. to Germany 2003–07; Special Adviser on int. energy- and climate issues, Ministry of Foreign Affairs 2007–10; currently Chair. Council of the Norwegian Defense Univ. Coll.; mem. Bd of Dirs Statoil ASA 2010–; Sr Advisor, Inst. of Political Science, Univ. of Oslo 2002–03; mem. Council for the Study of Power Distribution in Norway 1972–80, Standing Cttee on Finance 1986–89, on Foreign and Constitutional Affairs 1989–91, on Defence 1997–2000, Storting; Chair. Middle East Cttee 1997–2000, Socialist Int.; mem. North Atlantic Ass. 1997–2000. *Address:* Council of the Norwegian Defense University College, PO Box 800, Postmottak 2617, Lillehammer, Norway (office).

GODARD, Jean-Luc; French film director; b. 3 Dec. 1930, Paris; s. of Paul Godard and Odile Monad; m. 1st Anna Karina 1961 (divorced); m. 2nd Anne Wiazemsky 1967; ed Lycée Buffon and Faculté des Lettres, Paris; journalist and film critic; film director 1958–; Consul supérieur de la langue française 1989–; Chevalier, Ordre nat. du Mérite; Prix Jean Vigo for A bout de souffle 1960, Jury's Special Prize and Prix Pasinetti, Venice Festival 1962, Diploma of Merit,

Edin. Film Festival 1968 for Weekend, Grand Prix Nat. 1982, Grand Prix Nat. de la culture 1999, Hon. Acad. Award, Acad. of Motion Picture Arts and Sciences 2010. *Films:* Opération Béton 1954, Une femme coquette 1955, Tous les garçons s'appellent Patrick 1957, Charlotte et son Jules 1958, Une histoire d'eau 1958, A bout de souffle 1959, Le petit soldat 1960, Une femme est une femme 1961, Les sept péchés capitaux 1961, Vivre sa vie 1962, RoGoPaG 1962, Les carabiniers 1963, Le mépris 1963, Les plus belles escroqueries du monde 1963, Paris vu par ... 1963, Bande à part 1964, Une femme mariée 1964, Alphaville 1965, Pierrot le fou 1965, Masculin-féminin 1966, Made in USA 1966, Deux ou trois choses que je sais d'elle 1966, La chinoise 1967, Loin du Vietnam 1967, Weekend 1967, Le plus vieux métier du monde 1967, Vangelo '70 1967, Le gai savoir (TV) 1968, Un film comme les autres 1968, One Plus One 1968, One American Movie – 1 a.m. 1969, British Sounds 1969, Le vent d'est 1969, Lotte in Italia 1970, Vladimir et Rosa 1971, Tout va bien 1972, Numéro deux 1975, Ici et ailleurs 1976, Bugsy 1979, Sauve qui peut 1980, Passion 1982, Prénom Carmen 1983, Detective 1984, Je vous salue, Marie 1985, Soigne ta droite 1987, Aria (segment) 1987, Nouvelle Vague 1989, Allemagne neuf zero 1991, Hélas pour moi 1993, JLG/JLG 1995, Forever Mozart 1996, De l'origine du XXI^esiècle 2000, Eloge de l'amour 2001, Liberté et patrie 2002, Ten Minutes Older: The Cello 2002, Notre musique 2004, Vrai faux passeport 2006, Une Catastrophe 2008, Film Socialisme 2010. *Publication:* Introduction à une véritable histoire du cinéma 1980. *Address:* 26 ave Pierre 1er de Serbie, 75116 Paris, France; 15 rue du Nord, 1180 Roulle, Switzerland (home).

GODBER, John Harry, BEd, MA, PhD, FRSA; British playwright, film and theatre director and actor; *Senior Lecturer, Dance, Drama and Performance Studies Department, Liverpool Hope University;* b. 18 May 1956, Hemsworth, Yorks., England; s. of Harry Godber and Dorothy Godber; m. Jane Thornton; two d.; ed Minsthorpe High, Bretton Hall Coll., Wakefield, Univ. of Leeds; fmr Head of Drama, Minsthorpe High; Artistic Dir Hull Truck Theatre Co. 1984–; apptd Prof. of Contemporary Theatre, Liverpool Hope Univ. 2004, currently Sr Lecturer, Dance, Drama and Performance Studies Dept; fmr Prof. of Drama, Univ. of Hull; est. John Godber Co.; Hon. Lecturer, Bretton Hall Coll.; Hon. DLitt (Hull) 1988, (Lincoln) 1997, Hon. DUniv; Sunday Times Playwright Award 1981, Olivier Award 1984, Joseph Jefferson Award, Chicago 1988, Fringe First Winner (five times), BAFTA Awards for Best Schools Drama and for Best Original Drama 2005. *Plays:* Happy Jack 1982, September in the Rain 1983, Up 'n' Under (Laurence Olivier Comedy of the Year Award 1984) 1984, Bouncers (seven Los Angeles Critics' Awards 1986) 1985, Blood, Sweat and Tears 1986, Shakers, Teechers 1987, Salt of the Earth 1988, On the Piste 1990, Happy Families 1991, April in Paris 1992, The Office Party, Passion Killers 1994, Lucky Sods 1995, Dracula 1995, Gym and Tonic 1996, Weekend Breaks 1997, It Started with a Kiss 1997, Unleashed 1998, Perfect Pitch, Thick as a Brick (music by John Pattison) 1999, Big Trouble in Little Bedroom 1999, Seasons in the Sun 2000, On a Night Like This 2000, This House 2001, Departures 2001, Moby Dick 2002, Men of the World 2002, Reunion 2002, Next Best Thing 2007, Sold 2007, Our House 2008, Funny Turns 2009, 20,000 Leagues Under the Sea 2010; also radio plays and TV programmes. *Film:* Up 'n' Under (writer and dir) 1998. *Television:* The Ritz (BBC 2 series) 1987, The Continental (BBC Christmas Special), My Kingdom for a Horse (BBC film) 1991, Chalkface (BBC series) 1991, Bloomin' Marvellous (BBC comedy series) 1997, Thunder Road (BBC 4 film) 2001, Portas, Os 2005; has also written numerous episodes of Brookside, Crown Court and Grange Hill. *Leisure interests:* skiing, sport, literature, reading. *Address:* c/o Alan Brodie Representation Ltd, Paddock Suite, The Courtyard, 55 Charterhouse Street, London, EC1M 6HA, England (office); St Nicholas Swanland, North Ferriby, HU14 3QY, England (home). *Telephone:* (20) 7253-6226 (office); (1482) 633854 (home). *Fax:* (20) 7183-7999 (office). *E-mail:* lisa@alanbrodie.com (office); johnhgodber@hotmail.com (office). *Website:* www.alanbrodie.com (office); www.johngodber.co.uk.

GODDARD, Joseph Evan, DLS, MSc, JP; Barbadian industrial relations consultant and diplomatist; *Permanent Representative, United Nations;* b. 5 Aug. 1942; m. Nadine Pamela Goddard; one s. one d.; ed Ruskin Coll. and London School of Econs, UK; Gen. Sec. Caribbean Public Services Asscn 1982–97, Exec. Mem. 1997–2006; mem. Exec. Bd Public Services International (PSI) 1994–97, Regional Rep., PSI Public Sector Working Group 2003–06; Amb. and Perm. Rep. to UN, New York 2010–; mem. Bd Barbados Nat. Productivity Council 1996–2006, Barbados Airport Inc. 2000–06, Congress of Trade Unions and Staff Asscns of Barbados (CTUSAB) 1998–2006 (Vice-Pres. 2000–04); mem. Bd of Dirs Barbados Consumer Research Org. 2005–; Keys to City of Shanghai, Govt of China 2001; numerous awards, including Award of Excellence, Caribbean Congress of Labour 2007, Pride of Barbados Award 2007, CTUSAB Lifetime Award 2008. *Address:* Permanent Mission of Barbados to United Nations, 820 Second Avenue, 9th Floor, New York, NY 10017, USA (office). *Telephone:* (212) 551-4300 (office). *Fax:* (212) 986-1030 (office). *E-mail:* prun@foreign.gov.bb (office); barbados@un.int (office).

GODDARD, William Andrew, III, BS, PhD, FRSC; American chemist, materials scientist, applied physicist and academic; *Charles and Mary Ferkel Professor of Chemistry, Materials Science and Applied Physics and Director, Materials and Process Simulation Center, Beckman Institute, California Institute of Technology;* b. 29 March 1937, El Centro, Calif.; s. of William A. Goddard II and Barbara Worth Bright; m. Yvonne Amelia Goddard; one s. three d.; ed Univ. of California, Los Angeles, California Inst. of Tech.; Asst Prof. of Theoretical Chem., California Inst. of Tech. 1965, Assoc. Prof. and Prof. –1978, Prof. of Chem. and Applied Physics 1978–84, Dir NSF Materials Research Group 1984–90, Charles and Mary Ferkel Prof. of Chem. and Applied Physics 1984–2001, Charles and Mary Ferkel Prof. of Chem., Materials Science and Applied Physics 2001–, Dir Materials and Process Simulation Center, Beckman Inst. 1990–, Dir NSF Grand Challenges Applications Group 1992–97; World Class Univ. Prof., Energy Environment Water Susceptibility Grad. School, KAIST, Daejeon, S Korea 2009–13; Co-founder Molecular Simulations Inc. (now Accelrys) 1984 (Dir 1984–95, Chair. 1984–91), Schrödinger Inc. 1990 (Dir 1990–2000), Systine Inc. 2001 (Chair. 2003–), Allozyne 2004, QioMed 2010–; Chair. Material Science Advisory Bd; mem. Materials Research Soc., ACS, NAS 1984, Int. Acad. of Quantum Molecular Science 1988; Fellow, American Physical Soc. 1988, AAAS 1990, American Acad. of Arts and Sciences 2010; Hon. Philosophia Doctorem, Chem. (Uppsala) 2004; ACS Buck-Whitney Medal 1978, ACS Award for Computers in Chem. 1988, Calif. Inst. of Tech. Richard M. Badger Teaching Prize in Chem. 1995, Foresight Inst. Feynman Prize 1999, NASA Space Sciences Award 2000, 2009, 2012, ACS Richard Chase Tolman Prize

2000, ISI most Highly-Cited Chemist 1981–99, Inst. of Molecular Manufacturing Prize in Computational Nanotechnology Design 2002, ACS Award in Theoretical Chem. 2007, Award for Distinguished Scientific Achievement in Catalysis, 7th World Congress on Oxidation Catalysis 2013. *Publications:* 1,033 publs in scientific books and journals. *Address:* Beckman Institute (139–74), California Institute of Technology, 1200 East California Boulevard, Pasadena, CA 91125, USA (office). *Telephone:* (626) 395-2731 (office). *Fax:* (626) 585-0918 (office). *E-mail:* wag@wag.caltech.edu (office). *Website:* www.wag.caltech.edu (office).

GODDIO, Franck, BSc; American archaeologist; *Chairman, Franck Goddio Society;* b. 1947, Casablanca, Morocco; ed Ecole Nat. de la Statistique admin. Economique, Paris; adviser to various int. orgs; gained experience in marine archaeology in late 1970s; f. Institut Européen d'Archéologie Sous Marine, Paris 1987; Founder and Chair. Franck Goddio Soc.; excavated historically important sunken ships and discovered submerged ruins of Alexandria; Sr Visiting Lecturer, School of Archaeology, Univ. of Oxford 2009; Légion d'Honneur 2009. *Publications:* several books and scientific articles. *Address:* Franck Goddio Society, 3, Rue Bovy-Lysberg, 1204 Geneva, Switzerland (office). *Fax:* (509) 479-3653 (office). *E-mail:* info@franckgoddio.org (office). *Website:* www.franckgoddio.org (office).

GODFREY, Malcolm Paul Weston, CBE, MB, BS, FRCP; British medical practitioner (retd); b. 11 Aug. 1926, London; s. of Harry Godfrey and Rose Godfrey; m. Barbara Goldstein 1955; one s. two d. (one deceased); ed Hertford Grammar School, King's Coll., London, King's Coll. Hosp. Medical School; various appointments in Nat. Health Service 1950–60; Fellow in Medicine and Asst Physician, Johns Hopkins Hosp. Baltimore, Md 1957–58; HQ staff, MRC 1960–74; Dean, Royal Postgrad. Medical School, Hammersmith Hosp. 1974–83; Second Sec. MRC 1983–88; Queen's Hon. Physician 1987–90; Chair. Public Health Lab. Service Bd 1989–96, United Medical and Dental Schools of Guys and St Thomas' Hosps 1996–98; mem. Soc. of Scholars, Johns Hopkins Univ. (USA) 2000; Fellow, Royal Postgraduate Medical School 1985, Imperial Coll. School of Medicine 1999, King's Coll., London 2000; Pres. King's Coll. London Asscn 2002–04; Univ. of London Gold Medal 1950. *Publications:* articles on cardio-respiratory disorders in medical and scientific journals. *Leisure interests:* theatre, reading, current affairs, walking. *Address:* 17 Clifton Hill, St John's Wood, London, NW8 0QE, England (home). *Telephone:* (20) 7624-6335 (home). *Fax:* (20) 7328-9474 (home). *E-mail:* malcolmpgodfrey@talktalk.net (home).

GODINE, David R., MA, EdM; American publisher; *Founder-President, David R. Godine, Inc.;* b. 4 Sept. 1944, Cambridge, Mass; s. of Morton R. Godine and Bernice Beckwith; m. Sara Sangree Eisenman 1988; one s. one d.; ed Dartmouth Coll., Harvard Univ.; Founder-Pres. David R. Godine Inc. 1970–; mem. Bds Massachusetts Historical Soc., Massachusetts Horticultural Soc.; Fellow, Pierpoint Morgan Library; Dwiggins Award 1984. *Publication:* Renaissance Books of Science From the Collection of Albert E. Lownes (ed) 1970, The Red Pear Garden: Three Great Dramas of Revolutionary China 1973, 200 Years of American Sculpture 1976, The Field and Forest Handy Book: New Ideas for Out of Doors 2000, The Half-Life of An American Essayist (ed) 2008. *Leisure interests:* sailing, skiing. *Address:* David R. Godine, Inc., Fifteen Court Square, Suite 320, Boston, MA 02108-4715 (office); 196 School Street, Milton, MA 02186, USA (home). *Telephone:* (617) 451-9600 (office). *Fax:* (617) 350-0250 (office). *E-mail:* info@godine.com (office). *Website:* www.godine.com (office).

GODLEE, Fiona N., MB, BChir, FRCP; British physician, editor, writer and publisher; *Editor-in-Chief, British Medical Journal;* m.; two c.; apptd Asst Ed., British Medical Journal (BMJ) 1990, Editorial Dir, establishing open-access online publr BioMed Central, Current Science Group 2000–03, Head of Knowledge Div. BMJ Publishing Group 2003–04, Ed.-in-Chief British Medical Journal 2005–; Harkness Fellow, Harvard Univ. 1994; Co-Ed. Peer Review in Health Sciences; fmr Pres. World Asscn of Medical Eds; Chair., Cttee on Publication Ethics 2004–05. *Address:* BMJ Publishing Group Ltd, BMA House, Tavistock Square, London, WC1H 9JR, England (office). *Website:* www.bmjpg.com (office).

GODMANIS, Ivars, DrPhys; Latvian scientist and politician; b. 27 Nov. 1951, Rīga; s. of Teodors Godmanis and Ingrida Godmanis; m. Ramora Godmanè 1978; two s. one d.; ed Univ. of Latvia; engaged in scientific work since 1973; staff-mem. Inst. of Solid-State Physics, Univ. of Latvia 1973–86, Lecturer, Univ. of Latvia 1986–90; active involvement in Movt for Independence of Latvia, Deputy Chair., People's Front; Chair. Council of Ministers of Repub. of Latvia (Prime Minister) 1990–93; with commercial co. Software House 1994–95; Vice-Chair. Asscn of Commercial Banks of Latvia 1995–96; Pres. Latvia Savings Bank (jt stock co.) 1996–97; mem. Saeima (Parl.) 1998–; Minister of Finance 1998–99, of the Interior 2006–07, Prime Minister of Latvia 2007–09 (resgnd); Programme Man. JSC Radio SWH 2003–; Chair. Latvia's Way (Latvijas ceļš) 2004–07, Co-Chair. Latvian First Party/Latvian Way (Latvijas Pirmā Partija/Latvijas ceļš) 2007–; mem. Bd JSC Latvian Shipping Co. 1997–98, JSC Saliena Real 2002–04; Order of the Three Stars (Second Class); Commemorative medal for participation in the barricades of 1991. *Leisure interest:* tennis. *Address:* Latvian First Party/Latvian Way (Latvijas Pirmā Partija/Latvijas ceļš), Elizabetes iela 2, Rīga 1010, Latvia (office). *Telephone:* 6722-6070 (office). *Fax:* 6722-6831 (office). *E-mail:* info@lpplc.lv (office). *Website:* www.lpplc.lv (office).

GODOVSKY, Yan; Russian ballet dancer; *Assistant Ballet Artistic Director, Bolshoi Ballet;* b. Tbilisi, Georgia; ed Moscow Coll. of Choreography (now Moscow Acad. of Choreography); joined Bolshoi Theatre Co. 1993, becoming leading soloist, Asst Ballet Artistic Dir 2011–; Golden Mask Nat. Theatre Prize 2006, Ballet magazine Soul of Dance Prize 2008. *Roles danced include:* He-Devil (Nutcracker) 1993, Conrad (Tikhon Khrennikov's Love for Love) 1994, Peasant Pas de Deux (Giselle) 1994, Boy (La Sylphide) 1994, Jig (Don Quixote) 1994, Fool (Swan Lake) 1995, Pas d'Action (Giselle) 1997, Mime (Spartacus) 1997, Friend to Prince (Swan Lake) 1998, French Doll (Nutcracker) 1999, Nutcracker-Prince (Nutcracker) 2000, Alain (La Fille mal gardée) 2002, Magedaveya, Dance with drum (La Bayadère) 2002, Romeo (Romeo and Juliet) 2003, Tarantella 2004, Yan (Dmitry Shostakovich's Bolt) 2005, Soloist (Igor Stravinsky's Jeu de cards) 2005, Pas d'Esclaves (Le Corsaire) 2007. *Address:* Bolshoi Theatre Company, Moscow, Teatralnaya sq., 1, Russia (office). *Telephone:* (495) 292-92-70 (office). *Website:* www.bolshoi.ru (office).

GODREJ, Adi Burjor, MS; Indian industrialist; *Chairman, Godrej Group;* b. 3 April 1942, Bombay (now Mumbai); s. of Dr Burjor Pirojsha Godrej and Jai Burjor Godrej; m. Parmeshwar Mader 1966; one s. two d.; ed St Xavier's High School and Coll., Bombay, Massachusetts Inst. of Tech., USA; Chair. Godrej Group, Godrej Industries Ltd, Godrej Consumer Products Ltd, Godrej Properties Ltd, Godrej Hershey Ltd; mem. Bd of Dirs Godrej & Boyce Manufacturing Co. Ltd, Godrej Agrovet Ltd, Godrej International Ltd; fmr Chair. and Pres. Indian Soap & Toiletries Makers' Asscn, Central Org. for Oil Industry and Trade, Solvent Extractors' Asscn of India, Compound Livestock Feeds Mfrs' Asscn, Indo-American Soc., Governing Council of Narsee Monjee Inst. of Man. Studies; fmr mem. Dean's Advisory Council, MIT Sloan School of Man., Wharton Asian Exec. Bd; Chair. Indian School of Business; Pres.-Designate Confed. of Indian Industry; Patron Himalayan Club; Rajiv Gandhi Award 2002, Entrepreneur of the Year, Asia Pacific Entrepreneurship Awards 2010, Best Businessman of the Year, GQ Men of the Year Awards 2010, Chemexcil's Life Time Achievement Award 2010, AIMA-JRD Tata Corp. Leadership Award 2010, BMA Management Man of the Year Award 2010–11. *Leisure interests:* boating, waterskiing, windsurfing, horse riding, bridge. *Address:* Godrej Industries Ltd, Pirojshanagar, Eastern Express Highway, Vikhroli, Mumbai 400 079 (office); Aashraye Godrej House, 67-H Walkeshwar Road, Mumbai 400 006, India (home). *Telephone:* (22) 25188060 (office); (22) 25188010 (office); (22) 23642956 (home); (22) 23642956 (home). *Fax:* (22) 25188062 (office); (22) 23645159 (home). *E-mail:* abg@godrej.com (office); ab.godrej@godrejcp.com (office). *Website:* www.godrejindustries.com (office).

GODSELL, Robert (Bobby) Michael, BA, MA; South African business executive; b. 14 Sept. 1952, Boksburg; s. of Cyril H. Godsell and Winnefred Godsell (née Stephens); m. Gillian Hall 1975; three d.; ed Grosvenor Boys' High School, Univ. of Natal, Univ. of Cape Town; Deputy Prov. Leader Progressive Party, Natal 1969–70, Nat. Youth Chair. 1975–76; Dir Industrial Relations and Public Affairs, Anglo-American Corpn 1974–95, CEO Gold Div. 1995–2007, Deputy Chair. 1995–96, Chair. 1996–99, Dir (non-exec.) 1999–2008, Chair. and CEO AngloGold Ltd 2000–04, CEO AngloGold Ashanti (after Anglo merger with Ashanti Goldfields Co. Ltd) 2004–07; Chair. (non-exec.) Eskom Holdings Ltd 2008–09, World Gold Council 2001–02, Business Unity SA, Business Leadership SA, Freeworld Coatings; Co-Chair. Millennium Labour Council; Vice-Pres. Chamber of Mines 1991–97, Pres. 1992, 1997–98; Ind. Dir (non-exec.) Optimum Coal Holdings Ltd 2010–; fmr mem. Bd of Dirs (non-exec.) Standard Bank Group Ltd, Housing for Africa; mem. Nat. Econ. Forum 1994–, Nat. Planning Comm. 2010–; fmr mem. Buthelezi Comm.; Hon. Prof., Wits Business School. *Publications:* A Future South Africa: Visions, Strategies and Realities 1988 (co-ed.). *Leisure interest:* squash. *Address:* c/o Bd of Dirs, Optimum Coal Holdings Limited, First Floor, Marlborough Gate, Hyde Park Lane, Hyde Park, PO Box 411333, Johannesburg 2196, South Africa (office).

GODSOE, Peter C., OC, BSc, MBA, FCA; Canadian business executive; b. 2 May 1938, Toronto; s. of Joseph Gerald Godsoe and Margaret Graham Cowperthwaite; m. Shelagh Cathleen Reburn 1963; three c.; ed Univ. of Toronto, Harvard Univ., USA; fmr Deputy Chair. Bd, Pres., CEO and Dir Bank of Nova Scotia, Chair. CEO 1995–2004, also Chair. Bd of Dirs Bank of Nova Scotia Int. 1995–2004; Chair. Sobeys Inc., Fairmont Hotels and Resorts Inc. 2004–06; Vice Chair. Atlantic Inst. for Market Research; fmr Chair. and Dir Scotia Centre Ltd, Scotia Futures Ltd, Scotia Mortgage Corpn; fmr Vice-Chair. and Dir Bank of Nova Scotia Properties Inc., Scotia Properties Québec Inc., Scotia Realty Ltd; fmr Dir various Bank of Nova Scotia subsidiary cos, Alexander & Alexander Services Inc., Reed Stenhouse Cos Ltd, Nova Scotia Corpn, Scotiabank Jamaica Trust and Merchant Bank Ltd, West India Co. of Merchant Bankers Ltd; mem. Bd of Dirs Barrick Gold Corpn 2004–10, Ingersoll-Rand Co. Ltd 1998–, Onex Corpn 2004–, Rogers Communications Inc. 2004–, Templeton Emerging Markets Investment Trust PLC 2003–08, Canadian Council of Christians and Jews, Mount Sinai Hosp., Lonmin PLC 2001–10; fmr Chair. Canadian Bankers Asscn; Chancellor, Univ. of Western Ontario 1996–2000; Fellow, Inst. of Chartered Accountants; Hon. Commdr OJ 2004; Dr hc (Univ. of King's Coll.) 1993, (Concordia Univ.) 1995, (Univ. of Western Ontario) 2001, (Dalhousie Univ.) 2004; elected to Canadian Business Hall of Fame 2002, Ivey Business Leader Award, Univ. of Western Ontario 2005. *Address:* c/o Board of Directors, Rogers Communications Inc., 333 Bloor St. East, 10th Floor, Toronto, ON M4W 1G9, Canada,.

GODSON, Anthony; British fmr diplomatist and charity administrator; *Specialist Adviser, Foreign and Commonwealth Office;* b. 1 Feb. 1948, London, England; s. of the late Percival Lawrence Godson and Kathleen Elizabeth Godson (née Jennings); m. Maryan Jane Margaret Godson (née Hurst); joined FCO 1968, Attaché, Bucharest 1970–71, Third Sec., Kuala Lumpur 1972–73, Jakarta 1973–76, Pvt. Sec. to British High Commr, Canberra 1976–79, Cen. African Dept, FCO 1980–82, Second, later First Sec., UK Perm. Mission, New York 1983–86, First Sec. and Consul, Kinshasa 1987–88, Head of Indo-China Section, later Deputy Head of SE Asian Dept, FCO 1988–89, Deputy Head of Mission, Bucharest 1989–91, First Sec., UK Mission, Geneva 1992–95, Deputy Head of Eastern European and Cen. Asia Dept, FCO 1996–98, Counsellor, Later Deputy Head of Mission and Consul General, Jakarta 1998–2002, FCO 2003–04, High Commr to Mauritius (also accred as Amb. to the Comoros and Amb.-designate to Madagascar) 2004–07, Specialist Adviser, FCO 2012–; Exec. Dir Prospect Burma (charity) 2007–10. *Leisure interests:* playing tennis, skiing, walking, classical music, reading biographies, photography.

GODWIN, Gail Kathleen, PhD; American writer; b. 18 June 1937, Birmingham, Ala; d. of Mose Godwin and Kathleen Krahenbuhl; m. 1st Douglas Kennedy 1960 (divorced 1961); m. 2nd Ian Marshall 1965 (divorced 1966); ed Peace Jr Coll. Raleigh, NC and Univs of North Carolina and Iowa; news reporter, Miami Herald 1959–60; reporter and consultant, US Travel Service, London 1961–65; Editorial Asst Saturday Evening Post 1966; Fellow, Center for Advanced Study, Univ. of Illinois, Urbana 1971–72; Lecturer, Iowa Writers' Workshop 1972–73, Vassar Coll. 1977, Columbia Univ. Writing Program 1978, 1981; American specialist, USIS 1976; Guggenheim Fellow 1975–76; librettist for various productions; mem. PEN, Authors' Guild, Authors' League, Nat. Book Critics' Circle; American Acad. and Inst. of Arts and Letters Literature Award 1981. *Publications include:* novels including: The Perfectionists 1970, Glass People 1972, The Odd Woman 1974, Violet Clay 1978, A Mother and Two Daughters 1982, The Finishing School 1985, A Southern Family 1987, Father Melancholy's Daughter 1991, The Good Husband 1994, Evensong 1998, Evenings At Five 2003, Queen of the Underworld 2005,

Unfinished Desires 2009, Flora 2013; non-fiction: Heart 2001; The Making of A Writer: Journals (ed.) 1961–63 Vol. 1 2006, Vol. 2 2011; also short stories, uncollected stories, novellas and librettos. *Address:* PO Box 946, Woodstock, NY 12498-0946, USA (office). *E-mail:* gail@gailgodwin.com (office). *Website:* www .gailgodwin.com.

GOEDGEDRAG, Frits Martinus de los Santos, LLM; Dutch government official; b. 1 Nov. 1951, Aruba; m. Dulcie Yvonne Terborg; three s.; ed High School, Colegio Arubano, Catholic Univ. of Nijmegen; legal adviser, Dept of Legal and General Affairs 1977–81; Sec. to the Island Territory of Bonaire 1981–92; Sec. to Council of Govs 1981–92; Gov. of Island Territory of Bonaire 1992–98; Attorney Gen. 1998–2002; Gov. of Netherlands Antilles 2002–10 (last gov. before dissolution of Netherlands Antilles); Gov. of Curaçao 2010–12; Pres. Requisition Cttee Public Prosecutor, Application Comm. for the position of Dir of Dept of Justice; Pres. Judicial Governmental Del. to Netherlands 1998, to Belgium 2000, to Italy 2001; mem. Supervisory Bd Drug Rehabilitation Centre (Brasami), Curaçao, Selection Cttee for Public Servants Judicial Trainees (RAIO), and numerous other govt cttees; mem. Supervisory Bd Antillean Airlines Co., ALM, Cttee of Appeal of Football League of Bonaire, Bd Nat. Parks Foundation (Stinapa), Bonaire, Recompression Tanks Foundation, Zuster Maria Höppner Foundation, Jumpers basketball team, Bonaire; Hon. mem. Rotary Club of Curaçao 2004–; Kt, Order of Orange Nassau 1998; Naval Medal 'Almirante Luis Brion' for Distinguished Services Rendered to Venezuelan Navy 1994; Person of the Year, Bonaire Lions Club 1992. *Address:* c/o Ministry of Foreign Affairs, Bezuidenhoutseweg 67, POB 20061, 2500 EB, The Hague, Netherlands.

GOEHR, Alexander, MA; British composer and academic; *Professor Emeritus of Music, University of Cambridge;* b. 10 Aug. 1932, Berlin, Germany; s. of Walter Goehr and Laelia Goehr; m. 1st Audrey Baker 1954; m. 2nd Anthea Felicity Staunton 1972; m. 3rd Amira Katz; one s. three d.; ed Berkhamsted School, Royal Manchester Coll. of Music, Paris Conservatoire (with Olivier Messiaen) and privately with Yvonne Loriod; composer, teacher, conductor 1956–; held classes at Morley Coll., London; part-time post with BBC, being responsible for production of orchestral concerts 1960–; works performed and broadcast world-wide; awarded Churchill Fellowship 1968; Composer-in-Residence, New England Conservatory, Boston, Mass. 1968–69; Assoc. Prof. of Music, Yale Univ. 1969–70; Prof., West Riding Chair of Music, Univ. of Leeds 1971–76; Prof. of Music, Univ. of Cambridge 1976–99, Prof. Emer. 1999–, Fellow of Trinity Hall, Cambridge 1976–; Reith Lecturer 1987; Hon. Prof., Beijing Univ. 2001; Hon. mem. American Acad. and Inst. of Arts and Letters; Hon. ARCM 1976; Hon. FRNCM 1980; Hon. FRCM 1981; Hon. DMus (Southampton) 1973, (Manchester), (Nottingham) 1994, (Siena) 1999; Dr hc (Cambridge) 2000. *Works include:* Songs of Babel 1951, Sonata 1952, Fantasias 1954, Capriccio 1957, The Deluge 1957–58, La belle dame sans merci 1958, Four Songs from the Japanese 1959, Sutter's Gold 1959–60, Suite 1961, Hecuba's Lament 1959–61, A Little Cantata of Proverbs 1962, Two Choruses 1962, Virtutes 1963, Little Symphony 1963, Little Music for Strings 1963, Five Poems and an Epigram of William Blake 1964, Pastorals 1965, Piano Trio 1966, Arden muss sterben (Arden Must Die, opera) 1966, Warngedichte 1967, Romanza 1968, Naboth's Vineyard 1968, Nonomiya 1969, Paraphrase 1969, Symphony in One Movement 1970, Shadowplay 1970, Sonata about Jerusalem 1970, Concerto for Eleven Instruments 1970, Chaconne for Wind 1974, Lyric Pieces 1974, Metamorphosis/Dance 1974, Fugue on the Notes of the Fourth Psalm 1976, Romanza on the Notes of the Fourth Psalm 1977, Prelude and Fugue for Three Clarinets 1978, Chaconne for Organ 1979, Das Gesetz der Quadrille 1979, Babylon the Great is Fallen 1979, Behold the Sun 1984, Two Imitations of Baudelaire 1985, Symphony with Chaconne 1986, Eve Dreams in Paradise 1987, Carol for St Steven 1989, . . .in real time 1989, Sing, Ariel 1989, Still Lands 1990, Bach Variations 1990, The Death of Moses 1991, The Mouse Metamorphosed into a Maid 1991, Colossus or Panic 1992, I Said, I Will Take Heed 1993, Cambridge Hocket 1993, Arianna (opera) 1995, Schlussgesang 1997, Kantan (opera) 2000, Piano Quintet 2001, Second Musical Offering (GFH) 2002, Marching to Carcassonne 2003, Adagio (Autoporträt) 2003, Dark Days 2004, Fantasie 2005, Broken Lute 2006, Since Brass, Nor Stone (British Composer Award for Best Chamber Music Composition 2009) 2008, manere 2008, Broken Psalm 2009, TurmMusik/Tower Music 2009/10, from Shadow of Night 2009–10, Hymn to Night 2010, When Adam Fell 2010–11, Cities and Thrones and Powers 2011, Pomfret. The Dungeon of the Castle 2012, Largo Siciliano 2012, To These Dark Steps/The Fathers Are Watching 2012, . . .between the Lines/. . .zwischen den Zeilen 2013. *Address:* c/o Schott Music, 48 Great Marlborough Street, London, W1F 7BB, England. *E-mail:* promotions@ schott-music.com. *Website:* www.schott-music.com.

GOEI, Glen, BA, MA; Singaporean film and theatre director; *Associate Artistic Director, W!ld Rice Theatre Co.;* b. 22 Dec. 1962; ed Univ. of Cambridge, UK, New York Univ., USA; f. Mu-Lan Arts, London, Artistic Dir 1990–98; Creative Dir, Singapore Nat. Day Parade 2003, 2004, Singapore Pavilion for World Expo, Nagoya, Japan 2005; Assoc. Artistic Dir W!ld Rice Theatre Co.; Dir Dream Academy; Nat. Youth Council Award (Excellence) 1994. *Plays include:* with Mu-Lan Arts: Madame Mao's Memories 1991, 1993, Porcelain (London Fringe Awards Best Play, Best Production) 1992, The Magic Fundoshi (Best Comedy) 1993, 1994, Three Japanese Women 1993; in Singapore: Into the Woods 1994, Kampong Amber (Singapore Arts Festival headline event) 1994, Land of a Thousand Dreams 1995; with W!ld Rice: Blithe Spirit 2001, Boeing Boeing 2002, 2005, The Magic Fundoshi 2006, The Importance of Being Earnest 2009; with Dream Academy: Revenge of the Dim Sum Dollies 2004, The History of Singapore, The Little Shop of Horrors 2006. *Films:* Forever Fever (writer, dir and producer) 1998, The Blue Mansion 2009. *Address:* W!ld Rice Theatre Co, 3A Kerbau Rd, 219142, Singapore. *Telephone:* 6292-2695 (office). *Fax:* 6292-2249 (office). *E-mail:* info@wildrice.com .sg (office). *Website:* www.wildrice.com.sg (office).

GOEMAERE, Eric, MSc, MD; Belgian physician and international organization executive; ed Leuven Univ., Inst. of Tropical Medicine, Antwerp; fmr Head Mission in S Africa, Médecins Sans Frontières (MSF – Doctors Without Borders); est. training programme for primary health care, Univ. of Cape Town; Co-founder Jt Civil Soc. Monitoring Forum; fmr adviser to WHO; currently Lecturer, Univ. of Witwatersrand; Hon. DrSci (Univ. of Cape Town) 2008. *Address:* School of Public Health, Faculty of Health Sciences, University of Witwatersrand, Johannesburg,

South Africa. *Telephone:* (11) 717-2543. *Fax:* (11) 717-2084. *Website:* web.wits.ac .za/Academic/Health/PublicHealth.

GOENKA, Harsh Vardhan, MBA; Indian business executive; b. 10 Dec. 1957, Calcutta; s. of Rama Prasad Goenka and Sushila Goenka; m. Mala Sanghi 1977; one s. one d.; ed St Xavier's Coll., Calcutta, IMD (Int. Inst. of Managerial Devt), Lausanne, Switzerland; joined family business RPG Enterprises; Vice-Chair. Ceat Ltd; Chair. RPG Enterprises 1988–, RPG Life Science, KEC Int. Ltd, RPG Cables, Bayer (India) Ltd; Zensar Technologies Ltd; Dir (non-exec.) Bajaj Electricals; mem. Exec. Cttee Fed. of Indian Chambers of Commerce and Industry; Bd mem. IMD, Lausanne, Switzerland; fmr Pres. Indian Merchants' Chamber; mem. Bd of Govs Nat. Inst. of Industrial Eng. *Leisure interests:* sports, art. *Address:* RPG Enterprises Ltd, CEAT Mahal, 463 Dr Annie Besant Road, Worli Mumbai 400 025, India. *Telephone:* (22) 24930621 (office); (22) 23630873 (home). *Fax:* (22) 24938933 (office). *E-mail:* hgoenka@rpg.in (office). *Website:* www.rpg.in (office).

GOERENS, Charles; Luxembourg politician; *President, Sahel and West Africa Club, Organisation for Economic Co-operation and Development;* b. 6 Feb. 1952, Ettelbruck; m.; three c.; ed Lycée Technique Agricole; mem. Parl. (Northern Dist constituency) for Parti Démocratique 1979; mem. European Parl. 1982–84, 1994–99; Pres. Ass. of WEU (Interparliamentary European Security and Defence Ass.) 1987–90, 2004; Chair. Parti Démocratique 1989–94; Minister for Co-operation, Humanitarian Action and Defence and for the Environment 1999–2004, of Foreign Affairs 20–31 July 2004; Pres. Sahel and West Africa Club, OECD 2006–; mem. Consultative Ass. of Council of Europe. *Address:* Sahel and West Africa Club/OECD, 2 rue André-Pascal, 75775 Paris Cedex 16, France (office). *Telephone:* 1-45-24-89-87 (office). *Fax:* 1-45-24-90-31 (office). *E-mail:* swac .contact@oecd.org (office). *Website:* www.westafricaclub.org (office).

GOFF, Gregory J., BS, MBA; American business executive; *President and CEO, Tesoro Corporation;* ed Univ. of Utah; joined Conoco 1981, held several positions in transportation as well as in supply and trading, served internationally in Europe, Asia and Latin America, Sr Vice-Pres., Commercial, ConocoPhillips –2010; Pres. and CEO Tesoro Corpn 2010–. *Address:* Tesoro Corporation, 300 Concord Plaza Drive, San Antonio, TX 78216-6999, USA (office). *Telephone:* (210) 828-8484 (office). *Fax:* (210) 283-2045 (office). *E-mail:* info@tsocorp.com (office). *Website:* www.tsocorp.com (office).

GOFF, Martyn, CBE, OBE, FIAL, FRSA; British author and bookseller; *Executive Director and Chairman, Henry Sotheran Ltd;* b. 7 June 1923; s. of Jacob Goff and Janey Goff; ed Clifton Coll.; served in RAF 1941–46; worked in film industry 1946–48; bookseller 1948–70; established Booker Prize (later Man Booker Prize) 1969, Admin. 1970–2006, Chair. Advisory Cttee Man Booker Prize 2002–06, currently Pres. Booker Prize Foundation; CEO Book Trust 1970–88, Vice-Pres. 2000– (Deputy Chair. 1991–92, 1996–97, Chair. 1992–96); Fiction Reviewer, Daily Telegraph 1975–88, Non-fiction Reviewer 1988–; Dir and Exec. Chair. Henry Sotheran Ltd antiquarian bookseller 1988–; mem. Arts Council Literature Panel 1973–81, British Nat. Bibliography Research Fund 1976–88, British Library Advisory Council 1977–82, PEN Exec. Cttee 1978–, Exec. Cttee Greater London Arts Council 1982–88, Library and Information Services Council 1984–86; mem. Bd British Theatre Asscn 1983–85; Chair. Paternosters '73 Library Advisory Council 1972–74, New Fiction Soc. 1975–88, School Bookshop Asscn 1977–, Soc. of Bookmen 1982–84 (Pres. 1997–), 1890s Soc. 1990–99, Nat. Life Story Collections 1996–2004, Poetry Book Soc. 1996–99 (mem. Bd 1992–99), Wingate Scholarships 1988–2004, H. H. Wingate Foundation 1998–, Books for Keeps; Vice-Pres. Royal Overseas League 1996–; Dir Nat. Book League (mem. Prize Cttee 2008), Battersea Arts Centre 1992–97 (Trustee 1981–85); Trustee Cadmean Trust 1981–99, Nat. Literary Trust 1993–2004; Hon. FRSL 2002, Hon. FRS 2003; Hon. DLitt (Oxford Brookes) 2003; The Bookseller Services to Bookselling Award 2001. *Publications:* fiction: The Plaster Fabric 1957, A Season With Mammon 1958, A Sort of Peace 1960, The Youngest Director 1961, Red on the Door 1962, The Flint Inheritance 1965, Indecent Assault 1967, The Liberation of Rupert Bannister 1978, Tar and Cement 1988; non-fiction: A Short Guide to Long Play 1957, A Further Guide to Long Play 1958, LP Collecting 1960, Why Conform? 1968, Victorian and Edwardian Surrey 1972, Record Choice 1974, Royal Pavilion 1976, Organising Book Exhibitions 1982, Publishing 1988, Prize Writing: An Original Collection of Writings by Past Winners to Celebrate 21 Years of the Booker Prize (ed.) 1989. *Leisure interests:* travel, collecting pictures and books. *Address:* Henry Sotheran Ltd, 2 Sackville Street, London, W1S 3DP (office); 95 Sisters Avenue, London, SW11 5SW, England (home). *Telephone:* (20) 7734-1150 (office); (20) 7228-8164 (home). *Fax:* (20) 7434-2019 (office); (20) 7738-9893 (home). *Website:* www .sotherans.co.uk (office).

GOFF, Philip (Phil) Bruce, MA, MP; New Zealand politician; b. 22 June 1953, Auckland; s. of Bruce Charles Goff and Elaine Loyola Goff; m. Mary Ellen Moriarty 1979; two s. one d.; ed Papatoetoe High School, Univ. of Auckland, Nuffield Coll., Univ. of Oxford; Lecturer in Political Science, Auckland Univ.; field officer in Insurance Workers' Union; fmr Chair. Labour Youth Council; MP for Roskill 1981–90, 1993–96, for New Lynn 1996–99, for Mt Roskill 1999–; Minister of Housing, for the Environment, responsible for Government Life Insurance Corpn, in charge of the Public Trust Office 1986–87, of Employment, of Youth Affairs and Assoc. Minister of Educ. 1987–89, Minister of Tourism 1987–88, of Educ. 1989–90, of Foreign Affairs and Trade and of Justice 1999–2005, Minister of Defence 2005–08; Minister of Trade, of Pacific Island Affairs and for Disarmament and Arms Control Oct. 2005–08, of Corrections 2007–08; British Council Scholarship to Nuffield Coll. 1992; mem. Labour Party 1969–, Leader 2008–11, Leader of the Opposition 2008–11. *Leisure interests:* sports, gardening. *Address:* Executive Wing, Parliament Buildings, Wellington (office); Creightons Road RD 2, Papakura, Auckland, New Zealand (home). *Telephone:* (9) 624-2278 (office); (9) 292-8377 (home). *Fax:* (4) 624-1058 (office). *E-mail:* phil.goff@parliament.govt.nz (office). *Website:* www.labour.org.nz (office).

GOFF OF CHIEVELEY, Baron (Life Peer), cr. 1986, of Chieveley in the Royal County of Berkshire; Rt Hon. Lord Goff of Chieveley; **Robert (Lionel Archibald) Goff,** Kt, PC, DCL, FBA; British lawyer (retd); b. 12 Nov. 1926; s. of L.T. Goff; m. Sarah Cousins 1953; two s. (one deceased) two d.; ed Eton Coll., New Coll., Oxford; served in Scots Guards 1945–48 (commissioned 1945); called to the Bar, Inner Temple 1951; Bencher 1975; QC 1967; Fellow and Tutor, Lincoln Coll., Oxford

1951–55; in practice at the Bar 1956–75; a Recorder 1974–75; Judge of the High Court, Queen's Bench Div. 1975–82; Judge in charge of Commercial List and Chair. Commercial Court Cttee 1979–81; Chair. Council of Legal Educ. 1976–82, Vice-Chair. 1972–76, Chair. Bd of Studies 1970–76; Chair. Common Professional Examination Bd 1976–78; Chair. British Inst. of Int. and Comparative Law 1986–2001, Court of Univ. of London 1986–91, Sub-Cttee E (Law) of House of Lords Select Cttee on European Communities 1986–88; Chair. Pegasus Scholarship Trust 1987–2001; Pres. Bentham Club 1986, Chartered Inst. of Arbitrators 1986–91, Holdsworth Club 1988, British Inst. of Int. and Comparative Law 2001–; Hon. Prof. of Legal Ethics, Univ. of Birmingham 1980–81; Maccabean Lecturer 1983; Lionel Cohen Lecturer (Jerusalem) 1987; Cassel Lecturer (Stockholm) 1993; mem. Gen. Council of the Bar 1971–74; mem. Senate of Inns of Court and Bar 1974–82; Chair. Law Reform and Procedure Cttee 1974–76; Lord Justice of Appeal 1982–86; Lord of Appeal in Ordinary 1986–98; Sr Law Lord 1996–98; High Steward Oxford Univ. 1990–2001; Hon. Fellow, Lincoln Coll., Oxford, New Coll., Oxford, Wolfson Coll., Oxford; Hon. Fellow, American Coll. of Trial Lawyers 1997; Grand Cross, Order of Merit (Germany) 1999; Hon. DLitt (City) 1977, (Buckingham) 1989; Hon. LLD (Reading, London) 1990, (Bristol) 1996. *Publication:* The Law of Restitution (with Prof. Gareth Jones) 1966. *Address:* House of Lords, Westminster, London, SW1A 0PW, England (office).

GOGGIN, Brian J., MSc; Irish banking executive; ed Trinity Coll. Dublin; joined Bank of Ireland 1969, various sr man. roles within Bank of Ireland Group in USA, UK and Ireland, CEO Corp. and Treasury 1996, apptd to Court of Bank of Ireland 2000, CEO Wholesale Financial Services 2002–03, CEO Asset Man. Services 2003–04, Group Chief Exec. 2004–09 (resgnd), also Chair. Bristol & West PLC (subsidiary co.) 2005–; Pres. Irish Chapter, Ireland-US Council; Dir Post Office Ltd.

GOGGINS, Colleen A.; American business executive; *Worldwide Chairman, Consumer and Personal Care Group, Johnson & Johnson;* ed Kellogg School of Man., Northwestern Univ.; began working at Johnson & Johnson 1981, has held several sr posts, including Dir of Marketing, Johnson & Johnson GmbH, Germany 1990–92, Pres. Johnson & Johnson Canada 1992–94, Pres. Consumer Products Co. 1995–98, Co. Group Chair. 1998–2001, Worldwide Chair. Consumer and Personal Care Group and mem. Exec. Cttee, Johnson & Johnson 2001–; mem. Exec. Advisory Bd Center for Brand and Product Man., School of Business, Univ. of Wis.-Madison; ranked by Fortune magazine amongst the 50 Most Powerful Women in Business in US (37th) 2006, (39th) 2007, (24th) 2008, (19th) 2009, ranked by Forbes magazine amongst The World's 100 Most Powerful Women (78th) 2009. *Address:* Johnson & Johnson, 1 Johnson & Johnson Plaza, New Brunswick, NJ 08933, USA (office). *Telephone:* (732) 524-0400 (office). *Fax:* (732) 524-3300 (office). *Website:* www.jnj.com (office).

GOGOI, Tarun, BA, LLB; Indian lawyer and politician; *Chief Minister of Assam (Asom);* b. 1 April 1936, Rangajan Tea Estate, Jorhat Dist; s. of the late Kamaleswar Gogoi; m. Dolly Gogoi 1972; one s. one d.; ed Gauhati Univ.; mem. Jorhat Municipal Council 1968–71, Leader Assam Youth Community 1971; elected to Lok Sabha 1971–; Jt Sec. All India Congress Cttee 1976, Gen. Sec. 1985; Pres. Assam Pradesh Congress (I) Cttee 1986–1990, 1996–2001, Vice-Pres. 1991; Minister of Food 1991–93; Minister of State for Food Processing Industry 1993–95; mem. Assam Legis. Ass. 1997–98; Chief Minister of Assam (Asom) 2001–; fmr Chair. Assam Small Industrial Devt Corpn, Bharat Yuvak Samaj; fmr Dir Vayudoot; fmr Jt Sec. Jorhat Law Coll.; fmr Commdr Student Volunteer Corps; mem. Consultative Cttee, Ministry of Petroleum and Natural Gas 1998–99, Cttee on Railways 1999–2000, Bar Council Assam, Cttee on Govt Assurances, Cttee on External Affairs; Universal Smile Award 2009. *Leisure interests:* travelling, reading, gardening. *Address:* Office of the Chief Minister, Government of Assam, Assam Sachivalaya Complex, Dispur Guwahati 781 006 (office); Nazir Ali, Jorhat 785 001, India (home). *E-mail:* asmgovt@asm.nic.in (office). *Website:* www.assamgovt.nic.in (office).

GOH, Chok Tong, MA; Singaporean politician; *Emeritus Senior Minister and Senior Adviser, Monetary Authority of Singapore;* b. 20 May 1941, Pasir Panjang; s. of the late Goh Kah Khoon and of Quah Kwee Hwa; m. Tan Choo Leng 1965; one s. one d. (twins); ed Raffles Inst., Univ. of Singapore and Williams Coll., USA; with Singapore Admin. Service 1964–69, Neptune Orient Lines Ltd 1969–77; MP 1976–; Minister, Ministries of Trade and Industry, Health and Defence 1979–90, Deputy Prime Minister 1985–90; Prime Minister of Singapore 1990–2004; Sr Minister in Prime Minister's Office 2004–11, Emer. Sr Minister 2011–; Chair. Monetary Authority of Singapore 2004–11, Sr Adviser 2011–; mem. Central Exec. Cttee People's Action Party 1979–, Sec.-Gen. 1992–2004; Perm. mem. Pres.'s Council for Minority Rights; Patron for Advancement, Singapore Univ. of Tech. and Design 2012; Grand Knight Cordon (Special Class) of the Most Exalted Order of the White Elephant (Thailand) 1997, Hon. Companion of the Order of Australia 2005, Order of the Rising Sun (Japan) 2011; Medal of Honour, Nat. Trade Union Congress (NTUC) 1987, Distinguished Comrade of Labour Award 2001, Jawaharlal Nehru Award for Int. Understanding (India) 2004. *Leisure interests:* tennis, golf. *Address:* Monetary Authority of Singapore (MAS), 10 Shenton Way, MAS Bldg, Singapore 079117; Prime Minister's Office, Orchard Road, Istana, Singapore 238823 (office). *Telephone:* 62255577 (MAS); 62358577 (office). *Fax:* 62299491 (MAS); 67324627 (office). *E-mail:* Goh_Chok_Tong@pmo.gov.sg (office); webmaster@mas.gov.sg. *Website:* www.pmo.gov.sg (office); www.mas.gov.sg.

GOH, Kun, MS; South Korean politician; b. 2 Jan. 1938, Seoul; m.; three s.; ed Kyung Ki High School, Seoul Nat. Univ.; Pres. Gen. Students' Council, Seoul Nat. Univ. 1959; Asst Jr Official Ministry of Home Affairs 1962–65, Asst Dir Planning Office 1965–68; Dir Interior Dept Jeonbuk Prov. 1968–71; Commr New Village Movt 1971–73; Vice-Gov. Gangwon Prov. 1973; Gov. of S Jeolla Prov. 1975–79; Chief Sec. of Political Affairs to the Pres., Chong Wa Dae (The Blue House) 1979–80; Chief Adviser Korea Research Inst. for Human Settlement 1980; Minister of Transportation 1980–81, of Agric. and Marine Affairs 1981–82; Visiting Fellow, Harvard Univ. 1983; Visiting Prof. MIT 1984; mem. 12th Nat. Ass. 1985–88; Minister of Home Affairs 1987; Dir Local Admin. Bureau 1973–75; Mayor Seoul Metropolitan Govt 1988–90; Pres. Myong Ji Univ. 1994–97; Co-Pres. Korea Fed. for Environment Movt 1996–97; Prime Minister of Repub. of Korea 1997–98, 2003–04 (resgnd); Mayor of Seoul 1998–2002; Acting Pres. of Repub. of Korea March–May 2004; Pres. Transparency Int. Korea 2002–04 (resgnd); Hon. LLD

(Won Kwang Univ.) 1992, (Syracuse Univ.) 2001; Order of Service Merit (Blue Stripes) 1972, (Red Stripes) 1982; Outstanding Policy-Maker Award, Korea Univ. 2000, Transparency Int. Global Integrity Medal 2001, Polestar Order from the Mongolian Pres. 2002. *Address:* c/o Office of the Prime Minister, 77 Sejong-no, Jongno-gu, Seoul, Republic of Korea.

GOICOECHEA LUNA, Emilio Rafael José; Mexican business executive, politician and diplomatist; b. 22 Oct. 1948, Mazatlan, Sinaloa; ed Instituto Tecnológico y de Estudios Superiores de Monterrey; served as Pres. Confederación Nacional de Cámaras de Comercio (Confed. of Nat. Chambers of Commerce), Instituto Mexicano de Mercadotecnia A.C. (Mexican Marketing Inst.) and mem. Consejo Coordinador Empresarial (Entrepreneurial Coordinating Council), Confederación Patronal de la República Mexicana (Employers' Confed. of Mexico); fmr adviser/consultant to nat. orgs including Centro de Estudios Económicos del Sector Privado, Instituto Mexicano de Comercio Exterior, Instituto Mexicano del Seguro Social, Instituto del Fondo Nacional de la Vivienda para los Trabajadores, Fondo Nacional de Fomento al Turismo, Ferrocarriles Nacionales de México, Asociación Nacional de Importadores y Exportadores, Confederación Nacional de Cámaras Industriales; began political career as Senator 1994–2000, mem. Fed. Chamber of Deputies 2000–03, Under-Sec. of Tourism 2003, Chief of Staff to Pres. Vicente Fox 2004–06; Amb. to Canada 2007–09; mem. Partido Acción Nacional (mem. Nat. Exec. 1996–); Pres. Asscn of Scouts of Mexico; Acapulco Chamber of Commerce's Exec. of the Year, Key to the City of Miami, Inst. for Promotion of Free Enterprise Golden Eagle award.

GOIRIGOLZARRI TELLAECHE, José Ignacio, DEcon; Spanish banking executive; *President, Bankia SA;* b. 4 Feb. 1954, Bilbao; m.; two c.; ed Universidad de Deusto, Univ. of Leeds, England; joined the Banco de Bilbao 1978, worked in Strategic Planning, worked with Banco Bilbao Vizcaya Holdings, apptd Gen. Man. 1992, Man. Dir Retail Banking 1995–2000, Man. Dir Banco Bilbao Vizcaya Argentaria (BBVA) SA, US Div. 2000–01, Pres. and COO BBVA SA 2001–09, mem. Bd of Dirs 2001–09 (retd); Vice-Pres. Repsol YPF 2002–03; Dir and Pres. Bankia SA 2012–; Chair. Banco Financiero y de Ahorros 2012–; mem. Bd of Dirs Telefonica SA 2000–03. *Address:* Bankia SA, Pintor Sorolla nº 8, 46002 Valencia, Spain (office). *Website:* www.bankia.es (office).

GOKONGWEI, John L., Jr, MBA; Philippine business executive; *Founder and Chairman Emeritus, JG Summit Holdings Inc.;* b. 4 July 1926, Xiamen, China; m. Elizabeth Yu Gokongwei; one s. five d.; ed San Carlos Univ., Cebu, De La Salle Univ., Manila, Harvard Business School, USA; f. Amasia Trading (import co.) 1946; f. Universal Corn Products (corn milling plant) 1957, renamed Universal Robina Corpn 1966, currently Dir and Chair. Emer.; Dir and Chair. Emer. Robinsons Land Corpn, JG Summit Petrochemical Corpn; Chair. Emer. Robinsons Bank; Founder, JG Summit Holdings Inc., Chair. and CEO –2001, now Dir and Chair. Emer.; Chair. and CEO Robinsons Retail Holdings, Inc.; Chair. Gokongwei Brothers Foundation, Inc.; Deputy Chair. United Industrial Corpn Ltd, Singapore Land Ltd (Singland); mem. Bd of Dirs Oriental Petroleum and Minerals Corpn, A. Soriano Corpn, JG Summit Olefins Corpn, Cebu Air, Inc. *Address:* JG Summit Holdings, Inc., 44/F Robinsons Equitable Tower, ADB Avenue, corner Poveda Road, Ortigas Center, Pasig City, Philippines (office); JG Summit Holdings, Inc., 44/F Robinsons Equitable Tower, ADB Avenue, corner Poveda Road, Ortigas Center, Pasig City, Philippines. *Telephone:* (2) 6337631 (office). *Fax:* (2) 3952607 (office). *Website:* www.jgsummit.com.ph (office).

GOLAN, Menahem; Israeli film director and film producer; b. 31 May 1929, Tiberius; m.; three c.; ed Old Victoria, London, London Acad. of Music and Dramatic Art, New York Univ.; f. Noah Films with Yoram Globus (q.v.) 1963; Sr Vice-Pres. Cannon Group Inc. 1979–89; founder and Chair., CEO 21st Century Film Corpn 1989–96; co-partner Golan-Globus –2008; Israel Prize 1999. *Films include:* Over the Top, Delta Force, Over the Brooklyn Bridge, Enter the Ninja, The Magician of Lublin, Barfly, Surrender, Death Wish IV, Superman IV, Street Smart, Dancers, Eskimo Limon, 52 Pickup, Otello, The Assault, Hanoi Hilton, Cannon Movie Tales, Masters of the Universe, Duet for One, Tough Guys Don't Dance, Shy People, Hanna's War, The Rose Garden, Rope Dancing, The Phantom of the Opera, Armstrong, Kumite, Death Game, Crime and Punishment, Open Heart, Children of Wax, Days of Love, A Dangerous Dance, Rak Klavim Ratzim Hofshi. *Address:* 21st Century Film Corporation, 7000 West Third Street, Los Angeles, CA 90048, USA.

GOLANI, Rivka; Canadian violist and painter; b. 22 March 1946, Israel; d. of Jacob Gulnik and Lisa Gulnik; m. Jeremy Fox 1993; one s.; ed Univ. of Tel-Aviv; studied with Oedon Partos; concerts as soloist world-wide; has inspired many new works including viola concerti by Holloway, Hummel, Fontajn, Colgrass, Holmboe, Yuasa and Turner, solo works by Holliger, Holmboe and others; has collaborated with composers as a visual artist in presenting multimedia performances; art exhbns in Israel, UK, Germany and N America; Grand Prix du Disque 1985. *Recordings include:* three-album set of solo works by J. S. Bach. *Publication:* Birds of Another Feather (book of drawings). *Address:* Michael Brewer Artists Management, 8 Toynbee Close, Osbaston, Monmouth, NP25 3NU, Wales (office); c/o Margaret Barkman, 54 Long Point Drive, Richmond Hill, ON L4E 3W8, Canada (home). *Telephone:* (416) 722-6977 (home). *Fax:* (905) 773-6261 (home). *E-mail:* margaretbarkman@yahoo.com (home).

GOLD, Christina A.; Canadian business executive; ed Carleton Univ.; Founder, The Beaconsfield Group 1970–98; joined Avon Products, Inc. 1970, Pres. Avon Canada 1989–93, Pres. Avon North America 1993–97, Exec. Vice-Pres. of Global Devt 1997–98; Pres. and CEO Excel Communications 1999–2002; Pres. First Data Corpn (fmr parent co. of Western Union) 2002–06, Pres. and CEO Western Union Financial Services, Inc. 2006–10 (retd); mem. Bd of Dirs ITT Industries 1998–, New York Life Insurance Co. 2001–, Safe Water Network 2010–, IFF 2013–, Torstar Corpn 1998–2007; Batisseur hon. degree (Professional Business School of Montreal); named by Business Week amongst Top 25 US Managers 1996, ranked by Fortune magazine amongst the 50 Most Powerful Women in Business in the US (49th) 2003, (49th) 2006, (21st) 2008, (31st) 2009, ranked by Forbes magazine amongst The World's 100 Most Powerful Women (56th) 2007, (90th) 2008, (77th) 2009, Award of Distinction, Faculty of Commerce and Admin, Concordia Univ., Montreal.

GOLD, David; British business executive; *Owner and Chairman, Gold Group International;* b. 15 Jan. 1937, Stepney, East London; m.; two d.; Jt Owner (with brother Ralph) Gold Group International 1965–2008, sole Owner and Chair. 2008–, parent co. of retailer Ann Summers and lingerie chain Knickerbox, Gold Aviation, Greenwich House Properties, York Place and West Ham United Football Club; Chair. Birmingham City Football Club 1997–2009; acquired (with David Sullivan) 62% share of West Ham United Football Club, London 2010, Jt Chair. 2010–; Winner, Gozo Beacon 1979, Winner, Int. Malta Air Rally 1981, 1982 (runner up on three occasions). *Publication:* Pure Gold (with Bob Harris) 2005. *Leisure interests:* fixed wing pilot for 37 years, helicopter pilot for seven years. *Address:* Gold Group International, Gold Group House, Godstone Road, Whyteleafe, Surrey, CR3 0GG, England (office). *Telephone:* (1883) 629629 (office). *Fax:* (1883) 629220 (office). *Website:* www.davidgold.co.uk; www.whufc.com.

GOLD, Jack, BSc (Econ), LLB; British film director; b. 28 June 1930; m. Denyse Macpherson 1957; two s. one d.; ed Univ. of London; Asst Studio Man., BBC radio 1954–55; Ed. Film Dept, BBC 1955–60; Dir TV and film documentaries and fiction 1960–; Hon. Assoc., London Film School 2010. *Television films include:* Tonight, Death in the Morning (BAFTA Award) 1964, Modern Millionairess, Famine, Dowager in Hot Pants, World of Coppard (BAFTA Award 1967), Mad Jack (Grand Prix, Catholic Award, Monte Carlo Award) 1971, The Resistible Rise of Arturo Ui, Stockers Copper (BAFTA Award 1972), Catholics (Peabody Award) 1974, The Naked Civil Servant (Italia Prize, Int. Emmy, Critics Award, Desmond Davies Award 1976) 1976, Thank You Comrades 1978, A Walk in the Forest 1980, Merchant of Venice 1980, L'Elégance 1982, Praying Mantis 1983, Macbeth 1983, The Red Monarch 1983, The Tenth Man 1988, The Rose and the Jackal 1989, Ball Trap on Côte Sauvage 1989, The Shlemiel, The Shlemazi and The Doppess 1990, The War that Never Ends 1991, She Stood Alone 1991, The Last Romantics 1992, Spring Awakening 1995, Kavanagh QC 1995, 2001, Heavy Weather 1996, Mute of Malice 1997, Blood Money 1997, Into the Blue 1997, Care in the Community 1998, Goodnight Mr. Tom (Silver Hugo Award, Chicago 1998, BAFTA Award 1999) 1998, The Remorseful Day (BAFTA Award 2001) 2001, The John Thaw Story 2002, The Brief. *Theatre:* Council of Love, The Devil's Disciple, Danger Memory, This Story of Yours, Three Hotels, Crossing Jerusalem, 12 Angry Men. *Films include:* The Bofors Gun 1968, Mad Jack 1971, The National Health (Evening News Best Comedy Film 1973) 1973, Who? 1974, Man Friday 1975, Aces High (Evening News Best Film Award) 1976, The Medusa Touch 1977, The Sailor's Return (Karoly Vary Award, Martin Luther King Award, Monte Carlo Catholic Award, Monte Carlo Critics Award) 1978, Little Lord Fauntleroy (Christopher Award) 1981, A Lot of Happiness (Int. Emmy Award) 1983, Sakharov (Ace Award) 1984, Me and the Girls 1985, Murrow (Ace Award) 1986, Escape from Sobibor (Golden Globe Award) 1987, Stones for Ibarra 1988, The Lucona Affair 1993, Return of the Native 1994, Spring Awakening 1994, Into the Blue 1997. *Leisure interests:* music, reading, tennis.

GOLD, Phil, CC, OQ, BSc, MSc, MDCM, PhD, FRCP(C), MACP, FRSC; Canadian physician and academic; *Douglas G. Cameron Professor of Medicine and Professor of Physiology and of Oncology, McGill University;* b. 17 Sept. 1936, Montreal, Quebec; s. of the late Jack Gold and Rose Gold; m. Evelyn Katz; three c.; ed McGill Univ.; postgraduate training and research, The McGill Univ. Medical Clinic of The Montreal Gen. Hosp.; Medical Research Council of Canada Centennial Fellow 1967–68, Assoc. and Career Scientist 1969–80; Lecturer, Teaching Fellow, Asst and Assoc. Prof., Dept of Physiology and Dept of Medicine, McGill Univ. 1965–73, Prof. of Medicine and Clinical Medicine 1973–, of Physiology 1974–, of Oncology 1989–, Chair. Dept of Medicine 1985–90, Douglas G. Cameron Prof. of Medicine 1987–, Dir McGill Cancer Centre 1978–80, Sr Physician and Dir Clinical Research Centre, McGill Univ. Health Centre 1980–, Exec. Dir Clinical Research Centre, RIMUHC 1995–; Sr Physician, The Montreal Gen. Hosp. 1973–, Physician-in-Chief 1980–95, Sr Investigator Hosp. Research Inst.; Hon. Consultant, Royal Victoria Hosp., Montreal 1981–; mem. numerous professional socs, scientific research bds and orgs etc. including RSC, American Soc. for Clinical Investigation, Asscn of American Physicians; Hon. mem. Golden Key Int. Soc. 2012; Hon. DSc (McMaster); numerous honours and awards, including Sir Arthur Sims Commonwealth Travelling Professorship 1998, Carl Govesky Memorial Award 1999, 20th Anniversary of L'Actualité Medicale Award for Outstanding Contrib. to Medicine 2000, Montreal Gen. Hosp. Corpn Merit Award 2002, Queen's Golden Jubilee Medal 2002, honoured as Founding Dir of McGill Cancer Centre's 25th Anniversary 2003, Edwin F. Ullman Award, American Asscn of Clinical Chem. 2004, Award of Exception Merit, Canadian Soc. for Immunology 2004, Alpha Omega Achievement Medal, Alpha Omega Int. Dental Fraternity 2006, Isaak Walton Killam Award in Medicine of the Canada Council, Nat. Cancer Inst. of Canada R.M. Taylor Medal, Heath Medal of the MD Anderson Hosp., Inaugural Ernest C. Manning Foundation Award, Johann-Georg-Zimmerman Prize for Cancer Research, Medizinische Hochschule, Germany, Abbott Award (ISOBM), Japan, inauguration of Phil Gold Chair in Medicine, McGill Univ. Health Centre 2006, inducted into Canadian Medical Hall of Fame 2010, McGill Faculty of Medicine Global Award for Lifetime Achievement 2011, Queen's Diamond Jubilee Medal 2012, Lifetime Achievement Award, Dept of Oncology, McGill Univ. 2012, Prix du Québec, Wilder-Penfield 2013. *Publications:* 150 articles in professional journals since 1965. *Leisure interests:* photography, sailing, cinema, music, literature. *Address:* The Clinical Research Centre, Suite D13 173, Montreal General Hospital, 1650 Cedar Avenue, Montreal, QC H3G 1A4, Canada (office). *Telephone:* (514) 934-1934 (ext. 43061) (office). *Fax:* (514) 934-8338 (office). *E-mail:* phil.gold@mcgill.ca (office). *Website:* www.mcgill.ca (office).

GOLDBERG, RoseLee, BA, MA; South African art historian, author and curator; *Founding Director and Curator, Performa;* b. Durban; ed Univ. of the Witwatersrand, Courtauld Inst. of Art, London, UK; fmr Dir RCA Gallery, London; fmr Curator, The Kitchen, New York; Lecturer, New York Univ. 1987–; Founding Dir and Curator, Performa (arts org.), New York 2004–; frequent guest lecturer at Architectural Asscn and Tate Modern, London, California Inst. of the Arts, Guggenheim Museum, New York, Whitney Museum of American Art, Mori Museum, Tokyo, Yale Univ., Princeton Univ., Columbia Univ., Kyoto Univ. of Art and Design; regular contrib. to several magazines including Artforum; Chevalier des Arts et des Lettres. *Publications:* Performance Art: From Futurism to the Present 1979, Performance Since 1960 1998, Laurie Anderson 2000, Shirin Neshat 2002, Performa 2007, Performance Now: New Art, New Dance, New Media 2007. *Address:* Performa, 100 West 23rd Street, 5th Floor, New York, NY 10011, USA

(office). *Telephone:* (212) 366-5700 (office). *E-mail:* info@performa-arts.org (office). *Website:* 13.performa-arts.org (office).

GOLDBERG, Whoopi; American comedienne and actress; b. (Caryn Johnson), 13 Nov. 1955, New York, NY; d. of Robert Johnson and Emma Harris; m. 2nd Dave Claessen 1986 (divorced 1988); one m. 3rd Lyle Trachtenberg 1994 (divorced 1995); first stage appearance, aged 8, Hudson Guild Theater, New York; worked with Helena Rubinstein Children's Theater; moved to San Diego 1974; co-f. San Diego Repertory Theater, appeared in Mother Courage (Brecht) and Getting Out (Marsha Norman); moved to San Francisco, became mem. Blake St Hawkeyes Theater; toured USA in The Spook Show; co-wrote and appeared in Moms (one-woman show); Broadway debut, Lyceum Theater 1984; f. One Ho Productions (production co.) 1992; Grammy Award for Best Comedy Album 1985, Hans Christian Andersen Award for Outstanding Achievement by a Dyslexic, Mark Twain Prize for American Humor, Kennedy Center for Performing Arts 2001. *Plays include:* A Funny Thing Happened on the Way to the Forum, Ma Rainey's Black Bottom 2003. *Films include:* The Color Purple (Image Award from NAACP, Golden Globe Award, Hollywood Foreign Press Asscn), Jumpin' Jack Flash 1986, Burglar 1987, Fatal Beauty 1987, Ghost 1990, Soapdish 1991, Sarafina 1992, Sister Act 1992, The Player 1992, Made in America 1992, Alice 1993, Sister Act II 1993, Corrina Corrina 1993, The Lion King (voice) 1994, Boys on the Side 1994, Moonlight and Valentino, Bogus, Eddie, The Associate 1996, The Ghost of Mississippi 1996, How Stella Got Her Groove Back 1998, Deep End of the Ocean 1999, Girl Interrupted 1999, Rat Race 2001, Kingdom Come 2001, Monkeybone 2001, Golden Dreams 2001, Star Trek: Nemesis 2002, More Dogs Than Bones 2002, Good Fences 2003, Blizzard (voice) 2003, Pinocchio 3000 (voice) 2004, Jiminy Glick in La La Wood 2004, Racing Stripes (voice) 2005, Doogal (voice) 2006, Homie Spumoni 2006, Everyone's Hero (voice) 2006, Farce of the Penguins (voice) 2006, If I Had Known I Was a Genius 2007, Snow Buddies (video) (voice) 2008, Descendants (short) (voice) 2008, Madea Goes to Jail 2009, Stream (short) 2009, See You in September (uncredited) 2010, Toy Story 3 (voice) 2010, For Colored Girls 2010, A Little Bit of Heaven 2011, The Little Engine That Could (voice) 2011, The Contradictions of Fair Hope 2012, Teenage Mutant Ninja Turtles 2014, Black Dog, Red Dog 2014, Big Stone Gap 2014. *Television includes:* In the Gloaming 1997, Cinderella 1997, A Knight in Camelot 1998, Alice in Wonderland 1999, Jackie's Back! 1999, The Magical Legend of the Leprechauns 1999, What Makes a Family 2001, Call Me Claus 2001, It's a Very Merry Muppet Christmas Movie 2002, Good Fences 2003, Whoopi (series) 2003–04, Littleburg (series) 2004, Whoopi: Back to Broadway – The 20th Anniversary (film) 2005, Bear in the Big Blue House (series) 2005, So Notorious (series) 2006, Law & Order: Criminal Intent (series) 2006, Everybody Hates Chris (series) 2006, 30 Rock (series) 2007–09, Entourage (series) 2008, Life on Mars (series) (uncredited) 2008, A Muppets Christmas: Letters to Santa (film) 2008, The Cleaner (series) 2009, The Daly Show (series) 2012, The Middle (series) 2012, Suburgatory (series) (voice) 2012, Robot Chicken (series) (voice) 2012, 666 Park Avenue (series) 2012, Glee (series) 2012, Late Night with Jimmy Fallon (series) 2012–13, Once Upon a Time in Wonderland (series) (voice) 2013, Sensitive Men (film) 2013, A Day Late and a Dollar Short (film) 2014; producer, Hollywood Squares 1998–2002. *Address:* One Ho Productions, 375 Greenwich Street, Tribeca Film Center, New York, NY 10013; c/o Brad Cafarelli, Bragman/Nyman/Cafarelli, 9171 Wilshire Blvd, #300, Beverly Hills, CA 90210, USA.

GOLDBERGER, Marvin Leonard, PhD; American physicist and academic; *Professor Emeritus of Physics, University of California, San Diego;* b. 22 Oct. 1922, Chicago, Ill.; s. of Joseph Goldberger and Mildred Sedwitz Goldberger; m. Mildred C. Ginsburg 1945; two s.; ed Carnegie Inst. of Technology and Univ. of Chicago; Research Assoc. Radiation Lab., Univ. of Calif. (Berkeley) 1948–49, MIT 1949–50; Asst Prof., Univ. of Chicago 1950–57; Eugene Higgins Prof. of Physics, Princeton Univ. 1957–77, Chair. Physics Dept 1970–76, Joseph Henry Prof. of Physics 1977–78; Pres. Calif. Inst. of Tech. 1978–87; Dir Inst. for Advanced Study 1987–91; Prof. of Physics, UCLA 1991–93, Univ. of Calif., San Diego 1993–2000, Prof. Emer. 2000– (Dean Div. of Natural Sciences 1994–2000); Chair. Fed. of American Scientists 1971–72; mem. NAS, American Acad. of Arts and Sciences; Hon. ScD (Carnegie-Mellon Univ.) 1979, (Univ. of Notre Dame) 1979, (Brandeis Univ. 1991); Hon. LLD (Occidental Coll.) 1980; Hon. DHL (Hebrew Union Coll.) 1980, (Univ. of Judaism 1982; Dannie Heineman Prize for Mathematical Physics 1961. *Publication:* Collision Theory (with K. M. Watson) 1964. *Leisure interests:* running, tennis, cooking. *Address:* Department of Physics, 0354, University of California, San Diego, 9500 Gilman Drive, La Jolla, CA 92093-0354, USA (office). *E-mail:* mgoldberger@ucsd.edu (office). *Website:* physics.ucsd.edu (office).

GOLDBLUM, Jeff; American actor; b. 22 Oct. 1952, Pittsburgh; m. 1st Patricia Gaul (divorced); m. 2nd Geena Davis (q.v.) (divorced); studied at New York Neighborhood Playhouse. *Plays include:* The Pillowman (Broadway) 2005, The Prisoner of Second Avenue (Old Vic, London) 2010. *Films include:* Calif. Split 1974, Death Wish 1974, Nashville 1975, Next Stop Greenwich Village 1976, Annie Hall 1977, Between the Lines 1977, The Sentinel 1977, Invasion of the Bodysnatchers 1978, Remember My Name 1978, Thank God it's Friday 1978, Escape from Athena 1979, The Big Chill 1983, The Right Stuff 1983, Threshold 1983, The Adventures of Buckaroo Banzai 1984, Silverado 1985, Into the Night 1985, Transylvania 6-5000 1985, The Fly 1986, Beyond Therapy 1987, The Tall Guy 1989, Earth Girls are Easy 1989, First Born (TV) 1989, The Mad Monkey 1990, Mister Frost 1991, Deep Cover 1992, The Favour, the Watch and the Very Big Fish 1992, Father and Sons 1993, Jurassic Park 1993, Lushlife (TV) 1994, Future Quest (TV) 1994, Hideaway 1995, Nine Months 1995, Independence Day 1996, The Lost World 1997, Holy Man 1998, Popcorn 1999, Chain of Fools 2000, Angie Rose 2000, Cats and Dogs 2001, Igby Goes Down 2002, Dallas 362 2003, Spinning Boris 2003, Incident at Loch Ness 2004, The Life Aquatic with Steve Zissou 2004, Mini's First Time 2006, Fay Grim 2006, Man of the Year 2006, The Switch 2010, Zambezia 2012; producer Little Surprises 1995, Holy Man 1999, Pittsburgh 2006. *Address:* c/o The Gersh Agency 9465 Wilshire Blvd, 6th Floor, Beverly Hills, CA 90212 (office); c/o Keith Addis, Industry Entertainment, 955 Carrillo Drive Suite 300, Los Angeles, CA 90048, USA (office).

GOLDEMBERG, José, BSc, PhD; Brazilian physicist, academic and government official; b. 27 May 1928, Santo Angelo; ed Universidade de São Paulo, Univ. of Saskatchewan, Canada, Univ. of Illinois, USA; Asst Prof., Universidade de São

Paulo 1955, Assoc. Prof. 1955–67, Full Prof. of Physics 1967–, Dir Inst. of Physics 1970–78, Rector Universidade de São Paulo 1986–89; Research Assoc., High Energy Physics Lab., Stanford Univ., USA 1962–63; Assoc. Prof., Univ. of Paris (Orsay) 1964; Prof. of Physics, Univ. of Toronto, Canada 1972–73; Sr Research Assoc., Princeton Univ., USA several periods 1977–82; Visiting Prof., Woodrow Wilson School, Princeton Univ. 1993–94, Int. Acad. of the Environment, Geneva, Switzerland 1995, Center for Latin American Studies, Stanford Univ. 1996–97; Pres. Energy Co. of State of São Paulo 1983–86; Sec. of State for Science and Tech., Fed. Govt 1990–91; Minister of State for Educ., Fed. Govt 1991–92; Acting Sec. of State for Environment, Fed. Govt 1992; Sec. of State for the Environment, State of São Paulo 2002–06; Chair. Bd International Energy Initiative 1995–, World Energy Assessment 1998–; mem. Advisory Bd Alliance for Global Sustainability 1997–, Environmental Advisory Bd Asea Brown Boveri (ABB) 1998–, World Comm. on Dams 1998–, Nat. Council for Energy Policy of Brazil 1999–2001, Sustainable Energy Inst.; Pres. Brazilian Asscn for the Advancement of Science 1979–81; mem. Brazilian Acad. of Sciences, Third World Acad. of Science; Ordem Nacional Do Mérito Científico 1995; Hon. DSc (Technion – Israel Inst. of Tech.) 1991; Mitchell Prize for Sustainable Devt (co-recipient) 1991, José Goldemberg Chair in Atmospheric Physics est. at Tel-Aviv Univ. 1994, Volvo Environment Prize (co-recipient) 2000, Blue Planet Prize, Asahi Glass Foundation 2008. *Publications:* several books and numerous scientific papers on nuclear physics, environment and energy in professional journals. *Address:* Centro Nacional de Referência Em Biomassa, Iee, Av. Professor Luciano Gualberto 1289, Cidade Universitária, 05508-010 Sao Paulo, SP, Brazil (office). *Telephone:* (11) 34836983 (office). *Fax:* (11) 30912649 (office). *E-mail:* goldemb@iee.usp.br (office). *Website:* www.iee.usp.br (office).

GOLDENBERG SCHREIBER, Efrain; Peruvian business executive, lawyer and fmr politician; b. 28 Dec. 1929, Lima; s. of Aron Goldenberg and Charna Schreiber; m. Irene Pravatiner 1952; one s. four d.; ed San Andrés (fmrly Anglo-Peruvian) School, Universidad Nacional Mayor de San Marcos; Minister of Foreign Affairs 1993–94, Pres. Council of Ministers (Prime Minister) and Minister of Foreign Affairs 1994–95; work in pvt. sector 1995–99; Minister of Econ. and Finance 1999–2000; fmr Pres. Sociedad Nacional de Pesquería; fmr Dir Fondo para la Promoción de Exportaciones; fmr mem. Lima Jewish Community Asscn. *Address:* Miguel Dasso 144, Of. 2b, Lima 27, Peru (home). *Telephone:* (1) 4224291 (office). *E-mail:* efrain.goldenberg@gmail.com (office).

GOLDIE, Sue J., BS, MD, MPH; American medical researcher and professor of public health; *Roger Irving Lee Professor of Public Health, Director of the Center for Health Decision Science, Harvard School of Public Health and Director of the Harvard Institute for Global Health, Harvard University;* b. 14 Dec. 1961, Wash.; m. Dr Aaron Bradley Waxman 1986; two s.; ed Union Coll., Albany Medical Coll., Harvard Univ., Certificate, Nat. Bd of Examiners, Diploma, American Bd of Internal Medicine; Intern in Internal Medicine, Yale New Haven Hosp., Yale Univ. School of Medicine 1988–89, Resident in Internal Medicine 1989–91; Fellow, Agency for Health Care Research and Quality Policy, Harvard School of Public Health, Boston 1995–97; Attending Physician, Yale New Haven Hosp. 1990, Brigham and Women's Hosp. 1998; Clinical Asst Prof. of Medicine, Yale Univ. School of Medicine 1994–98; Instructor in Medicine, Harvard Medical School, Boston 1998, Asst Prof. of Health Policy and Health Decision Science, Harvard School of Public Health 1998, Roger Irving Lee Prof. of Public Health and Dir Center for Health Decision Science, Co-Dir Exec. Cttee, Harvard Inst. of Global Health, Cambridge, Mass 2007–10, Dir 2010–; Prin. Investigator, NIH, Centers for Disease Control and Prevention, Bill & Melinda Gates Foundation, Doris Duke Foundation; mem. Inst. of Medicine, NAS (mem. Bd of Global Health) 2009, Soc. of Medical Decision Making (Editorial Bd), American Program Directors of Internal Medicine, Soc. of Gen. Internal Medicine, American Coll. of Physicians; Everett Mendelsohn Excellence in Mentoring Award, Harvard Univ., Dana Scholar, Charles A. Dana Foundation 1981, Dana Fellow 1982–84, Charles P. Drumm and Harold C. Wiggers Merit Scholar 1984–88, Original Investigation Competition Award for innovative programmes in medical educ., American Program Directors of Internal Medicine 1995, Larry Lynn Award, Soc. of Gen. Internal Medicine 1998, MacArthur Fellow, John T. and Catherine MacArthur Foundation 2005, John Eisenberg Award 2009. *Publications:* more than 150 papers in professional journals. *Leisure interests:* Tae Kwon Do, skiing, climbing, training her two golden retrievers. *Address:* Center for Health Decision Science, Harvard School of Public Health, 2nd Floor, 718 Huntington Avenue, Boston, MA 02115-5924, (office); Harvard Institute for Global Health, 3rd Floor, 104 Mount Auburn Street, Cambridge, MA 02138, USA (office). *Telephone:* (617) 432-2010 (Boston) (office); (617) 495-8222 (Cambridge) (office). *Fax:* (617) 432-0190 (Boston) (office); (617) 495-8231 (Cambridge) (office). *E-mail:* sue_goldie@harvard.edu (office); chds@ hsph.harvard.edu (office); globalhealth@harvard.edu (office). *Website:* www.hsph .harvard.edu/faculty/sue-goldie (office); www.chds.hsph.harvard.edu (office); www .globalhealth.harvard.edu (office).

GOLDIN, Daniel S., BSc; American space agency official; *Chairman, Intellisis Corporation;* b. 23 July 1940, New York City; m. Judith Kramer; two d.; ed City Coll. of New York; research scientist, NASA Lewis Research Center, Cleveland 1962–67; joined TRW Space & Tech. Group, Redondo, Calif. 1967, Vice-Pres. and Gen. Man. –1992; Admin., NASA 1992–2001; Founder and Chair. Intellisis Corpn 2005–; mem. Bd of Dirs Lucent Technologies Inc. 2002–06; Distinguished Fellow, Council on Competitiveness 2001–; Fellow, American Inst. of Aeronautics and Astronautics; mem. Bd of Trustees Nat. Geographic Soc.; mem. Advisory Council Scripps Inst. of Oceanography; mem. Nat. Acad. of Engineers; numerous awards. *Address:* Intellisis Corporation, 10350 Science Center Drive, Suite 140, San Diego, CA 92121, USA (office). *Telephone:* (858) 909-5200 (office). *Fax:* (858) 909-5250 (office). *Website:* www.intellisis.com (office).

GOLDING, (Orrett) Bruce, BSc; Jamaican politician; b. 5 Dec. 1947; s. of Tacius Golding and Enid Golding (née Bent); m. Lorna Golding; one s. two d.; ed Jamaica Coll., Univ. of the W Indies; as a student served as Vice-Chair. Jamaica Labour Party (JLP) Constituency Exec. for West St Catherine and mem. Bd of Dirs, Nat. Lotteries Comm., selected as JLP parl. cand. for West St Catherine 1969, elected to JLP Cen. Exec. 1969, Co-founder Young Jamaica group 1970, elected as youngest-ever MP 1972, defeated in elections 1976, JLP Gen. Sec. 1974–84, Chair. 1984–95; apptd to Senate 1977, re-apptd 1980, Minister of Construction 1980–83; elected

MP for South Central St Catherine 1983, re-elected 1989, 1993; left JLP and f. Nat. Democratic Movt (NDM) 1995, Pres. 1995–2002, left NDM and rejoined JLP 2002, Chair. JLP 2003–05, Leader 2005–; Prime Minister 2007–11 (resgnd), also Minister of Planning and Devt and of Defence. *Radio:* host, Disclosure 2002. *Address:* Jamaica Labour Party, 20 Belmont Road, Kingston 5, Jamaica (office). *Telephone:* 929-1183 (office). *Website:* www.jamaicalabourparty.com (office).

GOLDMAN, William, MA; American author and screenwriter; b. 12 Aug. 1931, Chicago, Ill.; s. of M. Clarence Goldman and Marion Weil; m. Ilene Jones 1961 (divorced 1991); two d.; ed Oberlin Coll. and Columbia Univ.; Laurel Award for Lifetime Achievement in Screenwriting 1983. *Publications:* novels: The Temple of Gold 1957, Your Turn to Curtsy, My Turn to Bow 1958, Soldier in the Rain 1960, Boys and Girls Together 1964, The Thing of It Is 1967, No Way to Treat a Lady (under pseudonym Harry Longbaugh), Father's Day 1971, The Princess Bride 1973, Marathon Man 1974, Wigger 1974, Magic 1976, Tinsel 1979, Control 1982, The Silent Gondoliers 1983, The Color of Light 1984, Heat 1985, Brothers 1986; play: Blood, Sweat and Stanley Poole 1961 (with James Goldman); musical comedy: A Family Affair (with James Goldman and John Kander) 1962; non-fiction: Adventures in the Screen Trade 1983, Hype and Glory 1990, Four Screenplays 1995, Five Screenplays 1997, Which Lie Did I Tell? 2000; screenplays: Harper (Best Motion Picture Screenplay, Mystery Writers of America 1967) 1966, Butch Cassidy and the Sundance Kid (Acad. Award for best original screenplay 1970) 1969, Marathon Man 1976, All the President's Men (Acad. Award for best screenplay adaptation 1977) 1976, A Bridge Too Far 1977, Magic (Best Motion Picture Screenplay, Mystery Writers of America 1979) 1978, Heat 1985, Brothers 1987, The Princess Bride 1987, Year of the Comet 1992, Memoirs of an Invisible Man 1992, Chaplin 1992, Indecent Proposal 1993, Maverick 1994, The Ghost and the Darkness 1996, Absolute Power 1997, Hearts in Atlantis 2001, Dreamcatcher 2003. *Address:* Creative Artists Agency, 162 Fifth Avenue, 6th Floor, New York, NY 10010, USA (office). *Telephone:* (212) 277-9000 (office). *Fax:* (212) 277-9099 (office). *Website:* www.caa.com (office).

GOLDMARK, Peter Carl, Jr, BA; American newspaper executive and consultant; b. 2 Dec. 1940, New York; s. of Peter Carl Goldmark and Frances Charlotte Trainer; m. Aliette Marie Misson 1964; three d.; ed Harvard Univ.; worked for US Office of Econ. Opportunity, Washington; fmr teacher of history Putney School, Vt; employed in Budget Office, City of New York for four years, later Asst Budget Dir Program Planning and Analysis then Exec. Asst to the Mayor 1971; Sec. Human Services, Commonwealth of Mass. 1972–75; Dir of Budget, NY State 1975–77; Exec. Dir Port Authority of NY and NJ 1977–85; joined Times Mirror Co., Los Angeles 1985, fmr Sr Vice-Pres. Eastern Newspapers Div.; Pres. Rockefeller Foundation 1988–97; Chair. and CEO Int. Herald Tribune 1998–2003; Program Dir, Climate and Air Program, Environmental Defense Fund 2003–10; currently ind. consultant; columnist, Newsday; mem. Bd of Dirs Financial Accounting Foundation, Lend Lease Corpn, Whitehead Inst. for Biomedical Research. *Address:* Newsday, 235 Pinelawn Road, Melville, NY 11747, USA (office).

GOLDREICH, Peter, BSc, PhD; American scientist and academic; *Professor, School of Natural Sciences, Institute for Advanced Study;* b. 14 July 1939, New York; s. of Paul Goldreich and Edith Rosenfield Goldreich; m. Susan Kroll 1960; two s.; ed Cornell Univ.; Post-Doctoral Fellow, Univ. of Cambridge 1963–64; Asst Prof. Astronomy and Physics, UCLA 1964–66, Assoc. Prof. 1966; Assoc. Prof. of Planetary Science and Astronomy, Calif. Inst. Tech. 1966–69, Prof. 1969–81, Lee Du Bridge Prof. of Astrophysics and Planetary Physics 1981–2002, Prof. Emer. 2002–, Acting Chair. Div. of Geological and Planetary Sciences 1989; Prof., School of Natural Sciences, Inst. for Advanced Study, Princeton, NJ 2003–; Sackler Lecturer, Univ. of Toronto 1998, Harvard Univ. 2004; Harris Lecturer, MIT 2005; Andrew Dixon White Fellowship 1960–61; Fellow, NSF 1961–63, Nat. Acad. of Sciences, Nat. Research Council 1963–64, Sloan Foundation 1968; Regents Fellow, Smithsonian Inst. 1988–90; mem. NAS 1972–; Foreign mem. Royal Soc. 2004–; Hon. Woodrow Wilson Fellowship 1960–61; California Scientist of the Year Award 1981, Chapman Medal, Royal Astronomical Soc. 1985, Dirk Brouwer Award, American Astronomical Soc. 1986, Kuiper Prize, American Astronomical Soc. 1992, Gold Medal, Royal Astronomical Soc. 1993, Nat. Medal of Science 1995, Antoinette de Vaucouleurs Medal, Univ. of Texas 1999, Grande médaille, French Acad. of Sciences 2006, Shaw Prize, 2007. *Publications:* on planetary dynamics, pulsar theory, radio emission from Jupiter, galactic stability and interstellar masers. *Leisure interest:* competitive athletics. *Address:* School of Natural Sciences, Institute for Advanced Study (IAS), Princeton, NJ 08540 (office); California Institute of Technology, 1200 East California Boulevard, Pasadena, CA 91125 (office); 471 S Catalina Avenue, Pasadena, CA 91106, USA (home). *Telephone:* (609) 734-8016 (IAS) (office). *Fax:* (609) 951-4402 (IAS) (office). *E-mail:* pmg@nicholas.caltech.edu (office). *Website:* www.sns.ias.edu (office); www.gps .caltech.edu/faculty/goldreich/goldreich.html (office).

GOLDSMITH, Harvey, CBE; British music promoter; b. 4 March 1946, London; s. of Sydney Goldsmith and Minnie Goldsmith; m. Diana Goldsmith 1971; one s.; ed Christ's Coll. and Brighton Coll. of Tech.; joined Big O Posters, Kensington Market 1966; organized open-air free concerts, Parliament Hill Fields 1968; in partnership with Michael Alfandary opened Round House, London 1968; organized 13 Garden Party concerts at Crystal Palace, London 1969; merged with John Smith Entertainment 1970–75; formed Harvey Goldsmith Entertainment promoting rock tours by Elton John, Rolling Stones etc.; in partnership with Ed Simons, rescued Hotel Television Network 1983; formed Allied Entertainment Group as public co. 1984–86, returned to pvt. ownership 1986; subsidiary Harvey Goldsmith Entertainment promotes some 250 concerts per year; formed Classical Productions with Mark McCormack, promoting shows at Earls Court including Pavarotti concert and productions of Aida 1988, Carmen 1989, Tosca 1991; produced Bob Dylan Celebration, New York 1992, Mastercard Masters of Music (Hyde Park), The Eagles (Wembley), Three Tenors (Wembley), Lord of the Dance (world tour) 1996, Music for Montserrat (Royal Albert Hall), Boyzone (tour), Paul Weller (tour), Pavarotti (Manchester), Cirque du Soleil (Royal Albert Hall) 1997, Alegria (Royal Albert Hall), The Bee Gees (Wembley), Ozzfest (Milton Keynes Bowl), Paul Weller (Victoria Park) 1998; Chair. Nat. Music Day; Vice-Chair. Prince's Trust Bd; Vice-Pres. React 1989–; Trustee, Gret, Band Aid 1985–, Live Aid Foundation 1985–; Vice Pres.'s Club, London First, London Tourist Bd; Amb. for London Judges Award 1997; Chair. Ignition International 2006–; mem. Advisory Group Red Cross; Music

Industry Trust Award 2006. *Leisure interest:* golf. *Address:* Harvey Goldsmith Entertainments Ltd, 5th Floor, Langham House, 308 Regent Street, London, W1B 3AT, England (office). *Telephone:* (20) 7224-1992 (office). *Fax:* (20) 7224-0111 (office). *Website:* www.harveygoldsmith.com.

GOLDSTEIN, Jeffrey Alan, BA, MPh, PhD; American international civil servant, economist, government official and private equity investor; *Managing Director, Hellman & Friedman LLC;* b. 2 Dec. 1955, Pennsylvania; m. Nancy Coles; two s. one d.; ed Yale Univ., Vassar Coll., London School of Econs, UK; Research Asst, Brookings Inst., Washington, DC 1977–78; Int. Economist, Office of Int. Monetary Affairs, US Dept of Treasury, Washington, DC 1979; Consultant, Securities Group, New York 1980–81; Vice-Chair. Wolfensohn & Co. Inc., New York, then Co-Chair. BT Wolfensohn, New York 1984–99; Man. Dir and Chief Financial Officer, World Bank, Washington, DC 1999–2004; Man. Dir Hellman & Friedman LLC (pvt. equity firm) 2004–09, 2012–; Under-Sec. for Domestic Finance and Counselor to the Sec., US Dept of Treasury, Washington, DC 2009–11; mem. Bd LPL Financial, Advisory Bd Grosvenor Capital Management LLP 2012–, Council on Foreign Relations; mem. Bd of Trustees, Vassar Coll.; Virginia Swinburn Brownell Prize in Political Econ. Studies, Alexander Hamilton Award 2011. *Address:* 390 Park Avenue, 21st Floor, New York, NY 10022, USA (office). *Telephone:* (212) 871-6681 (office). *Fax:* (212) 871-6688 (office). *E-mail:* jgoldstein@hf.com (office). *Website:* www.hf.gov (office).

GOLDSTEIN, Joseph Leonard, MD; American geneticist, physician and academic; *Regental Professor, University of Texas Southwestern Medical Center at Dallas;* b. 18 April 1940, Sumter, SC; s. of Isadore E. Goldstein and Fannie A. Goldstein; ed Washington and Lee Univ., Lexington, Va, Univ. of Texas Southwestern Medical Center; Intern, then Resident in Medicine, Mass. Gen. Hosp., Boston 1966–68; Clinical Assoc., NIH 1968–70; Postdoctoral Fellow, Univ. of Washington, Seattle 1970–72; mem. Faculty, Univ. of Texas Southwestern Medical Center, Dallas 1972–, Paul J. Thomas Prof. of Medicine, Chair. Dept of Molecular Genetics 1977–, Harvey Soc. Lecturer 1977, Regental Prof. 1985–; Chair. Albert Lasker Medical Research Awards Jury 1996–; mem. Advisory Bd Howard Hughes Medical Inst. 1985–90, Chair. 1995–2002, Trustee 2002–; non-resident Fellow, The Salk Inst. 1983–93; mem. Scientific Advisory Bd Welch Foundation 1986–, Bd Dirs Passano Foundation 1985–, Bd Trustees Rockefeller Foundation 1994–, Bd of Scientific Govs, Scripps Research Inst. 1996–; mem. Editorial Bd Cell, Arteriosclerosis and Science; mem. NAS (mem. Council 1991–94), American Acad. of Arts and Sciences, American Philosophical Soc., Inst. of Medicine, Asscn of American Physicians, American Soc. of Clinical Investigation (Pres. 1985–86), American Soc. of Human Genetics, American Soc. of Biological Chemists, American Fed. of Clinical Research; Foreign mem. Royal Soc., London; Hon. DSc (Univ. of Chicago, Rensselaer Polytech. Inst., Washington and Lee Univ., Univ. of Paris-Sud, Univ. of Buenos Aires, Southern Methodist Univ., Univ. of Miami, Rockefeller Univ.); Heinrich-Wieland Prize 1974, ACS Pfizer Award in Enzyme Chem. 1976, Passano Award, Johns Hopkins Univ. 1978, Gairdner Foundation Award 1981, Award in Biological and Medical Sciences, New York Acad. of Sciences 1981, Lita Annenberg Hazen Award 1982, Research Achievement Award, American Heart Asscn 1984, Louisa Gross Horwitz Award 1984, 3M Life Sciences Award 1984, Albert Lasker Award in Basic Medical Research 1985, Nobel Prize in Physiology or Medicine 1985, Trustees' Medal, Mass Gen. Hosp. 1986, US Nat. Medal of Science 1988, Albany Medical Center Prize in Medicine and Biomedical Research 2003, Woodrow Wilson Award for Public Service 2005, Builders Science Award, Research America 2007. *Publication:* The Metabolic Basis of Inherited Disease (co-author) 1983. *Address:* Department of Molecular Genetics, University of Texas Southwestern Medical Center at Dallas, 5323 Harry Hines Boulevard, Dallas, TX 75390 (office); 3831 Turtle Creek Boulevard, Apt 22-B, Dallas, TX 75219, USA (home). *Telephone:* (214) 648-2141 (office). *Fax:* (214) 648-8804 (office). *E-mail:* jgoldstein@utsouthwestern.edu (office). *Website:* www8.utsouthwestern.edu/utsw/cda/dept14857/files/114532.html (office); www8.utsouthwestern.edu/utsw/home/research/molgen/index.html (office).

GOLDSTONE, David Joseph, CBE, LLB; British property executive; b. 21 Feb. 1929, Swansea, South Wales; s. of Solomon Goldstone and Rebecca Goldstone (née Degotts); one s. two d.; ed Dynevor Secondary School, Swansea and London School of Econs; admitted as solicitor 1955; legal practice 1955–66; Chief Exec. Regalian Properties PLC 1970–2001 Chair. 1990–2001; Dir Swansea Sound Commercial Radio 1974–95, London Welsh Rugby Football Club 1997–2001, Wales Millennium Centre; Chair. Coram Family 2001–05, now Hon. Vice-Pres.; fmr Chair. Swanbourne Development Services Ltd; currently Adviser to Minister for Health and Social Services and to Minister for Business, Enterprise, Technology and Science, Welsh Ass.; Special Adviser, Welsh Rugby Union; mem. Court of Govs LSE 1985–2009 (Fellow 1996), Gov. Emer. 2009–; mem. Bd Football Assocn of Wales 1970–72, Welsh Nat. Opera 1984–89, Univ. of London 1994– (Deputy Chair. 2002–); mem. Council Royal Albert Hall 1998–2006 (Hon. Vice-Pres. 2007–), Capital Advisory Group, Welsh Ass. Govt 2009–; Trustee, Civil Liberties Trust 2009–. *Leisure interests:* reading, sport. *Address:* Flat 4, Grosvenor Hill Court, 15 Bourdon Street, London, W1K 3PX (home); 19/20 Grosvenor Street, London, W1K 4NQ, England (office). *Telephone:* (20) 7499-4525 (home); (20) 7529-1603 (office). *E-mail:* djg@davstone.co.uk (office).

GOLDSTONE, Jeffrey, MA, PhD, FRS; British physicist and academic; *Cecil and Ida Green Professor Emeritus of Physics, Massachusetts Institute of Technology;* b. 3 Sept. 1933, Manchester, England; s. of Hyman Goldstone and Sophia Goldstone; m. Roberta Gordon 1980; one s.; ed Manchester Grammar School and Trinity Coll., Cambridge; Research Fellow, Trinity Coll., Cambridge 1956–60, Staff Fellow 1962–82; Univ. Lecturer, Applied Math. and Theoretical Physics, Univ. of Cambridge 1961–76, Reader in Math. Physics 1976; Prof. of Physics, MIT, USA 1977–83, Dir Center for Theoretical Physics 1983–89, Cecil and Ida Green Prof. of Physics 1983–2004, Cecil and Ida Green Prof. Emer. 2004–; Fellow, American Acad. of Arts and Sciences, American Physical Soc.; Hon. Fellow, Trinity Coll., Cambridge 2000; Heineman Prize, American Physical Soc. 1981, Guthrie Medal, Inst. of Physics 1983, Dirac Medal, Int. Centre for Theoretical Physics 1991. *Publications:* articles in scientific journals. *Address:* Department of Physics, 6-407, Massachusetts Institute of Technology, Cambridge, MA 02139, USA (office). *Telephone:* (617) 253-6263 (office); (617) 876-6027 (home). *Fax:* (617) 253-8674

(office). *E-mail:* goldston@mit.edu (office). *Website:* web.mit.edu/physics/people/faculty/goldstone_jeffrey.html (office).

GOLDSTONE, Richard J., LLB; South African judge; b. 26 Oct. 1938, Boksburg; m. Noleen Behrman 1962; two d.; ed King Edward VII School, Johannesburg and Univ. of Witwatersrand; admitted to Johannesburg Bar 1963, Sr Counsel 1976; Judge, Transvaal Supreme Court 1980–89; Judge, Appellate Div. Supreme Court of SA 1989–94; Justice, S African Constitutional Court 1994–2003; Chair. Comm. of Inquiry regarding Public Violence and Intimidation 1991–94; Prosecutor, Int. Criminal Tribunal for Fmr Yugoslavia and Int. Criminal Tribunal for Rwanda 1994–96; Nat. Pres. Nat. Inst. for Crime Prevention and Rehabilitation of Offenders 1982–99; Chair. cttee which drafted Valencia Declaration of Human Duties and Responsibilities 1998; mem. Ind. Int. Comm. on Kosovo 1999–2001, Int. Bar Asscn Task Force on Int. Terrorism 2001–; Head UN Fact Finding Mission on the Gaza Conflict 2009; mem. Council, Univ. of Witwatersrand 1988–94, Chancellor 1996–; Chair. Standing Advisory Cttee on Co. Law (Chair. 1991–), Exec. Cttee World ORT (Pres. 1997–); mem. UN Cttee of Inquiry into Iraq Oil for Food Programme (Volcker Cttee); Chair. Bd Human Rights Inst. of SA; Gov. Hebrew Univ. of Jerusalem 1982–; Chair. Bradlow Foundation 1989–; other professional appts; faculty mem. Salzburg Seminar 1996, 1998, 2001; Foreign mem. American Acad. of Arts and Sciences; Fellow Centre for Int. Affairs, Harvard Univ. 1989; Hon. mem. Bar Asscn of New York; Hon. Bencher Inner Temple, London; Hon. Fellow, St John's Coll. Cambridge; 19 hon. degrees including Hon. LLD (Cape Town) 1993, (Natal, Hebrew Univ. of Jerusalem, Witwatersrand) 1994, (Wilfred Laurier Univ.) 1995, (Tilburg Univ.) 1996, (Univ. of Glasgow, Notre Dame Univ.) 1997, (Univ. of Calgary) 1998, (Emory Univ.) 2001; several awards including Toastmasters Int. Communication and Leadership Award 1994, Int. Human Rights Award (American Bar Asscn) 1994. *Publication:* For Humanity – Reflections of a War Crimes Investigator. *Leisure interests:* reading, walking, wine. *Address:* PO Box 396, Morningside 2057 (home); 22 West Road South, Morningside, South Africa (home). *Fax:* (11) 8035472 (home). *E-mail:* rjgoldstone@iafrica.com (home).

GOLDSTRAW, Peter, MB, ChB, FETCS; British thoracic surgeon; *Professor of Thoracic Surgery, Imperial College London;* b. 1945; m. Denise Mary Bowyer 1968; one s. one d.; ed Univ. of Birmingham; Consultant Thoracic Surgeon, Royal Brompton Hospital 1979–, fmr Dir of Surgery, Head of Thoracic Surgery Section; civilian adviser to Royal Navy, RAF; fmr Hon. Consultant, Benenden Chest Hospital; Prof. of Thoracic Surgery, Imperial Coll., London; Chair. Int. Staging Cttee of Int. Asscn for the Study of Lung Cancer, UK Cardiothoracic Training Cttee; Nat. Rep. European Union of Medical Specialists; mem. Man. Bd European Bd of Thoracic and Cardiovascular Surgery; UK Rep. UEMS Section of Cardiothoracic Surgery; Chair. Cardiothoracic SHC; mem. Belgian Asscn for Cardio-Thoracic Surgery, Cardiothoracic Surgery Network, European Asscn for Cardio-Thoracic Surgery, European Soc. of Thoracic Surgeons, Soc. of Cardiothoracic Surgeons of Great Britain and Ireland, American Asscn for Thoracic Surgery, Soc. of Thoracic Surgeons; mem. Editorial Bd Thorax, Annals of Thoracic Surgery; Assoc. Ed. Lung Cancer; Clement Price-Thomas Award Royal Coll. of Surgeons of England 2004, Merit Award, Int. Asscn for the Study of Lung Cancer 2007, Lifetime Achievement Award, Soc. for Cardiothoracic Surgery in GB and Ireland 2010. *Publications:* contrib. to 44 textbooks on thoracic surgery; more than 200 articles in scientific journals; fmr Exec. Ed. Handbook of Staging in Thoracic Oncology. *Leisure interests:* sailing, fishing. *Address:* Imperial College London, South Kensington Campus, London, SW7 2AZ (office); Royal Brompton Hospital, Sydney Street, London, SW3 6NP, England (office). *Telephone:* (20) 7589-5111 (office). *E-mail:* p.goldstraw@imperial.ac.uk (office). *Website:* www1.ic.ac.uk/medicine/people/p.goldstraw (office).

GOLDSWORTHY, Andrew Charles, OBE, BA; British sculptor; b. 25 July 1956, Cheshire; s. of Fredrick Alan Goldsworthy and Muriel Goldsworthy (née Stanger); m. Judith Elizabeth Gregson 1982; two s. two d.; ed Bradford and Lancaster Art Colls; has exhibited in USA, France, Australia, Germany and Japan; numerous public and pvt. comms since 1984 including pieces for Grizedale Forest, Cumbria 1984, 1985, 1991, Enclosure, Royal Botanic Gardens, Edinburgh 1990, Seven Holes, Greenpeace, London 1991, Steel Cone, Gateshead 1991, Black Spring, Botanical Gardens, Adelaide 1992, Fieldgate, Poundridge, NY 1993, Laumeier Sculpture Park 1994, two pieces for Nat. Museum of Scotland, Edin. 1998; works represented in collections at Michael Hue-Williams Fine Arts Ltd, London, Galerie Lelong, New York and Paris, Haines Gallery, San Francisco, Galerij S65, Belgium, Springer and Winckler Galerie, Berlin; residency Yorks. Sculpture Park 1988; featured on Royal Mail Spring issue stamps 1995; Sr Lecturer in Fine Art and Craft, Univ. of Herts. 1996; Andrew D. White Prof.-at-Large, Cornell Univ., USA 2000–08; Visiting Prof., Crichton Coll., Univ. of Glasgow 2000–; collaborated with Cirque du Soleil, Montreal 1998; Hon. Fellow, Univ. of Cen. Lancs. 1995; mem. Cass Sculpture Foundation; Hon. BA (Bradford) 1993; North West Arts Award 1979, Yorks. Arts Award 1980, Northern Arts Award 1981, 1995, Scottish Arts Council Award 1988. *Dance:* Vegetal, with Regine Chopinot 1995, La danse du Temps, with Regine Chopinot and Ballet Atlantique 2000. *Film:* Two Autumns (for Channel 4) 1991, Rivers and Tides 2000. *Publications include:* A Collaboration with Nature 1989, Hand to Earth 1991, Touching North 1994, Stone 1994, Wood 1996, Time 2000, Passage 2005. *Leisure interests:* fishing, reading, listening to music.

GOLDTHORPE, John Harry, CBE, BA, FBA; British sociologist and academic; *Fellow Emeritus, Nuffield College, Oxford;* b. 27 May 1935, Barnsley, South Yorks.; s. of Harry and Lilian Eliza Goldthorpe; m. Rhiannon Esyllt Harry 1963; one s. one d.; ed Wath-upon-Dearne Grammar School, Univ. Coll. London, London School of Econs; Asst Lecturer, Dept of Sociology, Univ. of Leicester 1957–60; Fellow, King's Coll., Cambridge 1960–69; Asst Lecturer, then Lecturer in Faculty of Econs and Politics, Univ. of Cambridge 1962–69; Official Fellow, Nuffield Coll., Oxford 1969–2002, Fellow Emer. 2002–; mem. British Econ. and Social Research Council 1988–91; mem. Academia Europaea 1989; Foreign mem. Royal Swedish Acad. of Sciences 2001; Visiting Professorial Fellow, Centre for Longitudinal Studies, Inst. of Education, London; Hon. Fil. Dr (Stockholm Univ.) 1990; Helsinki Univ. Medal 1990. *Publications:* The Affluent Worker series (three vols) (with David Lockwood et al.) 1968–69, The Social Grading of Occupations (with Keith Hope) 1974, The Political Economy of Inflation (with Fred Hirsch, eds) 1978, Social Mobility and

Class Structure 1980, Order and Conflict in Contemporary Capitalism (ed. and contrib.) 1984, Die Analyse sozialer Ungleichheit: Kontinuität, Erneuerung, Innovation (with Hermann Strasser; ed. and contrib.) 1985, The Constant Flux: a Study of Class Mobility in Industrial Societies (with Robert Erikson) 1992, The Development of Industrial Society in Ireland (with Christopher T. Whelan; ed. and contrib.) 1992, On Sociology: Numbers, Narratives and the Integration of Research and Class Theory 2000 (second, two-vol. edn 2007). *Leisure interests:* lawn tennis, bird watching, computer chess, cryptic crosswords. *Address:* Nuffield College, Oxford, OX1 1NF (office); 32 Leckford Road, Oxford, OX2 6HX, England (home). *Telephone:* (1865) 278559 (office); (1865) 556602 (home). *Fax:* (1865) 278621 (office). *E-mail:* john.goldthorpe@nuffield.ox.ac.uk (office).

GOLDWASSER, Shafi, BS, MS, PhD; American/Israeli computer scientist and academic; *RSA Professor of Electrical Engineering and Computer Science, Massachusetts Institute of Technology;* b. 1958, New York, NY; m. Nir Shavit; two s.; ed Carnegie Mellon Univ., Univ. of California, Berkeley; Bantrel Postdoctoral Fellowship, MIT 1983, Asst Prof. 1983–87, Assoc. Prof. 1987–92, Prof. of Electrical Eng and Computer Science 1992–, RSA Prof. of Electrical Eng and Computer Science 1997–, Co-leader Cryptography and Information Security Group and mem. Complexity Theory Group within Theory of Computation Group and Computer Science and Artificial Intelligence Lab.; Prof. of Computer Science and Applied Math., Weizmann Inst. of Science 1993–; Fellow, American Acad. of Arts and Sciences 2001, NAS 2004, Nat. Acad. of Eng 2005, Int. Asscn for Cryptologic Research 2012; IBM Young Faculty Devt Award 1983–85, NSF Presidential Young Investigator Award 1987–92, NSF Award for Women in Science 1991–96, SIGACT Gödel Prize (co-recipient) 1993, 2001, Grace Murray Hopper Award, Asscn for Computing Machinery (ACM) 1996, RSA Award in Math. for Outstanding Math. Contribs to Cryptography 1998, Levenson Prize in Math., Weizmann Inst. 1999, Distinguished Alumnus Award in Computer Science and Eng, Univ. of California, Berkeley 2006, Athena Lecturer, ACM Cttee on Women in Computing 2008, Benjamin Franklin Medal in Computer and Cognitive Science 2010, IEEE Emanuel R. Piore Award 2011, ACM A.M. Turing Award (with Silvio Micali) 2012. *Publications:* numerous papers in professional journals. *Address:* Room 32-G682, Computer Science and Artificial Intelligence Laboratory, Massachusetts Institute of Technology, 77 Massachusetts Avenue, Cambridge, MA 02139, USA (office). *Telephone:* (617) 253-5914 (office). *E-mail:* shafi@csail.mit.edu (office). *Website:* www.csail.mit.edu/user/733 (office).

GOLIKOVA, Tatyana Alekseyevna; Russian economist and government official; *Minister of Health and Social Development;* b. 9 Feb. 1966, Mytischi, Moscow Region; m. Viktor Khristenko; ed Moscow Inst. of Nat. Economy (Plekhanov Inst.); served as economist in Ministry of Finance 1990–98, Head of Budget Dept 1998–99, 2007, Deputy then First Deputy Minister of Finance 1999–2007; Minister of Health and Social Devt 2007–; Medal of the Order of Merit to the Fatherland (First Degree) 2004; Medal of Honour 2006, Medal of Friendship 2006. *Address:* Ministry of Health and Social Development, 127994 Moscow, Rakhmanovskii pereulok 3/25, Russia (office). *Telephone:* (495) 628-44-53 (office). *Fax:* (495) 628-50-58 (office). *E-mail:* interdep@rosminzdrav.ru (office). *Website:* www .minzdravsoc.ru (office).

GOLITSYN, Georgy Sergeyevich; Russian physicist; b. 23 Jan. 1935, Moscow; s. of Sergei Golitsyn and Claudia Golitsyna; m. Ludmila Lisitskaya; two d.; ed Moscow State Univ.; Head of Lab., Head of Div., Dir Inst. of Atmospheric Physics, USSR (now Russian) Acad. of Sciences 1958–; Corresp. mem. USSR (now Russian) Acad. of Sciences 1979, mem. 1987, mem. Presidium 1988–2001; Chair. Council, Int. Inst. of Applied Systems Analysis 1992–97; main research on geophysical fluid dynamics, climate theory; A. Friedmann Prize, Demidov Prize, Alfred Wegener Prize. *Publications include:* Introduction to Dynamics of Planet Atmospheres 1973, Study of Convection with Geophysical Applications and Analogies 1980, Global Climate Catastrophes 1986, Convection of Rotating Fluids 1995, Dynamics of Natural Processes 2004. *Leisure interests:* history, art, literature. *Address:* A.M. Obukhov Institute of Atmospheric Physics, Russian Academy of Sciences, Pyzhyevsky per. 3, 119017 Moscow, Russia (office). *Telephone:* (495) 951-55-65 (office). *Fax:* (495) 953-16-52 (office). *E-mail:* mail_adm@ifaran.ru (office). *Website:* www.ifaran.ru (office).

GOLL, Gerhard; German lawyer, business executive and academic; b. 18 June 1942, Stuttgart; m.; two c.; ed Univs of Tübingen and Freiburg; Judge, Regional Court of Stuttgart; with Ministry of Culture of Baden-Württemberg 1972–75; joined Ministry of Finance of Baden-Württemberg 1975, Head of Centre 1976–77, Head of Gen. Office of Budget Dept 1977–78; Sec., CDU Group, Parl. of Baden-Wuerttemberg 1980; joined Landeskreditbank Baden-Württemberg 1982, mem. Bd of Dirs and Deputy CEO 1984; CEO Badenwerk AG, Karlsruhe 1993–97; joined Schwaben AG 1997, subsequently merged with Energie Baden-Württemberg (EnBW) AG, Chair. Energie Baden-Württemberg (EnBW) AG 1998–2003; currently Lecturer, Karlshochschule Int. Univ. *Address:* Karlshochschule International University, 76133 Karlsruhe, Germany (office). *Telephone:* (72) 11303500 (office). *E-mail:* info@karlshochschule.de (office). *Website:* www.karlshochschule .de (office).

GÖLLNER, Theodor, PhD, DrPhil, Habil.; German musicologist; *Professor Emeritus and Director, Commission of Music History, Bavarian Academy of Sciences;* b. 25 Nov. 1929, Bielefeld; s. of Friedrich Göllner and Paula Brinkmann; m. Marie Louise Martinez 1959; one s. one d.; ed Univs of Heidelberg and Munich; Lecturer, Univ. of Munich 1958–62, Asst Prof. 1962–67, Assoc. Prof. 1967; Prof., Univ. of Calif., Santa Barbara 1967–73; Prof. and Chair. Inst. of Musicology, Univ. of Munich 1973–97; Prof. Emer. and Dir Comm. of Music History, Bavarian Acad. of Sciences 1982–; mem. European Acad. of Sciences and Arts 1991–. *Publications:* Formen früher Mehrstimmigkeit 1961, Die mehrstimmigen liturgischen Lesungen 1969, Die Sieben Worte am Kreuz 1986, Et incarnatus est in Bachs h-moll-Messe und Beethovens Missa solemnis 1996, Die Tactuslehre in den deutschen Orgelquellen des 15. Jahrhunderts 2003, Münchner Veröffentlichungen zur Musikgeschichte (ed.) 1977–2006, Münchner Editionen zur Musikgeschichte 1979–97, Die psalmodische Tradition bei Monteverdi und Schütz 2006. *Address:* Institute of Musicology, University of Munich, Geschwister-Scholl-Platz 1, 80539 Munich (office); Bahnweg 9, 82229 Seefeld, Germany (home). *Telephone:* (1089) 21802364 (office). *E-mail:* TheodorGoellner@aol.com (home).

GOLODETS, Olga Yuryevna, PhD (Econ); Russian politician; *Deputy Chairman of the Government;* b. 1 June 1962, Moscow; ed Lomonosov Moscow State Univ.; Researcher at Cen. Research Lab. of Labour Resources, R&D Inst. of Labour and Russian Acad. of Sciences' Employment Problems Inst. 1984–97; Social Programmes Dir, Reformugol Foundation 1997–99; Dir Social Policy and Human Resources Dept, Mining and Metallurgical Co. Norilsk Nickel 1999–2001, Deputy Dir Gen. for Human Resources and Social Policy 2002–08; Deputy Gov. for Social Issues, Taimyr (Dolgano-Nenets) Autonomous Okrug 2001; Pres. All-Russian Inter-industry Asscn of Employers –Nat. Alliance of Nickel and Precious Metals Mfrs; Chair. Soglasiye Insurance Co. 2008–10; Deputy Moscow Mayor for Educ. and Healthcare and mem. Moscow City Govt 2010–12; Deputy Chair. of the Govt 2012–. *Address:* Office of the Chairman of the Government, 103274 Moscow, Krasnopresnenskaya nab. 2, Russia (office). *Telephone:* (495) 605-53-29 (office). *Fax:* (495) 605-52-43 (office). *E-mail:* duty_press@aprf.gov.ru (office). *Website:* www.government.ru (office); www.premier.gov.ru (office).

GOLU, Mihai, MA, PhD; Romanian politician and scientist; *Professor and Head, Department of Psychology, Spiru Haret University;* b. 4 March 1934, Bumbeşti-Pitic, Gorj Co.; s. of Ion Golu and Gheorghita Golu; m. Elena Filip 1957; two s.; ed Psychology Coll., Bucharest and Lomonosov Univs; worked as psychologist, Prof., Bucharest Univ.; Researcher, Carnegie-Mellon Univ., USA 1973–74; Deputy (ind. cand.) 1990–92, Party of Social Democracy 1992–96; Minister of Educ. and Science 1991–92, of Culture 1992–93; Deputy, Parl. Ass. of Council of Europe 1993–96; currently Prof. and Head, Dept of Psychology, Spiru Haret Univ.; Pres. Romanian Asscn of Psychologists 1990–2004, Nat. Soc. for Educ. 1993–; Vice-Pres. Nat. Foundation for Gifted Children and Young People 2004–; Nat. Comm. for UNESCO 1990–95; mem. Acad. of Scientists 1998–, New York Acad. of Science; Romanian Acad. Prize 1981, Pablo Picasso Medal, UNESCO 1991, Jan Amos Komenius Medal, Czech Acad. 1992, Nat. Merit Award 2004. *Publications:* Sensibility 1970, Principles of Cybernetic Psychology 1975, Dynamics of Personality 1993, Neuropsychology 2000, Fundamentals of Psychology 2000, General Psychology 2003; scientific papers and articles. *Leisure interests:* reading biographies of famous people, classical music. *Address:* Bulevardul Libertatii 22, Bloc 102, Scara 5, Apt. 89, Bucharest, Romania (home). *Telephone:* 318-77-91 (home). *E-mail:* mgolu@spiruharet.ro.

GOLUB, Harvey, BS; American business executive; b. 16 April 1939, New York; s. of Irving Golub and Pearl Fader; m. Roberta Glunts 1980; one s. and two s. one d. by previous m.; Jr Pnr, McKinsey & Co. Inc., New York 1967–74, Sr Pnr 1977–83; Pres. Shulman Air Freight, New York 1974–77; Sr Officer, American Express Co., New York 1983–84, Vice-Chair. 1990–93, CEO, Chair. 1993–2001; Chair., Pres. IDS Financial Services (now American Express Financial Advisors), Minn. 1984–90, Chair., CEO 1990–2001; Chair., Campbell Soup Co. 2004–09 (now Dir; Chair. American International Group (AIG) 2009–10 (resgnd); Chair. Ripplewood Holdings (pvt. equity firm), New York; fmr Chair. Reader's Digest Association Inc.; fmr mem. Bd of Dirs Dow Jones & Company; mem. Advisory Bd Miller Buckfire & Co. LLC, Marblegate Asset Management LLC. *Address:* Ripplewood Holdings, 1 Rockefeller Plaza, 32nd Fl., New York, NY 10020, USA (office). *Telephone:* (212) 582-6700 (office). *Fax:* (212) 582-4110 (office).

GOLUTVA, Alexander Alekseyevich; Russian cinematographer; b. 18 March 1948, Liepaya, Latvia; m.; one d.; ed Moscow State Univ.; fmr teacher; taught philosophy at Leningrad Ulyanov-Lenin Electro-technical Inst. (LETI) 1973–74; fmr Lecturer, Div. of Propaganda and Agitation, Petrograd Exec. CP Cttee 1974–80, then Instructor, then Head; consultant, House of Political Educ. 1980–83; Head of Sector, Div. of Culture, Leningrad Regional CP Cttee 1983–85; Ed.-in-Chief Lenfilm Film Studio 1985–87, Dir 1987–96; First Deputy Chair. State Cttee on Cinematography 1996–97, State Sec. then First Deputy Chair. 1997–99, Chair. 1999–2000; First Deputy Minister of Culture, Head of Cinema Dept 2000–04; mem. Presidential Council for Culture and Art; ORKF 'Kinotvar' Best Producer of Russia 1995, Badge of Honour of Russian Fed. 1998, Nika Prize of Russian Fed. 1995, 1999, 2000. *Films:* Taxi Blues 1990, Peculiarities of the National Hunt 1995, Khrustalyov, My Car! 1998, His Wife's Diary 2000. *Address:* c/o Cinema Departments, Ministry of Culture of Russian Federation, M. Gnezdnikovsky per. 7, 125009 Moscow, Russia.

GOLYSHEV, Vyacheslav Arkadevich, PhD; Uzbekistani government official; First Deputy Presidential Adviser for Econ. Affairs –2005; Deputy Prime Minister, Head of the Econ. Sector and Foreign Econ. Relations Sector, Minister of the Economy 2005. *Address:* c/o Ministry of the Economy, pr. Uzbekistanii 45a, 100003 Tashkent, Uzbekistan (office). *Telephone:* (71) 139-63-20 (office). *Fax:* (71) 132-63-72 (office). *E-mail:* mineconomy@mmes.gov.uz (office). *Website:* www.mineconomy .cc.uz (office).

GOMA, Col Louis Sylvain; Republic of the Congo politician and army officer; *Secretary General, Economic Community of Central African States;* b. 24 June 1941; ed Versailles and Saint-Cyr; Asst Dir of Mil. Engineers –1968; Chief of Staff of Congolese People's Nat. Army 1968, promoted Capt. 1968; mem. Parti Congolais du Travail (PCT) 1969, Cen. Cttee 1970, Special Gen. Staff of Revolution 1974, Political Bureau; Sec. of State for Defence 1969–70; Minister of Public Works and Transport 1970–74; promoted Maj. 1973; Chief of Gen. Staff of Armed Forces 1974; Prime Minister 1975–84, 1991, responsible for Plan 1975–79; mem. Council of State 1975–77; mem. PCT Mil. Cttee (Second Vice-Pres.) 1977–79; currently Sec. Gen. Econ. Community of Cen. African States; mem. Nat. Transitional Council 1997; Crans Montana Award 2010. *Address:* General Secretariat, Economic Community of Central African States, BP 2112, Libreville, Gabon (office). *Telephone:* 41-44-47-31 (office). *Fax:* 41-44-47-32 (office). *E-mail:* secretariat@ ceeac-eccas.org (office). *Website:* www.ceeac-eccas.org (office).

GOMARD, Bernhard, DJur; Danish lawyer and academic; *Professor of Law, Copenhagen Business School;* b. 9 Jan. 1926, Karise; s. of C. J. Gomard and Karen Gomard (née Magle); m. 1st 1974; one s.; m. 2nd Marianne Rosen 1994 (died 2000); ed Univ. of Copenhagen; Legal Adviser, Danish Dept of Justice 1950–58, Danish Atomic Comm. 1956–76, Danish Insurance Cos 1958–2002; Prof. of Law, Univ. of Copenhagen 1958–96; Prof. of Law, Copenhagen Business School 1996–; mem. Bd of Dirs Danske Bank 1974–96; mem. and Chair. numerous Govt cttees; mem. Danish Acad. of Sciences 1975, Academia Europaea 1989, Inst. of International Business Law and Practice; Hon. Prof., Univ. of Freiburg; Commdr, Order of

Dannebrog; Hon. DrIur (Univ. of Lund); Nordic Jurists Prize 1987, Oersted Medal 1995. *Publications:* articles and treatises on contract and company law, civil procedure, with particular emphasis on Danish law. *Leisure interests:* opera, French art and literature. *Address:* Centre for Financial Law, Copenhagen Business School, Solbjergvej 3, 1, 2000 Frederiksberg C (office); 3 Hammerensgade, 1267 Copenhagen K, Denmark (home). *Telephone:* 38-15-26-42 (office); 33-32-80-20 (home). *Fax:* 38-15-26-60 (office). *E-mail:* bg.ckk@cbs.dk (office).

GOMER, Robert, PhD; American chemist and academic; *Professor Emeritus, The James Franck Institute, University of Chicago;* b. 24 March 1924, Vienna, Austria; s. of Richard Gomer and Anne Olah 1955; one s. one d.; ed Pomona Coll. and Univ. of Rochester; Instructor, then Assoc. Prof., James Franck Inst. and Dept of Chem., Univ. of Chicago 1950–58, Prof. 1958–96, Dir James Franck Inst. 1977–83, Carl William Eisendrath Distinguished Service Prof. of Chem. 1984–96, Prof. Emer. 1996–; Assoc. Ed. Journal of Chemical Physics 1957–59, Review of Scientific Instruments 1963–65; mem. Editorial Bd Surface Science 1964–70; Consultant, Pres.'s Science Advisory Bd 1961–65; Chair. Editorial Bd Bulletin of the Atomic Scientists 1965–70, mem. Bd of Dirs. 1960–84; Assoc. Ed. Applied Physics 1974–89; Co-Ed. Springer Series in Chemical Physics 1978–; mem. Bd of Dirs Univs Space Research Asscn 1976–78; mem. Advisory Group JASON; mem. Advisory Cttee Directorate of Physical Sciences, Air Force Office of Scientific Research 1961–75; mem. NAS, American Acad. of Arts and Sciences, Leopoldina Akad. der Naturforscher; Bourke Lecturer, Faraday Soc. 1959; Kendall Award in Colloid or Surface Science, ACS 1975, Davisson-Germer Prize, American Physical Soc. 1981, M.W. Welch Award, American Vacuum Soc. 1989, A. Adamson Award, ACS 1996. *Publications:* more than 240 scientific articles; Field Emission and Field Ionization 1961. *Leisure interests:* skiing, music and literature. *Address:* University of Chicago, James Franck Institute, GCIS E225, 929 East 57th Street, Chicago, IL 60637-1454 (office); 4824 South Kimbark Avenue, Chicago, IL 60615-1916, USA (home). *Telephone:* (773) 834-9058 (office). *Fax:* (773) 834-5250 (office). *E-mail:* r-gomer@uchicago.edu (office). *Website:* jfi.uchicago.edu (office).

GOMERSALL, Sir Stephen John, Kt, KCMG, MA; British business executive and fmr diplomatist; *Chief Executive for Europe, Hitachi Ltd;* b. 17 Jan. 1948, Doncaster, S Yorks.; s. of Harry Raymond Gomersall and Helen Gomersall; m. Lydia Veronica Parry 1975; two s. one d.; ed Queens' Coll., Cambridge, Stanford Univ., USA; entered diplomatic service 1970; in Tokyo 1972–77; Rhodesia Dept, FCO 1977–79; Pvt. Sec. to Lord Privy Seal 1979–82; Washington, DC 1982–85; Econ. Counsellor, Tokyo 1986–90; Head of Security Policy Dept, FCO 1990–94, Dir Int. Security 1998–99; Deputy Perm. Rep., Perm. Mission to the UN 1994–98; Amb. to Japan 1999–2004; Chief Exec. for Europe, Hitachi Ltd 2004–; mem. Advisory Council, London Symphony Orchestra. *Leisure interests:* music, golf. *Address:* 24 Windsor Court, Moscow Road, London, W2 4SN, England (home). *Telephone:* (1628) 585705 (home). *Fax:* (1628) 585710 (home). *E-mail:* sjgomersall@hotmail.com (home); stephen.gomersall@hitachi-eu.com (office). *Website:* www.hitachi-eu.com (office).

GOMES, Aristides; Guinea-Bissau politician; *President, Partido Republicano para a Independência e o Desenvolvimento;* b. 8 Nov. 1954; s. of Lawrence Gomes and Hope Baticã Gomes Ferreira; ed Univ. of Paris VIII, France; Dir-Gen. Televisão Experimental da Guiné-Bissau 1990–92; fmr Minister of Planning and Int. Cooperation; Prime Minister 2005–07 (resgnd); Founder and Pres. Partido Republicano para a Independência e o Desenvolvimento 2008–; fmr mem. African Party for the Independence of Guinea and Cape Verde. *Address:* Partido Republicano para a Independência e o Desenvolvimento, Bissau, Guinea-Bissau (office).

GOMES, Daniel; Guinea-Bissau politician; *Minister of Energy and Industry;* fmr Spokesman, Partido Africano da Independência da Guiné e Cabo Verde (PAIGC); Minister of Defence 2004–05, Minister of the Presidency of the Council of Ministers, Social Communication and Parl. Affairs 2005–07, of Fisheries and the Maritime Economy 2007, of Energy and Industry 2012–. *Address:* Ministry of Energy, Industry and Natural Resources, CP 311, Bissau, Guinea-Bissau (office). *Telephone:* 3215659 (office). *Fax:* 3223149 (office).

GOMÈS, Philippe; New Caledonian politician; b. 27 Oct. 1958, Algiers, Algeria; mem. Congress 1988–99, 1999–2004; mem. Perm. Comm. 1988–89, 1990–95; Mayor of La Foa 1989–2008; mem. Govt responsible for Employment and Vocational Training 1999–2001; Pres. Agricultural Pricing Comm. 1995; Pres. South Prov. Ass. 2004–09; mem. L'Avenir Ensemble –2008, co-f. Calédonie Ensemble 2008; Pres. of the Govt, also responsible for Mining, Air Transport and Int. Affairs 2009–11. *Address:* c/o Présidence du Gouvernement, 8 route des Artifices, POB M2, 98849 Nouméa Cédex, New Caledonia (office). *Telephone:* 246536 (office). *Fax:* 273129 (office). *E-mail:* presidence@gouv.nc (office). *Website:* www.gouv.nc (office).

GOMES JÚNIOR, Carlos; Guinea-Bissau politician; b. 19 Dec. 1949, Bolama; s. of Carlos Domingos Gomes and Maria Augusta Ramalho; m. Salomea Neves; four c.; banker and businessman; elected to Parl. 1994–, First Vice-Pres. 1996; mem. African Party for the Independence of Guinea-Bissau 1991–, Sec. for Foreign Affairs and Int. Co-operation 1999–2002, Leader 2002–; Prime Minister of Guinea-Bissau May 2004–05, 2009–12; cand. in presidential election 2012. *Address:* c/o Partido Africano da Independência da Guiné e Cabo Verde (PAIGC), CP 106, Bissau, Guinea-Bissau.

GOMEZ, Jill, FRAM; British singer (soprano); b. 21 Sept. 1942, New Amsterdam, British Guiana; ed St Joseph's Convent, Trinidad, St Maur's Convent, Surrey, Royal Acad. of Music, Guildhall School of Music, studied with Luigi Ricci in Rome; operatic debut as Adina in L'Elisir d'Amore with Glyndebourne Touring Opera 1968 and has since sung leading roles with Glyndebourne Festival Opera including Mélisande, Calisto and Ann Truelove in The Rake's Progress; has appeared with The Royal Opera, ENO, English Opera Group, and Scottish Opera in roles including Pamina, Ilia, Fiordiligi, the Countess in Figaro, Elizabeth in Elegy for Young Lovers, Ann Trulove, Tytania, Lauretta in Gianni Schicchi and the Governess in The Turn of the Screw; cr. the role of Flora in Tippett's The Knot Garden, at Covent Garden 1970 and of the Countess in Thea Musgrave's Voice of Ariadne, Aldeburgh 1974; sang title role in Massenet's Thaïs, Wexford 1974 and Jenifer in The Midsummer Marriage with Welsh Nat. Opera 1976; cr. title role in William Alwyn's Miss Julie for radio 1977; performed Tatiana in Eugene Onegin

with Kent Opera 1977; Donna Elvira in Don Giovanni, Ludwigsburg Festival 1978; cr. title role in BBC world premiere of Prokofiev's Maddalena 1979; Fiordiligi in Così fan tutte, Bordeaux 1979; sang in première of the Eighth Book of Madrigals in Zürich Monteverdi Festival 1979; Violetta in Kent Opera's production of La Traviata, Edin. Festival 1979; Cinna in Lucio Silla, Zurich 1981; The Governess in The Turn of the Screw, Geneva 1981; Cleopatra in Giulio Cesare, Frankfurt 1981; Teresa in Benvenuto Cellini, Berlioz Festival, Lyon 1982, Leila in Les Pêcheurs de Perles, Scottish Opera 1982–83; Governess in The Turn of the Screw, ENO 1984; Helena in Glyndebourne's production of Britten's A Midsummer Night's Dream; Donna Anna in Don Giovanni, Frankfurt Opera 1985 and with Kent Opera 1988; Rosario in Goyescas by Granados 1988, Helena in Midsummer Night's Dream, London Opera 1990; cr. role of Duchess of Argyll in Thomas Adès's Powder Her Face, Cheltenham Int. Music Festival and London 1995; regular engagements including recitals in France, Austria, Belgium, Netherlands, Germany, Scandinavia, Switzerland, Italy, Spain, USA; festival appearances include Aix-en-Provence, Spoleto, Bergen, Versailles, Flanders, Netherlands, Prague, Edin. and BBC Promenade concerts; master-classes at Pears-Britten School, Aldeburgh, Trinity Coll. of Music, London, Dartington Summer Festival, Meridian TV. *Recordings include:* Vespro della Beata Vergine 1610 (Monteverdi), Ode for St, Cecilia's Day (Handel), Acis and Galatea (Handel), Admeto (Handel), A Child of Our Time (Tippett), three recital discs of French, Spanish and Mozart songs with John Constable, Quatre Chansons Françaises (Britten), Trois Poèmes de Mallarmé (Ravel), Chants d'Auvergne (Canteloube), Les Illuminations (Britten), Bachianas Brasileiras No. 5 (Villa Lobos), Cabaret Classics with John Constable, Knoxville-Summer of 1915 (Barber), South of the Border (Down Mexico Way...) arranged by Christopher Palmer for Jill Gomez, Britten's Blues (songs by Britten and Cole Porter); premiere recordings of Quatre Chansons Françaises (Britten), Cantiga – The Song of Inês de Castro commissioned by her from David Matthews, Seven Early Songs (Mahler), A Spanish Songbook (with John Constable), The Knot Garden (Tippett), Miss Julie (William Alwyn), Powder Her Face (Thomas Adès). *Address:* 16 Milton Park, London, N6 5QA, England (home).

GÓMEZ MONT URUETA, Fernando Francisco, LicenDer; Mexican lawyer and politician; b. 1963; s. of Felipe Gómez Mont; ed Escuela Libre de Derecho; mem. Cámara Federal de Diputados 1991–94, Chair. Justice Comm. 1991–94; adviser to Pres. Ernesto Zedillo 1994–2000; mem. Partido Acción Nacional, fmr mem. Nat. Exec. Council and Policy Comm., Rep. in Fed. Electoral Inst. –1995 (resgnd); Pnr, Zínser Esponda y Gómez Mont SC, (law firm), Mexico City 1995–2008; Sec. of Interior 2008–10. *Address:* c/o Secretariat of State for the Interior, Bucareli 99, Col. Juárez, 06069 México, DF, Mexico (office).

GOMEZ-PIMIENTA, Bernardo, MArch; Mexican architect and academic; *Director, School of Architecture, Universidad Anáhuac;* b. 18 Aug. 1961, Brussels, Belgium; s. of Jose Luis Gomez-Pimienta and Danielle Magar; m. Loredana Dall'Amico; one d. one s.; ed Universidad Anáhuac, Mexico City, Columbia Univ., New York, USA; draftsman, George Wimpey Contractors Ltd, London, UK 1980–81; fmr Co-Dir Ten Arquitectos; Dir Furniture Design, Visual Int. 1995–; Prof. of Architecture Universidad Iberoamericana 1987–89, Universidad Anáhuac 1989, Universidad Nacional Autónoma de México 1992–96, 1998–2002, Federico E. Marcial Chair of Architecture 2002; Visiting Prof., Southern Calif. Inst. of Architecture 1994, Univ. of Illinois at Urbana-Champaign 1996–97; currently Dir School of Architecture, Universidad Anáhuac; mem. Mexican Coll. of Architects 1990; mem. Editorial Bd and founding mem. Arquine Review 1997; mem. Bd Architecture Cttee, Colegio de Arquitectos de la Ciudad de Mexico AC 1998–; mem. Editorial Bd Periódico Reforma 2002; mem. Jury AIA Design Honour Awards (New Mexico) 1997, (Iowa) 1999, (San Juan) 1999, Premios Alfher 2000, Fere Ambiente, Frankfurt 2002, Il Bienal Nacional de Diseño 2003; mem. Academia Nacional de Arquitectura 2003, Nat. Creator System, Council for Culture and Arts; Knight of the Legion of Honor; Hon. Fellow, Royal Architectural Inst. of Canada; over 40 architectural awards from Mexico, USA, Ecuador, UK and Argentina. *Architectural works include:* House 'O' 1992, Televisa Services Bldg 1994, Museum of Natural History, Mexico City 1996, Nat. Centre of the Arts, Mexico City 1996, Casa IA 2001, Hotel Habita 2002, Educare 2002, Arquine 2002, Mesa Lupa 2002, Perchero Ti 2002, Mesa Lobe 2002, Silla IA 2002. *Publications include:* numerous books, monographs, periodicals, catalogues and reviews. *Address:* School of Architecture, Universidad Anáhuac, Apdo 10-844, 11000 México, DF Mexico (office). *Telephone:* (55) 5627-0210 (office). *Fax:* (55) 5589-9796 (office). *E-mail:* anahuac@anahuac.mx (office). *Website:* www.anahuac.mx/arquitectura (office).

GÓMEZ-POMPA, Arturo, DrSc; Mexican biologist, botanist and academic; *University Professor Emeritus and Distinguished Professor Emeritus of Botany, University of California, Riverside;* b. 1934, Mexico City; ed Universidad Nacional Autónoma de México (UNAM—Nat. Autonomous Univ. of Mexico); fmr Prof. of Botany, Univ. of California, Riverside, USA, fmr Univ. Prof. and Distinguished Prof. of Botany, now Univ. Prof. Emer. and Distinguished Prof. Emer. of Botany, fmr Dir Inst. of Univ. of California to Mexico and US (UC MEXUS); Founder and CEO Inst. for Research on Biotic Resources (INIREB), Xalapa, Veracruz; Head of Dept of Botany, UNAM-Inst. of Biology, Prof. of Ecology and Botany, Faculty of Nat. Univ.; Founder and first Pres. Asociación Mexicana de Jardines Botánicos, AC (Mexican Asscn of Botanic Gardens, AC) 1983; Pres. Bd El Edén Ecological Reserve, AC; mem. Bd American Inst. of Biological Sciences, Exec. Council Tyler Prize; mem. Awards Cttee Acad. of Sciences for the Developing World, Int. Scientific Advisory Bd INBio, Costa Rica; fmr Vice-Chair. Species Survival Comm. of Int. Union for Conservation of Nature (IUCN); fmr Pres. Int. Coordinating Council of UNESCO's MAB Programme; fmr mem. Bd of Govs The Nature Conservancy; Founder and Exec. Dir US-Mexico Foundation for Science; fmr mem. Advisory Cttee on Science, Space and Tech. of US House of Reps, Bd Smithsonian Inst., Washington, DC; Founder and mem. Bd Pronatura, AC; mem. acads of Mexico, Latin American, Third World and American Acad. of Arts and Sciences; Dr hc (Autonomous Univ. of Morelos); Medal of Merit, Univ. of Veracruz, Tyler Prize for Environmental Achievement, Chevron Conservation Medal, Luis Elizondo Prize in Science and Tech., Instituto Tecnológico de Estudios Superiores de Monterrey, Arca de Oro Medal (Netherlands) 1984, Alfonso L. Herrera Medal, Mexican Inst. of Renewable Natural Resources, Botanical Merit Medal, Botanical Soc. of Mexico. *Publications:* more than 200 scientific papers in professional journals on tropical ecology, ethnobotany, conservation and man. of tropical forests. *Address:* Center for Tropical Research (CITRO), University of Veracruz,

Antigua Hacienda Lucas Martín, Xalapa, Veracruz, Mexico (office). *Telephone:* (228) 104-9269 (office). *E-mail:* arturo.gomez-pompa@ucr.edu (office); floramex@ucr.edu (office). *Website:* www.ucr.edu (office); www.agomezpompa.org (office).

GOMORY, Ralph Edward, BA, MA, PhD; American mathematician, academic, business executive and foundation executive; *Research Professor, Stern School of Business, New York University;* b. 7 May 1929, Brooklyn Heights, NY; s. of Andrew L. Gomory and Marian Schellenberg; m. 1st Laura Secretan Dumper 1954 (divorced 1968); two s. one d.; m. 2nd Lilian Wu; ed Williams Coll., King's Coll., Cambridge and Princeton Univ.; Lt, USN 1954–57; Higgins Lecturer and Asst Prof., Princeton Univ. 1957–59; joined IBM 1959, Fellow 1964, filled various managerial positions including Dir Math. Science Dept, Dir of Research 1970–86, Vice-Pres. 1973–84, Sr Vice-Pres. 1985–89, mem. Corp. Man. Bd 1983–89, Sr Vice-Pres. for Science and Tech. 1986–89 (retd); Andrew D. White Prof.-at-Large, Cornell Univ. 1970–76; Pres. Alfred P. Sloan Foundation, New York 1989–2007, Pres. Emer. 2007–; Research Prof., Stern School of Business, New York Univ. 2008–; Dir Bank of New York 1986–88, Industrial Research Inst. 1986–91; mem. Bd of Dirs Washington Post Co. 1989–, Lexmark Int. Inc. 1991–; mem. NAS, Nat. Acad. of Eng, American Acad. of Arts and Sciences, Council on Foreign Relations, White House Science Council (1986–89), Visiting Cttee, Harvard Univ. Grad. School of Business 1995–; Fellow, Econometric Soc., American Acad. of Arts and Sciences 1973; Trustee, Hampshire Coll. 1977–86, Princeton Univ. 1985–89; Hon. DSc (Williams Coll.) 1973, (Polytechnic Univ.) 1987, (Syracuse Univ.) 1989, (Carnegie Mellon Univ.) 1989; Hon. LHD (Pace Univ.) 1986; Lanchester Prize, Operations Research Soc. of America 1964, John von Neumann Theory Prize 1984, Harry Goode Memorial Award 1984, IRI Medal 1985, IEEE Eng Leadership Recognition Award 1988, Nat. Medal of Science 1988, Presidential Award (New York Acad. of Sciences) 1992, Arthur M. Bueche Award, Nat. Acad. of Eng 1993, Heinz Award 1998, Madison Medal 1999, Harold Larnder Prize, Canadian Operational Research Soc. 2006. *Publications:* Global Trade and Conflicting National Interests 2001 (co-author); published more than 80 articles. *Address:* Leonard N. Stern School of Business, Kaufman Management Center, 44 West 4th Street, Room 8-179, New York, NY 10012 (office); 260 Douglas Road, Chappaqua, NY 10514, USA (home). *Telephone:* (212) 998-0100 (office). *E-mail:* rgomory@stern.nyu.edu (office). *Website:* www.stern.nyu.edu (office).

GOMRINGER, Eugen; Swiss poet and academic; b. 20 Jan. 1925, Cachuela Esperanza, Bolivia; s. of Eugen Gomringer and Delicia Rodriguez; m. 1st Klara Stöckli 1950; m. 2nd Nortrud Ottenhausen; five s. one d.; ed Kantonsschule, Zürich and Univ. of Berne; Sec. and Docent, Hochschule für Gestaltung, Ulm 1954–58; Art Dir Swiss Industrial Abrasives 1959–67; Man. Dir Schweizer Werkbund, Zürich 1961–67; Man. of Cultural Relations, Rosenthal AG, Germany 1967–85; Prof. of Aesthetics, Düsseldorf Art School 1976–90; Man. Int. Forum for Design, Ulm 1988–; co-f. first museum for concrete art in Ingolstadt 1992; f. Inst. für Konstruktive Kunst und Poesie IKKP Rehau 1999; Hon. Prof., Univ. of Zwickau; mem. Akad. der Künste, Berlin, PEN; Bayerischer Verdienstorden 2008. *Publications include:* several books of poetry and monographs in the art field; many publs for Concrete Poetry, beginning with Constellations, Bern 1953. *Leisure interests:* mountaineering, art collecting, farming, dogs. *Address:* Institute for Constructive Art and Concrete Poetry, Kirchgasse 4, 95111 Rehau, Germany (office). *Telephone:* 9283-899485 (office); 9283-1234 (home). *Fax:* 9283-899487 (office); 9283-1234 (home). *E-mail:* info@kunsthaus-rehau.de (office). *Website:* www.kunsthaus-rehau.de (office).

GOMUŁKA, Stanisław, DEcon; Polish economist and academic; *Chief Economist, Business Centre Club;* b. 10 Sept. 1940, Krężoły; s. of Władysław Gomułka and Zofia Gomułka; m. Joanna Gomułka; one s.; ed Warsaw Univ.; Dept of Econs, Warsaw Univ. 1962–65; Researcher, Dept of Econs, Århus Univ., Denmark 1970, 1973; Reader in Econs, LSE, London 1970–2005; Fellow, Netherlands Inst. for Advanced Studies 1980–81; Prof., Dept of Econs, Univ. of Pennsylvania, USA 1985–86; Fellow, Stanford Univ. 1986, Columbia Univ. 1987, Harvard Univ., USA 1989–90; Prof., Central European Univ., Dept of Econs 1995–2000; Prof., Natolin Coll. of Europe 1995–2000; Chief Economist, PZU Group (insurance co.) 2002–07; Under-Sec. of State, Ministry of Finance Jan.–April 2008; currently Chief Economist, Business Centre Club, Warsaw; econ. adviser to Polish govts 1989–2002, to Chair. Nat. Bank of Poland 1996–97, to Russian Govt 1991; fmr econ. adviser to IMF, OECD, EU; Corresp. mem. Polish Acad. of Sciences 2013; Dr hc (Poznań Econs Univ.). *Publications:* Inventive Activity, Diffusion and the Stages of Economic Growth 1971, Growth, Innovation and Reform in Eastern Europe 1986, Economic Reforms in the Socialist World (co-ed.) 1989, The Theory of Technological Change and Economic Growth 1990, Polish Paradoxes (co-ed.) 1990, Emerging from Communism – Lessons from Russia, China, and Eastern Europe (co-ed.) 1998, The Theory of Technological Change and Economic Growth (e-book) 2002, Transformacja polska, dokumenty i analizy, Vol. I 2010, Vol. II 2011, Vol. III 2013; chapters in some 50 books and numerous articles in professional journals. *Leisure interests:* chess, bridge, walks. *Address:* Business Centre Club, 00-136 Warsaw, Plac Żelaznej Bramy 10, Poland (office). *Telephone:* (22) 6253037 (office). *Fax:* (22) 6218420 (office). *E-mail:* stanislaw.gomulka@bcc.org.pl (office). *Website:* www.bcc.org.pl (office).

GONCHAR, Andrei Aleksandrovich; Russian mathematician; b. 21 Nov. 1931, Moscow; m.; two c.; ed Moscow State Univ.; Lecturer, Docent, Moscow State Univ. 1957–63, Scientific Sec. Dept of Math. 1964–65; Sr Researcher, Head of Div., then Deputy Dir V.A. Steklov Math. Inst. 1966–68; main scientific research carried out in complex analysis and approximations theory; Ed.-in-Chief Matematicheskiye Sborniki; Corresp. mem. USSR (now Russian) Acad. of Sciences 1974, mem. 1987, Vice-Pres. 1991–98; mem. Nat. Acad. of Math. *Publications:* numerous scientific publs on complex analysis and approximation theory, theory of analytical functions. *Address:* Russian Academy of Sciences, Department of Mathematics, Leninsky pr. 14, Moscow, Russia (office). *Telephone:* (495) 938-18-12 (office). *Fax:* (495) 135-0555 (office). *Website:* www.mi.ras.ru (office).

GONCHAR, Nikolai Nikolayevich, CEconSc; Russian politician; b. 16 Oct. 1946, Murmansk; m.; one d.; ed Moscow Energy Inst.; engineer, then head of div. Moscow City Council on research activities of students 1972–75; Head of Div. Research Inst. of Complex Devt of Nat. Econs of Moscow 1976–82; Deputy, then First Deputy Chair. Exec. Cttee of Deputies, Soviet of Bauman Region of Moscow 1987–89, Chair. 1990–91; Sec. Regional CPSU Cttee 1989–90; Deputy Chair.

Moscow City Soviet of People's Deputies 1990–91, Chair. 1991–93; mem. Council of Fed. 1993–95, Deputy Chair. Cttee on Budget and Financial Regulations 1994–95; mem. State Duma 1995–, mem. Cttee on Budget, Banks, Taxes and Finances 1995–. *Address:* State Duma, Okhotny Ryad 1, 103265 Moscow, Russia (office). *Telephone:* (495) 292-75-08 (office). *E-mail:* gonchar@duma.gov.ru (office). *Website:* www.duma.gov.ru (office).

GONCHIGDORJ, Radnaasumberel R., PhD, DSc; Mongolian politician and mathematician; b. 29 Dec. 1953, Tsakhir Dist, Arkhangai Prov.; s. of Radnaasumberel Gonchigdorj; m. Damdinsurengiin Hishigt 1977; two s. two d.; ed Mongolian State Univ., Inst. of Math., Belorussian Acad. of Sciences, Minsk; Lecturer in Math., Mongolian State Univ. 1975–88; Dir Inst. of Math., Mongolian Acad. of Sciences 1988–90; Chair. Exec. Cttee Mongolian Social Democratic Movt 1990; Chair. Mongolian Social Democratic Party 1994; Deputy to Great People's Hural 1990–92; Vice-Pres. of Mongolia and Chair. State Little Hural 1990–92; mem. State Great Hural 1992–96, Chair. 1996–2000; presidential cand. 2001. *Address:* c/o State Great Hural, Government House, Ulan Bator 12, Mongolian People's Republic. *Telephone:* (1) 326877. *Fax:* (1) 322866.

GÖNCZ, Árpád, LLD; Hungarian writer and fmr head of state; b. 10 Feb. 1922, Budapest; s. of Lajos Göncz and Ilona Heimann; m. Mária Zsuzsanna Göntér 1946; two s. two d.; ed Pázmány Péter University of Arts and Sciences, Budapest; early career as bank clerk with Nat. Land Credit Inst.; joined Ind. Smallholders, Landworkers and Bourgeois Party; leading positions in Ind. Youth Org.; Ed.-in-Chief Generation (weekly); sentenced in 1957 to life imprisonment as defendant in political Bibó trial; released under amnesty 1963; then freelance writer and literary translator, especially of English works; Pres. Hungarian Writers Fed. 1989–90, Hon. Pres. 1990–; Founding mem. Free Initiatives Network, Free Democratic Fed., Historic Justice Cttee; mem. Parl. 1990; Acting Pres. of Hungary May–Aug. 1990, Pres. of Hungary 1990–2000; Hon. KCMG 1991; Dr hc (Butler) 1990, (Connecticut) 1991, (Oxford) 1995, (Sorbonne) 1996, (Bologna) 1997; Attila József Prize 1983, Wheatland Prize 1989, Premio Meditteraneo 1991, George Washington Prize 2000, Vision for Europe Award 2000, Pro Humanitate Award 2001, Polish Business Oscar Award 2002, Corvinus Award, Europe Institute Foundation 2003, Saint Adalbert Prize for Peace, Freedom and Cooperation in Europe 2009. *Publications include:* Men of God (novel) 1974, Encounters (short stories) 1980, Homecoming and Other Stories (short stories) 1991, Hungarian Medea (play), Balance (play), Iron Bars (play), A Pessimistic Comedy (play), Persephone (play), political essays; translated more than 100 works, mostly by British and American authors, including James Baldwin, Edgar Lawrence Doctorow, William Faulkner, William Golding, Ernest Hemingway, William Styron, Susan Sontag, John Updike, Edith Wharton and others. *Leisure interests:* reading, walking. *Address:* Office of the Former President, 1055 Budapest, Kossuth tér 4, Hungary (office). *Telephone:* (1) 441-3550 (office). *Fax:* (1) 441-3552 (office).

GONDJOUT, Laure Olga, MA; Gabonese politician; b. 18 Dec. 1953, Paris, France; d. of Paul Gondjout, fmr Pres. of Supreme Court and fmr Pres. of Nat. Ass.; ed Catholic Univ. of Paris, Polytechnic of Central London, England; began career as translator; worked at African Devt Bank (ADB), Abidjan, mem. Bd of Dirs for Gabon, ADB, Libreville 1995–2001, returned to Gabon and served as adviser to Pres. 1984–2002, Secrétaire particulière to Pres. 2003; Minister Del. to Minister of State for Foreign Affairs 2006–07; Minister of Communication, Posts and the Digital Economy Dec. 2007–Feb. 2008, 2008–11, of Foreign Affairs, Co-operation, Francophone Affairs and Regional Integration Feb.–Oct. 2008; Gen. Sec. Children of Africa Foundation, Libreville. *Address:* c/o Ministry of Communication, Posts and the Digital Economy, Libreville, Gabon.

GONDWE, Goodall; Malawi politician and economist; *Minister of Economic Planning and Development;* fmr Gen. Man. Reserve Bank of Malawi; fmr Sr Vice Pres. and Acting Pres. African Devt Bank; Dir of African Div., IMF 1998; fmr Econ. Adviser to Pres. of Malawi; Minister of Finance 2004–09, of Local Govt and Rural Devt 2009–11, of Natural Resources, Energy and the Environment 2011–12, of Econ. Planning and Devt 2012–; Vice-Pres. Democratic Progressive Party 2011–. *Address:* Ministry of Development Planning and Cooperation, Capital Hill Circle, PO Box 30136, Lilongwe 3, Malawi (office). *Telephone:* 1788888 (office). *Fax:* 1788247 (office). *E-mail:* mepd@malawi.net (office). *Website:* www.malawi.gov.mw (office).

GONDWE, Michael M., MBA; Zambian business executive and central banker; *Chairman and Governor, Bank of Zambia;* ed Univ. of Zambia, Univ. of Virginia, USA, Moi Univ., Kenya Coll. of Accountancy, Advanced Man. Programme, Univ. of Oxford, UK; worked for Zambia Industrial Mining Corpn (ZIMCO) and Bank of Zambia –1986; served in sr positions in Eastern and Southern African Trade and Devt Bank (PTA Bank), a COMESA inst. 1986–2001, Pres. PTA Bank 2001–11; Chair. and Gov. Bank of Zambia 2011–; fmr Dir, Zep Re Pta Reinsurance Co., Athi River Mining Ltd, Gulf African Bank. *Address:* Bank of Zambia, Bank Square, Cairo Road, PO Box 30080, 10101 Lusaka, Zambia (office). *Telephone:* (211) 228888 (office). *Fax:* (211) 221722 (office). *E-mail:* pr@boz.zm (office). *Website:* www.boz.zm (office).

GONG, Ke; Chinese engineer, academic and university administrator; *President, Nankai University;* b. 1955, Beijing; ed Beijing Inst. of Tech., Tech. Univ. Graz, Austria; Prof., Tsinghua Univ. 1994, also Chair. Dept of Electronic Eng 1997, Dir Chinese Nat. Lab. on Microwave and Digital Communications 1998, Vice-Pres. Tsinghua Univ. 1999, also Dean, School of Information 2004, Dir Tsinghua Nat. Lab. for Information Science and Tech. 2005; Pres. Tianjin Univ. 2006–11, Nankai Univ. 2011–; Vice-Pres. Chinese Inst. of Electronics, Chinese Inst. of Communication, China Inst. of Measurement and Instrumentations; Exec. mem. China Asscn of Science and Tech., Tech. Advisory Cttee, Ministry of Industry and Informatization; Fellow, Russian Acad. of Aerospace Sciences 2002–; Pan Wen Yuan Foundation Award for Outstanding Research in 2006. *Publications:* author or co-author of more than 100 papers in wireless communication, radiowave propagation, digital TV transmission, microsatellites and their applications, etc. *Address:* Office of the President, Nankai University, 94 Weijin Road, Nankai District, Tianjin 300071, People's Republic of China (office). *Telephone:* (22) 27401631 (office). *Fax:* (22) 27401631 (office). *E-mail:* gongk@ieee.org (office). *Website:* www.nankai.edu.cn (office).

GONG, Yuzhi; Chinese politician; *Vice-President, China Anti-Cult Association;* b. 1929, Xiangtan, Hunan Prov.; ed Tsinghua Univ.; joined CCP 1948; researcher, CCP Cen. Cttee Propaganda Dept 1952–66; Deputy Office Dir Cttee for Editing and Publishing Works of Mao Zedong 1977–80; Deputy Dir CCP Cen. Cttee Party Documents Research Office 1982; Deputy Dir CCP Cen. Cttee Propaganda Dept 1988; mem. 5th to 8th CPPCC Nat. Cttee 1978–98 (Vice-Chair. Sub-cttee of Study 1993–98), Standing Cttee 9th CPPCC Nat. Cttee 1998–2003 (Vice-Chair. Sub-cttee of Cultural and Historical Data 1998–2003); Vice-Pres. CCP Cen. Cttee Cen. Party School 1994–96, Soc. of Research on History of CCP (Pres. 1999–), China Soc. of Dialectics of Nature, China Anti-Cult Asscn 2000–; Dir Research Centre for Theory of Building Socialism with Chinese Characteristics; Exec. Deputy Dir Cen. Party History Research Centre; fmr mem. Academic Council, Inst. of Philosophy, Chinese Acad. of Social Sciences; fmr Guest Prof., Beijing and Tsinghua Univs. *Publications:* Some Questions on the Law of Development for Natural Sciences, On Science, Philosophy and Society, From New Democracy to Primary Stage of Socialism. *Address:* c/o Central Committee of the Chinese Communist Party, Beijing, People's Republic of China.

GONO, Gideon; Zimbabwean central banker; *Governor, Reserve Bank of Zimbabwe;* b. 29 Nov. 1959; m. Hellin Gono; two d. one s.; began career with ZimBank; worked at Commercial Bank of Zimbabwe (re-named Jewel Bank), fmr CEO Jewel Bank; Gov. Reserve Bank of Zimbabwe 2003–; Head Univ. of Zimbabwe Council; fmr Chair. Zimbabwe Broadcasting Holdings; Dr hc (Univ. of Zimbabwe). *Address:* Reserve Bank of Zimbabwe, POB 1283, Harare, Zimbabwe (office). *Telephone:* (4) 703000 (office). *Fax:* (4) 706450 (office). *E-mail:* rbzmail@rbz.co.zw (office). *Website:* www.rbz.co.zw (office).

GONSALVES, Ralph E., PhD; Saint Vincent and the Grenadines politician and lawyer; *Prime Minister and Minister of Finance and National Security;* b. 1946; ed Univ. of West Indies, Victoria Univ. of Manchester, UK; called to Bar, Gray's Inn, London; practised law at Eastern Caribbean Supreme Court; fmr Lecturer, Depts of Govt, Political Science and Sociology, Univ. of W Indies; Leader United People's Movt (UPM) 1979–82, Movt for Nat. Unity (MNU) 1994–98; Leader United Labour Party (ULP); Prime Minister of Saint Vincent and the Grenadines and Minister of Finance, Planning, Econ. Devt, Labour and Information 2001–10, Minister of Nat. Security 2005–10, Prime Minister and Minister of Finance and Nat. Security 2010–. *Address:* Office of the Prime Minister, Administrative Building, 4th Floor, Bay Street, Kingstown, Saint Vincent and the Grenadines (office). *Telephone:* 451-2939 (office). *Fax:* 457-2152 (office). *Website:* pmosvg@caribsurf.com (office).

GONUL, Mehmet Vecdi; Turkish politician; b. 1939, Erzincan; m.; three c.; ed Faculty of Political Science, Ankara Univ.; participated in state training programme for recruiting dist govs 1967; Dist Gov. in several areas of Turkey 1967–76; Gov. of Kocaeli 1976–77, later of Izmir; Dir-Gen. of Nat. Security (Police) Directorate 1977–79; Gov. of Ankara 1979–88; Under-Sec. Ministry of the Interior 1988–91; apptd Head of State Court of Accounts 1991; elected MP for Kocaeli 1999–2001, Deputy Speaker of Parl. 1999–2001; joined AK Party 2001; Minister of Nat. Defence 2002–11; Del. to EU Parl. Ass. *Address:* c/o Ministry of National Defence, Milli Savunma Bakanlığı, 06100 Ankara, Turkey (office).

GONZALES, Alberto (Al) R., LLB; American lawyer and fmr government official; b. 4 Aug. 1955, San Antonio, Tex.; m. Rebecca Gonzales; three s.; ed Rice Univ., Harvard Law School; served in USAF 1973–75, attended USAF Acad. 1975–77; joined Vinson & Elkins LLP, Houston, Tex. 1982, Pnr –1994; Adjunct Prof. of Law, Univ. of Houston –1994; Gen. Counsel to Tex. Gov. George W. Bush 1994–97; Sec. of State for Tex. 1977–99; Justice of Supreme Court of Tex. 1999–2001; Legal Counsel to the White House 2001–04, Attorney Gen. 2004–07; Visiting Prof., Political Science Dept, Texas Tech Univ. 2009–; Special Legal Counsel to Houston Host Cttee for Summit of Industrialized Nations 1990; mem. Del. of American Council of Young Political Leaders to People's Repub. of China 1995, Mexico 1996; Pres. Houston Hispanic Bar Asscn 1990–91, Leadership Houston 1993–94; Chair. Comm. for Dist Decentralization, Houston Ind. School Dist 1994; mem. Bd of Dirs United Way of Tex. Gulf Coast 1993–94; mem. Cttee on Undergraduate Admissions, Rice Univ. 1994; mem. Bd State Bar of Tex. 1991–94, Bd of Trustees, Tex. Bar Foundation 1996–99; mem. American Law Inst. 1999–; mem. Republican Party; Hispanic Salute Award, Houston Metro Ford Dealers 1989, Outstanding Young Lawyer of Tex., Tex. Young Lawyers Asscn 1992, Presidential Citation, State Bar of Tex. 1997, Latino Lawyer of the Year, Hispanic Nat. Bar Asscn 1999, Distinguished Alumnus of Rice Univ. 2002, Harvard Law School Asscn Award 2002, Hispanic Scholarship Fund Alumni Hall of Fame 2003, Good Neighbour Award, US–Mexico Chamber of Commerce 2003, Pres.'s Award, US Hispanic Chamber of Commerce 2003, Pres.'s Award, League of United Latin American Citizens 2003. *Address:* c/o Political Science Department, Texas Tech University, 113 Holden Hall, Boston & Akron Streets, Lubbock, TX 79409-1015, USA. *Telephone:* (806) 742-3121. *Fax:* (806) 742-0850. *Website:* www.depts.ttu.edu/politicalscience.

GONZALES POSADA, Luis; Peruvian lawyer and politician; b. 30 July 1945, Pisco; fmr Legal Adviser, Banco Industrial, Corporación Financiera de Desarrollo, Electricidad del Perú and of Social Security Dept; mem. Bd of Dirs, Seguro Social Obrero, Seguro Social del Empleado, Empresa Nacional de Turismo del Perú, La Crónica, Futura and Visión Peruana publishing cos; Founder and Dir daily Hoy and the weekly Visión; has been on staff of La Tribuna, La Prensa, Correo and La Crónica; mem. Colegio de Abogados de Lima (Pres. Foreign Affairs Comm. 1999) and of Colegio de Periodistas de Lima; Minister of Justice 1985–86; currently mem. Congreso, Pres. 2007–08. *Address:* Congreso de la República del Perú, Palacio Legislativo, Plaza Bolívar. Avenue, Abancay s/n, Lima, Peru (office). *Telephone:* 311-7777 (home). *Website:* www.congreso.gob.pe (office).

GONZÁLEZ CASANOVA, Pablo, MA, PhD; Mexican researcher and academic; b. 11 Feb. 1922, Toluca; s. of Pablo González Casanova and Concepción del Valle; m. Natalia Henríquez Ureña 1947; three s.; ed El Colegio de México, Escuela Nacional de Antropología, Univ. Nacional Autónoma de México and Univ. de Paris, France; Asst Researcher, Inst. de Investigaciones Sociales, Univ. Nacional Autónoma de México (UNAM) 1944–50, Researcher 1950–52, Full-time Researcher 1973–78; Researcher, El Colegio de México 1950–54; Sec. Gen. Asscn of Univs 1953–54; Titular Prof. of Mexican Sociology, Escuela Nacional de Ciencias Políticas y Sociales, UNAM 1952–66, of Gen. Sociology 1954–58; Dir Escuela

Nacional de Ciencias Políticas y Sociales 1957–65, Full-time Titular Prof. 1964–65, Titular Prof. of Research Planning 1967–; Dir Inst. Investigaciones Sociales, UNAM 1966–70; Rector UNAM 1970–72, Prof. Emer. 1984–; Visiting Prof., Univ. of Cambridge, UK 1981–82; Pres. Admin. Cttee Facultad Latinoamericana de Ciencias Sociales, Santiago and Centro Latinoamericano de Investigaciones Sociales, Rio de Janeiro, UNESCO 1959–65; Consultant UN Univ. 1983–87; Dir Centro de Investigaciones Interdisciplinarias en Humanidades Univ. Nacional Autónoma de Mexico 1986; mem. Asscn Int. de Sociologues de Langue Française, Comité Int. pour la Documentation des Sciences Sociales, Acad. de la Investigación Científica; Pres. Asociación Latinoamericana de Sociología 1969–72; Dr hc (Universidad Autonoma de Queretaro) 2007; Nat. Award for Social Sciences 1984, José Martí Int. Prize, UNESCO 2003. *Publications:* El Poder al Pueblo 1985, El misoneísmo y la modernidad cristiana 1948, Satira del Siglo XVIII (with José Miranda) 1953, Una utopia de América 1953, La literatura perseguida en la crisis de la Colonia 1958, La ideología norteamericana sobre inversiones extranjeras 1955, Estudio de la técnica social 1958, La Democracia en México 1965, Las categorías del desarrollo económico y la investigación en ciencias sociales 1967, Sociología de la explotación 1969, América Latina: Historia de Medio Siglo 1925–1975 (two vols, ed.) 1977, Historia del Movimiento Obrero en América Latina, Siglo XX 1981, El Estado y los Partidos Políticos en México 1981, América Latina, Hoy 1990, El Estado y la Política en el Sur del Mundo 1994. *Address:* Peña Pobre 28, Tlalpan, México, DF 14050, Mexico. *Telephone:* 5506702.

GONZÁLEZ FERNÁNDEZ, Margarita Marlene; Cuban engineer and politician; *Minister of Labour and Social Security;* b. 20 July 1964; spent several years working in construction industry; Vice-Minister, Ministry of Labour and Social Security 2001–03, First Vice-Minister 2001–09, Minister of Labour and Social Security 2009–; mem. Communist Party of Cuba. *Address:* Ministry of Labour and Social Security, Calle 23, esq. Calles O y P, Vedado, Municipio Plaza de la Revolución, Havana, Cuba (office). *Telephone:* (7) 838-0022 (office). *E-mail:* webmaster@mtss.cu (office). *Website:* www.mtss.cu (office).

GONZÁLEZ GONZÁLEZ, (Jaime) Ignacio; Spanish politician; *President, Madrid Regional Government;* b. 19 Oct. 1960, Madrid; m.; three d.; ed Autonomous Univ. of Madrid; Under-Sec., Ministry of Culture, Educ. and Sports 1996–99; Sec. of State for Public Admin, Ministry of Public Admin 1999–2002; Sec. of State for Immigration, Ministry of Interior 2002–03, also Govt Commr for Foreigners and Immigration 2002–03; mem. Partido Popular (PP), Sec.-Gen., PP in Madrid 2011–, mem. PP Nat. Exec. Cttee; Vice-Pres. and Spokesperson, Madrid Regional Govt 2003–12, Pres. 2012–; Deputy, Ass. of Madrid (regional legislature) 2007–; Minister of Culture and Sports, Madrid Regional Govt 2009–12. *Address:* City Hall, Plaza de Cibeles, 28014 Madrid, Spain (office). *Telephone:* (91) 5216500 (office). *Website:* www.madrid.org/cs (office).

GONZÁLEZ MACCHI, Luis Angel; Paraguayan fmr head of state and lawyer; b. 13 Dec. 1947, Asunción; s. of Dr Saúl González and the late Julia Macchi; m. Susana Galli; two d.; ed Univ. Nacional de Asunción; fmr Pres. Nat. Congress; fmr Chair. Nat. Vocational Service, Ministry of Justice and Labour; Dir-Gen. and Pres. of Exec. Council, Servicio Nacional de Promoción Profesional (SNPP) 1993–98; Pres. Chamber of Senators –1999; Pres. of Paraguay March 1999–2003; sentenced to eight years in prison for fraud and embezzlement 2006, successfully appealed sentence; mem. Asociación Nacional Republicana—Partido Colorado. *Address:* c/o Asociación Nacional Republicana—Partido Colorado, Casa de los Colorados, 25 de Mayo 842, Asunción, Paraguay (office).

GONZÁLEZ MÁRQUEZ, Felipe; Spanish lawyer and politician; b. 5 March 1942, Seville; m. Mar García Vaquero; two s. one d.; ed lower and high school, school of law, continued studies at Catholic Univ. of Louvain, Belgium; on graduating from law school, opened first labour law office to deal with workers' problems in Seville 1966; mem. Spanish Socialist Youth 1962; mem. Spanish Socialist Party (Partido Socialista Obrero Español, PSOE) 1964–, mem. Seville Prov. Cttee 1965–69, Nat. Cttee 1969–70, mem. Exec. Bd 1970, First Sec. 1974–79, resgnd; re-elected Sept. 1979, then Sec.-Gen. –1997; mem. for Madrid, Congress of Deputies 1977–2004; Prime Minister of Spain and Pres. Council of Ministers 1982–96; fmr Chair. Socialist Parl. Group; fmr EU Special Rep. for Fed. Repub. of Yugoslavia; mem. Club of Madrid, Circle of Montevideo, InterAcción Council, Shimon Peres Int. Council for Peace, Japanese Bonsai Asscn; Grand Cross of the Order of Mil. Merit 1984; Order of Isabel the Catholic 1996; Golden Cross of Merit (Austria) 1997; Dr hc (Louvain) 1995, Charlemagne Prize 1993, Carlos V Prize, Academia Europaea 2000. *Publications:* What is Socialism? 1976, P.S.O.E. 1977, El futuro no es lo que era (with J. Cebrián) 20011, Memorias del Futuro 2003, Mi idea de Europa 2010, ¿Aún podemos entenernos? (with Miquel Roca) 2011. *Leisure interests:* reading, bonsai plants, jewellery. *Address:* c/o Partido Socialista Obrero Español (PSOE), Ferraz 68 y 70, 28008 Madrid (office); Fundación Progreso Global, Gobelas 31, 28023 Madrid, Spain. *Telephone:* (91) 5820444 (office). *Fax:* (91) 5820422 (office). *E-mail:* infopsoe@psoe.es (office). *Website:* www.psoe.es (office).

GONZÁLEZ PASTORA, Marco Antonio del Cármen, DScS, LLD; Nicaraguan international organization executive, academic and attorney; *Executive Secretary, Central American Commission for Environment and Development;* b. 16 July 1948, Jinotega; m. Gina Cuthbert; one d.; ed Nicaragua Nat. Univ., Friendship Univ., Moscow, Russia; fmrly with Rosenstiel School of Marine and Atmospheric Science, Univ. of Miami, Fla, USA; Exec. Sec. Comisión Centroamericana de Ambiente y Desarrollo (Cen. American Comm. for Environment and Devt—CCAD), Dir-Gen. for Environment of the Cen. American Integration System, mem. Tech. Cttee Técnico Asesor AEA and Rep. to World Labour Org.; Sr Adviser to Chair. of UN Gen. Ass.; mem. numerous cttees including IUCN Environmental Law Comm., Steering Cttee of Int. Inst. for Environmental Compliance and Enforcement (INECE); Del. to 10 Climate Change Convention Confs; Dr hc (Paulo Freire Univ.); World League of Environmental Lawyers Medal 2007, Academic Award from Autonomous Univ., Mexico. *Publications:* author of many articles and books on environmental law and policy issues, including Central American Manual of Environmental Law 2007, Nicaraguan Manual of Environmental Law 2009. *Address:* c. Verapaz C-32, Arcos de Santa Elena, Antiguo Cuscatlàn, San Salvador (office); Secretaría Ejecutiva de la Comisión Centroamericana de Ambiente y Desarrollo (SE-CCAD), Blvd Orden de Malta 470, Santa Elena, Antiguo Cuscatlàn, San Salvador, El Salvador (office). *Telephone:* 2248-8842 (office). *Fax:* 7888-9799 (office). *E-mail:* magonzalez@sica.int (office); magonzalezp2003@yahoo.com (home). *Website:* www.ccad.ws (office).

GONZÁLEZ RODRÍGUEZ, Francisco; Spanish banking executive; *Chairman and CEO, Banco Bilbao Vizcaya Argentaria SA;* b. 19 Oct. 1944, Chantada, Galicia; m.; two d.; ed Universidad Complutense de Madrid; began career as computer programmer, Nixdorf, Germany 1970s; fmrly with FG Inversiones Bursátiles; led restructuring and privatisation of Argentaria (collection of state banks) 1996, Argentaria merger with Banco Bilbao Vizcaya (BBA) 2000; Co-Chair. Banco Bilbao Vizcaya Argentaria (BBVA) SA 2000–02, Chair. and CEO 2002–, Chair. Fundación BBVA; Dir Inst. for Int. Finance; Global Counsellor The Conf. Bd; Gov. Red Cross, Guggenheim Museum Bilbao, Museo de Bellas Artes, Fundación Príncipe de Asturias, Real Instituto Elcano, Foundation for Terrorism Victims, Foundation for Help Against Drug Addiction; mem. European Financial Services Roundtable, Institut Européen d'Etudes Bancaires, IMF Capital Markets Consultative Group, Int. Monetary Conf. *Leisure interest:* golf. *Address:* Banco Bilbao Vizcaya Argentaria SA, Plaza San Nicolás 4, Bilbao 48005, Vizcaya, Spain (office). *Telephone:* (944) 875555 (office). *Fax:* (944) 876161 (office). *Website:* www.bbva.com (office); www.bbva.es (office).

GONZÁLEZ SEGOVIA, Roberto Eudez; Paraguayan politician; b. 1959, Piribebuy; m. Miriam Benítez de González; four c.; ed Universidad Nacional de Asunción; practised as lawyer from 1986; Legal Adviser, various nat. pvt. enterprises; participant, various congresses, seminars; mem. Students' Rights Centre UNA; Students' Rep. of Hon. Council Bd Law and Social Sciences UNA; apptd Minister of Home Affairs 2002; Minister of Nat. Defence –2007; Minister for Public Works and Communications 2008. *Address:* c/o Ministry of Public Works and Communications, Oliva y Alberdi, Asunción, Paraguay (office).

GONZI, Lawrence, LLD, KBE; Maltese politician and lawyer; *Senior Legal Partner, Gonzi & Associates, Advocates;* b. 1 July 1953, Valletta, Malta; s. of Louis Gonzi and Inez Gonzi (née Galea); m. Catherine Gonzi (née Callus); two s. one d.; ed Malta Univ.; practised law 1975–88; Speaker House of Reps 1988–92, 1992–96; MP (Nationalist Party) 1996–2013; Leader Nationalist Party 2004–13, Whip, Parl. Group 1997–99, Sec.-Gen. 1997–98; Shadow Minister and Opposition Spokesman for Social Policy 1996–98; Leader of the House and Minister for Social Policy 1998–99, Deputy Prime Minister and Minister for Social Policy 1999–2004, Prime Minister and Minister of Finance 2004–08, Minister of Home Affairs, Tourism and Local Govt and Parl. Affairs 2012–13; Gen. Pres. Malta Catholic Action 1976–86; Chair. Pharmacy Bd 1987–88, Nat. Comm. for Persons with Disabilities 1987–94 (Pres. 1994–96), Nat. Comm. for Mental Health Reform 1987–96, Electoral System (Revision) Comm. 1994–95, Chair., Mizzi Org. Bd of Dirs 1989–97; mem. Prisons Bd 1987–88; Hon. Companions of Honour (KUOM). *Address:* Gonzi & Associates, Advocates, 115B, Old Mint Street, Valletta VLT1515, Malta (office). *Telephone:* 20157000 (office). *Fax:* 20157010 (office). *E-mail:* lawrence.gonzi@gonzi.com.mt (office). *Website:* www.gonzi.com.mt (office).

GOOCH, Graham Alan, OBE; British professional cricket coach and fmr professional cricketer; b. 23 July 1953, Leytonstone, Essex; s. of the late Alfred Gooch and of Rose Gooch; m. Brenda Daniels 1976; three d.; ed Norlington Junior High School, Leytonstone, Redbridge Tech. Coll.; right-hand opening batsman, right-arm medium bowler; played for Essex 1973–97 (Capt. 1986–87, 1989–94), MCC 1975–2000, Western Prov. 1982–83, 1983–84; played in 118 Tests for England 1975–1994/95, 34 as Capt., scoring 8,900 runs (England record) (average 42.58) including 20 hundreds (highest score 333 and record Test match aggregate of 456 against India, Lord's 1990, becoming only batsman to score a triple century and a century in a first-class match) and holding 103 catches; scored 44,846 First-class runs (128 hundreds), average 49.01 and held 555 catches; toured Australia 1978–79, 1979–80, 1990–91 (Capt.) and 1994–95; 125 One-Day Ints, including 50 as Capt. (both England records), scoring 4,290 runs (average 36.98, highest score 142) including eight hundreds; mem. England Selection Cttee 1996–99; Man. England Tour to Australia 1998–99; Head Coach, Essex County Cricket Club 2001–05, specialist batting coach and commercial role 2005–; Wisden Cricketer of the Year 1980, mem. Fed. of Int. Cricketers Asscn Hall of Fame 2000. *Publications:* Testing Times 1991, Gooch: My Autobiography 1995. *Leisure interests:* squash, golf, football. *Address:* c/o Essex County Cricket Club, The County Ground, New Writtle Street, Chelmsford, Essex, CM2 0PG, England. *Telephone:* (1245) 252420. *E-mail:* administration.essex@ecb.co.uk. *Website:* www.essexcricket.org.uk.

GOOD, Anthony Bruton Meyrick, OBE, FID; British public relations consultant and marketing consultant; *Chairman, Cox and Kings (UK and India) Limited;* b. 18 April 1933, Sutton, Surrey, England; s. of Meyrick G. B. Good and Amy M. Trussell; m. (divorced); two d.; ed Felsted School, Essex; man. trainee, Distillers Group 1950–52; Editorial Asst Temple Press 1952–55; Public Relations Officer, Silver City Airways; Public Relations and Marketing Man., Air Holdings Group 1955–60; Founder and Chair. Good Relations Ltd (previously Good Relations Group PLC) 1961–89; Dir Cox and Kings Travel Ltd 1971–, Chair. 1975–; Chair. Good Relations (India) Ltd 1988–, Cox and Kings (UK and India) Ltd 1988–, Good Consultancy Ltd 1989–, Flagship Group 1999–2011, The Tranquil Moment Ltd 2000–07, Sage Organics 2000–09, Miller Insurance Group 2000–04, Outright Marketing and Distribution Ltd (fmrly Q-Link International Ltd) 2000–, Tulip Star Hotels Ltd 2000–, Relish Events Ltd 2001–06, Neutrahealth plc 2004–, Marlin Group Holdings plc 2012–; Dir (non-exec.), Arcadian International PLC 1995–98, Care First Group plc 1996–98, Gowrings PLC 2003–05, Obento Ltd 2004–, Indo-British Partnership Network 2005–, Benney Watches plc 2007–, I-Connections UK Ltd 2008–, DQ Entertainment plc 2008–13, Outright Communication Ltd 2009–, All About Brands plc 2010–12; Founder Dir International Motors; Dir UK India Business Council (India) Ltd 2005– (Chair. 2009–13); currently Adviser, Marks & Spencer PLC, Adam & Co. PLC, Early Learning Centre, Scottish & Newcastle PLC; Fellow, Inst. of Public Relations. *Leisure interests:* travel, reading, theatre. *Address:* Clench House, Wootton Rivers, Marlborough, Wilts., SN8 4NT, England (home). *Telephone:* (1672) 810126 (office); (1672) 810670 (home). *Fax:* (1672) 810869 (office); (1672) 810149 (home). *E-mail:* anthony.good@btinternet.com.

GOOD, Leonard, PhD; Canadian international organization official; ed Univ. of Toronto, Univ. of Western Ontario; taught econs at Univ. of Prince Edward Island; various positions in Canadian Dept of Energy 1979–87; Deputy Minister of

Environment 1989–93, 1998–99; Canada's Exec. Dir on Bd of IBRD (World Bank) 1994–98; Pres. Canadian Int. Devt Agency 1999–2003; Chair. and CEO Global Environment Facility 2003–06 (retd). *Address:* c/o Global Environment Facility Secretariat, 1818 H Street, NW, Washington, DC 20433, USA. *Telephone:* (202) 473-0508.

GOODALE, Rt Hon Ralph, PC, BA, LLB; Canadian politician; b. Wilcox, Sask.; m. Pamela Goodale; ed Univ. of Regina, Sask. and Univ. of Saskatchewan; MP for fed. constituency of Assiniboia 1974; Leader, Sask. Liberal Party 1980s; mem. Sask. Legis. Ass. 1986; apptd MP for Regina-Wascana 1993, 1997, 2000, 2004, 2006, 2008 and 2011; Minister of Agric. and Agri-Food 1993–97, of Natural Resources Canada 1997–2002, Minister of State and Leader of the Govt in House of Commons Jan.–May 2002, Minister of Public Works and Govt Services Canada, Minister responsible for the Canadian Wheat Bd, Fed. Interlocutor for Métis and Non-Status Indians, Minister responsible for Indian Residential Schools Resolution Canada, Minister responsible for Communication Canada and with regional responsibilities for Sask. and the North 2002–03, Minister of Finance 2003–06, Opposition House Leader, Liberal Party 2006–10, Deputy Leader 2010–. *Address:* House of Commons, Ottawa, ON K1A 0A6, Canada (office). *Telephone:* (613) 996-4743 (office). *Fax:* (613) 996-9790 (office). *E-mail:* ralph.goodale@parl.gc.ca (office); goodale@sasktel.net (office). *Website:* www.ralphgoodale.ca.

GOODALL, Sir (Arthur) David (Saunders), Kt, GCMG, KSG, MA; British diplomatist (retd); b. 9 Oct. 1931, Blackpool; s. of Arthur William Goodall and Maisie Josephine Byers; m. Morwenna Peecock 1962; two s. one d.; ed Ampleforth Coll., Trinity Coll., Oxford; army service in Kenya, Aden, Cyprus 1954–56; joined Foreign (now Diplomatic) Service 1956, served at Nicosia, Jakarta, Bonn, Nairobi, Vienna 1956–75, Head of Western European Dept, FCO 1975–79, Minister, Bonn 1979–82, Deputy Sec., Cabinet Office 1982–84, Deputy Under-Sec. of State, FCO 1984–87, High Commr in India 1987–92; Jt Chair. Anglo-Irish Encounter 1992–97; Pres. Irish Genealogical Research Soc. 1992–2010; Chair. Leonard Cheshire Foundation 1995–2000 (Chair. Int. Cttee 1992–95), British-Irish Asscn 1997–2002, Governing Body, Heythrop Coll., Univ. of London 2000–06, Advisory Cttee for Ampleforth Coll. 2004–10; Visiting Prof. in Irish Studies, Univ. of Liverpool 1996–2012; mem. Council Univ. of Durham 1992–2000, Vice-Chair. 1997–2000; Distinguished Friend of the Univ. of Oxford 2001; Hon. Fellow, Trinity Coll. Oxford 1992, Heythrop Coll. 2006; Hon. LLD (Hull) 1994. *Publications:* Remembering India 1997, Ryedale Pilgrimage 2000; contribs to The Tablet, The Ampleforth Journal, The Past, The Irish Genealogist, Parliamentary Brief. *Leisure interests:* painting in watercolours, reading, walking. *Address:* Greystones, Ampleforth, North Yorks., YO62 4DU, England (home).

GOODALL, Dame Jane, DBE, PhD; British primatologist, ethologist and anthropologist; *Founder, Jane Goodall Institute;* b. (Valerie Jane Morris-Goodall), 3 April 1934, London; d. of Mortimer Herbert Morris-Goodall and Vanne Morris-Goodall (née Joseph); m. 1st Hugo Van Lawick 1964 (divorced 1974); one s.; m. 2nd M. Derek Bryceson 1975 (died 1980); ed Uplands School, Univ. of Cambridge; Sec. Univ. of Oxford; Asst Sec. to Louis Leakey, worked in Olduvai Gorge, then moved to Gombe Stream Game Reserve (now Gombe Nat. Park), Tanzania 1960, camp became Gombe Stream Research Centre 1964, Dir of Research, Gombe Nat. Park 1972–2003; Scientific Dir Gombe Stream Research Centre 1967–2003; studied social behaviour of the Spotted Hyena, Ngorongoro Conservation Area 1968–69; Founder, mem. Bd of Dirs and Trustee, Jane Goodall Inst. for Wildlife Research, Educ. and Conservation, USA 1976–; Scientific Gov. Chicago Acad. of Sciences 1981–; Int. Dir ChimpanZoo (research programme involving zoos and sanctuaries world-wide), USA 1984–; Vice-Pres. Animal Welfare Inst., British Veterinary Asscn, UK 1987–; Dir Humane Soc. of the US 1989–; mem. Int. Advisory Bd of Teachers Without Borders, USA 2001–; mem. Bd Orangutan Foundation, USA 1994–, Save the Chimps/Center for Captive Chimpanzee Care 2000–, North American Bear Center 2001–; mem. Hon. Cttee Farm Sanctuary, USA 2001–; mem. Bd of Dirs Cougar Fund 2002–, The Many One Foundation, USA 2002–; mem. Advisory Panel World Summit on Sustainable Devt 2002, and numerous other advisory bds and cttees; Visiting Prof., Dept of Psychiatry and Program of Human Biology, Stanford Univ. 1971–75; Adjunct Prof., Dept of Environmental Studies, School of Veterinary Medicine, Tufts Univ. 1987–88; Assoc., Cleveland Natural History Museum 1990; Distinguished Adjunct Prof., Depts of Anthropology and Occupational Therapy, Univ. of Southern California 1990; A.D. White Prof.-at-Large, Cornell Univ., NY 1996–2002; Scientific Fellow, Wildlife Conservation Soc., USA 2002–; Trustee, L. S. B. Leakey Foundation 1974–, Jane Goodall Inst., UK 1988–, Jane Goodall Inst., Canada 1993–; mem. Explorer's Club, New York 1981, American Philosophical Soc. 1988, Soc. of Women Geographers, USA 1988, Deutsche Akad. der Naturforscher Leopoldina 1990, Academia Scientiarium et Artium Europaea, Austria 1991; Foreign mem. Research Centre for Human Ethology, Max Planck Inst. for Behavioural Physiology 1984; speaker on conservation issues, appearing on numerous TV shows including: 20/20, Nightline, Good Morning America; Hon. Foreign mem. American Acad. of Arts and Sciences 1972; Hon. Fellow, Royal Anthropological Inst. of GB and Ireland 1991; Hon. mem. Ewha Acad. of Arts and Sciences 2006; Ordre nat. de la Légion d'honneur 2006; 22 hon. degrees; numerous awards including Franklin Burr Award, Nat. Geographic Soc. 1963–64, Conservation Award, New York Zoological Soc. 1974, Order of the Golden Ark, World Wildlife Award for Conservation 1980, J. Paul Getty Wildlife Conservation Prize 1984, Albert Schweitzer Award, Int. Women's Inst. 1987, Nat. Geographic Soc. Centennial Award 1988, Anthropologist of the Year Award 1989, AMES Award, American Anthropologist Asscn 1990, Gold Medal, Soc. of Women Geographers 1990, Inamori Foundation Award 1990, Washoe Award 1990, Kyoto Prize in Basic Science 1990, Rainforest Alliance Champion Award 1993, Hubbard Medal for Distinction in Exploration, Discovery, and Research, Nat. Geographic Soc. 1995, Lifetime Achievement Award, In Defense of Animals 1995, Silver Medal, Zoological Soc. of London 1996, Tanzanian Kilimanjaro Medal 1996, Conservation Award, Primate Soc. of GB 1996, William Proctor Prize for Scientific Achievement Kilimanjaro 1996, Commonwealth Award for Public Service 1997, Royal Geographical Soc./Discovery Channel Europe Award for A Lifetime of Discovery 1997, Roger Tory Peterson Memorial Medal, Harvard Museum of Natural History 2001, 2007, Benjamin Franklin Medal in Life Science 2003, Award of Harvard Medical School Center for Health and the Global Environment 2003, Prince of Asturias Award for Tech. and Scientific Achievement 2003, Life Time Achievement Award,

Int. Fund for Animal Welfare 2004, UNESCO 60th Anniversary Gold Medal 2006, Lifetime Achievement Award, Jules Verne Adventures 2006, Hon. Medal of the City of Paris 2007, Lifetime Achievement Award, Heart of Green Awards 2011. *Films:* Miss Goodall and the Wild Chimpanzees 1963, Among the Wild Chimpanzees 1984, People of the Forest (with Hugo van Lawick) 1988, Chimpanzee Alert 1990, Chimps, So Like Us 1990, The Life and Legend of Jane Goodall 1990, The Gombe Chimpanzees 1990, Fifi's Boys 1995, My Life with the Wild Chimpanzees 1995, Chimpanzee Diary 1995, Animal Minds 1995, Jane Goodall: Reason For Hope 1999, Chimps R Us 2001, Jane Goodall's Wild Chimpanzees 2002, Jane Goodall's Return to Gombe 2004, Jane Goodall's State of the Great Ape 2004, Jane Goodall – When Animals Talk 2005, Jane Goodall's Heroes 2006. *Publications include:* My Friends the Wild Chimpanzees 1967, Innocent Killers (with H. van Lawick) 1971, In the Shadow of Man 1971, The Chimpanzees of Gombe: Patterns of Behavior (R. R. Hawkins Award for the Outstanding Tech., Scientific or Medical Book of 1986, The Wildlife Soc. (USA) Award for Outstanding Publ. in Wildlife Ecology and Man. 1986) 1986, Through a Window: 30 Years Observing the Gombe Chimpanzees 1990, Visions of Caliban (with Dale Peterson) (New York Times Notable Book for 1993, Library Journal Best Sci-Tech Book for 1993) 1993, Brutal Kinship (with Michael Nichols) 1999, 40 Years at Gombe 2000, Africa in My Blood: An Autobiography in Letters (ed. by Dale Peterson) 2000, Beyond Innocence: An Autobiography in Letters, the Later Years (ed. by Dale Peterson) 2001, Performance and Evolution in the Age of Darwin: Out of the Natural Order 2002, Ten Trusts: What We Must Do to Care for the Animals We Love (with Marc Bekoff) 2002, Hope for Animals and Their World: How Endangered Species Are Being Rescued from the Brink (with Thane Maynard and Gail Hudson) 2009; for children: Grub: The Bush Baby 1972, My Life with the Chimpanzees (Reading-Magic Award for Outstanding Book for Children 1989) 1988, The Chimpanzee Family Book (UNICEF Award for the Best Children's Book of 1989, Austrian State Prize for Best Children's Book of 1990) 1989, Jane Goodall's Animal World: Chimps 1989, Animal Family Series, Jane Goodall: With Love 1994, Dr. White (illustrated by Julie Litty) 1999, The Eagle & the Wren (illustrated by Alexander Reichstein) 2000, Chimpanzees I Love: Saving Their World and Ours 2001, Rickie and Henri: A True Story (with Alan Marks) 2004; numerous book chapters and articles in scientific journals. *Address:* The Jane Goodall Institute for Wildlife Research, Education and Conservation, 4245 North Fairfax Drive, #600, Arlington, VA 22203, USA (office). *Telephone:* (703) 682-9220 (office). *Fax:* (703) 682-9312 (office). *E-mail:* info@janegoodall.org (office). *Website:* www.janegoodall.org.

GOODE, Anthony William, MD, FRCS FACS; British surgeon; b. 3 Aug. 1945, Newcastle-upon-Tyne; s. of the late William Henry Goode and of Eileen Veronica Goode; m. Patricia Josephine Flynn 1987; ed Corby School and Univ. of Newcastle-upon-Tyne; held clinical surgical posts in Newcastle Hosps Group 1968–76; Univ. of London Teaching Hosps 1976–; Prof. of Endocrine and Metabolic Surgery, Univ. of London; Hon. Consultant Surgeon, Royal London Hosp.; Consultant Surgeon, Whitechapel and St Bartholomew's Hosp.; Hon. Prof., Centre for Biological and Medical Systems, Imperial Coll. London 1982–; Clinical Dir Helicopter Emergency Medical Service, London 1998–2000; Ed.-in-Chief Medicine, Science and the Law 1996–; Asst Sec., Gen. British Acad. of Forensic Science 1982–87, Pres. 1999–; Hon. Sec., British Asscn of Endocrine Surgeons 1983–96; Fellow, Royal Soc. of Medicine 1971–; American Coll. of Surgeons 2000; mem. Int. Soc. of Surgery 1984–, Int. Soc. of Endocrine Surgeons 1984–, New York Acad. of Sciences 1986–, MCC 1982–, Hunterian Soc. 1998 (Orator 1998), British Acad. of Forensic Sciences; Trustee, Smith and Nephew Foundation 1990–; Liveryman, Worshipful Soc. of Apothecaries of London; Freeman City of London 1992. *Publications:* numerous papers and articles on nutrition in surgical patients, endocrine diseases, metabolic changes in manned spaceflight and related topics. *Leisure interests:* cricket, music (especially opera), literature. *Address:* The Surgical Unit, The Royal London Hospital, Whitechapel, London, E1 1BB, England. *Telephone:* (20) 7601-7032 (office).

GOODE, Charles Barrington, AC, BCom (Hons), MBA; Australian business executive; b. 26 Aug. 1938; ed Scotch Coll., Melbourne, Melbourne Univ., Columbia Univ., USA; mem. Bd Dirs Australia and New Zealand Banking Group Ltd (ANZ) 1991–2010, Chair. 1995–2010; mem. Bd Dirs Woodside Petroleum Ltd 1988– (Chair. 1999–2007), Australian United Investment Co. Ltd (currently Chair.) 1990–, Diversified United Investment Ltd (currently Chair.) 1991–, The Ian Potter Foundation Ltd (currently Chair.) 1998–, Howard Florey Inst. of Experimental Physiology and Medicine (fmr Pres.); mem. Bd Dirs Singapore Airlines 1999–2006; fmr mem. Bd Dirs CSR, Pacific Dunlop, Legal & General Assurance, Oliver J. Nilsen Australia, Queensland Investment Corpn; fmr Pres. Inst. of Public Affairs; fmr mem. Council of Monash Univ., Finance Cttee of Australian Acad. of Science, Investment Cttee of Melbourne Univ. Grad. School of Man. Foundation; fmr Dir Melbourne Business School Foundation; Hon. LLD (Melbourne and Monash Univs) Melbourne Business School Award 2006. *Address:* c/o ANZ Centre, Level 9, 833 Collins Street, Melbourne 3008, Australia. *Telephone:* (3) 9683-9999. *E-mail:* media.relations@anz.com. *Website:* www.anz.com.au.

GOODE, Richard Stephen, DipMus, BSc; American pianist; *Co-Artistic Director, Marlboro Music;* b. 1 June 1943, New York City; m. Marcia Weinfeld 1987; ed Mannes Coll. of Music, Curtis Inst., studied with Nadia Reisenberg and Rudolf Serkin; debut, New York Young Concert Artists 1962; Carnegie Hall recital début 1990; mem. Boston Symphony Chamber Players 1967–69; Founding mem. Chamber Music Soc. of the Lincoln Center 1969–79, 1983–89; mem. Piano Faculty, Mannes Coll. of Music 1969–; concerts and recitals in USA, Europe, Japan, South America, Australia, Far East; has played with Baltimore, Boston, Chicago, Cleveland, New York, Philadelphia, Berlin Radio, Finnish Radio and Bamberg Symphony Orchestras, New York, Los Angeles, Baltimore, Orpheus, Philadelphia, ECO and Royal Philharmonic Orchestras; currently co-Artistic Dir with Mitsuko Uchida, Marlboro Music (series of chamber music festivals); Young Concert Artists Award, First Prize Clara Haskil Competition 1973, Avery Fischer Prize 1980, Grammy Award (with clarinettist Richard Stoltzman), Jean Gimbel Lane Prize Northwestern Univ. School of Music 2006. *Leisure interests:* book collecting, museums. *Address:* Marlboro Music, Box K, Marlboro, VT 05344 (office); Marlboro Music, 121 West 27th Street, Suite 703, New York, NY 10001 (office); 12 East 87th Street, Apt 5A, New York, NY 10128, USA (office). *Telephone:* (212) 581-5197 (NY) (office). *Fax:* (212) 581-4029 (NY) (office). *Website:* www.marlboromusic.org (office).

GOODE, Sir Royston (Roy) Miles, Kt, CBE, QC, LLD, FBA, FRSA; British fmr professor of law and author; *Emeritus Professor of Law and Fellow of St John's College, University of Oxford;* b. 6 April 1933, London; s. of Samuel Goode and Bloom Goode; m. Catherine A. Rueff 1964; one d.; ed Highgate School and Univ. of London; admitted as solicitor 1955; Partner, Victor Mishcon & Co. (solicitors) 1966–67; called to Bar, Inner Temple 1988, Hon. Bencher 1992–; Prof. of Law, Queen Mary Coll., London 1971–73, Crowther Prof. of Credit and Commercial Law 1973–89, Head of Dept and Dean of Faculty of Laws 1976–80, Dir and Founder, Centre for Commercial Law Studies 1980–89; Norton Rose Prof. of English Law, Univ. of Oxford 1990–98, Prof. Emer. 1998–; mem. Monopolies and Mergers Comm. 1981–86, Council of the Banking Ombudsman 1989–92; Chair. Pension Law Review Cttee 1992–93; mem. Council and Chair. Exec. Cttee JUSTICE 1994–96; Hon. Pres. Centre for Commercial Law Studies 1990–, Oxford Inst. of Legal Practice 1994–; Fellow St John's Coll. Oxford 1990–98 (Fellow Emer. 1998–); mem. Governing Council, Int. Inst. for Unification of Private Law (UNIDROIT) 1989–2003; mem. Crowther Cttee on Consumer Credit; Hon. Fellow, Queen Mary and Westfield Coll., London 1991–; Hon. DSc (London) 1997; Hon. LLD (Univ. of E Anglia) 2003. *Publications include:* Consumer Credit 1978, Commercial Law 1982 (2nd edn 1995, 3rd edn 2004), Legal Problems of Credit and Security 1982 (2nd edn 1988, 3rd edn 2003, 4th edn 2008), Payment Obligations in Commercial and Financial Transactions 1983, Proprietary Rights and Insolvency in Sales Transactions 1985, Principles of Corporate Insolvency Law 1990 (2nd edn 1997), Proprietary Rights and Insolvency in Sales Transactions (3rd edn 2010), Consumer Credit Law and Practice (looseleaf), Commercial Law in the Next Millennium; books on hire purchase; contribs. to Halsbury's Laws of England (4th edn). *Leisure interests:* chess, reading, walking, browsing in bookshops. *Address:* 42 St John Street, Oxford, OX1 2LH (home); St John's College, Oxford, OX1 3JP, England (office). *Telephone:* (1865) 515494 (home). *Fax:* (1865) 514744 (home). *E-mail:* roy.goode@sjc.ox.ac.uk (office).

GOODEN, Linda, BS; American business executive; *Executive Vice-President, Information Systems and Global Solutions, Lockheed Martin Corporation;* ed Youngstown State Univ., San Diego State Univ., Univ. of Maryland Univ. Coll., Exec. Program Manager course at Defense Systems Management Coll.; has held positions of increasing responsibility since joining Lockheed Martin Corpn, Vice-Pres. Software Support Services unit from 1994, later Pres. Information Tech., Exec. Vice-Pres. Information Tech. & Global Services –2007, Exec. Vice-Pres. Information Systems & Global Services, Gaithersburg, Md and Officer of Lockheed Martin Corpn 2007–; mem. Bd of Dirs ADP, Inc.; mem. Eisenhower Fellowships Bd of Trustees, Armed Forces Communications and Electronics Asscn International, Information Tech. Asscn of America, Univ. of Maryland's A. James Clark School of Eng, Prince George's Community Coll. Foundation; Hon. Doctor of Public Service (Univ. of Maryland Univ. Coll.) 2005; Federal 100 'Eagle' Award, Federal Computer Week 2002, Corp. Leadership Award, Women in Technology 2002, Black Engineer of the Year, U.S. Black Engineer and IT magazine 2006, Exec. of the Year, Greater Washington Govt Contractor Awards 2007, inducted into Maryland Business Hall of Fame 2008, named to Corporate Board Member magazine's Top 50 Women in Technology 2008, featured as one of Black Enterprise magazine's 100 Most Powerful Execs in Corp. America for 2009, ranked by Fortune magazine amongst the 50 Most Powerful Women in Business in the US (33rd) 2010–11, (34th) 2012, inducted into Career Communications Hall of Fame 2011. *Address:* Lockheed Martin Corporation, 6801 Rockledge Drive, Bethesda, MD 20817-1877, USA (office). *Telephone:* (301) 897-6000 (office). *Fax:* (301) 897-6704 (office). *E-mail:* info@lockheedmartin.com (office). *Website:* www.lockheedmartin.com (office).

GOODENOUGH, John Bannister, BA, PhD; American physicist, materials engineer and academic; *Professor of Mechanical and Electrical Engineering, University of Texas, Austin;* b. 25 July 1922, Jena, Germany; s. of Erwin R. Goodenough and Helen M. Lewis Goodenough; m. Irene J. Wiseman 1951; ed Yale Univ., Univ. of Chicago; Research Engineer, Westinghouse Electric Corpn 1951–52; Group Leader and Residential Physicist, Lincoln Lab., MIT 1952–76; helped develop computer memories for USAF; conducted ground-breaking research on behaviour of metal oxides; Prof. and Head of Inorganic Chem. Lab., Univ. of Oxford, UK 1976–86; Prof. of Mechanical and Electrical Eng, Univ. of Tex. 1986–, apptd Virginia H. Cockrell Centennial Chair in Eng; conducted research on energy and high-temperature superconductivity; mem. NAS, Nat. Acad. of Eng, ACS, AAAS, Acad. des Sciences de l'Inst. de France, RSC, Physical Soc. of Japan; Fellow, American Physical Soc.; Foreign Assoc., Indian Acad. of Sciences, Acad. de Ciencias Exactas, Físicas y Naturales, Spain; Foreign mem. Royal Soc., London; Centenary Lecturer, Royal Soc. of Chem. 1976; Hon. PhD (Univ. of Bordeaux) 1967, (Univ. of Santiago de Compostela) 2002; Solid State Chem. Prize, Royal Soc. of Chem. 1980, Von Hippel Award, Materials Research Soc. 1989, Sr Research Award, American Soc. for Eng Educ. 1990, Medal for Distinguished Achievement, Univ. of Pennsylvania 1996, John Bordeen Award, Mining, Metallurgy & Materials Soc. 1997, Olin Palladium Award, Electrochemical Soc. 1999, Japan Prize 2001, Hocott Award, Univ. of Tex. 2002, Enrico Fermi Award 2009, IEEE Medal for Environmental and Safety Technologies 2012, Nat. Medal of Science 2012, Nat. Alliance for Advanced Technology Batteries Lifetime Achievement Award 2012, Charles Stark Draper Prize, Nat. Acad. of Eng 2013. *Publications include:* Magnetism and the Chemical Bond 1963, Les Oxydes des métaux de transition 1973, Witness to Grace 2008, Solid Oxide Fuel Cell Technology: Principle, Performance, and Operation (with K. Huang) 2009; numerous articles in scientific journals. *Leisure interests:* travel, Episcopal Church. *Address:* University of Texas, Department of Mechanical Engineering and Materials Science, 204 East Dean Keeton Street, Stop C2200, Austin, TX 78712-1592, USA (office). *Telephone:* (512) 471-1646 (office). *Fax:* (512) 471-7681 (office). *E-mail:* jgoodenough@mail.utexas.edu (office). *Website:* www.engr.utexas.edu (office).

GOODFELLOW, Peter Neville, DPhil, FRS, FMedSci; British geneticist; *Senior Adviser, Abingworth Management Ltd;* b. 4 Aug. 1951; s. of Bernard Clifford Roy Goodfellow and Doreen Olga Goodfellow (née Berry); m. Julia Mary Lansdall 1972; one s. one d.; ed Univs of Bristol and Oxford; MRC Postdoctoral Fellow, Univ. of Oxford 1975–76; Jane Coffin Childs Postdoctoral Fellow, Stanford Univ. 1976–78; Sr Fellow, American Cancer Soc. 1978–79; Staff Scientist, Imperial Cancer Research Foundation 1979–83, Sr Scientist 1983–86, Prin. Scientist 1986–92; Arthur Balfour Prof. of Genetics, Univ. of Cambridge 1992–96; Sr Vice-Pres. of

Biopharmaceuticals and Neuroscience, Smithkline Beecham Pharmaceuticals 1996–2001, Sr Vice-Pres. Discovery Research, GlaxoSmithKline plc 2001–06; Visiting Scholar, Rockfeller Univ. 2007; currently Sr Adviser Abingworth Man. Ltd; Visiting Prof., Univ. of Kent, Univ. College London, Bristol Univ., Univ. of Hong Kong; fmr mem. Bd of Dirs Decode Genetics; mem. Bd of Advisers Beaton Inst., Max Plank Inst. Berlin; mem. Scientific and Clinical Advisory Bd Prosensa Therapeutics BV; mem. Bd Inst. of Cancer Research, Muscular Dystrophy Campaign; Amory Prize 1997, Louis Jeantet Prize. *Publications include:* The Mammalian Y Chromosome: Molecular Search for the Sex Determining Gene (co-ed.) 1987, Cystic Fibrosis (ed.) 1989, Molecular Genetics of Muscular Disease (co-ed.) 1989, Sex Determination and the Y Chromosone (co-ed.) 1991, Mammalian Genetics (co-ed.) 1992; numerous reviews and specialist articles in learned journals. *Leisure interests:* science, football. *Address:* Abingworth Management Ltd, 38 Jermyn Street, London SW1Y 6DN, England (office). *Telephone:* (20) 7534-1500 (office). *Fax:* (20) 7287-0480 (office). *Website:* www.abingworth.com (office).

GOODHART, Charles Albert Eric, CBE, PhD, FBA; British economist and academic; *Norman Sosnow Professor Emeritus of Banking and Finance, London School of Economics;* b. 23 Oct. 1936, London, England; s. of Sir A. L. Goodhart; m. Margaret (Miffy) Smith 1960; one s. three d.; ed Eton Coll., Trinity Coll., Cambridge, Harvard Univ., USA; Asst Lecturer, Dept of Econs, Univ. of Cambridge and Prize Fellow, Trinity Coll.; Economist, Dept of Econ. Affairs, London 1965–66; Lecturer, LSE 1966–68, Norman Sosnow Prof. of Banking and Finance 1985–2002, Prof. Emer. 2002–, mem. Financial Markets Group 1987– (Deputy Dir 2002–04), Hon. Fellow 2006; Adviser on Monetary Affairs, Bank of England 1968–85, External mem. Monetary Policy Cttee 1997–2000; Adviser to Gov. of Bank of England on Financial Regulation 2002–04; mem. Exchange Fund Advisory Council, Hong Kong 1988–97. *Publications include:* Money, Information and Uncertainty 1989, The Evolution of Central Banks 1985, The Central Bank and the Financial System 1995, The Emerging Framework of Financial Regulation (ed.) 1998, The Foreign Exchange Market (with R. Payne) 2000, Financial Crises, Contagion and the Lender of Last Resort (co-ed with G. Illing) 2002, Intervention to Save Hong Kong (with Lu Dai) 2003, Financial Development and Economic Growth (ed) 2004, House Prices and the Macroeconomy (with B. Hofmann) 2006, The Regulatory Response to the Financial Crisis 2009, The Basel Committee on Banking Supervision: A History of the Early Years, 1974–1997 2011. *Leisure interest:* sheep farming. *Address:* Financial Markets Group, Room R414, London School of Economics, Houghton Street, London, WC2A 2AE (office); 27 Abbotsbury Road, London, W14 8EL, England (home). *Telephone:* (20) 7955-7555 (office); (20) 7603-5817 (home). *Fax:* (20) 7371-3664 (home). *E-mail:* c.a.goodhart@lse.ac.uk (office). *Website:* fmg.lse.ac.uk (office).

GOODING, Cuba, Jr.; American actor; b. 2 Jan. 1968, Bronx, NY; s. of Cuba Gooding Sr and Shirley Gooding; m. Sara Kapfer; three c.; started as backup break dancer 1984; two Nat. Assen for the Advancement of Colored People (NAACP) Awards. *Television appearances include:* Kill or Be Killed 1990, Murder with Motive: The Edmund Perry Story 1992, Daybreak 1993, The Tuskegee Airmen 1995. *Films include:* Coming to America 1988, Sing 1989, Boyz N the Hood 1991, Gladiator 1992, A Few Good Men 1992, Hitz 1992, Judgement Night 1993, Lightning Jack 1994, Losing Isaiah 1995, Outbreak 1995, Jerry Maguire (Acad. Award, Best Supporting Actor 1997, Chicago Film Critics Award, Screen Actor Guild Award) 1996, The Audition 1996, Old Friends 1997, As Good As It Gets 1997, What Dreams May Come 1998, A Murder of Crows 1999, Instinct 1999, Men of Honor 2000, Pearl Harbor 2001, Rat Race 2001, In the Shadows 2001, Snow Dogs 2002, Boat Trip 2002, The Fighting Temptations 2003, Radio 2003, Home on the Range (voice) 2004, Shadowboxer 2005, Dirty 2005, Lightfield's Home Videos 2006, End Game 2006, Norbit 2007, Daddy Day Camp 2007, American Gangster 2007, Hero Wanted 2008, Lies and Illusions 2009, Wrong Turn at Tahoe 2009, Red Tails 2012. *Address:* c/o The Endeavor Agency, 9601 Wilshire Blvd., 10th Floor, Beverly Hills, CA 90212, USA.

GOODING, Valerie (Val) Francis, CBE, BA, CIMgt; British business executive; *Chairman, Premier Farnell plc;* b. 14 May 1950; d. of Frank Gooding and Gladys Gooding; m. Crawford Macdonald 1986; two s.; ed Leiston Grammar School, Suffolk, Univ. of Warwick, Kingston Univ.; Reservations Agent, British Airways PLC 1973–76, Man. Trainer 1977–80, Personnel Trainer 1980–83, Reservations Man. 1983–86, Head of Cabin Services 1987–92, Head of Marketing 1992–93, Dir of Business Units 1993–96, Dir Asia Pacific 1996; Man. Dir UK Operations, BUPA 1996–98, CEO 1998–2008; Chair. Premier Farnell plc 2011–; mem. BBC Exec. Bd; mem. Bd of Dirs J Sainsbury plc 2007–, Standard Chartered Bank plc 2005–, Lawn Tennis Assen, Home Office (UK); Pres. Int. Fed. of Health Plans 2003–04; fmr mem. Bd Assen of British Insurers; mem. Advisory Bd Univ. of Warwick Business School; Trustee, British Museum, Rose Theatre; Hon. DBA (Bournemouth) 1999; ranked by Fortune magazine amongst 50 Most Powerful Women in Business outside the US (21st) 2002, (32nd) 2003, (18th) 2004, (16th) 2005, (18th) 2006, (21st) 2007, ranked by the Financial Times amongst Top 25 Businesswomen in Europe (third) 2005, (third) 2006, (sixth) 2007. *Leisure interests:* theatre, travel, tennis, keeping fit, family life. *Address:* Office of the Chairman, Premier Farnell plc, Farnell House, Forge Lane, Leeds, LS12 2NE, England (office). *Website:* www .premierfarnell.com (office).

GOODISON, Sir Nicholas Proctor, Kt, PhD, FBA, FSA, FRSA; British stockbroker and banker; b. 16 May 1934, Radlett; s. of Edmund Harold Goodison and Eileen Mary Carrington Proctor; m. Judith Abel Smith 1960; one s. two d.; ed Marlborough Coll. and King's Coll., Cambridge; joined H. E. Goodison & Co. (now Quilter & Co. Ltd) 1958–88, partner 1962, Chair. 1975–88; mem. Council The Stock Exchange 1968–88, Chair. 1976–88; Pres. British Bankers Assen 1991–96; Pres. Int. Fed. of Stock Exchanges 1985–86; Chair. TSB Group PLC 1989–95, TSB Bank PLC 1989–2000, Deputy Chair. Lloyds TSB Group PLC 1995–2000; Dir (non-exec.) Corus Group PLC (fmrly British Steel PLC) 1989–2001 (Deputy Chair. 1993–99); Dir Ottoman Bank 1986–92; Dir Gen. Accident 1987–95; Trustee, Nat. Heritage Memorial Fund 1988–97; Vice-Chair. Bd of English Nat. Opera 1980–88 (Dir 1977–98); Chair. Nat. Art-Collections Fund 1986–2002, Courtauld Inst. 1982–2002, Crafts Council 1997–2005, Burlington Magazine Publs 2001–09; Nat. Life Story Collection 2003–; Hon. Keeper of Furniture, Fitzwilliam Museum, Cambridge; Pres. Furniture History Soc.; Pres. Walpole Soc.; Gov. Marlborough Coll. 1981–97; mem. Royal Comm. on Long-term Care of the Elderly 1997–99;

Leader and Author Goodison Review: Securing the Best for our Museums; Private Giving and Govt Support (HM Treasury) 2003; Sr Fellow, RCA 1991; Hon. FRIBA 1992; Hon. Fellow, King's Coll. Cambridge 2001, Courtauld Inst. of Art 2003, Royal Acad. of Arts; Chevalier, Légion d'honneur 1990; Hon. DLitt (City Univ.) 1985; Hon. LLD (Exeter) 1989; Hon. DSc (Aston Univ.) 1994; Hon. DArt (De Montfort Univ.) 1998; Hon. DCL (Univ. of Northumbria) 1999; Hon. DLit (Univ. of London) 2003. *Publications:* English Barometers 1680–1860 1968 (revised 1977), Ormolu: the Work of Matthew Boulton 1974 (revised as Matthew Boulton: Ormolu 2003), Hotspur: Eighty Years of Antiques Dealing (ed with Robin Kern) 2004, These Fragments 2005; many papers and articles on the history of furniture, clocks and barometers. *Leisure interests:* visual arts, history of furniture and decorative arts, music and opera, walking. *Address:* PO Box 2512, London, W1A 5ZP, England.

GOODLAD, Baron (Life Peer), cr. 2005, of Lincoln in the County of Lincolnshire; **Alastair Goodlad,** Kt, KCMG, PC, LLB, MA; British politician and fmr diplomatist; *Honorary President, Overseas Services Pensioners' Association;* b. 4 July 1943; s. of the late Dr John F. R. Goodlad and Isabel Goodlad (née Sinclair); m. Cecilia Hurst 1968; two s.; ed Marlborough Coll., King's Coll., Cambridge; MP for Norwich 1974–83, for Eddisbury 1983–99; Lord Commr of the Treasury 1981–84; Parl. Under-Sec. of State for Energy 1984–87; Comptroller HM Household 1989–90; Treas., HM Household and Deputy Chief Whip 1990–92; Minister of State for FCO 1992–95; Govt Chief Whip 1995–97; Shadow Sec. of State for Int. Devt 1997–98; High Commr to Australia 2000–05; mem. (Conservative), House of Lords 2005–, Chair. Constitution Cttee 2006–10, Merits of Statutory Instruments Cttee 2010–12, Secondary Legislation Scrutiny Cttee (fmrly Merits Cttee) 2012–; Chair. Asia House 2006–07, Britain-Australia Soc. 2006–07, Australian Opera Capital Fund, UK; Trustee, Sir Robert Menzies Memorial Trust; Hon. Pres., Overseas Services Pensioners' Assen 2012–. *Address:* House of Lords, Westminster, London, SW1A 0PW, England (office). *Telephone:* (20) 7219-3427 (office). *Website:* www.parliament.uk/biographies/lords/lord-goodlad/670 (office).

GOODLAD, John I., PhD; American academic; *President, Institute for Educational Inquiry;* b. 1920, N Vancouver, BC, Canada; s. of William Goodlad and Mary Goodlad; m. Evalene M. Pearson 1945; one s. one d.; ed Univs of British Columbia and Chicago; fmr school teacher, school prin. and Dir of Educ. in BC; consultant in curriculum, Atlanta (Ga) Area Teacher Educ. Service 1947–49; Assoc. Prof., Emory Univ. and Agnes Scott Coll. 1949–50; Prof. and Dir, Div. of Teacher Educ., Emory Univ. and Dir Agnes Scott Coll.–Emory Univ. Teacher Educ. Program 1950–56; Prof. and Dir, Center for Teacher Educ. Univ. of Chicago 1956–60; Dir Corinne A. Seeds Univ. Elementary School, UCLA 1960–84; Prof., Grad. School of Educ., UCLA 1960–85, Dean 1967–83; Dir of Research, Inst. for Devt of Educ. Activities Inc. 1966–82; Prof., Coll. of Educ., Univ. of Washington 1985, now Prof. Emer.; Founder and Pres. Inst. for Educational Inquiry 1992–; 20 hon. degrees; Harold W. McGraw Prize in Educ. 1999, ECS James Bryant Conant Award 2000, Brock Int. Prize in Educ. 2002, New York Acad. of Public Educ. Medal 2003, American Assen of School Admin Educ. Award 2004, ATE Distinguished Educator Award 2005, Horace Mann League Outstanding Friend of Public Educ. 2009, John Dewey Soc. Outstanding Achievement Award 2009. *Publications:* numerous books, chapters in books and articles in educational journals. *Leisure interests:* boating, fishing, walking. *Address:* Institute for Educational Inquiry, 117 East Louisa Street #371, Seattle, WA 98102, USA (office). *Telephone:* (206) 325-3010 (office). *Website:* www .ieiseattle.org (office).

GOODMAN, Elinor Mary; British political broadcaster and journalist; b. 11 Oct. 1946; d. of Edward Weston Goodman and Pamela Longbottom; m. Derek John Scott 1985; ed pvt. schools and secretarial coll.; Consumer Affairs Corresp. Financial Times newspaper 1971–78, Political Corresp. 1978–82; Political Corresp. Channel Four News (TV) 1982–88, Political Ed. 1988–2005; freelance journalist 2006–; Chair., Affordable Rural Housing Commission 2005–06; mem. Bd, Commission for Rural Communities. *Leisure interests:* riding, walking. *Address:* Commission for Rural Communities, John Dower House, Crescent Place, Cheltenham, Glos., GL50 3RA (office); Martinscote, Oare, Marlborough, Wilts. SN8 4JA, England (home). *Telephone:* (1242) 521381 (office). *E-mail:* info@ ruralcommunities.gov.uk (office). *Website:* www.ruralcommunities.gov.uk (office).

GOODMAN, John, BFA; American film actor; b. 20 June 1952, St Louis; m. Annabeth Hartzog 1989; one d.; ed Meramac Community Coll. and SW Missouri State Univ.; Broadway appearances in Loose Ends 1979, Big River 1985. *Films include:* The Survivors 1983, Eddie Macon's Run 1983, Revenge of the Nerds 1984, C.H.U.D. 1984, Maria's Lovers 1985, Sweet Dreams 1985, True Stories 1986, The Big Easy 1987, Burglar 1987, Raising Arizona 1987, The Wrong Guys 1988, Everybody's All-American 1988, Punchline 1988, Sea of Love 1989, Always 1989, Stella 1990, Arachnophobia 1990, King Ralph 1990, Barton Fink 1991, The Babe 1992, Born Yesterday 1993, The Flintstones 1994, Kingfish: A Story of Huey P. Long 1995, Pie in the Sky, Mother Night 1996, Fallen 1997, Combat! 1997, The Borrowers 1997, The Big Lebowski 1998, Blues Brothers 2000 1998, Dirty Work 1998, The Runner 1999, Bringing Out the Dead 1999, Coyote Ugly 2000, O Brother Where Art Thou 2000, The Adventures of Rocky and Bullwinkle 2000, One Night at McCool's 2000, Emperor's New Groove (voice) 2000, Happy Birthday 2001, My First Mister 2001, Storytelling 2001, Monsters Inc. (voice) 2001, Mike's New Car (voice) 2002, Dirty Deeds 2002, Masked and Anonymous 2003, The Jungle Book 2 (voice) 2003, Home of Phobia 2004, Clifford's Really Big Movie (voice) 2004, Beyond the Sea 2004, Marilyn Hotchkiss' Ballroom Dancing and Charm School 2005, Cars (voice) 2006, Evan Almighty 2007, Death Sentence 2007, Bee Movie (voice) 2007, Speed Racer 2008, Gigantic 2008, Confessions of a Shopaholic 2009, The Artist 2011, Trouble with the Curve 2012, Argo 2012. *Television includes:* The Mystery of Moro Castle, The Face of Rage, Heart of Steel, Moonlighting, Chiefs (mini-series), The Paper Chase, Murder Ordained, The Equalizer, A Streetcar Named Desire 1995, Kingfish: A Story of Huey P. Long 1995, Roseanne (series) (American Comedy Award for Funniest Male Performer in a TV Series — Leading Role 1989, 1990) 1988–97, Normal, Ohio (People's Choice Award for Favorite Male Performer in a New Television Series 2001) 2000, Pigs Next Door 2000, Father of the Pride (voice) 2004–05, Center of the Universe (series) 2004–05, Studio 60 on the Sunset Strip (Emmy Award for Outstanding Guest Actor in a Drama Series 2007) 2006, The Year Without a Santa Claus 2006, You Don't Know Jack 2010. *Address:* c/o Fred Specktor, CAA, 2000 Avenue of the Stars, Los Angeles, CA 90067, USA.

GOODMAN, Marian; American art gallery owner; *President, Marian Goodman Gallery;* b. New York, NY; ed Columbia Univ.; f. Multiples 1965, publr of prints, multiples and publs by artists including Richard Artschwager, John Baldessari, Dan Graham, Sol Lewitt, Roy Lichtenstein, Claes Oldenburg, Robert Smithson and Andy Warhol, worked with European artists, introducing early edns by Joseph Beuys, Marcel Broodthaers, Blinky Palermo and Gerhard Richte 1968–75; est. Marian Goodman Gallery, New York 1977, relocated 1981, currently Pres.; est. Galerie Marian Goodman, Paris 1999; hon. degree from CUNY Grad. Center 2012. *Address:* Marian Goodman Gallery, 24 West 57th Street, New York, NY 10019, USA (office); Galerie Marian Goodman, 79 rue du Temple, 75003 Paris, France (office). *Telephone:* (212) 977-7160 (New York) (office); 1-48-04-70-52 (Paris) (office). *Fax:* (212) 581-5187 (New York) (office); 1-40-27-81-37 (Paris) (office). *E-mail:* goodman@mariangoodman.com (office). *Website:* www.mariangoodman.com (office).

GOODNIGHT, James (Jim) H., PhD; American software industry executive; *CEO, SAS;* b. 6 Jan. 1943, Wilmington, NC; m. Ann Goodnight; three c.; ed NC State Univ., mem. faculty, NC State Univ. 1972–76, Adjunct Prof. 1976–; co-founder and co-owner, with John Sall, SAS Inst. Inc. (world's largest privately held software co.) 1976–, currently CEO; co-founder (with wife) Cary Acad. 1996; Fellow American Statistics Asscn. *Address:* SAS Institute Inc., 100 SAS Campus Drive, Cary, NC 27513-2414, USA (office). *Telephone:* (919) 677-8000 (office). *Fax:* (919) 677-4444 (office). *E-mail:* software@sas.com (office). *Website:* www.sas.com (office).

GOODWIN, Frederick (Fred) Anderson, LLB, CA, FCIB, FIB; British chartered accountant and banker; b. 17 Aug. 1958, Paisley; m. Joyce Elizabeth McLean 1990; two c.; ed Paisley Grammar School, Univ. of Glasgow; with Touche Ross & Co. 1979–95, Partner 1988–95; CEO Clydesdale Bank 1995–98, Yorkshire Bank 1997–98; Deputy CEO The Royal Bank of Scotland Group PLC 1998–2000, Group CEO and Exec. Dir 2000–08 (resgnd); Adviser, RMJM (architectural firm) 2010; Chair. The Prince's Trust; Dir (non-exec.) Bank of China Ltd; Fellow, Chartered Inst. of Bankers in Scotland 1996– (fmr Pres.); Hon. Fellow, London Business School 2008; knighted for services to banking 2004, knighthood cancelled and annulled 2012; Hon. LLD (St Andrews) 2004; Forbes Businessman of the Year 2002, No. 1 in Scotland on Sunday's Power 100 2003–06, European Banker of the Year 2003. *Leisure interests:* restoring classic cars, golf, Formula One racing fan, shooting. *Address:* c/o RMJM, 10 Bells Brae, Edinburgh, EH4 3BJ, Scotland. *E-mail:* edinburgh@rmjm.com (office).

GOODYEAR, Charles W. (Chip), BSc, MBA, FCPA; American business executive; b. 18 Jan. 1958; m. Elizabeth Goodyear; one s. one d.; ed Yale Univ., Wharton School of Finance, Univ. of Pennsylvania; Assoc. Kidder Peabody Co. 1983–85, Asst Vice-Pres. 1986–89; Vice-Pres. of Corp. Finance Freeport-McMoRan Copper & Gold Inc. 1989–93, Sr Vice-Pres. and Chief Investment Officer 1993–95, Exec. Vice-Pres. and CFO 1995–97; Pres. Goodyear Capital Corpn 1997–99; CFO BHP Group (BHP Billiton from 2001), London 1999–2001, Chief Devt Officer 2001–03, CEO, Melbourne, Australia 2003–07, Dir BHP Billiton Ltd and BHP Billiton PLC 2001–07; mem. Bd of Dirs Temasek Holdings Ltd, Singapore March–Oct. 2009; mem. Int. Council on Mining and Metals, Nat. Petroleum Council. *Leisure interests:* cycling, tennis, fishing, skiing.

GOOLSBEE, Austan Dean, PhD; American economist, academic and fmr government official; *Robert P. Gwinn Professor of Economics, Booth School of Business, University of Chicago;* b. 18 Aug. 1969, Waco, Tex.; s. of Arthur Goolsbee and Linda Goolsbee; m. Robin Winters 1997; two s. one d.; ed Milton Acad., Yale Univ., Massachusetts Inst. of Tech.; mem. Macro econ. Task Force for Polish Econ. Restructuring, Warsaw, Poland 1990; mem. Econ. Staff of Senator David Boren, Washington, DC 1991; Asst Prof. of Econs, Grad. School of Business, Univ. of Chicago 1995–99, Assoc. Prof. of Econs 1999–2001, Robert P. Gwinn Prof. of Econs, Booth School of Business 2001–; Staff Dir and Chief Economist, President's Econ. Recovery Advisory Bd, The White House, Washington, DC 2009–10, also mem. Council of Econ. Advisors, Chair. Council of Econ. Advisors 2010–11; Research Assoc., Nat. Bureau of Econ. Research 2001–; fmr columnist, Slate.com; columnist, New York Times 2006–; mem. Panel of Econ. Advisers to Congressional Budget Office 2007–; fmr Research Fellow, American Bar Foundation; Alfred P. Sloan Fellow 2000–02; Fulbright Scholar 2006–07; Peter Lisagor Award for Exemplary Journalism 2006. *Television:* History's Business (History Channel). *Address:* Booth School of Business, University of Chicago, 5807 South Woodlawn Avenue, Chicago, IL 60637, USA (office). *Telephone:* (773) 702-5869 (office). *Fax:* (773) 702-0458 (office). *E-mail:* goolsbee@ChicagoBooth.edu (office). *Website:* www.chicagogsb.edu (office).

GOONETILEKE, Air Chief Marshal W. D. R. M. J.; Sri Lankan air force officer; *Chief of Defence Staff;* b. 28 Feb. 1956; s. of Harry Goonetileke; m. Nelun Goonetileke; one s. one d.; ed St Peter's Coll., Bambalapitiya, Air Command and Staff Coll., USAF Air Univ., Alabama, USA, Pakistan Nat. Defence Coll.; joined Sri Lanka Air Force as Officer Cadet, Gen. Duties Pilot Br. 1978, rank of Pilot Officer 1979, served as Operational Pilot and CO, No. 03 Maritime Squadron and later No. 04 Helicopter Wing, several sr operational command appointments including Zonal Commdr, North Zone, later East Zone, Commdr Air Force Bases, Katunayake, Anuradapura and China Bay, Dir of Operations/Deputy Chief of Staff Operations, becoming 12th Commdr Sri Lanka Air Force 2006–11, rank of Air Chief Marshal 2009, Chief of Sri Lanka Defence Staff 2009–; Chair. Civil Aviation Authority 2009–; Uttama Seva Padakkama, Rana Wickrama Padak-kama, Vishista Seva Vibhushanaya (Distinguished Service Decoration). *Address:* Ministry of Defence, 15/5 Baladaksha Mawatha, PO Box 572, Colombo 03, Sri Lanka (office). *Telephone:* (11) 2430860 (office). *Fax:* (11) 2446300 (office). *E-mail:* webinfo@defence.lk (office). *Website:* www.defence.lk (office).

GOOSEN, Retief; South African golfer; b. 3 Feb. 1969, Polokwane (fmrly Pietersburg); s. of Theo Goosen; m. Tracy Goosen; one s. one d.; turned professional 1990; sr victories, Iscor Newcastle Classic 1991, Spoornet Classic 1992, Bushveld Classic 1992, Witbank Classic 1992, Mount Edgecombe Trophy 1993, Phillips South African Open 1995, Slaley Hall Northumberland Challenge 1996, Peugeot Open 1997, Dunhill Cup 1997, 1998 (both times with Ernie Els and David Frost), Novotel Perrier Open 1999, Lancome Trophy 2000, 2003, Scottish Open 2001, Telefonica Open 2001, EMC World Cup (with Ernie Els) 2001, WGC World Cup (with Ernie Els) 2001, US Open 2001, 2004, Johnnie Walker Classic 2002,

Dimension Data Pro-Am 2002, BellSouth Classic 2002, Chrysler Championship 2003, European Open 2004, The Tour Championship 2004, Nedbank Challenge 2004, Linde German Masters 2005, VW Masters 2005, Int. Tournament, South African Airways Open 2005; mem. Dunhill Cup team 1996–2000, World Cup team 1993, 1995, 2000, 2001, Presidents Cup team 2000, 2003, 2011, Iskandar Johor Open 2008, Africa Open 2009; Hon. mem. European Tour 2002–; f. Retief Goosen Acad. 2000; Hon. Patron, Make a Difference Charity, South African Disabled Golf Asscn; Springbok Colours Award 1990, Volvo Order of Merit 2001, 2002 (first non-European to retain title), Harry Vardon Trophy 2001, Goose Sauvignon Blanc 2008, Decanter World Wine Award 2009. *Leisure interests:* water skiing, wines. *Address:* IMG, McCormack House, Hogarth Business Park, Burlington Lane, Chiswick, London, W4 2TH, England (office). *E-mail:* angela.jones@imgworld.com (office). *Website:* www.retiefgoosen.com.

GOPAKUMAR, Rajesh, PhD; Indian physicist and academic; *Professor, Harish-Chandra Research Institute;* b. 1967, Trivandrum; m. Rukmini Dey; ed Indian Inst. of Tech., Kanpur, Princeton Univ., USA; Post-doctoral Fellow, Univ. of Calif., Santa Barbara 1997–98, Harvard Univ. 1998–2001; Visiting mem. Inst. of Advanced Study, Princeton, NJ 2001–05; Invited Lecturer, Strings, TIFR, Mumbai 2001, Collège de France, Paris 2004, Beijing 2006, Uppsala 2011; mem. Organizing Cttee Asia-Pacific School on String Theory, Seoul, S Korea 2001, 2004, 2005; currently Prof., Harish-Chandra Research Inst., Allahabad; mem. Adjunct Faculty, Indian Inst. of Tech., Kanpur, TIFR, Mumbai, Int. Centre for Theoretical Sciences, Bangalore; Founding mem. Global Young Acad. 2010; Fellow, Indian Acad. of Sciences 2009, Indian Nat. Science Acad. 2010; Best Graduating Student Award in Physics, Indian Inst. of Tech., Kanpur 1992, B. M. Birla Science Prize 2004, ICTP Prize 2006, Swarnajayanthi Fellowship 2006, S. S. Bhatnagar Award 2009. *Achievement:* discovered Gopakumar-Vafa invariants and Gopakumar-Vafa duality. *Publications:* numerous scientific papers in professional journals on string theory, particularly AdS/CFT correspondence, topological string theories, large N field theories and noncommutative field theories. *Address:* Harish-Chandra Research Institute, Chhatnag Road, Jhusi, Allahabad 211 019, India (office). *Telephone:* (532) 2274059 (office); (532) 2274370 (office). *Fax:* (532) 2567748 (office). *E-mail:* gopakumr@mri.ernet.in (office). *Website:* www.mri.ernet.in (office).

GOPAL, Satya; Indian civil servant and government official; *Chairman, Chandigarh Housing Board;* mem. Indian Admin. Service; Admin. Union Terri-tories of Dadra and Nagar Haveli and of Daman and Diu –2011; Chair. Chandigarh Housing Bd 2011–. *Address:* Chandigarh Housing Board, 8, Jan Marg, Sector 9, Chandigarh, 160017, India (office). *Telephone:* (172) 4601822 (office). *E-mail:* chb_chd@yahoo.com (office). *Website:* chandigarh.gov.in/chb_ppl.htm (office).

GOPALAKRISHNAN, Adoor; Indian filmmaker and writer; *Chairman, Public Broadcasting Trust of India;* b. 3 July 1941, Adoor, Kerala; s. of the late Madhavan Unnithan and Gouri Kunjamma; m. R. Sunanda 1972; one d.; ed Gandhigram Rural Univ., Film Inst. of India; mem. Working Group on Nat. Film Policy 1979–80; Dir Nat. Film Devt Corpn 1980–83; Faculties of Fine Arts, Univ. of Kerala, Calicut and Mahatma Gandhi Univs 1985–89; Chair. Film & Television Inst. of India 1987–89, 1993–96; Chair. 7th Int. Children's Film Festival of India 1991; currently Chair. Public Broadcasting Trust of India; mem. Advisory Cttee Nat. Film Archive of India 1988–90; Chair. Jury Singapore Int. Film Festival; mem. Jury, Int. Film Festival of India 1983, Venice Int. Film Festival 1988, Bombay Int. Film Festival 1990, Hawaii Int. Film Festival, Sochi Int. Film Festival, Alexandria Int. Film Festival, est. Chithralekha Film Soc., Chalachithra Sahakarana Sangham; Padma Shri 1984, Commdr des Arts et des Lettres 2003, Padma Vibhushan 2006; Hon. DLitt, Mahatma Gandhi Univ. 2006, (Univ. of Kerala) 2014, (Viswabharati Univ.) 2014; UNICEF Film Prize, OCIC Film Prize, Interfilm Prize, Dadasaheb Phalke Award 2004, Lifetime Achievement Award, Cairo, Denver and New Jersey int. film festivals, numerous other int. film awards. *Plays:* Vaiki Vanna Velicham, Ninte Rajyam Varunnu. *Films include:* Swayam-varam (Nat. Film Award) 1972, Kodiyettam (Nat. Film Award, Kerala State Film Award) 1977, Elippathayam (British Film Inst. Award, London Film Festival 1982, Nat. Film Award, Kerala State Film Award) 1981, Mukhamukham (Int. Film Critics' Prize, New Delhi, Nat. Film Award, Kerala State Film Award) 1984, Anantaram (Int. Film Critics' Prize, Karlovy Vary, Nat. Film Award, Kerala State Film Award) 1987, Mathilukal (Int. Film Critics' Prize, Venice, Nat. Film Award) 1989, Vidheyan (Int. Film Critics' Prize, Singapore, Nat. Film Award, Kerala State Film Award) 1993, Kathapurushan 1995 (Int. Film Critics' Prize, Mumbai, Nat. Film Award), Nizhalkkuthu 2002 (Int. Film Critics' Prize, Mumbai, Nat. Film Award), Naalu Pennungal (Nat. Film Award), Oru Pennum Randaanum (Kerala State Film Award), more than 24 short and documentary films. *Publications include:* plays: Vaiki vanna velicham 1961, Ninte rajyam varunnu 1963; books: The World of Cinema (Nat. Award for Best Book on Cinema 1984) 1983, The Experience of Cinema (Kerala State Award 2004), Film, Literature and Life 2005; screenplays of Rat-trap, Face to Face, Monologue and all 11 film collections of essays. *Leisure interest:* reading. *Address:* Darsanam, Thiruvananthapuram, 695 017 India. *Telephone:* (471) 551144; (471) 2446567. *E-mail:* adoorg@gmail.com. *Website:* www.adoorgopalakrishnan.com.

GOPALAKRISHNAN, S., MSc, MTech; Indian business executive; *CEO and Managing Director, Infosys Technologies;* ed Indian Inst. of Tech. (ITT), Madras; software engineer for Patni computer systems, Mumbai 1979, Asst Project Man. 1981; Co-founder and Dir Infosys Technologies, Bangalore 1981–, Tech. Dir –1987, Tech. Vice-Pres. KSA/Infosys, USA 1987–94, Head of Tech. Support Services 1994, Head of Client Delivery and Tech. 1996–98, fmr COO, Deputy Man. Dir –2006, Pres. and Jt Man. Dir 2006–07, CEO and Man. Dir 2007–; Chair. IIT Madras Growth Fund, Confed. of Indian Industry (CII) Nat. Cttee on E-commerce, Indian Inst. of Information Tech. and Man., Kerala; Vice Chair. Bd for Information Tech. Educ. Standards; Vice Chair. CII Southern Regional Council; mem. Asscn for Computing Machinery, IEEE, IEEE Computer Soc.; IIT Madras Distinguished Alumnus Award 1998. *Address:* Infosys Technologies, Plot No. 44 & 97A, Electronics City, Hosur Road, Bangalore 560 100, India (office). *Telephone:* (80) 28520261 (office). *Fax:* (80) 28520362 (office). *Website:* www.infy.com (office).

GOPALASAMY, V., (Vaiko), BA, MA, BL; Indian lawyer and politician; *Leader, Marumalarchi Dravida Munnetra Kazhagam;* b. 22 May 1944, Kallingappatti, Tamil Nadu; s. of Vaiyapuri Gopalasamy and Mariammal Gopalasamy; m. Renugadevi Gopalasamy; one s. two d.; ed St Xavier's Coll., Presidency Coll.,

B.L Law Coll.; Propaganda Sec. Dravida Munnetra Kazhagam (DMK) Party for Tirunelveli and Kanyakumari dists 1972–73, DMK Election Campaign Sec. 1984–93; mem. Rajya Sabha (Parl.) 1978–96, Lok Sabha (Parl.) 1998–04; Founder and Leader Marumalarchi Dravida Munnetra Kazhagam; arrested on charges of terrorism July 2002, Oct. 2008, released both times; Pres. Citizen's Forum for Rehabilitation of Physically Handicapped; f. Marumalarchi Blood Donors Asscn; Convener Voluntary Blood Donors Asscn, Tirunelveli 1983; Gold Medal in Econs. *Address:* AL-Block, New no 20, 4th Cross Street, 11th Main Road, Anna Nagar, Chennai 600 040; Marumalarchi Dravida Munnetra Kazhagam, 'Thayagam', 141 Rukmani Lakshmi Pathi Salai, Egmore, Chennai 600 008, India; Kalingappatti Village, Thiruvengadam, Tirunelveli District 627 724 India. *Telephone:* (44) 26214252; (46) 36282127. *Website:* www.mdmk.org.in.

GOPALASWAMI, N., MSc; Indian government official (retd); b. 21 April 1944, Needamangalam (then in Thanjavur dist), Tamil Nadu; ed St Joseph's Coll., Tiruchirappalli, Univ. of Delhi, Univ. of London, UK; mem. Indian Admin. Service 1966–, served in state of Gujarat in various capacities 1967–92, including Dist Magistrate in dists of Kutch and Kheda, Municipal Commr, Surat, Dir of Relief, Dir Higher Educ. and Jt Sec. (Home Dept) Govt of Gujarat, Man. Dir Gujarat Communication and Electronics Ltd, Vadodara, mem. (Admin and Purchase) Gujarat Electricity Bd, Sec. to Govt (Science and Tech. in Tech. Educ.) and Sec. Dept of Revenue; served Govt of India 1992–2004, worked as Adviser (Educ.) in Planning Comm., Jt Sec., Dept of Electronics, in charge of Software Devt and Industry Promotion Div. and also Head of Software Tech. Park of India Soc. and SATCOMM India Soc., Sec. Dept of Culture, Sec.-Gen. Nat. Human Rights Comm., Union Home Sec. –2004; Election Commr 2004–06, Chief Election Commr (with rank of Judge of the Supreme Court) 2006–09 (retd); mem. Delimitation Comm. 2005–; int. observer in USA during presidential election Nov. 2004, gen. elections in Mauritius July 2005; Prof. Mitra Gold Medal, Univ. of Delhi (first recipient) 1965. *Leisure interests:* listening to carnatic music (classical music from South India), photography. *Address:* 77 Lodhi Estate, New Delhi 110 003 (home); c/o Election Commission of India, Nirvachan Sadan, Ashoka Road, New Delhi 110 001, India. *Telephone:* (11) 24652424 (home).

GOPEE-SCOON, Paula, BSc, LLB (Hons); Trinidad and Tobago politician and business executive; b. 18 April 1958, Point Fortin; m. (divorced); three c.; ed St Joseph's Convent, San Fernando, Univ. of the West Indies, Cave Hill, Barbados, Univ. of London, UK; professional experience includes teaching (Point Fortin Intermediate Roman Catholic School), banking and finance (Republic Bank and Royal Bank of Trinidad and Tobago), along with sales, marketing and customer service (BioChem Trinidad and Tobago Ltd and Sunspots Plastics Ltd); MP (People's Nat. Movt—PNM) for Point Fortin 2007–; Minister of Foreign Affairs 2007–10; mem. Dyslexia Asscn Bursary Fund Cttee, St Joseph's Convent (Port of Spain) Support Group. *Leisure interests:* sports, Caribbean art and culture. *Address:* House of Representatives, Port of Spain (office); 66 Cherry Crescent, Westmoorings, Trinidad and Tobago (home). *Telephone:* (868) 648-1086 (office); (868) 637-1244 (home). *Fax:* (868) 648-1086 (office); (868) 637-1249 (home). *E-mail:* scoongp@gmail.com (home).

GOPINATH, Capt. G. R.; Indian airline executive and fmr army officer; *Chairman, Deccan Charters Ltd;* b. Gorur, Karnataka; m. Bhargavi Gopinath; two d.; ed Nat. Defence Acad., Indian Mil. Acad.; first army assignment during Bangladesh War 1971; f. Malnad Mobikes; launched India's first low-cost airline Air Deccan 2003; unsuccessful cand. in nat. parl. elections 2009; Founder-Chair. Deccan Charters Ltd 2009–; Chevalier, legion d'Honneur 2007; Rolex Int. Award 1996, Rajyotsava Award 2005, Personality of the Decade Award, K.G. Foundation, WIPRO PRSI Award, Sir M Visvesvaraya Memorial Award, Fed. of Karnataka Chambers of Commerce and Industry. *Publications:* Simply Fly: A Deccan Odyssey 2010. *Address:* Deccan Charters Ltd, G11, G Block Market, Hauz Khas, New Delhi 110 016 India (office). *Telephone:* (11) 26520035 (office); (11) 26520036 (office). *Fax:* (11) 26520034 (office). *E-mail:* delops@deccanair.com (office). *Website:* www .deccanair.com (office).

GOPINATH, Shyamala, MCom; Indian banker; *Chairperson, Advisory Board on Bank, Commercial and Financial Frauds, Central Vigilance Commission;* b. 20 June 1949; joined Reserve Bank of India 1972, held several positions including Exec. Dir 2003–04, Deputy Gov. 2004–11, on secondment to IMF 2001–03; Chair. Advisory Bd on Bank, Commercial and Financial Frauds, Central Vigilance Comm. 2012–; mem. Bd of Dirs Union Bank of India 1998–2001, Bank of Maharashtra 1994–96, State Bank of India Ltd 2004–, Nat. Housing Bank, Export-Import Bank of India; Ind. Dir (non-exec.) Ernst & Young 2011–; Ind. Dir, Indian Oil Corpn Ltd 2012–; Exec. Dir Nat. Stock Exchange of India Ltd 2012–; mem. Indian Advisory Bd Catalyst Inc.; Additional Ind. Dir (non-exec.) Tata Elxsi Ltd 2011–, GAIL (India) Ltd 2012–; fmr Del. Asian Clearing Union, BIS; Convenor and mem. Working Group on Financial Conglomerates; Assoc., Indian Inst. of Bankers. *Address:* Central Vigilance Commission, Satarkata Bhavan, A-Block, GPO Complex, INA, New Delhi 110 023, India (office). *Telephone:* (11) 24651001 (office). *Fax:* (11) 24651010 (office). *E-mail:* vigilance@nic.in (office). *Website:* cvc.nic.in (office).

GORA, Jo Ann M., MA, PhD; American sociologist, academic and university president; *President, Ball State University;* b. New York; m. Roy Budd; one s. one step-d.; ed Vassar Coll., Rutgers Univ.; prof. of sociology with specialization in criminology, medical sociology and organizational behaviour; Provost and Vice-Pres. for Academic Affairs, Old Dominion Univ. 1992–2001; Chancellor Univ. of Massachusetts, Boston 2001–04; Pres. Ball State Univ. 2004–; mem. Cttee on Leadership and Institutional Effectiveness, American Council on Educ.; mem. Bd Nat. Asscn of State Univs and Land Grant Colls; mem. Cen. Indiana Corp. Partnership 2004–; mem. Bd of Dirs Ball State Univ. Foundation, First Merchants Corpn, Ball Memorial Hosp., Muncie Innovation Connector, Muncie Symphony Orchestra; Dr hc (Yeungnam Univ., South Korea) 2008; Sagamore of the Wabash, Gov. of Ind. 2005, Torchbearer Award, Indiana Comm. for Women 2005, one of Women of Wonder, Indiana Minority Business Magazine 2008, 2009, Mira Trailblazer Award (TechPoint) 2009. *Publications:* The New Female Criminal: Empirical Reality or Social Myth?, Emergency Squad Volunteers: Professionalism in Unpaid Work; numerous articles in professional journals. *Leisure interests:* photography, tennis, golf, reading. *Address:* Office of the President, Ball State University, AD Building 101, Muncie, IN 47306, USA (office). *Telephone:* (765)

285-5555 (office). *Fax:* (765) 285-1461 (office). *E-mail:* president@bsu.edu (office). *Website:* cms.bsu.edu/about/administrativeoffices/president (office).

GÖRANSSON, Bengt; Swedish politician; b. 25 July 1932, Stockholm; ed Univ. of Stockholm; Reso Ltd (travel org.) 1960–71; Chair. Manilla School for the Deaf 1970–78; Head, Community Centre Asscn 1971; Chair. of Bd Nat. Theatre Centre 1974–82; mem. various official cttees; Chair. of Bd Fed. of Workers' Educational Asscn 1980–82; Minister for Cultural Affairs 1982–89, Minister of Educ. and Cultural Affairs 1989–91; Chair. Ansvar Insurance Co. 1991–97, Int. Inst. of Alcohol Policy 1996–99, Center for Biotechnology 1996–98, Parl. Cttee on Democracy 1997–2000; Chair. Dalhalla Festival Stage 1994–2002, Norden Asscn 2000–07; Dr hc (Gothenburg); 10GT Veteran Medal 1997, Illis quorum Govt Medal 2000, Royal Gold Medal 2008. *Leisure interests:* culture, politics, education, sports. *Telephone:* (8) 6616607 (home); (70) 5616608 (home). *E-mail:* bengt.goransson@ abfstockholm.se (office); a.b.goransson@telia.com (home).

GORBACH, Hubert; Austrian business executive and fmr politician; b. 27 July 1956, Frastanz; m.; one s. one d.; ed secondary school in Feldkirch and commercial Coll.; mil. service 1978, cadre and sergeant's training; Export Man., Elektra Bregenz 1978–79; Head of Dept, Authorized Agent, Co. Sec., mem. Bd Textilwerke Ganahl 1979–87; CEO Kolb GmbH 1987–93; mem. Bd prov. Hosp.-GmbH 1999–2003; mem. OW Cttee 2000–01; mem. Freiheitspartei Österreichs (FPÖ— Freedom Party Austria) 1975–2005; Prov. Sec. Ring freiheitlicher Jugend 1976–82, Gen. Sec. 1980–85, mem. Prov. Party Exec. 1975, Prov. Party Cttee 1984, Prov. Deputy Gen. Sec. 1984–92, Local Party Rep., Frastanz 1986–92, Dist Rep., Feldkirch 1988–92, Prov. Party Rep., Vorarlberg 1992–2004, mem. Party Leaders' Group 1980–92, Party Exec. 1980–85, Party Cttee 1992–2005, Deputy Gen. Sec. 2000–02; mem. Frastanz Dist Council 1985–92, Frastanz Local Council 1990–92; mem. State Parl. of Vorarlberg 1989–93, Vorarlberg Prov. Govt 1993–2003; Deputy Head of Prov. 1999–2003; Fed. Minister of Transport, Innovation and Tech. 2003–07; Vice-Chancellor of Austria 2003–07; Chair. Walter Klaus Holding 2007; Founder and Prin. Gorbach Consulting GmbH 2007–; Foundation mem. Bündnis Zukunft Österreich (BZÖ—Alliance Future Austria) 2005–, mem. Fed. Party Man.; Carinthian Order in Gold 2006. *Leisure interests:* skiing, horseriding (pres. prov. horseriding club), tennis, jogging, reading, wine culture, shooting, flying (pvt. pilot's licence). *Address:* Gorbach Consulting GmbH, Obere Lände 1, 6820 Frastanz, Austria (office). *Telephone:* (5522) 522-22-12 (office). *Fax:* (5522) 522-22-16 (office). *E-mail:* h.gorbach@gorbach-consulting.com (office). *Website:* www.gorbach-consulting.com (office).

GORBACHEV, Mikhail Sergeyevich; Russian organization official, politician and fmr head of state; *Leader, Union of Social Democrats;* b. 2 March 1931, Privolnoye, Krasnogvardeiskii Dist, Stavropol Krai; s. of Sergei Andreevich Gorbachev and Maria Panteleimonovna Gorbachev (née Gopcalo); m. Raisa Titarenko 1953 (died 1999); one d.; ed Faculty of Law, Moscow State Univ. and Stavropol Agricultural Inst.; began work as machine operator 1946; joined CPSU 1952; Deputy Head, Dept of Propaganda, Stavropol Komsomol (V. I. Lenin Young Communist League) Territorial Cttee 1955–56, Second, then First Sec. 1958–62; First Sec. Stavropol Komsomol City Cttee 1956–58; del. to CPSU Congress 1961, 1971, 1976, 1981, 1986, 1990; Party Organizer, Stavropol Territorial Production Bd of Collective and State Farms 1962; Head, Dept of Party Bodies of CPSU Territorial Cttee 1963–66; First Sec., Stavropol City Party Cttee 1966–68; Second Sec., Stavropol Territorial CPSU Cttee 1968–70, First Sec. 1970–78; mem. CPSU Cen. Cttee 1971–91, Sec. for Agric. 1978–85, Alt. mem. Political Bureau CPSU, Cen. Cttee 1979–80, mem. 1980–91, Gen. Sec., CPSU Cen. Cttee 1985–91; Deputy Supreme Soviet of USSR 1970–89 (Chair. Foreign Affairs Comm. of Soviet Union 1984–85), mem. Presidium 1985–88, Chair. 1988–89, Supreme Soviet of RSFSR 1980–90, elected to Congress of People's Deputies of USSR 1989, Chair. 1989–90; Pres. of USSR 1990–91; Head, Int. Foundation for Socio-Economic and Political Studies (Gorbachev Foundation) 1992–; Head Int. Green Cross/Green Crescent 1993–; presidential cand. 1996; Co-founder and Co-Chair. Social Democratic Party of Russia 2000–04 (resgnd); Founder and Leader, Union of Social Democrats 2007–; syndicated columnist for numerous newspapers world-wide 1992–; Hon. Citizen of Berlin 1992, Freeman of Aberdeen 1993; Order of Lenin (three times), Orders of Red Banner of Labour, Badge of Honour; Nobel Peace Prize 1990, Albert Schweitzer Leadership Award (jt recipient) 1992, Ronald Reagan Freedom Award 1992, Urania-Medaille (Berlin) 1996, Augsburg Peace Prize 2005. *Recording:* Peter and the Wolf: Wolf Tracks (Grammy Award, Best Spoken Word Album for Children (jtly) 2004) 2003. *Publications:* A Time for Peace 1985, The Coming Century of Peace 1986, Speeches and Writings 1986–90, Peace Has No Alternative 1986, Moratorium 1986, Perestroika: New Thinking for Our Country and the World 1987, The August Coup (Its Cause and Results) 1991, December 1991: My Stand 1992, The Years of Hard Decisions 1993, Life and Reforms 1995. *Leisure interests:* literature, theatre, music, walking. *Address:* The Gorbachev Foundation, 125167 Moscow, Leningradskii pr. 39/14, Russia (office). *Telephone:* (495) 945-74-01 (office). *Fax:* (495) 945-74-01 (office). *E-mail:* gf@gorby.ru (office). *Website:* www .gorby.ru (office); sdorg.ru (office).

GORBULIN, Volodomir Pavlovich, DTech; Ukrainian politician and space scientist; b. 17 Jan. 1939, Zaporozhya; ed Dniepropetrovsk State Univ.; fmr engineer and mechanic Pivdenne construction co., then jr researcher 1962–76; took part in devt of Cosmos space rockets; mem. Cen. Cttee CP 1977–; Head Rocket, Space and Aviation Tech. Sector 1980–; Head of Defence Complex Section, Cabinet of Ministers 1990–92; Dir-Gen. Ukrainian Nat. Space Agency 1992–94; Sec. Council on Nat. Security 1994–96, Council on Nat. Security and Defence 1996; Head of Supreme Econ. Council 1997–; Deputy Chair. Council on Problems of Science and Tech. Policy 1999; Chair. State Cttee of Defence-Industrial Complex 1999; Pres. Ukrainian Basketball Fed.; mem. Ukrainian Nat. Acad. of Sciences 1997–; USSR State Prize 1990, Ukrainian Nat. Acad. of Sciences Prize. *Leisure interests:* music, playing cards. *Address:* Office of the President, Bankovskaya str. 11, 252011 Kiev, Ukraine (office).

GORBUNOVS, Anatolijs; Latvian politician and fmr head of state; b. 10 Feb. 1942, Pilda, Riga Co.; s. of Valerians Gorbunovs and Aleksandra Gorbunova (née Mekša); m. Lidija Klavina; one s.; ed Riga Polytech. Inst., Moscow Acad. of Social Sciences; early job as builder on a state farm; Sr Mechanic, Riga Polytech. Inst. 1959–62; served in Red Army 1962–65; various posts in the structure of the Latvian CP 1974–88; Pres. of Latvia (Chair. Supreme Council of Latvia) 1988–93;

Chair. Saeima (Parl.) 1993–95; mem. Parl. for Latvijas ceļš (Latvian Way, now Latvian First Party/Latvian Way) –2002, Chair. Saeima Cttee on European Affairs Feb.–Aug. 1996; Minister of Environmental Protection and Regional Devt and Deputy Prime Minister 1996–98; Minister of Communications 1998, of Transport 1999–2004; Chair. Latvian–Russian Intergovernmental Comm. 1996. *Leisure interests:* hunting, gardening. *Address:* c/o Latvijas Pirmā Partija/Latvijas ceļš (Latvian First Party/Latvian Way), Elizabetes iela 2, Riga 1050, Latvia (office).

GORDEYEV, Aleksey Vassilyevich, CandEconSci; Russian economist and politician; *Governor of Voronezh;* b. 28 Feb. 1955, Frankfurt an der Oder, Germany; m.; one s. one d.; ed Acad. of Nat. Econs, USSR Council of Ministers; Sr Supervisor SU-4 Govt Glavmosstroi 1980–81, Chief Expert, Head of Div., then Deputy Head Dept of Glavagrostroi 1981–86; Deputy Dir-Gen. Moskva (agro-industrial co.), Moscow region 1986–92; Deputy Head of Admin., Lyubertsy Dist, Moscow region 1992–97; Head, Dept of Econs, mem. Exec. Bd Ministry of Agric. and Food 1997–98, First Deputy Minister of Agric. and Food 1998–99, Minister of Agric. 1999–2009, concurrently Deputy Chair. Govt of Russian Fed. 2000–04; Gov. of Voronezh 2009–; Merited Econ. of Russian Fed. *Address:* Office of the Governor, 394018 Voronezh, pl. Lenina 1, Russia (office). *Telephone:* (4732) 55-27-37 (office). *Fax:* (4732) 53-28-02 (office). *E-mail:* ogv@comch.ru (office). *Website:* www.govvrn.ru (office).

GORDEYEV, Viacheslav Mikhailovich; Russian ballet dancer and choreographer; *Artistic Director, Russian State Ballet Theatre of Moscow;* b. 3 Aug. 1948, Moscow; s. of Mikhail Gordeyev and Lyubov Gordeyeva; m. 2nd Maya Saidova 1987; one s. one d.; ed Moscow State Univ., State Inst. of Theatrical Arts; Leading Dancer, Bolshoi Theatre 1968–87; mem. CPSU 1977–90; Artistic Dir Russian State Ballet; Founder and Artistic Dir Russian State Ballet Theatre of Moscow 1984–; Head, Ballet Co. of Bolshoi Theatre 1995–97; Deputy of Duma, Moscow Area 2007–11; First Prize, Moscow Int. Ballet Competition 1973, USSR People's Artist 1984, Best Choreographer of the Year 1992–93 (Germany), Maurice Béjart Special Prize for Best Choreography 1992. Roles include: Prince, Désiré (Tchaikovsky's Nutcracker, Sleeping Beauty), Romeo (Prokofiev's Romeo and Juliet), Spartacus, Ferhat (Melnikov's Legend of Love), Albreht (Giselle), Basil (Minkus's Don Quixote), Prince (Tchaikovsky's Swan Lake). *Choreographic works:* Revived Pictures, Memory, Surprise Manoeuvres, or Wedding with the General and more than 30 choreographic compositions; own versions of classical ballets Paquita, Don Quixote and Walpurgisnacht, Nutcracker 1993, Last Tango (Bolshoi Theatre) 1996, Sleeping Beauty (Russian State Ballet) 1999, Cinderella (Russian State Ballet) 2001. *Leisure interests:* classical music, athletics, tennis. *Address:* Volgogradsky Prospekt 121, Moscow 109443 (office); Tverskaya str. 9, Apt 78, Moscow 103009, Russia (home). *Telephone:* (495) 379-94-82 (office); (495) 379-43-24 (office); (495) 629-13-36 (home). *Fax:* (495) 379-43-24 (office). *E-mail:* dilyarsb@gmail.com (office); dilyarsb@yandex.ru. *Website:* www.russballet.ru (office).

GORDHAN, Pravin Jamnadas, BPharm; South African pharmacist and politician; *Minister of Finance;* b. 12 April 1949, Durban; m. Vanitha Raju; two c.; ed Univ. of Durban Westville; mem. African Nat. Congress (ANC), fmr Sec., Operation Vula (ANC underground network); pharmacist, King Edward VII Hosp., Durban 1974–81 (expelled after detention by police); Exec. mem. Natal Indian Congress 1974–90; took part in Convention for Democratic South Africa (Codesa) 1991–94; mem. Nat. Ass. (Parl.) (ANC) 1994–98; Deputy Commr, South African Revenue Service 1998–99, Commr 1999–2009; Human Resources Dir, Telkom 1999; Minister of Finance 2009–; Chair. Council of World Customs 2000–06; Hon. DComm (Univ. of SA) 2007, Hon. LLD (Cape Town) 2007. *Address:* National Treasury, 40 Church Sq., Pretoria 0002, South Africa (office). *Telephone:* (12) 3238911 (office). *Fax:* (12) 3233262 (office). *E-mail:* dumisa.jele@treasury.gov.za (office). *Website:* www.treasury.gov.za (office).

GORDILLO, Elba Esther; Mexican union leader and politician; *President, Executive Committee, Sindicato Nacional de Trabajadores de la Educación;* b. 6 Feb. 1945, Comitán, Chiapas; joined Sindicato Nacional de Trabajadores de la Educación—SNTE (Nat. Union of Educ. Workers) 1960, held succession of full-time positions 1971–1989, Pres. SNTE 1989–1995, Head of Finance 1995, Pres. Nat. Exec. Cttee 2004–; elected to Chamber of Deputies 1979, re-elected 1985, 2003, Leader Partido Revolucionario Institucional (PRI) in Lower Chamber 2003; party elected to Senate 1994, Chair. Educ. Cttee; Pres. CNOP (org. that marshals pro-PRI orgs in movt) 1996–2003, Sec. Org. of the Nat. Exec. Council 1986–87, Gen. Sec. Council of Nat. Popular Orgs 1997–2002, Sec.-Gen. PRI 2003–05 (resgnd); co-founder Nueva Alianza party 2005. *Publications:* La construcción de un proyecto sindical 1995, El paseo de las Reformas, la batalla por México 2005. *Address:* Sindicato Nacional de Trabajadores de la Educación, República de Venezuela No. 44, Col. Centro, 5to. Piso., México, DF (office); c/o Nueva Alianza, Durango 199, Col. Roma, Del. Cuauhtémoc, 06700 México, DF, Mexico. *Telephone:* (55) 5704-7000 (office). *E-mail:* info@snte.org.mx (office). *Website:* www.snte.org.mx (office).

GORDIMER, Nadine, FRSL; South African writer; b. 20 Nov. 1923, Springs, East Rand, Gauteng Prov.; d. of Isidore Gordimer and Nan Myers; m. 2nd Reinhold Cassirer 1954 (died); one s. one d.; ed convent school; mem. African Nat. Congress 1990–; Vice-Pres. International PEN; Goodwill Amb. UNDP; mem. Congress of S African Writers; mem. jury Man Booker Int. Prize 2007; Hon. Fellow, American Acad. of Arts and Letters, American Acad. of Arts and Sciences; Hon. mem. American Inst. of Arts and Letters; Commdr, Ordre des Arts des Lettres 1987; Charles Eliot Norton Lecturer in Literature, Harvard Univ. 1994; Dr hc (Cambridge) 1992, (Oxford) 1994; WHSmith Literary Award 1961, Thomas Pringle Award, English Acad. of SA 1969, James Tait Black Memorial Prize 1971, Booker Prize (co-winner) 1974, Grand Aigle d'Or Prize (France) 1975, CNA Literary Award (S Africa) 1974, 1979, 1981, 1991, Scottish Arts Council Neil M. Gunn Fellowship 1981, Modern Language Asscn Award (USA) 1981, Premio Malaparte (Italy) 1985, Nelly Sachs Prize (Germany) 1985, Bennett Award (USA) 1987, Benson Medal, Royal Soc. of Literature 1990, Nobel Prize for Literature 1991, Primo Levi Award 2002, Mary McCarthy Award 2003, Bavarian State Premier's Hon. Award (part of the Corine Int. Book Prize), Grinzane Cavour Prize 2007. *Publications:* The Soft Voice of the Serpent (stories), The Lying Days (novel) 1953, Six Feet of the Country (stories) 1956, A World of Strangers (novel) 1958, Friday's Footprint (stories) 1960, Occasion for Loving (novel) 1963, Not For Publication (stories) 1965, The Late Bourgeois World (novel) 1966, South African

Writing Today (co-ed.) 1967, A Guest of Honour (novel) 1970, Livingstone's Companions (stories) 1972, The Black Interpreters (literary criticism) 1973, The Conservationist (novel) 1974, Selected Stories 1975, Some Monday for Sure (stories) 1976, Burger's Daughter 1979, A Soldier's Embrace (stories) 1980, July's People (novel) 1981, Something Out There (novella) 1984, A Sport of Nature (novel) 1987, The Essential Gesture (essays) 1988, My Son's Story (novel) 1990, Jump (short stories) 1991, Crimes of Conscience (short stories) 1991, None to Accompany Me (novel) 1994, Writing and Being (lectures) 1995, The House Gun 1997, Living in Hope and History: Notes on our Century (essays) 1999, The Pickup 2001, Loot and Other Stories 2003, Telling Tales (ed. and contrib.) 2004, Get A Life 2005, Beethoven was One-Sixteenth Black (short stories) 2007, Telling Times: Writing and Living 1954–2008 2010, Life Times: Stories 1952–2007 (collection) 2010, No Time Like the Present (novel) 2012. *Address:* c/o Linda Shaughnessy, AP Watt at United Agents LLP, 12–26 Lexington Street, London, W1F 0LE, England (office). *Telephone:* (20) 3214-0800 (office). *E-mail:* info@unitedagents.co.uk (office). *Website:* www.unitedagents.co.uk (office).

GORDIN, Yakov Arkadyevich; Russian writer and historian; b. 23 Dec. 1935, Leningrad; m.; one s.; ed Moscow Ore Inst.; freelancer specializing in ed. historical research of crisis situations in Russian political history of 18th–20th centuries; Dir and Co-Ed. Zvezda (literary journal), St Petersburg. *Publications:* numerous articles and books, including Space, The Death of Pushkin, The Events and People of 14 December, Between Slavery and Freedom, Duels and Duelists, Coup of the Reformers, etc. *Address:* Mokhovaya str. 36, Apt 24, 191028 St Petersburg, Russia (home). *Telephone:* (812) 273-05-27 (home). *E-mail:* ariev@cityline.spb.ru.

GORDON, Alexander G.; Russian actor and journalist; b. 20 Feb. 1964, Obninsk, Moscow region; m.; ed Shchukin Theatre School; actor, Ruben Simonov Studio Theatre 1987–89; emigrated to USA, worked as waiter, asst cameraman of RTN TV co.; Sr Corresp., WMNB Corpn 1989–93; staff mem. Vostok Entertainment Co. 1993–94; writer and narrator of TV shows New York, New York. . . (TV-6, Moscow); writer of some 100 TV programmes; returned to Russia 1997; staff mem. radio programme Silver Rain 1997–; Founder-mem. and Sec.-Gen. Party of Public Cynicism 1998–; writer and narrator of publicity programmes on ORT TV channel, including Treasury of Mistakes, Gordon (NTV); actor, Theatre of the Contemporary Play. *Film directed:* Shepherd of his Sheep. *Leisure interest:* football. *Address:* ORT TV channel, Koroleva str. 12, 103473 Moscow, Russia (office). *Telephone:* (495) 725-51-24 (office); (495) 217-94-27 (office). *Website:* www.gordon.ru.

GORDON, Sir Donald, Kt; South African/British business executive; *Honorary Life President, Liberty International PLC;* b. 24 June 1930, Johannesburg; s. of Nathan Gordon and Sheila Gordon; m. Peggy Cowan 1958; two s. one d.; ed King Edward VII School, Johannesburg; Chartered Accountant, Partner Kessel Feinstein 1955–57; Founder Liberty Life Asscn of Africa Ltd, Chair. 1957–99, Chair. Liberty Holdings Ltd 1968–99, Liberty Investors Ltd 1971–99, Guardian Nat. Insurance Co. Ltd 1980–99; Deputy Chair. Standard Bank Investment Corpn Ltd 1979–99, Premier Group Holdings Ltd 1983–96; Dir Guardbank Man. Corpn Ltd 1969–99, Guardian Royal Exchange Assurance PLC (UK) 1971–94, Charter Life Insurance Co. Ltd 1985–99, The South African Breweries Ltd 1982–99, Beverage & Consumer Industry Holdings Ltd 1989–99, GFSA Holdings Ltd 1990–94, Sun Life Corpn PLC (UK) 1992–95, Chair. Liberty Int. PLC (fmrly Transatlantic Holdings PLC) 1981–2005, Capital & Counties PLC (UK) 1982–94, Capital Shopping Centres PLC 1994–2005; Hon. Life Pres. Liberty Life; Hon. D.Econ.Sc. (Witwatersrand) 1991; Financial Mail Businessman of the Year 1965; Sunday Times Man of the Year 1969; Achiever of the Century in South Africa Financial Services (Financial Mail 1999); Business Statesman Award (Harvard Business School); London Entrepreneur of the Year 2000, Special Award for Lifetime Achievement 2001. *Leisure interests:* opera, ballet. *Website:* www.donaldgordon.org (office).

GORDON, Douglas Lamont, BA, MA; British artist; b. 20 Sept. 1966, Glasgow; s. of James Gordon and Mary Clements Gordon (née McDougall); ed Glasgow School of Art, Slade School of Art; works in video, film, photography and sculpture; solo exhibitions at Tate Liverpool 2000, Museum of Contemporary Art, Los Angeles 2001, Hayward Gallery, London 2002, Van Abbemuseum, Eindhoven 2003; curator "The Vanity of Allegory", Deutsche Guggenheim, Berlin 2005, Palais des Papes, Avignon 2008; Visiting Prof. Fine Art, Glasgow School of Art, Glasgow Univ. 1999–; fmr Visiting Prof. and John Florent Stone Fellow, Edinburgh Coll. of Art; Int. Juror, 65th Venice Film Festival 2008; Turner Prize 1996, Premio 2000 1997, Hugo Bass Prize 1998, Roswitha Haftmann Prize 2008. *Address:* c/o Gagosian Gallery, 17–19 Davies Street, London W1K 3DE, England.

GORDON, Ilene S., MSc, BSc; American business executive; *Chairman, President and CEO, Ingredion Inc.;* m.; two c.; ed Massachusetts Inst. of Tech.; served as Vice-Pres. of Operations, Tenneco Inc. 1994–97, Vice-Pres. and Gen. Man. Folding Carton Business 1997–99; Pres. Pechiney Plastic Packaging Inc. and Sr Vice-Pres. Pechiney Group 1999–2004; Pres. Food Packaging, Americas, Alcan Inc. 2004–06, Sr Vice-Pres. Alcan Inc. and Pres. and CEO Alcan Global Packaging 2006–07, Pres. and CEO Packaging, Rio Tinto Alcan 2007–09, mem. Exec. Cttee, Paris, France 2007–09; Chair., Pres. and CEO Corn Products International, Inc. (changed its name to Ingredion Inc. 2012) 2009–; ranked by Fortune magazine amongst the 50 Most Powerful Women in Business outside the US (34th) 2007, (37th) 2008, and in the US (42nd) 2011, (43rd) 2012. *Address:* Ingredion Inc., 5 Westbrook Corporate Center, Westchester, IL 60154, USA (office). *Telephone:* (708) 551-2600 (office). *E-mail:* info@ingredion.com (office). *Website:* www.ingredion.com (office).

GORDON, Jeff; American motor racing driver; b. 4 Aug. 1971, Vallejo, Calif.; s. of William Grinnell Gordon and Carol Ann Bickford; m. 1st Brooke Sealy 1994 (divorced 2002); m. 2nd Ingrid Vandebosch; one s. one d.; current team: Hendrick Motorsports; United States Auto Club (USAC) Rookie of the Year 1989; youngest USAC National Midget Champion 1990 (aged 19); NASCAR racing driver; winner USAC Silver Crown and Busch Series Rookie of the Year 1991; three Busch Series victories 1992; Winston Cup debut 1992 (Atlanta Speedway); Darlington Raceway winner 1995, 1996, 1997, 1998, 2002, 2007; 69 Winston Cup victories including: Brickyard 400 1994, 1998, 2001, 2004, Southern 500 1995, 1996, 1997, 1998, 2002, Daytona 500 1997, 1999, 2009; Rookie of the Year 1993; Winston Cup Champion

1995, 1997, 1998, 2001; Winston Million Champion 1997; record seven career victories on road courses; youngest driver to achieve 50 career victories 2000; over US \$50 million career winnings; f. Jeff Gordon Foundation charity for children 1999; launched Jeff Gordon Collection of Wines 2005; Co-founder Athletes for Hope 2007; Silver Buffalo Award 2009. *Publication:* (with Steve Eubanks) Jeff Gordon: Racing Back to the Front – My Memoir 2003. *Address:* Hendrick Motorsports, 4414 Pappa Joe Hendrick Blvd., POB 9, Harrisburg, NC 28075, USA. *Website:* www .jeffgordon.com (office); www.jeffgordonchildrensfoundation.org (office).

GORDON, Robert James, PhD; American economist and academic; *Stanley G. Harris Professor in the Social Sciences, Northwestern University;* b. 3 Sept. 1940, Boston, Mass; s. of Robert A. Gordon and Margaret S. Gordon; m. Julie S. Peyton 1963; ed Harvard Univ., Univ. of Oxford, UK, Massachusetts Inst. of Tech.; Assoc. Prof. of Econs, Harvard Univ. 1967–68, Univ. of Chicago 1968–73; Prof. of Econs, Northwestern Univ. 1973–87, Stanley G. Harris Prof. in the Social Sciences 1987–, Chair. Dept of Econs 1992–96; Fellow, Econometric Soc. 1977, American Acad. of Arts and Sciences 1997; John Simon Guggenheim Memorial Fellowship 1980–81, Lustrum Award, Erasmus Univ., Rotterdam 1999. *Publications:* The American Business Cycle: Continuity and Change 1986, The Measurement of Durable Goods Prices 1990, The Economics of New Goods 1997, Macroeconomics (ninth edn) 2003. *Leisure interests:* photography, gardening, mil. history, airline man. *Address:* Department of Economics, 349 Andersen Hall, Northwestern University, Evanston, IL 60208-0001 (office); 202 Greenwood Street, Evanston, IL 60201, USA (home). *Telephone:* (847) 491-3616 (office); (847) 869-3544 (home). *Fax:* (847) 491-7001 (office). *E-mail:* rjg@northwestern.edu (office). *Website:* faculty-web.at .northwestern.edu/economics/gordon/indexmsie.html (office).

GORDON-LEVITT, Joseph Leonard; American actor and director; b. 17 Feb. 1981, Los Angeles, Calif.; s. of Dennis Levitt and Jane Gordon; ed Van Nuys High School, Columbia Univ. School of General Studies, New York; joined a musical theatre group aged four and played the Scarecrow in a production of The Wizard of Oz; began career in commercials as a child before making his film debut in Beethoven 1992; f. online production co. hitRECord 2004. *Theatre includes:* a producer of the Broadway show Slava's Snowshow 2008. *Films include:* Beethoven 1992, A River Runs Through It 1992, Holy Matrimony 1994, Roadflower 1994, Angels 1994, The Juror 1996, Sweet Jane 1998, Halloween H20: 20 Years Later 1998, 10 Things I Hate About You 1999, Picking Up the Pieces 2000, Forever Lulu 2000, Manic 2001, Treasure Planet (voice) 2002, Latter Days 2003, Mysterious Skin 2004, Brick 2005, Havoc 2005, Shadowboxer 2005, The Lookout 2007, Stop-Loss 2008, Miracle at St. Anna 2008, The Brothers Bloom (uncredited) 2008, Killshot 2008, 500 Days of Summer 2009, Uncertainty 2009, Women in Trouble 2009, G.I. Joe: The Rise of Cobra 2009, Hesher 2010, Elektra Luxx 2010, Inception 2010, 50/50 2011, The Dark Knight Rises 2012, Premium Rush 2012, Looper 2012, Lincoln 2012, Don Jon's Addiction 2013. *Television includes:* Stranger on My Land (film) 1988, Settle the Score (film) 1989, Changes (film) 1991, Hi Honey – I'm Dead (film) 1991, Plymouth (film) 1991, The Powers That Be (series) 1992–93, Gregory K (film) 1993, Roseanne (series) 1993–95, The Great Elephant Escape (film) 1995, 3rd Rock from the Sun (series) 1996–2001, Numb3rs (series) – Sacrifice 2005. *Publications:* The Tiny Book of Tiny Stories Vol. 1 (book/CD/DVD package) 2011, Vol. 2 2012. *Address:* c/o Creative Artists Agency, 2000 Avenue of the Stars, Los Angeles, CA 90067, USA (office). *Website:* www.caa.com (office); www.hitrecord.org (office). *E-mail:* support@hitrecord.org (office).

GORDON-REED, Annette, AB, JD; American lawyer, academic and writer; *Charles Warren Professor of American Legal History, Harvard Law School;* m. Robert Reed; one s. one d.; ed Dartmouth Coll., Harvard Law School; fmr Assoc., Cahill Gordon & Reindel (law firm); fmr Counsel to New York City Bd of Corrections; Prof. of Law, New York Law School 1992–2010; Prof. of History, Rutgers Univ. 2007–10; Charles Warren Visiting Prof. of American Legal History, Harvard Law School 2009, Prof. of Law 2010–, Carol K. Pforzheimer Prof., Radcliffe Inst. for Advanced Study 2010–, Prof. of History 2010–, Charles Warren Prof. of American Legal History 2012–; mem. Bd of Trustees, Dartmouth Coll. 2010–; MacArthur Fellowship 2010, National Humanities Medal 2010. *Publications:* Thomas Jefferson and Sally Hemings: An American Controversy 1997, Vernon Can Read!: A Memoir (co-author) 2001, The Hemingses of Monticello: An American Family (Nat. Book Award, Pulitzer Prize for History 2009) 2008, Race on Trial: Law and Justice in American History (essays, ed.) 2009, Andrew Johnson: The American Presidents Series: The 17th President, 1865-1869 2011. *Address:* Griswold Hall 405, Harvard Law School, Cambridge, MA 02138, USA (office). *Telephone:* (617) 495-3894 (office). *E-mail:* agordonreed@law.harvard.edu (office). *Website:* www.law.harvard.edu (office).

GORDY, Berry, Jr; American music industry executive and songwriter; b. 28 Nov. 1929, Detroit; s. of Berry Gordy, Sr and Bertha Fuller Gordy; m. 1st Thelma Coleman (divorced 1959); m. 2nd Raynoma Mayberry Liles (divorced 1964); m. 3rd Grace Eaton 1990 (divorced 1993); eight c.; owned record store in Detroit 1955; composer and ind. producer during late 1950s; Founder, Jobete Music 1958, Tamla Records 1959, Motown Record Corpn 1961–88; fmr Chair. The Gordy Co.; Dr hc (Michigan State Univ., Occidental Coll.); American Music Award, Outstanding Contrib. to Music Industry 1975, inducted into Rock and Roll Hall of Fame 1990, Michigan Rock and Roll Legends Hall of Fame 2009, NARAS Trustees Award 1991. *Films include:* Lady Sings The Blues (exec. producer) 1972, Mahogany (dir) 1975, The Last Dragon (exec. producer) 1985. *Play:* Motown: The Musical (co-producer) 2013. *Recordings include:* as composer/producer: Reet Petite (Jackie Wilson), Shop Around (The Miracles), Do You Love Me? (The Contours), Try It Baby (Marvin Gaye), Shotgun (Junior Walker and The All-Stars), I Want You Back and ABC (The Jackson 5), Compilation: The Music, The Magic, The Memories of Motown 1995. *Publication:* To Be Loved 1994 (autobiography). *Address:* West Grand Media, 6255 Sunset Blvd, Suite 1110, Los Angeles, CA 90028, USA.

GORE, Albert (Al) Arnold, Jr; American financial services industry executive, academic and fmr politician; *Chairman, Generation Investment Management LLP;* b. 31 March 1948, Washington, DC; s. of the late Albert Gore, Sr and Pauline Gore (née LaFon); m. Mary E. Aitcheson 1970 (separated 2010); one s. three d.; ed Harvard and Vanderbilt Univs; served with US Army during Viet Nam war; investigative reporter, editorial writer, The Tennessean 1971–76; home-builder and land developer, Tanglewood Home Builders Co. 1971–76; livestock and tobacco farmer 1973–; Head of Community Enterprise Bd 1993–; mem. US House of Reps

1977–79; Senator from Tennessee 1985–93; Vice-Pres. of USA 1993–2001; Democratic cand. in presidential elections 2000; Lecturer, Middle Tennessee State Univ., Columbia Univ. 2001–, Visiting Prof., UCLA, Fisk Univ. 2001–; Vice-Chair. Metropolitan West Financial LLC 2001–; Sr Adviser, Google Inc. 2001–; Co-founder and Chair. Current TV (youth cable TV network) 2004–13; Co-founder and Chair. Generation Investment Management LLP (fund man. firm), Washington, DC and London, UK 2004–; Pnr, Kleiner, Perkins, Caulfield & Byers 2007–; mem. Bd of Dirs Apple Computer Inc.; Dr hc (Harvard) 1994, (New York) 1998; Webby Award 2005, UNEP Champion of the Earth Laureate 2007, Prince of Asturias Award for Int. Co-operation 2007, Nobel Peace Prize (shared with UN Intergovernmental Panel on Climate Change) 2007, Primetime Emmy Award for Current TV 2007, Dan David Prize 2008. *Film:* An Inconvenient Truth (Best Documentary Los Angeles Film Critics Asscn 2006, Nat. Soc. of Film Critics 2007, Acad. Award for Best Documentary Feature 2007) 2006. *Publications:* Earth in the Balance 1992, An Inconvenient Truth (Quill Award for History, Current Affairs or Politics) 2006, The Assault on Reason: How the Politics of Blind Faith Subvert Wise Decision-Making (Quill Award for History/Current Affairs/Politics 2007) 2007, Our Choice: A Plan to Solve the Climate Crisis 2009, Future 2013. *Address:* Generation Investment Management US LLP, 750 17th Street, 11th Floor, Washington, DC 20006, USA (office). *Telephone:* (202) 785-7400 (office). *Fax:* (202) 785-7401 (office). *Website:* www.generationim.com (office); www.algore.com.

GORE, Elizabeth McKee, BS, MS; American UN official; *Resident Entrepreneur, United Nations Foundation;* b. Tex.; ed Texas A&M Univ.; fmr financial devt assoc., A&M Foundation; fmr US Peace Corps volunteer, served in Bolivia; fmr Dir of Devt and Corp. Relations, Points of Light Foundation; Vice-Pres. Global Partnerships, UN Foundation –2013, f. grassroots efforts, including Nothing But Nets Girl Up and the Shot@Life global vaccines campaign, first Resident Entrepreneur, UN Foundation 2013–, Chair. Global Entrepreneurs Council, also manages partnerships with Fortune 100 cos and with the Bill and Melinda Gates Foundation; mem. leadership councils of Women's Philanthropy Inst. in The Center on Philanthropy at Indiana Univ., CLASSY Awards; mem. Advisory Bd SOMA (all-natural water filter co.). *Achievements include:* joined Summit on the Summit and climbed Mt Kilimanjaro to raise awareness for the global clean water crisis on behalf of the UN 2010. *Address:* United Nations Foundation, 1800 Massachusetts Avenue, NW, Suite 400, Washington, DC 20036, USA (office). *Telephone:* (202) 887-9040 (office). *Fax:* (202) 887-9021 (office). *E-mail:* press@unfoundation.org (office). *Website:* www.unfoundation.org (office).

GOREGLYAD, Valery Pavlovich, DrEconSci; Russian economist; *Auditor, Accounts Chamber;* b. 18 June 1958, Gluzk, Mogilev Region, Belarus; m. Yekaterina Goreglyad; two s.; ed Moscow Inst. of Aviation; fmrly with mil. space industry; Head Tourism Co. –1990; Peoples' Deputy, Russian Fed. 1990–93; mem. Council of Feds, Fed. Ass. 1994; Exec. Dir Cttee on Budget, Revenue and Banking Activity 1994–2000, Deputy Head 2001–; elected mem. (for Sakhalin region) Fed Council 2001–02 (resgnd), Leader Parl. Grouping Fed. 2002–03 (resgnd); Auditor, Accounts Chamber 2004–. *Publications:* The Budget as a Financial Regulator of Economic Development 2002; five monographs and various scholarly articles on macro-econ. analysis, problems of regional econ. devt, and innovative economy. *Leisure interests:* reading historical literature, tennis, basketball, football. *Address:* Accounts Chamber, 2 Zubovskaya str., GSP-2, 119992 Moscow, Russia (office). *Telephone:* (495) 986-05-09 (office). *Fax:* (495) 986-09-52 (office). *E-mail:* info@ach.gov.ru (office). *Website:* www.ach.gov.ru/about/gor.php (office).

GORELICK, Jamie Shona, BA, JD; American lawyer and fmr government official; *Partner, WilmerHale;* b. 6 May 1950, New York City; m. Richard Waldhorn 1975; two c.; ed Harvard Coll., Harvard Law School; attorney, Miller, Cassidy, Larroca & Lewin, Washington, DC 1975–79, 1980–83; Asst to US Sec. of Energy and Counselor to Deputy Sec., Washington, DC 1979–80; Gen. Counsel, US Dept of Defense 1993–94, Vice-Chair. Task Force on the Audit, Inspection and Investigation Components; Deputy Attorney Gen., US Dept of Justice 1994–97; Vice-Chair. Fannie Mae 1997–2003; Pnr, WilmerHale (law firm), Washington, DC 2003–, Co-Chair. Nat. Security and Govt Contracts Dept, Co-Chair. Public Policy and Strategy Practice, Pnr, Litigation Dept; Pres. DC Bar 1992–93, mem. Bd of Govs 1982–88; fmr Lecturer, Harvard Law School, fmr mem. Bd of Overseers, Overseers' Visiting Cttee; Raytheon Lecturer on Business Ethics, Bentley Coll. 2004; has served on numerous govt bds and comms including CIA Nat. Security Advisory Panel 1997–2005, Pres.'s Intelligence Review Panel 2001–02, Nat. Comm. on Terrorist Attacks upon the US 2002–04; mem. ABA, American Law Inst., Women's Bar Asscn, Council on Foreign Relations; mem. Bd of Dirs United Technologies Corpn 2000–, Schlumberger Ltd 2002–10, John D. and Catherine T. MacArthur Foundation, Amazon 2012–, Washington Legal Clinic for the Homeless, Carnegie Endowment for Int. Peace; Counsellor American Soc. of Int. Peace; Trustee Urban Inst.; Sec. of Energy Outstanding Service Award 1980, Women's Bar Asscn Woman Lawyer of the Year 1993, Sec. of Defense Distinguished Service Award 1994, Prominent Woman in Int. Law 1994, Equal Justice Works Outstanding Advocate of the Year 1997, Dir of Cen. Intelligence Award 1997, Radcliffe Coll. Alumnae Recognition Award 1997, Dept of Justice Edmund J. Randolph Award 1997, American Bar Asscn Margaret Brent Award 1997, Wickersham Award for Exceptional Public Service and Dedication to the Legal Profession 1998, American Jewish Cttee Judge Learned Hand Award 1999, NOW Legal Defense and Educ. Fund Aiming High Award 2002, DC Chamber of Commerce's Corp. Leadership Award 2003, Women's Bar Asscn Star of the Bar Award 2003. *Publications:* Destruction of Evidence (co-author) 1983. *Address:* Wilmer Hale, 1875 Pennsylvania Avenue NW, Washington, DC 20006, USA (office). *Telephone:* (202) 663-6500 (office). *Fax:* (202) 663-6363 (office). *E-mail:* jamie.gorelick@wilmerhale.com (office). *Website:* www.wilmerhale.com/ jamie_gorelick (office).

GORENAK, Vinko; Slovenian politician; b. Boharina, Zreče; ed Pedagogical Acad., Maribor, State Univ. of Maribor, Kranj; began working as an educator in School for Militia Cadets, Tacen 1977; Asst Chief of Police, Celje 1982–84, Commdr of Police 1984–89, also Head of the Police Inspectorate in Celje; adviser in office of Minister of the Interior 1990–91, at Ministry of Interior dealing with problems of organization and development of the police from 1990, government adviser in Office of the Minister of the Interior –1995, led service organization and personnel of the Ministry of Interior 1995–99, co-chaired working group that prepared the

Police Act (adopted 1998); Sr Lecturer in Organization and Police Work, Faculty of Organizational Sciences, State Univ. of Maribor, Kranj 1995–2003, Asst Prof. of Man. and Security orgs 2004–09; Assoc. Prof., Faculty of Criminal Justice, Univ. of Maribor 2009–; State Sec., Ministry of Interior on Police and Gen. Affairs 2000–04, Head of Dept of Security Analysis and Policy; State Sec., Ministry of Internal Affairs 2004–05; State Sec., Cabinet of Prime Minister Janez Janša 2008–11; mem. Slovenian Democratic Party (SDP) 1999–; Deputy in Nat. Ass. 2008–, Deputy for 7th constituency (Maribor) 2011–; Minister of Internal Affairs 2012–13. *Publications:* numerous scientific and professional articles on police management. *Address:* Slovenian Democratic Party (SDP), 1000 Ljubljana, Trstenjakova 8, Slovenia (office). *Telephone:* (1) 4345450 (office). *Fax:* (1) 4345452 (office). *E-mail:* tajnistvo@sds.si (office). *Website:* www.sds.si (office); www.vinkogorenak.net.

GORENSTEIN, Mark Borisovich; Russian conductor; *Chief Conductor and Artistic Director, State Academic Symphony Orchestra of Russia;* b. 16 Sept. 1946, Odessa, Ukraine; m. 2nd; one s.; ed Chişinău State Conservatory as violinist, Novosibirsk State Conservatory as conductor; violinist with Bolshoi Theatre Orchestra 1973–75, State Academic Symphony Orchestra 1975–84; Chief Conductor and Artistic Dir MAV Orchestra, Budapest, Hungary 1985–88; Chief Conductor Pusan City Symphony Orchestra, S Korea 1989–91; Founder, Chief Conductor and Artistic Dir New Russia State Symphony Orchestra 1992–2002, State Academic Symphony Orchestra of Russia 2002–; Honoured Art Worker of Russia. *Address:* Rublevskoye shosse 28, Apt 25, 121609 Moscow (home); Bolshaya Nikitskaya 13, 125009 Moscow, Russia. *Telephone:* (495) 202-06-25 (office); (495) 414-52-03 (home). *Fax:* (495) 202-10-06 (office); (495) 414-52-03 (home). *E-mail:* director@gaso.ru (office); gaso@inbox.ru (office). *Website:* www.gaso.ru (office).

GOR'KOV, Lev Petrovich, PhD, DPhysSc; Russian physicist and academic; *Professor, Science, Condensed Matter/Theory, National High Magnetic Field Laboratory, Florida State University;* b. 1929, Moscow; s. of Petr Ivanovich Gor'kov and Antonina Grigor'evna Gor'kov; m. Donara Chernikova 1965; two s. (one d. from 1st m.); ed Moscow Inst. of Mechanics; Jr then Sr Researcher, Inst. of Physical Problems 1953–64; Head of Sector, Inst. of Chemical Physics 1964–65; Head of Sector, L.D. Landau Inst. of Theoretical Physics 1965–88, Deputy Dir 1988–91; Prof. and Dept Head, Inst. for Physics and Tech. 1965–92; Prof., Science, Condensed Matter/Theory Program, Nat. High Magnetic Field Lab., Florida State Univ. 1992–; mem. Int. Program Cttee 5th Int. Conf. STRIPES 2006, Int. Program Cttee M2S-HTSC VIII 2006; Fellow, Russian Acad. of Sciences, American Physical Soc.; mem. NAS; Foreign Hon. mem. American Acad. of Arts and Sciences; Dr hc (New York Univ.), (Univ. of Illinois); Lenin Prize, L. D. Landau Prize, Bardeen Prize in Superconductivity, Eugene Feenberg Medal 2004. *Publications:* Gradient-Invariant Formulation of Superconductivity Theory and Identification of Superconducting Order Parameter (Gor'kov Equations) 1958, Gapless Superconductivity 1960, Methods of Quantum Field Theory in Statistical Physics 1962, Physical Phenomena in Organic Conductors and Superconductors 1984, Unconventional Superconductivity in Heavy Fermion Systems 1987, Phase Separation in High Tc Superconductors 1987, 2004, 2009, Phase Transitions in Di-Chalcogenids of Transition Metals 2011, Quantum Oscillations in Superconductors 2012; articles in scientific journals on phenomena in condensed matter physics, quantum mechanics and hydrodynamics. *Address:* A-310 NHMFL, Florida State University, 1800 East Paul Dirac Drive, Tallahassee, FL 32310-3706, USA (office). *Telephone:* (850) 644-4187 (office). *Fax:* (850) 644-5038 (office). *E-mail:* gorkov@magnet.fsu.edu (office). *Website:* www.magnet.fsu.edu (office).

GORMAN, James P., BA, MBA; Australian lawyer and business executive; *Chairman and CEO, Morgan Stanley;* b. 14 July 1958; m. Penny Gorman; two c.; ed Univ. of Melbourne, Columbia Univ., New York, USA; began career as attorney, Phillips Fox & Masel, Melbourne 1982–85; Partner, McKinsey & Co. 1992–97, Sr Partner 1997–99; Chief Marketing Officer, Merrill Lynch Inc. 1999–2001, Pres. US Private Client Relationship Group 2001–02, Pres. Global Private Client Group 2002–05, Exec. Vice Pres. Acquisitions, Strategy and Research 2005; Pres. and COO of Global Wealth Man., Morgan Stanley 2006–08, Co-Head of Corp. Strategy 2007–09, also Co-Pres. 2007–10, Pres. and CEO 2010–12, Chair. and CEO 2012–, also Chair. Morgan Stanley Smith Barney (jt venture) 2009–, Morgan Stanley Wealth Management; Trustee, Columbia Business School, Spence School; Co-Chair. Business Cttee, Metropolitan Museum of Art; mem. Bd Board of Overseers Columbia Business School; mem. Bd of Dirs Partnership for New York City; fmr mem. Bd Securities Industry and Financial Markets Asscn, Washington, DC, Chair. 2006; mem. Business Roundtable, Business Council. *Address:* Morgan Stanley, 1585 Broadway, New York, NY 10036, USA (office). *Telephone:* (212) 761-4000 (home). *Fax:* (212) 762-0575 (office). *E-mail:* mediainquiries@morganstanley.com (office). *Website:* www.morganstanley.com (office).

GORMAN, Joseph Tolle, BA, LLB; American business executive (retd); *Chairman, Glengary LLC;* b. 1937, Rising Sun, Ind.; m. Bettyann Gorman; ed Kent State Univ. and Yale Law School; Assoc., Baker, Hostetler & Patterson, Cleveland 1962–67; with Legal Dept TRW Inc., Cleveland 1968–69, Asst Sec. 1969–70, Sec. 1970–72, Vice-Pres. Sr Counsel, Automotive Worldwide Operations 1972–73, Vice-Pres. Asst Gen. Counsel 1973–76, Vice-Pres. Gen. Counsel 1976–80, Exec. Vice-Pres. Industrial and Energy Sector 1980–84, Exec. Vice-Pres., Asst Pres. 1984–85, Chair., Pres. and COO 1985–91, Chair., CEO 1988–2000; fmr CEO Moxahela Enterprises LLC; Founder Pnr, Glengary LLC 2002, currently Chair.; mem. Bd of Dirs Alcoa Inc.; fmr mem. Bd of Dirs Procter & Gamble Co., Nat. City Corpn, Imperial Chemical Industries plc, US-China Business Council, The Prince of Wales Int. Business Leaders Forum, United Way Services, The Business Roundtable; fmr Dir Soc. Corpn, Soc. Nat. Bank, Cleveland, Standard Oil Co.; mem. Council on Foreign Relations, Pres.'s Export Council, Pres.'s Advisory Group of the US Chamber of Commerce, The Business Roundtable's Policy and Planning Cttee, Nat. Bureau of Econ. Research, The Business Council, Cleveland Council on World Affairs, In Business-Higher Education Forum, Kent State Univ. Foundation, Yale Alumni Asscn; Trustee New Ohio Inst., Cleveland Clinic Foundation, Musical Arts Asscn, Cleveland Play House; Chair. Civic Vision 2000 and Beyond; fmr Chair. Leadership Cleveland, US-Japan Business Council; founding mem. Ohio Gov.'s Educ. Man. Council; Japan Prime Minister's Trade Award 1994. *Address:* Glengary LLC, 3201 Enterprise Parkway, Suite 430, Beachwood, OH 44122, USA (office). *Telephone:* (216) 378-9200 (office). *Website:* glengaryllc.wiredviews.com (office).

GORMLEY, Sir Antony Mark David, Kt, OBE, RA, MA, DFA, FRSA; British sculptor; b. 30 Aug. 1950, London, England; s. of Arthur J. C. Gormley and Elspeth Brauninger; m. Vicken Parsons 1980; two s. one d.; ed Ampleforth Coll., Trinity Coll., Cambridge, Cen. School of Arts and Crafts, London, Goldsmiths' Coll., Univ. of London and Slade School of Fine Arts, London; works in numerous collections, including Tate Gallery, London, Scottish Nat. Gallery of Modern Art, Moderna Museet, Stockholm, Neue Galerie, Kassel, Victoria and Albert Museum, London, British Council, Arts Council of Great Britain, Art Gallery of NSW, Sydney, Leeds City Art Galleries, Modern Art Museum of Fort Worth, Louisiana Museum of Modern Art, Humblebaek, Denmark, Irish Museum of Modern Art, Dublin, Sapporo Sculpture Park, Japan; Trustee, British Museum; Hon. Fellow, Goldsmith's Coll., Univ. of London 1998, RIBA 2001, Jesus Coll., Cambridge 2003, Trinity Coll., Cambridge 2003; Dr hc (Univ. of Central England) 1998, (Open Univ.) 2001, (Cambridge) 2003, (Newcastle) 2004, (Liverpool) 2006, (Univ. Coll., London) 2006; Turner Prize 1994, South Bank Art Award for Visual Art 1999, Bernhard Heiliger Award for Sculpture 2007, Praemium Imperiale Award for Sculpture 2013. *Publications include:* Antony Gormley 1995, Making an Angel 1998, Total Strangers 1999, Antony Gormley, Asian Field 2004, Material Engagements: Studies in Honour of Colin Renfrew/A Meeting of Minds: Art And Archeology 2004, Making Space 2005, Antony Gormley Inside Australia 2005, Asian Field: Makers & Made 2006, Antony Gormley 2007, Antony Gormley: Blind Light 2007, Antony Gormley: Bodies in Space 2007, Antony Gormley, SteidlMack 2007, Antony Gormley: Between You and Me, Kunsthal Rotterdam 2008, Antony Gormley, Museo De Arte Contemporaneo 2008, Ataxia Ii, Galerie Thaddaeus Ropac 2009, Antony Gormley, Kunsthaus Bregenz 2009, Antony Gormley: Another Singularity, Galleria Continua Beijing 2009, Antony Gormley: Aperture, Xavier Hufkens 2010, Antony Gormley (Modern Artists Series) 2010, One and Other: Antony Gormley 2010, Antony Gormley: Drawing Space 2010, Still Standing 2011, Horizon Field Hamburg 2012, Still Being 2012, Vessel 2012, according to a given mean 2013, Firmament and Other Forms 2013, Model 2013, Meter 2013. *Leisure interests:* walking, talking. *Address:* 15–23 Vale Royal (studio), London, N7 9AP, England. *Telephone:* (20) 7697-2180. *E-mail:* admin-work@antonygormley.com. *Website:* www.antonygormley.com.

GORMLY, Allan Graham, CMG, CBE; British business executive and chartered accountant; b. 18 Dec. 1937, Paisley, Scotland; s. of William Gormly and Christina Swinton Flockhart; m. Vera Margaret Grant 1962; one s. one d.; ed Paisley Grammar School; with Peat Marwick Mitchell & Co. 1956–61, Rootes Group 1961–65; joined John Brown PLC, apptd. Chief Exec. 1983, Dir Trafalgar House PLC (when it acquired John Brown PLC) 1986–95, CEO 1992–94; Deputy Chair. Royal Insurance Holdings PLC 1992–93, Chair. 1994–96 (mem. Bd 1990–96), Deputy Chair. Royal and Sun Alliance Insurance Group PLC 1996–98; Chair. BPB PLC 1997–2004 (Dir 1995–2004); Chair. Overseas Projects Bd 1989–91; Deputy Chair. Export Guarantees Advisory Council 1990–92; Dir Brixton PLC 1994–2003 (Chair. 2000–03), European Capital Co. 1996–99, Bank of Scotland 1997–2001; Dir (non-exec.) Nat. Grid. Co. 1994–95; Chair. Q-One Group Ltd 1999–2003; mem. British Overseas Trade Bd 1989–91, Top Salaries Review Body 1990–92; Dir Bd of Man., FCO 2000–04. *Leisure interests:* golf, music. *Address:* 56 North Park, Gerrards Cross, Bucks., SL9 8JR, England (home). *Telephone:* (1753) 885079 (home).

GÖRNE, Matthias; German singer (baritone); b. 1967, Weimar; ed Leipzig Univ. of Music and Theatre 'Felix Mendelssohn Bartholdy' with Prof. Hans-Joachim Beyer, then with Dietrich Fischer-Dieskau and Elisabeth Schwarzkopf; performed with the children's choir at Chemnitz Opera; sang in Bach's St Matthew Passion under Kurt Masur, Leipzig 1990; appearances with NDR Symphony Orchestra Hamburg; further engagements under Horst Stein, with Bamberg Symphony Orchestra and in Hindemith's Requiem under Wolfgang Sawallisch; concerts at Leipzig Gewandhaus under Helmuth Rilling and in Amsterdam and Paris; Lieder recitals and records with pianists Eric Schneider, Vladimir Ashkenazy, Alfred Brendel, and Christoph Eschenbach at Wigmore Hall, London, Carnegie Hall, New York, festivals in Edinburgh, Lucerne, and Salzburg; sang title role in Henze's Prinz von Homburg, Cologne 1992, Marcello in La Bohème at Komische Oper, Berlin 1993, Wolfram in Tannhäuser, Cologne 1996, Die Schöne Müllerin, Bath 1997; Papageno in Die Zauberflöte, Salzburg Festival 1997; Wozzeck at The Royal Opera House, Covent Garden 2002; role of Kasim in Henzes L'Upupa 2003, Salzburg Festival 2003, repeated in Teatro Real, Madrid 2004; Wozzeck at Saito Kinen Festival with Ozawa in 2004; Papageno at Metropolitan Opera 2005; debut at Vienna State Opera as Wolfram 2010; Bluebeard in Bartók's Duke Bluebeard's Castle at Saito Kinen Festival 2011 and Maggio Musicale in Florence 2012; debut as Kurwenal at Bavarian State Opera, Munich 2012; engaged for roles of Kurwenal, Amfortas, and Wozzeck at Vienna State Opera in 2013/14; concert performances with all major orchestras in Europe and US including Amsterdam Concertgebouworkest, Berliner Philharmoniker, Boston Symphony, Chicago Symphony, London Symphony, London Philharmonic, Los Angeles Philharmonic, New York Philharmonic, Orchestre de Paris; tour with Wiener Philharmoniker in 2011; Prof. of Lieder Interpretation, Schumann Hochschule, Dusseldorf 2001–2005. *Recordings include:* Matthäuspassion 1994, Winterreiss 1997, Entarte Musik, Arias, J.S. Bach Cantatas, Eisler's Deutsche Sinfonie, The Hollywood Songbook, Mahler's des Knaben Wunderhorn, Mendelssohn's Paulus Oratorio op. 36, Schubert's Schwanengesang, Die Schöne Müllerin, Winterreise, Goethe-Lieder, Messe D950, Liedrekreis, Schumann's Dichterliebe. *Address:* Michael Kocyan Artists Management, Alt-Moabit 104A, 10559 Berlin, Germany (office). *Telephone:* (30) 31004940 (office). *Fax:* (30) 31004984 (office). *E-mail:* artists@kocyan.de (office); info@matthiasgoerne.de (office). *Website:* www.kocyan.de (office); www.matthiasgoerne.de.

GORSKY, Alex, BS, MBA; American business executive; *Chairman and CEO, Johnson & Johnson;* ed US Mil. Acad., West Point, NY, Wharton School, Univ. of Pennsylvania; spent six years in US Army, finished mil. career with rank of Capt.; began Johnson & Johnson career as sales rep. with Janssen Pharmaceutical Inc. 1988, held posts of increasing responsibility in sales, marketing and management, Pres. Janssen Pharmaceutical Inc. 2001–03, Co. Group Chair. Johnson & Johnson's pharmaceuticals business in Europe, Middle East and Africa 2003–04; joined Novartis Pharmaceuticals Corpn, served as head of co.'s pharmaceuticals business in North America 2004–08; returned to Johnson & Johnson as Co. Group Chair. for Ethicon 2008–09, Worldwide Chair. Surgical Care Group and mem.

Exec. Cttee early 2009, Worldwide Chair. Medical Devices and Diagnostics Group Sept. 2009–11, Vice-Chair. Exec. Cttee 2011–12, mem. Bd of Dirs, CEO and Chair. Exec. Cttee Johnson & Johnson April 2012–, Chair. Bd of Dirs Dec. 2012–; represents Johnson & Johnson on Bd of AdvaMed (US trade asscn); Exec. Sponsor of two Johnson & Johnson affinity groups, Women's Leadership Initiative and Veteran's Leadership Council; mem. Bd Travis Manion Foundation; named Mentor of the Year by Healthcare Businesswomen's Asscn 2009. *Address:* Johnson & Johnson, 1 Johnson & Johnson Plaza, New Brunswick, NJ 08933, USA (office). *Telephone:* (732) 524-0400 (office). *Fax:* (732) 524-3300 (office). *E-mail:* info@jnj.com (office). *Website:* www.jnj.com (office).

GORTON, Slade, BA, LLB; American politician and lawyer; *Of Counsel, Policy and Public Law, K&L Gates LLP;* b. 8 Jan. 1928, Chicago, Ill.; s. of Thomas Slade Gorton and Ruth Gorton (née Israel); m. Sally Clark 1958; one s. two d.; ed Evanston High School, Ill., Dartmouth Coll., Columbia Univ. Law School, New York; US Army 1945–46, USAF 1953–56, retd Col, USAF Reserve; admitted to Bar, Wash. State 1953; mem. Wash. State House of Reps 1959–69, Majority Leader 1967–68; Wash. State Attorney Gen. 1969–81; Senator from Wash. 1981–87, 1989–2001; Pnr Davis, Wright & Jones, Seattle 1987–89; with Preston, Gates & Ellis 2001–, now K&L Gates LLP, currently Of Counsel; mem. Wash. State Law and Justice Comm. 1969–80 (Chair. 1969–70), State Criminal Justice Training Comm. 1969–80 (Chair. 1969–76), Pres.'s Consumer Advisory Council 1975–77, Nat. Asscn of Attorneys-Gen. 1969–80 (Pres. 1976–77), Nat. Comm. on Fed. Election Reform 2001–2002, Nat. Comm. on Terrorist Attacks (9/11 Comm.) 2002–04; mem. Bd of Dirs Fred Hutchinson Cancer Research Center 1987–2002; mem. War Powers Comm. 2006–08; Co-Chair. Nat. Transporation Policy Project, Bipartisan Policy Center 2008–; Wash. State Redistricting Commr 2011–12; Republican; Wyman Award for Outstanding Attorney Gen. in the US 1980, Citizen of the Year, Seattle-King Co. Realtors 2010. *Address:* K&L Gates LLP, 925 Fourth Avenue, Suite 2900, Seattle, WA 98104-1158 (office); 9435 NE 18th Street, Clyde Hill WA 98004, USA (home). *Telephone:* (206) 623-7580 (office); (425) 635-0829 (home). *Fax:* (206) 623-7022 (office). *E-mail:* slade.gorton@klgates.com (office); sladeg@msn.com (home). *Website:* www.klgates.com (office).

GORVY, Brett; British/American art dealer; *Chairman and International Head of Post-War and Contemporary Art and Deputy Chairman, Christie's International Plc;* b. London, England; m. Amy Gold 2001; one c.; began career as an arts journalist; joined Christie's auction house 1994, apptd, along with Amy Cappellazzo, Co-Head of Post-War Art and Contemporary Art 2001–11, Chair. and Int. Head 2011–; presided over sales of Warhol portrait of Mao for $17.2 million 2006, sale of Andy Warhol's 'Green Car Crash (Green Burning Car I)' for $71.72 million 2007, currently Deputy Chair. Christie's International Plc. *Address:* Christie's, 8 King Street, St James's, London, SW1Y 6QT, England (office); Christie's International, 20 Rockefeller Plaza, New York, NY 10020, USA (office). *Telephone:* (20) 7839-9060 (London) (office); (212) 636-2000 (New York) (office). *Fax:* (20) 7839-1611 (London) (office); (212) 636-2399 (New York) (office). *E-mail:* info@christies.com (office). *Website:* www.christies.com (office).

GOSDEN, Roger Gordon, PhD, DSc; British/American professor of medical sciences (retd) and writer; b. 23 Sept. 1948, Ryde, Isle of Wight, England; s. of the late Gordon Conrad Jason Gosden and Peggy Gosden (née Butcher); four s.; m. 2nd Lucinda Leigh Veeck 2004; ed Chislehurst and Sidcup Grammar School, London, Univs of Bristol and Cambridge; MRC Research Fellow, Univ. of Cambridge 1973–76; Population Council Fellow, Duke Univ., USA 1974–75; Lecturer in Physiology, Univ. of Edin. 1976–84, Sr Lecturer 1984–94; Prof. of Reproductive Biology, Univ. of Leeds 1994–99, Visiting Prof. 1999–2002; Research Dir and Prof., McGill Univ., Canada 1999–2001, Adjunct Prof. 2001–09; Howard and Georgeanna Jones Prof. of Reproductive Medicine and Scientific Dir, Eastern Virginia Medical School, USA 2001–04, Adjunct Prof., Old Dominion Univ., Va 2002–04; Prof. of Reproductive Medicine and of Reproductive Medicine in Obstetrics and Gynecology, Dir of Research in Reproductive Biology, Weill Medical Coll., Cornell Univ., New York 2004–10; writer and lecturer, Jamestowne Bookworks; pioneer in fertility conservation tech.; scientific adviser to industry and govt bodies (UK, The Netherlands, Canada); radio and TV broadcaster; lecturer and educator, including founding online master's degree programmes; int. conf. organizer; Distinguished Scientist Lecture, American Soc. of Reproductive Medicine 2001, Patrick Steptoe Lecturer, British Fertility Soc. 2003, Anne McLaren Lecturer 2011 and other awards, prizes and lectureships. *Publications:* Biology of Menopause 1985, Cheating Time 1996, Designer Babies 1999, Biology and Pathology of the Oocyte (with A. O. Trounson) 2003 (second edn 2012), Preservation of Fertility (with T. Tulandi) 2004; numerous articles in academic journals, magazines and newspapers. *Leisure interests:* writing, natural history, gardening. *Address:* 107 Paddock Lane, Williamsburg, VA 23188, USA (home). *E-mail:* roger.gosden@cantab.net (home). *Website:* www.jamestownebookworks.com (office).

GOŠEV, Petar, MA; Macedonian politician and fmr central banker; b. 5 Sept. 1948, Pirava; m.; two s.; ed Univ. of Skopje; with 11 Oktomvri Bus Co. 1971–73; mem. Council Macedonian Trade Union Fed. 1973–87 (econ. adviser 1973–84, Chief, Office of the Union Pres. 1977, mem. Presidency 1982–87); mem. Presidency, Cen. Cttee Union of Communists of Macedonia (renamed SKM–PDP 1990, Social Democratic Alliance of Macedonia 1991) 1986–89, Pres. 1989–91; Chief of the Del. of the Nat. Ass. in the Ass. of the fmr Socialist Fed. Repub. of Yugoslavia 1990; mem. Parl. 1990–2002; f. Democratic Party 1993, Pres. 1993–97; mem. Council Nat. Bank of Repub. of Macedonia 1993–97; Pres. Liberal-Democratic Party–LDP (formed from merger of Liberal Party and Democratic Party) 1997–99; Vice-Pres. Parl. Group of the Nat. Ass. to the Inter-Parl. Union 1998–2002; Vice-Pres. of Fmr Yugoslav Repub. of Macedonia and Minister of Finance 2002–04; Gov. Nat. Bank of Repub. of Macedonia 2004–11; mem. Bd of Govs EBRD; mem. Supervisory Bd Center of Excellence in Finance; mem. Vienna Econ. Forum. *Address:* c/o Office of the Governor, National Bank of Republic of Macedonia, Kuzman Josifovski Pitu Blvd 1, 1000 Skopje, Republic of Macedonia.

GOSLING, Ryan; Canadian actor and musician; b. 12 Nov. 1980; s. of Thomas Gosling and Donna Gosling; began acting at age 12 in The Mickey Mouse Club (American variety TV show); co-f. Dead Man's Bones (pop band). *Television:* Mickey Mouse Club 1993–95, Kung Fu: The Legend Continues 1996, The Adventures of Shirley Holmes 1996, Flash Forward 1996, Breaker High 1997–98, Nothing Too Good for a Cowboy 1998, Young Hercules 1998–99,

Hercules: The Legendary Journeys 1998–99, The Unbelievables 1999. *Films include:* Frankenstein and Me 1996, The Believer 2001, Murder by Numbers 2002, The Notebook 2004, Half Nelson (Independent Spirit Award for Best Male Lead, Nat. Bd of Review Award for Best Breakthrough Performance, Stockholm Film Festival Award for Best Actor) 2006, Lars and the Real Girl 2007, All Good Things 2010, Blue Valentine 2010, The Place Beyond the Pines 2012. *Address:* c/o IFA Talent Agency, 8730 Sunset Blvd, Suite 490, Los Angeles, CA 90069, USA (office).

GOSS, Porter J., BA; American politician and government official; *Co-Chairman, Office of Congressional Ethics;* b. 26 Nov. 1938, Waterbury, Conn.; s. of Richard Wayne Goss and Virginia Holland Goss (née Johnston); m. Mariel Goss; four c.; ed Yale Univ.; served US Army 1960–66; Clandestine Services Officer CIA 1962–71; co-founder and publisher Community Newspaper 1971–74; Sanibel, Fla, City Council 1974–82, apptd Mayor of Sanibel 1974–77; mem. Lee Co. Bd of Commr 1983–88; mem. US House of Reps 1989–2004, Chair. House Perm. Select Cttee on Intelligence, mem. House Rules Cttee, Select Cttee for Homeland Security; Dir CIA 2004–06 (resgnd); small business owner and co-founder of local newspaper, Sanibel, Fla 2006–08; Co-Chair. Office of Congressional Ethics, Washington, DC 2008–; mem. Book and Snake Soc., Ripon Soc.; Distinguished Service Award 2006. *Address:* Office of Congressional Ethics, US House of Representatives, 425 3rd Street, SW, Suite 1110, Washington, DC 20024, USA (office). *Telephone:* (202) 225-9739 (office). *Fax:* (202) 226-0997 (office). *Website:* oce.house.gov (office).

GOTCHEV, Dimitar Bonev; Bulgarian judge; b. 27 Feb. 1936, Sofia; s. of Maj.-Gen. Boncho Gotchev and Zdravka Gotchev; m. Jova Gotcheva-Cholakova 1976; one d.; ed Univ. of Sofia St Kliment Ochridsky; legal adviser 1959–66; Arbiter, State Court of Arbitration 1966–89; Judge, Supreme Court 1990, Judge, Head of Commercial Div. 1990, Deputy Chief Justice, Supreme Court 1993; Judge, Constitutional Court 1994–2004; Judge, European Court of Human Rights, Strasbourg 1992–98. *Leisure interests:* music, mountaineering, skiing. *Address:* c/o Constitutional Court of Republic of Bulgaria, Bul. Dondoukov 1, 1202 Sofia; Koslodui Str. N34, 1202 Sofia, Bulgaria (home). *Telephone:* (2) 940-23-31; (2) 31-54-25 (home).

GÖTHE, (Lars) Staffan; Swedish playwright, actor, director and academic; *Actor, Royal Dramatic Theatre, Stockholm;* b. 20 Dec. 1944, Luleå; s. of the late Thorsten Göthe and of Margit Grape-Göthe; m. Kristin Byström 1969; one s.; ed Acad. of Performing Arts, Gothenburg; actor and playwright, regional theatre of Växjö 1971, Folkteatern, Gothenburg 1974; Headmaster Acad. of Performing Arts, Malmö 1976; actor, Folkteatern, Gävleborg 1983; Dir The RTC Co. 1984–95; actor and playwright, Royal Dramatic Theatre, Stockholm 1995–2003, actor 2011–; Prof., Malmö Theatre Acad., Univ. of Lund 2003–11; Royal Medal Litteris et Artibus, Award of Royal Swedish Acad. 2005. *Plays:* En natt i februari 1972, Den gråtande polisen 1980, La strada dell'amore 1986, En uppstoppad hund 1986, Den perfekta Kyssen 1990, Arma Irma 1991, Boogie Woogie 1992, Blått Hus Med Röda Kinder 1995, Ruben Pottas Eländiga Salonger 1996, Ett Lysande Elände 1999, Temperance 2000, Byta Trottoar 2001, Stjärnan Över Lappland 2005, Kvart i femekot 2010. *Publication:* Lysande Eländen (complete works) 2004. *Address:* Vindragarvägen 8, 117 50 Stockholm, Sweden (home). *Telephone:* (8) 668-38-18 (office). *Website:* staffangothe@gmail.com (office).

GOTT, Karel; Czech singer; b. 14 July 1939, Plzeň; two d.; ed Prague Conservatory (studied under Prof. Karenin); mem. Semafor Theatre, Prague 1963–65; mem. Apollo Theatre, Prague, 1965–67; freelance artist 1967–; numerous foreign tours; charity concerts with Eva Urbanová 1998; CD Rocky mého mládí (Rocks of my Youth) 1999; exhbn of paintings, Bratislava 1999; f. and Chair. Interpo Foundation 1993–96; concerts in Carnegie Hall, New York, Expo, Hanover, Kremlin Palace, Moscow 2000; charity concerts in Czech Repub. after 2002 floods; Golden Nightingale trophy (annual pop singer poll 1963–66, 1968–81, 1983, 1989–90, 1997–2001), MIDEM Prize, Cannes 1967, MIDEM Gold Record 1969, Polydor Gold Record 1970, Supraphon Gold Record 1972, 1973, 1979, 1980, 1996, Music Week Star of the Year 1974 (UK) 1975, Artist of Merit 1982, Gold Aerial 1983, radio station BRT (Belgium) 1984, Nat. Artist 1985, Polydor Golden Pin (Germany) 1986, Czech Nightingale Trophy 1996, 1997, 1999, 2001, 2002 (28 times in total), Czech TV Prize 1997, 1999, Platinum Record (for duets with Lucia Bílá) 1998 and many other awards. *Radio:* presenter monthly show Radio Impuls 2002–. *Film appearance:* Luck from Hell. *Recordings include:* Vánoce ve zlaté Praze 1969, 42 největších hitů 1991, Věci blízké mému srdci 1993, Zázrak vánoční 1995, Belcanto 1996, Duety s Lucií Bilou 1997, Miluj 1997, Svátek svátků 1998, Rocky mého mládí 1999, Originální nahrávky ze 70.let 2000, Originální nahrávky ze 80.let 2000, Originální nahrávky ze 90.let 2000, Pokaždé 2002, Gott & Vondaáčková 2003, Lásko má 2004, Můj strážný anděl 2004, K. Gott zpívá hity K. Svobody 2005, Jsou svátky 2006, Má pouť 2006, Každý má svůj sen 2007, Zlatá Kolekce 2007, Zmírám láskou 2008, Leben 2009, Oslava 70 narozenin 2009, Frohe Weihnacht 2010, Sentiment 2011, Dotek lásky 2012. *Publication:* Why Painting is Important for Me 2001. *Address:* GOJA spol. s r.o., Pod Prusekem 3, 102 00 Prague 10, Czech Republic (office); Nad Bertramkou 18, 150 00 Prague 5, Czech Republic (home). *Telephone:* (2) 72658337 (office). *Fax:* (2) 72659265 (office). *E-mail:* goja@goja.cz (office). *Website:* www.goja.cz (office); www.karelgott.com; www.karel-gott.de.

GOTTI, Irv; American music company executive and producer; *CEO, The Inc. Records;* b. (Irv Lorenzo), Hollis, Queens, New York; m. Debbie Gotti; began music career as DJ Irv; fmr producer Island Def Jam Records, artistes produced include Ashanti, Charli Baltimore, Toni Braxton, DMX, Ja Rule, Jay-Z; currently CEO Murder Inc. Records, now known as The Inc. Records. *Recordings include:* Irv Gotti Presents. . . (series of albums). *Address:* c/o The Inc. Records, 2220 Colorado Avenue, Santa Monica, CA 90404, USA (office). *Website:* www.theincrecords.com (office).

GOTTLIEB, Robert Adams, BA; American editor and critic; b. 29 April 1931, New York; s. of Charles Gottlieb and Martha Gottlieb (née Kean); m. 1st Muriel Higgins 1952; m. 2nd Maria Tucci 1969; two s. one d.; ed Columbia Coll. and Univ. of Cambridge, UK; with Simon and Schuster 1955–68, Ed.-in-Chief 1965–68; Ed.-in-Chief Alfred A. Knopf 1968–87, Pres. 1973–87; Ed.-in-Chief The New Yorker 1987–92; now dance and book critic for New York Observer, New York Times, The New Yorker and New York Review of Books. *Publications:* Reading Jazz 1996, Reading Lyrics (co-author) 2000, George Balanchine – The Ballet Maker 2004,

Reading Dance (ed.) 2008, Sarah: The Life of Sarah Bernhardt 2010. *Leisure interests:* ballet, movies, reading. *Address:* 237 East 48th Street, New York, NY 10017-1538, USA (home).

GOTTSCHALK, Gerhard, Dr rer. nat; German microbiologist, academic and fmr organization administrator; *Professor of Genome Research, Georg-August-University of Göttingen;* b. 27 March 1935, Schwedt/Oder; s. of Gerhard Gottschalk and Irmgard Gottschalk (née Ploetz); m. Ellen-Marie Hrabowski 1960; two s. one d.; ed Humboldt Univ., Berlin and Georg-August-Univ., Göttingen; Research Assoc., Dept of Biochemistry, Univ. of Calif., Berkeley, USA 1964–66, Visiting Prof. 1978–79; Docent, Georg-August-Univ. of Göttingen 1967–70, Prof. of Microbiology 1970–2003, Rector 1975–76, Vice-Pres. 1979–81, Prof. of Genome Research 2003–; Visiting Prof., Dept of Bacteriology, Univ. of Calif., Davis 1972–73; Vice-Pres. Acad. of Science, Göttingen 1996, Pres. 1998–2000; Pres. ALLEA (All European Acads) 1998–2000; Pres. Union of German Acads of Sciences and Humanities 2003–07; Fed. Cross of Merit (Germany) 2005; Philip Morris Prize 1992, Emil von Behring Prize 2006. *Publications:* Bacterial Metabolism 1986, Biotechnologie 1986, Göttinger Gelehrte (co-ed. with K. Arndt and R. Smend) 2001, World of Bacteria 2009. *Address:* Institute of Microbiology and Genetics, University of Göttingen, Grisebachstrasse 8, 37077 Göttingen, Germany (office). *Telephone:* (551) 394041 (office). *Fax:* (551) 394195 (office); (5503) 999128 (home). *E-mail:* ggottsc@gwdg.de (office). *Website:* www.img.bio.uni-goettingen.de (office); wwwuser.gwdg.de/~ggottsc (home).

GOTTSCHALK, Helmut; German business executive; *Chairman of the Supervisory Board, DZ Bank AG;* mem. Supervisory Bd DZ Bank AG 2004–, Deputy Chair. 2008–10, Chair. 2010–, also Vice-Chair. Supervisory Bd DZ Beteiligungs GmbH & Co. KG (largest shareholder of DZ Bank); CEO Volksbank Herrenberg-Rottenburg eG 2003–, Deputy Chair. 2008–, Speaker of the Bd of Man. Dirs; Chair. of the Council, Baden-Württemberg Cooperative Asscn; mem. Bd of Dirs Fed. Asscn of German Cooperative Banks (BVR); Staufer Medal (Baden-Württemberg) 2010. *Address:* Deutsche Zentral-Genossenschaftsbank AG, Platz der Republik, 60265 Frankfurt am Main, Germany (office). *Telephone:* (69) 7447-01 (office). *Fax:* (69) 7447-1685 (office). *E-mail:* mail@dzbank.de (office). *Website:* www.dzbank.de (office).

GÖTZE, Wolfgang; German theoretical physicist and academic; b. 11 July 1937; Prof. for Theoretical Physics, Munich Univ. of Tech. 1970–2003, Prof. Emer. 2003–; Max-Planck-Medal, German Physical Soc. 2006, Tomassoni Award, Univ. of Rome (La Sapienza) 2006. *Publications:* Complex Dynamics of Glass-Forming Liquids 2009; numerous scientific papers in professional journals. *Address:* Room 3333, Institute for Theoretical Physics, Munich University of Technology 85748, Garching, Germany (office). *Telephone:* (89) 289-12360 (office). *Fax:* (89) 289-14641 (office). *E-mail:* wg@ph.tum.de (office). *Website:* www.physik.tu-muenchen.de/lehrstuehle/T37_wg/Welcome_e.html (office).

GOU, Terry Tai-Ming; Taiwanese electronics industry executive; *Chairman and CEO, Hon Hai Precision Industry Co. Ltd;* b. 8 Oct. 1950, Banqiao Township, Taipei Co.; m. 1st Serena Lin (died 2005); one s. one d.; m. 2nd Delia Tseng 2008; one s. one d.; f. Hon Hai Precision Industry Co. Ltd (trading name Foxconn; world's largest contract manufacturer) with 10 workers to make plastic parts for TV sets in a rented shed in Tucheng suburb of Taipei 1974, opened first factory in Shenzhen, China 1988, customers include HP, IBM, Apple, Inc., now Chair. and CEO; f. educational charity with first wife 2000; ranked by Forbes magazine amongst The World's Most Powerful People (55th) 2012, (48th) 2013. *Address:* Hon Hai Precision Industry Co. Ltd, 2 Zihyou Street, Tucheng City, Taipei County 236, Taiwan (office). *Telephone:* (2) 2268-3466 (office). *Fax:* (2) 2268-6204 (office). *E-mail:* webadmin@foxconn.com (office). *Website:* www.foxconn.com (office).

GOUBET, Cédric; French civil servant; *Principal Private Secretary to the President;* b. 12 May 1971, Cambrai; served as Chief of Staff to prefects Claude Guéant, Franche-Comté 1998–2002, Jean-Marie Rebière and Thierry Klinger, Finistère 2000–02; Chief of Staff to Minister of the Interior, Nicolas Sarkozy 2004, Tech. Adviser 2005–07; Prin. Pvt. Sec. to Pres. Nicolas Sarkozy 2007–. *Address:* Palais de l'Elysée, 55 rue du faubourg Saint-Honoré, 75008 Paris, France (office). *Telephone:* 1-42-92-81-00 (office). *Website:* www.elysee.fr (office).

GOUELI, Ahmed, BSc, MSc, MA, PhD; Egyptian professor of agricultural economics and international organization official; b. 22 March 1937, Behera; m.; two c.; ed Coll. of Agric.-Agricultural Univ. of Alexandria, Univ. of California, Berkeley, USA; Agricultural Engineer, Authority of Land Reclamation 1957–58; Research Assoc., Dept of Agricultural Econs, Univ. of California, Berkeley 1964–65; Asst Prof. of Agricultural Econs, Faculty of Agric., Ain Shams Univ., Egypt 1965–71; Assoc. Prof., Zagazig Univ., Egypt 1971–74, Prof. 1974–84, 1999–2000, Chair. of Dept of Agricultural Econs, Faculty of Agric. 1971–84; Prof. of Agricultural Econs, Faculty of Agric., Cairo Univ. 2000–; Gov. of Damietta 1984–91, of Ismailia 1991–94; mem. People's Ass. (Parl.) 1995–2000; Minister of Supply and Home Trade 1994–96, of Trade and Supply 1996–99; CEO and Chair. Bd of Dirs, Kingdom Agricultural Devt Co. 2000–01; Sec.-Gen. Council of Arab Econ. Unity 2000–10; Chair. Egyptian Asscn of Agricultural Econs 1990–, Egyptian Water Partnership 2003–; currently Chair. Cttee for Assessment of Nominees for Nat. Awards in Agricultural Disciplines, Acad. of Science and Tech.; mem. Bd of Trustees, Int. Maize and Wheat Improvement Centre (CIMMYT) 1986–92, The Formulation of the World Food Security Strategy Expert Team, FAO 1984, Food Reserves Stocks Research Team, FAO 1991, Int. Council for Food and Agricultural Policy 2002–, Foundation Cttee of the Arab Water Council 2005; mem. Acad. of Science and Tech. 1988–92, Egyptian Council of Sciences 1995–2000; currently mem. Soc. for Political Economy, Egyptian Asscn for Policy Analysis, Food and Agric. Council, Presidential Council for Econ. and Production Affairs; Nat. Award of Sciences 1991, Sciences and Arts Medal 1995, Haas Int. Award, Univ. of California 1997, Mubarak Award 2007. *Publications:* more than 50 research papers in scientific journals and at int. confs. *Address:* c/o Council of Arab Economic Unity, 1113 Corniche en-Nil, 4th Floor, PO Box 1, 11518 Cairo, Egypt. *Telephone:* (2) 25755045. *E-mail:* caeu@idsc.net.eg.

GOUGH, Barry Morton, SBStJ, MA, PhD, DLit, FRHistS, FKC; Canadian historian; *Adjunct Professor of History, The Royal Military College of Canada;* b. 17 Sept. 1938, Victoria, BC; s. of John Gough and Dorothy Mouncy Morton Gough; m. 1st B. Louise Kerr 1964 (divorced 1977); one s. one d.; m. 2nd Marilyn J. Morris 1981; two s.; ed Victoria High School, Victoria Coll., Univs of British Columbia and Montana, King's. Coll., London, UK; Prof. of History, Western Washington Univ. and Wilfrid Laurier Univ. 1972–2004, now Emer.; Adjunct Prof. of History and War Studies, Royal Mil. Coll. of Canada 1994–; Asst Dean of Arts and Sciences, Wilfrid Laurier Univ. 1999–2001; historian, Nuu Chah Nulth Tribal Council in Meares Island Case; Founding mem. Asscn for Canadian Studies in the US and Co-Dir and Archivist Center for Pacific Northwest Studies, Western Washington Univ., Bellingham, Wash. 1968–72; mem. Canadian Historical Asscn, Canadian Nautical Research Soc., Soc. for the History of Discoveries; Visiting Prof., Duke Univ., Univ. of British Columbia, Otago Univ., Natal Univ., ANU, and others; Pres. N American Soc. for Oceanic History, Canadian Nautical Research Soc.; Vice-Pres. Social Sciences Fed. of Canada; Ed. American Neptune: Maritime History and Arts 1995–2001; Fellow, King's Coll. London; twice Archives Fellow, Churchill Coll. Cambridge, UK; Curator, George Vancouver Exhibit, Vancouver Maritime Museum 2011; Order of St John of Jerusalem, Queen's Golden Jubilee Medal 2002, Queen's Diamond Jubilee Medal 2012, Lt-Gov. of BC Medal; The Roderick Haig-Brown, Keith Matthews, John Lyman, K. Jack Bauer, British Columbia Historical Fed. and other book prizes, Clio Prize, Canadian Historical Asscn, Lt Gov. of BC Medal for Historical Writing. *Television:* historical consultant, Dive Detectives: Lost Schooners War of 1812. *Publications:* Royal Navy and the Northwest Coast 1971, Distant Dominion 1980, Gunboat Frontier 1984, Journal of Alexander Henry the Younger 1988, 1992, The Northwest Coast 1992, Falkland Islands/Malvinas 1992, First Across The Continent: Sir Alexander Mackenzie 1997, Historical Dictionary of Canada 1999 (second edn 2011), HMCS Haida: Battle Ensign Flying 2001, Fighting Sail on Lake Huron and Georgian Bay 1812 2002, Through Water, Ice and Fire: Schooner Nancy of the War of 1812 2006, Fortune's a River 2007, Historical Dreadnoughts: Arthur Marder, Stephen Roskill and Battles for Naval History 2010, Introduction to William Robert Broughton Voyage of Discovery to the North Pacific 2010, Juan de Fuca's Strait: Voyages in the Waterway of Forgotten Dreams 2012; numerous reviews and articles. *Leisure interests:* golfing, jazz clarinet. *Address:* PO Box 5037, Victoria, BC V8R 6N3, Canada (home); 107 Pall Mall, London, SW1Y 5ER, England (home). *Telephone:* (250) 592-0800 (Victoria) (home); (519) 925-3958 (summer) (home). *E-mail:* bgough@wlu.ca (office); barrygough@shaw.ca (office).

GOUGH, Douglas Owen, MA, PhD, FRS, FInstP; British astrophysicist; *Professor Emeritus of Theoretical Astrophysics, University of Cambridge;* b. 8 Feb. 1941, Stourport; s. of Owen Albert John Gough and Doris May Gough (née Camera); m. Rosanne Penelope Shaw 1965; two s. two d.; ed Hackney Downs School, London, St John's. Coll., Cambridge; Research Assoc., JILA, Univ. of Colorado, USA 1966–67, Fellow Adjoint 1986–; NAS Sr Postdoctoral Research Assoc., New York 1967–69; mem. Grad. Staff, Inst. of Theoretical Astronomy, Univ. of Cambridge 1969–73, Lecturer in Astronomy and Applied Math., Inst. of Astronomy and Dept of Applied Math. and Theoretical Physics 1973–85, Reader in Astrophysics, Inst. of Astronomy 1985–93, Prof. of Theoretical Astrophysics 1993–2008, Prof. Emer. 2008–; Deputy Dir, Inst. of Astronomy 1993–99, Dir 1999–2004; Fellow, Churchill Coll. Cambridge 1972–; Hon. Prof. Astronomy, QMW London 1986–2006; Visiting Prof. of Physics, Stanford Univ., USA 1996–2010, now Consulting Prof. of Experimental Physics; Foreign mem. Royal Danish Acad. of Sciences and Letters 1998; James Arthur Prize, Harvard Univ. (USA) 1982, William Hopkins Prize, Cambridge Philosophical Soc. 1984, George Ellery Hale Prize, American Astronomical Soc. 1994, Mousquetaire d'Armagnac 2001, Eddington Medal, Royal Astronomical Soc. 2002, Gold Medal, Royal Astronomical Soc. 2010. *Publications:* Problems in Solar and Stellar Oscillations (ed.) 1983, Seismology of the Sun and the Distant Stars (ed.) 1986, Challenges to Theories of the Structure of Moderate-Mass Stars (co-ed. with J. Toomre) 1991, Equation-of-state and Phase-transition Issues in Models of Ordinary Astrophysical Matter (co-ed. with V. Čelebonović and W. Däppen) 2004, The Scientific Legacy of Fred Hoyle (ed.) 2005; more than 300 papers in the professional scientific literature. *Leisure interest:* cooking. *Address:* Institute of Astronomy, Madingley Road, Cambridge, CB3 0HA, England (office). *Telephone:* (1223) 337516 (office). *Fax:* (1223) 337523 (office). *E-mail:* douglas@ast.cam.ac.uk (office).

GOUGH, Piers William, CBE, RIBA, FRSA, RA; British architect; *Partner, CZWG Architects;* b. 24 April 1946; s. of Peter Gough and Daphne Mary Unwin Banks; m. Rosemary Elaine Fosbrooke Bates 1991; ed Architectural Asscn School of Architecture; Pnr, CZWG Architects, London 1975–; Pres. Architectural Asscn 1995–97 (mem. Council 1970–72, 1991); Commr English Heritage 2000, Comm. for Architecture and Built Environment 2007–; mem. Bd Stonehenge 2002–, Council of the Royal Acad. 2003–04; Trustee, Trinity Buoy Wharf, Chisenhale Gallery 1993–2002, Artangel 1994–2003, Kent Design Champion 2004–08; mem. RIBA Gold Medal Panel 2000; Hon. DUniv (Middlesex) 1999, (Queen Mary Coll.); Royal Fine Art Comm. Award, Building of the Year Award, British Sky Broadcasting 1998. *Television:* presenter, Shock of the Old (six-part series), Channel 4 2000. *Principal works include:* Phillips West 2, Bayswater 1976, Cochrane Square (Phase I), Glasgow 1987, China Wharf, Bermondsey 1988, Craft, Design and Tech. Bldg, Bryanston School 1988, Street-Porter House 1988, The Circle, Bermondsey 1990, Westbourne Grove Public Lavatories 1993, 1–10 Summers Street, Clerkenwell 1994, Leonardo Centre, Uppingham School 1995, Cochrane Square (Phase II), Glasgow 1995, 90 Wardour Street, Soho 1995, 19th and 20th Century Galleries, Nat. Portrait Gallery 1996, Suffolk Wharf, Camden Lock 1996–, Brindleyplace Café, Birmingham 1997, Bankside Lofts, London 1997, The Glass Building, Camden 1999, The Green Bridge, Mile End Park 2000, Office Edinburgh Park 2000, Tunnel Wharf Rotherhithe, London 2001, Allen Jones' Studio, Ledwell 2001, Samworth's Girls' Boarding House Uppingham School 2001, Bankside Cen. 2001, Suffolk Wharf, Camden Lock, London 2002, Fulham Island, London 2002, Queen Elizabeth Square and Crown Street Corner, Gorbials 2003–04, Regency Galleries, Nat. Portrait Gallery 2003, Bling Bling Bldg, Liverpool 2006, South Cen. Bldg 2006, Arsenal Masterplan 2000 including Vision 7 N7 2007, Drayton Park 2008, Canada Water Library 2009, Fortune Green, London 2010, Almeida Centre, London 2010, Queensland Road 2010, Maggie's Centre, Nottingham 2011. *Publication:* English Extremists 1988. *Leisure interest:* throwing parties. *Address:* CZWG Architects, 17 Bowling Green Lane, London, EC1R 0QB, England (office). *Telephone:* (20) 7253-2523 (office). *Fax:* (20) 7250-0594 (office). *E-mail:* p.gough@czwgarchitects.co.uk (office). *Website:* www.czwg.com (office).

GOULD, Andrew F., BA, FCA; British business executive; *Non-Executive Chairman, BG Group plc;* b. 17 Dec. 1946; ed Univ. of Wales, Cardiff; began career with Ernst & Young; joined Internal Audit Dept, Schlumberger Ltd, Paris 1975, various man. roles including Treas., Schlumberger Ltd, Pres. Sedco Forex, Wireline & Testing and Oilfield Services Products, Exec. Vice-Pres. Schlumberger Oilfield Services, later Pres. and CEO Schlumberger Ltd, mem. Bd of Dirs 2002–, Chair. and CEO 2003–11, Chair. 2011–12; Dir Rio Tinto plc, Rio Tinto Ltd; Dir (non-exec.) BG Group plc 2011–, Chair. 2012–. *Address:* BG Group plc, 100 Thames Valley Park, Reading, Berks., RG6 1PT, England (office). *Telephone:* (118) 935-3222 (office). *Fax:* (118) 935-3484 (office). *E-mail:* Box.info@bg-group.com (office). *Website:* www.bg-group.com (office).

GOULD, Bryan Charles, BCL, LLM, MA; New Zealand/British politician and academic; *Chairman, National Centre for Tertiary Teaching Research;* b. 11 Feb. 1939, Hawera, Taranaki, North Island, NZ; s. of Charles T. Gould and Elsie M. Gould (née Driller); m. Gillian A. Harrigan 1967; one s. one d.; ed Victoria and Auckland Univs, New Zealand and Balliol Coll., Oxford, UK; in diplomatic service, British Embassy, Brussels 1964–68; Fellow and Tutor in Law, Worcester Coll., Oxford 1968–74; MP for Southampton Test 1974–79, Dagenham 1983–94; presenter and reporter Thames TV 1977–83; Opposition Spokesman on Trade 1983–86, on Trade and Industry 1987–89, on the Environment 1989–92; mem. of Shadow Cabinet, Labour's Campaign Co-ordinator 1986–89; Shadow Heritage Sec. 1992 (resgnd); unsuccessful cand. for Labour Party leadership 1992; Vice-Chancellor Waikato Univ. 1994–2004; Visiting Fellow, Nuffield Coll., Oxford 2005–; Chair. Nat. Centre for Tertiary Teaching Excellence, NZ, Eastern Bay Primary Health Alliance; Companion, NZ Order of Merit; Hon. PhD (Waikato). *Publications include:* Monetarism or Prosperity? 1981, Socialism and Freedom 1985, A Future for Socialism 1989, Goodbye to All That (memoirs) 1995, The Democracy Sham 2006, Rescuing the New Zealand Economy 2008, Myths, Politicians and Money 2013. *Leisure interests:* food, wine, gardening. *Address:* 239 Ohiwa Beach Road, RD2, Opotiki 3198, New Zealand (office). *E-mail:* bgould@paradise.net.nz (office). *Website:* www.bryangould.net (office).

GOULD, Elizabeth, BA, MA, PhD; American psychologist and academic; *Professor of Psychology, Princeton University;* ed St John's Univ., Queens, NY, Univ. of California, Los Angeles; Postdoctoral Fellow in Neuroendocrinology, The Rockefeller Univ. 1989–92, Asst Prof. 1993–96; Asst Prof., Princeton Univ. 1997–2000, Prof. of Psychology 2000–, Co-Dir Neuroscience Certificate Program 2006–; mem. NSF Learning and Intelligence Systems KDI-LIS Review Cttee 1998–2000, NJ Gov.'s Council on Autism Grants Review Panel 2000–01; ad hoc reviewer for NIH 2000–04, mem. LAM NIH study section 2002–06, ad hoc reviewer for NIH grants 2002–, for NIH Pioneer Award, New Innovator Award Panel, K99 Award Panel 2008–; mem. Editorial Bd, Journal of Neuroscience, Neurobiology of Learning and Memory, Biological Psychiatry, Cell Stem Cell; an early investigator of adult neurogenesis in the hippocampus; Nat. Research Service Award Individual Postdoctoral Fellowship 1989–91, WinstonTri-Institutional (Rockefeller, Cornell, Sloan-Kettering) Fellowship 1991–92, American Paralysis Asscn Fellowship 1992–93, NARSAD (now The Brain & Behavior Research Foundation) Young Investigator Award 1994–96, Nat. Inst. of Mental Health FIRST Award 1994–99, NAS Troland Award 2000, NARSAD Distinguished Investigator Award 2006, Benjamin Franklin Award, Royal Soc. of the Arts 2009. *Publications:* Psychology Around Us 2010; numerous book chapters, reviews and papers in professional journals. *Address:* Psychology Department, Princeton University, Princeton, NJ 08540, USA (office). *Telephone:* (609) 258-4483 (office). *Fax:* (609) 258-1113 (office). *E-mail:* goulde@princeton.edu (office). *Website:* psych.princeton.edu/psychology/research/gould/index.php (office).

GOULD, Elliott; American actor; b. (Elliott Goldstein), 29 Aug. 1938, Brooklyn, New York; s. of Bernard Goldstein and Lucille Goldstein (née Gross); m. 1st Barbra Streisand (q.v.) 1963 (divorced 1971); one s.; m. 2nd Jenny Bogart 1973 (divorced 1975, remarried 1978); one s. one d.; ed Professional Children's School; made Broadway début in Rumple 1957; other appearances include Say Darling 1958, Irma La Douce 1960, I Can Get It For You Wholesale 1962, Drat! The Cat 1965, Alfred in Little Murders 1967; toured in The Fantastiks with Liza Minnelli; nat. tour Deathtrap, Luv with Shelley Winters; mem. Nat. Bd of Dirs, Screen Actors Guild; Hon. LLD (Univ. of West Los Angeles). *Films include:* The Confession 1966, The Night They Raided Minsky's 1968, Bob and Carol and Ted and Alice 1969, Getting Straight 1970, M*A*S*H 1970, The Touch 1971, Little Murders 1971, The Long Good-Bye 1972, Nashville 1974, I Will . . . I Will . . . For Now 1976, Harry and Walter Go to New York 1976, A Bridge Too Far 1977, Capricorn One (1978), The Silent Partner 1979, The Lady Vanishes 1979, Escape to Athens 1979, The Muppet Movie 1979, Falling in Love Again 1980, The Devil and Max Devlin 1981, Over the Brooklyn Bridge 1984, The Naked Face 1984, Act of Betrayal 1988, Dead Men Don't Die 1989, Secret Scandal 1990, Bugsy 1991, Wet and Wild Summer! 1992, Beyond Justice 1992, Hoffman's Hunger 1993, Amore! 1993, The Feminine Touch 1994, The Dangerous 1994, The Glass Shield 1994, Bleeding Hearts 1994, P.C.H. 1995, I Want Him Back! 1995, Cover Me 1995, Kicking and Screaming 1995, Let It Be Me 1995, Busted 1996, Amanda's Game 1996, A Boy Called Hate 1996, Johns 1996, Camp Stories 1997, The Big Hit 1998, American History X 1998, Playing Mona Lisa 2000, Picking Up the Pieces 2000, Boys Life 3 2000, Ocean's Eleven 2001, The Experience Box 2001, Puckoon 2002, Ocean's Twelve 2004, Open Window 2006, Ocean's Thirteen 2007, Saving Sarah Cain 2007, The Ten Commandments 2007, WordGirl 2007, The Deal 2008, The Caller 2008, Noah's Ark: The New Beginning 2009, Little Hercules in 3-D 2009, Expecting Mary 2010, Uncorked 2010. *TV appearances include:* Doggin' Around (BBC TV), Once Upon a Mattress (CBC), Friends, Kim Possible, Drop Dead Diva 2009, The Life & Times of Tim 2009. *Address:* c/o Cunningham, Escott, Dipene, 10635 Santa Monica Blvd., Suite 130, Los Angeles, CA 90025, USA. *Website:* www.elliottgould.net (office).

GOULIAN, Mehran, AB, MD; American physician and academic; *Professor Emeritus, School of Medicine, University of California, San Diego;* b. 31 Dec. 1929, Weehawken, NJ; s. of Dicran Goulian and Shamiram Mzrakjian; m. Susan Hook 1961; three s.; ed Columbia Coll. and Columbia Univ. Coll. of Physicians and Surgeons, Washington Univ. School of Medicine, Yale Univ. School of Medicine; Medical Internship, Barnes Hosp. 1954–55; Medical Residency, Mass. Gen. Hosp. 1958–59, 1960; Fellow in Medicine (Hematology), Yale Univ. School of Medicine 1959–60; Research Fellow in Medicine (Hematology), Harvard Univ. July–Dec.

1960, 1962–63, Instructor in Medicine 1963–65; Clinical and Research Fellow in Medicine (Hematology), Mass. Gen. Hosp. July–Dec. 1960, 1962–63, Asst in Medicine, 1963–65; Fellow in Biochemistry, Stanford Univ. School of Medicine 1965–67; Research Assoc. in Biochemistry, Univ. of Chicago and Argonne Cancer Research Hosp. 1967–69, Assoc. Prof. of Medicine 1967–70, Assoc. Prof. of Biochemistry 1969–70; Prof. of Medicine, Univ. of Calif., San Diego 1970–94, now Prof. Emer. *Leisure interest:* music. *Address:* 8433 Prestwick Drive, La Jolla, CA 92037, USA. *Telephone:* (858) 459-0088 (office). *E-mail:* mgoulian@ussd.edu (office).

GOULONGANA, Jean-Robert; Gabonese diplomatist and government official; *Managing Director, Caisse Nationale d'Assurance Maladie et de Garantie Sociale;* b. 30 April 1953, Lambarene; m.; three c.; ed Dakar Univ., Senegal, Aix-Marseille III Univ., France; Minister of Waters, Forests and the Environment 1990–91; Amb. to Italy 1992, to Belgium 1996; fmr Head, Gabonese Mission to EU, Brussels; Sec.-Gen. African, Caribbean and Pacific States 2000–05; Man. Dir Caisse Nationale d'Assurance Maladie et de Garantie Sociale (Nat. Social Insurance and Social Security) 2007–; Officier, Ordre du Mérite Maritime Gabonais. *Address:* Caisse Nationale d'Assurance Maladie et de Garantie Sociale, Libreville, Gabon (office).

GOUNARIS, Elias, LLM; Greek diplomatist; b. 7 Sept. 1941, Athens; s. of Panayotis Gounaris and Christine Gounaris; one s.; ed Univ. of Athens; served in Greek Navy 1964–66; Attaché, Ministry of Foreign Affairs, Athens 1966, Consul, New York 1969–73, Head of Section, Turkey-Cyprus Dept, Ministry of Foreign Affairs 1973, Sec., Perm. Mission of Greece to Int. Orgs, Geneva 1975, Counsellor 1976, Deputy Chief Minister, Embassy in Belgrade 1979–83, Head of the American Desk, Ministry of Foreign Affairs 1983–87, Minister-Counsellor, then Minister, Embassy in Bonn 1987–88, Minister Plenipotentiary 1988, Amb. to USSR 1988 (also accred to Mongolia) 1989–93, to UK (also accred to Iceland) 1993–96, Dir Dept of Eastern and Western Europe and Deputy Dir Gen. for Political Affairs, Ministry of Foreign Affairs 1996–97, Dir for Political Affairs 1997–99, Perm. Rep. to UN, New York 1999–2002; Chair. Cttee for the Environment and Sustainable Devt, Ministry of Foreign Affairs 2002–04; mem. Bd of Dirs OTE SA (Hellenic Telecommunications Org.), M.I. Maillis, Packaging Materials; Hon. Amb.; decorations from Austria, Finland, Germany, Greece, Italy, Spain, Ukraine and Russian Orthodox Church. *Address:* Akadimias Street 1, 106 71 Athens, Greece.

GOURDAULT-MONTAGNE, Maurice, BA, MA; French diplomatist; *Ambassador to Germany;* b. 16 Nov. 1953, Paris; ed Institut d'Etudes Politiques, Paris, Univ. of Paris Sorbonne IV, Univ. Paris-Assas, Institut Nat. des Langues et Civilisations Orientales (INALCO); joined Ministry of Foreign Affairs 1978, Desk Officer for Indian Affairs, Asia and Oceania Directorate 1979–81, First Sec., Embassy in New Delhi 1981–83, Special Adviser to Sec.-Gen., Ministry of Foreign Affairs 1984–86, Counsellor (Parl. and press) in pvt. office of Foreign Minister Jean-Bernard Raymond 1986–88, Counsellor (Political Affairs, Bilateral Relations), Embassy in Bonn 1988–91, Deputy Head of Press, Information and Communication Dept 1991–92, Deputy, then interim Spokesman, Ministry of Foreign Affairs 1992–93, Deputy Prin. Pvt. Sec. to Foreign Minister Alain Juppé 1993–95, Prin. Pvt. Sec. to Prime Minister Alain Juppé 1995–97, Personal Rep. of Pres. of France 1997–98, Amb. to Japan 1998–2002, Sr Diplomatic Counsellor to Pres. Chirac and G8 Sherpa 2002–07, Amb. to UK 2007–11, to Germany 2011–; Hon. LVO 1992, Hon. CMG 2004; Chevalier, Ordre nat. du Mérite 1998, Légion d'honneur 2001. *Address:* Embassy of France, Pariser Platz 5, 10117 Berlin, Germany (office). *Telephone:* (30) 590039000 (office). *Fax:* (30) 590039110 (office). *E-mail:* kanzlei@botschaft-frankreich.de (office). *Website:* www.ambafrance-de.org (office); www.botschaft-frankreich.de (office).

GOURGEON, Pierre-Henri, BSc, BEng, MSc; French airline executive and fmr civil servant; b. 28 April 1946; ed Ecole de Salon de Provence et de Tours, Ecole Polytechnique, Ecole Nationale Supérieure de l'Aéronautique, California Inst. of Tech., USA; held various positions in French Govt and French state-owned enterprises –1990; Dir Gen. French Civil Aviation Authority 1990–93; CEO Servair and several of its subsidiaries 1993–96; Exec. Man. Dir Air France SA 1993–97, Exec. Vice-Pres., Devt and Int. Affairs 1997–2008, Deputy CEO Air France-KLM 2004–08, Deputy COO 1998–2004, CEO Air France-KLM and Air France (subsidiary) 2009–13; Chair. and CEO Amadeus France/Estrel 1996–97; mem. Bd of Dirs and Vice-Chair. Amadeus Technology Group SA (fmrly Amadeus Global Travel Distribution SA) 1996, later Chair.; mem. Bd of Dirs Stria, Autoroutes Du Sud de La France 2002–, Soderi SAS Steria SA; mem. Bd of Dirs and Supervisory Bd, Man. and Gen. Partner, Groupe Steria SCA 2000–. *Address:* c/o Groupe Air France, 45 rue de Paris, 95747 Roissy CDG Cedex, France.

GOURISSE, Daniel, DèsSc; French administrator and professor of chemical engineering; *President, Centrale Histoire;* b. 13 March 1939, Charleville; s. of Robert Gourisse and Marie-Marguerite Lalle; m. Michèle Maës 1961; three s.; ed Ecole Centrale Paris; Laboratory Head, Commissariat à l'Energie Atomique (Atomic Energy Comm.) 1964–73, Tech. adviser to the Gen. Admin. 1973–76, Head, Chem. Eng Dept 1976–84, Prof. of Chem. Eng, Ecole Centrale des Arts et Manufactures, Paris 1969–78, Dir Ecole Centrale 1978–2003, Hon. Dir 2003–; Pres. Conf. des Grandes Ecoles 1985–93 (now Hon. Pres.), Office de robotique et de productique du Commissariat à l'énergie atomique 1985–89; Scientific Adviser to Dir du Cycle du Combustible 1990–2003; founder Pres. European Univ. Asscn TIME 1998–2001, Hon. Pres. 2001–; Pres. Centrale Histoire; Dr hc (Bauman Inst., Tech. Univ., Moscow); Officier, Légion d'honneur, Ordre nat. du Mérite; Commdr des Palmes académiques. *Publications:* Central Paris, The Great Turning 1968–2003 (co-author); many articles in int. journals. *Leisure interests:* history, music. *Address:* Association des Centraliens, 8 rue Jean Goujon, 75008 Paris (office); 12 avenue de la Cure d'Air, 91400 Orsay, France. *Telephone:* 1-56-43-68-00 (office); 6-07-31-82-52 (mobile) (office). *Fax:* 1-49-53-08-21 (office). *E-mail:* daniel.gourisse@centraliens.net (office). *Website:* centrale-histoire.centraliens.net (office).

GOUTARD, Noël; French business executive; *President, NG Investments;* b. 22 Dec. 1931, Casablanca, Morocco; s. of F. Antoine Goutard and M. Edmée Goutard (née Lespinasse); m. Dominique Jung 1964; one s. one d.; ed Lycée Louis le Grand, Paris, Univ. of Bordeaux and Pace Coll., New York; Vice-Pres. Frenville Co., New York 1954–60; Finance Exec., Warner Lambert Int., Morris Plains, NJ 1960–62; African Area Man. Pfizer Inc., New York 1962–66; Exec. Vice-Pres. Gevelot SA

Paris 1966–71; Pres. and COO Compteurs Schlumberger SA, Paris 1971–76; Exec. Vice-Pres. and mem. Bd of Dirs Chargeurs SA, Paris 1976–83; Exec. Vice-Pres. and COO Thomson SA, Paris 1983–84, Dir.-Gen. 1983–86; Pres.-Dir Gen. Valéo SA 1987–2000, Hon. Pres. 2000–01; Pnr, LBO France 2000–05; Pres. NG Investments 2000–; mem. Supervisory Bd Riber SA; fmr mem. Bd of Dirs Thomson CSF, Banque Thomson, Thomson-Brandt Armements, Imétal, Alcatel-Alsthom 1997–2001; Officier, Légion d'honneur. *Publications:* L'outsider, The Outsider Chronicles of a Patron Outside the Norm 2005. *Leisure interests:* tennis, travel, golf. *Address:* NG Investments, 90 avenue des Champs-Elysées, 75008 Paris, France (office). *E-mail:* ng.investments@wanado.fr (office).

GOUVEIA, Maria Teresa Pinto Basto; Portuguese politician; *Executive Director and Member, Board of Trustees, Fundação Calouste Gulbenkian;* b. 18 July 1946, Lisbon; d. of Afonso Patrício Gouveia and Maria Madalena d'Orey Ferreira Pinto Basto; m. Alexandre Manuel Vahia de Castro O'Neill de Bulhões (died 1986); one s.; ed Univ. of Lisbon; Sec. of State for Culture 1985–1990; elected mem. Parl. 1987, 1991, 1995, 2002; Sec. of State for Environment 1991–93, Minister for Environment 1993–95; mem. Bd of Govs and Exec. Cttee, European Cultural Foundation, Amsterdam 1996–2002; Vice-Pres. Foreign Affairs Parl. Cttee 2002–03; Minister of Foreign Affairs and Portuguese Communities Abroad 2003–04; fmr Pres. Cttee for Cultural Cooperation, Council of Europe, Strasbourg; mem. Gen. Council O Público newspaper 1990–91; Pres. Bd of Trustees Serralves Foundation, Oporto 2001–03; Exec. Dir and mem. Bd of Trustees Calouste Gulbenkian Foundation 2004–; Great Cross, Ordem de Cristo, Great Cross, Ordem Infante D. Henrique. *Address:* c/o Board of Trustees, Fundação Calouste Gulbenkian, Avenida da Berna, 45A, 1067-001 Lisbon, Portugal (office). *Telephone:* (217) 823306 (office). *Fax:* (217) 823088 (office). *E-mail:* tpgouveia@gulbenkian.pt (office). *Website:* www.gulbenkian.pt (office).

GOUYOU BEAUCHAMPS, Xavier; French television industry executive; *President, Citizenside;* b. 25 April 1937, Paris; s. of Charles Gouyou Beauchamps and Anne-Marie Coulombeix; m. 2nd Geneviève Decugis 1986; two s. (from previous marriage); ed Ecole St Joseph, Sarlat, Inst. d'études politiques and Ecole nat. d'admin; Dir of Staff Loiret Pref. 1964–66; Asst Head of Staff, Minister of Agric. 1966–68, Minister of Educ. 1968–69; Official Staff Rep., Minister of Econ. and Finance 1969–74; Press Sec. to the Pres. 1974–76; Prefect of Ardèche 1976–77; Pres. and Dir-Gen. SOFIRAD 1977–81; Pres. Télédiffusion de France 1986–92, Pres. Asscn des organismes français de radiodiffusion et de télévision (OFRT) 1990–92; Pres. French broadcasters' group (GRF) of European Union of Radio and TV (UER) 1990, Vice-Pres. UER 1990; Pres. Admin. Council Nat. Park of Port Cros, Sofipost 1992–94; Dir-Gen. France 3 1994–96, Chair. Bd of Dirs. 1998; Pres., Dir-Gen. France 2 and France 3 cos. 1996–99; Founder and Man. XGB Conseil 1999–; Co-founder IAM; Founder, Pres. and Dir-Gen. Antalis-TV 2001–06; Pres. Asscn des employeurs du service public de l'audiovisuel 1998; Pres. Citizenside 2007–; Pres. Cap24 –2010; Chevalier, Légion d'honneur, Officier, Ordre nat. du Mérite, Chevalier du Mérite agricole, Croix de la Valeur militaire. *Publication:* Le ministère de l'économie et des Finances, un Etat dans l'Etat? 1976. *Address:* 73 avenue Franklin D. Roosevelt, 75008 Paris, France (home). *Website:* www .citizenside.com (office).

GOVAN, Michael, BA; American museum curator; *Director and CEO, Los Angeles County Museum of Art;* b. 1963, Washington, DC; m. Katherine Ross; ed Williams Coll., Mass, Univ. of San Diego, studied Renaissance art in Italy; Acting Curator and Special Asst, Williams Coll. Museum of Art, organized Picasso and Rembrandt in 1986; Deputy Dir Solomon R. Guggenheim Museum, New York, Venice, Italy, Bilbao, Spain 1986–94; Pres. and Dir Dia Art Foundation, New York 1994–2006; Co-curator touring exhbn 'Dan Flavin: A Retrospective' organized by Dia Art Foundation in asscn with Nat. Gallery of Art, Washington, DC, which opened at Hayward Gallery, London, UK 2006; Wallis Annenberg Dir and CEO Los Angeles Co. Museum of Art 2006–; mem. Advisory Bd Eli and Edythe Broad Art Museum, Michigan State Univ. *Publication:* The Great Utopia: The Russian and Soviet Avant-Garde, 1915–1932. *Address:* Los Angeles County Museum of Art, 5905 Wilshire Blvd, Los Angeles, CA 90036, USA (office). *Telephone:* (323) 857-6000 (office). *Fax:* (323) 857-0098 (office). *E-mail:* publicinfo@lacma.org (office). *Website:* www.lacma.org (office).

GOVE, Ernesto Gouveia, MEconSc; Mozambican economist and central banker; *Governor, Banco de Moçambique;* b. 1957; m.; four c.; ed Eduardo Mondlane Univ., Maputo, Univ. of London, IMF and World Bank Insts, Swiss Central Bank Inst., Berne; joined Banco de Moçambique (central bank) 1976, various managerial positions in Foreign, Issuing and Treasury and Credit Depts and Documentation Centre, including Dir for Foreign Currency, Issuing and Treasury Operations –1991, Exec. Dir and mem. Bd 1991–, Deputy Gov. 1995–2006, Gov. 2006–; Lecturer, Eduardo Mondlane Univ. 1990–94; Alt. Gov. Islamic Devt Bank; fmr Chair. Bd of Dirs Sociedade de Noticias; fmr Chair. Fiscal Cttee Açucareira de Mafambisse (Mafambisse Sugar Co.). *Address:* Office of the Governor, Banco de Moçambique, Av. 25 de Setembro 1695, CP 423, Maputo, Mozambique (office). *Telephone:* 21354600 (office). *Fax:* 21323247 (office). *E-mail:* gpi@bancomoc.mz (office). *Website:* www.bancomoc.mz (office).

GOVE, Rt Hon. Michael Andrew, PC; British journalist, author and politician; *Secretary of State for Education;* b. 26 Aug. 1967, Edinburgh, Scotland; adopted; m. Sarah Vine; one s. one d.; ed state school educated in Aberdeen, Robert Gordon's Coll. (scholarship), Lady Margaret Hall, Oxford; fmr Pres. Oxford Union; following graduation worked as journalist for local and nat. newspapers, radio and TV; joined The Times as a leader writer 1996, has been its Comment Ed., News Ed., Saturday Ed. and Asst Ed., has also written a weekly column on politics and current affairs for The Times and contributed to the Times Literary Supplement, Prospect magazine and The Spectator; fmr Chair. Policy Exchange (think-tank); MP for Surrey Heath 2005–; Shadow Minister for Housing 2005–07; Shadow Sec. of State for Children, Schools and Families 2007–10; Sec. of State for Educ. 2010–; mem. (Select Cttees), European Scrutiny 2005–07; mem. Educ., Youth, Culture and Sport Council, Council of the EU 2010–; Conservative. *Film:* played the school chaplain in the family comedy A Feast at Midnight 1995. *Radio:* fmr regular panellist on BBC Radio 4's The Moral Maze. *Television:* has worked for BBC Today programme, On The Record, Scottish Television and Channel 4 monologue programme A Stab In The Dark; fmr regular panellist on Newsnight Review (BBC 2). *Publications include:* Michael Portillo: The Future of the Right 1995, The Price

of Peace 2000, A Blue Tomorrow – New Visions for Modern Conservatives (co-ed. with Edward Vaizey and Nicholas Boles) 2001, Celsius 7/7 2006. *Address:* Department for Education, Sanctuary Buildings, Great Smith Street, London, SW1P 3BT (office); House of Commons, Westminster, London, SW1A 0AA; Constituency Office, Curzon House, Church Road, Windlesham, Surrey, GU20 6BH, England. *Telephone:* (20) 7925-7510 (Dept) (office); (20) 7219-6804 (Westminster); (1276) 472468 (Windlesham). *Fax:* (20) 7925-6995 (Dept) (office); (20) 7219-4829 (Westminster); (1276) 451602 (Windlesham). *E-mail:* michael.gove@education.gsi.gov.uk (office), michael.gove.mp@parliament.uk; office@shca.org.uk. *Website:* www.education.gov.uk (office); www.parliament.uk/biographies/commons/michael-gove/35482; www.michaelgove.com.

GOVORUKHIN, Stanislav Sergeyevich; Russian politician, film director and actor; b. 29 March 1936, Berezniki, Sverdlovsk Region; m.; one s.; ed All-Union Inst. of Cinematography; with Odessa Film Studio 1967–89; Mosfilm Studio 1989–; active participant opposition movt since early 1990s; mem. State Duma (Homeland faction) 1993–, mem. Cttee on Security 1994–95, Chair. Cttee on Culture 1996–99; one of leaders of Democratic Party of Russia, Chair. Deputies of Democratic Party of Russia in State Duma 1995; Leader Bloc of Stanislav Govorukhin in elections to Duma 1995; presidential cand. 2000; elected Deputy to State Duma in by-elections 2005–. *Films include:* Vertical 1967, The Day of the Angel 1969, White Explosion 1970, The Life and Wonderful Adventures of Robinson Crusoe 1973, Smuggle 1975, A Wind of Hope 1978, The Place of Meeting Cannot Be Changed (TV) 1979, Adventures of Tom Sawyer 1981, In Search of Captain Grant, Drops of Champagne; Act in Assa, On First Breath; documentaries: It Is Impossible To Live So 1990 (Nica Prize), The Russia We Have Lost 1992, Aleksander Solzhenitsyn 1992, Great Criminal Revolution 1994, The Voroshilov Shooter 1998, Bless the Woman 2003, Not By Bread Alone 2005. *Publications:* Pirates of the 20th Century, Secrets of Madame Vong, Great Criminal Revolution; articles in periodicals. *Address:* State Duma, Okhotny Ryad 1, 103265 Moscow, Russia (office). *Telephone:* (495) 292-83-10 (office). *Fax:* (495) 292-94-64 (office). *E-mail:* govorukhin@duma.ru (home). *Website:* www.duma.ru (office); www.govoruhin.ru.

GOVORUN, Oleg Markovich; Russian government official; *Presidential Envoy to the Central Federal Okrug;* b. 15 Jan. 1969, Bratsk, Irkutsk region; m.; three s. one d.; ed Moscow State Forest Univ.; served in mil. 1987–89; Man.'s Asst, then Project Man., then specialist in GR Dept., Rosprom 1995–97; Vice-Pres. Alfa Bank 1997–2000; First Deputy Chief of Presidential Main Territorial Directorate 2000–04, Deputy Chief, Presidential Domestic Policy Directorate 2004–06, Chief 2006–11; Presidential Envoy to Cen. Federal Okrug 2011–; Deputy Chair. Presidential Council on Cossack Affairs 2009; mem. Council of Trustees, Moscow State Forest Univ. 2010; Order for Services to the Fatherland, IV degree, Medal of the Order for Services to the Fatherland, II degree. *Address:* Office of the Presidential Representative to the Central Federal Okrug, 103102 Moscow, Nikolskii per. 6, Russia (office). *Telephone:* (495) 206-12-76 (office). *E-mail:* malakhov_dm@gov.ru (office).

GOWAN, David John, CMG, MA; British fmr diplomatist; b. 11 Feb. 1949, Oxford, England; s. of Ivor Lyn Gowan and Gwendoline Alice Gowan (née Pearce); m. Marna Gowan; two s.; ed Nottingham High School, Ardwyn Grammar School, Balliol Coll., Oxford; Home Civil Service, Ministry of Defence and NI Office 1970–75; joined FCO 1975, Desk Officer, Near East and N Africa Dept 1975–76, full-time language training 1976–77, Second, later First Sec. (Commercial, later Chancery), Moscow 1977–88, Desk Officer, S Asian Dept, FCO 1981–82, Desk Officer, Soviet Dept 1982–84, Consul and Head of Chancery, Brasilia 1985–88, on loan to Cabinet Office 1988–89, Asst Head of Soviet Dept, FCO 1989–90, on loan to Cabinet Office (Counsellor) 1990–91, Counsellor (Commercial and Know How Fund), Moscow 1992–95, Counsellor and Deputy Head of Mission, Helsinki 1995–99, UK War Crimes Co-ordinator, FCO 1999, Minister and Deputy Head of Mission, Moscow 2000–03, Amb. to Serbia and Montenegro 2003–06 (retd); Sr Assoc. mem. St Antony's Coll., Oxford 1999–2000; mem. Bishop's Council and Synod of Diocese in Europe 2007–, Advisory Cttee Centre for East European Language–Based Area Studies 2007–, Council of Keston Inst. 2009; Chair. Russian Booker Cttee 2012–; Hon. Sr Research Fellow, Univ. of Birmingham 2008–10. *Publications:* pamphlets and articles on Russia, Serbia and Kosovo. *Leisure interests:* reading, walking, travel, theatre, music. *Address:* 8 Blackmore Road, Malvern, Worcs., WR14 1QX, England. *Telephone:* (1684) 565707. *E-mail:* david .gowan@btinternet.com.

GOWAN, James, FRCA, ARIBA; British architect; b. 18 Oct. 1925, Glasgow; s. of James Gowan and Isabella G. MacKenzie; m. Marguerite A. Barry 1947; two d.; ed Hyndland School, Glasgow, Glasgow School of Art and Kingston School of Art; pvt. practice 1956–, in partnership with James Stirling 1956–63, design of new hosp., Milan 1991, Techint Int. co. HQ offices, Milan 1999; tutor, Architectural Asscn, London 1958–60, 1970–72; Visiting Prof., Princeton Univ., USA 1965, Simón Bolívar Univ., Venezuela 1982, Heriot Watt Univ., Edin. 1990; Banister Fletcher Prof., Univ. Coll. London 1975; Sr Tutor, RCA 1983–86; exhbn of drawings at RIBA Heinz Gallery 1994, at Scottish Nat. Gallery of Modern Art 1994; other projects include hosp. buildings in Italy at Bergamo 2003, Milan 2005, Rossano 2009; master plan for expansion of Rossano 2010; Hon. Dr of Design (Kingston Univ.) 1996; Reynolds Memorial Award (with James Stirling) 1965. *Publications:* Projects: Architectural Association 1946–71, 1972, A Continuing Experiment 1975, James Gowan (monograph) 1978, Style and Configuration 1994, Modernity and Reinvention: The Architecture of James Gowan (by Ellis Woodman) 2008, Studies in British Art #21: Neo-Avant-Garde and Postmodern: Post-War Architecture in Britain and Beyond (ed by Mark Crinson and Claire Zimmerman) 2010; as subject: Stirling and Gowan: Architecture from Austerity to Affluence (Paul Mellon Centre for Studies in British Art) by Mark Crinson 2012. *Leisure interests:* drawing, reading. *Address:* 2 Linden Gardens, London, W2 4ES, England. *Telephone:* (20) 7229-0642. *Fax:* (20) 7792-9771.

GOWANS, Sir James Learmonth, Kt, CBE, MB, DPhil, FRS, FRCP, FRSA; British medical scientist and fmr administrator; b. 7 May 1924, Sheffield, Yorks., England; s. of John Gowans and Selma Josefina Ljung; m. Moyra Leatham 1956; one s. two d.; ed Trinity School, Croydon, King's Coll. Hosp. Medical School, Univ. of Oxford; Fellow, St Catherine's Coll., Oxford 1961–; Sec.-Gen. Human Frontiers Science Programme, Strasbourg 1989–93; Consultant, WHO Global Programme on AIDS 1987–88; Henry Dale Research Prof. of Royal Soc. 1962–77; Dir MRC

Cellular Immunology Unit 1963–77, mem. MRC 1965–69, Sec. (Chief Exec.) 1977–87, Chair. MRC Biological Research Bd 1967–69; mem. Advisory Bd for the Research Councils 1977–87; mem. Council and Vice-Pres. Royal Soc. 1973–75; Dir Celltech PLC 1980–87; Chair. European Medical Research Councils 1985–87; mem. Academia Europaea 1991; Foreign Assoc. NAS (USA); Hon. ScD (Yale) 1966, Hon. DSc (Chicago) 1971, (Birmingham) 1978, (Rochester, New York) 1987, Hon. MD (Edinburgh) 1979, (Sheffield) 2000, Hon. LLD (Glasgow) 1988, Hon. DM (Southampton) 1987; Gairdner Award, Ehrlich Prize, Feldberg Award, Royal Medal of Royal Soc., Wolf Foundation Prize in Medicine 1980, Medawar Prize, Galen Medal. *Publications include:* articles in scientific journals. *Leisure interest:* old books. *Address:* 75 Cumnor Hill, Oxford, OX2 9HX, England. *Telephone:* (1865) 862304. *E-mail:* jamesgowans@btinternet.com.

GOWARIKER, Ashutosh, BSc; Indian actor, film director, film producer and scriptwriter; *Founding Director, Ashutosh Gowariker Productions Pvt. Ltd;* b. 15 Feb. 1964, Mumbai; s. of Kishori Gowariker and Ashok Gowariker; m. Sunita Gowariker 1988; two s. ed Mithibai Coll., Mumbai; began career as model for commercials by Govind Mihalani and Jenny Pinto for Lifebuoy soap and Close-Up toothpaste; film acting debut in Holi 1984; directed first film Pehla Nasha 1993; directed five commercials for Coca-Cola 2001; Founding Dir Ashutosh Gowariker Productions Pvt. Ltd; mem. Acad. of Motion Picture Arts and Sciences 2004; Filmfare Award 2001, 2008, IIFA Award 2001, 2008. *Film appearances include:* Naam 1986, West Is West 1987, Salim Langde Pe Mat Ro 1989, Goonj 1989, Gawahi 1989, Indrajeet 1991, Jaanam 1992, Chamatkar 1992, Kabhi Haan Kabhi Naa 1993, Vazir 1994, Sarkarnama 1998. *Films directed include:* Pehla Nasha 1993, Baazi 1995, Lagaan: Once Upon a Time in India 2001, Swades 2004, Jodhaa Akbar 2007, What's Your Rashee 2009. *Television includes:* Kachchi Dhoop 1987, Circus 1990, Woh 1998, CID 1999. *Address:* Ashutosh Gowariker Productions Pvt. Ltd, 201, Kum Kum, 16th Road, Bandra, Mumbai 400 050, Maharashtra, India (office). *Telephone:* (22) 26044236 (office); (22) 26004687 (home). *Fax:* (22) 26487164 (office). *E-mail:* info@agppl.com; ashgow@hotmail.com (home). *Website:* www.agppl.com; www.ashutoshgowariker.com.

GOWDA, D(everagunda) V(enkatappa) Sadananda, BSc, LLB; Indian lawyer and politician; b. 18 March 1953, Dakshina Kannada, Karnataka; s. of Venkappa Gowda and Kamala Gowda; m. Datty Sadananda; one s.; ed St Philomena Coll., Putur, Udupi Vaikunta Baliga Coll. of Law; began practising law in Sullia and Puttur 1976; Pres. Karnataka Industries Staff Union 1977–82; Asst Public Prosecutor 1979–82; State Sec. Bharatiya Janata Party (BJP) Yuva Morcha, Karnataka 1983–88; mem. Staff Selection Cttee, State LD Bank 1989–90; Dir CAMPCO, Mangalore, Karnataka 1991–94; mem. Karnataka Legis. Ass. 1994–2004, Deputy Leader of Opposition 1999–2004, mem. Cttee for Energy, Fuel and Power 2001–02, mem. Public Undertaking Cttee 2002–03, Pres. Public Accounts Cttee 2003–04; State Sec., BJP Karnataka 2003–04, State Pres. 2006–; elected to 14th Lok Sabha 2004–06, to 15th Lok Sabha 2009–, mem. Cttee on Commerce, Sub-cttee Dept Related Parl. Standing Cttee on Commerce for Special Econ. Zones, House Cttee, Cttee on Science and Technology, Environment and Forests 2009; Chief Minister of Karnataka 2011–12. *Address:* Anugraha, K K Annex, Kumarakrupa Road, Bangalore 560 001, India (home). *Telephone:* (80) 22200635 (home). *E-mail:* sadanandagowda@yahoo.com. *Website:* www.sadanandagowda.com.

GOWER, David Ivon, OBE; British journalist, broadcaster and fmr professional cricketer; *Presenter, International Cricket, BSkyB;* b. 1 April 1957, Tunbridge Wells, Kent, England; s. of Richard Hallam Gower and Sylvia Mary Gower (née Ford); m. Thorunn Ruth Nash 1992; two d.; ed King's School, Canterbury and Univ. Coll., London; left-hand batsman; played for Leicestershire 1975–89 (Capt. 1984–86), Hampshire 1990–93; played in 117 Tests for England 1978–92, 32 as Capt., scoring then England record 8,231 runs (average 44.25, highest score 215) with 18 hundreds; toured Australia 1978–79, 1979–80, 1982–83, 1986–87, 1990–91; scored 26,339 First-class runs (average 40.08, highest score 228) with 53 hundreds; played in 114 One-Day Ints, scoring 3,170 runs (average 30.77, highest score 158); Sunday Express Cricket Corresp. 1993–95; Public Relations Consultant for cricket sponsorship, NatWest Bank 1993–2000; columnist, Sunday Telegraph 1995–98, The Sun 2000–02, Sunday Times 2002–; commentator, Sky TV cricket 1993–, presenter, Int. Cricket, BSkyB 1999–; commentator and presenter, BBC TV 1994–99; Trustee, David Shepherd Conservation Foundation; Hon. MA (Southampton Inst., Nottingham Trent Univ., Univ. of Loughborough); Hon. Blue (Herriott Watt Univ., Edinburgh); Wisden Cricketer of the Year 1979, Int. Cricketer of the Year 1982/83. *Television:* Team Capt., They Think It's All Over 1995–2003. *Publications:* With Time to Spare 1979, Heroes and Contemporaries 1983, A Right Ambition 1986, On the Rack 1990, The Autobiography 1992. *Leisure interests:* Cresta run, skiing, tennis, photography, wildlife conservation. *Address:* c/o Diana van Bunnens, Jon Holmes Media Ltd, 3 Wine Office Court, London, EC4A 3BY, England (office). *Telephone:* (1582) 469233 (office). *E-mail:* diana@jonholmesmedia.com (office). *Website:* www.jonholmesmedia.com (office).

GOWERS, Andrew, MA; British journalist, communications executive and consultant; *Global Head of Corporate Affairs, Trafigura;* b. 19 Oct. 1957, Reading, Berks.; s. of Michael Gowers and Anne Gowers; m. Finola Gowers (née Clarke); one s. one d.; ed Trinity School, Croydon and Univ. of Cambridge; grad. trainee, Reuters 1980, Brussels Corresp. 1981, Zurich Corresp. 1982, joined Foreign Desk, Financial Times (FT), London 1983, Agric. Corresp. 1984, Commodities Ed. 1985, Middle East Ed. 1987, Foreign Ed. 1992, Deputy Ed. 1994, Acting Ed. 1997, Ed. FT Deutschland (German Language Business Paper) 1999, Ed. FT 2001–05; columnist, Evening Standard, Sunday Times 2005–06; Leader Gowers' Review of Intellectual Property for UK Government 2005–06; Head of Corp. Communications (Europe and Asia), Lehman Brothers 2006–07, Global Co-head of Corp. Communications, Marketing and Brand Man. 2007–08; Interim Head of External Relations, London Business School 2008–09, Head of Group Media, BP PLC 2009–10; Dir of External Relations, Asscn for Financial Markets in Europe 2011–12; Head of Corp. Affairs, Trafigura 2013–. *Publications:* Arafat, The Biography (co-author) 1991, The Gowers Review of Intellectual Property 2006, Investing in Change (commissioning ed.) 2012. *Leisure interests:* film, opera, music, theatre, gastronomy, tennis. *Address:* 4 Holmdene Avenue, London, SE24 9LF, England (home). *Telephone:* (20) 7733-4125 (home). *E-mail:* andrewgowers@btinternet.com (office).

GOWERS, Sir (William) Timothy, Kt, PhD, FRS; British mathematician and academic; *Royal Society 2010 Anniversary Research Professor, Department of Pure Mathematics and Mathematical Statistics, University of Cambridge;* b. 20 Nov. 1963, Marlborough, Wilts., England; s. of (William) Patrick Gowers and Caroline (Molesworth) Maurice; m. 1st Emily Joanna Thomas 1988 (divorced 2007); two s. one d.; m. 2nd Julie Barrau 2008; one s.; ed Eton Coll., Trinity Coll., Cambridge; Lecturer, Univ. Coll. London 1991–94, Reader 1994–95; Fellow, Trinity Coll., Cambridge 1989–93, Lecturer Univ. of Cambridge 1995–98, Rouse Ball Prof. of Math. 1998–2010, Royal Soc. 2010 Anniversary Research Prof. 2010–; Hon. Fellow, Univ. Coll. London 1999; Jr Whitehead Prize, London Mathematical Soc. 1995, European Mathematical Soc. Prize 1996, Fields Medal 1998. *Publications include:* Mathematics: A Very Short Introduction 2002, The Princeton Companion to Mathematics (ed.) 2008; mathematical papers in various journals. *Leisure interest:* playing jazz piano. *Address:* Department of Pure Mathematics and Mathematical Statistics, Room C2.04, Centre for Mathematical Sciences, Wilberforce Road, Cambridge, CB3 0WB, England (office). *Telephone:* (1223) 337973 (office). *Fax:* (1223) 337920 (office). *E-mail:* W.T.Gowers@dpmms.cam.ac.uk (office). *Website:* www.dpmms.cam.ac.uk/~wtg10 (office); gowers.wordpress.com.

GOWON, Gen. Yakubu, PhD; Nigerian army officer, organization official and fmr head of state; *President and Chairman, Board of Trustees, Yakubu Gowon Center for National Unity and International Co-operation;* b. 19 Oct. 1934, Garam, Pankshin Div., Plateau State; s. of Yohanna and Saraya Gowon; m. Victoria Hansatu Zakari 1969; one s. two d.; ed St Bartholomew's School, Wusasa, Zaria, Govt Coll., Barewa, Zaria, Royal Mil. Acad., Sandhurst, Staff Coll., Camberley and Jt Services Staff Coll., Latimer, UK; Adjutant, Nigerian Army 1960; with UN Peacekeeping Force, Congo 1960–61, Jan.–June 1963; promoted Lt-Col and apptd Adjutant-Gen. Nigerian Army 1963; Chief of Staff 1966; Maj.-Gen. 1967; promoted Gen. 1971; Head of Fed. Mil. Govt and C-in-C of Armed Forces of Fed. Repub. of Nigeria 1966–75 (deposed in coup); studying at Univ. of Warwick, UK 1975–83, postgraduate 1978–82; Chair. Ass. of Heads of State, OAU 1973–74; Chair. Nigerian Nat. Oil and Chemical Marketing Co. 1996; founder, Pres., Chair. Bd of Trustees Yadubu Gowon Center for Nat. Unity and Int. Co-operation; Chair. Nigeria Prays; Assoc. Research Prof., Centre for Devt Studies, Univ. of Jos; fmr Chair. Arewa Consultative Forum (ACF); Chair. Trustees, Commonwealth Human Ecology Foundation 1986; Chair. Bd of Dirs Industrial And Gen. Insurance Co. Ltd (IGI); Lifetime Achievement Award, THISDAY 2007. *Publication:* Faith in Unity 1970. *Leisure interests:* squash, tennis, photography, pen-drawings. *Address:* Yakubu Gowon Center for National Unity and International Co-operation, POB 3995, Garki, Abuja (office); c/o Board of Directors, IGI, Plot, 741 Adeola Hopewell Street, Victoria Island, Lagos, Nigeria. *Telephone:* (9) 3140613 (office). *E-mail:* ygc@inforweb.abs (office). *Website:* www.yakubugowoncentre.org (office).

GOWRIE, Rt Hon. Alexander Patrick Greysteil Hore-Ruthven (Grey), The Earl of Gowrie, PC, BA, AM, FRSL; British/Irish politician, business executive and writer; *Chairman, The Fine Art Fund;* b. (Alexander Hore-Ruthven), 26 Nov. 1939; s. of the late Hon. A. H. P. Hore-Ruthven and Pamela Margaret Fletcher; m. 1st Xandra Bingley 1962 (divorced 1973); one s.; m. 2nd Adelheid Gräfin von den Schulenburg 1974; ed Eton Coll., Balliol Coll., Oxford and Harvard Univ., USA; Fellow and Tutor, Lowell House, Harvard Univ. 1965–68; Asst Prof., Emerson Coll., Boston 1967–68; Lecturer in English and American Literature, Univ. Coll. London 1969–72; a UK del. to UN 1971; a Lord-in-Waiting to HM the Queen 1972–74; Govt Whip, House of Lords 1972–74; Consultant, Thomas Gibson Fine Art 1974–79; Opposition Spokesman on Econ. Affairs and Adviser to Margaret Thatcher 1977–79; Minister of State, Dept of Employment 1979–81; Minister of State, Privy Council Office and Minister for the Arts 1983–84; mem. of Cabinet as Chancellor of the Duchy of Lancaster (retaining portfolio as Minister for the Arts) 1984–85; Chair. The Really Useful Group 1985–90, Sotheby's Europe 1985–94, Arts Council 1994–98, Magdi Yacoub Inst., Fine Art Fund 2002–; Dir Sotheby's Holdings Inc. 1985–98; Provost RCA 1986–95; Chair. Devt Securities 1995–99, Dir (non-exec.) 2005–2001; Dir (non-exec.) NXT PLC, ITG PLC 1998–2002. *Publications:* A Postcard from Don Giovanni (poems) 1972, The Genius of British Painting: The Twentieth Century 1975, Derek Hill: An Appreciation 1987, The Domino Hymn: Poems from Harefield 2005, Third Day: New and Selected Poems 2008. *Leisure interests:* the arts. *Address:* The Magdi Yacoub Institute, Science Centre, Harefield, Middx, England (office). *Telephone:* (20) 7828-4777 (office).

GOYAL, Naresh, BCom; Indian airline executive; *Chairman, Jet Airways (India) Ltd;* b. 23 Dec. 1950, Patiala, Punjab; s. of Chowdhury Jagdish Rai; m. Anita Goyal 1988; one s. one d.; ed Bikram Coll. of Commerce, Patiala; began career as ticketing and reservations clerk, Lebanese Int. Airlines 1967, various man. positions 1967–74; f. Jetair (Private) Ltd May 1974, f. Jet Airways (India) Private Ltd 1991, Chair. 1991–, Chair. JetLite 2007–; Owner, Tailwinds Holding Co.; mem. Bd of Govs Int. Air Transport Asscn 2004–06, 2008–10; AIMO Visvesvaraya Entrepreneurship Award 1993, Bharat Sarathi Samman Award 1995, Priyadarshni Acad. Award 2000, Ernst & Young Entrepreneur of the Year for Services Award 2000, Distinguished Alumni Award 2000, Aerospace Laurels 2000, 2004, ITFT Chandigarh Award of Excellence 2001, Qimpro Gold Standard Award 2001, Outstanding Asian-Indian Award, American Centre for Political Awareness 2003, BML Munjal Award 2006, Travel Entrepreneur of the Year, Travel Trade Gazette Travel Awards 2007, Man of the Year Award, Aviation Press Club 2008, Business Person of the Year, UK Trade and Investment 2008, Int. Entrepreneurs of the Year, UK Sec. of State for Transport 2009. *Address:* Jet Airways (India) Private Ltd, SM Centre, Andheri-Kurla Road, Andheri East, Mumbai 400 059, India (office). *Telephone:* (22) 56986111 (office). *Fax:* (22) 28501313 (office). *Website:* www.jetairways.com (office).

GOYDER, Richard J. B., AO, BCom; Australian business executive; *CEO and Managing Director, Wesfarmers Limited;* ed Univ. of Western Australia, Advanced Man. Program at Harvard Business School, USA; held several positions with Tubemakers of Australia Ltd; joined Wesfarmers Ltd 1993, Gen. Man., Business Devt 1994–96, Finance Dir, Wesfarmers Landmark Ltd 1996–99, Man. Dir, Wesfarmers Dalgety Ltd (subsequently became Wesfarmers Landmark Ltd) 1999–2002, mem. Bd of Dirs, Wesfarmers Ltd 2002–, Finance Dir, Wesfarmers Ltd 2002–04, Deputy Man. Dir and Chief Financial Officer 2004–05, CEO and

Man. Dir 2005–, mem. Bd of Dirs Gresham Partners Holdings Ltd and several Wesfarmers group subsidiaries and related cos; mem. Bd of Dirs Fremantle Football Club Ltd, Business Council of Australia, Univ. of Western Australia Business School Advisory Bd; Chair. Scotch Coll. Council; Council mem. Australian Business Arts Foundation; Advisory Council mem. Juvenile Diabetes Research Foundation; Fellow, Australian Inst. of Co. Dirs. *Address:* Wesfarmers Ltd, 11th Floor, Wesfarmers House, 40 The Esplanade, Perth, WA 6000, Australia (office). *Telephone:* (8) 9327-4211 (office). *Fax:* (8) 9327-4216 (office). *E-mail:* info@wesfarmers.com.au (office). *Website:* www.wesfarmers.com.au (office).

GOYTISOLO, Juan; Spanish writer; b. 5 Jan. 1931, Barcelona; m. Monique Lange 1978 (died 1996); ed Univs of Barcelona and Madrid; emigrated to France 1957; reporter, Cuba 1965; assoc. with Gallimard Publishing Co.; Visiting Prof. at various univs in USA; Premio Europalia de la Comunidad Europea 1985, Premio Nelly-Sachs, Dortmund 1993, Premio Octavio Paz de Poesía y Ensayo, Mexico 2002, Premio Juan Rulfo 2004, Nat. Prize for Spanish Letters 2008, Prix Formento 2012. *Writing for television:* Alquibla (series). *Publications:* fiction: Juegos de manos (trans. as The Young Assassins) 1954, Duelo en el Paraíso (trans. as Children of Chaos) 1955, El circo (El mañana efímero trilogy vol. one) 1957, Fiestas (El mañana efímero trilogy vol. two) 1958, La resaca (El mañana efímero trilogy vol. three) 1958, La isla 1961, La chanca 1962, Señas de identidad (trans. as Marks of Identity) 1966, Reivindicación del conde don Julián (trans. as Count Julian) 1970, Juan sin tierra (trans. as John the Landless) 1975, Colera de Aquines 1979, Makbara 1980, Paisajes después de la batalla (trans. as Landscapes After the Battle) 1982, Las virtudes del pájaro solitario (trans. as The Virtues of the Solitary Bird) 1988, La cuarentena (trans. as Quarantine) 1991, La saga de los Marx (trans. as The Marx Family Saga) 1993, Campos de Níjar 1993, Las semanas del jardín (trans. as The Garden of Secrets) 1997, Carajicomedia (trans. as A Cock-Eyed Comedy) 2000, Telón de boca 2003, El exiliado de aquí y allá (trans. as Exiled from Almost Everywhere) 2008; non-fiction: Crónicas Sarracinas (essays, trans. as Saracen Chronicles) 1982, Coto vedado (autobiography, trans. as Forbidden Territory) 1985, En los reinos de Taifa (autobiography, trans. as Realms of Strife) 1986, Cuaderno de Sarajevo (Premio francés Méditerranée) 1994, Reconocimiento (Gran Premio Proartes de Narrativa Iberoamericana) 1997, Pájaro que ensucia su propio nido (essays) 2001, Cinema Eden: Essays from the Muslim Mediterranean 2004, El Lucernario: La pasión crítica de Manuel Azaña 2004, La saga de los Marx 2005, Contra las sagradas formas 2007, Ensayos escogidos 2008; short stories, travel narratives, literary criticism, essays. *Address:* c/o Eland Publishing Ltd, Third Floor, 61 Exmouth Market, London, EC1R 4QL, England. *E-mail:* jgoytiso@sauce.pntic.mec.es.

GOZON, Richard C., BS; American business executive; *Chairman, AmerisourceBergen Corporation;* b. 9 Oct. 1938, Pittsburgh, Pa; m. Fran Gozon (neé Burmeister); three c.; ed Valparaiso Univ., Harvard Univ.; began career in paper industry at Nationwide Papers 1970–72; joined Alco Standard Group as Pres. Rourke-Eno Paper Co. 1972–78, Exec. Vice-Pres. Unisource Corpn 1978–79, Pres. 1979, Pres. and CEO Paper Corpn of America 1979–87, elected mem. Bd of Dirs Alco Standard Group 1984, Exec. Vice-Pres. and COO 1987–88, Pres. and CEO 1988–93; Exec. Vice-Pres. for Pulp, Paper and Packaging, Weyerhaeuser Co. 1994–2002; mem. Bd of Dirs AmeriSource Health Corpn 1994–2001, AmerisourceBergen Corpn 2001–, Chair. 2006–; mem. Bd of Dirs UGI Corpn 1989–2011, AmeriGas Partners LP 1998–2011, Triumph Group, Inc.; mem. Bd of Trustees, Thomas Jefferson Univ., currently Interim Pres. *Address:* AmerisourceBergen Corporation, 1300 Morris Drive, Suite 100, Chesterbrook, PA 19087, USA (office). *Telephone:* (610) 727-7000 (office). *Fax:* (610) 727-3600 (office). *E-mail:* info@amerisourcebergen.com (office). *Website:* www.amerisourcebergen.com (office).

GRAB, Christoph, PhD; Swiss physicist; *Senior Scientist, Institute for Particle Physics, Eidgenössische Technische Hochschule (ETH), Zürich;* Research and Fellowships carried: Univ. of California at Berkeley, USA, Stanford Univ. (SLAC), USA, CERN, Geneva, Switzerland, DESY, Hamburg, Germany, Paul Scherrer Inst., Switzerland; currently Sr Scientist, Inst. for Particle Physics, ETH, Zürich, Switzerland; Swiss Rep., High Energy Physics Computing Coordinating Cttee; mem. Particle Data Group, CMS Experiment, CERN, H1 Experiment, DESY. *Publications:* numerous publs in scientific journals. *Address:* ETH Zürich, Institute for Particle Physics, Hönggerberg HPK/F26, 8093 Zürich, Switzerland (office). *Telephone:* (1) 6332022 (office). *Fax:* (1) 6331233 (office). *E-mail:* christoph.grab@phys.ethz.ch (office). *Website:* www.ipp.phys.ethz.ch (office).

GRABAR-KITAROVIĆ, Kolinda, MA; Croatian diplomatist and politician; *Assistant Secretary General for Public Diplomacy, NATO;* b. 29 April 1968, Rijeka; m. Jakov Kitarović; two c.; ed Los Alamos High School, NM, USA, Univ. of Zagreb, Diplomatic Acad., Vienna, Austria, George Washington Univ., USA; lived in USA for part of her childhood; Asst, then Adviser, Dept for Int. Co-operation, Ministry of Science and Tech. 1992–93; Adviser, then Sr Adviser to Deputy Minister, Ministry of Foreign Affairs 1993–95, Head of Dept for N America 1995–97; Diplomatic Counsellor, Embassy in Ottawa 1997–98, Minister Counsellor 1998–2000; Minister Counsellor, Ministry of Foreign Affairs 2001–03; mem. Parl. 2003–08; Minister for European Integration 2003–05; Nat. Aid Co-ordinator 2004; Head Del. for negotiations on accession to EU 2005; Minister of Foreign Affairs and European Integration 2005–08; Amb. to USA 2008–11; Asst Sec. Gen. for Public Diplomacy, NATO, Brussels 2011–; mem. Croatian Democratic Union (Hrvatska demokratska zajednica), Deputy Campaign Dir, Sec.-Gen. for European Integration, mem. Cen. Cttee, Nat. Council, Presidency; Presidential Medal, George Washington Univ. *Leisure interests:* literature, educ. and protection of children, hiking and walks in nature, film. *Address:* Public Diplomacy Division, NATO, 1110 Brussels, Belgium (office). *Telephone:* (2) 707-41-11 (switchboard) (office). *E-mail:* grabarkitarovic.kolinda@hq.nato.int (office). *Website:* www.nato.int (office).

GRABINER, Baron (Life Peer), cr. 1999, of Aldwych in the City of Westminster; **Anthony Stephen Grabiner,** QC, LLM; British barrister and college principal; b. 21 March 1945, London, England; s. of the late Ralph Grabiner and Freda Grabiner (née Cohen); m. Jane Aviva Portnoy 1983; three s. one d.; ed Cen. Foundation Boys' Grammar School, London School of Econs; called to the Bar (Lincoln's Inn) 1968; Droop Scholar, Lincoln's Inn 1968; Jr Counsel to Dept of Trade 1976–81; QC 1981; Bencher 1989–; Treas. of Lincoln's Inn 2013–; Deputy High Court Judge, Chancery and Queen's Bench Divs 1998–; Vice-Chair. Court of Govs LSE 1993–98, Chair. 1998–2007; Head of Chambers One Essex Court 1994–;

Leader, HM Treasury Inquiry into Black Economy 1999–2000; Chair. (non-exec.) Arcadia Group 2002–; mem. Bd of Dirs (non-exec.) Wentworth Club 2005–, Next PLC 2002; mem. (Labour), House of Lords 1999–; Master of Clare Coll., Cambridge 2014–; mem. Advisory Bd Best Lawyers; mem. Financial Services Law Cttee, Bank of England 2002–05; Hon. Fellow, LSE 2009. *Publications:* Sutton and Shannon on Contracts 1970, The Informal Economy 2000. *Leisure interests:* golf, theatre. *Address:* One Essex Court, Temple, London, EC4Y 9AR, England (office). *Telephone:* (20) 7583-2000 (office). *Fax:* (20) 7583-0118 (office). *E-mail:* agrabiner@oeclaw.co.uk (office). *Website:* www.oeclaw.co.uk (office); www.parliament.uk/biographies/lords/lord-grabiner/2496.

GRACH, Eduard Davidovich; Russian violinist; b. 19 Dec. 1930, Odessa; s. of David Grach and Evelina Grach; m. 2nd Valentina Vasilenko 1990; one s. one d.; ed P. Stolyarsky Odessa School of Music, Moscow State Conservatory (pupil of A. Yampolsky); winner of int. competitions in Budapest (First Prize) 1949, J. Thibaud in Paris 1955, P. Tchaikovsky in Moscow 1962; solo performances since 1953 in most countries of Europe; performer of classical and contemporary concertos and sonatas for violin; participant in trio with pianist Y. Malinin and cellist N. Shakhovskaya 1960–70; first performer of a number of works by Russian composers dedicated to him, including concertos by A. Eshpai; Head of Violin Dept, Moscow State Conservatory; Founder and Artistic Dir Moskovia Chamber Orchestra 1994–; People's Artist of USSR 1987, 1990. *Leisure interest:* football. *Address:* Moscow State Conservatory, Bolshaya Nikitskaya str. 13/6, 125009 Moscow (office); 1st Smolensky per. 9, kv. 98, 121099 Moscow, Russia (home). *Telephone:* (495) 629-76-26 (office); (495) 241-21-57 (home). *Fax:* (495) 629-73-18 (office); (495) 241-21-57 (home). *E-mail:* spravka@mosconsv.ru (office). *Website:* www.mosconsv.ru (office).

GRACIAS, HE Cardinal Oswald Anthony Agnelo, DCL, DiplJur; Indian ecclesiastic; *Archbishop of Bombay;* b. 24 Dec. 1944, Bombay (now Mumbai); s. of Jervis Gracias and Aduzinda Gracias; ed St Michael's School Mumbai, St Xavier's Coll. Mumbai, Pontifical Urbanian Univ., Rome, Gregorian Univ., Rome; ordained priest of Bombay 1970; Chancellor Diocese of Jamshedpur and Sec. to Diocesan Bishop 1970–75; Auxiliary Bishop of Bombay and Titular Bishop of Bladia 1997–2000; Archbishop of Agra 2000–06, of Bombay 2006–; cr. Cardinal (Cardinal-Priest of San Paulo della Croce a 'Corviale') 2007; participated in Papal Conclave 2013; Sec.-Gen. Catholic Bishops' Conf. of India (CBCI) 1998–2002, Vice-Pres. 2008–10, Pres. 2010–, Chair. CBCI Comm. for Social Communication 2002–, CBCI Comm. for Law and Public Litigation 2002–; Sec.-Gen. Feds of Bishops' Conf. of Asia; Chair. Nat. Inst. of Social Communications, Research and Training, New Delhi 2002–; Pres. Canon Law Soc. of India 1987–91 and 1993–97; Vice-Chair. Vatican's Vox Clara Cttee (advises Congregation for Divine Worship and Sacraments on trans. of Latin liturgical texts into English) 2001–, consultor to Pontifical Council for Interpretation of Legis. Texts 1992–97, currently mem.; currently Pres. Catholic Bishops' Conf. of India; teaches Canon Law at Pius X Seminary, Mumbai and St Peter's Pontifical Inst., Bangalore. *Publications include:* Conciliation Code. *Address:* Archbishop's House, 21 Nathalal Parekh Marg, Mumbai 400 001, India (office). *Telephone:* (22) 22021093 (office); (22) 22021193 (office). *Fax:* (22) 22853872 (office). *E-mail:* diocesebombay@gmail.com (office). *Website:* www.archdioceseofbombay.org (office).

GRADE OF YARMOUTH, Baron (Life Peer), cr. 2011, of Yarmouth in the County of Isle of Wight; **Rt Hon. Michael Ian Grade,** CBE, FRTS; British broadcasting executive; b. 8 March 1943, London, England; s. of the late Leslie Grade; m. 1st Penelope Jane Levinson 1967 (divorced 1981); one s. one d.; m. 2nd Hon. Sarah Lawson 1982 (divorced 1991); m. 3rd Francesca Mary Leahy 1998; one s.; ed Stowe House, Bucks., St Dunstan's Coll., London; trainee journalist, Daily Mirror 1960, sports columnist 1964–66; theatrical agent, Grade Org. 1966; Jt Man. Dir London Man. and Representation 1969–73; Deputy Controller of Programmes (Entertainment), London Weekend TV 1973–77, Dir of Programmes and mem. Bd 1977–81; Pres. Embassy TV 1981–84; Controller BBC One 1984–86, Dir of Programmes BBC TV 1986–87; CEO Channel 4 1988–97; Chair. VCI PLC 1995–98; Chair. and CEO First Leisure Corpn 1997–98 (Dir 1991–2000, Chair. (non-exec.) 1995–97); Chair. Ind. Inquiry into Fear of Crime 1989, Devt Council, Royal Nat. Theatre 1997–; Deputy Chair. Soc. of Stars 1995–; Pres. TV and Radio Industries Club 1987–88, Newspaper Press Fund 1988–89, Entertainment Charities Fund 1994–, Royal TV Soc. 1995–97; Vice-Pres. Children's Film Unit 1993–; mem. Bd of Dirs ITN 1989–93, Open Coll. 1989–97, Delfont Macintosh Theatres Ltd 1994–99, Charlton Athletic Football Club 1997–, Jewish Film Foundation 1997–, New Millennium Experience Co. 1997–99, Camelot Group 2000–04, Digitaloctopus 2000–; Chair. Octopus 2000–04, Pinewood Studio Ltd 2000–, Hemscott.NET 2000–06, BBC 2004–06; Exec. Chair. ITV 2006–09, Chair. (non-exec.) 2009; Chair. (non-exec.) Ocado Group Plc 2006–13; Chair. (non-exec.) James Grant Group Ltd 2010–; Dir (non-exec.) SMG 2003–06; mem. Council, London Acad. of Music and Dramatic Art 1981–93, BAFTA 1981–82, 1986–88, 2004– (Fellow 1994), Milton Cttee, British Screen Advisory Council 1986–97, Gate Theatre, Dublin 1990–2004, Int. Council Nat. Acad. of TV Arts and Sciences 1991–97, Cities in Schools 1991–95, Cinema and TV Benevolent Fund 1993–2004, Nat. Comm. of Inquiry into Prevention of Child Abuse 1994–96, Royal Acad. of Dramatic Art 1996–2004, Royal Albert Hall 1997–2004, 300 Group, Press Complaints Comm. 2011–; mem. Bd of Govs BANFF TV Festival 1997–99; Trustee, Band Aid, Nat. Film and TV School, Virgin Health Care Foundation; mem. (Conservative) House of Lords 2011–; Hon. Prof., Thames Valley Univ. 1994; Hon. Treas. Stars Org. for Spastics 1986–92; Hon. LLD (Nottingham) 1997; Royal TV Soc. Gold Medal 1997. *Publication:* It Seemed Like a Good Idea at the Time (autobiog.) 1999. *Leisure interests:* entertainment, Charlton Athletic Football Club. *Address:* James Grant Group Ltd, 94 Strand on the Green, Chiswick, London, W4 3NN (office); House of Lords, Westminster, London, SW1A 0PW, England. *Telephone:* (20) 8742-4950 (office); (20) 7219-5353. *E-mail:* enquiries@jgg.co.uk (office). *Website:* www.jg-group.co.uk (office); www.parliament.uk/biographies/lords/michael-grade/51610.

GRADIN, Anita; Swedish politician (retd); b. 12 Aug. 1933, Hörnefors, Västerbotten Co.; m. Bertil Kersfelt; one d.; ed Coll. of Social Work and Public Admin., Stockholm and in USA; journalist 1950, 1956–58, 1960–63; with Swedish Union of Forest Workers and Log Drivers 1952; with Social Welfare Planning Cttee and Municipal Exec. Bd Cttee on Women's Issues, Stockholm 1963–67; mem. Exec. Cttee, Nat. Fed. of Social Democratic Women 1964–93, Vice-Chair. 1975–93; mem.

Stockholm City Council 1966–68; First Sec. Cabinet Office 1967–82; mem. SDP Exec. Cttee of Stockholm 1968–82; mem. Parl. 1968–92; Chair. Dist Br., Fed. of Social Democratic Women, Stockholm 1968–82; Chair. Swedish Union of Social Workers and Public Admin. 1970–81; Chair. Nat. Bd for Intercountry Adoptions 1973–80; del. Council of Europe 1973–82, Chair. Cttee on Migration, Refugees and Democracy 1978–82; Minister with responsibility for Migration and Equality Affairs 1982–86; Vice-Chair. Socialist International Women's Council 1983–86, Chair. Socialist International Women 1986–92, Vice-Chair. Socialist International 1986–92; Minister with responsibility for Foreign Trade and European Affairs 1986–91; Amb. to Austria, Slovenia and to UN insts including IAEA, UNIDO and UNRWA 1992–94; EC Commr for Migration, Home and Judicial Affairs 1995–99; Chair. Research Council of Social Science and Working Life 2001–04; Chair. of Stockholm Conf. on Viet Nam 1974–76, of Swedish Cttee for Viet Nam, Laos and Cambodia 1977–82, Sr Club, Foreign Office 2002; mem. Exec. Cttee of RFSU (Nat. Asscn for Sexual Enlightenment) and Otterfonden 1969–92; mem. EFTA del. 1991–92; mem. Bd Stockholm School of Econs, Women's Forum 2001–08, Comm. on Gene Medicine 2002–08; Cavalieri di Gran Croce (Italy) 1991, Das Grosse Goldene Ehrenzeichen am Bande (Austria) 1994, The King's Medal in the 12th Dimension with ribbon of the Royal Order of the Seraphim 1998, European of the Year 2007; Dr hc (Umeå Univ.) 2002; Marisa Bellizario European Prize (Italy) 1998; Pro Merito Medal, Council of Europe 1982, Wizo Woman of the Year 1986. *Leisure interests:* fishing, reading books, jazz music. *Address:* Fleminggatan 85, 11245 Stockholm, Sweden. *Telephone:* (8) 269872. *Fax:* (8) 269872. *E-mail:* gradin .kersfelt@telia.com.

GRADY, Monica Mary, CBE, BSc, PhD; British meteoritic scientist and academic; *Professor of Planetary and Space Sciences, Planetary and Space Sciences Research Institute, Open University;* b. Leeds, Yorks., England; m. Dr Ian Wright; ed Univs of Durham and Cambridge; Head of Div., Petrology and Meteoritics, Natural History Museum, London, Leader, Meteorites and Micrometeorites Programme, Curator Meteorite Collection, Ed. Catalogue of Meteorites 1991–2005; Prof. of Planetary and Space Sciences, Planetary and Space Sciences Research Inst., Open Univ., Milton Keynes 2005–; mem. UK Astrobiology Panel, UK Planetary Forum; mem. Particle Physics and Astronomy Council's Science Cttee 2005–07; Fellow, Meteoritical Soc., Royal Astronomical Soc., Mineralogical Soc.; Hon. Reader in Geological Sciences, University Coll., London; Asteroid (4731) Monicagrady named after her; Royal Inst. Christmas Lecturer 2003. *Publications:* Meteorites: Flux with Time and Impact Effects 1998, Catalogue of Meteorites 2000, Search for Life 2001, Meteorites (co-author) (second edn) 2002. *Address:* Faculty of Science, Planetary and Space Sciences Research Institute, Walton Hall, Milton Keynes, MK7 6AA, England (office). *Telephone:* (1908) 659251 (office). *Fax:* (1908) 858022 (office). *E-mail:* m.m.grady@open.ac.uk (office). *Website:* www.open .ac.uk/science (office).

GRAF, Hans; Austrian conductor and music director; *Music Director, Houston Symphony;* b. 15 Feb. 1949, Linz; m. Margarita Graf; one d.; ed Bruckner Conservatory, Linz, Acad. of Music, Graz; Music Dir Iraqi Nat. Symphony Orchestra 1975–76, Mozarteum Orchestra, Salzburg 1984–94, Calgary Philharmonic Orchestra 1995–2003 (Music Dir Laureate 2006–), Orchestre Nat. de Bordeaux-Aquitaine 1998–2004, Opéra de Bordeaux 1998–2004, Houston Symphony 2001–13 (Conductor Laureate 2013–); guest conductor with several orchestras including Vienna Symphony, Vienna Philharmonic, Orchestre Nat. de France, Leningrad Philharmonic, Pittsburgh Symphony, Boston Symphony, Royal Concertgebouw Orchestra, Deutsches Symphony Orchestra, Bavarian Radio Orchestra; mem. CM Artists, New York; Chevalier, Légion d'Honneur 2002, Grand Honour in Gold (Austria); First Prize, Karl Böhm Conductors Competition, Salzburg 1979. *Leisure interests:* literature, fine wine, jazz. *Address:* Houston Symphony, 615 Louisiana Street, Suite 102, Houston, TX 77002, USA (office). *Telephone:* (713) 224-4240 (office). *E-mail:* office@houstonsymphony.org (office). *Website:* www.houstonsymphony.org (office).

GRAF, Stefanie (Steffi) M.; German fmr professional tennis player; b. 14 June 1969, Mannheim; d. of Peter Graf and Heidi Graf; m. Andre Agassi (q.v.); one s. one d.; coached by her father; won Orange Bowl 12s 1981, European 14-and-under and European Circuit Masters 1982, Olympic demonstration event, LA; winner German Open 1986, French Open 1987, 1988, 1993, 1995, 1996, 1999; Australian Open 1988, 1989, 1990, 1994; Wimbledon 1988, 1989, 1991, 1992, 1993, 1995, 1996, US Open 1988, 1989, 1993, 1995, 1996, won ATP Tour World Championship 1996, German Open 1989, numerous women's doubles championships with Gabriela Sabatini, Federation Cup 1992; Olympic Champion 1988; ranked No. 1 Aug. 1987; named Official World Champion 1988; Grand Slam winner 1988, 1989; youngest player to win 500 singles victories as a professional Oct. 1991; 118 tournament wins, 23 Grand Slam titles; announced retirement Aug. 1999; Amb. World Wildlife Fund 1984–; Founder and Chair. Children for Tomorrow; Amb. of EXPO 2000; Olympic Order 1999, German Medal of Honour 2002. *Publication:* Wege Zum Erfolg 1999. *Leisure interests:* music, dogs, photography, art, reading. *Address:* Steffi Graf Ventures, 3883 Howard Hughes Pkwy, #8, Las Vegas, NV 89169, USA; Stefanie Graf Marketing GmbH & Co.KG, Gartenstrasse 1, 68723 Schwetzingen, Germany. *Website:* www.stefanie-graf.com (office).

GRAFTON, Sue, BA; American writer; b. 24 April 1940, Louisville, Ky; d. of C.W. Grafton and Vivian Harnsberger; m. 3rd Steven F. Humphrey; one s. two d. from previous marriages; ed Univ. of Louisville, Ky; worked as admissions clerk, cashier and clinic sec., St John's Hosp., Santa Monica, CA; receptionist, later medical educ. sec., Cottage Hosp., Santa Barbara, CA; Cartier Diamond Dagger Award, Crime Writers' Asscn 2008, named Grand Master, Mystery Writers of America 2009. *Television:* has written numerous films for TV, including Walking Through the Fire (Christopher Award) 1979, Sex and the Single Parent, Mark, I Love You, Nurse; also adaptations of Caribbean Mystery and Sparkling Cyanide by Agatha Christie. *Publications:* Keziah Dane 1967, The Lolly-Madonna War 1969, A is for Alibi 1982, B is for Burglar 1985, C is for Corpse 1986, D is for Deadbeat 1987, E is for Evidence 1988, F is for Fugitive 1989, G is for Gumshoe 1990, H is for Homicide 1991, I is for Innocent 1992, J is for Judgement 1993, K is for Killer 1994, L is for Lawless 1995, M is for Malice 1996, N is for Noose 1998, O is for Outlaw 1999, P is for Peril 2001, Q is for Quarry 2003, R is for Ricochet 2004, S is for Silence (RIO Award of Excellence 2007) 2006, T is for Trespass 2007, U is for Undertow 2009, V is for Vengeance 2011; Killer in the Family (jt author with S. Humphrey), Love on

the Run (jt author with S. Humphrey). *Leisure interests:* cats, gardening, good food. *Address:* PO Box 41447, Santa Barbara, CA 93140, USA (office). *Website:* www.suegrafton.com.

GRAHAM, Sir Alexander Michael, KStJ, GBE, JP, DCL, CBIM, FCII, FCIS, FRSA; British chartered insurance broker; b. 27 Sept. 1938, London; s. of Dr Walter Graham and Suzanne Simon; m. Carolyn Stansfeld 1964; three d.; ed St Paul's School; nat. service with Gordon Highlanders 1957–59; broker, Frizzell Group Ltd 1957–67, Dir 1967–73, Man. Dir 1973–90, Deputy Chair. 1990–92; Alderman, City of London 1979–, Sheriff 1986–87, Lord Mayor 1990–91; Chair. Nat. Employers Liaison Cttee for TA and Reserve Forces 1992–97; Chair. First City Insurance Brokers Ltd 1993–98; Chair. Council, Order of St John, Herts. 1993–2001; Chair. Bd of Trustees, Morden Coll. 1995–2013; Chair. Folgate Insurance Co. Ltd 1995–2002, Employment Conditions Abroad Ltd 1993–2005, Euclidian PLC 1994–2001, United Response 1994–2002; Pres. British Insurance Law Asscn 1994–96; Underwriting mem. of Lloyd's; Fellow Chartered Insurance Inst.; Liveryman Mercers' Co. 1971–, Master 1983–84; Vice-Pres. Royal Soc. of St George 1999–; Grand Cross Order of Merit (Chile); Order of Wissam Alouite Class 3 (Morocco). *Leisure interests:* golf, shooting, tennis, swimming, wine, music, calligraphy. *Address:* Walden Abbotts, Whitwell, Hitchin, Herts., SG4 8AJ, England (home). *Telephone:* (1438) 871997 (home). *Fax:* (1438) 871997 (home).

GRAHAM, Andrew Winston Mawdsley, MA; British economist and academic; *Master, Balliol College Oxford;* b. 20 June 1942, Perranporth, Cornwall; s. of Winston Mawdsley Graham; m. Peggotty Fawssett 1970; ed Charterhouse, St Edmund Hall, Oxford; Econ. Asst, Nat. Econ. Devt Office 1964, with Dept of Econ. Affairs 1964–66, Asst to Econ. Adviser to Cabinet 1966–68, Econ. Adviser to Prime Minister 1968–69; Fellow and Tutor in Econs, Balliol Coll. Oxford 1969–97, Estates Bursar 1978, Investment Bursar 1979–83, Vice-Master 1988, 1992–94, Acting Master 1997–2001, Master 2001–; Policy Adviser to Prime Minister (leave of absence from Balliol) 1974–76; mem. ILO/JASPA Employment Advisory Mission to Ethiopia 1982; Head of Commonwealth/Food Studies Group assisting Govt of Zambia 1984; Econ. Adviser to Shadow Chancellor of Exchequer 1988–92, to Leader of Opposition 1992–94; Tutor, Oxford Univ. Business Summer School 1971, 1972, 1973, 1976; Visiting Scholar, MIT 1994; Chair. St James Group (Econ. Forecasting) 1982–84, 1985–92; Dir, Scott Trust (owner of the Guardian and the Observer) 2005–; consultant, BBC 1989–92; mem. Bd Channel 4 TV 1998–2005; Founder and Acting Dir Oxford Internet Inst. 2001; mem. Media Advisory Cttee, Inst. for Public Policy Research 1994–97, Council of Man. Templeton Coll. Oxford 1990–96, Council of Oxford Univ. 2006–; Founder-mem. Editorial Bd Library of Political Economy 1982–94; Sr Fellow, Gorbachev Foundation of N America 1999–; Trustee, Foundation for Information Policy Research 1998–2001, Esmée Fairbairn Foundation 2003–05, Oxford Centre for Islamic Studies 2007–10; Hon. DCL (Oxon.) 2003. *Publications:* Government and Economies in the Postwar Period (ed.) 1990, Broadcasting, Society and Policy in the Multimedia Age (co-author) 1997; contribs to books on econs and philosophy. *Leisure interest:* windsurfing. *Address:* Balliol College, Oxford, OX1 3BJ, England (office). *Telephone:* (1865) 277710 (office). *E-mail:* master@balliol.ox.ac.uk (office). *Website:* www.balliol.ox.ac .uk (office).

GRAHAM, Billy (see Graham, William Franklin).

GRAHAM, Christopher (Chris) Forbes, MA, DPhil, FRS; British biologist and academic; b. 23 Sept. 1940; ed Univ. of Oxford; fmrly Jr Beit Memorial Fellow in Medical Research, Sir William Dunn School of Pathology; Lecturer, Dept of Zoology, Univ. of Oxford 1970–85, fmr Prof. of Animal Devt; Professorial Fellow, St Catherine's Coll., Oxford 1985–; mem. British Soc. for Cell Biology, British Soc. for Developmental Biology, Soc. for Experimental Biology, Genetical Soc. *Publication:* The Developmental Biology of Plants and Animals 1976 (co-ed.), Developmental Control in Plants and Animals 1984. *Address:* St Catherine's College, Oxford, OX1 3UJ, England.

GRAHAM, Daniel Robert (Bob), BA, LLD; American politician and academic; *Research Fellow, Belfer Center for Science and International Affairs, John F. Kennedy School of Government, Harvard University;* b. 9 Nov. 1936, Coral Gables, Fla; s. of Ernest R. Graham and Hilda Simmons; m. Adele Khoury 1959; four d.; ed Univ. of Fla and Harvard Law School; Vice-Pres. Sengra Devt Corpn 1963–79; Fla State Rep. from Coral Gables 1966–70; Fla State Senator from Coral Gables 1970–78; Gov. of Fla 1979–87, Senator 1986–2005; currently Research Fellow, Belfer Center for Science and Int. Affairs, John F. Kennedy School of Govt, Harvard Univ.; Audubon Soc. Conservation Award 1974. *Leisure interests:* golf, tennis and reading. *Address:* Belfer Center for Science and International Affairs, John F. Kennedy School of Government, 79 JFK Street, Cambridge, MA 02138, USA (office). *Telephone:* (617) 495-1400 (office). *Fax:* (617) 495-8963 (office). *Website:* bcsia.ksg.harvard.edu (office).

GRAHAM, Donald Edward, BA; American newspaper publisher; *Chairman and CEO, The Washington Post Company;* b. 22 April 1945, Baltimore, Md; s. of the late Philip L. Graham and of Katharine Meyer Graham; m. 1st Mary L. Wissler 1967 (divorced 2007); one s. three d.; m. 2nd Amanda Bennett 2012; ed Harvard Univ.; joined the Washington Post 1971, Asst Man. Ed. (Sports) 1974–75, Asst Gen. Man. 1975–76, Exec. Vice-Pres. and Gen. Man. 1976–79, Publr 1979–2000, Chair. 2000–08; CEO The Washington Post Co. 1991–, Chair. 1993–; fmrly reporter and writer for Newsweek. *Address:* The Washington Post, 1150 15th Street, NW, Washington, DC 20071, USA (office). *Telephone:* (202) 334-6000 (office). *E-mail:* twpcoreply@washpost.com (office). *Website:* www.washpostco.com (office).

GRAHAM, Rt Hon. Sir Douglas Arthur Montrose 'Doug', KNZM, PC, LLB, JP; New Zealand lawyer, fmr politician, company director and consultant; b. 12 Jan. 1942, Auckland; s. of Robert James Alister Graham and Patricia Kennedy Graham; m. Beverley Virginia Graham 1966; two s. one d.; ed Southwell School, Auckland Grammar School and Univ. of Auckland; practising lawyer since 1965; est. own practice 1968; barrister and solicitor of High Court of New Zealand; Lecturer in Legal Ethics, Univ. of Auckland 1973–83; MP (Nat. Party) for Remuera 1984–96 (seat abolished), list MP 1996–99; Minister of Justice 1990–99, of Cultural Affairs 1990–97, for Disarmament and Arms Control 1990–99, Minister in Charge of Treaty of Waitangi Negotiations on behalf of the Crown 1991–99, Minister of Courts 1995–97; Attorney Gen. 1997–99; co. dir and consultant 1999–; Dr hc (Waikato) 1999. *Publication:* Trick or Treaty? 1997. *Leisure interests:* reading, music, rugby football, gardening, travel. *Address:* 3A Martin Avenue, Remuera, Auckland, New Zealand (home). *Telephone:* (9) 524-2921 (home). *E-mail:* douglas .graham@xtra.co.nz.

GRAHAM, James (see Patterson, Harry).

GRAHAM, Jorie, BFA, MFA; American poet and academic; *Boylston Professor of Rhetoric and Oratory, Harvard University;* b. 9 May 1951, New York City; m. James Galvin; ed New York Univ. and Univ. of Iowa; Poetry Ed. Crazy Horse 1978–81, The Colorado Review 1990–; Contributing Ed., Boston Review, Conjunctions, Denver Quarterly; Asst Prof., Murray State Univ. 1978–79, Humboldt State Univ. 1979–81; Instructor, Columbia Univ. 1981–83; Bunting Fellow, Radcliffe Inst. 1982; staff mem. Writers' Workshop and Prof. of English, Univ. of Iowa 1983–1998; Chancellor, Acad. of American Poets 1997–2003; Boylston Prof. of Rhetoric and Oratory in the Dept of English and American Literature and Language, Harvard Univ. 1998–; mem. American Acad. of Arts and Letters 2003–; American Acad. of Poets Award 1977, Poetry Northwest Young Poets Prize 1980, Pushcart Prizes 1980, 1982, Ingram Merrill Foundation grant 1981, Great Lakes Colleges Asscn Award 1981, American Poetry Review Prize 1982, Guggenheim Fellowship 1983–84, John D. and Catherine T. MacArthur Foundation Fellowship 1990. *Publications:* Hybrids of Plants and of Ghosts 1980, Erosion 1983, The End of Beauty 1987, The Best American Poetry (ed. with David Lehman) 1990, Region of Unlikeness 1991, Materialism 1993, The Dream of the Unified Field (Pulitzer Prize in Poetry 1996) 1995, Errancy 1997, Swarm 1999, Never 2002, Overlord 2004, Sea Change 2008. *Address:* Department of English, Harvard University, 12 Quincy Street, Cambridge, MA 02138, USA (office). *Telephone:* (617) 495-2533 (office). *Fax:* (617) 496-8737 (office). *E-mail:* engdept@fas.harvard.edu (office). *Website:* www .fas.harvard.edu/~english (office).

GRAHAM, Lindsay O., BA, JD; American politician; *Senator from South Carolina;* b. 9 July 1955; s. of Florence James Graham and Millie Graham; ed D.W. Daniel High School, Clemson, SC, Univ. of South Carolina; served in armed forces, assignments including Operation Desert Shield and Desert Storm; legal career in USAF; Base Staff Judge Advocate, McEntire Air Nat. Guard Base, Eastover 1989–94; est. pvt. law practice 1988; asst attorney in Oconee Co.; mem. S Carolina House of Reps from 2nd Dist Oconee Co. 1992–94; mem. US Congress from 3rd Dist S Carolina 1994–2003, mem. Cttee on Educ. and the Workforce, on Judiciary, on Armed Services; Senator from S Carolina 2003–, mem. Appropriations, Armed Services, Budget, and Judiciary Cttees; Col Air Force Reserves 1995–, Sr Instructor for Judge Advocate Gen. (JAG) Corps; Republican. *Address:* 290 Russell Senate Office Building, Washington, DC 20510, USA (office). *Telephone:* (202) 224-5972 (office). *Website:* lgraham.senate.gov (office).

GRAHAM, Patricia Albjerg, PhD; American academic; *Warren Professor Emerita, Graduate School of Education, Harvard University;* b. (Patricia Parks Albjerg), 9 Feb. 1935, Lafayette, Ind.; d. of Victor L. Albjerg and Marguerite Hall Albjerg; m. Loren R. Graham 1955; one d.; ed Purdue and Columbia Univs; teacher, Deep Creek and Maury High Schools, Norfolk, Va 1955–58; Chair. History Dept, St Hilda's and St Hugh's School, New York 1958–60, part-time Coll. Adviser 1961–63, 1965–67; Lecturer, Indiana Univ., School of Educ., Bloomington 1964–65; Asst Prof., Barnard Coll. and Columbia Teacher's Coll., New York 1965–68, Assoc. Prof. 1968–72, Prof. 1972–74; Prof., Harvard Univ. Grad. School of Educ., Cambridge, Mass 1974–79, Warren Prof. 1979–2006, Prof. Emer. 2006–, Dean, Grad. School of Educ. 1982–91; Dean, Radcliffe Inst. and Vice-Pres. Radcliffe Coll., Cambridge, Mass 1974–77; mem. Bd of Dirs Josiah Macy Jr Foundation 1976–77, 1979–10; Dir Nat. Inst. of Educ. 1977–79; Chair. Bd Carnegie Foundation for the Advancement of Teaching 2009–; Vice-Pres. for Teaching, American Historical Asscn 1985–89; Pres. Nat. Acad. of Educ. 1985–89; Dir Spencer Foundation 1983–2000, Pres. 1991–2000; Dir Johnson Foundation 1983–2001, Hitachi Foundation 1985–2004; mem. AAAS (mem. Council 1993–96, Vice-Pres. 1998–2001), American Philosophical Soc. 1999–; mem. Bd of Dirs Center for Advanced Study in the Behavioral Sciences 2001–07; Dir Northwestern Mutual Life 1980–2005, Apache Corpn 2002–; Trustee, Cen. European Univ. 2002–; 14 hon. degrees; John Simon Guggenheim Award 1972–73, Woodrow Wilson Center Fellow 1981–82. *Publications:* Progressive Education: From Arcady to Academe, A History of the Progressive Education Association 1967, Community and Class in American Education, 1865–1918 1974, Women in Higher Education (co-ed. with Todd Furniss) 1974, S.O.S. Sustain Our Schools 1992, Accountability (with Richard Lyman and Martin Trow) 1995, Schooling America 2005. *Address:* Harvard University Graduate School of Education, Appian Way, Cambridge, MA 02138, USA (office). *Telephone:* (617) 496-4839 (office). *Fax:* (617) 496-3095 (office). *E-mail:* patricia_graham@harvard .edu (office).

GRAHAM, Shawn; Canadian politician; b. 22 Feb. 1968, Kent Co., NB; s. of Alan Graham; m. Roxanne Reeves; ed Univ. of New Brunswick, St Thomas Univ.; mem. (Riding of Kent) Legis. Ass. of NB 1998–2010; Caucas Chair. Liberal Party of NB 1998–2002, Leader 2002–10 (youngest Liberal leader and youngest Leader of the Official Opposition in Canada); Premier of NB, Pres. Exec. Council, Minister of Wellness, Culture and Sport, of Intergovernmental Affairs, Minister responsible for the Premier's Council on the Status of Disabled Persons 2006–10; Chair. Council of Fed. 2007–; Hon. LLD (Univ. of New Brunswick) 2009; Intelligent Community Visionary of Year Award, Intelligent Community Forum 2010. *Address:* c/o Office of the Premier, Centennial Building, 670 King Street, PO Box 6000, Fredericton, NB E3B 5H1, Canada (office).

GRAHAM, Stuart E., BSc; American construction industry executive; *Chairman, Skanska USA Building Inc.;* b. 1946; ed Holy Cross Univ.; Asst Field Supt, Sordoni Construction Co. 1969; Pres. Sordoni Skanska 1990–95, Pres. and CEO Slattery Skanska 1995–97, Pres. Skanska USA Inc. 1997–2001, Pres. and CEO Skanska AB 2002–08 (retd), currently Chair. Skanska USA Building Inc.; mem. Bd of Dirs Securitas AB 2005–, PPL Corpn 2008–; mem. and fmr Dir Construction Industry Round Table. *Address:* Skanska USA Building Inc., 1633 Littleton Road, Parsippany, NJ 07054, USA (office). *Telephone:* (973) 753-3500 (office). *E-mail:* info@skanskausa.com (office). *Website:* www.skanskausa.com (office).

GRAHAM, Susan; American singer (mezzo-soprano); b. 23 July 1960, Roswell, NM; ed Manhattan School of Music, Texas Technical Univ.; sang Massenet's Chérubin while a student; engagements with St Louis Opera as Erika in Vanessa,

Charlotte and at Seattle as Stephano in Roméo et Juliette; season 1989–90 included Chicago Lyric Opera debut as Annius in La Clemenza di Tito, Sonia in Argento's Aspern Papers at Washington, Dorabella and the Composer at Santa Fe; Carnegie Hall debut in Des Knaben Wunderhorn and Bernstein concert in New York; season 1990–91 as Octavian with San Francisco Symphony, Minerva in Monteverdi's Ulisse with San Francisco Opera, Berlioz's Beatrice at Lyon, Cherubino at Santa Fe; Mozart's C minor Mass under Edo de Waart and with Philadelphia Orchestra under Neville Marriner; season 1991–92 at Metropolitan as Second Lady, Cherubino, and Tebaldo in Don Carlos; L'Opera de Nice as Cherubino and Les Nuits d'Été in Lyon; Beethoven's 9th in Spain conducted by Marriner; Salzburg Mozart Week 1993, as Cecilio in Lucio Silla, Easter and Summer Festivals as Meg Page in Falstaff; season 1993–94 as Massenet's Chérubin and Dorabella at Covent Garden, Ascanio in Les Troyens at the Met, Annius in Tito at San Francisco and 1994 Salzburg Festival; Octavian for WNO, and Vienna State Opera and Marguerite in La Damnation de Faust for L'Opéra de Lyon; season 1995 as Dorabella and as Arianna in the premiere of the opera by Goehr at Covent Garden; season 1997 with Chérubin at Covent Garden and in Lucio Silla at Salzburg; sang Octavian at Covent Garden 2000; created Sister Helen Prejean in Jack Heggie's Dead Man Walking, San Francisco 2000; season 2001 as Mignon at Toulouse and Dorabella at the New York Met; Opera News Award 2005. *Recordings include:* Falstaff conducted by Solti, La Damnation de Faust conducted by Kent Nagano, Béatrice et Bénédict conducted by John Nelson, Stravinsky's Pulcinella, Charles Ives Songs (Grammy Award for Best Classical Vocal Performance 2005) 2004, Poèmes de l'amour 2005. *Address:* IMG Artists, Carnegie Hall Tower, 153 West 57th Street, 5th Floor, New York, NY 10019, USA (office). *Telephone:* (212) 994-3500 (office). *Fax:* (212) 994-3550 (office). *E-mail:* atreuhaft@imgartists.com (office). *Website:* www.imgartists.com (office); www .susangraham.com.

GRAHAM, William (Bill), BA, LLB, DJur; Canadian politician, lawyer and academic; *Chancellor, Trinity College, University of Toronto;* b. 1939, Montreal, PQ; m. Catherine Graham; one s. one d.; ed Upper Canada Coll., Trinity Coll., Univ. of Toronto, Univ. of Paris, France; practised law with Fasken and Calvin, made Pnr 1983; Prof. of Law, Univ. of Toronto, Dir Centre of Int. Studies, Chancellor, Trinity Coll. 2007–; Visiting Prof., Université de Montréal, McGill Univ.; fmr Pres. Alliance Française, Toronto; MP 1993–2007, Chair. Standing Cttee on Foreign Affairs and Int. Trade 1995–2002; Minister of Foreign Affairs 2002–04, of Nat. Defence 2004–06; Parl. Opposition Leader 2006; Chair. Atlantic Council of Canada 2007–12, Advisory Bd, Centre for Contemporary Int. History 2011–; Founding Pres. Inter-Parl. Forum of the Americas; Pres. Canadian Int. Council 2013–; fmr Vice-Pres. and Treas., Parl. Asscn of OSCE; mem. Inter-Parl. Council Against Anti-Semitism; Hon. Life mem. Canadian Council of Int. Law; Hon. Lt Col, Gov. Gen.'s Horse Guards 2007–, Hon. Col 2012–; Chevalier, Légion d'honneur, Ordre de la Pléiade, Ordre du mérite de l'Asscn des juristes de l'Ontario; Prix Jean-Baptiste Rousseaux, Médaille d'argent de la ville de Paris, Médaille d'or de l'alliance française. *Publications:* The Canadian Law and Practice of International Trade (co-author), International Law: Chiefly as Interpreted and Applied in Canada (co-ed.), New Dimensions in International Trade Law (co-author). *Address:* 1130-151 Bloor Street West, Toronto, ON M5S 1S4, Canada (office). *Telephone:* (416) 920-2205 (home). *Fax:* (416) 920-5140 (home). *E-mail:* dilys.williams@afai.ca (office).

GRAHAM, William (Billy) Franklin, Jr, BA, BTh; American evangelist; b. 7 Nov. 1918, Charlotte, North Carolina; s. of William Franklin Graham, Sr and Morrow Graham; m. Ruth M. Bell 1943 (died 2007); two s. three d.; ed Florida Bible Inst., Wheaton Coll.; ordained to Baptist Ministry 1939; Minister First Baptist Church, Western Springs, Ill. 1943–45; First Vice-Pres. Youth for Christ Int. 1945–50; Pres. Northwestern Schools, Minneapolis 1947–52; Founder, World Wide Pictures, Burbank, Calif.; worldwide evangelistic campaigns 1947–; messages featured on weekly Hour of Decision radio programme 1950–; also periodic crusade telecasts; Founder, Billy Graham Evangelistic Asscn 1950; Hon. Chair. Lausanne Congress on World Evangelization 1974; Hon. KBE 2001; Dr hc (Hungarian Calvinist Church, Christian Acad. of Theology) 1981; numerous awards, including Bernard Baruch Award 1955, Humane Order of African Redemption 1960, Gold Award, George Washington Carver Memorial Inst. 1964, Horatio Alger Award 1965, Int. Brotherhood Award Nat. Conf. of Christians and Jews 1971, Sylvanus Thayer Award, Asscn of Graduates of US Mil. Acad. 1972, Franciscan Int. Award 1972, Man of South Award 1974, Liberty Bell Award 1975, Templeton Prize 1982, Presidential Medal of Freedom 1983, William Booth Award 1989, Congressional Gold Medal 1996, Ronald Reagan Presidential Foundation Award 2000. *Publications include:* Peace with God 1953 (revised edn 1984), The Secret of Happiness 1955, My Answer 1960, World Aflame 1965, The Challenge 1969, The Jesus Generation 1971, Angels – God's Secret Agents 1975, How to be Born Again 1977, The Holy Spirit 1978, Till Armageddon 1981, Approaching Hoofbeats: The Four Horsemen of the Apocalypse 1983, A Biblical Standard for Evangelists 1984, Unto The Hills 1986, Facing Death and the Life After 1987, Answers to Life's Problems 1988, Hope for the Troubled Heart 1991, Storm Warning 1992 (revised edn 2001), Just As I Am (autobiog.) 1997, Hope for Each Day 2002, The Journey: How To Live by Faith in an Uncertain World 2006, Wisdom for Each Day 2008, Nearing Home 2011, The Heaven Answer Book 2012, The Reason for My Hope: Salvation 2013. *Address:* 1 Billy Graham Parkway, Charlotte, NC 28201-0001, USA (office). *Telephone:* (704) 401-2432 (office). *Fax:* (704) 401-3017 (office). *E-mail:* media@ bgea.org (office). *Website:* www.bgea.org (office).

GRAHAM-DIXON, Andrew, MA; British critic, writer and broadcaster; *Chief Art Critic, Sunday Telegraph;* b. 26 Dec. 1960, London; s. of Antony Philip Graham-Dixon and Suzanne Graham-Dixon (née Villar); m. Sabine Marie-Pascale Tilly 1986; one s. two d.; ed Westminster School, Christ Church Coll. Oxford, Courtauld Inst., London; Chief Arts Critic, The Independent 1986–98; arts writer and presenter, BBC TV 1992–, Presenter, The Culture Show, BBC 2 2006–; Curator Broken English, Serpentine Gallery, London 1992; Chief Arts Writer, Sunday Telegraph Magazine and columnist, In the Picture 1999–, Chief Art Critic, Sunday Telegraph 2005–; BP Arts Writer of the Year 1988, 1989, 1990; First Prize Reportage, Montreal Film & TV Festival 1992; Hawthornden Prize 1992. *Television includes:* Gericault 1992; TV documentary series: A History of British Art 1994, Renaissance 1999, 1,000 Ways of Getting Drunk in England 2001, Secret Lives of the Artists 2003, The Elgin Marbles 2004, The Secret of Drawing 2005, I,

Samurai 2006, The Art of Eternity 2007, The Art of Spain 2008, Travels with Vasari 2009, The Medici: Makers of Modern Art 2009, The Art of Russia 2010, The Art of Germany 2011, The Art of America 2011, Treasures of Heaven: The Art of Relics 2011, I Never Tell Anybody Anything: The Life and Work of Edward Burra 2011, Sicily Unpacked (with Giorgio Locatelli) 2012, Cash in China's Attic 2012. *Publications:* Howard Hodgkin: A Monograph 1994, A History of British Art 1996, Paper Museum 1996, Renaissance 1999, In the Picture 2002, Michelangelo and the Sistine Chapel 2008, Caravaggio: A Life Sacred and Profane 2010. *Leisure interests:* walking, snooker, football, existentialism, golf. *Address:* c/o Capel Land, 21 Wardour Street, London, W1D 6PS, England (office). *Telephone:* (20) 7734-2414 (office). *E-mail:* anita@algrade.demon.co.uk (office).

GRAHAM-SMITH, Sir Francis, Kt, PhD, FRS, FRAS; British professor of radio astronomy; *Professor Emeritus of Physics, University of Manchester;* b. 25 April 1923, Roehampton, Surrey; m. Elizabeth Palmer 1946; three s. one d.; ed Rossall School, Epsom Coll., Downing Coll., Cambridge; with Telecommunications Research Establishment 1943–46; Cavendish Lab. 1947–64; 1851 Exhbn 1951–52; Warren Research Fellow, Royal Soc. 1959–64; Prof. of Radio Astronomy, Univ. of Manchester 1964–74, 1981–87, Pro-Vice-Chancellor 1987, Dir Nuffield Radio Astronomy Labs 1981–88, Langworthy Prof. of Physics 1987–90, Prof. Emer. 1990–; Deputy Dir Royal Greenwich Observatory 1974–75, Dir 1976–81; Astronomer Royal 1982–90; Visiting Prof. of Astronomy, Univ. of Sussex 1975–81; Sec. Royal Astronomical Soc. 1964–71, Pres. 1975–77; Sec., Vice-Pres. Royal Soc. 1988–94; Fellow, Downing Coll., Cambridge 1953–64, Hon. Fellow 1970; Chair. Govs Manchester Grammar School 1987–98; Hon. DSc (Queens Univ., Belfast) 1986, (Keele) 1987, (Birmingham) 1989, (Nottingham) 1990, (Trinity Coll. Dublin) 1990, (Manchester) 1993, (Salford) 2003, (Liverpool) 2003; Royal Medal, Royal Soc. 1987, Glazebrook Medal, Inst. of Physics 1991. *Publications:* Radio Astronomy 1960, Optics (with J. H. Thomson) 1971, Pulsars 1977, Pathways to the Universe (with Sir Bernard Lovell) 1988, Introduction to Radioastronomy (with B. F. Burke) 1997, Pulsar Astronomy (with A. G. Lyne) 1990 (third edn 2006), Optics and Photonics (with T. A. King) 2000 (with T. A. King and D. Wilkins 2007). *Leisure interests:* gardening, beekeeping. *Address:* Old School House, Henbury, Macclesfield, Cheshire, SK11 9PH, England (home). *Telephone:* (1477) 571321 (office); (1625) 612657 (home). *E-mail:* fgs@jb.man.ac.uk (office); fgsegs@talktalk.net (home).

GRAINGE, Lucian Charles, CBE; British music industry executive; *Chairman and CEO, Universal Music Group;* b. 1960, London; m.; three c.; song promoter April Music/CBS, later Head Creative Dept 1979–82; Dir and Gen. Man. RCA Music Publishing 1982–84; Dir of A&R MCA Records 1984–86; est. PolyGram Music Publishing UK office 1986–93; Gen. Man. A&R and business affairs, Polydor 1993–97, Man. Dir 1997–2001, following merger of Polygram and Universal promoted to Deputy Chair. Universal Music UK 2001, Chair. and CEO 2001–05, Chair. and CEO Universal Music Group Int. 2005–10, CEO Universal Music Group 2010–; Co-Chair. BRITS Cttee 2003–05; Dir BPI; bd mem. Int. Fed. of Phonographic Industry; Music Industry Trusts Award 2008, Humanitarian Award, Foundation for Ethnic Understanding 2013, SAG-AFTRA American Scene Award 2013, Salute to Industry Icons Award, Recording Acad. 2013. *Address:* Universal Music Group, 2220 Colorado Avenue, Santa Monica, CA 90404, USA (office). *Telephone:* (310) 865-4000 (office). *Website:* www.universalmusic.com (office).

GRAINVILLE, Patrick; French novelist; b. 1 June 1947, Villers-sur-mer; s. of Jacques Grainville and Suzanne Grainville (née Laquerre); m. Françoise Lutgen 1971; ed Lycée Deauville, Sorbonne; Prof., Lycée de Sartrouville 1975–; mem. CNRS literature section 1975; literary critic for Le Figaro; Officier, Ordre nat. du Mérite, Ordre des Arts et des lettres. *Publications:* La toison 1972, La lisière 1973, L'abîme 1974, Les flamboyants (Prix Goncourt) 1976, La Diane rousse 1978, Le dernier viking 1980, Les fortresses noires 1982, La caverne céleste 1984, Le paradis des orages 1986, L'atelier du peintre 1988, L'orgie, La neige (Prix Guillaume le Conquérant) 1990, Colère 1992, Mathieu (jtly.) 1993, Les anges et les faucons 1994, Le lien 1996, Le tyran éternel 1998, Le tour de la fin du monde, Une femme me cache 2000, La joie d'Aurélie 2004, La main blessée 2005, Lumière du rat, 2008, Le Baiser de la pieuvre 2010. *Leisure interests:* travelling, making collages, sculpture. *Address:* c/o Editions du Seuil, 27 rue Jacob, 75261 Paris cedex 06, France.

GRAMEGNA, Pierre, DEA; Luxembourg politician and fmr diplomatist; *Minister of Finance;* b. 22 April 1958, Esch-sur-Alzette; m.; two c.; ed Univ. Panthéon-Assas (Paris 2), France; began career as correspondent, Républicain Lorrain; joined Ministry of Foreign Affairs (MFA) 1983, Political and Econ. Counsellor, Embassy in Paris 1988–92, Consul Gen. and Dir, Luxembourg Bd of Econ. Devt, San Francisco 1992, Amb. to Japan and Repub. of Korea 1996–2002, Dir of Int. Econ. Relations, MFA 2002–03; Dir-Gen., Luxembourg Chamber of Commerce 2003–13; Minister of Finance 2013–; fmr Dir several cos including Cargolux Airlines International SA (Pres. 2004–8), Bourse de Luxembourg SA, Société Nationale de Crédit et d'Investissement, LuxExpo Luxembourg, BGL-BNP Paribas Luxembourg SA. *Address:* Ministry of Finance, 3 rue de la Congrégation, 1352 Luxembourg, Luxembourg (office). *Telephone:* 247-82600 (office). *Fax:* 247-5241 (office). *Website:* www.mf.public.lu (office).

GRAMM, (William) Philip, PhD; American investment banker and fmr politician; *Vice-Chairman, UBS Warburg LLC;* b. 8 July 1942, Fort Benning, Ga; s. of Kenneth M. and Florence (Scroggins) Gramm; m. Wendy Lee 1970; two s.; ed Univ. of Georgia; mem. of Faculty, Dept of Econs, Texas A&M Univ. 1967–78, Prof. 1973–78; Pnr, Gramm & Assocs 1971–78; mem. US House of Reps, Washington, DC 1979–85; Senator from Texas 1985–2002, fmr Chair. Senate Steering Cttee, Banking, Housing and Urban Affairs Cttee; Vice-Chair. UBS Warburg LLC, Washington, DC 2003–; Republican. *Publications:* The Economics of Mineral Extraction 1980, Role of Government in a Free Society 1982; articles in professional journals. *Address:* UBS AG, Suite 1100, 1501 K Street, NW, Washington, DC 20005 (office); 2323 Bryan Street, Suite 2150, Dallas, TX 75201, USA (home). *Telephone:* (202) 585-4000 (office). *Website:* www.ubs.com (office).

GRAMMER, Kelsey; American actor and comedian; b. (Allen Kelsey Grammer), 21 Feb. 1955, St Thomas, US Virgin Islands; s. of the late Frank Allen Grammer, Jr and of Sally Grammer (née Cranmer); m. 1st Doreen Alderman 1982 (divorced

1990); one d. and one d. with Barrie Buckner; m. 2nd Leigh-Anne Csuhany 1992 (divorced 1993); m. 3rd Camille Donatacci 1997 (divorced 2011); one s. one d.; m. 4th Kayte Walsh 2011; ed Juilliard School; three-year internship with Old Globe Theatre, San Diego in late 1970s; worked at Guthrie Theater, Minneapolis, Minn. 1980; Broadway debut in Lennox in Macbeth 1981; Broadway musical debut playing role of Georges in revival of La Cage aux Folles 2010. *Films include:* Galaxies Are Colliding 1992, Down Periscope 1996, Anastasia (voice) 1997, The Real Howard Spitz 1998, New Jersey Turnpikes 1999, Standing on Fishes 1999, Toy Story 2 (voice) 1999, 15 Minutes 2001, The Big Empty 2003, Teacher's Pet (voice) 2004, The Good Humor Man 2005, Even Money 2006, X-Men: The Last Stand 2006, Swing Vote 2008, An American Carol 2008, Middle Men 2009, Fame 2009, Crazy on the Outside 2010, I Don't Know How She Does It 2011, Dorothy of Oz (voice) 2012. *Television includes:* Kennedy (mini-series) 1983, George Washington (mini-series) 1984, Cheers (series) 1984–93, Crossings (mini-series) 1986, Dance 'Til Dawn (film) 1988, Top of the Hill (film) 1989, 227 (series) 1989, The Simpsons (series) 1990–2010, Beyond Suspicion (film) 1993, Frasier (series) 1993–2004, The Innocent (film) 1994, London Suite (film) 1996, The Pentagon Wars (film) 1998, Just Shoot Me! (series) (narrator) 1998, Animal Farm (film) (voice) 1999, The Sports Pages (film) 2001, Mr. St. Nick (film) 2002, Benedict Arnold: A Question of Honor (film) 2003, Frasier: Analyzing the Laughter (film) 2004, A Christmas Carol (film) 2004, Kelsey Grammer Presents: The Sketch Show (series) 2005, The Kelsey Grammer Bill Zucker Comedy Hour (film) 2010, Hank (series) 2009–10, Boss (series) (Golden Globe Award for Best Actor in a TV Series 2012) 2011. *Address:* c/o WME Entertainment, 9601 Wilshire Boulevard, Beverly Hills, CA 90210, USA (office).

GRANDAGE, Michael, CBE; British theatre director; *Director, Michael Grandage Company;* b. 2 May 1962; ed Humphry Davy Grammar School, Cornwall, Cen. School of Speech and Drama; began theatre career as actor 1981–96; full-time dir 1996–, Assoc. Dir Sheffield Theatres (including Sheffield Crucible) 2000–05; Assoc. Dir Donmar Warehouse, London 2000–02, Artistic Dir 2002–12; Dir Michael Grandage Company 2012–; also Visiting Prof., Univ. of Sheffield; Pres. Central School of Speech and Drama; Dr hc (Univ. of Sheffield), (Sheffield Hallam Univ.); Best Dir (for As You Like It and Passion Play), Evening Standard Theatre Awards 2000, Best Dir (for As You Like It, Passion Play and Merrily We Roll Along), Critics Circle Awards; Theatre Award (for As You Like It), South Bank Show Awards, Best Dir (for Caligula), Laurence Olivier Awards 2004, Best Dir (for Don Carlos), Evening Standard Theatre Awards 2005, TMA Awards 2005, German-British Forum Award for promoting relations between England and Germany 2005, Sydney Edwards Award for Best Dir 2008, Managed Networks Best Dir, WhatsOnStage Awards 2014. *Plays directed include:* Almeida Theatre: The Jew of Malta (also nat. tour); Sheffield Theatres: The Doctor's Dilemma (also nat. tour); Sheffield Theatres: Don Carlos Carlos (Evening Standard Award Best Dir), Suddenly Last Summer (also Albery Theatre, London), A Midsummer Night's Dream, The Tempest (also Old Vic, London), Richard III, Don Juan, Edward II, The Country Wife, As You Like It (also Lyric Hammersmith), Twelfth Night, What the Butler Saw; Donmar Warehouse: Guys and Dolls (Olivier Award for Outstanding Musical Production), Good 1999, Passion Play (Evening Standard Award and Critics' Circle Award for Best Dir) 2000, Merrily We Roll Along (Evening Standard Award Best Dir) 2000, Privates on Parade 2001, The Vortex 2002, Caligula (Olivier Award Best Dir) 2003, After Miss Julie 2003, Pirandello's Henry IV 2004, Grand Hotel (Olivier Award for Outstanding Musical Production, Evening Standard Award Best Dir) 2004, The Wild Duck (Critics' Circle Awards for Best Dir) 2005, Don Juan in Soho 2006, Frost/Nixon (also Gielgud Theatre) 2006, The Cut 2006, John Gabriel Borkman 2007, Othello (Evening Standard and Critics' Circle Awards for Best Dir) 2008, The Chalk Garden (Evening Standard and Critics' Circle Awards for Best Dir) 2008, Red (Tony Award for Best Direction of a Play 2010, Drama Desk Award 2010) 2009, King Lear 2011, Luise Miller 2011, Richard II 2012; Adelphi Theatre: Evita 2006; Donmar at Wyndham's Theatre: Ivanov (Evening Standard and Critics' Circle Awards for Best Dir) 2008, Twelfth Night 2008, Madame de Sade 2009, Hamlet 2009; Royal Nat. Theatre: Danton's Death 2010; Michael Grandage Company: Privates on Parade 2012, Peter and Alice 2013, The Cripple of Inishmaan 2013 (also Broadway 2014), A Midsummer Night's Dream 2013, Henry V 2013. *Publication:* A Decade at the Donmar 2013. *Address:* Michael Grandage Company, Fourth Floor, Gielgud Theatre, Shaftesbury Avenue, London, W1D 6AR, England (office). *Telephone:* (20) 3582-7210 (office). *E-mail:* info@michaelgrandagecompany.com (office). *Website:* www.michaelgrandagecompany.com (office).

GRANDI, Filippo, BA; Italian UN official; b. 1957; ed State Univs of Venice and Milan, Gregorian Univ., Rome; joined UNHCR 1988, served in several countries, including Sudan, Syria, Turkey and Iraq following first Gulf War, also headed several emergency operations, including in Kenya, Benin, Ghana, Liberia, the Great Lakes Region of Cen. Africa, Yemen and Afghanistan, Field Coordinator for UNHCR and UN humanitarian activities in Democratic Repub. of the Congo during civil war 1996–97, Special Asst, then Chief of Staff, Exec. Office of UNHCR, Geneva 1997–2001, Chief of Mission of UN High Commr for Refugees 2001–04; Deputy Special Rep. of UN Sec.-Gen. responsible for Political Affairs, UN Assistance Mission in Afghanistan 2004–05; Deputy Commr-Gen. UNRWA 2005–10, Commr-Gen. 2010–13. *Address:* Ministry of Foreign Affairs, Piazzale della Farnesina 1, 00194 Roma, Italy (office). *Telephone:* (06) 36911 (office). *Fax:* (06) 3236210 (office). *E-mail:* ministero.affariesteri@cert.esteri.it (office). *Website:* www.esteri.it (office).

GRANDMONT, Jean-Michel, LèsL, PhD; French economist and researcher; *Director of Research, Centre de Recherche en Économie et Statistique;* b. 22 Dec. 1939, Toulouse; s. of Jancu Wladimir Grunberg and Paule Cassou; m. 1st Annick Duriez 1967 (divorced 1978); two d.; m. 2nd Josselyne Bitan 1979; ed Ecole Polytechnique, Paris, Ecole Nationale des Ponts et Chaussées, Paris, Université de Paris, Univ. of California, Berkeley, USA; Research Assoc., CNRS, Centre d'Etudes Prospectives d'Economie Mathématique Appliquées à la Planification (CEPREMAP) 1970–75, then Dir various research units, Dir of Research, CNRS and CEPREMAP 1987–96, Dir Research Unit, CNRS 928, Recherches Fondamentales en Economie Mathématique 1991–96, Dir of Research, CNRS and Centre de Recherche en Economie et Statistique 1996–; Assoc. Prof., Ecole Polytechnique, Palaiseau 1977–92, Prof. 1992–2004, Chair. Dept of Econs 1997–2000, 2003–04; Prof. (part-time), Yale Univ., USA 1987, 1989–91, 1994; Pres. Econometric Soc.

1990; Hon. mem. American Econ. Asscn, Foreign Hon. mem. American Acad. of Arts and Sciences 1992–; Chevalier, Légion d'honneur 2004, Officier, Palmes académiques 2004; Dr hc (Lausanne) 1990, (Keio Univ., Tokyo) 2007; Alexander von Humboldt Award 1992. *Publications:* Money and Value 1983, Nonlinear Economic Dynamics (ed.) 1987, Temporary Equilibrium (ed.) 1988; articles in scientific econ. journals. *Address:* CREST-CNRS, 15 blvd Gabriel Péri, 92245 Malakoff Cedex (office); 55 boulevard de Charonne, Les Doukas 23, 75011 Paris, France (home). *Telephone:* 1-41-17-78-04 (office); 1-43-70-37-28 (home). *Fax:* 1-41-17-60-46 (office). *E-mail:* grandmon@ensae.fr (office). *Website:* www.crest.fr/ses .php?user=2958 (office).

GRANGE, Sir Kenneth Henry, Kt, CBE; British industrial designer; *Visiting Professor, Design Products, Royal College of Art;* b. 17 July 1929; s. of Harry Alfred Grange and Hilda Gladys Grange (née Long); ed Willesden School of Arts and Crafts, London; tech. illustrator, Royal Engineers 1948–50; design asst, Arcon Chartered Architects 1948; Bronek Katz & Vaughan 1950–51; Gordon Bowyer & Partners 1951–54; Jack Howe & Partners 1954–58; industrial designer, Kenneth Grange Design Ltd (pvt. practice) 1958–72; Founding Partner, Pentagram Design 1972–2000; solo 'shows, Victoria and Albert Museum 1974, Tokyo 1985, 'Those That Got Away', London 2003; Pres. Chartered Soc. of Designers 1987–88; Master of Faculty, RDI 1985–87; currently Visiting Prof., Design Products, Royal College of Art; mem. Bd of Dirs Shakespeare Globe Centre 1997–2002; mem. Advisory Bd for Product Design, Design Council, Industrial Design Adviser 1971; Hon. Prof., Heriot-Watt Univ. 1987; Hon. DUniv (Heriot-Watt) 1986; Dr hc (RCA) 1985, (De Montfort Univ.) 1998, (Staffordshire Univ.) 1998; ten Design Council Awards, Duke of Edinburgh Award for Elegant Design 1963, Royal Designer for Industry, Royal Soc. of Arts 1969, Chartered Soc. of Designers Gold Medal 1996, Prince Philip Designers' Prize 2001. *Leisure interests:* building. *Address:* Design Products, Royal College of Art, Kensington Gore, London, SW7 2EU (office); 53 Christchurch Hill, London, NW3 1LG, England (home). *Telephone:* (20) 7590-4444 (office). *Fax:* (20) 7590-4500 (office). *E-mail:* design@rca.ac.uk (office). *Website:* www.rca.ac.uk (office).

GRANHOLM, Jennifer Mulhern, BA, JD; American lawyer, academic, presenter and fmr politician; *Distinguished Practitioner of Law and Public Policy, Richard and Rhoda Goldman School of Public Policy, University of California, Berkeley;* b. 5 Feb. 1959, Vancouver, BC, Canada; d. of Victor Ivar Granholm and Shirley Alfreda Granholm (née Dowden); m. Daniel Mulhern 1986; one s. two d.; ed San Carlos High School, Calif., Univ. of California, Berkeley, Harvard Univ. Law School; won Miss San Carlos beauty pageant; abandoned efforts to launch acting career 1980; held jobs as tour guide at Universal Studios, within customer service for Los Angeles Times and was first female tour guide at Marine World Africa USA, Redwood City, piloting boats with 25 tourists aboard; became US citizen 1980; worked for John Anderson's ind. run for Pres. 1980; law clerk, Sixth Circuit Court of Appeals, Detroit 1987–88; Exec. Asst Wayne Co. Exec., Detroit 1988–89; Asst US Attorney, Dept of Justice, Detroit 1990–94; Corp. Counsel, Wayne Co. 1994–99, Gen. Counsel Detroit/Wayne Co. Stadium Authority 1996–98; Attorney-Gen. of Mich. 1999–2002; Gov. of Mich. (first female gov.) 2003–11; Distinguished Practitioner of Law and Public Policy, Goldman School of Public Policy, Univ. of California, Berkeley 2011–; mem. Bd of Dirs Dow Chemical Co. 2011, Marinette Marine Corpn 2011; Sr Advisor on clean energy policies, Pew Charitable Trusts 2011; mem. transition team for presidency of Pres. Barack Obama 2008–09; Vice-Pres. YWCA Inkster, Mich. 1995; fmr Commr, Great Lakes Comm.; fmr mem. Midwestern Govs Asscn (Vice-Chair. 2008–09, Chair. 2009); mem. Detroit Bar Asscn, Leadership Detroit, Womens' Law Asscn, Inc. Soc. of Irish Lawyers, Bd Cyberstate.org, YWCA; Democrat; Commdr, Royal Order of the Polar Star (Sweden) 2010; Public Servant of the Year, Mich. Asscn of Chiefs of Police, Michigander of the Year, Michigan Jaycees, Woman of Achievement Award, YWCA 1997, named by Politico as one of The 50 Politicos to Watch 2010. *Television:* fmr contestant on daytime game show The Dating Game, announced as host, The War Room with Jennifer Granholm, Current TV. *Publications:* numerous articles in professional journals. *Leisure interests:* running, family. *Address:* Richard and Rhoda Goldman School of Public Policy, University of California, Berkeley, 2607 Hearst Avenue, Berkeley, CA 94720-7320, USA (office). *Telephone:* (510) 642-4670 (office). *Fax:* (510) 643-9657 (office). *Website:* gspp .berkeley.edu (office).

GRANIĆ, Mate, DrSc; Croatian politician and physician; *Chairman and CEO, Magra Ltd;* b. 19 Sept. 1947, Baska Voda; m. Jadranka Granic; one s. two d.; ed Zagreb Univ.; physician, Vuk Vrhovac Inst. for Diabetes Endocrinology and Metabolic Diseases, School of Medicine, Zagreb Univ. 1975–79; Head of Clinical Dept Vuk Vrhovac Inst. 1979–85; Prof., Deputy Dir 1985–89; Vice-Dean, Faculty of Medicine, Zagreb Univ. 1989, Dean 1990; mem. and Vice-Pres. Croatian Democratic Union (HDZ); Deputy Prime Minister 1991–99; concurrently Minister of Foreign Affairs 1993–2000; presidential cand. (HDZ) Jan. 2000; led splinter faction of HDZ to form Democratic Centre Party (Demokratski centar—DC) 2000, Pres. 2000–02, left DC and retd from public life 2003; arrested under corruption charges 2004, charges later dropped; foreign policy adviser to Croatian Party of Rights 2005–; f. MAGRA Ltd consulting co. 2004–. *Publications:* papers and articles on diabetes. *Address:* MAGRA Ltd, Petrinjska 61, Zagreb, Croatia (office). *Telephone:* (1) 4811180 (office); (1) 4810510 (office). *E-mail:* magra@magra-doo.hr (office). *Website:* www.magra-doo.hr (office).

GRANÖ, Olavi Johannes, PhD; Finnish geographer and academic; *Professor Emeritus of Geography, Turku University;* b. 27 May 1925, Helsinki; s. of Prof. Dr J. Gabriel Granö and Hilma Ekholm; m. Eeva Kaleva 1953; two d.; ed Turku, Helsinki and Copenhagen Univs; Asst Prof. of Geography, Helsinki Univ. and Helsinki School of Econs 1948–57; Assoc. Prof. of Geography, Turku Univ. 1958–61, Prof. 1962–88, Chancellor 1984–94, currently Prof. Emer. of Geography; Pres. Archipelago Research Inst. 1965–84; Pres. Finnish Nat. Research Council for Sciences 1964–69; Pres. Cen. Bd of Research Councils (Acad. of Finland) 1970–73; mem. Science Policy Council 1964–74; Pres. Advisory Cttee for Research of Nordic Council of Ministers 1976–82; Fellow Acad. of Finland 1980–; mem. Finnish Acad. of Science and Letters 1970; (Chair. 1993–95); mem. Royal Swedish Acad. of Sciences 1985, Academia Europaea 1989; Visiting Fellow, Clare Hall, Cambridge Univ. 1982; Hon. Corresp. mem. Royal Geographical Soc. (London) 1980; Hon. mem. Geographical Soc. of S. Sweden 1981, Geographical Soc. of Turku 1991,

Students' Union of Turku Univ. 1992, Geographical Soc. of Finland 2001, Finnish Soc. for the History of Science and Learning 2005; Hon. Pres. Finnish Inst. of Migration 1999; Hon. Fellow Acad. of Finland; Dr hc (Toruń, Poland) 1980, (Tartu, Estonia) 1989, (Åbo Academy, Turku) 1993; Finnish Geographical Soc. Fennia Medal 1988, Hon. award Finnish Acad. of Science and Letters 1993. *Publications:* scientific publications on geography, geology, history of science and science policy. *Address:* Department of Geography, Turku University, 20014 Turku (office); Sirppitie 1A, 20540 Turku, Finland (home). *Telephone:* (2) 3335595 (office); (2) 2370640 (home). *Fax:* (2) 3335896 (office). *E-mail:* olavi.grano@utu.fi (office); olavi .grano@nic.fi (home). *Website:* www.sci.utu.fi/maantiede (office).

GRANT, B. Rosemary, PhD, FRS; British evolutionary biologist and academic; *Senior Research Scholar and Professor Emeritus, Department of Ecology and Evolutionary Biology, Princeton University;* b. (Barbara Rosemary Matchett), 8 Oct. 1936, Arnside, Cumbria, England; m. Peter Raymond Grant; two d.; ed Univ. of Edinburgh, Uppsala Univ., Sweden; Research Assoc., Univ. of British Columbia, Canada 1960–64, Yale Univ. 1964–65, McGill Univ., Montréal, Canada 1973–77, Univ. of Michigan 1977–85; Research Scholar and Lecturer, Princeton Univ. 1985–96, Sr Research Scholar and Prof. 1997–, now Emer.; Visiting Prof., Univ. of Zurich, Switzerland 2002, 2003; Edward P. Bass Distinguished Visiting Prof., Yale Univ. 2010; Foreign Fellow, RSC 2004; mem. American Acad. of Arts and Sciences 1997, Gen. Ass. Charles Darwin Foundation 2002, American Philosophical Soc. 2010; carried out, with Peter R. Grant, extensive research into evolution, ecology and behaviour amongst Darwin's finches of the Galápagos Islands from 1973; Hon. Fellow, Deutsche Ornithologen-Gesellschaft 2003; Dr hc (McGill Univ.) 2000, (Universidad San Francisco, Quito) 2005; Hon. DSc (Ohio Wesleyan Univ.) 2012; (with Peter Grant) Leidy Medal, Acad. of Natural Sciences of Philadelphia 1994, E.O. Wilson Prize, American Soc. of Naturalists 1998, Darwin Medal, Royal Soc. of London 2002, Loye and Alden Miller Award, Cooper Ornithological Soc. 2003, Grinnell Award, Univ. of California, Berkeley 2003, A.I.B.S Outstanding Scientist Award 2005, Balzan Prize in Population Biology 2005, Darwin-Wallace Medal (bestowed every 50 years by the Linnean Soc. of London) 2008, Kyoto Prize, Inamori Foundation (co-recipient) 2009, Rosemary and Peter Grant Lecture series, Univ. of Zurich, inaugurated 2011. *Publications:* Evolutionary Dynamics of a Natural Population: The Large Cactus Finch of the Galápagos (with Peter R. Grant) (Wildlife Publication Award, The Wildlife Soc. 1991) 1989, How and Why Species Multiply: The Radiation of Darwin's Finches 2008, In Search of the Causes of Evolution. From Field Observations to Mechanisms (co-ed.) 2010; more than 70 publs in scientific journals. *Address:* Department of Ecology and Evolutionary Biology, Room 106, Eno Hall, Princeton University, Princeton, NJ 08544-1003, USA (office). *Telephone:* (609) 258-6290 (office). *Fax:* (609) 258-1334 (office). *E-mail:* rgrant@princeton.edu (office). *Website:* www.princeton.edu/eeb (office).

GRANT, Hugh, MSc, MBA; British bioengineering industry executive; *Chairman, President and CEO, Monsanto Company;* b. 23 March 1958, Larkhall, Scotland; ed Univs of Glasgow and Edinburgh, Int. Man. Centre, Buckingham; joined Monsanto as product devt rep. for co.'s agricultural business in 1981, led Monsanto's marketing, sales and tech. orgs in Europe and North America, later Man. Dir all Monsanto business units in SE Asia, Australia and NZ, later Exec. Vice-Pres. and COO Monsanto Co. –2003, Chair., Pres. and CEO 2003–, Chair. Exec. Cttee; mem. Int. Advisory Bd Scottish Enterprise, Civic Progress, Pres.'s Advisory Group of CropLife Int.; mem. Bd of Dirs PPG Industries Inc., Biotechnology Industry Org.; mem. Bd of Commrs St Louis Science Centre; mem. Bd of Trustees Donald Danforth Plant Science Centre, Washington Univ., St Louis; mem. CEO Council; Dr hc (Webster Univ.) 2009. *Address:* Monsanto Company, 800 North Lindbergh Boulevard, St Louis, MO 63167, USA (office). *Telephone:* (314) 694-1000 (office). *Fax:* (314) 694-8394 (office). *Website:* www.monsanto.com (office).

GRANT, Hugh John Mungo, BA; British actor; b. 9 Sept. 1960, London; s. of James Murray Grant and the late Fynvola Susan Grant (née Maclean); partner 1st Elizabeth Hurley 1987–2000; partner 2nd Jemima Khan 2004–07; one d.; ed Latymer Upper School, Hammersmith, New College, Oxford; acting in theatre, TV and films and producer for Simian Films; began career in theatre performing Jockeys of Norfolk (written with Chris Lang and Andy Taylor); Best Actor, Venice Film Festival (jtly with James Wilby q.v.) 1987, Golden Globe Award and BAFTA Award for Best Actor in Four Weddings and a Funeral 1995, Peter Sellers Award for Comedy, Evening Standard British Film Awards for Four Weddings 1995, Notting Hill 2000 and Bridget Jones' Diary 2002, Best British Actor, Empire Film Awards for Notting Hill 2000, About a Boy 2003, London Critics Circle Film Awards Best British Actor for About a Boy 2003, BAFTA/LA Stanley Kubrick Britannia Award 2003. *Films include:* White Mischief 1987, Maurice 1987, Lair of the White Worm 1988, La Nuit Bengali 1988, Impromptu 1989, Bitter Moon 1992, Remains of the Day 1993, Four Weddings and a Funeral 1994, Sirens 1994, The Englishman Who Went up a Hill But Came down a Mountain 1995, Nine Months 1995, An Awfully Big Adventure 1995, Sense and Sensibility 1995, Restoration 1996, Extreme Measures (for Simian Films) 1996, Mickey Blue Eyes (for Simian Films) 1998, Notting Hill 1999, Small Time Crooks 2000, Bridget Jones' Diary 2001, About a Boy 2002, Two Weeks' Notice 2002, Love Actually 2003, Bridget Jones: The Edge of Reason 2004, American Dreamz 2006, Music and Lyrics 2006, Did You Hear About the Morgans? 2009, The Boat that Rocked 2009, The Pirates! Band of Misfits (voice) 2012, Cloud Atlas 2012. *Leisure interest:* golf.

GRANT, Sir Ian D., Kt, CBE, FRAgS; British civil servant (retd) and business executive; farmed in Perthshire 1962–93; Scottish Commr, The Crown Estate 1996–2002, Chair. 2002–09; fmr Deputy Chair. Scottish & Southern Energy plc; Deputy Chair. NFU Mutual –2008; Chair. Scottish Exhbn Centre Ltd, Glasgow; fmr Pres. Nat. Farmers Union Scotland; fmr Chair. EC Cereals Working Party, Int. Fed. of Agricultural Producers Grains Cttee, Scottish Tourist Bd; fmr Dir (non-exec.) East of Scotland Farmers, Clydesdale Bank plc; Hon. DBA (Napier Univ., Edinburgh). *Address:* c/o The Crown Estate, 16 New Burlington Place, London, W1S 2HX, England. *Telephone:* (20) 7851-5000. *E-mail:* enquiries@thecrownestate .co.uk.

GRANT, Sir John Douglas Kelso, Kt, KCMG, BA; British diplomatist; b. 17 Oct. 1954; s. of Douglas Marr Kelso Grant and Audrey Stevenson Grant (née Law); m. Anna Maria Lindvall; one s. two d.; ed Edinburgh Acad., St Catharine's Coll., Cambridge; joined FCO 1976, W African Dept 1976–77, Third Sec. (later Second Sec.), Chancery, British Embassy, Stockholm 1977–80, Russian Language Training 1980–81, First Sec., Commercial, British Embassy, Moscow 1982–84, Desk Officer, Soviet Dept, FCO, London 1984–85, Press Office, FCO 1986–89, Press Spokesman (later First Sec. External Relations), UK Rep. Office, Brussels 1989–93, European Secr., Cabinet Office 1993–94, Counsellor, External Relations, UK Rep. Office, Brussels 1994–97, Prin. Pvt. Sec., Sec. of State's Office, London 1997–99, Amb. to Sweden 1999–2003, Perm. Rep. to EU 2003–07; Morgan Grenfell and Co. Ltd 1985–86; Exec. Vice-Pres., BG Group PLC 2009–. *Leisure interests:* walking, cross-country skiing. *Address:* BG Group plc, Thames Valley Park, Reading, Berks., RG6 1PT, England (office).

GRANT, Keith Frederick, NDD, ARCA; British landscape painter, muralist and lecturer; b. (Frederick Nall), 10 Aug. 1930, Liverpool; adopted s. of Charles Grant and Gladys Emma Grant; m. 1st Gisèle Barka Djouadi 1964 (divorced 1999); one s. (deceased) one d.; m. 2nd Hilde Ellingsen 2000; one d.; ed Bootle Grammar School, Willesden School of Art and RCA, London; State Scholarship to Norway 1960; Head of Fine Art Dept, Maidstone Coll. of Art, Kent 1968–71; Gulbenkian Award Artist-in-Residence, Bosworth Coll., Leics. 1973–75; mem. Fine Art Bd CNAA 1978–81; Head of Painting Dept, Newcastle Polytechnic 1979–81; Head of Dept of Art, The Roehampton Inst., London 1981–90, Artist-in-Residence 1990–95; Expedition Artist to Guyana 1991; Art Dir Operation Raleigh 1991–95; solo shows in London 1960– and shows in Iceland, Norway, France, Italy and Luxembourg; recorded volcanic eruption, Iceland 1973; painted launch of Ariane Rocket 1982; visited Soviet Union for Anglo-Soviet cultural exchange programme of the British Council 1979; other British Council tours to Cyprus 1976, Hungary, Cuba 1985 and Norway 1987; visited Sarawak 1984 and 1985; designed prints for use in Earthlife Foundation's Rainforest Campaign; designed book covers for 6 Peter Mattheissen works 1988–89; visited Greenland to study icebergs at Ilulissat (Jakobshavn); Guest Artist, Ben Gurion Univ. of the Negev and British Israel Art Foundation 1988; elected mem. Telemark Artists' Asscn, Norway 1996; mem. Royal Cambrian Acad. 2001; selected to inaugurate Artists' and Writers' Programme Antarctica 2001/2002 of the British Antarctic Survey; Silver Medal for Mural Painting, RCA 1958. *Works:* works in many public collections including Arts Council of GB, Nat. Gallery of NZ, Nat. Gallery of S Australia, Hamilton Art Gallery, Ontario, Trondheim Art Gallery, Norway, Contemporary Art Soc., Fitzwilliam Museum, Cambridge, Abbot Hall Gallery, Kendal, British Council, All Souls Coll. Oxford, Imperial Coll. London, Victoria and Albert Museum, Richmond College, London, Univ. of E Anglia, Haugesund Art Gallery, Norway, Nat. Gallery of Iceland; mural/mosaics, stained glass window, Charing Cross Hosp., London, Gateshead Metro Station; painting, Guildhall School of Music and Drama, London, Avaldsnes triptych, Karmøy Kommune, Norway; sculpture, Shaw Theatre, London; commissioned to paint triptych for Church of Kopervik, Karmøy, Norway 2004. *Publications:* journals and sketchbooks 1960s–, archived in Fitzwilliam Museum, Cambridge. *Leisure interests:* walking, music, travel and writing; member of Garrick Club, London. *Address:* Partridge Fine Arts PLC, 144–146 New Bond Street, London, W1S 2PF, England (office); Holmenvegen 43, PO Box 7, 3834 Gvarv, Telemark, Norway. *Telephone:* 35959795. *Fax:* 35959795. *E-mail:* kefreg@online.no. *Website:* www.keithgrant.co.uk.

GRANT, Sir Malcolm John, Kt, CBE, LLB, LLM, LLD, AcSS; New Zealand/British university administrator, barrister, environmental lawyer, academic and public servant; *Chairman, NHS England;* b. 29 Nov. 1947, Oamaru; s. of Frank Grant and Vera Grant; m. Christine Grant (née Endersbee) 1974; three c.; ed Univ. of Otago; barrister and solicitor, NZ 1969–; barrister, Middle Temple 1998–, Bencher 2004–; Lecturer in Law, Univ. of Southampton 1972–86; Prof. of Law and Vice-Dean, Univ. Coll. London 1986–91, Pres. and Provost 2003–13; Prof. of Land Economy, Univ. of Cambridge 1991–2003, Head, Dept of Land Economy 1993–2001, Pro-Vice-Chancellor 2002–03, Fellow, Clare Coll. 1991–; Specialist Adviser, Parl. Jt Cttee on Pvt. Bill Procedure 1987–88; Chair. Asscn of London Govt's Ind. Panel on Remuneration of Councillors in London 1998–2005, Agric. and Environment Biotechnology Comm. 2000–05, UK Ind. Steering Bd for Public Debate on Genetic Modification 2002–03, The Russell Group of UK Research Univs 2006–09, Standards Cttee, Greater London Authority 2004–08 (Ind. mem. 2000–08, Deputy Chair. 2001–04); UK Business Amb. 2008–; mem. Local Govt Comm. for England 1992–2002 (Deputy Chair. 1995–96, Chair. 1996–2002), Advisory Bd Environmental Law Foundation 1993–, The Ditchley Foundation 2003–11 (Gov. 2002–), Higher Educ. Funding Council for England 2008–, Econ. and Social Research Council 2008–11, Univ. Grants Cttee Hong Kong 2007–, Int. Council for Global Competitiveness of Russian Univs 2013–; Dir, Genomics England Ltd 2013–; Chair. NHS Commissioning Bd (known as NHS England since March 2013) 2011–; consultant, Singapore Govt 1992–98, UNESCO 1993–94; Ed. Encyclopedia of Planning Law and Practice (seven vols) 1981–2006, Consultant Ed. 2006–; Consultant Ed. Encyclopedia of Environmental Law (eight vols) 1993–; Trustee, Somerset House 2014–; Academician, Acad. of Learned Socs for the Social Sciences 2000; Hon. mem. Royal Town Planning Inst. 1993–, Royal Inst. of Chartered Surveyors 1995–; Hon. Life mem. NZ Resource Man. Law Asscn 1999–; Officier, Ordre nat. du Mérite 2004; Hon. LLD (Otago) 2006, (Univ. Coll. London) 2013. *Publications:* Planning Law Handbook 1981, Urban Planning Law 1982, Rate Capping and the Law 1984, The Local Government Finance Act 1988, Permitted Development 1989, The Concise Lexicon of Environmental Terms (co-author) 1995, Singapore Planning Law 1999, The Environmental Court Project: Final Report 2000; numerous articles on planning and environmental law, regulation of biotechnology, local govt structures, finance and political man., central-local govt relations, human rights, property and participation, and environmental dispute resolution. *Address:* Chairman's Office, NHS England, 4W20 4th Floor, Quarry House, Quarry Hill, Leeds, LS2 7UA, England (office). *Telephone:* (113) 825-1104 (office). *E-mail:* laurabanks1@nhs.net (office). *Website:* www.england.nhs.uk (office).

GRANT, Peter Raymond, PhD, FRS, FRSC, FLS, FAAS; British biologist and academic; *Class of 1877 Professor Emeritus of Zoology and Professor Emeritus of Ecology and Evolutionary Biology, Princeton University;* b. 26 Oct. 1936, London, England; s. of Frederick Thomas Charles Grant and Mavis Irene Grant; m. Barbara Rosemary Matchett 1962; two d.; ed Univ. of Cambridge and Univ. of British Columbia, Canada; Postdoctoral Fellowship, Yale Univ. 1964–65; Asst Prof. of Biology, McGill Univ., Canada 1965–68, Assoc. Prof. 1968–73, Prof. 1973–78; Prof., Univ. of Michigan 1978–85; Prof. of Biology, Princeton Univ. 1985–89, Class of 1877 Prof., Dept of Ecology and Evolutionary Biology 1989–, now

Emer.; Visiting Prof., Univs of Uppsala and Lund, Sweden 1981, Univ. of Uppsala 1985; Edward P. Bass Distinguished Visiting Prof., Yale Univ. 2010; Assoc. Ed., Ecology 1968–70, Evolutionary Theory 1973–, Biological Journal of the Linnean Society 1984–, Philosophical Transactions of the Royal Society of London 1990–93; mem. American Philosophical Soc. 1991, American Acad. of Arts and Sciences 1997, American Soc. of Naturalists (Pres. 1999, Past Pres. 2000), Soc. for the Study of Evolution, Ecological Soc. of America, Soc. for Behavioral Ecology; Foreign mem. Royal Soc. of Sciences, Uppsala 1993, NAS 2007; Fellow, American Ornithologists' Union; Hon. mem. Nuttall Ornithological Soc. 2004, American Soc. of Naturalists 2008, Gen. Ass., Charles Darwin Foundation 2010; Hon. Fellow, Deutsche Ornithologen-Gesellschaft 2003; Hon. Citizen, Puerto Bacquerizo, I. San Cristóbal, Galápagos 2005; Hon. PhD (Uppsala) 1986, (Zurich) 2008; Hon. DSc (McGill) 2000, (Universidad San Francisco, Quito, Ecuador) 2005, (Ohio Wesleyan Univ.) 2012; Brewster Medal, American Ornithologists' Union 1983, S. Guggenheim Memorial Fellowship 1985–86, Sr Visiting Research Fellowship, Jesus Coll., Oxford 1986, Leidy Medal, Acad. of Natural Sciences of Philadelphia (with B. R. Grant) 1994, Alexander von Humboldt Foundation Sr Scientist Research Prize 1996, E.O. Wilson Prize, American Soc. of Naturalists (with B. R. Grant) 1998, Convocation Address, McGill Univ. 2000, Charles Darwin Foundation Millenial Medal for Conservation in Galápagos 2000, Uppsala Univ. official inauguration of the Evolutionary Biology Centre, Plenary Address 2000, Darwin Medal, Royal Soc. (with B. R. Grant) 2002, Loye and Alden Miller Award, Cooper Ornithological Soc. (with B. R. Grant) 2003, Grinnell Award, Univ. of California, Berkeley 2003, Nobel Conf. XXXIX, Gustavus Adolphus Coll. 2003, Outstanding Scientist Award, American Inst. of Biological Sciences (with B. R. Grant) 2005, Balzan Prize in Population Biology (with B. R. Grant) 2005, Municipality of Puerto Ayora Science Award, I. Santa Cruz, Galápagos (with B. R. Grant) 2006, Darwin-Wallace Medal, Linnean Soc. (with B. R. Grant) 2009, Kyoto Prize in Basic Sciences (with B. R. Grant) 2009, Rosemary and Peter Grant Lecture series, Univ. of Zurich, inaugurated 2011. *Publications:* Ecology and Evolution of Darwin's Finches 1986, Evolutionary Dynamics of a Natural Population: The Large Cactus Finch of the Galápagos (with B. Rosemary Grant) (Wildlife Publication Award, The Wildlife Soc. 1991) 1989, Molds, Molecules and Metazoa: Growing Points in Evolutionary Biology 1992, Evolution on Islands (ed.) 1998, How and Why Species Multiply (with B. Rosemary Grant) 2008, In Search of the Causes of Evolution. From Field Observations to Mechanisms (co-ed.) 2010. *Leisure interests:* camping, hiking, music and reading. *Address:* Department of Ecology and Evolutionary Biology, Room 105, Eno Hall, Princeton University, Princeton, NJ 08544-003, USA (office). *Telephone:* (609) 258-5156 (office). *Fax:* (609) 258-1334 (office). *E-mail:* prgrant@princeton.edu (office). *Website:* www.princeton.edu/eeb (office).

GRANT, Richard E., BA; British actor; b. 5 May 1957, Mbabane, Swaziland; s. of the late Hendrick Grant and of Leonie Grant; m. Joan Washington; one d.; ed S Africa; grew up in Swaziland. *Stage appearances include:* Man of Mode 1988, The Importance of Being Earnest 1993, A Midsummer Night's Dream 1994, Otherwise Engaged 2005, My Fair Lady (Sydney Opera) 2008, God of Carnage 2009. *Films include:* Withnail and I 1986, How to Get Ahead in Advertising 1989, Warlock 1989, Henry and June 1990, Mountains of the Moon 1990, LA Story 1991, Hudson Hawk 1991, Bram Stoker's Dracula 1992, The Player 1993, The Age of Innocence 1993, Prêt à Porter 1995, Jack and Sarah 1995, Portrait of a Lady 1995, Twelfth Night 1995, The Serpent's Kiss 1996, Food of Love 1996, All For Love 1997, Spice World – The Movie 1997, The Match 1998, A Christmas Carol 1999, Trial and Retribution 1999, Little Vampires 1999, Hildegarde 2000, Gosford Park (Screen Actors Guild Best Actor 2001) 2001, Monsieur 'N' 2002, Tooth 2002, Bright Young Things 2003, The Story of an African Farm 2003, Colour Me Kubrick: A True…ish Story 2004, Wah-Wah (dir and writer) 2005, Corpse Bride (voice) 2005, Bustin' Bonaparte (video) 2005, Garfield: A Tail of Two Kitties (voice) 2006, Penelope 2006, Jackboots on Whitehall (voice) 2007, Love Hurts 2008, Cosi 2009, Zambezia (voice) 2010, The Iron Lady 2011. *TV appearances include:* Honest, Decent, Legal and True 1986, Here is the News 1989, Suddenly Last Summer 1992, Hard Times 1993, Karaoke 1996, A Royal Scandal 1996, The Scarlet Pimpernel 1998, Hound of the Baskervilles 2002, Posh Nosh 2003, Frasier 2004, Patrick Hamilton: Words, Whisky and Women (video) 2005, Home Farm Twins (series) 2005, Above and Beyond (mini-series) 2005, Marple: Nemesis 2006, Dalziel & Pascoe 2006, The Secret Policeman's Ball 2006, Freezing 2007, Mumbai Calling 2008, Dear Diaries 2009, History of Safari 2010. *Publications:* With Nails: The Film Diaries of Richard E. Grant 1995, Twelfth Night 1996, By Design – A Hollywood Novel 1998, The Wah-Wah Diaries: The Making of a Film 2006. *Leisure interests:* scuba diving, building dolls' houses, photography. *Address:* c/o Independent Talent, Oxford House, 76 Oxford Street, London, W1N 0AX, England (office). *Telephone:* (20) 7636-6565 (office). *Fax:* (20) 7323-0101 (office). *Website:* www.independenttalent .com (office); www.richard-e-grant.com (office).

GRAPSAS, Gen. Dimitrios; Greek military officer; b. 1948, Ypati; m.; two c.; ed Hellenic Army War Coll., Hellenic Nat. Defense Coll.; fmr Commdr Armored Reconnaissance Battalion, Chief of Staff of 96th Mil. Command, Asst Chief of Staff of Higher Mil. Command of Interior and Islands, Commdr XXV Armored Brigade, Army Corps Chief of Staff; Dir Training Div., then Training and Doctrine Directorate, Hellenic Army Gen. Staff 2002–03; Commdr XX Mechanized Infantry Div. 2003–04; promoted to Lt Gen. 2004; Commdr Higher Mil. Command of Interior and Islands 2005–06; Chief of Hellenic Army Gen. Staff 2006–07, Chief of Defence Staff 2007–09; Golden Cross, Order of Phoenix, Order of Merit, Kt Commdr, Order of Phoenix, Order of Merit, High Cross of the Order of Phoenix, High Cross of the Order of Merit; Medal for Mil. Valor, C Class, Medal for Mil. Valor, B Class, Outstanding Command Commendation Medal, B Class, Staff Officer Service Commendation Medal, B Class, Medal for Mil. Valor, A Class, Formation/Maj. Unit Commendation Medal, C Class, Outstanding Command Commendation Medal, A Class, Staff Officer Service Commendation Medal, A Class, Commendation Medal for Merit and Valor. *Address:* c/o Ministry of National Defence, Odos Mesogeion 227–231, 154 51 Athens, Greece.

GRAPSTEIN, Steven H., BS; American business executive; *Non-Executive Chairman, Tesoro Corporation;* ed Brooklyn Coll.; fmr Man. with Laventhol & Horwarth; Vice-Pres. Kuo Investment Co. and Subsidiaries –1992, CEO 1992–; mem. Bd of Dirs Tesoro Corpn 1992–, Chair. (non-exec.) 2010–, mem. Audit Cttee, Governance Cttee. *Address:* Tesoro Corporation, 300 Concord Plaza Drive, San Antonio, TX 78216-6999, USA (office). *Telephone:* (210) 828-8484 (office). *Fax:* (210)

283-2045 (office). *E-mail:* info@tsocorp.com (office). *Website:* www.tsocorp.com (office).

GRASS, Günter Wilhelm; German writer, poet and artist; b. 16 Oct. 1927, Danzig (now Gdańsk, Poland); m. 1st Anna Schwarz 1954 (divorced 1978); three s. one d.; m. 2nd Ute Grunert 1979; ed Conradinum, Danzig, Kunstakademie, Düsseldorf, Höchschule für Bildende Künste, Berlin; served in Luftwaffe 1944–45; adviser to Städtischen Bühnen Frankfurt am Main 1967–70; mem. Akad. der Künste, Berlin (Pres. 1983–86), American Acad. of Arts and Sciences; mem. Social Democratic Party (resgnd Dec. 1992); Dr hc (Kenyon Coll.) 1965, (Harvard) 1976; Lyric Prize, Süddeutscher Rundfunk 1955, Group 47 Prize 1959, Literary Prize, Asscn of German Critics 1960, Georg-Büchner Prize 1965, Theodor-Heuss Prize 1969, Int. Feltrinelli Prize 1982, Karel Čapek Prize 1994, Sonning Arts Prize (Denmark) 1996, Thomas Mann Prize 1996, Hermann Kestan Medal 1995, Nobel Prize for Literature 1999, Premio Príncipe de Asturias 1999. *Plays:* Beritten, hin und zurück 1954, Hochwasser 1954, Die bösen Köche 1957, Noch Zehn Minuten bis Buffalo 1957, Onkel, Onkel 1958, Zweiunddreissig Zähne 1959, Die Plebejer proben den Aufstand 1965, Davor 1968, Die Vogelscheuchen (ballet) 1970. *Publications:* Die Vorzüge der Windhühner (poems, prose and drawings) 1955, Die Blechtrommel (novel, trans. as The Tin Drum) (Award for Best Foreign Novel, France 1962) 1959, Gleisdreieck (poems and drawings) 1960, Katz und Maus (novella, trans. as Cat and Mouse) 1961, Hundejahre (novel, trans. as Dog Years) 1963, Ausgefragt (poems and drawings) 1967, Über das Selbstverständliche 1968, Örtlich betäubt (novel) 1969, Aus dem Tagebuch einer Schnecke 1972, Dokumente zur politischen Wirkung 1972, Mariazuehren (poems and drawings) 1973, Die Bürger und seine Stimme 1974, Der Butt (novel, trans. as The Flounder) 1976, Denkzettel 1978, Das Treffen in Telgte (novel, trans. as The Meeting in Telgte) 1979, Kopfgeburten oder Die Deutschen sterben aus (novel, trans. as Headbirths, or the Germans are Dying Out) 1980, Aufsätze zur Literatur 1980, Zeichnen und Schreiben Band I 1982, Widerstand lernen-Politische Gegenreden 1980–83 1984 Band II 1984, On Writing and Politics 1967–83 1985, Die Rättin (novel) 1986, Züngezeigen 1987, Werkansgabe (10 vols) 1987, Die Gedichte 1955–1986 1988, Deutscher Lastenausgleich: Wider das dumpfe Einheitsgebot 1990, Two States—One Nation? 1990, Vier Jahrzehnte: Ein Werkstattbericht (drawings and notes) 1991, Unkenrufe (novel, trans. as The Call of the Toad) 1992, Rede vom Verlust: Über den Niedergang der politischen Kultur im geiinten Deutschland 1992, Der Ruf der Kröte (novel) 1992, Studienausgabe (12 vols) 1994, Ein weites Feld (trans. as Too Far Afield) 1995, Fundsachen für Nichtleser (poems) 1997, Auf ein anderes Blatt 1999, Vom Abenteuer der Aufklärung (jtly) 1999, Mein Jahrhundert (trans. as My Century) 1999, Nie wieder schweigen 2000, Fünf Jahrzehnte 2001, Im Krebsgang (novel, trans. as Crabwalk) 2002, Telling Tales (contrib. to charity anthology) 2004, Letzte Tänze (watercolours and drawings) 2003, Beim Häuten der Zwiebel (trans as Peeling the Onion, autobiog.) 2006, Dummer August (poems) 2007, Die Box (trans. as The Box: Tales from the Darkroom) 2008, Grimms Wörter 2010, Unterwegs von Deutschland nach Deutschland. Tagebuch 1990 2012. *Leisure interest:* cooking. *Address:* Glockengiesserstrasse 21, 23552 Lübeck, Germany.

GRASSER, Karl-Heinz, MBA; Austrian business executive and fmr politician; b. 2 Jan. 1969, Klagenfurt; m. Fiona Pacifico Griffini 2005; one d.; ed Univ. of Klagenfurt; mem. Freedom Party (FPÖ), Spokesperson for Tourism and European Integration 1992, FPÖ Sec.-Gen. and Man. Dir Party Educational Centre 1993; Second Deputy Gov. Prov. of Carinthia 1994–98; Vice-Pres. for Human Resources and Public Relations, Magna Europe 1998; Man. Dir Sport Management International 1999; Fed. Minister of Finance 2000–07; mem. Karl Popper Foundation (mem. Man. Bd –1999); Dir Meinl Power Management Ltd. *Address:* c/o Mr M Wanless, Aztec Financial Services (Jersey) Limited, PO Box 730, 11-15 Seaton Place, St Helier, Jersey, JE4 0QH, Channel Islands.

GRASSLE, J. Frederick, BS, PhD; American biologist, ecology and academic; *Professor Emeritus of Benthic Ecology and Ocean Biogeography, Institute of Marine and Coastal Sciences, Rutgers University;* b. 14 July 1939; ed Yale and Duke Univs; Teaching Asst, Duke Univ. 1961–63, Research Asst 1963–64, NSF Oceanography Traineeship, Duke Univ. Marine Lab. 1964–66, NSF Predoctoral Fellowship 1965–66; Fulbright Scholar, Univ. of Queensland, Australia 1966–69; Instructor, Marine Ecology Course, Marine Biological Lab. 1972; Asst Scientist, Woods Hole Oceanographic Inst. 1969-73, Assoc. Scientist 1974–78, Sr Scientist 1978–89, Adjunct Scientist 1989–96; Prof. II and Founding Dir, Inst. of Marine and Coastal Sciences, Rutgers Univ. 1989–2008, Prof. II 2008–12, Prof. Emer. 2012–; mem. Editorial Bd, Journal of Marine Environmental Engineering 1991–2008, Marine Technology Society 1991–2000, Society for Conservation Biology 1991–2000, Marine Biodiversity 1996–2011; Fellow, AAAS, Explorers Club, Linnean Soc. of London; NSF Undergraduate Award, Woods Hole Oceanographic Inst. 1959, NSF Predoctoral Award, Duke Univ. Marine Lab. 1964, UNESCO-Cousteau Ecotechnie Chair in Coastal Resources 2004, Grand Prix des Sciences de la Mer Albert 1er de Monaco 2005, Tom Gagliano Leadership Award, New Jersey Shore Partnership 2007, Vision Award, Nat. Water Quality Monitoring Council 2008, Benjamin Franklin Medal in Earth and Environmental Science 2009, J. Frederick Grassle Science Symposium on Census of Marine Life, Royal Soc., London 2010, A.C. Redfield Lifetime Achievement Award, American Soc. of Limnology and Oceanography 2011, Int. Cosmos Prize, presented by Expo 90 Foundation to the Census of Marine Life Scientific Steering Cttee 2011, 12 marine animal species (*grasslei*) and two genera (*Grasslea*) named in his honour, Japan Prize (co-recipient) 2013. *Publications:* numerous papers in professional journals. *Address:* Institute of Marine and Coastal Sciences, 71 Dudley Road, New Brunswick, NJ 08901-8525, USA (office). *Telephone:* (848) 932-3450 (office). *Fax:* (732) 932-8578 (office). *E-mail:* grassle@marine.rutgers.edu (office). *Website:* marine.rutgers.edu (office).

GRASSLEY, Charles Ernest, BA, MA; American farmer, teacher and politician; *Senator from Iowa;* b. 17 Sept. 1933, New Hartford, Ia; s. of Louis Arthur Grassley and Ruth Corwin; m. Barbara Ann Speicher 1954; three s. two d.; ed Univs of Northern Iowa and Iowa; Instructor, Political Science, Drake Community Coll. 1962, Charles City Coll. 1967–68; mem. U.S House of Reps 1969–75; mem. US House of Reps from 3rd Dist of Ia 1975–81; Senator from Iowa 1981–, Chair. Senate Finance Cttee Jan.–June 2001, 2003–06 (Ranking mem. from 2007), mem. Judiciary (Ranking mem.), Finance, Budget, Agric., and Jt Tax Cttees, Senate

Caucus on Int. Narcotics Control (Co-Chair.), Senate Caucus on Foster Youth (Co-Chair.); mem. Farm Bureau, Butler Co., State of Iowa Historical Societies, Int. Asscn of Machinists 1962–71; Lifetime Achievement Award, Nat. Whistleblower Center 2007, American Council for Capital Formation Arena Award, Health Policy Hero Award, Nat. Research Center for Women and Families 2009 and several other awards. *Address:* 135 Hart Senate Office Building, Washington, DC 20510-0001, USA (office). *Telephone:* (202) 224-3744 (office). *Fax:* (202) 224-6020 (office). *Website:* grassley.senate.gov (office).

GRASSO, Richard A., BS; American fmr stock exchange executive; b. 26 July 1946, Jackson Heights, New York; m. Lorraine Grasso; four c.; ed Pace and Harvard Univs; served in numerous positions with New York Stock Exchange 1968–2003, Dir Listing and Marketing 1973–77, Vice-Pres. Corp. Services 1977–81, Sr Vice-Pres. Corp. Services 1981–83, Exec. Vice-Pres. Marketing Group 1983–86, Exec. Vice-Pres. Capital Markets 1986–88, Pres., COO 1988–93, Exec. Vice-Chair., Pres. 1993–95, Chair. CEO 1994–2003; f. Gladiator Holdings LLC (investment co.), New Jersey; Pres. World Fed. of Exchanges, Paris 2003; fmr Chair. Econ. Club, New York; fmr mem. Bd of Dirs Nat. Italian American Foundation, Washington DC Police Foundation, New York State Business Council, Congressional Medal of Honor Foundation, Centurion Foundation, Lower Manhattan Devt Corpn, New York City Police Foundation, New York City Public Private Initiatives, New York Univ.; mem. Bd of Dirs Computer Associates 1994–2002, Home Depot 2002–04, McCain 2000; Trustee, Stony Brook Foundation; fmr mem. Advisory Bd Yale School of Man. *Address:* 231 Piping Rock Road, Locust Valley, NY 11560-2504, USA.

GRATTAN, Michelle, AO, BA; Australian journalist, political commentator and academic; b. 30 June 1944, Melbourne; ed Univ. of Melbourne; Chief Political Corresp., The Age 1976–93, Political Ed. 1995–96, 2004–13, Political Commentator 2002–04; Ed. Canberra Times 1993–95; sr writer and columnist, Australian Financial Review 1996–98; Chief Political Corresp. Sydney Morning Herald 1999–2002, columnist 2002–04; Professorial Fellow, Univ. of Canberra 2013–; Assoc. Ed. (Politics) and Chief Political Corresp., The Conversation (website) 2013–; Adjunct Prof., School of Journalism and Communication, Univ. of Queensland; Graham Perkin Australian Journalist of the Year Award 1988, Walkley Award for Journalism Leadership 2006. *Publications:* Australian Prime Ministers (ed.) 2000, Reconciliation (ed.) 2000. *Address:* ANZSOG Institute for Governance, University of Canberra, Building 23, level B, University Drive South, Canberra ACT 2601 (office); 147 Mugga Way, Red Hill, Canberra, ACT 2603, Australia (home). *Telephone:* (2) 6201-2074 (office). *Website:* www .governanceinstitute.edu.au (office); theconversation.com (office).

GRAUBNER, Most Rev. Jan; Czech ecclesiastic; *Archbishop of Olomouc and Moravia;* b. 29 Aug. 1948, Brno; s. of Oldrich Graubner and Ludmila Graubner; ed Univ. of Olomouc; ordained priest 1973; ordained Bishop 1990; Auxiliary Bishop of Olomouc 1990–92, Archbishop of Olomouc and Moravia 1992–; Vice-Chair. Czech Bishops' Conf. 1991–2000, Chair. 2000–; Chair. Czech Catholic Charity 1991–; Chair. Palacky Univ., Olomouc; Sec. of Defense Meritorious Cross 2003, Order of St Floriana Fire Asscn (Bohemia, Moravia and Silesia) 2003, Order of TG Masaryk (Czech Republic) 2008. *Publications:* several books and articles. *Address:* Archdiocese of Olomouc, Wurmova 9, p. schr. 193, 77101 Olomouc, Czech Republic (office). *Telephone:* (58) 7405111 (office). *Fax:* (58) 5224840 (office). *E-mail:* arcibol@arcibol.cz (office). *Website:* www.ado.cz (office).

GRAUERT, Johannes (Hans), Dr rer. nat; German mathematician and academic; *Professor Emeritus, University of Göttingen;* b. 8 Feb. 1930, Haren/Ems; s. of Clemens Grauert; m. Marie-Luise Meyer 1956; one s. one d.; ed Univs of Mainz and Münster and ETH, Zürich; Inst. for Advanced Study, Princeton 1957–59; Inst. des Hautes Etudes, Paris 1959 (mem. Supervisory Bd 1976–82); Prof. Univ. of Göttingen 1959–95, Prof. Emeritus, 1995–; mem. Acad. of Science, Göttingen (Pres. 1994–96, mem. Acad. of Science and of Literature Mainz, Acad. Leopoldina (Halle Saale), Acad. Mediterranea Catania, Academia Europaea, Acad. of Bayern (von Staudt Prize 1991); Hon. Dr rer. nat (Bayreuth) 1989, (Bochum) 1990, (Bonn) 1990. *Publications:* ten books and numerous papers in leading journals. *Leisure interests:* pure mathematics, philosophy.

GRAUŽINIENĖ, Loreta; Lithuanian economist and politician; *Chairman (Speaker), Seimas (Parliament);* b. 10 Jan. 1963, Rokiškis; m.; two s.; ed Žiežmariai Secondary School (now Žiežmariai Gymnasium), Kaišiadorys Dist, Lithuanian Acad. of Agric. (now Aleksandras Stulginskis Univ.), Lithuanian Inst. of Accounting and Audit; accountant, Peat Devt Authority 1982–86; economist, Asscn of Public Utilities, accountant, Agricultural Machinery Asscn of Ukmergė, collective farm Žiburys, Ukmergė Dist 1986–92; Chief Accountant, several pvt. cos 1992–94; Lecturer, Vocational Agricultural School, Ukmergė (now Vocational Business School) 1994–2004; Owner, pvt. co. providing business operation analysis, accounting, audit and advisory services 1996–2004; mem. Labour Party 2003–, Chair. Cttee on Audit, mem. Cttee on Budget and Finance, Cttee on European Affairs, Comm. for Parl. Scrutiny of Operational Activities 2004–08, mem. Labour Party Political Group 2008–12, mem. Cttee on Audit, on European Affairs, Labour Party Political Group 2012–13, Chair. Labour Party 2013–; cand. in presidential election 2009; mem. Seimas (Parl.) 2004–, mem. Cttee on Social Affairs and Labour 2012–13, Cttee on Audit 2013, Cttee on European Affairs 2013, Chair. (Speaker) 2013–, mem. Bd of the Seimas 2013–, mem. Labour Party Political Group 2012–13, mem. Conf. of Chairs 2013–, Deputy Chair. Women's Parl. Group, Parl. Group for Welfare of the Child, mem. Parl. Group 'For Corruption-Free Lithuania', Parl. Group 'Aukštaitija', Parl. Group for Assisting Rural Communities and Farmers in Addressing Matters of Their Concern, Group for Inter-Parl. Relations with Georgia, Group for Inter-Parl. Relations with the Repub. of India, Group for Inter-Parl. Relations with the Repub. of Estonia, Chair. Seimas Del. to Ass. of Members of the Seimas of the Repub. of Lithuania, the Sejm and Senate of the Repub. of Poland, and the Verkhovna Rada of Ukraine 2013–; mem. Lithuanian Chamber of Auditors. *Leisure interests:* reading, outdoor leisure activities. *Address:* Seimas (Parliament), Gedimino pr. 53, 01109 Vilnius (office); Klaipėdos g. 7-43, 20130 Ukmergė m., Lithuania. *Telephone:* (5) 239-6001 (office); (5) 2396001. *Fax:* (5) 239-6330 (office). *E-mail:* loreta.grauziniene@lrs.lt (office). *Website:* www.lrs.lt (office).

GRAVEL, Mike, BS; American organization official and fmr politician; b. 13 May 1930, Springfield, Mass.; s. of Alphonse Gravel and Maria Gravel; m. 1st Rita

Martin 1959; m. 2nd Whitney Gravel; one s. one d.; ed Columbia Univ.; served in US Army 1951–54, served as adjutant in Communications Intelligence Services and Special Agent in Counter Intelligence Corps; real estate developer; mem. Alaska House of Reps 1962–66, Speaker 1965; Senator from Alaska 1969–81; f. Mike Gravel Resource Analysts, Anchorage, Alaska 1981–; Founder Philadelphia II and Direct Democracy (non-profit orgs), merged to create Democracy Foundation 1989; mem. Bd of Counselors, Center for Econ. and Social Justice; Hon. mem. Advisory Bd Student World Ass. *Publications:* Jobs and More Jobs, Citizen Power, The Pentagon Papers (ed.). *Address:* c/o The Democracy Foundation, 1600 North Oak Street, Suite 1412, Arlington, VA 22209-2757, USA.

GRAVES, Jennifer (Jenny), AO, BSc, MSc, PhD, FAA; Australian geneticist and academic; *Distinguished Professor, Institute of Molecular Science, La Trobe University;* b. 24 Dec. 1941, Adelaide; d. of Theo John Marshall and Ann Nicholls; m.; two d.; ed Univ. of Adelaide, Univ. of California, Berkeley, USA; Lecturer in Genetics, La Trobe Univ. 1971–91; Prof. of Genetics 1991–2001; Prof. of Comparative Genomics and Group Leader, Comparative Genomics Research Group and ARC Centre for Kangaroo Genomics, Research School of Biological Sciences, ANU 2001, now Prof. Emer.; currently Distinguished Prof., Inst. of Molecular Science, La Trobe Univ.; Thinker-in-Residence, Univ. of Canberra; Professorial Fellow, Univ. of Melbourne; Fulbright Scholar 1963–71, L'Oréal-UNESCO Women in Science Award (Asia/Pacific Laureate) 2006, Australian Thinker of the Year, Int. School of Thinking 2007. *Address:* Level 1, LIMS2, La Trobe University, Melbourne, VIC 3086 (office); Building 46, Research School of Biology, Australian National University, Acton, ACT 0200, (office); Building 10 level C, University of Canberra, University Drive, Bruce, ACT 2601, Australia (office). *Telephone:* (3) 9439-5109 (office). *E-mail:* J.Graves@latrobe.edu.au (office); jenny.graves@anu.edu.au (office). *Website:* www.latrobe.edu.au/scitecheng (office).

GRAVES, Rupert; British actor; b. 30 June 1963, Weston-Super-Mare, Somerset, England; s. of Richard Harding Graves and Mary Lousilla Graves (née Roberts); m. Suzanne Lewis 2000; three s. two d.; ed Wyvern Community School. *Theatre includes:* Killing Mr Toad, Sufficient Carbohydrates, Torch Song Trilogy, The Importance of Being Earnest, A Midsummer Night's Dream, Madhouse in Goa, Closer (Theatre World Award) 1999, The Elephant Man 2002. *Films include:* A Room With A View 1986, Maurice 1987, A Handful of Dust 1988, The Children 1990, The Plot To Kill Hitler 1990, Where Angels Fear To Tread 1991, Damage 1992, Royal Celebration 1993, The Madness of King George 1994, Sheltering Desert 1994, The Innocent Sleep 1995, Intimate Relations (Best Actor, Montreal Film Festival 1996) 1996, Different for Girls 1996, The Revengers' Comedies 1997, Mrs Dalloway 1997, Dreaming of Joseph Lees 1998, Room to Rent 2000, The Extremists 2001, Snake 2001, Rag Tale 2005, V for Vendetta 2006, Death at a Funeral 2007, Intervention 2007, The Waiting Room 2007, Made in Dagenham 2010, Fast Girls 2012. *Television includes:* Fortunes of War (mini-series) 1987, Open Fire (film) 1994, Doomsday Gun (film) 1994, The Tenant of Wildfell Hall (mini-series) 1996, The Blonde Bombshell (film) 1999, Cleopatra (mini-series) 1999, The Forsyte Saga (mini-series) 2002–03, The Forsyte Saga: To Let (mini-series) 2003, Charles II: The Power & the Passion (mini-series) 2003, A Waste of Shame: The Mystery of Shakespeare and His Sonnets (film) 2005, Son of the Dragon (mini-series) 2006, To Be First 2007, Clapham Junction (film) 2007, The Dinner Party (film) 2007, To Be First (film) 2007, Ashes to Ashes (series) 2008, Waking the Dead (series) 2008, Midnight Man (mini-series) 2008, God on Trial (film) 2008, Marple: A Pocket Full of Rye (film) 2008, Masterpiece Contemporary (series) 2008, The Good Times Are Killing Me (film) 2009, Garrow's Law (series) 2009–12, Wallander (series) 2010, Lewis (series) 2010, Law & Order: UK (series) 2010, New Tricks (series) 2010, Single Father (mini-series) 2010, Sherlock (series) 2010–12, Case Sensitive (series) 2011, Scott & Bailey (series) 2011, Death in Paradise (series) 2011, The Charles Dickens Show (series) 2012, Doctor Who (series) 2012, Secret State (series) 2012, Air Force One is Down (series) 2013, The White Queen (series) 2013. *Address:* c/o United Agents, 12–26 Lexington Street, London, W1F 0LE, England. *Telephone:* (20) 3214-0800. *Fax:* (20) 3214-0801. *E-mail:* info@unitedagents.co.uk. *Website:* unitedagents.co.uk; www.rupert-graves.com (office).

GRAVES, William Preston; American national organization official and fmr politician; *President and CEO, American Trucking Associations Inc.;* b. 9 Jan. 1953, Salina, Kan.; s. of William Graves and Helen Mayo; m. Linda Bohey 1990; one d.; ed Kan. Wesleyan Univ., Salina and Univ. of Kan.; Deputy Asst Sec. of State, Kan. 1980–85, Asst Sec. of State 1985–87, Sec. of State 1987–95; Gov. of Kan. 1995–2003; Pres. and CEO American Trucking Asscns Inc. 2003–; Trustee Kan. Wesleyan Univ. 1987–; mem. Bd of Dirs Int. Speedway Corpn; Republican. *Leisure interests:* running, reading, travel. *Address:* American Trucking Associations Inc., 950 North Glebe Road, Suite 210, Arlington, VA 22203, USA (office). *Telephone:* (703) 838-1700 (office). *Fax:* (703) 838-1994 (office). *Website:* www.truckline.com (office).

GRAY, Alasdair James; British writer and painter; b. 28 Dec. 1934, Glasgow, Scotland; s. of Alexander Gray and Amy Fleming; m. 1st Inge Sørensen (divorced); one s.; m. 2nd Morag McAlpine 1991; ed Glasgow School of Art; art teacher, Glasgow and Lanarkshire 1958–62; scene painter, Pavilion and Citizens' theatres 1962–63; freelance writer and painter 1963–76; artist recorder, People's Palace Local History Museum, Glasgow 1976–77; Writer-in-Residence, Univ. of Glasgow 1977–79; freelance writer and painter 1979–2001; Prof. of Creative Writing, Univ. of Glasgow 2001–2003; painter of mural decorations in Oran Mor Leisure Centre, Glasgow, 2003–; works in collections of People's Palace Local History Museum, Glasgow, Collin's Gallery, Strathclyde Univ., Hunterian Museum, Univ. of Glasgow; mural paintings in Palace Rigg Nature Reserve Exhibition Centre, New Cumbernauld, Abbot's House Local History Museum, Dunfermline, The Ubiquitous Chip Restaurant, Glasgow, Riverside Restaurant, Kirkfieldbank; mem. Soc. of Authors, Scottish Artists Union; Saltire Soc. Award 1981, Times Literary Supplement Award 1983, Whitbread and Guardian Awards 1992. *Radio plays include:* Quiet People 1968, The Trial of Thomas Muir 1970, Dialogue 1971, Homeward Bound 1973, The Loss of the Golden Silence 1973, McGrothy and Ludmilla 1993, Working Legs 1998. *Television plays include:* The Fall of Kelvin Walker 1967, The Man Who Knew about Electricity 1973, The Story of a Recluse 1987. *Works include:* has designed and illustrated several books including Shoestring Gourmet 1986, Songs of Scotland 1997. *Publications include:* The

Comedy of the White Dog (short story) 1979, Lanark: A Life in Four Books (novel) 1981, Unlikely Stories Mostly 1982, Janine (novel) 1984, The Fall of Kelvin Walker (novel) 1985, Lean Tales (co-writer) 1985, Five Scottish Artists (catalogue) 1986, Saltire Self-Portrait 4 (autobiographical sketch) 1988, Old Negatives (four verse sequences) 1989, Something Leather (novel) 1990, McGrotty and Ludmilla (novel) 1990, Poor Things (novel) 1992, Why Scots Should Rule Scotland (polemic) 1992, Ten Tales Tall and True (Short Stories) 1993, A History Maker (novel) 1994, Mavis Belfrage (novel) 1996, Working Legs (play) 1997, The Book of Prefaces 2000, Sixteen Occasional Poems 2000, A Study in Classic Scottish Writing 2001, The Ends of Our Tethers: 13 Sorry Stories 2003, How We Should Rule Ourselves (polemic, with Adam Tomkins) 2005, Old Men in Love 2007, A Gray Playbook (plays, Collected Verses 2010, A Life in Pictures (auto-biog.) 2010, Every Short Story 1951-2012 2012. *Leisure interests:* reading, walking. *Address:* c/o Zoe Waldie, 20 Powis Mews, London, W11 1JN, England (office); c/o Morag McAlpine, 2 Marchmont Terrace, Glasgow, G12 9LT, Scotland. *Telephone:* (141) 339-0093. *Website:* www.alasdairgray.co.uk.

GRAY, Allan, MBA; South African accountant and business executive; *Founder, Allan Gray Proprietary Ltd;* b. 1938, East London; m.; ed Rhodes Univ., Harvard Business School, USA; financial analyst with Fidelity Management and Research, Boston, USA 1965–73, becoming Portfolio Man., Fidelity Capital Fund; returned to Cape Town 1973, est. Allan Gray Investment Counsel 1973 (later Allan Gray Ltd, now Allan Gray Proprietary Ltd), largest privately-owned investment man. firm in S Africa); est. Orbis (int. investment group) 1988, London and Bermuda, later renamed Orbis Investment Management; f. Allan Gray Orbis Foundation (educational charity) 2007. *Address:* Allan Gray Proprietary Ltd, POB 51605, V&A Waterfront, Cape Town 8002, South Africa (office). *Telephone:* (21) 4152301 (office). *Fax:* (21) 4152492 (office). *E-mail:* info@allangray.co.za (office). *Website:* www.allangray.co.za (office).

GRAY, C. Boyden, BA, JD; American lawyer; b. Winston-Salem, N Carolina; ed Harvard Univ., Univ. of N Carolina, Chapel Hill; Ed.-in-Chief the Law Review, Univ. of N Carolina, Chapel Hill; service in US Marine Corps; clerk for Earl Warren, Chief Justice of US Supreme Court 1968–69; Partner, Wilmer, Cutler, Pickering, Hale and Dorr (law firm), Washington, DC 1969–81, 1993–2005; Legal Counsel to US Vice-Pres. George Bush 1981–89, Legal Counsel to Pres. George H. W. Bush 1989–93; Chair. Admin. Law and Regulatory Practice, ABA 2000–02; Amb. to EU, Brussels 2006–07, Special Envoy for EU Affairs Jan. 2008–09, Special Envoy for Eurasian Energy March 2008–09 fmr mem. Cttee to Visit the Coll. and Cttee on Univ. Devt, Harvard Univ.; Vice-Chair. Int. Advisory Bd Atlantic Council; mem. Bd of Dirs European Institute; Presidential Citizen's Medal, Univ., Distinguished Alumnus Award, Univ. of N Carolina Law School. *Address:* c/o Atlantic Council, 1101 15th Street, NW, 11th Floor, Washington, DC 20005, USA.

GRAY, Douglas, MA, FBA; British/New Zealand academic; *Professor Emeritus, Lady Margaret Hall, University of Oxford;* b. 17 Feb. 1930, Melbourne, Australia; s. of Emmerson Gray and Daisy Gray; m. Judith Claire Campbell 1959; one s.; ed Wellington Coll. NZ, Victoria Univ. of Wellington, Merton Coll., Oxford; Asst Lecturer, Victoria Univ. of Wellington 1952–54, Lecturer in English, Pembroke and Lincoln Colls, Univ. of Oxford 1956–61, Fellow in English, Pembroke Coll. 1961–80, J. R. R. Tolkien Prof. of English Literature and Language and Fellow, Lady Margaret Hall, Oxford 1980–97, Prof. Emer. 1997–, Hon. Fellow, Lady Margaret Hall 1997–; Hon. LittD (Victoria Univ. of Wellington) 1995. *Publications:* Themes and Images in the Medieval English Lyric 1972, A Selection of Religious Lyrics 1974, Robert Henryson 1979, Oxford Book of Late Medieval Verse and Prose (ed.) 1985, J. A. W. Bennett, Middle English Literature (ed.) 1986, From Anglo-Saxon to Early Middle English (jt ed.) 1994, Selected Poems of Robert Henryson and William Dunbar (ed.) 1998, Oxford Companion to Chaucer (ed.) 2003, Later Medieval English Literature 2008, From the Norman Conquest to the Black Death 2011, The Phoenix and the Parrot: Skelton and the Language of Satire 2012. *Leisure interests:* travel, walking. *Address:* 31 Nethercote Road, Tackley, Oxford, OX5 3AW, England (home). *Telephone:* (1869) 331319 (home).

GRAY, Harry Barkus, BS, PhD; American chemist and academic; *Arnold O. Beckman Professor of Chemistry and Founding Director, Beckman Institute, California Institute of Technology;* b. 14 Nov. 1935, Woodburn, Ky; m. Shirley Barnes 1957; two s. one d.; ed Western Kentucky Univ., Northwestern Univ. and Univ. of Copenhagen; Asst Prof. of Chem., Columbia Univ. 1961–63, Assoc. Prof. 1963–65, Prof. 1965–66; Prof. of Chem., California Inst. of Tech. 1966–, now Arnold O. Beckman Prof. and Founding Dir Beckman Inst.; mem. NAS, American Acad. of Arts and Sciences, American Philosophical Soc. 2000; Foreign mem. Royal Soc. 2000, Royal Danish Soc. of Science and Letters, Accad. dei Lincei 2008; Hon. FRSC 2005; Distinguished Visiting Prof., Univ. of Hong Kong 2005; Hon. DSc (Carleton Univ., Ottawa) 2001, (Univ. of South Carolina) 2003, (Copenhagen) 2003, (Edinburgh) 2006; Franklin Award 1967, Fresenius Award 1970, ACS Award in Pure Chem. 1970, Harrison Howe Award 1972, MCA Award 1972, Guggenheim Fellow 1972–73, ACS Award in Inorganic Chem. 1978, Remsen Award 1979, Tolman Award 1979, Centenary Medal 1985, Nat. Medal of Science 1986, Pauling Medal 1986, Calif. Scientist of the Year 1988, Alfred Bader Award 1990, Gold Medal, American Inst. of Chemists 1990, Waterford Prize 1991, Priestley Medal 1991, Gibbs Medal 1992, Linderstrøm-Lang Prize 1992, Chandler Medal, Columbia Univ. 1999, Harvey Prize, Technion-Israel Inst. of Tech. 2000, ACS George C. Pimentel Award 2001, ACS Kosalopoff Award, Auburn Univ 2001, ACS Oesper Award, Univ. of Cincinnati 2001, Nichols Medal 2003, Wheland Award, Univ. of Chicago 2003, NAS Award in Chemical Sciences 2003, Dwyer Medal, Univ. of New South Wales, Australia 2003, Benjamin Franklin Medal in Chem. 2004, Wolf Prize in Chem. 2004, RSC Wilkinson Medal 2004, City of Florence Prize in Molecular Sciences 2006, Antonini Award, SPP, Univ. of Rome 2008, Pupin Medal, Columbia Univ. 2008, Schulich Award, Technion-Israel Inst. of Tech. 2008, ACS Fellow 2009, Welch Award in Chem. 2009, Creativity Award, Univ. of Oregon 2010, Int. Award, Japan Soc. of Co-ordination Chem. 2010, Othmer Gold Medal, Chemical Heritage Foundation 2013. *Publications:* 17 books, including Electrons and Chemical Bonding 1965, Molecular Orbital Theory 1965, Ligand Substitution Processes 1966, Basic Principles of Chemistry 1967, Chemical Dynamics 1968, Chemical Principles 1970, Models in Chemical Science 1971, Chemical Bonds 1973, Electronic Structure and Bonding 1981, Molecular Electronic Structures 1980, Braving the Elements 1995; more than 730 research papers. *Leisure* *interests:* tennis, music. *Address:* Noyes Laboratory of Chemical Physics, 408 Beckman, California Institute of Technology, Mail Code 127-72, 1200 East California Blvd, Pasadena, CA 91125-0001 (office); 1415 East California Boulevard, Pasadena, CA 91106-4101, USA (home). *Telephone:* (626) 395-6500 (office); (626) 793-1978 (home). *E-mail:* hbgray@caltech.edu (office). *Website:* www.cce .caltech.edu/faculty/gray (office).

GRAY, Paul Edward, SB, SM, ScD; American electrical engineer and academic; *Professor Emeritus, Department of Electrical Engineering and Computer Science, Massachusetts Institute of Technology;* b. 7 Feb. 1932, Newark, NJ; s. of Kenneth F. Gray and Florence Gilleo; m. Priscilla W. King 1955; one s. three d.; ed Grover Cleveland High School, Caldwell, NJ and Massachusetts Inst. of Tech.; Faculty mem. in Electrical Eng, MIT 1960–71, 1990–2007, Dean, School of Eng 1970–71, Prof., Dept of Electrical Eng and Computer Science –2007, Prof. Emer. 2007–, Chancellor MIT 1971–80, Pres. 1980–90, mem. of Corpn 1990–2007, Chair., Dir 1990–97, Pres. Emer. 1990–; various trusteeships and other professional appointments; Corresp. mem. Nat. Acad. of Eng in Mexico; Fellow, American Acad. of Arts and Sciences, AAAS, IEEE, Nat. Acad. of Eng (Treas. 1994–2001); Grand Cordon, Order of the Sacred Treasure (Japan) 1993; hon. degrees from Wheaton Coll., Mass, Technical Univ., NS, Cairo Univ., Northeastern Univ., Rensselaer Polytechnic Inst., Drexel Univ.; IEEE Founders Medal 2010. *Publications:* The Dynamic Behavior of Thermoelectric Devices 1960, Introduction to Electronics 1967; co-author of six other books. *Address:* Massachusetts Institute of Technology, 77 Massachusetts Avenue, Cambridge, MA 02139 (office). *Telephone:* (617) 253-4665 (office). *Fax:* (617) 258-0529 (office). *E-mail:* pogo@mit.edu (office). *Website:* www.eecs.mit.edu (office).

GRAY, Robin Trevor, BAgrSc, DDA, CPM; Australian politician, company director and agricultural consultant; *Manager, Rutherglen Farms;* b. 1 March 1940, Vic.; s. of Rev. W. J. Gray; m. Judith F. Boyd 1965; two s. one d.; ed Box Hill High School, Dookie Agric. Coll., Univ. of Melbourne; teacher, Victoria Educ. Dept 1961, Middx Co. Council, UK 1964; agric. consultant, Colac, Victoria 1965, Launceston, Tasmania 1965–76; part-time Lecturer in Agric. Econs, Univ of Tasmania 1970–76; Deputy Leader of Opposition, Tasmania 1979–81, Leader of Opposition 1981–82, 1989–91, Premier 1982–89, Minister for Racing and Gaming 1982–84, for Energy 1982–88, for Forests 1984–86, for State Devt 1984–89, for Primary Industry and Sea Fisheries 1992–95, for Energy 1992–95, for TT-Line 1993–95; Chair. R. T. Gray and Assocs. Pty Ltd 1995–; Partner, Evers Gray 1996–2005; Dir Gunns Ltd 1996–, Gunns Plantations Ltd 2009–; Chair. Botanical Resources Australia Pty Ltd 1996–; Dir AMC Search Ltd 1996–. *Leisure interests:* cricket, golf, reading.

GRAY, Vincent C., BS; American politician; *Mayor of the District of Columbia;* b. 8 Nov. 1942, Washington, DC; m. Loretta Gray 1998 (died 1998); one s. one d.; ed Dunbar High School, George Washington Univ.; began political career with DC Asscn for Retarded Citizens (Exec. Dir); Dir DC Dept of Human Services 1991–94; Founding Exec. Dir Covenant House Washington 1994–2004; mem. Council of DC for Ward 7 2005–11, Chair. 2007–11, served on Cttees on Health, on Econ. Devt, on Human Services, on Educ., Libraries and Recreation, also apptd to chair Special Cttee on Prevention of Youth Violence; Mayor of DC 2011–; Democrat; Mayor's Distinguished Public Service Award, United Way Outstanding Service Community Award. *Address:* Office of the Mayor, John A. Wilson Building, 1350 Pennsylvania Avenue NW, Suite 316, Washington, DC 20004, USA (office). *Telephone:* (202) 727-6300 (office). *Fax:* (202) 727-8527 (office). *E-mail:* eom@dc.gov (office). *Website:* mayor.dc.gov (office); www.dccouncil.us/gray.

GRAYDON, Air Chief Marshal Sir Michael (James), Kt, GCB, CBE, FRAeS; British air force officer (retd), company director and consultant; *Chairman, Symbiotics Ltd;* b. 24 Oct. 1938, Kew, London, England; s. of James Graydon and Rita Alkan; m. Margaret Clark 1963; ed Wycliffe Coll. and RAF Coll., Cranwell; qualified flying instructor No. 1, Flight Training School, Linton-on-Ouse 1960–62; No. 56 Squadron 1962–64; No. 226 Operational Conversion Unit (Queen's Commendation) 1965–67; Flight Command, No. 56 Squadron 1967–69; RAF Staff Coll., Bracknell 1970; Personal Staff Officer to Deputy C-in-C Allied Forces Cen. Europe, Brunssum 1971–73; Operations, Jt Warfare, Ministry of Defence 1973–75; Nat. Defence Coll. Latimer 1976; Officer Commdg No. 11 Squadron, Binbrook 1977–79; Mil. Asst to Chief of Defence Staff 1979–81; Officer Commdg RAF Leuchars 1981–83, RAF Stanley, Falkland Islands 1983; Royal Coll. of Defence Studies 1984; Sr Air Staff Officer, 11 Group, Bentley Priory 1985–86; Asst Chief of Staff, Policy, SHAPE 1986–89; Air Officer Commdg-in-Chief, RAF Support Command 1989–91, HQ Strike Command 1991–92; Chief of Air Staff 1992–97; Air ADC to HM The Queen 1992–97; Chair. Symbiotics Ltd 2006–; Dir, Air Tanker 2001–09, Cassidian plc 2010–; Dir (non-exec.) Thales UK plc 2006–11; Pres. Battle of Britain Memorial Trust 1999–; Chair. Lincolnshire Br., English Speaking Union, Sutton's Hosp., Charterhouse 2006–, United Church Schools Group 2012–; Vice-Pres. Wycliffe Coll. 2011–; Gov. English Speaking Union 2011–; Vice-Patron Air Cadet Council 1999–; mem. Council, Air League; Pres. Royal British Legion Kyrenia Br.; Freeman, City of London 1995. *Publications:* contribs to professional journals. *Leisure interests:* golf, birdwatching, reading, flying. *Address:* 85B Charlwood Street, Pimlico, London, SW1V 4PB, England (office). *E-mail:* mikegraydon@clara.net (office).

GRAYFER, Valery I., CandTechSci; Russian oil industry executive; *Chairman, Lukoil;* b. 1929; ed I.M. Gubkin Moscow Oil Inst.; began career with Tatneft State Production Asscn 1952, various positions including Deputy Foreman, Chief Engineer, Deputy Head of Tatneft 1952–72; Head of Econ. Planning Directorate, USSR Ministry of Oil Industry 1972–85; Deputy Minister of Oil Industry and Head of Glavtyumenneftegaz State Production Asscn 1985–92; CEO OAO Russian Innovation Fuel and Energy Co. (RITEK) 1992–2009, Chair. 2010–; mem. Bd of Dirs and Chair. OAO Lukoil 2000–, OOO Burovaya Kompaniya Eurasia 2009–; Prof., Gubkin Russian State Oil and Gas Univ.; mem. Acad. of Mining Sciences; Honoured Oil and Gas Industrialist of the Russian SSR, Honoured Scientist of the Tatar ASSR; Order of Lenin, Order of the Red Banner of Labour, Order of Int. Friendship, Order of Service Rendered to the Country IVth Grade, Badge of Honour; Merited Worker of Science and Eng, Merited Worker of the Oil and Gas Industry, Lenin Prize, Russian Govt Prize. *Address:* OAO Lukoil, 11 Sretenski Boulevard, 101000 Moscow, Russia (office). *Telephone:* (495) 627-4444 (office). *Fax:*

(495) 625-7016 (office). *E-mail:* pr@lukoil.com (office). *Website:* www.lukoil.com (office).

GRAYLING, Rt Hon. Christopher (Chris) Stephen, PC, BA; British politician and fmr television executive; *Lord Chancellor and Secretary of State for Justice;* b. 1 April 1962, London; m. Susan Clare Dillistone 1987; one s. one d.; ed Royal Grammar School, High Wycombe, Sidney Sussex Coll., Cambridge; joined BBC News as a trainee 1985, Producer 1986–88, Business Devt Man., BBC Select 1991–93; Ed. on Business Daily programme, Channel 4 1988–91; ran several TV production cos, including managing corp. communications div. of Workhouse Ltd 1992–95, SSVC Group, Gerrards Cross 1995–97; Man. Consultant, Burson Marsteller 1997–2001; fmr mem. Social Democratic Party; contested Warrington South in Gen. Election as a Conservative 1997; Councillor, London Borough of Merton 1998–2002; MP for Epsom and Ewell 2001–10, for Epsom and Ewell (revised boundary) 2010–, Select Cttees: Transport, Local Govt and the Regions 2001–02, Transport, Local Govt and the Regions (Transport Sub-Cttee) 2001–02, Transport, Local Govt and the Regions (Urban Affairs Sub-Cttee) 2001–02, Transport 2002, Modernisation of the House of Commons 2005–06; Opposition Whip 2002; Shadow Spokesperson for Health 2002–03; Shadow Minister for Public Services, Health and Educ. 2003–04, for Higher Educ. 2004–05, for Health 2005; Shadow Leader of the House of Commons 2005; Ex-officio mem. House of Commons' Comm. 2005; Shadow Sec. of State for Transport 2005–07, for Work and Pensions 2007–09; Shadow Home Sec. 2009–10; Minister of State for Employment, Dept for Work and Pensions 2010–12; Lord Chancellor and Sec. of State for Justice (first non-lawyer as Lord Chancellor since 1558) 2012–; Conservative. *Publications include:* The Bridgewater Heritage: The Story of Bridgewater Estates 1983, A Land Fit for Heroes: Life in England After the Great War 1985, Holt's: The Story of Joseph Holt 1985, Just Another Star?: Anglo-American Relations Since 1945 (with Christopher Langdon) 1987, Insight Guide Waterways of Europe (contrib.) 1989. *Leisure interest:* Manchester United Football Club. *Address:* Ministry of Justice, Selborne House, 54 Victoria Street, London, SW1E 6QW (office); House of Commons, Westminster, London, SW1A 0AA, England (office). *Telephone:* (20) 3334-3555 (Dept) (office); (20) 7219-8194 (London) (office). *Fax:* (20) 3334-4455 (Dept) (office); (20) 7219-1763 (London) (office). *E-mail:* graylingc@parliament.uk (office). *Website:* www.justice.gsi.gov.uk (office); www.chrisgrayling.net.

GRAZER, Brian; American film company executive and film producer; *Principal, Imagine Entertainment;* b. 12 July 1951, Los Angeles; s. of Thomas Grazer and Arlene Grazer; m. 1st Theresa McKay; m. 2nd Corki Corman Grazer; one s. one d.; m. 3rd Gigi Levangie (divorced 2007); two s.; ed Univ. of Southern California School of Cinema and TV; Co-Chair. Imagine Films Entertainment; David O. Selznick Lifetime Achievement Award 2001, Lifetime Achievement Award, ShoWest 2003. *Films produced include:* Night Shift 1982, Splash 1984, Real Genius 1985, Spies Like Us (jtly) 1985, Armed and Dangerous (jtly) 1986, Like Father, Like Son (jtly) 1987, Parenthood 1989, Cry Baby (jtly) 1990, Kindergarten Cop 1990, Closet Land (jtly) 1991, The Doors (jtly) 1991, Backdraft (jtly) 1991, My Girl 1991, Far and Away (jtly) 1992, Housesitter 1992, Boomerang 1992, CB4 (jtly) 1993, For Love Or Money 1993, The Paper (jtly) 1994, My Girl 2 1994, Greedy 1994, The Cowboy Way 1994, Apollo 13 (jtly) (Daryl F. Zanuck Motion Picture Producer of the Year Award 1995) 1995, Sergeant Bilko 1996, Ransom 1996, Bowfinger 1999, Curious George 2000, Nutty Professor II: The Klumps 2000, How the Grinch Stole Christmas 2000, A Beautiful Mind 2001 (Academy Award 2002, four Golden Globe Awards), 8 Mile 2002, Intolerable Cruelty 2003, The Cat in the Hat 2003, Friday Night Lights 2004, Inside Deep Throat 2005, Cinderella Man 2005, Curious George (Daytime Emmy Award) 2006, Inside Man 2006, American Gangster 2007, Frost/Nixon 2008, The Da Vinci Code, Angels and Demons 2010, Changeling, Robin Hood 2010. *Television includes:* Sports Night (series) 1998, Felicity (series) 1998, From the Earth to the Moon (mini series) 1998, Student Affairs 1999, Wonderland (series) 2000, 24 (series) (Emmy Award) 2001–, The Beast (series) 2001, Miss Match (series) 2003, Arrested Development (series) 2003–, The Big House (series) 2004. *Address:* Imagine Films Entertainment, 9465 Wilshire Boulevard, Floor 7, Beverly Hills, CA 90212, USA (office). *Website:* www.imagine -entertainment.com.

GRAZIANO DA SILVA, José, BA, PhD; Brazilian/Italian agro-economist and international organization official; *Director-General, Food and Agriculture Organization (FAO);* b. 17 Nov. 1949, Urbana, Illinois, USA; m. Paola Ligasacchi; two c.; ed Univ. of São Paulo, State Univ. of Campinas, Univ. Coll., London, Univ. of California, Santa Cruz, USA; Prof., State Univ. of Campinas 1978–, also Chair of Master's and Doctoral Program in Econ. Devt, Space, and Environment at Inst. for Econs; coordinated the formulation of the "Zero Hunger" Program (Fome Zero) in 2001; Extraordinary Minister for Food Security 2003–04; Special Adviser to the Presidency of the Repub. 2004–06; Prof., State Univ. of Campinas and Chair of Master's and Doctoral Program in Econ. Devt, Space and Environment; Regional Rep. for Latin America and the Caribbean and Asst Dir-Gen. FAO 2006–11, Dir-Gen. 2011–; Ordem de Rio Branco; Paulista Medal for Scientific and Technological Merit, Brazilian Soc. of Rural Econs Prêmio Sober. *Publications include:* 26 books including O que é a questão agrária (What is the Agrarian Question?), De boias frias a empregados rurais (From Bóias Frias to Rural Workers). *Address:* Food and Agriculture Organization, Viale delle Terme di Caracalla, 00153 Rome, Italy (office). *Telephone:* (06) 5705-1 (office). *Fax:* (06) 5705-3152 (office). *E-mail:* fao-hq@ fao.org (office). *Website:* www.fao.org (office); www.grazianodasilva.org.

GRCIC, Konstantin, MA; German product designer; *Chairman, Konstantin Grcic Industrial Design;* b. 1965, Munich; ed Parnham Coll., Beaminster, UK, Royal Coll. of Art, London, UK; apprenticeship as cabinet maker, Parnham Coll. 1985–87; worked in studio of Jasper Morrison 1990; Founder-Chair. Konstantin Grcic Industrial Design, Munich 1991–; designed products for Progetto Ogetto collection of objects commissioned for Cappellini by Jasper Morrison and James Irvine 1992; collections at Museum of Modern Art, New York, Centre Pompidou, Paris, Die Neue Sammlung, Munich; Compasso d'Oro 2001. *Address:* Konstantin Grcic Industrial Design, Schillerstr 40, 80336 Munich, Germany (office). *Telephone:* (50) 79995 (office). *Fax:* (50) 79996 (office). *E-mail:* press@konstantin-grcic .com (office). *Website:* www.konstantin-grcic.com (office).

GREAVES, Derrick, ARCA; British artist; b. 5 June 1927, Sheffield; s. of Harry Greaves and Mabel Greaves; m. Mary Margaret Johnson 1951 (divorced 1991); two

s. one d.; m. 2nd Sally Butler 1994; ed RCA, London and British School at Rome; part-time teacher St Martins School of Art 1954–64, Maidstone Coll. of Art and Royal Acad. Schools 1960; Head of Printmaking, Norwich Coll. of Art 1983–91; first one-man exhbn, Beaux Arts Gallery 1953; subsequent one-man exhbns at Zwemmer Gallery 1958, 1960, 1962, 1963, Inst. of Contemporary Arts (ICA), London 1969, 1971, Bear Lane Gallery, Oxford 1970, 1973, Belfast 1972, Dublin 1972, Whitechapel Gallery 1973, Monika Kinley 1973, City Gallery, Milton Keynes 1975, Cranfield Inst. of Tech. 1978, Exposición Int. de la Plástica, Chile 1978, Gallerie Daniel Wahrenberger, Zurich, Switzerland 1996, James Hyman Fine Art, London 2003, 2005, 2007, 2008; group exhbns include Contemporary Arts Soc. 1956, Venice Biennale 1956, Pushkin Museum, Moscow 1957, Whitechapel Gallery 1963, Carnegie Int. Exhbn, Pa 1964, Haymarket Gallery 1974, Royal Acad. 1977, Graves Art Gallery, Sheffield 1980, Fischer Fine Art 1980, Mall Galleries, London 1981, Mappin Art Gallery 1986, Leeds Art Gallery 1986, Philadelphia Museum of Art 1986, Walker Art Gallery; Dr hc (Anglia Ruskin Univ.) 2008; Prize John Moore's Exhbn 1957, Belfast Open Painting Exhbn purchase prize 1962;. *Publications:* Derrick Greaves. Paintings 1958–80; numerous catalogues; Derrick Greaves – Kitchen Sink to Shangri-La (by James Hyman) 2008. *Address:* c/o James Hyman Fine Art, 5 Savile Row, London, SW1Y 6BU, England.

GREAVES, Robert F., BA; American health care industry executive; *Chairman, Health Net Inc.;* b. 1947, Los Angeles; m. Erika Greaves; ed California State Univ., Long Beach; held various man. positions at Blue Cross of Southern Calif., Allstate Insurance Co. –1982; Pres. Health Systems Int. (renamed Health Net Inc.) 1982, Co-Chair., Pres. and CEO –1995, Chair. 2004–; Founding Chair. The Calif. Wellness Foundation (TCWF) 1992, mem. Bd of Dirs 1992–; mem. Leadership Conf. Advisory Council, Schering Plough Pharmaceuticals, Bd of Dirs Health Net of Calif.; Founding mem. Bd of Govs, Calif. State Univ., Long Beach; fmr mem. Bd of Dirs March of Dimes Birth Defects Foundation, Blue Cross, Southern Calif.; Hon. mem. Bd of Trustees, Calif. State Univ. *Address:* Health Net Inc., 21650 Oxford Street, Woodland Hills, CA 91367, USA (office). *Telephone:* (818) 676-6000 (office). *Fax:* (818) 676-8591 (office). *Website:* www.health.net (office).

GREBENÍČEK, Miroslav, PhDr, CSc; Czech university lecturer and politician; b. 21 March 1947, Staré Město, Uherské Hradiště Dist; m.; one s. two d.; ed Masaryk Univ., Brno; worked as teacher at several schools; specialist with Regional Museum, Mikulov 1973–75; mem. CP of Czechoslovakia 1975; Lecturer, Masaryk Univ., Brno 1975–86, Reader 1986–89; Deputy to House of Nations (Fed. Ass. of ČSFR) 1990–92, mem. Presidium 1992; First Vice-Pres., Fed. of CP of Bohemia and Moravia and Party of the Democratic Left (following re-organization of former communist party) Aug.–Nov. 1991, Pres. 1991–92, Chair. Communist Party of Bohemia and Moravia (KSČM) 1993–2005; mem. Chamber of Deputies (Parl.) (KSČM) for Southern Moravia constituency 1996–, mem. Organizational Cttee of Parl. 1996–, Parl. Cttee for Petitions 1996–98, for Culture, Youth and Physical Training 1998–. *Publications:* monographs, articles and reviews focusing on the history of 19th and 20th centuries. *Address:* Poslanecká sněmovna, Sněmovní 4, 110 00 Prague 1 (office); Zlámalova 9, 692 01 Mikulov, Czech Republic (home). *E-mail:* grebenicekm@psp.cz (office).

GREBENNIKOV, Valery Vassil'yevich; Russian lawyer and politician; *Mayor of Volgograd;* b. 14 Oct. 1946; ed Lumumba Univ. of Peoples' Friendship; elected Deputy Chief State Arbiter, Russian Fed. 1990–91, Chief State Arbiter; mem. State Duma 1995–, mem. Our Home Russia Faction (Motherland – All Russia) 1999–; Vice-Chair., then Chair. Cttee on State Construction; First Deputy Chair. Duma Cttee for Civil, Criminal, Arbitration and Procedural Legislation; Deputy Head of Russian Del. to Parl. Ass. of Council of Europe (PACE); Mayor of Volgograd 2007–; Vice-Pres. OLBI co.; mem. Bd of Dirs Bank of Nat. Credit. *Address:* Office of the Mayor, 5 Volodarskogo str., 400131 Volgograd, Russia (office). *Telephone:* (8442) 33-16-82 (office). *Fax:* (8442) 38-54-66 (office). *E-mail:* kancelyaria@volgadmin.ru (office). *Website:* www.volgadmin.ru (office).

GREBENSHCHIKOV, Boris Borisovich; Russian musician and singer; b. 27 Nov. 1953, Leningrad; s. of Boris A. Grebenshchikov and Ludmila Grebenshchi-kova; m.; one s. two d.; ed Leningrad Univ.; worked as a computer programmer 1977–80; lead singer and guitarist of rock group Akvarium 1975–; music for films and sound track albums includes Assa 1988, Black Rose 1990; tours and recordings in USA, Canada, Great Britain, all-Russia tour 1991 (110 concerts in 68 cities); performances at Royal Albert Hall, London 2007, 2008; artist as a painter has taken part in various art exhbns throughout fmr USSR; Medal for Services to the Fatherland 2003; Triumph Prize (for outstanding achievements in Russian culture) 1998. *Radio:* presenter, Aerostat. *Recordings include:* albums: with Akvarium: Akvarium (USSR) 1987, Radio Africa 1987, Equinox 1988, Radio Silence 1989, Russian Album 1992, Kostroma Mon Amour 1994, Navigator 1995, Snow Lion 1996, Hyperborea 1997, Lilith 1998, Psi 1999, Sister Chaos 2002, Fisherman's Song 2003, Zoom, Zoom, Zoom 2005, Careless Russian Rover 2006, White Horse 2008, Pushkinskaya 10 2009. *Publications include:* Ivan and Danilo 1989, poetry and song lyrics, trans. of Indian and Tibetan religious works, three vols of Aerostat's Musical Encyclopedia. *Leisure interests:* music, painting, writing, religions, travelling. *Address:* 2 Marata Street, Apt. 3, 191025 St Petersburg, Russia. *Fax:* (812) 272-05-41. *E-mail:* bg@aquarium.ru. *Website:* www.aquarium .ru.

GRECEANÎI, Zinaida, MA; Moldovan economist and politician; b. 7 Feb. 1956; m.; two c.; ed Moldova State Univ.; various roles within finance and budget inspectorate 1974–91; Economist, then Prin. Economist, Dept of Int. Finance, Ministry of Finance 1995–97, various sr positions including Dir of World Bank Section 1997–2001; Vice-Minister of Finance 2001–02, Minister of Finance 2002–05; First Deputy Prime Minister 2006–08, Prime Minister 2008–09; mem. Parl. 2009–; fmr Gov. for Moldova to IMF; Order of Honour, Order of the Repub. *Address:* Parlamentul (The Parliament), 2073 Chişinău, bd. Ştefan cel Mare 105, Moldova (office). *Telephone:* (22) 23-33-52 (office). *Fax:* (22) 23-30-12 (office). *E-mail:* greceanii.zinaida@gmail.com (office). *Website:* www.parliament.md (office).

GRECH, Joe Debono; Maltese politician; b. 17 Sept. 1941, B'Kara; s. of Carmelo Debono and Giovanna Grech; m. Edith Vella; two c.; ed St Aloysius Coll.; mem. Gen. Workers, Union Rep. for Gozo 1971; Sec. Petrol and Chemicals Section 1973–76; fmr Pres. Nat. Exec. Socialist Youth Movt, Gen. Sec. 1967–76; fmr mem.

Nat. Exec. Labour Party, Propaganda Sec. 1971–88; Man. Nat. Cargo Handling Co., Interprint; MP 1976–; Minister of Parastatal and People's Investments May–Sept. 1983, of Agric. and Fisheries 1983–87, for Transport and Ports 1996–98; Deputy Leader Labour Party 1988; mem. Socialist Bureau, Council of Europe 1998–; Hon. Pres. Santa Venera Band Club. *Leisure interests:* reading, farming. *Address:* c/o Partit Laburista (Labour Party), National Labour Centre, Mile End Rd, Hamrun HMR 1717; 105 Fleur de Lys Road, B'kara, Malta. *Website:* parliament.gov.mt (office).

GRECH, HE Cardinal Prospero, OSA; Maltese ecclesiastic and academic; b. 24 Dec. 1925, Vittoriosa (Birgu); professed mem. of the Order of St Augustine 1944, ordained priest 1950; served for many years in Rome, mostly as mem. of community of Collegio Santa Monica; Prof. of Sacred Scripture at various univs in Rome, including the Biblicum and the Lateran and Gregorian Univs; Co-founder and first Pres. Patristic Inst., the Augustinianum; collaborated with numerous dicasteries of the Holy See, especially Congregation for the Doctrine of the Faith; cr. Cardinal (non-voting) (Cardinal-Deacon of Santa Maria Goretti) 2012. *Address:* International College of St Monica, Via S. Uffizio 1, Rome (office); Order of St Augustine, Via Paolo VI 25, 00193 Rome, Italy. *Telephone:* (06) 880061. *Fax:* (06) 68006299. *E-mail:* info@augustinians.net. *Website:* www.augustinians .net.

GRECO, Mario; Italian business executive; *Group CEO and Joint Managing Director, Assicurazioni Generali SpA;* b. 16 June 1959, Naples; ed Univ. of Rome, Rochester Univ., NY, USA; began career at McKinsey & Co. 1986, Partner 1992–94; Head of Claims Div., RAS 1995–96, Gen. Man. 1996–98, Man. Dir 1998–2000, CEO 2000–05; joined Allianz AG Vorstand 2004–05; CEO EurizonVita, Sanpaolo IMI Group 2005, CEO Eurizon Financial Group 2005–07; Deputy CEO of Global Life, Zurich Financial Services 2007–08, CEO and mem. Exec. Cttee 2008–10, CEO Gen. Insurance, Zurich Insurance Group 2010–12; Group CEO and Jt Man. Dir Assicurazioni Generali SpA 2012–; mem. Bd of Dirs Gruppo Editoriale L'Espresso, Indesit, Saras; Insurance CEO of the Year 2004. *Address:* Assicur-azioni Generali SpA, Piazza Duca degli Abruzzi 2, 34132 Trieste, Italy (office). *Telephone:* (40) 6711 (office). *Fax:* (40) 671600 (office). *E-mail:* info@generali.com (office). *Website:* www.generali.com (office).

GREEHEY, William (Bill) E., CPA; American oil industry executive; *Chairman, NuStar Energy L.P.;* b. Fort Dodge, Ia; ed St Mary's Univ., San Antonio, Tex.; began career as accountant, Price Waterhouse; fmr accountant, Exxon; fmr accountant, Coastal Gas Corpn, becoming Vice-Pres. and Controller, Pres. and CEO LoVaca (subsidiary co., Valero from 1980) 1973, CEO Valero Energy Corpn 1980–2006, Chair. 1980–2007, Chair. NuStar Energy L.P. (formerly Valero L.P.) 2001–; Founder Pres. Greehey Family Foundation 2004–; Chair. Haven for Hope; fmr Chair. San Antonio Econ. Devt Foundation; mem. Bd of Dirs Southwest Foundation for Biomedical Research; mem. Bd of Trustees United Way of San Antonio (fmr Chair.), Bexar County, St Mary's Univ., San Antonio; fmr mem. Nat. Exec. Bd Boy Scouts of America; Dr hc (St Mary's Univ.) 1998; Silver Beaver Award, Alamo Area Council 1987, Distinguished Alumnus, St. Mary's Univ. 1986, Entrepreneur of the Year Award 1993, Outstanding Philanthropist Award 1998, Int. Citizen of the Year Award, San Antonio World Affairs Council 1999, Horatio Alger Award 2000, Golden Plate Award, American Acad. of Achievement 2000, Good Scout Award 2001, Tex. Business Hall of Fame 2002, Outstanding Volunteer Fundraiser Award, Asscn of Fundraising Professionals 2009. *Address:* NuStar Energy L.P., 2330 North Loop 1604 W, San Antonio, TX 78248, USA (office). *E-mail:* webmaster@nustarenergy.com (office). *Website:* www.nustarenergy.com (office).

GREEN, Al; American soul singer and songwriter; b. 13 April 1946, Forrest City, Ark.; founder, The Creations 1964; singer, Al Green and The Soul Mates; f. of his own record label Hot Line Music Journal, 1967; purchased his own church, The Full Gospel Tabernacle in Memphis, Tenn. in late 1970s, became pastor; left secular music 1980, returned 1993; American Music Award, Favourite Soul/R&B Album 1974, Grand Prize, Tokyo Music Festival 1978, Al Green Day, Los Angeles 1978, Soul Train, Best Gospel Recording 1987, numerous Grammy awards include: Best Soul Gospel Performances 1982–85, 1988, 1990, Best Male Soul Performance 1987, Best R&B Performance by a Duo or Group (for Stay With Me with John Legend) 2009, Best Traditional R&B Vocal Performance (for You've Got All the Love I Need) 2009, Grammy Lifetime Achievement Award 2002. *Recordings include:* albums: Al Green Gets Next To You 1971, Let's Stay Together 1972, I'm Still In Love With You 1972, Green Is Blues 1973, Call Me 1973, Livin' For You 1974, Al Green Explores Your Mind 1975, Al Green Is Love 1975, Full of Fire 1976, Have A Good Time 1977, Truth 'n' Time 1978, The Belle Album 1978, Cream of Al Green 1980, The Lord Will Make A Way 1980, Higher Plane 1982, Precious Lord 1983, I'll Rise Again 1983, White Christmas 1983, Going Away 1986, Soul Survivor 1987, I Get Joy 1989, Al 1992, Love and Happiness 2001, I Can't Stop 2003, Everything's OK 2005, Lay it Down 2008. *Address:* Full Gospel Tabernacle, 787 Hale Road, Memphis, TN 38116, USA. *Telephone:* (901) 396-9192. *E-mail:* algreenmusic@hotmail.com; reverend@algreenmusic.com. *Website:* www .algreenmusic.com.

GREEN, Anthony Eric Sandall, RA; British artist; b. 30 Sept. 1939, Luton; s. of Frederick Sandall and Marie Madeleine Green (née Dupont); m. Mary Louise Cozens-Walker 1961; two d.; ed Highgate School, Slade School of Fine Art, Univ. Coll. London; Asst Art Master, Highgate School 1961–67; Harkness Fellowship, USA 1967–69; Fellow, Univ. Coll. London 1991; elected mem. New English Art Club 2003; held over 100 solo exhbns; works in public and pvt. collections world-wide; French Govt Scholarship, Paris 1960; Hon. RBA, Hon. ROI Exhibit of the Year RA Summer Exhbn 1977, Featured Artist RA Summer Exhbn 2003. *Publication:* A Green Part of the World (with Martin Bailey) 1984. *Leisure interests:* family, travel. *Address:* Mole End, 40 High Street, Little Eversden, Cambridge, CB23 1HE, England (home). *Telephone:* (1223) 262292 (home). *Fax:* (1223) 265656 (home).

GREEN, Dan, BA; American book publishing executive; *Literary agent, Pom Inc.;* b. 28 Sept. 1935, Passaic, New Jersey; s. of Harold Green and Bessie Roslow; m. Jane Oliphant 1959; two s.; ed Syracuse Univ.; Publicity Dir Dover Press 1957–58; Station WNAC-TV 1958–59; Bobbs-Merrill Co. 1959–62; joined Simon & Schuster Inc. 1962, Assoc. Publr 1976–80, Vice-Pres., Publr 1980–84; Pres. Trade Publishing Group 1984–85; Founder and Publr, Kenan Press 1979–80; CEO Grove Press and Weidenfeld & Nicolson, New York 1985–89; Pres. Kenan Books, New York 1989–; Literary agent, Pom Inc. (literary agency) 1989–. *Address:* Pom Inc., 21 Vista Drive, Great Neck, New York, NY 11021 (office); Kenan Books, 21 Vista Drive, Great Neck, New York, NY 11021, USA (home). *Telephone:* (516) 487-3441 (office). *E-mail:* dangreen@pomlit.com (office).

GREEN, Hon. Sir Guy Stephen Montague, Kt, AC, KBE, CVO, LLB; Australian administrator and judge; b. 26 July 1937, Launceston, Tasmania; s. of the late Clement Francis Montague and Beryl Margaret Jenour (née Williams) Green; m. Rosslyn Marshall 1963; two s. two d.; ed Launceston Church Grammar School and Univ. of Tasmania; admitted to Bar 1960; Partner Ritchie & Parker Alfred Green & Co. 1963–71; Pres. Tasmanian Bar Asscn 1968–70; Magistrate 1971–73; Chief Justice of Tasmania 1973–95; Lt-Gov. of Tasmania 1982–95; Gov. of Tasmania 1995–2003; mem. Faculty of Law Univ. of Tasmania 1974–85; Chair. Council of Law Reporting 1978–85; Chair. Tasmanian Cttee, Duke of Edinburgh's Award in Australia 1975–80; Dir Winston Churchill Memorial Trust 1975–85, Deputy Nat. Chair. 1980–85; Chancellor, Univ. of Tasmania 1985–95; Deputy Chair. Australian Inst. of Judicial Admin. 1986–88; Pres. St John Council 1984–92; Priory Exec. Officer, Order of St John in Australia 1984–91, Chancellor 1991–95; Deputy Prior St John Ambulance Australia 1995–; Administrator of the Commonwealth (Acting Gov.-Gen. of Australia) 2003; Hon. LLD (Univ. of Tasmania) 1996; Kt of Grace, Most Venerable Order of the Hosp. of St John of Jerusalem 1985. *Address:* 13 Marine Terrace, Battery Point, Tasmania 7004, Australia.

GREEN, Hamilton; Guyanese politician; *Mayor of Georgetown;* b. 9 Nov. 1934, Georgetown; s. of Wilfred Amelius Green and Edith Ophelia Dorothy Green; m. 1st Shirley Field-Ridley 1970 (died 1982); five s. three d.; m. 2nd Dr. Jennifer Veronica Basdeo 1990; two d.; ed Queen's Coll.; fmrly Gen. Sec., People's Nat. Congress, Minister of Works, Hydraulics and Supply, of Public Affairs, of Co-operatives and Nat. Mobilization, of Health, Housing and Labour; fmrly Vice-Pres. with responsibility for Public Welfare, Vice-Pres. with responsibility for Production; Vice-Pres. and Prime Minister of Guyana 1985–92; expelled from People's Nat. Congress 1992; f. political and environmental group Good And Green Guyana; Mayor of Georgetown 1994, 2004–; unsuccessful presidential cand. 1997; mem. Presiding Council, Universal Peace Fed. *Publication:* From Pain to Peace – Green 1953–1964 (series of lectures at Cyril Potter Coll. of Educ. 1986). *Leisure interests:* reading (history and philosophy), table tennis, boxing and fitness training. *Address:* City Hall, Regent Street, Georgetown (office); Plot 'D' Lodge, Georgetown, Guyana (home). *Telephone:* (2) 57870 (office). *Fax:* (2) 57871.

GREEN, Howard, MD, MSc; American medical school professor and scientist; *George Higginson Professor of Cell Biology, Harvard University Medical School;* b. 10 Sept. 1925, Toronto, Canada; s. of Benjamin Green and Rose M. Green; m. Rosine Kauffmann; ed Univ. of Toronto and Northwestern Univ., USA; Research Asst, Dept of Physiology, Northwestern Univ. 1948–50; Research Assoc. (Instructor), Dept of Biochemistry, Univ. of Chicago 1951–53; Instructor, Dept of Pharmacology, New York Univ. School of Medicine 1954; Capt., MC, US Army Reserve, Immunology Div., Walter Reed Army Inst. of Research 1955–56; Dept of Pathology, New York Univ. School of Medicine 1956–68, Prof. and Chair., Dept of Cell Biology 1968–70; Prof. of Cell Biology, MIT 1970–80; Chair. Dept of Physiology and Biophysics, Harvard Medical School 1980–86, Chair. Dept of Cellular and Molecular Physiology 1988–93, George Higginson Prof. of Cell Biology 1993–; mem. NAS, American Acad. of Arts and Sciences, Institut de France (Acad. des Sciences); Hon. Pres. Scientific Council, Institut Curie, Paris; Hon. Mem. Soc. of Investigative Dermatology, Japanese Soc. for Plastic and Reconstructive Surgery; Hon. Fellow, American Acad. of Microbiology; Chevalier, Légion d'honneur; Hon. DSc (Univ. of Connecticut, State Univ. of NY at Stony Brook); Hon. MD (Göteborg); Mr and Mrs J. N. Taub Int. Memorial Award for Psoriasis Research 1977; Selman A. Waksman Award in Microbiology 1978; Lewis S. Rosenstiel Award in Basic Medical Research 1980, Lila Gruber Research Award, American Acad. of Dermatology 1980, Passano Award 1985, Blaise Pascal Medal for Biology and Life Sciences 2007. *Publications:* numerous articles on cell biology, genetics, growth and differentiation. *Address:* Department of Cell Biology, Harvard Medical School, 240 Longwood Avenue, Boston, MA 02115 (office); 82 Williston Road, Brookline, MA 02146, USA (home). *Telephone:* (617) 432-0851 (office). *Fax:* (617) 432-0109 (office). *E-mail:* hgreen@hms.harvard.edu (office). *Website:* cellbio.med.harvard.edu/faculty/green (office).

GREEN, Malcolm Leslie Hodder, BSc, DIC, PhD, FRS; British chemist and academic; *Professor Emeritus of Inorganic Chemistry, University of Oxford;* b. 16 April 1936, Eastleigh, Hants.; s. of Leslie E. Green and Sheila Mary Green (née Hodder); m. Jennifer C. Green (née Bilham); three c.; ed Acton Tech. Coll., Univ. of London, Imperial Coll. of Science and Tech.; Postdoctoral Research Assoc. Fellow, Imperial Coll. of Science and Tech. 1959–60; Asst Lecturer in Inorganic Chem., Univ. of Cambridge 1960–63; Septcentuary Tutorial Fellow, Balliol Coll. 1963–89; Lecturer, Univ. of Oxford 1965–, Prof. of Inorganic Chem. and Head of Dept 1989–2003, Prof. Emer. 2003–; Visiting Prof., Univ. of Western Ontario, Canada 1971, Ecole de Chimie and Inst. des Substances Naturelles, Paris, France 1972, Harvard Univ., USA (A.P. Sloan Visiting Prof.) 1973, Wuhan Univ., China 1985; Distinguished Visiting Prof., Hong Kong Univ. 2004–12; Sr Research Fellow, British Gas Royal Soc. 1979–84, 1984–86; Head, Chem. Dept Cttee, Royal Soc. of Chem. (RSC) 1989–; Chair. Editorial Bd RCS Chemical Communication 1997–99; Co-founder Oxford Catalysts PLC 2004, mem. Bd of Dirs and mem. Scientific Advisory Panel 2006–08; mem. Editorial Bd several journals including Topics in Chemica, Communications, Catalysis, Organometallics, Nouveau Journal de Chimie, Journal of Organometallic Chemistry; mem. Bd Inst. of Applied Catalysis 1995–; Fellow, Corpus Christi Coll. Cambridge 1961, Balliol Coll. Oxford 1962–89, St Catherine's Coll. Oxford 1989–; invited to present numerous hon. lectures at int. univs; Hon. Prof., Wuhan Univ., China 2004; Dr hc (Lisbon, Portugal) 1997; Hon. DSc (Southampton) 2006; numerous awards, including RSC Corday-Morgan Medal 1974, Tilden Prize 1982, ACS Annual Award for Inorganic Chem. 1984, RSC Medal in Organometallic Chem. 1986, Gesellschaft Deutscher Chemiker Karl-Ziegler Prize 1992, Royal Soc. Davy Medal 1995, Univ. of NSW Frank Dyer Medal 1997, NW Univ. Fred Basolo Medal 1998, RSC Sir Geoffrey Wilkinson Medal 2000, Soc. française de Chimie Prix Franco-Britannique 2006. *Publications:* two books

and more than 700 publs. *Address:* Inorganic Chemistry Laboratory, University of Oxford, South Parks Road, Oxford, OX1 3QR (office); Oxford Catalysts, 115E Milton Park, Oxford, OX14 4RZ, England (office). *Telephone:* (1865) 272600 (office); (1235) 841700 (Oxford Catalysts) (office). *Fax:* (1865) 272690 (office); (1235) 841701 (Oxford Catalysts) (office). *E-mail:* malcolm.green@chem.ox.ac.uk (office); info@oxfordcatalysts.com (office). *Website:* research.chem.ox.ac.uk/malcolm-green .aspx (office); www.oxfordcatalysts.com (office).

GREEN, Martin Andrew, AM, BE, MEngSc, PhD, DEng, FRS, FAA, FTS, FIEEE; Australian scientist, academic and business executive; *Executive Research Director, Australian Centre for Advanced Photovoltaics;* b. 20 July 1948, Brisbane, Queensland; s. of Eric William Green and Gwendolyn Lorraine Green (née Horsfall); m.; two c.; ed Univ. of Queensland, McMaster Univ., Canada, Univ. of New South Wales; initiated Solar Photovoltaics Group at Univ. of New South Wales 1974–, currently Prof., School of Photovoltaic and Renewable Energy Eng, Dir Australian Centre for Advanced Photovoltaics; Hon. Pres., Guodian New Energy Research Inst., China; Pawsey Medal, Australian Acad. 1982, Award for Outstanding Achievement in Energy Research 1988, IEEE Cherry Award 1990, CSIRO External Medal 1992, IEEE Ebers Award 1995, Australia Prize 1999, Gold Medal, Spanish Eng Acad. 2000, Medal of Eng Excellence for Distinguished Achievement in the Service of Humanity, World Eng Fed., Hanover 2000, Millennium Award, World Renewable Congress 2000, Right Livelihood Award 2002, Karl Böer Solar Energy Medal of Merit Award, Univ. of Delaware 2003, World Tech. Award in Energy, The World Tech. Network 2004, SolarWorld Einstein Award 2007, ENI Renewable Energy Award 2009. *Publications:* five books, nine book chapters, numerous reports, patents and conference papers, and more than 300 papers in int. refereed journals on semiconductors, microelectronics and solar cells. *Address:* Room 108, School of Photovoltaic and Renewable Energy Engineering, Tyree Energy Technologies Building, University of New South Wales, Sydney, NSW 2052, Australia (office). *Telephone:* (2) 9385-4018 (office). *Fax:* (2) 9662-4240 (office). *E-mail:* m.green@unsw.edu.au (office). *Website:* www.pv.unsw.edu.au (office).

GREEN, Michael Boris, PhD, FRS; British physicist and academic; *Lucasian Professor of Mathematics, University of Cambridge;* b. 22 May 1946, London, England; s. of Absalom Green and Genia Green; m. Joanna Chataway; one d.; ed William Ellis School, London, Univ. of Cambridge; Post-doctoral Fellowship, Inst. for Advanced Study, Princeton, NJ, USA 1970–72, Univ. of Cambridge 1972–77; Science and Eng Research Council (SERC) Advanced Fellowship, Univ. of Oxford 1977–79; Lecturer, Queen Mary and Westfield Coll., London 1979–85, Prof. of Physics 1985–93; SERC Sr Fellowship 1986–91; John Humphrey Plummer Prof. of Theoretical Physics, Univ. of Cambridge 1993–2009, Lucasian Prof. of Math. 2009–; numerous fellowships at US and European Insts, including Distinguished Fairchild Fellowship, Calif. Inst. of Tech. 1990; Hon. DSc (Queen Mary, Univ. of London) 2004; Maxwell Medal, Inst. of Physics 1987, William Hopkins Prize, Cambridge Philosophical Soc. 1987, Dirac Medal, Int. Center for Theoretical Physics 1989, Dannie Heineman Prize, American Physical Soc. 2002, Dirac Medal and Prize, Inst. of Physics 2004, Naylor Prize, London Math. Soc. 2007. *Publications:* Superstring Theory (two vols, with J. H. Schwarz and E. Witten) 1987; numerous publs in scientific journals. *Leisure interests:* pottery, music. *Address:* DAMTP, Centre for Mathematical Sciences, University of Cambridge, Wilberforce Road, Cambridge, CB3 0WA, England (office). *Telephone:* (1223) 330884 (office). *Fax:* (1223) 765900 (office). *E-mail:* mbg15@damtp.cam.ac.uk (office). *Website:* www.damtp.cam.ac.uk (office).

GREEN, Michael Philip, MA, ADipPsy, UKCP; British psychotherapist and fmr business executive; b. 2 Dec. 1947, London; s. of Cyril Green and Irene Green; m. 1st Hon. Janet F. Wolfson 1972 (divorced 1989); two d.; m. 2nd Theresa Buckmaster 1990; three s. one d.; ed Haberdashers' Aske's School; Dir and Co-Founder, Tangent Industries Ltd 1968–; Chief Exec. Carlton Communications plc 1983–91, Chair. 1983–2004, Chair. Carlton TV Ltd 1991–94, Chair. ITV plc 2003–04, fmr Chair. ITN; Founder Tangent Charitable Trust 1984; mem. Bd of Dirs GMTV Ltd 1992–2004, Reuters Holdings PLC 1992–99, Getty Communications PLC 1997–98; Chair. The Media Trust 1997–2006; Trustee, Sainsbury Centre for Mental Health 2001–05; mem. British Asscn of Counselling and Psychotherapy; Hon. DLitt (City Univ.) 1999. *Leisure interests:* reading, bridge. *Address:* 21 South Street, London, W1K 2XB, England (office). *Telephone:* (20) 7663-6464 (office). *Fax:* (20) 7663-6364 (office). *Website:* www.21southstreet.com (office).

GREEN, Sir Philip, Kt; British retail executive; b. 15 March 1952, Croydon; m. Tina Green; took over family property co. 1973; bought Jean Jeanie 1985 (sold to Lee Cooper), Owen Owen 1994, Sports Division (sold to JJB Sports), Mark One 1996, Shoe Express 1997, Sears 1999, British Home Stores (Bhs) 2000, Arcadia Group (including Top Shop, Top Man, Miss Selfridge, Dorothy Perkins, Wallis, Evans and Burtons clothing chains) 2002; Chair. and CEO Amber Day (now What Everyone Wants) 1988–92; Owner, Taveta Investments; apptd to lead UK govt efficiency review 2010. *Address:* Arcadia Group, Colegrave House, 70 Berners Street, London, W1T 3NL, England. *Telephone:* (20) 7636-8040. *Fax:* (20) 7927-0577. *Website:* www.arcadiagroup.co.uk.

GREEN, William (Bill) D., BS (Econs), MBA; American management consultancy executive; m.; two c.; ed Dean Coll., Babson Coll.; joined Accenture Ltd 1977, various positions including Partner 1986, Head of Mfg Industry Group, Man.-Pnr of New England Operations, Head of Resources Operating Group 1997–99, CEO Communications & High Tech. Group 1999–2003, Country Man.-Dir, USA 2000–03, Dir 2001–13, COO Client Services 2003–04, CEO 2004–10, Exec. Chair. 2006–13; Co-Chair. Business Coalition for Student Achievement; mem. Nat. Govs Asscn's Complete to Compete Nat. Advisory Group, Business Higher Educ. Forum, The Business Council, G100; mem. Bd of Dirs The McGraw-Hill Cos; Trustee, Dean Coll.; Hon. LLD (Babson Coll.). *Address:* c/o Accenture Ltd, 1345 Avenue of the Americas, New York, NY 10105, USA. *E-mail:* info@accenture.com.

GREEN OF HURSTPIERPOINT, Baron (Life Peer), cr. 2010, of Hurstpierpoint in the County of West Sussex,; **Stephen Keith Green,** MSc; British banking executive and fmr government official; b. 7 Nov. 1948; m.; two d.; ed Univ. of Oxford, Massachusetts Inst. of Tech., USA; early career with Ministry of Overseas Devt; consultant, McKinsey & Co. 1977; joined Hongkong and Shanghai Banking

Corpn (HSBC) 1982, responsible for Corp. Planning, Group Treas., HSBC Holdings PLC 1992–98, Dir HSBC Bank PLC 1995, Exec. Dir Corp., Investment Banking and Markets 1998–2003, responsible for Group Corp. Banking Business 2002, Group Chief Exec. 2003–06, Group Chair. 2006–10, Chair. HSBC Bank plc, HSBC North America Holdings Inc. –2010, HSBC Private Banking Holdings (Suisse) SA –2010, Dir of HSBC France –2010, HSBC Bank plc, Hongkong and Shanghai Banking Corpn Ltd; Minister of State for Trade and Investment 2011–13; Govt Spokesperson, Dept for Business, Innovation and Skills 2011–13, FCO 2011–13 (retd); Chair. British Bankers' Asscn 2006–10, Prime Minister's Business Council for Britain 2009–10; Dir (non-exec.) BASF SE 2009–10; mem. House of Lords; mem. Bd of Trustees, British Museum 2005–10; Non-stipendiary minister with the Anglican Church, deacon 1987, priest 1988; Trustee, Archbishop of Canterbury's Anglican Communion Fund; Hon. Trustee, Peking Univ. *Publication:* Serving God? Serving Mammon? Christians and the Financial Market 1996, Good Value: Reflections on Money, Morality and an Uncertain World 2009. *Address:* House of Lords, London, SW1A 0PW, England (office). *Telephone:* (20) 7219-5353 (office). *Fax:* (20) 7219-5979 (office). *E-mail:* contactholmember@parliament.uk (office). *Website:* www.parliament.uk/biographies/lords/lord-green-of-hurstpierpoint/4191 (office).

GREENAWAY, David, BSc, MCom, DLitt; British economist, academic and university administrator; *Vice-Chancellor, University of Nottingham;* b. 20 March 1952, Glasgow, Scotland; s. of David Greenaway and Agnes Greenaway; m. Susan Elizabeth Hallam; two s.; ed Liverpool Polytechnic, Univs of Liverpool and Nottingham; Head of Dept of Econs, Univ. of Nottingham 1987, currently Prof. of Econs, Dean Faculty of Law and Social Sciences 1991–94, Univ. Pro-Vice-Chancellor (Vice-Pres.) 1994–2001, 2004–08, Vice-Chancellor (Pres.) 2008–; mem. Armed Forces Pay Review Body 1998–2010 (Chair. 2004–10), Sr Salaries Review Body 2004–10, Review of Uninsured Driving for Sec. of State for Transport 2005–06; Chair. Ind. Review of Postgraduate Medical Educ. and Training in the UK 2012–; f. Leverhulme Centre for Research on Globalisation and Econ. Policy 1998; Gov. Nat. Inst. of Econ. and Social Research; Chair. Scientific Advisory Council, Institut für Weltwirtschaft, Kiel Univ.; mem. Scientific Cttee European Trade Study Group; Man. Ed. The World Economy (journal); DL of Notts. 2009–; Hon. Fellow, Liverpool John Moores Univ.; Hon. Citizen of Ningbo, China 2012; Hon. Col, East Midlands Univs Officers' Training Corps 2013–. *Publications:* author or ed. of 40 books; 150 articles in learned journals. *Leisure interests:* football, cycling, reading. *Address:* Vice-Chancellor's Office, University of Nottingham, University Park, Nottingham, NG7 2RD, England (office). *Telephone:* (115) 951-3001 (office). *Fax:* (115) 951-3005 (office). *E-mail:* david.greenaway@nottingham.ac.uk (office). *Website:* www.nottingham.ac.uk/Economics/People/david.greenaway (office); www.nottingham.ac.uk/about/vice-chancellor/vice-chancellor.aspx (office).

GREENAWAY, Peter, CBE; British film director, writer and painter; b. April 1942, Newport, Gwent, Wales; m.; two d.; ed Forest School and Walthamstow Coll. of Art; trained as painter and first exhibited pictures at Lord's Gallery 1964; film ed. Cen. Office of Information 1965–76; began making own films in 1966, numerous curatorial exhbns, one-man shows and group shows in Europe, USA, Australia and Japan 1988–; currently Prof. of Cinema Studies, European Graduate School, Saas-Fee, Switzerland; Officier, Ordre des Arts et Lettres; BAFTA Award for Outstanding British Contrib. to Cinema 2014. *Films include:* Train, Tree 1966, Revolution, Five Postcards from Capital Cities 1967, Intervals 1969, Erosion 1971, H is for House 1973, Windows, Water, Water Wrackets 1975, Goole by Numbers 1976, Dear Phone 1977, 1–100, A Walk Through H (Hugo Award, Chicago), Vertical Features Remake 1978, Zandra Rhodes (Hugo Award, Chicago 1981) 1979, The Falls (BFI Award, L'Age d'Or Brussels) 1980, Act of God (Melbourne Short Film Prize, Sydney Short Film Prize) 1981, The Draughtsman's Contract 1982, Four American Composers 1983, Making a Splash 1984, Inside Rooms: 26 Bathrooms 1985, A Zed & Two Noughts 1986, The Belly of An Architect (Best Actor Prize, Chicago) 1987, Drowning by Numbers (Best Artistic Contribution Prize), Fear of Drowning, Death in the Seine 1988, A TV Dante Cantos 1–8, Hubert Bals Handshake 1989, The Cook, The Thief, His Wife and Her Lover 1989, Prospero's Books, M is for Man, Music, Mozart 1991, Rosa (Dance Screen Prize), Darwin 1992, The Baby of Macon 1993, The Stairs, Geneva 1994, The Pillow Book (La Distinction Gervais, Cannes, Best Film and Best Cinematographer, Sitges, Spain) 1995, Flying over Water 1997, 8½ Women 1999, The Death of a Composer: Rosa, a Horse Drama 1999, The Man in the Bath 2001, The Tulse Luper Suitcases, Part 1: The Moab Story 2003, The Tulse Luper Suitcases, Part 3: From Sark to the Finish 2003, The Tulse Luper Suitcases, Part 2: Vaux to the Sea 2004, A Life in Suitcases 2005, Nightwatching 2007, Rembrandt's J'Accuse (documentary) 2008. *Opera:* Rosa, a Horse Drama 1994, Writing to Vermeer 1999. *Publications include:* A Zed and Two Noughts 1986, Belly of an Architect 1987, Drowning By Numbers, Fear of Drowning 1988, The Cook, The Thief, His Wife and Her Lover 1989, Papers 1990, Prospero's Books 1991, Prospero's Subjects (picture book) 1992, Rosa, The Falls, The Baby of Macon 1993, The Draughtsman's Contract 1994, The Pillow Book 1996. *Address:* c/o European Graduate School, Building Steinmatte, 3906 Saas Fee, Switzerland; c/o The Vue, 387B King Street, London, W6 9NJ, England. *Fax:* (20) 8748-3597. *E-mail:* info@petergreenawayevents.com. *Website:* www.petergreenawayevents.com; www.egs.edu/faculty/petergreenaway.html.

GREENBERG, Jack M., BSc, JD, CPA; American business executive; *Chairman and Presiding Director, Western Union Company;* b. 1942; s. of Edith S. Scher; m. Donna Greenberg; one s. two d.; ed Depaul Univ.; with Arthur Young & Co. 1964–82; Chief Finance Officer and Exec. Vice-Pres. McDonald's Corpn 1982, Vice-Chair. 1992, Pres., CEO 1997–99, Chair., CEO 1999–2002 (retd), also Dir; Chair. and Presiding Dir. Western Union Co. 2006–; mem. Bd of Dirs The Allstate Corpn, Hasbro, Inc., Innerworkings, Inc., Manpower Inc., DePaul University (fmr Chair.), Field Museum, Chicago Metropolis 2020; Trustee, Inst. of Int. Educ., Ronald McDonald House Charities, Chicago Symphony Orchestra, Chicago Bar Foundation, Chicago Community Trust; mem. American Inst. of Certified Public Accountants, ABA, Illinois CPA Soc., Council of the World Econ. Forum, Chicago Commercial Club, Chicago Bar Asscn; Hon. Dir American-Israel Chamber of Commerce and Industry, Inc. of Metropolitan Chicago; Hon. DHumLitt (DePaul) 1999. *Address:* Western Union Company, 12500 East Belford Avenue, Englewood, CO 80112, USA (office). *Telephone:* (720) 332-1000 (office). *Fax:* (720) 332-4753 (office). *Website:* www.westernunion.com (office).

GREENBERG, Jeffrey W., AB, JD; American business executive; *CEO, Aquiline Holdings LLC;* b. 1952; s. of Maurice R. Greenberg and Corinne P. Zuckerman; m. 1st Nikki Finke (divorced 1982); m. 2nd Kimberly Greenberg; ed Brown Univ., Georgetown Univ. Law School; fmr Head of Property/Casualty, American Int. Group; joined Marsh & McLennan Risk Capital 1996, CEO Marsh and McLennan Cos 1999–2004, Chair. 2000–2004 (resgnd); Founder Chair. Aquiline Holdings LLC, currently also CEO Aquiline Capital Partners LLC; Chair. Conning Holdings Corpn; mem. Bd of Dirs Futurity First Insurance Group, Validus Holdings Ltd; mem. Bd of Overseers Joan and Sanford I. Weill Graduate School of Medical Sciences, Cornell Univ.; Trustee, Brookings Inst., Spence School, New York Presbyterian Hospital, Brookings Institution, Metropolitan Museum of Art; mem. Trilateral Comm., Council on Foreign Relations, Brown Univ. Corpn, Asscn of the Bar, New York. *Address:* Aquiline Holdings LLC, 535 Madison Avenue, 24th Floor, New York, NY 10022, USA (office). *Telephone:* (212) 624-9500 (office). *E-mail:* contact@aquiline-llc.com (office). *Website:* www.aquiline-llc.com (office).

GREENBERG, Maurice Raymond (Hank), LLB; American lawyer and insurance executive; *Chairman and CEO, C.V. Starr & Co.;* b. 4 May 1925; s. of Jacob Greenberg and Ada Greenberg (née Rheingold); m. Corinne Phyllis Zuckerman 1950; four c.; ed Univ. of Miami, New York Univ. Law School; service with US army in Second World War and Korean War, rising to rank of Capt.; admitted to NY Bar 1953; worked for Continental Casualty Co. 1952–60; joined American Int. Group (AIG) Inc. 1960, Pres. American Home Assurance Co. 1962–67, CEO AIG Inc. 1967–2005, Chair. 1989–2005; Vice-Pres., C.V. Starr & Co. 1960–65, Dir 1965–68, Pres. 1968–2005, CEO 1968–, Chair. 2005–; mem. The Business Roundtable, Pres.'s Advisory Cttee for Trade Policy and Negotiations; Chair. US–China Business Council, US–ASEAN Council on Business and Tech., US–Philippine Business Cttee, The Starr Foundation; Vice-Chair. Center for Strategic and Int. Studies, Council on Foreign Relations; Chair. Emer. and Gov. Soc. of the NY Hosp.; hon. degrees from New England School of Law, NY Law School, Bryant Coll., Middlebury Coll., Brown Univ., Pace Univ. *Publication:* The AIG Story 2013. *Address:* C.V. Starr and Co., 399 Park Avenue, New York, NY 10022, USA (office). *Telephone:* (212) 230-5050 (office). *Fax:* (212) 230-5092 (office). *Website:* www.cvstarrco.com (office).

GREENBERG, Robert R., PhD; American chemist; *Research Chemist and Group Leader, Chemical Science and Technology Laboratory, National Institute of Standards and Technology;* Research Chemist and Group Leader, Chemical Science and Tech. Lab., Nat. Inst. of Standards and Tech. (NIST) 1976–; Fellow, American Nuclear Soc. 1998, mem. Exec. Cttee Biology and Medicine Div. 2009; NIST Judson C. French Award 2003, NIST Bronze Medal 2007, Hevesy Medal, Journal of Radioanalytical and Nuclear Chemistry 2007. *Publications:* numerous scientific papers in professional journals on the devt of high accuracy/high precision nuclear analytical methods and quality assurance procedures, and application of these methods to certification of standard reference materials. *Address:* Analytical Chemistry Division (839), National Institute of Standards and Technology, 100 Bureau Drive, Stop 8395, Gaithersburg, MD 20899-8395, USA (office). *Telephone:* (301) 975-6285 (office). *Fax:* (301) 208-9279 (office). *E-mail:* robert.greenberg@nist.gov (office). *Website:* www.nist.gov (office).

GREENBLATT, Stephen J., BA, PhD; American academic; *Cogan University Professor of the Humanities, Harvard University;* b. 7 Nov. 1943, Cambridge, Mass; s. of Harry Greenblatt and Mollie Brown; three s.; m. Ramie Targoff 1998; ed Yale Univ., Pembroke Coll., Cambridge, UK; Asst Prof. of English, Univ. of Calif., Berkeley 1969–74, Assoc. Prof. 1974–79, Prof. of English 1979–97; Prof. of English, Harvard Univ. 1997–, Cogan Univ. Prof. of the Humanities 2000–; numerous visiting professorships; Fellow, American Acad. of Arts and Sciences, American Acad. of Arts and Letters, American Philosophical Soc., Wissenschaftskolleg zu Berlin; mem. Int. Asscn of Univ. Profs of English, Modern Language Asscn, Renaissance Soc. of America; Guggenheim Fellow 1975, 1983; Porter Prize 1969, British Council Prize 1982, James Russell Lowell Prize 1989, Distinguished Teaching Award, Erasmus Inst. Prize 2001, Mellon Distinguished Humanist Award 2002, Wilbur Cross Medal 2010. *Publications:* Three Modern Satirists: Waugh, Orwell and Huxley 1965, Sir Walter Raleigh: The Renaissance Man and his Roles 1970, Renaissance Self-Fashioning: From More to Shakespeare 1980, Allegory and Representation (ed.) 1981, Power of Forms 1982, Representing the English Renaissance 1988, Shakespearean Negotiations: The Circulation of Social Energy in Renaissance England 1988, Learning to Curse: Essays in Early Modern Culture 1990, Marvelous Possessions: The Wonder of the New World 1991, Redrawing the Boundaries of Literary Study in English 1992, New World Encounters 1992, The Norton Shakespeare (ed.) 1997, The Norton Anthology of English Literature (ed.) 2000, Practising New Historicism 2000, Hamlet in Purgatory 2001, Will in the World: How Shakespeare Became Shakespeare 2004, Cultural Mobility: A Manifesto 2009, Shakespeare's Freedom 2010; contribs to scholarly journals. *Address:* Department of English, Harvard University, Cambridge, MA 02138, USA (office). *Telephone:* (617) 495-2101 (office). *Fax:* (617) 496-8737 (office). *E-mail:* greenbl@fas.harvard.edu (office). *Website:* www.fas.harvard.edu/~english (office).

GREENBLATT, Terry; Israeli human rights activist; *Executive Director and CEO, Urgent Action Fund for Women's Human Rights;* spent 20 years in Israel as women's rights and anti-occupation activist; Co-founder Kol Ha-Isha (The Women's Voice) Center, Jerusalem and Shani (Israeli Women Against the Occupation); mem. Founder's Council, Community School for Women's Studies and Econ. Devt, Kufr Kara, Israel; fmr Dir Bat Shalom (Israeli nat. women's peace org.), Jerusalem Link; Exec. Dir and CEO Urgent Action Fund for Women's Human Rights 2008–; mem. Bd of Trustees, Sarvoyada Gandhi Foundation, India; Ms Magazine 'Woman of the Year' Award 2002, Italian Archivio Disarmo Colombe d'Oro per la Pace 2002, 'Dialogue on Diversity' Liberty Award, Washington, DC 2003. *Address:* Urgent Action Fund for Women's Human Rights, 3100 Arapahoe Ave., Suite 201, Boulder, CO 80303, USA (office). *Telephone:* (303) 442-2388 (office). *Fax:* (303) 442-2370 (home). *E-mail:* urgentact@urgentactionfund.org (office). *Website:* www.urgentactionfund.org (office).

GREENBURY, Sir Richard, Kt; British fmr retail executive director; b. July 1936; m. 1st Sian Eames Hughes (divorced); two s. two d.; m. 2nd Gabrielle Mary McManus 1985 (divorced 1996); remarried Sian Eames Hughes 1996; ed Ealing Co. Grammar School; jr man. trainee, Marks and Spencer 1953, Alt. Dir 1970, Dir

1972, Jt Man. Dir 1978–85, 1985–86; COO Marks and Spencer PLC 1986, CEO 1988–99, Chair. 1991–99; part-time mem. British Gas Corpn 1976–87; Dir (non-exec.) Metal Box PLC 1985–89, ICI 1992–96, Lloyds Bank (now Lloyds TSB Group) 1992–97, Zeneca 1993–99; mem. Supervisory Bd, Philips Electronics NV 1998–2010; Dir (non-exec.) UNIFI Inc. 1999–2002, Game PLC 2000–03; Dr hc (Ulster) 1993, (Greenwich) 1993, (Nottingham Trent) 1994, (City and Guilds of London Inst.) 1994, (UMIST) 1996, (London Business School) 1996, (Bradford) 1999. *Leisure interests:* playing tennis, music, reading, watching sport. *Address:* Ambarrow Wood, Ambarrow Lane, Sandhurst, Berks., GU47 8JE, England (home). *Telephone:* (1344) 776985 (office); (1344) 779305 (home). *Fax:* (1344) 776913 (office).

GREENE, Brian R., PhD; American physicist, writer and academic; *Professor of Mathematics and Physics, Columbia University;* b. 9 Feb. 1963, New York; s. of Alan Greene; m. Tracy Day; ed Harvard Univ., Univ. of Oxford, UK; Post-doctoral Fellow, Harvard Univ. 1987–90; Asst Prof., Cornell Univ. 1990, Assoc. Prof. 1995, later Prof.; currently Prof. of Math. and Physics, Columbia Univ., also Co-Dir Inst. for Strings, Cosmology, and Astroparticle Physics, Dir Theoretical Advanced Study Inst. 1996–; mem. Editorial Bd Physical Review D, Advance in Theoretical and Mathematical Physics. *Television:* The Theory of Everything 2003. *Publications:* journal papers: Duality in Calabi-Yau Moduli Space (with M. R. Plesser) 1990, Calabi-Yau Moduli Space, Mirror Manifolds and Spacetime Topology Change in String Theory (with P. S. Aspinwall and D. R. Morrison) 1994, Black Hole Condensation and the Unification of String Vacua (with D. R. Morrison and A. Strominger) 1995, Orbifold Resolution by D-Branes (with M. R. Douglas and D. R. Morrison) 1997, D-Brane Topology Changing Transitions 1998; books: The Elegant Universe (Aventis Prize for Science Books 2000) 1999, The Fabric of the Cosmos: Space, Time and the Texture of Reality 2004, Icarus at the Edge of Time 2008, The Hidden Reality: Parallel Universes and the Deep Laws of the Cosmos 2011. *Address:* 910 Pupin, MC 5210, Box 10, 538 West 120th Street, New York, NY 10027, USA (office). *Telephone:* (212) 854-3349 (office); (212) 854-4347 (office). *E-mail:* greene@phys.columbia.edu (office); greene@math.columbia.edu (office). *Website:* www.iscap.columbia.edu (office); www.columbia.edu/cu/physics (office).

GREENE, Graham Carleton, CBE, MA; British publisher; b. 10 June 1936, Berlin, Germany; s. of Sir Hugh Carleton Greene and Helga Mary Connolly; m. 1st Judith Margaret Gordon Walker 1957 (divorced); m. 2nd Sally Georgina Horton 1976 (divorced); one s.; also one step-s. one step-d.; ed Eton Coll. and Univ. Coll., Oxford; Dir Jonathan Cape Ltd 1962–90, Man. Dir 1966–88; Dir Chatto, Virago, Bodley Head and Jonathan Cape Ltd 1969–88, Chair. 1970–88; Chair. Random House UK Ltd 1988–90; Chair. Nation Pty Co. Ltd 1981–87, New Society 1984–86, Great Britain-China Centre 1986–97; British Museum Devt Trust 1986–93 (Vice-Chair. 1993–2004), British Museum Publications (now British Museum Co.) Ltd 1998–2002, Museums and Galleries Comm. 1991–96, Vice-Pres. 1997–; Dir Book Reps (NZ) Ltd 1971–88, CVBC Services 1972–88, Australasian Publishing Co. Ltd 1969–88 (Chair. 1978–88), Guinness Peat Group PLC 1973–87, Triad Paperbacks 1975–88, Greene King PLC 1979–, Statesman and Nation Publishing Co. 1980–85 (Chair. 1981–85), Statesman Publishing Co. Ltd 1980–85 (Chair. 1981–85), Random House Inc. 1987–88, Jupiter Int. Investment Trust PLC 1989–2001, Henry Sotheran Ltd 1990–, Ed Victor Ltd 1991–, Rosemary Sandberg Ltd 1991–2002, Libra KFT (Budapest) 1991–, London Merchant Securities PLC 1996–2007 (Chair. 2000–07); Dir Garsington Opera Ltd 1996–; mem. Bd of British Council 1977–88, Council of Publrs Asscn (Pres. 1977–79) 1969–88; Trustee, British Museum 1978–2002 (Chair. 1996–2002, Trustee Emer. 2002–), Open Coll. of the Arts 1990–97; mem. Int. Cttee of Int. Publrs Asscn 1977–88, Groupe des Editeurs de Livres de la CEE 1977–86 (Pres. 1984–86); Chevalier, Ordre des Arts et des Lettres; Hon. DLitt (Keele Univ.) 2002, Hon. DCL (Univ. E Anglia) 2002, Hon. DLitt (Buckingham) 2004. *Address:* D2 Albany, Piccadilly, London, W1J 0AP, England (home). *Telephone:* (20) 7734-0270 (home). *Fax:* (20) 7437-5251 (home). *E-mail:* grahamc.greene@virgin.net (home).

GREENE, Jack Phillip, PhD; American historian and academic; *Andrew W. Mellon Professor Emeritus in the Humanities, Johns Hopkins University;* b. 12 Aug. 1931, Lafayette, Ind.; s. of Ralph B. Greene and Nellie A. Greene (née Miller); m. 1st Sue L. Nuenswander 1953 (divorced 1990); one s. one d.; m. 2nd Amy Turner Bushnell 1990; ed Univ. of North Carolina, Indiana Univ. and Duke Univ., Durham, NC; History Instructor, Michigan State Univ., East Lansing 1956–59; Asst Prof. of History, Western Reserve Univ., Cleveland, OH 1959–62, Assoc. Prof. 1962–65; Visiting Assoc. Prof. and Visiting Ed., William and Mary Quarterly, Coll. of William and Mary, Williamsburg, Va 1961–62; Assoc. Prof. of History, Univ. of Mich., Ann Arbor 1965–66; Visiting Assoc. Prof. of History, Johns Hopkins Univ., Baltimore, Md 1964–65, Prof. 1966–75, Chair. Dept of History 1970–72, Andrew W. Mellon Prof. in Humanities 1975–, now Prof. Emer.; Distinguished Prof., Univ. of California, Irvine 1990–92; Harmsworth Prof. of American History, Univ. of Oxford 1975–76; Visiting Prof., Hebrew Univ. of Jerusalem 1979, École des Hautes Études en Sciences Sociales 1986–87; Freeman Prof., Univ. of Richmond, Va 1996; Sweet Prof., Michigan State Univ. 1997; Gast Prof., Frei Universität, Berlin 2009; mem. Inst. for Advanced Study 1970–71, 1985–86, American Philosophical Soc., American Acad. of Arts and Sciences; Corresp. mem. British Acad.; Fellow, Woodrow Wilson Int. Center for Scholars 1974–75, Center for Advanced Study in Behavioral Sciences 1979–80, Churchill Coll., Cambridge 1986–, Nat. Humanities Center 1987–88, 2009–10, Guggenheim Fellow 1964–65; John Carter Brown Library Fellow 1999–2000; several awards, including American Historical Asscn Award for Scholarly Distinction 2008. *Publications:* 32 books, including Quest for Power 1963, Diary of Colonel Landon Carter of Sabine Hall (two vols) 1965, Settlements to Society 1966, Colonies to Nation 1967, Reinterpretation of American Revolution 1968, All Men are Created Equal 1976, Colonial British America 1983, Encyclopedia of American Political History 1984, Peripheries and Center 1986, Political Life in Eighteenth Century Virginia 1986, Intellectual Heritage of the Constitutional Era 1986, Magna Carta for America 1986, American Revolution 1987, Pursuits of Happiness 1988, Selling the New World 1988, Encyclopedia of the American Revolution (co-ed.) 1991, Imperatives, Behaviors and Identities 1992, Intellectual Construction of America 1993, Negotiated Authorities 1994, Understanding the American Revolution 1995, Interpreting Early America 1996, Companion to the American Revolution 2000, Atlantic History: A Critical Appraisal 2009, Exclusionary Empire 2009, Constitutional Origins of the American Revolution 2010, Evaluating Empire and Confronting

Colonialism in Eighteenth-Century Britain 2013, Creating the British Atlantic 2013. *Leisure interests:* travel, cinema. *Address:* Department of History, The Johns Hopkins University, Baltimore, MD 21218 (office); 1974 Division Road, East Greenwich, RI 02898, USA (home). *Telephone:* (401) 884-5883 (home). *Fax:* (401) 884-5883 (home). *E-mail:* jpgreene@jhem.jhu.edu (office); jack_greene@brown.edu (home). *Website:* www.jhu.edu/~history (office).

GREENE, Mark I., MD, PhD, FRCP; Canadian pathologist and academic; *John Eckman Professor of Medical Science, University of Pennsylvania;* ed Univ. of Manitoba, Canada; MRC Fellow, Harvard Univ., Mass 1976–78, Asst Prof. of Pathology 1978–80, Assoc. Prof. 1980–85; Clinical Consultant in Medicine, Dana Farber Cancer Inst., Boston 1980–86; Head, Basic Research Unit of Immunology, Univ. of Pennsylvania 1986–, Head of Fundamental Research, Cancer Center 1987–, Vice-Chair. Dept of Pathology 1993–, currently Eckman Prof. of Medical Science; Newton Abraham Prof. of Biological Science, Univ. of Oxford; J. Allyn Taylor Int. Prize in Medicine, Robarts Research Inst. 2006. *Publications:* numerous scientific papers in professional journals on receptors, reoviruses, neu-growth factor receptors and T-cell receptors. *Address:* Immunology Graduate Group, University of Pennsylvania, 410 BRB II/III, Philadelphia, PA 19104-6160, USA (office). *Telephone:* (215) 898-2847 (office). *Fax:* (215) 746-5525 (office). *E-mail:* greene@reo.med.upenn.edu (office). *Website:* www.med.upenn.edu/immun/greene.shtml (office); www.uphs.upenn.edu/abramson/greene.html (office).

GREENE, Maurice; American professional athlete; b. 23 July 1974, Kansas City, Mo.; s. of Ernest Greene and Jackie Greene; ed Schlage High School and Park Coll., Kansas City; world record-holder indoor 50m (shared with Donovan Bailey) and 60m (as at end 2002); coached by John Smith 1996–; silver medal US Championships 60m 1995; gold medal US Indoor Championships 60 m 1997; gold medal US Championships 100m 1997; gold medal World Championships 100m 1997, 100m, 200m and 4×100m relay 1999, 100m 2001; Olympic gold medallist 100m and 4×100m 2000, bronze medal 100m 2004; set world record for 100m in Athens 1999 (9.79 seconds); f. Finish the Race Foundation. *Address:* HS International, 9871 Irvine Center Drive, Irvine, CA 92618, USA (office). *Telephone:* (949) 753-9153 (office). *Fax:* (949) 753-9253 (office). *E-mail:* maurice@hsi.net (office). *Website:* www.hsi.net (office).

GREENE, Moya, BA; Canadian civil servant and business executive; *Chief Executive, Royal Mail Group;* b. Newfoundland; one d.; ed Osgoode Hall Law School, Memorial Univ. of Newfoundland; joined Public Service of Canada as an immigration adjudicator, Ottawa 1979, later held positions in Dept of Labour and Privy Council Office, as Asst Deputy Minister for Transport Canada, oversaw privatization of Canadian Nat. Railway and deregulation of Canadian airline industry; Man. Dir of Infrastructure Finance and Public Pvt. Partnership, TD Securities 1996–2000; Sr Vice-Pres. and Chief Admin. Officer, Retail Products, Canadian Imperial Bank of Commerce 2000–03; Sr Vice-Pres., Operational Effectiveness, Bombardier 2003–04; Pres. and CEO EPO Inc.; Pres. and CEO Canada Post Corpn 2005–10; Chief Exec. Royal Mail Holdings Plc and Royal Mail Group Plc, UK (first foreigner and first woman, highest–paid UK civil servant) 2010–; mem. Bd of Dirs Purolator Courier, Tim Hortons (coffee shop chain); named by the National Post amongst the 100 Most Influential Women in Canada 2003, named by the Ivey School of Business as one of the Top 40 Female Corp. Execs in Canada 2004. *Address:* Royal Mail Group Plc, 148 Old Street, London, EC1V 9HQ, England (office). *Telephone:* (20) 7250-2888 (office). *Fax:* (20) 7250-2244 (office). *E-mail:* info@royalmailgroup.com (office). *Website:* www.royalmailgroup.com (office).

GREENE, Sally, MBA; British impresario and producer; *Chief Executive, Old Vic Productions plc;* b. 27 May 1954; d. of Basil Greene and Clare Tully; m. Robert Bourne; one s. one d.; ed St Maur's Convent, Weybridge and Guildhall School of Music and Drama; bought Richmond Theatre, Surrey 1986, programmed then restored theatre 1991; took over Criterion Theatre, Piccadilly 1992, restored theatre, re-opening it 1993; f. Criterion Productions PLC 1994; bought The Old Vic Theatre 1998, est. charitable trust to run it; Founder (with Kevin Spacey q.v.) and CEO Old Vic Productions plc 2000; Club Owner Ronnie Scott's, London 2005–. *Productions include:* Taking Sides, Criterion Theatre 1994, Hot House, Comedy Theatre 1994, Jack 1993, Cyrano de Bergerac, RSC 1995, Car Man, Old Vic 2000, Medea 2001, Life x 3, Old Vic 2001, Vagina Monologues, Ambassador's Theatre 2001–02. *Leisure interests:* piano, skiing, singing. *Address:* Old Vic Productions plc, Park House, 26 North End Road, London, NW11 7PT; The Old Vic, The Cut, London, SE1 8NB (office); Lindsay House, 100 Cheyne Walk, London, SW10 0DQ, England (home). *Telephone:* (20) 7401-3534 (office). *Fax:* (20) 7261-9161 (office). *E-mail:* s.greene@dial.pipex.com (home). *Website:* www.oldvicproductions.com (office).

GREENER, Sir Anthony Armitage, Kt, FCMA; British business executive; *Chairman, The Minton Trust;* b. 26 May 1940, Bowden; s. of William Greener and Diana Greener; m. Min Ogilvie 1974; one s. one d.; ed Marlborough Coll.; Marketing Man. Thames Board Mills 1969; Retail Controller, Alfred Dunhill Ltd (later Dunhill Holdings PLC) 1972, Dir 1974, Man. Dir 1975; Man. Dir United Distillers 1987–92; Dir Guinness PLC 1986–97, Jt Man. Dir 1989–91, Chief Exec. 1992–97, Chair. 1993–97; Co-Chair. Diageo PLC (after merger with Grand Metropolitan PLC) 1997–98, Chair. 1998–2000; Chair. University for Industry Ltd 2000–04, Qualifications and Curriculum Authority 2002–08; Deputy Chair. BT 2001–06; Chair. The Minton Trust, St Giles Trust 2009–; Dir Louis Vuitton Moet Hennessy 1989–97, Reed Int. 1990–93, Reed Elsevier 1993–98, Robert Mondavi 2000–04; mem. Bd United Learning Trust, Williams Sonoma 2007–, WNSGS 2007–. *Leisure interests:* skiing, sailing, gardening. *Address:* The Minton Trust, 26 Hamilton House, Vicarage Gate, London, W8 4HL, England (office). *Telephone:* (20) 7937-2048 (office). *Fax:* (20) 7937-2048 (office). *E-mail:* greenera@mintontrust.com (office).

GREENFIELD, Jerry; American business executive; *Co-founder, Ben & Jerry's Homemade Inc.;* b. 14 March 1951, Brooklyn, New York; m. Elizabeth Greenfield 1987; one s.; ed Calhoun High School, Merrick, NY, Oberlin Coll., OH; employed as lab technician, NY and NC –1976; Co-founder (with Ben Cohen) Ben & Jerry's Homemade Inc. 1977, opened first ice cream parlour in Burlington, Vt 1978; est. Ben & Jerry's Foundation to oversee donation of 7.5% of corp. profits to non-profit orgs; Founding mem. Businesses for Social Responsibility (org. which promotes socially responsible business practices); mem. New England Futures Project; James Beard Humanitarians of the Year Award 1993. *Leisure interests:* basketball, volleyball, spending time with family and friends. *Address:* Ben & Jerry's Homemade Inc., 30 Community Drive, South Burlington, VT 05403-6828, USA (office). *Telephone:* (802) 846-1500 (office). *Website:* www.benjerry.com (office); www.jerrygreenfield.com.

GREENFIELD OF OTMOOR, Baroness (Life Peer), cr. 2001, of Otmoor in the County of Oxfordshire; **Susan Adele Greenfield,** CBE, BA (Hons), MA, DPhil, FRSE; British pharmacologist; *Professor in Synaptic Pharmacology, University of Oxford;* b. 1 Oct. 1950; d. of Reginald Myer Greenfield and Doris Margaret Winifred Greenfield; m. Peter William Atkins 1991 (divorced 2005); ed Godolphin and Latymer School for Girls, St Hilda's Coll., Oxford; Dame Catherine Fulford Sr Scholarship, St Hugh's Coll. Oxford 1974; MRC Training Fellow, Univ. Lab. of Physiology, Oxford 1977–81; Collège de France, Paris; Royal Soc. Study Visit Award, 1978; MRC-INSERM French Exchange Fellow 1979–80; Jr Research Fellow, Green Coll. Oxford 1981–84, Lecturer in Synaptic Pharmacology 1985–96, currently Prof. in Synaptic Pharmacology; Dir Royal Inst. 1998–2010; Gresham Prof. of Physic, Gresham Coll. Oxford 1995–99; Visiting Fellow, Inst. of Neuroscience, La Jolla, Calif., USA 1995; Visiting Distinguished Scholar, Queen's Univ., Belfast 1996; Adelaide Thinker in Residence 2004–06; Chancellor Heriot-Watt Univ. 2006–; Co-founder Synaptica Ltd 1997, BrainBoost Ltd 2002; Dir (non-exec.) Britech Foundation Ltd 2002–06, Oxford Inspires Ltd 2002–05, Israel Britain Business Council 2002, Young Foresight Ltd 2003, Bank Leumi (UK) 2003–06, Cherwell Capital plc 2004–06, Enkephala Ltd 2005–; mem. Nat. Advisory Cttee on Cultural and Creative Educ. 1998–; Pres. Asscn for Science Educ. 2000; Vice-Pres. Asscn of Women in Science and Eng 2001; Fellow, Australian Davos Connection 2007, Science Museum 2010; Trustee, Science Museum, London 1998–2003; Hon. Fellow, St Hilda's Coll. Oxford, Cardiff Univ. 2000; Hon. FRCP 2000; numerous hon. doctorates; Chevalier, Légion d'honneur 2003; Michael Faraday Medal, Royal Soc. 1998, Woman of Distinction, Jewish Care 1998, Hon. Australian of the Year 2006, Science and Tech. Award, British Inspiration Awards 2010, Australian Soc. for Medical Research Medal 2010. *Radio includes:* Start the Week, Any Questions and other discussion programmes; presenter of Turn On, Turn Off series on drugs and the brain, Today Programme. *Television includes:* Dimbleby Lecturer 1999, author and presenter of Brain Story 'Landmark' (BBC 2 series of programmes on the brain) 2000, Big Ideas in Science, Channel 5 (UK). *Publications include:* numerous articles in learned journals; Mindwaves (co-ed. with C. B. Blakemore) 1987, Journey to the Centres of the Brain (with G. Ferry) 1994, Journey to the Centres of the Mind 1995, The Human Mind Explained (ed.) 1996, The Human Brain: A Guided Tour 1997, Brainpower (ed.) 2000, Brain Story 2000, Private Life of the Brain 2000, Tomorrow's People: How 21st Century Technology is Changing the Way We Think and Feel 2003, ID: The Quest for Identity in the 21st Century 2008. *Leisure interests:* squash, travel. *Address:* Department of Pharmacology, Mansfield Road, Oxford, OX1 3QT, England (office). *Telephone:* (1865) 271852 (office). *Fax:* (1865) 271853 (office). *E-mail:* sagpa@pharm.ox.ac.uk (office).

GREENGARD, Paul, PhD; American neuroscientist, biochemist and academic; *Vincent Astor Professor, Rockefeller University;* b. 11 Dec. 1925, New York; ed Johns Hopkins Univ., Baltimore; postdoctoral studies in Biochemistry, Univ. of London, Univ. of Cambridge, UK and NIH, Bethesda, Md 1953–59; Dir Dept of Biochemistry, Geigy Research Lab., Ardsley, NY 1959–67; Visiting Assoc. Prof. and Prof. of Pharmacology, Albert Einstein Coll. of Medicine, NY 1961–70; Prof. of Pharmacology and Psychiatry, Yale Univ. School of Medicine 1968–83; Vincent Astor Prof. and Head, Lab. of Molecular and Cellular Neuroscience, Rockefeller Univ., NY 1983–; mem. NAS, NARSAD Scientific Council; numerous awards and prizes including Dickson Prize and Medal in Medicine, Univ. of Pittsburgh 1977, New York Acad. of Sciences Award in Biological and Medicinal Sciences 1980, 1993, 3M Life Sciences Award, Fed. of American Socs for Experimental Biology 1987, NAS Award in the Neurosciences 1991, Lieber Prize for Outstanding Achievement in Schizophrenia Research 1996, Metropolitan Life Foundation Award for Medical Research 1998, Bristol-Myers Squibb Award for Distinguished Achievement in Neuroscience Research 1989, Nobel Prize for Medicine or Physiology (co-recipient) 2000. *Publications:* numerous publs and articles in journals. *Address:* Laboratory of Molecular and Cellular Neuroscience, The Rockefeller University, 1230 York Avenue, New York, NY 10021, USA (office). *Telephone:* (212) 327-8780 (office). *Fax:* (212) 327-7746 (office). *E-mail:* greengard@rockefeller.edu (office). *Website:* www.rockefeller.edu/research/abstract.php?id=53 (office); www.rockefeller.edu/labheads/greengard/greengard-lab.html (office).

GREENGRASS, Paul; British film and television director; b. 13 Aug. 1955, Cheam, Surrey; began career as an investigative journalist and award-winning documentary filmmaker; Pres. Directors UK 2008–; BAFTA Alan Clarke Award for Outstanding Creative Contrib. to Television 2005, British Independent Film Variety Award 2013. *Films directed include:* Resurrected (Interfilm and OCIC Jury Awards, Berlin Film Festival) 1989, Sophie's World, The Theory of Flight 1998, Bloody Sunday (also writer) (Golden Bear, Berlin Int. Film Festival) 2002, The Bourne Supremacy 2004, United 93 (Best Dir, Los Angeles Film Critics Asscn, Best Film, New York Film Critics' Circle Awards, Best Dir, Best British Producer, Best Film, London Film Critics' Circle Awards, BAFTA Award for Best Dir 2007) 2006, The Bourne Ultimatum 2007, Green Zone 2010, Captain Phillips 2013. *Television work includes:* World In Action, Food and Trucks and Rock and Roll, U2 – Anthem for the Eighties, Moscow Week, Coppers, What Ever Happened to Woodward and Bernstein, When The Lies Run Out (Chicago Film Festival Silver Medal) 1993, Kavanagh QC 1994, Open Fire (writer) 1994, The One That Got Away (also writer) 1996, The Fix (also writer) 1997, The Murder of Stephen Lawrence (also writer) 1999, Omagh (writer and producer) (BAFTA Award for Best Single Drama 2005) 2004. *Publication:* Spycatcher (with Peter Wright). *Address:* c/o CAA, 2000 Avenue of the Stars, Los Angeles, CA 90067, USA.

GREENING, Rt Hon. Justine, MBA; British politician; *Secretary of State for International Development;* b. 30 April 1969, Rotherham, S Yorks., England; ed Oakwood Comprehensive School, Univ. of Southampton, London Business School; Councillor, Epping Town Council 1998–2002; contested Ealing, Acton and Shepherd's Bush constituency 2001; trained as accountant and worked as Accountant/Finance Man. for, amongst others, Price Waterhouse Coopers, GlaxoSmithKline and Centrica plc –2005; MP for Putney 2005–10, for Putney, Roehampton and Southfields 2010–; Shadow Minister for the Treasury 2007–09, for Communities and Local Govt 2009–10; Econ. Sec., HM Treasury 2010–11; Sec. of State for Transport 2011–12, for Int. Devt 2012–; mem. The Bow Group 1998–, Political Officer 1999–2000; Vice-Chair. (Youth), Conservative Party 2005–10; mem. (Select Cttees), Work and Pensions 2005–07, Public Accounts 2010–; Conservative. *Address:* Department for International Development, 1 Palace Street, London, SW1E 5HE (office); House of Commons, Westminster, London, SW1A 0AA (office); Constituency Office, 3 Summerstown, London, SW17 0BQ, England (office). *Telephone:* (20) 7023-0000 (Dept) (office); (20) 7219-8300 (Westminster) (office); (20) 8946-4557 (Constituency Office) (office). *Fax:* (20) 7023-0012 (Dept) (office). *E-mail:* greeningj@parliament.uk; pssofs@dfid.gov.uk (office). *Website:* www.dfid.gov.uk (office); www.parliament.uk/biographies/commons/justine-greening/1555 (office); www.justinegreening.co.uk.

GREENSPAN, Alan, KBE, MA, PhD; American economist and central banker (retd) and business consultant; *President, Greenspan Associates LLC;* b. 6 March 1926, New York; s. of Herbert Greenspan and Rose Goldsmith; m. Andrea Mitchell 1997; ed New York and Columbia Univs; Pres., CEO Townsend-Greenspan & Co. Inc. 1954–74, 1977–87; mem. Nixon for Pres. Cttee 1968–69; mem. Task Force for Econ. Growth 1969, Comm. on an All-Volunteer Armed Force 1969–70, Comm. on Financial Structure and Regulation 1970–71; Consultant to Council of Econ. Advisers 1970–74, to US Treasury 1971–74, to Fed. Reserve Bd 1971–74; Chair. Council of Econ. Advisers 1974–77, Nat. Comm. on Social Security Reform 1981–83; Chair. Bd of Govs Fed. Reserve System 1987–2006; Founder and Pres. Greenspan Assocs (consulting firm), Washington, DC 2006–, advisor to Pimco (for fund man.) 2007–, to Deutsche Bank (for investment banking) 2007–; Adviser Paulson and Co., New York 2008–; mem. Sec. of Commerce's Econ. Comm.'s Cen. Market System Cttee 1972, GNP Review Cttee of Office of Man. and Budget, Time Magazine's Bd of Economists 1971–74, 1977–87, Pres.'s Econ. Policy Advisory Bd 1981–87, Pres.'s Foreign Intelligence Advisory Bd 1983–85, Exec. Cttee Trilateral Comm.; Sr Adviser, Brookings Inst. Panel on Econ. Activity 1970–74, 1977–87; Adjunct Prof., Grad. School of Business Man., New York 1977–87; mem. Bd of Dirs Council on Foreign Relations; Past Pres. and Fellow, Nat. Asscn of Business Economists; mem. Bd of Dirs Trans World Financial Co. 1962–74, Dreyfus Fund 1970–74, Gen. Cable Corpn 1973–74, 1977–78, Sun Chemical Corpn 1973–74, Gen. Foods Corpn 1977–86, J.P. Morgan & Co. 1977–87, Mobil Corpn 1977–87, Aluminum Co. of America (ALCOA) 1977–87; Hon. KBE 2002, Commdr, Légion d'honneur; Jefferson Award 1976, William Butler Memorial Award 1977, Presidential Medal of Freedom 2005. *Publications:* The Age of Turbulence: Adventures in a New World (memoirs) 2007, The Map and the Territory 2013. *Leisure interest:* golf. *Address:* Greenspan Associates LLC, 1133 Connecticut Avenue, Suite 810, NW, Washington, DC 20036, USA (office). *Telephone:* (202) 457-8250 (office).

GREENSPON, Edward B., BA, MA; Canadian journalist and editor; *Editor-in-Chief, The Globe and Mail;* b. 26 March 1957, Montreal; s. of Mortimer Greenspon and Rosalie Greenspon; m. Janice Neil 1984; three s.; ed Carleton Univ., Ottawa, London School of Econs, UK (Commonwealth Scholar); fmr paperboy for (now defunct) Montreal Daily Star; moved to London, UK to study; Business Reporter, The Globe and Mail 1986, European Business Corresp., London, returned to Canada 1989, Man. Ed. Report on Business section and Deputy Man. Ed. The Globe and Mail 1989–93, Ottawa Bureau Chief and Assoc. Ed. 1993–99, Exec. News Ed., Political Ed. and columnist for Ottawa region 1999–2002, Founding Ed. www.globeandmail.com, Ed.-in-Chief 2002–; Hyman Soloman Award for Excellence in Public Policy Journalism. *Publications:* Double Vision: The Inside Story of the Liberals in Power (co-author) (Douglas Purvis Award for best public policy book 1996) 1995, Searching for Certainty: Inside the New Canadian Mindset (with Darrell Bricker) 2001. *Address:* The Globe and Mail, 444 Front Street West, Toronto, ON M5V 2S9, Canada (office). *Telephone:* (416) 585-5000 (office). *Fax:* (416) 585-5085 (office). *E-mail:* egreenspon@globeandmail.ca (office). *Website:* www.globeandmail.com (office).

GREENSTOCK, Sir Jeremy (Quentin), Kt, GCMG, MA; British diplomatist; *Chairman, Gatehouse Advisory Partners;* b. 27 July 1943, Harrow, Middx, England; s. of the late John Wilfrid Greenstock and Ruth Margaret Logan; m. Anne Derryn Ashford Hodges 1969; one s. two d.; ed Harrow School and Worcester Coll., Oxford; Asst Master, Eton Coll. 1966–69; entered diplomatic service 1969, studied Arabic at MECAS 1970–72, served in Dubai 1972–74, Pvt. Sec. to Amb., Washington, DC 1974–78, with FCO (Planning, Personnel Operations Dept, Near East and N African Dept) 1978–83; Commercial Counsellor, Jeddah 1983–85, Riyadh 1985–86; Head of Chancery, Embassy in Paris 1987–90; Asst Under-Sec. of State, FCO 1990–93; Minister, Embassy in Washington, DC 1994–95; Deputy Under-Sec. of State, FCO 1995; Political Dir, FCO 1996–98; Perm. Rep. to UN, New York 1998–2003, Chair. UN Security Council Counter-Terrorism Cttee 2001–03; UK Special Rep. for Iraq 2003–04; Dir The Ditchley Foundation 2004–10; Special Adviser to BP Group 2004–10; Dir (non-exec.) De La Rue PLC 2005–13; Dir Lambert Energy Advisory 2010–, Chair. 2012–; Chair. Gatehouse Advisory Partners 2010–, UN Asscn-UK 2011–; Trustee, Int. Rescue Cttee (UK) 2006–12; Hon. Fellow, King's Coll. London, Worcester Coll. Oxford. *Leisure interests:* reading, travel, golf, skiing, listening to music, watching sport. *Address:* Gatehouse Advisory Partners Ltd, 1 Tudor Street, London, EC4Y 0AH, England (office). *Telephone:* (20) 7099-5533 (office). *E-mail:* info@gatehouseap.com (office). *Website:* www.gatehouseadvisorypartners.com (office).

GREENWOOD, Sir Brian Mellor, Kt, CBE, FRCP, FRS; British physician, biomedical research scientist and academic; *Manson Professor of Clinical Tropical Medicine, London School of Hygiene and Tropical Medicine;* b. 1938; spent ten years working in Nigeria and 15 years as Head of MRC Labs in the Gambia researching malaria and infections caused by capsulated bacteria such as the meningococcus (*Neissera meningitidis*); currently Manson Prof. of Clinical Tropical Medicine, London School of Hygiene and Tropical Medicine; Chalmers Medal, Royal Soc. of Tropical Medicine and Hygiene 1977, McKay Prize, American Soc. of Tropical Medicine and Hygiene 1991, Adesuyi Prize, West African Health Community 1995, Manson Medal, Royal Soc. of Tropical Medicine and Hygiene 2001, inaugural recipient, Hideyo Noguchi Africa Prize (Medical Research category) 2008, Canada Gairdner Global Health Award 2012. *Publications:*

numerous papers in professional journals. *Address:* London School of Hygiene and Tropical Medicine, Keppel Street, London, WC1E 7HT, England (office). *Telephone:* (20) 7299-4712 (office). *Fax:* (20) 7436-5389 (office). *E-mail:* brian .greenwood@lshtm.ac.uk (office). *Website:* www.lshtm.ac.uk (office).

GREENWOOD, Christopher, CMG, BA (Hons), MA, LLB (Hons); British lawyer, academic and judge; *Judge, International Court of Justice;* ed Wellingborough School, Northants., Magdalene Coll., Cambridge (Whewell Scholar in Int. Law); called to the Bar, Middle Temple, London 1978–79, Bencher 2003; in practice 1985–; QC 1999; Univ. Lecturer, Univ. of Cambridge 1981–96, Dir of Studies of Law, Magdalene Coll. 1981–96, Dean, Magdalene Coll. 1981–87, Tutor 1989–96, Fellow, Magdalene Coll. 1978–96; Prof. of Int. Law, LSE 1996–; numerous visiting professorships; Judge, Int. Court of Justice, The Hague 2009–; mem. Arbitration Tribunal, Perm. Court of Arbitration, Larsen v. Hawaiian Kingdom 2001, Panel of Arbitrators, Law of the Sea Convention, Panel of Arbitrators, Int. Centre for the Settlement of Investment Disputes; expert witness on int. law in arbitrations and proceedings in Canada, NZ and USA; mem. Editorial Cttee British Year Book of International Law, Year Book of International Humanitarian Law, Journal of Conflict and Security Law; mem. Council, British Br., Int. Law Asscn; mem. American Soc. of Int. Law 1979, British Inst. of Int. and Comparative Law, Int. Inst. of Humanitarian Law, Soc. of Public Teachers of Law. *Publications:* several books and numerous articles and other publs on int. law. *Address:* International Court of Justice, Peace Palace, Carnegieplein 2, 2517 KJ The Hague, The Netherlands (office). *Telephone:* (70) 302-2323 (office). *Fax:* (70) 364-9928 (office). *E-mail:* info@icj-cij.org (office). *Website:* www.icj-cij.org (office).

GREER, David Steven, MD; American medical specialist; *Dean and Professor Emeritus, Community Health Department, Brown University;* b. 12 Oct. 1925, Brooklyn, New York; s. of Jacob Greer and Mary Greer (née Zaslawsky); m. Marion Clarich 1950; one s. one d.; ed Pritzker School of Medicine, Univ. of Chicago, Univ. of Notre Dame; Intern, Yale-New Haven Medical Center 1953–54; Resident in Medicine, Univ. of Chicago Clinics 1954–57; specialist in internal medicine, Fall River, Mass. 1957–74; Chief of Staff, Dept of Medicine, Fall River Gen. Hosp. 1959–62; Medical Dir Earle E. Hussey Hosp., Fall River 1962–72; Chief of Staff, Dept of Medicine, Truesdale Clinic and Truesdale Hosp., Fall River 1971–74; Faculty mem. Tufts Univ. Coll. of Medicine, Boston, Mass. 1969–78; Faculty mem. Brown Univ. Program in Medicine 1973–75, Prof. of Community Health 1975–93, Prof. Emer. 1993–, Assoc. Dean 1974–81, Dean 1981–92, Dean Emer. 1992–; Acting Dir Generalist Physician Programs, AAMC 1993–94; Founder Dir Int. Physicians for Prevention of Nuclear War; Dir Stanley Street Treatment Center; mem. Bd of Trustees Bristol Community Coll., Univ. of Mass; mem. NAS Inst. of Medicine, Physicians and Lawyers for Nat. Drug Policy, Mass Medical Soc.; academic medical consultant 1993–; Cutting Foundation Medal for Service to Religion and Medicine 1976, Lifetime Achievement Award, Mass Medical Soc. 2007 and other awards. *Publications:* numerous articles on chronic disease, geriatrics, long-term care and health-care evaluation. *Leisure interest:* squash. *Address:* Public Health Program, Brown University, Box G-A, Providence, RI 02912, USA (office). *Telephone:* (401) 729-3100 (office). *E-mail:* David_Greer@ Brown.EDU (office).

GREER, Germaine, PhD; Australian feminist, author and broadcaster; b. 29 Jan. 1939, Melbourne, Vic.; d. of Eric Reginald Greer and Margaret May Greer (née Lafrank); ed Star of the Sea Convent, Vic., Melbourne, Sydney Univ., Univ. of Cambridge, UK; Sr Tutor in English, Sydney Univ. 1963–64; Asst Lecturer, then Lecturer in English, Univ. of Warwick, UK 1967–72, Prof. of English and Comparative Studies 1998–2003; lecturer throughout N America with American Program Bureau 1973–78, to raise funds for Tulsa Bursary and Fellowship Scheme 1980–83; Visiting Prof., Grad. Faculty of Modern Letters, Univ. of Tulsa 1979, Prof. of Modern Letters 1980–83, Founder-Dir of Tulsa Centre for the Study of Women's Literature, Founder-Ed. Tulsa Studies in Women's Literature 1981; Dir Stump Cross Books 1988–; Special Lecturer and Unofficial Fellow, Newnham Coll., Cambridge 1989–98; broadcaster/journalist/columnist/reviewer 1972–; Jr Govt Scholarship 1952, Diocesan Scholarship 1956, Sr Govt Scholarship 1956, Teacher's Coll. Studentship 1956, Commonwealth Scholarship 1964; numerous TV appearances and public talks including discussion with Norman Mailer in The Theatre of Ideas, New York; Dr hc (Univ. of Griffith, Australia) 1996, (Univ. of York, Toronto) 1999, (UMIST) 2000; hon. degrees (Melbourne) 2003, (Essex) 2003, (Anglia Polytechnic) 2003, (Sydney) 2005; Australian Living Treasure Nat. Trust Award Centenary Medal 2003. *Film appearance:* Rabbit Fever 2006. *Television:* The Late Review, Celebrity Big Brother. *Publications include:* The Female Eunuch 1969, The Obstacle Race: The Fortunes of Women Painters and Their Work 1979, Sex and Destiny: The Politics of Human Fertility 1984, Shakespeare (co-ed.) 1986, The Madwoman's Underclothes (selected journalism 1964–85) 1986, Kissing the Rod: An Anthology of 17th Century Women's Verse (co-ed.) 1988, Daddy, We Hardly Knew You (J. R. Ackerly Prize and Premio Internazionale Mondello) 1989, The Uncollected Verse of Aphra Behn (ed.) 1989, The Change: Women, Ageing and the Menopause 1991, The Collected Works of Katherine Philips, the Matchless Orinda, Vol. III: The Translations (co-ed.) 1993, Slip-Shod Sybils: Recognition, Rejection and The Woman Poet 1995, The Surviving Works of Anne Wharton (co-ed.) 1997, The Whole Woman 1999, John Wilmot, Earl of Rochester 1999, 101 Poems by 101 Women (ed.) 2001, The Boy 2003, Poems for Gardeners (ed.) 2003, Whitefella Jump Up The Shortest Way to Nationhood 2004, Shakespeare's Wife 2007, White Beech 2014; articles for Listener, Spectator, Esquire, Harper's Magazine, Playboy, Private Eye and other journals. *Leisure interest:* gardening. *Address:* c/o Aitken Alexander Associates Ltd, 18–21 Cavaye Place, London, SW10 9PT, England (office).

GREF, Herman Oskarovich; Russian politician, jurist and banker; *Chairman and CEO, Sberbank;* b. 8 Feb. 1964, Panfilovo, Pavlodar Region, Kazakh SSR, USSR; m. 1st Yelena; one s.; m. 2nd Yana 2004; one d.; ed Faculty of Law, Omsk State Univ., Faculty of Law, Leningrad State Univ.; Soviet Army service 1982–84; legal adviser, Cttee for Econ. Devt and Property, Petrodvoretz Dist Admin, Petrodvoretz, St Petersburg 1991–92; Chair. Property Cttee, concurrently Deputy Head, Petrodvoretz, St Petersburg Mayor's Office 1992–94; Deputy Chair., Dir Dept of Real Estate, First Deputy Chair. Cttee on Man. of Municipal Property, St Petersburg Admin 1994–97; Vice-Gov., Chair. Municipal Property Cttee, St Petersburg Admin 1997–98; mem. Exec. Bd Ministry of State Property, Russian

Fed. 1998, First Deputy Minister 1998–2000; Minister of Econ. Devt and Trade 2000–07; Chair. and CEO Sberbank (Savings Bank of Russian Fed.) 2007–; serves on bds and supervisory bds of several jt stock corpns and cos; Order for Distinguished Service (Grade IV), Officier, Légion d'honneur 2010; Citation from the Russian Pres. *Address:* Sberbank, 19 Vavilova Street, 117997 Moscow, Russia (office). *Telephone:* (495) 500-55-50 (office). *E-mail:* sbrf@sberbank.ru (office). *Website:* www.sberbank.ru (office).

GREGAN, George Musarurwa, BE; Australian rugby union player; b. 19 April 1973, Ndola, Zambia; m. Erica Gregan; three c.; ed St Edmund's Coll., Canberra, Univ. of Canberra; scrum half; plays for Randwick; has played for ACT Under-19s, ACT Under-21s, Australian Under-19s, Australian Under-21s, Australian Sevens, ACT Brumbies (120 state caps, 103 appearances in Super 12 competition) 1996–2007, RC Toulonnais 2007–08; 139 caps (world record) and 99 Test points for Australia (debut versus Italy in Brisbane) 1994–2007; won World Cup 1999 with Australia, Capt. nat. team 2002–07, took Australia to World Cup final 2003; sr tours to S Africa (for World Cup) 1995, Europe 1996, Argentina and UK 1996, France and England 1997, UK (for World Cup) 1999, UK and Europe 2001, 2002, 2003, 2004, 2005, 2006, 2007 (World Cup, France); f. George Gregan Foundation and launched epilepsy awareness campaign with slogan 'Get on the Team' 2004; Patron Brainwave Australia; Super 12 Player of the Tournament 1997, Int. Players' Asscn Player of the Year 2001, Australian Super 12 Player of the Year 2001, Wallaby Players' Player 2001, awarded the inaugural Rugby Medal for Excellence in 2001. *Leisure interests:* golf, skiing, good food and wine. *Address:* c/o Randwick District Rugby Union Football Club Inc., 102–104 Brook Street, Coogee, NSW 2034, Australia. *Telephone:* (2) 9665-7079. *Fax:* (2) 9664-5729. *E-mail:* office@georgegreganfoundation.com.au. *Website:* www.randwickrugby.com.au; www.georgegregan.com.

GREGER, Janet L., BS, MS, PhD; American academic and author; *Professor Emerita, University of Wisconsin;* b. 18 Feb. 1948, Illinois; d. of Harold Greger and Marjorie Greger; ed Univ. of Illinois, Urbana-Champaign and Cornell Univ.; Asst Prof., Purdue Univ. 1973–78; Asst Prof., then Assoc. Prof., Univ. of Wisconsin, Madison 1978–83, Prof. of Nutritional Sciences 1983–2003, Prof. Emer. 2003–, Assoc. Dean, Grad. School 1990–96, Assoc. Dean, Medical School 1996–98; Vice-Provost of Research and Grad. Educ. and Dean of Grad. School, Univ. of Connecticut 2002–05, Vice Provost for Strategic Planning 2005–07, also Prof., Dept of Nutritional Sciences; AAAS Congressional Sciences Eng Fellow 1984–85; mem. Bd of Man. COGR 1993–99; mem. Bd of Dirs AAALAC 1992–2003, NIH Panel on Regulatory Burden 1999–2002; mem. Council Soc. of Experimental Biology and Medicine 2002–05, NAS/NRC Cttees 1991–94, 1996–2000, 2003–07; AAAS Congressional Science and Eng Fellowship 1984–85; Excellence in Nutrition Educ. Award, American Soc. for Nutrition 2008, Public Safety Writers Award for unpublished novels 2013. *Publications:* Nutrition for Living 1985, 1988, 1991, 1994; more than 159 papers in scientific journals and books; author of medical thrillers and mysteries since 2007, including Coming Flu (novel) 2012, Murder: A New Way to Lose Weight (novel) 2013, Ignore the Pain (novel) 2013. *Leisure interests:* travel, reading, pet therapy. *Address:* 925 Desert Willow Court, Bernalillo, NM 87004, USA. *Telephone:* (505) 876-4832. *E-mail:* janet.greger@ comcast.net. *Website:* www.jlgreger.com.

GREGERSON, Peter K., BS, MD; American geneticist and academic; *Director, Robert S. Boas Center for Genomics and Human Genetics, Feinstein Institute for Medical Research;* ed Johns Hopkins Univ., Columbia Univ. Coll. of Physicians and Surgeons; originally trained as a rheumatologist; Prof. of Molecular Medicine, Hofstra North Shore-LIJ School of Medicine; Dir Robert S. Boas Center for Genomics and Human Genetics, The Feinstein Inst. for Medical Research; leads North American Rheumatology Consortium; mem. Asscn of American Physicians 2009; Pfizer Scholars Award for New Faculty 1988, Klemperer Medal, New York Academy of Medicine 2007, Distinguished Basic Investigator Award, American Coll. of Rheumatology 2007, Crafoord Prize, Royal Swedish Acad. of Sciences (co-recipient) 2013. *Publications:* numerous papers in professional journals. *Address:* The Feinstein Institute for Medical Research, 350 Community Drive, Manhasset, NY 11030, USA (office). *Telephone:* (516) 562-1542 (office); (516) 562-1134 (office). *E-mail:* peterg@nshs.edu (office). *Website:* www.feinsteininstitute.org/faculty/ peter-k-gregersen-md (office).

GREGG, Judd, AB, JD, LLM; American lawyer and politician; *Chairman, Public Advisory Board, New Hampshire Institute of Politics, Saint Anselm College;* b. 14 Feb. 1947, Nashua, NH; s. of the late Hugh Gregg and Catherine Warner Gregg; m. Kathleen MacLellan 1973; one s. two d.; ed Phillips Exeter Acad., Columbia and Boston Univs; admitted to NH Bar 1972; law practice, Nashua, NH; mem. NH Gov.'s Exec. Council 1978–80; mem. US House of Reps for 2nd NH Dist, Washington, DC 1981–89; Gov. of NH 1989–93; Senator from NH 1993–2011 (retd), Chair. Health, Educ., Labor and Pensions Cttee 2003–05, Budget Cttee 2005–07 (Ranking mem.); currently Chair. Public Advisory Bd New Hampshire Inst. of Politics, St Anselm Coll.; Republican. *Address:* Public Advisory Board, New Hampshire Institute of Politics, Saint Anselm College, 100 Saint Anselm Drive, Manchester, NH 03102, USA (office). *Telephone:* (603) 222-4100 (office). *Fax:* (603) 222-4112 (office). *E-mail:* nhiop@anselm.edu (office). *Website:* www.anselm.edu/ Institutes-Centers-and-the-Arts/NHIOP.htm (office).

GREGOIRE, Christine O'Grady, BA, JuD; American lawyer, politician and fmr state governor; b. 24 March 1947, Auburn, Wash.; m. Mike Gregoire; two d.; ed Univ. of Washington, Gonzaga Univ.; began career as law clerk in Spokane Office, Attorney Gen. for State of Washington 1976, became Asst Attorney Gen. working on child abuse and neglect cases 1977–81, Sr Asst Attorney Gen. and Man. Spokane Office 1981–82, Deputy Attorney Gen. (first woman) 1982–92, Attorney Gen. (first woman) 1992–2004; Gov. of Washington 2005–13; Dir Wash. Dept of Ecology 1988–92; Inaugural Chair. Bd of Dirs The Legacy Foundation 1999–2002; Pres. Nat. Asscn of Attorneys Gen. (NAAG) 1999–2000; Chair. Nat. Govs Asscn 2010–11; Democrat; Hon. DJur (Gonzaga Univ.) 1995; US Supreme Court Best Brief Award, Wash. ACORN Fair Lending Champion Award, Campaign for Tobacco-Free Kids Champion Award, Distinguished Alumna Award, Univ. of Wash. Coll. of Arts and Sciences, Friend of Children Award, Wash. State Parent-Teachers Asscn, Pathfinder Award, Tri-City Chamber of Commerce, Woman of Distinction Award, YWCA's 7th Annual Woman of Achievement Awards, Child Health Advocacy Award, American Acad. of Pediatrics, Distinguished Jurisprudence Award, Pacific Northwest Region of Anti-Defamation League, Excellence in Leadership Award, Nat. Leadership Conf. of Women Execs in State Govt, Woman in Govt Award, Good Housekeeping Magazine, Woman of the Year Award, American Legion Auxiliary, Award of Excellence, Wash. State Asscn of Local Public Health Officials, 2000 Special Recognition Award, Wash. State Nurses Asscn, selected by Working Mother Magazine as one of nation's 25 Most Influential Working Mothers, Myra Bradwell Award, Gonzaga Univ. School of Law, Wash. State Bar Asscn Bd of Govs' Award for Professionalism, NAAG Wyman Award, Gleitsman Award for Leadership in Public Health, Gov.'s Child Abuse Prevention Award. *Address:* c/o Office of the Governor, 416 Sid Snyder Avenue SW, Suite 200, PO Box 40002, Olympia, WA 98504-0002, USA.

GREGORIAN, Vartan, MA, PhD; American university administrator and professor of history; *President, Carnegie Corporation of New York;* b. 8 April 1934, Tabriz, Iran; s. of Samuel B. Gregorian and Shushanik G. Gregorian (née Mirzaian); m. Clare Russell 1960; three c.; ed Coll. Arménien, Stanford Univ.; Instructor, Asst Prof. and Assoc. Prof. of History, San Francisco State Coll. 1962–68; Assoc. Prof. of History, UCLA 1968, Univ. of Texas, Austin 1968–72 (Dir Special Programs 1970–72); Tarzian Prof. of Armenian and Caucasian History, Univ. of Pennsylvania 1972–80, Dean 1974–79, Provost 1978–80; Prof. of History and Near Eastern Studies, New York Univ. 1984–89; Prof., New School for Social Research, New York 1984–89; Pres. New York Public Library 1981–89; Pres. Brown Univ. 1989–97, mem. Nat. Humanities Faculty 1970–; Pres. Carnegie Corpn of New York 1997–; mem. Acad. of Arts and Letters 1989–, Historical Asscn, Asscn for Advancement of Slavic Studies, American Philosophical Soc.; John Simon Guggenheim Fellow 1971–72; Silver Cultural Medal Italian Ministry of Foreign Affairs 1977, Gold Medal of Honour City and Province of Vienna 1976, Ellis Island Medal of Honor 1986, American Acad. and Inst. of Arts and Letters Gold Medal for Service to the Arts 1989, Nat. Humanities Medal 1998, Eleanor Roosevelt Val-Kill Award 1999, Medal of Freedom 2004. *Publications:* The Emergence of Modern Afghanistan 1880–1946 1969; Islam: A Mosaic, Not a Monolith 2003, The Road to Home: My Life and Times 2003; numerous articles for professional journals. *Address:* Office of the President, Carnegie Corporation of New York, 437 Madison Avenue, New York, NY 10022, USA. *Telephone:* (212) 371-3200. *Fax:* (212) 223-8831 (office). *Website:* www.carnegie.org (office).

GREGORY, Joseph M., BA; American financial services industry executive; m. Niki Gregory; five c.; ed Hofstra Univ.; joined Lehman Brothers 1974, held various man. positions including in Fixed Income Div., Head, Mortgage Business 1980–91, Co-Head Fixed Income Div. 1991–96, Head Global Equities Div. 1996–2000, Chief Admin. Officer 2000–02, Co-COO 2002–04, Pres. and COO 2004–08, mem. Exec. Cttee 2004–, Chair. Lehman Brothers Foundation; mem. Nat. Advisory Bd The Posse Foundation Inc.; mem. Bd of Trustees Harlem Children's Zone; Trustee and mem. Finance, Endowment and Investment Cttees, Hofstra Univ. *Address:* Lehman Brothers Holdings Inc., 745 7th Avenue, New York, NY 10019, USA (office). *Telephone:* (212) 526-7000 (office). *Fax:* (212) 526-8766 (office). *Website:* www.lehman.com (office).

GREGSON, Sir Peter Lewis, Kt, GCB, MA, FRSA; British civil servant; b. 28 June 1936, Yorks., England; s. of Walter Henry Gregson and Lillian Margaret Gregson; ed Nottingham High School, Balliol Coll., Oxford and London Business School; Nat. Service 1959–61; official Bd of Trade 1961–68; Pvt. Sec. to the Prime Minister 1968–72; Asst Sec., Dept of Trade and Industry, also Sec. Industry, Industrial Devt Bd 1972–74; Under-Sec., Dept of Industry, also Sec., Nat. Enterprise Bd 1975–77; Under-Sec., Dept of Trade 1977–80, Deputy Sec. 1980–81; Deputy Sec., Cabinet Office 1981–85; Perm. Under-Sec. of State, Dept of Energy 1985–89; Perm. Sec., Dept of Trade and Industry 1989–96; Dir Scottish Power PLC 1996–2004, Woolwich PLC 1998–2000 (Chair. Woolwich Pension Fund Trust Co. Ltd 1999–2000). *Leisure interests:* gardening, listening to music. *Address:* 9 Lavender Court, 10 Greenways, Beckenham, Kent, BR3 3NG, England. *Telephone:* (20) 8650-5925.

GREGURIĆ, Franjo, DSc; Croatian politician; b. 12 Oct. 1939, Lobor, Zlata Bistrica; m. Jozefina Gregurić (née Abramović); one s. one d.; ed Univ. of Zagreb; early jobs working in chemical factories; Tech. Dir Radonia at Sisak; Dir-Gen. Chromos factory, Zagreb; rep. of Foreign Trade Co. Astra in Moscow, Gen. Dir Astra-Int. Trade, Zagreb –1990; Vice-Dir, then Dir Chamber of Econs, Zagreb; mem. Christian Democratic Union (CDU); Deputy Premier of Croatia 1990; Prime Minister 1991–92; mem. Sabor (Croatian Parl.) 1990–; Adviser to Pres. of Croatia 1992–, apptd Special Del. (with rank of Amb.) to Croat-Bosnian Fed. and Bosnia and Herzegovina 1997; Pres. Supervisory Bd ELKA kabeli d.o.o. 2004–; fmr Dir INA Co., Zagreb; Pres. Croatian Firefighting Asscn 1993–2000; numerous nat. and int. awards for econs. *Leisure interests:* oenology, pomology. *Address:* ELKA kabeli d.o.o., 10000 Zagreb, Koledovčina 1 (office); 41000 Zagreb, Ilica 49, Croatia. *Telephone:* (1) 2482600 (office). *Fax:* (1) 2404898 (office). *E-mail:* elka-marketing@ elka.hr (office). *Website:* www.elka.hr (office).

GREIČIUS, Vytautas, LLM; Lithuanian judge; *Judge, Division of Criminal Cases, Supreme Court;* b. 9 May 1949, Tauragè; m. Teresè Greičiuvienè; one d. two s.; ed Faculty of Law, Vilnius Univ.; judge, Ukmergè Dist People's Court 1976–90; Judge, Supreme Court of Lithuania 1990–94, Chair. Div. of Criminal Cases 1995–99, Pres. of Supreme Court 1999–2009, Judge, Div. of Criminal Cases 2009–. *Address:* Supreme Court, Gynejų 6, 01109 Vilnius, Lithuania (office). *Telephone:* (5) 2616594 (office). *Fax:* (5) 2627950 (office). *E-mail:* lat@lat.lt (office). *Website:* www.lat.lt (office).

GREIDER, Carolyn (Carol) Widney, BA, PhD; American molecular biologist and academic; *Daniel Nathans Professor and Director, Molecular Biology and Genetics, School of Medicine, Johns Hopkins University;* b. 15 April 1961, San Diego, Calif.; ed Univ. of California, Santa Barbara, Univ. of California, Berkeley; Fellow, Cold Spring Harbor Lab. 1988–90, Asst Investigator 1990–92, Assoc. Investigator 1992–94, Investigator 1994–97; Assoc. Prof. of Molecular Biology and Genetics, Johns Hopkins Univ. School of Medicine 1997–99, Prof. of Molecular Biology and Genetics 1999–2003, Prof. of Oncology 2001–, Acting Dir Dept of Molecular Biology and Genetics 2002–03, Daniel Nathans Prof. and Dir Dept of Molecular Biology and Genetics 2003–; mem. Editorial Bd Cancer Cell 2001–, Molecular Cancer Research 2003–; mem. NAS 2003, Inst. of Medicine 2010; Fellow, American Acad. of Arts and Sciences 2003, AAAS 2003, American Acad. of

Microbiology 2004; Regents Scholarship, Univ. of California 1981, Pew Scholar in the Biomedical Sciences 1990–94, Allied Signal Outstanding Project Award 1992, Gertrude Elion Cancer Research Award, American Asscn for Cancer Research 1994, Glenn Foundation Award, American Soc. for Cell Biology 1995, Cornelius Rhoads Award, American Asscn for Cancer Research 1996, Schering-Plough Scientific Achievement Award, American Soc. for Biochemistry and Molecular Biology 1997, Ellison Medical Foundation Sr Scholar 1998, Gairdner Foundation Award 1998, Passano Foundation Award 1999, Rosenstiel Award in Basic Medical Research 1999, Harvey Soc. Lecturer 2000, NAS Richard Lounsbery Award 2003, Lila Gruber Cancer Research Award 2006, The Wiley Prize in Biomedical Sciences 2006, Albert Lasker Award for Basic Medical Research (with Elizabeth Blackburn and Jack Szostak) 2006, Louisa Gross Horwitz Prize, Columbia Univ. 2007, Nobel Prize in Physiology or Medicine (with Elizabeth Blackburn and Jack Szostak) 2009, Paul Ehrlich and Ludwig Darmstaedter Prize (jtly) 2009. *Publications:* more than 90 scientific publs. *Address:* Department of Molecular Biology and Genetics, Johns Hopkins University School of Medicine, 617 Hunterian, 725 North Wolfe Street, Baltimore, MD 21205, USA (office). *Telephone:* (410) 614-6506 (office). *Fax:* (410) 955-0831 (office). *E-mail:* cgreider@jhmi.edu (office). *Website:* www.mbg.jhmi .edu (office); www.greiderlab.org (office).

GREIFELD, Robert, BA, MBA; American business executive and stock exchange official; *President and CEO, Nasdaq Stock Market Inc.;* b. 18 July 1957, Queens, New York; m. Julia Greifeld; two s. one d.; ed Iona Coll., Stern School of Business, NY Univ.; Pres. and COO, Automated Securities Clearance Inc. (ASC) 1991–99; created BRUT, trading consortium; Exec. Vice-Pres. SunGard Data Systems Inc. 1999, then Corp. Vice-Pres. and Group CEO; Pres. and CEO NASDAQ Stock Market Inc. 2003–; Chair. USA Track and Field Foundation 2004–; Vice Chair. Kennedy Center Corp. Fund Bd; mem. Bd of Dirs Partnership for New York City; Brother Arthur A. Loftus Award for Outstanding Achievement, Iona Coll. 2004. *Leisure interest:* running. *Address:* Nasdaq Stock Market Inc., 1 Liberty Plaza, New York, NY 10006, USA (office). *Telephone:* (212) 401-8700 (office). *Fax:* (212) 401-1024 (office). *Website:* www.nasdaq.com (office).

GREIG, Geordie Carron, MA, FRSA; British journalist; *Editor, Mail on Sunday;* b. 16 Dec. 1960, London, England; s. of Sir Carron Greig and Monica Greig (née Stourton); m. Kathryn Elizabeth Terry 1995; one s. two d.; ed Eton Coll. and St Peter's Coll., Oxford; reporter, South East London and Kentish Mercury 1981–83, Daily Mail 1984–85, Today 1985–87; reporter, The Sunday Times 1987–89, Arts Corresp. 1989–91, New York Corresp. 1991–95, Literary Ed. 1995–99; Ed. of Tatler 1999–2009; Ed., London Evening Standard 2009–12, Editorial Dir 2010–12, Dir 2012–; Editorial Dir, The Independent 2010–12, Dir 2012–; Ed. Mail on Sunday 2012–, Dir, Mail Newspapers 2012–. *Publications:* Louis and the Prince 1999, Breakfast with Lucian 2013. *Address:* Mail on Sunday, Northcliffe House, 2 Derry Street, London, W8 5TT, England (office). *Telephone:* (20) 3361-3001 (office). *Fax:* (20) 7937-6721 (office). *E-mail:* geordie.greig@mailonsunday.co.uk (office). *Website:* www.mailonsunday.co.uk (office).

GREINER, Walter Albin Erhard, PhD, FInstP, FRSA; German physicist; *Professor Emeritus of Physics, Institute for Theoretical Physics, Johann Wolfgang Goethe-Universität;* b. 29 Oct. 1935, Neuenbau/Thür; s. of Albin Greiner and Elsa Greiner (née Fischer); m. Bärbel Chun 1960; two s.; ed Univs of Frankfurt, Darmstadt and Freiburg; Research Asst, Univ. of Freiburg 1961–62; Asst Prof., Univ. of Md, USA 1962–64; Prof., Inst. of Theoretical Physics, Johann Wolfgang Goethe-Universität, Frankfurt 1965–, now Prof. Emer., Founding Director, Frankfurt Institute for Advanced Studies; Adjunct Prof., Vanderbilt Univ., Nashville, Tenn., USA and Oak Ridge Nat. Lab. Tenn. 1975–; Consultant, Gesellschaft für Schwerionenforschung, Darmstadt 1976–97; Chair. Program Advisory Bd Flerov Lab., Dubna; Ed. Int. Journal of Modern Physics 1975–89, European Ed. 1991–; Ed. Foundations of Physics, Heavy Ion Physics, Reports on Progress of Physics; Hon. Ed. Journal of Physics G 1985–90, Hon. Prof., Beijing Univ. 1988, Jilin Univ., People's Repub. of China 2001, Hon. mem. Lorand Eötvös Soc. (Budapest) 1989, Romanian Acad. of Science 1992; Officier, Palmes académiques 1998; Hon. DSc (Witwatersrand) 1982, Dr hc (Tel-Aviv) 1991, (Louis Pasteur Univ., Strasbourg) 1991, (Bucharest) 1992, (Lajos Kossuth Univ., Hungary) 1997, (Nantes) 2001, (Universidata Autonoma de México) 2001, (St Petersburg) 2001, (Jt Inst. of Nuclear Research, Dubna) 2002, (Bogoliubov Inst. of Theoretical Physics, Kiev) 2003; Max Born Prize, Inst. of Physics (UK) 1974, Otto Hahn Prize, Frankfurt 1982, Alex von Humboldt Medal 1998. *Publications:* Nuclear Theory (with Eisenberg) (in English and Russian, three vols) 1972, Lectures on Theoretical Physics (in five languages, 12 vols), Dynamics of Heavy-Ion Collisions (with Cindro and Ricci), Quantum Electrodynamics of Strong Fields (with B. Müller and J. Rafelski) 1985; Experimental Techniques in Nuclear Physics (with D.N. Poenarū), Handbook of Nuclear Properties (with D.N. Poenarū), Heavy Elements and Related Phenomena (with R.K. Gupta), Fundamental Issues in Elementary Matter 2000; more than 700 papers in nat. and int. journals. *Leisure interests:* music, mycology, fishing, walking, swimming. *Address:* Institut für Theoretische Physik and Frankfurt Institute for Advanced Studies, Johann Wolfgang Goethe Universität, Max van Laue Strasse 1, 600438 Frankfurt am Main, Germany (office). *Telephone:* (69) 79847525 (office). *Fax:* (69) 79847527 (office). *E-mail:* greiner@fias.uni-frankfurt.de (office).

GRENFELL, Baron, (Life Peer), cr. 2000, of Kilvey in the County of Swansea; **Julian Pascoe Francis St Leger Grenfell,** BA (Hons) Law; British politician; b. 23 May 1935, London; s. of the late 2nd Baron Grenfell of Kilvey; m. 1st Loretta Reali 1961 (divorced 1970); one d.; m. 2nd Gabrielle Raab 1970 (divorced 1987); two d.; m. 3rd Elizabeth Porter Scott 1987 (divorced 1992); m. 4th Dagmar Langbehn Debreil 1993; ed Eton Coll., King's Coll., Cambridge; Second Lt, King's Royal Rifle Corps 1954–56; Pres. Cambridge Union 1959; Capt. Queen's Royal Rifles (Territorial Army) 1963; TV journalist 1960–64; with World Bank 1965–95, Chief of Information and Public Affairs in Europe 1969–72, Deputy Dir European Office 1973–74, Special Rep. to the UN Orgs 1974–81, Adviser, HQ 1983–90, Head of External Affairs, European Office 1990–95; mem. UK del. to Council of Europe 1997–99; sat in House of Lords as Lord Grenfell of Kilvey 1976–99, cr. Life Peer 2000; Chair. House of Lords Sub-cttee on Econ. and Financial Affairs 1998, mem. Select Cttee on EU 1999, 2000–08, Chair. 2002–08; Prin. Deputy Chair. of Cttees 2002–08; Deputy Speaker; Labour 2002–10; Chevalier, Légion d'honneur 2005, Commdr, Order of Merit, Germany 2008, Commdr, Order of Crown of Belgium

2009, High Order of Merit, Croatia 2010. *Publications:* novels: Margot 1984, The Gazelle 2004. *Leisure interests:* 20th century European history, writing fiction. *Address:* House of Lords, Westminster, London, SW1A 0PW, England (office); 24 rue Chaptal, 75009 Paris, France (home). *Telephone:* (20) 7219-3601 (office); (1) 48-74-08-55 (home). *Fax:* (20) 7219-6715 (office); (1) 45-26-30-21 (home). *E-mail:* grenfellj@parliament.uk (office); juliang@noos.fr (home).

GRENIER, Jean-Marie René; French business executive; b. 27 June 1926, Paris; s. of Henri Grenier and Germaine Pissavy; m. Marie-Alix Bonnet de Paillerets 1958; three s. one d.; ed Lycée Fustel-de-Coulanges, Strasbourg, École Bossuet, Lycée Louis-le-Grand, Faculté de Droit, Paris and École des Hautes Études Commerciales, Paris; Deputy Dir Soc. des Usines Chimiques Rhône-Poulenc 1962, Dir 1970, Commercial Dir 1971; Dir Rhône-Poulenc SA 1977–82; Pres. Syndicat de l'industrie chimique organique de synthèse et biochimie 1975–84, Hon. Pres. 1984–; Chevalier, Ordre nat. du Mérite, Croix de la valeur militaire, Chevalier, Légion d'honneur. *Leisure interest:* tennis. *Address:* 39 rue de la Glacière, 75013 Paris (home); Le Moulin Pocancy (Marne), 51130 Pocancy, France (home). *Telephone:* 1-47-07-79-82 (home); (3) 26-70-93-15 (home). *E-mail:* jmrgrenier@wanadoo.fr (home).

GRENON, Thomas; French mining engineer, civil servant and museum director; *Director General, Muséum national d'Histoire naturelle;* began career in public service in Dept of Nuclear Energy and Raw Materials, Ministry of Industry 1989–91; with Foreign Econ. Relations Dept, Ministry of Finance 1991–93, responsible for relations with all countries arising from the break up of the Soviet Union, Head of Corp. Finance supervising financial institutions specializing in business financing: Nat. Credit CEPME (Credit Facilities for Small and Medium Enterprises) Sofaris French Soc. Guarantee financing SMEs), Regional Devt Cos) 1993–95; tech. adviser, Ministry of Culture and Communication, in charge of budget, social relations, large-scale works and new technologies 1995–97, projects completed include Nat. Library of France, the Grand Louvre and renovation of the Centre Pompidou; worked in private sector 1997–2002, successively Deputy CEO Financière Agache, Sec. Gen. AXA France, Investment Dir, Royal Bank of Scotland; CEO Museum of Science and Industry 2003–05; Gen. Man. Réunion des Musées Nationaux 2005–10; Dir Gen. Muséum nat. d'Histoire naturelle (Nat. Museum of Natural History) 2010–. *Address:* Muséum national d'Histoire naturelle, 57 rue Cuvier, 75005 Paris, France (office). *Telephone:* 1-40-79-30-00 (office). *E-mail:* info@mnhn.fr (office). *Website:* www.mnhn.fr (office).

GRENS, Elmars; Latvian molecular biologist and academic; *Scientific Director, Biomedical Research and Study Centre;* b. 9 Oct. 1935, Rīga; s. of Janis Grens and Melita Grene; m. Eva Stankevich 1957; one s. one d.; ed Latvian State Univ., researcher, Head of Lab., Research Dir, Inst. of Organic Synthesis, Latvian Acad. of Sciences 1958–90, Dir Inst. of Molecular Biology 1991–93; Scientific Dir Biomedical Research and Study Centre 1993–; mem. Latvian Acad. of Sciences, Academia Europaea. *Publications include:* more than 180 scientific articles on molecular biology of viruses, fine biotechnology and genetic eng. *Leisure interest:* downhill skiing. *Address:* Biomedical Research and Study Centre, Ratsupites 1, Rīga 1067, Latvia (office). *Telephone:* 6780-8003 (office). *Fax:* 6744-2407 (office). *E-mail:* grens@biomed.lu.lv (office).

GRETZKY, Wayne; Canadian fmr professional ice hockey player, sports industry executive and ice hockey coach; b. 26 Jan. 1961, Brantford, Ont.; s. of Walter Gretzky and Phyllis Gretzky; m. Janet Jones 1988; three s. two d.; joined Indianapolis Racers of World Hockey Assen (WHA) 1978 at age 17, immediately traded to Edmonton Oilers (WHA then merged with Nat. Hockey League—NHL), played 1979–88, traded to Los Angeles Kings, played 1988–96, traded to St Louis Blues 1996, signed as free agent NY Rangers, played 1996–99 (retd); NHL scoring records include 2,857 points, 894 goals, 1,963 assists; NHL Most Valuable Player (Hart Memorial Trophy) nine times 1980–88; NHL scoring champion (Art Ross Trophy) ten times 1981–87, 1990–91, 1994; Most Valuable Player Stanley Cup playoffs (Conn Smythe Trophy) 1985, 1988; Most Gentlemanly Player (Lady Byng Memorial Trophy) 1980, 1991, 1992, 1994, 1999; winner Stanley Cup with Edmonton (four times); winner Canada Cup 1984, 1987, 1991; mem. Canadian Olympic team 1998; Exec. Dir Team Canada Hockey Team 2002 (Olympics), 2004 (World Cup of Hockey); investor Los Acros Sports LLC, Man. Pnr Phoenix Coyotes, 1999–2009, Coach 2005–09; f. Wayne Gretzky Foundation 2002; Special Advisor Men's Nat. Hockey Team, Vancouver Winter Olympics 2010; Hon. LLD (Univ. of Alberta) 2000; Lester Patrick Trophy for Outstanding Service to Hockey in US 1994, voted Greatest Player in NHL History 1997, elected Hockey Hall of Fame 1999, Olympic Order from Int. Olympic Cttee 2002. *Films include:* The Flamingo Kid 1984, A Chorus Line 1985. *Publication:* Gretzky: An Autobiography (with Rick Reilly). *Address:* c/o Coyotes Hockey LLC, 9375 East Bell Road, Scottsdale, AZ 85260, USA.

GREY, Dame Beryl Elizabeth, DBE, CBE; British prima ballerina; *Patron, Royal Ballet Benevolent Fund;* b. (Beryl Elizabeth Groom), 11 June 1927, London, England; d. of Arthur Ernest Groom and Annie Elizabeth Groom; m. Sven Gustav Svenson 1950; one s.; ed Dame Alice Owens School, London, Madeline Sharp School, Royal Ballet School and de Vos School of Dance; debut at Sadler's Wells Co. 1941; Prima Ballerina with Royal Ballet until 1957; freelance int. prima ballerina from 1957; first full-length ballet Swan Lake on 15th birthday; appeared in leading roles of classical and numerous modern ballets including Giselle, Sleeping Beauty, Sylvia, Casse Noisette, Les Sylphides, Checkmate, Donald of the Burthens, Dante Sonata, Three Cornered Hat, Ballet Imperial, Lady and the Fool, Les Rendezvous; American, Continental, African, Far Eastern tours with Royal Ballet from 1945; guest artist European Opera Houses in Norway, Finland, Sweden, Denmark, Belgium, Romania, Germany, Italy, etc.; guest artist, South and Central America, Middle East, Union of South Africa, Rhodesia, Australasia; first foreign guest artist ever to dance with the Bolshoi Ballet in Russia 1957–58 (Moscow, Leningrad, Kiev, Tbilisi) and first to dance with Peking Ballet and Shanghai Ballet 1964; Dir-Gen. of Arts Educational Trust, London 1966–68; Artistic Dir London Festival Ballet 1968–79; produced and staged Giselle, Perth, Australia 1984, 1986, Sleeping Beauty, Royal Swedish Ballet, Stockholm 1985, 2002; Pres. Dance Council for Wales 1981–2004, East Grinstead Operatic Soc. 1986–, Keep-fit Soc. 1992–93; Vice-Pres. Fed. of Music Festivals 1985–, The Music Therapy Charity 1980–, Royal Acad. of Dancing 1981–; East Grinstead Music Arts Festival 1991–; Chair. Imperial Soc. Teachers of Dancing 1962–91, Pres. 1991–2001, Life Pres.

2002–, Fellow; Gov. Royal Ballet 1993, Vice-Chair. 1995–2002; Pres. All England Dance Competitions 2005–, British Ballet Org. 2010–; a Dir Birmingham Royal Ballet 1995–99, Royal Opera House, Covent Garden 1999–2003; Trustee, Royal Ballet Benevolent Fund 1983–2011 (Chair. 1992–2011, Patron 2011–), Dance Teachers' Benevolent Fund (Vice-Chair. 1987–2004), Discs 1994–2009; Vice-Patron British School of Osteopathy 1992–; Patron and Trustee, Dancers Resettlement Trust; Patron Benesh Inst., Language of Dance Centre, Lisa Ullman Travelling Scholarship Fund 1986–, Friends of Sadler's Wells 1991–, Furlong Hip Replacement (renamed Furlong Research Charitable Foundation) 1993– (Trustee 2005–09), Osteopathic Centre for Children 1992–, Sussex Opera and Ballet Soc. 2001–, Theatre Design Trust for Dance 1995–, Critics' Circle Dance Awards 2005–10, German Shepherd Dog Rescue 2010, Council for Dance Educ. and Training 2011–; Hon. DMus (Leicester) 1970, (Univ. of London) 1996; Hon. DLit (City of London Univ.) 1974, (Buckingham) 1993; Hon. DEd (CNAA) 1989; Hon. DArt (Bedford) 2010; Queen Elizabeth II Coronation Award, Royal Acad. of Dancing 1996, Critics Circle Service to Dance Award 2002, Lifetime Achievement Award Imperial Soc. of Teachers of Dancing 2004, Carl Alan Lifetime Achievement Award 2010. *Film:* Black Swan (stereoscopic) 1952. *Radio:* Desert Island Discs (three times); numerous programmes and interviews since 1950. *Television:* numerous appearances and interviews since early 1950s. *Publications:* Red Curtain Up 1958, Through the Bamboo Curtain 1965, My Favourite Ballet Stories (ed.) 1981. *Leisure interests:* piano playing, painting, swimming, opera.

GREY-JOHNSON, Crispin, BA, MA, PGCE; Gambian diplomatist, government official, development consultant and business consultant; *Chairman and CEO, St Mary's Holding Company (Gambia) Ltd;* b. 7 Dec. 1946, Banjul; m.; several c.; ed Methodist Girls High School, Methodist Boys High School, Gambia High School, McGill Univ., Montreal, Canada, Univ. of Oxford, UK, George Washington Univ., USA; Master, Sr Master, Head of Dept, Gambia High School, Banjul 1968–77; Assoc. Econ. Affairs Officer, UN Econ. Comm. for Africa (ECA) 1977–81, Econ. Affairs Officer 1981–90, Sr Regional Adviser 1990–94, Coordinator, Multi-disciplinary Regional Advisory Group, Addis Ababa, Ethiopia 1994–96; Man. Dir Galloryaa Farms Ltd, The Gambia 1996–97; High Commr to Canada and Amb. to USA, Brazil and Venezuela 1997–99; High Commr to Sierra Leone and Amb. to Côte d'Ivoire and Liberia 1999–2002; Perm. Rep. to UN, New York 2002–07; Sec. of State for Higher Educ., Research, Science and Tech. Feb.–Sept. 2007, 2008–11, for Foreign Affairs 2007–08; Chair. and CEO St Mary's Holding Co. (Gambia) Ltd 2011–, MCM Holding Co. (Sierra Leone) Ltd 2011–; involved in setting up African Inst. for Higher Tech. Training and Research, Kenya, Return of Skills Programme for Africa 1982–92; served as Vice-Pres. UN Gen. Ass. UN Exec. Bd on Comm. on Population and Devt; Chair Group of Friends of Guinea-Bissau, Group of Friends of Taiwan; served as Gen. Ass. Facilitator in negotiations on the resolution on the Prevention of Armed Conflict; served also on many UN Task Forces; mem. African Assen for Public Admin and Man., African Adult Educ. Assen, African Assen for Training and Devt; Millennium Medal in recognition of Services for Peace and Security (Repub. of The Gambia) 2001, Hon. Diploma (Guinea Bissau) 2004; Govt of Canada Special Commonwealth African Aid Programme Scholarship 1965–58, Govt of UK Overseas Devt Agency Scholarship 1970–71, UN Fellowship for Research at African Inst. for Econ. Devt and Planning, Dakar, Senegal 1973, USAID Agency for Int. Devt Fellowship 1980. *Publications:* The Employment Crisis in Africa: Issues in Human Resources Development Policy 1990; book chapters and articles on human resources devt. *Address:* St Mary's Holding Co. (Gambia) Ltd, PO Box 26, Banjul (office); 30 2nd Street East, Fajara, Banjul, The Gambia. *Telephone:* 449-6090 (home). *E-mail:* cgreyjohnson@hotmail.com (home).

GREY-THOMPSON, Baroness (Life Peer), cr. 2010, of Eaglescliffe in the County of Durham; **Tanni Carys Davina Grey-Thompson,** DBE, BA; British athlete; b. 26 July 1969, Cardiff, Wales; d. of Peter Alexander Harvey Grey and Sulwen Davina Grey (née Jones); m. Dr Ian Thompson 1999; one d.; ed St Cyres Comprehensive School, Penarth, Loughborough Univ. of Tech.; bronze medal for 400m wheelchair races, Seoul Paralympics 1988; gold medals for 100m, 200m, 400m and 800m wheelchair races, Barcelona Paralympics 1988; gold medal for 800m and silver medals for 100m, 200m, 400m wheelchair races, Atlanta Paralympics 1996; gold medals for 100m, 200m, 400m and 800m wheelchair races, Sydney Paralympics 2000, 100m and 400m wheelchair races, Athens Paralympics 2004; gold medals, women's wheelchair race, London Marathon 1992, 1994, 1996, 1998, 2001, 2002, bronze medal 1993, silver medals 1997, 1999, 2000, 2003; three gold medals and one silver medal at European Championships 2003; broke over 20 world records; Devt Officer, UK Athletics 1996–2001; apptd Cross Bench Peer, House of Lords 2010–; TV and radio presenter, conf. and motivational speaker, also numerous guest appearances; Pres. Welsh Assen of Cricketers with a Disability; Vice-Pres. Women's Sports Foundation, South Wales Region of Riding for the Disabled, Get Kids Going; Deputy Chair. UK Lottery Awards Panel (Sport); mem. The Sports Council for Wales's Nat. Excellence Panel, Sports Council for Wales Sportlot Panel, Minister of Sport Implementation Group for the Devt of Sport, Welsh Hall of Fame Roll of Honour 1992–; English Sports Council Lottery Awards Panel 1995–99, Sports Council for Wales 1996–2002, for UK Sport 1998–2003, Nat. Disability Council 1997–2000, Manchester Commonwealth Games Organising Council Assen 2002; mem. Elect Laureus World Sports Acad. 2001, mem. 2002–; Patron British Sports Leaders, British Sport Trust, Durham Sport Millennium Youth Games, Regain, Youth Sport Trust, Nat. Sports Medicine Inst. of UK, Shelter Cymru 2003 London Marathon, Lady Taverners, Nat. Blood Service; Vice-Patron Helen Rollason Cancer Care Appeal, Jubilee Sailing Trust 2002–; Hon. Fellow, Univ. of Wales Coll., Cardiff 1997, Univ. of Wales Inst., Cardiff 2001, Univ. of Swansea 2001, Coll. of Ripon and York St John 2001, Inst. of Leisure and Amenity Man. 2001, Univ. of Wales Coll., Newport 2003; Freeman, City of Cardiff 2003; Hon. DUniv (Staffordshire) 1998, (Southampton) 1998; Hon. LLD (Exeter) 2003; Dr hc (Surrey) 2000, (Leeds Metropolitan) 2001, (Wales) 2002, (Loughborough) 2002, (Heriot-Watt) 2004; Hon. Masters degree (Loughborough) 1994, (Teesside) 2001; Hon. MSc (Manchester Metropolitan) 1998; BBC Wales Sports Personality of the Year (three times), Sunday Times Sportswoman of the Year 1992, 2000, (Third Place) 2004, Royal Mail Best Female Performance of the Paralympic Games 1992, Panasonic Special Award 1992, Variety Club Disabled Sportswoman of the Year 1992, Welsh Sports Hall of Fame 1993, Sports Writers' Assen Female Disabled Athlete of the Year 1994, Sporting Ambassador 1998,

Sportswriters Award 2000, Third Place, BBC Sports Personality of the Year 2000, Helen Rollason Award for Inspiration, BBC Sports Personality of the Year 2000, Helen Rollason Award, Sunday Times Sports Woman of the Year 2000, Welsh Woman of the Year 2001, Welsh Sportswoman of the Year 2001, Pride of Britain Special Award 2001, awarded title of UK Sporting Hero by Sport UK 2001, Chancellor's Medal, Univ. of Glamorgan 2001, one of only four British sportswomen to appear in book, 50 British Sporting Greats 2002, Walpole Best British Sporting Achievement Award 2002, Commonwealth Games Sports Award for Best Female Disabled Athlete 2002, voted Third Greatest Briton of all time, 47th Placing in 100 Greatest Sporting Moments 2002, BBC Ouch disability website 2003, UK Sport Fair Play Award 2004, Sports Journalist UK Sport Award 2004. *Radio:* numerous appearances including as presenter The Rush Hour, BBC Radio Wales 1995–96, Sportfirst, BBC Radio 4, BBC Radio 5 Live 1995–96. *Television:* Presenter, From the Edge (BBC 2) 1998–2000, X-Ray (BBC Wales) 2002, BBC Manchester; guest appearances on BBC Question Time, Breakfast with Frost, The Weakest Link, Grandstand, A Question of Sport, Countryside; It's My Funeral, My Favourite Hymns, CBBC's Blue Peter, They Think It's All Over, and various lifestyle programmes such as Gloria Hunniford and GMTV. *Publication:* Seize the Day: My Autobiography 2001; contrib. to leading newspapers including Daily Mail and the Guardian and various magazines including Disability Now, Now Magazine, Woman's Realm, Hello, Best, Good Housekeeping, Ability Needs. *Leisure interests:* reading, IT. *Address:* House of Lords, London, SW1A 0PW (office); c/o Helen Williams, Creating Excellence, Equity House, 1st Floor, Knight Street, South Woodham Ferrers, Chelmsford, Essex, CM3 5ZL, England (office). *Telephone:* (1245) 328303 (office). *Fax:* (1245) 323512 (office). *E-mail:* helen@ creatingexcellence.co.uk (office). *Website:* www.creatingexcellence.co.uk (office).

GRI, Françoise; French business executive; *President and CEO, Manpower France;* b. 21 Dec. 1957, Agen (Lot-et-Garonne); ed École nationale supérieure d'informatique et de mathématiques appliquées de Grenoble (ENSIMAG); joined IBM as engineer in 1981, various man. positions both in France and abroad, Dir Sales and Marketing, E-Business Solutions, IBM Middle East and Africa 1996–2000, Dir Logistics Devt 2000–01, Dir Commercial Operations Jan.–Aug. 2001, Pres. and Dir-Gen. IBM France 2001–07; Pres. and CEO Manpower France, Paris 2007–; mem. Supervisory Bd Rexel 2010–; mem. Bd Edenred (fmrly Accor Services) 2010–; mem. Policy Bd Institut de l'Entreprise, Bd SFIB (French asscn of IT cos, now part of Alliance TICS), Ethics Cttee Mouvement des entreprises de France, Bd of Dirs École Centrale, Paris; Chevalier, Ordre nat. du Mérite 2004, Légion d'honneur 2009; ranked by Fortune magazine amongst the 50 Most Powerful Women in Business outside the US (24th) 2003, (33rd) 2004, (36th) 2005, (44th) 2006, (37th) 2007, (43rd) 2008, (42nd) 2009, (39th) 2010, (31st) 2011–12, one of Women in Business: Europe's Top 25 2004. *Publication:* Plaidoyer pour un Emploi Responsable (Plea for Responsible Employment) 2009. *Leisure interests:* travelling, cooking, gardening. *Address:* Manpower France – Immeuble Eureka, 13 rue Ernest Renan, 92729 Nanterre Cedex, France (office). *Telephone:* 1-57-66-11-64 (office). *Fax:* 1-57-66-19-35 (office). *E-mail:* catherine.morin@manpower.fr (office). *Website:* www.manpower.fr/emplois (office); www.francoisegri.com (office).

GRIER, Pam; American actress and writer; b. 26 May 1949, Winston-Salem, NC; d. of Clarence Ransom Grier and Gwendolyn (Sylvia) Samuels; mem. Acad. of Motion Picture Arts and Sciences. *Films:* The Big Doll House 1971, Women in Cages 1971, Big Bird Cage 1972, Black Mama, White Mama 1972, Cool Breeze 1972, Hit Man 1972, Twilight People 1972, Coffy 1973, Scream, Blacula, Scream! 1973, The Arena 1973, Foxy Brown 1974, Bucktown 1975, Friday Foster 1975, Sheba Baby 1975, Drum 1976, Greased Lightning 1977, Fort Apache: The Bronx 1981, Something Wicked This Way Comes 1983, Stand Alone 1985, The Vindicator 1986, On the Edge 1986, The Allnighter 1987, Above The Law 1988, The Package 1989, Class of 1999 1991, Bill and Ted's Bogus Journey 1991, Tough Enough, Posse 1993, Serial Killer 1995, Original Gangstas 1996, Escape from LA 1996, Mars Attacks! 1996, Strip Search 1997, Fakin' Da Funk 1997, Jackie Brown 1997, No Tomorrow 1998, Jawbreaker 1999, Holy Smoke 1999, In Too Deep 1999, Fortress 2 1999, Snow Day 2000, Wilder 2000, 3 A.M. 2001, Love the Hard Way 2001, Bones 2001, John Carpenter's Ghosts of Mars 2001, Undercover Brother 2002, The Adventures of Pluto Nash 2002, Baby of the Family 2002, Back in the Day 2005, Just Wright 2010, Mafia 2011, Larry Crowne 2011, Woman Thou Art Loosed: On the 7th Day 2012, The Man with the Iron Fists 2012. *Television includes:* Roots: The Next Generations (mini-series) 1979, Badge of the Assassin 1985, A Mother's Right: The Elizabeth Morgan Story 1992, Feast of All Saints (mini-series) 2001, 1st to Die 2003, The L Word (series) 2004–09, Smallville 2010. *Stage appearances:* Fool for Love, Frankie and Johnnie, In the Claire De Lune; Best Actress NAACP 1986. *Publication:* Foxy: My Life in Three Acts 2010. *Leisure interests:* skiing, scuba diving, western and English horseback riding, tennis.

GRIESINGER, Christian, BSc, PhD; German chemist and academic; *Director, Max-Planck Institute for Biophysical Chemistry;* b. 5 April 1960, Ulm; s. of Karl and Christa Griesinger; ed Univ. of Frankfurt; Research Fellow, Univ. of Frankfurt 1984–86; Research Fellow, ETH Zürich 1985, Postdoctoral Assoc. 1986–89; Co-Founder MRPHARM GmbH, Frankfurt 1998; Prof., Univ. of Frankfurt 1999–2000; Scientific mem. and Dir Max-Planck Inst. for Biophysical Chem., Göttingen 1999–, Man. Dir Max Planck Inst. for Biophysical Chem. 2007–08; Co-founder MODAG 2012; Assoc. Ed. Journal of Magnetic Resonance 1997–, FEBS Letters 2004–; mem. Council ISMAR (Int. Soc. for Magnetic Resonance) 2001, EUROMAR, Russel Varian Prize Cttee 2002–11, DFG Study Section: Basics of Biology and Medicine 2004–12; mem. German Chemical Soc. 1983– (mem. Nuclear Magnetic Resonance Group Exec. Cttee 1994–96, Chair. 1997–2000), Acad. of Sciences, Göttingen, Nat. Acad. of Sciences Leopoldina, Göttingen Research Council 2007–11, European Molecular Biology Org. 2011; Hon. Prof. of Physical Chem., Univ. of Göttingen 2001–; Hon. mem. Nat. Magnetic Resonance Soc. (India) 2009; Fonds der Chemischen Industrie Young Investigator Award 1989, Literature Prize 1996, Bavarian Acad. of Science Sommerfeld Prize 1997, Deutsche Forschungsgemeinschaft Leibniz Prize 1998, Otto Bayer Prize 2003, ERC advanced grant 2008, Elhuyar-Goldschmidt Prize, Royal Soc. of Spain and Gesellschaft Deutscher Chemiker 2011, Theodor Bücher Award Lecturer, Fed. of European Biochemical Socs 2012. *Address:* Abteilung 030, Max-Planck Institute for Biophysical Chemistry, Am Fassberg 11, 37077 Göttingen, Germany (office). *Telephone:* (551) 201-2201 (office). *Fax:* (551) 201-2202 (office). *E-mail:* cigr@nmr .mpibpc.mpg.de (office). *Website:* medusa.nmr.mpibpc.mpg.de (office).

GRIEVE, Rt Hon. Dominic Charles Roberts, PC, QC, BA; British barrister and politician; *Attorney General for England and Wales and Advocate General for Northern Ireland;* b. 24 May 1956, Lambeth, London, England; s. of Percy Grieve QC (MP for Solihull 1964–83) and Evelyn Raymonde Louise Mijouain; m. Caroline Hutton 1990; two s.; ed Lycée Français Charles de Gaulle, South Kensington, Westminster School, Magdalen Coll., Oxford, Polytechnic of Cen. London (now Univ. of Westminster); Pres. Oxford Univ. Conservative Asscn 1977; called to the Bar, Middle Temple 1980, Bencher 2005, QC 2008; Councillor, London Borough of Hammersmith and Fulham 1982–86; contested Norwood constituency 1987; MP for Beaconsfield, Bucks. 1997–2010, for Beaconsfield (revised boundary) 2010–, mem. (Select Cttees), Jt Cttee on Statutory Instruments 1997–2001, Environmental Audit 1997–2001; Opposition Spokesperson for Constitutional Affairs and Scotland 1999–2001, for Criminal Justice 2001–08; Shadow Attorney Gen. 2003–09; Shadow Home Sec. 2008–09; Shadow Sec. of State for Justice 2009–10; Attorney Gen. for England and Wales and Advocate Gen. for NI 2010–; Chair. Research Cttee, Soc. of Conservative Lawyers 1992–95, Finance and General Purposes Cttee 2006–; police station lay visitor 1990–96, Deputy Church Warden; mem. London Diocesan Synod of the Church of England 1994–2000; Conservative. *Leisure interests:* canoeing, boating on the Thames at weekends, mountain climbing, skiing, travel, fell-walking, scuba diving, architecture, art. *Address:* Attorney General's Office, 20 Victoria Street, London, SW1H 0NF (office); House of Commons, Westminster, London, SW1A 0AA; Constituency Office, Disraeli House, 12 Aylesbury End, Beaconsfield, Bucks., HP9 1LW, England. *Telephone:* (20) 7271-2405 (Attorney Gen.'s Office) (office); (20) 7219-6220 (Westminster); (1494) 673745 (Beaconsfield). *Fax:* (20) 7271-2432 (Attorney Gen.'s Office) (office); (1494) 670428 (Beaconsfield). *E-mail:* dominic.grieve@attorneygeneral.gsi.gov.uk (office); dominic.grieve.mp@parliament.uk; office@beaconsfieldconservatives.co.uk. *Website:* www.attorneygeneral.gov.uk (office); www.parliament.uk/biographies/ commons/dominic-grieve/25630; www.dominicgrieve.org.uk; www .beaconsfieldconservatives.co.uk.

GRIFFEY, George Kenneth (Ken), Jr; American professional baseball player (retd); b. 21 Nov. 1969, Donora, Pa; s. of Ken Griffey Sr (fmr professional baseball player); m. Melissa Griffey; one s.; one d.; ed Moeller High School, Cincinnati; outfielder; drafted by Seattle Mariners in first round (1st pick) of 1987 amateur draft, played 1987–2000, traded to Cincinnati Reds 2000–08, Chicago White Sox 2008, Seattle Mariners 2009–10 (retd); became 20th player to hit 500 career home runs June 2004, 630 home runs upon retirement 2010; mem. All Star team 13 times 1990–2000, 2004, 2007, Most Valuable Player in All-Star Game 1992; American League Gold Glove Award winner 10 times 1990–99; American League Most Valuable Player 1997; named to All-Century Team 1999. *Website:* www .swingman3.com.

GRIFFIN, Jasper, MA, FBA; British academic and writer; *Professor Emeritus of Classical Literature, Balliol College;* b. 29 May 1937, London; s. of Frederick William Griffin and Constance Irene Cordwell; m. Miriam Tamara Griffin (née Dressler) 1960; three d.; ed Balliol Coll., Oxford; Jackson Fellow, Harvard Univ. 1960–61; Dyson Research Fellow, Balliol Coll., Oxford 1961–63, Fellow and Tutor in Classics 1963–2004, Sr Fellow 2000–04, Univ. Reader 1989–2004, Public Orator 1992–2004, Prof. of Classical Literature 1992–2004, Prof. Emer. 2004–. *Publications:* Homer on Life and Death 1980, Snobs 1982, Latin Poets and Roman Life 1985, The Mirror of Myth 1985, Virgil 1986, Homer: The Odyssey 1987, The Art of Snobbery 1998, Homer 2002, Latin Poets and Roman Life 2008; Ed. The Oxford History of the Classical World 1986, The Iliad: Book Nine 1995, Sophocles Revisited: Essays Presented to Sir Hugh Lloyd-Jones 1999; contrib. to articles and reviews. *Leisure interests:* music, wine. *Address:* Balliol College, Oxford, OX1 3BJ, England (office). *Telephone:* (1865) 277777 (office). *Fax:* (1865) 277803 (office). *Website:* www.balliol.ox.ac.uk (office).

GRIFFIN, Michael, BSc, MSc, PhD; American physicist, engineer and academic; *King-McDonald Eminent Scholar and Professor of Mechanical and Aerospace Engineering and Director of Center for System Studies, University of Alabama;* b. 1 Nov. 1949; ed Johns Hopkins Univ., Catholic Univ. of America, Univ. of Maryland, Univ. of Southern Calif., Loyola Coll., George Washington Univ.; fmr Deputy for Tech., Strategic Defense Initiative Org.; Chief Engineer, Assoc. Admin. NASA 1990s; fmr Adjunct Prof. Univ. of Maryland, Johns Hopkins Univ., George Washington Univ.; fmrly with Orbital Sciences Corpn, positions including CEO Magellan Systems, Inc.; Pres. and COO In-Q-Tel –2004; Head Space Dept, Applied Physics Lab., Johns Hopkins Univ. 2004–05; Admin. NASA 2005–09; King-McDonald Eminent Scholar and Prof. of Mechanical and Aerospace Eng and Dir Center for System Studies, Univ. of Alabama, Huntsville 2009–; Fellow, American Inst. of Aeronautics and Astronautics (fmr Pres.); mem. Nat. Acad. of Eng, American Astronautical Soc., Int. Acad. of Astronautics; Co-owner Grumman Tiger; Hon. Chancellor, Florida Southern Coll. 2008; NASA Exceptional Achievement Medal, AIAA Space Systems Medal, Dept of Defense Distinguished Public Service Medal, Goddard Astronautics Award, Goddard Trophy, Nat. Space Club 2009, Rotary Nat. Award for Space Achievement, Space Center Rotary Club of Houston. *Publications:* Space Vehicle Design (co-author), numerous technical papers. *Address:* Shelby Center 135, Mechanical and Aerospace Engineering, Huntsville, AL 35899, USA (office). *Telephone:* (256) 824-5677 (office). *E-mail:* Michael.Griffin@uah.edu (office). *Website:* www.mae.uah.edu (office).

GRIFFITH, Alan Richard, MBA; American banker; b. 17 Dec. 1941, Mineola, NY; s. of Charles E. Griffith and Amalie Guenther; m. Elizabeth Ferguson 1964; one s. one d.; ed Lafayette Coll. and City Univ. of New York; Asst Credit Officer, Bank of New York 1968–72, Asst Vice-Pres. 1972–74, Vice-Pres. 1974–82, Sr Vice-Pres. 1982–85, Exec. Vice-Pres. 1985–88, Sr Exec. Vice-Pres. 1988–90, Pres. 1990–94, Vice-Chair. 1994–2005; US Chair. British-North American Cttee, Atlantic Council; fmr Chair. ALS Asscn, currently mem. Bd of Trustees; Trustee, Chesapeake Bay Foundation, Chesapeake Bay Maritime Museum; Hon. DJur 2001; Lafayette's George T. Woodring Volunteer of the Year Award 1999, inducted into Société d'Honneur 2005. *Address:* British-North American Committee, Atlantic Council, 1101 15th Street, NW, 11th Floor, Washington, DC 20005, USA (office). *Telephone:* (202) 463-7226 (office). *Fax:* (202) 463-7241 (office). *Website:* www.bnac.org (office).

GRIFFITH, Gavan, AO, QC, LLM, DPhil; Australian barrister and international arbitrator; b. 11 Oct. 1941, Melbourne; s. of F. E. Griffith; one s. three d.; ed

Melbourne Univ. and Magdalen Coll. Oxford; barrister 1963; Lincoln's Inn 1969; QC 1981; Solicitor-Gen. of Australia 1984–97; del. to UN Int. Trade Law Comm. (UNCITRAL) 1984–, Vice-Chair. 1987–88, 1994–95; Agent and Counsel for Australia at Int. Court of Justice 1989–95; mem. Perm. Court of Arbitration, The Hague 1987–99; mem. Intelsat Panel of Legal Experts 1988–97, Chair. 1993–94; del. Hague Conf. of Pvt. Int. Law 1992–97; Arbitrator, Int. Comm. for Settlement of Int. Disputes (ISCID) 1994–; Consultant, Office of Legal Counsel, UN, New York 1994–95; Dir Australian Centre for Int. Commercial Arbitration 1997–; mem. Council, Nat. Gallery of Australia 1986–92; Visiting Fellow, Magdalen Coll. Oxford 1973–74, 1976, 1980, 1995; Order of the Repub. of Austria 1997. *Publications:* contribs to various legal journals and books. *Leisure interest:* real tennis. *Address:* Essex Court Chambers, Lincolns Inn Fields, London, WC2A 3EG, England (office); 205 William Street, Melbourne, Vic. 3000, Australia (office). *Telephone:* (3) 9225-7658 (Australia) (office); (20) 7813-8000 (London) (office); (4) 1925-0666 (Australia) (home). *Fax:* (3) 9225-8974 (Australia) (office). *E-mail:* Griffithqc@aol.com (office). *Website:* www.listd.com.au (office); www.essxcourt.net (office).

GRIFFITH, Melanie; American actress; b. 9 Aug. 1957, New York; d. of Tippi Hedren and Peter Griffith; m. 1st Don Johnson 1975 (divorced 1976, remarried 1989, divorced 1993); one d.; m. 2nd Steven Bauer (divorced); m. 3rd Antonio Banderas 1996; one d.; ed Hollywood Professional School; co-founder (with Antonio Banderas) Green Moon Productions. *Films:* Night Moves 1975, Smile 1975, The Drowning Pool 1975, One on One 1977, Underground Aces 1979, Roar, Fear City, Body Double 1984, Something Wild 1986, Stormy Monday 1987, The Milagro Beanfield War 1988, Working Girl 1988, Pacific Heights 1990, Bonfire of the Vanities 1990, Shining Through 1991, Paradise 1991, A Stranger Amongst Us 1992, Close to Eden 1993, Born Yesterday 1993, Milk Money 1994, Nobody's Fool 1994, Now and Then, Two Much, Mulholland Falls 1996, Lolita 1996, Shadow of Doubt 1998, Celebrity 1998, Another Day in Paradise 1998, Crazy in Alabama 1999, Cecil B. Demented 2000, Forever Lulu 2000, Life with Big Cats 2000, Tart 2001, Stuart Little 2 (voice) 2002, The Night We Called It a Day 2003, Shade 2003, Tempo 2003, Have Mercy 2006, The Grief Tourist 2012. *Theatre:* Chicago (Broadway) 2003. *Television:* Once an Eagle (mini-series) 1976, Daddy, I Don't Like It Like This 1978, Steel Cowboy 1978, Carter Country (series) 1978–79, Starmaker 1981, She's in the Army Now 1981, Golden Gate 1981, Buffalo Girls 1995, Me & George (series) 1998, RKO 281 1999, Twins (series) 2005–06, Viva Laughlin 2007, Nip/Tuck 2010. *Address:* 501 Doheny Road, Beverly Hills, CA 90210; Green Moon Productions, 11718 Barrington Court, Los Angeles, CA 90041, USA. *Website:* www.melaniegriffith.com (office).

GRIFFITH-JONES, John; British business executive and banking regulator; *Non-Executive Chairman, Financial Conduct Authority;* ed Trinity Hall, Cambridge; worked at KPMG 1975–2012, spent 11 years in Audit and 15 years in Corp. Finance before becoming CEO of KPMG's UK firm and subsequently Chair. and Sr Partner of UK div. 2006–07; Jt Chair. KPMG Europe 2007–12; Dir (non-exec.), Financial Services Authority (FSA) and Deputy Chair. 2012–13, Chair. (non-exec.) Financial Conduct Authority (successor of FSA, along with Prudential Regulatory Authority) 2013–; fmr Chair. Every Child a Chance Trust; Vice-Chair. Nat. Numeracy Trust; mem. Advisory Bd Cambridge Judge Business School. *Address:* Financial Conduct Authority, 25 The North Colonnade, Canary Wharf, London, E14 5HS, England (office). *Telephone:* (20) 7066-1000 (office). *E-mail:* info@fca.org .uk (office). *Website:* www.fca.org.uk (office).

GRIFFITHS, Alan Gordon, BEcons, LLB; Australian trade union official, politician, entrepreneur and investment banker; b. 4 Sept. 1952, Melbourne; s. of Alan Griffiths and Joy Griffiths; m. Sandra Griffiths 1970; one s.; three d.; ed Traralgon High School, Victoria, Monash Univ.; with Maurice Blackburn and Co. solicitors 1979–82; trade union industrial officer, Federated Rubber and Allied Workers' Union of Australia 1982–83; Labor mem. House of Reps for Maribyrnong, Vic. 1983–96; Jt Parl. Cttee Nat. Crime Authority 1984–87; Chair. House Reps Standing Cttee, Legal and Constitutional Affairs 1987–90; Minister for Resources and Energy 1990–93, for Tourism 1991–93, for Industry, Tech. and Regional Devt 1993–94; Chair. Griffiths Group Int. Pty Ltd 1996–; Founder, Exec. Chair. and Prin., Quantm Ltd 1999–. *Leisure interests:* the arts, sport, politics, travel, sailing. *Address:* Level 4, 333 Flinders Lane, Melbourne, Vic. 3000, Australia (office). *Telephone:* (614) 1951-6775 (office). *E-mail:* alan.griffiths@griffithsgroup.biz (office). *Website:* www.quantm.net (office).

GRIFFITHS, Phillip Augustus, IV, BS, PhD; American mathematician and academic; *Professor of Mathematics Emeritus, Institute for Advanced Study, Princeton;* b. 18 Oct. 1938, Raleigh, NC; s. of Phillip Griffiths and Jeanette Griffiths (née Field); m. 1st Anne Lane Crittenden 1958 (divorced 1967); one s. one d.; m. 2nd Marian Jones; two d.; ed Wake Forest and Princeton Univs; Univ. of California, Berkeley, Miller Fellow 1962–64, 1975–76, Faculty mem. 1964–67; Visiting Prof., Princeton Univ. 1967–68, Prof. 1968–72; Prof., Harvard Univ. 1972–83, Dwight Parker Robinson Prof. of Math. 1983; Provost and James B. Duke Prof. of Math., Duke Univ. 1983–91; Guest Prof., Univ. of Beijing 1983; Dir Inst. for Advanced Study, Princeton 1991–2003, Prof. of Math. 2004–09, Prof. Emer. 2009–, Chair. Science Initiative Group 1999–; Sr Advisor, The Andrew W. Mellon Foundation 2001–; mem. Bd of Dirs Bankers Trust NY Corpn 1994–99, Oppenheimer Funds 1999–, GSI Group 2001–; Sec., Int. Math. Union 1999–2006; Carnegie Fellow, Carnegie Corpn of New York 2007; mem. Council on Foreign Relations 2002–; mem. Editorial Bd, Duke Mathematical Journal 1983–, Selecta Mathematica 1994–, Annals of Math Studies 2001–, Advances in Function Theory 2001–, MSRI and Nankai Book Series on Mathematics 2008–; mem. NAS 1979– (Distinguished Presidential Fellow for Int. Affairs 2002–), American Acad. of Arts and Sciences 1995, American Philosophical Soc. 1996; Foreign Assoc., Accad. Nazionale dei Lincei 2001, TWAS (Acad. of Sciences for the Developing World) 2001, Indian Acad. of Sciences 2003; Fellow, American Math. Soc. 2012; Ordem Nacional do Mérito Científico (Brazil) 2002; Hon. DSc (Duke Univ.) 2004; hon. degrees from Wake Forest, Angers, Oslo and Beijing Univs; Guggenheim Fellow 1980–82, Wolf Foundation Prize in Math. (co-recipient) 2008, Brouwer Prize 2008 and other awards and distinctions. *Publications:* some 15 books and monographs, including Entire Holomorphic Mappings in One and Several Complex Variables 1976, Principles of Algebraic Geometry (co-author) 1978, Rational Homotopy Theory and Differential Forms (co-author) 1981,

Exterior Differential Systems and the Calculus of Variations 1983, Topics in Transcendental Algebraic Geometry 1984, Introduction to Algebraic Curves 1989; 90 articles in professional journals. *Leisure interest:* sailing. *Address:* Fuld Hall 315, Institute for Advanced Study, Einstein Drive, Princeton, NJ 08540, USA (office). *Telephone:* (609) 734-8041 (office). *Fax:* (609) 951-4430 (office). *E-mail:* pg@ math.ias.edu (office). *Website:* www.ias.edu/people/faculty-and-emeriti/griffiths (office).

GRIFFITHS, Rachel; Australian actress; b. 18 Dec. 1968, Melbourne; ed Univ. of Melbourne. *TV includes:* Secrets (series) 1993, The Feds 1993, Jimeoin (series) 1994, Since You've Been Gone 1998, Very Annie Mary 2001, Six Feet Under (series) 2001–05, After the Deluge (mini-series) 2003, Plainsong 2004, Angel 2005, Brothers & Sisters (series) 2006–09, Comanche Moon (mini-series) 2008. *Films include:* Muriel's Wedding 1994, Small Treasures 1995, Cosi 1996, Children of the Revolution 1996, Jude 1996, To Have and to Hold 1996, Welcome to Woop Woop 1997, My Best Friend's Wedding 1997, My Son the Fanatic 1997, Among Giants 1998, Divorcing Jack 1998, Amy 1998, Hilary and Jackie 1998, Me Myself I 1999, Blow Dry 2001, Blow 2001, The Rookie 2002, The Hard Word 2002, Ned Kelly 2003, Step Up 2006, Beautiful Kate 2009, Rake 2010. *Address:* c/o William Morris Agency, One William Morris Place, Beverly Hills, CA 90212, USA.

GRIFFITHS, Terence (Terry) Martin, OBE; British snooker coach and fmr professional snooker player; b. 16 Oct. 1947, Llanelli, Wales; s. of Martin Griffiths and the late Ivy Griffiths; m. Annette Jones 1968; two s.; fmr postman, insurance salesman, miner and bus conductor; won Welsh Amateur Championship 1975, English Amateur Championship 1977, 1978; turned professional snooker player 1978; ranking title: Embassy World Championship 1979; non-ranking titles: Benson & Hedges Masters 1980, Benson & Hedges Irish Masters 1980, 1981, 1982, Classic 1982, UK Championship 1982, Pot Black 1984, Hong Kong Masters 1985, Belgian Classic 1986, Welsh Professional Championship 1985, 1986, 1988; team events: World Cup with Wales team 1979, 1980; Trickshot events: World Trickshot 1992, 1994; f. Terry Griffiths Matchroom 1987; Dir World Snooker 1999–2000; Coach: The Sportsmasters Network 2000–; regular snooker commentator on BBC TV. *Publications:* Championship Snooker, Complete Snooker, Griff. *Leisure interests:* golf, music, playing snooker. *Address:* Terry Griffiths Matchroom, Waunlanyrafon, Llanelli, Carmarthenshire, SA15 3AA, Wales. *Website:* www .terrygriffithssnooker.com.

GRIFFITHS, Trevor, BA; British playwright; b. 4 April 1935, Manchester; s. of Ernest Griffiths and Anne Connor; m. 1st Janice Elaine Stansfield 1961 (died 1977); one s. two d.; m. 2nd Gillian Cliff 1992; ed Univ. of Manchester; taught English language and literature 1957–65; Educ. Officer, BBC 1965–72; Dir Saint Oscar 1990, The Gulf Between Us 1992, Who Shall be Happy…? 1995, Food for Ravens 1997; BAFTA Writer's Award 1981. *Film scripts:* Reds (with Warren Beatty q.v., Writers Guild of America Best Original Screenplay 1981) 1981, Fatherland 1986. *Plays include:* Occupations 1970, Apricots and Thermidor 1970, Sam Sam 1972, The Party 1974, Comedians 1976, The Cherry Orchard 1977, Oi for England 1981, Real Dreams 1984, Piano 1990, The Gulf Between Us 1992, Thatcher's Children 1993, Who Shall Be Happy 1994, Camel Station 2001, A New World: A Life of Thomas Paine 2009, Habaccuc Dreams 2011. *Television includes:* All Good Men 1974, Absolute Beginners 1974, Through the Night 1975, Bill Brand 1976, Country 1981, Sons and Lovers 1982, The Last Place on Earth 1985, Hope in the Year Two 1994, Food for Ravens 1997 (Royal Television Soc. Best Regional Programme 1998, Gwyn A. Williams Special Award, BAFTA Wales 1998). *Radio:* These Are The Times: A Life of Thomas Paine (BBC Radio) 2008. *Publications:* Occupations, Sam Sam 1972, The Party 1974, Comedians 1976, All Good Men, Absolute Beginners, Through the Night, Such Impossibilities, Thermidor and Apricots 1977, Deeds (co-author), The Cherry Orchard (trans.) 1978, Country 1981, Oi for England, Sons and Lovers (TV version) 1982, Judgement Over the Dead 1986, Fatherland, Real Dreams 1987, Collected Plays for TV 1988, Piano 1990, The Gulf Between Us 1992, Hope in the Year Two, Thatcher's Children 1994, Plays One (Collected Stage Plays) 1996, Food for Ravens 1998, These Are The Times 2005, Theatre Plays One 2007, Theatre Plays Two 2007, Bill Brand 2010. *Address:* c/o United Agents, 12–26 Lexington Street, London, W1F 0LE, England (office). *Telephone:* (20) 3214-0800 (office). *Fax:* (20) 3214-0801 (office). *E-mail:* info@unitedagents.co.uk (office). *Website:* www.unitedagents.co.uk (office).

GRIFFITHS OF FFORESTFACH, Baron (Life Peer), cr. 1991, of Fforestfach in the County of West Glamorgan; **Brian Griffiths,** MSc; British banker; *Vice-Chairman, Goldman Sachs International;* b. 27 Dec. 1941; s. of Ivor Winston Griffiths and Phyllis Mary Griffiths (née Morgan); m. Rachel Jane Jones 1965; one s. two d.; ed Dynevor Grammar School and London School of Econs; Asst Lecturer in Econs, LSE 1965–68, Lecturer 1968–76; Dir Centre for Banking and Int. Finance, City Univ., London 1977–82, Prof. of Banking and Int. Finance 1977–85, Dean, City Univ. Business School 1982–85; Dir Bank of England 1984–86, mem. Panel of Acad. Consultants 1977–86; Head of Prime Minister's Policy Unit 1985–90; Chair. Centre for Policy Studies 1991–2000; Head School Examinations and Assessment Council 1991–93; Vice-Chair. Goldman Sachs International 1991–; Dir Thorn-EMI 1991–96, Herman Miller 1991–2011, HTV 1991–93, Times Newspapers Ltd 1991–, Servicemaster 1992–2007, Telewest 1994–98, English, Welsh and Scottish Railway 1996–2006; Chair. Trillium 1998–2001, Westminster Health Care 1999–2002, Land Securities Trillium 2001–09, Lambeth Fund 1997–2012; mem. (Conservative) House of Lords 1991–; Hon. Fellow, Trinity Coll., Carmarthen 1997, Swansea Inst. of Higher Educ. 2003, Sarum Coll. 2006; Hon. DSc (City Univ.) 1999, (Univ. Coll. of Wales) 2004. *Publications:* Is Revolution Change? (ed. and contrib.) 1972, Mexican Monetary Policy and Economic Development 1972, Invisible Barriers to Invisible Trade 1975, Inflation: The Price of Prosperity 1976, Monetary Targets (co-ed. with G. E. Wood) 1980, The Creation of Wealth 1984, Monetarism in the United Kingdom (co-ed. with G. E. Wood) 1984, Morality and the Market Place 1989, Globalization, Poverty and International Development 2007, Fighting Poverty Through Enterprise 2007. *Leisure interests:* the family, reading, ornithology. *Address:* House of Lords, Westminster, London, SW1A 0PW, England (office). *Telephone:* (20) 7219-5353 (office). *Website:* www .parliament.uk/biographies/lords/brian-griffiths/26521 (office).

GRIFFITHS OF GOVILON, Baron (Life Peer), cr. 1985, of Govilon in the county of Gwent; **William Hugh Griffiths,** Kt, MC, PC, BA, MA; British judge; b. 26 Sept. 1923; s. of late Sir Hugh Griffiths; m. 1st Evelyn Krefting 1949; one s. three d.; m. 2nd Baroness Brigstocke 2000; ed Charterhouse and St John's Coll. Cambridge; called to Bar, Inner Temple 1949, QC 1964; Treas. Bar Council 1968–69; Recorder of Margate 1962–64, Cambridge 1964–70; Judge, Queen's Bench Div., High Court of Justice 1971–80; Pres. Senate of Inns of Court and the Bar 1982–; a Lord Justice of Appeal 1980–85; a Lord of Appeal in Ordinary 1985–93; mem. ADR Chambers UK; Chair. Security Comm. 1985–92; Chair. Advisory Cttee on Legal Educ. and Conduct 1991–93; Judge, Nat. Industrial Relations Court 1973–74; mem. Advisory Council on Penal Reform 1967–70; Vice-Chair. Parole Bd 1976–77; Capt. Royal and Ancient Golf Club, St Andrew's; Pres. MCC (cricket) 1991, Bar Golf Club 1990–; mem. Chancellor's Law Reform Cttee 1976–93; Hon. mem. Canadian Bar Assen 1981, Hon. Fellow American Inst. of Judicial Admin. 1985, American Coll. of Trial Lawyers 1988; Hon. LLD (Wales) 1987, (De Montfort) 1993. *Leisure interests:* golf, fishing. *Address:* c/o House of Lords, London, SW1A 0PW; ADR Chambers UK & Europe, City Point, 1 Ropemaker Street, London, EC2Y 9HT, England. *Website:* www.adrchambers.co.uk.

GRIGOROVICH, Yuriy Nikolayevich; Russian balletmaster; *Artistic Director, Grigorovich Ballet Company;* b. 2 Jan. 1927, Leningrad; s. of K. A. Grigorovich-Rozay and N. E. Grigorovich; m. Natalya Igorevna Bessmertnova; ed Leningrad Choreographic School and Lunarcharski Inst. of Theatrical Art, Moscow; soloist, Kirov (now Mariinsky) Theatre 1946–64, Ballet-Master 1962–64; Chief Ballet Master, Bolshoi Theatre, Moscow 1964–95; Chief Choreographer, Artistic Dir Kremlin Palace of Congresses Ballet 1998; now works in various theatres in Russia and abroad; Ed.-in-Chief Soviet Ballet Encyclopaedia 1981; Founder and Artistic Dir Bolshoi Ballet Grigorovich Co. (now Grigorovich Ballet Co.) 1990–; Chair. Int. Choreography Assen; mem. Vienna Music Soc.; Hon. Chair. Int. Theatre Inst., Ukrainian Dance Acad.; Order Merit to Fatherland Third Degree 2004, Order of Merit for the Fatherland, 1st class 2011; Lenin Prize 1970, People's Artist of USSR 1973, USSR State Prize 1985, Hero of Socialist Labour 1986, Soul of Dance Prize (magazine Balet) 2001, Golden Mask for Honour and Dignity 2003. *Ballets include:* Stone Flower (Kirov-Mariinsky) 1957, Legend of Love (Kirov-Mariinsky) 1960, Sleeping Beauty (Bolshoi) 1963, Nutcracker (Bolshoi) 1966, Spartacus 1968, Swan Lake 1969, Ivan the Terrible 1975, Angara 1976, Romeo and Juliet (Paris) 1978, Giselle 1979, Golden Age (Bolshoi) 1982, Raymonda 1984, Bayaderka 1991, Elektra (Grigorovich Ballet co-produced with Melanin and Bobrov) 1992, La Fille Mal Gardée (Grigorovich Ballet) 1993, Le Corsaire (Bolshoi) 1994. *Address:* Sretenskii Blvd 6/1, Apt 9, Moscow, Russia (home). *Telephone:* (495) 925-6431 (home).

GRIGORYANTS, Sergey Ivanovich; Russian journalist and human rights activist; b. 12 May 1941, Kiev; s. of Ivan Arkadievich Grigoryants and Vera Sergeevna Shenberg; m. Tamara Vsevolodovna Grigoryants; one s. (died 1995) one d.; expelled from Moscow Univ. by KGB 1968; Founder and ed. Information Bulletin on violation of human rights in USSR 1982–83; imprisoned for political activities 1975–80, 1983–87; Founder, Ed. and Publr Glasnost magazine 1987–91, Glasnost Information Agency 1991–; Founder and fmr Chair. Public Fund Glasnost (now Glasnost Defence Foundation) 1990, organized regular conf. KGB Yesterday, Today, Tomorrow; Head of Centre on Information and Analysis, Russian Special Service 1993, Initiator of Int. Non-Governmental Tribunal on the War Crimes and Crimes Against Humanity in Chechnya; Co-Chair. Coalition for Support for Int. Criminal Court; Head of Glasnost-Caucasus Information Agency 2000–; Gold Pen of Freedom Award, Medal of Bayern Lantague. *Publications:* contribs to New York Times and Washington Post. *Leisure interests:* collecting paintings, antiques, early medieval artefacts. *Address:* Glasnost Defence Foundation, 119992 Moscow, GSP-2 Zubovsky Boulevard 4, Entrance of the Union of Journalists of Russia, Room 432, Russia (office). *Telephone:* (495) 637-44-20 (office). *Fax:* (495) 299-85-38 (office); (495) 637-49-47 (office). *E-mail:* fond@gdf.ru (office). *Website:* www.gdf.ru (office).

GRIGORYEV, Anatoly Ivanovich, DrMed; Russian biologist and space scientist; *Vice-President, Institute for Biomedical Problems;* b. 23 March 1943, Zhitomir region, Ukraine; s. of Ivan Grigoryevich Grigoryev and Olga Isakovna Grigoryeva; m. Dorokhova Bella Radikovna; two s.; ed 2nd Moscow Medical Inst.; Researcher, Sr Researcher, Head of Lab., Head of Div., Deputy Dir State Research Centre of Inst. for Biomedical Problems, USSR (now Russian) Acad. of Sciences 1966–; Dir 1988–, Vice-Pres. Inst. for Biomedical Problems 2007–; Chief Medical Commr, Russian Space Agency 1988–; Chief Medical Officer 1996–; Co-Chair. Jt Soviet-American Workgroup on Space Biology and Medicine 1989–92; Chair. Section on Sciences of Life, Int. Acad. of Astronautics 1989–93, Section of Space Medicine, Russian Acad. of Sciences 1991–; Scientific Council on Space Medicine, Russian Acad. of Medicine 1993–; Co-Chair. Int. Space Station (ISS) Multilateral Medical Policy Bd 2000–, Man. of Medical Support in space flights on ISS 2001–; Vice-Pres. Int. Acad. of Astronautics 1993–2003, Int. Astronautical Fed. 2004–, Int. Astronomic Fed. 2006–; mem. Co-ordination Council, Russian Fed. Ministry of Science and Tech. 1998–; Presidential Council on Science and Technologies 2004–; mem. Aerospace Medical Assen, USA 1991–, Int. Union of Physiological Sciences 1992–, Russian Acad. of Medicine 1993–, New York Acad. of Sciences 1994–, Int. Acad. of Sciences 1995–, Russian Acad. of Natural Sciences 1996–, Russian Acad. of Sciences 1997– (mem. Presidium 2001–, Academician-Sec. Biology Dept 2002–), Russian R. Tsyolkovsky Acad. of Cosmonautics 1997–; Order, Sign of Hon. 1976, Labour Red Banner 1982, Banner of Labour (DDR) 1985, Order For Merits to Motherland (IV Degree) 2003, Officier de la Légion d'honneur 2004; Dr hc (Lyon Univ.) 1989; USSR State Prize 1989, Russian Acad. of Medicine Prize 1996, Bointon Prize, American Astronautics Assen 1995, 1999, Struckhold Prize, American Aviacosmic Assen 1996, Françoise Xavier Banier Prize, Michigan Univ., USA 1999, S. Korolev and Yu. Gagarin Medals, USSR Fed. of Cosmonautics, Merited Worker of Science of Russia 1996, State Award of Russian Fed. 2001, Louis H. Bauer Founders Award, AMA 2001, IAA Team Achievement Award 2001, Silver Snoopy Award, NASA 2002, Ikarus Stair Medal, Russian Space Agency 2003, Award of Russian Govt 2003, Triumf Prize for achievements in medicine 2006. *Publications:* more than 400 scientific publs including seven monographs and 22 patents. *Leisure interests:* music, theatre, historical literature. *Address:* Institute for Biomedical Problems, Khoroshovskoye shosse 76A, 123007 Moscow, Russia (office). *Telephone:* (495) 195-23-63 (office). *Fax:* (495) 195-22-53 (office). *E-mail:* grigoriev@imbp.ru (office). *Website:* www.imbp.ru (office).

GRIGORYEV, Vladimir Viktorovich; Belarusian politician and diplomatist; b. 5 April 1941, Mogilev; m.; one s.; ed Belarus Agricultural Acad., Acad. of Social Sciences; began career with local newspaper 1957–58; Second Sec., Komsomol (All-Union Lenin Communist Union of Youth/VLKSM) Dist Cttee, Mogilev Br. 1958–62, 1966–68, First Sec. 1968–70, Instructor, Political Dept, Mogilev 1962–65, Head of Div., Mogilev Regional VLKSM Cttee 1965–66, Sec. VLKSM 1970–72, First Sec. Minsk Regional Cttee 1974, Moscow Regional Cttee 1974–80, Second Sec. Brest Regional Cttee 1980–83; Chair. Exec. Cttee, Brest Prov. Soviet of People's Deputies (Ass.) 1983–85; First Sec., Vitebsk Regional Cttee, Communist Party of Belarus (KPB) 1986–90; Chair. Vitebsk Prov. Soviet of People's Deputies 1990–91; Dir Gen. Dolomite Production Assen, Vitebsk 1992–96; fmr mem. Supreme Soviet of BSSR (Parl.); Amb. to Russia and Perm. Rep.to Eurasian Econ. Community 1997–2006; Order of the Red Banner of Labour, Order of the Fatherland. *Address:* c/o Ministry of Foreign Affairs, 220030 Minsk, vul. Lenina 19, Belarus.

GRILLI, Vittorio Umberto, MEconSc, PhD; Italian economist and politician; b. 19 May 1957, Milan; ed Univ. Luigi Bocconi, Milan, Rochester Univ., USA; Asst Prof., Dept of Econs,Yale Univ. 1986–90; Lecturer in Financial Econs, Birkbeck Coll., Univ. of London 1990–94; joined Ministry of Economy and Finance as mem. Council of Experts, Treasury Dept 1993, Dir-Gen., Dept of Econ. and Financial Analysis and Privatization 1994–2000, also Dir-Gen. of Public Debt and Treasury 1996–97, becoming Dir-Gen., Treasury Dept 2005–11; Deputy Minister of Finance 2011–12, Minister of Finance 2012–13; Vice-Pres. ECOFIN Econ. and Finance Cttee 2009, later Pres.; several fmr private sector roles including Man. Dir Credit Suisse First Boston, London, Pres. Istituto Italiano di Tecnologia, fmr Dir Cassa Depositi e Prestiti, Istituto Nazionale di Genetica Molecolare, Scuola Superiore Sant'Anna di Pisa, ENEL SpA, Alitalia, Artigiancassa SpA, CONSAP SpA, CONSIP SpA, WIND, European Investment Bank; mem. European Bruegel (think-tank), Brussels, Aspen Inst. Italia; Cavaliere di Gran Croce, Ordine al merito della Repubblica Italiana 2011; several awards including Medaglia d'Oro dell'Università Luigi Bocconi 1981, Premio Saint Vincent per l'Economia 1992, Premio Ezio Tarantelli for best economic idea 2004, Premio Bocconiano dell'anno 2005, Premio Guido Carli for best new financial initiative 2010. *Publications include:* numerous articles and books on topics of national and international economic policy. *Address:* c/o Ministry of the Economy and Finance, Via XX Settembre 97, 00187 Rome, Italy.

GRILLO, (Giuseppe Piero) Beppe; Italian comedian, actor and political activist; *Leader, Movimento 5 Stelle;* b. 21 July 1948, Genoa; s. of Enrico Grillo and Piera Grillo; originally trained as accountant; discovered as comedian and launched by Italian TV presenter Pippo Baudo; known for satirical monologues; presented several TV programmes until increasing level of political satire led to ostracism in press and on TV; numerous tours in Italy and abroad; increasingly involved with political activism 2005–; addressed European Parl., Brussels 2007; organized 'V' protest movt 2007; best known for blog beppegrillo.it; Founder Movimento 5 Stelle (Five Star Movt) 2010. *Tours include:* Energy and Information (tour of over 60 Italian towns and cities) 1995–96, Brain 1997, Soft Apocalypse 1998, Time Out 2000, The Great Transformation 2001, All is Well 2002–03, Black-Out - Facciamo Luce 2003–04. *Television includes:* Secondo Voi 1977–78, Luna Park 1979, Fantastico 1979, Te la do io l'America (four episodes) 1982, Te lo do io il Brasile (six episodes) 1984, Grillometro (Grillometer), Domenica In, Festival di Sanremo, Beppe Grillo Show (RAI 1) 1993. *Films:* Cercasi Gesù 1982, Scemo di Guerra 1985, Topo Galileo 1987. *Website:* beppegrillo.it (office).

GRILLO, Ulrich; German business executive; *President, Federation of German Industries;* b. 1959, Cologne; m.; two c.; ed Westfälische Wilhelms Univ., Münster; began career as trainee, Deutsche Bank AG, Duisburg; worked for Arthur Andersen & Co. Ltd (accounting firm), Frankfurt am Main 1987–89; with A.T.Kearney Ltd (man. consulting firm), Düsseldorf 1989–93; joined Rheinmetall Group 1993, eventually becoming Deputy Chair. Exec. Bd, Rheinmetall DeTec, Ratingen –2001, also Chair. STN ATLAS Elektronik, Bremen (subsidiary co.); mem. Exec. Bd Grillo-Werke AG (family-owned metal and chemicals co.), Duisburg 2001–, Chair. 2004–; Vice-Pres. Fed. of German Industries (BDI) 2011–12, Pres. 2013–; Pres. WirtschaftsVereinigung Metalle (German non ferrous-metals assen) 2006–12; Deputy Chair. Exec. Bd UVM Unternehmerverband der Metallindustrie, Duisburg; mem. Advisory Council Mercator School of Man., Univ. of Duisburg/Essen, Commerzbank AG, Frankfurt; mem. Supervisory Bd Klöckner & Co. SE, Duisburg, IKB Deutsche Industriebank AG, Düsseldorf; Order of Merit of North Rhine-Westphalia 2008. *Address:* BDI, Breite Straße 29, 10178 Berlin, Germany (office). *Telephone:* (0) 30 2028-0 (office). *E-mail:* info@bdi.eu (office). *Website:* www.bdi.de (office).

GRIMLEY EVANS, Sir John, Kt, MA, MD, FRCP, FFPHM, FMedSci; British physician and academic; *Professor Emeritus of Clinical Geratology, University of Oxford;* b. 17 Sept. 1936, Birmingham, England; s. of Harry Walter Grimley Evans and Violet Prenter Walker; m. Corinne Jane Cavender 1966; two s. one d.; ed King Edward's School, Birmingham, St John's Coll., Cambridge, Balliol Coll., Oxford; Visiting Scientist, Univ. of Michigan 1966–67; Research Fellow, Wellington, NZ 1967–70; Lecturer, Univ. of London 1970–71; Prof. of Geriatric Medicine, Univ. of Newcastle-upon-Tyne 1973–84; Prof. of Clinical Geratology, Univ. of Oxford 1985–2002, Emer. 2002–; Fellow, Green Coll., Oxford 1985–; Consultant Physician, Oxford Hosps 1985–; mem. MRC 1993–95, Chair. Health Services Research Bd 1990–95; Vice-Pres. Royal Coll. of Physicians 1993–95; Ed. Age and Ageing 1988–95, Oxford Textbook of Geriatric Medicine; Hon. Fellow, Royal Soc. of Medicine 2000; Harveian Orator, Royal Coll. of Physicians 1997, Ignatius Nascher Prize, City of Vienna 2005. *Publications:* papers on epidemiology and geratology. *Leisure interests:* literature, fly-fishing. *Address:* Green Templeton College, Oxford, OX2 6HG, England (office). *E-mail:* john.grimleyevans@gtc.ox.ac.uk (office).

GRIMMEISS, Hermann Georg, Dr rer. nat, Dipl.Phys; Swedish physicist and academic; *Professor Emeritus of Solid State Physics, University of Lund;* b. 19 Aug. 1930, Hamburg, Germany; s. of Georg Grimmeiss and Franziska März; m. Hildegard Weizmann 1956; one s. one d.; ed Oberschule Nördlingen and Univ. of Munich; Prof. of Solid State Physics, Head of Dept Univ. of Lund 1965–96, Prof. Emer. 1996–, Dean for Research 1993–96; Chair. Int. Conf. of the Physics of Semiconductors, Stockholm 1986; Chair. Nobel Symposium on Hetrostructures in

Semiconductors, Sweden 1996; mem. Programme Cttee for Physics-Math. Swedish Natural Science Research Council 1971–80; mem. Bd Swedish Nat. Cttee for Physics 1971–72, 1981–97; Prof. of Physics, Dir, Univ. of Frankfurt am Main 1973–74; mem. Cttee for Electronics, Swedish Bd for Tech. Devt 1978–80; mem. Bd Swedish-German Research Asscn 1980–2011; mem. Cttee Univ. Frankfurt/Oder (Germany) 1991–93; mem. Cttee for Science and Research, Brandenburg (Germany) 1993–95; Vice-Pres. RIFA (mem. Ericsson Group) 1981–83; Visiting Miller Prof., Univ. of California, Berkeley 1990; Dir Inst. of Semiconductor Physics, Frankfurt (Oder), Germany 1991–93; mem. Bd Einstein Forum, Potsdam, Germany 1993–; mem. Exec. Cttee European Materials Research Soc. 2001–, Pres. 2003–07; Vice-Pres. European Materials Forum 2004–; mem. Int. Prize Cttee Global Energy, Moscow 2002–09; Chair. Scientific Advisory Bd IHP GmbH Frankfurt/Oder 2003–12; ed. and co-ed. several int. journals; mem. Royal Physiographic Soc. Lund, Royal Swedish Acad. of Eng Sciences, Royal Swedish Acad. of Sciences, Societas Scéntarium Sennica; Fellow, American Physical Soc.; Hon. mem. Roland Eötvös Physical Soc. 1983, Ioffe Inst., St Petersburg, Russia 1998; Order of North Star 1969, Bundesverdienstkreuz 1 Klasse 1993, King's Medal of 8th Dimension with Blue Ribbon, Stockholm 1998; Ehrenurkunde, Potsdam, Germany 2009, Czochralski Award, Washaw 2009. *Publications:* more than 250 scientific publns in int. journals and books. *Leisure interests:* tennis, classical music. *Address:* Division of Solid State Physics, University of Lund, Box 118, 221 00 Lund, Sweden (office). *Telephone:* (46) 2227675 (office); (46) 140980 (home). *Fax:* (46) 2227675 (office); (46) 140980 (home). *E-mail:* hermann .grimmeiss@ftf.lth.se (office). *Website:* www.ftf.lth.se/staff/emeriti (office).

GRIMSHAW, Sir Nicholas Thomas, Kt, CBE, RA, FCSD, RIBA; British architect; b. 9 Oct. 1939, Hove; s. of Thomas Cecil Grimshaw and Hannah Joan Dearsley; m. Lavinia Russell 1972; two d.; ed Wellington Coll., Edinburgh Coll. of Art, Architectural Asscn School, London; Chair. Nicholas Grimshaw & Partners Ltd 1980–; Pres. Architectural Asscn; mem. Royal Acad. of Arts 1994–, Pres. 2004–2011; Assessor for British Construction Industry Awards, RIBA, Dept of Environment; Hon. FAIA; Hon. DLitt; Hon. BDA; awards and commendations include 19 RIBA awards 1975–2007; seven Financial Times Awards for Industrial Architecture 1977–95, 14 Structural Steel Design Awards 1969–2007, eight Civic Trust Awards 1978–96, eight British Construction Industry Awards 1988–2001, four Royal Fine Art Comm./Sunday Times Bldg of the Year Awards 1989–2004, five Concrete Soc. Awards 1995–2001, Constructa Preis for Industrial Architecture in Europe 1990, European Award for Steel Structures 1981, Quaternario Foundation Int. Awards for Innovative Tech. in Architecture, Gold Award 1993, Mies Van der Rohe Pavilion Award for European Architecture 1994, RIBA Bldg of the Year Award 1994, Design Innovation Award 1996, British Council for Offices Award 1996, Int. Brunel Award 1996, AIA (UK) Excellence in Design Award 2001, 2005, Leisure Property Award for Best Regeneration Scheme 2001, European Award for Aluminium in Architecture 2001, RIBA Lubetkin Prize for Outstanding Architecture outside the EU 2007. *Major projects include:* Channel Tunnel Terminal, Waterloo, London; British Pavilion for Expo '92, Seville, Berlin Stock Exchange and Communications Centre, British Airways Combined Operations Centre, Heathrow Airport, London, Financial Times Printing Plant, HQ for Igus GmbH, Cologne, Germany, head office and printing press for Western Morning News, Plymouth, BMW HQ, Bracknell, new satellite and piers, Heathrow Airport, Western Region HQ for RAC, Herman Miller Factory, Bath, Oxford Ice Rink, Gillingham Business Park, Research Centre for Rank Xerox, J. Sainsbury Superstore, Camden, London, redevelopment of Terminal One, Manchester Airport, New Teaching and Research Bldg, Univ. of Surrey, Regional HQ for Orange Telecommunications, Darlington, Railway Terminus, Pusan, Korea, redevelopment of Zürich Airport, Restoration of Paddington Station 1996, Restoration of Spa, new Bldg, Bath & E Somerset Council 1997, Ijburg Bridges, Amsterdam 2002, HQ for Lloyds TSB, Gresham Street, London 2002, Caixa Galicia Foundation, La Coruña, Spain, Exhbn Hall for Frankfurt Fair, Eden Project, Cornwall 2001, Nat. Space Science Centre, Leicester 2002, Rolls Royce Factory, Goodwood 2003, Experimental Media and Performing Arts Center for Rensselaer Polytechnic Inst., Troy, NY, USA, HQ for KPMG, Berlin, Southern Cross Station, Melbourne, Australia 2007, Newport City Footbridge, Wales 2007, Fulton Street Station, New York, Stansted Airport Generation 2, New Acad. Building, 24 Kingsway, for LSE 2008, London Southbank Univ. New Building, New Galleries for Queen's Museum of Art, New York, Museo del Acero, Monterrey, Mexico, Earthpark, Iowa, USA, ExCel London Phase 2 Devt, Garibaldi Republica Fashion and Events Bldg, Milan, Nirah visitor destination and research centre, Adelaide Univ. Project 2, St Botolph's Office Bldg, London, New York Housing Project, Miami Science Museum, New York Univ. Strategic Planning Initiative, Nyetimber Vineyard, Sussex, The Edge, Pulkovo Airport, St Petersburg 2007, Eco Hotel Concept, North America 2011, St Botolph Building, London 2011, Mobilizarte Mobile Pavilion, Brazil 2012, Cutty Sark conservation project, London 2012. *Publications:* Product and Process 1988, Structure, Space and Skin 1993, Architecture, Industry and Innovation 1995, Equilibium 2000, The Architecture of Eden 2003; articles for RSA Journal and RIBA Journal. *Leisure interests:* sailing, tennis. *Address:* Royal Academy of Arts, Burlington House, Piccadilly, London, W1J 0BD, England (office). *Telephone:* (20) 7300-8000 (office). *E-mail:* press .office@royalacademy.org.uk (office). *Website:* www.royalacademy.org.uk (office).

GRIMSON, Eric, BSc, PhD; Canadian engineer and academic; *Bernard Gordon Professor of Medical Engineering, Massachusetts Institute of Technology;* b. Regina, Sask.; ed Univ. of Regina, Massachusetts Inst. of Tech., USA; worked for more than 30 years at MIT, positions include Assoc. Dir Artificial Intelligence Lab. 1998–2003, Educ. Officer, Dept of Electrical Eng and Computer Science 2001–04, Head of Dept of Electrical Eng and Computer Science 2005–, Prof. of Computer Science and Eng, Bernard Gordon Prof. of Medical Eng 1998–; Lecturer on Radiology, Harvard Medical School and Brigham and Women's Hosp.; Fellow, Asscn for the Advancement of Artificial Intelligence (AAAI), IEEE. *Address:* MIT CSAIL, Stata Center, 77 Massachusetts Avenue, 32-D524, Cambridge, MA 02139, USA (office). *Telephone:* (617) 253-4645 (office). *Fax:* (617) 253-0572 (office). *E-mail:* welg@csail.mit.edu (office). *Website:* people.csail.mit.edu (office).

GRÍMSSON, Ólafur Ragnar, PhD; Icelandic fmr politician and head of state; *President;* b. 14 May 1943, Isafjörður; s. of Grimur Kristgeirsson and Svanhildur Ólafsdóttir; m. 1st Guðrún Katrín Thorbergsdóttir 1974 (died 1999); two d. (twins); m. 2nd Dorrit Moussaieff 2003; ed Reykjavik Higher Secondary Grammar School,

Univ. of Manchester, UK; Lecturer in Political Science, Univ. of Iceland 1970–88, Prof. 1973; involved in production of political TV and radio programmes 1966–70; mem. Bd Progressive Party Youth Fed. 1966–73, Exec. Bd Progressive Party 1971–73, Alt. mem. Althing representing East Iceland (Liberal and Left Alliance) 1974–75; Chair. Exec. Bd Liberal and Left Alliance 1974–75; mem. Althing for Reykjavik 1978–83; mem. People's Alliance, Chair. Parl. Group 1980–83, Leader 1987–95; Minister of Finance 1988–91; Pres. of Iceland 1996–; Chair. Cttee on Relocation of Public Institutes 1972–75, Icelandic Social Sciences Asscn 1975, Organizing Cttee Parl. Conf. of Council of Europe: 'North-South: Europe's Role' 1982-84, Parliamentarians for Global Action 1984–90 (also fmr Pres., mem. Bd 1990–96); Vice-Chair. Icelandic Security Comm. 1979–90; mem. Bd Icelandic Broadcasting Service 1971–75, Nat. Power Co. 1983–88; mem. Parl. Ass. Council of Europe 1980–84, 1995. *Address:* Office of the President, Stadastadur, Sóleyjargata 1, 150 Reykjavík, Iceland (office). *Telephone:* 5404400 (office). *Fax:* 5624802 (office). *E-mail:* president@president.is (office). *Website:* www.president.is (office).

GRIMSTONE, Gerry, MA, MSc; British banking executive; *Chairman, Standard Life plc;* b. 1950; ed Merton Coll. and Wolfson Coll., Oxford; held sr positions with Dept of Health and Social Security and HM Treasury –1986; with Schroders Investment Bank 1986–99, London, Hong Kong and New York, becoming Vice-Chair. Schroders' worldwide investment banking activities; mem. Bd of Dirs Standard Life Assurance Co. 2003–, Deputy Chair. Standard Life plc 2006–07, Chair. 2007–; Chair. (non-exec.) Candover Investments PLC, F&C Global Smaller Cos PLC, TheCityUK; Ind. Dir (non-exec.), Deloitte LLP; Lead Dir (non-exec.), Ministry of Defence; apptd as one of UK's Business Ambs by the Prime Minister 2009; Chair. Jt Audit Cttee, RAF Strike Command Bd; Trustee, The Queille Trust. *Address:* Standard Life House, 30 Lothian Road, Edinburgh, EH1 2DH, Scotland (office). *Telephone:* (131) 225-2552 (office). *Fax:* (131) 245-7990 (office). *E-mail:* info@standardlife.com (office). *Website:* www.standardlife.com (office).

GRIMWADE, Sir Andrew (Sheppard), Kt, CBE, BSc, MA, FAIM; Australian business executive; b. 26 Nov. 1930, Melbourne; s. of the late Frederick Grimwade and Gwendolen Grimwade; m. Barbara Gaerloch Kater 1959 (died 1990); one s.; ed Melbourne Grammar School, Trinity Coll., Melbourne Univ., Oriel Coll. Oxford, UK; Dir Commonwealth Industrial Gases Ltd 1960–90, Nat. Australia Bank Ltd 1965–85, IBM Australia 1975–82, Sony (Australia) 1975–82, Turoa Holdings Ltd 1975–82; Chair. Australian Consolidated Industries Ltd 1977–82; fmr Vice-Chair. Nat. Mutual Life 1988 (Dir 1970); mem. Australian Govt Remuneration Tribunal 1976–82; mem. First Australian Govt Trade Mission to China 1973; Pres. Walter and Eliza Hall Inst. of Medical Research 1978–92 (Bd mem. 1963–); Deputy Pres. Australiana Fund 1978–82; Trustee Nat. Gallery of Victoria (Pres. 1976–90), Trustee Emer. 1990–; mem. Felton Bequests Cttee 1973–, now Chair.; Trustee Victorian Arts Centre 1980–90; mem. Council for Order of Australia 1975–82. *Publication:* Involvement: The Portraits of Clifton Pugh and Mark Strizic 1969. *Leisure interests:* skiing, Santa Gertrudis cattle breeding, Australian art. *Address:* c/o National Gallery of Victoria, PO Box 7259, Melbourne, Victoria 8004, Australia.

GRINBERG, Ruslan Semyonovich, DrSc; Russian institute director and academic; b. 1946; Deputy Dir Inst. for Int. Econ. and Political Studies, Russian Acad. of Sciences, Moscow –2002, Dir 2002–05; Vice-Chair. ECAAR Russia (Economists Allied for Arms Reduction); mem. Russian-American Econ. Transition Group; Ed.-in-Chief The World of Transformations; Admin. Adviser to Gorbachev Foundation; Chair. Cttee of CIS, Nat. Investment Council, Expertise Council for CIS of Russian Fed. Trade and Industry Chamber; mem. Expertise Council Supreme Certifying Comm., Expertise Bd for Ministry of Economy; mem. Cultural Information and Research Centres Liaison in Europe (CIRCLE); Corresp. mem. Russian Acad. of Sciences. *Publications include:* Economic Sociodynamics (with Alexander Rubinstein) 2000, The New Russia – Transition Gone Awry 2001, Rational Behavior of the State 2003; more than 184 publns on econ. theory, credit and monetary policy in post-Socialist countries, integration and disintegration in post-Soviet states, the role of state in transformation economies. *Address:* c/o Institute for International Economic and Political Studies, Novocheryemushkinskaya 42A, Moscow 117418, Russia. *Telephone:* (495) 128-67-80. *Fax:* (495) 120-83-71. *E-mail:* imepi@transecon.ru. *Website:* www.imepi-eurasia.ru.

GRINDENKO, Tatyana Tikhonovna, Russian violinist; *Artistic Director, Moscow Academy of Ancient Music;* b. 29 March 1946, Kharkov, Ukraine; m. 1st Gidon Kremer (q.v.); m. 2nd Vladimir Martynov; ed Moscow State Conservatory; repertoire includes baroque, avant-garde, jazz, rock, experimental music; Co-founder (with A. Lyubimov) and Artistic Dir Moscow Acad. of Ancient Music; est. OPUS-POST ensemble 1999, participates in multimedia projects; various recordings for CD, radio and TV; First Prize and Golden Medal at World Int. Youth Competition in Bulgaria 1968, Winner at IV Int. Tchaikovsky Competition 1970, Winner at Wieniawski Competition in Poland 1972, People's Artist of Russia 2002, State Prize of the Russian Fed. 2003. *Leisure interest:* driving sports cars. *Address:* Moscow State Philharmonia, Tverskaya str. 31, 103050 Moscow, Russia (office). *Telephone:* (495) 253 7425 (home).

GRININ, Vladimir Mikhailovich; Russian diplomatist; *Ambassador to Germany;* b. 15 Nov. 1947; m.; one d.; ed Moscow State Univ. for Int. Relations, Diplomatic Acad., USSR Ministry of Foreign Affairs; mem. staff Ministry of Foreign Affairs 1971–, took part in Soviet-American disarmament and arms control negotiations, Geneva 1982–86, Embassy of USSR in GDR 1986–1990, in FRG 1990–1992, Dir 4th European Dept 1994–96, Dir Gen. Secr. (mem. Collegium) 2000–03; Amb. to Austria 1996–2000, to Finland 2003–06, to Poland 2006–10, to Germany 2010–. *Address:* Embassy of the Russian Federation, Unter den Linden 63–65, 10117 Berlin, Germany (office). *Telephone:* (30) 2291110 (office). *Fax:* (30) 2299397 (office). *E-mail:* info@russische-botschaft.de (office). *Website:* w (office).

GRINSTEIN, Gerald (Jerry), LLB; American business executive; *Strategic Director, Madrona Venture Group;* b. 1932, Seattle, WA; m.; four c.; ed Yale Coll., Harvard Law School; Counsel to merchant marine and transport subcttees., Chief Counsel, US Senate Commerce Cttee 1958–67; Admin. Asst to US Senator Warren Magnuson 1967–69; Pnr, Preston, Thorgrimson, Ellis & Holman 1969–73; Chair. Bd Western Air Lines Inc. LA 1983–84, Pres. and COO 1984–85, CEO 1985–86, Chair. and CEO 1986–87; Vice-Chair. Burlington Northern Inc., Fort Worth 1987–88, Pres., CEO 1989–90, Chair. 1990–96, CEO 1990–95; Pres., CEO Burlington Northern R.R. Co. 1989–90, Chair. 1990–96, CEO 1990–95; Chair.

Delta Airlines Inc. 1997–99, CEO 2004–07, currently CEO Emer.; Chair. (non-exec.) Agilent Techs. 1999–2002; Co-founder and Strategic Dir Madrona Investment Group, Seattle 1995–2003, 2007–; mem. Bd of Dirs Long Live the Kings, Univ. of Washington Foundation, Seattle Foundation, Foster School of Business, William D. Ruckelshaus Center; Founder mem. Bd of Dirs Foundation Bank 2000–; fmr mem. Bd of Dirs Seattle First Nat. Bank, Browning Ferris Industries Inc., Sundstrand Corpn, Expedia.com, Imperial Sugar Corpn, PACCAR Inc., The Brink's Co.; Trustee, Henry M. Jackson Foundation. *Address:* Madrona Venture Group, 1000 Second Avenue, Suite 3700, Seattle, WA 98104, USA (office). *Telephone:* (206) 674-3000 (office). *Fax:* (206) 674-8703 (office). *E-mail:* jerry@madronn.com (office). *Website:* www.madronna.com (office).

GRINT, Rupert Alexander Lloyd; British actor; b. 24 Aug. 1988, Herefords.; s. of Nigel Grint and Joanne Parsons; ed Richard Hale School, Hertford; first performed in school plays and with Top Hat Stage School (local theatre group). *Films include:* Harry Potter and the Philosopher's Stone 2001, Harry Potter and the Chamber of Secrets 2002, Thunderpants 2002, Harry Potter and the Prisoner of Azkaban 2004, Harry Potter and the Goblet of Fire 2005, Driving Lessons 2006, Harry Potter and the Order of the Phoenix 2007, December Boys 2007, Harry Potter and the Half-Blood Prince 2009, Harry Potter and the Deathly Hallows: Part 1 2010, Cherrybomb 2010, Wild Target 2010, Harry Potter and the Deathly Hallows: Part 2 2011. *Television:* Come Fly with Me (BBC) 2010. *Radio:* Baggy Trousers (series, BBC Radio 4) 2003. *Play:* Mojo (WhatsOnStage Award for the Dewynters London Newcomer of the year 2014) 2013. *Address:* Hamilton Hodell, Fifth Floor, 66-68 Margaret Street, London, W1W 8SR, England (office). *Telephone:* (20) 7636-1221 (office). *Fax:* (20) 7636-1226 (office). *E-mail:* info@hamiltonhodell.co.uk (office). *Website:* www.hamiltonhodell.co.uk (office).

GRINVALD, Amiram; Israeli neuroscientist and academic; *Director, Murray H. & Meyer Grodetsky Center for Research of Higher Brain Functions, Weizmann Institute of Science;* b. Kibbutz Ramat Hashofet; ed Weizmann Inst. of Science, Hebrew Univ., Hadassah School of Medicine, Yale Univ., USA; joined Dept of Neurobiology, Weizmann Inst. of Science 1978, currently Prin. Investigator, Israel, Helen and Norman Asher Professorial Chair in Brain Research and Dir Murray H. & Meyer Grodetsky Center for Research of Higher Brain Functions; Foreign Dir Max Planck Inst. for Medicine, Heidelberg, Germany; Guest Staff mem. Frontier Research Program, RIKEN, Japan; Visiting Prof., Lab. of Neurobiology, Rockefeller Univ. 1985–91; Research Staff mem. IBM Thomas J. Watson Research Center 1986–91; Alice and Joseph Brooks Int. Lecturer in Neurosciences, Harvard Medical School 2002; mem. Israel Acad. of Sciences and Humanities 1998; Koerber's Europe Prize 2000, Dan David Prize (co-recipient) 2004. *Publications:* numerous scientific papers in professional journals on functional optical imaging. *Address:* Department of Neurobiology, Weizmann Institute of Science, PO Box 26, Rehovot 76100, Israel (office). *Telephone:* (8) 9343833 (office). *Fax:* (8) 9342438 (office). *E-mail:* Amiram.Grinvald@weizmann.ac.il (office). *Website:* www.weizmann.ac.il/brain/grinvald (office).

GRIRA, Ridha, DEA, LèsSc; Tunisian politician; b. 21 Aug. 1955, Sousse; m.; two c.; ed Univ. Paris I (Pantheon-Sorbonne), Institut d'études politiques, Paris, Ecole Nationale d'Administration, France; held several sr admin. positions at the Prime Ministry including Special Adviser and Dir Gen. of Public Service; CEO Banque Arabe Tuniso-Libyenne de Développement et de Commerce 1991; fmr Sec. Gen., Ministry of Foreign Affairs; Sec. Gen. of Govt 1992–99; Minister of State-Administered Properties and Land Affairs 1999–2010, Minister of Nat. Defence 2010–11; mem. Rassemblement constitutionnel démocratique (RCD), mem. Cen. Cttee and Chair. RCD El Manar 2 Tunis Div. 1994–2011; Grand Cordon, Ordre de la République, Grand Officier, Ordre du 7 Novembre. *Address:* c/o Ministry of National Defence, blvd Bab Menara, 1030 Tunis, Tunisia.

GRISEZ, Germain, MA, PhL, PhD; American academic; *Professor Emeritus of Christian Ethics, Mount Saint Mary's University;* b. 30 Sept. 1929, University Heights, Ohio; m. Jeannette Selby 1951 (deceased); four c.; m. Mariazinha Rozario 2006; ed John Carroll Univ., Univ. Heights, Ohio, Dominican Coll. of St Thomas Aquinas, River Forest, Ill. and Univ. of Chicago; Asst Prof. to Prof., Georgetown Univ. Washington, DC 1957–72; part-time Lecturer in Medieval Philosophy, Univ. of Virginia, Charlottesville 1961–62; Special Asst to HE Cardinal O'Boyle, Archbishop of Washington 1968–69; consultant (part-time) Archdiocese of Washington 1969–72; Prof. of Philosophy, Campion Coll. Univ. of Regina, Canada 1972–79; Most Rev. Harry J. Flynn Prof. of Christian Ethics, Mount St Mary's Univ., Emmitsburg, Md 1979–2009, Prof. Emer. 2009–; mem. American Catholic Philosophical Asscn; Hon. DD (Mount St Mary's, Emmitsburg) 2009; Pro ecclesia et pontifice Medal 1972; Cardinal Wright Award for service to the Church 1983 and other awards. *Publications:* Contraception and the Natural Law 1964, Abortion: The Myths, the Realities and the Arguments 1970, Beyond the New Morality (with Russell Shaw) 1974, Free Choice (with others) 1976, Life and Death with Liberty Justice (with Joseph M. Boyle, Jr) 1979, The Way of the Lord Jesus, Vol. I, Christian Moral Principles (with others) 1983, Vol. II, Living a Christian Life (with others) 1993, Vol. III, Difficult Moral Questions (with others) 1997, Nuclear Deterrence, Morality and Realism (with J. Finnis and Joseph M. Boyle) 1987, Fulfilment in Christ (with Russell Shaw) 1991, Personal Vocation: God Calls Everyone by Name (with Russell Shaw) 2003, God: A Philosophical Preface to Faith 2005; numerous articles in learned journals. *Leisure interests:* resting and licking my wounds. *Address:* Mount Saint Mary's University, 16300 Old Emmitsburg Road, Emmitsburg, MD 21727-7799, USA (office). *Telephone:* (301) 447-5771 (office). *E-mail:* grisez@msmary.edu (office). *Website:* www.twotlj.org (office).

GRISHAM, John, BS, JD; American writer and lawyer; b. (John Ray Grisham, Jr), 8 Feb. 1955, Jonesboro, Ark.; s. of John Grisham, Sr and Wanda Grisham (née Skidmore); m. Renée Jones 1981; one s. one d.; ed Mississippi State Univ., Univ. of Mississippi Law School; called to the Bar, Miss. 1981; attorney in Southaven, Miss. 1981–90; mem. Miss. House of Reps 1984–90; f. Rebuild The Coast Fund; Lifetime Achievement Award, British Book Awards 2007. *Film screenplay:* The Gingerbread Man 1998. *Publications:* novels: A Time to Kill 1989, The Firm 1991, The Pelican Brief 1992, The Client 1993, The Chamber 1994, The Rainmaker 1995, The Runaway Jury 1996, The Partner 1997, The Street Lawyer 1998, The Testament 1999, The Brethren 2000, A Painted House 2001, Skipping Christmas 2001, The Summons 2002, The King of Torts 2003, Bleachers 2003, The Last Juror 2004, The

Broker 2005, Playing for Pizza 2007, The Appeal 2008, The Associate 2009, Ford County 2009, Theodore Boone: Kid Lawyer 2010, The Confession 2010, The Litigators 2011, Theodore Boone: The Abduction 2011, Calico Joe 2012, Theodore Boone: The Accused 2012, The Racketeer 2012, Sycamore Row 2013; short stories: Ford County 2009; non-fiction: The Wavedancer Benefit: A Tribute to Frank Muller (with Pat Conroy, Stephen King and Peter Straub) 2002, The Innocent Man: Murder and Injustice in a Small Town 2006. *Address:* c/o Doubleday & Co. Inc., 1540 Broadway, New York, NY 10036, USA. *Website:* www.jgrisham.com.

GRISHKOVETS, Yevgeny B.; Russian actor, stage director and playwright; b. 17 Feb. 1967, Kemerovo; m.; one s.; two d.; ed Kemerovo State Univ.; f. and artistic Dir Theatre Lozha 1990; Anti-Booker Prize 1999, Golden Mask Prize 2000, Nat. Triumph Prize 2000. *Films include:* The Stroll, Not by Bread Alone, The First Circle. *Stage productions include:* Winter, How I Have Eaten a Dog, Simultaneously, Notes of a Russian Traveller, Titanic, Po Po. *Publications include:* Gorod 2001, Kak ya syel sobaku 2003, Rubashka 2004, Reki 2005, Planka 2006. *Website:* grishkovets.com.

GROCHOLEWSKI, HE Cardinal Zenon, DCL; Polish ecclesiastic; *Prefect, Congregation for Catholic Education (for Seminaries and Institutes of Study);* b. 11 Oct. 1939, Bródki; s. of Stanisław Grocholewski and Józefa Grocholewski (née Stawińska); ed Archbishop's Seminary, Poznań, Pontifical Gregorian Univ., Rome, Studio Rotale, Rome; ordained priest 1963, worked in Christ the Redeemer Parish, Poznań 1963–66; studies in Rome 1966–72; Official of Supreme Tribunal of Apostolic Signatura 1972–82, Sec. 1982–98, Prefect 1998–99; Lecturer (later Prof.) in Canon Law, Pontifical Gregorian Univ. 1975–99 (currently Grand Chancellor), Pontifical Lateran Univ. 1980–89 and Studio Rotale 1986–98; consecrated Titular Bishop of Agropoli 1982; mem. Pontifical Cttee for Int. Eucharistic Congresses 1989–2001; promoted to Archbishop 1991; Prefect Congregation for Catholic Educ. (for Seminaries and Insts of Study) 1999–2005, 2005–13, 2013–; mem. Congregation for Bishops 1999–, Pontifical Council for Interpretation of Legis. Texts 2000–, Special Council Oceania, Secr. Gen. (Synod of Bishops); Congregation for the Doctrine of the Faith 2001–; cr. Cardinal (Cardinal-Priest of San Nicola in Carcere) 2001; participated in Papal Conclave 2005, 2013; Hon. Citizen of Trenton, NJ 1988, Princeton, NJ 1992, Agropoli, Italy 1992, Levoča, Slovakia 1997; Hon. mem. Pontifical Acad. of St Thomas Aquinas, Rome 2001; Dr hc (Acad. of Catholic Theology, Warsaw) 1998, (Catholic Univ. of Lublin) 1999, (Passau) 2001, (Glasgow) 2001, (Bratislava) 2002, (Catholic Univ. of Buenos Aires) 2002; Polonia *Semper* Fidelis Medal 1998, Grand Medal of St Gorazd, Slovakia 2000. *Publications:* De exclusione indissolubilitatis ex consensu matrimoniali eiusque probatione 1973, Documenta recentoria circa rem matrimonialem et processualem, Vol. I (with I. Gordon) 1977, Vol. II 1980; La filosofía del derecho en las enseñanzas de Juan Pablo II y otros escritos 2001; four books in Slovakian, Hungarian and Polish and co-author of numerous other books. *Leisure interest:* tourism. *Address:* Congregazione per l'Educazione Cattolica, Palazzo delle Congregazioni, Piazza Pio XII 3, 00193 Cittádel Vaticano, Rome (office); Palazzo della Cancelleria 1, 00186 Rome, Italy (home). *Telephone:* (06) 69884167 (office); (06) 69887546 (home). *Fax:* (06) 69884172 (office). *Website:* www.vatican.va/roman_curia/congregations/ccatheduc (office).

GROENING, Matthew (Matt), BA; American writer, cartoonist and screenwriter; b. 15 Feb. 1954, Portland, Ore.; s. of Homer Philip Groening and Margaret Ruth Wiggum; m. Deborah Lee Caplan (divorced 1999); two c.; ed Evergreen State Coll.; cartoonist drawing and writing Life in Hell syndicated weekly comic strip, Sheridan, Ore. 1980–; Pres. Matt Groening Productions, Inc., Los Angeles 1988–, Bongo Entertainment, Inc., Los Angeles 1993–; creator, Simpsons interludes, The Tracey Ullman Show 1987–89; creator and Exec. Producer The Simpsons TV show 1989–; Founder and Publr Bongo Comics Group; Founder and Publr Zongo Comics (including Jimbo 1995, Fleener 1996); cartoonist for TV cartoon Futurama 1999; mem. Int. Acad. of Digital Arts and Sciences 1998–; 11 Emmy Awards, Diamond Distribution Gem Award 1993; George Foster Peabody Award 1997, Reuben Award, Nat. Cartoonist Soc. 2002, British Comedy Award 2004. *Publications:* Love Is Hell 1985, Work Is Hell 1986, School Is Hell 1987, Childhood Is Hell 1988, Akbar and Jeff's Guide to Life 1989, Greetings from Hell 1989, The Postcards That Ate My Brain 1990, The Big Book of Hell 1990, The Simpsons Xmas Book 1990, Greetings from The Simpsons 1990, With Love from Hell 1991, The Simpsons Rainy Day Fun Book 1991, The Simpsons Uncensored Family Album 1991, The Simpsons Student Diary 1991, How to Go to Hell 1991, Maggie Simpson's Alphabet Book 1991, Maggie Simpson's Counting Book 1991, Maggie Simpson's Book of Colors and Shapes 1991, Maggie Simpson's Book of Animals 1991, The Road to Hell 1992, The Simpsons Fun in the Sun Book 1992, Making Faces with the Simpsons 1992, Bart Simpson's Guide to Life 1993, The Simpsons Ultra-Jumbo Rain-Or-Shine Fun Book 1993, Cartooning with the Simpsons 1993, Bongo Comics Group Spectacular 1993, Binky's Guide to Love 1994, Love Is Hell 10th Anniversary Edition 1994, Simpsons Comics Extravaganza 1994, Simpsons Comics Spectacular 1994, Bartman: The Best of the Best 1994, Simpsons Comics Simps-O-Rama 1995, Simpsons Comics Strike Back 1995, Simpsons Comics Wing Ding 1997, The Huge Book of Hell 1997, Bongo Comics, Binky's Guide to Love: A Little Book of Hell 2006, The Simpsons Forever–And Beyond! 2006, Will and Abe's Guide to the Universe 2007. *Address:* Matt Groening Productions, 9720 Wilshire Blvd, 3rd Floor, Beverly Hills, CA 90212, USA (office). *Telephone:* (310) 586-9800 (office).

GROENINK, Rijkman W. J., MBS, DrIur; Dutch banking executive; *Senior Partner, Atlas NV;* b. 25 Aug. 1949, Den Helder; m. Irene Verboon; four c.; ed Utrecht Univ., Univ. of Manchester, UK; joined Amro Bank 1974, apptd Head of Syndicated Loans 1978, Head of Int. Corp. Accounts, Int. Div. 1980–82, Man. Dutch Special Credit Dept 1982–86, Exec. Sr Pres. of Corp. Business 1986–90, mem. Man. Bd 1988–90, mem. Man. Bd ABN AMRO (following merger with ABN) 1990–2007, Chair. Man. Bd 2000–07; currently Sr Partner, Atlas NV, Belgium; Officer, Order of Orange-Nassau; Hon. MBA (Trieste); European Banker of the Year, Frankfurt 2006. *Leisure interests:* skiing, horse riding, farming, tennis, golf. *Address:* Chaussée de la Hulpe 120, 1000 Brussels, Belgium (office); Oud Over 4, 3632 VD Loenen aan den Vecht, Netherlands (home). *Telephone:* (294) 230258 (office); (2) 663-17-56 (Brussels) (office). *Fax:* (294) 230276 (office); (2) 663-17-60 (Brussels) (office). *E-mail:* rg@atlasinvest.eu (office); rijkman.groenink@vrederijk.nl (home).

GROMOV, Aleksey Alekseyevich; Russian diplomatist and government official; *First Deputy Chief of Staff, Presidential Executive Office;* b. 31 May 1960; m.; two c.; ed Moscow State Univ.; joined staff, USSR Ministry of Foreign Affairs 1982, Attaché, Embassy in Prague 1985–88, Sec., Office of the Deputy Minister 1988–91, First Sec., Gen. Office 1991–92, Consul, Russian Consulate Gen., Bratislava, Slovakia 1992–93, Counsellor, Embassy in Bratislava 1993–96; Head of Press Service of Russian Pres. 1996–2000, Press Sec. 2000–08, Deputy Chief of Staff of Presidential Exec. Office 2008–12, First Deputy Chief of Staff 2012–. *Address:* Office of the President, Staraya pl. 4, 103132 Moscow, Russia (office). *Telephone:* (495) 910-07-38 (office). *Fax:* (495) 910-07-38 (office). *Website:* www.kremlin.ru (office).

GROMOV, Col-Gen. Boris Vsevolodovich; Russian army officer and politician; b. 7 Nov. 1943, Saratov; m. 2nd Faina Gromov; two s. two adopted d.; ed Leningrad Gen. Troops School, Frunze Mil. Acad., Gen. Staff Acad.; mem. CPSU 1966–91; Commdr of platoon, co., Bn, Regt, div. 1965–87, Commdr 40 Army in Afghanistan 1987–89, Commdr of troops Kiev Command 1989–90, First Deputy Minister of Internal Affairs of USSR 1990–91, First Deputy Commdr of Armed Forces of CIS 1991–92, First Deputy Minister of Defence of Russia 1992–95; Chief Mil. Expert and Deputy Minister of Foreign Affairs 1995–97; mem. State Duma 1996–99, Chair. Sub-Cttee on Arms Control and Int. Security; Gov. of Moscow Oblast 2000–12; f. war veterans' movt, Fighting Fraternity (later Honour and Homeland) 1997–;; Hero of Soviet Union, Order in the Name of Russia 2004. *Publication:* Memoirs of the Afghan War 1994. *Leisure interests:* tennis, cycling. *Address:* Administration of Moscow Region, 103070 Moscow, Staraya Pl. 6, Russia (office). *Telephone:* (495) 623-24-13; (495) 206-68-62 (office); (495) 206-60-42 (office). *Fax:* (495) 928-98-12 (office). *E-mail:* amo@mosreg.ru (office). *Website:* www.mosreg.ru/gubernator; www.bgromov.ru.

GROMOV, Mikhail Leonidovich (Misha), PhD; Russian/French mathematician and academic; *Permanent Professor, Institut des Hautes Études Scientifiques;* b. 23 Dec. 1943, Boksitogorsk, USSR; s. of Leonid Gromov and Lea Rabinovitz; m. Margarita Gromov 1967; ed Univ. of Leningrad; Asst Prof., Univ. of Leningrad 1967–74; Prof., State Univ. of New York, Stony Brook, USA 1974–81; Prof., Univ. of Paris VI, France 1981–82; Perm. Prof., Institut des Hautes Etudes Scientifiques 1982–; Prof. of Math., Univ. of Maryland 1991–96; Jay Gould Prof. of Math., Courant Inst. of Math. Sciences, New York Univ. 1996–; Foreign Assoc. mem. NAS; Foreign mem. American Acad. of Arts and Sciences, Norwegian Acad. of Science and Letters, Royal Soc. 2011; Foreign Assoc., Acad. des Sciences, Institut de France, mem. 1997; Dr hc (Geneva) 1992; Moscow Math. Soc. Prize 1971, Oswald Veblen Prize for Geometry, American Math. Soc. 1981, Prix Elie Cartan, Acad. des Sciences, Paris 1984, Prix Union des Assurances de Paris 1989, Wolf Prize in Math. 1993, Leroy P. Steele Prize for Seminal Contrib. to Research 1997, Lobachevsky Medal 1997, Balzan Prize for Math. 1999, Kyoto Prize in Math. Sciences 2002, Frederic Esser Nemmers Prize in Math. 2004, Bolyai Prize 2005, Abel Prize 2009. *Publications:* Structures métriques pour les variétés riemanniennes 1981, Manifolds of nonpositive curvature. Progress in Mathematics 61 (co-author) 1985, Partial differential relations. Ergebnisse der Mathematik und ihrer Grenzgebiete 1986; papers in mathematical journals. *Address:* Institut des Hautes Études Scientifiques, 35 route de Chartres, 91440 Bures-sur-Yvette (office); 91 rue de la Santé, 75013 Paris, France (home). *Telephone:* 1-60-92-66-00 (office); 1-45-88-14-42 (home). *Fax:* 1-60-92-66-09 (office). *E-mail:* gromov@ihes.fr (office); mg65@nyu.edu. *Website:* www.ihes.fr/~gromov (office).

GROMYKO, Anatoly Andreyevich; Russian political scientist, historian and painter; *Professor, Moscow State University;* b. 15 April 1932, Borisov; s. of Andrei Gromyko (fmr head of state) and Lidia Dmitrievna Gromyko; m.; two s. one d.; ed Moscow State Inst. of Int. Relations at Ministry of Foreign Affairs (Diploma with Distinction in Foreign Relations and Int. Law); mem. CPSU 1956–91; First Sec., USSR Embassy in London 1961–65; Head of Int. Relations section, Inst. for African Studies, USSR (now Russian) Acad. of Sciences 1966–68, Dir of Inst. 1976–92, Head, Centre for Political Analysis –2010, Head of Section for US Foreign Policy, Inst. for the United States and Canada Studies 1968–73, Pres. Centre for Global and Strategic Studies 1992–94, Sr Researcher, Inst. for Security Studies 2010–; Minister Plenipotentiary, Embassy in Washington, DC 1973–74, in Berlin 1974–76; Prof., Moscow State Univ. 2010–; f. Russian Regional Public Org. 'For the Democratic Legal World Order and Support of the United Nations' 2003; Corresp. mem. Russian Acad. of Sciences 1981; mem. Royal Acad. of Morocco 1990, Russian Acad. of Political Science 1997, Russian Union of Painters 2007; USSR Order of Peoples' Friendship, Order of Peter the Great, First Rank 2007; Dr hc (Leipzig); USSR State Prize 1980, V.V. Vorovskiy State Prize, Italian Acad. Simba Prize. *Publications:* US Congress: Elections, Organization, Powers 1957, The 1,036 Days of President Kennedy 1968, The Foreign Policy of the USA: Lessons and Reality the 60's and 70's 1978, The Conflict in the South of Africa: International Aspects 1979, Africa: Progress, Problems, Prospects 1981, Masks and Sculpture of Sub-Saharan Africa 1984, New Thinking in the Nuclear Age 1984, Kennedy Brothers 1985, Breakthrough (ed.) 1986, Will We Survive? (with others) 1989, Andrei Gromyko: In the Kremlin's Labyrinth 1997, Metamorphoses 2002, The Flight of His Arrow 2009. *Leisure interest:* lawn tennis, painting. *Address:* Institute of Europe, Russian Academy of Sciences, 11/3 B Mokhovaya Str., Moscow 125993, Russia (office). *Telephone:* (495) 692-21-02 (office); (495) 436-85-24 (home). *Fax:* (495) 692-21-02 (office). *E-mail:* alexey@gromyko.ru (office). *Website:* www .gromyko.ru (office).

GRONDIN, Jean, OC, BA, MA, PhD, FRSC; Canadian philosopher and academic; *Professor, Department of Philosophy, University of Montreal;* b. 1955; ed Univ. of Montreal, Univs of Heidelberg and Tübingen, Germany; taught at Université Laval, Quebec City 1982–90, Univ. of Ottawa 1990–91; Prof., Dept of Philosophy, Univ. of Montreal 1991–; Guest Prof., Univs of Nice 1998, Lausanne 1998, 2000, Minsk 2001, 2003, Istituto Italiano per gli Studi Filosofici di Naples 2003, Universidad Centroamericana de San Salvador 2005, Ecole Normale Supérieure de Port-au-Prince 2008, Universidad del Norte Santo Tomás de Aquino (UNSTA) de Tucumán, Argentina 2009; Étienne Gilson Chair of Metaphysics, Univ. of Paris Feb.–March 2013; mem. Editorial Bd Archives de philosophie, Etudes philosophiques, Graduate Faculty Philosophy Journal, Dialogue, Philosophiques 1986–92, Symposium, Ars interpretandi. Giornale di ermeneutica giuridica, Theoros, Divinatio, Internationale Zeitschrift für Philosophie, Phainomena, Internatio-

nales Jahrbuch für Hermeneutik, Heidegger Jahrbuch, Studia Phaenomenologica, Heidegger Studies, Science et Esprit, Analogia, Studium, Vox philosophiae, Analecta hermeneutica, Horizontes filosóficos, Bulletin heideggérien des Archives de philosophie; specialist in the thought of Immanuel Kant, Hans-Georg Gadamer and Martin Heidegger; principal advocate for the work of Gadamer and Paul Ricoeur; prominent in contemporary hermeneutics and metaphysics; has also worked extensively on German idealism, metaphysics and the hermeneutics of Wilhelm Dilthey and Ricoeur; mem. Acad. des lettres et des sciences humaines, RSC 1998; Founding mem. and Vice-Pres. Soc. francophone de Philosophie de la religion 2011; Hon. mem. Fundación Miguel Lillo de Tucumán 2008; Hon. Prof., Pontificia Universidad Católica Argentina Santa Maria de los Buenos Aires 2011; Dr hc (UNSTA de Tucumán) 2008, (Universidad Nacional de Santiago del Estero) 2011; bursary from Alexander von Humboldt Foundation 1988–89, from Killam Foundation 1994–96, Konrad Adenauer Prize, Humboldt Foundation and the RSC 2010, Prix du Québec Léon-Gérin 2011, Killam Prize (Humanities), Canada Council for the Arts 2012, Prix André-Laurendeau 2012. *Publications include:* Hermeneutische Wahrheit? Zum Wahrheitsbegriff Hans-Georg Gadamers 1982 (second edn 1994), Le tournant dans la pensée de Martin Heidegger 1987 (second edn 2011), Kant et le problème de la philosophie: l'a priori 1989, Emmanuel Kant avant-après 1991, L'universalité de l'herméneutique 1993, L'horizon herméneutique de la pensée contemporaine 1993, Sources of Hermeneutics 1995, Hans-Georg Gadamer. Eine Biographie 1999, Introduction à Hans-Georg Gadamers 1999 (trans. as Einführung zu Gadamer 2000), Von Heidegger zu Gadamer 2001, Du sens de la vie 2003, L'herméneutique 2006, La philosophie de la religion 2009, À l'écoute du sens 2011, Introduction to Metaphysics 2012, Paul Ricœur 2013, Du sens des choses. L'idée de la métaphysique 2013; numerous papers in philosophical journals. *Address:* Department of Philosophy, University of Montreal, CP 6128, Succursale Centre-ville, Montreal, PQ H3C 3J7, Canada (office). *Telephone:* (514) 343-6111 (ext. 39896) (office). *Fax:* (514) 343-7899 (office). *E-mail:* jean.grondin@umontreal.ca (office). *Website:* www.philo.umontreal.ca/personnel/professeur/grondin-jean (office); jeangrondin.wordpress.com.

GRÖNEMEYER, Herbert; German actor, singer and composer; b. 12 April 1956, Goettingen; wrote first compositions for Bochum Schauspielhaus Theatre 1974; Musical Dir, actor Schauspielhaus 1975; European Hero 2005, eight ECHO Awards, Single of the Year Award 2003, Album of the Year Award 2008. *Film appearances include:* The Hostage 1975, Daheim unter Fremden 1979, Springtime Symphony 1983, Father and Sons 1988, Control 2007, The American 2010. *Theatre appearances include:* John, Paul, George, Ringo and Bert 1974, Spring Awakening 1976, The Winter's Tale 1978, The Merchant of Venice 1979, Big and Little 1982. *Albums include:* Ocean Orchestra 1978, Grönemeyer 1979, Stand der Dinge 2000, Mensch 2002, Zeit dass sich was dreht (Official 2006 FIFA World Cup Anthem) 2007, Was muss muss 2008. *Address:* ZBF Agentur, 80802 Munich, Germany (office). *Telephone:* (30) 89355081 (office). *E-mail:* groenland@groenemeyer.de. *Website:* www.groenemeyer.de.

GRÖNHOLM, Marcus; Finnish racing driver; b. 5 Feb. 1968, Finland; s. of Ulf Uffe Grönholm; m. Teresa Grönholm; three c.; with team Peugeot 1999–2005, team Ford 2006–07 (retd), came out of retirement to drive in selected rallies; rally debut Finland 1988, Scandinavia Rally Champion 1989, World Rally Championship (WRC) debut Sweden 1995; 16 WRC victories include Sweden 2000, 2002, 2003, 2006, 2007, Australia 2000, 2001, 2002, Finland 2000, 2001, 2002, 2004, 2005, 2006, 2007, Great Britain 2001, 2006, Cyprus 2002, New Zealand 2000, 2002, 2003, 2006, 2007, Argentina 2003, Greece 2007; Finnish junior champion 1988; WRC winner 2000, 2002; total WRC points 259; mem. Mensa Finland. *Address:* Team MGR Finland, Santapellontie 1, Espoo 02780, Finland (office). *Website:* www.mgr .fi (office).

GRONKIEWICZ-WALTZ, Hanna, LLD, PhD; Polish banker and lawyer; *Mayor of Warsaw;* b. 4 Nov. 1952, Warsaw; m.; one d.; ed Warsaw Univ.; mem. of academic staff, Warsaw Univ. 1975–; mem. Solidarity Trade Union 1980; expert on public and econ. law, Polish Parl. 1989; mem. of academic staff, Univ. of Cardinal Wyszy 1990–; Pres. Nat. Bank of Poland 1992–2000; Chair. Faculty, Solidarity Br. 1989–92; ind. cand. in presidential election 1995; Vice-Pres. EBRD 2001–05; mem. of Sejm (Parl.), Platforma Obywatelska Party 2005–; Mayor of Warsaw (first female) 2006–; Dr hc (Marie Curie-Skłodowska Univ., Lublin) 1999; Global Finance magazine award for Best Chair. of a Cen. Bank 1994, 1997, 1998, 1999, The Central European Award 1995, 1998, Życie Gospodarcze Award 1995, The Warsaw Voice Award 1995. *Publications:* Central Bank from Centrally Controlled Economy to Market Oriented Economy: Legal Aspects 1993, Economic Law (co-author) 1996; over 50 works and articles in econ. and financial journals. *Leisure interests:* American literature, classical music. *Address:* Office of the Mayor, pl. Defilad 1, 00-142 Warsaw, Poland (office). *Telephone:* (22) 6567830 (office). *Fax:* (22) 8270635 (office). *E-mail:* biuroprezydenta@warszawa.um.gov.pl (office).

GROS, Francisco Roberto André, BA; Brazilian banker, economist and business executive; *Chairman, Wilson, Sons Ltd;* b. 21 April 1942, Rio de Janeiro; s. of André Paul Adolphe Gros and Dulce Simões Corrêa Gros; m. 1st Sandra Mattmann 1968; m. 2nd Isabel Teixeira Mendes; two s. one d.; ed Woodrow Wilson School of Public and Int. Affairs, Princeton Univ., USA; worked at Kidder, Peabody & Co., USA 1972–75; Dir Multiplic Corretora 1975–77; Supt Gen. and Commr Securities Comm.—CVM 1977–81; Exec. Dir in charge of investment banking activities, Unibanco—Banco de Investimento do Brasil 1981–85; Exec. Dir Nat. Devt Bank 1985–87; Pres. Cen. Bank of Brazil Feb.–May 1987, 1991–92; Pres. and CEO Aracruz SA (eucalyptus pulp exporter) 1987–89; Founding Pnr and CEO BFC Banco SA, Rio de Janeiro 1989–91, 1993; Man. Dir Morgan, Stanley and Co., New York 1993–2000; Pres. and CEO Nat. Devt Bank 2000–01; Pres. and CEO Petroleo Brasileiro SA Jan.–Dec. 2002; Pres. and CEO Fosfertil SA 2003–07, now mem. Bd of Dirs; Pres. and CEO OGX Petroleo e Gas 2007–08, currently Vice-Chair.; Chair. Wilson, Sons Ltd 2009–; mem. Bd of Dirs Lojas Renner SA, Globex Utilidades SA, Energias do Brasil SA, Wellstream Holdings PLC, AGCO Corpn 2006–; Officier, Légion d'honneur, several Brazilian decorations. *Leisure interests:* travel, tennis, fishing. *Address:* Wilson, Sons Ltd, Clarendon House 2, Church Street, Hamilton, HM 11, Bermuda (office). *Website:* www.wilsonsons.com.br/ingles (office).

GROS, François; French biochemist; *Honorary Permanent Secretary, Institut de France;* b. 24 April 1925, Paris; s. of Alexandre Gros and Yvonne Haguenauer; m. 1st Françoise Chasseigne (divorced 1963); m. 2nd Danièle Charpentier 1964; three s.; ed Lycée Pasteur, Neuilly, Univs of Toulouse and Paris, Rockefeller Inst., Univ. of Illinois, USA; joined CNRS 1947, Researcher, Lab. Prof. J. Monod 1955, Head of Research 1959–62, Scientific Dir 1962–; Head, Dept, Inst. de Biologie Physico-chimique 1963–69; Prof., Faculté des Sciences de Paris 1968, Inst. Pasteur 1972, Collège de France (Chair in Cellular Biochemistry) 1973–1996; Dir Inst. Pasteur 1976–81, Dir of Biochemistry Unit 1981, Hon. Dir 1982–; Adviser to Prime Minister 1981–85; mem. EC's CODEST 1984–90; Pres. Asscn Franco-Israélienne pour la recherche scientifique et tech. 1983, Scientific Council of Asscn Française de lutte contre la myopathie 1987–; Scientific Council of Nat. Agency for Research into AIDS 1989–; Chief Ed. Bulletin de la Société de chimie biologique 1964; mem. Nat. Consultative Cttee on the Ethics of Life and Health Sciences 1990–94; mem. EU Ass. on Science and Tech. 1994–97; mem. Inst. de France 1979–, Perm. Sec. 1991–2000, Hon. Perm. Sec. 2001–; mem. Institut Français, Acad. des Sciences, Acad. of Athens, Indian Nat. Acad. Sciences 1990; Assoc. mem. Acad. Royale de Belgique, Russian Acad. of Sciences, Acad. of Medical Science, UK, American Acad. of Arts and Sciences; Grand Officier, Légion d'honneur 2014, Grand Officier, Ordre nat. du Mérite; several foreign decorations; Dr hc (Weizmann Inst., Israel); Gold Medal, Pontifical Acad. of Sciences 1964, Fondation Lacassagne Prize 1968, Charles Léopold Mayer Prize, Acad. des Sciences 1969, Alexander von Humboldt Prize 1990, Jawaharlal Nehru Medal, Indian Nat. Science Acad. 1999. *Publications:* Initiation à la biochimie (with others); Sciences de la vie et société (with others) 1979, Les secrets du gène 1986, La civilisation du gène 1989, L'ingénierie du vivant 1990, Regard sur la biologie contemporaine 1992, Memoires scientifiques – un demi-siècle de Biologie 2003, Une biologie pour le développement 2009, Les mondes nouveaux de la biologie 2012; over 300 articles in scientific journals (molecular biology, gene regulation, cell differentiation). *Leisure interests:* music, drawing. *Address:* Institut de France, 23 quai Conti, 75006 Paris (office); 102 rue de la Tour, 75116 Paris, France (home). *Telephone:* 1-44-41-45-57 (office); 1-45-03-40-91 (home). *Fax:* 1-44-41-43-74 (office). *E-mail:* nathalie.zajdman@academie-sciences.fr (office); francois.gros@academie-sciences.fr (office).

GROS, Philippe, BSc, MSc, PhD, FRSC; Canadian biochemist and academic; *James McGill Professor in Biochemistry, Rosalind and Morris Goodman Cancer Centre, McGill University;* ed Univ. of Montréal, McGill Univ.; post-doctoral studies, Harvard Medical School, MIT, USA; currently James McGill Prof. in Biochemistry, Rosalind and Morris Goodman Cancer Centre, McGill Univ., also Prin. Investigator, Life Sciences Complex; Int. Scholar, Howard Hughes Medical Inst.; Scientific Dir Canadian Genetic Diseases Network; f. three biotechnology firms, Phagetech, RGS Genome, Emerillon Therapeutics; Distinguished Scientist, Canadian Inst. of Health Research; Hon. LLD (St Francis Xavier Univ.), Hon. PhD (Helsinki); Michael Smith Award of Excellence 1994, Prix Wilder-Penfield 2008, Canada Council for the Arts Killam Prize 2009. *Publications:* more than 300 scientific papers. *Address:* Francesco Bellini Life Sciences Building, 3649 prom-enade Sir-William-Osler, Montréal, PQ HG3 0B1, Canada (office). *Telephone:* (514) 398-3747 (office). *E-mail:* philippe.gros@mcgill.ca (office). *Website:* www.mcgill.ca/biochemistry/department/faculty/gros (office).

GROSS, David Jonathan, BSc, PhD; American physicist and academic; *Director, Kavli Institute for Theoretical Physics, University of California, Santa Barbara;* b. 19 Feb. 1941, Washington, DC; m. Jacquelyn Savani; three d.; ed Hebrew Univ., Jerusalem, Israel, Univ. of Calif., Berkeley; Visiting Prof. CERN, Geneva, Switzerland 1968–69, 1993; Asst Prof., Princeton Univ. 1969–71, Assoc. Prof. 1971–73, Prof. 1973–86, Eugene Higgins Prof. of Physics 1986–95, Jones Prof. of Physics 1995–97, Jones Prof. of Physics Emer. 1997–; Visiting Prof. Ecole Normale Supérieure, Paris, France 1983, 1988–89, Hebrew Univ., Jerusalem, Israel 1984, Lawrence Radiation Lab., Berkeley, Calif. 1992; Dir Kavli Inst. for Theoretical Physics, Univ. of Calif., Santa Barbara 1997–, also Prof. 1997–; Frederick W. Gluck Prof. of Theoretical Physics 2001–; Rothschild Prof., Univ. of Cambridge, UK 2007; visiting lecturer at numerous int. univs; Dir Jerusalem Winter School 1999–; Assoc. Ed. Nuclear Physics 1972–; mem. Advisory Bd Inst. for Theoretical Physics 1983–87 (Chair. 1986); Chair. Solvay Scientific Cttee for Physics 2006–; mem. numerous review cttees; Fellow, Alfred P. Sloan Foundation 1970–74, American Physical Soc. 1974–, American Acad. of Arts and Sciences 1985–, NAS 1986–, AAAS 1987–, Indian Acad. of Science 2007–, Indian Nat. Science Acad. 2007–, Third World Acad. of Sciences 2007–; Hon. PhD (Univ. of Montpellier) 2000, (Hebrew Univ., Jerusalem) 2001, (São Paulo Univ.) 2006, (Ohio State Univ.) 2007, (Univ. of the Philippines) 2008, (De La Salle Univ., Manila) 2008; American Physical Soc. J. J. Sakurai Prize 1986, MacArthur Foundation Fellowship Prize 1987, Dirac Medal 1988, Technion-Israel Inst. of Tech. Harvey Prize 2000, European Physical Soc. High Energy and Particle Physics Prize 2003, Grande Médaille d'Or (France) 2004, Nobel Prize in Physics (co-recipient) 2004. *Address:* Kavli Institute for Theoretical Physics, University of California, Santa Barbara, Kohn Hall, 1219, Santa Barbara, CA 93106, USA (office). *Telephone:* (805) 893-7337 (office). *Fax:* (805) 893-2431 (office). *E-mail:* gross@kitp.ucsb.edu (office). *Website:* www.physics.ucsb.edu (office); www.kitp.ucsb.edu (office).

GROSS, William (Bill) H., MBA; American investment company executive; *Chief Investment Officer, Pacific Investment Management Company (PIMCO);* b. 1944, Middletown, Ohio; ed Duke Univ., Univ. of California, Los Angeles; served in USN; briefly played blackjack professionally in Las Vegas; Co-founder Pacific Invest-ment Management (PIMCO), Newport Beach, Calif. 1971, currently Chief Investment Officer managing PIMCO's Total Return Fund and several smaller funds; ranked by Forbes magazine amongst The World's Most Powerful People (59th) 2010, (54th) 2011, (51st) 2012, (55th) 2013. *Achievements include:* prom-inent philatelist, became third person (after Robert Zoellner in 1990s and Benjamin K. Miller pre-1925) to form complete collection of 19th century US postage stamps Nov. 2005; auctioned British, Scandinavian and Finnish philatelic collections to make various charitable donations 2005–08. *Publications:* Every-thing You've Heard About Investing Is Wrong! 1997, Bill Gross on Investing 1998. *Address:* Pacific Investment Management Company, LLC, 840 Newport Center Drive, Suite 100, Newport Beach, CA 92660, USA (office). *Telephone:* (949) 720-6000 (office). *Fax:* (949) 720-1376 (office). *E-mail:* presscenter@pimco.com (office). *Website:* www.pimco.com (office).

GROSSART, Sir Angus McFarlane McLeod, Kt, CBE, LLD, DLitt, D.L., FRSE; British merchant banker, lawyer and company director; *Chairman, Noble Grossart Ltd;* b. 6 April 1937; s. of William John White Grossart and Mary Hay Gardiner; m. Gay Thomson 1978; one d.; ed Glasgow Acad. and Gasgow Univ.; mem. Faculty of Advocates 1963; practised at Scottish Bar 1963–69; Chair. Noble Grossart Ltd Merchant Bankers, Edin. 1969–, Chair. 1990–; Chair. Scottish Investment Trust PLC 1975–2003; mem. Bd of Dirs of numerous cos including Royal Bank of Scotland PLC 1982– (Vice-Chair. 1996–), Scottish and Newcastle 1998–, Trinity Mirror PLC 1998–; Chair. Bd of Trustees Nat. Galleries of Scotland 1988–97; Deputy Chair. and Trustee Nat. Heritage Memorial Fund 1999–2005; Chair. Nat. Museum of Scotland 2006–12; Chair. Burrell Renaissance 2013–, and other public and charitable appointments; Hon. QC 2011; Hon. LLD (Glasgow) 1985, (Aberdeen) 2006, Hon. DBA (Strathclyde) 1998, Hon. DLitt (St Andrews) 2004; Livingstone Captain of Industry Award 1990, Lord Provost of Glasgow Award for public service 1994, Paolozzi Gold Medal 1997, Walpole Medal of Excellence 2003, Nat. Museum of Scotland Gold Medal. *Leisure interests:* golf, the applied and decorative arts, Scottish castle restoration. *Address:* Noble Grossart Ltd, 48 Queen Street, Edinburgh, EH2 3NR, Scotland (office). *Telephone:* (131) 226-7011 (office). *Fax:* (131) 226-6032 (office). *E-mail:* fionacairns@noblegrossart .co.uk (office).

GROSSER, Alfred; French academic, writer and journalist; *Professor Emeritus, Institut d'études politiques;* b. 1 Feb. 1925, Frankfurt, Germany; s. of Paul Grosser and Lily Grosser (née Rosenthal); m. Anne-Marie Jourcin 1959; four s.; ed Univs of Aix en Provence and Paris; Asst Dir UNESCO Office in Germany 1950–51; Asst Prof., Univ. of Paris 1951–55; Lecturer, later Prof., Inst. d'études politiques, Paris 1954, Prof. Emer. 1992–; Dir Studies and Research, Fondation nat. des Sciences politiques 1956–92; with Ecole des hautes études commerciales 1961–66, 1986–88, with Ecole Polytechnique 1974–95; Visiting Prof., Bologna Center, Johns Hopkins Univ. 1955–69, Stanford Univ. 1964–67; political columnist, La Croix 1955–65, 1984–, Le Monde 1965–94, Ouest-France 1973–, L'Expansion 1979–89; Pres. Centre d'information et de recherche sur l'Allemagne contemporaine 1982–, Eurocréation 1986–92 (Hon. Pres. 1992–); Vice-Pres. Int. Political Science Asscn 1970–73; mem. Bd L'Express 1998–2003; Grosses Verdienstkreuz mit Stern 1995 und Schulterband 2003, Grand Officier, Légion d'honneur 2001, Grand Croix, Ordre nat. du Mérite 2013; Dr hc (Univ. of Aston, UK) 2001, (European Univ. of Humanities, Belarus) 2001; Peace Prize, Union of German Publrs 1975, Grand Prix, Acad. des Sciences Morales et Politiques 1998, Prize "für das Lebenswerk", German newspapers asscn 2013. *Publications include:* L'Allemagne de l'Occident 1953, La démocratie de Bonn 1958, Hitler, la presse et la naissance d'une dictature 1959, La Quatrième République et sa politique extérieure 1961, La politique extérieure de la Ve République 1965, Au nom de quoi? Fondements d'une morale politique 1969, L'Allemagne de notre temps 1970, Les Occidentaux: Les pays d'Europe et les Etats Unis depuis la guerre 1978, Affaires extérieures: la politique de la France 1944–84, 1984 (updated 1989), L'Allemagne en Occident 1985, Mit Deutschen streiten 1987, Vernunft und Gewalt. Die französische Revolution und das deutsche Grundgesetz heute 1989, Le crime et la mémoire 1989 (revised 1991), Mein Deutschland 1993, Les identités difficiles 1996, Une Vie de Français (memoirs) 1997, Deutschland in Europa 1998, Les fruits de leur arbre: regard athée sur les Chrétiens 2001, L'Allemagne de Berlin 2002, La France, semblable et différente 2005, Die Früchte ihres Baumes 2005, La Joie et la Mort – Bilan d'une vie 2011, Die Freude und der Tod. Eine Lebensbilanz 2011. *Leisure interest:* music. *Address:* 8 rue Dupleix, 75015 Paris, France. *Telephone:* 1-43-06-41-82. *E-mail:* grosser.alfred@wanadoo.fr.

GROSSMAN, David, BA; Israeli writer; b. 25 Jan. 1954, Jerusalem; m. Michal Grossman; two s. (one deceased) one d.; ed Hebrew Univ., Jerusalem; Chevalier, Ordre des Artes et Lettres; Dr hc (KU Leuven) 2007; Children's Literature Prize, Ministry of Educ. 1983, Prime Minister's Hebrew Literature Prize 1984, Israeli Publishers' Asscn Prize for Best Novel 1985, Vallombrosa Prize (Italy) 1989, Nelly Sachs Prize (Germany) 1992, Prix Eliette von Karajan (Austria), Premio Grinzane (Italy), Premio Mondelo (Italy), Vittorio de Sica Prize (Italy), Marsh Award for Children's Literature in Translation (UK), Juliet Club Prize (Italy), Buxtehuder Bulle (Germany), Sapir Prize (Israel), Italian Critics Prize (Italy), Nelly Sachs Prize (Germany), Mane Sperber Prize (Austria), Bernstein Prize (Israel), Bialik Prize (Israel), Emet Prize (Israel) 2007, Friedenspreis des Deutschen Buchhandels (Germany) 2010, Prix Medicis (France) 2011. *Publications:* Hiyukh ha-gedi (trans. as The Smile of the Lamb) 1983, 'Ayen 'erekh–ahavah (trans. as See Under: Love) 1986, Ha-Zeman ha-tsahov (non-fiction, trans. as The Yellow Wind) 1987, Gan Riki: Mahazeh bi-shete ma'arakhot (play, trans. as Rikki's Kindergarten) 1988, Sefer hakikduk hapnimi (trans. as The Book of Intimate Grammar) 1991, Hanochachim hanifkadim (non-fiction, trans. as Sleeping on a Wire: Conversa-tions with Palestinians in Israel) 1992, The Zigzag Kid (in trans.) (Premio Mondelo, Premio Grinzane), Duel (in trans.), Be My Knife (in trans.) 2002, Someone to Run With (in trans.) 2003, Death as a Way of Life: Dispatches from Jerusalem (non-fiction, in trans.) 2003, Her Body Knows (novel, in trans.), Lovers and Strangers (novel, in trans.) 2005, Dvash Arayiot (trans. as Lion's Honey: The Myth of Samson) 2005, Writing in the Dark (essays in trans.) 2009, To the End of the Land (novel, in trans.) (Jewish Quarterly-Wingate Literary Prize 2011) 2010; also short stories, children's books, contribs to periodicals. *Address:* c/o Deborah Harris Agency, PO Box 8528, Jerusalem 91083, Israel (office). *E-mail:* deborah@thedeborahharrisagency.com (office).

GROSSMAN, Marc, BA, MSc; American diplomatist, government official and business executive; *Vice-Chairman, The Cohen Group;* b. Los Angeles, Calif.; ed Univ. of California, Santa Barbara, London School of Econs, UK; joined US Foreign Service 1976, overseas assignments included Political Officer, Mission to NATO, Brussels, Embassy in Budapest, various positions at Bureau of Near Eastern and South Asian Affairs, Dept of State; fmr Deputy Special Adviser to Pres. Carter; Deputy Dir of Pvt. Office of Sec.-Gen. of NATO Lord Carrington 1984–86; Exec. Asst to Deputy Sec. of State John C. Whitehead 1986–89; Prin. Deputy Asst Sec. of State for Political and Mil. Affairs 1989–93; Special Asst to Sec. of State and Exec. Sec. Dept of State 1993–94; Amb. to Turkey 1994–87; Asst Sec. of State for European Affairs 1997–2000; Dir-Gen. of Foreign Service and Dir of Human Resources 2000–01; Under-Sec. of State for Political Affairs 2001–05 (retd); Vice-Chair. The Cohen Group, Washington, DC 2005–11, 2013–; Special US Rep. for Afghanistan and Pakistan 2011–12. *Address:* The Cohen Group, 500 Eighth Street NW, Suite 200, Washington, DC 20004, USA (office). *Telephone:* (202) 863-7248 (office). *Fax:* (202) 863-7809 (office). *E-mail:* mgrossman@cohengroup.net (office). *Website:* www.cohengroup.net (office).

GROSSMAN, Mindy F.; American business executive; *CEO, HSN Inc.;* m.; one d.; ed George Washington Univ.; began career in menswear industry 1977; Vice-Pres. of Sales and Merchandising, Tommy Hilfiger Corpn 1987–91, Sr Vice-Pres. of Menswear, Warnaco Inc. 1991–94, Vice-Pres. of New Business, Polo Ralph Lauren Corpn 1994–95, Pres. and CEO Polo Jeans Co. 1995–2000; Vice-Pres. and Head of Global Apparel Business, Nike Inc. 2000–06; CEO of Retailing Div., IAC 2006–08, mem. Bd of Dirs and CEO HSN Inc. (fmrly IAC Retailing) 2008–; mem. Bd of Dirs Nat. Retail Fed., East Harlem School; Chair. Exec. Women in Fashion Advisory Bd, Fashion Inst. of Tech.; mem. Advisory Bd, J. Baker School of Retail at the Wharton School of Business; ranked by Forbes magazine amongst 100 Most Powerful Women (97th) 2009, (89th) 2011, (96th) 2012, (89th) 2013. *Address:* HSN Inc., 1 HSN Drive, St Petersburg, FL 33729, USA (office). *Telephone:* (727) 872-1000 (office). *Website:* www.hsni.com (office).

GROSSMANN, Jürgen R., Dr-Ing; German steel industry executive; b. 4 March 1952, Mülheim an der Ruhr; m. Dagmar Grossmann Sikorski 1985; three c.; ed Tech. Univs of Clausthal and Berlin, Göttingen Univ., Purdue Univ., USA; various man. positions at Klöckner-Werke AG Group 1980–93, mem. Exec. Bd 1991–93; Man. Pnr, Georgsmarienhütte GmbH 1993–97, Owner and Man. Dir Georgsmar-ienhütte Holding GmbH 1997–2006, Owner 2007–; Pres. and CEO RWE AG 2007–12; Chair. Supervisory Bd SURTECO AG; mem. Supervisory Bd BATIG Gesellschaft für Beteiligungen mbH, British American Tobacco (Industrie) GmbH, British American Tobacco (Germany) GmbH, Deutsche Bahn AG, Volkswagen AG, Hanover Acceptances Ltd; Bundesverdienstkreuz 1. Klasse; Dr hc (Purdue Univ., USA); Courage Award 1997, Prize of Lower Saxony 2001. *Address:* Georgsmar-ienhütte Holding GmbH, Elbchaussee 189, 22605 Hamburg, Germany (office). *E-mail:* juergen.grossmann@gmh-holding.de (office). *Website:* www.gmh-gruppe .de (office).

GROVE, Andrew (Andy) S., PhD; American engineer and business executive; *Senior Advisor, Intel Corporation;* b. 2 Sept. 1936, Budapest, Hungary; m. Eva Grove; two c.; ed City Coll. of New York and Univ. of California, Berkeley; with Fairchild Instrument & Camera Co. 1963–67; Pres. and COO Intel Corpn, Santa Clara, Calif. 1967–87, Pres. 1987–98, CEO 1987–98, Chair. 1998–2005, Sr Advisor 2005–; Lecturer, Grad. School of Business Stanford Univ.; Overseer, Int. Rescue Cttee; mem. Nat. Acad. of Eng; Fellow, IEEE; mem. Bd of Dirs Prostate Cancer Foundation; f. Grove Foundation; Nat. Chair of the Campaign, Univ. of Calif., San Francisco; Hon. DSc (City Coll. of NY) 1985, Hon. DEng (Worcester Polytechnic Inst.) 1989, Hon. LLD (Harvard Univ.) 2000; American Inst. of Chemists Award 1960, IEEE Achievement Award 1966, IEEE J.J. Ebers Award 1974, Certificate of Merit, Franklin Inst. 1975, Nat. Acad. of Eng 1979, Townsend Harris Medal, City Coll. of New York 1980, Hall of Fame Award, Information Industries Asscn 1984, Council of 100 Members, Ariz. State Univ. 1984, IEEE Eng Leadership Recogni-tion Award 1987, Enterprise Award, Business and Professional Advertising Asscn 1987, George Washington Award, American-Hungarian Foundation 1990, Citizen of the Year Award, World Forum of Silicon Valley 1993, Exec. of the Year Award, Univ. of Ariz. 1993, American Eng Asscn (AEA) Medal of Achievement Award 1993, Heinz Foundation Tech. Award 1995, John von Neumann Medal, American Hungarian Asscn 1995, Steinman Medal, City Coll. of New York 1995, Statesman of the Year Award, Harvard Business School 1996, Int. Achievement Award, World Trade Club 1996, IEEE 1997 Computer Entrepreneur Award 1997, Cinema Digital Technologies Award, Int. Film Festival 1997, CEO of the Year Award, CEO Magazine 1997, Tech. Leader of the Year Award, Industry Week 1997, Man of the Year, Time Magazine 1997, Distinguished Exec. of the Year, Acad. of Man. 1998, IEEE Medal of Honor 2000, Lifetime Achievement Award, Strategic Man. Soc. 2001, Most Influential Business Person of the Last Twenty-Five Years, Wharton School of Business and Nightly Business Report 2004, Ernest C. Arbuckle Award, Stanford Univ. Graduate School of Business 2004. *Publications:* High Output Management 1983, One-on-One With Andy Grove 1987, Only the Paranoid Survive 1996, Swimming Across (autobiography) 2001, Strategic Dynamics: Concepts and Cases (with Robert A. Burgelman) 2005. *Address:* Intel Corporation, PO Box 58119, 2200 Mission College Boulevard, Santa Clara, CA 95052, USA (office). *Telephone:* (408) 765-1904 (office). *Fax:* (408) 765-1739 (office). *Website:* www.intel.com (office).

GROYS, Boris Efimovich, PhD; Russian art critic, philosopher and academic; *Professor of Russian and Slavic Studies, New York University;* b. 19 March 1947, Berlin, Germany; ed high school in Leningrad, Univ. of Leningrad, Univ. of Münster, Germany; worked as research fellow at various scientific insts in Leningrad from 1971; Research Fellow, Inst. of Structural and Applied Linguis-tics, Univ. of Moscow 1976–81; participated in unofficial cultural scenes of Moscow and Leningrad, publishing in '37', 'Chasy' and other samizdat magazines; published essay 'Moscow Romantic Conceptualism' in art magazine A-YA in which he coined the term 'Moscow Conceptualism' 1979; emigrated to FRG to pursue various scholarships 1981; currently Prof. of Russian and Slavic Studies, New York Univ.; Sr Research Fellow, Acad. of Design, Karlsruhe, Germany; Prof. of Aesthetics, Art History and Media Theory, Acad. of Design/Centre for Art and Media Tech. (HfG/ZKM), Karlsruhe; Visiting Prof. at several univs in USA and Europe, including Univ. of Pennsylvania and Univ. of Southern California; mem. Asscn Internationale des Critiques d'Art; fmr Fellow, Internationales Forschungs-zentrum Kulturwissenschaften, Harvard Univ. Art Museum, Univ. of Pittsburg; Rector Acad. of Fine Arts, Vienna 2001; headed research programme Post-Communist Condition, in co-operation with Univ. of Karlsruhe and Fed. Cultural Foundation of Germany 2003–04; Andrei Belyi Prize, Frank Jewett Mather Award for Art Criticism from the College Art Asscn 2009. *Publications include:* The Total Art of Stalinism 1992, Dream Factory Communism 2004, Ilya Kabakov: The Man Who Flew into Space from His Apartment 2006, The Total Enlightenment: Conceptual Art in Moscow 1960–1990 2008, Art Power 2008, Wait to Wait – A Conversation (with Andro Wekua) 2009, Going Public 2010, History Becomes Form: Moscow Conceptualism 2010, The Communist Postscript 2010; video: Thinking in Loop: Three Videos on Iconoclasm, Ritual and Immortality 2008; more than 150 articles in several languages on modern and contemporary art and Russian art and intellectual history. *Address:* Department of Art History, New York University, 100 Washington Square East, Silver 303, New York, NY 10003, USA (office). *Telephone:* (212) 998-8180 (office). *E-mail:* groys@aol.com (office). *Website:* arthistory.as.nyu.edu/object/borisgroys.html (office); www.borisgroys .com.

GRUBBS, Robert H., PhD; American chemist and academic; *Victor and Elizabeth Atkins Professor of Chemistry, California Institute of Technology;* b. 27 Feb. 1942, nr Possum Trot, Ky; s. of Henry Howard Grubbs and Faye Atwood; ed Univ. of Florida and Columbia Univ., New York; Faculty Fellow, Columbia Univ. 1965–66, NIH Trainee 1966–68; NIH Postdoctoral Fellow, Stanford Univ., Calif. 1968–69; Asst Prof., Michigan State Univ. East Lansing 1969–73, Assoc. Prof. 1973–78; Prof. of Chem., Calif. Inst. of Tech., Pasadena 1978–90, Victor and Elizabeth Atkins Prof. of Chem. 1990–; Christensen Visiting Fellow, St Catherine's Coll., Oxford, UK 1997, Rayson Huany Visiting Lectureship in Chem., Hong Kong 2001; Tarrant Visiting Prof. of Organic Chem., Univ. of Florida, Gainesville 2004; mem. NRC Cttee Basic Scientific Research, US Army 1981–; mem. Advisory Panel, NSF ARI Program 1996–; mem. Alexander von Humbolt Asscn of America 1999–2000; mem. Advisory Bd, Center on Polymer Interfaces and Macromolecular Assemblies 1999–2000, Advanced Synthesis and Catalysis 2000–; Advisory Ed. Journal of Polymer Science, Polymer Chemistry 1999–; mem. Editorial Advisory Bd Catalysis Technology 1996–, Accounts of Chemical Research 2000–; mem. ACS 1964–; Fellow, American Acad. of Arts and Sciences 1994; Hon. MRIA (Science Section) 1999; Hon. Prof., Shanghai Inst. of Organic Chem., Chinese Acad. of Sciences 2001; Alfred P. Sloan Fellow 1974–76, Alexander von Humbolt Fellowship 1975, The Camille and Henry Dreyfus Teacher-Scholar Award 1975–78, ACS Nat. Award in Organometallic Chem. 1988, Arthur C. Cope Scholar Award 1990, George Willard Wheland Award, Univ. of Chicago 1992, ACS Award in Polymer Chem., Mobil Chemical Co. 1995, Nagoya Medal of Organic Chem. 1997, Fluka Prize – Reagent of the Year 1998, Mack Memorial Award, Ohio State Univ. 1999, Benjamin Franklin Medal in Chem., The Franklin Inst. 2000, Herman F. Mark Polymer Chem. Award, ACS POLY-The Dow Chemical Co. Foundation 2000, Cliff S. Hamilton Award, Univ. of Nebraska, Lincoln 2000, Herbert C. Brown Award for Creative Research in Synthetic Methods, ACS-Aldrich Chemical Co. and The Purdue Borane Research Fund 2001, Prelog Lecturer, ETH, Zürich 2001, Werner E. Bachmann Memorial Lecturer, Univ. of Michigan, Ann Arbor 2002, Edward Frankland Prize and Lecturer, Royal Soc. of Chem. 2002, Arthur C. Cope Award, ACS Div. of Organic Chem. 2002, ACS Award for Creative Research in Homogenous or Heterogeneous Catalysis, Shell Oil Foundation 2003, Richard C. Tolman Medal, Southern Calif. Section of ACS 2003, Pauling Award Medal, Oregon, Portland, Puget Sound Sections of ACS 2003, ACS Tetrahedron Prize for Creativity in Organic Chem. 2003, Priestly Lecturer, Pennsylvania State Univ. 2003, Ralph Hirschmann Lecturer, Univ. of Wisconsin, Madison 2003, Linus Pauling Distinguished Lecturer, Oregon State Univ. 2003, Gilman Lecturer, Iowa State Univ. 2003, Karabatsos Lecturer, Michigan State Univ. 2003, Nobel Prize for Chem. (jtly) 2005. *Publications:* more than 350 publs in scientific journals on design, synthesis and mechanistic studies of complexes that catalyse useful organic transformations. *Address:* Division of Chemistry and Chemical Engineering, California Institute of Technology, M/C 127-72, Pasadena, CA 91125, USA (office). *Telephone:* (626) 395-6003 (office). *Fax:* (626) 564-9297 (office). *E-mail:* rhg@caltech.edu (office). *Website:* www.chemistry.caltech.edu (office).

GRUBE, Rüdiger, BEng, DSci; German business executive; *Chairman of the Management Board and CEO, Deutsche Bahn AG;* b. 2 Aug. 1951, Hamburg; ed Hamburg Univ.; teaching post, Production and Eng. Dept, Univ. of Hamburg 1981–86; joined MMB (Messerschmitt-Bölkow-Blohm) GmbH (later Daimler-Benz Aerospace, DASA), Munich 1989, Head of Marketing, Sales and Int. Relations, Energy and Industrial Tech. Div. 1989–90, Head of Man. Office, Deutsche Airbus GmbH, Hamburg 1990–92, Head of Munich-Ottobrunn site, Daimler-Benz Aero-space AG, Munich 1992–94, Head of Aviation Staff Unit 1994–95, Dir of Corp. Planning and Tech., Deutsche Aerospace AG, Munich 1995, Sr Vice-Pres. and Head of Corp. Strategy, Daimler-Benz AG (later DaimlerChrysler AG) 1996–2000, mem. Man. Bd, responsible for corp. devt and all NE Asia activities and for group's entire global IT operations 2001–09, Sr Vice-Pres. for Corp. Devt 2000–09, also Chair. Supervisory Bd DaimlerChrysler Off-Highway GmbH, Chair. Daimler-Chrysler China Ltd, Beijing, Vice-Chair. Beijing Benz DaimlerChrysler Automo-tive (BBDC-A), mem. Advisory Bd DaimlerChrysler Fleetboard, DaimlerChrysler Aviation, mem. Supervisory Bd DaimlerChrysler Financial Services AG; Chair. (non-exec.) European Aeronautic Defence and Space Co. (EADS) NV 2004–09, also Chair. EADS Participations BV; Chair. Man. Bd and CEO Deutsche Bahn AG 2009–, concurrently Chair. Man. Bd DB Mobility Logistics AG; fmr Chair. Supervisory Bd MTU Friedrichshafen GmbH (now Tognum AG); mem. Bd of Dirs McLaren Group Ltd; mem. Supervisory Bd Hamburg Port Authority (HPA GmbH); fmr mem. Admin. Bd Hyundai Motor Co., Seoul, S Korea, Mitsubishi Motors Corpn, Tokyo, Japan. *Address:* Deutsche Bahn AG, Potsdamer Platz 2, 10785 Berlin, Germany (office). *Telephone:* (30) 297-61131 (office). *Fax:* (30) 297-61919 (office). *E-mail:* info@deutschebahn.com (office). *Website:* www .deutschebahn.com (office); www.bahn.de (office).

GRUBISICH, José Carlos, BEng, MBA; Brazilian business executive; *CEO, ETH Bioenergia SA;* b. 1957; m.; two c.; ed Escola Superior de Química Osvaldo Cruz, INSEAD, France; various man., marketing and advertising roles with Grupo Rhône Poulenc, Brazil and other countries, including Pres. Rhodia Brazil and Latin America 1997–2000, mem. Exec. Cttee and Global Vice Pres. 2000–02; Pres. Grupo Odebrecht 2002–; CEO Braskem SA (fmrly Copene Petroquímica do Nordeste SA) 2002–08, ETH Bioenergia SA 2008–; mem. Bd of Dirs UNICA Brazilian Sugarcane Industry Asscn. *Address:* ETH Bioenergia SA, Av. Nações Unidas, 8501, 26° andar, Edifício Eldorado Business Tower, 05425-070 São Paulo, Brazil (office). *Telephone:* 3096-8000 (office). *Website:* www.eth.com (office).

GRUBJEŠIĆ, Suzana; Serbian politician; b. 29 Jan. 1963, Sombor; ed Faculty of Political Sciences, Belgrade; Project Man., European Movt in Serbia 1996–97; Co-founder and Project Man. G17 Plus 1997–2003, Exec. Dir G17 Plus 2003–08, Vice-Pres. and Whip 2007–; mem. (G17 Plus) Serbian Parl. 2003–12, mem. Admin. Cttee and Cttee for European Integration, Head of Serbian Del. to Parl. Ass. of OSCE, Deputy Whip of Parl. Group United Regions of Serbia 2011–12; Deputy Prime Minister, responsible for European Integration 2012–13. *Address:* c/o Office of the Prime Minister, 11000 Belgrade, Nemanjina 11, Serbia. *E-mail:* kabinetpremijera@gov.rs.

GRUDZINSKI, Przemyslaw, PhD; Polish diplomatist, academic and writer; *Permanent Representative, Organisation for Economic Co-operation and Develop-*

ment; b. 30 Oct. 1950, Toruń; m.; two d.; ed Univ. of Nicolaus Copernicus, Toruń, Inst. of History, Polish Acad. of Sciences, Warsaw; Lecturer then Reader, Inst. of History, Polish Acad. of Sciences 1976–96; Adviser to Deputy Minister of Nat. Defence 1990; Dir Bureau of Research and Dir-Gen. Sejm (Parl.) 1991–92; Deputy Minister of Nat. Defence 1992–93; Prof., Marshall European Centre for Security Studies, Garmisch, Germany 1994–97, Coll. of Int. and Security Studies 2005; Under-Sec. of State, Ministry of Foreign Affairs 1997–2000, 2008–09; Amb. to USA 2000–05; Perm. Rep. to OSCE, Vienna 2009–; mem. Solidarity Movt 1980s; Founder-mem. Euro-Atlantic Asscn 1994, Council on Foreign Policy, Warsaw 1996; Fellow, American Council of Learned Socs 1978–80; Fulbright Fellow, Princeton Univ. 1988, Visiting Fellow 1978–80, 1988; Visiting Fellow, Univ. of Southern California, UCLA 1989. *Publications include:* The Future of Europe in the Ideas of Franklin D. Roosevelt 1933–1945 1987, Scientists and Barbarians: The Nuclear Policy of the United States 1939–45 1987, Theology of the Bomb: The Origins of Nuclear Deterrence Vols 1–3 1988, A Critical Approach to European Security: Identity and Institutions 1999, Państwo inteligentne. Polska w poszukiwaniu międzynarodowej roli 2008; numerous articles in professional journals. *Leisure interests:* walking, mountains. *Address:* Permanent Representative of Poland to the UN Office and OSCE in Vienna, Hietzinger Hauptstraße 42 C, 1130 Vienna, Austria (office). *E-mail:* wieden.onz.obwe.sekretariat@msz.gov.pl (office). *Website:* www.wiedenosce.polemb.net (office).

GRUEVSKI, Nikola, BEcons, MSc; Macedonian lawyer, economist and politician; *Prime Minister;* b. 31 Aug. 1970, Skopje; s. of Talo Gruevski and Nadezda Gruevski; m. Borkica Gruevska; one d.; ed SS Cyril and Methodius Univ., Skopje, St Clement Ohrid Univ., Bitola; with Credit Dept, Foreign Dept, then Currency Dealing, Balkanska Banka Skopje 1994–98, Liquidity, Plan, Analyses and Securities Dept 1995–96; with Metal Bank, Frankfurt, Germany 1996–97, MG Finance PLC, London, UK 1997, Flemings Private Asset Man. Ltd, London 1997–98; Minister without Portfolio, then Minister of Trade 1998–99; Minister of Finance 1999–2002; Pres. Econ. Council 2000–02; mem. Macedonian Parl. 2002–06; Adviser, Ministry of Finance, Serbia 2003; Pres., Internal Macedonian Revolutionary Org.-Democratic Party for Macedonian Nat. Unity (VMRO-DPMNE) 2003–; Prime Minister 2006–; Vice-Pres. Euro-Atlantic Council of the Repub. of Macedonia 2005–06; Pres. Broker's Asscn of Macedonia 1998, State Securities and Exchange Comm. 2000–02, Parl. Cttee for Co-operation with European Parl. 2002–04; financial affairs commentator, MTM TV, Skopje 1998–. *Publications:* The Macedonian Economy at a Crossroad: On the Way to a Healthier Economy 1998, The Way Out: Foreign Direct Investment, Economic Development and Employment 2007; numerous articles on econ. and political issues. *Leisure interests:* boxing, basketball, football. *Address:* Office of the Prime Minister, 1000 Skopje, Ilindenska bb, Former Yugoslav Republic of Macedonia (office). *Telephone:* (2) 3115389 (office). *Fax:* (2) 3112561 (office). *E-mail:* primeminister@primeminister.gov.mk (office). *Website:* www.vlada.mk (office).

GRUMBACH, Melvin Malcolm, MD, FAAP; American physician and academic; *Edward B. Shaw Distinguished Professor Emeritus of Pediatrics, School of Medicine, University of California, San Francisco;* b. 21 Dec. 1925, New York, NY; s. of Emanuel Grumbach and Adele Grumbach (née Weil); m. Madeleine F. Butt 1951; three s.; ed Columbia Coll. and Columbia Univ. Coll. of Physicians and Surgeons; Resident in Pediatrics, Babies' Hosp., Presbyterian Hosp., New York 1949–51; Visiting Fellow, Oak Ridge Inst. of Nuclear Studies 1952; Postdoctoral Fellow, Asst in Pediatrics, Johns Hopkins School of Medicine 1953–55; mem. Faculty, Columbia Univ. Coll. of Physicians and Surgeons 1955–65; Asst Attending Pediatrician, subsequently Assoc. Prof. of Pediatrics, Head of Pediatric Endocrine Div. and Postdoctoral Training Program in Pediatric Endocrinology, Babies' Hosp. and Vanderbilt Clinic, Columbia-Presbyterian Medical Center 1955–65; Prof. of Pediatrics and Chair. Dept, School of Medicine, Univ. of California, San Francisco (UCSF) 1966–86, first Edward B. Shaw Distinguished Prof. of Pediatrics 1983–, now Prof. Emer., Acting Dir Lab. of Molecular Endocrinology 1987–89; Dir Pediatric Service Univ. of Calif. Hosps 1966–86; Pres. Asscn of Pediatric Dept Chairmen 1973–75, Lawson Wilkins Pediatric Endocrine Soc. 1975–76, Western Soc. for Pediatric Research 1978–79, Endocrine Soc. 1981–82, American Pediatric Soc. 1989–90; Exec. Cttee Int. Soc. of Endocrinology 1984–92 (Hon. Pres. 2000–04); mem. Inst. of Medicine of NAS 1983–, NAS 1995–, Johns Hopkins Soc. of Scholars 2002–; Fellow, American Acad. of Pediatrics, AAAS 1985–, American Acad. of Arts and Sciences 1995–; Founding Scientific Patron Sir Graham Liggins Inst., Univ. of Auckland, NZ 2001; Hon. mem. Royal Soc. of Medicine, London, and other socs; Hon. DM (Geneva) 1991; Dr hc (Paris V) 2000, (Athens) 2008; Joseph M. Smith Prize, Columbia Univ. 1962, Career Scientist Award, Health Research Council, New York 1961–66, Silver Medal, Bicentenary Columbia Coll. of Physicians and Surgeons 1967, Borden Award, American Acad. of Pediatrics 1971, Robert H. Williams Distinguished Leadership Award, Endocrine Soc. 1980, Alumni Gold Medal, Columbia Coll. of Physicians and Surgeons 1988, Fred Conrad Koch Award, Endocrine Soc. 1992, Lifetime Achievement Award: Medical Educ., American Acad. of Pediatrics 1996, John Howland Award, American Pediatric Soc. 1997, Van Wyck Prize for Career Achievement, Lawson Wilkins Pediatric Endocrine Soc. 2006, UCSF Medal 2010 and many others. *Television:* NOVA: Sex Unknown (WBQH Boston) 2001. *Publications:* numerous scientific and clinical papers and monographs. *Leisure interests:* tennis, gardening, literature. *Address:* Department of Pediatrics (S672), University of California San Francisco School of Medicine, San Francisco, CA 94143-0434, USA (office). *Telephone:* (415) 476-2244 (office). *Fax:* (415) 476-8214 (office). *E-mail:* grumbach@peds.ucsf.edu (office). *Website:* www.medschool.ucsf.edu (office).

GRUNBERG, Arnon; Dutch writer; b. (Arnon Yasha Yves), 22 Feb. 1971, Amsterdam; ed Vossius Gymnasium; columnist, Volkskrant (newspaper); Constantijn Huygens Prize 2009. *Television:* anchor, RAM 2004–05. *Films include:* de Kut van Maria 1989. *Publications:* Blauwe Maandagen (novel, trans. as Blue Mondays) (Anton Wachter-prijs) 1994, Figuranten 1997, De troost van de slapstick (essays) 1998, Het veertiende kippetje 1998, Liefde is business 1999, Fantoompijn (novel, trans. as Phantom Pain) (AKO-Literatuurprijs) 2000, The Asylum Seeker (Bordewijk Prize, AKO-Literatuurprijs) 2003, Grunberg The Bible 2005, Tirza 2006, Amuse-Bouche (short stories, in trans.) 2008, Onze oom 2008, Huid en Haar 2010, De man zonder ziekte 2012. *Address:* c/o Arnon Grunberg Agency, Singel 262, Amsterdam, Netherlands. *E-mail:* info@arnongrunberg.com. *Website:* www.arnongrunberg.com.

GRÜNBERG, Peter, PhD; German physicist and academic; *Lead Research Scientist, Institut fuer Festkoerperforschung (IFF), Forschungszentrum Jülich;* ed Technische Universität Darmstadt, Universität zu Köln; Postdoctoral Fellow, Carleton Univ., Ottawa, Canada 1969–72; Research Scientist, IFF, Forschungszentrum Jülich 1972–, now Lead Research Scientist; Visiting Prof., Universität zu Köln, IMR, Tohoku Univ., Japan, JRCAT, Tsukuba Research Centre, Japan; mem. Max-Planck-Institut für Mikrostrukturphysik; American Physical Soc. Int. Prize for New Materials (jtly) 1994, Int. Union for Pure and Applied Physics Magnetism Award (jtly) 1994, Technologiepreis des Vereins der Freunde und Foerderer des Forschungszentrums Jülich 1996, Hewlett-Packard Europhysics Prize (jtly) 1997, Pres.'s Prize for Innovation and Advancement of Tech. 1998, Manfred-von-Ardenne Prize for Applied Physics, European Soc. of Thin Films 2004, European Inventor of the Year, Univ. and Research category, European Patent Office 2006, Wolf Foundation Prize for Physics (jtly) 2007, Stern-Gerlach Medal, German Physical Soc. 2007, Nobel Prize for Physics (jtly) 2007. *Address:* Forschungszentrum Jülich GmbH, Institut für Festkörperforschung, Jülich 52425, Germany (office). *Telephone:* (2461) 613286 (office). *Fax:* (2461) 614443 (office). *E-mail:* p.gruenberg@fz-juelich.de (office). *Website:* www.fz-juelich.de (office).

GRUNDHOFER, Jerry A.; American banker; *Chairman, Citibank NA;* b. 1944, Glendale, Calif.; m.; ed Loyola Marymount Univ., LA; began banking career in S Calif. 1967; Dir, Pres. and CEO Security Pacific Nat. Bank 1992, also Dir Security Pacific Corpn; Vice-Chair. and Dir BankAmerica Corpn –1993; joined Star Banc Corpn 1993, becoming Chair., Pres. and CEO –1998; CEO Firstar Corpn 1998–2001, Pres. and CEO US Bancorp (following acquisition of Firstar) 2001–06, also Chair. 2003–07, Chair. Emer. 2007–; Chair. (non-exec.) Citibank NA, New York 2009–, mem. Bd of Dirs Citigroup Inc. (parent co.) 2009–; mem. Bd of Dirs Ecolab 1999–; fmr mem. Bd of Dirs Bank of America NT&SA, Lehman Brothers Inc., The Midland Co.; Forbes Magazine Banker of the Year 1998, American Banker Magazine Banker of the Year 2000. *Address:* Office of the Chairman, Citibank NA, 399 Park Ave., New York, NY 10022, USA (office). *Telephone:* (212) 559-1000 (office). *Website:* www.citibank.com (office).

GRUNSFELD, John M., BSc, MSc, PhD; American scientist and fmr astronaut; *Deputy Director, Space Telescope Science Institute;* b. 10 Oct. 1958, Chicago, Ill.; s. of Ernest A. Grunsfeld III; m. Carol E. Schiff; two c.; ed Massachusetts Inst. of Tech., Univ. of Chicago; Visiting Scientist, Univ. of Tokyo 1980–81; Grad. Research Asst, Univ. of Chicago 1981–85, NASA Grad. Student Fellow 1985–87, W. D. Grainger Postdoctoral Fellow in Experimental Physics 1988–89; Sr Research Fellow, Calif. Inst. of Tech. 1989–92; scientist and astronaut with NASA 1992–2009, positions included Chief Computer Support Branch, Instructor and Chief Extravehicular Activity Branch, Chief Scientist 2003–04; veteran of four space flights, having logged over 45 days in space; Deputy Dir Space Telescope Science Inst. Baltimore, Md 2010–; mem. American Astronomical Soc., American Alpine Club, Experimental Aircraft Asscn, Aircraft Owners and Pilots Asscn; Distinguished Alumni Award, Alumni Service Award, Univ. of Chicago, Komarov Diploma 1995, NASA Space Flight Medals 1995, 1997, 1999, 2002, Exceptional Service Medals 1997, 1998, 2000, Korolov Diploma 1999, 2002, Distinguished Service Medal 2002, Constellation Award 2004, Space Logistics Medal, Soc. of Logistics Engineers 2006. *Leisure interests:* mountaineering, flying, sailing, bicycling, music. *Address:* Space Telescope Science Institute, 3700 San Martin Drive, Baltimore, MD 21218-2463, USA (office). *Telephone:* (410) 338-4700 (office). *E-mail:* grunsfeld@stsci.edu (office). *Website:* www.stsci.edu (office).

GRUSHKO, Alexander; Russian diplomatist and politician; *Permanent Representative, NATO;* b. 25 April 1955, Oslo, Norway; s. of the late Viktor Fedorovich Grushko; ed Moscow State Inst. of Int. Relations (MGIMO); father served in Oslo as trainee in Soviet embassy, family lived in Oslo 1954–58, returned to Oslo where his father was Second Sec. 1962–72, returned with his family to Moscow 1972; adviser, Soviet embassy in Brussels 1980–90s; Head of Russian del. at disarmament negotiations between USSR and NATO within framework of jt consultative group under Treaty on Conventional Armed Forces in Europe (CFE Treaty); Chief Adviser to Dept of Security and Disarmament Affairs, Ministry of Foreign Affairs mid-1990s, Deputy Dir Dept of European Cooperation 2002–03, Dir 2003–05, mem. Bd Ministry of Foreign Affairs 2003, rank of Amb. 2004, Deputy Minister of Foreign Affairs with responsibility for pan-European and Euro-Atlantic orgs 2005–12, Perm. Rep. to NATO, Brussels 2012–; Lecturer, MGIMO; Order of Friendship 2004. *Address:* Permanent Mission of Russia to NATO, Avenue de Fre, 66, 1180 Brussels, Belgium (office). *Telephone:* (2) 372-0359 (office). *E-mail:* info@natomission.ru (office); amrus.nato@skynet.be. *Website:* natomission.ru (office).

GRYAZNOVA, Alla Georgiyevna, DEcon; Russian economist and academic; *President, Financial University under the Government of the Russian Federation;* b. 27 Nov. 1937, Moscow; m. Viktor Kononov; one s.; ed Moscow Finance Coll., Moscow Inst. of Finance; served in several teaching positions at Moscow Inst. of Finance (now Financial Univ. under the Govt of the Russian Federation) including Asst, Lecturer, Sr Lecturer and Docent, Prof. 1964–74, Pro-rector on int. relations and research 1976–85, Rector 1985–2006, Pres. 2006–; Ed.-in-Chief Banking System in Russia; mem. New Way Movt 1995; First Vice-Pres. Guild of Financiers; Vice-Pres. Acad. of Man. and Market; mem. Acad. of Econ. Sciences, Int. Acad. of Informatics, Int. Acad. of Eurasia; Pres. Moscow Int. School of Finance and Banking; Hon. Prof., Moscow Int. Higher Business School (MIRBIS); Honoured Worker of Science of Russian Fed. *Publications:* over 200 articles on econ. problems. *Leisure interests:* tennis, ballet, volleyball, poetry. *Address:* Financial University under the Government of the Russian Federation, 125993 Moscow, Leningradsky prosp. 49, Russia (office). *Telephone:* (495) 157-56-61 (office). *Fax:* (495) 157-70-70 (office). *E-mail:* academy@fa.ru (office). *Website:* en.fa.ru (office).

GRYBAUSKAITĖ, Dalia, PhD; Lithuanian politician, diplomatist and head of state; *President;* b. 1 March 1956, Vilnius; ed Leningrad (now St Petersburg) Univ., USSR, Zhdanov Univ., Edmund A. Walsh School of Foreign Service, Georgetown Univ., Washington, DC, USA; Head, Dept for Science, Inst. of Econs 1990–91; Programme Dir, Govt of Repub. of Lithuania, Prime Minister's Office 1991; Dir European Dept, Ministry of Int. Econ. Relations 1991–93; Dir Econ. Relations Dept, Ministry of Foreign Affairs 1993–94; Chair. Comm. for Aid Coordination

(PHARE and G-24) 1993–94; Chief of Negotiations with EU on Free Trade Agreement 1993–94; Envoy Extraordinary and Minister Plenipotentiary, Mission of Lithuania to EU, Brussels 1994–95, Deputy Chief Negotiator on Europe Agreement with EU; Rep. of Nat. Aid Coordinator, Brussels 1994–95; Minister Plenipotentiary, Embassy in Washington, DC 1996–99; Deputy Minister of Finance 1999–2000, Chief Negotiator in Negotiations with IMF and World Bank; Deputy Minister of Foreign Affairs 2000–01; Deputy Head of Negotiations, Del. to EU; Minister of Finance 2001–04; EU Commr for Educ. and Culture 2004, for Financial Programming and the Budget 2004–09; Pres. of Lithuania 2009–; Commdr's Cross, Order of Grand Duke Gediminas 2003, Order of Vytautas the Great with the Golden Chain 2009, Commdr Grand Cross with Chain, Order of the Three Stars 2011, Kt Grand Cross, Royal Norwegian Order of St Olav 2011, Kt Grand Cross, Order of the Falcon (Iceland) 2011, Grand Officer, Order of Saint-Charles (Monaco) 2012; named Commissioner of the Year in the European Voice Europeans of the Year poll 2005, Glamour magazine Woman of the Year (USA) 2010, Charlemagne Prize (Germany) 2013. *Address:* Office of the President, S. Daukanto 3, Vilnius 01122, Lithuania (office). *Telephone:* (5) 266-4154 (office). *Fax:* (5) 266-4145 (office). *E-mail:* kanceliarija@prezidentas.lt (office). *Website:* www.president.lt (office).

GRYNSPAN, Rebeca, BS, MS; Costa Rican politician and UN official; *Under-Secretary-General and Associate Administrator, United Nations Development Programme (UNDP);* b. 1955; m.; one s. one d.; ed Univ. of Costa Rica, Hebrew Univ., Israel, Univ. of Sussex, UK; fmr Prof., Univ. of Costa Rica; fmr Researcher, Instituto de Investigaciones de Ciencias Económicas de Costa Rica; various ministerial level positions 1986–94; Vice-Pres., Repub. of Costa Rica 1994–98; joined UN, becoming Dir Mexican Div., ECLAC 2001–06, Asst Admin. and Regional Dir, UNDP Latin America and Caribbean Bureau 2006–09, Under-Sec.-Gen. and Assoc. Admin., UNDP 2010–; fmr Vice-Pres. Int. Food Policy Research Inst. *Address:* United Nations Development Programme, One United Nations Plaza, New York, NY 10017, USA (office). *Telephone:* (212) 906-5000 (office). *Fax:* (212) 906-5001 (office). *E-mail:* UNDP-newsroom@undp.org (office). *Website:* www.undp.org (office).

GRYTSENKO, Anatoliy P., MPA; Ukrainian government official and politician; b. 21 Sept. 1958, Kerch (Autonomous Repub. of Crimea); m. Olga A. Grytsenko; one s. one d.; ed Kalinin Crimean Agricultural Inst., Simferopol and Kharkov Regional Inst. of Public Admin; began career 1976; held various positions including Chair. Exec. Cttee Chistopolskiy town council of nat. deputies, Chair. Leninskaya Dist State Admin; Deputy, Verkhovna Rada (Parl.) of the Autonomous Repub. of Crimea 1994–; first Vice-Chair. Presidium of the Supreme Council, Autonomous Repub. of Crimea 1987–97, Chair. 1997–98, 2006–10; Chair. Verkhovna Rada Comm. on Local Self-Govt 1987–97; Order of Merit (Third Degree) of Ukraine, Order of Peter the Great (First Degree), Russia, Order of St Anthony and Feodosiy Pecherski, Ukrainian Orthodox Church. *Leisure interests:* hunting, sociopolitical journalism. *Address:* 95000 Simferopol, 18 K. Marksa Street, Autonomous Republic of Crimea, Ukraine (office). *Telephone:* (65) 254-42-55 (office). *Fax:* (65) 227-25-81 (office). *E-mail:* svr@rada.crimea.ua (office). *Website:* www.rada.crimea.ua (office).

GRYZLOV, Boris Vyacheslavovich, PhD; Russian engineer and politician; *Chairman of Supreme Council, United Russia (Yedinaya Rossiya);* b. 15 Dec. 1950, Vladivostok; s. of Vyacheslav Gryzlov; m. Ada Viktorovna Gryzlova; one s. one d.; ed Leningrad (now St Petersburg) Inst. of Electro-Tech. Communications; radio engineer, Heavy Duty Radio Industry Scientific Research Inst. (Comintern), took part in devt of communications systems –1977; Head of construction, later Dept Dir, Electron-pribor Production Co. 1977–96; Dir New Training Tech. Centre, Baltic State Tech. Univ. 1996–99; cand. in St Petersburg city elections; Pres. Interregional Business Co-operation Fund Devt of Regions 1999–; Chief of Staff for Leningrad Oblast Gov. cand. Viktor Zubkov 1999; Founder mem. Unity (Yedinstvo) Movt 1999, Head of St Petersburg Regional Br. 1999, Chair. Unity Political Council 2000, Chair. Supreme Council of United Russia (Yedinaya Rossiya) 2004–, Chair. United Russia 2005–08; mem. Gosudarstvennaya Duma (State Duma) 1999–2001, 2003–, Leader, Unity faction 2000–01, Chair. State Duma Dec. 2003–11; Minister of Internal Affairs 2001–03; Chair. Inter-Parl. Ass., Eurasian Econ. Community (Eurasec IPA); Perm. mem., Security Council of Russian Fed. *Leisure interests:* soccer and other sports. *Address:* United Russia (Yedinaya Rossiya), 129110 Moscow, Pereyaslavskii per. 4, Russia (office). *Telephone:* (495) 786-82-89 (office). *Fax:* (495) 975-30-78 (office). *E-mail:* portalrss@edinros.ru (office). *Website:* er.ru (office); www.gryzlov.ru.

GRYZUNOV, Sergey Petrovich; Russian academic and fmr journalist; *Professor, Department of Journalism, Moscow State Institute for International Relations;* b. 23 July 1949, Kuybyshev; m.; one s.; ed Moscow State Univ., Acad. of Public Sciences, Cen. Communist Party Cttee; worked for Ria-Novosti 1974–94, fmr ed. Novosti, then reviewer, then Deputy Head of Bureau, Yugoslavia; Deputy Chair. Cttee on Press April–Sept. 1994, Chair. 1994–95; mem. Pres. Yeltsin's Election Campaign March 1996; Vice-Pres. ICN Pharmaceutical Corpn 1996–2001; Vice-Pres. Moscow News Publrs 2001–03, Russian Asscn of Ind. Publishers 2004–05; fmr Deputy Gen. Dir Rumelco OOO; fmr Chair. Communications and Public Relations Cttee Novolipetsk Steel (NLMK); Ed.-in-Chief and Dir Gen. Novoe Russkoe Slovo Publishing House; Prof., Dept of Journalism, Moscow State Inst. for Int. Relations 2009–. *Leisure interests:* cooking, fishing, underwater swimming. *Address:* Department of Journalism, Moscow State Institute for International Relations, 119454 Moscow, Prospekt Vernadskogo, 76, Russia (office). *Telephone:* (495) 434-90-66 (office). *Website:* english.mgimo.ru (office).

GRZEŚKOWIAK, Alicja, PhD (Habil.); Polish lawyer, politician and academic; *Professor, Kujawy and Pomorze University;* b. 10 June 1941, Swirz, Lvov Prov., Ukrainian SSR, USSR; (husband deceased); one d.; ed Nicolaus Copernicus Univ., Toruń; research worker, Faculty of Law and Admin of Nicolaus Copernicus Univ., Toruń 1966–96, Prof. 1990; on staff, Catholic Univ. of Lublin (KUL) 1990, apptd Prof. of Criminal Law 1991, now Prof. Emer., mem. Scientific Council of John Paul II Inst.; Lecturer in Religious Law, Higher Ecclesiastic Seminary, Toruń 1994–2002; currently Prof., Kujawy and Pomorze Univ., Bydgoszcz; mem. Solidarity Trade Union 1980; Senator 1989–2001, Vice-Marshal of Senate 1991–93, Marshal 1997–2001, del. Parl. Ass. of the Council of Europe 1989–97, mem. 1991–97, Vice-Chair. Group of Christian Democrats 1992–97; mem. Social

Movt of Solidarity Election Action (RSAWS) 1998–2001; mem. Admin. Council of John Paul II Foundation, Vatican 1992–2002; consultant of Pontifical Council for the Family 1993; mem. Pontificia Academia Pro Vita; Founder Foundation of Assistance to Single Mothers, Toruń; Hon. mem. Asscn of Catholic Families; Dr hc (Acad. of Catholic Theology, Warsaw) 1995, (Holy Family Coll., Phila) 1998, (Int. Ind. Univ. of Moldova) 1999; Pro Ecclesia et Pontifice Medal 1991, Medal of 13th Jan. of Lithuanian Repub.; Dame of the Holy Sepulchre Friars of Jerusalem, Great Cross, Order of Crown (Belgium) 1999, Great Cross, Orden del Merito Civil (Spain). *Publications:* numerous scientific publs on penal law, human rights and family rights. *Leisure interests:* reading, listening to music. *Address:* Kujawy and Pomorze University, ul. Toruńska 55–57, 85-023 Bydgoszcz, Poland (office). *E-mail:* alicja.grzeskowiak@wp.pl (home). *Website:* www.kpsw.edu.pl (office).

GSTEIGER, Fredy, MBS; Swiss journalist and editor; *Diplomatic Correspondent, Schweizer Radio und Fernsehen (SRF);* b. 1962, Berne; ed Univ. of St Gallen, Switzerland, Univ. of Lyons, France and Univ. of Québec, Canada; fmr Econ. Journalist, Der Bunde, Berne; Foreign Ed., St Galler Tagblatt 1988–89; Middle East Ed., Die Zeit, Hamburg, Germany 1989–93, Paris Corresp. 1997–2001; Ed.-in-Chief Die Weltwoche, Zürich 1997–2001; Diplomatic Corresp., Schweizer Radio und Fernsehen (SRF) (formed after merger of Schweizer Radio DRS and and Schweizer Fernsehen 2011) 2002–; Bd mem. International Press Inst. *Publication:* Blocher: Ein unschweizerisches Phänomen 2002. *Leisure interests:* reading, travelling, swimming. *Address:* Schweizer Radio und Fernsehen, Kundendienst Fernsehstrasse 1-4, 8052 Zürich, Switzerland (office). *Telephone:* 443661111 (office). *Fax:* 443055088 (office). *E-mail:* srf@srf.ch (office). *Website:* www.srf.ch (office).

GU, Binglin, BEng, PhD; Chinese physicist, academic and fmr university administrator; *Professor of Physics, Tsinghua University;* b. 8 Oct. 1945, Harbin, Heilongjiang; ed Tsinghua Univ., Beijing, Univ. of Arhus, Denmark; mem. Faculty, Tsinghua Univ. 1970–, Assoc. Prof. of Physics, 1983–88, Prof. of Physics 1988–, Head, Dept of Physics 1994–2000, Dean Grad. School 2000–, Pres. Academic Degree Cttee 2001–, Vice-Pres. Tsinghua Univ. 2001–03, Pres. 2003–12; Visiting Prof., Tohoku Univ., Japan 1993–94; Sr Visiting Scholar, Notre Dame Univ., USA 1985–86; Dir Steering Cttee for Physics and Astronomy, Ministry of Educ.; Pres. Chinese Stereology Cttee; Vice-Pres. Chinese Physical Soc.; mem. and Dir of Physics and Astronomy Senate; mem. Academic Degree Cttee of the State Council, Nat. Science and Tech. Reward Cttee, Council of Asscn of Asia Pacific Physical Socs; Academician, Chinese Acad. of Science; Second Prize of Scientific Achievement, Ministry of Educ. 1988, 1990, 1994, 1998, Top Award for Excellent Teacher, Baosteel Educ. Fund 1998, First Prize, Chinese Univ. Nature Science 2000, Second Nat. Prize of Nature Science 2000, Second Prize of Scientific Achievement, City of Beijing 2002, Award for Scientific and Technological Progress, Ho Leung Ho Lee Foundation 2002, First LuXun Award, Tohoku Univ. 2004. *Publications:* more than 200 scientific papers in professional journals on the properties of complex materials and phenomena. *Address:* Department of Physics, Tsinghua University, Building of School of Science 2405, Beijing 100084, People's Republic of China (office). *Telephone:* (10) 62789973 (office). *Fax:* (10) 62781886 (office). *E-mail:* gubl@phys.tsinghua.edu.cn (office). *Website:* www.phys.tsinghua.edu.cn (office).

GU, Jianguo, Chinese steel industry executive; *President, Magang (Group) Holding Co Ltd;* b. 1954; many years with Ma'anshan Iron and Steel Co. Ltd (Masteel), Chair. Masteel 1993–95, Gen. Man. Magang (Group) Holding and Chair. Masteel 1995–99, currently Pres. Magang (Group) Holding Co. Ltd, Chair. and Exec. Dir Masteel. *Address:* Magang (Group) Holding, 8 Hong Qi Zhong Road, Maanshan City 243003, People's Republic of China (office). *Telephone:* (555) 2888158 (office). *Fax:* (555) 2887284 (office). *Website:* www.magang.com.cn (office).

GU, Jinchi; Chinese party and government official; *Chairman, Sino-Lithuanian Friendship Association;* b. 1932, Xiongxian Co., Hebei Prov.; joined CCP 1949; Deputy Sec. Beijing No. 1 Machine Tools Plant, CCP Party Cttee 1959–65; Sec. Long March Machine Tools Plant, CCP Party Cttee, Zigong City, Sichuan Prov. 1965–75, Sec. CCP City Cttee 1980–81; Vice-Mayor Zigong City 1980–81; Vice-Gov. Sichuan Prov. 1982–85; mem. 13th CCP Cen. Cttee 1987–92, 14th CCP Cen. Cttee 1992–97; Deputy Sec. Sichuan Prov. Cttee 1987–90; Sec. Gansu Prov. Cttee 1990–93, Sec. CCP Liaoning Prov. Cttee 1995–97; Deputy, 8th NPC 1993–98, mem. 9th Standing Cttee of NPC 1998–2003 (Vice-Chair. Internal Affairs and Judicial Cttee 1998–2003); Del., 15th CCP Nat. Congress 1997–2002; Chair. Sino-Lithuanian Friendship Asscn. *Address:* c/o Standing Committee of National People's Congress, Beijing, People's Republic of China.

GU, Liji, BEng, MEng; Chinese engineer and business executive; *Chairman of the Supervisory Board, China Ping An Insurance Corporation;* ed Tsinghua Univ., Univ. of Science and Tech. of China, Harvard Business School, USA; Man. Dir China Merchants Shekou Industrial Zone Co. Ltd –2008, Hoi Tung Marine Machinery Suppliers Ltd (Hong Kong) –2008, China Merchants Technology Group –2008; Chair. China Merchants Technology Holdings Co. Ltd –2008, Exec. Dir 2008–10, Exec. Dir China Merchants Technology Investment Co. Ltd, Shenzhen 2008–10; Man. Dir China Int. Marine Containers Co. Ltd –2008; Chair. and Pres. China Merchants Shekou Port Services Co. Ltd –2008; Vice-Chair. China Ping An Insurance Co. –2008, Ind. Supervisor and Chair. Supervisory Bd China Ping An Insurance Corpn 2009–; Dir China Merchants Bank, China Merchants Group Ltd –2008; Outside Dir Xiang Tan Electric Manufacturing Group Co. Ltd (XEMC) 2011–; expert on Applicable Electronics, Shenzhen Expert Asscn; Vice-Chair. Scientific Asscn of Shenzhen Nanshan Dist. *Address:* China Ping An Insurance Corporation, Ping An Building, Bagua No. 3 Road, Shenzhen 518029, Guangdong (office); Ping An Insurance (Hong Kong) Co. Ltd, 11th Floor, Dah Sing Financial Centre, 108 Gloucester Road, Wanchai, Hong Kong Special Administrative Region, People's Republic of China (office). *Telephone:* (755) 82262888 (Shenzhen) (office); 28271883 (Hong Kong) (office). *Fax:* (755) 82414817 (Shenzhen) (office); 28020018 (Hong Kong) (office). *E-mail:* IR@paic.com.cn (office). *Website:* www.pingan.com.cn (office).

GU, Songfen; Chinese aeronautical engineer; b. 1930, Suzhou, Jiangsu Prov.; ed Shanghai Jiaotong Univ.; engineer, Aeronautical Industry Admin. of Ministry of Heavy Industry; Group Leader Aerodynamic Group of Design Dept, Shenyang Aeroplane Mfg Factory; Vice-Chief Designer, Chief Designer, Vice-Pres. then Pres.

Aviation Science and Tech. Research Inst.; mem. 4th Presidium of Depts 2000–; responsible for jet fighter design; Chief Designer Shenyang Aeroplane Mfg Co.; Vice-Chair. Science and Tech. Cttee, China Aviation Industry Corpn; joined CCP 1981; Deputy, 7th NPC 1988–93, mem. 8th Standing Cttee of NPC 1993–98 (mem. Educ., Science, Culture and Health Cttee 1993–98), 9th Standing Cttee of NPC 1998–2003; Fellow, Chinese Acad. of Sciences 1991– (Deputy Dir Div. of Technological Sciences 1996–); mem. Chinese Acad. of Eng 1994–; Nat. Model Worker 1988, Gold Nat. Aeronautical Award 1992, Scientific and Technological Progress Award, Ho Leung Ho Lee Foundation 1995. *Address:* Shenyang Aeroplane Manufacturing Company, Shenyang, Liaoning Province, People's Republic of China (office).

GU, Xiulian; Chinese economist, politician and party and government official; b. 1936, Nantong, Jiangsu Prov.; ed public security cadre's school, Shenyang, Liaoning Prov., Public Security Bureau of Benxi City, Liaoning, Secondary Metallurgical School of Shenyang; joined CCP 1956; technician and cadre, Communist Youth League of China Metallurgical Corpn 1961–64; technician, Ministry of Textile Industry 1969; cadre, State Council 1970; Vice-Minister, State Planning Comm., State Council 1973–83; Alt. mem. Cen. Cttee, CCP 1977; Vice-Chair. Cen. Patriotic Sanitation Campaign Cttee, Cen. Cttee 1981–89; mem. 12th Cen. Cttee, CCP 1982–87, 13th Cen. Cttee CCP 1987–92, 14th Cen. Cttee CCP 1992–97, 15th Cen. Cttee CCP 1997–2002; Deputy Sec. CCP Prov. Cttee, Jiangsu 1982–89; Gov. of Jiangsu 1983–89; Minister of Chemical Industry 1989–98 (also Party Cttee Sec. at the Ministry); Deputy, 9th NPC 1998–2003, Vice-Chair. 10th NPC Standing Cttee 2003–; Vice-Pres. 7th, 8th and 9th Exec. Cttee, All-China Women's Fed. 1998–2003, Pres. 9th All-China Women's Fed. 2003–08; Vice-Pres. 3rd Council, China Women's Devt Fund 1999, Vice-Pres. China Women's Devt Fund 2001–. *Address:* c/o The All-China Women's Federation, 15 Jian Guo Men Nei Street, Beijing 100730, People's Republic of China. *Telephone:* (10) 65211639. *Fax:* (10) 65211156. *E-mail:* yzhch@women.org.cn; acwf@women.org.cn. *Website:* www.women.org.cn.

GU, Yingqi; Chinese politician; b. 1930, Xinmin, Liaoning; m.; two s. one d.; joined PLA 1948, CCP 1950; Vice-Minister of Public Health 1984–95; Chief Physician; Co-ordinator State Co-ordination of Control of Narcotics and Against Drugs 1987–90; Head of Del. to UN Int. Conf. on Drug Abuse and Illicit Trafficking 1987, to Signing of Sino-US Memorandum of Understanding on Co-operation and Control of Narcotic Drugs, Washington 1987, to UN Conf. for Adoption of a Convention Against Illicit Traffic in Narcotic Drugs and Psychotropic Substances 1988, to 17th Special Session of UN Gen. Ass. on Int. Co-operation against Drugs 1990, to 44th Gen. Ass. of WHO 1991, to Int. Conf. for Protection of War Victims, Geneva, Switzerland 1993, to 9th Session of Gen. Ass. of Int. Fed. of Red Cross and Red Crescent Socs, Birmingham, UK 1993; Conf. Chair. 15th Meeting of Nat. Drug Law Enforcement Agencies for Asia and Pacific 1990, 4th Asia and Pacific Red Cross and Red Crescent Conf., Beijing 1993; Head of Chinese Red Cross Del. to 26th Int. Conf. of Red Cross and Red Crescent, Geneva 1995; Pres. China Rural Hygiene Assoc 1986–, Chinese Assoc of Rehabilitation Medicine 1985–, Chinese Assoc of Hosp. Man.; Exec. Vice-Pres. Red Cross Soc. of China 1990–; Vice-Pres. Int. Fed. of Red Cross and Red Crescent Socs 1991–93. *Address:* c/o Red Cross Society of China, 53 Ganmian Hutong, Beijing 100010, People's Republic of China. *Telephone:* (10) 513-5838. *Fax:* (10) 512-4169.

GUAINO, Henri; French civil servant and economist; *Special Adviser to the President;* b. 11 March 1957, Arles; ed Institut d'études politiques de Paris, École nationale d'admin.; economist, Crédit Lyonnais 1982–86; Course Dir, École supérieure de commerce de Paris and École normale supérieure de Saint-Cloud 1984–87; Chief of Staff to Treasury Dir 1987–88; Asst Sec.-Gen. Club de Paris 1987–88; worked on Jacques Chirac's presidential campaign 1988; Head of Lectures, Institut d'études politiques de Paris 1988–2003; Head of Finance Research, Louis Dreyfus Group 1989–90; Chief of Staff to Dir-Gen., Mutuelle d'assurance des artisans 1990–93; Chief of Staff to Pres. of Nat. Ass., Philippe Séguin 1993; adviser to Minister of the Interior, Charles Pasqua 1994–95; Chief of Staff, Gen. Planning Commissariat 1995–98; Planning and Devt Adviser to Charles Pasqua for Hauts-de-Seine, Paris 1999–2000; Scientific Adviser, Agence pour la diffusion de l'information technologique 2002–04; Admin., Agence de l'environnement et de la maîtrise de l'énergie 2003; Chief Adviser, Cour des Comptes 2006–; Special Adviser, Pres. of the Repub., Nicolas Sarkozy 2007–. *Publications:* L'Étrange renoncement 1998, La France est-elle soluble dans l'Europe? (with Daniel Cohn-Bendit) 1999, La sottise des modernes 2002. *Address:* Palais de l'Élysée, 55 rue du faubourg Saint-Honoré, 75008 Paris, France (office). *Telephone:* 1-42-92-81-00 (office). *Website:* www.elysee.fr (office).

GUAN, Guangfu; Chinese politician and banker; b. 1931, Muling Co., Heilongjiang Prov.; ed Hubei Univ.; joined CCP 1948; Vice-Pres. Hubei Br. People's Bank of China 1971–78, Pres., Hubei Br. 1978–82; Sec. Hubei Prov. CCP Cttee 1983–94; Chair. Hubei Prov. 8th People's Congress 1993–2002; mem. 12th CCP Cen. Cttee 1982–87, 13th CCP Cen. Cttee 1987–92, 14th CCP Cen. Cttee 1992–97. *Address:* Shui Guo Hu, Wuhan, Hubei Province, People's Republic of China.

GUAN, Qiao; Chinese engineer; b. 2 July 1935, Taiyuan, Shanxi Prov.; ed Moscow Bauman Eng Inst., USSR; Fellow, Chinese Acad. of Eng 1994–; invented low-stress no-distortion welding method; mem. Council Chinese Acad. of Eng; Research Fellow and Vice-Chair. Science and Tech. Cttee, Beijing Aeronautical Manufacturing Tech. Research Inst. 1987–, also Head of Welding Dept and Vice-Chair. Academic Cttee; Adjunct Prof., Tsing Hua Univ. and Beijing Univ. of Aeronautics and Astronautics; Pres. Chinese Welding Soc. 1990–95; Vice-Pres. Int. Inst. of Welding 1992–95; Nat. Invention Prize (2nd Class) 1995, GuangHua Prize (1st Class) 1996, Int. Inst. of Welding Lifetime Achievement Award 1999. *Publications:* more than 50 technical papers published in Chinese, 25 papers in English and Russian. *Address:* Beijing Aeronautical Manufacturing Technology Research Institute, PO Box 863, 100024 Beijing, People's Republic of China (office). *Telephone:* (10) 8570-1243.

GUAN, Qing, PhD; Chinese engineer and business executive; *President, China State Construction Engineering Corporation Limited;* Vice-Pres. China Southwest Architectural Design & Research Inst. Corpn Ltd 1998–2003, Pres. 2003–06; Deputy Sec. Party Cttee 2006–07; Vice-Pres. China State Construction Engineer-

ing Corpn Ltd 2007–09, Vice-Chair. and Pres. China Construction Engineering Design Group Corpn Ltd 2009–11, Pres. China State Construction Engineering Corpn Ltd April–May 2011, mem. Bd of Dirs May–July 2011, Chair. July–Sept. 2011, Dir and Pres. Sept. 2011–, Chair. China Construction Engineering Design Group Corpn Ltd; Deputy Dir China Green Building Council. *Address:* China State Construction Engineering Corporation Ltd, CSCEC Mansion, 15 Sanlihe Road, Haidian District, Beijing 100037, People's Republic of China (office). *Telephone:* (10) 88082888 (office). *Fax:* (10) 88082888 (office). *E-mail:* info@cscec.com (office); ir@cscec.com.cn (office). *Website:* www.cscec.com (office).

GUARD, Mark Perrott, MA, RIBA, MRIAI, MCSD; Irish architect; *Principal, Mark Guard Architects;* b. 22 May 1952, Dublin; s. of Wilson Perrott Guard and Ethena Joy Wallace; ed Avoca School, Dublin, Univ. of Toronto, Royal Coll. of Art, London; worked for architectural, film and textile design cos in Ireland and UK 1969–73; emigrated to Canada 1973; architect, Toronto and Vancouver 1973–76; worked for Richard Rogers Partnership, Rick Mather Architects, Eva Jiricna Architects, London 1982–86; started pvt. practice in modernist residential design and devt of transformable spaces 1986; Prin. Mark Guard Design 1986–88, Mark Guard Assocs 1988–93, Mark Guard Architects 1993–; Dir Mark Guard Ltd 1998–; Dir Guard Tillman Pollock Ltd 2002–; mem. Royal Inst. of the Architects of Ireland (RIAI), Chartered Soc. of Designers (CSD); RIBA Regional Award for New House, London, W2 1992, for house refurbishment, London, NW6 1995, CSD Commendation for transformable flat, London, EC2 1993, for house refurbishment, London, NW6 1995, RIAI Commendation for new house, Galway 1993, RIBA Award for Houses and Housing for penthouse apartment, Paris 1997. *Address:* 161 Whitfield Street, London, W1T 5ET, England (office). *Telephone:* (20) 7380-1199 (office). *Fax:* (20) 7387-5441 (office). *E-mail:* mga@markguard.com (office). *Website:* www .markguard.com (office).

GUARDADO, Facundo; Salvadorean politician; b. 27 Nov. 1954, Arcatao, Dept of Chalatenengo; s. of Sixto Guardado and Herlinda Guardado; m. Carmen Cristina Alvarez Basso 1993; one s. three d.; ed fellowship to econ. seminars at Cen. American Business Admin. Inst. and Heredia Nat. Univ. of Costa Rica; co-operative movt leader 1972–; Sec.-Gen. Revolutionary Popular Bloc 1977; mem. Cen. Cttee Nat. Liberation Front (FMLN) in 1980s, mem. Political Comm. 1993, Campaign Man. 1997, Gen. Co-ordinator 1997–99; Counselor at San Salvador Majorship 1997–; presidential cand. 1999; Leader, Movimiento Renovador (split from FMLN 2002) 2002–03 (dissolved after elections 2003); mem. peace negotiations del. La Palma 1984, Ayagualo 1984, La Nunciatura 1987, Mexico 1991; Vice-Pres. Perm. Conf. of Political Parties of Latin America and the Caribbean; mem. Initiatives Group for Latin America; Pres. El Salvador XXI Century Foundation. *Publications:* Political and Social Struggles in El Salvador, Participation and Social Change, Evolution of the Democratic Process in El Salvador. *Leisure interests:* agriculture, football. *Address:* Paseo Miralvalle 155, Colonia Miralvalle, San Salvador (home); c/o Motocross #49, Colonia Monteverde, San Salvador, El Salvador (home). *Telephone:* 274-2104 (home).

GUARDIOLA I SALA, Josep (Pep); Spanish football manager and fmr professional footballer; *Manager, FC Bayern Munich;* b. 18 Jan. 1971, Santpedor, Barcelona, Catalonia; s. of Dolors and Valentí; m. Cristina Serra; one s. two d.; played as defensive midfielder for Barcelona B 1990–92, FC Barcelona 1990–2001 (472 appearances, scored 10 goals, Capt. 1997–2001), mem. team that won La Liga 1990–91, 1991–92, 1992–93, 1993–94, 1997–98, 1998–99, Copa del Rey 1996–97, 1997–98, Supercopa de España 1991, 1992, 1994, 1996, mem. of team that won European Cup 1991–92 (Barcelona's first), UEFA Cup Winners' Cup 1996–97, UEFA Super Cup 1992, 1997; also played for Brescia Calcio 2001–02, A.S. Roma 2002–03, Al-Ahli (Qatar) 2003–05, Dorados de Sinaloa (Mexico) 2005–06 (while attending managing school); served four-month ban for positive drug test while playing in Italy 2001, cleared of all charges on appeal 2007 and again 2009; played internationally for Spain U21 1991–92, Spain 1992–2001 (won Olympic Gold Medal 1992), Catalonia 1995–2005; following retirement as player, became coach of FC Barcelona B 2007–08 (won Tercera División 2007–08), First Team Man. FC Barcelona 2008–12, in first season won treble of La Liga 2008–09, Copa del Rey 2008–09 and Champions League (youngest-ever UEFA Champions League winning man.) 2008–09, won Supercopa de España against Athletic Club Bilbao 2009, UEFA Super Cup against Shakhtar Donetsk 2009, 2011, FIFA Club World Cup against Estudiantes 2009 (first ever sextuple of six competitions in six competitions in one year), 2011, won La Liga 2009–10, 2010–11, Supercopa de España 2009, 2010, 2011, UEFA Champions League 2010–11 (a record 13 trophies in four seasons making him the most successful coach in the club's history); Man. FC Bayern Munich 2013–; Bravo Award 1992, UEFA Euro Team of the Tournament 1992, 2000, Spain's Best Player, Olympic Games 1992, IFFHS World's Best Club Coach of the Year 2009, 2011, Don Balon Award for Best Coach of the Year 2009, 2010, 2011, Onze d'Or Coach of the Year 2009, 2011, Miguel Muñoz Trophy for Best Coach of the Year 2009, 2010, World Soccer Magazine World Manager of the Year 2009, 2011, UEFA Team of the Year Best Coach 2008–09, 2010–11, La Liga Coach of the Year 2009, 2010, 2011, Catalan of the Year Award 2009, FIFA Ballon d'Or Best Coach 2011, Gold Medal of the Royal Order of Sporting Merit 2010, Gold Medal of the Catalan parliament 2011, FIFA World Coach of the Year 2011. *Address:* FC Bayern München AG, Säbener Straße 51–57, 81547 Munich, Germany (office). *Telephone:* (89) 69931-0 (office); (89) 6427930 (office). *Fax:* (89) 644165 (office). *Website:* www.fcbayern.telekom.de/en/teams/trainer/16491.php (office).

GUARGUAGLINI, Pier Francesco, PhD; Italian aerospace industry executive; b. 25 Feb. 1937, Castagneto Carducci, Livorno; m.; three c.; ed Univ. of Pisa, Univ. of Pennsylvania, USA; Asst Lecturer in Nuclear Electronics, Univ. of Pisa 1961–63; Asst Lecturer in Radar Systems, Univ. of Rome 1963–78; joined Selenia SpA as Systems Analyst 1963, Dir of Research Devt 1970–74, Dir IT and Telecommunications Div. 1975–79, Dir and Man. Civil Div. 1979–81, Deputy Gen. Man. 1981–82, Co-Gen. Man. 1982; Gen. Man. Officine Galileo 1984–87, Man. Dir 1987–94; Man. Dir Oto Melara SpA and Breda Meccanica Bresciana SpA 1994–96; Head, Defence Sector Businesses, Finmeccanica SpA 1996–99, Chair. Alenia Marconi Systems NV (joint venture between Finmeccanica and BAE) 1998–2000, Chair. and CEO Finmeccanica SpA 2002–11, Chair. May–Dec. 2011 (resgnd); CEO Fincantieri Cantieri Navali Italiani 1999–2002; Lecturer, Univ. of Rome; Pres. AeroSpace and Defence Industries Assoc of Europe; mem. Shareholders' Steering

Cttee IJVC Horizon Ltd; mem. IEEE; Aviation Week and Space Technology Person of the Year. *Address:* c/o Finmeccanica SpA, Piazza Monte Grappa 4, Rome 00195, Italy . *E-mail:* info@finmeccanica.it.

GUARINI, Kathryn Wilder, BS, PhD; American scientist and academic; ed Yale and Stanford Univs; fmr Ed.-in-Chief The Yale Herald; joined IBM Research Div. as Research Staff mem. and Man. 45nm Front End Integration Group, Silicon Tech. Dept, IBM T.J. Watson Research Center, Yorktown Heights, NY 1999, currently on assignment in IBM Corp. Tech. working on tech. assessments for IBM Tech. Team; mem. IEEE, AAAS, Asscn for Women in Science; named to TR100 list of top 100 young innovators by MIT's Technology Review magazine 2003, World Tech. Award in Information Tech. (Hardware), The World Tech. Network (co-recipient) 2004. *Publications:* Scanning Probe Lithography (Microsystems, Vol. 7; with Hyongsok T. Soh and Calvin F. Quate) 2001; more than 45 tech. publs on CMOS device fabrication, three-dimensional integrated circuits, and novel nanofabrication techniques and applications; more than 15 US patents. *Address:* IBM Corporate Division, 294 Route 100, Somers, NY 10598, USA (office). *E-mail:* kwg@us.ibm.com (office). *Website:* www.watson.ibm.com (office).

GUARINI, Renato; Italian statistician, university rector and academic; b. 16 March 1932, Naples; ed Univ. of Naples; did research at Univ. of Cen. Bureau of Statistics 1957–75, held post of Head of Dept for Gen. Methodology and Econ. Statistics; fmr Prof. of Econ. Statistics, Univ. of Cagliari; Prof. of Econ., Univ. of Rome 'La Sapienza' 1976–, Pres. Course of Statistics and Econs 1988–95, Dean of Faculty of Statistics 1995–2004, Pro-Rector La Sapienza Univ. 1997–2004, Rector 2004–08; mem. Comm. for the Guarantee of Information Statistics at Presidency of Council of Ministers, Scientific Advisory Cttee of Nat. Research Council, Ministry of Educ., Univ. and Research for 'decrees area', Comm. for the Reform of the Nat. Statistical System which prepared DL 322/89; mem. Accad. Nazionale dei Lincei 2001; Kt Grand Cross, Order of Merit of the Italian Repub. 2006. *Publications:* numerous scientific papers in professional journals. *Address:* c/o Office of the Rector, Università degli Studi di Roma 'La Sapienza', Piazzale Aldo Moro 5, 00185 Rome, Italy (office). *Telephone:* (06) 49914180 (office). *E-mail:* info@uniroma1.it (office). *Website:* www.uniroma1.it (office).

GUBBAY, Hon. Mr Justice Anthony Roy, MA, LLM; Zimbabwean judge; b. 26 April 1932, Manchester, England; m. Wilma Sanger 1962 (died 2002); two s.; ed Univ. of Witwatersrand, S Africa, Univ. of Cambridge, UK; admitted to practice 1957; advocate in Bulawayo, S Rhodesia 1958, Sr Counsel 1974; Pres. Matabeleland and Midlands Valuations Bds; Nat. Pres. Special Court for Income Tax Appeals, Fiscal Court and Patents Tribunal; Vice-Chair. Bar Asscn; Judge of the High Court, Bulawayo 1977–83, Judge of the Supreme Court 1983; Chair. Legal Practitioners' Disciplinary Tribunal 1981–87, Law Devt Comm., Judicial Service Comm.; Chief Justice of Zimbabwe 1990–2001, retd 2001; mem. Perm. Court of Arbitration; Pres. Oxford and Cambridge Soc. of Zimbabwe; Patron Commonwealth Magistrates and Judges Asscn; mem. Advisory Bd of Commonwealth Judicial Educ. Inst., Commonwealth Reference Group on the Promotion of the Human Rights of Women and the Girl Child through the Judiciary; Hon. Fellow, Jesus Coll. Cambridge; Hon. Bencher of Lincoln's Inn (UK); Hon. mem. The Soc. of Legal Scholars (UK) 2004; Great Cross, Rio Branco Order (Brazil) 1999; Dr hc (Essex) 1994; Hon. LLD (London) 2002, (Witwatersrand) 2005; Peter Gruber Foundation Justice Award 2001. *Leisure interests:* classical music, philately, watching all forms of sport, travel. *Address:* 26 Dacomb Drive, Chisipite, Harare, Zimbabwe (home). *Telephone:* (4) 496882 (home). *E-mail:* supreme-court@gta.gov .zw (office); gubbay@zol.co.zw (home).

GUBBAY, Raymond, CBE, FRSA; British music promoter; *Chairman, Raymond Gubbay Ltd;* b. 2 April 1946, London, England; s. of the late David Gubbay and Ida Gubbay; m. Johanna Quirke 1972 (divorced 1988); two d.; ed Univ. Coll. School, Hampstead; concert promoter 1966–; Founder, Man. Dir and Chair. Raymond Gubbay Ltd 1966–; presents regular series of concerts at major London and regional concert halls including Royal Albert Hall, Royal Festival Hall, Barbican Centre, Symphony Hall Birmingham, Bridgewater Hall Manchester, Royal Concert Hall Glasgow and in Ireland, Belgium, Germany, Austria, Switzerland, Netherlands and Scandinavia; has presented productions of: (operas and operettas) The Ratepayer's Iolanthe 1984, Turandot 1991–92, La Bohème (centenary production) 1996, 2004, 2006, Carmen 1997, 2002, 2005, 2009, 2010, 2013, Madam Butterfly 1998, 2000, 2003, 2011, The Pirates of Penzance 1998–99, 2000, Tosca 1999, Aïda 2001, Cavalleria Rusticana and Pagliacci 2002; (ballets) Swan Lake 1997, 1999, 2002, 2004, 2007, 2010, 2013, Romeo and Juliet 1998, The Sleeping Beauty 2000; D'Oyly Carte Opera Co. seasons 2000–03, Follies 2003, On Your Toes 2004, Savoy Opera 2004, Showboat 2006, Carmen Jones 2007, Strictly Gershwin 2008, 2011, The King and I 2009, Aïda (new production) 2012; mem. Bd Royal Philharmonic Orchestra, Bd Govs Cen. School of Ballet; Hon. FRAM 1988, Hon. FTCL 2000, Gold Badge Award, British Acad. of Songwriters, Composers and Authors 2009. *Leisure interests:* living in France, reading. *Address:* Dickens House, 15 Tooks Court, London, EC4A 1QH, England (office). *Telephone:* (20) 7025-3750 (office). *E-mail:* info@raymondgubbay.co.uk (office). *Website:* www .raymondgubbay.co.uk (office).

GUBBINS, David, BA, PhD, FRS, FInstP, MMath; British geophysicist and academic; *Professor Emeritus of Geophysics, School of Earth and Environment, University of Leeds;* b. 31 May 1947, Southampton, Hants., England; s. of the late Albert Edmund Gubbins and of Joyce Lucy Gubbins (née Rayner); m. Margaret Stella McCloy 1972; one s. two d.; ed King Edward VI Grammar School, Trinity Coll., Cambridge; Visiting Research Fellow, Univ. of Colorado 1972–73; instructor, MIT 1973–74; Asst Prof., UCLA 1974–76; Asst Dir of Research, Dept of Geodesy and Geophysics, Univ. of Cambridge 1976–89; Fellow, Churchill Coll., Cambridge 1978–90; Head of Geophysics, Univ. of Leeds 1989–2001, Research Prof. of Earth Sciences, currently Prof. Emer. of Geophysics; Ed. Geophysical Journal of the Royal Astronomical Society 1982–90, Physics of the Earth and Planetary Interior 1990–2002; Fellow, American Geophysical Union 1985; Foreign mem. Norwegian Acad. of Arts and Sciences 2005; Hon. mem. European Geosciences Union; Murchison Medal, Geological Soc. of London 1998, Gold Medal, Royal Astronomical Soc. 2003, John Adam Fleming Medal, American Geophysical Union 2004, Chree Medal, Inst. of Physics 2005, Augustus Love Medal, European Geophysical Union 2007, Arthur Holmes Medal, European Geophysical Union 2009. *Publications:* Seismology and Plate Tectonics 1990, Time Series Analysis and Inverse

Theory for Geophysicists 2004, Encyclopedia of Geomagnetism and Paleomagnetism 2007; more than 100 articles in scientific journals. *Leisure interests:* sailing, walking. *Address:* School of Earth and Environment, University of Leeds, Leeds, LS2 9JT, England (office). *Telephone:* (113) 343-5255 (office). *Fax:* (113) 343-5259 (office). *E-mail:* d.gubbins@see.leeds.ac.uk (office). *Website:* www.see.leeds.ac.uk/ people/d.gubbins (office); homepages.see.leeds.ac.uk/~ear6dg (office).

GUBENKO, Nikolai Nikolayevich; Russian actor and theatrical director; b. 17 Aug. 1941, Odessa; m. Jeanna Bolotova; ed All-Union Inst. of Cinema; mem. CPSU 1987–91, Cen. Cttee 1990–91, CP of Russian Fed. 1992–2002, expelled from party 2002, Ind. 2002–; actor at Taganka Theatre, Moscow 1964–, Artistic Dir 1987–89; Founder and Head of Concord of Taganka actors 1993–; dir several films including The Orphans (Soviet entry Cannes Film Festival 1977), The Life of Holidaymakers (based on story by Ivan Bunin), Life…Tears…Love, Restricted Area 1988; stage appearances include Boris Godunov; USSR Minister of Culture 1989–91; mem. State Duma (Parl.) 1995–2003; Deputy Chair. Cttee for Culture 1997–1999, Chair. 1999–2003; Pres. Int. Asscn of Help for Culture 1992; fmr mem. USSR Presidential Council; RSFSR People's Artist 1985. *Films include:* produced: Mne dvadtsat let 1964, Kogda uletayut aisty 1965, Parol ne nuzhen 1967, Nachalo nevedomogo veka 1967, Parviyat kurier 1968, Dvoryanskoe gnezdo 1969, Direktor 1969, Prishyol soldat s fronta 1971, Yesli khochesh byt schastlivym 1974, Proshu slova 1975, They Fought for Their Country 1975, Podranki 1977; directed: Nastasiya i Fomka 1970, Bratya Makarovy 1970, Iz zhizni otdykhayushchikh 1980, I zhizn, i slyozy, i lyubov 1984, Zapretnaya zona 1988. *Television:* Isayev 2008. *Address:* 110270 Moscow, Franzenskaya nab. 46, Apt. 65, Russia.

GUDANOV, Dmitry Konstantinovich; Russian ballet dancer; b. 1975, Moscow; ed Moscow Academic School of Choreography; joined Bolshoi Theatre Ballet Co. as a corps-de-ballet dancer 1994, soloist 1997, leading soloist 2000–; took part in Bolshoi Theatre project New Choreography Workshop 2004; 1st Prize and Gold Medal 7th Int. Moscow Ballet Competition 1998, 1st Prize Int. Ballet Competition Paris 1998, Soul of Dance Prize, Ballet Magazine 2000, Merited Artist of the Russian Fed. 2005. *Ballet:* leading roles in Sleeping Beauty, Nutcracker, Le Mégère Apprivoisée, La Sylphide, Fantasia on the Theme of Casanova, Giselle, Romeo and Juliet, Symphony C-major (production of G. Balanchine), Heir in Hamlet (production of B. Eifman), Chopiniana 2003. *Address:* Bolshoi Theatre, Teatralnaya pl. 1, Moscow, Russia (office). *Website:* www.bolshoi.org (office). mariinsky.ru/en/ballet/gudanov05.

GUÐFINNSSON, Einar Kristinn; Icelandic politician; b. 2 Dec. 1955, Bolungarvík; s. of Guðfinnur Einarsson (deceased) and María K. Haraldsdóttir; m. Sigrún J. Þórisdóttir; three c.; ed Coll. of Isafjordur, Univ. of Essex, UK; fmr journalist; fmr CEO fisheries co.; mem. Parl. 1991–, fmr Chair. Fisheries Cttee, Econs and Trade Cttee, fmr mem. Finance Cttee, Social Cttee, Agric. Cttee, Parls Cttee for Foreign Affairs; fmr Chair. Icelandic Group, IPU; fmr Group Chair. Independence Party; Minister of Fisheries 2005–09 (resgnd), also of Agriculture 2007–09 (resgnd). *Address:* Independence Party, 105 Reykjavik, Iceland (office). *Telephone:* 5151700 (office). *Fax:* 5151717 (office). *E-mail:* xd@xd.is (office). *Website:* www.xd.is (office).

GUDMUNDSSON, Már, BA, MPh; Icelandic economist and central banker; *Governor, Central Bank of Iceland;* b. 1954; m.; three c.; ed Univs of Essex and Cambridge, UK, Univ. of Gothenburg, Sweden; joined Seðlabanki Íslands (Cen. Bank of Iceland) as economist 1980, later Head of Research and Man., Chief Economist 1994–2004, Gov. 2009–; Econ. Adviser to Minister of Finance 1988–91; IMF Adviser to Trinidad and Tobago 1998–99; Deputy Head, Monetary and Econ. Dept, BIS, Basel, Switzerland 2004–09. *Publications include:* several articles in books and econ. journals. *Address:* Office of the Governor, Central Bank of Iceland, Kalkofnsvegur 1, 150 Reykjavík, Iceland (office). *Telephone:* 5699600 (office). *Fax:* 5699605 (office). *E-mail:* sedlabanki@sedlabanki.is (office). *Website:* www .sedlabanki.is (office).

GUÉANT, Claude Henri; French civil servant, government official and lawyer; b. 17 Jan. 1945, Vimy; s. of Robert Guéant and Madeleine Guéant (née Leclercq); m. Rose-Marie Benoist 1969; two c.; ed Faculté de droit de Paris, Institut d'études politiques de Paris, École nationale d'admin, Paris; Cabinet Dir, Prefect of Finistère 1971–74; Sec.-Gen. for Econ. Affairs, Guadeloupe 1974–77; served in Ministry of the Interior 1977–81; apptd sous-préfet hors classe, worked in Centre region prefect 1981, then Sec.-Gen. Hérault Prefect, then Sec.-Gen. Hauts-de-Seine Prefect; Préfet Hautes-Alpes 1991–94; Dir-Gen. Nat. Police Force 1994–98; Préfet Franche-Comté region and Doubs 1998–2000, of Brittany region, Western defence zone and d'Ille-et-Vilaine 2000–02; Chief of Staff to Minister of the Interior Nicolas Sarkozy 2002–04, 2005–07; with Ministry of Finance 2004; campaign manager for presidential campaign of Nicolas Sarkozy 2007; Adviser, Secrétaire général de la Présidence de la République 2007–11; Minister of the Interior, the Overseas Possessions, the Territorial Collectivities and Immigration 2011–12; political adviser to Union for a Popular Movement (UMP); Chevalier, Légion d'honneur, Commdr, Ordre Nat. de Mérite. *Address:* 34 avenue Georges V, 75008 Paris (office); 3 rue Weber, 75116 Paris, France (home). *Telephone:* 1-47-20-57-11 (office); 6-08-26-44-04 (home). *Fax:* 1-47-20-57-98 (office). *E-mail:* cg@ gueantavocats.com (office).

GUEBUZA, Armando Emílio; Mozambican politician and head of state; *President;* b. 20 Jan. 1943, Murrupula, Nampula Prov.; joined Frente de Libertação de Moçambique (Frelimo) 1963; elected to Cen. Cttee 1966–, to Politburo 1977–; guerrilla commdr during war with Portugal, rising to rank of Lt-Gen.; Political Commissar 1970–; Minister of Home Affairs 1974–78, 1983–84, Deputy Minister of Defence 1978–81, Resident Minister 1981–84, Minister in the Office of the Pres. 1984–86, Minister of Transport and Communication 1986–94; Head of Frelimo Parl. Bench 1994–2002, Frelimo Sec.-Gen. June 2002–; Pres. of Mozambique 2005–; Head of Govt Del. to Rome peace talks 1992; Chair. two Comms for Burundi peace process under Julius Nyerere and Nelson Mandela. *Address:* Office of the President, Avda Julius Nyerere 1780, Maputo (office); Frente de Libertação de Moçambique (Frelimo), Rua Pereira do Lago 229, Maputo, Mozambique (office). *Telephone:* (1) 491121 (office). *Fax:* (1) 492065 (office). *E-mail:* gabimprensa@teldata.mz (office); sg@frelimo.org.mz (office). *Website:* www .presidencia.gov.mz (office); www.frelimo.org.mz (office).

GUÉDIGUIAN, Robert; French filmmaker; b. 3 Dec. 1953, L'Estaque, Marseille; m. Ariane Ascaride; producer associated with AGAT Films & Cie. *Films:* Fernand (writer) 1979, Le souffleur (writer, producer) 1985; writer, dir, producer: Dernier été (Prix Georges Sadoul) 1980, Rouge midi 1983, Ki lo sa? 1985, Dieu vomit les tièdes (TV) 1989, Marie-Jo et ses 2 amours 2002, Mon père est ingénieur 2004, Le Voyage en Arménie 2006; writer, dir: L'argent fait le bonheur (Prix Michel Kuhn, Rencontres européennes de Reims) 1992; producer: Un tour de manège, Montalvo et l'enfant, Variétés 1989, Le cri du cochon 1990, Suzanne Linke, Bali, les couleurs du divin 1992, Marseille, la vieille ville indigne 1993, Baudelaire modernité 1986, Vittel Design 1987 (Grand Prix, Vidéo Festival de Biarritz), Le coupeur d'eau 1989, En direct de l'être humain 1991, C'est trop con (Prix du Jury, Festival européen d'Angers) 1992, Ça se passe en Equateur, Que la vie est belle 1993, A la vie à la mort, Marius et Jeannette, La ville est tranquille 2001, Dernier des fous 2006, Sous les toits de Paris 2007, Romances de terre et d'eau 2002, Les Fautes d'orthographe 2004; producer, dir: Le Promeneur du champ de Mars 2005. *Address:* c/o AGAT Films & Cie., 52 rue Jean-Pierre Timbaud, 75011 Paris, France (office).

GUÉGUINOU, Jean, GCVO; French diplomatist; *President, Conseil Franco-Britannique;* b. 17 Oct. 1941; s. of Louis-Bernard Guéguinon and Jeanne-Rose Le Fur; ed Ecole Nat. d'Admin; with Press and Information Dept, Ministry of Foreign Affairs 1967–69; Second Sec., London 1969–71; Head of Mission, Ministry of State/Ministry of Defence 1971–73; Head of Cabinet and Counsellor 1973–76; Dir of Cabinet of Sec. of State reporting to Prime Minister 1976–77; Asst Dir for Southern Africa and Indian Ocean 1977–82; Consul-Gen., Jerusalem 1982–86; Dir Press and Information Service 1986–90; Amb. to Czechoslovakia 1990–92, to Czech Repub. 1993, to UK 1993–98, to the Holy See 1998–2000, Amb. to UNESCO 2003–07; Pres. French Section, Franco-British Council (Conseil Franco-Britannique); Pres. Culturesfrance 2009–10; Chair. Cttee de patronage, Franco-Scottish Asscn 2001; mem. Admin Council, Agence France-Presse 1986–90, Soc. of Friends of the Louvre 2000–, Arts florissants 2001–; Chevalier, Légion d'honneur, Ordre Nat. du Mérite; Commdr Order of St Gregory the Great. *Address:* Conseil franco-britannique 66, rue de Bellechasse, Paris 75007, France (office). *Telephone:* 1-42-75-79-83 (office). *E-mail:* conseilfrancobritannique@wanadoo.fr (office). *Website:* www.conseilfrancobritannique.info (office).

GUÉHENNO, Jean-Marie; French diplomatist and fmr UN official; *Arnold Saltzman Professor of Professional Practice in International and Public Affairs and Director, Center for International Conflict Resolution, School of International and Public Affairs, Columbia University;* b. 30 Oct. 1949, Boulogne-sur-Seine (Hauts-de-Seine); s. of the late Jean Guéhenno and of Annie Guéhenno (née Rospabé); m. Michèle Fahy Moss 1981; one d.; ed Lycée Montaigne and Lycée Louis-le-Grand, Paris, Ecole Normale Supérieure, Inst. d'Études Politiques, École Nat. d'Admin, Paris; mem. Court of Auditors 1976–2000, Sr Auditor 1993–2000; Dir Cultural Affairs, French Embassy in Washington, DC 1982–86; Dir Policy Planning Staff, Ministry of Foreign Affairs 1989–93; Amb. to WEU 1993–95; UN Under-Sec.-Gen. for Peacekeeping Operations, New York 2000–08; Chair. Bd Inst. for Higher Defence Studies, Paris 1998–2000; Non-resident Sr Fellow, Brookings Inst., Washington, DC, New York Univ. Center on Int. Cooperation; Arnold Saltzman Prof. of Professional Practice in Int. and Public Affairs and Dir Center for Int. Conflict Resolution, School of Int. and Public Affairs, Columbia Univ., New York 2012–, Assoc. Dir Arnold A. Saltzman Inst. for War and Peace Studies, directs the School's Int. Conflict Resolution specialization; UN Asst to Kofi Annan in his mission in Syria March–July 2012; Chair. Centre for Humanitarian Dialogue, Geneva, Switzerland; mem. Bd, Int. Crisis Group, European Council on Foreign Relations, Civilians in Conflict, French-Amertican Foundation; Officier, Légion d'honneur; Commdr, Bundesverdienstkreuz. *Publications:* La fin de la démocratie (English trans. The End of the Nation-State) 1993, L'avenir de la liberté – la démocratie dans la mondialisation 1999, Guide du maintien de la paix (co-author) 2006. *Leisure interests:* sailing, walking, tennis, reading, museums. *Address:* Room 1325, International Affairs Building, School of International and Public Affairs, Columbia University, 420 West 118th Street, New York, NY 10027, USA (office). *Telephone:* (212) 851-5952 (office). *E-mail:* jg3083@columbia.edu (office). *Website:* new.sipa.columbia.edu/faculty/jean-marie-gu-henno (office).

GUELAR, Diego Ramiro; Argentine lawyer and diplomatist; b. 24 Feb. 1950; m. Magdalena D. Custodio; three c.; Prof. of Sociology of Law, Univ. of Buenos Aires 1971; outlawed by mil. for political activities (nat. leader, Peronist Youth) 1972–73; attorney, Justicialist Party of Buenos Aires Prov. 1973–76; Prof., Faculties of Architecture and Law, Univ. of Buenos Aires 1973–76; outlawed for political activities 1976–78; nat. adviser of coordinator for Justicialist activities 1978–83; Vice-Pres. Comm. for Budget and Finance, Nat. Chamber of Deputies 1984; Sec.-Gen. bloc of Nat. Justicialist Deputies 1985; Ed. and Dir La Razón newspaper 1987; Head, Foundation for Growth Arrangement; Amb. to EC (now EU) 1989–96, to USA 1997–99, 2002; currently Head of Relaciones Institucionales, Propuesta Republicana (PRO); Consultant, GLE Consorcio de Cooperación, Buenos Aires; mem. Inst. for European-Latin American Relations, Center for Studies about Regional Integration, Center for Strategic Int. Studies, Argentine Council for Int. Relations. *Publications include:* Chronicles of Transition (collection), political and econ. works etc. *Address:* c/o Propuesta Republicana Alsina 1325, C1088AAI, Buenos Aires, Argentina (office). *E-mail:* info@pro.com.ar (office). *Website:* www .pro.com.ar (office).

GUELENGDOUKSIA OUAÏDOU, Nassour; Chadian politician; b. 1947; fmrly Sec.-Gen. in Office of the Pres.; Prime Minister of Chad 1997–99; Sec.-Gen. Econ. Community of Cen. African States (ECCAS) 2012–13; *Website:* www.ceeac-eccas .org.

GUÉNA, Yves René Henri; French fmr politician; b. 6 July 1922, Brest; m. Oriane de la Bourdonnaye 1945; five s. two d.; ed Ecole Nat. d'Administration, Paris; mem. Free French Forces 1940–45; Official in Morocco 1947, Maître des Requêtes, Conseil d'Etat 1957, Dir de Cabinet to M. Debré (Minister of Justice) 1958–59, Deputy Dir de Cabinet to M. Debré (Prime Minister) Jan.–July 1959; High Commr Ivory Coast 1959–60, Envoy Extraordinary (Dean of Diplomatic Corps) 1960–61; elected Deputy for Dordogne, Nat. Ass. 1962, 1967, 1968, 1973, 1974, 1978, lost seat 1981, re-elected 1986, lost seat 1988; elected Senator for Dordogne 1989; Vice-Pres. of Senate 1992–95, 1995–97; mem. Constitutional Council 1997–2004 (Pres. 1999–2004); Minister of Posts and Telecommunications 1967–68, 1968–69, of Information May–July 1968, of Transport 1973–74, of Industrial and Scientific Devt, March–May 1974; Deputy Sec.-Gen. UDR 1974,

Sec.-Gen. 1976; Political Adviser and Nat. Treasurer, RPR 1977–79; Mayor of Périgueux (Dordogne) 1971, re-elected 1977, 1983, 1989, 1995–97 (resgnd); Pres. Arab World Inst. 2004–06; Conseiller d'Etat 1972; Croix de guerre 1944, Médaille de la Résistance 1946, Grand Croix Légion d'honneur 2005. *Publications:* Historique de la communauté 1962, Maintenir l'état 1970, L'enjeu (in collaboration) 1975, Le temps des certitudes 1940–69 1982, Catilina ou la gloire dérobée 1984, Les cent premiers jours (co-author) 1985, Ecrits et discours (25 années de vie publique) 1987, Moi duc de Lauzun, citoyen Biron 1997, Ecrits et discours (II) 1999, Le Baron Louis 1999, Phèdre 2000 (play) 2000, Les Wendel-Trois siècles d'Histoire 2004, L'Histoire de France racontée à mes petits enfants, Vol. 1 2004, Vol. 2, 2005, Mémoires d'Outre-Gaulle 2010. *Address:* 13 rue René Bazin, 75016 Paris, France (home). *Telephone:* 1-45-24-25-28 (home).

GUENIN, Marcel André, PhD; Swiss scientist, academic and company director; *Honorary Professor, University of Geneva;* b. 17 July 1937, Geneva; s. of Léandré André and Isabelle Guenin-Bontempo; m. Ingrid Marina Selbach 1962; three s.; ed Eidgenössische Technische Hochschule Zürich, Univ. of Geneva and Harvard Univ., USA; Asst and Master Asst, Univ. of Geneva 1960–64; Research Assoc., Princeton Univ. 1964–66; Lecturer, Grad. Programme, Univs. of Lausanne, Neuchâtel and Geneva 1966–68; Asst Prof., Univ. of Geneva 1968–70, Professeur extraordinaire 1970–73, Professeur ordinaire 1973–2000, Hon. Prof. 2000–, Dir Dept of Theoretical Physics 1974–77, Dir Group of Applied Physics (GAP) 1993–2000, Vice-Rector Univ. of Geneva 1980–83, Rector 1983–87; Pres. PBG Pvt. Bank, Geneva 1987–89; Chair. Bd COGITAS 1988–94, E. & L. Schmidheiny Foundation 1992–2007; mem. Bd BBC Brown Boveri Ltd 1987–96, Brunet 1990–93, Lasarray 1990–93, Soc. d'Instruments de physique 1998–2000; Sec.-Gen. European Physical Soc. 1974–79, Fellow 1980; Sec. Swiss Physical Soc. 1975–79; mem. Bd Soc. Financière de Genève 1988–89; Founding mem. Int. Asscn of Math. Physicists; mem. American Physical Soc. *Publications:* three books and about 40 scientific publs. *Leisure interests:* skiing, sailing, music. *Address:* Applied Physics Group, University of Geneva, 20 Ecole de Medicine, 1211 Geneva 4 (office); 2B chemin des Manons, 1218 Grand-Saconnex (GE), Switzerland (home).

GUÉRARD, Michel Etienne; French chef, restaurateur and hotelier; *President and Director General, Compagnie Hôtelière et Fermière d'Eugénie les Bains;* b. 27 March 1933, Vétheuil; s. of Maurice Guérard and Georgine Guérard; m. Christine Barthelemy 1974; two d.; ed Lycée Pierre Corneille, Rouen; apprentice patissier, Mantes la Jolie; Head Patissier, Hotel Crillon, Paris; chef to brothers Clérico, Lido, Paris; created restaurant le Pot au Feu, Asnières (two Michelin stars); undertook complex renovation of hotel and thermal treatment centre Les Prés d'Eugénie (now three Michelin stars), Eugénie les Bains; consultant to Nestlé; opened first Comptoir Gourmand Michel Guérard; restored Chai de Bachen and produced a white Tursan, Baron de Bachen; Officier, Légion d'honneur, Ordre nat. du Mérite, Mérite Agricole, des Arts et des Lettres; Chevalier des Palmes académiques; Meilleur Ouvrier de France (MOF Patisserie) 1958. *Publications:* La Grande Cuisine Minceur 1976, La Cuisine Gourmande 1978, Mes Recettes à la TV 1982, Minceur Exquise 1989, Le Sud-Ouest Gourmand de Relais en Châteaux 1993, La Cuisine Gourmande des Juniors 1997, Le Jeu de l'Oie et du Canard 1998, La Cuisine à Vivre 2000, Comment Briller aux Fourneaux sans Savoir Faire Cuire un Oeuf 2010, Minceur Essentielle 2012. *Leisure interests:* antiques, painting, sketchbooks, food and wine. *Address:* Les Prés d'Eugénie, Place de l'Impératrice, 40320 Eugénie les Bains, France (office). *Telephone:* (5) 58-05-06-07 (office). *Fax:* (5) 58-51-10-10 (office). *E-mail:* direction@michelguerard.com (office). *Website:* www.michelguerard.com (office).

GUERIN, Orla, MBE, MA; Irish journalist; b. May 1966; d. of the late Patrick James Guerin and Monica Guerin; ed Coll. of Commerce, Dublin, Univ. Coll. Dublin; newscaster, presenter and Foreign Corresp. with Irish State TV, RTE, Dublin 1987–94; joined BBC TV as news corresp. 1995, Southern Europe Corresp. covering the Balkans and conflict in the Basque country 1996–2000, Middle East Corresp. 2001–05, Africa Corresp. 2006–08, Pakistan Corresp. 2008, now Middle East Corresp.; Hon. MBE 2004; Hon. DUniv (Essex) 2002; Dr hc (Dublin Inst. of Tech.) 2005, (Open Univ.) 2007, (Queen's Univ. Belfast) 2009; Hon. DLitt (Ulster) 2009; The Jacobs Award for Broadcasters (Ireland) 1992, London Press Club Broadcaster of the Year Award 2002, News and Factual Award, Women in Film and Television (UK) 2003, David Bloom Award 2009. *Address:* c/o BBC News, Broadcasting House, Portland Place, London, W1A 1AA, England (office). *Website:* www.bbc.co.uk (office).

GUERRA PASTORA, José Adán, PhD; Nicaraguan politician; b. 28 Oct. 1952, Managua; trained as lawyer; Acting Minister of Foreign Affairs 2000; Minister of Nat. Defence 2001–05; Pres. of Demining Comm.; mem. Office of Nat. Security; mem. Exec., Nat. Comm. for Disaster Prevention, Nat. Council of the War on Drugs; Simón Bolívar Democracy and Human Rights Award, WHINSEC. *Address:* c/o Ministry of National Defence, Casa de la Presidencia, Managua, Nicaragua (office).

GUERRAOUI, Abdellatif; Moroccan business executive and fmr government official; *Chairman, Auto Hall Group;* b. 10 July 1939, Safi; s. of Abdeslam Guerraoui and Oumhani Benazzouz; m. Laila Iaoufir 1968; one s. two d.; ed École nationale supérieure d'électronique, d'électrotechnique, d'informatique, d'hydraulique et des télécommunications, Toulouse, France; Chief of Staff, Computer Systems, Cherifien Office of Phosphates (OCP) 1964–70, Chief of Personnel Admin. Div. 1970–71, Sec.-Gen. OCP 1971–90, mem. Bd of Dirs –2000; Admin., Gen. Man. Moroccan-Saudi Investment Co. (ASMA-INVEST) 1991–93; Minister of Energy and Mines 1993–97, of Social Affairs, Health, Youth and Sports, Nat. Mutual Aid 1997–98; Pres. Bd Tharwa Finance 1999–2001; Wali of the Region Laayoune Boujdour Sakiat El Hamra 2001–02; Gen. Dir Agency for Promotion of Econ. and Social Devt Southern Provs 2002–03; CEO Soc. Maroc Emirats Arabes Unis de Développement (SOMED) 2003–06; Chair. Auto Hall Group 2004–; fmr Vice-Chair. Supervisory Bd Credit du Maroc; Trustee, Al Akhawayn Univ.; mem. Bd Three Cultures and Three Religions Foundation; Officier, Wissam El Arch Grade 1985, Commdr Nat. Order of Merit (Portugal) 2003; Throne Award from King of Morocco 1985. *Leisure interests:* classical literature, history, management, economy, futurology. *Address:* Auto Hall SA, 64 Avenue Lalla yacout, Casablanca (office); 45 rue Ksar El Badii, Hay El Hana, Préfecture Ain Chock-Hay Hassani, Casablanca 20200, Morocco (home). *Telephone:* (522) 460304 (office); (522) 303041 (home). *Fax:* (522) 318915 (office); (522) 318803 (home). *E-mail:* dg@autohall.ma (office). *Website:* www.autohall.ma (office).

GUERRERO PEÑARANDA, Ramiro; Bolivian lawyer and politician; *Attorney General;* ed Universidad San Francisco Xavier de Chuquisaca; practised law for 20 years; worked with peasant orgs and indigenous peoples with la Fundación Tierra; adviser to Federación de Campesinos, Consejo de Capitanes y Guaraníes de Chuquisaca; mem. Movimiento Al Socialismo 2006–07, was part of the Comm. on Land and Territory; apptd Judge of the then Supreme Court (Corte Suprema de Justicia) by Pres. Evo Morales 2010–12; Attorney Gen. 2012–. *Address:* c/o Ministry of Justice, Avenida 16 de Julio (El Prado) 1769, La Paz, Bolivia (office). *Telephone:* (2) 212-4725 (office). *Fax:* (2) 231-5468 (office). *E-mail:* ministerio@justicia.go.bo (office). *Website:* www.justicia.gob.bo (office).

GUERROUJ, Hicham al-; Moroccan professional athlete; b. 14 Sept. 1974, Berkane; set six world records indoors and outdoors 1997–99 (including 1,500m, 3:26.00, Rome, July 1998, one mile, 3:43.12, Rieti, July 1999, 2,000m, 4:44.79, Berlin, Sept. 1999); bronze medal, World Jr Championships 5,000m 1992; World Champion 1,500m 1997, 1999, 2001, 2003; Indoor World Champion 1500m 2001; silver medallist, 2000 Olympics, gold medalist 1,500m 2004 Olympics; winner IAAF Grand Prix Final 1,500m 2001, 2002; silver medallist World Championships 5,000m 2003; holder of outdoor world record for 1,500m, 2,000m and one mile, of indoor record for 1,500m and one mile; winner of 72 races from 75 starts 1996–2002; retd 2006; mem. IAAF Athletes Comm. 2003–, Int. Cttee Olympic Athletes Comm. 2004–, Culture and Olympic Educ. Comm. 2007–, Nominations Comm. 2010–; Cordon de Commandeur (Morocco) 2004, IAAF Male Athlete of the Year 2001, 2002, US Track and Field Male Athlete of the Year 2002, Prince of Asturias Award 2004. *Address:* c/o International Association of Athletics Federations, 17 rue Princesse Florestine, BP 359, MC 98007, Monaco (office).

GUESNERIE, Roger Sylvain Maxime Auguste, DèsSc (Econs); French economist; *Professor of Economics, Collège de France;* b. 17 Feb. 1943, Ste Gemmes Le Rt.; s. of Sylvain Guesnerie and Marie Chapelière; ed Lycée de Rennes, Ecole Polytechnique and Ecole Nat. des Ponts et Chaussées, Univ. of Toulouse; Research Assoc., Centre d'Études Prospectives et de Recherches en Economie Mathématique Appliquée à la Planification (CEPREMAP) 1967–81; Research Assoc., CNRS 1976, Research Dir 1978; Dir of Studies, Ecole des Hautes Etudes en Sciences Sociales (EHESS) 1979–; Dir Centre d'Études Quantitatives Comparatives (CEQC) 1981–82, Centre d'Études et de Recherches en Analyse Socio-économiques (CERAS) 1982–84, Asscn pour le Développement de la Recherche en Economie et Statistique (ADRES) 1989–94, Dir Delta (mixed research unit of CNRS-EHESS-ENS) 1988–2000, Fédération Paris Jourdan 2001–05; Lecturer, École Nationale des Ponts et Chaussées 1970–83, Paris X Nanterre 1972–73, École Polytechnique 1974–86, Institut d'Études Politiques de Paris 1975–78, Paris IX-Dauphine 1974–76; Prof., École Nationale de la Statistique et de l'Administration Economique 1978–84; Prof., LSE 1990–94; Prof. of Econs, Coll. de France 2000–; Vice-Pres. European Econ. Asscn 1992, Pres. 1993; Pres. Scientific Cttee CEPREMAP 1992–95, Select Cttee on Econ. and Social Sciences, Brussels 1992–95, Asscn of Applied Econometrics 1997–2001, Asscn Française de Science Economique 2002–03; Pres. of Bd Paris School of Econs 2008–; mem. Scientific Council EHESS 1985–91, Nat. Cttee CNRS 1987–91, European Asscn of Science and Tech. 1994–97, Research Council of Ecole Polytechnique 2000–02, Nat. Cttee on Social and Scientific Coordination 2001–02, Scientific Cttee Ecole Normale Supérieure 2001–05; Foreign Fellow, Churchill Coll., Univ. of Cambridge 1978; Fellow, Econometric Soc., Pres. 1996; Foreign mem. American Acad. of Arts and Sciences 2000–; Hon. Foreign mem. American Econ. Asscn 1997; Chevalier, Ordre du Mérite, Legion d'Honneur; Dr hc (Ecole des Hautes Etudes Commerciales) 2001; Silver Medal, CNRS 1994. *Publications:* La documentation Française, 2 vols (co-author), Modèles de l'economie publique 1980, A Contribution to the Pure Theory of Taxation 1995, L'Economie de marché 1996, Assessing Rational Expectations 1 2001, Assessing Rational Expectations 2 2005, L'économie de marché 2006, Ethique et changement climatique (co-author) 2009, La santé, par quels moyens, à quel prix (co-author) 2010, Pour une politique climatique globale 2010; about 100 articles in econ. journals. *Leisure interests:* cycling, jogging, walking. *Address:* Collège de France, 3 rue d'Ulm, 75005 Paris, France (office). *Telephone:* 1-44-27-16-43 (office). *Fax:* 1-43-13-63-10 (office). *E-mail:* roger.guesnerie@college-de-france.fr (office). *Website:* www.pse.ens.fr/guesnerie (office); www.delta.ens.fr (office).

GUEST, Christopher; American actor, film director and screenwriter; b. (Christopher Haden-Guest), 5 Feb. 1948, New York City; s. of Peter Haden-Guest, Baron of Saling in the Co. of Essex; m. Jamie Lee Curtis 1984; two c.; ed High School of Arts and Music, New York City, Bard Coll.; theatre debut in Room Service, Broadway 1970; writer and performer, Nat. Lampoon radio series 1970s; appeared as Tufnel on Lenny and the Squigtones (album) 1980; wrote script and music for film This is Spinal Tap (with Rob Reiner, Michael McKean and Harry Shearer) 1984, later toured as band Spinal Tap; writer and dir Morton & Hayes TV series 1991. *Films include:* The Hot Rock 1972, Lemmings 1973, Death Wish 1974, The Fortune 1975, Girlfriends 1978, The Last Word 1980, The Long Riders 1980, Heartbeeps 1981, Million Dollar Infield 1982, Blind Ambition 1982, This is Spinal Tap 1984, Little Shop of Horrors 1986, The Princess Bride 1987, Beyond Therapy 1987, Sticky Fingers 1988, The Big Picture 1989 (writer and dir), The Return of Spinal Tap 1992, Spinal Tap: Break Like the Wind 1992 (writer and dir), A Few Good Men 1992, Attack of the 50 Foot Woman 1993 (writer and dir), Waiting for Guffman (also writer and dir) 1996, Spinal Tap: The Final Tour 1998, Small Soldiers 1998, Almost Heroes (writer and dir) 1998, Catching Up with Marty DiBeri 2000, Best in Show (also writer and dir) 2000, A Mighty Wind (also writer and dir) 2003, Mrs Henderson Presents 2005, For Your Consideration (also writer and dir) 2006, Night at the Museum: Battle of the Smithsonian 2009, The Invention of Lying 2009. *Address:* c/o Sharon Sheinwold, United Talent Agency Inc., 9560 Wilshire Boulevard, Suite 500, Beverly Hills, CA 90212, USA (office). *Telephone:* (310) 273-6700 (office). *Fax:* (310) 247-1111 (office).

GUEST, John Rodney, DPhil, FRS; British molecular geneticist and academic; *Professor Emeritus of Microbiology, University of Sheffield;* b. 27 Dec. 1935, Leeds, Yorks., England; s. of Sidney R. Guest and D. Kathleen Guest (née Walker); m. Barbara M. Dearsley 1962; one s. two d.; ed Campbell Coll., Belfast, Univ. of Leeds, Trinity Coll., Oxford; Guinness Research Fellow, Univ. of Oxford 1960–65;

Research Assoc. and Fulbright Scholar, Stanford Univ., USA 1963, 1964; Lecturer in Microbiology, Univ. of Sheffield 1965–68, Sr Lecturer and Reader 1968–81, Prof. of Microbiology 1981–2000, Prof. Emer. 2000–; Science and Eng Research Council Sr Fellowship 1981–86; Royal Soc. Leeuwenhoek Lecturer 1995; Hon. mem. Soc. for Gen. Microbiology 2000. *Achievements:* cloned and sequenced genes of the Citric Acid Cycle, Aspartase, and discovered and characterized an Oxygen-responding Gene Regulator (FNR) in bacteria. *Publications:* research papers in scientific journals. *Leisure interests:* hill walking, beekeeping, family history. *Address:* Department of Molecular Biology and Biotechnology, University of Sheffield, Western Bank, Sheffield, South Yorks., S10 2TN, England (office). *E-mail:* j.r.guest@sheffield.ac.uk (home).

GUEVARA MANZO, Gloria, MBA; Mexican tourism industry executive and politician; *Secretary of Tourism;* b. 1967; ed Universidad Anáhuac, Kellogg School of Business, Northwestern Univ., USA; began career with NCR Corpn and AT&GIS Mexico; several years in tourism industry with Sabre Travel Network in Mexico and USA, including sales, training, customer service, operations and technology roles, becoming Technology Dir Customer Service and Operations, Sabre Travel Network Latin America and the Caribbean, later with Sabre Holdings, Southlake, Tex., Vice-Pres. and Gen. Dir Sabre Travel Network Mexico 2005–10; Sec. of Tourism 2010–, also Head of Mexican Tourism Bd. *Address:* Secretariat of State for Tourism, Avda Presidente Masaryk 172, Col. Chapultepec Morales, Del. Miguel Hidalgo, 11587 México DF, Mexico (office). *Telephone:* (55) 3002-6300 (home). *Fax:* (55) 1036-0789 (home). *E-mail:* atencion@sectur.gob.mx (office). *Website:* www.sectur.gob.mx (home).

GUEVARA OBREGÓN, Alberto José, MSc; Nicaraguan politician, economist and central banker; *President, Banco Central de Nicaragua;* b. 1963; m.; three c.; ed Carlos Fonseca Amador Univ., Catholic Univ. of Chile and Nat. Univ. of Nicaragua; fmr Prof. of Economics and Public Finance; held various positions at Banco Central de Nicaragua (cen. bank) 1999–2006, currently Pres., also Gov. Inter-American Development Bank; Minister of Finance and Public Credit 2007–12. *Address:* Banco Central de Nicaragua, Carretera Sur, Km 7, Apdos 2252/3, Zona 5, Managua, Nicaragua (office). *Telephone:* 2255-7171 (office). *Fax:* 2265-0561 (office). *E-mail:* oaip@bcn.gob.ni (office). *Website:* www.bcn.gob.ni (office).

GUHA, Ramachandra, MA, PhD; Indian writer and historian; b. 1958, Dehradun; s. of Subramaniam Rama Das Guha; m. Sujata Keshavan; two c.; ed St Stephen's Coll., Delhi, Delhi School of Econs, Indian Inst. of Man., Calcutta; taught at Yale Univ. and Stanford Univ., USA; Fellow, Wissenschaftskolleg zu Berlin, Germany 1994–95; fmr Arné Naess Chair. Univ. of Oslo; fmr Indo-American Community Visiting Prof., Univ. of California, Berkeley, Sundaraja Visiting Prof. in the Humanities, Indian Inst. of Science, Bangalore 2003; fmr columnist, The Telegraph of Calcutta; currently full-time writer; Trustee, New India Foundation; Padma Bhushan 2009; MacArthur Fellowship, Leopold-Hidy Prize, American Soc. of Environmental History 2001, Daily Telegraph Cricket Soc. Book of the Year 2002, Malcolm Adideshiah Award, R. K. Narayan Prize 2003. *Publications:* The Unquiet Woods: Ecological Change and Peasant Resistance in the Himalaya 1989, This Fissured Land: An Ecological History of India (co-author) 1992, Wickets in the East 1992, Social Ecology (co-ed.) 1994, Spin and Other Turns 1994, An Indian Cricket Omnibus (co-ed.) 1994, Ecology and Equity (co-ed.) 1995, Nature, Culture, Imperialism: Essays on the Environmental History of South Asia (co-author) 1996, Varieties of Environmentalism: Essays North and South (co-author) 1997, Savaging the Civilized – Verrier Elwin, his tribals and India 1999, An Anthropologist Among the Marxists, and other essays 2000, Environmentalism: A Global History 2000, Institutions and Inequalities: Essays in Honour of André Béteille (co-author) 2000, A Corner of a Foreign Field (Daily Telegraph Cricket Soc. Book of the Year 2002) 2001, The Picador Book of Cricket (ed.) 2001, An Indian Cricket Century (ed.) 2002, The Last Liberal and Other Essays 2004, The States of Indian Cricket 2005, How Much Should a Person Consume?: Thinking Through the Environment 2006, Nature's Spokesman: M. Krishnan and Indian Wildlife (ed.) 2007, India after Gandhi: The History of the World's Largest Democracy 2007, The Miracle That Is India 2007; contrib. essays, articles and reviews to magazines. *Address:* 22A Brunton Road, Bangalore 560 025 (home); c/o Marketing and Promotions Department, Penguin Books India Pvt. Ltd, 11 Community Centre, Panchsheel Park, New Delhi 110017, India (office). *E-mail:* publicity@in.penguingroup.com (office). *Website:* www.penguinbooksindia.com (office).

GUHA, Subhendu, PhD; American (b. Indian) scientist and academic; *Senior Vice-President and Chairman, United Solar Ovonic LLC;* b. Calcutta, India; ed Presidency Coll., Univ. of Calcutta, Univ. of Sheffield, UK; worked on semiconductors at Tata Inst. of Fundamental Research 1970–82; Sr Vice-Pres. Photovoltaic Tech., Energy Conversion Devices, USA 1982–90, Pres. United Solar Ovonic LLC (wholly-owned subsidiary) 2000–03, Pres. and COO 2003–07, Sr Vice-Pres. and Chair. 2007–, Co-founder United Solar Systems (jt venture co. with Canon Inc. of Japan) 1990; mem. Advisory Bd Nat. Center for Photovoltaics; Grand Award (Best of What's New), Popular Science 1996, Discover Magazine's Tech. Innovation Award 1997, R&D Magazine's R&D 100 Award 1998, Bright Light Award, US Dept of Energy, World Tech. Award in Energy, The World Tech. Network 2005. *Achievements include:* noted for pioneering work with amorphous silicon; leading inventor of flexible solar shingles for converting sunlight to electricity. *Publications:* more than 200 publs and 30 US patents on the science and tech. of amorphous silicon alloy solar cells. *Leisure interests:* reading, listening to music. *Address:* United Solar Ovonic LLC, 2956 Waterview Drive, Rochester Hills, MI 48309, USA (office). *Telephone:* (248) 293-0440 (office). *Fax:* (248) 844-1214 (office). *E-mail:* info@uni-solar.com (office). *Website:* www.uni-solar.com (office).

GUI, Shiyong; Chinese politician; b. Feb. 1935, Huzhou City, Zhejiang Prov.; ed Chinese People's Univ.; joined CCP 1956; Dir Econs Inst. of Chinese Acad. of Sciences; Deputy Ed.-in-Chief Renmin Ribao (People's Daily); Alt. mem. 13th CCP Cen. Cttee 1987–92, 14th CCP Cen. Cttee 1992–97; mem. State Planning Comm. and Vice-Dir Research Office of the State Council 1988; Vice-Chair. State Planning Comm. and Dir Econs Research Centre 1989; Vice-Pres. Nat. School of Admin. 1994–2000; mem. 15th CCP Cen. Cttee 1997–2002; mem. 9th NPC Standing Cttee 1998–2003; Chair. CPPCC Sub-Cttee of Cultural and Historical Data 2003–.

Address: Chinese People's Political Consultative Conference, Beijing, People's Republic of China.

GUICHOT FLIPO, Isabelle, MBA; French business executive; *President and CEO, Balenciaga SA– Gucci Group;* b. 1 Oct. 1964, Suresnes; m.; two c.; ed École des Hautes Études Commerciales School of Man., Paris; several sr positions over 19 years at Richemont SA including Commercial Sales Dir, Man. Dir Cartier SA, CEO Lancel, CEO Van Cleef & Arpels Int. 1999–2005; Dir of Business Devt, Gucci Group NV 2005–, Exec. Vice-Pres. 2007–, Pres. and CEO Sergio Rossi 2005–07, Balenciaga SA (subsidiary of PPR) 2007–; Chevalier, Légion d'honneur. *Address:* Balenciaga SA, 15 rue Cassette, 75006 Paris, France (office). *Telephone:* 1-56-52-17-17 (office). *Website:* www.guccigroup.com (office); www.balenciaga.com (office).

GUIG, Mohamed Lemine Ould, DIur; Mauritanian politician; *Minister Secretary General of the Presidency;* b. 1 July 1959, Oualata; fmr Dir of Higher Educ.; Prof., Nouakchott Univ. 1987–97, Dean, Faculty of Law and Econs 1990–92; Lecturer and Dir of Studies, Int. Inst. of Human Rights, Strasbourg 1989; Chargé de mission to Sec. of State in charge of Civil Affairs 1993–95; Dir of Higher Educ., Ministry of Nat. Educ. 1995–97; Prime Minister of Mauritania 1997–98; Pres. Cour des Comptes 1998–2001; Minister Sec.-Gen. of the Presidency 2001–03, 2008–; Commr for Food Security 2003–04; mem. Nat. Ass., Chair. Human Resources Cttee; Founder-mem. Asscn internationale des enseignants et chercheurs des droits de l'homme, Strasbourg; mem. Institut de Droit d'expression française, Paris. *Address:* c/o Office of the Prime Minister, Nouackchott, Mauritania. *Telephone:* 5241014 (office); 5252317 (office); 5252581 (office). *Fax:* 5293473 (office). *E-mail:* mloguig@yahoo.fr (office). *Website:* ouldguig.skyrock.com.

GUIGNABODET, Lily (Liliane), LèsL; French writer; b. (Lily Lea Graciani), 26 March 1939, Paris; d. of Moïse Graciani and Olympia N. Graciani; m. Jean Guignabodet 1961; one s. two d.; ed primary school in Sofia, Bulgaria, Lycée Jules Ferry, Paris, Sorbonne and Univ. of London, UK; Prof. of French, San José, USA 1961–62; Prof. of Literature, Arts and Culture, Ecole Technique d'IBM France 1966–69; author 1977–; mem. PEN Club Français, Soc. des Gens de Lettres, Acad. Européenne des Sciences, des Arts et des Lettres, Acad. Valentin; Prix George Sand 1977, Grand Prix du Roman, Acad. Française 1983, Grand prix du Roman, Ville de Cannes 1991. *Publications:* L'écume du silence 1977, Le bracelet indien 1980, Natalia 1983, Le livre du vent 1984, Dessislava 1986, Car les hommes sont meilleurs que leur vie 1991, Un sentiment inconnu 1998. *Leisure interests:* travel, photography, piano. *Address:* 55 rue Caulaincourt, 75018 Paris, France. *Telephone:* 1-46-06-09-86.

GUIGOU, Elisabeth Alexandrine Marie, LèsL; French politician; b. 6 Aug. 1946, Marrakesh, Morocco; d. of Georges Vallier and Jeanne Flecchia; m. Jean-Louis Guigou 1966; one s.; ed Lycée Victor Hugo, Marrakesh, Lycée Descartes, Rabat, Facultés des Lettres, Rabat and Montpellier, Faculté des Sciences Economiques, Montpellier and Ecole Nat. d'Admin; joined Ministry of Finance 1974, served in Office of the Treasury 1974–75, Office of Banks 1976–78, Office of Financial Markets 1978–79; Deputy Chair. Finance Cttee VIIth Plan 1975–78; Maître de Conférences, Inst. d'Etudes Politiques, Paris 1976; Financial Attaché, Embassy in London 1979–81; Head, Office for Europe, America and Asia, Treasury 1981; Tech. Counsellor, Office of Minister of Economy and Finance 1982–88; with Office of Pres. of Repub. 1988–90; Sec.-Gen. Interministerial Cttee on European Econ. Cooperation 1985–90; Minister Delegate for European Affairs 1990–93; mem. Regional Council of Provence Alpes Côte-d'Azur 1992–2002, European Parl. 1994–97; elected Deputy to Nat. Ass. for Vaucluse (Socialist Party) 1997; Minister of Justice 1997–2000, of Employment and Solidarity 2000–02. *Publications:* Pour les Européens 1994, Etre femme en politique 1997. *Address:* c/o Conseil Régional de Provence Alpes Côte d'Azur, 27 place Jules Guesde, 13481 Marseille Cedex, France.

GUILFOYLE, The Hon. Dame Margaret Georgina Constance, AC, DBE, LLB; Australian politician and accountant; b. 15 May 1926, Belfast, Northern Ireland; d. of William McCartney and Elizabeth Jane Ellis; m. Stanley Martin Leslie Guilfoyle 1952; one s. two d.; ed ANU; chartered sec. and accountant 1947–; Liberal mem. Senate for Victoria 1971–87; Minister for Educ. Nov.–Dec. 1975, for Social Security 1975–80, for Finance 1980–83; Deputy Chair. Mental Health Research Inst. 1988–2000, Infertility Treatment Authority 1996–2002; Chair. Judicial Remuneration Tribunal 1995–2001, Ministerial Advisory Cttee on Women's Health 1996–99, Australian Political Exchange Council 1996–2009; Dir Australian Children's TV Foundation 1989–2003; mem. Nat. Inquiry Concerning Human Rights of People with Mental Illness 1990–93; Fellow, Australian Soc. of Accountants; Fellow, Chartered Inst. of Secs and Administrators; mem. Review of the Australian Blood Banking and Plasma Product Sector 1999; Silver Jubilee Medal 1977, Centenary Medal 2003. *Leisure interests:* reading, opera. *Address:* 34/2 Malmsbury Street, Kew, Vic. 3101, Australia (home).

GUILIANI CURY, Hugo, BEcons; Dominican Republic journalist, banker, politician and diplomatist; ed Univ. of Miami, USA, Latin America Econ. Planning Inst., Chile, Man. Research Inst. of Admin. Science, Netherlands; fmr Minister of Industry and Commerc 2001–02, and of Finance 1984; fmr mem. Pres.'s Council of Econ. Advisers; currently Pnr, Guiliani Cury and Asociados, Santo Domingo; Dir Banco de Reservas de la Republica, Gov. Banco Central de la República Dominicana 1984–86; chief negotiator for Dominican Repub. agreements with IMF and World Bank 1985; fmr Tech. Dir Corpn of Enterprises; Prof. of Business and Econs, Univ. of Santo Domingo 1966–77; producer of weekly ¿Con los Guiliani Cury? TV programme 1997–2008; columnist, Hoy (daily newspaper) 1970–84; Amb. to USA 2002–04. *Publications:* nine books on econ. subjects. *Address:* Guiliani Cury & Asociados, Consultores Empresariales, Nicolas De Bari No. 8, Santo Domingo, Dominican Republic (office). *Telephone:* 472-0300 (office). *E-mail:* guilianicuryyasociados@hotmail.com (office). *Website:* www.hugogulianicury.com (office).

GUILLAUD, Adm. Édouard; French naval officer; *Chief of the Defence Staff;* b. 10 July 1953, Paris; s. of Jean-Louis Guillaud; m. Odile Dattin; ed Lycée Hector Berlioz, Vincennes, Ecole Sainte Geneviève, Versailles, Ecole navale, Ecole supérieure de guerre navale, École des applications militaires de l'énergie atomique, Centre des hautes études militaires, Institut des hautes études de Défense nationale; following graduation, served on escort ship Paimpolaise monitoring nuclear trials in Mururoa 1976–78, on SNLE L'Indomptable 1978, on

Le Redoutable 1978; took command of minesweeper Lobelia 1979; studies in gunnery and missiles 1980–81; exchange visit to USA early 1980s; served on aviso Amyot d'Inville and T47 class destroyers, Du Chayla and Kersaint, cruising off Iran and Lebanon 1981–84; worked on computer expert systems of nuclear aircraft carrier programme 1984–87; promoted to Capitaine de corvette 1985; took command of the BATRAL (Bâtiment de Transport Léger) Dumont d'Urville taking part in operations surrounding the Ouvéa cave hostage taking 1987–88; promoted to Capitaine de frégate 1989; obtained degree in nuclear eng 1990; served as manoeuvre officer on Clemenceau in Gulf War 1990–92; took command of light escort Enseigne de vaisseau Henry (F749) 1992–93; promoted to Capitaine de vaisseau 1996; Deputy then Programme Officer on nuclear aircraft carrier Charles De Gaulle 1993–97, Second Officer 1997–99, Capt. 1999–2001; supervised her trials and fittings; served as naval aid to Chief of the Personal Staff of Pres. of the Repub. 2002–04; Préfet maritime for the English Channel and North Sea 2004–06; promoted to Vice-Adm. 2006; Chief of Mil. Staff of Pres. of the Repub. 2006; promoted to Adm. 2007; Chief of Defence Staff (Chef d'État-Major des Armées) 25 Feb. 2010–; commanded French forces enforcing Libyan no-fly zone March–Oct. 2011; mem. Yacht Club of France, Cercle de la Mer; Grand Officier, Légion d'honneur; Officier, Ordre nat. du Mérite, Ordre du Mérite maritime; Médaille d'Outre-Mer; Médaille de la Défense nationale échelon bronze; Médaille de reconnaissance de la Nation; Croix du Mérite, Ordre de Malte. *Leisure interests:* spending time with his grandchildren, reading, art, history. *Address:* Office of the Chief of the Defence Staff, Ministry of Defence, 14 rue Saint Dominique, 75007 Paris, France (office). *Telephone:* 1-42-19-30-11 (office). *Fax:* 1-47-05-40-91 (office). *E-mail:* courrier-ministre@sdbc.defense.gouv.fr (office); presse@dicod.defense.gouv.fr (office). *Website:* www.defense.gouv.fr/ema/le-chef-d-etat-major (office).

GUILLAUD, Jean Louis; French television industry executive; *Honorary Chairman, TV France International;* b. 5 March 1929, Caen; s. of Marcel Guillaud and Suzanne Le Brun; m. 2nd Catherine Chichet 1978; one d.; one s. one d. from previous relationships; ed Inst. d'Etudes Politiques, Paris; political journalist, Soc. Générale de Presse 1953–58, Paris-Jour 1958–60, France-Soir and Nouveau Candide 1961–63; Ed.-in-Chief, ORTF 1963, Dir of TV News 1968–69; special assignment at Secr.-Gen. of Presidency of Repub. 1970–72; Dir of Regional Stations and Third Channel, ORTF 1972–74; Dir-Gen. TF1 1975–78, Pres., Dir-Gen. 1978–81; later TV Dir Hachette Group; Pres., Dir-Gen. Agence France Presse (AFP) 1987–90; Pres. Polycom SA 1988–90; Pres., Dir-Gen. HDSA 1990–95, Media Campus 1990–95; Pres. TV France Int. 1994–2009, Hon. Chair. 2009–, mem. Bd of Dirs; mem. (Admin. Council) Revue de Défense Nationale 1991–; Dir Int. Acad. of TV Arts & Sciences; Officier, Légion d'honneur, Officier, Ordre nat. du Mérite, Chevalier des Arts et des Lettres. *Television:* Island Child (produced) 1975. *Address:* 13 rue de la Mairie, 27140 Bazincourt-sur-Epte, France (home).

GUILLAUME, Gilbert; French judge; *Judge ad hoc, International Court of Justice;* b. 4 Dec. 1930, Bois-Colombes; s. of Pierre Guillaume and Berthe Guillaume; m. Marie-Anne Hidden 1961; one s. two d.; ed Univ. of Paris, Paris Inst. of Political Studies and Ecole Nat. Admin; mem. Council of State 1957; Legal Adviser, State Secr. for Civil Aviation 1968–79; French Rep. Legal Cttee of ICAO 1968–69, Chair. of Cttee 1971–75; Chair. Conciliation Comm. OECD 1973–78; Dir of Legal Affairs, OECD 1979; French Rep. Cen. Comm. for Navigation of the Rhine 1979–87, Chair. 1981–82; Dir of Legal Affairs, Ministry of Foreign Affairs 1979–87; Conseiller d'Etat 1981–96; Judge, Int. Court of Justice 1987–2005, Pres. 2000–03, Judge ad hoc 2006–; First Vice-Pres. Institut de droit int.; Counsel/agent for France in int. arbitration proceedings, numerous cases before European Courts etc.; mem. Perm. Court of Arbitration 1980–; currently mem. Acad. des Sciences Morales et Politiques; Arbitrator, OSCE, ICSID etc.; del. to numerous int. legal and diplomatic confs; Prof., Inst. of Political Studies, Univ. of Paris and other lecturing appointments; mem. Bd Hon. Eds Chinese Journal of International Law; mem. various legal asscns, insts etc.; Grand Officier, Légion d'honneur; Commdr des Arts et des Lettres; Chevalier, Ordre nat. du Mérite, du Mérite agricole, du Mérite maritime. *Publications:* numerous books and articles on admin. and int. law, including Terrorisme et droit international 1989, Les grandes crises internationales et le droit 1994, La Cour Internationale de Justice à l'aube du XXIème siècle 2003. *Address:* International Court of Justice, Peace Palace, 2517 KJ, The Hague, Netherlands (office); 36 rue Perronet, 92200 Neuilly-sur-Seine, France (home). *Telephone:* (70) 302-24-60 (office); 1-46-24-25-67 (home). *Fax:* (70) 302-24-09 (office); 1-47-45-67-84 (home). *E-mail:* g.guillaume@icj-cij.org (office); g.ma.guillaume@orange.fr (home).

GUILLAUME JEAN JOSEPH MARIE, HRH Prince; b. 11 Nov. 1981; s. of HRH Grand Duke Henri and HRH Grand Duchess Maria Teresa of Luxembourg; m. Countess Stéphanie de Lannoy 2012; ed Lycée Robert Schuman, RMA Sandhurst, England, Univ. of Durham, England; proclaimed Hereditary Grand Duke of Luxembourg 18 Dec. 2000; apptd army Lt by Grand-Ducal Decree 2002, apptd First Lt 2003; Chair. Kräizberg Foundation 2000–; Hon. Pres. Bd of Econ. Devt 2001–; Kt, Order of the Gold Lion of the House of Nassau 1981, Grand Cross, Order of Adolphe of Nassau 1999, Grand Cross, Order of the Oak Crown; Grand Officer (or 2nd Class), Order of the White Double Cross (Slovakia) 2005, Kt Grand Cross, Order of Merit of the Italian Repub. 2009, Grand Cross, Order of Orange-Nassau (Netherlands) 2012. *Leisure interests:* playing piano, enjoys football, swimming and volleyball. *Address:* Grand Ducal Palace, 2013 Luxembourg, Luxembourg (office). *Website:* www.gouvernement.lu.

GUILLEM, Sylvie; French ballet dancer; b. 23 Feb. 1965, Le Blanc Mesnil; joined Ecole de Danse, Paris Opera 1976; Ballet de l'Opéra as Quadrille 1981, promoted to Coryphée 1982, to Sujet 1983, Première Danseuse, later Etoile 1984; Prin. Guest Artist, Royal Ballet, London 1988–2007; choreographer, Giselle, Nat. Ballet of Finland 1999; Assoc. Artist, Sadler's Wells Theatre 2005–; Hon. CBE 2003; Commandeur des Arts et Lettres 1988, Médaille de Vermeil de la ville de Paris 1993, Chevalier, Légion d'honneur 1994, Gente Dame d'Honneur des Hospitaliers de Pomerol 2000, Officier, Légion d'honneur 2009, Prix Nijinski 2001, Golden Lion for Lifetime Achievement, Biennale Danza de Venice 2012. *Leading roles in:* Romeo and Juliet, Don Quixote, Raymonda, Swan Lake, Giselle, Notre Dame de Paris, Manon, Marguerite and Armand. *Created roles include:* Cendrillon, In the Middle, Somewhat Elevated, Magnificat, Le Martyre de Saint-Sébastien. *Created and produced:* Evidentia (TV) 1995; Prize for Excellence and Gold Medal, Varna Int. Dance Competition 1983, Prix Carpeau 1984, Hans Christian Andersen Award

1988, Arpège Prize (Lanvin perfumes) 1989. *Address:* c/o Sadler's Wells, Rosebery Avenue, London, EC1R 4TN, England. *Website:* www.sylvieguillem.com.

GUILLEMIN, Roger Charles Louis, BA, BSc, MD, PhD; American professor of medicine; *Distinguished Professor, The Salk Institute;* b. 11 Jan. 1924, Dijon, France; s. of Raymond Guillemin and Blanche Guillemin; m. Lucienne Jeanne Billard 1951; one s. five d.; ed Univs of Dijon and Lyons, France, Univ. of Montreal, Canada; Prosector of Anatomy, Univ. of Dijon Medical School 1946–47; Research Asst, Inst. of Experimental Medicine and Surgery, Univ. of Montreal 1949–51, Assoc. Dir and Asst Prof. of Experimental Medicine 1951–53; Asst Prof. of Physiology, Coll. of Medicine, Baylor Univ., Houston, Tex. 1953, Assoc. Prof. 1957, Prof. of Physiology and Dir Labs for Neuroendocrinology 1963–70, Adjunct Prof. of Physiology 1970–; Consultant in Physiology, Veterans' Admin. Hosp., Houston 1954–60, 1967–70; Lecturer in Experimental Endocrinology, Dept of Biology, W. M. Rice Univ., Houston 1958–60; Assoc. Dir, Dept of Experimental Endocrinology, Coll. de France, Paris, as jt appointment with Coll. of Medicine, Baylor Univ. 1960–63; Resident Fellow and Research Prof., The Salk Inst. for Biological Studies, San Diego, Calif. 1970–89, Dean 1972–73, 1976–77, Adjunct Prof. 1989–97, Distinguished Prof. 1997–; Distinguished Scientist, Whittier Inst. for Diabetes and Endocrinology, La Jolla 1989–93, Medical and Scientific Dir 1993–94; Adjunct Prof. of Medicine, Univ. of Calif., San Diego 1995–97; mem. NAS 1974–, American Acad. of Arts and Sciences, American Physiological Soc., Soc. for Experimental Biology and Medicine, Int. Brain Research Org., Int. Soc. for Research in Biology and Reproduction, Swedish Soc. of Medical Sciences, Acad. Nat. de Médecine, France, Acad. des Sciences, France, Acad. Royale de Médecine de Belgique, Belgium; Pres. The Endocrine Soc. 1986; Citoyen d'Honneur 1983, Officier, Légion d'honneur 1984; hon. degrees (Univ. of Rochester, NY) 1976, (Univ. of Chicago, Ill.) 1977, (Baylor Coll. of Medicine, Houston, Tex.) 1978, (Univ. of Ulm) 1978, (Univ. of Dijon) 1978, (Univ. Libre de Bruxelles) 1979, (Univ. de Montreal) 1979, (Univ. of Manitoba) 1984, (Univ. of Turin) 1985, (Kung Hee Univ., Seoul) 1986, (Univ. Paris VII) 1986, (Autónoma, Madrid) 1988, (McGill Univ.) 1988, (Barcelona, Spain) 1988, (Sherbrook Univ., Quebec) 1997, (Univ. Franche-Conté) 1999; Bonneau and La Caze Awards in Physiology, Acad. des Sciences 1957, 1960, Ayerst-Squibb Award American Endocrine Soc. 1970, Gairdner Award (Toronto) 1974, Lasker Foundation Award 1975, co-recipient of Nobel Prize in Physiology or Medicine with Andrew V. Schally (q.v.) for discoveries relating to peptide hormones 1977, Dickinson Prize in Medicine 1976, Passano Award in Medical Sciences 1976, Nat. Medal of Science 1977, Barren Gold Medal 1979, Dale Medallist, UK Soc. for Endocrinology 1980; numerous int. awards and lectureships. *Publications:* ed. or co-ed. three books on neuroendocrinology and pharmacology; History of Medicine: Neural Modulation of Immunity (co-author); author or co-author of over 700 tech. publs and reviews in scientific journals in USA, France, UK, Canada, USSR, Japan. *Leisure interests:* computer art, music, fine wines. *Address:* The Salk Institute, 10010 North Torrey Pines Road, La Jolla, CA 92037, USA (office). *Telephone:* (858) 453-4100 (office). *Fax:* (858) 625-0688 (office). *E-mail:* guillemin@salk.edu (office). *Website:* www.salk.edu (office).

GUILLÉN, Héctor (Tito); Honduran agricultural engineer, academic and politician; *Minister of Finance;* m. Dinorah Arambarry; two s.; ed Mississippi State Univ.; worked for several years in the sugar industry; Founder, School of Agric. and first Dean and Prof., Universidad de San Pedro Sula; Mayor of San Pedro Sula 1990–94; fmr Dir Organizacion de Desarollo Empresarial Femenino (ODEF, credit programme); mem. Congreso Nacional (Parl.) for Cortes constituency 2009–, Pres. Parl. Budget Comm.; Minister of Finance 2012–; mem. Partido Nacional. *Address:* Ministry of Finance, Edif. SEFIN, Avda Cervantes, Barrio El Jazmín, Tegucigalpa, Honduras (office). *Telephone:* 2222-0111 (office). *Fax:* 2238-2309 (office). *E-mail:* sgeneral@sefin.gob.hn (office). *Website:* www.sefin.gob.hn (office); www.titoguillen.com.

GUILLERY, Rainer W., PhD, FRS; British anatomist, neurobiologist and academic; *Honorary Emeritus Research Fellow, MRC Anatomical Neuropharmacology Unit, University of Oxford;* b. 28 Aug. 1929, Greifswald, Germany; s. of Eva Hackel and Hermann Guillery; m. Margot Cunningham Pepper 1954 (divorced 2000); three s. one d.; ed Univ. Coll., London; Asst Lecturer, Anatomy Dept, Univ. Coll. London 1953–56, Lecturer 1956–63, Reader 1963–64; Assoc. Prof., Dept of Anatomy, Univ. of Wisconsin, Madison, USA 1964–68, Prof. 1968–77, Visiting Prof. 1996–2002, Prof. Emer. 2002–; Prof., Dept of Pharmacological and Physiological Sciences and Chair. Cttee on Neurobiology, Univ. of Chicago, USA 1977–84; Dr Lee's Prof. of Anatomy, Univ. of Oxford, UK 1984–96, currently Hon. Emer. Research Fellow, MRC Anatomical Neuropharmacology Unit; Pres. Anatomical Soc. of GB and Ireland 1994–96; Ed.-in-Chief European Journal of Neuroscience 1988–92; Fellow, Hertford Coll. Oxford 1984–96 (Fellow Emer. 1996–), Univ. Coll. London 1987; Hon. Prof. of Anatomy, Chinese Univ., Hong Kong. *Publications:* Exploring the Thalamus (with M. S. Sherman) 2001–; contribs to Journal of Comparative Neurology, Journal of Neuroscience, Neuroscience, Brain Research, etc. *Leisure interests:* working with wood, growing fruit and vegetables, needlepoint embroidery. *Address:* MRC Anatomical Neuropharmacology Unit, Mansfield Road, Oxford, OX1 3TH, England (office). *E-mail:* rguiller@wisc.edu (office).

GUIMARÃES, Eduardo Augusto, PhD; Brazilian economist, academic and banking executive; b. 1946, Rio de Janeiro; ed Pontifícia Universidade Católica do Rio de Janeiro, Univ. of London, UK, Universidade Federal do Rio de Janeiro; fmr Man.-Dir Banespa; Pres. and CEO Banco do Brasil SA 2001–03; Prof. of Econs, Universidade Fed. do Rio de Janeiro; Sec., Int. Relations Curitiba, Brazil; currently mem. of Teaching Staff, Direito GV, São Paulo; mem. Advisory Bd Chamber of Arbitration. *Publications:* author of numerous articles on econs in scholarly and professional journals. *Address:* Direito GV, Rocha Street, 233 Bela Vista, São Paulo SP 01330-000 Brazil.

GUINDON, Yvan, PhD, CM, FRSC; Canadian scientist and academic; *President, Royal Society of Canada;* ed Université de Montréal; joined Merck Frosst Canada as Sr Research Chemist 1979, Dir Medicinal Chem. 1984–85, Sr Dir 1985–87; joined Bio-Méga as Scientific Dir 1987, Vice-Pres. Bio-Méga/Boehringer Ingelheim Research Inc. 1987–94; apptd CEO and Scientific Dir Institut de Recherches Cliniques de Montréal 1994; Prof., Dept of Chem., Université de Montréal; Adjunct Prof., Dept of Chem., McGill Univ.; Pres. Royal Soc. of Canada 2007–; Fellow, Chemical Inst. of Canada 1988; Lionel-Boulet Award 2006. *Publications:* more

than 100 papers in scientific journals. *Address:* Royal Society of Canada, 170 rue Waller Street, Ottawa, ON K1N 9B9, Canada (office). *Telephone:* (613) 991-6990 (office). *Fax:* (613) 991-6996 (office). *E-mail:* theacademies@rsc.ca (office). *Website:* www.rsc.ca (office).

GUINGONA, Teofisto T., Jr; Philippine lawyer, politician and writer; b. 4 July 1928, San Juan, Rizal; s. of Teofisto Guingona, Sr; m. Ruthie de Lara; two s. one d.; ed Ateneo de Manila Univ.; fmr Gov. Devt Bank of the Philippines and Pres. Chamber of Commerce of the Philippines; served as human rights lawyer 1970s; Founder SANDATA and Hon. Chair. of BANDILA; jailed in 1972 and 1978 for his opposition to marital law; fmr Chair. Comm. on Audit; Senator 1980s, Senate Pres. Pro-tempore and Majority Leader, Chair. Blue Ribbon Cttee, Senator 1998, Minority Leader; fmr Dir Mindanao Devt Authority; fmr Chair. Mindanao Labor Man. Advisory Council; fmr Exec. Sec. to Pres.; fmr Justice Sec.; Vice-Pres. of the Philippines 2001–04; Sec. of Foreign Affairs 2001–02; Pres. Lakas-Christian Muslim Democrats (Lakas—CMD) –2003 (resgnd; fmr adviser to Fernando Poe, Jr.

GUION DE MÉRITENS, Col Isabelle; French police officer and naval officer; *Head of the Coast Guard;* b. 1 Oct. 1962, Pau (Pyrénées-Atlantiques); m.; two c.; ed Écoles de Saint-Cyr Coëtquidan, École des officiers de la gendarmerie nationale, Collège interarmées de défense, Paris (now the École de guerre); officer of French Nat. Gendarmerie, first woman to join the officer corps of gendarmerie 1987, attained rank of Lt, assigned to 1st group of mobile armoured police in Versailles-Satory as Officer in Charge and became Commdr of Armoured Training Centre, assigned as Educ. Officer to School of Sub-officers of Gendarmerie in Montlucon for two years, took command of a co. for training 1993, then took command of a co. of departmental police in Montmorency, Head of the Officers section, Office of Training Br., Maisons-Alfort 1998–2001; became an Officer of Staff to the Gen. Inspection of Armies, Paris; Commdr and Chief of Staff of Gendarmerie School, Chaumont 2004–06; apptd Col of the Gendarmerie (first woman) 2006; took command of Gendarmerie in Yvelines; Head of the Coast Guard 2012–; first woman to be apptd to the rank of Gen. of Police 2013; Medal of Nat. Defence with Bronze Clip 1993, Chevalier, Ordre nat. du Mérite 2000, Chevalier, Légion d'honneur 2005. *Address:* Head of the Coast Guard, c/o Ministry of Defence and Veterans, 14 rue Saint Dominique, 75007 Paris, France (office). *Telephone:* 1-42-19-30-11 (office). *Fax:* 1-47-05-40-91 (office). *E-mail:* courrier-ministre@sdbc .defense.gouv.fr (office). *Website:* www.defense.gouv.fr/marine/organisation/les -forces/gendarmerie-maritime/la-gendarmerie-maritime (office).

GUJRAL, Satish; Indian painter and sculptor; b. 25 Dec. 1925, Jhelum, Pakistan; m. Kiran Gujral; ed Palacio Nationale de Belles Artes, Mexico, Sir J. J. School of Arts, Mumbai, Mayo School of Arts, Lahore; Order of the Crown (Belgium) 1984; Dr hc (Vishakapatnam Univ.) 1996, (Visva Bharti Univ., Santiniketan) 2000; Nat. Award, Lalit Kala Akademi 1956, 1957, 1974, Desikottama, Santiniketan 1989, Da Vinci Award for Life Time Achievement, Mexico 1989, Padma Vibhushan 1998, Lalit Kala Ratna Puraskar, Lalit Kala Akademi 2004, Amity Lifetime Achievement Award, Amity School of Fine Arts 2010. *Publication:* A Brush with Life (autobiography). *Address:* 16, Feroz Gandhi Road, New Delhi 110 024, India (home). *Telephone:* (11) 29832154 (home). *Fax:* (11) 29832093 (home). *E-mail:* mail@satishgujral.com; gujralalpna@gmail.com. *Website:* www.satishgujral.com.

GÜL, Abdullah, BA, PhD; Turkish politician and head of state; *President;* b. 29 Oct. 1950, Kayseri Prov.; s. of Ahmet Hamdi Gül and Adviye Gül; m. Hayrünnisa Gül; three c.; ed Istanbul Univ., Univ. of London, UK; participated in the foundation of the Dept of Eng, Sakarya Univ., Lecturer in Econs 1980–83, Assoc. Prof. of Econs 1991–; economist with Islamic Devt Bank, Jeddah 1983–91; mem. Parl. representing the Welfare Party (now outlawed) 1991, later WP Deputy Head of Foreign Affairs; held numerous ministerial posts including Minister of State for Foreign Affairs 1996–97, Spokesman for Welfare Party Govt, also mem. European Council; Founder-mem. and Deputy Chair. AK Parti (Justice and Devt Party) 2001–; mem. NATO Parl. Ass. 2001–02; Prime Minister of Turkey Nov. 2002–March 2003; Deputy Prime Minister and Minister of Foreign Affairs 2003–07; President of Turkey 2007–; Hon. mem., Council of Europe 2001–; hon. doctorates (Bourgas Free, Bulgaria) 2003, (Exeter, UK) 2005, (Baku State, Azerbaijan) 2007, (Dimitrie Cantemir Christian, Romania) 2008, (Kazan State, Tatarstan) 2008, (Northeastern, China) 2009; Pro-Merito Medal of the Council of Europe 2001. *Address:* President's Office, Cumhurbaşkanlığı Köşkü, Çankaya, Ankara, Turkey (office). *Telephone:* (312) 4702308 (office). *Fax:* (312) 4701316 (office). *E-mail:* cumhurbaskanligi@tccb.gov.tr (office). *Website:* www.cankaya.gov.tr (office); www .abdullahgul.gen.tr (home).

GULABZOI, Maj.-Gen. Sayed Muhammad; Afghan fmr army officer and politician; b. 1951, Paktia Prov.; fmr Communist gen.; mem. Khalq faction of CP, People's Democratic Party of Afghanistan, took part in overthrow of King Muhammad Zahir Shah 1973; close aide of Communist leader, Nur Muhammad Taraki; served as Interior Minister and Commdr Sarandoy (Defenders of the Revolution—nat. gendarmerie) for many years during Soviet occupation; spent 17 years in exile in Russia, returned to run in parl. elections 2004; mem. (Khost Province) Wolasi Jirga (House of the People—Lower House of Parl.) 2004–, mem. Internal Security Cttee. *Address:* Wolasi Jirga, Kabul, Afghanistan (office).

GULAMOV, Kadir Gafurovich, PhD; Uzbekistani nuclear physicist, academic and fmr government official; b. 17 Feb. 1945, Tashkent; m. two c.; Sr Scientific Researcher, Physical Tech. Inst., Tashkent, later Head of Lab. 1983–88; Prof. of Physics 1980–; Prof., Faculty of Physics, Tashkent State Univ.; Deputy Minister of Defence –2000, Minister of Defence 2001–05; Presidential adviser 2005–; currently Dir Gen. Scientific Asscn Physics, Uzbekistan Acad. of Sciences; Fellow, Islamic Acad. of Sciences 1995–; Corresp. mem. Uzbekistan Acad. of Sciences 1989–; Beruni State Prize (Uzbekistan) 1983, Independence Memorial Medal (Uzbekistan) 1992. *Publications:* over 250 publs in fields of high energy and nuclear physics. *Address:* c/o Uzbekistan Academy of Sciences, 70 Acad. Gulyamov str., 700047 Tashkent, Uzbekistan. *E-mail:* yuldashev@iae.tashkent.su. *Website:* www .uzsci.net/academy.

GULBINOWICZ, HE Cardinal Henryk Roman, DTheol; Polish ecclesiastic; *Archbishop Emeritus of Wrocław;* b. 17 Oct. 1923, Szukiszki (now Sukiškes in Lithuania); s. of Antoni Gulbinowicz and Waleria Gajewska; ed Metropolitan Higher Ecclesiastic Seminary, Vilnius and Białystok, Catholic Univ. of Lublin;

ordained priest, Vilnius, Lithuania 1950; Titular Bishop of Acci and Apostolic Admin. Archdiocese of Białystok, Vilnius 1970–76, Archbishop of Wrocław 1976–2004, Archbishop Emer. 2004–; mem. Congregation for the Evangelization of Nations, Congregation for Eastern Churches, Congregation Clergy Affairs; mem. Main Council Polish Episcopate and several episcopate cttees; High Chancellor Pontifical Faculty Theology, Wrocław; cr. Cardinal (Cardinal-Priest of Immacolata Concezione di Maria a Grottarossa) 1985–; Hon. Citizen of Wrocław 1996; Commdr's Cross with Star, Order of Polonia Restituta; Dr hc (Pontifical Faculty of Theology, Wrocław) 1995, (Agricultural Acad., Wrocław) 2000. *Publications:* more than 240 works on moral theology, ethics, ecumenism and history of the Polish Eastern Territories. *Address:* Kuria Metropolitalna, ul. Katedralna 13, 50-328 Wrocław, Poland (office). *Telephone:* (71) 327-11-11 (office). *Fax:* (71) 322-82-69 (office). *Website:* www.archidiecezja.wroc.pl (office).

GULEGHINA, Maria; Belarusian/Armenian/Ukrainian singer (soprano); b. Odessa, Ukraine; ed Odessa Conservatory (studied with Yevgeni Ivanov); professional debut, Minsk Opera Theatre 1986; only soprano to have performed title roles in 14 new productions at Teatro La Scala, including Manon Lescaut, Tosca, I Due Foscari, Un Ballo in Maschera, Macbeth; has performed over 130 times at Metropolitan Opera, New York, title roles in Aida, Tosca, Norma, Adriana Lecouvreur, Macbeth, Nabucco, Andrea Chenier, Pique Dame, etc. 1991–; frequently performs in all major opera houses world-wide, including Vienna State Opera, Covent Garden, Opera Bastille, Bavarian State Opera, Deutsche Opera Berlin, Mariinsky Theatre, Teatro Liceu, Teatro Colon, etc.; future engagements include Turandot and Nabucco at The Met, Nabucco and Tosca at Vienna State Opera, Tosca, Turandot and Andrea at Deutsche Opera, Berlin, Norma, Macbeth and Attila at Mariinsky Theatre; renowned for her portrayal of characters of Lady Macbeth and Abigaille; opera roles include title roles in Tosca, Aïda, Manon Lescaut, Norma, Fedora, Adriana Lecouvreur, Turandot, as well as Lady Macbeth in Macbeth, Abigaille in Nabucco, Leonora in Il Trovatore, Oberto in La Forza del Destino, Elvira in Ernani, Elisabetta in Don Carlo, Amelia in Simon Boccanegra, Un Ballo in Maschera, Lucrezia in I due Foscari, Desdemona in Otello, Santuzza in Cavalleria Rusticana, Maddalena in Andrea Chénier, Lisa in Pique Dame, Odabella in Attila, etc; first singer of 21st century to attempt to execute variations in da capo of cabaletta of Abigaille and of Odabella in Attila; dubbed 'Queen of Opera' and 'Russian Soprano with Verdi in her veins'; Hon. Bd mem. Int. Paralympic Cttee, UNICEF Int. Goodwill Amb.; Order of Holy Olga, from Patriarch Alexis of Russia; recipient of numerous prizes and awards, including First Prize All-Union Glinka Competition 1984, Giovanni Zanatello Prize for her debut at Arena di Verona 1997, Maria Zamboni Gold Medal, Gold Medal, Osaka Festival 1999, Bellini Prize 2001, Arte e Operosita nel Mondo Prize, Milan. *Radio:* many live broadcasts from the Met, La Scala, Vienna etc. *Television:* Nabucco (Vienna Met), Andrea Chenier, Tosca, Manon Lescaut, Macbeth (all at La Scala), Verdi Arias, Italian Arias (both for NHK), Macbeth and Il Trittico (the Met), Nabucco (Arena di Verona). *Recordings:* albums include: Tabarro, Oberto, Francesca di Rimini, Pique Dame, Passion of Verismo (live concert recording), Passion of Rachmaninov; video-audio includes: Tosca, Manon Lescaut, Macbeth (all at La Scala, Milan), Andrea Chenier, Nabucco (both at Metropolitan Opera, New York), Andrea Chenier (DVD, Teatro Communale di Bologna), Macbeth (DVD, Liceu in Barcelona), Nabucco with James Levine (DVD, Metropolitan Opera). *E-mail:* info@mariaguleghina.com. *Website:* www.mariaguleghina.com.

GULIYEV, Fuad Khalil-ogly; Azerbaijani politician; b. 6 July 1941, Baku; m.; two c.; ed Azerbaijani Inst. of Oil Chem.; worked in Belorussia in oil chemical industry; Chief Engineer, later Gen. Dir Air Conditioners Factory, Baku; First Deputy Prime Minister of Azerbaijan 1994–95; Prime Minister of Azerbaijan 1995–96; mem. Milli Majlis (Nat. Ass.) 1991–; mem. New Azerbaijan Party; Science and Technology Prize Azerbaijan 1986, Honoured Engineer of Azerbaijan 1991. *Address:* 7 Samed Vurgun Street, Baku, 370000, Azerbaijan (home). *Telephone:* (12) 4981541 (home) *Fax:* (12) 4335609 (home). *E-mail:* fkuliev@azintex.com (home).

GULLICHSEN, Johan Erik, MSc; Finnish professor of pulping technology and engineer; *President and Partner, Arhippainen, Gullichsen & Company;* b. 28 June 1936, Pihlava; s. of Harry Gullichsen and Maire Ahlström; m. Anna Ramsay 1958; one s. two d.; ed Abo Akademi, Helsinki Univ. of Tech.; Research Asst, FPPRI 1962–64; Project Engineer, EKONO 1964–70; Pres. and Partner, Arhippainen, Gullichsen & Co. 1970–; Prof. of Pulping Tech., Helsinki Univ. of Tech. 1989–2000; Chair. Bd A. Ahlstrom Corpn 1987–2007; fmr Chair. Bd A. Ahlstrom Oy, Dir Kymmene Oy; Hon. DTech (Abo Akademi) 1988; Engineer of the Year in Finland 1984, Marcus Wallenberg Prize 1986. *Publications:* tech. and scientific papers on pulping tech., econs and environmental control. *Leisure interest:* yachting. *Address:* Arhippainen, Gullichsen & Co., Palikaistentie 167, 31460 Hirsjärvi, Finland (office). *Telephone:* (8) 2721-5100 (office). *E-mail:* Johan.Gullichsen@agco.fi (office). *Website:* www.agco.fi/homepage.htm.

GULLIT, Ruud; Dutch sports commentator, fmr football manager and fmr professional footballer; b. (Ruud Dil), 1 Sept. 1962, Amsterdam; m. 1st Yvonne de Vries 1984–91; two d.; m. 2nd Christina Pensa 1994–2000; one s. one d.; m. 3rd Estelle Cruyff 2000; one s. one d.; defender/midfielder/striker; played for HFC Haarlem, Netherlands 1979–82 (won Eerste Divisie 1981), Feyenoord 1982–85 (won Eredivisie 1984, KNVB Cup 1984), PSV Eindhoven 1985–87 (won Eredivisie 1986, 1987), AC Milan, Italy 1987–93 (won Serie A 1988, 1992, 1993, Supercoppa Italiana 1988, 1992, UEFA Champions League 1989, 1990, UEFA Super Cup 1989, 1990, Intercontinental Cup 1989, 1990), 1994 (won Supercoppa Italiana 1994), Sampdoria 1993–94 (won Coppa Italia 1994, Lotto Cup 1993), 1994–95, Chelsea, UK 1995–98 (Man. 1996–98) (won FA Cup 1997); Man. Newcastle United 1998–99; Head Coach Feyenoord 2004–05, Los Angeles Galaxy, USA 2007–08 (resgnd); won four caps and scored one goal for Netherlands U21 team 1979, 66 caps and 17 goals for Netherlands sr team 1981–94, including one in European Championship final victory over Russia 1988, also won Nasazzi's Baton 1985, 1986; football pundit for BBC during Euro 96 tournament 1996, for ITV during FIFA World Cup 2006; currently presenter for Dutch TV and analyst for UEFA Champions League games on Sky Sports, UK; Netherlands Player of the Year (Second Level) 1981, Dutch Footballer of the Year 1984, Netherlands Cup Top Scorer (nine goals) 1984, Dutch Footballer of the Year 1986, Dutch Golden Shoe Winner1 1986, Netherlands League Silver Top Scorer (24 goals) 1986, European Footballer of the Year 1987,

World Footballer of the Year 1987, 1989, Dutch Sportsman of the Year 1987, FIFA World Player of the Year 1987, 1989, Onze d'Silver 1988, 1989, Silver, World Soccer Player of the Year 1988, Bronze, Best World Player of the Year, IFFHS 1988, Silver Ball, Boot European Championship (one goal) 1988, World Soccer Magazine World Footballer of the Year 1989, Silver, Best Player of the Year, UEFA 1989, Bronze, Best World Player of the Year, Int. Fed. of Football History and Statistics (IFFHS) 1989, Dream Team European Championship 1988, 1992, Bronze, World Soccer Magazine World Footballer of the Year 1993, Silver Ball, English League Player of the Year 1996, Best Player of the Year, Chelsea 1996, named in FIFA 100 2004. *Recordings:* modest hit in 1984 with the song Not the dancing kind 1984, No. 3 hit with anti-apartheid song South Africa in Dutch Top 40 together with the reggae band Revelation Time 1988. *Address:* c/o Sky Sports, British Sky Broadcasting Ltd, Grant Way, Isleworth, TW7 5QD, England (office). *Telephone:* (20) 7705-3000 (office). *E-mail:* football@skysports.com (office). *Website:* www.skysports.com (office).

GULLIVER, Stuart T.; British banking executive; *Group Chief Executive, HSBC Holdings;* joined HSBC 1980, has held several key roles in Group's operations world-wide, including in London, Hong Kong, Tokyo, Kuala Lumpur and UAE, Head of Treasury and Capital Markets in Asia-Pacific 1996–2002, Group Gen. Man. 2000–04, Head of Global Markets 2002–03, Co-Head Global Banking and Markets 2003–06, Head 2006–10, Group Man. Dir 2004–10, Chair. Europe, Middle East and Global Businesses April–Dec. 2010, Exec. Dir 2008–10, Chair. HSBC France 2009–, HSBC Bank Middle East Feb.–Dec. 2010, HSBC Private Banking Holdings (Suisse) SA 2010–, HSBC Bank plc April–Dec. 2010, Group Chief Exec. and Chair. Group Man. Bd, HSBC Holdings 2011–, Dir, The Hongkong and Shanghai Banking Corpn Ltd (Chair. 2011–), Deputy Chair. and mem. Supervisory Bd HSBC Trinkaus & Burkhardt AG 2006–11. *Address:* HSBC Holdings, 8 Canada Square, London, E14 5HQ, England (office); The Hongkong and Shanghai Banking Corporation Ltd, GPO Box 64, 1 Queen's Road Central, Hong Kong Special Administrative Region, People's Republic of China (office). *Telephone:* (20) 7991-8888 (London) (office); 2822-1111 (Hong Kong) (office). *Fax:* (20) 7992-4880 (London) (office); 2810-1112 (Hong Kong) (office). *E-mail:* pressoffice@hsbc.com (office). *Website:* www.hsbc.com.hk (office).

GULOIEN, Donald A., BCom; Canadian business executive; *President and CEO, Manulife Financial Corporation;* ed Univ. of Toronto; joined Manulife Financial Corpn as research analyst 1981, held several marketing roles in both the Canadian and US Divs, held leadership roles in both insurance and investment operations, Vice-Pres., US Individual Business 1990–91, led Manulife's Business Devt Unit 1994–2001, mem. Bd of Dirs, Sr Exec. Vice-Pres. and Chief Investment Officer 2001–09, Pres. and CEO 2009–, Chair. Exec. Cttee; mem. Bd of Dirs Canadian Life and Health Insurance Asscn, Geneva Asscn; mem. Mayor of Shanghai's Int. Business Leaders' Advisory Council, Canadian Council of Chief Execs, Young Presidents' Org.; fmr mem. Bd Children's Aid Soc. Foundation, ThinkFirst Foundation of Canada, LIMRA International; mem. Campaign Cabinet for the Rotman School of Man. and fmr mem. Governing Council, Dean's Advisory Cttee for School of Grad. Studies and Hart House Bd of Stewards, Univ. of Toronto; Arbor Award for contribs to Univ. of Toronto 1998, Int. Business Exec. of the Year, Canadian Chamber of Commerce 2012. *Address:* Manulife Financial Corpn, 200 Bloor Street East, Toronto, ON M4W 1E5, Canada (office). *Telephone:* (416) 926-3000 (office). *Fax:* (416) 926-5454 (office). *E-mail:* info@manulife.com (office). *Website:* www.manulife.com (office).

G'ULOMOV, Ravshan; Uzbekistani fmr central banker and government official; fmr Deputy Chair. Nat. Bank for Foreign Econ. Affairs of the Repub.; fmr First Deputy Chair. Cen. Bank; fmr Chair. Asaka Bank; fmr Exec. Dir Fund for Reconstruction and Devt in Uzbekistan; First Deputy Minister of Finance –2010; Minister of the Economy 2010–11, of Foreign Econ. Relations, Investments and Trade 2011–12. *Address:* c/o Ministry of Foreign Economic Relations, Investment and Trade, 100029 Tashkent, Shevchenko ko'ch. 1, Uzbekistan (office).

GULOMOVA, Dilbar Mukhammadkhonovna; Uzbekistani politician; ed Tashkent Textile Inst.; Deputy Prime Minister and Chair. Women's Cttee 1995–2004; currently Chair. Asscn Business Women of Uzbekistan. *Address:* 41 Afrosiyob str., 100008 Tashkent, Uzbekistan (office). *Telephone:* (71) 44-84-11 (office). *E-mail:* womancomitet@mail.ru (office).

GULYAEV, Yury Vasilievich, DPhys-MathSc; Russian physicist; *Director, Institute of Radioengineering and Electronics, Russian Academy of Sciences;* b. 18 Sept. 1935, Moscow; m.; two c.; ed Moscow Inst. of Physics and Tech.; jr researcher, sr researcher, Head of Lab., Vice-Dir Inst. of Radioengineering and Electronics, USSR (now Russian) Acad. of Sciences 1960–87, Dir 1988–; Corresp. mem. USSR (now Russian) Acad. of Sciences 1979, mem. 1984–, mem. Presidium 1992–; Chair. Saratov br., Russian Acad. of Sciences 1981–; mem. Russian Acad. of Natural Sciences; USSR People's Deputy 1989–91; mem. Polish Acad. of Sciences; Vice-Pres. World Fed. of Eng Orgs (WFEO); Pres. Russian A.S. Popov Scientific and Technical Soc. of Radioengineering, Electronics and Telecommunications; currently Pres. Int. Union of Scientific and Technical Socs and Unions of CIS; Fellow and Sr Mem. IEEE and Chair. IEEE Russian Section; Ed.-in-Chief Radiotekhnica i Electronica, Radio and Communications Technology, Photonics and Optoelectronics, Nonlinear Applied Dynamics; Hon. Prof., St Petersburg Electrotechnical Univ. LETI (ETU); Hewlett-Packard Europhysics Prize of European Physical Soc. 1979, State Prize of the USSR 1974, 1984, Konstantinov Prize of Russian Acad. of Sciences 1992, State Prize of Russian Fed. 1993, A.S. Popov Gold Medal of Russian Acad. of Sciences 1995. *Publications:* more than 100 articles, mainly on acoustic electronics, acoustic optics and spin-wave electronics. *Address:* Institute of Radioengineering and Electronics, Mokhovaya ul. 11-7, 125009 Moscow, Russia (office). *Telephone:* (495) 200-52-58 (office). *Fax:* (495) 203-84-14 (office). *E-mail:* gulyaev@cplire.ru (office). *Website:* www.cplire.ru (office).

GULYÁS, Dénes; Hungarian singer (tenor) and politician; b. 31 March 1954; s. of Dénes Gulyás and Mária Szitár; m. Judit Szekeres; two s. one d.; ed Liszt Ferenc Acad. of Music, Budapest; joined State Opera, Budapest 1978; debut as Rinuccio in Gianni Schicchi; debut in USA, Carnegie Hall and Avery Fisher Hall, New York: concert performances; numerous tours in the USA; teacher, Liszt Ferenc Music Conservatory; mem. Országgyülés (Parl.) (Fidesz) for Pest Co. 10th dist 2006–; 1st Prize, Parma 1979, won Luciano Pavarotti singing competition, Philadelphia 1981,

Holder of Liszt Prize, titled Merited Artist. *Repertoire includes:* Faust, des Grieux (Manon), Werther, Hoffman, Titus (La Clemenza di Tito), Percy (Anne Boleyn), Ernesto (Don Pasquale), Duke of Mantua (Rigoletto), Fenton (Falstaff), Ferrando (Così fan tutte), Don Ottavio, Tamino, Alfredo (La Traviata), Edgardo (Lucia di Lammermoor), Nemorino, Rodolfo (La Bohème), Tom Rakewell (The Rake's Progress). *Recordings include:* Caldara, Albinoni, Sammartini, Vivaldi: Magnificat, Erkel: Hunyadi László 1994. *Leisure interests:* riding, sailing, viticulture, catering, cooking, horse riding, sailing. *Address:* Országgyülés (National Assembly), 1055 Budapest, Kossuth Lajos tér 1–32 (office); 2094 Budapest, Nagykovácsi Pf. 93, Hungary. *Telephone:* (1) 441-4000 (office); (1) 131-2550 (office). *Fax:* (1) 441-5000 (office). *E-mail:* denes.gulyas@parlament.hu (office). *Website:* www.mkogy .hu (office); www.gulyasdenes.hu.

GULYAS, Diane H., BS; American chemical engineer and business executive; *President, Performance Polymers, E. I. du Pont de Nemours and Company;* b. Chicago, Ill.; ed Univ. of Notre Dame, Advanced Management Program, Wharton School, Univ. of Pennsylvania; joined DuPont in 1978, held a variety of sales, marketing, tech. and systems devt positions, primarily in DuPont Polymers 1978–88, European Business Man., Geneva, Switzerland, for Engineering Polymers, and Plant Supt, Mechelen, Belgium 1988–92, Exec. Asst to Chair. of Bd 1993–94, Global Business Dir Nylon Fibers New Business Devt and Global Zytel Eng Polymers 1997–2001, Vice-Pres. and Gen. Man. DuPont Advanced Fiber Businesses, Spruance Plant, Richmond, Va 1997–2003, Group Vice-Pres. Electronic and Communication Technologies Platform 2003–04, Chief Marketing and Sales Officer 2004–06, Group Vice-Pres. Performance Materials 2006–09, Pres. Performance Polymers 2009–; mem. Bd of Dirs Viasystems; mem. Strategic Planning and Advocacy Cttees Delaware Nature Soc.; mem. Bd of Dirs Ministry of Caring; fmr mem. Bd of Dirs United Way of Richmond; fmr mem. Exec. Cttee Virginia Business Council; ranked 48th by Fortune magazine amongst 50 Most Powerful Women in Business in the US 2006. *Address:* DuPont Performance Materials, 1007 Market Street, Wilmington, DE 19898, USA (office). *Telephone:* (302) 774-1000 (office). *Fax:* (302) 999-4399 (office). *Website:* www2.dupont.com (office).

GULZAR; Indian filmmaker, poet and lyricist; b. (Sampooran Singh Kalra), 18 Aug. 1936, Deena, Jhelum Dist (now in Pakistan); s. of Makhan Singh Kalra and Sujan Kaur; m. Rakhee Gulzar; one d.; came to Delhi following partition; started as poet and was associated with Progressive Writers Asscn; joined Bimal Roy Productions in 1961; first break as lyricist came when he wrote Mora Gora Ang Lai Lae for Bimal Roy's Bandini 1963; began writing for films for dirs Hrishikesh Mukherjee and Asit Sen; turned filmmaker with first film Mere Apne 1971; began partnership with Sanjeev Kumar; Lifetime Hon. Fellowship, Indian Inst. of Advanced Studies 2001; five Nat. Film Awards, more than 17 Filmfare Awards, including seven for Best Lyricist, Filmfare Lifetime Achievement Award 2002, Padma Bhushan 2004, Dada Saheb Phalke Award 2013. *Films directed:* Shriman Satyawadi (Asst Dir) 1960, Kabuliwala (Chief Asst Dir) 1961, Bandini (Asst Dir) 1963, Mere Apne 1971, Parichay 1972, Koshish 1972, Achanak 1973, Mausam (Nat. Award for Best Dir, Filmfare The Best Dir Award) 1975, Khushboo 1975, Aandhi (Storm) 1975, Kitaab (also Producer) 1977, Kinara (also Producer) 1977, Meera 1979, Sahira 1980, Namkeen 1982, Angoor 1982, Suniye 1984, Aika 1984, Ek Akar 1985, Ijaazat (Guest) 1987, Ghalib (TV) 1988, Libaas 1988, Lekin… (But…) 1990, Ustad Amjad Ali Khan 1990, Pandit Bhimsen Joshi 1992, Maachis 1996, Hu Tu Tu 1999. *Film roles include:* Jallianwalla Bagh 1979, Grihapravesh (The Housewarming) (as himself) 1979, Wajood (guest appearance as himself) 1998, Chachi 420 (uncredited cameo appearance during end credits) 1998, Raincoat (voice) 2004, Yuvraaj (special appearance) 2008. *Film dialogue or scripts:* Sangharsh 1968, Aashirwad (The Blessing) 1968, Khamoshi 1969, Anand 1970, Guddi (Darling Child) 1971, Mere Apne 1971, Koshish (Nat. Award for Best Screenplay) 1972, Bawarchi 1972, Namak Haraam (The Ungrateful) 1973, Achanak 1973, Mausam 1975, Khushboo 1975, Chupke Chupke 1975, Aandhi (Storm) 1975, Palkon Ki Chhaon Mein 1977, Meera 1979, Grihapravesh (The Housewarming) 1979, Khubsoorat (Beautiful) 1980, Basera 1981, Namkeen 1982, Angoor 1982, Masoom (Innocent) 1983, New Delhi Times 1986, Ek Pal (A Moment) 1986, Ijaazat (Guest) 1987, Mirza Ghalib (TV) 1988, Lekin… (But…) 1990, Rudaal (The Mourner) 1993, Maachis 1996, Chachi 420 1998, Hu Tu Tu 1999, Saathiya 2002, Dus Kahaniya 2007. *Film song lyrics:* Swami Vivekananda 1955, Shriman Satyawadi 1960, Kabuliwala 1961, Prem Patra (Love Letter) 1962, Bandini 1963, Purnima 1965, Sannata 1966, Biwi Aur Makan 1966, Do Dooni Char 1968, Aashirwad (The Blessing) 1968, Rahgir 1969, Khamoshi 1969, Anand 1970, Guddi (Darling Child) 1971, Anubhav (Experience) 1971, Seema 1971, Mere Apne 1971, Parichay 1972, Koshish 1972, Doosri Seeta 1974, Chor Machaye Shor 1974, Mausam 1975, Khushboo 1975, Aandhi (Storm) 1975, Shaque 1976, Palkon Ki Chhaon Mein 1977, Kinara 1977, Gharaonda (The Nest) 1977, Ghar (Home) 1978, Meetha (Sweet and Sour) 1978, Devata 1978, Gol Maal (Hanky Panky) 1979, Ratnadeep (The Jewelled Lamp) 1979, Grihapravesh (The Housewarming) 1979, Sitara 1980, Thodisi Bewafaii 1980, Swayamvar 1980, Khubsoorat (Beautiful India) 1980, Garam 1981, Basera 1981, Namkeen 1982, Angoor 1982, Sadma 1983, Masoom (Innocent) 1983, Ghulami 1985, Jeeva 1986, Ek Pal (A Moment) 1986, Ijaazat (Guest) (Nat. Award for Best Lyricist) 1987, Libaas 1988, Lekin… (But…) 1990, Maya Memsaab (Maya: The Enchanting Illusion) 1992, Rudaali (The Mourner) 1993, Mammo 1994, Daayraa (The Square Circle, USA) 1996, Maachis 1996, Aastha (Aastha in the Prison of Spring) 1997, Satya 1998, Dil Se… (From the Heart, USA) 1998, Chachi 420 1998, Hu Tu Tu 1999, Khoobsurat 1999, Fiza 2000, Aks 2001, Asoka (Ashoka the Great, USA) 2001, Filhaal… 2002, Leela 2002, Lal Salaam (Red Salute) 2002, Dil Vil Pyar Vyar 2002, Makdee (The Web of the Witch) 2002, Saathiya 2002, Chupke Se 2003, Pinjar (The Cage) 2003, Jaan-E-Mann 2006, Guru 2007, Slumdog Millionaire (Jai Ho) (Academy Award for Best Original Song 2009, Grammy Award for Best Song Written for Motion Picture, Television or Other Visual Media 2010) 2008, Kaminey 2009, Veer 2010, Ishqiya 2010, Striker 2010, Raavan 2010, 7 Khoon Maaf 2011, Chala Mussaddi… Office Office 2011, Teen Thay Bhai 2011, Jab Tak Hai Jaan 2012, Do Paise Ki Dhoop, Chaar Aane Ki Baarish 2012, Kya Dilli Kya Lahore 2012, Matru Ki Bijlee Ka Mandola 2013, Ek Thi Daayan 2013, Shoebite 2013, Dedh Ishqiya 2014. *Publications include:* poetry: Jaanam 1962, Kuch Aur Nazme 1980, Chand Pukhraj Ka 1995, Triveni 2001, Dhuan 2001, Raat Pashmine Ki 2002, Raat Chand Aur Main 2004, Selected Poems 2008, Yaar Julaahe 2009, 100 Lyrics 2009,

Selected Poems 2012; short stories: Raavi Paar 1999, Dhuaan (Sahitya Acad. Award 2003) 2001, Kharaashein 2003, Meelo Se Din 2013, Half a Rupee Stories 2013, My Favourite Stories: Boskys Panchatantra 2013; 12 books for children, including Ekta (Nat. Council for Educ. Research and Training Award 1989). *Leisure interests:* reading, writing, tennis, cricket. *Address:* Boskiyana, Pali Hill, Bandra (W), Mumbai 400 050, India (home). *Telephone:* (22) 6498351 (home).

GUMBEL, Bryant Charles, BA; American broadcaster; b. 29 Sept. 1948, New Orleans, La; s. of Richard Gumbel and Rhea LeCesne; m. June C. Baranco 1973; one s. one d.; ed Bates Coll.; writer, Black Sports (magazine), New York 1971, Ed. 1972; sportscaster, KNBC-TV, Burbank, Calif. 1972–76, Sports Dir 1976–81; sports host, NBC Sports 1975–82; co-host, Today Show, NBC 1982–97; host of Real Sports with Bryant Gumbel, Home Box Office (HBO) 1995–, Public Eye, CBS 1997, The Early Show 1999–2000, Flashpoints USA with Bryant Gumbel and Gwen Ifill PBS; play-by-play announcer NFL Network 2006–08; mem. Bd of Dirs United Negro Coll. Fund, United Way of New York City, Xavier Univ., Bates Coll.; recipient of three Emmy Awards and two Golden Mike Awards (LA Press Club); Edward R. Murrow Award (Overseas Press Club) 1988, Frederick D. Patterson Award (United Negro Coll. Fund), Martin Luther King Award (Congress of Racial Equality), three NAACP Image Awards, International Journalism Award (TransAfrica), Africa's Future Award (US Cttee for UNICEF); Dr hc (Bates Coll., Xavier Univ., Holy Cross Univ., Providence Coll., Clark Atlanta Univ.). *Address:* c/o Home Box Office, Inc., 1100 Avenue of the Americas, New York, NY 10036, USA (office). *Website:* www.hbo.com/realsports (office).

GUMBS, Walford Vincent, OBE, JP; Saint Christopher and Nevis politician and trade unionist; *Ombudsman of the Federation of Saint Christopher and Nevis;* b. 21 Dec. 1946; m. two s. one d.; ed Basseterre Senior School, Ruppin Inst. of Agric., Israel, ILO Int. Training Centre, Turin, Italy; customs clerk, St Kitts Sugar Factory Ltd, Basseterre 1965–70; Accounts Officer and Acting Man. Sun Island Clothes Ltd 1973–77; field officer, St Kitts-Nevis Trades and Labour Union 1970–73, Exec. Officer 1978–, Second Vice-Pres. 1979–89, First Vice-Pres. 1989–2000, Pres. 2000–05; Pres. Young Labour 1969–71, Vice-Chair. St Kitts-Nevis Labour Party 1992–96; apptd Senator (Labour Party) in Nat. Ass. 1989, Speaker Nat. Ass. 1995–2004; Ombudsman of the Fed. of Saint Christopher and Nevis 2008–; non-resident Amb.; Deputy Speaker, Org. of Eastern Caribbean State Ass. 2012. *Leisure interests:* sports, jogging, int. affairs. *Address:* Office of the Federal Ombudsman, West Independence Square Street, Basseterre (office); Shadwell Housing, Basseterre, Saint Christopher and Nevis (home). *Telephone:* 466-5697 (office); 466-9126 (office); 665-8230 (home). *Fax:* 466-2352 (office). *E-mail:* walfordgumbs@ymail.com (office).

GUNATHILAKA, Nandana; Sri Lankan politician; *Mayor of Panadura;* s. of M. D. S. Gunathilaka; ed Sri Sumangala Vidyalaya, Panadura, Univ. of Peradeniya; mem. Parl. for Kalutara Dist 2000–10; Chair. United People's Freedom Alliance (later People's Alliance) 2004–08; Gen. Sec. Nat. Freedom Front 2008–09; fmr mem., Politburo, mem. and presidential cand. Janatha Vimukthi Peramuna party (resgnd 2006); Minister of Tourism July–Nov. 2009; Mayor of Panadura 2011–. *Address:* c/o National Freedom Front, 377/4 Ratnarama Rd, Hokandara North, Sri Lanka.

GUND, Agnes, BA, MA; American art gallery administrator (retd) and philanthropist; *President Emerita, Museum of Modern Art;* b. 1938, Cleveland, Ohio; d. of George Gund Jr; m. 1st Albrecht Saalfield; one s. three d.; m. 2nd Daniel Shapiro 1987; ed Connecticut Coll., Harvard Univ.; Trustee, Museum of Modern Art (MOMA), New York 1976–, Pres. 1991–2002, now Pres. Emer., Chair. MOMA Int. Council, MoMA PS1 Contemporary Art Center; f. Studio in a School 1977; Chair. Mayor's Cultural Affairs Advisory Comm. of New York City; mem. Bd Chess in the Schools, Cleveland Museum of Art, Foundation for Contemporary Arts, Foundation for Art and Preservation in Embassies, Robert Rauschenberg Foundation, Socrates Sculpture Park; mem. Bd of Trustees of Nat. Council on the Arts 2011–, New York State Council on the Arts 2012–; fmr mem. Bd J. Paul Getty Trust; Founding Trustee, Agnes Gund Foundation; regular contrib. on the arts to the Huffington Post; Hon. Trustee, Cleveland Museum of Art, Ind. Curators Int., Museum of Contemporary Art, Cleveland; Dr hc (Hamilton Coll.) 1994, (Case Western Reserve Univ.) 1995, (Brown Univ.) 1996, (Kenyon Coll.) 1996, (Univ. of Illinois) 2002, (CUNY Grad. Center) 2007, (Bowdoin Coll.) 2012; Nat. Medal of Arts 1997, Arts Educ. Award 1999, Carnegie Medal of Philanthropy 2005. *Address:* c/o Museum of Modern Art, 11 West 53rd Street, New York, NY 10019, USA (office). *Website:* www.moma.org (office).

GUNDOGDYYEV, Gen.-Maj. Begench; Turkmenistani army officer and government official; *Minister of Defence;* m. Ayna Gundogdyyeva; fmr Defence and Mil. Attaché, Embassy in Washington, DC; Deputy Minister of Defence 2009–11, Minister of Defence 2011–; demoted in rank from Gen.-Maj. to Col following munitions explosion in Abadan July 2011, promoted to Gen.-Maj. again Jan. 2013. *Address:* Ministry of Defence, 744000 Asgabat, Galkynys kōç. 4, Turkmenistan (office). *Telephone:* (12) 40-27-64 (office). *Fax:* (12) 39-37-39 (office).

GUNESEKERA, Romesh, FRSL; British (b. Sri Lankan) writer and poet; b. 1954, Colombo; m. Helen; two d.; Writer-in-Residence, Somerset House, London 2010, First Story, Highgate Wood School; mem. Council, RSL 2010; Ranjana (Sri Lanka) 2005; New York Times Notable Book of the Year 1993, 2003, Yorkshire Post Best First Work Award 1994, Premio Mondello 1997, BBC Asia Award 1998. *Publications include:* Monkfish Moon (short stories) 1992, Reef (novel) 1994, The Sandglass (novel) 1998, Heaven's Edge (novel) 2002, The Match (novel) 2006, The Spice Collector (short stories), The Prisoner of Paradise (novel) 2012. *Address:* c/o Bill Hamilton, A.M. Heath & Co., 6 Warwick Court, Holborn, London, WC1R 5DJ, England (office). *Telephone:* (20) 7242-2811 (office). *Fax:* (20) 7242-2711 (office). *Website:* www.amheath.com (office); www.romeshgunesekera.com (home). *E-mail:* rg@romeshgunesekera.com (home).

GUNGAADORJ, Sharavyn, PhD; Mongolian politician and diplomatist; b. 2 May 1935, Ikh Khet soum, Dornogobi Aimak (Prov.); ed Acad. of Agriculture, USSR; Chief Agronomist, Amgalan State farm; agronomist, Dept of State Farms 1959–67; Instructor, Mongolian People's Revolutionary Party (MPRP) Cen. Cttee 1967–68; Deputy Minister for Agric.; head of fodder farm in Zabhan Aimak Prov.; Head of group, Ministry of Agric. 1968–80; First Deputy Minister for State Farms 1980–81; First Sec. Party Cttee of Selenge Aimak Prov. 1981–86; Minister for

Agric. 1986–90; Deputy Chair. Council of Ministers 1987–90; Alt. mem. MPRP Cen. Cttee 1981–86, mem. 1986–; Deputy to Great People's Hural (Ass.) 1981–89, Prime Minister (Chair. Council of Ministers) April–Sept. 1990, Counsellor to the Pres., Chair. of the Civic Council attached to the Pres. 1990–91; Amb. to Democratic People's Repub. of Korea and Kazakhstan 1991–96; fmr Pres. Co-operatives Asscn; Man. Dir Agropro Corpn; mem. Mongolian Acad. of Sciences; Hon. mem. Gentleman's Mil. Interest Club. *Address:* c/o Ministry of Food, Agriculture and Light Industry, Government Bldg 9, Enkh Taivny Örgön Chölöö 16a, Bayanzürkh District, Ulan Bator, Mongolia.

GUNN, James Edward, BS, PhD; American astrophysicist and academic; *Eugene Higgins Professor of Astrophysics, Princeton University; b.* 21 Oct. 1938, Livingstone, Tex.; s. of James Edward Gunn and Rhea Gunn (née Mason); m. Gillian Knapp; two c.; ed Rice Univ., Calif. Inst. of Tech., Pasadena; served with CE US Army Reserve 1967; Sr Space Scientist, Jet Propulsion Lab., Pasadena, Calif. 1966–69; Asst Prof., Princeton Univ. 1969–70, Eugene Higgins Prof. of Astrophysics 1980–; Asst Prof. then Prof. of Astrophysics, Calif. Inst. of Tech. 1970–80; taught at Univ. of Calif., Berkeley, Univ. of Wash., Univ. of Chicago, Rice Univ.; Deputy Prin. Investigator, Space Telescope Wide Field Camera/Planetary Camera, Hubble Space Telescope, NASA 1977; fmr Assoc. Dir Apache Point Observatory; fmr Project Scientist and Tech. Dir Sloan Digital Sky Survey; Fellow, Sloan Foundation 1972–76, MacArthur Foundation 1983; mem. Astronomical Survey Cttee; mem. NAS, American Astronomical Soc., American Philosophical Soc.; Dr hc (Univ. of Portsmouth) 2006; Heinemann Prize, American Astronomical Soc. 1988, Gold Medal, Royal Astronomical Soc. London 1994, Distinguished Alumni Award, Calif. Inst. of Tech. 2003, Cosmology Prize, Peter Gruber Foundation 2005, Craoford Prize, Royal Swedish Acad. of Sciences 2005, Henry Norris Russell Lectureship, American Astronomical Soc. 2005, Nat. Medal of Science 2009. *Publications:* numerous scientific papers in professional journals. *Address:* Department of Astrophysical Sciences, Princeton University, Peyton Hall, Room 113, Princeton, NJ 08544-0001, USA (office). *Telephone:* (609) 258-3802 (office). *Fax:* (609) 258-8226 (office). *E-mail:* jeg@astro.princeton.edu (office). *Website:* www .princeton.edu/astro (office).

GUNN, John Charles, CBE, MD, FRCPsych, FMedSci; British psychiatrist; *Professor Emeritus of Forensic Psychiatry, Institute of Psychiatry, King's College, London; b.* 6 June 1937, Hove; s. of Albert Gunn and Lily Hilda Gunn (née Edwards); m. Celia Willis 1959 (divorced 1986, died 1989); one s. one d.; m. 2nd Pamela Taylor 1989; ed Brighton, Hove and Sussex Grammar School, Reigate Grammar School, Birmingham Univ. Medical School; Consultant Psychiatrist, Bethlem Maudsley Hosp. 1971–2002; Dir Special Hosps Research Unit 1975–78; Prof. of Forensic Psychiatry, Inst. of Psychiatry, King's Coll., London 1978–2002, Emer. Prof. 2002–; Chair. Research Cttee, Royal Coll. of Psychiatrists 1976–80; fmr Chair. Faculty of Forensic Psychiatry; Chair. Academic Bd, Inst. of Psychiatry 1980–85; Chair. Forensic Specialist Cttee, Jt Cttee on Higher Psychiatric Training 1982–85; Consultant European Cttee for Prevention of Torture 1993–; Ed. Criminal Behaviour and Mental Health 1991–; mem. Ont. Govt Enquiry in Oakridge, Ont., Canada 1984–85, Home Sec.'s Advisory Bd on Restricted Patients 1982–91, Bethlem Maudsley Special Health Authority 1986–90, Royal Comm. on Criminal Justice 1991–93, Council, Royal Coll. of Psychiatrists 1997–2004; Foundation mem. Acad. of Medical Sciences 1998; Chair. Faculty of Forensic Psychiatry, Royal Coll. of Psychiatry 2000–04; mem. Royal Comm. on Criminal Justice, Parole Bd for England and Wales; Hon. Royal Mil. Police Asscn Bronze Medal 1970, H. B. Williams Travelling Professorship to Australasia 1985, Phillipe Pinel Award 1992. *Publications:* Violence 1973, Epileptics in Prison 1977, Psychiatric Aspects of Imprisonment 1978, Current Research in Forensic Psychiatry and Psychology (Vols 1–3) 1982–85, Forensic Psychiatry: Clinical, Legal and Ethical Issues 1993. *Leisure interests:* theatre, cinema, opera, walking, photography. *Address:* POB 725, Bromley, BR2 7WF, England (home). *Telephone:* (20) 8462-1751 (home). *Fax:* (20) 8462-0490 (home).

GUNNARSSON, Birgir Ísleifur; Icelandic politician, lawyer and central banker (retd); b. 19 July 1936, Reykjavík; s. of Gunnar Espólín Benediktsson and Jorunn Ísleifsdóttir; m. Sonja Backman 1956; one s. three d.; ed Univ. of Iceland; advocate to lower courts 1962, Supreme Court 1967; law practice 1963–72; Leader Heimdallur Youth Soc. 1959–62; Sec.-Gen. Youth Fed. of Independence Party 1959–62; mem. Reykjavík City Council 1962–82; Mayor of Reykjavík 1972–78; mem. Parl. for Reykjavík 1979–91; Second Deputy Speaker of Althing 1983–87; Minister for Culture and Educ. 1987–88; Chair. Cttee on Heavy Industry 1983–87; mem. Bd Nat. Power Co. 1965–91, Civil Aviation Bd 1984–87; Gov. Cen. Bank of Iceland 1991–2005, Chair. Bd of Govs 1994–2005; Commdr, Order of the Falcon, Order of Dannebrog (Denmark), Order of St Olav (Norway), Order of the White Rose (Finland), Grosse Verdienstkreuz (Germany). *Leisure interests:* music, the outdoor life. *Address:* Fjölnisvegur 15, 101 Reykjavík, Iceland (home). *Telephone:* 552-0628 (home). *E-mail:* birgirisl@simnet.is (office).

GUNNELL, Sally, OBE; British sports commentator, fmr professional athlete and motivational speaker; b. 29 July 1966, Chigwell, Essex; m. Jon Bigg 1992; three s.; ed Chigwell High School; specialized in hurdles; coached by Bruce Longdon; mem. Essex Ladies Athletic Club; competed 400m hurdles Olympic Games, Seoul 1988; second, 400m hurdles World Championship, Tokyo 1991; bronze medal, 400m relay, Olympic Games, Barcelona 1992; women's team capt., Olympic Games 1992–97; gold medal, 400m hurdles, Barcelona 1992; gold medal, 400m hurdles, World Championships 1993 (world record); gold medal, 400m hurdles European Championships, Helsinki 1994; gold medal, 400m hurdles, Commonwealth Games, Canada 1994; only woman in history to have held four gold medals concurrently – Olympic, World, European and Commonwealth (as at end of 2002); retd 1997; sports commentator BBC 1999–2006. *Publications:* Running Tall (with Christopher Priest) 1994, Be Your Best 2001. *Address:* Old School Cottage, School Lane, Pyecombe, W Sussex, England. *Telephone:* (1903) 815510. *Fax:* (1903) 813888. *E-mail:* sally@sallygunnell.com. *Website:* www .sallygunnell.com.

GUNNING-SCHEPERS, Louise J., PhD; Dutch medical scientist, academic and university administrator; *President of the Executive Board, University of Amsterdam; b.* 1951; ed Erasmus Univ.; worked at Univ. of Leuven and at Erasmus Univ.; served as policy staff mem. at Ministry of Health; apptd Prof. of Social Medicine, Academisch Medisch Centrum-Universiteit van Amsterdam

(AMC-UvA) 1991, mem. Exec. Bd AMC-UvA 1997–2001, also Vice-Dean, Pres. Exec. Bd, AMC-UvA and Dean Faculty of Medicine 2001–10, Univ. Prof. of Health and Society –2012, Pres. Exec. Bd, Univ. Amsterdam 2012–; Pres. Health Council of the Netherlands –2012; mem. Scientific Council for Govt Policy 1995–97, Bd Stichting Comité for Concertgebouw; Int. Adviser, Cambridge University Health Partners; Chair. Supervisory Bd Netherlands Genomics Initiative, Scientific Advisory Council Aids Fund; mem. Social Advisory Council of the Dutch Council for Secondary Educ.; Officer, Order of Orange-Nassau 2010. *Publications:* numerous papers in professional journals. *Address:* Executive Staff, University of Amsterdam, Spui 21, 1012 WX Amsterdam, The Netherlands (office). *Telephone:* (20) 525-2752 (office). *E-mail:* secretariaat-voorzitterCvB@uva.nl (office). *Website:* www.uva.nl (office).

GUNNLAUGSSON, Sigmundur Davíð, DPhil; Icelandic politician; *Prime Minister; b.* 12 March 1975, Reykjavík; s. of Gunnlaugur Sigmundsson and Sigríður G. Sigurbjörnsdóttir; m. Anna Sigurlaug Pálsdóttir; one d.; ed Univ. of Copenhagen, Univ. of Oxford, UK; early career as journalist with state broadcaster Ríkisútvarpið (RÚV) 2000–07; mem. Althingi (parl.) for Reykjavík N Constituency 2009–13, for NE Constituency 2013–, mem. Foreign Affairs Cttee 2009–13, Working Group on European Affairs 2010–13, mem. Icelandic del. to EFTA and EEA Parl. Cttees 2009–13, EU–Iceland Jt Parl. Cttee 2010–13; Prime Minister 2013–; mem. Progressive Party, Chair. 2009–. *Address:* Prime Minister's Office, Stjórnarráðshúsinu við Lækjartorg, 150 Reykjavík, Iceland (office). *Telephone:* 5458400 (office). *Fax:* 5624014 (office). *E-mail:* postur@for.stjr.is (office). *Website:* www.forsaetisraduneyti.is (office).

GUO, Gen. Boxiong; Chinese army officer; *Executive Deputy Chief, Headquarters of the General Staff, People's Liberation Army; b.* 1942, Liquan Co., Shaanxi Prov.; ed Mil. Acad. of the Chinese PLA; worker, No. 408 Factory, Xingping Co., Shaanxi Prov. 1958–61; joined PLA 1961, CCP 1963; Squad Leader 164th Regt, 55th Div., Army (or Ground Force), PLA Services and Arms 1961–66, Platoon Commdr 8th Co. 1964–65, mem. staff Propaganda Group 1965–66, mem. staff HQ 164th Regt, 55th Div., Combat Training Section 1966–70, Leader HQ 164th Regt, 55th Div., Combat Training Section 1970–71, Staff Officer, Deputy Head, later Head, later Divisional Chief-of-Staff 1971–81; Deputy Dir Combat Dept (HQ), Lanzhou Mil. Area Command 1982–83; Army Chief-of-Staff 1983–85; Deputy Chief-of-Staff Lanzhou Mil. Area Command 1985–90; Army Group Commdr 1990–93; Deputy Commdr Beijing Mil. Area Command 1993–97; rank of Lt Gen. 1995, Gen. 1999; Commdr Lanzhou Mil. Area Command 1997–99; Exec. Deputy Gen., PLA 1999–2001, Chief of Staff 1999–2002, Exec. Deputy Chief, HQ of Gen. Staff 2002–; mem. 15th CCP Cen. Cttee 1997–2002 (mem. Cen. Mil. Comm.), 16th CCP Cen. Cttee 2002–07 (Vice-Chair. Cen. Mil. Comm. 2002–07), 17th CCP Cen. Cttee 2007–12 (Vice-Chair. Cen. Mil. Comm. 2007–12), also mem. Politburo 2007–12; Deputy Sec. PLA HQ of Gen. Staff, CCP Party Cttee 1999–. *Address:* c/o Ministry of National Defence, 20 Jingshanqian Jie, Beijing 100009, People's Republic of China.

GUO, Dongpo; Chinese politician; *Chairman, Sub-committee for Hong Kong, Macao and Taiwan Compatriots and Overseas Chinese, Chinese People's Political Consultative Conference; b.* Aug. 1937, Jiangdu Co., Jiangsu Prov.; ed Beijing Inst. of Foreign Trade; joined CCP 1960; Deputy Div. Chief, China Council for the Promotion of Int. Trade 1972 (Sec. CCP Party Br.), Deputy Dir Printing House, Vice-Pres. China Council for the Promotion of Int. Trade (Sec. CCP Party Cttee) 1982, Pres. 1992; fmr Vice-Pres. China Chamber of Int. Commerce, Pres. 1995; Dir Macau Bureau of Xinhua News Agency 1990–95; Vice-Dir Drafting Cttee of the Basic Law of Macau Special Admin. Zone 1990; Pres. Econ. and Trade Coordination Cttee for the Two Sides of the Straits 1996; Dir Foreign Econ. and Trade Arbitration Comm. 1996; Dir Office of Overseas Chinese Affairs of the State Council 1997–2003; Vice-Pres. China Overseas Exchanges Asscn 1998–; mem. 7th CPPCC Nat. Cttee 1988–93, Standing Cttee 8th CPPCC Nat. Cttee 1993–98, Chair. Sub-cttee for Hong Kong, Macao and Taiwan Compatriots and Overseas Chinese 2003–; Alt. mem. 14th CCP Cen. Cttee 1992–97; mem. 15th CCP Cen. Cttee 1997–2002. *Address:* Chinese People's Political Consultative Conference, State Council, Beijing, People's Republic of China (office). *Website:* www.cppcc.gov .cn (office).

GUO, Guangchang, BA, MBA; Chinese business executive; *Chairman, Fosun Group; b.* 1967, Zhejiang Prov.; m.; one c.; ed Fudan Univ.; Co-founder Guangxin Consulting Co. 1989 (renamed Fosun Holdings Ltd 1993), Chair. Fosun Group 1994–, also CEO Fosun International and Chair. Fosun Pharmaceutical and Forte Land; Deputy Chair. Shanghai Chamber of Commerce 2002; policy adviser to Shanghai Municipal Govt 2000; co-funded Chinese Private Enterprise Pavilion, Shanghai World Expo 2010; fmr Standing Commissary of Ninth Exec. Council of Greater China Fed. of Industry and Commerce Cttee; mem. China Democratic League; Deputy, 10th NPC 2003–08, 11th NPC 2009–12, 12th NPC 2013–; several nat. awards, including Outstanding Pvt. Entrepreneur Award, Outstanding Youth Entrepreneurs of Shanghai 1997. *Address:* Fosun Group Head Office, No. 2 East Fuxing Road, Shanghai 200010, People's Republic of China (office). *Telephone:* (21) 63325858 (office). *Fax:* (21) 63325028 (office). *Website:* www.fosun.com (office).

GUO, Jinggang, BA, PhD; Chinese engineer and business executive; *Vice-Chairman and General Manager, Datong Coal Mine Group Company Limited; b.* July 1964, Zhongmu Co., Henan; ed Henan Polytechnic Univ.; technician, Lu'an Mining Bureau of Zhangcun Coal Mine 1987–89, Chief of Lu'an Mining Bureau of Zhangcun Coal Mine Man. Div. and Deputy Chief Asst 1989–93; Office Dir and Kaiyuan Co. Man., Ren Luan Mining Bureau of Zhangcun Coal Mine, Zhengzhou 1993–94, Deputy Dir Zhangcun Coal Mine, Luan Mining Bureau March–Dec. 1994, Deputy Dir Zhangcun Coal Mine and Lu'an Mining Bureau Chief Engineer 1994–96, Chief Engineer and Office Deputy Dir (Chair.), Ren Luan Mining Bureau 1996–98, mem. Party Cttee, Lu'an Mining Group Co. 1998–2006, Deputy Gen. Man. Lu'an Mining Group Co. 2006–11, mem. Standing Cttee of Party Cttee, Lu'an Mining Group Co. and Gen. Man. June–Sept. 2011, Vice-Chair. and Gen. Man. Datong Coal Mine Group Co. Ltd 2011–; mem. CCP 1994–. *Address:* Datong Coal Mine Group Co. Ltd, 11 Dongmen Street, Datong 037003, People's Republic of China (office). *Telephone:* (352) 7868200 (office). *Fax:* (352) 7868201 (office). *E-mail:* dtmkjt@dtcoalmine.com (office). *Website:* www.dtcoalmine.com (office).

GUO, Jinlong; Chinese politician; b. July 1947, Nanjing, Jiangsu Prov.; ed Nanjing Univ.; technician, Hydropower Bureau, Zhongxian Co., Sichuan Prov. 1969–73; coach, Physical Culture and Sports Cttee, Zhongxian Co., Sichuan Prov. 1973–79; joined CCP 1979; teacher, Publicity Dept, CCP Co. Cttee 1979–80; Deputy Sec. then Sec. Cultural Bureau of Zhongxian Co., Sichuan Prov. 1980–83; Deputy Sec. CCP Zhongxian Co. Cttee then Magistrate of Zhongxian 1983–85; Deputy Dir Rural Policy Research Office, CCP Sichuan Prov. Cttee, Deputy Dir Sichuan Prov. Rural Econ. Comm. 1985–87; Deputy Sec. then Sec. CCP Leshan City Cttee 1987–92; Deputy Sec. CCP Sichuan Prov. Cttee 1992–93; Deputy Sec. then Exec. Deputy Sec. CCP Tibetan Autonomous Region Cttee 1993–2000, Sec. 2000–04; Alt. mem. 15th CCP Cen. Cttee 1997–2002, mem. 16th CCP Cen. Cttee 2002–07, 17th CCP Cen. Cttee 2007–12, 18th CCP Cen. Cttee 2012–, 18th CCP Cen. Cttee Politburo 2012–; Acting Mayor of Beijing 2007–08, Mayor 2008–12 (resgnd), also Deputy Sec., CCP Municipal Cttee, Beijing Municipality 2007–12, Sec. 2012–; Deputy 11th NPC. *Address:* Chinese Communist Party Politburo, Quanguo Renmin Diabiao Dahui, Zhongguo Gongchan Dang, 1 Zhongnanhai, Beijing, People's Republic of China. *Website:* www.cppcc.gov.cn (office).

GUO, Ping, MA; Chinese business executive; *Deputy Chairman and Rotating CEO, Huawei Technologies Company Limited;* b. 1966; ed Huazhong Univ. of Science and Tech.; joined Huawei Technologies Co. Ltd 1988, served successively as an R&D project manager, Gen. Man. of Supply Chain, Dir of Huawei Exec. Office, Chief Legal Officer, Pres. Business Process & IT Man. Dept, Pres. Corp. Devt Dept, Chair. and Pres. Huawei Device, Corp. Exec. Vice-Pres. and Chair. Finance Cttee, Deputy Chair. and Rotating CEO, Huawei Technologies Co. Ltd Oct. 2012–March 2013, April–Sept. 2014. *Address:* Huawei Technologies Co. Ltd, Bantian, Longgang District, Shenzhen 518129, People's Republic of China (office). *Telephone:* (755) 28780808 (office). *E-mail:* hwtech@huawei.com (office). *Website:* www.huawei.com (office).

GUO, Shengkun; Chinese metallurgist and politician; *Minister of Public Security;* b. Oct. 1954, Jiangxi Prov.; ed Jiangxi Inst. of Metallurgy, Central South Univ., Hunan Prov.; joined CCP 1974; Technician and Section Chief, Machinery Dept, Ministry of Metallurgical Industry 1979–85, also Sec., CCP Party Br. 1979–85; Superintendent, China Nat. Nonferrous Metals Industry Corpn 1985–93, Deputy Man. 1997–98; Group Leader, Preparatory Group, Aluminium Corpn of China 2000–01, Gen. Man. 2001–04, also Sec., CCP Party Br. 2001–04; Deputy Sec., CCP Autonomous Regional Cttee, Guangxi Zhuang Autonomous Region 2004–07, Sec. 2007–12; Vice-Chair., Autonomous Region People's Govt, Guangxi Zhuang Autonomous Region 2004–07; Minister of Public Security 2012–; Dir Nat. Anti-Terror Work Leading Group 2013–; mem. State Council 2013–; alt. mem. 16th CCP Cen. Cttee 2002–07, 17th CCP Cen. Cttee 2007–12, mem. 18th CCP Cen. Cttee 2012–. *Address:* Ministry of Public Security, 14 Dongchangan Dajie, Dongcheng Qu, Beijing 100741, People's Republic of China. *Telephone:* (10) 66262114 (office). *Fax:* (10) 65136577 (office). *E-mail:* gabzfwz@mps.gov.cn (office). *Website:* www.mps.gov.cn (office).

GUO, Shuqing, BA, DJur; Chinese banking executive; *Chairman, China Securities Regulatory Commission;* b. 1956; ed Nankai Univ., Acad. of Social Sciences; Deputy Dir Econ. Research Centre, State Planning Comm. 1988–93; Dir, Gen. Planning and Experiment Dept, State Comm. for Econ. Restructuring 1993–96, Sec.-Gen. State Comm. for Econ. Restructuring 1996–98; Deputy Gov. Guizhou Prov. 1988–2001; Dir State Admin of Foreign Exchange 2001–05; Deputy Gov. People's Bank of China 2001–03; Chair. Huijin 2003–05; Chair. and Exec. Dir China Construction Bank 2005–11; Chair. China Securities Regulatory Comm. 2011–, also Sec. Party Cttee 2011–; mem. 10th CPPCC Nat. Cttee; Alt. mem. 17th CCP Cen. Cttee 2007–12, mem. 18th CCP Cen. Cttee 2012–; Visiting Fellow, Univ. of Oxford, UK 1986–87. *Address:* China Securities Regulatory Commission, Focus Place 19, Jin Rong Street, West District, Beijing 100033, People's Republic of China (office). *E-mail:* consult@csrc.gov.cn (office). *Website:* www.csrc.gov.cn (office).

GUO, Wenqing, BA, MBA; Chinese business executive; *Vice-Chairman and President, China Metallurgical Group Corporation;* b. Dec. 1964; ed Univ. of Science and Tech., Tsinghua Univ.; began career as teacher in Xinlong Co., Hebei Prov., then worked successively as a secretary of county's educational bureau, secretary of county's local govt, head of local govt secr., Deputy Admin. of Beiyingfang Co., Hebei Prov., Sec. of Admin. Office for Chengde Dist, Hebei Prov., Sec. of Admin. Office, Hebei Prov. Party Cttee; Deputy Dir-Gen. Hebei Prov. Highway Admin Comm. 1994–2002, served as Sec. CCP Cttee and Dir-Gen. (Chair. and Pres. Hebei Prov. Highway Devt Co. Ltd); Dir-Gen. Hebei Prov. Waterway Admin Comm. 2002; Sec. CCP Cttee, Exec. Dir and Vice-Pres. Road & Bridge International Co. Ltd 2002–08; Dir, Deputy CCP Cttee and Sec. Disciplinary Cttee China Metallurgical Group Corpn 2009–12, Vice-Chair. and Pres. China Metallurgical Group Corpn 2012–, also Deputy Sec. CCP Cttee. *Address:* China Metallurgical Group Corporation, 28 Shuguangxili, Chaoyang, Beijing 100028, People's Republic of China (office). *Telephone:* (10) 59869999 (office). *Fax:* (10) 59869988 (office). *E-mail:* mcc@mcc.com.cn (office). *Website:* www.mcc.com.cn (office).

GUO, Zhengqian; Chinese party and government official; b. Feb. 1933, Loning Co., Henan Prov.; ed People's Univ. of China; joined CCP 1949; Judicial Officer and Investigator, Public Security Bureau, Songxian Co., Henan Prov. 1947–49; fmr Deputy Section Chief, Commercial Dept, Hubei Prov.; Vice-Pres. Hubei Prov. Commercial School 1964–66; Deputy Dir then Dir Political Dept, Financial and Trade Office, Hubei Prov. 1964–66, Deputy Dir Financial and Trade Office 1980–83; Gov. Hubei Br., People's Construction Bank of China 1980–83; Deputy Gov. Hubei Prov. 1983–86, Acting Gov. Jan. 1986, Gov. May–Oct. 1986; Deputy Sec. Hubei Prov. CCP Cttee 1985–90; Gov. Hubei Provincial People's Govt 1986–90; Deputy Gov. People's Bank of China 1990–93; First Deputy Auditor-Gen. of People's Repub. of China 1993–94, Auditor-Gen. 1994–98; Sr Economist, concurrently Prof., People's Univ. of China; Del. 12th CCP Nat. Congress 1982–87, mem. 13th and 14th CCP Cen. Cttees 1987–97, Del. 15th CCP Nat. Congress 1997–2002; Deputy, 6th NPC 1983–88, 7th NPC 1988–93, mem. 9th Standing Cttee of NPC 1998–2003 (Vice-Chair. Financial and Econ. Cttee 1998–2003, Chair. Budgetary Work Cttee 1998–2003). *Leisure interests:* reading, swimming, tennis, table tennis. *Address:* c/o NPC Budgetary Work Committee, Beijing, People's Republic of China (office).

GUO MUSUN, Mooson Kwauk, BS, MS; Chinese scientist and academic; *Director Emeritus, Institute of Process Engineering, Chinese Academy of Sciences;* b. 9 May 1920, Hangyang; s. of Zung-Ung Kwauk and Za-Nan Chow; m. Huichun Kwei Kwauk 1950; two s. one d.; ed Univ. of Shanghai, Princeton Univ., USA; Prof., Inst. of Chemical Metallurgy (now Inst. of Process Eng), Chinese Acad. of Sciences 1956, Dir 1982–86, Dir Emer. 1986–; Visiting Prof., Ohio State Univ. 1989; Vice-Pres. Chemical Industry and Eng Soc. of China 1978–; Visiting Prof. Virginia Polytechnic Inst. and State Univ. 1986–87; mem. Chinese Acad. of Sciences 1981–; Pres. Emer. Chinese Soc. of Particuology 1986–; Corresp. mem. Swiss Acad. of Eng Sciences 1997–; Distinguished Scholar, CSCPRC Program, US Nat. Acad. of Science 1984, Davis-Swindin Memorial Lecturer, Univ. of Loughborough, UK 1985, Danckwerts Memorial Lecturer, Inst. of Dirs, London 1989, Int. Fluidization Award 1989. *Publications:* Fluidization: Idealized and Bubbleless, with Applications 1992, Fast Fluidization 1994, Geometric Mobiles 1998. *Leisure interests:* kites, mobiles. *Address:* Institute of Process Engineering, Chinese Academy of Sciences, Beijing, 100080, People's Republic of China (office). *Telephone:* (10) 6255-4241 (office); (10) 6255-4050 (home). *Fax:* (10) 6255-8065 (office). *E-mail:* mooson@home.ipe.ac.cn (office). *Website:* english.ipe.cas.cn/pe/cm/ 200906/t20090612_6012.html (office).

GUPTA, Modadugu V., PhD; Indian marine biologist; b. 17 Aug. 1939, Bapatla, AP; ed Univ. of Calcutta; Scientist, Indian Council of Agricultural Research 1962–76; Aquaculture and Breeding Expert, UN Econ. and Social Comm. for Asia and the Pacific (UN-ESCAP) 1977–86; Fish Culture Expert, FAO, Bangladesh 1986–89; Asst Dir Gen. WorldFish Center 1989–2004 (retd), Sr Research Fellow 2005–08; Research Co-ordinator, Int. Network on Genetics in Aquaculture 1996–2004; consultant to FAO, UNDP, World Bank, Asian Devt Bank, USAID, Danish Int. Devt Agency (DANIDA), Commonwealth Secr., etc.; chaired and organized numerous global and regional confs; currently consultant/adviser to several insts; Fellow of numerous scientific socs; Hon. Fellow, Asscn of Aquaculturists; Hon. DSc (Fisheries Univ., Mumbai), (G.B. Pant Univ. of Agric. and Tech., Pantnagar); World Food Prize Laureate 2005, Gold Medal, Asian Fisheries Soc., Life Time Award, World Aquaculture Soc., Medal of Indian Council of Agricultural Research. *Publications include:* more than 150 papers in books, journals and conf. proceedings. *Address:* C502, Aditya Elite, B.S. Maktha, Begumpet, Hyderabad 500 016, India (office). *Telephone:* (40) 23400229 (office); 98-66508555 (mobile) (office). *Fax:* (40) 23400229 (office). *E-mail:* guptamo2000@ yahoo.co.in (office).

GUPTE, Lalita Dileep, BEcons, MMS; Indian banking executive; b. 1948; m.; two c.; ed Univ. of Delhi, Univ. of Bombay, Jamnalal Bajaj Inst. of Man. Studies; joined ICICI Bank Ltd 1971, held various leadership positions in Corp. and Retail Banking, Strategy and Resources, and Int. Banking depts, Exec. Dir Bd of Dirs ICICI Ltd 1994–96, Deputy Man. Dir 1996–99, Jt Man. Dir and COO 2001–06, Chair. (non-exec.) ICICI Venture Funds Management Co. Ltd 2006–; mem. Advisory Bd RAND Center for Asia-Pacific Policy; mem. Bd of Dirs Bharat Forge Ltd 2006–, Kirloskar Brothers Ltd 2007–, FirstSource Solutions Ltd 2007–, Godrej Properties Ltd 2008–, HPCL-Mittal Energy Ltd, Swadhaar FinServe Pvt Ltd, Nokia 2007–, Alstom 2010–; Twenty-First Century for Banking Finance and Banking Award, Ladies Wing of Indian Merchants' Chamber 1997, ranked by Fortune magazine amongst 50 Most Powerful Women in Business outside the US 2001, 2002, (31st) 2003, Women Achievers Award, Women Grads Asscn 2001, Int. Women's Asscn Woman of the Year Award 2002, ranked 93rd by Forbes magazine amongst 100 Most Powerful Women 2006. *Leisure interest:* looking after her family. *Address:* ICICI Bank Ltd, ICICI Bank Towers, Bandra Kurla Complex, Mumbai 400 051, India (office). *Telephone:* (22) 26531414 (office). *Fax:* (22) 26531167 (office). *Website:* www.icicibank.com (office).

GURASSA, Charles Mark, BEcons, MBA, FRSA, FRAeS; British business executive; b. 1956, London; m.; c.; ed Christ's Coll., London, Univ. of York, Int. Man. Centre, Buckingham; joined Thomas Cook 1977, posts in New York, London, Hong Kong, Gen. Man. Retail Operations 1988–89; Sr Commercial Dir British Airways 1989–99; CEO Thomson Travel Group plc 1999–2000; Chair. TUI N Europe and Airline Group 2000–03, Exec. Dir TUI AG 2000–03; Chair. (non-exec.) 7days Ltd 2003–, Worldwide Excellerated Leasing Ltd 2004–, LOVEFiLM Int. 2006–, MACH S.a.r.l. 2007–, Phones 4u Ltd 2007–; Chair. Virgin Mobile PLC 2004–06; Chair. Nat. Trust Enterprises Ltd; Dir (non-exec.) Whitbread plc 2000–09; Trustee, Whizz-Kidz 2003–; mem. Bd of Trustees Nat. Trust Council; mem. Advisory Bd Alpitour, Univ. of York; mem. Comparable Bd Neos SPA, Thomson Travel Group (Holdings) Ltd; Travel Industry Hall of Fame 2003. *Leisure interests:* music, travel, theatre, sports. *Address:* LOVEFiLM International, 6 Portal Way, London, W3 6RU, England (office). *Telephone:* (20) 8896-8000 (office). *Fax:* (20) 8896-8111 (office). *Website:* www.lovefilm.com (office).

GURBANMYRADOV, Yolly; Turkmenistani politician and economist; b. 1960, Ashgabat; ed Turkmen State Inst. of Nat. Econ.; worker in construction co. 1977–82; Sr Econ., Deputy Head Ashgabat br. USSR State Bank 1982–87; Head of Div. of Banking Automation State Bank (Ashgabat) 1988; Deputy Head of Regional Dept, USSR Zhilsotsbank 1988–89; man. of div. Agroprombank 1989–90; Br. Man. USSR Vnesheconombank 1990–92; First Deputy Chair., then Chair. Bd of Dirs State Bank of Foreign Trade of Turkmenistan 1992–96; Dir Turkmenistan State Agency on Foreign Investments 1996–97; Deputy Chair. Turkmen Cabinet of Ministers, concurrently Chair. Interbanking Council 1997–99; Deputy Prime Minister of Turkmenistan 1999–2004. *Address:* c/o Cabinet of Ministers, Ashgabat, Turkmenistan (office).

GURDON, Sir John Bertrand, Kt, DPhil, FRS; British cell biologist; b. 2 Oct. 1933, Dippenhall, Hants., England; s. of W. N. Gurdon and E. M. Gurdon (née Byass); m. Jean Elizabeth Margaret Curtis 1964; one s. one d.; ed Edgeborough School, Eton Coll., Univ. of Oxford; Beit Memorial Fellow 1958–61; Gosney Research Fellow, California Inst. of Tech., USA 1961–62; Research Fellow, Christ Church, Oxford 1962–72, Departmental Demonstrator 1963–64, Lecturer, Dept of Zoology 1966–72; Visiting Research Fellow, Carnegie Inst., Baltimore, Md, USA 1965; mem. Scientific Staff, Medical Research Council, Molecular Biology Lab., Univ. of Cambridge 1971–83, Head of Cell Biology Div. 1979–83, John Humphrey Plummer Prof. of Cell Biology 1983–2001, Master Magdalene Coll. Cambridge 1995–2002, Fellow, Churchill Coll., Cambridge 1973–95; Fellow, Eton Coll. 1978–93; Fullerian Prof. of Physiology and Comparative Anatomy, Royal Inst.

1985–91; Pres. Int. Soc. for Developmental Biology 1990–94; Chair. Wellcome Cancer Campaign Inst., Univ. of Cambridge 1990–2001; Gov. The Wellcome Trust 1995–2000; Chair. Co. of Biologists 2001–; Foreign Assoc., NAS 1980, Belgian Royal Acad. of Science, Letters and Fine Arts 1984, French Acad. of Sciences 1990; Foreign mem. American Philosophical Soc. 1983, Inst. of Medicine (USA) 2003; Hon. Foreign mem. American Acad. of Arts and Sciences 1978; Hon. Student, Christ Church, Oxford 1985; Hon. Fellow, Magdalene Coll. Cambridge 2002, Churchill Coll. Cambridge 2007; Hon. DSc (Chicago) 1978, (Oxford) 1988, (Hull) 1998, (Glasgow) 2000, (Cambridge) 2007, (Bruxelles) 2010; Dr hc (Paris) 1982, (Santiago, Chile) 2012, (Rockefeller, USA) 2014; Albert Brachet Prize, Belgian Royal Acad. 1968, Scientific Medal of Zoological Soc. 1968, Dunham Lecturer, Harvard Medical School 1974, Feldberg Foundation Award 1975, Croonian Lecturer, Royal Soc. 1976, Paul Ehrlich Award 1977, Carter-Wallace Lecturer, Princeton Univ. 1978, Nessim Habif Prize, Univ. of Geneva 1979, CIBA Medal, Biochemical Soc. 1981, Comfort Crookshank Award for Cancer Research 1983, William Bate Hardy Triennial Prize, Cambridge Philosophy Soc. 1983, Charles Léopold Mayer Prize, Acad. des Sciences (France) 1984, Ross Harrison Prize, Int. Soc. for Devt Biology 1985, Royal Medal, Royal Soc. 1985, Emperor Hirohito Int. Biology Prize 1987, Wolf Prize for Medicine (jtly with Edward B. Lewis) 1989, Distinguished Service Award, Miami 1992, Jean Brachet Memorial Prize, Int. Soc. of Diffusion 2000, Conklin Medal, Soc. for Developmental Biology 2001, Copley Medal, Royal Soc. 2003, Rosenstiel Award 2009, Albert Lasker Basic Medical Research Award 2009, Nobel Prize in Physiology or Medicine (with Shinya Yamanaka) 2012. *Publication:* Control of Gene Expression in Animal Development 1974. *Leisure interests:* skiing, horticulture, lepidoptera. *Address:* Whittlesford Grove, Whittlesford, Cambridge, CB2 4NZ, England (home). *Telephone:* (1223) 334090 (office); (1223) 832674 (home).

GURFINKEL, Viktor Semenovich; Russian physiologist; *Senior Scientist, Oregon Health and Science University;* b. 2 April 1922; ed Kyrgyz State Medical Inst.; during World War II head div. of blood transfusion 19th Army 1941–45, chief dr hospital 1946–48; sr researcher, head of lab., Inst. of Orthopaedics 1949–58; head of lab. Inst. of Experimental Biology and Medical Siberian br. USSR Acad. of Sciences 1949–58; head of lab. Inst. of Biophysics USSR Acad. of Sciences 1960–67; head of lab. Inst. for Information Transmission Problems, Russian Acad. of Sciences; currently Sr Scientist, Oregon Health and Science Univ., USA; corresp. mem. USSR (now Russian) Acad. of Sciences 1987, mem. 1994; research in physiology of movements, space physiology and medicine; resident in USA 1999–; Hon. mem. American Physiological Soc.; Dr hc (Univ. of Arizona 1995); USSR State Prize 1970, R. Dow Prize (USA) 1990, Humboldt Foundation Award 1990. *Publications:* three books and numerous articles in scientific journals. *Leisure interest:* fishing. *Address:* Neurological Sciences Institute, Oregon Health and Science University, West Campus, 505 NW 185th Avenue, Beaverton, OR 97006, USA.

GURG, Easa Saleh al-, KCVO, CBE; United Arab Emirates diplomatist, banker, business executive and politician; *Chairman, Easa Saleh Al Gurg Group;* b. Dubai; m. Soraya Al Gurg; f. Easa Saleh Al Gurg Group 1960; Co-founder and Chair. Al Gurg Fosroc LLC 1975–; Dir Emirates Bank Group 1983–; Chair. Easa Saleh Al Gurg Group, Al Gurg Leigh's Pants LLC, Gulf Metal Foundry LLC, Arabian E-Lever LLC; Deputy Chair. Nat. Bank of Fujairah Bank; Dir Investcorp Bank EC, Emirates Merchant Bank Ltd, Emirates Bank International; Amb. to UK (also accred to Ireland) 1991–2009; sponsorship for grad. students, Oxford Centre for Islamic Studies. *Publications:* The Wells of Memory: An Autobiography 1999. *Address:* Easa Saleh Al Gurg Group, Easa Saleh Al Gurg Building, Baniyas Street, Deira, PO Box 325, Dubai, UAE (office). *Telephone:* (4) 2279666 (office). *Fax:* (4) 2278620 (office). *E-mail:* esag@algurg.ae (office). *Website:* www.algurg.com (office).

GURG, Raja Easa al-; United Arab Emirates business executive; *Managing Director, Easa Saleh Al Gurg Group;* b. Dubai; d. of Easa Saleh al-Gurg; Man. Dir Easa Saleh Al Gurg Group (ESAG); Pres. Dubai Business Women's Council; Deputy Chair. Dubai Healthcare City Authority; mem. Bd Dubai Chamber of Commerce & Industry, Dubai Women's Asscn; mem. Dubai Econ. Council, Arab Int. Women's Forum, Nat. Advisory Council, Coll. of Business Sciences; involved in philanthropic, social and charitable activities, notably with the Easa Saleh Al Gurg Charity Foundation; named by Forbes International as the fourth Most Powerful Arab Businesswoman 2006, Stevie Award for Women in Business 2011, World of Difference Award, Int. Alliance for Women (TIAW) 2009, ranked by Arabian Business amongst the Power 500: The Worlds's Most Influential Arabs (58th) 2012. *Address:* Easa Saleh Al Gurg Group, Al Gurg Tower I, Baniyas Street, Deira, PO Box 325, Dubai, United Arab Emirates (office). *Telephone:* (4) 2279666 (office). *Fax:* (4) 2278620 (office). *E-mail:* esag@algurg.ae (office). *Website:* www .algurg.com (office).

GURGENIDZE, Vladimer (Lado), MBA; Georgian/British banker and politician; b. 7 Dec. 1970, Tbilisi; m. Larissa Gurgenidze; three c.; ed Tbilisi State Univ., Middlebury Coll., VT, USA, Goizueta School of Business of Emory Univ.; began his investment banking career with CEE corp. finance arm of MeesPierson; Dir ABN AMRO Corp. Finance in Russia and CIS 1997–98, served in various sr capacities at ABN AMRO Corp. Finance, London, including as a Dir and Head of Mergers and Acquisitions in the Emerging European Markets 1998–2000 and as a Man. Dir and Head of Tech. Corp. Finance 2001–03; Man. Dir and Regional Man. for Europe, Putnam Lovell NBF (boutique investment banking firm) 2003–04; CEO Bank of Georgia 2004–06, Chair. Supervisory Bd 2006–; Chair. Supervisory Bd Galt & Taggart Securities, Galt & Taggart Capital; mem. Supervisory Bd Georgian Stock Exchange; Prime Minister of Georgia 2007–08. *Television:* hosted a reality TV show The Candidate on Rustavi 2 (Georgian version of Donald Trump's franchise The Apprentice) 2006. *Address:* c/o Chancellery of the Government, P. Ingorovka 7, 0105 Tbilisi, Georgia (office).

GURGULINO DE SOUZA, Heitor, BSc, Lic Math.; Brazilian academic, scientist and international organization official; b. 1 Aug. 1928, São Lourenço, Minas Gerais; s. of Arthur Gurgulino de Souza and Catarina Sachser de Souza; m. Lilian Maria Quilici; two c.; ed Mackenzie Univ., São Paulo, Aeronautics Inst. of Tech., Sao Jose dos Campos, Univ. of Kansas, Univ. of São Paulo; Instructor and Asst Prof., Physics Dept, ITA, São José dos Campos, São Paulo, Brazil 1951–57; Prof. of Physics, State Univ. of São Paulo (UNESP), Rio Claro Campus 1958–1990; Program Specialist, Inter-American Science Program, Pan American Union,

Washington, DC 1962–64; Head, Unit of Educ. and Research, Dept of Scientific Affairs, OAS, Washington, DC 1964–69; Rector, Fed. Univ. of São Carlos, State of São Paulo 1970–74; Dir Dept of Univ. Affairs, Ministry of Educ. and Culture, Brasília 1972–74; Chair. Inter-American Cttee on Science and Tech. (CICYT), Council for Educ., Culture, OAS, Washington, DC 1974–77; Vice-Pres. Fed. Council of Educ. of Brazil 1972–87; Dir CNPq (Nat. Council for Scientific and Tech. Devt), Brasília 1975–78, Special Adviser to Pres. 1979–80; Vice-Pres. International Asscn of Univ. Pres. 1985–87, 1999–2002, Sec.-Gen. 2008–11, Sec.-Gen. Emer. 2012; Pres. Grupo Universitario Latinoamericano (GULERPE), Caracas 1985–87; Rector UN Univ., Tokyo 1987–97; Special Adviser for Higher Educ. to Dir-Gen., UNESCO, Paris 1997–99; Vice-Rector Unilegis-Universidade do Legislativo Brasileiro, Fed. Senate, Brasília 2003–05; Pres. Asscn Virtual Educ. Brasil 2003–; mem. American Physical Soc. 1956–, Club of Rome 1996– (Vice-Pres. 2008–12), Brazilian Acad. of Educ. 2004–; mem. Nat. Order of Educational Merit, MEC, Brasília 1973, Commdr Order of Rio Branco, MRE, Brasília 1974, Commdr Order Infante Dom Henrique, Portugal 1990, Nat. Order of Scientific Merit, MCT 1996; Dr hc (Universidad Autnoma de Guadalajara) 1984, (Espírito Santo) 1986, (Universidade Federal de São Carlos, São Paulo) 2006, (IESB, Brasilia) 2008, Hon. DJur (California State Univ., USA) 1997, Great-Cross, MCT- MRE, Paris 2002, (Obirin Univ., Tokyo, Japan) 2010, (Osaka Univ. of Commerce, Japan) 2010; Tiradentes Medal, Govt of State of Minas Gerais, Brazil 2012. *Television:* producer, Educação Tesouro a Descobrir, Rêde Vida 2004–12; numerous inter-views. *Publications include:* Gamma Rays from the Proton Bombardment of Natural Silicon 1957, Science Policy (co-ed.) 1974; author of chapter on Brazil in International Encyclopedia of Higher Education 1978; several articles. *Leisure interests:* sailing, swimming, music. *Address:* S.Q.S. 116 Bloco B, Apto 501, Asa Sul, Brasília, DF, CEP 70386-020, Brazil (home). *Telephone:* (61) 3346-1414 (home); 61-8159-9091 (mobile). *Fax:* (61) 3346-0938 (home). *E-mail:* hgurgulino@ aol.com; heitorgurgulino@gmail.com (office).

GURIRAB, Theo-Ben, PhD; Namibian politician; *President, Inter-Parliamentary Union;* b. 23 Jan. 1939, Usakos; m. Joan W. Guriras; two s. one d.; ed Augustineum Training Coll., Okahandja, Temple Univ.; in exile 1962; Chief Rep. in N America for South West Africa People's Org. (SWAPO) 1971; Head of SWAPO's Mission, UN 1972–86; mem. of Senate, UN Inst. for Namibia, Lusaka; Sr Adviser to SWAPO Pres. during Resolution 435 negotiations; Minister of Foreign Affairs 1990–2000, Minister of Foreign Affairs, Information and Broadcasting 2000–02, Prime Minister 2002–05; Speaker, Nat. Ass. 2005–; Pres. Inter-Parliamentary Union (IPU) 2008–. *Address:* National Assembly, Windhoek, Namibia (office). *Telephone:* (61) 2882504 (office). *Fax:* (61) 231626 (office). *E-mail:* w.hanse@parliament.gov.na (office). *Website:* www.parliament.gov.na (office).

GURNEY, Albert Ramsdell, (Pete Gurney), MFA; American playwright and novelist; b. 1 Nov. 1930, Buffalo, NY; s. of Albert R. Gurney and Marion Gurney (née Spaulding); m. Mary F. Goodyear 1957; two s. two d.; ed Williams Coll., Yale School of Drama; joined MIT, Faculty of Humanities 1960–96, Prof. 1970–96; mem. American Acad. of Arts and Letters 2006, Theater Hall of Fame; Hon. DDL (Buffalo State Univ., Williams Coll.); Drama Desk Award 1971, American Acad. of Arts and Letters Award 1987, Lucille Lortel Award 1992, William Inge Award 2000, Theatre Hall of Fame 2005, Drama Desk Award 2011. *Publications include:* plays: The Dining Room, The Cocktail Hour, Love Letters, Later Life, A Cheever Evening, Sylvia, Overtime; Let's Do It!, The Guest Lecturer, Labor Day, Far East, Ancestral Voices 1999, Human Events 2000, Buffalo Gal 2001, The Fourth Wall 2002, Big Bill 2004, Mrs Farnsworth 2004, Indian Blood 2006, Crazy Mary 2007, A Light Lunch 2009, The Grand Manner 2010, Office Hours 2010, Black Tie 2011, Heresy 2012; novels: The Gospel According to Joe, Entertaining Strangers, The Snow Ball; opera libretto: Stawberry Fields 1999. *Address:* 40 Wellers Bridge Road, PO Box 150, Roxbury, CT 06783-1616, USA. *Telephone:* (860) 354-3692. *Fax:* (860) 354-3692. *E-mail:* a.r.gurney@charter.net. *Website:* argurney.com.

GUROV, Maj.-Gen. Aleksander Ivanovich, DJur; Russian civil servant and politician; b. 17 Nov. 1945, Shushkan-Olshanka, Tambov Dist; m. Yelena Nikolayevna Gurova; one s.; ed Moscow State Univ.; inspector Div. of Criminal Investigation, Vnukovo Airport 1970–74; mem. of staff Dept of Criminal Investigation, USSR Ministry of Internal Affairs 1974–78, Head of Dept for Struggle Against Organized Crime, Corruption and Drug Business; USSR People's Deputy 1990–93; First Deputy Head of Centre of Public Relations, Ministry of Security; Vice-Pres. Inform-Service; Head of Tepko-Bank (security service) 1994–98; Head of All-Russian Inst., Ministry of Internal Affairs 1998–99; Co-founder and Co.-leader Yedinstvo 1999; mem. State Duma 1999, Chair. Cttee on Security 2000. *Publications include:* Red Mafia; over 150 scientific articles on struggle against original crime.

GÜRRAGCHAA, Maj.-Gen. Jügderdemidiin; Mongolian politician, army officer and fmr cosmonaut; served in Mongolian Armed Forces, rank of Maj.-Gen.; first Mongolian (and second Asian) to travel to space 1981; Minister of Defence –2004; Hero of the Nation, Contribution to Space Research Award, Russian Fund for Space Research 2000. *Address:* c/o Ministry of Defence, Government Building 7, Dandaryn Gudamj, Bayanzürkh District, Ulan Bator 61, Mongolia (office).

GURRÍA TREVIÑO, José Ángel, BA, MA; Mexican economist, diplomatist and international organization official; *Secretary-General, Organisation for Economic Co-operation and Development;* b. 8 May 1950, Tampico, Tamaulipas; m. Dr Lulu Quintana; three c.; ed Universidad Nacional Autónoma de México, Univ. of Leeds, UK, Harvard Univ., USA; Perm. Rep. of Mexico to Int. Coffee Org., London 1976–78; held various positions in Fed. Electricity Comm., Nat. Devt Bank (Nafinsa), Rural Devt Fund and Office of Mayor of Mexico City; at Finance Ministry 1978–92; Pres. and CEO Bancomext (export-import bank) 1992–93, Nacional Financiera (nat. devt bank) 1993–94; Minister of Foreign Affairs 1994–98, of Finance and Public Credit 1998–2000; Sec.-Gen. OECD 2006–; Chair. External Advisory Group, IDB. *Address:* OECD, 2 rue André Pascal, 75775 Paris Cedex 16, France (office). *Telephone:* 1-45-24-82-00 (office). *Fax:* 1-45-24-88-26 (office). *E-mail:* secretary.general@oecd.org (office). *Website:* www.oecd.org (office).

GURRY, Francis, LLB, LLM, PhD; Australian lawyer and international organization official; *Director General, World Intellectual Property Organization;*

b. 17 May 1951, Melbourne, Vic.; s. of Raymond Paul Gurry and Eileen Gurry (née Galbally); m.; three c.; ed Univ. of Melbourne, Univ. of Cambridge, UK; articled clerk, then attorney-at-law, Arthur Robinson & Co., Melbourne 1974–76; admitted barrister and solicitor, Supreme Court of Vic. 1975; Sr Lecturer in Law, Univ. of Melbourne 1979–84; Visiting Prof. of Law, Univ. of Dijon, France 1982–83; attorney-at-law, Freehills, Sydney 1984; joined WIPO 1985, held various positions, including Deputy Dir Gen. 2003–08, Dir Gen. 2008–; Sec. Gen. Int. Union for the Protection of New Varieties of Plants (UPOV) 2008–; Chair. High-Level Cttee on Man., UN System Chief Execs Bd 2012–; Fellow, Australian Inst. of Int. Affairs 2012; Hon. Professorial Fellow, Univ. of Melbourne 2001; Hon. Prof., Peking Univ. 2009, Eurasian Nat. Univ. 2012; Hon. mem. Univ. Council of the Arts, Univ. of Alcala 2012; Alawite Commdr Wissam (Morocco) 2013; Dr hc (Univ. of World and Nat. Economy, Sofia, Bulgaria) 2009, (Nat. Tech. Univ. of Ukraine 'Kiev Polytechnic Inst.') 2010, (Haifa Univ.) 2010, (Renmin Univ.) 2010, (Univ. of Akron) 2011, (Acad. of Econ. Studies of Moldova) 2012; Yorke Prize, Univ. of Cambridge 1980. *Publications include:* Breach of Confidence 1984, International Intellectual Property System: Commentary and Materials (with Frederick Abbott and Thomas Cottier) 1999, Intellectual Property in an Integrated World Economy (with Frederick Abbot and Thomas Cottier) 2007; several book chapters and articles in professional journals. *Address:* World Intellectual Property Organization, PO Box 18, 34 chemin des Colombettes, 1211 Geneva 20, Switzerland (office). *Telephone:* (22) 3389428 (office). *Fax:* (22) 3388090 (office). *E-mail:* directorgeneral@wipo.int (office). *Website:* www.wipo.int (office).

GURSKY, Andreas; German photographer; b. 15 Jan. 1955, Leipzig; s. of Willy Gursky and Rosemarie Gursky; ed Folkwang School, Univ. of Essen, Düsseldorf Acad. of Art; studied under Hilla and Bernd Becher; known for highly textured feel in enormous photographs, often using a high point of view; Foreign Hon. mem. American Acad. of Arts and Letters 2007; lives and works in Düsseldorf; Citybank Photography Prize 1998, Wilhelm-Loth-Prize 2003, The Imperial Ring Art Prize of the City of Goslar 2008. *Address:* c/o Regen Projects, 633 North Almont Drive, Los Angeles, CA 90069, USA.

GURUNG, Lt-Gen. Chhatra Man Singh, BA; Nepalese army officer; b. 18 July 1952, Pulimarang VDC, Tanahu dist; ed Tribhuvan Univ., Command and Gen. Staff Course in USA, Sr Command Course in India, Strategic Studies on Nat. Security and Mil. Command in China; joined army 1971, commissioned as 2nd Lt, has held various positions including Chief of Staff Western Div., Dir of Mil. Training and Quarter Master Gen. and Chief of Gen. Staff; served as Mil. Attaché in UK and France; served in UN Interim Force in Lebanon; Divisional Chief Midwestern Div. 2006–07; Chief of Army Staff 2009–13. *Leisure interest:* Taekwondo. *Address:* c/o Office of the Chief of Army Staff, Ministry of Defence, Singha Durbar, Kathmandu, Nepal. *E-mail:* mod@mos.com.np.

GUSAU, Lt-Gen. (retd) Mohammed Aliyu; Nigerian army officer and government official; *Minister of Defence;* b. 18 May 1943, Gusau, Zamfara State; ed Royal Coll. of Defence Studies, UK; Commdr, 9th Infantry Brigade, Abeokuta 1976–78, Adjutant Gen., 2nd Mechanised Div. 1978–79, Dir of Personnel Services, Army HQ Oct.–Nov. 1979, Dir of Mil. Intelligence 1979–83, Dir, Defence Intelligence Agency and Acting Dir-Gen., Nat. Security Org. 1985–86, Coordinator on Nat. Security 1986–89; Gen. Officer Commanding 2nd Mechanised Div., Ibadan 1989–90, Chief of Admin, Defence HQ, Lagos 1990–92, Commdr, Nigerian Defence Acad., Kaduna 1992–93, Nat. Security Adviser 1993, Chief of Army Staff Aug.–Sept. 1993, Nat. Security Adviser 1999–2006, March–Sept. 2010; Minister of Defence 2014–; Chair. and CEO Alpha Public Affairs Consultancy 1993; mem. People's Democratic Party. *Address:* Ministry of Defence, Ship House, Central Area, Abuja, Nigeria (office). *Telephone:* (9) 2340534 (office). *Fax:* (9) 2340714 (office). *E-mail:* mamed@nigeria.gov.ng (office).

GUSENBAUER, Alfred, PhD; Austrian politician and business executive; *Chairman of the Supervisory Board, Strabag SE;* b. 8 Feb. 1960, Sankt Pölten, Lower Austria; ed High School in Wieselburg, Univ. of Vienna; Fed. Leader Sozialdemokratische Partei Österreichs (Social Democratic Party of Austria—SPÖ) Youth Wing, Socialist Youth (SJ) 1984–90, Chair. SPÖ in Ybbs an der Donau and mem. Lower Austria Party Exec. 1991, Chair. SPÖ 2000–08; Vice-Pres. Socialist Youth Int. (IUSY) 1985–89, Socialist Int. 1989; elected Deputy for Lower Austria to Bundesrat 1991, Chair. Cttee for Devt Co-operation 1996–99, Leader of SPÖ Group in Bundesrat 2000–07; Fed. Chancellor 2007–08; mem. Austrian del. to parl. meeting of Council of Europe 1991, Chair. Social Cttee of Council of Europe 1995–98; Sr Research Fellow, Econ. Policy Dept, Lower Austria Chamber of Labour 1990–99; Visiting Prof., Brown Univ.; Leitner Global Fellow, Columbia Univ. School of Int. and Public Affairs, New York, USA 2009–; Chair. Advisory Bd Signa Holdings 2009–; Chair. Supervisory Bd Strabag SE 2010–; mem. Supervisory Bd Alpine Holding 2009–10; Pres. Dr Karl Renner Inst., Austrian Inst. for Int. Affairs, Austrian-Spanish Chamber of Commerce; Chair. Bd of Trustees of pvt. foundation est. by Strabag's CEO, Hans Peter Haselsteiner 2010–. *Address:* Strabag SE, Donau-City-Straße 9, 1220 Vienna (office); Social Democratic Party of Austria, Löwelstrasse 18, 1014 Vienna, Austria. *Telephone:* (1) 22422-1000 (office); (1) 534-27-0. *Fax:* (1) 22422-1003 (office); (1) 535-96-83. *E-mail:* Alfred.Gusenbauer@spoe.at (office); HPH@strabag.com (office). *Website:* www.strabag.com (office); www.alfred-gusenbauer.at; www.spoe.at.

GUSEV, Pavel Nikolayevich; Russian journalist and publisher; *Editor-in-Chief, Moskovsky Komsomolets;* b. 4 April 1949, Moscow; s. of Nikolai Gusev and Alla Guseva; m. Yevgeniya Valeryevna Yefimova; three d.; ed Moscow Inst. of Geological Survey, Maxim Gorky Inst. of Literature; First Sec. Komsomol Cttee of Krasnaya Presnya Region of Moscow 1975–80; Exec. Cen. Komsomol Cttee 1980–83; Ed.-in-Chief Moskovsky Komsomolets (newspaper) 1983–; Minister, Govt of Moscow, Head of Dept of Information and Mass Media Jan.–Oct. 1992; press adviser to Mayor of Moscow 1992–95; Chair. Comm. for the Protection of Information and Freedom of the Word of the Public Chamber, Public Council of Fed. Agency of Culture and Cinematography 2007–; currently Pres. Moscow Confed. of Journalists; also Prof. of Journalism, International Univ., Moscow. *Plays:* I Love You, Constance (Moscow Gogol Theatre) 1993, Cardinal's Coat (Maly Theatre) 2002. *Leisure interests:* golf, books, trophy hunting. *Address:* Moskovsky Komsomolets, 1905 Goda 7, 123995 Moscow, Russia (office). *Telephone:* (499) 259-50-36 (office). *Fax:* (499) 259-46-39 (office). *E-mail:* info@mk.ru (office). *Website:* www.mk.ru (office).

GUSEV, Vladimir A., CandArts; Russian arts administrator; *Director, State Russian Museum;* b. 25 April 1945, Kalinin (now Tver); m. Mukhina Xenia Vladimizovna; one d.; ed U.E. Repin Inst. of Painting, Sculpture and Architecture, Leningrad; Exec. Sec. Leningrad br., Russian Fed. Union of Artists 1974–78; Sr Asst, Head of Dept, Deputy Dir for Science, State Russian Museum 1978–88, Dir 1988–; headed reconstruction of Mikhailovsky Castle, Marble Palace and Inzhenerny Castle in St Petersburg; mem. Comm. on State Prizes; Corresp. Mem. Russian Acad. of Fine Arts; Officier, Légion d'honneur 2004; Medal for Valiant Labour 1971, Honoured Cultural Worker of the Russian Fed. 1996, State Award in Literature and Art 2003, Commemorative medal for tricentenary of St Petersburg 2003. *Publications:* more than 60 contribs to various publs in Russian, English, German, French, Italian, Spanish 1986–2005. *Address:* State Russian Museum, Inzhenernaya 4, 191186 St Petersburg (office); Bolshaya Monetnaya Street, app. 9, 197101 St Petersburg, Russia (home). *Telephone:* (812) 595-42-40 (office). *Fax:* (812) 314-41-53 (office). *E-mail:* info@rusmuseum.ru (office). *Website:* www.rusmuseum.ru (office).

GUSINSKII, Vladimir Aleksandrovich; Russian/Spanish banker; b. 6 Oct. 1952, Moscow; m. Yelena Gusinskaya; three s.; ed Moscow Gubkin Inst. of Oil and Chem., A. Lunacharskii State Inst. of Theatrical Art; Dir cultural programme, Moscow Festival of Youth and Students 1982–85; Dir cultural programme, Goodwill Games in Moscow 1985–86; f. co-operative Infex, later transformed into Holding Most, now comprising more than 40 enterprises in the field of construction, construction materials production, real estate and trade operations, also Most-Bank est. 1991; Owner major non-state TV co. NTV, Segodnya (newspaper) 1992, radio station Ekho Moskvy, Obshcheye Delo weekly, weekly TV programme 7 Days, Russian Television International (RTVi); Dir-Gen. Holding Group Most 1989–97, concurrently Pres. Most-Bank 1992–97, Pres. Media-Most co. 1997–2001; Vice Pres. Asscn of Russian Banks, Chair. Council of Authorized Banks of the Govt of Moscow; Pres. Jewish Congress of Russia 1995–2001; arrested in Spain on Russian prosecutor's request for extradition Jan. 2000–01, released after request rejected; took up residence in Israel April 2001; acquired Spanish citizenship Feb. 2007. *Address:* Russian Television International (RTVi), 110 West 40th Street, New York, NY 10018, USA (office). *Telephone:* (212) 944-9899 (office). *E-mail:* info@rtvi.ru (office). *Website:* www.rtvi.ru (office).

GUS'KOVA, Yelena Yuryevna, DHist; Russian historian and political scientist; *Head, Contemporary Studies, Institute of Slavic and Balkan Studies, Russian Academy of Sciences;* b. 23 Sept. 1949, Moscow; m.; two d.; ed Moscow State Univ.; Head Centre of Contemporary Studies, Inst. of Slavic and Balkan Studies, Russian Acad. of Sciences; leading scientific employee INION Russian Acad. of Sciences; mem. Presidium Russian Asscn of Co-operation with the UN; Political and Policy Analyst UN HQ of Peace-keeping Operations in fmr Yugoslavia; mem. Serbian Acad. of Sciences and Arts; Outstanding Scientist of Russia, Njegosha Award (Bosnia & Herzegovina) 1997, 850th Anniversary Medal, Moscow 1997, NATO Medal for peace-making operations in Kosovo 2002. *Publications:* over 340 works on the history of Yugoslavia and recent crises in the Balkans, including History of Yugoslavian Crisis (1990–2000) 2001 (Moscow), 2003 (Belgrade). *Address:* Institute of Slavic and Balkan Studies, Russian Academy of Sciences, 112334 Moscow, Leninsky prosp. 32A, Russia (office). *Telephone:* (495) 938-58-61 (office). *Fax:* (495) 938-00-96 (office); (495) 420-94-20 (home). *E-mail:* centar@guskova.ru (office); eguskova@com2com.ru (home). *Website:* www.inslav.ru (office); www.guskova.ru (home).

GUSMAN, Mikhail Solomonovich; Russian journalist; *First Deputy Director-General, ITAR-TASS News Agency;* b. 23 Jan. 1950, Baku, Azerbaijan; m.; one s.; ed Baku Higher CPSU School, Azerbaijan Inst. of Foreign Languages; Deputy Chair. Cttee of Youth Orgs, Azerbaijan 1973–86; Head of Information Dept, then Head of Press Centre, USSR Cttee of Youth Orgs 1986–91; Head of Gen. Admin. of Information Co-operation INFOMOL 1991–95; Vice-Pres. International Analytic Press Agency ANKOM-TASS 1995–98; Head of Chief, Dept of International Co-operation, Public Contacts and Special Projects, ITAR-TASS News Agency 1998–99, Deputy Dir-Gen., First Deputy Dir-Gen. 1999–; Co-founder World Congress of Russian Press 1999; Exec. Dir World Asscn of Russian Press; Diploma of the USSR Supreme Soviet, numerous medals; Gold Medal for contrib. to devt of TV and radio, International Acad. of Radio and Television (Russia) 2007. *Leisure interests:* travelling, reading newspapers. *Address:* ITAR-TASS News Agency, Tverskoy Blvd 10-12, 103009 Moscow, Russia (office). *Telephone:* (495) 629-7925 (office). *Website:* www.itar-tass.com (office).

GUSMAN, Yuly S.; Russian film administrator, producer and scriptwriter; b. 8 Aug. 1943, Baku, Azerbaijan; s. of Solomon M. Gusman and Lola Yu. Barsuk; m. Valida Gusman; one d.; ed Baku State Medical Inst.; Artistic Dir Baku Theatre of Musical Comedy 1965–72; Dir Central House of Cinematographers, Azerbaijan State Theatre of Musical Comedy; Chair. Cinematography Centre 1988–2002; mem. State Duma 1993–95; Founder CEO Russian Jewish Congress 1996; Founder CEO Nika Award; Sec., Union of Cinematographers of Russia; mem. Bd of Dirs State Cttee on Cinematography; mem. Russian Union of Writers; Merited Worker of the Arts, Order of Friendship 2004. *Films include:* On One Fine Day 1977, Cottage for a Family 1978, Don't Be Afraid, I'm with You 1981, Nastya (actor) 1993, The Soviet Period Park 2006. *Address:* 103473 Moscow, Delegatskaya str. 11, apt 10, Russia (home). *Telephone:* (495) 284-31-45 (home).

GUSMÃO, José Alexandre (Xanana); Timor-Leste politician and fmr head of state; *Prime Minister;* b. (José Alexandre Guzmão), 20 June 1946, Laleia, Manatuto; m. 1st Emilia Batista 1969; one s.; m. 2nd Kirsty Sword 2000; ed Nossa Senhora de Fatima seminary, Dare; fmr poet, teacher and chartered surveyor; joined pro-independence Fretilin (Revolutionary Front of the Independence of Timor Leste) 1974, Commdr 1978, now retd; C-in-C FALINTIL (Nat. Liberation Armed Forces of Timor Leste) 1981; arrested by Indonesian troops and sentenced to life imprisonment (later commuted to 20 years) 1992; released August 1999; Pres. Nat. Council of Timorese Resistance 1999–2001; Chair. Timor Leste Nat. Council 2000–01; Pres. of Timor Leste 2002–07; Founder and Pres. Conselho Nacional de Reconstrução do Timor (Nat. Congress for Timorese Reconstruction, CNRT) 2007–; Prime Minister 2007–; Sakharov Prize for Freedom of Expression 1999. *Address:* Office of the Prime Minister, Palácio do Governo, Av. Presidente Nicolau Lobato, Dili, Timor Leste (office). *Telephone:* 7243559 (office). *Fax:*

3339503 (office). *E-mail:* mail@primeministerandcabinet.gov.tp (home). *Website:* www.pm.gov.tp (office).

GUSTAFSON, Kathryn, RLA, ASLA; American landscape architect; *Director, Gustafson Guthrie Nichol Limited and Gustafson Porter Limited;* b. Yakima, Wash.; ed Univ. of Washington, Seattle, Fashion Inst. of Tech., New York, Ecole Nat. Supérieure du Paysage, Versailles, France; moved to France 1973; environmental artist and landscape designer 1980–; Co-founder and Dir, Gustafson Guthrie Nichol Ltd, Seattle 2000–; Co-founder and Dir, Gustafson Porter Ltd 1997–; Licensed Landscape Architect, Wash., NY, USA, France; Licensed and Chartered Landscape Architect, UK; Hon. FRIBA 1999; Hon. Royal Designer for Industry, Royal Soc. for the Encouragement of Arts, Manufactures & Commerce 2001; Architectural Medal, Acad. d'Architecture, Paris 1993, Jane Drew Prize, London 1998, Chrysler Design Award, Chrysler Design Inst. 2001, Club Laureate, Rainier Club, Seattle, Wash. 2008, Design Medal, American Soc. of Landscape Architects 2008, Sckell Ring Award, Bayerische Akad. der Kunste 2009. *Address:* Gustafson Porter, Linton House, 39–51 Highgate Road, London, NW5 1RS, England (office). *Telephone:* (20) 7267-2005 (office). *Fax:* (20) 7485-9203 (office). *E-mail:* enquiries@gustafson-porter.com (office). *Website:* www.gustafson-porter .com (office); www.ggnltd.com (office).

GUSTAFSSON, Lars Erik Einar, DPhil; Swedish writer, philosopher and academic; *Jamail Distinguished Professor Emeritus in the Plan II Program, University of Texas;* b. 17 May 1936, Västerås; s. of Einar Gustafsson and Margaretha Carlsson; m. 1st Madeleine Gustafsson 1962; m. 2nd Dena Alexandra Chasnoff 1982; two s. two d.; m. 3rd Agneta Blomqvist 2005; ed Uppsala Univ.; Editor-in-Chief, Bonniers Litterära Magasin 1966–72; Research Fellow, Bielefeld Inst. of Advanced Studies 1980–81; Adjunct Prof., Univ. of Texas 1983–2006, Jamail Distinguished Prof. in the Plan II Program 1995, now Prof. Emer.; Aby Warburg Foundation Prof., Hamburg 1997; mem. Akad. der Wissenschaften und der Literatur, Mainz, Akad. der Künste, Berlin, Royal Swedish Acad. of Eng, Bayerische Akad. der schönen Künste, Munich; Fellow Berlin Inst. of Advanced Studies 2004–05; Officier des Arts et des Lettres; Kommendör des Bundesver-dienstzeichens, Literis et Artibus; Prix Charles Veillon, Heinrich Steffen Preis, Övralidspriset, Bellman Prize of Swedish Acad.; John Simon Guggenheim Memorial Prize of Poetry 1993. *Television:* 18th Century Pessimism (Swedish TV2), The Philosophers (syndicated). *Plays:* Celebration at Night, Zürich, Frankfurt, Berlin 1979. *Publications:* The Death of a Beekeeper 1978, Language and Lies 1978, Stories of Happy People 1981, Bernard Foy's Third Castle 1986, The Silence of the World before Bach (poems) 1988, Fyra Poeter 1988, Problemformu-leringsprivilegiet 1989, Det sällsamma djuret från norr 1989, The Afternoon of a Tiler 1991, Historien med Hunden 1993, The Tail of the Dog 1997, Windy 1999, A Time in Xanadu 2003. *Leisure interests:* painting, boating, tennis. *Address:* University of Texas, Waggener Hall, Room 413, Department of Philosophy, Austin, TX 78712 (office); PMB 317, 3112 Windsor Road, Austin, TX 78703, USA. *Telephone:* (512) 471-5632 (office). *E-mail:* lars.gustafsson@ownit.nu (office); lars .gustafsson@mail.utexas.edu (office). *Website:* www.utexas.edu/cola/depts/ philosophy (office); www.utexas.edu/cola/depts/germanic (office).

GUSTOV, Vadim Anatolyevich; Russian politician; b. 26 Dec. 1948, Kalinino, Vladimir Region; m.; two c.; ed Moscow State Inst. of Geological Prospecting, Leningrad Inst. of Politology; Head of uranium mines, Navoi Metallurgy Factory, Uzbekistan 1971–77; Head of mine, Phosphorite Kingisepp, Leningrad Region 1977–78; instructor, Head of Div., Kingisepp City CP Cttee 1978–86; First Deputy Chair. Kingisepp City Exec. Cttee 1986–87; Second Sec. Kingisepp City CP Cttee 1987–90; Chair. Kingisepp City Soviet 1990–91; Chair. Soviet of People's Deputies Leningrad Region 1991–93; mem. Council of Fed. of Russia, Chair. Cttee on CIS Cos 1993–98; Gov. Leningrad Region 1996–98; First Deputy Chair., Govt of Russian Fed. 1998–99; Rep. of Vladimir Region to Federation Council 2001; Chair. Cttee on CIS 2001; Order of Honour 1998. *Publications include:* Russia-CIS: The Path of Integration is Thorny but Tempting (co-author) 2002, Russia-CIS: Co-operation for Development and Progress 2007. *Leisure interests:* hunting, fiction, sports.

GUT, Rainer Emil; Swiss banker and business executive; *Honorary Chairman, Credit Suisse Group;* b. 24 Sept. 1932, Baar; s. of Emil Anton Gut and Rosa Gut (née Müller); m. Josephine Lorenz 1957; two s. two d.; ed Cantonal School of Zug; professional training in Switzerland, France and England; Gen. Pnr, Lazard Frères & Co., New York 1968–71; Chair. and CEO, Swiss American Corpn (Credit Suisse's US investment banking affiliate) 1971–73; mem. Exec. Bd Credit Suisse, Zürich 1973–77, Speaker of Exec. Bd 1977–82, Pres. Exec. Bd 1982–83, Chair. 1983–2000, Chair. Credit Suisse Group (fmrly CS Holding) 1986–2000, Chair. Credit Suisse First Boston, New York 1988–97, Chair. Credit Suisse First Boston Zürich 1997–2000, Hon. Chair. Credit Suisse Group 2000–; Chair. Nestlé SA 2000–05 (retd); Chair. and Del. Uprona (Canada) Ltd, Toronto 2000–; Vice-Pres. Gesparal, Paris 2000–; mem. Bd of Dirs L'Oréal, Paris, Pechiney SA, Paris, Sofina SA, Brussels. *Address:* Credit Suisse Group, PO Box 1, 8070 Zurich (office); Credit Suisse Group, Paradeplatz 8, 8001 Zurich (office); c/o Nestlé SA, Avenue Nestlé 55, 1800 Vevey, Switzerland. *Telephone:* (44) 212-16-16 (office). *Fax:* (44) 333-25-87 (office). *E-mail:* info@credit-suisse.com (office). *Website:* www.credit-suisse.com (office).

GUTERRES, António Manuel de Oliveira; Portuguese politician and UN official; *High Commissioner, United Nations High Commissioner for Refugees;* b. 30 April 1949, Lisbon; m. (wife died 1998); one s. one d.; ed Instituto Superior Técnico, Lisbon; trained as electrical engineer; joined Socialist Party 1974; Chief of Staff to Sec. of State for Industry 1974–75; fmr asst to several cabinet ministers; Pres. Municipal Ass. of Fundão 1979–95; Deputy to Ass. of the Repub. 1976–83, 1985–, Pres. several parl. comms, Pres. Socialist Parl. Group 1988–91; Strategic Devt Dir IPE (State Investment and Participation Agency) 1984–85; mem. Council of State 1991–; Leader of Socialist Party 1992–; Vice-Pres. Socialist Int. 1992–99, Pres. 1999–; Prime Minister of Portugal 1995–2001; High Commr, Office of the UN High Commr for Refugees 2005–; Coordinator Tech. Electoral Comm. 1980–87; Founder and Vice-Pres. Portuguese Asscn for the Defence of the Consumer 1973–74; mem. Asscn for Econ. and Social Devt 1970–96; ranked 64th by Forbes magazine amongst The World's Most Powerful People 2009. *Publications:* various books and articles for newspapers and magazines. *Leisure interests:* travel, history (especially Middle Ages), cinema, opera. *Address:* Office of the United Nations

High Commissioner for Refugees, CP 2500, 1211 Geneva 2 Dépôt, Switzerland (office). *Telephone:* (22) 7398254 (office). *Fax:* (22) 7397346 (office). *Website:* www .unhcr.org (office).

GUTERRES, Jose Luis; Timor-Leste politician and diplomatist; *Minister of Foreign Affairs and Co-operation;* m.; two c.; ed Univ. of Cambridge, UK, Univ. of the Western Cape, S Africa, Malaysia Inst. of Diplomacy and Foreign Relations, Inst. of Strategic and Int. Studies, Portugal; Founding mem. Frente Revolucio-nária do Timor Leste Independente (FRETILIN—Revolutionary Front for an Independent East Timor), mem. FRETILIN external del. 1974–, Rep. to Angola, also Perm. Rep. to Mozambique and FRETILIN Rep. to UN; Vice-Minister for Foreign Affairs and Co-operation 2002–03, Head of Timor-Leste del., Council of Ministers meeting, Comunidade dos Países de Língua Portuguesa, Brazil and ACP/EU meeting, Dominican Repub. July 2002, Timor-Leste Rep. to Sustainable Devt Summit, S Africa Aug. 2002; Amb. to USA and Perm. Rep. to UN, New York 2003–06; Minister of Foreign Affairs and Co-operation 2006–07, 2012–. *Address:* Ministry of Foreign Affairs and Cooperation, GPA Building 1, Ground Floor, Rua Avenida Presidente Nicolau Lobato, PO Box 6, Dili, Timor-Leste (office). *Telephone:* 3339600 (office). *Fax:* 3339025 (office). *E-mail:* administration@mnec .gov-tl.net (office). *Website:* www.mfac.gov.tp (office).

GUTERSON, David, BA, MFA; American author; b. 4 May 1956, Seattle, Wash.; s. of Murray Guterson and Shirley Guterson (née Zak); m. Robin Ann Radwick 1979; three s. two d.; ed Univ. of Washington, Brown Univ. *Publications:* The Country Ahead of Us, The Country Behind (short stories) 1989, Family Matters: Why Home Schooling Makes Sense 1992, Snow Falling on Cedars (PEN/Faulkner Award for Fiction 1994, Barnes & Noble Discovery Award, Pacific NW Booksellers Award 1995) 1994, East of the Mountains 1998, Our Lady of the Forest 2003, The Other 2008, Ed King 2011. *Address:* c/o Georges Borchardt Inc., 136 East 57th Street, New York, NY 10020, USA (office). *E-mail:* georges@gbagency.com (office).

GUTFREUND, Herbert, PhD, FRS; British academic; *Professor Emeritus of Physical Biochemistry, University of Bristol;* b. 21 Oct. 1921, Vienna, Austria; s. of Paul Gutfreund and Clara Gutfreund; m. Mary Kathleen Davies 1958; two s. one d.; ed Univs of Vienna, Austria and Cambridge, UK; Research Fellow, Univ. of Cambridge 1947–57; with Agricultural Research Council, Univ. of Reading 1957–64; Visiting Prof., Univ. of Calif. 1965, Max Planck Inst., Germany 1966, Dir Molecular Enzymology Lab. and Prof. of Physical Biochemistry, Univ. of Bristol 1967–86, Prof. Emer. 1986–; part-time Scholar in Residence, NIH, Bethesda, USA 1986–89; Scientific mem. (external) Max Planck Inst. for Medical Research 1987–; Fogarty Scholar, NIH, Washington, DC 1987–89. *Publications:* An Introduction to the Study of Enzymes 1966, Enzymes: Physical Principles 1972, Molecular Evolution 1981, Biothermodynamics 1983, Kinetics for the Life Sciences: Receptors, Transmitters and Catalysts 1995. *Leisure interests:* hill walking, reading, cooking. *Address:* Somerset House, Upton, Oxon., OX11 9JL, England (home). *Telephone:* (1235) 851468 (home). *E-mail:* h.gutfreund@bristol.ac .uk (home).

GUTH, Alan Harvey, PhD; American physicist and academic; *Victor F. Weisskopf Professor of Physics, Massachusetts Institute of Technology;* b. 27 Feb. 1947, New Brunswick, NJ; s. of Hyman Guth and Elaine Cheiten; m. Susan Tisch 1971; one s. one d.; ed Massachusetts Inst. of Tech.; Instructor, Princeton Univ. 1971–74; Research Assoc. Columbia Univ. New York 1974–77, Cornell Univ. 1977–79, Stanford Linear Accelerator Center, Calif. 1979–80; Assoc. Prof. of Physics, MIT 1980–86, Prof. 1986–89, Jerrold Zacharias Prof. of Physics 1989–91, Victor F. Weisskopf Prof. of Physics 1992–, Margaret MacVicar Faculty Fellow; Physicist, Harvard-Smithsonian Center for Astrophysics 1984–89, Visiting Scientist 1990–91; Alfred P. Sloan Fellow 1981; Fellow, American Physics Soc. (Chair. Astrophysics Div. 1989–90), AAAS, American Acad. of Arts and Sciences; mem. NAS, American Astronomical Soc.; Rennie Taylor Award, American Tentative Soc. 1991, Julius E. Lilienfeld Prize, American Physical Soc. 1992, Benjamin Franklin Medal for Physics, Franklin Inst. 2001, Cosmology Prize, Peter Gruber Foundation 2004, Isaac Newton Medal, British Inst. of Physics 2009. *Publications:* The Inflationary Universe: The Quest for a New Theory of Cosmic Origins 1998. *Address:* Center for Theoretical Physics, Room 6-209, Massachusetts Institute of Technology, 77 Massachusetts Ave, Cambridge, MA 02139-4307, USA (office). *Telephone:* (617) 253-6265 (office). *E-mail:* guth@ctp.mit.edu (office). *Website:* web .mit.edu/physics/facultyandstaff/faculty/alan_guth.html (office).

GUTHRIE, Michelle L., BA, BLL; Australian lawyer and business executive; *Director of Strategic Business Development for Japan and Asia Pacific, Google Inc.;* ed Univ. of Sydney; fmr lawyer, Allen, Allen and Hemsley, Sydney and Singapore; joined News Corpn 1994, becoming Gen. Counsel, BSkyB and News International, London, later Dir of Legal and Business Affairs, FOXTEL, Sydney; joined Star TV 2000, Sr Vice-Pres. Business Devt 2001–03, Exec. Vice-Pres. Regional Distribution and Business Devt June–Nov. 2003, CEO Nov. 2003–07; Man. Dir Providence Equity Partners LLC, Hong Kong 2007–10; currently Dir of Strategic Business Devt for Japan and Asia Pacific, Google Inc., Singapore; Chair. Plan International Hong Kong (charity); mem. Bd of Dirs Metro International SA; fmr mem. Bd of Dirs Phoenix Satellite Television, Hathway, China Network Systems, Balaji Telefilms Ltd. (STAR joint venture cos); fmr mem. Council of Govs Cable and Satellite Broadcasting Asscn of Asia; named Young Global Leader by the World Econ. Forum 2005, Veuve Clicquot Business Woman of the Year Award 2005. *Address:* Google Singapore, 8 Marina View, Singapore 018960 (office).

GUTHRIE, Roderick (Rod) I. L., BSc (Eng), PhD, ARSM, DIC, FRSC, FCAE, FCIM; British/Canadian metallurgist, engineer and academic; *Macdonald Professor and Director, McGill Metals Processing Centre, McGill University;* b. 12 Sept. 1941, Sutton Coldfield, West Midlands, England; s. of Lawrence Carr Guthrie and Norah Smith; ed Royal School of Mines, Imperial Coll., Univ. of London; currently Macdonald Prof. of Metallurgy, Dept of Mining and Materials Eng and Dir McGill Metals Processing Centre, McGill Univ., Montreal, Canada; Fellow, Canadian Acad. of Engineers, Canadian Inst. of Mining; research consultant to steel and aluminium industries; Hon. mem. Japan Iron and Steel Inst.; Distinguished mem. Iron and Steel Soc., Asscn for Iron and Steel Technologies; 24 Best Paper Awards, Queen's Golden Jubilee Medal 2002, 77th Howe Memorial Lecturer, Iron and Steel Soc., John Elliott Distinguished Lecturer, Iron and Steel Soc. 2003–04, Killam Prize for Eng 2006, NSERC Leo Derikx Award for collaborative research with industry. *Publications:* Engineering in Process Metallurgy, The Physical Properties of Liquid Metals, The Science and Practice of Steelmaking, and Steel Processing; more than 200 patents on topics ranging from metal delivery systems for high-speed strip casting processes, to improved aerodynamics for batch annealing furnaces and in-situ detection of inclusions in liquid aluminium, steel and magnesium; more than 450 scientific papers in professional journals. *Leisure interests:* long distance kayaking, running, cycling. *Address:* McGill Metals Processing Centre, 3610 University Street, M.H. Wong Building, 2M040, Montreal, PQ H3A 2B2, Canada (office). *Telephone:* (514) 398-1555 (office); (514) 398-5556 (office). *Fax:* (514) 398-4168 (office). *E-mail:* rod@ mmpc.mcgill.ca (office). *Website:* www.mmpc.mcgill.ca (office).

GUTHRIE, Roy David (Gus), AM, DSc, FTSE; Australian consultant, fmr vice-chancellor and professor of chemistry; *Director, Gus Guthrie Consulting;* b. 29 March 1934, England; s. of David Guthrie and Ethel Guthrie (née Kimmins); m. 2nd Lyn Fielding 1982; three s. from first m.; ed King's Coll., London; Research Officer, Shirley Inst. 1958–60; Asst Lecturer then Lecturer, Univ. of Leicester 1963–73; Lecturer then Reader, Univ. of Sussex 1963–73; Foundation Prof., Griffith Univ., Australia 1973–81, Pro-Vice-Chancellor 1980–81, Prof. Emer. 1981; Vice-Chancellor Univ. of Tech., Sydney 1986–96; Provost Insearch Educ. 1996–97; Dir Gus Guthrie Consulting 1996–; Sec.-Gen. Royal Soc. of Chem. 1982–85; Chair. Queensland Innovation Council 1999–2002, Buderim Foundation 2003–05; Pres. Coastal Caring Clowns 2001–06; mem. Council Univ. of the Sunshine Coast 1999–2005; Fellow, Acad. of Technological Sciences and Eng; Centenary Medal. *Publications:* Introduction to Carbohydrate Chemistry (with J. Honeyman); more than 130 research papers in learned chemical journals. *Leisure interests:* theatre, croquet, tai chi, caring clowning. *Address:* PO Box 285, Bli Bli, Qld 4560, Australia.

GUTHRIE OF CRAIGIEBANK, Baron (Life Peer), cr. 2001, of Craigiebank in the City of Dundee; **Charles (Ronald Llewelyn) Guthrie,** GCB, LVO, OBE, DL; British army officer and business executive; b. 17 Nov. 1938, London; s. of the late Ronald Guthrie and Nina Llewelyn; m. Catherine Worrall 1971; two s.; ed Harrow School and Royal Mil. Acad. Sandhurst; commissioned Welsh Guards 1959; served in BAOR, Aden; 22 Special Air Service (SAS) Regt 1965–69; Staff Coll. 1972; Mil. Asst (GSO2) to Chief of Gen. Staff, Ministry of Defence 1973–74; Brigade Maj., Household Div. 1976–77; CO, 1st Bn Welsh Guards, Berlin and NI 1977–80; Col, Gen. Staff, Mil. Operations, Ministry of Defence 1980–82; Commdr British Forces, New Hebrides 1980; 4th Armoured Brigade 1982–84; Chief of Staff 1st (British) Corps 1984–86; Gen. Officer Commdg NE Dist and Commdr 2nd Infantry Div. 1986–87; Asst Chief of Gen. Staff, Ministry of Defence 1987–89; Commdr 1st (British) Corps 1989–91; Commdr Northern Army Group 1992–93 and C-in-C BAOR 1992–94; Col Commdt, Intelligence Corps 1986–96; ADC Gen. to HM the Queen 1993–, Gold Stick to HM the Queen 1999–; Chief of Gen. Staff 1994–97, of the Defence Staff 1997–2001; Special Envoy to Pakistan 2001; Dir (non-exec.) N. M. Rothschild & Sons 2001–11, Petropavlovsk Colt, Gulf Keystone Petroleum; Chair. Hospital of St John & St Elizabeth, St John's Hospice; Col of the Life Guards 1999–; Chancellor Liverpool Hope Univ. 2013–; Pres. Action Medical Research, London Fed. of Youth Clubs; Freeman, City of London; Kt, Sovereign Mil. Order of Malta 1999; Commdr, Legion of Merit (USA) 2001. *Publication:* Just War: The Just War Tradition: Ethics in Modern Warfare (co-author) 2007. *Leisure interests:* tennis, opera. *Address:* PO Box 25439, London, SW1P 1AG, England.

GUTIERREZ, Carl T.C.; American computer industry executive and politician; b. 15 Oct. 1941, Agana Heights, Guam; s. of the late Tomas Taitano Gutierrez and of Rita Benavente Cruz; m. Geraldine Chance Torres; one s. two d.; ed S. San Francisco High School; service with USAF; est. first data processing centre in Guam; f. Carltom Enterprises 1971; Propr Carltom Consulting; elected Senator 1972, Speaker of Legislature; Gov. of Guam 1994–98, 1998–2003, indicted on allegations that he abused his power Dec. 2003, charges dismissed April 2004, indicted again over alleged use of Govt funds and personnel May 2004, acquited July 2004; Pres. Asscn of Pacific Island Legislatures; Chair. Guam Tax Code Comm., Cttee on Ways and Means; Vice-Chair. Cttee on Rules, Cttee on Tourism and Transportation; f. People Helping People 1994; Hon. Citizen (Belau); Hon. DHumLitt (World Acad. of Art and Sciences) 1985, Hon. DJur (Univ. of Guam) 1996; Eagle Award, Nat. Guard Bureau. *Leisure interests:* tennis, fishing, hunting. *Address:* c/o PO Box 2950, Agana, GU 96932-2950, USA.

GUTIERREZ, Carlos M.; American (b. Cuban) business executive and fmr government official; *Co-Chairman, Albright Stonebridge Group;* b. 4 Nov. 1953, Havana, Cuba; m.; three c.; ed Monterrey Inst. of Tech.; joined Kellogg de Mexico as sales rep. 1975, Supervisor, Latin America Marketing Services, Kellogg HQ, Mich. 1982–83, Man. Int. Marketing Services 1983–84, Gen. Man. Kellogg de Mexico 1984–89, Pres. and CEO Kellogg Canada Inc. 1989–90, Corp. Vice-Pres. Product Devt at Kellogg HQ 1990, Vice-Pres. Kellogg Co. and Exec. Vice-Pres. Sales and Marketing, Kellogg USA 1990–93, Exec. Vice-Pres. Kellogg USA and Gen. Man. Kellogg USA Cereal Div. 1993–94, Exec. Vice-Pres. Kellogg Co. and Pres. Kellogg Asia-Pacific 1994–96, Exec. Vice-Pres. Business Devt 1996–98, Pres. and COO 1998–99, elected to Bd of Dirs Jan. 1999, apptd CEO April 1999, Chair. 2000–04; US Sec. of Commerce, Washington, DC 2004–09; Co-Chair. Global Political Strategies div., APCO Worldwide Inc. 2010–11; Vice-Chair., Institutional Clients Group, Citigroup Inc. 2011–13, also mem. Sr Strategic Advisory Group; Vice-Chair. Albright Stonebridge Group 2013–14, Co-Chair. 2014–; Founder and Chair. Republicans for Immigration Reform 2012–; Nat. Trustee Univ. of Miami, also Visiting Scholar, Inst. for Cuban and Cuban American Studies; Trustee Meridian International Center; mem. Bd of Dirs US-Mexico Foundation, Occidental Petroleum Corpn, Met Life, Inc., Time Warner, Inc. *Address:* Albright Stonebridge Group, 1101 New York Avenue, NW, Suite 900, Washington, DC 20005, USA (office). *Website:* www.albrightstonebridge.com (office).

GUTIÉRREZ, Gustavo, DTheol, OP; Peruvian ecclesiastic and academic; *John Cardinal O'Hara Professor of Theology, Department of Theology, University of Notre Dame;* b. 8 June 1928, Lima; ed Univ. Nacional Mayor de San Marcos, Lima, Univ. Catholique de Louvain, Univ. de Lyon, Univ. Gregoriana and Inst. Catholique de Paris; ordained priest 1959; Adviser, Nat. Union of Catholic Students 1960; Prof. Catholic Univ. of Lima 1960; mem. Pastoral-Theological team, Latin American Conf. of Catholic Bishops (CELAM) 1967–68; currently John Cardinal O'Hara Prof. of Theology, Univ. of Notre Dame, USA; mem. Bd of Dirs Inst. Bartolomé Las Casas-Rímac 1974–, Concilium; Assoc. Vicar, Rímac, Lima

1980–; fmr Prin. Prof. Pontifical Univ. of Peru; Visiting Prof. and lecturer at univs, colls and seminaries in USA and elsewhere; mem. EATWOT (Ecumenical Asscn of Third World Theologians), American Acad. of Arts and Sciences, Peruvian Acad. of Language; Legion of Honor 1993, Master of the Order, Order Of Preachers 2009; Dr hc (Nijmegen) 1979, (Tübingen) 1985, (King's Coll., USA) 1989, (Haverford Coll., USA) 1990, (Fribourg, Germany) 1990, (San Marcos, Lima) 1991, (Montreal) 1993, (Universidad Nacional de Ingeniería, Peru) 1993, (State of NY) 1994, (Holy Cross, MA) 1994, (San Agustín Peru) 1995, (Catholic Theol. Union USA) 1995, (St Norbert Coll., USA) 1996, (St Michael, Canada) 1996, (Simón Bolívar, Peru) 1997, (Freiburg, Suiza) 1998, (Southern Methodist, USA) 2000, (Brown, USA) 2000; Príncipe de Asturias Award 2003, Niebuhr Medal, Elmhurst Coll. 2009. *Publications:* A Theology of Liberation 1971, The Power of the Poor in History 1980, We Drink from Our Own Wells: the Spiritual Journey of a People 1983, On Job, God-talk and the Suffering of the Innocent 1986, La Verdad los hará libres 1986, Dios o el Oro en las Indias 1989, El Dios de la Vida 1989, Entre las Calandrias 1990, En Busca de los Pobres de Jesucristo 1992, Compartir la Palabra 1995, Essential Writings (with Nikoloff) 1996, Densidad del Presente 1996. *Leisure interests:* swimming, literature. *Address:* University of Notre Dame, Department of Theology, 331 Malloy Hall, Notre Dame, IN 46556, USA (office); Instituto Bartolomé Las Casas-Rímac, Apartado 3090, Lima 100, Peru. *Telephone:* (574) 631-5366 (office). *E-mail:* Gustavo.A.Gutierrez.30@nd.edu (office). *Website:* www .nd.edu/~theo (office).

GUTIERREZ, Lino, MA; American diplomatist; b. Havana, Cuba; m. Miriam Gutierrez (née Messina); three d.; ed Univs of Miami and Alabama; social studies teacher, Dade County School System and Urban League, Miami 1973–75; joined US Foreign Service 1977, overseas assignments include at Embassies in Lisbon, Port-au-Prince, Grenada, Paris and Nassau, served as Officer-in-Charge of Nicaraguan Affairs, of Portuguese Affairs, Dir Office of Policy Planning, Coordination and Press, Bureau of Inter-American Affairs, Amb. to Nicaragua 1996–99, Prin. Deputy Asst Sec. for Western Hemisphere Affairs, Dept of State 1999–2001, Acting Asst. Sec. 2001–02; Int. Affairs Adviser, Nat. War Coll. 2002–03; Amb. to Argentina 2003–06; Founder and currently CEO Gutierrez Global LLC; Dept of State Distinguished Honor Award, Meritorious Honor Award. *Telephone:* (703) 909-0290 (office). *E-mail:* info@gutierrezglobal.com (office). *Website:* www.gutierrezglobal.com (office).

GUTIERREZ BORBÚA, Lucio Edwin; Ecuadorean politician and fmr head of state; b. 23 March 1957, Quito; m. Ximena Bohórquez; two c.; ed Army Polytechnic School, Inter-American Defense Coll., Washington, DC, USA; fmr pentathelete; fmr Col in army; staged Indian uprising against Pres. Jamil Mahuad 2000, sentenced to six months in a mil. prison; Pres. of Ecuador 2003–05 (resgnd); cand. in presidential elections 2009, 2013; Founder Partido Sociedad Patriótica 21 de Enero (PSP). *Address:* Partido Sociedad Patriótica 21 de Enero, Quito, Ecuador (office). *Website:* www.sociedadpatriotica.com (office).

GUTIÉRREZ GIRÓN, Edgar Armando; Guatemalan politician; b. 27 July 1960, Guatemala City; m. María Elena Aiza Meade de Gutiérrez; two s. three d.; political and econ. analyst in Guatemala and Central America 1982–; consultant for various int. agencies in Europe and USA; Co-Founder Asscn for the Advancement of the Social Sciences 1987, Coordinadora de ONG y Cooperativas 1992, Myrna Mack Foundation 1993; Co-ordinator-Gen. Interdiocesan Project 'Recuperación de la Memoria Histórica' 1995–98; Jt Ed. Periódico de Guatemala 1999; Sec. of Strategic Analysis 2000–02; Minister of Foreign Affairs 2002–04. *Publications include:* Centroamérica en el vórtice de la crisis 1986, Modelos heterogéneos en Centroamérica 1987, Guatemala: política exterior y estabilidad del Estado 1988, ¿Quién quiso asaltar el cielo? 1998, Sociedad civil y derechos humanos en la difícil transición guatemalteca 1998, Hacia un paradigma democrático del sistema de inteligencia en Guatemala 1999; poetry: Para conjurar su hechizo 1990, Al final de esta luna 1992, Memoria de la Muerte 1997.

GUTIÉRREZ IRIARTE, Waldo M.; Bolivian fmr government official; *Associated Consultant, International Institution for Economics and Business;* ed Univ. of Mayor Real y Pontificia de San Francisco Xavier de Chuquisaca, Univ. of New Mexico; fmr Deputy Minister of the Treasury; Minister of Finance 2005–06; currently Associated Consultant Int. Inst. for Econs and Business IIDEE. *Address:* International Institution for Economics and Business, Ed. Torre Ketal, Piso 3, Oficina 318 Calle 15, Calacoto, La Paz, Bolivia (office). *Telephone:* (2) 277-2170 (office). *Fax:* (2) 277-2170 (office). *Website:* www.iidee.net (office).

GUTIÉRREZ PEMBERTY, Javier Genaro, BEng, MEng; Colombian civil engineer, business executive and academic; *President and CEO, Ecopetrol SA;* b. 1951, Bogotá; m.; two c.; ed Universidad de los Andes in Bogotá, Int. Atomic Energy Agency, Argonne Nat. Lab., Illinois, USA, Escuela de Administración, Finanzas y Tecnología (EAFIT) Medellín; began career with Interconexión Eléctrica SA E.S.P. – ISA 1981, promoted to Man. of Planning Office, Gen. Man. ISA 1992–2007; Pres. and CEO Ecopetrol SA 2007–; Prof. of Statistics and Operations Research, Universidad de los Andes and Prof. of Operations Research with emphasis on Dynamic Programming, EAFIT; Portfolio Award (Best Corp. Leader category) 2002, Excellence Award (Internationalization category), América Economía Magazine 2005, acknowledged by Republica newspaper as one of the ten best executives of the year in Colombia 2005. *Address:* Ecopetrol SA, Carrera 13 No. 36 - 24, Bogotá, DC, Colombia (office). *Telephone:* (1) 2344000 (office). *Fax:* (1) 2344099 (office). *E-mail:* javier.gutierrez@ecopetrol.com.co (office). *Website:* www .ecopetrol.com.co (office).

GUTIONTOV, Pavel Semenovich; Russian journalist; b. 23 Jan. 1953; ed Moscow State Univ.; mem. of staff Moskovski Komsomolets 1970–75; fmr corresp. Komsomolskaya Pravda, then Head of Div. 1975–85; special corresp. Sovetskaya Rossiya 1985–87; political observer Izvestia; Co-Chair. Liberal Journalists Club –1997; Chair. Cttee for Defence of Freedom of Speech and Journalists' Rights; Sec. Russian Journalists' Union; winner of numerous professional prizes. *Publications:* Games in the Fresh Air of Stagnation 1990, Fate of Drummers 1997 and numerous articles. *Address:* Russian Journalists' Union, Zubovsky blvd 4, 119021 Moscow, Russia (office). *Telephone:* (495) 637-21-59 (office). *E-mail:* gutiontov@mail.ru (office).

GUTMAN, Lt-Gen. Albin; Slovenian military officer; b. 17 Dec. 1947, Novo Mesto; m.; one s. one d.; ed Univ. of Ljubljana; previous posts include Territorial-

Defence Municipal Staff, Novo Mesto, Defence Secr., Novo Mesto, Territorial-Defence Regional Staff, Dolenjska, Ministry of Defence; Chief of Armed Forces Gen. Staff 1993–96, 2006–09; Chief Defence Insp. 1998–2003; mil. adviser to Minister of Defence 2003–06; Silver Order of Freedom of Repub. of Slovenia, Order of Gen. Maister with Swords, Légion d'honneur; Manoeuvre Structure of Nat. Defence (MSNZ) Badge 1990, Defended Slovenia Badge, Slovenian Armed Forces Gold Medal, Slovenian Armed Forces Gold Plaque. *Address:* Ministry of Defence, 1000 Ljubljana, Vojkova 55, Slovenia (office). *Telephone:* (1) 4712211 (office). *Fax:* (1) 4712978 (office). *E-mail:* info@mors.si (office). *Website:* www.mors.si (office).

GUTMAN, Natalia Grigorievna; Russian/German cellist; b. 14 Nov. 1942; m. Oleg Kagan (deceased); three c.; ed Gnessin Music School, Moscow (under R. Shaposhnikov), Moscow Conservatory (under Prof. Kozolupova) and postgraduate studies in Leningrad (under Mstislav Rostropovich); tours include visits to Europe, USA and Japan, appearing with the Berlin Philharmonic Orchestra, Vienna Philharmonic Orchestra, London Symphony Orchestra, Orchestre Nat. de France and Orchestre de Paris; played chamber music in USSR and Europe with Eliso Virsaladze and Oleg Kagan; played sonatas, trios and quartets with Sviatoslav Richter; plays sonata and concerto written for her by Alfred Schnittke; solo tours include USA with USSR State Symphony Orchestra and Yevgeny Svetlanov, Italy with BBC Symphony and Yuri Temirkanov, USSR with Sir John Pritchard; performed with Royal Philharmonic Orchestra under Yuri Temirkanov, Royal Festival Hall, London, Concertgebouw, London Philharmonic, Munich Philharmonic, Berlin Philharmonic, Orchestre Nat. de France, Los Angeles Philharmonic under André Previn, Chicago Symphony under Claudio Abbado 1988–89; fmr teacher at Moscow Conservatory; Prof., Stuttgart Conservatory 1997–2004; f. Oleg Kagan Music Festival, Kreuth and Moscow; Winner, Vienna Student Festival Competition, Dvořák Competition, Prague, ARD Competition, Munich. *Address:* Natalia Gutman's Office, c/o Tallafocs els Ferros 7, 46012 Valencia, Spain. *Telephone:* 6-9380483 (mobile). *E-mail:* cellogutman@gmail.com.

GUTMANN, Amy, BA, MSc, PhD; American academic and university president; *President, University of Pennsylvania;* m. Michael W. Doyle; one d.; ed Harvard-Radcliffe Coll., London School of Econs, UK, Harvard Univ.; Asst Prof. of Politics, Princeton Univ. 1976–81, Assoc. Prof. 1981–86, Dir of Grad. Studies 1986–88, Prof. 1987–2004, Andrew W. Mellon Professorship 1987–90, Laurance S. Rockefeller Prof. of Politics 1990–2004, Founding Dir Univ. Center for Human Values 1990–95, 1998–2001, Dean of Faculty 1995–97, Academic Adviser to Pres. 1997–98, Provost 2001–04; Pres. Univ. of Pennsylvana and Christopher H. Browne Distinguished Prof. of Political Science, School of Arts and Sciences, Annenberg School for Communication, Grad. School of Educ. and Dept of Philosophy 2004–; Visitor, Inst. for Advanced Study, Princeton 1981–82; Visiting Rockefeller Faculty Fellow, Center for Philosophy and Public Policy, Univ. of Maryland 1984–85; Visiting Prof., John F. Kennedy School of Govt, Harvard Univ. 1988–89; Pres. American Soc. for Political and Legal Philosophy 2001–04; Chair. US Presidential Comm. for the Study of Bioethical Issues 2009–, APSA Charles Merriam Award Cttee 2012–, Re-accrediting Cttee for Brown Univ. 2009; mem. Bd of Dirs Salzburg Seminar 1987–90, Center for Policy Research in Educ. 1987–95, Exec. Cttee Assen of Practical and Professional Ethics 1990–2007, Bd and Exec. Cttee, Princeton University Press 1996–2004, Advisory Council, Kennedy School of Govt, Harvard Univ. 1996–2001, Bd and Exec. Cttee, Center for Advanced Study in the Behavioural Sciences, Stanford Univ. 1998–2005, Int. Advisory Bd Ethnicities 2000–, Academic Advisory Bd Inst. for Human Sciences, Vienna 2001, Advisory Bd Annenberg Public Policy Center Student Voices Project 2000–05, Bd of Govs Partnership for Public Service 2004–07, Service Nation Leadership Council 2008, Teach for America Champions' Bd 2010–, Exec. Cttee, Assen of American Univs 2011–, Presidents Circle, Nat. Council for Research on Women 2011, Comm. on the Humanities and Social Sciences, American Acad. of Arts and Sciences 2011–, Int. Advisory Council, The Israel Democracy Inst. 2012–; Ed. Univ. Center for Human Values Series, Princeton University Press 1992–2004; mem. Editorial Bd Teachers' College Record 1990–95, Cambridge Studies in Philosophy and Public Policy 1991–, Raritan 1995–, Journal of Political Philosophy 1995–, Handbook of Political Theory 1999–, Annual Reviews 2001–05; Chair. Bd of Trustees, Whig-Cliosophic Soc. 1985–88; mem. Nat. Constitution Center Bd of Trustees 2007–; Fellow, American Acad. of Arts and Sciences 1997, Nat. Acad. of Educ. 1997, American Philosophical Soc. 2005; W.E.B. Du Bois Fellow, American Acad. of Political and Social Science 2001–; Hon. DIur (Kalamazoo Coll.) 1992; Hon. LLD (Rochester) 2005, (Columbia Univ.) 2012; Hon. DLitt (Wesleyan Univ.) 2005; Nat. Endowment for the Humanities Summer Fellowship 1977, American Council of Learned Socs Fellowship 1978–79, Bicentennial Preceptorship, Princeton 1979–82, N American Soc. for Social Philosophy Book Award 1996–97, American Assen of Univ. Profs Betram Mott Award 1998, Kenneth Robinson Fellowship, Univ. of Hong Kong 1998–99, Spencer Foundation Sr Scholar Award 1999, Princeton Univ. Distinguished Teaching Award 2000, Harvard Univ. Centennial Award 2003, Carnegie Corpn Leadership Award 2009, Benjamin E. Mays Award, A Better Chance 2010. *Publications:* Liberal Equality 1980, Ethics and Politics: Cases and Comments (co-author) 1984, Democratic Education 1987, Democracy and the Welfare State (ed.) 1988, Multiculturalism and the Politics of Recognition (ed.) 1992, Democracy and Disagreement (co-author) 1996, Color Conscious: The Political Morality of Race (N American Soc. for Social Philosophy Book Award 1996–97, Gustavus Myers Center for the Study of Human Rights in N American Award 1997, Ralph J. Bunche Award, American Political Science Assen 1997) 1996, A Matter of Interpretation: Federal Courts and the Law (ed.) 1997, Work and Welfare (ed.) 1998, Freedom of Association (ed.) 1998, The Lives of Animals (ed.) 1999, Goodness and Advice (ed.) 2001, Identity in Democracy 2003, Why Deliberative Democracy? 2004, The Spirit of Compromise: Why Governing Demands It and Campaigning Undermines It 2012; as Chair of the Presidential Commission for the Study of Bioethical Issues: New Directions: The Ethics of Synthetic Biology and Emerging Technologies 2010, Moral Science: Protecting Participants in Human Subjects Research 2011, Research Across Borders: Proceedings of the International Research Panel of the Presidential Commission for the Study of Bioethical Issues 2011, Ethically Impossible: STD Research in Guatemala from 1946–48 2011; numerous chapters in books and articles in professional journals. *Address:* Office of the President, University of Pennsylvania, 1 College Hall, Philadelphia, PA 19104-6380, USA (office). *Telephone:* (215) 898-

7221 (office). *Fax:* (215) 898-9659 (office). *E-mail:* presweb@upenn.edu (office). *Website:* www.upenn.edu/president (office).

GUTMANN, Francis Louis Alphonse Myrtil; French diplomatist; *President of Scientific Council for Defence, Ministry of Defence;* b. 4 Oct. 1930, Paris; s. of Robert Gutmann and Denise (née Coulom) Gutmann; m. Chantal de Gaulle 1964; two s. one d.; ed Lycée Pasteur, Neuilly-sur-Seine; Head of Dept, Ministry of Foreign Affairs 1951–57; Asst Head Office of Sec. of State for Econ. Affairs 1955, mem. French Del. to Econ. and Social Council and to UN Gen. Ass. 1952–55, to Common Market Conf., Brussels 1956–57; Adviser Pechiney Co. 1957–59, Sec.-Gen. 1963, Dir 1970–71; Sec.-Gen. Fria 1960–62; mem. Governing Bd Pechiney-Ugine-Kuhlmann group 1962–78, Pres.-Dir-Gen. Ugine-Kuhlmann 1971–76, in charge of social affairs 1975–78; Pres. Alucam 1968–72; Pres. Frialco and Vice-Pres. Friguia 1977–81; Dir-Gen. French Red Cross 1980–81; Sec.-Gen. Ministry for External Relations 1981–85; Admin. representing the State, Paribas 1982–84, Gaz de France 1984–85, St Gobain 1982–85; Amb. to Spain 1985–88; Pres. Admin. Council Gaz de France 1988–93, Hon. Pres. 1993–; Pres. Fondation Méditerranéenne d'Etudes Stratégiques 1989–2000, Assoc. Eurogas-Union 1990–94, (Admin. Council) Institut Français du Pétrole (IFP) 1993–96; Vice-Pres. Mémoire et espoirs de la Résistance 1994–2000; attached to Ministry of Foreign Affairs 1996–; Pres. Scientific Council for Defence, Ministry of Defence 1998–; Dir French Red Cross 1992–2000; Officier, Légion d'honneur; Commdr, Ordre nat. du Mérite; Grand croix de l'ordre du Merité (Spain); numerous foreign awards. *Publications:* Les chemins de l'effort 1975, Le nouveau décor international 1994, Demain est un autre monde 2008, Changer de politique: une autre politique étrangère pour un monde différent? 2011. *Address:* 1–4 av. de Bois-Préau, 92500 Rueil-Malmaison, France (office). *Telephone:* 1-47-52-68-84 (office). *Fax:* 1-47-52-67-54 (office).

GUTZWILLER, Peter Max, LLM, DrIur; Swiss lawyer; *Counsel, Lenz & Staehelin;* b. 30 April 1941, Basle; s. of Max and Helly Gutzwiller; m. 1st Vreny Lüscher 1971 (divorced); one s.; m. 2nd Barbara Menzel; ed Univs of Basle and Geneva and Harvard Law School, USA; Assoc., Staehelin Hafter & Pnrs (now Lenz & Staehelin) 1970–76, Pnr 1977–2007, Counsel 2007–; mem. Bd of Int. Law Assen (Swiss Br.) 1975–; Sec. Swiss Assen of Int. Law 1976; Maj., Swiss Army 1979; Chair. Harvard Law School Foundation, Swiss Nat. Museum Foundation; mem. Bd of Dirs Beyer Chronometrie AG; mem. Soc. of Trust and Estate Practitioners, Chambers of Commerce China, Germany, GB, Munich, USA. *Publications:* Swiss International Divorce Law 1968, Von Ziel und Methode des IPR 1968, Arbeitsbewilligungen für Ausländer 1975, 1976, Grundriss des schweizerischen Privat- und Steuerrechtes (co-author) 1976, Schweizerisch-Deutsches Erbrecht (co-author) 2005, The Swiss Legal System, in: Switzerland Business and Investment Handbook 2006, Trusts für die Schweiz 2007, Über die Substanz der Urteilsfähigkeit 2008, Das schweizerische internationale Trustrecht im Lichte der Haager Trust-Konvention-eine Einführung 2008. *Leisure interests:* art collection (cartoons), music, travel. *Address:* Lenz & Staehelin, Bleicherweg 58, 8027 Zurich (office); Sonnenrain 15, 8700 Küsnacht, Switzerland (home). *Telephone:* 4508000 (office). *Fax:* 4508001 (office). *E-mail:* peter-max.gutzwiller@lenzstaehelin.com (office). *Website:* www.lenzstaehelin.com (office).

GUY, George (Buddy); American blues musician (guitar); b. 30 July 1936, Lettsworth, La; played with artists, including Slim Harpo, Lightnin' Slim; mem., Rufus Foreman Band; solo artist; mem. houseband, Chess Records, including sessions with Muddy Waters, Howlin' Wolf; musical partnership with Junior Wells; numerous live performances; numerous awards including 23 W.C. Handy Awards, Billboard Music Awards Century Award 1993, Nat. Medal of Arts 2003, Kennedy Center Honor 2012. *Recordings include:* albums: Blues From Big Bill's Copa Cobana 1963, A Man and The Blues 1968, This Is Buddy Guy 1968, Hold That Plane! 1972, I Was Walking Through The Woods 1974, Hot and Cool 1978, Got To Use Your House 1979, Dollar Done Fell 1980, DJ Play My Blues 1982, The Original Blues Brothers – Live 1983, Ten Blue Fingers 1985, Live At The Checkerboard, Chicago 1979 1988, Breaking Out 1988, Damn Right I Got The Blues (with Eric Clapton, Jeff Beck, Mark Knopfler) 1991 (Grammy Award 1992), My Time After Awhile 1992, Feels Like Rain 1993 (Grammy Award 1994), American Bandstand, Vol. 2 1993, Slippin' In 1994 (Grammy Award 1996), I Cry 1995, Live! The Real Deal 1996, As Good As It Gets 1998, Heavy Love 1998, Last Time Around 1998, The Real Blues 1999, 20th Century Masters – The Millennium Collection 2000, Sweet Tea 2001, Blues Singer 2003 (Grammy Award 2004), Bring 'Em In 2006, Skin Deep 2008, Living Proof 2010 (Grammy Award 2011); with Junior Wells: Buddy and The Juniors 1970, Buddy Guy and Junior Wells Play The Blues 1972, Drinkin' TNT and Smokin' Dynamite 1982, Alone and Acoustic 1991, Alive in Montreux 1992. *Address:* GBG Enterprises, 700 South Wabash Avenue, Chicago, IL 60605, USA (office). *Telephone:* (312) 427-0962 (office). *Fax:* (312) 427-5922 (office). *E-mail:* annie@buddyguy.com (office). *Website:* www.buddyguy.net.

GUYAUX, Joseph C., BS, MBA; American business executive; *Head of Retail Banking and President, PNC Financial Services Group;* ed Brown Univ., Univ. of Pittsburgh, Stonier Grad. School of Banking; joined PNC 1972, held several man. positions, Sr Vice-Pres. and Man. of Metropolitan Commercial Banking, Pittsburgh 1989–91, Pres. PNC's Northeast Pa 1991–93, Exec. Vice-Pres. and Retail Market Man. for the Pittsburgh market 1993–95, Sr Vice-Pres. and Man. PNC Private Bank 1995–97, Deputy Man. Consumer Banking business 1997, CEO 1997–2001, responsible for PNC's middle market, corp. finance, capital markets, asset-based lending, treasury man. and leasing businesses 2001–02, Pres. The PNC Financial Services Group 2002–, Head of Retail Banking 2005–; Chair. Civic Light Opera, Carnegie Museum of Natural History, Pittsburgh (also Life Trustee); mem. Bd of Dirs DQE Holdings LLC, Pittsburgh Cultural Trust, Highmark, Inc., Private Export Funding Corpn; mem. Bd of Dirs Emer. Duquesne Univ. 2009–. *Address:* The PNC Financial Services Group, 249 Fifth Avenue, Pittsburgh, PA 15222, USA (office). *Telephone:* (412) 762-2000 (office). *Fax:* (412) 762-7829 (office). *E-mail:* info@pnc.com (office). *Website:* www.pnc.com (office).

GUZY, Carol; American photographer; b. 7 March 1956, Bethlehem, Pa; m. Jonathan Utz; ed Northampton Co. Area Community Coll., Art Inst. of Fort Lauderdale; attended nursing school; intern then staff photographer Miami Herald 1980–88; staff photograpner, The Washington Post 1988–; notable assignments include coverage of volcanic eruption in Colombia, fall of communism, nomads in Mali, Rwandan exodus, famine in Ethiopia, civil war in Somalia, daily life in Haiti, and plight of Kosovo refugees; Pulitzer Prize 1986, 1995, 2000, 2011,

Photographer of the Year (Nat. Press Photographers Asscn) 1990, 1993, 1997, Robert F. Kennedy Memorial Prize 1997, eight White House Press Photographers Asscn's Photographer of the Year, Leica Medal of Excellence, Overseas Press Club Citation of Excellence and numerous other awards. *Address:* The Washington Post, 1150 15th Street, NW, Washington, DC 20071-0002, USA. *Website:* www .washingtonpost.com/wp-dyn/photo/bestofthepost/guzycarol.

GUZZANTI, Corrado; Italian actor, director, writer and satirist; b. 17 May 1965, Rome; s. of journalist and Senator Paolo Guzzanti; brother of Sabina and Caterina Guzzanti; began career as writer for his sister Sabina; debut as actor in roles for himself in Avanzi, hosted by Serena Dandini; collaborated with her in TV shows, including Tunnel, Maddecheaò, Pippo Chennedy Show and L'ottavo nano; famous for his satirical imitations of Italian politicians and personalities; also cr. several characters, including the Quelo (comical version of a New Age guru) and the poet Brunello Robertetti (satire of a typical Italian alleged intellectual); debut as film dir with Fascisti su Marte 2006. *Films include:* I Cammelli (The Camels) (voice) 1988, Prima le donne e i bambini 1992, DeGenerazione 1994, Und1c1/8ttavi (also writer and dir) 2000, Fascisti su Marte (Fascists on Mars) (also writer, dir and producer) 2006. *Television includes:* Scusate l'interruzione (series) 1990, Avanzi 1992 (series) 1991. *E-mail:* info@corradoguzzanti.it (office). *Website:* www .corradoguzzanti.it (office).

GVINDADZE, Dimitri; Georgian economist and politician; b. 23 Dec. 1973, Tbilisi; m. Maia Kvaliashvili; two d.; ed Tbilisi State Tech. Univ., Diplomatic Acad. of Paris, France, Int. Inst. of Social Studies, The Hague, Netherlands, John F. Kennedy School of Govt, Harvard Univ. and Financial Programming and Policy course at Int. Monetary Fund Inst., Washington, DC, USA; served in various positions at Ministry of Foreign Affairs 1994–2003; Deputy Minister of Finance 2005–11, Minister of Finance 2011–12. *Address:* c/o Ministry of Finance, 0114 Tbilisi, V. Gorgasali Str. 16, Georgia. *E-mail:* minister@mof.ge.

GVOZDENOVIĆ, Branimir (Brano), MSc; Montenegrin politician; *Minister of Sustainable Development and Tourism;* b. 1961, Bar; ed Univ. of Montenegro, Podgorica; Programmer, Republican Information Cttee 1986–89; Adviser for Devt of Information System, Republican Secr. for Devt 1989–90; Sr Adviser for Informatics 1990–91, Asst Dir 1991–95, Republican Devt Bureau; Asst Sec., Secr. for Devt 1995–99; Dir, Post of Montenegro Ltd 1999–2002; acting Minister of Maritime Affairs 2002, Deputy Prime Minister for Econ. Policy and Devt 2002–06, Minister of Econ. Devt 2006–09, of Urban Planning and Environment 2009–10, of Sustainable Devt and Tourism 2012–; Pres. of Bar Municipality 2002–03; Political Dir Democratic Party of Socialists of Montenegro (Demokratska Partija Socijalista Crne Gore) (DPS) 2011–12; Pres. Council of Montenegro Civil Aviation Agency 2012; Expo Italia Real Estate Award 2009. *Address:* Ministry of Sustainable Development and Tourism, 81000 Podgorica, St. 4. Proleterske 19, Montenegro (office). *Telephone:* (20) 446200 (office). *Fax:* (20) 446215 (office). *E-mail:* branimir .gvozdenovic@mrt.gov.me (office). *Website:* www.mrt.gov.me (office).

GWIN, Robert G., BS, MBA; American chartered financial analyst and business executive; *Chairman of the Supervisory Board, LyondellBasell Industries;* ed Univ. of Southern California, Fuqua School of Business at Duke Univ.; joined Prudential Capital in 1990, served at Prudential Capital Group (an asset management unit of The Prudential Insurance Co. of America) in merchant banking roles for ten years, including as its Man. Dir; joined Prosoft Learning Corpn (fmrly Prosoft training) in 2000, Consultant and Chief Financial Officer (CFO) 2000–04, Exec. Vice-Pres. 2001–04, Pres. and CEO 2002–04, Chair. 2002–06; CEO Community Broadband Ventures LP 2004–06; Vice-Pres. of Finance and Treas., Anadarko Petroleum Corpn 2006–08, Sr Vice-Pres. 2008–09, Exec. Vice-Pres. of Finance and CFO 2009–13; mem. Bd of Dirs Western Gas Holdings LLC (General Partner of Western Gas Partners LP) 2007–, Pres. 2007–09, CEO 2007–10, Chair. (non-exec.) 2009–13, Chair. Western Gas Equity Holdings, LLC 2012–; mem. Supervisory Bd, LyondellBasell Industries NV 2011–, Vice-Chair. (non-exec.) May–Aug. 2013, Chair. Aug. 2013–, Supervisory Dir of Lyondell Chemical Co. *Address:* LyondellBasell Industries, Weena 737, 3013 Rotterdam, The Netherlands (office). *Telephone:* (10) 275-55-00 (office). *E-mail:* info@lyondellbasell.com (office). *Website:* www.lyondellbasell.com (office).

GYAMTSHO, Lyonpo Pema, MAgrSc (Hons), PhD; Bhutanese agriculturalist and politician; *President, Druk Phuensum Tshogpa (DPT);* m.; one s. four d.; ed univ. in New Zealand, Eidgenössische Technische Hochschule (Swiss Fed. Inst. of Tech.), Zürich; worked in various fields, including rural devt, planning, project man. and research; fmr Deputy Resident Coordinator of Helvetas, resgnd to join politics; elected for Druk Phuensum Tshogpa (DPT) party from Chhoekhor-Tang constituency, Bumthang, Pres. DPT party 2013–; Minister of Agric. and Forests 2008–13; Founding Co-Chair. Bhutan Water Partnership; fmr mem. Planning Comm., Sustainable Devt Secr., Centre of Bhutan Studies, Forestry Devt Corpn Bd; while at ICIMOD, Nepal, travelled extensively and worked in several countries, including Afghanistan, China, Pakistan, India, Nepal and Mongolia on agric. and rural devt programmes. *Address:* Druk Phuensum Tshogpa (DPT), Chang Lam, Thimphu, Bhutan (office). *Telephone:* (2) 336336 (office). *Fax:* (2) 335845 (office). *E-mail:* dpt@druknet.bt (office). *Website:* www.dpt.bt (office).

GYAMTSHO, Lyonpo Thinley, BA; Bhutanese politician; b. 1952; ed Trashigang High School, St Joseph's Coll., India, Wellington Univ., NZ; Jt Dir Dept of Educ. 1985, Dir Dept of Nat. Budget and Accounts 1986, Dir of Educ. 1987–90, Dir Gen. 1990–94, Sec. 1994–96; Sec. Royal Civil Service Comm. 1996–98, Deputy Minister 1998; Minister of Home Affairs 1998–2003, of Educ. 2003–08; Red Scarf 1991, Orange Scarf 1998, Coronation Medal 1999. *Address:* c/o Education Division, Ministry of Health and Education, Tashichhodzong, PO Box 726, Thimphu, Bhutan. *Telephone:* 325146. *Fax:* 324823. *E-mail:* lyonpo_tg@hotmail.com. *Website:* www.education.gov.bt.

GYANENDRA BIR BIKRAM SHAH DEV, BA; Nepalese fmr ruler; b. 7 July 1974, Kathmandu; s. of the late King Mahendra Bir Bikram Shah and the late Crown Princess Indra Rajya Laxmi Devi Shah; brother of the late King Birendra Bir Bikram Shah Dev; m. Komal Rajya Laxmi Devi Shah 1970; one s. one d.; ed St Joseph's Coll., Darjeeling, India, Tribhuvan Univ. Kathmandu; King of Nepal 2001–08; Supreme Commdr Royal Nepalese Army –2006; made state visits to India 2002, China 2002; official visits to India 1976, Democratic People's Repub. of Korea 1978, Repub. of Korea 1987; other visits to India, Pakistan, China, Bhutan,

Thailand, Myanmar, Singapore, USA, USSR, UK, The Netherlands, Denmark, Germany, France, Italy, Switzerland, Saudi Arabia, Turkey, Yugoslavia, Romania, Hungary, Bulgaria, Czechoslovakia, Australia, New Zealand, Belgium, Spain, UAE, Austria, Canada, Iran; Chair. (currently Patron) Lumbini Devt Trust 1986–1991, King Mahendra Trust for Nature Conservation 1982–2001; Founding mem. 1001–Nature Trust 1986; Patron, Pushupati Area Devt Trust; Chancellor Tribhuvan Univ. and Mahendra Sanskrit Univ.; special interest in conservation and preservation of natural and man-made heritage; declared state of emergency, took over as Chair. of Council of Ministers Feb. 2005, relinquished power April 2006, stripped of most constitutional powers 2006, monarchy abolished May 2008; Hon. mem. Worlwide Fund for Nature; Grand Cross of the House Order of Orange (Netherlands) 1967, Kt Grand Cordon of the Most Exalted Order of the White Elephant (Thailand) 1979, Grand Cross Ordre nat. du Mérite 1983, Kt Grand Cross of the Most Distinguished Order of St Michael and St George 1986, Grand Cross of Order of Isabel la Católica (Spain) 1987, His Holy Majesty, King of the Lands of the Nepalese People and Kt of the Holy and Most Majestic Order of the Rose of Jordan, Sovereign of all Orders of the Kingdom of Nepal. *Leisure interests:* nature, reading, writing poetry.

GYELTSHEN, Dasho Rinzin; Bhutanese civil servant (retd); Chair. Royal Advisory Council (Zhung Kalyon) 1998–2008 (retd). *Address:* c/o Royal Advisory Council, Tashicho Dzong, Thimphu, Bhutan. *Telephone:* 322816. *E-mail:* rinzingyaltshen@hotmail.com.

GYIBUG, Puncog Cedain; Chinese politician; b. 1930, Tibet; Vice-Chair. of People's Govt of Tibet Autonomous Region 1983–; Deputy for Tibet to 7th NPC 1988. *Address:* People's Government of Tibet Autonomous Region, Lhasa, People's Republic of China.

GYLL, (John) Sören; Swedish business executive; b. 26 Dec. 1940, Skorped; s. of Josef Gyll and Gertrud Gyll; m. Lilly Margareta Hellman 1974; two s. one d.; Marketing Dir and Vice-Pres. Rank Xerox 1963–77; Pres. Uddeholms Sweden AB 1977–79, Exec. Vice-Pres. Uddeholms AB 1979–81, Pres. and CEO 1981–84; Pres. and CEO Procordia AB 1984–92; Pres. and CEO AB Volvo 1992–97, also Dir; fmr Chair. Pharmacia and Upjohn Inc.; fmr Chair. Gyttorp Cartridge Co.; Chair. Capedal AB, Genesis-IT AB; mem. Bd of Dirs Svenska Cellulosa Aktiebolaget SCA 1997–, Fenix Outdoor, SKF, Skanska, Topeja Holding, Scandinavian Touch, Medicover Holding, Askus AB, Oresa Ventures AB, Probi AB; mem. Bd of Dirs Junior Achievement and Young Entreprise Europe –2004; mem. European Advisory Bd, Schroder Salomon Smith Barney 2001; fmr Pres. Confederation of Swedish Enterprise; mem. Royal Acad. of Eng Sciences. *Leisure interests:* hunting, skiing.

GYLLENHAAL, Jake; American actor; b. 19 Dec. 1980, Los Angeles; s. of Stephen Gyllenhaal and Naomi Foner Gyllenhaal; brother of Maggie Gyllenhaal; ed Columbia Univ.; Nat. Arts Award 2006. *Films include:* City Slickers 1991, A Dangerous Woman 1993, Josh and S.A.M 1993, Homegrown 1998, October Sky 1999, Donnie Darko (Young Hollywood Award 2002, Chlotrudis Award 2003) 2001, Bubble Boy 2001, Lovely and Amazing 2001, The Good Girl 2002, Highway 2002, Moonlight Mile 2002, The Day After Tomorrow 2004, The Man Who Walked Between the Towers 2005, Brokeback Mountain (BAFTA Award for Best Actor in a Supporting Role 2006) 2005, Proof 2004, Jarhead 2005, Zodiac 2007, Rendition 2007, Brothers 2009, Prince of Persia: The Sands of Time 2010, Love and Other Drugs 2010, End of Watch 2012. *Plays include:* This Is Our Youth (New York and London) (Evening Standard Award). *Publication:* Between My Legs 2008. *Leisure interests:* woodworking, cooking. *Address:* WME, 9601 Wilshire Blvd, Beverly Hills, CA 90201, USA (office). *Website:* www.jakegyllenhaal.com.

GYLLENHAAL, Maggie, BA; American actress; b. 16 Nov. 1977, New York City; d. of Stephen Gyllenhaal and Naomi Foner Gyllenhaal; sister of Jake Gyllenhaal; m. Peter Sarsgaard 2009; ed Columbia Univ., Royal Acad. of Dramatic Arts, London. *Films include:* Waterland 1992, A Dangerous Woman 1993, Homegrown 1998, The Photographer 2000, Cecil B. DeMented 2000, Donnie Darko 2001, Riding in Cars with Boys 2001, Secretary (several awards including Boston Soc. of Film Critics Award for Best Actress) 2002, 40 Days and 40 Nights 2002, Adaptation 2002, Confessions of a Dangerous Mind 2002, Casa de los babys 2003, Mona Lisa Smile 2003, The Pornographer: A Love Story 2004, Criminal 2004, Happy Endings 2005, The Great New Wonderful 2005, Trust the Man 2005, SherryBaby 2006, Paris, je t'aime 2006, Monster House 2006, World Trade Center 2006, Stranger Than Fiction 2006, High Falls 2007, The Dark Knight 2008, Crazy Heart 2009, Nanny McPhee and the Big Bang 2010, Hysteria 2011, Won't Back Down 2012. *Television includes:* Shattered Mind 1996, Patron Saint of Liars 1998, Resurrection 1999, Shake, Rattle and Roll: An American Love Story 1999, Strip Search 2004. *Address:* c/o 200 Park Avenue South, 8th Floor, New York, NY 10003; c/o Creative Artists Agency, Inc., 9830 Wilshire Blvd., Beverly Hills, CA 90212-1825, USA. *Telephone:* (310) 288-4545. *Fax:* (310) 288-4800. *Website:* www.caa .com.

GYLLENHAMMAR, Pehr Gustaf, BLL; Swedish business executive; *Vice-Chairman Europe, Rothschild;* b. 28 April 1935, Gothenburg; s. of Pehr Gustaf Victor Gyllenhammar and Aina Dagny Kaplan; m. 1st Eva Christina Engellau 1959 (died 2008); one s. three d.; m. 2nd Christel Sofia Behrmann 2010 (divorced 2012); m. 3rd Lee Welton Croll 2013; ed Univ. of Lund, studied int. law in England, vocational studies in maritime law, USA, Centre d'Etudes Industrielles, Geneva; employed by Mannheimer & Zetterlöf (solicitors), Gothenburg 1959, Haight, Gardner, Poor & Havens (Admiralty lawyers), New York 1960, Amphion Insurance Co., Gothenburg 1961–64; Asst Admin. Man. Skandia Insurance Co., Stockholm 1965–66, Vice-Pres. Corporate Planning 1966–68, Exec. Vice-Pres. 1968, Pres. and CEO 1970; joined AB Volvo, Gothenburg 1970, Man. Dir and CEO 1971–83, Chair. of Bd and CEO 1983–90, Exec. Chair. Bd of Dirs 1990–93; Chair. Bd MC European Capital SA 1994–96; Chair. Swedish Ships Mortgage Bank 1976–2007, Procordia AB 1990–92; Sr Adviser Lazard Frères & Co. 1996–99, Man. Dir 2000–03; Chair. Cofinec NV 1996–2000; fmr Chair. CGU PLC (fmr Chair. CGNU after merger of CGU PLC and Norwich Union PLC, co. changed name to Aviva 2002); Vice-Chair. Europe, Rothschild 2003–; Chair. Investment AB Kinnevik (formed by merger of Industriförvaltnings AB Kinnevik and Invik & Co. AB) 2004–08, Majid Al Futtaim Group 2005–09, Arise AB 2007–; f. European Round Table of Industrialists 1982–93, European Financial Services Round Table

2003–06; Chair. London Philharmonic Trust 2006–11; mem. Bd of Dirs Skandinaviska Enskilda Banken 1979–94, United Technologies Corpn 1981–99, Kissinger Assocs, Inc. 1982–97, Pearson PLC 1983–97, Reuters Holdings PLC 1984–97, Philips Electronics NV 1990–96, Renault SA 1990–93 and numerous other cos and orgs; Trustee, Reuters (now Thomson Reuters) 1997–2012 (Chair. Trustees 1999–2012); mem. Royal Swedish Acad. of Eng Sciences 1974, Int. Advisory Cttee Chase Manhattan Bank 1972–95; Hon. Master, Bench of Inner Temple 2001; Officer (1st Class), Royal Order of Vasa 1973, Commdr, Order of the Lion of Finland 1977, Commdr, Ordre nat. du Mérite 1980, King's Medal (12th Size) with Ribbon, Order of the Seraphim 1981, Commdr, St Olav's Order 1984, Commdr, Order of the Lion of Finland (1st Class) 1986, Commdr, Légion d'honneur 1987, Kt Grand Officer, Order of Merit (Italy) 1987, Commdr, Order of Leopold 1989; Hon. DrMed (Gothenburg Univ.) 1981; Hon. DTech (Brunel) 1987; Hon. DrEng (Nova Scotia) 1988; Hon. DrScS (Helsinki) 1990; Hon. LLD (Vermont) 1993; Hon. Dr of Econs and Commercial Law (Gothenburg) 2003; Hon. DBA (Metropolitan Univ., London) 2004; Golden Award, City of Gothenburg 1981. *Publications:* Mot sekelskiftet på måfå (Towards the Turn of the Century at Random) 1970, Jag tror på Sverige (I Believe in Sweden) 1973, People at Work 1977, En industripolitik för människan (Industrial Policy for Human Beings) 1979, Fortsättning följer... (To Be Continued...) 2000. *Leisure interests:* golf, music, sailing. *Address:* Rothschild, New Court, St Swithin's Lane, London, EC4N 8AL, England (office). *Telephone:* (20) 7280-5000 (office). *Website:* www.rothschild.com (office).

GYLYS, Povilas, DSc (Econ); Lithuanian economist, academic and fmr politician; *Professor, Department of Economic Theory, Vilnius University;* b. 14 Feb. 1948, Didžiokai, Molėtai Region; m. Nijole Rezaitė 1969; two s.; ed Molėtai Secondary School and Vilnius Univ.; Lecturer, later Prof. of Econs, Vilnius Univ. 1969–92; Head, Dept of Int. Econ. Relations 1992, currently Prof., Dept of Econ. Theory (fmr Chair.), mem. Univ. Senate; mem. Parl. (Seimas) 1992–2000, mem. Lithuanian Democratic Labour Party Parl. Group 1996–2000, Cttee on Foreign Affairs 1998–2000, Comm. on Econ. Crimes Investigation 1999–2000, Seimas Del. to Parl. Ass. of Council of Europe 1999–2000); Minister of Foreign Affairs 1992–96; Ed.-in-Chief Ekonomika; mem. Council, Lithuanian Social Research Inst.; Expert, Lithuanian State Science and Studies Foundation. *Publications:* Economy, Antieconomy and Globalization; numerous articles and monographs. *Address:* Department of Economic Theory, Economics Faculty, Vilnius University, Sauletekio 9, 10222 Vilnius, Lithuania (office). *Telephone:* (5) 236-6147 (office). *E-mail:* povilas.gylys@ef.vu.lt (office); pogyly@lrs.lt (home). *Website:* www.ef.vu.lt (office).

GYMNASTIAR, Abdullah, (Aa Gym); Indonesian religious speaker and business executive; *Managing Director, MQ Corporation;* b. 30 Feb. 1962, Bandung; m. 1st Teteh Nini Gym; m. 2nd Alfarini Eridani; six c.; fmr student military leader; Commdr Regiment Students Acad. of Eng 1982; f. Daarut Tauhiid ('Home of the One God') movt 1990; Man. Dir MQ Corpn; business interests include 15 media cos.; frequent TV appearances as Islamic preacher. *Publications include:* Berani karena Benar, Jujur Kunci Sukses, Memberi dengan Gembira, Pantang Mengeluh, Percaya Diri, Semangat Tanpa Henti, Sayang Orang Tua. *Leisure interests:* diving, shooting, parachuting, singing country songs, riding. *Address:* MQ Corporation, Kompleks Pesantren Daarut Tauhiid, Jl. Gegerkalong Girang, Bangdung, 40154, Indonesia (office). *Telephone:* 22 2008844 (office). *Fax:* 22 2014543 (office). *E-mail:* info@mqmedia.com (office). *Website:* www.mqmedia.com (office).

GYOHTEN, Toyoo; Japanese economist and fmr banker; *President, Institute for International Monetary Affairs;* b. 1931, Yokohama; m.; one s. one d.; ed Univ. of Tokyo, Princeton Univ., USA; joined Ministry of Finance 1955; worked at Japan Desk, Asian Dept, IMF 1964–66; Special Asst to Pres. of Asian Devt Bank, Manila, Philippines 1966–69; Dir-Gen. Int. Finance Bureau 1984–86, Vice-Minister of Finance for Int. Affairs 1986–89; Visiting Prof., Grad. School of Business, Harvard Univ., USA 1990, Woodrow Wilson School, Princeton Univ. 1990–91, Univ. of St Gallen, Switzerland 1991; joined Bank of Tokyo Ltd (merged with Mitsubishi Bank Ltd 1996) 1991, Chair. 1992–96, Sr Adviser, Bank of Tokyo-Mitsubishi Ltd 1996, 2006–; Pres. Inst. for Int. Monetary Affairs 1995–; Chair. Working Party III, OECD, Paris 1988–90, Inst. of Int. Finance Inc., USA 1994–97; Special Adviser to Prime Minister Keizo Obuchi 1998; mem. Bd of Trustees, Princeton in Asia, USA 1989–, Advisory Panel, E African Devt Bank, Kampala, Uganda 1990–, Asia Pacific Advisory Cttee, New York Stock Exchange (now NYSE Next) 1990–, Int. Council, The Asia Soc., New York 1991–, Exec. Cttee of Trilateral Comm., New York, Paris and Tokyo 1991–, Group of Thirty, Washington, DC 1992–2009 (now Emer.), Council of Inst. Aspen France, Banking Advisory Group of IFC, Washington, DC 1992–; Founding mem. Int. Advisory Bd of Council on Foreign Relations, New York 1995–; Fulbright Scholar 1956–58. *Publication:* Changing Fortunes (with Paul Volcker) 1992. *Address:* Institute for International Monetary Affairs, 12F The Bank of Tokyo- Mitsubishi UFJ Ltd, Nihombashi Annex, 3-2 Nihombashi, Hongokucho, 1-Chome, Chuo-ku, Tokyo 103-0021, Japan (office). *E-mail:* info@iima.or.jp (office). *Website:* www.iima.or.jp (office).

GYSI, Gregor; German lawyer and politician; b. 16 Jan. 1948, Berlin; s. of the late Klaus Gysi and of Irene Gysi; m. 1st (divorced); two s.; m. 2nd; one d.; ed Humboldt Univ.; defence lawyer; elected Leader CP 1989, name changed to PDS (now known as Left Party), Parl. Leader; mem. Bundestag 1990–2002, 2005–; Deputy Mayor of Berlin and Senator for Econs, Labour and Women's Issues 2002; Founder mem. Cttee for Justice. *Publications:* Das Waris: Noch Lange Nicht (biog. notes) 1999, Ein Blick Zürück: Ein Schritt Nachvorn 2001. *Address:* Die Linke (Left Party), Karl-Liebknecht-Haus, Kleine Alexanderstr. 28, 10178 Berlin, Germany. *Telephone:* (30) 240090. *Fax:* (30) 2411046. *E-mail:* bundesgeschaeftsstelle@die-linke .de. *Website:* www.die-linke.de.

GYURCSÁNY, Ferenc; Hungarian business executive and politician; b. 4 June 1961, Pápa; m. 2nd Edina Bognár; two s.; m. 3rd Klára Dobrev; two c.; ed Faculty of Economy, Janus Pannonius Univ. of Sciences, Pécs; Sec. Pécs City Cttee, Communist Youth Alliance (KISZ) 1984–88, Pres. Univ. and Coll. Council, Cen. Cttee 1988–89, Vice-Pres. Democratic Youth Alliance (DEMISZ) 1989; Consultant, CREDITUM Financial Consultant Ltd 1990–92; Dir EUROCORP Int. Financial Inc. 1992; CEO ALTUS Investment and Assets Man. Inc. 1992–2002, Chair. 2002–03; Sr Adviser to Prime Minister Medgyessy 2002–03; mem. Nat. Exec. Cttee Hungarian Socialist Party (MSZP) 2003–, Chair. Győr-Moson-Sopron Co. Org. Feb.–Sept. 2004, Chair. MSZP 2007–09; Minister of Children, Youth and Sports 2003–04 (resgnd); Prime Minister of Hungary 2004–09 (resgnd). *Publication:* Útközben (On the Way, political essay) 2005. *Leisure interests:* running, skiing. *Address:* c/o Hungarian Socialist Party, 1081 Budapest, Köztársaság tér 26, Hungary (office).

H

HAACKE, Hans Christoph Carl, MFA; German artist and professor of art; *Professor Emeritus of Art, Cooper Union for the Advancement of Science and Art;* b. 12 Aug. 1936, Cologne; s. of Dr Carl Haacke and Antonie Haacke; m. Linda Snyder 1965; two s.; ed State Art Acad., Kassel; Asst Prof., Cooper Union for the Advancement of Science and Art, New York 1971–75, Assoc. Prof. 1975–79, Prof. 1979–2002, Prof. Emer. 2002–; Guest Prof., Hochschule für Bildende Künste, Hamburg 1973, 1994, Gesamthochschule, Essen 1979; Hon. DFA (Oberlin Coll.) 1991, (San Francisco Art Inst.) 2008; Dr hc (Bauhaus-Universität, Weimar) 1998; numerous awards including Golden Lion, Venice Biennale 1993. *Works include:* perm. sculptural installation in Reichstag Bldg (German Parl.), Berlin 2000, Denkzeichen Rosa Luxemburg, Berlin 2006. *Publications:* solo exhbn catalogues: Werkmonographie (with Edward F. Fry) 1972, Framing and Being Framed (co-author) 1975, *Nach* allen Regeln der Kunst 1984, Unfinished Business (co-author) 1987, Artfairismes 1989, Bodenlos (co-author) 1993, Obra Social (co–author) 1995, AnsichtsSachen/Viewing Matters 1999, Mia san mia (co-author) 2001, Hans Haacke (monograph, co-author) 2004, Hans Haacke – For Real, Works 1959–2006 2006; Libre-Echange (with Pierre Bourdieu) 1994; numerous articles and inter-views in int. art magazines. *Address:* Cooper Union for the Advancement of Science and Art, Cooper Square, New York, NY 10003, USA (office). *Telephone:* (212) 353-4200 (office). *Website:* www.cooper.edu (office).

HAAG, Rudolf, Dr rer. nat; German physicist; *Professor Emeritus in Theoretical Physics, Hamburg University;* b. 17 Aug. 1922, Tubingen; s. of Albert Haag and Anna Haag (née Schaich); m. 1st Kaethe Fues 1948 (died 1991); three s. one d.; m. 2nd Barbara Klie 1992; ed Tech. Univ., Stuttgart and Univ. of Munich; Prof. of Physics, Univ. of Illinois, USA 1960–66; Prof. of Theoretical Physics, Hamburg Univ. 1966–87, Prof. Emer. 1987–; Dr hc (Aix-Marseille) 1979; Max-Planck-Medal 1970, Henri Poincaré Prize 1997. *Publications:* Local Quantum Physics 1992; over 100 articles on fundamental physical theory. *Address:* Waldschmidtstrasse 4B, 83727 Schliersee Neuhaus, Germany (home). *Telephone:* 80267444 (home).

HAAK, Willem Elize (Pim), LLM; Dutch fmr chief justice; b. 19 April 1934, Haarlem; s. of Willem Adriaan Haak and Elisabeth Willemina H. ten Hooven; m. Cornelia Jacoba van Heek 1968; two s.; ed Univ. of Amsterdam; worked as advocate in Amsterdam until 1972; Dist Court Judge 1972–76; Justice, Amsterdam Court of Appeal 1976–79; Advocate Gen. to the Supreme Court 1979–81, Justice, Supreme Court 1981–92, Deputy Pres. 1992–99, Chief Justice 1999–2004; Chair. Advisory Bd Foundation of the Old Church Amsterdam 2004–09; Pres. Court of Appeals for the Gen. Comm. for the Navigation of the Rhine, Strasbourg 2004–07; Appointing Authority for the Iran-US Claims Tribunal, Perm. Court of Arbitration, The Hague 2009–13; mem. Advisory Bd Resolution Group (Effective Negotiation and Dispute Resolution), The Hague 2005–09; fmr Sec. Asscn of Dutch Lawyers; fmr Deputy Chair. Int. Law Inst.; fmr Pres. Appeals Tribunal, Dutch Inst. of Psychologists; fmr mem. Insurance Cos Supervisory Bd; fmr Pres. Bd Frits Lugt art collection; fmr Deputy Chair. Supervisory Bd, Institut Néerlandais, Paris; mem. Advisory Cttee on Endowed Chairs, Univ. of Amsterdam; mem. Perm. Appeals Tribunal of the Gen. Meeting of the Remonstrant Church; Kt, Order of the Dutch Lion, Commdr. Order Oranje-Nassau, Officier, Légion d'honneur. *Publications:* several articles and monographs on pvt. int. law, transport law, comparative law and criminal law. *Leisure interest:* mountain hiking. *Address:* Joh. Vermeerstraat 75, 1071 DN Amsterdam, The Netherlands. *Telephone:* (20) 6796935. *E-mail:* pimhaak@xs4all.nl.

HAAKON, HRH Crown Prince (Haakon Magnus), BSc; b. 20 July 1973; s. of HM King Harald V and HM Queen Sonja; m. Mette-Marit Tjessem Høiby 2001; one d. one s. one step-s.; ed Kristelig Gymnasium, Officers' Cand. School/Navy, Horten, Royal Norwegian Naval Acad., Bergen, Univ. of California at Berkeley, USA, LSE, UK; second-in-command, missile torpedo boat 1995–96; numerous official func-tions. *Leisure interests:* skiing, cycling, paragliding, sailing, theatre. *Address:* Royal Palace, 0010 Oslo, Norway (home). *Telephone:* (47) 2204-8700 (home). *Fax:* (47) 2204-8790 (home). *Website:* www.kongehuset.no (office).

HAAKONSEN, Bent, LLB; Danish diplomatist (retd); b. 10 Jan. 1936; m. Kirsten Haakonsen; one d.; joined Ministry of Foreign Affairs 1961; served Bonn 1964–67, Perm. Rep. to EEC, Brussels 1972–74; Amb. to Czechoslovakia 1978–79; Head, Danish del. to CSCE, Madrid 1980–81; Under-Sec. for Trade Relations 1983–86; Perm. Under-Sec. of State 1986–91; Perm. Rep. to UN, New York 1991–95; Amb. to Germany 1995–2001, to Sweden 2001–04; Pres. Franz Schubert Soc., Denmark. *Address:* Provstevænget 10, 4000 Roskilde, Denmark (home).

HAARDE, Geir H., MA; Icelandic politician and economist; b. 8 April 1951; m. Inga Jona Thordardottir; five c.; ed Brandeis Univ., Johns Hopkins Univ., Univ. of Minnesota, USA; teaching asst, Univ. of Minnesota, USA 1976–77; economist, Int. Dept, Cen. Bank of Iceland 1977–83; Lecturer, Econs Dept, Univ. of Iceland 1979–83; Special asst to Minister of Finance 1983–87; mem. Althing (Parl.) 1987–2009; mem. Foreign Affairs Cttee 1991–98, Chair. 1995–98; Minister of Finance 1998–2005; Minister of Foreign Affairs 2005–06; Prime Minister 2006–09 (resgnd); Chair. Youth Org. of Independence Party 1981–85, Chair. Parl. Group 1991–98, Vice-Chair. 1999–2005, Party Chair. 2005–09; Pres. Icelandic Group Inter-Parl. Union 1988–98, mem. Exec. Cttee 1994–98, Vice-Pres. 1996–97; mem. Control Cttee Nordic Investment Bank 1991–95; mem. Presidium Nordic Council 1991–98, Pres. 1995, Chair. Conservative Party Group 1995–97; Chair. Standing Cttee of Parliamentarians of Arctic Region 1995–98; Hon. LLD (Univ. of Minnesota) 2007; Alumni of the Year Award, Brandeis Univ., USA 2006. *Address:* Independence Party, Háaleitisbraut 1, 105 Reykjavík, Iceland (office). *Telephone:* 5151700 (office). *Fax:* 5151717 (office). *E-mail:* geir@haarde.is (office). *Website:* www.xd.is (office).

HAAS, Peter M., PhD; American political scientist and academic; *Professor of Political Science, University of Massachusetts, Amherst;* b. 23 Jan. 1955, Oakland; s. of Ernst B. Haas and Hildegarde Haas; m. Julie Zuckman; one s.; ed Univ. of Michigan, Massachusetts Inst. of Tech.; Visiting Asst Prof., Yale Univ. 1986; Marine Policy Research Fellow, Woods Hole Oceanographic Inst. 1986–87; Asst Prof. of Political Science, Univ. of Massachusetts, Amherst 1986–92, Assoc. Prof.

1992–98, Prof. 1998–; visiting positions, Univ. of Oxford, UK 2002, Brown Univ. 2002–03, Wissenschaftszentrum, Berlin 2009. *Publications include:* Saving the Mediterranean 1990, Institutions for the Earth 1993, Knowledge, Power and International Policy Co-ordination (ed.) 1997, The International Environment in the New Global Economy 2003, Emerging Forces in Environmental Governance 2004, Global Environmental Governance 2006, Controversies in Globalization 2012, Improving Global Environmental Governance 2013; articles and chapters on int. environmental politics and int. relations. *Address:* Department of Political Science, University of Massachusetts, 216 Thompson Hall, Amherst, MA 01003, USA (office). *Telephone:* (413) 545-6174 (office). *Fax:* (413) 545-3349 (office). *E-mail:* haas@polsci.umass.edu (office). *Website:* www.umass.edu/polsci (office).

HAAS, Richard John, BS, MFA; American artist; b. 29 Aug. 1936, Spring Green, Wis.; s. of Joseph F. Haas and Marie N. Haas; m. 1st Cynthia Dickman 1963 (divorced 1970); m. 2nd Katherine Sokolnikoff 1980; one s.; ed Univ. of Wisconsin-Milwaukee and Univ. of Minnesota; Instructor of Art, Univ. of Minn. 1963–64; Asst Prof. of Art, Michigan State Univ. 1964–68; Instructor in Printmaking, Bennington Coll. 1968–80, Fine Arts Faculty, School of Visual Arts 1977–81; Commr New York City Art 1976–79; Bd mem. Public Art Fund 1980–84, NY State Preservation League 1983–90; Gov. Skowhegan School of Painting and Sculpture 1980–; mem. Bd of Trustees, Hudson River Museum 1989–; Pres. Nat. Acad. of Design, New York 2009–11; Dir Abbey Mural Fund 2000–11; AIA Medal of Honor 1977, Municipal Art Soc. Award 1977, Nat. Endowment for the Arts Fellowship 1978, Guggenheim Fellowship 1983, Doris C. Freedman Award 1989, Fellowship, MacDowell Colony 2003, Individual Artist Award, Westchester Arts Council 2003, Yonkers Friends of the Arts Public Art Honoree 2003, Jimmy Ernst Award, American Acad. of Arts and Letters 2005. *Publication:* Richard Haas: An Architecture of Illusion 1981. *Leisure interests:* tennis, film. *Address:* c/o David Findlay Jr Gallery, 41 East 57th Street, #1120, New York, NY 10022, USA (office); 361 West 36th Street, 5A, New York, NY 10018, USA (office). *Telephone:* (212) 486-7660 (office); (212) 947-9868 (office). *Website:* www.davidfindlayjr.com (office); www.richardhaas.com (office); www.artnet.com (office). *E-mail:* haasnyc@aol.com (office).

HAAS, Robert Douglas, MBA; American business executive; *Chairman Emeri-tus, Levi Strauss & Company;* b. 3 April 1942, San Francisco; s. of the late Walter Haas and of Evelyn Danzig; m. Colleen Gershon 1974; one d.; ed Univ. of California, Berkeley and Harvard Univ.; with US Peace Corps, Côte d'Ivoire 1964–66; Assoc., McKinsey and Co. 1969–72; with Levi Strauss & Co., San Francisco 1973–, Sr Vice-Pres. (Corp. Planning and Policy) 1978–80, Pres. New Business Group 1980, Pres. Operating Groups 1980–81, Exec. Vice-Pres. and COO 1981–84, Pres. and CEO 1984–89, CEO and Chair. 1989–99, Chair. 1989–2008, Chair. Emer. 2008–; Hon. Dir San Francisco AIDS Foundation; Trustee, Ford Foundation; mem. Bd of Dirs Levi Strauss Foundation, Calif. Business Round-table, Stark County Veterans Service Comm.; White House Fellow 1968–69; fmr Berkeley Fellow; mem. Advisory Bd Haas School of Business, Stanford Humanities and Sciences Council, Stanford Humanities and Sciences Council; fmr mem. Bd of Dirs American Apparel Asscn; mem. Trilateral Comm., Council on Foreign Relations; fmr mem. Nat. Advisory Cttee League of Women Voters Educ. Fund; Hon. Trustee, Brookings Inst.; Chancellor's Award 1968, Nat. Leadership Coalition on AIDS Edward N. Brandt, Jr Award 1991, Ron Brown Award 1998, Cal Alumnus of the Year Award 2009. *Address:* Levi Strauss & Co., 1155 Battery Street, San Francisco, CA 94111, USA (office). *Telephone:* (415) 501-6000 (office). *Fax:* (415) 501-7112 (office). *Website:* www.levistrauss.com (office).

HAASAN, Kamal; Indian actor, filmmaker and screenwriter; b. 7 Nov. 1954, Paramakudi, Tamil Nadu; s. of D. Srinivasan and Rajalakshmi; m. 1st Vani Ganapathy 1978 (divorced 1988); m. 2nd Sarika 1988 (divorced 2002); partner Gouthami Tadimalla 2004; two c.; Owner, Rajkamal Int. (production co.); apptd Chair., Fed. of Indian Chambers of Commerce and Industry 2009; Dr hc (Sathyabama Deemed Univ.) 2005; Kalaimamani Award 1979, Padma Shri 1990, Abraham Kovoor National Award for Humanist Activities 2004, Chevalier Sivaji Ganesan Award for Excellence in Indian Cinema 2006, Living Legend Award, FICCI 2009, CNN-IBN Indian of the Year 2010, Hon. Award, Govt of Kerela 2010, Padma Bhushan 2014. *Films include:* Kalathur Kannamma (Nat. Film Award) 1960, Paadha Kannikkai 1962, Anandha Jodhi 1963, Mundram Pirai (Nat. Film Award) 1963, Maanavan 1969, Annai Velankanni 1971, Kanna Nalama 1972, Sollathaan Ninaikkiren 1973, Aval Oru Thodar Kathai 1974, Pattikkaattu Raja 1975, Moondru Mudichu 1976, Lalitha 1976, Oor Magal Marikkumo 1977, Satyavan Savithri 1977, Maro Charitra 1978, Madanolsavam 1978, Allaudinaum Arputha Vilakkum 1979, Azhiyadha Kolangal 1979, Maria, My Darling 1980, Natchathiram 1980, Thillu Mullu 1981, Kadal Meengal 1981, Do Dil Diwane 1981, Apoorva Raagangal (Filmfare Award) 1981, Agni Sakshi 1982, Moondram Pirai 1982, Moondram Pirai (Nat. Film Award) 1982, Sattam 1983, Thoongadhey Thambi Thoongadhey 1983, Sagara Sangamam (Filmfare Award, Nandi Award) 1983, Yeh Desh 1984, Raj Tilak 1984, Oru Kaidhiyin Diary 1984, Kaakki Sattai 1985, Mangamma Sabadham 1985, Dekha Pyar Tumhara 1985, Naanum Oru Thozhilali 1986, December Pookal 1986, Kadamai Kanniyam Kattupaadu 1987, Nayagan (Nat. Film Award) 1987, Pushpak (Filmfare Award) 1988, Sathya 1988, Daisy 1988, Indrudu Chandrudu (Filmfare Award for Best Actor, Nandi Award) 1989, Apoorva Sagodharargal (Filmfare Award) 1989, Chanakyan 1989, Michael Madhana Kamarajan 1990, My Dear Marthandan 1990, Guna 1991, Thevar Magan (also producer) (Filmfare Award, Nat. Film Award for Best Feature Film) 1992, Singaravelan 1992, Kalaignan 1993, Maharasan 1993, Nammavar 1994, Mahanadhi 1994, Kuruthipunal 1995, Sathi Leelavathi 1995, Avvai Shanmugi 1996, Indian (Nat. Film Award for Best Actor, Filmfare Award) 1996, Kaathala Kaathala 1998, Chachi 420 (also Dir) 1998, Hey Ram (also Dir and producer) (Filmfare Award for Best Actor) 2000, Aalavandhan 2000, Parthale Paravasam 2001, Panchathantiram Nala 2002, Pammal K. Sambandam 2002, Damayanthi 2003, Anbe Sivam 2003, Virumaandi (Best Asian Film Award, Puchon Int. Fantastic Film Festival) 2004, Mumbai Xpress 2005, Vettaiyaadu Vilaiyaadu 2006, Dasavathaaram (also writer) (Tamil Nadu State Film Award) 2008, Unnaipol Oruvan 2009, Four Friends 2010, Manmadan Ambu 2010, Vishwaroopam (also writer, dir and co- producer) (Nat. Film Award for Best Production Design and Best Choreography 2013) 2013, Vishwaroopam 2 2014. *Address:* 63, Luz Church Road, Mylapore, Chennai 600 004, India (home).

HAASIS, Heinrich; German banking executive and politician; *President, Deutscher Sparkassen- und Giroverband (German Savings Banks and Giro Association);* b. 21 April 1945, Balingen-Streichen (Baden-Wurttemberg); m.; two c.; ed Balingen Gymnasium, Albstadt-Ebingen Commercial Coll.; Mayor of Bisingen Dist 1971–81; mem. State Parl. (Landtag) for Zollernalb Dist 1976–2001, also Chair. Christian Democratic Union (CDU) Parl. Group and Head CDU Regional Party Group for Baden-Württemberg; mem. State Senate (Zollernalb Dist) 1981–91; Pres. Baden-Württemberg Asscn of Savings Banks 1991–, German Savings Banks and Giro Asscn, Berlin 2006–; Chair. Supervisory Bd Landesbank Baden-Württemberg (LBBW) –2008; Pres. European Savings Bank Group 2006–; Chair. DekaBank 2006–; Chair. Supervisory Bd Deutsche Sparkassen Leasing AG Man. 2006–, Supervisory Bd Foundation Schloss Neuhardenberg GmbH 2006–, Supervisory Bd Landesbank Berlin Holding AG 2007–; Chair. Bd of Trustees Savings Bank Foundation for Int. Cooperation Asscn 2006–; mem. Bd of Dirs Kreditanstalt für Wiederaufbau; mem. Bd of Gov. Fed. Financial Supervisory Authority (BaFin); Chair. Higher Council of Univ. of the Sparkassen finance group; Dist Chair. German Red Cross; mem. Bd Donors' Asscn for German Science, Bd of Trustees of German Sports Aid Foundation, Bd of Trustees of Cultural Foundation of countries eV, and numerous bds in other social and cultural orgs; Hon. Senator, Albstadt-Ebingen Univ. for Applied Science; Verdienstkreuz am Bande des Verdienstordens der Bundesrepublik Deutschland 1983, Verdienstkreuz 1. Klasse 1988, Großes Verdienstkreuz 1999; AMSEL-Landesverband Prize 2002. *Address:* Deutcher Sparkassen- und Giroverband E.V., Postfach 1429, Simrockstrasse 4, 53004 Bonn, Germany (office). *E-mail:* info@dsgv .de (office). *Website:* www.dsgv.de (office).

HAASS, Christian, Dr rer. nat; German biochemist and academic; *Professor of Neurobiochemistry, Ludwig Maximilians University of Munich;* b. 19 Dec. 1960, Mannheim; ed Univ. of Heidelberg; Postdoctoral Fellow, Center for Neurologic Diseases, Harvard Medical School, Boston, Mass, USA, Asst Prof. 1993–95; Assoc. Prof. of Molecular Biology, Cen. Inst. of Mental Health, Mannheim 1995–99; Prof. of Neurobiochemistry, Dept of Biomedicine I, Ludwig Maximilians Univ. of Munich 1999–, Head Lab. for Alzheimer's and Parkinson's Disease Research, German Center for Neurodegenerative Diseases, Prin. Investigator, Collaborative Research Center SFB 596 Molecular Mechanisms of Neurodegeneration; mem. Center for Integrated Protein Science Munich; Dr hc (Univ. of Zurich) 2010; awards from Heidelberg Soc. for Molecular Biology for diploma thesis 1986, doctoral thesis 1989, Organon Research Award, Award of Heidelberg Acad. of Sciences, Award of German Brain League, Int. Alois Alzheimer Award, Family Hansen Award, Ernst Jung Prize for Medicine 2002, Gottfried Wilhelm Leibniz Prize 2002, Potamkin Prize, American Acad. of Neurology 2002. *Publications:* Molecular Biology of Alzheimer's Disease: Genes and Mechanisms Involved in Amyloid Generation 1998; numerous articles in scientific journals. *Address:* Adolf-Butenandt-Institut, Lehrstuhl für Stoffwechselbiochemie, Ludwig-Maximilians-Universität, Schillerstraße 44, 80336 Munich, Germany (office). *Telephone:* (89) 218075-472 (office). *Fax:* (89) 218075-415 (office). *E-mail:* chaass@med.uni -muenchen.de (office). *Website:* www.med.uni-muenchen.de/haass (office).

HAASS, Richard N., BA, DPhil; American fmr government official and fmr diplomatist; *President, Council on Foreign Relations;* m.; two c.; ed Oberlin Coll., Ohio, Univ. of Oxford, UK; fmr legis. aide, US Senate; various posts in Dept of Defense 1979–80, Dept of State 1981–85, Special Asst to Pres. and Sr Dir for Near East and S Asian Affairs, Nat. Security Council 1989–93; Vice-Pres. and Dir of Foreign Policy Studies, Sydney Stein Jr Chair in Int. Security, Brookings Inst. –2001; Dir of Policy Planning, Dept of State 2001–03, US Co-ordinator for Afghanistan policy; fmr Special Envoy of Pres. George W. Bush to NI Peace Process; fmr Sr Fellow and Dir of Nat. Security Programs, Council on Foreign Relations, Pres. Council on Foreign Relations 2003–; mem. IISS (fmr Research Assoc.), Trilateral Comm.; Sr Assoc., Carnegie Endowment for Int. Peace; fmr Sol. M. Linowitz Visiting Prof. of Int. Studies, Hamilton Coll.; fmr Lecturer in Public Policy, Harvard Univ. Kennedy School of Govt; fmr consultant, NBC News; Presidential Citizen's Medal 1991, Dept of State Distinguished Honor Award 2003. *Publications:* The Reluctant Sheriff: The United States after the Cold War 1998, Economic Sanctions and American Diplomacy 1998, The Bureaucratic Entrepreneur: How to Be Effective in Any Unruly Organization 1998, Intervention: The Use of American Military Force in the Post-Cold War World 1999, The Opportunity: America's Moment to Alter History's Course 2005, War of Necessity, War of Choice: A Memoir of Two Iraq Wars 2009, Foreign Policy Begins at Home: The Case for Putting America's House in Order 2013; frequent contribs to foreign affairs journals. *Address:* Council on Foreign Relations, 58 East 68th Street, New York, NY 10021, USA (office). *Telephone:* (212) 434-9540 (office). *Fax:* (212) 434-9880 (office). *E-mail:* president@cfr.org (office). *Website:* www.cfr.org (office).

HAAVISTO, Heikki Johannes, MSc, LLM; Finnish politician; b. 20 Aug. 1935, Turku; s. of Johan Haavisto and Alli Svensson; m. Maija Rihko 1964; three s.; Head of Dept, Oy Vehnä Ab 1963–66; Sec.-Gen. Cen. Union of Agricultural Producers and Forest Owners in Finland (MTK) 1966–75, Pres. 1976–94; Vice-Pres. Int. Fed. of Agricultural Producers 1977–80, 1986–90, mem. Bd of Dirs 1984–86; mem. Cen. Council of Nordic Farmer Orgs (NBC), Pres. 1977, 1985–87; Chair. Del. of Finn Cooperative Pellervo (Confed. of Finnish Cooperatives) 1979–2000; mem. Admin. Council, Osuuskunta Metsäliitto, Vice-Chair. 1976–82, Pres. 1982–93; Vice-Chair. Admin. Council, OKO (Cen. Union of Cooperative Credit Banks) 1985–93; mem. Bd of Dirs Metsä-Serla Oy 1986–93; Pres. Admin. Council, Raisio Group 1987–96, Pres. Bd of Dirs 1997–2000; mem. Int. Policy Council on Agric. and Trade 1988–2000; Minister for Foreign Affairs 1993–95, for Devt Co-operation 1994–95; three hon. doctorates. *Address:* Hintsantie 2, 21200 Raisio, Finland. *Telephone:* (2) 4383020. *Fax:* (2) 4383499.

HABARUGIRA, Tharcisse; Democratic Republic of the Congo politician; fmr Deputy Minister of Security and Public Order, of Admin of Goma Territory –2006; Minister of Defence 2006–07. *Address:* c/o Ministry of Defence, Demobilization and War Veterans' Affairs, BP 4111, Kinshasa -Gombe, Democratic Republic of the Congo.

HABASHI, Wagdi George, BEng, MEng, PhD, FRSC; Canadian (b. Egyptian) engineer, academic and entrepreneur; *Professor, Department of Mechanical Engineering, McGill University;* b. 29 June 1946, Egypt; s. of Georges Habashi and Iris Banoub; one s. two d.; ed McGill Univ., Montreal, Cornell Univ., USA; Asst Prof., Dept of Mechanical Eng, Concordia Univ., Montreal 1975–79, Assoc. Prof. 1979–84, Prof. 1984–2000; Prof., Dept of Mechanical Eng, McGill Univ. 2000–, also Dir Computational Fluid Dynamics Lab.; Aerodynamics Consultant, Pratt & Whitney Canada 1977–2001, Research Fellow 2000–; Pres. and CEO Newmerical Technologies International 2000–; Ed.-in-Chief, International Journal of Computational Fluid Dynamics; mem. Ordre des ingénieurs du Québec 1975; Fellow, ASME 1996, Canadian Acad. of Eng 2002, Acad. of Science, AIAA 2009; Hon. Prof., Tongji Univ., Shanghai, People's Repub. of China; Chevalier, Ordre nat. du Québec 2012; Queen's Diamond Jubilee Medal 2012; British Asscn Medal for Great Distinction in Mechanical Eng 1967, E.W.R. Steacie Memorial Fellowship, Nat. Sciences and Eng Research Council 1988, Cray Gigaflop Award 1990, Computerworld Smithsonian Award 1991, Corp. Higher Educ. Forum Certificate of Merit for Distinguished Achievement in Furthering Univ.-Industry Research Co-Operation 1992, Pratt & Whitney Canada Tech. Partnership Award 1998, Sr Research Fellow Award, Concordia Univ. 1999, voted amongst the 10 top scientists in Montreal (only engineer) by The Gazette newspaper in its series, Montreal, The Year 2000, Lifetime Achievement Award, Computational Fluid Dynamics Soc. of Canada 2006, Hon. Pioneer Award, Pratt & Whitney Canada 2009, Killam Prize for Eng, Canada Council for the Arts 2009, James C. Floyd Award, Aerospace Industries Asscn of Canada 2010, McCurdy Award, Canadian Aerospace & Space Inst. 2011, Innovation-Inspiration Award 2012, Christophe Pierre Award for Research Excellence, McGill Univ. 2012. *Publications:* selected by Canadian Foundation for Innovation to write 'Essays by Leading Canadian Researchers' 2002; more than 400 publs in refereed scientific journals and at confs. *Address:* CFD Laboratory, Department of Mechanical Engineering, 688 Sherbrooke Street West, Suite 717, Montreal, QC H3A 2S6, Canada (office). *Telephone:* (514) 398-3747 (office). *E-mail:* wagdi.habashi@mcgill.ca (office). *Website:* people.mcgill.ca/wagdi.habashi (office); www.cfdlab.mcgill.ca/wordpress (office).

HABERMAS, Jürgen, DPhil, Habilitation; German academic and writer; *Professor Emeritus of Philosophy, University of Frankfurt;* b. 18 June 1929, Düsseldorf; m. Ute Habermas-Wesselhoeft 1955; one s. two d.; ed Univs of Bonn and Göttingen; Research Asst, Inst. für Soziale Forschung, Frankfurt 1956; Prof. of Philosophy, Univ. of Heidelberg 1961, of Philosophy and Sociology, Univ. of Frankfurt 1964; Dir Max Planck Inst., Starnberg, Munich 1971; Prof. of Philosophy, Univ. of Frankfurt 1983–94, Prof. Emer. 1994–; mem. Academia Europaea; Foreign mem. American Acad. of Arts and Sciences 1984, British Acad. of Science 1994; Hon. DD (New School for Social Research) 1984; hon. degrees from Hebrew Univ. (Jerusalem), Univs of Hamburg, Buenos Aires, Evanston (Northwestern), Utrecht, Athens, Bologna, Paris, Tel-Aviv, Cambridge, Harvard; Hegel Prize 1972, Sigmund Freud Prize 1976, Adorno Prize 1980, Geschwister Scholl Prize 1985, Leibniz Prize 1986, Sonning Prize 1987, Jaspers Prize 1997, Culture Prize of the State of Hesse 1999, Friedenspreis des deutschen Buchhandels 2001, Prince of Asturias Award for Social Science 2003, Kyoto Prize for Philosophy 2004, Holberg Int. Memorial Prize 2005, Bruno Kreisky Prize 2006, Staatspreis des landes Nordheim-Westfalen 2006, Int. Brunet Prize, Pamplona 2008, Ulysses Medal, Dublin 2010, Heinrich Heine Prize 2012, Erasmus Prize 2013. *Publications:* Strukturwandel der Öffentlichkeit 1962, Theorie und Praxis 1963, Erkenntnis und Interesse 1968, Legitimationsprobleme im Spätkapitalismus 1973, Theorie des kommunikativen Handelns 1981, Moralbewüsstsein und Kommunikatives Handeln 1983, Der Philosophische Diskurs ober Moderne 1985, Eine Art Schadensabwicklüng 1987, Nachmetaphysisches Denken 1988, Nachholende Revolution 1990, Texte und Kontexte 1991, Erläuterungen zur Diskursetnik 1991, Faktizität und Geltung 1992, Vergangenheit als Zukunft 1993, Die Normalität einer Berliner Republik 1995, Die Einbeziehung des Anderen 1996, Vom sinnlichen Eindruck zum symbolischen Ausdruck 1997, Die postnationale Konstellation 1998, Wahrheit und Rechtfertigung 1999, Zeit und Übergänge 2001, Kommunikatives Handeln und Detranszendentalisierte Vernunft 2001, Die Zukunft der Menschlichen Natur 2001, Zeitdiagnosen 2003, Der gespaltene Westen 2004, Ach Europa 2008, Philosophische Texte (five vols) 2009, Zür Verfassung Europas 2011, Nachmetaphysisches Denken II 2012. *Address:* Department of Philosophy, University of Frankfurt, Grüneburgplatz 1, 60629 Frankfurt am Main (office); Ringstrasse 8B, 82319 Starnberg, Germany (home). *Telephone:* (8151) 13537 (home). *Fax:* (8151) 13537 (home).

HABGOOD, Baron (Life Peer), cr. 1995, of Calverton in the County of Buckinghamshire; **Rt Rev. and Rt Hon. John Stapylton Habgood,** PC, MA, PhD, DD; British ecclesiastic (retd); b. 23 June 1927, Stony Stratford, Bucks., England; s. of Arthur Henry Habgood and Vera Chetwynd-Stapylton; m. Rosalie Mary Anne Boston 1961; two s. two d.; ed Eton Coll., King's Coll. Cambridge Univ. and Cuddesdon Coll., Oxford; Demonstrator in Pharmacology, Univ. of Cambridge 1950–53; Fellow, King's Coll. Cambridge 1952–55, Hon. Fellow 1984; Curate, St Mary Abbott's Church, Kensington 1954–56; Vice-Prin. Westcott House, Cambridge 1956–62; Rector, St John's Church, Jedburgh, Scotland 1962–67; Prin. Queen's Coll., Birmingham 1967–73; Bishop of Durham 1973–83; Archbishop of York 1983–95; Pres. (UK) Council on Christian Approaches to Defence and Disarmament 1976–95; Chair. WCCs' Int. Hearing on Nuclear Weapons 1981; mem. Council for Science and Society 1975–90, Council for Arms Control 1981–95; Moderator of Church and Soc. Sub-Unit, WCC 1983–90; Chair. UK Xenotransplantation Interim Regulatory Authority 1997–2003; Hon. DD (Durham) 1975, (Cambridge) 1984, (Aberdeen) 1988, (Huron) 1990, (Hull) 1991, (Oxford) 1996, (Manchester) 1996, (London) 2005; Hon. DUniv (York) 1996; Hon. DHL (York, Pa) 1995; Bampton Lecturer, Univ. of Oxford 1999, Gifford Lecturer, Univ. of Aberdeen 2000. *Publications:* Religion and Science 1964, A Working Faith 1980, Church and Nation in a Secular Age 1983, Confessions of a Conservative Liberal 1988, Making Sense 1994, Faith and Uncertainty 1997, Being a Person 1998, Varieties of Unbelief 2000, The Concept of Nature 2002. *Leisure interests:* carpentry, painting in oils. *Address:* 18 The Mount, Malton, N Yorks., YO17 7ND, England (home). *E-mail:* js.habgood@btinternet.com (home).

HABIB, Irfan, MA, DPhil; Indian historian; b. 1931; s. of Mohammad Habib and Sohaila; ed Aligarh Muslim Univ., New College Oxford, UK; Prof. of History, Aligarh Muslim Univ. 1969–91, Dir Centre for the Advanced Study of History

1975–77, 1984–94, Prof. Emer. 2007–; Jt Ed. Cambridge Economic History of India (journal); Radhakrishnan Lecturer, Oxford 1991; Jawaharlal Nehru Fellow 1968; Fellow, British Royal Historical Soc. 1997; Pres. Indian History Congress 1981; Chair. Indian Soc. for Historical Research 1987–93; mem. Indian Inst. of Advanced Studies, Shimla; Hon. DLitt, Banaras Hindu Univ. 2008; Watumull Prize, American Historical Asscn 1982, Padma Bhushan 2005, Muzaffar Ahmad Memorial Prize 2006. *Publications include:* The Agrarian System of Mughal India 1556–1707 1963, An Atlas of the Mughal Empire 1982, Essays in Indian History: Towards a Marxist Perception 1995, The Economic History of Medieval India: A Survey 2001, Confronting Colonialism: Resistance and Modernization Under Haidar Ali and Tipu Sultan 2002, Mauryan India 2004, The Cambridge Economic History of India 2005, Karl Marx on India 2006, Indian Economy, 1858–1914 2006, Medieval India: The Study of a Civilization 2008, Class, Caste and Colony: India from the Mughal Period to the British Raj 2010. *Address:* Badar Bagh, Civil Lines, Aligarh 202 992 (home); c/o Department of History, Aligarh Muslim University, Aligarh 202 002, India (office). *Telephone:* (571) 2705792 (office); (571) 2702620 (home). *Fax:* (571) 2701539.

HABIB, Vice-Adm. Muhammad Farid; Bangladeshi naval officer; *Chief of Naval Staff;* b. 1959, Tangail; joined Bangladesh Navy 1979, commands held include Cdre Commdg BN Flotilla (COMBAN), Cdre Commdg Khulna (COM-KHUL), Naval Admin. Authority Dhaka (Admin Dhaka), Asst Chief of Naval Staff (Personnel), Asst Chief of Naval Staff (Operations), Chief of Naval Staff 2013–. *Address:* Ministry of Defence, Gonobhaban Complex, Sher-i-Bangla Nagar, Dhaka 1207, Bangladesh (office). *Telephone:* (2) 8116955 (office). *E-mail:* modgob@bttb .net.bd (office). *Website:* www.mod.gov.bd (office); www.bdmilitary.com (office).

HABIB, Rafiq M.; Pakistani business executive; *Group Chairman, House of Habib;* Group Chair. House of Habib, includes Agriauto Industries Ltd, AuVitronics Ltd, Habib Insurance Co. Ltd, Indus Motor Co. Ltd, Makro Habib Pakistan Ltd, Metro Habib Cash & Carry Pakistan, Noble Computer Services (Pvt.) Ltd, Shabbir Tiles & Ceramic Ltd, Thal Ltd, Thal Ltd–Corp. Office, Thal Ltd–Eng Divs; Chancellor Habib Univ., Chair. Habib Univ. Foundation; multiple awards for leadership and industry innovation. *Address:* House of Habib, 2nd Floor, Jinnah C.H. Society, Sharea Faisal, Karachi 75350, Pakistan (office). *Telephone:* (21) 3431-2030 (office). *Fax:* (21) 3431-2314 (office). *E-mail:* hoh@hoh .net (office). *Website:* www.hoh.net (office).

HABIB, Randa, MA; Lebanese/French journalist; *Director and Head, Agence France Presse, Jordan;* b. 16 Jan. 1952, Beirut, Lebanon; d. of Farid Habib; m. Adnan Gharaybeh 1973; one s. one d.; ed French Lycée, Rio de Janeiro and Univ. of Beirut; corresp., Agence France Presse (AFP) 1980, Dir and Head of AFP Office, Amman 1987–; corresp., Radio Monte Carlo 1988–2006, columnist in local Jordanian papers, corresp. also for several int. publs and TV; Chair. Foreign Press Club, Jordan; mem. Bd of Dirs Jordan Media Inst.; Gov., Agence France Presse Foundation; mem. Bd Center to Protect Journalists; Chevalier, Ordre nat. du Mérite 2001, Légion d'honneur 2008; Médaille du Travail (France) 2000. *Publications:* Hussein père et fils, 30 années qui ont changé le Moyen-Orient 2007, Hussein and Abdullah Inside the Jordanian Royal Family 2010. *Leisure interests:* reading, swimming, painting. *Address:* Agence France Presse, Jebel Amman, 2nd Circle, PO Box 3340, Amman 11181, Jordan (office). *Telephone:* (6) 4642976 (office). *Fax:* (6) 4654680 (office). *E-mail:* randa.habib@afp.com (office). *Website:* www.afp.com (office).

HABIBIE, Bacharuddin Jusuf, DEng; Indonesian aviation engineer, politician and fmr head of state; b. 25 June 1936, Pare-Pare, South Sulawesi; m. H. Hasri Ainun Besari 1962 (died 2010); two s.; ed Bandung Inst. of Tech., Technische Hochschule, Aachen; Head of Research at Messerschmitt-Boelkow-Blohm, Hamburg, Germany 1966; Govt Adviser 1976; Chair., CEO, Pres. Indonesian State Aircraft Industry 1976–98; Minister of State for Research and Tech. 1978–98; Head of Agency for Tech. Evaluation and Application 1978–98; Chair., CEO, Pres. Indonesian Shipbuilding Industry 1978–98; Chair. Batam Industrial Devt 1978–98; Chair. Team for Defence Security Industrial Devt 1980–99; mem. Indonesian Parl. 1982–99; Chair., CEO, Pres. Small Arms and Munitions Industry 1983–98; Chair. Nat. Research Council 1984–; Vice-Chair. Bd of Patrons, Indonesian Strategic Industries 1988–; Chair. Agency for Strategic Industries 1989–98; Head of Indonesian Muslim Intellectuals Asscn 1990–; Vice-Pres. of Indonesia March–May 1998, Pres. 1998–99; Founder and Chair. Indonesian Aeronautics and Astronautics Inst.; Founder and Chair. Bd of Trustees, Habibie Center; mem. Royal Swedish Acad. of Eng Sciences, Acad. Nat. de l'Air et de l'Espace (France); Fellow, Royal Aeronautical Soc.; Gran Cruz del Mérito Aeronáutico con Distintivo Blanco (Spain) 1980, Grosses Bundesverdienstkreuz 1980, Dwidya Sistha Medal 1982, Grand Cross of the Order of Orange Nassau 1983, Grand Officier, Ordre nat. du Mérite; Dr hc (Univ. of Indonesia) 2010. *Publications:* Detik-Detik Yang Menentukan: Jalan Panjang Indonesia Menuju Demokrasi 2006; numerous scientific and tech. papers. *Address:* c/o Habibie Centre, Jl. Kemang Selatan No. 98, South Jakarta 12560, Indonesia. *Telephone:* (21) 7817211. *Fax:* (21) 7817212. *Website:* www.habibiecenter.or.id.

HABICHT, Werner, DPhil; German academic; *Professor Emeritus of English, University of Würzburg;* b. 29 Jan. 1930, Schweinfurt; s. of Wilhelm Habicht and Magda Habicht (née Müller); ed Univ. of Munich, Johns Hopkins Univ., Baltimore, USA, Univ. of Paris, France; Asst, Freie Universität, Berlin 1957–60, Univ. of Munich 1960–65; Prof. of English, Univ. of Heidelberg 1966–70, Univ. of Bonn 1970–78, Univ. of Würzburg 1978–95, Prof. Emer. 1995–; Visiting Prof., Univ. of Tex. at Austin 1981, Univ. of Colo. Boulder 1987, Ohio State Univ., Columbus 1988, Univ. of Cyprus 1995–96; mem. Akad. der Wissenschaften und der Literatur, Mainz, Bayerische Akad. der Wissenschaften; Pres. Deutsche Shakespeare-Gesellschaft West 1976–88, Vice-Pres. 1988–93; Hon. Vice-Pres. Int. Shakespeare Asscn 1996–. *Publications include:* Die Gebärde in englischen Dichtungen des Mittelalters 1959, Studien zur Dramenform vor Shakespeare 1968, Shakespeare and the German Imagination 1994, English and American Studies in German (ed.) 1968–82, Jahrbuch, Deutsche Shakespeare-Gesellschaft West (ed.) 1982–95, Literatur Brockhaus (three vols) (co-ed.) 1988; numerous articles on English literature and drama. *Address:* Allerseeweg 14, 97204 Höchberg, Germany (home). *Telephone:* (931) 49267 (home). *E-mail:* whabicht@t-online.de.

HABILA, Helon; Nigerian author and academic; *Faculty Member, Graduate Creative Writing Program, Department of English, George Mason University;* b. 17 Nov. 1967, Kaltungo, Gombe State; m. Susan Habila; three c.; ed Univ. of Jos, Univ. of East Anglia, UK; Lecturer in English and Literature, Fed. Polytechnic, Bauchi 1997–99; fmr contrib. to Hints magazine, Lagos; fmr Arts Ed. Vanguard (newspaper), Lagos; African Writing Fellow, Univ. of East Anglia, UK 2002–04; Chinua Achebe Fellow of Africana Global Studies, Bard Coll., New York, USA 2005–06; Faculty mem. Dept of English, Grad. Creative Writing Program, George Mason Univ., USA 2007–; Contributing Ed. Virginia Quarterly Review; First Prize, MUSON Festival Poetry Competition (for poem Another Age) 2000, Caine Prize for African Writing, UK (for short story Love Poems) 2001, Emily Balch Prize (for short story Hotel Malogo) 2008. *Publications:* Mai Kaltungo (biog.) 1997, Prison Stories (short stories) 2000, Waiting for an Angel (Commonwealth Prize for Best First Book, African Region 2003) 2001, Measuring Time (Virginia Library Foundation Fiction Prize 2008) 2007, Oil on Water 2010; ed. Granta Book of the African Short Story 2011; co-ed. New Writing 14 (British Council Anthology), Miracles, Dreams, and Jazz; short stories and poems in anthologies. *Address:* Graduate Creative Writing Program, Department of English, George Mason University, 4400 University Drive, MSN 3E4, Fairfax, VA 22030, USA (office); c/o DGA Ltd, 55 Monmouth Street, London, WC2H 9DG, England (office). *Telephone:* (703) 993-9553 (office); (20) 7240-9992 (office). *E-mail:* hngalaba@gmu.edu (office); david@davidgodwinassociates.co.uk (office). *Website:* english.gmu.edu (office); www.helonhabila.com; www.helonhabila.com (office). *Fax:* (20) 7395-6110 (office).

HABRAKEN, Nicolaas John; Dutch architect; *Professor Emeritus of Architecture, Massachusetts Institute of Technology;* b. 29 Oct. 1928, Bandung, Indonesia; s. of the late J. W. L. Habraken and J. L. S. Heyting; m. E. Marleen van Hall 1958; one s. one d.; ed Delft Tech. Univ.; architect, Lucas & Niemeyer (architects), Voorburg 1961–65; Dir Stichting Architecten Research, Voorburg 1965–66, Eindhoven 1966–75; Prof. and First Chair. Dept of Architecture, Eindhoven Tech. Univ. 1966–70, Prof. of Architecture 1966–75; Head, Dept of Architecture, MIT, USA 1975–81, Prof. of Architecture 1975–89, Prof. Emer. 1989–; Partner, Infill Systems, Delft 1986–99; Hon. mem. Architectural Inst. of Japan 1994; Kt, Order of the Dutch Lion 2003; Dr hc (Tech. Univ. Eindhoven) 2005; David Roell Prize 1979, King Fahd Award for Design and Research in Islamic Architecture 1985, ACSA Creative Achievement Award 1989, BKVB Nat. Architecture Award 1996, BNA (Dutch Architects' Asscn) Kubus Award of Merit 2003. *Publications include:* Supports: An Alternative to Mass Housing 1962, Transformations of the Site 1983, The Appearance of the Form 1985, The Structure of the Ordinary 1998, Palladio's Children 2005, Conversations with Form (co-author) 2014; research reports and numerous articles. *Address:* 63 Wildernislaan, 7313 BD Apeldoorn, Netherlands (home). *E-mail:* habraken@xs4all.nl (office). *Website:* www.habraken.com (office).

HABRÉ, Hissène; Chadian politician and fmr head of state; b. 1942, Faya-Largeau; formerly one of the leaders of the Front de Libération Nationale du Tchad (FROLINAT); head of Northern Armed Forces Command Council –1977; Leader of Forces Armées du Nord 1977; negotiated with Govt of Brig.-Gen. Félix Malloum 1978; Prime Minister 1978–79, resgnd after Kano peace agreement with FROLINAT forces led by Goukouni Oueddei March 1979; Minister of State for Defence and War Veterans in Provisional Govt April–May 1979; Minister of Defence 1979 (in conflict with Goukouni Oueddei in civil war, reported in exile 1980); Minister of Nat. Defence, Veterans and War Victims 1986–90; Pres. of Chad June–Oct. 1982, Pres. 1982–90 (ousted in coup); living in Cameroon 1990, in Senegal 1999–; indicted for complicity in torture by Senegalese Court, Feb. 2000 (case later dismissed), then under investigation by a Belgian court Feb. 2002; sentenced to death in absentia by Chadian court for war crimes and crimes against humanity 2008.

HACHETTE, Jean-Louis, LenD; French publisher; b. 30 June 1925, Paris; s. of Louis and Blanche (née Darbou) Hachette; m. Y. de Bouillé 1954; one s. two d.; ed Collège Stanislas, Paris and Faculté de Droit, Paris; joined Librairie Hachette (f. by great-grandfather in 1826) 1946 (now Hachette Livre); entire career spent with Librairie Hachette, Admin. Dir 1971–; Pres. Librairie Générale Française 1954–. *Leisure interests:* polo, golf, skiing.

HACKETT, Grant George, BCom, BL; Australian swimmer; b. 9 May 1980, Southport, Queensland; s. of Neville Hackett and Margaret Hackett; m. Candice Alley 2007; ed Merrimac State High School, Bond Univ., Gold Coast; mem. Miami Swim Club; Olympic Games, Sydney 2000: Gold Medal 1500m freestyle, 4×200m freestyle relay (heat swim); World Championships, Fukuoka 2001: Gold Medal 4×200m freestyle relay (world record), 1500m freestyle (world record time of 14:34.56), Silver Medal 400m freestyle, 800m freestyle; Commonwealth Games, Manchester 2002: Gold Medal 1500m freestyle, 4×200m freestyle relay, 4×100m freestyle relay (heat swim), Silver Medal 800m freestyle, 400m freestyle; Pan Pacific Games 2002: Gold Medal 1500m freestyle, 800m freestyle, 4×200m freestyle relay, 4×100m freestyle relay, Silver Medal 400m freestyle, 200m freestyle; World Championships, Barcelona 2003: Gold Medal 1500m freestyle, 800m freestyle, 4×200m freestyle relay, Silver Medal 400m freestyle; Olympic Games, Athens 2004: Gold Medal 1500m freestyle (Olympic record), Silver Medal 400m freestyle, 4×200m freestyle relay; Telstra Australian Swimming Championships 2005: Gold Medal 1500m freestyle, 800m freestyle, 400m freestyle, 200m freestyle; World Championships, Montreal 2005: Gold Medal 1500m freestyle, 800m freestyle (world record time of 7:38.65), 400m freestyle, Silver Medal 200m freestyle; World Championships, Melbourne 2007: Bronze Medal 400m freestyle; Olympic Games, Beijing 2008: Silver Medal 1500m freestyle (Olympic record, heat swim), Bronze Medal 4×200m freestyle relay; unbeaten at 1500m freestyle 1996–2007, first to swim under 15 minutes for the distance; won his first Nat. Championship 10km Open Water race 2007; Order of Australia Medal 2001; Australian Swimming Male Distance Swimmer of the Year 1998, 2002, 2003, 2004, Australian Sports Medal 2000, Centenary Medal 2000, Goodwill Games Ambassador 2001, Swimmer of the Year 2003, Telstra People's Choice Award 2004, Telstra Swimmer of the Year (with Ian Thorpe) 2004, Australian Export Awards Special Achievement Award 2004, World Swimmer of the Year 2005, Pacific Rim Swimmer of the Year 2005, Telstra Swimmer of the Year 2005, Telstra Swimmers' Swimmer of the Year 2005, Telstra Middle and Distance Swimmer of the Year 2005, 'The Don' Award, Sport Australia Hall of Fame 2005, Telstra Dolphins

Australian Swim Team Captain 2005. *Leisure interests:* surfing, fast cars, playing drums and guitar. *Address:* c/o Lisa Stallard, International Quarterback Pty Ltd, 24/76 Doggett Street, Newstead, Queensland 4006, Australia (office). *Telephone:* (7) 3252-2311 (office). *Fax:* (7) 3252-3411 (office). *E-mail:* lisa@iqsport.com.au (office). *Website:* www.iqsport.com.au (office).

HACKING, Ian MacDougall, CC, PhD, FRSC, FBA; Canadian academic; *Professor Emeritus, Collège de France;* b. 18 Feb. 1936, Vancouver, BC; s. of Harold Eldridge Hacking and Margaret Elinore MacDougall; m. 1st Laura Anne Leach 1962; m. 2nd Judith Polsky Baker 1983; one s. two d.; ed Univ. of British Columbia, Univ. of Cambridge, UK; Asst then Assoc. Prof., Univ. of British Columbia 1964–69; Univ. Lecturer in Philosophy, Univ. of Cambridge and Fellow of Peterhouse 1969–74; Prof., then Henry Waldgrave Stuart Prof. of Philosophy, Stanford Univ. 1975–82; Prof., Univ. of Toronto 1983–2003, Univ. Prof. 1991–2003, Prof. Emer. 2003–; Prof., Chair of Philosophy and History of Scientific Concepts Collège de France, Paris 2000–06, Prof. Emer. 2006–; Fellow American Acad. of Arts and Sciences 1991; Hon. Fellow, Trinity Coll., Cambridge 2000, Peterhouse, Cambridge 2002; Hon. LLD (Univ. of British Columbia) 2001, (McMaster Univ.) 2008, (Toronto) 2010; Hon. PhD (Univ. of Córdoba, Argentina) 2007; Molson Prize, Canada Council 2001, Killam Prize, Canada Council 2002, Holberg Int. Memorial Prize 2009. *Publications:* Logic of Statistical Inference 1965, Why Does Language Matter to Philosophy? 1975, The Emergence of Probability 1975, Representing and Intervening 1983, The Taming of Chance 1991, Le plus pur nominalisme 1993, Rewriting the Soul: Multiple Personality and the Sciences of Memory 1995, Mad Travelers 1998, The Social Construction of What? 1999, Probability and Inductive Logic 2001, Historical Ontology 2002. *Leisure interests:* walking, canoeing. *Address:* Philosophy Department, University of Toronto, 170 St George Street, Toronto, ON M5R 2M8, Canada (office). *E-mail:* ian.hacking@college-de-france.fr (office). *Website:* www.ianhacking.com.

HACKMAN, Gene; American actor; b. 30 Jan. 1930, San Bernardino, Calif.; s. of Eugene Ezra Hackman; m. 1st Fay Maltese 1956 (divorced 1985); m. 2nd Betsy Arakawa; one s. two d.; studied acting at the Pasadena Playhouse; Acad. Award for Best Actor, New York Film Critics' Award, Golden Globe Award, British Acad. Award, The French Connection, British Acad. Award, The Poseidon Adventure, Cannes Film Festival Award, Scarecrow, Nat. Review Bd Award, Mississippi Burning 1988, Berlin Film Award 1989, Acad. Award, The Unforgiven 1993, Cecil B. DeMille Award, Golden Globes 2003. *Films include:* Lilith 1964, Hawaii 1966, Banning 1967, Bonnie and Clyde 1967, The Split 1968, Downhill Racer 1969, I Never Sang For My Father 1969, The Gypsy Moths 1969, Marooned 1970, The Hunting Party 1971, The French Connection 1971, The Poseidon Adventure 1972, The Conversation 1973, Scarecrow 1973, Zandy's Bride 1974, Young Frankenstein 1974, The French Connection II 1975, Lucky Lady 1975, Night Moves 1976, Domino Principle 1977, Superman 1978, Superman II 1980, All Night Long 1980, Target 1985, Twice in a Lifetime 1985, Power 1985, Bat 21, Superman IV 1987, No Way Out 1987, Another Woman 1988, Mississippi Burning 1988, The Package 1989, The Von Metz Incident 1989, Loose Connections 1989, Full Moon in Blue Water 1989, Postcards from the Edge 1989, Class Action 1989, Loose Canons 1990, Narrow Margin 1990, Necessary Roughness 1991, Company Business 1991, The William Munny Killings 1991, The Unforgiven 1992, The Firm 1992, Geronimo, Wyatt Earp 1994, Crimson Tide, The Quick and the Dead 1995, Get Shorty, Birds of a Feather, Extreme Measures 1996, The Chamber 1996, Absolute Power 1996, Twilight 1998, Enemy of the State 1998, Under Suspicion 2000, Heist 2001, The Royal Tenenbaums (Golden Globe for Best Actor in a Musical or Comedy) 2001, Runaway Jury 2003, Welcome to Mooseport 2004. *Stage plays include:* Children From Their Games 1963, Cass Henderson in Any Wednesday 1964, Poor Richard, 1964, Death and the Maiden 1992. *Television includes:* many guest appearances on US series; also My Father, My Mother, CBS Playhouse 1968 and Shadow on the Land 1971, Under Suspicion 1999. *Publication:* Wake of the Perdido Star (with David Lenihan) 2000, Justice for None (co-author) 2004, Escape from Andersonville (co-author) 2009. *Address:* c/o Fred Specktor, Creative Artists Agency, 9830 Wilshire Boulevard, Beverly Hills, CA 90212; c/o Barry Haldeman, 1900 Avenue of the Stars, Suite 2000, Los Angeles, CA 90067, USA.

HACKNEY, Roderick (Rod) Peter, PhD, RIBA; British architect; *Managing Director, Rod Hackney and Associates Limited;* b. 3 March 1942, Liverpool, England; s. of William Hackney and Rose Hackney (née Morris); m. Christine Thornton 1964; one s.; ed John Bright's Grammar School, Llandudno, School of Architecture, Univ. of Manchester; Job Architect, Expo '67, Montreal, for monorail stations 1967; Housing Architect for Libyan Govt, Tripoli 1967–68; Asst to Arne Jacobsen, working on Kuwait Cen. Bank, Copenhagen 1968–71; est. practice of Rod Hackney Architect, Macclesfield 1972, architectural practices in Birmingham, Leicester, Belfast, Cleator Moor, Workington, Carlisle, Millom, Clitheroe, Manchester, Stirling, Burnley, Chesterfield and Stoke on Trent 1975–88, Man. Dir Rod Hackney and Assocs Ltd; Jt Dir with Tia Kansara, Kansara Hackney Ltd 2009–; Council mem. RIBA, including Vice-Pres. for Public Affairs and Vice-Pres. for Overseas Affairs 1978–84, Pres. 1987–89, mem. of Council 1991–, Vice-Pres. Int. Affairs 1992–94, Hon. Librarian 1998–2001; Council mem. Int. Union of Architects 1981–85, 1991–, Pres. 1987–90; Patron Llandudno Museum and Art Gallery 1988–2000; Pres. Snowdonia Nat. Park Soc. 1987–2003; Pres. North Wales Centre of The Nat. Trust 1990–2009; mem. Editorial Bd, UIA Journal of Architectural Theory and Criticism; Jury mem. Cembureau Award for Low Rise Housing in France 1982, for Prix Int. d'Architecture de l'Institut Nat. du Logement 1983; Pres. Young Architects Forum, Sofia 1985, Building Communities (Int. Community Architecture Conf.), London 1986; presentation of case for Int. Year of Shelter for the Homeless to all four party confs 1986; Chair. Times/RIBA Community Enterprise Scheme 1985–89, Trustees of Inner City Trust 1986–97, British Architecture Library Trust 1999–2001; Special Prof. in Architecture, Univ. of Nottingham 1987–91; Int. Adviser, Univ. of Manchester School of Architecture Centre for Int. Architectural Studies 1992–2000; adviser on regeneration and inner city problems in Sweden, Italy, UAE, Germany, Denmark, Libya, Canada and USA 1990–; consultant, World Architecture Review Agency 1992–; Adviser, Centre for Human Settlements Int. 1994–, Habitat Centre News Journal, India 1996; Chair. UN Habitat Award 2004–05, UN Habitat Awards, UAE 2004; Jt Chair., with Tia Kansara, Sustainability for Life 2009–; mem. Chartered Inst. of Building 1987–, Assc'n of Planning Supervisors 1996–2006; attained registration for BSI ISO9001 1996; Adviser, UN Int. Council for Caring Communities 1995–,

World Habitat Awards, Social Housing Foundation, Coalville, UK 2003–; RIBA Sr Conservation Architect 2011–; Hon. FAIA; Hon. Fellow, Fed. de Colegios de Arquitectos de la República Mexicana, United Architects of the Philippines, Royal Architectural Inst. of Canada, Indian Inst. of Architects, Architectural Soc. of China; Hon. Fellow, nat. architectural soc. in Spain; Hon. DLitt (Keele) 1989; Dept of Environment Good Design in Housing Award 1975, 1980, First Prize, for St Ann's Hospice, Manchester 1976, Prix Int. d'Architecture de l'Institut Nat. du Logement 1979–80, RICS/Times Conservation Award 1980, Civic Trust Award of Commendation 1980, 1981, 1984, Sir Robert Matthews Award (Honourable Mention), Int. Union of Architects 1981, Manchester Soc. of Architects Pres.'s Award 1982, Otis Award 1982, Gold Medal, Bulgarian Inst. of Architects 1983, Gold Medal, Young Architect of the Year, Sofia 1983, Grand Medal of Federación de Colegios de Arquitectos (Mexico) 1986, Commendation, Business Enterprise Award for Housing 1993, Citation for World Habitat Awards 1996, Stone Award 1996. *Plays:* Good Golly Miss Molly, Augustus Welby Northmore Pugin versus Charles Barry. *Films:* The Hackney Way, Tomorrow's World – Rod Hackney Community and Sustainability. *Dance:* Walking Towards the Hackney Way, It's a Climb, The Architect and the Child, Ganbappe Iwaki with Tia Kansara. *Musicals:* Good Golly Miss Molly – Sustainability and Community, The Child is the Architect, with G. Uis (Italy). *Radio:* panellist on Any Questions (BBC Radio 4), contrib. to Woman's Hour (BBC Radio 2), Today (BBC Radio 4), Newsnight (BBC Radio 4). *Television:* Consultant to Chapman Clarke Films' Forever England, Central TV 1995; TV features: Build Yourself a House 1974, Community Architecture (RAI, Italy) 1977, BBC Omnibus 1987. *Publications:* Highfield Hall, A Community Project 1982, The Good, the Bad and the Ugly 1990, Good Golly Miss Molly (musical play) 1991. *Leisure interests:* outdoor pursuits, walking, fossils, geology, travelling, ballooning, looking at buildings, talking at conferences, go-carting, painting, writing. *Address:* Rod Hackney and Assocs Ltd, St Peter's House, Windmill Street, Macclesfield, Cheshire, SK11 7HS (office); Kansara Hackney Ltd, St Peter's House, Windmill Street, Macclesfield, Cheshire, SK11 7HS, England (office). *Telephone:* (1625) 431792 (Rod Hackney and Assocs) (office); (1625) 431792 (Kansara Hackney) (office). *E-mail:* roderick.hackney@gmail.com (office); kansarahackney@gmail.com (office). *Website:* www.kansarahackney.com (office).

HACON, Christopher, BA, MS, PhD; American (b. British) mathematician and academic; *Professor of Mathematics, University of Utah;* b. 14 Feb. 1970, Manchester; m.; two s. one d.; ed Univ. of Pisa, Italy, Univ. of California, Los Angeles; Research Fellowship, CNR 1998; Math. Instructor, Univ. of Utah 1998–2000, Asst Prof. 2002–05, Assoc. Prof. 2005–08, Prof. 2008–; Asst Prof., Univ. of California, Riverside 2000–02; Sloan Fellowship 2003, American Math. Soc. Centennial Fellowship 2006; Clay Research Award, Clay Math. Inst. 2007, Cole Prize in Algebra (jtly), American Math. Soc. 2009. *Publications:* more than 40 papers in professional journals. *Address:* JWB 325, Department of Mathematics, University of Utah, 155 South 1400 East, Salt Lake City, UT 84112-0090, USA (office). *Telephone:* (801) 581-7429 (office). *Fax:* (801) 581-4148 (office). *E-mail:* hacon@math.utah.edu (office). *Website:* www.math.utah.edu (office).

HADAWAL, Khan Afzal, BA, LLB, MA, MSc; Afghan banker; *First Deputy Governor, Da Afghanistan Bank;* ed Int. Islamic Univ., Islamabad, Univ. Coll. London, UK; Project Devt Officer, Sanayee Devt Foundation, Kabul June–Aug. 2001; Legal Consultant, Islamic Foundation for Rehabilitation of Afghanistan Jan.–March 2002; Legal Adviser, Counter Narcotic Directorate, Nat. Security Council 2002; Head of Licensing and Regulations, Bearing Point Inc., USAID Da Afghanistan Bank (Cen. Bank) in Reformation Project 2002–03, Head of Legis. and Regulatory Section, Bearing Point Inc., USAID Da Afghanistan Bank Reformation Project 2003–05, Adviser to Gov. and Sec. Gen. Supreme Council of Da Afghanistan Bank 2005–09, Acting Gov. Da Afghanistan Bank –2009, First Deputy Gov. 2011–; Pres. and CEO Bank-e-Millie Afghan 2009–11; participated in numerous nat. and int. confs and headed several dels of Afghanistan. *Achievements include:* played key role in establishment of Financial Intelligent Unit in Afghanistan and in developing the legal framework for the country's banking sector. *Address:* Da Afghanistan Bank, Ibne Sina Wat, Kabul, Afghanistan (office). *Telephone:* (20) 2100302 (office). *Fax:* (20) 2100305 (office). *E-mail:* info@centralbank.gov.af (office); khan.afzal@centralbank.gov.af (office). *Website:* www .centralbank.gov.af (office).

HADDAD, Fawwaz, LLB; Syrian writer; b. 1947, Damascus; ed Univ. of Damascus. *Publications:* novels: Mosaic, Damascus '39 1991, Teatro 1949 1994, Al-Risala al-Akhira (trans. as The Last Letter) 1994, Surat al-Rawee (trans. as The Image of the Narrator) 1998, Al-Walad al-Jahel (trans. as The Ignorant Child) 2000, Al-Daghina wa al-Hawa (trans. as Rancour and Affection) 2001, Mersal al-Gharam (trans. as The Love Messenger) 2004, Mashhad Aber (trans. as A Fleeting Scene) 2007, Al-Mutarjim Al-Khayn (trans. as The Unfaithful Translator) 2008, Azef Munfared 'ala al-Piano (trans. as A Solo Performance on the Piano) 2009, God's Soldiers 2010. *Address:* c/o Riad El-Rayyes Books, Sanayeh, Union Building, Beirut, Lebanon (office). *E-mail:* info@elrayyesbooks.com (office). *Website:* www .elrayyesbooks.com (office).

HADDAD-ADEL, Gholam-Ali, MSc, PhD; Iranian politician; b. 1945, Tehran; m.; four c.; ed Univs of Tehran and Shiraz; Prof. of Literature and Philosophy, Univ. of Tehran; fmr Deputy Minister of Educ. and Training, of Culture and Islamic Guidance; fmr Exec. Dir Islamic Encyclopaedia Foundation; Head, Iranian Acad. of Persian Language and Literature –2004; elected to Majilis-e-Shura-e Islami (Parl.) for Tehran 2004–, Head, Islamic Iran Developers' Council (Etelat-e Abadgaran-e Iran-e Islami) in Parl. 2004–, Speaker, Majilis-e-Shura-e Islami 2004–08; mem. Supreme Cultural Revolutionary Council, Iranian Acad. of Persian Language and Literature, Expediency Discernment Council; helped start nat. scientific olympiads in Iran. *Address:* c/o Majlis-e-Shura-e Islami (Parliament), Tehran, Iran. *E-mail:* info@abadgaran.ir. *Website:* www.abadgaran.ir.

HADDON, Mark, MA; British writer and illustrator; b. 1962, Northampton; m. Sos Eltis; one s.; ed Merton Coll., Oxford, Edinburgh Univ.; positions at Mencap and other charity orgs; illustrator and cartoonist; painter; television work. *Screenwriting:* Microsoap (Royal Television Soc. Best Children's Drama), episodes of Starstreet, Fungus and the Bogeyman (adaptation). *Publications:* fiction: Gilbert's Gobstopper 1988, A Narrow Escape for Princess Sharon 1989, Toni and the Tomato Soup 1989, Agent Z Meets the Masked Crusader 1993, Gridzbi

Spudvetch! 1993, In the Garden 1994, On Holiday (aka On Vacation) 1994, At Home 1994, At Playgroup 1994, Titch Johnson 1994, Agent Z Goes Wild 1994, Agent Z and the Penguin from Mars 1995, Real Porky Philips 1995, The Sea of Tranquillity 1996, Secret Agent Handbook 1999, Ocean Star Express 2001, Agent Z and the Killer Bananas 2001, The Ice Bear's Cave 2002, The Curious Incident of the Dog in the Night Time (Booktrust Teenage Prize 2003, Guardian Children's Fiction Prize 2003, South Bank Show Best Book Prize 2004, Whitbread Best Novel and Book of the Year 2004, Commonwealth Writers Prize for best first book 2004, Soc. of Authors McKitterick Prize 2004, WHSmith Children's Book of the Year 2004, Waterstone's Literary Fiction award 2004) 2003, A Spot of Bother 2006, The Red House 2012; poetry: The Talking Horse and the Sad Girl and the Village Under the Sea 2005. *Address:* 4 Farndon Road, Oxford, OX2 6RS, England. *Website:* www.markhaddon.com.

HADI, Abd ar-Rabbuh Mansur al-; Yemeni politician, army officer and head of state; *President;* b. 1945, Al-Wadhee'a Region, Governorate of Abyan; m.; three s. two d.; ed Supreme Acad. of Nasser, Egypt, Sandhurst Mil. Acad., UK, Frunze Acad., fmr USSR; mem. staff, Armoured Brigades, Mil. Acad.; Dir of Combat Training, of Supply and Provisions; Deputy Chief of Staff, Supply and Provisions; apptd Adviser to Presidential Council 1990; Minister of Defence May–Oct. 1994; Vice-Pres. 1994–2012, acting Pres. 4 June–23 Sept. 2011, 23 Nov. 2011–24 Feb. 2012, Pres. of Yemen 25 Feb. 2012–; rank of Gen. 1994, Lt-Gen. 1997, currently Field Marshall; mem. General People's Congress, currently Vice-Chair.; Order of the First Grade Badge 1995; numerous medals including Medal of Honour of Mil. Service 1980. *Leisure interests:* reading, current affairs, public folklore, local and classical music, swimming. *Address:* Office of the President, San'a, Yemen (office). *Telephone:* (1) 272283. *Fax:* (1) 252803.

HADID, Dame Zaha, DBE, CBE; Iraqi architect; b. 31 Oct. 1950, Baghdad; ed American Univ. of Beirut, Architectural Asscn, London; fmr Partner, Office for Metropolitan Architecture; taught at Architectural Asscn, led her own studio –1987; Kenzo Tange Chair, Grad. School of Design, Harvard Univ. 1994; Sullivan Prof., Univ. of Chicago School of Architecture 1997; Guest Prof., Hochschüle für Bildende Künste, Hamburg 1997, Knolton School of Architecture, Ohio, Masters Studio, Columbia Univ., New York; Eero Saarinen Visiting Prof. of Architectural Design, Yale Univ., New Haven, CT 2002; currently Prof., Univ. of Applied Arts, Vienna; won competition for The Peak leisure complex, Hong Kong 1982 (project later cancelled); designed restaurant interior, Sapporo 1991 (first completed work); other winning designs include Kurfürstendamm, Berlin 1986, Düsseldorf Art and Media Centre 1992–93, Cardiff Bay Opera House, Wales 1994, Thames Water/ Royal Acad. Habitable Bridge, London 1996, Univ. of North London Holloway Road Bridge 1998, Wolfsburg Science Centre 2000, Maritime Ferry Terminal in Salerno 2000, Placa de les Artes in Barcelona 2001, One-north Masterplan for Singapore's Science Hub 2001, Ordrupgaard Museum Extension, Copenhagen 2001, Price Tower Art Center, Bartlesville, USA 2002, Departement de l'Herault Culture Sport Building, Montpellier, France 2003, High Speed Rail Station Napoli-Afragola, Naples 2003, masterplan for Beijing's Soho City, China 2003; designed British pavilion at Venice Biennale 2000; works included in perm. collections of MoMA, New York, MoMA, San Francisco, Deutsches Architektur Museum, Frankfurt; current projects include: public square and cinema complex, Barcelona, masterplan for Bilbao's Zorrozaurre dist, housing project in Florence, design for hotel in Madrid, social housing project 'Spittelau Viaduct', Vienna, major bridge structure in Abu Dhabi, Ice and Snow Installation, Lapland, Grand Théatre de Rabat, Morocco; Hon. FAIA 2000; Hon. mem. American Acad. of Arts and Letters 2000, Bund Deutsches Architekten 1998; Architectural Asscn Diploma Prize 1977, Gold Medal for Architectural Design 1982, RIBA Awards for Mind Zone, Millennium Dome 2000, AIA UK Chapter and Red Dot Awards for Terminus Honheim-Nord, Strasbourg 2002, Austrian State Architecture Prize and Tyrolian Architecture Award for Bergisel Ski Jump, Innsbruck 2002, Mies van der Rohe Award for Terminus Honheim-Nord, Strasbourg 2003, Pritzker Architecture Prize 2004, ranked by Forbes magazine amongst 100 Most Powerful Women (68th) 2007, (69th) 2008, Praemium Imperiale 2009, Stirling Prize 2010, ranked by Arabian Business amongst the Power 500: The Worlds's Most Influential Arabs (50th) 2011, (79th) 2012. *Major works include:* Vitra Fire Station, Germany 1991, LFone pavilion, Weil am Rhein, Germany 1993–99, housing project for IBA-Block 2, Berlin 1993, Mind Zone in Millennium Dome, Greenwich, London 1999, Tram Station and Car Park, Strasbourg 2001, Bergisel Ski Jump, Austria 2002, Lois & Richard Rosenthal Center for Contemporary Art, Cincinnati 2003, BMW Central Building, Leipzig 2005, Phaeno Science Center 2005, Ordrupgaard Museum Extension, Copenhagen 2005, Spittelau Viaducts Housing 2006, Maggie's Centre, Kirkcaldy 2006, E. Lopez de Heredia Wine Pavilion, Spain 2006, Nordpark Railway Stations, Innsbruck 2007, Chanel Mobile Art Pavilion 2008–10, Zaragoza Bridge Pavilion 2008, Neil Barrett Flagship Shop, Tokyo 2008, JS Bach Chamber Music Hall, Manchester 2009, Burnham Pavilion, Chicago 2009, Maxxi, Museum of XXI Century Arts, Rome 2009, Guangzhou Opera House, People's Repub. of China 2010, London Aquatics Centre 2011. *Publications include:* Zaha Hadid: The Complete Buildings and Projects 1998, Zaha Hadid, Opere e progetti 2002, Zaha Hadid Architektur 2003; numerous articles and monographs. *Address:* Studio 9, 10 Bowling Green Lane, London, EC1R 0BD, England (office). *Telephone:* (20) 7253-5147 (office). *Fax:* (20) 7251-8322 (office). *E-mail:* press@zaha-hadid.com (office). *Website:* www.zaha-hadid.com (office).

HADLEE, Sir Richard John, Kt, MBE; New Zealand fmr professional cricketer; *Director, New Zealand Cricket;* b. 3 July 1951, St Albans, Christchurch; s. of W. A. Hadlee (New Zealand cricketer); m. Dianne Hadlee; ed Christchurch Boys High School; middle-order left-hand batsman, right-arm fast-medium bowler; played for Canterbury 1971–72 to 1988–89, NZ 1972–90, Nottinghamshire 1978–87, Tasmania 1979–80; played in 86 Tests 1972/73–90, scoring 3,124 runs (average 27.16, highest score 151 not out) and taking then world record 431 wickets (average 22.29); first to take 400 Test wickets (at Christchurch in Feb. 1990 in his 79th Test); took five or more wickets in an innings a record 36 times in Tests; highest Test score 151 against Sri Lanka, Colombo 1987; best Test bowling performance 9/52 against Australia, Brisbane 1985–86; toured England 1973, 1978, 1983, 1986, 1990; scored 12,052 First-class runs (average 31.71, highest score 210 not out) including 14 hundreds, and took 1,490 wickets, including five or more in an innings 102 times; achieved Double (1,179 runs and 117 wickets) 1984; Level III Coach, Christchurch; NZ Cricket (NZC) Selection Man. 2000–08, Chair.

of Selectors, NZC 2000–08, Life mem. NZC 2010, Dir 2013–; NZC World Cup Project Man. for 2007 World Cup in West Indies; consultant, APL (American Premier Cricket League) 2009; Public Relations Amb. for Bank of New Zealand 1991–2007; Brand Amb. for Christchurch Int. Airport, Ecoglo, Shelter Box, Pingar, Domain Consulting, FernRidge; Founder and Patron The Sir Richard Hadlee Sports Trust 1990; Patron, Kidz Zipper, India New Zealand Business Council 2009–; int. after-dinner, seminar and conf. speaker; Hon. DLitt (Nottingham) 2008; Wisden Cricketer of the Year 1982, Winner, Winsor Cup on 13 occasions (including 12 consecutive years) for the most meritorious bowling performance of the season, NZ Sportsperson of the Year (Supreme Award) 1980, 1986, NZ Sportsman of the Year 1987, NZ Sportsman of the last 25 years (shared with Sir John Walker) 1987, NZ Sportsperson of the Decade 1989, chosen by Wisden as second greatest Test bowler of all time 2002, Bert Sutcliffe Medal for Services to New Zealand Cricket 2008, commemorated as one of the Twelve Local Heroes, and a bronze bust of him unveiled outside Christchurch Arts Centre 2009, inducted into ICC (Int. Cricket Council) Cricket Hall of Fame 2009, 12th Best Cricketer of all time in ESPN Legends Of Cricket, inducted into ICC/FICA World Cricket Hall of Fame 2009, Altiora Peto Medal, High School Old Boys Asscn (Christchurch Boys High School) 2009, inducted as a Canterbury Sporting Legend 2010. *Achievement:* aged 56, played in NZ Cricket Beach team that defeated England in the final against Australia 2008. *Publications include:* Hadlee on Cricket – The Essentials of the Game 1982, Rhythm and Swing (autobiog.) 1989, Soft Deliveries – A Century of Cricket Years 1996, Hard Knocks – A Selection of Cricket Capers 1997, Caught Out – Tales from The Pavilion 1998, Cricket – The Essentials of the Game 2000, Howzat! – Hadlee's Tales from the Boundary 2002, Changing Pace – A Memoir 2009. *Leisure interests:* movies, golf, gardening. *Address:* Box 78-061, Pegasus 7648, North Canterbury 7648, New Zealand (office). *Telephone:* (3) 920-0220 (office). *Fax:* (3) 920-0220 (office). *E-mail:* hadleerj@clear.net.nz (office). *Website:* www.hadlee.co.nz (office); www.hadlee.org.nz (office).

HADLEY, Stephen John, BA, JD; American lawyer and fmr government official; b. 13 Feb. 1947, Toledo; m. Ann Simon; two c.; ed Cornell Univ., Yale Law School; worked as an analyst for Comptroller, US Dept of Defense 1972–74; mem. Nat. Security Council staff 1974–77; Pnr, Shea and Gardner (law firm), Washington, DC 1977–2001; fmr Prin. The Scowcroft Group Inc. (consulting firm), Washington, DC; Counsel, Tower Comm. Special Review Bd 1986–87; Asst US Sec. of Defense for Int. Security Policy 1989–1993; sr foreign policy and defence policy adviser to George W. Bush during his first presidential campaign; Deputy Nat. Security Advisor 2001–05, Nat. Security Advisor 2005–09. *Address:* c/o National Security Council, Eisenhower Executive Office Building, 17th Street and Pennsylvania Avenue, NW, Washington, DC 20504, USA.

HAEFLIGER, Andreas; Swiss pianist; b. Berlin, Germany; ed Juilliard School, New York; studied with Herbert Stessin, twice won Gina Bachauer Memorial Scholarship; has appeared with many of world's leading orchestras in N America, Europe and Japan; numerous recital appearances including Great Performers Series, Lincoln Center, New York, Wigmore Hall, London and in Germany, Austria, France and Italy; has performed regularly at BBC Proms, London; performs in USA with Takacs String Quartet; performs frequently with baritone Matthias Goerner; Preis der Deutschen Schallplattenkritik (for recording of Schubert's Goethe Lieder). *Recordings include:* Mozart Piano Sonatas, Schumann's Davidsbündlertanze and Fantasiestücke, Schubert's Impromptus, music by Sofia Gubaidulina, Schubert's Goethe Lieder (with Matthias Goerne), Perspectives I–IV (including works by Schubert, Adès, Mozart and Beethoven). *Address:* Intermusica Artists Management Ltd, 36 Graham Street, Crystal Wharf, London, N1 8BZ, England (office). *Telephone:* (20) 7608-9900 (office). *Fax:* (20) 7490-3263 (office). *E-mail:* mail@intermusica.co.uk (office). *Website:* www.intermusica.co.uk (office).

HÆKKERUP, Nick, LLM, PhD; Danish politician; *Minister for Health and Prevention;* b. 3 April 1968, Fredensborg; s. of Klaus Hækkerup and Irene Hækkerup; m. Petra Freisleben Hækkerup; four c.; ed Univ. of Copenhagen; mil. service, Auderød Naval Coll.; Head of Section, Nat. Income Tax Tribunal 1994; mem. Hillerød Town Council 1994–2007, Mayor of Hillerød 2000–07; Lecturer, Univ. of Copenhagen 1998–2000; mem. Folketing (Parl.) for Nordsjællands Storkreds constituency 2007–, mem. Finance Cttee 2007–11, Fiscal Affairs Cttee 2007–11, Standing Orders Cttee 2009–10, Nat. Tax Bd 2007–09; Minister of Defence 2011–13, Minister for European Affairs 2013–14, Minister for Health and Prevention 2014–; Chair. Man. Cttee Danish Atlantic Treaty Asscn 2004–09; mem. Socialdemokraterne (Social Democrats), Vice-Chair. 2005–. *Publications include:* Udvikling i EU siden 1992 på de områder, der er omfattet af de danske forbehold (co-author) 2000, Controls and Sanctions in the EU Law 2001. *Address:* Ministry of Health, Holbergsgade 6, 1057 Copenhagen K, Denmark (office). *Telephone:* 72-26-90-00 (office). *Fax:* 72-26-90-01 (office). *E-mail:* sum@sum.dk (office). *Website:* www .sum.dk (office).

HAEMAMOOL, Uthis; Thai author; b. 10 Jan. 1975, Kaeng Khoi; ed Silpakorn Univ.; fmr short film maker; film reviewer, Movie Time magazine 2001–. *Films:* Pipop Buntoon, Dokmai Nai Tarng Puen (artistic dir). *Publications:* Luen: Joodjob Kong Name AunPenAuen 2001, Rabum Maytun 2005, Porimat Rampueng (short stories) 2005, Krajok Ngao/Ngao Krajok 2006, Mai Yorn Kuen (short stories) 2008, Lap Lae, Kaeng Khoi (The Brotherhood of Kaeng Khoi)) (Southeast Asian Writers Award 2009), Lak A-lai (The Nature of Regret) 2012. *Address:* c/o Somsri Hansirisawasdi, SEA Write Award, Public Relations Department, The Oriental Bangkok, 48 Oriental Avenue, Bangkok 10500, Thailand.

HAENNI, Tatjana; Swiss sports organization executive; *Head of Women's Competitions, Fédération Internationale de Football Association (FIFA);* Responsible Women's Football, Union of European Football Asscns (UEFA) 1994–98; Ed. Sat.1 1998–99; Man. Dir of Women's Football, FIFA 2001–07, Head of Women's Competitions 2008–; Chair. FC Zürich Frauen. *Address:* Fédération Internationale de Football Association, FIFA-Strasse 20, PO Box 8044, Zurich (office); FC Zürich Frauen, PO Box 3375, 8021 Zurich, Switzerland (office). *Telephone:* (43) 2227777 (FIFA) (office); (43) 5211212 (FC Zürich Frauen) (office). *Fax:* (43) 2227878 (FIFA) (office); (43) 5211213 (FC Zürich Frauen) (office). *E-mail:* haenni@ fcz-frauen.ch (office); info@fifa.com (office). *Website:* www.fifa.com (office); www.fcz .ch (office).

HAFEN, Ernst, PhD; Swiss geneticist and academic; *Professor, Institute of Molecular Systems Biology, Eidgenössische Technische Hochschule (ETH) Zürich;* b. 1956, St Gallen; ed Univ. of Basel; Research Asst, Biocenter Basel 1983; Postdoctoral Research Asst, Dept of Biochemistry, Univ. of California, Berkeley, USA 1984–86; Asst Prof. for Developmental Genetics, Univ. of Zürich 1987–94, Assoc. Prof. 1994–97, Full Prof. 1997–2005, Dir Zoological Inst. 2005; Dir ETH Zürich 2005–06; fmr mem. Nat. Research Council; fmr rep. profs at Council of Univ. of Zürich; mem. editorial bds of several major journals, including The EMBO Journal; helped develop jt centres of ETH and Univ. of Zürich, including SystemsX, Life Science Zurich, Life Science Learning Center Zürich; Co-founder and Scientific Advisor, The Genetics Co.; Ernst Jung Prize for Medicine, Jung-Stiftung für Wissenschaft und Forschung (co-recipient) 2005. *Publications:* numerous scientific papers in professional journals on developmental and cell biology. *Address:* Institute for Molecular Systems Biology, ETH Zürich, Wolfgang-Pauli-Strasse 16, 8093 Zürich, Switzerland (office). *Telephone:* (44) 633-36-88 (office). *Fax:* (44) 633-10-51 (office); (44) 633-11-41 (office). *E-mail:* hafen@imsb.biol .ethz.ch (office); ernst.hafen@imsb.biol.ethz.ch (office). *Website:* www.zool.uzh.ch (office).

HAFEZ, Suleiman al-, BA; Jordanian politician; *Minister of Finance;* b. 1941; ed Beirut Arab Univ. (br. of Alexandria Univ., Egypt); fmr Minister of Posts and Communications; fmr Minister of Energy; Minister of Finance 2012–; Chief Commr Electricity Regulatory Comm.; mem. Bd of Dirs of several orgs, including the Royal Jordanian, Jordan Electricity Authority, Civil Aviation Authority, Jordan Phosphate Mines Co., Jordan Cement Factories, Agricultural Credit Corpn. *Address:* Ministry of Finance, PO Box 85, King Hussein Street, Amman 11118, Jordan (office). *Telephone:* (6) 4646516 (office); (6) 4636321 (office). *Fax:* (6) 4618527 (office). *E-mail:* info@mof.gov.jo (office). *Website:* www.mof.gov.jo (office).

HAFFAR AL-HASSAN, Raya, MBA; Lebanese politician; b. 1967; m.; three c.; ed George Washington Univ., Washington DC, USA; mem. March 14 Alliance; mem. Future Movt; Minister of Finance 2009–11. *Address:* c/o Ministry of Finance, MOF Bldg, place Riad es-Solh, Beirut, Lebanon (office).

HAGAN, Kay Ruthven, BA, JD; American lawyer and politician; *Senator from North Carolina;* b. 26 March 1953, Shelby, N Carolina; m. Charles T. (Chip) Hagan, III; one s. two d.; ed Florida State Univ., Wake Forest Univ.; served in pvt. law practice as attorney for North Carolina Nat. Bank (now Bank of America) 1978–88; mem. N Carolina State Senate 1999–2003, Co-Chair. Pensions, Retirement and Aging Cttee, mem. Cttees on Appropriations and Base Budget, on Commerce, Small Business and Entrepreneurship, on Educ., on Finance, on Health Care; Senator from N Carolina 2009–; Democrat. *Address:* 521 Dirksen Senate Office Building, Washington, DC 20510, USA (office). *Telephone:* (202) 224-6342 (office). *Fax:* (202) 228-2563 (office). *Website:* hagan.senate.gov (office).

HAGEDORN, Jürgen, Dr rer. nat; German academic; *Professor Emeritus of Geography, University of Göttingen;* b. 10 March 1933, Hankensbüttel; s. of Ernst Hagedorn and Dorothea Schulze; m. Ingeborg A. Carl 1965; one d.; ed Hermann-Billung-Gymnasium, Celle, Tech. Hochschule Hanover and Univ. of Göttingen; Asst Lecturer, Univ. of Göttingen 1962–69, Dozent 1969–70, Prof. 1970–72, Prof. of Geography and Dir Inst. of Geography 1972–2001, now Prof. Emer.; mem. Göttingen Acad., Akad. Leopoldina. *Publications:* Geomorphologie des Uelzener Beckens 1964, Geomorphologie griechischer Hochgebirge 1969, Late Quaternary and Present-Day Fluvial Processes in Central Europe (ed.) 1995. *Address:* Jupiterweg 1, 37077 Göttingen, Germany (home). *Telephone:* (551) 21323 (home). *E-mail:* jhagedo@gwdg.de (office); a.j.hagedorn@arcor.de (home).

HAGÈGE, Claude, LèsL, TH; French linguist, author and academic; *Professor, Collège de France;* b. 1 Jan. 1936, Carthage, Tunisia; s. of Edmond Hagège and Liliane Taïeb-Hagège; ed Lycée Carnot, Tunis, Lycée Louis-le-Grand, Paris, Ecole Normale Supérieure, Paris, Harvard Univ. and Massachusetts Inst. of Tech., USA; diplômes de chinois, arabe, russe de l'Ecole Nationale des Langues Orientales, Paris; teacher, Lycée Carnot, Tunis 1959–61, Lycées Victor Duruy et Saint-Louis, Paris 1963–66; Prof. of Linguistics, Univ. of Poitiers 1971–87; Chief of Confs, Univ. of Paris XII Val-de-Marne 1971–74, Univ. of Paris IV 1976–78, Univ. of Paris III 1977–78; Dir of Linguistic Studies, Ecole Pratique des Hautes Etudes 1977; Prof., Collège de France 1988–; Hon. Dir of Studies, Ecole Pratique des Hautes Etudes, Paris; Officier, Ordre des Palmes académiques 1995, Chevalier, Ordre des Arts et des Lettres 1995, Officier, Légion d'honneur 2005; Prix Volney, Acad. des Inscriptions et Belles-Lettres 1981, CNRS Médaille d'or 1995, Prix du Mot d'or des langues 2003. *Publications:* La Structure des langues 1982, L'Homme de paroles (English trans.: The Dialogic Species 1990) (Grand Prix de l'Essai, Soc. des Gens de Lettres 1986, Prix de l'Académie Française 1986) 1985, Le Français et les siècles 1987, Le Souffle de la langue 1992, The Language Builder, An Essay on the Human Signature in Linguistic Morphogenesis 1993, L'Enfant aux deux langues 1996, Le Français, histoire d'un combat 1996, Halte à la mort des langues 2001 (English trans.: On the Death and Life of Languages 2009), Combat pour le français 2006, Dictionnaire amoureux des langues 2009, Contre la pensée unique 2012. *Address:* Collège de France, 11 place Marcelin Berthelot, 75231 Paris Cedex 05, France (office). *Telephone:* 1-44-27-17-03 (office). *Fax:* 1-44-27-13-29 (home). *E-mail:* claude.hagege@college-de-france.fr (office); claude-hagege@wanadoo.fr (home).

HAGEL, Charles (Chuck), BA; American politician; *Secretary of Defense;* b. 4 Oct. 1946, North Platte, Neb.; m. Lilibet Hagel (née Ziller); one s. one d.; ed Brown Inst. of Radio & Television, Minneapolis, Minn., Univ. of Nebraska at Omaha; served in Army 1967–68; Deputy Admin. Virginia 1981–82; Pres. and CEO World United Service Org. 1987–90; Pres. McCarthy & Co. 1991–96; Senator from Nebraska 1996–2009, mem. numerous Senate cttees including Chair. Senate Sub-cttee on Int. Econ. Policy, Export and Trade Promotion; Distinguished Prof. in the Practice of Nat. Governance, Edmund A. Walsh School of Foreign Service, Georgetown Univ. 2009–; Prof. Univ. of Nebraska at Omaha 2009–; Chair. Atlantic Council 2009–; Sec. of Defense 2013–; Co-Chair. Pres.'s Intelligence Advisory Bd; Founder-Dir Vanguard Cellular Systems Inc.; mem. Bd of Dirs Public Broadcasting Service (PBS), Chevron Corpn, Zurich Holding Co. of America; mem. Advisory Bd, Deutsche Bank Americas, Corsair Capital, M.I.C. Industries, Kaseman LLC; Sr Advisor McCarthy Capital Corpn; mem. American Legion, Veterans of Foreign Wars; Trustee, Omaha Chamber of Commerce; Republican; numerous awards including Cordell Hull Award 2003, Award for Distinguished Int. Leadership, Atlantic Council 2004, Woodrow Wilson Int. Center for Scholars Public Service Award 2005, Marlin Fitzwater Excellence in Public Communication Award 2005, US Chamber of Commerce 'Spirit of Enterprise' Award 2007, Millard E. Tydings Award for Courage and Leadership in American Politics, Univ. of Maryland 2008, Aspen Strategy Group Leadership Award 2008. *Publication:* America: Our Next Chapter. *Address:* Office of the Secretary of Defense, Department of Defense, 1400 Defense Pentagon, Washington, DC 20301-1400 (office); Atlantic Council, 1101 15th Street, NW, 11th Floor, Washington, DC 20005, USA (office). *Telephone:* (703) 571-3343 (Department of Defense) (office); (202) 778-4952 (Atlantic Council) (office). *Fax:* (703) 428-1982 (Department of Defense) (office); (202) 463-7241 (Atlantic Council) (office). *E-mail:* info@acus.org (office). *Website:* www.defense .gov (office); www.acus.org (office).

HAGEN, Carl I.; Norwegian politician; b. 6 May 1944, Oslo; s. of Ragnar Hagen and Gerd Gamborg Hagen; m. 1st Nina Aamodt 1970; m. 2nd Eli Engum Hagen 1983; one s. one d.; ed Inst. of Marketing, London; CEO Tate and Lyle 1970–74; Sec., Anders Lange Party 1973–74; mem. Stortinget (Norwegian Parl.) 1974–77, 1981–2009, Deputy Speaker 2005–09; consultant, Finansanalyse 1977–79; consultant on econ. policy 1979–81; Leader of Fremskrittspartiet (Progress Party) and Parl. Group 1978–2006; mem. Bd British Business Forum 1972, Norske Agenters Landsforbund 1972–74. *Publication:* Aerlighet Varer Lengst (autobiog.). *Leisure interests:* tennis, family, golf. *Address:* Fremskrittspartiet, PO Box 8903, Young-storget, 0028 Oslo, Norway. *E-mail:* postmottak.frp@stortinget.no. *Website:* www .frp.no.

HAGGIS, Paul; Canadian screenwriter, film director and film producer; b. 10 March 1953, London, Ont.; s. of Ted Haggis and Mary Haggis; m. 1st Deborah Rennard; m. 2nd Diane Christine Gettas; four c.; ed Fanshawe Coll.; directed and wrote plays for parents' Gallery Theatre, London, Ontario 1970s; co-founder Artists for Peace and Justice; Chair. of Film Programs, Canadian Film Centre, Toronto 2011–; mem. Bd of Dirs Environmental Media Asscn, Pres.'s Council of Defenders of Wildlife; mem. Advisory Bd Centre for the Advancement of Non-Violence; Valentine Davies Award, Writers' Guild of America 2001. *Films include:* Red Hot (screenwriter) 1993, Million Dollar Baby (screenwriter and producer) 2004, Crash (writer, dir and producer) (Acad. Award for Best Film 2006, Humanitas Prize 2006) 2005, Last Kiss (screenwriter) 2006, Flags of Our Fathers (screenwriter) 2006, Casino Royale (screenwriter) 2006, Letters from Iwo Jima (story) 2006, In the Valley of Elah (screenwriter, producer and dir) 2007, Quantum of Solace (writer) 2008, Next Three Days (screenwriter, producer and dir) 2010. *Television includes:* Due South (exec. producer and writer), creator Walker, Texas Ranger, Family Law (exec. producer and writer), EZ Streets (exec. producer and writer), creator The Black Donnellys 2007, Speechless 2008, Crash (exec. producer) 2008–09; writer numerous episodes in series. *Address:* c/o CAA, 9830 Wilshire Blvd., Beverly Hills, CA 90212-1825, USA.

HÄGGLUND, Gen. (retd) Gustav, MS (Pol.Sc.); Finnish army officer (retd); *Chancellor, The Order of the Cross of Liberty;* b. 6 Sept. 1938, Wyborg; m. Ritva Ekström; one s. two d.; ed Finnish Mil. Acad., Univ. of Helsinki, Finnish War Coll.; nat. mil. service 1957–58; commanded Finnish Bn UNEF II, Sinai 1978–79, Nyland Brigade, Finland 1984–85, UNDOF, Golan Heights 1985–86, UN Interim Force in Lebanon (UNIFIL), Lebanon 1986–88, South East Mil. Area Finland 1988–90; Chief of Defence Staff 1990–94, Chief of Defence 1994–2001; Chair. EU Mil. Cttee, Brussels 2001–04; US Army Command and Gen. Staff Coll. 1972–73; currently Chancellor The Order of the Cross of Liberty; Fellow, Harvard Univ. Center for Int. Affairs 1981–82; Legion of Merit (twice), Commdr, Legion d'honneur and about 50 others. *Publications:* Peace-making in the Finnish Winter War 1969, Northern Europe in Strategic Perspective 1974, US Strategy for Europe 1974, Parliamentary Defence Committees in Finland 1981, Modern US Cruise Missiles, an Evaluation 1982, Peace-keeping in a Modern War Zone 1990, Defence of Finland 2001, European Defence 2004, The Lion and the Dove (autobiog.) 2006 We Were Young Soldiers 2009, The Lucky Hunter 2010, Colorful Generals 2011. *Leisure interests:* hunting, shooting, roaming in the wilderness. *Address:* Ylänkötie 3n, 00650 Helsinki, Finland (home). *Telephone:* (9) 7242192 (office).

HAGIWARA, Toshitaka, LLM; Japanese business executive; *Senior Adviser, Komatsu Ltd;* b. Tokyo; ed Waseda Univ.; joined Komatsu Ltd 1969, mem. Bd of Dirs 1990–2007, Man. Dir 1995–97, Exec. Man. Dir 1997–99, Rep. Dir 1999–2007, Exec. Vice-Pres. 1999–2003, Chair. 2003–07, Sr Adviser 2007–; Pres. Financial Accounting Standards Foundation; Chair. Int. Financial Reporting Standards Council; Chair. Jt Cttee on Econ. Regulation, Nippon Keidanren; Co-Chair. Japan Business Fed.'s Econ. Law Cttee; mem. Bd of Dirs Yamato Holdings Co. Ltd 2009–, Zensho Holdings Co. Ltd 2010–; mem. Legislative Council, Ministry of Justice; Integrity Award 2010. *Address:* Komatsu Ltd, 2-3-6 Akasaka, Minato-ku, Tokyo 107-8414, Japan (office). *Website:* www.komatsu.com (office).

HAGUE, Rt Hon. William Jefferson, PC, MA, MBA, FRSL; British politician and writer; *Secretary of State for Foreign and Commonwealth Affairs;* b. 26 March 1961, Rotherham, Yorks.; s. of Timothy N. Hague and Stella Hague; m. Ffion Jenkins 1997; ed Wath-upon-Dearne Comprehensive School, Magdalen Coll. Oxford, Institut Européen d'Admin des Affaires (INSEAD), France; made nat. news aged 16 by speaking at Conservative Party's nat. conf. 1977; Pres. Oxford Union 1981; man. consultant, McKinsey & Co. 1983–88; political adviser, HM Treasury 1988; MP (Conservative) for Richmond, Yorks. 1989–; Parl. Pvt. Sec. to Chancellor of Exchequer 1990–93; Parl. Under-Sec. of State, Dept of Social Security 1993–94; Minister for Social Security and Disabled People, Dept of Social Security 1994–95; Sec. of State for Wales 1995–97; Leader of Conservative Party and Leader of the Opposition 1997–2001; Chair. Int. Democratic Union 1999–2001, now Deputy Chair.; Shadow Foreign Sec. and Sr mem. of the Shadow Cabinet 2005–10; Sec. of State for Foreign and Commonwealth Affairs 2010–; Econ. and Political Adviser, JCB PLC 2001–; Dir (non-exec.) AES Eng PLC 2001–; mem. Political Council of Terra Firma Capital Partners 2001–; Vice-Pres. Friends of the British Library; mem. Conservative Friends of Israel 1976–; The Spectator Parliamentarian of the Year Award 1998, Channel 4 Politician of the Year 2001, The Spectator Speech of the Year Award 2007, Trustees Award, Longman/History Today Awards 2008. *Publications:* William Pitt the Younger (biog.) (British Book Award for History Book of the Year 2005) 2004, William Wilberforce: The Life of the Great Anti-Slave Trade Campaigner 2007. *Leisure interests:* walking, judo, playing the piano. *Address:* Foreign and Commonwealth Office, King Charles Street, London, SW1A 2AH (office); House of Commons, Westminster, London, SW1A 0AA; Constituency Office, Unit 1, Omega Business Village, Thurston Road, Northallerton, DL6 2NJ, England. *Telephone:* (20) 7008-1500 (FCO) (office); (20) 7219-4611 (Westminster); (1609) 779093 (Northallerton). *Fax:* (1609) 778172 (Northallerton). *E-mail:* haguew@parliament.uk (office). *Website:* www.gov.uk/government/organisations/foreign-commonwealth-office (office); www.parliament.uk/biographies/commons/william-hague/25550; www.williamhague.org.uk.

HAHN, Carl Horst, Dr rer. pol; Austrian business executive; b. 1 July 1926, Chemnitz; m. Marisa Traina 1960; three s. one d.; Chair. of Bd, Continental Gummi-Werke AG 1973–81, Saurer AG 1983–99; Chair. Man. Bd, Volkswagen AG 1981–92, currently Chair. Emer., Volkswagen Group; mem. Supervisory Bd HAWESKO, Hamburg, Perot Systems 1993–, Dallas; mem. Int. Supervisory Bd Indesit Co., Fabriano; mem. Int. Advisory Bd, Textron, Wichity, Inst. de Empresa, Madrid; mem. Int. Advisory Cttee, Salk Inst., Calif.; Chair. Bd of Trustees, Kunstmuseum Wolfsburg; mem. Bd Mayo Clinic, Stiftung, Frankfurt, Lauder-Inst., Wharton School, Pa; Pres. German-Czech Chamber of Commerce 1993–99; several hon. doctorates. *Publication:* Meine Jahre mit Volkswagen. *Address:* Hollerplatz 1, 38440 Wolfsburg, Germany (office). *Telephone:* (5361) 26680 (office). *Fax:* (5361) 266815 (office). *E-mail:* carl.hahn@volkswagen.de (office). *Website:* www.carl-hahn.de.

HAHN, Erwin Louis, BS, PhD, FRS; American physicist and academic; *Professor Emeritus of Physics, University of California, Berkeley;* b. 9 June 1921, Sharon, Pa; s. of Israel Hahn and Mary Hahn; m. 1st Marian Ethel Failing 1944 (deceased); one s. two d.; m. 2nd Natalie Woodford Hodgson 1980; ed Juniata Coll. and Univ. of Illinois; Asst, Purdue Univ. 1943–44; Research Asst, Univ. of Illinois 1950; Nat. Research Council Fellow, Stanford Univ. 1950–51, Instructor 1951–52; Research Physicist, Watson IBM Lab., New York 1952–55; Assoc., Columbia Univ., New York 1952–55; Assoc., Univ. of Calif., Berkeley 1955, Asst Prof. 1955–56, Assoc. Prof. 1956–61, Assoc. Prof., Miller Inst. for Basic Research 1958–59, Prof. of Physics 1961–91, Prof. Emer. 1991–; Visiting Fellow, Brasenose Coll., Oxford 1960–61, 1981–82 (Hon. Fellow 1981–82); Miller Prof., Univ. of Calif. 1985–86; Eastman (Visiting) Prof., Balliol Coll. Oxford 1988–89; mem. NAS 1972; Assoc. mem. Slovenian Acad. of Sciences 1981; Foreign Assoc. mem. Acad. des Sciences (France) 1992; Fellow, American Acad. of Arts and Sciences, American Physical Soc., Int. Soc. of Electron Paramagnetic Spin Resonance; Foreign Fellow, Royal Soc. (UK) 2001, Physical Soc. (UK) 2001; discoverer of spin echoes; introduced pulsed nuclear magnetic resonance free precession spectroscopy; Hon. DSc (Juniata Coll.) 1966, (Purdue Univ., Indiana) 1975, (Warwick Univ., UK) 2007; Hon. Dr rer. nat (Stuttgart) 2001; Guggenheim Fellow 1961, 1970; Buckley Prize 1971, Int. Soc. of Magnetic Resonance Prize 1971, Alexander von Humboldt Foundation Award (FRG) 1976–77, Co-winner, Wolf Foundation Prize 1983/84, Calif. Inventors Hall of Fame 1984, The Berkeley Citation 1991, Comstock Prize (co-recipient), NAS (for research in radiation and electromagnetism) 1993, Russell Varian NMR Prize 2000, and other prizes and awards. *Publications:* Nuclear Quadruple Resonance Spectroscopy (with T.P. Das) 1958; articles in learned journals. *Leisure interests:* violin, chamber music. *Address:* Department of Physics, University of California, 257 Birge Hall, Berkeley, CA 94720-0001 (office); 69 Stevenson Avenue, Berkeley, CA 94708-1732, USA (home). *Telephone:* (510) 642-2305 (office); (510) 845-0082 (home). *Fax:* (510) 643-8497 (office); (510) 841-4618 (home). *E-mail:* hahn@physics.berkeley.edu (office). *Website:* physics.berkeley.edu/people/directory.php?id=239 (office).

HAHN, James Kenneth (Jim), BA, JD; American politician, lawyer and business executive; *Mediator, Alternative Resolution Centers;* b. 1951, Los Angeles; s. of Kenneth Hahn and Ramona Hahn (née Fox); divorced; one s. one d.; ed Lutheran High School, South LA, Pepperdine Univ.; Deputy City Prosecutor, LA City Attorney's Office 1975–79, City Controller of LA 1981–85, City Attorney of LA 1985–2001; Mayor of LA 2001–05; Man. Dir Chadwick Saylor and Co. Inc., LA 2005–07; Mediator, Alternative Resolution Centers 2007–; pvt. law practice in Marina del Rey, Calif. 1979–81; Democrat. *Address:* Alternative Resolution Centers, 1875 Century Park East, Suite 450, Los Angeles, CA 90067, USA (office). *Telephone:* (310) 284-8224 (office). *Fax:* (310) 284-8229 (office). *E-mail:* jhahn@arc4adr.com (office). *Website:* www.arc4adr.com (office).

HAHN, Johannes; Austrian politician and international organization official; *Commissioner for Regional Policy, European Commission;* b. 1957, Vienna; m. Marina Hahn; one s.; ed Univ. of Vienna; various man. posts in different business sectors in Austria 1985–92; Bd mem., later Chair. Novomatic AG 1997–2003; mem. Austrian People's Party (ÖVP), Chair. Viennese group, Youth Austrian People's Party 1980–85, Man. Dir ÖVP Vienna 1992–97, mem. Vienna City Council and Health Policy Spokesman of ÖVP Vienna 1996–2003, Deputy Chair. ÖVP Vienna 2002–04, Acting Chair. 2004–05, Chair. 2005–; mem. Vienna City Govt 2003–07; Fed. Minister for Science and Research 2007–09; Commr for Regional Policy, EC, Brussels 2010–. *Address:* European Commission, rue de la Loi 200, 1049 Brussels, Belgium (office). *Telephone:* (2) 299-11-11 (office). *Fax:* (2) 295-01-38 (office). *Website:* ec.europa.eu (office).

HAI, Musharaf; Pakistani business executive; *Country Business Manager, Citibank NA Pakistan;* ed London School of Econs, UK, Boston Univ., USA; joined Unilever 1983, several man. positions including Marketing Man., Co-ordinator for Detergents in East Asia-Pacific and Africa/Middle East regions, Unilever HQ, London 1993–96, responsible for Unilever Pakistan Ice Cream Div. 1996, later Dir Home & Personal Care Div., Sales Dir –2001, Chair. Unilever Pakistan (first woman head of a major multinational co. in Pakistan) 2001–06; Country Business Man. Citibank NA Pakistan, Karachi 2006–, also Head of Consumer Banking Pakistan; mem. Bd of Govs Lahore Univ. Man. Sciences, LEAD Pakistan 2003–; mem. Bd LEAD Pakistan 2003–; mem. Nat. Council Duke of Edinburgh's Award Programme Pakistan; mem. Man. Cttee Overseas Investors' Chamber of Commerce and Industry, Bd of Investment, Govt of Pakistan 2002–03; ranked by Fortune magazine amongst 50 Most Powerful Women in Business outside the US (46th) 2004. *Address:* Citibank NA Pakistan, State Life Building #1, 3rd Floor I.I. Chundrigar Road, Karachi, Pakistan (office). *Website:* www.citibank.com/pakistan (office).

HAIDALLA, Lt-Col Mohamed Khouna Ould; Mauritanian politician and army officer; b. 1940, La Güera; ed École Spéciale Militaire de Saint-Cyr; Chair. Mil. Cttee for Nat. Recovery (now Cttee for Nat. Salvation) 1978–84; Chief of Staff of Mauritanian Army 1978–79; Minister of Defence April–May 1979, 1980, Prime Minister 1979–80, Pres. of Mauritania 1980–84 (overthrown in coup); stood as unsuccessful cand. in presidential election 2003, 2007; arrested and charged with treason Nov. 2003, trial suspended Dec. 2003.

HAIDAR, Shoukria, MA, PhD; French/Afghan human rights activist and teacher; *President, NEGAR—Support Women of Afghanistan Association;* b. 11 Nov. 1957, Kabul; m.; ed Univ. of Nice, France; fmr ping-pong champion, Kabul; worked for IOC 1979–80; exile in France 1980–; various jobs in a bakery, dress-making workshop, Paris; Founding Pres. NEGAR—Support Women of Afghanistan Asscn 1996–; obtained French citizenship 1998; currently Prof. of Physical Educ., Collège d'Aulnay-sous-Bois; organiser and Speaker, Women on the Road to Afghanistan Conf., Dushanbe, Tajikistan 2000. *Address:* Negar—Soutien aux Femmes d'Afghanistan, BP 10, 25770 Franois, France (office). *Telephone:* 1-48-35-07-56 (office). *Fax:* 1-48-35-07-56 (office). *E-mail:* negar@wanadoo.fr (office). *Website:* www.negar-afghanwomen.org (office).

HAIDER, Maximilian, PhD; Austrian physicist and business executive; *Managing Director, Corrected Electron Optical Systems (CEOS) GmbH;* b. 23 Jan. 1950, Freistadt; ed Univ. of Kiel, Darmstadt Univ. of Tech.; Group Leader, Physical Instrumentation Program, European Molecular Biology Lab. (EMBL), Heidelberg 1989; co-f. CEOS (Corrected Electron Optical Systems) GmbH, Heidelberg 1996, Man. Dir 1996–; Hon. Prof., Karlsruher Institut für Technologie 2008; several awards, including Innovation Award of the State of Baden Württemberg (Rudolf Eberle Award) (jtly) 2005, Karl Heinz Beckurts Prize (jtly) 2006, Honda Prize (jtly) 2008, Wolf Prize in Physics (jtly) 2011. *Address:* CEOS GmbH, Englerstr. 28, 69126 Heidelberg, Germany (office). *Telephone:* (6221) 89467-0 (office). *Fax:* (6221) 89467-29 (office). *E-mail:* info@ceos-gmbh.de (office). *Website:* www.ceos-gmbh.de (office).

HAIDUC, Ionel, MSc, PhD; Romanian chemist and academic; *President, Romanian Academy;* b. 9 May 1937, Cluj; ed Babes-Bolyai Univ., Inst. of Fine Chemicals Tech., Moscow, Iowa State Univ., Univ. of Georgia, USA; Lab. Asst, Dept of Chem., Babes-Bolyai Univ. 1959–62, Asst 1962–64, Lecturer 1964–69, Reader 1969–73, Prof. 1979–, Prorector 1976–84, Rector 1990–93; NSF Visiting Scientist, Dept of Chem., Univ. of Georgia, USA 1992; EC Visiting Scientist, Univ. of Santiago de Compostela, Spain 1993; Visiting Scientist, Nat. Univ. of Singapore 2002; Visiting Prof., Instituto de Quimica, Universidad Nacional Autonoma de Mexico 1993–94, Instituto de Quimica, Universidade Federal de Sao Carlos, Brazil 1994, 2000, Univ. of Santiago de Compostela 1998, Univ. of Texas, El Paso 2000–01, 2004, Göttingen Univ., Germany 1998–99, 2002; Consultant Dept of Chem., Univ. of Texas, El Paso 1997, 2005; Visiting Lecturer, Columbia Univ., New York 2003; UNESCO Expert, Consulting Mission to Moldova 1999; Corresp. mem. Romanian Acad. 1990–, mem. 1991–, Pres. Transylvania Br. 1995–, mem. Grant Cttee 1996–, Vice-Pres. 1998–2000, Pres. 2006–; Bd mem. Nat. Council for Academic Research 1992–, Nat. Council for Academic Titles and Diplomas 1992–, Nat. Council for Academic Reform 1998; Pres. Consultative Coll., Nat. Agency for Research, Devt and Innovation 1998–2003; mem. Bd of Dirs Alliance of Univs for Democracy 1991–93; mem. Int. Council of Main Group Chem. 1993–; Founding mem. Nat. Foundation for Science and Arts; mem. Accad. Europaea 2002–; mem. Editorial Bd Synthesis and Reactivity in Inorganic and Metal-organic Chemistry, Main-Group Metal Chemistry, Metal-Based Drugs, Science and Engineering Ethics, Revue Roumaine de Chimie, Revista de Chimie; Hon. Citizen of Cluj-Napoca 1999, Hon. mem. Moldavian Acad. of Sciences 2002; Star of Romania 2000, Order of Honour (Moldova) 2006; Hon. Diploma (Moldavian Acad. of Sciences) 1999; Dr hc (Gh. Assachi Tech. Univ.) 2002, (Polytechnic Univ. of Timisoara) 2004; Fulbright Fellowship 1966, G. Spacu Prize, Romanian Acad. 1974, Pro Colaboratione Award, Hungarian Acad. of Sciences 1999, Romanian Chemical Soc. Prize 2004. *Publications:* Chemistry of Inorganic Ring Systems 1970, Basic Organometallic Chemistry (with J.J. Zuckerman) 1985, Chemistry of Inorganic Homo and Heterocycles 1987, Organometallics in Cancer Chemotherapy (with C. Silvestru) 1990, Supramolecular Organometallic Chemistry (with F.T. Edelmann) 1999; numerous contribs to academic journals. *Address:* Romanian Academy, 125 Calea Victoriei, sector 1, 010071 Bucharest, Romania (office). *Telephone:* (21) 28640 (office). *Fax:* (21) 16608 (office). *E-mail:* ihaiduc@chem.ubbcluj.ro (office). *Website:* www.academiaromana.ro (office).

HAIGNERÉ, Claudie, MD, PhD; French politician, astronaut, physician and rheumatologist; *Senior Adviser to the Director General, European Space Agency;* b. (Claudie André), 13 May 1957, Le Creusot (Saône-et-Loire); m. Jean-Pierre Haigneré; one d.; ed Faculté de Médecine, Dijon and Paris-Cochin, Faculté des Sciences, Paris-VII; physician, rheumatologist and researcher, Rheumatology Clinic and Rehab Dept, Cochin Hosp., Paris 1984–92; postgraduate researcher, Neurosensory Physiology Lab., CNRS 1985–90; cand. astronaut, French Space Agency (CNES) 1985; Science Co-ordinator Life Sciences experts aboard Antarés mission 1989–92; responsible for French and int. space physiology and medicine programmes, CNES Life Sciences Div., Paris 1990–92; backup cosmonaut for Altair mission, mem. ground team 1992; Co-ordinator Science Programme Cassiopée mission 1993–94; Co-ordinator French experts aboard Euromir mission 1994; Research Cosmonaut Cassiopée mission (first French woman in space) 1994–96; French Rep. Starsem, Moscow 1997; backup astronaut for Perseus mission, Crew Interface Co-ordinator, Mission Control Centre 1998–99; mem. European Astronaut Corps, ESA, Cologne 1999–; trainee Soyuz flight engineer for Andromède mission to Int. Space Station (first European woman on space station) 2001–; Minister for Research and New Technologies, Ministry of Youth, Nat. Educ. and Research 2002–04; Minister-Del. attached to the Ministry of Foreign Affairs, responsible for European Affairs 2004–05; Sr Adviser to Dir Gen. ESA 2005–; Vice-Pres. Int. Acad. of Astronautics; Perm. mem. French Acad. of Tech., French Sport Acad.; mem. Bd France Telecom, Sanofi, Fondation de France, Fondation L'Oréal, Cité des Sciences et de l'Industrie, Fondation Génial, Fondation Lacoste; mem. Acad. de l'Air et de l'Espace, Acad. des Sports, Acad. des Technologies; Hon. mem. Asscn Aéronautique et Astronautique de France, Soc. Française de Médecine Aéronautique et Spaciale; Commdr, Légion d'honneur, Chevalier, Ordre nat. du Mérite, Russian Order of Friendship, Russian Medal for Personal Valour,

Bundesverdienstkreuz; Dr hc (École Polytechnique Fédérale de Lausanne, Faculté Polytechnique de Mons). *Leisure interests:* contemporary art (painting, sculpture), reading, sports, especially gymnastics and golf. *Address:* European Space Agency, 8–10 rue Mario Nikis, 75738 Paris Cedex 15, France (office). *Telephone:* 1-53-69-74-13 (office). *Fax:* 1-53-69-73-69 (office). *E-mail:* claudie.haignere@esa.int (office). *Website:* www.esa.int (office).

HAIN, Rt Hon. Peter Gerald, PC, BSc, MPhil; British politician; b. 16 Feb. 1950, Nairobi, Kenya; s. of Walter Hain and Adelaine Hain; m. 1st Patricia Western 1975; two s.; m. 2nd Elizabeth Haywood 2003; ed Pretoria Boys High School, Emanuel School, Queen Mary Coll., London, Univ. of Sussex; noted anti-apartheid campaigner 1970s; Head of Research, Communication Workers' Union 1976–91; MP (Labour) for Neath 1991–; Labour Party Foreign Affairs Whip 1995–96; Shadow Employment Minister 1996–97; Parl. Under-Sec. of State, Welsh Office 1997–99; Minister of State, FCO 1999–2001; Minister for Energy and Competitiveness in Europe 2001; Minister of State for Europe, FCO 2001–02; Sec. of State for Wales 2002–08, 2009–10; Leader of the House of Commons 2003–05; Lord Privy Seal 2003–05; Sec. of State for Northern Ireland 2005–07, for Work and Pensions 2007–08; Shadow Sec. of State for Wales and Chair. of the Nat. Policy Forum 2010–12; Founding mem. Anti-Nazi League 1970s; Chair. Tribune magazine 1993–97; mem. Council for Nuclear Disarmament (CND), GMB Union, Friends of the Earth, Fabian Soc. *Publications include:* 20 publs, including Ayes to the Left: A Future for Socialism, Sing the Beloved Country, Mandela, Outside In (memoir). *Leisure interests:* soccer, cricket, rugby, motor racing. *Address:* House of Commons, Westminster, London, SW1A 0AA, England (office); Neath Constituency Office, 39 Windsor Road, Neath, SA11 1NB, Wales. *Telephone:* (20) 7210-3925 (London); (1639) 630152 (Neath). *Fax:* (20) 7219-3816 (London) (office); (1639) 641196 (Neath). *E-mail:* hainp@parliament.uk (office). *Website:* www.parliament.uk (office); www.peterhain.org.

HAJI-FAQI, Abdihakim Mohamoud; Somali diplomatist and politician; fmr diplomat, served in New York; Minister of Defence and Second Deputy Prime Minister 2010–14. *Address:* c/o Ministry of Defence, Mogadishu, Somalia.

HAJI-IOANNOU, Sir Stelios, Kt, BSc (Econ), MSc; British/Cypriot entrepreneur; *Founder and Chairman, easyGroup;* b. 14 Feb. 1967, Athens, Greece; s. of Loucas Haji-Ioannou and Nedi Haji-Ioannou; ed Doucas School, Athens, London School of Econs and Political Science, Cass Business School, UK; joined father's co., Troodos Maritime 1988, CEO –1991; Founder Cyprus Marine Environment Protection Asscn (CYMEPA) 1992; Founder and Chair. Stelmar Tankers, Athens and London 1992; Founder easyJet, London 1995 (Chair. 1995–2002), Founder and Chair. easyGroup 1998, Founder, easyCar 2000, easyBus 2004, easyHotel 2005, easyProperty 2012; Founder Stelios Philanthropic Foundation 2009; lives in Monaco; Hon. Gen. Consul of Cyprus to the Principality of Monaco; Dr hc (Liverpool John Moores Univ.), (Cass Business School), (Cranfield Univ.), (Newcastle Business School). *Leisure interest:* yachting. *Address:* easyGroup Holdings Ltd, Le Ruscino, 14 Quai Antoine 1er, 98000 Monaco (office). *Telephone:* 98-80-10-10 (office). *Fax:* 97-97-37-88 (office). *E-mail:* chairmansoffice@easygroup.co.uk (office); mlb@stelios.com (office). *Website:* www.easy.com (office); www.stelios.com (office).

HAJJAJ, Emad, BA; Palestinian cartoonist; b. 1967, Ramallah; ed Al Yarmouk Univ., Irbid; first cartoon published in Al Yarmouk Univ. newspaper (Sahafat Al Yarmouk) 1987, later worked for several newspapers including Akher Khabar, Al Ahali, Al Raseef, Al Bilad, Al Mustaqbal, Al Dustour, Al Rai; worked for Al Quds Al Arabi newspaper, London 1992; currently with Al Gahd, Amman; mem. Jordan Press Union 1999–, Cartoonists and Writers Syndicate, USA; Best Published Cartoon in the Arabic Media (for 'The Crying Arabic Camel') 2005, winner Arabic Press Award (Dubai Press Club) 2006. *Address:* c/o Al-Ghad, POB 3535, Amman 11821, Jordan (office). *E-mail:* emad@mahjoob.com (office). *Website:* www.mahjoob.com (office).

HAJJAJI, Najat al-, BA, MA; Libyan journalist, international organization official and diplomatist; b. 26 July 1952, Tripoli; d. of Mehdi al-Hajjaji and Ftitima al-Maghur; one d.; ed Univ. Libya, Egypt; Ed. Gen. Inst. for Journalism, Tripoli 1973–75; corresp., Alfajer Al-Jadid (daily newspaper) 1975–77; Dir of Foreign Relations and Training, Jamahiriya News Agency 1978–91; Minister Plenipotentiary, Perm. Mission to UN, Geneva 1992–98, Chargé d'affaires a.i. 1998–2000, Amb. and Perm. Rep. to UN, Geneva 2000–07; Vice-Pres. UN Human Rights Comm., Geneva 2001, Pres. 2003–05; Head of Del. to UN Human Rights Comm. and Sub-Comm. on Promotion and Protection of Human Rights 1993–2001; Leader Dels to Human Rights Treaty bodies 1993–2001; rapporteur, Main Cttee, World Conf. Against Racism, Racial Discrimination, Xenophobia and Related Intolerance, Durban 2001; Vice-Chair. Preparatory Cttee, World Summit on the Information Soc. 2002, Diplomatic Conf. on the Third Protocol Additional to the Geneva Conventions; mem. UN Special Committee to select winners of UN prize in field of human rights, Working Group on Mercenaries 2005; Pres. Council of Int. Org. for Migration 2006–07; apptd Chair. Durban II UN Human Rights Council, Geneva 2009; Hon. Rep. Int. Org. for Peace, Care and Relief Geneva 2003; Kuala Lumpur World Peace Conf. Award Malaysia 2003, Geneva Inst. for Human Rights 2004, Hon. Distinction, Arab Labour Org. 2004, Medal, Gen. Head of Dubai Police 2004, Medal, Int. Criminal Court on Rwanda, Arab Women Studies Centre Award, Dubai 2006. *Publications include:* wide range of articles on the promotion and protection of human rights and African affairs. *Leisure interests:* playing the piano, classical music, reading, sports. *Address:* c/o Permanent Mission of Libyan Arab Jamahiriya, 25 rue Richemond, 1202 Geneva, Switzerland (office).

HAJJRI, Abdulwahab Abdulla al-, LLM; Yemeni diplomatist; b. 1958; m.; three c.; ed Sana'a Univ., American Univ., Washington DC, USA, Al Azhar Univ., Cairo, Egypt; joined Ministry of Foreign Affairs 1980, Diplomatic Attaché, Political Dept, Sana'a 1980–82, Cultural Attaché, Cairo 1982–87, Washington, DC 1987–92, Counsellor, Cairo 1992–95, Minister Plenipotentiary, Embassy in Washington, DC 1995–97, Amb. to USA (also accred to Mexico and Venezuela) and Perm. Observer of Yemen to OAS 1997–2012. *Address:* Ministry of Foreign Affairs, PO Box 1994, San'a, Yemen (office). *Telephone:* (1) 276612 (office). *Fax:* (1) 286618 (office). *E-mail:* mofa1@mofa.gov.ye (office). *Website:* www.mofa.gov.ye (office).

HAJRAF, Nayef Falah al-; Kuwaiti academic and politician; Curriculum Coordinator, Coll. of Business Admin, Gulf Univ. for Science & Tech. 2002–04, Head

of Accounting Dept 2004–07, later Prof. of Accounting and Asst Vice-Pres. for Academic Services; Financial Adviser, Kuwait Stock Exchange 2003–04; Financial Adviser to UN Devt Programme, Ministry of Planning 2003–04, 2007–08; CEO First Abu Dhabi Co. for Real Estate Devt 2009; Commr, Kuwait Capital Markets Authority 2011–; Minister of Finance, of Educ. and Acting Minister of Higher Educ. 2012–13, Minister of Educ. and of Higher Educ. 2013; Chair. Kuwait Public Authority for Applied Educ. and Training. *Address:* c/o Ministry of Education, POB 7, Hilali St, 13001 Safat, Kuwait City, Kuwait.

HÄKÄMIES, Jyri, MSSc; Finnish business executive and politician; *Minister of Economic Affairs;* b. 30 Aug. 1961, Karhula; s. of Erkki Häkämies and Pirkko Häkämies; m. Tuija Arhosola; two s.; Communications Man. Kymen Viestintä Oy (newspaper publr) 1989–91; Sales Man. Kymen Sanomat (newspaper) 1991–94; Man. Dir Kymenlaakso Chamber of Commerce 1994–99; mem. Suomen Eduskunta (Parl.) (Nat. Coalition Party—NCP) 1999–, mem. NCP Communications Sec., Parl. Group 1987–89, Vice-Chair. (Parl. Group) 2003–06, Chair. 2006–; Minister of Defence 2007–11, also Minister at the Prime Minister's Office (ownership steering) 2007–11, Minister of Econ. Affairs 2011–; mem. Kotka City Council 2005–, Regional Council of Kymenlaakso Ass. (Chair. 2005–); mem. Supervisory Bd Port of Kotka Ltd (Chair. 2005–07), Sitra, The Finnish Innovation Fund 2006–07, Kymen Puhelin Oy 1998–2007; Vice-Pres. European People's Party 2003–06; mem. Council, Finland-Russia Soc. 2006–. *Leisure interests:* jogging, tennis, golf, skiing, reading. *Address:* Ministry of Employment and the Economy, Aleksanterinkatu 4, PO Box 32, 00170 Helsinki, Finland (office). *Telephone:* (10) 606000 (office). *Fax:* (9) 16062160 (office). *E-mail:* kirjaamo@tem.fi (office). *Website:* www.tem.fi (office).

HAKEEM, Abdul Rauf; Sri Lankan politician; *Leader, Sri Lanka Muslim Congress Party;* ed Royal Coll. Colombo; fmr First Sec. Sri Lanka Muslim Congress (SLMC) Working Cttee, Deputy Sec.-Gen., then Sec.-Gen., currently Leader SLMC; Minister of Internal and Int. Trade and Commerce, of Shipping Devt and of Muslim Religious Affairs –2001; Minister of Port Devt and Shipping and of Eastern Devt and Muslim Religious Affairs 2001–04, of Posts and Telecommunications 2007–09. *Address:* Sri Lanka Muslim Congress, Sama Mandiraya, 53 Vauxhall Lane, Colombo 2, Sri Lanka (office). *Telephone:* (11) 22431711 (office). *E-mail:* info@slmc.lk (office). *Website:* www.slmc.lk (office).

HAKIM, Nadey S., MD, PhD, FRCS, FACS; British surgeon and fmr international organization official; *Max Thorek Professor, International College of Surgeons;* b. 9 April 1958, Beirut, Lebanon; m. Nicole Hakim; four c.; ed René Descartes Univ., Paris, Mayo Clinic, Univ. of Minnesota, USA; Consultant Surgeon and Surgical Dir Transplant Unit, Hammersmith Hosp., London; Fellow, Int. Coll. of Surgeons 1987–, Max Thorek Prof. 2008–, fmr European Fed. Sec., fmr Sec. UK Section, WHO Rep., Pres. 2004–; Ed.-in-Chief Emer. Journal of International Surgery; Registered Sculptor, Royal Soc. of British Sculptors, American Soc. for Bariatric and Metabolic Surgery; Hon. Prof. of Surgery, Univ. of São Paolo, Ricardo Palma Peru Univ., Univ. of Bashkent; Hon. Prof., Univ. of Lyon, Hon. Fellow, Int. Coll. of Surgeons, Int. Medical Sciences Acad., Int. Napoleonic Soc.; Hon. Sec., Royal Soc. of Medicine; Grand Cross, Order of St John of Jerusalem, Bailiff of the Order of St John of Jerusalem, Kt of the Order of the Cedars (Lebanon); Makhzoumi Prize of Medical Excellence, Laureate, Faculty of Medicine, Paris, J. Wesley Alexander Prize for Outstanding Research in Transplantation 2007. *Music:* six Music Recordings (clarinet), USA. *Television:* Presenter, Insider programme (Channel 4) 2007. *Publications include:* author or editor of 23 textbooks; Transplantation Surgery (co-ed.), Introduction to Organ Transplantation (ed.), History of Organ and Cell Transplantation (co-ed.), Pancreas and Islet Transplantation (co-ed.), Haemostasis in Surgery (co-ed.), Composite Tissue Allograft (co-ed.), Atlas of Transplantation, Bariatric Surgery State of the Art, Hernias, Artificial Organs; more than 150 peer-reviewed papers. *Leisure Interests:* music, sculpture. *Address:* 10 Harley Street, London, W1G 7LG, England (office). *Telephone:* 7850-503297 (mobile) (office). *Fax:* (20) 7431-8497 (home). *E-mail:* nadey@globalnet.co.uk (home). *Website:* www.icsglobal.org (office).

HAKIMI, Eklil Ahmad; Afghan diplomatist; *Ambassador to USA;* b. 1968, Kabul; m.; three d.; ed Kabul Polytechnic Inst., California State Univ., Long Beach, USA; joined Ministry of Foreign Affairs 1992, served in various positions including policy formation and strategic planning 1998–2002; Adviser, Ind. Admin. Reform and Civil Service Comm., Office of the Vice-Pres. 2002–05; Amb. to People's Repub. of China (also accred to Mongolia and Viet Nam) 2005–09, to Japan 2009–10, Deputy Foreign Minister for Political Affairs 2010, Amb. to USA (also accred to Mexico, Brazil, Argentina and Colombia) 2011–. *Address:* Embassy of Afghanistan, 2341 Wyoming Avenue NW, Washington, DC 20008, USA (office). *Telephone:* (202) 483-6410 (office). *Fax:* (202) 483-6488 (office). *E-mail:* press@embassyofafghanistan.org (office). *Website:* www.embassyofafghanistan.org (office).

HÄKKÄNEN, Matti Klaus Juhani, LLM; Finnish diplomatist (retd); b. 21 July 1936, Helsinki; s. of Klaus Häkkänen and Kaiju Broms; m. Pirkko Hentola 1962; two s.; ed Univ. of Helsinki; served in Finnish Foreign Service Helsinki, Paris, New York, Moscow and Peking 1960–76; Amb. to Romania (also accred to Albania) 1976–80; Under-Sec. of State 1980–83; Amb. to Netherlands (also accred to Ireland) 1983–87, to Argentina (also accred to Chile and Uruguay) 1987–88, to France 1988–93, to Italy (also accred to Malta and San Marino) 1993–97, to Portugal (also accred to Morocco) 1997–2001; mem. Selection and Training Bd Finnish Foreign Ministry 2004–07; mem. Bd French-Finnish Chamber of Commerce 2005–08; First Lt, Finnish Naval Forces; Kt Commdr, Order of Lion of Finland, Grand Cross, Orange Nassau of the Netherlands, Officer, Black Star of France, Grand Cross, Nat. Merit of Italy, Kt Commdr, Ordre nat. du Mérite (France), Mil. Medal of Finland, Grand Cross, Order of Infante Dom Henrique (Portugal). *Publications:* Marshal Mannerheim in Portugal 1945, Mannerheimiana 2004. *Leisure interest:* tennis. *Address:* Töölönkatu 9, 00100 Helsinki, Finland. *Telephone:* (9) 497515; 50-5497895 (mobile). *E-mail:* matti.hakkanen@welho.com.

HÄKKINEN, Mika; Finnish fmr professional racing driver; *Brand Ambassador and Driver Manager, Aces Management Group;* b. 28 Sept. 1968, Helsinki; s. of Harri Häkkinen and Aila Häkkinen; five c.; fmrly go-kart driver, Formula Ford 1600 driver, Finnish, Swedish and Nordic Champion 1987; Formula 3 driver,

British Champion with West Surrey Racing 1990; Formula One driver Lotus 1991–93, McLaren 1993–2001; Grand Prix wins: European 1997, Australia 1998, Brazil 1998, 1999, Spain 1998, 1999, 2000, Monaco 1998, Austria 1998, 2000, Germany 1998, Luxembourg 1998, Japan 1998, 1999, Canada 1999, Malaysia 1999, Hungary 1999, 2000, Belgium 2000; Formula One World Champion 1998, 1999; took sabbatical at end of 2001, then announced retirement from Formula 1; driver for Mercedes in German Touring Car Championship 2004–07; Brand Amb. and Driver Man., Aces Management Group; mem. Laureus World Sports Acad.; Laureus Media Award 2009, Best Amb. for Sports (Finland). *Leisure interests:* karting, golf, music. *Address:* c/o Didier Coton, Aces Management Group, 23 Boulevard des Moulins, MC 98000 Monte Carlo, Monaco (office). *Telephone:* 93-50-08-80 (office). *Fax:* 93-50-08-90 (office). *E-mail:* didier.coton@aces-management .com (office).

HAKOPIAN, Vilen Paruirovich; Armenian university rector and neuropharmacologist; b. 1 May 1938, Garnahovit, Talin; s. of Paruir Hakopian and Inthizar Hakopian; m. Rosa Hovhannes Gasparian; one s. one d.; ed Yerevan Medical Inst.; Jr research worker, Biochem. Inst., Nat. Acad. of Sciences of Armenia 1961–65; Sr research worker and Asst, Dept of Pharmacology, Yerevan State Medical Univ. (YSMU) 1965–80, Prof. 1980–94, Dean of Foreign Students 1972–79, Dean of Medical Faculty 1979–83, Vice-Rector of Educational Affairs 1986–87, Rector of YSMU 1987–2006, Head Dept of Pharmacology 1994–; mem. Nat. Acad. of Sciences of Armenia, NAS (USA), Int. Union of Pharmacology (Belgium), Int. Pharmaceutical Fed. (Netherlands), Int. Information Acad., Moscow, Int. Higher Educ. Acad. of Sciences, Moscow, Int. Acad. of Ecology and Life Protection Sciences, St Petersburg; Fellow Scientific Council of Int. Coll. of Angiology, New York; Ed.-in-Chief Medical Science of Armenia; mem. Editorial Bd Experimental and Clinical Pharmacology (Moscow) 1993–, Int. Asscn of Pathophysiology (Moscow) 1991– and many other scientific bodies. *Publications:* nearly 200 works, including nine monographs. *Leisure interests:* chess, reading, geology, apiculture. *Address:* Department of Pharmacology, Yerevan State Medical University, 2 Koryun Street, 0025 Yerevan (office); Apt. 33, 28 Orbelli Street, Yerevan 375012, Armenia (home). *Telephone:* (10) 581802 (office). *Fax:* (10) 582532 (office). *Website:* www.ysmu.am (office).

HAKOSHIMA, Shinichi; Japanese newspaper executive; *Adviser, The Asahi Shimbun Company;* joined The Asahi Shimbun Co. (newspaper publr) 1962, posts included Chief of Econ. News section, Man. Ed. Tokyo Head Office, Exec. Man. Dir 1994, Pres. and CEO 1999–2005, Exec. Adviser –2005, Adviser 2005–; Dir NSK (Japanese Newspaper Publrs and Eds Asscn) 1999–2005, Chair. 2003–05. *Address:* The Asahi Shimbun Company, 5-3-2 Tsukiyi, Chuo-ku, Tokyo 104-8011, Japan (office). *Telephone:* (3) 5540-7724 (office). *Website:* www.asahi.com (office).

HALAIQA, Mohammad al-, BSc, PhD; Jordanian fmr government official; b. 20 May 1951, Al Shioukh; m.; ed Univ. of Jordan, Univ. of Leeds, UK; Gen. Man. of industrial co., Jordan 1981–87; Dir-Gen. Jordan Chamber of Industry 1990–92; Dir Industry and Mineral Resources Sector, Higher Council for Science and Tech. 1992–93, Asst Sec.-Gen. Higher Council for Science and Tech. 1993–94; Dir-Gen. Jordanian Export Devt and Commercial Centres Corpn (JEDCO) 1994–97; Sec.-Gen. Ministry of Trade and Industry 1997–2000; Deputy Prime Minister and Minister of Industry and Trade 2003–05; fmr Minister of Admin. Devt; fmr Senator; Pres. Jordan Chemical Soc. 1983–91, Union of Arab Chemists 1985–86, Jordanian Soc. for Quality 1997–99; fmr Pres. Arab Acad. for Banking and Financial Sciences.; led Jordanian del. to Free Trade Agreement negotiations with USA and to negotiations for Jordan's accession to WTO; mem. Bd of Dirs Jordan Valley Authority 1997–2000, Aqaba Region Authority 1997–2000, Social Security Corpn 1997–2000, Jordan Cement Factories Co. 1997–2000, Industrial Estates Corpn 1997–2000; mem. Bd of Trustees (fmr Chair.) Al Quds Coll.; mem. Econ. Consultative Council, Hashemite Royal Court; mem. Bd Trustees Princess Sumayya Coll. 1995–99, Faculty of Sciences, Hashemite Univ., Faculty of Sciences, Univ. of Jordan; mem. Higher Advisory Bd Talal Abu Ghazaleh Coll. of Business; Independence Medal of the First Order (Jordan), Al-Kawkab Medal of the Second Order. *Address:* c/o Board of Trustees, Al Quds College, Airport Road, POB 183334, Amman 11118, Jordan (office).

HALANE, Hussein; Somali economist and politician; *Minister of Finance;* fmr exec. with UN Children's Fund; various roles with Save the Children including Country Dir for Sudan 2007, Emergency Adviser in Haiti 2010; Minister of Finance 2010–11, 2014–. *Address:* Ministry of Finance, 1 Villa Somalia, 2525 Mogadishu, Somalia (office). *Telephone:* (5) 404240 (office). *Website:* www.mof .somaligov.net (office).

HALAS, Naomi J., BA, MA, PhD, DSc; American scientist and academic; *Stanley C. Moore Professor in Electrical and Computer Engineering and Professor of Biomedical Engineering, Chemistry, Physics and Astronomy, Rice University;* ed La Salle Coll., Bryn Mawr Coll., La Salle Univ.; Grad. Research Fellow, IBM T.J. Watson Research Center, Yorktown, NY 1983–86; Postdoctoral Assoc., Vanderbilt Univ. 1987, AT&T Bell Laboratories, Holmdel, NJ 1987–89; Asst Prof., Rice Univ. 1989–94, Assoc. Prof. 1994–99, Prof., Dept of Electrical and Computer Eng 1999–2001, Prof., Dept of Chem. 1999–, Stanley C. Moore Prof. in Electrical and Computer Eng 2001–, Founder and Dir Lab. for Nanophotonics 2004–, Prof., Dept of Biomedical Eng 2006–, Prof., Dept of Physics and Astronomy 2009–; Visiting Prof., Inst. of Physics, Chinese Acad. of Sciences; Co-founder Nanospectra Biosciences, Inc; Prin. Investigator of NSF-funded integrative grad. educ. and research training grant (IGERT) in Nanophotonics; Co-Chair. Gordon Research Conf. on Plasmonics 2008; Chair. Plasmonics Gordon Research Conf. 2010; mem. Advisory Bd Center for Integrated Nanotechnologies, Los Alamos Nat. Lab., Sandia Nat. Laboratories; mem. Keck Center for Gene Therapy, Univ. of Texas M.D. Anderson Cancer Center, Houston, Tex.; mem. Nanophotonics Program Cttee, IQEC 2009, Scientific Advisory Cttee, SPP4 (Int. Conf. on Plasmonics) 2009; mem. Editorial Advisory Bd Laser and Photonics Reviews 2009–, Nano Letters 2006–08 (Assoc. Ed. 2009–); Fellow, American Physical Soc. 2001, Optical Soc. of America 2003, AAAS 2005, Int. Soc. for Optical Eng (SPIE) 2007; Sr mem. IEEE 2004, Fellow 2008; mem. American Acad. of Arts and Sciences 2009, ACS; NSF Young Investigator 1992, Hershel M. Rich Invention Award: C60 Purification Method 1993, Hershel M. Rich Invention Award: Metal Nanoshells 1998, CRS-Cygnus award for outstanding grad. student research (co-recipient) 2000, Hershel M. Rich Invention Award: Photothermal Nanoshell-Polymer Drug Delivery

Material 2001, Hershel Rich Invention Award: Optically Active Nanoparticles for use in Therapeutic and Diagnostic Methods 2003, Chevy Trucks' 'Lone Star Hero' week of 10 Nov. 2003, Breast Cancer Research Program Innovator Award, US Army Medical Research and Material Command, Congressionally Funded Medical Research Programs, Dept of Defense (DoD) 2003, Nanotechnology Now's "Best Discovery of 2003" 2004, Woman of Achievement, YWCA, Houston 2005, Nanotech Brief's Nano 50 Innovator Award 2006, Esquire's Best and Brightest, Dec. 2006, NBIC Research Excellence Award, Univ. of Pennsylvania 2008, DoD Nat. Security Science and Eng Faculty Fellow 2009. *Achievements include:* best known in the field of plasmonics as the inventor of tunable nanoparticles with resonances spanning the visible and infrared regions of the spectrum. *Publications:* several book chapters and tech. reports and more than 200 papers in professional journals on the design and fabrication of optically responsive nanostructures, nanophotonics and plasmonics; 15 issued and pending patents. *Address:* Abercrombie Lab A237, Department of Electrical and Computer Engineering, Rice University, 6100 Main Street, MS 366, Houston, TX 77005-1892, USA (office). *Telephone:* (713) 348-5611 (office). *Fax:* (713) 348-5686 (office). *E-mail:* halas@rice.edu (office). *Website:* halas.rice.edu (office).

HALBERT, David D., BBA; American business executive; *Chairman, Caris Ltd;* m. Kathryn Ann Halbert; three c.; ed Abilene Christian Univ.; f. Halbert & Assocs Inc.; f. AdvancePCS, Chair., Pres. and CEO 1987–2004 (after merger with Caremark Rx); Founder and Chair. Caris, Ltd (investment partnership) 2004–; Co-founder Caris Foundation; Chair. Pathology Partners Inc.; fmr Ind. Dir Herbalife Ltd. *Leisure interest:* baseball. *Address:* Caris Ltd, 5215 North O'Connor Blvd, Suite 2650, Irving, TX 75039, USA (office). *Telephone:* (972) 590-2100 (office). *Fax:* (972) 590-2103 (office). *E-mail:* David.Halbert@carisltd.com (office). *Website:* www .carisltd.com (office).

HALBRON, Jean-Pierre; French business executive; *Member of the Executive Committee, Alcatel SA;* b. 31 Aug. 1936; ed Ecole Polytechnique, Paris, Corps des Mines, Inst. Français du Pétrole; various posts with Compagnie Financière 1963–82, including Gen. Man. 1968–74, CEO 1974–82; Finance Dir Rhône-Poulenc SA 1983, Deputy Man. Dir 1984–87; Gen. Man. CdF Chimie (later Orkem) 1987–90; Finance Dir Total SA 1990–92; Man. Dir Wasserstein Perella Corpn and Chair. Wasserstein Perella France 1992–95; Dir of Strategy and Finance, Alcatel SA 1995–97, Co-Dir-Gen. 1997–99, Financial Dir 1997–2001, Dir-Gen. 2000–02, mem. Exec. Cttee 2002–; fmr mem. Bd of Dirs Alstom SA, Electro Banque SA; mem. Strategic Cttee Agence France Trésor. *Address:* Office of the Executive Committee, Alcatel SA, 54 rue la Boétie, 75006 Paris, France (office). *Telephone:* 1-40-76-10-10 (office). *E-mail:* execoffice@alcatel-lucent.com (office). *Website:* www .alcatel.com (office).

HALDEMAN, Charles Edgar (Ed), Jr, AB, MBA, JD; American business executive; b. 29 Oct. 1948, Philadelphia, Pa; s. of Charles Edgar Haldeman, Sr and Betty Jane Haldeman; m. Barbara Haldeman; one s. two d.; ed Dartmouth Coll., Harvard Business School (Baker Scholar), Harvard Law School; Chartered Financial Analyst; began career at Cooke & Bieler, Inc. (affiliate of United Asset Management Corpn—UAM) 1974, held a series of sr exec. positions; Chair. and CEO Delaware Investments, and Pres. and COO UAM –2002; Co-Head of Investment Div., Putnam Investments 2002–03, Pres. and CEO Putnam Investments 2003–08, led sale of Putnam Investments to Power Financial Corpn Jan. 2007, mem. Putnam Funds' Board of Trustees 2004–09, Pres. Putnam Funds 2007–09, Chair. Putnam Investment Man., LLC (investment adviser for the Putnam Funds) 2008–09; CEO Freddie Mac (Federal Home Loan Mortgage Corpn) 2009–11 (retd); Chair. Bd of Trustees, Dartmouth Coll. 2007–10; fmr mem. Bd of Govs Investment Company Inst., Investment Counsel Asscn of America; named by CFA Magazine as One of the Most Influential CFA Institute Members 2006, named by Businessweek as one of their 50 Most Powerful People in Real Estate 2010. *Address:* c/o Freddie Mac, 8200 Jones Branch Drive, McLean, VA 22102-3110, USA. *E-mail:* info@freddiemac.com.

HALE OF RICHMOND, Baroness (Life Peer), cr. 2004, of Easby in the County of North Yorkshire; **Rt Hon. Brenda Marjorie Hale,** DBE, PC, MA; British judge, barrister and university chancellor; *Justice, The Supreme Court;* b. 31 Jan. 1945, Leeds, Yorks., England; d. of Cecil Frederick Hale and Marjorie Hale (née Godfrey); m. 1st Anthony John Christopher Hoggett 1968 (divorced 1992); one d.; m. 2nd Julian Thomas Farrand 1992; ed Richmond High School for Girls, Yorks., Girton Coll., Cambridge and Gray's Inn, London; Asst Lecturer, Faculty of Law, Univ. of Manchester 1966–68, Lecturer 1968–76, Sr Lecturer 1976–81, Reader 1981–86, Prof. 1986–89; Prof., King's Coll., London 1989–90; practice, Manchester Bar 1969–72; Asst Recorder 1982–89, Recorder 1989–94; Law Commr 1984–93; Judge of the High Court, Family Div. 1994–99; Lord Justice of Appeal 1999–2004, Lord of Appeal in Ordinary (first female Law Lord) 2004–09; Justice of the Supreme Court 2009–; Visiting Fellow, Nuffield Coll., Oxford 1997–2005; Chancellor Univ. of Bristol 2004–; Visitor, Girton Coll., Cambridge 2004–, Hon. Fellow 1996–2004; Pres. Asscn of Women Barristers 1998–2005, UK Asscn of Women Judges 2003–, Int. Asscn of Women Judges 2010–12; Ed. Journal of Social Welfare Law 1978–84; mem. Mental Health Review Tribunal for the North-West 1979–80, Council on Tribunals 1980–84; Chair. Nat. Family Conciliation Council 1989–93; mem. Judicial Studies Bd Civil and Family Cttee 1990–94, Human Fertilization and Embryology Authority 1990–93; Gov. Centre for Policy on Ageing 1990–93; Pres. Nat. Family Mediation 1994–; Man. Trustee Nuffield Foundation 1987–2002; Hon. FBA 2004; Hon. FRCPsych 2007; Hon. LLD (Sheffield) 1989, (London Guildhall) 1996, (Manchester) 1997, (Bristol) 2002, (Cambridge) 2005, (Hull) 2006, (King's Coll. London) 2007, (Oxford) 2007, (City) 2007, (Reading) 2007, (Coll. of Law) 2008, (West of England) 2009, (Huddersfield) 2009, (Sussex) 2009, (Salford) 2010, (Westminster) 2011; Hon. DUniv (Essex) 2005. *Publications:* Women and the Law (co-author) 1984, Parents and Children (fourth edn) 1993, From the Test Tube to the Coffin: Choice and Regulation in Private Life 1996, The Family Law and Society: Cases and Materials (sixth edn, co-author) 2009, Mental Health Law (fifth edn) 2010. *Leisure interests:* bridge, theatre, home. *Address:* The Supreme Court, Parliament Square, London, SW1P 3BD, England (office). *Telephone:* (20) 7960-1936 (office). *Fax:* (20) 7960-1961 (office). *E-mail:* justices@supremecourt.gsi.gov .uk (office). *Website:* www.supremecourt.gov.uk (office).

HALES, Antony John (Tony), CBE, BSc; British business executive; *Chairman, Canal and River Trust;* b. 25 May 1948, Blackpool, Lancs., England; s. of S. A.

Hales and M. J. Hales; m. Linda Churchlow 1975; three s. one d.; ed Repton School, Univ. of Bristol; Marketing Man. Cadbury Schweppes 1969–79; joined Allied Domecq 1979, Marketing Dir Joshua Tetley 1979–83, Man. Dir Hall's Oxford SW 1983–85, Man. Dir Taylor Walker 1985–87, Man. Dir Ansells 1987–89, Dir Allied Breweries, Chair. and CEO Allied Domecq Spirits and Wine (fmrly Hiram Walker Group) 1995; CEO J. Lyons 1989–91, Dir Allied Domecq (fmrly Allied-Lyons) PLC 1989–99, CEO 1991–99; Dir Hyder PLC 1994–97, Midland Bank PLC (now HSBC Bank) 1994–2001, Aston Villa PLC 1997–2006, David Halsall International 2000–06, Tempo Holdings Ltd 2000–01, Reliance Security Group 2001–05, Satellite Information Services Holdings 2002–10, IPF Group PLC 2006–, Welsh Nat. Opera 2010–, Capital and Regional plc 2011–; Chair. Naati 2001–08, Workspace Group PLC 2002–11, British Waterways 2005–12, NAAFI Pension Fund Trustees 2010–, Canal and River Trust 2012–. *Leisure interests:* football, theatre, opera. *Address:* Belvoir House, Edstone Court, Wooton Wawen, Henley in Arden, Warwicks., B95 6DD (home); Canal and River Trust, Station House, 500 Elder Gate, Milton Keynes, MK9 1BB, England (office). *E-mail:* thales_uk@yahoo .com (office). *Website:* canalrivertrust.org.uk (office).

HALEY, Nimrata (Nikki) Randhawa, BS; American business executive, politician and state governor; *Governor of South Carolina;* b. (Nimrata Randhawa), 20 Jan. 1972, Bamberg, S Carolina; d. of Dr Ajit Randhawa and Raj Randhawa of India; m. Michael Haley; one s. one d.; ed Clemson Univ., S Carolina; Accounting Supervisor, FCR Corpn (waste man. and recycling co.) 1994–96; joined her mother's business, Exotica International (clothing firm) as Chief Financial Officer 1996–2004; mem. Bd of Dirs Orangeburg Co. Chamber of Commerce 1998, Lexington Chamber of Commerce 2003; Treas. Nat. Asscn of Women Business Owners 2003–04, Pres. 2004 (also Pres. S Carolina Chapter); Chair. Friends of Scouting Leadership Div. campaign 2006; mem. SC House of Reps for 87th Dist 2005–10, Majority Whip 2006–10; Gov. of South Carolina 2011– (first female gov. of SC and second Indian-American gov. in the country); mem. Bd Lexington Medical Foundation 2004, Lexington Co. Sheriff's Foundation 2004–06, West Metro Republican Women, Lexington Rotary Club, Mount Horeb United Methodist Church, Nat. Rifle Asscn; Republican; named as one of The 50 Politicos to Watch, Politico 2010, The Politics 40 Under 40, TIME magazine 2010. *Address:* Office of the Governor, 1205 Pendleton Street, Columbia, SC 29201 (office); Governor's Mansion, 800 Richland Street, Columbia, SC 29201, USA (home). *Telephone:* (803) 734-2100 (office); (803) 737-3000 (home). *Fax:* (803) 734-5167 (office). *E-mail:* nikkihaley@gov.sc.gov (office). *Website:* www.governor.sc.gov (office).

HALÍK, Mgr Tomáš, ThD, PhDr; Czech philosopher, academic, ecclesiastic and writer; *Professor, Department of Philosophy of Religion, Charles University;* b. 1 June 1948, Prague; s. of Miroslav Halík and Marie Halík; ed Charles Univ., Prague, Pontifical Lateran Univ., Rome, Vatican City; psychologist, Inst. of Ministry of Industry 1972–89; clandestinely ordained priest, Erfurt, GDR 1978; psychotherapist, Univ. Apolináře Hosp., Prague 1984–90; involved in 'underground' RC Church as close co-worker with Cardinal Tomášek; Gen. Sec. Czech Bishops' Conf. 1990–93; consultant, Pontifical Council for Dialogue with non-believers, Vatican 1990–93; Prof. and Head, Dept of Philosophy of Religion, Faculty of Philosophy, Charles Univ., Rector Univ. Church, mem. Scientific Bd Centre for Theoretical Study Charles Univ. 1992–; Visiting Fellow, St Edmund's Coll. Cambridge, UK 2003; lectures in univs world-wide, including Oxford and Cambridge, UK and Harvard, USA; Pres. Czech Christian Acad.; adviser to Pres. Havel; mem. Academic Bd Palacký Univ. Olomouc 1994–, European Acad. of Sciences and Arts, Cttee of Wise Persons, COMECE (Commissio Episcopatuum Communitatis Europensis—Comm. of the Bishops' Confs of the EC), Brussels 2006–; Hon. mem. Church Law Soc., Hon. Prelate of His Holiness 2008; Kt's Cross, Order of Merit 2012; Konrad Adenauer Silver Medal 1995, Masaryk's Arts Acad. Prize 1997, Andrew Elias SVU Human Tolerance Award 2002, Communio et Progressio Cardinal König Prize (Austria) 2003, Prize for Literature 2006, Czech Soc. for Science and Art 2007, Polish Fenix Prize for the best work by a foreign author 2008, Truth and Justice Award 2009, Romano Guardini Prize 2010, Man of Reconciliation, Soc. of Christians and Jews 2010, Prize for the best theological book of Europe, European Soc. for Catholic Theology 2010, Golden Medal of St Adalbert 2010. *Television:* 18 TV films on the world's religions 2006–07. *Publications:* books in ten languages: O přítomnou církev a společnost 1992, Sedm úvah o slubě nemocným a trpícím 1993, Du wirst das Angesicht der erde erneuern: Kirche und Gesellschaft an der Schwelle zur Freiheit 1993, Víra a kultura 1995, Un proyecto de renovación espiritual 1996, Ptal jsem se cest 1997, Wyzwoleni, jesze nie wolni 1997, Mistica, anima della filosofia? 1999, Radzilem sie drógi 2001, Co je bez chvění, není pevné 2002, Oslovit Zachea 2003, Co nie jest chwiejne, jest nietrwałe 2004, Vzývám i nevzývám 2004, Noc zpovědník 2005, Prolínání světů 2006, Wzywany czy niewzywany 2006, Premówic do Zacheusza 2006, Zacheusz! 2006, Vzdáleným nablízku 2007, Dotkni se ran 2008, Blizu pola: Molk na Antarktiki 2008, Stromu zbývá naděje 2009, Cierpliwosc wobec Boga 2009, Divadlo pro anděly 2010, Dotknij ran 2010, A gyóntató éjszakája 2010, Drzewo ma jescze nadzieję 2010, Patience with God 2009, Geduld mit Gott 2010, Dotakni se ran 2010, Smířená různost 2011, Uvahy na prahu tisíciletí 2011, Nič zpovidnika 2011, Night of the Confessor 2012, Nachtgedanken eines Beichtvaters 2012, Chci, abys byl 2012, Przenikanie światów 2012, Vicino au iontani 2012, Blizu oddaljenim 2012, Těplelivist z Bogom 2012, Blizu oddaljenim 2012, Berühre die Wunden 2013, La Notte del Confessore 2013; more than 300 articles (some distributed secretly in Czechoslovakia before 1989). *Address:* Univerzita Karlova, ÚFaR FF UK, nám. Jana Palacha 2, 110 00 Prague 2 (office); Naprstkova 2, 110 00 Prague 1, Czech Republic (home). *E-mail:* tomas.halik@gmail.com (home). *Website:* www.halik.cz.

HALILOVIĆ, Safet; Bosnia and Herzegovina politician; Chair. Municipal Bd, Party of Democratic Action (Stranka Demokratske Akcije—SDA), Sarajevo 1994–; Pres. of Fed. of Bosnia and Herzegovina 2002–03, Minister of Civil Affairs 2003–07, of Human Rights and Refugees 2007–12. *Address:* c/o Ministry of Human Rights and Refugees, 71000 Sarajevo, trg Bosne i Hercegovine 1, Bosnia and Herzegovina (office).

HALIMAN, Trihatma Kusuma; Indonesian real estate executive; *President Director, Agung Podomoro Group JL;* b. 1952; s. of Anton Haliman; m.; two c.; joined family firm Agung Podomoro Group JL (real estate co.), Pres. Dir 1986–. *Address:* Agung Podomoro Group JL, Danau Sunter Blok M2 No. 7, Kompleks Podomoro, Sport Centre Sunter Agung, Jakarta Utara 14350, Indonesia (office). *Telephone:* (21) 6511435 (office). *Fax:* (21) 6511496 (office). *Website:* www .agungpodomoro.com (office).

HALL, Alan, PhD; British molecular biologist and academic; *Chairman, Cell Biology Program, Sloan-Kettering Cancer Institute;* b. 1952; ed Univ. of Oxford, Harvard Univ., USA; Postdoctoral Fellow, Univ. of Edinburgh 1977–79, Univ. of Zurich, Switzerland 1979; mem. staff, Inst. for Cancer Research 1980; Lecturer, Dept of Biochemistry and Molecular Biology, Univ. Coll., London 1992–2001, Prof. of Molecular Biology and Dir MRC Lab. for Molecular Cell Biology and Cell Biology Unit 2001–06; Chair. Cell Biology Program, Sloan-Kettering Cancer Inst., New York 2006–; Jt Winner Louis Jeantet Prize for Medicine 2005. *Publications:* numerous articles in scientific journals. *Address:* Memorial Sloan-Kettering Cancer Center, 1275 York Avenue, New York, NY 10021, USA (office). *Telephone:* (212) 639-2000 (office). *E-mail:* halla@mskcc.org (office). *Website:* www.mskcc.org (office).

HALL, Aleksander, MA; Polish historian and fmr politician; b. 20 May 1953, Gdańsk; m. Katarzyna Hall; ed Gdańsk Univ.; history teacher, Secondary School No 6, Gdańsk 1977; active in Acad. Pastoral Cure, Gdańsk in early 1970s; mem. Movt for Defence of Human and Civic Rights (ROPCIO) 1977–79; Ed. Bratniak 1977–81; Co-Founder and Leader, Young Poland Movt 1979; mem. Solidarity Trade Union 1980–; co-f. Cttee for Defence of Persons Imprisoned because of their Opinions, attached to Solidarity Trade Union 1980; mem. Regional Co-ordinative Comm. of Solidarity Trade Union, Gdańsk 1981–84; publicist, Przegląd Katolicki (Catholic Review) 1984–89, Polityka Polska (Polish Politics) 1982–89; mem. Primatial Social Council 1986–; mem. Civic Cttee attached to Lech Wałęsa (q.v.), Chair. Solidarity Trade Union 1988–90, Vice-Pres., Dziekania Political Thought Club 1988–89; participant in Round Table debates, mem. group for political reforms Feb.–April 1989; Minister-mem. Council of Ministers (for co-operation with political orgs and Asscns) 1989–90; Deputy to Sejm (Parl.) 1991–93, 1997–2001; Vice-Chair. Solidarity Election Action Parl. Caucus 1997–2000; Leader, Democratic Right Forum 1990–92; Co-founder and Leader Conservative Party 1992–96, mem. Conservative Peasant Party (SKL) 1996– (Conservative Peasant Party-New Poland Movt, SKL-RNP from 2002), mem. Bd and Political Council. *Publications:* Refleksje i polemiki, Wybór publicystyki politycznej 1989, Spór o Polskę 1993, Zanim będzie za późno 1994, Polskie patriotyzmy 1997, Pierwsza taka dekada 2000, Widziane z prawej strony 2000; numerous articles in Polish periodicals. *Leisure interests:* reading, history, politics, political thought and history of ideas, culture and history of France. *Address:* Stronnictwo Konserwatywno Ludowe-Ruch Nowej Polski—SKL-RNP, Pl. Dąbrowskiego 5, 00-065 Warsaw, Poland (office). *Telephone:* (22) 8278442 (office). *Fax:* (22) 8278441 (office). *E-mail:* webmaster@skl.org.pl (office). *Website:* www.skl-rnp.pl (office).

HALL, Brian, BSc, PhD, DSc, FRSC; Australian biologist and academic; *George S. Campbell Professor Emeritus of Biology and University Research Professor Emeritus, Dalhousie University;* ed Univ. of New England, Armidale, NSW; Asst Prof., Dalhousie Univ., Halifax, NS, Canada 1968–75, Full Prof. of Biology 1975–96, Chair. of Biology 1978–85, Faculty of Science Killam Prof. of Biology 1996–2001, fmr George S. Campbell Prof. of Biology, Killam Research Fellow 2003–05, now Prof. Emer. of Biology and Univ. Research Prof. Emer.; Fellow, Centre for Human Biology, Univ. of WA, Perth 1993–; mem. of several editorial bds including Journal of Craniofacial Genetics and Developmental Biology, International Journal of Developmental Biology, Evolution and Development; Assoc. Ed. Molecular and Developmental Evolution 1998–; Hon. mem. St Petersburg Soc. of Naturalists, Golden Key Int. Honor Soc. 2003, Foreign Hon. Mem. American Acad. of Arts and Sciences 2002; Fry Medal, Canadian Soc. of Zoologists 1994, Int. Craniofacial Biology Distinguished Scientist Award 1996, Alexander Kowalevsky Medal St Petersburg Soc. of Naturalists 2001, Killam Prize for Natural Sciences 2005. *Publications:* has written more than 250 scientific articles and more than 16 books including Evolutionary Development Biology (textbook), Neural Crest in Development and Evolution (1999), Homology: Hierarchical Basis of Comparative Biology 2000, Evolution and Development 2000. *Address:* Department of Biology, Life Science Center, Dalhousie University, 1355 Oxford Street, Halifax, NS B3H 4J1, Canada (office). *Telephone:* (902) 494-3515 (office). *Fax:* (902) 449-3737 (office). *E-mail:* Biology@Dal.ca (office). *Website:* biology.dal.ca/us/f/hall/hall.html (office).

HALL, Sir David Michael Baldock, Kt, KB, MB, BS, BSc, FRCP, FRCPCH; British paediatrician and academic; *Professor of Community Paediatrics, University of Sheffield;* b. 4 Aug. 1945; s. of Ronald Hall and Ethel Gwen Hall (née Baldock); m. Susan M. Luck 1966; two d.; ed Reigate Grammar School, St George's Hosp., Univ. of London; Sr Medical Officer, Baragwanath Hosp., Johannesburg, South Africa 1973–76; Sr Registrar, Charing Cross Hosp., London 1976–78; Consultant Paediatrician, St George's Hosp. 1978–93; Prof. of Community Paediatrics, Univ. of Sheffield 1993–; Fellow, Royal Coll. of Paediatrics and Child Health 1996–, Pres. 2000–03; retd 2005; Hon. FRCPE 1999; Hon. Prof. of Paediatrics, Univ. of Cape Town 2007–; Univ. of London Gold Medal. *Publications include:* Child with a Disability 1996, Health for All Children (fourth edn) 2003, Child Surveillance Handbook 2006; numerous articles in scientific journals. *Leisure interests:* horses, travel. *Address:* Storrs House Farm, Storrs Lane, Stannington, Sheffield, S Yorks., S6 6GY, England. *E-mail:* d.hall@ sheffield.ac.uk (office).

HALL, Donald Andrew, BA, BLitt, LHD, DLitt; American poet, writer and academic; b. 20 Sept. 1928, New Haven, Conn.; s. of Donald A. Hall and Lucy Hall (née Wells); m. 1st Kirby Thompson 1952 (divorced 1969); one s. one d.; m. 2nd Jane Kenyon 1972 (died 1995); ed Harvard Univ., Univ. of Oxford, Stanford Univ.; Jr Fellow, Harvard Univ. 1954–57; Asst Prof., Univ. of Michigan 1957–61, Assoc. Prof. 1961–66, Prof. of English 1966–75; Poetry Ed. Paris Review 1953–62; Consultant Harper & Row 1964–81; Poet Laureate of the USA 2006–07; Guggenheim Fellow 1963, 1972; mem. Authors' Guild, American Acad. of Arts and Letters; Univ. of Oxford Newdigate Prize for Poetry 1952, Acad. of American Poets Lamont Poetry Selection 1955, Edna St Vincent Millay Memorial Prize 1956, Longview Foundation Award 1960, Sarah Josepha Hale Award 1983, Leonore Marshal Award 1987, Los Angeles Times Book Award 1989, Poetry Soc. of America Robert Frost Silver Medal 1991, New Hampshire Writers and Publishers Project Lifetime Achievement Award 1992, New England Booksellers Asscn Award 1993, Ruth Lilly Prize 1994, Aiken Taylor Award for Modern American Poetry 2009, Nat.

Medal of Art 2011. *Publications:* poetry: Poems 1952, Exile 1952, To the Loud Wind and Other Poems 1955, Exiles and Marriages 1955, The Dark Houses 1958, A Roof of Tiger Lilies 1964, The Alligator Bride: Poems New and Selected 1969, The Yellow Room: Love Poems 1971, A Blue Wing Tilts at the Edge of the Sea: Selected Poems 1964–1974 1975, The Town of Hill 1975, Kicking the Leaves 1978, The Toy Bone 1979, The Twelve Seasons 1983, Brief Lives 1983, Great Day at the Cows' House 1984, The Happy Man 1986, The One Day: A Poem in Three Parts (Nat. Book Circle Critic's Award 1989) 1988, Old and New Poems 1990, The One Day and Poems (1947–1990) 1991, The Museum of Clear Ideas 1993, The Old Life 1996, Without: Poems 1998, The Painted Bed 2000, White Apples and the Taste of Stone: Selected Poems 1946–2006 2006, The Back Chamber 2011; children's books: Ox-Cart Man (Caldecott Medal 1980) 1979, Lucy's Christmas 1994, I Am the Dog, I Am the Cat 1994, Lucy's Summer 1995; short stories: The Ideal Bakery 1987, Willow Temple 2002; prose: Henry Moore: The Life and Work of a Great Sculptor 1966, Marianne Moore: The Cage and the Animal 1970, The Gentleman's Alphabet Book 1972, Writing Well 1973, Goatfoot Milktongue Twinbird: Interviews, Essays and Notes on Poetry 1970–76 1978, The Weather for Poetry: Essays, Reviews and Notes on Poetry 1977–81 1982, Poetry and Ambition: Essays 1982–1988 1988, Here at Eagle Pond 1990, Their Ancient Glittering Eyes 1992, Life Work 1993, Death to Death of Poetry 1994, Principal Products of Portugal 1995, Breakfast Served Any Time All Day 2003, The Best Day The Worst Day (biog.) 2005, Unpacking the Boxes: A Memoir of a Life in Poetry 2008, Christmas at Eagle Pond 2012, Essays After Eighty 2014; editor: Harvard Advocate Anthology 1950, The New Poets of England and America (with L. Simpson and R. Pack) 1957, Second Selection (with R. Pack) 1962, A Poetry Sampler 1962, Contemporary American Poetry 1962, Poetry in English (with W. Taylor) 1963, A Concise Encyclopaedia of English and American Poets and Poetry (with S. Spender) 1963, Faber Book of Modern Verse 1966, The Modern Stylists 1968, A Choice of Whitman's Verse 1968, Man and Boy 1968, Anthology of American Poetry 1969, Pleasures of Poetry 1971, A Writer's Reader (with D. Emblen) 1976, Remembering Poets: Reminiscences and Opinions: Dylan Thomas, Robert Frost, T. S. Eliot, Ezra Pound 1978, To Read Literature 1981, To Read Poetry 1982, Oxford Book of American Literary Anecdotes 1981, Claims for Poetry 1982, Oxford Book of Children's Verse in America 1985, To Read Fiction 1987, Anecdotes of Modern Art (with Pat Corrigan Wykes) 1990. *Leisure interest:* baseball.

HALL, Henry Edgar, PhD, FRS; British physicist and academic; *Emeritus Professor of Low Temperature Physics, University of Manchester;* b. 1928; s. of John A. Hall; m. Patricia A. Broadbent 1962; two s. one d.; ed Latymer Upper School, Hammersmith and Emmanuel Coll. Cambridge; Royal Soc. Mond Lab. Cambridge 1952–58; Sr Student, Royal Comm. for Exhbn of 1851, 1955–57; Research Fellow, Emmanuel Coll. Cambridge 1955–58; Lecturer in Physics, Univ. of Manchester 1958–61, Prof. of Low Temperature Physics 1961–95, Emer. Prof. 1995–; has held visiting professorships in Australia, USA and Japan; Simon Memorial Prize (with W. F. Vinen) 1963, Guthrie Medal and Prize, Inst. of Physics 2004. *Publications:* Solid State Physics 1974; papers in scientific journals. *Leisure interest:* mountain walking. *Address:* Schuster Laboratory, School of Physics and Astronomy, University of Manchester, Oxford Road, Manchester, M13 9PL, England (office). *Telephone:* (161) 275-4070 (office). *Fax:* (161) 275-4056 (office). *E-mail:* henry.hall@man.ac.uk (office). *Website:* www.physics.man.ac.uk (office).

HALL, Jeffrey C., PhD; American geneticist, biologist and academic; *Part-time Faculty Member, University of Maine;* b. 1945, Brooklyn, New York; ed Amherst Coll., Univ. of Washington, Seattle; Postdoctoral Researcher, California Inst. of Tech. –1974; apptd Faculty mem., Brandeis Univ., Waltham, Mass 1974; currently Part-time Faculty mem., Univ. of Maine; Louisa Gross Horwitz Prize 2011, Gairdner Int. Award 2012, Shaw Prize in Life Science and Medicine (co-recipient) 2013. *Achievements include:* cloned, with Michael Rosbash, the Period gene in *Drosophila melanogaster* controlling its biological rhythms 1984; also discovered that the mRNA and protein encoded by this gene show circadian oscillations. *Publications:* numerous papers in professional journals. *Address:* School of Biology and Ecology, 5751 Murray Hall, Orono, ME 04469, USA (office). *Telephone:* (207) 581-2540 (office). *Fax:* (207) 581-2537 (office). *Website:* www.umaine.edu (office).

HALL, Jerry; American model and actress; b. 2 July 1956, Gonzales, Tex.; d. of the late John P. Hall and Marjorie Sheffield; m. Mick Jagger (q.v.) 1990 (divorced 1999); two s. two d.; ed The Actors' Studio, New York, Nat. Theatre, London, UK, Open Univ.; moved to Paris aged 16, began modelling career in 1970s; numerous TV appearances, USA; stage debut in William Inge's Bus Stop, Lyric Theatre, London 1990; Contributing Ed. Tatler 1999–; contracts include Yves Saint Laurent, Revlon Cosmetics, L'Oréal Hair, Thierry Mugler; Judge, Whitbread Book Awards and WH Smith Travel Book Awards; mem. Leadership Group for Amnesty International; Amb. for Prince's Trust, Caldicott Foundation, Breast Cancer; Patron Richmond Theatre, Tate Museum, Campaign for Stowe School, Pink Ribbon Foundation, Frontline Homeopathy, WELLBEING, UNICEF, Human Rights Centre for Amnesty International; Patron and Spokesperson for Nat. Soc. for Prevention of Cruelty to Children; Vice-Pres. Kingston Theatre Trust; Trustee, Tate Modern; Hon. Chair. British Red Cross London Ball. *Plays include:* The Graduate, Gielgud Theatre, London 2000 (US tour 2003), Picasso's Women 2001, The Play What I Wrote 2002, The Vagina Monologues 2002 (US tour 2003), Benchmark, New End Theatre, Hampstead 2003, UK tour 2007, Bus Stop. *Films include:* Merci Docteur Rey, Willie and Phil 1980, Urban Cowboy 1980, Topo Galileo 1987, Let's Spend the Night Together, Running Out of Luck 1987, Hysteria! 2 (TV) 1989, The Emperor and the Nightingale, Batman 1989, 25 × 5: The Continuing Adventures of the Rolling Stones 1989, The Wall: Live in Berlin (TV) 1990, Bejewelled (TV) 1991, Freejack 1992, Princess Caraboo 1994, Savage Hearts 1995, Vampire in Brooklyn 1995, Diana and Me 1997, R.P.M. 1997, Being Mick (TV) 2001, Comic Relief: Say Pants to Poverty 2001, Tooth 2004, Enchantement (short) 2004, Gangster Kittens 2011. *Television includes:* Married with Children, Just Shoot Me, Saturday Night Live (host), The Clive James Show, French and Saunders, Jerry Hall's Gurus, Popetown, Art Deco, Annie Proulx, Way Out West, The Holiday Show, Lenny Goes to Town, Cluedo (six-part series) 2004, Kept 2005, Popetown (series) 2006, The Children's Party at the Palace (special) 2006, Hotel Babylon (series) 2007, The All Star Impressions Show (film) 2009, Money (series) 2010 contestant on Strictly Come Dancing (BBC) 2012. *Radio:* The Magic Flute (Classic FM), The Betty Grable Story (BBC Radio 3). *Publications:* Tall Tales 1985, Jerry Hall's Gurus 2004. *Leisure interests:* riding, swimming,

reading, playing piano, travelling. *Address:* c/o Elite Model Management Ltd, 3–5 Islington High Street, London, N1 9LQ (office); 12 Macklin Street, Covent Garden, London, WC2B 5EZ, England.

HALL, John L., PhD; American physicist and academic; *Professor Adjoint, Physics Department, University of Colorado;* b. Aug. 1934, Denver, Colo; s. of John Ernest Hall and Elizabeth Rae Hall (née Long); m. Marilyn Charlene Robinson; two s. one d.; ed Carnegie Inst. of Tech. (now Carnegie-Mellon Univ.), Pittsburgh, Pa; NRC Postdoctoral Fellow, Nat. Bureau of Standards (now Nat. Inst. of Standards and Tech.) 1961–62, Physicist 1962–71, apptd Sr Scientist 1971, currently Scientist Emer.; Lecturer, Physics Dept, Univ. of Colorado 1961–, Prof. Adjoint 2007–; Fellow, Jt Inst. for Lab. Astrophysics (now JILA) 1971–, American Physical Soc., Optical Soc. of America; mem. Acad. of Science; Légion d'honneur 2004; Dr hc (Université Paris Nord) 1989; Hon. DSc (Carnegie Mellon) 2006, (Glasgow) 2007, (Ohio State) 2008; Dept of Commerce Gold Medal 1969, (group) 1974, 2002, Samuel W. Stratton Award 1971, E. U. Condon Award 1979, Optical Soc. of America Charles Hard Townes Award (co-recipient) 1984, American Physical Soc. Davisson-Germer Prize 1988, Optical Soc. of America Frederic Ives Medal 1991, American Physical Soc. Arthur L. Shawlow Prize 1993, Allen V. Astin Measurement Science Award 2000, Optical Soc. of America Max Born Award 2002, Office of Personnel Man. Presidential Rank Award 2002, IEEE Soc. for Ultrasonic, FerroElectricity and Frequency Control I. I. Rabi Prize 2004, Nobel Prize in Physics (co-recipient) 2005. *Publications:* numerous articles in peer-reviewed journals, and 11 patents. *Leisure interests:* music, photography, electronic design, travel. *Address:* JILA, University of Colorado, 440 UCB, Boulder, CO 80309-0440, USA (office). *Telephone:* (303) 492-7843 (office). *Fax:* (303) 492-5235 (office). *E-mail:* jhall@jila.colorado.edu (office). *Website:* jila.colorado.edu/hall (office); www.Sci-TeksDiscoveryProgramforKids.org (office).

HALL, Most Hon. Sir Kenneth O., Kt, BA, MA, PhD, GCMG, OJ; Jamaican academic, university administrator and government official; b. 24 April 1941, Hanover, Jamaica; m. Rheima Holding; one d.; ed Univ. of the West Indies, Mona, Jamaica, Inst. of Int. Relations, Univ. of the West Indies, St Augustine, Trinidad, Queen's Univ., Canada; Prof. of History, State Univ. of NY (SUNY), Oswego, becoming Adjunct Prof. of Caribbean Studies, SUNY, Albany, also Prof. of American Studies, SUNY, Old Wesbury, Vice-Pres., Academic Affairs; Deputy Sec.-Gen. Caribbean Community (CARICOM) Secr. 1994–96; Pro-Vice-Chancellor and Prin. Univ. of the West Indies, Mona campus 1996–2006; Gov.-Gen. of Jamaica 2006–09; mem. Univ. Council of Jamaica; mem. Bd Dirs Bank of Jamaica; Chair. Caribbean Examinations Council 2003–07; Order of the Nation. *Address:* c/o King's House, Hope Road, Kingston 10, Jamaica (office).

HALL, Nigel John, MA, RA; British sculptor; b. 30 Aug. 1943, Bristol; s. of Herbert John Hall and Gwendoline Mary Hall (née Olsen); m. Manijeh Yadegar 1986; ed Bristol Grammar School, West of England Coll. of Art, Royal Coll. of Art, London; Harkness Fellowship to USA 1967–69; first solo exhbn, Galerie Givaudan, Paris 1967; represented in the following collections: Tate Gallery, London, Musée Nat. d'Art Moderne, Paris, Nat. Galerie, Berlin, Museum of Modern Art, New York, Australian Nat. Gallery, Canberra, Art Inst. of Chicago, Kunsthaus, Zurich, Tokyo Metropolitan Museum, Musée d'Art Moderne, Brussels, Louisiana Museum, Denmark, Nat. Museum of Art, Osaka, Museum of Contemporary Art, Sydney, Tel-Aviv Museum, others; sculpture commissioned for Thameslink Tunnel, London 1993, Bank of America, London 2003, Said Business School, Univ. of Oxford, 2005, Bank for Int. Settlements, Basel 2006; Jack Goldhill Prize for Sculpture, RA, London 2002. *Publications:* Nigel Hall: Other Voices, Other Rooms, Galerie Scheffel, Bad Homburg, Germany 2007, Nigel Hall: Sculpture and Works on Paper, Royal Acad. of Arts 2008. *Address:* 11 Kensington Park Gardens, London, W11 3HD, England. *Telephone:* (20) 8675-5945 (office); (20) 7727-3162 (home). *Fax:* (20) 7229-1852.

HALL, Peter Gavin, DPhil, FRS, FAA; Australian statistician and academic; *Professor of Statistics, University of Melbourne;* b. 20 Nov. 1951, Sydney; s. of William Holmen Hall and Ruby Violet Hall; m. Jeannie Jean Chien; ed Sydney Univ., Australian Nat. Univ., Univ. of Oxford, UK; Lecturer in Statistics, Univ. of Melbourne 1976–78, Prof. of Statistics 2006–; Lecturer in Statistics, ANU 1978–82, Sr Lecturer 1983–95, Reader 1986–88, Prof. 1988–2006; Centennial Professorship, LSE, UK 2000–02; Pres. Bernoulli Soc. for Math. Statistics and Probability 1999–2003; mem. Editorial Bd Annals of Statistics and several other journals; Corresp. Fellow, Royal Soc. of Edinburgh; Fellow, Inst. of Math. Statistics 1984, American Statistical Asscn 1996; Hon. Fellow, Royal Statistical Soc. 1989; Dr hc (Univ. Catholique de Louvain) 1997; Hon. DSc (Glasgow) 2005; Australian Math. Soc. Medal 1986, Rollo Davidson Prize, Univ. of Cambridge 1986, S.S. Wilks Lecture, Princeton Univ. 1988, Lyle Medal, Australian Acad. of Science 1989, Pitman Medal, Statistical Soc. of Australia 1990, Hannan Medal 1995, Kolmogorov Lecture, Vienna 1996, Invited Lecture, Int. Congress of Mathematicians, Berlin 1998, Matthew Flinders Medal and Lecture, Australian Acad. of Science 2006. *Publications:* Rates of Convergence in the Central Limit Theorem 1982, Introduction to the Theory of Coverage Processes 1988, The Bootstrap and Edgeworth Expansion 1992; over 400 papers in journals. *Address:* Centre for Mathematics and its Applications, 1163 JDMS Building, Australian National University, Canberra, ACT 0200 (office); Department of Mathematics and Statistics, University of Melbourne, Parkville, Vic. 3010; 6 Ramsay Place, Wanniassa, ACT 2903, Australia (home). *Telephone:* (2) 6125-3474 (Canberra) (office); (3) 8344-9682 (Melbourne) (office). *Fax:* (2) 6125-5549 (Canberra) (office); (3) 8344-4599 (Melbourne) (office). *E-mail:* Peter.Hall@maths.anu.edu.au (office); pghall@unimelb.edu.au (office). *Website:* wwwmaths.anu.edu.au/CMA (office); www.ms.unimelb.edu.au (office).

HALL, Sir Peter Geoffrey, Kt, MA, PhD, FBA; British geographer and academic; *Bartlett Professor of Planning and Regeneration, Bartlett School of Planning, University College London;* b. 19 March 1932, London, England; s. of Arthur Vickers and Bertha Hall (née Keefe); m. 1st Carla M. Wartenberg 1962 (divorced 1967); m. 2nd Magdalena Mróz 1967; ed Blackpool Grammar School, St Catharine's Coll., Cambridge; Asst Lecturer, Birkbeck Coll., Univ. of London 1956–60, Lecturer 1960–65; Reader in Geography with special reference to planning, LSE 1966–67; Prof. of Geography, Univ. of Reading 1968–89, Prof. Emer. 1989–; Prof. of City and Regional Planning, Univ. of California, Berkeley 1980–92, Prof. Emer. 1993–; Dir Inst. of Urban and Regional Devt 1989–92;

Special Adviser to Sec. of State for the Environment 1991–94; Bartlett Prof. of Planning and Regeneration, Bartlett School of Planning, Univ. Coll., London 1992–; mem. South East Econ. Planning Council 1966–79, Social Science Research Council 1974–80, Urban Task Force 1998–99; mem. Academia Europaea; Fellow, British Acad. 1983; Hon. Fellow, St Catherine's Coll. Cambridge 1988; 13 hon. degrees; Gill Memorial Prize, Royal Geographical Soc. 1968, Adolphe Bentinck Prize 1979, Founder's Medal, Royal Geographical Soc. 1988, Prix Vautrin Lud 2001, Gold Medal, Royal Town Planning Inst. 2003, Deputy Prime Minister's Lifetime Achievement Award 2005, Balzan Int. Prize 2005. *Publications:* approx. 40 books on urban questions authored, co-authored or edited, including The Industries of London 1962, London 2000 1963, Labour's New Frontiers 1964, Land Values (ed.) 1965, The World Cities 1966, Von Thünen's Isolated State (ed.) 1966, Theory and Practice of Regional Planning 1970, The Containment of Urban England 1973, Planning and Urban Growth 1973, Urban and Regional Planning 1974, Europe 2000 1977, Growth Centres in the European System 1980, Great Planning Disasters 1980, The Inner City in Context (ed.) 1981, Silicon Landscapes (ed.) 1985, Can Rail Save the City? 1985, High-Tech America 1986, Western Sunrise 1987, Cities of Tomorrow 1988, The Carrier Wave 1988, London 2001 1989, The Rise of the Gunbelt 1992, Technopoles of the World 1993, Sociable Cities 1998, Cities in Civilization 1998, Urban Future 21 2000, Working Capital 2002, The Polycentric Metropolis 2006, London Voices London Lives 2007. *Leisure interests:* reading, talking. *Address:* 12 Queens Road, London, W5 2SA (home); Bartlett School of Planning, University College London, Wates House, 22 Gordon Street, London, WC1H 0QB, England (office). *Telephone:* (20) 8997-3717 (home); (20) 8810-8723 (office). *Fax:* (20) 7679-7502 (office). *E-mail:* p.hall@ucl.ac.uk (office). *Website:* www.bartlett.ucl.ac.uk/planning (office).

HALL, Sir Peter Reginald Frederick, Kt, CBE, MA; British theatre director and film director; b. 22 Nov. 1930, Bury St Edmunds, Suffolk; s. of late Reginald Hall and Grace Hall; m. 1st Leslie Caron 1956 (divorced 1965); one s. one d.; m. 2nd Jacqueline Taylor 1965 (divorced 1981); one s. one d.; m. 3rd Maria Ewing (q.v.) 1982 (divorced 1989); one d.; m. 4th Nicola Frei 1990; one d.; ed Perse School and St Catharine's Coll., Cambridge; produced and acted in over 20 plays at Cambridge; first professional production The Letter, Windsor 1953; produced in repertory at Windsor, Worthing and Oxford Playhouse; two Shakespearean productions for Arts Council; Artistic Dir Elizabethan Theatre Co. 1953; Asst Dir London Arts Theatre 1954, Dir 1955–57; formed own producing co., Int. Playwright's Theatre 1957; Man. Dir Royal Shakespeare Co., Stratford-upon-Avon and Aldwych Theatre, London 1960–68 (resgnd). Assoc. Dir –1973; mem. Arts Council 1969–73; Co-Dir, Nat. Theatre (now Royal Nat. Theatre) with Lord Olivier April-Nov. 1973, Dir 1973–88; f. Peter Hall Co. 1988; Artistic Dir Glyndebourne 1984–90; Artistic Dir The Old Vic 1997; Wortham Chair in Performing Arts, Houston Univ., Tex. 1999; Chancellor, Kingston Univ. 2000–; fmr Dir Kingston Theatre, now Dir Emer.; Assoc. Prof. of Drama, Warwick Univ. 1964–67; Patron, Canon's Mouth; mem. Bd Playhouse Theatre 1990–91; acted in The Pedestrian (film) 1973; Hon. Fellow, St Catharine's Coll. Cambridge 1964; Chevalier, Ordre des Arts et des Lettres 1965; Dr hc (York) 1966, (Reading) 1973, (Liverpool) 1974, (Leicester) 1977, (Essex) 1993, (Cambridge) 2003; Hon. DSocSc (Birmingham) 1989; Hamburg Univ. Shakespeare Prize 1967, Evening Standard Special Award 1979, Evening Standard Award for Outstanding Achievement in Opera 1981, Evening Standard Best Dir Award for The Oresteia 1981, Evening Standard Best Dir Award for Antony and Cleopatra 1987, South Bank Show Lifetime Achievement Award 1998, Olivier Special Award for Lifetime Achievement 1999, New York Shakespeare Soc. Medal 2003, Lifetime Achievement Award, Theater Hall of Fame 2006. *Productions include:* Blood Wedding, The Immoralist, The Lesson, South, Mourning Becomes Electra, Waiting for Godot, Waltz of the Toreadors, Camino Real, Gigi, Love's Labours Lost, Cymbeline, Twelfth Night, A Midsummer Night's Dream, Coriolanus, Two Gentlemen of Verona, Troilus and Cressida, Ondine, Romeo and Juliet, The Wars of the Roses (London Theatre Critics' Award for Best Dir 1963), Becket, Cat on a Hot Tin Roof, The Rope Dancers (on Broadway), The Moon and Sixpence (opera, Sadler's Wells), Henry VI (parts 1, 2 and 3), Richard III, Richard II, Henry IV (parts 1 and 2), Henry V, Eh?, The Homecoming (London Theatre Critics' Award for Best Dir 1965, Antoinette Perry Award for Best Dir 1966), Moses and Aaron (opera, Covent Garden), Hamlet (London Theatre Critics' Award for Best Dir 1965), The Government Inspector, The Magic Flute (opera), Work is a Four Letter Word (film) 1968, Macbeth, Midsummer Night's Dream (film) 1969, Three into Two Won't Go (film) 1969, A Delicate Balance, Perfect Friday (film) 1971, La Calisto (opera, Glyndebourne Festival) 1970, The Knot Garden (opera, Covent Garden) 1970, Eugene Onegin (opera, Covent Garden) 1971, Old Times 1971, Tristan and Isolde (opera, Covent Garden) 1971, All Over 1972, Il Ritorno d'Ulisse (opera, Glyndebourne Festival) 1972, Alte Zeiten (Burgtheater, Vienna) 1972, Via Galactica (musical, Broadway) 1972, The Homecoming (film) 1973, Marriage of Figaro (opera, Glyndebourne) 1973, The Tempest 1973, Landscape (film) 1974, Akenfield (film) 1974, Happy Days 1974, No Man's Land 1975, Judgement 1975, Hamlet 1975, Tamburlaine the Great 1976, Don Giovanni (opera, Glyndebourne Festival) 1977, Volpone (Nat. Theatre) 1977, Bedroom Farce (Nat. Theatre) 1977, The Country Wife (Nat. Theatre) 1977, The Cherry Orchard (Nat. Theatre) 1978, Macbeth (Nat. Theatre) 1978, Betrayal (Nat. Theatre) 1978, Così Fan Tutte (opera, Glyndebourne) 1978, Fidelio (opera, Glyndebourne) 1979, Amadeus (Nat. Theatre) 1979, Betrayal (New York) 1980, Othello (Nat. Theatre) 1980, Amadeus (New York) (Tony Award for Best Dir 1981) 1980, Family Voices (Nat. Theatre) 1981, The Oresteia (Nat. Theatre) 1981, A Midsummer Night's Dream (opera, Glyndebourne) 1981, The Importance of Being Earnest (Nat. Theatre) 1982, Other Places (Nat. Theatre) 1982, The Ring (operas, Bayreuth Festival) 1983, Jean Seberg (musical, Nat. Theatre) 1983, L'Incoronazione di Poppea (opera, Glyndebourne) 1984, Animal Farm (Nat. Theatre) 1984, Coriolanus (Nat. Theatre) 1984, Yonadab (Nat. Theatre) 1985, Carmen (opera, Glyndebourne) 1985, (Metropolitan Opera) 1986, Albert Herring (opera, Glyndebourne) 1985, The Petition (New York and Nat. Theatre) 1986, Simon Boccanegra (opera, Glyndebourne) 1986, Salome (opera, Los Angeles) 1986, Coming in to Land (Nat. Theatre) 1986, Antony and Cleopatra (Nat. Theatre) 1987, Entertaining Strangers (Nat. Theatre) 1987, La Traviata (Glyndebourne) 1987, Falstaff (Glyndebourne) 1988, Salome (Covent Garden) 1988, Cymbeline (Nat. Theatre) 1988, The Winter's Tale (Nat. Theatre) 1988, The Tempest 1988, Orpheus Descending 1988, Salome (opera, Chicago) 1988, Albert Herring 1989, Merchant of Venice (Nat. Theatre) 1989, She's Been Away (TV) 1989, New Year

(opera, Houston and Glyndebourne) 1989, Born Again (musical) 1990, The Homecoming 1990, Orpheus Descending (film) 1990, Twelfth Night 1991, The Rose Tattoo 1991, Tartuffe 1991, The Camomile Lawn (TV) 1991, Four Baboons Adoring the Sun (New York) 1992,All's Well That Ends Well (RSC) 1992, The Gift of the Gorgon (RSC) 1992, The Magic Flute (LA) 1993, Separate Tables 1993, Lysistrata 1993, She Stoops to Conquer 1993, Piaf (musical) 1993, An Absolute Turkey (Le Dindon) 1994, On Approval 1994, Hamlet 1994, Jacob (TV) 1994, Never Talk to Strangers (film) 1995, Julius Caesar (RSC) 1995, The Master Builder 1995, The Final Passage (TV) 1996, The Oedipus Plays (Nat. Theatre at Epidaurus and Nat. Theatre) 1996, A School for Wives 1995, A Streetcar Named Desire 1997, The Seagull 1997, Waiting for Godot 1997, 1998, King Lear 1997, The Misanthrope 1998, Major Barbara 1998, Simon Boccanegra (Glyndebourne) 1998, Amadeus 1998, Kafka's Dick 1998, Measure for Measure (LA) 1999, A Midsummer Night's Dream (LA) 1999, Lenny (Queens Theatre) 1999, Amadeus (LA, NY) 1999, Tantalus (Denver, Colo) 2000, Japes 2000, Romeo and Juliet (LA) 2001, Japes 2001, Troilus and Cressida (NY) 2001, A Midsummer Night's Dream (Glyndebourne) 2001, Otello (Glyndebourne) 2001, Japes (Theatre Royal) 2001, The Royal Family (Theatre Royal) 2001, Lady Windermere's Fan (Theatre Royal) 2002, The Bacchai (Olivier Theatre) 2002, Design for Living (Theatre Royal, Bath) 2003, Betrayal (Theatre Royal, Bath) 2003, The Fight for Barbara (Theatre Royal, Bath) 2003, As You Like It (Theatre Royal, Bath) 2003, Cuckoos (Theatre Royal, Bath) 2003, The Marriage of Figaro (Lyric Opera of Chicago) 2003, Happy Days (Arts Theatre, London) 2003, Man and Superman (Theatre Royal, Bath) 2004, Galileo's Daughter (Theatre Royal, Bath) 2004, The Vortex 2007, An Ideal Husband 2008, Pygmalion 2009. *Publications:* The Wars of the Roses 1970, Shakespeare's three Henry VI plays and Richard III (adapted with John Barton), John Gabriel Borkman (English version with Inga-Stina Ewbank) 1975, Peter Hall's Diaries: The Story of a Dramatic Battle 1983, Animal Farm: a stage adaptation 1986, The Wild Duck 1990, Making an Exhibition of Myself (autobiog.) 1993, An Absolute Turkey (new trans. of Feydeau's Le Dindon, with Nicki Frei) 1994, The Master Builder (with Inga-Stina Ewbank) 1995, Mind Millie for Me (new trans. of Feydeau's Occupe-toi d'Amélie, with Nicki Frei), The Necessary Theatre 1999, Exposed by the Mask 2000, Shakespeare's Advice to the Players 2003. *Leisure interest:* music. *Address:* 48 Lamont Road, London, SW10 0HX, England. *E-mail:* phpetard@aol.com (office).

HALL, Philip David; British journalist and PR consultant; *Chairman, PHA Media;* b. 8 Jan. 1955; s. of Norman Philip Hall and Olive Jean Hall; m. Marina Thomson 1997; two c.; ed Beal Grammar School, Ilford; reporter, Dagenham Post 1974–77, Ilford Recorder 1977–80; Sub-Ed. Newham Recorder 1980–84, Weekend Magazine 1984–85; reporter, The People 1985–86, Chief Reporter 1986–89, News Ed. 1989–92; News Ed. Sunday Express 1992–93; Asst Ed. (Features) News of the World 1993–94, Deputy Ed. 1994–95, Ed. 1995–2000; with Max Clifford Assocs 2000–01; Ed.-in-Chief Hello! 2001–02; Founder and Chair. Phil Hall Assocs. (public relations) (now PHA Media) 2004–; mem. Press Complaints Comm. 1998–2000, 2002–. *Leisure interests:* golf, cinema, theatre, football. *Address:* PHA Media, 117 Wardour Street, London, W1F 0UN, England (office). *Telephone:* (20) 7025-1350 (office). *Fax:* (20) 7025-1351 (office). *E-mail:* info@pha-media.com (office). *Website:* www.pha-media.com (office).

HALL, Rev. Wesley Winfield; Barbadian church leader, politician, public relations consultant and fmr cricketer; b. 12 Sept. 1937, Glebe Land, Station Hill, St Michael; m. (divorced); four c.; ed Combermere School and Industrial Soc. London (personnel man.); right-arm fast bowler and lower-order right-hand batsman; took 192 wickets (average 26.38) in 48 Tests, best bowling (innings) 7/69, (match) 11/126; took 546 First-class wickets (average 26.14), best bowling (innings) 7/51; played amateur and professional cricket in England, Australia, NZ, India, Sri Lanka and throughout West Indies including 48 Test matches in which he took 192 wickets and first hat-trick by a West Indian 1961–69; Man. West Indies Cricket Team throughout West Indies and abroad 1983–85; Pres. West Indies Cricket Bd 2001–; trainee telegraphist, Cable and Wireless, Barbados 1955–60; Public Relations Consultant, Esso, Queensland, Australia 1960–63, British American Tobacco Co. Ltd (Trinidad and Tobago) 1968–78; Personnel and Public Relations Man. Banks Barbados Breweries Ltd 1975–85; Ind. Senator, Barbados Senate 1971–76, Opposition Senator 1981–86; Minister of Employment, Labour Relations and Community Devt 1986–88, of Tourism and Sports 1988–93, of Industrial Relations, Community Devt and Sports 1993–94; fmr mem. Bd of Dirs Stanford 20/20 Cricket Project; Life mem. MCC; Hon. Life mem. Barbados Football Asscn; Humming Bird Gold Medal 1987. *Publications:* Secrets of Cricket 1962, Pace Like Fire 1965. *Address:* c/o Ministry of Tourism and Sports, Harbour Road, St Michael, Barbados.

HALL OF BIRKENHEAD, Baron (Life Peer), cr. 2010, of Birkenhead in the County of Cheshire; **Anthony (Tony) William Hall,** CBE, MA, FRSA; British business executive; *Director-General, British Broadcasting Corporation;* b. 3 March 1951, Birkenhead, Merseyside, England; s. of Donald William Hall and Mary Joyce Hall; m. Cynthia Lesley Davis 1977; one s. one d.; ed King Edward's School, Birmingham, Birkenhead School, Merseyside, Keble Coll., Oxford; joined BBC as a news trainee 1973, News Ed. 1987–90, Dir News and Current Affairs 1990–93, Man. Dir News and Current Affairs 1993–96, Chief Exec. BBC News 1996–2001, Dir-Gen. 2013–; Chief Exec. Royal Opera House, London 2001–13; mem. Council Brunel Univ. 1999–2002; Fellow, Vice-Chair. Royal TV Soc. (Chair. 1998–2000); Dir (non-exec.) Customs and Excise 2002–05, Channel 4 TV (Deputy Chair. 2012–13); Chair. Sector Skills Council for the Creative and Cultural Industries 2004–09, Theatre Royal Stratford East, Cultural Olympiad 2009–, Mayor of London's Cultural Forum; Dir (non-exec.), London Organising Cttee of the Olympic Games 2009–12, Paul Hamlyn Foundation; Trustee, High House Production Park Ltd, British Council 2008–; Patron Newsworld 1999–2000; mem. (Crossbench) House of Lords 2010–; Hon. Visiting Fellow, City Univ. 1999–2000. *Publications include:* King Coal: A History of the Miners 1981, Nuclear Politics: The History of Nuclear Power in Britain 1986, articles in various periodicals. *Leisure interests:* reading, writing, church architecture, opera, walking in Dorset. *Address:* Office of the Director General, Broadcasting House, Portland Place, London, W1A 1AA (office); House of Lords, Westminster, London, SW1A 0PW, England. *Telephone:* (20) 7580-4468 (office). *Fax:* (20) 7637-1630 (office). *E-mail:* TonyHallandPA@bbc.co.uk (office); halla@parliament.uk (office). *Website:*

.bbc.co.uk (office); www.parliament.uk/biographies/lords/lord-hall-of-birkenhead/3765 (office).

HALLBERG, Anders, BScEd, MSc, PhD; Swedish chemist, academic and fmr university vice-chancellor; *Professor Emeritus of Medicinal Chemistry, Uppsala University;* b. 29 April 1945; ed Lund Univ.; teacher/Research Asst, schools in Sweden/Lund Univ. 1970–73; Asst Research Fellow, The Chemical Centre, Lund 1973–79; Research Scientist, Nobel Kemi, Karlskoga 1980; Research Assoc., Univ. of Arizona, Tucson 1980, Asst Prof. (Pharmacy) 1981–82; Assoc. Prof. (forskare, NFR grant), The Chemical Centre, Lund 1983–86; Assoc. Dir, Astra (now AstraZeneca), Lund 1986–88, Dir, Head of Medicinal Chem. 1988–90, Scientific Adviser, AstraZeneca Lund 1990–99, Scientific Adviser, AstraZeneca Mölndal 2000–06; Prof. of Medicinal Chem., Uppsala Univ. 1990–, Head, Dept of Organic Pharmaceutical Chem. 1991–2006, Dean for Research, Faculty of Pharmacy 1996–2002, Deputy Vice-Pres. (Medicine/Pharmacy) 2002–05, Deputy Vice-Chancellor Uppsala Univ. 2005–06, Vice-Chancellor 2006–11; Visiting Researcher and Prof. at univs in USA; Section Ed., European Journal of Pharmaceutical Sciences 1998–2005; mem. Bd Åbo Akademi Univ. Finland 2009–, Forskningsberedningen (Scientific Advisory Bd of the Govt) 2011–, Bd Baltic Sea Foundation 2012–, Bd Medivir AB 2012–, Bd Beijer Foundation 2012–; mem. Royal Soc. of Sciences, Uppsala 1994, Royal Soc. of Arts and Sciences, Uppsala 2004, Royal Physiographic Soc., Lund 2005, Royal Swedish Acad. of Sciences (KVA, class IV chemistry) 2006, Royal Swedish Acad. of Eng Sciences (IVA, class IV chemistry) 2007, Royal Patriotic Soc.; Hon. mem. Småland Student Nation, Upland Student Nation, Uppsala, Allmänna Sången, Uppsala Univ. Jazz Orchestra, Orpheus Drängar, Royal Academic Orchestra, Rotary International; Order of the Cross of Terra Mariana (Estonia) 2011; Dr hc (Univ. of Sherbrooke, Canada) 2009; Fabian Gyllenberg Award, Royal Physiographic Soc. for best PhD thesis 1981, Sr Individual Grant Award to Outstanding Sr Scientist 1998, first recipient of Nat. Swedish Prize in Organic Chem. (The Holmquist Prize) 2004, Oscar Carlsson Medal for Excellence, Swedish Chemical Soc. 2005, Best Teacher Prize, Pharmacy Student Union, Uppsala Univ. 2006, HM the King's Medal for Distinguished Achievements in Educ. and Research 2008, Gustav Adolf Medal (of the year 1924), Uppsala Univ. 2011, Hon. Medal (Förtjänstmedaljen) of Kuratorskonventet, Curator curatorum 2011, Hon. Medal of Uppsala County (Förtjänstmedaljen) from the Gov. 2011, Rudbeck Medal for Outstanding Achievements in Science, Uppsala Univ. 2013. *Publications:* more than 240 scientific papers on organic synthesis and the devt of new pharmaceuticals against infectious diseases such as HIV/AIDS, HCV and malaria. *Address:* Department of Medicinal Chemistry, BMC, Box 574, 751 23 Uppsala, Sweden (office). *Telephone:* (18) 471-42-84 (office). *Fax:* (18) 471-44-74 (office). *E-mail:* anders.hallberg@orgfarm.uu.se (office). *Website:* www.farmfak.uu.se/organisk (office).

HALLBERG, Paul Thure, Fil Lic; Swedish fmr library director; b. 10 Dec. 1931, Gothenburg; s. of the late Severin Hallberg and Eva Hallberg (née Theorell); m. Elisabeth Löfgren 1958; one s.; ed Göteborg Univ., Yale Univ., USA; Asst Teacher, Dept of English Language and Literature, Göteborg Univ. 1958–59; Librarian, Göteborg Univ. Library 1960–68, Head of Dept 1968–77, Dir 1977–96; Sec. Main Cttee for Scandia Plan 1964–65; Sec. Scandinavian Fed. of Research Librarians 1966–69, mem. Bd 1979–84; mem. Royal Soc. of Arts and Sciences in Göteborg 1977–99, Librarian and Publications Officer 1977–2005, Hon. mem. 1999–; mem. Nat. Bibliographic Council 1983–96; Chair. Swedish Cataloguing Cttee 1979–85; Chair. Steering Group of Swedish LIBRIS system 1992–96; mem. of Bd Nordic Council for Scientific Information and Research Libraries (NORDINFO) 1986–88; mem. Standing Cttee, International Fed. of Library Assocns and Insts, Section on Acquisition and Exchange 1977–85, mem. Standing Cttee, Section of Univ. Libraries and other Gen. Research Libraries 1985–93, Sec. 1985–89; Dr hc (Göteborg) 1997. *Publications include:* A Passage to China: Colin Campbell's Diary of the First Swedish East India Company Expedition to Canton 1732–33 (co-ed.) 1996, En ostindiefarande fältskärs berättelse. Carl Fredrik Adlers journal från skeppet Prins Carl 1753–56 (co-ed.) 2013; author and ed. of numerous books and articles on bibliography and librarianship. *Leisure interests:* music, gardening. *Address:* Orangerigatan 34, 412 66 Göteborg, Sweden (home). *Telephone:* (31) 40-23-18 (home). *E-mail:* paul.hallberg@ub.gu.se (office).

HALLIER, Hans-Joachim, DIur; German diplomatist; b. 25 April 1930, Offenbach; s. of Christian L. Hallier and Sophie Heberer; m. Almuth H. Frantz 1966; two s.; ed Lessing Gymnasium, Frankfurt and Univs of Frankfurt and Heidelberg, Western Reserve Univ., Cleveland, Ohio, USA; attaché, German NATO Del. Paris 1960–61; Second Sec., Djakarta 1962–66; First Sec., Tokyo 1966–69; Dir Cabinet of Foreign Minister, Bonn 1970–74; Amb. to Malaysia 1974–76, to Indonesia 1980–83, to Japan 1986–90, to the Holy See 1990–95; Dir-Gen. Foreign Office, Bonn 1983–86. *Publications:* Völkerrechtliche Schiedsinstanzen für Einzelpersonen und ihr Verhältnis zur innerstaatlichen Gerichtsbarkeit 1962, Zwischen Fernost und Vatikan (memoirs) 1999, Das Dorf – eine mecklenburgische Chronik 2001; books and research papers on int. law. *Address:* Eifelblick 11, 53619 Rheinbreitbach, Germany (home). *Telephone:* (2224) 5931 (home). *Fax:* (2224) 70183 (home). *E-mail:* poreta91@aol.com (home).

HALLIWELL, Geraldine (Geri) Estelle; British singer; b. 7 Aug. 1972, Watford; one d.; mem. (with Victoria Adams, Melanie Brown, Emma Bunton and Melanie Chisholm) Touch, later renamed The Spice Girls 1993–98, as 'Ginger Spice', reunion tour 2007–08; UN Goodwill Amb. 1998–; Prince's Trust Amb.; Patron Breast Cancer Care; solo artist 1998–; two Ivor Novello songwriting awards 1997, Smash Hits Award for Best British Band 1997, BRIT Award for Best Single (for Wannabe, with The Spice Girls) 1997, BRIT Award for Best Video (for Say You'll Be There, with The Spice Girls) 1997, for Best Performance of the last 30 years 2010, three American Music Awards 1998, Special BRIT Award for Int. Sales 1998. *Films include:* Spiceworld The Movie 1997, Fat Slags 2004. *Television appearances:* judge on Popstars – The Rivals (ITV 1) 2002, appearance in Sex and the City (HBO) 2003. *Recordings include:* albums: with The Spice Girls: Spice 1996, Spiceworld 1997, Greatest Hits 2007; solo: Schizophonic 1999, Scream If You Wanna Go Faster 2001, Passion 2005. *Publications include:* If Only (autobiography) 1999, Just for the Record (autobiography) 2002; Ugenia Lavender children's series: Ugenia Lavender 2008, Ugenia Lavender and the Terrible Tiger 2008, Ugenia Lavender and the Burning Pants 2008, Ugenia Lavender: Home Alone 2008, Ugenia Lavender and the Temple of Gloom 2008, Ugenia Lavender the

One and Only 2008. *Address:* c/o Red Light Management, 10-16 Scrutton Street, Ground Floor, Shoreditch, London, EC2A 4RU, England. *E-mail:* press@gerihalliwell.com. *Website:* blog.gerihalliwell.com; www.ugenialavender.com.

HALLSTRÖM, Lasse; Swedish film director; b. 2 June 1946, Stockholm; m. 1st Malou Hallström (divorced), one s.; m. 2nd Lena Olin, one d. *Films include:* A Lover and his Lass 1975, Abba – The Movie 1977, Father-to-be 1979, The Rooster 1981, Happy We 1983, My Life as a Dog 1985 (Film of the Year 1985), The Children of Bullerby Village 1986, More about the Children of Bullerby Village 1987, Once Around 1991, What's Eating Gilbert Grape (also co-exec. producer) 1993, Something to Talk About 1995, Lumière and Company 1995, The Cider House Rules 1999, Chocolat 2000, The Shipping News 2002, An Unfinished Life 2004, Casanova 2005, The Hoax 2006, Hachiko: A Dog's Story 2009, Dear John 2010, The Danish Girl 2010, Salmon Fishing in the Yemen 2011. *Promotional films include:* music videos for Abba including Waterloo 1974, Mamma Mia 1974, Money, Money, Money 1976, Summer Night City 1978, The Winner Takes It All 1980, When All Is Said and Done 1981, Head Over Heels 1982. *Address:* c/o David Nochimson, Ziffren, Brittenham, Branca, Fischer, Gilbert-Lurie, Stiffelman & Cook LLP, 1801 Century Park West, Los Angeles, CA 90067-6406; c/o Creative Arts Agency, 2000 Avenue of the Stars, Los Angeles, CA 90067, USA.

HALLÚ, Rubén Eduardo, BSc; Argentine veterinarian, academic and university administrator; *Rector, University of Buenos Aires;* b. 16 Jan. 1951; ed Univ. of Buenos Aires; fmr Assoc. Teacher and Dir of Basic Science, Faculty of Veterinary Sciences, Nat. Univ. of La Pampa, Santa Rosa; fmr Lecturer in Pharmacology, Nat. Univ. of Rosario; Assoc. Prof., later Prof. of Pharmacology, Univ. of Buenos Aires, also Sec. of Admin Supervision, Vice-Dean, Faculty of Veterinary Sciences 1994–2002, Dean 2002–, mem. Univ. of Buenos Aires Superior Bd 2002–, Rector Univ. of Buenos Aires 2006–. *Publications:* more than 50 research papers. *Address:* Office of the Rector, University of Buenos Aires, 430/444 Viamonte, 1053 Buenos Aires, Argentina (office). *Telephone:* (11) 4510-1100 (office). *Website:* www.uba.ar (office).

HALLYDAY, Johnny; French singer, musician (guitar) and actor; b. (Jean-Philippe Smet), 15 June 1943, Paris; s. of Léon Smet; m. 1st Sylvie Vartan; one s.; m. 2nd Elisabeth Etienne; m. 3rd Adeline Blondieu; m. 4th Laetitia Boudou 1996; one c. with Nathalie Baye; appeared on stage aged five; music hall tours with his cousin and her husband, American dancer Lee Halliday; numerous concerts; Chevalier, Légion d'honneur 1997, Officier, Ordre des Arts et des Lettres, Ordre de la Couronne (Belgium); Prix Cinématographique Jean-Gabin 2003. *Films include:* Les Diaboliques 1955, Les Parisiennes 1961, Un Coup dans l'aile 1963, D'où viens-tu, Johnny? 1964, A Tout casser 1968, Visa de censure 1968, Gli Specialisti 1970, Point de chute 1970, Malpertuis 1971, Pour une pomme 1972, L'Aventure, c'est l'aventure 1972, L'Animal 1977, Le Jour se lève et les conneries commencent 1981, Détective 1985, Conseil de famille 1986, Terminus 1987, The Iron Triangle 1989, La Gamine 1991, Pourquoi pas moi? 1999, Love Me 2000, L'Homme du train 2002, Crime Spree 2003, Les Rivières pourpres 2: Les anges de l'apocalypse 2004, Quartier VIP 2005, Jean-Philippe 2006, The Pink Panther 2 2009, Vengeance 2009. *Television:* David Lansky (series) 1989. *Recordings include:* albums: Retiens la nuit 1961, Whole Lotta Shakin' Goin' On 1962, Sings America's Rockin' Hits 1962, Les Bras en croix 1963, Da dou ron ron 1963, L'Idole des jeunes 1963, D'Où viens-tu Johnny? 1963, Le pénitencier 1964, Excuse-moi partenaire 1964, Noir c'est noir 1966, Je suis né dans la rue 1968, Que je t'aime 1969, Fils de personne 1971, Toute la musique que j'aime 1972, J'ai pleuré sur ma guitare 1973, Rock n' Roll Man 1974, Flagrant Delit 1975, Gabrielle 1975, Hamlet 1976, Johnny Hallyday Story: Palais des Sports 1976, J'ai oublié de vivre 1977, Le Bon temps du rock 'n' roll 1978, Ma gueule 1979, Pavillon de Paris 1979, Mon Amérique à moi 1981, Je suis victime de l'amour 1982, Signes extérieurs de richesse 1983, Nashville Blues 1984, Rock 'n' Roll Attitude 1985, Gang 1986, Mon p'tit loup 1988, Oh ma jolie Sarah 1988, La Peur 1988, Ses 32 premieres chansons 1988, Johnny à Bercy 1988, Mirador 1989, Ca ne change pas un homme 1991, Dans la chaleur de Bercy 1991, La Nuit Johnny 1993, Parc de Princes 1993, Deux étrangers 1993, Cheveux longs et idées courtes 1993, A tout casser 1993, Paroles d'hommes 1995, Rough Town 1996, Destination Vegas 1996, Aimer vivre 1997, Insolitudes 1997, Vie 1998, Stade de France 1998, Derrière l'amour 1998, Ce que je sais 1998, Sang pour sang 1999, Les rocks les plus terribles 1999, Ballades 1999, Solitude a deux 2000, Salut les copains 2000, Rock 'n' Slow 2000, Rock a Memphis 2000, Riviere ouvre ton lit 2000, Reve et amour 2000, Quelque part un aigle 2000, Pas facile 2000, La Generation perdue 2000, Chant 2000, Johnny 67 2000, Jeune homme 2000, Je t'aime, je t'aime, je t'aime 2000, Hollywood 2000, Halleluyah 2000, Entre Violence et Violon 2000, En V O 2000, En pieces detachees 2000, Country Folk Rock 2000, C'est la vie 2000, A Partir de maintenant 2000, La Terre promise 2000, À la vie, à la mort! 2002, Ma Vérité 2005, Le Cœur d'un homme 2007, Ça ne finira jamais 2008, Jamais seul 2011. *Publications include:* Johnny raconte Hallyday 1980, Johnny la forme (jtly) 1990, Déraciné (1943–1964) 1996. *Address:* c/o Camus and Camus Productions, 6 rue Daubigny, 75017 Paris, France. *Website:* www.johnnyhallyday.com.

HALONEN, Tarja Kaarina, LLM; Finnish politician, lawyer and fmr head of state; b. 24 Dec. 1943, Helsinki; d. of Vieno Olavi Halonen and Lyyli Elina Loimola; m. Pentti Arajärvi 2000; one d. from previous relationship with Kari Pekkonen; ed Univ. of Helsinki and Univ. of Kent at Canterbury, UK; lawyer, Lainvalvonta Oy 1967–68; social welfare officer, organizing Sec. Nat. Union of Finnish Students 1969–70; lawyer, Cen. Org. of Finnish Trade Unions 1970–2000; mem. Social Democratic Party 1971–2000; Parl. Sec. to Prime Minister Sorsa 1974–75; mem. Helsinki City Council 1977–96; mem. Parl. 1979–2000, Chair. Parl. Social Affairs Cttee 1984–87; Second Minister, Ministry of Social Affairs and Health 1987–90, for Nordic Co-operation 1989–91, of Justice 1990–91, for Foreign Affairs 1995–2000; Pres. of Finland (first woman) 2000–12; Chair. Int. Solidarity Foundation 1991–2000 (mem. Bd of Dirs), TNL Theatre Org., Council of Women World Leaders 2009–; Co-Chair. World Comm. on the Social Dimension of Globalization, ILO 2002–04; mem. Rep. Body of the Cooperative Retail Co. Elanto 1975– (mem. Supervisory Bd 1980–96), UNCTAD Panel of Eminent Persons 2005–06, Bd Oslo Centre for Peace and Human Rights 2006–, UN High-level Panel on Global Sustainability (Co-Chair. 2010–); hon. degrees (Univ. of Helsinki) 2000, (Helsinki School of Econs) 2001, (Ewha Womens Univ., Repub. of Korea) 2002, (Univ. of Kent) 2002, (Eötvös Loránd Univ., Budapest) 2004, Chinese Acad. of Forestry)

2002, (Finlandia Univ., USA) 2003, (Univ. of Turku) 2003, (Univ. of Bluefiels, Nicaragua) 2004, (Univ. of Tartu, Estonia) 2004, (State Univ. of Yerevan, Armenia) 2005, (Helsinki Univ. of Tech.) 2008, (Univ. of Minnesota, Duluth) 2008, (Theatre Acad., Helsinki) 2009, (Umeå Univ.) 2009, (Univ. of Helsinki) 2010, (Univ. of Kazan, Russia) 2010; ranked by Forbes magazine amongst The World's 100 Most Powerful Women (31st) 2004–05, (44th) 2006, (50th) 2007, (71st) 2008, (68th) 2009, (62nd) 2010. *Leisure interests:* art history, drawing, painting, the theatre, swimming. *Address:* c/o Office of the President, Mariankatu 2, 00170 Helsinki, Finland.

HALPERIN, Bertrand Israel, PhD; American physicist and academic; *Hollis Professor of Mathematicks and Natural Philosophy, Harvard University;* b. 6 Dec. 1941, Brooklyn, New York; s. of Morris Halperin and Eva Halperin; m. Helena Stacy French 1962; one s. one d.; ed George Wingate High School, Brooklyn, Harvard Coll. and Univ. of California (Berkeley); NSF Postdoctoral Fellow, Ecole Normale Supérieure, Paris 1965–66; mem. tech. staff, Bell Labs 1966–76; Prof. of Physics, Harvard Univ. 1976–, Chair. Dept of Physics 1988–91, Hollis Prof. of Mathematicks and Natural Philosophy 1992–; Assoc. Ed. Reviews of Modern Physics 1974–80; mem. NAS, American Acad. of Arts and Sciences, American Philosophical Soc.; Fellow, American Physical Soc.; Oliver Buckley Prize for Condensed Matter Physics 1982, Lars Onsager Prize 2001, Wolf Prize in Physics (jt recipient) 2003, Goettingen Akademie der Wissenschaften Dannie Heineman Prize 2007, Lars Onsager Medal and Lecture, Norwegian Univ. of Science and Tech. 2009. *Publications include:* about 250 articles in scientific journals. *Address:* Lyman Laboratory of Physics, Harvard University, 17 Oxford Street, Cambridge, MA 02138, USA (office). *Telephone:* (617) 495-4294 (office). *E-mail:* halperin@physics.harvard.edu (office). *Website:* www.physics.harvard.edu/people/facpages/halperin.html (office); cmtw.harvard.edu (office).

HALPERIN, (Donghi) Tulio, DPhil; Argentine historian and academic; *Muriel McKevitt Sonne Professor Emeritus, University of California, Berkeley;* b. 27 Oct. 1926, Buenos Aires; ed Univ. de Buenos Aires, Ecole Pratique des Hautes Etudes, Paris; Prof., Univ. Nac. del Litoral (Rosario, Argentina) 1955–61; Prof. Univ. de Buenos Aires 1959–66, Univ. of Oxford 1970–71; Prof., Univ. of Calif., Berkeley 1971, now Muriel McKevitt Sonne Prof. Emer.; fmr Lecturer, History Dept, Harvard Univ.; several hon. degrees; Clarence Haring Prize 1976, Universidad de Santiago de Chile Medal, Scholarly Distinction Award, American Historical Assen 1998. *Publications:* El Pensamiento de Echeverría 1951, Un Conflicto Nacional: Moriscos y Cristianos Viejos en Valencia 1955, El Río de la Plata al Comenzar el Siglo XIX 1960, Tradición Política Española e Ideología Revolucionaria de Mayo 1961, Historia de la Universidad de Buenos Aires 1962, Argentina en el Callejón 1964, Historia contemporánea de América Latina 1969, Hispanoamérica después de la Independencia 1972 (in English The Aftermath of Revolution in Latin America 1973), Revolución y guerra 1972 (in English Politics, Economics and Society in Argentina in the Revolutionary Period 1975), Jose Hernandez y Sus Mundos 1992, Argentina en el callejón 1995, Historia Contemporanea de America Latina (Contemporary History of Latin America) 1999, Historia de La Universidad de Buenos Aires 2002, La Argentina y La Tormenta del Mundo 2003, La República Imposible, 1930-1944 2004, Son Memorias 2008. *Address:* c/o Department of History, University of California, 3229 Dwinelle Hall, Berkeley, CA 94720-2550, USA (office).

HALPERN, Daniel, MFA; American editor and writer; b. 11 Sept. 1945, Syracuse, NY; s. of Irving Halpern and Rosemary Halpern; m. Jeanne Carter 1982; one d.; ed California State Univ. and Columbia Univ., New York; instructor in poetry and fiction workshops, New School of Social Research, New York 1971–76; Co-founder The Ecco Press (acquired by HarperCollins Publishers 1999) 1971, Ed.-in-Chief Antaeus magazine 1971–91, Editorial Dir 1991–94; Adjunct Prof., Columbia Univ. 1975–95; apptd Dir Nat. Poetry Series 1978; Visiting Prof., Princeton Univ. 1975–76, 1987–88; Nat. Endowment for the Arts Fellowship 1974, 1975, 1987; Robert Frost Fellowship, CAPS; Guggenheim Fellow 1988; numerous awards including Carey Thomas Award for Creative Publishing, Editor's Award 2009. *Publications:* poetry: Travelling on Credit 1972, Street Fire 1975, Life Among Others 1978, Seasonal Rights 1982, Tango 1987, Foreign Neon 1991, Selected Poems 1994, Antaeus 1970 1996, Something Shining 1998; ed. several anthologies including The Art of the Tale 1987, Reading the Fights 1990, Dante's Inferno: Translations by Twenty Contemporary Poets 1994, The Art of the Story 2000. *Leisure interest:* cooking. *Address:* c/o HarperCollins Publishers, 10 East 53rd Street, New York, NY 10022, USA.

HALPERN, Jack, PhD, FRS; American chemist and academic; *Louis Block Distinguished Service Professor, Department of Chemistry, University of Chicago;* b. 19 Jan. 1925, Poland; s. of Philip Halpern and Anna Sass; m. Helen Peritz 1949; two d.; ed McGill Univ., Montreal, Canada; NRC Postdoctoral Overseas Fellow, Univ. of Manchester, UK 1949–50; Prof. of Chem., Univ. of BC, Canada 1950–62; Nuffield Fellow, Univ. of Cambridge, UK 1959–60; Louis Block Distinguished Service Prof., Dept of Chem., Univ. of Chicago 1962–; External Scientific mem. Max Planck Inst. für Kohlenforschung, Mulheim, Germany 1983–; Visiting Prof. at various univs in USA, UK and Copenhagen; Chair. German-American Council 1993–96, Chair. Bd of Trustees 1996–99; numerous other lectureships, professional and editorial appointments; Fellow, American Acad. of Arts and Sciences; Dir American Friends of the Royal Soc. 2000–02; mem. Advisory Bd Humboldt Foundation Transatlantic Science and Humanities Program 2001–04; mem. NAS 1984– (mem. Council 1990–2001, Chair. Chem. Section 1991–93, Vice-Pres. 1993–2001); Hon. FRSC 1987; Cross of Merit (Germany) 1996; Hon. DSc (Univ. of BC) 1986, (McGill) 1997; ACS Award in Inorganic Chem. 1968, Royal Soc. of Chem. Award in Catalysis 1977, Humboldt Award 1977, Richard Kokes Award 1978, ACS Award for Distinguished Service in the Advancement of Inorganic Chem. 1985, Willard Gibbs Medal 1986, Bailar Medal 1986, German Chemical Soc. August Wilhelm von Hoffman Medal 1988, American Inst. of Chemists Chemical Pioneer Award 1991, Swiss Chemical Soc. Paracelsus Prize 1992, Basolo Medal 1993, Robert A. Welch Award 1994, ACS Award in Organometallic Chem. 1995, Int. Precious Metals Inst. Henry Alberts Award 1995. *Publications:* more than 250 scientific articles in various scientific journals. *Leisure interests:* art, music, theatre. *Address:* Department of Chemistry, University of Chicago, Chicago, IL 60637 (office); 5801 S Dorchester Avenue, Apartment 4A, Chicago, IL 60637, USA (home). *Telephone:* (773) 702-7095 (office); (773) 643-6837 (home). *Fax:* (773) 702-

8809 (office); (773)-324-9849 (home). *E-mail:* jhjh@uchicago.edu (office). *Website:* chemistry.uchicago.edu (office).

HALPERN, Sir Ralph (Mark), Kt, CBIM, FID; British business executive; b. 1938, London; s. of Bernard Halpern and Olga Halpern; m. Joan Halpern (divorced); one s. one d.; ed St Christopher School, Letchworth; fmr trainee Selfridges; joined Burton Group PLC 1961, Chief Exec. and Man. Dir 1978–90, Chair. 1981–90; Co-Founder Top Shop 1970; Chair. Halpern Assocs; Chair. CBI Marketing and Common Affairs Cttee 1984; Chair. Police and Community Partnership Group, E Surrey; fmr Hon. Prof., Univ. of Warwick; mem. CBI City-Industry Task Force 1986; mem. Pres.'s Cttee, Chair. British Fashion Council 1990–94; mem. Advisory Council Prince's Youth Business Trust 1991–92. *Leisure interest:* country pursuits.

HALQI, Wael Nader al-, MD; Syrian physician and politician; *Prime Minister;* b. 1964, Jasim, Dar'a Governorate; m.; four c.; ed Univ. of Damascus; Dir of primary health care, Jasim 1997–2000; Pres. Syrian Doctors' Syndicate 2010; Minister of Health 2011–12; Prime Minister 2012–; mem. Baath Arab Socialist Party, Sec.-Gen., Dar'a Br. 2000–04. *Address:* Office of the Prime Minister, rue Chahbandar, Damascus, Syria (office). *Telephone:* (11) 2226000 (office). *Fax:* (11) 2237842 (office).

HALSBAND, Frances, BA, MArch, FAIA; American architect; *Partner, Kliment Halsband Architects;* b. 30 Oct. 1943, New York City; m. Robert Kliment 1971; one s.; ed Swarthmore Coll., Columbia Univ., New York; worked at Mitchell & Giurgola Architects, New York 1968–72; Founding Pnr (with Robert Kliment), Kliment Halsband Architects, New York 1972–; fmr Dean School of Architecture, Pratt Inst.; Guest Lecturer, Ball State Univ., Univ. of California, Berkeley, Univ. of Cincinnati, Columbia Univ., Harvard Univ., Univ. of Illinois, North Carolina State Univ., Univ. of Maryland, Univ. of Pennsylvania, Rice Univ. and Univ. of Virginia; fmr Pres. New York Chapter, AIA, Architectural League of New York; fmr Commr New York City Landmarks Preservation Comm.; Chair. Cttee on Design, AIA 1999; mem. Architectural Review Bd of Fed. Reserve Bank; Architect Advisor, Corpn at Brown Univ.; fmr mem. Architctural Advisory Bd US Dept of State; AIA NY State Award of Merit, Interfaith Forum on Religion, Art and Architecture Design Award, Gen. Services Admin Design Award Citation, AIA New York Chapter Medal of Honour. *Architectural works include:* Roth Center for Jewish Life, Hanover, New Hampshire, Long Island Railroad Entrance Pavilion to Pennsylvania Station, New York. *Publications include:* articles in professional journals. *Address:* Kliment Halsband Architects, 322 Eighth Avenue, New York, NY 10001, USA (office). *Telephone:* (212) 243-7400 (office). *Fax:* (212) 633-9769 (office). *E-mail:* halsband@kliment-halsband.com (office). *Website:* www.kliment -halsband.com (office).

HALSE, Bengt Gösta, DEng; Swedish business executive; b. 2 Feb. 1943, Gothenburg; ed Chalmers Inst. of Tech., Gothenburg, Linköping Univ.; with Ericsson Group 1974–95; Pres. and CEO Saab AB 1995–2003; Chair. Comhem AB, Flexlink AB, IFK Gothenburg 2003–06; mem. Bd of Dirs Omhex AB, Teleca AB, TietoEnator 2004–09, Denel Ltd; fmr Chair. ACARE (Advisory Council for Aeronautical Research in Europe; mem. Advisory Bd Tracab; mem. Royal Swedish Acad. of Engineering Sciences, Royal Swedish Acad. of War Sciences; Hon. DrIng (Linköping Univ.) 1999; Hon. mem. Royal Swedish Soc. of Naval Sciences 2002; Hon. Fellow, Royal Aeronautical Soc., London 2001, Hon. Consul, Gothenburg 2008; King's Medal of the12th Dimension with Ribbon of the Order of the Seraphim 2004. *Address:* c/o Comhem AB, POB 43, 871 21, Härnösand, Sweden. *Telephone:* (734) 187105. *Fax:* (31) 930926.

HALSEY, Albert Henry, MA, PhD; British academic; *Professor Emeritus, University of Oxford;* b. 13 April 1923, London; s. of William T. Halsey and Ada Draper; m. Gertrude M. Littler 1949; three s. two d.; ed London School of Econs; research worker, Univ. of Liverpool 1952–54; Lecturer, Univ. of Birmingham 1954–62; Fellow, Centre for Advanced Study of Behavioral Sciences, Palo Alto, Calif. 1956–57; Prof. of Sociology, Univ. of Chicago 1959–60; Dir Barnett House and Fellow, Nuffield Coll., Oxford 1962–90; Prof. of Social and Admin. Studies, Univ. of Oxford 1978–90, Prof. Emer. 1990–; Sr Fellow British Acad. 1995; mem. Acad. Europaea 1992; Foreign mem. American Acad. of Arts and Sciences 1988; Hon. Fellow, Goldsmiths Coll. London 1992, LSE 1993, Royal Statistical Soc. 1999; Hon. DSc (Birmingham) 1987; Dr hc (Open Univ.) 1989; Hon. DLit (Warwick, Leicester) 1994, (Glamorgan) 1995. *Radio:* Reith Lecturer, BBC 1978. *Publications:* Origins and Destinations 1980, Change in British Society 1986, English Ethical Socialism (with Norman Dennis) 1988, The Decline of Donnish Dominion 1992, No Discouragement: an Autobiography of A. H. Halsey 1996, Education, Culture, Economy and Society 1997, British Social Trends: The Twentieth Century 2000, A History of Sociology in Britain: Science, Literature and Society 2004, Changing Childhood 2009. *Leisure interest:* gardening, painting. *Address:* Nuffield College, Oxford, OX1 1NF (office); 28 Upland Park Road, Oxford, OX2 7RU, England (home). *Telephone:* (1865) 278521 (office); (1865) 558625 (home).

HALSTEAD, Sir Ronald, Kt, CBE, MA, CBIM, FRSC, FRSA; British business executive; *President, Engineering Industries Association;* b. 17 May 1927, Lancaster, Lancs., England; s. of Richard Halstead and Bessie Harrison Halstead; m. 1st Yvonne Cecile de Monchaux 1968 (deceased); two s.; m. 2nd Susanne Eugenie Stoessl (died 2013); ed Queens' Coll., Cambridge; Research Chemist H.P. Bulmer & Co. 1948–53; Mfg Man. Macleans Ltd 1954–55; Factory Man. Beecham Products Inc., USA 1955–60, Asst Man. Dir Beecham Research Lab. Ltd 1960–62, Pres. Beecham Research Labs, Inc. (USA) 1962–64, Vice-Pres. Marketing, Beecham Products, Inc. (USA) 1962–64, Chair. Food and Drink Div. Beecham Group 1964–67; Chair. Beecham Products 1967–84, Man. Dir (consumer products) Beecham Group 1973–84, Chair. and Chief Exec. Beecham Group PLC 1984–85; Dir The Otis Elevator Co. Ltd 1978–83, Burmah Oil 1983–89; Dir (non-exec.) American Cyanamid Co. 1986–94, Davy Corpn PLC 1986–91, Gestetner Holdings PLC 1986–95; Dir Laurentian Financial Group PLC 1991–95; Chair. CAB Int. 1995–98; Deputy Chair. Tech. Colls Trust 1993–2006; Vice-Chair. Proprietary Assen of GB 1968–77; Pres. Nat. Advertising Benevolent Soc. 1978–80; Vice-Pres. Inst. of Packaging 1979–81, Pres. 1981–83; Dir British Steel Corpn 1979–86, Deputy Chair. 1986–94; Gov. Ashridge Man. Coll. 1970–2007, Vice-Chair. 1977–2007; Pres. Inc. Soc. of British Advertisers 1971–73; Chair. British Nutrition Foundation 1970–73, Council mem. 1967–79; Vice-Chair. Advertising Assen

1973–81; Vice-Chair. Food & Drink Industries Council 1973–76; Pres. Food Mfrs Fed. 1974–76; mem. CBI 1970–86, BIM 1972–77, Cambridge Univ. Appointments Bd 1969–73, Agric. Research Council 1978–84; Dir Nat. Coll. of Food Tech. 1977–78, Chair. of Bd 1978–83; Chair. Knitting Sector Working Group, NEDO 1978–90, Textile and Garment Working Group, 1991–93; Fellow, Inst. of Grocery Distribution 1979–, Marketing Soc. 1981–99; Trustee, Inst. of Econ. Affairs 1980–93; mem. Monopolies and Mergers Comm. Newspaper Panel 1980–92; mem. Industrial Devt Advisory Bd Dept of Trade and Industry 1983–93, Chair. 1984–93; Hon. Treas. and Dir, Centre for Policy Studies 1984–93; mem. Priorities Bd for Research and Devt in Agric. and Food, Ministry of Agric. Fish and Food 1984–87; Chair. Bd of Food Studies Univ. of Reading 1983–86; Pres. Eng Industries Asscn 1991–; mem. Monopolies and Mergers Comm. 1993–99; Council mem. European Policy Forum 1993–; Council mem. Univ. of Buckingham 1973–95, Univ. of Reading 1978–98; Council and Exec. Cttee mem., Imperial Soc. of Kts Bachelor 1985–2003; Chair. Conservative Foreign and Commonwealth Council 1995–; Gov. De Montfort Univ. (fmrly Leicester Polytechnic) 1989–97; Fellow, Inst. of Marketing 1975–, Vice-Pres. 1980–99; mem. Council, Food Mfrs Fed. Inc. 1966–85; Hon. Fellow, Inst. of Food Science and Tech., Inst. of Marketing, Queens' Coll. Cambridge 1985; Hon. DSc (Reading) 1982, (Univ. of Lancaster) 1987. *Leisure interests:* sailing, squash racquets, skiing. *Address:* Engineering Industries Association, 62 Bayswater Road, London, W2 3PS (office); 37 Edwardes Square, London, W8 6HH, England (home). *Telephone:* (20) 7298-6455 (office); (20) 7603-9010 (home). *Fax:* (20) 7298-6456 (office); (20) 7371-2595 (home). *E-mail:* head .office@eia.co.uk (office). *Website:* www.eia.co.uk (office).

HALVORSEN, Kristin; Norwegian politician; b. 2 Sept. 1960; m. Charlo Halvorsen; two c.; mem. Stortinget (Parl.) for Oslo 1989–, mem. Standing Cttee on Finance 1989–97, on Scrutiny and Constitutional Affairs 1997–2001, on Foreign Affairs 2001–05, mem. Parl. Del. in Connection with European Parl. 2001–05; Leader, Socialist Left Party of Norway 1997–; Minister of Finance 2005–09, of Educ. 2009–13; Observer UN Gen. Meeting 1985; Deputy mem. Cttee on Ex-Gratia Payment of Compensation 1996; mem. Consulting Agency Regarding EEC Matters 1997–2001. *Address:* c/o Ministry of Education, Akersgt. 44, POB 8119 Dep., 0032 Oslo, Norway (office).

HALYLOV, Muhammetnur; Turkmenistani geologist and government official; *Minister of the Petroleum and Gas Industry and Mineral Resources;* Dir Inst. of Geology, State Geological Co., TurkmenGeology –2013; Minister of the Petroleum and Gas Industry and Mineral Resources 2013–. *Address:* Ministry of the Petroleum and Gas Industry and Mineral Resources, 744000 Aşgabat, Arçabil Saýoly 56, Turkmenistan (office). *Telephone:* (12) 40-30-01 (office). *Fax:* (12) 40-30-44 (office). *E-mail:* ministryoilgas@online.tm (office). *Website:* www.oilgas.gov.tm (office).

HAMÁCEK, Jan; Czech politician; *Chairman, Poslanecká sněmovna (Chamber of Deputies);* mem. Poslanecká sněmovna (Chamber of Deputies) (Czech Social Democratic Party) 2006–, Deputy Chair. Foreign Affairs Cttee 2006–10, Chair. 2010–13, Head of Czech Del. to NATO Parl. Ass., Shadow Minister of Defence, Chair. Chamber of Deputies 2013–. *Publications:* articles on defence and world affairs have appeared in the Harvard International Review, US Atlantic Council, Europe's World. *Address:* Office of the Chairman, Poslanecká sněmovna (Chamber of Deputies), Sněmovní 4, 118 26 Prague 1, Czech Republic (office). *Telephone:* (2) 57173001 (office). *Fax:* (2) 57534472 (office). *E-mail:* hamacekj@psp.cz (office); posta@psp.cz (office). *Website:* www.psp.cz (office).

HAMAD, Abdul-Latif al-, BA; Kuwaiti international organization official, banker and politician; *Director General and Chairman, Arab Fund for Economic and Social Development;* b. 1936; m.; four c.; ed Claremont Coll., Calif. and Harvard Univ., USA; mem. Kuwaiti del. to UN 1962; Dir-Gen. Kuwait Fund for Arab Econ. Devt 1963–81; Dir The South & Arabian Gulf Soc. 1963–81, Assistance Authority for the Gulf and Southern Arabia 1967–81; Dir, then Man. Dir Kuwait Investment Co. 1963–71; Man. Dir Kuwait Investment Co. 1965–74; Chair. Kuwait Prefabricated Bldg Co. 1965–78, United Bank of Kuwait Ltd, London 1966–84; Exec. Dir Arab Fund for Econ. and Social Devt 1972–81, Dir Gen. and Chair. Bd of Dirs 1985–; Chair. Compagnie Arabe et Internationale d'Investisse-ments, Luxembourg 1973–81; Chair. Devt Cttee Task Force on Multilateral Devt Banks; mem. Bd of Trustees, Corporate Property Investors, New York 1975–; mem. Governing Body Inst. of Devt Studies, Sussex, UK 1975–87; mem. Ind. Comm. on Int. Devt Issues (Brandt Comm.) 1976–79; mem. Bd Int. Inst. for Environment and Devt, London 1976–80; Minister of Finance and Planning 1981–83; Gov. for Kuwait, World Bank and IMF 1981–83; mem. UN Cttee for Devt Planning 1982–91, Chair. 1987; mem. IFC Banking Advisory Bd Group 1987–, Advisory Group on Financial Flows for Africa (UN) 1987–88, South Comm. 1987–89, Group of Ten (African Devt Bank) 1987–, World Bank's Pvt. Sector Devt Review Group 1988–, UN Panel for Public Hearings on Activities of Transnational Corpns in S Africa and Namibia 1989–92, Bd Trustees of Stockholm Environment Inst. 1989–92, Comm. on Global Governance 1992–, Int. Finance Corpn, Banking Advisory Bd Group (World Bank), Bd of Kuwait Investment Authority, Group of Thirty Consultative Group on Int. Econ. and Monetary Affairs, Inc., Washington, DC; Trustee, Arab Planning Inst. *Address:* Arab Fund for Economic and Social Development, PO Box 21923, Safat 13080, Kuwait (office). *Telephone:* 4844500 (office). *Fax:* 4815760 (office). *E-mail:* hq@arabfund.org (office). *Website:* www .arabfund.org (office).

HAMAD, Seif Sharif, BA; Tanzanian politician and political scientist; *Secretary-General, Civic United Front;* b. 22 Oct. 1943, Pemba; s. of the late Sharif Hamad Shehe and Time Seif Haji; m. 1st Furtunah Saleh Mbamba 1971; m. 2nd Aweinah Sanani Massoud 1977; one s. four d.; ed King George VI Secondary School, Zanzibar, Univ. of Dar es Salaam; teacher, Lumumba Coll., Fidel Castro Coll. 1964–72; Asst to Pres. of Zanzibar 1975–77, Minister of Educ., Zanzibar 1977–80; mem. Tanzanian Parl. 1977–80; mem. Zanzibar House of Reps 1980–99; mem. Cen. Cttee Chama Cha Mapinduzi (CCM) Party 1977–88, Head Econ. and Planning Dept of CCM 1982–88; Chief Minister of Zanzibar 1984–88; political prisoner in Zanzibar 1989–91; Nat. Vice-Chair. Civic United Front 1992–, now Sec.-Gen.; presidential cand. in Zanzibar elections 2000, 2010; Chair. Gen. Ass. Unrepresented Nations and Peoples' Org. (UNPO) 1997–. *Leisure interests:* reading, swimming. *Address:* Civic United Front, Mtendeni Street at Malindi, PO Box 3637, Zanzibar (office); PO Box 10976, Dar es Salaam, Tanzania.

Telephone: (24) 2237446 (office); (51) 861009; (812) 787790; (811) 324886. *Fax:* (24) 2237445 (office); (51) 861010. *E-mail:* headquarters@cuftz.org (office). *Website:* www.cuftz.org (office).

HAMADA, Hiroshi; Japanese business executive; b. 28 April 1933, Kagoshima Prefecture; m.; three c.; ed Tokyo Univ.; Pres. Ricoh Co. Ltd 1983–96, Chair. 1996–2004, now Supreme Adviser; Chair. Keidanren Cttee on Human Resources Devt 2000; fmr Vice-Chair. Japan Business Fed.; Pres. Japan Business Machines and Information System Industries Asscn 1992–93; Dir UFJ Holdings; mem. Council, Japan Productivity Centre for Socio-Econ. Devt; Counselor, Sasakawa Peace Foundation; Officer, Légion d'honneur 1998; Blue Ribbon Medal 1991. *Address:* c/o Ricoh Company Limited, 15–5 Minami Aoyama 1–chome, Minato-ku, Tokyo 107–8544, Japan.

HAMADA, Junichi, BA, MA, PhD; Japanese academic and university adminis-trator; *President, University of Tokyo;* ed Faculty of Law, Univ. of Tokyo; has been closely connected with the Inst. of Journalism and Communication Studies (renamed the Inst. of Socio-Information and Communication Studies) at Univ. of Tokyo (Todai) throughout his career, Research Assoc. and Inst. Dir 1995–99, Dean of Interfaculty Initiative in Information Studies and Grad. School of Interdiscip-linary Information Studies 2000–02, Man. Dir and Exec. Vice-Pres. Univ. of Tokyo 2005–09, Pres. Univ. of Tokyo 2009–; served as a govt adviser. *Publications:* numerous papers in professional journals. *Address:* Office of the President, University of Tokyo, 7-3-1 Hongo, Bunkyo-ku, Tokyo, 113-8654, Japan (office). *Telephone:* (3) 3812-2111 (office). *E-mail:* info@u-tokyo.ac.jp (office). *Website:* www .u-tokyo.ac.jp/en/about/president.html (office).

HAMADA, Rick, BS; American business executive; *CEO, Avnet, Inc.;* ed San Diego State Univ.; joined Hamilton/Avnet Electronics as technical specialist in San Diego 1983, roles included sales and marketing, including serving as field sales rep., computer sales manager, sales unit dir, regional sales manager, Area Vice-Pres. and Vice-Pres. of Business Devt for Open Systems, Corp. Vice-Pres. Avnet, Inc. 1999–2002, Sr Vice-Pres. 2002–03, Global Pres. Avnet Computer Marketing 2003, Global Pres. Avnet Technology Solutions (formed from integration of Avnet Computer Marketing and Avnet Applied Computing) 2003–06, COO Avnet, Inc. 2006–10, Pres. and COO 2010–11, mem. Bd of Dirs and CEO 2011–; Chair. Global Tech. Distribution Council 2012–; mem. Advisory Bd Coll. of Business Admin, San Diego State Univ. 2009–; Avnet Chair.'s Award, twice named to Computer Reseller News' Top 25 Most Influential Channel Executives. *Address:* Avnet, Inc., 2211 South 47th Street, Phoenix, AZ 85034, USA (office). *Telephone:* (480) 643-2000 (office). *E-mail:* m@avnet.com (office). *Website:* www.avnet.com (office).

HAMADOU, Djida; Niger politician; Minister of Nat. Defence 2007–10; mem. Convention démocratique et social—Rahama (CDS). *Address:* c/o Ministry of National Defence, BP 626, Niamey, Niger (office).

HAMAGUCHI, Michinari, BMed, MD, PhD; Japanese physician, academic and university administrator; *President, Nagoya University;* b. 19 Feb. 1951; ed Nagoya Univ.; Research Assoc., Cancer Research Facility, School of Medicine, Nagoya Univ. 1980–83, Research Assoc., Pathological Control Research Facility 1983–84, Assoc. Prof., Pathological Control Research Facility 1984–93, Prof., Pathological Control Research Facility 1993–97, Dir Radioisotope Research Centre 1997–2001, Prof. 2001–02, Dir Pathological Control Research Facility, Grad. School of Medicine 2002–03, Prof., Centre for Neural Disease and Cancer 2003–04, Vice-Dir Grad. School of Medicine 2004–05, Dir Centre for Medical Educ. Research and Support, Grad. School of Medicine 2004–05, Dean, Grad. School of Medicine and School of Medicine 2005–09, Pres. Nagoya Univ. 2009–; Councillor, Japanese Cancer Asscn, Japanese Biochemical Soc., Japanese Soc. of Virology; mem. Japanese of Virology, Japanese Biochemical Soc., Japanese Cancer Asscn, American Soc. for Cell Biology, American Asscn of Cancer Research. *Publications:* numerous papers in professional journals on the molecular mechanism in cancer invasion and metastasis. *Leisure interests:* music appreciation, drawing, garden-ing. *Address:* Office of the President, Nagoya University, Furo-cho, Chikusa-ku, Nagoya 464-8601, Japan (office). *Telephone:* (52) 789-5111 (office). *Website:* www .nagoya-u.ac.jp/en/about-nu/president (office).

HÄMÄLÄINEN, Sirkka Aune-Marjatta, DSc (Econ); Finnish banker and economist; b. 8 May 1939, Riihimäki; d. of Martti Hinkkala and Aune Hinkkala; m. 1st Arvo Hämäläinen 1961; one s. one d.; m. 2nd Bo Lindfors 1999; ed Helsinki School of Econs and Business Admin.; Economist, Econs Dept, Bank of Finland 1961–72, Head of Office, Econs Dept 1972–79, Head of Dept 1979–81, Dir 1982–91, mem. Bd 1991–92, Gov. and Chair. Bd 1992–98; Dir Econs Dept, Ministry of Finance 1981–82; Chair. Bd of Dirs Financial Supervision Authority 1996–97; mem. Exec. Bd European Cen. Bank, Frankfurt 1998–2003; Docent, Adjunct Prof. of Econs Helsinki School of Econs and Business Admin 1991–2006; Dir Investor AB 2004–11, Sanoma Corpn 2004–; Chair. Finnish Nat. Opera 2007–; Vice-Chair. KONE Corpn 2004–; Foreign Academian, Real Academia de Ciencias Económicas y Financieras, Barcelona; Commdr, First Class of Order of the White Rose, Merit Medal, First Class of Order of the White Star (Estonia); Dr hc (Turku School of Econs and Business Admin.) 1995. *Publications include:* books, numerous articles, speeches. *Address:* Unioninkatu 45 B34, 00170 Helsinki, Finland (home). *Telephone:* 50-5021831 (mobile) (home). *E-mail:* sam.hamalainen@kolumbus.fi.

HAMARI, Julia; Hungarian/German singer (mezzo-soprano); b. 21 Nov. 1942, Budapest; d. of Sándor Hamari and Erzsébet Dokupil; ed Franz Liszt Music Acad. of Budapest, Hochschule für Musik, Stuttgart; debut as soloist, Bach's St Matthew Passion in Vienna under Karl Richter 1966; specializes in Rossini, Mozart, Bellini; lieder recitalist and oratorio performer; has appeared world-wide with conductors including Herbert von Karajan, Sergiu Celibidache, Rafael Kubelik, Georg Solti, Karl Böhm, Pierre Boulez, Carlo M. Giulini, Nikolaus Harnoncourt, Claudio Abbado, Riccardo Muti and Mariss Jansons; debut in USA as soloist with Chicago Symphony Orchestra 1967; opera debut at Salzburg Festival as Mercedes in Bizet's Carmen 1967 and as Carmen in Stuttgart 1968; has appeared with Deutsche Oper am Rhein in various baroque and classical operas; has appeared at major opera houses including La Scala, Covent Garden, Vienna State Opera, Metropolitan Opera; opera roles include Celia in La fedeltia premiata (J. Haydn), Orpheus (Gluck), Dorabella and Despina (Così fan tutte), Angelina in La Cenerentola (Rossini), Rosina in Il Barbiere di Siviglia (Rossini), Sesto in La clemenza di Tito (Mozart), Cherubino in Le Nozze di Figaro (Mozart), Sinaide in

Mosé in Egitto (Rossini), Romeo in I Capuleti ed I Montecchi (Bellini), Farnace in Mitridate (Mozart); Prof., Staatliche Hochschule für Musik, Stuttgart 1989–2009; performed in festivals of Edinburgh, Glyndebourne, Florence (Maggio Musicale), Netherlands (Schleswig-Holstein Musik, Schwetzingen); Offizierskreuz (Hungary) 2002; prizewinner, Erkel Int. Singing Competition, Budapest 1964, Kodály Prize 1987. *Recordings include:* Bach's St John and St Matthew Passion 2006, Bach's Mass in B Minor, Oratorios, Cantatas, Oberon by Weber, Il matrimonio segreto by Cimarosa, Giulio Cesare by Handel, Roméo et Juliette by Berlioz, Mozart's Requiem, Mass in C major by Beethoven, Ernani by Verdi, Tito Manlio, Cavalleria rusticana, Juditha Triumphans by Vivaldi, I Puritani by Bellini, Beethoven's 9th Symphony, Mahler's Second and Eighth Symphonies, Orpheus by Gluck, Stabat Mater by Haydn and Pergolesi, Don Sanche by F. Liszt, Mosé in Egitto by Rossini, Prima la musica by A. Salieri, Eugen Onegin (also video), Meistersinger, Zigeunerlieder 1967, Lieder 1969, Bartók Songs 1973, Nausikaa Lieder Recital 1982, Lieder der Romantik 1982–94, Handel German Arias 1990, Julia Hamari Operatic Recital 1983–2000. *Address:* Max Brod-Weg 14, 70437 Stuttgart, Germany (office). *Fax:* (711) 8403625 (home). *E-mail:* julia.hamari@live.de (home).

HAMBAYASHI, Toru; Japanese business executive; b. 7 Jan. 1937; Pres. Nichimen Corpn 2001–03, Chair. and Co-CEO, Nissho Iwai-Nichimen Holding Corpn (following merger) April 2003–04; Special Corp. Adviser, Sojitz Corpn; Int. Sr Econ. Consultant, The People's Govt of Shaanxi Prov. 2002–; Econ. Adviser, Heilongjiang Prov. 2004–; mem. Bd of Dirs Fast Retailing Co. Ltd 2005–, Maeda Corpn 2007–; Adviser, Asscn for Promotion of Int. Trade 2009–; mem. Bd World Forestry Center 2001; mem. Japan and Tokyo Chambers of Commerce and Industry. *Address:* c/o Board of Directors, Fast Retailing Company Limited, 717-1 Sayama, Yamaguchi City, Yamaguchi 754-0894, Japan.

HAMBLING, Maggi, CBE, OBE, Higher Diploma in Fine Art; British artist; b. 23 Oct. 1945, Sudbury, Suffolk; d. of Harry Leonard Hambling and Marjorie Rose Hambling; ed Hadleigh Hall School and Amberfield School, Suffolk, Ipswich School of Art, Camberwell School of Art, London, Slade School of Fine Art, London; studied painting with Lett Haines and Cedric Morris 1960–; tutor, Morley Coll., London; First Artist in Residence, Nat. Gallery, London 1980–81; Oscar Wilde memorial, Adelaide St, London 1998; Scallop-Benjamin Britten memorial, Aldeburgh, Suffolk 2003; The Brixton Heron, London SW4 2010; Boise Travel Award 1969, Arts Council Award 1977, Jerwood Prize (jtly) 1995, Marsh Award for Excellence in Public Sculpture (Scallop) 2005. *Publications:* Maggi and Henrietta 2001, Father 2001, Maggi Hambling – The Works and Conversations with Andrew Lambirth 2006, George Always 2009, The Sea 2009, You are the Sea 2009, The Aldeburgh Scallop 2010. *Leisure interest:* tennis. *Address:* Morley College, 61 Westminster Bridge Road, London, SE1 7HT, England (office). *Telephone:* (20) 7928-8501 (office); (20) 7450-1856 (office). *Fax:* (20) 7928-4074 (office). *Website:* www.maggihambling.com (office).

HAMBRECHT, Jürgen, DSc; German chemical industry executive; *Chairman of the Board of Executive Directors, BASF SE;* b. 1946, Reutlingen; m.; four c.; ed Univ. of Tübingen; joined BASF AG Polymer Lab. 1976, Head of Research and Purchasing, Lacke und Farben AG, Münster 1985–90, Pres. Eng Plastics Div. 1990–95, Pres. E Asian Div., Hong Kong 1995, mem. Bd of Exec. Dirs 1997–, Chair. BASF AG (renamed BASF SE Jan. 2008) 2003–; mem. Supervisory Bd Bilfinger Berger AG 2000–, Daimler AG, Lufthansa AG; Pres. German Chemical Industry Asscn 2003–; Vice-Pres. Fed. of German Industries (BDI); Chair. Asia Pacific Cttee of German Business (APA). *Address:* BASF SE, Carl-Bosch Str. 38, 67056 Ludwigshafen, Germany (office). *Telephone:* (621) 60-0 (office). *Fax:* (621) 60-42525 (office). *E-mail:* info@basf.de (office). *Website:* www.basf.de (office).

HAMBRO, Rupert Nicholas, FRSA; British private investor; *Chairman, J.O. Hambro Limited;* b. 27 June 1943, London, England; s. of the late Jocelyn Olaf Hambro and Anne Silvia Muir; m. Mary Robinson Boyer 1970; one s. one d.; ed Eton Coll., Aix-en-Provence Univ.; with Peat Marwick Mitchell & Co. 1962–64; joined Hambros Bank 1964, Dir 1969, Deputy Chair. 1980–83, Chair. 1983–86; Chair. J.O. Hambro Magan Ltd 1988–96, currently Chair. J.O. Hambro Ltd, Robinson Hambro 2010–, Hambro Perks Ltd 2012–; Chair. Asscn of Int. Bond Dealers 1979–82, Wiltons (St James's) Ltd 1987–2003, Mayflower Corpn PLC 1988–2004, Soc. of Merchants Trading to the Continent 1995–2009; mem. Bd of Dirs Anglo-American Corpn of SA Ltd 1981–97, Chatsworth House Trust Ltd 1982–2004, Racecourse Holdings Trust Ltd 1985–94, Telegraph Group Ltd 1986–2003, Sedgwick Group PLC 1987–92, Triton Europe PLC 1987–90, Hamleys PLC 1988–96 (Chair. 1989–94), Pioneer Concrete Holdings PLC 1989–99, Abel Hadden and Co. Ltd 1998–2001, Goldsmiths' Research Foundation 1998–, KBC Peel Hunt Ltd 2000–03, Bank Gutmann AG 2000–, Business for Sterling Ltd 2002–07, Open Europe Ltd 2006–07; mem. Int. Advisory Bd Montana AG, Vienna 1988–2000, CTR Group 1990–97, Fenchurch PLC 1993–97, Longshot PLC 1996–2007, Woburn Golf & Country Club Ltd 1998–2003, Third Space Group Ltd 1999–2007, The Walpole Cttee Ltd 2000–05, Jermyn Street Asscn 2000–03, Roland Berger and Partners Ltd 2000–02, Woburn Enterprises Ltd 2003–11, Cazenove & Loyd 2004–, Lovedean Ltd 2008–11, Sipsmith Ltd 2009–, Theo Fennell PLC 2009–13; mem. Int. Council US Information Agency 1988–; mem. Council RCA 2010–; Chair. of Trustees, Silver Trust 1987– (Patron 2005–08, Pres. 2008–), Boys' Club Trust 1991–2000, Chiswick House Trust 2005–11; Patron, Vice-Patron Royal Soc. of British Sculptors 1997; Patron British Asscn of Adoption and Fostering 2005–08, Pres. 2008–; Patron Asscn of British Designer Silversmiths 2006–; Treas. Nat. Art Collections Fund 1991–2003; Deputy Pres. Anglo-Danish Soc. 1987–; Chair. of Govs Museum of London 1998–2005, Co-Chair. Museum in Docklands 2003–05; Liveryman Co. of Goldsmiths 1994– (Prime Warden 2009–10); Trustee, Wallace Collection 2013–; Hon. Fellow, Univ. of Bath 1998, mem. Court of the Co. of Goldsmiths, Freeman Fishmongers' Co. 1969–; Kt of the Falcon (Iceland) 1986; Walpole Award for British Excellence 2005. *Leisure interests:* country pursuits. *Address:* J.O. Hambro Ltd, 19 Buckingham Gate, London, SW1E 6LB, England (office). *Telephone:* (20) 7399-9986 (office); (20) 7259-0101 (home). *E-mail:* rnhambro@joh.co.uk (office).

HAMBURG, Margaret A., MD; American physician, scientist and government official; *Commissioner, Food and Drug Administration;* b. Chicago, Ill.; d. of Dr David Hamburg and Dr Beatrix Hamburg; m.; two c.; ed Harvard Medical School; completed residency in internal medicine at what is now New York-Presbyterian Hosp./Weill Cornell Medical Center; conducted research on neuroscience at Rockefeller Univ.; studied neuropharmacology at Nat. Inst. of Mental Health; later focused on AIDS research as Asst Dir Nat. Inst. of Allergy and Infectious Diseases; Commr New York City Dept of Health and Mental Hygiene 1991–97; Asst Sec. for Policy and Evaluation, US Dept of Health and Human Services 1997–2001; Founding Vice-Pres. for Biological Programs, Nuclear Threat Initiative 2001–05, Sr Scientist 2005–09; Commr Food and Drug Admin, Silver Spring, Md 2009–; mem. Inst. of Medicine 1994; ranked by Forbes magazine amongst The World's 100 Most Powerful Women (21st) 2011, (61st) 2012, (59th) 2013. *Address:* Food and Drug Administration, 10903 New Hampshire Avenue, Silver Spring, MD 20993-0002, USA (office). *Telephone:* (888) 463-6332 (office). *E-mail:* margaret.hamburg@fda.hhs.gov (office). *Website:* www.fda.gov/AboutFDA/CommissionersPage (office).

HAMDALLAH, Rami, BA, MA, PhD; Palestinian academic and politician; *Interim Prime Minister;* b. 10 Aug. 1958, Anabta, West Bank; m.; three c. (deceased); ed Univ. of Jordan, Manchester Univ., UK, Lancaster Univ., UK; Instructor, Dept of English, An-Najah Nat. Univ. 1982–85, Chair., Dept of English 1988–92, Dean, Faculty of Arts 1992–95, Vice-Pres. for Academic Affairs, Colls of Humanities 1995–98, Pres. An-Najah Nat. Univ. 1998–; Sec.-Gen. Palestinian Central Elections Comm. 2002–13, Deputy Chair. 2011; Prime Minister 3–20 June 2013 (resgnd), Interim Prime Minister 20 June 2013–; mem. Fatah Movt. *Address:* Office of the Prime Minister, Ramallah, Palestinian Territories (office). *E-mail:* rhamdallah@pmo.pna.ps (office); info@pmo.gov.ps (office). *Website:* www.palestinecabinet.gov.ps (office).

HAMDAN, Mohammed, PhD; Jordanian mathematician and politician; *Professor, Engineering Sector, Higher Council for Science and Technology;* b. 3 Nov. 1934; m.; two c.; ed Cairo Univ., Egypt and Sydney Univ., Australia; Visiting Prof., Virginia Polytechnic Inst. and State Univ. 1969–71; Assoc. Prof. of Math., American Univ. of Beirut 1970–76, Prof. of Math. 1976–77, also at American Univ. of Cairo 1977–78; Prof. of Math., Dean Faculty of Sciences, Univ. of Jordan 1984–86; Pres. Yarmouk Univ. 1986–89; Minister of Educ. and Higher Educ. 1989–91, 1998; Pres. Hashemite Univ. 1991–98; fmr Sec.-Gen. Higher Council for Science and Tech., currently Prof., Eng Sector; mem. Bd of Dirs Nat. Energy Research Centre; mem. Int. Statistical Inst., American Statistical Asscn, Third World Acad. of Sciences, Jordan Acad. of Arabic Language, Union of Arab Physicists and Mathematicians; mem. Bd Trustees Hitteen, Ibn Khaldoun and Al-Razi Community Coll.; mem. Editorial Bd Int. Statistical Review, Arab Journal of Mathematics, Mu'tah Journal of Research and Studies and Research Journal, Univ. of Jordan; mem. Islamic Acad. of Sciences, mem. Council 1994–99. *Publications:* over 60 tech. papers. *Address:* The Higher Council for Science and Technology, PO Box, 36 Jubaiha, Amman, Jordan (office). *Telephone:* (6) 5340401 (office). *Fax:* (6) 5340589 (office). *E-mail:* mhamdan@hcst.gov.jo (office). *Website:* www.hcst.gov.jo (office).

HAMDANI, Smail; Algerian politician; b. 1930, Bordj Bou-Arreridj; m.; one c.; fmrly Govt Sec.-Gen., adviser to Presidency, Amb. to Scandinavia, Spain, France, to UNESCO, Sec.-Gen. at Foreign Ministry; mem. Council of the Nation; Prime Minister of Algeria 1998–99; fmr Lecturer, Ecole Nat. d'Admin; consultant and mem. Nat. Inst. for Strategic Studies; Chair. Algerian Asscn for Int. Relations. *Address:* c/o Office of the Prime Minister, rue Docteur Saâdane, Algiers, Algeria.

HAMED, Mongi, PhD; Tunisian international organization official and government official; *Minister of Foreign Affairs;* b. 23 April 1959, Sidi Bouzid; m.; three c.; ed Ecole Nat. d'Ingénieurs, Tunis, Univ. of Southern California, Harvard Univ., USA; with UN Secr., New York 1988–98, Head, Science, Tech. and ICT Div., UN Comm. on Science and Tech. for Devt (CSTD), Geneva 2001–13, Head of Cabinet of Sec.-Gen., UN Conf. on Trade and Devt (UNCTAD), Geneva 2012–13; Minister of Foreign Affairs 2014–. *Address:* Ministry of Foreign Affairs, ave de la Ligue des états arabes, 1030 Tunis, Tunisia (office). *Telephone:* (71) 847-500 (office). *Fax:* (71) 785-025 (office). *E-mail:* mae@diplomatie.gov.tn (office). *Website:* www.diplomatie.gov.tn (office).

HAMED FRANCO, Alejandro; Paraguayan academic, diplomatist and government official; b. 26 Feb. 1934, Asunción; ed Universidad de la República, Montevideo, Universidad Nacional de Asunción; fmr Prof., Universidad Católica, Universidad Nacional de Ciudad del Este; Asunción; fmr Docent, Universidad Nacional en Asunción; Amb. to Lebanon (also accred. to Qatar, Syria and Kuwait) –2008; Minister of Foreign Affairs 2008–09. *Publications include:* El Islán Diferente 2001, La Intifad Palestina an y su Poesía 2002, Los Arabes y sus Descendientes en el Paraguay 2002. *Address:* Ministry of Foreign Affairs, Juan E. O'Leary y Presidente Franco, Asunción, Paraguay (office). *Telephone:* (21) 49-4593 (office). *Fax:* (21) 49-3910 (office). *Website:* www.mre.gov.py (office).

HAMEED, Naseem; Pakistani athlete; b. 1988, Karachi; won 100m Gold Medal at South Asian Games, Dhaka 2010 gaining title of 'Fastest Woman in South Asia'; Pakistan Amb. of Sports 2010, Mobilink Jazz Brand Amb. 2010. *Address:* c/o Athletics Federation of Pakistan, Room No.123, Jinnah Stadium, Pakistan Sports Complex, Islamabad, Pakistan.

HAMELIN, Louis-Edmond, OC, MA, PhD, DèsSc, FRSC; Canadian researcher and consultant in polar affairs; b. 21 March 1923, St Didace; m. Colette Lafay 1951; one s. one d.; ed Laval Univ. and Univs of Grenoble and Paris, France; Prof., Laval Univ. 1951–78, Dir Inst. of Geography 1955–61, Founding Dir Centre for Northern Studies 1962–72; mem. Legis Ass., Yellowknife, Northwest Territories 1971–75; Rector Université de Québec, Trois-Rivières 1978–83; Gov. Int. Devt Research Centre, Ottawa 1984–88; Corresp., Inst. de France, Paris 1989; Ordre des francophones d'Amérique 1994, Grand Officier, Ordre nat. du Québec 1998; Dr hc (McGill, Ottawa, Waterloo, Sherbrooke, Montreal, Trois-Rivières); Léo-Pariseau Prize 1972, Pierre Chauveau Medal 1972, Gov.-Gen.'s Award 1976, Massey Medal 1976, Grand Prix Geography (Paris) 1977, Gloire de l'Escolle Medal 1982, Molson Foundation Prize (Canada) 1982, Human Sciences Prize (Québec) 1987, Léon-Gérin Prize 1987. *Publications include:* Illustrated Glossary of Periglacial Phenomena 1967, Atlas du Monde 1967, Canada: A Geographical Perspective 1973, Canadian Nordicity 1979, The Canadian North 1988, Obiou 1990, Le rang d'habitat 1993, Écho des pays froids 1996, Le Québec par des mots 2000–03 (electronic and printed versions, three vols), L'âme de la terre 2006. *Leisure interests:* writing, walking, sightseeing. *Address:* 1244 Rue Albert Lozeau,

Sillery, QC G1T 1H4, Canada. *Telephone:* (418) 683-0386. *E-mail:* louis-edmond
.hamelin@sittel.ca. *Website:* www.lehamelin.sittel.ca.

HAMID, Abdul, BA, LLB; Bangladeshi lawyer, politician and head of state;
President; b. 1 Jan. 1944, Kamalpur, Mithamain, Kishoreganj, Bengal Presidency,
British India; s. of the late Hazi Md. Tayebuddin and Tomiza Khatun; m. Rashida
Hamid; three s. one d.; ed Cen. Law Coll. under Univ. of Dhaka; imprisoned by
Pakistan Govt for taking part in student movt 1961; Gen. Sec. Student Union,
Gurudayal Coll., Kishoreganj 1963, Vice-Pres. 1965; Founder-Pres. Student
League Kishoreganj Sub-Div. 1964, Vice-Pres. Student League, Mymensingh
Dist 1966–67; imprisoned by Pakistan Govt 1968; joined Awami League 1969;
mem. Nat. Ass. of Pakistan from Mymensingh 18 constituency 1970; Chair.
recruiting camp in Meghalaya, India, during liberation war 1971, Commdr Sub-
Sector Kishoreganj, Bangladesh Liberation Force; mem. Constitutent Ass.,
Bangladesh 1972; mem. Jatiya Sangsad (Parl.) from Kishoreganj-5 constituency
1973–2013, Deputy Speaker 1996–2001, Deputy Leader of the Opposition
2001–06, Speaker July–Oct. 2001, 2009–13; Acting Pres. of Bangladesh (following
death of Zillur Rahman), Pres. 2013–; Pres. Kishoreganj Bar Asscn several times;
Swadhinata Padak 2013. *Address:* President's Secretariat, Old Sansad Bhaban,
Dhaka (office); Jatiyo Sangshad Bhaban, Dhaka, Bangladesh (office).

HAMIED, Yusuf K., PhD; Indian pharmaceuticals industry executive; *Chairman
and Managing Director, Cipla Limited;* b. 25 July 1936, Vilnius, Lithuania; s. of
Khwaja Abdul Hamied; m.; ed Cathedral and John Connon School, Bombay (now
Mumbai), Univ. of Cambridge, UK; raised in Bombay; began career as research
officer, Cipla Ltd 1960, Man. Dir 1976–, Chair. 1989–; Fellow, Christ's Coll.,
Cambridge; known outside India for defying large Western pharmaceutical cos in
order to provide generic AIDS drugs and treatments for other ailments primarily
affecting people in poor countries; Nat. Award, Dept of Science and Tech., Padma
Bhushan 2005, Indian of The Year in (Business category) CNN-IBN 2012. *Leisure
interest:* Western classical music. *Address:* Cipla Ltd, Mumbai Central, 289 J. B. B.
Marg, Mumbai 400 008, India (office). *Telephone:* (22) 23095521 (office). *Fax:* (22)
23070013 (office). *Website:* www.cipla.com (office).

HAMILTON, Andrew David, BSc MSc, PhD, FRS; British chemist, academic
and university administrator; *Vice-Chancellor, University of Oxford;* b. 3 Nov.
1952, Guildford, Surrey, England; m. Jennifer Hamilton; two s. one d.; ed Royal
Grammar School, Guildford, Univ. of Exeter, Univ. of British Columbia, Canada,
St John's Coll., Cambridge; post-doctoral researcher, Université Louis Pasteur,
Strasbourg 1980–81; Asst Prof., Dept of Chem., Princeton Univ. 1981–88; Assoc.
Prof., Dept of Chem., Univ. of Pittsburgh 1988–92, Prof. 1992–97, Chair. Dept of
Chem. 1994–97; Irénée duPont Prof. of Chem., Yale Univ. 1997–2004, Chair. Dept
of Chem. 1999–2003, Benjamin Silliman Prof. of Chem. 2004–09, Deputy Provost
for Science and Tech., Yale Univ. 2003–04, Provost Yale Univ. 2004–08; Vice-
Chancellor Univ. of Oxford 2009–, Hon. Fellow, Harris Manchester Coll., Kellogg
Coll.; mem. American Acad. of Arts and Sciences 2010; Fellow, AAAS 2004; ACS
Arthur C. Cope Scholar Award 1999, Int. Izatt Christiansen Award in Macrocyclic
Chem. 2011. *Leisure interest:* football. *Address:* Office of the Vice-Chancellor,
University Offices, Wellington Square, Oxford, OX1 2JD, England (office).
Telephone: (1865) 270242 (office). *Fax:* (1865) 270085 (office). *E-mail:* andrew
.hamilton@admin.ox.ac.uk (office); vice-chancellor@admin.ox.ac.uk (office).
Website: www.admin.ox.ac.uk/vc (office).

HAMILTON, Hon. Lee H., BA, JD; American research institute director and fmr
politician; *Director, Center on Congress, Indiana University;* b. 20 April 1931,
Daytona Beach, Fla; m. Nancy Ann Hamilton (née Nelson); one s. two d.; ed
DePauw Univ., Goethe Inst., Frankfurt, Germany, Indiana Univ. School of Law;
practised law in Chicago and Columbus, Ind. –1965; mem. US House of Reps from
Ind. 9th Dist 1965–99, served as Chair., ranking mem. Cttee on Int. Relations,
Chair. and Vice-Chair. Jt Econ. Cttee, Chair. Perm. Select Cttee on Intelligence,
Chair. Jt Cttee on Org. of Congress, Chair. Oct. Surprise Task Force, Chair. Select
Cttee to Investigate Covert Arms Transactions with Iran, Chair. Sub-Cttee on
Europe and Middle East 1970–93, mem. House Standards of Official Conduct
Cttee; Dir Woodrow Wilson Int. Center for Scholars 1999–2010; has served on
numerous panels and comms including Commr US Comm. on Nat. Security in the
21st Century (Hart-Rudman Comm.), Co-Chair. Baker-Hamilton Comm. to
Investigate Certain Security Issues at Los Alamos, Commr Carter-Baker Comm.
on Fed. Election Reform, Vice-Chair. Nat. Comm. on Terrorist Attacks Upon the
US (9-11 Comm.); mem. US Dept of Homeland Security Advisory Council; Co-
Chair. Ind. Task Force on Immigration and America's Future, Nat. Advisory Cttee
to Campaign for Civic Mission of Schools, Dept of Energy Blue Ribbon Comm on
America's Nuclear Future, Pres.'s Foreign Intelligence Advisory Bd; Co-Chair.
Iraq Study Group, US Inst. of Peace 2006–07; Prof. of Practice, School of Public and
Environmental Affairs, Indiana Univ., Dir Center on Congress, Distinguished
Scholar, School of Global and Int. Studies; Chevalier, Légion d'honneur 1984,
Grosses Verdienstkreuz 1985, Bundesverdienstkreutz 1999; Dr hc (DePauw
Univ.), (Hanover Coll.), (Detroit Coll. of Law), (Ball State Univ.), (Univ. of
Southern Ind.), (Wabash Coll.) (Union Coll.), (Marian Coll.), (American Univ.),
(Ind. Univ.), (Suffolk Univ.), (Ind. State Univ.), (Anderson Univ.), (Franklin Coll.),
(Shenandoah Univ.), (Bellarmine Univ.), (Georgetown Univ. School of Law), (St
Joseph's Coll.), (Illinois Coll.), (Manchester Coll.); Defense Intelligence Agency
Medallion 1987, CIA Medallion 1988, Indiana Univ. Inst. for Advanced Study
Distinguished Citizen Fellow 1994, Indiana Univ. Pres.'s Medal for Excellence
1996, Center for Nat. Policy Edmund S. Muskie Distinguished Public Service
Award 1997, American Political Science Asscn Hubert H. Humphrey Award 1998,
ABA CEELI Award 1998, Center for Civic Educ. Civitas Award 1998, US Dept of
Defense Medal for Distinguished Public Service 1998, Paul H. Nitze Award for
Distinguished Authority on Nat. Security Affairs 1999, Eisenhower Nat. Security
Series Award 2003, Franklin and Eleanor Roosevelt Inst. Freedom from Fear
Award (co-recipient) 2005, Dwight D. Eisenhower Medal for Leadership and
Service 2007, George C. Marshall Foundation Award 2007, Gerald R. Ford Medal
for Distinguished Public Service 2007, Churchill Award for Statesmanship 2007,
World Affairs Councils of America Chair.'s Award for Lifetime Achievement 2008,
Benjamin Harrison Presidential Site Advocating American Democracy Award
2011, 9/11 Tenth Anniversary Summit Distinguished Public Service Award 2011,
Chicago Council on Global Affairs Nat. Leadership Award 2012. *Publications:* A
Creative Tension: The Foreign Policy Roles of the President and Congress (with

Jordan Tama) 2002, How Congress Works and Why You Should Care 2004,
Without Precedent: The Inside Story of the 9/11 Commission (with Thomas H.
Kean) 2006, Strengthening Congress 2009. *Address:* Center on Congress, 1315
East Tenth Street, Suite 320, Bloomington, IN 47405-1701, USA (office).
Telephone: (812) 856-4706 (office). *E-mail:* congress@indiana.edu (office).
Website: www.centeroncongress.org (office).

HAMILTON, Lewis Carl Davidson, MBE; British racing driver; b. 7 Jan. 1985,
Stevenage, Herts.; ed John Henry Newman School; took up Karting 1993, Cadet
1993–97, Super One British Champion 1995, STP Champion 1995, Sky TV Kart
Masters Champion 1996, Five Nations Champion 1996, Jr Yamaha 1998, Super
One British Champion 1998, Jr Intercontinental A 1999, Italian Industrials
Champion 1999, Vice European Champion 1999, winner Trophy de Pomposa 1999,
Formula A 2000, European Champion 2000, World Cup Champion 2000, Karting
World Number 1, Formula Super A 2001, European Champion 2000; signed to
McClaren F1 Driver Devt Program 1998; participated in British Formula Renault
Winter Series 2001, Formula Renault 2002–03, Champion 2003, Third 2002;
competed for Manor Motorsport in Formula 3 Euroseries Championship 2004, for
ASM Formula 3 2005, Drivers' Champion 2005, Fifth 2004; joined ART Grand Prix
team and competed in GP2 Series 2006, Drivers' Champion 2006, Formula 1 debut,
Australian Grand Prix 2007, Formula 1 World Drivers' Champion Runner-up
2007, Champion (youngest Formula 1 Drivers' Champion) 2008; winner, Formula
1 World Championship 2008, Bahrain Grand Prix 2014; associated with McLaren
Mercedes Formula 1 team 2007–12, Mercedes AMG Petronas Formula 1 Team
2013–; British Club Driver of the Year 2003, Rookie Of The Year 2006–07,
Hawthorn Memorial Trophy 2007, 2008, British Competition Driver 2007, Int.
Racing Driver Award 2007, German GQ magazine Man of the Year 2007, UK
Sportsman of the Year 2007, BRDC Gold Star Award 2007, Walpole Award for
British Excellence 2007, Laureus World Breakthrough of the Year 2008. *Address:*
c/o 33 Ransomes Dock, 35–37 Parkgate Road, London, SW11 4NP, England (office);
Mercedes AMG Petronas Formula 1 Team, Operations Centre, Brackley, NN13
7BD, England (office). *Telephone:* (20) 7801-1919 (office). *Fax:* (20) 7801-1920
(office). *E-mail:* teamlh@xixentertainment.com (office); enquiries@mercedesamgf1
.com (office). *Website:* www.xixentertainment.com (office); www.mercedesamgf1
.com (office); www.lewishamilton.com (office).

HAMILTON, Linda; American actress; b. 26 Sept. 1956, Salisbury, Md; m. 1st
Bruce Abbott (divorced); m. 2nd James Cameron (q.v.) 1996 (divorced); one d.
Stage appearances: Looice 1975, Richard III 1977. *Films include:* T.A.G.: The
Assassination Game 1982, Children of the Corn 1984, The Stone Boy 1984, The
Terminator 1984, Black Moon Rising 1986, King Kong Lives! 1986, Mr Destiny
1990, Terminator 2: Judgment Day 1991, Silent Fall 1994, The Shadow Conspiracy
1997, Dante's Peak 1997, The Secret Life of Girls 1999, Skeletons in the Closet
2000, Wholey Moses 2003, Jonah 2004, Smile 2005, Missing in America 2005, In
Your Dreams 2008, Holy Water 2009, Refuge 2010, Bad Behavior 2012. *Television
includes:* Reunion 1980, Rape and Marriage: The Rideout Case 1980, The Secrets
of Midland Heights (series) 1980–81, King's Crossing (series) 1982, Country Gold
1982, Secrets of a Mother and Daughter 1983, Secret Weapons 1985, Club Med
1986, Beauty and the Beast (series) 1987–90, Go Toward the Light 1988, The Way
to Dusty Death 1995, A Mother's Prayer 1995, On the Line 1998, Point Last Seen
1998, The Color of Courage 1999, Sex & Mrs X 2000, A Girl Thing (mini-series)
2001, Bailey's Mistake 2001, Silent Night 2002, Take 3 2008, Home by Christmas
2006, The Line (series) 2008–09, Chuck (series) 2010–12. *Address:* United Talent
Agency, 5th Floor, 9560 Wilshire Boulevard, Beverly Hills, CA 90212, USA.

HAMILTON, Richard Streit, BA, PhD; American mathematician and academic;
Davies Professor of Mathematics, Columbia University; b. 1943, Cincinnati, Ohio;
ed Yale and Princeton Univs; has taught at Univ. of California, Irvine, Univ. of
California, San Diego and Cornell Univ.; currently Davies Prof. of Math.,
Columbia Univ.; mem. NAS 1999, American Acad. of Arts and Sciences 2003;
Oswald Veblen Prize in Geometry 1996, Clay Research Award 2003, Leroy P.
Steele Prize for a Seminal Contrib. to Research, American Math. Soc. 2009, Shaw
Prize in Math. Sciences (co-recipient) 2012. *Publications:* numerous papers in
professional journals. *Address:* Mathematics Department, Columbia University,
Room 522, MC 4424 2990 Broadway, New York, NY 10027, USA (office).
Telephone: (212) 854-4755 (office). *Fax:* (212) 854-8962 (office). *E-mail:*
hamilton@math.columbia.edu (office). *Website:* www.math.columbia.edu (office).

HAMM, Jonathan (Jon) Daniel; American actor; b. 10 March 1971, St Louis,
Mo.; s. of the late Daniel Hamm and Deborah Hamm; pnr Jennifer Westfeldt
1997–; ed John Burroughs School, Univ. of Missouri; fmr drama teacher, John
Burroughs School, Mo.; f. Points West Pictures (production co.) 2009; named
among Entertainers of the Year, Entertainment Weekly 2008. *Films include:*
Space Cowboys 2000, Kissing Jessica Stein 2001, We Were Soldiers 2002, Ira and
Abby 2006, The Ten 2007, The Day the Earth Stood Still 2008, A Single Man 2009,
Stolen 2009, Howl 2010, The Town 2010, Shrek Forever After 2010, Sucker Punch
2011, Friends with Kids 2012. *Television:* The Hughleys 2000, The Trouble with
Normal 2000, Providence 2000, Early Bird Special 2001, Gilmore Girls 2002, The
Division 2002, Charmed 2005, Point Pleasant 2005, CSI: Miami 2005, Related
2006, What About Brian 2006, The Unit 2006, The Sarah Silverman Program
2007, Mad Men (Golden Globe Award for Best Actor in TV Series Drama 2008,
Golden Nymph Award 2009, Screen Actors Guild Award for Outstanding
Performance by an Ensemble in a Drama Series 2009, 2010) 2007–, 30 Rock
(guest actor) 2009–10, Children's Hospital 2010, The Increasingly Poor Decisions
of Todd Margaret 2012. *Leisure interests:* ice hockey, baseball. *Address:* International Creative Management, 10250 Constellation Blvd., 9th Floor, Los Angeles,
CA 90067; Forward Entertainment, 9255 Sunset Blvd, Suite 805, Los Angeles, CA
90069, USA.

HAMM, Mariel Margret (Mia); American fmr professional footballer; b. 17
March 1972, Selma, Ala; m. 1st Christian Corry 1994 (divorced 2001); m. 2nd
Nomar Garciaparra 2003; twin d.; ed Lake Braddock Secondary School, Burke, Va,
Notre Dame High School, Wichita Falls, Tex., Univ. of North Carolina; centre
forward; with Washington Freedom 1987–2003; played for US nat. team (youngest
player aged 15) 1987–2004, represented USA at World Cup 1991 (gold medal),
1995 (bronze medal), 1999 (gold medal), 2003 (bronze medal), Olympic Games 1996
(gold medal), 2000 (silver medal), 2004 (gold medal), CONCACAF Cup 2002 (gold
medal); US coll. football's leading scorer (103 goals); 275 int. caps (second highest

total), 158 goals (world record); retd 2004; f. Mia Hamm Foundation (supports young female athletes and bone marrow research) 1999; won four NCAA Championships with Univ. of North Carolina 1989, 1990, 1992, 1993, Most Valuable Player (MVP) at Chiquita Cup 1994, US Soccer Athlete of the Year 1994, 1995, 1996, MVP at World Cup 1995, Women's Sports Foundation Athlete of the Year 1997, ESPN Outstanding Female Athlete 1998, FIFA Female Player of the Year 2001, 2002, inducted into Nat. Soccer Hall of Fame 2007. *Publications:* (with Aaron Heifetz) Go for the Goal: A Champions Guide to Winning in Soccer and Life 1999. *Leisure interests:* golf, basketball, reading, cooking. *Address:* c/o Mia Hamm Foundation, PO Box 56, Chapel Hill, NC 27514, USA. *Telephone:* (919) 544-9848. *Fax:* (919) 544-9878. *E-mail:* michelle@miafoundation.org. *Website:* www.miafoundation.org.

HAMM, Paul; American gymnast; b. (Paul Elbert Hamm), 24 Sept. 1982, Washburn, Wis.; s. of Sandy Hamm and Cecily Hamm; ed Univ. of Wisconsin; took up gymnastics in 1989, int. debut 1999; fifth place in team event Olympic Games, Sydney 2000; team silver medal World Championships 2001; team silver medal, bronze medal floor exercise World Championships 2002; gold medal horizontal bar World Cup 2002; gold medals floor exercise and individual all-round (first US male gymnast to win all-round gold medal at World Championships), team silver medal World Championships 2003; gold medal floor exercise World Cup 2003; gold medals vault and horizontal bar, silver medal floor exercise, bronze medals parallel bars and pommel horse World Cup 2004; gold medal individual all-round (first US male to win all-round Olympic gold medal), silver medals horizontal bar and team event Olympic Games, Athens 2004; American Cup 2007, 2008, Pacific Rim Championship 2008; mem. Team Chevron, Columbus OH; James E. Sullivan Award 2004. *Leisure interests:* playing tennis, cards, chess. *Address:* c/o Sheryl Shade, Shade Global, Inc., 10 East 40th Street, 48th Floor, New York, NY 10016, USA.

HAMMAMI, Hamma; Tunisian politician; *Leader, Parti communiste des ouvriers tunisiens (PCOT);* b. 8 Jan. 1952, El Aroussa; m. Radhia Nasraoui 1981; three d.; Co-founder and Leader, Parti communiste des ouvriers tunisiens (PCOT) (banned communist party); Dir El Badil (The Alternative) banned newspaper, fmr ed.; imprisoned for participation in student movt 1972–74, for membership in El Aamel Ettounsi (The Tunisian Worker) 1974–80, exiled in France, sentenced in absentia May 1987, returned to Tunisia, numerous arrests 1989–91, went into hiding Oct. 1992, tried in absentia Dec. 1992, arrested Feb. 1994, imprisoned June 1994–Nov. 1995, went into hiding, sentenced in absentia July 1999, emerged from hiding and imprisoned March–Sept. 2002, released a few months later. *E-mail:* pcot@albadil.org. *Website:* www.albadil.org.

HAMMEL, Eugene Alfred, AB, PhD; American demographer and academic; *Professor Emeritus, Department of Demography, University of California, Berkeley;* b. 18 March 1930, New York, NY; s. of William Hammel and Violet Brookes; m. Joan Marie Swingle 1951; ed Univ. of Calif., Berkeley; field work in archaeology and linguistics, Calif. 1947–51, in ethnography, Peru 1957–58, in archaeology and ethnography in New Mexico 1959–61, in ethnography in Mexico 1963, in Yugoslavia and Greece 1963, 1965–66; Asst Prof., Univ. of New Mexico 1959–61; Asst Prof., Univ. of Calif., Berkeley 1961–63, Assoc. Prof. 1963–66, Prof. 1966–93, Prof. of Anthropology and Demography 1978–93, Prof. Emer. 1993–, Dir Quantitative Anthropology Lab. 1974–90, Chair. Demography 1978–88; archival research in Yugoslavia, Hungary, Austria 1983–; mem. NAS; Guggenheim Fellow 1965–66; American Acad. of Arts and Sciences Award 1991. *Publications:* Wealth, Authority and Prestige in the Ica Valley, Peru 1962, Ritual Relations and Alternative Social Structures in the Balkans 1968, The Pink Yoyo: Occupational Mobility in Belgrade c. 1915–65 1969, Statistical Studies of Historical Social Structure (with Wachter and Laslett) 1978; approximately 180 articles. *Leisure interests:* hiking, guitar, carpentry, photography. *Address:* Department of Demography, University of California, 2232 Piedmont Avenue, Berkeley, CA 94720-2120, USA (office). *Telephone:* (415) 642-9800 (office). *E-mail:* gene@demog.berkeley.edu (office). *Website:* www.demog.berkeley.edu/~gene (office).

HAMMER, Bonnie, BA, MA; American television executive; *Chairman, Cable Entertainment and Cable Studios, NBCUniversal;* b. Queens, NY; m.; two c.; ed Boston Univ. Coll. of Communication and School of Educ.; began TV career at WGBH, Boston, produced This Old House and ZOOM series; later executive producer of Good Day! for Boston's ABC affiliate, WCVB; est. herself professionally in New York as a programming exec. at Lifetime Television, oversaw production of award-winning series of documentaries; Pres. Cable Entertainment and Cable Studios, NBCUniversal –2010, exec. responsibility for Syfy, USA Network 2004–, Chiller 2008–, Cloo 2008–, Universal HD 2008–, Universal Cable Productions 2008–, Chair. Cable Entertainment and Cable Studios, NBCUniversal 2011–, added exec. responsibility for E! Entertainment, E! Studios and G4; ranked by Fortune magazine amongst the 50 Most Powerful Women in Business in the US (45th) 2010, (36th) 2011, (33rd) 2012, ranked by Forbes magazine amongst The World's 100 Most Powerful Women (54th) 2011, (73rd) 2012, (61st) 2013. *Address:* NBCUniversal Media LLC, 30 Rockefeller Plaza, New York, NY 10112, USA (office). *Telephone:* (212) 664-4444 (office). *Fax:* (212) 664-4085 (office). *E-mail:* info@nbcuni.com (office). *Website:* www.nbcuni.com (office).

HAMMERGREN, John H., BA, MBA; American pharmaceuticals industry executive; *Chairman, President and CEO, McKesson Corporation;* b. 1959; ed Univ. of Minnesota, Xavier Univ., Cincinnati, Ohio; Vice-Pres. McKesson Health Systems 1996–97, Group Pres. 1997–99, Exec. Vice-Pres. McKesson Corpn Jan.–July 1999, Dir, Co-Pres. and Co-CEO 1999–2001, Pres. and CEO 2001–, Chair. 2002–, CEO Supply Man. Business Jan.–July 1999; mem. Bd of Dirs Hewlett Packard, Nadro SA de CV (Mexico); Chair. Healthcare Leadership Council 2009–10; mem. Business Council, Business Roundtable. *Publication:* Skin in the Game (co-author) 2008. *Address:* McKesson Corporate Headquarters, One Post Street, San Francisco, CA 94104, USA (office). *Telephone:* (415) 983-8300 (office). *Fax:* (415) 983-7160 (office). *E-mail:* corp.communications@mckesson.com (office). *Website:* www.mckesson.com (office).

HAMMES, Gordon G., PhD; American biochemist, academic and fmr university vice-chancellor; *Professor Emeritus and University Distinguished Service Professor Emeritus of Biochemistry, Medical Center, Duke University;* b. 10 Aug. 1934, Fond du Lac, Wis.; s. of Jacob Hammes and Betty (Sadoff) Hammes; m. Judith

Ellen Frank 1959; one s. two d.; ed Princeton Univ. and Univ. of Wisconsin; Postdoctoral Fellow, Max Planck Inst. für physikalische Chemie, Göttingen, FRG 1959–60; instructor, subsequently Assoc. Prof., MIT, Cambridge, Mass. 1960–65; Prof., Cornell Univ. 1965–88, Chair. Dept of Chem. 1970–75, Horace White Prof. of Chem. and Biochemistry 1975–88, Dir Biotechnology Program 1983–88; Prof., Univ. of Calif., Santa Barbara 1988–91, Vice-Chancellor for Academic Affairs 1988–91; Prof., Duke Univ., Durham, NC 1991–2008, Emer. 2008–, Vice-Chancellor Duke Univ. Medical Center 1991–98, Univ. Distinguished Service Prof. of Biochemistry 1996–2008, Emer. 2008–; mem. Physiological Chem. Study Section, Physical Biochemistry Study Section, Training Grant Cttee, NIH; mem. Bd of Counsellors, Nat. Cancer Inst. 1976–80, Advisory Council, Chem. Dept, Princeton 1970–75, Polytechnic Inst., New York 1977–78, Boston Univ. 1977–85; mem. Nat. Research Council, US Nat. Comm. for Biochemistry 1989–95; mem. ACS, American Soc. of Biochemistry and Molecular Biology (Pres. 1994–95), NAS, American Acad. of Arts and Sciences; Ed. Biochemistry 1992–2003; ACS Award in Biological Chem. 1967, William C. Rose Award, American Soc. of Biochemistry and Molecular Biology 2002. *Achievements:* ACS est. the Gordon G. Hammes Lecture annual award 2008. *Publications:* Principles of Chemical Kinetics, Enzyme Catalysis and Regulation, Chemical Kinetics: Principles and Selected Topics (with I. Amdur), Thermodynamics and Kinetics for the Biological Sciences 2000, Spectroscopy for the Biological Sciences 2005, Physical Chemistry for the Biological Sciences 2007; numerous learned articles. *Leisure interests:* music, tennis. *Address:* 11 Staley Place, Durham, NC 27705 (home); Department of Biochemistry, Duke University, Box 3711, Medical Center, Durham, NC 27710, USA (office). *Telephone:* (919) 684-8848 (office). *Fax:* (919) 684-9709 (office). *E-mail:* hamme001@mc.duke.edu (office). *Website:* medschool.duke.edu; www.biochem.duke.edu/modules/biochem_people/index.php?id=3 (office).

HAMMES, Michael Noel, MBA; American business executive; *Chairman, James Hardie Industries SE;* b. 25 Dec. 1941, Evanston, Ill.; s. of Ferdinand Hammes and Winifred Hammes; m. Lenore Lynn Forbes 1964; three s. two d.; ed Georgetown Univ., New York Univ.; Asst Controller, Ford Motor Ass. Div. 1974, Plant Man., Ford Wixom Assembly Plant 1975, Man. Program Planning, Ford Automotive Ass. Div. 1976, Dir Int. Business Planning, Int. Operations, Ford 1977, Man. Dir and Pres., Ford Motor Co. of Mexico 1979, Vice-Pres. Truck Operations, Ford of Europe 1983–86; Vice-Pres., Int. Operations, Chrysler Motors Corpn 1986–90; Pres. Worldwide Consumer Product Operations, Black and Decker Corpn 1990–93; Chair. and CEO Coleman Co. 1993–97; CEO Guide Corpn 1998–2000; Chair. and CEO Sunrise Medical Inc., Carlsbad, Calif. 2000–07, Chair. –2008; Chair. James Hardie Industries SE 2008–, Joerns Healthcare Inc.; mem. Bd of Dirs Johns Manville 1993–, Navistar Int. Corpn 1996–, DynaVox Mayer-Johnson, DeVilbiss, Int. Tech. Corpn; mem. Bd of Visitors, Georgetown Univ. School of Business. *Leisure interests:* skiing, tennis, golf, antique cars. *Address:* Office of the Chairman of the Supervisory Board, James Hardie Industries SE, Second Floor, Europe House, Harcourt Centre, Harcourt Street, Dublin 2, Ireland (office). *Telephone:* (1) 4116924 (office). *Fax:* (1) 4791128 (office). *Website:* www.jameshardie.com (office).

HAMMOND, Aleqa; Greenlandic politician; *Prime Minister, responsible for Foreign Affairs;* b. 23 Sept. 1965, Narsaq; ed in Ellekilde, Denmark, Arctic Coll., Iqaluit; Regional Co-ordinator for Greenland Tourism, Diskobugten 1993–95; Information Officer, Landsstyre Secr. 1995–96; worked for Nuuk Tourism 1996–99; Commr Inuit Circumpolar Conf. 1999–2003; Culture Co-ordinator Arctic Winter Games 2002; worked in Tourism and Culture, Sulisartut Høsjkoliat, Qaqortoq 2002–03; Head of Tourism, Qaqortoq 2004–05; mem. Parl. for the Social Democratic Siumut (Forward) party 2005–, Leader 2009–; Minister for Family Affairs and Justice 2005–07, of Finance and Foreign Affairs 2007–08 (resgnd); Prime Minister (first female), responsible for Foreign Affairs 2013–. *Address:* Siumut (Forward) Party, PO Box 357, 3900 Nuuk, Greenland (office). *Telephone:* 322077 (office). *Fax:* 322319 (office). *E-mail:* siumut@greennet.gl (office). *Website:* www.siumut.gl (office).

HAMMOND, Norman David Curle, MA, Dip. Class. Arch., PhD, ScD, FSA, FBA; British archaeologist and journalist; *Senior Fellow, McDonald Institute for Archaeological Research, University of Cambridge;* b. 10 July 1944, Brighton, Sussex, England; s. of William Hammond and Kathleen Jessie Howes; m. Jean Wilson 1972; one s. one d.; ed Varndean Grammar School, Peterhouse, Cambridge; Research Fellow, Centre of Latin American Studies, Cambridge 1967–71, Leverhulme Research Fellow 1972–75; Research Fellow, Fitzwilliam Coll. Cambridge 1973–75; Sr Lecturer, Univ. of Bradford 1975–77; Visiting Prof., Univ. of Calif., Berkeley 1977, Rutgers Univ., USA 1977–78, Assoc. Prof. 1978–84, Prof. of Archaeology 1984–88; Prof. of Archaeology, Boston Univ. 1988–2011, Prof. Emer. 2011–; Assoc. in Maya Archaeology, Peabody Museum, Harvard Univ. 1988–; Sr Fellow, McDonald Inst. for Archaeological Research, Univ. of Cambridge 2009–; Archaeology Corresp., The Times 1967–, Archaeology Ed. Times Literary Supplement 2009–11; Ed. South Asian Archaeology 1970–73, Afghan Studies 1976–79, International Congress of Americanists Archaeology Proceedings 1982–84; Consulting Ed. Library of Congress, USA 1977–89; Archaeological Consultant Scientific American 1979–95; Acad. Trustee, Archaeological Inst. of America 1990–93; mem. Council, Soc. of Antiquaries of London 1996–99; excavations and surveys in Libya and Tunisia 1964, Afghanistan 1966, Belize 1970–2002, Ecuador 1972–84; Fellow, Dumbarton Oaks, Washington, DC; Visiting Fellow, Worcester Coll. 1989, Oxford, Peterhouse, Cambridge, 1991, 1996, All Souls Coll., Oxford 2004, Clare Hall, Cambridge 2004; De Carle Distinguished Prof., Univ. of Otago 2013; Hon. DSc (Bradford) 1999; Curl Lecturer, Royal Anthropological Inst. 1985, British Archaeological Press Award 1994, 1998, Bushnell Lecturer, Univ. of Cambridge 1997, Stone Lecturer, Archaeological Inst. of America 1998, Willey Lecturer, Harvard Univ. 2000, Sackler Distinguished Lecturer, Metropolitan Museum of Art 2001, Soc. of Antiquaries Medal, London 2001, Reckitt Lecturer, British Acad. 2006, Aronui Lecturer, Royal Soc. of NZ 2011. *Publications include:* South Asian Archaeology (ed.) 1973, Mesoamerican Archaeology (ed.) 1974, Lubaantun: A Classic Maya Realm 1975, Social Process in Maya Prehistory (ed.) 1977, The Archaeology of Afghanistan (co-ed. with F. R. Allchin) 1978, Ancient Maya Civilisation 1982, Nohmul: Excavations 1973–83, 1985, Cuello: An Early Maya Community in Belize 1991, The Maya 2000; Archaeology Proc. 44th Congress of Americanists (Gen. Ed.) 1982–84; contribs to learned and other journals. *Leisure interests:* heraldry, genealogy, wine. *Address:* McDonald Institute for Archaeological Research, University of Cambridge, Downing Street,

Cambridge, CB2 3ER (office); Wholeway, Harlton, Cambridge, Cambs., CB23 1ET, England (home). *Telephone:* (1223) 262376 (home). *E-mail:* ndch1@cam.ac.uk (office). *Website:* www.mcdonald.cam.ac.uk (office); www.bu.edu/archaeology/people/hammond (office).

HAMMOND, Rt Hon. Philip, PC, BA; British politician; *Secretary of State for Defence;* b. 4 Dec. 1955, Epping, Essex; m. Susan Carolyn Williams-Walker 1991; one s. two d.; ed Shenfield School (now Shenfield High School), Brentwood, Univ. Coll., Oxford; joined medical equipment mfrs Speywood Laboratories Ltd 1977, Dir Speywood Medical Ltd 1981–83; Dir, Castlemead Ltd 1984–93; Partner, CMA Consultants 1993–95; Dir, Castlemead Homes 1994; various business interests, including house building and property, manufacturing, healthcare and oil and gas; various consulting assignments in Latin America for the World Bank, Washington, DC; consultant to Govt of Malawi 1995–97; contested Newham NE by-election 1994; MP for Runnymede and Weybridge 1997–; Opposition Spokesperson for Health and Social Services 1998–2001, for Trade and Industry 2001–02; Shadow Minister for Local and Devolved Govt Affairs 2002–05; Shadow Chief Sec. to the Treasury May–Dec. 2005, 2007–10; Shadow Sec. of State for Work and Pensions 2005–07; Sec. of State for Transport 2010–11, for Defence 2011–; Chair. East Lewisham Conservative Asscn 1989–96; mem. Greater London Area Exec. Council 1989–96; mem. (Select Cttees), Unopposed Bills (Panel) 1997–2004, Environment, Transport and Regional Affairs 1998, Environment, Transport and Regional Affairs (Transport Sub-Cttee) 1998, Trade and Industry 2002; mem. Transport, Telecommunications and Energy Council, Council of the European Council 2010–; Conservative. *Address:* Ministry of Defence, Floor 5, Main Building, Whitehall, London, SW1A 2HB (office); House of Commons, Westminster, London, SW1A 0AA; Constituency Office, Runnymede, Spelthorne and Weybridge, Conservative Association, 55 Cherry Orchard, Staines, TW18 2DQ, England. *Telephone:* (20) 7218-9000 (Ministry) (office); (20) 7218-2111 (Minister's pvt. office) (office); (1784) 453544 (Staines); (20) 7219-4055 (Westminster). *Fax:* (20) 7218-7140 (Minister's pvt. office) (office); (20) 7219-5851 (Westminster); (1784) 466109 (Staines). *E-mail:* defencesecretary@mod.uk (office); philip.hammond.mp@parliament.uk; office@runnymedeweybridgeconservatives.com. *Website:* www.mod.uk (office); www.parliament.uk/biographies/commons/philip-hammond/25564 (office); www.runnymedeweybridgeconservatives.com.

HAMMONDS, Bruce L., BS; American business executive (retd); b. 25 April 1948; m.; two c.; ed Univ. of Baltimore; began career as Br. Man. Pacific Finance Co.; COO MBNA Corpn 1991–2002, Pres. and CEO 2003–05, Chair. and CEO 2002–05; Pres. Global Card Services, Bank of America Corpn 2006–08; fmr Dir Financial Services Roundtable; Dir Database Business Roundtable, Chair. Roundtable's Educ. Cttee; mem. Bd of Trustees, Goldey-Beacom Coll. *Address:* 1275 South Ocean Blvd, Palm Beach, FL 33480, USA.

HAMMOUD, Mahmoud, BA, LLB; Lebanese politician and diplomatist; b. 1935; ed Lebanese Univ.; fmr secondary school teacher; fmr Amb. to UAE 1978–83, FRG 1983–85, USSR and Finland 1986–90, to UK 1990–99; Dir-Gen. State Econ. and Social Council 2000–; Minister of Foreign Affairs and Emigrants 2001–03, 2004–05, of Defence 2003–04. *Address:* c/o Ministry of Foreign Affairs and Emigrants, rue Sursock, Achrafieh, Beirut, Lebanon (office).

HAMNETT, Katharine Eleanor, CBE; British fashion designer; b. 16 Aug. 1947; d. of Group Capt. James Appleton; two s.; ed Cheltenham Ladies' Coll. and St Martin's School of Art; co-f. Tuttabankem (with Anne Buck) 1969–74; designed freelance in New York, Paris, Rome and London 1974–76; f. Katharine Hamnett Ltd 1979; launched Choose Life T-Shirt collection 1983; involved in Fashion Aid 1985; opening of first Katharine Hamnett shop, London 1986, followed by two more shops in 1988; production moved to Italy 1989; Visiting Prof., London Inst. 1997–; Hon. Prof., Cen. St Martin's Coll. of Art; Designer of the Year, Int. Inst. of Cotton 1982, British Fashion Industry Designer of the Year 1984, Menswear Designer of the Year Award, Bath Costume Museum 1984, Award for Export, British Knitting and Clothing Export Council 1988. *Publications:* various publs in major fashion magazines and newspapers. *Leisure interests:* travel, photography, gardening, archaeology. *Address:* Katharine E. Hamnett Head Office, Unit 3D, Aberdeen Studios, 22–24 Highbury Grove, London, N5 2EA, England (office). *E-mail:* info@katharinehamnett.com. *Website:* www.katharinehamnett.com (office).

HAMPE, Michael, DPhil; German stage and television director, actor and academic; *Professor, Hochschule für Musik und Tanz, Cologne;* b. 3 June 1935, Heidelberg; s. of Hermann Hampe and Annemarie Hampe; m. Sibylle Hauck 1971; one d.; ed Falckenberg Schule, Munich, Univs of Vienna and Munich, Syracuse Univ., USA; Deputy Dir Schauspielhaus, Zürich 1965–70; Dir Nat. Theatre, Mannheim 1972–75, Cologne Opera 1975–95, Salzburg Festival 1984–90, Dresden Music Festival 1992–2000; has directed opera at La Scala, Milan, Covent Garden, London, Paris Opera, Salzburg and Edin. Festivals, Munich, Stockholm, Cologne, Geneva, San Francisco, Sydney, Los Angeles, Buenos Aires, Tokyo; has directed drama at Bavarian State Theatre, Munich Schauspielhaus, Zürich, etc.; director and actor in film and TV; Prof., State Music Acad., Cologne and Cologne Univ.; mem. Bd European Acad. of Music, Vienna; theatre-bldg consultant; Prof., Hochschule für Musik und Tanz, Cologne; teaches at Vienna Univ., UCLA, Univ. of Southern California and Yale Univ., USA, Kunitachi Coll. of Music and Studio, New Nat. Theatre, Tokyo, Universität der Künste, Berlin; Bundesverdienstkreuz, Commendatore Ordine al Merito (Italy), Goldenes Ehrenzeichen des Landes Salzburg; Olivier West End Award 1983. *Productions include:* Don Giovanni, Così fan tutte, le Nozze di Figaro, Il Ritorno d'Ulisse in Patria, La Cenerentola for Salzburg Festival, Andrea Chénier for Royal Opera House, Covent Garden 1984, Il Barbiere di Siviglia for Royal Opera House, Covent Garden 1985, La Gazza Ladra for Cologne Opera 1987, L'Italiana in Algeri 1987, Die Meistersinger von Nürnberg 1988, Il Barbiere di Siviglia 1988, La Cenerentola for Royal Opera House, Covent Garden 1990, Così fan tutte 1989, Don Giovanni 1991, Falstaff at Schwetzingen Festival 1996, world premiere of Farinelli, oder die Macht des Gesangs at Karlsruhe 1998, Così fan tutte in Santiago and in Genoa, Fidelio for San Francisco Opera 2005, Die Zauberflöte at Megaron, Athens, Die Frau ohne Schatten for Helsinki Opera, Die Zauberflöte at New Nat. Theatre, Toyko, Dallas and San Diego, La clemenza di Tito for Washington Opera 2006, Così fan tutte at Teatro Colón, Buenos Aires 2006, Maometto II at Pesaro 2008, Trovatore at Semperoper, Dresden, Elektre, Aïda, Teatro Municipal, Santiago, etc. *Publications:* 20 Jahre Kölner Oper 1995, Alles Theater, Reden und Aufsätze 2000;

articles in newspapers and periodicals. *Address:* Carl Spitteler Strasse 105, 8053 Zürich, Switzerland.

HAMPEL, Sir Ronald Claus, Kt, MA; British business executive; *Chairman, International Stadia Group (ISG);* b. 31 May 1932, Shrewsbury; s. of Karl Victor Hugo Hampel and Rutgard Emil Klothilde Hauck; m. Jane Bristed Hewson 1957; three s. one d.; ed Canford School, Wimborne, Dorset, Corpus Christi Coll., Cambridge; 2nd Lt in Royal Horse Artillery 1950–51; joined ICI 1955, Vice-Pres. ICI Agrochemicals USA 1973–75, ICI Latin America 1975–77, ICI Gen. Man. Commercial 1977–80, Chair. ICI Paints 1980–83, ICI Agrochemicals 1983–85, Dir ICI 1985–99, COO ICI 1991–93, CEO ICI 1993–95, Chair. 1995–99; Chair. United News and Media (now United Business Media) 1999–2002; mem. Bd of Dirs Powell Duffryn 1983–88, Commercial Union 1987–95, British Aerospace 1989–2002, ALCOA 1995–, Teijin 1999–2004, TI Automotive 2007–09; Chair. Templeton Emerging Markets Investment Trust 2003–07, Int. Stadia Group (ISG) 2010–; Dir American Chamber of Commerce 1985–90; mem. Exec. Cttee British North America Cttee 1989–96, Listed Companies Advisory Cttee, London Stock Exchange 1996–99, Nomination Cttee, NY Stock Exchange 1996–99; mem. European Round Table 1995–99, UK Advisory Bd INSEAD 1994–99, Advisory Cttee Karlpreis Aachen 1997–2001; Vice-Pres. All England Lawn Tennis Club, mem. Exec. Cttee 1994–2007; Chair. Cttee on Corp. Governance 1995–97; Chair. Bd of Trustees Eden Project 2000–07; Hon. Fellow, Corpus Christi Coll. Cambridge 1997. *Leisure interests:* tennis, golf, skiing. *Address:* International Stadia Group, 3 Bentinck Mews, London, W1U 2AH, England (office). *Telephone:* (20) 7935-9518. *E-mail:* info@internationalstadiagroup.co.uk (office); rch@hampelrc.com. *Website:* www.isgworld.co.uk (office).

HAMPSHIRE, Susan, OBE; British actress and writer; b. 12 May 1942; d. of the late George Kenneth Hampshire and June Hampshire; m. 1st Pierre Granier-Deferre 1967 (divorced 1974); one s. one d. (deceased); m. 2nd Sir Eddie Kulukundis (q.v.) 1981; ed Hampshire School, Knightsbridge; Hon. DLitt (City Univ., London) 1984, (St Andrews) 1986, (Exeter) 2001, Hon. DArts (Pine Manor Coll., Boston, USA) 1994, Dr hc (Kingston) 1994; Emmy Award, Best Actress for The Forsyte Saga 1970, for The First Churchills 1971, for Vanity Fair 1973, E. Poe Prize du Film Fantastique, Best Actress for Malpertius 1972. *Stage roles include:* Expresso Bongo 1958, Follow that Girl 1960, Fairy Tales of New York 1961, Marion Dangerfield in Ginger Man 1963, Kate Hardcastle in She Stoops to Conquer 1966, On Approval 1966, Mary in The Sleeping Prince 1968, Nora in A Doll's House 1972, Katharina in The Taming of the Shrew 1974, Peter in Peter Pan 1974, Jeannette in Romeo and Jeannette 1975, Rosalind in As You Like It 1975, Miss Julie 1975, Elizabeth in The Circle 1976, Ann Whitefield in Man and Superman 1977, Siri Von Essen in Tribades 1978, Victorine in An Audience Called Edouard 1978, Irene in The Crucifer of Blood 1979, Ruth Carson in Night and Day 1979, Elizabeth in The Revolt 1980, Stella Drury in House Guest 1981, Elvira in Blithe Spirit 1986, Marie Stopes in Married Love, The Countess in A Little Night Music 1989, Mrs Anna in The King and I 1990, Gertie in Noel and Gertie 1991, The Countess of Marshwood in Relative Values 1993, Suzanna Andler in Suzanna Andler, Alicia Christie in Black Chiffon 1995–96, Sheila Carter in Relatively Speaking 2000–01, Felicity Marshwood in Relative Values 2002, Miss Shepherd in The Lady in the Van 2004–05, The Fairy Godmother in Cinderella, Wimbledon 2005–06, The Bargain 2007, Lady Kitty in The Circle 2008, Mrs Bennet in Pride and Prejudice 2009–10. *Television roles:* Andromeda in The Andromeda Breakthrough (series) 1962, Katy (series) 1962, Fleur Forsyte in The Forsyte Saga (mini-series) 1967, Becky Sharp in Vanity Fair (mini-series) 1967, Sarah Churchill, Duchess of Marlborough, in The First Churchills (mini-series) 1969, Baffled! 1973, Dr. Jekyll and Mr. Hyde 1973, Glencora Palliser in The Pallisers 1974, The Story of David 1976, Kill Two Birds 1976, Lady Melford in Dick Turpin 1981, Madeline Neroni in The Barchester Chronicles (mini-series) 1982, Martha in Leaving 1984, Martha in Leaving II 1985, Going to Pot 1985, Don't Tell Father (series) 1992, Esme Harkness in The Grand 1996–98, Miss Catto in Coming Home 1998–99, Miss Catto in Nancherrow 1999, Molly in Monarch of the Glen 1999–2005, Lucilla Drake in Sparkling Cyanide 2003, The Lady in the Van 2004, The Circle 2008, The Royal 2008–09, Bridge Celebrity Grand Slam 2009, Casualty 2011, 2013. *Films include:* The Woman in the Hall 1947, Idle on Parade (uncredited) 1959, Upstairs and Downstairs 1959, Expresso Bongo (uncredited) 1960, The Long Shadow 1961, During One Night 1961, The Three Lives of Thomasina 1964, Night Must Fall 1964, Wonderful Life 1964, Paris in August 1965, The Fighting Prince of Donegal 1966, Monte Carlo or Bust 1969, Malpertuis 1971, A Time for Loving 1971, Rogan, David Copperfield, Living Free 1972, Neither the Sea Nor the Sand 1972, Le fils 1973, Peccato mortale (aka Roses and Green Peppers) 1973, Bang! 1977. *Publications:* Susan's Story (autobiographical account of dyslexia) 1981, The Maternal Instinct, Lucy Jane at the Ballet 1985, Lucy Jane on Television 1989, Trouble Free Gardening 1989, Every Letter Counts 1990, Lucy Jane and the Dancing Competition 1991, Easy Gardening 1991, Lucy Jane and the Russian Ballet 1993, Rosie's First Ballet Lesson 1997. *Leisure interests:* gardening, music. *Address:* c/o Chatto & Linnit Ltd, 123A Kings Road, London, SW3 4PL, England (office). *Telephone:* (20) 7352-7722 (office).

HAMPSON, Christopher, CBE, BEng, MBA; Canadian/British business executive; b. 6 Sept. 1931, Montreal, Quebec; s. of Harold Ralph Hampson and Geraldine Mary Hampson (née Smith); m. Joan Margaret Cassils Evans 1954; two s. three d.; ed Ashbury Coll. School, Ottawa, McGill Univ., CEI Geneva, Switzerland; joined Canadian Industries Ltd (subsidiary of ICI) 1956, Vice-Pres., Dir 1973; seconded to ICI PLC as Gen. Man. Planning 1978, Sr Vice-Pres. Canadian Industries Ltd 1982, fmr CEO, Dir ICI Australia Ltd, Exec. Dir, mem. Bd ICI 1987–94; Chair. Yorks. Electricity Group 1995–97, RMC Group 1996–2002, British Biotech PLC 1998–2002; mem. bd The Environment Agency 1994–, Deputy Chair. 2000–01. *Leisure interests:* gardening, tennis, skiing. *Address:* 77 Kensington Court, London, W8 5DT, England. *Telephone:* (20) 7937-0325. *Fax:* (20) 7376-1906.

HAMPSON, Sir Stuart, Kt, MA; British civil servant and business executive; *Chairman and First Commissioner, The Crown Estate;* b. 7 Jan. 1947; s. of Kenneth Hampson and Mary Hampson; m. Angela McLaren 1973; one s. one d.; ed Royal Masonic School, Bushey, St John's Coll., Oxford; with Board of Trade 1969–72; FCO Mission to UN, Geneva 1972–74; Dept of Prices and Consumer Protection 1974–79; Dept of Trade 1979–82; with John Lewis Partnership PLC 1982–, Dir of Research and Expansion 1986, Deputy Chair. 1989–93, Chair. and

CEO 1993–2007; Chair. and First Commr The Crown Estate 2010–; Founding Deputy Chair. London First; Pres. Royal Agricultural Soc. of England 2005–06, Employee Ownership Assocn; chaired team tackling econ. renewal in deprived communities, one of Prince of Wales's Ambs in this area; Hon. DBA (Kingston Univ.) 1998. *Address:* The Crown Estate, 16 New Burlington Place, London, W1S 2HX, England (office). *Telephone:* (20) 7851-5000 (office). *E-mail:* enquiries@ thecrownestate.co.uk (office). *Website:* www.thecrownestate.co.uk (office); www .stuarthampson.co.uk.

HAMPSON, (Walter) Thomas, BA; American singer (baritone); b. 28 June 1955, Elkhart, Ind.; s. of Walter Hampson and Ruthye Hampson; one d.; ed Eastern Washington Univ., Fort Wright Coll., Music Acad. of West; with Düsseldorf Ensemble 1981–84; title role in Der Prinz von Homburg, Darmstadt 1982; debut in Cologne, Munich, Santa Fé 1982–84, Metropolitan Opera, New York, Vienna Staatsoper, Covent Garden 1986, La Scala, Milan, Deutsche Oper, Berlin 1989, Carnegie Hall, San Francisco Opera 1990; Artist-in-Residence, New York Philharmonic; has performed with Vienna Philharmonic, New York Philharmonic, London Philharmonic and Chicago Symphony orchestras; Special Advisor to the Study and Performance of Music in America, Library of Congress; f. The Hampsong Foundation 2003; mem. American Acad. of Arts and Sciences 2010–; Hon. mem. RAM 1996, Freunde der Wiener Staatsoper 2004, Wiener Konzerthausgesellschaft 2005; Chevalier des Arts et des Lettres, Officer of the Order Pro Merito Melitensi (Malta) 2006; Dr hc (Whitworth Coll., Washington, San Francisco Conservatory, Manhattan School of Music); Edison Prize, Netherlands 1990, 1992, Grand Prix du Disque 1990, 1996, Cannes Classical Award 1994, Echo Klassik 1995, EMI Artist of the Year 1997, Deutsche Schallplattenkritik Award 1999, Cecilia Award 2000, Diapason d'Or Award 2000; Citation of Merit, Vienna Kammersänger 1999, Edison Award for Life Achievement 2005, Grammy Award for Best Opera Recording 2006, Deutsche Schallplatten Prize 2008, Distinguished Artistic Leadership Award, Atlantic Council 2009, Award for Distinguished Achievement in the Arts, Third Street Music School Settlement 2009, Living Legend Award, Library of Congress 2010, Concertgebouw Prize 2011, Venetian Heritage Award 2013, inducted to Hall of Fame by Gramophone 2013. *Recordings include:* Schubert's Winterreise 1997, Das Lied von der Erde 1997, Belshazzar's Feast 1998, Operetta Album with London Philharmonic 1999, No Tenors Allowed: Opera Duets (with Samuel Ramey) 1999, Verdi Arias with Orchestra of the Age of Enlightenment 2001, Wagner's Tannhäuser 2002, Cole Porter's Kiss Me Kate 2002, Forbidden and Banished 2006, I Hear America Singing 2006, Simon Boccanegra 2006, Don Giovanni 2006, Doktor Faust 2007, Athanaël 2008, Mozart Gala From Salzburg 2008, Wondrous Free—Song of America II 2009, Mahler: Des Knaben Wunderhorn 2011, Brahms: Ein Deutsches Requiem 2011, Schubert: Winterreise 2011, Puccini: Tosca 2011, Verdi: La Traviata 2011. *Address:* c/o Centre Stage Artist Management, Stralauer Allee 1, Raum 1.11, 10245 Berlin, Germany (office); 1841 Broadway, Suite 1204, New York, NY 10023, USA (office). *Telephone:* (30) 520071762 (office); (212) 767-0074 (office). *Fax:* (20) 87425682 (office). *E-mail:* jonathan.letts@umusic.com (office); judith.neuhoff@umusic.com (office); info@thomashampson.com (office). *Website:* www.thomashampson.com (office); www.hampsong.com.

HAMPTON, Christopher James, CBE, MA, FRSL; British playwright; b. 26 Jan. 1946, Fayal, The Azores, Portugal; s. of Bernard Patrick and Dorothy Patience (née Herrington) Hampton; m. Laura Margaret de Holesch 1971; two d.; ed Lancing Coll., New Coll., Oxford; wrote first play When Did You Last See My Mother? 1964; Resident Dramatist, Royal Court Theatre 1968–70; freelance writer 1970–; Officier, Ordre des Arts et des Lettres 1998; Evening Standard Award for Best Comedy 1970, 1983, for Best Play 1986, Plays and Players London Critics' Award for Best Play 1970, 1973, 1985; Los Angeles Drama Critics' Circle Award 1974, Laurence Olivier Award for Best Play 1986, New York Drama Critics' Circle Award for Best Foreign Play 1987, Prix Italia 1988, Writers' Guild of America Screenplay Award 1989, Academy Award for Best Adapted Screenplay 1989, BAFTA Award for Best Screenplay 1990, Special Jury Award, Cannes Film Festival 1995, Tony Awards for Best Original Score (lyrics) and Best Book of a Musical 1995, Scott Moncrieff Prize 1997. *Plays:* When Did You Last See My Mother? 1964, Total Eclipse 1969, The Philanthropist 1970, Savages 1973, Treats 1976, Able's Will (TV) 1978, Tales from Hollywood 1983, Les Liaisons Dangereuses 1985, The Ginger Tree (adaptation) 1989, The Philanthropist/Total Eclipse/Treats 1991, White Chameleon 1991, Sunset Boulevard 1993, Alice's Adventures Underground (adaptation) 1995, Carrington 1995, The Secret Agent/Nostromo (adaptation) 1996, The Talking Cure 2002. *Translations include:* Marya (Babel) 1967, Uncle Vanya, Hedda Gabler 1970, A Doll's House 1971 (film 1974), Don Juan 1972, Tales from the Vienna Woods 1977 (film 1979), Don Juan Comes Back from the War 1978, The Wild Duck 1980, Ghosts 1983, Tartuffe 1984, Faith, Hope and Charity 1989, Art 1996, An Enemy of the People 1997, The Unexpected Man 1998, Conversations After a Burial 2000, Life × Three 2001, Three Sisters 2005, Embers 2006. *Directed:* (films) Carrington 1995, The Secret Agent 1996, Imagining Argentina 2003. *Opera libretto:* Waiting for the Barbarians (music by Philip Glass) 2005. *Publications:* When Did You Last See My Mother? 1967, Total Eclipse 1969 (film 1995), The Philanthropist 1970, Savages 1973, Treats 1976, Able's Will (TV) 1978, The History Man (TV adaptation of novel by Malcolm Bradbury) 1981, The Portage to San Cristobal of A.H. (play adaptation of novel by George Steiner) 1983, Tales from Hollywood 1983, The Honorary Consul (film adaptation of a novel by Graham Greene) 1983, Les Liaisons Dangereuses (adaptation of a novel by Laclos) 1985, Hotel du Lac (TV adaptation of a novel by Anita Brookner q.v.) 1986, The Good Father (film adaptation of a novel by Peter Prince) 1986, Wolf at the Door (film) 1986, Dangerous Liaisons (film) 1988, The Ginger Tree (adaptation of novel by Oswald Wynd, TV) 1989, White Chameleon 1991, Sunset Boulevard (book and lyrics with Don Black) 1993, Alice's Adventures Underground (with Martha Clarke) 1994, Carrington (film) 1995, Mary Reilly (film) 1996, The Secret Agent (film) 1996, Nostromo (screenplay) 1997, The Quiet American (film) 2002, Collected Screenplays 2002, The Talking Cure 2002. Hampton on Hampton 2005. *Leisure interests:* travel, cinema. *Address:* Casarotto Ramsay and Associates Ltd., Waverley House, 7–12 Noel Street, London, W1F 8GQ, England (office). *Telephone:* (20) 7287-4450 (office). *Fax:* (20) 7287-9128 (office). *E-mail:* info@casarotto.co.uk (office). *Website:* www.casarotto.co.uk (office).

HAMPTON, Sir Philip Roy, Kt, MA, MBA; British business executive; *Chairman, Royal Bank of Scotland Group plc;* ed Lincoln Coll. Oxford, Institut

Européen d'Admin des Affaires (INSEAD), Fontainebleau, France; qualified as chartered accountant 1978; began career as Auditor, Coopers & Lybrand, London and W Africa 1975–81; various positions in Mergers and Acquisitions, Business Restructurings and Capital Markets, Lazard Brothers 1981–86; seconded to Lazard Freres, New York and Paris 1986–90; Group Finance Dir British Steel plc 1990–95, British Gas plc 1995–97, BG Group plc 1997–2000, British Telecommunications (BT) plc 2000–02, Lloyds TSB plc 2002–04; Chair. J Sainsbury plc 2004–09; Deputy Chair. Royal Bank of Scotland Group plc Jan.–Feb. 2009, Chair. Feb. 2009–; Dir (non-exec.) RMC Group plc 2002–05, Belgacom SA (Belgian telecom group) 2004–, Anglo American plc 2009–; led Treasury review on govt red tape 2004–05; fmr Chair. UK Financial Investments Ltd (co. est. to manage UK Govt's shareholding in banks subscribing to its recapitalization fund); Assoc., Inst. of Chartered Accountants. *Address:* Royal Bank of Scotland Group plc, 42 St Andrew Square, Edinburgh, EH2 2YE, Scotland (office). *Telephone:* (131) 523-2033 (office). *Fax:* (131) 556-7468 (office). *E-mail:* info@rbs.com (office). *Website:* www .rbs.com (office).

HAMRAWI, Habib Chawki; Algerian broadcasting executive, international organization executive and diplomatist; *Ambassador to Romania;* b. 1 Aug. 1962; m.; four c.; ed Univ. of Algiers; Minister of Communication and Culture 1992, 1997–99, also Govt Spokesman 1997–99; journalist with Algerian Television (ENTV) 1997, Dir-Gen. 1999–2008; Pres. High Coordination Cttee of Arab Satellite Channel 2000–; Chair. Conférence Permanente de l'Audiovisuel Méditerranéen (CoPeAM) 2002–06; Pres. Exec. Council, Arab States Broadcasting Union (ASBU) 2004–08; Pres. Festival International du Film Arabe, Oran 2007–; Amb. to Romania 2009–; mem. Bd European Broadcasting Union. *Address:* Embassy of Algeria, 010663 Bucharest, Bd. Lascăr Catargiu 29, Sector 1, Romania (office). *Telephone:* (21) 2124185 (office). *Fax:* (21) 2115695 (office). *E-mail:* ambalgerie@ roumanie.eunet.ro (office).

HAMUD, Maj.-Gen. Mohamed Sheikh Hassan; Somali army officer and politician; *Minister of Defence;* fmr Dir, Somali Nat. Intelligence and Security Service; Minister of Defence 2014–. *Address:* Ministry of Defence, Mogadishu, Somalia (office). *Website:* www.mod.somaligov.net (office).

HAMUD, Muhammad Ali; Somali politician; Minister for Foreign Affairs and Int. Co-operation 2007–08, of Finance and Planning 2008–10. *Address:* c/o Ministry of Finance and Planning, Mogadishu, Somalia (office).

HAMUTENYA, Hidipo; Namibian politician; b. 1939; Minister of Trade and Industry 1990–2002; Minister of Foreign Affairs 2002–04. *Address:* c/o Ministry of Foreign Affairs, Government Buildings, Robert Mugabe Avenue, PMB 13347, Windhoek, Namibia (office).

HAMZA, Ahmed Amin, MSc, PhD; Egyptian physicist, academic and university administrator; *President, British University, Cairo;* b. 8 March 1941, Giza; s. of the late Amin Hamza and Hanim Abdel Meguid; m. Sahar Khalil 1968; three d.; ed Saaidiya Secondary School, Giza and Ain Shams Univ. Cairo; Head of Printing Dept, Cairo Dyeing & Finishing Co. 1962–72; Lecturer in Physics, Mansoura Univ. 1972–76, Assoc. Prof. 1994–99, Prof. of Experimental Physics 1999, Head of Dept of Physics 1984–86, Vice-Dean, Faculty of Science 1986–92, Vice-Pres. Univ. for Community and Environmental Devt 1992–94, now Prof. Emer.; Pres. Univ. of Mansoura 1994–2001; Vice-Pres. British Univ. 2005–08, Pres. 2008–; Scientific Consultant, Thebes Acad.; Assoc. Prof., Sana'a Univ., Yemen 1989–91; Assoc. Prof., UAE Univ. 1991–94; Postdoctoral Research Fellow, Univ. of Leeds 1976–77; Fellow, Royal Microscopical Soc. (Oxford) 1977–, Inst. of Physics (London) 1982–, African Acad. of Sciences 1995–; mem. Bd of Dirs Acad. of Scientific Research and Tech., Head Cttee of Pure and Applied Physics 2001–; mem. Nat. Cttee UNESCO, Advisory Cttee for Minister of Higher Educ. and Scientific Research; mem. Bd of Devt of Higher Educ. Supreme Council of Egyptian Univs; mem. Int. Soc. for Optical Eng 1989, New York Acad. of Sciences 1995, Egyptian Acad. of Sciences 1995, AAAS 1995–, Basic Science Council; Dr hc (Tech. Univ. of Liberec, Czech Repub.) 2000; Egyptian Nat. Award in Physics 1987, Sr Academic Prize and Certificate Distinction of the Univ. of Mansoura in Basic Sciences 1992, First-Class Medal for Distinction 1995, State Prize of Merit in Basic Sciences 1997, Certificate of Merit, Faculty of Science Ain Shams Univ., Mubarak Prize in Advanced Tech. Science 2005. *Publications:* Interferometry of Fibrous Materials (co-author) 1990; numerous publs in fields of interferometry, fibre optics, colour measurement and polymer physics. *Leisure interest:* playing football. *Address:* British University, Suez Desert Road, El Sherouk City, Cairo (office); Mansoura University, Faculty of Science, 60 El-Gomhoria Street, Mansoura (office); 6 Korash Street, 6th District, Nasr City, Cairo, Egypt (home). *Telephone:* (2) 26875892 (office); (50) 2259427 (office); (2) 22462549 (home). *Fax:* (2) 26875889 (office); (50) 247900. *E-mail:* ahamza@bue.edu.eg (home); scimphydept@mum.mans.eun.eg (office); hamzaaa@ idsc.net.eg (home). *Website:* www.bue.edu.eg (office); www.mans.edu.eg (office).

HAMZA, Bedri, MBA; Kosovo politician; *Minister of Finance;* b. 8 Nov. 1963, Klina e Epërme, Skënderaj/Srbica Municipality; m. Remzie Hamza; one s. two d.; ed Prishtina Univ., Tirana Univ., Albania; Head of Accounting and Finance, Lead Metallurgy Dept, KXMK Trepça Mining Complex 1987–90; engaged in pvt. business 1990–98; Dir of Public Services, Mitrovica Municipal Ass. 2000–03; Deputy Minister of Economy and Finance 2009–11, Minister of Finance 2011–; mem. Democratic Party of Kosovo (DPK); fmr Deputy Pres. DPK Mitrovica br. *Address:* Ministry of Finance, 10000 Prishtina, Sheshi Nënë Terezë, Kosovo (office). *Telephone:* (38) 20034101 (office). *E-mail:* abeqiri@mfe-ks.org (office). *Website:* www.mef-rks.org (office).

HAMZAH, Tengku Tan Sri Datuk Razaleigh (see Razaleigh).

HAMZÍK, Pavol, JUDr; Slovak academic, politician and diplomatist; *Ambassador to Ukraine;* b. 20 Aug. 1954, Trenčín; s. of Pavol Hamžík and Júlia Hamžíková; m. Dagmar Hamžíková (née Kiššová) 1976; two d.; ed Komensky Univ., Bratislava, Diplomatic Acad., Moscow; lawyer 1978–84; joined Czechoslovak Foreign Ministry 1984, Consul, Embassy in Copenhagen 1985–89; studied at Diplomatic Acad., Moscow 1989–91; Vice-Chair. del. to int. disarmament negotiations, Vienna 1991; mem. del. to CSCE 1991–92, Pres. CSCE Steering Group on crisis in Yugoslavia 1992, Head of Slovak del. to CSCE 1993, Head of Slovak Perm. Mission to CSCE 1993–94; Amb. to Germany 1994–96; Foreign Minister 1996–97; f. Party of Civic Understanding (SOP) 1998, Chair. 1999–2003; mem. Parl. 1998–2002, mem.

Defence and Security Cttee 2001–02; Vice-Prime Minister 1998–2001; mem. Convention for the Slovak Repub. on the Future of the EU 2001–02; Rep. of the Prime Minister during discussion of Lisbon Treaty 2007–08; Amb. to Ukraine 2009–; fmr Lecturer and mem. Scientific Bd, Faculty of Political Sciences and Int. Relations, Matej Bell Univ.; Golden Biatec, Informal Econ. Forum 2000. *Leisure interests:* history, skiing, literature, tennis. *Address:* Embassy of Slovakia, 01901 Kyiv, vul. Yaroslaviv Val 34, Ukraine (office); Žilinská 1, 81105 Bratislava, Slovak Republic (home). *Telephone:* (44) 272-03-10 (office); (2) 9079-09011 (home). *Fax:* (44) 272-32-71 (office). *E-mail:* emb.kiev@mzv.sk (office). *Website:* www.slovakia .kiev.ua (office).

HAN, Chang-woo; South Korean business executive; *Chairman and CEO, Maruhan Corporation;* b. 15 Feb. 1931, Samcheonpo City, Gyeongsangnam-do; ed Hosei Univ., Japan; moved to Japan 1947; Pres. Maruhan Corpn 1972–99, Chair. and CEO 1999–; Admin. Dir Han Tetsu Foundation; Dir Kyoto UNESCO Asscn; Admin Officer, Kyoto Chapter, UN Asscn of Japan; mem. R.I.D. 2650 Rotary Club of Kyoto Heian, Advisory Council on Democratic and Peaceful Unification; Chair. World Fed. of Korean Asscn of Commerce; Hon. Dir Kyungnam Univ., S Korea; Hon. Citizen of Mineyama-town, Kyoto where Maruhan was founded 1995, of Los Angeles, Calif. for contrib. to amity of Japan, USA and S Korea 1995; Cheongryong Medal (Order of Sports Merit, S Korea) 1987, Mugunghwa Medal (Order of Civil Merit, S Korea) 1995, Order of the Sacred Treasure, Gold Rays with Neck Ribbon (Japan) 1999, Medal for the Most Distinguished Service (Marshall Islands) 2004, Royal Order of Cambodia, Grand Cross with First Style Ribbons 2008; Hon. DEcon (Kyungnam Univ., S Korea) 1996, Hon. DBA (Pusan Nat. Univ., S Korea) 2006; Medal with Dark Blue Ribbon, Prime Minister of Japan 1972, Presidential Citation (18th Commerce and Industry Day, S Korea) 1991, 6th Korean Overseas Compatriots' Prize, KBS (S Korea) 1998, Goodwill Amb. of Arkansas (USA) 2003. *Address:* Maruhan Corporation, 231 Seiryu-cho, Demachi, Imadegawa, Kamigyo-ku, Agaru, Kyoto 602-0822, Japan (office). *Telephone:* (75) 252-0011 (office). *Fax:* (75) 252-0018 (office). *E-mail:* info@maruhan.co.jp (office). *Website:* www.maruhan .co.jp (office).

HAN, Changfu; Chinese politician; *Minister of Agriculture;* b. 1954, Heilongjiang Prov.; ed Renmin Univ. of China; joined CCP 1974, mem. Communist Youth League of China 1986–2001, mem. Cen. Cttee Standing Cttee 1990–2001; Deputy Dir, State Council Research Office 2003–06; Deputy Sec., CCP Jilin Prov. Cttee 2006–09; Acting Gov. Jilin Prov. 2006–07, Gov. 2007–09; Exec. Vice-Minister of Agric. 2001–03, Minister of Agric. 2009–; mem. 16th CCP Cen. Cttee Cen. Comm. for Discipline Inspection 2002–07; mem. 17th CCP Cen. Cttee 2007–12, 18th CCP Cen. Cttee 2012–. *Address:* Ministry of Agriculture, 11 Nongzhanguan Nanli, Chao Yang Qu, Beijing 100125, People's Republic of China (office). *Telephone:* (10) 59193366 (office). *Fax:* (10) 59192468 (office). *E-mail:* webmaster@agri.gov.cn (office). *Website:* www.agri.gov.cn (office).

HAN, Duk-soo, MA, PhD; South Korean politician and diplomatist; *Chairman, Korea International Trade Association;* b. 18 June 1949, Jeonju, N Jeolla Prov.; ed Seoul Nat. Univ., Harvard Univ., USA; Dir Policy Coordinate Div., Econ. Planning Bd 1980–82; Dir Bureau of Int. Trade Promotion, Ministry of Trade and Industry 1982–85, Dir Bureau of Industry Policy 1985–87, Dir Bureau of Machinery Industry 1987–89, Dir Gen. Small and Medium Enterprise Bureau 1989–90, Dir Gen. Industrial Policy Bureau 1990–92, Dir Gen. Electronics and Information Industry Bureau 1992–93; Presidential Sec. for Econ. Affairs 1993; Asst Minister for Planning and Man., Ministry of Trade and Industry 1994; Asst Minister, Int. Trade Affairs Bureau, Ministry of Trade, Industry and Energy (MOTIE) 1995–96, Vice Minister MOTIE 1997–98; Commr Korean Industrial Property Office 1996; Minister for Trade Affairs, Ministry of Foreign Affairs and Trade 1998–2000; Amb. to OECD 2001; Sr Presidential Sec. for Policy and Planning 2001, for Econ. Affairs Jan.–July 2002; Minister, Office for Govt Policy Co-ordination 2004–05; Deputy Prime Minister and Minister of Finance and the Economy 2005–06 (resgnd); Prime Minister 2007–08; Amb. to USA 2009–12; Pres. Korea Inst. for Industrial Econs and Trade 2003; Chair. Korea Int. Trade Asscn 2012–. *Address:* Korea International Trade Association, 511 Yeongdongdae-ro, Gangnam-gu, Seoul, South Korea (office). *Telephone:* (2) 1566-5114 (office). *E-mail:* kitainfo@kita.net (office). *Website:* www.kita.org (office).

HAN, Joon-ho, BA, PhD; South Korean energy industry executive; ed Seoul Nat. Univ., Kyunghee Univ.; Asst Minister, Ministry of Trade, Industry and Energy 1997–98; Admin. Korean Small and Medium Business Admin 2000–04; Chair., Pres. and CEO Korea Electric Power Corpn (KEPCO) 2004–06; fmr Chair. Korean Productivity Centre (KPC); Chief of Presidential Comm. on Small & Medium Enterprise 2003; mem. Pacific Basin Econ. Council. *Address:* c/o Korea Electric Power Corpn, 411 Yeongdong-daero, Gangnam-gu, Seoul 135-791, Republic of Korea.

HAN, Kwang-bok; North Korean politician; *Vice-Premier and Minister of the Electronics Industry;* b. 18 March 1946; ed Kim Chaek Univ. of Tech.; worked as an instructor and Chief Instructor at Comm. for the Metal Industry and Construction Equipment; Deputy Minister for the Electronics Industry –2009, Minister for the Electronics Industry 2009–; Vice-Premier 2010–; mem. Korean Workers' Party Cen. Cttee. *Address:* Ministry of the Electronics Industry, Pyongyang, Democratic People's Republic of Korea (office).

HAN, Mingzhi, MA; Chinese economist and business executive; *Chairman of the Board of Supervisors, China Merchants Group Limited;* ed Johns Hopkins Univ., USA; Exec. Dir, China Soc. for Finance and Banking; China Exec. Dir, IMF 1996–98; Deputy Dir, Int. Dept, People's Bank of China 1999–2003; Dir, Int. Dept, China Banking Regulatory Comm. 2003–10; Chair. Bd of Supervisors, China Merchants Group Ltd 2010–. *Address:* China Merchants Group Ltd, 40th Floor, China Merchants Building, 168–200 Conaught Road, Central, Hong Kong Special Administrative Region (office); China Merchants Bank Co. Ltd, 7088 Shen Nan Road, Futian District, Shenzhen 518040, Guangdong, People's Republic of China (office). *Telephone:* 25428288 (Hong Kong) (office); (755) 83198888 (Shenzhen) (office). *Fax:* 25448851 (Hong Kong) (office); (755) 83195109 (Shenzhen) (office). *E-mail:* cmhk@cmhk.com (office). *Website:* www.cmhk.com (office); www.cmbchina .com (office).

HAN, Myong-sook, BA, MA; South Korean politician; b. 24 March 1944, Pyeongyang; m. Park Sung-jun; ed Ewha Womans Univ.; mem. staff, Korea Christian Acad. 1974–79; jailed as a prisoner of conscience, Christian Acad. Case 1979–81; Lecturer, Dept of Women's Studies, Ewha Womans Univ. 1986–97, Visiting Researcher, Asian Center for Women's Studies 1996–2003; Lecturer, Dept of Women's Studies, Sungsim Womans Univ. 1988–94; Chair. of Special Cttee on Revision of Family Law, Korea Women's Asscns United Jan.–Dec. 1989, Co-rep. 1993–96; Pres. Korean Womenlink 1990–94; Chief Dir Korea Inst. for Environmental and Social Policies 1992; fmr Head, Presidential Comm. on Women's Affairs; mem. Nat. Ass. 2000–01, 2004–, mem. Unification, Foreign Affairs and Trade Cttee; Minister of Gender Equality 2001–03, of the Environment 2003–04; Prime Minister (first woman) 2006–07 (resgnd); Pres. Korean Parl. League on Children, Population and Environment 2004–06, Korea-Singapore Parliamentarians' Friendship Asscn June 2004; Pres. Exec. Cttee Asia-Pacific Parliamentarians' Conf. on Environment and Devt 2004–06; Vice-Pres. Korea–Japan Parl. League 2006–; mem. Exec. Cttee Seoul and Pyungyang Symposium Peace of Asian and Women's Role 1992–96; Co-rep., Viewers Alliance for Fair Broadcasting Policy Advisor 1993–94, Cttee for Interchange and Cooperation, Ministry of Unification 1993–94, Citizens' Asscn for Broadcasting Reform 1994–95; mem. Environmental Reservation Cttee, Ministry of Environment 1993–95, Anti-Corruption Cttee, Bd of Audit and Inspection 1993–95; fmr mem. Uri Party, mem. Cen. Standing Cttee April–Nov. 2005, Nat. Ass. Environment and Labour Cttee 2006–; currently mem. Democratic Party (fmrly United New Democratic Party), unsuccessful campaign to become party cand. for Pres. of South Korea 2007; Civil Merit Medal 1998; Order of Service Merit Medal (Blue Stripes) 2005; ranked 68th by Forbes magazine amongst 100 Most Powerful Women 2006. *Address:* c/o Democratic Party, 133-6, Youngdeungpo-dong, Youngdeungpo-gu, Seoul 150-036, Republic of Korea. *Website:* www.minjoo.kr.

HAN, Sang-beom, PhD; South Korean business executive; *Representative Director, President and CEO, LG Display Company Ltd;* b. 18 June 1955; ed Stevens Inst. of Tech.; fmr Head of IT Business Unit, LG.Philips LCD Co. Ltd, Vice-Pres. Panel 5 Factory and Manufacturing Tech. Centre 2001–06, Exec. Vice-Pres. LG.Philips LCD Co. Ltd 2006–09, Head of TV Business Div. 2009–12, Rep. Dir, Pres. and CEO LG Display Co. Ltd 2012–; Vice-Pres. Hynix Semiconductor Inc. *Address:* LG Display Co. Ltd, 65-228 Hangang-ro 3-ga, Seoul 140-716, South Korea (office). *Telephone:* (2) 3777-1010 (office). *E-mail:* info@lgdisplay.com (office). *Website:* www.lgdisplay.com (office).

HAN, Seung-soo, PhD; South Korean politician, economist, diplomatist and international organization official; b. 28 Dec. 1936, Chunchon, Kangwon Prov.; m. Hong Soja; two c.; ed Yonsei Univ., Seoul Nat. Univ. and Univ. of York, UK; taught econs at Univ. of York, UK 1965–68, Univ. of Cambridge 1968–70; Prof. of Econs, Seoul Nat. Univ. 1970–88; Sr Fulbright Scholar, Dept of Econs, Harvard Univ. 1985–86; Visiting Prof., Univ. of Tokyo 1986–87; fmr Distinguished Visiting Prof., Yonsei Univ.; served as advisor to Bank of Korea, Korea Export–Import Bank, Korea Industrial Bank, Korea Chamber of Commerce and Industry, Fed. of Korea Industries and Korea Int. Trade Asscn; consultant to World Bank and UN Econ. Comm. for Asia and the Pacific (ESCAP), seconded by World Bank as Financial Adviser to Govt of Jordan 1974–76; Pres. Korea Int. Econ. Asscn 1983–84; first Chair. Korea Trade Commr 1987–88; elected mem. of Nat. Ass., Repub. of Korea 1988–2004; Minister of Trade and Industry 1988–90; Amb. to USA 1993–94; Chair. Council of the Repub. of Korea Group of the Inter-Parl. Union (IPU); Chief of Staff to Pres. of Repub. of Korea 1994–95; Deputy Prime Minister and Minister of Finance and Economy 1996–97; Minister of Foreign Affairs and Trade 2001–02; Pres. 56th Session of UN Gen. Ass. 2001–02; Pres. Korean Water Forum 2004; UN Special Envoy for Climate Change 2007–08; Prime Minister of Repub. of Korea 2008–09; Chair. Global Green Growth Institute 2010–12; apptd Special Envoy of UN Sec.-Gen. on Climate Change; Founding Chair. UN High-Level Expert Panel on Water and Disaster/UNSGAB, mem. Sec.-Gen.'s High-level Panel on Global Sustainability; f. Korean Acad. of Industrial Tech. (KAITEC) 1989; Pres. Korea–Britain Soc., Korea–UK Forum for the Future, Alumni Asscn of the Grad. School of Public Admin of Seoul Nat. Univ.; mem. Bd of Dirs Standard Chartered PLC 2010–; mem. Royal Econ. Soc., Korean Econ. Asscn, Int. Inst. of Public Finance, Seoul Forum for Int. Affairs, Korean Council on Foreign Relations, Korean Soc. for Future Studies, Korean Asscn of Public Admin, Bretton Woods Club; Hon. Prof., Univ. of York, UK, Hon. KBE 2004; Order of Public Service Merit (First Class, Blue Stripes), Order of Industrial Merit (Bronze Tower), Order of Nat. Security Merit (Cheonsu Medal); Sixth European Communities Prize 1971, Columbia Law School/ Parker School Award for Distinguished Int. Service 1997. *Publications include:* Taxes in Britain and the EEC: The Problem of Harmonization (jtly) 1968, Britain and the Common Market (jtly) 1971, The Growth and Function of the European Budget 1971, The Health of Nations 1985; numerous articles in learned journals and press commentaries in both Korean and English. *Address:* Global Sustainability Panel Secretariat, Room A-300, 866 United Nations Plaza, United Nations Headquarters, New York, NY 10017, USA (office). *Website:* www.un.org/gsp.

HAN, Shao Gong; Chinese writer; b. 1 Jan. 1953, Chang Sha; s. of Han Ke Xian and Zhang Jing Xing; m. Liang Yu Li 1980; one d.; ed Hunan Teacher's Univ.; Council mem. Chinese Writers' Asscn 1984; Vice-Chair. Hunan Youth Union 1985; Chief Ed. of Hainan Review 1988; Pres. Hainan Literature Correspondence Coll. 1988; Chair. Hainan Writers Asscn 1995; mem. Standing Cttee CPPCC Hainan Prov. 1988; Chair. Hainan Artists' Asscn 2000; mem. Council Chinese Artists' Union 2001; Prize for Best Chinese Stories 1980, 1981, Newman Prize for Chinese Literature 2011. *Film:* The Deaf and Mute 1983. *Publications:* Biography of Ren Bi Shi 1979; (collections of short stories): Yue Nan 1981, Flying Across the Blue Sky 1983, New Stories 1986, Fondness for Shoes 1994, Red Apple is an Exception 1994; To Face the Mystical and Wide World (selection of articles) 1985, The Other Shore (selection of prose pieces) 1988, The Murder 1990, Pa Pa Pa and Seduction and Femme Femme Femme 1990–91, Homecoming 1992, The Play and Holy War 1993, Raving of a Pedestrian in the Night 1994, The Thought of the Sea 1994, Dictionary of Ma-Bridge (novel) 1995, Ma Qiao ci Dian 1997, Gui Qu Lai 2008; trans: The Unbearable Lightness of Being (Kundera) 1987, The Book of Disquiet (F. Pessoa) 1999, Collected Works (10 vols) 2001. *Leisure interest:* Chinese calligraphy. *Address:* Room 2-602, Hainan Teachers' University, Haikou 571100, Hainan (home); 1st Building, Hainan Plaza, 69 Guoxing Road, Haikou, People's Republic of China (office). *Telephone:* (898) 5882748 (home); (898) 5336231 (office). *Fax:* (898) 53328034 (office). *E-mail:* hanshaog@public.hk.hi.cn (home).

HAN, Sung-joo, PhD; South Korean academic and fmr politician; *President, Seoul Forum for International Affairs;* b. 1940; ed Seoul Nat. Univ. and Univ. of California, Berkeley; taught at CUNY, New York 1970–78, Columbia Univ., New York 1986–87, Stanford Univ., Calif. 1992; Distinguished Fellow, Rockefeller Brothers Fund 1986–87; fmr Vice-Chair. Int. Political Science Asscn; int. columnist, Newsweek 1984–93; Adviser to Govt on foreign affairs, nat. defence and unification since late 1970s; Minister of Foreign Affairs 1993–95; Prof. of Political Science and Pres. Ilmin Int. Relations Inst., Korea Univ. 1995–, fmr Acting Pres. Korea Univ.; UN Sec.-Gen.'s Special Rep. for Cyprus 1996–97; mem. UN Inquiry Comm. on the 1994 Genocide in Rwanda 1999; Amb. to USA 2003–05; Freeman Foundation Visiting Prof. in Asian Affairs, Claremont McKenna Coll., USA 2006; Pres. Seoul Forum for Int. Affairs; Deputy Chair. for Asia Pacific, Trilateral Comm.; Chair. East Asia Vision Group 2000–01; Co-Chair. Council for Security Co-operation in the Asia-Pacific; mem. Int. Panel on Democracy and Devt, Int. Bd of Govs The Peres Center for Peace; fmr mem. Bd Asia Pacific Foundation of Canada, Hon. Advisers of New Zealand's Asia 2000. *Publications include:* The Failure of Democracy in South Korea 1974, The US-South Korean Alliance 1983, The Division and Unification of Korea 1992, Choice for Korea in a World in Transition 1992, Korean Diplomacy in an Era of Globalization 1995, Korea in a Changing World 1995, Changing Values in Asia: Their Impact on Governance and Development (ed.). *Address:* Ilmin International Research Institute, Korea University, 5th Floor, Inchon Memorial Building, 5-1 Anam-dong, Seongbuk-Gu, Seoul 136-701, Republic of Korea (office). *Telephone:* (2) 923-2416/7 (office). *Fax:* (2) 927-5265 (office). *E-mail:* irikor@unitel.co.kr (office). *Website:* www.korea.ac.kr/~ilmin (office).

HAN, Wan-sang; South Korean fmr government official, professor of sociology and university administrator; *President, Korean National Red Cross;* b. 18 March 1936; s. of Han Young-Jik; m. 1966; three d.; ed in USA; Asst Prof., Coll. of Eng, Univ. of Tenn. 1967–69; Asst Prof, E. Carolina Univ 1969–70; Assoc. Prof. of Sociology, Seoul Nat. Univ. 1970–76, Prof., 1984–93; adviser to Kim Young Sam; Deputy Prime Minister and Minister of Unification 1993; Pres. Korea Nat. Open Univ. 1994–98; Pres. Sangji Univ. 1999–2001; First Deputy Prime Minister and Minister of Educ. and Human Resource Devt 2001–02; Pres. Hansung Univ. 2002–05; Pres. Korea Nat. Red Cross (KNRC) 2004–; Hon. Dr of Humanities (Emory Univ., Atlanta, Ga, USA) 1999. *Leisure interest:* tennis. *Address:* Office of the President, Korean National Red Cross, 32-3ka, Namsan-dong, Choong-Ku, 100-043 Seoul, Republic of Korea (office). *Telephone:* (2) 3705-3661–4 (office). *E-mail:* international@redcross.or.kr (office). *Website:* www.redcross.or.kr (office).

HAN, Zhaoshan; Chinese business executive; *Chairman and General Manager, Panpan Group Limited;* b. 1949, Yingkou, Liaoning Prov.; Vice-Dir Shuiyuan Township Agric. Machinery Factory, Yingkou 1970–83; founded Yingkou Great Wall Metal Product Factory 1983–92; Chair. and Gen. Man. Panpan Group Ltd 1992–, Panpan Security Industries Co. Ltd; took part as torchbearer during Olympic flame relay, Shenyang, Liaoning Prov. July 2008. *Leisure interest:* basketball. *Address:* Panpan Group Ltd, Yingkou, Liaoning Province, People's Republic of China (office).

HAN, Zheng, MA; Chinese economist and politician; *Secretary, CPC Municipal Committee, Shanghai Municipality;* b. April 1954, Cixi Co., Zhejiang Prov.; ed East China Normal Univ.; joined CCP 1979; served successively as Sec. CYLC Shanghai Chemical Industry Bureau Ctte 1982–86, Deputy Party Sec. Shanghai Chemical Eng School 1986–87, Party Sec. and Deputy Dir Shanghai No. 6 Rubber Shoes Factory 1987–88, Party Sec. and Deputy Dir Dazhonghua Rubber Factory 1988–90, Sec. Communist Youth League of China Shanghai Cttee 1991–92, Gov. Shanghai Luwan Dist 1992–93, Deputy Sec.-Gen. Shanghai Municipality 1995–97; Dir Shanghai Devt Planning Comm. –1998; mem. Standing Cttee CCP Shanghai Cttee and Vice-Mayor of Shanghai 1997–2002, Vice-Sec. CCP Shanghai Cttee May 2002, Exec. Vice-Mayor Oct. 2002, mem. 16th CCP Cen. Cttee 2002–07, Deputy Sec. CCP Shanghai Cttee and Mayor of Shanghai 2003–12, Acting Sec. CCP Shanghai Cttee 2006–07, Sec. 2012–; mem. 17th CCP Cen. Cttee 2007–12, 18th CCP Cen. Cttee 2012–, 18th CCP Cen. Cttee Politburo 2012–. *Leisure interest:* dancing. *Address:* CPC Municipal Committee, Shanghai Municipality, 1418 West Nanjing Road, Shanghai 200040, People's Republic of China (office).

HAN, Zhubin; Chinese politician and lawyer; b. Feb. 1932, Harbin, Heilongjiang Prov.; ed Beijing Econs Corresp. Univ.; train captain, Railway Admin, Harbin City 1946–50; joined CCP 1950; Dir Railway Admin, Liuzhou City, Guangxi Zhuang Autonomous Region, Railway Admin, Shanghai 1983–90; fmr Vice-Sec., then Sec. Communist Youth League, Liuzhou Railway Bureau Cttee, Dir 1975–83; Vice-Sec. CCP Group and Sec. CCP Cttee for Discipline Inspection, Ministry of Railways 1990–92; Minister of Railways 1993–98; Deputy Head Leading Group for Beijing-Kowloon Railway Construction 1993–; Procurator-Gen., Supreme People's Procuratorate 1998–2003; Pres. Chinese Asscn of Prosecutors 1998–2003; mem. 14th Cen. Cttee CCP 1992–97, 15th Cen. Cttee CCP 1997–2002 (Deputy Sec. Cen. Comm. for Discipline Inspection 1997–2002); Deputy, 8th NPC 1993–98. *Address:* c/o Chinese Association of Prosecutors, Beijing, People's Republic of China.

HANANIA, Daoud Anastas, MBBS, FRCS, FRSM, FRCSE; Jordanian surgeon and fmr army officer; *Consultant Cardiovascular Surgeon, Hanania Medical Center;* b. 1934, Jerusalem; m. Nada Pio; two c.; ed St Mary's Hosp. Medical School, Univ. of London, UK; joined Royal Jordanian Army 1951, Head of Royal Medical Services of Jordanian Armed Forces 1976–88, retd from army with rank of Lt-Gen. 1989; House Surgeon and Surgical Registrar, Royal Northern Hosp., London 1959–61; Fellow in Thoracic and Cardiovascular Surgery, Baylor Univ. Coll. of Medicine, Texas in 1960s; Dir King Hussein Medical Centre (KHMC), Jordan 1973–76, Chief of Cardiovascular Surgery 1973–92 (performed first heart transplant in the Arab world 1985); Dir-Gen. Nat. Medical Inst., Amman 1987–89; Clinical Prof. of Surgery, Jordan Univ. of Science and Tech. 1989; mem. Senate 1989–97, 2007–13; f. Arab Centre for Heart and Special Surgery (now Arab Medical Centre), Dir 1991–99; f. pvt. clinic, Hanania Centre, Amman; mem. Bd of Trustees, King Hussein Foundation 1999, Al Quds Univ.; elected Pres. for Life, Jordan Cardiothoracic Soc. 2005; Fellow, American Coll. of Surgeons 1971, American Coll. of Cardiology 1977, Int. Coll. of Angiology 1979; Hon. Fellow, Royal Coll. of Surgeons in Ireland 1980, Royal Coll. of Physicians and Surgeons of Glasgow 1988; Hon. KBE 1984, Légion d'honneur 1984, Nile Medal First Class (Sudan) 1986, Commdr (First Class), Royal Swedish Order 1989, Medal of the Banner/Bright Star of Taiwan; Ben Qurrah Award for Excellence in Medicine, Arab-American Medical Asscn-Houston 1998. *Leisure interests:* tennis, motor racing. *Address:* Hanania Medical Center, 13 Khalil Maz'al Street, Amman, Jordan (office).

HANAWA, Yoshikazu, BA; Japanese business executive; b. 14 March 1934, Tokyo; ed Tokyo Univ.; joined Nissan Motor Co. 1957, Pres. Nissan N America 1989, various marketing and planning positions, Exec. Vice-Pres. 1991–96, Pres. 1996–2000, CEO and Chair. 2000–03, Advisor and Hon. Chair. 2003–; mem. Bd of Dirs Renault Group –2005, Hoya Corpn. *Address:* c/o Nissan Motor Co., 6-17-1 Ginza chome, Chuo-ku, Tokyo 104-8023, Japan.

HANCE, James Henry, Jr, BA, MBA; American accountant and business executive; *Operating Executive, The Carlyle Group LP;* b. 16 Sept. 1944, St Joseph, Mo.; ed Westminister Coll., Washington Univ.; Partner, Price Waterhouse, Charlotte, NC 1968–85; Chair. Consolidated Coin Caterers Corpn 1985–86; Exec. Vice-Pres. and Chief Accounting Officer NCNB Corpn 1987–88; Chief Financial Officer, Bank of America Corpn 1988–2004, Vice-Chair. 1993–2005 (retd); mem. Bd of Dirs Sprint Nextel Corpn 2005–13, Chair. 2007–13; Sr Advisor, The Carlyle Group LP 2005–, Operating Exec. 2012–; mem. Bd of Dirs, Summit Properties Inc. 1994–, Caraustar Industries Inc. 1995–2003, Lance Inc. 1995–2003, Fon Group, Enpro Industries Inc. 2002–, Rayonier Inc. 2004–, Cousins Properties Inc. 2005–, Duke Energy Corpn 2005–, Morgan Stanley 2009–12, Ford Motor Co. (Ind. Dir) 2010–, Duke Energy Carolinas, LLC, American City Business Journals Inc., ACE Guaranty RE, ACE Capital RE Corpn; mem. Bd of Visitors, Duke Univ. Fuqua School of Business, Johnson C. Smith Univ.; Chairman of Trustees at North Carolina Blumenthal Performing Arts Center. Mr. Hance is a Trustee of Washington University and a Member of Washington University's National Council for the John M. Olin School of Business. In addition, he is a Director of The United Negro College Fund and The Foundation for the University of North Carolina at Charlotte as well as a Member of the Society of International Business Fellows; fmr Co-Chair. Advantage Carolina. *Address:* The Carlyle Group LP, 520 Madison Avenue, New York, NY 10022, USA (office). *Telephone:* (212) 813-4900 (office). *Fax:* (212) 813-4901 (office). *E-mail:* info@carlyle.com (office). *Website:* www.carlyle.com (office).

HANCHARYK, Uladzimir; Belarusian politician and trade union official; mem. Supreme Council –1996; Co-Founder Consultative and Coordinating Council of Democratic Forces (alliance of opposition parties cr. to contest Presidential elections) 2000; cand. in Presidential Elections 2001; requested the opening of criminal case to investigate malpractice during election, rejected by the Supreme Court 2001; Chair. Fed. of Trade Unions of Belarus –2001; denied registration as candidate in Chamber of Reps election 2004. *Address:* c/o Federation of Trade Unions of Belarus, Prospekt Masherova 21, 220126 Minsk, Belarus (office).

HANCOCK, Herbert (Herbie) Jeffrey, BA; American jazz pianist and composer; b. 12 April 1940, Chicago, Ill.; s. of Wayman Edward Hancock and Winnie Griffin; m. Gudrun Meixner 1968, one d.; ed Grinnell Coll., Roosevelt Univ., Manhattan School of Music, New School for Social Research; Owner and Publr Hancock Music Co. 1962–; Founder Hancock and Joe Productions 1989–; Pres. Harlem Jazz Music Center, Inc.; Creative Chair for Jazz, Los Angeles Philharmonic Orchestra 2010–; has performed with Chicago Symphony Orchestra 1952, Coleman Hawkins, Chicago 1960, Donald Byrd 1960–63, Miles Davis Quintet 1963–68; recorded with Chick Corea; mem. Nat. Acad. of Recording Arts and Sciences, Jazz Musicians Asscn, Nat. Acad. of TV Arts and Sciences, Broadcast Music; apptd UNESCO Goodwill Ambassador 2011; Prof., UCLA Univ. 2013–; numerous awards including Citation of Achievement, Broadcast Music, Inc. 1963, Jay Award, Jazz Magazine 1964, several awards from Black Music Magazine 1967–71, 5 MTV Awards, Grammy Award for Best Rhythm and Blues Instrumental Performance 1983, 1984, for Best Jazz Instrumental Composition (co-composer) 1987, Best Jazz Instrumental Performance 1995. *Albums include:* Takin' Off 1963, Succotash 1964, Maiden Voyage 1965, Speak Like a Child 1968, Fat Albert Rotunda 1969, Mwandishi 1971, Crossings 1972, Sextant 1972, Headhunters 1973, Thrust 1974, The Best of Herbie Hancock 1974, Man-Child 1975, The Quintet 1977, V.S.O.P. 1977, Sunlight 1978, An Evening with Herbie Hancock and Chick Corea In Concert 1979, Feets Don't Fail Me Now 1979, Monster 1980, Greatest Hits 1980, Lite Me Up 1982, Future Shock 1983, Sound System 1984, Perfect Machine 1988, Jamming 1992, Cantaloupe Island 1994, Tribute to Miles 1994, Dis Is Da Drum 1995, The New Standard 1996, Gershwin's World 1998 (Grammy Award), Night Walker 2000, Future 2 Future 2001, Directions in Music (with others) 2002, River: The Joni Letters (Grammy Awards for Best Album and Best Contemporary Jazz Album 2008) 2007, The Imagine Project 2010; with Miles Davis Quartet: Miles in the Sky, Nefertiti, Sorcerer, ESP, Miles Davis In Concert (My Funny Valentine), In A Silent Way, Jack Johnson, Seven Steps to Heaven; contrib. to Colour and Light – Jazz Sketches On Sondheim 1995. *Films:* composed film music for Blow Up 1966, The Spook Who Sat by the Door 1973, Death Wish 1974, A Soldier's Story 1984, Jo Jo Dancer, Your Life is Calling 1986, Action Jackson 1988, Colors 1988, Harlem Nights 1989, Livin' Large 1991; wrote score and appeared in film Round Midnight 1986 (Acad. Award Best Original Score 1986). *Publications include:* A Tribute to Miles 1994, Dis is Da Drum 1994, The New Standard 1996, I H with Wayne Shorter 1997, Gershwin's World 1998. *Address:* c/o Melinda Murphy, Hancock Music Company, 1250 North Doheny Drive, Los Angeles, CA 90069, USA (office). *Telephone:* (310) 273-3321 (office). *E-mail:* hhmusicco@herbiehancock.com (office). *Website:* www.herbiehancock.com (office).

HANDLER, Chelsea Joy; American television presenter, stand-up comedian, actress, model and author; *Host, Chelsea Lately;* b. 25 Feb. 1975, Livingston, NJ; d. of Melvin Handler and Sylvia Handler; moved from NJ to Los Angeles to pursue acting career 1984, became stand-up comic 1986; has performed nationwide as a stand-up comedian, appeared as regular on the Oxygen Network series Girls Behaving Badly and on other shows, including Weekends at the D.L., The Bernie Mac Show, My Wife and Kids, and The Practice; regular commentator on E! and Scarborough Country as well as a corresp. on The Tonight Show; hosted The Chelsea Handler Show April 2006 (two seasons); guest on Red Eye with Greg Gutfeld and The View; hosts own late night talk show Chelsea Lately on E! Cable Television Network 2007– (only second woman in TV history to host late-night talk show); host of MTV Video Music Awards 2010; writes column in Cosmopolitan and

UK celebrity magazine NOW; production co., Borderline Amazing Productions, produces Chelsea Lately; Bravo A-List Award for A-List Funny 2009, ranked 98th on Forbes Celebrity 100, ranked 91st on the Maxim Hot 100 2009, ranked by Forbes magazine amongst The World's 100 Most Powerful Women (33rd) 2010. *Films include:* National Lampoon Presents Cattle Call 2006, Hop 2011, This Means War 2012. *Television includes:* Spy TV 2001, The Plotters 2001, The Practice 2002, My Wife and Kids 2002, Girls Behaving Badly 2002, The Bernie Mac Show 2004, Weekends at the D.L. 2005, Dirty Famous (unsold pilot) 2005, Totally High 2005, The Chelsea Handler Show 2006, Red Eye with Greg Gutfeld 2007, Chelsea Lately 2007–, Comedy Central Presents (stand-up), In The MotherHood (webseries) 2007–08, The Good Wife 2009, Pretty Wild (producer) 2010, After Lately 2011–13, Whitney 2011, 2013, Are You There, Chelsea? 2012, Web Therapy 2013. *Publications:* three books on New York Times Best Seller List: My Horizontal Life: A Collection of One-Night Stands (memoir), Are You There, Vodka? It's Me, Chelsea (collection of humorous essays), Chelsea Chelsea Bang Bang 2010. *E-mail:* chelsea@chelseahandler.com (office). *Website:* www.eonline .com/on/shows/chelsea (office); www.borderlineamazingcomedy.com (office); chelseahandler.com.

HANDLEY, Joseph (Joe); Canadian politician and consultant; *Special Advisor, Pacific & Western Bank of Canada;* b. 9 Aug. 1943, Meadowlake, Saskatchewan; m. Theresa Handley; two c.; Asst Prof., Univ. of British Columbia and Univ. of Manitoba –1985; moved to NWT to assume position of Deputy Minister of Educ. with Govt of NWT 1985; Deputy Minister for Govt of NWT –1999; MLA for Weledeh 1999–, Minister of Finance, Chair. Financial Man. Bd and Minister Responsible for Workers' Compensation Bd 2000, Minister of Transportation and Minister Responsible for NWT Power Corpn 2001, Premier of NWT (retd) 2003–07; Special Advisor, Pacific & Western Bank of Canada 2007–; fmr Official Trustee and Chief Supt Frontier School Div., Manitoba; Queen's Golden Jubilee Medal 2002, Saskatchewan Medal for outstanding achievement 2005, Aboriginal Achievement Award 2008. *Address:* Pacific & Western Bank of Canada, 410 22nd Street E, Suite 950, Saskatoon, Sask. S7K 5T6, Canada (office). *Telephone:* (416) 203-0882 (office). *Website:* www.pwbank.com (office).

HANDOVER, Richard, CBE; British retail executive; b. 1946; joined W H Smith Group 1964, numerous man. posts within the group including Man. Dir, Our Price Music Ltd 1989, Man. Dir W H Smith News 1995, mem. Bd, W H Smith PLC 1995–2004, CEO 1997–2003, Chair. 2003–04; Chair. Alexon Group plc (now Irisa Group Ltd) 2008–11; Chair. Adult Learning Inspectorate 2001–07; Dir (non-exec.) Nationwide Building Soc. 2000–07, Royal Mail Holdings PLC 2003–11; mem. Bd of Trustees, Community Foundation for Wiltshire and Swindon. *Address:* c/o Community Foundation for Wiltshire and Swindon, Sandcliffe House, Northgate Street, Devizes, Wilts., SN10 1JJ, England.

HANDS, Terence David (Terry), CBE, BA; British theatre director; *Director, Clwyd Theatr Cymru;* b. 9 Jan. 1941, Aldershot; s. of Joseph Ronald and Luise Bertha Hands (née Köhler); m. 1st Josephine Barstow 1964 (divorced 1967); m. 2nd Ludmila Mikael 1975 (divorced 1980); one d.; partner Julia Lintott; two s.; m. 3rd Emma Lucia 2002; ed Woking Grammar School, Birmingham Univ., Royal Acad. of Dramatic Art (RADA), London; Founder-Dir Everyman Theatre, Liverpool 1964–66; Artistic Dir Theatregoround, RSC 1966; Assoc. Dir RSC 1967–77, Jt Artistic Dir 1978–86, Artistic Dir and Chief Exec. 1986–91, Dir Emer. 1991; Dir Clwyd Theatr Cymru 1997–; Consultant Dir Comédie Française 1975–80; Hon. Fellow Shakespeare Inst. 1990, Welsh Coll. of Music and Drama 2002, Glyndwr Univ. 2002; Chevalier, Ordre des Arts et Lettres; Hon. DLit (Birmingham) 1988, (Liverpool); Hon. LLD (Middx) 1997; Meilleur Spectacle de l'Année for Richard III 1972, for Twelfth Night 1976; Plays and Players Award for Henry VI 1977, Society of West End Theatre Award 1978 and 1984, Pragnell Shakespeare Award 1991, Evening Standard Best Dir Award 1993. *Productions:* over 50 plays with RSC, five with Comédie Française, two with Burgtheater, Vienna, one opera at Paris Opera House, one at Covent Garden, London, one at Bremen, 40 at Clwyd Theatr Cymru; Women Beware Women, Teatro Stabile di Genova, Italy; Arden of Faversham, Schauspielhaus, Zürich; Hamlet, Paris 1994, Merry Wives of Windsor, Oslo 1995, Kongsemnerne 1996, The Seagull 1998; recording: Murder in the Cathedral 1976; trans. (with Barbara Wright): The Balcony (Genet) 1971, Pleasure and Repentance 1976, Henry V (ed. Sally Beauman) 1976, Cyrano de Bergerac (TV). *Translation:* Hamlet, into French. *Address:* Clwyd Theatr Cymru, Mold, Flintshire, CH7 1YA, N Wales (office). *Telephone:* (1352) 756331 (office). *Fax:* (1352) 701558 (office). *E-mail:* terryhands@clwyd-theatre-cymru.co.uk (office). *Website:* www.clwyd -theatr-cymru.co.uk (office).

HANEDA, Katsuo; Japanese airline industry executive; *Executive Vice-President, Japan Airlines Corporation;* m. Teiko Haneda; ed Faculty of Econs, Keio Univ.; joined Japan Airlines Co. Ltd 1965, apptd mem. Bd of Dirs 1995, Man. Dir and Sr Vice-Pres., Passenger Marketing 2001–02, Vice-Pres. 2002–03, Pres. 2003–04, Exec. Vice-Pres. Japan Airlines Corpn (holding co. cr. following merger of Japan Airlines and Japan Air Systems 2004) 2004–, Pres. Japan Airlines Int. Co. 2004–, Sr Vice-Pres. Japan Airlines Domestic Co. Ltd 2004–. *Address:* Japan Airlines Corpn, 4-11, Higashi-shinagawa 2-chome, Shinagawa-ku, Tokyo 140-8605, Japan (office). *Telephone:* (3) 5769-6097 (office). *Fax:* (3) 5460-5929 (office). *E-mail:* info@jal.com (office). *Website:* www.jal.com (office).

HANEGBI, Tzahi, BA, LLB; Israeli politician; b. 1957, Jerusalem; m.; three c.; ed Hebrew Univ. of Jerusalem; served in an Israeli Defence Forces paratroopers unit 1974–77; Pres. Hebrew Univ. Student Union 1979–80, Nat. Union of Israeli Students 1980–82; Adviser to Minister of Foreign Affairs 1984–86; Bureau Dir, Prime Minister's Office 1986–88; mem. Likud Party, Knesset (Parl.) 1988–, mem. Knesset Foreign Affairs and Defence Cttee, Cttee on Constitution, Law and Justice, Knesset House Cttee, Cttee on Labour and Social Welfare, Cttee on Educ. and Culture 1988–92; Head (in rotation) Econ. Affairs Cttee; mem. Cttee on Constitution, Law and Justice 1992–96; Minister of Health 1996–97, Minister of Justice 1997–2001, of the Environment 2001–03, of Transport 2002–03, of Public Security 2003–04 (resgnd); left Likud party to join Kadima party Dec. 2005. *Address:* c/o Ministry of Public Security, POB 18182, Jerusalem 91181, Israel (office).

HANEKE, Michael; Austrian (b. German) film director and screenwriter; b. 23 March 1942, Munich, Germany; s. of Fritz Haneke and Beatrix von Degenschild;

ed Univ. of Vienna; fmr film critic; ed. and dramaturg, Südwestfunk (German TV) 1967–70; directed several stage productions in German, including Strindberg, Goethe and Heinrich von Kleist in Berlin, Munich and Vienna; debut as TV dir in 1973; directed first opera, Mozart's Don Giovanni, Paris 2006; currently Prof. of Directing, Univ. of Music and Performing Arts, Vienna. *Films include:* writer and dir: Der siebente Kontinent (The Seventh Continent) 1989, Benny's Video 1992, 71 Fragmente einer Chronologie des Zufalls (71 Fragments of a Chronology of Chance) 1994, Lumière et compagnie (Lumière and Company, segment 'Michael Haneke/Vienne') 1995, Funny Games 1997, Das Schloß (The Castle) 1997, Code inconnu: Récit incomplet de divers voyages (Code Unknown: Incomplete Tales of Several Journeys) 2000, La pianiste (The Piano Teacher) (Grand Prize, Best Actor and Actress Awards, Cannes Film Festival 2001) 2001, Le temps du loup (The Time of the Wolf) 2003, Caché (Hidden) 2005, Funny Games (remake) 2007, Das weiße Band (The White Ribbon) (Palme d'Or, Cannes Film Festival 2009) 2009, Amour 2012 (Palme d'Or, Cannes Film Festival 2012); actor: Charms Zwischenfälle (Charm's Incidents) 1996. *Television includes:* writer and dir: After Liverpool 1974, Sperrmüll 1976, Drei Wege zum See 1976, Lemminge, Teil 1 Arkadien 1979, Lemminge, Teil 2 Verletzungen 1979, Variation 1983, Wer war Edgar Allan? 1984, Fraulein 1986, Nachruf für einen Mörder 1991, Die Rebellion 1993. *Address:* Universität für Musik und darstellende Kunst Wien, Anton-von-Webern-Platz 1, 1030 Vienna, Austria.

HANEKOM, Derek; South African politician; *Deputy Minister of Science and Technology;* b. 13 Jan. 1953, Cape Town; m. Trish Hanekom; mem. African Nat. Congress (ANC); arrested 1977 for protesting against detentions, imprisoned for ANC activities 1983–86; in exile in Zimbabwe 1987–90; fmr ANC Co-ordinator of Land and Agricultural Devt; MP 1994–; Minister of Land Affairs 1994–99, of Agric. 1996–99; Chair. Man. Cttee Nat. Rural Devt Forum; Deputy Minister of Science and Tech. 2004–; mem. Bd of Dirs Land and Agric. Policy Centre; mem. Bd SEED; mem. Bd of Trustees Ahmed Kathrada Foundation; mem. Nat. Exec. Cttee African Nat. Congress; Free Market Award 2002. *Address:* Department of Science and Technology, Private Bag AGX894, Pretoria 0001, South Africa (office). *Telephone:* (12) 8436300 (office). *Website:* www.dst.gov.za (office).

HANGST, Jeffrey Scott, SB, SM, PhD; American physicist and academic; *Professor of Physics, University of Århus;* b. Pa; ed Massachusetts Inst. of Tech., Univ. of Chicago; Assoc. Prof., later Prof. Dept of Physics and Astronomy, Univ. of Århus; Physics Co-ordinator ATHENA Experiment, CERN, Geneva, Switzerland, Spokesperson, ALPHA Experiment 2004–; Fellow, American Physical Soc.; European Physical Soc. Accelerator Prize 1996. *Address;* Department of Physics and Astronomy, University of Århus, Ny Munkegade, Århus C 8000, Denmark (office). *Telephone:* 89-42-37-51 (office). *Fax:* 86-12-07-40 (office). *E-mail:* hangst@ phys.au.dk (office). *Website:* www.phys.au.dk (office).

HANIEL, Franz Markus; German engineer and business executive; *Chairman of the Supervisory Board, Franz Haniel & Cie. GmbH;* b. 1955; career in family-owned co. Franz Haniel & Cie. GmbH, Chair. Supervisory Bd 2003–04, 2007–; mem. Bd of Dirs Giesecke & Devrient GmbH; mem. Supervisory Bd BMW AG 2004–, Security Networks (Secunet) AG 2004–; mem. and Chair. Supervisory Bd Metro AG 2007–10, mem. 2011–, Chair. 2012–. *Address:* Franz Haniel & Cie. GmbH, Franz-Haniel-Platz 1, 47119 Duisberg, Germany (office). *Telephone:* (203) 806-0 (office). *Fax:* (203) 806-622 (office). *E-mail:* jstolle@haniel.de (office). *Website:* www.haniel.de (office).

HANIN, Roger; French actor and director; b. (Roger Paul Lévy), 23 Oct. 1925, Algiers; s. of Joseph Lévy and Victorine Hanin; m. 2nd Christine Gouze-Renal 1959; one d.; ed Faculté Mixte de Médecine et de Pharmacie, Algiers; Dir Pau Festival; producer, Lucrèce Borgia 1979 (play); author and producer, Argent mon bel amour (play) 1983; numerous stage and TV appearances, including Shakespearean roles; Chevalier, Ordre nat. du Mérite; Dramatic Art Grand Prize, Enghiem 1972, Médaille Achir, Algeria 2000. *Films include:* Le Protecteur (also dir) 1973, Big Guns 1974, L'Intrépide 1975, Le Faux Cul (also dir) 1975, Le coup de Sirocco, Le Sucre 1978, Le Grand Pardon 1981, La Baraka 1982, L'Etincelle 1984, La Galette du Roi 1985, Train d'enfer (also dir) 1985, Dernier été à Tanger 1986, La Rumba (also dir) 1987, L'Orchestre Rouge 1989, Jean Galmot, aventurier 1990, Le Grand Pardon II 1992, Le Nombril du Monde 1993, Soleil 1997. *Television includes:* Palace (miniseries) 1988, Les Grandes familles (miniseries) 1989, Navarro (series) 1989, L'Eternel mari 1993, Le Misanthrope 1994, Samson le magnifique 1995, Une femme explosive 1996, Maître Da Costa (series) 1997, La Femme du boulanger 1999, Bier: Anschlag auf das Oktoberfest 1999, Trilogie marseillaise: La Marius 2000, Fanny 2000, César 2000, Anibal 2000, L'Etrange monsieur Joseph 2001, Ne meurs pas 2003, Mademoiselle Navarro 2005, La femme et le pantin 2007, Brigade Navarro 2007. *Publications:* plays: Ciel, où sont passées les dattes de tes oasis? 1968, Virgule 1974; books: L'Ours en lambeaux 1981, Le Voyage d'Arsène 1995, Les Gants Blancs 1994, L'hotel de la vieille lune 1998, Dentelles 2000, Lettre à un ami mystérieux 2001. *Leisure interests:* basketball, table-tennis, water-polo, boxing. *Address:* 9 rue du Boccador, 75008 Paris, France.

HANIYA, Ismail Abd as-Salam Ahmad, BA; Palestinian politician; b. 1962, Gaza; m.; 12 c.; ed Islamic Univ. of Gaza; jailed by Israelis for three years, released 1992 and deported to Lebanon; returned to Gaza 1993; Dean, Islamic Univ. of Gaza 1993–97; Head of Office of Sheikh Ahmed Yassin (Hamas spiritual leader) 1997–2004; Prime Minister, Palestinian Nat. Authority (Hamas) 2006–07 (resgnd), March–June 2007 (under unity govt), also Minister of the Interior May–June 2007; currently self-declared as Prime Minister of Palestinian Nat. Authority (disputed). *Address:* c/o Islamic Resistance Movement (Hamas: Harakat al-Muqawama al-Islamiyya), Gaza Palestinian Autonomous Areas.

HANKEL, Wilhelm; German economist and professor; b. 10 Jan. 1929, Danzig; s. of Oskar and Jenny (née Schoffmann) Hankel; m. Uta Wömpner; three c.; ed Univ. of Mainz and Univ. of Amsterdam, Netherlands; worked in Cen. Planning Bureau of Netherlands Govt 1951; subsequently joined Deutsche Bundesbank; served in Ministry of Econ. Co-operation and later in Foreign Ministry 1954–57; with Berliner Bank, Berlin and Kreditanstalt für Wiederaufbau, Frankfurt am Main 1957–68; Dir Money and Credit Dept, Fed. Ministry of the Economy and Finance 1968–72; Pres. Hessische Landesbank, Girozentrale, Frankfurt am Main 1972–74; Lecturer, Univ. of Frankfurt 1966–70, Hon. Prof. 1971–; Monetary Adviser EEC, Brussels 1974–76; Visiting Prof., Harvard, Georgetown and Johns Hopkins Univs,

USA and Wissenschaftszentrum, Berlin; Verdienstorden der Bundesrepublik Deutschland. *Publications:* Die zweite Kapitalverteilung 1961, Währungspolitik 1971, Heldensagen der Wirtschaft oder schöne heile Wirtschaftswelt 1975, Der Ausweg aus der Krise 1976, Weltwirtschaft 1977, Caesar 1978, Gegenkurs, von der Schuldenkrise zur Vollbeschäftigung 1984, Keynes, Die Entschlüsselung des Kapitalismus 1986, Vorsicht, unser Geld 1989, Eine Mark für Deutschland 1990, Dollar und Ecu, Leitwährungen im Wettstreit 1992, Die sieben Todsünden der deutschen Vereinigung 1993, Das grosse Geldtheater 1995, Die Euro-Klage. Warum die Währungsunion scheitern muss (jtly.) 1998, Die Euro Lüge: Eine volkswirtschaftliche Märchen; various articles, lectures, etc. *Leisure interests:* literature, music. *Address:* Berghausenerstrasse 190, 53639 Königswinter 21, Germany. *Telephone:* (2244) 7447 (office). *Fax:* (2244) 82034 (office). *E-mail:* whankel@aol.com.

HANKEN, James, AB, PhD; American zoologist and academic; *Alexander Agassiz Professor of Zoology, Curator in Herpetology and Director, Museum of Comparative Zoology, and Professor of Biology, Department of Organismic and Evolutionary Biology, Harvard University;* b. 14 July 1952, New York City, NY; s. of William Hanken and Miriam Gertz; m. Sally Susnowitz 1984; one s. one d.; ed Univ. of California, Berkeley; Postdoctoral studies at Dalhousie Univ., NS, Canada; then Faculty position, Univ. of Colorado, Boulder; Prof. of Biology, Dept of Organismic and Evolutionary Biology and Faculty mem. Center for Health and the Global Environment, Harvard Medical School, Harvard Univ. 1999–, currently Alexander Agassiz Prof. of Zoology, Curator in Herpetology and Dir Museum of Comparative Zoology; Past Pres. Int. Soc. of Vertebrate Morphologists, American Soc. of Ichthyologists and Herpetologists; fmr Chair. Int. Bd of Dirs Declining Amphibian Populations Task Force; fmr Co-Chair. Scientific Advisory Bd Consortium for the Barcode of Life; mem. Soc. for Study of Evolution, Soc. for Integrative and Comparative Biology, Herpetologists League; Fellow, AAAS; von Hofsten Lecturer, Uppsala Univ., Sweden, Gompertz Lecture in Integrative Biology, Univ. of California, Berkeley. *Achievements include:* nature and scientific photographer whose photographs appear in several books, field guides and magazines, including Natural History, Geo, Audubon and National Geographic World. *Publications:* Skull, Vol. 1: Development 1993, Skull, Vol. 2: Patterns of Structural and Systematic Diversity 1993, Skull, Vol. 3: Functional and Evolutionary Mechanisms 1993; has edited four books and published more than 100 scientific papers in professional journals on the evolutionary morphology, development and systematics of vertebrates, especially amphibians. *Address:* Museum of Comparative Zoology, 26 Oxford Street, Cambridge, MA 02138, USA (office). *Telephone:* (617) 495-2496 (office). *Fax:* (617) 495-5667 (office). *E-mail:* hanken@oeb.harvard.edu (office). *Website:* www.oeb.harvard.edu/faculty/hanken/hanken-oeb.html (office); www.oeb.harvard.edu/faculty/hanken/public_html/index.html (office); eol.org/info/bio_jhanken.

HANKES, Sir Claude, KCVO; British strategist and financial adviser; b. 8 March 1949; with Robert Fleming & Co. Ltd 1972–77, Dir 1974–77; Chair. Man. Cttee Price Waterhouse and Partners 1983–89, Action Resource Centre 1986–91; Adviser to the Bd Corange (Boehringer Mannheim) 1988–94; mem. Gov. Council, Business in the Community 1986–91, Pres.'s Cttee 1988–91; Deputy Chair. Leutwiler and Partners Ltd 1992–96; Chair. Shaw & Bradley 1993–; Interim Chair. Roland Berger Strategy Consultants Ltd 2003–05; assisted Dr Fritz Leutwiler in his role as ind. mediator between S African Govt and foreign banks 1985–86; Nobel Ind. Report 1991; Chair. Advisory Cttee to Jordan on Strategic Econ. Policy Matters 1993–94; Adviser to Iraq 2003, to Iraq Governing Council 2003–04, to Iraq (on macro-strategic issues) 2005–06; Sr Adviser to Trade Bank of Iraq 2007–11; Chair. Global Interaction Cttee 2011–; Trustee, Windsor Leadership Trust 1998–2007 (Chair. 2000–07); Trustee and adviser, St George's House, Windsor Castle 2000–06, Hon. Fellow and Life mem. of the Council 2006–; Hon. Fellow, Corpus Christi Coll., Oxford, Coll. of St George, Windsor Castle 2002–06 (Hon. mem. 2006–). *Publications:* The Dangers of the Banking System: Funding Country Deficits 1975, Nobel Industrier Independent Report, Stockholm 1991. *Leisure interests:* hiking, surfing, photography. *Fax:* (20) 7016-9143 (office). *E-mail:* officesirclaude@gmail.com (office).

HANKS, Tom; American actor and film producer; b. 9 July 1956, Oakland, Calif.; m. 1st Samantha Lewes 1978 (divorced 1985); two c.; m. 2nd Rita Wilson 1988; two s.; ed California State Univ.; began acting career with Great Lakes Shakespeare Festival; mem. Acad. of Motion Picture Arts and Sciences, mem. Bd of Govs 2001–, Vice-Pres. 2005–09, First Vice-Pres. 2009–; American Film Inst. Lifetime Achievement Award 2002, BAFTA Award for Excellence in Film 2004, People's Choice Award 1995–96, 1999, 2002, 2004. *Films include:* He Knows You're Alone 1980, Splash 1984, Bachelor Party 1984, The Man with One Red Shoe 1985, Volunteers 1985, The Money Pit 1986, Nothing in Common 1986, Every Time We Say Goodbye 1986, Dragnet 1987, Big 1988, Punchline 1988, The 'Burbs 1989, Turner & Hooch 1989, Joe Versus the Volcano 1990, The Bonfire of the Vanities 1990, Radio Flyer (uncredited) 1992, A League of Their Own 1992, Sleepless in Seattle 1993, Philadelphia (Acad. Award for Best Actor 1994) 1993, Forrest Gump (Acad. Award for Best Actor 1995) 1994, Apollo 13 1995, Toy Story (voice) 1995, That Thing You Do (also dir) 1996, Turner & Hooch 1997, Saving Private Ryan 1998, You've Got Mail 1998, The Green Mile 1999, Toy Story 2 (voice) 1999, Cast Away (also producer) 2000, Road to Perdition 2002, My Big Fat Greek Wedding (producer) 2002, Catch Me If You Can 2003, The Ladykillers 2004, Connie and Carla (producer) 2004, The Terminal 2004, Elvis Has Left the Building 2004, The Polar Express (also exec. producer) 2004, Magnificent Desolation: Walking on the Moon 3D (documentary short) (voice) 2005, Da Vinci Code 2006, Cars (voice) 2006, Neil Young: Heart of Gold (producer) 2006, The Ant Bully (producer) 2006, Starter for Ten (producer) 2006, Charlie Wilson's War 2007, The Great Buck Howard 2008, Angels & Demons 2009, Beyond All Boundaries (short) (voice) 2009, Where the Wild Things Are (producer) 2009, Toy Story 3 (voice) 2010, Hawaiian Vacation (short) (voice) 2011, Larry Crowne 2011, Small Fry (short) (voice) 2011, Extremely Loud & Incredibly Close 2011, Cloud Atlas 2012, Captain Phillips 2013. *Television includes:* The Love Boat (series) 1980, Bosom Buddies (series) 1980–82, Taxi (series) 1982, Happy Days (series) 1982, Mazes and Monsters (film) 1982, Family Ties (series) 1983–84, Tales from the Crypt (series) 1992, Fallen Angels (series) 1993, Vault of Horror I (film) 1994, From the Earth to the Moon (mini-series, also exec. producer) 1998, West Point (series, producer) 2000, We Stand Alone Together (exec. producer) 2001, Scene by Scene (series) 2001, Band of Brothers (Emmy

Award for Outstanding Mini-series 2002, also exec. producer) 2001, My Big Fat Greek Life (exec. producer) 2003, Freedom: A History of Us (series documentary) 2003, Great Performances (series) (uncredited) 2003, We're with the Band (producer) 2005, Big Love (exec. producer) 2006–07, Late Show with David Letterman (series) 2009, The Pacific (mini-series) (exec. producer) 2010, Electric City (series short) 2012. *Plays:* Lucky Guy (Broadway) 2013. *Address:* 8383 Wilshire Blvd, Suite 500, Beverly Hills, CA 90211 (office); c/o Creative Artists Agency, 2000 Avenue of the Stars, Los Angeles, CA 90067, USA (office). *Telephone:* (424) 288-2000 (office). *Fax:* (424) 288-2900 (office). *Website:* www.caa.com (office).

HANLEY, Rt Hon. Sir Jeremy James, KCMG, PC, FCA, FCIS, FCCA; British business executive, politician and chartered accountant; b. 17 Nov. 1945, Amersham, Bucks.; s. of the late Jimmy Hanley and Dinah Sheridan; m. 1st Helene Mason 1968 (divorced 1973); one s.; m. 2nd Verna, Viscountess Villiers (née Stott) 1973; one s. one step d.; ed Rugby School; with Peat Marwick Mitchell & Co. 1963–66; Dir Anderson Thomas Frankel (ATF) 1969, Man. Dir ATF (Jersey and Ireland) 1970–73; Deputy Chair. The Financial Training Co. Ltd 1973–90; Sec. Park Place PLC 1977–83; Chair. Fraser Green Ltd 1986–90; Parl. Adviser to ICA 1986–90; Conservative MP for Richmond and Barnes 1983–97; Parl. Under-Sec. of State, Northern Ireland Office 1990–93; Minister for Health, Social Security and Agric. 1990–92, for Political Devt, Community Relations and Educ. 1992–93; Minister of State for the Armed Forces, Ministry of Defence 1993–94; Cabinet Minister without Portfolio 1995; Chair. Conservative Party 1994–95; Foreign Office Minister of State for the Middle East and Hong Kong 1995–97; Chair. AdVal Group PLC, Int. Trade and Investment Missions Ltd 1998–2002; Dir ITE Group PLC 1996–2010, GTECH Corpn, USA 2001–06; fmr Chair. Financial Reporting Council UK Corporate Governance Cttee; Dir Lottomatica SpA, Arab-British Chamber of Commerce 1998–2012, European Advisory Bd 2004–05, Calyon (fmrly Crédit Lyonnais) 2000–05, Nymex Europe Ltd 2005–08, Blue Hackle Ltd 2006–10, Willis Group Holdings Inc. 2006–; Chair. British Iran Chamber of Commerce 2000 (Vice-Pres. 2001–06), Brain Games Network PLC 2000–01; Deputy Chair. Langbar International 2006–; mem. British-American Parl. Group 1983–97, Anglo-French Parl. Group 1983–97, CPA 1983–97, IPU 1983–97, British-Irish Inter-Parl. Body 1990, Advisory Bd Talal Abu-Ghazaleh Int.; Vice-Chair. Nat. Anglo-West Indian Conservative Soc. 1982–83; Chair. Conservative Cands Assen 1982–83; mem. Bow Group 1974–97, European Movement 1974–97, Mensa 1968–; mem. Court of Assts, Worshipful Co. of Chartered Accountants, Master 2005–06; mem. Dyers' Co.; mem. Brixham Rotary Club, Brixham Yacht Club; Fellow, Assen of Chartered Certified Accountants; Freeman of the City of London 1989. *Leisure interests:* cookery, chess, cricket, languages, theatre, cinema, music. *Address:* Berry Head House, Victoria Road, Brixham, Devon, TQ5 9AR (home); 6 Butts Mead, Northwood, Middx, HA6 2TL, England (home). *Telephone:* (1803) 882317 (Devon) (home); (1923) 826675 (Middx) (home). *Fax:* (1923) 836447 (Middx) (home). *E-mail:* jeremy@hanley.com (home).

HANLON, Lt-Gen. Edward, BS, MS; American military officer (retd); *President, Raytheon International, Inc. Europe;* ed Southeastern Okla Univ., Pepperdine Univ., Univ. of Minn., Officer Candidates School, Quantico; commissioned Second Lt 1967; posts have included Exec. Officer and Fire Direction Officer 1st Bn, 13th Marines, Vietnam 1968–69, Asst S-3 Legal Officer and Public Affairs Officer, Marine Corps HQ 1969–72, Bn S-4 2nd Bn, later CO E Battery, 12th Marines 1973–74, Exec. Officer Training Support Co., CO Enlisted Instructor Co. and Exec. Officer Company M, The Basic School, Quantico 1974–77, Marine Officer Instructor and Exec. Officer, Naval Reserve Officers Training Course Unit, Univ. of Minn. 1977–80, Bn S-4 2nd Bn, Exec. Officer 3rd Bn and Div. Staff Sec., 1st Marine Div., Camp Pendleton 1981–84, CO 3rd Bn, 12th Marines 1984–85, Dir of Personal Services Marine Corps Recruit Depot, San Diego 1985–86, Asst Chief of Staff for Plans and Operations, HQ Fleet Marine Force Europe, London 1987–90, Atlantic Fleet Marine Officer 1990–92, CO 10th Marines, 2nd Marine Div. 1992–93, promoted to Brig.-Gen. 1993, Deputy Commdr Naval Striking and Support Forces Southern Europe, Naples, Italy 1993–96, promoted to Maj.-Gen. 1996, Dir Expeditionary Warfare Div. 1996–98, Commanding Gen. Marine Corps Base, Camp Pendleton 1998–2001, promoted to Lt-Gen. 2001, Commanding Gen. Marine Corps Combat Devt Command, Quantico and Deputy Commandant Combat Devt, Marine Corps HQ 2001–04; Mil. Rep. to NATO 2004–06; Pres. Raytheon International Inc. Europe 2007–; Defense Superior Service Medal with oak leaf, Legion of Merit with two gold stars, Defense Meritorious Service Medal, Meritorious Service Medal, Navy and Marine Corps Commendation Medal with Combat "V" and gold star, Combat Action Ribbon. *Address:* Raytheon International, 870 Winter Street, Waltham, MA, 02451, USA (office). *Website:* www.raytheon.com (office).

HANLON, Philip J., AB, PhD; American college administrator and mathematician; *President, Dartmouth College;* m. Gail Gentes; ed Dartmouth Coll., California Inst. of Tech.; Instructor of Applied Math., Massachusetts Inst. of Tech. 1981–83; Bantrell Fellow in Math., California Inst. of Tech. 1983–86; Assoc. Prof., Univ. of Michigan 1986–90, Prof. 1990–2013, Arthur F. Thurnau Prof. 1992–2013, D.J. Lewis Prof. of Math. 2001–13, Assoc. Dean for Planning and Finance, Coll. of Literature, Science and the Arts 2001–04, Assoc. Provost for Academic and Budgetary Affairs 2004–07, Vice-Provost for Academic and Budgetary Affairs 2007–10, Provost and Exec. Vice-Pres. for Academic Affairs 2010–13, mem. Exec. Cttee, Coll. of Literature, Science and the Arts 1994–97, mem. Univ. of Michigan Presidential Comm. on Undergraduate Studies 2000–01; Pres. Dartmouth Coll. 2013–; visiting positions: Center for Communications Research, Princeton 1984, 1986, 1990, Univ. of Oxford, UK 1988, Univ. of Strasbourg, France 1988, 1993, Institut des Hautes Études Scientifiques, Bures-sur-Yvette, France 1988, Mittag-Leffler Inst., Stockholm, Sweden 1992, Isaac Newton Inst., Univ. of Cambridge, UK 2001; Founder and Exec. Dir Michigan Math Scholars Program 1996–99, Chair. Planning Cttee 1997–99; Prin. Organizer of six-month programme on Symmetric Functions at Isaac Newton Inst., Univ. of Cambridge 2001; Chair. Presidential Task Force on Multidisciplinary Learning and Team Teaching, Univ. of Michigan 2004–05, mem. Bd of Dirs Univ. of Michigan Hosps and Health Centers 2010–, Bentley Historical Library 2010–12; mem. Nat. Security Agency Advisory Bd 1994–2007, mem. Math. Sub-panel 1994–, Chair. 1994–2006; Chair. Mathematical Reviews Editorial Cttee 1992–95; mem. Editorial Bd Transactions of the American Mathematical Society 1992–2000, Journal of Algebraic Combinatorics 1993–, Electronic Journal of Combinatorics

1996–; mem. Council of American Math. Soc. 1992–95, FOCUS Advisory Cttee 1989–93, 2007; NSF Presidential Young Investigator Award 1987–92, Alfred P. Sloan Fellowship 1986–88, Prin. Speaker, American Math. Soc. 1988, Henry Russel Award 1990, Plenary Speaker, Canadian Math. Soc. 1992, John Simon Guggenheim Fellowship 1992, Michigan Soc. of Fellows 1993–96, Literature, Science and the Arts Excellence in Educ. Award 1997. *Publications include:* more than 60 papers in professional journals on algebraic combinatorics, discrete probability, bioinformatics and theoretical computer science. *Address:* Office of the President, Dartmouth College, 207 Parkhurst Hall, Hanover, NH 03755, USA (office). *Telephone:* (603) 646-2223 (office). *Fax:* (603) 646-2266 (office). *E-mail:* president's.office@dartmouth.edu (office). *Website:* www.dartmouth.edu/ ~president (office).

HANNAH, Daryl; American actress; b. 3 Dec. 1960, Chicago, Ill.; ed Univ. of California, Los Angeles; studied with Stella Adler; studied ballet with Marjorie Tallchief; appeared on TV in Paper Dolls. *Films:* The Fury 1978, The Final Terror, Hard Country, Blade Runner, Summer Lovers, Splash, The Pope of Greenwich Village, Reckless, Clan of the Cave Bear, Legal Eagles, Roxanne, Wall Street, High Spirits, Steel Magnolias, Crazy People, At Play in the Fields of the Lord, Memoirs of an Invisible Man, Grumpy Old Men, Attack of the 50 ft Woman, The Tie That Binds, Grumpier Old Men 1995, Two Much 1996, The Last Days of Frankie the Fly 1996, Wild Flowers 1999, My Favorite Martian 1999, Dancing at the Blue Iguana 2000, Cord 2000, Speedway Junky 2001, Jackpot 2001, A Walk to Remember 2002, Hard Cash 2002, Northfork 2002, Kill Bill Vol. I 2003, Kill Bill: Vol. 2 2004, Yo puta 2004, Silver City 2004, Careful What You Wish For 2004, Love is the Drug 2006, Keeping Up with the Steins 2006, Olé 2006, The Poet 2007, The Cycle 2008, Vice (also producer) 2008, Shannon's Rainbow 2009, The Cycle 2009, A Closed Book 2010, S.O.S Love! The Million Dollar Contract 2011, The Hot Flashes 2013; Dir, Writer, Producer: The Last Supper (Berlin Int. Film Festival Jury Award for Best Short) 1994; Dir: A Hundred and One Nights 1995. *Play:* The Seven Year Itch 2000. *Address:* dhlovelife, 1112 Montana Avenue, #721, Santa Monica, CA 90403; Columbia Plaza Producers, Building 8-153, Burbank, CA 91505, USA. *E-mail:* dhlovelife@yahoo.com.

HANNAH, John; British actor; b. 23 April 1962, Glasgow; s. of John Hannah and Susan Hannah; m. Joanna Roth; two c.; ed Royal Scottish Acad. of Music and Drama; fmrly electrician; worked with Workers' Theatre Co. *Television includes:* Bookie 1987, Brond 1987, Paul Calf's Video Diary 1993, Milner 1994, Faith 1994, Pauline Calf's Wedding Video 1994, McCallum (series) 1995, Out of the Blue (series) 1995, Truth or Dare 1996, Circles of Deceit: Kalon 1996, The Love Bug 1997, Rebus: Black and Blue 2000, Rebus: The Hanging Garden 2000, Rebus: Dead Souls 2001, Dr. Jekyll and Mr. Hyde 2002, MDs (series) 2002, Amnesia 2004, Rebus: Mortal Causes 2004, Marple: 4.50 from Paddington 2004, Cold Blood 2005, Ghost Son 2006, New Street Law 2006–07, Kidnap and Ransom 2011, Touch of Cloth 2012. *Films include:* Harbour Beat 1990, Four Weddings and a Funeral 1994, The Final Cut 1995, Madagascar Skin 1995, The Innocent Sleep 1996, The James Gang 1997, Sliding Doors 1998, Resurrection Man 1998, So This Is Romance? 1998, The Mummy 1999, The Hurricane 1999, The Intruder 1999, Circus 2000, Pandaemonium 2000, The Mummy Returns 2001, Before You Go 2002, I'm with Lucy 2002, I Accuse 2003, Male Mail 2004, The Last Legion 2007, The Mummy: Tomb of the Dragon Emperor 2008, Spartacus: Blood and Sand 2010,. *Address:* c/o William Morris Agency, Inc., 1 William Morris Place, Beverly Hills, CA 90212, USA.

HANNAY OF CHISWICK, Baron (Life Peer), cr. 2001, of Chiswick, of Bedford Park in the London Borough of Ealing; **David Hugh Alexander Hannay,** GCMG, CH, MA, DLitt; British diplomatist; *Member, House of Lords;* b. 28 Sept. 1935, London; s. of Julian Hannay and Eileen Hannay; m. Gillian Rosemary Rex 1961; four s.; ed Craigflower School, Torryburn, Fife, Scotland, Winchester Coll. and New Coll. Oxford; Second Lt, King's Royal Irish Hussars 1954–56; Persian language student, Foreign Office and British Embassy, Tehran 1959–61; Oriental Sec., British Embassy, Kabul 1961–63; Second Sec., Eastern Dept, Foreign Office, London 1963–65; Second, then First Sec., UK Del. to EC, Brussels 1965–70, First Sec. UK Negotiating Team 1970–72; Chef de Cabinet to Sir Christopher Soames, Vice-Pres. EC Comm. 1973–77; Counsellor, Head of Energy, Science and Space Dept, FCO, London 1977–79, Counsellor, Head of Middle East Dept 1979, Asst Under-Sec. of State (EC) 1979–84; Minister, Embassy in Washington, DC 1984–85; UK Perm. Rep. to EC 1985–90, to UN 1990–95; British Govt Special Rep. for Cyprus 1996–2003; Prime Minister's Personal Envoy to Turkey and EU Special Rep. for Cyprus 1998; Life Peer (Ind.), House of Lords 2001–; mem. UN Sec. Gen.'s High Level Panel on Threats, Challenges and Change 2003–04, House of Lords EU Select Cttee 2002–06, 2008–14, House of Lords Inter-Governmental Orgs Cttee 2007–08; Chair. Int. Advisory Bd EDHEC 2003–09, UN Asscn of the UK 2006–11; Vice-Chair. All Party Parl. Group on Europe 2006–, Chair. on UN 2011–; Jt Convenor, All-Party Parl. Group on Global Security and Non-Proliferation 2007–; Dir (non-exec.) Chime Communications 1996–2006, Aegis 2000–03; mem. Court and Council, Univ. of Birmingham 1998–2006, Pro-Chancellor 2001–06; mem. Council of Britain in Europe 1999–2005; mem. Council Univ. of Kent 2009–; mem. Centre for European Reform 1997–; mem. Top Level Group on Nuclear Disarmament and Nonproliferation 2011–; mem. Bd Salzburg Seminar 2002–05, TANGGUH Int. Advisory Panel 2002–09, Advisory Bd Judge Business Schools 2004, GPW & Co. 2011–; Gov. Ditchley Foundation 2005–; Hon. Fellow, New Coll. Oxford; Hon. DLitt (Birmingham). *Publication:* Britain's Entry into the European Community: Report on the Negotiations (ed.) 1970–72, Cyprus: The Search for a Solution 2004, A More Secure World: Our Shared Responsibility (UN Panel Report) 2004, New World Disorder: The UN After the Cold War 2008, Britain's Quest for a Role: a Diplomatic Memoir from Europe to the UN 2012. *Leisure interests:* gardening, travel, photography. *Address:* 3 The Orchard, London, W4 1JZ, England (home). *Telephone:* (20) 8987-9012 (home). *Fax:* (20) 8987-9012 (home).

HANNIBALSSON, Jón Baldvin, MA (Econ); Icelandic politician, diplomatist and academic; b. 21 Feb. 1939, Ísafjörður; s. of Hannibal Valdimarsson and Sólveig Ólafsdóttir; m. Bryndís Schram 1959; one s. three d.; ed Menntaskólinn í Reykjavík, Univ. of Edinburgh, UK, Nationalökonomiska Inst., Stockholm, Sweden, Univ. of Iceland and Harvard Univ., USA; teacher in secondary school, Reykjavik 1964–70; journalist, Frjáls thjóð, Reykjavik 1964–67; Founder and

Rector Ísafjörður Coll. 1970–79; Chief Ed. Althýðublaðið, Reykjavik 1979–82; mem. Althingi (Parl.) 1982–98; Chair. SDP 1984–96; Minister of Finance 1987–88, for Foreign Affairs and Foreign Trade 1988–95, led negotiations with EU on European Econ. Area 1989–94; Chair. Council of Ministers, EFTA 1989, 1992, 1994; Amb. to USA (also accred to Mexico, Brazil, Chile and Argentina) 1998–2002, to Finland (also accred to Estonia, Latvia, Lithuania and Ukraine) 2002–05; Univ. Lecturer, Univ. of Iceland 2005–06, Univ. of Bifrost 2005–06; writer and frequent commentator on current affairs; Hon. Citizen of Vilnius, Lithuania 1996; Hon. mem. Bd Baltic Devt Forum; Order of Terra Marina, Estonia 1996, Order of Grand Duke Gediminas, Lithuania 1996, Order of Pres. of Latvia 1996, Order of Prince Trpimir and Croatian Morning Star 2001, Presidential Order of Merit (Slovenia). *Film:* Those Who Dare (documentary) 2011. *Television:* Dialogue with Jón Baldvin (Stod 2) 1997, Hans Kristján Arnason: Iceland and the Surrounding World through the Eyes of Jón Baldvin Hannibalsson (HKA) 2001. *Publications include:* Who Owns Iceland? 1985. Economic Strategy for Social-Democrats (co-author) 1986, The Icelandic Tax Reform 1987, The Age of Extremes – Reflections of 22 Icelanders at the Dawn of a New Millennium (co-ed. with Gunnar Q. Schram) 2000, Iceland and the Baltic Nations' Struggle for the Restoration of Independence 1988–91 2001, Iceland in the New Century (co-author) 2001, Expectations and Disappointments of the 20th Century 2001, Tilhugalíf (Honeymoon; political memoirs) 2002, The Welfare State and Its Enemies 2004, The Baltic Road to Freedom: The Western Response to The Restoration of Independence of the Baltic States 2005, Iceland and the Current Economic Crisis – Political Implications and the Way Forward 2009, Iceland and the European Union 2009, Iceland's Triple Crisis – Are There Lessons to be Learned? 2010, The Solidarity of Small Nations 2010, The Future of Enlargement, European Strategy Forum 2010, The First Decade of the 21st Century in Retrospect: To Be or Not to Be – A Republic at a Crossroads 2011. *Leisure interests:* reading, swimming, travel. *Address:* Alfhóll v/ Engjaveg, 270 Mosó, Iceland. *Telephone:* 566-6362; 895-6362. *E-mail:* jon.baldvin@ simnet.is. *Website:* www.jbh.is.

HANOOMANJEE, Hon. Santi Bai; Mauritian politician and civil servant; *Minister of Health and Quality of Life;* b. 15 Nov. 1952, Vacoas; m.; three d.; ed Queen Elizabeth Coll., Univ. of Mauritius; worked in Electoral Commrs' Office, Ministry of Educ. and Cultural Affairs, Ministry of Employment, Ministry of Internal Communications, Prime Minister's Office, Ministry for Women's Rights, Child Devt and Family Welfare, Ministry of Civil Service Affairs, Ministry of Agric. and Natural Resources, Ministry of Finance and Econ. Devt; retd as Perm. Sec. 2005; joined MSM Party 2005; mem. of Nat. Ass. for Constituency No. 14 Savanne-Black River 2005–10; Minister of Health and Quality of Life 2010–; Chair. Farmers' Service Corpn 1996–2005, Sugar Planters' Mechanical Pool Corpn 1996–2001, Tea Bd 1996–2005, Mauritius Sugar Authority 2001–05; First Chair. Mauritius Revenue Authority 2005–05; mem. Nat. Women's Council, Nat. Children's Council, Mauritius Sugar Industry Research Inst., Film Devt Corpn, Mauritius Sugar Bulk Terminal Corpn. *Leisure interests:* social work, promoting women's interests, reading, cooking. *Address:* Ministry of Health and Quality of Life, 5th Floor, Emmanuel Anquetil Building, Port Louis, Mauritius (office). *Telephone:* 201-2175 (office). *Fax:* 208-7222 (office). *E-mail:* moh@mail.gov.mu (office). *Website:* www.gov.mu/portal/site/mohsite (office).

HANRAHAN, Paul T., MBA; American energy industry executive; b. 1957; ed Harvard Business School, US Naval Acad.; active service in USN; various man. roles with AES Corpn in USA, Europe and Asia including Gen. Man. AES Transpower Inc. 1990–93, Exec. Vice-Pres., CEO and Sec. AES China Generating Co. (Chigen) 1993–95, Pres. and CEO 1995–98, Vice-Pres. AES 1994–97, Sr Vice-Pres. 1997, CEO and Exec. Vice-Pres. 1997–2002, Pres. and CEO 2002–11; mem. Bd of Dirs Corn Products Int. Inc. 2006–, Seven Seas Water Corpn 2012–. *Address:* c/o Board of Directors, Seven Seas Water Corporation, 14400 Carlson Circle, Tampa, FL 33626, USA (office).

HANS-ADAM II, HSH Prince of Liechtenstein (Duke of Troppau and Jägerndorf, Count of Rietberg); b. 14 Feb. 1945, Zürich, Switzerland; s. of the late Prince Franz Josef II and Princess Gina; m. Countess Marie Aglaë Kinsky von Wchinitz und Tettau 1967; three s. (including Hereditary Prince Alois Philipp Maria) one d.; ed Schottengymnasium, Vienna, School of Econs and Social Sciences, St Gallen, Switzerland; Chief Exec. of Prince of Liechtenstein Foundation 1970–84; took over exec. authority of Liechtenstein Aug. 1984; transferred exec. power to Hereditary Prince Alois Aug. 2004. *Address:* Schloss Vaduz, 9490 Vaduz, Principality of Liechtenstein. *E-mail:* office@fuerstenhaus.li (office). *Website:* www.fuerstenhaus.li.

HÄNSCH, Theodor Wolfgang, MSc, PhD; German physicist and academic; *Carl Friedrich von Siemens Professor of Physics and Director, Max-Planck-Institut für Quantenoptik, Ludwig-Maximilians-Universität München;* b. 30 Oct. 1941, Heidelberg; s. of Karl Hänsch and Marta Hänsch; ed Helmholtz-Gymnasium, Heidelberg, Univ. of Heidelberg; Asst Prof. Inst. of Applied Physics, Univ. of Heidelberg 1969–70; NATO Postdoctoral Fellow, Stanford Univ. 1970–72, Assoc. Prof. of Physics 1972–75, Prof. of Physics 1975–86; Dir Max-Planck-Institut für Quantenoptik 1986– (Exec. Dir 1993–96, 2003–04), Carl Friedrich von Siemens Prof. of Physics, Ludwig-Maximilians-Universität München 1986–, Chair. Physics Dept 2001–02; Chair. Int. Science Council, King Abdullah Inst. of Nanotechnology; Visiting Prof., College de France 1978, Univ. of Kyoto 1979, Univ. of Florence 1979, 1995, Fudan Univ. 1982, Ecole Normale Superieure, Paris 1992; Gordon Moore Distinguished Scholar 2001; Qatar Foundation Distinguished Lecturer, Texas A&M Univ.; Consultant, Scientific Advisory Bd Cold Quanta Inc. 2007; Fellow, American Physical Soc., Optical Soc. of America; mem. Editorial Bd Applied Physics B, Physics in Perspective, Springer Series in Optical Sciences, Laser Physics Review; mem. American Acad. of Arts and Sciences, Bavarian Acad. of Arts and Sciences, Berlin-Brandenburg Acad. of Sciences; Hon. Citizen, City of Garching 2006, City of Florence, Italy 2007; Hon. mem. Optical Soc. of America 2008, German Physical Soc. 2011; Hon. Prof., Nat. Chiang Tung Univ., Hsinchu, Taiwan 2010; Hon. Chair. Prof., Univ. System of Taiwan 2010; Bayerischer Maximiliansorden, Grand Officer Cross (Order of Merit) 2006, Grosses Bundesverdienstkreuz mit Stern 2007; Dr hc (Univ. of St Andrews) 2006, (Free Univ., Berlin) 2006, (Bar-Ilan-Univ.) 2008; Calif. Museum of Science and Industry Calif. Scientist of the Year 1973, Alexander von Humboldt Sr US Scientist Award 1977, Freie Universität Berlin Otto Klung Prize 1980, NAS Cyrus B. Comstock Prize

1983, American Physical Soc. Herbert P. Broida Prize 1983, Optical Soc. of America William F. Meggers Award 1985, Franklin Inst. Michelson Medal 1986, Italgas Prize for Research and Innovation 1987, Deutsche Forschungsgemeinschaft Gottfried Wilhelm Leibniz Preis 1988, King Faisal Int. Prize for Science 1989, Einstein Medal for Laser Science 1995, American Physical Soc. Arthur L. Schawlow Prize for Laser Science 1996, Philip Morris Research Prize 1998, 2000, Deutsche Physikalische Gesellschaft Stern-Gerlach Medal 2000, Laser Inst. of America Arthur L. Schawlow Award 2000, European Physical Soc. Quantum Electronics and Optics Prize 2001, Int. Union of Pure and Applied Physics SUNAMCO Medal 2001, Italian Nat. Acad. of Sciences Matteucci-Medal 2002, Alfried Krupp Prize for Science 2002, IEEE I. I. Rabi Award 2005, Optical Soc. of America Frederic Ives Medal 2005, Otto-Hahn-Prize for Chem. and Physics 2005, Nobel Prize in Physics (jtly) 2005, De Scientia et Humanitate Meritis Medal 2007, Carl Friedrich von Siemens Prize and Chair 2007, Ioannes Marcus Marci Medal, Czech Spectroscopic Soc. 2007, Garbsen Ring, City of Garbsen 2007, Rudolf Diesel Gold Medal, German Inst of Interventions 2007, Orden Pour Le Mérite für Wissenschaften und Künste (Germany) 2008, James Joyce Award 2009, Sayling Wen Excellent Lecture Award, Nat. Central Univ., Taiwan 2010, Bavarian Constitution Medal in Gold, Order of Merit 2010, Advanced Grant, European Research Council 2010. *Publications:* more than 620 scientific articles. *Address:* c/o G. Gschwendtner, Schellingstr. 4/III, 80799 Munich, Germany (office). *Telephone:* (89) 2180-3212 (office). *Fax:* (89) 285192 (office). *E-mail:* t.w.haensch@physik.uni-muenchen.de (office). *Website:* www.mpq.mpg.de/~haensch (office).

HANSEID, Einar; Norwegian journalist (retd); b. 19 Nov. 1943, Sandefjord; m. Mari Onsrud 1977; two s.; reporter, Sandefjords Blad 1965; News Ed. Dagbladet 1974; Chief Ed. Hjem & Fritid 1982; Man. Ed. Verdens Gang 1984, Chief Ed. 1987–93; Chief Ed. Aftenposten 1994–2003; Counselor, Schibsted Group. *Address:* Schibsted Asa, Apotekergaten 10, 0180 Oslo, Norway.

HANSEN, Barbara C., PhD; American professor of physiology and university administrator; *Director, Obesity, Diabetes and Aging Resource and Center for Preclinical Research and Professor of Internal Medicine and Pediatrics, University of South Florida;* b. 24 Nov. 1941, Boston, Mass; d. of Reynold Caleen and Dorothy Richardson Caleen; m. Kenneth D. Hansen 1976; one s.; ed Univ. of California, Los Angeles, Univ. of Pennsylvania and Univ. of Washington, Seattle; Research Fellow, Univ. of Pennsylvania Inst. of Neurosciences 1966–68; Asst and Assoc. Prof., Univ. of Washington 1971–76; Prof. and Assoc. Dean, Univ. of Michigan, Ann Arbor 1977–83; Assoc. Vice-Pres. of Academic Affairs and Research and Dean of Grad. School, Southern Illinois Univ., Carbondale 1983–85; Vice-Pres. for Grad. Studies and Research, Univ. of Maryland, Baltimore 1986–90, Prof. of Physiology 1990, Dir Obesity and Diabetes Research Center 1990, also Dir Obesity, Diabetes and Aging Animal Resource and Dir of Research, Joslin Clinic; currently Dir Obesity, Diabetes and Aging Resource and Center for Preclinical Research and Prof. of Internal Medicine and Pediatrics, Univ. of South Florida, Tampa; Pres. Int. Asscn for Study of Obesity 1987–90, N American Asscn for Study of Obesity 1984–85, American Soc. of Clinical Nutrition 1995–96; mem. NAS Inst. of Medicine, Chair. Section 3 Membership Cttee 2012–. *Publications include:* Controversies in Obesity (ed.) 1983, The Commonsense Guide to Weight Loss for People with Diabetes 1998, The Metabolic Syndrome X 1999; book chapters and articles in learned journals. *Leisure interests:* sailing, scuba diving, golf, reading. *Address:* Center for Obesity, Diabetes & Aging, University of South Florida, 12901 Bruce B Downs Blvd. Tampa, FL 33612, USA (office). *Telephone:* (813) 974-7394 (office). *Fax:* (813) 905-9883 (office). *E-mail:* bhansen@health.usf.edu (office). *Website:* health.usf.edu/medicine/internalmedicine/index.htm (office).

HANSEN, James E., BA, MS, PhD; American space scientist, environmental scientist, academic and research institute director; *Director, National Aeronautical and Space Administration (NASA) Goddard Institute for Space Studies;* b. 29 March 1941, Denison, Ia; ed Univ. of Iowa; NASA Grad. Traineeship 1965–66; NAS-NRC Resident Research Assoc., Goddard Inst. for Space Studies (GISS), New York 1967–69, Staff mem./Space Scientist, GISS, Man. GISS Planetary and Climate Programs 1972–81, Dir NASA Goddard Inst. for Space Studies 1981–; NSF Postdoctoral Fellow, Leiden Observatory, Netherlands 1969; Research Assoc., Columbia Univ., New York 1969–72, Adjunct Assoc. Prof., Dept of Geological Sciences 1978–85, Adjunct Prof. of Earth and Environmental Sciences 1985–; Co-Prin. Investigator, AEROPOL Project (airborne terrestrial infrared polarimeter) 1971–74; Co-Investigator, Voyager Photopolarimeter Experiment 1972–85; Prin. Investigator, Pioneer Venus Orbiter Cloud-Photopolarimeter Experiment 1974–78, Co-Investigator 1974–94; Prin. Investigator, Galileo (Jupiter Orbiter) Photopolarimeter Radiometer Experiment 1977–2000, Earth Observing System Interdisciplinary Investigation: Interannual Variability of Earth's Carbon, Energy and Water Cycles 1989–2000; best known for his research in climatology, his testimony on climate change to congressional cttees in 1980s that helped raise awareness of global warming issue, and his continuing advocacy of action to limit impacts of climate change; mem. NAS 1996; Fellow, American Geophysical Union 1992; Goddard Special Achievement Award (Pioneer Venus) 1977, NASA Group Achievement Award (Voyager, Photopolarimeter) 1978, NASA Exceptional Service Medal (Radiative Transfer) 1984, Nat. Wildlife Fed. Conservation Achievement Award 1989, NASA Presidential Rank Award of Meritorious Exec. 1990, Alumni Achievement Award, Univ. of Iowa 1991, NASA Group Achievement Award (Galileo, Polarimeter/Radiometer) 1993, William Nordberg Achievement Medal, Goddard Space Flight Center 1996, Editor's Citation for Excellence in Refereeing for Geophysical Research Letters 1996, NASA Presidential Rank Award of Meritorious Exec. 1997, Alumni Fellow, Univ. of Iowa 2000, GISS Best Scientific Publication (peer vote): 'Global warming – alternative scenario' 2000, John Heinz Environment Award 2001, Roger Revelle Medal, American Geophysical Union 2002, GISS Best Scientific Publication (peer vote): 'Soot climate forcing' 2004, GISS Best Scientific Publication (peer vote): 'Earth's Energy Imbalance' 2005, Duke of Edinburgh Conservation Medal, World Wildlife Fund (WWF) 2006, Laureate, Dan David Prize 2007, Leo Szilard Lectureship Award, American Physical Soc. 2007. *Publications:* Storms of my Grandchildren 2009; also numerous scientific papers in professional journals on radiative transfer in planetary atmospheres and interpretation of remote sounding of atmospheres, devt of global climate models, analysis of climate change, current climate trends, and projections of man's impact on climate. *Address:* NASA Goddard Institute for Space Studies, 2880 Broadway, New York, NY 10025 (office); 750 Armstrong Hall,

Columbia University, 2880 Broadway, New York, NY 10025, USA (office). *Telephone:* (212) 678-5500 (office). *Fax:* (212) 678-5622 (office). *E-mail:* jhansen@giss.nasa.gov (office); james.e.hansen@nasa.gov (office). *Website:* www.giss.nasa.gov (office).

HANSEN, John Mark, BA, MPhil, PhD; American political scientist, academic and university dean; *Charles L. Hutchinson Distinguished Service Professor, Department of Political Science and Dean, Social Sciences Division, University of Chicago;* ed Univ. of Kansas, Yale Univ.; Asst Prof. in Political Science, Univ. of Chicago 1986–92, Assoc. Prof. 1992–94, Prof. 1994–, Chair. Dept of Political Science 1995–98, Assoc. Provost for Educ. and Research 1998–, William R. Kenan Jr Prof. in Political Science –2001, currently Charles L. Hutchinson Distinguished Service Prof. and Dean of Social Sciences Div.; Prof. of Govt, Harvard Univ. 2001; Fellow, American Acad. of Arts and Sciences 2003; mem. Bd of Overseers, American Nat. Election Studies; Heinz Eulau Award, American Political Science Asscn for the Best Article Published in the American Political Science Review in 1998, 1999. *Publications:* Mobilization, Participation and Democracy in America (with Steven Rosenstone) (Outstanding Book Award, Nat. Conf. of Black Political Scientists 1995) 1993, Gaining Access: Congress and the Farm Lobby, 1919–1981 1991; numerous papers and articles on interest groups, citizen activism, public opinion, public budgeting and politicians' inferences from the outcomes of elections. *Address:* Office of the Dean, Social Sciences Division, 1126 E 59th Street, SS 110, Chicago, IL 60637, USA (office). *Telephone:* (773) 702-8798 (office). *Fax:* (773) 702-9029 (office). *E-mail:* jhansen@uchicago.edu (office). *Website:* www.uchicago.edu (office).

HANSEN, Kai Aaen, MSc(Econ); Danish central banker and international civil servant; b. 26 Nov. 1942, Hadsten; s. of Hans Helge Hansen and Kathrine Elisabeth Hansen; m. Ann Marie Skovløv 1970; ed Univ. of Århus; economist, Danmarks Nationalbank (Cen. Bank of Denmark) 1972–77, Asst Head of Dept 1980–82, Head of Dept 1985–91, Dir 1992–97, 2000–11, Consultant 2011–; economist, OECD, Paris 1977–80; Econ. Adviser, IMF, Washington, DC 1983–85, Exec. Dir 1998–2000; Deputy Chair. Nordic Comm. on Money Transmission 1981–83; mem. UN Informal Group on Money Transmission 1981–83, Govt Comm. on Money Transmission 1982–83, Econ. Ministry Cttee on Econ. Policies 1987–91, on Econ. and Monetary Union Issues 1996–97; Alt. mem. EU Comm. of Cen. Bank Govs 1991–94, European Monetary Comm. 1987–93; Alt. Council mem. European Monetary Inst. 1994–97; Chair. Nordic-Baltic Monetary and Financial Alt. Cttee 2000–04, Nordic-Baltic Cttee on IMF Governance 2005–06; mem. Int. Relations Cttee, European Cen. Bank 2000–, Sub-cttee on Int. Monetary and Finance Insts, EU/EFC 2000–; Asst Prof. (part-time), Copenhagen School of Econs 1974–77, 1980–83; Kt, First Degree, Order of Dannebrog. *Publications:* The International Monetary System, an Essay to Interpretation (with Erik Hoffmeyer) 1991, Pengepolitiske Problem-stillinger (with Erik Hoffmeyer) 1993. *Leisure interest:* history. *Address:* Danmarks Nationalbank, Havnegade 5, 1093 Copenhagen, Denmark (office). *Telephone:* 33-63-60-70 (office). *Fax:* 33-63-71-29 (office). *E-mail:* kah@nationalbanken.dk (office). *Website:* www.nationalbanken.dk (office).

HANSEN, Lars Peter, BS, PhD; American economist and academic; *David Rockefeller Distinguished Service Professor in Economics, Statistics, Department of Economics, University of Chicago;* b. 26 Oct. 1952; m. Grace Tsiang; one c.; ed Univ. of Minn., Utah State Univ.; Asst Prof., Carnegie-Mellon Univ. 1978–80, Assoc. Prof., Grad. School of Industrial Admin 1980–81; Visiting Assoc. Prof., Univ. of Chicago 1981–82, Prof. 1984–90, Homer J. Livingston Prof. in Econs 1990–97, Homer J. Livingston Distinguished Service Prof., Dept of Econs 1997–2008, David Rockefeller Distinguished Service Prof. in Econs, Statistics and the Coll. 2008–, Dir of Grad. Studies, Dept of Econs 1988–94, Chair. Dept of Econs 1998–2002, Research Dir Becker Friedman Inst.; Visiting Assoc. Prof., MIT 1983; Visiting Prof., Dept of Econs, Harvard Univ. 1986, Stanford Univ. 1989–90, Univ. of Chicago Grad. School of Business 2003–05; Project Dir, Macroeconomic Modeling and Systemic Risk Research Initiative; fmr Co-Ed. Econometrics, Journal of Political Economy; Research Assoc., Econs Research Center, N.O.R.C. 1984–; mem. Bd Govs, The Stevanovich Center for Financial Math.; mem. American Acad. of Arts and Sciences; Fellow, Sloan Foundation 1982, Econometric Soc. 1985 (First Vice-Pres. 2006), NAS; Distinguished Fellow, Macro Finance Soc.; Guggenheim Fellow, Frisch Prize (co-winner), Econometric Soc. 1984, Faculty Award for Excellence in Grad. Teaching, Univ. of Chicago 1997–98, Erwin Plein Nemmers Prize in Econs 2006, CME Group-MSRI Prize in Innovative Quantitative Applications 2008, Nobel Prize in Econs (with Eugene Fama and Robert Shiller) 2013. *Achievements include:* inventor of statistical technique GMM or Generalized Method of Moments 1982. *Publications:* author or co-author of numerous articles and books, including Robust Control and Economic Model Uncertainty (with Thomas J. Sargent); co-ed. Handbook of Financial Econometrics. *Address:* Department of Economics, University of Chicago, 1126 East 59th Street, Chicago, IL 60637, USA (office). *Telephone:* (773) 702-8170 (office); (773) 702-3908 (Asst) (office). *Fax:* (773) 702-8490 (office). *E-mail:* lhansen@uchicago.edu (office). *Website:* larspeterhansen.org (office).

HANSEN, Mogens Herman, DPhil; Danish reader in classical philology; *Associate Professor, The SAXO Institute, University of Copenhagen;* b. 20 Aug. 1940, Copenhagen; s. of Herman Hansen and Gudrun Maria (née Heslet) Hansen; m. Birgitte Holt Larsen; one s.; ed Univ. of Copenhagen; Research Fellow, Inst. of Classics, Univ. of Copenhagen 1967–69, Lecturer in Classical Philology 1969–88, Reader in Greek 1989–, currently Assoc. Prof., The SAXO Inst.; Dir The Copenhagen Polis Centre 1993–2005; Visiting Fellow, Wolfson Coll., Cambridge, UK 1974; Visiting Prof., Univ. of Melbourne, Australia 1988, Univ. of British Columbia, Canada 2001; mem. Inst. for Advanced Study, Princeton, NJ, USA 1983; Corresp. Fellow, Deutsches Archaeologisches Institut 1995, British Acad. 1997; Fellow, Royal Danish Acad. of Sciences and Letters 1987; Kt of the Dannebrog; Einar Hansen Stipendium 2000, Fordyce Mitchel Memorial Lecturer 2004, Gad Rausing Prize for outstanding research in the humanities 2007, Royal Swedish Acad. 1997; Fellow, Royal Danish Acad. of Sciences and Letters 1987 1987, British Acad. Lecturer 2010. *Publications include:* The Sovereignty of the People's Court in 4th Century Athens 1974, Eisangelia 1975, Aspects of Athenian Society 1975, Apagoge, Endeixis and Ephegesis 1976, The Athenian Ecclesia I 1983, II 1989, Demography and Democracy 1985, The Athenian Assembly 1987, The Athenian

Democracy in the Age of Demosthenes 1991, Acts of the Copenhagen Polis Centre I 1993, II 1995, III 1996, IV 1997, V 1998, VI 1999, VII 2005, Papers from the Copenhagen Polis Centre I 1994, II 1995, III 1996, IV 1997, V 2000, VI 2002, VII 2004, VIII 2007, A Comparative Study of Thirty City-State Cultures 2000, A Comparative Study of Six City-State Cultures 2002, An Inventory of Archaic and Classical Poleis 2004, The Tradition of Ancient Greek Democracy and Its Importance for Modern Democracy 2005, The Shotgun Method – The Demography of the Ancient Greek City-State 2006, Polis – An Introduction to the Ancient Greek City-State 2007, Démocratie Athénienne – démocratie moderne: Tradition and influences. Fondation Hardt Entretiens sur l'Antiquité Classique 2009; more than 150 articles in int. journals on Athenian democracy and ancient Greek constitutional history. *Leisure interests:* playing the flute, writing poetry, book binding. *Address:* The SAXO Institute, University of Copenhagen, Njalsgade 80, 2300 Copenhagen S (office); Wilhelm Marstrandsgade 15, 2100 Copenhagen Ø, Denmark (home). *Telephone:* 35-32-91-03 (office); 35-26-15-88 (home). *E-mail:* mhh@hum.ku.dk (office). *Website:* saxoinstitute.ku.dk (office).

HANSENNE, Michel, DenD; Belgian politician; b. 23 March 1940, Rotheux-Rimiere; MP 1974–89; Minister of French Culture 1979–81, of Employment and Labour 1981–88, for Civil Service 1988–89; Dir-Gen. Int. Labour Org., Geneva 1989–98; MEP 1999–. *Publication:* Emploi, les scénarios du possible. *Address:* European Parliament, Plateau du Kirchberg, B.P. 1601, 2929, Luxembourg. *E-mail:* mhansenne@europarl.eu.int.

HANSKI, Ilkka A., BSc, LicBiol, DPhil; Finnish zoologist, ecologist and academic; *Professor of Ecology and Evolutionary Biology, University of Helsinki;* b. 14 Feb. 1953, Lempäälä; m.; ed Univ. of Helsinki, Univ. of Oxford, UK; worked at Acad. of Finland 1978–88, 1991–92; Docent, Univ. of Helsinki 1981–3, Univ. of Joensuu 1983; Acting Prof. of Zoology, Univ. of Helsinki 1988–91, Prof. of Zoology 1993–, also Prof. of Ecology and Evolutionary Biology; Academy Prof., Acad. of Finland 1996–; Foreign mem. Royal Swedish Acad. of Sciences 2000, Royal Soc.; Hon. FRS 2005; Hon. Fellow, NAS 2006 Balzan Prize for Ecological Sciences 2000, Crafoord Prize, Royal Swedish Acad. of Sciences 2011. *Publications:* numerous papers in professional journals. *Address:* Metapopulation Research Group, Department of Ecology and Evolutionary Biology, PO Box (Viikinkaari 1), University of Helsinki, 00014 Helsinki, Finland (office). *Telephone:* (9) 191-57745 (office). *Fax:* (9) 191-57694 (office). *E-mail:* ilkka.hanski@helsinki.fi (office). *Website:* www.helsinki.fi/~ihanski (office).

HANSON, Curtis; American film director and screenwriter; b. 24 March 1945, Los Angeles, Calif.; s. of Wilbur Hale Bill Hanson and Beverly June Hanson; Ed. Cinema magazine; began film career as screenplay writer; mem. Bd Govs Acad. of Motion Picture Arts and Sciences 2001–; Hon. Chair. UCLA Film and TV Archive. *Films directed:* The Arousers 1970, Sweet Kill (also screenplay) 1972, Little Dragons (also co-producer) 1977, Losin' It 1983, The Bedroom Window (also screenplay) 1988, Bad Influence 1990, The Hand that Rocks the Cradle 1992, The River Wild 1994, LA Confidential 1998, The Children of Times Square (TV film), Wonder Boys 1999, 8 Mile 2002, In Her Shoes (also producer) 2005, Lucky You 2007, Chasing Mavericks 2012. *Screenplays:* The Dunwich Horror 1970, The Silent Partner 1978, White Dog 1982, Never Cry Wolf 1983. *Television:* Hitchcock: Shadow of a Genius (actor) 1999, Three Rivers 2010. *Address:* United Talent Agency, 9560 Wilshire Boulevard, Floor 5, Beverly Hills, CA 90212, USA.

HANSON, Sir John Gilbert, KCMG, CBE, MA; British fmr government official and fmr university college warden; *Honorary Fellow, Green Templeton College, Oxford;* b. 16 Nov. 1938, Sheffield, Yorks., England; s. of Gilbert F. Hanson and Gladys Kay; m. Margaret Clark 1962 (died 2003); three s.; ed Manchester Grammar School, Wadham Coll. Oxford; War Office 1961–63; British Council, Madras, India 1963–66; Middle East Centre for Arab Studies, Lebanon 1966–68; British Council, Bahrain 1968–72, London HQ 1972–75, Dir British Council, Iran and Cultural Counsellor, Embassy in Tehran 1975–79, Controller (Finance), British Council, London 1979–82; Royal Coll. of Defence Studies 1983; Dir British Council, India and Minister (Cultural), High Comm. in New Delhi 1984–88; Deputy Dir-Gen. British Council 1988–92, Dir-Gen. 1992–98; Warden Green Templeton Coll., Oxford 1998–2006; Chair. Trustees, British Skin Foundation 1997–2002, Bahrain-British Foundation 1997–2002; mem. Gov. Council, SOAS 1991–99, Univ. of London 1996–98; Pres. UK Council for Overseas Student Affairs 1999–2001; Trustee, Charles Wallace (India) Trust 1998–2000; Patron GAP 1989–98; Hon. Fellow, Wadham Coll., Oxford 1997, St Edmund's Coll., Cambridge 1998, Green Templeton Coll., Oxford; Hon. Freeman, The Girdlers Co. 2010; Hon. DLitt (Oxford Brookes) 1995, (Lincolnshire & Humberside) 1996, (Greenwich) 1996; Great Gold Medal, Comenius Univ. (Slovakia) 1997. *Leisure interests:* music, sport, foreign affairs. *Address:* c/o Green Templeton College, 43 Woodstock Road, Oxford, OX2 6HG, England. *Telephone:* (1865) 274770 (office).

HANSON, Margus, PhD; Estonian politician and academic; b. 6 Jan. 1958, Tartu; m.; two s. one d.; ed Tartu Secondary School No. 2, Leningrad Inst. of Financial Economy, Tartu State Univ.; engineer, Lab. of Educational Sociology, Tartu Univ. 1981–84, Asst to Chair of Finance and Credit 1984–87, Sr Lecturer 1990–91, Lecturer and Assoc. Prof. of Public Finance, Inst. of Econ. Policy and Public Economy 1992–94; Chair. Bd Estonian Commercial Bank of Industry and Construction 1995–96; Head of Tartu Br., Tallinn Bank 1996–97; mem. Tartu City Council 1996, 1999, 2002; Deputy Mayor of Tartu 1997–2003; mem. Riigikogu (Parl.) 2003–, mem. Nat. Defence Cttee; Minister of Defence 2003–04 (resgnd); professional training courses with Bank of Finland 1990–91, World Bank and Soros Foundation 1992, Austrian Bankers Club 1995, Estonian Banking Asscn, Barcelona 1996; mem. Eesti Reformierakond (Estonian Reform Party), Tartu Rotary Club. *Address:* Riigikogu, Lossi plats 1A, 15165 Tallinn, Estonia (office). *Telephone:* 631-6572 (office). *Fax:* 631-6334 (office). *E-mail:* margus.hanson@riigikogu.ee (office). *Website:* www.riigikogu.ee (office).

HANSSON, Ardo Hillar, BA (Hons), MA, PhD; Estonian academic and central banker; *Governor, Bank of Estonia;* b. 15 July 1958, Chicago, Ill., USA; m.; two s.; ed Semiahmoo Senior Secondary School and Univ. of British Columbia, Canada, Harvard Univ., USA; Research Asst, Univ. of British Columbia 1980–82, Lecturer, Dept of Econs 1987–90; Research Asst, Harvard Univ. 1984–87; Researcher, WIDER Inst./Jeffrey D. Sachs & Assocs, United Nations Univ. 1990–92; short-term econ. adviser to the govts and central banks of Poland, Slovenia, Mongolia

and Ukraine 1990–96; Adviser to Minister of Foreign Affairs 1991–92; Alt. mem. Monetary Reform Cttee of the Repub. of Estonia 1992; Econ. Adviser to the Prime Minister of Estonia 1992–94, 1997; Researcher, Stockholm School of Econs 1992–96; Head of Working Group on Econ. Co-operation, Council of the Baltic Sea States 1993–94; mem. Supervisory Bd Eesti Pank (Bank of Estonia) 1993–98, Gov. 2012–; Economist for Poland and the Baltic States, World Bank 1998–99, Sr Economist for Lithuania 1999–2000, Sr Economist for Yugoslavia 2000–02, Lead Economist for Serbia and Montenegro 2002–03, Lead Economist for the Western Balkans 2003–08, Chief of Econ. Policy Unit in China 2008–12; mem. Bd Estonian Railways 1997; Order of the White Star (Third Class) 1998; Luup magazine Person of the Year 1997. *Address:* Bank of Estonia (Eesti Pank), Estonia pst. 13, Tallinn 15095, Estonia (office). *Telephone:* 668-0810 (office). *Fax:* 668-0836 (office). *E-mail:* info@eestipank.ee (office). *Website:* www.eestipank.ee (office).

HANWAY, H. Edward, BA, MBA, CPA; American insurance executive; b. 1951; m. Ellen Hanway; three c.; ed Loyola Coll. of Baltimore, Widener Univ.; joined CIGNA Corpn 1978, Pres. CIGNA Int. 1989–96, mem. Bd of Dirs 1992–, Pres. CIGNA HealthCare 1996–99, Pres. Cigna Corpn 1999–2008, COO 1999–2000, CEO Jan. 2000–, Chair. Dec. 2000–09; mem. Bd of Dirs Philadelphia Orchestra, Council for Affordable Quality Healthcare 2000– (Treas. 2000–01, Chair. 2001–02), Alliance for Health Reform, Marsh & McLennan Companies, Inc. (Ind. Dir) 2010–; fmr mem. Bd of Dirs America's Health Insurance Plans; mem. Bd of Advisors March of Dimes Foundation; mem. Pennsylvania and American Insts of Certified Public Accountants; Trustee, Loyola Coll. of Baltimore, Eisenhower Exchange Fellowships; Outstanding Alumnus Award, Loyola Coll. of Baltimore 2002. *Address:* Marsh & McLennan Companies Inc., 1166 Avenue of the Americas, New York, NY 10036, USA (office). *Telephone:* (212) 345-5000 (office). *Fax:* (212) 345-4808 (office). *E-mail:* info@mmc.com (office). *Website:* www.mmc.com (office).

HAO, Bailin; Chinese physicist and academic; *Professor, Department of Physics, Fudan University;* b. 26 June 1934, Beijing; s. of Hao Kingsheng and Zhao Weimei; m. Zhang Shuyu 1959; one s. one d.; ed Kharkov State Univ., Ukraine; Research Asst, Inst. of Physics, Academia Sinica 1959–63, Research Assoc. 1963–78, Research Prof. 1978–2005 (Dir Inst. of Theoretical Physics 1990–94); Prof., Fudan Univ. 2005–; mem. Chinese Acad. of Sciences 1980–; External Faculty mem., Santa Fe Inst., NM, USA 2002–03, 2005–11; mem. Third World Acad. of Sciences 1995; Science and Tech. Progress Award 1987, Nat. Award in Natural Science 1993, 2000, Chinese Acad. of Sciences Award 1992, 1999, He-Liang-He-Li Award in Physics 2001, Nat. SciTech Award 2007. *Publications:* 10 books, including Applied Symbolic Dynamics and Chaos 1998; 130 scientific papers on theoretical physics, computational physics, nonlinear science and theoretical life science. *Leisure interest:* reading classical Chinese poems. *Address:* c/o Institute of Theoretical Physics, 55 Zhongguancun East Road, Beijing 100190 (office); Apartment 1601, Building A801, Huangzhaung Complex, Academy of Sciences, Haidian District, Beijing 100190, People's Republic of China (home). *Telephone:* (10) 62541807 (office); (10) 82661757 (home). *Fax:* (10) 62562587 (office). *E-mail:* hao@mail.itp.ac.cn (office). *Website:* www.itp.ac.cn/~hao (office).

HAOMAE, William Ni'i; Solomon Islands politician; b. 26 Nov. 1960, Mou Village, Small Malaita; m. Filistas T. Haomae; two s. two d.; ed East-West Centre, Honolulu; early govt posts include Information Officer, Prime Minister's Office, Press Sec. to the Prime Minister, Foreign Affairs Information Officer, Ministry of Foreign Affairs, Dir of Information Dept, Prime Minister's Office; mem. Parl. from Small Malaita, Malaita Prov. 1993–, mem. Parl. House Cttee July–Dec. 2007, Foreign Relations Cttee 2006–07; Minister for Culture, Tourism and Aviation 1994–97, for Police and Justice 2000–01; Deputy Prime Minister and Caretaker Minister for Nat. Unity, Reconciliation and Peace Aug.–Dec. 2001; Minister for Police and Nat. Security April–May 2006; Minister of Foreign Affairs, External Trade and Immigration 2007–10. *Leisure interests:* reading, gardening, fishing, soccer. *Address:* c/o Ministry of Foreign Affairs, External Trade and Tourism, PO Box G26, Honiara, Solomon Islands (office).

HAQ, Gen. Ehsan-ul-; Pakistani army officer; b. 22 Sept. 1949; ed Command and Staff Coll., Quetta, Nat. Defence Coll., Islamabad; first commissioned Army Air Defence Regt 1969, fmr Head of Mil. Intelligence, promoted to Lt-Gen. 2001, to Gen. 2004, Chair. Jt Chiefs of Staff Cttee 2004–07, Dir-Gen. Inter-Services Intelligence; Hilal-e-Imtiaz (Mil.). *Address:* c/o Joint Staff Headquarters, Chaklala, Rawalpindi, Pakistan. *Telephone:* (51) 8462336.

HAQ, Maulvi Anwar ul-; Pakistani lawyer and judge; practising lawyer of High Court and Supreme Court for many years; served as judge of Lahore High Court for 10 years; Deputy Attorney-Gen. during premiership of Mian Nawaz Sharif 1990s; one of judges of Lahore High Court who took oath on Provisional Constitutional Order of Gen. Pervez Musharraf in violation of Supreme Court verdict of 3 Nov. 2007, received notice of court contempt and tendered his resignation following Supreme Court verdict declaring 3 Nov. steps as extraconstitutional; Attorney-Gen. 2010–12. *Address:* c/o Office of the Attorney General, Supreme Court of Pakistan, Constitution Avenue, Islamabad, Pakistan.

HAQQANI, Husain, BA, MA; Pakistani journalist and diplomatist; b. 1 July 1956, Karachi; ed Univ. of Karachi; started career as journalist, wrote numerous articles on nat. and int. politics published by Pakistan's leading newspapers Jang (Urdu) and Dawn (English); worked in Hong Kong as East Asian Corresp. for London-based Arabia – the Islamic World Review 1980–84; wrote extensively on Muslims in China and East Asia and Islamic political movts in aftermath of Iranian Revolution of 1979; Pakistan and Afghanistan Corresp. for Far Eastern Economic Review 1984–88; covered Pakistani politics, India-Pakistan relations and war in Afghanistan; contributed to Voice of America radio 1984–86; syndicated columnist for The Indian Express, Gulf News, Oman Tribune, Daily Star (Bangladesh) and The Nation (Pakistani newspaper); Special Asst to Chief Minister, Punjab 1988–90; served as main Opposition Spokesman, represented Opposition at int. forums, including in negotiations with US Govt; organized past. election campaign for IJI alliance led by Nawaz Sharif 1988; Special Asst to Prime Minister Ghulam Mustafa Jatoi 1990, Special Asst and Prin. Spokesman of Prime Minister Nawaz Sharif 1990–92, represented Prime Minister in talks with US Govt over imposition of sanctions in retaliation for Pakistan's nuclear programme; Amb. to Sri Lanka 1992–93; worked in parl. election campaign for Peoples Democratic Front led by Mohtarma Benazir Bhutto 1993, Spokesman for Prime

Minister Benazir Bhutto with rank of Minister of State, and Fed. Sec. for Information and Broadcasting 1993–95; Chair. House Building Finance Corpn 1995–96; Assoc. Prof. for Int. Relations, Boston Univ. 2004–; Co-Chair. Project on Islam and Democracy, Hudson Inst., Washington, DC 2004–; Ed. Current Trends in Islamists Ideology (journal) 2004–; Visiting Scholar, Carnegie Endowment for Int. Peace, Washington DC 2002–05; Professional Lecturer, School of Advanced Int. Studies, Johns Hopkins Univ., Washington, DC 2003–04; Amb. to USA 2008–11 (resgnd); mem. South Asia Council, Asscn of Asian Studies 2007. *Publications:* Pakistan Between Mosque and Military 2005; numerous book chapters and articles and more than 390 op-ed articles in newspapers and magazines 2000–; articles have been published in The Wall Street Journal, The New York Times, Boston Globe, Financial Times, International Herald Tribune, South China Morning Port, Indian Express, The Hindu, Toronto Globe and Mail, The Ottawa Citizen, Arab News, The New Republic, Gulf News and Le Monde. *Address:* Ministry of Foreign Affairs, Constitution Avenue, Islamabad (office). *Telephone:* (51) 9210335 (office). *Fax:* (51) 9207600 (office). *Website:* www.mofa.gov.pk (office).

HARA, Hiroshi, DArch; Japanese architect and academic; *Professor Emeritus, University of Tokyo;* b. 9 Sept. 1936, Kawasaki, Kanagawa Pref.; ed Univ. of Tokyo; mem. generation of avant-garde New Wave architects; developed unique anthropological approach and theories of design from studies of vernacular architecture and indigenous settlements; conducted research trips in Europe, Asia and Africa; Asst Prof., then Prof., Inst. of Industrial Science, Univ. of Tokyo 1969–97, Prof. Emer. 1997–; cr. so-called 'reflection houses' in 1970s; began receiving commissions for large public bldgs 1980s; developed style of 'architecture of modality' whereby bldgs became metaphors of 'cities with the city' late 1980s; began designing 'modal spaces of consciousness' inspired by electronic and information technologies 1990s; began designing futuristic spaceship-like urban-scale projects late 1990s; Victor L. Regnier Chair in Architecture, Dept of Architecture, Kan. State Univ., USA 2004–05; Murano Togo Prize 1986, Suntory Arts and Science Prize 1988. *Publications:* Hiroshi Hara (co-author) 1993, The Floating World of Architecture (co-author) 2001; numerous monographs, chapters in books and articles in professional journals. *Address:* c/o Department of Architecture, Faculty of Engineering, the University of Tokyo, 7-3-1 Hongo, Bunkyo-ku, Tokyo 113-8654, Japan.

HARA, Kazuo; Japanese film director; b. 8 June 1945, Yamaguchi; m. Sachiko Kobayashi; known for creating films that blur the distinction between documentary films and fiction films, so-called 'action documentaries'; co-f. Shissō Productions 1971. *Films include:* Sayonara CP (Goodbye, CP) 1972, Gokushiteki erosu: Renka 1974 (Extreme Private Eros: Love Song 1974) 1974, Umi to dokuyaku (The Sea and Poison: Asst Dir) 1986, Yuki Yukite shingun (The Emperor's Naked Army Marches On: KNF Award, Director's Guild of Japan New Director's Award 1986, Caligari Film Award, Berlin Film Festival 1987) 1986, Sen no Rikyu (Death of a Tea Master: Asst Dir) 1989, Shikibu monogatari (Mount Aso's Passions: Chief Asst Dir) 1989, Zenshin shosetsuka (A Dedicated Life) 1994, Fukai kawa (Deep River: Second Unit Dir) 1995, Watashi no Mishima 1999, Mata no hi no Chika 2005, Kaitei Mikan no Kawa Mairu 2009. *Television include:* National Kid 1960, Air in Summer Kôhen: Ametsuchi-Universe 2005, ETV Tokushû 2007. *Address:* Shisso Productions, 1-15-16-202 Shinjuku, Shinjuku-ku, Tokyo 160-0022, Japan.

HARABIN, Štefan, DJur; Slovak judge and politician; *President, Supreme Court;* b. 4 May 1957, Lubica; m.; four c.; ed Univ. of Pavel Jozef Šafárik, Košice; Judge, Dist Court, Poprad 1983–90, Regional Court, Košice 1990–91; Judge of the Supreme Court 1991–98, Pres. of the Supreme Court 1998–2003, 2009–, Chair. Criminal Panel 2003–06; Head of Penal Dept, Section of Justice Admin., Ministry of Justice 1991–92; Pres. of Senate and Penal Bd 1996–98; Pres. Judicial Council 2002–03; Deputy Prime Minister and Minister of Justice 2006–09. *Address:* Supreme Court of the Slovak Republic, Župné nám. 13, 814 90 Bratislava, Slovakia (office). *Telephone:* (2) 5935-3111 (office). *Fax:* (2) 5441-1535 (office). *Website:* www.nssr.gov.sk (office).

HARAD, George Jay, BA, MBA; American business executive; b. 24 April 1944, Newark, NJ; s. of Sidney Harad and Irma Harad; m. Beverly Marcia Harad 1966; one s. one d.; ed Franklin & Marshall Coll., Harvard Business School; Admin. Asst to Sr Vice-Pres. Housing Group, Boise Cascade Corpn 1971–72, Finance Man. Boise Cascade Realty Group 1972–76; Man. Corp. Devt, Boise Cascade Corpn 1976–80, Dir Retirement Funds 1980–82, Vice-Pres. Controller 1982–84, Sr Vice-Pres., Chief Financial Officer 1984–89, Exec. Vice-Pres., Chief Financial Officer 1989–90, Exec. Vice-Pres. Paper 1990–91, Pres., COO 1991–94, Pres., CEO 1994–95, Chair. Bd and CEO 1995–2004; Chair. Harad Capital Management LLC 2004–; Exec. Chair. OfficeMax Inc. 2004–05 (retd); mem. Bd of Dirs Clorox Co. 2006–; George F. Baker Scholar, Harvard Univ. 1970–71; Frederick Roe Fellow, Harvard Univ. 1971; Executive Papermaker of the Year Award, PaperAge Magazine 2001. *Leisure interests:* golf, skiing. *Address:* c/o Board of Directors, Clorox Company, 1221 Broadway, Oakland, CA 94612-1888, USA.

HARADA, Akihiko; Japanese business executive; fmr Pres. and Rep. Dir Maxvalu Tohoku Co. Ltd and Maxvalu Nishinihon Co. Ltd; Chair. Aeon Co. Ltd 2008–11. *Address:* c/o AEON Co. Ltd, 1-5-1 Nakase, Mihama-ku, Chiba-shi, Chiba 261-8515, Japan. *E-mail:* info@aeon.info.

HARADA, Minoru; Japanese religious leader; *President, Soka Gakkai;* b. 8 Nov. 1941, Tokyo; s. of Eiji Harada and Yuriko Harada; m. Kimie Harada 1968; two s.; ed Univ. of Tokyo; with Soka Gakkai (Buddhist network), Japan 1953–, Head of Student Div. 1973–76, Head of Youth Div. 1976–77, Vice-Pres. 1977–2001, Sec.-Gen. 1984–2006, Vice-Gen. Dir 2001–06, Pres. 2006–, Vice-Pres. Soka Gakkai International 2003–07, Deputy Pres. 2007–. *Leisure interests:* reading, watching sports. *Address:* Soka Gakkai Headquarters, 32 Shinano-machi, Shinjuku-ku, Tokyo 160-8583 Japan (office). *Telephone:* (3) 3353-7111 (office). *Website:* www.sgi.org (office).

HARADINAJ, Ramush, MBA; Kosovo politician and fmr guerrilla leader; *President, Alliance for the Future of Kosovo;* b. 3 July 1968, Gllogjan/Gloḍane, nr Deçan/Dečani; m. 1st one s.; m. 2nd Anita Haradinaj; two s. one d.; ed High School, Gjakovë/Ðakovica, Faculty of Law, Univ. of Prishtina, American Univ. of Kosovo (associated with Rochester Inst. of Tech.); nat. mil. service in Yugoslav People's Army 1987; emigrated to Switzerland 1991; returned to Kosovo 1998; Commdr

Kosovo Liberation Army 1998–99; Co-founder and Pres. Aleanca për Ardhmërinë e Kosovës (Alliance for the Future of Kosovo) 2001–; Prime Minister of Kosovo Dec. 2004–March 2005 (resgnd); acquitted of war crimes by Int. War Crimes Tribunal, The Hague 3 April 2008; asked by Ugandan Rebel Group 'Allied Democratic Forces' to mediate peace talks with Cen. Govt in Kampala Feb. 2009; re-arrested to face a partial retrial 21 July 2010, trial began 2011, acquitted for a second time 29 Nov. 2012. *Address:* Alliance for the Future of Kosovo (Aleanca për Ardhmërinë e Kosovës), 10000 Prishtina, Bulevardi i Dëshmorëve 49, Kosovo (office). *Telephone:* (38) 544188 (office). *E-mail:* info@aak-ks.com (office). *Website:* www.aak-ks.com (office).

HARAGUCHI, Kazuhiro; Japanese politician; b. 2 July 1959, Saga Pref.; ed Tokyo Univ., Matsushita Inst. of Govt and Man., Chigasaki; elected mem. Saga Prefectural Ass. (LDP) 1987, served two terms; mem. House of Reps for Saga No. 1 constituency 1996–, Sr Dir Parl. Cttee on Internal Affairs and Communications; mem. Shinshinto (New Frontier Party) –1998, mem. Democratic Party of Japan (DPJ) 1998–; Minister of Internal Affairs and Communications and Minister of State for Promotion of Regional Sovereignty 2009–10. *Address:* c/o Ministry of Internal Affairs and Communications, 2-1-2, Kasumigaseki, Chiyoda-ku, Tokyo 100-8926, Japan (office).

HARALD V, HM The King of Norway; b. 21 Feb. 1937, Skaugum; s. of the late King Olav V and Crown Princess Märtha; m. Sonja Haraldsen 1968 (now HM Queen Sonja); one s. (HRH Crown Prince Haakon) one d.; ed Oslo Katedralskole, Cavalry Officers' Cand. School, Mil. Acad. and Balliol Coll. Oxford; lived in Washington, DC 1940–45; has participated in many int. sailing competitions representing Norway at Olympic Games several times; undertook frequent official visits abroad while Crown Prince; succeeded his father, King Olav V 17 Jan. 1991. *Address:* Royal Palace, 0010 Oslo, Norway. *Telephone:* 22-04-87-00. *Website:* www.kongehuset.no.

HARASZTI, Miklós; Hungarian writer, journalist, human rights advocate, international organization executive and academic; b. 1945, Jerusalem, Israel; ed Budapest Univ.; co-f. Hungarian Democratic Opposition Movt 1976; Ed. samizdat periodical Beszélo 1980; participated in roundtable negotiations on transition to free elections 1989; mem. Hungarian Parl. 1990–94; currently Lecturer, Budapest Study Center, Univ. of California; Rep. on Freedom of the Media, OSCE 2004–10; Dr hc (Northwestern Univ., USA) 1996. *Publications:* A Worker in a Worker's State, The Velvet Prison (both translated into several languages); several essays have been published in The New York Times and The Washington Post. *Address:* Budapest Study Center KHT, Eötvös Loránd University, Pazmany Peter setany 1/A, 1117 Budapest, Hungary (office).

HARBERGER, Arnold C., PhD; American economist and academic; *Professor, Department of Economics, University of California, Los Angeles;* b. 27 July 1924, Newark, NJ; s. of Ferdinand C. Harberger and Martha L. Bucher; m. 1958; two s.; ed Univ. of Chicago; Asst Prof., Johns Hopkins Univ., Baltimore, Md 1949–53; Assoc. Prof., Univ. of Chicago 1953–59, Prof. 1959–76, Gustavus F. and Ann M. Swift Distinguished Service Prof. 1976–91, Prof. Emer. 1991–; Prof. of Econs, UCLA 1984–; Pres. Western Econ. Asscn 1988–89, American Econ. Asscn 1997; consultant to numerous econ. govt depts and int. orgs; Fellow, Econometric Soc. 1967, American Acad. of Arts and Sciences 1969; mem. NAS 1989. *Publications:* Project Evaluation 1972, Taxation and Welfare 1974, World Economic Growth 1984. *Address:* 8283 Bunche Hall, University of California at Los Angeles, 405 Hilgard Avenue, Los Angeles, CA 90095 (office); 136 Buckskin Road, Bell Canyon, CA 91307, USA (home). *Telephone:* (310) 825-1011 (office). *Fax:* (310) 825-9528 (office). *E-mail:* harberger@econ.ucla.edu (office). *Website:* econweb.sscnet.ucla.edu (office).

HARBI, Mohammed; Algerian politician, historian and academic; b. 16 June 1933, El-Arrouch; s. of Brahimi Harbi; m. (divorced); c.; ed Sorbonne; joined Parti du people algérien 1948; various posts with Front de Libération Nationale (FLN) 1954–62, including Leader, French Div. 1957, Dir FLN cabinet 1959, FLN Rep. in Cairo 1960, Del. Evian Accord negotiations 1961; Adviser to Pres. Ahmed Ben Bella 1963; Founding mem. Organisation de la résistance populaire 1965; imprisoned 1964–71, house arrest 1971; fled to France 1973; Lecturer in Sociology, Univ. de Paris-V, Prof. of History, Paris-VII 1974. *Publications include:* Aux origines du Front de libération nationale 1975, FLN: Mirage et réalité 1980, L'Algérie et son destin, La guerre commence en Algérie; Mémoires politiques Tome 1: 1945–1962 (first volume of his political memoirs) 2001.

HARBINSON, Stuart Wreford, OBE, JP; British lawyer and international organization official; b. 1948; m.; one s.; ed Univ. of Cambridge; Perm. Rep. to WTO, Geneva 1994–2002, Chair. Gen. Council 2001–02, Chair. Special Sessions of WTO Cttee on Agric. 2002–03, Chief of Staff, Office of the Dir-Gen 2002–05, Special Adviser to Dir-Gen 2005–07; fmr Chair. special sessions of negotiations on agriculture, working party on Tonga accession; currently working on projects with UNCTAD Secr., Geneva; fmr Adviser, Winston & Strawn LLP (law firm), Geneva; Special Adviser Fipra 2012–; fmr Chair. Int. Textiles and Clothing Bureau; Gold Bauhinia Star 2002. *Address:* Fipra, 62 rue Liotard, 1203 Geneva, Switzerland (office). *Telephone:* (450) 03-5857 (office).

HARBISON, Peter, MA, DPhil, MRIA, FSA; Irish archaeologist, art historian and editor; *Honorary Academic Editor, Royal Irish Academy;* b. 14 Jan. 1939, Dublin; s. of Dr James Austin Harbison and Sheelagh Harbison (née McSherry); m. Edelgard Soergel 1969 (died 2008); three s.; ed St Gerard's School, Bray, Glenstal, Univ. Coll. Dublin and Univs of Marburg, Kiel and Freiburg, Germany; awarded travelling scholarship by German Archaeological Inst. 1965; archaeological officer, Irish Tourist Bd 1966–84, editorial publicity officer 1984–86, Ed. Ireland of the Welcomes (magazine) 1986–95; Sec. Friends of the Nat. Collections of Ireland 1971–76; mem. Council, Royal Irish Acad. 1981–84, 1993–96, 1998–2001, 2004–, Vice-Pres. 1992–93, 2006–07, Hon. Academic Ed. 1997–; Prof. of Archaeology, Royal Hibernian Acad. of Arts; Chair. Nat. Monuments Advisory Council 1986–90, Dublin Cemeteries Cttee 1986–89, 1996–2002, Bunratty Castle Ownership and Furniture Trusts 2004–; Vice-Pres. for Leinster, Royal Soc. of Antiquities of Ireland 2005–07; Guest Prof., Univ. of Vienna summer 2004; Corresp. mem. German Archaeological Inst.; Hon. mem. Royal Hibernian Acad. of Arts 1998, Royal Inst. of Architects of Ireland; Hon. Fellow, Trinity Coll., Dublin 2000. *Publications include:* Guide to National Monuments of Ireland 1970, The

Archaeology of Ireland 1976, Irish Art and Architecture (co-author) 1978, Pre-Christian Ireland (Archaeological Book of the Year Award 1988) 1988, Pilgrimage in Ireland 1991, Beranger's Views of Ireland 1991, The High Crosses of Ireland 1992, Irish High Crosses 1994, Ancient Ireland (with Jacqueline O'Brien) 1996, Ancient Irish Monuments 1997, Beranger's Antique Buildings of Ireland, L'Art Médiéval en Irlande 1998, Spectacular Ireland 1999, The Golden Age of Irish Art 1999, The Crucifixion in Irish Art 2000, Cooper's Ireland 2000, Our Treasure of Antiquities 2002, Treasures of the Boyne Valley 2003, Ireland's Treasures 2004, Beranger's Rambles in Ireland 2004, A Thousand Years of Church Heritage in East Galway 2005, William Burton Conyngham and his Irish Circle of Antiquarian Artists 2012; articles in books and journals. *Leisure interests:* music, travel, wining, dining, cruising. *Address:* 5 St Damian's, Loughshinny, Skerries, Co. Dublin (home); Royal Irish Academy, 19 Dawson Street, Dublin 2, Republic of Ireland (office). *Telephone:* (1) 8490940 (home); (1) 6762570 (office). *Fax:* (1) 6762346 (office). *E-mail:* p.harbison@ria.ie (office). *Website:* www.ria.ie (office).

HARCOURT, Geoffrey Colin, AO, PhD, LittD, FASSA, AcSS; Australian/British economist and academic; *Emeritus Fellow, Jesus College and Reader Emeritus in the History of Economic Theory, University of Cambridge;* b. 27 June 1931, Melbourne, Vic.; s. of Kenneth and Marjorie Harcourt (née Gans); m. Joan Bartrop 1955; two s. two d.; ed Univ. of Melbourne, Univ. of Cambridge, UK; Lecturer in Econs, Univ. of Adelaide 1958–62, Sr Lecturer 1962–65, Reader 1965–67, Prof. (Personal Chair) 1967–85, Prof. Emer. 1988–; Lecturer in Econs and Politics, Univ. of Cambridge 1964–66, 1982–90, Reader in the History of Econ. Theory 1990–98, Reader Emer. 1998–; Dir of Studies in Econs and Fellow, Trinity Hall, Cambridge 1964–66, Fellow and Lecturer in Econs, Jesus Coll., Cambridge 1982–98, Fellow Emer. 1998–, Pres. 1988–92; Leverhulme Exchange Fellow, Keio Univ., Tokyo 1969–70; Visiting Fellow, Clare Hall, Cambridge 1972–73; Visiting Prof., Univ. of Toronto, Canada 1977, 1980, Univ. of Melbourne 2002; Visiting Fellow, ANU 1997; Visiting Professorial Fellow, Univ. of New South Wales 2010–; Pres. Econ. Soc. of Australia and New Zealand 1974–77; mem. Council Royal Econ. Soc. 1990–95, Life mem. 1998–; Distinguished Fellow, Econ. Soc. of Australia 1996, History of Econs Soc., USA 2004, European Soc. for the History of Econ. Thought 2004, History of Econ. Thought Soc. of Australia 2012; Academician, Acad. of Learned Socs for the Social Sciences 2003; Fellow, Acad. of the Social Sciences in Australia 1971 (Exec. Cttee mem. 1974–77); Hon. Fellow, Queen's Coll., Melbourne 1998, Sugden Fellow 2002; Hon. Prof., Univ. of NSW 1997, 1999; Hon. mem. European Soc. for the History of Economic Thought 2004; Hon. LittD (De Montfort Univ.) 1997; Hon. DCom (Melbourne) 2003; Hon. Dr rer. pol (Fribourg) 2003; Wellington Burnham Lecturer, Tufts Univ., Medford, Mass 1975, Edward Shann Memorial Lecturer, Univ. of Western Australia 1975, Newcastle Lecturer in Political Economy, Univ. of Newcastle 1977, Acad. Lecturer, Acad. of the Social Sciences in Australia 1978, G.L. Wood Memorial Lecturer, Univ. of Melbourne 1982, John Curtin Memorial Lecturer, ANU 1982, Special Lecturer in Econs, Univ. of Manchester 1984, Lecturer, Nobel Conf. XXII, Gustavus Adolphus Coll., Minn. 1986, Laws Lecturer, Univ. of Tennessee at Knoxville 1991, Donald Horne Lecturer 1992, Sir Halford Cook Lecturer, Queen's Coll., Univ. of Melbourne, Kingsley Martin Memorial Lecturer, Cambridge 1996, Colin Clark Memorial Lecturer, Brisbane 1997, Bernard Hesketh Lecturer, Univ. of Minn., Kansas City 2006, Veblen-Commons Award, Asscn for Evolutionary Econs (USA) 2010. *Publications:* Economic Activity (with P. H. Karmel and R. H. Wallace) 1967, Readings in the Concept and Measurement of Income (co-ed.) 1969 (second edn with R. H. Parker and G. Whittington 1986), Capital and Growth, Selected Readings (co-ed.) 1971, Some Cambridge Controversies in the Theory of Capital 1972, The Microeconomic Foundations of Macroeconomics (ed.) 1977, The Social Science Imperialists, Selected Essays (ed. Prue Kerr) 1982, Keynes and his Contemporaries (ed.) 1985, Controversies in Political Economy, Selected Essays of G. C. Harcourt (ed. Omar Hamouda) 1986, International Monetary Problems and Supply-Side Economics: Essays in Honour of Lorie Tarshis (co-ed.) 1986, On Political Economists and Modern Political Economy, Selected Essays of G. C. Harcourt (co-ed.) 1992, Post-Keynesian Essays in Biography: Portraits of Twentieth Century Political Economists 1993, The Dynamics of the Wealth of Nations. Growth, Distribution and Structural Change: Essays in Honour of Luigi Pasinetti (co-ed.) 1993, Income and Employment in Theory and Practice. Essays in Memory of Athanasios Asimakopulos (co-ed.) 1994, Capitalism, Socialism and Post-Keynesianism. Selected Essays of G. C. Harcourt 1995, A 'Second Edition' of The General Theory (two vols, co-ed.) 1997, 50 Years a Keynesian and Other Essays 2001, Selected Essays on Economic Policy 2001, L'Economie rebelle de Joan Robinson (ed.) 2001, Joan Robinson: Critical Assessments of Leading Economists (five vols, co-ed.) 2002, Editing Economics: Essays in Honour of Mark Perlman (co-ed.) 2002, Capital Theory (three vols, co-ed.) 2005, The Structure of Post-Keynesian Economics: The Core Contributions of the Pioneers 2006, Joan Robinson (with Prue Kerr) 2009, On Skidelsky's Keynes and Other Essays 2012, The Making of a Post-Keynesian Economist 2012; more than 350 articles, chapters and reviews. *Leisure interests:* bike riding, politics, reading, watching cricket, gossip. *Address:* Room 411, School of Economics, University of New South Wales, High Street, Kensington, NSW 2052, Australia (office). *Telephone:* (2) 9385-8829 (office). *E-mail:* gch@unsw.edu.au (office).

HARDADÓTTIR, Oddný G.; Icelandic teacher and politician; b. 9 April 1957; began career as math. teacher, Akureyri Jr Coll. and later Suðurnesja Comprehensive, Keflavík 1994, Prin. 2005; Project Man., Ministry of Educ. 2001–03; Mayor of Garði 2006–09; mem. Althingi (Parl.) for South Constituency 2009–, mem. Educ. and Gen. Affairs Cttee, Special Cttee on Standing Orders of Althingi; Minister of Finance 2011–12; mem. Icelandic Del. to IPU (apptd Vice-Chair. 2011); mem. Social Democratic Alliance, Chair. SDA Parl. Group 2011–. *Address:* Social Democratic Alliance—SDA, Hallveigarstíg 1, 101 Reykjavík, Iceland (office). *Telephone:* 4142200 (office). *Fax:* 4142201 (office). *E-mail:* samfylking@samfylking .is (office). *Website:* www.samfylking.is (office).

HARDCASTLE, Jack Donald, CBE, MA, MChir, FRCS, FRCP; British surgeon and academic; *Emeritus Professor of Surgery, University of Nottingham;* b. 3 April 1933, Yorks.; s. of Albert Hardcastle and Bertha Hardcastle (née Ellison); m. Rosemary Hay-Shunker 1965; two c.; ed Emmanuel Coll., Cambridge; House Physician, London Hosp. 1959–60; House Surgeon, Hammersmith Hosp., London 1961–62; Research Asst London Hosp. 1962, Lecturer in Surgery 1963, Registrar in Surgery 1964, Registrar in Surgery, Thoracic Unit 1965, Sr Registrar 1965, Sr

Lecturer 1968; Sr Registrar St Mark's Hosp., London 1968; Prof. of Surgery, Univ. of Nottingham 1970–98, Prof. Emer. 1998–; Lead Clinician, Mid-Trent Cancer Network 1998–2005; Sir Arthur Sims Commonwealth Travelling Prof., Royal Coll. of Surgeons 1985; Mayne Visiting Prof., Univ. of Brisbane, Australia 1987, Univ. of Melbourne 2001; Dir of Educ. Royal Coll. of Surgeons 1993–98, mem. Council 1987–99, Vice-Pres. 1995–97, Dir of Overseas Office 1996–99; Pres. Surgical Section Royal Soc. Medicine 1981, Pres. Coloproctology Section, Royal Soc. 1983, Pres. Asscn of Surgical Oncology 1992–93; Pres. Surgical Research Soc. 1995–96; Hon. Fellow, Royal Coll. of Physicians and Surgeons (Glasgow), Asscn of Coloproctology; Huntarian Orator 1998, Royal Coll. of Surgeons (England) Gold Medal 1999. *Publications include:* Isolated Organ Perfusion (with H. D. Ritchie) 1973; articles in professional journals. *Leisure interests:* golf, gardening. *Address:* Field House, 32 Marlock Close, Fiskerton, Notts., NG25 0UB, England (home). *Telephone:* (1636) 830316 (home). *Fax:* (1636) 830316 (home). *E-mail:* hardcastlejdr@aol.com.

HARDIE, (Charles) Jeremy (Mawdesley), CBE, BPhil (Econs), ACA; British business executive; b. 9 June 1938; s. of Sir Charles Hardie; m. 1st Susan Chamberlain 1962 (divorced 1976); two s. two d.; m. 2nd Xandra, Countess of Gowrie 1978 (divorced 1994); one d.; m. 3rd Kirsteen Margaret Tait 1994; ed Winchester Coll. and New Coll., Oxford; Nuffield Coll., Oxford 1966–67; Jr Research Fellow, Trinity Coll., Oxford 1967–68; Fellow and Tutor in Econs Keble Coll., Oxford 1968–75; Pnr, Dixon Wilson & Co. 1975–82; Deputy Chair. Monopolies and Mergers Comm. –1975; Dir (non-exec.) W. H. Smith Group 1988– (Deputy Chair. 1992–94, Chair. 1994–99); Chair. Nat. Provident Inst. 1980–89, Alexander Syndicate Man. Ltd 1982–95, Radio Broadland Ltd 1983–85; fmr Chair. David Mann Underwriting Agency Ltd; mem. Bd of Dirs Alexanders Discount Co. Ltd 1978–87, John Swire and Sons Ltd 1982–98, Alexanders Laing & Cruickshank Gilts Ltd 1986–87, Butler Foundation 1988–94, Northdor Holdings 1989–93; Chair. Centre for Econ. Policy Research 1984–89, Blanc Brasseries PLC, China Dialogue, Esmée Fairbairn Foundation 2003–07; currently Commr UK Drug Policy Comm.; also currently Research Assoc. Centre for Philosophy of Natural and Social Science, LSE; other business and public appointments; parl. cand. Norwich South, (SDP) 1983, (SDP/Alliance) 1987; Trustee, Somerset House, Int. House, Butler Foundation 1988–94; Hon. Fellow, Keble Coll. *Leisure interests:* sailing, skiing.

HARDIE BOYS, Rt Hon. Sir Michael, GNZM, GCMG, QSO, PC; New Zealand fmr Governor-General and fmr judge; b. 6 Oct. 1931, Wellington; s. of Justice Reginald Hardie Boys and Edith May Hardie Boys (née Bennett); m. Edith Mary Zohrab 1957; two s. two d.; ed Wellington Coll., Victoria Univ. of Wellington; barrister, solicitor with pvt. practice 1950–80; Councillor, then Pres., Wellington Dist Law Soc. 1974–79; Judge, High Court 1980–89, Court of Appeal 1989–95; Gov.-Gen. of New Zealand 1996–2001; mem. Legal Aid Bd (Chair.); Hon. Bencher of Gray's Inn; Hon. Fellow, Wolfson Coll., Cambridge; KStJ; Hon. LLD (Victoria Univ., Wellington) 1997. *Leisure interest:* the outdoors. *Address:* 387A Te Moana Road, Waikanae 5036, New Zealand (home).

HARDING, James; British editor and journalist; *Director of News and Current Affairs, BBC;* ed St Paul's School, London, Trinity Coll., Cambridge; learnt Japanese and moved to Japan, worked as speechwriter in office of Chief Cabinet Sec. Koichi Kato early 1990s; worked in Japan unit of EC; joined Financial Times (FT) 1994, posted to Shanghai bureau (first European newspaper since 1949 revolution) 1996–99, returned to UK as Media Ed. 1999–2002, Chief of Washington, DC bureau 2002–05, Business and City Ed. The Times 2006–07, Ed. The Times 2007–12 (resgnd); Dir of News and Current Affairs, BBC 2013–; est. justdosomething.net jtly with Common Purpose civic action group (online service that links professionals with non-exec. positions in local schools, prisons, hosps and nat. charities). *Publication:* Alpha Dogs: How Spin became a Global Business 2008. *Address:* Office of the Director of News and Current Affairs, BBC Broadcasting House, Portland Place, London, W1A 1AA, England (office). *Website:* www.bbc.co.uk/news (office).

HARDING, Marshal of the RAF Sir Peter Robin, GCB, DSc, FRAeS, FRSA; British air force officer (retd) and business executive (retd); b. 2 Dec. 1933, London; s. of Peter Harding and Elizabeth Kezia Clear; m. Sheila Rosemary May 1955; three s. one d.; ed Chingford High School; joined RAF 1952; pilot, numerous appointments in fighter, light bomber, strike/attack, reconnaissance and helicopters; Air Officer Commanding Number 11 Group 1981–82; Vice-Chief Air Staff 1982–84, of Defence Staff 1985; Air Officer Commdg-in-Chief, RAF Strike Command and C-in-C UK Air Forces (NATO) 1985–88; Chief of Air Staff 1988–92, Chief of Defence Staff 1993–94; ADC to HM the Queen 1975, Air ADC to HM the Queen 1988–92; Deputy Chair. GEC-Marconi Ltd 1995–98; Chair. Thorlock Int. Ltd 1998–2000, Merlyn Int. Assocs Ltd 1995–2002, Sienna Cancer Diagnostics Ltd 2003–05; Council mem. Winston Churchill Memorial Trust 1990–2008; Cttee mem. Leonard Cheshire Conflict Recovery Centre 1996–05; Vice-Pres. The Guild of Aviation Artists 1994–; mem. Pilgrims Soc. of GB; Liveryman Guild of Air Pilots and Navigators; Fellow and Hon. Companion, Royal Aeronautical Soc. 1989; Commdr, Legion of Merit (USA); CB 1980, KCB 1982, GCB 1988; Hon. DSc (Cranfield Inst. of Tech.) 1990. *Leisure interests:* ten grandchildren, swimming, piano, bridge, birdwatching and shooting (normally separately), the Beefsteak and Garrick clubs. *E-mail:* alice_merlyn@btinternet.com (home).

HARDY, Sir David William, Kt, CBIM, FCA, FILT; British business executive; b. 14 July 1930, Wilmslow, Cheshire; s. of the late Brig. John H. Hardy; m. Rosemary Collins 1957; one s. one d.; ed Wellington Coll. and Harvard Business School, USA; with Funch Edye Inc. and Imperial Tobacco, USA 1954–70; HM Govt Coordinator of Industrial Advisers 1970–72; Group Finance Dir Tate & Lyle Ltd 1972–77; Dir Ocean Transport & Trading PLC 1977–83; Dir Globe Investment Trust PLC 1976–90, Exec. Chair. 1983–90; Chair. Ocean Inchcape 1980–83, London Park Hotels 1983–87, Docklands Light Railway 1984–87, Swan Hunter 1986–88, MGM Assurance 1986–99, London Docklands Devt Corpn 1988–92, Europa Minerals 1991–94, Bankers Trust Investment Man. Ltd 1992–94, Burmine 1992–96, James Fisher 1992–93, Y. J. Lovell 1994–99; Dir (non-exec.) Imperial Tobacco Group 1996–2001, Milner Estates 1996–99, Sons of Gwalia 1996–98, Hanson 1991–2001, Ciba Geigy 1991–96, J. Devenish 1991–93; mem. Financial Services Practitioner Forum 2001–; numerous other directorships, professional appointments etc.; Chair. of Trustees Nat. Maritime Museum 1995–2005; Chair.

Transport Research Foundation 1996–2007; Fellow, Chartered Inst. of Transport; Hon. LLD (Greenwich) 2003. *Address:* Crow Horne House, Nine Mile Ride, Wokingham, Berks., RG40 3GA, England (home). *Telephone:* (1344) 773131 (home). *Fax:* (20) 7584-0086 (home). *E-mail:* seahardy@aol.com (office).

HARDY, Françoise; French singer, writer and astrologer; b. 17 Jan. 1944, Paris; m. Jacques Dutronc 1981; one s.; ed Inst. La Bruyère, Faculté des Lettres de Paris; solo recording artist 1962–; lyricist for musicians, including Diane Tell, Julien Clerc, Khalil Chahine, Guesch Patti and composer-arranger Alain Lubrano; also worked as model and actor; presents Horoscope RTL. *Films include:* Château en suède 1963, I Ragazzi dell'hully-gully 1964, Questo pazzo, pazzo mondo della canzone 1965, What's New, Pussycat 1965, Altissima pressione 1965, Une balle au coeur 1966, Europa canta 1966, Grand Prix 1966, Le Lapin de Noël (TV) 1967, Les Colombes 1972, Émilie Jolie (TV) 1980. *Recordings include:* albums: Françoise Hardy 1965, The Yeh-Yeh Girl from Paris 1965, Ma jeunesse fout le camp 1967, Comment te dire adieu 1968, Françoise Hardy en anglais 1969, Je vous aime 1969, Soleil 1970, La Question 1971, Et si je m'en vais avant toi 1972, Love Songs 1972, Message personnel 1973, Star 1977, J'écoute de la musique saoûle 1978, Gin Tonic 1980, Vingt ans vingt titres 1993, Blues 1995, Le Danger 1996, Maison ou j'ai grandi 1996, Clair obscur 2000, En Resume 2000, If You Listen 2000, Ce petit coeur 2004, Tant de Belle Choses 2005, Parenthèses 2006, La Pluie sans parapluie 2010, L'Amour fou 2012. Message personnel 2013. *Publications include:* Le Grand livre de la vierge (with B. Guenin), Entre les lignes, entre les signes (with Anne-Marie Simond) 1986, Françoise Hardy présente L'Astrologie universelle 1986, Notes secrètes (with E. Dumont) 1991, 35 Succès 1992, Les Rythmes du Zodiaque 2003, Le Désespoir des Singes et Autres Bagatelles 2008, Entre les lignes entre les signes 2009. *Leisure interest:* reading, especially books dealing with spirituality. *Address:* c/o VMA, 20 avenue Rapp, 75007 Paris (office); 13 rue Hallé, 75014 Paris, France (office). *E-mail:* info@vma.fr (office). *Website:* www.francoise-hardy.com (office).

HARDY, Jessica Adele; American swimmer; b. 12 March 1987, Long Beach, Calif.; d. of George Hardy and Denise Robinson; ed Wilson Classical High School, Long Beach, Univ. of California, Berkeley; competed for two years at Univ. of California, Berkeley, four-time NCAA Champion; turned professional 2007; World Championships (long course), Montreal 2005: silver medal, 4×100m medley, 50m breaststroke, 100m breaststroke, Melbourne 2007: 50m breaststroke, silver medal, 4×100m medley, Shanghai 2011: gold medal, 50m breaststroke, silver medal, 4×100m freestyle, Barcelona 2013: gold medal, 4×100m medley, bronze medal, 50m breaststroke, 100m breaststroke; World Championships (short course): Manchester 2008: gold medal, 50m breaststroke, 100m breaststroke, 4×100m medley, Shanghai 2006: silver medal, 4×100m medley, bronze medal, 50m breaststroke, Dubai 2010: silver medal, 4×100m freestyle, 4×100m medley; Pan Pacific Championships, Victoria 2006: gold medal, 4×100m medley, 50m breaststroke, 50m freestyle, 4×100m freestyle, 4×100m medley; withdrew from US Olympic Team for Beijing Olympics for one year following a failed drugs test 2008; swam in London Olympics 2012 4×100m medley relay; coach: Dave Salo; Female High School Swimmer of the Year, Swimming World magazine 2004, 2005, Female World Cup Overall Winner 2009. *Leisure interests:* surfing, scuba diving, water polo. *Address:* c/o Evan Morgenstein, Premier Management Group, LLC, 115 Crescent Commons, Suite 250, Cary, NC 27518, USA (office). *E-mail:* evan@pmgsports.com (office). *Website:* pmgsports.com/jessicahardy; www.jessicahardy.net.

HARDY, John Philips, MA, DPhil; Australian fmr professor of English; b. 1 Jan. 1933, Brisbane, Qld; s. of E. A. Hardy and N. A. Hardy (née Philips); m. 1st 1961 (divorced); three s. one d.; m. 2nd 1992; ed Church of England Grammar School, Brisbane, Univ. of Queensland and Univ. of Oxford, UK; Fellow, Magdalen Coll. Oxford 1962–65; Asst Prof., Univ. of Toronto, Canada 1965–66; Prof. of English, Univ. of New England, Armidale, NSW, Australia 1966–72, ANU 1972–87; Foundation Prof. of Humanities and Social Sciences, Bond Univ. 1988–94; Sec. Australian Acad. of the Humanities 1981–88; Harold White Hon. Fellow, Nat. Library of Australia 1992; Australian Centenary Medal; Queensland Rhodes Scholar 1957. *Publications:* Reinterpretations: Essays on Poems by Milton, Pope and Johnson 1971, Samuel Johnson 1979, Jane Austen's Heroines 1984, Stories of Australian Migration (ed.) 1988, Terra Australis to Australia (co-ed.) 1989, European Voyaging towards Australia (co-ed.) 1990. *Leisure interests:* films. *Address:* 40/2A Hollywood Avenue, Bondi Junction, Sydney, NSW 2022, Australia.

HARDY, Robert, CBE, MA (Oxon.), FSA; British actor and author; b. 29 Oct. 1925; s. of the late Maj. Henry Harrison Hardy and Edith Jocelyn Dugdale; m. 1st Elizabeth Fox 1952 (divorced); one s.; m. 2nd Sally Pearson 1961 (divorced 1986); two d.; ed Rugby School, Magdalen Coll., Oxford; Trustee, Royal Armouries 1984–95; Consultant, Mary Rose Trust 1979–, Trustee 1991–; Master of Worshipful Co. of Bowyers 1988–90; Trustee, then Patron, Battlefields Trust; mem. Battlefields Panel of English Heritage; Hon. DLitt (Reading) 1990, (Durham) 1997, (Portsmouth) 2006. *Films include:* How I Won the War, Yellow Dog, Dark Places, Young Winston, Ten Rillington Place, Le Silencieux, Gawain and the Green Knight, The Spy Who Came In From The Cold, La Gifle, Robin Hood, The Shooting Party, Paris by Night, War and Remembrance, Mary Shelley's Frankenstein, Sense and Sensibility, Mrs Dalloway, The Tichborne Claimant 1998, An Ideal Husband 1999, The Gathering 2001, Harry Potter and the Chamber of Secrets 2002, Harry Potter and the Prisoner of Azkaban 2004, Harry Potter and the Goblet of Fire 2005, Lassie 2005, Goodbye Mr Snuggles 2006, Harry Potter and the Order of the Phoenix 2007. *Theatre:* theatre appearances 1949– include four seasons of Shakespeare at Stratford-on-Avon, two at Old Vic; world tours include Henry V and Hamlet, USA; numerous appearances London and Broadway theatres 1952–; Winston Churchill in Celui Qui a Dit Non, Palais des Congrès, Paris 1999–2000. *Television:* writer and presenter of numerous programmes 1952– including The Picardy Affair, The History of the Longbow, Heritage, Horses in our Blood, Gordon of Khartoum etc.; other TV appearances have included Prince Hal and Henry V in Age of Kings, Prince Albert in Edward VII, Sgt. Gratz in Manhunt, Malcolm Campbell in Speed King, Winston Churchill in the Wilderness Years, Siegfried Farnon in All Creatures Great and Small, Twiggy Rathbone and Russell Spam in Hot Metal, the Commandant in The Far Pavilions, Sherlock Holmes, Inspector Morse, Middlemarch, Castle Ghosts, Gulliver's Travels, Midsomer Murders, Tenth Kingdom, Justice in Wonderland, Lucky Jim, Shackleton. *Publications:* Longbow 1976, The Great Warbow (with Matthew Strickland) 2005. *Leisure interests:*

making and shooting longbows, most country pursuits. *Address:* c/o Chatto & Linnit Ltd, 123A Kings Road, London, SW3 4PL, England (office). *Telephone:* (20) 7352-7722 (office). *Fax:* (20) 7352-3450 (office).

HARE, Sir David, Kt, MA, FRSL; British playwright and theatre director; b. 5 June 1947, Hastings, Sussex; s. of Clifford Theodore Rippon Hare and Agnes Cockburn Gilmour; m. 1st Margaret Matheson 1970 (divorced 1980); two s. one d.; m. 2nd Nicole Farhi 1992; ed Lancing Coll., Jesus Coll., Cambridge; Literary Man. and Resident Dramatist, Royal Court 1969–71; Resident Dramatist, Nottingham Playhouse 1973; f. Portable Theatre 1968, Joint Stock Theatre Group 1975, Greenpoint Films 1983; Assoc. Dir Nat. Theatre 1984–88, 1989–; UK/US Bicentennial Fellowship 1978; Hon. Fellow, Jesus Coll. Cambridge 2001; Officier, Ordre des Arts et des Lettres 1997; Evening Standard Drama Award 1970, John Llewellyn Rhys Prize 1974, BAFTA Best Play of the Year 1978, New York Critics' Circle Awards 1983, 1990, 1997, 1999, Golden Bear Award for Best Film 1985, Evening Standard Drama Award for Best Play 1985, Plays and Players Best Play Awards 1985, 1988, 1990, City Limits Best Play 1985, Drama Magazine Awards Best Play 1988, Laurence Olivier Best Play of the Year 1990, 1996, Time Out Award 1990, Dramalogue Award 1992, Time Out Award for Outstanding Theatrical Achievement 1998, Outer Critics' Circle Award 1999, Drama League Award 1999, Drama Desk Award 1999, Joan Cullman Award 1999, PEN Pinter Prize 2011. *Plays:* Slag, Hampstead 1970, Royal Court 1971, New York Shakespeare Festival (NYSF) 1971, The Great Exhibition, Hampstead 1972, Brassneck (with Howard Brenton q.v.), Nottingham Playhouse 1973 (also Dir), Knuckle, Comedy Theatre 1974, Fanshen, Inst. of Contemporary Arts 1975, Hampstead 1975, Nat. Theatre 1992, Teeth 'n' Smiles, Royal Court 1975 (also Dir), Wyndhams 1976 (also Dir), Plenty, Nat. Theatre 1978 (also Dir), NYSF and Broadway 1982 (also Dir), Albery 1999, A Map of the World, Nat. Theatre 1983 (also Dir) NYSF 1985 (also Dir), Pravda: A Fleet Street Comedy (with Howard Brenton), Nat. Theatre 1985 (also Dir), The Bay at Nice, Nat. Theatre 1986 (also Dir), The Secret Rapture, Nat. Theatre 1988, NYSF and Broadway 1989 (also Dir), Racing Demon, Nat. Theatre 1990, 1993, Broadway 1995, Murmuring Judges, Nat. Theatre 1992, 1993, The Absence of War, Nat. Theatre 1993, Skylight, Nat. Theatre 1995, Wyndhams and Broadway 1996, Vaudeville 1997, Amy's View, Nat. Theatre 1997, Aldwych 1998, Broadway 1999, The Judas Kiss, Almeida and Broadway 1998 (Dir on radio only), Via Dolorosa, Royal Court 1998 (also acted), Almeida and Broadway 1999 (also acted), My Zinc Bed, Royal Court 2000 (also Dir), The Breath of Life, Theatre Royal, Haymarket 2002, The Permanent Way, Nat. Theatre 2003, Stuff Happens, Nat. Theatre 2004, The Vertical Hour (Music Box Theatre, Broadway) 2006, Gethsemane, Nat. Theatre 2009. *Plays adapted:* The Rules of the Game, Nat. Theatre 1971, Almeida 1992, The Life of Galileo, Almeida 1994, Mother Courage and Her Children, Nat. Theatre 1995, Ivanov, Almeida and Broadway 1997 (Dir on radio only), The Blue Room, Donmar and Broadway 1998, Theatre Royal 2000, Platonov, Almeida 2001, The House of Bernarda Alba, Lorca 2005. *Plays directed:* Christie in Love, Portable Theatre 1969, Fruit, Portable Theatre 1970, Blowjob, Portable Theatre 1971, England's Ireland, Portable Theatre 1972 (Co-Dir), The Provoked Wife, Palace, Watford 1973, The Pleasure Principle, Theatre Upstairs 1973, The Party, Nat. Theatre 1974, Weapons of Happiness, Nat. Theatre 1976, Devil's Island, Joint Stock 1977, Total Eclipse, Lyric 1981, King Lear, Nat. Theatre 1986, The Designated Mourner, Nat. Theatre 1996, Heartbreak House, Almeida 1997. *Radio play:* Murder in Samarkand 2010. *TV screenplays:* Man Above Men (BBC) 1973, Licking Hitler (BBC) 1978 (also Dir), Dreams of Leaving (BBC) 1979 (also Dir), Saigon: Year of the Cat (Thames) 1983 (also Assoc. Producer), Heading Home (BBC) 1991 (also Dir), The Absence of War (BBC) 1995. *Film screenplays:* Wetherby 1985 (also Dir), Plenty 1985, Paris by Night 1989 (also Dir), Strapless 1990 (also Dir), Damage 1992, The Secret Rapture 1993 (also assoc. producer), Via Dolorosa 2000 (also actor), The Hours (adaptation of Michael Cunningham's novel) 2001, Lee Miller 2003, The Corrections (adaptation of Jonathan Franzen's novel) 2005. *Film directed:* The Designated Mourner 1996 (also Producer). *Opera libretto:* The Knife, New York Shakespeare Festival 1988 (also Dir). *Publications:* Writing Lefthanded 1991, Asking Around 1993, Acting Up: A Diary 1999, Obedience, Struggle and Revolt (collection of speeches) 2005. *Address:* c/o Casarotto Ramsay & Associates Ltd, Waverley House, 7–12 Noel Street, London, W1F 8GQ, England (office). *Telephone:* (20) 7287-4450 (office). *Fax:* (20) 7287-9128 (office). *E-mail:* info@casarotto.co.uk (office). *Website:* www.casarotto.co.uk (office).

HARE DUKE, Rt Rev. Michael Geoffrey, MA; British fmr ecclesiastic; *Honorary Health Care Chaplain, Perth Royal Infirmary;* b. 28 Nov. 1925, Calcutta, India; s. of the late R. A. Hare Duke and Dorothy Holmes; m. Grace Lydia Frances McKean Dodd 1949; one s. three d.; ed Bradfield Coll., Berks., Trinity Coll., Oxford, Westcott House, Cambridge; Sub-Lt RNVR 1944–46; ordained Deacon 1952, Priest 1953; Curate St John's Wood, London 1952–56; Vicar St Mark's, Bury 1956–62; Pastoral Dir Clinical Theology Asscn 1962–64; Vicar St Paul's, Daybrook 1964–69; Bishop of St Andrew's, Dunkeld and Dunblane 1969–94; Chair. Age Concern Scotland 1994–2000, Nat. Forum on Older Volunteers 2000–03; Patron RSVP (Scotland) 2003–; Hon. Health Care Chaplain, Perth Royal Infirmary 2002–; Hon. DD (St Andrew's). *Publications:* Understanding the Adolescent 1969, The Break of Glory 1970, Freud 1972, Good News 1976, Stories, Signs and Sacraments in the Emerging Church 1982, Praying for Peace: Reflections on the Gulf Crisis 1991, Hearing the Stranger: Reflections, Poems and Hymns 1994, One Foot in Heaven 2001; contrib. to various newspapers and journals. *Leisure interests:* writing and broadcasting. *Address:* 2 Balhousie Avenue, Perth, PH1 5HN, Scotland (home). *Telephone:* (1738) 622642 (home). *Fax:* (1738) 622642 (home). *E-mail:* bishmick@blueyonder.co.uk (home).

HARGROVE, Basil (Buzz), OC; Canadian trade union official (retd); *Distinguished Visiting Professor, Ted Rogers School of Management, Ryerson University;* b. 8 March 1944, Bath, NB; s. of Percy Hargrove and Eileen Doucet; m. Denise Small; mem. Canadian Auto Workers (CAW) Cttee Chrysler Canada 1965–75, Nat. Rep. 1975–78, Asst to Pres. and Dir CAW 1978–92, Nat. Pres. CAW 1992–2008 (retd); Vice-Pres. Exec. Cttee Canadian Labour Congress; Ombudsman Nat. Hockey League Players Asscn Feb.–Nov. 2009; currently Distinguished Visiting Prof., Ted Rogers School of Man., Ryerson Univ., Toronto; Fellow, Centennial Coll.; Dr hc (Brock Univ.) 1998, (Univ. of Windsor) 2003, (Wilfred Laurier Univ.) 2004, (Ryerson Univ.) 2006, Univ. of New Brunswick) 2008, (Queen's Univ.) 2009. *Publication:* Labour of Love 1998, Laying It on the Line: Driving a Hard Bargain in

Challenging Times 2009. *Address:* Ted Rogers School of Management, Ryerson University, 350 Victoria Street, Toronto, ON M5B 2K3, Canada (office). *Telephone:* (416) 979-5000 (office). *Website:* www.ryerson.ca/tedrogersschool (office).

HARGROVE, Roy; American jazz musician (trumpet); b. 16 Oct. 1969, Waco, Texas; ed Booker T. Washington School for Visual and Performing Arts, Dallas, Berklee School of Music, Boston, New School Univ., New York; toured Europe and Japan, playing with established jazz artists; formed own quintet and made debut solo record 1989; f. Roy Hargrove's Big Band 1995; formed The RH Factor 2003–. *Recordings include:* albums: Tenors Of Our Time 1994, Family 1995, Damn! 1995, Parker's Mood: Tribute to Charlie Parker 1995, The Main Ingredient 1996, Angel Eyes 1996, Crisol: Habana 1997, Jazz 'Round Midnight 1998, I Remember Miles 1998, Moment to Moment 2000, Directions In Music (Celebrating Miles Davis and John Coltrane) 2002, Hard Groove 2003, Nothing Serious 2006, Distractions (with The RH Factor) 2006, Emergence 2009. *E-mail:* contact@vervemusicgroup.com. *Website:* www.vervemusicgroup.com.

HARIB, Mohammed Saeed; United Arab Emirates animator; *Founder, Lammtara Pictures;* b. 1978, Dubai; ed Northeastern Univ., Boston, USA; began career as Art Dir, Tech. and Media Free Zone Authority, Dubai 2005; f. Lammtara Pictures Sept. 2005; created Freej (Middle East's first computer animated TV series), first broadcast Sept. 2006; CEO Magazine Young CEO of the Year 2008, Dubai Int. Film Festival Muhur Award for Best UAE Talent 2008. *Address:* Lammtara Pictures, Dubai Media City, PO Box 502274, Dubai, United Arab Emirates (office). *Telephone:* (4) 3757478 (office). *Fax:* (4) 4290949 (office). *E-mail:* info@lamtarapictures.com (office). *Website:* www.lammtarapictures.com (office).

HARIHARAN, BSc, LLB; Indian singer; b. 3 April 1955, Mumbai; s. of the late Ananthasubramani Iyer ('H. A. S. Mani') and Shrimati Alamelu; m. Lalita 1994; two s.; ed SIES Coll., trained in Hindustani music with Ustad Ghulam Mustafa Khan; signed by the late music dir Jaidev to sing for Hindi film Gaman following success in singing competition 1977; toured concert circuit and performed on TV for several serials, e.g. Junoon; recorded several successful ghazal albums for which he wrote the scores; sang in several Hindi movies such as Sahibaan, Lamhe, Raam Nagari, Dard Ke Rishte, Zamana, Sindoor, Rangeela, Bombay, Pardes, Traffic Signal, Muukhbir; debut singing in Tamil in film Roja 1993; sang more than 1000 Tamil songs; All-India Sur Singaar Competition Prize 1977, UP State Award 1977, Best Male Playback Singer, Tamil Nadu State Govt Film Awards 1995, Nat. Award for Best Male Playback Singer 1998, Padma Shri 2004, Yesudas Award 2004, Dinanath Mangeshkar Award 2010. *Albums include:* Shamakhana, Sukoon 1983, Dil Nasheen 1988, Reflections 1989, The Very Best of Hariharan (compilation) 1989, Hariharan In Concert 1989, Dil Ki Baat 1990, My Favourite Hits (compilation) 1990, Hazir 1992, Abshaar-e-Ghazal (Gold), Gulfam (Double Platinum) (Diva Award for Best Album of the Year 1994) 1994, Saptarishi 1995, Paigham 1995, Qaraar, Visaal 1996, Halka Nasha, Jashn 1996, Colonial Cousins (first Indian act to be featured on MTV Unplugged, also won MTV Indian Viewers' Choice Award and US Billboard Award) 1996, Aathwan Sur – The Other Side of Naushad 1998, 2009, Kaash (Screen Videocon Award for Best Non-film Album 2000) 2000, Swar Utsav 2001. *Films include:* Power of Women. *Leisure interests:* film, travel, antique collecting, football. *Address:* 101 (1st Floor), Legacy Tower, Powai Vihar Complex, Powai, Mumbai 400 076, India (home). *Telephone:* (22) 25701673 (office). *Fax:* (22) 25704619 (office). *E-mail:* singerhari@gmail.com (office). *Website:* www.hariharan.co (office).

HARIRI, Ayman Rafik; Lebanese business executive; *Vice-Chairman and Deputy CEO, Saudi Oger Limited;* s. of the late Rafik Hariri (assassinated fmr Prime Minister of Lebanon); brother of Saad ed-Din Hariri (fmr Prime Minister of Lebanon); m.; one c.; ed Georgetown Univ., Washington, DC, USA; began career with Intelsat (satellite provider); currently mem. Bd of Dirs, Vice-Chair. and Deputy CEO Saudi Oger Ltd; Chair. Epok (software co.); Dir Cell C, South Africa (mobile telephone co.); ranked by Arabian Business magazine as one of the world's 100 most influential Arabs in their annual Power list 100 2009–11, also ranked sixth in the CEO Middle East's list of the Arab world's most influential leaders in property, selected as the Best Executive in the Construction Sector in Saudi Arabia 2010, 2011, ranked No. 1 in the Construction Week Power 100 List for 2011, ranked by Arabian Business amongst the Power 500: The World's Most Influential Arabs (80th) 2012. *Address:* Saudi Oger Ltd, PO Box 1449, Riyadh 11431, Saudi Arabia (office). *Telephone:* (1) 477-3115 (office). *Fax:* (1) 477-0079 (office). *E-mail:* ccd@saudioger.com (office). *Website:* www.saudioger.com (office).

HARIRI, Nazek; Lebanese foundation executive; *President, Hariri Foundation;* b. (Nazek Audeh), widow of Rafik Hariri (fmr Prime Minister of Lebanon); four s. one d. three step-c.; supports Lebanese fashion designers and works for several charitable causes, including Children's Cancer Center of Lebanon, Int. Osteoporosis Foundation, Chronic Care Center, Muslim Inst. for Orphanages; Pres. Hariri Foundation; Amb. of Int. Osteoporosis Foundation 2003–; unanimously chosen to head all social and charitable orgs est. by her husband in Lebanon following his assassination 2005; campaigned for step-son Saad in Lebanese elections. *Address:* c/o Hariri Foundation, Beirut, Lebanon (office). *E-mail:* info@rafichariri.org (office). *m.i.s@hariri-foundation.org.lb* (office). *Website:* www.nazekhariri.net; www.hariri-foundation.org.lb (office).

HARIRI, Saad ed-Din; Lebanese/Saudi Arabian business executive and politician; *Leader, Tayyar al-Mustaqbal (Movement of the Future);* b. 18 April 1970, Riyadh, Saudi Arabia; s. of the late Rafik Hariri and Nidal al-Bustani; m. Lara Bashir Al Adem 1998; two s. one d.; ed McDonough School of Business, Georgetown Univ., Washington, DC, USA; Marketing Man. Sipco Saudi Industrial Paints Co., Riyadh 1993; fmr Chair. Exec. Cttee Oger Telecom, also Gen. Man. Saudi Oger Ltd and Dir Oger International Entreprise de Travaux Internationaux; Chair. Omnia Holdings; Dir and Chair. Saraya Holdings, UAE; returned to Lebanon 2005; Leader, Tayyar al-Mustaqbal (Movement of the Future) 2005–; Prime Minister 2009–11. *Address:* Tayyar al-Mustaqbal (Movement of the Future), PO Box 123, Koraytem, Hamra, Beirut, Lebanon (office). *Telephone:* (3) 375442 (office). *Fax:* (1) 375442 (office). *E-mail:* info@almustaqbal.org (office). *Website:* www.almustaqbal.org (office); www.saadhariri.com.

HARISH, Michael, BA; Israeli economist and politician; b. 28 Nov. 1936, Romania; s. of Joseph Harish and Esther Harish; m. Edith Normand 1963; three s. one d.; ed Hebrew Univ.; Sec.-Gen. Labour Party's Student Org. 1961–63; Dir and

Chair. Int. Dept Israel Labour Party 1967–82, Sec.-Gen. Israel Labour Party 1989–92; Minister of Industry and Trade 1992–96; mem. Knesset 1974–96, Deputy Chair. Defence and Foreign Affairs Cttee 1984–88, Chair. Finance Cttee 1988–89, Co-Chair. Jt Science and Tech. Cttee; Chair. Israel Centre for Energy Policy; mem. several ministerial cttees including Econ. Affairs, Immigrants' Absorption, Devt Areas, Jerusalem Affairs; mem. Cttee for co-ordinating activities between Govt and the Jewish Agency and the Zionist Org.; fmr Pres. Me Harish Enterprises Ltd; mem. Public Council for Soviet Jewry. *Leisure interests:* sport, music. *Address:* 5 Mishmar Hayarden Street, Givatayim, 53582, Israel (home). *Telephone:* (3) 571-5233 (home). *Fax:* (3) 571-5233 (home). *E-mail:* meharish@internet-zahav.net.il.

HARKIANAKIS, Stylianos, DD; Australian ecclesiastic; *Primate, Greek Orthodox Church of Australia;* b. 29 Dec. 1935, Rethymnon, Crete, Greece; ed Theological School of Halki, Univ. of Athens; Deacon Constantinople (Istanbul) 1957; priest, Rethymnon 1958; Abbot Holy Patriarchal Monastery of Vlatadon, Thessaloniki 1966; Pres. Patriarchal Inst. of Patristic Studies; Lecturer, Univ. of Thessaloniki 1969–75, Univ. of Sydney 1975–85; Titular Bishop of Miletoupolis 1970; Exarch of Mount Athos 1970–75; Visiting Prof., Univ. of Regensberg 1973; Archbishop Greek Orthodox Church of Australia 1975, Primate 1975–; Co-Chair. official theological dialogue between Roman Catholic and Orthodox Churches 1980–2003; Chair. Standing Conference of Canonical Orthodox Churches, Australia; Dean, St Andrew's Greek Orthodox Theological Coll. 1986–, currently Lecturer in Systematic Theology; Prof., Sydney Coll. of Divinity; mem. jt official comm. of theological dialogue between Orthodox and Anglicans 1970; Dr hc (Univ. of Lublin) 1985; Gottfried von Herder Prize (Vienna) 1973, Award for Poetry (Acad. of Athens) 1980, Golden Cross of St Andrew (Constantinople), Golden Cross of Holy Sepulchre, Archdiocese of Thyateira; awarded Key to City of Adelaide 1995. *Publications include:* The Infallibility of the Church in Orthodox Theology 1965, The Constitution 'De Ecclesia' of the Second Vatican Council 1969, Orthodoxy and Catholicism, Incarnations of Dogma 1996, For Present and Future 1999, 37 vols of poetry (in Greek), over 70 theological essays in periodicals. *Leisure interests:* poetry, reading, swimming, walking. *Address:* 242 Cleveland Street, Redfern, Sydney 2016, Australia. *Telephone:* (612) 9698-5066. *Fax:* (612) 9698-5368.

HARKIN, Thomas (Tom) R., JD; American lawyer and politician; *Senator from Iowa;* b. 19 Nov. 1939, Cumming, Ia; s. of Patrick Harkin and Frances Harkin; m. Ruth Raduenz 1968; two d.; ed Iowa State Univ. and Catholic Univ. of America Law School; admitted to Iowa bar 1972; served in USN 1962–67, Naval Reserve 1968–74; Attorney, Polk Co., Ia Legal Aid Soc. 1973; mem. US House of Reps, Washington, DC 1975–85; Senator from Iowa 1985–, Chair. Cttee on Agric., Nutrition, and Forestry 2001–03, Cttee on Health, Educ., Labor and Pensions 2009–; fmr mem. Bd of Dirs Iowa Consumers League; mem. Small Business Cttee, Democratic Steering Cttee; Democrat. *Publication:* Five Minutes to Midnight 1990. *Address:* 731 Hart Senate Office Building, Washington, DC 20510, USA (office). *Telephone:* (202) 224-3254 (office). *Fax:* (202) 224-9369 (office). *Website:* harkin.senate.gov (office).

HARLEY, Ian; British finance executive; articled clerk, Touche Ross & Co. 1972; later with Corp. Planning Dept, Morgan Crucible Ltd; joined Abbey Nat. building Soc. (later Abbey Nat. PLC) 1977, Financial Analyst then various Sr Man. posts with Finance, Treasury and Retail Divs., Reg. Man. for the SE, Retail Operations Div. 1984–86, Commercial Man. for Business Devt 1986, Group Financial Controller 1986–88, Asst Gen. Man. of Finance 1988–91, Finance Dir of Retail Operations 1991–92, Operations Dir Jan.–Oct. 1992, Group Treas. and Chief Exec. Abbey Nat. Treasury Services PLC 1992–98, Finance Dir and mem. Bd 1993–2002, CEO 1998–2002; mem. Bd of Dirs British Energy Group PLC and British Energy Holdings PLC 2004–09, Rentokil Initial plc, Remploy; Gov. Whitgift Foundation; Vice-Pres. Nat. Deaf Children's Soc.; fmr Chair. Asscn for Payment Clearing Services.

HARLIN, Renny; Finnish film director; b. 1958, Helsinki; m. Geena Davis (q.v.) (divorced); ed Univ. of Helsinki Film School; f. Midnight Sun Pictures (production co.). *Films:* Born American (debut) 1986, Prison, A Nightmare on Elm Street IV: The Dream Master, Die Hard 2, The Adventures of Ford Fairlane, Rambling Rose (producer only), Cliffhanger, Speechless (co-producer only), Cutthroat Island (also producer), The Long Kiss Goodnight (also producer) 1996, Deep Blue Sea 1999, Blast from the Past (producer) 1999, Exorcist: The Beginning 2004, Mindhunters (also producer) 2004, The Covenant 2006, Cleaner 2007, 12 Rounds 2009. *Films for television include:* Freddy's Nightmares 1990, T.R.A.X. 2000. *Address:* c/o Alan Gasmer, William Morris Agency, 1 William Morris Place, Beverly Hills, CA 90212, USA (office). *Fax:* (310) 440-9167 (office). *E-mail:* nikki@midnightsunpictures.com (office); renny@rennyharlin.com. *Website:* www.midnightsunpictures.com (office); www.rennyharlin.com.

HÄRMÄLÄ, Jukka, BSc; Finnish business executive; b. 1946; ed Helsinki School of Econs; joined Enso-Gutzeit Oy 1970, Dir of Finance 1981–83, Vice-Pres. and Gen. Man., Sawmill Div. 1983–84, Pres. and COO Enso Oyj 1988–92, Chair., Pres. and CEO 1992–98, CEO Stora Enso Oyj (following merger) 1999–2007; mem. Bd Finnish Forest Industries Fed.; fmr Vice-Chair. Finnlines; mem. European Round Table of Industrialists.

HARMAN, Gilbert Helms, BA, PhD; American academic and writer; *James S. McDonnell Distinguished University Professor of Philosophy, Princeton University;* b. 26 May 1938, East Orange, New Jersey; s. of William H. Harman, Jr and Marguerite Page; m. Lucy Newman 1970; two d.; ed Swarthmore Coll., Harvard Univ.; faculty mem. Dept of Philosophy, Princeton Univ. 1963–, apptd Stuart Prof. of Philosophy 1971, Co-Dir Cognitive Science Lab. 1986–2000, currently James S. McDonnell Distinguished Univ. Prof. of Philosophy; mem. American Philosophical Asscn, Philosophy of Science Asscn, Soc. for Philosophy and Psychology, American Psychological Soc., Linguistic Soc. of America, American Acad. of Arts and Sciences 2005; Fellow, Cognitive Science Soc. 2002, Asscn for Psychological Science 2011; Jean Nicod Prize 2005, Behrman Award 2009. *Publications:* Semantics of Natural Language (co-ed. with Donald Davidson) 1971, Thought 1973, On Noam Chomsky (ed.) 1974, The Logic of Grammar (ed. with Donald Davidson) 1975, The Nature of Morality: An Introduction to Ethics 1977, Change in View: Principles of Reasoning 1986, Skepticism and the Definition of Knowledge 1990, Conceptions of the Human Mind (ed.) 1993, Moral Relativism and Moral Objectivity (with Judith Jarvis Thomson) 1996, Reasoning, Meaning and Mind

1999, Explaining Values and other Essays in Moral Philosophy 2000, Reliable Reasoning: Induction and Statistical Learning Theory 2007, An Elementary Introduction to Statistical Learning Theory (with Sanjeev Kulkarni) 2011; contrib. to scholarly journals. *Address:* Department of Philosophy, Princeton University, 1879 Hall, Room 118, Princeton, NJ 08544-1006 (office); 106 Broadmead Street, Princeton, NJ 08540, USA (home). *Telephone:* (609) 258-4289 (office). *Fax:* (609) 258-1502 (office). *E-mail:* harman@princeton.edu (office). *Website:* www.princeton.edu/~harman (office).

HARMAN, Rt Hon. Harriet Ruth, PC, QC; British solicitor and politician; *Deputy Leader and Chairman, Labour Party;* b. 30 July 1950, London, England; d. of the late John Harman and of Anna Spicer; m. Jack Dromey 1982; two s. one d.; ed St Paul's Girls' School and Univ. of York; Brent Community Law Centre 1975–78; Legal Officer, Nat. Council for Civil Liberties 1978–82; MP for Peckham 1982–97, for Camberwell and Peckham 1997–; Shadow Chief Sec. to Treasury 1992–94; Shadow Spokesperson on Employment 1994–95, on Health 1995–96, on Social Security 1996–97; Sec. of State for Social Security 1997–98; Solicitor-Gen., Law Officers Dept 2001–05; Minister of State, Dept of Constitutional Affairs 2005–07; Leader, House of Commons, Lord Privy Seal, Minister for Women and Sec. of State for Equalities 2007–10; Deputy Leader and Chair. Labour Party 2007–, Interim Leader and Chair. Labour Party and Leader of the Opposition May–Sept. 2010; Deputy Leader of the Opposition and Shadow Sec. of State for Int. Devt 2010–. *Publications:* Sex Discrimination in Schools 1977, Justice Deserted: The Subversion of the Jury 1979, The Century Gap 1993. *Address:* House of Commons, Westminster, London, SW1A 0AA (office); Labour Party, 39 Victoria Street, London, SW1H 0HA, England (office). *Telephone:* (20) 7219-3000 (office); (870) 590-0200 (Labour) (office). *Fax:* (20) 7802-1234 (Labour) (office). *E-mail:* harmanh@parliament.uk (office); info@new.labour.org.uk (office). *Website:* www.harrietharman.org (office); www.labour.org.uk (office); www.parliament.uk (office).

HARMAN, Sir John, Kt, BSc, FRSA; British teacher, lecturer and civil servant; *Chairman, Environment Agency;* b. 30 July 1950, Leeds, Yorks.; s. of John Edward Harman and Patricia Josephine Harman (née Mullins); m. Susan Harman; one s. three d.; ed St George's Coll., Weybridge, Univ. of Manchester and Huddersfield Coll. of Educ.; teacher and lecturer –1997; elected to W Yorks. Metropolitan Co. Council 1981–86; elected to Kirklees Metropolitan Co. Council 1986, Leader 1986–99; first Leader Regional Ass. for Yorks. and Humberside 1999–2000; mem. Bd Environment Agency 1996, later Deputy Chair., currently Chair.; Co-Chair. Sustainable Building Task Group 2004–05; Vice-Chair. Asscn of Metropolitan Authorities 1992–97; Deputy Leader Labour Group and Chair. Local Govt Asscn Urban Comm. 1997–2000; Local Govt Adviser to UK Del. to the Earth Summit, Rio de Janeiro 1992; Founder-Chair. UK Local Agenda 21 Steering Group; mem. Math. Asscn, Child Poverty Action Group; Chair. Kirklees Stadium Devt Ltd; Dir Energy Savings Trust, Nat. House Building Council, Aldersgate Group; mem. SITA UK Advisory Bd; Trustee, Nat. Coal Mining Museum for England, Forum for the Future, Inst. for European Environmental Policy, One Community Foundation; Hon. Fellow, ICE, Chartered Inst. of Waste Man., Chartered Inst. of Water and Environmental Mans, Soc. for the Environment; Hon. DCL. *Leisure interests:* music, gardening, Huddersfield Town Football Club. *Website:* www.environment-agency.gov.uk (office).

HARMOKO, Haji; Indonesian politician and journalist; *Co-ordinator of Advisers, Partai Golongan Karya;* b. 7 Feb. 1939, Kertosono, E Java; ed Sr High School, Kediri, E Java and Inst. of Nat. Defence (LEMHANAS), Jakarta; journalist, Merdeka (magazine and daily) 1960–65; Ed. Api (daily); Man. Ed. Merdeka and Chief Ed. Merdiko 1966–68; Chief Ed. Mimbar Kita 1968–69; Gen. Man., Chief Ed. Pos Kota (daily); mem. Bd of Film Censors 1974; mem. Press Council 1975; Chief Ed. Warna Sari 1976–83; mem. House of Reps and People's Consultative Ass. and Head of International and Mass Media Div. of Functional Group (GOLKAR) 1978, Pres. and Chair., then Co-ordinator of Advisers, Partai Golongan Karya 1993–; Head of Advisory Bd of Newspaper Publrs Asscn 1979–84; mem. Exec. Bd Press and Graphics Asscn 1980–84; Minister of Information 1983–97; Speaker People's Consultative Ass. and House of Reps 1997–2001. *Address:* c/o People's Consultative Assembly, Jalan Gatot Subroto 6, Jakarta, Indonesia.

HARNEY, Mary, BA; Irish politician; b. 1953, Ballinasloe, Co. Galway; ed Presentation Convent, Clondalkin, Co. Dublin and Trinity Coll. Dublin; mem. Seanad Éireann (youngest ever Senator) 1977–81; mem. Dublin Co. Council 1979–91; TD 1981–, Co-founder Progressive Democrats 1985, Deputy Leader Progressive Democrats 1993, then Leader and Spokesperson on Justice, Equality and Law Reform; Minister for Environmental Protection 1989–92; Tánaiste (Deputy Prime Minister) and Minister for Enterprise, Trade and Employment 1997–2004, Tánaiste 2004–07, Minister for Health and Children 2004–11. *Address:* Constituency Office, Clondalkin, Dublin 22, Ireland (office). *Website:* www.maryharney.ie.

HARNISH, Reno L., III, MA; American academic and fmr diplomatist; *Director, Center for the Environment and National Security, Scripps Institution of Oceanography;* b. 21 Jan. 1949, Norman, Okla; m. Leslie Harnish; one s. one d.; ed San Diego State Univ., American Univ., Massachusetts Inst. of Tech.; worked as research asst at American Enterprise Inst., as int. economist at US Dept of Treasury and as clerk for US Congressman Dave Martin of Neb.; served as Environment, Science and Tech. Counselor, Embassy in Rome, Econ. and Commercial Counselor, Embassy ino GDR, in Office of Developed Country Trade, US State Dept, as Econ. Officer, Embassy in Vienna, as Political Officer, Status Liaison Office, Saipan and as Econ. Commercial Officer, Embassy in Lagos; led US policy on Cen. Asian politics and scientific cooperation with New Independent States, US State Dept 1992–95; fmr Deputy Chief of Mission, Stockholm, then Cairo, fmr Chief of Mission, US Office, Pristina, Amb. to Azerbaijan 2004–06, Gen. Chair. WIREC 2008 Interagency Leadership Group 2006, Prin. Deputy Asst Sec. of State, Bureau of Oceans and Int. Environmental and Scientific Affairs 2006–09; Dir Center for Environment and Nat. Security, Scripps Inst. of Oceanography, San Diego 2009–; mem. Threat Reduction Advisory Cttee, Dept of Defense; Order of Malta; twice honoured for Presidential Meritorious Service and once for State Dept Distinguished Service, multiple Sr Performance Pay Awards, Meritorious Honor Award, two Superior Honor Awards. *Leisure interests:* golf, tennis, skiing, reading, gardening. *Address:* Scripps Institution of Oceanography, 8602 La Jolla Shores Drive, La Jolla, CA 92037, USA (office). *Telephone:* (858) 534-2542 (office). *E-mail:* rharnish@ucsd.edu (office). *Website:* www.scripps.ucsd.edu (office).

HARNONCOURT, Nikolaus; Austrian cellist and conductor; b. 6 Dec. 1929, Berlin, Germany; s. of Eberhard and Ladislaja Harnoncourt (née Meran); m. Alice Hoffelner 1953; three s. one d.; ed Matura Gymnasium, Graz, Acad. of Music, Vienna; cellist mem. of Vienna Symphony Orchestra 1952–69; solo concerts on viola da gamba; int. debuts 1966; Prof., Mozarteum and Inst. of Musicology, Univ. of Salzburg 1972–93; founder-mem., Concentus Musicus, Ensemble for Ancient Music 1953; as conductor has performed in leading concert halls worldwide, including in Amsterdam, Berlin, Vienna, Zürich, London, New York, Tokyo and at the Salzburg Festival; Officier de la Légion d'honneur 2012; several hon. doctorates including Hon. DMus (Edin.) 1987; Erasmus Prize (jtly) 1980, H. G. Nägeli Medal, Zürich 1983, Polar Prize, Stockholm 1994, Ernst von Siemens Music Prize 2002, Grammy Award (for recording of Bach's St Matthew Passion) 2002, Kyoto Prize (arts and philosophy category, for life's work) 2005, Gramophone Lifetime Achievement Award 2009, RPS Gold Medal 2012. *Recordings include:* more than 450 recordings with period instruments and music from 1200–1950; many works with Concentus Musicus, notably Handel's Messiah, Mozart's early symphonies, Bach's Brandenburg Concertos and Cantatas, Beethoven symphonies with Chamber Orchestra of Europe, Mozart and Schubert symphonies with Concertgebouw Orchestra Amsterdam, recordings with Berlin and Vienna Philharmonic Orchestras, Arnold Schoenberg Choir. *Publications include:* Musik als Klangrede, Wege zu einem neuen Musikverständnis 1982, Der musikalische Dialog 1983, Was ist Wahrheit 1995, Mozart-Dialoge 2005, Töne sind höhere Worte 2007. *Leisure interests:* cultural history, woodwork. *Address:* 38 Piaristengasse, 1080 Vienna (home); c/o Styriarte, Steirische Kulturveranstaltungen GmbH, Sackstraße 17, 8010 Graz, Austria (office). *Website:* www.harnoncourt.info.

HAROCHE, Serge, PhD; French physicist and academic; *Chair of Quantum Physics and Administrator, Collège de France;* b. 11 Sept. 1944, Casablanca, Morocco; s. of Albert Haroche and Valentine Haroche (née Roublev); m. Claudine Haroche (née Zeligson); two c.; ed École Normale Supérieure and Université Pierre et Marie Curie, Paris; left Morocco and settled in France 1956; worked at CNRS, Paris as research scientist 1967–71, Chargé de recherches 1971–73, Maître de recherches 1973–75; Visiting Scholar, Stanford Univ., USA 1972–73, 1976, 1979; Maître de conferences, École Polytechnique, Paris 1973–84; apptd Prof., Paris VI Univ. 1975; Visiting Scientist, MIT, USA 1979; Visiting Prof., Harvard Univ., USA 1981; Prof. (part-time), Yale Univ., USA 1984–93; Professeur de Physique, Université Pierre et Marie Curie 1975–2001; Prof., École Normale Supérieure 1982–2001, mem. Institut Universitaire de France 1991–2001, Head of Dept of Physics 1994–2000; Prof., Collège de France and holder of the Chair of Quantum Physics 2001–, Admin. 2012–; mem. Soc. Française de Physique, European Physical Soc., Acad. des Sciences 1993, European Acad. of Sciences 2009; Foreign Assoc., Brazilian Acad. of Sciences 2009, NAS 2010; mem. American Physical Soc. 1988, Fellow 1990; Officier, Légion d'honneur, Gra Cruz Ordem Nacional Do Merito Cientifico (Brazil) 2007; Prix Aimé Cotton, Soc. Française de Physique 1971, Loeb Lecturer, Harvard Univ. 1980, Grand Prix de Physique Jean Ricard, Soc. Française de Physique 1983, Einstein Prize for Laser Science (Industrial and Univ. Research Affiliates) 1988, Humboldt Award (Germany) 1992, Michelson Medal, Franklin Inst., Philadelphia 1993, EPS travelling lecturer 1993–94, Manne Siegbahn Lecture, Stockholm 2000, Tomassoni Award, La Sapienza Univ., Rome 2001, Quantum Electronics Prize, European Physical Soc. 2002, Quantum Communication Award, Int. Org. for Quantum Communication, Measurement and Computing and Tamagawa Univ. (Japan) 2002, Charles Hard Townes Award, Optical Soc. of America 2007, CNRS Gold Medal 2009, Advanced Research Grant, European Research Council 2009, Herbert Walther Award, German Physical Soc. and Optical Soc. of America 2010, Nobel Prize in Physics (jtly with David J. Wineland) for "ground-breaking experimental methods that enable measuring and manipulation of individual quantum systems" 2012. *Achievements include:* principally known for proving quantum decoherence by experimental observation, while working with colleagues at École Normale Supérieure 1996. *Publications include:* Laser Spectroscopy, Proceedings of the Second International Conference, Megève (co-ed.) 1975, Frontiers in Laser Spectrscopy, Proceedings of Les Houches Summer School, Session XXVII (co-ed.) 1977, Atomic Physics 11, Proceedings of the 11th International Conference in Atomic Physics (co-ed.) 1989, La physique quantique 2004, Exploring the Quantum: Atoms, Cavities and Photons (with Jean-Michel Raimond) 2006; more than 240 papers in professional journals. *Address:* Collège de France, 11 place Marcelin Berthelot, 75231 Paris Cedex 05 (office); Département de Physique de l'Ecole Normale Supérieure, 24 rue Lhomond, 75005 Paris, France (office). *Telephone:* 1-44-32-34-20 (office). *Fax:* 1-44-32-34-94 (office). *E-mail:* haroche@lkb.ens.fr (office). *Website:* www.college-de-france.fr/site/en-serge-haroche (office).

HAROON, Abdullah Hussain; Pakistani diplomatist and politician; b. 21 Oct. 1950, Karachi; ed Karachi Grammar School, Univ. of Karachi; began career in public service as Election Co-ordinator for Pakistan Muslim League 1970; Councillor, Karachi Metropolitan Corpn 1979–85; Trustee Karachi Port Trust 1980–82; mem. Prov. Ass. of Sindh 1985–88, Speaker 1985–86, Leader of Opposition 1986–88; Consultant, Pakistan Herald Publication Ltd 1988–89; fmr del. to UN Gen. Ass.; Amb. and Perm. Rep. to UN, New York 2008–12; mem. Bd of Govs Inst. of Business Admin, Karachi 1996–99; mem. Bd of Dirs Karachi Electric Supply Corpn 1997–99; Chair. Griffith Coll., Karachi 1999–2005; Pres. Pakistan-China Business Forum 1999–2004, English Speaking Union of Pakistan, Sindh Club (youngest pres.). *Address:* Ministry of Foreign Affairs, Constitution Avenue, Islamabad, Pakistan (office). *Telephone:* (51) 9210335 (office). *Fax:* (51) 9207600 (office). *Website:* www.mofa.gov.pk (office).

HAROUN, Mahamat-Saleh; Chadian film director and former journalist; b. 1961, Abéché; ed Conservatoire Libre du Cinéma, Paris, Institut Technique de Bordeaux. *Films include:* Maral Tanié 1994, Goi Goi 1995, A Tea in the Sahel, Bord'Africa 1995, Soitgui Kouyate 1996, Un griot moderne, Bye Bye Africa 1999 (film prizes in Venice 1999, Zanzibar 2000, M-Net All African Awards 2000), Abouna 2002, Dry Season 2006, Sexe, gombo et beurre salé 2008, A Screaming Man (Grand Prix du Jury, Cannes Film Festival) 2010.

HAROUTUNIAN, Gagik G., DL; Armenian politician and lawyer; *Chairman, Constitutional Court;* b. 1948, Geghashen; three c.; ed Yerevan State Univ.;

Lecturer, Yerevan Inst. of Industry 1975–77; in Yugoslavia 1977–78; on staff Cen. Cttee Armenian CP 1982–88; Head of Dept 1988–90; joined nationalist opposition 1990; Deputy Chair. Armenian Parl. 1990–91; Vice-Pres. of Armenia 1991–95; Acting Chair. Council of Ministers (Prime Minister) 1991–92; Chair. Constitutional Court 1996–; Pres. Int. Conf. of Constitutional Control Organs of New Democracy States; Council Pres. Centre of Constitutional Law; mem. Int. Asscn of Constitutional Law, Comm. for Democracy through Law, Council of Europe. *Publications:* 23 monographs, including Constitutional Review (with A. Mavčič) 1999, 2002; 150 scientific works. *Address:* Constitutional Court, Marshal Baghramian Avenue 10, 0019 Yerevan (office); Avan, Quchak Quarter, Apt 11, Yerevan, Armenia (home). *Telephone:* (10) 58-81-30 (office). *Fax:* (10) 52-99-91 (office). *E-mail:* armlaw@concourt.am (office). *Website:* www.concourt.am

HAROUTUNIAN, Michael; Armenian army officer and government official; b. 10 Feb. 1946, Sagiyan village, Shemakhin; m.; three c.; ed Frunze Mil. Acad. and Mil. Acad. of the Soviet Armed Forces; early career in Soviet Army, posts included CO of reconnaissance unit, Deputy Chief of Staff, Head of Reconnaissance Dept; Sr Instructor of Reconnaissance Unit, Military Acad. of the Soviet Armed Forces 1988–92; enlisted in Armed Forces of Armenia 1992; Head of Operations Dept and Deputy Head, Chief of Staff 1992–93; First Deputy Head, Chief of Staff of Armed Forces 1993–94, Chief of Staff of Armed Forces and First Deputy Minister of Defence 1994–2007, Minister of Defence 2007–08; 'Service to the Motherland', Second Degree (USSR), Combat Cross, Second Degree (Armenia), Vardan Mamikonyan (Armenia), Combat Cross, Second Degree (NKR), Legion of Honor (USA), Combat Service, First Degree (Armenia), 'For the Service to the Motherland', First Degree (Armenia), Marshal Baghramyan decoration, Ministry of Defence, 'For Perfect Service', First and Second Degrees, Ministry of Defence, Andranik Ozanyan decoration, Ministry of Defence, 'Coat of Arms', Ministry of Defence, Nominal Weapon, Ministry of Defence, 'For Strengthening Combat Collaboration', Ministry of Defence, Russian Fed. *Address:* c/o Ministry of Defence, G. Shaush Street 60, Yerevan 0088, Armenia.

HARPER, Charles Michel (Mike), MBA; American business executive (retd); b. 26 Sept. 1927, Lansing, Mich.; s. of Charles F. Harper and Alma Michel; m. Joan F. Bruggema 1950; one s. three d.; ed Purdue Univ., Univ. of Chicago; with General Motors Corpn, Detroit, Mich. 1950–54; with Pillsbury Co., Minneapolis, Minn. 1954–74, Group Vice-Pres. Poultry, Food Service and Venture Businesses 1970–74; Exec. Vice-Pres., COO and Dir Conagra Inc., Omaha 1974–76, Chair. and CEO 1976–92, Chair. 1992–93; CEO RJR Nabisco Holdings Inc. 1993–95, Chair. 1995–96; mem. Bd of Dirs Norwest Corpn, Valmont Industries, Inc., Peter Kiewit Sons Inc.; several hon. degrees. *Address:* 6625 State Street, Omaha, NE 68152, USA. *Telephone:* (402) 571-6612. *Fax:* (402) 571-2151. *E-mail:* olemike27@gmail.com (office).

HARPER, Judson Morse, BS, MS, PhD; American academic administrator (retd), consultant and academic; b. 25 Aug. 1936, Lincoln, Neb.; s. of Floyd Harper and Eda Harper; m. Patricia A. Kennedy 1958; three s.; ed Iowa State Univ., with General Mills 1963–70, latterly Man. for New Business Ventures in Research Div.; Prof. of Chemical and Bioresource Eng, Colorado State Univ. 1970–2002, Prof. Emer. 2004–, Vice-Pres. for Research and Information Tech. 1982–2000, Interim Pres. 1989–90, Special Asst to Pres. 2000–04; consultant 1974–2010; Fellow, Inst. of Food Technologists 1992, AAAS 1995; Fulbright-Hayes Scholar 1978–79; Food Eng Award 1983, Int. Award, Inst. of Food Technologists 1990, Charles A. Lory Public Service Award, Colorado State Univ. 1993, Professional Achievement Award, Iowa State Univ. 1986; named Harper Research Complex, Colorado State Univ. 2000. *Publications include:* Extrusion of Foods 1981, Extrusion Cooking 1989; 91 refereed publs; holder of six US patents. *Leisure interests:* walking, gardening, reading. *Address:* 1818 Westview Road, Fort Collins, CO 80524, USA (home). *Telephone:* (970) 222-0357 (office); (970) 493-1191 (office). *Fax:* (970) 493-1191 (office). *E-mail:* judson.harper@colostate.edu (office).

HARPER, Stephen, MA; Canadian politician and economist; *Prime Minister;* b. 20 April 1959, Toronto; m. Laureen Teskey; one s. one d.; ed Richview Collegiate Inst., Univ. of Calgary; Chief Aide to Jim Hawkes MP 1985; Exec. Asst to Deborah Grey MP 1989, Chief Adviser and Speech Writer –1993; founding mem. Reform Party; MP (Calgary West) 1993–97, 2002; Vice-Pres. Nat. Citizens Coalition 1997, later Pres.; Leader Canadian Alliance 2002; Leader of the Opposition 2002–06; Co-founder Conservative Party of Canada 2003, Leader 2004–, Prime Minister of Canada 2006–; mem. Queen's Privy Council for Canada. *Address:* Office of the Prime Minister, Langevin Block, 80 Wellington Street, Ottawa, ON K1A 0A2 (office); Conservative Party of Canada, 130 Albert Street, Suite 1720, Ottawa, ON K1P 5G4, Canada (office). *Telephone:* (613) 941-6888 (PM) (office); (613) 755-2000 (office). *Fax:* (613) 941-6900 (PM) (office); (613) 755-2001 (office). *E-mail:* pm@pm .gc.ca (office); info@conservative.ca (office). *Website:* www.pm.gc.ca (office); www .conservative.ca (office).

HARPPRECHT, Klaus Christoph; German/French author, television producer, journalist and editor; b. 11 April 1927, Stuttgart; s. of Christoph Harpprecht and Dorothea Harpprecht (née Bronisch); m. Renate Lasker 1961; ed Evangelical Theological Seminary, Blaubeuren, Württemberg and Univs of Tübingen, Munich and Stuttgart; jr and Bonn Corresp., Christ und Welt 1948–53; commentator and corresp., RIAS Berlin (Rundfunk im amerikanischen Sektor), Sender Freies Berlin and Westdeutscher Rundfunk, Cologne 1953–61; America Corresp., Zweites Deutsches Fernsehen 1962–65; Publr, S. Fischer Verlag and Ed. Der Monat 1966–71; consultant and chief speech writer to Chancellor Willy Brandt 1972–74; Ed. GEO magazine, Hamburg 1978–79; now ind. writer; Chevalier, Légion d'honneur; Theodore Wolff Award 1965, Drexel Award 1966, Medienpreis der Gesellschaft für Deutsche Sprache 2002, City of Hamburg Lessing Prize 2010, Theodor Wolff Lebenswerk Award 2011. *Radio:* regular contribs to political and cultural programmes. *Television:* about 100 documentary films. *Publications include:* The East German Rising 1954, Viele Grüsse an die Freiheit 1964, Beschädigte Paradiese 1966, Willy Brandt: Portrait 1970, L'Evolution Allemande 1978, Der Fremde Freund Amerika: Eine Innere Geschichte 1982, Amerikaner: Freunde, Fremde, Ferne Nachbarn 1984, Amerika: die Geschichte seiner Eroberung (with Thomas Hoepker) 1986, Georg Forster – oder die Liebe zur Welt 1987, Das Ende der Gemuetlichkeit 1987, Die Lust der Freiheit. Deutsche Revolutionaere in Paris 1989, Die Leute von Port Madeleine – Dorfgeschichten aus der Provence (with Hans Hillmann) 1989, Welt-Anschauung Reisebilder 1991,

Thomas Mann. Eine Biographie 1995, Schreibspiele: Bemerkungen zur Literatur 1996, Mein Frankreich – eine schwierige Liebe 1999, Dieu est-il encore français? 2000, Im Kanzleramt: Tagebuch der Jahre mit Willy Brandt 2000, Harald Poelchau – Ein Leben im Widerstand 2004, Die Gräfin: Marion Dönhoff. Eine Biographie 2008, Arletty und ihr deutscher Offizier 2011. *Leisure interests:* music, literature, history. *Address:* 16 Clos des Palmeraies, 83420 La Croix-Valmer, France. *Telephone:* (4) 94-79-60-76. *Fax:* (4) 94-54-20-30. *E-mail:* klausharpprecht@aol.com.

HARRACH, Péter; Hungarian politician; b. 2 Nov. 1947, Budapest; m.; three c.; ed Catholic Univ. of Budapest; joined Christian Democratic People's Party (KDNP) 1989, specialist on church policy, Pres. KDNP Budapest Zugló district 1990–97, Pres. Budapest co-ordinating org. 1993–94, Nat. Vice-Pres. 1995–97 (resgnd), Parl. Group Deputy Leader 2006, Leader 2010–; mem. Parl. 1998–; Vice-Pres. Hungarian Christian Democratic Alliance (MKDSZ) 1997–2000, Co-Pres. 2000–04, Pres. 2004–; pastoral assistant at several parishes –1990; official in charge of secular affairs Secr. of Hungarian Catholic Bishops' Conf. 1990–98; mem. Budapest Zugló (District XIV) Ass. 1990–98; mem. Budapest Municipal Ass. 1994–98; Minister for Social and Family Affairs 1998–2002; Deputy Speaker Nat. Ass. 2002; mem. (as MKDSZ del.) Exec. of Alliance of Young Democrats (FIDESZ); Pres. Szob constituency FIDESZ-Hungarian Civic Alliance 2004–06. *Address:* Hungarian National Assembly, 1357 Budapest, Kossuth tér 1–3, Hungary (office). *Telephone:* (1) 441-4000 (office); (1) 441-4408 (office). *Fax:* (1) 441-4414 (office). *Website:* www.parlament.hu (office).

HARRELL, Lynn; American cellist; *Professor of Cello, Shepherd School of Music, Rice University;* b. 30 Jan. 1944, New York; s. of Mack Harrell and Marjorie Fulton; m. Linda Blandford 1976; one s. one d.; ed Juilliard School of Music, New York and Curtis Inst. of Music, Philadelphia; principal cellist, Cleveland Orchestra (under George Szell) 1963–71; now appears as soloist with the world's major orchestras; Piatigorsky Prof. of Cello, Univ. of Southern California 1987–93; Prof. of Int. Cello Studies, RAM, London 1988–93, 1993–95; Artistic Dir LA Philharmonic Inst. 1988–92; Music Adviser, San Diego Symphony Orchestra 1988–89; soloist, Memorial Concert for Holocaust Victims, Vatican 1994; Prof. of Cello, Shepherd School of Music, Rice Univ. 2002–; collaborations with Anne-Sophie Mutter, André Previn; two Grammy Awards. *Recordings include:* works by J. S. Bach, Beethoven, Bloch, Boccherini, Brahms, Bruch, Debussy, Dutilleux, Dvořák, Elgar, Fauré, Haydn, Herbert, Hindemith, Lalo, Mendelssohn, Prokofiev, Rachmaninov, Rosza, Saint-Saëns, Schoenberg, Schubert, Schumann, Shostakovich, Strauss, Tchaikovsky, Villa-Lobos, Vivaldi, Walton. *Leisure interests:* chess, fishing, golf, writing. *Address:* Opus 3 Artists, 470 Park Avenue South, 9th Floor North, New York, NY 10016, USA (office); 2271 Alice Pratt Brown Hall, Rice University, Houston, TX 77005-1892, USA (office). *Telephone:* (212) 584-7500 (office); 713-348-4854 (office). *Fax:* (646) 300-8200 (office). *E-mail:* eblackburn@opus3artists.com (office). *Website:* www.opus3artists.com (office); www.ruf.rice.edu/~musi/facultybios/ harrell (office).

HARRELSON, Woodrow (Woody) Tracy, BA; American actor; b. 23 July 1961, Midland, Tex.; m. Laura Louie 2008; three d.; ed Hanover Coll.; Founder, Voice Yourself (website). *Theatre includes:* The Boys Next Door, Two on Two (author, producer, actor), The Zoo Story (author, actor), Brooklyn Laundry, Furthest from the Sun (also playwright), On An Average Day (Comedy Theatre, London) 2002, Night of the Iguana (Lyric Theatre, London) 2005–06. *Television includes:* Cheers (series) 1985–93, Bay Coven 1987, Killer Instinct 1988, Mother Goose Rock 'n' Rhyme 1990, Will & Grace (series) 2001, Game Change (film) 2012, True Detective (series) 2014. *Films include:* Wildcats 1986, Cool Blue 1988, Doc Hollywood 1991, Ted and Venus 1991, White Men Can't Jump 1992, Indecent Proposal 1993, I'll Do Anything 1994, The Cowboy Way 1994, Natural Born Killers 1994, Money Train 1995, The Sunchaser 1996, The People vs Larry Flynt 1996, Kingpin 1996, Wag the Dog 1997, Welcome to Sarajevo 1997, The Thin Red Line 1998, Palmetto 1998, The Hi-Lo Country 1998, EdTV 1999, Play It to the Bone 1999, American Saint 2001, Scorched 2003, Anger Management 2003, She Hate Me 2004, After the Sunset 2004, The Big White 2005, North Country 2005, The Prize Winner of Defiance, Ohio 2005, A Prairie Home Companion 2006, Free Jimmy (voice) 2006, A Scanner Darkly 2006, The Grand 2007, The Walker 2007, No Country for Old Men 2007, Battle in Seattle 2007, Transsiberian 2008, Sleepwalking 2008, Semi-Pro 2008, Surfer, Dude 2008, Management 2008, Seven Pounds 2008, The Messenger 2009, Zombieland 2009, 2012 2009, Defendor 2010, Bunraku 2010, The Hunger Games 2012, Seven Psychopaths 2012, Now You See Me 2013, Out of the Furnace 2013, The Hunger Games: Catching Fire 2013. *Leisure interests:* sports, juggling, writing, chess. *Address:* c/o Creative Artists Agency, 9830 Wilshire Boulevard, Beverly Hills, CA 90212, USA. *Website:* www.voiceyourself.com.

HARRIES OF PENTREGARTH, Baron (Life Peer), cr. 2006, of Ceinewydd in the County of Dyfed; **Richard Douglas Harries,** DD, FKC, FRSL, FLSW; British ecclesiastic; *Honorary Professor of Theology, King's College London;* b. 2 June 1936, Eltham, London, England; s. of Brig. W. D. J. Harries and G. M. B. Harries; m. Josephine Bottomley 1963; one s. one d.; ed Wellington Coll., Royal Mil. Acad., Sandhurst, Selwyn Coll., Cambridge, Cuddesdon Coll., Oxford; Lt, Royal Corps of Signals 1955–58; Curate, Hampstead Parish Church 1963–69; Chaplain, Westfield Coll. 1966–69; Lecturer, Wells Theological Coll. 1969–72; Warden, Salisbury and Wells Theological Coll. 1971–72; Vicar, All Saints, Fulham, London 1972–81; Dean, King's Coll., London 1981–87, Fellow and Hon. Prof. of Theology; Bishop of Oxford 1987–2006; Prof. of Divinity, Gresham Coll., London 2008–12, Prof. Emer. 2012–; Vice-Chair. Council of Christian Action 1979–87, Council for Arms Control 1982–87; Chair. Southwark Ordination Course 1982–87, Shalom, End Loans to South Africa (ELSTA) 1982–87, Christian Evidence Soc.; Chair. Church of England Bd of Social Responsibility 1996–2001; Consultant to the Archbishops on Jewish-Christian Relations 1986–92; Chair. Council of Christians and Jews 1993–2001, House of Lords select Cttee on Stem Cell Research 2001–02; Visiting Prof., Liverpool Hope Coll. 2002; mem. (Crossbench) House of Lords 2006–; mem. Home Office Advisory Cttee for Reform of Law on Sexual Offences 1981–85, Bd Christian Aid 1994–2001, Royal Comm. on Lords Reform 1999–, Nuffield Council of Bioethics 2002–06, Human Fertilisation and Embryology Authority 2003–09, Parl. Select Cttee on Privacy and Superinjunctions 2012; Trustee, Multi-Faith School Trust, Woolf Inst., Cambridge; Fellow, Learned Soc. of Wales 2011; Hon. Fellow, Selwyn Coll., Cambridge, St Anne's Coll. Oxford; Hon. FMedSci 2004; Hon.

Fellow, Soc. of Biology 2009; Hon. DD (London) 1996; Hon. DUniv (Oxford Brookes) 2001, (Open Univ.), (Huddersfield) 2008; Sir Sigmund Steinberg Award 1989, Pres.'s Medal, British Acad. 2012. *Radio:* regular broadcaster, particularly on BBC Radio 4's Today Programme. *Publications include:* Prayers of Hope 1975, Turning to Prayer 1978, Prayers of Grief and Glory 1979, Being a Christian 1981, Should Christians Support Guerrillas? 1982, The Authority of Divine Love 1983, Praying Round the Clock 1983, Seasons of the Spirit (co-ed.) 1984, Prayer and the Pursuit of Happiness 1989, Reinhold Niebuhr and the Issues of Our Time (ed.) 1986, Christianity and War in a Nuclear Age 1986, C. S. Lewis: The Man and His God 1987, Is There a Gospel for the Rich? 1992, Art and the Beauty of God 1993, The Value of Business and its Values (co-author) 1993, Questioning Faith 1995, A Gallery of Reflections 1995, In the Gladness of Today 2000, Christianity: Two Thousand Years (co-ed.) 2000, God Outside the Box: Why Spiritual People Object to Christianity 2002, After the Evil: Christianity and Judaism in the Shadow of the Holocaust 2003, The Passion in Art 2005, The Re-Enchantment of Morality 2008, Faith in Politics? – Rediscovering the Christian Roots of Our Political Values 2010, Questions of Life and Death 2010, Reinhold Niebuhr and Contemporary Politics (co-ed.) 2010; contrib. to several books; numerous articles. *Leisure interests:* theatre, literature, sport. *Address:* House of Lords, Westminster, London, SW1A 0PW, England (office). *Telephone:* (20) 7219-2910 (office). *E-mail:* harriesr@ parliament.uk (office). *Website:* www.parliament.uk/biographies/lords/richard -harries/26680 (office).

HARRINGTON, Anthony Stephen; American lawyer, consultant and fmr diplomatist; *President and CEO, Albright Stonebridge Group;* b. 9 March 1941, Taylorsville, NC; s. of Atwell Lee Harrington and Louise Harrington (née Chapman); m. Hope Reynolds 1971; two s.; ed Univ. of North Carolina, Duke Univ.; Sr Pnr, Hogan & Hartson (law firm), Washington, DC, now Sr Advisor; Amb. to Brazil 2000–01; Pres. and CEO Stonebridge Int. LLC (now Albright Stonebridge Group LLC (investment and consulting group); fmr mem. Bd of Dirs PRE Holdings, Inc.; fmr Chair. Pres.'s Intelligence Oversight Bd; Vice-Chair. Pres.'s Foreign Intelligence Advisory Bd 1994–99; Co-Chair. Advisory Council Brazil Inst. of Woodrow Wilson Int. Center for Scholars, Brazil-US Business Council; mem. Bd of Dirs Center for Democracy; mem. Bd of Trustees Kenan Inst. for Pvt. Enterprise; fmr mem. Comm. on the Roles and Capabilities of the US Intelligence Community; co-founder Telecom USA (long-distance telephone co.); Founder and Dir Ovation; Order of Rio Branco, Grand Cross (Brazil). *Leisure interests:* politics, tennis, gardening, reading. *Address:* Albright Stonebridge Group, 555 Thirteenth Street, NW, Suite 300, West Columbia Square, Washington, DC 20004-1109 (office); Ratcliffe Manor, 7768 Ratcliffe Manor Lane, Easton, MD 21601, USA (home). *Telephone:* (202) 637-8600 (office). *Fax:* (202) 637-8615 (office). *E-mail:* info@albrightstonebridge.com (office). *Website:* www.albrightstonebridge.com (home).

HARRINGTON, Padraig; Irish professional golfer; b. 31 Aug. 1971, Dublin; m. Caroline Harrington 1997; two s.; turned professional 1995, joined European Tour 1996, PGA Tour 2005; European Tour wins include Spanish Open 1996, Brazil Sao Paulo 500 Years Open 2000, BBVA Turespana Masters de Madrid 2000, Volvo Masters 2001, Dunhill Links Championship 2002, 2006, BMW Asian Open 2003, Deutsche Bank Open 2003, Omega Hong Kong Open 2004, Linde German Masters 2004, Irish Open 2007; major tournament wins include Open Championship 2007, 2008, PGA Championship 2008; PGA Tour wins include Honda Classic 2005, Barclay's Classic 2005; other wins include Irish PGA Championship 1998, 2004, 2005, 2007, 2008, Target World Challenge 2002, Dunlop Phoenix Tournament 2006, Hassan II Trophy, Morocco 2007; represented Europe in Ryder Cup 1999, 2002, 2004, 2006, 2008; f. Padraig Harrington Charitable Foundation 2005; European Order of Merit 2006, European Tour Golfer of the Year 2007, 2008, European Tour Shot of the Year 2008, AGW Trophy 2007, 2008, Hon. Mem. European Tour 2007, PGA of America Player of the Year, US PGA Tour Player of the Year 2008. *Address:* c/o IMG, McCormack House, Burlington Lane, Chiswick, London, W4 2TH, England. *Telephone:* (20) 8233-5300 (office). *Fax:* (20) 8233-5268 (office). *E-mail:* katie.powell@imgworld.com (office). *Website:* www .padraigharrington.com (home).

HARRIS, Edward Allen (Ed), BFA; American actor; b. 28 Nov. 1950, Englewood, NJ; s. of Bob L. Harris and Margaret Harris; m. Amy Madigan; one c.; ed Columbia Univ., Univ. of Oklahoma, Calif. Inst. of Arts. *Stage appearances include:* A Streetcar Named Desire, Sweet Bird of Youth, Julius Caesar, Hamlet, Camelot, Time of Your Life, Grapes of Wrath, Present Laughter, Fool for Love (Obie Award 1983), Prairie Avenue (LA Drama Critics Circle Award 1981), Scar 1985 (San Francisco Critics Award), Precious Sons 1986 (Theater World Award), Simpatico 1994, Taking Sides 1996, Wrecks 2005. *Films include:* Coma 1978, Borderline 1978, Knightriders 1980, Creepshow 1981, The Right Stuff 1982, Swing Shift 1982, Under Fire 1982, A Flash of Green 1983, Places in the Heart 1983, Alamo Bay 1984, Sweet Dreams 1985, Code Name: Emerald 1985, Walker 1987, To Kill a Priest 1988, Jacknife 1989, The Abyss 1989, State of Grace 1990, Paris Trout 1991, Glengarry Glen Ross 1992, Needful Things 1993, The Firm 1993, China Moon 1994, Milk Money 1994, Apollo 13 1995, Just Cause 1995, Eye for an Eye 1995, The Rock 1996, Absolute Power 1997, Stepmom 1998, The Truman Show 1998, The Third Miracle 1999, Waking the Dead 2000, The Prime Gig 2000, Pollock (also producer and dir) 2001, Enemy at the Gates 2001, Buffalo Soldiers 2001, A Beautiful Mind 2001, Just a Dream (voice) 2002, The Hours 2002, Masked and Anonymous 2003, The Human Stain 2003, Radio 2003, Dirt Nap 2005, Winter Passing 2005, A History of Violence (Nat. Film Critics Supporting Actor Award) 2005, Copying Beethoven 2006, Gone Baby Gone 2007, Cleaner 2007, National Treasure Book of Secrets 2007, Touching Home 2008, Appaloosa (also dir) 2008, Once Fallen 2010, The Way Back 2010, Virginia 2010, Salvation Boulevard 2011, That's What I Am 2011, Man on a Ledge 2012, Sweetwater 2013, Phantom 2013, Snowpiercer 2013, Pain & Gain 2013, Look of Love 2013. *Television includes:* Gibbsville – Trapped 1976, The Amazing Howard Hughes 1977, The Seekers 1979, The Aliens are Coming 1980, The Last Innocent Man 1987, Running Mates 1992, The Stand 1994, Riders of the Purple Sage 1996, Empire Falls 2005, Game Change (film) (Golden Globe Award for Best Performance by an Actor in a Supporting Role in a Series, Mini-Series or Motion Picture Made for Television 2013) 2012. *Address:* c/o Rick Kurtzman, CAA, 15260 Ventura Blvd, Suite 940, Sherman Oaks, CA 91403, USA (office).

HARRIS, Emmylou; American singer; b. 2 April 1947, Birmingham, Ala; m. 1st Brian Ahern; m. 2nd Paul Kennerley 1985; two d.; ed Univ. of North Carolina; singer 1967–, toured with Fallen Angels Band in USA and Europe; Pres. Country Music Foundation 1983–; Fellow, American Acad. of Arts and Sciences 2009–; Grammy Awards 1976, 1977, 1980, 1981, 1984, 1987, 1992, 1996, Country Music Asscn Female Vocalist of the Year 1980, Grammy Award for Best Female Country Vocal Performance (for The Connection) 2006. *Recordings include:* albums: Gliding Bird 1969, Pieces of the Sky 1975, Elite Hotel 1976, Luxury Liner 1977, Quarter Moon in a Ten-Cent Town 1978, Blue Kentucky Girl 1979, Light of the Stable 1979, Roses In The Snow 1980, Evangeline 1981, Cimarron 1981, Last Date 1982, White Shoes 1983, The Ballad of Sally Rose 1985, Thirteen 1986, Trio (with Dolly Parton and Linda Ronstadt) (Acad. of Country Music Album of the Year 1988) 1987, Angel Band 1987, Bluebird 1989, Brand New Dance 1990, Duets (with Nash Ramblers) 1990, At The Ryman 1992, Cowgirl's Prayer 1993, Songs of the West 1994, Wrecking Ball 1995, Portraits 1996, Nashville 1996, Spyboy 1998, Red Dirt Girl 2000, Singin' with Emmylou Harris (vol. I) 2000, Anthology 2001, Stumble Into Grace 2003, All the Roadrunning (with Mark Knopfler) 2006, Neil Young Heart of Gold 2006, All I Intended to Be 2008, Hard Bargain 2011, Old Yellow Moon (with Rodney Crowell) (Grammy Award for Best Americana Album 2014) 2013. *Address:* 1025 16th Ave South, Suite 202, Nashville, TN 37212-2328, USA (office).

HARRIS, Sir Henry, Kt, FRS, FRCP, FRCPath; British cell biologist; *Regius Professor Emeritus of Medicine, University of Oxford;* b. 28 Jan. 1925; s. of Sam Harris and Ann Harris; m. Alexandra Brodsky 1950; one s. two d.; ed Sydney Boys High School, Univ. of Sydney, Lincoln Coll., Oxford; Dir of Research, Cancer Research Campaign, Sir William Dunn School of Pathology, Oxford 1954–59; Visiting Scientist, NIH, USA 1959–60; Head, Dept of Cell Biology, John Innes Inst. 1960–63; Prof. of Pathology, Univ. of Oxford 1963–79, Regius Prof. of Medicine 1979–92, Prof. Emer. 1992–; Head of the Sir William Dunn School of Pathology, Oxford 1963–94; Corresp. mem. Australian Acad. of Science; Foreign mem. Max Planck Soc.; Foreign Prof., Coll. de France; Hon. mem. American Asscn of Pathologists, German Soc. of Cell Biology; Foreign Hon. mem. American Acad. of Arts and Sciences; Hon. Fellow, Cambridge Philosophical Soc.; Hon. FRCPath (Australia); Hon. DSc (Edinburgh); Hon. MD (Geneva, Sydney); Feldberg Foundation Award; Ivison Macadam Memorial Prize; Prix de la Fondation Isabelle Decazes de Nöue for cancer research, Madonnina Prize for Medical Research; Katherine Burkan Judd Award of the Memorial-Sloan Kettering Cancer Center; Medal of Honour, Univ. of Pavia, Royal Medal of the Royal Soc., Osler Medal of the Royal Coll. of Physicians. *Publications:* Nucleus and Cytoplasm 1968, Cell Fusion 1970, La fusion cellulaire 1974, The Balance of Improbabilities 1987, The Cells of the Body 1995, The Birth of the Cell 1999, Things Come to Life 2002, Remnants of a Quiet Life 2006; papers on cellular physiology and biochemistry in various scientific books and journals and some fiction. *Leisure interests:* history and literature. *Address:* c/o Sir William Dunn School of Pathology, South Parks Road, Oxford, OX1 3RE, England. *Telephone:* (1865) 275500. *Fax:* (1865) 275501.

HARRIS, Isaiah (Ike), Jr; American business executive; *Chairman, CIGNA Corporation;* Pres. BellSouth Enterprises, Inc. 2004–05; Pres. and CEO AT&T Advertising & Publishing – East (fmr BellSouth Advertising and Publishing Group) 2005–07; mem. Bd of Dirs CIGNA Corpn 2005–, Vice-Chair. July–Dec. 2009, Chair. Dec. 2009–; mem. Bd of Dirs Deluxe Corpn 2004–11; Ind. Trustee, Wells Fargo Advantage Funds 2008–. *Address:* CIGNA Corpn, 2 Liberty Place, 1601 Chestnut Street, Philadelphia, PA 19192, USA (office). *Telephone:* (215) 761-1000 (office). *Fax:* (215) 761-5515 (office). *E-mail:* info@cigna.com (office). *Website:* www.cigna.com (office).

HARRIS, Jeff, CA; British business executive; *Chairman, Cookson Group PLC;* b. 1948; began career as accountant with two auditing firms; Chief Accountant, Alliance UniChem PLC 1985, Finance Dir 1986, then Deputy CEO then CEO, Chair. 2001–05; Chair. Filtrona PLC 2005–, Cookson Group PLC 2010–; mem. Bd of Dirs Bunzl PLC –2010, Andreae-Noris Zahn 1999–2007, Associated British Foods May 2003–07; Hon. DBA (Kingston Univ.). *Address:* Cookson Group PLC, 165 Fleet Street, London EC4A 2AE, England (office). *Telephone:* (0780) 220000 (office). *Fax:* (0207) 820100 (office). *E-mail:* info@cookson.co.uk (office). *Website:* www.cookson.co.uk (office).

HARRIS, Kamala D., JD; American lawyer and government official; *Attorney-General of California;* b. 20 Oct. 1964, Oakland, Calif.; d. of Donald Harris and Shyamala Gopalan; ed Howard Univ., Washington, DC, Univ. of California, Hastings Coll. of Law; spent many years in Prosecutor's Office, including Deputy Dist Attorney, Alameda Co., Calif. 1990–98, Man. Attorney, Career Criminal Unit, San Francisco Dist Attorney's Office 1998–2000, Chief of Community and Neighborhood Div., Office of San Francisco City Attorney 2000–04, Dist Attorney of San Francisco 2004–10, Attorney-Gen. of Calif. 2011–. *Publications:* Smart on Crime: A Career Prosecutor's Plan to Make Us Safer 2009. *Address:* Attorney-General's Office, California Department of Justice, PO Box 944255, Sacramento, CA 94244-2550, USA (office). *Telephone:* (916) 322-3360 (office). *Website:* oag.ca .gov (office).

HARRIS, Sir Martin Best, Kt, CBE, PhD, DL; British administrator and fmr university vice-chancellor; b. 28 June 1944, Ruabon, Wales; s. of William Best Harris and Betty Evelyn Harris (née Martin); m. Barbara Mary Daniels 1966; two s.; ed Devonport High School, Plymouth, Queens' Coll., Cambridge, School of Oriental and African Studies, Univ. of London; Lecturer in French Linguistics, Univ. of Leicester 1967–72; Prof. of Romance Linguistics 1976–87, Pro-Vice-Chancellor 1981–87; Vice-Chancellor, Univ. of Essex 1987–92, Univ. of Manchester 1992–2004; Chair. Cttee of Vice-Chancellors and Prins 1997–99; mem. Univ. Grants Cttee 1984–87, Chair. Northern Ireland Cttee 1985–87; Chair. Northern Ireland Cttee, Univs Funding Council 1987–91, Nat. Curriculum Working Group on Modern Languages 1989–90, HEFCE/CVCP Review of Postgraduate Educ. 1995–96, Clinical Standards Advisory Group 1996–99, North West Univs Asscn 1999–2001, Higher Educ. Careers Advisory Services Review 2000–01, Manchester: Knowledge Capital 2003–08; Deputy Chair. Northwest Dent Agency 2002–08; Pres. Clare Hall, Cambridge Univ. 2008–13; mem. Bd Universities' Superannuation Scheme 1991–, Deputy Chair. 2004–06, Chair. 2006–; Dir Office of Fair Access 2004–12; Chair. of Govs, Centre for Information on Language Teaching 1990–96; Crown Gov. SOAS

1990–93; Gov. Anglia Polytechnic Univ. 1989–93; mem. High Council, European Univ. Inst., Florence 1992–97, Comm. for Health Improvement 1999–2002; DL (Greater Manchester) 1997; Hon. mem. Royal Northern Coll. of Music 1996; Hon. Fellow, Queens' Coll., Cambridge 1992, Bolton Inst. 1996, Univ. of Central Lancashire 1999; Hon. LLD (Queen's Univ., Belfast) 1992; Hon. DUniv (Essex) 1993; Hon. DLitt (Salford) 1995, (Manchester Metropolitan) 2000, (Leicester) 2003, (Lincoln) 2003, (Ulster) 2004, (Manchester) 2004, (UMIST) 2004, (Keele) 2006, (Exeter) 2008, (Plymouth) 2009, (London) 2013. *Publications include:* The Evolution of French Syntax 1978, The Romance Languages (with N. Vincent) 1988; numerous articles in anthologies and professional journals. *Leisure interests:* gardening, walking. *Address:* Universities Superannuation Scheme, Royal Liver Building, Liverpool, L3 1PY, England (office). *Telephone:* (151) 227-4711 (office). *Fax:* (151) 236-3173 (office). *E-mail:* postbox@uss.co.uk (office). *Website:* www.uss .co.uk (office).

HARRIS, Michael, BSc, PhD; American mathematician and academic; *Professor of Mathematics, Université de Paris 7 Denis Diderot;* ed Princeton and Harvard Univs; held positions at Brandeis Univ. 1977–94, Prof. 1989–94; Prof., Université de Paris 7 Denis Diderot 1994–; mem. Institut Universitaire de France 2001; Sloan Fellowshiop 1982, Grand Prix Sophie Germain de l'Acad. des Sciences 2006, Clay Research Award, Clay Math. Inst. (co-recipient) 2007. *Publications:* more than 60 publs in professional journals. *Address:* Centre de Mathématiques de Jussieu, Université Paris 7 Denis Diderot, Case Postale 7012, 2 place Jussieu, 75251 Paris Cedex 05, France (office). *Telephone:* 1-44-27-86-78 (office). *E-mail:* harris@math .jussieu.fr (office). *Website:* people.math.jussieu.fr/~harris (office).

HARRIS, Michael (Mike) Deane, ICD.D; Canadian business executive, consultant and fmr politician; *Senior Business Advisor, Fasken Martineau DuMoulin LLP;* b. 23 Jan. 1945, Toronto, Ont.; s. of Deane Harris and Hope Harris; m. Laura Marie Harris; two s.; ed Inst. of Corp. Dirs; fmr school teacher, School Bd Trustee and School Bd Chair. Nipissing Bd of Educ.; began career in tourism and recreation industry owning ventures including tourist resort and ski centre; first elected to Ont. Legislature as MPP for Nipissing 1981, Minister of Natural Resources and Energy 1985, Premier of Prov. of Ont. 1995–2002; Leader of Conservative Party 1990–2002; fmr Sr Business Advisor, Cassels Brock & Blackwell LLP; currently Sr Business Advisor, Fasken Martineau DuMoulin LLP; mem. Bd of Dirs Chartwell Seniors Housing Reit 2003– (Chair.), Canaccord Financial Inc. 2004–, FirstService Corpn 2006–, Route1 Inc. 2009– (Chair.), Element Financial 2010–, Tim Horton Childrens' Foundation; Sr Fellow, Fraser Inst., Vancouver; Hon. DLitt (Nipissing Univ.) 2010; Nat. Citizens' Coalition Freedom Medal 1996, E.P. Taylor Award of Merit, Standardbred Canada 2000, Tax Fighter of the Year Award, Canadian Taxpayer's Fed. 2000, Paul Harris Award, Rotary Club of North Bay 2008, Harris Learning Library, Nipissing Univ. 2011. *Leisure interests:* golf, skiing, bridge. *Address:* Fasken Martineau DuMoulin LLP, 2400-333 Bay Street, Toronto, ON M5H 2T6, Canada (office). *Telephone:* (416) 865-4535 (office). *Fax:* (416) 364-7813 (office). *E-mail:* mharris@fasken.com (office). *Website:* www.fasken.com (office).

HARRIS, Robert Dennis, FRSL; British journalist and writer; b. 7 March 1957, Nottingham; s. of the late Dennis Harris and Audrey Harris; m. Gill Hornby 1988; two s. two d.; ed Univ. of Cambridge; Pres. Cambridge Union; Dir and reporter, BBC 1978–86; Political Ed. Observer 1987–89; columnist, Sunday Times 1989–92, 1996–97. *Publications include:* non-fiction: A Higher Form of Killing (with Jeremy Paxman) 1982, Gotcha! 1983, The Making of Neil Kinnock 1984, Selling Hitler 1987, Good and Faithful Servant 1990; novels: Fatherland 1992, Enigma 1995 (film 2001), Archangel 1998, Pompeii 2003, Imperium 2006, The Ghost 2007, Lustrum 2009, Conspirata 2010, The Fear Index 2011, An Officer and a Spy (Popular Fiction Book of the Year, Specsavers Nat. Book Awards) 2013. *Leisure interests:* collecting books, walking. *Address:* Old Vicarage, Church Street, Kintbury, RG17 9TR, England (home).

HARRIS, Rolf, CBE, OBE, MBE, AM; Australian entertainer and painter; b. 30 March 1930, Bassendean, Perth, WA; s. of C. G. Harris and A. M. Harris (née Robbins); m. Alwen Hughes 1958; one d.; ed Perth Modern School, Univ. of Western Australia, Claremont Teachers' Coll.; champion swimmer as an adolescent and young adult; represented Australia at seven World Fairs 1969–85; painted an official portrait of Queen Elizabeth II, which was the subject of a special episode of Rolf on Art 2005; Hon. mem. Royal Soc. of British Artists; King of Moomba 1975; Dr hc (Univ. of East London) 2007, (Liverpool Hope Univ.) 2010; Australian Centenary Medal 2001, inducted into Australian Recording Industry Asscn Hall of Fame 2008, BAFTA Fellowship 2012. *Television includes:* Eurovision Song Contest UK Commentator 1967, The Rolf Harris Show (BBC) 1967–71, Rolf on Saturday (BBC) 1977–79, Rolf's Cartoon Time (BBC) 1981–87, Rolf's Cartoon Club (HTV) 1989–93, Animal Hospital (BBC) 1994–2004, Rolf's Amazing World of Animals (BBC) 1997–, Bligh of the Bounty—World Navigator 1998–99, Rolf on Art (BBC) 2001–, Rolf's Golden Jubilee, Royal Albert Hall (BBC) 2003, Rolf Harris Star Portraits (BBC) 2004–07, Have I Got News for You 2009–, Penguin Island 2010–. *Singles include:* Tie Me Kangaroo Down Sport 1960, Sun Arise 1962, Two Little Boys 1969, Stairway to Heaven 1993. *Achievements include:* 110 yards backstroke jr champion of Australia 1946. *Publications:* Rolf Harris Picture Book of Cats 1978, Your Cartoon Time 1986, Win or Die 1989, Your Animation Time 1991, Personality Cats 1992, Me and You and Poems Too 1993, Can You Tell What It Is Yet (autobiog.) 2001, Rolf on Art 2002. *Leisure interests:* painting and portraiture, photography, wood carving, lapidary. *Address:* c/o Billy Marsh and Associates, 174–178 North Gower Street, London, NW1 2NB, England (office). *Website:* www .rolfharris.com (office).

HARRIS, Stephen E., MS, PhD; American physicist and academic; *Kenneth and Barbara Oshman Professor, Department of Applied Physics, Stanford University;* b. 29 Nov. 1936, Brooklyn, New York; s. of Henry Harris and Anne Alpern Harris; m. Frances J. Greene 1959; one s. one d.; ed Rensselaer Polytechnic, Troy, New York and Stanford Univ.; Prof. of Electrical Eng, Stanford Univ. 1963–79, of Electrical Eng and Applied Physics 1979–88, Kenneth and Barbara Oshman Prof. 1988–, Dir Edward L. Ginzton Lab. 1983–88, Chair. Dept of Applied Physics 1993–96; Stephen E. Harris Endowed Prof., Texas A&M Univ. 2005; Guggenheim Fellowship 1976–77; Fellow, Optical Soc. of America 1968, IEEE 1972, American Physical Soc. 1975, American Acad. of Arts and Sciences 1995; mem., Nat. Acad. of Eng, NAS; A. Noble Prize 1965, McGraw Research Award 1973, Sarnoff Award

1978, Davies Medal 1984, C.H. Townes Award 1985, Einstein Prize 1991, Quantum Electronics Award 1994, Frederic Ives Medal 1999, Arthur L. Schawlow Prize in Laser Science 2002, Harvey Prize 2007. *Achievements include:* holds 16 US patents. *Publications:* articles in professional journals. *Leisure interests:* skiing, jogging, hiking. *Address:* Edward L. Ginzton Laboratory, Stanford University, 450 Via Palou, Stanford, CA 94305, USA (office). *Telephone:* (650) 723-0224 (office). *Fax:* (650) 725-4115 (office). *E-mail:* seharris@ee.stanford.edu (office). *Website:* www.-ee.stanford.edu/seharris (office).

HARRIS, Thomas; American writer; b. 11 April 1940, Jackson, Tenn.; s. of William Thomas Harris, Jr and Polly Harris; m. (divorced); one d.; ed Baylor Univ.; worked on news desk at Waco News-Tribune newspaper; mem. staff, Associated Press, New York City 1968–74. *Publications:* Black Sunday 1975, Red Dragon 1981, The Silence of the Lambs (Bram Stoker Best Novel Award) 1988, Hannibal 1999, Hannibal Rising 2007. *Address:* c/o Janklow & Nesbit Associates, 445 Park Avenue, New York, NY 10022, USA. *Website:* www.randomhouse.com/features/ thomasharris.

HARRIS, Timothy Sylvester, BSc, MSc, PhD; Saint Christopher and Nevis politician; *Minister of International Trade, Industry, Commerce, Agriculture, Marine Resources, Consumer Affairs and Constituency Empowerment;* b. 1964, Tabernacle; two d.; ed Cayon High School, Basseterre Sr High School, Univ. of the West Indies, Cave Hill and Sr Augustine, Concordia Univ., Montreal, Canada; worked at Social Security Office, Wellington Ltd and S.L. Horsford & Co. Ltd; mem. Labour Party, Constituency Sec. and Constituency Rep. on Nat. Exec. Bd, mem. Young Labour Advisory Cttee and Youth Co-ordinator, currently Chair. St Kitts-Nevis Labour Party; mem. Parl. 1993–; Minister of Agric., Lands and Housing 1995–2000, of Foreign Affairs and Educ. 2000–04, of Foreign Affairs, Int. Trade, Industry, Commerce and Consumer Affairs 2004–10, of Int. Trade, Industry, Commerce, Agric., Marine Resources, Consumer Affairs and Constituency Empowerment 2010–; Victor Cooke Prize, Univ. of W Indies, Post Graduate Award, Cen. Bank of Trinidad and Tobago, Concordia/UWI Post Graduate Award. *Publications:* several articles in journals. *Leisure interests:* cricket, tennis, swimming, basketball, dominoes, travel. *Address:* Ministry of International Trade, Industry, Commerce, Agriculture, Marine Resources, Consumer Affairs and Constituency Empowerment, Basseterre (office); Tabernacle, St Kitts (home). *Telephone:* (869) 467-1008 (office); (869) 467-1014 (office); (869) 465-7768 (home). *Fax:* (869) 465-2556 (office). *E-mail:* timskb@yahoo.co.uk (home).

HARRISON, Alistair, CMG, CVO; British diplomatist and government official; *Marshal of the Diplomatic Corps;* b. 14 Nov. 1954, Guisborough, North Yorks., England; m. Sarah Harrison 1996; one s. two d.; ed Newcastle Royal Grammar School, Univ. Coll., Oxford, Univ. of London; joined Defence Dept, FCO 1977; Third, then Second Sec., Embassy in Warsaw 1979–82; First Sec. Cyprus/Malta Desk, FCO 1982–84, Pvt. Sec. to Parl. Under-Sec. 1984–87; First Sec., Perm. Mission to UN, New York 1987–92; Deputy Head of Middle East Dept, FCO 1992–95; Deputy Head of Mission, Embassy in Warsaw 1995–98; Foreign Policy Adviser, European Comm. 1998–2000; Counsellor and Head of Chancery, Perm. Mission to UN, New York 2000–03; Head of UN Dept, then Head of Int. Orgs Dept 2003–05; High Commr to Zambia 2005–08; Head of Zimbabwe Unit, FCO 2008; Gov. of Anguilla 2009–13; Marshal of the Diplomatic Corps 2014–. *Leisure interests:* music, skiing, sailing, tennis, bridge, golf. *Address:* The Lord Chamberlain's Office, Royal Household, Buckingham Palace, London, SW1A 1AA, England. *Website:* www.royal.gov.uk.

HARRISON, Sir David, Kt, CBE, ScD, FREng, FRSC, FIChemE, CCMI, FRSA, FRSCM; British chemist and academic; b. 3 May 1930, Clacton-on-Sea, Essex, England; s. of Harold David Harrison and Lavinia Wilson; m. Sheila Rachel Debes 1962; one s. one d. (one s. deceased); ed Bede School, Sunderland, Clacton County High School, Selwyn Coll., Univ. of Cambridge; Lecturer in Chemical Eng, Univ. of Cambridge 1956–79, Fellow, Selwyn Coll. 1957–, Sr Tutor 1967–79, Master of Selwyn Coll. 1994–2000, Chair. Faculty of Eng 1994–2001, mem. Council, Univ. of Cambridge 1967–75, 1995–2000, Chair. Faculty Bd of Educ. 1976–78, Deputy Vice-Chancellor 1995–2000, Pro-Vice-Chancellor 1997; Vice-Chancellor Univ. of Keele 1979–84, Univ. of Exeter 1984–94; Visiting Prof. of Chemical Eng, Univ. of Delaware, USA 1967, Univ. of Sydney, Australia 1976; Hon. Ed. Transactions, Inst. of Chemical Engineers 1972–78; Chair. Bd Trustees, Homerton Coll., Cambridge 1979–2010, Council Ely Cathedral 2001–, Univs' Cen. Council for Admissions 1984–91, Church & Associated Colls Advisory Cttee of the Polytechnics and Colls Funding Council 1989–91, Cttee of Vice-Chancellors and Prins of UK 1991–93, Shrewsbury School 1989–2003, Advisory Cttee on Safety of Nuclear Installations 1993–99, Eastern Arts Bd 1994–98, Arts Council of England 1996–98; Dir Salters' Inst. of Industrial Chem. 1993–; Vice-Pres. Inst. of Chemical Engineers 1989, Pres. 1991–92; Fellow, Royal Acad. of Eng, Royal School of Church Music; Liveryman, Salters' Co. 1998; Hon. DUniv (Keele) 1992, (York) 2008; Hon. DSc (Exeter) 1995; George E. Davis Medal, Inst. of Chemical Engineers 2001. *Publications include:* Fluidized Particles (with J. F. Davidson) 1963, Fluidization (with J. F. Davidson) 1971, Fluidization (with J. F. Davidson and R. Clift) 1985. *Leisure interests:* music, tennis, hill walking, good food. *Address:* 7 Gough Way, Cambridge, Cambs., CB3 9LN, England (home). *Telephone:* (1223) 359315 (home). *E-mail:* sirdavidharrison@yahoo.co.uk (home).

HARRISON, James (Jim) Thomas, BA, MA; American writer and poet; b. 11 Dec. 1937, Grayling, Mich.; s. of Winfield Sprague Harrison and Norma Olivia Harrison (née Wahlgren); m. Linda May King 1960; two d.; ed Michigan State Univ.; Asst Prof. of English, SUNY at Stony Brook 1965–66; NEA grant 1967–69, Guggenheim Fellowship 1968–69. *Film screenplays:* Cold Feet (with Tom McGuane) 1989, Revenge (with Jeffrey Fishkin) 1990, Wolf (with Wesley Strick) 1994. *Publications:* fiction: Wolf: A False Memoir 1971, A Good Day to Die 1973, Farmer 1976, Legends of the Fall 1979, Warlock 1981, Sundog 1984, Dalva 1988, The Woman Lit by Fireflies 1990, Sunset Limited 1990, Julip 1994, The Road Home 1998, The Beast God Forgot to Invent 2000, True North 2004, The Summer He Didn't Die 2005, Returning to Earth 2007, The English Major 2008, The Farmer's Daughter: Novellas 2010, The Great Leader 2011, The River Swimmer 2013; poetry: Plain Song 1965, Locations 1968, Walking 1969, Outlyer and Ghazals 1971, Letters to Yesinin 1973, Returning to Earth 1977, New and Selected Poems, 1961–81 1982, The Theory and Practice of Rivers 1986, After Ikkyu and Other Poems 1996, The Shape of the Journey 1998, Braided Creek: A Conversation in

Poetry 2003, Livingston Suite 2005, Saving Daylight 2006; non-fiction: Just Before Dark 1991, The Raw and the Cooked: Adventures of a Roving Gourmand 2001.

HARRISON, Patricia De Stacy, BA, MA,; American government official and broadcast executive; *President and CEO, Corporation for Public Broadcasting;* b. Brooklyn, New York; m. Emmett Bruce Harrison; three c.; ed American Univ.; mem. Pres.'s Export Council 1990, fmr mem. Exec. Cttee; mem. US Trade Rep.'s Service Policy Advisory Council 1992; Co-Chair. Republican Nat. Cttee 1997–2001; Asst Sec. for Educ. and Cultural Affairs, US Dept of State, Washington, DC 2001–05, Acting Under-Sec. for Public Diplomacy and Public Affairs 2004; Pres. and CEO Corpn for Public Broadcasting, Washington, DC 2005–; Founding Pnr, E. Bruce Harrison Co. (public relations agency) 1973–96; Founder and Pres. Nat. Women's Econ. Alliance; fmr Pres. Capital Press Women; fmr Chair. Guest Services Inc., Int. Cttee, Small Business Advisory Council, Small Business Admin; Visiting Fellow John F. Kennedy School of Govt 1992, Inst. for Public Service, Annenberg Public Policy Center 2000; est. Partnerships for Learning initiative; Dr hc (American Univ. of Rome) 2002; Entrepreneur of the Year, Arthur Young Co. and Venture Magazine 1988, Northwood Inst. Distinguished Woman Award 1989, Hispanic Heritage Leadership Award 1998, Global Women's Leadership Award 1999, Woman of the Year Award, New York Black Republican Council 1999, Sec.'s Distinguished Service Award. *Publications:* A Seat at the Table: An Insider's Guide for America's New Women Leaders, America's New Women Entrepreneurs 1986. *Address:* Corporation for Public Broadcasting, 401 Ninth Street, NW, Washington, DC 20004-2129, USA (office). *Telephone:* (202) 879-9600 (office). *Website:* www.cpb.org (office).

HARRISON, Sir Terence, Kt, BSc, DL, FREng, FIMechE, FIMARE; British business executive (retd); b. 7 April 1933; s. of the late Roland Harrison and Doris Wardle; m. June Forster 1956; two s.; ed A. J. Dawson Grammar School, Co. Durham, West Hartlepool and Sunderland Tech. Colls. and Univ. of Durham; marine eng apprenticeship, Richardson's Westgarth, Hartlepool 1949–53; mil. service, Nigeria 1955–57; Clarke Chapman Ltd, Gateshead 1957–77, Man. Dir 1976–77; Northern Eng Industries 1977, Chief Exec. 1983–86, Exec. Chair. 1986–89; Dir Rolls-Royce PLC 1989–96, Chief Exec. 1992–96; Dir (non-exec.) Alfred McAlpine PLC 1995–2002, Chair. 1996–2002; Hon. DEng (Newcastle) 1991; Hon. DTech (Sunderland) 1995; Hon. DSc (Durham) 1996. *Publications:* technical papers. *Leisure interests:* golf, fell walking. *Address:* 2 The Garden Houses, Whalton, Northumberland, NE61 3HB, England (home). *Telephone:* (1670) 775400 (home). *Fax:* (1670) 775291 (home).

HARRISON, Tony; British poet, dramatist and director; b. 30 April 1937, Leeds, Yorks.; s. of Harry Ashton Harrison and Florence Horner (née Wilkinson); m. Sian Thomas; ed Leeds Grammar School and Univ. of Leeds; Hon. DPhil (Athens); Hon. DLitt (Leeds); Cholmondeley Award for Poetry, Geoffrey Faber Memorial Award, European Poetry Translation Prize, Whitbread Poetry Prize 1993, Mental Health Award 1994, Prix Italia 1994, Northern Rock Foundation Writers' Award 2004, PEN/Pinter Prize 2009, Wilfred Owen Award for Poetry 2008, European Prize for Literature (Strasbourg) 2011. *Plays include:* Aikin Mata (with J. Simmons) 1965, The Misanthrope (version of Molière's play) 1973, Phaedra Britannica (version of Racine's Phèdre) 1975, The Passion 1977, Bow Down 1977, The Bartered Bride (libretto) 1978, The Oresteia (trans.) 1981, The Mysteries 1985, The Trackers of Oxyrhynchus 1990, The Common Chorus 1992, Square Rounds 1992, Poetry or Bust 1993, The Kaisers of Carnuntum 1995, The Labourers of Herakles 1995, The Prince's Play 1996, Fire and Poetry 1999, Hecuba 2005, Fram 2008. *Writing for TV and film includes:* Yan Tan Tethera 1983, The Big H 1984, 'V' 1987, Loving Memory 1987, The Blasphemers' Banquet 1989, The Gaze of the Gorgon 1992, Black Daisies for the Bride 1993, A Maybe Day in Kazakhstan 1994, The Shadow of Hiroshima 1995, Prometheus 1998, Crossings 2002. *Publications include:* poetry: Earthworks 1964, Newcastle is Peru 1969, The Loiners 1970, Poems of Palladas of Alexandria (ed. and trans.) 1973, From the School of Eloquence and Other Poems 1978, Continuous 1981, A Kumquat for John Keats 1981, US Martial 1981, Selected Poems 1984, Fire-Gap 1985, 'V' 1985, Dramatic Verse, 1973–1985 1985, 'V' and Other Poems 1990, A Cold Coming: Gulf War Poems 1991, The Gaze of the Gorgon and other poems 1992, The Shadow of Hiroshima and other film/ poems 1995, Permanently Bard 1995, Laureate's Block and other poems 2000, Under the Clock 2005, Collected Poems 2007, Collected Film Poetry 2007; collections of plays: Plays 1 1985, Theatre Works 1973–1985 1986, Plays 2 2002, Plays 3 1996, Plays 4 2002, Plays 5 2004, Hecuba 2005, Fram 2008.

HARRISON, Wayne David, BA; Australian theatre director and producer; b. 7 March 1953, Melbourne; s. of Lindsay Graham Harrison and Florence Rosina Cannell; ed Christian Brothers' Coll., Melbourne, Univ. of Melbourne, Univ. of New South Wales; Dramaturge, Sydney Theatre Co. 1981–86; Asst Dir Northside Theatre Co., NSW 1987–89; Artistic Dir Sydney Theatre Co. 1990–99; Creative Dir Back Row Int., London and Clear Channel Entertainment Europe 1999–2001; Creative Dir New Year's Eve celebration, Sydney 2005–07, Closing Ceremony 2006 Melbourne Commonwealth Games, Helpmann Awards for Live Performance 2007; mem. Advisory Bd Alex Buzo Co. *Plays directed include:* Alone it Stands, Mum's The Word for Mollison Productions 2002, The Return of Houdini for City Theatre, Reykjavik 2005, Sunset Boulevard for The Production Company, Melbourne 2005, End of The Rainbow for Ensemble Theatre, Sydney Opera House and MTC, Melbourne 2005, Just Macbeth for Bell Shakespeare Co. 2008, Absinthe and Desir for Spiegelworld Productions 2008, The Normal Heart, A Little Night Music, Shadowlands, Into the Woods, The Gift of the Gorgon, Much Ado About Nothing, Two Weeks with the Queen, Dead White Males, Heretic, Medea, Amy's View. *Address:* c/o Advisory Board, Alex Buzo Company, POB 833, Kingsford, NSW 2032, Australia (office).

HARRISON, William Burwell, Jr, AB; American banker; b. 12 Aug. 1943, Rocky Mount, NC; s. of William Burwell and Katherine Spruill; m. Anne MacDonald Stephens 1985; two d.; ed Univ. of N Carolina, Chapel Hill; trainee Chemical Bank, New York 1967–69, Mid-South Corpn and corresp. banking group 1969–74, West Coast corp. and corresp. banking group 1974–76, Dist Head and Western Regional Co-ordinator San Francisco 1976–78, Regional Co-ordinator and Sr Vice-Pres. London 1978–82, Sr Vice-Pres. and Divisional Head, Europe 1982–83, Exec. Vice-Pres. US corp. div. New York 1983–87, Group Exec., banking and corporate finance group 1987–90, Vice-Chair. institutional banking 1990–2000; Vice-Chair. Global Bank 1992–2000; Vice-Chair. Manhattan Corpn (then Chase Manhattan Corpn)

New York 1995–2000, Pres. and CEO 1999–2000, Chair. and CEO 2000, Pres. JPMorgan Chase (following merger) 2000–04, CEO 2000–05, Chair. 2001–06; mem. investment advisory cttee, Aurora Capital Partners 2008–. *Leisure interests:* athletics, travel. *Address:* c/o Aurora Capital Partners, 10877 Wilshire Boulevard, Suite 2100, Los Angeles, CA 90024, USA (office).

HARRISS, Gerald Leslie, MA, DPhil, FBA; British historian and academic; b. 22 May 1925, London; s. of W. L. Harriss and M. J. O. Harriss; m. Margaret Anne Sidaway 1959; two s. three d.; ed Chigwell School, Essex, Magdalen Coll., Oxford; war service in RNVR 1944–46; Univ. of Oxford 1946–53; Lecturer, Durham Univ. 1953–65, Reader 1965–67; Fellow and Tutor in History, Magdalen Coll., Oxford 1967–92, Fellow Emer. 1992–, Reader in Modern History, Univ. of Oxford 1990–92. *Publications:* King, Parliament and Public Finance in Medieval England 1975, Henry V: the Practice of Kingship (ed.) 1985, Cardinal Beaufort 1988, K. B. McFarlane, Letters to Friends (ed.) 1997, Shaping the Nation: England 1360–1461 2005. *Address:* Fairings, 2 Queen Street, Yetminster, Sherborne, Dorset, DT9 6LL, England (home).

HARRY, Deborah (Debbie) Ann; American singer and actress; b. 1 July 1945, Miami, Fla; d. of Richard Smith and Catherine Harry (Peters); ed Centenary Coll.; singer and songwriter, rock group Blondie 1975–83, reformed 1997; awarded Gold, Silver and Platinum records. *Singles include:* Heart of Glass, Call Me, Tide is High, Rapture. *Recordings:* albums: with Blondie: Blondie 1976, Plastic Letters 1977, Parallel Lines 1978, Eat to the Beat 1979, Autoamerican 1980, The Hunter 1982, Rapture 1994, No Exit 1999, Livid 2000, The Curse of Blondie 2003; solo: Koo Koo 1981, Rockbird 1986, Def, Dumb and Blonde 1989, Debravation 1993, Virtuosity (with the Heads) 1995, Necessary Evil 2007. *Film appearances:* The Foreigner 1978, Unmade Beds 1980, Union City 1980, New York Beat Movie 1981, Videodrome 1983, Forever, Lulu 1987, Satisfaction 1988, Hairspray 1988, New York Stories 1989, Tales from the Darkside: The Movie 1990, Dead Beat 1994, Drop Dead Rock 1995, Heavy 1995, Cop Land 1997, Six Ways to Sunday 1997, Joe's Day 1998, Zoo 1999, Red Lipstick 2000, Deuces Wild 2000, Spun 2002, Try Seventeen 2002, My Life Without Me 2003, A Good Night to Die 2003, Tulse Luper Suitcases, Part 1: The Moab Story 2003, Patch 2005, I Remember You Now 2005, Elegy 2007. *Television appearances:* Saturday Night Live, The Muppet Show, Tales from the Darkside, Wiseguys. *Theatre:* Teaneck Tanzi, The Venus Flytrap. *Address:* Tenth Street Entertainment, 700 San Vicente Boulevard, Suite G410, West Hollywood, CA 90069, USA (office). *Website:* www.blondie.net; www .deborahharry.com.

HART, Ann Weaver, MA, PhD; American professor of educational administration and university administrator; *President, University of Arizona;* b. Salt Lake City, Utah; m. Randy B. Hart; four d.; ed Univ. of Utah; began career teaching math., English and history at Cottonwood High School and Bonneville Jr High, Salt Lake City 1971–74; Prof. Farrer Jr High School, Provo, Utah 1983–84; Asst Prof., Educational Admin Dept, Univ. of Utah 1984, held various positions including Prof. of Educational Leadership, Assoc. Dean, then Dean of Grad. School of Educ., Accreditation Liaison Officer and Special Asst to Pres. –1998; Provost, Vice-Pres. for Academic Affairs and Faculty mem., Claremont Grad. Univ., Calif. 1998–2002; Pres. Univ. of New Hampshire 2002–06; Pres. Temple Univ., Phila 2006–12; Pres. Univ. of Arizona 2012–, also Prof. of Educational Policy Studies and Practice, College of Educ.; fmr Pres. Western Asscn of Grad. Schools; fmr Chair. Research Cttee Grad. Record Examination, Educational Testing Service; fmr Ed. Educational Administration Quarterly; mem. Asscn of American Universities, Asscn of Public Land Grant Universities, Arizona State Bd of Educ., Campus Research Corporation, Greater Phoenix Leadership, Southern Arizona Leadership Council, Tucson Regional Economic Opportunities, Chairman's Circle, Udall Foundation; fmr mem. Bd of Dirs Citizens Bank of New Hampshire; awards from Univ. Council for Educational Admin 1992, Business and Professional Women's Foundation 1995, Utah Women's Forum, Univ. of Utah Distinguished Alumna Humanities 2004, Business New Hampshire Magazine (Ten Most Powerful People in NH) 2006, Jack Culbertson Award in Educational Admin, Univ. Council for Educational Admin, Outstanding Professional Award, Business and Professional Women's Foundation, PoWeR Award, Professional Women's Roundtable, Champion of Diversity and Access Award, Urban STEM Strategy Group 2009, Outstanding Community Service Award, Network for Teaching Entrepreneurship. *Publications:* The Principalship: A Theory of Professional Learning and Practice (co-author) 1996, Designing and Conducting Research (co-author) 1996; more than 85 refereed journal articles and book chapters, five books and edited vols and numerous articles in pubs on leadership succession and development, work redesign and organizational behaviour in educational organizations, and academic freedom. *Leisure interests:* cross-country hiking, camping in Wind River Range, Wyo., kayaking, bicycling. *Address:* Office of the President, Administration Building, Room 712, 1401 East University Boulevard, PO Box 210066, Tucson, AZ 85721-0066, USA (office). *Telephone:* (520) 621-5511 (office). *Fax:* (520) 621-9323 (office). *E-mail:* president@email.arizona.edu (office). *Website:* president .arizona.edu (office).

HART, Gary, BA, BD, JD, DPhil, LLB; American politician and lawyer; *Of Counsel, Coudert Brothers LLP;* b. 28 Nov. 1936, Ottawa, Kan.; m. Lee Ludwig 1958; one s. one d.; ed Bethany Coll., Okla, Yale Univ.; assisted in John F. Kennedy Presidential Campaign 1960; called to Bar 1964; Attorney, US Dept of Justice and Special Asst to Sec., US Dept of Interior 1964–67; voluntary organizer, Robert F. Kennedy Presidential Campaign 1968; legal practice, Denver, Colo 1967–70, 1972–74; Nat. Campaign Dir, George McGovern Democratic Presidential Campaign 1970–72; Senator for Colorado 1975–86; with Davis, Graham & Stubbs, (law firm) Denver 1985; Of Counsel, Coudert Brothers LLP 1988–; co-Chair. US Comm. on Nat. Security for the 21st Century (Hart-Rudman Comm.) 1998–2000; fmr mem. Bd of Commrs, Denver Urban Renewal Authority; fmr mem. Park Hill Action Cttee. *Publications:* Right From the Start, A New Democracy 1983, The Double Man (with W. S. Cohen), 1985, America Can Win 1986, The Strategies of Zeus 1987, Russia Shakes the World 1991, The Minutemen: Restoring an Army of the People 1998, The Fourth Power: An Essay Concerning A Grand Strategy for the United States in the 21st Century 2004, The Thunder and the Sunshine: Four Seasons in a Burnished Life 2010. *Address:* Coudert Brothers LLP, One Market Spear Street Tower, Suite 2100, San Francisco, CA 94105-1126, USA (office).

Telephone: (415) 267-6200 (office). *Fax:* (415) 977-6110 (office). *Website:* www.coudert.com (office).

HART, Graeme, MBA; New Zealand business executive; b. 1955; m.; two c.; ed Univ. of Otago; f. Rank Group Australia Pty Ltd (pvt. investment co.), Auckland, has acquired several cos including Burns, Philp & Co. Ltd (food products), Carter Holt Harvey (forest products), Evergreen Packaging Inc. (packaging equipment co.), SIG Holding (drink carton manufacturer), Alcoa Packaging & Consumer Group (now Reynolds Packaging Group). *Address:* Rank Group Ltd, Level 12, 132 Quay Street, Auckland 1001, New Zealand (office).

HART, Michael, CBE, PhD, DSc, FRS, FInstP; British academic; *Visiting Professor of Physics, University of Bristol;* b. 4 Nov. 1938, Bristol; s. of Reuben H. V. Hart and Phyllis M. Hart (née White); m. Susan M. Powell 1963; three d.; ed Cotham Grammar School, Bristol and Univ. of Bristol; Research Assoc., Dept of Materials Science and Eng, Cornell Univ. 1963–65; Dept of Physics, Univ. of Bristol 1965–67, Lecturer in Physics 1967–72, Reader 1972–76; Sr Resident Research Assoc., Nat. Research Council, NASA Electronics Research Center, Boston, Mass 1969–70; Special Adviser, Cen. Policy Review Staff 1975–77; Wheatstone Prof. of Physics, King's Coll. London 1976–84; Prof. of Physics, Univ. of Manchester 1984–93, Prof. Emer. of Physics 1993–; Visiting Prof. of Applied Physics, De Montfort Univ. 1993–98, Hon. Prof. in Eng, Univ. of Warwick 1993–1995; Science Programme Co-ordinator (part-time), Daresbury Lab. Science and Eng Research Council 1985–88; Chair. Nat. Synchrotron Light Source, Brookhaven Nat. Lab., USA 1995–2000; Visiting Prof. of Physics, Univ. of Bristol 2000–; Bertram Eugene Warren Award, American Crystallographic Asscn 1970, Charles Vernon Boys Award, Inst. of Physics 1971. *Publications:* contribs to learned journals. *Leisure interests:* flying kites, cookery. *Address:* Department of Physics, University of Bristol, Bristol, BS8 1TL (office); 2 Challoner Court, Merchants Landing, Bristol, BS1 4RG, England (home). *Telephone:* (117) 921-5291 (home). *E-mail:* michael.hart8@btopenworld.com (home).

HART, Oliver D'Arcy, PhD; British/American economist and academic; *Andrew E. Furer Professor of Economics, Harvard University;* b. 9 Oct. 1948, London, England; s. of Philip D'Arcy Hart and Ruth Meyer; m. Rita B. Goldberg 1974; two s.; ed Univs of Cambridge and Warwick and Princeton Univ., USA; Lecturer in Econs, Univ. of Essex 1974–75; Asst Lecturer, then Lecturer in Econs, Univ. of Cambridge 1975–81; Prof. of Econs, LSE 1981–85, BP Centennial Visiting Prof. 1992–93, 1997–; Prof. of Econs, MIT 1984–93; Prof. of Econs, Harvard Univ. 1993–97, Andrew E. Furer Prof. of Econs 1997–; Fellow, American Acad. of Arts and Sciences; Corresp. Fellow, British Acad. 2000; Hon. DPhil (Basle) 1994; Hon. DSc (Econ) (London Business School) 2011; Hon. LLD (Warwick) 2012; Dr hc (Free Univ. of Brussels) 1992, (Copenhagen Business School) 2009, (Paris-Dauphine) 2009. *Publications include:* Firms, Contracts, and Financial Structure 1995; numerous articles in professional journals. *Address:* Department of Economics, Littauer 220, Harvard University, Cambridge, MA 02138, USA (office). *Telephone:* (617) 496-3461 (office). *E-mail:* ohart@harvard.edu (office). *Website:* economics.harvard.edu/faculty/hart (office).

HART, Stanley Robert, BS, MS, PhD; American geochemist and academic; *Scientist Emeritus, Woods Hole Oceanographic Institution;* b. 20 June 1935, Swampscott, Mass; s. of Robert W. Hart and Ruth M. Hart; m. 1st Joanna Smith 1956 (divorced 1976); m. 2nd Pamela Shepherd 1980; one s. two d.; ed Massachusetts Inst. of Tech., California Inst. of Tech.; Fellow, Carnegie Inst. of Washington 1960–61, mem. staff 1961–75; Visiting Prof., Univ. of Calif., San Diego 1967–68; Prof. of Geology and Geochemistry, MIT 1975–89; Sr Scientist, Woods Hole Oceanographic Inst. 1989–2007, Scientist Emer. 2007–; mem. NAS; Fellow, American Geophysical Union, Geological Soc. of America, European Asscn of Geochemistry, Geochemical Soc., European Union of Geosciences, American Acad. of Arts and Sciences; Dr hc (Paris) 2005; Goldschmidt Medal, Geochemical Soc. 1992, Hess Medal, American Geophysical Union 1997, Columbus O'Donnell Iselin Chair for Excellence in Oceanography, NAS Arthur L. Day Prize and Lectureship 2007. *Publications:* more than 235 articles in scientific journals. *Leisure interests:* woodworking, fishing, running. *Address:* Woods Hole Oceanographic Institution, Woods Hole, MA 02543 (office); 4671 East Madera Vista Road, Green Valley, AZ 85614, USA (home). *Telephone:* (508) 524-2019 (office); (520) 625-4543 (office). *Fax:* (508) 457-2175 (office). *E-mail:* shart@whoi.edu (office). *Website:* www.whoi.edu/science/GG/people/shart (office).

HART OF CHILTON, Baron (Life Peer), cr. 2004, of Chilton in the County of Suffolk; **Garry Richard Rushby Hart,** LLB, FRSA; British solicitor; *Chancellor, University of Greenwich;* b. 29 June 1940, London, England; s. of Dennis George Hart and Evelyn Mary Hart; m. 1st Paula Lesley Shepherd 1966 (divorced 1986); two s. one d.; m. 2nd Valerie Elen Mary Davies 1986; two d.; ed Northgate Grammar School, Ipswich, Univ. Coll., London; solicitor, Herbert Smith 1966–70, Partner 1970–98, Head of Property Dept 1988–97; Special Expert Adviser to Sec. of State for Constitutional Affairs and Lord Chancellor 1998–2007; Chancellor Univ. of Greenwich 2008–; mem. House of Lords Select Cttee on Merits of Statutory Instruments, House of Lords Select Cttee on the Constitution, Leaders Group Rules of Conduct for Mems of the House of Lords (The Eames Group) 2009, House of Lords Appointments Comm. 2010–; mem. Hon. Degrees and Fellowships Cttee and Research Governance Cttee, Univ. Coll. London, Project & Devt Cttee, Victoria & Albert Museum, Devt Council of Almeida Theatre; Trustee, Architecture Foundation 1997–2005 (Deputy Chair. 2000–05), Almeida Theatre 1997–2004 (Chair. 1997–2002), British Architectural Library Trust 2000–; Fellow, Univ. Coll., London 2001; Hon. FRIBA 2000. *Publications include:* Blundell & Dobry's Planning Applications Appeals and Procedures (co-ed. 4th and 6th edns) 1990, 1996. *Leisure interests:* travel, conservation, talking. *Address:* House of Lords, Westminster, London, SW1A 0PW, England (office). *Telephone:* (20) 7226-5431 (office). *E-mail:* hartofchilton@btinternet.com (office). *Website:* www.parliament.uk/biographies/lords/lord-hart-of-chilton/3675 (office).

HARTARTO SASTRO SUNARTO, AO, BE; Indonesian politician and engineer; b. 30 May 1932, Delanggu, Cen. Java; s. of Sastro Sunarto; m. Hartini Hartarto; three s. two d.; ed Univ. of Indonesia Bandung School of Chemical Eng and Univ. of NSW, Australia; Head, Expansion Project, Leces Paper Mill 1960, Dir Leces Paper Co. 1961–64, Pulp & Paper Holding Co. 1964–66; on staff of Dir-Gen. for Basic Chemical Industries, Ministry of Industry 1966, Dir-Gen. 1979; Chair. Gresik

Petrochemical Co. 1978–83, Tonasa Cement Co. 1978–93, PT Asean Aceh Fertilizer Co. 1978–83, Rekayasa Eng & Contracting Co. 1981–83; mem. The People's Consultative Ass. 1983; Leader and Chair. Indonesian Ministerial Del., APEC Ministerial Meeting, ASEAN Econ. Ministers Meeting, Indonesia-Malaysia-Singapore Growth Triangle; Minister of Industry 1983–93, Co-ordinating Minister for Industrial and Trade 1993–95, for Production and Distribution 1995–98, 1998–99, for Devt Supervision and State Admin. Reform, also acting as Co-ordinating Minister for Econ., Finance and Industry; currently Chair. Foundation of Indonesian Inst. of Tech.; Life Deputy Gov. American Biographical Inst. Research Asscn; Life Sec. Gen. United Cultural Convention, USA 2004–; Groot Kruis, Order Van Oranje Nassau (Netherlands) 1966; Grosse Verdienstkreuz mit Stern und Schulterband (FRG) 1984; Grand Cordon of Order of Al-Istliqlal (Jordan) 1988; Grand Order of Mugunghwa (South Korea) 1992; Kt Commdr's Cross (Austria) 1996; Bohdan Khmelnitsky Order, First Degree (Ukraine) 1997; Hon. DLitt (Univ. of Nagpur, India) 1992, (Nanyang Technological Univ. of Singapore) 1995; Hon. DSc (NSW) 1993, (Bandung Inst. of Tech.) 1996; Dr hc (Erasmus Univ., Netherlands and Bernard Mandeville Foundation, Rotterdam) 1995; Satya Lancana Pembangunam 1974, Bintang Mahaputera Adipradana 1987, Medal of Veteran Legion 1991, Productivity Award, Int. Productivity Network, Rutgers State Univ. of New Jersey 1992, Bintang Republik Indonesia Utama 1998. *Publication:* Industrialisation and the Development of Agriculture Sector and Services to Achieve the Indonesian Vision 2030 2006. *Leisure interest:* world history. *Address:* 34–36 Tirtayasa, Kebayoran Baru, Jakarta 12160, Indonesia (home). *Telephone:* (21) 7260073 (home); (21) 7203049. *Fax:* (21) 72222206 (home).

HÄRTER, Hans-Georg; German engineer and business executive; *CEO, ZF Group;* b. 2 May 1945, Bensheim; ed Berlin Tech. School, Meersburg Acad.; trained as machine fitter; certified as state-approved mechanical engineer (industrial production); joined ZF Passau GmbH, Passau 1973, Head of Dept, Value Analysis/Methods 1982–87, Head of Specialist Dept, Value Analysis/Methods 1987–90, Sr Head of Tech. Cost Budgeting 1990, Deputy Group Vice-Pres., ZF Passau GmbH, Passau 1990–91, Group Vice-Pres. 1991–94, mem. Bd of Man. ZF Group Off-Road Driveline Tech. and Axle Systems Div., Marine Propulsion Systems Business Unit and Production Tech. 1994–2002, mem. Bd of Man., ZF Group Powertrain and Suspension Components, Div. Business Unit Aftermarket Trading, Asian Pacific Region and CEO ZF Sachs AG, Schweinfurt 2002–06, Exec. Vice-Pres., ZF Group 2006–07, CEO 2007–. *Address:* ZF Friedrichshafen AG, Graf-von-Soden-Platz 1, 88046 Friedrichshafen, Germany (office). *Telephone:* (7541) 77-0 (office). *Fax:* (7541) 77-908000 (office). *E-mail:* postoffice@zf.com (office). *Website:* www.zf.com (office).

HARTERY, Nicky, CEng, MBA, FIEI; Irish engineer and business executive; *Chairman, CRH plc;* fmr Pres. and CEO Verbatim Corpn, USA; Exec. Vice-Pres., Eastman Kodak –2000; Vice-Pres. of Manufacturing and Business Operations, Europe, Middle East and Africa operations, Dell Inc. 2000–08; Dir (non-exec.) CRH plc 2004–, Chair. 2012–; Chief Exec. Prodigium (consulting co.); Dir (non-exec.), Musgrave Group plc, Eircom Ltd; Fellow, Inst. of Engineers of Ireland. *Address:* CRH plc, Belgard Castle, Clondalkin, Dublin 22, Ireland (office). *Telephone:* (1) 4041000 (office). *Fax:* (1) 4041007 (office). *E-mail:* mail@crh.com (office). *Website:* www.crh.com (office).

HARTL, Franz-Ulrich, MD, DrMed (Habil.); German biochemist and academic; *Professor of Cellular Biochemistry and Managing Director, Max Planck Institute for Biochemistry;* b. 10 March 1957, Essen; ed Univs of Heidelberg and Munich; Postdoctoral Fellow, Inst. of Physiological Chem., Univ. of Munich 1985–86, Group Leader Inst. of Physiological Chem. 1987–89, 'Akademischer Rat', Inst. of Physiological Chem. 1990–91; Postdoctoral Fellow, UCLA and Fellow, Deutsche Forschungsgemeinschaft (German Research Council) 1989–90; Assoc. mem. Program in Cellular Biochemistry and Biophysics, Sloan-Kettering Inst., New York 1991–92, mem. (with tenure) 1993–97, William E. Snee Chair of Cellular Biochemistry 1995; Assoc. Prof. of Cell Biology and Genetics, Grad. School of Medical Science, Cornell Univ., NY 1991–92, Prof. 1993–97; Assoc. Investigator, Howard Hughes Medical Institute 1994–97; Prof. of Cellular Biochemistry and Dir, Max Planck Inst. for Biochemistry, Martinsried 1997–, Man. Dir 2002; mem. European Molecular Biology Org. 1998, German Acad. of Sciences Leopoldina 2002, Bavarian Acad. of Sciences 2004; Foreign mem. Acad. of Science of Nordrhein-Westfalen 1997; Fellow, AAAS 2010, American Acad. of Microbiology 2012; Hon. Prof., Univ. of Munich 1997; Foreign Hon. mem. American Acad. of Arts and Sciences 2000; Hon. mem. Japanese Biochemical Soc. 2008; Order of Merit 2011; Vinci Award, LVMH Science for Art competition 1996, Lipmann Award, American Soc. of Biochemistry and Molecular Biology 1997, Academy Prize, Acad. of Science of Berlin-Brandenburg 1999, Wilhelm Vaillant Research Prize 2000, Gottfried Wilhelm Leibniz-Prize, Deutsche Forschungsgemeinschaft 2002, Feldberg Prize 2003, Gairdner Foundation Int. Award 2004, Ernst Jung Prize for Medicine, Jung-Stiftung für Wissenschaft und Forschung (co-recipient) 2005, Stein and Moore Award, Protein Soc. 2006, Koerber European Science Award 2006, Wiley Prize in Biomedical Sciences 2007, Lewis S. Rosenstiel Award 2008, Louisa Gross Horwitz Prize 2008, Otto Warburg Medal, German Soc. for Biochemistry and Molecular Biology (GBM) 2009, van Gysel Prize for Biomedical Research in Europe 2010, Dr H.P. Heineken Prize for Biochemistry and Biophysics, Royal Netherlands Acad. of Arts and Sciences 2010, Albert Lasker Basic Medical Research Award 2011, Massry Prize 2011, Heinrich Wieland-Prize, Boehringer Ingelheim Foundation 2011, Shaw Prize in Life Science and Medicine 2012, Tabor Research Award 2013. *Publications:* numerous scientific papers in professional journals. *Address:* c/o Evelyn Frey-Royston, Max Planck Institute of Biochemistry, Department of Cellular Biochemistry, Am Klopferspitz 18, 82152 Martinsried, Germany (office). *Telephone:* (89) 8578-2244 (office). *Fax:* (89) 8578-2211 (office). *E-mail:* uhartl@biochem.mpg.de (office); efrey@biochem.mpg.de (office). *Website:* www.biochem.mpg.de/en/rd/hartl (office).

HARTLAND, Michael (see James, Michael Leonard).

HARTLEY, Frank Robinson, DSc, FRSC, CCMI; British chemist; b. 29 Jan. 1942, Epsom, Surrey; s. of Sir Frank Hartley and Lydia May England; m. Valerie Peel 1964; three d.; ed Kings Coll. School, Wimbledon, Magdalen Coll., Oxford; Post-doctoral Fellow, Commonwealth Scientific and Industrial Research Org., Div. of Protein Chem., Melbourne, Australia 1966–69; ICI Research Fellow and Tutor in Physical Chem., Univ. Coll., London 1969–70; Lecturer in Inorganic Chem., Univ. of Southampton 1970–75; Prof. of Chem. and Head of Dept of Chem. and Metallurgy, Royal Mil. Coll. of Science, Shrivenham 1975–82, Acting Dean 1982–84, Prin. and Dean 1984–89; fmr Man. Dir CIT Holdings Ltd; Dir (non-exec.) T&N PLC 1989–98, Nat. Westminster Bank Eastern Region Advisory Bd 1990–92, Kalon PLC 1994–99, Kenwood PLC 1995–99; Vice-Chancellor Cranfield Univ. 2000–06; Asscn of Commonwealth Univs Sr Travelling Fellow 1986; Special Adviser on Defence Systems to the Prime Minister 1988–90; Specialist Adviser to House of Lords Select Cttee on Science and Tech. 1993–94; Chair. AWE Academic Council 1998–2001; currently Chair. Sr Council for Devon, Teignmouth; fmr mem. Int. Advisory Bd Kanazawa Acad. of Science and Tech., Japan; Dir Shuttleworth Trust 1994–97; Trustee, Lorch Foundation 1994–; fmr mem. Advisory Panel AWE Corp.; fmr DL Beds.; Hon. FRAeS; Hon. Life mem. Cranfield Students Asscn. *Publications:* The Chemistry of Platinum and Palladium (Applied Science) 1973, Elements of Organometallic Chemistry (Chemical Soc.) 1974, Solution Equilibria (with C. Burgess and R. M. Alcock) 1980; The Chemistry of the Metal Carbon Bond (Vols 1–5) 1983–89, Supported Metal Complexes 1985, Brasseys New Battlefield Weapons Systems and Technology series 1988– (Ed.-in-Chief), The Chemistry of Organophosphorus Compounds Vols 1–4 1990–96, Chemistry of the Platinum Group Metals 1991; papers in inorganic, co-ordination and organometallic chem. in major English, American and Australian journals. *Leisure interests:* cliff walking, golf, swimming, gardening. *Address:* c/o Senior Council for Devon, PO Box 210, Harberton, Totnes, Devon, TQ9 9DA (office); Cranfield Students Association, Building 114, Cranfield University, Cranfield, Beds., MK43 0AL, England (office). *Telephone:* (1226) 776452 (office). *E-mail:* f.r.hartley@cranfield.ac .uk (office). *Website:* www.seniorcouncildevon.org.uk (office); www.cranfield.ac.uk (office).

HARTLEY, Hal, (Ned Rifle), BA; American film director, producer and script-writer; b. 3 Nov. 1959, Lindenhurst, NY; s. of Harold Hartley and Eileen Hartley (nee Flynn); m. Miho Nikaido 1996; ed Massachusetts Coll. of Art, State Univ. of New York-Purchase Film School; worked with Action Productions; f. True Fiction Pictures 1984 (now Possible Films); Visiting Lecturer, Harvard Univ. 2001–04; Fellow, American Acad. Berlin 2004; Chevalier Ordre des Arts et des Lettres 1996. *Films:* Kid 1984, Home of The Brave 1986, The Cartographer's Girlfriend 1987, Dogs 1988, The Unbelievable Truth 1990, Trust 1991, Simple Men 1992, From a Motel 6 1993, Iris 1993, The Only Living Boy in New York 1993, Flirt 1993, Amateur (Young Filmmakers Award 1994) 1994, Henry Fool (Best Screenplay Award, Cannes Film Festival 1998) 1997, The Book of Life 1998, Monster 2000, Kimono 2000, No Such Thing 2001, The Girl from Monday 2004, Fay Grim 2006. *Television films:* Surviving Desire 1989, Achievement 1991, Ambition 1991, Flirt 1993, Opera No. 1 1994, NYC 3/94 1994, The New Math(s) 2000, Kimono 2001. *E-mail:* info@possiblefilms.com (office). *Website:* www.possiblefilms.com (office).

HÄRTLING, Peter; German writer and journalist; b. 13 Nov. 1933, Chemnitz; s. of Rudolf Härtling and Erika Härtling (née Häntzschel); m. Mechthild Maier 1959; two s. two d.; ed Gymnasium (Nürtingen/Neckar); childhood spent in Saxony, Czechoslovakia and Württemberg; journalist 1953–; Literary Ed. Deutsche Zeitung und Wirtschaftszeitung, Stuttgart and Cologne; Ed. Der Monat magazine 1962–70, also Co-publisher; Ed. and Man. Dir S. Fischer Verlag, Frankfurt 1968–74, Ed. Die Väter; mem. PEN, Akad. der Wissenschaften und der Literatur Mainz, Akad. der Künste Berlin, Deutsche Akad. für Sprache und Dichtung Darmstadt; Hon. Prof. 1996; Grosses Bundesverdienstkreuz 1996; Hon. DPhil 2001; Dr hc (Giessen) 2002; Literaturpreis des Deutschen Kritikerverbandes 1964, Literaturpreis des Kulturkreises der Deutschen Industrie 1965; Literarischer Förderungspreis des Landes Niedersachsen 1965, Prix du meilleur livre étranger, Paris 1966, Gerhart Hauptmann Preis 1971, Deutscher Jugendbuchpreis 1976, Stadtschreiber von Bergen-Enkheim 1978–79, Hölderlin-Preis 1987, Lion-Feuchtwanger-Preis 1992, Stadtschreiber von Mainz 1995, Leuschner-Medaille des Landes Hessen 1996, Eichendorff-Preis 1999, Deutsche Jugendbuchpreis 2001, Deutscher Bücherpreis 2002. *Publications:* Yamins Stationen (poetry) 1955, In Zeilen zuhaus (essays) 1957, Palmström grüsst Anna Blume (essays) 1961, Spielgeist-Spiegelgeist (poetry) 1962, Niembsch oder Der Stillstand (novel) 1964, Janek (novel) 1966, Das Familienfest (novel) 1969, Gilles (play) 1970, Ein Abend, Eine Nacht, Ein Morgen (novel) 1971, Neue Gedichte 1972, Zwettl – Nachprüfung einer Erinnerung (novel) 1973, Eine Frau (novel) 1974, Hölderlin (novel) 1976, Anreden (poetry) 1977, Hubert oder Die Rückkehr nach Casablanca (novel) 1978, Nachgetragene Liebe (novel) 1980, Die dreifache Maria 1982, Vorwarnung 1983, Sätze von Liebe 1983, Das Windrad (novel) 1983, Ich rufe die Wörter zusammen 1984, Der spanische Soldat oder Finden unter Erfinden 1984, Felix Guttmann (novel) 1985, Waiblingers Augen (novel) 1987, Die Mösinger Pappel 1987, Der Wanderer (novel) 1988, Briefe von drinnen und draußen (poetry) 1989, Herzwand (novel) 1990, Brüder unter Schwestern: Tagebuch eines Synodalen 1991, Schubert (novel) 1992, Bozena (novel) 1994, Schumanns Schatten (novel) 1996, Grosse, Kleine Schwester (novel) 1998, Hoffmann oder Die vielfältige Liebe (novel) 2001, Leben lernen (autobiog.) 2004, Die Lebenslinie (autobiog.) 2005, Das ausgestellte Kind: Mit Familie Mozart unterwegs 2007, O'Bär an Enkel Samuel: Eine Erzählung mit fünf Briefen 2008, Dorther: Reisen aus dem Gedächtnis 2009, Leicht geworden für Gedankenflüge 2010, Liebste Fenchel: Das Leben der Fanny Hensel-Mendelssohn in Etüden und Intermezzi 2011. *Address:* Finkenweg 1, 64546 Mörfelden-Walldorf, Germany. *Telephone:* (6105) 6109 (office). *Fax:* (6105) 74687 (office). *E-mail:* peter@haertling.de (office). *Website:* www.haertling.de.

HARTMAN, George Eitel, MFA, FAIA; American architect; *Principal Emeritus, Hartman-Cox Architects;* b. 7 May 1936, Fort Hancock, NJ; s. of George E. Hartman and Evelyn Ritchie; m. 1st Ann Burdick 1965 (divorced 2000); one s. one d.; m. 2nd Ian Cigliano 2001; ed Princeton Univ.; with Keyes Lethbridge & Condon Architects 1960–64; own pvt. practice George E. Hartman 1964–65, Hartman-Cox Architects 1965–; mem. US Comm. of Fine Arts 1990–93, Architectural Advisory Bd, Foreign Bldg Office, Dept of State 1991–, currently Prin. Emer.; taught in Catholic Univ., North Carolina State Univ., Univ. of Maryland; fmr Pres. Washington Chapter AIA; mem. Bd of Dirs Arthur C. Clarke Foundation; Fellow, American Acad. Rome; Co-publr Acad. Press; mem. Comm. of Fine Arts; AIA Nat. Honor Awards 1970, 1971, 1984, 1988, 1989, 2005 and numerous other awards. *Buildings include:* US Embassy, Kuala Lumpur 1979, 1001 Pennsylvania Avenue, Washington, DC 1979, HEB HQ, San Antonio, Tex. 1982, Chrysler Museum, Norfolk, NJ 1984, Georgetown Univ. Law Library 1989, Market Square,

Washington, DC 1990, 800 N Capital Street, Washington, DC 1990, 1200 K Street and 154 K Street, Washington, DC 1991. *Leisure interest:* sailing. *Address:* Hartman Cox Architects, 1074 Thomas Jefferson Street, NW, Washington, DC 20007 (office); 1657 31st Street, Washington, DC 20007, USA (home). *Telephone:* (202) 333-6446 (office); (202) 333-1657 (home). *E-mail:* inquiries@hartmancox.com (office). *Website:* www.hartmancox.com (office).

HARTMANN, Peter C., DPhil; German historian and academic; *Professor Emeritus of General and Modern History, University of Mainz;* b. 28 March 1940, Munich; s. of Alfred Hartmann and Manfreda Knote; m. Beate Just 1972; two s. two d.; ed . Univs of Munich and Paris; Research Assoc. Deutsches Historisches Institut, Paris 1970–81; Privatdozent, Munich 1979; Prof. Univ. of Passau 1982; Prof. of Gen. and Modern History, Univ. of Mainz 1988–2005, currently Prof. Emer.; held Chair of Educ. and Modern History, Johannes Gutenberg Univ. of Mainz; mem. Bd Franco-German Cultural Foundation; mem. Historical Comm. of Bavarian History, Bavarian Acad. of Sciences; Sr Phili. KDStV Aenania, Munich 2005–; Chevalier des Palmes académiques 2001, Bundesverdienstkreuz a. Bande 2012; Hon. DUniv (Paris); Strasbourg Int. Prize. *Publications:* Pariser Archive, Bibl. u. Dok.zentren 1976, Geld als Instrument europäischer Machtpolitik im Zeitalter des Merkantilismus 1978, Das Steuersystem der europäischen Staaten am Ende des Ancien Regime 1979, Karl Albrecht-Karl VII: Glücklicher Kurfürst, Unglücklicher Kaiser 1985, Französische Geschichte 1914–1945, Französische Verfgeschichte der Neuzeit (1450–1980), Ein Überblick 1985 (second edn 2003), Bayerns Weg in die Gegenwart: Vom Stammesherzogtum bis zur Freistaat heute 1989 (third edn 2012), Der Jesuitenstaat in Südamerika 1609–1768 1994, Franz. Könige u. Kaiser der Neuzeit 1994, Regionen in der Frühen Neuzeit 1994 (second edn 2006), Der Mainzer Kurfürst als Reichskanzler 1996, Der Bayerische Reichskreis (1500–1803) 1997, Kurmainz, das Reichskanzleramt und der Reich 1998, Geschichte Frankreichs 1999 (fourth edn 2007), Geschichte aktuell, hg. v.K. Amann 2000, Reichskirche, Kurmainz und Reichserzkanzleramt 2001, Die Jesuiten 2001 (second edn 2008), Kulturgeschichte des Heiligen Römischen Reiches 1648 bis 1806 Verfassung, Religion und Kultur 2001 (second edn 2011), Die Mainzer Kurfürsten d. Hauses Schönborn 2002, Religion und Kultur im Europa d.17 u.18 Jahrhunderts 2004 (second edn 2006), Das Heilige Römische Reich deutscher Nation in der Neuzeit 1485–1806 2005, Kleine Mainzer Stadtgeschichte 2005 (second edn 2011), Das Hl Röm. Reich u. sein Ende 2006, Münchens Weg in d. Gegenwart 2008, Bayer.-cgines. Beziehungen 2008, Der Dreißigjähr. Krieg 2010, Bayern in Lateinamerika 2011. *E-mail:* peterclaushartmann@gmx.de.

HARTMANN, Ulrich; German business executive; b. 7 Aug. 1938, Berlin; m.; two c.; legal studies in Munich, Berlin and Bonn; auditor, Treuarbeit AG, Düsseldorf 1967–71; Asst to Man. Bd Deutsche Leasing AG, Frankfurt 1971–72; Corp. Counsel, VEBA Kraftwerke Ruhr AG, Gelsenkirchen 1973–75; Head, Bd Office and Public Relations, VEBA AG, Düsseldorf 1975–80; mem. Man. Bd Nordwestdeutsche Kraftwerke AG, Hamburg 1980–85, PreussenElektra AG, Hanover 1985–89; mem. Man. Bd VEBA AG 1989, Chief Finance Officer 1990–93, CEO and Chair. 1993; Chair. Supervisory Bd E.ON AG 2003–11, also Chair. Exec. Cttee and Finance and Investment Cttee; Chair. Supervisory Bd of major group cos and Münchener Rückversicherungs-Gesellschaft AG, Munich, RAG Aktiengesellschaft, Essen, Degussa AG 1998; Consul-Gen. of Norway 1993; Dir (non-exec.) Cable and Wireless PLC, London; mem. or fmr mem. Supervisory Bd Daimler-Benz AG, Stuttgart, Deutsche Lufthansa AG –2010, Cologne, Hochtief AG, Essen, IKB Deutsche Industriebank AG, Düsseldorf, Münchener Rückversicherungs-Gesellschaft AG, Munich. *Address:* c/o E.ON SE, E.ON-Platz 1, 40479 Düsseldorf, Germany (office).

HARTONO, Michael (Bambang), (Oei Wie Siang) Indonesian business executive; *Joint Chief Executive, PT Djarum;* s. of Oei Wie Gwan; brother of Robert Budi Hartono; m.; four c.; joined family co. PT Djarum (clove cigarette mfr) 1981, now Co-Propr and CEO (with brother); major shareholder (via FarIndo Investments, Mauritius Ltd) PT Bank Central Asia Tbk (BCA) 1998–. *Address:* PT Djarum, Jl Aipda K. S. Tubun 2C/57, Jakarta, Indonesia (office). *Telephone:* (21) 5346901 (office). *Fax:* (21) 5346892 (office). *Website:* www.djarum.co.id (office).

HARTONO, Robert Budi, (Oei Wie Tjhong), Indonesian business executive; *Joint Chief Executive, PT Djarum;* s. of Oei Wie Gwan; brother of Michael (Bambang) Hartono; m.; three s.; joined family co. PT Djarum (clove cigarette mfr) 1981, now Co-Propr and CEO (with brother); major shareholder (via FarIndo Investments, Mauritius Ltd) PT Bank Central Asia Tbk (BCA) 1998–. *Leisure interest:* badminton. *Address:* PT Djarum, Jl Aipda K. S. Tubun 2C/57, Jakarta, Indonesia (office). *Telephone:* (21) 5346901 (office). *Fax:* (21) 5346892 (office). *Website:* www.djarum.co.id (office).

HARTSHORN, Michael Philip, DPhil, FRSNZ; British/New Zealand chemist and academic; *Professor Emeritus of Chemistry, University of Canterbury;* b. 10 Sept. 1936, Coventry, England; m. Jacqueline Joll 1963; four s.; ed Imperial Coll. of Science and Tech., London, University Coll., Oxford; Lecturer in Chem., Univ. of Canterbury, NZ 1960–66, Sr Lecturer 1966–68, Reader 1968–72, Prof. 1972–97, Prof. Emer. 1996–; Fulbright Visiting Prof., Cornell Univ., New York 1966–67; Guest Prof., Lund Univ., Sweden 1991–92, 1995, 1997; Fürth Visiting Lecturer, Royal Soc. of Edinburgh 1991; Wilsmore Fellow Melbourne Univ. June–July 1996; Fellowship NZ Inst. of Chem. 1969; Hector Medal, Royal Soc. of NZ 1973. *Publications:* approx. 255 scientific papers, Steroid Reaction Mechanisms (with D. N. Kirk) 1968. *Leisure interests:* reading, music, gardening. *Address:* 29 Clare Road, Merivale, Christchurch 8001, New Zealand (home). *Telephone:* (3) 3556-450 (home). *Fax:* (3) 3558-357 (home). *E-mail:* michael.hartshorn@canterbury.ac.nz (office). *Website:* www.chem.canterbury.ac.nz (office).

HARTUNG, Harald; German poet, academic and critic; b. 29 Oct. 1932, Herne; s. of Richard Hartung and Wanda Hartung; m. Freia Schnackenburg 1979; two s.; secondary school teacher 1960–66; Prof., Pädagogische Hochschule Berlin 1971–80, Tech. Univ. Berlin 1971–98 (retd); mem. Akad. der Künste, Berlin, PEN; Literature Promotion Prize of the Berlin Art Prize 1979, Annette von Droste-Hulshoff Prize 1987, Int. Poetry Prize Chianti Ruffino Antico Fattore 1999, Prize of the Frankfurt anthology 2002, Würth Prize for European Literature 2004, Johann Heinrich Merck Prize 2009, Literatur Prize Ruhr 2012. *Publications:* Experimentelle Literatur und Konkrete Poesie 1975, Das Gewöhnliche Licht 1976,

Augenzeit 1978, Deutsche Lyrik seit 1965 1985, Traum im Deutschen Museum 1986, Luftfracht 1991, Jahre mit Windrad 1996, Masken und Stimmen 1996, Jahrhundertgedächtnis.Deutsche Lyrik im 20.Jahrhundert 1998, Machen oder Entstehenlassen 2001, Langsamer träumen 2002, Aktennotiz meines Engels 2005, Ein Unterton von Glück – Über Dichter und Gedichte 2007, Wintermalerei. Gedichte 2010, Der Tag vor dem Abend 2012. *Address:* Rüdesheimer Platz 4, 14197 Berlin, Germany.

HARTWELL, Leland H., BS, PhD; American geneticist; *President and Director Emeritus, Fred Hutchinson Cancer Research Center;* b. 30 Oct. 1939; s. of Ernest Hartwell and Marjorie Taylor Hartwell; m. Theresa Naujack-Hartwell; ed California Inst. of Technology, MIT, Salk Inst. for Biological Studies; Assoc. Prof. Univ. of Calif. 1965–68; Assoc. Prof., then Prof., Univ. of Washington 1968–2010; Pres. and Dir Fred Hutchinson Cancer Research Center 1997–2010, Pres. and Dir Emer. 2010–; Faculty, Virginia G. Piper Chair of Personalized Medicine Arizona State Univ. 2009–, Chief Scientist Biodesign Inst. 2010–, Prof., Ira A. Fulton School of Eng 2010–; Prof., American Cancer Soc.; Chair. Scientific Advisory Board Canary Foundation; mem. Nat. Advisory Bd BioLab 2000–; mem. Bd of Sponsors Fed. of American Scientists; mem. Editorial Bd Molecular and Cellular Biology, Journal of Cell Biology 1988–91, Molecular Biology of the Cell 1991–93; mem. NAS 1987–, American Soc. of Microbiology, American Acad. of Microbiology, Genetics Soc. of America, American Soc. for Cell Biology, American Asscn for Cancer Research, American Acad. of Arts and Sciences; numerous awards including General Motors Sloan Award 1991, Gairdner Foundation Int. Award 1992, Genetics Soc. of America Medal 1994, Louisa Gross Horwitz Prize 1995, Albert Lasker Basic Medical Research Award 1998, Nobel Prize in Medicine (jtly) 2001, Medal of Merit 2003, Komen Brinker Award for Scientific Distinction. *Publications:* co-author of several books. *Leisure interests:* health care. *Address:* Fred Hutchinson Cancer Research Center, 1100 Fairview Avenue North, D1-060 Seattle, WA 98109-1024, USA (office). *Telephone:* (206) 667-5000 (office). *Fax:* (206) 667-5268 (office). *E-mail:* lhartwel@fhcrc.org (office); externalrel@fhcrc.org (office). *Website:* www.fhcrc.org

HARTZENBERG, Ferdinand, DSc; South African fmr politician; b. 8 Jan. 1936, Lichtenburg; s. of Ferdinand Hartzenberg; m. Magdalena Judith de Wet 1962; two s.; ed Sannieshof, Hoër Volkskool, Potchefstroom and Univ. of Pretoria; mem. Parl. for Lichtenburg; Leader Conservative Party of SA (CPSA) 1993–2004; Deputy Minister of Devt 1976; Minister of Educ. and Training 1979–82.

HARUTIUNIAN, Arayik; Azerbaijani economist and politician; *Prime Minister of the 'Republic of Nagornyi Karabakh';* b. 14 Dec. 1973, Stepanakert (Xankändi), Nagornyi Karabakh Autonomous Oblast, Azerbaijan SSR, USSR; m.; two c.; ed Physics and Math. School, Stepanakert, Inst. of Nat. Economy, Yerevan, Artsakh State Univ.; entered defence forces of Nagornyi Karabakh Repub. (NKR) 1992, active participation in several operations; Asst to the Minister of Finance and Economy (NKR) 1995–97; banking exec., Askeran br. of Hayagrobank 1997–99, Stepanakert br. of Hayagrobank 1999–2004; Deputy of NKR Nat. Ass. 2005–; Leader of Azat Hayrenik party, head of Hayrenik faction; Prime Minister of the 'Repub. of Nagornyi Karabakh' 2010–. *Address:* Office of the Prime Minister of the 'Republic of Nagornyi Karabakh', 374430 Stepanakert, Petrvari 20 poghots 1, Nagornyi Karabakh, Azerbaijan (office). *Telephone:* (47) 94-32-14 (office). *Fax:* (47) 94-32-14 (office). *E-mail:* info@gov.nkr.am (office). *Website:* gov.nkr.am (office).

HARVEY, Anthony; British film editor and film director; b. 3 June 1931, London; s. of Geoffrey Harrison and Dorothy Leon; ed Royal Acad. of Dramatic Art, London; joined Crown Film Unit 1949; started career as film ed. *Films include:* films ed: Private's Progress 1956, On Such a Night 1956, Happy Is the Bride 1957, Brothers in Law 1957, I'm All Right Jack 1959, Carlton-Browne of the F.O. 1959, The Millionairess 1960, The Angry Silence 1960, The Angry Silence 1960, Lolita 1962, The L-Shaped Room 1962, Dr. Strangelove 1964, The Spy Who Came In from the Cold 1965, Dutchman 1967, The Whisperers 1967; films directed: Dutchman 1967, The Lion in Winter (Directors Guild of America Award) 1968, They Might Be Giants 1971, The Abdication 1974, Players 1979, Eagle's Wing 1979, Richard's Things 1980, Grace Quigley 1984. *Television includes:* The Glass Menagerie 1973, The Disappearance of Aimee 1976, The Patricia Neal Story 1981, Svengali 1983, This Can't Be Love 1994. *Leisure interest:* gardening. *Address:* c/o Arthur B. Greene, Maris, Paneth & Shron, 622 Third Avenue, New York, NY 10017, USA.

HARVEY, HE Cardinal James Michael, DCL; American ecclesiastic and diplomatist; *Archpriest of the Basilica di San Paolo fuori le Mura;* b. 20 Oct. 1949, Milwaukee, Wis.; ed St Francis Seminary, Pontifical North American Coll., Rome, Pontifical Ecclesiastical Acad.; ordained priest, Archdiocese of Milwaukee 1975; entered diplomatic service of the Holy See 1980, served as attaché in Apostolic Nunciature in Dominican Repub. 1980–81, Sec. 1981–82, worked at Secr. of State 1982–97, Assessor of Secr. of State 1997–98; Titular Bishop of Memphis (Egypt) 1998–2003, Titular Archbishop of Memphis 2003–; Prefect of the Papal Household 1998–2012; Archpriest of Basilica di San Paolo fuori le Mura 2012–; cr. Cardinal (Cardinal-Deacon of San Pio V a Villa Carpegna) 2012; mem. Congregation for Causes of Saints 2012–, Admin of Patrimony of the Apostolic See 2013–, Congregation for Evangelization of Peoples 2013–; Kt Grand Cross, Order of Merit of the Italian Rep. 1999. *Address:* Roman Curia, 00120 Città del Vaticano, Rome, Italy (office). *Telephone:* (06) 69880800 (office); (06) 69880802 (office). *Fax:* (06) 69880803 (office). *E-mail:* info@basilicasanpaolo.org (office); spbasilica@org.va (office). *Website:* www.vatican.va/various/basiliche/san_paolo/index_en.html (office).

HARVEY, Richard, FIA; British insurance industry executive; *Non-Executive Chairman, PZ Cussons Plc;* b. 1951, Gloucestershire; m. Kay Harvey; joined Norwich Union 1992, various sr man. posts in NZ and UK, fmr Dir, Group CEO 1998–2000, Deputy Group CEO Aviva PLC (following merger) 2000–01, CEO 2001–07; Chair. (non-exec.) PZ Cussons PLC 2010–; Dir Asscn of British Insurers 2001–05; mem. Bd of Dirs Jardine Lloyd Thompson PLC 2009–; mem. Audit, Nominations and Remuneration Cttees. *Address:* PZ Cussons, Manchester Business Park, 3500 Aviator Way, Manchester, M22 5TG, England (office). *Telephone:* (16) 1435-1000 (office). *E-mail:* pzweb.general@pzcussons.com (office). *Website:* www.pzcussons.com (office).

HARWIT, Martin Otto, BA, MA, PhD; American (b. Czechoslovak) astrophysicist, academic and fmr museum director; *Professor Emeritus of Astronomy,*

Cornell University; b. 9 March 1931, Prague, Czechoslovakia; s. of Felix Michael Haurowitz and Regina Hedwig Haurowitz (née Perutz); m. Marianne Mark; three c.; ed English High School for Boys, Istanbul, Bronx High School of Science, New York, Oberlin Coll., Univ. of Michigan, Massachusetts Inst. of Tech.; moved with family to Istanbul, Turkey aged eight, to USA aged 15; served in US Army 1955–57; carried out postdoctoral research on theoretical astrophysical problems with Fred Hoyle at Univ. of Cambridge, UK 1960–61; postdoctoral researcher, Cornell Univ. 1961, mem. astronomy faculty 1962, visited Naval Research Lab. with Herbert Friedman's group 1963–64, returned to Cornell 1964, worked with Aerobee rockets to conduct infrared astronomy from space, built several rocket payloads with liquid nitrogen, helium-cooled telescopes and infrared detectors, went into airborne infrared astronomy working on NASA's Learjet and Kuiper flying observatories, co-pioneered infrared spectroscopy and made many near- and far-infrared observations, developed the Hadamard Transform technique of multislit spectroscopic imaging, co-f. and co-directed doctoral programme in the history and philosophy of science and tech. at Cornell, Prof. Emer. of Astronomy 1988–; one of original planners of NASA's Great Observatories programme; NAS/ Czechoslovak Acad. of Sciences Exchange Fellow, Prague 1969–70; Mission Scientist, ESA Infrared Space Observatory 1985, ESA Herschel Space Observatory; Science Team mem., NASA Submillimeter Wave Astronomy Satellite Project and Vision Mission Far-Infrared and Submillimeter Interferometer study; Dir Smithsonian Nat. Air and Space Museum, Washington, DC 1987–95; External mem. Max Planck Soc., Germany 1979; Adriaan Blaauw Visiting Prof., Univ. of Groningen, Netherlands 2002; Distinguished Fellow, Inst. of Advanced Study, Durham Univ., UK 2007; Hon. DSc (Oberlin Coll.) 2011; Alexander von Humboldt Sr US Scientist Award (Germany) 1976–77, Bruce Medal, Astronomical Soc. of the Pacific 2007. *Publications:* Astrophysical Concepts 1973 (translated into Chinese) (fourth edn 2006), Hadamard Transform Optics (with Neil J. A. Sloane) 1979, Cosmic Discovery: The Search, Scope and Heritage of Astronomy 1981 (translated into German and French), Treasures of the National Air and Space Museum 1995, An Exhibit Denied – Lobbying the History of Enola Gay (translated into Japanese) 1996, The Extragalactic Background and its Cosmological Implications (with M. G. Hauser) 2001. *Address:* 511 H Street SW, Washington, DC 20024, USA (office). *Telephone:* (202) 479-6877 (office). *E-mail:* harwit@verizon.net (office). *Website:* astro.cornell.edu (office).

HARWOOD, Sir Ronald, Kt, CBE, FRSL; British author and playwright; b. (Ronald Horwitz), 9 Nov. 1934, Cape Town, South Africa; s. of the late Isaac Horwitz and Isobel Pepper; m. Natasha Riehle 1959; one s. two d.; ed Sea Point Boys' High School, Cape Town and Royal Acad. of Dramatic Art; actor 1953–60; author 1960–; Artistic Dir Cheltenham Festival of Literature 1975; presenter, Kaleidoscope, BBC Radio 1973, Read All About It, BBC TV 1978–79, All The World's A Stage, BBC TV; Chair. Writers' Guild of GB 1969; Visitor in Theatre, Balliol Coll. Oxford 1986; Pres. PEN (England) 1989–93, Int. PEN 1993–97; Gov. Cen. School of Speech and Drama; mem. Council Royal Soc. of Literature 1998–2001, Chair. 2001–04; Trustee, Booker Foundation 2002; Chevalier des Arts et Lettres 1996; Hon. DLitt (Keele) 2002; New Standard Drama Award 1981, Drama Critics Award 1981, Molière Award for Best Play, Paris 1993. *TV plays include:* The Barber of Stamford Hill 1960, Private Potter (with Casper Wrede) 1961, The Guests 1972, Breakthrough at Reykjavik 1987, Countdown to War 1989. *Screenplays include:* A High Wind in Jamaica 1965, One Day in the Life of Ivan Denisovich 1971, Evita Perón 1981, The Dresser 1983, Mandela 1987, The Browning Version 1994, Cry, Beloved Country 1995, Taking Sides 2002, The Pianist 2002 (Acad. Award for Best Adapted Screenplay 2003), The Statement 2003, Being Julia 2004, Oliver Twist 2005, Le Scaphandre et le Papillon (BAFTA Award for Best Adapted Screenplay 2008) 2007, Love in the Time of Cholera 2007, The Diving Bell and the Butterfly 2007, Australia 2008, Quartet 2012. *Plays include:* Country Matters 1969, The Good Companions (musical libretto) 1974, The Ordeal of Gilbert Pinfold 1977, A Family 1978, The Dresser 1980, After the Lions 1982, Tramway Road 1984, The Deliberate Death of a Polish Priest 1985, Interpreters 1985, J. J. Farr 1987, Ivanov (from Chekhov) 1989, Another Time 1989, Reflected Glory 1992, Poison Pen 1994, Taking Sides 1995, The Handyman 1996, Equally Divided 1998, Quartet 1999, Mahler's Conversion 2002, An English Tragedy 2007. *Publications include:* fiction: All the Same Shadows 1961, The Guilt Merchants 1963, The Girl in Melanie Klein 1969, Articles of Faith 1973, The Genoa Ferry 1976, César and Augusta 1978, Home 1993; non-fiction: Sir Donald Wolfit, CBE: His Life and Work in the Unfashionable Theatre (biog.) 1971; editor: A Night at the Theatre 1983, The Ages of Gielfud 1984, Dear Alec: Guinness at Seventy-Five 1989, The Faber Book of the Theatre 1994; vols of essays and short stories. *Leisure interest:* cricket. *Address:* Judy Daish Associates, 2 St Charles Place, London, W10 6EG, England (office). *Telephone:* (20) 8964-8811 (office).

HASAN, Abdulkasim Salad; Somali fmr head of state; b. 1942; Minister of Industry, of Trade, of Labour, of Information and of the Interior 1973–1990; Pres. of Somalia 2000–04. *Address:* c/o Office of the President, People's Palace, Mogadishu, Somalia (office).

HASAN, Khandaker Mahmud-ul, MA, LLM; Bangladeshi international organisation official, fmr judge and diplomatist; *President, Arbitral Tribunal, Commonwealth Secretariat;* b. 27 Jan. 1939; s. of the late Khandaker Mohammed Hasan; enrolled as Supreme Court advocate 1963, Judge of the High Court 1991–2002, Appellate Div. 2002, apptd Chief Justice, Supreme Court 2003; Amb. to Iraq 1980–82; mem. Arbitral Tribunal Commonwealth Secr. 2005–08, Pres. 2009–; fmr Chair. Fed. Insurance Co.; fmr Int. Assoc. American Bar Asscn; fmr part-time Lecturer, Dhaka Univ.; fmr mem. Governing Body Cen. Law Coll.; fmr mem. Bangladesh Bar Council; mem. Del. Islamic Foreign Ministers Conf. Baghdad, Iraq 1981, Non-Aligned Labour Ministers Conf. Baghdad, Iraq 1981; Hon. Sec., Bangladesh Inst. of Law and Int. Affairs 1975–80, Hon. Dir 1982–85. *Publications:* several articles. *Address:* Commonwealth Secretariat Arbitral Tribunal, Marlborough House, Pall Mall, London, SW1Y 5HX, England (office). *Telephone:* (20) 7747-6181 (office). *Fax:* (20) 7747-6449 (office). *E-mail:* csat@commonwealth.int (office). *Website:* www.thecommonwealth.org (office).

HASAN, Masuma, MA, PhD; Pakistani diplomatist and academic; *Chair, Pakistan Institute of International Affairs;* ed Univ. of Cambridge, UK, Univ. of Karachi; mem. Faculty, Nat. Inst. of Public Admin, Karachi 1967–81, Dir 1991–94, 1997–99; Dir Public Admin Research Centre, Govt of Pakistan, Islamabad

1981–84, Dir-Gen., Man. Services Div., Islamabad and Karachi 1984–90; Perm. Rep. to UN, IAEA, UNIDO and other int. orgs, Vienna 1994–97, Chair., Group of 77, UN in Vienna 1996, Amb. to Australia (also accred to Slovenia and Slovakia) 1994–97; Cabinet Sec., Islamabad 2000–01; Chair., Pakistan Inst. of Int. Affairs; Pres. Aurat Foundation. *Publication:* Pakistan in a Changing World 1978. *Address:* Pakistan Institute of International Affairs, Aiwan-e-Sadar Road, PO Box 1447, Karachi 74200 (office); Aurat Foundation, House #12, Street No. 12, F-7/2, Islamabad 44000, Pakistan (office). *Telephone:* (51) 2608956-8 (Islamabad) (office); (21) 35686069 (Karachi) (office). *Fax:* (51) 2608955 (Islamabad) (office); (21) 35686069 (Karachi) (office). *E-mail:* headoffice@af.org.pk (Islamabad) (office); masumahasan@hotmail.com (office); info@piia.org.pk (Karachi) (office). *Website:* www.af.org.pk/mainpage.htm (Islamabad) (office); www.piia.org.pk (Karachi) (office).

HASANI, Baqir Husain, BSc, LLB; Iraqi/Italian diplomatist (retd); b. 12 Feb. 1915, Baghdad; ed Columbia Univ., USA and Law Coll., Baghdad Univ.; Dir of Commerce and Registrar of Patents, Trade Marks and Companies, Ministry of Econs, Iraq 1947–51; Dir-Gen. of Contracts and Econ. Research, Devt Bd 1951–54; Dir-Gen. of Income Tax, Ministry of Finance 1954–55; Dir-Gen. and Chair. Bd of Dirs Tobacco Monopoly Admin. 1955–59; Envoy Extraordinary and later Amb. to Austria 1959–63; Chair. Bd of Govs IAEA 1961–62; Special Adviser to Dir-Gen. IAEA, Vienna 1963–66, 1970–76; Adviser to Saudi Arabian Mission in Vienna 1978–81; consultant on Middle Eastern Affairs 1985–; mem. numerous govt cttees and del. to the UN and to int. confs; Lecturer, Coll. of Business Admin., Coll. of Pharmacy, Mil. Staff Coll.; Rafidain Decoration, Austrian Grand Golden Decoration. *Publications:* numerous articles in newspapers and magazines. *Leisure interests:* collecting stamps and coins, composing poetry. *Address:* Via Civelli 9, 21100 Varese, Italy (home); 7 Ashenden Road, Guildford, Surrey, GU2 7UU, England (home). *Telephone:* (0332) 229633 (Italy) (home); (1483) 838371 (England) (home).

HÄSÄNLI, Cämil Poladxan oğlu, PhD; Azerbaijani historian, academic and politician; b. 15 Jan. 1952, Agalikend, Bilasuvar Rayon, Azerbaijan SSR; ed Azerbaijan State Univ., Southern Illinois Univ., USA; worked as history teacher in Tazakend village, Jalilabad Rayon; Lecturer, Baku br. of Cen. Lenin Museum 1976–77; entered doctoral courses at Baku State Univ. 1977, Docent 1990–, Dean of New and Modern History of Europe and Americas Dept 1992–94, now Prof.; Adviser to Pres. of Azerbaijan April–Sept. 1993; mem. Pres.'s Expert Council of High Accreditation Comm. of Azerbaijan 1994–2004; elected Deputy to Nat. Ass. 2000; Deputy Chair. Azerbaijan Popular Front Party; unsuccessful cand. (Nat. Council of Democratic Forces bloc), presidential election 9 Oct. 2013; participated in research projects at Humboldt Univ. of Berlin 2013; mem. Azerbaijan Nat. Acad. of Sciences, North American Soc. for Middle Eastern Studies 1998. *Publications include:* Black Shadow of White Dots: Soviet Totalitarism in Azerbaijan in 1920–1930 1991, Azerbaijan Republic in the International Relations System 1993, History of Azerbaijan (co-author) 1995, Azerbaycan Tarihi: Türkiye Yardımından Rusya İşgaline Kadar (1918–1920), 1998, History of Azerbaijan: From Turkey's Help to Russian Occupation (1918–1920) 1998, South Azerbaijan: Between Tehran, Baku and Moscow 1998, History: From the Past to the Future 1998, South Azerbaijan: Place of Beginning of the Cold War 1999, Soviet-American-British Confrontation in South Azerbaijan 2001, South Azerbaijan: Beginning of the Cold War 2003, USSR–Turkey: Cold War Arena 2005, Soğuk Savaşın İlk Çatışması: İran Azerbaycanı 2005, First Confrontation of the Cold War: Iranian Azerbaijan 2005, At the Dawn of the Cold War: The Soviet-American Crisis over Iranian Azerbaijan, 1941–1946 2006, USSR-Iran: Azerbaijani Crisis and the Beginning of the Cold War 2006, USSR-Turkey: From Neutrality to Cold War 2008, National Question in Azerbaijan: Political Leadership and Intelligence 2008, Khrushchev's Thaw and the National Question in Azerbaijan, 1954–1959 2009, Diplomatic History of the Azerbaijan Republic (in three vols), Vol. 1 The Foreign Policy of the Azerbaijan Democratic Republic (1918–1920) 2010, Stalin and the Turkish Crisis of the Cold War, 1945–1953 2011, Azerbaijan and the Russian Revolution: A Difficult Path to Independence, 1917–1920 2011, Sovet dövründä Azärbaycanın Xarici Siyasäti (1920–1939) 2012, Foreign Policy of the Republic of Azerbaijan, 1918–1920: The Difficult Road to Western Integration 2013. *Address:* c/o Azerbaijan Popular Front Party (Azärbaycan Xalq Cabhasi Partiyası), 1152 Baku, Milli Mäclis, Mehti Hussein küç. 2, Azerbaijan (office). *Telephone:* (12) 498-07-94 (office). *E-mail:* faiq73@mail.ru (office). *Website:* www.camilhasanli.com.

HASANOV, Ramiz Ayvaz oglu; Azerbaijani government official and fmr diplomatist; *Chairman, State Committee on Standardization, Metrology and Patents;* b. 20 Aug. 1961; m.; two c.; ed Faculty of Int. Law, Moscow State Inst. of Int. Relations, USSR; worked in various Govt ministries responsible for foreign trade issues; First Deputy Chair. Azcontrakt Open Jt Stock Co. 1983–2004; Amb. to Georgia 2004–05; Chair. State Cttee on Standardization, Metrology and Patents 2005–; Co-Chair. EuroAsian Interstate Council for Standardization, Metrology and Certification. *Address:* State Committee on Standardization, Metrology and Patents, Mardanov Gardashlary str. 124, 1147 Baku, Azerbaijan (office). *Telephone:* (12) 449-99-59 (office). *Fax:* (12) 440-52-24 (office). *E-mail:* azs@azstand.gov.az (office). *Website:* www.azstand.gov.az (office).

HÄSÄNOV, Col-Gen. Zakir; Azerbaijani politician and fmr army officer; *Minister of Defence;* b. 6 June 1959, Astara; m.; two c.; ed Baku High Army Commanders School; served in Soviet Armed Forces units in Germany 1980–85; worked in Altay Mil. Registration and Enlistment Office, Siberia Mil. Region of USSR Ministry of Defence 1985–93; served in Main Office of Border Troops, Nat. Ministry of Security, Azerbaijan 1993–2003, Chief of Office of Int. Relations of State Border Service 2003; Deputy Minister of Interior and Commdr of Internal Troops 2003–13; Minister of Defence 2012–; attained rank of Maj.-Gen. 2003, Col-Gen. 2013; Order of Azerbaijan Flag 2004; Medal for Distinguished Service in the Border 1998, Medal for Distinguished Services 2002. *Address:* Ministry of Defence, 1139 Baku, Azärbaycan pr., Azerbaijan (office). *Telephone:* (12) 439-41-89 (office). *Fax:* (12) 492-92-50 (office).

HASEEB, Khair El-Din, BA, MSc, PhD; Iraqi economist and statistician; *Director-General, Centre for Arab Unity Studies;* b. 1 Aug. 1929, Mosul; m. 1955; one s. two d.; ed Univ. of Baghdad, London School of Econs and Univ. of Cambridge, UK; civil servant, Ministry of Interior 1947–54; Head of Research and Statistics Dept, Iraqi Oil Co. 1959–60; Full-time Lecturer, Univ. of Baghdad

1960–61, Part-time 1961–63; Dir-Gen. Iraqi Fed. of Industries 1960–63; Gov. and Chair. Cen. Bank of Iraq 1963–65; Pres. Gen. Org. for Banks 1964–65; Acting Pres. Econ. Org., Iraq 1964–65; Assoc. Prof., Dept of Econs, Univ. of Baghdad 1965–71, Prof. of Econs 1971–74; mem. Bd of Dirs Iraq Nat. Oil Co. 1967–68; Chief, Programme and Co-ordination Unit and Natural Resources, Science and Tech. Div. UN Econ. Comm. for Western Asia, then Lebanon and Iraq 1974–76 and 1976–83; Acting Dir-Gen. Centre for Arab Unity Studies, Lebanon 1978–83, Dir-Gen. 1983–; Chair. Bd of Trustees and Dirs Arab Cultural Foundation, London 1987; Chair. Bd of Trustees Arab Org. for Translation, Lebanon 1999–. *Publications:* The National Income of Iraq 1953–1961, 1964, Workers' Participation in Management in Arab Countries (in Arabic) 1971, Sources of Arab Economic Thought in Iraq 1900–71 (in Arabic) 1972, Arab Monetary Integration (co-ed.) 1982, Arabs and Africa (ed.) 1985, The Future of the Arab Nation 1991, Arab-Iranian Relations (ed.) 2002, The Future of Iraq: Occupation, Resistance, Liberation and Democracy 2004, Planning Iraq's Future: A Detailed Project to Rebuild Post-Liberation Iraq (ed.) 2006, An Overview of Arab Concerns: Arab Nationalism, Arab Unity; The Centre for Arab Unity Studies; The Arab Intellectual and Democracy 2008, The Future of the Arab Nation: Challenges and Options 2012; numerous articles. *Leisure interests:* swimming, tennis. *Address:* Centre for Arab Unity Studies, 'Beit Al-Nahda' Bldg, Basra Street, PO Box 113-6001, Hamra, Beirut 2034 2407, Lebanon (office). *Telephone:* (1) 750084 (office); (1) 740631 (home). *Fax:* (1) 750088 (office). *E-mail:* info@caus.org.lb (office). *Website:* www.caus.org.lb (office).

HASEGAWA, Itsuku; Japanese architect; *Founder, Itsuku Hasagawa Atelier;* b. 1941, Shizuoka Pref.; ed Kanto Gakuin Univ., Tokyo Inst. of Tech.; worked for Kiyonori Kikutate 1964–69; researcher Dept of Architecture, Tokyo Inst. of Tech. 1969–71, Asst to Prof. Kazuo Shinohara 1971–78; est. Itsuku Hasagawa Atelier 1979; Lecturer, Waseda Univ. 1988, Tokyo Inst. of Tech. 1989, Niigata Univ. 1993, Tokyo Denki Univ. 1995; Visiting Prof., Grad. School of Design, Harvard Univ., USA 1992, Kanto Gakuin Univ. 2001; Hon. FRIBA 1997; Hon. FAIA 2006; hon. degree (Univ. Coll. London) 2001; Japan Inter-Design Forum Award 1986, Japan Cultural Design Award 1986, First Prize, Competition for Sumida Cultural Centre 1990, First Prize, Competition for Shiogama City Town Centre 1995, Int. Young Generation Award 1998, Avon Arts Award. *Architectural works include:* House in Kuwahara, Matsuyama 1980, Aono Bldg, Matsuyama 1982, Bizan Hall (Architectural Inst. of Japan Prize for Design) 1986, Shonandai Cultural Centre, Fujisawa, Kanagawa (BCS Award, Bldg Constructors Soc. 1992) 1987–90, STM House, Shibuya-ku, Tokyo 1991, Sumida Culture Factory 1994, Oshima-Machi Picture Book Museum, Toyama (Public Building Award 2000) 1994, Yamanashi Fruit Garden 1995, Imai Newtown Housing, Nagano (Olympic Village) 1998, Niigata City Performing Arts Centre (Japan Art Acad. Award 2000, BCS Award, Bldg Constructors Soc. 2001, Public Bldg Award 2004) 1998, Fukuroi Workshop Centre, Shizuoka 2001, Centre in Shizuoka 2004, Taisei Jr High and High School, Shizuoka 2004, Ohota Project 2005, Suzu Performing Arts Center, Ishikawa 2006, Shizuoka Univ. of Welfare 2006. *Publications include:* Itsuko Hasegawa 1997, The Equipment of Life 1999, Island Hopping 2000; articles in professional journals. *Address:* Itsuku Hasagawa Atelier, 1-9-7 Yushima, Bunkyo-ku, Tokyo 113-0034, Japan (office). *Telephone:* (3) 3818-5470 (office). *Fax:* (3) 3818-1821 (office). *E-mail:* ihasegawa@ihasegawa.com (office). *Website:* www.ihasegawa.com (office).

HASEGAWA, Kaoru, BEcons; Japanese business executive; b. 15 April 1924, Hyogo; m. Shizue Hasegawa 1952; one s. one d.; ed Naval Acad. of Japan, Gakushuin Univ.; joined Rengo Co. Ltd 1952, Gen. Man. Corp. Planning Dept 1960, Man. Dir 1962, Sr Man. Dir 1970, Exec. Vice-Pres. 1973, Pres. and CEO 1984, fmr Chair.; Pres. Japan Corrugated Case Asscn 1986; Vice-Chair. Japan Paper Asscn 1995; consultant on overseas Devt, China Packaging Tech. Asscn 1999. *Publications include:* Two Lives: My Personal History, Cultural and Economic Dialogues: Learning from the History and Wisdom of Europe.

HASEGAWA, Toru; Japanese automotive industry executive; *President, Nissan Motor Company Ltd, Thailand;* joined Yamaha Motor Co. Ltd 1960, various positions including export agent, Dir of Procurement 1970s, Dir of European Operations, Netherlands 1990, Sr Man. Dir –2001, Pres. and Rep. Dir, Yamaha Motor Co. Ltd 2001–04, fmr Chair. and Dir; currently Pres. Nissan Motor Co. Ltd Thailand, Regional Vice-Pres. Asia and Oceania Operations; fmr mem. Bd of Dirs Int. Business Dept Fuji Kiko Co. Ltd, Euroland.com AB. *Address:* Nissan Motor Company Limited, 74 Moo, 2 Bangna Trad Km 21 Srisajarakea Yai Bangsaothong, Samutprakarn 10540, Thailand (office). *Website:* www.nissan.co.th (office).

HASELSTEINER, Hans Peter, MA, PhD; Austrian business executive and fmr politician; *Chairman of the Management Board and CEO, Strabag SE;* b. 1 Feb. 1944, Wörgl; ed Vienna Univ. of Econs and Business Admin; mil. service 1963–64; univ. studies 1964–70; worked for auditing and tax consultancy firm, Perfekta GmbH, Vienna 1970–74; joined ILBAU AG as mem. Supervisory Bd 1972, mem. Man. Bd and CEO group parent co. 1974–94, Chair. Man. Bd Bauholding Strabag AG (Bauholding Strabag SE from 2004, Strabag SE from 2006) 1998–; mem. Parl. and Vice-Chair. Liberal Forum 1994–98; Chair. Fachverband der Bauindustrie (Austrian Construction Industry Asscn), Vienna 2002–. *Address:* Strabag SE, Donau-City-Straße 9, 1220 Vienna, Austria (office). *Telephone:* (1) 22422-1000 (office). *Fax:* (1) 22422-1003 (office). *E-mail:* HPH@strabag.com (office). *Website:* www.strabag.com (office).

HASELTINE, William A., PhD; American scientist and academic; *Chairman and CEO, Haseltine Associates Ltd;* b. 17 Oct. 1944, St Louis, Missouri; s. of William R. Haseltine and Jean Adele Ellsberg; m. 1st Patricia Gercik; m. 2nd Gale Hayman 1991; two c.; ed Univ. of California, Harvard Univ.; Prof., Dana-Farber Cancer Inst., Harvard Medical School and Harvard School of Public Health 1976–93, fmr Chair. Div. of Cancer Pharmacology, Div. of Human Retrovirology; f. Human Genome Sciences Inc. (HGS) 1992, Chair. and Chief Exec. 1993–2004; currently Chair. and CEO Haseltine Associates Ltd; currently Chair. Haseltine Global Health LLC; Pres. William A. Haseltine Foundation for Medical Sciences and the Arts; Co-Chair. President's Council Cold Spring Harbor Lab.; Chair. Berkeley Center of Synthetic Biology; Pres. William A. Haseltine Foundation for Medical Sciences and Arts; Adjunct Prof. Scripps Research Inst.; Scientific Advisor HealthCare Ventures; Founder, fmr Ed.-in-Chief Journal of AIDS Research and Retrovirology; Founder Journal of Regenerative Medicine; Founder and Ed. on-line journal E-Biomed; est. seven biotechnology cos; Speaker Global Conf. Milken

Inst. 2005; Advisor Colorado Music Educ. Asscn; mem. Bd One World Health; mem. CEO Council New York Acad. of Science; mem. Reliance Innovation Council Reliance Industries Ltd; mem. Chairman's Circle Asia Soc.; mem. Council on Foreign Relations, Trilateral Comm.; mem. Leadership Council David H. Koch Inst. for Integrative Cancer Research at MIT; numerous awards and honours for his achievements in science, medicine and business. *Achievements include:* holder of more than 50 patents for his discoveries. *Publications:* over 250 scientific publs. *Address:* Reliance Industries Limited, Reliance Innovation Council, Makers Chambers-IV, Nariman Point, Mumbai 400 021, India (office). *Telephone:* (22) 22785000 (office). *Website:* www.ril.com (office).

HASHEL, Mohammed Y. al-, BSc, MBA, PhD; Kuwaiti economist and central banker; *Governor and Chairman, Central Bank of Kuwait;* b. 28 April 1974; ed Kuwait Univ., Emory Univ., USA, Old Dominion Univ.; mem. Kuwait Stock Exchange Cttee 2008–11; Deputy Gov., Central Bank of Kuwait 2009–12, Gov. and Chair. 2012–; Alt. Gov. of Kuwait at IMF and Arab Monetary Fund; Chair. Kuwait Inst. of Banking Studies; Co-Chair. Financial Stability Bd Regional Consultative Group for Middle East and N Africa; mem. Governing Bd Int. Islamic Liquidity Man.; mem. Council Islamic Financial Services Bd; mem. Higher Council of Planning and Devt, Higher Petroleum Council; mem. Bd of Dirs Kuwait Investment Authority, Gulf Monetary Council. *Address:* Office of the Governor, Central Bank of Kuwait, POB 526, 13006 Safat, Abdullah al-Salem St, Kuwait City, Kuwait (office). *Telephone:* 22449200 (office). *Fax:* 22464887 (office). *E-mail:* cbk@cbk.gov.kw (office). *Website:* www.cbk.gov.kw (office).

HASHIM, Ali; Maldivian business executive and politician; helped establish Maldives Stock Exchange 2007, Man. Dir 2007–08; Minister of Finance and Treasury 2008–10; mem. Maldivian Democratic Party, fmr Vice-Chair. *Address:* c/o Ministry of Finance and Treasury, Ameenee Magu, Malé 20-379, Maldives.

HASHIM AL-KADER, Fawzia; Eritrean politician; *Minister of Justice;* women's rights campaigner; fought as soldier in Eritrean wars of independence in 1970s; Minister of Justice 1991–. *Address:* Ministry of Justice, POB 241, Asmara, Eritrea (office). *Telephone:* (1) 127739 (office). *Fax:* (1) 126422 (office).

HASHIMI, Tariq al-, MA; Iraqi politician; b. 1942, Baghdad; ed Al-Mustansiriyah Univ.; attended Mil. Acad. 1959–62, pursued mil. career –1975; instructor, Leadership Acad. 1975; Iraq Br. Man., Arab Shipping Co. 1979–81, moved to Kuwait, served as Dir-Gen., Arab Shipping Co. –1990; returned to Iraq 1990; mem. Iraqi Islamic Party, fmr mem. Planning Cttee and Shura Council, Sec.-Gen. –2009; Second Vice-Pres. of Iraq 2006–11, First Vice-Pres. 2011, currently living in exile in Istanbul, Turkey, faced trial in absensia 2012. *E-mail:* info@alhashimi.org (office). *Website:* alhashimi.org (office).

HASHIMOTO, Toru; Japanese lawyer and politician; *Mayor of Osaka;* b. 29 June 1969, Hatagaya, Shibuya; m. Noriko Hashimoto; three s. four d.; ed Waseda Univ.; mem. Osaka Bar Asscn 1996–; f. Hashimoto Law Office 1998, currently Partner; became well-known giving legal advice on local radio and TV programmes in Kansai area, including programmes Super Morning (TV Asahi) and Gyōretsu no Dekiru Hōritsu Sōdanjo (The Legal Advisory Office that People Queue Up For, NTV); Gov. Osaka Pref. 2008–11 (youngest gov. in Japan); Mayor of Osaka 2011–; Founding Pres. Osaka Restoration Asscn ('One Osaka') 2010–. *Address:* Office of the Mayor, 3-20 Nakanoshima 1-chome, Kita-ku, Osaka 530-8201, Japan (office). *Telephone:* (6) 6208-7231 (office). *Fax:* (6) 6202-6950 (office). *Website:* www.city .osaka.lg.jp/contents/wdu020/seisakukikakushitsu (office).

HASHMI, (Aurangzeb) Alamgir, MA, DLit; Pakistani academic, poet, writer, editor and translator and broadcaster; b. 15 Nov. 1951, Lahore; ed Univ. of Louisville, USA, Univ. of Punjab; Instructor and Tutor in English, Govt Coll., Lahore 1971–73; Lecturer, Forman Christian Coll., Lahore 1973–74; Davidson Int. Visiting Scholar, Univ. of North Carolina 1974–75; Lecturer in English, Univ. of Louisville 1975–78, Univ. of Zürich and Volkshochschule, Zürich 1980–85; Asst Prof. of English, Univ. of Bahawalpur, Pakistan 1979–80; Lecturer in English, Univ. of Basel, Univ. of Bern 1982; Prof. of English and Commonwealth Literature, Univ. of Geneva, Univ. of Fribourg 1985; Assoc. Prof. of English, Int. Islamic Univ., Islamabad 1985–86; Foundation Chair, Prof. of English and Head, Dept of English, Univ. of Azad Jammu and Kashmir, Muzaffarabad 1986–87; Visiting Prof. of English, Govt Postgraduate Coll., Islamabad 1986; Research Prof. of English, American, African and Comparative Literature, Quaid-i-Azam Univ., Islamabad 1986–2000; Prof./Ed., PIDE, Quaid-i-Azam Univ. Campus, Islamabad 1988–2011; Course Dir, Foreign Service Training Inst. and Acad., Islamabad 1988–; Prof. of English and Comparative Literature, Univ. of Iceland 2000; Founder and Chair. Standing Int. Cttee on English in S Asia 1989–; Founder and Chair. Townsend Poetry Prize Cttee 1986–; Judge, Commonwealth Writers Prize 1990, nat. literature prizes, Pakistan Acad. of Letters 1998–; jury mem., Neustadt Int. Prize for Literature; Ed., Advisory Ed., Editorial Adviser and referee for numerous int. scholarly and literary journals and book series; thesis supervisor and external examiner for many univs world-wide; broadcaster, lecturer, scriptwriter, translator, ed. for Radio Pakistan and Pakistan TV 1968–; adviser, Nat. Book Council of Pakistan 1989–95, Nat. Book Foundation 1993–; Judge, Prime Minister's Award for Literature; Founding Pres. The Literature Podium; mem. Council Asscn for Commonwealth Studies, Bd of Govs Pakistan Acad. of Letters; mem. Poetry Soc., Associated Writing Programs, Asscn for Asian Studies, New York Acad. of Sciences, Council on Nat. Literatures, Asscn for Commonwealth Literature and Language Studies, Int. Asscn of Univ. Profs of English, Modern Language Asscn of America; Fellow, Int. Centre for Asian Studies, Int. PEN; Rockefeller Foundation Fellow; Life Fellow, Pakistan Acad. of Letters; Hon. LittD (Luxembourg, San Francisco); First Prize, All Pakistan Creative Writing Contest 1972, Patras Bokhari Award, Pakistan Acad. of Letters 1985, Roberto Celli Memorial Award 1994, inscribed in Academic Roll of Honour, Govt Coll., Lahore, Certificate of Merit, Univ. of the Punjab, Lahore, Pres. of Pakistan's Award for Pride of Performance (Medal for Literature); numerous other academic and literary distinctions, prizes and citations from different countries. *Publications:* poetry: The Oath and Amen: Love Poems 1976, America is a Punjabi Word 1979, An Old Chair 1979, My Second in Kentucky 1981, This Time in Lahore 1983, Neither This Time/Nor That Place 1984, Inland and Other Poems 1988, The Poems of Alamgir Hashmi 1992, Sun and Moon and Other Poems 1992, Others to Sport with Amaryllis in the Shade 1992, A Choice of Hashmi's Verse 1997, The Ramazan

Libation: Selected Poems 2003; other: Pakistani Literature (two vols; ed., second edn as Pakistani Literature: The Contemporary English Writers) 1978, Ezra Pound 1983, Commonwealth Literature 1983, The Worlds of Muslim Imagination (ed.) 1986, The Commonwealth, Comparative Literature and the World 1988, Pakistani Short Stories in English (ed.) 1992, Postindependence Voices in South Asian Writings (co-ed.) 2001, Your Essence, Martyr (ed.) 2011; contrib. to many books, journals and periodicals. *Leisure interests:* walking, cricket, music, films. *Address:* 1542 Service Road West, G-11/2, Islamabad, Pakistan. *E-mail:* alamgirhashmi@yahoo.co.uk.

HASHMI, Makhdoom Javed; Pakistani politician; *President, Pakistan Tehreek-e-Insaf;* b. 1 Jan. 1948, Multan; m.; two d.; fmr Fed. Minister for Labour, Minister for Health and Population Welfare 1997–99; mem. Pakistan Muslim League (Nawaz); apptd Parl. Leader 1999, fmr Acting Pres.; mem. Alliance for the Restoration of Democracy 2003; arrested Oct. 2003, sentenced to 23 years in prison for inciting mutiny in the army, forgery and defamation April 2004, released Aug. 2007; Pres. Pakistan Tehreek-e-Insaf 2012–. *Address:* Pakistan Tehreek-e-Insaf, Central Secretariat, House No. 2, Street No. 84, Sector G-6/4, Islamabad, Pakistan (office). *Telephone:* (51) 2270744 (office). *Fax:* (51) 2873893 (office). *Website:* www .insaf.pk (office).

HASHMI, Moneeza, MEd, MA; Pakistani television executive; *General Manager, International Relations, HUM TV Eye Television Network;* b. (Moneeza Gul Faiz), 22 Aug. 1946, Simla; d. of Faiz Ahmad Faiz; m. Humair Hashmi; two s.; ed Univ. of Hawaii, USA, Punjab Univ., Lahore; Program Man., Pakistan TV (PTV), Lahore 1974–81, Man. Educational TV 1982–88, Gen. Man. 1988–2003, Director of Programmes 2003–04; Gen. Man. Int. Relations, HUM TV Eye Television Network, Lahore 2005–; Chair. Asia-Pacific Media AIDS Initiative; Co-founder Himmat Soc. (charity); mem. Bd of Govs Omar Asghar Khan Devt Foundation; Grad. Award 2000, 2001, Commonwealth Broadcasting Award Citation 2002, Pres. of Pakistan's Pride of Performance 2002, Fatima Jinnah Award 2004. *Television includes:* Khwateen Time (Exec. Producer). *Leisure interests:* travelling, reading. *Address:* HUM TV, Office #102, 1st Floor, Siddique Centre, Gulberg, Lahore; 102-H Model Town, Lahore, Pakistan (home). *Telephone:* (42) 5884324 (home). *Fax:* (42) 5782007 (office); (42) 5884866 (home). *E-mail:* moneezahashmi@yahoo.co.uk (office).

HASHWANI, Sadruddin; Pakistani business executive; *Chairman, Hashoo Group;* m.; two s. three d.; business ventures in cotton, petroleum, hotel industry, real estate, trading, and property devt 1950–; f. Hashwani Hotels Ltd, Net 21; Founder and Chair. Hashoo Group. *Address:* Hashoo Group, PEC Building Ataturk Ave G-5/2, POB 1670, Islamabad, Pakistan. *Telephone:* (51) 2272890 (office). *Fax:* (51) 2274812 (office). *E-mail:* info@hashoogroup.com (office); hashwani@net21pk.com (office). *Website:* www.hashoogroup.biz (home).

HASKINS, Baron (Life Peer), cr. 1998; of Skidby in the County of the East Riding of Yorkshire; **Christopher Robin Haskins,** BA; Irish business executive; *Chairman of Council and Pro-Chancellor, Open University;* b. 30 May 1937, Dublin; s. of Robert Brown Haskins and Margaret Elizabeth Haskins (née Mullen); m. Gilda Susan Horsley 1959; three s. two d.; ed St Columba's Coll., Dublin, Trinity Coll., Dublin; with Ford Motor Co. 1960–62; joined Northern Foods PLC 1962, Chair. 1986–2002 (retd); mem. Culliton Irish Industrial Policy Review Group 1991–92, Ind. Comm. Social Justice 1992–94, UK Round Table on Sustainable Devt 1995–98, CBI's Pres. Cttee 1996–99, Hampel Cttee on Corp. Governance 1996–97; Chair. Better Regulation Task Force 1997–2002, Express Dairies 1998–2002, DEFRA (Dept for Environment, Food and Rural Affairs) Review Group 2002–03; Dir Lawes Agricultural Trust, Yorkshire TV 2002–; Dir Yorkshire and Humber Regional Devt Agency 1998–; mem. New Deal Task Force 1997–2001, Yorkshire Forward 1998–; Co-ordinator Rural Recovery 2001–03; Chair. European Movement 2004–; Chair. of Council and Pro-Chancellor Open Univ. 2005–; hon. degrees (Leeds Metropolitan Univ., Dublin, Essex, Nottingham, Hull, Huddersfield, Lincoln, Cranfield, Bradford). *Leisure interests:* farming, watching cricket, writing, politics. *Address:* Quarryside Farm, Main Street, Skidby, nr Cottingham, East Yorks., HU15 6TG, England (home). *Telephone:* (1482) 842692 (home). *Fax:* (1482) 845249 (home). *E-mail:* gshaskins@aol.com (home). *Website:* www.open.ac .uk (office).

HASKINS, Sam (Samuel Joseph); British photographer, designer and author; b. 11 Nov. 1926, Kroonstad, South Africa; s. of Benjamin G. Haskins and Anna E. Oelofse; m. Alida Elzabé van Heerden 1952; two s.; ed Helpmekaar School and Witwatersrand Tech. Coll., Johannesburg, Bolt Court School of Photography (now London Coll. of Communication), London; Ind. Photographic Studio: Johannesburg 1953–68, London 1968–2002, Sydney 2002–; Sr External Assessor, Photographic Course, London Coll. of Printing 1975–82; 500-image slide show set to music, presented as entertainment to photographic confs in over 50 cities, 50+ solo exhbns on four continents, 14 int. group exhbns; work featured in perm. collection of V&A Museum, London and Nat. Portrait Gallery, Australia; Prix Nadar (France) for Cowboy Kate and Other Stories 1964, Israel Museum Award, Int. Art Book Contest Award 1969, Gold Medal Award for Haskins Posters, New York 1974, Kodak Book of the Year Prize 1980 for Photo Graphics. *Publications:* Five Girls 1962, Cowboy Kate and Other Stories 1964, African Image 1966, November Girl 1967, Haskins Posters 1972, Photo Graphics 1980, Sam Haskins à Bologna 1984, Fashion Etcetera 2009; portfolios in most major int. photographic magazines. *Leisure interests:* vintage car restoration and rallying, books, music, horticulture, collecting antiques and design icons, carpentry. *Address:* The Sam Haskins Partnership, PO Box 1197, NSW 2576, Australia (office). *Telephone:* (2) 4862-1453 (home). *E-mail:* sam@haskins.com (office). *Website:* www.haskins.com (office); www.samhaskinsblog.com (office).

HASLAM, William Edward (Bill), BA; American business executive, politician and state governor; *Governor of Tennessee;* b. 23 Aug. 1958, Knoxville, Tenn.; s. of Jim Haslam and Cynthia Haslam (née Allen); m. Crissy Garrett 1981; two s. one d.; ed Webb School of Knoxville, Emory Univ.; began working as teenager part-time in family business, Pilot Corpn (petroleum co. f. by his father), Knoxville, following graduation, returned to Knoxville to work for Pilot, later became Pres. and Dir (co. runs nationwide Pilot Flying J chain of truck stops and Pilot Food Mart convenience stores); left Pilot to become Mayor of Knoxville 2003–10; Gov. of Tenn. 2011–; fmr CEO SAKS Direct (e-commerce and catalogue div. of Saks Fifth

Avenue); Co-owner Tennessee Smokies (minor league baseball team); mem. Bd Advisory Council on Historical Preservation 2008–, Tennessee Tech. Devt Corpn 2008–; Chair. East Tennessee Center for Non-Profit Man.; Chair. and Pres. Project GRAD; Chair. Exec. Cttee Young Life of Knoxville; Campaign Chair. Foothills Land Conservancy; Vice-Chair. Knoxville Museum of Art; fmr mem. Bd Cornerstone Foundation and World Vision, Emerald Avenue Youth Foundation, Diversity Task Force of Nine Counties, One Vision; mem. Salvation Army (Chair.), United Way of Greater Knoxville; Elder, Cedar Springs Presbyterian Church; mem. Mayors Against Illegal Guns Coalition –2009 (resgnd), Nat. Rifle Asscn; Republican. *Leisure interests:* bicycling, running. *Address:* Office of the Governor, 1st Floor, State Capitol, Nashville, TN 37243-0001, USA (office). *Telephone:* (615) 741-2001 (office). *Fax:* (615) 532-9711 (office). *E-mail:* bill.haslam@tn.gov (office). *Website:* www.state.tn.us/governor (office); www.tn.gov/governor (office).

HASLER, Adrian; Liechtenstein economist and politician; *Head of Government and Minister of Finance;* b. 11 Feb. 1964; m. Gudrun Hasler-Elkuch; two s.; ed Univ. of St Gallen, Switzerland; Dir, Control Dept, Balzers AG 1992–96; Head of Finance Group and Deputy Dir Verwaltungs- und Privat-Bank AG, Vaduz 1996–2004; Chief of Nat. Police Force 2004–13; mem. Landtag (Parl.) (FBP) 2001–04, mem. Finance Cttee 2001–04; Head of Govt and Minister of Finance 2013–; mem. Progressive Citizens' Party (FBP). *Address:* Regierungsgebäude, Peter-Kaiser-Pl. 1, Postfach 684, 9490 Vaduz, Liechtenstein (office). *Telephone:* 2366111 (office). *Fax:* 2366022 (office). *E-mail:* info@regierung.li (office). *Website:* www.liechtenstein.li (office).

HASLER, Otmar; Liechtenstein politician; b. 28 Sept. 1953; m. Traudi Hasler-Hilti; two s. two d.; ed secondary school-teaching diploma from Fribourg Univ.; teacher, Realschule, Eschen 1979–2001; Pres. Progressive Citizens' Party of Liechtenstein (FBP) 1993–95, mem. Exec. Cttee 1993–; mem. Parl. 1989–2001, Vice-Pres. 1993–94, 1996–2001, Pres. 1995; Prime Minister of Liechtenstein, also responsible for Govt Affairs, Finance, Construction and Public Works 2001–09 (resgnd); Pres. newly founded Liechtenstein Sr Citizens' Org. 1999–; mem. Historical Soc., Liechtenstein Art Soc., Liechtenstein Senior Educational Asscn. *Leisure interests:* reading, music, hiking. *Address:* c/o Progressive Citizens' Party, Aeulestrasse 56, Postfach 1213, 9490 Vaduz, Liechtenstein (office).

HASNEDL, Jerry, AA; American business executive; ed Northland Coll., Thief River Falls, Minn.; mem. Bd of Dirs CHS 1995, served as Sec.-Treas., chaired Capital Cttee and served as mem. Govt Relations Cttee, Chair. CHS 2011–12, also Chair. Exec. Cttee and Chair. CHS Foundation; mem. and fmr Dir Northwest Grain (CHS retail business); mem. Bd of Dirs Cooperative Network. *Address:* c/o CHS, PO Box 64089, St Paul, MN 55164-0089, USA. *E-mail:* info@chsinc.com.

HASQUIN, Hervé, PhD; Belgian historian, academic and politician; *Permanent Secretary, Académie Royale des Sciences, des Lettres et des Beaux-Arts de Belgique;* b. 31 Dec. 1942, Charleroi; s. of René-Pierre Hasquin and Andrée Jacquemart; m. Michèle Nahum 1986; one s.; Dean, Faculty of Arts and Philosophy, Université Libre de Bruxelles 1979–82, Rector 1982–86, Chair. Bd of Dirs 1986–95, Pres. Inst. for Religious and Secular Studies 1987–; Head French-speaking network Scientific Information and Technological Devt 1986–87; Vice-Pres. Parti Réformateur Libéral (PRL) 1986–89, Gen. Sec. 1990–92, Head PRL Group, Council of Brussels, Capital Region 1991–; Senator 1988–95; Regional Deputy, Brussels 1989–99; Minister of Environmental Planning, Town Planning and Transport, Brussels Capital Region 1995–99; Minister-Pres. of French-speaking Community of Belgium responsible for Int. Relations 1999–2004; Prés. de la Fédération MR du Hainaut 2000–04; Fed. Deputy 2003–07; Perm. Sec. Acad. Royale des Sciences, des Lettres et des Beaux-Arts de Belgique 2008–; Chair. Centre de l'Egalité des Chances et Contre le racisme 2008–11; mem. Acad. Royale de Belgique 2002, Academia Toscana Di Scienze e Lettre 'La Colombaria'; Sociétaire hc, Acad. des Sciences et des Arts 2000; Chevalier, Légion d'honneur 1989, Commdr, Order of Leopold II 1984, Order of the Lion (Senegal) 1987, Grand Officer, Order of Leopold 1999, Grand Cross, Order of the Crown 2004; Dr hc (Cluj, Romania); Royal Acad. of Belgium Prize 1990, Literary Prize of French-speaking Community Council 1981, Prix ALUMNI Fondation universitaire and other prizes. *Publications:* La Wallonie: Le Pays et les Hommes, Histoire de la Laïcité principalement en Belgique et en France, La Wallonie, son histoire 1999, Dictionnaire d'histoire de Belgique: Vingt siècles d'institutions. Les hommes. Les faits 1988, Dictionnaire d'histoire de Belgique: Les Hommes, les institutions, les faits, le Congo Belge et le Ruanda–Urundi 2000; Les séparatistes wallons et le gouvernement de Vichy (1940–43), Acad. royale de Belgique lecture 2003, Louis XIV – Face à l'Europe du Nord 2005, Joseph II – Catholique anticlerical et réformateur impatient 2007, Population, commerce et religion au siècle des lumières 2008, Les catholiques belges et la franc-maconnerie. De la 'rigidite Ratzinger' a la transgression 2011, Les pays d'islam et la Franc-maçonnerie 2013; about 150 articles and papers in Belgian and foreign learned journals. *Leisure interests:* writing, teaching, football, cycling, cinema. *Address:* Académie royale des sciences, des lettres et des beaux-arts de Belgique, Palais des Académies, 1 rue Ducale, 1000 Brussels (office); Rue du Long Bois 1, 7830 Graty Silly, Belgium (home). *Telephone:* (2) 550-22-12 (office). *Fax:* (2) 550-22-05 (office). *E-mail:* herve.hasquin@cfwb.be (office). *Website:* www.academieroyale.be (office); www.hasquin.be.

HASSAN, Az-Zobeir Ahmed al-; Sudanese politician; Minister of Finance and Nat. Economy –2008. *Address:* c/o Ministry of Finance and National Economy, POB 735, Khartoum, Sudan (office).

HASSAN, Fred, BSc, MBA; American (b. Pakistani) health industry executive; *Chairman, Bausch & Lomb;* b. 12 Nov. 1945, Multan, Pakistan; m. Noreen Hassan; one s. two d.; ed Imperial Coll. of Science and Tech., Univ. of London, UK, Harvard Business School; raised in Lahore where his father was a civil servant and his mother a women's rights activist; joined Sandoz Pharmaceuticals (now Novartis) in 1972, Head, US Pharmaceuticals 1984; Exec. Vice-Pres. Pharmaceutical and Medical Products, Wyeth (fmrly American Home Products), Head, Genetics Inst. (wholly-owned subsidiary), mem. Bd of Dirs 1995–97; CEO and mem. Bd of Dirs Pharmacia & Upjohn 1997–2001, Chair. and CEO Pharmacia Corpn (formed following merger of Monsanto and Pharmacia & Upjohn cos) 2001–03; Chair. and CEO Schering-Plough Corpn 2003–09; Sr Advisor Warburg Pincus LLC 2009–; Chair. Bausch & Lomb (Warburg Pincus is majority owner) 2010–; Pres. Int. Fed. of Pharmaceutical Mfrs Asscns; mem. Bd of Dirs Avon

Products, Inc., CIGNA Corpn, TimeWarner Inc. 2009; fmr Chair. Bd of Dirs Pharmaceutical Research and Manufacturers of America (PhRMA), HealthCare Inst. of New Jersey; CEO-of-the-Year in the Global Pharmaceutical Industry, Financial Times 1999. *Address:* Bausch & Lomb World Headquarters, One Bausch & Lomb Place, Rochester, NY 14604-2701, USA (office). *Telephone:* (585) 338-6000 (office). *Fax:* (585) 338-6007 (office). *Website:* www.bausch.com (office).

HASSAN, Jafar Abed A., MSc, PhD; Jordanian diplomatist and politician; *Minister of Planning and International Co-operation;* b. 1968, Khreibet al Souq; ed Grad. Inst. of Int. and Devt Studies, Univ. of Geneva, Switzerland, Boston Univ., Harvard Business School, USA, American Coll., Paris, France; joined Foreign Service 1991; fmr Head of Human Rights Issues and Humanitarian Affairs, Perm. Mission to UN, Geneva 1995–99; fmr Personal Asst to Dir of Nat. Security, Royal Palace, Jordan; Dir Israel Section, Ministry of Foreign Affairs –2001, Deputy Chief of Mission, Embassy in Washington, DC 2001–06; Dir Int. Affairs Dept, Royal Hashemite Court 2006–09; Minister of Planning and Int. Co-operation 2011–. *Address:* Ministry of Planning and International Co-operation, PO Box 555, Amman 11118, Jordan (office). *Telephone:* (6) 4644466 (office). *Fax:* (6) 4642247 (office). *E-mail:* mop@mop.gov.jo (office). *Website:* www.mop.gov.jo (office).

HASSAN, Jean-Claude Gaston; French banker and public servant; b. 11 Nov. 1954, Tunis, Tunisia; s. of Charles Hassan and Yvonne Lellouche; m. Françoise Benhamou 1981; two s. one d.; ed Lycée de Mutuelleville, Tunis, Lycée Louis-le-Grand, Paris, Ecole normale supérieure, Ecole nat. d'admin; mem. Conseil d'Etat, Auditeur 1981, Counsel 1985; Tech. Adviser to Office of Minister of Social Affairs and Nat. Solidarity 1984–85; Deputy Dir-Gen. Banque Stern 1986–89, Dir-Gen. 1989–92; Dir-Gen. Banque Worms 1992–94; rejoined Conseil d'Etat 1994–2000, 2002; Conseiller pour l'euro de Laurent Fabins, Ministry of the Econ., Finance and Industry 2000–02; Conseiller d'État 2005–; mem. Cttee de règlement des différends de la CRE, Comm. de Régulation de l'Energie 2006–. *Address:* Commission de Régulation de l'Energie, 2 rue du Quatre-Septembre, 75084 Paris Cedex 02 (office); Conseil d'Etat, Palais-Royal, 75100 Paris 01 SP, France (office). *E-mail:* wemmestre@cre.fr (office). *Website:* www.cre.fr (office).

HASSAN, M.A.; Bangladeshi pharmaceuticals industry executive; *Chairman and Managing Director, Aristopharma Ltd;* f. Aristopharma Ltd 1986, currently Chair. and Man. Dir; apptd Vice-Pres. Bangladesh Asscn of Pharmaceutical Industries 2007. *Address:* Aristopharma Ltd, 7 Purana Paltan Line, Dhaka 1000, Bangladesh (office). *Telephone:* (2) 93516913 (office). *Fax:* (2) 8317005 (office). *E-mail:* apl@aristopharma.com (office). *Website:* www.aristopharma.com (office).

HASSAN, Maggie, BA, JD; American lawyer, politician, state governor and business executive; *Governor of New Hampshire;* b. 27 Feb. 1958, Boston, Mass; m. Thomas Hassan; two c.; ed Brown Univ., Northeastern Univ. School of Law; attorney, Palmer & Dodge (law firm) 1985–92; Assoc. Gen. Counsel for Brigham and Women's Hosp./Partners Healthcare 1993–96; attorney, Sullivan, Weinstein & McQuay (law firm) 1996–; apptd by Gov. Jeanne Shaheen as citizen adviser to Advisory Cttee to Adequacy in Educ. and Finance Comm. 1999; unsuccessful cand. for New Hampshire Senate 2002; mem. New Hampshire Senate from 23rd Dist 2005–10, served as Asst Democratic Whip, Pres. Pro Tempore and Majority Leader; Gov. of New Hampshire 2013–; Democrat. *Address:* Office of the Governor, State House, 107 North Main Street, Concord, NH 03301, USA (office). *Telephone:* (603) 271-2121 (office). *Fax:* (603) 271-7640 (office). *Website:* www.governor.nh.gov (office).

HASSAN, Mohamed Hag Ali, BSc, MSc, PhD; Sudanese mathematician, academic and international organization official; *Executive Director, Academy of Sciences for the Developing World;* b. 21 Nov. 1947, Elgetina; m.; three c.; ed Univ. of Newcastle-upon-Tyne, Univ. of Oxford, UK; Sr Lecturer, Dept of Math. Sciences, Univ. of Khartoum 1974, Assoc. Prof. 1979, Prof. –1986, Dean of Math. Sciences 1985–86; Fulbright Research Fellow 1984; Exec. Dir Third World Acad. of Sciences (now Acad. of Sciences for the Developing World) Trieste, Italy 1983–; Sec.-Gen. Third World Network of Scientific Orgs 1988–2006; Pres. Network of African Science Acads 2001–; Dir of Secr., InterAcademy Panel 2001–, Co-Chair. 2010–; Chair. Co-ordinating Council Comm. on Science and Tech. for Sustainable Devt in the South 1995–, Hon. Presidential Advisory Council for Science and Tech. (apptd by Pres. of Nigeria) 2001–, Advisory Bd UN Univ./Inst. of Natural Resources in Africa 2003–; mem. Bd of Dirs Int. Science Programs 1998–, Science Initiative Group 2004–; Fellow, Third World Acad. of Sciences 1985–, African Acad. of Sciences 1985– (Pres. 2000–), Islamic Acad. of Sciences 1992– (mem. Council 1999–); Corresp. mem. Académie Royale des Sciences d'Outre, Belgium 2001–; Foreign Fellow, Pakistan Acad. of Sciences 2002–; mem. World Acad. of Arts and Sciences 2005–; Foreign mem. Lebanese Acad. of Sciences 2006–; Comendator, Ordem Nacional de Mérito Científico, Brazil 1996–; Cavaliere Ufficiale dell'Ordine al Merito della Repubblica Italiana, Italy 2003–; Classe da Grã-Cruz na Ordem Nacional do Mérito Científico, Brazil 2005–; Hon. mem. Colombian Acad. of Exact Sciences 1996–, Palestine Acad. of Science and Tech. 2005–. *Publications:* over 40 scientific papers and over 30 articles on applied math. *Address:* Office of the Executive Director, Academy of Sciences for the Developing World, ICTP Campus, Strada Costiera 11, 34014 Trieste, Italy (office); African Academy of Sciences, PO Box 24916, Nairobi, Kenya. *Telephone:* (40) 2240382 (office). *Fax:* (40) 224559 (office). *E-mail:* mhassan@twas.org (office). *Website:* twas.ictp.it (office).

HASSAN, Tan Sri Mohamed Sidek bin Haji, BEcon, MBA; Malaysian civil servant (retd) and business executive; *Chairman, Petroliam Nasional Berhad (PETRONAS);* b. 24 June 1951, Pekan, Pahang; ed Univ. of Malaya, New Hampshire Coll., USA; began career in Admin. and Diplomatic Service as an Asst Dir, Int. Trade Div., Ministry of Trade and Industry 1974–77, Asst Trade Commr, Embassy in Tokyo 1977–80, served in Implementation Coordination Unit of Prime Minister's Dept, initially as Prin. Asst Dir, later promoted to Deputy Dir, Project Analysis Sector and subsequently as Deputy Dir of Research in same dept 1980–84, held positions in Ministry of Int. Trade and Industry including Malaysia's Trade Commr in Sydney, Deputy Dir in Policy and Research, Deputy Dir (Operations) in Int. Trade Div., Minister Counsellor of Econ. Affairs at Malaysian Trade Commr's Office, Washington, DC, Dir of Multilateral Relations Div., Deputy Sec.-Gen. (Trade), Ministry of Int. Trade and Industry 2001–04, Sec.-Gen. 2004–06, Chief Sec. to the Govt 2006–12; mem. Bd of Dirs and Chair. Petroliam Nasional Berhad (PETRONAS) 2012–; Pres. Int. Islamic Univ. Malaysia

2008–. *Address:* Petroliam Nasional Berhad (PETRONAS), Tower 1, PETRONAS Twin Towers, Kuala Lumpur City Centre, Kuala Lumpur 50088, Malaysia (office). *Telephone:* (3) 20515000 (office). *Fax:* (3) 20265050 (office). *E-mail:* webmaster@petronas.com.my (office). *Website:* www.petronas.com.my (office).

HASSAN, Sabir Muhammad, BSc, MA, PhD; Sudanese fmr central banker; b. 1 Jan. 1945, Dongola; ed Univ. of Khartoum, Syracuse Univ., NY, USA; Financial Insp., Export Section Exchange Control Dept, Bank of Sudan, Khartoum 1968–71, Deputy Man., Export Section 1972–76, Chair. and Gov., Bank of Sudan 1993–96, Gov. Cen. Bank of Sudan 1998–2011; Teaching Asst, Econs Dept Syracuse Univ. 1978–81; part-time Lecturer, Econs Dept, Islamic Univ. of Omdurman 1982–83, The Bank Inst., Khartoum 1982–83, Econs Dept, Univ. of Khartoum 1992–93; consultancy work, including Financial Analysis and Project Evaluation 1982–83; Advisor to Exec. Dir of IMF, Washington, DC 1983–90; State Minister, Ministry of Finance 1996–98; Chair. Commercial Bank's Portfolio for Agricultural Schemes, Commercial Bank Cttee for Exchange Rate Determination; Sec.-Gen. Islamic Soc. of Upstate NY 1978; Pres. Dar Al-Higra Mosque, Washington, DC 1985–86; mem. Bd of Dirs North American Islamic Trust 1986–. *Publication:* Money Supply and Inflation in the Sudan (co-author) 1970–1981.

HASSAN, Syed Munawar, MScS; Pakistani politician; *President, Jamaat-e-Islami Pakistan;* b. Aug. 1944, Delhi, British India; ed Karachi Univ.; migrated with his family from Delhi to Karachi following Partition 1947; Ed. coll. magazine; joined Nat. Students Fed., elected Pres. 1959; became acquainted with activists of Islami Jamiat-e-Talaba (IJT) Pakistan and studied writings of Mawlana Sued Abul A'ala Mawdudi, joined IJT 1960, elected Pres. of its Karachi Univ. Unit, Karachi City Unit and became mem. Cen. Exec. Council, became all-Pakistan Pres. 1964–67; Research Asst, Islamic Research Acad., Karachi 1963, Sec. Gen. 1969; Man. Ed. monthlies The Criterion, The Universal Message, Karachi; mem. Jamaat-e-Islami Pakistan 1967–, served in Karachi unit as Asst Sec., Sec., Deputy Amir and Amir of the city, elected to Cen. Shura and Exec. Council, Asst Sec. Gen. Jamaat-e-Islami Pakistan 1992–93, Sec. Gen. 1993–2009, represented Jamaat at several platforms, including United Democratic Front and Pakistan Nat. Alliance, heads several planning and research bodies within Jamaat, Amir (Pres.) Jamaat-e-Islami Pakistan 2009–; cand. in Nat. Ass. elections 1977. *Address:* Jamaat-e-Islami Pakistan, Mansoorah, Multan Rd, Lahore 54570, Pakistan (office). *Telephone:* (42) 5419504 (office). *Fax:* (42) 5419505 (office). *E-mail:* uroobah@pol.com.pk (office). *Website:* www.jamaat.org (office).

HASSAN, Tayem; Syrian actor; b. 1976, Tartous; m. Dima Bayaa 2004; two c.; ed Higher Inst. of Dramatic Arts, Damascus; début appearance in TV series Kan yama kan (Once Upon a Time) 1999; has since appeared in several Arabic series, with particular success in Egypt. *Television series:* Al-Zir Salem (The Philanderer Salem) 2000, Nizar Qabbani (Best Actor's Award, Cairo Festival for Arab Media) 2005, Al-Malek Farouq (King Farouk) (Best Actor's Award, Cairo Festival for Arab Media) 2007, Zaman al A'ar (Time of Disgrace), Al Intizar 2008, Conflict on the Sand 2008, Abid Karman 2010. *Films:* Molouk el Tawa'ef, Rabie'Qortoba, Saladin 2001, Taifas 2005, The Waiting 2006, Meccano 2009. *Address:* c/o Middle East Broadcasting Center, POB 76267, Dubai, United Arab Emirates (office). *E-mail:* infotv@mbc.ae (office). *Website:* www.mbc.net (office).

HASSAN BIN TALAL, HRH Prince, GCVO, MA; b. 20 March 1947, Amman; s. of Talal of Jordan and Zein al Sharaf Talal; m. Sarvath Khujista Akhter Banu 1968; one s. three d.; ed Harrow School, England, Christ Church, Univ. of Oxford; brother of the late Hussein ibn Talal, King of Jordan and heir to the throne until the changes in succession announced by the late King Hussein Jan. 1999; fmrly acted as Regent during absence of King Hussein; Ombudsman for Nat. Devt 1971–; Founder Royal Scientific Soc. of Jordan 1970, Royal Acad. for Islamic Civilization Research (Al AlBait) 1980, Arab Thought Forum 1981, Forum Humanum (now Arab Youth Forum) 1982, Royal Inst. for Inter-Faith Studies 1994; Co-Chair. Independent Comm. on Int. Humanitarian Issues; Founder, Pres. Higher Council for Science and Tech.; Pres. Club of Rome 1999–2007, Fed. for Martial Arts, Polo and Squash; Moderator World Conf. of Religions for Peace; Co-Patron Islamic Acad. of Sciences; joined Soldiers of Peace project 2003; Amb. Islamic Educational, Scientific and Cultural Org. 2006; co-f. Int. Cultures Foundation; Founder, Pres. Foundation for Inter-religious and Intercultural Research and Dialogue, Foundation for Interreligious and Intercultural Research and Dialogue; Pres. Emer. World Conf. of Religions for Peace; Chair. Arab Thought Forum; mem. Bd of Dirs Nuclear Threat Initiative 2002–; Co-Pres. Int. Tolerance Foundation for Humanities and Social Studies 2006–; Co-founder Parliament of Cultures 2002, Partners in Humanity 2003; Int. Patron, Rights and Humanity; mem. Advisory Council Research of the Center for Democracy and Community Devt 2010; Hon. Gen. of Jordan Armed Forces, Hon. Fellow, Royal Soc. of Edinburgh 2008; Kt of Grand Cross of Order of Merit (Italy) 1983, Order of Al Hussein bin Ali 1987, Grand Decoration of Honour in Gold with Sash 2004; Hon. PhD (Econ.) (Yarmouk) 1980, Hon. DSc (Bogazici Univ., Turkey) 1981, Hon. Dr Arts and Sciences (Jordan) 1987, Hon. DCL (Univ. of Durham) 1990, Dr hc (Ulster) 1996, (Moscow State Inst. for Int. Relations) 1997, (Bilkent Univ.) 1999, (Univ. of York) 2002, (Faculdades Metropolitanas Unidas) 2006, (Eötvös Loránd Univ.) 2007, Hon. LLB (Univ. of Hertfordshire) 2000, Hon. DTheol (Eberhard-Karls-Univ.) 2001, Hon. DIur Int. Islamic Univ. of Islamabad) 2005, (Univ. of Calgary) 2008; Medal of Pres. of Italian Repub. 1982, Gandhi/King/Ikeda Community Builders Medal and Torch of Nonviolence 2001, Distinguished Foreign Visitor Award 2002, Rabbi Marc H. Tanenbaum Award 2003, Abraham Fund Pioneer of Co-existence Award 2003, Eternal Flame Award 2005, Abraham Geiger Award 2008, Peace Prize 2008, inducted into Académie des Sciences Morales et Politiques of Institut de France 2008. *Publications:* A Study on Jerusalem 1979, Palestinian Self-Determination 1981, Search for Peace 1984, Christianity in the Arab World 1994, Continuity, Innovation and Change 2001, To be a Muslim 2003, In Memory of Faisal I: The Iraqi Question 2003, El Hassan bin Talal Collected Works: Volume One 2007. *Leisure interests:* polo, squash, scuba diving, mountaineering, archaeology, karate, taekwondo, helicopter piloting, skiing. *Address:* The Royal Palace, Amman, Jordan. *Telephone:* 64649186 (office). *Fax:* 64634755 (office). *E-mail:* majlis@majliselhassan.org (office). *Website:* www.elhassan.org (office).

HASSAN MARICAN, Tan Sri Dato Sri Mohamed, FCA; Malaysian oil industry executive; *President and CEO, Petroliam Nasional Berhad (PETRONAS);* b. 1952, Sungai Petani, Kedah; m. Puan Sri Datin Sri Noraini Mohd Yusoff; ed Sekoleh

Rendah Ibrahim, Malay Coll., Kuala Kangsar; began career as articled clerk, Touche Ross & Co., London 1972, later becoming Audit Man.; Accountant, Tetuan Hanfiah Raslan & Mohamed/Touche Ross & Co., Kuala Lumpur 1980, Pnr 1981–89; Sr Vice-Pres., Finance, Petroliam Nasional Berhad (PETRONAS) 1989, Pres. and CEO 1995–; Chair. Engen Ltd; Dir Pergaanan Kemajuan Negeri Kedah 1986–94; Dir Malaysia-Thailand Jt Authority; mem. Int. Investment Council for Repub. of SA, Commonwealth Business Council, World Econ. Forum Council of 100 Leaders; fmr mem. council Majlis Amanah Rakyat, Malaysian Accounting Standards Bd, Kumpulan Wang Amanah Pencen Investment Panel; Darjah Sultan Mahmud Terengganu Yang amat Terpuji 1992, Bintang Darjah Seri Paduka Mahkota Terengganu 1996, Panglima Setia Mahkota 1997, Panglima Negara Bintang Sarawak 2003; Commdr Légion d'honneur (France) 2000; DEng hc (Univ. Malaya) 2001; Vietnamese Govt Friendship Medal 2001. *Address:* Petroliam Nasional Berhad (PETRONAS), Tower 1, PETRONAS Twin Towers, 50088 Kuala Lumpur, Malaysia (office). *Telephone:* (603) 20265000 (office). *Fax:* (603) 20265050 (office). *Website:* www.petronas.com.my (office).

HASSANI, Hajim al-, PhD; Iraqi politician; b. 1954, Kirkuk; ed Mosul Univ., Univs of Nebraska and Conn., USA; moved to USA 1979; Researcher, Dept of Agricultural and Resource Econs, Univ. of Conn. 1990; Head of American Investment and Trading Co., Claremont, Calif. 1991–2003; active mem. of Iraqi Islamic Party (IIP) in exile; returned to Iraq following invasion 2003; worked for Iraqi Interim Governing Council 2003; Leader IIP 2003–04; involved in negotiating unsuccessful cease-fire between US forces and insurgents in Fallujah April 2004; Minister of Industry and Minerals 2004; Speaker Transitional Nat. Ass. 2005–07; currently Sr Aide to Prime Minister Nouri al-Maliki. *Address:* c/o Office of the Prime Minister, Baghdad, Iraq.

HASSANOV, Hassan Aziz Oglu, PhD; Azerbaijani politician and diplomatist; *Ambassador to Poland;* b. 20 Oct. 1940, Tbilisi, Georgia; s. of Aziz Hassanov and Ruhsara Adjalova; m. 1964; one s. one d.; ed Azerbaijan Polytech. Inst., Higher Party School, Azerbaijan State Pedagogical Univ.; mem. various student groups 1958–61; Chair. Baku Student Council 1960–63; with Lenin Young Communists League (Komsomol) Orgs of Yasamal region of Baku 1961–66; with Komsomol Cen. Cttee, Moscow, 1967–69; with Construction Section, Cent. Cttee, Azerbaijan CP 1971–75; First Sec. CP, Sabail region, then of Communist Party of Sumgayit and Gandja cities 1975–81; mem. Azerbaijan Supreme Soviet (Parl.) 1977–95, USSR Supreme Soviet 1979–84; Sec., Cent. Cttee Communist Party, Azerbaijan (Ideology) 1981, (Construction and Transport) 1983–90, (Econ.) 1989; first Prime Minister of the Repub. of Azerbaijan 1990–1992; Perm. Rep. to UN 1992–93; Minister of Foreign Affairs 1993–98; mem. of Mili Mejlis (Parl.) 1995–2000; Amb. to Hungary 2004–10, to Poland 2010–; mem. Security Council 1993–98. *Play:* Letter from Brussels (Azerbaijan State Drama Theatre) 2001. *Publications:* more than 100 articles on Azerbaijani economy, policies, diplomacy and history. *Leisure interests:* art, music, history, politics, chess. *Address:* Azerbaijani Embassy, 03-941 Warsaw, ul. Zwycięców 12, Poland (office); Gendjler Meydani 3, Baku 370001; Apt. 36, 9 Istiglad Str., Baku 370001 Azerbaijan (home). *Telephone:* (22) 6162188 (office); (12) 4927744 (home); (12) 4929114. *Fax:* (22) 6161949 (office); (12) 4651038; (12) 4988480. *E-mail:* warsaw@mission.mfa.gov.az (office); Ggassuhov@hotmail.com. *Website:* www.azembassy.pl (office).

HASSELL, Michael Patrick, CBE, MA, PhD, DSc, FRS; British professor of insect ecology; *Honorary Distinguished Research Fellow, Imperial College, London;* b. 2 Aug. 1942, Tel-Aviv, Israel; s. of Albert Hassell and Ruth Hassell; m. 1st Glynis M. Everett 1966; m. 2nd Victoria A. Taylor 1982; three s. one d.; ed Whitgift School, Croydon, Clare Coll., Cambridge and Oriel Coll., Oxford; Visiting Lecturer, Univ. of California, Berkeley 1967–68; NERC Research Fellowship, Hope Dept of Entomology, Oxford 1968–70; Lecturer, Dept of Zoology and Applied Entomology, Imperial Coll., London 1970–75, Reader 1975–79, Prof. of Insect Ecology, Dept of Biology 1979–, Deputy Head, Dept of Biology 1984–92, Head 1993–2001; Prin. Faculty of Life Sciences 2001–04; Dir Imperial Coll., Silwood Park 1988–2007, Dean 2004–07, Hon. Distinguished Research Fellow 2007–; Storer Life Sciences Lecturer, Univ. of California, Davis 1985; Pres. British Ecological Soc. 1998–99; Chair. Nat. Biodiversity Network 2011–; Ed.-in-Chief, Proceedings B of the Royal Society 2008–; Assoc. Ed. Researches in Population Ecology; mem. Editorial Bd Journal of Theoretical Biology; mem. Bd of Reviewing Eds Science; mem. Council of Zoological Soc. of London, Chair. Awards Cttee; Trustee, Natural History Museum 1999–2004; Fellow, Academia Europaea 1998; Hon. mem. British Ecological Soc. 2012; Scientific Medal, Zoological Soc. 1981, Gold Medal, British Ecological Soc. 1994, Weldon Prize, Univ. of Oxford 1995. *Publications:* Insect Population Ecology (with G. C. Varley and G. R. Gradwell) 1973, The Dynamics of Competition and Predation 1975, The Dynamics of Arthropod Predator-Prey Systems 1978, The Spatial and Temporal Dynamics of Host-Parasitoid Interactions 2000; numerous publs on population ecology. *Leisure interests:* walking, natural history. *Address:* Biology, Silwood Park, Ascot, Berks., SL5 7PY (office); Barnside, Buckland Brewer, Bideford, Devon, EX39 5NF, England (home). *E-mail:* m.hassell@imperial.ac.uk (office).

HASSELMO, Nils, (Nicholas Hazel), PhD; American (b. Swedish) fmr university president and fmr association executive; b. 2 July 1931, Köla, Sweden; s. of Wilner Hasselmo and Anna Backlund; m. 1st Patricia Tillberg 1958 (died 2000); two s. one d.; m. 2nd Ann Die 2003; ed Uppsala Univ., Augustana Coll. Rock Island, Illinois and Harvard Univ.; Asst Prof. of Swedish, Augustana Coll. 1958–59, 1961–63; Visiting Asst Prof. in Scandinavian Studies, Univ. of Wisconsin 1964–65; Assoc. Prof. of Scandinavian Language and Literature, Univ. of Minnesota 1965–70, Dir Center for North West European Languages and Area Studies 1970–73, Prof. of Scandinavian Language and Literature 1970–73, Assoc. Dean and Exec. Officer, Coll. of Liberal Arts 1973–78, Vice-Pres. for Admin. and Planning 1980–83, Pres. Univ. of Minnesota 1988–97; Prof. of English and Linguistics and Sr Vice-Pres. for Academic Affairs and Provost, Univ. of Arizona 1983–88; Pres. Asscn of American Univs 1998–2006; mem. Bd of Dirs Swedish Council 1978– (Chair. 1999–2001), Nat. Asscn of State Univs and Land-Grant Colls (Chair. 1994–95), Carnegie Foundation for the Advancement of Teaching; mem. numerous other orgs; Royal Order of North Star (Sweden); Dr hc (Uppsala) 1979, (North Park Univ., Chicago) 1992, (Augustana Coll., Illinois) 1995, elected memberships in the Royal Gustavus Adolphus Acad. and other scholarly socs in Sweden; recipient of many honours and awards, including King Carl XVI Gustaf Bicentennial Gold Medal. *Publications* include: Murder in Mountain Lion Canyon 2009, The Cyrus Cylinder 2012, Wrath (as Nicholas Hazel); articles and reviews in the field of linguistics. *Leisure interests:* reading, music, hiking. *Address:* 5960 East Placita Alta Reposa, Tucson, AZ 85750-1058, USA. *Telephone:* (520) 299-8792. *Fax:* (520) 299-0833. *E-mail:* nilshasselmo@comcast.net. *Website:* www.nilshasselmo.com; www.nicholashazel .com.

HASSINK, Martinus J.; St Maarten accountant and politician; *Minister of Finance;* Asst Accountant, Moret & Limperg (later Ernst & Young), Amsterdam 1974–77, Curaçao 1977–81; Accountant, Van Dien+Co (later PriceWaterhouse-Coopers) 1981; Dir Dat-Acc NV 1986; Dir KPMG Accountants 1989; Vice-Pres. USFilter Enerserve Group 1998; fmr Pnr, Hassink & Roos Accounting and Financial Advisory Services; Dir and freelance consultant Baker Tilly St Maarten BV 2012; Interim Dir of Resources, Island Govt of St Maarten 2000; Minister of Finance 2013–. *Leisure interests:* gardening, photography, writing, drawing. *Address:* Ministry of Finance, Government Administration Building, POB 943, Clem Labega Square, Philipsburg, St Maarten (office). *Telephone:* 542-2233 (office). *Website:* www.sintmaartengov.org/Government/Ministryoffinance (office).

HASSON, Maurice; French/Venezuelan violinist; *Professor of Violin, Royal Academy of Music, London;* b. 6 July 1934, Berck-Plage, Pas de Calais; m. Jane Hoogesteijn 1969; one s. three d.; ed Conservatoire Nat. Supérieur de Musique, Paris, further studies with Henryk Szeryng; concert artist in major concert halls world-wide, also in TV and radio performances; Prof., RAM, London 1986–; Hon. mem. RAM; Orden Andrés Bello (First Class), Orden Tulio Febres Cordero (Venezuela), refused Orden Francisco de Miranda (First Class) as a political statement against Pres. Hugo Chavez of Venezuela, Médaille de Vermeil de la Ville de Paris; First Prize Violin, Prix d'Honneur and First Prize Chamber Music, Conservatoire Nat. Supérieur de Musique, Paris 1950, Int. Prize Long Thibaut 1951, Int. Prize, Youth Festival, Warsaw 1955, Grand Prix Musique de Chambre 1957. *Recordings include:* Concerto No. 1 (Paganini), Concerto No. 2 (Prokofiev), Debussy Sonatas, Fauré Sonatas, Concerto No. 1, Scottish Fantasy (Bruch), Concerto for 2 and 4 violins (Vivaldi), Double Concerto (Bach), Concerto (Brahms), Brilliant Showpieces for the Violin, Tzigane (Ravel), Rondo Capriccioso (Saint Saëns), Poème (Chausson), Gypsy Airs (Sarasate), Violin Concerto (Castellanos-Yumar), Sonata (Franck), virtuoso pieces. *Leisure interests:* reading, painting, politics. *Address:* 18 West Heath Court, North End Road, London, NW11 7RE, England. *Telephone:* (20) 8458-3647. *E-mail:* jdehasson@btinternet.com.

HASTE, Andy; British insurance executive; *Deputy Chairman, Lloyd's;* b. 1962; fmrly with National Westminster (NatWest) Bank, Head Consumer Loans Products Div., NatWest US operations 1992–95, Pres. US consumer credit business 1995–99; Pres. and CEO Global Consumer Finance Group, GE Capital; CEO AXA Sun Life (also Exec. Dir AXA UK) 1999–2003; Group CEO Royal & Sun Alliance Group (also mem. Main Bd Dirs Royal & Sun Alliance) 2003–12; Deputy Chair. Lloyd's 2012–; mem. Bd Dirs Asscn of British Insurers 2003–11, ITV PLC 2008–. *Address:* Lloyd's, One Lime Street, London, EC3M 7HA, England (office). *Telephone:* (20) 7327-1000 (office). *E-mail:* enquiries@lloyds.com (office). *Website:* www.lloyds.com (office).

HASTERT, (J.) Dennis, BA, MS; American business executive and fmr politician; b. 2 Jan. 1942, Aurora, Ill.; s. of Jack Hastert and Naomi Hastert; m. Jean Kahl 1973; two s.; ed Wheaton Coll., Ill., Northern Illinois Univ.; teacher, Yorkville High School, Ill., also wrestling coach 1964–80; mem. Ill. House of Reps, Springfield 1980–86; mem. 100th–105th Congresses from 14th Dist Ill. 1987–2007 (resgnd), mem. Commerce Comm., Govt Reform and Oversight Comm.; Speaker of House of Reps 1999–2007; Sr Advisor Dickstein Shapiro LLP 2008–; Republican; Grand Cordon of the Order of the Rising Sun (Japan) 2010. *Leisure interest:* wrestling. *Address:* Dickstein Shapiro LLP, 1825 Eye Street, NW, Washington, DC 20006-5403, USA (office). *Telephone:* (202) 420-4401 (office). *E-mail:* hastertd@ dicksteinshapiro.com (office). *Website:* www.dicksteinshapiro.com (office).

HASTINGS, Sir Max Macdonald, Kt, FRSL, FRHistS; British writer and broadcaster; b. 28 Dec. 1945, London; s. of Macdonald Hastings and Anne Scott-James (Lady Lancaster); m. 1st Patricia Edmondson 1972 (divorced 1994); one s. (and one s. deceased) one d.; m. 2nd Penelope Grade 1999; ed Charterhouse and Univ. Coll., Oxford; reporter, London Evening Standard 1965–67, 1968–70; Fellow, US World Press Inst. 1967–68; reporter, current affairs, BBC Television 1970–73; freelance journalist, broadcaster and author 1973–; columnist, Evening Standard 1979–85, Daily Express 1981–83, Sunday Times 1985–86; Ed. Daily Telegraph 1986–95, Dir 1989–95, Ed.-in-Chief 1990–95; Ed. Evening Standard 1996–2002; Dir Evening Standard Ltd 1996–2002; columnist Daily Mail 2002–; book reviewer Sunday Times 2006–; mem. Press Complaints Comm. 1990–92; Trustee Liddell Hart Archive, King's Coll. London 1988–2004, Nat. Portrait Gallery 1995–2004; Pres. Council for the Protection of Rural England 2002–07; Hon. Fellow, King's Coll. London 2004; Hon. DLitt (Leicester) 1992, (Nottingham) 2005; Journalist of the Year 1982, Reporter of the Year 1982, Somerset Maugham Prize for Non-fiction 1979, Ed. of the Year 1988, Royal United Services Inst. Westminster Medal 2008, Pritzker Mil. Library Literature Award for Lifetime Achievement 2012, èStoria Festival Friuladria Prize 2014. *Television:* documentaries: Ping-Pong in Peking 1971, The War About Peace 1983, Alarums and Excursions 1984, Cold Comfort Farm 1985, The War in Korea (series) 1988, We Are All Green Now 1990, Spies (in series Cold War) 1998, Churchill and His Generals (series) 2003, The Falklands Legacy 2012, The Necessary War 2014. *Publications:* America 1968: The Fire, The Time 1968, Ulster 1969, The Struggle for Civil Rights in Northern Ireland 1970, Montrose: The King's Champion 1977, Yoni: Hero of Entebbe 1979, Bomber Command 1979, The Battle of Britain (with Lee Deighton) 1980, Das Reich 1981, Battle for the Falklands (with Simon Jenkins) 1983, Overlord: D-Day and the Battle for Normandy 1984, Victory in Europe 1985, The Oxford Book of Military Anecdotes (ed.) 1985, The Korean War 1987, Outside Days 1989, Scattered Shots 1999, Going to the Wars 2000, Editor (memoir) 2002, Armageddon: The Battle for Germany 1944–45 2004, Warriors: Extraordinary Tales from the Battlefields 2005, Country Fair 2005, Nemesis: The Battle for Japan 1944–45 2007, Finest Years: Churchill as Warlord, 1944–45 2009, Did You Really Shoot the Television? A Family Fable 2010, All Hell Let Loose 2011, Catastrophe 2013. *Leisure interests:* shooting, fishing. *Address:* c/o PFD, Drury House, 34–43 Russell Street, London, WC2B 5HA, England (office). *Telephone:* (20)

7344-1000 (office). *Fax:* (20) 7836-9539 (office). *E-mail:* info@pfd.co.uk (office). *Website:* www.pfd.co.uk (office).

HASUMI, Shigehiko, MA, PhD; Japanese film critic, academic and fmr university administrator; *Professor Emeritus, University of Tokyo;* b. 29 April 1936, Tokyo; s. of Shigeyasu Hasumi; m. Marie Chantal Hasumi; ed Dept of Literature, Univ. of Tokyo, Univ. of Paris, France; began publishing film criticism in Cinema 69 1968; work influenced by Cahiers du Cinéma and post-structuralism; Ed.-in-Chief Lumiére 1985–88; began academic career as Asst Lecturer, Univ. of Tokyo, held positions successively as Asst Prof., fmr Prof. of Pedagogics, now Prof. Emer., Head of Pedagogics Dept 1993–95, Vice-Chancellor 1995–97, Chancellor 1997–2001; fmr Vice-Chair. Asscn of East Asian Research Univs; fmr Asst Prof., Rikkyo Univ.; Hon. Founder Sino-Japanese Cultural Research Centre Nanjing Univ. 2001; Dr hc (Asian Inst. of Tech.). *Publications:* Portrait of a Common Artist, The Argument Against Japanese, Statement of Superficial Critique, Maxime Du Camp: The Invention of Mediocrity, The Director Yasujirou Ozu; chapters in books. *Address:* c/o Office of the Chancellor, University of Tokyo, 7-3-1 Hongo, Bunkyo-ku, Tokyo 113-8654, Japan.

HATA, Tsutomu; Japanese politician; *Special Representative, Democratic Party of Japan;* b. 24 Aug. 1935, Tokyo; ed Seijo Univ.; fmr bus tour operator; elected to House of Reps 1969; fmr Parl. Vice-Minister of Posts and Telecommunications, Agric., Forestry and Fisheries; fmr Minister of Agric., Forestry and Fisheries; Chair. Liberal-Democratic Party (LDP) Research Comm. on the Election System; fmr Minister of Finance 1991–92; left LDP to found Shinseito (New Life Party), Pres. 1993–94, Shinseito dissolved 1994 (merged with eight others to form New Frontier Party); Leader Good Governance Party 1998 (merged with two others to form Democratic Party of Japan—DPJ); currently Special Rep. Standing Officers Council of DPJ; Deputy Prime Minister and Minister of Foreign Affairs 1993–94; Prime Minister of Japan May–June 1994. *Address:* Nagata-cho 2-2-1, Chiyoda-ku, Tokyo 100-8981; House of Representatives, Tokyo, Japan. *Telephone:* (3) 3508-7324 (office). *Fax:* (3) 3508-5080 (office); (3) 3239-3055 (home). *E-mail:* t-hata@nifty .com (office). *Website:* www.t-hata.com (office).

HATAB, Abdul Karim Mahoud al-, (Abu Hattem); Iraqi guerrilla leader; b. 1958, Amara; ed religious school; fmr fighter with peshmerga (Kurdish guerrilla group); imprisoned, Abu Ghraib prison, Baghdad 1980–86; guerrilla leader 1990–, leader Hizbullah of Iraq. *Address:* Hizbullah of Iraq, Amara, Iraq.

HATANO, Yoshio, BA; Japanese university administrator and fmr diplomatist; *Chancellor;* b. 3 Jan. 1932, Tokyo; s. of Keizo Hatano and Tatsuko Hatano; m. Sumiko Shimazu 1961; one s. one d.; ed Tokyo Univ., Princeton Univ., USA; joined Foreign Ministry 1953, held various positions including Dir Econ. Affairs, Asian Affairs and Treaties Bureaux, Personnel Div., Gen. Co-ordination Div.; First Sec., Embassy, London 1970; Counsellor, Embassy, Jakarta 1971; Minister, Embassy, Washington, DC 1979, Envoy Extraordinary and Minister Plenipotentiary 1981; Dir-Gen. Middle Eastern and African Affairs Bureau, Dir-Gen. for Public Information and Cultural Affairs, Ministry of Foreign Affairs 1982–87; Perm. Rep. to int. orgs in Geneva 1987–90; Perm. Rep. to UN, New York 1990–94; Pres. Foreign Press Center 1994; Pres. Gakushuin Women's Coll. 2003–06, Chancellor 2006–. *Television:* regular mem. of Wake Up panel, Yomiuri TV. *Leisure interests:* golf, opera. *Address:* 3-20-1 Toyama, Shinjuku-ku, Tokyo (office); 2-14-13 Hiroo, Shibuya-ku, Tokyo, Japan (home). *Telephone:* (3) 3203-1906 (office); (3) 3407-0463 (home). *Fax:* (3) 3203-8373 (office); (3) 3407-0463 (home). *E-mail:* gwc-off@ gakushuin.ac.jp (office). *Website:* www2.gwc.gakushuin.ac.jp (office).

HATCH, Marshall Davidson, AM, BSc, PhD, FRS, FAA; Australian research scientist (retd); b. 24 Dec. 1932, Perth; s. of Lloyd D. Hatch and Alice Dalziel; m. 2nd Lyndall Langman 1983; two s.; ed Newington Coll., Sydney Univ., Univ. of California, USA; Research Scientist, CSIRO 1955–59; Post-doctoral Fellow, Univ. of California 1959–61; Research Scientist, Colonial Sugar Refining Co. Ltd 1961–70; Chief Research Scientist, Div. of Plant Industry, CSIRO, Canberra 1970–98; Pres. Australian Soc. of Plant Physiologists 1980–81; Foreign Assoc. NAS 1990; Hon. Research Fellow, CSIRO 1998–2008; Dr hc (Göttingen) 1993, (Queensland) 1997; Clark Medal, Royal Soc. of North South Wales 1973, Lemberg Medal, Australian Biochemical Soc. 1974, Charles Kettering Award for Photosynthesis, American Soc. of Plant Physiologists 1980, Rank Award, Rank Foundation 1981, Int. Prize for Biology, Japan Soc. for Promotion of Science 1991. *Publications include:* Historical Records of Australian Science (co-author); over 165 review articles, chapters in books and research papers in scientific journals relating to the mechanism and function of c-4 photosynthesis. *Leisure interests:* reading, skiing, cycling, hiking. *Address:* 34 Dugdale Street, Cook, ACT 2614, Australia. *Telephone:* (2) 6251-5159. *E-mail:* halhatch@bigpond.com.

HATCH, Orrin Grant, BS, JD; American lawyer and politician; *Senator from Utah;* b. 22 March 1934, Homestead Park Pa; s. of Jesse Hatch and Helen Kamm Hatch; m. Elaine Hansen 1957; three s. three d.; ed Brigham Young Univ., Univ. of Pittsburgh; journeyman metal lather; Pnr, Thomson, Rhodes & Grigsby (law firm) 1962–69; Sr Vice-Pres. and Gen. Counsel, American Minerals Man. and American Minerals Fund Inc., Salt Lake City, Utah 1969–71; Pnr, Hatch & Plumb (law firm), Salt Lake City 1976; Senator from Utah 1977–, Chair. Senate Labor and Human Resources Cttee 1981, Senate Judiciary Cttee 1995–2001, Jt Cttee on Taxation, Cttee on Indian Affairs, Sub Cttee on Taxation, mem. Senate Cttee on Finance, Senate Cttee on Intelligence 1977–; Co-Chair. Federalist Soc.; mem. Bd of Dirs Holocaust Memorial Museum; mem. Bd of Advisors Becket Fund for Religious Liberty, Close Up Foundation, Defenders of Property Rights; mem. Nat. Bd of Advisors Washington Legal Foundation; Band Man. Free Agency; Republican; Hon. Co-Chair. Afghanistan Relief Cttee; numerous hon. degrees; 111th Congress Tax Fighter Award, Nat. Tax-Limitation Cttee. *Publications include:* ERA Myths and Realities 1983, Good Faith under the Uniform Commercial Code, Higher Laws: Understanding the Doctrines of Christ 1995, Square Peg: Confessions of a Citizen Senator (autobiography) 2002, articles in legal journals. *Leisure interests:* wrestling, basketball, music. *Address:* 104 Hart Senate Office Building, Washington, DC 20510, USA (office). *Telephone:* (202) 224-5251 (office). *Fax:* (202) 224-6331 (office). *Website:* hatch.senate.gov (office).

HATHAWAY, Anne; American actress; b. 12 Nov. 1982, Brooklyn, NY; d. of Gerald Hathaway and Kate McCauley; m. Adam Shulman 2012; ed Vassar Coll., New York Univ. *Films include:* The Princess Diaries 2001, The Other Side of

Heaven 2001, The Cat Returns 2002, Nicholas Nickleby 2002, Ella Enchanted 2004, The Princess Diaries 2: Royal Engagement 2004, Hoodwinked! 2005, Havoc 2005, Brokeback Mountain 2005, The Devil Wears Prada 2006, Becoming Jane 2007, Get Smart 2008, Passengers 2008, Rachel Getting Married 2008 (Nat. Bd of Review Award for Best Actress, SE Film Critics Award for Best Actress), Bride Wars 2009, Valentine's Day 2010, Alice in Wonderland 2010, Love and Other Drugs 2010, The Dark Knight Rises 2012, Les Misérables (Golden Globe Award for Best Supporting Actress in a Motion Picture 2013, BAFTA Award for Best Supporting Actress 2013, Academy Award for Best Supporting Actress 2013) 2012. *Television:* Get Real (series) 1999–2000, The Simpsons (two episodes) 2009–10, Family Guy 2010. *Address:* c/o Creative Artists Agency, 2000 Avenue of the Stars, Los Angeles, CA 90067, USA (office). *Telephone:* (424) 288-2000 (office). *Fax:* (424) 288-2900 (office). *Website:* www.caa.com (office).

HATOYAMA, Kunio; Japanese politician; b. 13 Sept. 1948, Tokyo; s. of Iichiro Hatoyama; ed Univ. of Tokyo; mem. House of Reps (Fukuoka Dist 6th) 1976–; fmr Parl. Vice-Minister for Educ., mem. Liberal-Democratic Party (LDP) –1993, 2000–, Dir Educ. Div., Chair. Cttee on Educ., House of Reps, Cttee on Rules and Admin Feb. 2002, Special Cttee on Response to Armed Attacks Oct. 2002, LDP Cttee on Harmony Between Nature and People March 2004; mem. Renaissance Party 1993; Founding mem. Democratic Party of Japan 1996; Minister of Educ. 1991–92, of Labour May–June 1994, of Justice 2007–08, of Internal Affairs 2008–09; mem. Japan-Korea Parliamentarians' Union. *Address:* Liberal-Democratic Party (LDP), 1-11-23, Nagata-cho, Chiyoda-ku, Tokyo, 100-8910 Japan. *Telephone:* (3) 3581-6211 (office). *E-mail:* koho@ldp.jimin.or.jp (office). *Website:* www.jimin.jp (office); www.hatoyamakunio.org.

HATOYAMA, Yukio, PhD; Japanese politician; b. 11 Feb. 1947, Tokyo; brother of Kunio Hatoyama; ed Tokyo Univ., Stanford Univ., USA; Asst Prof., Senshyu Univ. 1981; Pvt. Sec. to Iichiro Hatoyama, House of Councillors 1983; elected to House of Reps as mem. Parl. for Hokkaido 9th Dist 1986–, Parl. Vice-Minister, Hokkaido Devt Agency 1990, Vice-Chief Sec. to Hosokawa Cabinet 1993; mem. New Party Sakigake 1993, Chief Sec. New Party Sakigake Perm. Cttee 1994; Jt Leader Democratic Party of Japan (DPJ) 1996–97, Sec.-Gen. 1997, Deputy Sec.-Gen. 1998–99, Pres. of DPJ 1999–2002, currently Sec.-Gen.; Prime Minister of Japan 2009–10 (resgnd); Vice-Chair. Japan-Russia Soc.; mem. House of Reps Standing Cttee on Science and Tech.; Chair. Touch Football Asscn of Japan; ranked 35th by Forbes magazine amongst The World's Most Powerful People 2009. *Leisure interests:* touch football, tennis, karaoke, computers. *Address:* Democratic Party of Japan, 1-11-1 Nagata-Cho, Chiyoda-ku, Tokyo 100-0014, Japan (office). *Telephone:* (3) 3595-9960 (office). *Fax:* (3) 3595-7318 (office). *E-mail:* dpjnews@dpj.or.jp (office). *Website:* www.dpj.or.jp (office).

HATTERSLEY, Baron (Life Peer), cr. 1997, of Sparkbrook in the County of West Midlands; **Roy Sydney George Hattersley,** PC, BSc (Econ.), FRSL; British politician, writer and broadcaster; b. 28 Dec. 1932; s. of the late Frederick Roy Hattersley and Enid Hattersley (née Brackenbury); m. Molly Loughran 1956; ed Sheffield City Grammar School, Univ. of Hull; journalist and health service exec. 1956–64; mem. Sheffield City Council 1957–65; MP for Sparkbrook Div. of Birmingham 1964–97; Parl. Pvt. Sec. to Minister of Pensions and Nat. Insurance 1964–67; Dir Campaign for European Political Community 1965; Jt Parl. Sec. Dept of Employment and Productivity 1967–69; Minister of Defence for Admin 1969–70; Opposition Spokesman for Defence 1970–72, for Educ. 1972–74, for the Environment 1979–80, for Home Affairs 1980–83, on Treasury and Econ. Affairs 1983–87, on Home Affairs 1987–92; Minister of State for Foreign and Commonwealth Affairs 1974–76; Sec. of State for Prices and Consumer Protection 1976–79; Deputy Leader of the Labour Party 1983–92; Pres. Local Govt Group for Europe 1998–; Public Affairs Consultant, IBM 1971, 1972; columnist, Punch, The Guardian, The Listener 1979–82; Visiting Fellow, Inst. of Politics, Harvard Univ. 1971, 1972, Nuffield Coll., Oxford 1984–; Labour; Hon. LLD (Hull) 1985; Dr hc (Aston) 1997. *Publications:* Nelson – A Biography 1974, Goodbye to Yorkshire – A Collection of Essays 1976, Politics Apart – A Collection of Essays 1982, Press Gang 1983, A Yorkshire Boyhood 1983, Choose Freedom: The Future for Democratic Socialism 1987, Economic Priorities for a Labour Government 1987, The Maker's Mark (novel) 1990, In That Quiet Earth (novel) 1991, Skylark's Song (novel) 1994, Between Ourselves (novel) 1994, Who Goes Home? 1995, Fifty Years On 1997, Buster's Diaries: As Told to Roy Hattersley 1998, Blood and Fire: The Story of William and Catherine Booth and their Salvation Army 1999, A Brand from the Burning: The Life of John Wesley 2002, The Edwardians 2004, Borrowed Time: The Story of Britain Between the Wars 2007, David Lloyd George: The Great Outsider 2010; contrib. to newspapers and journals. *Leisure interests:* watching cricket and football, writing. *Address:* House of Lords, Westminster, London, SW1A 0PW, England (office). *Telephone:* (20) 7219-3000 (office).

HATTON, Stephen Paul, BComm; Australian politician; b. 28 Jan. 1948, Sydney; s. of Stanley J. Hatton and Pauline Hatton (née Taylor); m. 1st Deborah J. Humphreys 1969 (divorced 1993); three s. one d.; m. 2nd Cathy Huyer 1995; one d.; ed Univ. of New South Wales; Personnel Officer, James Hardie & Co. Pty Ltd 1965–70; Industrial Officer Nabalco Pty Ltd 1970–75; Exec. Dir NT Confed. of Industries and Commerce Inc. 1975–83; elected NT Legislative Ass. (Nightcliff) 1984, Minister for Lands, Conservation, Ports and Fisheries, Primary Production 1983–84, for Mines and Energy, Primary Production 1986, for Health and Community Services 1989, for Conservation 1989, for Industries and Devt and for Trade Devt Zone and Liquor Comm. 1990–91, for Lands, Housing and Local Govt and Minister for Aboriginal Devt 1992, for Constitutional Devt 1994, Attorney-Gen., Minister for Educ. for Constitutional Devt 1995–96, for Sport and Recreation 1995–97, for Correctional Services 1996–97, for Parks and Wildlife 1996–97, for Ethnic Affairs 1996–97; Chief Minister for NT 1986–88. *Leisure interest:* sport. *Address:* Shop 5, Nightcliff Shopping Centre, Pavonia Way, Nightcliff, NT 0810, Australia.

HAUB, Christian; American retail executive; *Executive Chairman, Great Atlantic & Pacific Tea Company Inc. (A&P);* b. 1964; s. of Erivan Haub; ed Universitat Wien; joined Great Atlantic & Pacific Tea Co. Inc. 1998, Pres. and CEO 1998–2000, Exec. Chair. 2000–, Interim Pres. and CEO 2009–10; Pres. Super Market Service Corpn; Partner, Co-CEO Tengelmann Group Germany; mem. Bd of Dirs Metro Inc. 2006–; Trustee, St Joseph's Univ.; Grand Marshal 2009. *Address:* Great Atlantic & Pacific Tea Company Inc., 2 Paragon Drive, Montvale, NJ 07645, USA (office). *Telephone:* (201) 573-9700 (office). *Fax:* (201) 571-8719 (office). *Website:* www.aptea.com (office).

HAUB, Erivan Karl; German retail industry executive; *Chairman of the Board, Tengelmann Warenhandelsgesellschaft;* b. 29 Sept. 1932, Meal; s. of Elizabeth Haub; m. Helga Otto 1958; three s.; ed Univ. of Hamburg; with Tengelmannhausebank, Frankfurt 1979; co-owner Kaiser's Kaffee Geschäft AG; fmr CEO Tengelmann Warenhandelsgesellschaft, food retailer with supermarkets and outlets in several countries and majority shareholder in Great Atlantic and Pacific Tea Co. (A&P), currently Chair. Bd, Man. Partner; mem. Advisory Bd Arbeitsgemeinschaft der Lebensmittelfilialbetriebe, Bonn; Erivan K. Haub Exec. Conf. Center and Erivan K. Haub School of Business, St Joseph's Univ. are named after him; Distinguished Service Cross First Class, Order of Merit of the Fed. Repub. of Germany; Dr hc (St Joseph's Univ.) 1992; Earth Day Int. Award, Dr Leo M. Goodman Award, American Chamber of Commerce 1996. *Address:* Tengelmann Warenhandelsgesellschaft KG, Wissollstrasse 5-43, 45478 Mülheim an der Ruhr, Germany (office). *Telephone:* (208) 58067601 (office). *Fax:* (208) 58066401 (office). *Website:* www.tengelmann.de (office).

HAUER, Rutger; Dutch actor; b. 23 Jan. 1944, Amsterdam; m. 1st Heidi Merz (divorced); m. 2nd Ieneke Hauer 1985; f. Rutger Hauer Starfish Asscn; Golden Heron 2004, Career Achievement Award, Golden Calf Culture Award 2008. *Films include:* Turkish Delight 1973, The Wilby Conspiracy 1975, Keetje Tippel 1975, Max Havelaar 1976, Mysteries 1978, Soldier of Orange 1978, Woman Between Dog and Wolf 1979, Spetters 1980, Nighthawks 1981, Chanel Solitaire 1981, Blade Runner 1982, Eureka 1982, Outsider in Amsterdam 1983, The Osterman Weekend 1983, A Breed Apart 1984, Ladyhawke 1984, Flesh and Blood 1985, The Hitcher 1986, Wanted Dead or Alive 1986, The Legend of the Holy Drinker 1989, Salute of the Juggler, Ocean Point, On a Moonlit Night, Split Second, Buffy the Vampire Slayer, Past Midnight, Nostradamus, Surviving the Game, The Beans of Egypt Maine, Angel of Death, New World Disorder 1999, Wilder 2000, Lying in Wait 2000, Partners in Crime 2000, Jungle Juice 2001, Flying Virus 2001, I Banchieri di Dio 2002, Scorcher 2002, Warrior Angels 2002, Confessions of a Dangerous Mind 2002, In the Shadow of the Cobra 2004, Tempesta 2004, Never Enough 2004, Sin City 2005, Batman Begins 2005, Mirror Wars: Reflection One 2005, Minotaur 2006, Mentor 2006, Goal II: Living the Dream 2007, 7eventy 5ive 2007, Moving McAllister 2007, Spoon 2008, Magic Flute Diaries 2008, Bride Flight 2008, The Rhapsody 2008, Dazzle 2009, Barbarossa 2009, Happiness Runs 2009, The 5th Execution 2010, Life's a Beach 2010, Hobo With a Shotgun 2010. *TV Films include:* Angel of Death 1994, Menin 1998, The 10th Kingdom 2000, Salem's Lot 2004, The New Poseidon Adventure 2005, The Prince of Motor City 2008. *Publications:* All Those Moments 2007. *Address:* Rutger Hauer Starfish Association, Via Tulipani, 2, 20146 Milan, Italy (office). *E-mail:* rhinfo1@rutgerhauer.org (office). *Website:* www.rutgerhauer.org (office).

HAUFF, Volker, Dr rer. pol; German politician and business consultant; b. 9 Aug. 1940, Backnang; s. of Richard Hauff and Ilse Hauff (née Dieter); m. Ursula Irion 1967; two s.; ed Free Univ. of Berlin; with IBM Deutschland, Stuttgart 1971–72; Sec. of State to Fed. Minister for Research and Tech. 1972–78; Fed. Minister for Research and Tech. 1978–80, of Transport 1980–82; mem. Bundestag 1969; mem. Social Democratic Party (SPD) 1959, Vice-Pres. Parl. Group 1983; Mayor of Frankfurt 1989–91; with Axel Springer Verlag AG 1992–94; with KPMG Deutsche Treuhand-Gesellschaft AG 1995–98, mem. Bd KPMG Germany 1999–2001; Sr Vice-Pres. Bearing Point GmbH 2003–08, mem. Supervisory Bd 2005–08; Chair. German Council for Sustainable Devt 2001–10; fmr mem. UN World Comm. on Environment and Devt; Bundesverdienstkreuz mit Stern und Schulterband. *Publications:* Programmierfibes – Eine verständliche Einführung in das Programmieren digitaler Automaten 1969, Wörterbuch der Datenverarbeitung 1966, Für ein soziales Bodenrecht 1973, Modernisierung der Volkswirtschaft 1975, Politik als Zukunftsgestaltung 1976, Damit der Fortschritt nicht zum Risiko wird 1978, Sprachlose Politik 1979, Global Denken – Lokal Handeln 1992. *Leisure interests:* modern art, cooking. *Address:* c/o German Council for Sustainable Development, GTZ Potsdamer Platz 10, 10785 Berlin, Germany.

HĂULICĂ, Dan; Romanian art critic; b. 7 Feb. 1932, Iași; s. of Neculai Hăulică and Lucreția Hăulică; m. Cristina Isbășescu 1971; one d.; ed Coll. of Philology, Iași, N. Grigorescu Fine Arts Inst., Bucharest; Reader, Iași Coll. of Philology 1954–56; Ed. Literary Magazine, Bucharest 1956–58; Researcher, Inst. for Literary History and Theory of the Romanian Acad. 1958–63; Deputy Ed.-in-Chief Secolul 20 (journal) 1963–67, Ed.-in-Chief 1967; Prof., N. Grigorescu Coll. of Fine Arts, Bucharest 1965; Pres. Int. Asscn of Art Critics (AICA) 1981–84, Hon. Pres. 1984–; Chair. Conseil audiovisuel mondial pour l'édition et la recherche sur l'art (CAMERA) 1986; UNESCO consultant; Amb. to UNESCO 1990–; mem. European Soc. of Culture 1988, European Acad. of Sciences, Letters and Arts 1987; Chair. Int. Confs on Arts, TV and Problems of the Image: Paris, UNESCO 1981, Biennale di Venezia 1982, Sophia Antipolis, Moscow-Tashkent 1982, Helsinki 1983, Caracas 1983, Delphi 1984, Lisbon, Gulbenkian 1984, Paris 1986, Prague 1987, Alger-Tipasa 1987; Chair. Int. Jury of the Arts Film Festivals, Montreal 1984, Le Carnival et la Fête, Nice 1985, Politiques Culturelles et Télévision, Paris 1986; mem. leading bds Romanian Writers' Union, Romanian Fine Arts Union; Prize of the Romanian Fine Arts Union 1967, Prizes of the Romanian Writers' Union 1974, 1984; Prize of the Romanian Film Studio Al. Sahia, Great Prize of the Romanian Fine Arts Union 1975; Grand Prix Int. de la meilleure revue d'art (Festival Int. d'Art de Beaubourg) Paris 1987. *Works include:* Peintres roumains (UNESCO, Vol. I 1963, Vol. II 1965), Brancusi ou l'anonymat du génie 1967, Critică și cultură (Criticism and Culture) 1967, Calder, Variations sur le thème Homo Faber 1971, Geografii spirituale (Spiritual Geographies) 1973, Nostalgia sintezei (The Nostalgia for Synthesis) 1984. *Address:* Str. Docenților 26, 71311 Bucharest, Romania (home).

HÄUPL, Michael, DPhil; Austrian politician; *Mayor and Governor of Vienna;* b. 14 Sept. 1949, Altlengbach; m. Helga Häupl; two c.; ed Bundesrealgymnasium, Krems a.d. Donau, Univ. of Vienna; scientific worker, Natural History Museum, Vienna 1975–83; mem. SPÖ (Austrian Socialist Party), Chair. VSSTÖ (Asscn of Austrian Socialist Students) 1975–77, mem. Ottakring Party Cttee 1978–, various appointments in SPÖ Youth Div. (JG) 1978–84, elected Chair. Vienna JG and fmr Vice-Chair. Nat. JG; mem. Vienna Regional Legislature 1983–88; City Councillor for Environment and Sport 1988–94; fmr Chair. SPÖ Regional Cttee; Mayor and

888

Gov. of Vienna 1994–; Chair. Council of European Municipalities and Regions 2004–; Pres. Austrian Asscn of Cities and Towns; Dir Austria Vienna Football Club. *Leisure interest:* football. *Address:* Rathaus, Rathausplatz 1, Stiege 5, 1 Vienna 1010, Austria (office). *Telephone:* (1) 4000-8111 (office). *Fax:* (1) 4000-8111 (office). *E-mail:* buergermeister@magwien.gv.at (office); michael.haeupl@wien.gv .at (office). *Website:* www.wien.gv.at (office).

HAUSER, Claude, Lic. Oec., MBA; Swiss business executive; ed Collège Calvin, Geneva, Univ. of Geneva, Univ. of Lausanne, Columbia Univ., New York and Stanford Univ., Calif., USA; Controlling Montres Universal, Geneva 1966–67; various roles at Migros, Geneva 1967–76, Man.-Dir 1976–2000, Chair. Migros-Genossenschafts-Bund and Fed. of Migros Cooperatives, Zürich 2000–12; Chair. Clinique G-Beaulieu SA, Migros Beteiligungen AG; mem. Bd of Dirs CIES/CGF (Consumer Goods Forum), Paris, Fondation Signal de Bougy. *Address:* c/o Federation of Migros Cooperatives, Limmatstrasse 152, 8005 Zürich, Switzerland. *E-mail:* media@migros.ch.

HAUSIKU, Marco Mukoso; Namibian politician; b. 25 Nov. 1953, Kapako; m.; ed Bunya Roman Catholic Mission School, Rundu Secondary School, Dobra Training Coll., Augustineum Training Coll.; teacher, Katutura Secondary School 1977–89; mem. SWAPO Windhoek Br. Exec. Cttee 1977–89, mem. Cen. Cttee and Polit-Bureau 1991; Election Dir Kavango and Tsumkwe Area 1989; Minister of Lands, Resettlement and Rehabilitation 1990, of Works, Transport and Communication 1992, of Prisons and Correctional Services 1995, of Labour 2002, of Foreign Affairs 2004–10; Founding mem. and Pres. Namibia Nat. Teachers Union 1988. *Leisure interests:* reading, watching television, listening to music. *Address:* c/o Ministry of Foreign Affairs, Government Buildings, Robert Mugabe Avenue, PMB 13347, Windhoek, Namibia (office).

HÄUSLER, Gerd; German business executive; *CEO, Bayerische Landesbank;* ed Univ. of Frankfurt, Univ. of Geneva, Switzerland; with Deutsche Bundesbank 1978–96, mem. Exec. Bd and Cen. Bank Council 1994–96; mem. Bd of Man. Dirs Dresdner Bank AG, Frankfurt 1996–2000; Chair. Dresdner Kleinwort Benson, London, UK 1997–2000; Counsellor and Dir of Int. Capital Markets Dept, IMF 2001–06, credited with creation of Global Financial Stability Report, represented the Fund at the Financial Stability Forum; Vice-Chair. and Man. Dir Financial Insts Group and Sovereign Debt Advisory practice, Lazard 2006–08; joined RHJ International as a Bd Dir and Sr Adviser 2008; Deputy Chair. Supervisory Bd Bayerische Landesbank 2008–10, CEO Bayerische Landesbank 2010–; Chair. Supervisory Bd DKB Deutsche Kreditbank AG 2013–; served as outside dir on bds of various cos (Airbus Germany, RWE Solutions, ARBED SA and ESSO Germany); mem. Group of Thirty (think tank) 1996–. *Address:* Bayerische Landesbank Girozentrale, Briennerstrasse 18, 80333 Munich, Germany (office). *Telephone:* (89) 2171-01 (office). *Fax:* (89) 2171-23-578 (office). *E-mail:* info@bayernlb.de (office). *Website:* www.bayernlb.de (office).

HAUSMAN, Jerry Allen, AB, BPhil, DPhil; American economist and academic; *John and Jennie S. MacDonald Professor, Massachusetts Institute of Technology;* b. 5 May 1946, Weirton, W Va; s. of Harold Hausman and Rose Hausman; m. Margaretta Stone; one s. one d.; ed Brown Univ., Univ. of Oxford, UK; served in US Army Corps of Engineers 1968–70; Visiting Scholar, Dept of Econs, MIT 1972–73, Asst Prof. 1973–76, Assoc. Prof. 1976–79, Prof. 1979–, John and Jennie S. MacDonald Prof. 1992–; numerous visiting positions including Visiting Prof., Harvard Univ. 1982–83, Harvard Business School 1986–87, univs of Washington, Oxford, Sydney, Wuhan, Beijing, Xiamen, Uppsala, ANU, Ecole Normale Super-ieure, Univ. of W Australia, Univ. Coll. London, Sorbonne; Research Assoc., Nat. Bureau of Econ. Research 1979–; Assoc. Ed. numerous journals including Bell Journal of Economics 1974–83, Journal of Public Economics 1982–98, Journal of Applied Econometrics 1985–93; mem. Cttee on Nat. Statistics 1985–90, Nat. Acad. of Social Insurance 1990; Fellow, Econometric Soc. 1979, American Acad. of Arts and Sciences 1991; Hon. Prof., Xiamen Univ. 2005; Hon. Fellow, Nuffield Coll., Oxford 2008; Econometric Soc. Frisch Medal 1980. *Publications:* numerous papers on econometrics and applied microeconomics. *Address:* MIT Department of Economics, 50 Memorial Drive Building E52, Room 271D, Cambridge, MA 02142-1347, USA (office). *Telephone:* (617) 253-3644 (office). *Fax:* (617) 253-1330 (office). *E-mail:* jhausman@mit.edu (office). *Website:* economics.mit.edu/faculty/ hausman (office).

HAUSNER, Jerzy, PhD; Polish politician, economist and academic; b. 6 Oct. 1949, Swinovjscie; m. Maria Hausner; two d.; ed Kraków Econ. Acad.; began career as Lecturer on Econs, Kraków Econ. Acad. 1972–94; Sec. Regional Kraków Cttee Polish United Workers' Party 1986–89; Dir-Gen. Office of the Prime Minister and Adviser to Deputy Prime Minister 1994–96; Commr for Social Security Reform 1997–2001; Minister of Labour and Social Policy 2001–03; Deputy Prime Minister and Minister of the Economy, Labour and Social Policy 2003–04; Deputy Prime Minister and Minister of the Economy and Labour 2004–05; Chair. of Econs and Public Admin, Cracow Univ. of Econs; mem. Monetary Policy Council, Nat. Bank of Poland 2010–; mem. Polish Econ. Asscn, Scientific Asscn of Org. and Man., European Asscn for Evolutionary Political Economy; Cross of Merit 1996, Kt's Cross of Polonia Restituta Order 1996; Nat. Educ. Comm. Medal 1996, 75th Anniversary Medal of Kraków Econ. Acad. 2001. *Publications:* more than 90 articles in scientific journals. *Leisure interests:* mountain walking, music, soccer. *Address:* Monetary Policy Council, National Bank of Poland, ul. Świętokrzyska 11/ 21, 00-919 Warsaw, Poland (office). *Telephone:* (22) 6531000 (office). *Fax:* (22) 6208518 (office). *Website:* www.nbp.p (office).

HAUSSLER, David, BA, MS, PhD; American computer scientist and academic; *Distinguished Professor of Biomolecular Engineering and Director, Center for Biomolecular Science and Engineering, University of California, Santa Cruz;* ed Connecticut Coll., New London, Conn., California Polytechnic State Univ. at San Luis Obispo, Univ. of Colorado at Boulder; Asst Prof. of Math. and Computer Science, Univ. of Denver, Colo 1982–86; Asst Prof. of Computer Science, Univ. of California, Santa Cruz (UCSC) 1986–89, Assoc. Prof. 1989–93, Prof. 1993–2004, Dir Center for Biomolecular Science and Eng 1999–, Distinguished Prof. of Biomolecular Eng 2004–, Dir Training Program in the Systems Biology of Stem Cells 2005–, mem. Chancellor's Millennium Cttee 1997–98; Investigator, Howard Hughes Medical Inst. 2000–; Affiliate, Crown Coll.; mem. Univ. of California System-Wide Life Science Informatics Working Group 1998–; Scientific Co-Dir

California Inst. for Quantitative Biosciences (QB3) 2000–; Assoc. Ed. Machine Learning 1988–97, Journal of Computational Biology 1996–, Public Library of Science Computational Genomics 2005–; mem. Editorial Bd, Journal of Artificial Intelligence Research 1993–95, Journal of Neurocomputing 1995–2002, Neural Computing Surveys 1996–2002, Drug Discovery Today 2001–; mem. NAS 2006; Fellow, American Asscn of Artificial Intelligence 1992, California Acad. of Sciences 2001, AAAS 2003, American Academy of Arts and Sciences 2006; Julia Bower Math. Award, Connecticut Coll. 1975, Math. Award, California Polytechnic State Univ. at San Luis Obispo 1979, Grad. Student Research Award, Univ. of Colorado at Boulder 1982, Univ. of California Presidential Chair of Computer Science 2000–03, Scientist of the Year, Research and Development Magazine 2001, Featured Scientist, Incyte Genomics 2001, UCSC Faculty Research Lecturer 2001–02, Distinguished Scientist of the Year Award, Boston Biomedical/Clinical Ligand Assay Soc. 2003, Tech Award Laureate, San Jose Tech Museum of Innovation 2003, Allen Newell Award, Asscn for Computing Machinery (ACM) and American Asscn for Artificial Intelligence (AAAI) 2004, Distinguished Eng Alumni Award, Univ. of Colorado, Boulder 2005, AAAI Classic Paper Award, for "Quantifying the inductive bias in concept learning" 1986 2005, World Tech. Award in Information Tech. (Software), The World Tech. Network 2005, Dickson Prize in Science, Carnegie Mellon Univ. 2006, Sr Scientist Accomplishment Award, Int. Soc. for Computational Biology 2008. *Publications:* Proceedings of the First Workshop on Computational Learning Theory (co-ed.) 1988, Proceedings of the Second Workshop on Computational Learning Theory (co-ed.) 1989, Proceed-ings of the Fifth ACM Workshop on Computational Learning Theory (co-ed.) 1992; numerous scientific papers in professional journals. *Address:* University of California, Santa Cruz, 1156 High Street, MS: CBSE/ITI Engineering 2 Building, Suite 501, Santa Cruz, CA 95064, USA (office). *Telephone:* (831) 459-2105 (office). *Fax:* (831) 459-1809 (office). *E-mail:* haussler@soe.ucsc.edu (office). *Website:* www .cbse.ucsc.edu/staff/haussler.shtml (office).

HAUSSMANN, Helmut, DEcon, Dr rer. pol; German politician; *Honorary Professor of International Management, University of Erlangen-Nürnberg;* b. 18 May 1943, Tübingen; s. of Emil Haussmann and Elisabeth Rau; m. Dr Margot Scheu 1980; business exec. 1968–71; Research and Academic Asst, Univ. of Erlangen-Nuremberg 1971–75; joined FDP 1969; mem. Bad Urach Town Council, FDP Dist Chair., Reutlingen 1975–80; mem. Deutscher Bundestag 1976–2002; Econ. Cttee 1977–88; mem. FDP Fed. Exec. Cttee 1978; Ombudsman FDP Econs Cttee 1980; Econ. Spokesman, FDP Parl. Party 1980–84; Vice-Chair. FDP in Land Baden-Württemberg 1983–88, 1995–; Sec.-Gen. FDP 1984–88; Fed. Minister of Econ. Affairs 1988–91; mem. Foreign Affairs Cttee and Spokesman on EC Policy 1991–2002; Hon. Prof. of Int. Man., Univ. Erlangen-Nürnberg 1996–; Chair. Asia-Europe Foundation 1997–98; Chair. Advisory Bd Gemini Exec. Search GmbH. *Leisure interests:* reading, tennis and golf. *Address:* Lehrstuhl für Internationales Management, Lange Gasse 20, 90403 Nuremberg, Germany (office). *E-mail:* internationales.management@wiso.uni-erlangen.de. *Website:* www.helmut -haussmann.de.

HAVEL, Jiři, Dr Ing., CSc, PhD; Czech politician and academic; b. 20 Aug. 1957, Prague; m. (wife died 1994); three s.; ed Univ. of Econs, Prague, Inst. of Econ. Studies, Charles Univ.; worked at Univ. of Econs, Prague 1982–91; Specialist in Econ. Institutions, Capital Markets and Econ. Policy, Inst. of Econ. Studies, Charles Univ. 1991–, also Head, Dept of Macroeconomics and Econometrics, mem. Scientific Bd 2002–; corp. governance consultant 1990–; has served as Bd mem. of various jt stock cos including SPIF, Česká Spořitelna, Paramo, Komerční Banka, Telecom, Unipetrol; Deputy Chair. then Chair. of Exec. Cttee Nat. Property Fund 1999–2001; Deputy Prime Minister Responsible for the Economy 2006; mem. European Parl. (Party of European Socialists) 2009–; fmr mem. CP, participated in establishment of Ind. Left party, later involved with Convent of Democratic Left, joined Czech Social Democratic Party (ČSSD) 1997, Vice-Pres. Econ. Cttee, Speaker for Educ.; mem. Czech Econ. Soc., Vice-Chair 2001–04; fmr mem. Academic Bd Inst. of Finance and Admin; mem. Grant Agency of Czech Repub., Accreditation Comm., Ministry of Educ., Youth and Sports. *Publications:* numer-ous academic and other publications. *Address:* European Parliament, Bât. Altiero Spinelli 14G103, 60, rue Wiertz, Brussels, Belgium; Institute of Economic Studies, Charles University, 110 00 Prague 1, Opletalova 26, Czech Republic (office). *Telephone:* 222112325 (office). *E-mail:* jiri.havel@europarl.europa.eu; havel@mbox .fsv.cuni.cz (office). *Website:* ies.fsv.cuni.cz (office).

HAVEL, Richard Joseph, MD, FAAS; American physician and academic; *Professor Emeritus, Cardiovascular Research Institute, University of California, San Francisco;* b. 20 Feb. 1925, Seattle, Wash.; s. of Joseph Havel and Anna Fritz; m. Virginia J. Havel 1947; three s. one d.; ed Reed Coll., Portland, Ore., Univ. of Oregon Medical School and Cornell Univ. Medical Coll.; Asst in Biochem. Univ. of Ore. Medical School 1945–49; Asst Resident in Medicine, New York Hospital 1950–51, Chief Resident in Medicine 1952–53; Instructor Cornell Univ. Medical Coll. 1952–53; Clinical Assoc. Nat. Heart Inst. 1953–54, Research Assoc. 1954–56; Asst Prof. of Medicine, Univ. of Calif., San Francisco 1956–59, Assoc. Prof. 1959–64, Prof. of Medicine 1964, Chief Metabolism Section 1967–77, Dir Cardiovascular Research Inst. 1973–92, now Prof. Emer.; Dir Arteriosclerosis Specialized Center of Research 1970–96; Ed. Journal of Lipid Research 1972–75; mem. Editorial Bd, Journal of Arteriosclerosis 1980–; mem. Food and Nutrition Bd, Nat. Research Council 1983 (Chair. 1987–90); mem. NAS, Inst. of Medicine, American Acad. of Arts and Sciences, American Soc. of Clinical Nutrition, Asscn of American Physicians, American Soc. for Clinical Investigation; Fellow American Inst. of Nutrition; Fellow, AAAS; T. Smith Award, AAAS 1960, Bristol-Myers Award for nutrition research 1989, McCollum Award 1993, Gold Medal Charles Univ. (Czech Repub.) 1996, Mayo Soley Award 1997. *Publications:* over 300 scientific articles and book chapters. *Address:* University of California, Cardio-vascular Research Institute, San Francisco, CA 94143-0130, USA (office).

HAVIGHURST, Clark Canfield, JD; American legal scholar; *William Neal Reynolds Professor Emeritus of Law, Duke University;* b. 25 May 1933, Evanston, Ill.; s. of Harold Canfield and Marion Clay Havighurst (née Perryman); m. Karen Waldron 1965; one s. one d.; ed Princeton and Northwestern Univs; Research Assoc., Duke Univ. School of Law 1960–61; pvt. practice, Debevoise, Plimpton, Lyons & Gates, New York 1958, 1961–64; Assoc. Prof. of Law, Duke Univ. 1964–68, Prof. 1968–86, William Neal Reynolds Prof. 1986–2005, Prof. Emer. 2005–;

Interim Dean Duke Univ. School of Law 1999; numerous other professional appointments; mem. Inst. of Medicine, NAS. *Publications:* Deregulating the Health Care Industry 1982, Health Care Law and Policy 1988 (second edn 1998), Health Care Choices: Private Contracts as Instruments of Health Reform 1995; articles on regulation in the health services industry, the role of competition in the financing and delivery of health care and anti-trust issues arising in the health care field. *Address:* Box 90360, Duke University School of Law, Durham, NC 27708 (office); 1109 Fearrington Post, Pittsboro, NC 27707, USA (home). *Telephone:* (919) 613-7061 (office); (919) 542-5084 (home). *E-mail:* hav@law.duke.edu (office). *Website:* www.law.duke.edu (office).

HAWASS, Zahi, PhD; Egyptian archaeologist and Egyptologist; b. 28 May 1947, Damietta; ed Alexandria Univ., Cairo Univ., Univ. of Pennsylvania, USA; Inspector of Antiquities of Middle Egypt, Tuna El-Gebel and Mallawi 1969, Italian Expedition, Sikh Abada, Minia 1969, Edfu-Esna, Egypt 1969, Pennsylvania Yale Expedition at Abydos 1969, Western Delta at Alexandria 1970, Embaba, Giza 1972–74, Abu Simbel 1973–74, Pennsylvania Expedition, Malkata, Luxor 1974, Giza Pyramids (for Boston Museum of Fine Arts) 1974–75; First Inspector of Antiquities, Embaba and Bahariya Oasis 1974–79, Chief Inspector 1980, Gen. Dir 1987–98; Gen. Dir Saqqara and Bahariya Oasis 1987–98; apptd Archaeological Site Man. Memphis 1991; Under-Sec. of State for Giza Monuments 1998–2002; apptd Sec.-Gen. of the Supreme Council of Antiquities 2002; Goodwill Amb. to Japan 2008; Minister of State for Antiquities Affairs Jan.–July 2011; Dir of numerous excavations, conservation projects and discoveries including tombs of the pyramid builders at Giza and the Valley of the Golden Mummies in Bahariya; numerous consultancy roles; mem. Bd Egyptian Nat. Museum 1996–; Trustee, Egyptian Nat. Museum; Sound and Light Co. 1990; mem. German Archaeological Inst. 1991–, Russian Acad. of Natural Sciences 2001–, Austrian Archaeological Inst.; Explorer-in-Residence Nat. Geographic 2001; mem. of numerous cttees; Officier, Ordre des Arts et des Lettres 2007, Commdr, Order of Merit (Italy) 2008, Grand Decoration of Honour in Silver with Star (Austria), Order of the Sun (Peru); Hon. PhD (American Univ., Cairo) 2005, Dr hc (Catholic Univ. of Santo Domingo, Dominican Republic) 2009, (Bansomdejchaopraya Rajabhat Univ., Thailand) 2009, (Univ. of Veliko Tarnovo, Bulgaria) 2010, (New Univ. of Lisbon) 2011; Grantee Mellon Fellowship, Univ. of Pennsylvania, Presidential Medal 1988, Golden Plate Award, American Acad. of Achievement 2000, Distinguished Scholar of the Year Asscn of Egyptian-American Scholars 2000, Silver Medal Russian Acad. of Natural Sciences 2001, Achievement Award Mansoura Univ. 2002, named one of Five Distinguished Egyptians Egyptological Soc. of Spain 2002, Paestum Archaeology Award 2006, named amongst Top 100 Most Influential People of the Year by Time magazine 2005, Emmy Award Nat. Acad. of Television Arts and Sciences 2006, World Tourism Award 2008, Medal of the Spanish Order of Arts and Culture 2009, Personality of the Year Award 2010, Cape Breton Univ./Canadian International Coll. Special Award 2010. *Television:* numerous appearances in documentaries and features on Egypt including BBC, CNN, Discovery Channel, History Channel, National Geographic, The Learning Channel. *Publications:* Valley of the Golden Mummies 2000, Silent Images: Women in Pharaonic Egypt 2000, Secrets from the Sand 2003, Hidden Treasures of Ancient Egypt 2004, The Curse of the Pharaohs (children's book), Tutankhamun and the Golden Age of the Pharaohs 2005, Mountains of the Pharaohs 2006, The Great Book of Ancient Egypt: In the Realm of the Pharaohs 2006, The Royal Tombs of Egypt 2006, The Archeaeology and Art of Ancient Egypt: Essays in Honor of David B. O'Connor 2007, Pyramids: Treasures, Mysteries, and New Discoveries in Egypt 2007, Treasures of Ancient Egypt 2007, King Tutankhamun: The Treasures of the Tomb 2007, Tutankhamun: The Golden King and the Great Pharaohs 2008, Royal Mummies: Immortality in Ancient Egypt 2008, Wonders of the Horus Temple: The Sound and Light of Edfu 2011; numerous papers on Egyptology and archaeology. *Address:* 42 Aden Street, Mohandiseen, Cairo, Egypt (home). *E-mail:* pyramiza2004@yahoo.com. *Website:* www.drhawass.com.

HAWK, Tony; American professional skateboarder; b. 12 May 1968, San Diego, Calif.; s. of Frank Hawk and Nancy Hawk; descendant of Henry Hudson, discoverer of the Hudson River; m. 1st Cindy Dunbar 1990 (divorced 1994); one s.; m. 2nd Erin Lee 1996 (divorced 2004); two s.; finished in top five in Van's/Offshore Amateur State Finals (Calif.) in boys 11–13 div. 1980; turned professional aged 14, mem. Powell Peralta's Bones Brigade; pioneered modern vertical skateboarding; First, Rusty Harris Series final contest: vert discipline 1982, Del Mar Spring Nationals (Calif.): vert 1983, NSA-Del Mar Skatepark (Calif.): vert 1984, Transworld Skateboard Championships (Vancouver, BC, Canada): vert 1986; Second, Vision Skate Ecape: vert 1988; Third, X Games: vert best trick 2002, First, vert doubles (with Andy MacDonald) 2002; has entered an estimated 103 professional contests, won 73, placed second in 19; est. children's skate clothing co. Hawk Clothing 1998, acquired by Quiksilver 2000; has accomplished numerous historic tricks including ollie 540, kickflip 540, varial 720 and first 900 degree spin (at 1999 X Games after 11 failed attempts, winning the Best Trick competition); retd from competitive skateboarding 1999; launched Boom Boom HuckJam, a 24-city arena tour featuring world's best skateboarders, BMX bike riders and Motocross riders performing choreographed routines 2002; est. Tony Hawk Foundation; voted Best Vert Skater by readers of Transworld Skateboarding magazine. *Film roles in:* Thrashin' 1986, Police Academy 4: Citizens on Patrol 1987, Gleaming the Cube 1989, Destroying America (video) 2001, CKY 3 (video) 2001, Collage (video) (stunts) 2001, xXx 2002, Haggard: The Movie 2003, Lords of Dogtown 2005. *Television includes:* The Contest 1989, MTV Sports & Music Festival 3: Skate Trick 1999, Reunion X 2004; cameo roles in Cyberchase, Rocket Power, The Simpsons, Max Steel, Sifl and Olly and CSI: Miami, and in films such as Jackass: The Movie, The New Guy, Max Keeble's Big Move, and Dogtown and Z-Boys; hosted documentary, Video Game Invasion. *Publication:* Hawk–Occupation: Skateboarder (autobiog.) 2000, Tony Hawk: Professional Skateboarder 2002, Between Boardslides and Burnout: My Notes from the Road 2002, How Did I Get Here? 2010. *Address:* THI, 1611-A South Melrose Drive, #362, Vista, CA 92081; c/o Terra McGibbon, Tony Hawk Foundation, 1611-A South Melrose Drive, #360, Vista, CA 92081, USA. *Telephone:* (760) 477-2479. *E-mail:* info@tonyhawk.com; questions@tonyhawkfoundation.org; tony@clubtonyhawk.com. *Website:* www .tonyhawk.com.

HAWKE, Allan, PhD; Australian diplomatist, business executive and university chancellor; ed Australian Nat. Univ.; with Australian Public Service 1974–91;

Deputy Sec. Dept of Defence 1991–93; Chief of Staff to Prime Minister 1993–94; Deputy Sec. Dept of Prime Minister and Cabinet 1994; Sec. Dept of Veterans' Affairs 1994–96; Sec. Dept of Transport and Regional Services 1996–99; Sec. of Defence 1999–2001; Head of Secr. for Review of Aboriginal and Torres Strait Islander Comm. 2001–03; Amb. to New Zealand 2003–06; Chancellor ANU, Canberra 2006–10; currently Chair. Civil Aviation Safety Authority Board; *Website:* www.casa.gov.au.

HAWKE, Ethan; American actor and writer; b. 6 Nov. 1970, Austin, Tex.; s. of James Steven Hawke and Leslie Carole Hawke; m. 1st Uma Thurman (q.v.) 1998 (divorced 2004); m. 2nd Ryan Shawhughes; one d.; ed New York Univ.; co-f. Malaparte Theatre Co.; Co-Founder and Sponsor New York Public Library Young Lions Fiction Award; inducted into Tex. Film Hall of Fame 2004; Michael Mendelson Award for Outstanding Commitment to the Theater. *Theatre appearances include:* Casanova 1991, A Joke, The Seagull 1992, Sophistry, Henry IV (Broadway) 2003, Hurlyburly 2005, The Coast of Utopia 2006, The Cherry Orchard 2009, The Winter's Tale 2009, A Lie of the Mind (dir) 2010. *Films include:* Explorers 1985, Dead Poets Society 1989, Dad 1989, White Fang 1991, Mystery Date 1991, A Midnight Clear 1992, Waterland 1992, Alive 1993, Rich in Love 1993, Straight to One 1993 (dir), Reality Bites 1994, Quiz Show 1994, Floundering 1994, Before Sunrise 1995, Great Expectations, Gattaca, Joe the King 1999, Hamlet 2000, Tape 2001, Waking Life 2001, Training Day 2001, The Jimmy Show 2001, Before Sunset 2004, Taking Lives 2004, Assault on Precinct 13 2005, Lord of War 2005, The Hottest State 2006, Fast Food Nation 2006, Before the Devil Knows You're Dead 2007, What Doesn't Kill You 2008, New York, I Love You 2009, Daybreakers 2009, Brooklyn's Finest 2010, The Woman in the Fifth 2011, Sinister 2012. *Television:* Moby Dick 2010. *Publication:* The Hottest State 1996, Ash Wednesday 2002. *Address:* c/o Malaparte Theatre Company, 545 8th Avenue, New York, NY 10018, USA.

HAWKE, Gary Richard, CNZM, DPhil, FRSNZ; New Zealand economic historian and academic; *Professor Emeritus, Victoria University of Wellington*; b. 1 Aug. 1942, Napier; s. of Vyvyan Nesbitt Hawke and Jean Avis Hawke (née Carver); m. Helena Joyce Powrie 1965; two s.; ed Victoria Univ. of Wellington, Balliol and Nuffield Colls, Oxford, UK; Lecturer, Victoria Univ. of Wellington 1968–70, Reader 1971–73, Prof. of Econ. History 1974–2008, Prof. Emer. 2008–, Head, School of Govt 2003–08; Dir Inst. of Policy Studies 1987–97; visiting appointments at Stanford Univ., USA 1972–73, All Souls Coll., Oxford, UK 1977–78, Japan Foundation 1993, Japan Soc. for Promoting Knowledge 1994; Chair. NZ Planning Council 1986–91; Fellow, Inst. of Public Admin of NZ 2008; Sr Fellow, NZ Inst. of Econ. Research (NZIER); Distinguished Fellow, New Zealand Asscn of Economists 2005; Companion, NZ Order of Merit 2009; NZIER-QANTAS Award for Econs 1998. *Publications include:* Railways and Economic Growth 1970, Between Governments and Banks 1973, Economics for Historians 1980, The Making of New Zealand 1985, The Thoroughbred Among Banks (co-author) 1997, Innovation and Independence: The Reserve Bank of New Zealand 1973–2002 2006. *Leisure interests:* classical music, armchair criticism. *Address:* New Zealand Institute of Economic Research, PO Box 3479, Wellington 6140 (office); 7 Voltaire Street, Karori, Wellington, New Zealand (home). *Telephone:* (4) 470-1806 (office); (4) 476-9109 (home); 27-5635794 (mobile). *Fax:* (4) 472-211 (office). *E-mail:* gary.hawke@ vuw.ac.nz (office). *Website:* www.vuw.ac.nz (office).

HAWKE, Robert (Bob) James Lee, AC, BA, LLB, BLitt; Australian politician and fmr trade union official; b. 9 Dec. 1929, Bordertown, S Australia; s. of A. C. Hawke; m. 1st Hazel Masterson 1956 (divorced 1995); one s. two d.; m. 2nd Blanche d'Apulget 1995; ed Univs of Western Australia and Oxford; Rhodes scholar 1953; Research Officer, Australian Council of Trade Unions 1958–70, Pres. 1970–80; Sr Vice-Pres. Australian Labor Party 1971–73, Pres. 1973–78, Leader 1983–91; MP for Wills, Melbourne 1980–92; Prime Minister 1983–91, mem. Nat. Exec. 1971–91; reporter 1992; Business Consultant 1992; Adjunct Prof. Research School of Pacific Studies and Social Sciences, ANU 1992–95; Hon. Visiting Prof. in Industrial Relations Sydney Univ.; mem. Advisory Council of Inst. for Int. Studies, Stanford Univ., Calif.; Chair. Cttee of Experts on mem. of Educ. Int. 1993–; Sydney City Mission Fundraising Task Force; Dir Quantum Resources Ltd 1996–; mem. Bd Reserve Bank of Australia 1973–83, Governing Body ILO 1972–80; mem. Australian Council for Union Training, Australian Population and Immigration Council; mem. Australian Manufacturing Council 1977, Nat. Labour Consultative Council 1977–92, Australian Refugee Advisory Council; Patron Australia-China Sports Friendship Cttee 2000; Hon. Fellow, Univ. Coll., Oxford 1984; Dr hc (Nanjing) 1986; Hon. DPhil (Hebrew Univ. of Jerusalem) 1987; Hon. LLD (Univ. of NSW) 1987; UN Media Peace Prize 1980. *Publication:* The Hawke Memoirs 1994. *Leisure interests:* tennis, golf, cricket, reading. *Address:* Suite 1, Level 13, 100 Williams Street, Sydney, NSW 2001, Australia.

HAWKEN, Paul; American environmental activist, entrepreneur, journalist and author; *Executive Director, Natural Capital Institute*; b. 8 Feb. 1946; f. or co-f. cos or software cos specializing in proprietary content man. tools, including Smith & Hawken (garden and catalogue retailer) and several first natural food cos in USA relying solely on sustainable agricultural methods; Head of PaxIT, PaxTurbine, PaxFan (three cos associated with Pax Scientific, a research and devt co. focused on energy-saving technologies that apply biomimicry to fluid dynamics); Founder and Exec. Dir Natural Capital Inst., Sausalito, Calif.; fmr mem. Bd numerous environmental orgs, including Point Foundation (publr of Whole Earth Catalogs), Center for Plant Conservation, Trust for Public Land, Friends of the Earth, Nat. Audubon Soc.; five hon. doctorates; Esquire Magazine Award for the Best 100 People of a Generation 1984, California Inst. of Integral Studies Award 'For Ongoing Humanitarian Contributions to the Bay Area Communities', Cine Golden Eagle Award in video for the PBS programme 'Marketing' from Growing a Business, Metropolitan Home Design 100 Editorial Award for the 100 best people, products and ideas that shape our lives, American Horticultural Soc. Award for commitment to excellence in commercial horticulture, Corp. Conscience Award, Council on Econ. Priorities 1990, Small Business Admin Entrepreneur of the Year 1990, Design in Business Award for environmental responsibility, American Center for Design, Creative Visionary Award, Int. Soc. of Industrial Design, Utne 'One Hundred Visionaries Who Could Change Our Lives' 1995, Western Publications Asscn Maggie Award for 'Natural Capitalism' as the best Signed Editorial/Essay in 1997, World Council for Corp. Governance 2002, Green Cross Millennium

Award for Individual Environmental Leadership 2003. *Achievements include:* has given keynote addresses to Liberal Party of Canada, King of Sweden at his inaugural Environmental Seminar, American Booksellers' Asscn, Urban Land Inst., SRI International, Harvard Univ., Stanford Univ., Wharton School, Cornell Univ., Prime Minister of NZ's Conf. on Natural Capitalism, US Dept of Commerce, Australian Business Council, Yale Univ. and Yale Univ. Commencement, Univ. of California, Berkeley Commencement, French Ministry of Agric., AAAS, Prince of Wales Conf. on Business and the Environment at Univ. of Cambridge, Commonwealth Club, Herman Miller, Nat. Wildlife Fed., State of Washington, American Soc. of Landscape Architects, AIA, American Inst. of Graphic Arts, American Solar Energy Asscn, Apple Computer, World Business Council for Sustainable Devt, Cleveland City Club, Conf. Bd, US Forest Service, Ontario Hydro, Environment Canada, Environmental Protection Agency, and several hundred others. *Television:* host and producer of 17-part PBS series based on his book Growing a Business, shown in 115 countries. *Publications:* author or co-author of numerous articles, op-eds, papers, as well as seven books, including The Next Economy 1983, Growing a Business 1987, The Ecology of Commerce (voted No. 1 coll. text on business and the environment by profs in 67 business schools 1998) 1993, Natural Capitalism: Creating the Next Industrial Revolution (with Amory Lovins) 1999, Blessed Unrest: How the Largest Movement in the World Came Into Being, and Why No One Saw it Coming 2007; writings have appeared in Harvard Business Review, Resurgence, New Statesman, Inc., Boston Globe, Christian Science Monitor, Mother Jones, Utne Reader, Orion, and more than 100 other publs. *Address:* Natural Capital Institute, 3 Gate Five Road, Suite B, Sausalito, CA 94965, USA (office). *Telephone:* (415) 332-2860 (office). *Fax:* (415) 331-6242 (office). *E-mail:* info@paulhawken.com (office). *Website:* www.naturalcapital.org (office); www.paulhawken.com.

HAWKER, Graham Alfred, CBE, CIMgt, FCCA, FRSA; British business executive; b. 12 May 1947; s. of Alfred Hawker and Sarah Rebecca Bowen; m. Sandra Ann Evans 1967; one s. one d.; ed Bedwelty Grammar School; trainee accountant, Caerphilly Dist Council 1964–66; accountant, Abercarn Dist Council 1966–67, Chief Accountant 1967–68, Deputy Treas. 1968–70; Chief Auditor, Taf Fechan Water Bd 1970–74; Audit Man. Welsh Water Authority 1974–78, Div. Finance Man. 1978–84, Chief Accountant 1984–86, Dir Planning and Devt 1986–87, Finance 1987–89; Dir Finance Welsh Water PLC 1989–91, Group Man. Dir 1991–93, Chief Exec. Hyder (fmrly Welsh Water) PLC 1993–2000; Chair. Dwr Cymru Ltd 1993–2000, Hyder Consulting (fmrly Acer) 1993–2000, Swalec 1996–2000; Dir (non-exec.) Bank of England 1998–2000; Chair. BITC (Wales) 1994–2000; fmr Dir Welsh Devt Agency, Deputy Chair. 1998–2000, CEO 2000–04; Chair. New Deal Task Force Advisory Cttee (Wales) 1997–98; mem. New Deal Advisory Cttee (UK) 1997–98; mem. CBI Council, Wales 1994–97, Prince of Wales Review Cttee on Queen's Awards 1999; Fellow, Inst. of Certified Accountants; Hon. Fellow, Univ. of Wales, Cardiff 1999; Dr hc (Univ. of Glamorgan) 1996, Hon. DL (Gwent) 1998; Prince of Wales Ambassador's Award for Corp. Social Responsibility 1999. *Leisure interests:* family, walking, wine, career.

HAWKES, John; American actor; b. (John Marvin Perkins), 11 Sept. 1959, Alexandria, Minn.; s. of Pete Perkins and Patricia Perkins. *Television includes:* Wings 1994, Shaughnessy 1996, ER 1997, Buffy the Vampire Slayer 1998, The X-Files 1999, The Practice 2000, 24 2001, Taken 2002, Deadwood 2004–06, CSI: Crime Scene Investigation 2007, Eastbound & Down 2009–10, Lost 2010. *Films include:* Future-Kill 1985, Scary Movie 1989, From Dusk Till Dawn 1996, Rush Hour 1998, The Perfect Storm 2000, Buttleman 2002, Me and You and Everyone We Know 2005, American Gangster 2007, Wasteland 2009, Small Town Saturday Night 2010, Winter's Bone (several awards including San Diego Film Critics Soc. Award for Best Supporting Actor, San Francisco Film Critics Circle Award for Best Supporting Actor) 2010, Lincoln 2012, The Sessions 2012. *Address:* c/o Innovative Artists, 1505 10th St, Santa Monica, CA 90401, USA (office). *Telephone:* (310) 656-0400 (office). *Website:* www.innovativeartists.com (office).

HAWKING, Stephen William, CH, CBE, BA, PhD, FRS; British theoretical physicist, applied mathematician, academic and author; *Director of Research, Department of Applied Mathematics and Theoretical Physics, University of Cambridge;* b. 8 Jan. 1942, Oxford; s. of Dr F. Hawking and Mrs E. I. Hawking; m. Jane Wilde 1965 (divorced); two s. one d.; m. 2nd Elaine Mason 1995 (divorced 2007); ed St Albans School, Univ. Coll., Oxford, Trinity Hall, Cambridge; Research Fellow, Gonville and Caius Coll., Cambridge 1965–69, Fellow for Distinction in Science 1969–; Research Asst, Inst. of Astronomy, Cambridge 1972–73; Research Asst, Dept of Applied Math. and Theoretical Physics, Univ. of Cambridge 1973–75, Reader in Gravitational Physics 1975–77, Prof. 1977–79, Lucasian Prof. of Applied Math. 1979–2009, Dir of Research 2009–; Distinguished Research Chair, Perimeter Inst. for Theoretical Physics, Waterloo, Ont., Canada 2009–; mem. Inst. of Theoretical Astronomy, Cambridge 1968–72; mem. Papal Acad. of Science 1986; Foreign mem. American Acad. Arts and Sciences 1984; Hon. Fellow, Univ. Coll., Oxford 1977, Trinity Hall, Cambridge 1984; Hon. FRSA; several hon. degrees; Eddington Medal 1975, Pontifical Acad. of Sciences Pius XI Gold Medal 1975, Cambridge Philosophical Soc. William Hopkins Prize 1976, Wolf Foundation Prize for Physics 1988, Inst. of Physics Maxwell Medal 1976, Royal Soc. Hughes Medal 1976, Albert Einstein Award 1978, Royal Astronomical Soc. Gold Medal 1985, Inst. of Physics Paul Dirac Medal and Prize 1987, Sunday Times Special Award for Literature 1989, Britannica Award 1989, RSA Albert Medal 1999, Royal Soc. Copley Medal 2006, Fonseca Prize 2008, Presidential Medal of Freedom 2009. *Publications:* The Large Scale Structure of Spacetime (with G. F. R. Ellis) 1973, General Relativity: An Einstein Centenary Survey (co-ed. with W. Israel) 1979, Is the End in Sight for Theoretical Physics?: An Inaugural Lecture 1980, Superspace and Supergravity: Proceedings of the Nuffield Workshop (co-ed. with M. Rocek) 1981, The Very Early Universe: Proceedings of the Nuffield Workshop (co-ed.) 1983, 300 Years of Gravitation (with W. Israel) 1987, A Brief History of Time: From the Big Bang to Black Holes 1988, Hawking on the Big Bang and Black Holes 1992, Black Holes and Baby Universes and Other Essays 1993, The Cambridge Lectures: Life Works 1995, The Nature of Space and Time (with Roger Penrose) 1996, The Universe in a Nutshell (Aventis Prize 2002) 2001, The Theory of Everything: The Origin and Fate of the Universe 2002, The Future of Spacetime (co-ed.) 2002, On the Shoulders of Giants 2002, A Briefer History of Time (with Leonard Mlodinow) 2005, George's Secret Key to the Universe (children's fiction) (with Lucy Hawking) 2007, The Grand Design (with Leonard

Mlodinow) 2010; also individual lectures, contrib. to scholarly books and journals. *Leisure interest:* opera. *Address:* Department of Applied Mathematics and Theoretical Physics, Centre for Mathematical Sciences, University of Cambridge, Wilberforce Road, Cambridge, CB3 0WA, England (office). *Telephone:* (1223) 337843 (office). *Website:* www.damtp.cam.ac.uk (office); www.hawking.org.uk.

HAWKINS, Jeff, BS; American business executive, computer scientist and inventor; b. 1 June 1957, Long Island, Huntingdon, New York; s. of Robert Hawkins; m.; two d.; ed Cornell Univ.; various key tech. positions with Intel Corpn 1979–82; Vice-Pres. of Research, GriD Systems Corpn 1982–92; f. Palm Computing 1994, invented PalmPilot (hand held computer) 1994; Co-founder, Handspring Inc., fmr Chair. and Chief Product Officer and fmr Chief Tech. Officer Palm Inc. (after Handspring merger with Palm Inc.); Founder Redwood Neuroscience Inst. (now Redwood Center for Theoretical Neuroscience) 2002, fmr Exec. Dir and Chair., now mem. Advisory Bd; f. Numenta (medical tech. firm) 2005; mem. Scientific Bd of Dirs Cold Spring Harbor Lab., New York; mem. Advisory Bd Secular Coalition for America; mem. Nat. Acad. of Eng 2003–; PC Magazine Lifetime Achievement Award for Tech. Excellence 2000, Cornell Univ. Entrepreneur of the Year 2000. *Publications:* On Intelligence: How a New Understanding of the Brain will Lead to the Creation of Truly Intelligent Machines 2004. *Leisure interests:* sailing, music, family. *Address:* Numenta, Inc., 811 Hamilton Street, Redwood City, CA 94063, USA (office). *Telephone:* (650) 369-8282 (office). *Fax:* (650) 369-8283 (office). *Website:* www.numenta.com (office).

HAWLEY, Christine, CBE, AADipl, RIBA, FRSA; British architect; *Dean, The Bartlett School;* began career with Dept of the Environment, UK Govt; worked for Pearson Int. Architects, London; fmr Pnr Yorke Rosen Cook & Hawley Architects; f. Christine Hawley Architects, London 1998; fmrly Lecturer, Architectural Asscn and Head School of Architecture, Univ. of E London; currently Dean The Bartlett School, Head Faculty of the Built Environment and Prof. of Architectural Studies, Univ. Coll. London; Visiting Chair. of Design, Tech. Univ. of Vienna, Austria and Univ. of Oslo, Norway; currently Adviser UK Govt Comm. for Architecture and the Built Environment; lectured extensively throughout USA, Europe and Far East; RIBA Teaching Award. *Architectural works include:* Social Housing for Int. Bau Austellung, Berlin, Canteen, Städel Acad., Frankfurt, Osaka Folly, Japan, Exhbn Pavilions at Osaka and Nagoya Expo, Pfaffenberg Museum Ext., Bad Deutsch-Altenberg, Austria, Kitagata Housing Reconstruction, Gifu, Japan, Museum for Roman Remains, Carnuntum, Austria. *Publications include:* chapters in books The Architect: Reconstructing Her Practice 1996, The Architect: Women in Contemporary Architecture 2001; numerous articles in professional journals. *Address:* The Bartlett School, Wares House, 22 Gordon Street, London, WC1H 0QB, England (office). *Telephone:* (20) 7679-7505 (office). *Fax:* (20) 7679-7453 (office). *E-mail:* c.hawley@ucl.ac.uk (office). *Website:* christinehawleyarchitects.co.uk; www.bartlett.ucl.ac.uk (office).

HAWLEY, John F., BA, PhD; American astronomer, astrophysicist and academic; *Professor and Associate Dean for the Sciences, College of Arts and Sciences, University of Virginia;* ed Haverford Coll., Univ. of Illinois; Bantrell Fellow, California Inst. of Tech. 1984–87; Asst Prof., Univ. of Virginia 1987–93, Assoc. Prof. 1993–99, Prof. 1999–, Chair. Dept of Astronomy 2006–12, Assoc. Dean for the Sciences, Coll. of Arts and Sciences 2012–; Helen B. Warner Prize, American Astronomical Soc. 1993, Shaw Prize in Astronomy (co-recipient) 2013. *Publications:* Foundations of Modern Cosmology; numerous papers in professional journals on accretion disks and related phenomena. *Address:* Associate Dean's Office, PO Box 400772, University of Virginia, Charlottesville, VA 22904 (office); Astronomy Main Office, PO Box 400325, University of Virginia, Charlottesville, VA 22904-4325, USA. *Telephone:* (434) 924-4648 (Dean's Office) (office); (434) 924-7494 (Astronomy Main Office) (office). *Fax:* (434) 924-1317 (Dean's Office) (office); (434) 924-1304 (Astronomy Main Office) (office). *E-mail:* jh8h@virginia.edu (office). *Website:* www.astro.virginia.edu/~jh8h (office).

HAWLEY, Robert, CBE, PhD, DSc, CEng, CPhys, FRSE, FREng, FInstP, FIMechE, FIEE; British business executive and engineer; b. 23 July 1936, Wallasey, The Wirral; s. of William Hawley and Eva Hawley; m. 1st Valerie Clarke 1961 (divorced); one s. one d.; m. 2nd Pamela Swan; ed Wallasey Grammar School, Wallasey Tech. Coll., Birkenhead Tech. Coll. and King's Coll., Univ. of Durham; joined C.A. Parsons 1961, Electrical Designer, Generator Dept 1964, Chief Electrical Eng 1970, Dir of Production and Eng 1973–74; Dir of Production and Eng NEI Parsons 1974, Man. Dir 1976; Man. Dir Power Eng Group, NEI PLC 1984–88, Man. Dir Operations 1989–92; Main Bd Dir Rolls Royce PLC 1989–92; Chief Exec. Nuclear Electric PLC 1992–95, British Energy PLC 1995–97; Chair. Taylor Woodrow PLC 1999–2003; mem. Bd of Dirs Colt Telecom 1998–; Chair. Eng Council 1999–2002, Particle Physics and Astronomy Research Council 1999–2002, Rocktron 2001; Pres. IEE 1996–97; Adviser HSBC Investment Bank PLC; Chair. Council Univ. of Durham; Master Worshipful Co. of Engineers 2005–06; Order of Diplomatic Service Gwanghwa Medal 1999, IEE Honorary Fellowship 2003. *Publications:* Dielectric Solids (co-author) 1970, Conduction and Breakdown in Mineral Oil 1973, Fundamentals of Electromagnetic Field Theory 1974, Vacuum as an Insulator. *Leisure interests:* philately, gardening. *Address:* Summerfield, Rendcomb, nr Cirencester, Glos., GL7 7HB (home); 823 Whitehouse Apartments, 9 Belvedere Road, London, E1 9AT, England (home). *Telephone:* (20) 7265-2340 (office); (1285) 831610 (Cirencester) (home); (20) 7620-3145 (London) (home). *Fax:* (20) 7265-2341 (office); (1285) 831801 (Cirencester) (home); (20) 7620-3144 (London) (home). *E-mail:* robert.hawley@btinternet.com (home).

HAWN, Goldie; American actress and film producer; b. 21 Nov. 1945, Washington, DC; d. of Edward Rutledge Hawn and Laura Hawn; m. 1st Gus Trikonio 1969 (divorced); m. 2nd Bill Hudson (divorced); one s. one d. (Kate Hudson); pnr, Kurt Russell, one s.; ed American Univ., Washington, DC; began career as chorus-line dancer, World's Fair, New York 1964; Pnr, Hawn/Sylbert Movie Co. with Anthea Sylbert 1984–95; Co-founder Cosmic Entertainment (production co., fmrly Cherry Alley Productions) 2003; f. Goldie Hawn Inst., Bright Light Foundation 2003 (renamed Hawn Foundation 2005). *Stage appearances include:* Romeo and Juliet (Williamsburg), Kiss Me Kate, Guys and Dolls (New York). *Television series include:* Good Morning World (series) 1967, Rowan and Martin's Laugh-In 1968–70, Goldie and Kids—Listen to Us. *Films include:* Cactus Flower 1969, There's a Girl in My Soup 1970, $ 1971, Butterflies are Free 1972, The Girl from Petrovka 1974, The Sugarland Express 1974, Shampoo 1975, The

Duchess and the Dirtwater Fox 1976, Foul Play 1978, Viaggio con Anita 1979, Private Benjamin (also producer) 1980, Seems Like Old Times 1980, Best Friends 1982, Swing Shift 1984, Protocol (also producer) 1984, Wildcats (also producer) 1986, Overboard 1987, Bird On A Wire 1990, Deceived 1991, CrissCross 1992, Housesitter 1992, Death Becomes Her 1992, The First Wives Club 1996, Everybody Says I Love You 1996, The Out Of Towners 1999, Town and Country 2001, The Banger Sisters 2003. *Publications:* A Lotus Grows in the Mud (with Wendy Holden) 2005, 10 Mindful Minutes 2011. *Address:* c/o Alan Nevins, Renaissance Literary & Talent, PO Box 17379, Beverly Hills, CA 90209, USA. *Telephone:* (323) 848-8305. *E-mail:* Alan@RenaissanceMgmt.Net. *Website:* thehawnfoundation.org.

HAWTHORNE, M(arion) Frederick, BA, PhD; American chemist and academic; *Director, International Institute of Nano and Molecular Medicine, University of Missouri;* b. 1928, Fort Scott, Kan.; ed Missouri School of Mines and Metallurgy, Pomona Coll., Univ. of California, Los Angeles; began career as Postdoctoral Assoc. in Physical-Organic Chem., Iowa State Univ.; Sr Research Chemist, Rohm & Haas Co., Huntsville, Ala, Head of Lab. –1962; Prof., Univ. of California, Riverside 1962–69; Prof., UCLA 1969–98, Univ. Prof. of Chem. 1998–2006; Founder-Dir Int. Inst. of Nano and Molecular Medicine, Univ. of Missouri 2006–, Curators' Distinguished Prof. 2010; Visiting Lecturer at several int. univs, including Distinguished Visiting Prof., Ohio State Univ. 1990; Assoc. Ed. Inorganic Chemistry 1966–69, fmr Ed.-in-Chief; mem. Editorial Advisory Bd Bioconjugate Chemistry; mem. NAS 1973, American Acad. of Arts and Sciences 1975; Fellow, AAAS 1980, Japan Soc. for the Promotion of Science 1986, ACS 2009; Hon. DSc (Pomona Coll.) 1974; numerous awards, including Alfred P. Sloan Research Fellowship 1963, Univ. of California, Riverside Chancellor's Award for Research 1968, UCLA McCoy Award for Contribs to Chem. 1972, ACS Award in Inorganic Chem. 1973, USAF Meritorious Civilian Service Medal 1986, ACS Richard C. Tolman Medal 1986, Boron USA Award 1988, Alexander von Humboldt Foundation Award for Sr US Scientists 1990, Bailar Medal 1991, Chemical Pioneer Award 1994, Willard Gibbs Medal 1994, Seaborg Medal 1997, Basolo Medal 2001, King Faisal Int. Prize for Science (co-recipient) 2003, Monie A. Ferst Award 2003, ACS Priestley Medal 2009, Senate of the State of Missouri Resolution of Appreciation for Scientific Achievements 2009, Boron in the Americas Pioneer Award 2012, Nat. Medal of Science 2012. *Publications:* 10 book chapters, more than 500 research papers, 30 patents. *Address:* International Institute of Nano and Molecular Medicine, University of Missouri, 1514 Research Park Drive, Columbia, MO 65211-3450, USA (office). *Telephone:* (573) 882-7016 (office). *Fax:* (573) 884-6900 (office). *E-mail:* hawthornem@health.missouri.edu (office). *Website:* www .nanomed.missouri.edu (office).

HAXHINASTO, Edmond; Albanian politician and diplomatist; b. 16 Nov. 1966, Tirana; ed Univ. of Tirana, Int. Devt Exec. Center, Brdo, Slovenia, Woodrow Wilson School of Public and Int. Affairs, Princeton Univ., NJ, USA; Head of Foreign Relations, Kuvendi Popullor (Parl.) 1991–92; worked in pvt. sector 1993–97; Head of Co-ordination Dept, Office of the Prime Minister 1997–99, Diplomatic Adviser to Prime Minister 2000–01; Chargé d'affaires a.i., Embassy in Belgrade, Yugoslavia 2001–02; Chief of Cabinet, Ministry of Foreign Affairs 2002–03; Adviser to Ilir Meta (mem. Int. Comm. on the Balkans) 2004–05; Co-founder Inst. for Peace, Devt and Integration, Tirana 2004; mem. Socialist Movt for Integration, becoming Int. Sec., Head of Nat. Cttee and Vice-Chair. 2004–09; Deputy Minister of Public Works and Transport 2009–10; Minister of Foreign Affairs 2010–12; Deputy Prime Minister 2011–13; Minister of Economy, Trade and Energy 2012–13. *Address:* c/o Ministry of Economy, Trade and Energy, Bulevardi Dëshmorët e Kombit 2, 1001, Tirana, Albania. *E-mail:* kabineti@mete.gov.al.

HAY, John, AC, PhD; Australian university administrator; *Chairman, Australian Learning and Teaching Council;* m. Barbara Hay; three s. one d.; ed Univ. of Western Australia, Univ. of Cambridge, UK; fmr Chair of English, Head of Dept, Deputy Chair. Academic Bd, Univ. of Western Australia; fmr Dean of Arts, Chair. Nat. Key Centre, Sr Deputy Vice-Chancellor Monash Univ.; Vice-Chancellor and Pres. Deakin Univ. 1992–95; Vice-Chancellor and Pres. Univ. of Queensland 1996–2008, now Prof. Emer.; Chair. Group of Eight 2002–03, Universitas 21 2003–, Carrick Inst. for Learning and Teaching in Higher Educ., Australian Learning and Teaching Council, Queensland Inst. of Medical Research, Spring-field Health City, Martin Inst.; Chair. Bd of Trustees, Queensland Art Gallery; currently Deputy Chair. Library Council Nat. Library of Australia; Fellow, Australian Coll. of Educators, Australian Inst. of Man., Australian Acad. of Humanities, Australian Coll. of Educators; mem. Judging Panel Prime Minister's Literary Awards 2010; mem. Higher Educ. Review Reference Group 2002, City Planning and Econ. Devt; Hon. DLitt (Deakin, Univ. of Western Australia), Hon. LLD (Univ. of Queensland); Centenary Medal 2003. *Address:* Australian Learning and Teaching Council, Level 14, Centennial Plaza Building, C 300 Elizabeth Street, Surry Hills, 2010, Australia (office). *Telephone:* (2) 8667-8500 (office). *Fax:* (2) 8667-8515 (office). *Website:* www.altc.edu.au (office).

HAY, Lewis, III, BS, MS; American business executive; *Advisor, Clayton, Dubilier & Rice, LLC;* b. 1955, Pennsylvania; m. Sherry Hay; three c.; ed Lehigh Univ., Carnegie Mellon Univ.; Man. Trainee US Steel Corpn, Pittsburgh 1977–80; Pnr Strategic Planning Assocs (later Mercer Man. Consulting) 1982–91; Chief Financial Officer US Foodservice Inc. 1991–99; joined NextEra Energy as Vice-Pres., Finance and Chief Financial Officer 1999, Pres. NextEra Energy Resources LLC 2000–01, Pres. and CEO NextEra Energy, Inc. 2001–06, Chair. 2002, Exec. Chair. –2013, also Chair. Florida Power & Light Company and NextEra Energy Resources, LLC (subsidiaries), Chief Financial Officer Florida Power & Light Co. (FPL) Inc. 1999–2000, Pres. FPL Energy 2000–01, Pres. FPL Group 2001–06, Chair. and CEO 2002–08; Advisor, Clayton, Dubilier & Rice LLC 2014–; fmr Chair. Edison Electric Inst., Inst. of Nuclear Power Operations; mem. Bd of Dirs Capital One Financial Corpn, Harris Corpn, WellPoint, Inc.; mem. Business Bd of Advisors, Tepper School of Business, Carnegie Mellon Univ., Presidential Consultation Cttee, Carnegie Mellon Energy Futures Inst., President's Council on Jobs and Competitiveness 2011–12; Ernst & Young Florida Lifetime Achieve-ment Award 2010, CEO of the Year, Energy Biz Magazine 2011. *Address:* Clayton, Dubilier & Rice, LLC, 375 Park Avenue, 18th Floor, New York, NY 10152, USA (office). *Website:* www.cdr-inc.com (office).

HAY, Marianne, BSc, DipEd; British banking executive; *Head of Private Banking, Europe, Americas and MENA (Middle East and North Africa), Standard Chartered Private Bank;* ed Univ. of Edinburgh; completed qualification of Inst. of Bankers in Scotland; began career as an analyst with Bank of Scotland, Edinburgh; later Portfolio Manager, Ivory & Sime; later Dir of Martin Currie; joined Morgan Stanley, New York in institutional investment man. business 1993, Co-Head of Global Emerging Markets 1995–99, Chief Investment Officer, Pvt. Wealth Man. 1999, later Head of Pvt. Wealth Man. Europe and the Middle East, fmr mem. European Exec. Cttee, Dir, Morgan Stanley International Ltd, Morgan Stanley Quilter, fmr Chair. Morgan Stanley Iberia, fmr mem. Bd of Dirs Morgan Stanley's UK and Swiss Banks; fmr CEO Citi Global Wealth Man., Europe; currently Head of Pvt. Banking, Europe, Americas and MENA (Middle East and North Africa), Standard Chartered Private Bank; fmr mem. European Diversity Council; ranked by Fortune magazine amongst the 50 Most Powerful Women in Business outside the US (28th) 2010. *Address:* Standard Chartered Private Bank, 1 Basinghall Avenue, London, EC2V 5DD, England (office). *Telephone:* (20) 7885-8300 (office). *Fax:* (20) 7885-8333 (office). *E-mail:* info@standardchartered.com (office). *Website:* www.privatebank.standardchartered.com (office).

HAYAISHI, Osamu, MD, PhD; Japanese fmr institute director, medical scientist and academic; b. 8 Jan. 1920, Stockton, Calif., USA; s. of Jitsuzo Hayaishi and Mitsu Hayaishi; m. Takiko Satani 1946; one d.; ed Osaka High School, Osaka Univ.; Asst Prof., Dept of Microbiology, Washington Univ. School of Medicine, St Louis, Mo., USA, 1952–54; Chief, Toxicology, Nat. Inst. of Arthritis and Metabolic Diseases, NIH, Bethesda, Md, USA 1954–58; Prof., Dept of Medical Chem. 1958–83, Prof., Dept of Molecular Biology, Inst. for Chemical Research, Kyoto Univ. 1959–76; Prof. Dept of Physiological Chem. and Nutrition, Univ. of Tokyo 1970–74; Prof. Inst. of Scientific and Industrial Research, Osaka Univ. 1975–76; Dean Faculty of Medicine, Kyoto Univ. 1979–81; Prof. Emer. Kyoto Univ. 1983–; Pres. Osaka Medical Coll. 1983–89; Dir Osaka Bioscience Inst. 1987–98, Dir Emer. 1998–, now Chair. Bd of Trustees; mem. Scientific Council Int. Inst. of Cellular and Molecular Pathology (Belgium) 1979–; Foreign Assoc. NAS 1972; Dunham Lecture (Harvard) 1980, Pfeizer Lecture, Albert Einstein School of Medicine 1980; mem. Japan Acad. 1974, New York Acad. of Sciences 1975; Foreign Hon. mem. of American Acad. of Arts and Sciences 1969; Hon. mem. American Soc. of Biological Chemists 1974, Int. Soc. on Clinical Entymology 1988, Soc. for Free Radical Research 1988; Hon. Citizen of Kyoto 1984; Int. Hon. Citizen of New Orleans, USA 1990; 1st Order of Merit, Grand Cordon of Sacred Treasure; Hon. DSc (Michigan) 1980; Hon. MD (Karolinska Institutet, Sweden) 1985; Dr hc (Padua) 1988; Award of Japan Soc. of Vitaminology 1964, Award of Matsunaga Science Foundation 1964, Asahi Award for Science and Culture 1965, Award of Japan Acad. 1967, Order of Culture 1972, Award of Fujiwara Science Foundation 1975, Médaille de Bronze de la Ville de Paris 1975, CIBA Foundation Gold Medal 1976, Louis and Bert Freedman Foundation Award for Research in Biochemistry 1976, Deutsche Akad. der Naturforscher Leopoldina (FRG) 1978, Jiménez Díaz Memorial Award (Spain) 1979, Wolf Foundation Prize in Medicine, Israel 1986, Jaroslav Heyrovský Gold Medal, Czechoslovak Acad. of Sciences 1988, Special Achievement Award, Miami Biotech. Winter Symposium 1989, Distinguished Lecturer in Neuroscience Awards, La State Univ. Medical Center, USA 1990, Distinguished Visitor Awards, Univ. of New Orleans, USA 1990; 4th Vaajasalo Lecture, 5th Nordic Neuroscience Meeting, Finland 1991, Invited Lecture, Founding Congress of World Fed. of Sleep Research Socs, France 1991, Luigi Musajo Award, Italy 1995, Distinguished Scientist Award, World Fed. of Sleep Research Socs, 3rd Int. Congress, Germany 1999. *Publications:* Oxygenases 1962, Molecular Mechanisms of Oxygen Acti-vation 1974, Molecular Oxygen in Biology 1974 and 510 scientific reviews and articles. *Leisure interest:* golf. *Address:* Osaka Bioscience Institute, 6-2-4 Furuedai Suita, Osaka 565-0874 (office); 159-505 Kageyukoji-cho, Shimotachiuri-agaru, Muromachi-dori, Kamigyo-ku, Kyoto 602-8014, Japan (home). *Telephone:* (6) 6872-4833 (office); (75) 417-2751 (home). *Fax:* (6) 6872-4818 (office); (75) 417-2752 (home). *E-mail:* hayaishi@obi.or.jp (office). *Website:* www.obi.or.jp/index2.html (office).

HAYAMA, Kanji; Japanese construction industry executive; ed Univ. of Tokyo; joined Taisei Corpn 1960, Vice-Pres. 1997–2001, Pres., CEO and Rep. Dir 2001–07, fmr Chair. and Rep. Dir –2008; Chair. Japanese Civil Contractors Asscn; mem. Bd Japan Productivity Center for Socio-Econ. Devt. *Address:* c/o Taisei Corporation, 25–1 Nishi-Shinjuku-ku, Tokyo 163-0606, Japan.

HAYASHI, Fumiko; Japanese business executive and politician; *Mayor of Yokohama;* ed Aoyama High School, Tokyo; began career working for Toray and Matsushita Electric; salesperson, Honda 1977–87; joined BMW Japan as Br. Man. 1987, Sales Man. –1999, Pres. BMW Tokyo 2003–05; Pres. Fahren Tokyo, Volkswagen Group Japan 1999–2003; CEO Daiei Inc. 2005–07, Chair. 2005–07, Adviser 2005–07, Vice-Chair. 2007; Chair. Tonichi Carlife Group Inc. and Pres. Tokyo Nissan Auto Sales Co. Ltd 2008; Mayor of Yokohama 2009–; ranked by Fortune magazine amongst 50 Most Powerful Women in Business outside the US (tenth) 2005, (29th) 2006, ranked by Forbes magazine amongst 100 Most Powerful Women (66th) 2005, (39th) 2006. *Website:* www.city.yokohama.lg.jp/ex/mayor (office).

HAYASHI, Motoo; Japanese politician; b. 3 Jan. 1947, Chiba Pref.; m.; one s. one d.; ed Univ. of Nihon; elected to Chiba Prefectural Ass. 1983; mem. House of Reps (10th Electoral Dist of Chiba Pref.) 1989–; Parl. Sec. Vice-Minister of Transport 1998–2003; Vice-Minister of Land 2003–05, Chair. Ministry of Land, Infrastruc-ture and Transport 2005–08; Minister of State, Chair. Nat. Public Safety Comm., and Minister of State in charge of Okinawa and Northern Territories and Disaster Man. 2008–09; First Deputy Sec.-Gen. LDP 2007–. *Publication:* Pursuing Dreams – The Near Future of a Metropolitan Area Airport. *Leisure interests:* walking, reading. *Address:* Liberal-Democratic Party, 1-11-23, Nagata-cho, Chiyoda-ku, Tokyo 100-8910, Japan (office). *Telephone:* (3) 3581-6211 (office). *E-mail:* koho@ldp .jimin.or.jp (office). *Website:* www.jimin.jp (office).

HAYASHI, Naoki, BA; Japanese business executive; *Chairman, AEON Company Limited;* ed Keio Univ.; joined AEON Co. Ltd 1970, Gen. Man. Gen. Affairs 1990–96, Gen. Man. Kanto Regional operations, Jusco Co. Ltd 1996–98, Gen. Man. Exec. Sec. Office 1996–98, Man. Dir from 1998, Exec. Vice-Pres. AEON Co. Ltd (fmrly Jusco Co. Ltd) 1998–2008, Sr Exec. Officer 2004–06, Exec. Vice-Pres. Shopping Centre Devt Business 2006–08, CEO Shopping Centre Devt Business,

Exec. Officer and Vice-Pres. AEON Co. Ltd 2008–11, Dir, AEON Mall Co. Ltd 2007–, Chair. 2008–11. Chair. AEON Co. Ltd 2011–; Pres. and CEO Yozo Tai; Chair. Diamond City Co. Ltd 2006–; Vice-Chair. Japan Council of Shopping Centers 2008–; Non-Ind. and Non-Exec. Dir, AEON Co. (Malaysia) Berhad 2009–. *Address:* AEON Co. Ltd, 1-5-1 Nakase, Mihama-ku, Chiba-shi, Chiba 261-8515, Japan (office). *Telephone:* (4) 3212-6042 (office). *Fax:* (4) 3212-6849 (office). *E-mail:* info@aeon.info (office). *Website:* www.aeon.info (office).

HAYASHI, Yoshimasa, LLB, MPA; Japanese lawyer and politician; *Minister of Agriculture, Forestry and Fisheries;* b. 19 Jan. 1961; s. of Yoshiro Hayashi; m.; one d.; ed Univ. of Tokyo, Kennedy School of Govt, Harvard Univ., USA; Asst to US Congressman Steve Neal, Washington, DC 1991, also Int. Affairs Intern at Office of US Senator William Roth; worked in pvt. for Mitui & Co. Ltd, Tokyo, Sanden Koutsu Co., Yamaguchi, Yamaguchi Godo Gas Co., Keefe Co., Washington, DC; mem. House of Councillors (LDP) for Yamaguchi Pref. 1995–, Leader Pro-Whaling League; Sec., Ministry of Finance 1999–2000; Deputy Minister, Cabinet Office 2006–07; Minister of Econ. and Fiscal Policy 2008–09; Minister of Agriculture, Forestry and Fisheries 2012–. *Address:* Ministry of Agriculture, Forestry and Fisheries, 1-2-1, Kasumigaseki, Chiyoda-ku, Tokyo 100-8950, Japan (office). *Telephone:* (3) 3502-5517. *Fax:* (3) 3592-7697 (office). *Website:* www.maff.go.jp (office).

HAYASHI, Yujiro, PhD, DEng; Japanese university administrator and academic; Lecturer, Kanazawa Univ. 1970–71, Asst Prof. 1971–81, Prof. of Mechanical Systems Eng 1981–99, fmr Pres. Kanazawa Univ.; mem. Science Council of Japan; fmr Auditor Japan Inst. of Science and Tech.; fmr mem. Bd of Dirs Asscn of Nat. Univs. *Address:* Science Council of Japan, 7-22-34 Roppongi, Minato-ku, Tokyo 106-8555, Japan (office). *Telephone:* (33) 403-3793 (office). *Fax:* (33) 403-1260 (office). *Website:* www.scj.go.jp (office).

HAYAT, Sardar Sikander; Pakistani politician; b. 1 June 1934, Karela Majhan; s. of Sardar Fateh Mohammad Khan Karelvi; ed Gordon Coll., Rawalpindi, Univ. Law Coll., Lahore; practised law in Kotli 1958; mem. Kolti local council for eight years; elected to first Azad Jammu and Kashmir Legis. Ass. 1970; Minister of Revenue, Forests and Finance 1972–74; Pres. All Pakistan Jammu and Kashmir Conf. 1976–88; Prime Minister Azad Jammu and Kashmir 1985–89, 2001–05; Pres. Azad Jammu and Kashmir 1991–96; fmr Pres. Bar Asscn Kotli.

HAYAT, Makhdoom Syed Faisal Saleh, MA; Pakistani politician; m.; one s. one d.; ed Aitchison Coll., FC Govt Coll., Lahore, King's Coll. London, UK; elected to Nat. Ass. 1977–; Sr mem. Cen. Exec. Cttee, Pakistan People's Party 1987–; fmr Sr Minister for Home and Services and Gen. Admin., Punjab Cabinet; Minister of Commerce, Industries and Local Govt –2002, of the Interior, Narcotics Div., Control and Capital Admin. and Devt Divs 2002–04, Minister of the Environment 2006–07; mem. Nat. Security Council; Pres. Pakistan Football Fed. *Leisure interests:* squash, cricket, riding. *Address:* c/o Ministry of the Environment, Local Government and Rural Development, Block 4, Old Naval Headquarters, Civic Centre, G-6, Islamabad, Pakistan. *Telephone:* (51) 9224578.

HAYDEN, Matthew Lawrence; Australian professional cricketer; b. 29 Oct. 1971, Kingaroy, Queensland; m. Kellie Hayden; left-hand opening batsman; teams: Queensland 1991–, Hampshire 1997, Northamptonshire 1999–2000, Australia 1993–2009 (Capt. Australia A 2000–01, Australia 1993–2009); First-class debut: 1991/92; Test debut: Australia vs S Africa, Johannesburg 4–8 March 1994; One-Day Int. (ODI) debut: Australia vs England, Manchester 19 May 1993; T20I debut: England vs Australia, Southampton 13 June 2005; 103 tests for Australia, scored 8,625 runs (average 50.73) with 30 hundreds, highest score 380 (fmr world record, against Zimbabwe, Perth, Australia 9–10 Oct. 2003); scored 24,603 runs (average 52.57) with 79 hundreds in First-class cricket; 161 ODIs, scored 6,133 runs (average 43.80) with ten hundreds, highest score 181 not out (highest score by an Australian); first Australian to score 1,000 runs in debut season 1991/92; six centuries in seven consecutive innings in 1993/94; shared in Queensland record 2nd wicket partnership (with Martin Love) vs Tasmania 1995/96; second highest run-scorer for Australia in a calendar year 2001 (1,391 runs); ranked World No. 1 Batsman 2003; four consecutive double century first-wicket partnerships (with Justin Langer) for Australia (world record); Queensland's most prolific century-maker (24); mem. Australia's World Cup winning side 2003; Founder, The Hayden Way; Mercantile Mutual Cup Player of the Year 1998/99, 1999/2000, Allan Border Medal 2002, Wisden Cricketer of the Year 2003, ODI Player of the Year 2007, QLD Sportsman of the Year 2007. *Address:* The Hayden Way, PO Box 4134, Gumdale, Queensland 4154, Australia (office). *Telephone:* (7) 3245-1765 (office). *Fax:* (7) 3245-3392 (office). *E-mail:* team@thehaydenway.com (office). *Website:* www.thehaydenway.com (office).

HAYDEN, Michael R., MB, ChB, PhD, FRCP(C), FRSC; South African geneticist and academic; *Director and Senior Scientist, Centre for Molecular Medicine and Therapeutics, University of British Columbia;* began scientific career with investigations of Huntington disease and discovery of neuroendocrine abnormalities; later work contributed to understanding and gene identification of atherosclerosis, Huntington disease and inherited lipid disorders; currently Prin. Investigator and Univ. Killam Prof., Dept of Medical Genetics, Univ. of British Columbia, Dir and Sr Scientist, Centre for Molecular Medicine and Therapeutics, Canada Research Chair in Human Genetics and Molecular Medicine; founder of three biotechnology cos, including Aspreva Pharmaceuticals Inc.; Order of British Columbia 2009; Prix Galien (Canada) 2007, Canada's Health Researcher of the Year: Canadian Insts of Health Research Michael Smith Prize in Biomedical and Clinical Research 2008, Canada Gairdner Wightman Award for leadership in medical science in Canada 2011, Killam Prize in Health Sciences, Canada Council for the Arts 2011. *Publications:* numerous papers in professional journals. *Address:* Room 3025, Centre for Molecular Medicine and Therapeutics, Child and Family Research Institute, 950 West 28th Avenue, Vancouver, BC V5Z 4H4, Canada (office). *Telephone:* (604) 875-3535 (office). *Fax:* (604) 875-3819 (office). *E-mail:* mrh@cmmt.ubc.ca (office). *Website:* www.cmmt.ubc.ca (office).

HAYDEN, Gen. Michael Vincent, BA, MA; American air force officer and fmr government official; b. 17 March 1945, Pittsburgh; s. of Harry Hayden Sr and Sadie Hayden; ed N Catholic High School, Duquesne Univ., Pittsburgh, Academic Instructor School, Squadron Officer School, Air Command and Staff Coll., Air War Coll., Maxwell AF Base, Ala, Defense Intelligence Agency, Bolling AF Base,

Washington DC, Armed Forces Staff Coll., Norfolk, Va; rank of Second Lt 1967–70; Analyst and Briefer, Strategic Air Command HQ, Offnut AF Base, Neb. 1970–72; promoted to First Lt 1970, to Capt. 1971; Chief Current Intelligence Div., 8th AF HQ, Andersen AF Base, Guam 1972–75; Academic Instructor and Commdt of Cadets, ROTC Program, St Michael's Coll., Winooski, Vt 1975–79; promoted to Maj. 1980; Chief of Intelligence, 51st Tactical Fighter Wing, Osan Air Base, S Korea 1980–82; Air Attaché, Embassy in Sofia, Bulgaria 1984–86; promoted to Lt–Col 1985; Politico-Mil. Affairs Officer, Strategy Div., USAF HQ, Washington, DC 1986–89, Chief, Sec. of AF Staff Group 1991–93; Dir for Defense Policy and Arms Control, Nat. Security Council 1989–91; promoted to Col 1990; Dir Intelligence Directorate, US European Command HQ, Stuttgart, Germany 1993–95; promoted to Brig. Gen. 1993; Special Asst to Commdr, Air Intelligence Agency HQ, Kelly AF Base Oct.–Dec. 1995, Commdr 1996–97, Dir Jt Command and Control Warfare Center 1996–97; Deputy Chief of Staff, UN Command and US Forces Korea, Yongsan Army Garrison, S Korea 1997–99; promoted to Lt Gen. 1999; Dir Nat. Security Agency 1999–2005, Chief, Cen. Security Service, Fort George G. Meade, Md 1999–2005; promoted to Gen. 2005; Prin. Deputy Dir, Nat. Intelligence, Washington, DC 2005–06; Dir CIA 2006–09; Defense Distinguished Service Medal, Defense Superior Service Medal with oak leaf cluster, Legion of Merit, Bronze Star Medal, Meritorious Service Medal with two oak leaf clusters, AF Commendation Medal, AF Achievement Medal. *Address:* c/o Central Intelligence Agency, Office of Public Affairs, Washington, DC 20505, USA.

HAYDEN, Hon. William (Bill) George, AC, BEcons; Australian fmr politician, fmr police officer and farmer; b. 23 Jan. 1933, Brisbane, Queensland; m. Dallas Broadfoot 1960; one s. three d. (one deceased); ed Brisbane State High School, Queensland Secondary Correspondence School, Univ. of Queensland; Queensland State Public Service 1950–52; mem. Queensland Police Force 1953–61; mem. Fed. Parl. for Oxley 1961–88; Parl. Spokesman on Health and Welfare 1969–72, Treas. 1975; Minister for Social Security 1972–75, for Foreign Affairs 1983–88, for Foreign Affairs and Trade 1987–88; Gov.-Gen. Commonwealth of Australia 1989–96 (retd); Leader Parl. Labor Party (Opposition) 1977–83; Adjunct Prof., Queensland Univ. of Tech. 1996; Chair. Editorial Cttee Quadrant Journal 1998–2004; Resident Visiting Fellow, Jane Franklin Hall, Univ. of Tasmania 2000; mem. The Gen. Sir John Monash Foundation Asscn of Fmr Mems of the Parl. of Australia, Queensland Retd Police Asscn Inc.; Patron Australian Inst. of Int. Affairs (Queensland Br.), Australian Fabian Soc. (Queensland Br.); Hon. FRACP 1995; KStJ; Commdr, Order of the Three Stars (Latvia); Gwanghwa Medal (Korean Order of Diplomatic Merit); Hon. LLD (Queensland) 1990; Hon. DUniv (Central Queensland) 1992; Hon. DLitt (Southern Queensland) 1997; Dr hc (Griffith) 1990; Australian Humanist of the Year 1996. *Publication:* Hayden: An Autobiography 1996. *Address:* Level 13, Waterfront Place, 1 Eagle Street, Brisbane, Queensland (office); GPO Box 7829, Waterfront Place, Brisbane, Queensland 4001, Australia. *Telephone:* (7) 3229-3500 (office). *Fax:* (7) 3229-3499 (office). *E-mail:* wdhayden@bigpond.net.au (office).

HAYEK, Nayla; Swiss/Lebanese business executive and horse breeder; *Chairman, Swatch Group Ltd;* b. 1951, Switzerland; d. of the late Nicolas Hayek. Chair. Swatch Group Ltd; m. Roland Weber (divorced); one s.; Adviser, Swatch Group Middle East, Dubai, then hired as employee, est. Tiffany Watch Co. Ltd 2008, mem. Bd of Dirs Swatch Group 1995–, Vice-Chair. May–June 2010, Chair. 2010–; CEO Harry Winston, Inc. 2013–; mem. Bd of Dirs Belenos Clean Power Holding Ltd, Hayek Group, Rivoli Investments LLC, Dubai; mem. World Arabian Horse Org.; Owner, Hanaya Stud, Schleinikon, Switzerland; serves as int. Arabian horse judge; Dr hc (European Univ., Montreux); ranked by Arabian Business amongst the Power 500: The World's Most Influential Arabs (33rd) 2013. *Address:* Swatch Group Limited, Seevorstadt 6, PO Box 2501, 2501 Biel, Switzerland (office). *Telephone:* 3436811 (office). *Fax:* 3436911 (office). *Website:* www.swatchgroup.com (office); www.hanaya.ch.

HAYEK, Salma; Mexican actress; b. (Salma Valgarma Hayek-Jimenez), 2 Sept. 1966, Coatzacoalcos, Veracruz; m. François-Henri Pinault 2009; one d.; Pres. and Chief Exec. Ventanazul (production co.) 2007–; Kt, Ordre national de la Légion d'honneur 2012. *Films include:* Mi vida loca 1993, Miracle Alley 1995, Desperado 1995, Four Rooms 1995, Fair Game 1995, From Dusk Till Dawn 1996, Fled 1996, Fools Rush In 1997, Breaking Up 1997, Follow Me Home 1997, The Velocity of Gary 1998, 54 1998, Wild Wild West 1999, Dogma 1999, Frida 2002 (also producer), Death to Smoochy 2002, Once Upon a Time in Mexico 2003, Hotel 2003, After the Sunset 2004, Ask the Dust 2006, Lonely Hearts 2006, Across the Universe 2007, Cirque Du Freak: The Vampire's Assistant 2009, Grown Ups 2010, Americano 2011, La chispa de la vida 2011, Puss in Boots (voice) 2011, The Pirates! Band of Misfits (voice) 2012, Savages 2012, Here Comes the Boom 2012. *Television appearances include:* The Hunchback 1997, In the Time of the Butterflies 2001, The Maldonado Miracle (Daytime Emmy Award for Outstanding Directing in a Children/Youth/Family Special 2004) 2003, 30 Rock 2006, Ugly Betty (also exec. producer) 2006–07. *Address:* William Morris Agency, 1325 Avenue of the Americas, New York, NY 10019-6047, USA.

HAYES, Francis Mahon, BA, DPA, BL; Irish lawyer, consultant and fmr diplomatist; *Member, Permanent Court of Arbitration;* b. 2 March 1930, Cork; s. of Francis Mahon Hayes and Aileen Hayes (née Walsh); m. Kathleen O'Donoghue 1958; one s. three d.; ed Univ. Coll., Dublin and King's Inns, Dublin; Asst Legal Adviser, Dept of Justice 1957–65; Asst Legal Adviser, First Sec. Dept of Foreign Affairs 1965–70, Legal Adviser, Counsellor 1970–74, Legal Adviser, Asst Sec. 1974–77; Amb. to Denmark, Norway and Iceland 1977–81; Perm. Rep. to UN Office at Geneva 1981–87; Deputy Sec. Gen. Dept of Foreign Affairs 1987–89; Perm. Rep. to UN, New York 1989–95; mem. Int. Law Comm. 1986–91, The (Irish) Constitution Review Group 1995–96, Advisory Task Force on Immigrants 2001–02, Perm. Court of Arbitration, The Hague 2005–; Prime Minister's Alt. Rep. on EU Charter of Human Rights Convention 1999–2000; freelance consultant on int. and legal affairs. *Publication:* The Law of the Sea 2011. *Leisure interests:* reading, theatre, music, films, watching sport, golf. *Address:* Tara, 28 Knocknashee, Goatstown, Dublin 14, Ireland (home). *Telephone:* (1) 2983787 (home). *Fax:* (1) 2983787 (home).

HAYES, Roger Peter, BSc (Econ), MA, DBA; British public relations executive, company director, lecturer and trainer; *Senior Counsellor, APCO Worldwide;* b. 15 Feb. 1945, Hampton, Richmond upon Thames, England; s. of Peter Hall and

Patricia Hall; m. Margaret Jean Eales 1974; one s.; ed Isleworth Grammar School, Univ. of London, Univ. of Southern California, USA, Henley Business School; Reuters Corresp., Paris and London 1967–72; Vice-Pres. and Dir Buson-Marsteller 1972–79; Man. P.A. Consulting Group 1979–83; Dir Corp. Communications, Thorn-EMI PLC 1983–87; Chair. Hayes-MacLeod; Sec.-Gen. Int. Public Relations Asscns (Bd mem. 1984–88); Dir (non-exec.) IT World 1985–; fmr Int. Dir Perception Man., Perception International; Chair. Int. Foundation for Public Affairs Studies 1986–89; Dir-Gen. British Nuclear Industry Forum 1993–97; Vice-Pres. (Public Affairs and Govt Relations) Ford of Europe 1991–93; Pres. Int. Public Relations Asscn 1997, now mem. Emer.; Dir Int. Inst. of Communications 1997–; Dir (non-exec.) Echo Communications Research Group 1999–2009, Communications Ethics Ltd; Group CEO British Amusements Catering Trades Asscn 2004–, Amusements Trades Exhbns Ltd 2004–; currently Sr Counsellor, APCO Worldwide, postings to S Africa and India; Assoc. Faculty mem. Henley Business School; Fellow, Chartered Inst. of Public Relations. *Publications:* (co-author) Corporate Revolution 1986, Experts in Action 1988, Systematic Networking 1996. *Leisure interests:* books, music, cinema, int. politics, tennis, travel. *Address:* 75 Ellerby Street, London, SW6 6EU, England (home). *Telephone:* (20) 7526-3600 (office); (20) 7731-1255 (home). *Fax:* (20) 7323-9623 (office). *E-mail:* roger_p_hayes@yahoo.co.uk (home); rhayes@apcoworldwide.com (office).

HAYES, William, MA, PhD, DPhil; Irish physicist and fmr university administrator; b. 12 Nov. 1930, Killorglin, Co. Kerry; s. of Robert Hayes and Eileen Tobin; m. Joan Ferriss 1962 (died 1996); two s. one d.; ed Univ. Coll., Dublin and St John's Coll., Oxford; Official Fellow, St John's Coll. Oxford 1960–87, Prin. Bursar 1977–87, Pres. 1987–2001; Univ. Lecturer in Physics, Univ. of Oxford 1962–87; Dir Clarendon Lab. Oxford 1985–87; Pro-Vice-Chancellor, Univ. of Oxford 1990–2001; Chair. Curators of Oxford Univ. Chest 1992–2000; Sr Foreign Fellow, NSF, Purdue Univ., USA 1963–64; Visiting Prof., Univ. of Ill., USA 1971; mem. Tech. Staff, Bell Labs, New Jersey, USA 1974; Hon. MRIA 1998, Hon. Fellow, St John's Coll. Oxford 2001–; Hon. DSc (Nat. Univ. of Ireland) 1988, (Purdue Univ.) 1996. *Publications include:* Scattering of Light by Crystals (with R. Loudon) 1978, Defects and Defect Processes in Non-Metallic Solids (with A. M. Stoneham) 1985; research papers in professional journals. *Leisure interests:* walking, reading, listening to music. *Address:* 91 Woodstock Road, Oxford, OX2 6HL, England (home). *E-mail:* w.hayes1@physics.ox.ac.uk (office).

HAYMAN, Baroness (Life Peer), cr. 1996, of Dartmouth Park in the London Borough of Camden; **Rt Hon. Helene Valerie Hayman,** GBE, PC, MA; British politician; *Member, General Medical Council;* b. 26 March 1949, Wolverhampton, West Midlands; d. of the late Maurice Middleweek and Maude Middleweek; m. Martin Heathcote Hayman 1974; four s.; ed Wolverhampton Girls' High School, Newnham Coll., Cambridge; Pres. Union, Newnham Coll. Cambridge 1969; with Shelter: Nat. Campaign for the Homeless 1969–71; mem. staff, Social Services Dept, London Borough of Camden 1971–74; MP for Welwyn and Hatfield 1974–79 (Baby of the House 1974–79); Deputy Dir Nat. Council for One Parent Families 1974; Jr Minister, Dept for Environment, Transport and the Regions and Dept for Health 1997–99; Minister of State in the House of Lords for Agric., Fisheries and Food 1999–2001; mem. (Crossbench) House of Lords 1996–, elected first ever Lord Speaker of the House of Lords 2006–11, Pres. America Group 2007–; mem. Royal Coll. of Gynaecologists Ethics Cttee 1982–97, Univ. Coll. London/Univ. Coll. Hosp. Cttee on Ethics of Clinical Investigation 1987–97 (Vice-Chair. 1990–97), Univ. Coll. London 1992–97, Human Fertilisation and Embryology Authority, Gen. Medical Council; Chair. Whittington Hosp. NHS Trust 1992–97, Cancer Research UK 2001–04, Specialised Health Care Alliance 2004–06, Human Tissue Authority 2005; mem. Bd Roadsafe 2001–05 (Patron 2006–), Review Cttee of Privy Counsellors of the Anti-terrorism, Crime and Security Act 2002–04; Pres. Commonwealth Parl. Asscn (UK Br.) 2006–11; Trustee, Royal Botanical Gardens, Health and Educ. Trust, Sabin Vaccine Inst., Malaria Consortium; mem. Bd Disasters Emergency Cttee 2013–; mem. Exec. Cttee Commonwealth Parl. Asscn; Hon. Pres. British Group, Inter-Parl. Union 2006–11; Copy of the Key of the City of Tirana on the occasion of her state visit to Albania 2010; Hon. Fellow, Newnham Coll., Cambridge; several hon. degrees from British univs. *Address:* House of Lords, Westminster, London, SW1A 0PW, England (office). *Telephone:* (20) 7219-5083 (office). *E-mail:* haymanh@parliament.uk (office).

HAYMAN, Walter Kurt, MA, ScD, FRS; British mathematician and academic; *Professor Emeritus and Senior Research Fellow, Department of Mathematics, Imperial College London;* b. 6 Jan. 1926, Cologne, Germany; s. of Franz Samuel Haymann and Ruth Therese Hensel; m. 1st Margaret Riley Crann 1947 (died 1994); three d.; m. 2nd Waficka Katifi 1995 (died 2001); m. 3rd Marie Jennings 2007; ed Gordonstoun School and Univ. of Cambridge; Lecturer, King's Coll., Newcastle and Fellow, St John's Coll., Cambridge 1947; Lecturer 1947–53 and Reader, Univ. of Exeter 1953–56; Visiting Lecturer, Brown Univ., USA 1949–50, Stanford Univ. summer 1950, 1955, American Math. Soc. 1961; first Prof. of Pure Math., Imperial Coll. of Science and Tech., London 1956–85, Dean Royal Coll. of Science 1978–81, Prof. Emer. 1985–, Sr Research Fellow 1995–; Prof. Univ. of York 1985–93, Prof. Emer. 1993–; mem. London Math. Soc.; mem. Cambridge Philosophical Soc.; Fellow, Imperial Coll. 1989; Foreign mem. Finnish Acad. of Science and Letters, Accad. dei Lincei; Corresp. mem. Bavarian Acad. of Science; first organizer (with Margaret Hayman) of British Math. Olympiad 1964–68; Hon. DSc (Exeter) 1981, (Birmingham) 1985, (Giessen) 1992, (Uppsala) 1992, (Nat. Univ. of Ireland) 1997; First Smiths Prize 1948, shared Adams Prize, Univ. of Cambridge 1949, Junior Berwick Prize 1955, Sr Berwick Prize 1964, de Morgan Medal, London Math. Soc. 1995. *Publications:* Multivalent Functions 1958, 1994, Meromorphic Functions 1964, Research Problems in Function Theory 1967, Subharmonic Functions I 1976, II 1989; and over 200 articles in various scientific journals. *Leisure interests:* music, travel, television. *Address:* Department of Mathematics, Room 6M43, Imperial College, London, SW7 2AZ (office); Cadogan Grange, Bisley, Stroud, Glos., GL6 7AT, England (home). *Telephone:* (20) 7594-8535 (office); (1452) 770545 (home). *Fax:* (20) 7594-8517 (office). *Website:* www.ma.ic.ac.uk (office).

HAYMET, A. D. J. (Tony), BSc, PhD, DSc; Australian/American chemist, environmental scientist, academic, research institute director and business executive; *Distinguished Professor and Director and Vice-Chancellor Emeritus, Scripps Institution of Oceanography;* ed Sydney Grammar School, Univ. of Sydney,

Univ. of Chicago, USA; Postdoctoral Research Fellow, Lyman Lab. of Physics, Harvard Univ. 1981–83; Asst Prof. of Chem., Univ. of California, Berkeley 1983–88; Assoc. Prof. of Chem., Univ. of Utah 1988–91, Prof. of Chem. 1991, Adjunct Prof. of Chem. 1991–95; Deputy Dir for Physical Sciences, UniServe*Science, CAUT Center for Educational Software in Science, Univ. of Sydney, Australia 1994–97, Prof. of Chem. (Established Chair of Theoretical Chem.), Univ. of Sydney 1991–98, Visiting Prof. in School of Chem. 1998–99; Affiliated Faculty mem. W. M. Keck Center for Computational Biology 1998–2002; Affiliate Staff Scientist, Pacific Northwest Nat. Lab., PASS 1996–2002; Chair. Physical Chem. Div., Univ. of Houston, Tex. 1998–2001, Founder Univ. of Houston Environmental Modeling Inst. 2000–02, Distinguished Univ. Prof. of Chem. 1998–2002; mem. Advisory Bd Environmental Inst. of Houston 2001–02; mem. Founding Group, WA Marine Science Inst. 2005–06; mem. Bd of Dirs CRC for Antarctic Climate and Ecosystems 2003–06, Western Australian Marine Science Inst.; seconded as CSIRO Dir of Science and Policy 2005–06, Chief of CSIRO Marine Research, then Marine & Atmospheric Research 2006; Dir Scripps Inst. of Oceanography, Univ. of California, San Diego 2006–12, Vice-Chancellor for Marine Sciences and Dean of Grad. School of Marine Sciences, Univ. of California, San Diego 2006–12; Co-founder, mem. Bd and fmr Chair. CleanTECH, San Diego 2007–; Strategic Advisor (part time), Pegasus Capital Advisors 2010–; Special Counsel (part time), Phillips & Assocs 2012–; Visiting Research Fellow, ANU Research School of Chem. 1993; Australian Acad. of Science Fellowship to Japan 1994; Visiting Prof. of Chemical Eng and Petroleum Refining, Colorado School of Mines, Golden, Colo, USA 1997; Chair. Partnership for the Observation of Global Oceans (POGO); Chair. Ocean Global Agenda, Council Ocean Council, World Econ. Forum 2012–13, Vice-Chair. 2013–14; Vice-Chair. VCAT, Nat. Inst. of Standards and Tech. 2008–13; mem. Chemical Educ. Sub-cttee Australian Acad. of Science 1997–98, Advisory Editorial Bd PhysChemComm 1998–2001; Fellow, Royal Australian Chemical Inst. 1992; Hon. Research Prof. of Chem., Univ. of Tasmania 2002–06; Sr Knox Prize, Sydney Grammar School 1973, Levey Scholarship for Chem. I and Physics I and Iredale Prize for Chem. II 1974–75, C.S.R. Chemicals Prize for Chem. and Union Carbide Prize for Chem. 3 1976–77, Univ. Medal and First Class Honours in Theoretical Chem. 1977, Masson Medal, Royal Australian Chemical Inst. 1977, NSF Presidential Young Investigator 1985–90, Alfred P. Sloan Research Fellow 1986–89, Rennie Medal, Royal Australian Chemical Inst. 1988, Student Distinguished Service Award, Univ. of Utah 1990, Antarctic Service Medal, US Dept of Navy and NSF 1994, Distinguished Young Chemist Award, Fed. of Asian Chemical Socs 1997, Woolmers Lecturer in Chemical Educ., Univ. of Tasmania 1997, Excellence Award in Oceanography, Werner Petersen Foundation 2013. *Publications:* more than 170 scientific papers in professional journals; numerous op-ed pieces in leading newspapers. *Address:* Integrative Oceanography Division, Scripps Institution of Oceanography, University of California, San Diego, MC 0209, 9500 Gilman Drive, La Jolla, CA 92093-0209, USA (office). *Telephone:* (858) 534-2083 (office). *Fax:* (858) 453-0167 (office). *E-mail:* haymet@ucsd.edu (office). *Website:* scripps.ucsd.edu/profiles/thaymet (office).

HAYNES, Desmond Leo; Barbadian politician and fmr professional cricketer; *Special Adviser, Cricket Committee, West Indies Cricket Board;* b. 15 Feb. 1956, Holders Hill, St James; m. Dawn Haynes 1991; ed Fed. High School, Barbados; right-hand opening batsman, teams: Barbados 1976–95 (Capt. 1990–91), Scotland (Benson & Hedges Cup) 1983, Middx 1989–94, W Prov. 1994–97; played in 116 Tests for West Indies 1977–94 (four as Capt.), scoring 7,487 runs (average 42.29, highest score 184) including 18 hundreds; played in 238 One-Day Ints, scoring record 8,648 runs (average 41.37, highest score 152 not out) including record 17 hundreds; scored 26,030 First-class runs (average 45.90, highest score 255 not out) including 61 hundreds; formed partnership with Gordon Greenidge for West Indies cricket team in Test cricket during 1980s, between them they managed 16 century stands, four in excess of 200, pair made 6,482 runs while batting together in partnerships, the highest total for a batting partnership in Test cricket history; toured England 1979 (World Cup), 1980, 1983 (World Cup), 1984, 1988, 1991; Chair. Barbados Cricket Asscn Sr Selection Panel 1999–2001; elected Senator in Parl. 2001; fmr Chair. Nat. Sports Council; fmr Pres. Carlton Cricket Club; fmr Sec. West Indies Players' Asscn; currently Special Adviser, Cricket Cttee, West Indies Cricket Bd; a Wisden Cricketer of the Year 1991. *Leisure interest:* playing golf. *Address:* West Indies Cricket Board Inc., PO Box 616 W, St John's, Antigua (office). *Telephone:* 481-2450 (office). *Fax:* 481-2498 (office). *E-mail:* wicb@windiescricket.com (office). *Website:* www.windiescricket.com (office).

HAYRIKYAN, Paruyr; Armenian lawyer and nationalist leader; *President, Union for National Self-Determination party;* b. 5 July 1949, Yerevan; s. of Arshavir Hayrikyan and Zaruhi Abrahamyan; m. Susanna Avakian; one s. five d.; ed Yerevan State Univ.; founder and leader of democracy movts in USSR; leading role in Nat. United Party of Armenia (reformed on principle of independence through referendum and renamed Union for Nat. Self-Determination (UNSD) 1987) 1968–; sentenced to imprisonment for various nationalist activities 1969–73, 1974–87, with latest arrest after mass demonstrations in Yerevan in 1988; deprived of Soviet citizenship 1989, deported from USSR, citizenship restored 1990; elected to Parl. 1990; cand. for Presidency of Armenia Oct. 1991; fmrly Chair. Union for Nat. Self-Determination (also 1991–96), now Pres. UNSD; Adviser to Pres. of Armenia 1998–99; Chair. Comm. on Human Rights in Presidential Admin. 1998–2002; Pres. Constitutional Reform Comm. 1998–99; Prefect of Goris and Goris Region 1992; elected Pres. int. org. Democracy and Independence, Paris 1989, Prague 1990; has also written nationalistic, freedom-fighting and lyrical songs; Nat. Council to Support Democracy Movements in the USSR Democracy Award (USA) 1990, First Prize (Lyrical Category) for 'The Bird of Love', Pan-Armenian Sayat Nova Song Competition 2001, Conservative Political Action Conf. Honoree and Guest Speaker, Hagop Megapart Medal, Nat. Library of Armenia 2009, Parl. Club (Geragun Horurt) First Medal for Democracy and Human Rights 2010. *Compositions:* albums: Zimvori Avotka (Soldier's Prayer) album (composer, performer, producer) 1988, Hayastan (Armenia) 2002. *Publications:* Independence (weekly newspaper) 1987, Knight of Freedom 1989; collection of articles, songs, poems, interviews and memoirs 1989; poetry collections: Freedom Songs 1996, And Thus Until Death 1997, Three Annals on the Road to Independence, The Human Rights Point of View of the Election Committee of the Armenian Republic 2000, The Representative Coefficient of the Voters or the True Equality of the Voters 2002, Democracy by Word and Act 2002, The Strategically Victorious National

Organization 2002, Formula of States' Democracy 2003, Armenian People on the Border of 2003–2004 2004, Cooperation for the Main Issues of Democracy 2004, On the Quest of Light (autobiog.) 2004, With Faith and Love (filmscript) 2004, Complete Democracy 2008. *Address:* Union for National Self-Determination, Grigor Lusavorichi Street 15, 375013 Yerevan (office); Tpagrichneri 9, Apt 102, Yerevan, Armenia (home). *Telephone:* (10) 36-94-46 (office); (10) 58-94-85 (home). *Fax:* (10) 57-38-70 (office). *E-mail:* aim@aimusd.org (office). *Website:* www.aimusd .org (office).

HAYS, Hon. Daniel (Dan), BA, LLB; Canadian lawyer, politician and business executive; *Partner, Norton Rose Canada LLP;* b. 24 April 1939, Calgary; s. of Harry Hays; m. Kathy Hays; three d.; ed Univ. of Alberta and Univ. of Toronto; Senator for Alberta 1984–2007, Deputy Leader of the Govt in the Senate 1999–2001, Speaker of the Senate 2001–06, Leader of the Opposition 2006–07; mem. Liberal Party of Canada, Pres. 1994–98; currently Partner Norton Rose Canada LLP; Chair. Canada-Japan Inter-Parl. Group 1994–99, Asia-Pacific Parl. Forum 1994–99; fmr Pres. Canadian Hays Converter Asscn; fmr mem. Bd of Dirs CBC, Calgary Dist Foundation, Rotary Club of Calgary; mem. Advisory Council Canadian Defence and Foreign Affairs Inst.; mem. Law Soc. of Alberta, Bar Asscn, Canadian Tax Foundation; mem. Rotary Club, Trustee, Rotary Challenger Park Soc.; Hon. Col King's Own Calgary Regt; Grand Cordon, Order of the Sacred Treasure (Japan), Ordre de la Pléiade. *Leisure interests:* downhill skiing, horseback riding, films. *Address:* Norton Rose Canada LLP, Suite 3700, 400 3rd Avenue SW, T2P 4H2, Canada (office). *Telephone:* (403) 267-8338 (office). *Fax:* (403) 264-5973 (office). *E-mail:* dan.hays@nortonrose.com (office). *Website:* www .nortonrose.com (office).

HAYTHORNTHWAITE, Richard (Rick), SM, MA; British business executive; b. Dec. 1956; m.; one s. one d.; ed Colston's School, Bristol, Queen's Coll., Oxford; joined British Petroleum 1978, exploration geologist, then Man. Magnus Oilfield, Pres. Venezuela and other group posts until 1995; Corp. and Commercial Dir Premier Oil PLC 1995–97; joined Blue Circle Industries PLC 1997, CEO Heavy Bldg Materials Asia and Europe, CEO 1999–2001; CEO Invensys PLC 2001–05; mem. Bd of Dirs MasterCard Inc. 2006–, currently Chair.; Chair. Network Rail Ltd 2009–12; Chair. Centre for Creative Communications, Almeida Theatre, Southbank Centre; mem. Bd of Dirs Cookson Group 1999–2003, Imperial Chemical Industries PLC, Lafarge SA 2001–03, Land Securities Group PLC 2008–09, British Council; fmr Gen. Man. BP Exploration Inc.; fmr Pres. PetroSaudi Int. Ltd; fmr Pres. Almeida Theatre; Trustee, Nat. Museum of Science and Industry; Sloan Fellow, MIT; Adviser and Pnr, Star Capital Partners Ltd 2006–08. *Leisure interests:* travel, tennis, skiing, theatre, visual arts. *Address:* c/o Office of the Chairman, Network Rail Limited, Kings Place, 90 York Way, London, N1 9AG, England.

HAYWARD, Anthony Bryan (Tony), BSc, PhD, CCMI, FRSE; British business executive; *Interim Chairman, Glencore Xstrata plc;* b. 21 May 1957, Slough, Berks.; m. Maureen Hayward; one s. one d.; ed Univs of Edinburgh and Birmingham; joined BP plc 1982, various tech. and commercial posts with BP Exploration, London, Aberdeen, France, China and Glasgow, later Exploration Man., Colombia, Pres. BP Exploration Venezuela 1995–97, Dir BP Exploration, London 1997–99, Group Vice-Pres. and mem. Upstream Exec. Cttee 1999–2000, Group Treas. 2000–02, Exec. Vice-Pres. and CEO Exploration and Production 2003–07, Exec. Dir BP 2003–07, Group Chief Exec. 2007–10 (resgnd), Dir (non-exec.) TNK-BP, Moscow 2010–13; Dir (sr ind. non-exec.) Corus Group plc 2002–; Dir, Glencore International plc (merged with Xstrata plc to form Glencore Xstrata plc May 2013) 2011–, Interim Chair. 2013–; Chair. CompactGTL 2013–; Dir (non-exec.) Tata Steel; mem. Advisory Bd Citibank 2000–03, Tsinghua, MIT Energy; mem. Business Council of Britain; Chair. GLOBE CEO Forum for Climate Change; Trustee, Emirates Foundation; Companion, Chartered Man. Inst. 2005; Dr hc (Univs of Edinburgh, Aston, Birmingham); hon. degree from Robert Gordon Univ. 2013; honoured as a "distinguished leader" by Univ. of Birmingham 2013. *Leisure interests:* sailing, skiing, triathlons, watching sport. *Address:* Glencore Xstrata plc, Baarermattstrasse 3, 6340 Baar, Switzerland (office). *Telephone:* (41) 7092000 (office). *Fax:* (41) 7093000 (office). *E-mail:* info@glencorexstrata.com (office). *Website:* www.glencorexstrata.com (office).

HAZ, Hamzah, BA; Indonesian politician; b. 15 Feb. 1940, Ketapang, W Kalimantan; m. (two wives); twelve c.; ed Sr Econ. High School, Ketapang, Tanjungpura Univ.; newspaper journalist, Pontianak; teacher of econs, Tanjungpura Univ.; mem. W Kalimantan Prov. Legis. Council 1968–71; mem. Nahdlatul Ulama (NU; later amalgamated into United Devt Party – PPP), Leader PPP 1999–; mem. House of Reps 1971–; fmr State Minister of Investment, Co-ordinating Minister for People's Welfare and Eradication of Poverty; Vice-Pres. of Indonesia 2001–04. *Leisure interest:* music. *Address:* Jalan Tegalan No. 27, Matraman, Jakarta Timur, Indonesia (home). *Telephone:* (21) 8581327 (home).

HAZANAVICIUS, Michel; French film director and screenwriter; b. 29 March 1967, Paris; m. Bérénice Bejo; two c.; two c. (with Virginia Lovisone). *Films include:* as co-writer: Delphine 1, Yvan 0 1996, Le clone 1998, Les Dalton 2004; as screenwriter and dir: Mes amis 1999, OSS 117: Cairo, Nest of Spies 2006, OSS 117: Lost in Rio 2009, The Artist (Academy Award for Best Dir 2012, BAFTA Awards for Best Dir, and for Best Original Screenplay 2012, Australian Acad. of Cinema and TV Arts Award for Best Direction –Int. 2012, César Award for Best Dir 2012, Directors Guild Award for Outstanding Achievement in Directing in a Theatrical Release 2012) 2011. *Television includes:* Derrick contre Superman 1992, Ca détourne 1992, La Classe américaine 1993, C'est pas le 20 heures 1994, Les films qui sortent le lendemain dans les salles de cinema 1996. *Address:* c/o La Petite Reine, 20 rue de Saint Pétersbourg, 75008 Paris, France (office). *Telephone:* (1) 44-90-73-90 (office). *Fax:* (1) 44-90-73-99 (office). *E-mail:* thomas.langmann@ lapetitereine.fr (office); ombeline.marchon@lapetitereine.fr (office).

HAZARE, Anna; Indian social worker; b. (Kisan Baburao Hazare), 15 June 1937, Bhingar, Bombay Prov., British India; s. of Baburao Hazare and Laxmibai Hazare; served in the army 1960–75; worked on Ralegan Siddhi model village rural devt project 1975–; known for his contrib. to Watershed Devt Programme, Right To Information Act; prominent leader in Indian Anti-Corruption Movt 2011; Indira Priyadarshini Vrikshamitra Award 1986, Man Of The Year Award 1988, Krishi Bhushana Award 1989, Padmashree 1990, Padma Bhushan 1992, UNEP's Roll Of Honour—Global 500 Forum 1993, Vivekananda Seva Puraskar 1994, Shiromani Award 1996, Mahaveer Puraskar 1997, Care Int. Award 1998, Jana Seva Puraskar 1998, Rotary Int. Manav Seva Puraskar 1998, Nat. Integration Award 1999, Diwaliben Mehta Award 1999, Paul Mittal Nat. Award 2000, Giants Int. Award 2000, Basavshri Prashasti Award 2000, Transparency Int. Integrity Award 2003, Jit Gill Memorial Award for Outstanding Public Service, World Bank 2008, NDTV Indian of the Year (jt winner) 2011; Dr hc (Gandhigram Rural Univ.) 2005. *Publications include:* Mahiticha Adhikar, Gramsabha, Ration, Nirbhay Bano, Majhe Gaon Majhe Tirth. *Address:* Ralegan Siddhi Pariwar, Ralegan Siddhi, Parner, Ahmednagar 414 302, India (office). *Telephone:* (24) 88240401 (office). *Fax:* (24) 88240581 (office). *E-mail:* annahazare1@gmail.com; info@annahazare.org (office). *Website:* www.annahazare.org (office).

HAZARIKA, A. K., BE; Indian engineer and business executive; *Director (Onshore), Oil and Natural Gas Corporation;* ed Assam Eng Coll.; grad. trainee, Oil and Natural Gas Corpn (ONGC) 1976, first assignment was as driller (cementing) in Assam, then transferred to Mumbai 1995, Head of Multi-disciplinary Team, Mumbai High Redevelopment Projects, Head of Well Services, Mumbai 2002, Exec. Dir and Chief of Well Services 2003, Dir (Onshore) 2004–, Chair. and Man. Dir Feb.–Oct. 2011, also Dir (Exploration); Chair. Mangalore Refinery and Petrochemicals Ltd Feb.–Nov. 2011, also Dir (Onshore); apptd Chair. ONGC TERI Bio-technology Ltd, Exhibition Cttee Petrotech 2010; Chair. Working Group for Underground Coal Gasification, Office of Principal Scientific Adviser, Govt of India; mem. Bd of Dirs ONGC Videsh Ltd 2004–, Tripura Power Co.; Rep. Oil and Gas Sub-cttee, Int. M2M (Methane to Market) Partnership, US Environmental Protection Agency; mem. Soc. of Petroleum Engineers, New Delhi; mem. Governing Council, Petroleum Fed. of India; Drilling Engineer of the Year 1990, Soc. of Petroleum Engineers Pres.'s Award, Greening of Oil and Gas Business Award 2010. *Address:* Oil and Natural Gas Corporation, Tel Bhavan, Dehradun 248 003, Uttarakhand, India (office). *Telephone:* (13) 52759561 (office). *Website:* www.ongcindia.com (office).

HAZELTINE, Richard Deimel, MS, PhD; American physicist and academic; *Chairman, Department of Physics, College of Natural Sciences, University of Texas;* b. 12 June 1942, Jersey City, NJ; s. of the late Alan Hazeltine and of Elizabeth Barrett Hazeltine; m. Cheryl Pickett 1964; one s. one d.; ed Harvard Coll. and Univ. of Michigan; mem. Inst. for Advanced Study 1969–71; Research Scientist, Univ. of Texas 1971–82, then Prof. of Physics 1986, Asst Dir Inst. for Fusion Studies 1982–86, Acting Dir 1987–88, 1991, Dir 1991–2002, currently Chair. Dept of Physics, Coll. of Natural Sciences; fmr Assoc. Ed. Reviews of Modern Physics; fmr Ed. Physical Review, Physics of Fluids; Fellow, American Physical Soc., AAAS, Atomic Energy Research Foundation; mem. Fusion Energy Sciences Cttee US Dept of Energy; mem. Bd of Physics and Astronomy, NRC. *Publications include:* Plasma Confinement (with J. D. Meiss) 1992, Framework of Plasma Physics (with F. Waelbroeck) 1998; more than 140 articles in scientific journals. *Address:* University of Texas, Institute for Fusion Studies, 1 University Station C1500, Austin, TX 78712-0262, USA (office). *Telephone:* (512) 471-4307 (office). *Fax:* (512) 471-6715 (office). *E-mail:* rdh@physics.utexas.edu (office). *Website:* www .physics.utexas.edu (office).

HAZEN, Paul Mandeville, MBA; American banker and business executive; *Chairman, Accel-KKR;* b. 1941, Lansing, Mich.; m.; ed Univ. of Ariz. and Univ. of Calif., Berkeley; Asst Man. Security Pacific Bank 1964–66; Vice-Pres. Union Bank 1966–70; Chair. Wells Fargo Realty Advisors 1970–76; with Wells Fargo Bank, San Francisco 1979–98, Exec. Vice-Pres. and Man. Real Estate Industries Group 1979–80, mem. Exec. Office 1980, Vice-Chair. 1980–84, Pres. and COO 1984–94, Chair. 1995–98, also Dir; Pres. and Treas. Wells Fargo Mortgage & Equity Trust 1977–84; with Wells Fargo & Co. (parent), San Francisco 1978–2001, Exec. Vice-Pres., then Vice-Chair., Pres., COO and Dir 1978–95, CEO 1995–98, Chair. 1998–2001; currently Chair. Accel-KKR, KKR Financial Corpn, Sr Advisor Kohlberg Kravis Roberts; Deputy Chair. and Lead Ind. Dir Vodafone Group plc 2000–06; mem. Bd of Dirs Applied Predictive Technologies, Safeway, Inc., Xstrata AG, Prosper Marketplace, Inc.; Trustee, Wells Fargo Mortgage and Equity Trust. *Address:* Accel-KKR, 2500 Sand Hill Road, Suite 300, Menlo Park, CA 94025, USA (office). *Telephone:* (650) 289-2460 (office). *Fax:* (650) 289-2461 (office). *E-mail:* inquiries@accel-kkr.com (office). *Website:* www.accel-kkr.com (office).

HAZIM, His Beatitude Ignatius IV; Lebanese ecclesiastic; *Greek Orthodox Patriarch of Antioch and All the East;* b. 1920, Mharde; ed Beirut Univ. and Institut Saint-Serge, Paris; Dir of a secondary Theological Inst., Beirut, Lebanon; Co-founder Orthodox Youth Movt 1949; Rector of Theological Inst. Balamand Monastery then elected Bishop of Lattakia, Syria 1966, took up post 1970; Greek Orthodox Patriarch of Antioch and All the East (with jurisdiction over Syria, Lebanon, Iran and Iraq) 1979–; f. Balamand Orthodox Theological Seminary, fmr Dean; several times Pres. Middle East Council of Churches, Geneva; Founder Univ. of Balamand, Lebanon 1987, Pres. Bd of Trustees; lectures in European and Middle-Eastern univs. *Publications:* La résurrection et l'homme d'aujourd'hui and in Arabic: I Believe, The Telling of Your Word Enlightens, Words on Pastoral Matters, The Church in the Middle East (trans. of the work by Père Corbon), God's Design (trans. of the work by Suzanne de Dietrich). *Address:* Patriarcat Grec-Orthodoxe, PO Box 9, Damascus, Syria (office). *Telephone:* (11) 5424400 (office). *Fax:* (11) 5424404 (office). *E-mail:* info@antiochpat.org (office). *Website:* www .antiochpat.org (office).

HAZZARD, Shirley, FRSL; Australian/American writer; b. 30 Jan. 1931, Sydney, Australia; d. of Reginald Hazzard and Catherine Hazzard; m. Francis Steegmuller 1963 (died 1994); ed Queenwood School, Sydney; Special Operations Intelligence, Hong Kong 1947–48; UK High Commr's Office, Wellington, NZ 1949–50; UN, New York (Gen. Service Category) 1952–61; novelist and writer of short stories and contrib. to The New Yorker 1960–; Guggenheim Fellow 1974; mem. American Acad. of Arts and Letters, American Acad. of Arts and Sciences; Hon. Citizen of Capri 2000; American Acad. of Arts and Letters Award in Literature 1966, First Prize, O. Henry Short Story Awards 1976, Nat. Book Critics Award for Fiction, USA 1981, Boyer Lecturer, Australia 1984, 1988, Clifton Fadiman Medal for Literature 2001, Nat. Book Award for Fiction 2003, William Dean Howells Medal, American Acad. of Arts and Letters 2005. *Publications include:* short stories: Cliffs of Fall 1963; novels: The Evening of the Holiday 1966, People in Glass Houses 1967, The Bay of Noon 1970, The Transit of Venus (Nat. Critics Circle Award for

Fiction 1981) 1980, The Great Fire (Nat. Book Award for Fiction) 2003, Australia (Miles Franklin Prize 2004) 2004; non-fiction: Defeat of an Ideal: A Study of the Self-destruction of the United Nations 1973, Countenance of Truth: The United Nations and the Waldheim Case 1990, Greene on Capri (memoir) 2000, Ancient Shore: Dispatches from Naples (with Francis Steegmuller) 2009. *Leisure interest:* parthenophile.

HE, Chunlin; Chinese politician; b. Aug. 1933, Wuxi City, Jiangsu Prov.; ed Northeast China Agricultural Coll.; joined CCP 1951; technician, engineer, then Deputy Section Chief and Section Chief, Chinese Acad. of Agricultural Mechanization Sciences 1962–66; clerk, Org. Dept, CCP Hebei Prov. Cttee 1966–67; Deputy Chief, Science and Tech. Div., Agricultural Machinery Research Inst., First Ministry of Machine-Building Industry 1972–78; Chief, Comprehensive Div., Survey and Research Section, Ministry of Agricultural Machinery 1979–80, Dir, Gen. Office and of Survey and Research Section 1980–82; Dir Special Econ. Zones Office of State Council 1984–93; Deputy Sec.-Gen. State Council 1988–98 (Deputy Sec. CCP Leading Party Group 1988–91); Head, Nat. Leading Group for Suppressing Smuggling 1993; mem. State Leading Group for Science and Tech. 1996; mem. Hong Kong Special Admin. Region Preparatory Cttee, Govt Del. at Hong Kong Hand-Over Ceremony 1997; Sec.-Gen. 9th Standing Cttee of NPC 1998–2003, Chair. Internal and Judicial Affairs Cttee of 10th NPC 2003–08, Chair. Credentials Cttee 2003–08; mem. 14th CCP Cen. Cttee 1992–97, 15th CCP Cen. Cttee 1997–2002. *Address:* State Council, Beijing, People's Republic of China.

HE, Guangwei; Chinese civil servant; Deputy Dir China Nat. Tourism Admin. 1986–95, Dir 1995. *Address:* China National Tourism Administration, 9A Jian Guo Men Nei Dajie, Beijing 100740, People's Republic of China. *Telephone:* (10) 65138866. *Fax:* (10) 65122096.

HE, Guangyuan; Chinese state official; b. 1930, Anxin Co., Hebei Prov.; ed No. 9 Middle School, Hebei Mil. Dist, PLA Beijing Mil. Region; joined CCP 1945, PLA 194; Deputy Dir Forging Sub-Plant, Changchun No. 1 Motor Vehicle Plant, Changchun City, Jilin Prov. 1956–66, Dir 1966; criticized and denounced in Cultural Revolution 1966–70; Vice-Mayor of Changchun City 1980–82; Vice-Minister of Agricultural Machinery 1980 (Deputy Sec. CCP Leading Party Group); Vice-Minister of Machinery and Electronics Industry 1982–88, Minister 1988–93, of Machine-Building Industry 1993–96; Alt. mem. 12th CCP Cen. Cttee 1982–87, 13th Cen. Cttee 1987–92; mem. 14th CCP Cen. Cttee 1992–97; mem. Standing Cttee, 8th CPPCC 1993–98, 9th CPPCC 1998–2003, Chair. Motions Cttee 9th CPPCC Nat. Cttee 1998–2003. *Address:* c/o National Committee of Chinese People's Political Consultative Conference, 23 Taipingqiao Street, Beijing, People's Republic of China.

HE, Guoqiang; Chinese politician; b. Oct. 1943, Xiangxiang Co., Hunan Prov.; ed Beijing Chemical Eng Inst.; joined CCP 1966; fmr technician, later Dir Synthesizing Workshop, Lunan Chemical Fertilizer Plant, Shandong Prov. (Sec. CCP Party Br. 1967–78), later Deputy Dir Lunan Chemical Fertilizer Plant, Deputy Chief Engineer 1978–80; Dir Control Office, Deputy's Govt, Shandong Prov. 1980–82; Deputy Dir-Gen. and CCP Sec. Shandong Petro-Chemical Dept 1982–84, Dir-Gen. 1984–86; mem. of the Standing Cttee of CCP Shandong Provincial Cttee, Vice-Sec., Sec. CCP Ji'nan City Cttee 1986; Vice-Minister of Chemical Industry 1991–96; Vice-Sec. CCP Fujian Provincial Cttee, Acting Gov. Fujian Prov. 1996–97, Gov. 1997–99; Sec. CCP Chongqing Municipal Cttee 1999–2002; mem. 12th CCP Cen. Cttee 1982–87, 13th CCP Cen. Cttee 1987–92, 14th CCP Cen. Cttee 1992–97, 15th CCP Cen. Cttee 1997–2002, 16th CCP Cen. Cttee 2002–07 (Head of Org. Dept and mem. Secr. of Politburo 2002–07), 17th CCP Cen. Cttee 2007–12, Politburo Standing Cttee 2007–12; Sec. Cen. Comm. for Discipline Inspection 2007–12). *Address:* c/o Central Commission for Discipline Inspection, Central Committee of the Chinese Communist Party, Beijing, People's Republic of China (office).

HE, Jiuchang; Chinese business executive; *General Manager, Shaanxi Yanchang Petroleum (Group) Company Limited;* fmr Deputy Dir Gen., Devt and Reform Comm. of Shaanxi Prov.; Dir, Gen. Man. and Deputy Sec. of Party Cttee, Shaanxi Yanchang Petroleum (Group) Co. Ltd 2013–. *Address:* Shaanxi Yanchang Petroleum (Group) Co. Ltd, 75 Keji Road, Xi'an 710075, Shaanxi, People's Republic of China (office). *Telephone:* (29) 88899666 (office). *Fax:* (29) 88899669 (office). *E-mail:* webmaster@sxycpc.com (office). *Website:* www.sxycpc.com (office).

HE, Kang, BSc; Chinese politician; b. 26 Feb. 1923, Hebei Prov.; m. Miao Shixia 1945; two s.; m. 2nd Yu Junmin 1993; ed Agric. Coll. of Guangxi Univ.; Chief Dir of Agric. and Forestry under Shanghai Mil. Control Cttee 1949–50; Deputy Head Dept of Agric. and Forestry under E China Mil. and Political Cttee 1950–52; Dir Dept of Special Forestry of Ministry of Forestry 1952–54; Dir Dept of Tropical Plants, Ministry of Agric. 1955–57; Dir S China Tropical Crop Science Research Inst. and Tropical Crop Coll. 1957–72; Deputy to 3rd NPC 1965–75; Deputy Dir Gen. Bureau of Land Reclamation, Guangdong Prov. 1972–77; Vice-Minister of Agric., Deputy Dir Nat. Planning Comm., Deputy Dir Nat. Comm. on Agric. 1978–82; mem. 12th CCP Cen. Cttee 1982–87, 13th Cen. Cttee 1987–93; mem. 8th NPC Standing Cttee 1993–98; Minister of Agric. 1983–90; Vice-Chair. Nat. Cttee, China Asscn for Science and Tech. 1986–96; Vice-Chair. Nat. Agric. Regional Planning Cttee 1979–90; Pres. Chinese Village & Township Enterprises Asscn 1990–2000, Chair. China-Bangladesh Friendship Ass256 1993–; Vice-Chair. Zhongkai Inst. of Agric. Tech.; Hon. DUniv (Maryland, USA) 1986; World Food Prize 1993. *Publications:* Agricultural Reform and Development in China, Rubber Culture in Northern Tropical Area (ed. and writer). *Leisure interests:* photography, listening to music, reading. *Address:* c/o Ministry of Agriculture, 11 Nongzhanguan Nanli, Chaoyang Qu, Beijing 100026, People's Republic of China (office). *Telephone:* (10) 64192406 (office). *Fax:* (10) 64192468 (office). *E-mail:* heyu@agri .gov.cn (office).

HE, Luli; Chinese politician and paediatrician; b. 7 June 1934, Jinan, Shandong Prov.; d. of the late He Siyuan and He Yiwen; m. Rong Guohuang 1958 (died 1989); two s.; ed Beijing Coll. of Medicine; paediatrician, Beijing Children's Hosp. 1957–, Beijing No. 2 Hosp. 1988–96; Deputy Head, People's Govt, Xicheng Dist, Beijing 1984–88; Vice-Mayor Beijing Municipality 1988–96; Vice-Chair. Cen. Cttee, 7th Revolutionary Cttee of the Chinese Kuomintang (RCCK) 1988–92, Vice-Chair. Women and Youth Cttee, RCCK 1988–96, Chair. Beijing Municipal Cttee 1988–93, Chair. Cen. Cttee of 8th RCCK 1992–97, Chair. Cen. Cttee of 9th RCCK

1997–2002; Pres. Cen. Acad. of Socialism 1999–; mem. CPPCC 8th Nat. Cttee 1993–98, Vice-Chair. 1996–98; Vice-Chair. Standing Cttee of 9th NPC 1998–2003, of 10th NPC 2003–08; Vice-Pres. Exec. Cttee of All China Women's Fed. 1993–; apptd Pres. China Population Welfare Foundation 2000; mem. Govt Del. at Macao Hand-Over Ceremony, Macao Special Admin. Region Preparatory Cttee 1999; Hon. Vice-Pres. Red Cross Soc. of China 1999; honoured as Nat. March 8 Red-Banner Bearer 1994. *Address:* Central Academy of Socialism, Beijing 100081, People's Republic of China (office).

HE, Ping; Chinese news agency executive; *Editor-in-Chief, Xinhua News Agency;* b. 1957; ed Beijing Univ.; Deputy Ed.-in-Chief, Xinhua News Agency 1982–2007, Vice-Pres. 1993–2007, Ed.-in-Chief 2007–; mem. 18th CCP Central Cttee Central Comm. for Discipline Inspection 2012–. *Address:* Xinhua, 20F Dacheng Plaza, 127 Xhuanwumen Street West, Beijing 100031, People's Republic of China (office). *E-mail:* xxp69@xinhuanet.com (office). *Website:* (office).

HE, Maj.-Gen. Qizong; Chinese army officer; b. 1943, Yingshan Co., Sichuan Prov.; joined PLA 1961; joined CCP 1965; Deputy Commdr Kunming Mil. Region 1979–85; Chief of Staff of Div. 1982–83, Div. Commdr 1983, Deputy Commdr of Army 1983–84, Commdr 1984–85, Deputy Chief of Gen. Staff, PLA 1985; Alt. mem. 13th CCP Cen. Cttee 1987–92; Alt. mem. 14th Cen. Cttee 1992–97; Deputy Commdr Nanjing Mil. Region 1993–; rank of Maj.-Gen. 1988. *Address:* People's Liberation Army General Staff Headquarters, Beijing, People's Republic of China.

HE, Wenbo; Chinese engineer and business executive; *President, Baosteel Group Corporation;* mem. CCP; Dir, Vice-Pres. and mem. CCP Cttee of Shanghai Baosteel Group Corpn 1998–, Dir Baoshan Iron & Steel Co. Ltd 2000–01, Dir, Vice-Pres. and Standing mem. CCP Cttee of Shanghai Baosteel Group Corpn and Dir of Baoshan Iron & Steel Co. Ltd 2001–05, Vice-Pres. and Standing mem. CCP Cttee of Baosteel Group Corpn and Dir of Baoshan Iron & Steel Co. Ltd 2005–06, Standing mem. CCP Cttee of Baoshan Iron & Steel Co. Ltd 2006–08, Dir, Pres., Standing mem. CCP Cttee of Baosteel Group Corpn and Dir and Standing mem. CCP Cttee of Baoshan Iron & Steel Co. Ltd 2008–, Vice-Chair. Baoshan Iron & Steel Co. Ltd 2009–, Chair. and Sec. CCP Cttee of Baoshan Iron & Steel Co. Ltd 2010–. *Address:* Baosteel Group Corporation, Baosteel Tower, 370 Pudian Road, Shanghai 200122 (office); Office of the Board of Directors, Baoshan Iron & Steel Co. Ltd, Baosteel Administrative Centre, 885 Fujin Road, Baoshan District, Shanghai 201990, People's Republic of China. *Telephone:* (21) 58350000 (office); (21 26647000. *Fax:* (21) 68404832 (office); (21) 26646999. *E-mail:* info@baosteel.com (office); ir@baosteel.com. *Website:* www.baosteel.com (office).

HE, Xiangjian; Chinese business executive; *Chairman, Midea Investment Holding Co. Ltd;* b. 1941, Guangdong Prov.; m.; one s.; co-founded with 23 neighbours (fmr rice-farmers and fishermen) Beijiao Neighbourhood Plastic Production Team 1968 (renamed Midea 1981), Chair. and CEO Guangdong Midea Electric Appliances Co. Ltd 2001–12, currently Chair. Midea Investment Holding Co. Ltd. *Address:* Guangdong Midea Electric Appliances Co. Ltd, Midea Industrial City, Shunde District, Foshan 528311, Guangdong, People's Republic of China (office). *Telephone:* (757) 26338823 (office). *Fax:* (757) 26651991 (office). *E-mail:* inquiry@midea.com.cn (office). *Website:* www.midea.com.cn (office).

HE, Yong; Chinese politician; b. Oct. 1940, Qianxi Co., Hebei Prov.; ed Tianjin Univ.; joined CCP 1958; technician, Metering Office, No. 238 Factory 1968–70, Production Sec., Head Office 1970–75, Dir Political Dept 1975–78 (mem. Standing Cttee of CCP Party Cttee 1975–78), Dir No. 238 Factory 1978–83 (Deputy Sec. CCP Party Cttee 1978–83); Deputy Dir Office of Science, Tech. and Industry for Nat. Defence, Hubei Prov. 1983–85; Dir-Gen. Personnel Dept, Ministry of Ordinance Industry 1985–86; Deputy Head, Org. Dept of CCP Cen. Cttee 1986–87, Dir Bureau of Party and Govt Personnel Engaged in Foreign Affairs 1986–87; Vice-Minister of Supervision 1987–98, Minister 1998–2002; mem. Standing Cttee of 14th CCP Cen. Comm. for Discipline Inspection 1992–97, mem. 15th CCP Cen. Cttee 1997–2002 (Deputy Sec. Cen. Comm. for Discipline Inspection 1997–2002), 16th CCP Cen. Cttee 2002–07 (mem. Politburo Secr. 2002–07, Deputy Sec. Standing Cttee of Cen. Comm. for Discipline Inspection 2002–07); mem. 17th CCP Cen. Cttee 2007–, Deputy Sec. Cen. Comm. for Discipline Inspection 2007–. *Address:* c/o Zhongguo Gongchan Dang (Chinese Communist Party), Beijing, People's Republic of China.

HE, Zhenliang; Chinese government official (retd); b. 29 Dec. 1929, Zhejiang Prov.; m. 1953; one s. one d.; ed Aurora Univ., Shanghai; Sec.-Gen. Chinese Cttee 1982–86, Vice-Pres. 1986–89, Pres. 1989–94, Hon. Pres. 1994–; Dir Int. Liaison Dept, State Comm. of Physical Culture and Sports 1982–85, Vice Minister 1985–94; Vice-Pres. Int. Ass. for the Nat. Org. of Sports 1984; mem. IOC 1981–, Exec. Bd 1985–89, 1994–98, 1999–, Vice-Pres. 1989–93, Pres. Cultural Comm. 1995–99, Pres. Cultural and Olympic Education Comm. 2000–; Vice-Chair. All-China Sports Fed. 1986, Councillor 1997–; mem. CPPCC 1988–92, Standing Cttee of CPPCC 1993–98; Pres. Athletic Asscn of People's Repub. of China 1992–96, Rowing Asscn of People's Repub. of China 1986–, Rowing Fed. of Asia 1990–94. *Address:* 9 Tiyuguan Road, Beijing, People's Republic of China.

HE, Zhiqiang; Chinese government official and engineer; b. 1934, Lijiang Co., Yunnan Prov.; ed Chongqing Univ.; joined CCP 1956; Deputy Chief Engineer, Yunnan Prov. Geological Bureau 1979–83, Deputy Dir 1985; Vice-Gov. of Yunnan Prov. 1983–85, Gov. 1985–98; Deputy Sec., CCP 6th Yunnan Prov. Cttee 1995–; NPC Deputy for Yunnan Prov.; Alt. mem. 13th CCP Cen. Cttee 1987–92, mem. 14th CCP Cen. Cttee 1992–97; Del., 15th CCP Nat. Congress 1997–2002; mem. Standing Committee of 9th CPPCC 1998–2003; Chinese Population Prize 1996. *Address:* Yunnan Provincial Government, 5 Wuchua Shan Road, Kunming City, Yunnan Province, People's Republic of China.

HE, Zuoxiu; Chinese physicist; b. 27 July 1927, Shanghai; m. Qing Chengrui 1962; one s.; ed Shanghai Jiaotong Univ., Tsinghua Univ.; researcher, Beijing Modern Physics Inst. and Atomic Energy Inst., Academia Sinica 1951–80; Deputy Dir Theoretical Physics Inst., Academia Sinica 1978–84, mem. Dept of Math. and Physics, Academia Sinica 1980–; fmr mem. Standing Cttee CPPCC. *Publications:* A New Possible Quantum Field Theory of Composite Particles, (with Falung Gong), From Theory of Elementary Chi to Particle Physics, Wind Power – the most realistic and best choice for sustainable devt of China 2004; more than 200 published papers. *Address:* Theoretical Physics Institute, PO Box 2735, Beijing

100080, People's Republic of China (office). *Telephone:* (10) 62569352 (office). *Fax:* (10) 62562587 (office). *E-mail:* qcr@itp.ac.cn (office); lijing@itp.ac.cn. *Website:* itp.ac.cn.

HEAD, Tim David, BA; British artist; b. 22 Oct. 1946, London; s. of Percy Head and Muriel Head; m. Vivian Katz 1973; two d.; ed Dept of Fine Art, Univ. of Newcastle-upon-Tyne, St Martin's School of Art, London; Lecturer, Goldsmith's Coll. School of Art, London 1971–79; Lecturer, Slade School of Fine Art, Univ. Coll. London 1976–; Fellowship at Clare Hall and Kettle's Yard, Cambridge 1977–78; Gulbenkian Foundation Visual Arts Award 1975, First Prize, John Moores Liverpool Exhbn 15, Walker Art Gallery, Liverpool 1987, Wellcome Trust Artist's Residency, Dept of Biochemistry, Oxford Univ. 2006–07. *Commissions:* Sculpture, Nat. Museum of Photography, Film and TV, Bradford, Yorks. 1985, Floor Design, Science Museum, London 1995 Installation, Chatham Historic Dockyard, Rochester, Kent, Sculpture, Dance Performance with Laurie Booth Co. 1997–98, Light Rain, Artezium Arts and Media Centre, Luton 1998, A Hard Day's Night (CD ROM) 2000 www.eyestorm.com; Artistic Dir Eurythmics Peace Tour 1999. *Address:* c/o The Slade School of Fine Art UCL, Gower Street, London WC1E 6BT, England. *E-mail:* info@timhead.net (home). *Website:* www.timhead.net (home).

HEAL, (Barbara) Jane, PhD, FBA; British academic; *Professor Emerita and Fellow, St John's College, University of Cambridge;* b. 21 Oct. 1946, Oxford; d. of William Calvert Kneale and Martha Kneale (née Hurst); m. John Gauntlett Benedict Heal 1968 (divorced 1987); one s. one d.; ed Oxford High School for Girls, New Hall, Cambridge; Research Fellow, Newnham Coll., Cambridge 1971–74; Harkness Fellow of the Commonwealth Fund, Visiting Fellow, Princeton Univ. and Univ. of Calif., Berkeley, USA 1974–76; Lecturer in Philosophy, Univ. of Newcastle upon Tyne 1976–86, Univ. of Cambridge 1986–96, Reader in Philosophy 1996–99, Prof. 1999, now Prof. Emer. and Fellow, St John's Coll., Pres. St John's Coll. 1999–2003; mem. Aristotelian Soc., Pres. 2001–02. *Publications include:* Fact and Meaning 1989, Mind, Reason and Imagination 2003. *Address:* St John's College, Cambridge, CB2 1TP, England (office). *Telephone:* (1223) 338668 (office); (1223) 314317 (home). *E-mail:* jane.heal@phil.cam.ac.uk (office). *Website:* www.phil.cam.ac.uk (office).

HEALD, Rt Hon. Oliver, PC; British barrister and politician; *Solicitor General for England and Wales;* b. 15 Dec. 1954, Reading, Berks.; m. Christine Whittle; one s. two d.; ed Reading School, Pembroke Coll., Cambridge; called to the Bar, Middle Temple 1977; practising barrister in London and East Anglia 1979–95; contested Southwark and Bermondsey constituency in Gen. Election 1987; MP for North Hertfordshire 1992–97, for North East Hertfordshire 1997–2010, for North East Hertfordshire (revised boundary) 2010–, mem. Select Cttees: Administration 1998–2000, Modernization of the House of Commons 2003–05, Work and Pensions 2007–12, Selection 2009–10, Standards and Privileges 2010–12, Ecclesiastical Cttee 2010–12, Jt Cttee on the Draft House of Lords Reform Bill 2011–12; Parl. Pvt. Sec. to Sir Peter Lloyd as Minister of State, Home Office 1994, to William Waldegrave as Minister of Agric., Fisheries and Food 1994–95; sponsored Pvt. Mem.'s Bill Insurance Companies (Reserves) Act 1995; Parl. Under-Sec. of State, Dept of Social Security 1995–97; Opposition Whip 1997–2000; Opposition Spokesperson for Home Affairs 2000–01, for Health 2001–02; Shadow Minister for Work and Pensions 2002–03; Shadow Leader of the House 2003–05; mem. House of Commons' Comm. 2003–05; Shadow Sec. of State for Constitutional Affairs 2004–07; Shadow Chancellor of the Duchy of Lancaster 2005–07; Solicitor Gen. for England and Wales 2012–; Chair. North Hertfordshire Conservative Asscn 1984–86; mem. Southwark and Bermondsey Conservative Asscn, Pres. 1993–98, Patron 1998–; Chair. Exec. Soc. of Conservative Lawyers 2008–12, Exec. Parl. Resources Unit; mem. Cttee on Standards in Public Life 2008–; mem. Council of Europe 2008–; Conservative. *Address:* Solicitor General's Office, 20 Victoria Street, London, SW1H 0NF (office); House of Commons, Westminster, London, SW1A 0AA, England (office). *Telephone:* (20) 7271-2406 (Solicitor Gen.'s Office) (office); (20) 7219-6354 (Westminster) (office). *Fax:* (20) 7271-2429 (Solicitor Gen.'s Office) (office). *E-mail:* oliver.heald@attorneygeneral.gsi.gov.uk (office); oliver.heald.mp@parliament.uk (office). *Website:* www.oliverhealdmp.com.

HEALEY, Baron (Life Peer), cr. 1992, of Riddlesden in the County of West Yorkshire; **Denis Winston Healey,** PC, CH, MBE, FRSL, MA, DPhil; British politician; b. 30 Aug. 1917, Mottingham; s. of William Healey; m. Edna May Edmunds 1945 (died 2010); one s. two d.; ed Bradford Grammar School and Balliol Coll., Oxford; Maj., Royal Engineers 1945; Sec. Labour Party Int. Dept 1945–52; MP 1952–92; Sec. of State for Defence 1964–70; Chancellor of the Exchequer 1974–79; Opposition Spokesman for Treasury and Econ. Affairs 1979–80, for Foreign and Commonwealth Affairs 1980–87; Chair. Interim Ministerial Cttee of IMF 1977–79; Deputy Leader of Labour Party 1980–83; Pres. Birkbeck Coll. London 1993–99, Corelli Ensemble 2011; Hon. Fellow, Balliol Coll. Oxford 1980; Freeman of Leeds 1991; Grand Cross of Order of Merit (FRG) 1979; Hon. DLitt (Bradford) 1983; Hon. LLD, (Sussex) 1989, (Leeds) 1991. *Publications:* The Curtain Falls 1951, New Fabian Essays 1952, Neutralism 1955, Fabian International Essays 1956, A Neutral Belt in Europe 1958, NATO and American Security 1959, The Race Against the H Bomb 1960, Labour Britain and the World 1963, Healey's Eye (photographs) 1980, Labour and a World Society 1985, Beyond Nuclear Deterrence 1986, The Time of My Life (autobiog.) 1989, When Shrimps Learn to Whistle (collection of essays) 1990, My Secret Planet 1992, Denis Healey's Yorkshire Dales 1995, Healey's World (photographs) 2002. *Leisure interests:* music, painting, literature, photography. *Address:* House of Lords, Westminster, London, SW1A 0PW, England (office). *Telephone:* (20) 7219-3546 (office); (1323) 870028 (home).

HEALEY, Rt Hon. John, PC, BA; British politician; b. 13 Feb. 1960, Wakefield, West Yorks., England; m. Jackie Bate 1993; one s.; ed Lady Lumley's Comprehensive School, Pickering, St Peter's School, York, Christ's Coll., Cambridge; worked in voluntary sector at MIND, Royal Nat. Inst. for the Deaf, Royal Asscn for Disability and Rehabilitation 1984–90; journalist, house magazines (public relations co.) 1990–92; Head of Communications, MSF (trade union) 1992–94; Campaigns Dir TUC 1994–97; fmr part-time tutor, Open Univ. Business School; MP (Labour) for Wentworth 1997–2010, for Wentworth and Dearne 2010–, mem. Employment Select Cttee, Parl. Pvt. Sec. to Chancellor of the Exchequer, Parl. Under-Sec. of State for Adults Skills, Dept for Educ. and Skills, Financial Sec. to Treasury 2005–07, Local Govt Minister, Dept for Communities and Local Govt 2007–09, Minister of State for Housing and Planning 2009–10; Shadow Minister for Housing May–Oct. 2010, Shadow Sec. of State for Health Oct. 2010–11; Vice-Pres. Local Govt Asscn 2010–11. *Address:* House of Commons, London, SW1A 0AA (office); Wentworth and Dearne Parliamentary Office, 79 High Street, Wath upon Dearne, Rotherham, S63 7QB, England. *Telephone:* (1709) 875943 (Rotherham). *Fax:* (1709) 874207 (Rotherham). *E-mail:* john.healey.mp@parliament.uk (office); hartleyi@parliament.uk (office). *Website:* www.parliament.uk/biographies/commons/john-healey/25567 (office); www.johnhealeymp.co.uk (office).

HEALEY, Melanie L., BS; American business executive; *Group President, North America and Global Hyper-Super-Mass Channel, Procter & Gamble Company;* b. 5 April 1961, Rio de Janeiro, Brazil; m.; two c.; ed Univ. of Richmond, Va; Asst Brand Man. S.C. Johnson & Sons 1983–86, Brand Man. and Marketing Man. Johnson & Johnson 1987–90; Brand Man. for Phebo Soap, Procter & Gamble, Brazil 1990–92, Marketing Man. for Pampers 1992–93, for Personal Cleansing and Fabric Softeners, Procter & Gamble, Mexico 1993–95, Marketing Dir for Health Care, Procter & Gamble, Brazil 1995–97, for Health and Hair Care 1997–98, Feminine Care 1998, Gen. Man. Feminine Care Latin America 1998–2001, Feminine Care N America 2001, Vice-Pres. and Gen. Man. 2001–05, Pres. Global Feminine Care 2005–06, Global Feminine Care and Adult Care 2006–07, Group Pres. Global Feminine and Health Care 2007–09, Group Pres., North America 2009–11, Group Pres., North America and Global Hyper-Super-Mass Channel 2011–, fmr Chair. P&G Fine Arts Fund Corp. Campaign; mem. Bd of Dirs Verizon Communications Inc.; fmr mem. Bd of Dirs Bacardi Ltd; mem. Bd Grocery Mfrs Asscn, Cincinnati-Northern Kentucky Int. Airport; mem. Bd of Trustees Univ. of Richmond; mem. Women's Capital Club of Cincinnati; Founding mem. Women's Leadership Initiative, United Way of Greater Cincinnati, Cincinnati Women's Exec Forum; fmr mem. Bd of Dirs Fine Arts Fund of Greater Cincinnati, Univ. of Richmond Alumni Asscn; YWCA Career Woman of Achievement Award 2007, ranked by Fortune magazine amongst the 50 Most Powerful Women in Business in the US (45th) 2007, (37th) 2008, (15th) 2009, (13th) 2010–11, (11th) 2012, named in The Wall Street Journal's 50 Women to Watch list 2007, named in Advertising Age's Women to Watch list 2008, ranked by Forbes magazine amongst The World's 100 Most Powerful Women (84th) 2009. *Address:* Procter & Gamble Co., 1 Procter & Gamble Plaza, Cincinnati, OH 45202, USA (office). *Telephone:* (513) 983-1100 (office). *Website:* www.pg.com (office).

HEALY, Thomas William, AO, MSc, PhD, FAA; Australian chemist and academic; *Professor Emeritus, Particulate Fluids Processing Centre, Department of Chemical and Biomolecular Engineering, University of Melbourne;* b. 1 June 1937; s. of W. T. Healy and C. M. Healy; m. Beverley Healy 1960; four s.; ed St Kilda, Univ. of Melbourne and Columbia Univ., New York, USA; Lecturer in Materials Science, Univ. of California, Berkeley 1963–65, Visiting Assoc. Prof. 1970; Queen Elizabeth II Fellow, Univ. of Melbourne 1965–67, Sr Lecturer in Physical Chem. 1967–75, Reader 1976–77, Prof. 1977–98, Prof. Emer. 1998–, Professorial Fellow 1999–, Deputy Chair. School of Chem. 1979–81, Assoc. Dean (Research and Grad. Studies), Faculty of Science 1983–84, Dean 1985–90, mem. Council Univ. of Melbourne 1985–88, Dir Advanced Mineral Products Special Research Centre 1991–99, Vice-Pres. Academic Bd 1994–96, Pres. and Pro-Vice-Chancellor 1997–98, Deputy Dir Particulate Fluids Processing Centre (ARC), Dept of Chemical and Biomolecular Eng 2000–04 (Chair. Scientific Bd 2005), mem. Bd Ian Potter Museum of Art 2004; Sr Visiting Research Fellow, Univ. of Bristol, UK 1975; Visiting Sr Research Scientist, ICI Corp. Colloid Group, Runcorn, Cheshire, UK 1981; Fulbright Sr Scholar, Inst. of Colloid and Surface Science, Clarkson Univ., Potsdam, NY, USA 1981; Visiting Prof., Columbia Univ., New York 2001; mem. Council Australian Research Council (ARC) 1993–, Chair. Institutional Grants Cttee 1995–96, mem. Planning and Review Cttee ARC-ANU Review of the Inst. of Advanced Studies 1994–95, Research Grants Appeals Cttee 1998–2004; Vice-Pres. Victorian Br. Royal Australian Chemical Inst. (RACI) 1983, Pres. 1984, mem. Cttee 1972–74, 1976, 1982–85, mem. Exec. Council RACI 1984; Deputy Chair. Victorian Univs and Schools Examination Bd Science Standing Cttee 1977–79, Course Advisory Cttee, Bendigo, Victorian Inst. of Colls of Advanced Educ.; mem. numerous review bds; Dir UniMelb Ltd 1990–92; part-time consultant to Geopeko Pty Ltd, Australia Mt Morgan Mines Pty Ltd, Australia Peko Wallsend Pty Ltd, BHP Co. Ltd Australia, Monier Ltd, ICI (Australia) Ltd, Tioxide (Australia) Pty Ltd, Burnie, Tasmania and Tioxide International Ltd, Teeside, UK, ICI UK Ltd, ICI Glidden Paints USA, Orica Pty Ltd, Lachlan Resources Pty Ltd NSW, Davies Ryan & De Boos, Corr Pavey Whiting & Byrne, Kitchener Mines Pty Ltd, Supreme Court of NSW, Mallesons, Brisbane, Sienna, NSW; Gov. Ian Potter Foundation 1990–; Chair. Australian Landscape Trust 1995–; mem. Australasian Inst. of Mining and Metallurgy, Royal Soc. of Chem. (Faraday Div.), Soc. of Sigma XI, Council Victorian Inst. of Marine Sciences 1986; mem. and Founding Cttee mem. Int. Asscn of Colloid and Interface Scientists 1979–, Div. of Colloid and Surface Chem., Chemical Soc. of Japan; mem. Editorial Advisory Bd Journal of Colloid and Interface Science 1969–74, Advances in Colloid and Interface Science 1975–; Founding Ed. and Regional Ed. Colloids and Surfaces 1979–83, mem. Editorial Advisory Bd 1979–; mem. Editorial Bd Langmuir 1987–96, Current Opinion in Colloid and Interface Science 1995–; Fellow, Australian Acad. of Science 1975, RACI 1975, Australian Acad. of Technological Sciences and Eng; Foreign Assoc., US Nat. Acad. of Eng 2008; Hon. DSc (Melbourne) 1999; ACS Certificate of Merit 1967, RACI Rennie Medal 1968, Grimwade Prize, Univ. of Melbourne 1974, RACI Hartung Youth Lecturer 1979, Chemical Soc. (London) Lecturer 1980, Freundlich Centennial Lecturer, ACS 55th Colloid Symposium 1981, Liversidge Lecturer, Australia and NZ Asscn for the Advancement of Science Festival of Science 1985, RACI-ICI (Australia) Inaugural Bicentennial Lectureship 1988, Plenary Lecturer, Papua New Guinea Inst. of Chem., Fifth Congress 1988, Plenary Lecturer IACIS Conf., Hakone, Japan 1989, Plenary Lecturer, R.K. Her Symposium, ACS, Washington DC 1990, A.E. Alexander Lectureship, RACI and Univ. of Sydney 1991, Royal Soc. of Vic. Medallist 1992, Plenary Lecturer XVIth Int. Minerals Processing Congress, Sydney 1993, Plenary and Foreign Guest Lecturer, 46th Nat. Colloid Symposium, Japanese Chemical Soc., Tokyo, Japan 1993, Plenary and Foreign Guest Lecturer, Mineral Processing: Recent Advances and Future Trends, Kanpur, India 1995, Plenary and Foreign Guest Lecturer, NEPTIS-5 Conf., Kyoto, Japan 1996, Plenary and Foreign Guest Lecturer, 5 Australian Japan Symposia on Colloid and Surface Chem., Fukuoka,

Japan 1998, Ian Wark Medal and Lecture, Australian Acad. of Science 1999, T.G.H. Jones Memorial Lecturer, Univ. of Queensland 2001, T.H. Healy Award est. by School of Chem., Univ. of Melbourne to commemorate his distinguished career 2002, Impact Faraday Partnership Annual Lecture, Royal Chemical Inst. of GB 2003, Australian Centenary Medal 2003, RACI 40 Year Membership Award 2003, Sr Australian of the Year (Victorian Finalist) 2004, Australasian Inst. of Mining and Metallurgy 40 Year Membership Award 2005, Sir Eric Rideal Medal, RSC-UK Soc. of Chemical Industry Jt Award 2010. *Publications:* more than 200 research papers in physical chem., colloid and surface science, process eng and mineral processing. *Leisure interests:* sailing, golf, reading. *Address:* Particulate Fluids Processing Centre, Department of Chemical and Biomolecular Engineering, University of Melbourne, Melbourne, Vic. 3010 (office); 473 Dryburgh Street, North Melbourne, Vic. 3051, Australia (home). *Telephone:* (3) 8344-6481 (office); (3) 9078-2160 (home). *Fax:* (3) 8344-6233 (office). *E-mail:* tomhealy@unimelb.edu.au (office). *Website:* www.pfpc.unimelb.edu.au (office).

HEALY, Tom; Irish stock exchange executive; *CEO, Abu Dhabi Securities Exchange;* ed Trinity Coll., Dublin; early career with Export Board and Industrial Devt Agency; Chief Exec. Irish Stock Exchange 1987–2007 (retd), oversaw Irish Stock Exchange's demerger from London Stock Exchange 1995; CEO Abu Dhabi Securities Exchange 2007–; int. consultancy and advisory assignments included IBRD, EU, USAID; active involvement with World Fed. of Exchanges and Fed. of European Securities Exchanges; mem. Securities Inst., UK. *Address:* Abu Dhabi Securities Exchange, Al Ghaith Tower, Hamdan Street, POB 54500, Abu Dhabi, United Arab Emirates (office). *Telephone:* (2) 627-7777 (office). *Fax:* (2) 627-0300 (office). *E-mail:* thealy@adsm.ae (office). *Website:* www.adsm.ae (office).

HEAP, Sir Robert Brian, Kt, KBE, CBE, BSc, MA, PhD, ScD, FRS, CChem, FRSC, FSB; British research scientist and academic; *Research Associate, Centre of Development Studies, University of Cambridge;* b. 27 Feb. 1935, Derbyshire, England; s. of the late Bertram Heap and Eva M. Melling; m. Marion P. Grant 1961; two s. one d.; ed New Mills Grammar School, Univ. of Nottingham and King's Coll., Cambridge; Univ. Demonstrator, Cambridge 1960; Lalor Research Fellow, ARC Babraham, Cambridge, staff mem. 1964, Head, Dept of Physiology 1976, Head Cambridge Research Station 1986; Dir of Research, Agricultural and Food Research Council Inst. of Animal Physiology and Genetics Research, Cambridge and Edinburgh 1989–93, Dir of Science, Biotechnology and Biological Sciences Research Council 1991–94, Dir of Research, Babraham Inst. 1993–94; UK Rep., NATO Science Cttee, Brussels 1997–2005; Visiting Prof., Univ. of Nairobi 1974; Visiting Research Fellow, Murdoch Univ. 1976; Special Prof., Univ. of Nottingham 1988–2008; Visiting Prof., Univ. of Guelph, Canada 1990; Visiting Sr Fellow, School of Clinical Medicine, Univ. of Cambridge 1994–2002, Babraham Inst. 1995; Master St Edmund's Coll., Cambridge 1996–2004; Research Assoc., Centre of Devt Studies, Univ. of Cambridge 2013–; fmr Ed. Philosophical Transactions of the Royal Society, Series B; Pres. Inst. of Biology 1996–98, Int. Soc. of Science and Religion 2006–08; Pres. European Acads Science Advisory Council 2010–13; Chair. Trustees Academia Europaea; mem. Council Royal Soc. 1994–2001 (Foreign Sec. and Vice-Pres. 1996–2001), Nuffield Council on Bioethics 1997–2001; Fellow, Soc. of Biology; other professional appointments and distinctions; Hon. FZS; Hon. Fellow, Royal Agricultural Soc. of England 1995, Templeton-Green Coll. Oxford, St Edmund's Coll. Cambridge, Korean Acad. of Science; Hon. DSc (Nottingham) 1994, (St Andrews) 2007; Hon. DUniv (York) 2001. *Publications:* papers on reproductive biology, endocrinology, growth, lactation, science policy and biotechnology in biological and medical journals. *Leisure interests:* music, walking, travel. *Address:* St Edmund's College, Cambridge, CB3 0BN (office); Lincoln House, 8 Fendon Road, Cambridge, CB1 7RT, England (home). *Telephone:* (1223) 248509 (home). *E-mail:* rbh22@cam.ac.uk (office). *Website:* www.b4fa.org (office).

HEARN, Loyola; Canadian politician and diplomatist; *Ambassador to Ireland;* b. Renews, Newfoundland; m. Maureen Hearn; one s. one d.; ed Memorial Univ., Univ. of New Brunswick; elected mem. Newfoundland House of Ass. for St Mary's the Capes, Newfoundland 1982–93; Minister of Educ. for Newfoundland and Labrador 1985–89; left politics and returned to teaching in Renews 1993–2000; MP 2000–08 (re-elected for new riding of St John's South-Mount Pearl 2004), House Leader for Progressive Conservative Party (later first House Leader for new Conservative Party of Canada following merger with Canadian Alliance parties), also held several critic roles, including lead critic for Fisheries and Oceans; Minister of Fisheries and Oceans and Regional Minister for Newfoundland and Labrador 2006–08; Ambassador to Ireland 2010–. *Address:* Embassy of Canada, 7–8 Wilton Terrace, 3rd Floor, Dublin 2, Ireland (office). *Telephone:* (1) 2344000 (office). *Fax:* (1) 2344001 (office). *E-mail:* dubln@international.gc.ca (office). *Website:* www.canadainternational.gc.ca/ireland-irlande (office).

HEARNE, Sir Graham James, Kt, CBE; British business executive and solicitor; *Chairman, Catlin Group Limited;* b. 23 Nov. 1937, Birmingham; s. of Frank Hearne and Emily Hearne (née Shakespeare); m. Carol Jean Brown 1961; one s. three d.; ed George Dixon Grammar School, Birmingham; admitted solicitor 1959; with Pinsent & Co. Solicitors 1959–63, Fried, Frank, Harris, Shriver & Jacobson Attorneys, New York 1963–66, Herbert Smith & Co., Solicitors 1966–67, Industrial Reorganization Corpn 1967–68, N. M. Rothschild & Sons Ltd 1968–77; Finance Dir Courtaulds Ltd 1977–81; Chief Exec. Tricentrol 1981–83; Group Man. Dir Carless, Capel & Leonard 1983–84; Chair. Catlin Group Ltd 2003–; Chair. Braemar Seascope Group PLC; Deputy Chair. Gallaher Group PLC; Chief Exec. Enterprise Oil PLC 1984–91, Chair. 1991–2002; mem. Bd of Dirs N. M. Rothschild & Sons Ltd, Courtaulds PLC 1991–98, Invensys (fmrly BTR) PLC 1998–2003, Novar (fmrly Caradon) PLC 1999–2005, Rowan Companies Inc. 2004–, Stratic Energy Corpn 2005–; High Sheriff of Greater London 1995–96. *Address:* Catlin Group Limited, 3 Minster Court, Mincing Lane, London, EC3R 7DD, England (office). *Telephone:* (20) 7626-0486 (office). *Fax:* (20) 7623-9101 (office). *E-mail:* catlininfo@catlin.com (office). *Website:* www.catlin.com (office).

HEARNS, Thomas; American fmr professional boxer; b. 18 Oct. 1958, Grand Junction, Tenn.; m. Rena Hearns; four c.; as amateur won 147 of 155 fights, Amateur Athletic Union (AAU) national and Golden Gloves 147–pound championships 1977; turned professional Nov. 1977 winning 28 straight fights before winning World Boxing Assn (WBA) welterweight championship knocking out Pepino Cuevas 1980; lost title on technical knockout to Sugar Ray Leonard 1981; won World Boxing Council (WBC) super welterweight championship beating

Wilfred Benitez 1982, beat Roberto Duran to win WBA version 1984; as middleweight lost to Marvelous Marvin Hagler for world middleweight championship 1985; won WBC world light-heavyweight championship from Dennis Andries and WBC middleweight championship beating Juan Roldan 1987; won World Boxing Org. (WBO) super-middleweight championship by beating James Kinchen 1988; rematch with Leonard ending in draw 1989; won WBA light-heavyweight championship 1991, lost it to Ivan Barkley 1992; won North American Boxing Fed. (NABF) cruiserweight title 1995, won Int. Boxing Org. (IBO) version 1999, lost IBO title to Uriah Grant 2000; in professional career won 59 of 64 fights (46 by knockout) with one draw. *Television include:* Who's the Boss? 1987. *Address:* 19244 Bretton Drive, Detroit, MI 48223, USA. *Website:* www .tommyhearns.com.

HEARST, George Randolph, Jr; American communications industry executive; *Chairman, The Hearst Corporation;* b. 13 July 1927, San Francisco; s. of George Randolph Hearst and Blanche Wilbur; m. 1st Mary Thompson 1951 (died 1969); two s. two d.; m. 2nd Patricia Ann Bell 1969 (divorced 1985); mem. staff, Los Angeles Examiner newspaper 1948–50, San Francisco Examiner 1954–56, Los Angeles Evening Herald-Express 1956 (Business Man. 1957, Publr 1960); Publr Los Angeles Herald-Examiner 1962; Vice-Pres. The Hearst Corpn 1977–96, Chair. 1996–; Pres. The Hearst Foundation; Dir William Randolph Hearst Foundation. *Address:* The Hearst Corporation, 959 8th Avenue, New York, NY 10019, USA (office). *Telephone:* (212) 649-2148 (office). *Fax:* (212) 649-2108 (office). *Website:* www.hearstcorp.com (office).

HEATHER-LATU, Brenda Patricia, LLB, BA; Samoan/New Zealand barrister and solicitor; *Partner, Latu Lawyers, Barristers & Solicitors;* b. 23 Dec. 1961, Wellington, New Zealand; d. of Cuthbert Stanley Heather and Winnie Anesi Heather; m. George Latu; one s. one d.; ed Wellington Girls Coll., Victoria Univ. of Wellington; solicitor, Ministry of Educ., New Zealand 1987–88; Asst Crown Counsel, Crown Law Office, Wellington, New Zealand 1988–91, Crown Counsel 1991–96; Prin. State Solicitor, Office of the Attorney-Gen., Apia, Samoa 1996–97; Attorney-Gen. of Samoa 1997–2006; currently Partner, Latu Lawyers, Barristers & Solicitors, Apia Samoa. *Publications include:* Pacific Islands AIDS Trust Education Prevention Programme 1993. *Leisure interests:* Samoan culture and traditions, pacific migration, geneology. *Address:* Latu Lawyers, Barristers & Solicitors, Ground Floor, ANZ House, PO Box 3619, Apia, Samoa (office). *Telephone:* 30364 (office). *Fax:* 30365 (office). *E-mail:* heather-latu@latulaw.com (office); latu@latulaw.com (office).

HEATON, Brian Thomas, DPhil, DSc, CChem, FRSC; British chemist and academic; *Professor Emeritus, University of Liverpool;* b. 16 Feb. 1940, Broughton-in-Furness, Cumbria, England; s. of William Edwin Heaton and Mabel Heaton (née Benson); m. Wendy Janet Durrant 1964; three d.; ed Ulverston Grammar School, Hatfield Polytechnic, Univ. of Sussex; Lecturer in Chem., Univ. of Kent at Canterbury 1968–81, Sr Lecturer 1981–84, Reader 1984, Prof. 1984–85; Grant Prof. of Inorganic Chem., Univ. of Liverpool 1985–2004, Prof. Emer. 2005–, Head of Dept of Chem. 1988–97; Chair. SERC Inorganic Cttee 1990–93; Sec. and Treas. Dalton Div., RSC 1990–93; Leverhulme Foundation Research Fellowship 1997; Visiting Prof., Univ. Louis Pasteur, Strasbourg 2001, Univ. of Heidelberg, Germany 2003, Inst. of Chemical and Eng Sciences, Singapore 2007–10, Nat. Univ. of Singapore 2008; Nuffield Foundation Research Fellowship 1981–82, RSC Tilden Lectureship and Prize 1986, Japanese Soc. for Promotion of Science Fellowship 1989, First Prize, Dept of Trade and Industry 1996, Leverhulme Foundation Research Fellowship 1997–98, RSC Award for research on platinum metals 2002. *Publications:* several books, including Mechanisms in Homogeneous Catalysis (ed.) 2005; numerous articles in professional journals. *Leisure interests:* rugby, walking, listening to and playing music, eating and drinking (especially wine). *Address:* Department of Chemistry, University of Liverpool, PO Box 147, Liverpool, L69 7ZD (office); 44 Graham Road, West Kirby, CH48 5DW, England (home). *Telephone:* (151) 632-3206. *E-mail:* bth@liv.ac.uk (office). *Website:* www.liv .ac.uk/chemistry (office).

HEATON, Frances Anne, BA, LLB; British barrister and financial services industry executive; *Chairman, Schroders Pension Trustee Limited;* b. (Frances Anne Whidborne), 11 Aug. 1944, Winchester, Hants., England; d. of John Ferris Whidborne and Marjorie Annie Maltby; m. Martin Heaton 1969; two s.; ed Trinity Coll., Dublin; with Dept of Econ. Affairs 1967–70; joined HM Treasury 1970, Asst Sec. 1979–80; seconded to S. G. Warburg & Co. Ltd 1977–79; with Corp. Finance Div., Lazard Bros & Co. Ltd 1980–2001, Exec. Dir 1987–2001, Chair. Lazard London Dirs' Pension Scheme 2006–; Chair. Schroders Pension Trustee Ltd 2008–; Dir (non-exec.) W.S. Atkins PLC 1990–2003 (Deputy Chair. (non-exec.)) 1996–2003, BUPA 1998–2001, World Pay Group PLC 2000, Fountain GB Ltd 2001, Legal & General Group plc 2001–10, AWG PLC 2002–07, Jupiter Primadona Growth Trust 2005–, BMT Ltd 2007–, Bank of England 1993–2001; Dir Gen. Take-overs and Mergers Panel 1992–94; mem. Cttee on Standards in Public Life 1997–2005. *Leisure interests:* bridge, gardening, riding. *Address:* Tagents Farm, Graffham, Petworth, West Sussex, GU28 0NL. *Telephone:* (1798) 867282. *E-mail:* fah@carillon.co.uk (office).

HEBEISH, Ali Ali, DSc, PhD; Egyptian chemist and academic; *Professor Emeritus, National Research Centre, Cairo;* b. 21 Dec. 1936, Mehalla El-Kubra, Gharbia; m.; two c.; ed Cairo Univ., Gujarat Univ.; Research Fellow Nat. Research Centre, Cairo 1960–61, other research positions 1962–74, Assoc. Prof. 1974–79, Prof. 1979–84, Prof. Emer. 1996–; Under-Sec. of State Office of the Pres., Acad. of Scientific Research and Tech., Cairo 1985–88, Vice-Pres. 1988–91, Pres. 1992–96; Pres. Egyptian Asscn for Scientific Culture 1993–, Egyptian Textile Soc. 1993–; Chair. Egyptian Syndicate for Science Profs 1994–2011; Vice-Pres. Egyptian Science Union; Fellow, Alexander von Humboldt Foundation 1973–75, African Acad. of Sciences, Third World Acad. of Sciences, Islamic Acad. of Sciences; mem. Research and Devt Council; mem. Bd Egyptian Acad. of Science; mem. IFSTAD Council 1992–96; mem. Acad. of Sciences for Developing World's Arab Regional Office; Order of Science and Art, First Class 1974, Order of the Repub. Second Class 1983; Dr hc (Leberec) 1995; State Prize for Chem. 1972, Production Prize 1985, 1990, TWNSO First Prize in Tech. 1990, State Merit Prize 1995, The Nile Prize 2004. *Achievements include:* holds 13 patents. *Publications:* over 580 publs. *Address:* 26 El-Basra Street, Mohandseen, Dokki, Cairo (home); National

Research Centre, Tahrir Street, Dokki, Giza, Egypt. *Telephone:* 3357807 (office); 37499125 (home). *Fax:* 33363261 (office). *E-mail:* alihebeish@hotmail.com (office).

HECHE, Anne; American actress; b. 25 May 1969, Aurora, Ohio; d. of Donald Heche and Nancy Heche; m. Coleman Laffoon 2001; one s. *Films include:* An Ambush of Ghosts 1993, The Adventures of Huck Finn 1993, A Simple Twist of Fate 1994, Milk Money 1994, I'll Do Anything 1994, The Wild Side 1995, Pie in the Sky 1995, The Juror 1996, Walking and Talking 1996, Donnie Brasco 1997, Volcano 1997, Subway Stories, Wag the Dog 1997, Six Days Seven Nights 1998, A Cool Dry Place 1998, Psycho 1998, The Third Miracle 1999, Auggie Rose 2001, John Q 2002, Prozac Nation 2003, Birth 2004, Sexual Life 2005, Suffering Man's Charity 2006, Toxic Skies 2008, The Other Guys 2010, Cedar Rapids 2011, That's What She Said 2012. *Television includes:* (series) Another World; (films) O Pioneers! 1992, Against the Wall 1994, Girls in Prison 1994, Kingfish: A Story of Huey P. Long 1995, If These Walls Could Talk 1996, If These Walls Could Talk 2 (dir and screenwriter), One Kill 2000, Gracie's Choice 2004, The Dead Will Tell 2004, True 2005, Everwood (series) 2004–05, Silver Bells 2005, Fatal Desire 2006, Men in Trees (series) 2006–07, Hung 2009–10, Blackout 2012. *Publication:* Call Me Crazy: A Memoir 2001. *Address:* c/o United Talent Agency 9560 Wilshire Blvd, Beverly Hills, CA 90212, USA (office). *Website:* www.anneheche.com.

HECHTER, Daniel; French couturier; b. 30 July 1938, Paris; s. of Raymond Hechter and Rosy Mendelsohn; m. 1st Marika Stengl Diez Deaux (deceased); one d.; m. 2nd Jennifer Chambon 1973; ed Lycées Voltaire and Chaptal, Paris; designer 1954–; designer House of Pierre d'Alby 1959–62; first women's collection 1962, first men's collection 1968, first perfume line 1989; sold label to Miltenberger Otto Aulbach 1999; founder and Dir-Gen. Vêtements Hechter 1962–; Pres. Fed. Française du Pret-à-Porter Féminin 1984–87; Pres. Festival de la Mode 1987; Pres. Strasbourg Racing Club 1987; fmr Vice-Pres. Etoile-Carouge football club; co-founder Paris Saint-Germain football club; inventor of Pret-a-Porter or ready-to-wear fashion. *Publications:* Le Boss 2000. *Leisure interests:* football, tennis, swimming, skiing, curling, golf. *Address:* SMB SA, rue de Maurapans, BP 87504, 25075 Besançon, Cedex 09, France. *Website:* www.daniel-hechter.com.

HECK, Richard Fred, BS, PhD; American chemist and academic; *Willis F. Harrington Professor Emeritus, University of Delaware;* b. 15 Aug. 1931, Springfield, Mass; ed Univ. of California, Los Angeles; two periods of postdoctoral research at ETH, Zurich, Switzerland, then at UCLA; took position with Hercules Corpn, Wilmington, Del. 1957; Prof. of Chem., Dept of Chem. and Biochemistry, Univ. of Delaware 1971–89 (retd), remains Willis F. Harrington Prof. Emer.; annual lectureship at Univ. of Delaware named in his honour 2004, Wallace H. Carothers Award 2005, Herbert C. Brown Award for Creative Research in Synthetic Methods 2006, Nobel Prize in Chem. (jtly with Ei-ichi Negishi and Akira Suzuki) "for palladium-catalyzed cross couplings in organic synthesis" 2010. *Achievements include:* best known for the Heck Reaction (sometimes called the Mizoroki-Heck Reaction) developed during the 1960s and 1970s, which uses the metal palladium to catalyse organic chemical reactions that couple aryl halides with alkenes and is widely used for the creation of carbon–carbon bonds in the synthesis of organic chemicals. *Publications:* numerous papers in scientific journals. *Address:* Department of Chemistry and Biochemistry, University of Delaware, Newark, DE 19716, USA (office). *Telephone:* (302) 831-1247 (office). *Fax:* (302) 831-6335 (office). *E-mail:* 03267@udel.edu (office). *Website:* www.udel.edu/nobelprize/#2010 (office).

HECKER, Zvi, BArch; Israeli architect; b. 31 May 1931, Kraków, Poland; m. Deborah Houchman 1957; one s. one d.; ed Kraków Polytechnic School of Architecture, Israel Inst. of Tech., Haifa and Avni Acad., Tel-Aviv; worked in office of Arieh Sharon and Benjamin Idelson, Tel-Aviv 1957–58; in partnership with Eldar Sharon, Tel-Aviv 1959–65, with Alfred Neumann, Tel-Aviv 1960–68; Visiting Prof., Laval Univ., Québec, Canada 1968–69, Adjunct Prof. 1969–72; Visiting Lecturer, McGill Univ., Montreal and Univ. of Pennsylvania 1969–72; pvt. practice, Tel-Aviv 1972–, Berlin 1991–; work includes housing projects, synagogues, public bldgs etc.. *Publications:* exhbn catalogues, articles in professional journals. *Address:* Oranienburger Straße 41, 10117 Berlin, Germany (office); 19 Elzar Street, 65157 Tel-Aviv, Israel. *Telephone:* (30) 275-82-670 (office). *Fax:* (30) 275-82-677 (office). *E-mail:* berlin@zvihecker.com (office). *Website:* www.zvihecker.com (office).

HECKMAN, James Joseph, PhD; American economist and academic; *Henry Schultz Distinguished Service Professor of Economics, University of Chicago;* b. 19 April 1944, Chicago, Ill.; s. of John Heckman and Bernice Heckman; m. Lynne Pettler Heckman; one s. one d.; ed Colorado Coll. and Princeton Univ.; systems engineer, Martin-Marietta Aerospace 1965; Jr Economist, Council of Econ. Advisors 1967; Adjunct Asst Prof., New York Univ. 1972; Asst Prof., Columbia Univ. 1970–73, Assoc. Prof. 1973–74; Assoc. Prof. of Econs, Univ. of Chicago 1973–77, Prof. of Econs 1977–, Henry Schultz Prof. of Econs 1985–95, Henry Schultz Distinguished Service Prof. of Econs 1995–, Prof., Irving Harris School of Public Policy 1990–, Dir Center For Evaluation of Social Programs 1991–; A. Whitney Griswold Prof. of Econs, Yale Univ. 1988–90, Irving Fisher Prof. 1984, Prof. of Statistics 1990–, Lecturer, Yale Law School 1989–90, Alfred Cowles Distinguished Visiting Prof., Cowles Foundation 2008–; Research Assoc., Nat. Bureau of Econ. Research 1971–85, 1987–, Harry Scherman Fellow 1972–1973; consultant, RAND Corpn 1975–76; Social Science Research Council Training Fellow 1977–78; Guggenheim Fellow 1978–79; Fellow, Center for Advanced Study in the Behavioral Sciences, Stanford Univ. 1978–79; Research Assoc., Nat. Opinion Research Center; Econs Research Center 1979–; Sr Research Fellow, American Bar Foundation 1991–; Pres.-elect Midwest Econs Asscn 1996–97, Pres. 1998; Fellow, Econometric Soc. 1980, American Acad. of Arts and Sciences 1985, American Statistical Asscn 2001; mem. NAS 1992–; Co-Ed. Journal of Political Economy 1981–87; Assoc. Ed. Journal of Econometrics 1977–83, Journal of Labor Economics 1982–, Review of Economic Studies 1982–85, Econometric Reviews 1987–, Journal of Economic Perspectives 1989–96; mem. Editorial Bd Review of Economics and Statistics 1994–; Dir Econs Research Center, Univ. of Chicago 2001–; Pres. Western Econs Asscn 2005–06; Lifetime mem. Irish Econ. Asscn 2009; Fellow, Int. Statistical Inst. 2007, AAAS 2009; Hon. Prof., Univ. of Tucuman 1998, Huazhong Univ., China 2001, Huazhong Univ. 2001, Univ. of Chile 2002, Wuhan Univ. 2003, Universidad Autónoma del Estado de México 2003, Bard Coll., Univ. of Montreal 2004, Pontifical Univ. of Chile 2009; Hon. mem. Latin and Caribbean

Econ. Assgn 1999; Gold Medal, Pres. of Italian Repub. 2008; Hon. MA (Yale) 1989; Hon. PhD (Colo Coll.) 2001; Hon. DUniv (Chile) 2002, (UAEM, Mexico) 2003; John Bates Clark Medal, American Econs Assgn 1983, First Annual Louis T. Benezet Distinguished Alumnus Award, Colo Coll. 1985, Nobel Prize in Econs 2000, Statistician of the Year, Chicago Chapter, American Statistical Assgn 2002, Jacob Mincer Award, Soc. of Labour Econs 2005, Dennis Aigner Award 2005, 2007, Distinguished Contrib. Public Policy for Children, Soc. for Research in Child Devt 2009. *Publications include:* Longitudinal Analysis of Labor Market Data (co-ed.) 1985, Performance Standards in A Government Bureaucracy (ed collection), Lecture Notes on Longitudinal Data Analysis (co-author) 1997, Inequality in America: What Role for Human Capital Policy? (co-ed.) 2003, Law and Employment: Lessons From Latin America and the Caribbean (co-author) 2003, Handbook of Econometrics (co-ed.), Vol. 5 2001, Vol. 6 2007, Global Perspectives on the Rule of Law (co-ed.) 2010; more than 260 articles in professional journals. *Address:* Department of Economics, University of Chicago, 1126 East 59th Street, Chicago, IL 60637, USA (office). *Telephone:* (773) 702-0634 (office). *Fax:* (773) 702-8490 (office). *E-mail:* j-heckman@uchicago.edu (office); hiraic@uchicago.edu (office). *Website:* jenni.uchicago.edu (office).

HECKMANN, Fritz-Jürgen; German lawyer and business executive; *Chairman of the Supervisory Board, HeidelbergCement;* m.; two c.; ed Univ. of Konstanz, Univ. of St Gallen, Switzerland; lectured in commercial law at Univ. of Konstanz; worked in tax advice office –1983; with Kees Hehl Heckmann commercial law firm, Stuttgart 1983–, Pnr 1985–; currently Chair. Supervisory Bd HeidelbergCement; holds mandates in supervisory and advisory bodies, including Hübner GmbH, Kassel, Infoman AG, Stuttgart, Drews Holding AG, Schrozberg, Neue Pressegesellschaft mbH & Co. KG (Südwestpresse Group), Ulm, LTG Holding GmbH & Co. KG, Stuttgart, Paul Hartmann AG, Heidenheim, SWMH Südwestdeutsche Medien Holding GmbH (Stuttgarter Zeitung/Stuttgarter Nachrichten Group), Stuttgart. *Address:* HeidelbergCement, Berliner Strasse 6, 69120 Heidelberg, Germany (office). *Telephone:* (6221) 481-0 (office). *Fax:* (6221) 481-554 (office). *E-mail:* info@heidelbergcement.com (office). *Website:* www.heidelbergcement.com (office).

HEDEGAARD, Connie, MA; Danish journalist, politician and international organization official; *Commissioner for Climate Action, European Commission;* b. 15 Sept. 1960, Copenhagen; m. Jacob Andersen two c.; ed Holbæk Pvt. Lower Secondary School, Stenhus Upper Secondary School, Univ. of Copenhagen; mem. Folketing (Det Konservative Folkeparti—Conservative Party) for Copenhagen Co. constituency 1984–90, 2005–07, for Greater Copenhagen constituency 2007–, Spokeswoman on Defence Policy 1987–89; journalist, Berlingske Tidende newspaper 1990–94; Head of News Bulletin Service, Radioavisen, Danish Broadcasting Corpn 1994–98, Anchorwoman with DR 2 1998–2004; regular columnist, Politiken daily newspaper 1998–2004; Minister for the Environment 2004–07, for Nordic Co-operation 2005–07, of Climate and Energy 2007–10, for the UN Climate Change Conf. in Copenhagen 2009; Commr for Climate Action, EC, Brussels 2010–; Chair. Conservative Students in Metropolitan Region 1981–82, Centre for Cultural Co-operation with the Developing Countries 1998–2001, Man. Cttee Ministry of Culture's Devt Fund 2001–02, Man. Cttee BUSTER children's film festival 2002–; Nat. Chair. Denmark's Conservative Students 1983–84; Pres. Atlantic Assgn of Young Political Leaders 1985–87; mem. Council of Reps of Danish Atlantic Treaty Assgn 1986–; Bd Democracy Foundation 1990–95, Man. Cttee Centre for Tech. Supported Teaching (Center for Teknologistøttet Undervisning) 1995–98, Cttee on Public Information Policy 1996–97, Year 2000 Foundation (Ár 2000-Fonden) 1999–2000; KLF/Kirke & Mediers Scholarship Grant 2001, Culture Prize, Popular Educ. Assgn 2002, Nat. Press Club of Denmark Prize 2003, Ebbe Munck Award 2003, Publicist Award 2003, chosen by Time magazine amongst 100 Most Influential People in the World 2009. *Publications:* contrib. to various books. *Address:* European Commission, rue de la Loi 200, 1049 Brussels, Belgium (office); Høyrups Alle 24, 2900 Hellerup, Denmark (home). *Telephone:* (2) 299-11-11 (office). *Fax:* (2) 298-86-06 (office). *E-mail:* kirsten.winther@ec.europa-eu (office). *Website:* ec.europa.eu (office); www.conniehedegaard.dk.

HEDELIUS, Tom Christer, MBA; Swedish banker; b. 3 Oct. 1939, Lund; s. of Curt Hedelius and Brita (Påhlsson) Hedelius; m. Ulla Marianne Ericsson 1964; three s.; ed Univ. of Lund; industrial expert, Svenska Handelsbanken 1967–69, Credit Man. 1969–74, Head, Regional Unit (Stockholm City) 1974–76, Head, Cen. Credit Dept 1976–78, Pres. 1978–, Chair. of Bd 1991–2001; Chair. Bd AB Industrivärden, Bergman & Beving AB, Svenska AB Le Carbone, Anders Sandrews Stiftelse, Addtech. AB 2001–, Lagercrantz Group AB 2001–; mem. Bd Svenska Cellulosa AB, AB Volvo; Hon. Chair. Svenska Handelsbanken; Hon. DEcon (Umeå) 1989. *Address:* AB Industrivärden, Box 5403, 11484 Stockholm (office); Sturegatan 38, 11436 Stockholm, Sweden (home). *Telephone:* (8) 6666400. *Fax:* (8) 6616235.

HEDGES, Robert Ernest Mortimer, PhD; British archaeologist and academic; *Professor of Archaeological Science, University of Oxford;* b. 1944; ed High Wycombe Royal Grammar School, Univ. of Cambridge; Fellow, St Cross Coll., Oxford, reappointed a Lecturer in Archaeology 1994–; now Prof. of Archaeological Science, School of Archaeology and Emer. Fellow, St Cross Coll., Deputy Dir Research Lab. for Archaeology and the History of Art –2009; Royal Medal, Royal Soc. 2008. *Publications:* numerous papers in professional journals. *Address:* Research Laboratory for Archaeology and the History of Art, Dyson Perrins Building, South Parks Road, Oxford, OX1 3QY, England (office). *Telephone:* (1865) 285230 (office). *Fax:* (1865) 285220 (office). *E-mail:* robert.hedges@rlaha.ox.ac.uk (office). *Website:* www.arch.ox.ac.uk/RH1.html (office).

HEEGER, Alan J., PhD; American physicist and academic; *Professor of Physics and Materials Engineering, University of California, Santa Barbara;* b. 22 Jan. 1936, Sioux City, Ia; m. Ruth Heeger; two s.; ed Univ. of California, Berkeley; Prof. of Physics, Univ. of Calif., Santa Barbara 1982–, Dir Inst. for Polymers and Organic Solids 1982–2000, Prof. of Physics and Materials Engineering 1987–; Adjunct Prof. of Physics, Univ. of Utah 1988–, Chief Scientist 1999–; Pres. UNIAX Corpn 1990–94, Chair. 1990–99, Chief Tech. Officer 1999–; Co-founder and Chair. Brite Inc.; Co-founder and Vice-Chair. Cynvenio, Cytomx Therapeutics; Venture Pnr, NGEN LLC; mem. Bd of Dirs Konarka Techs Inc., QTL Biosystems; mem. Advisory Bd Science and Eng Festival, Clipper Windpower PLC; Foreign mem. Korean Acad. of Science and Tech. 2001; mem. Russian Acad. of Sciences,

American Physical Soc. 1968; Fellow, Alfred P. Sloan Foundation 1963–65; Guggenheim Foundation 1968–69; Hon. DrSc (Univ. of Mons) 1992, (Abo Akademie Univ.) 1998, DTheol (Univ. of Linköping) 1996; Oliver E. Buckley Prize 1983, John Scott Medal 1989, Balzan Prize for Science of Non-Biological Materials 1995, Nobel Prize for Chem. (jt recipient) 2000 for pioneering work on conductive polymers. *Achievements include:* holds several patents. *Address:* Department of Physics, Broida 4415, University of California, Santa Barbara, CA 93106-9530 (office); UNIAX Corporation, 6780 Cortona Drive, Santa Barbara, CA 93117, USA. *Telephone:* (805) 893-3184 (office). *Fax:* (805) 893-4755 (office). *Website:* www.cpos .ucsb.edu (office).

HEEMSKERK, Hubertus (Bert), BEcons; Dutch banker; *Vice-Chairman, Bank Sarasin & Co. Ltd;* b. 13 April 1943, Noordwijerhoud; ed High School A, Heemstede, Testimonium Europa Inst., Maastricht, Philosophy-Theology Hochschule, Frankfurt, Eberhard Karls Univ., Tübingen, Univ. Catholique, Paris, Nederlandse Economische Hogeschool, Rotterdam; Merger Mediation/Int. Acquisitions, AMRO Bank 1969–72, Head Account Man. 1972–74, Area Man., Germany, Scandinavia and Far East 1974–75, AMRO Bank Rep., Tokyo, Japan 1975–76, Head Area Man. (Europe) Amsterdam 1976–78, Dir AMRO Bank, Dubai 1978–79, Regional Man., Europe, AMRO Bank, Amsterdam 1979–80, Regional Man., Europe 1980–83, Co. Dir AMRO Bank, London, UK 1983–87, Head of Int. Commercial Banking Div., Head of Int. Group Strategy and Project Group Dir of Gen. Affairs 1988, Head of Merger Secr., AMRO-Generale, Dir Gen. Netherlands, ABN AMRO Netherlands 1988–91; Chair. Exec. Bd, F. van Lanschot Bankiers NV 1991–2002; Chair. Exec. Bd Rabobank Group 2003–09; mem. Bd of Dirs and Vice-Chair. Bank Sarasin & Co. Ltd, Basel, Switzerland; mem. Bd of Liquidators of Stock Exchange Asscn, mem. Governing Bd; mem. Advisory Council Amsterdam, Inst. of Finance; mem. Supervisory Bd Stock Exchange Foundation, VADO Beheer BV, Koninklijke Boskalis Westminster NV, Ecoconcern BV; mem. Bd of Man. European Asscn for Banking and Financial History eV (EABH); mem. AMREF Trust Fund, London; mem. Recommending Cttee AMREF Flying Doctors Netherlands, Passionata Foundation (literary journal in Rotterdam), Ronald McDonald Children's Fund, Special Olympics Nederland Foundation; Chair. Finance and Banking Museum. *Address:* Bank Sarasin & Co. Ltd, Elisabethenstrasse 62, PO Box, 4002 Basel, Switzerland (office). *Telephone:* (61) 277-77-77 (office). *Fax:* (61) 272-02-05 (office). *E-mail:* info@sarasin.com (office). *Website:* www.sarasin.com (office).

HEFFER, Simon James, MA, PhD; British journalist and writer; *Editor, Mail Comment Online, and Columnist, Daily Mail;* b. 18 July 1960, Chelmsford, Essex; s. of the late James Heffer and of Joyce Mary Clements; m. Diana Caroline Clee 1987; two s.; ed King Edward VI School, Chelmsford and Corpus Christi Coll., Cambridge; medical journalist 1983–85; freelance journalist 1985–86; Leader Writer, Daily Telegraph 1986–91, Deputy Political Corresp. 1987–88, political sketch writer 1988–91, political columnist 1990–91, Deputy Ed. 1994–96; Deputy Ed. The Spectator 1991–94; columnist, Evening Standard 1991–93, Daily Mail 1993–94, 1995–2005; Assoc. Ed. Daily Telegraph 2005–11; Ed. Mail Comment Online 2011–, columnist, Daily Mail 2011–; Fellow Commoner, Corpus Christi Coll., Cambridge 2010; Charles Douglas-Home Prize 1993. *Publications:* A Tory Seer (co-ed. with C. Moore) 1989, A Century of County Cricket (ed.) 1990, Moral Desperado: A Life of Thomas Carlyle 1995, Power and Place: The Political Consequences of King Edward VII 1998, Like the Roman: The Life of Enoch Powell 1998, Nor Shall My Sword; The Reinvention of England 1999, Vaughan Williams 2000, The Great British Speeches 2007, Strictly English: The Correct Way to Write and Why It Matters 2010, A Short History of Power 2011. *Leisure interests:* cricket, music, ecclesiology, bibliophily. *Address:* The Daily Mail, 2 Derry Street, London, W8 5TT, England (office). *Telephone:* (20) 7938-6000 (office). *E-mail:* simon.heffer@ dailymail.co.uk (office). *Website:* www.dailymail.co.uk (office).

HEFNER, Hugh Marston, BS; American publisher; *Chairman Emeritus, Playboy Enterprises, Inc.;* b. 9 April 1926, Chicago, Ill.; s. of Glenn L. Hefner and Grace Hefner (née Swanson); m. 1st Mildred Williams 1949 (divorced 1959); one s. one d.; m. 2nd Kimberley Conrad 1989 (divorced 2010); two s.; m. 3rd Crystal Harris 2012; ed Univ. of Illinois; Ed.-in-Chief Playboy Magazine 1953–, Oui Magazine 1972–81; Chair. Emer. Playboy Enterprises 1988–; Pres. Playboy Club Int. Inc. 1959–86; Int. Press Directory Int. Publisher Award 1997. *Leisure interests:* cinema, jazz. *Address:* Playboy Enterprises Inc., 680 North Lake Shore Drive, Chicago, IL 60611, USA (office). *Telephone:* (312) 751-8000 (office). *Fax:* (312) 751-2818 (office). *Website:* www.playboyenterprises.com (home).

HEGARTY, Anthony Francis, PhD, DSc, MRIA; Irish chemist and academic; *Professor and Chair of Organic Chemistry, University College Dublin;* b. 5 Aug. 1942, Cork; s. of Daniel F. Hegarty and Patricia Doyle; m. Ann M. Fleming 1967; two s. two d.; ed Univ. Coll. Cork (Nat. Univ. of Ireland) and Univs of Paris, France and California, USA; Lecturer in Chem., Univ. Coll. Cork 1970–79; Prof. and Chair. of Organic Chem., Univ. Coll. Dublin (UCD) 1980–, Head of Dept 1980–83, 1986–89, 1996–99, Dean of Postgraduate Studies 1989–96, mem. Governing Body of UCD 1990–2005, Chair. Bd for Funded Research and Research and Scholarship Bd 1995–2004, Vice-Pres. for Research at UCD 1998–2004; Visiting Prof., Brandeis Univ. 1975, Kuwait Univ. 1983, Univ. of Paris VII 1987; Chair. Nat. Trust for Ireland 1984–87, Royal Soc. of Chem. in Ireland 1987–90; Deputy Chair. Irish Research Council for Science, Eng and Tech. 2001–; mem. Senate Nat. Univ. of Ireland 1992–; Council mem. Royal Irish Acad. 1982–96, 2003–, Sec. for Science 1986–88, Treas. 1988–96. *Publications:* 184 papers in int. journals in area of organic reaction mechanisms and bioorganic chem. *Leisure interests:* sailing, walking, classical music. *Address:* School of Chemistry and Chemical Biology, University College Dublin, Belfield, Dublin 4, Ireland (office). *Telephone:* 87-2201014 (mobile). *Fax:* (1) 7161178 (office). *E-mail:* f.hegarty@ucd.ie (office). *Website:* www.ucd.ie/chem/hegarty (office).

HEGAZI, Al-Mursi al-Sayid, MEconSc, PhD; Egyptian economist, academic and government official; ed Univ. of Alexandria, Univ. of Connecticut, USA; Asst Prof., Dept of Public Finance, Univ. of Alexandria 1986–96, Chair. Dept of Public Finance 2003–08, Prof. Emer. 2008–; Asst, later Assoc. Prof., Dept of Econs, King Abdul-Aziz Univ., Qassim, Saudi Arabia 1990–95, Chair. Dept of Econs 1995–96; Chair. Dept of Public Finance, Beirut Arab Univ., Lebanon 1997–99, Dean, Faculty of Commerce 1999–2001; Minister of Finance Jan.–May 2013. *Address:* c/o Ministry of Finance, Ministry of Finance Towers, Cairo, Egypt.

HEGEDÜS, Loránt, DTheol; Hungarian ecclesiastic; *President, Bishop of Laszlo Ravasz Association;* b. 1930, Hajdunánás; s. of Géza Hegedüs and Magdolna Szabó; m. Zsuzsa Illés; two s. two d.; ed Theological Acad., Budapest, Basel, Princeton Univ., USA; Asst Minister, Bicske, Budapest 1956, Komló Nagykörös, Alsónémedi 1954–63, Hidas 1963–65; Minister, Hidas 1965–68, Szabadság tér, Budapest 1983–96, Kálvin tér, Budapest 1996–2005; Bishop 1990–2002; Prof. 1993–; Bishop, Consultative Synod, Hungarian Reformed Churches 1995–2004; Acting Chair. Hungarian Presbyterian Churches Ecumenical Council 1994; mem. Presidium of European Churches Conf. 1992–97, Council of Hundreds 1997–; Pres. Bishop of László Ravasz Asscn 2002–; Hon. Prof., Budapest, Veszprém; Dr hc (Cluj, Kolozsvár, Romania); Bocskai Díj Award 1997. *Publications include:* Aspekte der Gottesfrage 1979, Nyitás a Végtelenre (Opening for Eternity) 1989, The Concept of Transcendence 1991, Testvérek, menjünk bátran! (Brethren, Let Us Go On) 1992, Kálvin teologiája (Calvin's Theology) 1996, Isten szuverenitása és az ember felelőssége (The Sovereignty of God and the Responsibility of Man) 1996, Jézus és Europa (Jesus and Europe) 1998, Ujjángiánus és értékteologia (Neo-Kantian and Value Theology in Hungary) 1998, Isten kezében a történelem (History in God's Hand) 1998, Házasság (Wedding) 1998, Magyar reformatus millénium (Hungarian Reformed Millennium) 2001, 1 Mózes Huszonkettő 2001, Apokalipszis 2005, Prédikator Könyve 2005, Apokalipszisből megmentő emlekezés (Zakarias) 2006, Püspöki jelentések 1991–2002 2007. *Leisure interests:* reading, listening to music. *Address:* Szabadság tér 2, 1054 Budapest, Hungary. *Telephone:* (1) 311-8695. *Fax:* (1) 311-8695. *E-mail:* dr.hegeduslorant@freemail.hu (home).

HEIDE, Ola Mikal, MSc, DrAgr; Norwegian botanist and academic; *Professor Emeritus of Botany, Norwegian University of Life Sciences;* b. 26 April 1931, Trondenes; s. of Hans Kr. Heide and Marit Heide; m. Gerd Lillebakk 1955; three s. two d.; ed Agricultural Univ. of Norway and Univ. of Wisconsin; Research Fellow, Agric. Univ. of Norway 1961–70; Prof. of Plant Sciences, Makerere Univ. of Kampala, Uganda 1970–72; Prof. of Plant Physiology, Univ. of Tromsö 1972–76; Prof. of Botany, Agric. Univ. of Norway (renamed Norwegian Univ. of Life Sciences 2005) 1976–, Head, Dept of Biology and Nature Conservation 1990–95, Rector 1978–83; Vice-Chair. Agric. Research Council of Norway 1979–84; mem. Norwegian Acad. of Sciences, Royal Soc. of Sciences of Uppsala 1991, Finnish Acad. of Science and Letters 1994; Pres. Scandinavian Soc. of Plant Physiology 1976–82, 1988–94, Fed. of European Socs of Plant Physiology 1988–90; Kellogg Foundation Fellowship 1965; Norsk Varekrigsforsikrings Fund Science Prize 1968. *Publications include:* more than 150 primary scientific publs in the fields of plant physiology and ecophysiology. *Leisure interests:* sport, especially cross country skiing and running. *Address:* Norwegian University of Life Sciences, Dept of Ecology and Nature Resource Management, 1432 As (office); Skogvegen 34, 1430 Ås, Norway (home). *Telephone:* 64-96-53-86 (office); 64-94-16-01 (home). *Fax:* 64-96-58-01 (office). *E-mail:* ola.heide@umb.no (office). *Website:* www.umb.no (office).

HEIDEN, Eric A., MD; American orthopaedic surgeon, fmr speed skater and fmr professional cyclist; *Assistant Professor-Sports Medicine, Davis Medical Group, University of California;* b. 14 June 1958, Madison, Wis.; m. Karen Drews 1995; ed Univ. of Wis., Stanford Medical School; competed in Winter Olympics, Innsbruck, Austria 1976, Lake Placid, New York 1980 (five gold medals for men's speed skating, became first athlete ever to win five gold medals in a single Winter Olympics); winner, three consecutive World Speed Skating Championships 1977–79 (set new world records for 3,000m 1978, 1,000m 1978); retd from speed skating 1980; became professional cyclist 1981, winner US Professional Cycling Championships 1985; took part in Tour de France 1986; currently Asst Prof., Univ. of Calif., Davis Sports Medicine Clinic, Sacramento, Calif.; also affiliated to Intermountain Medical Centre, LDS Hospital, Park City Medical Centre; US speed skating team physician, Winter Olympics 2002, 2006; Fellow, American Sports Medicine Inst. 1996–97; mem. American Acad. of Orthopedic Surgeons; Sullivan Award for Best US Amateur Athlete 1980, UPI Int. Athlete of the Year 1980, USOC Sportsman of the Year 1980, inducted into Olympic Hall of Fame 1983, Bicycling Hall of Fame 1999. *Publication:* Faster, Better, Stronger 2008. *Address:* UC Davis Medical Group-Sports Medicine, 2805 J Street, Suite 300, Sacramento, CA 95815, USA (office). *Telephone:* (916) 734-6805 (office). *E-mail:* eric.heiden@ ucdmc.ucdavis.edu (office). *Website:* www.ucdmc.ucdavis.edu (office).

HEIFETZ, Zvi; Israeli lawyer and diplomatist; b. USSR; m. Sigalia Heifetz; seven c.; ed Tel-Aviv Univ.; family exiled from Latvia to Siberia during World War II; following high school, served in army for seven years in Intelligence, now a Maj. in the Reserves, instructor in cadet school; est. law practice in Tel-Aviv; went to USSR in 1989; fmr legal advisor to Prime Minister's Office on Soviet matters; Vice-Chair. Ma'ariv (Israel's second-largest publishing group) 1999, Chair. Tower Records 2001; Hon. Consul of Latvia to Israel –2004, Amb. to UK 2004–07; adviser and spokesman for Defense Ministry dealing with Russian-language media; mem. Bd of Dirs Hadera Paper Ltd 2012–, Clal Industries and Investments Ltd 2012–; mem. Israel Bar Asscn. *Address:* c/o Board of Directors, Clal Industries and Investments Ltd, 3 Azrieli Center, 45th Floor, Tel-Aviv 67023, Israel.

HEIGHTON, Steven, MA; Canadian author; b. 14 Aug. 1961, Toronto, Ont.; ed Silverthorn Coll. Inst., Queen's Univ.; Ed. Quarry magazine 1988–94; Writer-in-Residence, Concordia Univ. 2002–03; Jack McLelland Writer-in-Residence, Massey Coll., Univ. of Toronto 2004; participating author, American Movements II course, Univ. of New Orleans 2006; instructor Summer Literature Seminars, Herzen Univ., Russia 2007; Writer-in-Residence Univ. of Ottawa 2009, Royal Mil. Coll., Kingston 2010; Fellow, Cambridge Literary Seminars 1997; Ed. Quarry Magazine 1988–94; Gerald Lampert Award for Best First Book of Poetry 1990, Air Canada Award 1990, Gold Medal for Fiction, Nat. Magazine Awards 1992, 2007, 2009, Petra Kenney Prize 2002, Gold Medal for Poetry, Nat. Magazine Awards 2003, K. M. Hunter Award (Literature Category) 2010. *Publications include:* Stalin's Carnival (poetry) 1989, Foreign Ghosts (travelogue/poetry) 1989, Flight Paths of the Emperor (stories) 1992, The Ecstasy of Skeptics (poetry) 1994, On earth as it is (stories) 1995, The Admen Move on Lhasa: Writing and Culture in a Virtual World (essays) 1997, The Shadow Boxer (novel) 2000, Musings: An Anthology of Greek-Canadian Literature (co-ed.) 2003, The Address Book (poetry) 2004, Afterlands (novel) 2006, Patient Frame (poetry) 2010, Every Lost Country (novel) 2010; poetry, fiction and critical articles in various periodicals and anthologies, including London Review of Books, Poetry, Tin House, New York Times Book Review, Best English Stories, Best Canadian Stories, Poetry London,

Brick, etc. 1984–. *Address:* c/o Anne McDermid Agency, 83 Willcocks Street, Toronto, ON M5S 1C9, Canada (office). *E-mail:* anne@mcdermidagency.com (office); sheighton@kos.net (office). *Website:* www.mcdermidagency.com (office); www.stevenheighton.com.

HEIKAL, Mohamed Hassanein; Egyptian journalist; b. 1923; m.; three s.; reporter, The Egyptian Gazette 1943, Akher Sa'a magazine 1945; Ed. Al-Akhbar daily newspaper 1956–57; Ed. Al-Ahram 1957–74, Chair. Bd of Dirs 1959–74; mem. Cen. Cttee, Arab Socialist Union 1968–74; Minister of Information and Foreign Affairs April–Oct. 1970; arrested Sept. 1981, released Nov. 1981. *Publications:* Nahnou wa America 1967, Nasser: The Cairo Documents 1972, The Road to Ramadan 1975, Sphinx and Commissar 1979, The Return of the Ayatollah 1981, Autumn of Fury 1983, Cutting the Lion's Tail 1986, Suez Through Egyptian Eyes 1986, Boiling Point 1988, (The) Explosion 1990, Illusions of Triumph 1992, Arms and Politics 1993, Secret Channels 1996.

HEILBRONNER, François; French government official and business executive; b. 17 March 1936, Paris; s. of Paul Heilbronner and Elsie Schwob; m. Nathalie Ducas 1966; two s. two d.; ed Lycée Charlemagne, Paris, Inst. d'Etudes Politiques, Paris and Ecole Nat. d'Admin; Insp. des Finances 1964; apptd to Secr. of Interministerial Cttee on Questions of European Econ. Cooperation 1966, Deputy Sec.-Gen. 1969–72; Adviser to Minister of Foreign Affairs 1968–69; Deputy Dir Office of Minister of Agric. 1972–73, Dir 1973–74; Econ. and Financial Adviser to Prime Minister Jacques Chirac 1974, Deputy Dir of Office of Prime Minister Chirac 1975–76, 1986; Insp.-Gen. des Finances 1983; Pres. Groupe des assurances nationales (Gan) 1986, Banque pour l'industrie française, Phénix Soleil SpA (Italy) (now Gan Italia SpA) 1986–94; consultant, FH Conseil 1995–; Pres. HL Gestion 1997–99; Man. Dir REFCO HL Securities 1999–2000; Chair. and CEO Arbel 2001; mem. Bd of Dirs Fondation Médecins sans Frontières; Chevalier, Légion d'honneur, du Mérite maritime, Officier, Ordre nat. du Mérite; Commdr du Mérite agricole. *Address:* 27 rue d'Edimbourg, 75008 Paris, France.

HEIMANN, John G.; American investment banker; *Senior Advisor, Financial Stability Institute, Bank for International Settlements;* fmr NY State Supervisor of Banking and Commr of Housing and Community Devt; Comptroller of the Currency 1977–81; also served as first Chair. Fed. Financial Insts Examination Council and Acting Chair. Fed. Deposit Insurance Corpn; joined Warburg Paribas Becker-AG Becke 1981; Founding Chair. Financial Stability Inst. (jt initiative of BIS and Basel Cttee on Banking Supervision) 1999–2000, Sr Advisor 2002–; mem. Emer. Group of Thirty Consultative Group on Int. Econ. and Monetary Affairs, Inc. (G-30), Washington, DC. *Address:* Financial Stability Institute, Bank for International Settlements, 4002 Basel, Switzerland (office). *Telephone:* (61) 280-99-89 (office). *Fax:* (61) 280-91-00 (office). *E-mail:* fsi@bis.org (office). *Website:* (office).

HEIN, Christoph; German novelist and playwright; b. 8 April 1944, Heinzendorf, Schlesien; ed Gymnasium Berlin, Univ. of Leipzig, Humboldt Univ., Berlin; dramatist and playwright, Volksbühne Berlin 1971–79; author 1979–; Chevalier, Ordre des Arts et des Lettres; Heinrich Mann-Preis der Akad. der Künste Berlin 1982, (westdeutscher) Kritikerpreis für Literatur Berlin 1983, Literaturpreis Hamburg 1985, Lessing Prize 1989, Stefan Andres Prize, Schweich 1989, Erich Fried Prize, Vienna 1990, Ludwig Mülheims Prize 1992, Berliner Literaturpreis der Stiftung Preussische Seehandlung 1992, Norddt. Literaturpreis 1998, Peter-Weiss-Preis 1998, Solothurner Literaturpreis 2000, Premio Grinzane Cavour Turin 2002, State Prize for European Literature Austria 2002, Schiller-Gedächtnispreis 2004, Verdi Literaturpreis 2004. *Plays:* Schlötel oder Was solls 1974, Cromwell 1980, Lassalle fragt Herrn Herbert nach Sonja 1981, Die wahre Geschichte des Ah Q 1983, Passage 1987, Die Ritter der Tafelrunde 1989, Randow 1994, Bruch 1998, Himmel auf Erden 1998, In Acht und Bann 1998, Mutters Tag 2000, Noach (opera) 2001, Zur Geschichte des menschlichen Herzens 2002. *Publications:* fiction: Einladung zum Lever Bourgeois (stories) 1980, Nachfahrt und früher Morgen (juvenile) 1980, Der fremde Freund (novel) (trans. as The Distant Lover) 1982, Horns Ende (novel) 1985, Das Wildpferd unterm Kachelofen (juvenile) 1985, Der Tangospieler (novel) (trans. as The Tango Player) 1989, Die Vergewaltigung (stories) 1991, Matzeln 1991, Das Napoleonspiel (novel) 1993, Exekution eines Kalbes und andere Erzählungen 1994, Von allem Anfang an (novel) 1997, Willenbrock (novel) 2000, Mama ist gegangen (juvenile) 2003, Landnahme (trans. as Settlement) 2004, In seiner frühen Kindheit ein Garten (novel) 2005, Frau Paula Trosseau (novel) 2007; non-fiction: Die wahre Geschichte des Ah Q (plays/essays) 1984, Schlötel oder Was solls (essays) 1986, Öffentlich arbeiten. Essays und Gespräche 1987, Die fünfte Grundrechenart. Aufsätze und Reden 1986–1989 1990, Als Kind habe ich Stalin gesehen (essays/speeches) 1990, Die Mauern von Jerichow 1996. *Address:* c/o Suhrkamp-Verlag, Postfach 10 19 45, 60019 Frankfurt am Main, Germany.

HEINÄLUOMA, Eero; Finnish politician; *Speaker of Parliament;* b. 4 July 1955, Kokkola; s. of Heimo Olavi Heinäluoma and Aino Maria Heinäluoma; m. Satu Orvokki Siitonen-Heinäluoma; mem. Parl. for Uusimaa constituency 2003–07, for Helsinki constituency 2007–, mem. Defence Cttee 2003, Foreign Affairs Cttee 2003–, Deputy mem. Cttee for the Future 2003, Vice-Chair. and mem. Parl. Supervisory Council 2003–05, Chair. Social Democratic Parl. Group 2010–11, Speaker of Parl. 2011–; Minister of Finance 2005–07, Deputy Prime Minister 2006–07; Sec. Finnish Social Democratic Party 2002–05, Chair. 2005–08; mem. Helsinki City Council 2008–. *Address:* Parliament of Finland, Eduskunta, 00102 Helsinki, Finland (office). *Telephone:* (9) 4321 (office); (9) 432-3058. *E-mail:* eero .heinaluoma@parliament.fi (office). *Website:* www.eduskunta.fi (office).

HEINDORFF, Michael, MA; German artist; b. 26 June 1949, Braunschweig; s. of Hans Heindorff and Sigrid Bootz (née Hampe); m. Monica Buferd 1983 (died 2002); one s. one d.; ed Art Coll. and Univ. of Braunschweig, Royal Coll. of Art, London, UK; has been represented in numerous group exhbns internationally 1976–, also numerous solo exhbns 1977–; Sr Tutor in Painting, RCA 1980–99, Hon. Fellow 2001; various comms 1986–; Life mem. Chelsea Arts Club 1988–; John Moore's Liverpool Award 10 1976, Schmidt-Rotluff Prize 1981, Villa Massimo Prize 1981. *Art exhibitions include:* Drawn to Seeing, London 1995, Drawn to Seeing II, touring Germany 1999–2001, Guildhall Art Gallery, London 2002, Deutsche Bank, London 2003. *Leisure interests:* gardening, walking. *Address:* 2 Shrubland Road, London, E8 4NN, England. *Telephone:* 7773-429774 (mobile). *E-mail:* heindorff@ aol.com. *Website:* www.londonartscafe.org.uk/shows/mh/index.htm.

HEINE, Volker, MSc, PhD, FRS, FInstP; British theoretical physicist and fmr academic; b. 19 Sept. 1930, Germany; m. Daphne Hines 1955; one s. two d.; ed Wanganui Collegiate School, Otago Univ., New Zealand, Univ. of Cambridge; Demonstrator, Lecturer and Reader, Univ. of Cambridge 1958–76, Prof. in Theoretical Physics 1976–97; Visiting Prof., Univ. of Chicago 1965–66; Visiting Scientist, Bell Labs, USA 1970–71; Fellow, Clare Coll. Cambridge 1960–; Foreign mem. Max Planck Gesellschaft; Fellow, American Physical Soc.; Maxwell Medal, Inst. of Physics, Royal Medal, Royal Soc., Dirac Medal, Inst. of Physics, Max Born Medal, Inst. of Physics and German Physical Soc. 2001. *Publications include:* Group Theory in Quantum Mechanics 1960, Solid State Physics (Vol. 24) 1970, (Vol. 35) 1980; articles in Journal of Physics, Physical Review etc. *Address:* Cavendish Laboratory, JJ Thomson Avenue, Cambridge, CB3 0HE, England (office). *Telephone:* (1223) 768151 (office).

HEINEMAN, David (Dave) Eugene, BS; American fmr army officer, politician and state governor; *Governor of Nebraska;* b. 12 May 1948, Falls City, Neb.; s. of Jean Heineman and Irene Heineman; m. Sally Ganem 1977; one s.; ed US Mil. Acad., West Point; fmr Capt. in US Army; fmr Chief of Staff for Congressman Hal Daub; fmr Fremont Area Office Man. for Congressman Doug Bereuter; Neb. State Treas. 1995–2001; Lt Gov. of Neb. 2001–05, Dir of Homeland Security for Neb. (mem. Homeland Security Advisory Council 2004), Chair. Neb. Information Comm., Presiding Officer Neb. Legislature; US Sec. of Agric., Washington, DC 2005; Gov. of Nebraska 2005–; Chair. Nat. Govs Asscn 2011–12; Republican. *Address:* Office of the Governor, PO Box 94848, Lincoln, NE 68509-4848, USA (office). *Telephone:* (402) 471-2244 (office). *Fax:* (402) 471-6031 (office). *Website:* www.governor.nebraska.gov (office).

HEINONEN, Olavi Ensio, LLD; Finnish judge; b. 12 Sept. 1938, Kuopio; s. of Eino Ensio Heinonen and Aili Vesa; m. Marjatta Rahikainen 1962; two s. two d.; ed Univ. of Helsinki; Asst Prof. of Law, Univ. of Helsinki 1969–70; Justice, Supreme Court of Finland 1970–86; Parl. Ombudsman 1986–89; Chief Justice, Supreme Court of Finland 1989–2001 (retd); Grand Cross, Order of White Rose of Finland; Hon. LLD (Turku). *Publications:* books and articles on criminal justice and criminal policy. *Leisure interests:* cycling, basketball. *Address:* c/o Supreme Court, Pohjoisesplanadi 3, PO Box 301, 00171 Helsinki, Finland.

HEINRICH, Martin Trevor, BS; American politician; *Senator from New Mexico;* b. 17 Oct. 1971, Fallon, Nev.; s. of Peter C. Heinrich and Shirley A. Heinrich (née Bybee); m. Julie Heinrich; two c.; ed Univ. of Missouri, Univ. of New Mexico; served as Exec. Dir Cottonwood Gulch Foundation; f. public affairs consulting firm; mem. Albuquerque City Council 2003–07, City Council Pres. 2006; apptd by Gov. Bill Richardson to state's Natural Resources Trustee 2006; mem. US House of Reps for 1st Congressional Dist of NM 2009–13, mem. Cttee on Armed Services, Cttee on Natural Resources; Senator from New Mexico 2013–; Democrat. *Address:* United States Senate, Washington, DC 20510, USA (office). *Telephone:* (202) 224-3121 (office). *Website:* www.senate.gov (office); www.martinheinrich.com.

HEINRICHT, Frank, DrIng; German business executive; *Chairman of the Board of Management, Schott AG;* b. 1962, Berlin; m.; three c.; ed Tech. Univ. of Berlin; trainee programme, TEMIC Semiconductors 1992, held several man. positions, including Project Man. and Plant Man., apptd Gen. Man. for Integrated Circuits 1995, later Head of Integrated Circuits Div., responsible for subsidiaries in Germany, France, UK and USA, CEO TEMIC Semiconductor Group 1998–2003; Chief Operating and Tech. Officer and mem. Bd of Man., Heraeus Holding GmbH 2003–13, Chair. Bd of Man. 2008–13; Chair. Bd of Man. Schott AG 2013–; mem. Supervisory Bd Würth Group, Sennheiser Electronic GmbH & Co. KG; First Deputy Chair. German Materials Soc. (DGM). *Address:* Schott AG, Hattenbergstraße 10, 55122 Mainz, Germany (office). *Telephone:* (6131) 66-0 (office). *Fax:* (6131) 66-2000 (office). *E-mail:* info@schott.com (office). *Website:* www .schott.com (office).

HEINS, Thorsten, MSc; German telecommunications executive; *President and CEO, BlackBerry;* b. 29 Dec. 1957, Gifhorn; ed Univ. of Hanover; CEO of various business divns in the communication business, Chief Tech. Officer and mem. Group Bd Siemens Communications Group, Siemens AG –2007; Sr Vice-Pres., Handheld Business Unit, Research In Motion (name changed to BlackBerry 2013) 2007–09, COO Product Eng 2009–11, COO Product and Sales 2011, mem. Bd of Dirs, Pres. and CEO 2012–; mem. Bd of Dirs Canadian German Chamber of Industry and Commerce Inc. *Address:* Board of Directors, BlackBerry, 295 Phillip Street, Waterloo, ON N2L 3W8, Canada (office). *Telephone:* (519) 888-7465 (office). *Fax:* (519) 888-7884 (office). *E-mail:* info@blackberry.com (office). *Website:* www .blackberry.com (office).

HEISBOURG, François, FRSA; French academic and business executive; *Special Adviser, Fondation pour la Recherche Stratégique;* b. 24 June 1949, London, England; s. of Georges Heisbourg and Hélène Pinet; m. Elyette Levy 1989; two s.; ed Coll. Stanislas, Paris, Inst. d'Etudes Politiques, Cycle Supérieur d'Aménagement et d'Urbanisme, Ecole Nat. d'Admin; Asst to Dir of Econ. Affairs, Ministry of Foreign Affairs 1977–78; policy planning staff, Ministry of Foreign Affairs 1978–79; First Sec. Perm. Mission of France to UN 1979–81; Int. Security Adviser to Minister of Defence 1981–84; Vice-Pres. Thomson Int. 1984–87; Dir IISS, London 1987–92, Chair. 2001–; Sr Vice-Pres. Matra Défense Espace 1992–98; Head French Interministerial Group on teaching and of research in, strategic and int. affairs; Chair. Geneva Centre for Security Policy 1998–; Dir Fondation pour la Recherche Stratégique, Paris 2001–05, Special Adviser 2005–; mem. Royal Soc. for Encouragement of Arts, Manufacture and Commerce; Chevalier, Légion d'honneur, Ordre nat. du Mérite, Grosses Verdienstkreuz (Germany), Commdr, Ordre de la Couronne de Chêne (Luxembourg), Merito Militar (Spain). *Publications:* La Puce, les Hommes et la Bombe (with P. Boniface) 1986, Les Volontaires de l'an 2000 1995, The Future of Warfare 1997, European Defence: Making it Work 2000, Hyperterrorisme: La Nouvelle Guerre 2001, Le fin d'Occident? – Les Etats Unis, l'Europe et le Moyen Orient 2005; numerous articles in int. media and scholarly journals. *Leisure interests:* hiking, chess, collecting atlases. *Address:* Fondation pour la Recherche Stratégique, 27 rue Damesme, 75013 Paris, France (office). *Telephone:* 1-43-13-77-80 (office). *Fax:* 1-43-13-77-78. *E-mail:* f.heisbourg@frstrategie.org (office); heisbour@noos.fr (home). *Website:* www.frstrategie.org (office).

HEITKAMP, Mary Kathryn (Heidi), BA, JD; American lawyer and politician; *Senator from North Dakota;* b. 30 Oct. 1955, Mantador, North Dakota; m. Dr Darwin Lange; two s.; ed Univ. of North Dakota, Lewis and Clark Coll.; attorney, US Environmental Protection Agency 1980–81; attorney, Office of ND State Tax Commr 1981–86; Tax Commr of North Dakota 1986–92; Attorney Gen. of ND 1993–2000; unsuccessful cand. on Democratic-NPL ticket for State Gov. 2000; Dir Great Plains Synfuels Plant, Dakota Gasification Co. 2001; Senator from North Dakota 2013–; Democrat. *Address:* United States Senate, Washington, DC 20510, USA (office). *Telephone:* (202) 224-3121 (office). *Website:* www.senate.gov (office).

HEITSCH, Ernst, DPhil; German classicist and academic; *Professor of Classical Linguistics, University of Regensburg;* b. 17 June 1928, Celle; s. of Ernst Heitsch and Luise Meineke; m. Paula Sötemann 1961; two s. one d.; ed Univ. of Göttingen; Univ. Lecturer in Classical Linguistics, Univ. Göttingen 1960–66, Prof. 1966–67; Prof. of Classical Linguistics, Univ. of Regensburg 1967–; mem. Akad. der Wissenschaften und der Literatur zu Mainz, Akad. der Wissenschaften zu Göttingen, Deutsches Archäologisches Institut. *Publications:* Die griechischen Dichterfragmente der römischen Kaiserzeit I und II 1963–65, Epische Kunstsprache und Homer 1968, Parmenides 1974, 1995, Parmenides und die Anfänge der Erkenntniskritik und Logik 1979, Xenophanes 1983, Antiphon aus Rhamnus 1984, Willkür und Problembewusstsein in Platons Kratylos 1984, Platon über die rechte Art zu reden und zu schreiben 1987, Überlegungen Platons im Theaetet 1988, Wege zu Platon 1992, Platon Phaidros 1993, 1997, Geschichte und Situationen bei Thukydides 1996, Gesammelte Schriften I 2001, II 2002, III 2003, Platon Apologie 2002, 2004, Dialoge Platons vor 399? 2002, Platon und die Aufänge seines dialektischen Philosophierens 2004, Geschichte und Personen bei Thukydides 2007, Platon Hippias Major 2011, Eine Episode aus der Geschichte des Wahrheitsbegriffs 2011, Vision als Offenbarüng? 2012; numerous articles in periodicals. *Leisure interest:* sailing. *Address:* Mattinger Strasse 1, 93049 Regensburg, Germany (home). *Telephone:* (941) 31944 (home).

HEKMATYAR, Gulbuddin; Afghan politician and fmr guerrilla leader; b. 1947, Imam Saheb, Kunduz Prov.; ed Kabul Univ.; mem. Muslim Youth 1970; imprisoned 1972–73; fled to Pakistan 1973; Leader Hizb-i Islami Mujahidin Movt against Soviet-backed regime; Prime Minister of Afghanistan 1993–94, 1996–97; returned from exile in Iran 1998; currently Leader, Hizb-i Islami Gulbuddin.

HELD, Heinz Joachim, DrTheol; German theologian and fmr bishop; b. 16 May 1928, Wesseling/Rhein; s. of Heinrich Held and Hildegard Röhrig; m. Anneliese Novak 1959 (died 2002); one s. three d.; m. Barbara Mauritz 2003; ed Wuppertal, Göttingen, Heidelberg, Bonn and Austin, Tex.; Research Asst, Wuppertal Theological Seminary 1952, 1953–56; parish pastor, Friedrichsfeld/Niederrhein 1957-64; Prof. of Theology, Buenos Aires Lutheran Seminary 1964–68; Pres. River Plate Evangelical Church, Buenos Aires 1968–74; mem. Cen. Cttee World Council of Churches 1968–91, Moderator of Cen. Cttee and Exec. Cttee 1983–91; Pres. Dept of Ecumenical Relations and Ministries Abroad of the Evangelical Church in Germany 1975–93; Bishop 1991; Chair. Council of Christian Churches, FRG 1982–88, 1992–95; Hon. DrTheol (Lutheran Theological Univ., Budapest) 1985; Hon. DD (Acad. of Ecumenical Indian Theology and Church Admin., Chennai) 1988. *Publications:* Matthew as Interpreter of the Miracle Stories 1960 (English trans. 1963), Von Nairobi nach Canberra.EKD und ÖRK im Dialog 1975–1991 1994/1996, Den Reichen wird das Evangelium gepredigt 1997, Ökumene im Kalten Krieg 2000, Der Ökumenische Rat der Kirchen im Visier der Kritik 2001, Einsichten und Ausblicke 2008. *Leisure interests:* stamp collecting, amateur music (piano), photography. *Address:* Bussilliatweg 32, 30419 Hanover, Germany (home). *Telephone:* (511) 2714308 (home). *E-mail:* heijo.held@htp-tel.de (home).

HELD, Richard (Dick) M., MA, PhD; American neuroscientist, psychologist and academic; *Professor Emeritus, Massachusetts Institute of Technology;* b. 10 Oct. 1922, New York City, NY; s. of Lawrence Walter Held and Tessie Klein Held; m. Doris Bernays 1951; three c.; ed Columbia and Harvard Univs and Swarthmore Coll.; Research Asst Dept of Psychology, Swarthmore Coll. 1946–48; Research Asst, Teaching Fellow and NIH Postdoctoral Fellow, Dept of Psychology, Harvard Univ. 1949–53; Instructor, Asst Prof., Assoc. Prof., Prof. and Chair. Dept of Psychology, Brandeis Univ. 1953–62; mem. Inst. for Advanced Study, Princeton 1955–56; Sr Research Fellow, NSF and Visiting Prof., Dept of Psychology, MIT 1962–63, Prof., Dept of Psychology 1963–93, Dept Chair. 1977–86, Prof. Emer. 1994–; Research Prof. of Vision Science, New England Coll. of Optometry 1995–2008; numerous other professional appointments; mem. NAS and many other learned socs; Fellow, American Acad. of Arts and Sciences; Dr hc (Free Univ. of Brussels) 1984, (New England Coll. of Optometry); Glenn A. Fry Award 1979, H.C. Warren Medal 1983, Kenneth Craik Award 1985, Galileo Award 1996. *Publications:* several hundred publications. *Leisure interests:* tennis, theatre, visual arts. *Address:* New England College of Optometry, 424 Beacon Street, Boston, MA 02115, USA (office). *Telephone:* (617) 369-0180 (office); (617) 491-7218 (home). *Fax:* (617) 369-0188 (office). *E-mail:* heldd@neco.edu (home); helddr@yahoo.com (home).

HELENIUS, Ari, PhD; Finnish biochemist and academic; *Professor, Institute of Biochemistry, Eidgenössische Technische Hochschule Zürich;* b. 3 Sept. 1944, Oulu; ed Univ. of Helsinki; fmr Staff Scientist, European Lab. for Molecular Biology, Heidelberg, Germany, later Assoc. Prof.; Prof., Dept of Cell Biology, Yale Univ., New Haven, Conn., USA 1983–97 (Chair. Dept 1992–97); Prof., Inst. of Biochemistry, ETH, Zürich, Switzerland 1997–; mem. American Soc. for Cell Biology, Finnish Soc. of Sciences and Letters, European Molecular Biology Org.; Komppa Prize 1973, Ernst Prize for Medicine 2003, The Schleiden Medal in Cell Biology 2003, Marcel Benoist Prize 2007, Govt Medal 2007. *Publications:* numerous publs in scientific journals on membrane biology, virology and protein chem. *Leisure interests:* literature, hiking. *Address:* Institute of Biochemistry, Building HPM, Room E6.3, ETH Hönggerberg, 8093 Zürich, Switzerland (office). *Telephone:* (44) 6326817 (office). *Fax:* (44) 6321269 (office). *E-mail:* ari.helenius@bc .biol.ethz.ch (office). *Website:* www.bc.biol.ethz.ch (office).

HELFT, Jorge Santiago; Argentine arts foundation director; b. 10 June 1934, France; s. of the late Jacques Helft and Marianne Loevi; m. Mariana Eppinger 1955; three s.; ed New York Univ. and Columbia Univ., USA; lived in Paris until 1940, New York 1940–47, Buenos Aires 1947–; business exec. with Continental

Grain Co. 1956–74, Vesuvio SA 1974–82; Trustee and Dir Fundación Antorchas 1985–93, Fundación Lampadia, Vaduz, Liechtenstein; Pres. Fundación San Telmo 1980–; Founding mem. and mem. Bd of Dirs Fundación Teatro Colón 1978–; fmr mem. Int. Council of Museum of Modern Art; Oficial, Ordem de Rio Branco (Brazil). *Leisure interests:* arts and music. *Address:* Defensa 1364 (1143), Buenos Aires, Argentina (home).

HELINSKI, Donald Raymond, PhD, FAAS; American biologist and academic; *Professor Emeritus, Section of Molecular Biology, University of California, San Diego;* b. 7 July 1933, Baltimore, Md; s. of George L. Helinski and Marie M. Helinski; m. Patricia M. Doherty 1962; one s. one d.; ed Univ. of Maryland, Case Western Reserve Univ., Cleveland, Ohio, Stanford Univ.; US Public Health Service Postdoctoral Fellow, Stanford Univ., Calif. 1960–62; Asst Prof., Princeton Univ., NJ 1962–65; Assoc. Prof., Dept of Biology, Univ. of California, San Diego 1965–70, Prof. 1970 then Research Prof., Chair. Dept of Biology 1979–81, Dir Center for Molecular Genetics 1984–95, Assoc. Dean of Natural Sciences 1994–97, now Prof. Emer., Section of Molecular Biology; Public Health Service Predoctoral Fellow, Western Reserve Univ. 1957–59; Fellow, American Soc. of Microbiology; mem. NIH Advisory Cttee on DNA Recombinant Research 1975–78; mem. NAS, AAAS, American Acad. of Microbiology; Assoc. mem. European Molecular Biology Org. *Publications:* more than 180 publs and 50 review articles in the fields of biochemistry, molecular genetics and microbiology. *Address:* Department of Biology, Division of Biological Sciences, University of California, San Diego, 9500 Gilman Drive, La Jolla, CA 92093 (office); 8766 Dunaway Drive, La Jolla, CA 92037, USA (home). *Telephone:* (858) 534-3638 (office); (858) 453-2758 (home). *Fax:* (858) 534-0559 (office). *E-mail:* dhelsinki@ucsd.edu (office); helinski@biomail.ucsd .edu (office). *Website:* biology.ucsd.edu/faculty/helinski.html (office).

HELL, Stefan W., Dr rer. nat; German scientist; *Director, Department of NanoBiophotonics, Max Planck Institute for Biophysical Chemistry;* b. 1962; m. Anna Hell; two s.; ed Univ. of Heidelberg; worked at European Molecular Biology Lab., Heidelberg 1991–93; Sr Researcher, Univ. of Turku, Finland 1993–96; Visiting Scientist, Univ. of Oxford, UK 1994; apptd to Max Planck Inst. for Biophysical Chemistry, Göttingen 1997, Dir Dept of NanoBiophotonics 2002–; Dir High Resolution Optical Microscopy Research Group, German Cancer Research Centre; Prize of the Int. Comm. in Optics 2000, Carl Zeiss Research Award 2002, Innovation Award of the German Fed. Pres. 2006, Julius Springer Award for Applied Physics 2007. *Publications:* more than 100 publs in refereed journals. *Address:* Max Planck Institute for Biophysical Chemistry, Am Faßberg 11, 37077 Göttingen, Germany (office). *Telephone:* (551) 2012501 (office). *Fax:* (551) 2011222 (office). *E-mail:* shell@gwdg.de (office). *Website:* www.gwdg.de (office).

HELLAWELL, Keith, QPM, MSc, LLD; British police officer and business executive; *Chairman, Sports Direct International PLC;* b. 18 May 1942, Yorks.; s. of Douglas Hellawell and Ada Alice Hellawell; m. Brenda Hey 1963; one s. two d.; ed Kirkburton Secondary Modern School, Dewsbury Tech. Coll., Cranfield Inst. of Tech. and London Univ.; worked for five years as a miner before joining Huddersfield Borough Police; progressed within W Yorks. Police to Asst Chief Constable; Deputy Chief Constable of Humberside 1985–90, Chief Constable of Cleveland Police 1990–93, Chief Constable of W Yorks. Police 1993–98; first UK Anti-Drugs Co-ordinator 1998–2001; Adviser to Home Sec. on Int. Drug Issues 2001; Asscn of Police Officers Spokesman on Drugs; mem. Advisory Council on the Misuse of Drugs, Bd Community Action Trust; Chair. Catapult Presentations Ltd, Airshelter 2009–; Chair. Goldshield Group PLC 2006–09, Dynamic Change 2006–10, Sports Direct Int. PLC 2009–; mem. Bd of Dirs Universal Vehicles Group Ltd, Evans PLC 1998–99, Dalkia PLC 2006–09, Mortice PLC 2008–; fmr Trustee, Nat. Soc. for the Prevention of Cruelty to Children; mem. Editorial Advisory Bd Journal of Forensic Medicine; Dr hc (Leeds Metropolitan Univ.) 1997, (Huddersfield Univ.) 1998, Hon. LLD (Univ. of Bradford) 1998. *Publication:* The Outsider (autobiog.) 2002. *Leisure interests:* gardening, design, reading. *Address:* Sports Direct International PLC, Unit A, Brook Park East, Shirebrook, NG20 8RY, England (office). *Telephone:* (84) 5129-9200 (office). *Website:* www.sports-direct -international.com (office).

HELLBERG, Klaus; Finnish politician and business executive; *Chairman, Supervisory Board, Neste Oil Oyj;* b. 1945, Porvoo; mem. Eduskunta (Finnish Parl.) for Uusimaa constituency (Suomen Sosialidemokraatinen Puolue/Finnish Social Democratic Party); Chair. Supervisory Bd Neste Oil Oyj 2007–; mem. Supervisory Bd Fortum Corpn; mem. Finnish Council for Environment and Natural Resources. *Address:* Neste Oil Oyj, Keilaranta 8, PO Box 95, 00095 Espoo, Finland (office). *Telephone:* (10) 45811 (office). *Fax:* (10) 4584442 (office). *Website:* www.nesteoil.com (office).

HELLER, Dean A., BBA; American stockbroker and politician; *Senator from Nevada;* b. 10 May 1960, Castro Valley, Calif.; s. of Charles Alfred 'Jack' Heller and Janet Heller (née MacNelly); m. Lynne Heller; four c.; ed Carson High School, Univ. of Southern California; moved to Carson City, Nev. 1961; worked as stockbroker and broker/trader on Pacific Stock Exchange; moved back to Carson City; Chief Deputy Nev. State Treas. –1991; mem. Nev. State Ass. representing Carson City 1991–95; Sec. of State of Nev. 1995–2007; mem. US House of Reps for 2nd Congressional Dist of Nev. 2007–11, mem. House Ways and Means Cttee, Vice-Chair. Western Caucus; apptd Senator from Nevada by Gov. Brian Sandoval to a vacant seat created by the resignation of John Ensign 2011–; Founding Bd mem. Boys and Girls Club of Western Nevada, Western Nevada Community Coll. Foundation; Advisory Bd mem. Nevada's Foster Grandparent programme; Republican. *Address:* 361A Russell Senate Office, Washington, DC 20510, USA (office). *Telephone:* (202) 224-6244 (office). *Fax:* (202) 228-6753 (office). *Website:* heller.senate.gov (office).

HELLER, Jeffrey M. (Jeff), BBA; American information technology industry executive (retd); m. Carol Heller; one s. one d.; ed Univ. of Texas, Austin; served in US Marine Corps as jet pilot 1960–66, attained the rank of Capt.; joined Electronic Data Systems Corpn's Systems Eng Devt Program 1968, worked as systems engineer in medicare field in Pa, Calif., Ia, Ind., New York and Boston, worked on a New York Stock Exchange sales study 1970, man. of a regional data center, Dallas 1972, Regional Man. of Healthcare, eastern USA 1973–74, Corp. Vice-Pres. 1974–79, Head of Tech. Services 1979–84, led a project for General Motors, Detroit 1984–87, Sr Vice-Pres. 1987–96, Pres. and COO 1996–2000, Vice Chair.

1996–2002, 2006–08, Pres. 2003–06; mem. Bd of Dirs Mutual of Omaha 1998–; Trustee, Southwestern Medical Foundation; fmr mem. Bd of Dirs Dallas Symphony Asscn, Trammell Crow Co., Cotton Bowl Athletic Asscn, Temple-Inland; mem. Men's Athletics Council, Univ. of Tex.; fmr mem. Chancellor's Council, Eng Foundation Advisory Council, McCombs School of Business Advisory Council, Devt Bd; mem. Longhorn Foundation. *Address:* c/o Board of Directors, Mutual of Omaha, 3333 Farnam Street, Omaha, NE 68175, USA.

HELLER, Margot; British gallery curator; *Director, South London Gallery;* Dir South London Gallery 2001–, five exhbns each year profile the work of est. int. figures including Tom Friedman, Mark Dion, Rivane Neuenschwander, Alfredo Jaar and Superflex, as well as that by younger and mid-career British artists including Eva Rothschild and Ryan Gander, gallery's live art and film programme has included presentations by Rachel Gomme, Nathaniel Mellors, Gail Pickering, OMSK and Gisele Vienne, and occasional large scale off-site projects have included those by On Kawara in Trafalgar Square 2004 and Chris Burden at Chelsea Coll. of Art Parade Ground 2006, presented Omer Fast, Ryan Gander, Tatiana Trouvé and Alfredo Jaar 2010. *Publications include:* Incommunicado (with Tom McCarthy). *Address:* South London Gallery, 65 Peckham Road, Camberwell, London, SE5 8UH, England (office). *Telephone:* (20) 7703-6120 (office). *E-mail:* mail@southlondongallery.org (office). *Website:* www.southlondongallery.org (office).

HELLER, Michał Kazimierz; Polish professor of philosophy of science and ecclesiastic; b. 12 March 1936, Tarnów; ed Inst. of Theology, Tarnów; ordained priest 1959; Catholic Univ. of Lublin, Pontifical Acad. of Theology, Kraków, Extraordinary Prof. 1985, Ordinary Prof. 1990, currently Prof. of Cosmology and Philosophy of Science; Jt mem. Vatican Astronomical Observatory; Rector Inst. of Theology, Tarnów; Ordinary mem. Pontifical Acad. of Sciences, Rome 1991; mem. Petersburg Acad. of Sciences 1997, Int. Astronomical Union, Int. Soc. for General Relativity and Gravitation, European Physical Soc., Int. Soc. of the Study of Time, Polish Physical Soc., Polish Astronomical Soc., Science Soc. of Catholic Univ. of Lublin; Dr hc (Acad. of Mining and Metallurgy, Kraków) 1996; Templeton Prize 2008. *Publications:* The Singular Universe – An Introduction to the Classical Singularity Theory 1991, Theoretical Foundations of Cosmology – Introduction to the Global Structure of Space-Time 1992, Physics of Space-Time and Motion 1993, The New Physics and a New Theology 1996, To Catch Passing Away 1997, Quantum Cosmology 2001, The Beginning is Everywhere 2002, and over 600 publs on relativistic physics, cosmology, history and philosophy of science and relations between science and theology and articles in journals. *Address:* Papieska Akademia Teologiczna, Wydział Filozoficzny, ul. Franciszkańska 1, 30-004 Kraków, Poland (office). *E-mail:* mheller@wsd.tarnow.pl (office); mheller@alumn.wsd.tarnow.pl (home).

HELLMAN, Peter S., MBA, BEcons; American business executive; b. 16 Oct. 1949, Cleveland, Ohio; s. of Arthur Cerf Hellman and Joan Alburn; m. Alyson Dulin Ware 1976; one s. one d.; ed Hobart Coll. and Case Western Reserve Univ.; with The Irving Trust Co., New York 1972–79; Financial Planning Assoc., BP America 1979–82, Man. Financial Planning 1982–84, Dir, Operations Analysis 1984–85, Asst Treas. 1985–86, Corp. Treas. 1986–89; Vice-Pres. and Treas. TRW Inc. 1989–91, Exec. Vice-Pres. and Chief Financial Officer 1991–94, Exec. Vice-Pres. and Asst Pres. 1994–95, Pres. and COO 1995–2000; Exec. Vice-Pres. and Chief Financial Officer Nordson Corpn, Ohio 2000–04, Pres. and Chief Financial and Admin. Officer 2004–08; mem. Bd of Dirs Qwest Communications 2000–, Baxter Int. 2005–, Owens-Illinois Inc. 2007–, Goodyear Tire and Rubber Co. 2010–, Nordson Corpn 2001–08; mem. Cleveland Clinic Foundation Urological Inst. Advisory Cttee; Trustee, Baxter Int., Case Western Reserve Univ., Lifebank Lorain Co. Community Coll. Foundation, Western Reserve Acad. *Address:* c/o Board of Directors, Baxter International, One Baxter Parkway, Deerfield, IL 60015-4625, USA.

HELLSTRÖM, Mats, MA; Swedish politician and diplomatist; b. 12 Jan. 1942, Stockholm; m. Elisabeth Hellström; two c.; ed Univ. of Stockholm; Lecturer in Econs, Univ. of Stockholm 1965–69; mem. Parl. 1968, 1969–96, mem. Exec. Cttee Social Democratic Party Youth League 1969–72; mem. Bd Social Democratic Party 1969–96; Special Adviser, Ministry of Labour 1973–76; Minister of Foreign Trade at Ministry of Foreign Affairs 1983–86; Minister of Agric. 1986–91, for Foreign Trade and European Union Affairs 1994–96; Amb. to Germany 1996–2001; Gov. Stockholm Co. 2002–06; Chair. Nordic Folk High School Biskops-Arnö; mem. High Level Advisory Group of Global Subsidies Initiative 2005–, Advisory Bd Globe Forum 2008–; Sr Advisor, Plantagon 2009–, Magnusson (Baltic Sea region law firm) 2010–, GAIA Leadership 2010–. *Publications:* A Seamless Globe? A Personal Story of the Uruguay Round in GATT 1999, Östersjömat 2005. *Address:* Nytorgsgatan 19A, 116 22 Stockholm, Sweden (home). *Telephone:* (70) 610-41-43 (office); (8) 640-80-50 (home). *E-mail:* mats.hellstrom@bfrex.se (office).

HELLWIG, Fritz, DPhil Habil; German economist and fmr politician; b. 3 Aug. 1912, Saarbrücken; s. of Friedrich Hellwig and Albertine Hellwig (née Christmann); m. Dr Margarete Werners 1939; two s. one d.; ed Marburg, Vienna and Berlin Univs; staff mem. Saarbrücken Chamber of Industry and Commerce 1933–39; Dir Saarwirtschaftsarchiv 1936–39; Man. Dist Orgs of Iron and Steel Industry at Düsseldorf and Saarbrücken, 1940–43; war service 1943–47; Econ. Adviser and Dir Deutsches Industrieinstitut, Cologne 1951–59; Substitute del., Consultative Ass. of Council of Europe 1953–56; mem. Bundestag 1953–59, Chair. Econ. Affairs Cttee 1956–59; mem. European Parl. 1959; mem. of High Authority of the European Coal and Steel Community, Luxembourg 1959–67; Vice-Pres. Comm. of the European Communities, Brussels 1967–70; Exec. mem. Bd of German Shipowners Asscn 1971–73; Hon. Prof., Univ. of Trier (for History of Cartography 1990; Grosses Bundesverdienstkreuz mit Stern und Schulterband 1971; Int. Charlemagne Prize, Aachen (with EEC Comm.) 1969. *Publications:* Westeuropas Montanwirtschaft, Kohle und Stahl beim Start der Montan-Union 1953, Saar zwischen Ost und West, Die wirtschaftliche Verflechtung 1954, 10 Jahre Schumanplan 1960, Gemeinsamer Markt und Nationale Wirtschaftspolitik 1961, Montanunion zwischen Bewährung und Belastung 1963, Politische Tragweite der europäischen Wirtschaftsintegration 1966, Das schöne Buch und der Computer 1970, Die Forschungs- und Technologiepolitik der Europäischen Gemeinschaften 1970, Verkehr und Gemeinschaftsrecht: Seeschiffahrt und Europäische Wirtschaftsgemeinschaft 1971, Die deutsche Seeschiffahrt: Strukturwandel und künftige Aussichten 1973, Zur älteren Kartographie der Saargegend I

1977, II 1981, Alte Pläne von Stadt und Festung Saarlouis 1980, Die Hogenberg-Geschichtsblätter 1983, Landkarten der Pfalz am Rhein (with W. Reiniger and K. Stopp) 1984, Mittelrhein und Moselland im Bild alter Karten 1985, Überwindung der Grenzen. Robert Schuman zum Gedenken 1986, Caspar Dauthendeys Karte des Herzogtums Braunschweig 1987, Europäische Integration aus historischer Erfahrung (Ein Zeitzeugengespräch mit Michael Gehler) 2004. *Leisure interests:* collecting old maps, views and illustrated books. *Address:* Klosterbergstrasse 117C, 53177 Bonn, Germany (home). *Telephone:* (228) 322017 (home).

HELLYER, Hon. Paul Theodore, PC, BA; Canadian politician; b. 6 Aug. 1923, Waterford, Ont.; s. of Audrey S. Hellyer and Lulla M. Anderson; m. 1st Ellen Jean Ralph (died 2004); two s. one d.; m. 2nd Sandra Bussiere (née Meades) 2005; ed Waterford High School, Curtiss Wright Tech. Inst., California and Univ. of Toronto; Fleet Aircraft Manufacturing Co., Fort Erie 1942–44; RCAF 1944–45; Owner, Mari-Jane Fashions, Toronto 1945–56; Treas. Curran Hall Ltd 1950, Pres. 1951–62; Pres. Trepil Realty Ltd 1951–62; Pres. Hendon Estates Ltd 1959–62; mem. House of Commons 1949–57, 1958–74, Parl. Asst to Minister of Nat. Defence 1956–57, Assoc. Minister April–June 1957, Minister of Nat. Defence 1963–67, of Transport 1967–69, responsible for Central Mortgage and Housing Corpn 1968–69; Chair. Task Force on Housing and Urban Devt 1968; Acting Prime Minister 1968–69; joined Progressive Conservative Party July 1972; rejoined Liberal Party 1982; Leader Canadian Action Party 1997–2004; Opposition Spokesman on Industry, Trade and Commerce 1973; Distinguished Visitor, Faculty of Environmental Studies, York Univ. 1969–70; Founding Chair. Action Canada 1971; syndicated columnist, Toronto Sun 1974–84; Exec. Dir Canada UNI Asscn 1991–95; Fellow, Royal Soc. for Encouragement of the Arts. *Publications:* Agenda – A Plan for Action 1971, Exit Inflation 1981, Jobs For All – Capitalism on Trial 1984, Canada at the Crossroads 1990, Damn the Torpedos 1990, Funny Money – A Common Sense Alternative to Mainline Economics 1994, Surviving the Global Financial Crisis – The Economics of Hope for Generation X 1996, Arundel Lodge – A Little Bit of Old Muskoka 1996, The Evil Empire: Globalization's Darker Side 1997, Stop – Think 1999, Goodbye Canada 2001, One Big Party – To Keep Canada Independent 2003. *Leisure interests:* swimming, skin and scuba diving, stamp collecting. *Address:* Suite 506, 65 Harbour Square, Toronto, ON M5J 2L4, Canada (home). *Telephone:* (416) 850-1375 (office); (416) 366-4092 (home). *Fax:* (416) 850-1486 (office). *E-mail:* phellyer@sympatico.ca (office). *Website:* www.paulhellyerweb.com.

HELME, Mart; Estonian diplomatist and politician; *Chairman, Estonian Conservative People's Party;* b. 31 Oct. 1949, Parnu; m. Sirje Helmega Helme; ed Tartu Univ.; Eesti Raamat Publishing House 1973–75; reporter Harju Elu (newspaper) 1975–77; Sr Ed. Literature section Pioneer magazine 1977–86; farmer 1986–89; publisher 1989–91; Acting Dir Union of Publishers of Estonia, political observer Paeveleht (daily) 1991–93; Head, Fourth Bureau (Asia, Africa, S America) Political Dept, Ministry of Foreign Affairs Feb.–May 1994; Head of Third Bureau (Russia, CIS, E and Cen. Europe) Political Dept, Ministry of Foreign Affairs 1994–95; Amb. to Russian Fed. 1995–2000; apptd Vice-Chancellor Ministry of Foreign Affairs 1999; fmr Counsellor to Minister of Agric.; fmr Dir Research Center Free Europe; Chair. Nat. Conservative Party-Farmers' Ass.; cand. for People's Union in elections for European Parl. 2004; Advisor to Tunne Kelam 2005–09; currently Chair. Estonian Conservative People's Party (Eesti Konservatiivseks Rahvaerakonnaks); Lecturer, International University Audentes (now merged with Tallinn School of Econs and Business Admin) 2001–. *Publications include:* Chinese Stories, Two Swords, Lembitu: Estonians' Uncrowned King. *Address:* Estonian Conservative People's Party (Eesti Konservatiivseks Rahvaerakonnaks), Pärnu mnt. 30–5, Tallinn 10141, Estonia (office). *Telephone:* 616-1790 (office). *Fax:* 616-1791 (office). *E-mail:* erl@erl.ee (office).

HELMFRID, Staffan, PhD; Swedish geographer and academic; *Professor Emeritus of Human Geography, University of Stockholm;* b. 13 Dec. 1927, Stockholm; s. of Hartwig E. W. Helmfrid and Greta Helmfrid (née Kristiansson); m. Antje Teichmann 1954; three d.; ed Stockholm Univ.; Asst, Dept of Geography, Stockholm Univ. 1951, Asst Prof. 1955–62, Assoc. Prof. 1962–67, Research Fellow 1967–69, Prof. of Human Geography 1969–92, Prof. Emer. 1992–, Dean of Faculty of Social Sciences 1970, Pro-Rector (Vice-Pres.) Stockholm Univ. 1974, Rector 1978–88; Chair. Bank of Sweden Tercentenary Foundation 1980–86, Fulbright Comm. in Sweden 1984–85, Swedish Nat. Cttee of Geography 1988–94; mem. Standing Conf. on Univ. Problems (CC-PU), Council of Europe 1983–88; mem. Royal Acad. of Letters, History and Antiquities (Sec.-Gen. 1993–98), Royal Acad. of Sciences (Vice-Pres. 1988–91), Academia Europaea; Hon. Corresp. mem. Royal Geographical Soc., London 1995; Kt, Royal Order of North Star; Dr hc (Helsinki) 1986; HM Gold Medal, 12th size, Lord in Waiting 1987, Great Gold Medal, Royal Acad. of Letters, History and Antiquities 1999, Höpken Gold Medal, Royal Acad. of Sciences 2000, Vitus Behring Medal, Royal Danish Geographical Soc. 2002, Gösta Berg Medal, Royal Patriotic Soc. 2010, Olaus Magnus Medal, Swedish Cartographic Soc. 2012. *Publications:* Östergötland Västanstäng. Studien über die ältere Agrarlandschaft und ihre Genese 1962; books and articles on agrarian and historical geography; textbooks on geography and social science, National Atlas of Sweden. *Leisure interests:* mountain hiking, local history. *Address:* Department of Human Geography, Stockholm University, 106 91, Stockholm (office); Björkhags-vägen 40, 186 35 Vallentuna, Sweden (home). *Telephone:* (8) 51-17-48-33 (home). *E-mail:* staffan.helmfrid@swipnet.se (home).

HELØE, Leif Arne; Norwegian dentist and fmr politician; *Senior Researcher, Norwegian Institute for Urban and Regional Research;* b. 8 Aug. 1932, Harstad; m. Berit Heløe; two s. one d.; ed Univ. of Oslo; school and dist dentist, Harstad region 1957; Prof. of Community Dentistry, Univ. of Oslo 1975; mem. Harstad City Council 1960–69, mem. Municipal Exec. Bd 1968–69, Mayor of Harstad 1968–69; proxy mem. Storting (Parl.) 1965–73; Minister of Health and Social Affairs 1981–86; Dir-Gen. Norwegian Research Council for Science and Humanities 1988–91; Co-Gov. of Troms 1991–2000; Prof. (part-time), Norwegian Inst. for Urban and Regional Research 2000, Sr Researcher 2013–; Commdr, Order of the Finnish Lion 1996. Dr hc of Dentistry (Kupio) 1982, (Lund) 1984. *Address:* Rosenborggaten 5, 0356 Oslo, Norway (home). *Telephone:* 22-95-89-64 (office); 23-36-75-99 (home). *Fax:* 22-60-77-74 (office). *E-mail:* leif.heloe@nibr.no (office); arn-helo@online.no.

HELSØ, Gen. Hans Jesper; Danish army officer; b. 9 July 1948, Copenhagen; m. Pernille Vibeke Helsø; four c.; nat. service 1968, rank of Sergeant 1969, 2nd Lt 1970, 1st Lt 1974; Gun Position Officer, Fire Direction Officer, Battery Exec. Officer, Battery Commdr, Kings Artillery 1974–78; Co. Exec. Officer UNFICYP 1979; Capt. 1979; Staff Officer, Logistic Br. LANDZEALAND 1979–82, Procurement Br. CHODDEN 1983–87, NATO Office, Ministry of Defence 1987–90; rank of Maj. 1986, Lt-Col 1990; Bn Commdr, 1st and 2nd ARTY-Bn, Kings Artillery 1990–92; DCOS Plans and Policy, Army Operational Command 1992–94; rank of Col 1994; CO Kings Artillery 1994–96; Commdr Bihac Area, UNPROFOR 1995; CO 1st Zealand Brigade 1996–98; rank of Maj.-Gen. 1998; Commdr Army Operational Command 1998–2000; rank of Lt-Gen. 2000; Deputy Chief of Defence 2000–02, Chief of Defence 2002–08; rank of Gen. 2002; Grand Cross, Order of Dannebrog, Badge of Honour for Good Service in the Army, Badge of Honour, Danish Reserve Officers' Org., Grand Officier, Ordre nat. du Mérite, Order of the Cross of the Eagle, Commdr, Légion d'honneur; UN Medals, UNFICYP and UNPROFOR, Medal for Support to Latvia's membership of NATO. *Address:* c/o Defence Command, PO Box 2153, 1016 Copenhagen K, Denmark (office). *Telephone:* 45-67-30-00 (office). *Fax:* 45-89-07-48 (office). *E-mail:* fko-fc@mil.dk (office). *Website:* www.forsvaret.dk (office).

HELTAU, Michael; Austrian actor and singer; *Kammerschauspieler, Burgtheater, Vienna;* b. 5 July 1933, Ingolstadt; s. of Georg Heltau and Jakobine Heltau; ed gymnasium and Reinhardt Seminar; appeared at Würzburg and Bayerische Staatstheater, Munich 1953, Schillertheater, Berlin and Hamburg Schauspielhaus 1964–68, Theater in der Josefstadt, Vienna 1957–69, Volkstheater, Vienna 1970, Salzburg Festival 1965–75, Théâtre du Châtelet, Paris 1986; Kammerschauspieler, Burgtheater, Vienna 1972–, Doyen of the Burgtheater; noted for appearances in Shakespearean roles including Hamlet, Romeo, Richard II, Henry VI, Schnitzler's Anatol, von Hofmannsthal's Der Schwierige, Schiller's Wallenstein, etc.; second career as singer, especially songs of Jacques Brel (in German) and Viennese songs; numerous one-man shows on stage and TV; Hon. mem. Vienna Burgtheater 2003, Vienna Volksoper 2004; Austrian Cross of Honour (First Class) for Science and Art, Order of Merit (Germany) 2006; Karl Skraup Prize, Kainz Medal/Goldener Rathausmann, Gold Award of City of Vienna Nestroy Life Achievement Award 2005. *Films include:* Verlobung Am Wolfgangsee 1956, Der Letzte Mann 1956, Die Liebe Familie 1957, Lemkes Sel. Witwe 1957, Wiener Luft 1958, Das Weite Land 1970, Reigen 1974. *Publication:* Auf d'Nacht Herr Direktor! Momente aus dem Milieu (co-author) 2012. *Leisure interests:* reading, swimming. *Address:* Sulzweg 11, 1190 Vienna, Austria.

HELY-HUTCHINSON, Timothy Mark, MA; British publisher; *Group Chief Executive, Hachette UK;* b. 26 Oct. 1953, London; s. of Earl of Donoughmore and Countess of Donoughmore (née Parsons); ed Eton Coll. and Univ. of Oxford; Man. Dir Macdonald & Co. Ltd (publrs) 1982–86, Headline Book Publishing PLC 1986–93; Group Chief Exec. Hodder Headline Ltd 1993–, Dir W. H. Smith PLC 1999–, Chair. W. H. Smith News Ltd 2002–04, Group Chief Exec. Hachette Livre UK Ltd 2004–; mem. International Bd Hachette Livre and Dir Hachette Book Group USA; Venturer of the Year (British Venture Capital Asscn) 1990, Publr of the Year (British Book Awards) 1992. *Leisure interests:* opera, racing, bridge. *Address:* Hachette UK, 338 Euston Road, London, NW1 3BH, England (office). *Telephone:* (20) 7873-6011 (office). *Fax:* (20) 7873-6012 (office). *Website:* www .hachette.co.uk (office).

HEMINGER, Gary R., BA, MBA; American oil company executive; *President and CEO, Marathon Petroleum Corporation;* ed Tiffin Univ., Univ. of Dayton, Ohio, Wharton School Advanced Man. Program, Univ. of Pennsylvania; joined Marathon Petroleum 1975, spent five years in various financial and admin. roles, three years in London, UK as Audit Supervisor of the Brae Project, Pres. Marathon Pipe Line Co. 1995–96, Man., Business Devt and Jt Interest, Marathon Oil Co. 1996–98, Vice-Pres. Business Marathon Ashland Petroleum LLC (Marathon Petroleum Co. LLC from 2005, Marathon Petroleum Co. LP from 2010) 1998–99, Sr Vice-Pres., Business Devt 1999–2001, Exec. Vice-Pres., Supply, Transportation and Marketing 2001, Pres. Marathon Petroleum Co. LLC (Marathon Petroleum Co. LP from 2010, wholly owned subsidiary of Marathon) and Exec. Vice-Pres., Downstream, Marathon Oil Corpn 2001–11, mem. Exec. Cttee, Pres. and CEO 2011–; worked with Emro Marketing for eight years in several marketing and commercial roles, Vice-Pres. Western Div. Emro Marketing (Speedway SuperAmerica LLC) 1991; Chair. Bd of Trustees, Tiffin Univ.; Past Chair. American Petroleum Inst. Downstream Cttee, Louisiana Offshore Oil Port; mem. Bd of Dirs Fifth Third Bancorp; mem. Bd of Dirs and Exec. Cttee Nat. Petrochemical and Refiners Asscn; mem. Oxford Inst. for Energy Studies, US-Saudi Arabian Business Council Exec. Cttee. *Address:* Marathon Petroleum Corporation, Corporate Headquarters, 539 South Main Street, Findlay, OH 45840, USA (office). *Telephone:* (419) 422-2121 (office). *Fax:* (419) 425-7040 (office). *E-mail:* info@marathonpetroleum.com (office). *Website:* www.marathonpetroleum.com (office).

HEMINGFORD, 3rd Baron of Watford in the County of Hertford (cr. 1943); **(Dennis) Nicholas Hemingford,** (Nicholas Herbert), MA, FRSA; British journalist; b. (Dennis Nicholas Herbert), 25 July 1934, Watford, Herts., England; s. of Dennis George Ruddock Herbert, 2nd Baron Hemingford and Elizabeth McClare (née Clark); m. Jennifer Mary Toresen Bailey 1958; one s. three d.; ed Oundle School, Clare Coll., Cambridge; Sports Desk, Reuters 1956–57, Diplomatic Desk 1957–60, Washington, DC Bureau 1960–61; Asst Washington Corresp., The Times 1961–65, Middle East Corresp. 1965–69, Deputy Features Ed. 1969–70; Ed. Cambridge Evening News 1970–74; Editorial Dir Westminster Press 1974–91, Deputy Chief Exec. 1991–95; Pres. Guild of British Newspaper Eds 1980–81, Media Soc. 1982–84; Hon. Sec. Asscn of British Eds 1985–95; mem. E Anglian Regional Cttee, Nat. Trust 1983–2000, Chair. 1990–2000; Gov. Bell Educational Trust 1985–90; mem. Council Europa Nostra 1999–2005, Culture Cttee, UK Comm., UNESCO 1999–2003; Pres. Huntingdonshire Family History Soc.; mem. Council Friends of the British Library 2005–11, 2013–; Hon. mem. Soc. of Eds 1999; Hon. Sr mem. Wolfson Coll., Cambridge; Liveryman, Grocers' Co.; Jt Self-Publisher of the Year Award, Self-Publishing Awards 2010. *Publications:* Jews and Arabs in Conflict 1969, Press Freedom in Britain (with David Flintham) 1991, Successive Journeys (First Prize for Non-Fiction, Nat. Self-Publishing Awards 2010) 2008. *Leisure interests:* Egyptian War 1882, family history, computers, sport. *Address:* The Coach House, 4 Common Lane, Hemingford Abbots, Huntingdon,

Cambs., PE28 9AN, England (home). *Telephone:* (1480) 466234 (home). *Fax:* (1480) 380275 (home). *Website:* nicholas-herbert.co.uk (home).

HEMINGWAY, Wayne, MBE, BSc; British designer; b. 19 Jan. 1961, Morecambe, Lancs.; s. of Billy Two Rivers (Mohawk Indian chief); m. Gerardine Hemingway; two s. two d.; ed Univ. Coll., London; together with wife started in business with market stall in Camden, London; cr. footwear, clothing and accessory label Red or Dead 1992 (now non-exec. Chair.); collection retailed through eight Red or Dead shops in UK and three Red or Dead shops in Japan and wholesaled to int. network of retailers; jt venture with Pentland Group PLC 1996–; f. hemingwaydesign 1999; designed new wing for Inst. of Directors 2001; current design and consultancy projects include an award-winning 800-unit housing estate, carpet design, wall coverings and menswear; Chair. Building for Life, South Coast Design Forum; Prof., Northumbria Univ.; Fellow, Blackburn Coll.; Hon. Prof., Univ. of Northumbria; Hon. MA (Surrey); Dr hc (Wolverhampton), (Stafford); Street Designers of the Year, British Fashion Awards 1996, 1997, 1998, Housing Development of the Year 2005, Hero to Animals Award 2010. *Television:* appeared in various TV programmes including The Art Show for Channel 4, The Noughties…Was That It? 2009, Late Review 2010. *Publications:* Red or Dead: The Good, the Bad and the Ugly (with Gerardine Hemingway) 1998, Kitsch Icons 1999, Just Above the Mantelpiece 2000, Mass Market Classics The Home 2003; articles in newspapers and journals. *Address:* Hemingway Design, 15 Wembley Park Drive, Wembley, Middx, HA9 8HD, England (office). *Telephone:* (20) 8903-1074 (office). *Fax:* (20) 8903-1076 (office). *E-mail:* hemingway@tesco.net (office). wayne@hemingwaydesign.co.uk (office).

HEMMING, John Henry, CMG, MA, DLitt, FSA; British/Canadian writer and publisher; *Joint Chairman, Hemming Group Ltd;* b. 5 Jan. 1935, Vancouver, BC; s. of H. Harold Hemming, OBE, MC and Alice L. Hemming, OBE; m. Sukie Babington-Smith 1979; one s. one d.; ed Eton Coll., UK, McGill Univ. and Univ. of Oxford, UK; Dir and Sec. Royal Geographical Soc. 1975–96; Jt Chair. Hemming Group Ltd 1976–; Chair. Brintex Ltd, Newman Books Ltd; explorations in Peru and Brazil 1960, 1961, 1971, 1972, 1986–88, led Maracá Rainforest Project, Brazil (largest ever Amazon research programme by a European country) 1987–88; Hon. Fellow, Magdalen Coll. Oxford 2004; Commdr, Order of Southern Cross (Brazil) 1998, Grand Cross, Order of Merit (Peru) 2007; Hon. DLitt (Oxford) 1981, Dr hc (Warwick) 1989, (Stirling) 1991; Pitman Literary Prize 1970, Christopher Award (USA) 1971, Founder's Medal, Royal Geographical Soc. 1989, Bradford Washburn Medal, Boston Museum of Science 1989, Mungo Park Medal, Royal Scottish Geographical Soc. 1988, Special Award, Instituto Nacional de Cultura (Peru) 1996, Citation of Merit, Explorers' Club (New York) 1997. *Publications:* The Conquest of the Incas 1970, Tribes of the Amazon Basin in Brazil (with others) 1973, Red Gold: The Conquest of the Brazilian Indians 1978, The Search for El Dorado 1978, Machu Picchu 1982, Monuments of the Incas 1983, Change in the Amazon Basin (two vols) (ed.) 1985, Amazon Frontier: The Defeat of the Brazilian Indians 1987, Maracá 1988, Roraima, Brazil's Northernmost Frontier 1990, The Rainforest Edge (ed.) 1993, Royal Geographical Society Illustrated (ed.) 1997, The Golden Age of Discovery 1998, Die If You Must: Brazilian Indians in the Twentieth Century 2003, Tree of Rivers: The Story of the Amazon 2007. *Leisure interests:* travel, writing. *Address:* 10 Edwardes Square, London, W8 6HE (home); Hemming Group Ltd, 32 Vauxhall Bridge Road, London, SW1V 2SS, England (office). *Telephone:* (20) 7602-6697 (home); (20) 7973-6634 (office). *Fax:* (20) 7233-5049 (office). *Website:* www.hgluk.com (office); www.johnhemming.net.

HEMMINGSEN, Ralf, MD, DrMed; Danish psychiatrist, academic and university rector; *Rector (Vice-Chancellor), University of Copenhagen;* b. 12 Oct. 1949; ed Univ. of Copenhagen; research training and clinical training as consultant in psychiatry 1975–76; Sr Lecturer in Psychiatry, Univ. of Copenhagen 1978–80, 1984–95, Prof. of Psychiatry 1995–, Dean of Faculty of Health Sciences 2002–05, Rector Univ. of Copenhagen 2005–, Chair. Faculty Jt Cttee 2002–05, Faculty Occupational Health Cttee 2002–05, Man. Forum, Copenhagen Univ. Hosp. (KUHL) 2002–05, Copenhagen Tech Transfer Consortium 2003–05, mem. Main Jt Cttee 2002–05, Steering Group for Univ. of Copenhagen's Value Process 2003–05, Human Resources Policy Cttee 2004–05; Consultant in Psychiatry, Frederiksberg Hosp. 1986; Medical Dir Bispebjerg Hosp. 1986–2002; Chair. Danish Soc. for Biological Psychiatry 1997–2000; mem. Danish Medicolegal Council 1992–; mem. Bd The Medical Soc. in Copenhagen 1991–97; mem. Danish Psychiatric Soc. (Chair. 1986–90); mem. European Soc. for Clinical Investigation (Pres. 1983–87); Kt of the Dannebrog 2007; Gold Medal, Univ. of Copenhagen. *Publications:* more than 150 papers in scientific journals. *Address:* Rector's Office, University of Copenhagen, Nørregade 10, PO Box 2177, 1017 Copenhagen K, Denmark (office). *Telephone:* 35-32-26-12 (office). *E-mail:* rektor@adm.ku.dk (office). *Website:* www .ku.dk (office).

HEMSLEY, Stephen J.; American business executive; *President and CEO, UnitedHealth Group;* ed Fordham Univ.; fmr Man. Partner, Chief Financial Officer and Head of Strategy, Tech., and Operating Professional Service Lines, Arthur Andersen and Co.; Sr Exec. Vice-Pres. UnitedHealth Group 1997–98, COO 1998–2006, Pres. 1999–, mem. Bd of Dirs 2000–, CEO 2006–. *Address:* UnitedHealth Group, PO Box 1459, Minneapolis, MN 55440-1459, USA (office). *Telephone:* (952) 936-1300 (office). *E-mail:* info@unitedhealthgroup.com (office). *Website:* www.unitedhealthgroup.com (office).

HEN, Józef, (Korab), Polish writer and playwright; b. 8 Nov. 1923, Warsaw; s. of Rubin Cukier and Ewa Cukier; m. Irena Hen 1946; one s. one d.; self-educated; Lecturer, Sorbonne, France 1993 and Univ. of Warsaw 1995–96; mem. Acad. des Sciences, Belles Lettres et des Beaux Arts, Bordeaux, France; mem. Polish PEN Club; Great Literary Prize of Warsaw. *Film screenplays include:* Krzyż walecznych (Cross of Valour) 1959, Kwiecień (April) 1961, Nikt nie woła (Nobody's Calling) 1961, Bokser i śmierć (The Boxer and Death), Prawo i pięść (Law and the Fist) and Don Gabriel. *Screenplays for TV serials:* Życie Kamila Kuranta (The Life of Kamil Kurant) 1983, Crimen and Królewskie Sny (Royal Dreams) 1987. *Theatre plays:* Ja, Michał z Montaigne (I, Michel de Montaigne) 1984, Justyn! Justyn!, Popołudnie kochanków (Lovers' Afternoon) 1994. *Publications include:* Skromny chłopiec w haremie (A Modest Boy in a Harem) 1957, Kwiecień (April) 1960 (Book of the Year 1961), Teatr Heroda (Herod's Theatre) 1966, Twarz pokerzysty (Pokerface) 1970, Oko Dajana (Dayan's Eye, as Korab) 1972, Yokohama 1973, Crimen 1975, Bokser i śmierć (The Boxer and Death) 1975, Ja, Michał z Montaigne

(I, Michel de Montaigne) 1978, Milczące między nami (Silent between Us) 1985, Nie boję się bezsennych nocy (I'm Not Afraid of Sleepless Nights), 3 books 1987, 1992, 2001, Królenskie sny (Royal Dreams) 1989, Nikt nie woła (Nobody's Calling) 1990, Nowolipie 1991, Odejście Afrodyty (Aphrodite's Departure) 1995, Najpiękniejsze lata (The Most Beautiful Years) 1996, Niebo naszych ojcow (Sky of Our Fathers 1997, Błazen – wielki mąż (Jester – The Great Man) (ZAiKS Book of the Year Award 1999) 1998, Mójprzyjaciel Król (My Friend the King) (Booker's Club Book of the Year Award 2005) 2003, Bruliony profesora T. (The Bloch-notes of Professor T.) 2006, Ping-pomgista (The Ping-pongist) 2008, Dziennik na nowy wiek (A Diary for the New Age) 2009, Szóste, najmlodsze (The Sixth, The Youngest) 2012. *Leisure interests:* historical and literary monographs, watching sports programmes on television, films. *Address:* Al. Ujazdowskie 8 m. 2, 00-478 Warsaw, Poland (home). *Telephone:* (22) 629-19-03 (home). *E-mail:* jozef.hen@gmail.com (home).

HENARE, Tau; New Zealand politician; b. 29 Sept. 1960, Auckland; m.; five c.; ed Hillary Coll.; Advisory Officer in Maori Devt, Waitakere City Council 1988–90; Youth Educ. Co-ordinator, Race Relations Conciliator, Advisory Officer, Dept of Internal Affairs 1990–94; MP for Northern Maori (now Te Tai Tokerau) 1993–; Minister of Maori Affairs 1997–99, for Racing, Assoc. Minister for Sport, Fitness and Leisure; Deputy Leader NZ First Party, Spokesperson on Cultural Affairs and Treaty of Waitangi Negotiations; mem. Bd of Dirs Te Pataka Ohanga Ltd 2004–05; Host, Newstalk ZB; mem. Clerical Workers' Union 1984–88. *Address:* Parliament Office, Private Bag 18888, Parliament Buildings, Wellington 6160, New Zealand (office). *Telephone:* (4) 817-9999 (office). *Fax:* (4) 471-2551 (office). *Website:* www.parliament.nz (office).

HENAULT, Gen. (retd) Raymond Roland (Ray), CD, BA, MSc; Canadian fmr armed forces officer and business executive; *Chairman of the Board and Strategic Executive Advisor, ADGA Group Inc.;* b. 26 April 1949, Winnipeg, Manitoba; s. of Roland Henault and Sylvia Henault; m. Loraine Anne Henault; ed Univ. of Man., Nat. Defence Coll., Kingston, Ontario, École Supérieure de Guerre Aérienne, Paris, France; began career in Canadian Armed Forces 1968; training at Canadian Force Base (CFB) Borden, Ontario and Gimili, Man.; CF-101 Voodoo Pilot, 425 Squadron, CFB Bagotville, Québec 1971; Flying Instructor, Musketeer, CFB Portage la Prairie 1972–74; Air Traffic Controller, CFB Bagotville 1974–76; Twin Huey Helicopter Pilot, 408 Squadron, CFB Edmonton, Alberta 1976–80; Staff Officer Aviation, 5 Canadian Brigade Group HQ, CFB Valcartier 1980–81; Twin Huey Flight Commdr, 430e Escardon, CFB Valcartier 1981–83; École supérieure de Guerre aérienne, Paris, France, 1983–85; Head of Doctrine and Int. Programs, Directorate of Land Aviation, Nat. Defence HQ, Ottawa 1985; Project Dir Canadian Forces Light Helicopter Project, Ottawa 1985–87; Commdg Officer 444(CA) Tactical Helicopter Squadron, CFB Lahr, Germany 1987–89; Sr Staff Officer Requirements, Air Command HQ, Winnipeg 1989–90; Base Commdr, CFB Portage la Prairie 1990–92; Deputy Commdr 10 Tactical Air Group, CFB Montreal 1992–93, Commdr 1994–95; Chief of Staff Operations, Air Command HQ 1995–96; Chief of Staff J3 and Dir-Gen. Mil. Plans and Operations, Nat. Defence HQ 1996–97; Acting Deputy Chief of Defence Staff 1997, Asst Chief of Air Staff 1997–98, Deputy Chief of Defence Staff 1998–2001, Chief of Defence Staff 2001–05; Chair. Mil. Cttee NATO 2005–08 (retd); Pres. Canadian Defence Asscns Inst.; promoted to Brigadier-Gen. 1994, Maj.-Gen. 1997, Lt-Gen. 1998, Gen. 2001; currently Chair. and Strategic Exec. Advisor, ADGA Group Inc.; Commdr Order of Mil. Merit, Canadian Meritorious Service Cross, Commdr Légion d'honneur, Most Venerable Order of St John of Jerusalem, US Legion of Merit, Czech Cross of Merit, NATO Meritorious Service Medal, Ukrainian Medal of Honour, Commdr's Cross, Hungarian Order of Merit, Commdr, Belgian Order of the Grand Croix; Hon. LLD (Univ. of Man.), Hon. PhD (Royal Military Coll. of Canada) 2005. *Address:* ADGA Group Inc., 116 Albert Street, Suite 600, Ottawa, ON K1P 5G3, Canada (office). *Telephone:* (613) 237-3022 (office). *Fax:* (613) 237-5359 (office). *E-mail:* rhenault@adga.ca (office). *Website:* www.adga.ca (office).

HENDE, Csaba, PhD; Hungarian lawyer and politician; *Minister of Defence;* b. 5 Feb. 1960, Szombathely; m.; twin d.; ed Nagy Lajos Secondary Grammar School, Szombathely, Eötvös Loránd Univ.; worked as attorney trainee at Attorneys' Asscn, Szombathely 1984–91; Parl. Sec., Head of Legal Dept and Cabinet Sec., Ministry of Defence 1991–94; worked as attorney in Szombathely 1994–98; mem. Gen. Ass. of Szombathely 1990; mem. Parl. (Magyar Demokrata Fórum—MDF) 1993–96, (Country List) 2002–06, for Vas Co. 2006–; Political State Sec., Ministry of Justice 1998–2002; asked by Pres. Viktor Orbán to be Nat. Coordinator of the Civic Circles 2002–05; Notary for Legislation during inaugural session of Parl. 2005–10; mem. Nat. Security Cttee 2009–; Minister of Defence 2010–; mem. MDF 1988–2004, Pres. MDF org. in Szombathely 1990–91, Nat. Commr for Ethics 1993–96, mem. party presidency 1996–2002, Nat. Vice-Pres., then Gen. Vice-Pres. 1999–2002; incl. June–Dec. 2004; mem. Fidesz—Hungarian Civic Alliance (Fidesz—Magyar Polgári Szöevetség) 2004–; mem. Apáczai Csere János Foundation Advisory Bd 1990–97; col in army reserve. *Leisure interest:* cycling. *Address:* Ministry of Defence, 1055 Budapest, Balaton u. 7–11 (office); Ministry of Defence, 1885 Budapest, Pf.: 25, Hungary (office). *Telephone:* (1) 474-1155 (office). *Fax:* (1) 474-1285 (office). *E-mail:* miniszter@hm.gov.hu (office); minister@hm.gov.hu (office). *Website:* www.kormany.hu/en/ministry-of-defence (office).

HENDERSON, Sir Denys (Hartley), Kt, MA, LLB, FRSA; British business executive and solicitor; b. 11 Oct. 1932, Colombo, Sri Lanka; s. of the late John Hartley Henderson and Nellie Henderson (née Gordon); m. Doreen Mathewson Glashan 1957; two d.; ed Aberdeen Grammar School and Univ. of Aberdeen; Commercial Asst ICI 1957–58, Chair. Paints Div. 1977–80, Main Bd Dir 1980, Deputy Chair. 1986–87, Chair. 1987–95; Chancellor Univ. of Bath 1993–98; Chair. Zeneca Group PLC 1993–95; mem. Bd of Dirs Barclays Bank PLC 1983–97, Barclays PLC 1985–97, RTZ Corpn PLC 1990–96, Rank 1994–2001 (Chair. 1995–2001), MORI, Dalgety PLC 1996–98 (Chair. 1997–98), AZ Electronic Materials; mem. Law Soc. of Scotland; Chair. Court of Govs of Henley Man. Coll. 1989–96; mem. Pres.'s Cttee, CBI 1987–96; First Crown Estate Commr 1995–2002; Trustee, The Natural History Museum 1989–98; Chair. Univ. of Aberdeen Quincentenary Appeal Cttee 1993–96; Pres. and Chair. Bd British Quality Foundation 1993–97; Hon. Fellow, City and Guilds of London Inst. 1990; Hon. DUniv (Brunel) 1987, (Strathclyde) 1993, Hon. LLD (Aberdeen) 1987, (Nottingham) 1990, (Manchester) 1991, (Bath) 1993, Hon. DSc (Cranfield Inst. of Tech.)

1989, (Teesside) 1993; Soc. of Chemical Industry Centenary Medal 1993. *Leisure interests:* family life, swimming, reading, travel, gardening and "unskilled but enjoyable" golf.

HENDERSON, Donald Ainslie, MD, MPH; American physician, epidemiologist and academic; *Professor of Medicine and Public Health and Resident Scholar, Center for Biosecurity, University of Pittsburgh Medical Center;* b. 7 Sept. 1928, Cleveland, Ohio; s. of David A. Henderson and Grace E. McMillan; m. Nana I. Bragg 1951; two s. one d.; ed Oberlin Coll., Univ. of Rochester and Johns Hopkins Univ.; Intern, Mary Imogene Bassett Hosp., Cooperstown, NY 1954–55, Resident 1957–59; various posts at Communicable Diseases Center, Dept of Health, Educ. and Welfare 1955–66, Chief Smallpox Eradication Program 1965–66; Chief Medical Officer, WHO Smallpox Eradication 1966–77; Prof. of Epidemiology and Int. Health, Johns Hopkins Univ. Bloomberg School of Public Health 1977–2003, Dean 1977–90, Dir Civilian Biodefense Studies Center 1998–2001, now Univ. Distinguished Service Prof. and Dean Emer.; Prof. of Medicine and Public Health, Univ. of Pittsburgh Medical Center 2003–, Resident Scholar, Center for Biosecurity (now for Health Security) 2003–; Assoc. Dir, Office of Science and Tech. Policy, Exec. Office of the Pres. 1991–93; Deputy Asst Sec. Dept of Health and Human Services, Washington, DC 1993–95, Sr Scientific Adviser 1993–95; Dir Office of Public Health Preparedness, Dept of Health and Human Services 2001–03, Sr Scientific Adviser 2003–; mem. numerous professional socs, cttees and advisory panels; 16 hon. degrees; Presidential Medal of Freedom 2002, Kt Grand Cross, Govt of Thailand 2006, Ordre of Brilliant Star with Grand Cordon, Repub. of China 2013; Nat. Medal of Science 1986, Japan Prize 1988, Edward Jenner Medal, Royal Soc. of Medicine, recipient of numerous scientific awards and recognitions from orgs in USA, Canada, UK, Japan, Brazil, Uruguay, Switzerland, People's Repub. of China, Ethiopia, Afghanistan, Germany, Australia, India and Pakistan. *Publications:* more than 250 articles dealing primarily with smallpox eradication, epidemiology and immunization. *Address:* Center for Health Security, University of Pittsburgh Medical Center, Pier IV Building, Suite 210, 621 East Pratt Street, Baltimore, MD 21202 (office); 3802 Greenway, Baltimore, MD 21218, USA (home). *Telephone:* (443) 573-3323 (office); (410) 614-9438 (home). *Fax:* (443) 573-3305 (office); (410) 889-6514 (home). *E-mail:* dahzero@aol.com (office); dahzero@aol.com (home). *Website:* upmchealthsecurity.org (office).

HENDERSON, Frederick A. (Fritz), BBA, MBA; American automotive industry executive; b. 29 Nov. 1958, Detroit; m. Karen Henderson; two d.; ed Lake Orion High School, Mich., Ross School of Business, Univ. of Michigan, Harvard Business School, Harvard Univ.; with General Motors (GM) since 1984, GM Vice-Pres. and Man. Dir GM do Brasil (covering GM operations in Brazil, Argentina, Paraguay and Uruguay) 1997–2000, Group Vice-Pres. and Pres. GM-LAAM (Latin America, Africa and Middle East) 2000–02, Pres. GM Asia Pacific, Singapore 2002–04, Chair. GM Europe, Zurich, Switzerland 2004–06, Vice-Chair. and Chief Financial Officer 2006–09, Pres. and CEO General Motors Corpn (following Chapter 11 bankruptcy reorganization) 2009; Group Vice-Pres. of Finance, GMAC Financial Services (fmrly General Motors Acceptance Corpn), Detroit 1992–97. *Achievements include:* pitched for Univ. of Michigan Wolverines baseball team. *Address:* c/o General Motors Corporation, 300 Renaissance Center, Detroit, MI 48265-3000, USA.

HENDERSON, Richard, PhD, FRS; British molecular biologist; *Programme Leader, Laboratory of Molecular Biology, Medical Research Council;* b. 19 July 1945, Edinburgh, Scotland; s. of John W. Henderson and Grace S. Henderson (née Goldie); m. 1st Penelope Fitzgerald 1969 (divorced 1988); one s. one d. (one d. deceased); m. 2nd Jade Li 1995; ed Hawick High School, Boroughmuir Secondary School, Univs of Edinburgh and Cambridge; professional interest in structure and function of protein molecules, especially in biological membranes; Helen Hay Whitney Postdoctoral Fellow, Yale Univ., USA 1970–73; Fellow, Darwin Coll. Cambridge 1982–2012; mem. research staff, MRC Lab. of Molecular Biology 1973–, Dir 1996–2006, Programme Leader 2006–; Scientific Founder Heptares Therapeutics 2007; Foreign Assoc. NAS; Ernst Ruska Prize for Electron Microscopy 1981, Lewis S. Rosenstiel Award, Brandeis Univ. 1991, Louis Jeantet Award 1993, Gregori Aminoff Award 1999. *Publications:* numerous scientific articles in books and journals. *Leisure interests:* canoeing, wine. *Address:* MRC Laboratory of Molecular Biology, Francis Crick Avenue, Cambridge, CB2 0QH, England (office). *Telephone:* (1223) 267065 (office). *Fax:* (1223) 268305 (office). *E-mail:* rh15@mrc-lmb.cam.ac.uk (office). *Website:* www2.mrc-lmb.cam.ac.uk/group-leaders/h-to-m/richard-henderson (office); www2.mrc-lmb.cam.ac.uk/groups/rh15 (office).

HENDRICKS, Barbara Ann, BSc, BMus; Swedish (b. American) singer (soprano); b. 20 Nov. 1948, Stephens, Ark., USA; d. of M. L. Hendricks and Della Hendricks; m. Ulf Englund 1978; one s. one d.; ed Univ. of Nebraska-Lincoln and Juilliard School of Music, New York, studying with Jennie Tourel; operatic debut, San Francisco Opera (L'Incoronazion di Poppea) 1976; has appeared with opera companies of Boston, Santa Fe, Glyndebourne, Hamburg, La Scala (Milan), Berlin, Paris, Los Angeles, Florence and Royal Opera, Covent Garden (London), Vienna; recitals in most major centres in Europe and America; has toured extensively in USSR and Japan; concert performances with all leading European and US orchestras; has appeared at many major music festivals including Edinburgh, Osaka, Montreux, Salzburg, Dresden, Prague, Aix-en-Provence, Orange and Vienna; nominated Goodwill Amb. for Refugees at UNHCR 1987; Founder Barbara Hendricks Foundation for Peace and Reconciliation 1998; Hon. mem. Inst. of Humanitarian Law, San Remo, Italy 1990; Commdr des Arts et des Lettres 1986, Chevalier, Légion d'honneur 1992; Hon. DMus (Nebraska Wesleyan Univ.) 1988, Dr hc (Univ. of Louvain, Belgium) 1990, 1993, (Juilliard School, New York) 2000; Prince of Asturias Foundation Award 2000, Lions Club International Award for the Defense of Human Rights 2001, Premio Internacional Xifra Heras, Univ. of Gerona, Spain 2004, La Medaille D'Or de la ville de Paris 2004. *Film appearances:* La Bohème 1988, The Rake's Progress 1994. *Recordings:* nearly 90 recordings. *Leisure interest:* reading. *Address:* B H Office, Fondberg Produktion, Dalagatan 48, 11324, Stockholm, Sweden (office). *E-mail:* bh.office@bluewin.ch (office). *Website:* www.barbarahendricks.com (office).

HENDROPRIYONO, Lt-Gen. (retd) Abdullah Mahmud; Indonesian politician; b. 1945, Jakarta; ed AMN Military Acad.; mil. career with Kopassus Unit, including several tours of combat duty in Kalimantan 1960s and 1970s, in East

Timor 1975; sr positions in Bais (Indonesian mil. intelligence agency) 1990s, Jakarta Area Commdr 1993–94; Minister of Transmigration and Resettlement 1998–99; Head of Nat. Intelligence Agency (BIN) 2001–04; also owner of a law firm; Bintang Mahaputera Indonesia Adipradana, Bintang Kartika Eka Paksi Nararya Prestasi, Satya Lencana Bhakti. *Address:* c/o Office of the Co-ordinating Minister for Political Affairs, Security and Social Welfare, Jalan Medan Merdeka Barat 15, Jakarta 10110, Indonesia (office).

HENDRY, Sir David Forbes, Kt, PhD, FBA, FRSE; British economist and academic; *Professor of Economics, University of Oxford;* ed London School of Econs; Lecturer, then Reader, later Prof. of Econs, LSE –1982; Prof. of Econs, Univ. of Oxford 1982–, Head of Dept of Econs 2001–07, Professorial Fellow, Nuffield Coll. Oxford; Fellow, Econometric Soc., Journal of Econometrics; Hon. Vice-Pres. Royal Econ. Soc.; Hon. Fellow, Int. Inst. of Forecasters; Foreign Hon. mem. American Acad. of Arts and Sciences, American Econ. Asscn. *Publications:* Econometrics and Quantitative Economics (co-ed.) 1984, PC-NAIVE, An Interactive Program for Monte Carlo Experimentation in Econometrics. Version 6.0 (co-author) 1991, PcGive 7: An Interactive Econometric Modelling System (co-author) 1992, Econometrics: Alchemy or Science? 1993, 2001, Co-integration, Error Correction and the Econometric Analysis of Non-Stationary Data (co-author) 1993, Dynamic Econometrics 1995, The Foundations of Econometric Analysis (co-author) 1995, Forecasting Economic Time Series (co-author) 1998, Forecasting Non-stationary Economic Time Series (co-author) 1999, Nonlinear Econometric Modeling in Time Series. Proceedings of the Eleventh International Symposium in Economic Theory (co-ed.) 2000, Automatic Econometric Model Selection (co-author) 2001, Empirical Econometric Modelling Using PcGive Volumes I, II and III (co-author) 2001, GiveWin: An Interface to Empirical Modelling (2nd edn) (co-author) 2001, Interactive Monte Carlo Experimentation in Econometrics Using PcNaive (co-author) 2001, Understanding Economic Forecast (co-author) 2001, A Companion to Economic Forecasting (co-author) 2002, General to Specific Modelling (co-author) 2004, Econometric Modeling: A Likelihood Approach (co-author) 2007; numerous papers in professional journals on time series econometrics and the econometrics of the demand for money, the theory of forecasting and on automated model building. *Address:* Nuffield College, New Road, Oxford, OX1 1NF, England (office). *Telephone:* (1865) 278587 (office). *E-mail:* david.hendry@economics.ox.ac.uk (office); david.hendry@nuffield.ox.ac.uk (office). *Website:* www.nuff.ox.ac.uk/users/hendry (office); www.economics.ox.ac.uk (office).

HENDRY, Stephen Gordon, MBE; British professional snooker player; b. 13 Jan. 1969, South Queensferry, Edinburgh, Scotland; s. of Gordon J. Hendry and Irene Anthony; m. Amanda Elizabeth Teresa Tart 1995; two s.; ed Inverkeithing High School; began playing snooker aged 12; won Scottish U-16 Championship 1983; appeared on BBC's Junior version of Pot Black 1983; won Scottish Amateur Championship 1984, 1985; youngest ever entrant in World Amateur Championship 1984; turned professional 1985 (youngest ever); winner of 74 titles (36 ranking, 38 non-ranking), including Scottish Professional 1986, 1987, 1988, Grand Prix 1987, 1990, 1991, 1995, Australian Masters 1987, British Open 1988, 1991, 1999, 2003, New Zealand Masters 1988, Masters 1989, 1990, 1991, 1992, 1993, 1996, Scottish Masters 1989, 1990, 1995, UK Championship 1989, 1990, 1994, 1995, 1996, Dubai Duty Free Classic 1989, 1990, 1993, Continental Airlines London Masters 1989, 1990, Embassy World Championship 1990, 1992, 1993, 1994, 1995, 1996, 1999, Pontins Professional 1990, 1991, Indian Challenge 1991, Matchroom League 1991, 1992, Irish Masters 1992, 1997, 1999, Regal Welsh 1992, 1997, 2003, Scottish Open 1993, 1997, 1999, European Challenge 1992, 1993, European Open 1993, 1994, 2001, European League 1994, 1995, Top Rank Classic 1994, Charity Challenge 1995, 1997, Thailand Masters 1998, Red Bull Super Challenge 1998, Malta Grand Prix 1998, 2001, Champions Cup 1999, Premier League Snooker 2000, 2004, Malta Cup 2005, Legends of Snooker 2009; team events: World Doubles (with Mike Hallett) 1987, Mita/Sky World Masters Men's Doubles (with Mike Hallett) 1991, World Cup (with team Scotland) 1996, Nations Cup (with team Scotland) 2001; holds the most world ranking titles (36) and most competitive century breaks (762); second only to Ronnie O'Sullivan for the most competitive 147 breaks with 10 in total; announced retirement May 2012; Dr hc (Stirling) 2000; World Professional Billiards and Snooker Assen (WPBSA) Young Player of the Year 1988, BBC Scotland Sports Personality of the Year 1987, 1996, WPBSA Player of the Year 1990, 1991, 1992, 1993, 1995, 1996, WPBSA Performance of the Year 1995, MacRoberts Trophy 2001. *Publication:* Snooker Masterclass 1994. *Leisure interests:* golf, poker, music, Formula 1, Heart of Midlothian (Hearts) Football Club. *Address:* Stephen Hendry Snooker Club, 275 Brook Street, Preston, PR1 7NH, England (office). *Telephone:* (1772) 824861 (office). *E-mail:* info@stephenhendrysnookerclub.co.uk (office). *Website:* www .stephenhendrysnookerclub.co.uk (office).

HENG, Swee Keat, MA, MPA; Singaporean government official; *Managing Director, Monetary Authority of Singapore;* ed Univ. of Cambridge, UK, Kennedy School of Govt, Harvard Univ., USA; fmr Sr Police Officer; Dir of Higher Educ., Ministry of Educ. –1997; served in Prime Minister's Office as Prin. Pvt. Sec. to then Sr Minister Lee Kuan Yew 1997–2000; Deputy Sec. (Trade), Ministry of Trade and Industry 2000–01, concurrently CEO Trade Devt Bd 2001, Perm. Sec. 2001–05; Man. Dir (Designate) Monetary Authority of Singapore March–June 2005, Man. Dir June 2005–; Overseas Singapore Police Force Scholar, Gold Medal in Public Admin 2001. *Address:* Monetary Authority of Singapore, 10 Shenton Way, MAS Building, Singapore City, 079117, Singapore (office). *Telephone:* 6225-5577 (office). *Fax:* 6229-9491 (office). *E-mail:* webmaster@mas.gov.sg (office). *Website:* www.mas .gov.sg (office).

HENG SAMRIN; Cambodian politician; *Chairman, National Assembly of Cambodia;* b. 25 May 1934, Prey Veng Prov.; Political Commissar and Commdr of Khmer Rouge 4th Infantry Div. 1976–78; led abortive coup against Pol Pot and fled to Viet Nam 1978; Pres. Nat. Front for Nat. Salvation of Kampuchea 1978; Pres. People's Revolutionary Council 1979 (took power after Vietnamese invasion of Kampuchea); Chair. Council of State of Cambodia 1991; Sec. Gen. People's Revolutionary Party of Kampuchea (KPRP) 1981–91, Vice-Chair. 1998–2006; Chair. Nat. Ass. of Cambodia 2006–; mem. Politburo of Cambodia 1991–; Hon. Chair. Cambodian People's Party 1993. *Address:* National Assembly of Cambodia, Sothearos Boulevard Khan Daun Penh, Phnom Penh, Cambodia (office). *Tele-*

phone: (23) 427768 (office). *Fax:* (23) 427769 (office). *Website:* www.national -assembly.org.kh (office).

HENIN, Justine; Belgian professional tennis player (retd); b. 1 June 1982, Liège; d. of José Henin and the late Françoise Henin; m. Pierre-Yves Hardenne 2002 (divorced 2007); right-handed, one-handed backhand; winner, French Open Jr Championship 1997; turned professional 1 Jan. 1999; semi-finalist, French Open 2001, winner 2003, 2005, 2006, 2007; finalist, Wimbledon 2001, 2006, semi-finalist 2002, 2003; semi-finalist, Australian Open, 2003, winner 2004, finalist 2010; winner, US Open 2003, 2007; winner, WTA Championships 2006, 2007; Gold Medal, Olympic Games, Athens 2004; retd from professional tennis 14 May 2008; returned from retirement Jan. 2010, retd again 2011; 503 career singles wins, 109 defeats, 47 career doubles wins, 35 defeats; 43 singles WTA titles, two doubles titles; highest ranking (singles): World No. 1 20 Oct. 2003. *Address:* c/o Vincent Stavaux, Place Riva Bella 12/5, 1420 Braine L'Alleud, Belgium.

HÉNIN, Pierre-Yves, PhD; French academic, university administrator and economist; *President, Université Paris I (Panthéon Sorbonne);* b. 11 April 1946, St-Aubin, Saône et Loire; m.; four c.; ed Faculté de Droit et de Sciences Economiques de Paris, Université Paris I (Panthéon Sorbonne); Research Dir ISEA, CNRS 1967–71; Prof. Université d'Orléans 1972–75; Founder and Dir Macroéconomie et Analyse des Déséquilibres research centre, Université Paris I (Panthéon Sorbonne) 1974–1990, Prof. Université Paris I (Panthéon Sorbonne) 1975–, Dir UER 1978–82, 1985–90, Vice-Pres. Scientific Council 1982–89, 1993–, Pres. Université Paris I (Panthéon Sorbonne) 2004–; Consultant to Ministry of Research and Tech. 1985–86; Dir CEPREMAP 1991–2004; mem. Scientific Council Ecole Nationale des Statistiques et de l'Admin Economique 1980–86; Vice-Pres. Assen Française de Sciences Economiques 1994–95, Pres. 1995–97; Chevalier de l'Ordre Nationale du Mérite 1993, Chevalier des Palmes Académiques 1998, Chevalier de la Légion d'Honneur 2002; AFSE Thesis Prize 1970, Le Nouvel Economiste Economist of the Year 1996. *Publications include:* Macrodynamics: Fluctuations And Growth 1986, Advances in Equilibrium Business Cycles Research 1995, Should we Rebuild Built-in Stabilizers? 1997 and several other books and articles. *Address:* Office of the President, Université Paris I (Panthéon Sorbonne), 12 place du Panthéon, 75231 Paris Cedex 05, France (office). *Telephone:* 1-44-07-80-00 (office). *E-mail:* Pierre-Yves.Henin@univ-paris1.fr (office). *Website:* www.univ -paris1.fr (office).

HENKEL, Hans-Olaf; German business executive; *Honorary Professor of International Management, University of Mannheim;* b. 14 March 1940, Hamburg; four c.; joined Int. Business Machines (IBM), Germany 1962, Pres. IBM Germany 1987–89, Vice-Pres. IBM Corpn 1989–95, CEO IBM Europe 1993–95; Pres. Bundesverband der Deutschen Industrie 1995–2000; Pres. Leibniz Gemeinschaft 2001–05; Hon. Prof. of Int. Man., Univ. of Mannheim 2000–; mem. Supervisory Bd Altira, Bayer AG, Continental AG, Daimler Luft- und Raumfahrt Holding AG, SMS GmbH, Ringier AG; mem. Amnesty Int.; Co-founder Konvent für Deutschland; Dr hc (Tech. Univ. of Dresden) 1991; Commdr, Légion d'honneur; WWF Environmental Manager of the Year 1991, Wirtschaftswoche magazine Innovation Award, Corine Writers' Award, Ludwig-Erhard Award, Cicero 'Best Business Speaker' Award, Deutscher Mittelstandspreis 2006, Hayek Medal 2007. *Publications:* Jetzt oder nie, Die Macht der Freiheit, Die Ethik des Erfolgs, Die Kraft des Neubeginns, Der Kampf um die Mitte, Die Abwracker, Rettet unser Geld. *Leisure interests:* sailing, jazz. *Address:* Friedrichstrasse 166, 10117 Berlin, Germany (office). *Telephone:* (30) 200597701 (office). *Fax:* (30) 200597729 (office). *E-mail:* petra.ziemer@baml.com (office).

HENKELMAN, R. Mark, PhD, FRSC; Canadian biophysicist and academic; *University Professor, Department of Medical Biophysics and Medical Imaging, University of Toronto;* Prof., Dept of Medical Biophysics and Medical Imaging, Univ. of Toronto, Univ. Prof. 2005–, also Canada Research Chair in Imaging Technologies in Human Disease and Preclinical Models; Dir Mouse Imaging Centre (MICe), The Hosp. for Sick Children; Sr Scientist in Physiology & Experimental Medicine programme, SickKids; Gold Medal, Int. Soc. of Magnetic Resonance in Medicine 1998, Killam Prize in Health Sciences, Canada Council for the Arts 2010. *Publications:* more than 300 papers in professional journals. *Address:* Mouse Imaging Centre, The Hospital for Sick Children, Toronto Centre for Phenogenomics, 25 Orde Street, Toronto, ON M5T 3H7, Canada (office). *Telephone:* (647) 837-5820 (office); (647) 837-5821 (office). *Fax:* (647) 837-5832 (office). *E-mail:* mhenkel@phenogenomics.ca (office). *Website:* medbio.utoronto.ca/ faculty/henkelman.html (office).

HENLEY, Elizabeth (Beth) Becker, BFA, PhD; American playwright and actress; b. 8 May 1952, Jackson, Mississippi; d. of Charles and Lydy Henley; one s.; ed Southern Methodist Univ., Univ. of Illinois; New York Drama Critics Circle Best Play Award 1981, George Oppenheimer/Newsday Playwriting Award 1980–81. *Film:* screenplays: Nobody's Fool 1986, Crimes of the Heart 1986, Miss Firecracker 1989, Signatures 1990, Revelers 1994, Impossible Marriage 1998. *Publications:* plays: Crimes of the Heart (Pulitzer Prize for Drama 1981) 1978, The Wake of Jamey Foster 1982, Am I Blue 1982, The Miss Firecracker Contest 1984, The Lucky Spot 1987, The Debutante Ball 1988, Abundance 1990, Signatures 1990, Beth Henley: Monologues for Women 1992, Control Freaks 1993, Revelers 1994, Collected Plays: Volume I, 1980–1989 2000, Collected Plays: Volume II, 1990–1999 2000, Family Week 2000, Ridiculous Fraud 2006.

HENLEY, Jeffrey O., BA, MBA; American computer software industry executive; *Chairman, Oracle Corporation;* ed Univ. of California, Santa Barbara, Univ. of California, Los Angeles; fmr Controller of Int. Operations, Fairchild Camera and Instruments; fmr Dir of Finance, Memorex Corpn; fmr Exec. Vice-Pres., Chief Financial Officer, Saga Corpn, Pacific Holding Co.; Exec. Vice-Pres. and Chief Financial Officer, Oracle Corpn 1991–2004, mem. Bd Dirs 1995–, Chair. 2004–, mem. Exec. Man. Cttee; Chair. Mid-Pacific Region Trustees, Boys & Girls Clubs of America; mem. Bd Dirs CallWave Inc.; mem. Bd Govs Boys and Girls Clubs of America; mem. Chancellor's Advisory Council and Int. Advisory Council, Eng Coll., Univ. of California, Santa Barbara; mem. Advisory Bd InTouch Technologies; UCLA Anderson School's Outstanding Alumnus Award 2004. *Address:* Oracle Corpn, 500 Oracle Parkway, Redwood City, CA 94065-1675, USA (office). *Telephone:* (650) 506-7000 (office). *Fax:* (650) 506-7200 (office). *E-mail:* info@oracle .com (office). *Website:* www.oracle.com (office).

HENNEKENS, Charles H., MD, DrPH; American epidemiologist and academic; *Sir Richard Doll Research Professor, College of Medicine, Florida Atlantic University;* ed Cornell Univ. Medical Coll. and Harvard School of Public Health; Epidemic Intelligence Officer, US Public Health Service, Dada Co., Fla 1969–71; Asst Prof. of Epidemiology, Univ. of Miami School of Medicine 1972–74; Asst Prof. of Medicine, Harvard Univ. 1975–81, Assoc. Prof. of Medicine and Clinical Epidemiology 1981–88, Prof. of Medicine and Preventive Medicine 1990–99; Physician, Brigham and Women's Hosp. 1982–92, Sr Physician 1992–93, Prof. of Medicine and Head of Div. of Preventive Medicine 1993–99; Visiting Epidemiologist, Univ. of Oxford, UK 1978–79; Prof. of Medicine & Epidemiology and Public Health, Univ. of Miami School of Medicine, Fla 1999; Co-Dir Cardiovascular Research, Mount Sinai Medical Center-Miami Heart Inst., Miami Beach, Fla 2001–04; currently Sir Richard Doll Research Prof., Charles E. Schmidt Coll. of Biomedical Science, Florida Atlantic Univ.; Clinical Prof., Nova Southeastern Univ.; fmr Pres. Soc. for Epidemiologic Research; Pres. American Epidemiological Soc.; Visiting Fellow, Green Coll. Univ. of Oxford 2000–; Fellow, American Coll. of Preventive Medicine, American Coll. of Epidemiology; mem. Asscn of American Physicians, Food and Nutrition Bd; fmr Ed.-in-Chief American Journal of Preventive Medicine; Founding Ed.-in-Chief Annals of Epidemiology; mem. Preventive Medicine Residency Advisory Cttee Health Dept, External Advisory Bd Cardiovascular Research Inst. 2003–; Hon. FACC; Hon. DSc (Univ. of Medicine and Dentistry) 1996, (City Univ.) 1997; Bruce Award, American Coll. of Physicians, Lilienfeld Award American Coll. of Epidemiology, Duncan Clark Award, Lewis Atterbury Conner Lectureship Award, Jan J. Kellermann Memorial Award, Sr Int. Aspirin Award, First Public Health Physician of the Year Award, inducted into Hall of Fame, American Asscn of Clinical Chemistry 2007. *Publications:* Epidemiology in Medicine (co-author) 1987, Clinical Trials in Cardiovascular Disease: A Companion to Braunwald's Heart Disease (co-author) 1999 and several other books. *Address:* Florida Atlantic University, 777 Glades Road, Boca Raton, FL 33431, USA (office). *Telephone:* (561) 297-4074 (office). *Fax:* (561) 297-3843 (office). *E-mail:* chenneke@fau.edu (office). *Website:* www.med.fau.edu (office).

HENNEKINNE, Loïc; French diplomatist and business executive; b. 20 Sept. 1940, Caudéran, Gironde; s. of Michel Hennekinne and Elisabeth Declemy; m. 2nd Marie Bozelle 1987; one d.; two s. (by first m.); ed Ecole Nat. d'Admin; First Sec., embassies in Viet Nam 1969–71, Chile 1971–73; Minister-Counsellor, Japan 1979–81; Del. for External Action, Ministry of Industry 1981–82; Dir of Cabinet of Minister of Research and Industry 1982; Dir of Personnel and Admin Ministry of Foreign Affairs 1983–86; Amb. to Indonesia 1986–88; Gen. Sec. summit conf. of Western industrialized nations, Paris 1989; Diplomatic Adviser to Pres. Mitterrand 1989–91; Amb. to Japan 1991–93; Inspector-Gen. of Foreign Affairs 1993–96; Amb. to Canada 1997–98; Sec.-Gen. Ministry of Foreign Affairs (with rank of Amb. of France) 1998–2002; Amb. to Italy 2002–05; Adviser to Pres. PlaNet Finance France 2007–12, also Head of Confs; numerous int. decorations, including Officier, Ordre nat. du Mérite, Commdr, Légion d'honneur, Grand' Ufficiale Ordine Naz. al Merito della Repub. Italiana, Ordine Bernardo O'Higgins. *Leisure interest:* tennis. *Address:* 15 avenue Frochot, 75009 Paris, France. *Telephone:* 1-42-82-03-38; 6-74-76-65-25 (mobile). *E-mail:* loic.hennekinne@laposte.net.

HENNEQUIN, Denis, BA, MA; French business executive; *Chairman and CEO, Accor SA;* b. 8 June 1958; m.; three c.; ed Université Panthéon-Assas, Paris; began career at McDonald's as Asst Dir of a Paris-based restaurant, promoted to Restaurant Man. Dir, later held numerous positions within the co., including Training and Recruitment Consultant, Field Service Consultant, Dir of Franchising, Dir of Operations and Regional Man. for Paris and the surrounding suburbs, Pres. and Man. Dir McDonald's France 1996–2005, Pres. McDonald's Europe Ltd (first non-American) 2005–10; joined Bd of Accor (hotels group) as Ind. Dir 2009, Exec. Dir Accor SA 2010–11, Chair. and CEO 2011–. *Leisure interests:* motorcycles, rock music. *Address:* Accor SA, Corporate Headquarters, Immeuble Odyssey, 110 avenue de France, 75210 Paris Cedex 13, France (office). *Telephone:* 1-45-38-86-00 (office). *E-mail:* info@accor.com (office). *Website:* www.accor.com (office).

HENNESSEY, Keith, BAS, MPP; American economist and government official; *Director, National Economic Council;* ed Stanford Univ., Calif., John F. Kennedy School of Govt, Harvard Univ., Mass; Program Designer, Symantec Corpn, Cupertino, Calif. 1990–92; Research Asst, Bipartisan Comm. on Entitlement and Tax Reform 1994–95; Health Economist, Budget Cttee, US Senate 1995–97, Policy Dir for Senate Majority and Senator Trent Lott 1997–2002; Deputy Asst to US Pres. for Econ. Policy and Devt and Deputy Dir Nat. Econ. Council 2002–07, Asst to US Pres. for Econ. Policy and Devt and Dir Nat. Econ. Council 2007–. *Address:* The White House Office, 1600 Pennsylvania Avenue, NW, Washington, DC 20500, USA (office). *Telephone:* (202) 456-1414 (office). *Fax:* (202) 456-2461 (office). *E-mail:* vice_president@whitehouse.gov (office). *Website:* www.whitehouse.gov/nec (office).

HENNESSY, Edward Lawrence, Jr, BS; American business executive (retd); b. 22 March 1928, Boston, Mass; s. of Edward L. Hennessy and Celina Mary Doucette; m. Ruth F. Schilling 1951; one s. one d.; ed Fairleigh Dickinson Univ., Rutherford, NJ and New York Univ. Law School; Asst Controller, Textron 1950–55; Group Controller, Eastern Electronics Group, Lear Siegler Inc. 1956–60; Controller, Int. Electronic Corpn, Int. Telephone & Telegraph Corpn (ITT) 1960–61, Controller, Corporate Staff 1961–62, Controller, ITT Europe 1962–64; Dir of Finance, Europe, Middle East and Africa, Colgate Palmolive Co. 1964–65; Vice-Pres. Finance, Heublein Inc. 1965–68, Sr Vice-Pres. Admin. and Finance 1969–72; Dir United Technologies Corpn 1972–79, Sr Vice-Pres. Finance and Admin. 1972–77, Exec. Vice-Pres., Group Vice-Pres. Systems & Equipment Group and Chief Financial Office 1977–79; Chair. and CEO AlliedSignal Corpn (now Honeywell) 1979–93 (retd); mem. Bd of Dirs Bank of New York, Wackenhut Corpn, Avanir Pharmaceuticals, Automatic Data Processing, Northeast Utilities, Lockheed Martin Corpn, Coast Guard Foundation, Powertrusion 2000; Trustee, Fairleigh Dickinson Univ. (fmr chair.), Catholic Univ. of America; Officier Légion d'honneur 1991, Kt of Malta (Vatican) 1981, Kt of St Gregory (Vatican) 1984, Hilal-i-Quaid-i-Azam (Pakistan) 1985, Kt of the Holy Sepulchre (Vatican) 1986. *Leisure interests:* sailing, tennis, reading, golf. *Address:* PO Box 3000 R, Morristown, NJ 07960 (office); 500 Island Drive, Palm Beach, FL 33480, USA (home). *Telephone:* (973) 455-4811 (office); (561) 655-0107 (home). *Fax:* (973) 455-2973 (office).

HENNESSY, John L., BE, MS, PhD; American computer scientist and university administrator; *President, Stanford University;* b. 1953; ed Villanova Univ., State Univ. of New York at Stony Brook; apptd Asst Prof. of Electrical Eng, Stanford Univ. 1977, Full Prof. 1986–, inaugural Willard R. and Inez Kerr Bell Prof. of Electrical Eng and Computer Science 1987–2004, Dir Computer Systems Lab. 1983–93, Chair. Computer Science 1994–96, Dean, School of Eng 1996–99, Provost, Stanford Univ. 1999–2000, Pres. 2000–, inaugural holder of Bing Presidential Professorship 2005; a pioneer in computer architecture, particularly RISC (Reduced Instruction Set Computer); Co-founder MIPS Computer Systems (now MIPS Technologies) 1984; mem. Bd of Dirs Atheros Communications 1998– (currently Chair.), Cisco Inc. 2002–, Google Inc. 2004–, Daniel Pearl Foundation; mem. Bd of Govs Partnership for Public Service; First Int. Advisor, Trinity Coll./Univ. Coll. Dublin; mem. Academic Advisory Council Coll. of Eng Cornell Univ., Computer Science Dept Princeton Univ.; mem. Cttee on Research Univs Nat. Research Council; mem. NAS, Nat. Acad. of Eng, American Philosophical Soc. 2008; Fellow, American Acad. of Arts and Sciences, Asscn for Computing Machinery, IEEE, Computer History Museum 2007; Hon. Fellow, Foreign Policy Asscn 2010; several Hon. degrees; IEEE John von Neumann Medal 2000, ASEE Benjamin Garver Lamme Award 2000, ACM Eckert-Mauchly Award 2001, Seymour Cray Computer Eng Award 2001, NEC C&C Prize for lifetime achievement in computer science and eng 2004, Founders Award, American Acad. of Arts and Sciences 2005, Lifetime Achievement Award, Silicon Valley Leadership Group 2009, Ulysses Medal, Univ. Coll. Dublin 2009, Morris Chang Exemplary Leadership Award, Global Semiconductor Alliance 2010, IEEE Medal of Honor 2012. *Publications include:* Computer Organization and Design: The Hardware/Software Interface, Computer Architecture: A Quantitative Approach. *Address:* Office of the President, Building 10, Inner Quad, Stanford University, Stanford, CA 94305-2061, USA (office). *Telephone:* (650) 723-2481 (office). *Fax:* (650) 725-6847 (office). *E-mail:* president@stanford.edu (office); hennessy@stanford.edu (office). *Website:* president.stanford.edu (office); www.stanford.edu/~hennessy (office).

HENNESSY, Patrick; Irish diplomatist; *Ambassador to United Arab Emirates;* fmr Counsellor, Embassy in Washington, DC; fmr Amb. to Israel; Dir Gen., Dept of Foreign Affairs –2009; Amb. to Italy 2009–13, Amb. to UAE 2013–. *Address:* Embassy of Ireland, 1–2 Khalifa al-Suwaidi Development, 19th Street (off 32nd Street), al-Bateen Area, Abu Dhabi, United Arab Emirates (office). *Telephone:* (2) 4958200 (office). *Fax:* (2) 6819233 (office). *E-mail:* irishvisaofficedubai@gmail.com (office). *Website:* www.embassyofireland.ae (office).

HENNIS-PLASSCHAERT, Jeanine Antoinette; Dutch politician; *Minister of Defence;* b. 7 April 1973, Heerlen; m. Erik-Jan Hennis; one s.; ed St Antonius Coll., Gouda, European Secretarial Acad., Utrecht; began career with Directorate-Gen. for Enlargement, EC, Brussels, including two years working for EC in Riga, Latvia; consultant for KPMG, Amstelveen 2000–02; Political Asst to Amsterdam Municipal Exec. Bd 2002–04; MEP (VVD—People's Party for Freedom and Democracy) 2004–10; mem. House of Reps (VVD) 2010–12; Minister of Defence 2012–. *Address:* Ministry of Defence, Plein 4, POB 20701, 2500 ES The Hague, Netherlands (office). *Telephone:* (70) 3188188 (office). *Fax:* (70) 3187888 (office). *E-mail:* defensievoorlichting@mindef.nl (office). *Website:* www.rijksoverheid.nl/ministeries/def (office).

HENRETTA, Deborah (Deb) A., BA, MA; American business executive; *Group President, Global Beauty Care, The Procter & Gamble Company;* b. 1 May 1961, Rochester, NY; two d. one s.; ed St Bonaventure Univ., Syracuse Univ.; intern, WXXI Channel 21, Rochester, NY 1982, WOKR Channel 13, Rochester, NY 1982–85; brand asst, Procter & Gamble 1985–86, Asst Brand Man. Bold/Dawn 1986–88, Brand Man. Cheer 1988–91, Assoc. Advertising Man. Tide 1991–93, Marketing Dir Laundry Products, Procter & Gamble North America 1993–96, Gen. Man. Fabric Conditioners, Procter & Gamble North America 1996–98, Gen. Man. Fabric Conditioners and Bleach, Procter & Gamble Worldwide 1998–99, Vice-Pres. Global Strategic Planning and Design, Laundry Fabric Conditioners/Bleach 1999, Vice-Pres. North America Baby Care 1999–2001, Pres. Global Baby Care 2001–04, Pres. Global Baby and Adult Care 2004–05, Pres. ASEAN/Australasia/India 2005–07, Group Pres., Asia 2007–11, Group Pres., Asia and Global Speciality Channel 2011–12, Group Pres., Skin Care, Cosmetics and Personal Care 2012, Group Pres., Global Beauty Care 2012–; mem. Bd of Dirs WCET/Channel 48 1997–2001, Chair. Strategic Planning Cttee 1998–2001; mem. Conf. Cincinnati Women 1988–90, Advisory Cttee Newhouse School, Syracuse Univ. 1998–, Advisory Council for Children's Day Care Center 1999–2002, Oversight Cttee for Children's Day Care Center 1999–, Strategy and Marketing Cttee Children's Hosp. of Cincinnati 2000–, Bd of Trustees for Children's Hosp. 2001–, YWCA Career Women of Achievement Steering Cttee 2002–, The Committee of 200 2003–, Bd of Trustees St Bonaventure Univ. 2003–; mem. Alexis de Tocqueville Soc. of the United Way 2001–; led P&G's Advancement of Women effort (which won P&G the Catalyst Award 1998) 1994–2000; Univ. Wall of Fame 2000, ranked by Fortune magazine amongst the 50 Most Powerful Women in Business in the US (34th) 2002, (34th) 2003, (41st) 2004, and amongst the 50 Most Powerful Women in Business outside the US (23rd) 2007, (24th) 2008, (19th) 2009, (20th) 2010, (19th) 2011, (17th) 2012, YWCA Career Women of Achievement Award 2002, YWCA Acad. of Career Women 2002, Advertising Age magazine Women to Watch 2003, Advertising Age Top Ten Who Made Their Mark on Marketing 2004, ranked by Forbes magazine amongst The World's 100 Most Powerful Women (86th) 2009. *Address:* The Procter & Gamble Co., 238A Thomson Road, #21- 09/10, Novena Square, Tower A, Singapore City 307684, Singapore (office). *Telephone:* 6824-5800 (office). *Fax:* 6824-6309 (office). *E-mail:* henretta.da@pg.com (office). *Website:* www.pg.com (office).

HENRI ALBERT FÉLIX MARIE GUILLAUME, HRH Grand Duke of Luxembourg, LèsScPol; b. 16 April 1955, Château de Betzdorf; s. of Jean Benoît Guillaume Marie Robert Louis Antoine Adolphe Marc d'Aviano, HRH fmr Grand Duke of Luxembourg and the late Princess Josephine-Charlotte of Belgium; m. Maria Teresa Mestre 1981; four s. (including Prince Guillaume Jean Joseph Marie) one d.; ed Royal Mil. Acad. Sandhurst, Univ. of Geneva; mem. State Council 1980–98; apptd Lt Rep. of Grand Duke March 1998; succeeded father as Grand Duke of Luxembourg Oct. 2000; Chair. Bd of Econ. Devt, Galapagos Darwin Trust Luxembourg; Pres. Organizing Cttee, Int. Trade Fairs of Luxembourg; mem. Mentor Foundation, Int. Olympic Cttee; Hon. Maj., Parachute Regt; Grand

Master, Order of the Gold Lion of the House of Nassau, Grand Master, Mil. and Civil Order of Adolphe of Nassau, Grand Master, Order of the Oak Crown, Grand Master, Order of Merit of the Grand Duchy of Luxembourg; Hon. Dr rer. pol (Trier); Hon. DHumLitt (Sacred Heart); Hon. LLD (Miami), Hon. DEcon (Khon Kaen). *Leisure interests*: reading, listening to classical music, skiing, swimming, water skiing, tennis, hunting. *Address*: Grand Ducal Palace, 2013 Luxembourg, Luxembourg (office). *Website*: www.gouvernement.lu.

HENRICH, Dieter, DrPhil; German philosopher and academic; *Professor Emeritus of Philosophy, University of Munich*; b. 5 Jan. 1927, Marburg; s. of Hans Harry Henrich and Frieda Henrich; m. Dr Bettina von Eckardt 1975; two d.; ed Univ. of Heidelberg; Prof., Freie Univ. Berlin 1960–65, Univ. of Heidelberg 1965–81; now Prof. Emer. of Philosophy, Univ. of Munich; Visiting Prof., Columbia Univ. 1968–72, Univ. of Mich. 1969, Harvard Univ. 1973–86, Tokyo Univ. 1979, Yale Univ. 1987; mem. Heidelberg and Bavarian Acads; Hon. Prof., Humboldt Univ., Berlin 1997; Hon. Foreign mem. American Acad. of Arts and Sciences; Maximilians Orden für Kunst und Wissenschaft 2007; Hon. DTheol (Münster) 1999, (Marburg) 2002; Hon. DrPhil (Jena) 2005; Hoelderlin Prize 1995, Hegel Prize 2003, Kant Prize 2004, German Language Award 2006, Leopold Lucas Prize 2008, Kuno Fischer Prize, Univ. of Heidelberg 2008. *Publications*: Der ontologische Gottesbeweis 1960, Fichtes ursprüngliche Einsicht, 1967, Hegel im Kontext 1971, Identität und Objektivität 1976, Fluchtlinien 1982, Der Gang des Andenkens 1986, Konzepte 1987, Ethik zum nuklearen Frieden 1990, Konstellationen 1991, Der Grund im Bewusstsein 1992, The Moral Image of the World 1992, The Unity of Reason 1994, I. C. Diez 1997, Bewusstes Leben 1999, Versuch über Kunst und Leben 2001, Fixpunkte 2003, Between Kant and Hegel 2003, Grundlegang aus dem Ich 2004, Die Philosophie im Prozess der Kultur 2006, Denken und Selbstsein 2007, Die Philosophie in der Sprache 2007, Endlichkeit und Sammlung des Lebens 2009, Werke im Werden 2011. *Address*: Gerlichstrasse 7A, 81245 Munich, Germany. *Telephone*: (89) 8119131. *E-mail*: dieter.henrich@lrz.uni-muenchen.de.

HENRIKSON, C(arl) Robert (Rob), BA, JD; American insurance industry executive; b. 1947; m. Mary Henrikson; two s.; ed Univ. of Pennsylvania, Emory Univ., Wharton School Advanced Management Program; more than 30 years with MetLife Inc., holding numerous sr man. positions, COO 2004–06, Pres. 2004–11, mem. Bd of Dirs 2005–11, Chair. and CEO 2006–May 2011, Chair. June–Dec. 2011; mem. Bd of Dirs American Council of Life Insurers, The Ron Brown Award for Corp. Leadership, New York Botanical Garden; apptd by Pres. Obama to President's Export Council 2010; Bd mem. Emer. American Benefits Council; mem. Bd and fmr Chair. Financial Services Forum, American Council of Life Insurers; mem. Nat. Bd of Advisors, Morehouse School of Medicine; Chair. S.S. Huebner Foundation for Insurance Educ., Emory Univ.; mem. Emory Law School Council, Emory Campaign Steering Cttee; mem. Bd The New York Botanical Garden, New York Philharmonic, Partnership for New York City; Trustee, American Museum of Natural History; fmr mem. Cttee on Econ. Dev't Subcommittee on Social Security Reform; fmr adviser and consultant various Congressional and US Dept of Labor hearings; fmr del. Nat. Summit on Retirement Savings; Alumni Trustee, Emory Law School's Bd of Trustees 2007; Distinguished Alumni Award, Emory Law School 2006. *Address*: c/o MetLife Inc., 2701 Queens Plaza North, Long Island City, NY 11101-4015, USA. *E-mail*: info@metlife.com.

HENRÍQUEZ, Roberto C.; Panamanian business executive and politician; *Minister of the Presidency*; b. 4 Dec. 1950, Panamá City; ed Universidad Santa Maria La Antigua; Co-owner Compañía Atlas SA (co. with interests in commercial, industrial and real estate sectors) 1972–; mem. Cámara de Comercio, Industrias y Agricultura de Panamá, Sr Vice-Pres. 1990–91, Chair. Econ. Research Centre 1989; Deputy Minister of Foreign Trade 2000, Minister of Trade and Industry 2009–11, Minister of Foreign Affairs 2011–12, of the Presidency 2012–; mem. Asociación Panameña de Ejecutivos de Empresas, Pres. 1984, 1985; Vice-Pres. Nat. Council of Private Enterprise 1985; mem. Cambio Democrático. *Address*: Ministry of the Presidency, Palacio de Las Garzas, Corregimiento de San Felipe, Apdo 2189, Panamá 1, Panama (office). *Telephone*: 527-9600 (office). *E-mail*: ofasin@presidencia.gob.pa (office). *Website*: www.presidencia.gob.pa (office).

HENRY, André Armand; French teacher, trade union official and politician; b. 15 Oct. 1934, Fontenoy-le-Château; s. of Alice Henry; m. Odile Olivier 1956; one s. one d.; ed Cours Complémentaire de Bains-les-Bains, Ecole normale d'instituteurs, Mirecourt; teacher, Fontenoy-le-Château 1955–56, Thaon-les-Vosges 1956–69; began trade union career with Syndicat Nat. des Instituteurs (SNI), Training Coll. Rep. (Vosges) 1954, mem. Exec. Comm. (Vosges) 1955–69, Asst Sec.-Gen. 1960–63, Sec.-Gen. 1963–69, mem. Nat. Council, SNI 1965–74, Perm. Sec. 1969–74; in charge of youth, then gen. admin. section of SNI; mem. Fed. Council, in charge of culture, youth and leisure sections, Fédération de l'education nationale (FEN) 1971, Perm. Sec. and Sec.-Gen. 1974–81; Minister for Free Time 1981–83; Délégué Général à l'économie sociale 1983–; Chair. and Man. Dir Caisse Nat. de l'Energie 1984–87; Inspecteur Général de l'administration de l'education nat. 1989–95; Nat. Vice-Pres. Asscn laïque pour l'éducation, la formation, la prévention et l'autonomie (ALEFPA) 1995–2001, Pres. 2001–06; Délégué départemental de l'education nationale; Vice-Pres. Mission Laïque française 1997–2002; Hon. Pres. ALEFPA 2006–; Commdr, Ordre du Mérite; Chevalier, Légion d'honneur, Chevalier des Palmes académiques. *Publications*: Danier l'école 1971, Serviteurs d'état (two vols) 1988, Conquérir l'avenir 1992, Le Ministre qui voulait changer la vie 1996. *Leisure interests*: football, volleyball, photography, flying light aircraft. *Address*: 1 bis rue de l'Espérance, 94000 Créteil, France (home). *Telephone*: 1-48-99-37-79 (office), (6) 11-87-30-51 (home). *E-mail*: andre.h@cegetel.net (home).

HENRY, Charles Bradford (Brad), BA, JD; American lawyer and politician; *Of Counsel, Lester, Loving & Davies, PC*; b. 10 July 1963, Shawnee, Okla; s. of Charles Henry; m. Kimberley Blain; three d.; ed Shawnee High School, Univ. of Oklahoma; econs teaching asst, Univ. of Oklahoma, Norman 1983–85; staff researcher, Oklahoma State Senate, Oklahoma City 1984, mem. 1992–2002; legal asst, Henry Henry & Henry, Shawnee 1985; Okla/Cleveland Co. Coordinator Robert Henry for Attorney General campaign 1986; law clerk, Andrews Davis Legg Bixler Milsten & Murrah, Oklahoma City 1987; legal intern, Cleveland Co. Legal Aid Office, Norman 1987–88; Pres. Brad Henry Oil Co., Inc., Shawnee 1987–89; Commr, Univ. of Oklahoma Election Comm. 1987–88; called to Okla Bar 1988, US Dist Court (We. Dist) Okla, US Court of Appeals (10th Circuit); assoc. attorney, Andrews Davis Legg Bixler Milsten & Price 1988–89; attorney, City of Shawnee

1989–2002; est. law firm Henry, Canavan & Hopkins PLLC; mem. Okla State Senate 1992–2002, Chair. Senate Judiciary Cttee; Gov. of Okla 2003–11; of Counsel, Lester, Loving & Davies, PC, Edmond, Okla 2011–; mem. Bd of Dirs Gateway to Prevention and Recovery, Inc.; mem. Asscn of Trial Lawyers of America, ABA, American Inns of Court, Pottawatomie Co. Bar Asscn (Pres. 1991), Okla Bar Asscn, Shawnee Chamber of Commerce, Jaycees, Lions, Norman Chamber of Commerce; mem. Bd Govs, Univ. Oklahoma 1982–84, Bd of Trustees, St Gregories Coll., Govs' Council, Health Project, Bipartisan Policy Center, Washington, DC 2011–; Democrat; Letzeiser Gold Medal, Univ. of Oklahoma, Outstanding Young Oklahoman 1997, Charles Dick Medal of Merit, Nat. Guard Asscn of US 2010. *Address*: Lester, Loving & Davies, PC, 1701 South Kelly Avenue, Edmond, OK 73013-3018, USA (office). *Telephone*: (405) 844-9900 (office). *Fax*: (405) 844-9958 (office). *E-mail*: info@lldlaw.com (office). *Website*: www.lldlaw.com (office).

HENRY, Graham, BEd; New Zealand professional rugby union coach; b. 8 June 1946, Christchurch; m. Raewyn Henry; two s. one d.; ed Christchurch Boys High School, Univ. of Otago, Massey Univ.; played rugby union for Canterbury and cricket for Otago in the Plunket Shield; became a secondary school geography and physical education teacher 1969; taught at Auckland Grammar School 1973–81, coached first XV; Deputy Headmaster, Kelston Boys' High School 1982–87, Headmaster 1987–96, coached first XV; first major role as coach of Auckland prov. rugby team 1992–97, won Nat. Prov. Championship 1993, 1994, 1995, 1996; also coached the Blues in the Super 12, won title 1996, 1997, runner-up 1998; won title again as technical adviser 2003; left NZ to coach Wales (first ever Lions' coach from outside Home Nations) 1998–2002, became highest paid rugby union coach in the world, coached team to 11 consecutive victories; apptd coach of British and Irish Lions for their unsuccessful tour to Australia 2001; left Wales following record defeat to Ireland (54–10) in Six Nations 2002; returned to NZ and apptd defensive coach of the Blues during Super 12 season 2003; coach of New Zealand rugby team (All Blacks) 2004–11, began career with wins over Rugby World Cup 2003 winners England in NZ in both Tests 2004, coached All Blacks in 3–0 series defeat of British and Irish Lions 2005, to Tri-Nations victories 2005, 2006, 2007, 2008, 2010, to second ever Grand Slam over the four Home Nations 2005, lost to France (20–18) in World Cup quarterfinal 2007, coached All Blacks to win Rugby World Cup defeating France 8–7 in final 2011, coached All Blacks to 88 wins in 103 Tests (140 matches); announced retirement as coach of New Zealand 1 Nov. 2011; Int. Rugby Bd (IRB) Int. Coach of the Year 2005, 2006, 2008, 2010, 2011. *Address*: c/o New Zealand Rugby Union, PO Box 2172, Wellington 6140, New Zealand. *Telephone*: (4) 499-4995. *Fax*: (4) 499-4224. *E-mail*: info@nzrugby.co.nz. *Website*: www.nzru.co.nz.

HENRY, Lenny, CBE, BA (Hons); British comedian, actor, writer and television presenter; b. (Lenworth Henry), 29 Aug. 1958; m. Dawn French (q.v.) (divorced 2010); one d.; Monaco Red Cross Award, The Golden Nymph Award (for Alive and Kicking) 1992, BBC Personality of the Year, Radio and Television Industry Club 1993, Golden Rose of Montreux Award for Lenny in Pieces (Christmas Special) 2000, Lifetime Achievement Award for Ongoing Performance UK Comedy Awards 2003. *Tours include*: Loud!, UK and Australia 1994, 1995, Large!, UK, Australia and NZ 1998, Have You Seen This Man tour 2001, So Much Things to Say, Wyndhams Theatre 2003, tour 2004, Where You From? tour 2007–08, Othello regional tour and West End (London Evening Standard Theatre Award for Outstanding Newcomer 2009) 2009. *Films include*: True Identity 1991, Mirrormask 2004, Harry Potter and the Prisoner of Azkaban 2004, MirrorMask 2005, Penelope 2006. *Radio*: Lenny and Will Acts 1 & 2 2006, Anansi Boys 2007, Rudy's Rare Records series 1 & 2 2008–09, Bad Faith 2008, What's So Great About? 2008. *Television includes*: New Faces (debut) 1975, Tiswas 1978–81, Three of a Kind 1981–83, The Lenny Henry Show 1984–85, 1987–88, Comic Relief 1985–, Lenny Henry Tonite! 1986, Coast to Coast 1990, Alive and Kicking 1991, Bernard and the Genie 1991, In Dreams 1992, The Real McCoy 1992, Chef (title role) (three series) 1993–96, Lenny Hunts the Funk, New Soul Nation, White Goods 1994, Funky Black Shorts 1994, Comic Relief, Lenny Go Home 1996, British Acad. Awards (host) 1997, Lenny's Big Amazon Adventure 1997, Lenny Goes to Town 1998, The Man 1999, Hope and Glory 1999–2000, Lenny's Atlantic Adventure 2000, Lenny in Pieces (Christmas Special) 2000, Lenny in Pieces (Christmas Special) 2001, Lenny Henry – This is My Life 2003, Lenny Henry in Pieces series 2 2003, The Lenny Henry Show 2004, Berry's Way 2006, Lenny's Britain 2007, Lennyhenry.tv 2008, Big & Small 2008–09, Happy Birthday OU 2009. *Videos*: Lenny Henry Live and Unleashed 1989, Lenny Henry Live and Loud 1994. *Publications*: The Quest for the Big Woof (autobiography) 1991, Charlie and the Big Chill (children's book) 1995. *Leisure interests*: R'n'B, HipHop, Funk, reading, tennis, comics, family. *Address*: c/o PBJ Management Ltd, 5 Soho Square, London, W1D 3QA, England (office). *Telephone*: (20) 7287-1112 (office). *Fax*: (20) 7287-1191 (office). *E-mail*: general@pbjmgt.co.uk (office). *Website*: www.pbjmgt.co.uk (office).

HENRY, Pierre; French composer; b. 9 Dec. 1927, Paris; s. of Georges Henry and Germaine Mazet; m. Isabelle Warnier 1971; one d. and one s. from previous m.; ed Conservatoire Nat. Supérieur de Musique and studies with Nadia Boulanger, Olivier Messiaen and Félix Passerone; head of group researching concrete music, ORTF 1950–58; Founder and Dir Studio Apsome 1959–; Founder Assen for Electro-acoustic Composition and Research 1972; cr. Son et Recherche Assen 1982; Commdr, Légion d'honneur, Officier, Ordre nat. du Mérite, Commdr des Arts et des Lettres; Grand Prix, Acad. du Disque 1966, Grand Prix, Acad. Charles Cros 1970, Grand Prix nat. de la Musique 1985, Grand Prix de la Musique Symphonique (Sacem) 1987, Victoires de la Musique 1998, Grand Prix Karl Sczuka 1997, etc. *Works include*: Symphonie pour un homme seul 1950, Messe de Liverpool 1967, Messe pour le temps présent 1970, Nijinsky, clown de Dieu (ballet by Maurice Béjart) 1973, Dieu, action de voix, de sons et de gestes (spectacular, Lille 1977, Paris 1978), Hommage à Beethoven 1979, Les noces chymiques, rituel féerique en 12 journées (Opéra comique) 1980, Paradis perdus 1982, Berlin, symphonie d'une grande ville (film, concert) 1987, Livre des morts égyptien 1988, Une maison de sons 1990, Maldoror-Feuillation 1992, L'homme à la caméra (film/concert) 1993, Une ample comédie à cent actes divers: Hommage à La Fontaine 1995, Intérieur/Extérieur 1996, Schubert 97 (1997), Histoire naturelle 1997, La Xème remix 1998, L'homme au microphone 1999, Tam tam du merveilleux 2000, Concerto sans orchestre 2000, Phrases de Quatuor 2000, Poussière de Soleils 2001, Dracula 2002, Requiem profane 2000, Carnet de Venise 2002, Labyrinthe 2003, Faits divers 2003,

Duo 2003, Lumières 2003, Metamorphoses d'Ovide 2004, Voyage initiative 2004, Comme une symphonie 2005, Grande Toccata 2006, Variance 2006, Utopia 2007, Pulsations 2007, Trajectoire 2007, Pleins jeux 2007, Un Monde lacéré 2008, Miroirs du temps 2008, Capriccio 2009, Envol 2010, Empreintes 2010, L'Art de la fugue odyssée 2011, Paroxysmes 2011. *Publication:* Pierre Henry's House of Sounds. *Address:* 32 rue Toul, 75012 Paris, France. *E-mail:* sonre@wanadoo.fr.

HENRY, Thierry Daniel; French professional footballer; b. 17 Aug. 1977, Les Ulis, Essonne, Paris; m. Nicole Merry 2003 (divorced 2007); one d.; striker/winger; signed as schoolboy player, Versailles football club; youth player, CO Les Ulis 1983–89, US Palaiseau 1989–90, Viry-Châtillon 1990–92, Clairefontaine 1992, Monaco 1992–94; sr player, Monaco 1994–99 (won Ligue 1 1996–97, French Super Cup 1997), Juventus, Italy 1999, Arsenal, England 1999–2007 (winner FA Cup 2002, 2003, 2005, Premiership 2002, 2004, Community Shield 2002, 2004, Capt. of team 2005–07), 2012 (on loan), Barcelona, Spain 2007–10 (won La Liga 2008/09, 2009/10, Copa del Rey 2008/09, UEFA Champions League 2008/09, Supercopa de España 2009, UEFA Super Cup 2009, FIFA Club World Cup 2009); with New York Red Bulls 2010– (won MLS Eastern Conf. 2010, Atlantic Cup 2011, Walt Disney World Pro Soccer Classic 2010, Emirates Cup 2011), Capt. 2011–; mem. French nat. team 1997–2010 (winner FIFA World Cup 1998, UEFA European Football Championship 2000, FIFA Confederations Cup 2003), Capt. 2008–10; mem. UNICEF-FIFA squad; Chevalier, Légion d'honneur 1998; Premier League 10 Seasons Awards 1992/93–2001/02, UNFP Ligue 1 Young Player of the Year 1996–97, PFA Players' Player of the Year 2002–03, 2003–04, PFA Team of the Year 2000–01, 2001–02, 2002–03, 2003–04, 2004–05, 2005–06, FWA Footballer of the Year 2002–03, 2003–04, 2005–06, Premier League Golden Boot 2001–02, 2003–04, 2004–05, 2005–06, Golden Boot Landmark Award 10 2004–05, Golden Boot Landmark Award 20 2004–05, Premier League Goal of the Season 2002–03, UEFA Team of the Year 2001, 2002, 2003, 2004, 2006, MLS Best XI 2011, Onze d'Or 2003, 2006, European Golden Boot 2003–04, 2004–05, French Player of the Year 2000, 2003, 2004, 2005, 2006, IFFHS World's Top Goal Scorer of the Year 2003, FIFA FIFPro World XI 2006, FIFA World Cup All-Star Team Germany 2006, FIFA Confederations Cup Golden Ball France 2003, FIFA Confederations Cup Golden Shoe France 2003, UEFA European Football Championship Team of the Tournament 2000, FIFA 100 2004, Time 100 Heroes & Pioneers No. 16 2007, inducted into English Football Hall of Fame 2008, MLS Best XI 2011. *Website:* www .newyorkredbulls.com.

HENRY de VILLENEUVE, Xavier, LenD; French banker; b. 8 July 1932, Quintin; s. of Jacques Henry de Villeneuve and Yvonne de la Motte de la Motte Rouge; m. Simone de Vigneral 1963; two s. one d.; ed Ecole des Frères, Quintin, Coll. des Cordeliers, Dinan, Coll. St Charles, St Brieuc and Faculté de Droit, Rennes; joined Banque de Bretagne 1959, Asst Dir-Gen. 1971, Dir-Gen. 1979, Pres. and Man. Dir 1986; Pres. and Man. Dir, Banque de la Cité 1978–82, Pres. 1983–85, Hon. Pres. Admin. 1991; Pres. Comm. des Affaires Sociales of Assen Française des Banques 1988, Pres. Compagnie Financière de Participation 1988, Ronceray 1991–93, ACLPME 1995–98, ACLPME Finances 1997–98; Vice-Pres. Assen d'Eloge 1995–96, Résidences ACL 1997–98; fmr Pres. Diocesan Cttee of Catholic Educ., Nanterre (Codiec 92); Chevalier, Légion d'honneur, des Arts et Lettres, Ordre du Saint-Sépulcre de Jérusalem. *Publication:* Contes et nouvelles des quatre vents. *Leisure interests:* the arts, reading, old wars, hunting. *Address:* 19 rue de la Convention, 75015 Paris (home); Kerbic, 22200 Pommerit-le-Vicomte, France (home).

HENRYSSON, Haraldur; Icelandic judge; b. 17 Feb. 1938, Reykjavik; s. of Henry Alexander Hálfdanarson and Gudrun Thorsteinsdottir; m. Elisabet Kristinsdóttir 1972; one s.; ed Reykjavik High School, Univ. of Iceland; Asst Judge 1964–73; Judge, Criminal Court, Reykjavik 1973–89; fmr Judge Supreme Court, Pres. 1996–97; Chair. Cttee Investigating Accidents at Sea 1973–83; Pres. Nat. Life Saving Assen 1982–90; Vice-mem. Althing 1967–71; Kt Grand Cross of Icelandic Falcon. *Leisure interest:* outdoor sports. *Address:* Hæstirettur Islands, Domhus v. Arnarhol, 150 Reykjavik, Iceland. *Telephone:* 510-3030. *Fax:* 562-3995. *Website:* www.haestirettur.is.

HENSHER, Philip Michael, BA, PhD, FRSL; British writer; b. 20 Feb. 1965, London, England; ed Lady Margaret Hall, Oxford, Jesus Coll., Cambridge; clerk, House of Commons 1990–96; Chief Book Reviewer, The Spectator 1994–; Art Critic, Mail on Sunday 1996–; columnist, The Independent; mem. RSL (mem. of Council 2000–); Somerset Maugham Award 1996. *Publications:* Other Lulus 1994, Kitchen Venom 1996, Pleasured 1998, The Bedroom of the Mister's Wife (short stories) 1999, The Mulberry Empire 2002, The Fit 2004, The Northern Clemency 2008, King of the Badgers 2011; other: libretto for opera Powder Her Face, by Thomas Adès. *Address:* c/o AP Watt at United Agents LLP, 12–26 Lexington Street, London, W1F 0LE, England (office); 83A Tennyson Street, London, SW8 3TH, England (home). *Telephone:* (20) 3214-0800 (office). *Fax:* (20) 3214-0801 (office). *E-mail:* info@unitedagents.co.uk (office). *Website:* www.apwatt.co.uk (office).

HEPPELL, (Thomas) Strachan, CB; British public service official; *Chairman, Audit Advisory Committee, European Medicines Agency;* b. 15 Aug. 1935, Teesside; s. of the late Leslie Heppell and Doris Potts; m. Felicity Rice 1963; two s.; ed Acklam Hall Grammar School, Middlesbrough and Queen's Coll. Oxford; Asst Prin. Nat. Assistance Bd (NAB) 1958; Prin. NAB, Cabinet Office, Dept of Health and Social Security (DHSS) 1963; Asst Dir of Social Welfare, Hong Kong 1971–73; Asst Sec. DHSS 1973, Under-Sec. 1979; Deputy Sec. DHSS, Dept of Health 1983–95; Chair. Man. Bd European Medicines Agency 1994–2000, Chair. Audit Advisory Cttee 2005–; Chair. European Inst. for Health 2007–10; Consultant Dept of Health 1995–2000; Chair. Family Fund Trust 1997–2003; Visiting Fellow, LSE 1996–2000; mem. Broadcasting Standards Comm. 1996–2002. *Publications:* contribs to pubs on social security, social welfare, health and pharmaceuticals. *Address:* European Medicines Agency, 7 Westferry Circus, Canary Wharf, London, E14 4HB, England. *Website:* www.emea.europa.eu (office).

HERAEUS, Jürgen, PhD; German business executive; *Chairman of the Supervisory Board, Heraeus Holding GmbH;* b. 1936, Hanau; m.; five d.; ed Univ. of Munich; joined family firm Heraeus Holding GmbH 1964, lived in USA for two years and worked for several Heraeus subsidiaries, mem. Bd of Man. 1970–, Head of Finance 1970, Vice-Chair. Bd of Man. 1977–83, Chair. 1983–2000, Chair.

Supervisory Bd 2000–, Chair. Shareholders' Cttee 2000–; Chair. TEUTONIA Zementwerk AG, Lafarge Roofing GmbH; Chair. and mem. Supervisory Bd GEA Group AG, Messer Group GmbH 2001–, MG Technologies AG 2003–; mem. Admin. Bd Argor-Heraeus SA, Switzerland; Special Adviser CVC Capital Partners; Sr Adviser to WTO Cttee in Shanghai and Chair. Working Group on China, Asia Pacific Cttee of German Business (APA), Berlin 1998–; mem. Bd of Dirs Buderus AG, EPCOS AG, Heidelberger Druckmaschinen AG, IKB Deutsche Industriebank, Schmalbach-Lubeca AG; mem. Presidium, Bundesverbandes der Deutschen Industrie (Fed. of German Industries) 1990–; mem. Advisory Bd Technische Universität, Darmstadt 2001–, Chair. 2007–; Chair. Kathinka Platzhoff Foundation; Hon. Chair. German UN Children's Fund, UNICEF. *Address:* Heraeus Holding GmbH, Postfach 1561, 63405 Hanau (office); Heraeus Holding GmbH, Heraeusstrasse 12–14, 63450 Hanau, Germany (office). *Telephone:* (6181) 35-0 (office). *Fax:* (6181) 35-35-50 (office). *E-mail:* pr@heraeus.com (office). *Website:* www.heraeus.com (office).

HERBEN, Mathieu (Mat); Dutch politician; b. 15 July 1952, The Hague; m.; one d.; journalist for internal publications, Ministry of Defence 1977–87, Chief Ed. 1990–2002; Ed.-in-Chief, Manna (catholic newspaper) 1987–90; various roles with Orde van Vrijmetselaren (freemasons' lodge) 1993–97; Leader, Lijst Pim Fortuyn (LPT) May–Aug. 2002, Parl. Leader May 2002, Leader LPF Advisory Council Aug. 2002. *Publications:* Vijftig jaar vrijmetselaarij. *Leisure interests:* classical music, reading, nature. *Address:* Tweede Kamer der Staten-Generaal, Fractie Lijst Pim Fortun, Postbus 20018, 2500 EA The Hague, Netherlands (office). *Telephone:* (70) 318-5846 (office). *Fax:* (70) 318-5847 (office). *E-mail:* m.herben@tk.parlement.nl (office). *Website:* www.lijstpimfortuyn.nl (office).

HERBERT, Adam, BA, MPA, PhD; American university administrator and professor of public administration; *Professor Emeritus, Indiana University;* b. Muskogee, Okla; m. Karen Herbert; ed Univs of Southern Calif. and Pittsburgh; White House Fellow in Ford Admin 1974, served as Special Asst to US Sec. of Health, Educ. and Welfare; Special Asst to US Under-Sec. of Housing and Urban Devt 1975; academic positions at Univ. of Southern Calif., Howard Univ., Va Polytechnic Inst. and State Univ., Univ. of Pittsburgh; fmr Dean School of Public Affairs and Services and Vice-Pres. for Academic Affairs, Fla Int. Univ.; fmrly Regents Prof. and Founding Exec. Dir, The Fla Center for Public Policy and Leadership, Univ. of N Fla, also Univ. Pres. 1989–98; Chancellor of State Univ. System of Fla 1998–2000; Prof. of Public Admin and Political Science, and Pres. Indiana Univ. 2003–07, currently Prof. Emer.; Sr Consultant Michael L. Buckner Law Firm 2009–; led transition team for Gov.-Elect Jeb Bush 1998; Co-Chair. Gov. Bush's Reading Priority Transition Team 2002; fmr Pres. Nat. Asscn of Schools of Public Affairs and Admin; Chair. Jacksonville Chamber of Commerce 1993; served as Fla Commr, Comm. on Educ.; mem. Bd of Dirs Indiana Univ. Foundation –2010, St Joe Corpn; mem. Nat. Acad. of Public Admin (NAPA), Knight Foundation Comm. on Intercollegiate Athletics, Fla Fed. Judicial Nominating Comm. *Address:* c/o Indiana University, 107 South Indiana Avenue, Bloomington, IN 47405-7000, USA (office).

HERBERT, Rt Rev. Christopher William, BA, MPhil, PhD; British ecclesiastic (retd); b. 7 Jan. 1944, Lydney, Glos., England; s. of Walter Herbert and the late Hilda Dibben; m. Janet Turner 1968; two s.; ed Monmouth School, Univ. of Wales, Lampeter, Univ. of Bristol and Wells Theological Coll., Univ. of Leicester; Curate, St Paul's, Tupsley, Hereford 1967–71; Adviser in Religious Educ., Diocese of Hereford 1971–76, Dir of Educ. 1976–81; Vicar, St Thomas on the Bourne, Diocese of Guildford 1981–90, Dir of Post-Ordination Training 1984–90; Archdeacon of Dorking 1990–95; Bishop of St Albans 1995–2009; Hon. Citizen, Fano, Italy; Hon. DLitt (Hertfordshire); Hon. DArts (Bedfordshire). *Publications include:* Be Thou My Vision 1985, This Most Amazing Day 1986, The Question of Jesus 1987, Alive to God 1987, Ways Into Prayer 1987, Help in Your Bereavement 1988, Prayers for Children 1993, Pocket Prayers 1993, The Prayer Garden 1994, Words of Comfort 1994, A Little Prayer Diary 1996, Pocket Prayers for Children 1999, Pocket Prayers for Commuters 2009, Health 2012; contrib. to Edinburgh Companion to the Bible and the Arts 2014. *Leisure interests:* cycling, reading, writing, walking, art history. *Address:* 1 Beacon Close, Farnham, Surrey, GU10 4PA, England. *Telephone:* (1252) 795600. *E-mail:* cwherbert7@gmail.com. *Website:* www .threeabbeys.me.uk.

HERBERT, Gary Richard; American business executive, politician and state governor; *Governor of Utah;* b. 7 May 1947, American Fork, Utah; s. of Paul Peters and Carol Peters; adopted s. of Duane Barlow Herbert; m. Jeanette Snelson; three s. three d.; ed Orem High School, served two-year mission for the Church of Jesus Christ of Latter-day Saints in Eastern Atlantic States Mission, later attended Brigham Young Univ.; served for six years as mem. Utah Army Nat. Guard, becoming a staff sergeant; est. real estate firm, Herbert & Assocs Realtors in Orem, and a child-care service with his wife, The Kids Connection; Commr on Utah Co. Comm. 1990–2004; fmr Pres. Utah Asscn of Counties, Utah Asscn of Realtors; campaigned for Republican nomination for Gov. of Utah Nov. 2003, running mate of Jon Huntsman April 2004, Lt-Gov. of Utah 2005–09, served as Chair. of 13 statewide comms, including Comm. on Volunteers and Comm. on Civic and Character Educ. and the Emergency Man. Admin. Council, Gov. of Utah 2009–; mem. Bd Provo Orem Chamber of Commerce, Utah Water Conservancy Dist; Republican. *Address:* Office of the Governor, Utah State Capitol Complex, 350 North State Street, Suite 200, PO Box 142220, Salt Lake City, UT 84114-2220, USA (office). *Telephone:* (801) 538-1000 (office). *Fax:* (801) 538-1528 (office), (801) 538-1557 (office). *E-mail:* gherbert@utah.gov (office). *Website:* www.utah.gov/governor (office).

HERBISH, Suleiman Jasir Al-, BA, MEconSc; Saudi Arabian international organization official; *Director-General, OPEC Fund for International Development;* b. 6 Nov. 1942, Ar-Rass; m. Dr May Al-Jasser; four c.; ed Trinity Univ., San Antonio, Tex., USA, Univ. of Cairo, Egypt; fmr Dir Saline Water Conversion Corpn, Saudi Co. for Precious Metals; fmr Asst Deputy Minister; fmr Chair. Nat. Shipping Co. of Saudi Arabia, Saudi Arabian Oil Texaco Ltd (later renamed Saudi Arabian Chevron Co.), Arabian Drilling Co.; Gov. for Saudi Arabia, OPEC, Vienna 1990–2003; Dir-Gen. OPEC Fund for Int. Devt 2003–; head of numerous Saudi Arabian dels to int. confs and negotiations on energy-related issues; Commdr, Ordre Nat. Ivoirien (Côte d'Ivoire) 2009, Commdr, Order of Wissam Al Alaoui (Morocco) 2009, Chevalier, Ordre Nat. (Burkina Faso) 2011, Medal of Nat.

Recognition (Mauritania) 2012, Order of the Two Niles, First Degree (Sudan) 2013, Golden Medal of Merit and Excellence (Palestine) 2013, Grand Decoration of Honour in Silver with Sash (Austria) 2013, Nat. Order of Merit (Côte d'Ivoire) 2013; Congressional Medal of Achievement (Philippines) 2005, Prix de la Fondation, Crans Montana Forum 2007, Anania Shirakatsi Medal (Armenia) 2009. *Address:* OPEC Fund for International Development, PO Box 995, 1011 Vienna, Austria (office). *Telephone:* (1) 51564 (office); (1) 51164 (office); (1) 51166 (office); (1) 51165 (office). *Fax:* (1) 513-92-38 (office). *E-mail:* info@ofid.org (office). *Website:* www.ofid.org (office).

HERBST, John Edward; American diplomatist; *Coordinator, Office for Reconstruction and Stabilization, State Department;* ed School of Foreign Service, Georgetown Univ., Fletcher School of Law and Diplomacy; worked in embassies in Moscow and Saudi Arabia; Dir Office of Ind. States and Commonwealth Affairs; Dir Office of Regional Affairs, Near East Asia Bureau; Political Counsellor, Embassy in Tel-Aviv; Deputy Dir for Econs, Office of Soviet Union Affairs; Dir for Policy, Nat. Security Council; Prin. Deputy to Amb.-at-Large for the New Ind. States; Consul-Gen. Jerusalem 1997–2000; Amb. to Uzbekistan 2000–03, to Ukraine 2003–06; Coordinator, Office for Reconstruction and Stabilization, US State Dept 2006–. *Address:* Office of the Coordinator for Reconstruction and Stabilization, US State Department, 2201 C Street, NW, Washington, DC 20520; 8355 Thompson Road, Annandale, VA 22003, USA (home). *Telephone:* (202) 663-0323 (office). *Fax:* (202) 663-0327 (office). *E-mail:* scrs_info@state.gov (office). *Website:* www.state.gov/s/crs (office).

HERCUS, Luise Anna, AM, PhD, FAHA; Australian academic; *Visiting Fellow in Linguistics, School of Language Studies, Australian National University;* b. (Luise Anna Schwarzschild), 16 Jan. 1926, Munich, Germany; d. of Alfred Schwarzschild and Theodora Schwarzschild; m. Graham Robertson Hercus 1954 (died 1974); one s.; ed Univ. of Oxford, UK and Australian Nat. Univ., Canberra; Tutor and Lecturer, St Anne's Coll., Oxford 1946–54; Research Fellow, Univ. of Adelaide 1965–68; Sr Lecturer in Asian Studies, ANU 1969–71, Reader 1972–91, now Visiting Fellow in Linguistics; work conducted recording nearly extinct Aboriginal languages 1963–. *Publications:* The Languages of Victoria: A Late Survey 1969, The Bagandji Language 1982, This is What Happened, Historical Narratives by Aborigines (co-ed.) 1986, Nukunu Dictionary 1992, Wembawemba Dictionary 1992, Paakantyi Dictionary 1993, The Wirangu Language of the West Coast of South Australia 1999; articles on Middle Indo-Aryan and on oral traditions of S Australian Aborigines, The Arabana – Wangkangurru Language, The Land is a Map (with F. Hodges, J. Simpson) 2002, Two Rainbow Serpents Travelling: Mura Track Stories from the 'Corner Country' (with Jeremy Beckett) 2009, Aboriginal Placenames: Naming and Re-Naming the Australian Landscape (with Harold Koch) 2009, The Mathi Group of Languages (with Barry Blake, Stephen Moray and Edward Ryan), ongoing work on writing up Wangkangurru Song Cycles (not as open publs), so far completed The Story of Wurru the Crane, The Arabana-Wangkangurru Emu History, The Seven Sisters History in the Lake Eyre Basin, The Fire History. *Leisure interest:* raising orphaned marsupials. *Address:* School of Language Studies, Baldessin Precinct Building 110, Australian National University, Canberra, ACT 0200 (office); Kintala via Gundaroo, Dick's Creek Road, NSW 2620, Australia (home). *Telephone:* (2) 6236-8145 (home). *Fax:* (2) 6125-4779 (office). *E-mail:* luise.hercus@anu.edu.au (office); luiseh@dodo.com.au (home).

HERCUS, Dame (Margaret) Ann, DCMG, BA, LLB; New Zealand politician, diplomatist and international consultant; b. 24 Feb. 1942, Hamilton; d. of Horace Sayers and Mary Sayers (née Ryan); m. John Hercus; two s.; ed Univs of Auckland and Canterbury; Lawyer and Staff Training Officer, Beath & Co., Christchurch 1969–70; mem. Price Tribunal and Trade Practices Comm. 1973–75; Deputy Chair. Commerce Comm. 1975–78; Chair. Consumer Rights Campaign 1975; MP for Lyttelton 1978–87, Opposition Spokesperson on Social Welfare, Consumer Affairs and Women's Affairs 1978–84; Minister of Social Welfare, Police and Women's Affairs 1984–87; Perm. Rep. to UN, New York 1989–90; int. consultant 1991–98; Chief of Mission, UN Force in Cyprus 1998–99; mem. Bd of Dirs Television New Zealand Ltd 2002–05 (resgnd); Labour. *Leisure interests:* collecting original New Zealand prints, theatre, reading. *Address:* 209 Collingwood Street, Nelson 7010, New Zealand. *E-mail:* ajhercus@clear.net.nz.

HERFKENS, Eveline L.; Dutch diplomat, politician and UN official; b. 1952, The Hague; ed Leiden Univ.; Policy Officer for Devt Cooperation, Ministry of Foreign Affairs 1976–81; mem. Lower House of Parl. 1981–90; Treasurer and mem. Cttee of Parliamentarians for Global Action 1985–96; mem. Econ. Cttee, Parliamentary Ass. of Council of Europe 1986–89, also Jt Organiser North-South Campaign; Exec. Dir World Bank, Washington, DC 1990–96; Amb. and Perm. Rep. to UN, Geneva 1996–98; Minister for Devt Co-operation 1998–2002; Exec. Coordinator Millennium Devt Goals Campaign, UN, NY 2002–06, Special Adviser 2006–07; fmr Chair. Evert Vermeer Foundation, Dutch Fair Trade Org.; fmr mem. Council of the Labour Party (PvdA), Devt Cttee of Netherlands Council of Churches; mem. Bd of Dirs International Partnership for Microbicides 2008–. *Address:* c/o Board of Directors, International Partnership for Microbicides, 8401 Colesville Road, Suite 200, Silver Spring, MD 20910, USA.

HÉRIARD DUBREUIL, Dominique; French business executive; b. 6 July 1946, Paris; d. of André Hériard Dubreuil and Anne-Marie Hériard Dubreuil (née Renaud); m. Alain-Pierre Jacquet 1975; one d.; ed Univ. of Paris II (Panthéon-Assas) and Inst. des Relations Publiques; press attaché, Havas Conseil 1969–72; est. public relations dept for Ogilvy & Mather 1972; Programme Head, Hill & Knowlton 1973–75; Founder, Pres. and Man. of Agence Infoplan 1978–87; Man. Dir E. Rémy Martin & Cie SA 1988–, Chair. 1990–, CEO Rémy Cointreau 1998–2004, Chair. 2001–12;, currently Chair. Cointreau SAS; Pres. Fed. of Wine and Spirit Exporters of France 1992–94; Pres. Comite Colbert 1994–98, Vinexpo 1998; mem. Supervisory Bd Vivendi; Chevalier, Légion d'honneur, Officier, Ordre nat. du Mérite; ranked by Fortune magazine amongst the 50 Most Powerful Women in Business outside the US (28th) 2004, (24th) 2004, (30th) 2005, (38th) 2006, (42nd) 2007–08, (41st) 2009. *Leisure interest:* visual arts. *Address:* Rémy Cointreau, 21 boulevard Haussman, 75009 Paris, France (office). *Telephone:* 1-44-13-44-13 (office). *Fax:* 1-44-13-44-66 (office); 1-45-62-82-52 (office). *E-mail:* dominique

.heriard.dubreuil@remy-cointreau.com (office). *Website:* www.remy-cointreau.com (office).

HERINCX, Raimund (Raymond Frederick); British singer (bass-baritone) and voice teacher and therapist; b. 23 Aug. 1927, London; s. of Florent Herincx and Marie Cheal; m. Margaret J. Waugh (known as Astra Blair) 1954; one s. two d.; ed Thames Valley Grammar School and Univ. of London; studied singing in Antwerp, Brussels, Barcelona and London with Giovanni Valli, Samuel Worthington and Harold Williams 1949–53; Educ. Officer, Household Cavalry 1946–48; mem. Royal Opera House chorus; joined Welsh Nat. Opera 1956; Prin. Baritone, Sadler's Wells Opera 1957–67; debut Royal Opera House, Covent Garden 1968; joined Metropolitan Opera House, New York 1976, subsequently appeared in most major US opera houses mainly in works of Wagner and Richard Strauss; opera and concert appearances in South America 1976–81; many operatic performances in Europe in Wagner's Ring Cycle and other helden baritone roles; frequent European appearances 1974–87 in concert performances of British composers Elgar, Britten, Tippett, Walton and Vaughan-Williams; last professional performances: opera: Dalua in Rutland Boughton's The Immortal Hour, Glastonbury Festival 1998; concert: Verdi's Requiem, Wells Cathedral 2001; Prof. of Voice RAM 1970–77; Sr Visiting Prof. and Voice Teacher, North East of Scotland Music School 1979–; voice therapist 1979–; voice teacher Trinity Coll. of Music, London 1993–95; Lecturer, Univ. Coll., Cardiff 1984–87; Music Critic for Music and Musicians; Hon. RAM 1971; Hon. DMus (Aberdeen) 1991; Opera Medal, Int. Music Awards 1968. *Leisure interests:* Artists' Asscn Against Aids, vineyard man., plant breeding (begonias and geraniums), wine and its history, wildfowl. *Address:* North East of Scotland Music School, Dorothy Hately Music Centre, 21 Huntly Street, Aberdeen, AB10 1TJ, Scotland (office). *Telephone:* (1224) 649685 (office). *Fax:* (1224) 649685 (office). *E-mail:* nesms@dsl.pipex.com. *Website:* www.nesms.org.uk.

HERING, Jürgen; German librarian; b. 15 Sept. 1937, Chemnitz; s. of the late Karl Hering and Margot Hering (née Schubert); m. Inge Rich 1961; one s. two d.; ed Univs of Stuttgart, Munich and Tübingen; Library Asst Stuttgart Univ. Library 1968, Library Adviser 1971, Sr Library Adviser 1972, Librarian 1974, Chief Librarian 1975–96; Chief Librarian Sächsische Landesbibliothek–Staats and Dresden Univ. Library 1997–2003 (retd); Chair. Verein Deutscher Bibliothekare 1979–83, First Deputy Chair. 1983–85; Geschäftsführer Max-Kade-Stiftung Stuttgart 1982–, Wissenschaftlicher Beirat Bibliothek für Zeitgeschichte, Stuttgart 1986–99, Kuratorium Deutsches Bibliotheksinstitut Berlin 1990–95; mem. Exec. Cttee German Libraries Asscn 1992–95 (Chair. 1989–92); Adviser, Stiftung Preussischer Kulturbesitz 1999–2003; Hon. Prof., School of Eng, Econs and Culture 1999; Verdienstorden des Freistaates Sachsen 2003, Cross of Merit (Germany) 2009, Verdienstkreuz am Bande des Verdienstordens der Bundesrepublik Deutschland 2009; Dr Josef Bick Ehrenmedaille (Austria) 1992, Saxon Merit Award 2003. *Leisure interests:* photography, travel. *Address:* Eichenparkstrasse 34, 70619 Stuttgart, Germany (home). *Telephone:* (711) 473944 (home). *Fax:* (711) 47059770 (home). *E-mail:* juergen.k.hering@web.de.

HERKERT, Craig R., BS, MBA; American business executive; b. 1959; ed St Francis Coll., Northern Illinois Univ.; first job as teenager at Jewel-Osco; spent 23 years with Albertsons and American Stores, held positions including Exec. Vice-Pres., Marketing, and Pres., Acme Markets; Pres. and CEO The Americas, Wal-Mart –2009; Pres. and CEO Supervalu Inc. 2009–12; Vice-Pres. Distribucion y Servicio SA; mem. Exec. Cttee Minnesota Business Partnership; mem. Bd and Exec. Cttee Food Marketing Inst.; mem. The Business Council (nat. org. of CEOs), Bd of the Council of the Americas. *Address:* c/o Supervalu Inc., 11840 Valley View Road, Eden Prairie, MN 55344, USA. *E-mail:* info@supervalu.com

HERKSTRÖTER, Cornelius Antonius Johannes, BSc; Dutch business executive; b. 21 Aug. 1937, Venlo; m. Regina Maria Haske 1959; two s. one d.; ed Erasmus Univ. Rotterdam; qualified as chartered accountant; joined Billiton as business economist 1967, following acquisition of Billiton by Shell Petroleum, apptd. Head Dept Financial and Econ. Affairs 1971, various sr posts in Billiton cos, Switzerland and Netherlands 1972–80, Area Co-ordinator SE Asia, Shell Int. Petroleum Co. Ltd 1980, Vice-Pres. (Finance) Shell Française SA 1982, Chair. Bd of Man. Deutsche Shell AG 1985, Regional Co-ordinator Europe, Dir Shell Internationale Petroleum Mij. BV 1988, Man. Dir The Shell Petroleum Co. Ltd, Chair. Supervisory Bd Shell Nederland BV, Group Man. Dir 1989, Chair. Supervisory Bd Deutsche Shell AG 1990, Dir Shell UK Ltd; Chair. Bd of Dirs Billiton Int. Metals BV 1991; Pres. NV Koninklijke Nederlandsche Petroleum Maatschappij (Royal Dutch Petroleum Co.) 1992–98; mem. Supervisory Bd ING Groep N.V. 1998–2007, Chair. 1999–2007; fmr Chair. Public Advisory Council Tinbergen Inst.; fmr Chair. Supervisory Council Erasmus Univ.; Prof. Int. Man. Amsterdam Univ.; Trustee, Int. Accounting Standards Cttee; mem. Supervisory Bd DSM Special Products BV, Hollandsche Beton Group NV; mem. Int. Advisory Bd CNOOC Ltd; mem. Advisory Council Robert Bosch GmbH; Verdienstkreuz (First Class) (Germany), Kt Order of Netherlands Lion. *Leisure interests:* reading, music, photography. *Address:* c/o Supervisory Board, ING Groep N.V., ING House, Amstelveenseweg, 500 1081 KL Amsterdam, Netherlands.

HERMAN, Alexis M.; American politician and administrator; *Chairman and CEO, New Ventures LLC;* b. 16 July 1947, Mobile, Ala; m. Dr Charles Franklin 2000; ed Xavier Univ.; with Recruitment and Training Program Inc., US Dept of Labor, New York City 1971–72, Consulting Supervisor 1973–74; Nat. Dir Minority Women's Employment Program 1974–77; Dir Women's Bureau, US Dept of Labor, Washington, DC 1977–81; Founder A.M. Herman & Assocs, Washington, DC 1981, Pres. and CEO 1985–93; Chief of Staff and Deputy Chair. Democratic Nat. Convention Cttee –1991, CEO 1991–92; Deputy Dir Clinton-Gore Presidential Transition Office 1992–93; Asst to Pres. of USA; Public Liaison Dir White House 1993–96; Sec. of Labor 1997–2000; Chair. and CEO New Ventures LLC (corp. consulting firm) 2001–; mem. Sodexo Advisory Bd, Toyota Advisory Bd on Diversity 2001–; mem. Bd of Dirs Cummins Inc. 2001–, MGM Resorts International 2002–, Entergy Corpn 2003–, Coca-Cola Company 2007–; mem. Nat. Council of Negro Women, Ron Brown Foundation; Sara Lee Front Runner Award 1999. *Address:* New Ventures LLC, 1333 H Street, NW, Washington, DC 20005, USA.

HERMAN, Richard, BA, PhD; American mathematician, academic and university administrator; *Chancellor, University of Illinois at Urbana-Champaign;* m.

Susan Herman; three c.; ed Stevens Inst. of Tech., Univ. of Maryland; began teaching career as Lecturer in Math., UCLA; joined Pennsylvania State Univ. 1972, Chair. Dept of Math. 1986–90; Dean, Coll. of Computer, Math. and Physical Sciences, Univ. of Maryland 1990–98; Provost and Vice Chancellor for Academic Affairs, Univ. of Illinois at Urbana-Champaign 1998–2005, Chancellor 2005–; Chair. Council of Pres.'s of Univs Research Asscn Inc.; mem. Pres. Bush's Council of Advisors on Science and Tech.; mem. American Acad. of Arts and Sciences 2008–. *Address:* Office of the Chancellor, University of Illinois at Urbana-Champaign, 317 Swanlund Administration Building, 601 E. John Street, Champaign, IL 61820, USA (office). *Telephone:* (217) 333-1000 (office). *Website:* oc.illinois.edu/index.html (office).

HERMANI MELONI, Gen. (retd) Remigio; Peruvian government official; Head of Nat. Bureau of Criminal Investigation (DIRINCRI) 2001–02; Chief of Security, Office of the Comptroller Gen. 2002–08; Minister of the Interior 2008–09 (resgnd). *Address:* c/o Ministry of the Interior, Plaza 30 de Agosto 150, San Isidro, Lima, Peru (office).

HERMANN, Valerie; French business executive; *CEO, Yves Saint Laurent;* three d.; Gen. Man. John Galliano –2005; CEO Yves Saint Laurent (acquired by the Gucci Group, the luxury div. of the PPR Group, in 1999) 2005–; ranked by Fortune magazine amongst the 50 Most Powerful Women in Business outside the US (48th) 2009. *Address:* Yves Saint Laurent, 7 avenue George V, 75008 Paris, France (office). *Telephone:* 1-41-43-30-38 (office). *E-mail:* info@ysl.com (office). *Website:* www.ysl.com (office).

HERMANS, Christopher, MA; Botswana banker; b. 23 Dec. 1936, Cape Town, South Africa; s. of Henry Hodgson Hermans and Marjorie Stanhope Hermans; m. 1st Janet Gallagher 1960 (divorced 1987); one s. two d.; m. 2nd Vonna Deulen 1987; two d.; ed Diocesan Coll., Rondebosch, Cape Town, Trinity Coll., Oxford, Howard Univ., Wash., Vanderbilt Univ., Nashville, Tenn.; Asst Sec. for Devt, Bechuanaland Protectorate Admin. 1961–66; Perm. Sec., Ministry of Devt Planning, Botswana Govt 1966–70, Ministry of Finance and Devt Planning 1970–75; Gov. Bank of Botswana 1975–77, 1987–99; Sr Planning Adviser/Loan Officer, World Bank 1977–82, CEO Thailand and Indonesia Programs Div., 1982–84; CEO World Bank Regional Mission, Bangkok 1984–87; Presidential Order of Meritorious Service. *Leisure interests:* tennis, wildlife, windsurfing, gardening. *Address:* c/o Bank of Botswana, PO Box 712, Gaborone, Botswana.

HERMASSI, Abdelbaki; Tunisian politician; Minister of Culture, Youth and Leisure –2004; Minister of Foreign Affairs 2004–05. *Address:* c/o Ministry of Foreign Affairs, ave de la Ligue des états Arabes, Tunis, Tunisia (office).

HERMASZEWSKI, Gen. Mirosław; Polish astronaut and air force officer (retd); b. 15 Sept. 1941, Lipniki (now Ukraine); s. of the late Roman Hermaszewski and of Kamila Hermaszewska; m. Emilia Hermaszewska 1965; one s. one d.; ed Air Force Officers' School, Dęblin, Karol Sverchevski Mil. Acad., Gen. Staff Acad., Warsaw, Voroshilov Mil. Acad., Moscow; served in Nat. Air Defence 1964–76; 1st class pilot 1966, supersonic MiG-21 pilot 1967, flight leader 1971–72, Deputy Squadron Leader 1972–75, Regt Commdr 1975–76; master's class pilot; in Cosmonauts' Training Centre, Zvezdnoy Gorodok, nr Moscow 1976–78; space flight on board Soyuz-30 and space-station Salyut-6 June–July (7 days 22 hours 2 minutes and 59 seconds) 1978; service in HQ of Nat. Air Defence 1978–80; Chief of Shkola Orlyat High Aviation School 1982–85; Second-in-Command, Air Forces and Air Defence of Polish Repub. 1990–91; Commdr Air Force Officers' School, Dęblin 1984–90; Adviser for Polish Sec. of Defence 2009; mem. Space Research Cttee of Polish Acad. of Sciences 1978–, Asscn of Space Explorers 1985–; Pres. Gen. Bd Polish Astronautical Soc. 1983–87; Maj.-Gen. 1988; Pres. Nat. Council of Aviation 1998–2000; Gold Cross of Merit 1976, Cross of Grunwald Order (1st Class) 1978, Gold Star of Hero of USSR 1978, Order of Lenin 1978, Mil. Champion Pilot 1978, Cosmonaut of Polish People's Repub. 1978, Int. Order of Smile 1991. *Leisure interests:* science fiction novels, sailing, hunting, sports, dogs. *Address:* ul. Czeczota 25, 02-607 Warsaw, Poland. *Website:* www.hermaszewski.com.

HERNÁDI, Zsolt, BEcons; Hungarian business executive; *Chairman and CEO, MOL Group;* b. 1960; ed Budapest Univ. of Econ. Sciences; various posts with Kereskedelmi és Hitelbank Rt. 1989–94, becoming Deputy Gen. Man. 1992–94; CEO Cen. Bank of Hungarian Savings Cooperatives 1994–2001, Dir 1994–2002; Dir MOL Group 1999–, Chair. 2000–, CEO 2001–; mem. Corp. Governance and Remuneration Cttee; Dir Hungarian Banking Asscn 1995–2001, Panrusgas; mem. European Round Table of Industrialists 2001–; Hon. Citizen of Corvinus Univ. of Budapest 2009. *Address:* MOL Hungarian Oil and Gas Plc, 1117 Budapest, Október huszonharmadika u. 18, Hungary (office). *Telephone:* (1) 209-0000 (office). *Website:* www.mol.hu (office).

HERNÁNDEZ ALCERRO, Jorge Ramón; Honduran lawyer, politician and diplomatist; *Ambassador to USA;* b. 29 Aug. 1948; m.; two c.; ed Inst. Européen de Hautes Etudes Internationales, France, Univ. of Nice and Universidad Nacional Autónoma de Honduras; fmr attorney and lecturer at Univ. Nacional Autónoma de Honduras; fmr Judge, Inter-American Court of Human Rights; fmr Gen. Sec. Inovación y Unidad Party, Deputy to Nat. Ass. and Deputy to Nat. Congress; fmr Deputy Foreign Minister; Amb. and Perm. Rep. to UN, New York 1987–89; Amb. on Special Assignment in Latin America, USA and at UN Gen. Ass. 1990–94; Minister of the Interior and Justice 2002–06; Amb. to USA 2010–. *Address:* Embassy of Honduras, 3007 Tilden Street NW, Suite 4-M, Washington, DC 20008, USA (office). *Telephone:* (202) 966-2604 (office). *Fax:* (202) 966-9751 (office). *E-mail:* embassy@hondurasemb.org (office). *Website:* www.hondurasemb.org (office).

HERNÁNDEZ ALVARADO, Juan Orlando; Honduran lawyer, business executive, politician and head of state; *President;* b. 28 Oct. 1968, Gracias; s. of Juan Hernández Villanueva and Elvira Alvarado Castillo; m. Ana García Carías; one s. three d.; ed Universidad Nacional Autónoma de Honduras, State Univ. of New York, USA; business interests include coffee production in Gracias, hotels and broadcasting cos; Asst to First Sec. of Congreso Nacional (Parl.) 1990–94; Lecturer in constitutional law, Universidad Nacional Autónoma de Honduras –1999; mem. Congreso Nacional for Lempira 1998–2014, Pres. 2010–13; Pres. of Honduras 2014–; mem. Partido Nacional. *Address:* Office of the President, Palacio José Cecilio del Valle, Boulevard Francisco Morazán, Tegucigalpa, Honduras (office).

Telephone: 2290-5010 (office). *Fax:* 2231-0097 (office). *E-mail:* diseloalpresidente@presidencia.gob.hn (office).

HERNÁNDEZ COLÓN, Rafael, AB, LLB; Puerto Rican lawyer and fmr politician; b. 24 Oct. 1936, Ponce; s. of Rafael Hernández Matos and Dorinda Colón Clavell; m. 1st Lila Mayoral 1959 (died 2003); three s. one d.; m. 2nd Nelsa López 2004; ed Valley Forge Mil. Acad., Wayne Pa, Johns Hopkins Univ., Univ. of Puerto Rico Law School; pvt. law practice 1959–69, 1977–84; Assoc. Commr of Public Service 1960–62; Lecturer in Law, Catholic Univ. of Puerto Rico 1961–65; Sec. of Justice 1965–67; Senator at Large, Popular Democratic Party 1968; Pres. of Senate 1969–73; Leader of Popular Democratic Party 1969; Gov. of Puerto Rico 1972–76, 1989–93; Trustee, Carnegie Foundation for Int. Peace; Founder Fundación Biblioteca Rafael Hernández Colón; mem. Inter-American Bar Asscn, Club of Rome; Great Cross of Isabel la Católica (Spain) 1987, Order of El Libertador (Venezuela) 1987; Dr hc (Johns Hopkins Univ.), (Catholic Univ. of Puerto Rico); Harvard Foundation Award 1987, Spirit of Caribbean Award 1987, Olympic Order Award 1989, Principe de Asturias de las Letras Award 1991. *Publications:* Text on Civil Procedure 1968 and many articles on topics of law. *Address:* Fundación Biblioteca Rafael Hernández Colón, PO Box 2030, Ponce, PR 00733-2030, Puerto Rico (office). *Telephone:* (787) 259-0421 (office). *Fax:* (787) 844-8400 (office). *E-mail:* info@rafaelhernandezcolon.org. *Website:* www.rafaelhernandezcolon.org (office).

HERRERA, Paloma; Argentine ballet dancer; b. 21 Dec. 1975, Buenos Aires; d. of Alberto Herrera and Marisa Herrera; ed Teatro Colón, Buenos Aires, Minsk Ballet School, School of American Ballet; joined American Ballet Theater (ABT) corps de ballet; roles in Sleeping Beauty, Don Quixote and La Bayadère; soloist, ABT 1992, prin. dancer 1995–; leading role in How Near Heaven (cr. for her by Twyla Tharp q.v.; 1994; other notable roles include Clara in The Nutcracker, Medora in Le Corsaire, Kitri in Don Quixote, Juliet in Romeo and Juliet 1995; Int. Prize Gino Tani 1997, Top Ten Dancers of the Twentieth Century, Dance Magazine 1999, Leader of the Millennium, Time Magazine and CNN 1999, Konex Platinum Prize, Ballerina of the Decade 1989-1999, Buenos Aires, Argentina 1999, Maria Ruanova Award 2000, NY Immigrant Achievement Award 2001. *Address:* American Ballet Theater, 890 Broadway, New York, NY 10003 (office); One Lincoln Plaza, 20 West 64th Street, Apt F, New York, NY 10023, USA (home); Billinghurst 2553, 10 Piso Dto, CP 1425 Buenos Aires, Argentina. *Website:* www.palomaherrera.com; www.abt.org.

HERRERA ARAYA, Marvin; Costa Rican politician and international organization executive; *Secretary-General, Coordinación Educativa y Cultural Centroamericana;* Deputy Minister of Public Educ. 1978–81; mem. Inter-American Cttee on Educ., OAS 1980–82; Deputy to Legis. Ass. 1982–86; Minister of Public Educ. 1990–94; mem. Higher Council of Educ. 1999–2003; Sec.-Gen. Coordinación Educativa y Cultural Centroamericana 2003–. *Address:* Coordinación Educativa y Cultural Centroamericana, 100m norte de la Nunciatura, Casa 8815, Rohrmoser, San José, Costa Rica (office). *Telephone:* 232-2891 (office). *Fax:* 232-2891 (office). *E-mail:* sgcecc@racsa.co.cr (office). *Website:* www.sica.int/cecc (office).

HERRERA FLORES, Jordy Hernán; Mexican economist and politician; b. 24 Jan. 1974; ed Universidad Iberoamericana; subject teacher in Dept of Econs, Universidad Iberoamericana 1996–2003; Dir Gen. Liaison H. Congress of the Social Devt Secr. Jan.–Nov. 2001; Sec. to Dir Gen. of Banobras April–Sept. 2003; Pvt. Sec. to the Sec. of Energy 2003–04; Dir Gen. Investment Promotion Unit, Ministry of Energy 2004–05; Undersecretary of Energy Planning and Technological Devt, Ministry of Energy 2006–10; Sec. of State for Energy 2011–12; CEO Pemex Gas and Basic Petrochemicals 2010–11, CEO Petróleos Mexicanos (PEMEX) 2011–12; mem. Partido Acción Nacional. *Address:* Partido Acción Nacional (PAN), Avenida Coyoacán 1546, Col. del Valle, Del. Benito Juárez, 03100 México DF, Mexico (office). *Telephone:* (55) 5200-4000 (office). *E-mail:* correo@cen.pan.org.mx (office). *Website:* www.pan.org.mx (office).

HERRERA NICOLALDE, Fausto Eduardo, MBA; Ecuadorian economist and government official; *Minister of Finance;* ed Pontificia Universidad Católica del Ecuador, INCAE Business School, Costa Rica; Jr Consultant, Inter-American Devt Bank 2002–03; several roles within Ministry of Economy and Finance including Coordinator of Studies and Macroeconomic Programming 2003–06, Asst Sec. for Econ. Policy 2005–06, Asst Sec. for Fiscal Consistency 2007–08, Adviser to Nat. Sec., Nat. Secr. for Planning and Devt (SENPLADES) 2009, Adviser to Minister of Finance 2010, Asst Sec. for Fiscal Relations 2012, Vice-Minister of Finance 2012–13, Minister of Finance 2013–. *Address:* Ministry of Finance, Avda 10 de Agosto 1661 y Bolivia, Quito, Ecuador (office). *Telephone:* (2) 399-8300 (office). *Fax:* (2) 250-5256 (office). *E-mail:* mefecuador@finanzas.gob.ec (office). *Website:* www.finanzas.gob.ec (office).

HERRERA NIETO, Gen. Nelson; Ecuadorean government official, fmr diplomatist and fmr army officer; fmr Dir of Educ. for the Army; fmr Dir Instituto de Altos Estudios Nacionales; fmr Commdr Aerial Brigade of the Army; fmr Amb. to Mexico; fmr Pres. INVEREC; Minister of Nat. Defence 2004–05; fmr mem. Instituto Panamericano de Geografía e Historia. *Address:* c/o Ministry of National Defence, Exposición 208, Quito, Ecuador.

HERRERO ACOSTA, Fernando, MA, PhD; Costa Rican government official; b. 15 Dec. 1952, San José; s. of Fernando Herrero Acosta Serrano and Isabel Sanchez Flor; m. Isabel Flor Rodríguez Céspedes 1975; ed Univ. of New York, Univ. of Costa Rica; Prof., Cen. American and the Caribbean Nat. Univ. 1975–2005; Adviser to Minister of Nat. Planning and Econ. Policy 1984; Consultant and Dir of Devt Alternatives, Oikos Economic Advisers 1984–87; Econ. Adviser to the Pres. of Costa Rica 1988, Deputy Minister of Nat. Planning and Econ. Policy 1988–89, Deputy Minister of Finance 1989–90, Minister of Finance 1994–96, 2010–12; Amb. to OAS 1996–98, also Amb. to American Council for Integral Devt; Exec. Dir PROCESOS (research and consulting group concerned with devt of democracy in Cen. America and the Caribbean) 1998–2005; Prof., Universidad Nacional 2000–05; Gov. Gen. Public Services Regulatory Authority 2006–10; mem. Consultant Bd Cen. American Inst. for Fiscal Studies. *Publications include:* several books and articles. *Address:* c/o Ministry of Finance, Edif. Antigüo Banco Anglo, Avda 2a, Calle 3a, San José, Costa Rica (office).

HERRERO RODRIGUEZ DE MIÑON, Miguel, LPh, PhD; Spanish politician and barrister; *Permanent Councillor of State*; b. 18 June 1940; s. of Miguel Herrero and Carmen Rodríguez de Miñon; m. Cristina de Jáuregui; one s. two d.; ed Univs of Madrid, Oxford, Luxembourg, Geneva, Paris and Louvain; Lecturer in Int. Law, Univ. of Madrid 1963–65; Sr Legal Adviser to Spanish Admin 1966; Gen. Sec. Ministry of Justice 1976; mem. Parl. 1977–93; Leader, Parl. Group of Unión de Centro Democrático in Govt 1980–81; Deputy Leader of Parl. Group of AP, major opposition group in Parl. 1982–87; Magistrate, Constitutional Court, Andorra 2001–08; Perm. Councillor of State 2009–; mem. Trilateral Comm. 1982–2004, State Council of Spain; mem. Real Academia de Ciencias Morales y Políticas 1991–; Gran Cruz de Isabel la Católica, Gran Cruz de San Raimundo de Peñafort, Orden Mérito Constitucional, Creu San Jordi, G. Off. Merito (Italy), Collar Merito Civil; Dr hc (UNED, Leon). *Publications:* several books on constitutional law and int. relations. *Leisure interests:* collecting old books, hunting. *Address:* Calle Mayor 79, 28013 Madrid, Spain (office). *Telephone:* (91) 5166203 (office). *E-mail:* miguel .herrerominon@consejo-estado.es (office).

HERRMAN, Ernie; American business executive; *President, The TJX Companies, Inc.*; joined TJX as a buyer 1989, held a series of sr merchandising positions of increasing responsibility, Exec. Vice-Pres. of Merchandising at Marmaxx 2001–04, COO Marmaxx of TJX Companies 2004–05, Exec. Vice-Pres. TJX 2004–05, Pres. and COO T.J. Maxx, Pres. The Marmaxx Group 2005–08, Sr Exec. Vice-Pres. TJX 2007–11, Group Pres. 2008–11, Pres. The TJX Companies, Inc. 2011–. *Address:* The TJX Companies, Inc., 770 Cochituate Road, Framingham, MA 01701, USA (office). *Telephone:* (508) 390-1000 (office). *Fax:* (508) 390-2828 (office). *E-mail:* info@tjx.com (office). *Website:* www.tjx.com (office).

HERRMANN, Wolfgang A., Dipl. Chem. Univ., Dr rer. nat; German chemist, academic and university administrator; *Professor of Chemistry and President, Technische Universität München;* b. 18 April 1948, Kehlheim/Donau, Bavaria; ed Donau-Gymnasium Kelheim, Bavaria, Technische Hochschule München, Univ. of Regensburg; Research Fellow, Penn State Univ., USA 1975–76; Assoc. Prof., Univ. of Regensburg 1979–81; Prof., Univ. of Frankfurt 1982–85; Prof. of Chem., Technische Universität München 1985–, Dean of Science Faculty 1988–90, Univ. Pres. 1995–; Chair. Scientific Council, VIAG AG, Bonn 1991–96; fmr Visiting Prof. at numerous int. univs, including Strasbourg, Bordeaux, Rennes and Toulouse, France, Rijksuniversiteit Utrecht, Netherlands, Texas A&M Univ., USA; mem. Editorial Bd numerous publs, including Journal of Cluster Science 1988–94, Journal of Molecular Catalysis 1994–2000, Angewandte Chemie 1999–, Catalysis Letters 1999–; Chair. Supervisory Bd Deutsches Museum, Munich 1998–, Bayerische Rektorenkonferenz (Bavarian Univ. Rectors Conf.) 2002–04; Founding Chair. Universität Bayern e.V. 2004–05; mem. Int. Advisory Council, King Abdullah Univ. of Science and Tech., Saudi Arabia 2007–, Governing Bd European Inst. of Innovation and Tech. 2008–, Zukunftsrat (Future Council of the Bavarian Govt) 2010–; mem. Supervisory Bd Evonik Industries AG 2008–; mem. Deutsche Akad. der Naturforscher 1995–, Royal Swedish Acad. of Eng Science 2011–; Fellow, Japanese Soc. for Promotion of Science 1992; Fed. Cross of Merit 1997, Chevalier, Légion d'honneur 2000, Bavarian Order of the Constitution 2005, Bavarian Order of Merit 2006, Bavarian Maximilian Order of Science and Art 2012; Hon. DrSc (Univ. Claude Bernard, Lyon) 1990, (Univ. Veszprém, Hungary) 1995, (Univ. of South Carolina, USA) 1999, (Lisbon) 2002, (Rennes) 2003, (Nanjing Univ., China) 2003, (Univ. of Timişoara, Romania) 2005, (Frankfurt) 2006, (Texas A&M Univ.) 2006, (Baumann Univ., Moscow) 2006, (Tiflis Univ., Georgia) 2009; Otto-Klung Award for Chem. 1982, Gottfried Wilhelm Leibniz Prize, German Research Foundation 1987, Alexander von Humboldt Award 1989, Otto Bayer Award 1990, Max Planck Research Award (co-recipient) 1991, Pino Medal, Italian Chemical Soc. 1994, Wilhelm Klemm Award, German Chemical Soc. 1995, Luigi Sacconi Medal 2000, Werner Heisenberg Medal 2000, ACS Award in Organometallic Chemistry 2004, Univ. Manager of the Year, Financial Times Deutschland, Centrum für Hochschulentwicklung 2009, Goldene Bürgermedaille of Freising 2010, President of the Year, Deutscher Hochschulverband 2012. *Address:* Hochschulpräsidium, Technische Universität München, Arcisstr. 21 80333 München (office); Lehrstuhl für Anorganische Chemie, Technische Universität München, Lichtenbergstrassse 4, Garching bei München 85747, Germany (office). *Telephone:* (89) 28922200 (office); (89) 28913080 (office). *Fax:* (89) 28923399 (office); (89) 28913473 (office). *E-mail:* wolfgang.herrmann@ch.tum.de (office); praesident@tum.de (office). *Website:* portal.mytum.de/tum/praesident/index_html (office); aci.anorg.chemie.tu-muenchen.de/wah (office).

HERSCHBACH, Dudley Robert, BS, MS, AM, PhD, FRSC; American chemist and academic; *Professor Emeritus, Harvard University;* b. 18 June 1932, San José, Calif.; s. of Robert Dudley Herschbach and Dorothy Edith Beer; m. Georgene Lee Botyos 1964; two d.; ed Stanford and Harvard Univs; Asst Prof., Univ. of Calif., Berkeley 1959–61, Assoc. Prof. 1961–63; Prof. of Chem., Harvard Univ. 1963–76, Frank B. Baird, Jr Prof. of Science 1976–2003, Chair. Chemical Physics Program 1964–77, Chair. Dept of Chem. 1977–80, mem. Faculty Council 1980–83, Co-Master of Currier House 1981–86, currently Prof. Emer.; Chair. Bd of Trustees Science Service; Prof. Texas A&M Univ. 2005–; fmr Chair. Soc. for Science and Public; Assoc. Ed., Journal of Physical Chem. 1980–88; Scientific Advisor Aerodyne Corpn; Chair. Society for Science and the Public 1992–2010; mem. Bd of Dirs Center for Arms Control and Non-Proliferation; mem. Bd of Sponsors Fed. of American Scientists, Bulletin of Atomic Scientists; mem. Advisory Bd USA Science and Eng Festival; Junior Fellow, Harvard Soc. of Fellows 1957–59; Guggenheim Fellowship 1968; Fellow, American Acad. of Arts and Sciences, NAS, American Philosophical Soc.; Hon. Life mem. Asscn for Women in Science; Hon. DSc (Toronto) 1977, (Adelphi) 1990; Nobel Prize for Chem. (jtly) 1986, ACS Pure Chem. Prize 1965, ACS Pauling Medal 1978, Polanyi Medal, Royal Soc. of Chem. 1981, Langmuir Prize, American Physical Soc. 1983, Nat. Award of Science 1991, Sierra Nevada Distinguished Chemist Award 1993, Kosolapoff Medal 1994, William Walker Prize 1994, President's Award, Council of Scientific Soc. 1999, Distinguished Eagle Scout Award. *Publications:* more than 400 research papers. *Leisure interests:* viola, running. *Address:* Department of Chemistry and Chemical Biology, Harvard University, 12 Oxford Street, Cambridge, MA 02138, USA. *Telephone:* (617) 495-3218 (office). *Fax:* (617) 495-4723 (office). *E-mail:* herschbach@chemistry.harvard.edu (office). *Website:* www.chem.harvard.edu/herschbach (office).

HERSH, Seymour Myron, BA; American journalist and writer; b. 8 April 1937, Chicago; m. Elizabeth Sarah Klein 1964; two s. one d.; ed Univ. of Chicago; Chicago City News Bureau 1959; corresp. United Press International 1962–63, Associated Press 1963–67, The New Yorker 1992–; mem. of staff, New York Times 1972–79; nat. corresp. Atlantic Monthly 1983–86; Pulitzer Prize for Int. Reporting 1970, George Polk Memorial Awards 1970, 1973, 1974, 1981, 2004, Scripps-Howard Public Service Award 1973, Sidney Hillman Award 1974, John Peter Zenger Freedom of the Press Award 1975, Los Angeles Times Book Prize 1983, Nat. Book Critics Circle Award 1983, Investigative Reporters and Editors Prizes 1983, 1992, Nat. Magazine Award 2004, George Orwell Award 2004. *Publications:* Chemical and Biological Warfare: America's Hidden Arsenal 1968, My Lai 4: A Report on the Massacre and Its Aftermath 1970, Cover-Up: The Army's Secret Investigation of the Massacre at My Lai 1972, The Price of Power: Kissinger in the Nixon White House (Nat. Book Critics Circle Award, Los Angeles Times Book Prize) 1983, The Target is Destroyed: What Really Happened to Flight 007 and What America Knew About It 1986, The Samson Option: Israel's Nuclear Arsenal and America's Foreign Policy 1991, The Dark Side of Camelot 1997, Against All Enemies: Gulf War Syndrome: The War Between America's Ailing Veterans and Their Government 1999, Chain of Command: The Road from 9/11 to Abu Ghraib 2004; contribs to various magazines. *Address:* 3214 Newark Street NW, Washington, DC 20008-3345, USA (home).

HERSHEY, Barbara; American actress; b. 5 Feb. 1948, Hollywood, Calif.; d. of William H. Herzstein; one s.; m. Stephen Douglas 1992 (divorced 1995); ed Hollywood High School; debut in TV series The Monroes. *Films include:* With Six You Get Eggroll 1968, Heaven with a Gun 1969, The Last Summer 1969, The Liberation of L.B. Jones 1970, The Baby Maker 1970, The Pursuit of Happiness 1971, Dealing: Or the Berkeley-to-Boston Forty-Brick Lost-Bag Blues 1972, Boxcar Bertha 1972, Love Comes Quietly 1973, The Crazy World of Julius Vrooder 1974, You and Me 1975, Diamonds 1975, Trial by Combat 1976, The Last Hard Men 1976, The Stuntman 1980, The Entity 1981, Americana 1981, Take This Job and Shove It 1981, The Right Stuff 1983, The Natural 1984, Hannah and Her Sisters 1986, Hoosiers 1986, Tin Men 1987, Shy People 1987 (Best Actress, Cannes Film Festival), The Last Temptation of Christ 1988, A World Apart 1988 (Best Actress, Cannes Film Festival), Beaches 1988, Tune in Tomorrow 1990, Paris Trout 1990, The Public Eye 1991, Defenseless 1991, Swing Kids 1993, Splitting Heirs 1993, Falling Down 1993, A Dangerous Woman 1994, Last of the Dogmen 1995, Portrait of a Lady 1996, The Pallbearer 1996, A Soldier's Daughter Never Cries 1998, Frogs for Snakes 1999, Drowning on Dry Land 1999, Breakfast of Champions 1999, Lantana 2001, 11:14 2003, Riding the Bullet 2004, The Bird Can't Fly 2007, Love Comes Lately 2007, Childless 2008, Black Swan 2010. *Television includes:* Just a Little Inconvenience, A Killing in a Small Town (Emmy and Golden Globe Awards 1990), The Bible 1993, Return to Lonesome Dove 1993, Portrait of a Lady 1996, A Soldier's Daughter Never Cries 1998, Frogs for Snakes 1998, The Staircase 1998, Breakfast of Champions 1999, Passion 1999, Chicago Hope (series) 1999–2000, Daniel Deronda 2002, Hunger Point 2003, The Stranger Beside Me 2003, Paradise 2004, The Mountain (series) 2004–05, Anne of Green Gables: A New Beginning 2008. *Address:* c/o Suzan Bymel, Bymel O'Neill Management, N Vista, Los Angeles, CA 90046 (office); c/o Jenny Rawlings, CAA, 9830 Wilshire Boulevard, Beverly Hills, CA 90212, USA.

HERSHKO, Avram, MD, PhD; Israeli biochemist and academic; *Professor, Faculty of Medicine, Technion-Israel Institute of Technology;* b. 31 Dec. 1937, Hungary; s. of Moshe Hershko and Shoshana Margit Hershko; m. Judith Leibowitz Hershko 1963; three s.; ed Hebrew Univ. of Jerusalem; prisoner in Nazi concentration camp; emigrated to Israel with parents 1950; mil. service as physician in Israeli army 1965–67; postdoctoral fellowship in San Francisco 1969–71; Prof., Faculty of Medicine, Technion-Israel Inst. of Tech. 1980–; studied protein degradation at biochemical level with Aaron Ciechanover (q.v.) and Irwin Rose 1977–90; studies roles of protein degradation in the control of cell division 1990–; mem. Scientific Advisory Bd Oramed Pharmaceuticals; Dr hc (Hebrew Univ.) 2009; Weizmann Prize for Sciences 1987, Israel Prize in biochemistry 1994, Gairdner Int. Award, Canada 1999, Albert Lasker Basic Medical Research Award 2000, Louisa Gross Horwitz Prize, Columbia Univ. 2001, Wolf Prize for Medicine (with Alexander Varshavsky q.v.) 2001, Nobel Prize in Chemistry (with Aaron Ciechanover and Irwin Rose) 2004. *Publications:* co-author of several books. *Address:* Faculty of Medicine, Technion-Israel Institute of Technology, Haifa 31096, Israel (office). *Telephone:* (4) 8295344 (office). *E-mail:* hershko@tx.technion .ac.il (office). *Website:* www1.technion.ac.il (office).

HERSOV, Basil Edward, DMS, BA (Hons), MA, FRSA, FID, FSAIM; South African business executive (retd); b. 18 Aug. 1926, Johannesburg; s. of Abraham Sundel (Bob) Hersov and Gertrude Hersov (née Aronson); m. Antoinette Herbert 1957; two s. two d.; ed Michaelhouse, Natal, Christ's Coll., Cambridge, UK; pilot in S African Air Force 1944–46; joined Anglovaal Ltd as Learner Official on gold mine 1949, later holding a number of sr positions with Anglovaal Group: Deputy Chair. 1970, Chair. and Man. Dir 1973–98; Chair. Hartebeestfontein Gold Mining Co. Ltd, Anglovaal Industries Ltd, The Associated Manganese Mines of SA Ltd; mem. bd of many other cos within and outside Anglovaal Group; Dir Mutual and Fed. Insurance Co. Ltd; Pres. and Fellow, Inst. of Dirs (SA); Hon. Pres., mem. Council, South Africa Foundation; Gov. Rhodes Univ. Bd of Trustees, Business South Africa, Nat. Business Initiative; Fellow, S African Inst. of Man., S African Inst. of Mining and Metallurgy; Hon. Col, 21 Squadron, SAAF Doyen, SAAF Hon. Cols 1980, Liveryman Guild of Air Pilots & Navigators 2009; Decoration for Meritorious Service; Hon. LLD (Rhodes); Witwaterstand Univ. Award for Business Excellence 1984, Brig. Stokes Memorial Award, S African Inst. of Mining and Metallurgy 1996. *Leisure interests:* skiing, horse racing, tennis, flying, sailing. *Address:* Springwaters, Box 65097, Benmore 2010 (home); PO Box 846, Saxonwold 2132, South Africa (office). *Telephone:* (11) 447-5510 (office). *Fax:* (11) 883-4006 (home); (86) 652-8936 (office). *E-mail:* basilh@hersov.co.za (home).

HERTELEER, Adm. (retd) Willy Maurits; Belgian naval officer (retd); *President,* ; b. 1 Oct. 1941, Assenede; m. Jacqueline Liekens 1962 (deceased); one s. three d.; ed Royal Cadet School, Brussels, Merchant Navy Acad., Belgian Staff Coll., Brussels, Ecole Supérieure de Guerre Navale, Paris; commissioned Belgian Navy 1962, as ensign served on minesweepers and a supply/command ship 1963–68, became mine warfare specialist 1969–70, Staff Officer, Mine Countermeasures,

Operational Command 1970–72; Commdr coastal minesweeper 1975, ocean minesweeper/hunter 1978, (instructor Belgian-Dutch School for Mine Warfare, Ostend between these postings); rank of Lt-Commdr 1979; apptd to Planning section, Belgian Naval Staff, also mem. Naval Bd, NATO Mil. Standardization Agency 1979–82; Second-in-Command frigate Westdiep 1982–84, CO 1984–85; Asst Chief of Staff Operations, Naval Operations Command 1986, Chief of Staff 1986–87; Head Belgian-Dutch School for Mine Warfare 1987–89; mem. Audit Team, Belgian Naval Staff, Brussels 1989, Staff Officer, Operations 1990, Commdr Naval Operations 1990–92; rank of Rear-Adm. 1992; joined Gen. Staff HQ, Brussels 1992, Chief of Naval Staff 1993–95; rank of Vice-Adm. 1995; Chief of the Gen. Staff 1995–2002; retd 2003; Pres. Koninklijk Werk IBIS (school for boys) 2005–, EuroDefense Belgium 2008–; promoted to Aide to King Albert II 1999; Belgische Nationale Orden – Grootkruis in de Kroonorde, Commdr in de Leopoldorde, Belgische Militaire Eretekens, Militair Kruis 1ste Klasse, Buitenlandse Orden, Commdr, Légion d'honneur, Commdr, Legion of Merit (USA), Grand Officier, Ordre de Mérite du Grand-Duché de Luxembourg, Commdr, Order of Merit of the Repub. of Poland, Commdr, Ordre Nat. du Benin, Grootofficier 'Merito Naval' (Brazil), La Medaille du Mérite Naval (France), Grand Cross (Repub. of Hungary), Liberation Medal, Third Degree (Kuwait), Liberation Medal with Palm (Saudi Arabia). *Address:* Koninklijk Werk IBIS, 1 Prinses Elisabethlaan, 8450 Bredene, Belgium (office). *Telephone:* (2) 742-62-09 (IBIS) (office); (59) 50-86-39 (EuroDefense Belgium) (office). *Fax:* (59) 32-69-47 (home). *E-mail:* willy@herteleer.eu (office). *Website:* www.ibisschool.be (office); eurodefense-belgium.eu (office).

HERTRICH, Rainer, BCom; German fmr aerospace industry executive; b. 6 Dec. 1949, Ottengrün; m.; two c.; ed Tech. Univ. of Berlin, Univ. of Nuremberg; apprenticeship and business training, Siemens AG 1969–71; Information Processing Supervisor controlling Dept, Mil. Aircraft Div., Messerschmitt-Bölkow-Blohm (MBB) GmbH 1977, Head Controlling Dept MBB Service Div., Ottobrunn 1978–83, Chief Financial Officer 1983–84, Head Controlling and Finance Dept, MBB Dynamics Div. 1984–87, Chief Financial Officer and mem. Div. Man., MBB Marine and Special Products Div. 1987–90; Head Divisional Controlling, Cen. Controlling Section, Deutsche Aerospace AG, Dasa (now European Aeronautic Defence and Space Co.—EADS) 1990–91, Sr Vice-Pres., Corp. Controlling, Dasa 1991–96, Head Aeroengines Business Unit, Dasa, Pres. and CEO Motoren- und Turbinen-Union München (MTU München) GmbH, mem. Exec. Cttee Dasa 1996–2000, Pres. and CEO DaimlerChrysler Aerospace (Dasa) AG 2000, CEO EADS 2000–05 (Head of Aeronautic Div. 2004–05); Pres. BDLI (German aerospace industries asscn) 2001–05; Officier Légion d'honneur. *Address:* c/o EADS Deutschland GmbH, CCICP, 81663 Munich, Germany.

HERTZ, Noreena, BA, MBA, PhD; British economist, academic and writer; *Fellow, Judge Business School, University of Cambridge;* b. 24 Sept. 1967, London; ed Univ. Coll., London, Univ. of Cambridge, Wharton School of the Univ. of Pennsylvania, USA; attended business school in USA; helped establish first Leningrad (now St Petersburg) stock exchange 1991; Int. Finance Corpn adviser to Russian Govt on econ. reforms 1992; fmr head of research team working on prospects for regional econ. co-operation in the Middle East; fmr Distinguished Fellow and Assoc. Dir Centre for Int. Business and Man., Judge Inst. of Man. Studies, Univ. of Cambridge, currently Fellow, Judge Business School; also currently Duisenberg Prof. of Globalization, Sustainability and Finance, Duisenberg School of Finance, Erasmus Univ.; Belle van Zuylen Chair of Global Political Economy, Utrecht Univ. April–Sept. 2005; attended World Econ. Forum 2002; regular commentator on TV and radio. *Television includes:* documentary film of her book The Silent Takeover (Channel 4) 2001. *Publications include:* Russian Business in the Wake of Reform (doctoral thesis) 1996, The Silent Takeover: Global Capitalism and the Death of Democracy 2001, IOU: The Debt Threat and Why We Must Defuse It 2004; contribs to New Statesman, the Observer, the Guardian and the Washington Post. *Address:* Judge Business School, Trumpington Street, Cambridge, CB2 1AG, England (office). *Telephone:* (20) 7724-0829 (office). *Fax:* (20) 7724-1726 (office). *E-mail:* noreenah@yahoo.com (office). *Website:* www.jbs.cam.ac.uk (office).

HERTZBERGER, Herman; Dutch architect and academic; *Principal, Architectuurstudio HH;* b. 6 July 1932, Amsterdam; m. J. C. Van Seters 1959; one s. two d.; ed Delft Tech. Univ.; pvt. practice, Architectuurstudio HH, Amsterdam 1958–; Co-Ed. (Dutch) Forum 1959–63; teacher, Acad. of Architecture, Amsterdam 1965–69; Prof. of Architectural Design, Tech. Univ. of Delft 1970–99; Prof., Univ. of Geneva 1986–93; Chair. Berlage Inst., Amsterdam 1990–95; guest teacher at univs/architectural insts in Argentina, Austria, Belgium, Brazil, Croatia, Cyprus, Denmark, France, Germany, Greece, Ireland, Israel, Italy, Japan, Mexico, the Netherlands, Norway, Slovenia, S Korea, Spain, Switzerland, Taiwan, UK, USA; Hon. mem. Royale de Belgique 1975, Bund Deutscher Architeckten 1983, Akad. der Künste 1993, Accad. delle Arti del Disegno, Florence 1995, Acad. d'Architecture de France 1997, Bond van Nederlandse Architecten 2002, Architectural Asscn, London 2013; Hon. FRIBA 1991; Hon. Fellow, Royal Incorporation of Architects in Scotland 1996; Hon. FAIA 2004; Kt, Order of Oranje Nassau 1991, Companion, Order of the Dutch Lion; Hon. DUniv (Geneva) 2001; numerous prizes and awards including Architectural Award of the Town of Amsterdam 1968, Eternit Award 1974, Fritz Schumacher Award 1974, Architecture Award of the City of Amsterdam 1985, Premio Europa 1991, BNA Award 1991, Concrete Award 1991, Prix Rhénan 1993, Architecture Award, City of Breda 1998, Premios Vitruvio 98 Trayectoria Internacional 1998, Dutch School Bldg Award 2000, Leone d'oro (Venice) 2002, Architecture Award, City of Apeldoorn 2004, Oeuvre Award for Architecture of the Netherlands Foundation for Visual Arts, Design and Architecture 2004, Dutch School Building Award 2004, Arie Keppler Award 2005, Architecture Award of the Citizens of Apeldoorn 2006, RIBA Royal Gold Medal 2012. *Major works include:* 14 primary schools, six extended school complexes and four secondary schools in the Netherlands since 1966, office bldg 'Centraal Beheer', Apeldoorn 1972, housing for old and disabled people 'De Drie Hoven', Amsterdam 1974, music centre 'Vredenburg', Utrecht 1978, urban renewal 'Haarlemmer Houttinen', Amsterdam 1982, office bldg Ministry of Social Welfare and Employment, The Hague 1990, Theatre Centre Spui, The Hague 1993, library and art and music centre, Breda 1993, Chassé Theater, Breda 1995, Theater Markant, Uden 1996, residential bldgs, Haarlem 1996, Düren, Germany 1996, Berlin 1997, extension to Vanderveen Department Store, Assen 1997, YKK Dormitory Guesthouse, Kurobe City, Japan 1998, Bijlmer Monument (with

Georges Descombes) 1998, residential area 'Merwestein Noord', Dordrecht 1999, Waterhouse, Middelburg 2002, Il Fiore office bldg, Maastricht 2002, MediaPark office bldgs and residential complex, Cologne 2004, CODA museum, library and municipal archives, Apeldoorn 2004, Theatre and Congress Centre ORPHEUS, Apeldoorn 2004, Head Office, Waternet, Amsterdam 2005, Faculty, FNSI Univ. of Amsterdam 2009, NHL Univ., Leeuwarden 2009, Faculty of Science, Univ. of Utrecht 2011, Primary and Junior School, Rome, Italy 2012. *Publications:* Homework for More Hospitable Form (Dutch) Forum XXIV 1973, Herman Hertzberger 1959–86 Bauten und Projekte/Buildings and Projects/Bâtiments et Projets (co-author) 1987, Lessons for Students in Architecture 1991, Herman Hertzberger Projekte/Projects 1990–1995 1995, Chassé Theater 1995, Herman Hertzberger: View of Projects of 1960–1997 (co-author) 1997, Space and the Architect: Lessons for Students in Architecture part II 2000, Articulations 2002, Cultuur onder Dak: Shelter for Culture – Herman Hertzberger and Apeldoorn 2004, De theaters van Herman Hertzberger 2005, Waternet Doubeltower 2006, Hertzberger's Amsterdam 2007, Space and Learning 2008, The Schools of Herman Hertzberger 2009. *Leisure interest:* music. *Address:* Architectuurstudio HH, Gerard Doustraat 220, PO Box 74665, 1070 BR Amsterdam, Netherlands (office). *Telephone:* (20) 6765888 (office). *Fax:* (20) 6735510 (office). *E-mail:* office@ahh.nl (office). *Website:* www.ahh.nl (office).

HERVÉ, Edmond; French politician; *Senator;* b. 3 Dec. 1942, La Bouillie, Côtes du Nord; s. of Marcel Hervé; m. Jeannine Le Gall 1978; two s. one d.; Prof. of Constitutional Law, Rennes Univ.; Conseiller Général, Ille-et-Vilaine 1973–82; Mayor of Rennes 1977–2008, Hon. Mayor 2008–; Pres. regional hosp. centre and univ. hosp. centre, both in Brittany 1977–; fmr Minister of Health; Minister Del. to Minister of Industry for Energy 1981–83; Sec. of State for Health 1983–86; Regional Councillor, Brittany 1986–88; Deputy for Ille-et-Vilaine to Nat. Ass. 1986–2002; Pres. Dist Urbain de l'agglomeration rennaise (Audiar) 1989, Conf. permanente du tourisme urbain 1989–95, Hon. Pres. 1995–; Chair. Conf. de villes de l'arc atlantique 2000–; Senator 2008–; mem. Conseil de Surveillance du Crédit local de France 1990, City Scientific Cttee on Science and Industry of La Villette 1990, Nat. Council on Towns and Urban Social Devt 1991, Parti Socialiste. *Address:* 21 Quai Lamennais, 35000 Rennes, France (office). *Telephone:* (2) 99-78-27-10 (office). *Fax:* (2) 99-35-18-96 (office). *E-mail:* e.herve@senat.fr (office). *Website:* senateurs-socialistes35.fr (office); www.senat.fr (office).

HERZ, Robert (Bob) H., BEcons, CPA, CA; American financial executive; *Chairman, Financial Accounting Standards Board;* ed Univ. of Manchester, UK; accountant, Price Waterhouse 1974–96, Pricewaterhouse Coopers 1998–2002, becoming Sr Partner 1998 and mem. Global and US Bds; Chair. Financial Accounting Standards Bd 2002–; Sr Tech. Partner, Coopers & Lybrand 1996; fmr Chair. AICPA SEC Regulations Cttee, Transnational Auditors Cttee, Int. Fed. of Accountants; fmr mem. Emerging Issues Task Force, American Accounting Asscn Financial Accounting Standards Cttee. *Publications:* The Value Reporting Revolution: Moving Beyond the Earnings Game (jt author). *Address:* Financial Accounting Standards Board, 401 Merritt 7, PO Box 5116, Norwalk, CT 06856–5116, USA (office). *Telephone:* (203) 847-0700 (office). *Fax:* (203) 849-9714 (office). *E-mail:* rhherz@fasb.org (office). *Website:* www.fasb.org (office).

HERZOG, Jacques, DipArch; Swiss architect; b. 1950, Basel; ed Swiss Federal Tech. Univ. (ETH), Zurich; Asst to Prof. Dolf Schnebli, ETH, Zurich 1977; f. architectural practice Herzog & De Meuron (with Pierre de Meuron, q.v.) 1978; Prof. of Architecture and Design, ETH 1999–; Visiting Prof., Harvard Univ., Cambridge, Mass, USA 1989, Tulane Univ., New Orleans 1991; (all jtly with Pierre de Meuron q.v.) Architecture Prize, Berlin Acad. of Arts 1987, Andrea Palladio Int. Prize for Architecture, Vicenza, Italy 1988, Pritzker Architecture Prize 2001, Praemium Imperiale 2007. *Principal works include:* Blue House, Oberwil 1979–80, Photostudio Frei, Weil am Rhein 1981–82, Sperrholz Haus, Bottmingen 1984–85, Apartment Bldg, Hebelstr. 11, Basel 1984–88, Wohn- und Geschäftshaus Schwitter, Basel 1985–98, Goetz Art Gallery, Munich 1989–92, Wohn- und Geschäftshaus Schützenmattstr., Basel 1992–93, Dominus Winery, Napa Valley, Yountville, Calif. 1995–97, Tate Gallery Extension (Tate Modern), Bankside, London (RIBA Gold Medal 2007) 1995–99, Cultural Centre and Theatre, Zurich 1996, Ricola Marketing Bldg, Laufen 1998, Laban Centre for Dance, London (Stirling Prize) 2003, M. H. de Young Memorial Museum, San Francisco 2005, Walker Art Center expansion, Minneapolis, Minnesota 2005, Beijing Nat. Stadium, China (Lubetkin Prize 2009) 2008. *Works in progress include:* Prada Headquarters, New York, Miami Art Museum, São Paulo Companhia de Dança Brazil, Kolkata Museum of Modern Art, India, as well as projects in UK, France, Germany, Italy, Spain and Japan. *Address:* Herzog & de Meuron Architekten, Rheinschanze 6, 4056 Basel, Switzerland (office). *Telephone:* (61) 3855757 (office). *Fax:* (61) 3855758 (office). *E-mail:* info@herzogdemeuron.com (office).

HERZOG, Roman, DJur; German politician and fmr head of state; b. 5 April 1934, Landshut; m. Christiane Krauss 1958; ed Univ. of Munich, Freie Univ., Berlin and Hochschule für Verwaltungswissenschaft, Speyer; mem. Bd Evangelische Kirche in Deutschland Chamber for Public Accountability 1971–80; Rep. of Rhineland-Palatinate in Bundestag 1973–78; Chair. Evangelical Working Party, CDU/CSU 1978–83; Minister for Culture and Sport, Baden-Württemberg 1978–80, for Interior 1980–83; mem. Fed. Cttee CDU 1979–83; Vice-Pres. Fed. Constitutional Court 1983–87, Pres. 1987–94; Pres. of Germany 1994–99; Chair. Bd of Trustees Stiftung Brandenburger Tor 1999–; Chair. Bd of Trustees Konrad Adenauer Foundation 2000–; Hon. Prof. Hochschule für Verwaltungswissenschaft, Speyer, Univ. of Tübingen; Hon. DCL (Oxford) 1996; Hon. Citizen of Berlin 1999, of Bonn 1999; Karlspreis 1997, Ludger-Westrick-Preis 1999, Forum-Kiedrich-Preis 2000. *Publications include:* Kommentar zur Grundgesetz (co-author) 1968, Staaten der Frühzeit: Ursprünge und Herrschaftsformen 1988. *Address:* Postfach 860445, 81631 Munich (office); Schloss Bellevue, Spreeweg 1, 10557 Berlin, Germany (home). *Telephone:* (228) 2001 (office).

HERZOG, Werner; German film director; b. 5 Sept. 1942, Munich; f. Werner Herzog Filmprodukiion 1963. *Films include:* Signs of Life 1967, Even Dwarfs Started Small 1970, Fata Morgana 1971, The Land of Darkness and Silence 1971, Aguirre Wrath of God 1973, The Enigma of Kaspar Hauser 1974, The Great Ecstasy of Woodcutter Steiner 1974, How Much Wood Would a Woodchuck Chuck 1976, Heart of Glass 1976, Stroszek 1976–77, Woyzeck 1979, Nosferatu 1979, Le pays du silence et de l'obscurité 1980, Fitzcarraldo 1982, Where the Green Ants

Dream 1984, Cobra Verde 1987, Les Gauloises 1988, Echos aus einem düstern Reich 1990, Scream from Stone 1991, Lektionen in Finsternis 1992, Glocken aus der Tiefe 1993, Little Dieter Needs to Fly 1997, Wings of Hope 1998, Mein liebster Feind - Klaus Kinski 1999, Pilgrimage 2001, Invincible 2001, Ten Minutes Older: The Trumpet 2002, Wheel of Time 2003, The White Diamond 2004, Grizzly Man (Dirs Guild of America Best Dir Documentary 2006) 2005, The Wild Blue Yonder 2005, Rescue Dawn 2006, Mister Lonely 2006, Encounters at the End of the World 2008, Bad Lieutenant: Port of Call New Orleans 2009, My Son, My Son, What Have Ye Done 2009, Happy People: A Year in the Taiga (co-dir), Cave of Forgotten Dreams 2010, Ode to the Dawn of Man (short) 2011, Into the Abyss 2011, Death Row (TV documentary) 2012, Jack Reacher 2012. *Opera directed includes:* Lohengrin (Bayreuth Festival) 1987, Tannhäuser (Houston Grand Opera) 2001, Die Zauberflöte (Baltimore Opera) 2001, Parsifal (Palau de les Arts, Valencia) 2008. *Publications:* Conquest of the Useless: Reflections from the Making of Fitzcarraldo, Of Walking In Ice 2007. *Address:* Werner Herzog Filmproduktion, Türkenstrasse 91, 80799 Munich, Germany.

HESBURGH, Rev. Theodore M., STD; American ecclesiastic and fmr university administrator; *President Emeritus, University of Notre Dame;* b. 25 May 1917, Syracuse; s. of Theodore Hesburgh and Anna Hesburgh; ed Univ. of Notre Dame, Gregorian Univ., Rome and Catholic Univ. of America; ordained priest of Congregation of Holy Cross 1943; joined Univ. of Notre Dame 1945, Head of Theology Dept 1948–49, Exec. Vice-Pres. of Univ. 1949–52, Pres. 1952–87, Pres. Emer. 1987–; mem. US Comm. on Civil Rights 1957–72 (Chair. 1969–72), President's Comm. on All-Volunteer Armed Force, Carnegie Comm. on the Future Structure and Financing of Higher Educ., Comm. on the Future of Pvt. and Ind. Higher Educ. in New York State, Presidential Clemency Bd 1974–75; Perm. Rep. of Holy See to Int. Atomic Energy Agency, Vienna 1957; Pres. Int. Fed. of Catholic Univs; Pres. Bd of Overseers Harvard Univ. 1994–95; Trustee, Rockefeller Foundation, Chair. Bd of Trustees 1977–82, Carnegie Foundation for Advance-ment of Teaching (Pres. 1963–64); Chair. Acad. Council, Ecumenical Inst. for Advanced Theological Studies in Jerusalem; Chair. with rank of Amb. US Del. to UN Conf. on Science and Tech. for Devt 1977–79; Chair. Select Comm. on Immigration and Refugee Policy 1979–81; Chair. Kt Comm. on Intercollegiate Athletics 1990–96; mem. Bd of Dirs US Inst. of Peace 1991, War and Peace Foundation; fmr mem. Bd of Dirs American Council on Educ.; Fellow, American Acad. of Arts and Sciences; mem. Advisory Council TechnoServe 2008–, Nuclear Age Peace Foundation; mem. Advisory Bd Opportunity Int.; Co-founder People for the American Way; Hon. mem. KÖHV Alpenland 1961, Hon. Trustee, Inst. of Int. Educ.; 150 hon. degrees; USN Distinguished Service Medal, Presidential Medal of Freedom 1964, Jefferson Award 1976, Sylvanus Thayer Award, US Military Acad. 1980, F. Sadlier Dinger Award 1982, Congregational Gold Medal 2000, NCAA President's Gerald R. Ford Award 2004. *Film:* Rudy 1993. *Publications:* God and the World of Man 1950, Patterns for Educational Growth 1958, Thoughts for Our Times 1962, More Thoughts for Our Times 1965, Still More Thoughts for Our Times 1966, Thoughts IV 1968, Thoughts V 1969, The Humane Imperative: A Challenge for the Year 2000 1974, The Hesburgh Papers: Higher Values in Higher Education 1979, God, Country, Notre Dame 1990, Travels with Ted and Ned 1992. *Address:* 1315 Hesburgh Library, University of Notre Dame, Notre Dame, IN 46556, USA (office). *Telephone:* (219) 631-6882 (office). *Website:* www.nd.edu/aboutnd/about/history/hesburgh_bio.shtml (office).

HESELTINE, Colin S., BEcons; Australian diplomatist and international organization official; *Co-Chairman, Asia Pacific Exchange and Cooperation Foundation;* b. 1947; m.; two d.; ed Monash Univ.; joined Dept of External Affairs, Canberra 1969, served in Embassy in Santiago, Chile 1970–75, in Madrid 1975–80, Chinese language training 1981–82, Minister and Deputy Head of Mission, Embassy in Beijing 1982–85, Dir, China Investment Project, Dept of Industry, Tech. and Resources, Victorian Govt 1985–87, Minister and Deputy Head of Mission, Embassy in Beijing 1988–92, Rep. (Head of Mission), Australian Commerce and Industry Office, Taipei 1992–97; Asst Sec., Maritime South East Asia Br. (covering Indonesia, Malaysia, Singapore, Philippines), Dept of Foreign Affairs and Trade 1997–98, First Asst Sec., North Asia Div. 1998–2001; Amb. to South Korea 2001–05; Deputy Exec. Dir APEC Secr. 2006, Exec. Dir 2007–08; Co-Chair. Asia Pacific Exchange & Cooperation Foundation 2011–. *Address:* Asia Pacific Exchange and Cooperation Foundation, 01-01, Section A, Liangmaqiao DRC, 22 Dongfang East Road, Chaoyang District, Beijing 100600, People's Republic of China (office). *Telephone:* (10) 85322403 (office). *Website:* www.apecf.org (office).

HESELTINE, Baron (Life Peer), cr. 2001, of Thenford in the County of Northamptonshire; **Rt Hon. Michael Ray Dibdin Heseltine,** PC, CH; British politician and publisher; *Chairman, Haymarket Group;* b. 21 March 1933, Swansea, Wales; s. of the late Col Rupert Heseltine and Eileen Ray Heseltine; m. Anne Edna Harding Williams 1962; one s. two d.; ed Shrewsbury School, Pembroke Coll., Oxford; Pres. Oxford Union 1954; Chair. Haymarket Press 1965–70, 1999–2009; MP for Tavistock 1966–74, for Henley 1974–2001; Parl. Sec. Ministry of Transport 1970; Parl. Under-Sec. of State, Dept of the Environment 1970–72; Minister of Aerospace and Shipping 1972–74; Opposition Spokesman for Industry 1974–76, for the Environment 1976–79; Sec. of State for the Environment 1979–83, 1990–92, for Defence 1983–86, Sec. of State for Industry and Pres. of the Bd of Trade 1992–95; Deputy Prime Minister and First Sec. of State 1995–97; Dir Haymarket Publishing Group 1997–, Chair. 2001–; Pres. Asscn of Conservative Clubs 1982–83, Chair. Conservative Mainstream 1998–2006; Pres. Quoted Companies Alliance Int. Advisory Council 2000–03, Anglo-China Forum 1998–2001; Pres. Conservative Group for Europe 2001–04; Vice-Pres. Royal Horticultural Soc. 2009; Chair. Regional Devt Fund Advisory Cttee 2010–; Fellow, Chartered Inst. of Man. 1998, The 48 Group Club 2003; Hon. Fellow, Pembroke Coll. Oxford 1986, Leeds Metropolitan Univ. 1989, Univ. of Wales (Swansea) 2001; Hon. FRIBA 1991; Freedom of the City of Liverpool 2012; Hon. LLD (Liverpool) 1990; Hon. DBA (Bedfordshire) 2003; Pres.'s Medal, Inst. of Public Relations 1998, Gold Medal, Inst. of Sheet Metal Eng 1999, PPA Marcus Morris Award 2003, Lifetime Achievement Award, Nat. Business Awards 2005, Publicity Club of London Cup 2005. *Publications:* Reviving the Inner Cities 1983, Where There's a Will 1987, The Challenge of Europe: Can Britain Win? 1988 (Bentinck Prize 1989), Life in the Jungle (memoirs) 2000. *Address:* House of Lords, Westminster, London,

SW1A 0PW (office). *Telephone:* (20) 8267-4213 (office). *Website:* www.parliament.uk/biographies/lords/michael-heseltine/26639 (office).

HESS, John B., BA, MBA; American energy industry executive; *CEO, Hess Corporation;* b. 5 April 1954; s. of Leon Hess and Norma Hess; m. Susan Elizabeth Kessler; ed Harvard Univ.; joined Amerada Hess Corpn (now Hess Corpn) 1977, mem. Bd of Dirs 1978–, Sr Vice-Pres. –1986, Sr Exec. Vice-Pres. 1986–95, Chair. and CEO 1995–2013, CEO 2013–; mem. US Sec. of Energy's Advisory Bd 1999–2002, Nat. Petroleum Council at US Dept of Energy; Vice-Chair. Lincoln Center for the Performing Arts, Inc., Dir 2007–; Dir, Nat. Advisory Board of J.P. Morgan Chase & Co. 1991–, Deerfield Acad. 2004–, The Dow Chemical Company 2006–13, Trilateral Comm. 2009–, NYC2012, Inc, Kohlberg Kravis Roberts & Co. 2011–, KKR Management LLC 2011–; mem. Bd of Trustees, Wildlife Conservation Soc./New York Zoo 1991–, United Cerebral Palsy Research and Educational Foundation; Trustee, The Mount Sinai Hosp. 1988–, New York Public Library 2008–, Center for Strategic and Int. Studies, Inc.; mem. Dean's Advisors of Harvard Business School 2001–, The Business Council of the Council of Foreign Relations 2003–. *Address:* Hess Corporation, 1185 Avenue of the Americas, New York, NY 10036, USA (office). *Telephone:* (212) 997-8500 (office). *Fax:* (212) 536-8390 (office). *E-mail:* info@hess.com (office). *Website:* www.hess.com (office).

HESSE, Daniel (Dan) Ryan, BA, MS, MBA; American telecommunications executive; *CEO, Sprint Corporation;* b. 18 Oct. 1953, Fort Belvoir, Va; s. of Richard Joseph Hesse and Ellen Louise Hesse (née Seidell); m. Diane Yvette Canaday 1990; ed Univ. of Notre Dame, Cornell Univ., Massachusetts Inst. of Tech.; worked for 23 years with AT&T Corpn, becoming Sales Vice-Pres. 1990–91, Pres. and CEO AT&T Network Systems International 1991–95, Sr Vice-Pres. Online Services Group 1996, Exec. Vice-Pres. 1997–2000, Pres. and CEO AT&T Wireless Services Inc. 1997–2000; Chair., Pres. and CEO Terabeam Corpn 2000–04; CEO Local Telecommunications Div., Sprint Nextel Corpn 2005–06, CEO Sprint Nextel Corpn 2007– (renamed Sprint Corpn 2013); Chair., Pres. and CEO Embarq Corpn 2006–07; mem. Bd Dirs Nokia Inc. 2005–, VF Corpn 2001–, Better Business Bureau Online, CTIA (Wireless Asscn), Clearwire Corpn; Gov. Boys & Girls Club of America; mem. Business Advisory Council, Mendoza Coll. of Business, Univ. Notre Dame; mem. MIT's Soc. of Sloan Fellows, Univ. of Notre Dame's E.F. Sorin Soc., Cornell Univ. Dean's Soc.; appointed by President Obama to the National Security Telecommunications Advisory Committee; Brooks Thesis Prize, MIT 1990, Ellis Island Medal of Honor, named Most Influential Person in Mobile Technology by LAPTOP magazine, RCR Magazine Wireless Industry Person of theYear, Wireless Business and Tech. Magazine Exec. of the Year, Wireless Week magazine's Leadership Award, named by Junior Achievement of Middle America to Greater Kansas City Business Hall of Fame 2010, recognized by Ingram's magazine as Kansas City's Best CEO 2010, John J. Sullivan, Jr Foundation Humanitarian Award of The Irish Museum and Cultural Center of Kansas City 2010. *Address:* Sprint Corporation, 6200 Sprint Parkway, Overland Park, KS 66251, USA (office). *Telephone:* (703) 433-4000 (office). *E-mail:* boardinquiries@sprint.com (office). *Website:* www.sprint.com (office).

HESSELS, Jan-Michiel, LLM, MA; Dutch business executive; *Chairman of the Supervisory Board, Royal Philips Electronics; Chairman, NYSE Euronext Inc.;* b. 21 Dec. 1942, The Hague; m. Elisabeth Hillen; three c.; ed Univ. of Leiden, London School of Econs, UK, Wharton School of Finance, Univ. of Pennsylvania, USA; with S.G. Warburg & Co., London, Overseas Devt Bank, Geneva, McKinsey & Co. Inc., New York and Amsterdam 1967–73; Corp. Treas., Akzo NV 1973–77, Pres. Akzo Ltda (Brazil and Argentina), São Paulo 1977–82, Exec. Vice-Pres. Akzona Inc., Asheville, NC, USA 1982–85; CEO NV Deli Universal, Rotterdam 1985–90; CEO Vendex International NV/Royal Vendex KBB NV 1990–2000; mem. Supervisory Bd Royal Philips Electronics 1999–, currently Chair.; Chair. Supervisory Bd Euronext NV 2000–07, Chair. NYSE Euronext Inc. (following merger with NYSE Group) 2007–; Chair. Risk and Capital Cttee, Fortis NV; mem. Bd of Dirs Amsterdam Airport Schiphol Group NV (Chair. Audit Cttee –2006), Schiphol Airport Devt Corpn (Chair.), SC Johnson Europlant NV (Chair.); Chair. 'Stichting Particuliere Historische Buitenplaatsen' (Dutch Asscn of Pvt. Historical Estates), Nat. Cttee 'Rembrandt 400'; mem. Supervisory Bd BAM 1988–93, Dillards Department Stores Inc. 1990–98, Barnes & Noble Inc. 1990–2000, Yule Catto PLC 1991–98, Royal Vopak NV 1993–2005, Amsterdam Exchange 1997–, Laurus 1998–2004, B&N Com, Inc. 1999–2003, Heineken NV; mem. Int. Advisory Bd Morgan Stanley –2006, The Blackstone Group, SC Johnson Corpn; Chair. Election Platform Cttee, CDA 2002–03; mem. Bd of Trustees and Chair. Rijksmuseum, Amsterdam 1996–2003; mem. Bd and Chair. Medisch Centrum, Haaglanden 1992–2003; Chair. Dutch Retail Asscn (RND) 1991–98; mem. Bd Nat. Fund 4 and 5 May; Chair. Queen Juliana School, São Paolo, Brazil. *Address:* Royal Philips Electronics, Breitner Center, HBT 14.12, Amstelplein 2, 1096 BC Amsterdam, Netherlands (office); NYSE Euronext, 11 Wall Street, New York, NY 10005, USA (office). *Telephone:* (20) 597-71-22 (Amsterdam) (office); (212) 656-3000 (New York) (office). *Fax:* (20) 597-71-20 (Amsterdam) (office). *Website:* www.philips.com (office); www.nyse.com (office).

HESTER, James McNaughton, DPhil; American academic administrator; b. 19 April 1924, Chester, Pa; s. of James Montgomery Hester and Margaret Hester (McNaughton); m. Janet Rodes 1953; three d.; ed Princeton and Oxford Univs; Capt., US Marine Corps 1943–46, 1951–52; Civil Information Officer, Fukuoka Mil. Govt Team, Japan 1946–47; Rhodes Scholar, Oxford Univ. 1947–50; Asst to American Sec. to Rhodes Trustees, Princeton 1950; Asst to Pres., Handy Assocs. Inc. (Management Consultants) NY 1953–54; Account Supervisor, Gallup & Robinson Inc. 1954–57; Provost, Brooklyn Center, LI Univ. 1957–60, Vice-Pres., Trustee, LI Univ.; Prof. of History, Exec. Dean Arts and Sciences, Dean Grad. School of Arts and Sciences, New York Univ. 1960–61, Trustee 1962, Pres. 1962–75; Rector, UN Univ., Tokyo 1975–80; Pres. New York Botanical Garden 1980–89, Harry Frank Guggenheim Foundation; mem. Bd of Dirs Union Carbide Corpn 1963–96, Alliance Fund and related funds 1983; Chair. Pres. Nixon's Task Force on Priorities in Higher Educ. 1969; mem. Asscn of American Rhodes Scholars 1962; Pres. Harry Frank Guggenheim Foundation 1989–2004; Trustee, Lehman Foundation 1973; Hon. LLD (Princeton, Moorehouse Coll., Hofstra Univ., Lafayette Coll., Hahnemann Medical Coll., Fordham); Hon. LHD (Hartwick Coll., Pace Univ., Colgate, Pittsburgh, New York); Hon. DCL (Alfred Univ.); Chevalier, Légion d'honneur, First Class Order of the Sacred Treasure 1981. *Portraits:* of

Mary Bunting at Harvard Club, NY and of James Evans at Center Coll., Danville, Ky. *Leisure interest:* painting. *Address:* 25 Cleveland Lane, Princeton, NJ 08540, USA (home). *Telephone:* (609) 921-6727.

HESTER, Ronald Ernest, PhD, DSc, FRSC; British chemist and academic; *Professor Emeritus of Chemistry, University of York;* b. 8 March 1936, Slough, Bucks., England; s. of Ernest Hester and Rhoda Lennox; m. Bridget Maddin 1958; two s. two d.; ed Royal Grammar School, High Wycombe, Univs of London and Cambridge and Cornell Univ., USA; Asst Prof., Cornell Univ. 1962–65; Lecturer, Sr Lecturer, Reader, Univ. of York 1965–85, Prof. of Chem. 1985–2001, Prof. Emer. 2001–; European Ed. Biospectroscopy 1994–2005; Jt Ed. Issues in Environmental Science and Technology 1994–; mem. Council and various bds, Science and Eng Research Council. *Publications:* Physical Inorganic Chemistry 1964, Understanding Our Environment 1986, Advances in Spectroscopy (26 vols) 1975–98, Spectroscopy of Biological Molecules 1991, Issues in Environmental Science and Technology 1994–; more than 300 research papers in int. journals. *Leisure interests:* skiing, tennis, golf, travel. *Address:* Department of Chemistry, University of York, York, YO10 5DD, England (office). *Website:* www.york.ac.uk/chemistry/staff/academic/emeritus/rhester (office).

HESTER, Stephen, BA; British banking executive; worked for Credit Suisse First Boston, holding various Investment Banking roles until becoming Chief Financial Officer 1996, then Global Head of Fixed Income Div. –2002; Finance Dir, later COO Abbey National plc 2002–04; mem. Bd of Dirs and Chief Exec. The British Land Company PLC 2004–08; Group Chief Exec. and Exec. Dir Royal Bank of Scotland Group plc 2008–13; Trustee, The Foundation and Friends of the Royal Botanical Gardens, Kew. *Address:* c/o The Royal Bank of Scotland Group plc, Group Secretariat, Business House F, Gogarburn, Edinburgh, EH12 1HQ, Scotland.

HETFIELD, James Alan; American singer and musician (guitar); b. 3 Aug. 1963, Downey City, CA; s. of Virgil Hetfield and Cynthia Hetfield; fmr mem. Obsession, Leather Charm; mem. and lead singer heavy rock group, Metallica 1981–; worldwide tours and concert appearances; American Music Award for Favorite Heavy Metal Artist (with Metallica) 1993, Grammy Award for Best Metal Performance (for My Apocalypse) 2009. *Film:* Some Kind Of Monster (Independent Spirit Award for Best Documentary 2005) 2004. *Recordings include:* albums: Kill 'Em All 1983, Ride The Lightning 1984, Master Of Puppets 1986, …And Justice For All 1988, The Good, The Bad And The Live 1990, Metallica 1991, Load 1996, Reload 1997, Early Days 1997, S&M (live) 1999, St Anger 2003, Death Magnetic 2008; singles: Whiplash 1985, Garage Days Revisited 1987, Creeping Death 1990, Harvester Of Sorrow 1988, One (Grammy Award for Best Heavy Metal Performance) 1989, Stone Cold Crazy (Grammy Award for Best Heavy Metal Performance) 1991, Jump In The Fire 1991, The Unforgiven (Grammy Award for Best Heavy Metal Performance 1992) 1991, Enter Sandman 1991, Nothing Else Matters 1992, Wherever I May Roam 1992, Sad But True 1992, Until It Sleeps 1996, Hero Of The Day 1996, Mama Said 1996, King Nothing 1997, The Memory Remains 1997, Fuel 1998, Turn The Page 1998, Whisky In The Jar (Grammy Award for Best Hard Rock Performance 2000) 1999, Die Die My Darling 1999, No Leaf Clover 2000, I Disappear 2000, Call Of The Ktulu (Grammy Award for Best Rock Instrumental Performance) 2001, St Anger 2003, Death Magnetic 2008. *Address:* Q-Prime Inc., 729 Seventh Avenue, 16th Floor, New York, NY 10019, USA (office). *Telephone:* (212) 302-9790 (office). *Fax:* (212) 302-9589 (office). *Website:* www.metallica.com.

HEUER, Rolf Dieter, PhD; German physicist; *Director General, European Organization for Nuclear Research (CERN);* b. 24 May 1948, Boll; ed Univ. of Stuttgart, Univ. of Heidelberg; worked on OPAL experiment, CERN, Geneva 1984–98, Dir-Gen. CERN 2009–; Prof., Univ. of Hamburg 1998; worked on JADE experiment, Deutsches Elektronen-Synchrotron (DESY), Hamburg, Research Dir for high-energy physics, DESY 2004–09. *Address:* European Organization for Nuclear Research (CERN), Geneva 23, Switzerland (office). *Telephone:* 22-76-761-11 (office). *Fax:* 22-76-765-55 (office). *Website:* consult.cern.ch (office).

HEWAGE, Thosapala; Sri Lankan civil servant and diplomatist; *Ambassador to Nepal;* b. 19 Feb. 1949, Kalawana; s. of U. Hewage; m. Thilaka Hewage; one s. one d.; Sec., Ministry of Environment and Natural Resources 1999, Ministry of Urban Devt and Water Supply c. 2005, to Ministry of Enterprise Devt and Investment Promotion c. 2007, to Ministry of Ports and Aviation c. 2008; Amb. to Nepal 2009–. *Leisure interests:* sports. *Address:* Embassy of Sri Lanka, 'Shah Villa', Chundevi Road, Maharajgunj, PO Box 8802, Kathmandu, Nepal (office). *Telephone:* (1) 4720623 (office); (1) 4720213 (office). *Fax:* (1) 4720128 (office). *E-mail:* lankaemb@wlink.com.np (office); info@slembktm.com (office). *Website:* www.slembktm.com (office).

HEWISH, Antony, PhD, FRS, FRAS; British radio astronomer and academic; *Professor Emeritus of Radio Astronomy, University of Cambridge;* b. 11 May 1924, Fowey, Cornwall; s. of the late Ernest W. Hewish and Grace F. L. Hewish (née Pinch); m. Marjorie E. C. Richards 1950; one s. one d.; ed King's Coll., Taunton and Gonville and Caius Coll., Cambridge; war service 1943–46; Research Fellow, Gonville and Caius Coll., Cambridge 1951–54, Supernumerary Fellow 1956–61; Univ. Asst Dir of Research 1953–61, lecturer 1961–69; Fellow, Churchill Coll. Cambridge 1962–; Reader in Radio Astronomy, Univ. of Cambridge 1969–71, Prof. 1971–89, Prof. Emer. 1989–; Prof. Royal Inst. 1977; Vikram Sarabhai Prof., Ahmedabad 1988; Head, Mullard Radio Astronomy Observatory, Cambridge 1982–88; mem. Belgian Royal Acad. of Arts and Sciences 1989; mem. Emer. Academia Europaea 1996; Foreign Fellow, Indian Nat. Science Acad.; Foreign Hon. mem. American Acad. of Arts and Sciences 1977, Hon. Fellow, Indian Inst. of Electronics and Telecommunication Engineers 1985, Hon. Citizen of Kwangju, S Korea 1995; Hon. ScD (Leicester) 1976, (Exeter) 1977, (Manchester) 1989, (Santa Maria, Brazil) 1989, (Cambridge) 1996, (Univ. Teknologi Malaysia) 1997; Hamilton Prize (Cambridge) 1951, Eddington Medal, Royal Astronomical Soc. 1968, Boys Prize, Inst. of Physics 1970, Dellinger Medal, Int. Union of Radio Science 1972, Hopkins Prize, Cambridge Philosophical Soc. 1972, Michelson Medal 1973, Franklin Inst. 1973, Holweck Medal and Prize, Soc. Française de Physique 1974, Nobel Prize for Physics (jtly with Sir Martin Ryle) 1974, Hughes Medal, Royal Soc. 1977, Vainu Bappu Prize, Indian Nat. Science Acad. 1998. *Achievements:* discovery of pulsars, first ground-based measurements of the solar wind, and discovery of enhanced speed from the solar pole. *Publications:* Seeing Beyond

the Invisible, Pulsars as Physics Laboratories (ed.), numerous papers in scientific journals. *Leisure interests:* listening to good music, gardening, cliff walking. *Address:* Cavendish Laboratory, Madingley Road, Cambridge, CB3 0HE (office); Pryor's Cottage, Kingston, Cambridge, CB3 7NQ, England (home). *Telephone:* (1223) 337299 (office); (1223) 262657 (home). *Fax:* (1223) 354599 (office). *E-mail:* ah120@mrao.cam.ac.uk (office). *Website:* www.mrao.cam.ac.uk (office).

HEWITT, Lleyton Glynn; Australian professional tennis player; b. 24 Feb. 1981, Adelaide, S Australia; s. of Glynn Hewitt and Cherilyn Rumball; m. Bec Cartwright 2005; one s. two d.; turned professional 1998; became youngest-ever season-ending World No. 1 following Masters Cup victory over Pete Sampras (q.v.) 2001; winner, Davis Cup 1999, 2003, finalist 2000, 2001; winner, 29 singles titles (including US Open 2001, Wimbledon 2002), two doubles titles (including US Open 2000), Tennis Masters Cup (now called the ATP World Tour Finals) 2001, 2002, Indian Wells 2002, 2003, Queen's Club Championship 2006, BMW Open 2009, Gerry Weber Open 2010, Brisbane International 2014; finalist, Australian Open 2005; quarterfinalist, French Open 2001, 2004; coached by Peter Smith 997–98, Darren Cahill 1998–2001, Jason Stoltenberg 2001–03, Roger Rasheed 2003–07, Scott Draper Jan. 2007, Tony Roche 2007–09, Nathan Healey 2009–10, Brett Smith Aug.–Nov. 2010, Tony Roche Nov. 2010–, Peter Luczak 2013–; ATP Player of the Year Award 2001, 2002, Most Popular South Australian Award 2001, Australia's Athlete of the Year Award 2002, ESPY Best Male Tennis Player 2002, Young Australian of the Year 2003, Vogue Australia Sportsman of the Year Award 2003, Most Popular South Australian Award 2003, Young Australian of the Year Award 2003, Newcombe Medal (most outstanding Australian player) 2013. *Leisure interests:* Australian Rules football, golf. *Address:* Lleyton Hewitt Marketing, Suite 35, 209 Toorak Road, South Yarra, Vic. 3141, Australia. *Website:* www.lleytonandbechewitt.com.

HEWITT, Patricia Hope, MA (Cantab.), MA (Oxon.); British/Australian company director and fmr politician; *Chair, UK India Business Council;* b. 2 Dec. 1948, Canberra, ACT, Australia; d. of Sir (Cyrus) Lenox (Simson) Hewitt and Alison Hope Hewitt; m. William Birtles 1981; one s. one d.; ed Church of England Girls' Grammar School, Canberra, Australia, Australian Nat. Univ., Newnham Coll. Cambridge; Public Relations Officer, Age Concern 1971–73; Women's Rights Officer, Nat. Council for Civil Liberties (now Liberty) 1973–74, Gen. Sec. 1974–83; Labour Party cand. Leicester E, gen. elections 1983; Press and Broadcasting Sec. to Leader of Opposition 1983–88, Policy Co-ordinator 1988–89; Sr Research Fellow, Inst. for Public Policy Research 1989, Deputy Dir 1989–94; Visiting Fellow, Nuffield Coll. Oxford 1992–; Head, then Dir of Research, Andersen Consulting (now Accenture) 1994–97; Labour MP for Leicester W 1997–2010, mem. Select Cttee on Social Security 1997–98; Econ. Sec. to the Treasury 1998–99, Minister of State, Dept of Trade and Industry 1999–2001, Sec. of State for Trade and Industry 2001–05; Minister for Women 2001–05; Sec. of State for Health 2005–07; mem. Bd of Dirs BT Group plc 2008–, currently Sr Ind. Dir; Chair. UK India Business Council 2010–; mem. Bd of Dirs Eurotunnel Group 2010–; mem. Asia Pacific Advisory Cttee, Barclays Group plc 2010–12; mem. UK India Round Table 2009–, Asia Task Force 2010–; Hon. Fellow, London Business School 2004. *Publications:* Civil Liberties, the NCCL Guide (co-ed.) 1977, The Privacy Report 1977, Your Rights at Work 1981, The Abuse of Power 1981, Your Second Baby (co-author) 1990, About Time: The Revolution in Work and Family Life 1993. *Leisure interests:* reading, theatre, music, gardening. *Address:* UK India Business Council, 12th Floor, Millbank Tower, 21–24 Millbank, London, SW1P 4QP, England (office). *Telephone:* (20) 7592-3040 (office). *E-mail:* patricia.hewitt@ukibc.com (office). *Website:* www.ukibc.com (office).

HEWSON, John Robert, AO, BEcons, MA, PhD; Australian academic, business executive and fmr politician; *Chairman, The John Hewson Group;* b. 28 Oct. 1946, Sydney, NSW; s. of Donald Hewson and of the late Eileen Isabella Hewson (née Tippett); m. 1st Margaret Hewson; two s. one d.; m. 2nd Carolyn Judith Hewson 1988; m. 3rd Jessica Wilson 2007; one d.; ed Univ. of Sydney, Univ. of Saskatchewan, Canada and Johns Hopkins Univ. USA; Research Officer, Bureau of Census and Statistics, Treasury 1967–68; Teaching Fellow, Dept of Econs, Univ. of Saskatchewan 1968–69; Teaching Asst, Dept of Political Economy, Johns Hopkins Univ. 1969–71; Consultant and Economist IMF 1969–74; Research Economist Reserve Bank of Australia 1975–76; Econ. Adviser to Fed. Treas. 1976–77, 1978–81, Chief of Staff 1981–82; Prof. of Econs, Univ. of NSW 1978–87, Head School of Econs 1983–87; MP for Wentworth, Fed. Parl. 1987–95; Shadow Minister for Finance 1988–89, Shadow Treas. 1989–90; Leader of the Liberal Party and Leader of the Opposition 1990–94; Shadow Minister for Industry, Commerce, Infrastrucutre and Customs 1994–95; Dean, Grad. School of Man., Macquarie Univ. 2002–04; Consultant Hill Samuel Australia 1982–85; mem. Advisory Council ABN AMRO Australia Ltd 1998–2004 (Chair. 1995–98); Chair. The John Hewson Goup Pty Ltd 1995–, Network Entertainment Ltd 1996–97, Chair. Churchill Funds Man. 1996–99, subsequently GRD 2000–04, Australian Bus Mfg Co. Ltd (now Universal Bus Co. Pty Ltd) 1999–, Global Renewables Ltd 2000–04, Strategic Capital Man. Pty Ltd 2000–04, Belle Property Pty Ltd 2000–03, Investment Advisory Cttee Australian Olympic Foundation 2001, RepuTex Advisory Cttee 2003–04, X Capital Health 2004–, The Freehand Group 2004–; Special Advisor to Under-Sec. UN 2006; Chair. Pisces Group; Chair. Osteoporosis Australia Council 1997–, Arthritis Research Taskforce 2003–, Business Leaders Forum on Sustainable Devt 2003–, Gen. Security Australia Insurance Brokers Pty Ltd; Foundation Dir Macquarie Bank Ltd 1985–87; Dir and Vice-Chair. TV Shopping Network Ltd 1996–98; Deputy Chair. Miniproc Ltd 1998–2000; Pres. Arthritis Foundation of Australia 1997–2002; mem. Bd of Dirs Moran Health Care Group 1998–2001; mem. Bd of Dirs Positive Ageing Foundation 1999–2003; Patron, Australian Corp. Games; mem. Trilateral Comm. 2005–, External Advisory Group, Group Training Australia; weekly columnist, Australian Financial Review 1998–; Fellow, Australian Inst. of Co. Dirs, Hong Kong Man. Asscn; Hon. Trustee, Cttee of Econ. Devt of Australia; Centenary Medal. *Television:* Frontline 2004, Enough Rope with Andrew Denton 2006, The Gruen Transfer 2010. *Publications:* Liquidity Creation and Distribution in the Eurocurrency Market 1975, The Eurocurrency Markets and their Implications: A New View of International Monetary Problems and Monetary Reform (jtly) 1975, Offshore Banking in Australia 1981, innumerable articles in professional journals. *Leisure interests:* gardening, jazz, theatre, sport, cars, motor sports. *Address:* Level 10, 1

Market Street, Sydney, NSW 2000, Australia (office). *Telephone:* (2) 9372-9764 (office). *Fax:* (2) 9372-0364 (office). *E-mail:* john.hewson@horwath.com (office).

HEWSON, Marillyn A., BS, MEcons; American business executive; *President and CEO, Lockheed Martin Corporation;* b. Junction City, Kan.; m. James Hewson; two s.; ed Univ. of Alabama, Columbia Business School and Harvard Business School Exec. Devt Programs; joined Lockheed Martin 1983, held several corp. exec. roles, including Sr Vice-Pres. Corp. Shared Services, Vice-Pres. Global Supply Chain Man. and Vice-Pres. Corp. Internal Audit, Pres. and Gen. Man. Kelly Aviation Center, LP (affiliate of Lockheed Martin) 2004–07, Pres. Lockheed Martin Logistics Services Jan.–Feb. 2007, Exec. Vice-Pres. Global Sustainment for Lockheed Martin Aeronautics 2007–08, Pres. Lockheed Martin Systems Integration, Owego, NY 2008–09, Exec. Vice-Pres. Electronic Systems, Lockheed Martin Corpn 2010–12, Pres. and COO Lockheed Martin Corpn 2012, mem. Bd of Dirs 2012–, Pres. and CEO 2013–; Chair. Sandia Corpn 2010–13; mem. Bd of Dirs Carpenter Technology Corpn 2002–06, DuPont; mem. USO Bd Govs, Economic Club of Washington, DC, Univ. of Alabama's Culverhouse Coll. of Commerce and Business Administration Bd of Visitors, Congressional Medal of Honor Foundation; Chair. Steering Cttee, Defense Industry Initiative; ranked by Fortune magazine amongst the 50 Most Powerful Women in Business in the US (32nd) 2010, (27th) 2011, (19th) 2012, ranked by Forbes magazine amongst The World's 100 Most Powerful Women (34th) 2013. *Address:* Lockheed Martin Corporation, 6801 Rockledge Drive, Bethesda, MD 20817-1877, USA (office). *Telephone:* (301) 897-6000 (office). *Fax:* (301) 897-6704 (office). *E-mail:* info@lockheedmartin.com (office). *Website:* www.lockheedmartin.com (office).

HEWSON, Paul (see BONO).

HEY, John Denis, MA, MSc; British economist, statistician and academic; *Professor of Economics and Statistics, University of York;* b. 26 Sept. 1944, Tynemouth, N Tyneside, England; s. of G. B. Hey and E. H. Hey; m. Marlene Bissett 1968 (divorced 1997); one s. two d.; ed Univs of Cambridge and Edinburgh; econometrician, Hoare & Co. London 1968–69; Lecturer in Econs, Univ. of Durham 1969–74, Univ. of St Andrew's 1974–75; Lecturer in Econ. Statistics, Univ. of York 1975, Sr Lecturer, Prof. of Econs and Statistics 1984– (part-time 1998–), Co-Dir Centre for Experimental Econs 1986–2005; Prof. Ordinario, Univ. of Bari 1998–2005, LUISS, Rome, Italy 2005–10; Hon. Prof. of Econs and Econometrics, Univ. of Vienna. *Publications:* Statistics in Economics 1974, Uncertainty in Microeconomics 1979, Economics in Disequilibrium 1981, Data in Doubt 1984, Experiments in Economics 1991, Experimental Economics (ed.) 1995, Economics of Uncertainty 1997, Intermediate Microeconomics 2003. *Leisure interests:* walking, opera, music. *Address:* Department of Economics and Related Studies, University of York, Heslington, York, YO1 5DD, England (office). *Telephone:* (1904) 433786 (office). *Fax:* (1904) 433759 (office). *E-mail:* jdh1@york.ac.uk (office). *Website:* www -users.york.ac.uk/~jdh1 (office).

HEYHOE FLINT, Baroness (Life Peer), cr. 2011, of Wolverhampton in the County of West Midlands; **Rachel Heyhoe Flint,** MBE, OBE, DL; British sports business executive, broadcaster and fmr int. cricketer; b. 11 June 1939, Wolverhampton; d. of Geoffrey Heyhoe and Roma Heyhoe (née Crocker); m. Derrick Flint 1971; one s.; ed Wolverhampton Girls' High School and Dartford Coll. of Physical Educ.; Head of Physical Educ., Wolverhampton Municipal Grammar School 1960–62, Northicote School 1962–64; mem. England Women's Cricket Team 1960–84, Capt. 1966–78, unbeaten in six Test series, captained winning England team, Women's Cricket World Cup, England 1973; mem. England Hockey Team 1964; County Squash Player 1964–68; County Golfer 1982–84; Journalist Wolverhampton Express and Star 1965–72; Sports Writer Daily Telegraph 1967–84; Sports Ed. Wolverhampton Chronicle 1969–71; first woman sports reporter, ITV 1972; freelance public relations consultant to La Manga Club (Spain), Wolverhampton Wanderers Football Club 1980– (mem. Bd 1997–2004); Vice-Pres. Wolves Football Club 2005–, Dir of Public Relations; mem. Marketing Cttee MCC 2003–, mem. MCC Gen. Cttee (first woman) 2004–, Trustee, MCC; Pres. Lady Taverners 2001–; mem. (Conservative) House of Lords 2011–; Hon. Fellow, Univ. of Wolverhampton; Hon. Life mem. MCC 1999–; Hon. DUniv (Bradford), (Leeds Metropolitan), Hon. DSc (Univ. of Greeenwich); Best After-Dinner Speaker Award, Guild of Professional Toastmasters 1972, inducted into ICC (Int. Cricket Council) Cricket Hall of Fame (first woman) 2010. *Cricketing achievements:* right-handed batsman, right arm leg spin bowler; played in 22 Women's Test cricket matches, with batting average of 45.54 in 38 innings; scored three Test centuries, including highest score of 179 against Australia at the Oval 1976 (then a world record), earning a draw to save series by batting for more than 8½ hours; captained first England women's team to play at Lord's in Women's Ashes series 1976; also hit first six in a women's Test match, against Australia at the Oval 1963; played her last Test match in series against West Indies 1979, but went on to play in Women's Cricket World Cup 1982. *Publications include:* Just for Kicks 1966, Women's Hockey 1975, Fair Play (with Netta Rheinberg) 1976, Heyhoe (autobiog.) 1977. *Leisure interests:* golf, cricket, watching all sports. *Address:* Danescroft, Wergs Road, Tettenhall, Wolverhampton, WV6 9BN; House of Lords, Westminster, London, SW1A 0PW, England. *Telephone:* (20) 7219-5353 (London); (7771) 977416 (mobile). *Fax:* (1902) 765111 (Wolverhampton). *E-mail:* heyhoe@ wolves.co.uk (office).

HEYMAN, David; British film producer; b. 26 July 1961; ed Hill House London, Westminster School, London, Harvard Univ., USA; began career as production runner for film producers Milos Forman and David Lean; Creative Exec. Warner Bros, Los Angeles 1986–89, Vice-Pres. United Artists 1989; now working as ind. producer; returned to UK 1997, f. Heyday Films 1997; Showest Producer of the Year 2003. *Films produced include:* Juice, The Daytrippers, Harry Potter and the Philosopher's Stone 2001, Harry Potter and the Chamber of Secrets 2002, Harry Potter and the Prisoner of Azkaban 2004, Harry Potter and the Goblet of Fire 2005. *Address:* Heyday Films, 5 Denmark Street, London, WC2H 8LP, England (office). *Telephone:* (20) 7836-6333 (office). *Fax:* (20) 7836-6444 (office). *E-mail:* office@ heydayfilms.com (office).

HEYMANN, Daniel, PhD; Argentine economist and academic; *Professor of Economics and Director, Instituto Interdisciplinario de Economía Política de Buenos Aires (IIEP BAIRES), University of Buenos Aires;* b. 30 Dec. 1949, Buenos Aires; s. of Gunther Heymann and Marta Weil; m. Cristina Bramuglia 1976; two s.;

ed Coll. Français de Buenos Aires, Univ. of Buenos Aires and Univ. of Calif. Los Angeles; Asst Prof., Univ. of Buenos Aires 1973–75, Prof. of Econs 1987–, Dir Instituto Interdisciplinario de Economía Política de Buenos Aires (IIEP BAIRES) 2012–; Research Asst, ECLAC, Buenos Aires 1974–78, Sr Economist 1987–2010; Prof. of Econs, Instituto Torcuato Di Tella, Buenos Aires 1982–2003; Prof. of Econs, Univ. of La Plata 2004–; Prof. of Econs, Univ. of San Andres 2010–; Pres. Argentine Political Economy Asscn 2008–10; mem. Argentine Acad. of Econ. Sciences; Academic Distinction Prize in Econs, Univ. of Buenos Aires 2009. *Publications:* Fluctuations of the Argentine Manufacturing Industry 1980, Three Essays on Inflation and Stabilization 1986, The Austral Plan 1987, Distributive Conflict and the Fiscal Deficit: Some Inflationary Games (co-author) 1991, Fiscal Inconsistencies and High Inflation (co-author) 1994, On the Interpretation of the Current Account 1994, High Inflation (co-author) 1995, Business Cycles from Misperceived Trends (co-author) 1998, Price Setting in a Schematic Model of Inductive Learning (co-author) 1999, Learning about Trends: Spending and Business Fluctuations in Open Economies (co-author) 2001, Inconsistent Behavior and Macroeconomic Disturbances 2002, Great Expectations and Hard Times: The Argentine Convertibility (co-author) 2003, Land-Rich Economies, Education and Economic Development (co-author) 2008, Macroeconomics of Broken Promises 2009, Behavioral Heuristics and Market Patterns in a Bertrand Edgeworth Game (co-author) 2011. *Address:* Faculty of Economics, Universidad de Buenos Aires, Avenida Córdoba 2122, CP 1120 AAQ, Buenos Aires, Argentina (office). *Telephone:* (11) 4725-6969 (office); (11) 4374-4448 (office). *E-mail:* dheymann@udesa.edu.ar (office); dheymann@econ.uba.ar (office). *Website:* web.econ.uba.ar (office).

HEYMANN, Klaus; German business executive; *Chief Executive Officer, Naxos;* m. Takako Nishizaki; one s.; Export Advertising and Promotion Man., Max Braun AG 1961–62; with The Overseas Weekly, Frankfurt 1962–67, ran Hong Kong Office 1967–69; f. Pacific Mail-Order System 1969; organized classical concerts in Hong Kong; mem. Bd Hong Kong Philharmonic Orchestra, later Chair. Fund-Raising Cttee; Founder and CEO Naxos; Chair. HNH Int. Ltd; Hon. Gen. Man. Hong Kong Philharmonic Orchestra. *Address:* Naxos Rights International Ltd, Level 11, Cyberport 1, 100 Cyberport Road, Hong Kong Special Administrative Region (office); HNH International Ltd, 6/F, Sino Industrial Plaza, 9 Kai Cheung Road, Kowloon Bay, Hong Kong Special Administrative Region, People's Republic of China (office). *Telephone:* 27607818 (office). *Fax:* 27601962 (office). *Website:* www.naxos.com (office).

HEYZER, Noeleen, PhD; Singaporean international organization official; *Special Adviser of the Secretary General for Timor-Leste, United Nations;* m.; two d.; ed Univ. of Singapore, Univ. of Cambridge, UK; Fellow and Research Officer, Inst. of Devt Studies, Univ. of Sussex, UK 1979–81; with Social Devt Div., ESCAP, Bangkok, Thailand early 1980s; Dir Gender and Devt Programme, Asian and Pacific Devt Centre, Kuala Lumpur, Malaysia 1984–94; Co-ordinator for the Asia-Pacific NGO Working Group for the UN Fourth World Conf. on Women, Beijing, People's Repub. of China; Exec. Dir UN Devt Fund for Women (UNIFEM) 1994–2007; Exec. Sec. ESCAP 2007–13; Special Adviser of the Sec.-Gen. for Timor-Leste, UN 2013–; Convener Int. Women's Comm. for a Just and Sustainable Palestinian-Israeli Peace; mem. Bd Pres. Ahtisaari's Crisis Man. Initiative; mem. High-Level Commonwealth Comm. on Respect and Understanding; New Millennium Distinguished Visiting Scholar, Columbia Univ.; Chair. Consortium Advisory Group, Research Programme on Women's Empowerment in Muslim Contexts; has served on bds of several humanitarian orgs including Devt Alternatives with Women for a New Era, the Global South, ISIS, Oxfam, Panos and Soc. for Int. Devt; Global Tolerance Award for Humanitarian Service, Friends of the UN 2000, Lifetime Achievement Award, Inst. for Leadership Devt 2000, Woman of Distinction Award, UN NGO Cttee 2003, Leadership Award, Mount Sinai Hosp., New York 2004, Leadership Award, UN Asscn Greater Boston 2004, Dag Hammarskjöld Medal 2004, NCRW Women Who Make a Difference Award 2005. *Publications include:* Gender, Economic Growth and Poverty, The Trade in Domestic Workers, Working Women in South-East Asia. *Address:* United Nations, New York, NY 10017, USA (office). *Telephone:* (212) 963-1234 (office). *Fax:* (212) 963-4879 (office). *Website:* www.un.org (office).

HIATT, Fred, BA; American journalist; *Editorial Page Editor, The Washington Post;* b. 30 April 1955, Washington, DC; s. of Howard Haim Hiatt and Doris Bieringer; m. Margaret Shapiro; three c.; ed Harvard Univ.; City Hall reporter, Atlanta Journal-Constitution 1979–80; reporter, The Washington Star 1981; Virginia Reporter, The Washington Post 1981–83, Pentagon Reporter 1983–86, NE Asia Co-Bureau Chief 1987–90, Moscow Co-Bureau Chief 1991–95, Editorial Page Ed. 1996–. *Publications:* The Secret Sun: A Novel of Japan 1992 (novel), If I Were Queen of the World 1997 (children's book), Baby Talk 1999. *Address:* The Washington Post, 1150 15th Street, NW, Washington, DC 20071, USA (office). *Telephone:* (202) 334-6000 (office). *E-mail:* twpcoreply@washpost.com (office). *Website:* www.washingtonpost.com (office).

HIBRI, Fuad el-, BA, MA; American/Lebanese business executive; *Executive Chairman, Emergent BioSolutions Inc.;* b. 2 March 1958, Hildesheim, Germany; s. of Ibrahim el-Hibri and Liane el-Hibri; ed Yale Univ., Stanford Univ., USA; Man., Mergers and Acquisitions dept, Citibank, New York and Jeddah, Saudi Arabia; Chair. East West Resources Corpn 1990–2004, Pres. 1990–2004; Founder Emergent BioSolutions Inc. 1998, CEO 1998–2012, now Exec. Chair., Chair. and CEO BioPort Corpn 1998–2004 (co. acquired by Emergent); Chair. Digicel Holdings Ltd (telecommunications co.) 2000–06, Pres. 2000–05; Chair. El-Hibri Charitable Foundation; mem. Bd of Dirs US Chamber of Commerce; mem. Bd of Trustees International Biomedical Research Alliance, National Health Museum, American Univ.; mem. Advisory Bd Yale Healthcare Conference; f. El Hibri Peace Educ. Prize; Rene Moawad Foundation Distinguished Community Service and Achievement Award 2007, Ernst & Young Entrepreneur of the Year for Greater Washington 2009, Int. Leadership Award, World Trade Center Inst. 2010, Biotech CEO of the Year, World Vaccine Congress 2011, Exec. of the Year, Tech Council of Maryland 2012, Shining Stars Award, Dar Al-Aytam 2012, Citation for Public Service by Hon. US Senator Barbara A. Mikulski 2012. *Address:* Office of the Chairman, Emergent BioSolutions, 2273 Research Boulevard, Suite 400, Rockville, MD 20850, USA (office). *Telephone:* (301) 795-1800 (office). *Fax:* (301) 795-1899 (office). *Website:* ebsi.com (office).

HICK, Graeme Ashley, MBE; British (b. Zimbabwean) cricket coach and fmr professional cricketer; *High Performance Coach, Centre of Excellence, Cricket Australia;* b. 23 May 1966, Salisbury (now Harare); s. of John Hick and Eve Hick; ed Banket Primary School, Prince Edward Boys' High School; right-hand batsman, off-break bowler, slip fielder; teams: Zimbabwe 1983–86, Worcs. 1984–2008 (Capt. 2000–02), Northern Dists 1987–89, Queensland 1990–91, Chandigarh Lions (Indian Cricket League) 2008; scored his first hundred when aged six (for Banket primary school); youngest player (aged 17) to appear in 1983 World Cup and youngest to rep. Zimbabwe; 65 Tests for England 1991–2001, scoring 3,383 runs (average 31.32, highest score 178), including six hundreds, and took 23 wickets; played in 120 One-Day Ints for 3,846 runs (average 37.33, highest score 126 not out); played in 526 First-class matches, scoring 41,112 runs (average 52.23, highest score 405 not out) including 136 hundreds and 709 catches; youngest to score 2,000 First-class runs in a season (1986); scored 1,019 runs before June 1988, including a record 410 runs in April; fewest innings for 10,000 runs in county cricket (179); youngest (24) to score 50 First-class hundreds; toured Australia 1994–95; mem. England World Cup Squad 1996, 1999; scored 315 not out against Durham June 2002 – highest championship innings of the season; surpassed Graham Gooch's record for the most matches in all forms of the game combined 2008; retd from county cricket at end of 2008 season; apptd Coach, Malvern Coll. 2008; later coach for cricket at Barbados 2009 Sports Camp; High Performance Coach, Cricket Australia's Centre of Excellence 2013–; Wisden Cricketer of the Year 1987, Walter Lawrence Trophy 1988, Indian Cricket Cricketer of the Year 1993. *Publication:* My Early Life (autobiog.) 1992. *Leisure interests:* golf, tennis, squash, indoor hockey, cinema, television, listening to music. *Address:* Cricket Australia Centre of Excellence, c/o Queensland Cricket, Allan Border Field, 1 Bogan Street, Breakfast Creek, Qld 4010, Australia (office); c/o Worcestershire County Cricket Club, County Ground, New Road, Worcester, Worcs., WR2 4QQ, England. *Telephone:* (7) 3292-3100 (Queensland Cricket) (office). *Fax:* (7) 3262-9160 (Queensland Cricket) (office). *E-mail:* qldc@qldcricket.com.au (office). *Website:* www.cricket.com.au/about-us/high-performance-cricket/about/about-ca-centre-of-excellence; www.wccc.co.uk.

HICKENLOOPER, John Wright, BA, MS; American business executive, politician and state governor; *Governor of Colorado;* b. 7 Feb. 1952, Narberth, Pa; m. Helen Thorpe; one s.; ed Wesleyan Univ.; exploration geologist, Buckhorn Petroleum, Denver, Colo 1981–86; turned entrepreneur, owned restaurants in lower downtown area of Denver, Colo (LoDo) late 1980s; Co-founder The Wynkoop Brewing Co. microbrewery 1988–98; Mayor of Denver 2003–11; Gov. of Colorado 2011–; fmr mem. Mayors Against Illegal Guns Coalition; Co-founder CultureHaus, Chinook Fund; mem. Bd of Dirs Colorado Business Cttee for the Arts, Denver Metro Convention and Visitors Bureau, Denver Art Museum, Denver Civic Ventures, Volunteers for Outdoor Colorado; Democrat; named by TIME magazine as one of Top Five Big-City Mayors of America 2005, names as one of Top Public Officials of Year, Governing magazine 2005. *Address:* Office of the Governor, 136 State Capitol, Denver, CO 80203-1792, USA (office). *Telephone:* (303) 866-2471 (office). *Fax:* (303) 866-2003 (office). *Website:* www.colorado.gov/governor (office).

HICKEY, John; Papua New Guinea politician; mem. Parl. (Nat. Alliance Party) 2002–, Chair. Public Accounts Cttee 2003–05; Minister of Finance and Nat. Planning and Monitoring 2005–07, of Agric. and Livestock 2007–11. *Address:* c/o Department of Agriculture and Livestock, PO Box 2033, Port Moresby 121, NCD, Papua New Guinea (office).

HICKS, Kenneth C., MBA; American retail executive; *President and Chief Merchandising Officer, J.C. Penney Company, Inc.;* ed US Mil. Acad., Harvard Business School; worked for McKinsey and Co. (man. consultancy firm); fmr Sr Vice-Pres. and Gen. Merchandise Man. May Department Stores; fmr Exec. Vice-Pres. and Gen. Merchandise Man. Home Shopping Network; fmr Pres. Payless Shoes Inc.; Pres. and COO Stores and Merchandise Operations, J.C. Penney Co. Inc. 2002–05, Pres. and Chief Merchandising Officer 2005–. *Address:* J.C. Penney Co. Inc., 6501 Legacy Drive, Plano, TX 75024-3698, USA (office). *Telephone:* (972) 431-1000 (office). *Fax:* (972) 431-9140 (office). *E-mail:* info@jcpenney.net (office). *Website:* www.jcpenney.net (office).

HIDALGO, Anne, DEA; French (b. Spanish) politician and fmr civil servant; *Mayor of Paris;* b. 19 June 1959, San Fernando, Andalusia, Spain; m. Jean-Marc Germain; ed Univ. Jean Moulin Lyons 3, Univ. Paris Ouest Nanterre La Défense; worked as civil servant 1984–2011, including in Inspection du travail (Labour Inspectorate) 1984–93, Professional Training Div., Dept of Labour 1993–95, Mission to ILO, Geneva 1995–96; Officer, Human Resources Directorate, Compagnie générale des eaux (later renamed Vivendi then Vivendi Universal) 1996–97; Adviser to cabinet office of Minister of Employment and Solidarity 1997–98; Technical Adviser to cabinet office of Sec. of State for Women's Rights and Vocational Training 1998–2000, to cabinet office of Minister of Justice 2000–02; mem. Conseil de Paris for 15th arrondissement 2001; First Deputy Mayor of Paris 2001–14, Mayor of Paris 2014–; mem. Conseil régional d'Ile-de-France 2004–; mem. Parti socialiste 1994–; Commdr, Order of Isabella the Catholic (Spain) 2010, Chevalier, Ordre nat. de la Légion d'honneur 2012. *Address:* Hôtel de Ville, 29 rue de Rivoli, 75004 Paris, France (office). *Telephone:* 1-42-76-40-40 (office). *Website:* www.paris.fr (office); www.anne-hidalgo.net (office).

HIDAYAT, Bambang, PhD, FAAS; Indonesian astronomer and academic; *Professor Emeritus, Bandung Institute of Technology (ITB);* b. 18 Sept. 1934, Kundus, Cen. Java; s. of Soedirgo Dhonomidjojo; m. Estiti Bambang Hidayat (died 1995); two s.; ed Case Inst. of Tech., Cleveland; Dir Bosscha Observatory 1968–83; Asst Prof. of Astronomy, Bandung Inst. of Tech. (ITB) 1968, Assoc. Prof. 1974, Prof. 1976–2004, Prof. Emer. 2004–; fmr Chair. Indonesian–Dutch Astronomy Programme; Chair. Indonesian–Japan Astronomy Programme 1980–94, Consortium of Science and Mathematics; Vice-Pres. Int. Astronomical Union 1994–2000; f. Indonesian Astronomical Soc. 1978, co-f. Indonesian Physics Soc.; mem. American Astronomical Soc., Royal Astronomical Soc., Indonesian Inst. of Sciences 1991, Nat. Research Council, Indonesian Nat. Acad. of Sciences, Royal Comm. Al Albait Univ., Jordan 1993; Fellow, Islamic Acad. of Sciences; Habibie Award 2003. *Publications:* several astronomy textbooks and more than 40 scientific papers. *Address:* Institut Teknologi Bandung (ITB), Jalan Tamansari 64, Bandung 40116 (office); Indonesian Institute of Sciences, Jl. Jendral Gatot Subroto no. 10, PO Box 250, Jakarta, Indonesia (office). *Telephone:* (22) 2500935 (office); (21) 5251542

(office). *Fax:* (22) 2500935 (office); (21) 5207226 (office). *E-mail:* info-center@itb.ac .id (office); bhidayat@as.itb.ac.id; hidayatbambang@yahoo.com; bhidayat07@ hotmail.com. *Website:* www.itb.ac.id (office).

HIDAYAT, Taufik; Indonesian badminton player; b. 10 Aug. 1981, Bandung, West Java; s. of Aries Harris and Enok Dartilah; m. Armidianti Gumelar; one d.; winner Djarum Indonesia Open 1999, 2000, 2002, 2003, 2004, Singapore Open 2005; Gold Medal Athens Olympics 2004, XIV World Championships, Anaheim 2005; Bintang Jasa Utama (First Class Merit Star). *Leisure interests:* travelling, football. *Address:* Taufik Hidayat Management (THForce), Rasuna Office Park Blok MO-03, Jl. HR. Rasuna Said, Kuningan, Jakarta, 12960, Indonesia (office). *Telephone:* (81) 116-8909 (office). *E-mail:* info@taufik-hidayat.com (office); melatikarina@th-force.com (office). *Website:* www.taufik-hidayat.com (office).

HIDE, Raymond, CBE, MA, ScD, CPhys, FRS, FInstP; British research geophysicist and academic; *Honorary Senior Research Investigator, Imperial College London;* b. 17 May 1929, Doncaster, Yorks.; s. of the late Stephen Hide and Rose Edna Hide (née Cartlidge); m. Phyllis Ann Licence 1958; one s. two d.; ed Percy Jackson Grammar School, Doncaster, Univs of Manchester and Cambridge; Research Assoc. in Astrophysics, Yerkes Observatory, Univ. of Chicago, USA 1953–54; Sr Research Fellow, Gen. Physics Div. AERE, Harwell 1954–57; Lecturer in Physics, King's Coll., Univ. of Durham 1957–61; Prof. of Geophysics and Physics, MIT 1961–67; Head of Geophysical Fluid Dynamics Lab., Chief Scientific Officer (Individual Merit), Meteorological Office, Bracknell 1967–90; Gresham Prof. of Astronomy, Gresham Coll., City of London 1985–90; Dir Robert Hooke Inst. and Visiting Prof. of Physics, Univ. of Oxford 1990–92, Research Prof., Dept of Physics 1992–94, Prof. Emer. of Physics 1994–; Sr Research Investigator, Imperial Coll., London 2000–, now Hon.; Visiting Prof., Dept of Math., Univ. Coll., London 1969–84; Adrian Visiting Fellow, Univ. of Leicester 1981–83; Fellow, Jesus Coll., Oxford 1983–97, Hon. Fellow 1997–; mem. Council, Royal Soc. of London 1988–90; mem. Pontifical Acad. of Sciences, American Acad. of Arts and Sciences, Academia Europaea, Royal Astronomical Soc. (Pres. 1983–85), Royal Meteorological Soc. (Pres. 1974–76, Hon. mem. 1989), European Geophysical Soc. (Pres. 1982–84, Hon. mem. 1988), American Geophysical Union, Inst. of Physics, Int. Astronomical Union and numerous other socs and cttees; Chair. British Nat. Cttee for Geodesy and Geophysics, UK Chief Del. to Int. Union of Geodesy and Geophysics 1979–85; Hon. Fellow, Gonville and Caius Coll., Cambridge 2001, Jesus Coll., Oxford 1997; Hon. DSc (Leicester) 1985, (Manchester) 1994, (Paris) 1995; Charles Chree Medal and Prize of Inst. of Physics 1975, Holweck Medal and Prize, Société Française de Physique and Inst. of Physics 1982, Gold Medal, Royal Astronomical Soc. 1989, William Bowie Medal, American Geophysical Union 1997, Hughes Medal, Royal Soc. 1998, L.F. Richardson Medal, European Geophysical Soc. 1999, Symons Gold Medal, Royal Meteorological Soc. 2003. *Publications:* numerous scientific articles and papers. *Address:* Room 6M33, Department of Mathematics, Imperial College, London, SW7 2BZ, England (office). *Telephone:* (20) 8873-3366 (home). *E-mail:* r.hide@ic.ac.uk (office); arhide@ntlworld.com (home). *Website:* www2.imperial.ac .uk/mathematics (office); www3.imperial.ac.uk/people/r.hide (office).

HIDE, Rodney, QSO, MSc; New Zealand politician; b. 1956, Oxford, North Canterbury; ed Univs of Canterbury and Lincoln, Montana State Univ., USA; fmrly rig worker on North Sea oil rig, truck driver; fmr Lecturer, Centre for Resource Man. and Dept of Econs, Univ. of Lincoln, UK; Founding Chair. Assoc of Consumers and Taxpayers 1993; Founding Pres. and first Pres. ACT New Zealand 1994, Vice-Pres. 2000–04, Leader 2004–11; elected list MP 1996, ACT Spokesman for Finance 1996–, ACT Rep., Finance and Expenditure Select Cttee 1996–; ACT cand. for Epsom 1999, 2002; MP for Epsom 2005–11 (retd); Minister of Local Govt 2008–11, of Regulatory Reform 2008–11, Assoc. Minister of Commerce 2008–11; 'Backbencher of the Year' New Zealand Herald 2001, 'Opposition MP of the Year' Dominion 2001, 'Leader of the Opposition' North and South 2002, 'Politician of the Year' Dominion 2003. *Publications:* The Power to Destroy 1999; HideSight column for Nat. Business Review 1989–99; HideSight email newsletter published by rodneyhide.com 2003–, My Year of Living Dangerously 2007.

HIÉGEL, Catherine; French actress; b. 10 Dec. 1946, Montreuil; d. of Peter Hiégel; partner Richard Berry; one d.; ed Conservatoire nat. supérieur d'art dramatique; as a child, sang with André Claveau in Viens danser avec papa (Come and Dance with Dad) 1956; studied with Charon Jacques and Jean Darnel and began stage career at Théâtre des Bouffes-Parisiens; joined Comédie-Française 1969, worked with directors including Philippe Adrien, Patrice Chéreau, Dario Fo, Jorge Lavelli, Joel Jouanneau, Jacques Lassalle, Jean-Paul Roussillon in the classical and contemporary repertoire; Assoc. mem. Comédie-Française 1976, Dean (Doyen) 2008–09, Hon. mem. 2010–; Prof., Conservatoire nat. supérieur d'art dramatique 1998–. *Plays at Comédie-Française include:* Le Dépit amoureux (Molière) 1969, Le Jeu de l'amour et du hasard (Marivaux) 1969, Le Malade imaginaire (Molière) 1969, 1971, 1972, 1973 (toured to USSR) 2001, 2006, Dom Juan (Molière) 1970 (toured to USA, Canada and London), 1971, George Dandin (Molière) 1970, 1972, 1973, L'Impromptu de Versailles (Molière) 1971, 1973, Les Femmes savantes (Molière) 1971, 1973, Cœur à deux (Foissy 1972 (toured in Italy)), Les Fausses Confidences (Marivaux) 1972, Electre (Giraudoux) 1972, Amphitryon (Molière) 1973, L'Ile des esclaves (Marivaux) 1973, Les Précieuses ridicules (Molière) 1973, 2007, 2009, Henri IV (Pirandello) 1974, Maître Puntila et son valet Matti (Brecht) 1976, Cyrano de Bergerac (Rostand) 1976, Les Acteurs de bonne foi (Marivaux) 1977, Les Trois Sœurs (Chekhov) 1979, Le roi se meurt (Ionesco) 1980, La locandiera (Goldoni) 1981, 1983, Le Bourgeois gentilhomme (Molière) 1985, Le Médecin malgré lui (Molière) 1990, Maman revient pauvre orphelin (Grumberg) 1994, Le Shaga (Duras) 1995, Les Bonnes (Genet) 1997, Mère Courage et ses enfants (Brecht) 1998, Savannah bay (Duras) 2002, 2003, 2004, Les Papiers d'Aspern (Jean Pavans after Henry James) 2003, 2004, Tartuffe (Molière) 2005, Il Campiello (Goldoni) 2007, 2009, Une confrérie de farceurs (Faivre) 2007, Les Joyeuses Commères de Windsor (Shakespeare) 2009, Mystère Bouffe et fabulages (Fo) 2010, Les Fausses (Aristophanes) 2010. *Other plays include:* Quai Ouest (Koltès), Théâtre Nanterre-Amandiers 1986, Une visite inopportune (Copi), Théâtre nat. de la Colline, Nouveau Théâtre d'Angers 1988, La Veillée (Norén), Théâtre nat. de la Colline (Prix du Syndicat de la critique for Best Comedienne 1989) 1989, Arloc (Kribus), Théâtre nat. de la Colline 1996, Les Présidentes (Schwab), Théâtre nat. de Chaillot 1998, J'étais dans ma maison et j'attendais que la pluie vienne (Lagarce), Théâtre de la Cité internationale (Prix du Syndicat de la critique for Best Comedienne 2005) 2005, Objet perdu (Keene), Théâtre de la Commune 2006, La Mère (Zeller), De beaux lendemains (Banks), Théâtre des Bouffes du Nord 2011, Tout doit disparaître (Pessani), Festival d'Avignon 2011, Moi je crois pas! (Grumberg), Théâtre du Rond-Point 2012. *Plays directed at Comédie-Française:* Le Misanthrope (Molière) (co-directed with Jean-Luc Boutté) 1975, Les Femmes savantes (Molière), Comédie-Française au Théâtre de la Porte Saint-Martin 1987, Purgatoire (Minyana) 1994, La Demoiselle de la poste (Pokas) 1996, L'Âge d'or (Feydeau) 1998, George Dandin (Molière) 1999, Le Retour (Pinter) 2000, L'Avare (Molière) 2009. *Other plays directed:* Je danse comme Jésus Christ sur le vaste océan (after Alfred de Musset), Conservatoire nat. supérieur d'art dramatique 2011, Le Bourgeois gentilhomme (Molière), CADO 2011. *Films include:* L'état de grâce 1986, Life is a Long Quiet River 1988, Widow's Walk 1988, La petite amie 1988, My Life Is Hell 1991, Gazon maudit 1995, La serva amorosa 1996, Fred 1997, L'autre côté de la mer 1997, Hygiène de l'assassin 1999, Les après-midi de Laura (short) 2000, Les côtelettes 2003, Secret défense 2008, He Is My Girl 2009, Un baiser papillon 2011, Adieu Berthe 2012. *Television includes:* films: Spéciale dernière 1967, Le bourgeois gentilhomme 1968, Les précieuses ridicules 1972, Georges Dandin 1973, Chez les Titch 1974, La confession d'un enfant du siècle 1974, Ondine 1975, Le roi se meurt 1978, Les acteurs de bonne foi 1979, La folle de Chaillot 1980, Les trois soeurs 1980, Une page d'amour 1980, Créanciers 1981, La locandiera 1982, La corruptrice 1994, Le mangeur de lune 1994, Youth Without God 1996, Mylène 1996, Le malade imaginaire 2002, Les précieuses ridicules 2009; series: Le théâtre de la jeunesse – L'homme qui a perdu son ombre 1966, Au théâtre ce soir – Aux quatre coins 1970, Ferbac – Ferbac et la festin de miséricorde 1994, Julie Lescaut – Le secret des origines 1996. *Address:* c/o Comédie-Française, 1er Arrondissement, 75001 Paris, France. *Telephone:* 1-44-58-13-16. *E-mail:* informations@comedie-francaise.org. *Website:* www.comedie-francaise.fr.

HIERRO LÓPEZ, Luis; Uruguayan politician, teacher and journalist; b. 6 Jan. 1947, Montevideo; s. of Luis Hierro Gambardella and Celia Lopez; m. Ligia Armitran; four c.; journalist 1965–84; history teacher 1968–73; researcher, Museo Histórico Nacional 1974–84; mem. Nat. Exec. Cttee Colorado Party and Nat. Convention 1982–98, Chamber of Deputies (Pres. 1989) 1985–94; Chair. Cttees on the Constitution, Gen. Legislation and Admin and Human Rights, Special Cttee dealing with proposed anti-corruption legislation, Uruguayan Section of Jt Parl. Cttee of MERCOSUR; Senator, Colorado Party 1995–97; Vice-Pres. of Uruguay 2001–05. *Publications:* Diario del Uruguay (co-author) 1975, Battle y la Reforma del Estado 1978. *Address:* c/o Office of the Vice-President, Casa de Gobierno, Edif. Libertad, Avda Luis Alberto de Herrera 3350, esq. Avda José Pedro Varela, Montevideo, Uruguay (office).

HIESINGER, Heinrich, Dr-Ing; German business executive; *Chairman of the Executive Board, ThyssenKrupp AG;* b. 25 May 1960, Bopfingen; ed Tech. Univ. of Munich; Research Asst, Tech. Univ. of Munich 1986–92; held various positions in various countries in the Power Transmission and Distribution Group of Siemens 1992–2000, Pres. Power Transmission and Distribution Group 2000–03, Pres. and CEO Siemens Building Technologies AG, Zug, Switzerland 2003–07, mem. Man. Bd Siemens AG 2007–10, CEO Industry Sector of Siemens and Head of Cen. Dept Corp. Information Tech. 2008–10; Vice-Chair. Exec. Bd ThyssenKrupp AG 2010–11, Chair. 2011–. *Address:* ThyssenKrupp AG, PO Box, 45063 Essen (office); ThyssenKrupp AG, ThyssenKrupp Allee 1, 45143 Essen, Germany (office). *Telephone:* (201) 844-0 (office). *Fax:* (201) 844-536000 (office). *E-mail:* info@thyssenkrupp.com (office). *Website:* www.thyssenkrupp.com (office).

HIGGINS, Chester, Jr, BS; American photographer; *Staff photographer, New York Times;* b. Nov. 1946, Lexington, Ky; s. of Varidee Loretta Young Higgins Smith and step-s. of Johnny Frank Smith; m. 1st Renelda Walker (divorced); one s. one d.; m. 2nd Betsy Kissam; ed Tuskegee Inst., Ala (now Tuskegee Univ.); became photographer 1967; photographer for Look magazine 1970; part-time photography instructor, New York Univ. School of Fine Arts 1975–78; staff photographer, New York Times 1975–; photographs have appeared in ARTNews, Look, New York Times Magazine, Life, Newsweek, Fortune, Ebony, Essence, Archaeology; Fellow, Int. Center for Photography, Ford Foundation, Nat. Endowment for the Arts, Rockefeller Foundation, Andy Warhol Foundation; collections, The Museum of Modern Art (MoMA), New York; UN Award, Graphics Magazine Award, American Graphic Design Award, Art Dirs of New York Award. *Publications include:* Student Unrest at Tuskegee Institute 1968, Black Woman 1970, Drums of Life 1974, Some Time Ago: A Historical Portrait of Black Americans 1850–1950 1980, Feeling the Spirit: Searching the World for the People of Africa 1994, Elder Grace: The Nobility of Aging 2000, Echo of the Spirit: A Visual Journey 2004; numerous reviews and articles in journals. *Address:* 57 South Portland Avenue, Brooklyn, New York, NY 11217-1301, USA (office). *Telephone:* (718) 625-2474. *E-mail:* chesterhiggins@mindspring.com (office). *Website:* www.chesterhiggins.com.

HIGGINS, Christopher Francis, BSc, PhD, FRSE, FRSA, FMedSci; British academic and university administrator; *Vice-Chancellor and Warden, University of Durham;* b. 1955, Cambridge, England; s. of Philip Higgins; pnr; five d.; ed Raynes Park Comprehensive, London, Royal Coll. of Music, London, Durham Univ., University of California, Berkeley, USA; Lecturer, then Reader in Molecular Genetics, Univ. of Dundee 1981–88, Prof. 1988–89; Dir of Research Labs, Imperial Cancer Research Fund (now Cancer Research UK), Inst. of Molecular Medicine 1989–94, Nuffield Prof. and Head, Dept of Clinical Biochemistry 1994–98; Dir Clinical Science Centre, MRC 1998–2007; Head of Div., Faculty of Medicine, Imperial Coll. London 1998–2007; Scientific Adviser, House of Lords Select Cttee on Stem Cells 2001–02; Vice-Chancellor and Warden, Durham Univ. 2007–; Chair. Spongiform Encephalopathy Advisory Cttee; mem. Exec. Bd Assen of Medical Charities; fmr Bd mem. Acad. of Medical Sciences, Biotechnology and Biological Sciences Research Council; mem. Human Genetics Comm.; Trustee, Kennedy Inst. for Rheumatology; Hugh Bean Prize, Royal Coll. of Music, CIBA Medal, British Biochemical Soc., Fleming Award, Soc. for Gen. Microbiology. *Publications:* numerous articles in academic journals. *Address:* Office of the Vice-Chancellor, University of Durham, University Office, Durham, DH1 3HP, England (office). *Telephone:* (191) 334-6214 (office). *E-mail:* vice.chancellor@durham.ac.uk (office). *Website:* www.dur.ac.uk/vice.chancellor (office).

HIGGINS, Desmond G., PhD; Irish biologist/biochemist and academic; *Professor of Bioinformatics and Principal Investigator, Conway Institute of Biomolecular*

and Biomedical Research, University College Dublin; ed Trinity Coll. Dublin; Postdoctoral Researcher, Sharp. Lab., Dept of Genetics, Trinity Coll. Dublin 1985–90; Staff Scientist, European Molecular Biology Lab. (EMBL), Heidelberg, Germany 1990–94; Staff Scientist and Group Leader, EMBL/EBI, Hinxton, UK 1994–96; Statutory Lecturer, Dept of Biochemistry, Univ. Coll. Cork 1997–2003; Prof. of Bioinformatics and Prin. Investigator, Conway Inst. of Biomolecular and Biomedical Research, Univ. Coll. Dublin 2003–, Conway Fellow; mem. Royal Irish Acad. *Publications:* numerous articles in scientific journals. *Address:* Bioinformatics Department, Conway Institute of Biomolecular and Biomedical Research, University College Dublin, Belfield, Dublin 4, Ireland (office). *Telephone:* (1) 7166833 (office). *Fax:* (1) 7166701 (office). *E-mail:* des.higgins@ucd.ie (office). *Website:* www.ucd.ie/conway (office); bioinf.ucd.ie (home).

HIGGINS, Jack (see Patterson, Harry.)

HIGGINS, John, MBE; British professional snooker player; b. 18 May 1975, Wishaw, N Lanarkshire, Scotland; m. Denise Higgins; two s. one d.; winner, Mita/Sky World Masters – Junior (Under 16) 1991; turned professional 1992; won first tournament by defeating Dave Harold 9–6 in final of Grand Prix 1994; first teenager to win three ranking events in a season 1994–95; winner (ranking tournaments), Grand Prix 1994, 1999, 2005, 2008, British Open 1995, 1998, 2001, 2004, Int. Open 1995, 1996, German Open 1995, 1997, European Open 1997, World Snooker Championship 1998, 2007, 2009, 2011, UK Championship 1998, 2000, 2010, China Int. 1999, Welsh Open 2000, 2010, 2011; runner-up (ranking tournaments), Welsh Open 1995, 1998, Grand Prix 1995, 1997, British Open 1996, UK Championship 1996, 2009, Scottish Open 1998, World Snooker Championship 2001, Irish Masters 2003, LG Cup 2003, Malta Cup, 2006, China Open 2006, 2009; winner (non-ranking tournaments), Charity Challenge 1998, 1999, Masters 1999, 2006, Premier League Snooker 1999, Irish Masters 2000, 2002, Scottish Masters 2001, Champions Cup 2001, Euro-Asia Masters Challenge 2007, Scottish Open Championship 2008, Hainan Classic 2011, Scottish Professional Championship 2011; winner (minor ranking tournaments), Ruhr Championship 2010; winner (Pro-am tournaments), World Series of Snooker – Tournament in Saint Helier 2008, World Series of Snooker – Tournament in Moscow 2008; winner (team events), World Cup (with Team Scotland) 1996, Nations Cup (with Team Scotland) 2001; has won 24 ranking titles and made more than 400 competitive century breaks, including five maximum 147 breaks; ninth player to win World Championship title three or more times; ranked World No. 1 1998–99, 1999–2000, 2007–08, 2010–11; Patron, The Dalziel Centre hospice 2010; World Snooker Player of the Year, World Snooker Awards 2011, Snooker Journalists Player of the Year, World Snooker Awards 2011. *Leisure interests:* Celtic Football Club, Everton Football Club, playing poker, playing golf, enjoys gourmet food and cooking. *Address:* c/o World Snooker, Second Floor, Albert House, 111–117 Victoria Street, Bristol, BS1 6AX, England (office). *Telephone:* (117) 317-8200 (office). *Fax:* (117) 317-8300 (office). *E-mail:* info@worldsnooker.com (office). *Website:* www.worldsnooker.com (office).

HIGGINS, Dame Julia Stretton, DBE, BA, DPhil, FRS, FREng; British polymer scientist and academic; *Professor of Polymer Science and Senior Research Investigator, Department of Chemical Engineering and Chemical Technology, Imperial College London;* b. 1 July 1942, London, England; d. of George Stretton Downes and Sheilah Stretton Downes; ed Ursuline Convent School, Wimbledon, Somerville Coll. Oxford; physics teacher, Mexborough Grammar School 1966–68; Research Assoc., Univ. of Manchester 1968–72, Centre de Recherche sur les Macromolécules, Strasbourg, France 1972–73; physicist, Institut Laue-Langevin, Grenoble, France 1973–76; Lecturer, Chemical Eng Dept, Imperial Coll., London 1976–85, Reader in Polymer Science 1985–89, Prof. of Polymer Science and Sr Research Investigator 1989–, Dir Grad. School in Eng and Physical Sciences 2002–06, Prin. Faculty of Eng 2006–; Dean City and Guilds Coll. 1993–97; Chair. UK Eng and Physical Sciences Research Council 2003–07; Pres. BAAS; Foreign Sec. and Vice-Pres. Royal Soc. 2001–; Foreign mem. Nat. Acad. of Eng, USA. *Publications:* more than 200 articles in scientific journals. *Leisure interests:* theatre, opera, travel. *Address:* Department of Chemical Engineering and Chemical Technology, ACE Building, Room 510, Imperial College, London, SW7 2BY, England (office). *Telephone:* (20) 7594-5565 (office). *Fax:* (20) 7594-5638 (office). *E-mail:* j.higgins@imperial.ac.uk (office); j.higgins@ic.ac.uk (office). *Website:* www3.imperial.ac.uk/people/j.higgins (office).

HIGGINS, Michael D., BComm, MA; Irish politician, writer and head of state; *President;* b. 18 April 1941, Limerick; m. Sabina Coyne; three s. one d.; ed Univ. Coll. Galway, Indiana Univ., USA and Univ. of Manchester, UK; fmr Lecturer in Sociology and Politics, Univ. Coll. Galway; Senator 1973–77; mem. Galway Co. Council 1974–85; Alderman, Galway Borough Council 1974–85, Mayor of Galway 1982–83; mem. Galway City Council 1985–93; TD 1981–82, 1987–2011; Chair. The Labour Party 1978–87; Pres. 2003–11, Spokesperson on Foreign Affairs; Minister for Arts, Culture and the Gaeltacht 1994–97; Pres. of Ireland 2011–; Pres. European Council of Culture Ministers 1996. Council of Broadcasting Ministers 1996, Galway United Football Club; fmr Visiting Prof., Univ. of Southern Illinois; mem. Sociological Assen of Ireland, American Sociological Assen, PEN, Irish Writers' Union; Patron, Amnesty Int; Hon. Adjunct Prof., Univ. Coll. Galway; Sean McBride Peace Prize, Int. Peace Bureau, Helsinki 1992, Robert Adams Medal 1993, Kilkenny Award for Contrib. to Arts 1997. *Television:* The Other Emerald Isle. *Publications:* Poetry: Betrayal 1990, The Season of Fire 1993, An Arid Season 2004; numerous papers on cultural and political issues. *Leisure interests:* sports, writing. *Address:* Office of the President, Áras an Uachtaráin, Phoenix Park, Dublin 8 (office); Aimhirgin, Circular Road, Rahoon, Galway; Letteragh, Rahoon, Galway, Ireland (home). *Telephone:* (1) 6171000 (office); (1) 528500 (home). *Fax:* (1) 6171001 (office); (1) 528501 (home). *E-mail:* webmaster@president.ie (office). *Website:* www.president.ie (office).

HIGGINS, Baroness; Rosalyn, DBE, JSD, QC, FBA; British judge and fmr professor of international law; b. 2 June 1937; d. of the late Lewis Cohen and Fay Inberg; m. Rt Hon. Sir Terence L. (now Lord) Higgins 1961; one s. one d.; ed Burlington Grammar School, London, Girton Coll., Cambridge and Yale Law School, USA; UK Intern, Office of Legal Affairs, UN 1958; Commonwealth Fund Fellow 1959; Visiting Fellow, Brookings Inst. Washington, DC 1960; Jr Fellow in Int. Studies, LSE 1961–63; staff specialist in int. law, Royal Inst. of Int. Affairs 1963–74; Visiting Fellow, LSE 1974–78; Prof. of Int. Law, Univ. of Kent at

Canterbury 1978–81; Prof. of Int. Law, LSE 1981–95; Judge (first woman), Int. Court of Justice 1995–2009, Pres. 2006–09; mem. UN Cttee on Human Rights 1985–95; Visiting Prof., Stanford Univ. 1975, Yale Univ. 1977; Vice-Pres. American Soc. of Int. Law 1972–74, British Inst. of Int. and Comparative Law 2002–; Ordre des Palmes académiques 1988; Dr hc (Paris XI); Hon. DCL (Dundee) 1992, (Durham, LSE) 1995, (Cambridge, Sussex, Kent, City Univ., Greenwich, Essex) 1996, (Birmingham, Leicester, Glasgow) 1997, (Nottingham) 1999, (Bath, Paris II, Sorbonne) 2001, (Oxford) 2002, (Reading) 2003; Yale Law School Medal of Merit 1997, Manley Hudson Medal (ASIC) 1998, Harold Weig Medal, New York Univ. 1995, Prize of Int. Balzan Foundation 2007. *Publications include:* The Development of International Law Through the Political Organs of the United Nations 1963, Conflict of Interests 1965, The Administration of the United Kingdom Foreign Policy Through the United Nations 1966, Law in Movement – Essays in Memory of John McMahon (co-ed., with James Fawcett) 1974, UN Peacekeeping: Documents and Commentary: (Vol. I) Middle East 1969, (Vol. II) Asia 1971, (Vol. III) Africa 1980, (Vol. IV) Europe 1981, Problems and Process – International Law and How We Use It 1994; articles in law journals and journals of int. relations. *Leisure interests:* sport, cooking, eating. *Address:* c/o International Court of Justice, Peace Palace, 2517 KJ The Hague, Netherlands. *Telephone:* (70) 302-2415.

HIGGINS, Stuart; British journalist; *Managing Director, Stuart Higgins Communication;* b. 26 April 1956; m. Jenny Higgins; one s. one d.; ed Chase School for Boys, Filton Tech. Coll., Arblaster's of Bristol, Cardiff Coll. of Food, Tech. and Commerce; Dist reporter, The Sun, Bristol 1979, fmr NY corresp., Royal reporter, Features Ed., Exec. News Ed., Deputy Ed. 1991–93, Ed. 1994–98; public relations consultant 1998–; Founder and Man. Dir Stuart Higgins Communications 1999–; Acting Ed. News of the World 1993–94; mem. Bd of Dirs Project Associates; Vincent Fairfax Fellow, St James Ethics Centre. *Television:* Grow Your Own (produced), Bush Telegraph Water Challenge (produced). *Address:* Stuart Higgins Communications, One Brewers Green, Buckingham Gate, London, SW1H 0RH, England. *Telephone:* (20) 7096-5814. *E-mail:* hannah@stuart-higgins.com (office). *Website:* www.stuart-higgins.com.

HIGGS, Matthew; British artist and curator; *Director, White Columns Gallery;* b. 1964, Wakefield, W Yorks.; m. Anne Collier; ed Blackburn School of Art, Newcastle-upon-Tyne Polytechnic; began career with advertising agency, London 1988; f. Imprint 93 (publishing imprint) 1993; fmr teacher, RCA and Goldsmiths Coll., London; Curator, Wattis Inst. for Contemporary Arts, California Coll. of Arts and Crafts, San Francisco, USA 2001–04; Dir White Columns Gallery, New York 2004–; collaborator, Creative Growth Art Center, Oakland; Assoc. Dir of Exhbns, Inst. of Contemporary Art, London; mem. jury, Turner Prize 2006; Wingate Artists Award 1996. *Address:* White Columns Gallery, 320 West 13th Street, New York, NY 10014, USA (office). *Telephone:* (212) 924-4212 (office). *Fax:* (212) 645-4764 (office). *E-mail:* info@whitecolumns.org (office). *Website:* www.whitecolumns.org (office).

HIGGS, Peter Ware, CH, PhD, FRS, FRSE; British theoretical physicist; *Professor Emeritus of Theoretical Physics, University of Edinburgh;* b. 29 May 1929, Newcastle-upon-Tyne, England; s. of Thomas W. Higgs and Gertrude M. Higgs (née Coghill); m. Jo Ann Williamson 1963; two s.; ed Cotham Grammar School, Bristol and King's Coll., London; Sr Research Fellow, Univ. of Edinburgh 1955–56; ICI Research Fellow, Univ. Coll. London 1956–57, Imperial Coll. London 1957–58; Lecturer in Math., Univ. Coll. London 1958–60; Lecturer in Math. Physics, Univ. of Edinburgh 1960–70, Reader 1970–80, Prof. of Theoretical Physics 1980–96, Prof. Emer. 1996–; Fellow, King's Coll. London 1998; Hon. FInstP 1998; Hon. Fellow, Univ. of Swansea 2008; Hon. DSc (Bristol) 1997, (Edin.) 1998, (Glasgow) 2002, (King's Coll., London) 2009, (Univ. Coll., London) 2010, (Cambridge) 2012, (Heriot-Watt) 2012, (Durham) 2013, (Manchester) 2013; Hughes Medal, Royal Soc. 1981, Rutherford Medal, Inst. of Physics 1984, James Scott Prize, Royal Soc. of Edin. 1994, Paul Dirac Medal and Prize, Inst. of Physics 1997, High Energy and Particle Physics Prize, European Physical Soc. 1997, Royal Medal, Royal Soc. of Edin. 2000, Wolf Prize in Physics 2004, Oskar Klein Medal, Swedish Royal Acad. of Sciences 2009, Sakurai Prize, American Physical Soc. 2010, Edinburgh Award 2011, Nonino Prize 2013, Edinburgh Medal 2013, Nobel Prize in Physics (jtly with François Englert) 2013. *Publications include:* numerous papers in scientific journals. *Leisure interests:* walking, swimming, listening to music. *Address:* 2 Darnaway Street, Edinburgh, EH3 6BG, Scotland. *Telephone:* (131) 225-7060; (131) 650-5248. *E-mail:* p.w.higgs@ed.ac.uk (office). *Website:* www.ph.ed.ac.uk/higgs (office).

HIGUCHI, Takeo; Japanese business executive; *Representative Director, Chairman and CEO, Daiwa House Industry Company Ltd;* joined Daiwa House Industry 1963, Dir 1984–, Pres. Daiwa Danchi 1993–2001, Pres. Daiwa House Industry Co. Ltd 2001–04, Rep. Dir, Chair. and CEO 2004–; mem. Bd of Dirs Kansai Int. Public Relations Promotion Office (KIPPO) 2004–; fmr Dir Konica Minolta Holdings Inc., now Outside Dir Konica Minolta Business Solutions USA Inc.; Chair. Osaka Symphoniker Soc. 2006, Japan Fed. of Housing Orgs 2009; Vice-Chair. Osaka Chamber of Commerce and Industry 2005. *Address:* Daiwa House Industry Company Ltd, 3-3-5 Umeda, Kita-ku, Osaka 530-8241, Japan (office). *Telephone:* (6) 6346-2111 (office). *Fax:* (6) 6342-1419 (office). *E-mail:* info@daiwahouse.com (office). *Website:* www.daiwahouse.com (office); www.daiwahouse.co.jp (office).

HIGUCHI, Tomio; Japanese insurance executive; joined Nichido Fire & Marine Insurance Co. Ltd 1965, various sr positions include Dir 1993–95, Man.-Dir 1995–98, Sr Man.-Dir 1998–2000, Vice-Pres. 2000–01, Pres. and Sr Gen. Man. of Marketing and Sales Promotion HQ 2001–02, Chair. and Pres. 2002–04; Chair. Millea Holdings Inc. (following merger between Nichido Fire & Marine Insurance Co. and Tokio Marine 2004) 2004–07; fmr mem. Bd of Dirs Transatlantic Holdings Inc. *Address:* c/o Millea Holdings Inc., Otemachi First Square, West Tower, 1-5-1 Otemachi, Chiyoda-ku, Tokyo 100-0004, Japan.

HIJAB, Riyad Farid; Syrian politician; b. 1966, Deir ez-Zor; m.; four c.; Gov. of Quneitra Governorate 2008–11, of Latakia Governorate 2011; Minister of Agric. 2011–12; Prime Minister June–Aug. 2012; mem. al-Baath Arab Socialist Party.

HILBORN, Ray, BA, PhD, FRSC; Canadian/American marine biologist and academic; *Professor, School of Aquatic and Fishery Sciences, University of Washington, Seattle;* b. 31 Dec. 1947; ed Grinnell Coll., Ia, Univ. of British Columbia; Research Scholar, Int. Inst. for Applied Systems Analysis, Laxenburg, Austria 1974–75; Policy Analyst, Depts of Environment and Fisheries, Govt of Canada 1975–80; Hon. Lecturer, Inst. of Animal Resource Ecology, Univ. of British Columbia 1975–80, Adjunct Assoc. Prof. 1980–85; Sr Fisheries Scientist, Tuna and Billfish Program, South Pacific Comm., Noumea, New Caledonia 1985–87, Prof., School of Aquatic and Fishery Sciences, Univ. of Washington, Seattle 1987–; mem. Bd of Reviewing Eds, Science 2006–; mem. Editorial Bd, Natural Resource Modeling 1993–, Reviews in Fish Biology and Fisheries 1993–, Fish and Fisheries 1999–, New Zealand Journal of Marine and Freshwater Research 2003–, Canadian Journal of Fisheries and Aquatic Sciences 2002–; Award of Excellence, American Fisheries Soc. 2005, Volvo Environment Prize, Volvo Environment Foundation (co-recipient) 2006, Outstanding Achievement Award, American Inst. of Fisheries Research Biologists 2008. *Publications:* Adaptive Environmental Assessment and Management (co-author) 1978, Quantitative Fisheries Stock Assessment: Choice, Dynamics and Uncertainty (co-author) 1992 (also translated into Russian), Biomass Dynamics Models. FAO Computerized Information Series (Fisheries). No. 10 (co-author) 1996, The Ecological Detective: Confronting Models with Data (co-author) 1997, Bayesian Stock Assessment Methods in Fisheries. FAO Computerized Information Series (Fisheries) No. 12 (co-author) 2002, Overfishing: What Everyone Needs to Know 2012; numerous scientific papers in professional journals. *Address:* School of Aquatic and Fishery Sciences, University of Washington, Box 355020, Seattle, WA 98195-5020, USA (office). *Telephone:* (206) 543-3587 (office). *Fax:* (206) 685-7471 (office). *E-mail:* rayh@u.washington.edu (office). *Website:* www.fish.washington.edu (office).

HILDEBRAND, Philipp M., BA, MA, DPhil; Swiss banking executive; b. 19 July 1963; m. Kashya Hildebrand; one d.; ed Univ. of Toronto, Grad. Inst., Geneva, Switzerland, Univ. of Oxford, UK; raised in Switzerland and USA; worked as a bellhop at a hotel in Davos, Switzerland, where he met many leading European bankers; began career at World Econ. Forum, Geneva 1994; joined Moore Capital Management, London, UK 1995, Pnr 1997–2000; Chief Investment Officer, Vontobel Group 2000–01; mem. Exec. Cttee and Chief Investment Officer, Union Bancaire Privée, Geneva 2001–03; mem. Governing Bd and Head of Dept III (Financial Markets, Banking Operations, Information Tech.), Swiss Nat. Bank 2003, Vice-Chair. Governing Bd and Head of Dept II (Finance, Cash, Financial Systems, Security) 2007–10, Chair. Governing Bd and Head of Dept I (Econ. Affairs, Int. Affairs, Legal and Property Services), Zurich 2010–11 (resgnd); Visiting Prof. of Econs, Grad. Inst. of Int. Studies 2002–; Chair. of the Deputies of the Group of Ten (G10) 2006–07; Pres. Foundation Bd of Int. Centre for Monetary and Banking Studies, Geneva; apptd to Strategic Cttee of French Debt Man. Office (Agence France Trésor) 2006; mem. Bd of Dirs BIS, Basel; represents Switzerland in both the Steering Cttee and the Plenary of Financial Stability Bd; mem. Group of Thirty Consultative Group on Int. Econ. and Monetary Affairs, Inc. (G-30), Washington, DC 2008–; awarded Visiting Fellowships at European Univ. Inst., Florence, Italy 1992, Center for Int. Affairs, Harvard Univ., USA 1993. *Achievements include:* fmr mem. Swiss nat. swimming team. *Address:* c/o Swiss National Bank, Börsenstrasse 15, PO Box, 8022 Zurich, Switzerland.

HILDENBERG, Humphrey; Suriname economist and government official; ed Univ. of Groningen, The Netherlands; with Nationale Ontwikkelings Bank (NOB) 1981–92, 1996–2000; Minister of Finance 1992–96, 2000–10. *Address:* c/o Ministry of Finance, Tamarindelaan 3, Paramaribo, Suriname (office).

HILDENBRAND, Werner; German economist and academic; *Professor of Economics, University of Bonn;* b. 25 May 1936, Göttingen; Lecturer, Univ. of Heidelberg 1964–66; Visiting Asst Prof., Univ. of Calif., Berkeley 1966–67, Visiting Assoc. Prof. 1967–68; Research Prof., Univ. of Louvain, Belgium 1968–76; Prof. of Econs, Univ. of Bonn 1969–; Visiting Prof. of Econs, Univ. of Calif., Berkeley and Stanford Univ. 1970, Univ. of Calif., Berkeley 1973–74, Visiting Ford Prof., Univ. of Calif., Berkeley 1985–86, European Univ. Inst., Florence 1989–, Univ. of Calif., San Diego 1986–91; European Chair., Coll. de France 1993–94; Fellow, Econometric Soc. 1972; mem. Rhein-West Akad. der Wissenschaften 1981–, Academia Europaea 1985–, Berlin-Brandenburgischen Akad. der Wissenschaften 1993–; Foreign Hon. mem. American Acad. of Arts and Sciences 2005–; Dr hc (Univ. Louis Pasteur Strasbourg) 1988, (Bern) 2002, (Manchester) 2007; Leibniz-Preis Deutsche Forschungsgemeinschaft 1987, Max-Planck-Forsch-Preis 1995, Alexander-von-Humboldt-Preis 1997, Gay-Lussac-Preis 1997. *Publications:* Core and Equilibria of a Large Economy 1974, Lineare ökonomische Modelle (with K. Hildenbrand) 1975, Introduction to Equilibrium Analysis (with A. Kirman) 1976, Equilibrium Analysis (with A. Kirman) 1988, Market Demand: Theory and Empirical Evidence 1994; numerous papers. *Address:* University of Bonn, Wirtschaftstheorie II, Lennestr. 37, 53113 Bonn (office); Buchbitze 21, 53797 Lohmar, Germany (home). *Telephone:* (228) 739242 (office); (2246) 4339 (home). *Fax:* (228) 737940 (office); (2246) 16610 (home). *E-mail:* with2@uni-bonn.de (office). *Website:* www.wiwi.uni-bonn.de/fgh/ (office).

HILDNER, Rolf; German banking executive; b. 16 Nov. 1945, Wiesbaden; joined Wiesbadener Volksbank eG 1964, mem. Bd of Dirs 1977, Chair. Bd of 1987–2010 (retd); mem. Supervisory Bd SGZ Bank (now DZ Bank AG) 1990, Chair. 1995–2001, Vice-Chair. Supervisory Bd DZ Bank AG 2001–08, Chair. 2008–10; apptd Vice-Pres. IHK Wiesbaden 1985; mem. Supervisory Bd R+V Leben and R+V Versicherung AG; mem. Fed. Council, Co-operative Asscn, Frankfurt, apptd Bd mem. 1993, apptd Chair. 1997; mem. Fed. Council, Fed. Asscn of German Co-operative Banks (BVR), apptd Bd mem. 1994. *Address:* c/o Wiesbadener Volksbank eG, Schillerplatz 4, 65185 Wiesbaden, Germany.

HILFIGER, Tommy; American fashion designer; b. (Thomas Jacob Hilfiger), 24 March 1951, Elmira, NY; m. 1st Susie Hilfiger (divorced); four c.; m. 2nd Dee Ocleppo 2008; one s.; ed Elmira Free Acad.; opened first store, People's Place, Elmira, NY 1969; owned ten clothes shops throughout NY by 1978; moved to NY City to became full-time designer 1979; launched own sportswear label 1984; acquired fashion business from Mohan Muranji, cr. Tommy Hilfiger Inc. 1989, Pres. 1982–89, Vice-Chair. 1989–94, Hon. Chair. 1994–2003, now Prin. Designer; mem. Bd Fresh Air Fund, Race to Erase Multiple Sclerosis; f. Tommy Hilfiger Corp. Foundation 1995; From the Catwalk to the Sidewalk Award, VH-1 Fashion and Music Awards 1995, Menswear Designer of the Year, Council of Fashion Designers of America 1995, Parsons School of Design, Designer of the Year Award 1998. *Publication:* Iconic America: A Roller-Coaster Ride through the Eye-Popping

Panorama of American Pop Culture (with George Lois) 2007. *Leisure interests:* fishing, scuba diving, skiing. *Address:* Tommy Hilfiger USA Inc., 601 West 26th Street, New York, NY 10001, USA (office). *Telephone:* (212) 549-6000 (office). *Website:* www.tommy.com (office).

HILL, (Hugh) Allen (Oliver), PhD, FRS, FRSC; British chemist and academic; *Professor Emeritus of Bioinorganic Chemistry, University of Oxford;* b. 23 May 1937; ed Queen's Univ., Belfast; moved to Oxford 1962, Fellow, The Queen's Coll. 1965–, now Prof. Emer. of Bioinorganic Chem., Univ. of Oxford, Hon. Fellow, The Queen's Coll. and Wadham Coll.; Interdisciplinary Award, Chemistry and Electrochemistry of Transition Metals Medal, RSC Robinson Award, Breyer Medal, Royal Australian Chemical Inst., Mullard Award and Royal Medal, Royal Soc. "for his pioneering work on protein electrochemistry, which revolutionised the diagnostic testing of glucose and many other bioelectrochemical assays" 2010, Landmark blue plaque in Oxford 2012. *Publications:* numerous papers in professional journals. *Address:* Inorganic Chemistry Laboratory, South Parks Road, Oxford, OX1 3QR, England (office). *Telephone:* (1865) 272639 (office). *Fax:* (1865) 272690 (office). *E-mail:* allen.hill@chem.ox.ac.uk (office); allen.hill@oxford-biosensors.com (office). *Website:* research.chem.ox.ac.uk/allen-hill.aspx (office).

HILL, Anita F., BS, JD; American legal scholar and academic; *Professor of Social Policy, Law and Women's Studies, Heller School for Social Policy and Management, Brandeis University;* b. 30 July 1956, Lone Tee, Okla; d. of Albert Hill and Emma Hill; ed Oklahoma State Univ., Yale Univ. Law School; admitted to DC Bar 1980; Assoc., Wald, Harkrader & Ross, Washington, DC 1980–81; Special Counsel to Asst Sec., Office for Civil Rights, US Dept of Educ. 1981–82; Adviser to Chair. of Equal Employment Opportunity Comm. 1982–83; Asst Prof., Oral Roberts Univ. 1983–86; Prof., Coll. of Law, Univ. of Oklahoma 1986–97; Visiting Prof., Univ. of California Inst. for the Study of Social Change 1997; Prof. of Social Policy, Law and Women's Studies, Heller Grad. School, Brandeis Univ. 1997–; Visiting Scholar, Wellesley Coll., Newhouse Center for the Humanities and Wellesley Centers for Women 2007; Dr hc (Simmons Coll.) 2001, (Dillard Univ.) 2001, (Smith Coll.) 2003, (Lasell Coll.) 2007, (Massachusetts Coll. of Liberal Arts) 2010; Alphonse Fletcher Sr Fellowship Award 2005, Ford Hall Forum First Amendment Award 2008. *Publications include:* Race, Gender and Power in America: The Legacy of the Hill-Thomas Hearings 1995, Speaking Truth to Power (on her testimony of sexual harassment during US Senate confirmation hearings of Supreme Court nominee Clarence Thomas 1991) 1997; articles on int. commercial law, bankruptcy and civil rights. *Address:* Heller 374, Heller School for Social Policy and Management, Brandeis University, 415 South Street, Waltham, MA 02454-9110, USA (office). *Telephone:* (781) 736-3896 (office). *E-mail:* ahill@brandeis.edu (office). *Website:* heller.brandeis.edu (office).

HILL, Anthony, (Achill Redo); British artist; b. 23 April 1930, London; s. of Adrian Hill and Dorothy Whitley; m. Yuriko Kaetsu 1978; ed Bryanston School, St Martin's School of Art, Cen. School of Arts and Crafts; works in nat. collections in UK, USA, France, Israel, Denmark, Brazil; Leverhulme Fellowship, Dept of Math., Univ. Coll. 1971–72, Hon. Research Assoc. 1972–; mem. The London Math. Soc. 1979–; First Prize, Norwegian Print Biennale 1999. *Publications:* Data: Directions in Art, Theory and Aesthetics (ed.) 1968, Duchamp: Passim 1994; numerous articles in art and math. journals. *Leisure interest:* erotology. *Address:* 24 Charlotte Street, London, W1T 2ND, England (office). *Telephone:* (20) 7436-8820 (office). *E-mail:* achillredo@tiscali.co.uk.

HILL, Bonnie Guiton, BA, MS, EdD; American business executive; *President, B. Hill Enterprises LLC;* b. 30 Oct. 1941, Springfield, Ill.; d. of Henry Frank Brazelton and Zola Elizabeth Brazelton (née Newman); m. Walter Hill, Jr; one d.; ed Mills Coll., California State Univ., Hayward, Univ. of California, Berkeley; Admin. Asst to Presidential Special Asst, Mills Coll., Oakland, Calif. 1970–71, Admin. Asst to Asst Vice-Pres. 1972–73, Student Services Counsellor, Adviser to Resuming Students 1973–74, Asst Dean of Students, Interim Dir Ethnic Studies, Lecturer 1975–76; Exec. Dir Marcus A. Foster Educational Inst. 1976–79; Admin. Man. Kaiser Aluminium & Chemical Corpn 1979–80; Vice-Pres. and Gen. Man. Kaiser CTR, Inc. 1980–84; Vice-Chair. Postal Rate Comm., Washington, DC 1985–87; Asst Sec. for Vocational and Adult Educ., US Dept of Educ. 1987–89; Special Adviser to Pres. Bush for Consumer Affairs 1989–90; Pres. and CEO Earth Conservation Corps, Washington, DC 1990–91; Sec., State and Consumer Services Industry, State of Calif. 1991–92; Dean McIntire School of Commerce, Univ. of Virginia, Charlottesville 1992–97; Vice-Pres. The Times Mirror Co. Ltd 1997–2000; Co-founder and COO Icon Blue, Inc. (marketing consultancy) 2001–; Sr Vice-Pres. Communications and Public Affairs, LA Times newspaper 1998–2001, Pres. and CEO The Times Mirror Foundation 1997–2001; Pres. B. Hill Enterprises LLC (consulting firm) 2001–; mem. Bd of Dirs The Home Depot Co., Hershey Foods Corpn, AK Steel Holding Corpn, Choice Point, Inc., The Nat. Grid Group PLC 2001–, Albertsons, Inc., Yum! Brands 2003–; mem. Nat. Advisory Panel, Inst. for Research on Women and Gender, Stanford Univ.; mem. LA Urban League, United Way of Greater LA, Goodwill Industries of Southern Calif.; Nat. Women's Econ. Alliance Foundation Dirs' Choice Award, YWCA Tribute to Women in Int. Industry Award, Angeles Girl Scouts Council Grace Award, Anti-Defamation League Deborah Award. *Address:* Icon Blue, 5670 Wilshire Boulevard, Suite 600, Los Angeles, CA 90036, USA (office). *Telephone:* (323) 634-5301 (office). *Fax:* (323) 634-5314 (office). *E-mail:* info@iconblue.com (office). *Website:* www.iconblue.com (office).

HILL, Rt Rev. Christopher John, BD, MTh; British ecclesiastic; *Bishop of Guildford;* b. 10 Oct. 1945; s. of Leonard Hill and Frances Hill; m. Hilary Ann Whitehouse 1976; three s. one d.; ed Sebright School, Worcs., King's Coll., London; ordained (Diocese of Lichfield) 1969; Asst Chaplain to Archbishop of Canterbury for Foreign Relations 1974–81, Sec. for Ecumenical Affairs 1981–89; Anglican Sec. Anglican-Roman Catholic Int. Comm. I and II 1974–91; Anglican-Lutheran European Comm. 1981–82; Chaplain to Queen 1987–96; Canon Residentiary of St Paul's Cathedral, London 1989–96; Area Bishop of Stafford, Diocese of Lichfield 1996–2004, Hon. Canon, Lichfield Cathedral 1996–2004; Bishop of Guildford 2004–; Clerk of Closet, Royal Household 2005–; mem. Gen. Synod 1999–, House of Bishops 1999–; mem. Church of England-German Churches Conversations 1987–89, Church of England-Nordic-Baltic Conversations 1989–93, Church of England Legal Advisory Comm. 1991–, Faith and Order Advisory Group of Gen. Synod 1997–2010 (Vice-Chair. 1998–2010); mem. Council for Christian Unity

1992–97 (Chair. 2008–), Faith and Order Comm. 2010–, Anglican-Roman Catholic Int. Comm. III 2011–; Co-Chair. London Soc. of Jews and Christians 1991–96, Church of England-French Protestant Conversations 1993–98; Vice-Chair. Ecclesiastical Law Soc. 1993–2002, Chair. 2002–; Chair. Cathedrals' Precentors Conf. 1994–96, Women Bishops' Group 2005–06; Anglican Co-Chair. Meissen Theological Conf. 1999–2001; Vice-Pres. Conf. of European Churches 2009–; mem. London Soc. for the Study of Religion 1990–2000, Working Party on Women in the Episcopate 2001–04 (Vice-Chair. 2003–04), Liturgical Comm. 2003–, Clergy Discipline Comm. 2004–06, Theological Group 2006; Assoc., King's Coll. London, mem. Council 2010–; Lay mem. Council King's Coll.; mem. House of Lords 2010–; Hon. Canon, Canterbury Cathedral 1982–89; Relton Prize for Theology 1967. *Publications:* Anglicans and Roman Catholics: the Search for Unity (co-ed.), The Documents in the Debate. A Retrospect on the Papal Decision on Anglican Orders 1896 (co-ed.) 1996; ecumenical articles. *Leisure interests:* music, walking, reading. *Address:* Willow Grange, Woking Road, Guildford, Surrey, GU4 7QS, England (home). *Telephone:* (1483) 590500 (home). *Fax:* (1483) 590501 (home). *E-mail:* bishop.christopher@cofeguildford.org.uk (office). *Website:* www.cofeguildford.org.uk (office).

HILL, Christopher R., MA; American university administrator and fmr diplomatist; *Dean, Josef Korbel School of International Studies, University of Denver;* b. 1952, Little Compton, RI; m.; three c.; ed Bowdoin Coll., Maine, Naval War Coll.; with Peace Corps in Cameroon 1974; joined Foreign Service 1977, overseas assignments in Yugoslavia, Albania, S Korea and Poland; Sr Country Officer for Polish Affairs, Dept of State; Amb. to Macedonia 1996–99, to Poland 2000–04, to S Korea 2004–05; Asst Sec. Bureau of E Asian and Pacific Affairs 2005–09; Amb. to Iraq 2009–; Head of US del. to Six-Party Talks on N Korean nuclear issue 2005; Special Envoy to Kosovo 1998–99; fmr Sr Dir Southeast European Affairs, Nat. Security Council; Dean, Josef Korbel School of Int. Studies, Univ. of Denver 2010–; several State Dept awards including Robert S. Frasure Award and Distinguished Service Award, Building Bridges Award, Pacific Century Inst. 2008. *Address:* Josef Korbel School of International Studies, University of Denver, 2201 South Gaylord Street, Denver, CO 80208 (office); University of Denver, 2199 S. University Blvd, Denver, CO 80208, USA (office). *Telephone:* (303) 871-2539 (office). *Fax:* (303) 871-2456 (office). *Website:* www.du.edu/korbel (office).

HILL, Damon Graham Devereux, OBE; British fmr racing driver, company director and television presenter; b. 17 Sept. 1960, Hampstead, London; s. of the late Graham Hill (fmr Formula One world champion) and of Bette Hill; m. Georgie Hill 1988; two s. two d.; ed Haberdashers' Aske's School, London; first drove a car aged five; first drove in motorcycle racing 1979; driver with Canon Williams team 1993, Rothmans Williams Renault team 1994–96, Arrows Yamaha team 1997, Benson and Hedges Jordan team 1998–99; first motor racing victory in Formula Ford 1600, Brands Hatch 1984; first Formula One Grand Prix, Silverstone 1992; winner, Italian Grand Prix 1993, 1994, Belgian Grand Prix 1993, 1994, 1998, Hungarian Grand Prix 1993, 1995, Spanish Grand Prix 1994, British Grand Prix 1994, Portuguese Grand Prix 1994, Japanese Grand Prix 1994, 1996, Argentine Grand Prix 1995, 1996, San Marino Grand Prix 1995, 1996, Australian Grand Prix 1995, 1996, French Grand Prix 1996, Brazilian Grand Prix 1996, German Grand Prix 1996, Canadian Grand Prix 1996; third place, Drivers' World Championship 1993, second place 1994, 1995, Formula One World Champion 1996; 84 Grand Prix starts, 22 wins, 20 pole positions, 19 fastest laps, 42 podium finishes; retd end of 1999 season; Co-founder and Chair. P1 International 2000–; Pres. British Racing Drivers' Club 2006–11; Dir, Hill Sport Ltd; analyst for Sky F1 HD channel 2012–; British Competition Driver of the Year Autosport Awards 1995, BBC Sports Personality Award 1994, 1996, numerous racing awards. *Publications:* Damon Hill Grand Prix Year 1994, Damon Hill: My Championship Year 1996, F1 Through the Eyes of Damon Hill. *Leisure interests:* family, reading. *Address:* c/o British Racing Drivers' Club, Silverstone Circuit, Towcester, Northants. NN12 8TN, England. *E-mail:* enquiries@brdc.co.uk.

HILL, David Rowland; British government adviser; b. 1948, Birmingham; partner Hilary Coffman; ed King Edward's School, Birmingham, Brasenose Coll., Oxford; began career as industrial relations officer, Unigate Dairies, Birmingham; fmr press aide to Labour MP Roy Hattersley; Dir of Communications and Chief Media Spokesperson, Labour Party 1991–98; Labour cand. for Burton-on-Trent (unsuccessful), Sr Labour Party Press Spokesman during 2001 election campaign; Dir of Communications, Prime Minister's Office 2003–07; mem. Bd of Dirs Good Relations (public relations co.) 1998–2003, Bell Pottinger Group 2007–. *Leisure interest:* football. *Address:* c/o Board of Directors, Bell Pottinger Group, 6th Floor, Holborn Gate, 330 High Holborn, London, WC1V 7QD, England.

HILL, Sir Geoffrey William, Kt, MA, FAAAS; British poet, critic and academic; *Professor of Poetry, University of Oxford;* b. 18 June 1932; s. of William George Hill and Hilda Beatrice Hill; m. 1st Nancy Whittaker 1956 (divorced 1983); three s. one d.; m. 2nd Alice Goodman 1987; one d.; ed County High School, Bromsgrove and Keble Coll., Oxford; mem. academic staff, Univ. of Leeds 1954–80, Prof. of English Literature 1976–80; Univ. Lecturer in English and Fellow, Emmanuel Coll., Cambridge 1981–88; Univ. Prof. and Prof. of Literature and Religion, Boston Univ. 1988–2006, Emer. 2006–, Co-Dir Boston Univ. Editorial Inst. 1998–2004; Prof. of Poetry, Univ. of Oxford 2010–; Churchill Fellow, Univ. of Bristol 1980; Clark Lecturer, Trinity Coll., Cambridge 1986; Tanner Lecturer, Brasenose Coll., Oxford 2000; Assoc. Fellow, Centre for Research in Philosophy and Literature, Univ. of Warwick 2003; Empson Lecturer, Univ. of Cambridge 2005; Fellow, American Acad. of Arts and Sciences 1996; Hon. Fellow, Keble Coll., Oxford 1981, Emmanuel Coll., Cambridge 1990; Hon. DLitt (Leeds) 1988, (Warwick) 2007, (Bristol) 2009, (Oxford) 2010, Hon. LittD (Cambridge) 2010; Whitbread Award 1971, RSL Award (W.H. Heinemann Bequest) 1971, Loines Award, American Acad. and Inst. of Arts and Letters 1983, Ingram Merrill Foundation Award in Literature 1985, Kahn Award 1998, T.S. Eliot Prize, Ingersoll Foundation 2000, Truman Capote Award for Literary Criticism 2009. *Publications:* poetry: Poems 1952, For the Unfallen (Gregory Award 1961) 1959, Preghiere 1964, King Log (Hawthornden Prize 1968, Geoffrey Faber Memorial Prize 1970) 1968, Mercian Hymns (Alice Hunt Bartlett Award) 1971, Somewhere is Such a Kingdom: Poems 1952–71 1975, Tenebrae (Duff Cooper Memorial Prize 1979) 1978, The Mystery of the Charity of Charles Péguy 1983, Collected Poems 1985, New and Collected Poems 1952–1992 1994,

Canaan 1996, The Triumph of Love 1998, Speech! Speech! 2000, The Orchards of Syon 2002, Scenes from Comus 2005, Without Title 2006, Selected Poems 2006, A Treatise of Civil Power 2007, Oraclau/Oracles 2010, Clavic 2011, Odi Barbare 2012, Broken Hierarchies: Poems 1952–2012 2013; poetic drama: Henrik Ibsen's Brand: a version for the English stage 1978 (produced at Nat. Theatre, London 1978); criticism: The Lords of Limit: essays on literature and ideas 1984, The Enemy's Country 1991, Style and Faith 2003, Collected Critical Writings 2008. *Address:* Faculty of English Language and Literature, University of Oxford, St Cross Building, Manor Road, Oxford, OX1 3UL, England (office). *Telephone:* (1865) 271055 (office). *Fax:* (1865) 271054 (office). *Website:* www.english.ox.ac.uk (office).

HILL, Jay, PC; Canadian politician; b. 27 Dec. 1952, British Columbia; fmr Pres. BC Grain Producers Asscn and Dir for Grain, BC Fed. of Agric.; mem. Parl. for Prince George–Peace River 1993–2010; mem. Reform Party of Canada 1993–2000, Canadian Alliance 2000–03, Conservative Party of Canada 2003–; Chief Govt Whip 2006–08; Leader of the Govt in the House of Commons 2008–10. *Address:* c/o Office of the Leader of the Government in the House of Commons, 4th Floor, 14 Metcalfe Street, Ottawa, ON K1A 0A3, Canada (office). *Website:* www.jayhillmp.com.

HILL, Jonah; American actor, comedian, screenwriter and producer; b. (Jonah Hill Feldstein), 20 Dec. 1983, Los Angeles, Calif.; s. of Richard Feldstein and Sharon Lyn; ed Crossroads School, Santa Monica, New School Univ., New York; wrote and performed plays in East Village, New York. *Films include:* I Heart Huckabees 2004, The 40-Year-Old Virgin 2005, Grandma's Boy 2006, Click 2006, Accepted 2006, 10 Items or Less 2006, Knocked Up 2007, Evan Almighty 2007, Rocket Science 2007, Superbad 2007, Strange Wilderness 2008, Forgetting Sarah Marshall 2008, Just Add Water 2008, Emerson Park 2008, Funny People 2008, The Invention of Lying 2008, Get Him to the Greek 2010, Cyrus 2010, Megamind (voice) 2010, Moneyball 2011, Dragons: Gift of the Night Fury (short) 2011, The Sitter 2011, 21 Jump Street 2012, The Watch 2012, Django Unchained 2012, This Is the End 2013, The Wolf of Wall Street 2013, The Lego Movie 2014, True Story 2014, 22 Jump Street 2014, How to Train Your Dragon 2 (voice) 2014; as producer: Brüno 2008. *Television includes:* NYPD Blue 2004, Campus Ladies 2006, Clark and Michael 2007, Human Giant 2007, Reno 911 2009, The Simpsons (guest voice) 2009, Legend of the Boneknapper Dragon (short) 2010, Allen Gregory (series co-creator, exec. producer, voice artist) 2011–12. *Address:* c/o WME Entertainment, 9601 Wilshire Boulevard, Beverly Hills, CA 90210-5213, USA. *Telephone:* (310) 285-9000. *Fax:* (310) 285-9010. *Website:* www.wma.com.

HILL, Lynn, BS; American rock climber; b. (Carolynn Marie Hill), 1961, Detroit, Mich.; one s.; ed Staffs. State Univ. of NY, New Paltz, NY; began climbing aged 14; won over 30 int. climbing titles during 1980s; f. Lynn Hill Rock Climbing Camps; first person to free climb Nose route on El Capitan, Yosemite Valley, Calif. 1993, later free climbed the route in 23 hours in 1994, feat not repeated by any other climber until 2005; winner Survival of the Fittest TV competition (for times). *Main achievements:* competition winner, Troubat 1987, 1988, 1989, Worldwide indoor competition, Grenoble 1987, Arco Rock Master 1987, 1990, 1992, Bercy 1988, 1990, World Cup (jt winner) 1991, Stopped Competition 1993. *Film appearances include:* Extreme, Free Climbing the Nose, La Maitresse du Vide (French version). *Publications:* Climbing Free: My Life in the Vertical World (autobiography) 2002. *Address:* Lynn Hill Rock Climbing Camps, PO Box 383, Eldorado Springs, CO 80025, USA (office). *Telephone:* (303) 919-3223. *E-mail:* lynn@lynnhillblogs.com. *Website:* www.lynnhillclimbs.com; lynnhillblogs.com.

HILL, Michael William, MA, MSc, MRSC, FIInfSc, FCILIP, FRSA; British fmr information consultant, research chemist and library director; b. 27 July 1928, Ross-on-Wye, Herefords., England; s. of Geoffrey Hill and Dorothy Hill; m. 1st Elma Jack Forrest (died 1967); one s. one d.; m. 2nd Barbara Joy Youngman; ed King Henry VIIIth School, Coventry, Nottingham High School, Lincoln Coll., Oxford; Research Chemist, Laporte Chemicals Ltd 1953–56; Tech. and Production Man., Morgan Crucible Group 1956–64; Asst Keeper, British Museum 1964–68, Deputy Librarian Nat. Reference Library of Science and Invention (NRLSI) 1965–68, Keeper 1968–73; Dir, Science Reference Library, British Library 1973–86; Assoc. Dir Science, Tech. and Industry, British Library 1986–88; fmr Chair. Circle of State Librarians; fmr Vice-Pres. Int. Asscn of Tech. Univ. Libraries; Co-founder European Council of Information Asscns; Hon. Pres. Fed. Int. d'Information et de Documentation 1985–90 (Hon. Fellow 1992–), Hon. Fellow European Council of Information Asscns 1996–. *Publications include:* Patent Documentation (with Wittmann and Schiffels) 1979, Michael Hill on Science, Technology and Information 1988, National Surveys of Library and Information Services: 2: Yugoslavia (with Tudor Silovic), National Information Policies and Strategies 1994, The Impact of Information on Society 1998; Jt Series Ed. Saur Guides to Information Sources. *Leisure interests:* golf, theatre, music, Scottish dancing. *Address:* Jesters, 137 Burdon Lane, Cheam, SM2 7DB, England. *Telephone:* (20) 8642-2418.

HILL, Robert Murray, BA, BLL, LLM; Australian politician and diplomatist; *Chairman, Australian Carbon Trust;* b. 1946, Adelaide, S Australia; m.; four c.; ed Scotch Coll., Univ. of Adelaide, Univ. of London; barrister and solicitor 1970–; Liberal Party Campaign Chair. 1975–77, Chair., Constitutional Cttee 1977–81; Vice-Pres. Liberal Party, S Australian Div. 1977–79, State Pres. of S Australia Div. 1985–87; mem. Fed. Exec. of Liberal Party 1985–87, 1990–2006; Senator for S Australia 1981–2006; shadow portfolios in opposition include Foreign Affairs –1993, Defence 1993–94, Public Admin 1993–94, Educ., Science, Tech. 1994–96, Leader of Opposition in Senate 1993–96, Leader of Govt in Senate 1996–2006; Fed. Minister for Environment 1996–98, for Environment and Heritage 1998–2001, of Defence 2001–06; Perm. Rep. to UN, New York 2006–09; Chair. Australian Carbon Trust, Brisbane 2009–; mem. Law Soc. of S Australia. *Leisure interests:* law reform, Australian and Asian history, legal and environmental educ., the arts. *Address:* Australian Carbon Trust, c/o Department of Climate Change and Energy Efficiency, GPOB 854, Canberra, ACT 2600, Australia (office). *Telephone:* (2) 6159-7000 (office). *E-mail:* communications@climatechange.gov.au (office). *Website:* www.climatechange.gov.au/government/initiatives/aust-carbon-trust.aspx (office).

HILL OF OAREFORD, Baron (Life Peer), cr. 2010, of Oareford in the County of Somerset; **Rt Hon. Jonathan Hopkin Hill,** PC, CBE; British politician and business executive; *Leader of the House of Lords and Chancellor of the Duchy of Lancaster;* b. 24 July 1960; s. of Rowland Louis Hill and Paddy Marguerite Henwood; m. Alexandra Jane Nettelfield 1988; one s. two d.; ed Highgate School, London, Trinity Coll., Cambridge; worked in Conservative Party Research Dept 1985–86; special adviser to Kenneth Clarke at Dept of Employment, Dept of Trade and Industry and Dept of Health 1986–89; worked for Lowe Bell Communications 1989–91; worked at the Number 10 Policy Unit 1991–92, Political Sec. to Prime Minister John Major 1992–94; Sr Consultant, Bell Pottinger Group 1994–98; Co-founding Dir, Quiller Consultants 1998; Parl. Under-Sec. of State for Schools and Govt Spokesperson, Dept for Educ. 2010–13; Leader of the House of Lords and Chancellor of the Duchy of Lancaster 2013–; mem. (Conservative) House of Lords 2010–. *Address:* House of Lords, Westminster, London, SW1A 0PW, England (office). *Telephone:* (20) 7219-5353 (office). *Fax:* (20) 7219-5979 (office).

HILL WELLS, Susan Elizabeth, (Susan Hill), CBE, BA, MA, FRSL; British writer and playwright; b. 5 Feb. 1942, Scarborough, Yorks., England; d. of the late R. H. Hill and Doris Hill; m. Prof. Stanley W. Wells 1975; two d. (and one d. deceased); ed grammar schools in Scarborough and Coventry and King's Coll. London; literary critic, various journals 1963–; numerous plays for BBC 1970–; Fellow, King's Coll. London 1978; presenter, Bookshelf, BBC Radio 1986–87; Founder and Publr Long Barn Books 1996–. *Publications:* The Enclosure 1961, Do Me a Favour 1963, Gentleman and Ladies 1969, A Change for the Better 1969, I'm the King of the Castle 1970, The Albatross 1971, Strange Meeting 1971, The Bird of the Night 1972, A Bit of Singing and Dancing 1973, In the Springtime of the Year 1974, The Cold Country and Other Plays for Radio 1975, The Ramshackle Company (play) 1981, The Magic Apple Tree 1982, The Woman in Black 1983 (stage version 1989), One Night at a Time (for children) 1984, Through the Kitchen Window 1984, Through the Garden Gate 1986, Mother's Magic (for children) 1986, The Lighting of the Lamps 1987, Lanterns Across the Snow 1987, Shakespeare Country 1987, The Spirit of the Cotswolds 1988, Can it be True? (for children) 1988, Family (autobiog.) 1989, Susie's Shoes (for children) 1989, Stories from Codling Village (for children) 1990, I've Forgotten Edward (for children) 1990, I Won't Go There Again (for children) 1990, Pirate Poll (for children) 1991, The Glass Angels 1991, Beware! Beware! 1993, King of Kings 1993, Reflections from a Garden (with Rory Stuart) 1995, Contemporary Women's Short Stories (co-ed. with Rory Stuart) 1995, Listening to the Orchestra (short stories) 1996, The Second Penguin Book of Women's Short Stories 1997, The Service of Clouds 1998, The Boy Who Taught the Beekeeper to Read and Other Stories 2003, The Various Haunts of Men 2004, The Pure in Heart 2005, The Risk of Darkness 2006, The Man in the Picture 2007, Desperate Diary of a Country Housewife (non-fiction) 2007, The Battle for Gullywith (for children) 2008, The Beacon 2008, The Man in the Picture 2008, The Vows of Silence 2008, Howards End is On the Landing 2009, The Small Hand 2010, The Betrayal of Trust 2011, A Kind Man 2011. *Address:* c/o Sheil Land, 52 Doughty Street, London, WC1N 2LS, England (office). *E-mail:* vgreen@sheilland.co.uk (office); mail@susan-hill.com. *Website:* www.susan-hill.com.

HILLE, Bertil, BS, PhD; American physiologist, neurobiologist, biophysicist and academic; *Professor of Physiology and Biophysics, School of Medicine, University of Washington;* b. 10 Oct. 1940, New Haven, Conn.; m. Merrill Burr Hille; two s.; ed Yale Univ., The Rockefeller Univ.; Asst Prof., Dept of Physiology and Biophysics, Univ. of Washington School of Medicine 1968–71, Assoc. Prof. 1971–74, Prof. 1974–; mem. NAS 1986–, AAAS, Physiological Soc., Soc. for Neuroscience; Fellow, American Acad. of Arts and Sciences 1998–, Acad. of Medicine 2002–, Biophysical Soc.; Dr hc (Rockefeller Univ.) 2008; Louisa Gross Horwitz Prize for Biology or Biochemistry, Columbia Univ. (co-recipient) 1996, Albert Lasker Award for Basic Medical Research (co-recipient) 1999, Gairdner Int. Award, Gairdner Foundation (Canada) (co-recipient) 2001. *Publications:* Ion Channels of Excitable Membranes 1984, 1991, 2001; more than 150 publs in scientific journals on cell signalling by ion channels, neurotransmitters and hormones acting through G-protein coupled receptors and intracellular calcium, phosphoinositide messengers. *Address:* Department of Physiology and Biophysics, University of Washington School of Medicine, G-424 HSB, Box 357290, Seattle, WA 98195-7290, USA (office). *Telephone:* (206) 543-8639 (office). *Fax:* (206)-685-0619 (office). *E-mail:* hille@u.washington.edu (office).

HILLEL, Daniel, BA, MA, PhD; Israeli (b. American) water and soil scientist and academic; *Senior Research Scientist, NASA Goddard Institute for Space Studies;* b. 1930, Los Angeles, Calif.; ed American univs, Hebrew Univ. of Jerusalem; family emigrated to Palestine 1931; worked for Israeli Ministry of Agric.; Founding mem. Sde Boker kibbutz in Negev desert, where he worked as a surveyor; began developing the concept behind drip irrigation late 1950s; undertook missions to Burma 1956 and later to arid regions in Africa, Asia, S America and Australia; served as Head of Agricultural Research Service, Soil and Water Inst. of Israel, later consulted with governmental agencies in various countries; fmr Prof., Hebrew Univ. of Jerusalem, Univ. of Massachusetts, Columbia Univ.; also worked with int. orgs including World Bank, FAO, US Agency for Int. Devt, IAEA; currently Sr Research Scientist, NASA Goddard Inst. for Space Studies, The Earth Inst. at Columbia Univ., New York; Hon. DSc (Guelph Univ., Canada) 1992; Chancellor's Medal, Univ. of Massachusetts 1982, Guggenheim Fellowship and grant 1993, World Food Prize 2012. *Publications:* 21 books, including Soil and Water: Physical Principles and Processes 1971, Computer Simulation of Soil-Water Dynamics: A Compendium of Recent Work 1977, Applications of Soil Physics 1980, Fundamentals of Soil Physics 1980, Negev, Land, Water, and Life in a Desert Environment 1982, Introduction to Soil Physics 1982, Efficient Use of Water in Irrigation: Principles and Practices for Improving Irrigation in Arid and Semiarid Regions 1987, Out of the Earth: Civilization and the Life of the Soil 1992, The Rivers of Eden: The Struggle for Water and the Quest for Peace in the Middle East 1994, Environmental Soil Physics: Fundamentals, Applications, and Environmental Considerations 1998, Climate Change and the Global Harvest: Potential Impacts of the Greenhouse Effect on Agriculture 1998, Salinity Management for Sustainable Irrigation: Integrating Science, Environment, and Economics 2000, Introduction to Environmental Soil Physics 2003, Soil in the Environment: Crucible of Terrestrial Life 2007, The Natural History of the Bible: An Environmental Exploration of the Hebrew Scriptures 2007, Climate Variability and the Global Harvest: Impacts of El Niño and Other Oscillations on Agroecosystems 2008; more than 200 papers in professional journals. *Address:* NASA Goddard Institute for Space Studies, 2880 Broadway, New York, NY 10025, USA (office).

Telephone: (212) 678-5508 (office). *E-mail:* dh244@columbia.edu (office). *Website:* www.giss.nasa.gov/staff/dhillel.html (office).

HILLEL, Shlomo; Israeli politician; *President, The Society for the Preservation of Heritage Sites in Israel;* b. (Selim Hillel), 9 April 1923, Baghdad, Iraq; s. of Aharom Hillel and Hanini Hillel; m. Tmima Rosner 1952; one s. one d.; ed Herzliah High School, Tel-Aviv and Hebrew Univ., Jerusalem; mem. Ma'agan Michael Kibbutz 1942–58; Jewish Agency for Palestine—mission to countries in Middle East 1946–48, 1949–51; Israel Defence Forces 1948–49; Prime Minister's Office 1952–53; mem. of Knesset 1953–59, 1974–; Amb. to Guinea 1959–61, to Côte d'Ivoire, Dahomey, Upper Volta and Niger 1961–63; mem. Perm. Mission to UN with rank of Minister 1964–67; Asst Dir-Gen. Ministry of Foreign Affairs 1967–69; Minister of Police 1969–77; Co-ordinator of political contacts with Arab leadership in administered territories 1970–77; Minister of the Interior June–Oct. 1974, 1996–97; Chair. Ministerial Cttee for Social Welfare 1974–77, Cttee of the Interior and Environment 1977–81, of Foreign Affairs and Defence 1981–84; Perm. Observer to Council of Europe 1977–84; Speaker of the Knesset 1984–88; Chair. Sephardi Fed. 1976–; World Chair. Keren Hayesod United Israel Appeal 1989–98; Pres. Soc. for Preservation of Historical Sites in Israel 1996–; Chair. Zalman Shazar Center, Jerusalem; Commdr Nat. Order of Repubs of Ivory Coast, Upper Volta and Dahomey; Dr hc (Hebrew Univ.) 1995, (Ben-Gurion Univ.) 1997, (Tel-Aviv) 1998; Israel Prize for Life Achievement 1998. *Publication:* Operation Babylon 1988. *Leisure interests:* tennis, gardening. *Address:* 4 Shalom Aleichem str., Ra'anana 43368, Israel (home). *Telephone:* (3) 5057179 (office); (9) 7741789 (home). *Fax:* (3) 5034828 (office); (9) 7741788 (home). *E-mail:* s-t-h@zahav.net.il (home).

HILLEN, Johannes Stefanus Joseph (Hans); Dutch politician and fmr journalist; b. 17 June 1947, The Hague; m.; three c.; ed State Univ. of Utrecht; spent 14 years as journalist with Nederlandse Publieke Omroep (Netherlands Public Broadcasting), including as Desk Ed., NOS Studio Sport 1969–73, Foreign Ed., NOS Journaal (nat. TV news broadcast) 1973–77, Political Journalist, NOS Journaal, The Hague 1977–83; worked as social studies teacher in secondary schools in Hilversum and Bussum 1973–77; Dir of Information, Ministry of Finance 1983; mem. Tweede Kamer (House of Reps, lower house of Parl.) 1990–2002; mem. Eerste Kamer (Senate, upper house) 2007–; Minister of Defence 2010–12; mem. Christian Democratic Alliance (CDA), Parl. Party Sec. 1998–2001; fmr Chair. Health Care Insurance Bd; fmr columnist, Elsevier Weekblad, Katholiek Nieuwsblad; mem. Exec. Bd VNO-NCW (Confed. of Netherlands Industry and Employers); Chair. Centrum voor Merk en Communicatie (Centre for Brands and Communication); Special mem. Research Council for Security 2006–08; Chair. Friends of the Metropole Orchestra Foundation 2007–. *Address:* c/o Ministry of Defence, Plein 4, POB 20701, 2500 ES The Hague, Netherlands.

HILLEN, John, BA, MA, MBA, PhD; American consultant, fmr diplomatist and army officer (retd); *President, Global Strategies Group (USA) LLC;* ed Duke Univ., King's Coll. London, Univ. of Oxford, UK, Cornell Univ.; served 12 years as US Army officer; fmr Pres. American Man. Systems; fmr COO Island ECN; mem. US Comm. on Nat. Security/21st Century 1999; Defense Policy Advisor and Speechwriter for Pres. George W. Bush 2000; Asst Sec. of State for Political-Mil. Affairs, US State Dept 2005–07; Pres. Global Strategies Group (USA) LLC 2007–; mem. Chief of Naval Operations Exec. Panel (fed. advisory comm. for head of USN); fmr Contributing Ed., Nat. Review magazine; fmr Consultant, ABC News; mem. Young Pres.s' Org. (YPO); Life Mem. Council of Foreign Relations, Veterans of Foreign Wars; Founding mem. Henry Crown Fellows, Aspen Inst. 1997; Trustee IISS, Cttee on Econ. Devt in the US; fmr mem. Bd, Foreign Policy Research Inst., Univ. of Philadelphia; Bronze Star, Operation Desert Storm 1991. *Publications:* Blue Helmets: The Strategy of UN Military Operations 1998, Future Visions for US Defense Policy (ed.) 2001; numerous articles in leading journals and newspapers. *Address:* Global Strategies Group (USA) LLC, 1667 K Street, NW, Washington, DC 20006, USA. *Telephone:* (202) 223-4399 (office). *Website:* www .globalgroup.com (office).

HILLER, István, PhD; Hungarian academic and politician; b. 7 May 1964, Sopron; m. Julianna Hillerné Farkas; two c.; ed Eötvös Loránd Univ., Karls-Ruprecht Univ., Germany; Asst Lecturer, Eötvös Loránd Univ. 1989–94, Sr Lecturer 1994–2001, Prof. 2001–02; Founding mem. Hungarian Socialist Party (MSZP) 1989, Deputy Pres. MSZP Nat. Bd 1998–, Vice-Pres. MSZP 2003–04, Pres. 2005–07; mem. Parl. 2002–; Parl. State Sec., Ministry of Educ. 2002–03; Minister of Cultural Heritage 2003–05, of Educ. and Culture 2006–10; Researcher, Historical Inst., Univ. of Vienna 1995, 1997; Chevalier, Ordre des Arts et des Lettres, Cavaliere di Gran Croce (Italy), Große Verdienstkreuz (Germany); Professor of the Year, Eötvös Loránd Univ. 1999. *Address:* c/o Ministry of Education and Culture, 1055 Budapest, Szalay u. 10–14, Hungary (office). *Website:* www.hiller.hu (office).

HILLER, Susan, MA; American/British artist; b. 7 March 1940, New York City; d. of Paul Hiller and Florence Ehrich; m. David Coxhead 1962; one s.; ed Smith Coll. and Tulane Univ.; Residency, Karolyi Foundation, Vence, France 1968, Ministère des Beaux Arts, Morocco 1969; moved to UK 1969; Lecturer, Slade School of Art, London 1982–91; Artist-in-Residence, Univ. of Sussex 1975; Distinguished Visiting Prof. of Fine Art, California State Univ., Long Beach 1988; Visiting Arts Council Chair., UCLA 1991, 1992; Prof. of Art, Dept of Fine and Applied Arts, Univ. of Ulster, Belfast 1986–91; Baltic Prof. of Fine Art, Univ. of Newcastle 1999–2002; Residency, Couvent des Recollets, Paris 2005; works in public collections, including Tate Gallery, London, Ludwig Museum, Cologne, Israel Museum, Jerusalem, Arts Council of GB, Henie-Onstad Kunstsenter, Oslo, Tokyo Metropolitan Museum of Photography, Victoria & Albert Museum, London, Seibu Saison Corpn, Japan, Nat. Gallery of Art of S Australia, Adelaide, Henry Moore Sculpture Collection, Leeds City Museum and Art Gallery, Imperial War Museum, London, Contemporary Art Soc., London, Museum of London, MAG Collection, Ferens Museum and Art Gallery, Hull, John Creasy Collection, Salisbury, UK; Hon. Fellow, Dartington Coll. of Arts 1998; Gulbenkian Foundation Visual Artist's Award 1976, 1977, Greater London Arts Asscn Bursary 1981, Nat. Foundation for the Arts Fellowship (USA) 1982, Visual Arts Board Travelling Fellowship (Australia) 1982, Guggenheim Fellowship 1998, DAAD Fellowship, Berlin 2002, Kulturstiftung des Bundes, Halle, Germany 2003. *Art works include:* Hand Grenades 1969–72, Dedicated to the Unknown Artists 1972–76, Measure by

Measure 1973–, Sisters of Menon 1972, Dream Mapping 1974, Monument 1980–81, Midnight Self Portraits 1980–89, Inside a Cave Home 1983, Belshazzar's Feast 1983–84, Magic Lantern 1987, The Secrets of Sunset Beach 1987, An Entertainment 1990–91, From the Freud Museum 1991–97, Wild Talents 1997, Split Hairs: The Art of Alfie West 1998, Psi Girls 1999, Witness 2000, What every gardener knows 2003, Clinic 2004, The J Street Project: Film Index 2002–05, Psychic Archaeology 2005. *Publications include:* The Myth of Primitivism (ed.) 1991, After the Freud Museum 1995, Dreams – Visions of the Night (co-author) 1996, Thinking about Art: Conversations with Susan Hiller 1996, Dream Machines 1999, Witness 2000, Split Hairs: The Art of Alfie West (with David Coxhead) 2004. *Address:* 83 Loudoun Road, London, NW8 0DQ, England (office). *Telephone:* (20) 7372-0438 (office). *E-mail:* studioassist@artesian.org.uk (office). *Website:* www .susanhiller.org (office).

HILLIER, Bevis, FRSA, FRSL; British writer and editor; b. 28 March 1940, Redhill, Surrey; s. of the late Jack Ronald Hillier and of Mary Louise Palmer; ed Reigate Grammar School, Magdalen Coll., Oxford; Editorial Staff, The Times 1963–68, Antiques Corresp. 1970, Deputy Literary Ed. 1980–82; Ed. British Museum Soc. Bulletin 1968–70; Guest Curator, Minn. Inst. of Arts 1971; Ed. The Connoisseur 1973–76; Co-founder and Chair., The Twentieth-Century Soc. (fmrly The Thirties Soc.) 1979; Exec. Ed., Sunday Telegraph magazine 1982–83, Features Ed. 1983–84; Columnist and Assoc. Ed., Los Angeles Times 1984–88; Ed. Sotheby's Preview 1990–93; Vice-Pres., Betjeman Soc. 1988–2006, Pres. 2006–; Hon. DLitt (Univ. of Winchester) 2009. *Publications:* Master Potters of the Industrial Revolution: The Turners of Lane End 1965, Pottery and Porcelain 1700–1914 1968, Art Deco of the 1920s and the 1930s 1968, Posters 1969, Cartoons and Caricatures 1970, The World of Art Deco 1971, 100 Years of Posters 1972, Austerity-Binge 1975, Art Deco Style, A Tonic to the Nation: The Festival of Britain (co-ed.) 1951 1976, The New Antiques 1977, Greetings from Christmas Past 1982, The Style of the Century 1900–1980 1983, John Betjeman: A Life in Pictures 1984, Young Betjeman 1988, Early English Porcelain 1992, John Betjeman: New Fame, New Love 2002, Betjeman: The Bonus of Laughter 2004, John Betjeman: The Biography 2006, The Wit and Wisdom of G K Chesterton 2010. *Leisure interests:* piano, collecting, awarding marks out of ten for suburban front gardens. *Address:* Maggie Noach Literary Agency, 7 Peacock Yard, Iliffe Street, London, SE17 3LH, England (office). *Telephone:* (20) 7708-3073 (office). *E-mail:* info@mnla.co.uk (office). *Website:* www.mnla.co.uk (office).

HILLIER, Gen. (retd) Rick J., BSc; Canadian army officer (retd); b. Newfoundland and Labrador; m.; two s.; ed Memorial Univ. of Newfoundland; posted to 8th Canadian Hussars 1976, Royal Canadian Dragoons 1979; staff officer, Army HQ, Montréal, Nat. Defence HQ, Ottawa; Canadian Deputy Commdg Gen. 1998–2000; Commdr Multinational Div. (Southwest), Bosnia-Herzegovina; Asst Chief of the Land Staff –2003, Chief of the Land Staff 2003–05, Chief of Defence Staff 2005–08; Commdr Int. Security Assistance Force, Kabul, Afghanistan Feb.–Aug. 2004; Chancellor, Memorial Univ. of Newfoundland 2008–, co-f. Project Hero (scholarship programme) 2009; Chair. TELUS Atlantic Canada Community Bd 2008–; Strategic Advisor, Gowling Lafleur Henderson LLP, (law firm), Ottawa 2009–. *Address:* Gowling Lafleur Henderson LLP, 160 Elgin Street, Suite 2600, Ottawa, ON K1P 1C3, Canada (office). *Telephone:* (613) 233-1781 (office). *Fax:* (613) 563-9869 (office). *Website:* www.gowlings.com (office); www.generalhillier.com.

HILLS, Carla Anderson, AB, LLD; American lawyer and fmr government official; *Chairman and CEO, Hills and Company;* b. 3 Jan. 1934, Los Angeles; d. of Carl Anderson and Edith Anderson (née Hume); m. Roderick Maltman Hills 1958; one s. three d.; ed Stanford Univ., Calif., St Hilda's Coll., Oxford, UK, Yale Law School; Asst US Attorney, Civil Div., LA, Calif. 1958–61; Pnr, Munger, Tolles, Hills & Rickershauser (law firm) 1962–74; Adjunct Prof., School of Law, UCLA 1972; Asst Attorney-Gen. Civil Div., US Dept of Justice 1974–75; Sec. of Housing and Urban Devt 1975–77; Pnr, Latham, Watkins & Hills (law firm) 1978–86, Weil, Gotshal and Manges, Washington 1986–88; Mudge Rose Gutherie Alexander & Ferdon 1994; Chair., CEO Hills & Co. (consulting firm) 1993–; US Trade Rep., Exec. Office of the Pres. 1989–93; Co-Chair. Alliance to Save Energy 1977–89; Vice-Chair. Bar of Supreme Court of the US, Calif. State and DC Bars, Council Section of Anti-trust Law, ABA 1974, American Law Inst. 1974–, Fed. Bar Asscn (LA Chapter, Pres. 1963), Women Lawyers Asscn (Pres. 1964), LA Co. Bar Asscn, Chair. of various cttees including Standing Cttee on Discipline, Calif. 1970–74; mem. Bd Dirs American Int. Group (AIG), Lucent Technologies Inc., Bechtel Enterprises, Trust Co. of the West Group Inc., AOL Time-Warner Inc. 1993–2006, Chevron Corp. 1993–; mem. Carnegie Comm. on the Future of Public Broadcasting 1977–78, Sloan Comm. on Govt and Higher Educ. 1977–79, Advisory Cttee Woodrow Wilson School of Public and Int. Affairs 1977–80, Yale Univ. Council 1977–80, Fed. Accounting Standards Advisory Council 1978–80, Trilateral Comm. 1977–82, 1993–, American Cttee on East–West Accord 1977–79, Int. Foundation for Cultural Cooperation and Devt 1977, Editorial Bd, Nat. Law Journal 1978, Calif. Gov.'s Council of Econ. Policy Advisers 1993–, Council on Foreign Relations 1993–; Co-Chair. Int. Advisory Bd, Center for Strategic and Int. Studies; Chair. Nat. Cttee on US-China Relations 1993–; Contributing Ed. Legal Times 1978–88; Fellow, American Bar Foundation 1975; Trustee, Pomona Coll. 1974–79, Norton Simon Museum of Art 1976–80, Brookings Inst. 1977, Univ. of Southern Calif. 1977–78; Advisor, Annenberg School of Communications, Univ. of Southern Calif. 1977–78; Chair. Urban Inst. 1983; Dir Time Warner 1993–2006, AIG –2006; Vice-Chair. Interamerican Dialogue 1997–; mem. Bd Trustees Asia Soc., Inst. for Int. Econs, Americas Soc.; Dr hc (Pepperdine Univ.) 1975, (Washington Univ., St Louis, Mo.) 1977, (Mills Coll., Calif.) 1977, (Lake Forest Coll.) 1978, (Williams Coll.), (Notre Dame Univ.), (Wabash Coll.). *Publications:* Federal Civil Practice (co-author) 1961, Antitrust Adviser (ed. and co-author) 1971. *Leisure interest:* tennis. *Address:* Hills & Company, 1120 20th Street NW, Suite 200 North, Washington, DC 20036 (office); 3125 Chain Bridge Road NW, Washington, DC 20016, USA (home). *Telephone:* (202) 822-4700 (office). *Fax:* (202) 822-4710 (office). *E-mail:* CAHills@hillsandco.com (office). *Website:* www.hillsandco.com (office).

HILLY, Hon. Francis Billy, BA; Solomon Islands business executive and politician; b. 20 July 1948, Emu Harbour, Rannoga; ed King George VI Secondary School, Univ. of the South Pacific; joined pre-independence govt working under Solomon Mamaloni; later worked for a pvt. co. in Gizo; mem. Parl. for Ranogga/ Simbo Constituency 1976–84, 1993–, Chair. Public Accounts Cttee 2004–05, Parl.

House Cttee 2006–07; fmr Premier of Western Prov.; Prime Minister of the Solomon Islands 1993–94; Leader of the Opposition 1994–95, 2004–06; govt-nominated cand. for position of Prime Minister June 2000; Minister for Commerce, Industry and Employment May–Aug. 2006 (dismissed), 2007–10, for Finance and Treasury May–Aug. 2010; also served for periods as Minister for Home Affairs and as Minister for Health and Medical Services and Deputy Prime Minister. *Address:* c/o Ministry for Finance and Treasury, PO Box 26, Honiara, Solomon Islands (office).

HILMER, Frederick G., AO, LLB, LLM, MBA; Australian university administrator and academic; *President and Vice-Chancellor, University of New South Wales;* ed Sydney Univ., Univ. of Pennsylvania, Wharton School of Finance, USA; mem. Higher Educ. Council 1987–93; Dean and Prof. of Man., Australian Grad. School of Man., Univ. of New South Wales 1989–98, Pres. and Vice-Chancellor Univ. of New South Wales 2006–; CEO John Fairfax Holdings Ltd 1998–2005; fmr Chair. Commonwealth Higher Educ. Council; Chair. Nat. Competition Policy Review Cttee 1992–93, Group of Eight (Go8, coalition of Australia's leading research univs) 2011–, U21 (global network of research-intensive univs) 2013–; fmr Joseph Wharton Fellow, Wharton School of Finance; Fellow Hon. mem. CPA Australia 2010; John Storey Medal, Australian Inst. of Man. 1991. *Publications:* several books, including When The Luck Runs Out: The Future for Australians at Work 1985, New Games/New Rules: Work in Competitive Enterprises 1989, Strictly Boardroom: Improving Governance to Enhance Company Performance 1993, Management Redeemed: Debunking the Fads that Undermine Our Corporations (co-author) 1996, The Fairfax Experience – What the Management Texts Didn't Teach Me 2007; articles in the fields of gen. man., industrial relations, and competition law and policy. *Address:* Office of the President and Vice-Chancellor, University of New South Wales, Sydney, NSW 2052, Australia (office). *Telephone:* (2) 9385-2788 (office). *Fax:* (2) 9385-1949 (office). *E-mail:* vice-chancellor@unsw .edu.au (office). *Website:* www.unsw.edu.au (office).

HILSKÝ, Martin, PhD; Czech translator, reciter and academic; *Professor of English Literature, Charles University;* b. 8 April 1943, Prague; s. of Václav Hilský and Vlasta Hilská; m. Kateřina Hilská; two s. one d.; ed Charles Univ., Prague, Univ. of Oxford, UK; Asst Prof., Charles Univ., Prague 1965, Prof. of English Literature 1993–, Dir Inst. of English & American Studies 1988–98; Jr Research Fellow, Univ. of Oxford 1968–69; mem. Czech Modern Language Asscn (Chair. 1993–96), European Soc. for Study of English, PEN Club; also performer at Czech Radio 3, Vltava, Czech TV; Hon. OBE 2001, Hon. MBE 2002; IREX grant, USA 1985, Jungmann Translation Prize 1997, Tom Stoppard Award 2003. *Achievements:* Shakespeare translations performed throughout the Czech Repub. *Publications:* Současný britský román (Contemporary British Fiction) (Rector's Prize) 1991, Modernisté (The Modernists 1995), Od Poea k postmodernismu (essays) (From Poe to Postmodernism 1993), Od slavíka k papouškovi (co-author, essays) (Nightingales and Parrots 2003), Když ticho mluví (Languages of Silence 2007), Rozbité zrcadlo (The Broken Mirror 2009), Shakespeare a jeviště svět (Shakespeare and Theatrum Mundi 2011); over 80 papers on English and American literature; translations of Shakespeare (plays and poems), Thornton Wilder's Our Town 1978, Peter Shaffer's Amadeus 1981, James Goldman's Lion in Winter 1988, Peter Barnes's Red Noses 1991, J. M. Synge's The Playboy of the Western World 1996; Complete Works of Shakespeare (in Czech) 2011; Ed. dual language edn of Shakespeare plays and poems (six vols). *Leisure interests:* literature, theatre, arts, good wine, skiing, jogging, gardening. *Address:* Room 110, Department of English and American Studies, Faculty of Philosophy and Arts, Charles University, Jana Palacha 2, 116 38 Prague (office); Tychonova 10, 160 00 Prague 6, Czech Republic (home). *Telephone:* (2) 221619341 (office); (2) 607560926 (home). *E-mail:* hilsky@ volny.cz (office). *Website:* ualk.ff.cuni.cz/staff/martin-hilsky.

HILSUM, Cyril, CBE, PhD, FRS, FREng, FIET, FIEEE; British research scientist and academic; *Visiting Professor, University College London;* b. 17 May 1925, London, England; s. of Ben Hilsum and Ada Hilsum; m. Betty Hilsum 1947 (died 1987); one d. (one d. deceased); ed Raines School, London and Univ. Coll., London; HQ Admiralty 1945–47; Admiralty Research Lab., Teddington 1947–50; Services Electronics Research Lab., Baldock 1950–64; Royal Signals and Radar Establishments, Malvern 1964–83; Visiting Prof., Univ. Coll., London 1988–; Chief Scientist, Gen. Electric Co. (GEC) Research Labs 1983–85; Dir of Research, GEC PLC 1985–92, Corp. Research Adviser 1992–; Pres. Inst. of Physics 1988–90; mem. Science and Eng Research Council 1984–88; Fellow, Royal Acad. of Eng, Inst. of Eng and Tech.; Hon. FInstP; Hon. DEng (Sheffield) 1992, (Nottingham Trent) 1998; recipient of several awards. *Publications:* Semiconducting III-V Compounds 1961; over 100 scientific and tech. papers. *Leisure interests:* tennis, chess, ballroom dancing. *Address:* 12 Eastglade, Pinner, Middx, HA5 3AN, England. *Telephone:* (20) 8866-8323. *E-mail:* cyrilhilsum@aol.com.

HILSUM, Lindsey, BA (Hons); British journalist; *International Editor, Channel 4 News (UK);* b. 3 Aug. 1958; d. of Cyril Hilsum and Betty Hilsum; ed Univ. of Exeter; joined Oxfam working in Guatemala and Haiti 1979; began journalism career freelance reporting from Mexico and the Caribbean 1980; worked for three years as Information Officer for UNICEF, Nairobi; covered events in E Africa for BBC and The Guardian newspaper 1986–89; Sr Producer, BBC World Service 1990–93, reported from Rwanda, Middle East, Mexico, S Africa, S Pacific; Diplomatic Corresp., Channel 4 News 1996–2003, Int. Ed. 2003–, China Corresp. 2006–08; regular contrib. to Granta, Observer, Sunday Times; Amnesty International Awards 1997, 2004, TV News Award 2004, Royal Television Soc. Specialist Journalist of the Year 2003, Emmy Award for coverage of fall of Saddam Hussein (co-recipient) 2004, Royal Television Soc. TV Journalist of the Year Award 2005, James Cameron Award 2005, Women in Film and Television Award 2005, Foreign Press Asscn Award 2010, Charles Wheeler Award 2011, One World Journalist of the Year 2011, Political Studies Asscn Award 2011. *Publication:* Sandstorm: Libya in the Time of Revolution 2012. *Leisure interests:* bird watching, horse riding. *Address:* c/o Knight Ayton Management, 35 Great James Street, London, WC1N 3HB, England (office); Channel 4 News, ITN, 200 Grays Inn Road, London, WC1X 8XZ, England (office). *Telephone:* (20) 7831-4400 (office); (20) 7430-4606 (office). *Fax:* (20) 7831-4455 (office); (20) 7430-4607 (office). *E-mail:* sueayton@knightayton.co.uk (office); c4foreign@itn.co.uk (office). *Website:* knightayton.co.uk (office); www.channel4.com/news (office).

HILTON, Janet, ARNCM, FRCM; British clarinettist; *Professor of Clarinet, Royal College of Music;* b. 1 Jan. 1945, Liverpool, England; d. of H. Hilton and E. Hilton; m. David Richardson 1968; two s. (one deceased) one d.; ed Belvedere School, Liverpool, Royal Northern Coll. of Music, Vienna Konservatorium; BBC concerto debut 1963; appearances as clarinet soloist with major British orchestras including Royal Liverpool Philharmonic, Scottish Nat., Scottish Chamber, City of Birmingham Symphony Orchestra (CBSO), Bournemouth Symphony, Bournemouth Sinfonietta, City of London Sinfonia, BBC Scottish and Welsh Symphony, BBC Philharmonic; guest at Edinburgh, Aldeburgh, Bath, Cheltenham, City of London Festivals, BBC Henry Wood Promenade concerts; appearances throughout Europe and N America; Prin. Clarinet Scottish Chamber Orchestra 1974–80, Kent Opera 1984–88; teacher Royal Scottish Acad. of Music and Drama 1974–80, Royal Northern Coll. of Music 1983–87; Head of Woodwind, Birmingham Conservatoire 1992–; Prof. of Clarinet, Royal Coll. of Music, London 1998–, Head of Woodwind 1998–2010; Prof., Univ. of Central England 1993; Dir Camerata Wind Soloists; several recordings for Chandos, including all of Weber's music for clarinet with the CBSO, Lindsay Quartet and Keith Swallow, the Nielsen and Copland Concertos with the Scottish Nat. Orchestra, Stanford Clarinet Concerto with Ulster Orchestra, Mozart Clarinet Quintet with the Lindsay Quartet 1998; works composed for her by Iain Hamilton, John McCabe, Edward Harper, Elizabeth Maconchy, Alun Hoddinott, Malcolm Arnold; Reger Clarinet Sonatas with Jakob Fichert, piano 2009; int. master classes in Paris, Vienna, Wrocław, Singapore, Hong Kong, USA (Chicago, Indiana and Michigan); Hon. Fellow, Birmingham Conservatoire 2009. *Recordings:* Dedications—concertos by McCabe, Harper, Maconchy and Hoddinott with BBC Scottish Symphony Orchestra, Reger Clarinet Sonatas with Jakob Fichert, piano. *Leisure interests:* cookery, reading. *Address:* Royal College of Music, Prince Consort Road, London, SW7 2BS (office); Holte End, Whitehall Lane, Checkendon, RG8 0TN, England (home). *Telephone:* (1491) 682853 (home). *E-mail:* jhilton@rcm.ac.uk (office). *Website:* www.impulse-music.co .uk/hilton.htm (home).

HIMELFARB, Alexander (Alex), PhD; Canadian sociologist, academic and diplomatist; *Director, The Glendon School of Public and International Affairs, York University;* b. 1947; m. Frum Himelfarb; ed Univ. of Toronto; Prof. of Sociology, Univ. of New Brunswick 1972–81; Head, Unified Family Court Project, Dept of Justice 1979–81; joined Dept of Solicitor-Gen. 1981, held several positions including Dir-Gen. Planning and Systems Group; other public service posts have included Exec. Dir Nat. Parole Bd, Asst Sec. to Cabinet for Social Policy Devt, Privy Council Office, Assoc. Sec. Treasury Bd, Head, Fed. Task Force on Social Union; Deputy Minister of Canadian Heritage 1999–2002; Clerk of Privy Council and Sec. to Cabinet 2002–06; Amb. to Italy 2006–09 (also accred to Albania and San Marino and as High Commr to Malta); Dir The Glendon School of Public and Int. Affairs, York Univ. 2009–. *Address:* The Glendon School of Public and International Affairs, York University, 2275 Bayview Avenue, Toronto, ON M4N 3M6, Canada (office). *Telephone:* (416) 487-6706 (office). *E-mail:* publicaffairs@ glendon.yorku.ca (office). *Website:* www.glendon.yorku.ca (office); www.alexsblog .ca.

HIMMELFARB, Gertrude, PhD, FBA, FRHistS; American historian, academic and writer; *Professor Emeritus, City University of New York;* b. 8 Aug. 1922, New York; d. of Max Himmelfarb and Bertha Himmelfarb (née Lerner); m. Irving Kristol 1942; one s. one d.; ed Brooklyn Coll., City University of New York, Univ. of Chicago, Girton Coll., Cambridge; Distinguished Prof. of History, Graduate School, CUNY 1965–88, Prof. Emer. 1988–; Fellow, American Philosophical Soc., American Acad. of Arts and Sciences, Royal Historical Soc.; Fellow, Guggenheim Foundation 1955–56, 1957–58, Nat. Endowment for the Humanities 1968–69, American Council of Learned Socs 1972–73, Rockefeller Foundation 1980–81, American Acad. of Arts and Sciences; Fellow, Woodrow Wilson Int. Center 1976–77, Trustee, 1985–96; numerous hon. degrees including Hon. DHumLitt (Boston) 1987, (Yale) 1990, Hon. DLitt (Smith Coll.) 1977; Rockefeller Foundation Award 1962–63, Nat. Humanities Medal 2004. *Publications:* Lord Acton: A Study in Conscience and Politics 1952, Darwin and the Darwinian Revolution 1959, Victorian Minds 1968, On Liberty and Liberalism: The Case of John Stuart Mill 1975, The Idea of Poverty 1984, Marriage and Morals Among the Victorians 1986, The New History and the Old 1987, Poverty and Compassion: The Moral Imagination of the Late Victorians 1991, On Looking Into the Abyss: Untimely Thoughts on Culture and Society 1994, The De-Moralization of Society from Victorian Virtues to Modern Values 1995, One Nation, Two Cultures 1999, The Road to Modernity: The British, French and American Enlightenments 2004, The Moral Imagination 2006, The Jewish Odyssey of George Eliot 2009, The People of the Book: Philosemitism in England, from Cromwell to Churchill 2011; ed: Essay on Population (by Thomas Robert Malthus) 1960, Essays on Politics and Culture (by John Stuart Mill) 1962, On Liberty (by John Stuart Mill) 1974, Memoir on Pauperism (by Alexis de Tocqueville) 1997, Jews and Gentiles (by Milton Himmelfarb) 2007, The Spirit of the Age: Victorian Essays 2007, The Neoconservative Persuasion (by Irving Kristol) 2011. *Address:* 2510 Virginia Avenue, NW, Washington, DC 20037-1902, USA (home).

HINAULT, Bernard; French fmr professional cyclist; b. 14 Nov. 1954, Yffiniac, Côtes du Nord; s. of Joseph and Lucie (Guernion) Hinault; m. Martine Lessard 1974; two s.; competitive cycling début 1971; French jr champion 1972; French champion 1978; world champion 1980, third 1981; winner, Tour de France 1978, 1979, 1981, 1982, 1985, Tour d'Italie 1980, 1982, 1985, Tour d'Espagne 1978, 1983, Grand Prix des Nations 1978, 1982, 1984, Luis Puig Trophy 1986, Coors Classic, USA 1986 and many other int. racing events; retd from racing 1986; fmr Technical Adviser, fmr External Relations Dir Tour de France; fmr Sports Dir French team; fmr Dir-Gen. Ouest Levure; Chevalier, Légion d'honneur, Ordre Nat. du Mérite. *Publications:* Moi, Bernard Hinault (with others) 1979, Le Pentolou des souvenirs, Cyclisme sur route, technique, tactique, entraînement, Vélo tout terrain, découverte, technique et entraînement. *Address:* c/o Fédération française de cyclisme, Bâtiment Jean Monet, 5 rue de Rome, 93561 Rosny-sous-Bois, cedex; c/o Ouest Levure, 7 rue de la Sauvaie, 21 Sud-est, 35000 Rennes, France.

HINCH, Edward John, PhD, FRS; British academic; *Professor of Fluid Mechanics, University of Cambridge;* b. 4 March 1947, Peterborough; s. of Joseph Edward Hinch and Mary Grace Hinch (née Chandler); m. Christine Bridges 1969; one s. one d.; ed Univ. of Cambridge; Fellow, Trinity Coll., Cambridge 1971–; Asst

Lecturer, Univ. of Cambridge 1972–75, Lecturer 1975–94, Reader in Fluid Mechanics 1994–98, Prof. 1998–; Fellow, American Physical Soc. 1997–; Assoc. Ed. Letters of Physics of Fluids; mem. Editorial Bd Physics of Fluids, Journal of Non-Newtonian Fluid Mechanics, Granular Matter; Trustee, Isaac Newton Trust 2000–07; mem. Int. Science Cttee 2006, 2008, 2010; mem. EPSRC Coll. in Mathematics, Francqui Prize Cttee 2006; Chevalier, Ordre nat. du Mérite 1997; Dr hc (l'INP Toulouse) 2010 APS Fluid Dynamaics Prize 2010, Euromech Fluid Mechanics Prize 2010. *Publications:* Perturbation Methods 1991; various papers in learned journals on fluid mechanics and its application. *Address:* Department of Applied Mathematics and Theoretical Physics, Centre for Mathematical Sciences, Wilberforce Road, Cambridge, CB3 0WA (office); Trinity College, Cambridge, CB2 1TQ, England. *Telephone:* (12) 2333-7864 (office); (12) 2333-8427. *Fax:* (12) 2333-8564; (12) 2376-5900 (office). *E-mail:* e.j.hinch@damtp.cam.ac.uk (office); ejh1@cam.ac.uk (office). *Website:* www.damtp.cam.ac.uk (office).

HINCHCLIFFE, Peter Robert Mossom, CVO, CMG, MA; British diplomatist (retd) and academic; b. 9 April 1937, Mahableshwar, India; s. of Peter Hinchcliffe and Jeannie Hinchcliffe; m. Archbold Harriet Siddall 1965; three d.; ed Radley Coll., Trinity Coll., Dublin; British Army 1955–57; HMOCS, Aden Protectorate 1961–67; First Sec., FCO 1969–71; mem. UK Mission to UN 1971–74; Head of Chancery, British Embassy, Kuwait 1974–76, FCO 1976–78, Deputy High Commr, Dar es Salaam 1978–81, Consul Gen., Dubai 1981–85; Head of Information Dept, FCO 1985–87; Amb. to Kuwait 1987–90; High Commr in Zambia 1990–93; Amb. to Jordan 1993–97; Chair. Hutton and Paxton Community Council 2001–07; Adjunct Fellow, Curtin Univ., Perth, WA 2001–04; Sr Reseach Fellow, Queens Univ., Belfast 1997–2002; Hon. Fellow, Univ. of Edinburgh 1997–2009. *Publications:* Time to Kill Sparrows (anthology of diplomatic verse) 1999, History of Conflicts in the Middle East Since 1945 (third edn) 2007, Without Glory in Arabia: End of British Rule in Aden 1960–67 2006, Jordan: A Hashemite Legacy (2nd edn) 2009. *Leisure interests:* golf, cricket, hill walking, writing poetry. *Address:* Old Bakery, Willis Wynd, Duns, Scottish Borders, TD11 3AD, Scotland. *Telephone:* (1361) 883315.

HINCK, Walter, DPhil; German academic; *Professor of Modern German Language and Literature, University of Cologne;* b. 8 March 1922, Selsingen; s. of Johann Hinck and Anna Hinck (née Steffens); m. Sigrid Graupe 1957; one d.; ed Univ. of Göttingen; Prof. of Modern German Language and Literature, Literary Criticism, Univ. of Cologne 1964–; mem. Rheinisch-Westfälischen Akad. der Wissenschaften 1974– (Vice-Pres. 1986–87), Sektion Bundesrepublik Deutschland des Internationalen PEN-Clubs 1986–; Kasseler Literaturpreis 1992, Preis der Frankfurter Anthologie 2003. *Publications:* Die Dramaturgie des späten Brecht 1959, Das deutsche Lustspiel des 17. und 18. Jahrhunderts und die italienische Komödie 1965, Die deutsche Ballade von Bürger bis Brecht 1968, Das moderne Drama in Deutschland 1973, Von Heine zu Brecht—Lyrik im Geschichtsprozess 1978, Goethe—Mann des Theaters 1982, Germanistik als Literaturkritik 1983, Heinrich Böll: Ausgewählte Erzählungen 1984, Das Gedicht als Spiegel der Dichter 1985, Theater der Hoffnung, Von der Aufklärung bis zur Gegenwart 1988, Die Wunde Deutschland, Heinrich Heines Dichtung 1990, Walter Jens. Un homme de lettres 1993, Magie und Tagtraum. Das Selbstbild des Dichters in der deutschen Lyrik 1994, Geschichtsdichtung 1995, Im Wechsel der Zeiten: Leben und Literatur (autobiog.) 1998, Jahrhundertchronik, Deutsche Erzählungen des 20. Jahrhunderts 2000, Stationen der deutschen Lyrik von Luther bis in die Gegenwart. 100 Gedichte mit Interpretation 2000, Literatur als Gegenspiel. Essays zur deutschen Literatur von Luther bis Böll 2001, Selbstannäherungen. Autobiographien im 20. Jahrhundert von Elias Canetti bis Marcel Reich-Ranicki 2004, Romanchronik des 20. Jahrhunderts 2006, Wahmehmung des Lebens: Vom Schreiben im Nebenberuf 2008. *Address:* Reduitstr. 23, 76829 Landau/Pfalz, Germany. *Website:* www.walter-hinck.de.

HINDE, Robert Aubrey, CBE, BSc, MA, DPhil, ScD, FRS; British biologist, psychologist and academic; *Fellow, St John's College, University of Cambridge;* b. 26 Oct. 1923, Norwich; s. of Ernest B. Hinde and Isabella Hinde; m. 1st Hester Cecily Coutts (divorced); two s. two d.; m. 2nd Joan Stevenson 1971; two d.; ed Oundle School, St John's Coll., Cambridge, Balliol Coll., Oxford; pilot, RAF Coastal Command 1940–45; Curator, Ornithological Field Station, Dept of Zoology, Univ. of Cambridge 1950–64, Fellow, St John's Coll., Cambridge 1951–54, 1958–89, 1994–, Master 1989–94; Royal Soc. Research Prof. 1963–89; Hon. Dir MRC Unit of Devt and Integration of Behaviour 1970–89; Hitchcock Prof., Univ. of California 1979; mem. Academia Europaea 1990; Foreign Hon. mem. AAAS 1974; Hon. Fellow, American Ornithologists' Union 1976; Hon. Foreign Assoc. NAS 1978; Hon. Fellow, Royal Coll. of Psychiatry 1988, British Psychological Soc. 1981, Balliol Coll. Oxford 1986, Trinity Coll., Dublin 1990; Hon. FBA 2002; Hon. ScD (Univ. Libre, Brussels) 1974, (Nanterre) 1978, (Gothenburg) 1991; Dr hc (Stirling) 1991, (Edin.) 1992, (Western Ont.) 1996, (Oxford) 1998; Croonian Lecturer, Royal Soc. 1990, Frink Medal, Zoological Soc. of London 1992, Royal Medal, Royal Soc. 1996, Soc.'s Medal, Asscn for the Study of Animal Behaviour 1997 and numerous other awards. *Publications:* Animal Behaviour: A Synthesis of Ethology and Comparative Psychology 1966, Social Behaviour and Its Development in Sub-human Primates 1972, Biological Bases of Human Social Behaviour 1974, Towards Understanding Relationships 1979, Ethology 1982, Primate Social Behaviour 1983, Individuals, Relationships and Culture 1987, Relationships: A Dialectical Perspective 1997, Why Gods Persist 1999 (revised edn 2009), Why Good is Good 2002, War No More (co-author) 2003, Bending the Rules 2007, Ending War 2008; ed. or co-ed.: Bird Vocalizations (co-ed.) 1969, Short-term Changes in Neural Activity and Behaviour (co-ed.) 1970, Constraints on Learning (co-ed.) 1973, Growing Points in Ethology (co-ed.) 1976, Social Relationships and Cognitive Development (co-ed.) 1985, Relationships Within Families (co-ed.) 1988, Aggression and War: Their Biological and Social Bases (co-ed.) 1988, Education for Peace (co-ed.) 1991, Co-operation and Prosocial Behaviour (co-ed.) 1991, The Institution of War (ed.) 1991, War: A Cruel Necessity? (co-ed.) 1994; numerous articles in learned journals. *Leisure interests:* ornithology, reading, walking. *Address:* St John's College, Cambridge, CB2 1TP, England (office). *Telephone:* (1223) 339356 (office). *Fax:* (1223) 337720 (office). *E-mail:* rah15@cam.ac.uk (office). *Website:* www.joh.cam.ac.uk/contact/fellows (office).

HINDERY, Leo Joseph, Jr, MBA; American business executive; *Managing Partner, InterMedia Partners, LLP;* b. 31 Oct. 1947, Springfield, Ill.; s. of Leo

Joseph Hindery and E. Marie Whitener; m. 1st Deborah Diane Sale 1980; one d.; m. 2nd Patti Wheeler; one s.; ed Seattle Univ. and Stanford Univ. Business School; US Army 1968–70; Asst Treas., Utah Int., San Francisco 1971–80; Treas. Natomas Co., San Francisco 1980–82; Exec. Vice-Pres. Finance Jefferies and Co., LA 1982–83; Chief Finance Officer, AG Becker Paribas, New York 1983–85; Chief Officer, Planning and Finance, Chronicle Publishing Co., San Francisco 1985–88; Man. Gen. Pnr, Intermedia Partners, San Francisco 1988–97; Pres. TCI Cable Vision 1998–2000; Chair. and CEO Global Crossing Ltd March–Sept. 2000; Chair. The YES Network 2001–04; currently Man. Pnr, InterMedia Partners, LLP (investment firm); currently Exec.-in-Residence, Columbia Business School, Columbia Univ.; Chair. Economy/ Smart Globalization Initiative New America Foundation; Pres. HL Capital Inc.; fmr Chair. Nat. Cable TV Asscn; fmr Pres. and CEO Tele-Communications Inc. (now AT& T Broadband); Vice-Chair. HELP Comm. 2003–07; Sr Econ. Policy Advisor to presidential cand. John Edwards 2006–08; Econ. Advisor to Pres. Barack Obama; Co-Chair. Task Force on Jobs Creation; mem. Bd of Dirs Library of Congress Trust Fund, Minority Media & Telecommunications Council, Paley Center for Media and Teach for America, Daniels Fund, Global Business Council on HIV/AIDS, Milano School of New School Univ., Teach for America, Victory Junction Gang Camp, West Virginia Media Holdings LLC; mem. Bd of Visitors, Grad. School of Journalism, Columbia Univ.; Founder Jobs First 2012; mem. Bd Huffington Post Investigative Fund; mem. Council on Foreign Relations; Hon. mem. Bd of Dirs The Cable Center; Chapel of Four Chaplains Legion of Honor Award 2004; Hon. DHumLitt (Emerson Coll.), (Rabbinical Coll. of America); Foundation Award, Int. Radio and TV Soc. 1998, Executive Achievement Award, Nat. Asscn of Minorities in Cable 1998, President's Award 1998, Joel A. Berger Award 1998, Distinguished Vanguard Award for Leadership, Nat. Cable TV Asscn 1999, inducted into the Hall of Fame, Minority Media and Telecom Council 2002, Oates-Shrum Leadership Award, Gay and Lesbian Victory Fund 2002, Man of the Year Award, Kidney and Urology Foundation of America 2004, Chapel of Four Chaplains Legion of Honor Award 2004, Founders Award, Asia Society 2005. *Publications:* The Biggest Game of All 2003, It Takes a CEO 2005. *Leisure interest:* golf, racing. *Address:* InterMedia Advisors, LLC, 405 Lexington Avenue, 48th Floor, New York, NY 10174, USA (office). *Telephone:* (212) 503-2850 (office). *Website:* www.intermediaadvisors.com (office).

HINDLIP, 6th Baron of Hindlip in the County of Worcester and of Alsop-en-le-Dale in the County of Derby (cr. 1886); **Charles Henry Allsopp;** British business executive; b. 5 April 1940; s. of the late Baron Hindlip and Cecily Valentine Jane Borwick; m. Fiona Victoria Jean Atherley McGowan 1968; one s. three d.; ed Eton Coll.; served in Coldstream Guards 1959–62; joined Christie's 1962, Gen. Man. New York 1965–70, Chair. 1996–2002; fmr mem. Bd of Dirs Christie Manson & Wood, Deputy Chair. 1985–86, Chair. 1986–96; fmr Chair. Christie's Int. *Leisure interests:* painting, shooting, skiing. *Address:* c/o Christie's International Plc, 8 King St., St. James's, London, SW1Y 6QT; 32 Maida Avenue, London, W2 1ST; Lydden House, King's Stag, Sturminster Newton, Dorset, DT10 2AU, England.

HINDS, Samuel Archibald Anthony, BSc; Guyanese politician; *Prime Minister;* b. 27 Dec. 1943, Mahaicony, E Coast, Demerara; m. Yvonne Zereder Burnett 1967; three c.; ed Queen's Coll. Georgetown and Univ. of New Brunswick; various positions with Bauxite Co., Linden, Guyana 1967–92; mem. Science and Industry Cttee Nat. Science Research Council 1973–76; fmr Chair. Guyanese Action for Reform and Democracy (GUARD); Prime Minister of Guyana 1992–97, 1997–99, 2001–; also Minister of Public Works and Communication; leader CIVIC (special political movt of business people and execs). *Address:* Office of the Prime Minister, Oranapai Towers, Wights Lane, Georgetown (office); CIVIC, New Garden Street, Georgetown, Guyana. *Telephone:* 227-3101 (office). *Fax:* 226-7573 (office). *E-mail:* pmoffice@sdnp.org.gov.gy (office).

HINDUJA, Gopichand Parmanand; British (b. Indian) business executive; *Co-Chairman, Hinduja Group;* b. 29 Feb. 1940; s. of Parmanand Deepchand Hinduja and Jamuna Parmanand Hinduja; brother of Srichand Hinduja; m. Sunita Hinduja; two s. one d.; ed Jai Hind Coll., Mumbai; joined family business 1958; Pres. Hinduja Foundation and Hinduja Group of Cos 1962, now Co-Chair., Chair. Hinduja Automotive Limited, UK, Head of Hinduja Group Operations in Iran –1978; Chair. of Gurnanank Trust, Tehran; mem. Advisory Council, Hinduja Cambridge Trust 1991, Advisory Cttee Prince's Trust, Duke of Edin. Fellowship; Patron Balaji Temple, Swaminaryan Hindu Mission, London; Hon. LLD (Univ. of Westminster) 1996; Hon. DEcon (Richmond Coll.). *Leisure interests:* music, trekking, swimming. *Address:* Hinduja House, 171, Dr. Annie Besant Road, Worli, Mumbai 400 018 India (office). *Telephone:* (22) 24960707 (office). *E-mail:* gph@hindujagroup.com (office). *Website:* www.hindujagroup.com (office).

HINDUJA, Srichand Parmanand; Indian business executive; *Chairman, Hinduja Group;* b. 28 Nov. 1935, Shikarpur, Sindh (now in Pakistan); s. of Parmanand Deepchand Hinduja and Jamuna Parmanand Hinduja; brother of Gopichand Hinduja; m. Madhu Srichand Hinduja; two d.; ed Nat. Coll., Mumbai, Davar Coll. of Commerce, Mumbai; joined family business 1952, Chair. Hinduja Group of Cos 1962–, Chair. Hinduja Bank of Switzerland, Hinduja Foundations; Global Co-ordinator IndusInd 1962; Pres. IndusInd Int. Fed. 1996; mem. Advisory Council, Dharam Hinduja Indic Research Centres in Columbia, USA and UK, Advisory Council, Hinduja Cambridge Trust, Corpn of Mass. Gen. Hosp., Duke of Edinburgh's Award Fellowship; patron Centre of India–US Educ., Asia Soc.; Hon. LLD (Univ. of Westminster) 1996; Hon. DEcon (Richmond Coll.) 1997. *Publications include:* Indic Research and Contemporary Crisis 1995, Conceptualiser of Series of Paintings Theorama 1995, The Essence of Vedic Marriage For Success and Happiness 1996. *Leisure interests:* tennis, volleyball, cricket, Indian classical music. *Address:* Hinduja Group, Hinduja House, 171, Dr. Annie Besant Road, Worli, Mumbai 400 018, India (office). *Telephone:* (22) 24960707 (office). *Website:* www.hindujagroup.com (office).

HINE, Air Chief Marshal Sir Patrick, (Paddy), Kt, GCB, GBE, FRAeS, CBIM; British air force officer (retd); b. 14 July 1932, Chandlers Ford, Hants., England; s. of Eric Graham Hine and Cecile Grace Hine (née Philippe); m. Jill Adèle Gardner 1956; three s.; ed Peter Symonds School, Winchester; fighter pilot and mem. RAF 'Black Arrows' and 'Blue Diamonds' Formation Aerobatic Teams 1957–62; Commdr No. 92 Squadron 1962–64 and 17 Squadron 1970–71, RAF Germany Harrier Force 1974–75; Dir RAF Public Relations 1975–77; Asst Chief of Air Staff for Policy 1979–83; C-in-C RAF Germany and Commdr NATO's 2nd Allied Tactical Air Force 1983–85; Vice-Chief of the Defence Staff 1985–87; Air mem. for Supply and Org., Air Force Bd 1987–88; Air Officer Commdg-in-Chief, Strike Command, C-in-C UK Air Forces 1988–91; Jt Commdr British Forces in Gulf Conflict, Aug. 1990–April 1991; with reserve force, rank of Flying Officer 1991–; Mil. Adviser to British Aerospace 1992–99; defence and aerospace consultant 1999–2005; mem. Royal and Ancient Golf Club St Andrews 1995–, Capt. 2010–; mem. Sr Golfers Soc., RAF Club; Kt Grand Cross, Order of Bath 1989; Kt Grand Cross, Most Excellent Order of British Empire 1991; King of Arms of the Order of British Empire 1997–2010; England Boy Int. 1948, 1949, Hampshire Co. Championship 1949, Carris Trophy 1949, Brabazon Trophy 1949. *Television:* The Gulf War 1996. *Leisure interests:* golf, mountain walking, skiing, photography, caravanning, travel. *Address:* Royal and Ancient Golf Club, St Andrews, Fife, KY16 9JD, Scotland (office). *Telephone:* (13) 3446-0000 (office). *Fax:* (13) 3446-0001 (office). *Website:* www.randa.org (office).

HINGIS, Martina; Swiss professional tennis player; b. 30 Sept. 1980, Košice, Czechoslovakia; d. of Karol Hingis and Mélanie Molitor; competed in first tennis tournament 1985; family moved to Switzerland aged eight; winner French Open Jr championship 1993, Wimbledon Jr Championship 1994; turned professional and won first professional tournament Filderstadt (Germany) 1996; winner Australian Open 1997 (youngest winner of a Grand Slam title), 1998, 1999 (singles and doubles), beaten finalist 2000, 2001, 2002; won US Open 1997, beaten finalist 1998, 1999; Wimbledon singles champion 1997; Swiss Fed. Cup Team 1996–98; semifinalist US Open 2001; won 85 tournament titles, including five Grand Slam singles and ten doubles titles; elected to WTA Tour Players' Council 2002; retd 2002, returned to WTA Tour 2006; won Italian Open 2006; won Qatar Ladies Open, Doha 2007; retd 2007; with Lindsay Davenport, won Wimbledon Ladies' Invitation Doubles title 2011, 2012, 2013; won women's doubles with Sabine Lisicki, Sony Open, Miami 2014 (first title win since Doha 2007); spent a total of 209 weeks as World No. 1; took part in dancing competition Strictly Come Dancing on BBC TV, UK 2009; WTA Tour Most Impressive Newcomer 1995, Most Improved Player 1996, Player of the Year 1997, Associated Press Female Athlete of the Year 1997, selected as Player of the Year by WTA Tour, Int. Tennis Fed. and Tennis magazine 1997, BBC Overseas Sports Personality of the Year 1997, first female athlete to feature on cover of GQ men's magazine June 1998, WTA Tour Doubles Team of the Year with Jana Novotná 1998, WTA Tour Doubles Team of the Year with Anna Kournikova 1999, one of five female tennis players named to the 2000 Forbes magazine Power 100 in Fame and Fortune list at No. 51 2000, WTA Tour Diamond ACES Award 2000, elected to Tour Players' Council 2002, World Comeback of the Year Award, Laureus World Sports Awards 2006, Meredith Inspiration Award for inspiring women around the world, Family Circle Cup/Family Circle magazine 2007, inducted into International Tennis Hall of Fame 2013. *Leisure interests:* horse-riding, roller-blading, skiing, swimming, going to musicals. *Address:* c/o AM Seidenbaum 17, 9377 Truebbach, Switzerland.

HINGORANI, Narain G., PhD, DSc; Indian/American engineer and consultant; b. 15 June 1931, Pakistan; m. Joyce Hingorani; ed Baroda Univ., Univ. of Manchester Inst. of Science and Tech.; worked for Bombay Electricity Bd 1953–55; moved to UK to study 1955; Lecturer, Univs of Loughborough and Salford, UK 1960s; Sr Scientist, Bonneville Power Admin 1968–74; mem., later Vice-Pres. Electrical Systems Div., Electric Power Research Inst., Palo Alto, Calif. 1974–94; ind. consultant; mem. Nat. Acad. of Eng; Life Fellow, IEEE; considered father of flexible alternating current transmission systems (FACTS) and custom power innovations; IEEE Lamme Medal, Uno Lamm Award, IEEE Power Eng Soc., IEEE Power Eng Soc. renamed its FACTS and Custom Power Awards as the Nari Hingorani FACTS Award and the Nari Hingorani Custom Power Award 2004, Benjamin Franklin Inst. Bower Award and Prize for Achievement in Science 2006, Franklin Inst. Laureate 2006. *Publications include:* HVDC Transmission (co-author) 1960, Understanding FACTS Flexible AC Transmission (co-author) 2000. *Address:* 26480 Weston Drive, Los Altos Hills, CA 94022, USA (office). *Telephone:* (650) 941-5240 (home). *E-mail:* nhingorani@aol.com (home).

HINSHAW, Virginia S., BS, MS, PhD; American medical researcher, academic and university administrator; *Chancellor Emeritus and Professor of Tropical Medicine, Infectious Diseases and Pharmacology, University of Hawaii at Manoa;* m. Bill Hinshaw; two s.; ed Auburn Univ.; Clinical and Research Microbiologist, Medical Coll. of Virginia 1967–68; Research Virologist, Univ. of California, Berkeley 1974; Research Assoc., Div. of Virology, St Jude Children's Research Hosp., Memphis, Tenn. 1974–83, 1984–85; one year sabbatical, Harvard Medical School 1983–84; Assoc. Prof. of Virology, Dept of Pathobiological Sciences, School of Veterinary Medicine, Univ. of Wisconsin 1985–88, Prof. 1988–92, Interim Assoc. Dean, Research and Grad. Studies 1992–93, Assoc. Vice-Chancellor 1994–95, Vice-Chancellor, Research, Dean of Grad. School 1995–2001; Provost and Exec. Vice-Chancellor, Univ. of California, Davis 2001–07, also Prof. of Virology, Dept Internal Medicine, School of Medicine 2001–07, Prof. of Virology, Dept of Pathology, Microbiology, Immunology, School of Veterinary Medicine 2001–07; Chancellor, Univ. of Hawaii at Manoa 2007–12, Chancellor Emer. and Prof. of Tropical Medicine, Infectious Diseases and Pharmacology 2012–. *Address:* Department of Tropical Medicine, Medical Microbiology and Pharmacology, John A. Burns School of Medicine, 651 Ilalo Street, BSB 402F, Honolulu, HI 96813, USA (office). *Telephone:* (808) 692-1215 (office). *E-mail:* vhinshaw@hawaii .edu (office). *Website:* blog.hawaii.edu/tropicalmedicine (office).

HINSON, David R.; American airline executive; b. 2 March 1933; m. Ursula Hinson; three c.; fighter pilot, USN 1956–60, airline and eng pilot 1960–72; founder, Dir Midway Airlines Inc. 1979–91, Chair., CEO 1985–91; Admin. US Fed. Aviation Admin (FAA) 1993–96; Chair. Bd of Visitors, Air Safety Foundation, Aircraft Owners and Pilots Assen (AOPA); mem. Bd Nat. Air and Space Museum, Washington, DC; mem. Nat. Aeronautic Assen; Hon. mem. Advisory Bd Flight Safety Foundation; Operations Award, Aviation Week and Space Tech. 1997. *Leisure interests:* aviation history, collecting aviation art. *Address:* c/o Board of Visitors, Air Safety Foundation, AOPA, 421 Aviation Way, Frederick, MD 21701; c/o Board of Directors, National Air and Space Museum, 6th and Independence Avenue, SW, Washington, DC 20560, USA.

HINTERHÄUSER, Markus; Austrian conductor; b. 30 March 1958, La Spezia, Italy; ed Vienna Conservatory with Elisabeth Leonskaja, Mozarteum Univ. of Salzburg with Oleg Maisenberg; has performed as pianist in orchestral concerts, as recitalist and also in chamber concerts in major concert halls including Carnegie Hall, New York, the Muiskverein and Konzerthaus, Vienna, La Scala, Milan; festival appearances including Salzburg Festival, Schubertiade in Hohenems, Lucerne Festival, Wien Modern, Festival d'Automne, Holland Festival, Berlin Festival; performed with Arditti Quartet; worked with Brigitte Fassbaender as lied accompanist; known for interpretation of Second Viennese School and 20th century works, especially works by Luigi Nono, Karlheinz Stockhausen, Morton Feldman, John Cage, Galina Ustwolskaja and György Ligeti; worked with Christoph Marthaler, Johan Simons and Klaus Michael Grüber on music theatre productions; Co-founder, with Tomas Zierhofer-Kin, Zeitfluβ series as part of Salzburg Festival 1993–2001; fmr Artistic Dir Zeit-Zone Project, Vienna Festival; Concert Dir Salzburg Festival 2006–11, Artistic Dir 2011; apptd Dir Wiener Festwochen (Vienna Festival). *Recordings include:* several radio and TV record-ings and CDs of entire piano works of Schoenberg, Berg and Webern as well as compositions by Feldman, Nono, Scelsi, Ustvolskaya and Cage. *Address:* c/o Salzburger Festspiele, Hofstallgasse 1, 5020 Salzburg; Wiener Festwochen Lehárgasse 11, 1060 Vienna, Austria. *Telephone:* (662) 8045-0 (Salzburg); (1) 589-22-0 (Vienna). *Fax:* (1) 589-22-49 (Vienna). *E-mail:* info@salzburgfestival.at; festwochen@festwochen.at. *Website:* www.salzburgerfestspiele.at.

HINTIKKA, Jaakko, PhD; Finnish/American philosopher and academic; *Profes-sor of Philosophy, Boston University;* b. 2 Jan. 1929, Vantaa; ed Univ. of Helsinki; Jr Fellow, Harvard Univ. 1956–59; held professorial appointments at Univ. of Helsinki, Acad. of Finland and Fla State Univ.; mem. staff, Stanford Univ. 1965–82; Prof. of Philosophy, Boston Univ. 1990–; known as main architect of game-theoretical semantics and of interrogative approach to inquiry; Commdr Grand Cross, Order of the Lion of Finland 2011; Dr hc (Liège) 1984, (Jagiellonian Univ. of Kraków) 1995, (Uppsala) 2000, (Oulu) 2002, (Turku) 2003, (Bucharest) 2010; John Locke Lectureship, Univ. of Oxford 1964, Hägerström Lectureship, Uppsala Univ. 1983, Immanuel Kant Lectureship, Stanford Univ. 1985, Wihuri Int. Prize 1976, Guggenheim Fellowship 1979–80, Rolf Schock Prize in Logic and Philosophy 2005, Barwise Prize 2011. *Publications:* author or co-author of more than 30 books and monographs in nine languages; five vols of selected papers appeared 1996–2003; ed. or co-ed. 17 vols; more than 300 scholarly papers. *Address:* Department of Philosophy, Boston University, Office STH 502, 745 Commonwealth Avenue, Boston, MA 02215, USA (office). *Telephone:* (617) 353-2571 (office). *Fax:* (617) 353-6805 (office). *E-mail:* hintikka@bu.edu (office). *Website:* www.bu.edu/philo/people/faculty/full-time/jaakko-hintikka (office).

HINTON, Geoffrey E., BA, PhD, FRS, FRSC; British/Canadian computer scientist and academic; *Professor, Department of Computer Science, University of Toronto;* ed Univs of Cambridge and Edinburgh, UK; Research Fellow, Cognitive Studies Program, Univ. of Sussex, UK 1976–78; Visiting Scholar, Program in Cognitive Science, Univ. of California, San Diego, USA 1978–80, Visiting Asst Prof., Psychology Dept Jan.–June 1982; Scientific Officer, MRC Applied Psych-ology Unit, Cambridge 1980–82; Asst Prof. then Assoc. Prof., Computer Science Dept, Carnegie-Mellon Univ., Pittsburgh, USA 1982–87; Prof., Computer Science Dept, Univ. of Toronto, Canada 1987–98, 2001–, Univ. Prof. 2006–; Founding Dir Gatsby Computational Neuroscience Unit, University Coll., London 1998–2001; fmr mem. Editorial Bd Neural Computation, The Journal of Machine Learning Research; mem. Editorial Bd Artificial Intelligence, Cognitive Science, Machine Learning; Fellow, Canadian Inst. for Advanced Research 1987–98, 2004–(14), Asscn for the Advancement of Artificial Intelligence 1991, Cognitive Science Soc. 2003; Hon. Foreign mem. American Acad. of Arts and Sciences 2003; Hon. DSc (Edinburgh) 2001, (Sussex) 2011; David Marr Memorial Lecturer, King's Coll., Cambridge 1986, Weigand Lecturer, Univ. of Toronto 1987, Sun Annual Lecturer, Univ. of Manchester (eight lectures) 1989, Fourth Annual Hebb Lecturer, Dalhousie Univ., Halifax, NS 1989, St Andrews Easter Lecturer, Univ. of St Andrews (six lectures) 1991, Benjamin Meaker Lecturer, Univ. of Bristol (five lectures) 1992, Broadbent Lecturer, London 1993, Herzberg Lecturer, Ottawa 1993, Rockwood Memorial Lecture, Univ. of California, San Diego 1995, 1998, 2010, David E. Rumelhart Prize Lecturer, Edinburgh 2001, Pinkel Lecturer, Univ. of Pennsylvania 2003, Graham Lecturer, Univ. of Toronto 2006, Ian Howard Lecturer, York Univ. 2009, Ed Posner Lecturer, NIPS-09, Vancouver 2009, 'Big Thinkers' Lecturer, Yahoo, San Jose 2010, Hans-Lukas Teuber Lecturer, MIT 2010; Sr Award, IEEE Signal Processing Soc. 1990, ITAC/NSERC Award for Academic Excellence 1992, IEEE Neural Networks Pioneer Award 1998, The David E. Rumelhart Prize 2001, IJCAI Research Excellence Award 2005, Gerhard Herzberg Canada Gold Medal 2011, Killam Prize (co-recipient), Canada Council for the Arts 2012. *Publications:* Parallel Models of Associative Memory 1981 (revised second edn 1989), Proceedings of the Connectionist Models Summer School (co-ed.) 1988, Proceedings of the Connectionist Models Summer School (co-ed.) 1990, Connectionist Symbol Processing (special issue of the Journal of Artificial Intelligence issued as a book) 1991, Unsupervised Learning: Foundations of Neural Computation (co-ed.) 1999; numerous papers in professional journals. *Address:* Department of Computer Science University of Toronto, Pratt 290G, 6 King's College Road, Toronto, ON M5S 3G4, Canada (office). *Telephone:* (416) 978-7564 (office). *Fax:* (416) 978-1455 (office). *E-mail:* hinton@cs.toronto.edu (office). *Website:* www.cs.toronto.edu/~hinton (office).

HINZPETER KIRBERG, Rodrigo; Chilean lawyer and politician; b. 27 Oct. 1965, Santiago; m. Joyce Ventura Nudman; three s.; ed Pontifical Catholic Univ. of Chile; fmr Prof. of Civil Law, Pontifical Catholic Univ. of Chile; fmr consultant and dir of several cos; served as lawyer with Simpson Thacher & Bartlett, New York, USA; fmr Partner, Bofill Mir & Alvarez Jana Hinzpeter Abogados, Santiago; campaign manager for presidential cand. Sebastián Piñera 2005–06; Minister of the Interior 2010–11, of Interior and Public Security 2011–12, of Nat. Defence 2012–14; Founding-mem. Renovación Nacional, Nat. Sec. and First Vice-Pres. 2001–04, mem. Political Comm.; mem. Chilean Bar Asscn. *Publication:* La hipoteca 1993. *Address:* c/o Ministry of National Defence, Edif. Diego Portales 22°, Villavicencio 364, Santiago, Chile (office).

HIRAI, Kazuo (Kaz), BLibArts; Japanese entertainment industry executive; *President and CEO, Sony Corporation;* b. 22 Dec. 1960, Tokyo; ed Int. Christian Univ., Tokyo; hired at CBS/Sony Inc. (now Sony Music Entertainment (Japan) Inc.) 1984, involved in marketing int. music within Japan, promoted until Head of

Sony Computer Entertainment (int. business affairs office), joined Sony Computer Entertainment America 1995, Vice-Pres. Corp. Exec. Group 2006–07, Pres. Sony Computer Entertainment Inc. (SCEI) 2006–07, also COO SCEI 2006–07, Pres. and Group CEO SCEI 2007–11, Corp. Exec. Officer and Exec. Vice-Pres. Sony Corpn (following reorganization of electronics and game businesses into Consumer Products & Devices Group (CPDG) and Networked Products & Services Group (NPSG) 2009), concurrently Pres. NPSG 2009–11, Rep. Corp. Exec. Officer and Exec. Deputy Pres. Sony Corpn (following reorganization of consumer electronics, game and networked service businesses into Consumer Products & Services Group 2011) 2011–12, Pres. and CEO Sony Corpn 2012–; also Pres. Consumer Products & Services Group and Chair. SCEI, Chair. Sony Computer Entertainment 2011–; noted by Entertainment Weekly as one of the most powerful executives in the world 2006. *Address:* Sony Corporation, 1-7-1 Konan, Minato-ku, Tokyo 108-0075, Japan (office). *Telephone:* (3) 6748-2111 (office). *Fax:* (3) 6748-2244 (office). *E-mail:* info@sony.net (office). *Website:* www.sony.net (office).

HIRANO, Hirofumi; Japanese politician; *Minister of Education, Culture, Sports, Science and Technology;* b. 19 March 1949, Wakayama Pref.; ed Chuo Univ., Tokyo; joined Matsushita Electric Industrial Co. (now Panasonic Corpn) 1971, becoming Exec. mem. Matsushita Electric Union 1988–94; fmr Chief Sec. to Masao Nakamura (Socialist House of Reps mem.); Adviser to Japanese Electrical Electronic and Information Union; mem. House of Reps for Osaka No. 11 constituency 1996–, Sr Dir Parl. Cttee on Fundamental Nat. Policies; mem. Democratic Party of Japan (DPJ) 1998–, currently Deputy Sec.-Gen., Dir DPJ Bureau of Internal Affairs and Communications, DPJ Research Bureau, Deputy Chair. DPJ Admin Cttee, Diet Affairs Cttee; Chief Cabinet Sec. 2009–10; Minister of Educ., Culture, Sports, Science and Tech. 2012–. *Address:* Ministry of Education, Culture, Sports, Science and Technology, 3-2-2, Kasumigaseki, Chiyoda-ku, Tokyo 100-8959, Japan (office). *Telephone:* (3) 5253-4111 (office). *Fax:* (3) 3595-2017 (office). *Website:* www.mext.go.jp (office).

HIRANO, Hiroshi; Japanese insurance industry executive; Pres. Yasuda Fire and Marine Insurance Co. Ltd –2003, Pres. and CEO Sompo Japan Insurance Inc. (following merger) 2002–06; Pres. Sompo Japan Environment Foundation; Vice-Chair. Gen. Insurance Asscn of Japan; Dir Japan Telework Asscn. *Address:* c/o Sompo Japan Insurance Inc., 26-1 Nishi-Shinjuku 1-chome, Shinjuku-ku, Tokyo 160-8338, Japan (office).

HIRANO, Nobuyuki; Japanese business executive; *President, CEO and Representative Director, Mitsubishi UFJ Financial Group, Inc.;* joined The Mitsubishi Bank Ltd 1974, Non-Bd mem. Dir, The Bank of Tokyo-Mitsubishi Ltd (BTM) 2001–04, Exec. Officer, Mitsubishi Tokyo Financial Group, Inc. (MTFG) 2004–05, Non-Bd mem. Man. Dir BTM May–June 2005, Man. Dir BTM and Dir of MTFG June–Oct. 2005, Dir of Co. Oct. 2005–06, Man. Dir Bank of Tokyo-Mitsubishi UFJ Ltd (BTMU) 2006–08, Sr Man. Dir BTMU 2008–09, Deputy Pres. BTMU and Managing Man. of Co. 2009–10, Dir of Co. 2010–, Deputy Pres. of Co. 2010–12, Pres. BTMU and Dir of Co. 2012–13, Pres. and CEO Mitsubishi UFJ Financial Group, Inc. 2013–. *Address:* Mitsubishi UFJ Financial Group, Inc., 7-1, Marunouchi 2-chome, Chiyoda-ku, Tokyo 100-8330, Japan (office). *Telephone:* (3) 3240-8111 (office). *Fax:* (3) 3240-8203 (office). *E-mail:* info@mufg.jp (office). *Website:* www.mufg.jp (office).

HIRANO, Shin-ichi, BEng, MEng, DEng; Japanese university administrator; *President, National Institution for Academic Degrees and University Evaluation;* b. 7 Aug. 1942, Aichi Pref.; ed Nagoya Univ.; Research Assoc., Research Lab. of Eng Materials, Tokyo Inst. of Tech. 1970–76, Assoc. Prof. 1976–78; Assoc. Prof., School of Eng, Nagoya Univ. 1978–83, Prof. 1983–97, Prof., Grad. School of Eng 1997–2004, Dir Research Center for Advanced Energy Conversion 1999–2002, Dir Center for Cooperative Research in Advanced Science and Tech. 2002–03, Dean Grad. School of Eng and School of Eng 2003–04, Pres. Nagoya Univ. 2004–09; Pres. Nat. Inst. for Academic Degrees and Univ. Evaluation 2009–; Zhiyuan Prof., Special Pres. Advisory, Shanghai Jiao Tong Univ.; Einstein Chair Prof., Chinese Acad. of Sciences 2008; fmr Adjunct Prof. of Materials Science and Eng, Pennsylvania State Univ.; mem. Man. Council Insts of Natural Sciences; mem. World Acad. of Ceramics; ACerS Fellow, affiliated with Basic Science and Electronics Divs; Pres. Int. Ceramic Fed. 1997–99; fmr Pres. Asia-Oceania Ceramic Fed.; fmr Pres. Ceramic Soc. of Japan; Trustee, Japan Univ. Accreditation Asscn; Fellow, American Ceramic Soc. 1989, Distinguished Life mem. 2006–; Dr hc (Shanghai Jiao Tong Univ.); Soc. Award, Tokai Chemical Industry Soc. 1982, Soc. Award, Powder and Powder Metallurgy Soc. of Japan 1984, Academic Award, Ceramic Soc. of Japan 1986, Academic Award, Chemical Soc. of Japan 1989, Richard M. Fulrath Award, American Ceramic Soc. 1989, Memorial Award, Ceramic Soc. of Japan 1991, Int. Prize, Japanese Fine Ceramic Asscn 2000. *Publications:* numerous scientific papers in professional journals on inorganic materials chem. *Address:* National Institution for Academic Degrees and University Evaluation, 1-29-1 Gakuen-nishimachi Kodaira-shi, Tokyo 187-8587, Japan (office); School of Chemistry and Chemical Engineering, Shanghai Jiao Tong University (SJTU), Shanghai 200240, People's Republic of China. *Telephone:* (42) 307-1500 (office); (21) 34203058 (SJTU) (office). *Fax:* (42) 307-1552 (office). *Website:* www.niad.ac.jp (office); scce.sjtu.edu.cn:8000 (office).

HIRANO, Toshio, MD, PhD; Japanese medical scientist, academic and university administrator; ed Osaka Univ.; Visiting Fellow, NIH, USA 1973–76; mem. Medical Staff, Dept of Internal Medicine, Osaka Prefectural Habikino 1978–80; Assoc. Prof., Dept of Biochemistry, Inst. for Medical Immunology, School of Medicine, Kumamoto Univ. 1980–84; Assoc. Prof., Div. of Immunology, Inst. for Molecular and Cellular Biology, Osaka Univ. 1984–89, Prof., Div. of Molecular Oncology, Biomedical Research Centre, Faculty of Medicine 1989–2001, Dir Biomedical Research Centre 1997–99, Prof., Dept of Molecular Oncology (Lab. of Developmental Immunology), Grad. School of Medicine 2001–11, Prof., Lab. of Developmental Immunology, Grad. School of Frontier Biosciences 2002–11, mem. Council, Osaka Univ. 2003–04, 2007–08, Dean, Grad. School of Frontier Biosciences 2004–06, Prof., Lab. of Developmental Immunology, WPI Immunology Frontier Research Centre 2007–11, Dean, Grad. School of Medicine 2008–11, Pres. Osaka Univ. 2011–; mem. Science Council of Japan 2011–; mem. Council for Science and Tech. Policy, Cabinet Office 2012–14; Sandoz (now Novartis) Prize for Immunology (Switzerland) 1992, Osaka Science Prize (Japan) 1997, Academic Award, Mochida Memorial Foundation (Japan) 1998, Fujihara Award 2004,

Medical Award, Japan Medical Asscn 2005, The Emperor's Purple Ribbon Medal 2006, The Crafoord Prize 2009, Japan Prize 2011. *Achievements include:* discovery of the interleukin-6 (IL-6) gene 1986, clarification of the role of this gene in chronic inflammatory and auto-immune diseases. *Publications:* Signal Transducers and Activators of Transcription (STATs): Activation and Biology (co-ed.) 2003; several book chapters and more than 250 papers in peer-reviewed journals. *Address:* Office of the President, Osaka University, 1-1 Yamadaoka, Suita, Osaka 565-0871, Japan (office). *Telephone:* (6) 6850-6585 (office). *Fax:* (6) 6850-6589 (office). *E-mail:* hirano@ist.osaka-u.ac.jp (office). *Website:* www.osaka-u.ac.jp (office).

HIRANUMA, Takeo; Japanese politician; fmr Parl. Vice-Minister of Finance; Deputy Chair. LDP Policy Research Council, Chair. LDP Nat. Org. Cttee; mem. House of Reps; Minister of Transport 1995–96; Minister of Int. Trade and Industry 2000–01, of Economy, Trade and Industry 2001–03. *E-mail:* info@hiranuma.org. *Website:* www.hiranuma.org.

HIRAOKA, Hideo; Japanese lawyer and politician; *Minister of Justice;* b. 14 Jan. 1954; m.; two s.; ed Univ. of Tokyo; held various positions in Ministry of Finance 1976–88, including Section Chief Nat. Tax Agency Corp. Tax Dept, Dir-Gen. Tokai Finance Bureau, Dir-Gen. Tokyo Regional Taxation Bureau; fmr Counsellor, Cabinet Legislation Bureau; fmr First Sec., Embassy in Delhi; admitted to the bar 1998; mem. House of Reps (Democratic Party of Japan) for Yamaguchi No 2 Dist 2000–; fmr Sr Vice Minister of Internal Affairs, Sr Vice Minister for Cabinet Office 2010, Sec. of State for Internal Affairs and Communications 2010–11, Minister of Justice 2011–. *Leisure interest:* Igo (traditional board game). *Address:* Ministry of Justice, 1-1-1, Kasumigaseki, Chiyoda-ku, Tokyo 100-8977, Japan (office). *Telephone:* (3) 3580-4111 (office). *Fax:* (3) 3592-7011 (office). *E-mail:* webmaster@moj .go.jp (office). *Website:* www.moj.go.jp (office); www.hiraoka-hideo.jp.

HIRASHIMA, Osamu; Japanese construction industry executive; Pres. and CEO Taisei Corpn 2000, Chair. –2007, fmr Sr Advisor and Rep. Dir; Chair. Japan Fed. of Construction Contractors 2001–04; fmr Vice-Chair. Bd of Councillors, Japan Fed. of Econ. Orgs (KEIDANREN); fmr mem. Bd of Dirs Japan Productivity Center for Socio-Econ. Devt (JPC-SED), Japan Accreditation Bd for Conformity Assessment (JAB). *Address:* c/o Taisei Corporation, 25-1 Nishi-Shinjuku, Shinjuku-ku, Tokyo 163-0606, Japan.

HIRONAKA, Heisuke, PhD; Japanese mathematician and academic; *Professor Emeritus, Department of Mathematics, Harvard University;* b. 9 April 1931, Yamaguchi-ken; m. Wakako Hironaka; two c.; ed Kyoto Univ. and Harvard Univ., USA; mem. staff, Harvard Univ. following graduation, later Prof. of Math., now Prof. Emer.; Dir Research Inst. for the Math. Sciences, Kyoto Univ. 1983–85, Visiting Scholar, 1991–92; Prof. of Math. Seoul Nat. Univ. South Korea; Pres. Yamaguchi Univ. 1996–2002, Univ. of Creation, Art, Music and Social Work; Foreign Assoc. Acad. des sciences 1981–; mem. Japan Acad.; f. Japan Asscn for Mathematical Sciences 1984; currently lives in Japan; active in fund-raising for math. educ.; Order of Culture (Japan) 1975; Fields Medal, Int. Congress of Mathematicians, Nice, France 1970, Japan Acad. Award 1970. *Publications include:* Formal Functions and Formal Imbeddings (co-author) 1967, Introduction to the Theory of Infinitely Near Singular Points 1974, The Theory of the Maximal Contact (co-author) 1975, Desingularization Theorems (co-author) 1977, Geometric Singularity Theory (co-ed.) 2004, numerous articles in math. journals on complex analysis and singularity theory. *Leisure interest:* music. *Address:* Department of Mathematics, Office 325, Harvard University, One Oxford Street, Cambridge, MA 02138, USA (office). *Telephone:* (617) 495-2171 (office). *Fax:* (617) 495-5132 (office). *E-mail:* hironaka@math.harvard.edu (office). *Website:* www .math.harvard.edu (office).

HIRONO, Mazie Keiko, BA, JD; American (b. Japanese) lawyer and politician; *Senator from Hawaii;* b. 3 Nov. 1947, Fukushima Pref., Japan; d. of Hirono Matabe and Sato Laura Chie; m. Leighton Kim Oshima; one d.; ed Kaimuki High School, Univ. of Hawaii, Manoa, Georgetown Univ.; came to US 1955, naturalized 1959; Deputy Attorney Gen., State of Hawaii (Anti-Trust Div.) 1978–80; mem. Hawaii House of Reps from the 12th Dist 1981–83, from the 20th Dist 1983–85, from the 32nd Dist 1985–93, from the 22nd Dist 1993–95; with Shim, Tam, Kirimitsu & Naito (law firm) 1984–88; Lt Gov. of Hawaii 1994–2002; cand. for Office of Gov. 2002; mem. US House of Reps for the 2nd Congressional Dist of Hawaii 2007–13, mem. Cttee on Educ. and the Workforce, Cttee on Ethics, Cttee on Transportation and Infrastructure; Senator from Hawaii (first female Senator from HI, first Asian-American woman elected to the Senate, first US Senator born in Japan, first Buddhist US Senator) 2013–; Chair. Consumer Protection and Commerce Cttee 1987–92, Hawaii Policy Group, Nat. Comm. on Teaching and America's Future, Gov.'s Task Force on Science and Tech., Nuuanu YMCA, Honolulu 1982–84, Moiliili Community Center, Honolulu 1984; Deputy Chair. Democratic Nat. Cttee 1997; Co-Chair. Susan G. Komen Race for the Cure; Co-founder University Connections; Leader Pre-Plus (public–pvt. partnership providing opportunities for pre-school children); mem. US Supreme Court Bar, Hawaii Bar Asscn, Hawaii Public Television Bd, Japanese American Nat. Museum Bd, Women's Health Hawaii Advisory Bd; Democrat; Legislator of the Year 1984, Georgetown Univ. Law Center Alumni Achievement Award 2001. *Address:* United States Senate, Washington, DC 20510, USA (office). *Telephone:* (202) 224-3121 (switchboard) (office). *Website:* www.senate.gov (office).

HIROSE, Hiroshi; Japanese business executive; *Vice-Chairman, Sumitomo Chemical Company Ltd;* served as Man. Exec. Officer, Gen. Affairs Dept and Head of Investor Relations and Public Relations Dept, Sumitomo Chemical Co. Ltd, Dir and Pres. Sumitomo Chemical Co. Ltd –2011, Vice-Chair. and Chair. Internal Control Cttee 2011–; Outside Dir Inabata & Co. Ltd. *Address:* Sumitomo Chemical Co. Ltd, 27-1, Shinkawa 2-chome, Chuo-ku, Tokyo 104-8260, Japan (office). *Telephone:* (3) 5543-5102 (office). *Fax:* (3) 5543-5901 (office). *E-mail:* info@ sumitomo-chem.co.jp (office). *Website:* www.sumitomo-chem.co.jp (office).

HIROSE, Naomi; Japanese business executive; *President, Tokyo Electric Power Company (TEPCO), Inc.;* spent most of career in Sales, Tokyo Electric Power Co. (TEPCO), Inc., served as Chief of Kanagawa br. and its Marketing and Customer Relations Dept, later in charge of compensating victims of the accident at Fukushima No. 1 nuclear power plant that occurred in March 2011, Man. Dir TEPCO –2012, Pres. 2012–. *Address:* Tokyo Electric Power Co., Inc., 1-1-3 Uchisaiwai-cho, Chiyoda-ku, Tokyo 100-8560, Japan (office). *Telephone:* (3) 4216-

1111 (office). *Fax:* (3) 4216-2539 (office). *E-mail:* info@tepco.co.jp (office). *Website:* www.tepco.co.jp (office).

HIRSCH, Georges-François; French opera administrator and government official; *Director General, Artistic Creation, Ministry of Culture;* b. 5 Oct. 1944, Paris; s. of Georges Hirsch; stage-hand, Théâtre des Capucines 1960; later stage man. Théâtre de la Culture de l'Ile de France; Dir Théâtre de Limoges 1969–74; directed various productions especially in USA 1974–79; Lyric Arts Prof. Int. Summer Acad. of Nice 1974–80; Dance Admin. Paris Opéra 1979–82; mem. directing team, RTLN 1982–83; Dir Théâtre des Champs-Elysées 1983–89; Gen. Admin. Opéra Bastille 1989–92, Opéra de Paris (Garnier Bastille) 1991–92; mem. council CSA 1993–96; Dir-Gen. Orchestre de Paris 1996–2008; Chair. Syndicat nat. des orchestres et théâtres lyriques subventionnés de droit privé 1999–2008; Vice-Chair. French Assocn of Orchestras 2000–08; Dir Music, Theatre, Dance and Entertainment, Ministry of Culture 2008–10, Dir Gen. Artistic Creation 2010–; Officier, Légion d'honneur, Chevalier, Ordre nat. du Mérite, Commdr des Arts et Lettres. *Address:* Ministry of Culture and Communication, 3 rue de Valois, 75001 Paris, France (office). *Telephone:* 1-40-15-80-00 (office). *Fax:* 1-40-15-81-72 (office). *E-mail:* point.culture@culture.fr (office). *Website:* www.culture.gouv.fr (office).

HIRSCH, Judd, BS; American actor; b. 15 March 1935, Bronx, New York; s. of Joseph S. Hirsch and Sally Kitzis; m. 1st Elissa 1956 (divorced 1958); m. 2nd Bonni Sue Chalkin 1992 (divorced 2005); two s. one d.; ed City Coll. of New York; has appeared in numerous TV plays, series, films etc.; mem. Screen Actors Guild, AEA, AFTRA. *Stage appearances include:* Barefoot in the Park 1966, Knock Knock 1976 (Drama Desk Award), Scuba Duba 1967–69, King of the United States 1972, Mystery Play 1972, Hot L Baltimore 1972–73, Prodigal 1973, Chapter Two 1977–78, Talley's Folly 1979 (Obie Award), The Seagull 1983, I'm Not Rappaport 1985–86 (Tony Award), Conversations with My Father (Tony Award) 1992, A Thousand Clowns 1996, Below the Belt 1996, Death of a Salesman 1997, Art 1998, I'm Not Rappaport (revival) 2002, Sixteen Wounded 2004. *Films include:* King of the Gypsies 1978, Ordinary People 1980, Without a Trace 1983, Teachers 1984, The Goodbye People 1984, Running on Empty 1988, Independence Day 1996, Man on the Moon 1999, A Beautiful Mind 2002, Zeyda and the Hitman 2004, Brother's Shadow 2006, Polish Bar 2010. *Television appearances include:* Delvecchio (series) 1976–77, Taxi (series) 1978–83 (Emmy Award 1981, 1983, Medallion Award 2007), Dear John (series) 1988–92 (Golden Globe Award 1989), George and Leo (series) 1997, Regular Joe (series) 2003, Who Killed the Federal Theatre 2003, Street Time (series) 2003, Law and Order: Criminal Intent (series) 2003, Numbers (series) 2005–10, Studio 60 on the Sunset Strip (series) 2006, Tom Goes to the Mayor (series) 2006, American Dad! (series) 2009, The Whole Truth (series) 2010, Warehouse 13 (series) 2010, numerous appearances in TV episodes and movies. *Address:* c/o J. Wolfe Provident Financial Management, 2850 Ocean Park Blvd, Santa Monica, CA 90405, USA.

HIRSCH, Leon C.; American business executive; b. 20 July 1927, Bronx, New York; s. of the late Roslyn Hirsch and Isidor Hirsch; m. 2nd Turi Josefsen 1969; two s. one d. from 1st m.; ed Bronx School of Science; Chair. and CEO US Surgical Corpn 1964–2000; Founder JHK Investments, LLC, invested in Jarvik Heart, Inc., Chair. 2001–; inventor and developer of Auto Suture surgical staplers; Chair. Advisory Bd American Soc. of Colon and Rectal Surgeons Research Foundation; mem. American Business Conf.; fmr mem. Bd of Dirs Americans for Medical Progress; Trustee Emer., Boston Univ.; Gordon Grand Fellow, Yale Univ. 1993; Hon. DSc (Univ. of Illinois) 1994, Hon. DHumLitt (Quinnipiac Coll.) 1998; Michelangelo D'Oro Children of the World Award 1994, Surgery Award Nessim Habif, Univ. of Geneva. *Leisure interests:* fishing, horseback riding, skiing, tennis. *Address:* JHK Investments, LLC, 1 Gorham Island Road, Westport, CT 06880-3212, USA.

HIRSCH, Sir Peter Bernhard, Kt, MA, PhD, FRS; British scientist and academic; *Professor Emeritus of Metallurgy, University of Oxford;* b. 16 Jan. 1925, Berlin, Germany; s. of Ismar Hirsch and Regina Meyersohn; m. Mabel A. Kellar (née Stephens) 1959; one step-s. one step-d.; ed Univ. of Cambridge; Lecturer in Physics, Univ. of Cambridge 1959–64, Reader 1964–66; Fellow, Christ's Coll., Cambridge 1960–66; Isaac Wolfson Prof. of Metallurgy, Univ. of Oxford 1966–92, Prof. Emer. 1992–; Fellow, St Edmund Hall 1966–92, Fellow Emer. 1992–; Chair. Metallurgy and Materials Cttee, SRC 1970–73; mem. Council, Inst. of Physics 1968–72, Inst. of Metals 1968–73, Electricity Supply Research Council 1969–82, Council for Scientific Policy 1970–72, Metals Soc. Council 1978–82, Council Royal Soc. 1977–79; Royal Soc. UK-Canada Lecture 1992; mem. Bd (part-time) UKAEA 1982–94, Chair. 1982–84; mem. Tech. Advisory Cttee Advent 1982–89; Dir Cogent 1985–89, Rolls-Royce Assocs 1994–98; mem. Bd of Dirs OMIA 2000–01; mem. Tech. Advisory Cttee Monsanto Electronic Materials 1985–88; Chair. Isis Innovation Ltd 1988–96, Tech. Advisory Group on Structural Integrity 1993–2002, Materials and Processes Advisory Bd Rolls-Royce PLC 1996–2000; Fellow, Imperial Coll., London 1988; Assoc. mem. Royal Acad. of Sciences, Letters and Fine Arts of Belgium 1996; Foreign Assoc. Nat. Acad. of Eng, USA 2001; Hon. Fellow, St Catharine's Coll., Cambridge 1982, Royal Microscopical Soc. 1977, Christ's Coll., Cambridge 1978, Japan Soc. of Electron Microscopy 1979, Japan Inst. of Metals 1989, Inst. of Materials 2002, Hon. mem. Spanish Electron Microscopy Soc., Materials Research Soc., India 1990, Chinese Electron Microscopy Soc. 1992, Foreign Hon. mem. American Acad. of Arts and Sciences 2005; Hon. DSc (Newcastle Univ.) 1979, (City Univ.) 1979, (Northwestern Univ.) 1982, (East Anglia Univ.) 1983, Hon. DEng (Liverpool) 1991, (Birmingham) 1993; Rosenhain Medal, Inst. of Metals 1961, Boyes' Prize, Inst. of Physics and Physical Soc. 1962, Clamer Medal, Franklin Inst. 1970, Wihuri Int. Prize 1971, Hughes Medal of the Royal Soc. 1973, Platinum Medal of the Metals Soc. 1976, Royal Medal of Royal Soc. 1977, A. A. Griffith Medal, Inst. of Materials 1979, Arthur Von Hippel Award, Materials Research Soc. 1983, Wolf Prize in Physics (jtly) 1984, Distinguished Scientist Award, Electron Microscopy Soc. of America 1986, Holweck Prize, Inst. of Physics and French Physical Soc. 1988, Gold Medal, Japan Inst. of Metals 1989, Acta Metallurgica Gold Medal 1997, Heyn Medal of German Soc. for Materials Science 2002, Lomonosov Gold Medal, Russian Acad. of Sciences 2006. *Publications:* Electron Microscopy of Thin Crystals (co-author) 1965, The Physics of Metals, 2, Defects (ed.) 1975, Progress in Materials Science, Vol. 36 (co-ed.) 1992, Topics in Electron Diffraction and Microscopy of Materials (ed.) 1999, Fracture, Plastic Flow and Structural Integrity (co-ed.) 2000, Methods for the Assessment of

the Structural Integrity of Components and Structures (co-ed.) 2003; and numerous articles in learned journals. *Leisure interest:* walking. *Address:* Department of Materials, University of Oxford, Room 10.06, 21 Banbury Road, Oxford, OX1 3PH (office); 104A Lonsdale Road, Oxford, OX2 7ET, England (home). *Telephone:* (1865) 273700 (office); (1865) 273773 (office); (1865) 559523 (home). *Fax:* (1865) 273789 (office). *E-mail:* peter.hirsch@materials.ox.ac.uk (office). *Website:* www.materials.ox.ac.uk/peoplepages/hirsch.html (office).

HIRSCH, Robert Paul; French actor; b. 26 July 1925, L'Isle Adam, Val-d'Oise, Île-de-France; s. of Joachim Hirsch and Germaine Anne Raybois; mem. Comédie Française 1952–74; Brig. d'honneur 1992; Officier des Arts et des Lettres; Prix Jean-Jacques Gautier 1987, César Award 1990, Molière Award 1992, 1997, 1999, 2007. *Stage appearances include:* La belle aventure, Le prince travesti, Monsieur de Pourceaugnac, Les temps difficiles, La double inconstance, Le dindon, Amphitryon, Britannicus, Crime et Châtiment, La faim et la soif, Monsieur Amilcar, L'abîme et la visite, Le Piège, Deburau, Chacun sa vérité, Les dégourdis de la 11e 1986, Mon Faust 1987, Moi, Feuerbach 1989, Le Misanthrope (Molière Awards 1992) 1992, Une Folie 1993, Le bel air de Londres (Molière Awards 1999) 1998, Le gardien 2006. *Films include:* Les Intrigantes 1954, Votre dévoué Blake 1954, En effeuillant la marguerite 1956, Notre Dame de Paris 1956, La Bigorne 1958, Mimi Pinson 1958, Maigret et l'affaire Saint-Fiacre 1959, 125 rue Montmartre 1959, Adieu Philippine 1962, Pas question le samedi 1965, Monnaie de singe 1966, Martin Soldat 1966, Toutes folles de lui 1967, Les Cracks 1968, Appelez-moi Mathilde 1969, Traitement de choc 1973, Chobizenesse 1975, La Crime 1983, Hiver 54, l'abbé Pierre (César Awards 1990) 1989, Mon homme 1996, Mortel transfert 2001, Une affaire privée 2002. *Television includes:* La Nuit des rois 1962, Georges Dandin 1973, Tartuffe 1975, Trente ans ou La vie d'un joueur 1975, Les Papas naissent dans les armoires 1979, Deburau 1982, Sarah 2003, Volpone 2003. *Leisure interests:* painting, dancing. *Address:* Agence JFPM, 11 rue Chanez, 75016 Paris; 1 place du Palais Bourbon, 75007 Paris, France.

HIRSCH BALLIN, Ernst, LLD; Dutch lawyer and judge; *Minister of the Interior and Kingdom Relations;* b. 15 Dec. 1950, Amsterdam; s. of Ernst D. Hirsch Ballin and Maria Koppe; m. Pauline van de Grift 1974; two c.; ed Univ. of Amsterdam; mem. Faculty of Law, Amsterdam Univ. 1974–77; Legal Expert, Ministry of Justice 1977–81; Prof. of Constitutional and Admin. Law, Tilburg Univ. 1981–89, Prof. of Int. Law 1994–; Minister of Justice and Netherlands Antillean and Aruban Affairs 1989–94, Minister of Justice 2006–10, of the Interior and Kingdom Relations 2010–; mem. Parl. (Christian Democrat; Lower House) 1994–95, (Upper House) 1995–2000; Councillor of State 2000–; Pres. Admin. Jurisdiction Div. Council of State 2003–06; mem. Royal Netherlands Acad. of Science 2005; Kt, Order of the Dutch Lion; Grand Cross, Order of the Chest Crown (Luxembourg); Grand Cross, Orden del Libertador (Venezuela); Chevalier de la Légion d'honneur; Kt Order of Holy Sepulchre of Jerusalem; G. A. van Poelje Prize 1980. *Publications:* Publiekrecht en beleid 1979, Rechtsstaat en beleid 1992; 300 other publs on int. and comparative law, legal theory, constitutional and admin. law. *Leisure interests:* Brazilian music, philosophy, tennis. *Address:* Ministry of the Interior and Kingdom Relations, Schedeldoekshaven 200, POB 20011, 2500 EA The Hague (office); Council of State, PO Box 20019, 2500 EA The Hague (office); Bruggenrijt 12, 5032 BH Tilburg, Netherlands (home). *Telephone:* (70) 4266426 (office); (70) 4264657 (office). *Fax:* (70) 3639153 (office); (13) 5920687 (home). *E-mail:* info@minbzk.nl (office). *Website:* www.minbzk.nl (office).

HIRSCHFIELD, Alan J., BS, MBA; American business executive; b. 10 Oct. 1935, Oklahoma City, Okla; ed Univ. of Oklahoma, Harvard Univ.; Vice-Pres. Allen and Co. 1959–67; Vice-Pres. (Finance) and Dir Warner Bros Seven Arts Inc. 1967–68; Vice-Pres. and Dir American Diversified Enterprises Inc. 1968–73; Pres. and CEO, Columbia Pictures Industries Inc. 1973–79; Consultant, Warner Communications Inc. 1979; Vice-Chair. and COO 20th Century-Fox Film Corpn 1979–81, Chair., CEO and COO 1981–84; CEO Data Broadcasting Corpn 1990–2000; Co-Chair. Interactive Data Corpn 1992–2006, Co-CEO 1992–99; mem. Bd of Dirs 2000; Chair. Cantel Medical Corpn 1988–2009; Pres. Norman Hirschfield and Co. 2000–; mem. Bd of Dirs Carmike Cinemas, Inc. 2002–, Peregrine Systems, Inc. 2003–, Leucadia Nat. Corpn 2004–13,; fmr mem. Bd of Dirs Motion Picture Assocn of America, Nat. Museum of the American Indian; Vice-Chair. JNet Enterprises 2000; Trustee, Cancer Research Inst. (Sloan-Kettering), Dana-Farber Cancer Inst. *Address:* Norman Hirschfield & Company, 3490 Clubhouse Drive, Suite 206, Wilson, WY 83014, USA.

HIRSCHHORN, Thomas; Swiss artist; b. 16 May 1957, Bern; ed Schule für Gestaltung, Zurich; moved to France and joined Grapus, Parisian collective of communist graphic designers 1984; first solo exhbn at Bar Floréal, Paris 1986; influenced by Kurt Schwitters and Andy Warhol; translates leftist ideals into sculptural displays combining everyday materials such as aluminium foil, tape, board, plastic, and paper with wide array of cultural references; represented Switzerland at the Venice Biennale 2011; lives and works in Paris; Preis für Junge Schweizer Kunst 1999, Marcel Duchamp Prize 2000, Rolandpreis für Kunst im öffentlichen Raum 2003, Joseph Beuys Prize 2004, Beaux-Arts magazine Art Award 2005, Prix Aica 2006. *Major works include:* FlugplatzWelt/World Airport, Venice Biennale 1999, Battle Monument, Documenta XI, Kassel 2002, Gramsci Monument 2013; works on display in Kunstsammlung Nordrhein-Westfalen, Dusseldorf, S.M.A.K. (Stedelijk Museum voor Actuele Kunst), Ghent, Tate Modern, London, Walker Art Center, Minn., Art Inst. of Chicago, La Caixa, Barcelona, Centre Pompidou, Paris, Musée Précaire Albinet Aubervilliers 2004; and in major contemporary art museums in LA, Miami, New York, Philadelphia, Boston, Amsterdam, Porto, Basel, Munich, Marseille, Bordeaux, Paris, Santiago de Compostela, Zurich. *Publications:* Parkett #57 (co-author) 2000, Material: Public Works – The Bridge 2000 2001, Bataille Maschine (with M. Steinweg) 2003. *Address:* c/o Stephen Friedman Gallery, 25–28 Old Burlington Street, London, W1S 3AN, England. *Telephone:* (20) 7494-1434. *Fax:* (20) 7494-1431. *E-mail:* info@stephenfriedman.com. *Website:* www.stephenfriedman.com.

HIRST, Damien; British artist; b. 1965, Bristol; m. Maia Norman; three s.; ed Goldsmiths Coll., London; winner Turner Prize 1995; ranked first in ArtReview magazine's Power 100 list 2005, ranked 11th 2006; various other awards. *Television:* Channel 4 documentary about Damien Hirst and Exhbn at Gagosian Gallery, directed by Roger Pomphrey 2000. *Publication:* I Want to Spend the Rest of My Life Everywhere, One to One, Always, Forever 1997, Theories, Models,

Methods, Approaches, Assumptions, Results and Findings 2000. *Leisure interests:* losing myself, pub lunches. *Address:* c/o White Cube, Hoxton Square, London, N1 6PB, England. *Telephone:* (20) 7930-5373. *E-mail:* enquiries@science.ltd.uk (office).

HIRST, Paul Heywood, MA; British academic; *Emeritus Professor of Education, University of Cambridge;* b. 10 Nov. 1927, Huddersfield; s. of Herbert Hirst and Winifred Hirst; ed Huddersfield Coll., Trinity Coll., Cambridge and Univ. of London; school teacher of math. 1948–55; Lecturer and Tutor, Dept of Educ., Univ. of Oxford 1955–59; Lecturer in Philosophy of Educ., Inst. of Educ., Univ. of London 1959–65; Prof. of Educ., King's Coll., Univ. of London 1965–71; Prof. of Educ. and Head Dept of Educ., Univ. of Cambridge 1971–88, Emer. Prof. 1988–; Fellow, Wolfson Coll., Cambridge 1971–88, Fellow Emer. 1988–; Visiting Prof., Univs of British Columbia, Alberta, Malawi, Otago, Melbourne, Sydney, Puerto Rico, London 1988–; Vice-Chair. Cttee for Educ., CNAA 1975–81, Chair. Cttee for Research 1988–92; Chair. Univs Council for Educ. of Teachers 1985–88; Pres. Philosophy of Educ. Soc. 2012; mem. Swann Cttee on Educ. of Children of Ethnic Minorities 1981–85; Hon. DEd (CNAA) 1992; Hon. DPhil (Cheltenham and Gloucester Coll. of Higher Educ.) 2000; Hon. DLitt (Huddersfield) 2002. *Publications:* The Logic of Education (with R. S. Peters) 1970, Knowledge and the Curriculum 1974, Moral Education in a Secular Society 1974, Educational Theory and its Foundation Disciplines (ed.) 1983, Initial Teacher Training and the Role of the School (with others) 1988, Philosophy of Education: Major Themes in the Analytic Tradition (four vols) (co-ed.) 1998; numerous articles in educational and philosophical journals. *Leisure interest:* music (especially opera). *Address:* Flat 3, 6 Royal Crescent, Brighton, BN2 1AL, England (home). *Telephone:* (1273) 684118 (home).

HISLOP, Ian David, BA (Hons); British editor, writer and broadcaster; *Editor, Private Eye magazine;* b. 13 July 1960; s. of the late David Atholl Hislop and of Helen Hislop; m. Victoria Hamson 1988; one s. one d.; ed Ardingly Coll. and Magdalen Coll., Oxford; joined Private Eye (satirical magazine) 1981, Deputy Ed. 1985–86, Ed. 1986–; columnist, The Listener magazine 1985–89, The Sunday Telegraph 1996–2003; TV critic, The Spectator 1994–96; Underhill Exhbn; Violet Vaughan Morgan Scholarship; BAFTA Award for Have I Got News for You 1991, Editors' Editor, British Soc. of Magazine Eds 1991, Magazine of the Year, What the Papers Say 1991, Editor of the Year, British Soc. of Magazine Eds 1998, Award for Political Satire, Channel 4 Political Awards 2004, Award for Political Comedy, Channel 4 Political Awards 2006. *Radio:* The News Quiz (BBC Radio 4) 1985–90, Fourth Column 1992–96, Lent Talk 1994, Gush (scriptwriter, with Nick Newman) 1994, Words on Words 1999, The Hislop Vote (BBC Radio 2) 2000, A Revolution in 5 Acts (BBC Radio 4) 2001, The Real Patron Saints (BBC Radio 4) 2002, The Choir Invisible 2003, A Brief History of Tax (BBC Radio 4) 2003, Blue Birds over the White Cliffs of Dover (BBC Radio 4) 2004, Are We Being Offensive Enough? (BBC Radio 4) 2004, Looking for Middle England (BBC Radio 4) 2006. *TV scriptwriting:* Spitting Image (with Nick Newman; ITV) 1984–89, The Stone Age (with Nick Newman) 1989, Briefcase Encounter (with Nick Newman) 1990, Harry Enfield's Television Programme (with Nick Newman) 1990–92, Harry Enfield and Chums (with Nick Newman) 1994–98, Mangez Merveillac (with Nick Newman) 1994, Dead on Time (with Nick Newman) 1995, Gobble (with Nick Newman; BBC 1) 1996, Sermon from St Albions (ITV Granada) 1998, Songs and Praise from St Albions (with Nick Newman; ITV Granada) 1999, Confessions of a Murderer (with Nick Newman) 1999, My Dad's the Prime Minister (with Nick Newman; BBC) 2003, 2004. *TV performer:* Have I Got News for You (BBC 2) 1990–2000, (BBC 1) 2000–. *TV presenter:* Canterbury Tales (Channel 4) 1996, School Rules (Channel 4) 1997, Pennies from Bevan (Channel 4) 1998, Great Railway Journeys East to West (BBC) 1999, Who Do You Think You Are? (BBC 2) 2004, Not Forgotten (Channel 4) 2005, Not Forgotten: Shot at Dawn (Channel 4) 2007, Scouting for Boys (BBC 4) 2007. *Publications:* various Private Eye collections 1985–, contribs to newspapers and magazines on books, current affairs, arts and entertainment. *Address:* Private Eye, 6 Carlisle Street, London, W1D 3BN, England (office). *Telephone:* (20) 7437-4017 (office). *Website:* www.private-eye.co.uk (office).

HITAM, Tan Sri Dato' Musa bin; Malaysian politician (retd) and international organization official; *Chairman, World Islamic Economic Foundation;* b. 18 April 1934, Johor; ed English Coll., Johor Baharu Univ. of Malaya and Univ. of Sussex, UK; Assoc. Sec. Int. Student Conf. Secr. (COSEC), Leiden 1957–59; civil servant 1959–64; Political Sec. to Minister of Transport 1964; mem. Parl. 1968–90; Asst Minister to Deputy Prime Minister 1969; studied in UK 1970, subsequently lectured at Univ. of Malaya; Chair. Fed. Land Devt Authority 1971; Deputy Minister of Trade and Industry 1972–74; Minister of Primary Industries 1974–78, of Educ. 1978–81; Deputy Prime Minister and Minister of Home Affairs 1981–86; Deputy Pres. UMNO 1981–86; Special Envoy to UN 1990–91; Malaysia's Chief Rep. to UN Comm. on Human Rights 1993–98; Special Envoy of the Prime Minister to Commonwealth Ministerial Action Group 1995–; Chair. World Islamic Economic Foundation; Chair. Suhakam, (Malaysian Human Rights Comm.) 1999–2002; currently Chair. Lion Industries Corpn Berhad, UMLand Bhd, Sime Darby Berhad; mem. International Advisory Council, Brookings Doha Center. *Address:* Office of the Chairman, World Islamic Economic Foundation, 2nd Floor, Kompleks Antarabangsa Jalan Sultan Ismail, 50250 Kuala Lumpur, Malaysia (office). *Telephone:* (3) 2145-5500 (office). *E-mail:* enquiry@wief.org (office). *Website:* wief.org (office).

HITCHCOCK, Karen R., BS, PhD; American biologist, academic and university administrator; ed St Lawrence Univ., Univ. of Rochester; fmr Postdoctoral Fellow, Webb-Waring Inst. for Medical Research, Univ. of Colo Medical Centre; fmr George A. Bates Prof. of Histology and Chair Dept of Anatomy and Cellular Biology, Tufts Univ.; Assoc. Dean for Basic Sciences, Research and Grad. Studies, School of Medicine, Tex. Tech Health Sciences Center 1985–87; fmr Vice-Chancellor for Research, Dean of Grad. Coll., Prof. of Anatomy and Cell Biology, of Biological Sciences, Univ. of Ill. at Chicago; Vice-Pres. of Academic Affairs, Univ. of Albany, State Univ. of NY 1991–95, Pres. 1996–2004; Prin. and Vice-Chancellor Queen's Univ., Kingston, Ont., Canada 2004–08; Special Advisor, Park Strategies, LLC 2010–; Nat. Science Foundation Professorship for Women in Science and Eng 1983–84; fmr Pres. American Asscn of Anatomists; fmr mem. Nat. Bd of Medical Examiners; Dr hc (Albany Medical Coll., St Lawrence Univ.); Marketer of Excellence Award, New York Capital Region Chapter, American Marketing Asscn

2002, Capital Region Business Hall of Fame 2004, Woman in the Media Award, Women's Press Club of New York State 2004. *Publications:* numerous works on cell and developmental biology. *Address:* Park Strategies LLC, 101 Park Avenue, Suite 2506, New York, NY 10178, USA (office). *Telephone:* (212) 883-5608 (office). *Website:* www.parkstrategies.com (office).

HITCHENS, Theresa Ann; American journalist, editor, defence research director and international organization official; *Director, United Nations Institute for Disarmament Research (UNIDIR);* b. 11 Aug. 1959; served internships with Senator John Glenn (Democrat–Ohio) and with NATO Parl. Ass., Brussels; worked at Inside Washington Publrs on group's environmental and defence-related newsletters 1983–88; first Brussels Bureau Chief, Defense News 1989–93, Ed. Defense News 1998–2000; fmr Dir of Research, British American Security Information Council, Washington, DC and London; Dir Center for Defense Information (CDI), World Security Inst., Washington, DC –2008, led CDI's Space Security Project in co-operation with Secure World Foundation; Dir UN Inst. for Disarmament Research (UNIDIR), Geneva 2009–; mem. (ex officio) UN Sec.-Gen.'s Advisory Bd on Disarmament Matters. *Publications include:* Growing Pains: The Debate on the Next Round of NATO Enlargement (with Tomas Valasek) 2002, Future Security In Space: Charting a Cooperative Course 2004, European Military Space Capabilities: A Primer (with Tomas Valasek) 2006; numerous articles on space and nuclear arms control issues, military, defence industry and NATO affairs. *Address:* United Nations Institute for Disarmament Research, Palais des Nations, 1211 Geneva 10, Switzerland (office). *Telephone:* (22) 9174293 (office). *Fax:* (22) 9170176 (office). *E-mail:* thitchens@unog.ch (office). *Website:* www.unidir.org (office).

HITE, Shere D., MA, PhD; American/German cultural historian, writer and researcher; b. 1942, St Joseph, Mo.; m. Friedrich Hoericke 1985; ed Univ. of Florida, Columbia Univ., Nihon Univ., Japan; Dir feminist sexuality project NOW, New York 1972–78; Dir Hite Research Int., New York 1978–; Researcher, The Hite Reports, 1976, 1981, 1987, 1996, 2006; fmr instructor in female sexuality, New York Univ.; lecturer Harvard Univ., McGill Univ., Columbia Univ., also numerous women's groups, int. lecturer 1977–89, currently Visiting Prof., Nihon Univ., Japan; mem. Advisory Bd Foundation of Gender and Genital Medicine, Johns Hopkins Univ.; Consultant Ed. Journal of Sex Education and Therapy, Journal of Sexuality and Disability; mem. NOW, American Historical Asscn, American Sociological Asscn, AAAS, Acad. of Political Science, Women's History Asscn, Soc. for Scientific Study of Sex, Women's Health Network; Prof., Maimonides Univ. 2003; f. Nike Prize for Women's Non-Fiction Writing, Frankfurt 1997; Hon. Prof. Chongqing Medical Univ., China 2004; Award for Distinguished Contribs, American Asscn of Sex Educators, Counsellors and Therapists 1988. *Publications:* Sexual Honesty: By Women For Women 1974, The Hite Report: A Nationwide Study of Female Sexuality 1976, The Hite Report on Male Sexuality 1981, Hite Report on Women and Love: A Cultural Revolution in Progress 1987, Good Guys, Bad Guys (with Kate Colleran) 1989, Women as Revolutionary Agents of Change: The Hite Reports and Beyond 1993, The Hite Report on the Family: Growing Up Under Patriarchy 1994, The Divine Comedy of Ariadne and Jupiter 1994, The Hite Report on Hite: A Sexual and Political Autobiography 1996, How Women See Other Women 1998, Sex and Business 2000, Shere Hite Reader 2004, Oedipus Revisited: Sexual Behaviour in the Human Male Today 2005, Shere Hite Reader: Sex, Globalisation and Private Life 2006. *Leisure interests:* answering e-mails, writing weekly columns for int. newspapers. *Website:* www .hiteresearchfoundation.org.

HJELM-WALLÉN, Lena, MA; Swedish politician; *Chairman, International Institute for Democracy and Electoral Assistance;* b. 14 Jan. 1943, Sala; d. of Gustaf Hjelm and Elly Hjelm; m. Ingvar Wallén 1965; one d.; ed Uppsala Univ.; teacher in Sala 1966–69; active in Social Democratic Youth League; mem. Parl. 1969–2002; elected to 2nd Chamber of Parl. 1968; mem. Exec. Cttee Västmanland br. of Socialdemokratiska Arbetarepartiet (Social Democratic Labour Party—SDLP) 1968, mem. SDLP Parl. Exec. 1976–82, SDLP Spokeswoman on Schools, mem. Bd SDLP 1978–87, SDLP Spokeswoman on Educ. 1991–94; Minister without Portfolio, with responsibility for schools 1974–76; Minister of Educ. and Cultural Affairs 1982–85, of Int. Devt Co-operation 1985–91, of Foreign Affairs 1994–98; Deputy Prime Minister of Sweden 1998–2002; Govt Rep. to EU Convention on Future of Europe; Chair. Int. Inst. for Democracy and Electoral Assistance (IDEA) 2003–, European Forum for Democracy and Solidarity, Olof Palme International Center; Trustee Raoul Wallenberg Inst. 2003–, International Crisis Group. *Leisure interests:* nature, books, gardening, family. *Address:* International IDEA, Strömsborg, 103 34 Stockholm, Sweden (office). *Telephone:* (8) 698-37-00 (office). *Fax:* (8) 20-24-22 (office). *E-mail:* info@idea.int (office). *Website:* www.idea.int (office).

HJÖRNE, Peter Lars; Swedish newspaper editor and publisher; *Editor-in-Chief, Göteborgs-Posten;* b. 7 Sept. 1952, Gothenburg; s. of Lars Hjörne and Anne Gyllenhammar; m. 2nd Karin Linnea Tufvesson Hjörne 1995; five d.; ed Göteborgs Högre Samskola and Univ. of Gothenburg; Man. Trainee John Deere Co., USA 1978–79; Exec. Asst Göteborgs-Posten 1979–82, Deputy Man. Dir 1983–85, Man. Dir 1985–93, Owner, Publr and Ed.-in-Chief 1993–. *Leisure interests:* sailing, literature, music, art. *Address:* Göteborgs-Posten, Polhemsplatsen 5, 405 02 Gothenburg, Sweden (office). *Telephone:* 31-62-40-00 (office). *Fax:* 31-15-76-92 (office). *E-mail:* peter.hjorne@gp.se (office). *Website:* www.gp.se (office).

HLA, Maj.-Gen. Tun; Myanma politician; b. 11 July 1951, Yangon; s. of U Tin Ngwe and Daw Khin Kyi; m. Daw Khin Than Win; two c.; ed Defence Services Acad., Pyin-Oo-Lwin; fmr Deputy Dir.-Gen. Myanmar Police Force; fmr Gov. Bank of Myanmar; Minister of Finance and Revenue 2003–11; General Service Medal, People's War Medal, State Peace and Tranquility Medal, Maing Yan/Me Tha Waw Battle Star, Distinguished Service Medal, Service Medal. *Leisure interests:* golf, painting. *Address:* No. 28, Pan Wah Street, Kamayut Tsp., Yangon, Myanmar (home).

HLAWITSCHKA, Eduard, Dr Habil.; German academic; *Professor, University of Munich;* b. 8 Nov. 1928, Dubkowitz; s. of Ernst Hlawitschka and Emilie Tschwatschal; m. Eva-Marie Schuldt 1958; one s. one d.; ed Univs of Rostock, Leipzig, Freiburg and Saarbrücken; Prof., Univ. of Düsseldorf 1969, Univ. of Munich 1975–; Pres. Sudetendeutsche Akad. der Wissenschaften und Künste

1991–94; Sudetendeutscher Kulturpreis für Wissenschaft 1987, Prix de Liechtenstein, Conf. Int. de Généalogie et d'Héraldique 1991. *Publications:* Franken, Alemannen, Bayern und Burgunder in Oberitalien 1960, Studien zur Äbtissinnenreihe von Remiremont 1963, Lotharingien und das Reich an der Schwelle der deutschen Geschichte 1968, Die Anfänge des Hauses Habsburg-Lothringen 1969, Libri memoriales 1 1970, Vom Frankenreich zur Formierung der europäischen Staaten- und Völkergemeinschaft 840–1046 (1986), Untersuchungen zu den Thronwechseln der ersten Hälfte des 11. Jahrhunderts und zur Adelsgeschichte Süddeutschlands 1987, Stirps Regia 1988, Dubkowitz im Böhmischen Mittelgebirge 1997, Andechser Anfänge 2000, Konradiner-Genealogie, unstatthafte Verwandtenehen und spätottonisch-frühsalische Thronbesetzungspraxis 2003, Die Ahnen der hochmittelalterlichen deutschen Könige, Kaiser und ihrer Gemahlinnen Bd I (Vols 1 & 2) 2006, Bd II 2009, Bd III 2013. *Address:* Panoramastrasse 25, 82211 Herrsching/Ammersee, Germany. *Telephone:* (70) 81524991.

HO, Chih-Chin, BA, PhD; Taiwanese economist, academic and government official; b. 16 June 1952; ed Nat. Taiwan Univ., Univ. of Michigan; Economist, Okla State Resources Planning Bd, USA; Sr Researcher, Sentencing Comm., US Dept of Justice 1988–90; Sr Economist, US Internal Revenue Service 1990–98, Prin. Economist 1998–2003; Prof., Dept of Econs, Nat. Taiwan Univ. 2003–06, Dir 2004–06; mem. Kuomintang (KMT) Party; Minister of Finance 2006–08 (resgnd). *Address:* c/o Kuomintang (KMT) Party, 11 Jongshan South Road, Taipei 100, Taiwan (office). *Telephone:* (2) 23121472 (office). *Fax:* (2) 23434561 (office). *Website:* www.kmt.org.tw (office).

HO, Ching, BEng, MSc; Singaporean business executive; *Executive Director and CEO, Temasek Holdings (Private) Ltd;* b. 1953, d.-in-law of Lee Kuan Yew (Minister Mentor); m. Brig.-Gen. (retd) Lee Hsien Loong (Prime Minister of Singapore) 1985; four c.; ed Nat. Univ. of Singapore, Stanford Univ., USA; began career as engineer at Ministry of Defence with System Integration Man. Team –1986; Pres. and CEO Singapore Technologies (state defence contractor) –2002; Exec. Dir Temasek Holdings (has stakes in more than 40 cos, including Singapore Airlines, SingTel, DBS Bank, SMRT Corpn, Neptune Orient Lines, Keppel Corpn, SembCorp Industries, Singapore Technologies, PSA Corpn, Singapore Power) 2002–; Hon. Fellow, Inst. of Engineers, Singapore; Distinguished Engineering Alumnus Award, Nat. Univ. of Singapore 1995; Public Admin Silver Medal 1985, Public Service Star 1996, Medal of Commendation (Gold) Award for her support of the work of unions and for safeguarding workers' interests in Singapore 2009. *Address:* Temasek Holdings (Private) Ltd, 60B Orchard Road, #06–18, Tower 2, The Atrium, Singapore 238891 (office). *Telephone:* (65) 6828-6828 (office). *Fax:* (65) 6821-1188 (office). *E-mail:* enquiry@temasek.com.sg (office). *Website:* www.temasek.com.sg (office).

HO, Edmund H. W., BA; Chinese business executive and politician; b. 13 March 1955; s. of Ho Yin and Chan Keng; m.; one s. one d.; ed York Univ., Canada; chartered accountant and certified auditor 1981–; worked for accounting firm in Toronto, Ont. 1981–82; Gen. Man. Tai Fung Bank 1983, CEO 1999; mem. CPPCC 1986–; elected Deputy to NPC 1988, elected to 8th and 9th Standing Cttees; mem. Legis. Ass. of Macao 1988–, Vice-Pres. 1988–99; Vice-Pres. Macao Chamber of Commerce; Chair. Macao Asscn of Banks 1985–; Chief Exec. Macao Special Admin. Region (MSAR) May 1999–2009; Vice-Chair. 11th CPPCC 2010–; Vice-Chair. All-China Fed. of Industry and Commerce, Econ. Council of the Macao Govt, Kiang Wu Hosp. Bd of Charity, Tung Sin Tong Charitable Inst.; Vice-Pres. Drafting Cttee of the Basic Law of the MSAR 1988, Consultative Cttee of the Basic Law of the MSAR 1989, Preparatory Cttee of the MSAR 1998; Convenor of Land Fund Investment Comm. of the MSAR; Chair. Bd of Dirs Univ. of Macao; Vice-Chair. Bd of Dirs Jinan Univ., Guangzhou; Pres. Exec. Cttee Macao Olympic Cttee; Pres. Macao Golf Asscn; Founding mem. Macau Management Asscn;*Website:* www.cppcc.gov.cn.

HO, Pansy, BA; Hong Kong business executive; *Managing Director, Shun Tak Holdings;* b. 1962; d. of Dr Stanley Ho; ed Univ. of Santa Clara, USA; fmrly with high soc. events promotion co.; joined Shun Tak Group (cr. by father Stanley Ho in 1972) 1995, Exec. Dir 1995–99, Man. Dir (oversaw establishment of Macau Tower Convention and Entertainment Centre 2001) 1999–, also CEO Shun Tak-China Travel Shipping Investments Ltd (oversaw merger between shipping operations of Shun Tak and China Travel Services 1999) 1999–; CEO and Dir Melco Int. Devt Ltd; Dir Air Macau Corpn, Asia TV Ltd, Sociedade de Turismo e Diversões de Macau; entered into jt venture with MGM MIRAGE of Las Vegas, Nev. to build and operate MGM Grand Macau hotel and casino resorts 2005–; mem. Cttee CPPCC of Guangdong Prov.; Founding Hon. Adviser and Bd Dir Univ. of Hong Kong Foundation for Educational Devt and Research; mem. Advisory Council The Better Hong Kong Foundation; ranked by Fortune magazine amongst 50 Most Powerful Women in Business outside the US (31st) 2002, (46th) 2003, (49th) 2004, (39th) 2005, (42nd) 2006, (36th) 2007. *Address:* Shun Tak Holdings Ltd, Penthouse 39/F, West Tower, Shun Tak Centre, 200 Connaught Road Central, Hong Kong Special Administrative Region, People's Republic of China (office). *Telephone:* (852) 2859-3111 (office). *Fax:* (852) 2857-7181 (office). *E-mail:* enquiry@shuntakgroup.com (office). *Website:* www.shuntakgroup.com (office).

HO, Stanley Hung Sun, OBE; Chinese (Hong Kong) business executive; *Group Executive Chairman, Shun Tak Holdings Ltd;* b. 25 Nov. 1921, Hong Kong; m.; 17 c.; ed Univ. of Hong Kong; Group Exec. Chair. Shun Tak Holdings Ltd (operator of world's largest jetfoil fleet); Founder and Man. Dir Sociedade de Turismo e Diversões da, (SARL—tourism and entertainment, banking, property, airport and airline); Man. Dir Sociedade de Jogos de Macao, SA; Pres. Real Estate Developers' Asscn 1984–; Chair. Univ. of Hong Kong Foundation for Educational Devt and Research 1995–; mem. Court of Univ. of Hong Kong 1982–, Council 1984–; Vice-Patron Community Chest 1986–; Vice-Chair. Basic Law Drafting Cttee, Macao Special Admin. Region (MSAR) 1988–93, Vice-Chair. Preparatory Cttee, MSAR 1988–99; mem. Selection Cttee for First Govt of Hong Kong Special Admin. Region 1996–97; mem. Standing Cttee 9th CPPCC Nat. Cttee 1998–2003; Co-Chair. Cttee Franklin Delano Roosevelt Memorial Comm. 1994–97; mem. Econ. Council of Macao SAR 2000–; Hon. Citizen of Beijing 2001; Comendador da Ordem de Benemerência (Portugal) 1970; Comendador da Ordem de Infante Dom Henrique (Portugal) 1981; CStJ 1983; Chevalier, Légion d'honneur 1983, Grande-Oficial da Ordem do Infante Dom Henrique (Portugal) 1985, Order of the Sacred Treasure (Japan) 1987, Equitem Commendatorem Ordinis Sancti Gregorii Magni

1989, Darjah Dato Seri Paduka Mahkota Perak (Malaysia) 1990, Grä-Cruz, Ordem do Mérito (Portugal) 1990, Medalha Naval de Vasco da Gama (Portugal) 1991, Cruz de Plata de la Medalla de la Solidaridad (Spain) 1993, Grä-Cruz, Ordem do Infante Dom Henrique (Portugal) 1995, Hon. Order of the Crown of Terengganu Darjah Seri' Paduka Mahkota Terengganu (Malaysia) 1997, Nuno Gonçalo Vieira Matias (Portugal) 1999; Hon. DScS (Univ. of Macao) 1984, (Univ. of Hong Kong) 1987; Global Award for Outstanding Contrib. for the Devt of Int. Trade and Relations, Priyadashni Acad. (India) 2000, Gold Medal of Merit in Tourism (Portugal) 2001. *Leisure interests:* ballroom dancing, swimming, playing tennis. *Address:* Shun Tak Holdings Ltd, 39/F, West Tower, Shun Tak Centre, 200 Connaught Road Central, Hong Kong Special Administrative Region, People's Republic of China (office). *Telephone:* (852) 28593111 (Hong Kong) (office); (853) 566065 (Macao) (office). *Fax:* (852) 28581014 (Hong Kong) (office); (853) 371981 (Macao) (office).

HO, Tao, BA, MArch, LHD; Chinese architect, urban planner and artist; b. 17 July 1936, Shanghai; s. of Ping-Yin Ho and Chin-Hwa Chiu; m. 1st Chi-Ping Lu 1960, one s. two d.; m. 2nd Irene Lo 1978, one d.; ed Pui Ching Middle High School, Hong Kong 1950–56, Williams Coll., Williamstown, Mass. and Harvard Univ., USA; Research Asst, Albright-Knox Art Gallery, Buffalo, NY 1959; Architectural Asst to Walter Gropius 1963–64; Visiting Lecturer, Fine Arts Dept, Chinese Univ., Hong Kong 1965–67; f. own practice, Taoho Design Architects, Hong Kong 1968–; Co-founder, Hong Kong Arts Centre 1969, Chair. Visual Arts Cttee, Hong Kong Arts Centre 1972–77; Visiting Critic, Harvard Univ. Grad. School of Design 1975; External Examiner of Art, Chinese Univ., Hong Kong 1975–79; Visiting Critic, Design Dept, Hong Kong Polytechnic 1979–; Hon. Lecturer, School of Architecture, Hong Kong Univ. 1979–; Chair. Hong Kong Designers Asscn 1981; Hon. Adviser, City Hall Museum, Hong Kong 1981–; Chinese Govt Adviser for Hong Kong Affairs 1995; mem. Bd of Architects, Singapore 1981–; Assoc. mem. Chartered Inst. of Arbitrators 1979–; Core mem. Asian Planning and Architectural Consultants Ltd 1975–; Founder and Dir Vision Press Ltd, Hong Kong 1982–; Fellow, Hong Kong Inst. of Architects 1971–; mem. Singapore Inst. of Architects 1988, Ordre des Architectes, France, 1992; Founding mem. Hong Kong Artists' Guild 1987; f. Philharmonic Soc. of Hong Kong Professionals 1991; has organized more than 20 exhbns for Hong Kong Arts Centre 1972–; Arthur Lehman Fellow, Harvard Univ. 1960–63; Forum Fellow of World Econ. Forum at Davos 1997–2001; Justice of Peace of Hong Kong 1997–; mem. Political Consultative Cttee of Pudong, Shanghai 2001; Hon. FAIA 1988–; Hon. Fellow, Philippines Inst. of Architects 1993–; Hon. DHumLitt (Williams Coll., Mass., USA) 1979; Design Merit Award (Chinese Manufacturers' Asscn), Silver Medal (Hong Kong Inst. of Architects), Bicentennial Medal (Williams Coll., USA). *Radio:* 17-programme weekly radio series 'Tao Ho on Music' for RTHK 1987; regular panellist on 'Free as the Wind' (RTHK) 1997–. *Major works include:* Hong Kong Govt Pavilion, CMA Exhbn, Hong Kong 1969; Hong Kong Int. Elementary School 1975, Hong Kong Arts Centre 1977, residential devt, Shouson Hill, Hong Kong (with K. C. Lye) 1979, planning and rban design of Chinese cities Xiamen, Qingdao and Harigzhou 1985–86, 6A Bowen Road Apt 1983 (HKIA Silver Medal), Bayview Residential Devt 1988, (HKIA Design Award), Hong Kong Baptist Coll. Redevelopment 1988–89; revitalization of Western Market, Hong Kong 1992; Eng Bldg, Chinese Univ. of Hong Kong 1993; renovation of Hong Kong Govt House 1993; designed commemorative stamps for Hong Kong Govt 1975; commissioned by SWATCH to design art clock tower to represent Hong Kong at 1996 Olympic Games, Atlanta; solo painting exhbns at China Art Gallery, Beijing 1993, La Maison de Verre, Paris 1993, Hong Kong Univ. Museum 1995, Villa Turque, La Chaux-de-Fonds, Switzerland; China Construction Bank Head-quarters, Beijing 1998, Giant Panda Habitat, Hong Kong 1999, Pentecostal Holiness Wing Kwong Church (including stained glass design), Hong Kong 2000, Industrial and Commercial Bank Data Centre, Beijing 2002; light sculpture 'BIG BANG' created for new HQ of World Econ. Forum, Geneva. *Publications:* Taoho Building Dreams 2000; numerous papers on theory and practice of art and architecture. *Leisure interests:* collecting art, writing about art, listening to music, painting, reading in cosmology and philosophy of science, sculpture. *Address:* 8/B, 499 King's Road, North Point, Hong Kong Special Administrative Region, People's Republic of China. *Telephone:* (852) 28118780. *Fax:* (852) 28110337. *Website:* www.taoho.com (office).

HO LAU YUNG, Lawrence, BA; Canadian (b. Hong Kong Chinese) business executive; *Chairman and CEO, Melco International Development Ltd;* b. 1977; s. of Stanley Ho; m. Sharen Lo; ed Univ. of Toronto; fmrly worked for Jardine Fleming, Citibank and iAsia (online stock trader); bought Melco (family-held firm) 2001, Chief Man. Dir Melco International Development Ltd 2001–06, Chair. and CEO 2006–, also Co-Chair. and CEO Melco PBL Entertainment (Macau) Ltd; mem. Nat. Cttee CPPCC; Chair. Macau International Volunteers Asscn, Bd of Govs Canadian Chamber of Commerce in Hong Kong, The Chamber of Hong Kong Listed Cos; mem. Bd of Dirs, mem. Exec. Cttee, Vice-Patron, The Community Chest of Hong Kong; mem. Science and Technology Council of Macau Special Admin. Region Govt; mem. All China Youth Fed., Macau Basic Law Promotional Asscn; Hon. Lifetime Dir Chinese Gen. Chamber of Commerce of Hong Kong, Hon. Patron Macau Canadian Chamber of Commerce, Hon. Pres. Asscn of Property Agents and Real Estate Developers of Macau; Dr hc (Edinburgh Napier Univ., Scotland) 2009; named Best CEO, Institutional Investor 2005, Leader of Tomorrow, Hong Kong Tatler 2005, Dir of the Year, Hong Kong Inst of Dirs 2005, Fifth China Enterprise Award for Creative Businessmen. *Address:* Melco International Development Limited, 38th Floor, The Centrium, 60 Wyndham Street, Central, Hong Kong Special Administrative Region, People's Republic of China (office). *Telephone:* 31513777 (office). *E-mail:* info@melco-group.com (office). *Website:* www.melco-group.com (office).

HOAGLAND, Edward, AB; American author; b. 21 Dec. 1932, New York, NY; s. of Warren Eugene Hoagland and Helen Kelley Morley; m. 1st Amy J. Ferrara 1960 (divorced 1964); m. 2nd Marion Magid 1968 (died 1993); one d.; ed Harvard Univ.; Faculty mem. New School for Social Research, New York 1963–64, Rutgers Univ. 1966, Sarah Lawrence Coll., Bronxville, NY 1967, 1971, CUNY 1967, 1968, Univ. of Iowa 1978, 1982, Columbia Univ. 1980, 1981, Brown Univ. 1988, Bennington Coll., Bennington, Vt 1987–2005, Univ. of California, Davis 1990, 1992, Beloit Coll., Wis. 1995; Gen. Ed. Penguin Nature Library 1985–2004; Houghton Mifflin Literary Fellow 1954; American Acad. of Arts and Letters Travelling Fellow 1964; Guggenheim Fellow 1964, 1975; mem. American Acad. of Arts and Letters,

American Acad. of Arts and Sciences; Longview Foundation Award 1961, O. Henry Award 1971, Brandeis Univ. Citation in Literature 1972, New York State Council on Arts Award 1972, American Acad. of Arts and Letters Harold D. Vursell Memorial Award 1981, Nat. Endowment for the Arts Award 1982, NY Public Library Literary Lion Award 1988, Nat. Magazine Award 1989, Lannan Foundation Literary Award 1993, Boston Public Library Literary Lights Award 1995, John Burroughs Medal 2012. *Publications:* Cat Man 1956, The Circle Home 1960, The Peacock's Tail 1965, Notes from the Century Before: A Journal from British Columbia 1969, The Courage of Turtles 1971, Walking the Dead Diamond River 1973, The Moose on the Wall: Field Notes from the Vermont Wilderness 1974, Red Wolves and Black Bears 1976, African Calliope: A Journey to the Sudan 1979, The Edward Hoagland Reader 1979, The Tugman's Passage 1982, City Tales 1986, Seven Rivers West 1986, Heart's Desire 1988, The Final Fate of the Alligators 1992, Balancing Acts 1992, Tigers and Ice 1999, Compass Points 2001, Hoagland on Nature 2003, Early in the Season 2008, Sex and the River Styx 2011, Alaskan Travels: Far-Flung Tales of Love and Adventure 2012, Children Are Diamonds (novel) 2013; numerous essays and short stories. *Address:* POB 51, Barton, VT 05822 (office); POB 615, Edgartown, MA 02539, USA (home). *Telephone:* (508) 627-8803 (office).

HOAGLAND, Richard Eugene, AB, MA, MFA; American diplomatist; *Deputy Chief of Mission, Embassy in Islamabad;* b. Fort Wayne, Ind.; ed Univ. of Virginia, Univ. of Grenoble, France; taught English as a foreign language in Zaïre 1974–76, and African literature at Carter-Woodson Inst. of African and Afro-American Studies, Univ. of Virginia; joined Foreign Service 1985, now career mem. Sr Foreign Service with rank of Minister-Counselor, foreign assignments have included Russia (Press Spokesman for the Embassy), Uzbekistan, Pakistan (twice), has also served in State Dept's Bureau of Intelligence and Research (Lead Analyst for Afghanistan 1989–91), US Deputy Special Envoy for Afghanistan 1991–92, Dir Office of Public Diplomacy, Bureau of S Asian Affairs and Special Adviser to Nat. Security Council for public diplomacy on Afghanistan 1999–2001, Dir Office of Caucasus and Cen. Asian Affairs, Bureau of Europe and Eurasian Affairs 2001–03, Amb. to Tajikistan 2003–06, Chargé d'affaires a.i., Embassy in Ashgabat, Turkmenistan 2007–08, Amb. to Kazakhstan 2008–11, Deputy Chief of Mission, Embassy in Islamabad 2011–; two Meritorious Honor Awards, three Superior Honor Awards, several Group Honor Awards, Presidential Performance Awards. *Address:* US Embassy, Diplomatic Enclave, Ramna 5, PO Box 1048, Islamabad, Pakistan (office). *Telephone:* (51) 2080000 (office). *Fax:* (51) 2276427 (office). *E-mail:* infoisb@state.gov (office). *Website:* islamabad.usembassy .gov (office).

HOARE, Sir Charles Antony Richard, Kt, MA, FRS, FREng; British computer scientist; *Consultant Principal Researcher, Microsoft Research Ltd;* b. 11 Jan. 1934, Colombo, Ceylon (now Sri Lanka); s. of the late Henry S. M. Hoare and Marjorie F. Hoare; m. Jill Pym 1962; two s. one d.; ed Dragon School, Oxford, King's School, Canterbury, Merton Coll., Oxford, Unit of Biometry, Oxford and Moscow State Univ.; with Elliott Brothers (London) Ltd 1960–68; Prof. of Computing Science, Queen's Univ., Belfast 1968–77; Prof. of Computation, Univ. of Oxford 1977–93; James Martin Prof. of Computing 1993–99, Prof. Emer. 1999–; Sr Researcher, Microsoft Research Ltd 1999–, now Consultant Prin. Researcher; Fellow, Wolfson Coll. 1977–99; mem. Academia Europaea; Foreign mem. Accad. dei Lincei, Italy; Corresp. mem. Bavarian Acad. of Sciences; Assoc. mem. US Nat. Acad. of Eng; Distinguished Fellow, British Computer Soc.; Fellow, Royal Acad. of Eng; Fellow, Royal Soc.; Hon. Fellow, Kellogg Coll. Oxford 1998, Darwin Coll. Cambridge 2001, Merton Coll. Oxford; Hon. DSc (Univ. of Southern Calif., Warwick, Pennsylvania, Queen's, Belfast); Hon. DUniv (York) 1989, (Essex) 1991, (Bath) 1993, (Oxford Brookes) 2000, (Queen Mary & Westfield Coll., London) 2005, (Heriot Watt) 2007, (Athens) 2007, (Warsaw) 2012, (Madrid) 2013; A.M. Turing Award 1980, Harry Goode Memorial Award, Faraday Medal 1985, Kyoto Prize 2000, John von Neuman Medal 2011, Sigplan Distinguished Achievement Award 2011. *Publications:* Structured Programming (co-author) 1972, Communicating Sequential Processes 1985, Essays in Computing Science 1989, Unifying Theories of Programming (co-author) 1998. *Leisure interests:* walking, music, jigsaws, reading, travel, gardening. *Address:* Microsoft Research Ltd, 21 Station Road, Cambridge, CB1 2FB, England (office). *Telephone:* (1223) 479800 (office). *Fax:* (1223) 479999 (office).

HOBBS, Franklin (Fritz) W., BA, MBA; American business executive; *Chairman, Ally Financial Inc.;* ed Harvard Coll., Harvard Univ.; fmr Pres. and CEO Dillon, Read & Co. Inc.; fmr Chair. UBS AG's Warburg Dillon, Read & Co. Inc. unit; currently adviser to One Equity Partners LLC (manages investments and commitments for JPMorgan Chase & Co.); CEO Houlihan Lokey Howard & Zukin –2009; mem. Bd of Dirs and Chair. GMAC Financial Services (renamed Ally Financial Inc. 2010) 2009–; mem. Bd of Dirs Lord Abbett & Co., Molson Coors Brewing Co. *Address:* Ally Financial Inc., 200 Renaissance Center, Detroit, MI 48265-2000, USA (office). *Telephone:* (313) 556-5000 (office). *Fax:* (815) 282-6156 (office). *E-mail:* info@ally.com (office). *Website:* www.ally.com (office).

HOBDAY, Sir Gordon (Ivan), Kt, PhD, FRSC, CChem, DL; British business executive (retd); b. 1 Feb. 1916, Derbyshire; s. of the late Alexander Thomas Hobday and Frances Cassandra Hobday (née Meads); m. 1st Margaret Jean Joule 1940 (died 1995); one d.; m. 2nd Patricia Shaw (née Birge) 2002; ed Long Eaton Grammar School, Univ. Coll., Notts.; joined The Boots Co. Ltd 1939, Dir of Research 1952–68, Deputy Man. Dir 1968–70, Man. Dir 1970–72, Chair. 1973–81; Dir The Metal Box Co. Ltd 1976–81, Lloyds Bank 1981–86; Deputy Chair. Price Comm. 1977–78; Chair. Cen. Ind. TV Co. Ltd 1981–85; Chancellor Univ. of Nottingham 1979–91 (Pres. of the Council 1973–82); Pres. Portland Coll. 1990–93; Lord Lt and Keeper of the Rolls for Notts. 1983–91; Hon. LLD. *Leisure interests:* handicrafts, gardening.

HOBERMAN, Brent, MA; British business executive; ed Univ. of Oxford; Sr Consultant, Media and Telecoms Spectrum Strategy Consultants, LineOne; Gen. Man., Head of Business Devt and Founder mem. QXL; co-f. with Martha Lane Fox (q.v.) and CEO lastminute.com 1998–2006, Chair. and Chief Strategy Officer 2006–07, Consultant 2007–; Dir (non-exec.) Guardian Media Group 2007–; Chair. (non-exec.) Wayn.com (travel and social networking site) 2007–; Exec. Chair. mydeco.com (home design website) 2007–; Advisor Twitter Partners 2009–; Gov. Univ. of the Arts, London. *Address:* Guardian Media Group PLC, Kings Place, 90

York Way, London, N1 9GU, England (office). *Telephone:* (20) 3353-2000 (office). *Website:* www.gmgplc.co.uk (office).

HOBSON, Mellody, BA; American investment management executive; *President, Ariel Investments LLC;* b. 3 April 1969, Chicago; ed St Ignatius Coll. Prep., Woodrow Wilson School of Int. Relations and Public Policy, Princeton Univ.; joined Ariel Capital Man. LLC (now Ariel Investments) 1991, Pres. 2000–, also Chair. Bd of Trustees Ariel Investment Trust; financial analysis contrib., Good Morning America, ABC; appearances on CNN, WGN-TV; mem. Bd of Dirs Field Museum, Chicago Public Library, Chicago Public Educ. Fund, Sundance Inst., Tellabs Inc., DreamWorks Animation SKG Inc., Estée Lauder Cos Inc., Starbucks Corpn, Groupon 2011–; term mem. New York Council on Foreign Relations; mem. Econ. Club of Chicago, Commercial Club of Chicago, Young Pres.'s Org.; Trustee Princeton Univ.; Global Leader of Tomorrow, World Econ. Forum, Davos 2001. *Address:* Ariel Investments LLC, 200 East Randolph Drive, Suite 2900, Chicago, IL 60601, USA (office). *Telephone:* (312) 726-0140 (office). *Fax:* (312) 726-7473 (office). *E-mail:* email@arielinvestments.com (office). *Website:* www .arielinvestments.com (office).

HOCH, Orion, PhD; American business executive; b. 21 Dec. 1928, Canonsburg, Pa; m. 1st Jane Lee Ogan 1952 (died 1978); one s. two d.; m. 2nd Catherine Nan Richardson 1980; one s.; ed Carnegie Mellon Univ., UCLA and Stanford Univ.; engaged in research and devt Hughes Aircraft 1952–54; various positions, Electron Devices Div. Litton Industries Inc. 1957–68, Vice-Pres. Litton Components Group 1968–70, Corp. Vice-Pres. Litton Industries Inc. 1970, Sr Vice-Pres. 1971, Deputy Head, Business Systems and Equipment Group 1973–74, Pres. Advanced Memory Systems (later Intersil Inc.) 1974–81, Pres. Litton Industries Inc. 1982–88, Dir and COO 1982, CEO 1986–93, Chair. 1988–94, Chair. Emer. 1994–; mem. Bd of Dirs UNOVA Inc. 1982–2001; fmr mem. Bd of Dirs Bessemer Group Inc., Honeywell Measurex Corpn; Chair. Exec. Cttee Western Atlas Inc. 1994–98; Trustee, Carnegie Mellon Univ. *Address:* 55 Melanie Lane, Atherton, CA 94027, USA.

HOCHHUTH, Rolf; German playwright; b. 1 April 1931; m.; three s.; fmr publisher's reader; Resident Municipal Playwright, Basel 1963; mem. PEN of FRG. *Publications include:* plays: Der Stellvertreter: Ein christliches Trauerspiel (The Deputy, a Christian Tragedy) 1963, The Employer 1965, The Soldiers 1966, Anatomy of Revolution 1969, The Guerrillas 1970, The Midwife 1972, Lysistrata and NATO 1973, The Survivor 1981, Alan Turing 1987, Judith 1984, The Immaculate Conception 1989, Wessis in Weimar 1993, McKinsey is Coming 2004; novel: A Love in Germany 1980. *Address:* Agentur Hegmann, Essener Str. 32, 45529 Hattingen, Germany (office). *Telephone:* (23) 2443157 (office). *E-mail:* ahegmann@web.de (office). *Website:* www.hegmann.de.tt (office); www.rolf -hochhuth.de.

HOCHMAIR, Ingeborg, PhD; Austrian electrical engineer and entrepreneur; *CEO, MED-EL;* b. 17 Jan. 1953, Vienna; d. of Kurt Desoyer and Elisabeth Desoyer; m. Erwin Hochmair; four c.; ed Vienna Univ. of Tech.; spent a semester abroad in Karlsruhe, then worked as an Asst at Inst. of Gen. Electrical Eng and Electronics, Vienna; Fulbright Scholar, Stanford Univ. 1979; partnered with 3M 1981–88; Co-founder and CEO MED-EL 1989–; Dr hc (Innsbruck Medical Univ.) 2010; Holzer-Prize, Vienna Tech. Univ. 1979, Leonardo da Vinci Award 1980, Sandoz Prize 1984, Entrepreneur of the Year 1995, Veuve Clicquot Business Woman of the Year 1995, Wilhelm Exner Medal 1996, Lasker–DeBakey Clinical Medical Research Award (co-recipient) 2013. *Achievements include:* co-developed, with Erwin Hochmair, the first multi-channel microelectronic cochlear implant 1977. *Address:* MED-EL Medical Electronics, Fürstenweg 77A, 6020 Innsbruck, Austria (office). *Telephone:* (512) 57788 (office). *Fax:* (512) 293381 (office). *E-mail:* office@medel .com (office). *Website:* www.medel.com (office).

HOCHSCHILD, Eduardo; Peruvian mining industry executive; *Executive Chairman, Hochschild Mining plc;* s. of Luis Hochschild; ed Tufts Univ., Boston, USA; joined Hochschild Mining Group as Safety Asst, Arcata Unit 1987, Head of Group 1998–2006, Exec. Chair. 2006–, oversaw listing of co. on London Stock Exchange 2006; Vice-Chair. Cementos Pacasmayo SAA; mem. Bd of Dirs COMEX Peru, Banco de Crédito del Perú, Sociedad Nacional de Minería y Petróleo, Asian Pacific Econ. Council Business Advisory Cttee, Conferencia Episcopal Peruana, Pacífico Peruano Suiza, TECSUP, Universidad Nacional de Ingeniería, Universidad de Ciencias Aplicadas. *Address:* Hochschild Mining plc, Pasaje El Carmen, #180, Surco, Lima, 33, Peru (office). *Telephone:* (1) 3172000 (office). *Website:* www .hochschildmining.com (office).

HOCKEY, Joseph (Joe) Benedict, BA, LLB; Australian lawyer and politician; *Treasurer;* b. 2 Aug. 1965, Sydney; m. Melissa Babbage; two s. one d.; ed Univ. of Sydney; fmr banking and finance lawyer, Corrs Chambers Westgarth; fmr Dir of Policy to Premier of NSW; mem. House of Reps (Parl.) for N Sydney 1996–, Man. of Opposition Business in the House 2007–09; Minister for Financial Services and Regulation 1998–2001, for Small Business and Tourism 2001–04, for Human Services 2004–07, also Minister assisting Minister for Workplace Relations 2006–07, Minister for Employment and Workplace Relations and Minister assisting Minister for Public Service Jan.–Dec. 2007; Shadow Minister for Health and Ageing 2007–08, for Finance, Competition Policy and Deregulation 2008–09, Shadow Treasurer 2009–13, Treasurer 2013–; mem. Liberal Party of Australia. *Address:* Department of the Treasury, Langton Crescent, Parkes, ACT 2600, Australia (office). *Telephone:* (2) 6263-2111 (office). *Fax:* (2) 6273-2614 (office). *E-mail:* department@treasury.gov.au (office). *Website:* ww.treasury.gov.au (office); jbh.ministers.treasury.gov.au.

HOCKFIELD, Susan, BA, PhD; American neuroscientist, academic and fmr university administrator; *President Emerita, Massachusetts Institute of Technology;* b. 24 March 1951; m. Prof. Thomas N. Byrne, MD 1991; one d.; ed Horace Greeley High School, Chappaqua, NY, Univ. of Rochester, Georgetown Univ. School of Medicine; Postdoctoral Fellow, Univ. of California, San Francisco 1979–80; Jr Staff Investigator, Cold Spring Harbor Lab. 1980–82, Sr Staff Investigator 1982–85, Dir Summer Neurobiology Program 1985–97; Asst Prof., Section of Neurobiology, Yale Univ. School of Medicine 1985–89, Dir of Grad. Studies, Section of Neurobiology 1986–94, Assoc. Prof. 1989–94, Prof. 1994–2004, Dean Grad. School of Arts and Sciences 1998–2002, William Edward Gilbert Prof. of Neurobiology 2001–04, Provost 2003–04; Prof. of Neuroscience, MIT 2004–, Pres. (first woman) MIT 2004–12, Pres. Emer. 2012–; Marie Curie Visiting Prof.,

John F. Kennedy School of Govt, Harvard Univ. 2012–; mem. Editorial Bd Learning and Memory 1993–, NeuroImage 1994–; mem. Bd of Dirs General Electric Co. 2006–, Lord Foundation of Massachusetts 2005–, Nat. Math and Science Initiative 2007–, World Econ. Forum 2008–; mem. Leadership Council, The Climate Group 2009–; mem. Bd of Overseers Boston Symphony Orchestra 2006–; Trustee Carnegie Corpn of New York 2006–; Corpn mem. Woods Hole Oceanographic Inst. 2006–; mem. Soc. for Neuroscience, NIH Nat. Advisory Neurological Disorders and Stroke Council 2002–04; Trustee, Cold Spring Harbour Lab.; Life mem. Council on Foreign Relations 2007; Fellow, American Acad. of Arts and Sciences 2004, AAAS 2005; Affiliated Fellow, American Acad. of Rome 2012; Hon. MRIA 2010; Hon. mem. Asscn of Alumni and Alumnæ of the Massachusetts Inst. of Tech. 2010; Hon. DSc (Cold Spring Harbor Lab., Watson School of Biological Sciences) 2006, (Brown Univ.) 2006, (Mount Sinai School of Medicine, New York Univ.) 2009, (Univ. of Edinburgh) 2009; Dr hc (Tsinghua Univ.) 2006, (jtly by New Univ. of Lisbon, Technical Univ. of Lisbon and Univ. of Porto, Portugal) 2009, (Univ. Pierre and Marie Curie, Paris) 2010; Charles Judson Herrick Award, American Asscn of Anatomists 1987, Wilbur Lucius Cross Medal, Yale Univ. 2003, Meliora Citation for Career Achievement, Univ. of Rochester 2003, Sheffield Medal, Yale Univ. 2004, Golden Plate Award, Acad. of Achievement 2005, Amelia Earhart Award, Women's Union 2005, Citation Award, Midwest Research Inst. 2006, America's Best Leaders honoree, U.S. News & World Report and the Center for Public Leadership, John F. Kennedy School of Govt 2009, Edison Achievement Award 2010, Pinnacle Award for Lifetime Achievement, Greater Boston Chamber of Commerce 2013. *Publications:* Molecular Probes of the Nervous System – Selected Methods for Antibodies and Nucleic Acid Probes (co-author) 1993; numerous book chapter and scientific papers and reviews in professional journals and articles for the Boston Globe; six US patents 1997–2009. *Address:* Office of the President, Massachusetts Institute of Technology, 77 Massachusetts Avenue, Building 3-207, Cambridge, MA 02139-4307, USA (office). *Telephone:* (617) 253-0148 (office). *Fax:* (617) 253-3124 (office). *E-mail:* president-emerita@mit.edu (office). *Website:* hockfield.mit.edu (office).

HOCKING, John, LLB; Australian lawyer and UN official; *Assistant Secretary-General, Registrar, International Criminal Tribunal for the former Yugoslavia;* b. 6 Aug. 1957; one c.; ed Monash Univ., Sydney Univ., Univ. of London, UK; fmr Legal and Policy Adviser, OECD, Special Broadcasting Service (nat. multi-cultural television and radio broadcaster), British Film Inst., Australian Film Comm.; served as Legal Assoc. to Justice Michael Kirby (fmr Pres. of Court of Appeal, Judge of High Court); joined Int. Criminal Tribunal for the fmr Yugoslavia (ICTY) 1997, served as Sr Legal Officer for Appeals Chambers of both ICTY and Int. Criminal Tribunal for Rwanda, Deputy Registrar, ICTY 2004–09, Asst Sec.-Gen. and Registrar 2009–, Asst Sec.-Gen. and Registrar, Mechanism for International Criminal Tribunals 2012–; barrister, Lincoln's Inn, UK, Supreme Court of Victoria, Supreme Court of NSW. *Address:* International Criminal Tribunal for the former Yugoslavia, PO Box 13888, 2501 EW, The Hague, Netherlands (office). *Website:* www.icty.org (office).

HOCKNEY, David, OM, CH, RA; British artist, stage designer and photographer; b. 9 July 1937, Bradford, Yorks.; s. of the late Kenneth Hockney and Laura Hockney; ed Bradford Grammar School, Bradford Coll. of Art, Royal Coll. of Art, London; taught at Maidstone Coll. of Art 1962, Univ. of Iowa 1964, Univ. of Colorado 1965, UCLA 1966 (Hon. Chair. of Drawing 1980), Univ. of California, Berkeley 1967; has travelled extensively in Europe and USA; many works now housed in Salts Mill, Saltaire, nr Bradford; mem. Advisory Bd Standpoint (political magazine) 2008–; Assoc. mem. Royal Acad. 1985; Foreign Hon. mem. American Acad. of Arts and Sciences 1997; Freedom of the City of Bradford 2000; Hon. PhD (Aberdeen) 1988, (Royal Coll. of Art) 1992; Hon. DLitt (Oxford) 1995, (Leeds) 2000, (Cambridge) 2007; hon. degree from Acad. of Fine Arts, Florence 2003; Guinness Award 1961, Graphic Prize, Paris Biennale 1963, First Prize 8th Int. Exhbn of Drawings and Engravings, Lugano 1964, prize at 6th Int. Exhbn of Graphic Art, Ljubljana 1965, Cracow 1st Int. Print Biennale 1966, First Prize, 6th John Moores Exhbn 1967, Hamburg Foundation Shakespeare Prize 1983, Progress Medal, Royal Photographic Soc. 1988, Praemium Imperiale, Japan Art Asscn 1989, Fifth Annual Gov.'s Award for Visual Arts in Calif. 1994, Kulturpreis, Deutsche Gesellschaft für Photographie E.V. 1997, Mario Tamayo Award for Outstanding Dedication in the Visual Arts, Los Angeles Contemporary Exhbns 1998, Charles Wollaston Award, Royal Acad. of Arts, Summer Exhbn, London 1999, Commendation by the Gov. of Calif., Gray Davis, for Efforts on Behalf of People Living with HIV/AIDS 1999, Centenary Medal, Royal Photographic Soc. 2003, Lorenzo De' Medici Lifetime Career Award, Florence Biennale 2003, Orthopaedic Ward at The Yorkshire Clinic, W Yorks. named 'The Hockney Ward' 2003, La Rosa D'Oro Award, Palermo, Italy 2004, Bannister Fletcher Award 2004. *Film:* A Bigger Splash (autobiographical documentary) 1974. *Stage design:* set: Ubu Roi, Royal Court Theatre, London 1966, Rake's Progress, Glyndebourne 1975, Die Zauberflöte, Glyndebourne 1978, La Scala 1979, Nightingale, Covent Garden 1983, Varii Capricci, Metropolitan Opera House, New York 1983, Tristan and Isolde, LA Music Centre Opera, LA 1987, Turandot, Lyric Opera 1992–, San Francisco 1993, Die Frau Ohne Schatten, Covent Garden, London 1992, LA Music Centre Opera 1993, The Performing Arts Museum, Melbourne (Green Room Award for Stage Design in Opera 1997) 1997; costume and set: Les Mamelles de Teresias, Metropolitan Opera House, New York 1980, L'Enfant et les sortilèges, Metropolitan Opera House, New York 1980, Parade, Metropolitan Opera House, New York 1980, Oedipus Rex, Metropolitan Opera House, New York 1981, Le Sacre du Printemps, Metropolitan Opera House, New York 1981, Le Rossignol, Metropolitan Opera House, New York 1981. *Radio:* guest ed., Today programme (BBC Radio 4) to air his views as a pro-tobacco campaigner Dec. 2009. *Publications:* Hockney by Hockney 1976, David Hockney, Travel with Pen, Pencil and Ink (autobiog.) 1978, Paper Pools 1980, Photographs 1982, China Diary (with Stephen Spender), 1982, Hockney Paints the Stage 1983, David Hockney: Cameraworks 1984, Hockney on Photography: Conversations with Paul Joyce 1988, David Hockney: A Retrospective 1988, Hockney's Alphabet (ed. by Stephen Spender) 1991, That's the Way I See It (autobiog.) 1993, Off the Wall: Hockney Posters 1994, David Hockney's Dog Days 1998, Hockney on Art: Photography, Painting and Perspective 1999, Hockney on 'Art': Conversation with Paul Joyce 2000, Secret Knowledge: Rediscovering the Lost Techniques of the Old Masters (British Book Design and Production Award 2002) 2001, Hockney's Pictures 2004; illustrated Six

Fairy Tales of the Brothers Grimm 1969, The Blue Guitar 1977, Hockney's Alphabet 1991; contributed original sketches to launch edn of Standpoint magazine June 2008. *Address:* c/o 7508 Santa Monica Boulevard, Los Angeles, CA 90046-6407, USA. *Website:* www.hockneypictures.com.

HODDLE, Glenn; British football manager and fmr professional footballer; *Director, The Glenn Hoddle Academy;* b. 27 Oct. 1957, Hayes, Middx; s. of Derek Hoddle and Teresa Roberts; m. Christine Anne Stirling (divorced 1999); one s. two d.; ed Burnt Mill School, Harlow; attacking midfielder; played for Tottenham Hotspur 1975–87 (won UEFA Cup 1984, FA Cup 1981, 1982, FA Community Shield 1981), AS Monaco, France 1988–91 (won Ligue 1 Title 1987–88, French Cup 1991), Swindon Town (also Man.) 1991–93, Chelsea (also Man.) 1993–95; won 12 Under-21 caps and 53 full caps on England nat. team 1979–88, played in World Cup 1982 and 1986, Man. 1996–99 (won Tournoi de France 1997); Man. Chelsea 1996, Southampton 2000–01, Tottenham Hotspur 2001–03, Wolverhampton Wanderers 2004–06; Founder and Dir The Glenn Hoddle Acad. (first ind., professional football acad. offering alternative to professional club system) 2008–; football pundit for Sky TV. *Publications:* Spurred to Success (autobiography), Glenn Hoddle: The 1998 World Cup Story 1998. *Leisure interests:* tennis, golf, reading. *Address:* c/o The Glenn Hoddle Academy, Barceló Montecastillo Resort, Ctra. Arcos, km 6 11406 Jerez de la Frontera, Cádiz, Spain. *E-mail:* info@glennhoddleacademy.com. *Website:* www.glennhoddleacademy.com.

HODEL, Donald Paul, JD; American lawyer (retd) and fmr government official; *Chairman Emeritus, Summit Power Group Inc.;* b. 23 May 1935, Portland, Ore.; s. of Philip E. Hodel and Theresia R. (Brodt) Hodel; m. Barbara B. Stockman 1956; two s. (one deceased); ed Harvard Coll. and Univ. of Oregon; admitted to Ore. Bar 1960 (retd 2008); Attorney, Davies, Biggs, Strayer, Stoel & Boley 1960–63; Georgia Pacific Corpn 1963–69; Deputy Admin., Bonneville Power Admin. 1969–72, Admin. 1972–77; Pres. Nat. Elec. Reliability Council, Princeton, NJ 1978–80; Pres. Hodel Assocs. Inc. 1978–81; Under-Sec. Dept of Interior 1981–83; Sec. of Energy 1982–85, of the Interior 1985–89; Founder and Chair. Summit Power Group Inc. 1989–, currently Chair. Emer.; Pres. and CEO Focus on the Family 2003–05; Republican. *Address:* c/o Summit Power Group, LLC, 83 South King Street, Suite 200, Seattle, WA 98104, USA (office). *Telephone:* (206) 780-3551 (office). *E-mail:* info@summitpower.com (office). *Website:* www.summitpower.com (office).

HODGE, Daniel Robert; Curaçao banker and politician; b. 23 Oct. 1959; ed Erasmus Universiteit Rotterdam, Netherlands; Man. Dir Curaçaose Postspaarbank (PSB Bank) NV 2002–12; Prime Minister 2012–13. *Address:* c/o Office of the Prime Minister, Fort Amsterdam 17, Willemstad, Curaçao (office).

HODGE, Sir James William, KCVO, CMG, MA; British diplomatist; *Chairman, Society of Pension Consultants;* b. 24 Dec. 1943; s. of the late William Hodge and Catherine Hodge (née Carden); m. Frances Margaret Coyne 1970; three d.; ed Holy Cross Acad., Edin., Univ. of Edin.; entered FCO 1966, Rhodesia Political Dept 1966–67, Second Sec. (Information), Tokyo 1967–72, FCO Marine and Transport Dept 1972–73, UN Dept 1973–75, First Sec. (Devt and Later Chancery), Lagos 1975–78, FCO Personnel Operations Dept 1978–81, First Sec. (Econ.) and later Counsellor (Commercial), Tokyo 1981–86, Head of Chancery, Copenhagen 1986–90, FCO Security Dept 1990–93, attached to Royal Coll. of Defence Studies 1994; Minister Consular Gen. and Deputy Head of Mission, Beijing 1995–96; Amb. to Thailand 1996–2000; Consul-Gen. to Hong Kong Special Admin. Region, People's Repub. of China (concurrently non-resident Consul-Gen. to Macao) 2000–03; Chair. Soc. of Pension Consultants 2007–, Foreign and Commonwealth Office Asscn; Deputy Chair. Asia House; mem. Cen. Council of Royal Over-Seas League; Advisor to Mansion House Scholarship Scheme; Hon. DIur (Univ. of Liverpool) 2004. *Leisure interests:* books, music. *Address:* Foreign and Commonwealth Office Association, Room KG/117, King Charles Street, London, SW1A 2AH; Society of Pension Consultants, St Bartholomew House, 92 Fleet Street, London, EC4Y 1DG, England (office). *Telephone:* (20) 7353-1688 (office). *Fax:* (20) 7353-9296 (office). *E-mail:* info@spc.uk.com (office). *Website:* www.spc.uk.com (office); www.fcoa.org.uk (office).

HODGE, Patricia Ann; British actress; b. 29 Sept. 1946, Grimsby, Lincs.; d. of the late Eric Hodge and Marion Phillips; m. Peter Owen 1976; two s.; ed Wintringham Girls' Grammar School, Grimsby, St Helen's School, Northwood, Middx, Maria Grey Coll. (now West London Inst. of Higher Educ.), Brunel Univ., Twickenham, London Acad. of Music and Dramatic Art (LAMDA); Eveline Evans Award for Best Actress LAMDA, Olivier Award for Best Supporting Actress 1999; Hon. DLitt (Hull) 1996, (Brunel) 2001, (Leicester) 2003. *Stage appearances include:* No-one Was Saved, All My Sons, Say Who You Are, The Birthday Party, The Anniversary, Popkiss, Two Gentlemen of Verona, Pippin, Maudie, Hair, The Beggar's Opera, Pal Joey, Look Back in Anger, Dick Whittington, Happy Yellow, The Brian Cant Children's Show, Then and Now, The Mitford Girls, As You Like It, Benefactors, Noel and Gertie, Separate Tables, The Prime of Miss Jean Brodie, A Little Night Music (Royal Nat. Theatre), Heartbreak House 1997, Money (Royal Nat. Theatre) (Laurence Olivier Theatre Award for Best Supporting Actress 2000) 1999, Summer-folk (Royal Nat. Theatre) 1999, Noises Off (Royal Nat. Theatre and tour) 2000–01, His Dark Materials (Royal Nat. Theatre) 2004, Boeing Boeing 2007, The Country Wife 2008, The Clean House 2008, Calendar Girls 2008. *Film appearances:* The Disappearance, Rosie Dixon—Night Nurse, The Waterloo Bridge Handicap, The Elephant Man, Heavy Metal, Betrayal, Sunset, Just Ask for Diamond, The Secret Life of Ian Fleming, The Leading Man 1996, Prague Duet 1996, Jilting Joe 1997, Before You Go 2002. *Television appearances:* Valentine, The Girls of Slender Means, Night of the Father, Great Big Groovy Horse, The Naked Civil Servant, Softly, Softly, Jackanory Playhouse, Act of Rape, Crimewriters, Target, Rumpole of the Bailey, The One and Only Mrs Phyllis Dixey, Edward and Mrs Simpson, Disraeli, The Professionals, Holding the Fort, The Other 'Arf, Jemima Shore Investigates, Hayfever, The Death of the Heart, Robin of Sherwood, O.S.S., Sherlock Holmes, Time for Murder, Hotel du Lac, The Life and Loves of a She Devil, Rich Tea and Sympathy 1991, The Cloning of Joanna May 1991, The Legacy of Reginald Perrin 1996, The Moonstone 1996, The People's Passion (film) 1999, The Falklands Play (film) 2002, Waking the Dead (series) 2002, Sweet Medicine (series) 2003, Agatha Christie Marple: The Sittaford Mystery (film) 2006, Hustle (series) 2007, Maxwell 2007, Miranda 2009–. *Address:* c/o Independent Talent Group Ltd, Oxford House, 76 Oxford Street, London, W1D

1BS, England (office). *Telephone:* (20) 7636-6565 (office). *Fax:* (20) 7323-0101 (office). *Website:* www.independenttalent.com (office).

HODGES, Jim, BA, JD; American consultant and fmr state governor; *Partner, McGuireWoods LLP;* b. 19 Nov. 1956, Lancaster, SC; m. Rachel Gardner; two s.; ed Davidson Coll., Univ. of South Carolina; Lancaster Co. Attorney 1983–87; Pnr, Thomas, Goldsmith, Folks and Hodges 1983–90; mem. SC House of Reps 1986–97; Gen. Counsel Springs Co. 1990–98; Gov. of South Carolina 1999–2002; Founder, CEO and Man. Dir Hodges Consulting Group 2003–09; Pnr, Covington Lobdell and Hickman LLP 2003–08; currently Pnr, McGuireWoods LLP; Sr Advisor, McGuire Woods Consulting LLC; Chair. Southern Growth Policies Bd; Chair. Southern Tech. Council; Chair. Business Partnership School of Business, Univ. of South Carolina; mem. Bd of Dirs Park City Center for Public Policy; mem. Bd of Advisors Imadgen, Strategic Partnerships LLC, Public Insight LP; Dr hc (Univ. of South Carolina), (South Carolina State Univ.), (Winthrop Univ.), (Francis Marion Univ.); Legislator of the Year, SC Chamber of Commerce 1993, Compleat Lawyer Silver Medallion 1994, Guardian of Small Business Award, Nat. Fed. of Ind. Businesses 1996, Special Service Award, Common Cause 1998. *Address:* McGuireWoods LLP, 2001 K Street, NW, Suite 400, Washington, DC 20006-1040, USA (office). *Telephone:* (202) 857-1700 (office). *Fax:* (202) 857-1737 (office). *E-mail:* jhodges@mwcllc.com (office). *Website:* www.mcguirewoods.com (office).

HODGKIN, Sir Howard, Kt, CH, CBE, DLitt; British painter; b. 6 Aug. 1932; m. Julia Lane 1955; two s.; ed Camberwell School of Art and Bath Acad. of Art; Trustee, Tate Gallery 1970–76, Nat. Gallery 1978–85; British rep., Venice Biennale 1984; works in many public collections including Tate Gallery, London, Museum of Modern Art, New York, Nat. Gallery of Washington, Metropolitan Museum of Art, New York, Nat. Gallery of S Australia, Adelaide, Walker Art Center, Minneapolis; mem. Cttee Nat. Art Collections Fund 1989–90; Hon. Fellow, Brasenose Coll., Univ. of Oxford 1988, London Inst. 1999; Hon. DLitt (Birmingham) 1997, (Oxford) 2000; Tate Gallery Turner Prize 1985, Shakespeare Prize, Alfred Toepfer Stiftung FVS, Germany 1997. *Address:* c/o Gagosian Gallery, 6–24 Britannia Street, London, WC1X 9JD, England. *Website:* www.howardhodgkin.org.uk (office).

HODGKINSON, Sir Mike, Kt, BA; British business executive; b. 7 April 1944, Essex; m.; three c.; ed Hornchurch Grammar School, Nottingham Univ.; Ford Grad. Training Programme 1965; Finance and Admin. Dir Leyland Cars (Eng Div.) 1973–77; Man. Dir Land Rover 1978–82; Man. Dir Express Dairy Group 1985; CEO GM Foods Europe, Grand Metropolitan Group 1986–91; Group Airports Dir BAA 1992–99, CEO 1999–2003; Chair. The Post Office 2003–07; mem. Bd of Dirs (non-exec.) Crossrail Limited, Dublin Airport Authority plc, Nyras, Transport for London, Tui Travel plc (Deputy Chair.); mem. ACI World Gov. Bd, Advisory Bd Essex Econ. Partnership 2001–; Chair. Hayes West Drayton Partnership. *Leisure interests:* golf, theatre. *Address:* c/o Board of Directors, Nyras, 5th Floor, 40 Queen Street, London, EC4R 1HN, England.

HODGSON, Pete; New Zealand politician; b. 1950, Whangarei; m.; two s.; ed Massey Univ.; fmrly worked as Veterinary Surgeon in New Zealand and UK; mem. New Zealand Labour Party 1976–; MP for Dunedin N 1990–2011; Minister of Energy, Fisheries, Forestry, Research Science and Tech. 1999–2004, Minister for Crown Research Insts, Assoc. Minister of Econ., Industry and Regional Devt and Assoc. Minister of Foreign Affairs and Trade 1999–2005; Minister of Transport, of Commerce, for Land Information, of Statistics and Assoc. Minister of Health 2004–05, Minister of Health 2005–07, of Econ. Devt, Tertiary Educ. and Minister of Research, Science and Tech. 2007–08. *Address:* c/o Ministry of Economic Development, POB 1473, 33 Bowen Street, Wellington, New Zealand.

HODGSON, Thomas R., BS, MS, MBA; American business executive; *Chairman, Idenix Pharmaceuticals, Inc.;* b. 17 Dec. 1941, Lakewood, Ohio; s. of Thomas J. Hodgson and Dallas L. Hodgson; m. Susan Cawrse 1963; one s. two d.; ed Purdue Univ., Univ. of Michigan and Harvard Univ. Business School; Devt Engineer, DuPont 1964; Assoc., Booz-Allen & Hamilton 1969–72; with Abbott Labs 1972–99, Gen. Man. Faultless Div. 1976–78, Vice-Pres. and Gen. Man. Hosp. Div. 1978–80, Pres. Hosp. Div. 1980–83, Group Vice-Pres. and Pres. Abbott Int. Ltd 1983–84, Exec. Vice-Pres. 1985–90, Pres. and COO Abbott Labs Oct. 1990–99 (retd); mem. Bd of Dirs Idenix Pharmaceuticals Inc. 2002–, Chair. 2012–; Visiting Prof., Purdue Univ. 1996; mem. Bd of Dirs The St. Paul Travelers Inc. 1997–, Intermune, Inc. 2003–; Dr hc (Purdue Univ.). *Leisure interests:* skiing, scuba, wind-surfing, racquetball, tennis, kayaking. *Address:* Idenix Pharmaceuticals, Inc., 320 Bent Street, 4th Floor, Cambridge, MA 02141-2025, USA (office). *Telephone:* (617) 995-9800 (office). *Website:* www.idenix.com (office).

HOEFDRAAD, Gillmore; Suriname economist and central banker; *Governor, Centrale Bank van Suriname;* b. 1962; coordinator of Caribbean Programme, Center for Latin American Monetary Studies, Mexico –1999; Sr Economist with IMF 1999–2010; Gov. Centrale Bank van Suriname 2010–. *Achievements include:* fmr champion chess player, represented Suriname at Chess Olympiad, Lucerne 1982. *Address:* Office of the Governor, Centrale Bank van Suriname, 18–20 Waterkant, POB 1801, Paramaribo, Suriname (office). *Telephone:* 473741 (office). *Fax:* 476444 (office). *E-mail:* info@cbvs.sr (office). *Website:* www.cbvs.sr (office).

HØEG, Peter, MA; Danish writer; b. 1957, Copenhagen; m.; two d.; ed Univ. of Copenhagen; worked as sailor, ballet dancer, athlete and actor before becoming full-time writer; f. Lolwe Foundation 1996. *Publications:* Forestilling om det Tyvende århundrede (trans. as The History of Danish Dreams) 1988, Fortællinger om natten (trans. as Tales of the Night; short stories) 1990, Frk. Smillas fornemmelse for sne (trans. as Miss Smilla's Feeling for Snow) 1992, De måske egnede (trans. as Borderliners) 1994, Kvinden og aben (trans. as The Woman and the Ape) 1996, Den stille pige (trans. as The Quiet Girl) 2006. *Address:* c/o Rosinante, Købmagergade 62, Postbox 2252, 1019 Copenhagen K, Denmark (office). *Telephone:* 33-41-18-00 (office). *E-mail:* rosinante@rosinante.dk (home). *Website:* www.rosinante.dk (office).

HOEVEN, John, BA, MBA; American banker and politician; *Senator from North Dakota;* b. 13 March 1957, Bismarck, N Dakota; m. Mical (Mikey) Laird; one s. one d.; ed Dartmouth Coll., Northwestern Univ. Business School; Exec. Vice-Pres. First Western Bank, Minot 1986–93; Pres. and CEO Bank of North Dakota 1993–2000; Gov. of N Dakota 2000–10; Senator from N Dakota 2011–, mem.

Appropriations Cttee 2011–, Energy and Natural Resources Cttee 2011–; mem. Souris Valley Humane Soc.; Chair. Interstate Oil & Gas Compact Comm., Govs' Ethanol Coalition, Midwestern Govs Asscn, Health and Human Services Cttee, and Ntural Resources Cttee, Nat. Govs Asscn, Minot Area Devt Corpn; Trustee, Bismarck State Coll.; mem. Bd of Dirs First Western Bank & Trust, North Dakota Bankers Asscn, North Dakota Small Business Investment Co., North Dakota Econ. Devt Asscn, Bismarck YMCA, Harold Schafer Leadership Center; Dir Minot Kiwanis Club; Republican. *Address:* 120 Russell Senate Office Building, Washington, DC, 20510, USA (office). *Telephone:* (202) 224-2551 (office). *Fax:* (202) 224-7999 (office). *Website:* hoeven.senate.gov (office).

HOFFALT, Josua; French ballet dancer; *Star Dancer (Étoile), Ballet de l'Opéra National de Paris;* b. 1984; ed Dance School of the Paris Opera, Nanterre; began dancing aged eight, took private lessons with Colette Armand, then with Dir of Nat. Ballet of Marseille, aged ten; mem. Ballet of Paris Opera 2002–, promoted to Prin. Dancer 2009–, named Star Dancer (Étoile) by Dir Nicolas Joel 2012–; Silver Medal (Junior category), Int. Ballet Competition, Varna 2003, (Senior category, pas de deux with Mathilde Froustey) 2004, Prix du Cercle Carpeaux 2004, Prix de l'AROP 2009. *Ballet roles include:* Drosselmeyer in The Nutcracker, title role in Romeo and Juliet,Gaston Rieux in The Lady of the Camellias, the Prince in The Sleeping Beauty, Beranger in Raymonda, Frederick Lemaître and Lacenaire in Les Enfants du Paradis, Solor in La Bayadère, Frantz in Coppélia. *Address:* Ballet de l'Opéra National de Paris, Palais Garnier, 8 rue Scribe, 75009 Paris, France. *E-mail:* info@operadeparis.fr. *Website:* www.operadeparis.fr.

HOFFMAN, Alan Jerome, AB, PhD; American mathematician and educator; *IBM Fellow Emeritus, T.J. Watson Research Center, IBM;* b. 30 May 1924, New York, NY; s. of Jesse Hoffman and Muriel Hoffman; m. 1st Esther Walker 1947 (died 1988); two d.; m. 2nd Elinor Hershaft 1990; ed George Washington High School, Columbia Univ.; mem. US Army Signal Corps 1943–46; mem. Inst. for Advanced Study 1950–51; Mathematician, Nat. Bureau of Standards 1951–56; Scientific Liaison Officer, Office of Naval Research, London 1956–57; Consultant, Gen. Electric Co. 1957–61; Adjunct Prof., CUNY 1965–75; Research Staff mem. T.J. Watson Research Center, IBM 1961–2002, IBM Fellow 1977–2002, IBM Fellow Emer. 2002–; Visiting Prof., Yale Univ. 1975–80, Rutgers Univ. 1990–96, Georgia Inst. of Tech. 1992–93; Consulting Prof., Stanford Univ. 1981–91; Founding Ed., Linear Algebra and Its Applications; mem. NAS; Fellow, New York Acad. of Sciences, American Acad. of Arts and Sciences, INFORMS; Hon. DSc (Technion) 1986; Von Neumann Prize, Operations Research Soc. and Inst. of Man. Science 1992, Founders Award, Math. Programming Soc. 2000. *Publications:* Selected Papers of Alan Hoffman 2003; numerous articles in math. journals. *Address:* T.J. Watson Research Center, IBM, Box 218, Yorktown Heights, NY 10598, USA (office). *Telephone:* (203) 273-6065 (office). *E-mail:* ajh@us.ibm.com (office). *Website:* www.research.ibm.com/people/a/ajh (office).

HOFFMAN, Alfred, Jr, MBA; American business executive and fmr diplomatist; m. Dawn Hoffman; five c.; ed US Mil. Acad., West Point and Harvard Business School; served as fighter pilot in USAF; Founder and Chair. WCI Communities, Inc.; Nat. Co-Chair. and Fla State Finance Chair. for George W. Bush presidential campaign; Co-Chair. Finance for Presidential Inaugural Cttee and Nat. Finance Chair. Republican Nat. Cttee 2001, 2003–04; Chair. Fla Victory 2002, Fla Inaugural Cttee 2003; Finance Chair. Fla Gov. Jeb Bush's campaign 1998, 2002; Chair. Fla Educ. Foundation, Fla Council on Econ. Educ., Fla Council of 100 2001–03; Amb. to Portugal 2005–07; Co-f. Hoffman Development Group; Founding Chair. Clearwater's Ruth Eckerd Performing Arts Center; Vice-Chair. Tampa Bay Performing Arts Hall; Founding Dir Council for Educational Change, Bd Fla Chamber of Commerce; f. Tampa Bay Polo Club, Chair. for 15 years; Trustee, Fla Arts Council, Nat. Council of Advisors, Center for the Study of the Presidency and Congress. *Leisure interest:* polo. *Address:* Hoffman Development Group, PO Box 14638, North Palm Beach, FL 33408, USA (office). *Telephone:* (561) 844-0404 (office). *Fax:* (561) 844-6233 (office). *Website:* hoffmandevgroup.com (office).

HOFFMAN, Darleane Christian, BS, PhD; American nuclear chemist and academic; *Faculty Senior Scientist, Nuclear Science Division, Lawrence Berkeley National Laboratory;* b. 8 Nov. 1926, Terril, Ia; d. of Carl Christian and Elverna Christian; m. Marvin Hoffman 1951; one s. one d.; ed Iowa State Univ., Ames; Researcher, Oak Ridge Nat. Lab. 1952–53; Researcher, Los Alamos Nat. Lab. 1953–84, becoming Assoc. Group Leader and later Leader, Nuclear Chem. Div., Isotope and Nuclear Chem. Div.; Prof. of Chem., Univ. of California, Berkeley 1984–91, Prof. Emer. 1991–93, Prof., Grad. School 1993–, now Emer.; Faculty Sr Scientist and Group Leader, Heavy Element, Nuclear and Radiochemistry Group, Lawrence Berkeley Nat. Lab. 1984–96, Faculty Sr Scientist and Co-Group Leader 1996–2001, Faculty Sr Scientist, Nuclear Science Div. 2002–; Dir Seaborg Inst. for Transactinium Science 1991–96; Fellow, Norwegian Acad. of Science and Letters 1990, American Acad. of Arts and Sciences 1998; Hon. Int. mem. Japan Soc. of Nuclear and Radiochemistry 2004; Dr hc (Clark Univ.) 2000, (Univ. of Bern) 2001; Alumni Citation Merit, Iowa State Univ. 1978, Guggenheim Fellow 1978–79, ACS Award for Nuclear Chem. 1983, Distinguished Achievement Award, Iowa State Univ. 1988, ACS Garvan Medal 1991, US Nat. Medal of Science 1997, ACS Priestley Medal 2000, Women in Science and Tech. Hall of Fame 2000, Alpha Chi Sigma Hall of Fame 2002, Sigma Xi Procter Prize 2003, Lifetime Achievement Award, Radiochemistry Soc. 2003, Hevesy Medal Award 2011, Invited Lecturer, organizer of Symposia celebrating 100th Anniversary of Marie Curie's 1911 Nobel Prize in Chem. 2011, ACS Western Regional Meeting Symposium Honoree 2013. *Publications:* The Transuranium People: The Inside Story (co-author) 2000; more than 280 articles in books and scientific journals. *Leisure interests:* swimming, music. *Address:* Nuclear Science Division, MS70R0319, Lawrence Berkeley National Laboratory, One Cyclotron Road, Berkeley, CA 94720, USA (office). *Telephone:* (510) 486-4474 (office). *Fax:* (510) 486-7444 (office). *E-mail:* dchoffman@lbl.gov (office). *Website:* chem.berkeley.edu/faculty/emeriti/hoffman/index.php (office).

HOFFMAN, Dustin Lee; American actor; b. 8 Aug. 1937, Los Angeles, Calif.; s. of Harry Hoffman; m. 1st Anne Byrne 1969 (divorced); two d.; m. 2nd Lisa Gottsegen 1980; two s. two d.; ed Santa Monica City Coll.; worked as an attendant at a psychiatric inst.; demonstrator, Macy's toy dept; first stage role in Yes is for a Very Young Man (Sarah Lawrence Coll., Bronxville, NY); Broadway debut in A Cook for Mr. General 1961; Founder Punch Productions; Fellow, American Acad. of Arts and Sciences 2009–; Officier, Ordre des Arts et des Lettres; Britannia Award (BAFTA) 1997, Golden Globe Lifetime Achievement Award 1997, American Film Inst. Lifetime Achievement Award 1999, Kennedy Center Honor 2012. *Other stage appearances in:* Harry, Noon and Night 1964, Journey of the Fifth Horse (Obie Award) 1966, Star Wagon 1966, Fragments 1966, Eh? (Drama Desk, Theatre World, Vernon Rice Awards) 1967, Jimmy Shine 1968, Death of a Salesman 1984, The Merchant of Venice 1989; Asst Dir A View from the Bridge; Dir All Over Town 1974. *Films include:* The Tiger Makes Out 1966, Madigan's Millions 1966, The Graduate 1967, Midnight Cowboy 1969, John and Mary 1969, Little Big Man 1970, Who is Harry Kellerman...? 1971, Straw Dogs 1971, Alfredo Alfredo, Papillon 1973, Lenny 1974, All the President's Men 1975, Marathon Man 1976, Straight Time 1978, Agatha 1979, Kramer vs. Kramer (Acad. Award 1980, New York Film Critics Award) 1979, Tootsie (New York Film Critics Award, Nat. Soc. of Film Critics Award) 1982, Ishtar 1987, Rain Man (Acad. and Golden Globe Awards) 1988, Family Business 1989, Dick Tracy 1990, Hook 1991, Billy Bathgate 1991, Hero 1992, Outbreak 1995, American Buffalo, Sleeper 1996, Wag the Dog 1997, Mad City 1997, Sphere 1997, The Messenger: the Story of Joan of Arc 1999, Being John Malkovich 1999, Moonlight Mile 2002, Confidence 2003, Runaway Jury 2003, Finding Neverland 2004, I Heart Huckabees 2004, Meet the Fockers 2004, Racing Stripes (voice) 2005, The Lost City 2005, Perfume: The Story of a Murderer 2006, Stranger Than Fiction 2006, Mr. Magorium's Wonder Emporium 2007, Kung Fu Panda (voice) 2008, Last Chance Harvey 2009, Little Fockers 2010. *TV appearance in:* Death of a Salesman 1985. *Leisure interests:* tennis, piano, photography, reading. *Address:* Punch Productions, 1926 Broadway, Suite 305, New York, NY 10023; PO Box 492359, Los Angeles, CA 90049-8359; c/o The Endeavor Agency, 9601 Wilshire Blvd., 10th Floor, Beverly Hills, CA 90212, USA. *Telephone:* (212) 595-8800 (Punch Productions).

HOFFMAN, Jerzy; Polish film director; b. 15 March 1932, Kraków; m. (deceased); one d.; ed All-Union State Inst. of Cinematography, Moscow; has directed 27 documentaries with Edward Skórzewski including Remembrance of Kalwaria (Oberhausen and Florence Film Festival awards), Two Aspects of God, and others 1955–62; mem. Acad. of Fine Arts, Ukraine; Great Cross with Star, Order of Polonia Restituta; numerous Polish and int. film prizes including Minister of Culture and Arts Prize (four times). *Films include:* Gangsters and Philanthropists (feature film debut with Edward Skórzewski) 1962, Colonel Wolodyjowski (also wrote screenplay) 1969, Mazowsze 1971, The Deluge 1973, Leper 1976, The Quack 1981, Medicine Man, Beautiful Stranger 1993, With Fire and Sword (also wrote screenplay) (Polish Eagles for Best Film Producer 2000) 1999, Sienkiewicz Trilogy 2004; documentary: Ukraine 2005. *Leisure interests:* historical books, bridge, cooking, swimming. *Address:* Zodiak Jerzy Hoffman Production, ul. Puławska 61, 02-595 Warsaw, Poland (office). *Telephone:* (22) 845-20-47 (office).

HOFFMAN, Mat; American professional BMX rider; b. 9 Jan. 1972, Edmond, Okla; entered Freestyle BMX circuit as amateur aged 13, quickly rose to top of amateur class and turned professional aged 16; considered the greatest vert-ramp rider in history of BMX; Founder and Owner Hoffman Bikes, Hoffman Sports Asscn/Hoffman Promotions and Hoffman Enterprises, Inc.; first rider to perform 900 degree spin in competition and take backflip to vert; came out of retirement to compete in Summer X-Games 2002 and won Bronze Medal, also landed no-handed 900 for first time in competition resulting in Silver Medal; set record for highest air jump 26 feet 6 inches (8.07m) on 24-foot (7.31m) ramp (jump listed in 2004 Guinness Book of World Records as High Air World Record holder for BMX bike) 2002; creator of Mat Hoffman's Crazy Freakin Stunt Show for Universal Studios, Orlando, Fla 2003, 2005; involved in several film projects, including Keep Your Eyes Open, IMAX film Ultimate X, xXx, Jackass – The Movie; host of series of behind-the-scenes segments for Tomb Raider 2 2003; appeared in video games such as Mat Hoffman BMX, Mat Hoffman BMX 2, and Tony Hawk Pro Skater 4; participated in Tony Hawk's (q.v.) Boom Boom Huck Jam 2002, 2003, 2005; Vice-Pres. Int. BMX Freestyle Fed.; US BMX Freestyle Fed.; Lifetime Achievement Award, ESPN Action Sports and Music Awards 2002. *Television:* has produced, directed and hosted several TV series for ESPN including Kids in the Way, HBtv, Mat's World, a nine-episode segment on X-2day and the CFB Series; mem. cast of MTV's Trippin' 2005. *Publications:* The Ride of My Life (autobiog.) 2002. *Address:* c/o Brian Dubin, William Morris Agency, 1325 Avenue of the Americas, New York, NY 10019, USA. *Telephone:* (212) 903-1184. *E-mail:* bd@wma.com. *Website:* www.mathoffman.com.

HOFFMAN, Reid Garrett, BS, MSt (Oxon.); American business executive; *Executive Chairman, LinkedIn;* b. 5 Aug. 1967, Stanford, Calif.; s. of William Parker Hoffman, Jr and Deanna Ruth Rutter; m. Michelle Yee; ed The Putney School, Coll., Stanford Univ., Univ. of Oxford, UK; Sr User Experience Architect, Apple Computer 1994–96; Dir of Product Man. and Devt, Fujitsu Software Corpn 1996–97; Co-founder, Bd mem. and Vice-Pres., Product Socialnet.com 1997–2000; Exec. Vice-Pres. PayPal 2000–02; Co-founder, Chair. and CEO LinkedIn 2003–07, Chair. and Pres., Products LinkedIn 2007–08, Chair. and CEO 2008–09, Exec. Chair. 2009–; Angel Investor, Aufklarung LLC 2000–09; Chair. Westcoast Advisory Bd, Questbridge 2008–; Partner, Greylock, Menlo Park, Calif. 2009–; mem. Bd of Dirs PayPal 1998–2000, Grassroots 2003–09, Vendio 2003–10, Six Apart 2003–10, Tagged 2005–10, Mozilla Corpn 2005–, Kiva.org 2005–, Zynga 2008–; mem. Bd of Advisors, Lulan LLC 2003–09, Center for Citizen Media 2006–07; mem. Provost Council, College Eight, Univ. of California, Santa Cruz 2006–; Marshall Scholarship and Dinkelspiel Award, Stanford Univ., Matthew Arnold Memorial Prize (Proxime Accessit), SD Forum Visionary Award, Henry Crown Fellowship, named 17th on Fast Company's list of the 100 Most Creative People In Business 2010, shared the Ernst and Young US Entrepreneur of the Year Award 2011, honoured by the World Affairs Council and Global Philanthropy Forum 2012, David Packard Medal of Achievement Award, TechAmerica 2012, ranked by Forbes magazine amongst The World's Most Powerful People (71st) 2012, (65th) 2013. *Publication:* The Startup of You: Adapt to the Future, Invest in Yourself, and Transform Your Career (with Ben Casnocha) 2012. *Address:* LinkedIn, 2029 Stierlin Court, Mountain View, CA 94043, USA (office). *Telephone:* (650) 687-3600 (office). *E-mail:* press@linkedin.com (office). *Website:* www.linkedin.com/reidhoffman (office).

HOFFMANN, Claus Dieter; German business executive; *Chairman of the Supervisory Board, Energie Baden-Württemberg AG;* b. 1942; fmrly with Robert Bosch GmbH, becoming Chief Financial Officer –2002; Man. Partner, H + H Senior Advisors GmbH; Chair. Supervisory Bd Energie Baden-Württemberg AG 2006–; mem. Supervisory Bd ING Group 2003–, Bauerfeind AG, Jowat AG, De Boer Group; Chair. Charlottenklinik Foundation; Chair. Bd of Trustees (Vereinigung der Freunde), Stuttgart Univ.; mem. Foundation Council Japanisch-Deutsches Zentrum Berlin. *Leisure interest:* golf. *Address:* Energie Baden-Württemberg AG, Durlacher Allee 93, 76131 Karlsruhe, Germany (office). *Telephone:* (7) 21-63-00 (office). *Fax:* (7) 21-63-126-72 (office). *E-mail:* info@enbw.com (office). *Website:* www.enbw.com (office).

HOFFMANN, Gleisi Helena; Brazilian lawyer and politician; b. 6 Sept. 1965, Curitiba, Paraná; d. of Júlio Hoffmann and Getúlia Agda; m. Paulo Bernardo; one s. one d.; fmr Sec. of State, Mato Grosso do Sul State; fmr Muncipal Sec., City of Londrina; mem. Pres. Lula da Silva's transition team 2002; Dir of Finance, Itaipu (hydroelectric dam) 2003–06; unsuccessful cand. for Mayor of Curitiba 2008; mem. Senate for Paraná Feb.–June 2011; Cabinet Chief June 2011–14; mem. Partido dos Trabalhadores 1989–; fmr Pres. Paraná Regional Br. *Address:* c/o Partido dos Trabalhadores, SCS, Quadra 2, Bloco C, Edif. Toufic, Sala 256, 70302-000 São Paulo, Brazil.

HOFFMANN, Jules A., PhD; French (b. Luxembourg) biologist and academic; *Research Director and Member, Board of Administration, Centre national de la recherche scientifique (CNRS);* b. 2 Aug. 1941, Echternach, Luxembourg; m. Daniele Hoffmann; two c.; ed Louis Pasteur Univ., Strasbourg, France, Philipps Univ., Marburg, Germany; Research Asst, CNRS 1964–68, Research Assoc. 1969–74, Research Dir 1974–, Dir, CNRS Immune Response and Devt in Insects Lab. 1978–2005, Dir, Inst. of Molecular and Cellular Biology 1994–2006, also mem. CNRS Bd of Admin; Researcher, Gen. Biology Lab., Univ. of Strasbourg 1975–, Dir 1978, also currently Prof., Univ. of Strasbourg; Pres. Acad. des Sciences 2007–08; mem. Acad. française, German Acad. of Sciences Leopoldina, Academia Europaea, European Molecular Biology Org.; Foreign Assoc. NAS, American Acad. of Arts and Sciences, Russian Acad. of Sciences; Chevalier, Légion d'honneur; numerous awards, including William B. Coley Award 2003, Robert Koch Prize in Immunology 2004, Lewis S. Rosenstiel Award (jtly) 2010, Keio Medical Science Prize (with Shizuo Akira) 2011, Gairdner Award for Medical Research 2011, Shaw Prize in Life Science and Medicine (jtly) 2011, CNRS Gold Medal 2011, Nobel Prize in Physiology or Medicine (jtly) 2011. *Publications:* author or co-author of 250 publs, ed of numerous vols. *Address:* UPR 9022 du CNRS, Institut de Biologie Moléculaire et Cellulaire, 15 rue René Descartes, 67084 Cedex, Strasbourg, France (office). *Telephone:* 3-88-71-70-77 (office). *Fax:* 3-88-60-69-22 (office). *E-mail:* j.hoffmann@ibmc.u-strasbg.fr (office). *Website:* www.cnrs.fr (office).

HOFFMANN, Baron (Life Peer), cr. 1995, of Chedworth in the County of Gloucestershire; **Rt Hon. Leonard Hubert Hoffmann,** Kt, MA, PC; British judge; b. 8 May 1934; s. of B.W. Hoffmann and G. Hoffmann; m. Gillian Sterner 1957; two d.; ed South African Coll. School, Cape Town, Univ. of Cape Town and Queen's Coll. Oxford; Advocate, Supreme Court of S Africa 1958–60; called to Bar, Gray's Inn, London 1964, Bencher 1984; QC 1977; Judge, Courts of Appeal of Jersey and Guernsey 1980–85; Judge, High Court of Justice, Chancery Div. 1985–92; Lord Justice of Appeal 1992–95; a Lord of Appeal in Ordinary 1995–2009; Judge, Court of Final Appeal, Hong Kong Special Admin. Region 1997–; Chair. Financial Markets Law Cttee, Bank of England; Law Prof. and Consultant, Queen Mary Coll., Univ. of London; Arbitrator and Mediator, Brick Court Chambers, London; Dir ENO 1985–90, 1991–94; Stowell Civil Law Fellow, Univ. Coll. Oxford 1961–73; Pres. British-German Jurists Asscn 1991–; Hon. Fellow, Queen's Coll. Oxford 1992; Hon DCL (City) 1992, (Univ. of West of England) 1995. *Publication:* The South African Law of Evidence 1963. *Address:* House of Lords, London, SW1A 0PW (office); Surrey Lodge, 23 Keats Grove, London, NW3 2RS, England. *Telephone:* (20) 7219-6067 (office). *E-mail:* hoffmannl@parliament.uk (office).

HOFFMANN, Luc, DPhil; Swiss biologist; b. 23 Jan. 1923, Basel; s. of Dr Emanuel Hoffmann and Marie-Anne Hoffmann (née Stehlin); m. Daria Razumovsky 1953 (died 2002); one s. three d.; ed Gymnasium Basel and Flim, Grisons, Univ. of Basel; f. Station Biologique de la Tour du Valat 1954, Man. Dir 1954–84, Chair. of Bd Fondation Tour du valat 1974–2003, Hon. Pres. 2004–; f. World Wildlife Fund (WWF) (later World Wide Fund for Nature) 1961, Vice-Pres. of Bd 1961–88 (Exec. Vice-Pres. 1971–78), Vice-Pres. Emer. 1989–; Vice-Pres. of Bd Int. Union for Conservation of Nature (IUCN) 1966–69; Dir Int. Wildfowl Research Bureau (IWRB) 1962–69; Hon. Dir Wetlands Int. (fmrly IWRB); Vice-Pres. Wildfowl Trust 1979, Hon. Life Fellow 1983; mem. Exec. Cttee Int. Council for Bird Preservation (ICBP) 1984–90; f. Fondation Int. du Banc d'Arguin (FIBA) 1985, Pres. 1985–2000, Hon. Pres. 2000–; Vice-Pres. Bd of Dirs Hoffmann-La Roche and Co., Basel 1990–96; Pres. WWF France 1996–2000, Hon. Pres. 2001–; Founder and Pres. MAVA Foundation for Nature Conservation 1997, Pres. Emer. 2010–; Fellow, American Ornithologists Union 2004; Hon. mem. Schweizerische Gesellschaft für Vogelkunde + Vogelschutz 2010; Commdr Order of the Golden Ark (Netherlands) 1989, Croix du Mérite pour les Sciences et les Arts (Austria), Chevalier, Légion d'honneur (France) 1989, Officier, Ordre du Mérite Nat. de la République Islamique de Mauritanie 1998, Officier de l'Honneur (Greece) 1998, Medal of Isabelle the Catholic (Spain) 2009, Officier, Légion d'Honneur (France) 2010; Dr hc (Basel) 1990, (Thessaloniki) 1992; Kaj Curry-Lindhal Award, Waterbird Soc. 1994, Duke of Edin. Conservation Medal 1999, Intecol Int. Wetland Award 2004, European Prize for Culture, European Foundation for Culture 2004, John C. Philipps Memorial Medal, IUCN 2004, Byron Antipas Medal, Hellenic Soc. for the Protection of Nature 2005, Hon. Ramsar Award (Romania) 2012. *Publications:* Camargue (with K. Weber) 1968; more than 60 publs in the fields of ornithology, wetland ecology and conservation. *Leisure interests:* contemporary art, bird watching. *Address:* La Tour du Valat, Le Sambuc, 13200 Arles, France (office); Le Petit Essert, 1147 Montricher, Switzerland (home). *Telephone:* (4) 90-97-20-13 (office); (21) 8645977 (home). *Fax:* (4) 90-97-20-19 (office); (21) 8644230 (home). *E-mail:* l.hoffmann@tourduvalat.org (office). *Website:* www.tourduvalat.org (office); luchoffmanninstitute.org (office).

HOFFMANN, Maja; Swiss art collector, art patron, filmmaker, impresario and entrepreneur; *President, Kunsthalle Zürich;* b. 1956; d. of Luc Hoffmann and the late Daria Hoffmann-Razumovsky; ed New School and New York Univ., USA; Founder LUMA Foundation, Arles France 2004, supports initiatives in Switzerland and around the world, including Center for Curatorial Studies at Bard Coll.

and New Museum of Contemporary Art in New York (mem. Bd); also supports several art-based int. initiatives and institutional projects, including Kunsthalle Basel and Kunst-Werke Berlin, Fotomuseum Winterthur, Palais de Tokyo in Paris, Venice Biennale, Artangel and Serpentine Gallery, London; Pres. Kunsthalle Zürich; Vice-Pres. Council of Emanuel Hoffmann Foundation, Basel; Trustee, Tate Gallery, London. *Film:* produced documentary film Jean-Michel Basquiat: The Radiant Child 2010. *Address:* Kunsthalle Zürich, Limmatstrasse 270, 8005 Zürich, Switzerland (office). *Telephone:* (44) 272-15-15 (office). *Fax:* (44) 272-18-88 (office). *E-mail:* info@kunsthallezurich.ch (office). *Website:* www .kunsthallezurich.ch (office).

HOFFMANN, Roald, PhD; American chemist and academic; *Frank H.T. Rhodes Professor Emeritus of Humane Letters, Department of Chemistry and Chemical Biology, Cornell University;* b. (Roald Safran), 18 July 1937, Złoczów, Poland; s. of Hillel Safran and Clara Rosen, step-s. of Paul Hoffmann; m. Eva Börjesson 1960; one s. one d.; ed Columbia and Harvard Univs; Jr Fellow, Soc. of Fellows, Harvard Univ. 1962–65; Assoc. Prof., Dept of Chem. and Chemical Biology, Cornell Univ. 1965–68, Prof. 1968–74, John A. Newman Prof. of Physical Science 1974–96, currently Frank M. Rhodes Prof. Emeritus of Humane Letters; mem. NAS, USSR (now Russian) Acad. of Sciences, Societas Scientarum Fennica 1986, Int. Acad. of Quantum Molecular Science; Foreign mem. Royal Soc., Indian Nat. Acad. of Sciences, Royal Swedish Acad. of Sciences; Fellow, American Acad. of Arts and Sciences, American Philosophical Soc.; Hon. DTech (Royal Inst. of Technology, Stockholm) 1977, Hon. DSc (Yale) 1980, (Columbia) 1982, (Hartford) 1982, (City Univ. of New York) 1983, (Puerto Rico) 1983, (Uruguay) 1984, (La Plata) 1984, (Colgate) 1985, (State Univ. of New York at Binghamton) 1985, (Ben Gurion Univ. of Negev) 1989, (Lehigh) 1989, (Carleton) 1989, (Maryland) 1990, (Arizona) 1991, (Bar-Ilan Univ.) 1991, (Central Florida) 1991, (Athens) 1991, (Thessaloniki) 1991, (St Petersburg) 1991, (Barcelona) 1992, (Northwestern Univ.) 1996, (The Technion) 1996, (Durham) 2000 and others; ACS Award 1969, Fresenius Award 1969, Harrison Howe Award 1969, Annual Award of Int. Acad. of Quantum Molecular Sciences 1970, Arthur C. Cope Award, ACS 1973, Linus Pauling Award 1974, Nichols Medal 1980, Nobel Prize in Chem. (shared with Kenichi Fukui) 1981, Inorganic Chem. Award, ACS 1982, Nat. Medal of Science 1984, Nat. Acad. of Sciences Award, in Chemical Sciences 1986, Priestley Medal 1990, Pimentel Award in Chemical Educ. 1996, Lomonosov Gold Medal, Russian Acad. of Sciences 2011, Linus Pauling Legacy Award 2012, Harvard Centennial Medal, James T. Grady-James H. Stack Award for Interpreting Chem., and several others. *Plays:* Oxygen (with Carl Djerassi) 2001, Should've 2006, Something That Belongs To You 2009. *Publications:* Conservation of Orbital Symmetry 1969, The Metamict State 1987, Solids and Surfaces: A Chemist's View of Bonding in Extended Structures 1988, Gaps and Verges 1990, Chemistry Imagined (co-author) 1993, The Same and Not the Same 1995, Old Wine, New Flasks (co-author) 1997, Memory Effects 1999, Soliton 2002, Catalísta (Spanish) 2002. *Address:* Department of Chemistry and Chemical Biology, Cornell University, Baker Laboratory, Room 226, Ithaca, NY 14853-1301, USA (office). *Telephone:* (607) 255-3419 (office). *Fax:* (607) 255-5707 (office). *E-mail:* rh34@cornell.edu (office). *Website:* chemistry .cornell.edu/faculty/detail.cfm?netid=rh34 (office); www.roaldhoffmann.com.

HOFFMEYER, Erik, MSc (Econ), Dr polit.; Danish economist, academic and business executive; b. 25 Dec. 1924, Rårup, Jylland; s. of Skat Hoffmeyer (Bishop of Århus Diocese) and Aase f. Thejll; m. 1st Eva f. Kemp 1949; m. 2nd Lise Rafaelse; ed Århus Cathedral School, Univ.; took refuge in Sweden during occupation of Denmark 1943–45; first worked at Danmarks Nationalbank 1951–59, Chair. Bd of Govs 1965–94, Rep. of Gov. for Denmark to IMF 1965–94; Rockefeller Fellowship 1954–55; Lecturer in Econs, Univ. of Copenhagen 1956, Prof. of Econs 1959–62; Adjunct Prof., Southern Univ. 1998–2003; Chair. EIB 1973–77; mem. Cttee of Govs of Cen. Banks of the European Communities 1973–93, Chair. 1975–76, 1979–81, 1991–92; Deputy Chair. Danish Export Financial Corpn 1975–94; employed by Merrill Lynch & Co. in various capacities 1984–2003, most recently as Chair. Global Financial Insts Practice; mem. Bd of Dirs several publicly traded corpns; Chair. Social Econ. Soc. 1951–53, Econ. Council 1962–65, Acad. of Tech. Sciences 1963, Research Jt Cttee 1965–72, Bd of C.L. David Foundation and Collection 1967, Office of Construction Mortgage Fund 1969–72, Council of European Monetary Inst. 1994, Advisory Cttee of Environmental Support Fund for Eastern European Countries 1995–; Pres. Psychiatric Foundation 1996–, Laurits Andersen Foundation 1982–90; mem. Bd Nat. Econ. Asscn 1960–66, Danish Securities Council 1996–2001, Politiken Foundation 1996–; Chair. Foundation for Trees and Environment Protection 1979–, Alzheimer Asscn Research Foundation; mem. Group of Thirty Consultative Group on Int. Econ. and Monetary Affairs, Inc. (G-30), Washington, DC 1984 (now mem. Emer.), King Frederik VII Foundation 1985– (Chair. 1987–); Order of Merit in Gold 1994. *Publications:* Dollar Shortage and the Structure of U.S. Foreign Trade 1958, Price Stability and Full Employment 1960, Structural Changes on the Money and Capital Markets, 1960, The Theory of Economic Welfare and the Welfare State 1962, Industrial Growth 1963, Monetary History of Denmark 1968, The International Monetary System 1992, Monetary Policy Issues 1993, Decision Making for European Economic and Monetary Union 2000; contribs to Nationaloekonomisk Tidsskrift and int. econ. journals. *Address:* c/o The Group of Thirty, 1726 M Street, NW, Suite 200, Washington, DC 20036, USA.

HOGAN, Joseph M., BS, MS (Business Admin); American business executive; *CEO, ABB Group worldwide and ABB Ltd;* b. 7 May 1957; m. Lisa Hogan; three c.; ed Geneva Coll., Robert Morris Univ.; Sales, Marketing and Product Devt roles with GE Plastics, USA 1985–90, Business Leader, Lexan Europe, GE Plastics, Netherlands 1990–93, Gen. Man. Americas Marketing, GE Plastics, USA 1994–96, Staff Exec., GE Corp., USA 1996–98, Pres. and CEO, GE Fanuc Automation N America 1998–2000, Exec. Vice-Pres. and COO GE Medical Systems, USA 2000, Pres. and CEO GE Healthcare, USA and UK 2000–08; CEO ABB Group worldwide and ABB Ltd, Switzerland 2008–. *Address:* ABB Ltd, Affolternstrasse 44, 8050 Zurich, Switzerland (office). *Telephone:* (43) 317-71-11 (office). *Fax:* (43) 317-44-20 (office). *E-mail:* info@abb.com (office). *Website:* www.abb.com (office).

HOGAN, Mark T., BSc, MBA; American automobile industry executive; *President, Dewey Investments LLC;* b. 15 May 1951, Chicago; ed Univ. of Ill., Harvard Univ.; joined General Motors (GM) 1973, Factory Analyst, Electro-Motive Div., Chicago 1973–77, several analytical and supervisory positions, GM Financial

Staff 1977–81, Sr Admin. for Forward Business Planning, Fisher Body Div. 1981–82, Dir of Material, Labour and Forecast Section, Comptroller's Staff 1982–83, Dir Treasurer's Office, Detroit 1983–84, Group Dir Public Affairs Staff, Chevrolet-Pontiac-Canada Group 1984–86, Gen. Man. and Comptroller, New United Motor Mfg Inc. 1986–88, Group Dir of Business Planning, Truck and Bus Group 1988–92, Exec. Dir of Planning, N American Operations (NAO) 1992–94, Exec. Dir NAO Planning and Corp. Information Man. 1994, Pres. and Man.-Dir GM do Brasil, Group Vice-Pres. e-GM 1999–2004, Group Vice-Pres. for Advanced Vehicle Devt 2001–04; Pres. Magna Int. Inc. 2004–07; Pres. and CEO Vehicle Production Group, LLC 2008–10; Pres. Dewey Investments LLC 2010–; Advisor, Toyota Motor Corpn 2010–; mem. Bd of Dirs Visteon Corpn 2010–. *Address:* Dewey Investments LLC, 39533 Woodward Ave., Bloomfield Hills, MI 48304-5095, USA.

HOGAN, Paul, AO; Australian film actor; b. 8 Oct. 1940, Lightening Ridge; m. 1st Noelene Hogan (divorced 1989); five c.; m. 2nd Linda Kozlowski 1990; one s.; ed Parramatta High School; fmr rigger on Sydney Harbour Bridge; filmed TV specials on location in England 1983; commercials for Australian Tourist Comm., Fosters Lager; Australian of the Year 1985. *Films:* Crocodile Dundee (Golden Globe Award) 1986, Crocodile Dundee II 1989, Almost An Angel 1993, Lightning Jack 1994, Flipper 1996, Sorrow Floats 1997, Crocodile Dundee in Los Angeles 2001, Strange Bedfellows 2004. *TV:* The Paul Hogan Show 1973, Hogan in London 1975, Anzacs (miniseries) 1985. *Address:* c/o Silverstream Management, Level 4 350 Kent Street, Sydney, NSW 2001, Australia (office).

HOGE, James Fulton, Jr, BA, MA; American academic and editor; *Chairman, Human Rights Watch;* b. 25 Dec. 1935, New York, NY; m. Kathleen Lacey Hoge; ed Yale Univ., Univ. of Chicago, Harvard Univ.; Ed. Foreign Affairs (journal) 1992–2010, Peter G. Peterson Chair 1997–2010; fmr Ed.-in-Chief Chicago Sun-Times newspaper, then Publr and Pres. NY Daily News; fmr Dir Council on Foreign Relations; Chair. Human Rights Watch 2010–; mem. Bd of Dirs Int. Center for Journalists (ICFJ) 1992–, currently Chair.; mem. Bd of Dirs Center for Global Affairs, New York Univ.; Congressional Fellow, American Political Science Asscn 1962; Fellow, John F. Kennedy School of Govt Harvard Univ. 1991; Sr Fellow, Freedom Forum Media Studies Columbia Univ. 1992; Dir Foundation for Civil Society; mem. American Council on Germany, Program Cttee of American Ditchley Foundation; Dr hc (Columbia Coll.) 1985; Public Service Award, Univ. of Chicago 1973, Award for Contributions to Journalism, The Better Govt Asscn of Chicago 1975, Public Service Award, The Citizens Cttee for New York City 1985, six Pulitzer Prizes (to Chicago Sun Times while Ed. and Publr), Pulitzer Prize to New York Daily News while Publr). *Television:* The Threat of Terrorism (documentary writer and narrator). *Publications include:* The American Encounter: The United States and the Making of the Modern World (co-ed.) 1997, How Did This Happen? Terrorism and the New War (co-ed.) 2001; numerous articles, reviews and chapters in journals, newspapers and books. *Address:* Office of the Chairman, Human Rights Watch, 350 Fifth Avenue, 34th Floor, New York, NY 10118-3299, USA (office). *Telephone:* (212) 290-4700 (office). *Website:* www.hrw.org (office).

HOGG, Sir Christopher Anthony, Kt, MA, MBA; British business executive; *Chairman, Financial Reporting Council;* b. 2 Aug. 1936, London; s. of Anthony Wentworth Hogg and Monica Mary Gladwell; m. 1st Anne Patricia Cathie 1961 (divorced 1997); two d.; m. 2nd Dr Miriam Stoppard 1997; ed Marlborough Coll., Trinity Coll., Oxford and Harvard Business School, USA; Nat. Service, Parachute Regt 1955–57; Research Assoc. Institut pour l'Etude des Méthodes de Direction de l'Entreprise (business school), Lausanne, Switzerland 1962–63; with Philip Hill, Higginson, Erlangers Ltd (later Hill Samuel & Co. Ltd) 1963–66; staff mem. Industrial Reorganisation Corpn 1966–68; joined Courtaulds Group 1968, Man. Dir 1971, Dir (non-exec.) British Celanese Ltd 1971–72, Chair. 1972–75, Dir Courtaulds Ltd 1973–96, a Deputy Chair. 1978–80, Chief Exec. 1979–91, Chair. Courtaulds PLC 1980–96, Courtaulds Textiles PLC 1990–95; Deputy Chair. Allied Domecq 1995–96, Chair. 1996–2002; Dir (non-exec.) Reuters Group PLC 1984–2004 (Chair. 1985–2004), SmithKline Beecham PLC 1993–2000, GlaxoSmithKline 2000–04 (Chair. 2002–04); Air Liquide SA 2000–05; Chair. Financial Reporting Council 2006–; Chair. (non-exec.) Royal Nat. Theatre 1995–2004; Trustee, Ford Foundation 1987–99; mem. Dept of Industry Industrial Devt Advisory Bd 1976–81, Cttee of Award for Harkness Fellowships 1980–86, Int. Council J.P. Morgan 1988–, Court, Bank of England 1992–96; Hon. Fellow, Trinity Coll. Oxford 1982, London Business School 1992, City and Guilds of London Inst. 1992; Hon. FCSD 1987; Foreign Hon. mem. American Acad. of Arts and Sciences 1991; Hon. DSc (Cranfield Inst. of Tech.) 1986, (Aston) 1988; BIM Gold Medal 1986, Centenary Medal, Soc. of Chemical Industry 1989, Hambro Businessman of the Year 1993. *Publication:* Masers and Lasers 1962. *Leisure interests:* theatre, reading, walking. *Address:* Financial Reporting Council, 5th Floor, Aldwych House, 71–91 Aldwych, London, WC2B 4HN, England (office). *Telephone:* (20) 7492-2388 (office). *Fax:* (20) 7492-2399 (office). *E-mail:* c.hogg@frc.org.uk (office). *Website:* www.frc.org.uk (office).

HOGG, James C., OC, FRSC, MD, MSc, PhD; Canadian pathologist and academic; *Professor Emeritus of Pathology, University of British Columbia;* b. 3 Dec. 1935, Winnipeg; ed Univ. of Manitoba, McGill Univ., Montreal; Medical Officer, Royal Canadian Air Force 1963–66; specialist training in pathology, Mass Gen. Hosp., Boston and Royal Victoria Hosp., Montreal; Asst Prof. of Pathology, McGill Univ. 1971, Miranda Fraser Prof. of Comparative Pathology 1975–77; joined Univ. of British Columbia (UBC) and St Paul's Hosp., Vancouver 1977 (first full-time prof. based at St Paul's), co-f. pulmonary research lab. (later renamed UBC James Hogg Centre for Cardiovascular and Pulmonary Research), Prin. Investigator, UBC James Hogg Research Centre, currently Prof. Emer. of Pathology, UBC; Canadian Medical Hall of Fame 2010, American Soc. for Investigative Pathology Chugai Award 2003, Canada Gairdner Wightman Award 2013. *Publications:* more than 300 papers in peer-reviewed literature. *Address:* UBC James Hogg Research Centre, St Paul's Hospital, Room 166, 1081 Burrard Street, Vancouver, BC V6Z 1Y6, Canada (office). *Telephone:* (604) 806-8346 (office). *Fax:* (604) 806-8351 (office). *Website:* www.hli.ubc.ca (office).

HOGG, Baroness (Life Peer), cr. 1995, of Kettlethorpe in the County of Lincolnshire; **Sarah Elizabeth Mary Hogg;** British economist; b. 14 May 1946; d. of Lord Boyd-Carpenter; m. Rt Hon. Douglas M. Hogg QC, MP 1968; one s. one d.; ed St Mary's Convent, Ascot and Lady Margaret Hall, Oxford Univ.; staff writer, The Economist 1967, Literary Ed. 1970, Econs Ed. 1977; Econs Ed. Sunday Times 1981; Presenter, Channel 4 News 1982–83; Econs Ed. and Deputy Exec. Ed. Finance and Industry, The Times 1984–86; Asst Ed. and Business and City Ed. The Independent 1986–89; Econs Ed. The Daily Telegraph 1989–90; Head Policy Unit, 10 Downing Street (rank Second Perm. Sec.) 1990–95; Chair. London Econs 1997–99 (Dir 1995–97), Frontier Econs 1999–; mem. Int. Advisory Bd, Nat. Westminster Bank 1995–97, Advisory Bd, Bankinter 1995–98, House of Lords Select Cttee on Science and Tech. 1995–98, House of Lords Select Cttee on Monetary Policy 2000, Council, Royal Econ. Soc. 1996–, Council, Hansard Soc. 1995–99; Dir London Broadcasting Co. 1982–90, Royal Nat. Theatre 1988–91, Foreign & Colonial Smaller Cos Investment Trust 1995–2002 (Chair. 1997–2002), Nat. Provident Inst. 1996–99, GKN 1996– (Deputy Chair. 2003–), 3i Group 1997–2010 (Deputy Chair. 2000, Chair. 2002–10), P&O 1999–2000, P&O Princess Cruises 2000–03, Carnival Corpn & Carnival PLC 2003–, Martin Currie Portfolio Investment Trust 1999–02; Gov. BBC 2000–04, Centre for Econ. Policy Research 1985–92, London Business School 2004–, Financial Reporting Council 2004–; Fellow, Eton Coll. 1996–; Hon. Fellow, Lady Margaret Hall, Oxford 1994; Hon. MA (Open Univ.) 1987; Hon. DPhil (Loughborough Univ.) 1992; Hon. DL (Lincoln) 2001; Hon. DSc (City Univ.) 2002; Wincott Foundation Financial Journalist of the Year 1985. *Publication:* Too Close to Call (with Jonathan Hill) 1995. *Address:* House of Lords, Westminster, London, SW1A 0PW, England.

HOGNESS, David Swenson, PhD; American geneticist and academic; *Rudy J. and Daphne Donohue Munzer Professor Emeritus in the School of Medicine, Stanford University;* b. 1925; ed California Inst. of Tech.; Post-doctoral fellowship at Institut Pasteur, France 1952; joined faculty of Washington Univ.; held various chairs at Stanford Univ. 1955–59, currently Rudy J. and Daphne Donohue Munzer Prof. Emer. in the School of Medicine; Int. Prize for Biology, Japan Soc. for the Promotion of Science 2007. *Publications:* numerous scientific papers in professional journals on the study of gene structure in higher eukaryotes, the developmental genetics of the fruit fly *Drosophila melanogaster* and how the hormone ecdysone acts to regulate metamorphosis in *Drosophila*. *Address:* Stanford University School of Medicine, 300 Pasteur Drive, Stanford, CA 94305, USA (office). *Telephone:* (650) 723-6166 (office). *E-mail:* tran@cmgm.stanford.edu (office). *Website:* med.stanford.edu (office).

HOGWOOD, Christopher Jarvis Haley, CBE, MA, FRSA; British musician, conductor, musicologist and keyboard player, writer, editor and broadcaster; *Andrew D. White Professor-at-Large, Cornell University;* b. 10 Sept. 1941, Nottingham, Notts.; s. of Haley Evelyn and Marion Constance Hogwood (née Higgott); ed Univ. of Cambridge, Charles Univ., Prague, Czechoslovakia (now Czech Repub.); keyboard continuo, Acad. of St Martin-in-the-Fields 1965–76, keyboard soloist 1970–76, consultant Musicologist 1971–76; Founder-mem. Early Music Consort of London 1965–76; writer and presenter, The Young Idea (BBC Radio 3) 1972–82; Founder and Dir Acad. of Ancient Music 1973–2006, Dir Emer. 2006–; mem. Faculty of Music, Univ. of Cambridge 1975–; Artistic Dir King's Lynn Festival 1976–80; Dir Handel and Haydn Soc., Boston, USA 1986–2001, Conductor Laureate 2001–; Dir of Music, St Paul Chamber Orchestra, Minn., USA 1987–92, Prin. Guest Conductor 1992–98; Visiting Artist, Harvard Univ. 1988–89, Tutor, Mather House 1991–93; Artistic Adviser, Australian Chamber Orchestra 1989–93; Artistic Dir Summer Mozart Festival, Nat. Symphony Orchestra, USA 1993–2001; Assoc. Dir Beethoven Acad., Antwerp 1998–2002; Prin. Guest Conductor, Kammerorchester Basel, Switzerland 2000–06; Kayden Visiting Artist, Learning from Performers Programme, Harvard Univ. 2001; Prin. Guest Conductor, Orquesta Ciudad de Granada 2001–04, Orchestra Sinfonica di Milano Giuseppe Verdi 2003–06; Chief Guest Conductor, Poznán Philharmonic Orchestra, Poland 2011–; Int. Prof. of Early Music Performance, RAM, London 1992–2008; Visiting Prof., Dept of Music, King's Coll., London 1992–96; Gresham Prof. of Music, Gresham Coll. 2010–; Andrew D. White Prof.-at-Large, Cornell Univ., USA 2012–; Series Ed. Music for London Entertainment 1983–97; Chair. Advisory Cttee and Gen. Ed. Francesco Geminiani Opera Omnia, Ut Orpheus Edizioni 2008–; mem. Editorial Cttee C.P.E. Bach Edn (Md) 1986–98, Chair. Advisory Bd C.P.E. Bach Complete Works 1999–; mem. Editorial Bd Early Music (Oxford Univ. Press) 1993–97, Early Music Performers, Peacock Press 2002, Bd Eds Bohuslav Martinů Foundation 2003–, Advisory Panel, Eighteenth-Century Music, Cambridge Univ. Press 2003; Pres. Early Music Wales 1996–, Nat. Music Assen (NEMA) 2000, The Handel Inst. 2000–; Hon. Prof. of Music, Univ. of Keele 1986–90, Univ. of Cambridge 2002–08 (Hon. Prof. Emer. 2008–); Hon. Fellow, Jesus Coll., Cambridge 1989, Pembroke Coll., Cambridge 1992; Hon. mem. RAM 1995; Freeman, Worshipful Co. of Musicians 1989; Hon. DMus (Keele) 1991, (Cantab.) 2008, (RCM) 2013; Hon. PhD (Zurich) 2007; Winner, Yorkshire Post Music Book Award 1984, Walter Willson Cobbett Medal, Worshipful Co. of Musicians 1986, UCLA Award for Artistic Excellence 1996, Scotland on Sunday Music Prize, Edin. Int. Festival 1996, Distinguished Musician Award, Inc. Soc. of Musicians 1997, Martinů Medal, Bohuslav Martinů Foundation, Prague 1999; Handel & Haydn Soc. named its Fellowship 'The Christopher Hogwood Historically Informed Performance Fellowship' 2001, Regione Liguria per il suo contributo all'arte e alla filogia della musica 2003, Halle Hon. Handel Prize 2008, 'Musa' Polimnia, XLV Premio Internazionale, 'Le Muse', Florence 2010, Artist of the Year, Beijing Music Festival 2010, Harrison Medal, Soc. for Musicology in Ireland 2011. *Publications include:* Music at Court 1977, The Trio Sonata 1979, Haydn's Visits to England 1980, Music in Eighteenth-Century England (co-author) 1983, Handel 1984, Holmes' Life of Mozart (ed.) 1991, The Keyboard in Baroque Europe (ed.) 2003; many edns of musical scores; contribs to The New Grove Dictionary of Music and Musicians 1980 and 2001; numerous articles and recordings. *Address:* 10 Brookside, Cambridge, Cambs., CB2 1JE, England (home). *Telephone:* (1223) 363975 (home). *Fax:* (1223) 327377 (home). *E-mail:* office@hogwood.org (office). *Website:* www.hogwood.org.

HOHLER, Erla Karine Bergendahl, DPhil, FSA; Norwegian archaeologist, art historian and academic; *Professor Emerita, Institute of Archaeology, Art History and Numismatics, Oslo University;* b. 20 Nov. 1937, Oslo; m. Christopher Hohler 1961; three c.; ed Univ. of Oslo, Courtauld Inst., London; Asst Prof. Inst. of Art History, Univ. of Oslo 1975, Prof. Inst. of Archaeology, Art History and Numismatics 1993, currently Prof. Emer.; Keeper Medieval Dept, Univ. Museum of Nat. Antiquities, Oslo 1987; Prof. of Art History Univ. of Tromsø 1994; mem. Soc. of Antiquaries of London 1986, Det Norske Videnskapsakademi 1994. *Publications:* The Capitals of Urnes Church 1975, Stavkirkene 1981, Stilentwicklung in

der Holzkirchen Architektur 1981, Norwegian Stave Church Carving 1989, Norwegian Stave Church Sculpture I-II 1999, Catalogue Raisonné 1999, Painted Altar Frontals of Norway I-III 2004. *Address:* Lyder Sagens Gt. 23, 0358 Oslo (home); Universitetets Kulturhistoriske Museer, Frederiks Gt. 3, 0164 Oslo, Norway (office). *Telephone:* 22-46-57-32 (home); 22-85-95-36 (office). *E-mail:* erla .hohler@ukm.uio.no (office). *Website:* www.khm.uio.no (office).

HØJ, Peter, MSc, PhD, FTSE; Danish scientist, academic and university administrator; *Vice-Chancellor and President, University of Queensland;* ed Univ. of Copenhagen; Man. Dir Australian Wine Research Inst., Adelaide 1997–2004; CEO Australian Research Council 2004–07; Vice-Chancellor and Pres. Univ. of South Australia 2007–12; Vice-Chancellor and Pres. Univ. of Queensland 2012–; mem. Bd CSIRO; Deputy Chair. Universities Australia –2012, Lead Vice-Chancellor Research; pvt. mem. Prime Minister's Science Eng and Innovation Council 1999–2004, ex-officio mem. 2006–07; Foreign mem. (Natural Sciences Class) Royal Danish Acad. of Sciences and Letters; Fellow, Australian Acad. of Technological Sciences and Eng; Hon. DUniv (Copenhagen); Centenary Medal 2002. *Address:* Office of the Vice-Chancellor, Level 4, Brian Wilson Chancellery, University of Queensland, Brisbane, Qld 4072, Australia (office). *Telephone:* (7) 3365-1300 (office). *Fax:* (7) 3365-1266 (office). *E-mail:* vc@uq.edu.au (office). *Website:* www.uq.edu.au/about/vice-chancellor (office).

HOJAMUHAMMEDOV, Baymyrat; Turkmenistani hydrogeologist and government official; *Deputy Chairman of the Government, responsible for the Oil and Gas Sector and Fisheries;* b. 15 Nov. 1961, Așgabat, Turkmen SSR, USSR; s. of Geldymyrat Hojamuhammedov and Aynagozel Hojamuhammedov; m.; two s. two d.; ed Ordxhonikidze Moscow Geology Inst.; Hydrogeologist, Turkmen Research Inst. 1984–86; Sr Scientist, Turkmenistan Geology Scientific Research Inst. 1991–93; Sr Hydrogeologist, Turkmengeologiya 1993–97; Head of Gas Export Dept, Turkmennefigas State Trade Corpn 1997, later Deputy Chair. Nat. Clearing Center; Head of Gas Export Dept, Turkmengas 2006–07; Head of Investments and Mineral Resources, Ministry of Petroleum 2007, Minister of Petroleum, Natural Gas and Mineral Resources 2007–09, Deputy Chair. of Govt 2009–, responsible for Petroleum and Natural Gas 2009–11, for the Oil and Gas Sector and Fisheries 2011–. *Address:* Office of the President and the Council of Ministers, 744000 Așgabat, Galkynyș köç. 20, Turkmenistan (office). *Telephone:* (12) 35-45-34 (office). *Fax:* (12) 35-51-12 (office). *E-mail:* nt@online.tm (office). *Website:* www .turkmenistan.gov.tm (office).

HOLBOROW, Leslie Charles, QSO, BPhil, MA; New Zealand fmr university vice-chancellor; *Professor Emeritus, Victoria University of Wellington;* b. 28 Jan. 1941, Auckland; s. of George Holborow and Ivah V. Holborow; m. Patricia L. Walsh 1965 (died 2012); one s. two d.; ed Henderson High School, Auckland Grammar School, Univ. of Auckland and Univ. of Oxford, UK; Jr Lecturer, Univ. of Auckland 1963; Lecturer, Sr Lecturer, Univ. of Dundee (until 1967 Queen's Coll. Univ. of St Andrew's) 1965–74; Prof. of Philosophy, Univ. of Queensland, Brisbane 1974–85, Pres. Professorial Bd 1980–81, Pro-Vice-Chancellor (Humanities) 1983–85; Vice-Chancellor, Victoria Univ. of Wellington 1985–98, Prof. Emer. 1998–; Chair. NZ Vice-Chancellors' Cttee 1990, 1996; Council mem. Assen of Commonwealth Univs 1990–91, 1996; Pres. Australasian Assen of Philosophy 1977; Nat. Pres. NZ Inst. of Int. Affairs 1987–90, Standing Cttee 2002–13; Chair. Bd NZ Univs Acad. Audit Unit 2003–09, Lilburn Residence Trust; mem. NZ Cttee for Pacific Econ. Cooperation 1986–94, Educ. Sub-cttee of NZ Nat. Comm. for UNESCO 1996–99; Trustee, NZ String Quartet 1990–2011; mem. Bd NZ School of Dance 2010–; Hon. LLD (Victoria Univ. of Wellington) 1998. *Publications:* articles in philosophical journals and on New Zealand foreign policy. *Leisure interests:* golf, tramping, listening to music. *Address:* 16 Ames Street, Paekakariki 5034, New Zealand. *Telephone:* (4) 905-9886. *E-mail:* holborowles@gmail.com.

HOLBROOK, Harold (Hal) Rowe, Jr; American actor; b. 17 Feb. 1925, Cleveland, Ohio; s. of Harold Rowe Holbrook, Sr and Aileen Holbrook (née Davenport); m. 1st Ruby Holbrook 1945 (divorced 1965); one s. one d.; m. 2nd Carol Eve Rossen 1966 (divorced 1983) one d.; m. 3rd Dixie Carter 1984 (died 2010); ed Culver Academies, Denison Univ.; served in US Army in World War II, stationed in Newfoundland; performed a one-man show as Mark Twain 1954; mem. Valley Players, Holyoke, Mass 1941–62, performed at Mountain Park Casino Playhouse, Mountain Park, and performed Mark Twain Tonight to open the season 1957; sent by State Dept on a European tour, which included appearances behind the Iron Curtain; first played role of Mark Twain Off-Broadway 1959; Tony Award, Drama Desk Award. *Films include:* The Group 1966, Wild in the Streets 1968, The People Next Door 1970, The Great White Hope 1970, They Only Kill Their Masters 1972, Jonathan Livingston Seagull (voice) (uncredited) 1973, Magnum Force 1973, The Girl from Petrovka 1974, All the President's Men 1976, Battle of Midway 1976, Julia 1977, Rituals 1977, Capricorn One 1977, Natural Enemies 1979, The Fog 1980, The Kidnapping of the President 1980, Creepshow 1982, Girls Nite Out 1982, The Star Chamber 1983, Wall Street 1987, The Unholy 1988, Fletch Lives 1989, The Firm 1993, Acts of Love 1996, Cats Don't Dance (voice) 1997, Hercules (voice) 1997, Eye of God 1997, Hush 1998, Walking to the Waterline 1998, Judas Kiss 1998, Rusty: A Dog's Tale 1998, The Florentine 1999, The Bachelor 1999, Waking the Dead 2000, Men of Honour 2000, The Life and Adventures of Santa Claus (voice) 2000, The Majestic 2001, Purpose 2002, Seventh Day Documentary 2002, Country Music: The Spirit of America IMAX 2003, Shade 2003, Into the Wild 2007, Killshot 2008, That Evening Sun 2009, Flying Lessons 2010, Good Day for It 2011, Water for Elephants 2011, Lincoln 2012, Promised Land 2012, Savannah 2012. *Television includes:* The Brighter Day (series) 1954–59, Mr. Citizen (series) 1955, Preview Tonight (series) – The Cliff Dwellers 1966, The Glass Menagerie (film) 1966, Mark Twain Tonight (series) 1967, Coronet Blue (series) 1967, Off to See the Wizard (series) – Wild World (narrator) 1968, The F.B.I. (series) – The Fraud 1969, The Bold Ones: The Lawyers (series) – The Whole World Is Watching 1969, The Name of the Game (series) – The Perfect Image 1969, Disneyland (series) – The Wacky Zoo of Morgan City: Part 1, Part 2 1970, The Bold Ones: The Senator (series) (Outstanding Lead Actor - Drama Series, Primetime Emmy Awards 1971) 1970–71, Travis Logan, D.A. (film) 1971, Suddenly Single (film) 1971, Goodbye, Raggedy Ann (film) 1971, Appointment with Destiny (series) – Surrender at Appomattox (narrator) 1972, That Certain Summer (film) 1972, Pueblo (film) (Primetime Emmy Awards: Outstanding Lead Actor in a Miniseries or a Movie 1974, Actor of the Year 1974) 1973, Lincoln (mini-series) (Primetime

Emmy Awards Outstanding Lead Actor in a Miniseries or a Movie 1976) 1974–75, Great Performances (series) 1975–77, 33 Hours in the Life of God (film) 1976, Our Town (film) 1977, Tartuffe (film), Host (uncredited) 1978, The Awakening Land (mini-series) 1978, Murder by Natural Causes (film) 1979, The Legend of the Golden Gun (film) 1979, When Hell Was in Session (series) 1979, Off the Minnesota Strip (film) 1980, Omnibus (series) 1980, The Killing of Randy Webster (series) 1981, Celebrity (mini-series) 1984, George Washington (mini-series) 1984, The Three Wishes of Billy Grier (film) 1984, North and South Part 1 (mini-series) 1985, Behind Enemy Lines (film) 1985, Under Siege (film) 1986, Dress Gray (film) 1986, North and South Part 2 (mini-series) 1986, Designing Women (series) 1986–89, Plaza Suite (film) 1987, The Fortunate Pilgrim (mini-series) 1988, Emma: Queen of the South Seas (mini-series) 1988, I'll Be Home for Christmas (film) 1988, Day One (film) 1989, Sorry, Wrong Number (film) 1989, Evidence of Love (film) 1990, Evening Shade (series) 1990–94, Bonds of Love (film) 1993, A Perry Mason Mystery: The Case of the Lethal Lifestyle (film) 1994, A Perry Mason Mystery: The Case of the Grimacing Governor (film) 1994, A Perry Mason Mystery: The Case of the Jealous Jokester (film) 1995, She Stood Alone: The Tailhook Scandal (film) 1995, Innocent Victims (film) 1996, The Battle of the Alamo (documentary) (narrator) 1996, Great Soldiers (film) 1997, All the Winters That Have Been (film) 1997, The Third Twin (film) 1997, My Own Country (film) 1998, Beauty (film) 1998, A Place Apart (film) 1999, The Outer Limits (series) – Final Appeal 2000, Family Law (series) – One Mistake 2000, The Legend of the Three Trees (film) (voice) 2001, Haven (film) 2001, The West Wing (series) 2001–02, Becker (series) 2002, The Street Lawyer (film) 2003, Hope & Faith (series) – A Room of One's Own 2005, The Cultivated Life: Thomas Jefferson and Wine (film) (voice) 2005, Captain Cook's Extraordinary Atlas (film) 2009, Sons of Anarchy (series) 2010, The Event (series) 2010–11, Rectify (series) 2012–13. *Address:* c/o Abrams Artists Agency L.A., 9200 Sunset Blvd, 11th Floor, Los Angeles, CA 90069, USA (office).

HOLBROOK, Karen A., BS, MS, PhD; American biologist, academic and university administrator; *USF System Sr. Vice President for Global Affairs & International Research and Professor of Molecular Medicine, University of South Florida;* ed Univ. of Wisconsin, Univ. of Washington, Seattle; Teaching Asst, Zoology, Univ. of Wisconsin 1963–66; Instructor of Biology, Ripon Coll. 1966–69, Instructor, Upward Bound Program 1967; Instructor, NSF Summer Inst. 1969; Teaching Asst, Biological Structure, Univ. of Washington 1969–72, Instructor, Biological Structure, School of Medicine 1972–75, Asst Prof., Biological Structure, Adjunct Asst Prof., Dermatology 1975–79, assoc. Prof., Biological Structure, Adjunct Assoc. Prof., Dermatology 1979–84, Assoc. Chair. Biological Structure 1981–85, Prof., Biological Structure, Adjunct assoc. Prof., Dermatology 1984–93, Assoc. Dean, Scientific Affairs 1985–94; Prof. of Anatomy and Dermatology, Vice-Pres. for Research and Dean Grad. School, Univ. of Florida 1993–98; Prof. of Cell Biology, Sr Vice-Pres. for Academic Affairs and Provost Univ. of Georgia 1998–2002, Medical Coll. of Georgia Adjunct Prof. of Anatomy, Cell Biology and Medicine 1998–2002; Prof. of Internal Medicine—Dermatology, Ohio State Univ. 2002–07, Prof. of Physiology and Cell Biology 2002–07, Pres. Ohio State Univ. 2002–07; fmrly Vice-Pres. for Research and Innovation, now System Sr Vice-Pres. for Global Affairs and Int. Research and Prof. of Molecular Medicine, Univ. of South Florida 2007–; mem. Bd of Dirs Health Byrd Alzheimer's Inst.; Sr Fellow, Dermatology, Univ. of Wash. 1976–79; Assoc. Ed. Journal of Investigative Dermatology 1987–92, Journal of Investigative Dermatology 1997–; mem. Editorial Bd Journal of Investigative Dermatology 1978–82, Journal of Pediatric Dermatology 1982–89, American Journal of Anatomy 1983–92, Medicine Northwest 1985–87, Journal of Investigative Dermatology 1992–97, The Anatomical Record 1993–96; mem. Editorial Advisory Bd University Business magazine 2003–; mem. AAAS, American Soc. for Cell Biology, American Asscn of Anatomists, Soc. for Investigative Dermatology, Soc. for Pediatric Dermatology, American Civilization Seminar, Univ. of Florida; Hon. Mem. Epsilon Lambda Chi Alpha Engineering Leadership Circle, Nat. Bd Medical Coll. of Pennsylvania; Distinguished Mem. Nat. Soc. for Collegiate Scholars; Hon. DSc (Punjab Agricultural Univ.) 2006; Kung Sun Oh Memorial Prize, Yonsei Medical College, Seoul, S Korea 1994, 34th Annual Marion Spencer Fay Nat. Bd Award to a Distinguished Woman Physician/Scientist, Medical Coll. of Pennsylvania 1996, Pinkus Award, American Soc. of Dermatopathology 1997, Distinguished Contrib. to Research Admin Award, Soc. of Research Admins Int. 2002, Director's Award, Ohio Dept of Alcohol and Drug Addiction Services 2003, The Women's Center Leadership Award 2004, Acad. for Leadership Award, Harding-Evans Foundation 2004, Pres.'s Leadership Group Award, US Dept of Educ., Higher Educ. Center for Alcohol and Other Drug Abuse and Violence Prevention 2004, Women in Higher Educ. Award, Nat. Panhellenic Conf. Foundation, Inc. 2005, YWCA Women of Achievement Award 2006, Sixth Annual Empowered Woman Award, Columbus Women Pres.'s Org. 2006. *Films:* Prenatal Diagnosis of Inherited Skin Disease, Video Journal of Dermatology 1990, Fetal Skin Sampling, Dialogs in Dermatology 1994. *Publications:* more than 30 book chapters and more than 150 scientific papers in professional journals. *Address:* c/o University of South Florida, Health Byrd Alzheimer's Institute, 4001 East Fletcher Avenue, Tampa, FL 33613, USA.

HOLDEN, Bob, BS; American fmr politician; *Vice-Chairman, Midwest US–China Association;* m. Lori Hauser; two s.; ed Southwest Missouri State Univ., Harvard Univ.; fmr Admin. Asst to Congressman Richard Gephardt (q.v.), St. Louis; mem. Mo. House of Reps 1983–89; Mo. State Treas. 1993, Gov. of Mo. 2001–04; mem. Bd Fund Commrs, Mo. State Employees Retirement System, Mo. Rural Opportunities Council, Holden Scholarship Fund, Leadership St Louis, Council of State Govts, Nat Asscn State Treas.; Vice-Chair. Mo. Cultural Trust; Vice-Chair. Midwest US–China Asscn 2005–. *Address:* Midwest US–China Association, 20 North Clark Street, Suite 750, Chicago, IL 60602, USA (office). *Telephone:* (773) 909-2168 (office). *Fax:* (773) 281-4812 (office). *Website:* www.midwestuschina.org (office).

HOLDER, Eric H., Jr., BA, JD; American lawyer, judge and government official; *Attorney-General;* b. 21 Jan. 1951, New York; s. of Eric Holder and Miriam R. Yearwood; m. Dr Sharon Malone; three c.; ed Columbia Coll., Columbia Law School; Trial Attorney, Public Integrity Section, US Dept of Justice 1976–88, US Attorney 1993–97, US Deputy Attorney-Gen. 1997–2001, Attorney-Gen. 2009–; Pnr, Covington & Burling (law firm), Washington, DC 2001–; Assoc. Judge Superior Court, Washington, DC 1988–93. *Address:* Department of Justice, 950 Pennsylvania Avenue, NW, Washington, DC 20530-0001, USA (office). *Telephone:*

(202) 514-2000 (office). *Fax:* (202) 307-6777 (office). *E-mail:* askdoj@usdoj.gov (office). *Website:* www.usdoj.gov (office).

HOLDER, Rt Rev. John Walder Dunlop, BA, STM, PhD; Barbadian ecclesiastic; *Bishop of Barbados;* b. 16 Feb. 1948, Barbados; m. Betty Lucas-Holder; one s.; ed Codrington Coll., Barbados, Univ. of the West Indies, The School of Theology (Univ. of the South), King's Coll., London, UK; ordained priest 1975; tutor in Biblical Studies, Codrington Coll. 1977–81, Lecturer 1984–93, Acting Prin. Sept.–Dec. 1988, Sr Lecturer 1993–99, Deputy Prin. 1999–; Visiting Lecturer in Religious Studies, Erdiston Teacher Training Coll., Barbados; Lecturer in Biblical Studies, Lay Training Programme, Diocese of Barbados 1984–90; Visiting Lecturer, Barbados Community Coll. 1985; Visiting Sabbatical Prof., Gen. Theological Seminary, New York March–May 1988; Chair. Ministry of Educ. Cttee on Religious and Moral Educ. Syllabus for the primary schools of Barbados 1992–94; Visiting Lecturer, Bucknell Univ. Summer Programme 1996–98; Curate St George's Cathedral, St Vincent, West Indies 1975–77; Asst Priest, St John's Parish Church, Barbados 1977–81, Priest-in-Charge 1990–92; Hon. Chaplain, Univ. Church of Christ the King, London 1981–84; Asst Priest, St Michael's Cathedral, Barbados 1984–86, St Augustine 1986–89, Priest-in-Charge 1989–90; Priest-in-Charge, St Mark and St Catherine, Barbados 1992–93, St Mark 1993–94, Holy Trinity 1994–95, Holy Cross 1995–; Hon. Canon Diocese of Barbados 1996; Bishop of Barbados 2000–; Long and Dedicated Service Award, Codrington Coll. 1994. *Television:* Religion in Barbados During the First Twenty-Five Years of Independence 1966–91 CBC 1990, CBC presentation on professions 1994. *Publications:* Christian Commitment 1985, Set the Captives Free: The Challenge of the Biblical Jubilee 1887, A Layman's Guide to the Bible (Vols I & II) 1989, The Intertestamental Period 1994, Biblical Reflections on the Book of Hosea 1999. *Address:* Diocesan Office, Mandeville House, Henry's Lane, St Michael (office); Leland, Philip Drive, Pine Gardens, St Michael, Barbados (home). *Telephone:* 426-2761 (office); 435-0466 (home). *Fax:* 426-0871 (office). *E-mail:* bishop_holder@sunbeach.net (office).

HOLDGATE, Sir Martin Wyatt, Kt, CB, MA, PhD, FSB; British biologist and academic; b. 14 Jan. 1931, Horsham, Sussex, England; s. of the late Francis W. Holdgate and Lois M. Holdgate (née Bebbington); m. Elizabeth M. Weil (née Dickason) 1963; two s.; ed Arnold School, Blackpool and Queens' Coll., Cambridge; Research Fellow, Queens' Coll., Cambridge 1953–56; Jt Leader, Gough Island Scientific Survey 1955–56; Lecturer in Zoology, Univ. of Manchester 1956–57, Univ. of Durham 1957–60; Leader, Royal Soc. Expedition to Southern Chile 1958–59; Asst Dir of Research, Scott Polar Research Inst., Cambridge 1960–63; Chief Biologist, British Antarctic Survey 1963–66; Deputy Dir (Research), The Nature Conservancy (UK) 1966–70; Dir Central Unit on Environmental Pollution, Dept of Environment 1970–74; Dir Inst. of Terrestrial Ecology 1974–76; Dir-Gen. of Research, Dept of Environment 1976–81; Chief Scientist and Deputy Sec. (Environment Protection), Dept of Environment and Chief Scientific Adviser, Dept of Transport 1981–88; Dir-Gen. Int. Union for Conservation of Nature and Natural Resources 1988–94; Pres. Zoological Soc. of London 1994–2004; Co-Chair. Intergovernmental Panel on Forests, UN Comm. on Sustainable Devt 1995–97; mem. Royal Comm. on Environmental Pollution 1994–2002; Chair. Int. Inst. for Environment and Devt 1994–2000, Governing Council, Arnold School 1997–2004; Pres. Freshwater Biological Asscn 2002–10; Fellow, Soc. of Biology (UK); Hon. mem. British Ecological Soc. 1996, Int. Union for the Conservation of Nature and Natural Resources 2000; Commdr, Order of the Golden Ark 1991; Hon. DSc (Durham) 1991, (Sussex) 1993, (Lancaster) 1995, (Queen Mary, London) 2006; Bruce Medal, Royal Soc. of Edinburgh and Royal Scottish Geog. Soc. 1964, Silver Medal, UNEP 1983, UNEP Global 500 1988, Patrons Medal, Royal Geographical Soc. 1992, Livingstone Medal, Royal Scottish Geographical Soc. 1993, Int. Conservationist of the Year Award, Nat. Wildlife Fed. (USA) 1992. *Publications include:* Mountains in the Sea: The Story of the Gough Island Expedition 1958, A Perspective of Environmental Pollution 1979, From Care to Action: Making a Sustainable World 1996, The Green Web: A Union for World Conservation 1999, Penguins and Mandarins 2003, The Story of Appleby in Westmoreland 2006, Arnold: The Story of a Blackpool School 2009. *Leisure interests:* natural history, local history. *Address:* Fell Beck, Hartley, Kirkby Stephen, Cumbria, CA17 4JH, England (home). *Telephone:* (1768) 372316 (home). *E-mail:* martin@holdgate.org.

HOLDREN, John Paul, SB, SM, PhD; American environmental scientist, academic and government official; *Assistant to the President for Science and Technology and Director, Office of Science and Technology, Executive Office of the President;* b. 1 March 1944, Sewickley, Pa; s. of Raymond Andrew Holdren and Virginia June Holdren (née Fuqua); m. Cheryl Edgar 1966; one s. one d.; ed Massachusetts Inst. of Tech., Stanford Univ.; Assoc. Engineer, Performance Analysis, Lockheed Missiles and Space Co., Sunnyvale, Calif. Summer 1965, Sr Assoc. Engineer, Re-Entry Aerodynamics Summer 1966, Consultant in Re-Entry Physics 1966–67; Research Asst, Inst. for Plasma Research, Stanford Univ. 1969–70; Physicist, Theory Group, Magnetic Fusion Energy Div., Lawrence Livermore Nat. Lab. 1970–73 (on leave 1972–73); Sr Research Fellow, Div. of Humanities and Social Sciences and Environmental Quality Lab., California Inst. of Tech. 1972–73; Asst Prof. of Energy and Resources, Univ. of California, Berkeley 1973–75, Assoc. Prof. 1975–78, Acting Chair. Energy and Resources Group 1982–83, Fall 1990, Vice-Chair. 1983–96 (on leave 1987–88), Chair. of Grad. Advisors, Energy and Resources Group 1988–96, Prof. of Energy and Resources 1978–96, Class of 1935 Prof. of Energy 1991–96, Prof. Emer. of Energy and Resources 1996–; Teresa and John Heinz Prof. of Environmental Policy and Dir Science, Tech. and Public Policy Program, Belfer Center for Science and Int. Affairs, Kennedy School of Govt, Harvard Univ. 1996–2008, also Prof. of Environmental Science and Policy, Dept of Earth and Planetary Sciences, mem. Bd of Tutors, undergraduate concentration in Environmental Science and Public Policy; Asst to Pres. Obama for Science and Tech. and Dir Office of Science and Tech., Exec. Office of the Pres. 2009–; Visiting Scholar, Woods Hole Research Center 1992–94, Distinguished Visiting Scientist and Vice-Chair Bd of Trustees 1994–2005, Dir-Designate 2004–05, Dir 2005–08; Guest Prof., Tsinghua Univ., Beijing, People's Repub. of China 2008; Pres.-elect AAAS 2005, Pres. 2006, Chair. 2007; Chair. Exec. Cttee Pugwash Conf. on Science and World Affairs 1987–97, NAS Cttee on Int. Security and Arms Control 1994–2005 (mem. 1993–2005); mem. Pres. Clinton's Cttee of Advisors on Science and Tech. 1994–2001; Co-Chair. Nat. Comm. on Energy Policy 2002–07; mem. NAS, Nat. Acad. of Eng, American Acad.

of Arts and Sciences, Council on Foreign Relations; Foreign mem. Royal Soc. of London; Dr hc (Univ. of Puget Sound, Colorado School of Mines, Clark Univ., Univ. of Rome, Univ. of the Dist of Columbia); MacArthur Prize Fellowship 1981–86, Volvo Environment Prize 1993, Tyler Prize for Environment 2000, John Heinz Prize for Public Policy 2001, gave acceptance speech for Nobel Peace Prize on behalf of Pugwash Conf. on Science and World Affairs 1995. *Publications:* numerous scientific papers in professional journals on global environmental change, energy technology and policy, nuclear proliferation, and science and technology policy. *Address:* Office of Science and Technology Policy, NEOB 5230, The White House, Washington, DC 20502, USA (office). *Telephone:* (202) 456-6064 (office). *Fax:* (202) 456-6021 (office). *E-mail:* jholdren@ostp.eop.gov (office). *Website:* www.ostp.gov (office).

HOLENDER, Ioan; Romanian opera house director; b. 18 July 1935, Timisoara; m.; two s. one d.; ed Timisoara Polytechnic Inst., Vienna Conservatory; expelled from Romanian higher educ. system on political grounds 1956; worked as tennis trainer and stage dir's asst 1956–59; moved to Vienna and began singing studies 1960; opera singer, Vienna and Klagenfurt 1962–66; joined Starka Theater Agency 1966, later took control of agency and renamed it Holender Opera Agency; Gen. Sec. Vienna Staatsoper and Vienna Volksoper 1988–92, Dir Vienna Volksoper 1992–96, Gen. Dir Vienna Staatsoper 1992–2010; Guest Lecturer, Univ. of Vienna, Donau-Universität Krems 2008–; Artistic Adviser, Teatro Massimo Bellini, Catania 2008–; Artistic Consultant, Metropolitan Opera 2010–; hon. mem. Romanian Acad., Hon. Citizen of Timisoara; Vienna Municipality Golden Medal of Merit, Golden Medal for Services to Vienna Community, Grand Golden Hon. Medal of Austrian Repub., Austrian Hon. Cross for Science and Art, First Class, Officier, Ordre des Artes et des Lettres; Dr hc (Gheorge Dima Music Acad.); Vienna Philharmonic Franz Schalk Gold Medal. *Publications:* Ioan Holender: Der Lebensweg des Wiener Staatsoperndirektors (autobiog.) 2001. *Address:* c/o Metropolitan Opera, Lincoln Center, New York, NY 10023, USA (office). *Telephone:* (212) 799-3100 (office). *Website:* www.metoperafamily.org/metopera (office).

HOLIDAY, Eugene Bernard; St Maarten economist; *Governor;* b. 14 Dec. 1962; s. of Eugene Bernard Holiday Sr and Leone Cassandra Holiday-Marsham; m. Marie Louise Holiday-Hasell; ed Oranje School, Philipsburg, Milton Peters Coll., Catholic Univ. Brabant, Netherlands; analyst and policy adviser, Central Bank of the Netherlands Antilles 1987–89, Head of Research and Monetary Policy Dept 1989–91, Coordinator Monetary and Econ. Affairs 1991–94, Deputy Dir of Monetary and Econ. Affairs 1994–95; Man. Dir Windward Island Airways International Ltd 1995–98; Pres. Princess Juliana Int. Airport Exploitatie-maatschappij NV, St Maarten 1998–2010; Gov. of St Maarten (first Gov. following dissolution of Netherlands Antilles) Oct. 2010–. *Leisure interests:* sports, especially NBA basketball, tennis and golf. *Address:* Office of the Governor, Government Administration Bldg, Clem Labega Sq., POB 943, Philipsburg, St Maarten (office). *Telephone:* 542-6085 (office). *Fax:* 542-4172 (office). *E-mail:* dircab@governorsxm .com (office). *Website:* www.governorsxm.com (office).

HOLLÁN, R. Susan, MD; Hungarian professor of haematology; *Consultant, National Institute of Haematology and Blood Transfusion;* b. 26 Oct. 1920, Budapest; d. of Dr Henrik Hollán and Dr. Malvin Hornik; m. Dr György Révész; one s. one d.; ed Univ. Medical School, Budapest; intern, Rokus Hosp., Budapest 1945–50; Research Fellow, Univ. Medical School, Budapest 1950–54; Science Adviser, Inst. for Experimental Medical Research 1954–91; Dir Nat. Inst. of Haematology and Blood Transfusion 1959–85, Dir-Gen. 1985–90, Consultant 1990–; Prof. of Haematology, Postgraduate Medical School 1970–90; Corresp. mem. Hungarian Acad. of Sciences 1973, mem. 1982– (mem. of Presidium 1976–84); fmr Pres. Int. Soc. of Haematology and Vice-Pres. Int. Soc. of Blood Transfusion; mem. WHO Global AIDS Research Steering Cttee; mem. WHO Expert Cttee on Biological Standardization; mem. Clinical and Immunological Work Cttee of Hungarian Acad. of Sciences; Pres. Bd of Special Cttee for Clinical Sciences; Exec. mem. Hungarian Medical Research Council; Ed.-in-Chief Hungarian Medical Encyclopaedia and Haematologia (quarterly); mem. HSWP Cen. Cttee 1975–89; Foreign Corresp. mem. Soc. de Biologie, Collège de France, Paris; Vice-Pres. Nobel Prize Award, Int. Physicians Prevention of Nuclear War 1983–89; Hon. mem. American Soc. of Hematology, Polish Soc. of Haematology, German Soc. of Haematology (FRG), Purkinje Soc. (Czechoslovakia), Turkish Soc. of Haematology, All-Union Scientific Soc. of Haematology and Blood Transfusion (USSR); Hon. Pres. Hungarian Soc. of Human Genetics; Hungarian Academic Award 1970, State Prize 1974, Socialist Hungary Medal. *Publications:* Basic Problems of Transfusion 1965, Haemoglobins and Haemoglobinopathies 1972, Genetics, Structure and Function of Blood Cells 1980, Management of Blood Transfusion Services 1990; over 300 papers in Hungarian and int. medical journals. *Leisure interests:* fine arts, sport. *Address:* Daróczi ut 24, 1113 Budapest (office); Palánta u. 12, 1025 Budapest, Hungary (home). *Telephone:* (1) 372-4210 (office); (1) 326-0619 (home). *Fax:* (1) 372-4352. *E-mail:* hollan@ella.hu (office).

HOLLAND, Agnieszka; Polish film director and screenwriter; b. 28 Nov. 1948, Warsaw; m. Laco Adamik; one d.; ed FAMU film school, Prague; Asst to Krzysztof Zanussi in filming of Illumination 1973; Dir first TV film 1973; subsequently worked in theatre in Kraków; Co-Dir (with Jerzy Domaradzki and Paweł Kędzierski) film Screen Test 1977; co-scripted Wajda's film Rough Treatment 1978; also worked with Wajda on A Love in Germany, Man of Marble, Man of Iron, The Orchestra Conductor, Korczak, Danton 1982; wrote screenplay for Yurke Bocayevicz's Anna; has also made documentaries for French TV; directs plays for TV theatre (with Laco Aolamik); mem. Polish Film Asscn, European and American Acad. Award; Robert L. Hess Scholar in Residence, Brooklyn Coll. 2005; Officer's Cross, Order of Polonia Restituta 2001; Las Vegas Film Festival Award 1999. *Achievements include:* retrospective of films held at Museum of Modern Art, New York 2008–09. *Films directed include:* Provincial Actors (Critics' Award, Cannes 1980) 1979, The Fever (Gdańsk Golden Lions 1981) 1980, The Lonely Woman 1981, Angry Harvest (Germany) 1985, To Kill a Priest (France) 1987, Europa, Europa (Germany, France) 1990, (Golden Globe 1991) Olivier, Olivier (France) 1992, The Secret Garden (USA) 1993, Red Wind (USA) 1994, Total Eclipse (England, France) 1995, Washington Square (USA) 1996, The Third Miracle (USA) 1999, Golden Dreams 2001, Shot in the Heart (TV, USA) 2001, The Wire (three TV series episodes)

2002–08, Julie Walking Home (Poland–Canada–Germany) 2002, Cold Case (four TV series episodes) 2004–09, Veronica Mars (TV series) 2004, Prawdziwa historia Janosika i Uhorcika (co-dir) 2005, Copying Beethoven 2006, Janosik: A True Story 2009, In Darkness 2011. *Television includes:* A Girl Like Me: The Gwen Araujo Story (film) 2006, Burning Bush (mini-series) 2013; directed several episodes of series The Wire, Cold Case, The Killing, Treme. *Play:* Dybuk (Polish TV) 1999. *Publications:* Magia i pieniadze (Magic & Money) – Conversations with Maria Komatowska, ZNAK Poland 2002. *Address:* c/o Agence Nicole Cann, 1 rue Alfred de Vigny, 75008 Paris, France (office).

HOLLAND, Julian (Jools) Miles, OBE; British musician (piano, keyboard) and broadcaster; b. 24 Jan. 1958, London; s. of Derek Holland and June Rose Lane; one s. two d.; m. Christabel McEwen 2005; ed Invicta Sherington School, Shooters' Hill School; pianist 1975–78; Founder-mem. Squeeze 1974–81, 1985–90; regular tours and concerts; formed The Jools Holland Big Band 1987, later renamed The Rhythm and Blues Orchestra 1991–; BBC Radio 2 Jazz Artist of the Year 2006. *Films:* Spiceworld: The Movie 1997, Milk (wrote score) 1999. *Radio:* presenter BBC Radio 2 1997–. *Television:* The Tube (presenter) 1981–86, Walking to New Orleans (writer, producer and presenter, documentary) 1985, The Groovy Fellas (actor and writer) 1988, Juke Box Jury (presenter) 1989–90, Saturday Night (co-presenter New York NBC music show with David Sanborn) 1989, The Happening 1990, Mr Roadrunner (writer and producer, film) 1991, Later with Jools Holland (presenter) 1993–, Hootenanny (presenter for 13th time, New Year's Eve 2005), Name That Tune, Don't Forget Your Toothbrush, Beat Route (writer and producer, film) 1998, Jools Meets The Saint (writer and producer) 1999, Jools' History of the Piano 2002. *Recordings include:* albums: with Squeeze: Squeeze 1978, Cool for Cats 1979, Argy Bargy 1980, East Side Story 1981, Cosi Fan Tutti Frutti 1985, Babylon and On 1987, Frank 1989, Tom Jones and Jools Holland 2004, Swinging the Blues, Dancing the Ska 2005; solo: A World of his Own 1990, Full Complement 1991, A–Z of the Piano 1992, Live Performance 1994, Solo Piano 1994, Sex and Jazz and Rock and Roll 1996, Lift the Lid 1997, Sunset Over London 1999, Hop the Wag 2000, Small World, Big Band – Friends 2001, Small World, Big Band Vol. 2 – More Friends 2002, Small World, Big Band Vol. 3 2003, Moving Out to the Country (with Rhythm & Blues Orchestra) 2006, The Informer 2008, Rocking Horse (with Rhythm & Blues Orchestra) 2010. *Publications:* Beat Route 1998, The Hand That Changed Its Mind 2004, Barefaced Lies and Boogie-Woogie Boasts (autobiog.) 2007. *Leisure interests:* sketching, giving advice. *Address:* One-Fifteen, 1 Prince of Orange Lane, Greenwich, London, SE10 8JQ, England (office); Helicon Mountain Ltd, Helicon Mountain, Station Terrace Mews, London, SE3 7LP, England (office). *Telephone:* (20) 8293-0999 (office); (20) 8858-0984 (office). *Fax:* (20) 8293-4555 (office). *Website:* www.joolsholland.com.

HOLLANDE, François Gérard Georges; French politician and head of state; *President;* b. 12 Aug. 1954, Rouen (Seine-Maritime); fmr partner Valerie Trierweiler; three s. one d. with fmr partner Ségolène Royal; ed École des Hautes Études Commerciales de Paris, Institut d'Études Politiques de Paris, École Nat. d'Admin, Strasbourg; fmr Councillor, Cour des comptes; mem. Ussel City Council 1983–89; Deputy for Corrèze (1ère) in Nat. Ass. 1988–93, 1997–2012, mem. Defence Comm.; Deputy Mayor of Tulle 1989–95, mem. Tulle City Council 1995–2001, Mayor of Tulle 2001–08; mem. Limousin Regional Council March 1992, 1998–2001; Pres. Conseil Gen. Corrèze 2008–; First Sec. Parti socialiste (PS) 1997–2008; mem. European Parl. July–Dec. 1999; Pres. of France 2012–, Co-Prince of Andorra 2012–; ranked by Forbes magazine amongst The World's Most Powerful People (14th) 2012, (18th) 2013. *Address:* Office of the President, Palais de l'Elysée, 55–57 rue du Faubourg Saint Honoré, 75008 Paris, France (office). *Telephone:* 1-42-92-81-00 (office). *Fax:* 1-47-42-24-65 (office). *Website:* www.elysee .fr (office).

HOLLANDER, Samuel, OC, PhD, FRSC; British/Canadian/Israeli economist and academic; *University Professor Emeritus, University of Toronto;* b. 6 April 1937, London, England; s. of Jacob Hollander and Lily Bernstein; m. Perlette Kéroub 1959; one s. one d.; ed Gateshead Talmudical Acad., Hendon Tech. Coll., Kilburn Polytechnic, London School of Econs, Princeton Univ., NJ; emigrated to Canada 1963; Asst Prof., Univ. of Toronto 1963–67, Assoc. Prof. 1967–70, Prof. 1970–84, Univ. Prof. 1984–98, Univ. Prof. Emer. 1998–; Research Dir, Univ. of Nice (CNRS) 1999–2000; Visiting Prof., Florence Univ., Italy 1973–74, Univ. of London 1974–75, Hebrew Univ., Jerusalem 1979–80, 1988, La Trobe Univ., Melbourne, Australia 1985, Auckland Univ., NZ 1985, 1988, Sorbonne, Paris 1997, Nice Univ., France 2001, Ben Gurion Univ., Israel 2000–06; several guest lectureships; emigrated to Israel 2000; Hon. LLD (McMaster) 1999; Fulbright Fellowship 1959; Guggenheim Fellowship 1968–69; Social Science Fed. of Canada 50th Anniversary Book Award 1990, Thomas Guggenheim Prize in History of Economic Thought 2011. *Publications:* The Sources of Increased Efficiency 1965, The Economics of Adam Smith 1973, The Economics of David Ricardo 1979, The Economics of J. S. Mill 1985, Classical Economics 1987, Ricardo–The New View: Collected Essays I 1995, The Economics of T. R. Malthus 1997, The Literature of Political Economy: Collected Essays II 1998, John Stuart Mill on Economic Theory and Method: Collected Essays III 2000, Jean-Baptiste Say and the Classical Canon in Economics 2005, The Economics of Karl Marx 2008, Friedrich Engels and Marxian Political Economy 2011, Essays on Classical and Marxian Political Economy: Collected Essays IV 2013. *Address:* Department of Economics, Ben Gurion University of the Negev, 84105, Beer Sheva (office); 2 Rehov Sapir, 8906627 Arad, Israel (home). *Telephone:* 54-9474846 (mobile); 8-9771664 (home). *Fax:* 7-6472941 (office). *E-mail:* sholland@bgu.ac.il (office). *Website:* www.ec.bgu.ac .il (office); www.samuel-hollander.com.

HOLLEIN, Max; Austrian fine arts administrator, curator and director; *Director, Schirn Kunsthalle Frankfurt, Städel Museum and Liebieghaus Sculpture Collection;* b. 1969, Vienna; ed Wirtschaftsuniversität Wien, Universität Wien; Project Dir for Exhbns, Solomon R. Guggenheim Museum, New York 1995, Exec. Asst to the Dir 1996–98, Chief of Staff and Man. of European Relations 1998–2000; Commr and Curator American Pavilion, Seventh Biennale of Architecture, Venice 2000; Dir Schirn Kunsthalle Frankfurt 2001–, Städel Museum, Frankfurt 2006, Liebieghaus-Museum alter Plastile, Frankfurt 2006; Commr Austrian Pavilion, Biennale of Visual Art, Venice 2005; mem. Bd Dirs Kulturveranstaltungen des Bundes in Berlin GmbH; mem. Bd of Trustees Neue Galerie, New York. *Publications:* Zeitgenössische Kunst und der Kunstmarktboom (Contemporary

Art and the Boom on the Art Market) 1999, Unternehmen Kunst: Entwicklungen und Verwicklungen (The Business of Art) 2006. *Address:* Schirn Kunsthalle Frankfurt, Römerberg, 60311 Frankfurt (office); Städel Museum, Dürerstrasse 2, 60596 Frankfurt, Germany (office). *Telephone:* (69) 299882-111 (office); (69) 605098-100 (office). *Fax:* (69) 299882-240 (office); (69) 605098-198 (office). *E-mail:* welcome@schirn.de (office); *Website:* www.schirn.de (office); www .staedelmuseum.de (office).

HÖLLER, Carsten, DHabil; Belgian artist; b. 1961, Brussels; ed Univ. of Kiel, Germany; began his artistic career in 1988; uses his training as a scientist in his work as an artist, concentrating particularly on the nature of human relationships and demanding viewer participation; rejected any specific artistic identity, creating works that range from films, drawings, architectural plans and photographs to performances, sculptures and installations; works are most frequently devoted to chemically analysing the nature of human emotions; has collaborated with many other artists, notably with German artist Rosemarie Trockel, with whom, for Documenta X, they together created A House for Pigs and People 1997, in which people and pigs share the same physical space; works include: Addina 1997, Valerio I and II 1998, The Forest, Light Wall 2000, Solandra Greenhouse (garden filled with the Solandra maxima vine); lives and works in Fasta, Sweden. *Address:* c/o Casey Kaplan Gallery, 525 West 21st Street, New York, NY 10011, USA.

HOLLICK, Baron (Life Peer), cr. 1991, of Notting Hill in the Royal Borough of Kensington and Chelsea; **Clive Richard Hollick,** BA; British business executive; b. 20 May 1945, Southampton, Hants., England; s. of Leslie George Hollick and Olive Mary Hollick (née Scruton); m. Susan Mary Woodford 1977; three d.; ed Univ. of Nottingham; joined Hambros Bank 1968, Dir 1973; CEO MAI PLC (fmrly Mills & Allen Int. PLC) 1974–96, Shepperton Studios 1976–84, Garban Ltd (USA) 1983–97, United Business Media PLC 1996–2005; Man. Dir Kohlberg Kravis Roberts UK 2005–; Partner, GP Bullhound 2011–; mem. Int. Advisory Bd Jefferies 2011–; mem. Bd of Dirs Logica PLC 1987–91, Meridian Broadcasting 1991–96, British Aerospace 1992–97, Anglia TV Ltd 1994–97, TRW Inc. 2000–03, Diageo PLC 2001–11, Honeywell Int. 2003–, Pro Siebensat1 AG 2007–, BMG Music Rights Management 2009–; mem. Nat. Bus Co. 1984–91, Applied Econs Dept Advisory Cttee Univ. of Cambridge 1989–97, Financial Law Panel 1993–97; Special Adviser to Dept of Trade and Industry 1997–98; mem. (Labour), House of Lords 1991–, mem. Select Cttee on Econ. Affairs 2010–; Chair. South Bank Centre, London 2002–08; Chair. SBS NV 2005–07; Founder and Trustee, Inst. for Public Policy Research 1988–; Hon. LLD (Nottingham) 1993. *Leisure interests:* cinema, countryside, reading, tennis, theatre. *Address:* House of Lords, Westminster, London, SW1A 0PW, England. *Telephone:* (20) 7221-6746 (office). *E-mail:* hollickrc@ parliament.uk (office). *Website:* www.parliament.uk/biographies/lords/lord -hollick/2732 (office).

HOLLIDAY, Charles O. (Chad), Jr, BS; American engineer and business executive; *Chairman, Bank of America Corporation;* b. 9 March 1948, Nashville, Tenn.; s. of Charles O. Holliday, Sr and Ann Hunter; m. Ann Holliday; two s.; ed Univ. of Tennessee; joined DuPont Fibers Dept as engineer, Old Hickory, Tenn. 1970, Business Analyst, Wilmington, Del. 1974, later product planner, Asst Plant Man., Seaford, Del. 1978, joined DuPont Corp. Planning Dept 1984, Global Business Man. for Nomex 1986, Global Business Dir for Kevlar 1987, Dir of Marketing DuPont Chemicals and Pigments Dept 1988, Vice-Pres., then Pres. DuPont Asia-Pacific 1990, Chair. 1995, Sr Vice-Pres. DuPont 1992, Exec. Vice-Pres. and mem. Office of Chief Exec., E.I. du Pont de Nemours & Co. 1995, Dir 1997–2009, Pres. 1997–2009, CEO 1998–2008, Chair. 1999–2009 (retd); Chair. Bank of America Corpn 2009–; Chair. Catalyst; mem. Bd of Dirs DuPont Photomasks Inc., Deere & Co. 2007–; Chair. US Council on Competitiveness; fmr Chair. Business Roundtable's Task Force for Environment, Tech. and Economy, World Business Council for Sustainable Devt, The Business Council, Soc. of Chemical Industry (American Section); Founding mem. Int. Business Council; mem. Chancellor's Advisory Council for Enhancement, Univ. of Tennessee, Knoxville; Sr mem. Inst. of Industrial Engineers; mem. Nat. Acad. of Eng; Dr hc (Polytechnic Univ., Brooklyn, NY, Washington Coll., Chestertown, Md). *Publication:* Walking the Talk (co-author). *Address:* Bank of America Corporate Center, 100 North Tryon Street, Charlotte, NC 28255, USA (office). *Telephone:* (704) 386-1845 (office). *Fax:* (704) 386-6699 (office). *E-mail:* info@ bankofamerica.com (office). *Website:* www.bankofamerica.com (office).

HOLLIDAY, Sir Frederick (George Thomas), Kt, CBE, FIBiol, FRSE; British zoologist, business executive and fmr university vice-chancellor; b. 22 Sept. 1935; s. of the late Alfred Holliday and Margaret Holliday; m. Philippa Davidson 1957; one s. one d.; ed Bromsgrove County High School and Univ. of Sheffield; Fisheries Research Training Grant (Devt Comm.), Marine Lab. Aberdeen 1956–58, Scientific Officer 1958–61; Lecturer in Zoology, Univ. of Aberdeen 1961–66; Prof. of Biology, Univ. of Stirling 1967–75, Deputy Prin. 1972, Acting Prin. 1973–75; Prof. of Zoology, Univ. of Aberdeen 1975–79; Vice-Chancellor and Warden, Univ. of Durham 1980–90; Dir Shell UK 1980–99; mem. Bd Northern Investors Ltd 1984–90, BRB 1990–94 (Chair. BR (Eastern) 1986–90), Union Railways 1992–97, Lyonnaise des Eaux 1996–97, Suez Lyonnaise des Eaux 1997–, Wise Speke PLC 1997–98, Brewin Dolphin PLC 1998–; mem. Northern Regional Bd Lloyd's Bank 1985–91, Chair. 1986–89, Deputy Chair. 1989–91; Independent Chair. Jt Nature Conservation Cttee 1991; Chair. Northumbrian Water Group plc 1993–2006, Council, Water Aid 1995–97, Northern Venture Trust plc 1996–2009, Go-Ahead Group PLC 1997–2002; mem. Bd of Dirs Northern 2 VCT plc; Pres. British Trust for Ornithology 1996–2001; Vice-Pres. Freshwater Biological Asscn, Marine Biological Asscn; Chair. South Bank Centre 2002–; Hon. DUniv (Stirling) 1984; Hon. DSc (Sheffield) 1987, (Cranfield) 1991; Hon. DCL (Durham) 2002. *Publications:* Wildlife of Scotland (ed. and contrib.) 1979; numerous publs on fish biology and wildlife conservation in Advanced Marine Biology, Fish Physiology, Oceanography and Marine Biology etc. *Leisure interests:* walking, gardening, ornithology. *Address:* c/o Board of Directors, Northern 2 VCT plc, Northumberland House, Princess Square, Newcastle upon Tyne, NE1 8ER, England.

HOLLIDAY, Steven J., BSc; British business executive; *Chief Executive, National Grid PLC;* b. 1957; m.; three c.; ed Univ. of Nottingham; 19 years with Exxon Group; fmrly Exec. Dir British Borneo Oil & Gas PLC; Group Dir, UK and Europe, Nat. Grid PLC 2001–02, Head of Electricity and Gas Transmission

Businesses 2002–03, Group Dir responsible for UK Gas Distribution and Business Services 2003–06, Deputy CEO April–Dec. 2006, Chief Exec. 2007–, Chair. Exec. Cttee; Dir (non-exec.) Marks & Spencer Group PLC 2004–; Chair. UK Business Council for Sustainable Energy, Technician Council; mem. Bd of Trustees, Dirs for Business in the Community, Infrastructure UK. *Address:* National Grid PLC, 1–3 Strand, London, WC2N 5EH, England (office). *Telephone:* (20) 7004-3000 (office). *Fax:* (20) 7004-3004 (office). *E-mail:* corpcomms@ngrid.com (office). *Website:* www .nationalgrid.com (office).

HOLLIGER, Heinz; Swiss oboist and composer; b. 21 May 1939, Langenthal; m. Ursula Holliger; ed in Berne, Paris and Basel under Emile Cassagnaud (oboe) and Pierre Boulez (composition); Prof. of Oboe, Freiberg Music Acad. 1965–; has appeared at all the major European music festivals and in Japan, USA, Australia, Israel, etc.; conducted Chamber Orchestra of Europe, London 1992, London Sinfonietta 1997; Composer-in-Residence, Lucerne Festival 1998; recorded over 80 works, mainly for Philips and Deutsche Grammophon; recipient of several int. prizes. *Compositions include:* Der magische Tänzer, Trio, Siebengesang, Wind Quintet, Dona nobis pacem, Pneuma, Psalm, Cardiophonie, Kreis, String Quartet, Atembogen, Die Jahreszeiten, Come and Go, Not I. *Recording:* Koechlin's Vocal works with orchestra (Midem Classical Award for Vocal Recitals 2006). *Address:* c/o Colbert Artists Management, 111 West 57th Street, New York, NY 10019, USA; Konzertgesellschaft, Hochstrasse 51/Postfach, 4002 Basel, Switzerland.

HOLLINGHURST, Alan James, BA, MLitt, FRSL; British novelist, poet, short story writer and translator; b. 26 May 1954, Stroud, Glos., England; s. of the late James Kenneth Hollinghurst and Elizabeth Lilian Hollinghurst (née Keevil); ed Canford School, Dorset, Magdalen Coll., Oxford; Asst Ed., Times Literary Supplement 1982–84, Deputy Ed. 1985–90, Poetry Ed. 1991–95; Visiting Prof., Univ. of Houston, Tex., USA 1998; Old Dominion Fellow, Princeton Univ., NJ, USA 2004; Hon. Fellow, Magdalen Coll., Oxford 2013; Hon. DLitt (Univ. Coll. London) 2012; Newdigate Prize 1974. *Publications:* Confidential Chats with Boys (poems) 1982, The Swimming-Pool Library (novel) (Somerset Maugham Award 1989, American Acad. of Arts and Letters E.M. Forster Award 1989) 1988, Bajazet, by Jean Racine (trans.) 1991, The Folding Star (novel) (James Tait Black Memorial Prize) 1994, New Writing 4 (co-ed. with A. S. Byatt) 1995, The Spell (novel) 1998, Three Novels, by Ronald Firbank (ed.) 2000, A. E. Housman: Poems Selected by Alan Hollinghurst (ed.) 2001, The Line of Beauty (novel) (Man Booker Prize for Fiction) 2004, The Stranger's Child (novel) (Galaxy Nat. Book Award for UK Author of the Year) 2011, Prix du meilleur livre étranger (France) 2011, Bérénice, by Jean Racine (trans.) 2012. *Leisure interests:* music, architecture. *Address:* c/o Antony Harwood Ltd, 103 Walton Street, Oxford, OX2 6EB, England (office).

HOLLINGS, Ernest (Fritz), BA, LLB, JD; American fmr politician and lawyer; b. 1 Jan. 1922, Charleston, SC; s. of Adolph G. Hollings and Wilhelmine D. Meyer; m. 2nd Rita Liddy 1971; two s. two d. (by previous m.); ed Charleston Public Schools, The Citadel and Univ. of South Carolina; served in US Army 1942–45; admitted to S Carolina Bar 1947; mem. S Carolina House of Reps 1948–54, Speaker *pro tem.* 1951–53; Lt-Gov. of S Carolina 1955–59, Gov. of S Carolina 1959–63; law practice, Charleston 1963–66; Senator from S Carolina 1966–2005 (retd); Chair. Democratic Senatorial Campaign Cttee 1971–73; mem. Hoover Comm. on Intelligence Activities 1954–55, Pres.'s Advisory Comm. on Intergovernmental Relations 1959–63, on Federalism 1981; mem. Senate Cttees on Appropriations, Commerce, Budget, Chair. Budget Cttee 1980, Commerce Cttee 1982; currently Distinguished Visiting Prof. of Law, Charleston School of Law; fmr mem. Democratic Policy Cttee, Office of Tech. Assessment, Nat. Ocean Policy Study; mem. Advisory Bd Hollings Cancer Center, Medical Univ. of South Carolina; Democrat; numerous awards. *Publication:* The Case against Hunger: A Demand for a National Policy 1970. *Address:* Charleston School of Law, 81 Mary Street, Charleston, SC 29403, USA (office). *Website:* www.charlestonlaw.edu.

HOLLINGWORTH, Rt Rev. Peter, AC, OBE, MA, DipSocialStudies, ThL, FAIM; Australian ecclesiastic; b. 10 April 1935, Adelaide; m. Kathleen Ann Turner 1960; three d.; ed Trinity Coll. Univ. of Melbourne; Deacon-in-Charge then Priest-in-Charge, St Mary's, N Melbourne 1960–64; Chaplain to the Brotherhood of St Laurence 1964–90, Assoc. Dir 1970, later Dir of Social Services, Exec. Dir 1980–90; Hon. Curate, St Silas's, North Balwyn, later Hon. Curate at St Faith's, Burwood and Priest-in-Charge, St Mark's, Fitzroy; recipient of travelling bursary 1967; elected Canon, St Paul's Cathedral 1980; Bishop of the Inner City 1985–90, Archbishop of Brisbane 1990–2001; Gov.-Gen. of the Commonwealth of Australia 2001–03; Prior to Order of St John of Jerusalem; Chair. Int. Year of Shelter for the Homeless, Nat. Cttee of Non-Governmental Orgs 1986–88, Anglican Social Responsibilities Comm. of Gen. Synod 1990–98, Anglicare in diocese of Brisbane; Pres. Victorian Council of Social Services 1969; mem., Hon. Chair. Centenary of Fed. Council, Constitutional Convention (as non-parl. Rep.); Fellow, Trinity Coll. Melbourne; Hon. LLD (Monash Univ.) 1986, (Melbourne) 1990; Hon. DUniv (Griffith Univ.) 1993, (Queensland Univ. of Tech.) 1994, (Cen. Queensland) 1995; Hon. DLitt (Univ. of Southern Queensland) 1999; Victorian Rostrum Award of Merit 1985, Advance Australia Award 1988, Paul Harris Fellowship, Rotary Club 1989, Australian of the Year 1992, Nat. Living Treasure of Australia (Nat. Trust) 1997. *Publications:* The Powerless Poor 1972, The Poor: Victims of Affluence? 1974, Australians in Poverty 1979, Kingdom Come 1991, Public Thoughts of an Archbishop 1996. *Leisure interests:* swimming, Australian Rules football, theatre, reading, music. *Address:* POB 18081, Collins Street East, Melbourne, Victoria, 8003, Australia (office). *Telephone:* (3) 8633-3990 (office). *Fax:* (3) 9671-3954 (office). *E-mail:* amanda.dinsdale@pmc.gov.au (office).

HOLLIS, Brenda Joyce, JD; American lawyer and UN official; *Chief Prosecutor, Special Court for Sierra Leone, United Nations;* ed Bowling Green State Univ., Ohio, Univ. of Denver; Sr Trial Attorney, Int. Criminal Tribunal for the Fmr Yugoslavia (ICTY) 1994–2001; Expert Legal Consultant on int. law and criminal procedure 2001–07, trained judges, prosecutors and investigators at courts and int. tribunals in Indonesia, Iraq and Cambodia, also assisted victims of int. crimes in Democratic Repub. of the Congo and in Colombia to prepare submissions requesting investigations by Int. Criminal Court in The Hague; consultant to Office of the Prosecutor 2002–03, 2006, Prin. Trial Attorney, Office of the Prosecutor 2007–, responsible for leading legal team prosecuting fmr Liberian Pres. Charles Taylor; Chief Prosecutor, Special Court for Sierra Leone, UN 2010–. *Achievements include:* served as lead counsel in several historic prosecutions, led case in which rape was charged as torture, and was lead counsel in the preparation of the case against fmr Serbian Pres. Slobodan Milosevic. *Address:* The Special Court for Sierra Leone, Jomo Kenyatta Road, New England, Freetown, Sierra Leone (office); The Special Court for Sierra Leone, PO Box 19536, 2500 CM The Hague, The Netherlands (office). *Telephone:* (22) 297000 (Freetown) (office); (70) 515-9750 (The Hague) (office). *Fax:* (22) 297001 (Freetown) (office); (70) 322-2711 (The Hague) (office). *E-mail:* scsl-mail@un.org (office). *Website:* www.sc-sl.org (office).

HOLLOWAY, Bruce William, AO, PhD, DSc, FAA; Australian geneticist and academic; *Professor Emeritus, Monash University;* b. 9 Jan. 1928, Adelaide, S Australia; s. of Albert Holloway and Gertrude C. Walkem; m. Brenda D. Gray 1952; one s. one d.; ed Scotch Coll., Adelaide, Univ. of Adelaide, California Inst. of Tech., USA, Univ. of Melbourne; Lecturer in Plant Pathology, Waite Agric. Research Inst. 1949–50; Research Fellow in Microbial Genetics, John Curtin School of Medicine, ANU 1953–56; Sr Lecturer 1956–60, then Reader in Microbial Genetics, Univ. of Melbourne 1956–67; Foundation Prof. of Genetics, Monash Univ. 1968–93, Head, Dept of Genetics and Developmental Biology 1968–93, Prof. Emer. 1993–, Chair. Bd CRC for Vertebrate Biological Control 1994–99; Dir, Master Classes, Crawford Fund 1994–2004; Visiting Lecturer in Microbiology and Fellow, MIT, USA 1962–63; Sec. Biological Sciences, Australian Acad. of Science 1982–86; Visiting Prof., Univ. of Newcastle-upon-Tyne 1977–78; Chair. Nat. Biotechnology Program Research Grants Scheme 1983–86; mem. Industry and Research Devt Bd 1986–89; Kathleen Barton-Wright Lecturer, Soc. for Gen. Microbiology, UK 1998; Fellow, Australian Acad. of Science 1979, Australian Acad. of Technological and Eng Sciences 1993; Hon. Professorial Fellow, Monash Univ. 1994–2001; 50th Anniversary Research Award, Monash Univ. 2008. *Publications:* more than 190 papers on genetics and microbiology in scientific journals and conf. proceedings. *Leisure interests:* music, reading, tennis. *Telephone:* (3) 9836-5515 (home). *Fax:* (3) 9836-6869 (home). *E-mail:* hollowab@ozemail.com.au (home).

HOLLOWAY, Rt Rev. Richard Frederick, BD, STM, FRSE; British ecclesiastic (retd); b. 26 Nov. 1933, Glasgow, Scotland; s. of Arthur Holloway and Mary Holloway; m. Jean Holloway 1963; one s. two d.; ed Kelham Theological Coll., Edinburgh Theological Coll., Univ. of London (External), Union Theological Seminary, New York, USA; Curate, St Ninian's, Glasgow 1959–63; Priest-in-Charge, St Margaret's and St Mungo's, Gorbals, Glasgow 1963–68; Rector, Old St Paul's, Edin. 1968–80, Church of the Advent, Boston, Mass 1980–84; Vicar, St Mary Magdalen's, Oxford 1984–86; Bishop of Edinburgh 1986–2000; Primus, Scottish Episcopal Church 1992–2000; Prof. of Divinity, Gresham Coll., London 1997–2001; Chair. Jt Bd Scottish Arts Council, Scottish Screen 2006–10; mem. Human Fertilisation and Embryology Authority 1991–97, Broadcasting Standards Comm. 2001–04; Hon. DUniv (Strathclyde) 1994, (Open Univ.), (Stirling) 2010; Hon. DD (Aberdeen) 1994, (Glasgow) 2001; Hon. DLitt (Napier) 2001; Hon. LLD (Dundee) 2008; Dr hc (Royal Conservatoire of Scotland) 2012. *Radio:* Cover Stories (BBC) 2003, 2004, Divine Comedy (BBC) 2003, Sunday Morning with Richard Holloway (BBC). *Television:* Holloway's Road (BBC) 2000, The Sword and the Cross (BBC) 2003, Art and Soul (BBC) 2005. *Publications include:* Beyond Belief 1981, The Killing (Winifred M. Stanford Award) 1984, Paradoxes of Christian Faith and Life 1984, The Sidelong Glance 1985, The Way of the Cross 1986, Seven to Flee, Seven to Follow 1986, Crossfire 1988, Another Country, Another King 1991, Who Needs Feminism? 1991, Anger, Sex, Doubt and Death 1992, The Stranger in the Wings 1994, Churches and How To Survive Them 1994, Behold Your King 1995, Limping Towards the Sunrise 1996, Dancing on the Edge 1997, Godless Morality 1999, Doubts and Loves 2001, On Forgiveness 2002, Looking in the Distance 2004, Between the Monster and the Saint: Reflections on the Human Condition 2008, Leaving Alexandria: A Memoir of Faith and Doubt 2012. *Leisure interests:* walking, movies, reading, cooking. *Address:* 6 Blantyre Terrace, Edinburgh, EH10 5AE, Scotland. *Telephone:* (131) 446-0696. *E-mail:* richard@docholloway.org.uk.

HOLLOWAY, Robin Greville, PhD, DMus; British composer, writer and fmr academic; b. 19 Oct. 1943, Leamington Spa; s. of Robert Charles Holloway and Pamela Mary Holloway (née Jacob); ed St Paul's Cathedral Choir School, King's Coll. School, Wimbledon, King's Coll., Cambridge, New Coll., Oxford; Lecturer in Music, Univ. of Cambridge 1975, Reader in Musical Composition 1999, Prof. of Musical Composition 2001–11; Fellow, Gonville and Caius Coll., Cambridge 1969. *Compositions include:* Garden Music (Opus 1) 1962, First Concerto for Orchestra 1969, Scenes from Schumann (Opus 13) 1970, Evening with Angels (Opus 17) 1972, Domination of Black (Opus 23) 1973, Clarissa (opera) (Opus 30) 1976, Second Concerto for Orchestra (Opus 40) 1979, Brand (dramatic ballad) (Opus 48) 1981, Women in War (Opus 51) 1982, Seascape and Harvest (Opus 55) 1983, Viola Concerto (Opus 56) 1984, Peer Gynt 1985, Hymn to the Senses for chorus 1990, Serenade for strings 1990, Double Concerto (Opus 68), The Spacious Firmament for chorus and orchestra (Opus 69), Violin Concerto Opus 70 1990, Boys and Girls Come Out To Play (opera) 1991, Winter Music for sextet 1993, Frost at Midnight (Opus 78), Third Concerto for Orchestra (Opus 80) 1994, Clarinet Concerto (Opus 82) 1996, Peer Gynt (Opus 84) 1984–97, Scenes from Antwerp (Opus 85) 1997, Gilded Goldberg for two pianos 1999, Symphony 1999, Missa Caiensis 2001, Cello Sonata 2001, Spring Music (Opus 96) 2002, String Quartet No. 1 2003, String Quartet No. 2 2004. *Recordings:* Fantasy Pieces (Opus 16) 1971, Sea Surface Full of Clouds chamber cantata, Romanza for violin and small orchestra (Opus 28) 1974–75, Second Concerto for Orchestra (Opus 40) 1978–79, Horn Concerto (Opus 43) 1979–80, Third Concerto for orchestra (Opus 80) 1981–90, Violin Concerto (Opus 70) 1990, Gilded Goldberg (Opus 86) 1992–97, Missa Caiensis, Organ Fantasy 1993–2001, Woefully Arrayed 1999, Fourth Concerto for Orchestra 2003–05, Reliquary – Scenes from the life of Mary Queen of Scots enclosing an instrumentation of Robert Schumann's 'Gedichte der Königin Maria Stuart' 2009–10, Andante and Variations 2010, Fifth Concerto for Orchestra (Opus 107) 2011, Trio for Oboe, Violin, Piano 2011, String Quartet No. 4 2011, C'est l'extase (after Debussy) for soprano and orchestra 2012, Europa and the Bull for tuba and orchestra 2013. *Publications include:* Debussy and Wagner 1978, On Music: Essays and Diversions 1963–2003 2004; numerous articles and reviews. *Leisure interests:* cities, architecture, books. *Address:* Finella, Queen's Road, Cambridge, CB3 9AH, England (home). *Telephone:* (1223) 335424. *E-mail:* rgh@robinholloway.info. *Website:* www.robinholloway.info.

HOLM, Erik, MA, PhD; Danish foundation director and political economist; *Director, Eleni Nakou Foundation;* b. 6 Dec. 1933, Hobro; s. of Carl Holm and Anne Margrethe Holm (née Nielsen); m. Anne Jacoba Kevliken 1960 (died 1984); two s. two d.; ed Univ. of Copenhagen; economist, Cen. Statistical Office, Copenhagen 1961–65; Lecturer in Econs, Univ. of Copenhagen 1962–65, in Political Science 1971–81; economist, IMF, Washington, DC 1965–69; Sr Economist, Ministry of Econ. Affairs, Copenhagen 1969–72; Adviser on European Affairs to Prime Minister 1972–82; Prin. Adviser (econ. and financial affairs), EC Comm., Brussels 1982–87; Visiting Scholar, Inst. of Int. Studies, Univ. of Calif., Berkeley 1987–89; Dir Eleni Nakou Foundation, London 1989–; Kt of the Dannebrog. *Publications:* Stabilitet og Uligevagt 1986, Money and International Politics 1991, Union eller Nation 1992, Europe, a Political Culture? Fundamental Issues for the 1996 IGC 1994, The European Anarchy: Europe's Hard Road into High Politics 2001; articles in Danish and int. publs on European econ. and political affairs. *Address:* Vester Søgade 24, 1601 Copenhagen (home); Xylografensvej 4, 3220 Tisvildeleje, Denmark (Summer) (home). *Telephone:* 40-46-37-75 (home). *E-mail:* erik-holm@mail.dk (home).

HOLM, Sir Ian, Kt, CBE; British actor; b. 12 Sept. 1931, Ilford, Essex; s. of Dr James Harvey Cuthbert and Jean Wilson Cuthbert; m. 1st Lynn Mary Shaw 1955 (divorced 1965); two d.; one s. one d. (with Bee Gilbert); m. 2nd Sophie Baker 1982 (divorced 1986); one s.; m. 3rd Penelope Wilton 1991 (divorced); one step-d.; ed Chigwell Grammar School, Essex, RADA (Royal Acad. of Dramatic Art); joined Shakespeare Memorial Theatre 1954; Worthing Repertory 1956; on tour with Lord Olivier in Titus Andronicus 1957; mem. RSC 1958–67; Laurence Olivier Award 1998, Evening Standard Award for Best Actor 1993 and 1997. *Roles include:* Puck, Ariel, Lorenzo, Henry V, Richard III, The Fool (in King Lear), Lennie (in The Homecoming); appeared in Moonlight 1993, King Lear 1997, Max in The Homecoming 2001. *Films include:* Young Winston, Oh! What a Lovely War, Alien, All Quiet on the Western Front, Chariots of Fire, The Return of the Soldier, Greystoke 1984, Laughterhouse 1984, Brazil 1985, Wetherby 1985, Dance with a Stranger 1985, Dreamchild 1985, Henry V 1989, Another Woman 1989, Hamlet 1990, Kafka 1991, The Hour of the Pig 1992, Blue Ice 1992, The Naked Lunch 1992, Frankenstein 1993, The Madness of King George 1994, Loch Ness 1994, Big Night 1995, Night Falls on Manhattan 1995, A Life Less Ordinary 1996, The Sweet Hereafter 1997, The Fifth Element 1997, eXistenZ 1998, Simon Magus 1998, Esther Kahn 1999, Joe Gould's Secret 1999, Beautiful Joe 1999, From Hell 2000, The Emperor's New Clothes 2000, The Lord of the Rings – The Fellowship of the Ring 2001, The Lord of the Rings – The Return of the King 2003, Garden State 2004, The Day After Tomorrow 2004, The Aviator 2004, Strangers with Candy 2005, Chromophobia 2005, Lord of War 2005, Renaissance (voice) 2006, O Jerusalem 2006, The Treatment 2006, Ratatouille (voice) 2007, The Hobbit: An Unexpected Journey 2012. *Television appearances include:* The Lost Boys 1979, We, the Accused 1980, The Bell 1981, Strike 1981, Inside the Third Reich 1982, Mr. and Mrs. Edgehill 1985, The Browning Version 1986, Game, Set and Match 1988, The Endless Game 1989, The Last Romantics 1992, The Borrowers 1993, The Deep Blue Sea 1994, Landscape 1995, Little Red Riding Hood 1996, King Lear 1997, Alice Through the Looking Glass 1998, Animal Farm (voice) 1999, The Miracle Maker (voice) 2000, The Last of the Blonde Bombshells 2000, D-Day 6.6.1944 (voice) 2004. *Publication:* Acting My Life (autobiog.) 2004. *Leisure interests:* tennis, walking. *Address:* The Peggy Thompson Office, 296 Sandycombe Road, Kew, Richmond, Surrey, TW9 3NG (office); c/o Markham & Froggatt Ltd, Julian House, 4 Windmill Street, London, NW1T 2HZ, England (office).

HOLM, Richard H., PhD; American academic and chemist; *Higgins Research Professor of Chemistry, Harvard University;* b. 24 Sept. 1933, Boston, Mass.; m. Florence L. Jacintho 1958; four c.; ed Univ. of Massachusetts and Massachusetts Inst. of Tech.; Asst Prof. of Chem., Harvard Univ. 1960–65; Assoc. Prof. of Chem., Univ. of Wisconsin 1965–67; Prof. of Chem., MIT 1967–75, Stanford Univ. 1975–80; Prof. of Chem., Harvard Univ. 1980–83, Higgins Research Prof. 1983–, Chair. Dept of Chem. 1983–86; mem. American Acad. of Arts and Sciences, NAS; Hon. AM; Hon. DSc (twice); Chemical Sciences Award 1993, several awards for research in inorganic chem. *Publications:* numerous research papers in professional journals in the fields of inorganic chem. and biochemistry. *Address:* Department of Chemistry, Harvard University, Cambridge, MA 02138 (office); 483 Pleasant Street, #10, Belmont, MA 02418, USA (home). *Telephone:* (617) 495-0853 (office). *Fax:* (617) 496-9289 (office). *E-mail:* holm@chemistry.harvard.edu (office). *Website:* bioinorg.harvard.edu/~rhhgroup (office).

HOLM, Stefan Christian; Swedish high jumper; b. 25 May 1976, Forshaga; s. of Johnny Holm and Elisabeth Holm; m. Anna; one s.; Silver Medal Swedish Championships 1994–96, European Indoor Championships 2002, European Championships 2002, World Championships 2003; Gold Medal Swedish Indoor Championships 1997–2004, Swedish Championships 1998–2005, Goodwill Games 2001, World Indoor Championships 2001, 2003, 2004, Athens Olympics 2004, European Indoor Championships 2005; winner IAAF Grand Prix 2002, World Athletics Final 2004; ranked No. 1, Athletics Ints World Ranking 2002, 2004, Track & Field News World Ranking 2001, 2002, 2004; mem. Kils AIK Friidrottsklubb. *E-mail:* stefan.holm@scholm.com. *Website:* www.scholm.com.

HOLM-NIELSEN, Lauritz Broder, MSc; Danish botanist, academic and university administrator; *Special Advisor to the Senior Management, Aarhus University;* b. 8 Nov. 1946, Nordby; m. Helle Holm-Nielsen; two s. one d.; ed Aarhus Univ.; Asst Prof. of Botany, Aarhus Univ. 1972–75, Assoc. Prof. 1975–86, Dir Botanical Inst. 1983–85, Rector Aarhus Univ. 2005–13, Special Advisor to the Sr Man. 2013–; Prof., Universidad Católica, Quito, Ecuador 1979–81; Rector Danish Research Acad. 1986–93; Lead Higher Educ. Specialist, The World Bank 1993–2005; Chair. Danish Science Research Council 1985–87, Danish Council for Devt Research 1990–93, Danish Strategic Environment Research Programme 1991–2004; Vice-Chair. Danish Research Comm. 2000–01; Pres. Nordic Acad. for Advanced Study 1991–93, Euroscience 2012–; Vice-Pres. European Univ. Asscn 2012–; Fellow, The Linnean Soc., London, Danish Acad. of Natural Sciences, Acad. of Tech. Sciences; mem. Africa Comm. 2008–09, Danish Prime Minister's Growth Forum 2009–11, Nordic Univs Asscn 2008–, The Learned Soc.; Hon. mem. Instituto Ecuatoriano de Ciencias Naturales; Commdr, Star of the Order of Dannebrog, Gran Oficial del Orden Gabriela Mistral (Chile), Commdr, Order of the Dannebrog 2012. *Publications:* more than 130 research publs. *Address:* AU

Forskning og Talent – International Centre, Aarhus University, Høegh-Guldbergs Gade 4, 8000 Aarhus C, Denmark (office). *Telephone:* 23-38-21-26 (mobile) (office). *E-mail:* lhn@adm.au.dk (office). *Website:* www.au.dk (office).

HOLMES, Andrew S., BA, AM, PhD, FRS, FIET, MIEEE; British electronics engineer and academic; *Professor of Micro-Electro-Mechanical Systems, Imperial College London;* ed Univ. of Cambridge, Imperial Coll. London; Research Assoc., Dept of Electrical and Electronic Eng, Imperial Coll. London 1991–93, Jt Research Fellowship in Microengineering with Imperial Coll. and Rutherford Appleton Lab. 1993–95, apptd Lecturer, Imperial Coll. London 1995, currently Prof. of Micro-Electro-Mechanical Systems (MEMS); Co-founder and Dir, Microsaic Systems plc (Imperial Coll. spin-off) 2001–; mem. IEEE; Fellow, Inst. of Eng and Tech.; Royal Medal, Royal Soc. 2012. *Publications include:* more than 150 journal and conference papers. *Address:* Optical and Semiconductor Devices Research Group, Department of Electrical and Electronic, Room 701, South Kensington Campus, London, SW7 2AZ, England (office). *Telephone:* (20) 7594-6239 (office). *Fax:* (20) 7594-6308 (office). *E-mail:* a.holmes@imperial.ac.uk (office). *Website:* www .imperial.ac.uk/people/a.holmes (office).

HOLMES, Dame Kelly, DBE, MBE (Mil); British fmr athlete and business executive; *President, Commonwealth Games England;* b. 19 April 1970, Pembury, Kent; d. of step-father Michael Keith Norris and Pamela Thomson (née Norman); ed Hugh Christie Comprehensive School, Tonbridge, Kent; mem. Tonbridge, Ealing, Southall and Middlesex Athletics Clubs; competes primarily in 800m. and 1,500m events; won English Schools' titles then Recreation Asst 1986–87, Nursing Asst 1987–88; joined Army as Physical Training Instructor 1988–97; 12 major championship medals include silver medal, 1,500m European Championships 1994, gold medal, 1,500m Commonwealth Games 1994, bronze medal, 800m. silver medal, 1,500m World Championships 1995, silver medal, 1,500m Commonwealth Games 1998, bronze medal, 800m. Olympic Games, Sydney 2000, bronze medal, 800m European Championships 2002, gold medal, 1,500m Commonwealth Games 2002, silver medal, 1,500m World Indoor Championships 2003, silver medal, 800m World Championships 2003, gold medal, 800m, gold medal, 1,500m Olympic Games, Athens 2004; 1,500m, European Cup results include second 1994, first 1995, first 1997; 800m European Cup results include second 1996, fourth 2002; third 1,500m World Cup 2003; Amateur Athletics Asscn titles include 800m 1993, 1995, 1996, 1999, 2000, 2001, indoors 800m 2001, UK 800m 1993, 1997, 1,500m 1994, 1996, 2002; Founder and Dir Double Gold Enterprises Ltd 2004–; Dir Nat. School Sport Champion 2006–08; Pres. Commonwealth Games England 2009–; Chair. Dame Kelly Holmes Legacy Trust 2008–; twelve Dr hc including (Kent, Leeds Metropolitan) 2005; European Athlete of the Year 2004, BBC Sports Personality of the Year 2004, winner, Performance of the Year Award, IAAF Gala 2004, Laureus World Sports Woman of the Year Award 2005. *Publications include:* My Olympic Ten Days (with Richard Lewis) 2004, Black, White and Gold 2006, Get Your Kids Fit 2007, Katy the Shooting Star 2008, Just Go for It 2011. *Address:* Double Gold Enterprises Ltd (office). *E-mail:* info@doublegold.co.uk (office). *Website:* www.kellyholmes.co.uk.

HOLMES, Kenneth Charles, MA, PhD, FRS; British research biophysicist and academic (retd); b. 19 Nov. 1934, London; s. of Sidney C. Holmes and Irene M. Holmes (née Penfold); m. Mary Lesceline Scruby 1957; one s. three d.; ed Chiswick Co. School, St John's Coll., Cambridge and Birkbeck Coll., London; Research Asst, Birkbeck Coll., London 1955–59; Research Assoc., Children's Hosp., Boston 1960–62; mem. scientific staff, MRC Lab. of Molecular Biology, Cambridge 1962–68; Dir Dept of Biophysics, Max-Planck-Inst. for Medical Research, Heidelberg 1968–2003; Prof. of Biophysics, Univ. of Heidelberg 1972–99; mem. European Molecular Biology Org. 1968, Heidelberger Akad. der Wissenschaften 1994; Corresp. mem. Nordrhein-Westfälische Akad. der Wissenschaften, Düsseldorf; Gabor Medal, Royal Soc. of London 1997, European Latsis Prize 2000, Gregori Aminoff Prize, Royal Swedish Acad. of Sciences 2001. *Publications:* articles in scientific books and journals. *Leisure interests:* rowing, singing. *Address:* Max-Planck-Institute for Medical Research, Abt. Biophysik, Jahnstrasse 29, 69120 Heidelberg (office); Mühltalstrasse 117B, 6900 Heidelberg, Germany (home). *Telephone:* (6221) 486270 (office); (6221) 471313 (home). *E-mail:* holmes@ mpimf-heidelberg.mpg.de (office). *Website:* www.mpimf-heidelberg.mpg.de/ ~holmes (office).

HOLMES, Larry; American fmr boxer; b. 3 Nov. 1949, Cuthbert, Ga; s. of John Holmes and Flossie Holmes; m. Diana Holmes; one s. four d.; amateur boxer 1970–73; 22 amateur fights, 19 wins; lost by disqualification to Duane Bobick in finals of American Olympic trials 1972; won World Boxing Council (WBC) version of world heavyweight title from Ken Norton June 1978; made nine defences, all won inside scheduled distance (breaking previous record held by Joe Louis); became first man to stop Muhammad Ali Oct. 1980; stripped of WBCl version 1983; lost Int. Boxing Fed. version to Michael Spinks 1985, beaten again by Spinks 1986; defeated by Mike Tyson (q.v.) in attempts to win World Boxing Asscn, WBC and Int. Boxing Fed. heavyweight titles 1988; beaten by Evander Holyfield (q.v.) for World Boxing Asscn, WBC and Int. Boxing Fed. heavyweight titles 1992; by Oliver McCall for WBC heavyweight title 1995; was undefeated for record 13 years; career record 69 wins, (44 KOs), six defeats; runs an Internet casino business. *Leisure interests:* food, sport and self-education. *Address:* Larry Holmes Enterprises Inc., 91 Larry Holmes Drive, Suite 200, Easton, PA 18042, USA (office). *Telephone:* (610) 253-6905 (office). *E-mail:* larryholmes@larryholmes.com (office). *Website:* www.larryholmes.com (office).

HOLMES, Richard Gordon Heath, OBE, MA, FBA, FRSL; British writer, poet and academic; b. 5 Nov. 1945, London; s. of Dennis Patrick Holmes and Pamela Mavis Gordon; partner Rose Tremain; ed Downside School, Churchill Coll., Cambridge; literacy features writer, The Times 1967–92; Visiting Fellow, Trinity Coll., Cambridge 2000; Prof. of Biographical Studies, Univ. of East Anglia 2001–07; Hon. DLitt (East Anglia) 2000, (Tavistock Inst.) 2001, (Kingston Univ.) 2008; Somerset Maugham Award 1977, James Tait Black Memorial Prize 1994, Whitbread Book of the Year Prize 1989, Duff Cooper Prize 1998. *Radio:* BBC Radio: Inside the Tower 1977, To the Tempest Given 1992, The Nightwalking (Sony Award) 1995, Clouded Hills 1999, Runaway Lives 2000, The Frankenstein Project 2002, A Cloud in a Paper Bag 2007. *Publications:* Thomas Chatterton: The Case Re-Opened 1970, One for Sorrows (poems) 1970, Shelley: The Pursuit 1974, Shelley on Love (ed.) 1980, Coleridge 1982, Nerval: The Chimeras (with Peter Jay)

1985, Footsteps: Adventures of a Romantic Biographer 1985, Mary Wollstonecraft and William Godwin (ed.) 1987, Kipling: Something Myself (ed. with Robert Hampson) 1987, Coleridge: Early Visions 1989, Dr Johnson and Mr Savage 1993, Coleridge: Selected Poems (ed.) 1996, The Romantic Poets and Their Circle 1997, Coleridge: Darker Reflections 1998, Sidetracks: Explorations of a Romantic Biographer 2000, Classic Biographies (series) 2004–, Insights: The Romantic Poets and Their Circle 2005, The Age of Wonder (Nat. Book Critics' Circle Award for General Nonfiction 2009, Royal Soc. Prize for Science Books 2009) 2008. *Address:* c/o HarperCollins, 77–85 Fulham Palace Road, Hammersmith, London, W6 8JB, England.

HOLMES, Roger; British business executive; *Managing Director, Change Capital Partners;* began career with McKinsey & Co.; joined Kingfisher Group 1994, Finance Dir B&Q (subsidiary co.) 1994, becoming Man. Dir Woolworths and later CEO Kingfisher Electrical Retailing Div. –2000; joined Marks & Spencer Group PLC as Head of UK Retail Sales 2001–02, CEO 2002–2004; Man. Dir Change Capital Pnrs (pvt. equity firm) 2004–. *Address:* Change Capital Partners, 2nd Floor, College House, 272 Kings Road, London, SW3 5AW, England (office). *Telephone:* (20) 7808-9110 (office). *Fax:* (20) 7808-9111 (office). *E-mail:* rholmes@ changecapitalpartners.com (office). *Website:* www.changecapitalpartners.com (office).

HOLMES À COURT, Janet Lee, AC BSc, FAHA, HFAIB; Australian business executive and arts patron; b. 1943, Perth; m. Robert Holmes à Court (died 1990); three s. one d.; ed Perth Modern School and Univ. of Western Australia; fmr science teacher; Exec. Chair. Heytesbury Pty Ltd (family-owned co. which includes Heytesbury Beef Ltd, Vasse Felix (Vineyards), Heytesbury Thoroughbreds, John Holland Group and Key Transport) –2005 (retd); Chair. John Holland Group 1991–, West Australian Symphony Orchestra, Australian Children's Television Foundation, Australian Urban Design Research Centre of WA; mem. Bd of Dirs Vision 2020 Australia, Rio Tinto WA Future Fund, Australian Nat. Acad. of Music, Australian Chamber Orchestra, Australian Major Performing Arts Group, Chamber of Arts and Culture WA; f. Holmes à Court Gallery, Cowaramup 2000; Pro-Chancellor, Univ. of Western Australia 1990–94; fmr mem. Senate, Murdoch Univ., Univ. of Western Australia; mem. Bd Man. Festival of Perth; Founding Patron, Black Swan Theatre Company; Patron, Parks Forum, Manning Clark House; Hon. Fellow, Australian Inst. of Building; three hon. doctorates; British Business Woman of the Year 1996, Corporate Citizenship Award, Woodrow Wilson International Center for Scholars 2009. *Leisure interest:* the arts. *Website:* www .heytesbury.com.au; www.holmesacourtgallery.com.au.

HOLNESS, Andrew Michael, BSc, MSc; Jamaican politician; *Leader of the Opposition;* b. 22 July 1972, Spanish Town; m. Juliet Holness; two s.; ed Univ. of the West Indies; Exec. Dir Voluntary Org. for Uplifting Children (non-govt org.) 1994–96; Personal Asst to Leader of the Opposition Edward Seaga 1995–97; MP for West Central St Andrew 1997–, Opposition Spokesperson on Land and Devt 1999–2002, on Housing 2002–05, on Educ. 2005–07; Minister of Educ. 2007–11, Minister with responsibility for Electoral Matters and Leader of Govt Business in Parl. 2008–11, Prime Minister and Minister of Defence and of Educ. 2011–12; Leader of the Opposition 2012–; mem. Jamaica Labour Party, Leader 2011–. *Leisure interests:* chess, jogging, cycling, table tennis. *Address:* Jamaica Labour Party, 20 Belmont Rd, Kingston 5, Jamaica (office). *Telephone:* 929-1183 (office). *E-mail:* join@jamaicalabourparty.com (office). *Website:* www.jamaicalabourparty .com (office).

HOLOMISA, Maj.-Gen. Bantubonke Harrington, (Bantu); South African politician and army officer; *President, United Democratic Movement;* b. 25 July 1955, Mqandull, Transkei; s. of the late Chief B. Holomisa; m. Tunyelwa Dube 1981; one s. one d.; ed Army Coll. of South Africa; joined Transkei Defence Force 1976, Lt Platoon Commdr 1978–79, Capt. Training Wing Commdr 1979–81, Lt-Col Bn Command 1981–83, Col SS01 Operations and Training 1984–85, rank of Brig., Chief of Staff, Transkei Defence Force 1985–87, Commdr 1987–94; Leader of Transkei 1987–94; mem. African Nat. Congress Nat. Exec. Cttee 1994; Deputy Minister of Environmental Affairs, Govt of Nat. Unity 1994–96; Pres. United Democratic Movt 1997–; several mil. medals. *Publications:* Future Plan for South Africa, Comrades in Corruption (booklet). *Leisure interests:* soccer, rugby, cricket, athletics, wildlife gaming resorts. *Address:* PO Box 15, Parliament, Cape Town 8000 (office); PO Box 26290, Arcadia 0007, South Africa (home). *Telephone:* (21) 4033921 (Cape Town) (office); (12) 3210010 (Pretoria) (office); (82) 5524156 (Pretoria) (home). *Fax:* (21) 4032525 (Cape Town) (office); (12) 3210014 (Pretoria) (home). *E-mail:* holomisa@udm.org.za (home); bholomisa@holomisa.org.za (office). *Website:* www.udm.org.za (office).

HOLONYAK, Nick, Jr, MS, PhD; American physicist and academic; *John Bardeen Endowed Chair in Electrical and Computer Engineering and Physics, University of Illinois;* b. 3 Nov. 1928, Zeigler, Ill.; ed Univ. of Illinois, Urbana-Champaign; Researcher, Bell Labs 1954–55; Soldier (draftee), US Army Signal Corps 1955–57; Consulting Scientist, General Electric Co., Syracuse, NY 1957–63; Prof., Dept of Electrical and Computer Eng, Univ. of Illinois, Urbana-Champaign 1963–, John Bardeen Endowed Chair Prof. of Electrical and Computer Eng and Physics 1993–; mem. NAS 1984, Nat. Acad. of Eng, IEEE, American Physical Soc.; Foreign mem. Russian Acad. of Sciences 1999; Fellow, American Acad. of Arts and Sciences 1984, Int. Eng Consortium 1995, AAAS 2003; Charter Fellow, Nat. Acad. of Inventors 2013; Hon. mem. Ioffe Physical-Tech. Inst., Petersburg 1992; Hon. DSc (Northwestern Univ.) 1992; Hon. DEng (Notre Dame Univ.) 1994; Cordiner Award, General Electric 1962, IEEE Morris N. Liebmann Award 1973, John Scott Award, City of Philadelphia 1975, GaAs Symposium Award with Welker Medal 1976, IEEE Jack A. Morton Award 1981, Solid State Science and Tech. Award, Electrochemical Soc. 1983, IEEE Edison Medal 1989, Nat. Medal of Science 1990, Charles Hard Townes Award, Optical Soc. of America 1992, NAS Award for the Industrial Application of Science 1993, ASEE Centennial Medal 1993, 50th Anniversary Award ('Inventing America's Future'), American Electronics Asscn 1993, John Bardeen Award, The Minerals, Metals, and Materials Soc. 1995, Japan Prize 1995, Optical Soc. of America Nick Holonyak, Jr Award est. in his honour 1997, IEEE Third Millennium Medal 2000, Frederic Ives Medal, Optical Soc. of America 2002, Global Energy Int. Prize 2003, IEEE Medal of Honor 2003, Nat. Medal of Tech. 2003, Washington Award, Western Soc. of Engineers 2004, Lemelson-MIT Prize 2004, MRS Von Hippel Award 2004, Energy Conservation

Award, Izaak Walton League of America Ill. Div. 2004, Laureate, Lincoln Acad. of Illinois 2005, inducted into US Consumers Electronics Hall of Fame 2006, US Inventors Hall of Fame 2008, The Eng at Illinois Hall of Fame 2010, Eng and Sciences Hall of Fame (Dayton) 2011, Chancellor's Medallion, Univ. of Illinois, Urbana-Champaign 2012, LED Pioneer Awards of Strategies Unlimited 2013, Outstanding Achievement for Global SSL Devt, Beijing, People's Repub. of China 2013. *Achievements:* inventor of the light emitting diode (LED); co-inventor (with Milton Feng) of the transistor laser; holder of 56 patents, inventor of shorted-emitter symmetrical switch (TRIAC). *Publications:* Semiconductor Controlled Rectifiers 1964, Physical Properties of Semiconductors 1989; more than 580 papers in scientific journals. *Address:* University of Illinois at Urbana-Champaign, 1406 West Green Street, Urbana, IL 61801-2918, USA (office). *Telephone:* (217) 333-4149 (office). *E-mail:* nholonya@illinois.edu (office). *Website:* www.ece.uiuc.edu (office).

HOLROYD, Sir Michael de Courcy Fraser, Kt, CBE, CLit; British writer; *President Emeritus, Royal Society of Literature; b.* 27 Aug. 1935, London; s. of Basil Holroyd and Ulla Holroyd (née Hall); m. Margaret Drabble 1982; ed Eton Coll.; Chair. Soc. of Authors 1973–74, Nat. Book League 1976–78; Pres. English Centre of PEN 1985–88; Chair. Strachey Trust 1990–95, Public Lending Right Advisory Cttee 1997–2000, Royal Soc. of Literature 1998–2001 (Pres. 2003–10, Pres. Emer. 2010–); Vice-Pres. Royal Literary Fund 1997–; mem. Arts Council (Chair. Literature Panel) 1992–95; Gov. Shaw Festival Theatre, Niagara-on-the-Lake 1993–; Pres. Stephen Spender Trust 1998–; Trustee Laser Foundation 2001–03; Hon. DLitt (Ulster) 1992, (Sheffield, Warwick) 1993, (East Anglia) 1994, (LSE) 1998, (Sussex) 2009; Saxton Memorial Fellowship 1964, Bollingen Fellowship 1966, Winston Churchill Fellowship 1971, Irish Life Arts Award 1988, Heywood Hill Prize 2001, David Cohen Prize for Literature 2005, Golden Pen Award 2006, The Sheridan Morley Prize 2009. *Publications include:* Hugh Kingsmill: A Critical Biography 1964, Lytton Strachey: A Critical Biography 1967–68 (new edn 1994, Prix du Meilleur Livre Etranger 1996), A Dog's Life (novel) 1969, The Best of Hugh Kingsmill (ed) 1970, Lytton Strachey by Himself: A Self-Portrait (ed) 1971, Unreceived Opinions (essays) 1973, Augustus John 1974–75 (new edn 1996), The Art of Augustus John (with Malcolm Easton) 1974, The Genius of Shaw (ed) 1979, The Shorter Strachey (ed with Paul Levy) 1980, William Gerhardie's God's Fifth Column (ed with Robert Skidelsky) 1981, Peterley Harvesst: The Private Diary of David Peterley (ed) 1985, Bernard Shaw: Vol. 1: The Search for Love 1988, Vol. II: The Pursuit of Power 1989, Vol. III: The Lure of Fantasy 1991, Vol. IV: The Last Laugh 1992, Vol. V: The Shaw Companion 1992, Bernard Shaw 1997 (one-vol. biog.), Basil Street Blues 1999, Works on Paper: The Craft of Biography and Autobiography 2002, Mosaic: Portraits in Fragments 2004, A Strange Eventful History: The Dramatic Lives of Two Remarkable Families (James Tait Black Memorial Prize for Biography) 2008, A Book of Secrets 2010, On Wheels 2012. *Leisure interests:* music, stories. *Address:* c/o AP Watt at United Agents LLP, 12–26 Lexington Street, London, W1F 0LE, England (office). *Telephone:* (20) 3214-0800 (office). *Fax:* (20) 3214-0801 (office). *E-mail:* info@unitedagents.co.uk (office). *Website:* www.apwatt.co.uk (office).

HOLST, Per; Danish film producer; *b.* 28 March 1939, Copenhagen; s. of Rigmor Holst and Svend Holst; m. 1st Anni Møller Kjeldsen 1962–72; m. 2nd Kristina Holst 1976; four s.; joined Nordisk Film 1957; film man. and copywriter, WA Advertising Agency 1962; returned to Nordisk Film 1965; f. Per Holst Filmproduktion ApS 1965; numerous film awards including Palme d'Or, Cannes Film Festival and Acad. Award (Oscar) for Pelle the Conqueror 1988. *Films:* Afskedens Time 1967, Benny's Bathtub 1967, Kaptajn Klyde og Hans Venner vender tilbage 1981, The Tree of Knowledge 1982, Zappa 1983, Beauty and the Beast 1983, The Boy Who Disappeared 1984, Twist and Shout 1984, Element of Crime 1984, Up on Daddy's Hat 1985, Coeurs Flambés 1986, Pelle the Conqueror 1987, The Redtops 1988, Aarhus by Night 1989, Sirup 1990, War of the Birds 1990, Cassanova 1990, The Hideaway 1991, Pain of Love 1992, Jungle Jack 1993, All Things Fair 1995, Barbara 1998, Let's Get Lost 1998, Bornholms Stemme 2000, I Am Dina 2002, Ondskan 2003. *Leisure interest:* golf. *Address:* Nordisk Film, Mosedalvej 14, 2500 Valby, Denmark. *Website:* www.nordiskfilm.com.

HOLT, Dame Denise Mary, DCMG, CMG, BA; British diplomatist; *Chairman, M&S Bank; b.* 1 Oct. 1949, Vienna, Austria; d. of William Dennis Mills and Mary Johanna Shea; m. David Holt 1987; one s.; ed New Hall School, Chelmsford, Univ. of Bristol; grew up in Russia, Japan, Lebanon, the Netherlands, Iran and Bulgaria; joined British Diplomatic Service 1970; Desk Officer for Spain, Portugal and Gibraltar, FCO; First Sec., Embassy in Dublin 1984–88; Head of Section, Dept of Cen. America and Mexico 1988–90; First Sec., Embassy in Brasilia 1990–93; Deputy Dir Dept of Cen. Asia 1993–94; Deputy Dir of Personnel 1996–98, Dir 2001–02; Counsellor, Embassy in Dublin 1998–2001; Amb. to Mexico 2002–05, to Spain (also accred to Andorra) 2007–09; Dir Migration and Overseas Territories 2005–07; Chair. Anglo-Spanish Soc. (now the BritishSpanish Soc.) –2013; Chair. M&S Bank 2013–, Dir, Marks & Spencer Savings and Investments Ltd 2013–, Marks & Spencer Unit Trust Management Ltd 2013–; mem. Bd of Dirs Ofqual; Dir (non-exec.), HSBC Bank plc 2011–, Scottish Power Renewables 2011–; mem. NHS Pay Review Body, Office of Manpower Econs; Ind. Chair. Nominations Cttee, Alzheimer's Soc.; mem. Man. Council, Canada Blanch Centre for Contemporary Spanish Studies, LSE; Robin Humphrey Fellow, School of American Studies, Univ. of London; Hon. LLD (Bristol) 2012. *Leisure interests:* spending time with family and friends, reading, cooking. *Address:* M&S Bank, Kings Meadow, Chester, CH99 9FB, England (office). *Telephone:* (1244) 879080 (office). *E-mail:* ddpholt@aol.com (home); info@marksandspencer.com (office). *Website:* bank.marksandspencer.com (office).

HOLT, Sir James Clarke, Kt, DPhil, FBA, FSA; British historian and academic; *b.* 26 April 1922, Bradford, Yorks.; s. of the late Herbert Holt and Eunice Holt; m. Alice Catherine Elizabeth Suley 1950 (died 1998); one s.; ed Bradford Grammar School and Queen's Coll., Oxford; served in army 1942–45; Harmsworth Sr Scholar, Merton Coll., Oxford 1947–49; Lecturer, Univ. of Nottingham 1949–62, Prof. of Medieval History 1962–66; Prof. of History, Univ. of Reading 1966–78, Dean of Faculty of Letters and Social Sciences 1972–76; Professorial Fellow, Emmanuel Coll., Cambridge 1978–81, Prof. of Medieval History, Univ. of Cambridge 1978–88, Master of Fitzwilliam Coll., Cambridge 1981–88; Visiting Prof., Univ. of Calif., Santa Barbara, USA 1977; Visiting Hinkley Prof., Johns

Hopkins Univ., USA 1983; Raleigh Lecturer, British Acad. 1975; Visiting Prof., Japan 1986; mem. Advisory Council on Public Records 1974–81; Pres. Royal Historical Soc. 1980–84; Vice-Pres. British Acad. 1986–88; Pres. Lincoln Record Soc. 1987–96, Pipe Roll Soc. 1999–; Corresp. Fellow Medieval Acad. of America; Hon. Fellow, Emmanuel Coll. 1985–, Fitzwilliam Coll. 1988–, The Queen's Coll. 1996–, Merton Coll., Oxford 2001–; Hon. DLitt (Reading) 1984, (Nottingham) 1996; Comendador de la Orden del Mérito Civil 1988. *Publications:* The Northerners: A Study in the Reign of King John 1961, Praestia Rolls 14–18 John 1964, Magna Carta 1965, The Making of Magna Carta 1966, Magna Carta and the Idea of Liberty 1972, The University of Reading: The First Fifty Years 1977, Robin Hood 1982, War and Government in the Middle Ages (ed. with John Gillingham), Magna Carta and Medieval Government 1985; Hand-list of Acta Henry II and Richard I surviving in British Repositories (with Richard Mortimer) 1986, Domesday Studies (ed.) 1987, Colonial England 1066–1215 1997, Jersey 1204 (with Judith Everard) 2004; papers in English Historical Review, Past and Present, Economic History Review, trans. Royal Historical Soc. *Leisure interests:* music, mountain-eering, cricket, fly-fishing. *Address:* 5 Holben Close, Barton, Cambridge, CB23 7AQ, England. *Telephone:* (1223) 332041 (office); (1223) 264923 (home).

HOLTEN, Kasper Bech; Danish theatre, opera and film director; *Director of Opera, The Royal Opera; b.* 1973, Copenhagen; ed Univ. of Copenhagen; worked as an Asst Dir to John Cox, David Pountney and Harry Kupfer; mem. Danish Music Council 1995–99, Danish Radio and TV Council 2000–08; Artistic Dir Arhus Sommeropera Festival 1997–2000; Artistic Dir Royal Danish Opera 2000–11, led move into Copenhagen's new opera house 2005; Assoc. Prof., Copenhagen Business School 2007–; Dir of Opera, The Royal Opera, Covent Garden 2011–; has staged more than 60 productions of opera, drama, operetta and musical theatre in Denmark, Sweden, Norway, Finland, Iceland, France, Austria, Latvia, USA and Russia; production of Wagner's Ring in Copenhagen 2003–06, other key produc-tions include Le nozze di Figaro, Theater an der Wien, Tannhäuser, Copenhagen, A Clockwork Orange, Stockholm, My Fair Lady, Copenhagen and Die Tote Stadt, Helsinki, Don Giovanni, Covent Garden 2014; mem. Bd European Acad. of Music Theatre. *Film:* Juan (writer and dir) 2010. *Address:* c/o Ian Stones, Harrison/Parrott Ltd, 5–6 Albion Court, London, W6 0QT, England; Royal Opera House, Bow Street, Covent Garden, London, WC2E 9DD, England (office). *Telephone:* (20) 7313-3504; (20) 7240-1200 (office). *Fax:* (20) 7221-5042. *E-mail:* ian.stones@harrisonparrott.co.uk. *Website:* www.harrisonparrott.com (office); www.roh.org.uk (office); www.holten.com.

HOLTON, A. Linwood, Jr, BA, LLB; American lawyer and fmr politician; *Partner, McCandlish Holton, PC; b.* 21 Sept. 1923, Big Stone Gap, Va; s. of Abner Linwood Holton and Edith Holton (née Van Gorder); m. Virginia Harrison Rogers 1953; two s. two d.; ed public schools in Big Stone Gap, Washington and Lee Univ. and Harvard Law School; fmr Pnr, Eggleston, Holton, Butler and Glenn (law firm); served submarine force during Second World War; fmr Chair. Roanoke City Republican Cttee; Vice-Chair. Va Republican State Cen. Cttee 1960–69; del. to Republican Nat. Convention 1960, 1968, 1972; mem. Nat. Nixon for Pres. Cttee 1967, Regional Co-ordinator for Nixon for Pres. Cttee; Gov. of Va 1970–74; Asst Sec. of State for Congressional Relations, US Dept of State, Washington, DC 1974–75; Pnr, Hogan and Hartson (law firm) 1975–78; Vice-Pres. and Gen. Counsel American Council Insurance, Washington, DC 1978–84; Chair. Burket Miller Center for Public Affairs, Univ. of Va 1979–; Pres. Supreme Court Historical Soc. 1980–89; Chair. Metropolitan Washington Airports Authority 1987–93; Pnr, McCandlish Holton PC (law firm), Richmond 1994–; Pres. Center for Innovative Tech., Herndon, Va 1988–94. *Address:* McCandlish Holton PC, PC, 1111 East Main Street, Suite 1500, PO Box 796, Richmond, VA 23218 (office); 3883 Black Stump Road, Weems, VA 22576, USA (home). *Telephone:* (804) 775-3817 (office); (804) 435-0604. *Fax:* (804) 775-3800 (office). *E-mail:* lholton@lawmh.com (office). *Website:* www.lawmh.com (office).

HOLTON, Gerald, PhD; American physicist, historian of science and academic; *Mallinckrodt Professor of Physics and Professor of the History of Science Emeritus, Harvard University; b.* 23 May 1922, Berlin, Germany; s. of Dr Emanuel Holton and Regina Holton; m. Nina Rossfort 1947; two s.; ed Harvard Univ.; Harvard Univ. staff, officers' radar course and Lab. for Research on Electro-Acoustics 1943–45, various faculty posts 1945–, Mallinckrodt Prof. of Physics and Prof. of History of Science 1975–2011, Emer. 2011–; Visiting Prof., MIT 1976–94; NSF Faculty Fellow, Paris 1960–61; Exchange Prof., Leningrad Univ., USSR 1962; Founder and Ed.-in-Chief, Daedalus 1958–61; mem. Council, History of Science Soc. 1959–61, Pres. 1982–84; Visiting mem. Inst. for Advanced Study, Princeton, NJ 1964, 1967; mem. NAS Cttee on Communication with Scholars in the People's Repub. of China 1969–72, US Nat. Comm. on IUHPS 1982–88 (Chair. 1988); mem. German-American Acad. Council Kuratorium 1997–2000; mem. Bd Govs, Ameri-can Inst. of Physics 1969–74; Fellow, Center for Advanced Study in Behavioral Sciences, Stanford, Calif. 1975–76; mem. US Nat. Comm. on UNESCO 1975–80, Library of Congress Council of Scholars 1979–98, US Nat. Comm. on Excellence in Educ. 1981–83, Advisory Bd Nat. Humanities Center 1989–93; mem. Editorial Bd Collected Papers of Albert Einstein; Nat. Assoc., NAS; Fellow, American Physical Soc. (Chair. Div. of History of Physics 1992–93), American Acad. of Arts and Sciences (mem. Council 1991–95), American Philosophical Soc., AAAS, Acad. Internationale d'Histoire des Sciences (Vice-Pres. 1982–89), Deutsche Akad. der Naturforscher Leopoldina, Acad. Internationale de Philosophie des Sciences; Ehrenkreuz 1. Klasse (Repub. of Austria); eight hon. degrees; Robert A. Millikan Medal 1967, Herbert Spencer Lecturer, Univ. of Oxford 1979, Jefferson Lecturer 1981, Oersted Medal 1980, Guggenheim Fellowship 1980–81, McGovern Medal 1985, Andrew Gemant Award 1989, George Sarton Medal 1989, Bernal Prize 1989, Joseph Priestley Award 1994, Joseph H. Hazen Prize of the History of Science Soc. 1998, Abraham Pais Prize, American Physical Soc. 2008. *Film:* People and Particles (co-producer), The Life of Enrico Fermi (co-producer). *Publications:* Introduction to Concepts and Theories in Physical Science 1952, Project Physics Course (co-author) 1970, 1981, Thematic Origins of Scientific Thought 1973, 1988, Scientific Imagination 1978, Limits of Scientific Inquiry (ed.) 1979, Albert Einstein, Historical and Cultural Perspectives (ed.) 1982, The Advancement of Science and its Burdens 1986, Science and Anti-Science 1993, Einstein, History and Other Passions 1995, Gender Differences in Science Careers (co-author) 1995, Who Succeeds in Science? The Gender Dimension (co-author) 1995, The Scientific Imagination 1998, Physics, the Human Adventure (co-author) 2001, Ivory Bridges:

Connecting Science and Society (co-author) 2002, Understanding Physics (co-author) 2002, Victory and Vexations in Science 2005, What Happened to the Children Who Fled Nazi Persecution (co-author) 2006, Helping Young Refugees and Immigrants Succeed (co-author) 2010. *Leisure interests:* music, kayaking. *Address:* 64 Francis Avenue, Cambridge, MA 02138 (home); Jefferson Physical Laboratory, Harvard University, Cambridge, MA 02138, USA (office). *Telephone:* (617) 868-9003 (home); (617) 495-4474 (office). *Fax:* (617) 495-0416 (office). *E-mail:* holton@physics.harvard.edu (office). *Website:* www.physics.harvard.edu/people/facpages/holton.html (office).

HOLTZMAN, Wayne Harold, MS, PhD; American psychologist and academic; *Hogg Professor Emeritus in Psychology and Education, University of Texas;* b. 16 Jan. 1923, Chicago, Ill.; s. of Harold H. Holtzman and Lillian Manny; m. Joan King 1947; four s.; ed Northwestern and Stanford Univs; Asst Prof., Univ. of Texas at Austin 1949–53, Assoc. Prof. 1954–59, Prof. of Psychology 1959–, Dean Coll. of Educ. 1964–70, Hogg Prof. of Psychology and Educ. 1964–93, Prof. Emer. 1993–; Assoc. Dir Hogg Foundation for Mental Health 1955–64, Pres. 1970–93, Special Counsel 1993–2003; Dir Science Research Assocs 1974–89, Population Resource Center 1980–; Pres. Int. Union of Psychological Science 1984–88; other professional affiliations: Faculty Research Fellow, Social Science Research Council 1953–54, Center for Advanced Study in Behavioral Sciences 1962–63; Hon. LHD (Southwestern) 1980. *Publications:* Tomorrow's Parents (with B. Moore) 1964, Computer Assisted Instruction, Testing and Guidance 1971, Personality Development in Two Cultures (with others) 1975, Introduction to Psychology 1978, School of the Future (with others) 1992, History of the International Union of Psychological Science (with others) 2000. *Leisure interests:* travel, photography, gardening. *Address:* 3300 Foothill Drive, Austin, TX 78731, USA (home). *Telephone:* (512) 471-5041 (office); (512) 452-8296 (home). *E-mail:* wayne.holtzmann@mail.utexas.edu. *Website:* www.psy.utexas.edu (office).

HOLUM, John D., BS, JD; American lawyer and fmr government official; b. 4 Dec. 1940, Highmore, S Dak; m. Barbara P. Pedersen; one d.; ed Northern State Teachers' Coll. and George Washington Univ.; on staff of Senator George McGovern, US Senate Foreign Relations Cttee 1965–79; mem. Policy and Planning Staff, US State Dept 1979–81; attorney, O'Melveny & Myers 1981–93; defence and foreign policy adviser to Gov. Bill Clinton during 1992 presidential campaign; Exec. Dir 1992 Democratic Nat. Convention; Dir Arms Control and Disarmament Agency 1993–98, Sr Advisor for Arms Control and Int. Security Affairs 1998–2000; Under-Sec. of State for Arms Control and Int. Security 2000–01; Vice-Pres. Int. and Govt Affairs, Atlas Air Inc. 2000–03; mem. Center for Nonproliferation Studies Int. Advisory Bd. *Leisure interests:* flying, scuba diving, playing bluegrass and country music. *Address:* 1009 Bay Ridge Avenue, No. 122, Annapolis, MD 21403, USA.

HOLYFIELD, Evander; American professional boxer; b. 19 Oct. 1962, Atlanta, Ga; s. of Anna Laura Holyfield; won Bronze Medal at 1984 Olympic Games; won World Boxing Asscn (WBA) cruiserweight title 1986, Int. Boxing Fed. cruiserweight title 1987, World Boxing Council (WBC) cruiserweight title 1988; world heavyweight champion 1990–92, 1993–94, 1996–99 (following defeat of Mike Tyson q.v. Nov. 1996), defended title against Tyson 1997 (Tyson disqualified); defended IBF heavyweight title against Michael Moorer 1997; defended WBA and IBF titles and contested WBC title, against Lennox Lewis (q.v.) March 1999, bout declared a draw; lost to Lennox Lewis Nov. 1999; 2000–01 WBA heavyweight champion; career record 38 wins, eight defeats, two draws; suspended by NY State Boxing Comm. after defeat by Larry Donald Nov. 2004; f. Real Deal Record Label 1999; f. Holyfield Foundation to help inner-city youth; Espy Boxer of the Decade 1990–2000. *Leisure interests:* all kinds of music, American football. *Address:* Holyfield Management, 794 Evander Holyfield Highway, Fairburn, GA 30213, USA (office). *Telephone:* (770) 460-6807 (office). *Website:* www.evanderholyfield.com (office).

HOLZER, Jenny, BFA, MFA; American artist; b. 29 July 1950, Gallipolis, Ohio; d. of Richard Vornholt Holzer and Virginia Beasley Holzer; m. Michael Andrew Glier 1984; one d.; ed Ohio Univ., Rhode Island School of Design, Whitney Museum of American Art Ind. Study Program; became working artist in New York 1977; special projects and comms since 1978 include Green Table, Univ. of Calif., San Diego 1993, Lustmord, Süddeutsche Zeitung Magazin, No. 46, Germany, Black Garden, Nordhorn, Germany 1994, Allentown Benches, Allentown, Pa 1995, Erlauf Peace Monument, Erlauf, Austria 1995, installation at Schiphol Airport, Amsterdam, Netherlands 1995, Biennale di Firenze, Florence, Italy 1996, installation for Hamburger Kunsthalle, Hamburg, Germany 1996, perm. installation at Guggenheim Museum, Bilbao, Literaturhaus Munich, Germany, Oskar Maria Graf Memorial 1997, Kunsthalle Zürich, Switzerland, Telenor HQ, Norway 2002, Univ. of Pennsylvania 2003, Paula Hodersohn—Becker Museum 2005, Lawrence Convention Center, Pittsburgh 2005, SDtora Torget, Karlstad 2005; Fellow American Acad., Berlin 2000; Resident, American Acad. Rome 2003; Hon. DArts (Ohio Univ.) 1994, (Williams Coll.) 2000, (Rhode Island School of Design) 2003, (New School Univ.) 2005; Golden Lion Award for Best Pavilion, 44th Venice Biennale, Italy 1990, Gold Medals for Title and Design, Art Directors' Club of Europe 1993, Skowhegan Medal for Installation, New York 1994, Crystal Award, for outstanding contrib. to cross-cultural understanding, World Econ. Forum, Switzerland 1996, Kaiserring, City of Goslar 2002, Urban Visionaries Award, The Cooper Union 2006; Chevalier, Ordre des Arts et Lettres 2002. *Publications:* A Little Knowledge 1979, Black Book 1980, Eating Through Living 1981, Truisms and Essays 1983. *Leisure interests:* reading, riding. *Address:* c/o Cheim and Read Gallery, 547 West 25th Street, New York, NY 10001; 80 Hewitts Road, Hoosick Falls, NY 12090, USA. *Telephone:* (518) 686-9323. *Fax:* (518) 686-9019. *E-mail:* jh@jennyholzer.com. *Website:* www.jennyholzer.com.

HOMBACH, Bodo; German business executive and fmr politician; *Managing Director, WAZ Media Group;* b. 19 Aug. 1952, Mülheim; m. 1977; ed Düsseldorf Polytechnic, Duisberg Comprehensive Univ., Hagen Correspondence Univ.; fmrly trainee telecommunications worker, youth affairs spokesman and youth worker; Personal Asst to Chair. of German TU Confed. (DGB) North Rhine Westphalia 1974; Educ. Policy Sec. Educ. and Science TU North Rhine Westphalia 1976, Regional Dir 1977; Deputy Regional Dir German Social Democratic Party (SPD) North Rhine Westphalia 1979, Regional Dir 1981–91; Sr Election Campaign Man., 1979–91; Deputy Chair. Mülheim Dist 1993, Deputy Chair. Niederrhein Dist 1998;

Fed. Minister Without Portfolio and Head Fed. Chancellery 1998–99; mem. North Rhine Westphalia Landtag 1990–98, Chair. Parl. Inquiry Comm. 1992–94, Parl. Econ. Affairs Spokesman 1994–98, State Minister for Econ. SMEs, Tech. and Transport 1998; Dir Marketing, Org. and Corp. Strategy Preussag Handel GmbH (fmrly Salzgitter Stahl AG) 1991, Man. Dir Preussag Trade Ltd 1992–98, mem. Bd Preussag Int. GmbH 1995–98; Special Co-ordinator of the Stability Pact for S Eastern Europe 1999–2001; Man. Dir WAZ (Westdeutschen Allgemeine Zeitung) Media Group 2002–; Chair. Initiativkreis Ruhr 2011–. *Publications include:* Die SPD von innen (with Horst Becker) 1983, Die Zukunft der Arbeit, Aufruf für eine Geschichte des Volkes in Nordrhein-Westfalia, Die Lokomotive in voller Fahrt der Räder wechseln, Anders Leben, Sozialstaat 2000, Die Kraft der Region: Nordrhein-Westfalia in Europa, The Politics of the New Centre 2002; numerous articles in books. *Address:* Zeitungsverlagsgesellschaft E. Brost und J. Funke GmbH & Co., Friedrichstr. 34-38, 45123 Essen, Germany (office). *Telephone:* (201) 804-0 (office). *Website:* www.waz-mediengruppe.de (office).

HOME, 15th Earl of, cr. 1605; **David Alexander Cospatrick Douglas-Home,** Kt, CVO, CBE, MA; British banker; *Chairman, Coutts & Company Limited;* b. 20 Nov. 1943, Coldstream, Scotland; s. of the late Rt Hon. Alexander Frederick, Lord Home of the Hirsel and Elizabeth Hester Alington; m. Jane Margaret Williams-Wynne; one s. two d.; ed Eton Coll., Christ Church, Oxford; Dir Morgan Grenfell & Co. Ltd (now Deutsche Securities Ltd) 1974–99; Chair. Coutts & Co. 1999–2013; Chair. Coutts Bank (Switzerland) Ltd (now Coutts & Co. Ltd) 2000–; Chair. MAN Ltd 2000–10, Grosvenor Group Ltd 2007–10; Pres. British Malaysian Soc. 2001–; mem. Bd of Dirs Dubai Financial Services Authority 2005–10; Adviser, Southern Capital, Singapore; Trustee The Grosvenor Estate 1993–2010; Opposition Frontbench Spokesperson for Trade, House of Lords 1997–98, for the Treasury 1997–98; Kt Companion, Order of the Thistle 2013. *Leisure interest:* outdoor activities. *Address:* House of Lords, London, SW1A 0PW (office); Coutts & Co., 440 Strand, London, WC2R 0QS (office); 43 Chelsea Towers, Chelsea Manor Street, London, SW3 5PN, England (home). *Telephone:* (20) 7219-3168 (House of Lords) (office); (20) 3730-1690 (office); (20) 7352-9060 (home). *Fax:* (20) 7753-1066 (office). *Website:* www.coutts.com (office).

HOMER-DIXON, Thomas F., BA, PhD; Canadian political scientist, academic and writer; *Centre for International Governance Innovation Chair of Global Systems, Balsillie School of International Affairs, University of Waterloo;* b. 1956, Victoria, BC; m. Sarah Wolfe; one s. one d.; ed Carleton Univ., Ottawa, Massachusetts Inst. of Tech., USA; jobs in construction, forestry and petroleum industries in western Canada and as leader of nat. student org. based in Ottawa 1975–83; research position with Project Athena, MIT, Cambridge, Mass 1983–89; consultant, World Resources Inst., Washington, DC 1983–89; Prin. Investigator, Univ. of Toronto 1990–93, Dir Peace and Conflict Studies Program, Univ. Coll. 1990–2001, Asst Prof. of Political Science, Univ. of Toronto 1993–98, Assoc. Prof. 1998–2006, Prof. 2006–08, George Ignatieff Chair of Peace and Conflict Studies 2007–08, Dir Trudeau Centre for Peace and Conflict Studies 2001–07; Prof., Faculty of Arts, and Centre for Environment and Business, Faculty of Environment, Univ. of Waterloo, Ont. 2008–, Centre for Int. Governance Innovation Chair of Global Systems, Balsillie School of Int. Affairs 2008–; Adjunct Research Fellow, Center of Science and Int. Affairs, Kennedy School of Govt, Harvard Univ. 1986–88; SSRC/MacArthur Foundation Dissertation Fellowship in Int. Peace and Security 1986–88; Visiting Scholar, Aspen Inst. 1994; Assoc. Fellow, Canadian Inst. for Advanced Research 1995–; Postdoctoral Fellowship, Social Sciences and Humanities Research Council of Canada 1989–90, Northrop Frye Award, Univ. of Toronto 1999, Outstanding Performance Award, Univ. of Waterloo 2010. *Publications:* Science in Society: Its Freedom and Regulation (co-ed.) 1982, Ecoviolence: Links Among Environment, Population, and Security (co-ed.) 1998, Environment, Scarcity, and Violence (Lynton Keith Caldwell Prize, American Political Science Asscn 2000) 1999, The Ingenuity Gap (Gov.-Gen.'s Non-fiction Award, Canada Council for the Arts 2001) 2000, The Upside of Down: Catastrophe, Creativity, and the Renewal of Civilization (Nat. Business Book Award 2007) 2006, Carbon Shift: How the Twin Crises of Oil Depletion and Climate Change Will Define the Future (co-ed.) 2009; numerous book chapters, and articles in learned journals and newspapers. *Address:* Balsillie School of International Affairs, c/o Centre for International Governance Innovation, 57 Erb Street West, Waterloo, ON N2L 6C2, Canada (office). *Telephone:* (519) 888-4567 (ext. 38750) (office). *E-mail:* tad@homerdixon.com (office). *Website:* www.balsillieschool.ca; www.homerdixon.com.

HOMMELHOFF, Peter, DrIur; German lawyer, accountant and fmr university rector; *Partner, KPMG AG;* b. 1942, Hamburg; ed law studies in Berlin, Tübingen and Freiburg Univs, Univ. of Bochum; in-house legal adviser, Preußen Elektrizitäts AG, Hanover 1972; Academic Research Asst, Univ. of Bochum (Chair for German and European Commercial and Econ. Law) 1974; Chair of Civil Law, Commercial and Econ. Law, Univ. of Bielefeld 1981; part-time judge, Higher Regional Court (Oberlandesgericht), mem. Special Div. for Commercial and Co. Law 1983, Hamm –1990, Karlsruhe 1993–98; Dean Faculty of Law, Univ. of Heidelberg 1993–95, Partnership Commr Exchange Relations between Univ. of Heidelberg and Jagiellonian Univ. of Kraków –2002, Chair. Company Law Asscn (Gesellschaftsrechtliche Vereinigung) 1998–2001, mem. and Deputy Chair. Heidelberg Univ. Council 2000–01, Rector Ruprecht-Karls Univ. of Heidelberg 2001–07; Pnr, KPMG AG, Frankfurt 2007–; mem. Bd of Examiners for Chartered Accountants, Ministry of Econ. Affairs, North Rhine-Westphalia –2001, Ministry of Econ. Affairs, Baden-Württemberg 1986, Extended Bd in Asscn of Profs of Civil Law 1995; Expert for Civil, Econ. and Labour Law, German Research Asscn (Deutsche Forschungsgemeinschaft) 1996–2001; fmr Deputy Chair. Professional Bd of Advisors, Max Planck Inst. for Intellectual Property, Competition and Tax Law, Munich; Vice-Pres. Council of Acad. Pres (Hochschulrektorenkonferenz); Speaker for the Univs 2002; mem. Scholarly Bd of Advisors, German Railway Corpn (Deutsche Bahn AG) and of its Strategic Council 1999, Speaker of Legal Bd of Advisors 2006; mem. Professional Bd of Advisors, Max Planck Inst. for Foreign and Int. Pvt. Law, Hamburg; mem. Editorial Bd Journal for Business and Corporate Law (Zeitschrift für Unternehmens- und Gesellschaftsrecht, ZGR), Man. Ed. 1997; Max Planck Research Prize for Int. Cooperation 1997, Medal of Honour, Jagiellonian Univ. of Kraków 1999, Leo Baeck Prize, Cen. Council of Jews in Germany 2005; Hon. DrIur (Jagiellonian Univ. of Kraków) 2002, (Univ. of Montpellier I) 2005. *Publications:* more than 300 publs in professional journals. *Address:* KPMG AG, Marie-Curie-Straße 30, 60439 Frankfurt am Main, Germany (office). *Telephone:* (69) 9587-3311 (office). *E-mail:* phommelhoff@kpmg.com (office). *Website:* www.kpmg.de (office).

HOMMEN, Jan H. M.; Dutch business executive; b. 29 April 1943, 's-Hertogenbosch; Controller, Alcoa Nederland BV, Drunen 1970–74, Financial Dir 1974–78, Corp. Finance Man. Aluminum Co. of America (Alcoa), Pittsburgh 1978–79, Asst Treas. 1979–86, Vice-Pres. and Treas. 1986–91, Exec. Vice-Pres. and Chief Financial Officer 1991–97; Vice-Chair., Chief Finance Officer and mem. Bd of Man. Koninklijke Philips Electronics NV 1997–2005; mem. Supervisory Bd ING Group NV 2005–09, Chair. 2008–09, Chair. Exec. Bd (CEO) 2009–13, also fmr Chair. Man. Bds Banking and Insurance; mem. Supervisory Bd TNT NV 1998–2009, Chair. 2005–09; Chair. Supervisory Bd Reed Elsevier 2005–09, Academisch Ziekenhuis Maastricht, TiasNimbas Business School; Chair. Med-Quist, USA –2006; mem. Bd of Dirs Campina BV; mem. Bd Royal Concertgebouw Orchestra; Officer, Order of Orange-Nassau 2005, Commdr, Order of Orange-Nassau 2013. *Address:* c/o ING Group NV, Amsterdamse Poort, Bijlmerplein 888, 1102 MG Amsterdam, The Netherlands.

HONDA, Katsuhiko, LLB; Japanese tobacco industry executive; b. 12 March 1942, Kagoshima Pref.; ed Univ. of Tokyo; joined Japan Tobacco and Salt Public Corpn 1965, Vice-Pres. Corp. Planning Div. 1989–92, Man. Dir Human Resources Div. 1992–94, Exec. Dir Personnel and Labor Relations 1994–95, Exec. Dir Tobacco Business 1995–96, Exec. Vice-Pres. Tobacco Business 1996–98, Sr Exec. Vice-Pres., Japan Tobacco Inc. 1998–2000, Pres., Rep. Dir and CEO 2000–06, mem. Bd of Dirs 2006–. *Address:* c/o 2–1 Toranomon 2-chome, Minato-ku, Tokyo 105-8422, Japan (office). *Website:* www.jti.co.jp (office).

HONDA, Keiko, BA, MBA; Japanese international organization official and consultant; *Vice-President Designate, Multilateral Investment Guarantee Agency;* ed Ochanomizu Univ., Univ. of Pennsylvania, USA; fmr consultant, Bain and Co., Financial Analyst, Lehman Brothers; joined McKinsey and Co. 1989, mem. Bd of Dirs McKinsey and Co., Japan –2013; Vice-Pres. Multilateral Investment Guarantee Agency July 2013–; Visiting Assoc. Prof. of Corp. Finance, Hitotsubashi Univ. 2002–03; Lecturer, Chuo Business School 2002–05; Vice-Chair. Cttee on Promotion of EPAs/FTA, Keizai Doyukai (Japan Asscn of Corp. Execs); mem. Bd of Dirs Japanese Foundation for Cancer Research; mem. Council for Promotion of Regulatory Reform 2004–10, Business Accounting Council 2012–; mem. jury, Cartier Women's Initiative Award. *Publications include:* M&A and Strategic Alliances 1998, Turnaround 2004, Valuation. *Address:* Multilateral Investment Guarantee Agency, 1818 H Street, NW, Washington, DC 20433, USA (office). *Telephone:* (202) 458-2538 (office). *Fax:* (202) 522-0316 (office). *Website:* www.miga .org (office).

HONDROS, Ernest Demetrios, CMG, DSc, FRS; British scientist and academic; *Visiting Professor, Department of Materials, Imperial College London;* b. 18 Feb. 1930, Kastellorizo, Dodecanese, Greece; s. of Demetrios Hondros and Athanasia Paleologos; m. Sissel Kristine Garder-Olsen 1968; two s.; ed Univ. of Melbourne, Australia, Univ. of Paris; CSIRO Tribophysics Lab., Melbourne 1955–59; Research Fellow, Laboratoire de Chimie Minérale, Univ. of Paris 1959–62; Sr Research Fellow, Nat. Physical Lab. 1962, Prin. Research Fellow 1965, Sr Prin. Research Fellow 1974, Supt Materials Div. 1979–85; Dir Petten Establishment, EC (now EU) Jt Research Centre, Netherlands 1985–95, Dir Inst. for Advanced Materials 1989–95; Visiting Prof., Dept of Materials, Imperial Coll. of Science, Tech. and Medicine 1988–; Hon. mem. Soc. Française de Metallurgie; Hon. DSc (Univ. of London) 1997; Rosenhain Medal, Howe Medal, Griffiths Medal, Hatfield Memorial Lecturer, Univ. of Sheffield 1986. *Publications include:* Energetics of Solid-Solid Interfaces 1969, Grain Boundary Segregation (with M. P. Seah) 1973. *Leisure interest:* reading, writing. *Address:* 37 Ullswater Crescent, London, SW15 3RG, England. *Telephone:* (20) 8549-9526. *Fax:* (20) 8549-9526. *E-mail:* edhondros@ gmail.com.

HONG, Guofan; Chinese molecular biochemist; b. Dec. 1939, Ningbo, Zhejiang Prov.; ed Fudan Univ., Shanghai; researcher, Biochemical Research Inst., Chinese Acad. of Sciences 1964–; researcher, MRC Molecular Biological Lab., UK 1979–83; Research Prof., Shanghai Insts for Biological Sciences; coordinated Chinese Rice Genome Program 1992–98; Fellow, Chinese Acad. of Sciences 1997–; Dir Nat. Genetics Research Centre 1993–; now Prof., Coll. of Pharmaceuticals and Biotechnology, Tianjin Univ.; Fellow, Acad. of Sciences for the Developing World 1993–; Ho Leung Ho Lee Foundation Life Sciences Award 2006. *Address:* Shanghai Institutes for Biological Sciences, 320 Yue Yang Road, Shanghai 200031; Chinese Academy of Sciences, 17 Zhongguacun Lu, Beijing 100864, People's Republic of China (office). *Telephone:* (21) 54920000 (office). *Fax:* (21) 54921011 (office). *E-mail:* gfhong@sibcb.ac.cn. *Website:* www.sibcb.ac.cn.

HONG, Hu; Chinese politician; b. June 1940, Jinzhai Co., Anhui Prov.; ed Beijing Eng Inst.; joined CCP 1965; fmr technician, later Deputy Chief, Dye Plant, Jilin Chemical Industry Co.; fmr Workshop Chief, Liming Chemical Industry Factory, Qinghai Prov. (Vice-Chair. CCP Revolutionary Cttee); fmr Head, Comprehensive Planning Div., 2nd Bureau, Ministry of Chemical Industry; fmr Div. Chief, Planning Bureau, State Machine-Building Industry Comm.; Deputy Sec.-Gen., Sec.-Gen. State Comm. for Econ. Restructuring 1982–91; Vice-Minister, State Comm. for Econ. Restructuring 1991–98; Vice-Gov. Jilin Prov. (also Acting Gov.) 1998–99, Gov. 1999–2004; mem. Comm. of Securities of the State Council 1992–98; mem. CCP Cen. Cttee for Discipline Inspection 1992; mem. 15th CCP Cen. Cttee 1997–2002, 16th CCP Cen. Cttee 2002–07; Del., 10th NPC 2003–08, Vice-Chair. 10th NPC Law Cttee 2005; holds title of Outstanding CCP Mem. at State Organs Level 2002–. *Address:* National People's Congress Law Committee, Beijing, People's Republic of China (office).

HONG, Jae-hyong; South Korean politician; *Vice-Speaker, Kuk Hoe (National Assembly);* b. Cheongju, N Chungcheong Prov.; ed Seoul Nat. Univ.; joined Foreign Exchange Bureau, Ministry of Finance 1963; later worked at IBRD, Washington, DC; Admin., Korean Customs Admin.; Pres. Export-Import Bank of Korea, Korea Exchange Bank; Minister of Finance 1993; Deputy Prime Minister, Minister of Finance and Econs 1994–96; mem. Kuk Hoe (Nat. Ass.) (Democratic Party) for Cheongju, N Chungcheong Prov. 2000–, Vice-Speaker Kuk Hoe 2010–. *Address:* Democratic Party, 13-17, Yeouido-dong, Yeongdeungpo-gu, Seoul 150-701, South Korea (office). *Telephone:* (2) 1577-7667 (office). *Fax:* (2) 2630-0145 (office). *E-mail:* help@undp.kr (office). *Website:* minjoo.kr (office).

HONG, Qi, PhD; Chinese economist and business executive; *Vice-Chairman and President, China Minsheng Banking Corporation Limited;* b. 1957; fmr Man. Dir Beihai Br. of Bank of Communications; fmr Deputy Dir Securities Research Inst. of Renmin Univ. of China; fmr Section Chief, Head Office of the People's Bank of China; fmr Vice-Pres. and Gen. Man. Beijing Admin. Dept, China Minsheng Banking Corpn Ltd, currently Vice-Chair., Pres. and Sec. CCP Cttee. *Address:* China Minsheng Banking Corporation Ltd, 2 Fuxingmennei Avenue, Beijing 100873, People's Republic of China (office). *Telephone:* (10) 68946790 (office). *E-mail:* webmaster@cmbc.com.cn (office). *Website:* www.cmbc.com.cn (office).

HONG, Song-nam; North Korean politician; b. 1924, Kangwon Prov.; ed Kimilsung Univ.; Chief of a Korean Workers' Party Cen. Cttee Dept 1970; Deputy Premier and Chair. State Planning Comm. 1973, 1986; Assoc. mem., Politburo 1982, Sec. of Party chapter, S. Pyongan Prov. 1982, Full mem. of Politburo and First Deputy Premier 1986, Assoc. mem. 1989; Acting Premier of the Democratic People's Repub. of Korea Feb. 1997–Sept. 1998, Premier Sept. 1998–2003. *Address:* c/o Office of the Premier, Pyongyang, Democratic People's Republic of Korea (office).

HONJO, Tasuku, MD, PhD; Japanese molecular biologist and academic; *Professor, Department of Immunology and Genomic Medicine, Graduate School of Medicine, Kyoto University;* b. 27 Jan. 1942, Kyoto; s. of Shoichi Honjo and Ryu Honjo; m. Shigeko Kotani 1969; one s. one d.; ed Ube High School and Kyoto Univ.; Fellow, Carnegie Inst. of Washington, Baltimore, Md, USA 1971–73; Visiting Fellow and Assoc., Lab. of Molecular Genetics, NIH 1973–74; Asst Prof., Dept of Physiological Chem. and Nutrition, Faculty of Medicine, Univ. of Tokyo 1974–79; Prof., Dept of Genetics, Osaka Univ. School of Medicine 1979–84; Prof., Dept of Immunology and Genomic Medicine, Grad. School of Medicine, Kyoto Univ. 1984–, Dir Center for Molecular Biology and Genetics 1988–97, Dean, Faculty of Medicine, Kyoto Univ. 1996–2000, 2002–04; Science Adviser, Ministry of Educ., Culture, Sports, Science and Tech. (MEXT) 1999–2003; Dir Japan Soc. for the Promotion of Science, Research Centre for Science Systems 2004–06; Exec. mem. Council for Science and Tech. Policy, Cabinet Office 2006–12; Chair. Shizuoka Prefectural Univ. Corpn 2012–; mem. Leopoldina German Acad. of Natural Scientists 2003, Japan Acad. 2006; Foreign Assoc., NAS 2001; Hon. mem. American Asscn of Immunologists; Order of Culture from the Emperor of Japan 2013; Noguchi Hideyo Memorial Award for Medicine 1981, Asahi Award 1981, Erwin von Baelz Prize 1985, Takeda Medical Prize 1988, Behring-Kitasato Prize 1992, Imperial Prize and Japan Acad. Prize 1996, Person of Cultural Merit Award by Japanese Govt 2000, Robert Koch Prize 2012. *Publications:* Molecular Biology of B Cell 2003. *Leisure interest:* golf. *Address:* Department of Immunology and Genomic Medicine, Graduate School of Medicine, Kyoto University, Yoshida, Sakyo-ku, Kyoto 606-8501, Japan (office). *Telephone:* (75) 753-4371 (office). *Fax:* (75) 753-4388 (office). *E-mail:* honjo@mfour.med.kyoto-u.ac.jp (office). *Website:* www2.mfour.med.kyoto-u.ac.jp/E_Home.htm (office).

HONKAPOHJA, Seppo Mikko Sakari, DSocSc; Finnish economist, banker and fmr academic; b. 7 March 1951, Helsinki; m. Sirkku Anna-Maija Honkapohja 1973; one s. one d.; ed United World Coll. of the Atlantic, UK, Univ. of Helsinki; Scientific Dir Yrjö Jahnsson Foundation 1975–87; Prof. of Econs, Turku School of Econs and Business Admin 1987–91, Prof.-at-Large (Docent) 1992–; Prof.-at-Large (Docent) of Econs, Univ. of Helsinki 1981–91, Acting Prof. of Econs (Econometrics) 1985–87, Prof. of Econs 1992–; Visiting Lecturer and Scholar, Harvard Univ., USA 1978–79; Visiting Assoc. Prof. of Econs, Stanford Univ., USA 1982–83; Sr Fellow, Acad. of Finland 1982–83, Acad. Prof. 1989–95, 2000–04; Prof. of Int. Macroeconomics, Univ. of Cambridge, UK 2004–08, Professorial Fellow, Clare Coll. 2004–08; mem. Bd Bank of Finland 2008–; Man. Ed. Scandinavian Journal of Economics 1984–88; Ed. European Economic Review 1993–98; mem. Bd Finnish Econ. Asscn 1989–91, Finnish Soc. for European Studies 1994–2000; mem. Council, European Econ. Asscn 1985–86, 1999–2003, mem. Exec. Cttee 2004–06; Vice-Chair. Kansallis Foundation for Financial Research 1989–96; mem. Governing Body, The Finnish Cultural Foundation 1994–, Chair. 1997–2001, mem. Supervisory Bd 2003–; mem. Supervisory Bd, Okopankki Ltd 1996–, Chair 1997–2007; mem. Finnish Acad. of Science and Letters, Academia Europaea; Fellow, Econometric Soc., European Econ. Asscn; Jaakko Honko Medal, Helsinki School of Econs and Business Admin 1998, Yrjo Jahnsson Foundation Anniversary Prize 2004. *Publications:* Limits and Problems of Taxation 1985; ed. several books including The State of Macroeconomics 1990, Macroeconomic Modelling and Policy Implications 1993, Learning and Expectations in Macroeconomics 2001; numerous articles in journals. *Leisure interest:* fishing. *Address:* Bank of Finland, PO Box 160, 00101, Helsinki, Finland (office). *Telephone:* (10) 8312015 (office). *Website:* www.bof.fi (office).

HONOHAN, Patrick, BA, MA, MSc, PhD, MRIA; Irish economist, academic and central banker; *Governor, Central Bank of Ireland;* b. Oct. 1949, Dublin; m.; one s.; ed Univ. Coll., Dublin, London School of Econs, UK; Sec.'s Dept, IMF 1971–73, Visiting Scholar, Research Dept 1996; Temporary Lecturer in Econs, LSE, UK 1974; Economist, Research and Int. Relations Dept, Cen. Bank of Ireland 1976–80, Sr Economist 1980–84; Econ. Advisor to the Taoiseach (Prime Minister), Dr Garret FitzGerald 1981–82, 1984–86; Visiting Asst Prof., Dept of Econs, Univ. of California, San Diego, USA 1982–83; Coll. Lecturer, Dept of Political Economy, Univ. Coll. Dublin 1986–87; Visiting Fellow, Dept of Statistics, ANU, Australia 1987; Sr Economist, World Bank, Washington, DC, USA 1987–90, Lead Economist, Devt Research Group 1998–2002, Advisor, Financial Policy and Strategy Dept 2001–02, Sr Advisor, Financial Sector Policy 2002–07; Research Prof. and Dir Banking Research Centre, Econ. and Social Research Inst., Dublin 1990–98; Research Fellow, Centre for Econ. Policy Research, London 1992–; Prof. of Int. Financial Econs and Devt, Dept of Econs and Inst. for Int. Integration Studies, Trinity Coll. Dublin 2007–, Professorial Fellow 2008–; Gov. Cen. Bank of Ireland 2009–; mem. Governing Council, European Cen. Bank; Council mem. Irish Econ. Asscn 1993–2002 (Pres. 1998–2000), Econ. and Social Research Inst. 2006– (mem. Audit Cttee 2007–), Foundation for Fiscal Studies 2004–, Statistical and Social Inquiry Soc. of Ireland 2007–; mem. Nat. Econ. and Social Council 1995–98; mem. Royal Irish Acad. 2002, mem. Audit Cttee 2005–06. *Address:* Central Bank & Financial Services Authority of Ireland, PO Box 559, Dame Street, Dublin 2, Ireland (office). *Telephone:* (1) 2246000 (office). *Fax:* (1) 6716561 (office). *E-mail:* info@centralbank.ie (office); phonohan@tcd.ie. *Website:* www.centralbank.ie (office).

HONORÉ, Sandra; Trinidad and Tobago diplomatist and UN official; *Special Representative and Head of the Stabilization Mission in Haiti, United Nations;* b. 1955, Tunapuna; m.; one c.; ed Univs of Besançon and Bordeaux, France; several years' service with Ministry of Foreign Affairs (MFA) including postings to Brazil 1983–88, USA 1997–2000, Special Asst to Chief of OAS Electoral Observation Mission to Haiti 1995–96, Chief of Staff, Office of OAS Asst Sec.-Gen. 2000–05, Dir CARICOM and Caribbean Affairs Div. 2005, Chief of Protocol, MFA 2007, Amb. to Costa Rica –2012; UN Special Rep. and Head of UN Stabilization Mission in Haiti (MINUSTAH) 2013–. *Address:* MINUSTAH, Boulevard Toussaint Louverture et Clercine 18, Port-au-Prince, Haiti (office). *Telephone:* 2229-6700 (office). *Website:* www.un.org/en/peacekeeping/missions/minustah (office); www.minustah.org (office).

HONSCHEID, Klaus, PhD; German particle physicist and academic; *Professor, Department of Physics, Ohio State University;* ed Univ. of Bonn, Germany; Research Assoc., Univ. of Bonn 1988–89; Research Assoc., Cornell Univ., USA 1990–92; Asst Prof., Ohio State Univ. 1993–96, Assoc. Prof. 1996–2000, Prof. of Physics 2000–; mem. Center of Cosmology and Astro Particle Physics (CCAPP) Science Bd 2006–, Dark Energy Survey Project (DES) Man. Cttee 2007–, IEEE Computer Applications in Nuclear and Plasma Sciences (CANPS) Tech. Cttee 2008–; Alexander von Humboldt Foundation Lynen Fellow 1990–92; Alfred P. Sloan Research Fellow 1995–97; Fellow, American Physical Soc. 2005; Coll. of Arts and Sciences PhD Award (Univ. of Bonn) 1989, Alfred P. Sloan Foundation Fellowship 1995–96, Alumni Award for Distinguished Teaching, Ohio State Univ. 2004. *Publications:* numerous publs in scientific journals on particle and high-energy physics. *Address:* 3054 Physics Research Building, 191 West Woodruff Ave, Columbus, OH 43210, USA (office). *Telephone:* (614) 292-3287 (office). *Fax:* (614) 292-8261 (office). *E-mail:* kh@mps.ohio-state.edu (office). *Website:* www.physics.ohio-state.edu (office).

HOOD, Amy, BA, MBA; American business executive; *Chief Financial Officer, Microsoft Corporation;* m.; several d.; ed Duke Univ., Harvard Univ.; worked at Goldman Sachs & Co. in various roles including investment banking and capital markets groups; joined Microsoft 2002, held positions in Server and Tools Business and Corp. Finance Org., Vice-Pres. and Chief Financial Officer, Microsoft Business Div. –2013, Chief Financial Officer, Microsoft Corpn 2013–; ranked by Forbes magazine amongst The World's 100 Most Powerful Women (63rd) 2013. *Address:* Microsoft Corporation, 1 Microsoft Way, Redmond, WA 98052-8300, USA (office). *Telephone:* (425) 882-8080 (office). *Fax:* (425) 936-7329 (office). *E-mail:* info@microsoft.com (office). *Website:* www.microsoft.com (office).

HOOD, Brenda; Grenadian social worker and politician; *Parliamentary Secretary, Ministry of Tourism, Culture, and Civil Aviation with responsibility for Culture;* ed York Univ., Canada; fmr Chair. Nat. Coalition on the Rights of the Child, Grenada Adoption Bd; fmr Exec. Dir Grenada Save the Children Fund; mem. Parl. 1999–2003, Senator 2003–, Minister of State for Housing, Women's Affairs and Social Security 1999, Minister of Social Security, Nat. Insurance Scheme, Gender and Family Affairs 1999–2003, Minister of Tourism, Civil Aviation, Culture and the Performing Arts 1999–2007, Minister of Communications, Works and Transport 2007–08; Parliamentary Sec., Ministry of Tourism, Culture, and Civil Aviation with responsibility for Culture 2013–; mem. Exec. Cttee Inter-Parl. Forum of the Americas (FIPA); mem. New Nat. Party. *Address:* Ministry of Tourism, Civil Aviation and Culture Ministerial Complex, 4th Floor, Botanical Gardens, Tanteen, St George's, Grenada (office). *Telephone:* 440-0366 (office). *Fax:* 440-0443 (office). *E-mail:* tourism@gov.gd (office). *Website:* www.grenada.mot.gd (office).

HOOD, Hon. (Ignatius Joachim) Karl; Grenadian politician; b. 27 Oct. 1954, Happy Hill, St George's; s. of Anthony Percival Hood and Constance Hood (née Antoine); m. Hermione Hood; two c.; ed West Indies School of Theology, Trinidad, Nyack Coll., NY, USA; trained as optician and Minister of Religion; mem. House of Reps for St George South East; fmr Minister for Labour, Social Security and Ecclesiastical Affairs; fmr Minister of Health; Minister of Foreign Affairs 2010–12; mem. Nat. Democratic Congress. *Address:* c/o Ministry of Foreign Affairs, Ministerial Complex, Fourth Floor, Botanical Gardens, Tanteen, St George's, Grenada.

HOOD, John, BE, MPhil PhD; New Zealand engineer, foundation executive and fmr university administrator; *President and CEO, The Robertson Foundation;* ed Univ. of Auckland, Univ. of Oxford, UK; held various sr positions with Fletcher Challenge Ltd, including Head of Paper, Bldg and Construction Divs 1980–98; Vice-Chancellor Univ. of Auckland 1998–2004, Univ. of Oxford 2004–09; Pres. and CEO The Robertson Foundation 2010–; fmr Visiting Lecturer, Dept of Civil Eng, Univ. of Auckland; Chair. NZ Vice-Chancellors' Cttee, The Knowledge Wave Trust, Universitas 21 Ltd 2002–04; fmr Chair. Tonkin & Taylor Ltd; fmr Dir Universitas 21 Global, ASB Bank Ltd, ASB Group, Fonterra Cooperative Group Ltd; fmr mem. Prime Minister's Growth and Innovation Advisory Bd, Prime Minister's Enterprise Council; Chair. Prime Minister's Think Tank on High Performance Sport 1996; fmr Gov. and mem. Exec. Bd, NZ Sports Foundation; fmr NZ Sec., The Rhodes Trust; fmr Trustee Asia 2000 Foundation, King's School (also Gov.); Rhodes Scholarship. *Address:* 101 Park Avenue, 48th Floor, New York, NY 10178 (office); The Robertson Foundation, 300 Maynard Street, Ann Arbor, MI 48104-2212, USA (office). *Telephone:* (734) 663-8088 (office). *E-mail:* john.hood@robertsfoundation.org (office). *Website:* www.robertsonfoundation.org (office).

HOOD, Leroy Edward, MD, PhD; American biologist, academic and entrepreneur; *President, Institute for Systems Biology;* b. 10 Oct. 1938, Missoula, Mon.; s. of Thomas Edward Hood and Myrtle Evylan Wadsworth; m. Valerie A. Logan 1963; one s. one d.; ed California Inst. of Tech. and Johns Hopkins School of Medicine; NIH Predoctoral Fellowship, California Inst. of Tech. 1963–64; NIH Postdoctoral Fellowship 1964–67; Sr Investigator, Immunology Branch, GL&C, NCI, NIH, Bethesda, Md 1967–70; Asst Prof. of Biology, California Inst. of Tech. 1970–73, Assoc. Prof. 1973–75, Prof. 1975–77, Bowles Prof. of Biology 1977–92, Chair. Div. of Biology 1980–89, Dir Cancer Center 1981; Gates Prof. and Chair of Molecular Biotechnology, Univ. of Washington 1992–99; Dir NSF Science and Tech. Center for Molecular Biotechnology 1989–2000; Founder and Pres. Inst. for Systems Biology 1999–; Co-founder P4 Medicine Inst. (P4Mi) 2010; mem. IOM, NAS, Nat. Acad. of Eng, American Acad. of Arts and Sciences, AAAS, American Assscn of

Immunologists, American Philosophical Soc., American Soc. for Clinical Investigation, American Soc. of Biological Chemists, Asscn of American Physicians, Int. Soc. of Molecular Evolution, Soc. for Integrative and Comparative Biology; Fellow, American Acad. of Microbiology; Hon. DSc (Montana State) 1986, (Mount Sinai School of Medicine, CUNY) 1987, (Univ. of British Columbia) 1988, (Univ. of Southern California) 1989, (Wesleyan) 1992, (Whitman Coll.) 1995, (Bates Coll.) 1999, (Penn State) 2001, (Zhejiang Univ., Tsinghua Univ., China) 2004, (Medical Coll. of Wisconsin) 2005, (Coll. of Wooster) 2007; Hon. DHumLitt (Johns Hopkins) 1990, (Loyola) 2005, (Yale) 2010; Albert Lasker Basic Medical Research Award 1987, Commonwealth Award of Distinguished Service 1989, Cetus Award for Biotechnology 1989, American Coll. of Physicians Award 1990, Ciba-Geigy/Drew Award 1993, Lynen Medal 1994, Distinguished Alumnus Award, Johns Hopkins Univ. 1994, Beckman Lecturer Award 1998, Distinguished Service Award, American Asscn for Clinical Chem. 1998, Kyoto Prize in Advanced Technologies 2002, Economists Award for Innovation in Biosciences 2002, Lemelson-MIT Prize 2003, World Tech. Award for Biotechnology 2003, American Asscn for Pathology Award for Excellence in Clinical Diagnosis 2004, Heinz Award for Tech. and Econ. Devt 2006, Inventors Hall of Fame 2007, Kistler Prize 2010, Fritz J. and Dolores H. Russ Prize, Nat. Acad. of Eng 2011, Nat. Medal of Science 2011. *Publications:* co-author of six books on immunology, biochemistry, molecular biology, genetics and the human genome project and of more than 650 papers in learned journals. *Leisure interests:* mountaineering, running, exercise, photography, reading. *Address:* Institute for Systems Biology, 1441 N34 Street, Seattle, WA 98103, USA (office). *Telephone:* (206) 732-1202 (office). *Fax:* (206) 732-1254 (office). *E-mail:* lhood@systemsbiology.org (office). *Website:* www.systemsbiology.org (office).

HOODA, Bhupinder Singh, BA, LLB; Indian politician, agriculturist and lawyer; *Chief Minister of Haryana;* b. 15 Sept. 1947, Sanghi, Rohtak Dist; s. of Choudhary Ranbir Singh; m. Asha Hooda 1976; one s. one d.; ed Punjab Univ., Chandigarh, Univ. of Delhi; Pres. Block Congress Cttee, Kiloi, Haryana 1972–77; Sr Vice-Pres. Haryana Pradesh Youth Congress 1982–83, Pres. 1982–83; Chair. Panchayat Samiti, Rohtak 1983–87, Panchayat Parishad, Haryana 1984–87; mem. Lok Sabha 1991–, mem. Cttee on Agric. 1996–97, 1998–99, on Subordinate Legislation 1998–99; mem. All India Congress Cttee 1992–; mem. Exec. Congress Parl. Party 1994–; Convenor Haryana Congress Parl. Group 1994–96; Pres. Haryana Pradesh Congress Cttee 1996–2002; mem. Consultative Cttee Ministry of Communication 1998–99, Cttee on Subordinate Legislation; mem. Haryana Vidhan Sabha 2000–, Leader of the Opposition 2002–04; Leader Haryana Legislature Party 2005–; Chief Minister of Haryana 2005–; Pres. All India Young Farmers Asscn, Haryana, Khadi and Village Industries Comm. Employees Union; Dir, New Bank of India 1989–92; Patron Nat. Khadi and Village Industries Bd Employees Fed.; Founder-mem. and Working Pres. All India Freedom Fighters' Successors' Org.; Working Pres. Nat. Fed. of Railway Porters, Vendors and Bearers; Sec. Jat Educ. Soc., Rohtak, Farmers' Parl. Forum 1991–; mem. Man. Cttee, D.A.V. Educational Soc., Hasangarh, Haryana; National Law Day Award 2009. *Leisure interests:* reading, sports. *Address:* Kothi No. 1, Sector 3, Chandigarh (office); Matu Ram Bhawan, Model Town, Delhi Road, Rohtak, Haryana (home); Haryana Vidhan Sabha Bhawan, Sector 1 Chandigarh 160 001 India. *Telephone:* (172) 2749394 (office); (1262) 42283 (home). *Fax:* (1262) 212030 (home). *E-mail:* cm@hry.nic.in (office); hoodabhupindersingh@hry.nic.in (office). *Website:* www.haryana.nic.in/government/cmbio (office); www.haryanaassembly.gov.in.

HOOGENDOORN, Piet; Dutch business executive; b. 1946; ed Netherlands Inst. of Registeraccountants; worked as public auditor; Man. Partner Deloitte & Touche Netherlands 1990–2001; Vice-Chair. Deloitte Touche Tohmatsu Global Bd 1999–2000, Chair. July 2000–07; Pres. Royal NIvRAm (professional org. of Dutch accountants); mem. Supervisory Bd ING Groep NV 2007–, Nyenrode Univ.; mem. Bd Netherlands Foundation for Annual Reporting. *Address:* ING House, Amstelveenseweg 500, 1081 Amsterdam, Netherlands (office).

HOOKER, (Charles Raymond) Charlie; British sculptor and academic; *Course Leader, MA Fine Art and Research Initiative Leader, Faculty of Arts, University of Brighton;* b. 1 June 1953, London; s. of Raymond C. Hooker and Daphne Hooker; Partner Margery Jane Forest Taylor; ed Purley Grammar School, Croydon Coll. of Art and Brighton Polytechnic; Founder mem. The Artistics (music ensemble) 1972–75, 2B Butlers Wharf (art space) 1974–75; Visiting Lecturer, Chelsea, Croydon, Winchester, Trent, Cardiff, Central, Brighton, Newport, Newcastle, Camberwell Schools of Art/Polytechnics 1977–; part-time Lecturer, Brighton Polytechnic 1990–92; External Examiner, Chelsea School of Art 1995–; Sr Lecturer, Camberwell Coll. 1990–92; Sr Lecturer/Area Leader—Sculpture, Univ. of Brighton 1992–; Artist in Residence, Amherst Jr and Hatcham Wood Secondary Schools 1985; Co-ordinator, Artists' Open Week, Camberwell School of Art 1989; works in Arts Council collection and pvt. collections and perm. public outdoor work in UK; Art/Science projects with Science Museum, London and Herstmonceux Science Centre 1995; Subject Leader for Sculpture and Critical Fine Art Practice, Univ. of Brighton, currently Course Leader, MA Fine Art and Research Initiative Leader, Faculty of Arts. *Audio recordings:* Restricted Movement 1982, Transitions 1984, Charlie Hooker and Performers 1987, Wave-Wall/Dust and a Shadow 1991 for Audio Arts, Separate Elements 1992. *Leisure interest:* walking. *Address:* School of Art Design and Media, University of Brighton, Grand Parade, Brighton, BN2 0JY, England (office). *Telephone:* (1273) 643068 (office). *Fax:* (1273) 643041 (office). *E-mail:* charlie.hooker234@btinternet.com. *Website:* www.charliehooker.co.uk.

HOOKER, Morna Dorothy, MA, PhD, DD; British theologian and academic; *Lady Margaret's Professor Emerita of Divinity, University of Cambridge;* b. 19 May 1931, Surrey, England; d. of P. F. Hooker and L. Hooker (née Riley); m. Rev. Dr W. D. Stacey 1978 (died 1993); one step-s. two step-d.; ed Univs of Bristol and Manchester; Research Fellow, Durham Univ. 1959–61; Lecturer in New Testament, King's Coll. London 1961–70, Fellow 1979–; Lecturer in Theology, Univ. of Oxford 1970–76, Keble Coll., Oxford 1972–76; Fellow, Linacre Coll., Oxford 1970–76, Hon. Fellow 1980–; Visiting Fellow, Clare Hall, Cambridge 1974; Lady Margaret's Prof. of Divinity, Univ. of Cambridge 1976–98, Prof. Emer. 1998–, Fellow, Robinson Coll. 1977–; Visiting Prof., York St John Univ.; Jt Ed. Journal of Theological Studies 1985–2005; Visiting Prof., McGill Univ., Canada 1968, Duke Univ., USA 1987, 1989; Pres. Studiorum Novi Testamenti Societas 1988–89; Hon. DLitt (Bristol) 1994; Hon. DD (Edinburgh) 1997; Burkitt Medal 2004. *Publica-*

tions: Jesus and the Servant 1959, The Son of Man in Mark 1967, Pauline Pieces 1979, Studying the New Testament 1979, The Message of Mark 1983, Continuity and Discontinuity 1986, From Adam to Christ 1990, A Commentary on the Gospel According to St Mark 1991, Not Ashamed of the Gospel 1994, The Signs of a Prophet 1997, Beginnings: Keys that Open the Gospels 1997, Paul: A Short Introduction 2003, Endings 2003. *Leisure interests:* molinology, music, walking. *Address:* Robinson College, Cambridge, CB3 9AN, England (office). *Telephone:* (1223) 339100 (office). *Fax:* (1223) 351794 (office). *E-mail:* mdh1000@cam.ac.uk (office).

HOOKER, Steven; Australian athlete; b. 16 July 1982, Melbourne, Vic.; s. of Bill Hooker (represented Australia in 800m and 4×400m at 1974 Commonwealth Games) and Erica Hooker (1972 Olympian and Commonwealth Games long jump silver medallist 1978); pole vaulter; finished fourth at World Jr Championships, Santiago, Chile 2000; Gold Medal, Commonwealth Games, Melbourne 2006; finished fifth at World Athletics Final, Stuttgart 2006; finished first at World Cup, Athens 2006; Bronze Medal, World Athletics Final, Stuttgart 2007, World Indoor Championships, Valencia 2008; set personal best of 6.00m in Perth, WA Jan. 2008; Gold Medal, Olympic Games, Beijing 2008 (set new Olympic record of 5.96m), first Australian male track and field gold medallist since 1968. *Address:* c/o Australian Athletics Federation, Suite 22, Fawkner Towers, 431 St Kilda Road, Melbourne, Vic. 3004, Australia. *Telephone:* (3) 98203511. *Fax:* (3) 98203544. *E-mail:* info@athletics.org.au. *Website:* www.athletics.org.au.

HOOKWAY, Sir Harry Thurston, Kt, PhD; British administrator and librarian; b. 23 July 1921, London; s. of William Hookway and Bertha Hookway; m. Barbara Butler 1956; one s. one d.; ed Trinity School of John Whitgift and Univ. of London; Asst Dir Nat. Chem. Lab. 1959; Dir UK Scientific Mission (N America), Scientific Attaché, Embassy in Washington, DC, Scientific Adviser, High Comm., Ottawa, Canada 1960–64; Head, Information Div. Dept of Scientific and Industrial Research 1964–65; Chief Scientific Officer, Dept of Educ. and Science 1966–69, Asst Under-Sec. of State 1969–73; Deputy Chair. and Chief Exec. British Library Bd 1973–84; Pro-Chancellor Loughborough Univ. of Tech. 1987–93; mem. Royal Comm. on Historical Monuments (England) 1981–88; Chair. Publrs Data Bases Ltd 1984–87, LA Publishing Ltd 1986–89; Pres. The Library Asscn 1985; Dir Arundel Castle Trustees 1976–89; Hon. Fellow, Inst. of Information Scientists, Hon. FLA; Hon. LLD; Hon. DLitt; Gold Medal Int. Asscn of Library Asscns 1985. *Publications:* papers in learned and professional journals. *Leisure interests:* music, travel. *Address:* 3 St James Green, Thirsk, North Yorks., YO7 1AF, England.

HOOLEY, Christopher, PhD, FRS; British academic; b. 7 Aug. 1928, Edinburgh; s. of Leonard Joseph Hooley and Barbara Hooley; m. Birgitta Kniep 1954; two s.; ed Abbotsholme School and Corpus Christi Coll. Cambridge; Capt., Royal Army Educational Corps 1948–49; Fellow, Corpus Christi Coll. 1955–58; Lecturer in Math., Univ. of Bristol 1958–65; Prof. of Pure Math., Univ. of Durham 1965–67; Prof. of Pure Math., Wales Univ., Coll. of Cardiff (fmrly Univ. Coll. Cardiff) 1967–95, Distinguished Research Prof. 1995–, Head of Dept of Math. 1988–96, Dean of Faculty of Science 1973–76, Deputy Prin. Univ. Coll. Cardiff 1979–81, Wales Univ. Coll. of Cardiff 1991–94; Visiting mem. Inst. for Advanced Study, Princeton, NJ, USA on several occasions since 1970, Institut des Hautes Etudes Scientifiques, Paris 1984; Adam's Prize, Cambridge 1973, Sr Berwick Prize, London Math. Soc. 1980. *Publications:* Applications of Sieve Methods to the Theory of Numbers 1976, Recent Progress in Analytic Number Theory (ed. with H. Halberstam) 1981. *Leisure interests:* antiquities and classic cars. *Address:* Rushmoor Grange, Backwell, Bristol, BS19 3BN, England. *Telephone:* (1275) 462363.

HOON, Rt Hon. Geoffrey William, PC, MA; British politician and lawyer; b. 6 Dec. 1953; s. of Ernest Hoon and June Hoon; m. Elaine Ann Dumelow 1981; one s. two d.; ed Jesus Coll., Cambridge; labourer at furniture factory 1972–73; Lecturer in Law, Univ. of Leeds 1976–82; Visiting Prof. of Law, Univ. of Louisville, USA 1979–80; called to the Bar, Gray's Inn 1978; in practice in Nottingham 1982–84; MEP for Derbyshire 1984–94, mem. Legal Affairs Cttee 1984–94; MP for Ashfield 1992–2010; Opposition Whip 1994–95, Opposition Spokesman on Information Tech. 1995–97; Parl. Sec., Lord Chancellor's Dept 1997–98, Minister of State 1998–99, Sec. of State for Defence 1999–2005, Leader of the House of Commons 2005–06, Minister for Europe, FCO 2006–07, Parl. Sec. to the Treasury and Chief Whip 2007–08, Sec. of State for Transport 2008–09; Vice-Chair. and Gov. Westminster Foundation 1994–97; mem. Labour Party; US Dept of Defense Distinguished Public Service Award 2004. *Leisure interests:* cinema, cricket, football, music. *Address:* 8 Station Street, Kirby-in-Ashfield, Notts., NG17 7AR, England (home). *Telephone:* (1623) 720399 (home). *Fax:* (1623) 720398 (home). *E-mail:* contact@geoffhoonmp.co.uk (office). *Website:* www.geoffhoonmp.co.uk (office).

HOOPER, Thomas (Tom) George; British television and film director; b. 1972, London, England; s. of Richard Hooper and Meredith Hooper; ed Westminster School, London, University Coll., Oxford; early experience as dir whilst student as mem. Oxford Univ. Dramatic Soc.; began directing TV commercials, later directed episodes of various series for BBC and Granada TV. *Films:* Red Dust (IFFI Special Jury Award Special Award) 2004, Elizabeth I (Emmy Award for Outstanding Directing for a Miniseries, Movie or Dramatic Special) 2005, The Damned United 2009, The King's Speech (Dir's Guild of America Award for Outstanding Directorial Achievement in Motion Pictures 2010, London Film Critics' Circle Award for British Director of the Year 2010, Academy Award for Best Dir 2011) 2010, Les Misérables 2012. *Television:* Painted Faces (short) (Channel 4) 1992, four episodes of Byker Grove (Children's BBC series) 1997, EastEnders (BBC One) 1998–2000, Cold Feet (Granada TV) 1999, Love in a Cold Climate (mini-series) 2001, Daniel Deronda (mini-series) 2002, Prime Suspect 6: The Last Witness (Granada TV) 2003, Elizabeth I (mini-series) (Primetime Emmy Award for Outstanding Directing for a Miniseries, Movie or Dramatic Special 2006) 2005, Longford (film) (BAFTA for Best Single Drama 2007) 2006, John Adams (mini-series) 2008. *Address:* c/o Independent, Oxford House, 76 Oxford Street, London, W1D 1BS, England (office). *Telephone:* (20) 7636-6565 (office). *Fax:* (20) 7323-0101 (office). *E-mail:* info@independenttalent.com (office). *Website:* www.independenttalent.com (office).

HOPE, Christopher David Tully, MA, FRSL; South African writer; b. 26 Feb. 1944, Johannesburg; s. of Dudley Mitford Hope and Kathleen Mary Hope; m. Eleanor Marilyn Margaret Klein; two s.; ed Natal Univ., Univ. of the Witwatersrand; Founder Franschhoek Literary Festival 2007; mem. Soc. of Authors; Cholmondeley Award 1972, David Higham Award 1981, Int. PEN Award 1983, Whitbread Award 1986, CNA Literary Award (S Africa) 1989, Travelex Travel Writer of the Year 1997. *Publications include:* A Separate Development 1981, Private Parts 1982, The King, the Cat and the Fiddle (with Yehudi Menuhin) 1983, Kruger's Alp (Whitbread Prize for Fiction 1985) 1984, The Dragon Wore Pink 1985, The Hottentot Room 1986, Black Swan 1987, White Boy Running 1988, My Chocolate Redeemer 1989, Moscow! Moscow! 1990, Serenity House 1992, The Love Songs of Nathan J. Swirsky 1993, Darkest England 1996; poetry: Cape Drives 1974, In the Country of the Black Pig 1981, Englishman 1985, Me, the Moon and Elvis Presley 1997, Signs of the Heart 1999, Heaven Forbid 2002, Brothers Under the Skin 2003, My Mother's Lovers 2006, The Garden of Bad Dreams 2008, Shooting Angels 2011; contrib. to TLS, London Magazine, Les Temps Modernes, BBC, Guardian. *Leisure interest:* getting lost. *Address:* Rogers, Coleridge & White Ltd, 20 Powis Mews, London, W11 1JN, England (office). *Telephone:* (20) 7221-3717 (office). *Fax:* (20) 7229-9084 (office). *E-mail:* christopher1hope@gmail.com.

HOPE-CROSBY, Polly, FRSA; British artist, designer, author and photographer; b. (June Maryann Stockwell), 21 June 1933, Colchester, Essex, England; d. of Gen. Sir Hugh Stockwell and Lady Stockwell; m. 1st John Hope 1953; one s.; m. 2nd Theo Crosby 1990; ed Heatherley, Chelsea and Slade Schools of Art; trained as a classical ballet dancer; has completed various commissions, including pointillist mural for Barbican Centre, London, four life-size terracotta figures for Shakespeare's Globe Theatre; collaborated on bldg Shakespeare's Globe Theatre; made Millennium vestments for Wakefield Cathedral 1999–2000; numerous other public works; works with several composers writing librettos; has composed Greek song cycles; has written film scripts, novels, short stories, verse plays, made videos, films and animated films and operas, all of which have been published and produced. *Animated film:* Memories, Memories 1995. *Productions include:* Bran's Singing Head (music by Geoffrey Alvarez) 1996, Il Giardino degli Uccelli (one act opera, music by Quentin Thomas) 1999, Death of Lord Byron (one act opera, music by Quentin Thomas) 2000, The Bird Garden, Oper-am-Rhein, Düsseldorf (sets, libretto and book), design for Kiss Me Kate for Deutsch Oper-am-Rhein 2005, Tanks; production and design of own operas in major opera houses. *Plays include:* Freedom and Death 1992, General Hughie 1993, Tanks. *Artistic works:* many embroideries for Church of England, chasubles, altar frontals, tapestries, public works on many continents. *Publications include:* Here Away From it All 1969, Us Lot 1970, The Immaculate Misconception 1972, A Baker's Dozen of Greek Folk Songs 1994, Songs My Parrot Taught Me 1994, Egyptian Love Songs and Songs for Aphrodite 1998, Il Giardino degli Uccelli 1999, The Bird Garden 2002, Three True Stories 2010. *Leisure interests:* music, sitting in the sun, sleeping. *Address:* 5A Heneage Street, Spitalfields, London, E1 5LJ, England (home). *Telephone:* (20) 7247-3450 (home). *Fax:* (20) 7247-3450 (home). *E-mail:* polly@doxy.demon.co.uk (office). *Website:* www.hopeart.com (office).

HOPE OF CRAIGHEAD, Baron (Life Peer), cr. 1995, of Bamff in the District of Perth and Kinross; **Rt Hon. James Arthur David Hope,** Kt, KT, PC, BA, LLB, FRSE; British judge; b. 22 June 1938, Edinburgh, Scotland; s. of Arthur Henry Cecil Hope and Muriel Ann Neilson Hope; m. Katharine Mary Kerr 1966; two s. one d.; ed The Edinburgh Acad., Rugby School, St John's Coll., Cambridge, Univ. of Edinburgh; nat. service, Seaforth Highlanders 1957–59; admitted to Faculty of Advocates, to practise at Scottish Bar 1965; Standing Jr Counsel to Bd of Inland Revenue in Scotland 1974–78; apptd QC in Scotland 1978; Advocate-Depute, Crown Office, Edinburgh 1978–82; Chair. and Legal Chair. Medical Appeal Tribunals 1985–86; Dean Faculty of Advocates 1986–89; Lord Justice Gen. of Scotland and Lord Pres. of Court of Session 1989–96; mem. (Cross-Bench), House of Lords 1995–; a Lord of Appeal in Ordinary 1996–2009; Deputy Pres. The Supreme Court 2009–13; Chair. Sub-cttee E (Law and Insts), House of Lords Select Cttee on the EU 1998–2001; Pres. Stair Soc. 1993–2013, Int. Criminal Lawyers Asscn 2000, Commonwealth Magistrates' and Judges' Asscn 2003–06; Chancellor Univ. of Strathclyde 1998–2013, Prof. Emer. of Law 2013–; Hon. Prof. of Law, Univ. of Aberdeen 1994–; Hon. Fellow, St John's Coll., Cambridge 1995, American Coll. of Trial Lawyers 2000; Hon. LLD (Aberdeen) 1991, (Strathclyde) 1993, (Edin.) 1995, (Glasgow) 2013; Hon. DUniv (Strathclyde) 2013. *Publications:* Gloag & Henderson's Introduction to the Laws of Scotland (co-ed.) 1968, (asst ed.) 1980, 1987, 2001, Armour on Valuation for Rating (co-ed.) 1971, 1985, The Rent (Scotland) Act (co-author) 1984, 1986, Stair Memorial Encyclopaedia of Scots Law (contrib.). *Leisure interests:* walking, ornithology, music. *Address:* House of Lords, Westminster, London, SW1A 0PD, England (office); 34 India Street, Edinburgh, EH3 6HB, Scotland (home). *Telephone:* (20) 7219-0620 (office); (131) 225-8245 (home). *E-mail:* hopejad@parliament.uk (office). *Website:* www.parliament.uk/biographies/lords/lord-hope-of-craighead/2004 (office).

HOPE OF THORNES, Baron (Life Peer), cr. 2005, of Thornes in the County of West Yorkshire; **Rt Rev. and Rt Hon. David Michael Hope,** KCVO, PC, BA, DPhil; British ecclesiastic (retd); b. 14 April 1940, Wakefield, Yorks., England; s. of Jack Hope and Florence Hope; ed Wakefield Grammar School, Univ. of Nottingham, Linacre Coll., Oxford; Curate, St John's, Tuebrook, Liverpool 1965–70; Chaplain, Church of Resurrection, Bucharest 1967–68; Vicar, St Andrew's, Warrington 1970–74; Prin. St Stephen's House, Oxford 1974–82; Warden, Community of St Mary the Virgin, Wantage 1980–87; Vicar, All Saints', Margaret Street, London 1982–85; Bishop of Wakefield 1985–91, of London 1991–95; Archbishop of York 1995–2005; Vicar of St Margaret's, Ilkley, W Yorks. 2005–06 (retd); Prelate of the Order of the British Empire 1991–95; Dean of the Chapels Royal 1991–95; mem. (Crossbench) House of Lords 2005–, Court of Ecclesiastical Causes Reserved 2006–; Gov., Giggleswick School, Settle, N Yorks.; Trustee, Skipton Building Society Charitable Foundation, Walsingham Coll. (Yorkshire Properties) Ltd; Hon. Asst Bishop, Diocese of Bradford 2006; Hon. Fellow, Linacre Coll., Oxford; Hon. DD (Nottingham, Hull). *Publications:* The Leonine Sacramentary 1971, Living the Gospel 1993, Signs of Hope 2001. *Address:* House of Lords, Westminster, London, SW1A 0PW (office); 35 Hammerton Drive, Hellifield, Skipton, N Yorks., BD23 4LZ, England (home). *E-mail:* dmhhellifield@gmail.com (office).

HOPFIELD, John Joseph, AB, PhD; American scientist and academic; *Howard A. Prior Professor Emeritus of Molecular Biology, Princeton University;* b. 15 July 1933, Chicago, Ill.; s. of John Joseph Hopfield and Helen Staff Hopfield; m. Mary Waltham; three c.; ed Swarthmore Coll., Cornell Univ.; mem. tech. staff, Bell Labs 1958–60, 1973–89; Research Physicist, École Normale Supérieure, Paris 1960-61; Asst/Assoc. Prof. of Physics, Univ. of California, Berkeley 1961–64; Prof. of Physics, Princeton Univ. 1964–80, Eugene Higgins Prof. of Physics 1979–80, Prof., Dept of Molecular Biology 1997–, Howard A. Prior Prof. of Molecular Biology 2001–08, now Emer.; Roscoe Gilkey Dickinson Prof. and Prof. of Chem. and Biology, Calif. Inst. of Tech. 1980–97; Chair. NAS Cttee on Publication 1995–98, Selection Cttee, Burroughs-Wellcome Fund Interfaces Program 1997–99; mem. NASA Tycho Study Group on the nature of the lunar surface 1965–67, Strategic Mil. Panel of PSAC 1971–73, American Physical Soc. (APS) Study on Solar Photoelectricity 1977–78, Neurosciences Research Program 1978–89, Solar Photovoltaic Energy Advisory Cttee 1980–82, Advisory Council, Keck Grad. Inst. of Applied Life Sciences 1997–2001, NAS Cttee Bio 2010: Undergraduate Biology Educ. for Future Scientists 2000–02; Pres. APS 2006; mem. American Acad. of Arts and Sciences, NAS, American Philosophical Soc.; Trustee, Battelle Memorial Inst. 1982–2006, Neuroscience Research Inst. 1986–87, Harvey Mudd Coll. 1990–96, Huntington Medical Research Inst. 1991–96; Hon. DSc (Swarthmore Coll.) 1992, (Univ. of Chicago) 2007; Alfred Sloan Fellow 1962–64, Guggenheim Fellow, Univ. of Cambridge, UK 1969, APS Oliver E. Buckley Prize 1969, John and Catherine T. MacArthur Award 1983–88, APS Prize in Biophysics 1985, Michelson-Morley Award, Case-Western Univ. 1988, The Wright Prize, Harvey Mudd Coll. 1989, California Scientist of the Year, California Museum of Science and Industry 1991, IEEE Neural Network Pioneer Award 1997, Helmholtz Award, Int. Neural Network Soc. 1999, Dirac Medal and Prize, Int. Centre for Theoretical Physics, Trieste 2001, Pender Award, Moore School of Eng, Univ. of Pennsylvania 2002, Albert Einstein World Award of Science, World Cultural Council 2005, IEEE Rosenblatt Award 2009, Swarz Prize for Theoretical and Computational Neuroscience, Soc. for Neuroscience 2012, among others. *Achievements include:* most widely known for his invention of the associative neural network, the Hopfield Model 1982. *Publications:* more than 190 scientific papers in professional journals. *Address:* Lewis-Sigler Institute for Integrative Genomics, Princeton University, Carl Icahn Laboratory, Princeton, NJ 08544, USA (office). *Telephone:* (609) 258-1239 (office). *Fax:* (609) 258-7599 (office). *E-mail:* hopfield@princeton .edu (office). *Website:* genomics.princeton.edu/hopfield/Biography.html (office).

HOPKINS, Sir Anthony, Kt, CBE; American (b. British) actor; b. (Philip Anthony Hopkins), 31 Dec. 1937, Margam, Port Talbot, Wales; s. of Richard Hopkins and Muriel Hopkins; m. 1st Petronella Barker 1967 (divorced 1972); one d.; m. 2nd Jennifer Lynton 1973 (divorced 2002); m. 3rd Stella Arroyave 2003; ed Cowbridge Grammar School, S Wales, Welsh Coll. of Music and Drama, Cardiff, Royal Acad. of Dramatic Art; mil. training and service: clerk Royal Artillery Unit, Bulford 1958–60; joined Manchester Library Theatre, Asst Stage Man. 1960; then at Nottingham Repertory Co.; joined Phoenix Theatre, Leicester 1963; then Liverpool Playhouse, then Hornchurch Repertory Co.; joined Nat. Theatre Co. 1967; Film debut The Lion in Winter 1967; film, TV, stage actor in UK and USA 1967–, in USA 1974–84; Hon. RAM 1979; Hon. Fellow, St David's Coll., Lampeter 1992; BAFTA Fellowship 2008; Hon. DLitt (Univ. of Wales) 1988; Commdr, Ordre nat. des Arts et Lettres; US Film Advisory Bd Special Career Achievement Award for US Work 1994, BAFTA (US) Britannia Award for Outstanding Contrib. to the Int. Film and TV Industry 1995, Golden Globe Cecil B. DeMille Award 2006, and numerous others world-wide. *Stage appearances include:* title role in Macbeth, Nat. Theatre 1972, Dr Dysart in Equus, Plymouth Theatre, New York 1974, 1975, Huntingdon Hartford Theatre, Los Angeles (also Dir) 1977, Prospero in The Tempest, Los Angeles 1979, Old Times, New York 1983, The Lonely Road, Old Vic Theatre, London 1985, Pravda, Nat. Theatre Stage Actor of the Year, Soc. of West End Theatres Award, The Observer Award) 1985, King Lear (title role), Nat. Theatre 1986, Antony and Cleopatra (title role), Nat. Theatre 1987, M. Butterfly 1989, August (also Dir) 1994. *Films include:* The Lion in Winter 1967, The Looking Glass War 1967, Claudius in Hamlet 1969, When Eight Bells Toll 1969, Torvald in A Doll's House 1972, The Girl from Petrovka 1973, Juggernaut 1974, A Bridge Too Far 1976, Audrey Rose 1976, International Velvet 1977, Magic 1978, The Elephant Man 1979, A Change of Seasons 1980, Capt. Bligh in The Bounty 1983, The Good Father 1985, 84 Charing Cross Road (Best Actor, Moscow Film Festival) 1987, The Old Jest 1987, A Chorus of Disapproval 1988, The Tenth Man 1988, Desperate Hours 1989, The Silence of the Lambs (BAFTA Award and Acad. Award for Best Actor) 1990, Spotswood 1990, One Man's War 1990, Howard's End 1991, Freejack 1991, Bram Stoker's Dracula 1991, Chaplin 1992, The Trial 1992, The Innocent 1992, The Remains of the Day (BAFTA Award for Best Actor) 1992, Shadowlands 1993, Legends of the Fall 1993, The Road to Wellville 1993, August (also Dir) 1994, Nixon 1995, Surviving Picasso 1995, The Edge 1996, The Mask of Zorro 1997, Meet Joe Black 1998, Amistad 1998, Instinct 1999, Titus 1999, Mission Impossible 2, Hannibal 2001, Hearts in Atlantis 2001, The Devil and Daniel Webster 2001, Bad Company 2002, Red Dragon 2002, Human Stain 2003, Alexander 2004, Proof 2004, The World's Fastest Indian 2005, All the King's Men 2006, Bobby 2006, Slipstream 2007, Fracture 2007, Beowulf (voice) 2007, The City of Your Final Destination 2007, Where I Stand: The Hank Greenspun Story (documentary) (voice) 2008, Immutable Dream of Snow Lion (short) 2008, The City of Your Final Destination 2009, The Wolfman 2010, The Third Rule (short) 2010, You Will Meet a Tall Dark Stranger 2010, Bare Knuckles 2010, The Rite 2011, Thor 2011, 360 2011, Hitchcock 2012. *Television includes:* A Heritage and its History, A Company of Five 1968, The Three Sisters, The Peasants Revolt 1969, title roles in Dickens, Danton, Astrov in Uncle Vanya, Hearts and Flowers 1970, Pierre in War and Peace (BAFTA TV Actor Award 1972) 1971–72, title role in Lloyd George 1972, QB VII 1973, A Childhood Friend, Possessions, All Creatures Great and Small, The Arcata Promise 1974, Dark Victory, The Lindbergh Kidnapping Case (Emmy Award) 1975, Victory at Entebbe 1976, title role in Kean 1978, The Voyage of the Mayflower 1979, The Bunker (Emmy Award), Peter and Paul 1980, title role in Othello, Little Eyolf, The Hunchback of Notre Dame 1981, A Married Man 1982, Strangers and Brothers 1983, Old Times, The Arch of Triumph, Mussolini and I, Hollywood Wives, Guilty Conscience 1984, Blunt (role of Guy Burgess) 1987, Heartland 1989, Across the Lake (Donald Campbell) 1989, Great Expectations (Magwitch) 1989, To Be the Best 1990, A Few Selected Exits (Gwyn Thomas) 1993, Big Cats 1993, American Masters (series documentary) – Tony Bennett: The Music

Never Ends (narrator) 2007. *Leisure interests:* music, playing the piano, reading philosophy and European history. *Address:* c/o Creative Artists Agency, 2000 Avenue of the Stars, Los Angeles, CA 90067, USA; c/o The Peggy Thompson Office, 296 Sandycombe Road, Kew, Surrey, TW9 3NG, England (office). *Telephone:* (424) 288-2000. *Fax:* (424) 288-2900. *Website:* www.caa.com.

HOPKINS, Bernard; American professional middleweight boxer; b. 15 Jan. 1965, Philadelphia; ed Germantown High School; 95 victories and four defeats as an amateur; spent four years in jail for armed robbery when 17; turned professional on 11 Oct. 1988 (defeated by Clinton Mitchell); suffered second defeat versus Roy Jones, Jr, in world title bout on 22 May 1993; won Int. Boxing Fed. world title defeating Segundo Mercado on 29 April 1995; added World Boxing Council belt defeating Keith Holmes on 14 April 2001 and World Boxing Asscn title defeating Felix Trinidad on 29 Sept. 2001; undisputed middleweight champion of the world with 19 title defences (middleweight record), defeating Oscar de la Hoya on 19 Sept. 2004 in Las Vegas; light heavyweight champion of the world after defeating Antonio Tarver in Atlantic City on 10 June 2006; defeated Ronald Wright 2007, lost to Joe Calzaghe 2008, defeated Kelly Pavlik 2008, defeated Enrique Ornelas 2009, defeated Roy Jones Jr 2010, drew to Jean Pascal 2010; won 51 fights, including 32 knockouts, five defeats, two draws. *Address:* c/o Swanson Communications, 1025 Vermont Avenue, NW, Suite 1005, Washington, DC 20005, USA (office). *Telephone:* (202) 783-5500 (office). *Fax:* (202) 783-5516 (office). *E-mail:* contact@swansonpr.com (office). *Website:* www.swansonpr.com (office).

HOPKINS, Godfrey Thurston; British photojournalist and writer; b. 16 April 1913, London; s. of Sybil Beatrice Bately and Robert Thurston Hopkins; m. Grace Fyfe Robertson 1955; one s. one d.; ed Salesian RC School, Burwash, Sussex, Montpelier Coll., Brighton, Brighton Coll. of Art; trained as magazine illustrator, then as photographer; photographer with RAF Italy and N Africa 1939–45; freelance photographer in Europe 1946–49; mem. staff Picture Post, assignments world-wide 1949–57 and particular interest in aspects of British life; worked for London advertising agencies 1958–68; tutor, Studies in Photojournalism, Guildford School of Photography, W Surrey Coll. of Art and Design 1970–78; work in public collections including Victoria and Albert Museum, Arts Council, Museum of London, Metropolitan Museum of Art, New York, Helmut Gernsheim Collection, Switzerland, J. Paul Getty Museum, USA, Museum of Photographic Arts, San Diego, CA, USA, The Hulton-Getty Archive, London; Encyclopaedia Britannica Award (twice). *Publication:* Thurston Hopkins 1977. *Leisure interests:* painting, writing. *Address:* Wilmington Cottage, Wilmington Road, Seaford, East Sussex, BN25 2EH, England (home). *Telephone:* (1323) 897656 (home). *Fax:* (1323) 897656 (home). *E-mail:* gracerobertson@btinternet.com (home).

HOPKINS, Sir Michael John, Kt, CBE, RA, FRIBA; British architect; *Founding Partner, Hopkins Architects Partnership LLP;* b. 7 May 1935, Poole, Dorset; s. of the late Gerald Hopkins and Barbara Hopkins; m. Patricia Wainwright 1962; one s. two d.; ed Sherborne School, Architectural Asscn and RIBA; partnership with Norman Foster 1969–75; Founding Pnr, Michael Hopkins & Partners (now Hopkins Architects Partnership LLP), London 1976–; Consultant Architect, Victoria & Albert Museum 1985; Vice-Pres. Architectural Asscn 1987–93, Pres. 1997–99; mem. Royal Fine Art Comm. 1986–99; Trustee Thomas Cubitt Trust 1987–, British Museum 1993–; mem. RIBA Council, London Advisory Cttee to English Heritage, Architectural Advisory Group, Arts Council; Hon. mem. Bund Architekten; Hon. FAIA 1996; Hon. Fellow, Royal Incorporation of Architects of Scotland 1996; Hon. DLitt (Nottingham) 1995; Hon. DTech (London Guildhall); RIBA Award 1977, 1980, 1988, 1989, 1994, 1996; Civic Trust Award 1979, 1988, 1990, 1997; Financial Times Award 1980, 1982; Structural Steel Award, 1980, 1988; Royal Acad. Architectural Award 1982, co-winner (with wife Patricia Hopkins) RIBA Gold Medal for Architecture 1994. *Major works include:* Patera Bldg System 1984, Research Centre for Schlumberger, Cambridge 1984, Bicentenary Stand, Lord's Cricket Ground 1987, redevelopment of Bracken House for Ohbayashi Corpn 1987–91, R&D Centre, Solid State Logic 1988, Glyndebourne Opera House 1987–94, Portcullis House, Westminster 1989–2000, Westminster Underground Station 1990–99, The William Younger Centre 1990–99, Office Bldg for IBM at Bedfont Lakes, The Queen's Bldg, Emmanuel Coll., Cambridge 1993–95, Dynamic Earth, Edinburgh 1990–99, Jubilee Campus, Nottingham 1996–99, Saga Group Headquarters 1994–99, Hampshire Co. Cricket Club 1994–2001, Wildscreen @ Bristol 2,000 1996–99, Goodwood Racecourse 1997–2001, Haberdashers' Hall 1996–2002, The Forum, Norwich 1996–2001, Manchester City Art Gallery 1994–, Nat. Coll. of School Leadership, Nottingham 2000–02, London 2012 Velodrome 2011, Siemens Headquarters, Munich 2011, WWF-UK Headquarters, Woking 2013, Univ. of East London: Stratford Library 2013, Dubai Int. Finance Centre 2014, etc. *Leisure interests:* sailing, Catureglio, Blackheath. *Address:* Hopkins Architects, 27 Broadley Terrace, London, NW1 6LG (office); 49A Downshire Hill, London, NW3 1NX, England (home). *Telephone:* (20) 7724-1751 (office); (20) 7435-1109 (home). *Fax:* (20) 7723-0932 (office); (20) 7794-1494 (home). *E-mail:* mail@hopkins.co.uk (office). *Website:* www.hopkins.co.uk (office).

HOPKINS, Patricia (Patty) Anne, Lady Hopkins; British architect; *Partner, Hopkins Architects;* b. 7 April 1942, Staffs.; d. of Denys Wainwright; m. (now Sir) Michael Hopkins 1962; one s. one d.; ed Wycombe Abbey School, Architectural Asscn, London; Founding Pnr, Michael Hopkins and Pnrs (now Hopkins Architects) 1976–; Assessor for Civic Trust Award Schemes 1993–2000; Gov. Queen's Coll., Harley St 1998–; mem. Arts Council Nat. Lottery Advisory Bd 1994–99, Architectural Asscn 150 Campaign Bd 1994–99; Trustee Nat. Gallery, London 1998–; Hon. Fellow, Royal Inst. of Architects in Scotland 1996, American Inst. of Architects; Hon. DTech (London Guildhall) 1996. *Architectural works include:* Hopkins House, Hampstead (RIBA Award 1997) 1996, Hopkins Office, Marylebone 1985, Fleet Velmead School, Hants (RIBA Award, Civic Trust Award 1988) 1986, Victoria and Albert Museum (Consultant Architect and Masterplan) 1988, Glyndebourne Opera House (RIBA Award, Royal Fine Art Comm. Award 1994, Civic Trust Award, FT Award 1995) 1994, Queen's Bldg, Emmanuel Coll. Cambridge (RIBA Award, Royal Fine Art Comm. Award 1996) 1995, Jewish Care Home for the Elderly 1996, Preacher's Court, Charterhouse 2000, Wildscreen at Bristol (Civic Trust Award, DTLR Urban Design Award 2001) 2001, Manchester Art Gallery 2002, Haberdasher's Hall 2002. *Leisure interests:* family and friends at Catureglio and Blackheath. *Address:* Hopkins Architects, 27 Broadley Terrace,

London, NW1 6LG (office); 49A Downshire Hill, London, NW3 1NX, England (home). *Telephone:* (20) 7724-1751 (office); (20) 7794-1494 (home). *Fax:* (20) 7723-0932 (office); (20) 7794-1494 (home). *E-mail:* patty.h@hopkins.co.uk (office). *Website:* www.hopkins.co.uk (office).

HOPKINS, Paul Jeffrey, BA, PhD; American academic; *Founder and President, UMA Institute for Tibetan Studies;* b. 30 Sept. 1940, Providence, RI; s. of Charles E. Hopkins and Ora Adams; m. Elizabeth S. Napper 1983 (divorced 1989); ed public school in Barrington, RI, Pomfret School, Conn., Harvard Univ., Univ. of Wisconsin and Lamaist Buddhist Monastery of America; Asst Prof. of Religious Studies, Univ. of Virginia 1973–77, Assoc. Prof. 1977–89, Prof. 1989–2005, Prof. Emer. of Tibetan Buddhist Studies 2005–, Dir Center for South Asian Studies 1979–82, 1985–94; Founder and Pres. UMA Inst. for Tibetan Studies 1973–, Inst. for Asian Democracy 1994–; Visiting Prof., Univ. of British Columbia 1983–84; Yehan Numata Distinguished Visiting Prof. of Buddhist Studies, Univ. of Hawaii 1995; Chief Interpreter to Dalai Lama (q.v.) on overseas tours 1979–89, 1996; Fulbright Scholar, India and Germany 1971–72, India 1982, Taiwan 2002–03; Leverett Poetry Prize 1963. *Achievements include:* organized and directed the Nobel Peace Laureates Conf., Univ. of Virginia 1998. *Publications include:* Meditation on Emptiness 1973, Emptiness Yoga 1987, Fluent Tibetan 1993, Emptiness in the Mind-Only School of Buddhism 1999, Mountain Doctrine: Tibet's Fundamental Treatise on Other-Emptiness and the Buddha Matrix 2006; Tantric Techniques 2009; author or trans. of 43 other books, including 15 in collaboration with the Dalai Lama; more than 25 articles. *Leisure interests:* meditation, walking in woods, video, films. *Website:* uma-tibet.org (office); haa.ddbc.edu.tw (office).

HOPP, Dietmar, MS; German software industry executive; m.; two c.; ed Univ. of Karlsruhe; fmrly with IBM; co-f. SAP AG (software co.), CEO 1988–98, Chair. Supervisory Bd 1998–2003, mem. 2003–05; f. Dietmar Hopp Stiftung (charitable foundation) 1996. *Leisure interests:* beer, golf. *Address:* Dietmar Hopp Stiftung, Raiffeisenstraße 51, 68789 St Leon-Rot, Germany. *Telephone:* (6227) 8608550. *Fax:* (6227) 8608571. *E-mail:* info@dietmar-hopp-stiftung.de. *Website:* www .dietmar-hopp-stiftung.de.

HOPPE, Dominique; French international organization official; *President, Assemblée des fonctionnaires francophones des organisations internationales;* b. 24 Nov. 1959, Longwy; ed Lycée Alfred Mézières, Univ. of Nancy, Institut d'études politiques de Paris (Sciences Po), Stanford Univ. and Harvard Business School, USA; began career as int. civil servant at European Patent Office, Munich, Germany 1984, later Admin.; Vice-Pres. Asscn des Fonctionnaires Internationaux Français des Pays-Bas since its creation, Pres. 2006–07; Pres. Assemblée des fonctionnaires francophones des organisations internationales (French-speaking int. civil servants) 2007–; Pres. Cuperior Council of Int. Civil Servants in the Netherlands 2008–; mem. MENSA International 1994–; gives confs and courses on Management of Multicultural Environments at Harvard Business School and Sciences Po, Paris to several multilateral insts, including the UN, Int. Court of Justice, Int. Criminal Court, OPCW, European Space Agency, Europol and Eurojust, amongst others; elected, with Abdou Diouf, Francophone of the Year 2011. *Publications include:* articles in the French press for Le Monde and Le Post; technical reviews. *Address:* Assemblée des fonctionnaires francophones des organisations internationales, Sir Winston Churchilllaan 289F39, 2288 DB Rijswijk, Belgium (office). *E-mail:* affoimonde@gmail.com (office). *Website:* www .affoi.org (office).

HOPWOOD, Sir David Alan, Kt, MA, PhD, DSc, FRS, FIBiol; British geneticist and academic; *Fellow Emeritus, John Innes Centre;* b. 19 Aug. 1933, Kinver, Staffs., England; s. of Herbert Hopwood and Dora Grant; m. 1962 Joyce Lilian Bloom; two s. one d.; ed Purbrook Park County High School, Hants., Lymm Grammar School, Cheshire, St John's Coll., Cambridge; John Stothert Bye-Fellow, Magdalene Coll., Cambridge 1956–58, Research Fellow, St John's Coll. 1958–61, Univ. Demonstrator 1957–61; Lecturer in Genetics, Univ. of Glasgow 1961–68; Prof. of Genetics, Univ. of E Anglia, Norwich 1968–98, Prof. Emer. 1999–; Head of Genetics Dept, John Innes Centre 1968–98, Fellow Emer. 1999–; fmr Pres. Genetical Soc. of GB; Foreign Fellow, Indian Nat. Science Acad.; Pres. Soc. for Gen. Microbiology 2000–03; Hon. Prof., Chinese Acad. of Medical Science, Inst. of Microbiology and Plant Physiology, Chinese Acad. of Sciences, Huazhong Agricultural Univ., Wuhan, China, Jiaotong Univ., Shanghai, Guangxi Univ., Nanning; Hon. mem. Hungarian Acad. of Sciences, Soc. for Gen. Microbiology, Spanish Soc. of Microbiology; Hon. Fellow, UMIST, Magdalene Coll. Cambridge, St John's Coll. Cambridge; Dr hc (ETH), (Zurich), (Univ. of East Anglia), (Norwich), (Athens); Medal for Research in New Bioactive Compounds, Kitasato Inst. (Japan) 1988, Hoechst Award for Research in Antimicrobial Chemotherapy, American Soc. for Microbiology 1988, Chiron Biotech. Award, American Soc. for Microbiology 1992, Mendel Medal, Czech Acad. of Sciences 1995, Gabor Medal, Royal Soc. 1995, Stuart Mudd Prize Int. Union of Microbiological Sciences 2002, Ernst Chain Medal Imperial Coll., London 2003, Andre Lwoff Prize, Fed. of European Microbiology Socs 2003, Prize Lecturer, Soc. for Gen. Microbiology 2011. *Publications:* Genetics of Bacterial Diversity (co-ed. with K. F. Chater) 1989, Streptomyces in Nature and Medicine: The Antibiotic Makers 2007; 270 articles and chapters in scientific journals and books. *Leisure interests:* gardening, cooking, natural history. *Address:* John Innes Centre, Norwich Research Park, Colney, Norwich, NR4 7UH (office); 244 Unthank Road, Norwich, NR2 2AH, England (home). *Telephone:* (1603) 450000 (office). *Fax:* (1603) 450778 (office). *E-mail:* david.hopwood@jic.ac .uk (office). *Website:* www.jic.ac.uk/profile/david-hopwood.asp (office).

HOR, Nam Hong, LLB, ML; Cambodian diplomatist and politician; *Deputy Prime Minister and Minister of Foreign Affairs and International Co-operation;* b. 15 Nov. 1935, Phnom-Penh; m.; five c.; ed Univ. of Phnom-Penh, Univ. of Paris, L'Ecole Royale d'Admin, France; Embassy in Paris 1967–73; Amb. to Cuba 1973–75; Khmer Rouge prisoner 1975–79; Vice-Minister of Foreign Affairs 1980–82; Amb. to fmr USSR 1982–89; Minister of Foreign Affairs 1990–93; Amb. to France 1993–98; Minister of Foreign Affairs and Int. Co-operation 1998–, Deputy Prime Minister 2003–; mem. Nat. Ass. 1998–; mem. Supreme Nat. Council of Cambodia 1991–93; mem. Cambodian People's Party (CPP); Grand Officer of Monisaraphon, Grand Cross, Royal Order of Cambodia, Grand Collier, Royal Order of Cambodia, Grand Officer, Ordre nat. du Mérite, Grand Cross of the Most Exalted Order of the White Elephant (Thailand). *Leisure interests:* reading, swimming, gymnastics. *Address:* Ministry of Foreign Affairs and International Co-

operation, 3 rue Samdech Hun Sen, Khan Chamkarmon, Phnom-Penh, Cambodia (office). *Telephone:* (23) 214441 (office). *Fax:* (23) 216144 (office). *E-mail:* mfaicinfo@mfaic.gov.kh (office). *Website:* www.mfaic.gov.kh (office).

HORBULIN, VolodymyrVolodymyr Pavlovych, DTech; Ukrainian politician and space scientist; *President, Council for Foreign and Security Policy;* b. 17 Jan. 1939, Zaporozhya; ed Dnipropetrovsk State Univ.; with CB Yuzhnoye (Southern Design Bureau), Dnipropetrovsk 1962–77; mem. admin. staff, Cen. Cttee CP of Ukraine 1977–90, Chief of Missile and Aviation Section 1980; Gen. Dir Nat. Space Agency 1992; Sec. Nat. Security Council, Adviser to Pres. on nat. security issues 1994, Sec. Nat. Security and Defence Council 1996–99; Chair. State Comm. for Defence and Industrial Complex 2000–02; Asst to Pres. of Ukraine for Nat. N Security Issues 2002–03; Deputy Head of State Comm. for Reformation and Devt of Armed Forces of Ukraine 2003–05; Adviser to Pres. of Ukraine and Acting Head of Prin. Service of Defence Policy at Secr. of Pres. of Ukraine 2005–06; Sec., Nat. Security and Defence Council of Ukraine 2006; Adviser to Pres. of Ukraine 2006; Founder and Pres. Council for Foreign and Security Policy, Kiev 2009; fmr Head Ukraine-NATO Inter-Agency Comm.; mem. Ukrainian Nat. Acad. of Sciences 1997–; Order of Red Banner of Labour 1976, 1982, First Class Order of Yaroslav the Wise 1997; Ukrainian Nat. Acad. of Sciences Prize 1988, USSR State Prize 1990. *Publications include:* Road to Security: Ukrainian Fata Morgana (co-author) 2010. *Leisure interests:* music, literature, theatre. *Address:* Council for Foreign and Security Policy, 13 Chokolivsky blvd, Kiev 03186, Ukraine (office). *Telephone:* (44) 229-13-21 (office). *E-mail:* info@cfsp.org.ua (office). *Website:* www.cfsp.org.ua.

HORI, Kosuke; Japanese politician; mem. House of Reps 1979–; fmr Chair. LDP Diet Affairs Cttee; Parl. Vice-Minister for Agric., Forestry and Fisheries; fmr Minister for Educ.; Minister of Home Affairs, Chair. Nat. Public Safety Comm. 1999–2000; Chair. LDP Policy Research Council 2008–. *Address:* Liberal-Democratic Party (LDP) (Jiyu-Minshuto), 1-11-23, Nagata-cho, Chiyoda-ku, Tokyo 100-8910, Japan (office). *Telephone:* (3) 3581-6211 (office). *Fax:* (3) 5511-8855 (office). *E-mail:* koho@ldp.jimin.or.jp (office). *Website:* www.jimin.jp (office).

HORLOCK, Sir John Harold, Kt, ScD, FRS; British university administrator and engineer; b. 19 April 1928, Edmonton, Enfield, England; s. of Harold E. Horlock and Olive M. Horlock; m. Sheila J. Stutely 1953; one s. two d.; ed Latymer School, Edmonton and St John's Coll., Cambridge; design engineer, Rolls-Royce Ltd 1949–51; Demonstrator, Lecturer in Eng, Univ. of Cambridge 1952–58, Prof. of Eng 1967–74; Harrison Prof. of Mech. Eng, Univ. of Liverpool 1958–67; Vice-Chancellor, Univ. of Salford 1974–80, Open Univ. 1981–90; Fellow, Open Univ. 1991–; Treas. and Vice-Pres. Royal Soc. 1992–97; Pro-Chancellor UMIST 1995–2001; Pres. Asscn for Science Educ. 1999; Fellow, Royal Acad. of Eng; Hon. Fellow, UMIST, St John's Coll. Cambridge, Royal Aeronautical Soc. 2003; Hon. DSc (Heriot Watt, Salford, CNAA, East Asia, De Montfort, Cranfield); Hon. DEng (Liverpool), Hon. DUniv (Open Univ.); IMechE Hawksley Gold Medal, ASME R.T. Sawyer Award 1997, ICE Ewing Medal 2001, Isabe Achievement Award 2003. *Publications include:* Axial Flow Compressors 1958, Axial Flow Turbines 1967, Actuator Disc Theory 1978, Thermodynamics and Gas Dynamics of I.C. Engines (ed.) Vol. I 1982, Vol. II 1986, Cogeneration: Combined Heat and Power 1987, Combined Power Plants 1992, Advanced Gas Turbine Cycles 2003, An Open Book 2004, Energy–Resources, Utilisation and Policies 2009. *Leisure interests:* music, sport. *Address:* 2 The Avenue, Ampthill, Bedford, Beds., MK45 2NR, England. *Telephone:* (1525) 841307. *E-mail:* john.horlock1@btinternet.com.

HORN, Heinz, Dr rer. pol; German business executive; b. 17 Sept. 1930, Duisberg; s. of Heinrich and Elisabeth (née Eckernkamp) Horn; m.; two s. two d.; ed Univ. of Frankfurt, Univ. of Munster; fmrly with Mannesmann for six years; Financial Dir, Erschweiler Bergweks-Verein 1965–68, mem. Bd and later Pres. 1974–83; mem. Bd, Krupp 1968–72; Deputy Chair. of the Bd, Ruhrkohle AG, Essen 1983–85, Chair. Man. Bd 1985–95; Chair. Supervisory Bd Rütgerswerke AG, EBV 1989–95.

HORN, Paul M., PhD; American physicist, academic and electronics industry executive; *Senior Vice Provost for Research, New York University;* b. NY; ed Clarkson Coll. of Tech., Univ. of Rochester; trained as solid state physicist; Asst, then Assoc. Prof., Dept of Physics, James Franck Inst., Univ. of Chicago 1973–79; joined IBM Corpn 1979, various positions include Vice-Pres. and Lab. Dir of Almaden Research Centre, San Jose, Sr Vice-Pres. and Dir of Research 1996–2007; Distinguished Scientist in Residence, New York Univ. 2007–09, Sr Vice Provost for Research 2009–; fmr Assoc. Ed. Physical Review Letters; mem. Council on Competitiveness, Govt Univ. Industry Research Roundtable, Univ. of Calif., Berkeley Industrial Advisory Bd, Gallaudet Univ. Advisory Bd; Fellow, American Physical Soc., Grad. Fellow, Nat. Science Foundation; mem. Bd of Trustees, Clarkson Univ. 1998–, NY Hall of Science, Cttee for Econ. Devt; Alfred P. Sloan Research Fellowship 1974–78, Bertram Eugene Warren Award, American Crystallographic Asscn 1988, Distinguished Leadership Award, NY Hall of Science 2000, Hutchison Medal, Univ. of Rochester 2002, Pake Prize, American Physical Soc. 2002, Golden Kt Award, Clarkson Univ. 2004. *Publications:* over 85 scientific and technical papers. *Address:* Office of the Senior Vice Provost for Research, Bobst Library, 70 Washington Square South, 1224, New York, NY 10012, USA (office). *Telephone:* (212) 998-3228 (office). *Fax:* (212) 995-4121 (office). *E-mail:* paul.horn@nyu.edu (office). *Website:* www.research.ibm.com (office).

HORNBY, Andrew (Andy) H., MA, MBA; British business executive; b. 21 Dec. 1967, Scarborough, North Yorks.; m. Cathy Hornby; ed St Peter's Coll., Oxford, Harvard Business School, USA; worked for Boston Consulting Group for three years; held sr line man. posts with Blue Circle; worked at ASDA plc 1996–99, held posts of Dir of Corp. Devt, Retail Man. Dir, Man. Dir of George, ASDA's clothing business; Chief Exec. Halifax Retail 1999–2001, Chief Exec. Retail Div., HBOS plc (after merger between Halifax and Bank of Scotland) 2001–05, COO Retail Div. 2005–06, Chief Exec. HBOS plc 2006–08 (resgnd); Group Chief Exec. Alliance Boots 2009–11; Dir (non-exec.) GUS/Home Retail Group 2002–09. *Address:* c/o Alliance Boots GmbH, Baarerstrasse 78, 6300 Zug, Switzerland; c/o Boots UK, 1 Thane Road West, Nottingham, Notts., NG2 3AA, England. *E-mail:* enquiries@ allianceboots.com.

HORNBY, Nick; British journalist and novelist; b. 1957, London; William Hill Sports Book of the Year Award 1992, Writers' Guild Best Fiction Book Award 1995, American Acad. of Arts and Letters E. M. Forster Award 1999, WHSmith Fiction

Award 2002, London Award 2003. *Recordings:* wrote lyrics for Ben Folds album, Lonely Avenue 2010. *Publications:* Contemporary American Fiction (essays) 1992, Fever Pitch (memoir) 1992, (screenplay) 1997, My Favourite Year: A Collection of New Football Writing (ed.) 1993, High Fidelity (novel) 1995, Speaking With the Angel (ed.) 2000, About a Boy (novel) 2000, How to be Good (novel) 2001, 31 Songs (non-fiction) 2003, A Long Way Down 2005, The Complete Polysyllabic Spree (collected columns) 2006, Slam (juvenile fiction) 2007, Juliet, Naked 2009, More Baths, Less Talking (non-fiction) 2012; contrib. to Sunday Times, TLS, Literary Review, New York Times, New Yorker, the Believer. *Address:* United Agents, 12–26 Lexington Street, London, W1F 0LE, England (office). *Telephone:* (20) 3214-0800 (office). *Fax:* (20) 3214-0801 (office). *E-mail:* info@unitedagents.co.uk (office). *Website:* unitedagents.co.uk (office).

HORNE, Marilyn; American singer (mezzo-soprano); b. 16 Jan. 1934, Bradford, Pa; d. of Bentz Horne and Berneice Horne; m. 1st Henry Lewis (divorced); one d.; ed Univ. of Southern California with William Vennard; debut as Hata in The Bartered Bride, Guild Opera Co. 1954; performed with several German opera cos in Europe 1956; has since appeared at Covent Garden, London, San Francisco Opera, Chicago Lyric Opera, La Scala, Milan, Metropolitan Opera, New York; repertoire includes Eboli in Don Carlo, Marie in Wozzeck, Adalgisa in Norma, Jane Seymour in Anna Bolena, Amneris in Aida, Carmen, Rosina in Il Barbiere di Siviglia, Fidès in Le Prophète, Mignon, Isabella in L'Italiana in Algeri, Romeo in I Capuletti ed i Montecchi, Tancredi in Tancredi, Orlando in Orlando Furioso, Malcolm in La Donna del Lago, Calbo in Maometto II; retd from singing 1999, with galas in New York and San Francisco 1998; f. Marilyn Horne Foundation to coach and encourage young singers 1993; mem. Faculty, Music Acad. of the West 1995–, Dir Voice Program 1997–; Fellow, American Acad. of Arts and Sciences 2009–; numerous hon. doctorates, including Hon. DMus (Univ. of Pittsburgh) 2005; Nat. Medal of Arts 1992, Kennedy Center Honor 1995, Musical American Musician of the Year 1995, Classic FM Gramophone Award for Lifetime Achievement 2005, Opera News Award 2008, Nat. Endowment for the Arts Opera Award 2009. *Publications:* My Life (autobiog., with Jane Scovell), The Song Continues (autobiog., with Jane Scovell) 2005. *Leisure interests:* needlepoint, swimming, reading, sightseeing. *Address:* Voice Program, Music Academy of the West, 1070 Fairway Road, Santa Barbara, CA 93108, USA (office). *E-mail:* info@musicacademy.org (office). *Website:* www.musicacademy.org (office).

HORNER, Christian, OBE; British sports executive and fmr racing car driver; *Team Principal, Red Bull Racing;* b. 16 Nov. 1973, Leamington Spa, Warwicks.; began career in motorsport after winning a Formula Renault scholarship 1991; competed in British Formula Renault Championship with Manor Motorsport 1992, finished season as a race winner and highest placed rookie; moved up to British Formula Three, debut with the Fortec team 1994; moved to Alan Docking Racing team 1995, to TOM'S team 1996; also raced in British Formula Two 1996; moved up to Formula 3000 and f. Arden team 1997, Team Prin. for GP2 Series team Arden Motorsport; stayed in F3000 for 1998, retired from active racing at end of season; continued with team in F3000 as the owner, signed Viktor Maslov and Marc Goossens for 1999 season, signed Tomáš Enge and Björn Wirdheim 2002, Enge replaced by Townsend Bell, Wirdheim won title 2003; won both drivers' and constructors' championship titles in F3000 with Vitantonio Liuzzi and Robert Doornbos 2004; was brought into Formula One by Red Bull Racing team (youngest of team prins 2005), team's first podium finish at Monaco Grand Prix 2006, currently Team Prin. for Red Bull Racing, team won Constructors' Championship 2010, 2011, 2012. *Address:* Red Bull Racing, Bradbourne Drive, Tilbrook, Milton Keynes, Bucks., MK7 8BJ, England (office). *E-mail:* info@redbullracing.com (office). *Website:* www.redbullracing.com (office).

HORNER, James; American film music composer; b. 14 Aug. 1953, Los Angeles, Calif.; ed Royal Coll. of Music, London, Univ. of S Carolina, Univ. of Calif. at Los Angeles. *Film scores include:* The Lady in Red, Battle Beyond the Stars, Humanoids from the Deep, Deadly Blessing, The Hand, Wolfen, The Pursuit of D. B. Cooper, 48 Hours, Star Trek II: The Wrath of Khan, Something Wicked This Way Comes, Krull, Brainstorm, Testament, Gorky Park, The Dresser, Uncommon Valor, The Stone Boy, Star Trek III: The Search for Spock, Heaven Help Us, Cocoon, Volunteers, Journey of Natty Gann, Commando, Aliens, Where the River Runs Black, The Name of the Rose, An American Tail (Grammy Award for song Somewhere Out There), P.K. and the Kid, Project X, Batteries Not Included, Willow, Red Heat, Vibes, Cocoon: The Return, The Land Before Time, Field of Dreams, Honey I Shrunk the Kids, Dad, Glory (Grammy Award for instrumental composition), I Love You to Death, Another 48 Hours, Once Around, My Heroes Have Always Been Cowboys, Class Action, The Rocketeer, An American Tail: Fievel Goes West, Thunderheart, Patriot Games, Unlawful Entry, Sneakers, Swing Kids, A Far Off Place, Jack the Bear, Once Upon a Forest, Searching for Bobby Fischer, The Man Without a Face, Bopha!, The Pelican Brief, Clear and Present Danger, Legend of the Fall, Braveheart, Casper, Apollo 13, Jumanji, Courage Under Fire, Ransom, To Gillian on Her 37th Birthday, Titanic (Acad. Award, Grammy Award), Mighty Joe Young, The Mask of Zorro, Deep Impact, Perfect Storm, A Beautiful Mind, The Chumscrubber 2005, House of Sand and Fog, Troy, The Forgotten, All the King's Men 2006, The Boy in the Striped Pyjamas 2008, The Amazing Spider-Man 2012. *Address:* c/o Gorfaine Schwartz Agency, 13245 Riverside Drive, Suite 450, Sherman Oaks, CA 91423, USA.

HORNHUES, Karl-Heinz, Dr rer. pol; German international organization official and fmr politician; *Honorary President, Deutsche Afrika Stiftung e.V.;* b. 10 June 1939, Stadtlohn; m. Ellen Buss 1965; two s.; ed Univ. of Münster; adviser, Catholic Adult Educ. Centre, Ludwig-Windthorst-Hause, Holthausen 1966–71, Dir 1970–71; Educ. and Teaching Dir Hofmann-La Roche AG, Grenzbach 1971; Assoc. Prof. of Social Econs and Political Science 1974, Prof. 1977; mem. Bundestag 1972–2002; Deputy Chair. of CDU/CSU Parl. Party in Bundestag in charge of foreign policy, defence policy and European affairs 1989–94; Chair. Foreign Affairs Cttee 1994–98; Chair. German Del., Ass. of WEU 1998–2002; Pres. Deutsche Afrika Stiftung e.V. (German Africa Foundation) 1987–2010, Hon. Pres. 2010–; Kommendeurkreuz 1999. *Address:* Deutsche Afrika Stiftung e.V., Ziegelstraße 30, 10117 Berlin, Germany (office). *Telephone:* (30) 28094727 (office). *Fax:* (30) 28094728 (office). *Website:* www.deutsche-afrika-stiftung.de (office).

HORNSBY, Claude (Chip) A. S.; American business executive; m. Lynn Hornsby, three c.; ed Virginia Polytechnic and State Univ.; joined Ferguson

Enterprises Inc. as man. trainee 1982 (bought by Wolseley PLC), Pres. and CEO 2001–05, CEO US Plumbing and Heating Div., Wolseley PLC, which incorporates Ferguson, Familian Northwest and US operations of Westburne, acquired in 2001, CEO, North America, Wolseley PLC 2005–09, mem. Bd of Dirs Wolseley PLC 2001–09, Group Chief Exec. 2006–09; Dir (non-exec.). Virginia Co. Bank; mem. Visitors Bd Christopher Newport Univ. 2001–; mem. Nat. Asscn of Wholesaler-Distributors (currently Chair.), Southern Wholesalers Asscn, American Supply Asscn, Virginia Tech. Pamplin Advisory Council; Rector for Christopher Newport Univ. *Address:* c/o Wolseley PLC, Parkview 1220, Arlington Business Park, Theale, West Berks., RG7 4GA, England. *Telephone:* (118) 929-8700. *Fax:* (118) 929-8701. *E-mail:* info@wolseley.com. *Website:* www.wolseley.com.

HOROVITZ, Joseph, MA, BMus, FRCM; British composer and conductor; *Professor of Composition, Royal College of Music;* b. 26 May 1926, Vienna, Austria; ed New Coll., Oxford and Royal Coll. of Music (RCM), London and studied with Nadia Boulanger, Paris; resident in UK 1938–; Music Dir Bristol Old Vic 1949–51; Conductor Festival Gardens Orchestra and open-air ballet, London 1951; Co-Conductor Ballets Russes, English season 1951–52; Assoc. Dir Intimate Opera Co. 1952–63; Asst Conductor Glyndebourne Opera 1956; Prof. of Composition, RCM 1961–; mem. Council, Composers' Guild 1970–, Performing Right Soc. 1969–96; Pres. Int. Council of Composers and Lyricists, Int. Fed. of Socs of Authors and Composers 1981–89; Cross of Honour for Science and Art, First Class (Austria) 2007; Commonwealth Medal Composition 1959, Leverhulme Music Research Award 1961, Gold Order of Merit of Vienna 1996, Nino Rota Prize (Italy) 2002, Cobbett Medal for services to chamber music, Worshipful Co. of Musicians 2008. *Compositions:* 12 ballets including Alice in Wonderland, Les Femmes d'Alger, Miss Carter Wore Pink, Concerto for Dancers; opera: Ninotchka; one-act operas: The Dumb Wife, Gentlemen's Island; concertos for violin, trumpet, jazz-piano (harpsichord), oboe, clarinet, bassoon, percussion, tuba; other orchestral works include Horizon Overture, Jubilee Serenade, Sinfonietta for Light Orchestra, Fantasia on a Theme of Couperin, Toy Symphony; brass band music includes a euphonium concerto, Sinfonietta, Ballet for Band, Concertino Classico, Theme and Co-operation, The Dong with a Luminous Nose; music for wind band includes a divertimento Bacchus on Blue Ridge, Windharp, Fête Galante, Commedia dell'Arte, Dance Suite and Ad Astra in commemoration of the Battle of Britain; choral music includes Samson, Captain Noah and his Floating Zoo (Ivor Novello Award for Best British Music for Children 1976), Summer Sunday, Endymion, Sing Unto the Lord a New Song, three choral songs from As You Like It; vocal music includes Lady Macbeth (mezzo-soprano and piano) and works for the King's Singers (e.g. Romance); chamber music includes five string quartets, oboe sonatina, oboe quartet and clarinet sonatina; contribs to Hoffnung Concerts: Metamorphoses on a Bed-Time Theme and Horrortorio for chorus, orchestra and soloists; numerous scores for theatre productions, films and TV series (Ivor Novello Award for Best TV Theme of 1978 for the series Lillie); productions of Son et Lumière include St Paul's Cathedral, Canterbury Cathedral, Brighton Pavilion, English Harbour, Antigua, Bodiam Castle, Chartwell. *Address:* Royal College of Music, Prince Consort Road, London, SW7 2BS, England (office). *Website:* www .rcm.ac.uk (office).

HORROCKS, Jane; British actress; b. 18 Jan. 1964, Lancs.; d. of John Horrocks and Barbara Horrocks; partner Nick Vivian; one s. one d.; ed Royal Acad. of Dramatic Art, London. *Stage appearances include:* The Rise and Fall of Little Voice, Cabaret, Absurd Person Singular 2007, The Good Soul of Szechuan 2008, Aunt Dan and Lemon 2009, Annie Get Your Gun 2009. *Films include:* The Dressmaker 1988, Getting It Right 1989, The Wolves of Willoughby Chase 1989, The Witches 1990, Memphis Belle 1990, Life is Sweet (Best Supporting Actress, LA Critics Award) 1990, Deadly Advice 1994, Second Best 1994, Some Kind of Life 1995, Combination Skin (short) (voice) 1996, Bring Me the Head of Mavis Davis 1997, Little Voice 1998, Faeries (voice) 1999, Lion of Oz (voice) 2000, Discover Spot (video) (voice) 2000, Chicken Run (voice) 2000, Born Romantic 2000, Christmas Carol: The Movie 2001, Last Rumba in Rochdale (short) 2002, Wheeling Dealing (short) 2004, Look I'm Talking (video short) 2005, Corpse Bride (voice) 2005, Brothers of the Head 2005, Garfield 2 (voice) 2006, Tinker Bell (video) (voice) 2008, Tinker Bell and the Lost Treasure (voice) 2009, Tinker Bell and the Mysterious Winter Woods 2010, The Itch of the Golden Nit (short) (voice) 2011, Sunshine on Leith 2012. *Television includes:* Screenplay (series) 1987–92, First Sight (series) 1987, The Storyteller (series) 1988, The Ruth Rendell Mysteries (series) 1988, The Fifteen Streets (film) 1989, Heartland (film) 1989, The Jim Henson Hour (series) 1989, Victoria Wood (series) 1989, Smith & Jones (series) 1990, Boon (series) 1990, Came Out, It Rained, Went Back in Again (film) 1991, Screen One (series) 1991, Nona (film) 1991, Red Dwarf (series) 1992, Absolutely Fabulous 1992–2012, Bad Girl 1992, Roots (film) 1992, Cabaret (film) 1993, Suffer the Little Children (film) (Royal TV Soc. Award) 1994, Butter (short) 1994, Self Catering (film) 1994, Performance (series) 1995, Crapston Villas (series) 1995–98, Nightlife (film) 1996, Tales from the Crypt (series) 1996, Never Mind the Horrocks (special) 1996, Wyrd Sisters (mini-series) 1997, The Blobs (series) 1997, Hunting Venus (film) 1999, Foxbusters (series) 1999, The Flint Street Nativity (film) 1999, Hooves of Fire (short) 1999, Watership Down (series) 1999–2000, Mirrorball 2000, Little Big Mouth (series) 2001, Ivor the Invisible (film) 2001, Linda Green (series) 2002, Legend of the Lost Tribe (short) 2002, Monkey Trousers (film) 2004, Who Do You Think You Are 2005, Happy Birthday, Peter Pan (special documentary) 2005, Jericho (series) 2005, Fifi and the Flowertots (series) 2005–06, The Street (series) 2006, Little Princess (series) 2006, The Amazing Mrs Pritchard (series) 2006, Robbie the Reindeer in Close Encounters of the Herd Kind (short) 2007, Gracie! (film) 2009, The Road to Coronation Street (film) 2010, Coming Up (series) 2011, This is Jinsy (series) 2011, Trollied (series) 2011, True Love (series) 2012, Trollied 2011–13. *Address:* c/o United Agents, 12–26 Lexington Street, London, W1F 0LE, England (office). *Telephone:* (20) 3214-0800 (office). *Fax:* (20) 3214-0801 (office). *E-mail:* info@unitedagents.co.uk (office). *Website:* www.unitedagents.co.uk (office).

HORTA-OSÓRIO, António, MBA; Portuguese banking executive and academic; *Group Chief Executive, Lloyds Banking Group;* m.; three c.; ed Universidade Católica Portuguesa, Institut Européen d'Admin des Affaires (INSEAD), France, Harvard Business School, USA; began career at Citibank Portugal, later Head of Capital Markets; also Asst Prof., Universidade Catolica Portuguesa; then worked for Goldman Sachs in New York and London; joined Grupo Santander as Chief

Exec. Banco Santander de Negocios Portugal 1993, later CEO Banco Santander Brazil –2000, CEO Santander Totta 2000–06, Chair. 2006–11, also Exec. Vice-Pres. Grupo Santander and mem. Man. Cttee, Dir (non-exec.) Santander UK 2004–10, Chief Exec. 2006–10; Exec. Dir Lloyds Banking Group plc Jan. 2011–, Group Chief Exec. March 2011–; fmr Dir (non-exec.) Court of the Bank of England; Henry Ford II Prize, INSEAD. *Leisure interests:* tennis, scuba diving. *Address:* Lloyds Banking Group plc, 25 Gresham Street, London, EC2V 7HN, England (office). *Telephone:* (20) 7626-1500 (office). *Fax:* (20) 7356-2049 (office). *E-mail:* info@lloydsbankinggroup.com (office). *Website:* www.lloydsbankinggroup.com (office).

HORTEFEUX, Brice, LenD; French politician; b. 11 May 1958, Neuilly-sur-Seine; s. of Claude Hortefeux and Marie-Claude Hortefeux (née Schuhler); m. Valérie Dazzan 2000; three c.; ed Inst. of Political Studies, Paris, Univ. Paris X–Nanterre; Territorial Admin. 1986–94; mem. Regional Council, Auvergne 1992–2007; Chief of Cabinet of Minister for Budget and Communications 1993–95; Govt Spokesperson 1993–95; fmr mem. Political Cttee Rassemblement pour la République 1998–2002; currently mem. Union pour un Mouvement Populaire (UMP), mem. Political Cttee 2002–; MEP 1999–2005; Adviser to Minister of Interior and Security, later to Minister of Finance, Economy and Industry 2002–04; Minister-Del. for Territorial Collectivities 2005–07; Minister of Immigration, Integration, Nat. Identity and Co-Devt 2007–09, of Labour, Social Relations, the Family, Solidarity and Urban Affairs 2009, of the Interior, the Overseas Possessions and Territorial Collectivities and of Immigration 2009–11. *Publication:* Jardin à la française, plaidoyer pour une république de proximité 2003. *Leisure interest:* tennis. *Address:* c/o Ministry of the Interior, the Overseas Possessions and Territorial Collectivities and of Immigration, place Beauvau, 75008 Paris, France.

HORTON, Donald R.; American real estate executive; *Chairman, D. R. Horton Inc.;* m. Marty Horton; two s.; ed Univ. of Cen. Ark., Univ. of Okla.; took over father's Marshall, Ark. real estate business 1971; f. D. R. Horton Inc., Fort Worth, Tex. 1978, Pres. 1991–98, Chair. 1991–; Distinguished Alumni Award, Univ. of Cen. Ark. 2004. *Address:* D.R. Horton, Inc., 301 Commerce Street, Suite 500, Fort Worth, TX 76102, USA (office). *Telephone:* (817) 390-8200 (office). *Fax:* (817) 436-6717 (office). *Website:* www.drhorton.com (office).

HORTON, Frank Elba, MS, PhD; American academic and university administrator; *President Emeritus, University of Toledo;* b. 19 Aug. 1939, Chicago; s. of Elba E. Horton and Mae P. Prohaska; m. Nancy Yocom 1960; four d.; ed Western Illinois and Northwestern Univs; mem. Faculty, Univ. of Iowa 1966–75, Prof. of Geography 1966–75, Dir Inst. of Urban and Regional Research 1968–72, Dean of Advanced Studies 1972–75; Vice-Pres. for Acad. Affairs and Research, Southern Illinois Univ. 1975–80; Chancellor Univ. of Wisconsin, Milwaukee 1980–85; Pres. Univ. of Oklahoma 1985–88; Pres. Emer. 1999–; Prin. Horton and Assocs 1999–; Trustee Toledo Symphony Orchestra 1989–, Toledo Hosp. 1989–, Public Broadcasting Foundation, NW Ohio 1989–93, Soc. Bank and Trust 1990–; Vice-Chair. Toledo Chamber of Commerce 1991–93; mem. Bd Dirs Inter-State Bakeries, GAC Corpn; Interim Pres. Southern Illinois Univ. 2001; Interim Dean School of Biological Sciences, Univ. of Missouri 2002–03, Exec. Consultant to the Provost, Univ. of Missouri, Kansas City 2003–04. *Publications:* Geographic Perspectives on Urban Systems with Integrated Readings (with B. J. L. Berry) 1970, Urban Environmental Management Planning for Pollution Control 1974. *Leisure interests:* hiking, skiing, golf, jogging. *Address:* Horton & Associates, 13171 East Saddlerock Road, Tucson, AZ 85749 (office); 288 River Ranch Circle, Bayfield, CO 81122, USA (home). *Telephone:* (970) 884-2102 (office); (970) 884-2102 (home). *E-mail:* fehorton@attglobal.net (office).

HORTON, Richard C., BSc, MB, FRCP, FMedSci; British physician; *Editor, The Lancet;* b. 29 Dec. 1961, London; ed Univ. of Birmingham; Visiting Prof., London School of Hygiene and Tropical Medicine; Asst Ed., The Lancet (medical journal) 1990, North American Ed. 1993, Ed. 1995–; Chair. Royal Coll. of Physicians' Working Party on Physicians and Pharmaceutical Industry; Pres. US Council of Science Editors 2005–06; Bd mem. Health Metrics Network; Hon. Prof., London School of Hygiene and Tropical Medicine, Univ. Coll. London, Univ. of Edinburgh; Edinburgh Medal for professional achievements 2007. *Publications include:* non-fiction: Preventing Coronary Artery Disease (with Martin Kendall) 1997, How to Publish in Biomedicine 1997, Second Opinion: Doctors and Diseases 2003, Health Wars: On the Global Front Lines of Modern Medicine 2003, MMR: Science and Fiction 2004; contrib. to New York Review of Books, London Review of Books, The Lancet, journals. *Address:* The Lancet, 32 Jamestown Road, London, NW1 7BY, England (office). *Telephone:* (20) 7424-4910 (office). *Fax:* (20) 7424-4911 (office). *E-mail:* richard.horton@lancet.com (office). *Website:* www.lancet.com (office).

HORTON, Thomas W., BBA, MBA; American business executive; *Chairman, American Airlines Group, Inc. and American Airlines;* b. Hampton, Va; ed Baylor Univ., Cox School of Business, Southern Methodist Univ.; joined AMR Corpn (parent co. of American Airlines) 1985, held several sr financial positions, including Vice-Pres. and Controller, Vice-Pres. responsible for airline's Europe business, based in London, UK 1998–2000, Sr Vice-Pres. and Chief Financial Officer (CFO) AMR 2000–06, Exec. Vice-Pres., Finance and Planning, and CFO AMR and American Airlines 2006–10, Pres. AMR Corpn and American Airlines 2010–13, Chair. and CEO 2011–13, Chair. American Airlines Group, Inc. (following merger with US Airways Group) and American Airlines 2013–; joined AT&T Corpn as CFO 2002, Vice-Chair. and CFO –2006; Chair. oneworld® Alliance; mem. Bd of Dirs Qualcomm, Inc.; mem. Exec. Bd Cox School of Business, Southern Methodist Univ. *Address:* American Airlines Group, Inc., PO Box 619616, DFW Airport, TX 75261-9616 (office); American Airlines Group, Inc., 4333 Amon Carter Boulevard, Fort Worth, TX 76155, USA (office). *Telephone:* (817) 963-1234 (office). *Fax:* (817) 967-9641 (office). *E-mail:* info@aa.com (office). *Website:* www.aa.com (office).

HORVITZ, H. Robert, MA, PhD; American biologist and academic; *David H. Koch Professor of Biology, Massachusetts Institute of Technology;* b. 8 May 1947; ed Harvard Univ.; Asst Prof. of Biology, MIT 1978, Assoc. Prof. 1981, Prof. 1986–, now David H. Koch Prof.; Investigator, Howard Hughes Medical Inst. 1988–; also currently Neurobiologist and Geneticist, Mass Gen. Hosp., Boston; mem. NAS

1991–, Inst. of Medicine; Fellow, American Acad. of Arts and Sciences, American Acad. of Microbiology; numerous awards and honours including Spencer Award in Neurobiology 1986, US Steel Foundation Award in Molecular Biology 1988, Hans Sigrist Award 1994, Gairdner Foundation Int. Award 1999, Segerfalk Award 2000, Bristol-Myers Squibb Award for Distinguished Achievement in Neuroscience 2001, Genetics Soc. of America Award 2001, Nobel Prize in Physiology or Medicine (jtly) 2002. *Address:* Department of Biology, Room 68-425, Massachusetts Institute of Technology, 77 Massachusetts Avenue, Cambridge, MA 02139, USA (office). *Telephone:* (617) 253-4671 (office). *Fax:* (617) 253-8126 (office). *E-mail:* horvitz@mit .edu (office). *Website:* web.mit.edu/biology/www/facultyareas/facresearch/horvitz .shtml (office); web.mit.edu/horvitz/www (office); www.hhmi.org/research/ investigators/horvitz_bio.html.

HORWICH, Arthur L., AB, MD; American biologist and academic; *Eugene Higgins Professor of Genetics and Pediatrics, Yale School of Medicine;* b. 1951, Oak Park, Ill.; ed Brown Univ.; postdoctoral research, Salk Inst. for Biological Studies, La Jolla, Calif.; Intern and Resident, Pediatrics, Yale Univ. School of Medicine 1975–78, Postdoctoral Fellow 1981–84, apptd Asst Prof., Dept of Genetics 1984, currently Eugene Higgins Prof. of Genetics and Pediatrics; Investigator, Howard Hughes Medical Inst. 1990–; mem. NAS 2003; Hans Neurath Award, Protein Soc. 2001, Gairdner Int. Award 2004, Stein and Moore Award, Protein Soc. 2006, Wiley Prize in Biomedical Science 2007, Rosenstiel Award 2008, Louisa Gross Horwitz Prize 2008, Massry Prize, Keck School of Medicine, Univ. of Southern California 2011, Albert Lasker Basic Medical Research Award 2011, Shaw Prize 2012. *Publications:* numerous papers in professional journals. *Address:* Yale School of Medicine, 145 Boyer Center for Molecular Medicine, 295 Congress Avenue, New Haven, CT 06510, USA (office). *Telephone:* (203) 737-4431 (office). *Fax:* (203) 737-1761 (office). *E-mail:* arthur.horwich@yale.edu (office). *Website:* bbs.yale.edu/ people/arthur_horwich.profile (office); medicine.yale.edu/labs/horwich/www (office).

HOSEIN, Mainul, BA; Bangladeshi barrister, newspaper executive and politician; *Chairman, Editorial Board, The Daily Ittefaq;* b. Jan. 1940, Pirojpur (then Barisal) Dist; s. of the late Tafazzal Hossain; ed Dhaka Univ., studied law in London, UK; joined Middle Temple, London; called to Bar 1965; represented The Daily Ittefaq (f. by his father), Ed. 1969–73, Chair. Editorial Bd 1973–; mem. Commonwealth Press Union, London; practised law at Dhaka High Court 1965; mem. official del. to China on occasion of Nat. Day 1969; attended CPU Conf., Zimbabwe 1988; MP for village constituency at Bhandaria, Pirojpur (Barisal) 1973–75, resgnd in protest over changes to electoral system; Pres. Bangladesh Sangbadpatra Parishad (asscn of newspaper owners); mem. Press Council; Deputy Head Press Comm. 1984; Pres. Bangladesh Supreme Court Bar Asscn 2000–01; Hon. Adviser to Caretaker Govt, in charge of Ministry of Law, Justice and Parl. Affairs, of Parl. Secr., of Ministry of Housing and Public Works, of Ministry of Land and of Ministry of Information 2007–08. *Address:* The Daily Ittefaq, 1 Ramkrishna Mission Road, Dhaka, Bangladesh (office). *Telephone:* (2) 7122660 (office). *Fax:* (2) 7122651 (office). *E-mail:* rahat.khan@ittefaq.com (office). *Website:* www.ittefaq .com (office).

HOSKING, Geoffrey Alan, PhD, FBA, FRHistS; British historian and academic; *Professor Emeritus of Russian History, School of Slavonic and East European Studies, University College London;* b. 28 April 1942, Troon, Ayrshire, Scotland; s. of Stuart Hosking and Jean Smillie; m. Anne Lloyd Hirst 1970; two d.; ed Maidstone Grammar School, Moscow State Univ., Kings Coll., Cambridge, St Antony's Coll., Oxford; Lecturer in Govt, Univ. of Essex 1966–71, Lecturer in History 1972–76, Sr Lecturer and Reader in History 1976–84; Prof. of Russian History, School of Slavonic and East European Studies, Univ. Coll. London 1984–99, 2004–07, Prof. Emer. of Russian History 2007–, Leverhulme Research Prof. 1999–2004, Deputy Dir School of Slavonic and East European Studies 1996–98; Visiting Prof. in Political Science, Univ. of Wisconsin-Madison, USA 1971–72, Slavisches Institut, Univ. of Cologne, Germany 1980–81; mem. Inst. for Advanced Studies, Princeton, USA 2006–07; mem. Booker Prize Jury for Russian Fiction 1993; Dr hc (Russian Acad. of Sciences) 2000; LA Times History Book Prize 1986, US Ind. Publrs History Book Prize 2001, Alex Nove Book Prize 2008. *Radio:* BBC Reith Lectures 1988. *Publications include:* The Russian Constitutional Experiment 1973, Beyond Socialist Realism 1980, The First Socialist Society: A History of the Soviet Union from Within 1985, The Awakening of the Soviet Union 1990, The Road to Post-Communism: Independent Political Movements in the Soviet Union 1985–91 (with J. Aves and P. Duncan) 1992, Russia: People and Empire (1552–1917) 1997, Myths and Nationhood (co-ed. with George Schöpflin) 1997, Russian Nationalism Past and Present (co-ed. with Robert Service) 1998, Reinterpreting Russia (co-ed. with Robert Service) 1999, Russia and the Russians: A History 2001, Rulers and Victims: The Russians in the Soviet Union 2006, Trust: Money, Markets and Society 2010, Russian History: A Very Short Introduction 2012, Trust: A History 2014. *Leisure interests:* music, walking, chess. *Address:* School of Slavonic and East European Studies, University College London, Gower Street, London, WC1E 6BT (office); Flat 15, Julian Court, 150 Camden Road, London, NW1 9HU, England (home). *Telephone:* (20) 7267-5543 (home). *E-mail:* geoffreyhosking@mac.com (office).

HOSODA, Hiroyuki, LLB; Japanese politician; *Acting Executive Secretary-General;* b. 5 April 1944, Matsue City, Shimane Pref.; ed Faculty of Jurisprudence, Tokyo Univ.; joined Ministry of Int. Trade and Industry (MITI) 1967, Dir Price Policy Div., Industrial Policy Bureau 1985–86; Dir Washington Office, Japan Nat. Oil Corpn, USA 1983–85; elected mem. House of Reps for Shimane Constituency 1990–; Parl. Vice-Minister for Econ. Planning 1994–97; Dir Transport Div., Liberal Democratic Party (LDP) 1997–98, Dir Foreign Affairs Div. 1998–99, Deputy Sec.-Gen. LDP 2001, Dir-Gen. Election Bureau 2001–02, Sec.-Gen. 2008–09; Parl. Sec. for Int. Trade and Industry 1999–2001, currently Acting Exec. Deputy Sec.-Gen.; Minister of State for Okinawa and Northern Territories Affairs, for Science and Tech. Policy, and for Information Tech. Policy 2002–03; Deputy Chief Cabinet Sec. 2003; Minister of State for Gender Equality and Chief Cabinet Sec. 2004–05; currently Pres., Japan Contract Bridge League. *Leisure interests:* bridge. *Address:* Liberal-Democratic Party–LDP (Jiyu-Minshuto), 1-11-23, Nagata-cho, Chiyoda-ku, Tokyo 100–8910, Japan (office). *Telephone:* (3) 3581-6211 (office). *E-mail:* koho@ldp.jimin.or.jp (office). *Website:* www.jimin.jp (office).

HOSOI, Susumu; Japanese business executive; *Representative Director and President, Isuzu Motors Ltd;* joined Isuzu Motors Ltd 1973, has led operations in USA and Asia, has overseen divs including Corp. Planning, Finance, and Supplier Relations, Dir 2002, Vice-Pres. 2006, Exec. Vice-Pres. 2006–07, Pres. March 2007–. *Address:* Isuzu Motors Ltd, 26-1 Minami 6-chome, Shinagawa-ku, Tokyo 140-8722, Japan (office). *Telephone:* (3) 5471-1141 (office). *Fax:* (3) 5471-1043 (office). *E-mail:* info@isuzu.com (office). *Website:* www.isuzu.com (office).

HOSOKAWA, Morihiro; Japanese politician; b. 14 Jan. 1938, Tokyo; m. Kayoko Hosokawa; one s. two d.; ed Sophia Univ., Tokyo; reporter, The Daily Asahi Shimbun; mem. House of Councillors 1971–83; Gov. of Kumamoto 1983–91; Founder and Chair. Japan New Party 1992; mem. House of Reps 1993; Prime Minister 1993–94; fmr mem. LDP; retd from politics 1998; Chair. Eisei-Bunko Foundation. *Leisure interests:* pottery, skiing, golf.

HOSPITAL, Janette Turner, (Alex Juniper), MA; Australian/American writer and academic; *Carolina Distinguished Professor of English and Distinguished Writer-in-Residence, University of South Carolina;* b. 12 Nov. 1942, Melbourne, Vic.; d. of Adrian Charles Turner and Elsie Turner; m. Clifford Hospital 1965; one s. one d.; ed Univ. of Queensland and Queen's Univ., Canada; high school teacher, Queensland 1963–66; librarian, Harvard Univ. 1967–71; Lecturer in English, St Lawrence Coll., Kingston, Ont., in maximum and medium-security fed. penitentiaries for men 1971–82; professional writer 1982–; Writer-in-Residence and Lecturer, Writing Program, MIT 1985–86, 1987, 1989, Writer-in-Residence, Univ. of Ottawa, Canada 1987, Univ. of Sydney, Australia 1989, Queen's Univ. at Herstmonceux Castle, UK 1994; Adjunct Prof. of English, La Trobe Univ., Melbourne 1990–93; Visiting Fellow and Writer-in-Residence, Univ. of East Anglia, UK 1996; O'Connor Chair. in Literature, Colgate Univ., Hamilton, NY 1999; Carolina Distinguished Prof. of English and Distinguished Writer-in-Residence, Univ. of S Carolina 1999–; Hon. DUniv (Griffith Univ., Qld) 1995; Hon. DLitt (Univ. of Queensland) 2003; Gold Medal, Nat. Magazine Awards (Canada) 1991 (for travel writing), First Prize, Magazine Fiction, Foundation for the Advancement of Canadian Letters 1982, Patrick White Award for lifetime literary achievement (Australia) 2003. *Publications:* The Ivory Swing (Seal First Novel Award 1982) 1982, The Tiger in the Tiger Pit 1983, Borderline 1985, Charades 1988, The Last Magician 1992, Oyster 1996, Due Preparations for the Plague (Qld Premier's Literature Award 2003) 2003; short story collections: Dislocations (Fellowship of Australian Writers Fiction Award 1988) 1986, Isobars 1990, Collected Stories 1995, North of Nowhere, South of Loss 2003, Forecast: Turbulence (Steele Rudd Award for Best Collection of Short Stories, 2012) 2011; as Alex Juniper: A Very Proper Death 1991, Orpheus Lost 2007. *Leisure interests:* hiking, music, opera, gardening. *Address:* Department of English, University of South Carolina, Welsh Humanities Office Building, Room 504, Columbia, SC 29208, USA (office); c/o Barbara Mobbs, PO Box 126, Edgecliff, Sydney, NSW 2027, Australia; c/o Elaine Markson, Literary Agent, 44 Greenwich Avenue, New York, NY 10011, USA (office). *Telephone:* (803) 777-2186 (office). *E-mail:* hospitjt@mailbox.sc.edu (office). *Website:* artsandsciences.sc.edu/engl (office); www.janetteturnerhospital.com.

HOSS, Nina; German actress; b. 7 July 1975, Stuttgart; d. of Willi Hoss, co-founder German Green Party, and actress Heidemarie Rohweder; ed Drama School 'Ernst Busch', Berlin; stage debut aged 14; first major success in title role of Bernd Eichinger's A Girl Called Rosemarie 1996; close collaboration with dir Christian Petzold; ensemble mem. Deutsches Theater, Berlin 1998–, appeared as Medea; mem. jury, Locarno Int. Film Festival 2009, Berlin Int. Film Festival 2011; Amb. of Terre des Femmes, fighting against female genital cutting, supports the Make Poverty History campaign; Shooting Stars Award, European Film Promotion at Berlin Int. Film Festival 2000. *Films include:* And Nobody Weeps for Me 1996, Feuerreiter 1998, Der Vulkan 1999, Naked 2002, Epstein's Night 2002, Something to Remind Me (Adolf Grimme Award) 2003, Wolfsburg (Adolf Grimme Award in Gold 2005) 2003, The White Massai (Bavarian Film Award for Best Actress 2005) 2005, Atomised 2006, Leben mit Hannah 2006, Yella (Silver Bear for Best Actress, Berlin Int. Film Festival 2007, German Film Award 2008) 2007, Das Herz ist ein dunkler Wald 2007, The Anarchist's Wife 2008, Jerichow 2008, We Are the Night 2010, Summer Window 2011, Barbara 2012. *Television includes:* The Girl Rosemarie (film) 1996, Liebe deine Nächste! 1998, Die Geiseln von Costa Rica (film) 2000, Toter Mann (film) 2001, Emilia Galotti (film) 2002, Leonce und Lena (film) 2003, Bloch (series) 2004, History (series) 2008, Kinotipp (series) 2008, Eine Frau in Berlin – Anonyma (series) 2010, Die Akte Kleist (film) (voice) 2011.

HOSS, Selim al-, MBA, PhD; Lebanese professor of economics and fmr politician; b. 20 Dec. 1929; s. of Ahmad El-Hoss and Wadad Hoss; m. Leila Hoss (died 1990); one d.; ed American Univ. of Beirut, Indiana Univ., USA; teacher, later Prof. of Business, American Univ. of Beirut 1955–69; Financial Adviser, Kuwait Fund for Arab Econ. Devt, Kuwait 1964–66; Pres. Banking Supervision Comm. 1967–73; Chair. and Gen. Man. Nat. Bank for Industrial Devt 1973–76; Prime Minister 1976–80, remaining as Prime Minister in caretaker capacity July–Oct. 1980, Minister of the Econ. and Trade and Information 1976–79, of Industry and Petroleum 1976–77, of Labour, Fine Arts and Educ. 1984–85 (resgnd); Adviser to Arab Monetary Fund, Abu Dhabi, UAE 1983; Chair. Banque Arabe et Int. d'Investissement, Paris 1982–85; Head, Arab Dinar Study Group, Arab Monetary Fund 1984–85; Minister of Educ. 1985–87; Head, Arab Experts Team commissioned by Arab League 1986–87; Prime Minister 1987–90, also Minister of Foreign and Expatriate Affairs; elected Deputy to Parl. 1992–2000; Pres. of Council of Ministers (Prime Minister of Lebanon) 1976–80, 1987–90, 1998–2000; mem. Bd of Trustees, American Univ. of Beirut 1991–; mem. Consultative Council, Int. Bank for the Middle East and North Africa 1992–; Higher Nat. Decoration of Lebanon; Jamal Abdul Nasser Award. *Publications:* The Development of Lebanon's Financial Markets 1974, Lebanon: Agony and Peace 1982 and 17 books in Arabic; numerous articles on econs and politics. *Leisure interest:* reading. *Address:* Aisha Bakkar, Beirut, Lebanon (office). *Telephone:* 736000 (office); 736001 (home). *Fax:* 354929 (office). *E-mail:* amirhamawi@salimelhoss.com (office). *Website:* www.salimelhoss.com (office).

HOSSAIN, Muzammel, MA, LLB, LLM; Bangladeshi lawyer, academic and judge; *Chief Justice, Supreme Court;* b. 17 Jan. 1948; s. of the late Alhaz Ahmed Hossain and of Asia Akther Khatun; ed Univ. of Dhaka, Sheffield Univ., UK; Advocate, Dist Court 1971, High Court Div., Supreme Court 1978, apptd Judge

1998, Judge of Appellate Div. 2009, Chief Justice of Supreme Court 2011–; Chair. Judicial Service Pay Comm. 2010; Lecturer, Faculty of Law, Univ. of Miadiguri, Nigeria; Prof. (part-time), City Law Coll., Dhanmandi Law Coll., Bhuiyan Acad., Dhaka. *Address:* Supreme Court of Bangladesh, Ramna, Dhaka 1000, Bangladesh (office). *Telephone:* (2) 9562941 (office). *Fax:* (2) 9565058 (office). *E-mail:* registrar@supremecourt.gov.bd (office). *Website:* www.supremecourt.gov.bd (office).

HOSSAIN, Shah Moazzem, MA; Bangladeshi politician; b. 10 Jan. 1939, Munsigonj Dist; m. Begum Saleha Hossain (died 2009); one s. one d.; ed Dhaka Univ.; Gen. Sec. East Pakistan Students League 1959–60, Pres. 1960–63; Chair. the All-Party Action Cttee 1962; political prisoner for several years between 1953 and 1978; Chief Whip, Bangladesh Parliament 1972–73; co-f. Democratic League 1976, Gen. Sec. 1977–83; Minister of Land Admin. and Land Revenue 1973–75, in charge of Ministry of Labour and Manpower 1984–85, of Information 1985–86, of Local Govt, Rural Devt and Co-operatives 1986–88, of Labour and Manpower 1988–90, of Food 1990; Deputy Prime Minister 1987–90; mem. Bangladesh Jatiyatabadi Dal (Bangladesh Nationalist Party). *Publication:* Nitta Keragarey 1976. *Address:* c/o Bangladesh Jatiyatabadi Dal (Bangladesh Nationalist Party), 28/1 Naya Paltan, VIP Rd, Dhaka 1000, Bangladesh.

HOSSAIN, Suhrab; Bangladeshi diplomatist; *High Commissioner to Pakistan;* ed Univ. of Dhaka; joined Foreign Service 1973, held numerous posts including Amb. to Uzbekistan, to Thailand, High Commr to Canada, also served in diplomatic missions in Bangkok, Birmingham, Dakar, Ottawa, Paris, High Commr to Pakistan 2010–. *Address:* Bangladesh High Commission, House No. 1, Street No. 5, F-6/3, Islamabad, Pakistan (office). *Telephone:* (51) 2279260 (office). *Fax:* (51) 2279266 (office). *E-mail:* bdhcisb@yahoo.com (office). *Website:* www.bdhcpk.org (office).

HOSSEIN, Robert; French actor and director; b. 30 Dec. 1927, Paris; s. of Amin Hossein and Anna Mincovschi; m. 1st Marina de Poliakoff 1955 (divorced); two s.; m. 2nd Caroline Eliacheff 1962 (divorced); one s.; m. 3rd Candice Patou 1976; one s.; stage actor, dir and playwright, film dir and producer, scriptwriter and actor; Chair. and Man. Dir Sinfonia Films 1963–; founder and Dir Théâtre Populaire de Reims and of Théâtre-Ecole de Reims 1971; Artistic Dir Théâtre de Paris-Théâtre Moderne 1975–, Théâtre Marigny 2000–08; Commdr, Ordre nat. du Mérite, Officier, Légion d'honneur, Commdr des Arts et des Lettres; Prix Orange 1963, Médaille de Vermeil de la Ville de Paris, Molière d'honneur 1995, Prix Grand siècle Laurent Perrir 2000. *Plays include:* La neige était sale, Haute surveillance, Les voyous (writer), La P. respectueuse, Huis-Clos, Vous qui nous jugez (writer), Les six hommes en question (co-writer with Frédéric Dard and producer), La moitié du plaisir (producer), Crime et châtiment, Les bas-fonds, Roméo et Juliette, Pour qui sonne le glas, La maison des otages, Hernani (produced for the Comédie Française) 1974, La maison de Bernada (produced at the Odéon) 1975, Le cuirassé Potemkine (dir at Palais des Sports) 1975, Des souris et des hommes, Shéhérazade (ballet) 1975, Procès de Jeanne d'Arc (producer) 1976, Pas d'orchidées pour Miss Blandish (producer and actor) 1977, Notre-Dame de Paris (producer) 1978, Le cauchemar de Bella Manningham (producer) 1978, Danton et Robespierre (producer) 1979, Lorna et Ted 1981, Un grand avocat 1983, Les brumes de Manchester 1986, Liberty or Death and the Heritage of the French Revolution (Dominique Prize for Best Dir) 1988, Dans la nuit la liberté (producer) 1989, Cyrano de Bergerac (producer) 1990, Jésus était son nom 1991, Les bas-fonds 1992, Je m'appelais Marie-Antoinette 1993, La nuit du crime (producer and actor) 1994, Angélique, Marquise des anges (director and actor) 1995, Ouragan sur le Caine 1997, La Vie en bleu 1997, Surtout ne coulez pas (producer) 1997, De Gaulle, celui qui a dit non (producer) 1999, Jésus, la Résurrection 2000, Coupable ou non coupable 2001, Lumières et ténèbres 2002. *Films include:* Quai des blondes, Du rififi chez les hommes, Crime et châtiment, Toi le venin (script-writer and producer), Le jeu de la vérité (writer), Le goût de la violence (script-writer and producer), Le repos du guerrier, Le vice et la vertu, Les yeux cernés, Angélique marquise des anges, Banco à Bangkok, Le vampire de Düsseldorf, Le tonnerre de Dieu, La seconde vérité, J'ai tué Raspoutine (writer and producer), Indomptable Angélique, Don Juan 1973, Prêtres interdits, Le protecteur, Le faux cul 1975, Les uns et les autres, Le professionnel 1981, Les Misérables (producer) 1982, Un homme nommé Jésus (director) 1983, Jules César 1985, Les brumes de Manchester 1986, Un homme et une femme, vingt ans déjà 1986, Les Enfants du désordre 1989, L'Affaire 1994, la Nuit du Crime 1994, L'Homme au masque de cire 1996, Vénus beauté 1999, Gialloparma 1999, San Antonio 2004. *Television includes:* Les Uns et les autres (miniseries) 1983, Le Juge (miniseries) 2005. *Publications:* La sentinelle aveugle 1978, Nomade sans tribu 1981, En désespoir de cause (memoirs) 1987, La Nostalgie (autobiog.) 2001. *Leisure interest:* skiing. *Address:* c/o Mme Ghislaine de Wing, 10 rue du Docteur Roux, 75015 Paris, France.

HOSSEINI, Sayed Shamseddin; Iranian politician; fmr Dir-Gen. for Econ. Studies, Ministry of Commerce; fmr Deputy Minister of Welfare and Social Security; Sec., Working Group for Econ. Transformation –2008; Minister of Econ. Affairs and Finance 2008–13. *Address:* c/o Ministry of Economic Affairs and Finance, Sour Esrafil Avenue, Nasser Khosrou Street, Tehran 11149-43661, Iran (office).

HOSSEINI, Seyed Safdar, BA, PhD; Iranian politician; b. 1954, Khuzestan; ed Shiraz Univ.; Minister of Labour and Social Affairs 2001–04; Minister of Econ. Affairs and Finance 2004–05. *Address:* c/o Ministry of Economic Affairs and Finance, Sour Esrafil Avenue, Nasser Khosrou Street, Tehran 11149-43661, Iran (office).

HOSTETTER, Amos Barr, Jr, BA, MBA; American media executive; *Chairman, Pilot House Associates, LLC;* b. 12 Jan. 1937, New York City; s. of Amos Barr Hostetter and Leola Hostetter (née Conroy); m.; three c.; ed Amherst Coll., Harvard Univ.; Asst to Vice-Pres. of Finance, American and Foreign Power Co., New York 1958–59; investment analyst, Cambridge (Mass.) Capital Corpn 1961–63; Co-founder and Exec. Vice-Pres. Continental Cablevision Inc., Boston, Mass 1963–80, Pres. and CEO 1980–85, Chair. and CEO (co. renamed MediaOne) 1985–96, CEO MediaOne Inc., Boston 1996–2000, returned as Bd mem.; Chair. AT&T Broadband and Internet Services (BIS) 1999–2003; Chair. Pilot House Assocs LLC 1997–; Founder and mem. Bd of Dirs and Exec. Cttee, Cable-Satellite Public Affairs Network (C-SPAN) 1979– (fmr Chair.); Founding Chair. and mem. Exec. Cttee, Cable in the Classroom; mem. Bd of Dirs Commodities Corpn,

Princeton, NJ, Corpn for Public Broadcasting, Washington, DC 1975–79, The Walter Kaitz Foundation 1981–; Corporator, Perkins School for the Blind, Watertown, Mass 1982–; mem. Bd Overseers Museum of Fine Arts, Boston 1987–; mem. Nat. Cable TV Asscn (Dir 1965–75, 1982–, Nat. Chair. 1973–74), Amherst Coll. Soc. of Alumni (Pres. 1982–84, Exec. Comm. 1982–, Chair. 1987–), Int. Radio and TV Soc.; Trustee, various mutual funds, Massachusetts Financial Services 1985–, Children's TV Workshop, New York 1980–, New England Medical Center Hosp., Boston 1981–, Nantucket Conservation Foundation 1986–, Amherst Coll. (Chair. –2005), WGBH-TV (currently Chair.), Colonial Williamsburg Foundation 2005–; named Cablevision Magazine Man of the Year 1972, Nat. Cable TV Asscn Larry Boggs Award 1975, named to Broadcasting magazine's Hall of Fame 1991, Cable Television Public Affairs Asscn Beacon Award 1991, Cable Television Admin and Marketing Soc. 'Grand TAM Award' 1993, Walter Kaitz Foundation Award 1993, Harvard Business School Alumni Achievement Award 1994, Mass Telecommunications Council Hall of Fame 2000. *Address:* Pilot House Assocs LLC, The Pilot House, Lewis Wharf, Boston, MA 02110, USA (office).

HOU, Hsiao-hsien; Taiwanese film director; b. 8 April 1947, Meihsien, Canton Prov.; ed Taipei Nat. Acad. of Arts Film and Drama Dept; worked as an electronic calculator salesman; entered film industry in 1973; asst to several directors from 1974; Chair. Asian Film Soc. *Films include:* Chiu shih liu-liu-te t'a (Cute Girl) 1981, Feng-erh t'i-t'a-ts'ai (Cheerful Wind) 1982, Tsai na ho-pan ch'ing-ts'ao-ch'ing (Green Grass of Home) 1982, Erh-tzu-te ta wan-ou (The Sandwich Man) 1983, Feng-kuei-lai-te jen (The Boys from Fengkuei/All the Youthful Days) 1983, Tung-tung-te chia-ch'i (A Summer at Grandpa's) 1984, T'ung-nien wang-shih (The Time to Live and the Time to Die) 1985, Lien-lien feng-ch'en (Dust in the Wind/Rite of Passage) 1986, Ni-lo-ho nü-erh (Daughter of the Nile) 1987, Pei-ch'ing ch'eng-shih (A City of Sadness) 1989 (winner of Golden Lion at the Venice Film Festival), Three Times 2005, Flight of the Red Balloon 2006.

HOU, Jianguo, BS, MS, PhD; Chinese chemist, academic and university administrator; *President, University of Science and Technology of China;* b. 29 Oct. 1959, Fujian; ed Univ. of Science and Technology of China; Visiting Scientist, Lab. of Electron Microscopy, Inst. of Crystallography, USSR Acad. of Sciences 1988; Post-doctor, Material Science Div., Lawrence Berkeley Lab. and Dept of Physics, Univ. of California at Berkeley, USA 1991–93; Research Assoc., Dept of Chemistry, Oregon State Univ., USA 1993–95; Prof., School of Science, Univ. of Science and Tech. of China 1995–, also Univ. Pres. 1999–; Vice-Pres. Hefei Nat. Lab. for Physical Sciences; mem. Chinese Acad. of Sciences 2003–; mem. 11th NPC Standing Cttee 2008–13; US Overseas Chinese Physics Asscn Achievement in Asia Award 2002 (co-winner), Holeung Ho Lee Advancement Prize 2007, Tan Kah Kee Science Prize in Chem. 2008. *Address:* Office of the President, University of Science and Technology, Hefei 230026, People's Republic of China (office). *Telephone:* (10) 82649026 (office). *Fax:* (10) 82649027 (office). *E-mail:* wlxbcp@aphy.iphy.ac.cn (office). *Website:* www.ustc.edu.cn/en (office).

HOU, Rick; Solomon Islands banker and politician; *Minister for Finance and Treasury;* b. (Rick Houenipwela), 8 Aug. 1958; with Central Bank of Solomon Islands 1983–2008, beginning as Internal Auditor, Gov. –2008; Chair. Solomon Airlines 2007–08; Sr Adviser to Exec. Dir, World Bank Group, Washington, DC 2008; MP (Democratic Party) for Small Malaita constituency 2010–, mem. Bills and Legislation Cttee, Public Accounts Cttee; Shadow Minister for Finance and the Treasury 2010; Minister for Public Service April–Nov. 2011, for Finance and Treasury Nov. 2011–. *Address:* Ministry of Finance and Treasury, POB 26, Honiara, Solomon Islands (office). *Telephone:* 24102 (office). *Fax:* 28619 (office). *E-mail:* psfinance@pmc.gov.sb (office).

HOU, Runyu; Chinese orchestral conductor; b. 6 Jan. 1945, Kunming; s. of Hou Zhu and Zhu Bangying; m. Su Jia 1971; one s. one d.; ed Music Middle School of Shanghai Conservatory, Shanghai Conservatory, Musikhochschule, Cologne, Germany and Mozarteum, Salzburg, Austria; started playing piano aged seven, debut, Kunming 1954; Prin. Conductor Shanghai Symphony Orchestra 1990; Headmaster, Xiamen Music School 2002–; debut Carnegie Hall, New York 1990; currently conductor, East China Normal Univ. (ECNU) Orchestra and Chair. Music Dept; Hon. mem. Richard Wagner Asscn, Cologne. *Leisure interests:* sport, literature. *Address:* 105 Hunan Road, Shanghai (office); RD. 1601 No. 12 Lane 125, Cao Xi Road, Shanghai, People's Republic of China. *Telephone:* (21) 64690942 (office); (21) 315234747 (home). *E-mail:* rhou@gmx.net (home).

HOU, Yifan; Chinese chess player; b. 27 Feb. 1994, Xinghua, Taizhou; d. of Hou Xuejian; ed Nat. Chess Centre, Beijing; started playing chess aged six; first major tournament at Chinese Team Chess Championship (Men's), Tianjin 2003; first Fédération Int. des Échecs (FIDE, World Chess Fed.) rating of 2168 2004; took part aged 12 in FIDE Women's World Championship, Yekaterinburg 2006 and Chess Olympiad, Turin 2006 (youngest ever player); China's youngest ever Nat. Women's Champion 2007; other titles include Woman FIDE Master 2004, Woman Grandmaster 2007, Int. Master 2008, Women's World Chess Champion (after winning Women's World Championship in Hatay, Turkey aged 16) 2010–; Best Sportsperson of the Year in China (non-Olympic category) 2011. *Address:* c/o FIDE Secretariat, 9 Siggrou Avenue, Athens, Greece.

HOU, Yunde, DMSc; Chinese virologist; b. 13 July 1929, Changzhou, Jiangsu Prov.; ed Tongji Univ. Medical Coll., Russian Inst. of Medical Sciences; Fellow Chinese Acad. of Eng; Dir Inst. of Virology, Chinese Acad. of Preventive Medicine 1985–; Dir WHO Virus Research Centre, researching para-influenza and the structure and function of virus gene; Vice-Pres. Chinese Acad. of Eng 1994–98; Dir Nat. Key Research Lab. for Virogenetic Eng 1998–; Dir Nat. Eng Research Center for Viral Bio-technology (NERC-VBT) 1998–; now Dir Inst. of Virology, Chinese Acad. of Preventive Medicine; Chair. Bd of Tri-Prime Gene 1998–; Assoc. Chief Ed. Chinese Medical Sciences Journal; 21 prizes including one First Prize and two Second Prizes of Nat. Science and Tech. Advancement Award, He Liang & He Li Medical Prize 1994, China Medical Science Award 1996. *Publications:* nine monographs and over 400 scientific treatises. *Address:* Virology Research Institute, Chinese Academy of Preventative Medical Science, 100 Yingxin Street, Xuanwu District, Beijing 100052, People's Republic of China (office). *Telephone:* (10) 63529224 (office). *Fax:* (10) 63532053 (office). *E-mail:* engach@mail.cae.ac.cn (office).

HOU, Zongbin; Chinese administrator; b. 1929, Nanhe Co., Hebei Prov.; one s. one d.; joined CCP 1946; Vice-Gov., Gansu Prov. 1983–88; Deputy Sec. of Gansu Prov. CP 1986–88; Deputy Sec. Shaanxi Prov. CP 1989–90; Gov. Shaanxi Prov. 1989–90; Sec. Henan Prov. CP 1990–92; a Deputy Sec. Cen. Comm. for Discipline Inspection; Chair. Internal Affairs and Judicial Cttee of 9th NPC 1998–2003; mem. 14th CCP Cen. Cttee 1992–97. *Address:* c/o Standing Committee of National People's Congress, Beijing, People's Republic of China.

HOUBEN, Francine M. J., MSc; Dutch architect, company director and academic; *Director of Mecanoo Architects and Professor in Architecture and Aesthetics of Mobility, Delft University of Technology;* b. 2 July 1955, Sittard; m.; one s. two d.; ed Delft Univ. of Tech.; Founding Partner, Döll-Houben-Steenhuis architecten 1980–84; Dir Mecanoo architecten, Delft 1984–; Prof. in Architecture and Aesthetics of Mobility, Delft Univ. of Tech. 2000–; Visiting Prof., Philadelphia Univ., USA 1990, Univ. of Calgary, Canada 1992, Berlage Inst., Amsterdam 1994, Univ. of Oxford, UK 1994, Università della Svizzera Italiana, Mendrisio, Switzerland 2000–01, Harvard Univ., USA 2007; Dir/Curator First Int. Architecture Biennale Rotterdam 1997–2000; columnist, Het Financieele Dagblad 2006–; mem. Bd Netherlands Architecture Inst. 1990–92, Int. Design Cttee, London, UK 1990–92, Fine Art, Design and Architecture Fund 1990–2006, Forum for Urban Renewal 2003–, Int. Film Festival, Rotterdam 2005–; mem. Supervisory Bd Kröller Museum, Otterlo 2005–; jury mem. for awards in Netherlands, Turkey, Germany, USA, UK, Canada; appeared in TV documentaries; Hon. FRIBA 2001, Hon. FRAIC 2007; numerous awards include Rotterdam-Maaskant Prize for Young Architects 1987, Nieuwe Maas Prize for Housing Hillekop, Rotterdam 1990, Berlagevlag Award for Offices for Gravura Lithographers, The Hague 1993, Auszeichnung Guter Bauten and Hugo Häring Prize Bund Deutscher Architekten for Experimental Housing Int. Gartenbau Ausstellung, Stuttgart, Germany 1993/1994, Jhr Victor de Stuerspenning for Herdenkingsplein housing project, Maastricht 1994, Scholenbouwprijs 1996, 2003, Nat. Staalprijs and Corus Construction Award for the Millennium for Library at Delft Tech. Univ. 1996/2000, Bouwkwaliteitsprijs, Rotterdam 2000, TECU Architecture Award and Dutch Building Prize for Nat. Museum of Heritage, Arnhem 2000/2003, Gezichtsbepalend 3 Culture Award Prov. of South Holland 2005, Building Quality Award for Montevideo Rotterdam 2006. *Publications include:* Mecanoo architecten (with P. Volland and L. Waaijers) 1998, Maliebaan, een huis om in te werken 2000, Composition, Contrast, Complexity 2001, Mobility – A Room with a View 2002. *Address:* Mecanoo architecten, Postbus 3277, 2601 DG Delft, Netherlands (office). *Telephone:* (15) 279-81-00 (office). *Fax:* (15) 279-81-11 (office). *E-mail:* francine .houben@mecanoo.nl (office). *Website:* www.mecanoo.nl (office).

HOUEIJ, Muhammad Ali al–; Libyan economist and politician; fmr oil economist, responsible for man. overseas investments; Sec. of the Gen. People's Cttee for Finance 2004–06, 2007–09; Asst Sec. of the Gen. People's Cttee (Deputy Prime Minister) 2006–07; Sec. for Industry, the Economy and Trade 2009–11. *Address:* c/o Secretariat for Industry, the Economy and Trade, PO 4779, Tripoli, Libya (office).

HOUELLEBECQ, Michel, DipAgr; French novelist, poet and film director; b. 26 Feb. 1958, Réunion; s. of René Thomas and Lucie Ceccaldi; m. 1st 1980 (divorced); one s.; m. 2nd Marie-Pierre Gauthier 1998; ed Institut Nat. Agronomique Paris-Grignon; fmr Admin. Sec., French Nat. Ass.; first works (poetry) published in Nouvelle Revue de Paris 1986; Grand Prix Nat. des Lettres Jeune Talent 1998. *Music:* Présence Humaine 2000. *Films include:* Cristal de souffrance 1978, Déséquilibres 1982, La rivière 2001, La Possibilité d'une île 2008. *Publications include:* H.P. Lovecraft (Contre le monde, contre la vie) 1991, Rester vivant 1991, La poursuite de bonheur (Prix Tristan Tzara) 1992, Extension du domaine à la lutte 1994, Le sens du combat (Prix de Flore) 1996, Interventions, Les Particules élémentaires (Prix Novembre, Int. Impac Dublin Literary Prize) 1998, Renaissance 1999, Lanzarote 2000, Plateforme 2002, La Possibilité d'une île (Prix Interallié) 2005, Ennemis Publics (with Bernard-Henri Lévy) 2008, La Carte et le Territoire (Prix Goncourt) 2010. *Address:* c/o Editions Flammarion, 1 place de l'Odéon, 75006 Paris, France.

HOUGH, Stephen Andrew Gill, CBE, MMus, GMus, FRNCM, PPRNCM; British pianist, composer and writer; b. 22 Nov. 1961, Heswall, Cheshire, England; ed Chetham's School of Music, Royal Northern Coll. of Music (RNCM) and Juilliard School, New York, USA; guest performer with Berlin Philharmonic, London Symphony, New York Philharmonic, Cleveland, Philadelphia, Los Angeles Philharmonic, Boston Symphony, NHK Symphony, Chicago Symphony, Philharmonia, Royal Philharmonic and London Philharmonic Orchestras; Visiting Prof., RAM; Int. Chair of Piano, RNCM; regular appearances with other orchestras and as recitalist in USA, Europe, Australia, Far East and at int. music festivals including Verbier, Salzburg, Aldeburgh, Edinburgh, BBC Proms, Mostly Mozart, Ravinia, Blossom, Tanglewood, Hollywood Bowl, La Roque d'Anthéron; regular blog for The Telegraph website; Hon. RAM; Hon. DMus; Dayas Gold Medal, RNCM, Terence Judd Award 1982, Naumburg Int. Piano Competition 1983, Gramophone Record of the Year 1996, 2002, MacArthur Foundation Fellowship 2001, Jean Gimbel Lane Prize 2007, Gramophone Gold Disc 2008, Royal Philharmonic Soc. Award for Best Instrumentalist 2010. *Compositions:* Transcriptions, Suite R-B and Other Enigmas, Piano Album, songs and choral works 2005, Viola Sonata 2000, Piano Pieces, The Loneliest Wilderness: Elegy for Cello and Orchestra 2005, Mass of Innocence and Experience 2006, Missa Mirabilis 2007, The Bible as Prayer 2007, Un Piccolo Sonatina, Threnody for Guitar, Three Grave Songs, Was mit den Tranen Geschieht: trio for flute or piccolo, bassoon or contrabassoon and piano, Herbstlieder for baritone and piano, Requiem Aeternum (after Victoria) for string sextet, Other Love Songs for SATB solo voices and piano duet, Sonata for piano (Broken Branches) 2011, Piano Sonata No. 2 (Notturno Luminoso), Bridgewater for bassoon and piano, Missa Mirabilis (orchestral version) 2012, Sonata for cello and piano (Les Adieux) 2013. *Recordings include:* complete Beethoven violin sonatas (with Robert Mann), Hummel piano concertos, recitals of Liszt and Schumann, Brahms concerto Nos 1 and 2, The Piano Album Vols I, II, Britten Music for One and Two Pianos, Scharwenka and Sauer concertos, Grieg, Liszt, Rubinstein cello sonatas (with Steven Isserlis), Brahms violin sonatas (with Robert Mann), York Bowen piano music, Franck piano music, Mompou piano music, Liebermann piano concertos, Mendelssohn piano and orchestral works, Schubert sonatas and New York Variations, Brahms clarinet trio, The New Piano

Album, Liszt sonata, Mozart piano and wind quintet, Brahms F minor sonata, Saint-Saëns Complete Music for Piano and Orchestra (Gramophone Gold Disc Award and CD of the Year), English Piano Album, Hummel piano sonatas, Chopin ballades and scherzos, Rachmaninov and Franck cello sonatas (with Steven Isserlis), Rachmaninov piano concertos (with Dallas Symphony and A. Litton) (Classical BRIT Critics' Award 2005, Classic FM Gramophone Editor's Choice Award 2005) 2004, Brahms, Dvořák and Suk 2005, Liszt Années de Pèlerinage (Suisse), Brahms cello sonatas with Stephen Isserlis, Children's Cello with Steven Isserlis, Beethoven and Mozart piano and wind quintets with the Berlin Philharmonic Wind Quintet, Stephen Hough's Spanish Album, Tsontakis Man of Sorrows, Brahms piano quintet with the Takacs Quartet, complete Tchaikovsky works for piano and orchestra with Minnesota Orchestra and Osmo Vanska, Stephen Hough in Recital, Chopin: Late Masterpieces, Chopin Complete Waltzes (Diapason d'Or de l'Année 2011), Liszt and Grieg Concertos 2011, Broken Branches (compositions by Stephen Hough) 2011, Stephen Hough's French Album 2012, Two Brahms Piano Concertos 2013, In the Night recital 2014. *Leisure interests:* reading, writing, painting. *Address:* c/o Harrison Parrott, 5–6 Albion Court, London, W6 0QT, England (office). *Telephone:* (20) 7229-9166 (office). *Fax:* (20) 7221-5042 (office). *E-mail:* info@harrisonparrott.co.uk (office); houghwebsite@ gmail.com (office). *Website:* www.harrisonparrott.co.uk (office); www .stephenhough.com; blogs.telegraph.co.uk/culture/author/stephenhough.

HOUGHTON, James Richardson, AB, MBA; American business executive; b. 6 April 1936, Corning, NY; s. of the late Amory Houghton and Laura Richardson Houghton; m. May Kinnicutt 1962; one s. one d.; ed St Paul's School, Concord, NH, Harvard Coll. and Harvard Univ. Grad. Business School; worked in investment banking, Goldman, Sachs and Co., New York 1959–61; in production and finance, Corning Glass Works, Danville, Ky and Corning, New York 1962–64; Vice-Pres. and Area Man., Corning Glass Int., Zurich and Brussels 1964–68; Vice-Pres. and Gen. Man. Consumer Products Div., Corning Glass Works (Corning Inc. 1989–), Corning, New York 1968–71, Vice-Chair. of Bd 1971–83, Chair. and CEO 1983–96, 2002–05, Chair. 2005–07 (retd); fmr mem. Bd of Dirs Exxon Mobil, Corning Inc., Metropolitan Life Insurance Co.; fmr Trustee Corning Glass Works Foundation, Corning Museum of Glass, Metropolitan Museum of Art, Pierpont Morgan Library; mem. Harvard Corpn 1995–2010; mem. Council on Foreign Relations, The Business Council.

HOUGHTON, Sir John, Kt, CBE, MA, DPhil, FRS; British physicist; *Honorary Scientist, Hadley Centre, Meteorological Office;* b. 30 Dec. 1931, Dyserth, Clwyd, Wales; s. of Sidney Houghton and Miriam Houghton (née Yarwood); m. 1st Margaret E. Broughton 1962 (died 1986); one s. one d.; m. 2nd Sheila Thompson 1988; ed Rhyl Grammar School and Jesus Coll., Oxford; Research Fellow, Royal Aircraft Establishment. Farnborough 1954–57; Lecturer in Atmospheric Physics, Univ. of Oxford 1958–62, Reader 1962–76, Prof. 1976–83, Fellow, Jesus Coll. 1960–83, Hon. Fellow 1983–; Dir Appleton, Science and Eng Research Council 1979–83; Chair. Earth Observation Advisory Cttee, ESA 1980–93; Chair. Jt Scientific Cttee, World Climate Research Prog. 1981–83; Dir-Gen. Meteorological Office 1983–90, Chief Exec. 1990–91; mem. Exec. Cttee WMO 1983–91, Vice-Pres. 1987–91; Pres. Royal Meteorological Soc. 1976–78; Chair. (or Co-Chair.) Scientific Assessment Working Group, Intergovernmental Panel on Climate Change 1988–2002, Royal Comm. on Environmental Pollution 1992–98, Jt Scientific and Tech. Cttee, Global Climate Observing System 1992–95; mem. UK Govt Panel on Sustainable Devt 1994–2000; Chair. The John Ray Initiative 1997–2007, Pres. 2007–; Hon. Scientist, Rutherford Appleton Lab. 1992–, Hadley Centre 2002–; Trustee, Shell Foundation 2000–; mem. Academia Europaea; Fellow, Optical Soc. of America, Learned Soc. of Wales; Hon. FRIBA 2001; Hon. mem. Royal Meteorological Soc., American Meteorological Soc.; Hon. DSc (Univ. of Wales) 1991, (Stirling) 1992, (East Anglia) 1993, (Leeds) 1995, (Heriot-Watt) 1997, (Greenwich) 1997, (Glamorgan) 1998, (Reading) 1999, (Birmingham) 2000, (Gloucestershire) 2001, (Hull) 2002, (Oxford) 2006; Hon. LLD (Dalhousie, Canada) 2010; Charles Chree Medal and Prize, Inst. of Physics 1979, Rank Prize for opto-electronics (jt recipient) 1989, Glazebrook Medal, Inst. of Physics 1990, Symonds Gold Medal, Royal Meteorological Soc. 1991, Bakerian Lecturer, Royal Soc. 1991, Global 500 Award, UNEP 1994, Gold Medal, Royal Astronomical Soc. 1995, Int. Meteorological Org. Prize 1998, Japan Prize 2006, Albert Einstein Science Award, World Cultural Council 2009. *Publications:* Infra Red Physics (with S. D. Smith) 1966, The Physics of Atmospheres 1977 (revised edn 2003), Remote Sounding of Atmospheres (with F. W. Taylor and C. D. Rodgers) 1984, Does God Play Dice? 1988, The Search for God: Can Science Help? 1995, Global Warming: The Complete Briefing 1997 (revised edn 2003). *Address:* Hadley Centre, Meteorological Office, Exeter, Devon, EX1 3PB, England (office).

HOUGHTON, Michael, PhD; American virologist and academic; *Canada Excellence Research Chair in Virology, University of Alberta;* ed Kings Coll. London, UK; Vice-Pres. Hepatitis C Research, Chiron Corpn, Emeryville, Calif. 1982–2007; Chief Scientific Officer, Epiphany Biosciences, Calif. 2007–10; Canada Excellence Research Chair in Virology, Univ. of Alberta 2010–, also Prof., Dept of Medical Microbiology and Immunology; Lasker Award for Clinical Medical Research 2000. *Achievements include:* headed research team that discovered Hepatitis C virus in 1987 and cloned it in 1989. *Publications:* numerous articles in scientific journals. *Address:* Department of Medical Microbiology and Immun-ology, University of Alberta, Faculty of Medicine and Dentistry, 6-010 Katz Group-Rexall Centre for Health Research, Edmonton, AB T6G 2E1, Canada (office). *Telephone:* (780) 248-1888 (office). *Fax:* (780) 492-7521 (office). *E-mail:* michael .houghton@ualberta.ca (office). *Website:* www.mmi.med.ualberta.ca (office).

HOUK, Kendall N., AB, MS, PhD, FRSC; American chemist and academic; *Saul Winstein Chair in Organic Chemistry, University of California at Los Angeles;* b. 27 Feb. 1943, Nashville, Tenn.; ed Harvard Univ.; Instructor, Harvard Extension School 1966–68; Asst Prof., Louisiana State Univ. 1968–72, Assoc. Prof. 1972–75, Prof. 1975–80; Visiting Prof., Princeton Univ. 1974–75; Prof., Univ. of Pittsburgh 1980–85; Prof. of Chem., UCLA 1986–, Chair. 1991–94, Saul Winstein Chair in Organic Chem. 2009–, mem. UCLA Molecular Biology Inst. 2010–; Dir NSF Chem. Div. 1988–90; Visiting Lecturer at numerous univs, including Lady Davis Fellow and Visiting Prof., Technion (Israel Inst. of Tech.) 2000; mem. Int. Acad. of Quantum Molecular Science 2003–; Sr Ed. Accounts of Chemical Research; mem. Editorial Advisory Bd of several learned journals including Central European

Journal of Chemistry, Chinese Journal of Chemistry, Chemical and Engineering News; mem. NAS 2010; Fellow, AAAS 1988, American Acad. of Arts and Sciences 2002; Hon. Dr rer. nat (Essen) 1999; ACS Akron Section Award 1983, Arthur C. Cope Scholar Award 1988, James Flack Norris Award 1991, Schroedinger Medal 1998, Richard C. Tolman Medal 1999, ACS Award for Computers in Chemical and Pharmaceutical Research 2003, ACS Arthur C. Cope Award 2010, RSC Robert Robinson Award 2012, UCLA Soc. of Postdoctoral Scholars Mentoring Award 2013, UCLA Glenn T. Seaborg Medal 2013. *Leisure interest:* cycling. *Address:* Depart-ment of Chemistry and Biochemistry, UCLA, 607 Charles E. Young Drive East, Box 951569, Los Angeles, CA 90095-1569, USA (office). *Telephone:* (310) 206-0515 (office). *Fax:* (310) 206-1843 (office). *E-mail:* houk@chem.ucla.edu (office). *Website:* www.chem.ucla.edu/houk (office).

HOUNGBÉDJI, Adrien; Benin lawyer and politician; *Leader, Parti du renouveau démocratique;* sentenced to death in absentia March 1975 after alleged involvement in attempted coup; mem. Nat. Ass. 1991–, Speaker 1991–96; Prime Minister 1996–98; Leader, Parti du renouveau démocratique (PRD). *Address:* Parti du renouveau démocratique, Immeuble Babo Oganla, 01 BP 1157, Porto-Novo, Benin (office). *Telephone:* 21-30-07-57 (office).

HOUNGBO, Gilbert Fossoun, BA; Togolese politician and UN official; ed Université de Lomé; worked at Price Waterhouse Canada; mem. UNDP Strategic Man. Team and Dir of Finance and Admin, then Chief of Staff UNDP, New York 2003–05; Asst Sec.-Gen., Asst Admin. of UNDP and Dir of UNDP's Regional Bureau for Africa 2005–08; Prime Minister of Togo 2008–12 (resgnd); mem. Canadian Inst. of Chartered Accountants. *Address:* c/o Office of the Prime Minister, Palais de la Primature, BP 1161, Lomé, Togo.

HOUNSOU, Djimon; Benin actor and fmr fashion model; b. 24 April 1964, Cotonou. *Films include:* Without You I'm Nothing 1990, Unlawful Entry 1992, Stargate 1994, The Small Hours 1997, Amistad 1997, Ill Gotten Gains 1997, Deep Rising 1998, Gladiator 2000, The Middle Passage Narrator 2000, The Tag 2001, Dead Weight 2002, The Four Feathers 2002, In America (Independent Spirit Award) 2002, Heroes 2002, Biker Boyz 2003, Lara Croft Tomb Raider: The Cradle of Life 2003, Blueberry 2004, Constantine 2005, Beauty Shop 2005, The Island 2005, Blood Diamond 2006, Eragon 2006, Never Back Down 2008, Push 2009. *Television includes:* ER (series) 1999, Alias (series) 2003–04.

HOUSE, Karen Jo Elliott, BJ; American publishing executive, journalist and academic; *Senior Fellow, Belfer Center for Science and International Affairs, Kennedy School of Government, Harvard University;* b. (Karen Jo Elliott), 7 Dec. 1947, Matador, Tex.; d. of Ted Elliott and Bailey Elliott; m. 1st Arthur House 1975 (divorced 1983); m. 2nd Peter Kann 1984; one s. three d.; ed Univ. of Texas at Austin and Harvard Univ. Inst. of Politics, Cambridge, Mass; Educ. Reporter, Dallas Morning News 1970–71, with Washington, DC bureau 1971–74; Regulatory Corresp., Wall Street Journal 1974–75, Energy and Agric. Corresp. 1975–78, Diplomatic Corresp. 1978–83, Asst Foreign Ed. 1984, Foreign Ed. 1984–89; Vice-Pres. Dow Jones Int. Group 1989–95, Pres. 1995–2006, Vice-Pres. and mem. Exec. Cttee Dow Jones & Co. 2002, Sr Vice-Pres. 2002–06; Publr The Wall Street Journal 2002–06; Sr Fellow, Belfer Center for Science and Int. Affairs, Kennedy School of Govt, Harvard Univ. 2006–; Public Del., US Mission to UN 2008; Dir German-American Council 1988–, Council on Foreign Relations 1987–98, Cttee to Protect Journalists; Trustee, Boston Univ.; Vice-Chair. Bd of Trustees, RAND; Fellow, American Acad. of Arts and Sciences; Dr hc (Lafayette Coll., Pa) 1992, (Boston Univ.) 2003; Georgetown Univ. Edward Weintal Award 1980, Nat. Press Club Edwin Hood Award 1982, Univ. of Southern California Distinguished Achieve-ment Award 1983, Pulitzer Prize in Int. Reporting for coverage of Middle East 1984, Overseas Press Club Bob Considine Award 1984, 1988, Pulitzer Prize for International Reporting 1984, Univ. of Texas Distinguished Alumnus Award 1992, ranked by Forbes magazine amongst 100 Most Powerful Women (54th) 2004, (73rd) 2005. *Publications:* On Saudi Arabia: Its People, Past, Religion, Fault Lines – and Future 2012. *Leisure interest:* tennis. *Address:* Belfer Center, Kennedy School of Government, 79 John F. Kennedy Street, Cambridge, MA 02138, USA (office). *Telephone:* (609) 921-8923 (home). *Fax:* (609) 921-2041 (home). *E-mail:* karenehouse@gmail.com (home).

HOUSER, Sam; British computer games industry executive; *President, Rockstar Games;* s. of Geraldine Moffat; started career as in-house music video dir BMG Entertainment; Head int. product devt BMG Interactive Div. –1998; Co-Founder and Pres. Rockstar Games 1998–, also Vice-Pres. Worldwide Product Devt, Take-Two Interactive Software Inc. *Address:* Rockstar Games, 622 Broadway, New York, NY 10012, USA (office). *Telephone:* (646) 536-2842 (office). *Fax:* (646) 536-2926 (home). *Website:* www.rockstargames.com (office).

HOUSHIARY, Shirazeh, BA; British (b. Iranian) sculptor; b. 15 Jan. 1955, Shiraz, Iran; ed Tehran Univ., Chelsea School of Art and Cardiff Coll. of Art; sculptor at the Lisson Gallery, London; Jr Fellow, Cardiff Coll. of Art 1979–80; Prof., London Inst. 1997–; comms include Art for the World with UNICEF 2002; lives and works in London. *Address:* c/o Lisson Gallery London Ltd, 67 Lisson Street, London, NW1 5DA, England; c/o Lehmann Maupin Gallery, 540 West 26th Street, New York, NY 10001, USA. *Telephone:* (20) 7724-2739 (London); (212) 255-2923 (New York). *Fax:* (20) 7724-7124 (London). *E-mail:* info@lehmannmaupin .com. *Website:* www.lehmannmaupin.com.

HOUSLAY, Miles Douglas, BSc, PhD, FRSE, FMedSci, CBiol, FIBiol, FRSA; British biochemist, molecular pharmacologist and academic; *Managing Director and CEO, BioGryffe Consulting Ltd;* b. 20 June 1950; s. of Doug Houslay and Mollie Houslay; m. Rhian Houslay; ed The Grammar School, Brewood, Staffs., Univ. Coll., Cardiff, King's Coll., Cambridge; ICI Postdoctoral Research Fellow, Univ. of Cambridge 1974–76, Research Fellow, Queen's Coll. 1975–76; Lecturer in Biochemistry, UMIST 1976–82, Reader 1982–84; Prof., Gardiner Chair of Biochemistry, Univ. of Glasgow 1984–2011; Prof. (part time), Chair of Pharma-cological Innovation, King's Coll. London 2011–; Prof. (part time), Strathclyde Inst. of Pharmacology and Biomedical Sciences, Univ. of Strathclyde 2012–; Burroughs Wellcome Fund Visiting Prof. (USA) in Basic Medical Sciences 2000; Man. Dir and CEO BioGryffe Consulting Ltd 2011–; Co-founder BioTheryX Inc., USA, Chair. Scientific Advisory Bd 2009–; Ed.-in-Chief, Cellular Signalling 1987–; Deputy Chair. Editorial Bd Biochemical Journal 1983–86; mem. Editorial Bd Progress in Growth Factor Research 1988–93; external assessor, Univ. of Malaysia 1991–95;

Pres. Conferences Jacques Monod (France) 1998; Chair. Gordon Research Conf. on Cyclic Nucleotide Phosphodiesterases 1998; mem. Cttee Biochemical Soc. 1982–86; mem. MRC Cell Bd 1989–94, Chair. MRC Cell Bd Research Grant Cttee A 1990–92, British Heart Foundation Research Grant Panel 1996–98; mem. Scottish Home and Health Dept Research Cttee 1991–94, Wellcome Trust Biochemistry Cell Biology Grant Panel 1996–2000, Scientific Advisory Bd Celgene Corpn, USA 2002–05, Scientific Advisory Bd Fission Pharmaceuticals, USA 2007–11; Selby Fellow, Australian Royal Soc. 1984; Trustee, British Heart Foundation 1996–2000; Hon. Sr Research Fellow, California Metabolic Research Foundation, La Jolla, USA 1980–91; Colworth Medal, Biochemical Soc. 1985, Joshua Lederberg Society Prize, Celgene Corpn 2012. *Publications:* Dynamics of Biological Membranes; more than 450 scientific articles. *Leisure interests:* walking, music, driving. *E-mail:* miles.houslay@glasgow.ac.uk (office). *Website:* www.biogryffeconsulting .co.uk (office).

HOVANNISIAN, Raffi K., BA, MALD, JD; Armenian politician; *Chairman, Heritage Party (Zharangutyun);* b. 20 Nov. 1959, Fresno, Calif., USA; eldest s. of Prof. Richard Hovannisian and Dr Vartiter Hovannisian; m. Armenouhi Hovannisian; four s. one d.; ed Georgetown Univ. Law Center, Univ. of California, Berkeley and Los Angeles, Fletcher School of Law and Diplomacy, Tufts Univ., USA; Lecturer in Armenian History, Tufts Univ. 1981–82; fmr Int. Lawyer and Civil Litigator, Hill, Farrer and Burrill, Whitman & Ransom, Stroock & Stroock & Lavan, and Coudert Brothers 1985–89; Founder and Dir Armenian Bar Asscn 1989–90; Project Dir, Armenian Ass. of America Earthquake Relief 1990–91; first Minister of Foreign Affairs, Repub. of Armenia 1991–92; Founding Dir Armenian Centre for Nat. and Int. Studies, Yerevan State Univ. 1993–; Chief, Dept of Information and Publications March–April 1998; Exec. Chair. 'Hayastan' All-Armenian Fund 1998; mem. Parl. and Chair. Heritage Party (Zharangutyun) 2007–; took part in public hunger strike in Freedom Square, Yerevan in protest against Pres. Sarkissian and his govt March 2011; runner-up cand. in presidential election Feb. 2013; relinquished US citizenship to be eligible to become an Armenian citizen 2001; Justin Turner Prize for Outstanding Honors Thesis. *Publications:* numerous treatises, monographs, essays and articles in Armenian, Russian, American, European and Middle Eastern publs. *Address:* Heritage Party (Zharangutyun), 0002 Yerevan, Moscovian Street 31, Armenia (office). *Telephone:* (10) 53-69-13 (office). *Fax:* (10) 53-26-97 (office). *E-mail:* office@heritage.am (office). *Website:* www.heritage.am (office).

HOVE, Andrew C., Jr; American banker and financial services industry executive; b. 9 Nov. 1934, Minden, Neb.; s. of the late Andrew C. Hove and Rosalie Vopat; m. Ellen Matzke 1956; one s. two d.; ed Univ. of Nebraska and Univ. of Wisconsin Grad. School of Banking; served in USN 1956–60, Neb. Nat. Guard 1960–63; Officer, Minden Exchange Bank & Trust Co. 1960–81, Chair. and CEO 1981–90, Vice-Chair. then Acting Chair. 1990–2001; currently Sr Adviser to Chair. CEO Promontory Financial Group LLC; mem. Bd of Dirs Sovereign Bancorp Inc. 2001–, Great Western Bancorporation, Inc. 2001–07, Saline State Bank. *Address:* c/o Office of the Chairman and CEO, Promontory Financial Group LLC, 1201 Pennsylvania Avenue, NW, Washington, DC 20004, USA.

HOVE, Chenjerai, BA; Zimbabwean journalist and writer; b. 9 Feb. 1956, Zvishavane; s. of R. Muza Hove and Jessie Muza Hove; m. Thecla Hove 1978; three s. two d.; ed Gweru Teacher's Coll.; high school teacher 1978–81; Ed. Mambo Press, Gweru 1981; Sr Ed. Zimbabwe Publishing house, Harare 1985; Ed. Cultural Features, Interpress Service 1988; Writer-in-Residence, Univ. of Zimbabwe 1991–94; Visiting Prof., Lewis and Clark Coll., Oregon, USA 1995; full-time writer 1999–; in exile in France 2002–; Fellow, International Writers Project, Brown Univ. 2007–08; Democracy and Freedom of Speech in Africa Prize, Berlin 2001. *Publications include:* Swimming in Floods of Tears (co-author) 1983, Red Hills of Home 1985, Bones (Zimbabwe Book Publishers Literary Award 1988, Noma Award for Publishing in Africa 1989) 1988, Shebeen Tales 1989, Shadows 1991, Guardians of the Soil 1996, Ancestors 1996, Shebeen Tales: Messages from Harare 1997, Rainbows in the Dust 1997, Palaver Finish (essays) 2003, Blind Moon 2004, The Keys of Ramb 2004, Homeless Sweet Home: A Memoir of Miami 2011. *Leisure interests:* gardening, reading, snooker, table tennis.

HOVERS, Joannes Coenradus Maria, PhD; Dutch business executive; b. 29 July 1943, Beek; m. Ineke van der Heijde 1971; three s.; ed Michiel Lyceum, Geleen, Tilburg Univ.; with Océ NV 1967–76, Chair. Bd of Exec. Dirs 1998; Chair. Man. Bd Teewen Group (bldg materials), later Chair. Man. Bd Synres (synthetic resins) 1976–83; fmr Chair. of Exec. Bd Nederlandsche Apparatenfabriek NV; mem. Man. Bd Stork NV 1983–88, Exec. Vice-Pres. Man. Bd 1988–89, CEO Man. Bd 1989–98; Chair. Comm. of Int. Econ. Relations; Supervisory Dir De Nederlandsche Bank NV, Hoechst AG, Koninklijke Grolsch NV, Ericsson Telecommunicatie BV; mem. Supervisory Bd TIAS Training Inst., Gooi-Noord Regional Hosp.; Asscn of European Man. Publrs Award 1973. *Address:* c/o Nederlandsche Apparatenfabriek NV, Parallelweg 2, 7141 DC Groenlo, Gelderland, Netherlands.

HOWAI, Larry, BSc; Trinidad and Tobago accountant and politician; *Minister of Finance;* m. Anu Howai; ed Univ. of the West Indies; CEO First Citizens Bank 1996–2012; Minister of Finance 2012–; fmr Chair. Nat. Gas Co.; fmr Pres. Bankers Asscn of Trinidad and Tobago; fmr Dir of numerous cos including Trinidad and Tobago Unit Trust Corpn, Home Mortgage Bank, Nat. Energy Corpn of Trinidad and Tobago, St Lucia Electricity Co. Man. Dir Investment, Commonwealth Business Council Ltd; Dir United Way of Trinidad and Tobago, Habitat for Humanity; fmr mem. Finance and General Purposes Cttee, Univ. of the West Indies; fmr Dir and Chair. of Audit Cttee, Guardian Media Ltd; Fellow, Inst. of Banking of Trinidad and Tobago; Caribbean Banking Excellence Award. *Address:* Ministry of Finance, Eric Williams Finance Bldg, Level 18, Independence Square, Port of Spain, Trinidad and Tobago (office). *Telephone:* 627-9700 (office). *Fax:* 627-5882 (office). *E-mail:* comm.finance@gov.tt (office). *Website:* www.finance.gov.tt (office).

HOWARD, Alan Mackenzie, CBE; British actor; b. 5 Aug. 1937, London; s. of the late Arthur John Howard and of Jean Howard (Compton Mackenzie); m. 1st Stephanie Hincheliffe Davies 1965 (divorced 1976); m. 2nd Sally Beauman 2004; one s.; ed Ardingley Coll.; nat. service with RAF in Germany 1956–58; stage hand, Asst Stage Man., actor, Belgrade Theatre Coventry 1958–60; London West End debut, Duke of York's Theatre in Roots 1959; played in London at Royal Court,

Arts, Mermaid, Strand, Phoenix theatres, also outside London 1960–65; with RSC 1966–, Assoc. Artist 1967–; Plays and Players London Theatre Critics Most Promising Actor Award 1969, Best Actor Award 1977; Soc. of West End Theatre Managers Best Actor in a Revival Award 1976, 1978; Evening Standard Drama Award for Best Actor 1978, 1981; Variety Club of Great Britain Best Actor Award 1980. *Plays include:* Twelfth Night, Revenger's Tragedy, As You Like It, The Relapse, King Lear, Troilus and Cressida, Much Ado About Nothing, Bartholomew Fair, Dr. Faustus, Hamlet, Midsummer Night's Dream, Enemies, Man of Mode, The Balcony, The Bewitched, Henry IV Parts 1 and 2, Henry V, Wild Oats, Henry VI Parts 1, 2 and 3, Coriolanus, Antony and Cleopatra, Children of the Sun, Richard II, Richard III, The Forest, Good 1981, 1982–83, Breaking the Silence 1985, The Silver King 1990, Scenes from a Marriage 1990, Pygmalion 1992, Macbeth 1993, La Grande Magia 1995, Rosencrantz and Guildenstern Are Dead 1995, Oedipus Plays 1996, Waiting for Godot 1997, King Lear 1997, Khludov in Flight 1998, The Play About the Baby 1998, Sloper in the Heiress 2000, Lulu 2001, Gates of Gold 2002, Keepers of the Flame 2003, The Hollow Crown, The Hollow Crown 2005. *Films include:* Victim 1961, The Password is Courage 1962, The V.I.Ps 1963, The Americanisation of Emily 1964, The Heroes of Telemark 1965, Work is a Four Letter Word 1968, Royal Flash 1975, Oxford Blues 1984, The Return of the Musketeers 1989, The Cook, The Thief, His Wife And Her Lover 1989, Strapless 1989, Dakota Road 1991, The Secret Rapture 1994, The Lord Of The Rings: The Fellowship of the Ring (voice) 2001, The Lord of the Rings: The Two Towers (voice) 2002, The Lord of the Rings: The Return of the King (voice) 2003. *Television includes:* A Perfect Spy 1987, David Copperfield 2000. *Leisure interests:* reading, music. *Address:* c/o Julian Belfrage Associates, 3rd Floor, 9 Argyll Street, London, W1F 7TG, England (office). *Website:* www.alanhoward.org.uk (office).

HOWARD, Sir David Howarth Seymour, Bt , MA, DSc; British business executive; *Chairman, Charles Stanley & Company, Stockbrokers;* b. 29 Dec. 1945, Lincoln; s. of Sir Edward Howard, Bt; m. Valerie Picton Crosse 1968; two s. two d.; ed Radley Coll., Worcester Coll., Oxford; Chair. Charles Stanley & Co., Stockbrokers 1971–; Pro-Chancellor and Chair. City Univ. 2003–08; Pres., Chartered Man. Inst. 2008–10; mem. Sutton London Borough Council 1974–78; Common Councilman, City of London 1972–86, Alderman 1986–, Sheriff 1997–98, Lord Mayor of London 2000–01; Master, Gardeners' Co. 1990–91; Hon. Fellow, Chartered Inst. for Securities and Investment. *Leisure interest:* gardening. *Address:* Office of the Chairman, Charles Stanley & Co. Ltd, 25 Luke Street, London, EC2A 4AR, England (office). *Telephone:* (20) 7739-8200 (office). *Fax:* (20) 7739-7798 (office).

HOWARD, James Kenneth (Ken), RA, RWS, RWA, ARCA, PPNEAC; British painter; *Professor of Perspective, Royal Academy of Arts;* b. 26 Dec. 1932, London; s. of Frank Howard and Elizabeth Howard; m. 1st Ann Popham (divorced 1974); m. 2nd Christa Gaa (née Köhler; died 1992); m. 3rd Dora Bertolutti 2000; ed Kilburn Grammar School, Hornsey School of Art, Royal Coll. of Art; British Council Scholarship to Florence 1958–59; taught in various London art schools 1959–73; Official Artist for Imperial War Museum, NI 1973, 1978; painted for British Army in NI, Germany, Cyprus, Oman, Hong Kong, Brunei, Nepal, Canada, Norway, Belize, Beirut 1973–83; Prof. of Perspective, Royal Acad. of Arts 2004–; works in public collections including Plymouth City Art Gallery, Ulster Museum, Imperial War Museum, Nat. Army Museum, Hove City Art Gallery, Guildhall Art Gallery; comms for UN, BAOR, Stock Exchange, London, States of Jersey, Banque Paribas, Drapers Co., Royal Hosp. Chelsea, Richard Green 2003; Pres. NEAC 1998–2003; Hon. mem. Royal Inst. of Oil Painters, Royal Soc. of British Artists; First Prize Lord Mayor's Art Award 1965, Hunting Group Award 1982, Sparkasse Karlsruhe 1983, Prizewinner John Moores 1978, Annual Critics' Prize, New English Art Club 2000. *Publications:* The Paintings of Ken Howard 1992, Ken Howard: A Personal Viewpoint 1998. *Leisure interests:* opera, cinema. *Address:* St Clements Studio, Paul Lane, Mousehole, Cornwall, TR19 6TR; 8 South Bolton Gardens, London, SW5 0DH, England (home); 6262 Canareggio, Venice, Italy (home). *Telephone:* (1736) 731596 (Cornwall) (office); (20) 7373-2912 (London) (home); (41) 5202277 (Italy) (home). *Fax:* (20) 7244-6246 (home).

HOWARD, Hon. John Winston, AC, LLB; Australian lawyer and fmr politician; b. 26 July 1939, Sydney, NSW; s. of Lyall Falconer Howard and Mona Jane Howard; m. Alison Janette Parker 1971; two s. one d.; ed Univ. of Sydney; solicitor to Supreme Court, NSW 1962; Partner, Sydney solicitors' firm 1968–74; Liberal MP for Bennelong, NSW, Fed. Parl. 1974–2007; Minister for Business and Consumer Affairs 1975–77, Minister Assisting Prime Minister 1977, Fed. Treas. 1977–83; Deputy Leader of Opposition 1983–85, Leader 1985–89; Shadow Minister for Industrial Relations, Employment and Training, Shadow Minister Assisting the Leader on the Public Service and Chair. Manpower and Labour Market Reform Group 1990–95; Prime Minister of Australia 1996–2007; mem. State Exec., NSW Liberal Party 1963–74; Vice-Pres., NSW Div., Liberal Party 1972–74; Fed. Parl. Leader Liberal Party 1985–1989, 1995–2007; Order of Merit 2012, Grand Cordon, Order of the Rising Sun (Japan) 2013; US Presidential Medal of Freedom 2009. *Leisure interests:* reading, cricket, tennis. *Address:* GPO Box 36, Sydney, NSW 2001, Australia.

HOWARD, Sir Michael Eliot, Kt, OM, CH, CBE, MC, MA, DLitt, FBA, FRHistS; British historian; *Regius Professor Emeritus of Modern History, University of Oxford;* b. 29 Nov. 1922, London; s. of the late Geoffrey Eliot Howard and of Edith Howard (née Edinger); civil pnr Mark James; ed Wellington Coll., Christ Church, Oxford; served in army 1942–45; Asst Lecturer, Lecturer in History, King's Coll., London 1947–53; Lecturer, Reader in War Studies, Univ. of London 1953–63; Prof. of War Studies, Univ. of London 1963–68; Fellow in Higher Defence Studies, All Souls Coll., Oxford 1968–77; Chichele Prof. of the History of War, Univ. of Oxford 1977–80; Regius Prof. of Modern History, Univ. of Oxford 1980–89, Prof. Emer. 1989–; Robert A. Lovett Prof. of Mil. and Naval History, Yale Univ. 1989–93; Leverhulme Lecturer 1996; Lee Kuan Yew Distinguished Visitor, Nat. Univ. of Singapore 1996; Founder and Pres. Emer. Int. Inst. for Strategic Studies; mem. The Literary Soc. (Pres. –2004); Foreign mem. American Acad. of Arts and Sciences; Hon. Fellow, Oriel Coll., Oxford 1990; Hon. Student Christ Church 1990; Order of Merit; Hon. LittD (Leeds) 1979; Hon. DLitt (London) 1988; Duff Cooper Memorial Prize 1961, Wolfson Foundation History Award 1972, NATO Atlantic Award 1989, Chesney Memorial Gold Medal, Royal United Services Inst., Samuel Eliot Morison Prize, Soc. for Mil. History 1992, Paul Nitze Award, Center for Naval

Analysis 1994, Political Book Prize, Friedrich Ebert Stiftung 2002. *Publications include:* The Coldstream Guards 1920–1946 (with John Sparrow) 1951, Disengagement in Europe 1958, Wellingtonian Studies 1959, The Franco-German War 1961, The Theory and Practice of War 1965, The Mediterranean Strategy in the Second World War 1967, Studies in War and Peace 1970, Grand Strategy, Vol. IV (in UK History of Second World War) 1972, The Continental Commitment 1973, War in European History 1976, Clausewitz on War (trans. with Peter Paret) 1976, War and the Liberal Conscience 1978, Restraints on War (ed.) 1979, The Causes of Wars 1983, Clausewitz 1983, Strategic Deception: British Intelligence in the Second World War 1990, The Lessons of History (essays) 1991, The Oxford History of the Twentieth Century (co-ed. with W. R. Louis) 1998, The Invention of Peace 2000, The First World War 2001, Captain Professor: A Life in War and Peace 2006, Liberation or Catastrophe?: Reflections on the History of the Twentieth Century 2007. *Leisure interests:* music, gardening. *Address:* The Old Farm, Eastbury, Hungerford, Berks., RG17 7JN, England (home). *Telephone:* (1488) 71387 (home). *Fax:* (1488) 71387 (home). *E-mail:* michaelhoward@xlninternet.co.uk (home).

HOWARD, Ron; American film director, film producer and actor; *Principal, Imagine Entertainment;* b. 1 March 1954, Duncan, Okla.; s. of Rance Howard and Jean Howard; m. Cheryl Alley 1975; two s. two d.; ed Univ. of Southern Calif. and Los Angeles Valley Coll.; Co-founder and Prin. Imagine Entertainment 1986–; National Medal of Arts 2003. *Films directed include:* Night Shift 1982, Splash 1984, Cocoon 1985, Gung Ho 1986, Return to Mayberry 1986, Willow 1988, Parenthood 1989, Backdraft 1991, Far and Away (also co-producer) 1992, The Paper 1994, Apollo 13 1995 (Outstanding Directorial Achievement in Motion Picture Award from Directors' Guild of America (DGA) 1996), How the Grinch Stole Christmas 2000, A Beautiful Mind (Acad. Awards for Best Dir and Best Film (producer) 2002, DGA Best Dir Award 2002) 2001, The Missing 2003, Cinderella Man 2005, The Da Vinci Code 2006, Frost/Nixon 2008, Angels & Demons 2009, The Dilemma 2011. *Film appearances include:* The Journey 1959, Five Minutes to Live 1959, Music Man 1962, The Courtship of Eddie's Father 1963, Village of the Giants 1965, Wild County 1971, Mother's Day, American Graffiti 1974, The Spikes Gang, Eat My Dust 1976, The Shootist 1976, More American Graffiti 1979, Leo and Loree (TV), Act of Love 1980, Skyward 1981, Through the Magic Pyramid (Dir, exec. producer) 1981, When Your Lover Leaves (co-exec. producer) 1983, Return to Mayberry 1986, Ransom 1996, Ed TV 1999. *Television includes:* (series) The Andy Griffith Show 1960–68, The Smith Family 1971–72, Happy Days 1974–80 and many other TV appearances. *Address:* Creative Artists Agency, 2000 Avenue of the Stars, Los Angeles, CA 90067, USA (office).

HOWARD OF LYMPNE, Rt Hon. Baron (Life Peer), cr. 2010, of Lympne in the County of Kent; **Michael Howard,** PC, CH, QC; British politician and barrister; *Chairman of the Advisory Board, Diligence, Europe;* b. (Michael Hecht), 7 July 1941, Gorseinon, NW Swansea, Wales; s. of Bernard Howard (originally Hecht, name anglicized from Romanian 1947) and Hilda Howard (née Kershion); m. Sandra Clare Paul 1975; one s. one d. one step-s.; ed Llanelli Grammar School, Peterhouse Coll., Cambridge; Pres. Cambridge Union 1962; called to Bar, Inner Temple 1964, Master of the Bench of Inner Temple 1992; Jr Counsel to the Crown (Common Law) 1980–82; a Recorder 1986–; Conservative Parl. cand., Liverpool (Edge Hill) 1966, 1970; Chair. Bow Group 1970–71; MP for Folkestone and Hythe 1983–2010; Parl. Pvt. Sec. to Solicitor-Gen. 1984–85; Under-Sec. of State, Dept of Trade and Industry, Minister for Corp. and Consumer Affairs 1985–87; Minister of State, Dept of the Environment 1987–88, Minister of Water and Planning 1988–90; Sec. of State for Employment 1990–92, for the Environment 1992–93, Home Sec. 1993–97; Opposition Front-Bench Spokesman on Foreign and Commonwealth Affairs 1997–99; Shadow Chancellor of the Exchequer 2001–03; Leader of the Conservative Party and Leader of the Opposition 2003–05; mem. House of Lords Appointments Comm. 2010–; Chair. Advisory Bd Diligence, Europe 2006–; Chair. (non-exec.) Northern Racing Ltd, Luup Ltd; Deputy Chair. (non-exec.) Entrée Gold Inc.; Dir, Luup International Ltd; Dir (non-exec.) Helphire Group PLC, Orca Exploration Group Inc., Global Switch (UK) Ltd; Hon. Patron Univ. Philosophical Soc. 2007–. *Leisure interest:* watching football and films, reading, walking. *Address:* Diligence, Inc., 10th Floor, One Canada Square, Canary Wharf, London, E14 5AB, England (office). *Telephone:* (20) 7516-0007 (office). *Fax:* (20) 7516-0004 (office). *E-mail:* howardm@parliament.uk (office); london@diligence.com (office); webcontact@michaelhoward.org (office). *Website:* www.diligence.com (office); www.michaelhoward.org.

HOWARTH, Elgar, ARAM, DMus, FRCM, FRNCM; British musician (trumpet), conductor and composer; b. 4 Nov. 1935, Cannock, Staffs.; s. of Oliver Howarth and Emma Wall; m. Mary Bridget Neary 1958; one s. two d.; ed Eccles Grammar School and Manchester Univ./Royal Northern Coll. of Music (jt course); orchestral player 1958–70; Chair. Royal Philharmonic Orchestra 1968–70; Prin. Guest Conductor Opera North 1985–88; freelance orchestral conductor 1970–; Musical Adviser Grimethorpe Colliery Brass Band 1972–; compositions: Trumpet Concerto 1968, Trombone Concerto 1962, Music for Spielberg 1984, Songs for BL for brass band; Fellow, Welsh Coll. of Music and Drama; Hon. FRNCM 1999; Hon. Fellow Royal Coll. of Music 2001, Univ. Coll. Salford; Hon. DUniv (en. England, York); Hon. DMus (Keele) 1996, (York) 2000; Hon. DLitt (Salford) 2003; Eddison Award 1977, Olivier Award for Outstanding Achievement in Opera 1997. *Leisure interests:* hypochondria, cricket, football. *Address:* c/o Andrew Rosner, Allied Artists, 42 Montpelier Square, London, SW7 1JZ, England (office). *Telephone:* (20) 7589-6243 (office). *Fax:* (20) 7581-5269 (office). *E-mail:* info@alliedartists.co.uk (office). *Website:* www.alliedartists.co.uk (office).

HOWATCH, Susan, LLB; British writer; b. 14 July 1940, Leatherhead, Surrey; d. of G. S. Sturt and Ann Sturt; m. Joseph Howatch 1964 (separated 1975); one d.; ed Sutton High School, King's Coll., London; emigrated to USA 1964, lived in Ireland 1976–80, returned to UK 1980; first book published 1965; Fellow, King's Coll. London 1999–; f. Starbridge Lectureship in Theology and Natural Science Univ. of Cambridge 1992; Winifred Mary Stanford Memorial Prize 1991; Hon. DLit (Hope Coll., Mich., USA) 2012. *Publications:* novels: The Dark Shore 1965, The Waiting Sands 1966, Call in the Night 1967, The Shrouded Walls 1968, April's Grave 1969, The Devil on Lammas Night 1970, Penmarric 1971, Cashelmara 1974, The Rich are Different 1977, Sins of the Fathers 1980, The Wheel of Fortune 1984, Glittering Images 1987, Glamorous Powers 1988, Ultimate Prizes 1989, Scandalous Risks 1991, Mystical Paths 1992, Absolute Truths 1994, A Question of

Integrity (revised title: The Wonder Worker) 1997, The High Flyer 1999, The Heartbreaker 2003. *Leisure interest:* theology. *Address:* Aitken Alexander Associates Ltd, 18–21 Cavaye Place, London, SW10 9PT, England (office). *Telephone:* (20) 7373-8672 (office). *Fax:* (20) 7373-6002 (office). *E-mail:* reception@aitkenalexander.co.uk (office). *Website:* www.aitkenalexander.co.uk (office).

HOWDEN, Timothy Simon; British business executive; b. 2 April 1937, London; s. of Phillip Alexander Howden and Rene Howden; m. 1st Penelope Mary Howden 1958 (divorced 1984); two s. one d.; m. 2nd Lois Chesney 1999; ed Tonbridge School; 2nd Lt, RA 1955–57; Factory Man., Floor Treatments, SA, then Sales, UK 1957–62; on staff of Reckitt & Colman in France, FRG and UK, ending as Dir Reckitt & Colman Europe 1962–73; Dir RH.M. Flour Mills 1973–75, Man. Dir RH.M. Foods Ltd 1975–80, Chair. and Man. Dir British Bakeries Ltd 1980–85, Planning Dir RH.M. PLC 1985–89, Man. Dir RH.M. PLC 1989–92; Group Chief Exec. for Europe, The Albert Fisher Group 1992–96, CEO for N America 1996–97; Chair. Zwetshost Ltd 2001–04, Benchmark Dental Holdings Ltd 2001–04; Dir (non-exec.) SSL International PLC 1994–2004, Finning International Inc. 1998–2007, Hyperion Insurance Group Ltd 2000–10; Assoc. Dir Mahendra British Telecom Ltd 2000–03. *Leisure interests:* skiing, scuba diving, tennis, sailing, opera. *Address:* Flat 72, Berkeley House, Hay Hill, London, W1J 8NT, England (home). *Telephone:* (20) 7355-1608 (home). *E-mail:* timlwe@btinternet.com (office).

HOWE, Brian Leslie, AM, MA; Australian politician and academic; *Professional Associate, Center for Public Policy, University of Melbourne;* b. 28 Jan. 1936, Melbourne; s. of John Percy Howe and Lilian May Howe; m. Renate Morris 1962; one s. two d.; ed Melbourne Univ., McCormick Theological Seminary, Chicago; worked as Uniting Church Minister, Melbourne and Morwell, Victoria; fmr Sr Lecturer in Sociology and Chair. Dept of Social and Political Studies, Swinburne Inst. of Tech., Melbourne; joined Australian Labor Party 1961; MP for Batman, House of Reps. 1977–96; Minister for Defence Support 1983–84, for Social Security and assisting the Prime Minister for Social Justice 1984–90, for Health, Housing and Community Services and assisting the Prime Minister for Social Justice 1990–93, for Housing, Local Govt and Community (now Human) Services 1993–94, for Housing and Regional Devt 1994–96; Deputy Prime Minister 1991–95; Minister assisting the Prime Minister for Commonwealth Relations 1991–93; Professional Assoc. Centre for Public Policy and Dept of Social Work, Univ. of Melbourne 1996–; Visiting Research Fellow Woodrow Wilson School of Public Policy and Int. Affairs 1997, 1998; fmr Chair. Caucus Econs Cttee; fmr mem. Caucus Resources Cttee, Urban and Regional Affairs Cttee, House of Reps. Standing Cttee on the Environment, Jt House Cttee on Publs; Fellow Queen's Coll., Univ. Melbourne 2000. *Leisure interests:* Australian Rules football, tennis, films, reading. *Address:* Centre for Public Policy, 2/234 Queensberry Street, Carlton, Vic. 3053 (office); 6 Brennand Street, North Fitzroy, Vic. 3068, Australia (home). *Telephone:* (3) 8344-9469 (office); (3) 9489-4787 (home). *Fax:* (3) 9349-4442 (office); (3) 9482-3202 (home). *E-mail:* bhowe@unimelb.edu.au (office). *Website:* www.ssps.unimelb.edu.au (office).

HOWE, Geoffrey Michael Thomas, MA; British solicitor and business executive; *Chairman, Nationwide Building Society;* b. 3 Sept. 1949, Cambridge, Cambs.; s. of Michael Edward Howe and Susan Dorothy Howe (née Allan); m. Karen Mary Webber (née Ford); two d.; ed Manchester Grammar School, St John's Coll., Cambridge; with Stephenson Harwood law firm 1971–75 (qualified as solicitor 1973); joined Clifford Chance 1975, apptd Partner, Corp. Dept 1980, Man. Partner 1989–97; Dir and Gen. Counsel, Robert Fleming Holdings Ltd 1998–2000; Dir J.P. Morgan, Fleming Overseas Investment Trust PLC 1999–2008; Chair. Railtrack Group PLC March–Oct. 2002; Dir (non-exec.) Jardine Lloyd Thompson Group PLC 2002– (currently Chair.), Investec PLC 2003–10, Close Brothers Group PLC 2011–; mem. Bd of Dirs Nationwide Building Society 2005–, Chair. 2007–. *Leisure interests:* opera, wine, paintings. *Address:* Nationwide Building Society, Pipers Way, Swindon, Wilts., SN38 1NW, England (office). *Telephone:* (1793) 656789 (office). *Fax:* (1793) 455341 (office). *E-mail:* geoffreymt.howe@lineone.net (home); info@nationwide.co.uk (office). *Website:* www.nationwide.co.uk (office).

HOWE OF ABERAVON, Baron (Life Peer), cr. 1992, of Tandridge in the County of Surrey; **(Richard Edward) Geoffrey Howe,** CH, PC, QC; British politician and lawyer; b. 20 Dec. 1926, Port Talbot, Glam.; s. of the late B. Edward Howe and of E. F. Howe; m. Elspeth R. M. Shand (cr. Baroness Howe of Idlicote 2001) 1953; one s. two d.; ed Winchester Coll. and Trinity Hall, Cambridge; called to the Bar, Middle Temple 1952, Bencher 1969; Deputy Chair. Glamorgan Quarter Sessions 1966–70; MP for Bebington 1964–66, for Reigate 1970–74, for East Surrey 1974–92; Solicitor-Gen. 1970–72; Minister for Trade and Consumer Affairs 1972–74; Opposition Spokesman for Social Services 1974–75, for Treasury and Econ. Affairs 1975–79; Chancellor of the Exchequer 1979–83; Sec. of State for Foreign and Commonwealth Affairs 1983–89; Lord Pres. of the Council, Leader of House of Commons and Deputy Prime Minister 1989–90; Visitor SOAS Univ. of London 1991–2001; Special Adviser on European and Int. Affairs to int. law firm Jones, Day, Reavis & Pogue 1991–2000; Herman Phleger Visiting Prof. Stanford Law School, USA 1992–93; Pres. GB-China Centre 1992–, Consumers Asscn (renamed Which?) 1992–, Acad. of Experts 1993–2003; Chair. Framlington Russian Investment Fund 1994–2003; a Gov. IMF 1979–83; Chair. Int. Cttee 1983, Steering Cttee Tax Law Rewrite Project 1996–2003, Trustees Thomson Foundation 2004–; fmr Pres. British Overseas Trade Bd; Dir Sun Alliance and London Insurance Group 1974–79, BICC 1991–97, Glaxo 1991–96; Dir EMI Ltd 1974–79, AGB Research Ltd 1974–79; mem. Int. Advisory Councils, J. P. Morgan 1992–2001, Stanford Univ. Inst. for Int. Studies 1991–2000, Fuji Wolfensohn Int. European Advisory Bd 1996–98, Carlyle European Advisory Bd 1996–2001, Fuji Bank Advisory Council 1999–2003; Patron UK Metric Asscn (UKMA) 2002–, Pres. 2005–; Conservative; Hon. Fellow, American Bar Foundation 2000; Hon. Fellow, Trinity Hall 1992, SOAS, London 2003; Grand Cross Order of Merit (Portugal) 1987, (Germany) 1992; Order of Ukraine for Public Service 2001; Hon. LLD (Wales) 1988, LSE 2004, (Glamorgan) 2004; Hon. DCL (City Univ.) 1993; Joseph Bech Prize 1993, Paul Harris Fellow, Rotary International 1995. *Publication:* Conflict of Loyalty 1994; Bow Group booklets (co-author): Houses to Let 1956, Work for Wales 1959. *Leisure interest:* photography, contemporary history, fmrly mountain climbing. *Address:* House of Lords, Westminster, London, SW1A 0PW, England (office). *Telephone:* (20) 7219-6986 (office). *Fax:* (20) 7219-0587 (office). *E-mail:* howeg@parliament.uk (office).

HOWELL OF GUILDFORD, Baron (Life Peer), cr. 1997, of Penton Mewsey in the County of Hampshire; **David Arthur Russell Howell,** PC, BA; British journalist, economist and politician; *President, The Royal Commonwealth Society;* b. 18 Jan. 1936, London, England; s. of the late Col Arthur Howell and of Beryl Howell; m. Davina Wallace 1967; one s. two d.; ed Eton Coll., King's Coll., Cambridge (Foundation Scholar); Lt Coldstream Guards 1954–56; Econ. Section, HM Treasury 1959, resgnd 1960; Leader-writer, The Daily Telegraph 1960; Chair. Bow Group 1961–62; fmr Crossbow; MP for Guildford 1966–97; a Lord Commr of Treasury 1970–71; with Civil Service Dept 1970–72; Parl. Under-Sec. Dept of Employment 1971–72; Minister of State, NI Office 1972–74, Dept of Energy Jan.–Feb. 1974; Sec. of State for Energy 1979–81, for Transport 1981–83; Chair. House of Commons Foreign Affairs Cttee 1987–97, One Nation Group of Conservative MPs 1987–97, European Cttee on Common Foreign and Security Policy 1999–2000; Opposition Spokesman on Foreign and Commonwealth Affairs 2000–10, Deputy Leader of the Opposition 2005–10, Minister of State and Govt Spokesperson, FCO 2010–12; Chair. UK–Japan 2000 Group 1989–2001; Dir Conservative Political Centre 1964–66; Dir Monks Investment Trust 1992–2005, John Laing Investments PLC 1997–2002; Advisory Dir UBS-Warburg 1996–2000; Sr Adviser, Japan Cen. Railway Co. 2001–; European Adviser, Mitsubishi Electric BV; Adviser to Kuwait Investment Office; Pres. The Royal Commonwealth Soc. 2013–, Energy Industries Council 2013–; Chair. Council of Commonwealth Socs; mem. Governing Bd Centre for Global Energy Studies; Visiting Fellow, Nuffield Coll., Oxford 1993–2001; Gov. Sadler's Wells Trust 1995–98; Trustee, Shakespeare's Globe Theatre 2000–06, Duke of Edinburgh's Commonwealth Study Conf.; Grand Cordon of the Order of the Sacred Treasure (Japan) 2001; Richards Prize 1959. *Publications:* Principle in Practice (co-author) 1960, The Conservative Opportunity 1965, Freedom and Capital 1981, Blind Victory 1986, The Edge of Now 2000, Out of the Energy Labyrinth 2008, Old Links and New Ties 2013. *Leisure interests:* family life, writing. *Address:* House of Lords, Westminster, London, SW1A 0PW, England (office). *Website:* www.parliament.uk/biographies/lords/lord-howell-of-guildford/993 (office); www.lordhowell.com.

HOWELLS, Rt Hon. Kim Scott, PC, BA, PhD; British broadcaster, writer, painter and fmr politician; b. 27 Nov. 1946, Merthyr Tydfil, Wales; s. of Glanville James Howells and Joan Glenys Howells (née Edwards); m. Eirlys Howells; three c.; ed Mountain Ash Grammar School, Hornsey Coll. of Art, Cambridge Coll. of Art and Tech., Univ. of Warwick; lecturer 1975–79; Official Research Officer, Coalfield History Project, Nat. Union of Miners (NUM) 1979–82, research officer and journal ed., NUM S Wales Area 1982–89; writer and broadcaster 1986–89; Labour MP for Pontypridd 1989–2010, Opposition Spokesman on Devt and Co-operation 1993–94, for Home Affairs 1994–95, for Foreign and Commonwealth Affairs 1994–95, for Trade and Industry 1995, Parl. Under-Sec. of State for Lifelong Learning, Dept for Educ. and Employment 1997–98; Minister for Consumers and Corp. Affairs, Dept for Trade and Industry 1998–2001; Minister for Tourism, Broadcasting and Media, Dept of Culture, Media and Sport 2001–03; Minister of State for Transport 2003–04, for Further and Higher Educ. and Lifelong Learning 2004–05, for the Middle East and South Asia, FCO 2005–08; mem. Welsh Affairs Select Cttee 1989–90, mem. Environmental Select Cttee 1990–92, mem. Public Accounts Cttee 1992–93, 1993–94, Chair. Intelligence and Security Cttee 2008–10; mem. British Mountaineering Council; Hon. Fellow, Univ. of Wales Inst. Cardiff; Dr hc (Anglia Ruskin Univ.), (Univ. of Glamorgan). *Television:* Framing Wales: History of Art in Wales in the 20th Century (BBC 2) 2011. *Leisure interests:* painting, mountaineering, cycling, jazz, gardening. *Address:* 16 Tyfica Road, Pontypridd, Wales (home). *Telephone:* (1443) 402551 (home). *E-mail:* kim.howells@hotmail.co.uk (office).

HOWIE, Archibald, CBE, PhD, FRS; British research physicist and academic; *Fellow, Churchill College, University of Cambridge;* b. 8 March 1934, Kirkcaldy, Scotland; s. of Robert Howie and Margaret Marshall McDonald; m. Melva Jean Scott 1964; one s. (deceased), one d.; ed Kirkcaldy High School, Univ. of Edinburgh, California Inst. of Tech., USA, Univ. of Cambridge; ICI Research Fellow, Cavendish Lab. and Research Fellow, Churchill Coll., Cambridge 1960–61, Demonstrator in Physics, Cavendish Lab. 1961–65, Teaching Fellow and Dir of Studies in Physics, Churchill Coll. 1961–86, Lecturer 1965–79, Reader 1979–86, Professorial Fellow 1986–2001, Pensioner Fellow 2001–, Head of Dept of Physics 1989–97; part-time consultant, Union Carbide Corpn 1977–78, World Bank China Univ. Devt Programme 1984, Norwegian Research Council 1986; Dir (non-exec.) NPL Man. Ltd 1995–2001; Pres. Royal Microscopical Soc. 1984–86, Int. Fed. of Socs for Electron Microscopy 1999–2002; Hon. FRSE 1995; Hon. Fellow, Royal Microscopical Soc. 1978, Japanese Microscopy Soc. 2003; Hon. mem. Electron Microscopy Soc. of America 1991, Chinese Electron Microscopy Soc. 2000; Hon. Prof., Univ. of York 2009–; Hon. Dr of Physics (Bologna) 1989, (Thessaloniki) 1995, (York) 2011; C.V. Boys Prize (co-recipient), Guthrie Medal, Inst. of Physics 1992, Hughes Medal (co-recipient), Royal Soc. 1988, Distinguished Scientist Award, Electron Microscopy Soc. of America 1991, Royal Medal, Royal Soc. 1999. *Publications:* Electron Microscopy of Thin Crystals (co-author) 1965 and numerous articles on electron microscopy and related subjects in scientific journals. *Leisure interest:* making wine. *Address:* Cavendish Laboratory, J J Thomson Avenue, Cambridge, CB3 0HE (office); 194 Huntingdon Road, Cambridge, CB3 0LB, England (home). *Telephone:* (1223) 337335 (office); (1223) 570977 (home). *Fax:* (1223) 363263 (office). *E-mail:* ah30@cam.ac.uk (office). *Website:* www.phy.cam.ac.uk (office).

HOWIE, J. Robert, BA, BCL, QC; Canadian politician and lawyer; b. 29 Oct. 1929, Fredericton, NB; s. of James R. Howie and Mary L. Pond; m. Nancy Goulding 1955; one s. three d.; ed Univ. of New Brunswick; solicitor, Oromocto 1962–72; Clerk of the New Brunswick Legislature 1970–72; mem. House of Commons for Fredericton 1972–88; Minister of State (Transport) 1979–80, 1984–88; Presiding mem. Veterans' Appeal Bd 1990–93; lawyer in pvt. practice 1993; mem. Bd of Govs, Univ. of New Brunswick 2003–; Progressive Conservative. *Leisure interests:* curling, hockey, theatre, swimming, writing. *Address:* 678 Churchill Row, Fredericton, NB E3B 1P6, Canada (home). *Telephone:* (506) 455-9320 (home). *Fax:* (506) 455-6256 (office). *E-mail:* jrh@nbnet.nb.ca (office).

HOXHAJ, Enver; Kosovo political scientist, academic and politician; *Minister of Foreign Affairs;* m. Remzije Hoxhaj; one s. one d.; ed Univ. of Prishtina, Univ. of Vienna; Scientific Researcher, Univ. of Vienna and Head of Research Team on the Balkans, Ludwig Boltzmann Inst. für Menschenrechte, Vienna 1996–2000; Fellow, LSE Centre for Study of Global Governance 2003–04; Founder Kosovar Research and Documentation Inst. –2004 (resgnd); mem. Democratic Party of Kosovo (DPK) 2004–; mem. Kosovo Del. to negotiations on Comprehensive Settlement of Kosovo's Status 2005–07; Assoc. Prof., Dept of Political Science, Univ. of Prishtina 2006–; Minister of Educ., Science and Tech. 2008, also Head, Parl. Comm. for Educ., Culture and Youth; Minister of Foreign Affairs 2011–; guest lecturer at many int. univs including Univ. of Oxford, Univ. Coll. London, Johns Hopkins Univ., Columbia Univ. *Address:* Ministry of Foreign Affairs, 10000 Prishtina, Ndërtesa e Qeverisë, Rruga Nënë Terezë, Kosovo (office). *Telephone:* (38) 213963 (office). *Fax:* (38) 213985 (office). *E-mail:* enver.hoxhaj@rks-gov.net (office); mfa@rks-gov.net (office). *Website:* www.mfa-ks.net (office).

HOY, Sir Christopher Andrew (Chris), Kt, MBE, BSc (Hons); British cyclist; b. 23 March 1976, Edinburgh, Scotland; m. Sarra Kemp 2010; ed George Watson's Coll., Edinburgh, Univ. of St Andrews, Univ. of Edinburgh; track cyclist representing GB team at four Olympic Games 2000, 2004, 2008, 2012, World and European Championships 1996–2012, World Cup Team 1997–2012, and Scotland Team at three Commonwealth Games, Kuala Lumpur 1998, Manchester 2002, Melbourne 2006; most successful Scottish Olympian ever; multiple World and Olympic Champion; first Briton to win three medals in a single Olympic games since Henry Taylor in 1908; most successful Olympic male cyclist of all time; raced BMX (Scotia BMX 1984–86, GT Factory BMX Team 1986–91) and was ranked 2nd in Britain, 5th in Europe and 9th in the world; sponsored by Slazenger and Kwik-Fit and competed in GB, Europe and USA; also rowed for Scottish jr team, coming second in British Championships with Grant Florence in coxless pairs 1993; also played rugby as part of his school's team; joined his first cycling club, Dunedin Cycling Club 1992–94; joined City of Edinburgh Racing Club and began concentrating on track cycling 1994–2001; set sea-level kilometre record of 1:00.711 seconds by winning gold at Athens Olympics 2004; set second fastest time ever (58.880) in attempt on world record for the kilometre May 2007; set record of 24.758 seconds for 500m flying start; World Championships: Silver Medal, Team sprint, Berlin 1999, Manchester 2000, Bronze Medal, Team sprint, Antwerp 2001, Gold Medals, 1km time trial and Team sprint, Copenhagen 2002, Bronze Medal, Team sprint, Stuttgart 2003, Gold Medal, 1km time trial, Bronze Medal, Team sprint, Melbourne 2004, Gold Medal, Team sprint, Bronze Medal, 1km time trial, Los Angeles 2005, Gold Medal, 1km time trial, Silver Medal, Team sprint, Bordeaux 2006, Gold Medals, Keirin and 1km time trial, Silver Medal, Team sprint 2007, Gold Medals, Sprint and Keirin, Silver Medal, Team sprint, Manchester 2008, Gold Medal, Keirin, Copenhagen 2010, Bronze Medal, Team sprint, Copenhagen 2010, Gold Medal, Keirin, Silver Medal, Team Sprint and Silver Medal, Sprint, Apeldoorn, Netherlands 2011, Gold Medal, Keirin and Bronze Medal, Sprint, Melbourne 2012; Commonwealth Games: Gold Medal, 1km time trial, Bronze Medal, Team sprint (with Craig MacLean and Ross Edgar), Manchester 2002, Bronze Medal, 1km time trial, Gold Medal, Team sprint (with Craig MacLean and Ross Edgar), Melbourne 2006; Olympic Games: Silver Medal, Team sprint (with Craig MacLean and Jason Queally), Sydney 2000, Gold Medal, 1km track time trial, Athens 2004, Gold Medal, Team sprint (with Jason Kenny and Jamie Staff), Gold Medal, Keirin, Gold Medal, Sprint, Beijing 2008, Gold Medal, Team sprint (with Jason Kenny and Philip Hindes), London 2012; raced for Team Athena 2001–03, Team Persil 2004, Team Wolfson Microelectronics/Miller 2005–07, Team Sky+ HD 2008–13; Amb. for 2012 Summer Olympics in London; announced retirement from competitive cycling April 2013; Hon. PhD (Edinburgh) 2005, (Heriot-Watt) 2005, (St Andrews) 2009; BBC Sports Personality Team of the Year 2000, 2008, Glenfiddich Scottish Sports Personality 2002, Edinburgh City Council Civic Reception 2002, 2007, Commonwealth Games Council Scottish Sports Personality 2003, 2004, 2005, 2007, BBC Scottish Sports Personality of the Year 2003, Radio Forth Sports Personality 2004, cyclingnews.com Track Cyclist of the Year 2005, Glasgow Sportsperson of the Year 2007, BBC Sports Personality of the Year 2008, inducted into Univ. of Edinburgh's Sports Hall of Fame 2009, The Sir Chris Hoy Velodrome built for the 2014 Commonwealth Games in Glasgow is named in his honour. *Publication:* Chris Hoy: The Autobiography 2009. *Address:* c/o British Cycling, Stuart Street, Manchester, M11 4DQ, England. *Telephone:* (161) 274-2000. *Fax:* (161) 274-2001. *E-mail:* info@chrishoy.com; admin@chrishoy.com. *Website:* www.britishcycling.org.uk; www.chrishoy.com.

HØYEM, Tom, MA; Danish politician, teacher, journalist and business executive; *Headmaster, European School, Karlsruhe;* b. 10 Oct. 1941, Nykøbing, Falster; s. of Ove Charles Høyem and Karen Høyem; m. 1st Inge-Lise Bredelund 1969 (died 2000); one s. one d.; m. 2nd Gerlinde Martin 2002; ed Univ. of Copenhagen, Univ. of Bergen, Norway; schoolteacher 1960–64; teacher, Skt Jørgens Gymnasium 1964–80; Sr Master, Foreningen Norden, Sweden 1967–68; business exec. 1968–; co-founder, Chair. Centre Democratic Party 1973; Asst Prof. of Danish Language and Literature, Univ. of Stockholm 1975–79; Foreign corresp., Berlingske Tidende, Sweden 1975–80; headmaster Høng Gymnasium 1979; Sec. of State for Greenland 1982–87; Headmaster European School, Culham 1987–94, Munich 1994–2000, Karlsruhe 2000–; mem. (Liberal) Karlsruhe Town Council 2004–; Co-founder European Folk High School, Møn, Denmark and of similar insts in Sicily, Austria, Ireland and Luxembourg; Leader of European Movt West Zeeland, Denmark 1980–82; election observer in Albania and Bosnia 1996; Goodwill Amb. for Copenhagen; mem. Ausländerbeirat, Munich 1997–2000; OSCE observer of elections in Bosnia, Albania, Montenegro, Ukraine and Palestine; Hon. Pres. European Inst., Luxembourg 1983; Kt of the Dannebrog. *Publications:* Avisens spisesseddel-avisens ansigt 1975, Tabloidetik i Norden 1976, Mulighedernes Samfund (co-author) 1985, Laegaest 1985, Dagens Grønland 1986, There is Something Wonderful in the State of Denmark 1987, Gud, Konge, Faedreland 1987, Nordisk i Europa 1988, From My Office 1999, Danmark 2020 (co-author) 2004. *Leisure interests:* politics, reading, golf, walking. *Address:* European School, Albert-Schweitzer-str. 1, 76139 Karlsruhe, Germany. *Telephone:* (721) 680090 (office). *Fax:* (721) 6800950 (office). *E-mail:* hmtm@eursc.org (office). *Website:* www .eskar.org (office).

HOYER, Steny Hamilton; American politician; b. 14 June 1939, New York City; s. of Steen Hoyer; m. Judy Pickett (died 1997); three d.; ed Suitland High School, Md, Univ. of Maryland, College Park, Georgetown Univ. Law Center, Washington, DC; fmr intern for US Senator Daniel Brewster from Md; mem. Md State Senate for Prince George's Co. 1966–81, Pres. State Senate 1975–81 (youngest in state history); mem. Bd of Higher Educ. 1978–81; mem. US House of Reps for Md 5th Congressional Dist 1981–, Deputy Majority Whip 1987–89, Chair. Democratic Caucus 1989–94, fmr Co-Chair. (and current mem.) Democratic Steering Cttee, Chief Cand. Recruiter for House Democrats 1995–2000, House Democratic Minority Whip 2002–06, 2011–; Sr mem. House Appropriations Cttee, mem. Transportation, Treasury and Housing Sub-cttee, Labor, Health and Human Services, Educ., and Related Agencies Sub-cttee, House Majority Leader 2007–11; mem. Bd of Trustees St Mary's Coll. of Md; Democrat; Congressional Leadership Award, Epilepsy Foundation 2002. *Address:* 1705 Longworth House Office Building, Washington, DC 20515, USA (office). *Telephone:* (202) 225-4131 (office). *Fax:* (202) 225-4300 (office). *Website:* www.hoyer.house.gov (office).

HRISTOV, Kalin, MEconSc; Bulgarian economist and politician; b. 1971, Pleven; ed Univ. of Nat. and World Economy (UNWE), Sofia; Asst Prof., Econs Dept, UNWE 1977–2000, Chief Asst Prof., Finance Dept 2001–04; Researcher, Exchange Rate Issues Project, Bank of England Sept.–Dec. 2001; Expert, Econ. Research and Forecasting Directorate, Bulgarian Nat. Bank (BNB) 1997–2001, mem. BNB Investment Cttee 2002–, Adviser to Deputy Gov. in charge of Issue Dept 2002–03, Adviser to BNB Gov. 2003–09, mem. BNB Governing Council and Deputy Gov. in charge of Issue Dept 2009–13; Minister of Finance (in caretaker govt) March–May 2013; mem. Monetary Policy Cttee, European Central Bank 2005–; Chair. Governing Council, Bulgarian Macroeconomics Asscn; mem. Governing Council, Inst. of Market Economy. *Publications:* several publs in Bulgaria and abroad on macroeconomics, monetary policy, currency and adoption of the euro. *Address:* c/o Ministry of Finance, 1040 Sofia, ul. G. S. Rakovski 102, Bulgaria.

HRUŠOVSKÝ, Pavol, JUDr; Slovak politician; b. 9 June 1952, Veľká Maňa, Nové Zámky Dist; ed Comenius Univ., Bratislava; worked in various econ. orgs as a lawyer 1980s; Head of the Legal Dept, Jednota SD co-operative, Nitra 1989; Head of Dist Council, Nitra 1992; mem. Christian Democratic Movt (Krestanskode-mokratické hnutie) 1989–, Leader 2000–; co-opted as a Deputy of Fed. Ass. (Parl.) of Czechoslovakia 1989, elected as a Deputy of the Ass. 1990, mem. Constitutional, Foreign Relations and Mandate and Immunity Cttees; mem. Nat. Council of the Slovak Republic (Parl.) 1992–, mem. Constitutional and Mandate and Immunity Cttees, Deputy Speaker 1998–2002, 2010–, Speaker 2002–06; parl. cand. for Slovak Democratic Coalition 1998, mem. of coalition 1998–99, Deputy Leader of the movt for Domestic Politics 1999–2000. *Address:* National Council of the Slovak Republic (Národná rada Slovenskej republiky), Námestie Alexandra Dubčeka 1, 812 80 Bratislava, Slovakia (office). *Telephone:* (2) 5972-1111 (office). *Fax:* (2) 5441-9529 (office). *E-mail:* pavol_hrusovsky@nrsr.sk (office). *Website:* www.nrsr.sk (office).

HRŮZA, Jiří, Ing.Arch, CSc; Czech architect and urban planner; *Senior Lecturer, Technical University, Prague;* b. 31 May 1925, Prague; s. of the late Václav Hrůza and of Františka Hrůza; m. 1st Emilie Hrůza (died 1991); one s. (deceased) one d.; m. 2nd Marta Opplová; ed Faculty of Architecture, Tech. Univ., Prague; with City Planning Office 1961–90; Chief Designer Master Plan of Prague 1961–91, Master Plan of Colombo, Sri Lanka 1978; Chief Specialist, Terplan, AS 1990–98; Guest Lecturer, Charles Univ. and Acad. of Graphic and Plastic Arts 1991; currently Sr Lecturer Inst. of Urbanism, Technical Univ., Prague; Founding mem. Int. Soc. of City and Regional Planners 1965; Corresp. mem. German Acad. for Town Planning 1993, German Acad. of Urban and Regional Planning (DASL) 1994; Hon. mem. Czech Soc. for Urban and Regional Planning; Medal of Univ. in Coimbra 1966, Medal for Merits of the City of Prague 1969, Medal 'The Spirit of Detroit' 1969, Herder's Prize, Univ. of Vienna 1979, Havlicek's Prize, Union of Czech Architects 1985, Vladimíra Karfík's Prize, City of Zlin 2011. *Publications:* Czech Towns 1960, Theory of Towns 1965, International History of City Development (co-author) 1972, The City of Prague 1990, The Development of Urban Planning, Vols 1 and 2 1996, The World of Architecture (second edn) 2003, City Builders 2011. *Leisure interests:* foreign languages, history, classical literature, theory and history of architecture and urban design. *Address:* Institute of Urbanism of Technical University, Thákurova 9, 16634 Prague 6 (office); K Matěji 18, 16000 Prague 6, Czech Republic (home). *Telephone:* (2) 24354986 (office); (2) 33334645 (home). *Fax:* (2) 24310185 (office). *E-mail:* hruza-praha@volny.cz (home); dubna@sa.cvut.cz (office).

HRYSHCHENKO, Kostyantyn Ivanovich; Ukrainian politician and diploma-tist; b. 28 Oct. 1953, Kyiv; m. Nataliya Ihorivna Hryshchenko; one d.; ed Moscow State Inst. of Int. Relations, USSR; staff mem., UN Secr., New York, USA 1976–80; various positions in Ministry of Foreign Affairs, USSR 1981–91; various positions in Arms Control and Disarmament Directorate, Ministry of Foreign Affairs, Kyiv 1992–95; Deputy Foreign Minister 1995–98; Amb. to Belgium, the Netherlands and Luxembourg, Head of Mission to NATO and Perm. Rep. to OPCW, The Hague, Netherlands 1998–2000; Amb. to USA 2000–03; Minister of Foreign Affairs 2003–05, 2010–12; Counsellor of Prime Minister 2006–07; First Deputy, Nat. Security and Defence Council (RNBO) 2008; Amb. to Russia 2008–10; Chair. UN Advisory Bd on Disarmament Matters 2003; Co-founder Republican Party of Ukraine 2004, Vice-Chair. 2004–; Vice-Prime Minister 2012–14 (resgnd); mem. Foundation Council, Geneva Centre for Security Policy 1995–98; fmr mem. Coll. of Commrs of UN Monitoring, Verification and Inspection Comm. (UNMOVIC); Order of Merit, Third Class 1998, Second Class 2003, several foreign decorations. *Address:* c/o Office of the Cabinet of Ministers, 01008 Kyiv, vul. M. Hrushevskoho 12/2, Ukraine. *E-mail:* web@kmu.gov.ua.

HRYTSENKO, Anatoliy Stepanovych, DTechSci; Ukrainian government official and political analyst; b. 1957, Cherkasy oblast; ed Kyiv School of Higher Mil. Aviation Eng and Acad. of Armed Forces; Lecturer, Kyiv Higher School of Mil. Aviation Eng; fmr Head, Problem-Analytical Dept, Science-Research Centre, Armed Forces of Ukraine; fmr Head, Dept for Mil. Security and Construction, Nat. Scientific Research Centre for Defence Techs; Head, Analytical Apparatus, Nat. Security and Defence Council 1997–99; Pres. Center for Econ. and Political Studies 1999–2005; Minister of Defence 2005–07; mem. People's Union Our Ukraine party. *Address:* People's Union Our Ukraine, 04070 Kyiv, vul. Borychiv Tik 22A, Ukraine (office). *Telephone:* (44) 206-60-95 (office). *E-mail:* tak@ua.org.ua (office). *Website:* www.razom.org.ua (office).

HSIAO, Hsin-Huang Michael, BA, MA, PhD; Taiwanese academic; *Director, Institute of Sociology, Academia Sinica, Taiwan;* b. (Hsiao Hsin-Huang), 26 Dec.

1948, Taipei; m. Yu-Hyang Lee Hsiao; two s.; ed Nat. Taiwan Univ., State Univ. of New York at Buffalo; Assoc. Research Fellow, Inst. of Ethnology, Academia Sinica 1979–83, Research Fellow 1983–95, Distinguished Research Fellow 2011–, Chair. 1980–82, Deputy Dir 1989–94; Dir Program for SE Asian Area Studies 1996–2001; Dir Asia-Pacific Research Program 2001–02; Exec. Dir Centre for Asia-Pacific Area Studies, Academia Sinica 2003–09, Dir Inst. of Sociology 2009–; Assoc. Prof., Dept of Sociology, Nat. Taiwan Univ. 1980–84, Prof. 1984–; Sr Prof., Grad. Inst. of Sociology, Nat. SYS Univ., Kaohsiung Univ. 2009–; Chair Prof., Coll. of Hakka Studies, Nat. United Univ. 2007–09, Coll. of Hakka Research, Nat. Cen. Univ. 2010–11, Visiting Chair Prof., Leiden Univ., The Netherlands; Visiting Prof., Ritsumeikan Univ., Japan; Int. Assoc., Inst. on Culture, Religion and World Affairs, Boston Univ. 1990–; Nat. Policy Adviser to Pres. of Taiwan 1996–2006; Hon. Sr Research Fellow, Hong Kong Inst. of Asia-Pacific Studies, Chinese Univ. of Hong Kong 1999–; Pres. Taiwanese Sociological Asscn 1992–93, Taiwan Asscn of Southeast Asian Studies 2004–09; mem. Bd of Dirs Public TV Service 1998–2001, Nat. Culture and Art Foundation 1998–2001, 2007–; mem. Nat. Unification Council 1997–2000; Councillor Nat. Council on Sustainable Devt, Exec. Yuan of Taiwan 1999–2008; Pres. Inst. of Nat. Devt 2000–02, Adviser 2002–; Councillor, Govt Reform Council, Office of the Pres. of Taiwan 2002–03; Man. Dir Asia Foundation in Taiwan 2003–; standing supervisor, Taiwan Foundation for Democracy 2003–09; mem. editorial bd several Taiwanese and int. journals; Fulbright Sr Visiting Scholar, Center for Asian Devt Studies, Boston Univ. and Fairbank Center for East Asian Research, Harvard Univ. 1983–84; Visiting Prof., Dept of Sociology and Center for Int. Studies, Duke Univ. 1988; Dr Hu Shi Visiting Chair Prof. Sinological Inst., Leiden Univ., Netherlands 1994; Distinguished Research Award, Nat. Science Council, Exec. Yuan of Taiwan 1990–91, 1992–94, Distinguished Int. Alumni Award, State Univ. of New York at Buffalo 2005. *Publications:* more than 100 books, including Exploration of the Middle Classes in Southeast Asia (ed.) 2003, Chinese Enterprise, Transnationalism and Identity (co-ed.) 2003, Sustainable Taiwan 2011 (co-ed.) 2003, Taiwan and Southeast Asia: Go-South Policy and Vietnamese Brides (ed.) 2004, Green Blueprint: Toward Local Sustainable Development in Taiwan (in Chinese, co-ed.) 2005, Taiwan's New Paradigms (in Chinese, co-author) 2006, Asian New Democracies: The Philippines, South Korea and Taiwan Compared (ed.) 2006, Capital Cities in Asia-Pacific: Primacy and Diversity (co-ed.) 2007, Asia-Pacific Peace Watch 2008, Non-Profit Sector: Organization and Practice 2009, 2011, Rise of China: Beijing's Strategies and Implications for the Asia-Pacific 2009, Cross-Border Marriages with Asian Characteristics (co-ed.) 2009, Changing Faces of Hakka in Southeast Asia: Singapore and Malaysia (ed.) 2011, The Social History of Ethnic Groups in Taiwan (in Chinese, co-author) 2011, The Social History of Surnames and Lineages in Taiwan (in Chinese, co-author) 2011; 150 book chapters and more than 144 journal articles in the fields of sociology of devt, civil society and democracy, environmental sociology, and the middle classes in Asia-Pacific. *Leisure interests:* gardening, classical music, travel, film. *Address:* Institute of Sociology, Academia Sinica, Nankang, Taipei, Taiwan (office). *Telephone:* (2) 2652-5140 (office); (2) 2652-5068 (office); (2) 2691-3880 (home). *Fax:* (2) 2788-8911 (office); (2) 2652-5060 (office); (2) 2691-3895 (home). *E-mail:* michael@gate.sinica.edu.tw (office). *Website:* www.ios.sinica.edu.tw (office).

HSIEH, Frank Chang-ting, LLM; Taiwanese politician; b. 18 May 1946, Taipei; ed Nat. Taiwan Univ., Kyoto Univ., Japan; practised as attorney 1969–81; Defence Counsel in Kaohsiung Incident 1990; mem. Taipei City Council 1981–88; mem. Cen. Standing Cttee, Democratic Progressive Party (DPP) 1986–96, Legislator 1989–96, Chair. Cen. Review Cttee 1996–98, DPP Vice-Presidential cand. 1996, Chair. DPP 2000–02, Jan.–March 2008; Mayor of Kaohsiung 1998–2005; Premier of Taiwan 2005–06; cand. for Mayor of Taipei 2006; DPP Presidential cand. 2008 elections. *Address:* Democratic Progressive Party (DPP), 10/F, 30 Beiping East Road, Taipei 10051, Taiwan (office). *Telephone:* (2) 23929989 (home). *Fax:* (2) 23929989 (office). *E-mail:* foreign@dpp.org.tw (office). *Website:* www.dpp.org.tw (office).

HSIEH, Hsiang-chuan, BS, MS, PhD; Taiwanese academic and politician; b. 12 Dec. 1944; ed Nat. Taiwan Univ., Univ. of Wisconsin, USA; Postdoctoral Fellow, Dept of Biochemistry, Florida State Univ. 1974–77; Investigator, Inst. of Dental Research, Univ. of Alabama 1977–82; Visiting Specialist, Nat. Science Council, Exec. Yuan 1982–84, Dir-Gen. Dept of Planning and Evaluation 1984–86, Dept of Life Sciences 1986, Deputy Dir-Gen. Hsinchu Science-based Industrial Park Admin 1989–96, Deputy Minister 1996–2001, Convener, Economy and Tech. Div., Nat. Policy Foundation 2003–08, Sec.-Gen. Exec. Yuan 2008–09, concurrently Gov. Fujian Prov. 2008. *Address:* c/o Office of the Secretary-General, Executive Yuan, 1, Section 1, Jhongsiao East Road, Jhongjheng District, Taipei 10058, Taiwan (office).

HSIUNG, Ming-Ho, MA; Taiwanese business executive; *President and Co-CEO, Cathay Life Insurance Company Limited;* ed Univ. of Iowa, USA; Pres. and Co-CEO Cathay Life Insurance Co. Ltd 2008–, mem. Bd of Dirs Cathay Financial Holdings. *Address:* Cathay Life Insurance Co. Ltd, 296 Jen Ai Road, Section 4, Taipei 10639, Taiwan (office). *Telephone:* (2) 2755-1399 (office). *Fax:* (2) 2704-1485 (office). *E-mail:* info@cathlife.com.tw (office); service@cathayholdings.com.tw (office). *Website:* www.cathlife.com.tw (office).

HSÜ, Kenneth Jinghwa, MA, PhD; Swiss scientist, inventor and writer; *President, Kenneth Hsü IHC Technology Ltd; Professor Emeritus, ETH Zürich; Director, KJH Centre, Beijing National Institute of Geosciences;* b. (Jinghwa Hsü), 28 June 1929, China; s. of Sin-wu Hsü and Su-lan; m. 1st Ruth Grunder 1958 (deceased); two s. one d.; m. 2nd Christine Eugster 1966; one s.; m. 3rd Susan Milan 2005; ed Chinese Nat. Univ., Nanking, Ohio State Univ., Univ. of California, Los Angeles, USA and ETH, Zürich; Research Geologist and Research Assoc., Shell Devt Co., Houston, Tex. 1954–63; Assoc. Prof., State Univ. of New York, Binghamton, NY 1963–64; Assoc. Prof., Univ. of Calif., Riverside 1964–67; Prof., Swiss Fed. Inst. of Tech. (ETH), Zürich 1967–94, Prof. Emer. 1994–; Pres. Kenneth Hsü IHC Tech. Ltd, Beijing 2004–; Prof., Nanjing Univ. 2004–; Pres. Int. Asscn of Sedimentologists 1978–82; Chair. Int. Marine Geology Comm. 1980–89; Dir Kenneth Center for ZHC Devt, Beijing Nat. Inst. of Geosciences 2004–; Foreign assoc. mem. NAS, Acad. Sinica, Taiwan; Fellow, Inst. of Advanced Studies, Berlin, Germany 1995–96; Assoc. Fellow, Third World Acad. of Sciences; Hon. Prof., Chinese Acad. of Sciences, Univ. Coll. London; Hon. mem. Int. Asscn of

Sedimentologists; Dr hc (Nanjing Univ.) 1994; Wollaston Medal, Geological Soc. of London; Twenhofel Medal, American Sedimentological Soc., Penrose Medal, Geological Soc. of America, President's Award, American Asscn of Petroleum Geologists, Alumnus of the Century, Nanjing Univ., Int. Writer of the Year, IBC 2003. *Publications:* Ein Schiff revolutioniert die Wissenschaft 1982, The Mediterranean was a Desert 1984, The Great Dying 1986, Challenger at Sea 1994, Geology of Switzerland 1995, Tectonic Facies Map of China 1996, Geologic Atlas of China 1998, Klima macht Geschichte 2000, Mozart in Love (in Chinese) 2003, Physics of Ledimen trilogy 2004; other books and more than 400 scientific articles. *Leisure interest:* Chinese aerophilately. *Address:* Oakcombe, Marley Common, Haslemere, Surrey, GU27 3PT, England (home). *Telephone:* (1) 3621462 (office); (1428) 641457 (home). *E-mail:* kenjhsu@aol.com (home).

HSU, Li-Teh, LLM, MPA; Taiwanese politician and business executive; *Chairman, Global Investment Holdings Co., Ltd;* b. 6 Aug. 1931, Loshan County, Honan; m.; two s.; ed Taiwan Prov. Coll. of Law and Commerce, Nat. Chengchi Univ. and Harvard Univ.; Dir Fifth Dept Exec. Yuan 1972–76; Admin. Vice-Minister of Finance 1976–78; Commr Dept of Finance, Taiwan Prov. Govt 1978–81; Minister of Finance 1981–84, of Econ. Affairs 1984–85; Chair. Lien-ho Jr Coll. of Tech., Global Investment Holding Co. Ltd 1986–88; Chair. Finance Comm. Cen. Cttee Kuomintang 1988–93; Deputy Sec.-Gen. and Exec. Sec. Policy Coordination Comm. Cen. Cttee Kuomintang 1990–93; Vice-Premier of Taiwan 1993–97; Founder and Chair. Global Investment Holdings Co., Ltd 1988–, also Chair. Prudence Venture Investment Corpn. *Address: . E-mail:* info@gih.com.tw. *Website:* www.cidc.com.tw.

HSU, Sheng-Hsiung (Rock); Taiwanese business executive; *Chairman, Compal Electronics;* ed Nat. Taiwan Normal Univ.; Chair. Compal Electronics, Inc. 1984–; Chair., Exec. Dir. Man. Dir, Gen. Man. and other sr positions in more than 30 technological cos in Taiwan, including Kinpo Electronics Inc., AcBel Polytech Inc., Cal-Comp Electronics & Communications Co., Vibo Telecom Inc. as well as China Productivity Center; Vice-Chair. Straits Exchange Foundation; Deputy Dir-Gen. Chinese Nat. Fed. of Industries; Nat. Policy Advisor under the Office of the Pres.; Advisor, Exec. Yuan; Hon. Dir-Gen. Taiwan Electrical & Electronic Mfrs' Asscn, Importers & Exporters Asscn of Taipei; Hon. PhD (Nat. Taiwan Normal Univ.) 2008; Nat. Quality Award (Individual), Ministry of Econ. Affairs 1999, named as one of Nat. Taiwan Normal Univ.'s Outstanding Alumni for 2005, Exceptional Accomplishment Award, 7th Industrial Sustainable Excellence Awards 2006. *Address:* Compal Electronics Inc., 581 Ruiguang Road, Neihu District, Taipei 11492, Taiwan (office). *Telephone:* (2) 87978588 (office). *Fax:* (2) 26585001 (office). *E-mail:* info@compal.com (office). *Website:* www.compal.com (office).

HSU, Shui-Teh, MA; Taiwanese politician; b. 1 Aug. 1931, Kaohsiung City; m. Yang Shu-hua; two s.; ed Nat. Taiwan Normal Univ., Nat. Chengchi Univ. and Japan Univ. of Educ.; official, Pingtung County Govt 1968–70, Kaohsiung City Govt 1970–75; Commr Dept of Social Affairs, Taiwan Provincial Govt 1975–79; Dir Dept of Social Affairs, Cen. Cttee, Kuomintang 1979, fmr Sec.-Gen.; Sec.-Gen. Kaohsiung City Govt 1979–82; Mayor of Kaohsiung 1982–85, of Taipei 1985–88; Minister of the Interior 1988–91; Rep. Taipei Econ. and Culture Rep. Office in Japan 1991–93; Pres. Examination Yuan 1996–2002; Hon. LLD (Lincoln Univ.) 1985. *Publications:* The Childhood Education of Emile, My Compliments— Recollections of Those Days Serving as Kaohsiung Mayor, A Thousand Sunrises and Midnights, My Scoopwheel Philosophy, A Study of Welfare Administration for the Aged, several works on psychology and educ. *Address:* c/o Office of the President, Examination Yuan, No.1, Shiyuan Road, Wenshan Dist., Taipei 11601, Taiwan.

HU, Chunhua, BA; Chinese politician; *Secretary, CCP Provincial Committee, Guangdong Province;* b. 1963, Wufeng Co., Hubei Prov.; ed Beijing Univ., CCP Cen. Cttee Central Party School; joined CCP 1983; Man., Ministry of Human Resources and Social Security, Tibet Lhasa Hotel, Tibet Autonomous Region 1985–87; Deputy Commr, Admin Office, Nyingchi, Tibet Autonomous Region 1992–95; Deputy Sec., CCP Autonomous Prefectural Cttee, Lhokha Pref., Tibet Autonomous Region 1995–97; Vice-Chair. All-China Youth Fed. 1997–2001; Commr, Standing Cttee, CCP Autonomous Regional Cttee, Tibet Autonomous Region 2001–07; First Sec., Communist Youth League of China Cen. Cttee 2007–08; Gov. Hebei Prov. (China's youngest gov.) 2008–09; Deputy Sec., Hebei CCP Provincial Cttee 2009; Sec., Inner Mongolia Autonomous Regional CCP Cttee 2009–12, Chair., Standing Cttee, Regional People's Congress, Inner Mongolia Autonomous Region 2010–; Sec., CCP Provincial Cttee, Guangdong Prov. 2012–; mem. 17th CCP Cen. Cttee 2007–12, 18th CCP Cen. Cttee 2012–, also mem. 18th CCP Cen. Cttee Politburo 2012–. *Address:* Chinese Communist Party Politburo, Quanguo Renmin Diabiao Dahui, Zhongguo Gongchan Dang, 1 Zhongnanhai, Beijing, People's Republic of China. *Website:* cpc.people.com.cn (office).

HU, Fuguo; Chinese politician and engineer; b. 1937, Changzi Co., Shanxi Prov.; ed Fuxin Mining Coll.; Dir Xishan Coal Mining Admin. of Shanxi Prov., 1978–82, Gov. (a.i.) of Shanxi Prov. 1992–93; Sec. CCP 6th Shanxi Prov. Cttee 1993–99; Chair. CCP 7th Shanxi Prov. Cttee 1994; Vice-Minister of Coal Industry 1982–88; Vice-Minister of Energy 1988; mem. State Econ. Examination Cttee 1983; mem. 14th CCP Cen. Cttee 1992–97, 15th CCP Cen. Cttee 1997–2002. *Address:* c/o Shanxi Provincial Committee of CCP, Taiyuan, People's Republic of China.

HU, Han, PhD; Chinese academic; b. 1924; s. of Hu Yen Bo and Xiao Shi Xun; m. Dong Yu Shen; one d.; ed Central Univ., Zhongqing; Lab. of Genetics and Breeding, Dept of Biology Univ. of Leningrad, USSR; Asst Prof., Inst. of Genetics, Academia Sinica 1964–78, Assoc. Prof. 1977–87, Dir 1978–96, Prof. 1992–; Chair. of Scientific Cttee of State Key Lab. of Plant Cell & Chromosome Eng; Vice-Pres. Genetics Soc. of China 1978–91; Ed. Science in China and Chinese Sciences Bulletin 1978–91, Theoretical Applied Genetics 1978–91, Plant Science 1992–2000; Nat. Science Congress Prize 1978, Major Prize, Academia Sinica 1978, Holeung Ho Lee Foundation Life Sciences Prize 2006. *Publications:* (co-ed.) Haploids of Higher Plants in Vitro 1986, Plant Somatic Genetics and Crop Improvement 1988, Plant Cell Manipulation and Breeding 1990, numerous articles on androgenesis in cereals and chromosome eng of pollen-derived plants in wheat. *Address:* Institute of Genetics, Academia Sinica, Bei Sha Tan Building, Beijing 100101, People's Republic of China.

HU, Houkun, (Ken Hu), BSc; Chinese business executive; *Deputy Chairman and Rotating CEO, Huawei Technologies Company Ltd;* b. 1967; ed Huazhong Univ. of Science and Tech.; joined Huawei 1990, served successively as Pres. of Marketing and Sales Dept in China, Pres. of Latin America Region, Pres. of Global Sales Dept, Chief Sales and Service Officer, Chief Strategy and Marketing Officer, Chair. Corp. Global Cyber Security Cttee, Chair. Huawei USA, Corp. Exec. Vice-Pres., Chair. Human Resources Cttee, Deputy Chair. and Rotating CEO, Huawei Technologies Co. Ltd April–Sept. 2013, Oct. 2014-March 2015. *Address:* Huawei Technologies Co. Ltd, Bantian, Longgang District, Shenzhen 518129, People's Republic of China (office). *Telephone:* (755) 28780808 (office). *E-mail:* hwtech@ huawei.com (office). *Website:* www.huawei.com (office).

HU, Huaibang, PhD; Chinese economist and banking executive; *Chairman, China Development Bank Corporation;* b. 1955, Henan Prov.; ed Shaanxi Inst. of Finance and Econs; worked at Shaanxi Inst. of Finance and Econs 1982–97; successively Vice-Prin. and Prin. China Finance Coll. 1997–2000; Deputy Gen. Man. People's Bank of China (PBC), Chengdu Br., Gen. Man. PBC, Xi'an Br. and concurrently Deputy Dir of State Admin of Foreign Exchange, Shaanxi Br. 2000–03; Dir, Working Dept of Supervisory Cttee and Commr of Discipline Inspection, China Banking Regulatory Comm. (CBRC) 2003–07; Chair. Bd of Supervisors China Investment Corpn 2007–08; Exec. Dir and Chair. Bank of Communications 2008–13; Chair. China Development Bank Corpn 2013–; Alt. mem. 18th CCP Cen. Cttee 2012–. *Address:* China Development Bank Corpn, 29 Fuchengmenwai Street, Xicheng District, Beijing 100037, People's Republic of China (office). *Telephone:* (10) 6830-6688 (office). *Fax:* (10) 6830-6699 (office). *E-mail:* info@bcdb.com.cn (office). *Website:* www.cdb.com.cn (office).

HU, Jason Chih-chiang, DPhil; Taiwanese politician and academic; *Mayor of Taichung City;* b. 15 May 1948, Yungchi Co., Kirin Prov., China; m. Shirley S. Hu; one s. one d.; ed Nat. Chengchi Univ., Univ. of Southampton, Univ. of Oxford; Exec. Sec. Nat. Union of Students 1966–68; led del. to UN World Youth Asscn 1970; fmr instructor Inst. of Int. Studies, Univ. of SC, USA; taught Oxford Overseas Studies Programme 1982–83, Research Fellow, St Antony's Coll., Oxford, UK 1985; Assoc. Prof., Nat. Sun Yat-sen Univ. 1986–90; Deputy Dir Sun Yat-sen Centre for Policy Studies 1986–90; Deputy Dir First Bureau, Office of the Pres., concurrently Presidential Press Sec. 1991; Dir-Gen. Govt Information Office and Govt Spokesman 1991–96; Rep. of Taipei Econ. and Cultural Office, Washington, DC; Minister of Foreign Affairs 1997–99; Presidential Campaign Man., Kuomintang 1999–2000, Dir Cultural and Communication Affairs Cen. Cttee. 2000–01, Deputy Sec.-Gen. 2001; Mayor of Taichung City 2001–; Dr hc (Southampton) 1997; Best Govt Spokesman Award 1993, Top Ten Chinese Award 1994, Outstanding Professional Achievement Award 1996. *Publications include:* Say Yes to Taiwan! 1997, Quiet Revolution (in Chinese) 1996; many other books in Chinese. *Address:* No. 99, Sec 3, Taiwan Boulevard Road, Taichung, Taiwan (office). *Telephone:* (2) 2228-8211 (office). *Fax:* (2) 2229-1136 (office). *E-mail:* 10001@taichung.gov.tw (office). *Website:* www.tccg.gov.tw (office).

HU, Jia; Chinese platform diver (retd); b. 10 Jan. 1983, Wuhan, Hubei Prov.; joined Guangdong prov. team 1994, nat. team 1998; winner 10m. Platform Synchronized, World Championships, Fukuoka 2001, Grand Prix, Southern Cross 2003; winner 10m. Platform, Grand Prix, Bangkok 2000, Grand Prix, USA Diving 2001; Silver Medal 10m. Platform, Platform Synchronized, Sydney Olympics 2000; Gold Medal 10m. Platform, Athens Olympics 2004; retd from diving 2009. *Leisure interests:* music, computers, travelling. *Address:* c/o China Swimming Association, 5 Tiyuguan Road, Chongwen District, Beijing 100763, People's Republic of China (office). *Telephone:* (10) 67020332 (office). *Fax:* (10) 67020320 (office). *Website:* (office).

HU, Jiangchao; Chinese business executive; *Chairman, Zhejiang Materials Industry Group Corporation;* Legal Rep., Zhejiang Southeast Electric Power Co. Ltd; Chair. Zhejiang Provincial Energy Group Corpn, currently Chair. Zhejiang Materials Industry Group Corpn. *Address:* Zhejiang Materials Industry Group Corporation, 56 West Huancheng Road, Hangzhou 310006, Zhejiang Prov., People's Republic of China (office). *Telephone:* (571) 87054509 (office). *Fax:* (571) 87054509 (office). *E-mail:* office@zjmi.com (office). *Website:* www.zjmi.com (office).

HU, Jintao; Chinese engineer and fmr head of state; b. 21 Dec. 1942, Jixi, Anhui Prov.; m. Liu Yongqing; two c.; ed Tsinghua Univ., Beijing; joined CCP 1964; postgraduate and political instructor, Water Conservancy Eng Dept, Tsinghua Univ. 1964–65, researcher 1965–68; Sec. Gansu Prov. Construction Cttee, Deputy Dir 1974–75, Vice-Chair. 1980–82; Chair. All-China Youth Fed. 1982–84; Sec. Gansu Prov. Br. Communist Youth League 1982; Sec. Communist Youth League 1982–84, First Sec. 1984–85; mem. Standing Cttee, 6th NPC, mem. Presidium and mem. Standing Cttee, CPPCC 6th Nat. Cttee 1983–98; Sec. CCP Prov. Cttee, Guizhou 1985–88, Tibet 1988–92; Vice-Pres. of People's Repub. of China (PRC) 1998–2003, Pres. 2003–13; Gen. Sec. CCP 2002–12; Vice-Chair. Cen. Mil. Comm. of PRC 1999–2002, Chair. 2005–; mem. 12th CCP Cen. Cttee 1982–87, 13th CCP Cen. Cttee 1987–92, 14th CCP Cen. Cttee 1992–97 (mem. Secr. and Standing Cttee of Politburo 1992–97), 15th CCP Cen. Cttee 1997–2002 (mem. Secr. and Standing Cttee of Politburo 1992–97, Vice-Chair. Cen. Mil. Comm. 1997–2002), 16th CCP Cen. Cttee 2002–07 (Gen. Sec. 2002–07, Vice-Chair. Cen. Mil. Comm. 2002–05, Chair. 2005–07, mem. Standing Cttee of Politburo 2002–07); Gen. Sec. 17th CCP Cen. Cttee 2007–12 (mem. Standing Cttee of Politburo 2007–12, Chair. CCP Cen. Mil. Comm. 2007–12); Pres. Cen. Party School 1993–; ranked by Forbes magazine amongst The World's Most Powerful People (second) 2009, (first) 2010, (third) 2011. *Address:* c/o Office of the President, Great Hall of the People, West Edge, Tiananmen Square, Beijing, People's Republic of China (office). *Website:* www.gov .cn (office).

HU, Kehui; Chinese lawyer; b. Feb. 1944, Anshun, Guizhou Prov.; ed Southwest Univ. of Political Science and Law; joined CCP 1971; Chief Procurator of Guizhou Prov. People's Procuratorate 1993–98; Deputy Procurator-Gen., Supreme People's Procuratorate 1998–2009; Vice-Pres. Chinese Asscn of Public Prosecutors. *Address:* c/o Supreme People's Procuratorate, Beijing, People's Republic of China.

HU, Maoyuan; Chinese automobile industry executive; *Chairman, SAIC Motor Corporation Limited;* b. April 1951, Shanghai; ed Fudan Univ.; began career in automotive industry 1968; mem. CCP 1980–; Man. Dir Shanghai Tractor Factory 1983; served as Deputy Gen. Man. and Asst to Gen. Man. of Shanghai Automotive and Tractor Industry Jt Business Co., Asst to Gen. Man., Deputy Gen. Man., Vice-Pres. Shanghai Automotive Industry Corpn (SAIC), Deputy Gen. Man. Shanghai Automotive Co. Ltd and Gen. Man. Shanghai General Motors Automotive Co. Ltd, Vice-Pres. 1991–99, later Pres., Vice-Sec. Party Cttee of Shanghai SAIC (Group), currently Chair. and Sec. Party Cttee of SAIC (Group), also Chair. and Sec. Party Cttee of SAIC Motor Corpn Ltd and Chair. HUAYU Automotive Systems Co. Ltd; State Model Worker, State Advanced Individual in Quality Man., Excellent Party Mem. of Shanghai Municipality, Master of Operation and Man. in Machinery Industry, CCTV Award for People of Economy. *Publication:* Dialogue with the World. *Address:* SAIC Motor Corporation Ltd, 487 Weihai Road, Shanghai 200041, People's Republic of China (office). *Telephone:* (21) 22011888 (office). *Fax:* (21) 22011777 (office). *E-mail:* info@saicgroup.com (office). *Website:* www.saicgroup.com (office).

HU, Ping; Chinese government official; b. 1930, Jiaxing Co., Zhejiang Prov.; ed Jiangsu Industry Inst.; joined CCP 1950; Vice-Gov. of Fujian 1981–83; Sec. CCP Prov. Cttee Fujian 1982; Deputy Sec. CCP Prov. Cttee, Fujian 1982; Dir Fujian Cttee for Econ. Reconstruction 1983; Alt. mem. 12th CCP Cen. Cttee 1982–87; mem. 13th CCP Cen. Cttee 1987–92; Sec. CCP Prov. Cttee 1982–83; Acting Gov. of Fujian 1983, Gov. 1983–87 (removed from post); Vice-Minister, State Planning Comm. 1987–88; Minister of Commerce 1988–93; Dir Special Econ. Zones Office 1993–96; Chair. Bd of Regents, Overseas Chinese Univ. 1986. *Address:* c/o Ministry of Commerce, 45 Fuxingmen Nei Dajie, Beijing 100801, People's Republic of China.

HU, Qiheng; Chinese scientist and public official; *Chairman, Internet Society of China;* b. 15 June 1934, Beijing; d. of Shu Wei Hu and Wen Yi Fan; m. Yuan Jian Lian 1959; one s. one d.; ed Moscow Inst. of Chemical Machinery, USSR; Dir Inst. of Automation, Academia Sinica 1980–89; Vice-Pres. Chinese Acad. of Sciences 1988–96; mem. Nat. Cttee, 8th and 9th CPPCC 1993–; Vice-Pres., China Asscn for Science and Tech. 1996–; Chair. Internet Soc. of China 2001–; mem. UN Working Group on Internet Governance 2004; Visiting Research Prof., Case Western Reserve Univ., USA 1980–82; mem. Chinese Acad. of Eng; Outstanding Woman of China 1984, Award for contrib. to Nat. Hightech. Programme 863 1996. *Publications:* book chapters in Advances in Information Systems Science 1986; Processing of Pattern-Based Information, Parts I and II (with Yoh Han Pao). *Leisure interests:* reading novels, growing flowers, pets (kittens and guinea-pigs), bicycling, computer drawing. *Address:* Internet Society of China, No.13, West Chang'an Avenue, Beijing 100804, People's Republic of China. *Telephone:* (10) 66068552 (office). *Fax:* (10) 68512458 (office). (10) 66418201 (office). *E-mail:* isc@isc.org.cn (office).

HU, Qili; Chinese politician; *Chairman, Song Qingling Foundation;* b. 1929, Yulin Co., Shaaxi Prov.; m.; one s. one d.; ed Beijing Univ.; joined CCP 1948; Sec. Communist Youth League (CYL) Cttee, Beijing Univ. 1954; Vice-Chair. Students' Fed. 1954; mem. Standing Cttee, Youth Fed. 1958; Sec. CYL 1964, 1978; Vice-Chair. Youth Fed. 1965; purged 1967; Vice-Pres. Tsinghua Univ., Beijing 1976; Sec. CYL 1978; Chair. Youth Fed. 1979–80; mem. Standing Cttee, 5th CPPCC 1979–83; Mayor, Tianjin 1980–82; Sec. CCP Cttee, Tianjin 1980–82; Dir Gen. Office Cen. Cttee CCP 1982–87; Vice-Chair. Cen. Party Consolidation Comm. 1983–89; mem. Presidium, 1st session 7th NPC; Vice-Minister of Electronics Industry and Machine-Building Industry 1991–93; Minister of Electronics Industry 1993–98; Deputy Head, State Leading Group for Information 1996; Chair. Song Qingling Foundation 1998–; mem. 12th CCP Cen. Cttee 1982–87, 13th CCP Cen. Cttee 1987–92 (mem. Politburo 1982–89, Politburo Standing Cttee 1987–89, Sec. Secr. CCP 1982–89), mem. 14th CCP Cen. Cttee 1992–97; Vice-Chair. 9th Nat. Cttee of CPPCC 1998–2003. *Leisure interests:* tennis, cycling. *Address:* Song Qingling Foundation, A12F, Zhejiang Plaza, No. 29 Anzhen Xili, Chaoyang District, Beijing, People's Republic of China (office).

HU, Shuli; Chinese journalist and media executive; *Editor-in-Chief, Caixin Media Co Ltd and Caixin Century Weekly;* b. 1953, Beijing; d. of Cao Qifeng and Hu Lingsheng; m. Miao Di 1982; ed Renmin Univ. of China; began career as Asst Ed., Reporter and Int. Ed., Worker's Daily 1982; Int. Ed. China Business Times 1992–95, Chief Reporter 1995; Founding Ed. Caijing (finance and econs magazine) 1998–2009 (resgnd); Ed.-in-Chief Caixin Media Co. Ltd and Caixin Century Weekly 2009–; Dean, School of Communication and Design, Sun Yat-sen Univ. 2009–; Knight Journalism Fellow, Stanford Univ. 1994; Fellow, China Media Project, Univ. of Hong Kong; World Press Review Int. Ed. of the Year 2003, Harvard Univ. Nieman Foundation Louis Lyons Award for Conscience and Integrity in Journalism 2007. *Publications include:* New Financial Time, Reform Bears No Romance, The Scenes Behind American Newspapers. *Address:* Caixin Media Company Limited, Floor 15/16, Tower A, Winterless Center, No.1 Xidawanglu, Chaoyang District, Beijing 100026, People's Republic of China (office). *Website:* english.caixin.com (office).

HU, Xiaolian; Chinese central banker; *Deputy Governor, People's Bank of China;* b. 1958; ed People's Bank of China Grad. School; held various positions at State Admin of Foreign Exchange, including Deputy Dir then Dir Policy Research Office, Deputy Dir Law and Regulation Dept, Deputy Dir Reserves and Man. Dept, Deputy Dir State Admin of Foreign Exchange 2001–07, Dir 2007–09; Deputy Gov. People's Bank of China 2009–; Alt. mem. 17th CCP Cen. Cttee 2007–12, 18th CCP Cen. Cttee 2012–. *Address:* People's Bank of China, 32 Chengfang Jie, Xicheng Qu, Beijing 100800, People's Republic of China (office). *Telephone:* (10) 66194114 (office). *Fax:* (10) 66195370 (office). *E-mail:* master@pbc.gov.cn (office). *Website:* www.pbc.gov.cn (office).

HU TSU TAU, Richard, PhD; Singaporean politician and business executive; *Chairman, CapitaLand Ltd;* b. 30 Oct. 1926; m. Irene Tan Dee Leng; one s. one d.; ed Anglo-Chinese School, Univ. of California, Berkeley, USA, Univ. of Birmingham, UK; Lecturer in Chemical Eng, Univ. of Manchester, UK 1958–60; joined Shell (Singapore and Malaysia) 1960, Dir Marketing and Gen. Man. Shell (KL) 1970, with Shell Int. Petroleum Co., Netherlands 1973, Chief Exec. Shell Cos (Malaysia) 1974, Chair. and Chief Exec. Shell Cos (Singapore) 1977, Chair. 1982; Man. Dir The Monetary Authority of Singapore and Man. Dir Govt of Singapore Investment Corpn Pte. Ltd 1983–84, Chair. The Monetary Authority of Singapore, Chair. Bd of Commrs of Currency 1985; elected MP (People's Action Party) 1984; Minister for Trade and Industry Jan.–May 1985, for Health 1985–87, for Finance

1985–2001, of Nat. Devt 1992; Chair. CapitaLand Ltd 2004–, Fullerton Financial Holdings Pte Ltd; mem. Bd of Dirs Govt of Singapore Investment Corpn (GIC) Real Estate Pte Ltd (fmr Chair.), Buildfolio; Chancellor, Singapore Management Univ. 2002–10. *Leisure interests:* golf, swimming. *Address:* CapitaLand Ltd, 168 Robinson Road, #30-01, Capital Tower, Singapore 068912 (office). *Telephone:* 68233200 (office). *Fax:* 68202202 (office). *E-mail:* ask-us@capitaland.com (office). *Website:* www.capitaland.com (office).

HUA, Jun-Duo; Chinese diplomatist and government official; Amb. to India –2006; Commr-Gen. World Expo 2010 Shanghai China 2006. *Address:* c/o Executive Committee, 2010 Shanghai World Leisure Expo, No. 3588, Pudong Rd, Shanghai 200125, People's Republic of China (office).

HUA, Qingshan, MEng; Chinese economist and banking executive; *Chairman of the Board of Supervisors, Bank of Communications;* ed Hunan Univ.; served successively at Nat. Gen. Labour Union, Dept of Labour and Gen. Office of State Council 1979–94; Asst to Pres. of Bank of China 1994–98, Deputy Pres. 1998–2007, Exec. Dir 2004–07, Dir (non-exec.) Bank of China Hong Kong (Holdings) Ltd 2002–07; joined Bank of Communications June 2007, Chair. Bd of Supervisors Aug. 2007–. *Address:* Bank of Communications, 188 Yin Cheng Zhong Lu, Shanghai 200120, People's Republic of China (office). *Telephone:* (21) 95559 (office). *E-mail:* info@bankcomm.com (office). *Website:* www.bankcomm.com (office).

HUANG, An-Lun, MM, FTCL; Canadian (b. Chinese) composer; b. 15 March 1949, Guangzhou City, Guangdong Prov.; s. of Huang Fei-Li and Zhao Fang-Xing; m. Ouyang Rui-Li 1974; one s.; ed Central Conservatory of Music, Beijing, Univ. of Toronto, Canada, Trinity Coll. of Music, London and Yale Univ., USA; started piano aged five; studied with Shaw Yuan-Xin and Chen Zi; works have been widely performed in China, Hong Kong, Philippines, northern Africa, Australia, Europe, USA and Canada; Resident Composer, Cen. Opera House of China 1976–; Pres. Canadian Chinese Music Soc., Ont. 1987–96; Fellowship in Composition, Trinity Coll. of Music, London 1983; Yale Alumni Asscn Prize, Yale Univ. 1986; Skills for Change New Pioneer Award, Ontario 2004. *Compositions:* operas: Flower Guardian Op. 26 1979, Yeu Fei Op. 37 1986 and 6 others; symphonic, chamber, vocal, choral and film music, including: Symphonic Concert Op. 25, Symphonic Overture, The Consecration of the Spring in 1976 Op. 25a 1977, Piano Concerto in G Op. 25b 1982, Symphony in C Op. 25c 1984, The Sword (symphonic poem) Op. 33 1982, Easter Cantata (text by Semuel Tang) Op. 38 1986; Psalm 22-A Cantata in Baroque Style Op. 43c 1988, Piano Concerto in G; ballets: The Little Match Girl Op. 24 1978, A Dream of Dun Huang Op. 29 1980, The Special Orchestra Album 1997. *Leisure interests:* reading, sport. *Address:* 15 Carlton Road, Markham, Ont., L3R 17E, Canada (office); The Central Opera House of China, Zuojia Zhuang, Out of Dongzhimen Gate, Beijing, People's Republic of China. *Telephone:* (416) 423-6396.

HUANG, Chih-Fang, BA; Taiwanese diplomatist and politician; b. 14 Sept. 1958; ed Nat. Taiwan Univ.; Officer, Taipei Rep. Office, UK 1985–86; Officer, Dept of N American Affairs, Ministry of Foreign Affairs (MoFA), Exec. Yuan 1986–91; Sec. Congressional Liaison Div., Taipei Econ. and Cultural Rep. Office in USA 1991–96; Chief, Section 1, Dept of N American Affairs (DNAA), MoFA 1996–99; Sr Specialist, and concurrently Chief of Section 1, DNAA 1999; Sr Specialist, Dept of Policy Planning, Mainland Affairs Council (MAC), Exec. Yuan 1999, Sr Researcher, MAC 1999, Deputy Dir Dept of Information and Liaison, MAC 2001–02; Dir-Gen. Dept of Public Affairs, Office of the Pres. 2002–04, Deputy Sec.-Gen., Office of the Pres. 2004–06; Minister of Foreign Affairs 2006–08; mem. Democratic Progressive Party. *Address:* Democratic Progressive Party, 10/F, 30 Beiping East Road, Taipei 10051, Taiwan (office). *E-mail:* foreign@dpp.org.tw (office). *Website:* www.dpp.org.tw (office).

HUANG, Da, MA; Chinese economist and academic; b. 22 Feb. 1925, Tianjin; s. of Shu-ren and Gao Huang; m. Shu-zhen Luo 1952; two s.; ed Northern China United Univ.; Dir Finance Dept Renmin Univ. of China 1978–83, Vice-Pres. 1983–91, Pres. 1991–94; mem. NPC, NPC Cttee on Finance & Econ. 1993–98; mem. and head of econ. group, Academic Degrees Cttee of the State Council 1988–; mem. Monetary Policy Cttee of People's Bank of China 1997–; Dir Expert Advisory Cttee on Humanities and Social Sciences Studies, State Educ. Comm. 1997–; in charge of Eighth 5-Year Plan 1991–95; Vice-Chair. Chinese Soc. for Finance and Banking 1984–95 (Chair. 1995), Chinese Soc. for Public Finance 1983, Chinese Soc. for Prices 1986, Chinese Soc. for Materials Circulation 1990; Vice-Pres. China Enterprise Man. Asscn and the Securities Asscn of China 1987; Council mem., Chinese Asscn for Int. Understanding 1982; Chair. Chinese Cttee on Econs Educ. Exchange with USA 1985. *Publications:* Money and Money Circulation in the Chinese Socialist Economy 1964, Socialist Fiscal and Financial Problems 1981, Introduction to the Overall Balancing of Public Finance and Bank Credit 1984, The Price Scissors on the Price Parities Between Industrial and Agricultural Products 1990, The Economics of Money and Banking 1992, Macro-economic Control and Money Supply 1997. *Leisure interest:* calligraphy. *Address:* c/o Office of the President, Renmin University of China, Beijing 100872, People's Republic of China.

HUANG, Daren; Chinese mathematician, academic and university administrator; b. 1945, Zhejiang Prov.; ed Zhejiang Univ.; Visiting Scholar, Dept of Math., Univ. of South Carolina, USA 1985–86; Vice-Pres., Zhejiang Univ. 1992–98; Vice-Pres. Zhongshan Univ. (Sun Yat-sen Univ.) 1998–99, Pres. 1999–2010; Progress in Science and Tech. Award, Nat. and Prov. Awards for Excellence in Teaching. *Publications:* over 100 research papers on math. *Address:* c/o Office of the President, Sun Yat-sen University, Guangzhou 510275, Guangdong Province, People's Republic of China (office).

HUANG, Fanzhang; Chinese economist; *Senior Adviser, China Reform Forum;* b. 8 Feb. 1931, Jiang-Xi; s. of Qi-Kun Huang and Yun-Jin Hua; m. Yue-Fen Xue 1959; two s.; ed Peking Univ.; Researcher, Inst. of Econs, Chinese Acad. of Social Science (CASS) 1954–, Sr Researcher and Prof. 1979–, Deputy Dir 1982–85; Visiting Scholar, Harvard Univ. 1980–82, Stockholm Univ. 1982; Exec. Dir for China, IMF 1985–86; Visiting Research Assoc. Center for Chinese Studies, Univ. of Mich. 1986–87; Consultant to World Bank 1987–88; Dir Dept of Int. Econ. Studies, State Planning Comm. 1988–90; Vice-Pres. Acad. of Macro-Economic Research, State Devt and Reform Comm. 1990–97, Sr Researcher 1997–; Vice-Chair. China Reform

Forum 1997–2008, Sr Adviser 2008–; CASS Prize 1985. *Publications include:* Modern Economics in Western Countries (with others) 1963, The Evolution of Socialist Theories of Income Distribution 1979, Swedish Welfare State in Practice and its Theories 1987, The Reform in Banking System and The Role of Monetary Policy in China 1989, China's Exploration of the Theories of Economic Reform in the Last Ten Years (1979–89) 1991, Stock Ownership, Privatization, Socialization and Other Topics 1992, Foreign Direct Investment in China Since 1979 1992, East Asian Economics: Development, Prospects for Co-operation and China's Strategy 1993, China's Transitional Inflation 1994, China's Use of Foreign Direct Investment and Economic Reform 1995, Selected Works of Huang Fan-Zhang (1980–93) 1995, White Paper on East Asian Economies 1996, Economic Globalization and Financial Supervision In Internationalization 1998, Whither Will the East Asian Economies Go? 1999, China's Reform: Opening to the Outside and Its International Environment 2002, China's New Road of Industrialization and its Peaceful Rise 2004, The Blue Book on East Asian Economies 2000–05 2006, 30 Years of Institutional Innovation and Theoretical Innovation: In Memory of 30th Anniversary of Reform & Open Policy 2008. *Leisure interest:* classical music. *Address:* Apartment 801, Building 13, Mu-Xi-Di, Bei-Li, Beijing 100038, People's Republic of China (home). *Telephone:* (10) 63261950 (home). *Fax:* (10) 63908071 (home). *E-mail:* huangfz@hotmail.com (home). *Website:* www.chinareform.org (office).

HUANG, Guangyu, (Wong Kwong Yu); Chinese business executive; b. 1969, Shantou, Guangdong Prov.; brother of Huang Junqin; m. Du Juan; left high school 1987, moved to Beijing with older brother Huang Junqin, took out small bank loan and began selling household appliances; Founder and Chair. GOME Appliances (fmrly China Eagle Group Co. Ltd, name changed to GOME 1993) 1987–2010, GOME Electrical Appliances Holdings Ltd 1987–2010; convicted of bribery, insider trading and illegal foreign exchange dealings, sentenced to 14 years in prison 2010.

HUANG, Huang; Chinese party official; b. 1933, Lianshui Co., Jiangsu Prov.; joined PLA 1946, CCP 1949; Leading Sec. CCP Cttee, Anhui Prov. 1983–86; mem. 12th CCP Cen. Cttee 1985–87; mem. Presidium 6th NPC 1986–88; Deputy Gov. Jianxi Prov. 1987–90; Sec. CCP 7th Ningxia Hui Autonomous Regional Cttee 1990–; Political Commissar 1990–96; mem. 14th CCP Cen. Cttee 1992–97.

HUANG, Jack; Taiwanese editor and newspaper executive; s. of Y. P. Huang and Nancy Huang, co-founders of The China Post; Publr and Ed. The China Post. *Address:* The China Post, 8 Fu Shun Street, Taipei 10452, Taiwan (office). *Telephone:* (2) 2596-9971 (office). *Fax:* (2) 2595-7962 (office). *E-mail:* cpost@msl .hinet.net (office); info@mail.chinapost.com.tw (office). *Website:* www.chinapost .com.tw (office).

HUANG, James C. F., BA; Taiwanese government official; b. 14 Sept. 1958, Tainan City; m. Charlene Ting; one s. two d.; ed Nat. Taiwan Univ.; Officer Dept of N American Affairs, Ministry of Foreign Affairs 1986, Officer Secr. 1989, Section Chief, First Section 1996, Asst Deputy-Gen. and Section Chief, First Section 1999; Sec., Congressional Liaison Div., Taipei Econ. and Cultural Rep. Office, USA 1991; Asst Deputy-Gen. Dept of Policy and Planning, Mainland Affairs Council, Exec. Yuan 1999, Sr Researcher, Mainland Affairs Council 2000, Deputy Dir-Gen. Dept of Information and Liaison, Mainland Affairs Council 2001; Dir-Gen. Dept of Public Affairs, Office of the Pres. 2002, Deputy Sec.-Gen. to the Pres. 2004; Minister of Foreign Affairs 2006–08 (resgnd). *Address:* c/o Ministry of Foreign Affairs, 2 Kaitakeland Boulevard, Taipei 100, Taiwan (office).

HUANG, Jianxin; Chinese film director; b. 1954, Shenxian, Hebei Prov.; ed Northwest Univ., Beijing Motion Picture Acad. *Films include:* as director: The Black Cannon Incident (Golden Rooster Best Director Award 1986) 1985, Samsara, Lun Hui (Golden Rooster Best Director Award) 1989, Stand Straight, Don't Collapse 1993, Back to Back, Face to Face 1994, Signal Left, Turn Right 1996, Surveillance 1997, Shuibuzhao (Can't Fall Asleep) 1998, Shei Shuo Wo Bu Zaihu (Who Says I Don't Care?) 2001; as producer: 2 Young 2005. *Address:* Xian Film Studio, Xian, People's Republic of China.

HUANG, Junqin, (Wong Chung-yam); Chinese business executive; b. Shantou, Guangdong Prov.; brother of Huang Guangyu; moved to Beijing with younger brother Huang Guangyu, took out small bank loan and began selling household appliances; f. Gome brand for their electronics business 1987; moved into real estate industry, two brothers later separated and Junqin obtained assets of real estate business; f. Towercrest Group, later Chair.; Chair. Shandong Jintai Group Co. 2002; convicted of fraud and insider dealing, served three and a half years in prison 2010–12.

HUANG, Pi-twan, BA, MA, PhD; Taiwanese academic and politician; b. 14 Nov. 1945; ed Nat. Taiwan Univ., Univ. of Wisconsin, USA; Assoc. Prof. and Chair. Dept of Foreign Languages and Literature, Nat. Sun Yat-sen Univ. 1980–92; Deputy Dir Nat. Chiang Kai Shek Cultural Center 1992–95; Chair. Dept of Foreign Languages and Literature, Nat. Chi Nan Univ. 1995–97, Dean, Coll. of Humanities 2000; Dir Dept of Higher Educ., Ministry of Educ., Exec. Yuan 1997–2000; Pres. Tainan Nat. Univ. of the Arts 2000–06; Minister of the Council for Cultural Affairs 2008–12; Hon. Fellow, Univ. of Wisconsin 1989–90. *Address:* c/o Council for Cultural Affairs, 30-1 Beiping East Road, Taipei 10051, Taiwan (office).

HUANG, Rayson Lisung, CBE, JP, DPhil, DSc, LLD, FRCPE; Singaporean university teacher and administrator; b. 1 Sept. 1920, Shantou, China; s. of Rufus Huang and Roseland Huang; m. Grace Wei Li 1949 (deceased); two s.; ed Munsang Coll., Hong Kong, Univ. of Hong Kong, Univ. of Oxford, UK; Demonstrator in Chem., Nat. Kwangsi Univ., Kweilin, China 1943; Postdoctoral Fellow and Research Assoc., Univ. of Chicago 1947–50; Lecturer in Chem., Univ. of Malaya, Singapore 1951–54, Reader in Chem. 1955–59; Prof. of Chem., Univ. of Malaya, Kuala Lumpur 1959–69, Dean of Science 1962–65; Vice-Chancellor Nanyang Univ., Singapore 1969–72, Univ. of Hong Kong 1972–86; Pres. Asscn of Southeast Asian Insts of Higher Learning 1970–72, 1981–83; Chair. Council, Asscn of Commonwealth Univs 1980–83; unofficial mem. Legis. Council of Hong Kong 1977–83; Vice-Chair. Council, Shantou Univ., China 1987–94; mem. Drafting Cttee and Vice-Chair. Consultative Cttee for Basic Law of the Hong Kong Special Admin. Region of the People's Repub. of China 1985–90; Life mem. of Court, Univ. of Hong Kong; Life mem. Bd Trustees Rayson Huang Foundation, Kuala Lumpur; Dir Ming Pao Enterprise Corpn Ltd, Hong Kong 1990–94; Fellow, Royal Coll. of Physicians, Edinburgh 1986–; Honorary Trustee, Croucher Foundation; Order of the Rising Sun (Japan) 1986; Hon. DSc (Hong Kong) 1968; Hon. LLD (E Asia, Macao) 1986. *Publications:* The Chemistry of Free Radicals 1974, A Lifetime in Academia (autobiog.) 2000; about 50 research papers on chemistry of free radicals, molecular rearrangements and synthetic oestrogens. *Leisure interests:* opera, ballet, concerts, violin-playing. *Address:* Raycrest II, 10 The Stables, Selly Park, Birmingham, B29 7JW, England (home). *Telephone:* (121) 472-0180 (home).

HUANG, Shuxian; Chinese politician; *Minister of Supervision;* b. 1955, Yangzhong; ed Nanjing Univ.; began career as jr cultural official and CCP Party Sec. in Yangzhong County, Jiangsu Prov.; Chinese Communist Youth League Prov. Sec., Jiangsu Prov. 1985; Minister of Supervision 2013–; Dir Nat. Bureau of Corruption Prevention 2013–; Deputy Sec., 17th CCP Cen. Cttee Cen. Comm. for Discipline Inspection 2007–12, 18th CCP Cen. Cttee Cen. Comm. for Discipline Inspection 2012–; mem. 18th CCP Cen. Cttee 2012–. *Address:* Ministry of Supervision, 2 Guanganmen Nan Jie, Xuanwu Qu, Beijing 100053, People's Republic of China (office). *Telephone:* (10) 59595320 (office). *E-mail:* jcbfwxx@mos .gov.cn (office). *Website:* www.mos.gov.cn (office).

HUANG, Tianwen; Chinese business executive; b. 1955; Pres. Sinosteel Corpn 2003–11, Deputy Sec. Party Cttee CCP; Co-organizer Fourth Chinese Iron and Steel Traders' Conf., An'shan 2009. *Address:* c/o Sinosteel Corpn, Sinosteel International Plaza, 8 Haidian Street, Beijing 100080, People's Republic of China.

HUANG, Tiao-kuei, MA; Taiwanese insurance industry executive; ed Nat. Tsing Hua Univ., Swiss Insurance Training Centre, Switzerland; fmrly Exec. Vice-Pres. Cathay Life Insurance Co. Ltd, Pres. –2008, also fmr Pres. Cathay Financial Holdings; fmr Man.-Dir Life Insurance Asscn of Repub. of China, Chair. 2003; mem. Int. Insurance Soc. *Address:* c/o Cathay Life Insurance Company Ltd, 296 Jen Ai Road, Section 4, Taipei 10639, Taiwan. *Telephone:* (22) 755-1399.

HUANG, Zhendong; Chinese politician; b. 1941, Dafeng Co., Jiangsu Prov.; ed Nanjing Navigation Eng School, Shanghai Shipping Inst.; Sr Engineer at Research Fellow level, Nanjing Navigation Eng School 1962; entered workforce, Admin. Bureau, Qinhuangdao Harbour, Hebei Prov. 1963, Deputy Chief of Planning Div. and Deputy Dir Admin. Bureau 1963–82, Dir 1982; joined CCP 1981; Vice-Minister of Communications 1985–88, Minister 1991–2003 (Sec. CCP Leading Party Group, Ministry of Communications 1991); Gen. Man. State Communications Investment Co. 1988–91; Chair. China Merchants' Steam Navigation Group Ltd 1991; mem. 14th CCP Cen. Cttee 1992–97, 15th Cen. Cttee 1997–2002, 16th CCP Cen. Cttee 2002–07; Sec. Chongqing CCP Municipal Cttee 2002–05; Chair. Standing Cttee Chongqing Municipal People's Congress 2003–06. *Address:* c/o Zhongguo Gongchan Dang (Chinese Communist Party), 1 Zhong Nan, Beijing, People's Republic of China.

HUANG, Zhiquan; Chinese politician; b. Feb. 1942, Tongxiang, Zhejiang Prov.; ed Zhejiang Agricultural Univ.; joined CCP 1979; Div. Head and Deputy Dir Jiangxi Prov. Planning Comm. 1984–91, Dir 1991–93; Asst Gov. Jiangxi Prov. 1991–93, Vice-Gov. 1993–2001, Gov. 2001–06; Deputy Sec. CCP Jiangxi Prov. Cttee 1995–; mem. 15th CCP Cen. Cttee 1997–2002, 16th CCP Cen. Cttee 2002–07. *Address:* c/o Jiangxi Provincial People's Government, 5 Beijing West Road, Nanchang 330046, People's Republic of China (office).

HUBBARD, Allan (Al) Brooks, BA, MA, JD; American business executive and fmr government official; *CEO, E&A Industries Inc.;* b. 8 Sept. 1947, Jackson, Tenn.; m. Kathryn Hubbard (née Fortune) 1979; one s.; ed Vanderbilt Univ., Harvard School of Business Admin, Harvard Law School; Co-founder and CEO E&A Industries Inc., Indianapolis 1983–; Deputy Chief of Staff to Vice-Pres. Dan Quayle 1990–92, fmr Dir Pres.'s Council on Competitiveness; Asst to Pres. for Econ. Policy and Dir Nat. Econ. Council 2005–07 (resgnd); Trustee Emer., Hudson Inst. *Address:* E&A Industries Inc., 101 West Ohio St, Suite 1350, Indianapolis, IN 46204, USA (office). *Telephone:* (317) 684-3150 (office). *Fax:* (317) 681-5068 (office). *Website:* www.eaindustries.com (office).

HUBBARD, John, BA; American painter; b. 26 Feb. 1931, Ridgefield, Conn.; s. of G. Evans Hubbard and Dorothea Denys Hubbard; m. Caryl Whineray 1961; one s. one d.; ed Milton Acad., Harvard Univ. and Art Students' League; served in US Army in Counter-Intelligence 1953–56; designed decor and costumes for Le Baiser de la Fée, Dutch Nat. Ballet 1968, Midsummer, Royal Ballet, London 1983 and Sylvia Pas de Deux, Royal Ballet, London 1985; mem. Advisory Panel, Tate Gallery, St Ives 1993–2000; also works as gardener, making parterres for Waddesdon Manor in 2000 etc.; Astra Award (Garden Design) 1992, Jerwood Prize 1996. *Television:* The South Bank Show 1981, Flowering Passions 1992, Gardens of the World 2005. *Publications:* Second Nature 1984, The Tree of Life 1989. *Leisure interests:* walking, gardening. *Address:* Chilcombe House, Chilcombe, Bridport, Dorset, DT6 4PN, England (home); c/o Marlborough Fine Art, 6 Albemarle Street, London, W1S 4BY, England (office). *Telephone:* (1308) 482234 (home); (20) 7629-5161 (office). *E-mail:* john@johnhubbard.com (home); mfa@ marlboroughfineart.com (office). *Website:* johnhubbard.com; www .marlboroughfineart.com (office). *Fax:* (20) 7629-6338 (office).

HUBBARD, Richard (Dick), ONZM, B Tech; New Zealand business executive and fmr politician; Chair. Hubbard Foods Ltd 1988–; Mayor of Auckland 2004–07; Founding Chair. NZ Businesses for Social Responsibility (now The Sustainable Business Network); Dir Outward Bound NZ; councillor, Massey Univ.; Trustee, NZ Nat. Parks and Conservation Foundation; Fellow, NZ Inst. of Food Science and Tech., NZ Inst. of Man.; Dr hc (Massey Univ.). *Leisure interests:* climbing, motorcycling, photography. *Address:* Hubbard Foods Ltd, PO Box 24-395, Royal Oak, Auckland 1345, New Zealand (office). *Fax:* (9) 634-6070 (office). *E-mail:* email@hubbards.co.nz (office). *Website:* www.hubbards.co.nz (office).

HUBBARD, R(obert) Glenn, PhD; American economist, academic and fmr government official; *Russell L. Carson Professor of Finance and Economics and Dean, Graduate School of Business, Columbia University;* b. 4 Sept. 1958, Apopka, Fla; m. Constance Pond Hubbard; two s.; ed Univ. of Cen. Florida, Harvard Univ.; Asst Prof. of Econs, Northwestern Univ. 1983–88; Prof. of Finance and Econs, Grad. School of Business, Columbia Univ. 1988–, Russell L. Carson Prof. of Finance and Econs 1994–, Sr Vice-Dean 1994–97, Co-Dir Entrepreneurship Program 1998–2004, Dean 2004–; Deputy Asst Sec. for Tax Policy, US Treasury Dept, Washington, DC 1991–93; Chair. Pres. Council of Econ. Advisers, White

House 2001–03; Visiting Scholar, American Enterprise Inst., Washington, DC; econ. advisor to Mitt Romney campaign for Republican nomination for Pres. 2008; Visiting Prof. of Business Admin, Harvard Business School 1997–98; mem. Bd of Dirs ADP Inc. 2004–, KKR Financial Corpn 2004–, BlackRock Closed-End Funds 2004–, MetLife 2007–; Chair. Econ. Policy Cttee OECD 2001–03, Econ. Club of New York 2008–; Co-Chair. Cttee on Capital Markets Regulation 2006–; Life Mem. Council on Foreign Relations 2007–; mem. Advisory Bd Nat. Center for Addiction and Substance Abuse 2004–; mem. Panel of Econ. Advisors, Fed. Reserve Bank of New York 1993–2001, 2007–, Panel of Academic Advisors, Tax Foundation 2003, American Council for Capital Formation 2003–; Fellow, Nat. Asscn of Business Economists 2005; Nat. Soc. of Professional Engineers Award, Univ. of Cen. Florida, Northwestern Univ. Associated Student Govt Teaching Awards 1985, 1986, 1987, John M. Olin Fellowship, Nat. Bureau of Econ. Research 1987–88, Distinguished Alumnus Award, Univ. of Cen. Florida 1991, Exceptional Service Award, US Treasury Dept 1992, Best Paper Award for Corp. Finance, Western Finance Asscn 1998, Alumni Hall of Fame, Univ. of Cen. Florida 2000, Michelle Akers Award for Distinguished Service, Univ. of Cen. Florida 2001, Exceptional Service Award, The White House 2002,; William F. Butler Memorial Award, New York Asscn of Business Economists 2005. *Television:* commentator, Nightly Business Report (PBS) 2003–. *Radio:* commentator, Marketplace, Nat. Public Radio 2003–. *Publications:* as co-author: Healthy, Wealthy and Wise: Five Steps to a Better Health Care System 2005, Principles of Economics 2006, The Aid Trap: Hard Truths About Ending Poverty 2009; commentator for press titles including Business Week, Wall Street Journal, New York Times, Financial Times, Washington Post, Nikkei, Daily Yomiuri; books: Money, the Financial System and the Economy 1994; over 100 scholarly articles. *Address:* Graduate School of Business, Columbia University, 3022 Broadway, New York, NY 10027, USA (office). *Telephone:* 212-854-2888 (office). *Fax:* 212-932-0545 (office). *E-mail:* rgh1@columbia.edu (office). *Website:* www.columbia.edu (office).

HUBBARD, Thomas C.; American business executive and fmr diplomatist; *Senior Director for Asia, McLarty Associates;* b. 1943, Ky; m. Joan Magnusson Hubbard; two c.; ed Univ. of Ala; joined Foreign Service 1965, Political/Econ. Officer, Embassy in Santo Domingo 1966, Econ./Commercial Officer, Fukuoka, Japan, with Political Section, Embassy in Tokyo 1971, Econ. Officer, Japan Desk, Dept of State 1973–75, Exec. Sec. to Del., then Energy Advisor, Perm. Mission to OECD, Paris 1975–78, with Political Section, Embassy in Tokyo 1978–81, Dir Training and Liaison Staff, Bureau of Personnel, State Dept, Deputy Dir, Philippine Desk 1984–85, Country Dir 1985–87, Deputy Chief of Mission, Embassy in Kuala Lumpur 1987, Minister-Counsellor, Sr Foreign Service 1989, Minister and Deputy Chief of Mission, Embassy in Manila 1990–93, Deputy Asst Sec., East Asian and Pacific Affairs, Dept of State 1993–96, Amb. to Philippines 1996–2000, Prin. Deputy Asst Sec. of State for E Asian and Pacific Affairs 2000–01, Amb. to Repub. of Korea 2001–04, Sr Advisor, Akin Gump Strauss Hauer & Feld LLP, Washington, DC 2004; currently Sr Dir for Asia, McLarty Associates; Chair. Korea Soc. 2009–; mem. Advisory Council Korea Econ. Inst.; Dr hc (Univ. of Maryland), (Univ. of Alabama). *Address:* McLarty Associates, 900 Seventeenth Street, NW, Suite 800, Washington, DC 20006, USA (office). *Telephone:* (202) 419-1420 (office). *E-mail:* info@maglobal.com (office). *Website:* www.maglobal.com (office).

HUBER, Bernd, DHabil; German economist, university president and academic; *President, Ludwig Maximilian University (LMU) of Munich;* b. 20 May 1960, Wuppertal; m.; two c.; ed Univs of Giessen and Würzburg; Lecturer in Econs, Univ. of Würzburg 1985–89, Akademischer Rat 1989–94, on leave of absence 1993–; Visiting Prof., Univ. of Bochum (Vertretung einer C-3 Professur) 1993–94, Univ. of Dresden April–July 1994, Univ. of Munich (Lehrstuhlvertretung) April–July 1994; currently Prof. of Econs, Ludwig Maximilian Univ. (LMU) of Munich, Pres. 2002–; Bavarian Order of Merit 2007. *Publications:* Staatsverschuldung und Allokationseffizienz – Schriften zur öffentlichen Verwaltung und öffentlichen Wirtschaft 1990, Optimale Finanzpolitik und zeitliche Inkonsistenz, Studies in Contemporary Economics 1996, Chancen und Grenzen föderalen Wettbewerbs – ifo Beiträge zur Wirtschaftsforschung (co-author) 2000, Die Einwohnergewichtung auf Länderebene im Länderfinanzausgleich – ifo Beiträge zur Wirtschaftsforschung (co-author) 2000; numerous articles on public finance, govt and debt, European fiscal and monetary integration, int. taxation and labour markets. *Address:* University Executive Board, Ludwig-Maximilians-Universität München, Leopoldstr. 3, 80802 Munich, Germany (office). *Telephone:* (89) 2180-2412 (office). *Fax:* (89) 2180-3656 (office). *E-mail:* huber.sekretariat@lrz.uni-muenchen.de (office); presidium@lmu.de (office). *Website:* www.uni-muenchen.de (office); www.en.uni-muenchen.de/about_lmu/index.html (office).

HUBER, Erwin; German politician; b. 26 July 1946, Reisbach, Lower Bavaria; m.; two c.; ed Univ. of Munich; started career at Bavarian state finance office 1963; joined Bavarian State Ministry of Finance 1970; fmr Borough and Dist Chair., Junge Union (Young Conservative Party); mem. Borough Council and Cttee, Dingolfing-Landau 1972–78; mem. Bavarian Landtag (Parl.) 1978–, Chair. Parl. Cttee on Devt and Environmental Affairs 1986–87; State Minister and Head of State Chancellery 1994–95, 1998–2005, State Minister of Finance 1995–98, Minister of State for Fed. Matters and Admin. Reform 2003–05, for Economy 2005–; Deputy Sec.-Gen. CSU party 1987–88, Sec.-Gen. 1988–94, Dist Chair., Lower Bavaria 1993–2007, Party Leader 2007–08 (resgnd). *Address:* c/o Büro des Vorsitzenden, Nymphenburger Straße 64, 80335 Munich, Germany (office).

HUBER, Robert, Dr rer. nat, FRS; German biochemist and academic; *Director Emeritus, Max-Planck-Institut für Biochemie;* b. 20 Feb. 1937, Munich; s. of Sebastian Huber and Helene Huber; m. Christa Huber 1960; two s. two d.; ed Tech. Univ. Munich; Dir Max-Planck-Inst. für Biochemie 1972–2005, Dir Emer. 2006–; fmr External Prof. then Assoc. Prof., Munich Tech. Univ. 1976–; Visiting Prof., Univs of Barcelona, Singapore, Duisburg-Essen, Cardiff; Ed. Journal of Molecular Biology 1976–; Scientific mem. Max-Planck-Gesellschaft; mem. Bavarian Acad. of Sciences, Accad. Nazionale dei Lincei and numerous socs; Fellow, American Acad. of Microbiology; Assoc. Fellow Third World Acad. of Sciences, Trieste, Italy; Foreign Assoc. NAS; numerous hon. professorships; Grosse Verdienstkreuz mit Stern und Schulterband 1997; mem. Orden pour le Merite für Wissenschaften und Künste; Dr hc (Louvain) 1987, (Ljubljana) 1989, (Tor Vergata, Rome) 1990, (Lisbon) 2000, (Barcelona) 2000, (Tsinghua Univ., Beijing) 2003; E.K. Frey Prize, German Surgical Soc. 1972, Otto Warburg Medal, Soc. for Biological Chem. 1977,

Emil von Behring Prize, Univ. of Marburg 1982, Keilin Medal, Biochemical Soc., London, Richard Kuhn Medal, Soc. of German Chemists 1987, Nobel Prize in Chemistry (jtly) 1988, E.K. Frey-E. Werle Medal 1989, Kone Award, Asscn of Clinical Biochemists 1990, Sir Hans Krebs Medal 1992, Bayerischer Maximiliansorden für Wissenschaft und Kunst 1993, Linus Pauling Medal 1993, Distinguished Service Award, Miami Winter Symposia 1995, Max Tishler Prize, Harvard Univ. 1997, Max Bergmann Medal, Max-Bergmann-Kreises zur Förderung der peptidchemischen Forschung 1997, Röntgenplakette der Stadt Remscheid-Lennep 2004, Premio Citta di Firenze sulle Scienze Molecolari 2004. *Leisure interests:* hiking, biking, skiing. *Address:* Max-Planck-Institut für Biochemie, Am Klopferspitz 18, 82152 Martinsried, Germany (office). *Telephone:* (89) 85782678 (office). *Fax:* (89) 85783516 (office). *E-mail:* huber@biochem.mpg.de (office). *Website:* www.biochem.mpg.de/xray (office).

HUBER-HOTZ, Annemarie; Swiss politician; b. 16 Aug. 1948, Baar, Canton Zug; m.; three c.; ed Univ. of Geneva, Swiss Fed. Inst. of Tech., Zürich; fmr Head Secr. Dept for German Law, Faculty of Law, Univ. of Geneva; translator, ILO, Geneva 1973–75; mem. staff Regional Planning Office, Canton of Zug 1976–77; Asst to Sec.-Gen. Fed. Ass. 1978–81, Dir Scientific Services 1989–99, Sec.-Gen. 1992–99; Chancellor of the Swiss Confed. 2000–07; mem. Radical Free Democratic Party. *Address:* c/o Federal Chancellery, Bundeshaus-West, 3003 Berne, Switzerland (office).

HUBERT, Jean-Paul, BA, BCL, MIA, DPolSci, PhD; Canadian lawyer, diplomatist, international organization executive and academic; b. 16 Dec. 1941, Grand-Mère, QC; s. of Jean-Paul Hubert and Cécile Hubert (née Laperrière); m. 1st Mireya Melgar 1967 (divorced 1995); two s. one d.; m. 2nd Florence Fournier 1995; ed Laval Univ., McGill Univ., Columbia Univ., New York, Univ. of the Sorbonne, Paris, Moncton (New Brunswick) Univ.; with Dept of Foreign Relations and Int. Trade, Canadian Diplomatic Service, Ottawa 1971–72, Second Sec., Vice-Consul for Spain and Morocco, Madrid 1972–74, Legal Affairs Div., Ottawa 1974–76, Personnel Div. 1976–78, First Sec. and Consul, Havana 1978–81, Political Counsellor and Rep., Agency for Cultural and Tech. Co-operation, Paris 1991–95, Econ. and Treaty Law Div., Ottawa 1985–86, Fed. Co-ordinator for La Francophonie 1986–88, Amb. to Mauritania, Guinea, Guinea-Bissau, Cape Verde and Senegal 1988–90, High Commr to the Gambia 1988–90, Prime Minister's Personal Rep. for La Francophonie 1988–90, Embassy in Dakar 1988–90, first Amb. and Perm. Rep. of Canada to OAS, Washington, DC 1990–93, Sr Advisor, Commonwealth La Francophonie/Hemispheric Affairs, Ottawa 1993–94, Prime Minister's Personal Rep. for La Francophonie, Ottawa, Brussels 1994–98, Amb. to Belgium and Luxembourg 1994–98, to Argentina and Paraguay 1998–2001, to Switzerland and Liechtenstein 2001–05, Amb. and Perm. Observer of Canada to the Council of Europe 2001–05; elected mem. Inter-American Juridical Cttee, OAS 2004–12, Pres. 2005–07; Interim Pres. Int. Centre for Human Rights and Democratic Devt (Rights & Democracy) 2007–08; Designated Order of La Pleiade, Int. Asscn of French-Speaking Parliamentarians 1989. *Leisure interest:* genealogy, trekking.

HUBERT, Yves; French engineer and banking executive; *Chairman of the Supervisory Board, Caisse Nationale des Caisses d'Epargne;* early career with Rohm and Haas chemical co.; Chair. Supervisory Bd, Caisse d'Epargne de Picardie 1992–2007, Chair. Supervisory Bd, Caisse Nationale des Caisses d'Epargne 2007–, also Chair. Steering and Supervisory Bd Caisse d'Epargne de Picardie. *Address:* Caisse Nationale des Caisses d'Epargne, 50 avenue Pierre Mendès, 75201 Paris Cedex 13, France (office). *Telephone:* 1-58-40-40-02 (office). *Fax:* 1-58-40-50-30 (office). *E-mail:* info@groupe.caisse-epargne.com (office). *Website:* www.groupe.caisse-epargne.com (office).

HÜBNER, Danuta, PhD; Polish politician and economist; *Chairman, Committee on Regional Policy, European Parliament;* b. 8 April 1948, Nisko; two d.; ed Warsaw School of Econs; researcher, Main School of Planning and Statistics, Warsaw (now Warsaw School of Econs) 1971–, Deputy Dir Research Inst. for Developing Countries, Warsaw School of Econs 1981–87, Deputy Dir Inst. for Devt and Strategic Studies 1991–94; Deputy Ed.-in-Chief Ekonomista (bi-monthly) 1991–97; Ed.-in-Chief Gospodarka Narodowa (monthly) 1994–97; Under-Sec. of State Ministry of Industry and Trade 1994–96; Sec. Cttee for European Integration 1996–97, 2001–04; Sec. of State for European Integration 1996–97; Head, Chancellery of the Pres. of Poland 1997–98; Econ. Adviser to Pres. of Poland 1998–2001; Deputy Exec. Sec. UN Econ. Comm. for Europe 1998–2000, Exec. Sec. 2000–01, UN Under-Sec.-Gen. 2000–01; Sec. of State, Ministry of Foreign Affairs 2001–04; Minister for European Affairs 2003–04; EU Commr without Portfolio 2004, for Regional Policy 2004–09; mem. European Parl. 2009–, Chair. Cttee on Regional Policy; Chair. Council for Social Planning 1996–98; mem. Exec. Cttee European Asscn of Devt Research and Training Insts 1987–96, Nat. Statistics Council 1995–97, Scientific Bd Econ. Sciences Inst., Polish Acad. of Science 1996–98; Hon. LLB (Univ. of Sussex) 2005; Dr hc (Univ. of Nat. and World Economy, Sofia) 2007, (Univ. of Poznań) 2010. *Address:* European Parliament, Rue Wiertz 60, 1047 Brussels, Belgium (office). *Telephone:* (2) 283-71-92 (office). *E-mail:* danuta.huebner@ep.europa.eu (office). *Website:* www.danuta-huebner.pl.

HUCKABEE, Michael Dale, BA; American politician, ecclesiastic and fmr state official; b. 24 Aug. 1955, Hope, Ark.; m. Janet McCain 1974; three s. one d.; ed Ouachita Baptist Univ., Arkadelphia, Ark., Southwestern Baptist Theological Seminary, Fort Worth; ordained to ministry 1974; pastor, various Baptist churches 1974–, Beech St 1st Baptist Church, Texarkana, Ark. 1986–; Lt Gov. State of Ark. 1994–96, Gov. of Arkansas 1996–2007; Founder, Past-Pres. American Christian TV System, Pine Bluff; Pres. Ark. Baptist Convention 1989–91; columnist weekly newspaper Positive Alternatives; unsuccessful cand. for Republican nomination for Pres. of US 2007–08. *Address:* 1800 Center Street, Little Rock, AR 72206, USA (home).

HUCKLE, Alan, MA; British diplomatist (retd); *Research Analyst, Foreign and Commonwealth Office;* b. 15 June 1948, Penang, Malaya; s. of the late Albert Huckle and Ethel Huckle; m. Helen Huckle 1973; one s. one d.; ed Rugby School, Univ. of Warwick; with Civil Service Dept (CSD) 1971–74; Asst Pvt. Sec. to Sec. of State for NI, Belfast 1974–75, Machinery of Govt Div., CSD 1975–78; Political Affairs Div., NI Office 1978–80; with FCO 1980–83; Exec. Dir British Information Services, New York, USA 1983–87; Head of Chancery, Manila 1987–90; Deputy

Head, Arms Control and Disarmament Dept, FCO 1990–92; Counsellor and Head of Del. to CSCE, Vienna 1992–96; Head, Dept Territories Regional Secr., Bridgetown 1996–98; Head, OSCE/Council of Europe Dept, FCO 1998–2001; Head, Overseas Territories Dept, FCO and Commr (non-resident) British Antarctic Territory and British Indian Ocean Territory 2001–04; Gov. of Anguilla 2004–06; Gov. of Falkland Islands and Commr S Georgia and S Sandwich Islands 2006–10; Research Analyst, FCO 2012–; Chair. Chagos Conservation Trust 2011–13, Falkland Islands Asscn 2011–; Leverhulme Trust Scholar, British School at Rome Scholar 1971. *Leisure interests:* armchair mountaineering, hillwalking. *Address:* OTD, WH2.306, Foreign and Commonwealth Office, King Charles Street, London, SW1A 2AH, England (office). *Telephone:* (20) 7008-3164 (office). *Website:* www.gov.uk/government/organisations/foreign-commonwealth -office (office).

HUCKNALL, Michael (Mick) James, BA; British singer and songwriter; b. 8 June 1960, Manchester; pnr Gabriella Wesberry; one d.; ed Manchester Polytechnic; fmrly with own punk band, Frantic Elevators 1979; founder mem. and lead singer, Simply Red 1984–2009; numerous world tours; co-f. reggae music label, Blood and Fire 1992; mem. Govt Task Force on the Music Industry 1997–; founded record label, Simplyred.com 2003–; solo artist 2009–; Hon. MSc (UMIST) 1997; BRIT Award for Best British Band 1991, 1992, Best Male Solo Artist 1992, Ivor Novello Songwriter of the Year Award 1992, Mobo Award for Outstanding Achievement 1997, Manchester Making it Happen Award 1998. *Recordings include:* albums: with Simply Red: Picture Book 1985, Early Years 1987, Men and Women 1987, A New Flame 1989, Stars 1991, Life 1995, Blue 1997, Love and the Russian Winter 1999, It's Only Love 2000, Home 2003, Simplified 2005, Stay 2007, Simply Red 25 2008, Songs of Love 2010; solo: Tribute to Bobby 2008, American Soul 2012. *Address:* c/o Creative Artists Agency, 2000 Avenue of the Stars, Los Angeles, CA 90067, USA (office); simplyred.com, PO Box 6215, Basildon, SS14 0AN, England. *Telephone:* (424) 288-2000 (office); (20) 8969-2498 (office). *Fax:* (424) 288-2900 (office); (20) 8969-2506 (office). *Website:* www.caa.com (office); www .simplyred.com; www.mickhucknall.com. *E-mail:* info@simplyred.com (office).

HUCKSTEP, Ronald Lawrie, CMG, MA, FRCS, FRCSE, FRACS; British/ Australian consultant orthopaedic surgeon, academic, writer and inventor; *Professor Emeritus, University of New South Wales;* b. 22 July 1926, Chefoo (now Yantai), China; s. of Herbert George Huckstep and Agnes Huckstep (née Lawrie-Smith); m. Ann Macbeth 1960; two s. one d.; ed Cathedral School, Shanghai, Queens' Coll., Cambridge, Middlesex, Royal Nat. Orthopaedic and St Bartholomew's Hosps, London; Registrar and Chief Asst, Orthopaedic Dept, St Bartholomew's Hosp. and various surgical appointments, Middx and Royal Nat. Orthopaedic Hosps 1952–60, Hunterian Prof., Royal Coll. of Surgeons 1959–60; Lecturer, Sr Lecturer and Reader in Orthopaedic Surgery, Makerere Univ., Kampala, Uganda 1960–67, Prof. 1967–72; Hon. Consultant Orthopaedic Surgeon, Mulago and Mengo Hosps and Round Table Polio Clinic, Kampala 1960–72; Hon. Orthopaedic Surgeon to all Govt and Mission hosps in Uganda and Adviser on Orthopaedic Surgery to Ministry of Health, Uganda 1960–72; Prof. and Head, Dept of Traumatic and Orthopaedic Surgery, Univ. of North South Wales 1972–92 and fmr Rotating Chair., School of Surgery; Chair. Dept of Traumatic and Orthopaedic Surgery and Dir of Accident Services, Prince of Wales/Prince Henry Hosps 1972–92, Consultant Orthopaedic Surgeon, Royal S Sydney and Sutherland Hosps, Sydney 1974–92; Prof. Emer. of Traumatic and Orthopaedic Surgery, Univ. of North South Wales and Consultant Orthopaedic Surgeon, Prince of Wales and Prince Henry Hosps 1993–; Visiting Prof., Univ. of Sydney 1995–; Sr Medical Disaster Commdr, Dept of Health, North South Wales and Chair. and mem. of various disaster and emergency cttees in Australia 1972–; Vice-Pres. Australian Orthopaedic Asscn 1982; Pres. Coast Medical Asscn, Sydney 1985–86; Corresp. Ed. British and American Journals of Bone and Joint Surgery 1965–72, Injury, British Journal of Accident Surgery 1972; mem. Traffic Authority of North South Wales 1982–2008; Consultant to Archives of Orthopaedic Surgery 1984; Founder World Orthopaedic Concern 1973; Patron Medical Soc. of Univ. of North South Wales 1976; numerous orthopaedic inventions including Huckstep nail, hip, femur, knee, shoulder, humerus, staple, circlip, plate, bone screw, caliper, wheelchairs and skelecasts; Hon. Dir Orthopaedic Overseas, USA 1978, Hon. Fellow, Western Pacific Orthopaedic Asscn 1968, Asscn of Surgeons of Uganda 1993, Hon. Adviser, Rotary Int., The Commonwealth Foundation, WHO and UN on starting services for the disabled in developing countries 1970–; Hon. MD (Univ. of North South Wales) 1988; Irving Geist Award, Int. Soc. for Rehabilitation of the Disabled 1969, Melsome Memorial Prize, Cambridge 1948, Raymond Horton Smith Prize, Cambridge 1957, Betts Memorial Medal, Australian Orthopaedic Asscn 1983, James Cook Medal, Royal Soc. of North South Wales 1984, K.L. Sutherland Medal, Australian Acad. of Tech. Sciences 1986, Paul Harris Fellow and Medal, Rotary International and Rotary Foundation 1987, Humanitarian Award (Orthopaedics Overseas, USA) 1991, Vocational Service Award, Rotary Club of Sydney 1994, Australian Centenary Medal 2003, Eyre-Brook Medal, World Orthopaedic Concern 2009. *Film includes:* Polio in Uganda 1966. *Publications include:* Typhoid Fever and Other Salmonella Infections 1962, A Simple Guide to Trauma 1970 (fifth edn) 1994, Poliomyelitis: A Guide for Developing Countries, Including Appliances and Rehabilitation 1975, A Simple Guide to Orthopaedics 1993, Picture Tests – Orthopaedics and Trauma 1994; numerous book chapters and papers. *Leisure interests:* photography, designing orthopaedic appliances and implants, swimming and travel. *Address:* 108 Sugarloaf Crescent, Castlecrag, Sydney, NSW 2068, Australia (home). *Telephone:* (612) 9958-1786 (home). *Fax:* (612) 9967-2971 (home). *E-mail:* rlh333@optusnet.com.au. *Website:* www.worldortho.com.

HUDA, A. T. M. Shamsul, BA, MA, MPA, PhD; Bangladeshi civil servant; b. 10 July 1943; ed Univ. of Dhaka, Syracuse Univ., USA; Asst Commr, Cadre of the Civil Service of Pakistan 1966–68; Sub-Div. Officer, in sub-dist in present Bangladesh and Pakistan 1968–71; Deputy Dir (Food), Punjab, West Pakistan 1971; Additional Deputy Commr 1971–72; Deputy Sec., Establishment Div. 1972–75, 1979–82; Research Asst World Bank, Washington, DC, USA 1978–79, Maxwell School, Syracuse Univ. 1978–79; Deputy Sec., Ministry of Agric. and Forests 1981–82, Jt Sec. 1982–84, Project Coordinator, Bangladesh Jute Seed Project 1982–84, Project Dir, Agricultural Man. Devt Programme 1981–84; mem. Directing Staff, Bangladesh Public Admin Training Centre 1984–88; Jt Sec., Ministry of Irrigation, Water Devt and Flood Control 1988–91, Additional Sec. and Chair. Bangladesh Water Devt Bd 1991–92; Man. Dir Bangladesh Agricultural

Devt Bank 1992–94; Sec., Banking Div., Ministry of Finance 1994–96; Sec., Ministry of Water Resources 1996–2000 (retd); Chief Election Commr 2007–12. *Publications include:* The Small Farmer and the Problem of Access 1983, Coordination in Public Administration in Bangladesh 1987, Sustainability of Projects for Higher Agricultural Education: A Case Study of Bangladesh Agricultural University 1988. *Address:* c/o Election Commission Secretariat, Block-5/6, Sher-e-Bangla Nagar, Dhaka 1207, Bangladesh.

HUDEČEK, Václav; Czech violinist; b. 7 June 1952, Rozmital pod Třemšínem; m. Eva Trejtnarova 1977; ed Acad. of Performing Arts, Prague, studied with David Oistrakh in Moscow; debut with Royal Philharmonic Orchestra in London 1967; soloist with Czech Philharmonic Orchestra 1984–90, Royal Philharmonic Orchestra, London, Berlin Philharmonic, Leipzig Gewandhaus Orchestra, NHK Orchestra of Tokyo; concert tours in Europe, Japan and USA since London debut, and tours in Europe, USA, Japan and Australia; founded School for Talented Young Violinists in Czech Repub.; mem. Central Cttee, Union of Czech Composers and Concert Artists; mem. Asscn of Czech Musicians; Award for Outstanding Labour 1978, Artist of Merit of Czechoslovakia 1980, Supraphon Gold Record Prize 1994, recognized by Pres. Vaclav Klaus through the Nat. Award for Achievement in the Area of Culture and the Arts 2007, Award of the City of Prague 2012. *Recordings:* Bach: Concertos, Bravo Vivaldi, Czech Christmas – Eva Urbanová, Drdla/ Sarasate/Hubay/Lehár/Ravel, Dvorák: Compositions for Violin and Piano, Dvorák: Concerto for Violin and Orchestra in A minor, Op. 53, Guitar: Prague Guitar Concertos, Haydn: Sitkovetsky, Davidovich, Hudeček play Haydn, Mendelssohn-Bartholdy/Sibelius: Violin Concertos, Mozart: The Famous Violin Concertos, Music for Weddings, P.I. Tchaikovsky, J. Sibelius: Violin Concertos, Paganini: Hudeček and Brabec play Paganini, Prokofjev/Tchaikovsky, Souvenir, Václav Hudeček – Violin Recital, Supraphon Stars 2000, Tartini/Paganini/Gragnani/ Giuliani, Triny – Gipsy Streams, Trojan: Suites from the Films, Violin: Hudeček Il Giardino di Musica, Vivaldi: Concertos for Various Instruments, Vivaldi: Le Quattro Stagioni (Record of the Year 1992). *Address:* Londynskà 25, 120 00 Prague 2, Czech Republic. *Telephone:* (323) 640225 (home). *E-mail:* violin@vaclav-hudecek .cz. *Website:* www.vaclav-hudecek.cz.

HUDES, Quiara Alegría, BA, MFA; American playwright and teacher; m. Ray Beauchamp; one d.; ed Yale Univ., Brown Univ.; raised in W Philadelphia; resident writer, New Dramatists; Visiting Writer, Theater Dept, Wesleyan Univ., Middletown, Conn., teacher of advanced intensive course in playwriting 2011–12; mem. Bd Philadelphia Young Playwrights; United States Artists Fellow 2010, Roe Green Award 2012. *Plays include:* Yemaya's Belly (Clauder Prize 2003, Paula Vogel Award in Playwriting 2003, Kennedy Center/ACTF Latina Playwriting Award 2003), Elliot, a Soldier's Fugue 2007, In the Heights (book for musical) (Tony Award for Best Musical 2008, Lucille Lortel Award 2008, Outer Critics Circle Award for Best Musical 2008) 2008, 26 Miles 2009, Barrio Grrrl! 2009, Water by the Spoonful (Pulitzer Prize for Drama 2012) 2011. *Publications include:* Yemaya's Belly 2008, Welcome to My Neighborhood! A Barrio ABC (co-author) 2010, 26 Miles 2011, Water by the Spoonful 2012, Elliot, A Soldier's Fugue 2012. *Address:* c/o John Buzzetti, William Morris Endeavor Entertainment, 1325 Avenue of the Americas, New York, NY 10019, USA (office). *Telephone:* (212) 903-1166 (office). *E-mail:* jbuzzetti@wmeentertainment.com (office). *Website:* www .wmeentertainment.com (office).

HUDSON, Hugh; British film director and producer; b. 25 Aug. 1936; s. of the late Michael Donaldson-Hudson and Jacynth Ellerton; m. 1st Susan Caroline Michie 1977; one s.; 2nd Maryam d'Abo 2003; ed Eton Coll.; numerous awards and prizes. *Films include:* The Tortoise and the Hare 1967, Chariots of Fire 1980 (five BAFTA Awards, four Acad. Awards, other awards), Greystoke: The Legend of Tarzan (also producer) 1984, Revolution 1985 (BFI Anthony Asquith Award for Music), Lost Angels 1989, Lumière et compagnie 1996, A Life So Far 1999, I Dreamed of Africa 2000, Revolution Revisited 2008; numerous documentaries, political films (for Labour Party) and over 600 advertisements. *Address:* Hudson Film Ltd, 24 St Leonard's Terrace, London, SW3 4QG, England (office). *Telephone:* (20) 7730-0002 (office). *Fax:* (20) 7730-8033 (office). *E-mail:* hudsonfilm@aol.com (office).

HUDSON, Jennifer Kate; American singer and actress; b. 12 Sept. 1981, Chicago; one s.; ed Dunbar Vocational Career Acad.; solo artist and actress 2003–; American Idol contestant 2004; Soul Train Sammy Davis Jr Award for Entertainer of the Year 2007. *Television includes:* American Idol (contestant) 2004, Smash 2013. *Films:* Dreamgirls (Satellite Award for Best Actress in a Supporting Role 2006, NYFCC Award for Best Supporting Actress 2006, Screen Actors Guild Award for Outstanding Performance by a Female in a Supporting Role 2007, Image Award for Outstanding Supporting Actress in a Motion Picture 2007, Golden Globe for Best Performance by an Actress in a Supporting Role in a Motion Picture 2007, Critics Choice Award for Best Supporting Actress 2007, BET Award for Best Actress 2007, BAFTA Award for Best Actress in a Supporting Role 2007, Academy Award for Best Performance by an Actress in a Supporting Role 2007) 2006, Sex and the City 2008, Winged Creatures (aka Fragments) 2008, The Secret Life of Bees 2008, Winnie 2011, The Three Stooges 2012, The Inevitable Defeat of Mister and Pete 2013. *Recordings include:* albums: Jennifer Hudson (Grammy Award for Best R&B Album 2009) 2008, I Remember Me 2011. *Address:* Arista Records, 550 Madison Avenue, New York, NY 10022, USA (office). *Website:* www .jenniferhudsononline.com.

HUDSON, Linda Parker, BS; American business executive; *President and CEO, BAE Systems, Inc.;* b. 22 Aug. 1950; ed Univ. of Florida; began career at Harris Corpn, Melbourne, Fla as research and devt engineer 1972–76; joined Ford Aerospace and Communications Corpn, Newport Beach, Calif. 1976, led reliability engineering and quality assurance orgs and was programme man. on a multibillion dollar production programme; held a variety of sr man. positions in production operations, programme man. and business devt in the defence industry 1985–99, beginning with Martin Marietta, led orgs through the Lockheed Martin merger and a subsequent divestiture to General Dynamics; served for seven years as an officer and Vice-Pres. of General Dynamics Corpn, later Pres. General Dynamics Armament and Tech. Products, Charlotte, NC; Pres. Land and Armaments operating group, BAE Systems, Inc. 2007–10, Pres. and CEO BAE Systems, Inc. (US-based, wholly owned subsidiary of BAE Systems plc, London, UK) 2010–, Exec. Dir BAE Systems, Inc. Bd and BAE Systems plc Bd and mem. Exec. Cttee BAE Systems plc; mem. United Service Orgs Worldwide Bd Govs,

Asscn of the US Army Council of Trustees, Blue Star Families Bd of Dirs, Univ. of Florida Foundation Bd, Advisory Bd for the Women in Eng Program at the Univ. of Maryland; mem. N Carolina and Washington, DC chapters of the Int. Women's Forum and C200 (global org. of women business leaders); mem. Alumni and Athletic Asscns of Univ. of Florida and mem. Advisory Bd Coll. of Eng; Dr hc (Worcester Polytechnic Inst.) 2011; Distinguished Alumnus, Univ. of Florida and mem. Industrial and Systems Eng Hall of Fame, ranked by Fortune magazine amongst the 50 Most Powerful Women in Business in the US (43rd) 2009, (37th) 2010, (34th) 2011, (38th) 2012, Woman of the Year Distinguished Service Award, United Service Orgs 2011. *Address:* BAE Systems, Inc., 1101 Wilson Blvd, Suite 2000, Arlington, VA 22209, USA (office). *Telephone:* (301) 838-6000 (office); (703) 312-6100 (office). *Fax:* (301) 838-6925 (office). *E-mail:* baesystemsinfo@baesystems .com (office). *Website:* www.baesystems.com/WorldwideLocations/UnitedStates (office).

HUE, Robert; French politician and nurse; b. 19 Oct. 1946, Cormeilles-en-Parisis; s. of René Hue and Raymonde Gregorius; m. Marie-Edith Solard 1973; one s. one d.; ed Coll. d'Enseignement Technique and Ecole d'Infirmier; mem. Young Communists 1962; mem. French CP 1963–, mem. Secr. Fed. of Val d'Oise 1970–77, mem. Cen. Cttee 1987, mem. Politburo 1990, Nat. Sec. 1994–2001, Pres. 2001, Chair. 2001–03, Senator 2004; cand. of CP in French presidential election 1995, 2002; Mayor of Montigny-les-Cormeilles 1977–; Conseiller-Général Val d'Oise 1988–97; Deputy for Argenteuil-Bezons 1997–; mem. European Parl. 1999–2000; Pres. Nat. Asscn of Communist and Republican elected mems 1991–94, Fondation Gabriel Péri 2003–. *Publications:* Histoire d'un village du Parisis des origines à la Révolution 1981, Du village à la ville 1986, Montigny pendant la Révolution 1989, Communisme: la mutation 1995, Il faut qu'on se parle 1997, Communisme: un nouveau projet 1999, Qui êtes-vous? 2001. *Leisure interests:* reading, painting, cinema, music (jazz and rock), walking, judo. *Address:* SENAT, 15 rue de Vauginard, 75291 Paris Cedex 06, France (office). *E-mail:* fondation@gabrielperi.fr (office).

HUERTA, Dolores C.; American trade union official; *First Vice-President Emerita, United Farm Workers of America;* b. 10 April 1930, New Mexico; d. of Juan Fernandez and Alicia Chavez; 11 c.; ed Delta Community Coll., Univ. of the Pacific; fmr teacher at grammar school; Founding mem. Stockton Chapter, Community Service Org. (campaigned against segregation and police brutality) 1955–62; Founder Agricultural Workers Asscn 1960; est. (with Cesar Chavez) Nat. Farm Workers Asscn 1962; during Delano Grape Strike 1965–70, merger of Nat. Farm Workers Asscn and Agricultural Workers Organizing Cttee to form United Farm Workers Organizing Cttee (UFWOC) 1966; negotiated UFWOC contract with Schenley Wine Co. (first time a negotiating cttee comprised of farmworkers negotiated collective bargaining agreement with agric. corpn in USA) 1966; co-f. (with Cesar Chavez) Robert F. Kennedy Medical Plan, Juan De La Cruz Farm Worker Pension Fund, Farm Workers Credit Union, Nat. Workers Service Center, Inc.; currently First Vice-Pres. Emer. United Farm Workers of America (AFL–CIO), Vice-Pres. Coalition for Labor Union of Women, Vice-Pres. AFL–CIO Calif.; mem. Bd Fund for the Feminist Majority, Democratic Socialists of America, Latinas for Choice, Fairness in Media Reporting, Center for Voting and Democracy; Founder and Pres. Dolores Huerta Foundation 2002–; Hon. PhD (New Coll. of San Francisco) 1990, (San Francisco State Univ.) 1993, (SUNY New Palz Univ.) 1999; Dr hc (California State, Northridge) 2003, (Wayne State) 2004, (SUNY School of Law) 2004, (North Texas) 2005, (Princeton) 2006; Calif. State Senate Outstanding Labor Leader Award 1984, inducted into Nat. Women s Hall of Fame 1993, American Civil Liberties Union Roger Baldwin Medal of Liberty Award 1993, Eugene V. Debs Foundation Outstanding American Reward 1993, Ellis Island Medal of Freedom Award 1993, Consumers Union Trumpeter's Award, Eleanor Roosevelt Human Rights Award 1998, Community of Christ Int. Peace Award (jtly) 2007. *Achievements include:* instrumental in passage of legislation allowing voters right to vote in Spanish language 1961; lobbied for end to 'captive labour' Bracero Programme 1962; instrumental in securing Aid For Dependent Families for un- and under-employed, and disability insurance for farm workers in Calif. 1963; negotiated contracts to establish first health and benefit plans for farmworkers; led consumer boycotts resulting in enactment of Agricultural Labor Relations Act 1974; lobbied against fed. guest worker programmes resulting in Immigration Act 1985. *Address:* c/o Dolores Huerta Foundation, PO Box 2087, Bakersfield, CA 93303, USA (office). *Website:* www.doloreshuerta.org (office).

HUERTAS MEJÍAS, Antonio, BA; Spanish business executive; *Chairman and CEO, MAPFRE SA;* b. 18 Jan. 1964, Villanueva de la Serena (Badajoz); ed Univ. of Salamanca; Man. IT Trames, MAPFRE Mutualidad Functional Area 1990–94, Regional d. MAPFRE Mutualidad in Asturias and Extremadura 1994–98, Exec. Vice-Chair. MAPFRE Praico 1998–2000, Gen. Man. 2000–04, Chair. and CEO 2001–04, Gen. Man. MAPFRE Mutualidad and Chief Exec. MAPFRE's Motor Unit 2005–06, Chair. Exec. Cttee MAPFRE Mutualidad 2005–06, Exec. Vice-Chair. MAPFRE Agricultural 2006–08, Chair. MAPFRE Box Health 2006–08, Chair. Gen. Insurance 2006–08, Chair. MAPFRE Automotive 2006–08, Health Box Chair. MAPFRE SA 2006–08, Chair. MAPFRE Seguros Generales SA 2006–08, Car Chair. MAPFRE SA 2006–08, Chair. MAPFRE Familiar SA 2006–10 Chair. Exec. Cttee 2006–10, mem. Bd of Dirs and Steering Cttee 2006–11, mem. Bd of Dirs MAPFRE Vida SA 2007–12, mem. Exec. Cttee 2009–12, Chair. Ascat General Insurance 2010–11, mem. Bd of Dirs and Exec. Cttee MAPFRE Familiar SA 2011–12, Third Vice-Chair. Bd of Dirs and Steering Cttee MAPFRE SA 2011–12, Chair. MAPFRE Estate 2011–12, Chair. MAPFRE's Domestic Insurance Div. 2011–12, Chair. Bd of Dirs and Steering Cttee MAPFRE SA 2012–, Chief Exec. MAPFRE Network 2006–, Chief Exec. of the Corp. Area for Technologies and Operating Procedures 2006–, First Vice-Chair. UNESPA 2011–, CEO Int. Insurance and Global Business Divs 2012–; mem. Bd of Dirs Spanish Insurance Compensation Consortium 2012–; mem. Bd of Trustees, Fundación MAPFRE 2006–; mem. Advisory Bd Spanish Gen. Directorate for Insurance and Pension Funds 2011–, Business Council for Competitiveness 2012–. *Address:* MAPFRE SA, Carretera de Pozuelo-Majadahonda 52, 28220 Majadahonda, Madrid, Spain (office). *Telephone:* (91) 581-11-00 (office). *Fax:* (91) 581-11-34 (office). *E-mail:* info@mapfre.com (office). *Website:* www.mapfre.com (office).

HUFFINGTON, Arianna, MA; Greek/American writer and columnist; *President and Editor-in-Chief, Huffington Post Media Group;* b. (Arianna Stassinopoulou),

15 July 1950, Athens, Greece; d. of Konstantinos Stassinopoulos and Elli Stassinopoulou (née Georgiadi); m. fmr Republican congressman Michael Huffington 1986 (divorced 1997); two d.; ed Girton Coll., Cambridge, UK; moved to England aged 16; fmr Pres. Cambridge Union 1971; moved to London and lived with journalist and broadcaster Bernard Levin; moved to USA 1980; nationally syndicated columnist and author; provided political coverage of Nat. Elections for Comedy Central 1996; co-f. Americans for Fuel Efficient Cars; spokesperson Detroit Project 2003; ind. cand. for Gov. in Calif. recall election 2003; Founder and Ed.-in-Chief The Huffington Post (news website) 2005–11, Pres. and Ed.-in-Chief Huffington Post Media Group 2011– (after acquisition of Huffington Post by AOL); guest appearances on numerous TV shows including Larry King Live, The O'Reilly Factor, Hannity & Colmes, Oprah, Nightline, Inside Politics, Good Morning America, The Today Show; mem. Bd Points of Light Foundation, A Place Called Home; mem. Bd Trustees Archer School for Girls; mem. Advisory Bd Council on American Politics, George Washington Univ.; mem. Bd Reform Inst.; ranked 12th by Forbes magazine in its first ever list of the Most Influential Women In Media 2009, ranked 42nd in the Guardian's Top 100 in Media List 2009, ranked by Forbes magazine amongst The World's 100 Most Powerful Women (28th) 2010, (31st) 2011, (29th) 2012, (56th) 2013. *Publications include:* The Female Woman 1973, After Reason 1978, Maria Callas: The Woman Behind the Legend 1981, Pablo-Picasso: Creator and Destroyer 1988, The Gods of Greece 1993, The Fourth Instinct 1994, Greetings from the Lincoln Bedroom 1998, How to Overthrow the Government 2000, Pigs at the Trough: How Corporate Greed and Political Corruption are Undermining America 2003, Fanatics and Fools 2004, On Becoming Fearless… In Love, Work, and Life 2007, Right is Wrong: How the Lunatic Fringe Hijacked America, Shredded the Constitution, and Made Us All Less Safe 2008, Third World America: How Our Politicians Are Abandoning the Middle Class and Betraying the American Dream 2010. *Address:* The Huffington Post, 1158 26th Street, PO Box 428, Santa Monica, CA 90403, USA (office). *E-mail:* arianna@ariannaonline.com (office). *Website:* www.huffingtonpost.com (office).

HUG, Michel, PhD; French civil engineer; b. 30 May 1930, Courson; s. of René Hug and Marcelle Hug (née Quenee); m. Danielle Michaud; one s. two d.; ed Ecole Polytechnique, Ecole Nationale des Ponts et Chaussées, Univ. of Iowa; joined Electricité de France 1956, various positions at the Chatou Research and Test Centre 1956–66, Regional Man. (Southern Alps) 1967–68, Research and Devt Man. 1969–72, Planning and Construction Man. 1972–82; Gen. Man. Charbonnages de France (French Coal Bd) 1982–86; Prof. of Fluid Mechanics, Ecole Nationale des Ponts et Chaussées 1963–80; Chair. Bd Ecole Nationale Supérieure d'Electrotechnique, d'Electronique, d'Informatique et d'Hydraulique de Toulouse 1980–90; Chair. Bd CdF Chimie 1985–86; Deputy Admin. Org. des Producteurs d'Energie Nucléaire (OPEN) 1992–2000; mem. Applications Cttee of Acad. des Sciences 1987; Foreign mem. US Nat. Acad. of Eng 1979–; mem. American Nuclear Soc.; Hon. mem. Int. Assoc. of Hydraulics Research; Lauréat de l'Institut (Prix des Laboratoires) 1964; Commdr Ordre nat. du Merite 1980; Officier, Légion d'honneur 1977; Officier des Palmes académiques (Ministry of Educ.) 1986; Chevalier des Arts et Lettres 1981, du Mérite agricole. *Publications:* Mécanique des fluides appliquée aux problèmes d'aménagement et d'énergétique 1975, Organiser le changement dans l'entreprise—une expérience à E.D.F. 1975. *Leisure interests:* tennis, shooting, swimming, flying. *Address:* Design Stratégique, BP 2, 78290 Croissy-sur-Seine, France (office). *E-mail:* michel.hug@neuf.fr (office).

HUGHES, Anthony Vernon, MA; Solomon Islands banking executive and civil servant; b. 29 Dec. 1936, England; s. of Henry Norman Hughes and Marjorie Hughes; m. 1st Carole Frances Robson 1961 (divorced 1970); one s.; m. 2nd Kuria Vaze Paia 1971; one s. one d. two adopted d.; ed Queen Mary's Grammar School, Walsall, England, Pembroke Coll., Oxford and Bradford Univ.; Commr of Lands, Registrar of Titles, Solomon Islands 1969–70, Head of Planning 1974–76, Perm. Sec. Ministry of Finance 1976–81, Gov. Cen. Bank 1982–93; Devt Sec., Gilbert and Ellice Islands 1971–73; Regional Econ. Adviser UN Econ. and Social Comm. for Asia and the Pacific 1994–99; currently freelance econ. man. consultant; Cross of Solomon Islands 1981. *Publications:* numerous articles on land tenure, econ. planning, devt admin, foreign investment, expecially jt ventures, with special emphasis on small countries. *Leisure interests:* working outside, sculling, sailing. *Address:* PO Box 486, Honiara, Solomon Islands (home).

HUGHES OF STRETFORD, Baroness (Life Peer), cr. 2010, of Ellesmere Port in the County of Cheshire; **Rt Hon. Beverley Hughes,** PC, MSc; British politician; *Shadow Spokesperson for Children and Education, House of Lords;* b. 30 March 1950; d. of the late Norman Hughes and of Doris Hughes; m. Tom McDonald 1973; one s. two d.; ed Ellesmere Port Girls' Grammar School, Univs of Manchester and Liverpool; probation officer, Merseyside –1976; Research Assoc., Univ. of Manchester 1976–81, Lecturer 1981–93, Sr Lecturer and Head of Dept 1993–97; Councillor, Trafford Metropolitan Borough Council 1986–97, Council Leader 1995; MP (Labour) for Stretford and Urmston 1997–2010, mem. Select Cttee on Home Affairs 1997–98; Parl. Pvt. Sec. to Hilary Armstrong, Minister for Local Govt and Housing 1998–99, Parl. Under-Sec. of State, Dept of the Environment, Transport and the Regions 2000–02; Minister of State for Immigration, Citizenship and Counter-Terrorism 2002–04, for Children, Young People and Families 2005–07, for Children and Youth Justice 2007–09 (resgnd); mem. (Labour), House of Lords 2010–, Shadow Spokesperson for Children and Educ. 2011–. *Leisure interests:* walking, jazz. *Address:* House of Lords, Westminster, London, SW1A 0PW, England (office). *Telephone:* (20) 7219-0956 (office). *E-mail:* hughesb@parliament .uk (office). *Website:* www.parliament.uk/biographies/lords/baroness-hughes-of -stretford/459 (office).

HUGHES, Rev. Gerard Joseph, MA, STL, PhD; British ecclesiastic and academic; *Tutor in Philosophy, Campion Hall, University of Oxford;* b. 6 June 1934, Wallington, Surrey; s. of Henry Hughes and Margaret Hughes; ed St Aloysius Coll. Glasgow, London Inst. of Educ., Campion Hall, Univ. of Oxford, Heythrop Coll., Oxford and Univ. of Michigan, USA; Chair. Dept of Philosophy, Heythrop Coll., Univ. of London 1973–96, Vice-Prin. 1986–98; mem. Senate and Academic Council, Univ. of London 1987–96; Vice-Prov. British Prov. of SJ 1982–88; Austin Fagothey Prof. of Philosophy, Univ. of Santa Clara, Calif. 1988, 1992; Master, Campion Hall, Oxford 1998–2005, Tutor in Philosophy 2005–; Hon. DLit (London) 2009. *Publications:* Authority in Morals 1978, Moral Decisions 1980, The Philosophical Assessment of Theology (ed.) 1987, The Nature of God

1995, Aristotle on Ethics 2001, Is God to Blame? 2007, Fidelity without Fundamentalism 2010. *Leisure interests:* music, crosswords, walking, gardening. *Address:* Campion Hall, Oxford, OX1 1QS, England (office). *Telephone:* (1865) 286111 (office). *E-mail:* gerard.hughes@campion.ox.ac.uk (office).

HUGHES, H. Richard, FRIBA; British architect; *Voluntary Guide, Tate Britain and Tate Modern, London;* b. 4 July 1926, London, England; s. of Maj. Henry Hughes and Olive Hughes (née Curtis); m. 1st Anne Hill 1951 (died 2006); one s. two d.; m. 2nd Anna Kavya (née Strouts) 2009; ed Kenton Coll., Nairobi, Kenya, Hilton Coll., Natal, SA, Architectural Asscn School of Architecture, London; Corporal in Kenya Regt attached to Royal Engineers 1945–46; Asst Architect, Kenya and Uganda 1950–51; Architect, Hartford, Conn., USA 1953–55, Nairobi, Kenya 1955–57; Prin. Richard Hughes and Partners 1957–86; Chair. Kenya Br., Capricorn Africa Soc. 1958–61, Environment Liaison Cen. 1976–78, Lamu Soc. 1977–79; UNEP Consultant on Human Settlements 1978; UN Cen. for Human Settlements Consultant on bldg materials, construction tech. in developing countries 1979; Ed., Fireball Intl. 1986–92; mem. Exec. Cttee, Friends of the Elderly, London 1987–92; mem. Zebra Housing Asscn Bd, London 1988–98, Trustee, Zebra Trust, London 1988–2012 (Vice-Chair. 1994); Voluntary Guide, Tate Britain and Tate Modern, London 1987–; NADFAS Lecturer 1995–2006. *Publications:* Habitat Handbook (co-author with Graham Searle) 1982, In the Frame 1989, Living Paintings Trust Albums of Architecture for the Blind (ed.) 1991, 1994, Capricorn – David Stirling's Second African Campaign 2003; contribs to books on architecture and articles in New Commonwealth, Architectural Review, Architects Journal and Modern Painters. *Leisure interests:* collecting modern art, dinghy sailing. *Address:* 47 Chiswick Quay, London, W4 3UR, England.

HUGHES, Hubert Benjamin; Anguillan politician; *Chief Minister;* b. 1933; Chief Minister of Anguilla 1994–2000, 2010–, also Minister of Finance, Econ. Devt and Tourism 2010–; Leader, Anguilla United Movt; mem. House of Ass. for Dist 6, Road South constituency. *Address:* Office of the Chief Minister, The Secretariat, POB 60, The Valley, Anguilla (office). *Telephone:* 497-2518 (office). *Fax:* 497-3389 (office). *E-mail:* chief-minister@gov.ai (office).

HUGHES, John Lawrence, BA; American publisher; b. 13 March 1925, New York; s. of John C. Hughes and Margaret Kelly; m. Rose M. Pitman 1947; three s. one d.; ed Yale Univ.; reporter, Nassau Review Star, Rockville Centre, Long Island, NY 1949; Asst Sr Ed., Pocket Books, Inc. New York 1949–59; Vice-Pres. Washington Square Press 1958; Sr Ed., Vice-Pres. and Dir William Morrow & Co. 1960–65, Pres. and CEO 1965–85; Pres. The Hearst Trade Book Group 1985–87, Chair. and CEO 1988–90, Ed.-at-Large, Group Adviser 1990; Consultant and Ed.-at-Large HarperCollins Publrs, NY 1999–2001; Trustee, Yale Univ. Press, Pierpont Morgan Library and Museum, Library of America, Acad. of American Poets; mem. Bd Asscn of American Publishers 1986–90 (Chair. 1988–90); mem. Bd Nat. Book Awards 1982–94 (Chair. 1988–89); mem. Publrs Hall of Fame 1989. *Leisure interest:* golf. *Address:* PO Box 430, Southport, CT 06890, USA (home). *Telephone:* (203) 259-8957 (home). *Fax:* (203) 259-8142 (home). *E-mail:* lawrencehughes@earthlink.net (home).

HUGHES, Karen, BA, BFA; American communications consultant, fmr political adviser and fmr diplomatist; *Worldwide Vice-Chairman, Burson-Marsteller;* b. 27 Dec. 1956, Paris, France; d. of Harold Parfitt and Patricia Parfitt; m. Jerry Hughes; one s. one step-d.; ed Southern Methodist Univ.; TV news reporter, KXAS-TV, Dallas/Fort Worth, Tex. 1977–84; press coordinator for Reagan-Bush presidential campaign 1984; fmr Exec. Dir Republican Party of Tex.; Communications Dir for George W. Bush (while Gov. of Tex. and for presidential campaign) 1995–2000, Counselor to the President 2001–02, left Bush admin to return to Tex. July 2002, Sr Advisor to White House 2003–04, returned to full-time service with Bush campaign Aug. 2004; Under-Sec. of State for Public Diplomacy and Public Affairs with rank of Amb., US State Dept 2005–07 (resgnd); Worldwide Vice-Chair. Burson-Marsteller (communications consultancy), Austin, Tex. 2008–; mem. West Point Bd of Visitors 2008–; ranked by Forbes magazine amongst 100 Most Powerful Women (18th) 2004. *Publication:* Ten Minutes from Normal 2004. *Address:* Burson-Marsteller, 98 San Jacinto, Suite 1450, Austin, TX 78701-3232, USA (office). *Telephone:* (512) 879-0990 (office). *Fax:* (512) 879-0999 (office). *Website:* www.burson-marsteller.com (office).

HUGHES, Leslie Ernest, MB, DS, FRCS, FRACS; Australian surgeon and academic; *Professor Emeritus of Surgery, College of Medicine, University of Cardiff, Wales;* b. 12 Aug. 1932, Parramatta; s. of Charles J. Hughes and Vera D. Hughes (née Raines); m. Marian Castle 1955; two s. two d.; ed Parramatta High School and Univ. of Sydney; surgical trainee, Sydney 1955–59; Registrar, Derby and London, UK 1959–61; British Empire Cancer Research Campaign Research Fellow, King's Coll. Hosp., London 1962–63; Reader in Surgery, Univ. of Queensland 1964–71; Eleanor Roosevelt Int. Scholar, Roswell Park Memorial Inst., Buffalo, NY 1969–71; Prof. of Surgery, Univ. of Wales Coll. of Medicine, Cardiff 1971–92, Prof. Emer. 1992–; Visiting Prof., Univs of Queensland, Allahabad, Sydney, Witwatersrand, Cairo, Melbourne, Lund, Albany, New York and NSW; Pres. Welsh Surgical Soc. 1991–93, Surgical Research Soc. 1992–94; Chair. Editorial Cttee, European Journal of Surgical Oncology 1992–97; Pres. History of Medicine Soc. of Wales 1999–2000; Hon. Fellow, Asscn of Coloproctology of GB and Ireland 2000. *Publications:* Benign Disorders and Diseases of the Breast (third edn) 2008; more than 200 papers and book chapters dealing mainly with tumour immunology, disease of the breast, inflammatory bowel disease, surgical oncology, surgical pathology and wound healing. *Leisure interests:* history, gardening, travel. *Address:* 1 Park View Apartments, 74 Lake Road East, Cardiff, CF23 5NN, Wales.

HUGHES, Louis R., MBA; American business executive; *Chairman and CEO, GBS Laboratories LLC;* b. 10 Feb. 1949, Cleveland, OH; m. Candice Ann Hughes 1972; two c.; ed Gen. Motors Inst. Flint, Mich. and Harvard Univ.; began career with Gen. Motors on financial staff in New York; Asst Treas 1982; Vice-Pres. of Finance, Gen. Motors of Canada 1985–86; Vice-Pres. for Finance, Gen. Motors (Europe) Zürich 1987–89; Chair., Man. Dir Adam Opel AG 1989–92; Exec. Vice-Pres. Gen. Motors Corpn (responsible for int. operations) 1992–; Pres. Gen. Motors (Europe) AG 1992–94; Chair. Bd Saab Automobile AB 1992; Pres. Gen. Motors Int. Operations, Inc., Switzerland 1994–98; Exec. Vice-Pres. New Business Strategies,

Gen. Motors Corpn, Detroit 1998–2000; Pres. and COO Lockheed Martin 2000; Chair. Maxager Technology Inc. 2000–08; Chief of Staff, Afghanistan Reconstruction Group, US State Dept 2004–05; Chair. and CEO GBS Laboratories LLC 2005–; Exec. Advisor Pnr, Wind Point Partners; mem. Bd of Dirs ABB 2003–, Akzo Nobel (Netherlands), Sulzer (Switzerland), Alcatel-Lucent (France); mem. Supervisory Bd Deutsche Bank 1993–2000; Pres. Swiss-American Chamber of Commerce; Chair. European Council of American Chambers of Commerce; mem. British Telecom US Advisory Bd; Order of Merit (Germany). *Leisure interests:* skiing, mountain climbing, antiques. *Address:* GBS Laboratories LLC, 2325 Dulles Corner Blvd, Suite 500, Herndon, VA 20171, USA (office).

HUGHES, Mervyn Gregory; Australian fmr professional cricketer; b. 23 Nov. 1961, Euroa, Vic.; s. of Ian Hughes and Freda Hughes; m. Sue Hughes 1991; one d.; right-arm fast bowler and right-hand lower-order batsman; played for Victoria 1981–95, Essex 1983; played in 53 Test matches for Australia 1985–94, taking 212 wickets (average 28.38) and scoring 1,032 runs (average 16.64, highest score 72 not out), took hat-trick v. W Indies, Perth 1988; toured England 1989, 1993; played in 33 One-Day Ints, taking 38 wickets (average 29.34), best bowling (innings) 4/44; played in 165 First-class matches, taking 593 wickets (average 29.39), best bowling (innings) 8/87 and scoring 2,649 runs (average 17.54); replaced Allan Border as a selector for Australian cricket team June 2005; Wisden Cricketer of the Year 1994. *Film:* has done some acting, portraying Ivan Milat in comedy movie, Fat Pizza. *Leisure interests:* golf, relaxing at home, going to the beach, Australian Rules, basketball. *Address:* c/o Cricket Australia, 90 Jolimont Street, Jolimont, Vic. 3002, Australia. *Telephone:* (3) 9653-9999. *E-mail:* info@crickettas.com.au; events@crickettas.com.au. *Website:* www.cricket.com.au.

HUGHES, Sean Patrick Francis, MS, FRCS, FRCSEd (Orth.), FRCSI; British surgeon and academic; *Professor Emeritus of Orthopaedic Surgery, Imperial College London;* b. 2 Dec. 1941, Farnham, Surrey; s. of Patrick Hughes and Kathleen E. Hughes; m. Felicity M. Anderson 1971; one s. two d.; ed Downside School and St Mary's Hosp. Medical School, Univ. of London; Asst Lecturer in Anatomy, St Mary's Hosp. Medical School 1969; Research Fellow, Mayo Clinic, USA 1975; Sr Registrar in Orthopaedics, Middlesex Hosp., London 1977; Sr Lecturer in Orthopaedics, Royal Postgraduate Medical School, London 1979, Prof. of Orthopaedic Surgery, Royal Postgraduate Medical School (became part of Imperial Coll. School of Medicine) 1991–96, Prof. of Orthopaedic Surgery, Imperial Coll. London 1996–2006, Prof. Emer. 2006–, Head of Div. Surgery, Anaesthetics and Intensive Care 1996–2004, Hon. Consultant, Imperial Coll. Health Care Trust 2007–; Prof. of Orthopaedic Surgery, Univ. of Edinburgh 1979–91; Hon. Consultant, Orthopaedic Surgeon Hammersmith Hosps 1991–2006; Clinical Dir Surgery and Anaesthetics, Hammersmith Hosps NHS Trust 1998–2002; Medical Dir, Ravenscourt Park Hosp., Hammersmith Hosps NHS Trust 2002–07; Rahume Darwood Prof., E Africa 1993, Patrick Kelly Visiting Prof., Mayo Clinic 2000; Vice-Pres. Royal Coll. of Surgeons of Edinburgh 1994–97; Fellow, Royal Coll. of Surgeons in Ireland; Hon. Civilian Consultant to RN, Hon. Consultant 1994–; Aris and Gale Lecturer, Royal Coll. of Surgeons 1976, Walter Mercer Medal, British Orthopaedic Asscn 2004. *Publications:* textbooks and scientific publications on orthopaedics, particularly bone blood flow, musculoskeletal infection, fractures and management of spinal disorders. *Leisure interests:* sailing, golf, walking, skiing, opera, ballet, watching Tottenham Hotspur, running. *Address:* Department of Surgery, Imperial College London Hammersmith Hospital, Du Cane Road, London, W12 0HS (office); The Old Dairy, Maugersbury, Cheltenham, Glos. GL54 1HR, England (home). *Telephone:* (1451) 870234 (home). *E-mail:* s.hughes@imperial.ac.uk (office).

HUGHES, Simon Henry Ward, PC, MA; British politician and barrister; *Minister of State for Justice;* b. 17 May 1951, Cheshire, England; s. of the late James Henry Annesley Hughes and of Sylvia Hughes (née Ward); ed The Cathedral School, Llandaff, Christ Coll., Brecon, Selwyn Coll., Cambridge, Inns of Court School of Law; called to The Bar, Inner Temple 1974; trainee, EEC, Brussels 1975–76; trainee and mem. Secr., Directorate and Comm. on Human Rights, Council of Europe, Strasbourg 1976–77; practising barrister 1978–; Vice-Chair. Bermondsey Liberal Asscn 1981–83; MP for Southwark and Bermondsey 1983–97 (Liberal 1983–88, Liberal Democrat 1988–97), for Southwark N and Bermondsey 1997–2010, for Bermondsey and Old Southwark 2010–; Vice-Chair. Parl. Youth Affairs Lobby 1984–; Vice-Pres. Southwark Chamber of Commerce 1987– (Pres. 1984–87); Liberal Spokesman on the Environment 1983–87, 1987–88; Alliance Spokesman on Health Jan.–June 1987; Liberal Democrat Spokesperson on Educ. and Science 1988–90, on Environment 1988–94, on Natural Resources 1992–94, on Community and Urban Affairs and Young People 1994–95, on Social Welfare 1995–97, on Health 1995–99, on Home Affairs 1999–2003, on Constitutional Affairs and Attorney-Gen. 2006–07, on the House of Commons 2007–08, on Energy and Climate Change 2009–10, cand. for London Mayor 2004, Deputy Leader Liberal Democrat Party 2010–; Minister of State for Justice 2013–; Chair. Liberal Party Advisory Panel on Home Affairs 1981–83; mem. Accommodation and Works Select Cttee 1992–97; mem. Southwark Area Youth Cttee, Anti-Apartheid Movt; mem. Liberal Democrat Party, (Pres. 2004–08); Hon. Fellow, South Bank Univ. *Publications:* Across the Divide 1986, Pathways to Power 1992. *Leisure interests:* music, sport, theatre, the outdoors. *Address:* House of Commons, Westminster, London, SW1A 0AA (office); Constituency Office, 4 Market Place, London, SE16 3UQ; 6 Lynton Road, Bermondsey, London, SE1 5QR, England (home). *Telephone:* (20) 7219-6256 (office). *Fax:* (20) 7219-6567 (office). *E-mail:* simon@simonhughes.org.uk (office). *Website:* www.parliament.uk/biographies/commons/simon-hughes/194 (office); www.simonhughes.org.uk (office).

HUH, Chang-soo, MBA; South Korean business executive; *Chairman, GS Holdings Corporation;* m.; two c.; ed Korea Univ., St Louis Univ., USA; joined LG Group strategic planning office 1977, worked in LG International and LG Chemical, Man. Dir LG International Hong Kong and Tokyo offices 1982–86, Exec. Vice-Pres. LG Industrial Systems 1992–95, Chair. LG Cable 1995–2001, with LG Engineering and Construction 2002–04, Chair. GS Holdings Corpn (conglomerate of 59 affiliate cos spun off from LG Group in 2004) 2004–, mem. Exec. Bd; f. J.K. Huh Foundation (charity); Chair. Fed. of Korean Industries 2010–; Dr hc (St Louis Univ.) 2007. *Leisure interest:* football fan. *Address:* GS Holdings Corpn, 23 F, GS Tower, 679 Yoksam Dong, Gangnam Gu, Seoul, South Korea (office). *Telephone:* (2)

2005-1114 (office). *Fax:* (2) 2005-8181 (office). *E-mail:* info@gsholdings.com (office). *Website:* www.gsholdings.com (office).

HUH, Jin-soo, BBA, MBA; South Korean business executive; *Vice-Chairman and CEO, GS Caltex Corporation;* b. 1953, Busan; ed Korea Univ., George Washington Univ., USA; joined GS Caltex Corpn in 1986, has held positions of increasing responsibility in the co., Vice-Chair. and CEO 2013–. *Address:* GS Caltex Corporation, 679 Yeoksam-dong, Seoul 135-985, South Korea. *Telephone:* (2) 2005-1114 (office). *Fax:* (2) 2005-8181 (office). *E-mail:* info@gscaltex.com (office). *Website:* www.gscaltex.com (office).

HUHNE, Christopher (Chris) Murray Paul-, BA (Hons); British politician; b. 2 July 1954, Westminster, London, England; s. of Peter Paul-Huhne and Ann Muray; m. Vicky Pryce 1984 (divorced 2011); two s. one d. two step-d.; ed Westminster School, Magdalen Coll., Oxford (Demy Scholar), Univ. of the Sorbonne, Paris; edited Isis student magazine at Oxford; served on Exec. of Oxford Univ. Labour Club; financial and econ. journalist at the Guardian, Independent and the Economist for 19 years, also Business Ed. The Independent and The Independent on Sunday; undercover freelance reporter in India during Prime Minister Indira Gandhi's emergency when western journalists had been expelled; also worked for Liverpool Daily Post and Liverpool Echo and The Economist; f. Sovereign Ratings IBCA 1994; Man. Dir Fitch IBCA 1997, Vice-Chair. Fitch Ratings 1999–2003; contested Reading East constituency (Social Democratic Party-Liberal Alliance) 1983, Oxford West and Abingdon 1987; MEP for SE England 1999–2005; MP for Eastleigh, Hants. 2005–10, for Eastleigh (revised boundary) 2010–13 (resgnd); Liberal Democrat Shadow Chief Sec. to the Treasury 2005–06, Shadow Sec. of State for Environment, Food and Rural Affairs 2006–07, Shadow Home Sec. 2007–10, Shadow Sec. of State for Justice and Lord Chancellor 2008–09; Sec. of State for Energy and Climate Change 2010–12; Chair. Press and Broadcasting Policy Panel 1994–95; Econ. Adviser, Gen. Election 1997; mem. Econ. Policy Comm. 1998; Advisory Bd mem. Centre for Reform 1998–; Jt Chair. Policy Panel on Global Stability, Security and Sustainability 1999–2000; Chair. Expert Comm. of Britain's Adoption of the Euro 1999–2000, Comm. on Public Services 2001–02; contested Liberal Democrat leadership 2006, 2007; mem. Council of the EU, Environment Council 2010–13, Transport, Telecommunications and Energy Council 2010–13, European Movt, Green Lib Dems, Asscn of Liberal Democrat Trade Unionists, Nat. Union of Journalists; Liberal Democrat; Jr and Sr Wincott Awards for Financial Journalist of the Year 1980, 1989, respectively. *Publications:* Debt and Danger (with Lord Lever of Manchester) 1985, Both Sides of the Coin (with James Forder) 1999; contrib.: Orange Book 2004, The City in Europe and the World 2005; articles for the Financial Times, The Guardian, The Independent and New Statesman. *Address:* c/o House of Commons, Westminster, London, SW1A 0AA, England. *E-mail:* chris@chrishuhne.org.uk. *Website:* www .chrishuhne.org.uk.

HUI, Ann; Chinese film director; b. 23 May 1947, Anshan, Liaoning Prov.; ed Hong Kong Univ., London Film School; moved to Hong Kong aged five; fmr asst to film director Hu Jingquan; joined TVB and began career making TV documentaries and features; joined Ind. Comm. for Anti-Corruption 1977, made seven TV episodes for drama series (two of which were banned); joined RTHK (Govt TV network) 1978, directed three segments of Beneath the Lion Rock (series); acted in The River 1998, 2001; Lifetime Achievement Award, Asian Film Awards 2012. *Films include:* The Secret 1979, The Spooky Bunch 1980, Boy From Vietnam (TV feature), The Story of Woo Viet (TV feature) 1981, The Boat People (TV feature) (Official Selection at Cannes Film Festival, Best Film, Hong Kong Film Awards) 1982, Love in a Fallen City 1984, The Romance of Book and Sword/Princess Fragrance 1987, Starry is the Night 1988, Song of the Exile (Best Film, Asian Pacific Film Festival and Rimini Film Festival) 1990, Zodiac Killers 1991, My American Grandson 1991, A Boy and His Hero 1993, The Day the Sun Turned Cold (exec. producer) (Best Film, Tokyo Int. Film Festival) 1994, Ah Kam 1996, Opium War (assoc. producer) 1997, Ordinary Heroes 1999, Black Mask (screenwriter) 1999, Summer Show (Silver Bear Award, Berlin Film Festival), Ordinary Heroes, Visible Secret 2002, July Rhapsody 2002, Jade Goddess of Mercy 2003, The Postmodern Life of My Aunt 2006, The Way We Are (Hong Kong Film Award 2009) 2008, Night and Fog 2009, All About Love 2010, A Simple Life 2011. *Publications include:* The Secret 1979, Boat People 1982, Romance of Book and Sword 1987, Yakuza Chase 1991, Summer Snow 1995.

HUI, Liangyu; Chinese politician and economist; b. Oct. 1944, Yushu Co., Jilin Prov.; ed Jilin Agricultural School, Party School of CCP Jilin Prov. Cttee; clerk, Agricultural Bureau and Personnel Supervision Bureau, Yushu Co. 1964–68; joined CCP 1966; clerk and Deputy Head, CCP Revolutionary Cttee (Political Dept), Yushu Co. 1969–72; Deputy Dir Org. Dept, CCP Yushu Co. Cttee 1972–74; Deputy Sec. CCP Yushu Co. Cttee 1974–77; Deputy Dir Jilin Prov. Agricultural Bureau, Prov. Agricultural and Animal Husbandry Dept; Deputy Sec. CCP Leading Group 1977–84; Deputy Sec. CCP Baichengzi Prefectural Cttee, Commr Baichengzi Admin. Office 1984–85; elected mem. Standing Cttee CCP Jilin Prov. Cttee 1985; Dir Rural Policy Research Office, Dir Rural Work Dept CCP Jilin Prov. Cttee 1985–87; apptd Vice-Gov. Jilin Prov. 1987; Deputy Dir CCPCC Policy Research Office 1990; Deputy Sec. CCP Hubei Prov. Cttee 1992; Chair. 1993 Hubei Prov. CPPCC Cttee, Deputy Sec. CCP Anhui Prov. Cttee and Acting Gov. Anhui Prov. 1994–95, Gov. 1995–98; Sec. CCP Anhui Prov. Cttee 1998, Sec. CCP Jiangsu Prov. Cttee 1999–2002; Rep. 15th CCP Congress; Alt. mem. 14th CCP Cen. Cttee, mem. 15th CCP Cen. Cttee 1997–2002, 16th CCP Cen. Cttee 2002–07, 17th CCP Cen. Cttee 2007–12, also mem. Politburo 2007–12; Rep. of 7th, 8th and 9th NPC; Vice-Premier, State Council 2003–13. *Address:* c/o State Council, Beijing, People's Republic of China.

HUI SI-YAN, Rafael, MPA; Hong Kong government official; ed Harvard Univ., USA; joined Civil Service 1970, Admin. Officer 1971, with Ind. Comm. Against Corruption 1977–79, Deputy Sec.-Gen. Unofficial Mems of the Exec. and Legis. Councils Office 1985–86, Deputy Sec. for Econ. Services 1986–90, for Works 1990–91, Dir New Airport Projects Co-ordination Office 1991, Commr for Transport 1992–95, Sec. for Financial Services 1995–2000; Man. Dir Mandatory Provident Fund Schemes Authority 2000–03; Dir Kowloon Motor Bus Holdings Ltd 2004–05; Chief Sec. for Admin, Hong Kong Special Admin. Region 2005–07; Vice-Chair. Hong Kong Arts Festival Soc. 2001–05; mem. Exec. Cttee Hong Kong Philharmonic Soc. Ltd 2004–05; Steward Hong Kong Jockey Club 2002; Justice of

the Peace 1986, Hon. Sec. Hong Kong Int. Film Festival Soc. Ltd 2004–05; Gold Bauhinia Star 1998. *Address:* c/o Executive Council, Central Government Offices, Lower Albert Road, Central, Hong Kong Special Administrative Region, People's Republic of China (office).

HUILLARD, Xavier; French construction industry executive; *Chairman and CEO, Vinci;* b. 27 June 1954; ed École Polytechnique, École Nationale des Ponts et Chaussées; served as civil servant in a local Public Works and Planning Dept and in Ministry for Infrastructure's Dept of Int. Business; joined SGE as Dir of Int. Business at SOGEA 1996, Chair. 1997–2000; Chair. Vinci Construction 2000–02, Sr Exec. Vice-Pres. Vinci and Chair. Vinci Energies 2002, mem. Bd of Dirs and CEO Vinci 2006–, Chair. 2010–, also Chair. VINCI Concessions 2006–; Chair. Institut de l'Entreprise 2011–. *Address:* Vinci, 1 cours Ferdinand de Lesseps, 92851 Rueil-Malmaison Cedex France (office). *Telephone:* 1-47-16-35-00 (office). *Fax:* 1-47-51-91-02 (office). *E-mail:* contact.internet@vinci.com (office). *Website:* www.vinci.com (office).

HUISGEN, Rolf, PhD; German chemist and academic; *Professor Emeritus of Organic Chemistry, University of Munich;* b. 13 June 1920, Gerolstein, Eifel; s. of Edmund Huisgen and Maria Flink; m. Trudl Schneiderhan 1945 (died 2010); two d.; ed Univs of Bonn and Munich; Lecturer, Univ. of Munich 1947–49, Full Prof. of Organic Chem. 1952–88, Prof. Emer. 1988–; Assoc. Prof., Univ. of Tübingen 1949–52; Rockefeller Fellow, USA 1955; numerous guest professorships, USA, Israel, Japan, Spain and Switzerland; mem. Bavarian Acad. of Science, Deutsche Akad. der Naturforscher Leopoldina; Foreign Assoc. NAS, Washington; Corresp. mem. Real Acad. de Ciencias Exactas, Madrid, Heidelberg Acad. of Sciences, Polish Acad. of Sciences, Chemical Soc. of Japan; Hon. FRSC, London; Hon. mem. American Acad. of Arts and Sciences, Soc. Chimique de France, Pharmaceutical Soc. of Japan, Gesellschaft Deutscher Chemiker, Accad. Nazionale dei Lincei (Italy), Istituto Lombardo, Polish Acad. Sciences; Hon. Prof., Univ. of St Petersburg; Bavarian Order of Merit 1982, Bavarian Maximilian Order for Science and Art 1984; Hon. Dr rer. nat (Freiburg) 1977, (Erlangen-Nuremberg) 1980, (Würzburg) 1984, (Regensburg) 1985, (Tech. Inst., St Petersburg) 1993, (Freie Univ., Berlin) 2010; Dr hc (Univ. Complutense de Madrid) 1975; Liebig Medal, Gesellschaft Deutscher Chemiker 1961, Médaille Lavoisier, Soc. Chimique de France 1965, ACS Roger Adams Award in Organic Chem. 1975, Otto Hahn Award for Chem. and Physics 1979, Adolfo Quilico Medal, Italian Chemical Soc. 1987 and other awards. *Publications:* The Adventure Playground of Mechanisms and Novel Reactions (autobiog.) 1994; more than 600 research papers on organic reaction mechanisms and cycloadditions. *Leisure interests:* modern art, archaeology. *Address:* Kaulbachstr. 10, 80539 Munich (home); Department Chemie, Universität München, Butenandtstr. 5–13, 81377 Munich, Germany (office). *Telephone:* (89) 218077712 (office); (89) 281645 (home). *E-mail:* rolf.huisgen@cup .uni-muenchen.de (office). *Website:* www.cup.uni-muenchen.de (office).

HUITFELDT, Anniken; Norwegian politician; b. 1969; m.; three c.; ed London School of Econs, UK, Univ. of Oslo; Pres. Labour Youth League, Ullensaker municipality 1985–88; mem. Bd Labour Youth League, Akershus Co. 1986–90, Sec. 1988–89, mem. Bd Labour Youth League 1990–94, Vice-Pres. 1994–96, Pres. 1996–2000; Student Rep., Akershus Co. School Bd 1986–88; Pres. Nordic Socialist Youth League 2000; Vice-Pres. Int. Union of Socialist Youth 2000–01; mem. Housing Comm. 2000–02; Researcher, Inst. for Applied Social Science 2000–05; mem. Cen. Exec. Cttee Det norske Arbeiderparti (DnA—Norwegian Labour Party) 2002–; mem. Parl. (DnA) for Akershus Co. 2005–; First Deputy Chair. Standing Cttee for Educ., Research and Church Affairs 2005–; Head of DnA women's network 2007–; Minister of Children and Equality 2008–09, of Culture 2009–12, of Labour and Social Inclusion 2012–13; mem. Cen. Exec. Cttee of the Norwegian School Students' Union 1987–88, Comm. for Gen. Educ. Subjects 1987–89, Gender Equality Cttee, Ullensaker municipality 1987–91, School Cttee, Akershus Co. 1989–95, Falstad Memorial and Human Rights Centre 2000–05, Save the Children Norway 2001–07, Comm. on Quality in Basic Educ. 2001–03, Bd of Norwegian Org. for Asylum Seekers 2003–05. *Address:* c/o Ministry of Culture, Akersgata 59, PO Box 8030 Dep., 0030 Oslo, Norway (office). *E-mail:* anniken.huitfeldt@kud.dep.no (office).

HUIZENGA, (Harry) Wayne; American business executive; *Chairman, Huizenga Holdings, Inc.;* b. 29 Dec. 1939, Evergreen Park, Ill.; s. of G. Harry Huizenga and Jean Huizenga (née Riddering); m. Martha Jean Pike 1972; three s. one d.; ed Calvin Coll.; Vice-Chair., Pres., COO Waste Man. Inc., Oak Brook, Ill. 1968–84; Prin. and Chair. Huizenga Holdings, Inc., Fort Lauderdale, Fla 1984–; Chair. and CEO Blockbuster Entertainment Corpn, Fort Lauderdale 1987–94; Owner Florida Marlins, Miami 1992–99, Miami Dolphins, Dolphin Stadium; Chair. Boca Resorts Inc. 1996–, Auto Nation Inc. 1995–2002, Extended Stay America Inc.; mem Bd Dirs Republic Services, ANC Rental Corpn; mem. Team Republican Nat. Cttee, Washington, DC 1988–90; Man of Year, Billboard/Time Magazine 1990 and numerous other awards. *Leisure interests:* golf, collecting antique cars. *Address:* Huizenga Holdings, Inc., 450 E. Las Olas Boulevard, Suite 1500, Fort Lauderdale, FL 33301, USA (office). *Telephone:* (954) 627-5000 (office). *Fax:* (954) 627-5050 (office).

HULCE, Thomas (Tom) Edward; American actor and producer; b. 6 Dec. 1953, Detroit, Mich.; ed North Carolina School of Arts. *Plays include:* Broadway: The Rise and Rise of Daniel Rocket 1982, Eastern Standard 1988, A Memory of Two Mondays, Equus, A Few Good Men 1990, Spring Awakening (producer) (Tony Award) 2007; London: The Normal Heart, Hamlet. *Films:* September 30th 1955, National Lampoon's Animal House, Those Lips Those Eyes, Amadeus 1985, Echo Park 1985, Slam Dance 1987, Nicky and Gino 1988, Parenthood 1989, Shadowman, The Inner Circle, Fearless, Mary Shelley's Frankenstein 1994, Wings of Courage 1995, The Hunchback of Notre Dame (voice) 1996, Home at the End of the World (producer) 2004, Stranger Than Fiction 2006. *Television includes:* Emily Emily, St Elsewhere, Murder in Mississippi 1990, Black Rainbow, The Heidi Chronicles (Emmy Award) 1995. *Address:* c/o CAA, 9830 Wilshire Boulevard, Beverly Hills, CA 90212, USA.

HULL, Brett; American (b. Canadian) professional ice hockey player (retd); b. 9 Aug. 1964, Belleville, Ont., Canada; s. of Bobby Hull; ed Univ. of Minnesota-Duluth; right-winger; played two seasons for Univ. of Minn.-Duluth; began professional career with Calgary Flames of National Hockey League (NHL) 1986, traded to St Louis Blues, played 1988–1998, signed as free agent Dallas Stars, played 1998–2001 (team won Stanley Cup 1999), signed as free agent for Detroit Red Wings, played 2001–04 (team won Stanley Cup 2002), signed as free agent for Phoenix Coyotes 2004–05 (retd); All-Star games appearances 1989, 1990, 1991, 1992, 1993, 1994, 1995, 1997, 2001, All-Star First Team 1990, 1991, 1992; led the NHL in goals with 72 1989/90, with 86 1990/91 (2nd highest total, record for a right-winger); 3rd highest goal total in NHL history (741); 3rd fastest to 600 goals (900 games); 494 goals in 1990s (record); record 17 consecutive seasons of 20 goals or more, including 13 seasons of 30 or more; represented USA at Canada Cup 1991–92, World Cup 1996–97, 2004, Winter Olympics 1998, 2002; Exec. Dallas Stars 2006–07, Co-Gen. Man. 2007–09, Exec. Vice-Pres. 2009–; studio analyst NHL on NBC TV 2006; WCHA Freshman of the Year 1984/85, NHL Lady Byng Trophy 1989/90, NHL Most Valuable Player 1990/91, NHL Lester B. Pearson Award 1990/91, Gold Medal at World Cup 1996 (and named in All-Tournament Team), USA Hockey Distinguished Achievement Award 2003, inducted into Hockey Hall of Fame 2009. *Address:* Dallas Stars, L.P., 2601 Avenue of the Stars, Frisco, TX 75034, USA (office). *Telephone:* (214) 387-5500 (office). *Fax:* (214) 387-5610 (office). *Website:* www.dallasstars.com (office).

HULME, Keri; New Zealand novelist; b. 9 March 1947, Christchurch; ed Canterbury Univ., Christchurch; worked as tobacco picker, fish and chip cook, TV dir and woollen mill worker and studied law, before becoming full-time writer 1972; Writer-in-Residence Otago Univ. 1978, Univ. of Canterbury, Christchurch 1985; Katherine Mansfield Memorial Award 1975, Maori Trust Fund Prize 1978, East-West Centre Award 1979, Mobil Pegasus Prize 1984, Chianti Ruddino Regional Award 1987. *Publications include:* The Bone People (New Zealand Book of the Year Award 1984, Booker Prize 1985) 1984, Te Kaihau 1987, Homeplaces 1989, Strands (poems) 1992, Bait 1996, Te Whenua Te Iwi 1987, Homeplaces 1989, Stonefish 2004. *Leisure interests:* fishing, painting, reading.

HULSE, Russell Alan, PhD; American research physicist; *Principal Research Physicist, Plasma Physics Laboratory, Princeton University;* b. 28 Nov. 1950; s. of Alan Earle Hulse and Betty Joan Wedemeyer; ed The Cooper Union, New York and Univ. of Massachusetts; worked at Nat. Radio Astronomy Observatory 1975–77; researcher at Plasma Physics Lab., Princeton Univ. 1977–80, Prin. Research Physicist 1992–, Head of Advanced Modelling Sciences Lab. 1994–; Fellow, American Physical Soc. 1993, Distinguished Resident Fellow, Princeton Univ. 1994; Nobel Prize in Physics (jt winner) 1993. *Publications:* papers in professional journals and conf. proceedings in fields of pulsar astronomy, controlled fusion plasma physics and computer modelling. *Leisure interests:* cross-country skiing, canoeing, nature photography, bird watching, other outdoor activities, target shooting, music. *Address:* Princeton Plasma Physics Laboratory, PO Box 451, Princeton, NJ 08543, USA (office). *Telephone:* (609) 799-4268 (home). *E-mail:* rhulse@pppl.gov (office). *Website:* www.pppl.gov (office).

HULTQVIST, Bengt Karl Gustaf, DrSci; Swedish space physicist; *Professor Emeritus, Swedish Institute of Space Physics;* b. 21 Aug. 1927, Hemmesjö; s. of Eric Hultqvist and Elsa Hultqvist; m. Gurli Gustafsson 1953; two s. one d.; ed Univ. of Stockholm; Dir Kiruna Geophysical Observatory 1956–73, Kiruna Geophysical Inst. 1973–87, Swedish Inst. of Space Physics 1987–94 (currently Prof. Emer.), Int. Space Science Inst., Berne, Switzerland 1995–99; Sec.-Gen. Int. Asscn of Geomagnetism and Aeronomy 2001–09; Chair. Swedish Space Science Cttee 1972–97, Swedish Nat. Cttee for Geodesy and Geophysics 1980–94, EISCAT Council 1987–88, Nordic Soc. for Space Research 1989–92, Space Science Advisory Cttee, ESA 1998–2000, and others; Kt of the Northern Star Award 1965; Royal Swedish Acad. of Science Prize 1968, 1972, Gold Medal, Royal Swedish Acad. of Eng Sciences 1988, King's Medal 1991, Berzelius Medal, Royal Swedish Acad. of Science 1994, Julius Bartels Medal, European Geophysical Soc. 1996, Haunes Alfvén Medal, European Geophysical Soc. 2002, and other awards. *Publications include:* Introduction to Geocosmophysics 1967, High Latitude Space Plasma Physics (ed.) 1983, Space, Science and I 1997, Magnetospheric Plasma Sources and Losses (ed.) 1999; more than 200 scientific papers on radiation and space physics. *Address:* Grönstensv. 2, 981 40 Kiruna, Sweden (home); Swedish Institute of Space Physics, Box 812, 981 28 Kiruna (office). *Telephone:* (980) 843-40 (home); (980) 790-60 (office). *Fax:* (980) 790-50 (office). *E-mail:* hultqv@irf.se (office); hultqv@irf.se (home).

HUMAIDHI, Badr Mishari al-, BA; Kuwaiti economist and government official; b. 23 Oct. 1948; ed Kuwait Univ.; Lecturer of Econs, Kuwait Univ. 1972–74; Econ. Expert, Operations Dept, Kuwaiti Fund for Arab Econ. Devt 1974–78, Deputy Dir-Gen. 1981–86, Dir-Gen. 1986–; Minister of Finance 2006–08; Bd mem. Arab Gulf Program for Supporting UN Devt Orgs 1981, Arab Fund for Social and Econ. Devt 1986, Arab Planning Institute; fmr Deputy Gov. World Bank, Int. Fund for Agricultural Devt for Kuwait. *Address:* c/o Ministry of Finance, POB 9, 13001 Safat, al-Morkab Street, Ministries Complex, Kuwait City, Kuwait (office).

HUMALA TASSO, Lt-Col (retd) Ollanta Moisés, BA, MA; Peruvian politician and army officer (retd) and head of state; *President;* b. 27 June 1963, Lima; m. Nadine Humala Tasso; c.; ed Colegio Franco Peruano, Universidad Católica; began mil. career 1982, officer 1984; formed clandestine group within army called Militares etnocaceristas 1989; promoted to Capt. 1991, to Major 1996, to Lt-Col 2000; led uprising against then Pres. Alberto Fujimori in Tacna 2000, imprisoned but pardoned; Exec. Dir of Mobilisation, Ministry of Nat. Defence, Sedena 2001; Mil. Attaché, Embassy in Paris 2003, in Seoul 2004; Leader Partido Nacionalista Peruano and unsuccessful presidential cand. Unión por el Perú 2006; Pres. of Peru 2011–; Cross of Military Merit, Officer level 1996, Cross of Military Merit, Commander level 2001. *Address:* Office of the President, Jirón Carabaya, cuadra 1 s/n, Anexo 1105-1107, Lima (office); Partido Nacionalista Peruano, Avda Arequipa 3410, Lima 27, Peru (office). *Telephone:* (1) 7168600 (Office of the President) (office); (1) 4223592 (Partido Nacionalista Peruano) (office). *Fax:* (1) 4449168 (Office of the President) (office). *E-mail:* atencionciudadana@pcm.gob.pe (office). *Website:* www.pcm.gob.pe (office); www.partidonacionalistaperuano.com (office).

HUMAM, Muhammad Awad bin, BSc; Yemeni economist and central banker; *Governor, Central Bank of Yemen;* b. 26 Dec. 1944, Hadramout; ed American Univ. of Beirut, Lebanon; Dir of Research and Statistics, Nat. Bank of Yemen 1978–90; joined Central Bank of Yemen 1990, Deputy Gov., Foreign Operations and Research Dept –2003, Gov. 2010–. *Address:* Office of the Governor, Central Bank of Yemen, POB 59, Ali Abd al-Mughni Street, San'a, Yemen (office). *Telephone:* (1) 274314 (office). *Fax:* (1) 274360 (office). *E-mail:* cbyh@y.net.ye (office). *Website:* www.centralbank.gov.ye (office).

HUME, Cameron R.; American lawyer and diplomatist; b. 1947; m.; four d.; ed Princeton Univ., American Univ. School of Law; joined Foreign Service 1970, early assignments included Vice-Consul in Palermo, Adviser on Human Rights, US Mission to UN, mem. planning staff, Sec. of State, Desk Officer for South Africa; Political Counsellor in Damascas and Beirut; Dir Foreign Service Inst. field school, Tunis –1986; Advisor on Middle East, Mission to UN 1986–90, Sr Advisor 1990–91; Deputy Chief of Mission, Holy See and US Rep. to Mozambique Peace Talks 1991–94; Minister Counsellor for Political Affairs, Mission to UN 1994–97; Amb. to Algeria 1997–2000; Special Advisor to Perm. Rep. to UN 2000–01; Amb. to South Africa 2001–05, Chargé d'affaires a.i. to Sudan 2005–07, Amb. to Indonesia 2007–10; consultant to various interests in Indonesia, including Sinar Mas Group 2010–; Fellow, Council on Foreign Relations 1975–76, Harvard Univ. Center for Int. Affairs 1989–90; Guest Scholar, US Inst. of Peace 1994. *Publications include:* The United Nations, Iran and Iraq: How Peacemaking Changed 1994, Ending Mozambique's War 1994, Mission to Algiers: Diplomacy by Engagement 2006; numerous articles on diplomacy. *Address:* US Department of State, 2201 C Street NW, Washington, DC 20520, USA (office). *Telephone:* (202) 647-4000 (office). *Fax:* (202) 647-6738 (office). *Website:* www.state.gov (office).

HUME, Gary, RA; British artist; b. 9 May 1962, Tenterden, Kent; ed Goldsmiths Coll., Univ. of London; mem. RA Summer Exhbn Selection Cttee 2002; Jerwood Painting Prize 1997. *Publications include:* Gary Hume: Carnival 2005, Gary Hume: Yardwork 2009, Gary Hume: Other Criteria 2009, Gary Hume: The Wonky Wheel 2013. *Address:* c/o Matthew Marks Gallery, 522 West 22nd Street, New York, NY 10011, USA (office). *Telephone:* (212) 243-0200 (office). *Fax:* (212) 243-0047 (office). *E-mail:* info@matthewmarks.com (office). *Website:* matthewmarks.com (office).

HUME, John, MA; British teacher and fmr politician; *Tip O'Neill Chair, University of Ulster;* b. 18 Jan. 1937, Londonderry, N Ireland; s. of Samuel Hume and Anne Hume (née Doherty); m. Patricia Hone 1960; two s. three d.; ed St Colomb's Coll., Londonderry, St Patrick's Coll., Maynooth, Nat. Univ. of Ireland; Research Fellow, Trinity Coll.; Assoc. Fellow, Centre for Int. Affairs, Harvard Univ., USA; Founder mem. Credit Union in NI, Pres. 1964–68; non-violent civil rights leader 1968–69; rep. Londonderry in NI Parl. 1969–72, in NI Ass. 1972–73; Minister of Commerce, Powersharing Exec. 1974; rep. Londonderry in NI Convention 1975–76; MEP 1979–2004; Leader, Social Democratic and Labour Party (SDLP) 1979–2001; mem. NI Ass. 1982–86; MP for Foyle 1983–98; mem. for Foyle, NI Ass. 1998–2005 (Ass. suspended 2002–07); currently Tip O'Neill Chair., Univ. of Ulster; mem. SDLP New Ireland Forum 1983–84, Irish Transport and Gen. Workers Union, Bureau of European Parl. Socialist Group 1979, Regional Policy and Regional Planning Cttee 1979, EEC, Socialist Co-Chair. Intergroup on Minority Cultures and Languages; Co-Leader Int. Democratic Observers for 1986 Philippines Election; mem. Advisory Cttee on Pollution of the Sea (ACOPS) 1989; Sponsor, Irish Anti-Apartheid Movt; Club Pres. Derry City FC; Freedom, City of Cork 2004; Légion d'honneur; Dr hc (Massachusetts) 1985, (Catholic Univ. of America) 1986, (St Joseph's Univ., Phila) 1986, (Univ. of Mass., Catholic Univ. of America, Washington, DC, Tusculum Coll., Tenn.); Hon. LLD (Queen's) 1995, (Wales) 1996; Hon. DLitt (Ulster) 1998; shared Nobel Peace Prize 1998; Martin Luther King Award 1999, Gandhi Peace Prize 2002. *Publication:* Politics, Peace and Reconciliation in Ireland 1996. *Address:* Faculty of Social Sciences, University of Ulster, Magee Campus, Derry, BT48 7JL, Northern Ireland (office). *Telephone:* (28) 71375575 (office). *E-mail:* j.hume@ulster.ac.uk.

HUMER, Franz B., LLD, MBA; Swiss/Austrian pharmaceutical industry executive; *Chairman, Roche Holding Limited;* b. 1 July 1946; ed Univ. of Innsbruck, Institut Européen d'Admin des Affaires (INSEAD), Paris; ICME, Zurich 1971–73; Asst to Vice-Pres., Schering-Plough Corpn 1973–81; Area Man., S Europe, Glaxo Holdings PLC 1981, later becoming Dir of Marketing Devt, Man. Dir Glaxo Pharmaceutical Ltd, UK Dir Glaxo Holdings PLC –1995; joined F. Hoffman-La Roche Ltd 1995, Dir Roche Holding Ltd 1995–, Head of Pharmaceuticals Div. 1995–, COO 1996–98, CEO Roche Holding Ltd 1998–2008, Chair. 2001–; Chair. (non-exec.) Diageo Plc 2008–; mem. Bd Dirs Chugai Pharmaceuticals, Japan (Roche subsidiary); mem. Int. Advisory Bd Allianz SE; Vice-Chair. Swiss Business Fed., EFPIA (trade asscn); Dir Project Hope (charity); mem. European Round Table of Industrialists (ERT), JPMorgan Int. Council, Int. Business Leaders' Advisory Council for the Mayor of Shanghai, Bd Univ. of Salzburg, Int. Advisory Bd Nat. Centre for Missing and Exploited Children (also Vice-Chair.); Chair. Friends of Phelophepa Foundation, Switzerland, Humer Stiftung, INSEAD; Dr hc (Basel), Hon. DSc (London School of Pharmacy). *Address:* Roche Holding Ltd, Grenzacherstrasse 124, 4070 Basel, Switzerland (office). *Telephone:* (61) 688-11-11 (office). *Fax:* (61) 691-93-91 (office). *E-mail:* info@roche.com (office). *Website:* www.roche.com (office).

HUMMES, HE Cardinal Cláudio, OFM; Brazilian ecclesiastic; *Prefect Emeritus, Congregation for the Clergy;* b. 8 Aug. 1934, Montenegro; s. of Pedro Adão Hummes and Maria Frank Hummes; ordained priest of Order of Friars Minor 1958; Titular Bishop of Carcabia 1975; Coadjutor Bishop of Santo André, São Paulo March–Dec. 1975, Bishop of Santo André 1975–96, Archbishop of Fortaleza, Ceara 1996–98, of São Paulo 1998–2006; cr. Cardinal (Cardinal-Priest of Sant'Antonio da Padova in Via Merulana) 2001; participated in Papal Conclave 2005, 2013; Prefect for the Congregation for the Clergy 2006–10, Prefect Emer. 2010–. *Address:* c/o Palazzo delle Congregazioni, Piazza Pio XII, 3, 00193 Rome, Italy (office).

HUMPHRIES, (John) Barry, AO, CBE; Australian entertainer and author; b. 17 Feb. 1934, Kew, Melbourne, Vic.; s. of J. A. E. Humphries and L. A. Brown; m. 1st Brenda Wright 1955 (divorced 1957); m. 2nd Rosalind Tong 1959 (divorced 1970); two d.; m. 3rd Diane Millstead 1979 (divorced 1989); two s.; m. 4th Lizzie Spender 1990; ed Melbourne Grammar and Univ. of Melbourne; repertory seasons at Union Theatre, Melbourne 1953–54, Phillip Street Revue Theatre, Sydney 1956, Demon Barber Lyric, Hammersmith 1959, Oliver, New Theatre 1960; one-man shows (author and performer): A Nice Night's Entertainment 1962, Excuse I 1965, Just a Show 1968, A Load of Olde Stuffe 1971, At Least You Can Say That You've Seen It 1974, Housewife Superstar 1976, Isn't It Pathetic at His Age 1979, A Night with Dame Edna 1979, An Evening's Intercourse with Barry Humphries 1981–82,

Tears Before Bedtime 1986, Back with a Vengeance, London 1987–88, Look at Me When I'm Talking to You 1993–94, Edna: The Spectacle 1998, Dame Edna: The Royal Tour, San Francisco 1998, Remember You're Out 1999, My First Last Tour 2008, All About Me (Broadway) 2010, Eat, Pray, Laugh (farewell tour) 2012; numerous plays, films and broadcasts, including The Hobbit: An Unexpected Journey 2012; best-known for his comic characterizations of Dame Edna Everage, Sir Les Patterson and Sandy Stone; Pres. Frans de Boewer Soc. (Belgium); Vice-Pres. Betjeman Soc. 2001–; Dr hc (Melbourne Univ.), (Griffith Univ.) 1994, Hon. LLD (Melbourne) 2003; Douglas Wilkie Medal 1975, Comedy Performance of the Year, Soc. of West End Management, London (now known as the Laurence Olivier Awards) 1979, TV Personality of the Year 1990, Golden Rose of Montreux, Sir Peter Ustinov Award for Comedy, Banff World Television Festival 1997, Honoured Artists Award, Melbourne City Council 1997, British Comedy Awards – Lifetime Achievement Award 1999, Special Tony Award for a live theatrical event at the 55th Annual Tony Awards for Dame Edna: The Royal Tour 2000, Special Achievement Award by the Outer Critics Circle for The Royal Tour 2000, Best Play, National Broadway Theatre Awards for The Royal Tour 2000, J.C. Williamson Award for his life's work in the live performance industry 2007, Oldie of the Year for "his wonderful split personality which has entertained us for so many years" 2011, WhatsOnStage Award for Best Solo Performance (for Eat Pray Laugh!) 2014. *Publications include:* Bizarre 1964, Innocent Austral Verse 1968, The Wonderful World of Barry McKenzie (with Nicholas Garland) 1970, Bazza Holds his Own (with Nicholas Garland) 1972, Dame Edna's Coffee Table Book 1976, Les Patterson's Australia 1979, Treasury of Australian Kitsch 1980, A Nice Night's Entertainment 1981, Dame Edna's Bedside Companion 1982, The Traveller's Tool 1985, The Complete Barry McKenzie 1988, My Gorgeous Life: The Autobiography of Dame Edna Everage 1989, The Life and Death of Sandy Stone 1991, More Please: An Autobiography (J.R. Ackerley Prize for Autobiography 1993) 1992, Women in the Background (novel) 1996, My Life As Me (autobiog.), Handling Edna (biog.) 2010. *Leisure interests:* reading second-hand booksellers' catalogues in bed, inventing Australia. *Address:* c/o Claire Nightingale, PBJ Management, 22 Rathbone Street, London, W1T 1LA, England (office). *Telephone:* (20) 7287-1112 (office). *Fax:* (20) 7287-1191 (office). *E-mail:* general@pbjmgt.co.uk (office). *Website:* www.pbjmgt.co.uk (office).

HUMPHRY, Richard George, AO, FCA, FCPA, FAICD, A Fin, MACS; Australian business executive and fmr stock exchange official; *Advisor, Morgan Stanley Australia Ltd;* b. 24 Feb. 1939, Perth; s. of Arthur D. Humphry and Enid G. Humphry; m. Rose Friel 1961; one s. one d.; ed Univ. of Western Australia; computer programmer in public service 1967–77; Asst Sec. Supply Computer Systems Br. 1978–79, Accounting Devt Br. 1979–81; Asst Sec. Defence Br. Commonwealth Dept of Finance 1981–82; First Asst Sec. Financial Man. and Accounting Policy Div. 1982–85; Deputy Sec. Commonwealth Dept of Aboriginal Affairs 1985; Auditor-Gen., Victoria 1986–88; Dir Gen. Premier's Dept of NSW 1988–94; Chair. Audit and Compliance Cttee, State Super Financial Services 1992–2001; Dir State Super Financial Services 1992–2001; Chair. NSW Financial Institutes Comm. 1994–99; Man. Dir and CEO Australian Stock Exchange 1994–2004; currently Advisor to Morgan Stanley Australia Ltd; Chair. Australian Financial Insts Comm. 1996–2000 (Dir 1992–96); Dir Garvan Medical Research Foundation 1997; Pres. Commonwealth Remuneration Tribunal 1998; Ind. Reviewer Govt Information Tech. Outsourcing Initiative 2000; mem. Bd of Dir UGL Ltd 2004–, HSBC Bank Australia Ltd, BUPA Australia Pty Ltd, BUPA Australia Holdings Pty Ltd, BUPA Australia Health Pty Ltd, MBF Alliances Pty Ltd, MBF Travel Pty Ltd, MBF Foundation Ltd, O'Connell Street Associates Pty Ltd; Deputy Chair. Taronga Conservation Soc. Australia; Deputy Chair. Zoological Parks Bd, NSW 1998; mem. Advisory Bd Nat. Office for Information Economy 1997–98, Financial Sector Advisory Cttee Taskforce 1998–, Foreign Affairs Council 2000; Business Council of Australia 2000; mem. Australian Computing Soc., Australasian Inst. of Banking and Finance; Fellow, Australian Soc. of Certified Practising Accountants, Australian Inst. of Co. Dirs; Int. Fed. of Accountants Award 1988, Accountant of the Year (Public Sector Div.) 1989, Best Financial Services Exec. (Australian Banking and Finance Awards) 2000. *Leisure interests:* bush walking, reading, scuba diving. *Address:* Morgan Stanley Australia Ltd, Level 39, Chifley Tower 2 Chifley Square, Sydney, NSW 2000, Australia (office). *Telephone:* (2) 9770-1111 (office). *Fax:* (2) 9770-1101 (office). *Website:* www .morganstanley.com/about/offices/australia.html (office).

HUMPHRYS, John; British broadcaster; b. 17 Aug. 1943; s. of Edward George Humphrys and Winifred Matthews; m. (divorced); two s. one d.; ed Cardiff High School; Washington Corresp., BBC TV 1971–77, Southern Africa Corresp. 1977–80, Diplomatic Corresp. 1981; presenter, BBC Nine O'Clock News 1981–87; presenter, BBC Radio 4 Today Programme 1987–, On the Record, BBC TV 1993–, The John Humphrys Interview (Radio 4) 1995, On the Ropes (Radio 4), Mastermind (TV) 2003–; Hon. Fellow, Cardiff Univ. 1998; Hon. DLitt (Dundee) 1996; Hon. MA (Univ. of Wales) 1998; Hon. LLD (St Andrews) 1999; Sony Gold for News Journalist of the Year 2007, Sony Radio Acad. Award for Radio Journalism of the Year 2013. *Publications:* Devil's Advocate 1999, Lost for Words: The Mangling and Manipulation of the English Language 2004, Beyond Words 2006, In God We Doubt: Confessions of an Angry Agnostic 2007. *Leisure interests:* cello, trees, books, farming, music. *Address:* Today Programme, BBC Radio 4, Broadcasting House, London, W1A 1AA, England. *Website:* www.bbc.co.uk/programmes/b006qj9z.

HUN SEN, BA, PhD; Cambodian politician; *Prime Minister;* b. 5 Aug. 1952, Stoeung Trang District, Kompang-Cham Prov.; m. Bun Rany 1975; three s. three d.; ed Lycée Indra Devi, Phnom Penh, Univ. of Phnom Penh, Nat. Political Acad., Hanoi; joined Khmer Rouges 1970, rising to Commdt; in Viet Nam with pro-Vietnamese Kampucheans 1977, returned to Kampuchea (now Cambodia) after Vietnamese-backed take-over; Founding mem. United Front for the Nat. Salvation of Kampuchea 1978; Minister for Foreign Affairs 1979–85; Deputy Prime Minister 1981–85; Chair. Council of Ministers of Cambodia (Prime Minister) 1985–91, Second Prime Minister Royal Govt of Cambodia 1993–98, Prime Minister of Cambodia 1998–; Vice-Pres. Cambodian People's Party (CPP); mem. Russian Acad. of Sciences 2002–, Bar Asscn of Cambodia 2004–; Hon. mem. ASEAN Eng Fed. 2002; Hon. PhD (Southern Calif. Univ.) 1995, (Iowa Wesleyan Coll.) 1996; Dr hc (Dankook Univ., S Korea) 2001, (Ramkhamhaeng, Thailand) 2001, (Irish Int. Univ.) 2004, (Univ. of Cambodia) 2004, (Soon Chun Hyang Univ., S Korea) 2006, (Rajabhat Univ., Thailand) 2006, (Hanoi Nat. Univ. of Educ.) 2007; awarded title

Samdech by the King of Cambodia, World Peace Award, Int. Peace Center 'Lifting Up the World with a Oneness-Heart' Award 2001, Irish Int. Univ. Medal of Excellence 2004, U Thant Peace Award 2005. *Address:* Council of Ministers, Russian Federation Blvd, Phnom Penh, Cambodia (office). *Telephone:* (12) 804442 (office). *Fax:* (23) 880624 (office). *E-mail:* ocm@cambodia.gov.kh (office). *Website:* www.ocm.gov.kh (office).

HUNAIDI, Rima Khalaf, MA, PhD; Jordanian foundation executive, fmr government official and fmr UN official; *CEO, Mohammed bin Rashid Al Maktoum Foundation;* ed American Univ. of Beirut, Lebanon and Portland State Univ., Ore., USA; started career as Lecturer, Dept of Econs, Portland State Univ. 1979; Dir-Gen. Jordan Export Devt and Commercial Centers Corpn and Dir-Gen. for Investment Promotion Dept, Amman 1990–93; Minister of Industry and Trade 1993–95, of Planning 1995–98; Senator, Jordanian Upper House 1997–2000; Deputy Prime Minister 1999–2000; mem. Jordanian Econ. Consultative Council; Asst Sec.-Gen. and Dir UNDP Regional Bureau for the Arab States 2000–07; CEO Mohammed bin Rashid Al Maktoum Foundation, Dubai 2008–; mem. Bd of Dirs Centre for Global Devt; mem. Advisory Bd UN Democracy Fund; Grand Cordon of the Order of Al-Kawkab Al-Urduni (The Star of Jordan) 1995. *Address:* Mohammed bin Rashid Al Maktoum Foundation, PO Box: 214444, Building No. 26, 7th Floor, Dubai Healthcare City, Dubai, United Arab Emirates (office). *Telephone:* (4) 3299999 (office). *Fax:* (4) 3687777 (office). *Website:* www.mbrfoundation.ae (office).

HUNAITI, Abdelrahim A., BSc, MSc, PhD; Jordanian biochemist, academic and university administrator; *President, Mutah University;* b. Feb. 1952, Abu Alanda; m.; four c.; ed Univ. of Jordan, California State Univ., Washington State Univ., USA; Teaching Asst Wash. State Univ. 1980–81, Research Asst 1981–83; Asst Prof., Yarmouk Univ. 1983–87, Assoc. Prof. 1987–92, Chair. Dept of Biological Sciences 1989–91, Prof. 1992–93; Visiting Prof., Gar Younis Univ. 1991–92; Dean of Academic Research and Grad. Studies, Mu'tah Univ. 1993–94, Asst to Univ. Pres. for Admin. Affairs 1993–94, Foundation Dean Faculty of Agric. 1994–95, Vice-Pres. for Admin. Affairs and Projects 1994–96, for Academic Affairs 1996–98, for Faculties of Sciences Affairs 1998–2000; Vice-Pres. for Academic Affairs, Philadelphia Univ. 2000–04; Pres. Univ. of Jordan 2004–07; Pres. Higher Educ. Accreditation Comm. 2007–08; Pres. Hashemite Univ. 2008–12; Pres. Mutah Univ. 2012–; mem. Higher Educ. Accreditation Council 1997–2004, Dir-Gen. Nov.–Dec. 2004; mem. Editorial Bd Yarmouk Applied and Engineering Scientific Journal 2000–; mem. Jordanian Biological Sciences Soc., Jordanian Environmental Pollution Soc., Int. Soc. for Free Radical Research in Medicine, Biology and Chem., Arab Biophysics Union, New York Acad. of Sciences; Von Humboldt Fellow 1992; Abdel Hamid Shouman Prize for Young Arab Scientists 1990. *Publications:* Laboratory Manual for Experimental Biochemistry 1986, Biochemistry (Arabic) (co-author) 1993, General Science (Arabic) (co-author) 1993, Science and Technology in the Arab World (co-author) 2002. *Address:* Mutah University, Karak 61710, Jordan (office). *Telephone:* 7-99088080 (office). *E-mail:* hunaiti2001@yahoo.com (office). *Website:* www.mutah.edu.jo (office).

HÜNER, Tomáš, DipEng; Czech business executive, engineer and government official; *Vice-Chairman, ČEZ Group;* b. 26 June 1959, Ostrava; s. of Julius Hüner and Olga Hüner; m. Katerina Trnková; two d.; ed Brno Univ. of Tech.; engineer at power station Dětmarovice 1984–94; Chair. and CEO Severomoravská energetika, a.s. 1994–2004; consultant for AP&P 2002; CEO ČEZ Group distribution cos in Bulgaria (following merger between Severočeská energetika, Severomoravská energetika, Středočeská energetická, Východočeská energetika and Západočeská energetika) 2004–06, currently Vice-Chair.; Vice-Minister of Industry and Trade and manager of Industry and Energy Sector 2006–; Chair. Supervisory Bd Aliatel a.s.; Chair. Energetika Vítkovice a.s., ePRIM, a.s.; Vice-Chair. Supervisory Bd Union Group a.s. *Publications include:* Chronicle of Corporate Heads, Historica Prague (Publr); papers in specialist journals. *Leisure interests:* skiing, tennis, surfing. *Address:* ČEZ a.s., Hlavni Sprava, Duhova 2/1444, 140 53 Prague 4 (office); ul. Přátelství 269/15, 73601 Havirov, Czech Republic (home). *Telephone:* (2) 71131111 (office); (6) 96415491 (home). *Fax:* (2) 71132001 (office). *E-mail:* tomas .huner@cez.cz (office). *Website:* www.cez.cz (office).

HUNG, Huang; Chinese magazine publisher, television presenter and writer; *CEO, China Interactive Media Group;* b. 1961, Beijing; d. of Hong Junyan and Zhang Hanzhi; m. Chen Kaige 1989 (divorced); ed Vassar Coll., USA; returned to Beijing following educ. in USA 1983; began career as investment consultant; Chief Rep., Metallgesellschaft AG, Beijing 1986–96; Exec. Dir Standard International Management Ltd 1996–2000; currently CEO China Interactive Media Group, magazines published include iLook (relaunched 2006), Time Out Beijing, Chinese-language Seventeen; began writing China Chic (English-language column) in China Daily 2009–, also now writes column for Daily Beast website; author of popular blog on Sina.com; launched retail venture with BNC (Brand New China), Sanlitun, Beijing 2010. *Film:* co-wrote and starred in ind. film Perpetual Motion 2005. *Publications:* My Abnormal Life as a Publisher (autobiog), Conversation with Mom. *Address:* China Interactive Media Group, 2 Jiuxian Qiao Lu, PO Box 80, Beijing 100015, People's Republic of China (office). *Telephone:* (10) 6436 2098 (office). *Fax:* (10) 9437 2837 (home).

HUNGERFORD, John Leonard, MA, MB, BChir, FRCS, FRCOphth; British ophthalmologist and ocular oncologist; *Consultant Ophthalmic Surgeon, St Bartholomew's Hospital;* b. 12 Sept. 1944; s. of Leonard Harold Hungerford and Violet Miriam Hungerford (née Bickerstaff); m. Yvonne Carole Rayment 1987; one d.; ed The Glyn School, Epsom, Gonville and Caius Coll. Cambridge, Charing Cross Hosp. Medical School; consultant surgeon, Moorfields Eye Hosp. 1983–; Consultant Ophthalmic Surgeon, St Bartholomew's Hosp. 1983–; Vice-Pres. Int. Soc. for Ocular Oncology 2001; Ridley Medal 1998, Gregg Medal 2001. *Publications:* several publs on ocular cancer. *Leisure interests:* travel, reading, music, gardening, architecture. *Address:* Department of Ophthalmology, St Bartholomew's Hospital, West Smithfield, London, EC1A 7BE (office); 114 Harley Street, London, W1N 1AG, England (office). *Telephone:* (20) 7601-7158 (St Bartholomew's Hospital) (office); (20) 7935-1565 (office). *Fax:* (20) 7601-7863 (St Bartholomew's Hospital) (office); (20) 7224-1752 (office). *E-mail:* john.hungerford@moorfields.nhs.uk (office); john.hungerford@btopenworld.co.uk (home). *Website:* www .bartsandthelondon.nhs.uk/ourservices/ophthalmology.asp (office).

HUNKAPILLER, Michael W., PhD; American scientist and business executive; *Partner, Alloy Ventures;* b. 1949; ed Oklahoma Baptist Univ., California Inst. of Tech.; joined Research and Devt Dept of Applied Biosystems Inc. 1983, Exec. Vice-Pres. 1995, Gen. Man. 1995–97; Vice-Pres. PE Corpn 1995–97, Sr Vice-Pres. and Pres. of Applied Biosystems Div. 1997–98, Pres. Appled Biosystems Group 1998–2004 (retd); Pnr, Alloy Ventures (investment capital firm) 2004–; Dir ACLARA Biosciences Inc. 2000; mem. Bd of Dirs Fluidigm Corpn 2005–; mem. of numerous professional socs. *Publications:* more than 100 publs. *Address:* Alloy Ventures, 400 Hamilton Avenue, 4th Floor, Palo Alto, CA 94301, USA (office). *Telephone:* (650) 687-5000 (office). *Fax:* (650) 687-5010 (office). *E-mail:* info@alloyventures.com (office). *Website:* www.alloyventures.com (office).

HUNKIN, John S.; Canadian banking executive (retd); ed York Univ.; joined Canadian Imperial Bank of Commerce (CIBC) 1969, various man. positions becoming Pres. Investment and Corp. Banking Div. (known as CIBC World Markets from 1997), Dir 1993–, Pres. and CEO CIBC 1999–2004, CEO 2004–05 (retd); fmr Gov. Council for Canadian Unity, York Univ.; mem. Bd of Dirs York Univ. Foundation, St Michael's Hosp. Foundation, Centre for Addiction and Mental Health Foundation; mem. Advisory Council, Schulich School of Business, York Univ.; mem. Conf. Bd of Canada; Trustee, Li Ka Shing [Canada] Foundation, Centre for Addiction and Mental Health. *Address:* c/o Board of Directors, York University Foundation, West Office Building, 4700 Keele Street, Toronto ON M3J 1P3, Canada.

HUNT, Helen Elizabeth; American actress; b. 15 June 1963, LA; d. of Gordon Hunt and Jane Hunt; m. Hank Azaria 1999 (divorced); f. Hunt-Tavel Productions (production co.). *Stage appearances include:* Been Taken, Our Town, The Taming of the Shrew, Methusalem. *Films include:* Rollercoaster 1977, Girls Just Want to Have Fun 1985, Peggy Sue Got Married 1986, Trancers 1985, Waiting to Act 1985, Project X 1987, Stealing Home 1988, Miles from Home 1988, The Frog Prince 1988, Next of Kin 1989, Trancers II 1991, The Waterdance 1992, Only You 1992, Bob Roberts 1992, Mr Saturday Night 1992, Sexual Healing 1993, Kiss of Death 1995, Twister 1996, As Good As It Gets (Acad. Award for Best Actress) 1997, Pay It Forward 2000, Dr. T and the Women 2000, Cast Away 2000, What Women Want 2000, The Curse of the Jade Scorpion 2001, A Good Woman 2004, Bobby 2006, Then She Found Me (also dir) 2007, Every Day 2009, The Sessions 2012. *Television includes:* Swiss Family Robinson 1975, St Elsewhere (series) 1984–86, Mad About You (series, Emmy Award 1996, 1997, Golden Globe Award 1997) 1992–99, Empire Falls 2005. *Address:* Hunt-Tavel Productions, 10202 West Washington Blvd., Astaire 2410, Culver City, CA 90232, USA. *Telephone:* (310) 244-3144.

HUNT, James Baxter, Jr, BA, MS, JD; American lawyer and fmr politician; *Attorney, Womble, Carlyle, Sandridge & Rice PLLC;* b. 16 May 1937, Guilford Co., NC; s. of James Baxter Hunt and Elsie Hunt (née Brame); m. Carolyn Joyce Leonard 1958; one s. three d.; ed North Carolina State Univ., Univ. of North Carolina; called to Bar of NC 1966; Econ. Adviser to Govt of Nepal for Ford Foundation 1964–66; Pnr, Kirby, Webb and Hunt (law firm) 1966–72, Poyner and Spruill, Raleigh, NC 1985–93; Attorney, Womble, Carlyle, Sandridge & Rice PLLC 2001–; Lt-Gov. of North Carolina 1973–77, Gov. of North Carolina 1977–85, 1993–2000; Founder and Chair. Hunt Inst. for Educational Leadership and Policy, Univ. of North Carolina, Chapel Hill; fmr Chair. Nat. Bd for Professional Teaching Standards; Democrat; 1st Annual Harry S. Truman Award Nat. Young Democrats 1975, Soil Conservation Honors Award 1986, Outstanding Govt Leader in US Conservation, Nat. Wildlife Fed. 1983 and numerous other awards. *Address:* Womble, Carlyle, Sandridge & Rice PLLC, 150 Fayetteville Street Mall, Suite 2100, Raleigh, NC 27602, USA (office). *Telephone:* (919) 755-2105 (office). *Fax:* (919) 755-6089 (office). *Website:* www.wcsr.com (office).

HUNT, Jay; Australian broadcasting executive; *Chief Creative Officer, Channel 4;* ed Lady Eleanor Holles School, Hampton, Middx, St John's Coll., Cambridge; joined BBC as researcher on Breakfast News 1989, becoming Output Ed., later Producer Newsnight –1998, Sr Producer Panorama 1998, Ed. One O'Clock News and Six O'Clock News 1999, Exec. Producer for Daytime TV 2002–03, BBC Controller Daytime and Early Peak –2007, Controller BBC One 2008–11; Dir of Programmes, Channel Five 2007; Chief Creative Officer, Channel 4 2011–. *Address:* Channel 4, 124 Horseferry Road, London, SW1P 2TX, England (office). *Website:* www.channel4.com (office).

HUNT, Rt Hon. Jeremy Richard Streynsham, PC, BA (Hons); British politician; *Secretary of State for Health;* b. 1 Nov. 1966, Godalming, Surrey, England; s. of Adm. Sir Nicholas Hunt and Meriel Eve Givan; m. Lucia Hunt 2009; one s.; ed Charterhouse School, Godalming, Magdalen Coll., Oxford; Pres. Oxford Univ. Conservative Asscn 1987; worked for a man. consultancy firm before going to Japan for two years to teach English and learn Japanese; co-f. Profile PR (public relations agency); co-f. Hotcourses (educational publishing business); set up a charity to help AIDS orphans in Africa; MP for SW Surrey 2005–10, for SW Surrey (revised boundary) 2010–, mem. Int. Devt Select Cttee 2005–06; Shadow Minister for Disabled People 2005–07; Shadow Sec. of State for Culture, Media and Sport 2007–10; Sec. of State for Culture, Olympics, Media and Sport 2010–12, for Health 2012–; mem. Educ., Youth, Culture and Sport Council, Council of the EU 2010–; Conservative. *Address:* Department of Health, Richmond House, 79 Whitehall, London, SW1A 2NS (office); House of Commons, Westminster, London, SW1A 0AA; SW Surrey Conservative Association, 2 Royal Parade, Tilford Road, Hindhead, Surrey, GU26 6TD, England. *Telephone:* (20) 7210-5202 (Dept) (office); (20) 7219-6813 (Westminster); (1428) 609416 (Hindhead). *Fax:* (1428) 607498 (Hindhead). *E-mail:* jeremy.hunt@dh.gsi.gov.uk (office); huntj@parliament.uk. *Website:* www.dh.gov.uk (office); www.parliament.uk/biographies/commons/jeremy-hunt/35446; www.hotcourses.com; www.hotcoursesfoundation.org; www.jeremyhunt.org.

HUNT, Rt Hon. Jonathan Lucas, ONZ, PC, MA; New Zealand politician and diplomatist; b. 2 Dec. 1938, Lower Hutt; s. of H. Lucas Hunt and A. Z. Hunt; ed Auckland Grammar School, Auckland Univ.; teacher, Kelston Boys' High School 1961–66; tutor, Univ. of Auckland 1964–66; MP for New Lynn 1966–2005; Jr Govt Whip 1972, Chair. of Cttees and Deputy Speaker of House of Reps 1974–75, Acting Speaker 1975; Labour Opposition Spokesman on Health 1976–79, Constitution and Parl. Affairs 1978–81; Sr Opposition Whip 1980–84; Shadow Minister of Broadcasting 1982; Minister of Broadcasting and Postmaster-Gen. 1984–87,

Minister of State 1987–89, Leader of the House 1987–90, Minister of Broadcasting 1988–90, for Tourism 1988–89, of Housing 1989, of Communications Jan.–Oct. 1990; Sr Opposition Whip 1990–96, Shadow Leader of the House 1996–99; Speaker, House of Reps 1999–2005; High Commr to UK and Nigeria and Amb. to Ireland 2005–08. *Leisure interests:* music, int. affairs, cricket, literature. *Address:* c/o Ministry of Foreign Affairs and Trade, Private Bag 18901, Wellington, New Zealand.

HUNT, Linda; American actress; b. 2 April 1945, Morristown, NJ; ed Interlochen Arts Acad., Mich. and Goodman Theater and School of Drama, Chicago; has appeared on Broadway and in films 1975–. *Plays include:* Down by the River 1975, A Metamorphosis in Miniature (Obie Award) 1982, Top Girls (Obie Award) 1983, Little Victories 1983, Aunt Dan and Lemon 1985, Cherry Orchard 1988; Broadway appearances: Ah, Wilderness! 1975, End of the World 1984. *Films include:* Popeye 1980, The Year of Living Dangerously (Acad. Award for Best Supporting Actress) 1983, Dune 1984, The Bostonians 1984, Eleni 1985, Silverado 1985, Waiting for the Moon 1987, She-Devil 1989, Kindergarten Cop 1990, If Looks Could Kill 1991, Rain Without Thunder 1993, Twenty Bucks. 1993, Younger and Younger 1993, Prêt-a-Porter 1994, Pocahontas (voice) 1995, Eat Your Heart Out 1997, Amazon (voice) 1997, The Relic 1997, Out of the Past 1998, Pocahontas II: Journey to a New World (voice) 1998, The Century (narrator) 1999, Dragonfly 2002, Yours, Mine & Ours 2005, Stranger Than Fiction 2006, Once Upon a Tide (narrator) 2008, The Crooked Eye (narrator) 2009. *Address:* William Morris Endeavor, One William Morris Place, Beverly Hills, CA 90212, USA (office). *Telephone:* (310) 859-4000 (office). *Fax:* (310) 859-4462 (office). *Website:* www.wma.com (office).

HUNT, Sir Richard Timothy (Tim), Kt, PhD, FRS; British biologist; b. 19 Feb. 1943, Neston, Wirral; s. of Richard William Hunt and Kit Rowland; m. Mary Collins; two d.; ed Dragon School, Oxford, Magdalen Coll. School, Oxford and Univ. of Cambridge; Research Fellow in Biochemistry, Univ. of Cambridge 1970–81, Univ. Lecturer 1982–90; Prin. Scientist, Cancer Research UK 1990–2010; Officier, Légion d'honneur 2002; Nobel Prize for Physiology or Medicine 2001. *Publications:* Molecular Biology of the Cell – Problems Book (co-author), The Cell Cycle: An Introduction (co-author); papers in cell and molecular biology. *Address:* Rose Cottage, Ridge, Herts., EN6 3LH (home); Cancer Research UK, Clare Hall Laboratories, South Mimms, Herts., EN6 3LD, England (office). *Telephone:* (1707) 646484 (home); (1707) 625981 (office). *E-mail:* tim.hunt@cancer.org.uk (office). *Website:* www.cancer.org.uk (office).

HUNT, Swanee, MA, PhD; American research institute director, diplomatist and academic; *Director, Women and Public Policy Program, Harvard University;* b. Dallas, Tex.; d. of H. L. Hunt; m. Charles Ansbacher; three c.; civic leader and philanthropist; led community efforts on public educ., mental health services and affordable housing in Denver, Colo; Founder Women's Foundation of Colo; co-dir half-way house for the mentally ill; Founder Hunt Alternatives (pvt. foundation addressing issues of poverty and discrimination), Chair. Inclusive Security: Women Waging Peace; Amb. to Austria 1993–97; hosted negotiations and int. symposia on efforts to secure peace in Balkans; launched Vienna Women's Initiative 1997; Dir Women and Public Policy Program (WAPPP), John F. Kennedy School of Govt, Harvard Univ. 1997–, also Adjunct Eleanor Roosevelt Lecturer in Public Policy; mem. Council on Foreign Relations; Contrib. Ed. The American Benefactor; syndicated columnist Scripps Howard news service; awards and hons from Anti-Defamation League, Inst. for Int. Educ., American Mental Health Asscn, Nat. Women's Forum, named Woman of Peace, Together for Peace Foundation, Rome, Italy. *Publications include:* This Was Not Our War: Bosnian Women Reclaiming the Peace 2004, Half Life of a Zealot 2006; articles in professional journals and US and int. newspapers. *Leisure interests:* photography, music (composed The Witness Cantata, performed in Washington DC), poetry, hiking, running marathons. *Address:* Women and Public Policy Program (WAPPP), John F. Kennedy School of Government, Harvard University, 79 JFK Street, Cambridge, MA 02138 (office); Inclusive Security: Women Waging Peace, 2040 S Street, NW, Washington, DC 20009, USA (office). *Telephone:* (617) 995-1950 (office); (202) 403-2000 (office). *Fax:* (617) 496-6154 (office); (202) 299-9520 (office). *E-mail:* swanee_hunt@huntalternatives.org (office); information@womenwagingpeace.net (office). *Website:* www.ksg.harvard.edu/wappp (office); www.womenwagingpeace.net (office).

HUNT OF KINGS HEATH, Baron (Life Peer), cr. 1997, of Birmingham in the County of West Midlands; **Philip Alexander Hunt,** OBE, BA, PC; British politician; *Deputy Leader of Opposition, House of Lords;* b. 19 May 1949, Birmingham; m.; five c.; ed City of Oxford High School, Oxford School and Univ. of Leeds; joined Oxford Regional Hosp. Bd 1972; with Nuffield Orthopaedic Centre 1974; Sec. Edgware and Hendon Community Health Council 1975–79; joined Nat. Asscn of Health Authorities 1978, Dir 1990; mem. House of Lords 1997–; apptd Govt Whip and Spokesman on Educ. and Employment and Health, House of Lords 1998; Parl. Under-Sec. of State, Dept of Health 1999–2003, 2007, Dept for Work and Pensions 2005–07, Ministry of Justice 2007–08; Minister of State, Dept for the Environment, Food and Rural Affairs 2008–09; Minister of State, Dept of Energy and Climate Change 2008–10; Deputy Leader, House of Lords 2008–10, Deputy Leader of Opposition 2010–; mem. Oxford City Council 1973–79, Birmingham City Council 1980–82; Jt Chair. All Party Care and Public Health Group 1997–98; Vice-Chair. All Party Group on AIDS 1997–98; Dr hc (Birmingham) 2005. *Leisure interests:* swimming, Birmingham City Football Club, music. *Address:* House of Lords, Westminster, London, SW1A 0PW, England (office). *Telephone:* (20) 7238-0681 (office).

HUNT OF WIRRAL, Baron (Life Peer), cr. 1997, of Wirral in the County of Merseyside; **Rt Hon. David James Fletcher Hunt,** PC, MBE; British lawyer, politician and business executive; *Chairman, Press Complaints Commission;* b. 21 May 1942; ed Liverpool Coll., Univ. of Bristol; practising solicitor and Partner, Beachcroft Wansbroughs (now Beachcroft LLP) 1968–, Sr Partner 1995–2005, currently Chair. Financial Services Div.; contested Bristol South constituency 1970, Kingswood 1974; MP (Conservative) for Wirral 1976–83, for Wirral W 1983–97; Opposition Spokesman for Shipping and Shipbuilding 1977–97; Parl. Pvt. Sec. to John Nott as Sec. of State for Trade 1979–81, for Defence 1981; Asst Whip 1981–83; Govt Whip 1983–84; Parl. Under-Sec. of State, Dept of Energy 1984–87; Deputy Chief Whip (Treas. of HM Household) 1987–89; Minister for Local Govt and Inner Cities 1989–90; Sec. of State for Wales 1990–93, 1995, for

Employment 1993–94; Chancellor of the Duchy of Lancaster and Minister for Public Service and Science 1994–95; Opposition Spokesperson for Business, Enterprise and Regulatory Reform/Business, Innovation and Skills, House of Lords 2008–10; Chair. Press Complaints Comm. 2011–; Vice-Chair. Bristol Conservative Asscn 1970; Chair. Nat. Young Conservatives 1972–73; Vice-Pres. European Conservative and Christian Democratic Youth Community 1974–76; Vice-Chair. Conservative Party 1983–84; Pres. Tory Reform Group 1991–97, Patron 1997–; Chair. British Youth Council 1971–74; mem. South West Econ. Planning Council 1972–76, Govt Advisory Cttee on Pop Festivals 1972–75; Pres. British Youth Council 1978–80; Gov., English Speaking Union 1998–, Deputy Chair. 2000–05, Chair. 2005–11, Int. Chair. 2008–11; Chair. Professional Standards Bd, Chartered Insurance Inst. 2004–06, Pres. 2007–08; Chair. (non-exec.) McDonald's Education Co. 2009–, Lending Standards Bd 2011–; Gov., European Youth Foundation, Strasbourg 1972–75; Chair. British Atlantic Group of Young Politicians 1979–81; Pres. Atlantic Asscn for Young Political Leaders 1981–83; Dir, Asscn of Conservative Clubs, Parl. Cttee against Anti-Semitism; Dir, Case Management Soc.; Vice-Pres. Holocaust Educational Trust; Deputy Pres. Royal Soc. for the Prevention of Accidents (RoSPA); Trustee and Churchwarden, St Mary Magdalene Church, Chewton Mendip, Somerset; mem. (Conservative) House of Lords 1997–; Hon. LLD (Bristol) 2008; jt winner The Observer Mace debating competition for Univ. of Bristol 1995. *Address:* Press Complaints Commission, Halton House, 20/23 Holborn, London, EC1N 2JD (office); House of Lords, Westminster, London, SW1A 0PW, England (office). *Telephone:* (20) 7831-0022 (PCC) (office); (20) 7219-6688 (House of Lords) (office). *Fax:* (20) 7831-0025 (PCC) (office). *E-mail:* complaints@pcc.org.uk (office). *Website:* www.pcc.org.uk (office).

HUNTE, Julian Robert, OBE; Saint Lucia politician, diplomatist and sport administrator; *President, West Indies Cricket Board;* b. 14 March 1940, Castries; Mayor of Castries 1970–71; joined St Lucia Labour Party 1978, Leader 1984–96; mem. Parl. 1987–96; fmr Chair. Standing Conf. of Popular Democratic Parties of the Eastern Caribbean; Perm. Rep. to UN, New York –2001, 2004–06 (resgnd); currently Chair. and Dir The Julian R. Hunte Group of Cos; Minister of Foreign Affairs, Int. Trade and Civil Aviation 2001–04; Pres. of 58th Session, UN Gen. Ass. 2003–04; fmr Pres. St Lucia Cricket Asscn, Windward Islands Cricket BD; Pres. W Indies Cricket Bd 2007–; Knight of the Grand Cross Pian Order from Pope John Paul II 2004. *Address:* West Indies Cricket Board Inc., PO Box 616 W, St John's, Antigua. *Telephone:* 481-2450 (office). *Fax:* 481-2498 (office). *E-mail:* wicb@windiescricket.com (office). *Website:* www.windiescricket.com (office).

HUNTER, Anthony (Tony) Rex, MA, PhD, FRS, FRSA; British/American molecular biologist and cell biologist; *American Cancer Society Professor, The Salk Institute;* b. 23 Aug. 1943, Ashford, Kent, England; s. of Ranulph Rex Hunter and Nellie Ruby Elsie Hitchcock; m. 1st Philippa Charlotte Marrack 1969 (divorced 1974); m. 2nd Jennifer Ann Maureen Price 1992; two s.; ed Felsted School, Essex and Gonville and Caius Coll., Cambridge; Research Fellow, Christ's Coll., Cambridge 1968–71, 1973–75; Research Assoc., Salk Inst., San Diego, Calif. 1971–73, Asst Prof. 1975–78, Assoc. Prof. 1978–82, Prof. 1982–, American Cancer Soc. Prof. 1992–2008, Dir Salk Cancer Center 2008–, Renato Dulbecco Chair. in Cancer Research 2011–; Adjunct Assoc. Prof., Div. of Biology, Univ. of Calif., San Diego 1979–82, Adjunct Prof. 1982–; mem. Inst. of Medicine 2004–, American Philosophical Soc. 2006–; Assoc. mem. European Molecular Biology Org. 1992; Foreign Assoc. mem. NAS 1998; Fellow, American Acad. of Arts and Sciences 1992, American Asscn for Cancer Research Acad. 2013; American Business Foundation for Cancer Research Award 1988, Katharine Berkan Judd Award (Memorial Sloan-Kettering Cancer Center) 1992, Hopkins Medal (Biochemical Soc.) 1994, Gairdner Foundation Int. Award 1994, General Motors Cancer Research Foundation Mott Prize 1994, Feodor Lynen Medal 1999, J. Allyn Taylor Int. Prize in Medicine 2000, Keio Medical Science Prize 2001, Sergio Lombroso Award in Cancer Research 2003, City of Medicine Award 2003, American Cancer Soc. Medal of Honor 2004, Kirk A. Landon Prize for Basic Cancer Research, American Asscn for Cancer Research 2004, Prince of Asturias Award for Scientific and Tech. Research 2004, Louisa Gross Horwitz Prize 2004, Daniel Nathans Memorial Award 2005, Wolf Foundation Prize in Medicine 2005, Pasarow Award in Cancer Research 2006, American Soc. of Biochemistry and Molecular Biology, Herbert Tabor Award 2007, Clifford Prize for Cancer Research 2007, Hon. Medal, Signal Transduction Soc. 2011, Einstein Prof., Chinese Acad. of Sciences 2013. *Publications include:* more than 525 papers and journal articles. *Leisure interests:* whitewater rafting, desert camping. *Address:* Molecular and Cell Biology Laboratory, The Salk Institute, 10010 North Torrey Pines Road, La Jolla, CA 92037-1099 (office); 4578 Vista de la Patria, Del Mar, CA 92014-4150, USA (home). *Telephone:* (858) 453-4100 (ext. 1385) (office); (858) 792-1492 (home). *Fax:* (858) 457-4765 (office). *E-mail:* hunter@salk.edu (office). *Website:* www.salk.edu/faculty/hunter .html (office); pingu.salk.edu/~hunter (office).

HUNTER, Holly, BFA; American actress; b. 20 March 1958, Conyers, Ga; d. of Charles Hunter and Opal M. Catledge; m. Janusz Kaminski (q.v.) 1995; two c. (twins) with Gordon MacDonald; ed Carnegie-Mellon Univ.; Dir Calif. Abortion Rights Action League; Emmy Award for TV production Roe vs. Wade 1989; Best Actress Award, American TV Awards, for cable TV production of The Positively True Adventures of the Alleged Texas Cheerleader Murdering Mom 1993; Best Actress Award, Cannes Film Festival Award 1993 and Acad. Award 1994 for role in The Piano. *Theatre:* on Broadway: Crimes of the Heart, The Whale of Jamey Foster, The Miss Firecracker Contest; other: A Weekend Near Madison, The Person I Once Was, Battery (all in New York), A Lie of the Mind (Los Angeles), By the Bog of Cats (Wyndham's Theatre, London) 2004 and regional productions. *Films include:* The Burning 1981, Swing Shift 1984, Broadcast News 1987, Raising Arizona 1987, End of the Line 1988, Miss Firecracker 1989, Always 1989, Animal Behavior 1989, Once Around 1990, The Piano 1993, The Firm 1993, Home for the Holidays 1995, Copycat 1995, Crash 1996, A Life Less Ordinary 1997, Living Out Loud 1998, Jesus' Son 1999, Timecode 2000, Things You Can Tell Just by Looking at Her 2000, Woman Wanted 2000, O Brother, Where Art Thou? 2000, Moonlight Mile 2002, Thirteen 2003, Levity 2003, The Incredibles (voice) 2004, Little Black Book 2004, Nine Lives 2005, The Big White 2005, Won't Back Down 2012. *Television includes:* Roe vs. Wade 1989, The Positively True Adventures of the Alleged Texas Cheerleader-Murdering Mom 1993, Harlan County War 2000, When Billie Beat Bobby 2001, Saving Grace (series) 2007–09. *Address:* c/o International Creative Management, 8942 Wilshire Blvd, #219, Beverly Hills, CA 90211, USA.

HUNTER, Howard O., AB, JD; American lawyer, academic and university administrator; *Professor of Law, Singapore Management University;* m. Susan Frankel 1971; one d.; ed Yale Univ.; admitted to the Bar of Ga 1971; mem. Faculty of Law, Emory Univ. 1976–2004, Asst Prof. 1976–79, Assoc. Prof. 1979–82, Prof. 1982–2004, Dean School of Law 1989–2001, Interim Provost and Exec. Vice-Pres. for Academic Affairs 2001–03, Prof. of Law and Dean Emer. 2005–; Pres. Singapore Man. Univ. 2004–10, Prof. of Law 2010–; Fulbright Sr Scholar, Univ. of Sydney Law School 1988; Recurring Visiting Prof. of Law, Cen. European Univ., Budapest 1999–; Visiting McWilliam Prof. of Commercial Law, Univ. of Sydney 2004; mem. Bd of Dirs Workforce Devt Authority of Singapore 2005–, Singapore Int. Chamber of Commerce 2005–, Enterprise Challenge of Singapore 2005–, Nat. Research Foundation of Singapore 2006–, American Arbitration Asscn 2006–, Building and Construction Authority 2009–; mem. Bd of Dirs Ga Volunteer Lawyers for the Arts Inc. 1975–89 (Pres. 1985–87, mem. Bd of Advisers 1997); mem. Chief Justice's Comm. on Professionalism 1990–2004; mem. Ga Supreme Court Comm. on Indigent Defense 2000–; mem. Editorial Bd Journal of Contract Law 1988–; mem. American Law Inst., ABA, Asscn of American Law Schools; Hon. Prof. of Law Hong Kong Univ. 1986; Bar and Media Award 1980, Supreme Court of Georgia Amicus Curiae Award 1998. *Publications include:* Recent Reforms in Swedish Higher Education (co-author) 1980, Universities and Community Service: Concepts and Problems 1980, Modern Law of Contracts, Law in Perspective: The Integrative Jurisprudence of Harold J. Berman (ed.) 1996, numerous journal articles. *Address:* School of Law, Singapore Management University, 60 Stamford Road, Level 4, 178900, Singapore (office). *Telephone:* 68085180 (office). *Fax:* 68280805 (office). *E-mail:* howardhunter@smu.edu.sg (office). *Website:* www.smu .edu.sg (office).

HUNTER, Larry D.; American television executive; *Executive Vice-President and General Counsel, The DIRECTV Group;* Corp. Vice-Pres. The DIRECTV Group, Inc. 1998–2001, Chair. and CEO DIRECTV Japan 1998–2001, Sr Vice-Pres., The DIRECTV Group, Inc. 2001–04, Assoc. Gen. Counsel 2001–02, Gen. Counsel 2002–, Exec. Vice-Pres. and Gen. Counsel 2004–09, 2009–, Interim CEO 2009. *Address:* The DIRECTV Group, Inc., 2230 East Imperial Highway, El Segundo, CA 90245, USA (office). *E-mail:* info@directv.com (office). *Website:* www.directv.com (office).

HUNTER, Robert John, AM, PhD, FAA; Australian research chemist and academic; *Honorary Associate Professor, School of Chemistry, University of Sydney;* b. 26 June 1933, Abermain; s. of Ronald Hunter and Elizabeth Dixon; m. Barbara Robson 1954 (divorced 1995); one s. one d.; ed Cessnock High School, New South Wales, New England Univ. Coll., Univ. of Sydney; secondary school teacher 1953–54; Tech. Officer, CSIRO 1954–57, Research Officer 1960–64; Lecturer, Univ. of Sydney 1964, Assoc. Prof. of Physical Chem. 1972–90, Head, School of Chem. 1987–90, Hon. Research Assoc. 1990–94, Hon. Assoc. Prof. 1994; Dir Colloidal Dynamics Pty Ltd 1988–96; Chair. Nat. Science and Industry Forum 1991–93; Pres. Int. Asscn of Colloid and Interface Scientists 1992–94; Nat. Pres. Scientists for Global Responsibility (fmrly Scientists Against Nuclear Arms) 1986–88, 1990–92, 1996–2008; Archibald Olle Prize 1982, 1993, Alexander Memorial Lecturer 1987, Liversidge Lecturer, Royal Soc. of New South Wales 1988, to Australia and New Zealand Acad. for Advancement of Science 2001. *Publications include:* Chemical Science 1976, Zeta Potential in Colloid Science 1981, Foundations of Colloid Science, (Vol. I) 1987, (Vol. 2) 1989, (second edn) 2001, Introduction to Modern Colloid Science 1993; author or co-author of about 100 research papers. *Leisure interests:* music, drama, reading, lawn bowls. *Address:* School of Chemistry, Building F11, University of Sydney, Sydney, NSW 2006 (office); 26/20A Austin Street, Lane Cove, NSW 2066, Australia (home). *Telephone:* (2) 9427-6261 (home). *E-mail:* Robert.hunter@sydney.edu.au (office); sgr@hotkey .net.au (home). *Website:* www.chem.usyd.edu.au/research/hunter.html (office).

HUNTSMAN, Jon Meade, Sr, BA, MBA; American chemical industry executive; *Chairman, Huntsman International LLC;* b. 21 June 1937, Blackfoot, Ida; m. Karen Haight 1959; nine c.; ed Univ. of Pennsylvania Wharton School, Univ. of Southern California; family moved to Palo Alto, Calif. 1950; salesman for egg-producing co., LA 1961; set up side-business selling repackaged music recordings 1964; Pres. Dolco Packaging (jt venture between egg business and Dow Chemical) 1967–70; Co-founder and CEO Huntsman Container Corpn 1970–80; Assoc. Admin. Dept of Health, Educ. and Welfare and later Special Asst to Pres. Nixon 1970; Founder, Chair. and CEO Huntsman Chemical Corpn, Salt Lake City, UT 1982; est. with Dow Chemical Co. a plastic, glass and aluminium-recycling programme in US Nat. Parks 1990; f. Huntsman Packaging 1992; est. Huntsman Cancer Inst., Univ. of UT, Salt Lake City 1993; Founder and Chair. Huntsman Corpn 1994–, all Huntsman operating entities brought under man. of Huntsman Corpn 1996–; Texas Gov.'s Award for Environmental Excellence 1996. *Address:* Huntsman International LLC, 500 Huntsman Way, Salt Lake City, UT 84108, USA (office). *Telephone:* (801) 584-5700 (office). *Fax:* (801) 584-5781 (office). *Website:* www.huntsman.com (office).

HUNTSMAN, Jon Meade, Jr, BA; American business executive, politician and diplomatist; *Chairman, Huntsman Cancer Institute;* b. 26 March 1960, Redwood City, Calif.; s. of Jon Huntsman, Sr and Karen Huntsman (née Haight); m. Mary Kaye Cooper; two s. three d. two adopted d.; ed Univs of Utah and Pennsylvania; served as missionary for the Church of Jesus Christ of Latter-day Saints (Mormon) in Taiwan; fmr White House Staff Asst to Pres. Ronald Reagan; served as Deputy Asst Sec. of Commerce for Trade Devt, then Deputy Asst Sec. of Commerce for E Asian and Pacific Affairs, then US Amb. to Singapore (youngest amb. in more than a century) under Pres. George H. W. Bush; served as Deputy US Trade Rep./US Trade Amb. for Asia, South Asia and Africa under Pres. George W. Bush; currently Chair. and CEO Huntsman Family Holdings Co. LLC (holding co. for Huntsman Corpn, fmr Chair. Exec. Cttee); Gov. of Utah 2005–09 (resgnd); Amb. to People's Repub. of China 2009–11 (resgnd); cand. for Republican US presidential nomination 2012; first Pres. and CEO Huntsman Cancer Foundation, responsible for organizing and funding of Huntsman Cancer Inst. (Chair. 2012–), Univ. of Utah; mem. Bd of Dirs Ford Motor Co. 2012–, Caterpillar Inc. 2012–; fmr Bd mem. Intermountain Health Care, ARUP Laboratories; fmr Br. Dir San Francisco Fed. Reserve Bank Bd; Founding Dir Pacific Council on Int. Policy; fmr mem. Bd

Brookings Inst. Asia Policy Board, Asia Soc., New York, Nat. Bureau of Asian Research; fmr mem. Int. Advisory Council, Singapore Econ. Devt Bd, Nat. Bd, Juvenile Diabetes Foundation; fmr Chair. KSL's Family Now Campaign, Envision Utah, Utah Opera; fmr Vice-Chair. Coalition for Utah's Future; fmr mem. Advisory Bd, Univ. of Utah School of Business, Nat. Govs Asscn; fmr Trustee, Univ. of Pennsylvania; fmr Chair. Western Govs Asscn; Distinguished Fellow, Brookings Inst., Washington, DC 2012; Hon. Dr of Public Service (Snow College) 2005, Hon. DSc (Westminster College) 2008, Hon. DHumLitt (Univ. of Utah) 2010, Hon. LLD (Univ. of Pennsylvania) 2010, Hon. Dr of Law (Southern New Hampshire Univ.) 2011; Distinguished Eagle Scout Award, Boy Scouts of America 2007. *Address:* Huntsman Cancer Institute, 2000 Circle of Hope, Salt Lake City, UT 84112, USA (office). *Telephone:* (801) 585-0303 (office). *E-mail:* public.affairs@hci.utah.edu (office). *Website:* www.huntsmancancer.org (office); www.jon2012.com.

HUO, Lianhong, BEng; Chinese economist and business executive; *General Manager and President, China Pacific Insurance (Group) Company Ltd;* ed Cen.-South Inst. of Mining and Metallurgy; Deputy Man. Insurance Dept, Hainan br., Bank of Communications –1993; joined China Pacific Insurance (Group) Co. Ltd 1993, held numerous positions, including Gen. Man. Hainan and Beijing brs, Exec. Vice-Pres. China Pacific Insurance (Group) Co. Ltd –2000, mem. Bd of Dirs, Gen. Man. and Pres. 2000–, Dir, China Pacific Insurance Life Insurance Co. Ltd, Chair. China Pacific Property Insurance Co. Ltd, China Pacific Asset Management Co. Ltd. *Address:* China Pacific Insurance (Group) Co. Ltd, 190 Yincheng Zhong Road, Shanghai 200120, Shanghai Province, People's Republic of China (office). *Telephone:* (21) 58776688 (office). *Fax:* (21) 68870922 (office). *E-mail:* info@cpic.com.cn (office). *Website:* www.cpic.com.cn (office).

HUPPERT, Herbert Eric, MA, MSc, MS, PhD, ScD, FRS; Australian scientist and academic; *Professor of Theoretical Geophysics and Director, Institute of Theoretical Geophysics, University of Cambridge;* b. 26 Nov. 1943, Sydney; s. of Leo Huppert and Alice Huppert (née Neumann); m. Felicia Ferster 1966; two s.; ed Sydney Boys High School, Univ. of Sydney, Australian Nat. Univ. and Univ. of California, San Diego, USA; ICI Research Fellow, Univ. of Cambridge 1968–69, Asst Dir Research Dept Applied Math. and Theoretical Physics 1970–81, Univ. Lecturer 1981–88, Reader Geophysical Dynamics 1988–89, Prof. of Theoretical Geophysics and Dir Inst. of Theoretical Geophysics 1989–, Fellow, King's Coll., Cambridge 1970–; Prof. of Math., Univ. of NSW 1991–95; BP Venture Unit Sr Research Fellow 1983–89; fmr Visiting Research Scientist, Univ. of Calif., USA, Univ. of Canterbury, NZ, Univ. of NSW, ANU, MIT, USA, Univ. of Western Australia, Woods Hole Oceanographic Inst., USA, California Inst. of Tech., USA; Vice-Chair. Scientists for the Release of Soviet Refuseniks 1985–88, Co-Chair. 1988–92; mem. Council NERC 1993–98, Scientific Council, The Earth Centre 1995–, Council Royal Soc. 2001–03; Ed. Journal of Soviet Jewry 1986–92; Assoc. Ed. Journal of Fluid Mechanics 1971–90; mem. Editorial Bd Philosophical Transactions of the Royal Society A 1994–99, Reports on Progress in Physics 1997–2000; Fellow, American Geophysical Union 2002, American Physical Soc. 2004; Evnin Lecturer, Princeton Univ. 1995, Mid-West Mechanics Lecturer 1996–97, Henry Charnock Distinguished Lecturer 1999, Smith Industries Lecturer, Univ. of Oxford 1999, Nat. Acad. of America's Arthur L Prize and Lectureship 2005, Distinguished Israel Pollak Lecturer of Technion 2005, William Hopkins Prize, Cambridge Philosophical Soc. 2005, Murchison Medal, London Geological Soc. 2007, Bakerian Lecturer, Royal Soc. 2011. *Achievement:* played squash for Cambridgeshire 1970–72. *Publications:* more than 230 papers on fluid motions associated with the atmosphere, oceans, volcanoes and the interior of the Earth. *Leisure interests:* his children, squash, mountaineering, lawn tennis, music, travel. *Address:* Institute of Theoretical Geophysics, Department of Applied Mathematics and Theoretical Physics, University of Cambridge, Centre for Mathematical Sciences, Wilberforce Road, Cambridge, CB3 0WA (office); 46 De Freville Avenue, Cambridge, CB4 1HT, England (home). *Telephone:* (1223) 337853 (office); (1223) 356071 (home). *Fax:* (1223) 765900 (office). *E-mail:* heh1@esc.cam.ac.uk (office). *Website:* www.itg.cam.ac.uk/people/heh (office).

HUPPERT, Isabelle Anne Madeleine; French actress; b. 16 March 1953, Paris; d. of Raymond Huppert and Annick Beau; m. Ronald Chammah 1982; two s. one d.; ed Lycée de St-Cloud, Ecole nat. des langues orientales vivantes; Pres. Comm. d'avances sur recettes 1994–; several theatre appearances including Mary Stuart (London) 1996, 4.48 Psychose (Paris) 2002; Pres. Cannes Film Festival Jury 2009; Chevalier, Légion d'honneur 1999, Officier 2009, Chevalier, Ordre nat. du Mérite 1994, Officier 2005; Stanislavsky Award 2008. *Theatre:* 4.48 Psychosis (New York) 2005. *Films include:* Le bar de la Fourche, César et Rosalie, Les valseuses, Aloïse, Dupont la joie, Rosebud, Docteur Françoise Gailland, Le juge et l'assassin, Le petit Marcel 1976, Les indiens sont encore loin 1977, La dentellière (BAFTA for Most Promising Newcomer) 1978, Violette Nozière (Cannes Film Festival Best Actress Award 1978) 1978, Les soeurs Brontë 1979, Loulou 1980, Sauve qui peut (la vie), Les Héritières 1980, Heaven's Gate 1980, Coup de Torchon 1981, La Dame aux Camélias 1981, Les Ailes de la Colombe 1981, Eaux Profondes 1981, Passion, travail et amour, La Truite 1982, Entre Nous 1984, My Best Friend's Girl 1984, La Garce 1984, Signé Charlotte, Sac de noeuds 1985, Cactus 1986, Sincerely Charlotte 1986, The Bedroom Window 1986, The Possessed 1988, Story of Women 1989, Milan Noir 1990, Madame Bovary 1991, Malina 1991, Après l'amour 1992, La Séparation 1994, Amateur 1994, L'Inondation 1994, La Cérémonie (César Best Actress Award) 1995, Les Affinités électives 1996, Rien ne va plus 1997, Les Palmes de M. Schutz 1997, L'Ecole de la chair 1998, Merci pour le chocolat 2000, Les Destinées sentimentales 2000, La Fausse suivante et Saint-Cyr 2000, La Pianiste (Best Actress, Cannes Film Festival) 2001, 8 Femmes 2002, Deux 2002, La Vie promise 2002, Le Temps du loup 2003, Ma Mère 2004, I Heart Huckabees 2004, Les Soeurs fâchées 2004, Gabrielle (Venice Film Festival Special Lion) 2005, L'Ivresse du pouvoir, Nue Propriété 2006, L'Amour caché 2007, Médée miracle 2007, Home 2008, The Sea Wall 2008, Villa Amalia 2009, White Material 2009, Copacabana 2010, Sans queue ni tête 2010, Special Treatment 2010, My Little Princess 2011, My Worst Nightmare 2011, Dubaï Flamingo (voice, uncredited) 2012, Captive 2012, Amour 2012, In Another Country 2012, Lines of Wellington 2012, Dormant Beauty 2012, Dead Man Down 2013, The Disappearance of Eleanor Rigby: His 2013, The Disappearance of Eleanor Rigby: Hers 2013, Tip Top 2013, Abus de Faiblesse 2013, La religieuse 2013. *Television:* Law & Order: Special Victims Unit (series) 2010, As Linhas de Torres Vedras (mini-series) 2012.

Publication: Madame Deshoulières 2001. *Address:* c/o VMA, 20 avenue Rapp, 75007 Paris, France. *Telephone:* 1-43-17-37-00. *E-mail:* info@vma.fr. *Website:* www.vma.fr.

HÜPPI, Rolf; Swiss financial services industry executive; b. 25 April 1943, Uznach; joined Zurich Financial Services 1963, Man. India Office 1964–70, Zurich Office 1970–72, Regional Man. US Office, Pittsburgh 1972–74, mem. Group Exec. Bd 1983–, CEO for US Br. 1983–87, Deputy COO 1987–88, COO 1988–91, Pres. and CEO 1991–98; mem. Bd of Dirs Zurich Insurance Co. 1993–2002, Chair. 1995–2002; Chair. and CEO Zurich Financial Services Group (following merger) 1998–2002 (resgnd); f. Rolf Hüppi AG, Zurich 2002; Founder, Pres. and CEO ParaLife Holding AG (micro-insurance co. operating in developing countries) 2006–; Chair. Advisory Bd The Peninsula Group LLC; Int. Counselor, Center for Strategic and Int. Studies, Washington, DC; Batten Fellow, Darden Business School, Charlottesville, Va 2004; Dr hc (Universidad Autonoma de Guadalajara). *Address:* Rolf Hüppi AG, Gartenstrasse 33, 8002 Zürich, Switzerland; c/o Advisory Board, The Peninsula Group LLC; 1010 Wisconsin Avenue, NW, Suite 620, Washington, DC 20007, USA (office). *E-mail:* info@peninsulagrouplllc.com. *Website:* peninsulagrouplllc.com.

HUR, Dong-soo, BS, MS, PhD; South Korean chemical engineer and business executive; *Chairman, GS Caltex Corporation;* b. 13 July 1943; ed Bosung Senior High School, Yonsei Univ., Univ. of Wisconsin, USA; mil. service 1961–63; Research Engineer, Chevron Research Co., USA 1971–73; joined GS Caltex Corpn 1973, Special Asst to Jt Rep. Dirs 1973–78, Vice-Pres. and Deputy Refinery Man. 1978–81, Vice-Pres., Planning/Project and Construction 1981–84, Exec. Vice-Pres., Corp. Planning/Crude Oil/Supply and Distribution 1984–87, Exec. Vice-Pres., Planning and Manufacturing 1987–91, Pres. and COO GS Caltex Corpn 1991–93, Pres. and CEO 1994–97, Vice-Chair. and CEO 1998–2002, Chair. and CEO 2003–12, Chair. 2013–, Chair. GS Caltex Foundation 2006–; Chair. Korea Petroleum Asscn 1994–95, Korea Baduk Asscn 2001–, Korea Business for Sustainable Devt 2002–, Cttee on Consumer Complaints Man. System 2005–, Korea Cttee on the Korea-China-Japan Business Forum 2005–, Korea-Oman Friendship Asscn 2007–; Head of Business Dialogue, Presidential Cttee on Green Growth 2009–; Auditor, Global Green Growth Inst. 2010–; Order of Industrial Service Merit, Bronze Tower 1995, Order of Industrial Service Merit, Gold Tower 2000, Order of Civil Merit, Mugunghwa Medal 2005, Order of Culture Merit, Geumgwan 2012; Industrial Service Medal 1985, Award for Energy Entrepreneur, Korea Resource Econs Asscn 2003. *Address:* GS Caltex Corporation, 679 Yeoksam-dong, Seoul 135-985, Republic of Korea (office). *Telephone:* (2) 2005-1114 (office). *Fax:* (2) 2005-8181 (office). *E-mail:* info@gscaltex.com (office). *Website:* www.gscaltex.com (office).

HUR, Won-joon, BSc; South Korean business executive; *Vice-Chairman, Hanwha Chemical Corpn;* b. 19 May 1956; ed Pusan High School, Yonsei Univ., Seoul; joined Hanwha Chemical 1968, Head of Research, Hanwha Group Research Centre, 1982–89, Head of Business Devt Div., Hanwha Chemical Corpn, 1989–92, Head of Tech. Planning Div. 1992–97, Head of New Business Devt Div. 1997–98, Head of Restructuring Team 1998–2001, Chief Planning, Tech. and Information Officer 2001, Pres. and CEO 2002–09, Vice-Chair. 2009–; Chair. Korea Petro-chemical Industry Asscn 2007–10, Korea Responsible Care Council 2004–06; Order of Industrial Service Merit, Ivory Tower 2000. *Address:* Hanwha Chemical Corpn, Hanwha Building, 1 Changgyo-Dong, Chung-Ku, Seoul 100-797, Republic of Korea (office). *Telephone:* (2) 729-2700 (office).

HURD, Mark Vincent, BA; American computer industry executive; *President, Oracle Corporation;* b. 1 Jan. 1957, Flushing, NY; m. Paula Kalupa; ed Baylor Univ.; various positions with NCR 1980–2005, including Vice-Pres. Worldwide Marketing and Americas Professional Services Div., Sr Vice-Pres. Teradata Solutions Group 1998–2000, COO Teradata Div., Pres. NCR 2001–05, COO 2002–03, CEO 2003–05; CEO and Pres. Hewlett-Packard Co. 2005–10 (resgnd), Chair. 2006–10; Pres. Oracle Corpn 2010–; mem. Bd of Dirs News Corpn; mem. Computer Systems Policy Project. *Address:* Oracle Corporation, 500 Oracle Parkway, Redwood Shores, CA 94065, USA (office). *Telephone:* (650) 506-7000 (office). *Fax:* (650) 506-7200 (office). *E-mail:* info@oracle.com (office). *Website:* www.oracle.com (office).

HURD OF WESTWELL, Baron (Life Peer), cr. 1997, of Westwell in the County of Oxfordshire; **Douglas Richard Hurd,** CH, CBE, PC, BA (Hons); British politician, diplomatist, banker and author; b. 8 March 1930, Marlborough, Wilts.; s. of the late Anthony Hurd, Baron Hurd and Stephanie Corner; m. 1st Tatiana Elizabeth Michelle Eyre 1960 (divorced 1982); three s.; m. 2nd Judy Smart 1982 (died 2008); one s. one d.; ed Eton Coll., Trinity Coll., Cambridge; fmr Pres. Cambridge Union Soc.; joined diplomatic service 1952; served in Beijing 1954–56, UK Mission to UN 1956–60, Pvt. Sec. to Perm. Under-Sec. of State, Foreign Office 1960–63, in British Embassy, Rome 1963–66; joined Conservative Research Dept 1966, Head of Foreign Affairs Section 1968; Pvt. Sec. to Leader of the Opposition 1968–70, Political Sec. to the Prime Minister 1970–74; MP for Mid-Oxon 1974–83, for Witney 1983–97; Opposition Spokesman on European Affairs 1976–79, Minister of State, FCO 1979–83, Home Office 1983–84; Sec. of State for NI 1984–85; Home Sec. 1985–89; Sec. of State for Foreign and Commonwealth Affairs 1989–95; mem. Constitutional Comm. 1998–99, Royal Comm. on the Reform of the House of Lords 1999–2001, House of Lords Appointments Comm. 2000–10; Deputy Chair. NatWest Markets 1995–98; Dir NatWest Group 1995–99; Chair. British Invisibles 1997–2000; Deputy Chair. Coutts and Co. 1998–2010; cand. for Conservative Leadership 1990; Chair. Prison Reform Trust 1997–2001 (Pres.), Booker Prize Cttee 1998, Archbishop of Canterbury's Review 2000–01, Council for Effective Dispute Resolution 2001–04; Sr Adviser to Hawkpoint Partners Ltd 1999–; Pres. Montrose Strategic Consultancy, London; Chair. Advisory Council, FIRST Magazine (Forum For Decision Makers) (int. affairs org.), London; High Steward Westminster Abbey 2000–10; Pres. German-British Forum; Co-Pres. Royal Inst. Int. Affairs 2002–10; Vice-Pres. Falkland Islands Asscn 1996–2000 (Pres. 2000–), Commonwealth Parl. Asscn (UK Br.); mem. Global Leadership Foundation, Top Level Group of UK Parliamentarians for Multilateral Nuclear Disarmament and Non-proliferation 2009–; f. charity, Crime Concern 1988 (merged with young people's charity Rainer to become Catch22 2008); Fellow, Nuffield Coll. Oxford; Hon. DLitt (Aston) 2009, (Brunel) 2009; Spectator Award for Parliamentarian of the Year 1990. *Publications:* non-fiction: The Arrow War 1967,

An End to Promises 1979, The Search for Peace 1997, Memoirs 2003, Robert Peel, a Biography 2007, Choose Your Weapons: The British Foreign Secretary (with Edward Young) 2010, Disraeli: Or, the Two Lives (with Edward Young) 2013; fiction: Send Him Victorious (with Andrew Osmond) 1968, The Smile on the Face of the Tiger 1969, Scotch on the Rocks (with Andrew Osmond) 1971, Truth Game 1972, Vote to Kill 1975, War Without Frontiers (with Andrew Osmond) 1982, Palace of Enchantments (with Stephen Lamport) 1985, The Last Day of Summer 1992, The Shape of Ice 1998, Ten Minutes to Turn the Devil (short stories) 1999, Image in the Water 2001. *Leisure interests:* writing, broadcasting. *Address:* House of Lords, Westminster, London, SW1A 0PW, England (office).

HURFORD, Peter John, OBE, MusB, MA, FRCO; British organist; b. 22 Nov. 1930, Minehead, Somerset, England; s. of Hubert John Hurford and Gladys Winifred James; m. Patricia Mary Matthews 1955; two s. one d.; ed Blundell's School, Royal Coll. of Music (Open Foundation Scholar), Jesus Coll., Cambridge (Organ Scholar) and pvt. studies with André Marchal, Paris; commissioned into Royal Signals 1954–56; debut, Royal Festival Hall, London 1956; Organist and Choirmaster, Holy Trinity Church, Leamington Spa 1956–57; Dir of Music, Bablake School, Coventry 1956–57; Master of the Music, Cathedral and Abbey Church of St Alban 1958–78; freelance concert and recording organist 1978–98; Visiting Prof., Coll. Conservatory of Music, Cincinnati, USA 1967–68, Univ. of Western Ontario, Canada 1976–77; Acting Organist, St John's Coll. Cambridge 1979–80; Visiting Artist-in-Residence, Sydney Opera House 1980–82; Prof., RAM 1982–88; John Betts Fellow, Univ. of Oxford 1990–92; Decca recording artist 1977–; concerts in USA, Canada, Australia, NZ, Japan, Far East, Eastern and Western Europe 1958–98; f. St Albans Int. Organ Festival 1963, Artistic Dir 1963–78, Hon. Pres. 1978–; Pres. Inc. Assen of Organists 1995–97; mem. Council Royal Coll. of Organists 1964–2003, Pres. 1980–82; Fellow, Royal School of Church Music 1977; Hon. FRCM 1987; Hon. Fellow in Organ Studies, Univ. of Bristol 1997–98; Hon. Fellow, Jesus Coll. Cambridge 2006; Hon. RAM 1982; Hon. DMus (Baldwin-Wallace Coll., Ohio, USA) 1981, (Bristol) 1992; Hon. DArts (Univ. of Hertfordshire) 2007; Gramophone Award 1979, Royal Coll. of Organists Medal 2013. *Compositions include:* organ music; Suite – Laudate Dominum, Chorale Preludes; choral music: The Communion Service, Series III, The Holy Eucharist, Rite 2 (for American Episcopal Church), music for the Daily Office, miscellaneous anthems, songs, carols, etc. *Recordings include:* complete organ works of J.S. Bach, Handel, F. Couperin, P. Hindemith, music of Franck, Mendelssohn; numerous recitals for BBC, including 34 commentated programmes of J.S. Bach's complete organ works 1980–82, Bach organ music cycle (Herald Angel Critics Award), 50th Edin. Int. Festival 1997. *Publications:* Making Music on the Organ 1988; contrib. to journals, numerous forewords. *Leisure interest:* hill walking, wine, silence. *Address:* Broom House, St Bernard's Road, St Albans, Herts., AL3 5RA, England.

HURLEY, Elizabeth Jane; British model, actress and fashion designer; b. 10 June 1965; d. of the late Roy Leonard Hurley and of Angela Mary Hurley; m. Arun Nayar 2007 (divorced); one s. (from previous relationship); produced several films starring Hugh Grant under their jointly-owned production co. Simian Films; represents Estée Lauder as 'spokesmodel' 1994–; toured USA and other countries with the late Evelyn Lauder, raising funds and awareness for The Breast Cancer Research Foundation; owns 400-acre organic farm in Glos.; launched Elizabeth Hurley Beach fashion collection 2005; honoured by Landmark Foundation and awarded the Humanitarian Award for fundraising efforts 2009. *Films include:* Aria 1987, The Skipper 1990, The Long Winter of 39 1992, Passenger 57 1992, Mad Dogs and Englishmen 1995, Austin Powers: International Man of Mystery (ShoWest Award for Best Supporting Actress 1997) 1997, My Favourite Martian 1999, Austin Powers: The Spy Who Shagged Me 1999, The Weight of Water 2000, Bedazzled 2000, Double Whammy 2001, Dawg 2002, Method 2004, The Last Guy on Earth 2006. *Television:* title role in Christabel (film) 1988, Rumpole of the Bailey (series) 1988, Inspector Morse 1988, Act of Will (series) 1989, Death Has a Bad Reputation (film) 1990, The Orchid House (series) 1991, The Good Guys (series) 1992, The Young Indiana Jones Chronicles (series) 1992, Sharpe's Enemy (film) 1994, The Shamrock Conspiracy (film) 1995, Harrison: Cry of the City (film) 1996, Samson and Delilah (film) 1996, Wonder Woman (film) 2011, Gossip Girl (series) 2011. *E-mail:* ducotyG@unitedtalent.com (office); office@elizabethhurley .com (office). *Address:* PO Box 16, Cirencester, Glos., GL7 9GH, England. *Website:* www.elizabethhurley.com.

HURN, David; British photographer and lecturer; b. 21 July 1934, Redhill, Surrey, England; s. of Stanley Hurn and Joan Maynard; m. Alita Naughton 1964 (divorced 1971); one d.; ed Hardy's School, Dorchester and Royal Mil. Acad., Sandhurst; Asst Photographer to Michael Peto and George Vargas, Reflex Agency, London 1955–57; freelance photographer for The Observer, Sunday Times, Look, Life, etc. 1957, working from Wales 1971; mem. Magnum Photos co-operative agency, New York, Paris, London and Tokyo 1967–; Editorial Adviser Album Photographic magazine, London 1971; Head, School of Documentary Photography, Gwent Coll. of Higher Educ., Newport, Gwent 1973–90; Distinguished Visiting Artist and Adjunct Prof., Arizona State Univ., USA 1979–80; mem. Photographic Cttee, Arts Council of GB 1972–77, Arts Panel 1975–77, CNAA 1978–87; works in collections of Welsh Arts Council, Arts Council of GB, British Council, Bibliothèque Nationale, Paris, Int. Center of Photography, New York, San Francisco Museum of Modern Art, Museum of Modern Art, New York and others; Hon. Fellow, Univ. of Wales 1997; Welsh Arts Council Award 1971, Imperial War Museum Arts Award 1987–88, Kodak Photographic Bursary 1975, UK/USA Bicentennial Fellowship 1979–80, Bradford Fellow 1993–94, Arts Council of Wales Bursary 1995. *Publications:* David Hurn: Photographs 1956–1976 1979, On Being a Photographer 1997, Wales: Land of My Father 2000, On Looking at Photographs 2000, Living in Wales 2003, Writing the Picture 2010. *Leisure interests:* music, looking, meeting people. *Address:* c/o Magnum Photos, 63 Gee Street, London, EC1V 3RS, England (office); Prospect Cottage, Tintern, Monmouthshire, NP16 6SG, Wales. *Telephone:* (20) 7490-1771 (office); (1291) 689358. *Fax:* (20) 7608-0020 (office). *E-mail:* london@magnumphotos.com (office); hurn@tintern.u-net.com (office). *Website:* www.magnumphotos.com (office).

HURST, Sir Geoffrey Charles, Kt, MBE; British professional football manager, fmr professional footballer and business executive; b. 8 Dec. 1941, Ashton-under-Lyne, Lancs.; s. of Charles Hurst and Evelyn Hurst; m. Judith Harries 1964; three d.; striker; player, West Ham United 1957–72 (won UEFA Cup Winners Cup 1965,

FA Cup 1964, Int. Soccer League 1963), Stoke City 1972–74, West Bromwich Albion 1975–76, Seattle Sounders 1976, Cork Celtic 1976; player and Man. Telford United 1976–79; Man. Chelsea 1979–81; won 49 caps and scored 24 goals for England nat. team 1966–72, scored hat-trick in victory over W Germany, World Cup 1966 (only player to do so in a World Cup final); Dir Aon Warranty Group 1995–; currently Dir of Football, McDonald's fast food chain; Patron Ludlow Town Football Club; inducted into English Football Hall of Fame 2004. *Publication:* 1966 and All That 2001, World Champions 2006. *Leisure interests:* sport in general, family. *Address:* c/o Dave Davies, PO Box 99, Hockley, Essex, SS5 4TB, England (office). *Telephone:* (1702) 202036 (office). *Fax:* (871) 871-2065 (office). *E-mail:* dave@football1966.com (office); david@geoffhurst.net (office). *Website:* www .geoffhurst.net (office).

HURT, John, CBE; British actor; b. (John Vincent Hurt), 22 Jan. 1940, Chesterfield, Derbyshire, England; s. of Rev. Arnould Herbert and Phyllis Hurt (née Massey); m. 1st Annette Robertson; m. 2nd Donna Peacock 1984 (divorced 1990); m. 3rd Jo Dalton 1990 (divorced 1995); two s.; m. 4th Anwen Rees Meyers 2005; ed The Lincoln School, Lincoln and Royal Acad. of Dramatic Art; began as painter; stage debut, Arts Theatre, London 1962; Dir United British Artists 1982; Fellow, British Film Inst. 2009–; Richard Harris Award for Outstanding Contrib. to British Film, British Ind. Film Awards 2003, BAFTA Film Award for Outstanding British Contribution to Cinema 2012. *Stage appearances include:* Chips With Everything, Vaudeville Theatre 1962, The Dwarfs, Arts 1963, Hamp (title role), Edinburgh Festival 1964, Inadmissible Evidence, Wyndhams 1965, Little Malcolm and his Struggle against the Eunuchs, Garrick 1966, Belcher's Luck (RSC), Aldwych 1966, Man and Superman, Gaiety, Dublin 1969, The Caretaker, Mermaid 1972, The Only Street, Dublin Festival and Islington 1973, Travesties (RSC), Aldwych and The Arrest, Bristol Old Vic 1974, The Shadow of a Gunman, Nottingham Playhouse 1978, The London Vertigo, Dublin 1991, A Month in the Country, Albery 1994, Krapp's Last Tape, New Ambassadors Theatre 2000, Gate Theatre, Dublin 2001, Afterplay, Gielgud Theatre 2002. *Films include:* The Wild and the Willing 1962, A Man for All Seasons 1966, Sinful Davey 1968, Before Winter Comes 1969, In Search of Gregory 1970, Mr Forbush and the Penguins 1971, 10 Rillington Place, Little Malcolm 1974, The Disappearance, The Shout, Alien, Midnight Express (British Acad. Best Supporting Actor Award 1978, Golden Globe Best Supporting Actor Award 1978, Variety Club Best Actor Award 1978) 1978, Heaven's Gate 1980, The Elephant Man (British Acad. Best Actor Award 1980, Variety Club Best Film Actor Award 1980) 1980, Champions (Evening Standard Best Actor Award 1984) 1983, The Hit (Evening Standard Best Actor Award 1984) 1984, Rocinante 1986, Aria 1987, White Mischief 1987, Scandal 1988, From the Hip 1989, Frankenstein Unbound, The Field 1989, King Ralph 1991, Lapse of Memory 1991, Dark at Noon 1992, Monolith 1994, Even Cowgirls Get the Blues 1994, Rob Roy 1994, Two Nudes Bathing (Cable Ace Award 1995) 1995, Dead Man 1996, Wild Bill 1996, Love and Death on Long Island 1998, The Love Letter 1999, Krapp's Last Tape 1999, Lost Souls 2000, Night Train 2000, Captain Corelli's Mandolin 2001, Harry Potter and the Philosopher's Stone 2001, Tabloid 2001, Bait 2001, Crime and Punishment 2002, Miranda 2003, Dogville (voice) 2003, Hellboy 2004, The Proposition 2004, Manderlay 2005, V for Vendetta 2006, Perfume: The Story of a Murderer (voice) 2006, The Oxford Murders 2007, Indiana Jones and the Kingdom of the Crystal Skull 2008, Hellboy II: The Golden Army 2008, Outlander 2008, An Englishman in New York 2009, The Limits of Control 2009, 44 Inch Chest 2009, Brighton Rock 2010, Harry Potter and the Deathly Hallows: Part 1 2010, Regret Not Speaking 2011, Melancholia 2011, Harry Potter and the Deathly Hallows: Part 2 2011, 23 Degrees, 5 Minutes (short) 2011, Tinker, Tailor, Soldier, Spy 2011, In Love with Alma Cogan 2011, Immortals 2011, Jayne Mansfield's Car 2012. *Television includes:* The Waste Places 1968, Nijinsky: God of the Dance (Best Television Actor 1975) 1975, The Naked Civil Servant (British Acad. Award 1975, Emmy Award 1978) 1975, Caligula in I, Claudius 1976, Treats 1977, Raskolnikov in Crime and Punishment 1979, Poison Candy 1988, Deadline 1988, Journey to Knock 1991, Red Fox (Best Actor Monte Carlo TV Awards 1991) 1991, Six Characters in Search of an Author 1992, Prisoner in Time 1995, Saigon Baby 1995, Alan Clark Diaries 2004, Hellboy: Sword of Storms (voice) 2006, Merlin (series) (voice) 2008–11, The Gruffalo (voice) 2009, An Englishman in New York 2009, The Confession (series) 2011, The Gruffalo's Child (film) 2011, Labyrinth (series) 2012. *Address:* c/o Julian Belfrage Associates, 3rd Floor, 9 Argyll Street, London, W1F 7TG, England (office).

HURT, William; American actor; b. 20 March 1950, Washington, DC; m. 1st Mary Beth Hurt 1971 (divorced 1982); m. 2nd Heidi Henderson 1989 (divorced 1992); two s.; ed Tufts Univ., Juilliard School; appeared with Ore. Shakespeare Festival production of Long Day's Journey Into Night; mem. Circle Repertory Co.; recipient of first Spencer Tracy Award 1988, for outstanding screen performances and professional achievement. *Stage appearances include:* Henry V 1976, Mary Stuart, My Life, Ulysses in Traction, Lulu, Fifth of July, Childe Byron, The Runner Stumbles, Hamlet, Hurlyburly, Beside Herself 1989, Ivanov 1991. *Films include:* Altered States 1980, Eyewitness 1981, Body Heat 1981, The Big Chill 1983, Gorky Park 1983, Kiss of the Spider Woman (Best Actor Award Cannes Film Festival 1985, Acad. Award for Best Actor 1985) 1985, Children of a Lesser God 1986, Broadcast News 1987, A Time of Destiny 1988, The Accidental Tourist 1989, I Love You to Death 1990, The House of Spirits 1990, Alice 1990, The Doctor 1991, Until the End of the World 1991, Mr. Wonderful 1993, The Plague 1993, Trial by Jury 1994, Second Best 1994, Jane Eyre 1995, Secrets Shared With a Stranger, Smoke 1995, A Couch in New York 1996, Michael 1996, Loved 1997, Lost in Space 1998, One True Thing 1998, The Proposition 1998, Dark City 1998, The 4th Floor 1999, The Big Brass Ring 1999, Sunshine 1999, Do Not Disturb 1999, The Simian Line 2000, The Contaminated Man 2000, AI: Artificial Intelligence 2001, The Flamingo Rising 2001, Rare Birds 2001, Changing Lanes 2002, Au plus pres du paradis 2002, Tuck Everlasting 2002, Tulse Luper Suitcases: The Moab Story 2003, Blue Butterfly 2004, The Village 2004, A History of Violence 2005, Syriana 2005, The King 2005, Neverwas 2005, The Legend of Sasquatch (voice) 2006, Beautiful Ohio 2006, The Good Shepherd 2006, Mr. Brooks 2007, Into the Wild 2007, Vantage Point 2008, The Incredible Hulk 2008, Endgame 2009, The Countess 2009, Robin Hood 2010. *Television includes:* The Flamingo Rising 2001, Master Spy: The Robert Hanssen Story 2002, Frankenstein (miniseries) 2004, Hunt for Justice 2005, Damages (series) 2009. *Address:* 88 SW Century Drive, #348, Bend, OR

97702-1047; c/o Creative Artists Agency, 9830 Wilshire Blvd, Beverly Hills, CA 90212-1825, USA. *Telephone:* (310) 288-4545. *Fax:* (310) 288-4800.

HURTADO LARREA, Osvaldo, BrerPol, DIur; Ecuadorean fmr head of state; *President, Corporation for Development Studies (CORDES);* b. 26 June 1939, Chambo, Chimborazo Prov.; s. of Agustín Hurtado and Elina Larrea de Hurtado; m. Margarita Pérez Pallares; three s. two d.; ed Catholic Univ. of Quito; f. Ecuadorian Christian Democratic Party 1964; Pres. of Congress 1966; Prof. of Political Sociology, Catholic Univ., Quito; Dir Instituto Ecuatoriano de Desarrollo Social (INEDES) 1966; Under-Sec. of Labour 1969; Sub-Dean, Faculty of Econs and Dir Inst. of Econ. Research, Catholic Univ., Quito 1973; invited to form part of World Political Council of Christian Democracy 1975; joined with other political groups to form Popular Democracy 1978; Pres. Org. of Christian Democrats of America, Vice-Pres. Int. Christian Democrats; Pres. Comm. to prepare Law of Referendum of Elections and Political Parties 1977; Vice-Pres. of Ecuador and Pres. Consejo Nacional de Desarrollo (Nat. Devt Council) 1979–81; Pres. of Ecuador 1981–84; Pres. Nat. Ass. 1998; Pres. CORDES (org. for study of Latin American Devt problems), Quito; fmr Vice-Pres. Inst. for European Latin-American Relations, Madrid; mem. Council of ex-Pres, Atlanta, Interamerican Dialogue, Washington, DC (Co-Pres, Bd of Dirs), The Carter Center, Atlanta, Club de Madrid, Foro de Biarritz, Emerging Markets Forum, Washington, DC, Foro Iberoamericano; mem. comm. that prepared the environmental reports Nuestra Propia Agenda 1990, Amazonía Sin Mitos 1992 and Amanecer en los Andes 1997 at request of IDB and UNDP; Dr hc (Georgetown); various foreign decorations. *Publications:* numerous essays and several books about Ecuadorian politics, sociology and economy, including El Poder Político en el Ecuador (Political Power in Ecuador) 1977, Los Costos del Populismo 2006, Las Costumbres de los Ecuatorianos 2007; academic work about Latin America gathered in several books published in collaboration with other authors in many countries. *Leisure interests:* tennis, gardening. *Address:* CORDES, Suecia 277 y Av. Los Shyris, Edificio Suecia Piso 2, PO Box 17-17-307, Quito, Ecuador (office). *Telephone:* (5932) 2455701 (office). *Fax:* (5932) 2446414 (office). *E-mail:* cordes2@cordes.org (office). *Website:* www.cordes.org (office).

HUSA, Karel; American composer and conductor; b. 7 Aug. 1921, Prague, Czech Repub.; s. of the late Karel Husa and Bozena Husova; m. Simone Husa (née Perault); four d.; ed Prague Conservatory of Music, Prague Acad. of Music, Paris Conservatory of Music, Ecole normale de musique de Paris; composer, conductor in Paris, guest conductor with European orchestras, Kappa Alpha Prof. of Music, Cornell Univ. 1954, Asst Prof. 1954, Assoc. Prof. 1957, Prof. 1961; conductor of the univ. orchestras, teacher of composition (retd 1992), guest conductor with American orchestras and lecturer; Prof., School of Music, Ithaca Coll. 1967–86; mem. Belgian Royal Acad. of Arts and Sciences 1974–, American Acad. of Arts and Letters 1994–; hon. degrees include Coe Coll. 1976, Cleveland Inst. of Music 1985, Ithaca Coll. 1986, Baldwin-Wallace Coll. 1991, St Vincent Coll. 1995, Hartwick Coll. 1997, New England Conservatory 1998, Masaryk Univ., Brno 2000, Acad. of Musical Arts, Prague 2000; Pulitzer Prize 1969, Sudler Prize 1984, Friedheim Award 1985, Grawemeyer Award 1993, Guggenheim Award 1964, 1965, Sousa Order of Merit 1985, Czech Repub. Medal of Merit (First Class) 1995, Medal of Honor of the City of Prague 1998. *Dance:* Monodrama (ballet) for Butler Ballet, Indiana 1976, The Steadfast Tin Soldier for Boulder Philharmonic, Colorado 1974, The Trojan Women for Louisville Ballet, Kentucky 1980. *Film:* Young Generation 1946, Gen, Prague 2001, Karel Husa Comes Home 2002. *Music:* Music for Prague 1968, Apotheosis of this Earth 1972, four string quartets; concertos for piano, brass quintet, organ, viola, violin, cello, saxophone, percussion, trumpet, orchestra; symphonies (Mosaiques, Fantasies); chamber music includes quintets for wind, brass, works for piano, sonatas for violin, music for band. *Publications:* Music for Prague; Apotheosis of this Earth; Concerto for Orchestra; The Trojan Women; An American Te Deum; Concerto for Sax and Winds; Concerto for Wind Ensemble; Les couleurs fauves, Cayuga Lake; Four Quartets; Twelve Moravian Songs; Sonata a Tre; Symphony No. 1; Evocation de Slovaquie; Serenade. *Leisure interests:* painting, poetry, tennis. *Address:* c/o Stanton Management, 25 Cimarron Road, Putnam Valley, NY 10579, USA (office). *Telephone:* (620) 563-7312 (office). *E-mail:* TDStanton@StantonMgt.com (office).

HUSAR, Cardinal Lubomyr, MA, DTheol; Ukrainian ecclesiastic; *Major Archbishop, Ukrainian Catholic Church;* b. 26 Feb. 1933, Lviv; ed St Basil Coll., Stamford, Catholic Univ. of America, Washington DC, St Josaphat Seminary, Washington DC, Fordham Univ., USA; ordained priest 1958; consecrated Bishop 1977; Auxiliary Bishop of the Greater Archiepiscopate of Lviv of the Ukrainians 1996–2001, Major Archbishop Jan. 2001–; cr. Cardinal 2001. *Address:* PO Box B-125, 01001 Kyiv, Ukraine (office). *Telephone:* (44) 278-61-84 (office). *Website:* www.ugcc.org.ua (office).

HUSBANDS, Sir Clifford Straughn, Kt, GCMG, CHB, QC; Barbadian barrister and fmr judge; b. 5 Aug. 1926; s. of Adam Straughn Husbands and Ada Augusta (née Griffith); m. Ruby Parris 1959; one s. two d.; ed Parry School, Harrison Coll., Middle Temple, Inns of Court, London, UK; called to Bar, Middle Temple 1952; in pvt. practice, Barbados 1952–54; Acting Deputy Registrar, Barbados 1954; Legal Asst to Attorney-Gen., Grenada 1954–56; magistrate, Grenada 1956–57, Antigua 1957–58; Crown Attorney, Magistrate and Registrar, Montserrat 1958–60; Acting Crown Attorney, St Kitts-Nevis-Anguilla 1959, Acting Attorney-Gen. 1960; Asst to Attorney-Gen., Barbados 1960–67 (legal draftsman 1960–63); Dir Public Prosecutions, Barbados 1967–76; QC Barbados 1968; Judge, Supreme Court, Barbados 1976–91; Justice of Appeal 1991–96; Gov.-Gen. of Barbados 1996–2011 (retd); Chief Scout, Barbados Scouts Asscn 2006–; Kt of St Andrew, Order of Barbados 1995, Kt of Grace, Order of St John 2004; Queen's Silver Jubilee Medal 1977, Paul Harris Fellowship Award 2001. *Leisure interests:* music, swimming, photography, cricket.

HUSH, Noel S., PhD, AO, FAA, FRS; Australian/British chemist and academic; *Professor Emeritus, University of Sydney;* b. 1924; ed Univ. of Sydney; began career as Lecturer in Physical Chem., Univ. of Manchester, UK 1950; faculty mem., Univ. of Bristol 1955–71; Foundation Prof. of Theoretical Chem., Univ. of Sydney 1971–89, currently Convenor, Molecular Electronics Group and Prof. Emer.; Fellow, Australian Chemical Inst.; mem. American Acad. of Arts and Sciences; Australian Acad. of Science Flinders Medal, Royal Soc. of Chem. Centenary Medal, Australian Acad. of Science David Craig Medal, Royal

Australian Chemical Soc. Physical Chem. Medal, Australian Federation Medal, Welch Award in Chem. 2007, Ahmed Zewail Award 2013. *Address:* School of Chemistry, University of Sydney, Building F11, Sydney, NSW 2006, Australia (office). *Telephone:* (2) 9351-4504 (office). *Fax:* (2) 9351-3329 (office). *E-mail:* hush_n@chem.usyd.edu.au (office). *Website:* www.chem.usyd.edu.au (office).

HUSSAIN, Ahmed Faiz; Maldivian judge; *Chief Justice of the Supreme Court;* fmr Civil Court Judge; apptd to Supreme Court, Chief Justice 2010–. *Address:* Supreme Court of the Maldives, Theemuge Orchid Magu, Malé, Maldives (office). *Telephone:* 3009990 (office). *Fax:* 3008554 (office). *E-mail:* info@supremecourt.gov .mv (office). *Website:* www.supremecourt.gov.mv (office).

HUSSAIN, Altaf, BPharm; Pakistani politician; *Leader, Muttahida Qaumi Movement;* b. 17 Sept. 1953, Karachi; s. of Nazir Hussain and Khurshid Begum; m.; ed Karachi Univ.; Founder and Leader Muttahida Qaumi Movt (MQM); in exile in UK since 1992. *Address:* MQM International Secretariat, 54–58, First Floor, Elizabeth House, High Street, Edgware, Middx, HA8 7EJ, England (office). *Telephone:* (20) 8905-7300 (office). *Fax:* (20) 8952-9282 (office). *E-mail:* mqm@mqm .org (office). *Website:* www.mqm.org (office).

HUSSAIN, Chaudhry Amir, BA, BL; Pakistani barrister and politician; b. 22 June 1942, Jammu and Kashmir; s. of Chaudhry Diwan Ali; m.; ed Punjab Univ.; mem. Pakistan Muslim League (QA); mem. Nat. Ass. for NA-111, Sialkot constituency 1985–2002, Chair. Standing Cttee on Law, Justice, Human Rights and Parl. Affairs 1997–99, mem. Standing Cttee on Science and Tech. 1997–99, Speaker of Nat. Ass. 2002–08; Parl. Sec. for Law and Justice 1985–88; Fed. Minister for Law, Justice and Parl. Affairs 1990–91, for Parl. and Youth Affairs 1991–93; signatory of first Asscn of Asian Parls for Peace (AAPP) Conf. held in Dhaka 1999; Leader of Pakistan Parl. Del. Exec. Council Meeting of AAPP, Beijing 2003; Leader and mem. Pakistan Parl. and Official Dels to USA, UK, Saudi Arabia, Dubai, UAE, Egypt, Malta, Canada, Nicaragua, Libya, Sri Lanka, Democratic People's Repub. of Korea, Thailand, Philippines, S Africa, Namibia, Bangladesh, Russian Fed., Turkey, Kuwait, Morocco, Japan, Belgium, Chile, China, India, Algeria, France, Mexico, Switzerland and Malaysia; Pres. AAPP 2004–05. *Leisure interests:* reading, farming. *Address:* National Assembly of Pakistan, Parliament House, Islamabad (office); House No. 22, Ministers' Enclave, Sector F-5, Islamabad, Pakistan (home). *Telephone:* (51) 9221082 (office). *Fax:* (51) 9221106 (office). *E-mail:* assembly@na.gov.pk (office). *Website:* www.na.gov.pk (office).

HUSSAIN, Chaudhry Shujaat; Pakistani politician; *President, Pakistan Muslim League;* b. 27 Jan. 1946; s. of Chaudhry Zahoor Elahi; m.; two s. one d.; ed Forman Christian Coll., Lahore and Univ. of London, UK; mem. Majlis-e-Shoora 1982–85; mem. Nat. Ass. 1985–, Leader of Opposition 1988–90; Fed. Minister for Information and Broadcasting 1986, for Industries and Production 1987–88, of the Interior 1990–93, 1997–99, of Narcotics Control 1997–99; Pres. Pakistan Muslim League 2004–; Prime Minister of Pakistan June–Aug. 2004; Hon. Consul-Gen. to Repub. of Korea 1982–; Order of Diplomatic Service Merit Ueung-in-Metal. *Address:* Pakistan Muslim League, PML House, F-7/3, Islamabad, Pakistan (office).

HUSSAIN, Ishrat, MA, PhD; Pakistani economist and central banker (retd) and university administrator; *Dean and Director, Institute of Business Administration Karachi;* b. 17 June 1941, Allahabad, India; s. of the late Rahat Husain and Khursheed Rahat Husain; m. Shahnaz Husain; two d.; ed Williams Coll., Boston Univ. and Grad. Exec. Devt Programme (Harvard, Stanford and INSEAD); mem. Staff Sr Managerial, Planning and Devt Dept and Finance Dept, Govt of Sindh; Additional Deputy Commr for Devt, Chittagong, Bangladesh; mem. Govt of Pakistan's Panel of Economists; Adjunct Prof. of Econs, Karachi Univ., Dir Poverty and Social Policy Dept; IBRD Resident Rep. for Nigeria 1986, Chief Economist for Africa, IBRD 1991–94, Chief Economist for E Asia and Pacific Region 1995, also Chief Debt and Int. Finance Div., Dir for Cen. Asian Repubs; Gov. State Bank of Pakistan 1999–2005; Chair. Nat. Comm. for Govt Reforms with rank of Fed. Minister 2006–08; Dean and Dir Inst. of Business Administration, Karachi 2008–; Hilal-e-Imtiaz 2003; Central Bank Gov. of the Year in Asia Award, The Banker magazine (first Pakistani Gov. to receive award) 2005, Jinnah Award 2005, Special Gold Medal, Federation of Pakistan Chambers of Commerce and Industry 2005, Lifetime Achievement Award, Asian Banker Magazine Singapore 2006. *Publications:* Dollars, Debts, and Deficits, Pakistan: The Economy of an Elitist State, The Political Economy of Reforms: Case Study of Pakistan, Adjustment in Africa: Lessons from Case Studies: Dealing with Debt Crisis, African External Finance in the 1990s, The Economy of Modern Sindh; numerous articles and papers on debt, external finance and adjustment issues. *Leisure interests:* reading and writing economics, poetry. *Address:* Office of the Dean, Institute of Business Administration, University Road, Karachi 75270 (office); 98/II Street 16, D.H.A. Phase VI, Karachi, Pakistan (home). *Telephone:* (21) 35245291. *E-mail:* ihusain@iba.edu.pk (office). *Website:* www.iba.edu.pk (office); ishrathusain.iba.edu.pk.

HUSSAIN, Mamnoon; Pakistani business executive, politician and head of state; *President;* b. 2 March 1940, Agra, British India; ed Inst. of Business Admin, Karachi; family migrated to Karachi following the partition of India 1949; fmr Pres. Karachi Chamber of Commerce and Industry; Gov. of Sindh June–Oct. 1999, term of office cut short by mil. coup d'état; official nominee of Pakistan Muslim League in presidential election July 2013, Pres. of Pakistan 2013–. *Address:* Office of the President, Aiwan-e-Sadr, Islamabad, Pakistan (office). *Telephone:* (51) 9206060 (office). *Fax:* (51) 9208046 (office). *E-mail:* publicmail@president.gov.pk (office). *Website:* www.presidentofpakistan.gov.pk (office).

HUSSAIN, Nasser, OBE, BSc; British sports commentator and fmr professional cricketer; b. 28 March 1968, Madras (now Chennai), India; s. of Jawad (Joe) Hussain; m. Karen Hussain; two s.; ed Forest School, Walthamstow, Durham Univ.; right-hand higher middle-order batsman, right-hand leg-break bowler; played for Essex 1987–2004 (Capt. 1999), England 1989–2004 (Capt. 1999–2003), MCC 1991; youngest-ever batsman to represent Essex Under-15 Schools 1980; England Test debut against W Indies, Kingston 1990; Capt. England 'A' team in tour of Pakistan 1990; scored first Test centuries at Edgbaston and Trent Bridge against India 1996 and career-best 207 against Australia at Edgbaston 1997; played in 96 Tests, scoring 5,764 runs (average 37.18) including 14 centuries; played in 88 One-Day Ints, scoring 2,332 runs (average 30.28, highest score 115) including one century; scored 20,698 First-class runs (average 42.06) including 52 centuries; cricket commentator, Sky Sports 2005–; Cricket Writers' Club Young Cricketer of the Year Award 1989, Wisden Cricketer of the Year 2003. *Publication:* The Autobiography 2004, Playing with Fire (British Sports Book Awards) 2005. *Leisure interests:* golf, football (Leeds United fan); reading. *Address:* c/o The England and Wales Cricket Board, Lord's Cricket Ground, London, NW8 8QZ; Sky Sports, British Sky Broadcasting Ltd, Grant Way, Isleworth, TW7 5QD, England (office). *Telephone:* (20) 7432-1200; (20) 7705-3000 (office). *Fax:* (20) 7286-5583. *E-mail:* cricket@skysports.com (office). *Website:* www.ecb.co.uk; www.skysports .com (office).

HUSSAIN, Baron (Life Peer), cr. 2011, of Luton in the County of Bedfordshire; **Qurban Hussain;** British employment adviser and politician; b. Kashmir, Pakistan; m.; came to live in UK 1971; joined trade union movt and served as a Sec. for Luton TUC 1994–96; campaigned against Iraq war and joined Liberal Democrats 2003; Liberal Democrat Councillor, Luton Borough Council 1996–99, 2003–, mem. Council Exec., held portfolios of Citizenship, Community, Youth and Leisure Services as well as Equality and Social Inclusion 2003–07, Deputy Leader of Luton Borough Council 2005–07, currently Deputy Leader of Liberal Democrat Group; unsuccessful Parl. cand. for Luton South in Gen. Elections 2005, 2010. *Address:* Luton Borough Council, Town Hall, George Street, Luton, Beds., LU1 2BQ (office); House of Lords, Westminster, London, SW1A 0PW; 49 Claremont Road, Luton, Beds., LU4 8LY, England (home). *Telephone:* (1582) 546000 (office); (1582) 618919 (home); (20) 7219-5353 (House of Lords). *Fax:* (20) 7219-5979 (House of Lords). *E-mail:* qurban.hussain@ntlworld.com. *Website:* www.luton.gov.uk (office).

HUSSAIN, Rana Tanveer; Pakistani politician; *Minister of Defence Production;* b. 10 Jan. 1949; s. of the late Haji Muhammad Anwar; mem. Nat. Ass. (Pakistan Muslim League) for Sheikhupura-II NA-132 constituency; fmr Minister of Defence Production in the cabinet of Yousaf Raza Gillani; Minister of Defence Production 2013–; convicted of corruption by the Nat. Accountability Bureau. *Address:* Ministry of Defence, Pakistan Secretariat, No. II, Rawalpindi 46000, Pakistan (office). *Telephone:* (51) 9271107 (office). *Fax:* (51) 9271113 (office). *E-mail:* tahir@mod.gov.pk (office). *Website:* www.mod.gov.pk (office).

HUSSAIN, Rashad, MA, JD, MPA; American lawyer and government official; *Special US Envoy to the Organization of the Islamic Conference;* b. 1978, Wyoming; s. of Mohammad Hussain and Ruqaya Hussain; ed Univ. of North Carolina, Yale Univ. Law School, Kennedy School of Govt, Harvard Univ.; fmr ed. Yale Law Journal; fmr Legis. Asst, US House of Reps Judiciary Cttee; fmr trial attorney, US Justice Dept; fmr clerk to Damon J. Keith, US Court of Appeals for Sixth Circuit; Deputy Assoc. Counsel to Pres. Barack Obama 2009–10; Special US Envoy to OIC 2010–; Fellow, Paul and Daisy Soros Fellowships for New Americans 2003. *Address:* Organization of the Islamic Conference, Medina Rd, Sary St, POB 178, Jeddah 21411, Saudi Arabia (office). *Telephone:* (2) 690-0001 (office). *Fax:* (2) 275-1953 (office). *E-mail:* info@oic-oci.org (office). *Website:* www.oic-oci.org (office).

HUSSAIN, Prince Sharif Ali bin al-, MA; *Leader, Constitutional Monarchy Movement;* b. 1956, Baghdad; s. of Sharif Al Hussain bin Ali and Princess Badia; cousin of the late King Faisal II; m.; ed schools in Lebanon, univ. in UK; royal family in exile following revolution 1958–; childhood spent in Lebanon and UK; began career in investment banking, London; currently Leader Constitutional Monarchy Movt (a mem. of Iraqi Nat. Congress—INC); returned to Iraq to make claim to the throne June 2003. *Leisure interest:* fencing. *Telephone:* (1) 778-2897 (office). *Fax:* (1) 778-0199 (office). *Website:* www.iraqcmm.org (office).

HUSSAIN, Zakir; Indian musician (tabla), producer, actor and composer; b. 9 March 1951, Mumbai; s. of Ustad Alla Rakha Qureshi; m. Antonia Minnecola; ed St Michael's High School, St Xavier's Coll., Maharashtra; plays with Ali Akbar Khan, Birju Maharaj, Ravi Shankar, Shivkumar Sharma; formed band Shanti with Aashish Khan 1970; formed band Shakti with John McLaughlin and L. Shankar 1975; first professional concert 1963; also formed percussion group, Rhythm Experience, Diga Rhythm Band, Making Music, Planet Drum with Mickey Hart, Tabla Beat Science, Sangam with Charles Lloyd and Eric Harland; f. Moment! Records 1992–; composed music for opening ceremony, Summer Olympic Games, Atlanta, USA 1996; Old Dominion Fellow, Humanities Council, Princeton Univ., Prof. of Indian classical music, Dept of Music 2005–06; Visiting Prof., Stanford Univ. 2007; commissioned by Indian Govt to compose anthem to celebrate 60 years of Indian independence 2007; Padma Shri 1988, Indo-American Award 1990, Sangeet Natak Akademi Award 1991, Nat. Heritage Fellowship, USA 1999, Padma Bhushan 2002, Kalidas Samman 2006, Grammy Award (best contemporary world music) 2009. *Films include:* soundtracks: Apocalypse Now 1979, Heat and Dust 1983, Miss Beatty's Children 1992, Little Buddha 1993, In Custody 1993, Saaz 1997, Gaach 1998, Zakir and his Friends 1998, Vaanaprastham 1999, Everybody Says I'm Fine 2001, The Mystic Masseur 2001, Mr and Mrs Iyer 2001, The Speaking Hand: Zakir Hussain and the Art of the Indian Drum 2003, One Dollar Curry 2004, The Way of Beauty 2006, Parzania 2005, For Real 2006, The Rhythm Devils Concert Experience 2008. *Recordings include:* albums: Making Music 1987, Planet Drum (with Mickey Hart) (Grammy Award for Best World Music Album) 1992, Tabla Duet (with Ustad Alla Rakha) 1988, Zakir Hussain And The Rhythm Experience 1991, Venu 1972 1991, Essence Of Rhythm 1998, Drums of India 2003, Raag Chandrakauns 2004, Sangam (with Charles Lloyd) 2006, Global Drum Project (with Mickey Hart, Zakir Hussain, Sikiru Adepoju, Giovanni Hidalgo) 2007, The Melody of Rhythm - Triple Concerto and Music for Trio (with Béla Fleck, Edgar Meyer) 2009. *Address:* c/o Kevin Kastrup, IMG Artists, Carnegie Hall Tower, 152 West 57th Street, 5th Floor, New York, NY 10019, USA (office). *Telephone:* (212) 994-3500 (office). *Fax:* (212) 994-3550 (office). *E-mail:* artistsny@imgartists.com (office); kkastrup@imgartists.com (office); dshultz@imgartists.com (office). *Website:* www.imgartists.com (office); www.zakirhussain.com.

HUSSEIN, Maj.-Gen. Abd ar-Rahim Muhammad; Sudanese politician; *Minister of National Defence;* career in Armed Forces; attained rank of Maj.-Gen.; Minister of Interior 1998; Minister of Presidential Affairs –2001; Minister of Internal Affairs 2001–04; Minister of Nat. Defence 2005–. *Address:* Ministry of National Defence, POB 371, Khartoum, Sudan (office). *Telephone:* (183) 774910.

HUSSEIN, Bishar Abdirahman, BA; Kenyan diplomatist and international organization official; *Director-General, International Bureau, Universal Postal Union;* ed Univ. of Nairobi; man. trainee, Kenya Posts and Telecommunications

Corpn 1984; Postmaster-Gen., Postal Corpn of Kenya 1999; Amb. to UAE 2002–08; Chair UPU Congress, Geneva 2008, Council of Admin, UPU 2008–12, UPU Strategy Conf., Nairobi 2010, Dir-Gen. Int. Bureau, UPU 2013–. *Address:* International Bureau, Universal Postal Union, Case postale 312, 3000 Berne 15, Switzerland (office). *Telephone:* 313503111 (office). *Fax:* 313503110 (office). *Website:* www.upu.int (office).

HUSSEIN, HRH Princess Haya bint al-, MA; Jordanian philanthropist and athlete; b. 3 May 1974; d. of HM King Hussein I of Jordan (died 1999) and HM Queen Alia al-Hussein of Jordan (died 1977); sister of HRH Prince Ali Bin al-Hussein and Abir Muhaisen; m. HH Sheikh Muhammad bin Rashid al-Maktoum 2004; one d.; ed Badminton Boarding School for Girls, Bristol, Bryanston School, Dorset and St Hilda's Coll. Oxford, UK; selected to represent Jordan in Equestrian Sport (show jumping) age 13; winner Jordanian Nat. Show Jumping Championships 1986, 1987, 1989, 1990, 1992; first female to qualify and compete in Equestrian, Pan Arab Games, Damascus, Syria 1992; trained by Paul Darragh and Alian Storme as show-jumping and flat-race jockey, Co. Meath, Ireland 1995–96; cr. int. competing team, Team Harmony 1996; winner of 33 int. classes, 6 grand prix and one Volvo World Cup Qualifier 1996; trained with Paul Schockemohle, Muhlen, Germany 1997–99, Hans Horn, Ootmarsum, The Netherlands 1999, Katie Monahan Prudent and Alice Debany Clero, Paris, France 2000; qualified for Olympic Games Sydney (first female Arab flag-bearer at Olympic Games and first Arab woman to compete in Equestrian) 2000; signed commercial contract with Loro Piana, Italy 2000; qualified for World Championships, Jerez, Spain (first Arab woman to qualify and compete) 2002; Rep. of Jordan to Int. Equestrian Fed. (FEI), Chair. Middle E and Western Asian Sub-Group 1992–96, Pres. FEI 2006–; Pres. Queen Alia Foundation for Hearing and Speech Impaired, Children's Dental Health Care Soc. (SMILE), Jordanian Women's Qualifying and Training Center, Haya Art's and Cultural Center for Child Dev't; Pres. and Founder Int. Athletes Cultural Asscn; Chair. Int. Humanitarian City, Dubai; Athlete Amb. for Right to Play, for Olympic Aid, for Innocence in Danger; mem. IOC 2007–; mem. Advisory Bd Just World Int.; Founder and Chair. Takiyet Um Ali (org. addressing issues of poverty) 2003–; UN Messenger of Peace 2007–; Goodwill Amb. for WFP 2005–07; Hon. Pres. Land Transport and Mechanical Union, Hon. Pres. Int. Sports and Solidarity Foundation; Bronze Medal, Pan Arab Games 1992, voted Athlete of the Year by Jordanian public 1993, nominated Athlete of the Year by Arab BBC Radio 1994, Equestrian Personality of the Year, Spanish Equestrian Fed. 1996, Int. Golden Helm Award, Int. Asscn of Golden Helmsmen of Tourism 2000, nominated Legendary Woman by Int. Femmes Mythique Asscn. *Publications:* biog. of the late King Hussein I. *Leisure interests:* camping, water skiing, tennis, sailing, photography, art, camel racing. *Address:* Office of HRH Princess Haya bint al-Hussein, PO Box 111888, World Trade Center Complex, Convention Center Building, 5th Floor, Dubai, United Arab Emirates (office). *Telephone:* (4) 3292333 (office). *Fax:* (4) 3292555 (office). *E-mail:* info@hrhoffice.ae (office). *Website:* www.princesshaya .net.

HUSSEIN, Dato' Seri Hishammuddin bin Tun, LLB, LLM; Malaysian lawyer and politician; *Minister of Defence and Acting Minister of Transport;* b. 5 Aug. 1961; s. of Tun Hussein Onn (fmr Prime Minister); m. Yang Mulia Tengku Datin Seri Panglima Marsilla Tengku Abdullah; ed Malay Coll. Kuala Kangsar, Univ. of Wales, Aberystwyth, London School of Econs, UK; early career as lawyer with law firms Skrine & Co., Kuala Lumpur and Lee Hishammuddin (now Lee Hishammuddin Allen & Gledhill); mem. Dewan Rakyat (House of Reps, parl.) for Tenggara 1995–2003, for Sembrong 2003–, Parl. Sec. for Int. Trade and Industry 1995; Deputy Minister of Main Industry 1997, Minister of Youth and Sport 1999–2004, of Educ. 2004–09, of Home Affairs 2009–13, of Defence 2013–, also Acting Minister of Transport 2013–; mem. United Malays Nat. Org. (UMNO), Vice-Pres. 2009–. *Address:* Ministry of Defence, Wisma Pertahanan, Jalan Padang Tembak, 50634 Kuala Lumpur, Malaysia (office). *Telephone:* (3) 26921333 (office). *Fax:* (3) 26914163 (office). *E-mail:* portal@mod.gov.my (office). *Website:* www.mod.gov.my (office).

HUSSEIN, Muhammad al-, PhD; Syrian politician; fmr Chair. Econ. Bureau, Govt Exec.; Minister of Finance 2003–11 (resgnd with rest of cabinet at Pres.'s request following popular protests). *Address:* c/o Ministry of Finance, BP 13136, rue Jule Jammal, Damascus, Syria (office). *Telephone:* (11) 2211300 (office). *Fax:* (11) 2224701 (office). *E-mail:* mof@net.sy (office). *Website:* www.syrianfinance.org (office).

HUSSEIN, Col Nur Hassan, (Nur Adde); Somali lawyer, police officer and politician; b. 1938, Mogadishu; from Abgal sub-clan of Hawiye clan; ed Mogadishu Nat. Univ., Fiscal Law School, Rome; started his career as customs officer in 1958, rose through ranks to become Interpol Liaison Officer in Somalia and finally Chief Police Officer in charge of planning and training under fmr regime of Mohamed Siad Barre until the latter's ousting in 1991, served as Attorney Gen. –1991; Sec.-Gen. Somali Red Crescent Soc. 1991–2007; Prime Minister 2007–09. *Address:* c/o Office of the Prime Minister, Mogadishu, Somalia (office).

HUSSEY, Michael Edward Killeen; Australian professional cricketer; b. 27 May 1975, Morley, WA; m. Amy Hussey; four c. opening batsman; left-handed batsman; right-arm medium pace bowler; plays for Western Australia (Vice-Capt.) 1994–, Northants. 2001–03, Glos. 2004, Australia 2004–13, Durham 2005, Chennai Super Kings 2008–, Perth Scorchers 2011–; First-class debut: 1994/95; Test debut: Australia v West Indies, Brisbane 3–6 Nov. 2005; One-Day Int. (ODI) debut: Australia v India, Perth 1 Feb. 2004; T20I debut: NZ v Australia, Auckland 17 Feb. 2005; has played in 78 Tests, taken 7 wickets and scored 6,183 runs (19 centuries, 29 half-centuries), highest score 195, average 51.52, best bowling (innings) 1/0, (match) 2/2; ODIs: 185 matches, took 2 wickets and scored 5,442 runs, highest score 109 not out, average 48.15; T20Is: 38 matches, scored 721 runs, highest score 60 not out, average 37.94; announced retirement from int. cricket 29 Dec. 2012; One-Day Int. Player of the Year 2006. *Address:* c/o Western Australian Cricket Association, WACA Ground, PO Box 6045, Nelson Crescent, East Perth, WA 6892, Australia (office). *Telephone:* (8) 9265-7222. *Fax:* (8) 9265-7275. *E-mail:* info@waca.com.au. *Website:* www.waca.com.au.

HUSTON, Anjelica; American actress; b. 8 July 1951, Los Angeles, Calif.; d. of the late John Huston and Enrica Huston (née Soma); m. Robert Graham 1992 (died 2008). *Films include:* Sinful Davey, A Walk with Love and Death 1969, The Last

Tycoon 1976, The Postman Always Rings Twice 1981, Swashbuckler, This is Spinal Tap 1984, The Ice Pirates 1984, Prizzi's Honor (Acad. Award for Best Supporting Actress 1985, New York and Los Angeles Film Critics' Awards 1985), Gardens of Stone, Captain Eo, The Dead, Mr North, A Handful of Dust, The Witches, Enemies, A Love Story, The Grifters, The Addams Family, Addams Family Values, The Player, Manhattan Murder Mystery, The Crossing Guard 1995, The Perez Family 1995, Buffalo '66 1997, Phoenix 1997, Ever After 1998, Breakers 1999, The Golden Bowl 2001, The Royal Tenenbaums 2002, Blood Work 2002, The Man from Elysian Fields 2002, Daddy Day Care 2003, The Life Aquatic with Steve Zissou 2004, These Foolish Things 2006, Art School Confidential 2006, Material Girls 2006, Seraphim Falls 2006, The Darjeeling Limited 2007, Choke 2008, Tinker Bell (voice) 2008, Spirit of the Forest (voice) 2008, The Kreutzer Sonata 2008, When in Rome 2010, Horrid Henry: The Movie 2011, 50/50 2011, The Big Year 2011, TinkerBell and the Secret of the Wings (voice) 2012; films directed: Bastard Out of Carolina 1996, Agnes Browne 1999. *Stage appearances include:* Tamara, Los Angeles 1985. *Television appearances include:* The Cowboy and the Ballerina (NBC-TV film) 1984, Faerie Tale Theatre, A Rose for Miss Emily (PBS film), Lonesome Dove (CBS mini-series), The Mists of Avalon (TNT mini-series) 2001, Iron Jawed Angels (Best Supporting Actress in a Series, Miniseries or TV Movie, Golden Globe Awards 2005) 2004, Riding the Bus with My Sister (dir) 2005, Covert One: The Hades Factor 2006, Medium (series) 2008–09, Smash (series) 2012–13. *Address:* ICM, 10250 Constellation Boulevard, Beverly Hills, CA 90067, USA.

HUSTVEDT, Siri, PhD; American poet, novelist and essayist; b. 19 Feb. 1955, Northfield, Minn.; d. of the late Lloyd Hustvedt and of Ester Vegan Hustvedt; m. Paul Auster 1981; one d.; ed Columbia Univ.; worked as ed. and trans.; Gabarron Int. Award for Thought and Humanities 2012. *Publications:* Reading to You (poems) 1982, The Blindfold (novel) 1992, The Enchantment of Lily Dahl (novel) 1996, Yonder: Essays 1998, What I Loved (novel, Prix des Libraires de Québec) 2003, Mysteries of the Rectangle (essays) 2005, A Plea for Eros (essays) 2006, The Sorrows of an American (novel) 2008, The Shaking Woman or a History of My Nerves (non-fiction) 2010, The Summer Without Men (novel) 2011, Living, Thinking, Looking 2012, The Blazing World (novel) 2014; contrib. to Paris Review, Modern Painters, The Guardian, The Yale Review, Conjunctions, Neuropsychoanalysis, Seizure: The European Journal of Epilepsy, Clinical Neurophysiology and numerous other publs; fiction translated into more than 30 languages. *Address:* c/o Amanda Urban, ICM Partners, 750 Fifth Avenue, New York, NY 10019, USA (office). *Telephone:* (212) 556-5600 (office). *Fax:* (212) 556-5665 (office). *Website:* sirihustvedt.net.

HUTAPEA, Eva Riyanti; Indonesian business executive; *President Director, PT Usaha Kita Makmur Indonesia;* b. 26 Dec. 1952; m. Bunbunan Hutapea; three d.; ed School of Econs, Univ. of Indonesia; trained as accountant; fmr auditor; joined Salim Group 1982, owner of Indofood, worked through Indofood ranks to become CEO and Pres. Dir 1999–2004 (retd); Pres. Dir PT Usaha Kita Makmur Indonesia (UKM Way) 2004–; Deputy Chair. Indonesian Chamber of Commerce and Industry (KADIN) for the field of Small and Medium Enterprises and Cooperatives; mem. Advisory Council Nat. Bd of the Indonesian Employers Asscn (APINDO); Deputy Chair. Exec. Council Indonesian Inst. of Commrs and Dirs; Dir Gen. Instant Ramen Mfrs Asscn 1999–2001. *Address:* RP Suroso No. 6, Gondangdia Lama, Jakarta 10350, Indonesia. *Telephone:* (21) 31909730 (office).

HUTCHEON, Linda Ann Marie, OC, MA, PhD, FRSC; Canadian writer and academic; *University Professor Emeritus, University of Toronto;* b. (Linda Bortolotti), 24 Aug. 1947, Toronto, Ont.; d. of Roy Bortolotti and Elisa Rossi; m. Michael Alexander Hutcheon 1970; ed Univ. of Toronto, Cornell Univ., USA; Asst. Assoc. and Full Prof. of English, McMaster Univ. 1976–88; Prof. of English and Comparative Literature, Univ. of Toronto 1988–96, Distinguished Univ. Prof. 1996–2010, Univ. Prof. Emer. 2010–; mem. Modern Language Asscn of America, American Acad. of Arts and Sciences; Hon. LLD 1995, Hon. DLitt 1999, 2000, 2005, 2007, 2008, 2011; Killam Prize 2005, Molson Prize 2010. *Publications include:* Narcissistic Narrative 1980, Formalism and the Freudian Aesthetic 1984, A Theory of Parody 1985, A Poetics of Postmodernism 1988, The Canadian Postmodern 1988, The Politics of Postmodernism 1989, Splitting Images 1991, Irony's Edge 1995, A Theory of Adaptation 2006, Opera: Desire, Disease, Death (with Michael Hutcheon) 1996, Bodily Charm: Living Opera (with Michael Hutcheon), 2000, Opera: The Art of Dying (with Michael Hutcheon), 2004. Ed.: Other Solitudes 1990, Double-Talking 1992, Likely Stories 1992, A Postmodern Reader 1993, Rethinking Literary History: A Forum on Theory 2002; contribs to Diacritics, Textual Practice, Cultural Critique and other journals. *Leisure interests:* piano, cycling, hiking. *Address:* Department of English, University of Toronto, Toronto, ON M5R 2M8, Canada (office). *Telephone:* (416) 978-6616 (office). *Fax:* (416) 978-2836 (office). *E-mail:* l.hutcheon@utoronto.ca (office). *Website:* individual.utoronto.ca/lindahutcheon (office).

HUTCHINGS, Graham John, BSc, PhD, DSc, FRS; British chemist and academic; *Professor of Physical Chemistry and Director, Cardiff Catalysis Institute, Cardiff University;* b. 3 Feb. 1951; ed Univ. Coll., London; with ICI Petrochemicals Div. 1975–84, Tech. Officer, Research Dept, Wilton, Teeside 1975–78, Plant Man. and Production Support Man., Oil Works, Teeside 1978–81; Sr Research Officer, AECI, Modderfontein, SA (seconded) 1981–83, Chief Research Officer 1983–84; Lecturer, Univ. of the Witwatersrand, SA 1984–86, Sr Lecturer in Chem. 1986–87, Prof. 1987, Visiting Prof. 1987–90, 2002–, Visiting Research Assoc. 1990–93; Asst Dir Leverhulme Centre for Innovative Catalysis, Univ. of Liverpool 1987–94, Deputy Dir and Prof. 1994–97; Prof. of Physical Chem. and Head of School, Cardiff Univ. 1997–2006, Distinguished Research Prof. 2006–, Dir Cardiff Catalysis Inst. 2008–, Pro Vice-Chancellor Research 2010–12; Visiting Scientist, Institut de Recherches sur la Catalyse, CNRS, Villeurbanne France 1992–93; Prof.-in-Residence, Université Pierre et Marie Curie, Paris 2003–04; Visiting Prof., Tokyo Metropolitan Univ., Japan 2010–; Adjunct Prof., Louisiana State Univ. 2010–; Ed.-in-Chief Catalytic Science 1996–; Ed. Applied Catalysis Newsbrief 1997–, Journal of Catalysis 2005–; Corresp., Newsbrief section, Applied Catalysis B 1994–; mem. Editorial Bd, Catalysis Today 1994–, Catalysis Letters 1994–, Topics in Catalysis 1994–, Advances in Catalysis 2007–, Gold Bulletin 2007–, Green Chemistry 2009–, Catalysis Science and Technology 2010–, Proceedings of the Royal Society A 2012–, Scientific Reports 2013–; mem. Strategy and Tech. Advisory Bd on Sustainability for Chem. Innovation Knowledge Transfer Network 2007–; RAE panel mem. for Chem. (Panel 18) 2005–08; mem. Faraday Div. Council, RSC 2008–, Pres. Faraday Div. 2012–15; Chair. SCORE 2010–13; REF Panel mem. and Deputy Chair. for Chem. (Panel B8) 2011–14; mem. Sasol (SA) Heterogeneous Catalysis Advisory Bd 2000–09, NIOK Int. Review Group 2000, 2006, 2010 (Chair.); mem. Fachbeirat of Fritz-Haber-Institut, Berlin 1999–2015, Academia Europaea 2010; Founding Fellow, Learned Soc. of Wales; Langmuir Distinguished Lecturer Award, Div. of Colloid and Surface Science, ACS 1996, DGMK 2001 – Kolleg Lectureship, Germany 2001, Entech Medal, Inst. of Chemical Engineers (IChemE) 2004, RSC Award for Heterogeneous Catalysis 2004, François Gault Lecturer, European Fed. of Catalysis Socs 2006, IChemE Impact Award for Applied Catalysis 2005, RSC Green Chem. Lecturer 2007, IChemE Environwise Award for Green Chem. 2007, Winner, Dow Methane Challenge 2008, RSC Award for Surfaces and Interfaces 2009, IChemE Sustainability Award 2009, IPMI Henry J. Albert Award 2011, France Great Britain Chem. Prize 2011, Dechema Alvin Mittasch Award 2012, Heinz Heinemann Award, Int. Asscn of Catalysis Socs 2012, Distinguished Visiting Lecturer, Catalysis Soc. of South Africa 2013, Davy Medal, Royal Soc. 2013. *Publications:* 14 edited books and more than 570 articles in professional journals; 42 patents. *Address:* School of Chemistry, Cardiff University, Main Building, Park Place, Cardiff, CF10 3AT, Wales (office). *Telephone:* (29) 2087-4059 (office). *Fax:* (29) 2087-4030 (office). *E-mail:* hutch@cardiff.ac.uk (office). *Website:* www.cardiff.ac.uk/chemy (office).

HUTCHINSON, (John) Maxwell, AADipl; British architect, broadcaster and writer; *Director, The Hutchinson Studio Architects;* b. 3 Dec. 1948; s. of the late Frank M. Hutchinson and Elizabeth R. M. Wright; ed Oundle, Scott Sutherland School of Architecture, Aberdeen and Architectural Asscn School of Architecture; Founder Hutchinson & Partners (Chartered Architects) 1972, Chair. Hutchinson & Partners Architects Ltd 1987–92; Dir The Hutchinson Studio Architects 1992–, SMC Group PLC; Visiting Prof. of Architecture, Queen's Univ., Belfast 1988–93; Special Prof. of Architectural Design, Univ. of Nottingham 1993–96; Visiting Prof., Univ. of Westminster 1997–2001; Chair. Permarock Products Ltd, Loughborough 1985–96, London Br. Elgar Soc. 1987–93, East Midlands Arts Bd 1991–94, British Architectural Library Trust 1991–99, Schools of Architecture Accreditation Bd 1991–97; Chair. Industrial Bldg Bureau 1988–91; Founder and Life Pres. Architects for Aid 2005–; Vice-Chair. Construction Industry Council 1990–91; mem. Council RIBA 1978–93, Sr Vice-Pres. 1988–89, Pres. 1989–91; Church Warden Our Most Holy Redeemer, Clerkenwell 2007–; mem. Council Royal School of Church Music 1997–2000; regular broadcaster on TV and radio; freelance writer; Hon. Fellow, Univ. of Greenwich 1990, Royal Soc. of Ulster Architects 1992, Univ. Coll. London 2008 Hon. Dr of Design (Robert Gordon Univ.) 2007. *Television:* presenter of major series including No. 57 – The History of a House (Channel 4), Demolition Detectives (Channel 4), Maxwell's Hidden Treasures (ITV 1), Prefabs and Palaces, Pure Inventions, Mod Cons (Discovery Channel), How to Rescue a House (BBC 2), Songs of Praise (BBC 1). *Compositions:* The Kibbo-Kift 1979, The Ascent of Wilberforce 111 1984, Requiem in a Village Church 1988, Christmas Cantata 1990. *Publications:* The Prince of Wales, Right or Wrong: An Architect Replies 1989, Number 57 – The Story of a House 2003; contrib. to How to Rescue a House 2005. *Leisure interests:* composing, travel, beer, music. *Address:* 17 Chart Street, London, N1 6DD, England (office). *Telephone:* (20) 7273-9288 (office). *E-mail:* info@hutchinsonstudio.co.uk (office). *Website:* www.hutchinsonstudio.co.uk.

HUTH, John E., AB, PhD; American physicist and academic; *Donner Professor of Science, Department of Physics, Harvard University;* b. 16 March 1958, London, UK; ed Princeton Univ., Univ. of California, Berkeley; Postdoctoral Scientist, Fermi Nat. Accelerator Lab. (Fermilab), Batavia, Ill. 1985–88, Wilson Fellow 1988–91, Staff Scientist 1990–93, mem. Fermilab Physics Advisory Panel 1993–97; Prof. of Physics, Harvard Univ. 1993–2003, Chair., Dept of Physics 2003–07, Donner Prof. of Science 2007–; mem. 'Godparent Cttee' on the discovery of the top quark 1993–94; mem. Project Oversight Bd of LHC Grid Computing Project 2002–; mem. Steering Cttee Brookhaven Nat. Lab. Science and Tech. 1998–2006; mem. Dark Energy Task Force 2005–06; Fellow, American Physical Soc. 1993–. *Publications include:* numerous articles in scientific journals. *Address:* Physics Department, Harvard University, Lyman 236, 17 Oxford Street, Cambridge, MA 02138, USA (office). *Telephone:* (617) 495-8144 (office). *Fax:* (617) 495-0416 (office). *E-mail:* huth@physics.harvard.edu (office). *Website:* huhepl.harvard.edu/~huth (office). www.physics.harvard.edu (office).

HUTT, Peter Barton, BA, LLB, LLM; American lawyer; *Senior Counsel, Covington & Burling LLP;* b. 16 Nov. 1934, Buffalo, NY; s. of Lester Ralph Hutt and Louise Rich Fraser; m. Catherine Adams Hutt; ed Phillips Exeter Acad., Yale, Harvard and New York Univs; Assoc., Covington & Burling LLP (law firm) 1960–68, Pnr 1968–71, 1975–2004, Sr Counsel 2004–; Lecturer on Food and Drug Law, Harvard Law School 1994–, Stanford Law School 1998; Chief Counsel, US Food and Drug Admin. 1971–75; Counsel, Soc. for Risk Analysis, American Coll. of Toxicology; Chair. Alcoholic Beverage Medical Research Foundation 1986–92; Vice-Chair. Legal Action Center, New York 1984–2003, Foundation for Biomedical Research 1988–; mem. Inst. of Medicine, NAS 1970–, Advisory Bd, Tufts Center for Study of Drug Devt 1976–99, Univ. of Virginia Center for Advanced Studies 1982–, Nat. Cttee on New Drugs for Cancer and AIDS 1988–90, Inst. of Medicine Round Table on Drugs and Vaccines against AIDS 1988–95, Nat. Acad. of Public Admin's Panel on restructuring NIH 2004–06, Nat. Inst. of Allergy and Infections Disease Working Group on Div. of AIDS 2005–06; mem. Bd of Dirs numerous cos; mem. Advisory Bd of numerous other scientific, academic and financial orgs; Underwood-Prescott Award, MIT 1977, and numerous other honours and awards. *Publications:* Dealing with Drug Abuse (with Patricia M. Wald) 1972, Food and Drug Law: Cases and Materials (with Richard A. Merrill) 1980, 1991, 2007. *Leisure interests:* research on the history of govt regulation of food and drugs. *Address:* 124 South Fairfax Street, Alexandria, VA 22314 (home); Covington & Burling LLP, 1201 Pennsylvania Avenue NW, Washington, DC 20004, USA (office). *Telephone:* (202) 662-5522 (office). *Fax:* (202) 778-5522 (office). *E-mail:* phutt@cov.com (office).

HUTTON, Baron (Life Peer), cr. 1997, of Bresagh in the County of Down; **Rt Hon. (James) Brian Edward Hutton,** PC; British fmr judge; b. 29 June 1931, Belfast, Northern Ireland; s. of the late James Hutton and Mabel Hutton; m. 1st Mary

Gillian Murland 1975 (died 2000); two d.; 2nd Rosalind Ann Nickols 2001; two step-s. one step-d.; ed Shrewsbury School, Balliol Coll. Oxford; Queen's Univ. of Belfast; called to NI Bar 1954, QC (NI) 1970, Bencher, Inn of Court of NI 1974, Sr Crown Counsel 1973–79, Judge of High Court of Justice 1979–88, Lord Chief Justice of NI 1988–97; a Lord of Appeal in Ordinary 1997–2004; mem. Jt Law Enforcement Comm. 1974, Deputy Chair. Boundary Comm. for NI 1985–88; Pres. NI Asscn for Mental Health 1983–90; Visitor, Univ. of Ulster 1999–2004; Chair. of Inquiry into death of Dr David Kelly 2003–04; Hon. Fellow, Balliol Coll., Oxford; Hon. Bencher Inner Temple, King's Inns, Dublin; Hon. LLD (Queen's Univ. of Belfast, Univ. of Ulster). *Address:* House of Lords, Westminster, London, SW1A 0PW, England (office). *Telephone:* (20) 7219-3202 (office).

HUTTON, Timothy; American actor; b. 16 Aug. 1960, Malibu, Calif.; s. of Jim Hutton and Maryline Hutton; m. Debra Winger (q.v.) 1986 (divorced); one s. *Plays:* Prelude to a Kiss, Broadway 1990, Babylon Gardens 1991. *Television appearances include:* Zuma Beach 1978, Best Place to Be, Baby Makes Six, Sultan and the Rock Star, Young Love, First Love, Friendly Fire 1979, Aldrich Ames: Traitor Within 1998, Nero Wolfe Mystery (series) 2001–02, WW3 2001, 5ive Days to Midnight (mini series) 2004, Avenger 2006, Kidnapped 2006–07, Leverage 2008. *Films include:* Ordinary People (Oscar for Best Supporting Actor) 1980, Taps 1981, Daniel 1983, Iceman 1984, Turk 1985, The Falcon and the Snowman 1985, Made in Heaven 1987, A Time of Destiny 1988, Everybody's All-American 1988, Betrayed 1988, Torrents of Spring 1990, Q & A 1990, The Temp 1993, The Dark Half 1993, French Kiss 1995, City of Industry, Scenes From Everyday Life 1995, The Substance of Fire 1996, Mr and Mrs Loving 1996, Beautiful Girls 1996, City of Industry 1997, Playing God 1997, Deterrance 1998, The General's Daughter 1999, Just One Night 2000, Deliberate Intent 2000, Deterrence 2000, Lucky Strike 2000, Sunshine State 2002, Secret Window 2004, Kinsey 2004, Turning Green 2005, Last Holiday 2006, Stephanie Daley 2006, The Kovak Box 2006, Heavens Fall 2006, Falling Objects 2006, Off the Black 2006, The Good Shepherd 2006, The Last Mimzy 2007, The Killing Room 2008, The Alphabet Killer 2008. *Address:* c/o The Endeavor Agency, 9601 Wilshire Boulevard, Beverly Hills, CA 90210, USA.

HUTTON, Will Nicholas, MBA; British writer and broadcaster; b. 21 May 1950, London; s. of the late William Hutton and Dorothy Haynes; m. Jane Atkinson 1978; one s. two d.; ed Chislehurst and Sidcup Grammar School, Univ. of Bristol and Institut Européen d'Admin des Affaires (INSEAD), Fontainebleau, France; with Phillips & Drew (stockbrokers) 1971–77; Sr Producer Current Affairs, BBC Radio 4 1978–81; Dir and Producer The Money Programme, BBC 2 1981–83; Econs Corresp. Newsnight, BBC 2 1983–88; Ed. European Business Channel 1988–90; Econs Ed. The Guardian 1990–95, Asst Ed. 1995–96; Ed. The Observer 1996–98, Ed.-in-Chief 1998–2000; Chief Exec. The Work Foundation (fmrly The Industrial Soc. –2002) 2000–08, now Chair, Big Innovation Centre; Gov. LSE 2000–; Prin. Hertford Coll., Oxford; contrib. The Observer, The Guardian, Financial Times; Hon. DLitt (Kingston) 1995, (De Montfort) 1996; Political Journalist of the Year, What the Papers Say 1993. *Publications:* The Revolution That Never Was: An Assessment of Keynesian Economics 1986, The State We're In 1994, The State to Come 1997, The Stakeholding Society 1998, The World We're In 2002, The Writing on the Wall: China and the West in the 21st Century 2007, Them and Us: Politics, Greed and Inequality—Why We Need a Fair Society 2010. *Leisure interests:* family, reading, squash, tennis, cinema, writing. *Address:* The Work Foundation, 21 Palmer Street, London, SW1H 0AD (office); 34 Elms Avenue, London, N10 2JP, England (home). *Telephone:* (20) 7976-3565 (office). *E-mail:* pa@theworkfoundation.com (office). *Website:* www.theworkfoundation.com (office).

HUTTON OF FURNESS, Baron (Life Peer), cr. 2010, of Aldringham in the County of Cumbria; **John Hutton,** PC, BCL, MA; British politician; *Adviser, Eversheds LLP;* b. 6 May 1955; m. Heather Rogers 2004; four s. (one deceased) one d.; ed Westcliffe High School, Essex, Magdalen Coll., Oxford; Research Assoc., Templeton Coll. 1980–81; Sr Lecturer in Law, Newcastle Polytechnic (now Univ. of Northumbria) 1981–92; unsuccessful cand. for MP for Penrith and the Border 1987, for MEP for Cumbria and N Lancs. 1989; MP for Barrow and Furness 1992–2010; Parl. Pvt. Sec. to Margaret Beckett 1997–98; Parl. Under-Sec. of State, Dept of Health 1998–99, Minister of State for Health 1999–2005; Chancellor of the Duchy of Lancaster and Minister for the Cabinet Office 2005; Sec. of State for Work and Pensions 2005–07, for Business, Enterprise and Regulatory Reform 2007–08, for Defence 2008–09; mem. Home Affairs Select Cttee 1994–97; Chair. Labour Parl. Cttees for Defence 1992–94, for Home Affairs 1994–97, for Home Affairs, Trade and Industry, for the Treasury 1997–2001; Adviser, Eversheds LLP (law firm) 2009–; Trustee, Furness Animal Refuge; Chair. Welfare and Park Home Owners All-party Subject Group 1995–97; Chair. British Latin American Group 1997. *Leisure interests:* football, cricket, films, music, history. *Address:* c/o Eversheds LLP, 1 Wood Street, London, EC2V 7WS, England (office). *Telephone:* (20) 7919-4500 (office). *Website:* www.eversheds.com (office).

HUXLEY, George Leonard, MA, FSA, MRIA; British scholar; *Honorary Professor, Classics, Trinity College, Dublin and Adjunct Professor, Mathematics and Greek, National University of Ireland;* b. 23 Sept. 1932, Leicester; s. of Sir Leonard Huxley and Lady (Molly) Huxley; m. Davina Iris Best 1957; three d.; ed Blundell's, Magdalen Coll., Oxford (Demy); commissioned into Royal Engineers 1951; Acting Operating Supt, Longmoor Mil. Railway 1951; Fellow, All Souls Coll., Oxford 1955–61; Prof. of Greek, Queen's Univ., Belfast 1962–83, Prof. Emer. 1988–; Hon. Pres. Classical Asscn of Ireland 1999–2000; Dir Gennadius Library, American School of Classical Studies, Athens 1986–89; mem. Exec. NI Civil Rights Asscn 1971–72; mem. Man. Cttee ASCSA 1991–; mem. Irish Advisory Bd, Inst. of Irish Studies, Univ. of Liverpool 1996–2005; Hon. Prof., Trinity Coll., Dublin 1989–; Adjunct Prof. Math. and Greek, Nat. Univ. of Ireland Maynooth 2008–; Sr Vice-Pres. Fédération Int. des Sociétés d'Etudes Classiques 1984–89; Irish mem. Humanities Cttee of European Science Foundation 1978–86; Vice-Pres. Royal Irish Acad. 1984–85, 1997–98, Hon. Librarian 1990–94, Special Envoy 1994–99, Sr Vice-Pres. 1999–2000; mem. Int. Comm. Thesaurus Linguae Latinae, Munich 1999–2000; mem. Editorial Bd Dictionary of Mediaeval Latin from Celtic Sources 2001–10; Patron Irish Inst. of Hellenic Studies, Athens 1998–; Keynote Speaker XVI Int. Congress on Classical Archaeology, Boston 2003; Hon. Freeman of Kythera 2012; Hon. LittD (Dublin) 1984, Hon. DLitt (Belfast) 1996, Hon. DLit (Nat. Univ. of Ireland Maynooth) 2013; mem. Acad. Europaea 1990–; Cromer Greek Prize 1963. *Publications:* Early Sparta 1962, Achaeans and Hittites 1960,

The Early Ionians 1966, Greek Epic Poetry 1969, Kythera (co-author) 1972, Pindar's Vision of the Past 1975, On Aristotle and Greek Society 1979, Homer and the Travellers 1988; articles on Hellenic, Byzantine, mathematical and railway subjects. *Address:* Classics, Trinity College, Dublin 2, Ireland (office); Forge Cottage, Church Enstone, Oxfordshire, OX7 4NN, England (home). *Telephone:* (1608) 677595 (home).

HUXLEY BARKHAM, Selma de Lotbinière, CM; British/Canadian historical geographer and writer; b. 8 March 1927, London, England; d. of Michael Huxley and Ottilie Huxley (née de Lotbinière Mills); m. John Brian Barkham 1954 (died 1964); two s. two d.; Asst, Cttee on Geographical Names, Royal Geographical Soc., UK 1949; Librarian, Arctic Inst. of N America, Montréal 1951–54; Founder African Students Asscn 1960s; prepared and presented brief to Royal Comm. on Bilingualism and Biculturalism which was deemed instrumental in bringing French immersion to Canadian public school system; Founding mem., French Section, Citizens' Cttee on Children; helped Edgar Demers start first French Canadian theatre group for children in the Outaouais, 'La compagnie des Trouvères' 1960s; researcher for Historic Sites of Canada (including Louisbourg) 1964–68; teacher, Instituto Anglo-Mexicano, Guadalajara, Mexico until moving to Spain 1969–72; discovered the presence of 16th century Basque whaling settlements and shipwrecks in harbours of Belle Isle, and found earliest civil documents written in Canada 1972–87; Royal Canadian Geographical Soc. grant to lead first expedition to identify 16th century Basque whaling sites in Labrador including what is now the Red Bay Nat. Historic Site 1977; led teams of underwater and land archaeologists to these sites; worked for Public Archives of Canada in Spain 1973–85; Social Sciences and Humanities Research Council of Canada grant for publ. of documents relating to Basques in Newfoundland and Labrador 1984–86; mem. Advisory Cttee, Museo Naval de San Sebastian 1992–, Advisory Cttee For Red Bay, Labrador, Nat. Historic Site 1996–; advocates Basque Nat. Trust for the Preservation of Basque Architecture 1993–; Co-founder Northern Peninsula Heritage Soc. 1997–; elected mem. Réal Sociedad Bascongada de Amigos del País 1981; Fellow, Wings WorldQuest 2009; numerous publs, lectures and confs; Hon. Consul of Bilbao, Bilbao Chamber of Commerce (first woman) 1992; Order of Canada 1981; Dr hc (Memorial Univ. of Newfoundland) 1993, (Univ. of Windsor, Ont.) 1985; Gold Medal, Royal Canadian Geographical Soc. (first woman) 1980, Award for Culture, Fundación Sabino Arana, Bilbao 1999, City of St John's, Newfoundland named one of its streets 'Barkham Street' 1999, Queen's Golden Jubilee Medal 2002. *Publications include:* Los Vascos en el Marco Atlántico Norte, Siglos XVI y XVII, Itsasoa (Vol. 3) 1987, The Basque Coast of Newfoundland 1989. *Leisure interests:* languages, bird watching. *Address:* 7 Chapel Street, Chichester, West Sussex, PO19 1BU, England; 23 Des Estacades, Cantley, QC J8V 3J3, Canada. *E-mail:* orianabarkham@ncf.ca.

HUYGENS, Robert Burchard Constantijn, PhD; Dutch professor of medieval Latin (retd); b. 10 Dec. 1931, The Hague; m. Caroline Sprey 1962; one s. two d.; ed Leiden Univ.; army service 1952–54; Lecturer in Medieval Latin, Univ. of Leiden 1964, Prof. 1968–96; Fellow, Dumbarton Oaks, Washington, DC 1982, Inst. for Advanced Study, Jerusalem 1983–84, Inst. for Advanced Study, Princeton, NJ 1986–87, Herzog August Bibliothek, Wolfenbüttel 1987; mem. Royal Netherlands Acad., Soc. des Antiquaires de France, Monumenta Germaniae Historica; Past Pres. Rotary Club, Leiden. *Publications include:* Jacques de Vitry 1960, Accessus ad Auctores 1970, Vézelay 1976, William of Tyre 1986, Berengar of Tours 1988, Guibert of Nogent 1992, Serta mediaevalia 2000, Ars edendi 2001, Christian of Stavelot 2008, Mary of Oignies 2012. *Address:* Witte Singel 28, 2311 BH Leiden, Netherlands (home). *Telephone:* (71) 5143798 (home).

HUYGHE, Pierre; French artist; b. 11 Sept. 1962, Paris; ed École Nationale Supérieure des Arts Decoratifs, Paris; works in a variety of media from film and video to public interventions; represented France at the Venice Biennale (pavilion, Le Château de Turing) 2001; Artist in Residency, DAAD (German Academic Exchange Service), Berlin 1999–2000; Prof. of Art and Philosophy, European Grad. School, Saas-Fee, Switzerland 2008–; Special Award, Jury of the Venice Biennial 2001, Hugo Boss Prize, Guggenheim Museum 2002, Prix du meilleur artiste français, Beaux-Arts Magazine Art Awards 2005. *Address:* c/o Marian Goodman Gallery, 24 West 57th Street, New York, NY 10019, USA. *Telephone:* (212) 977-7160. *Fax:* (212) 581-5187. *E-mail:* goodman@mariangoodman.com. *Website:* www.pierrehuyghe.com (office).

HUYGHEBAERT, Jan, BA, DrIur; Belgian business executive; b. 1945; ed Univ. of Antwerp, Catholic Univ. of Louvain; Attaché, Science Policy Programme 1970–74; Adviser, Cabinet of Prime Minister Leo Tindemans 1974–78; Alderman, Port of Antwerp 1978–85; Pres. Exec. Cttee Kredietbank NV (forerunner of KBC) 1985–91, Chair. Almanij NV (holding co. of KBC) 1991–2005, Chair. KBC Group NV (following merger of Almanij and KBC) 2005–11, fmr Chair. KBC Bank, KBC Insurance; Chair. Kredietbank Luxembourg; fmr mem. Coudenberg group (Belgian think tank). *Address:* c/o KBC Group NV, Havenlaan 2, Brussels 1080, Belgium. *E-mail:* info@kbc.be.

HVIDT, Gen. (retd) Christian, DFC; Danish air force officer (retd) and business executive; *Chairman, Rovsing A/S;* b. 15 July 1942, Copenhagen; m. 1st; three c.; m. 2nd Jane Hvidt; two step-c.; flying service (F-100 Super Sabre) 1962–69; test pilot on F-35 Draken at SAAB factories, Linköping, Sweden 1969–72; Deputy Squadron Commdr (F-35 Draken) 1972–74; Br. Chief Tactical Air Command, Denmark 1975–79; Squadron Commdr First Danish F-16 Squadron, Air Station Skrydstrup 1979–83; staff officer and Br. Chief Plans and Policy Div., HQ Chodden 1983–87; CO Air Station Karup 1987–88; Chief of Staff, Tactical Air Command, Denmark 1989–90; Deputy Chief of Staff, Plans and Policy, Operations, Budget and Finance, HQ, Chodden 1991–93; Perm. Danish Rep., NATO Mil. Cttee 1994–96; Chief of Staff, HQ Chodden 1996; Chief of Defence 1996–2002; Chair. Rovsing A/S 2006–; Grand Cross of the Order of Dannebrog, Danish Air Force Badge of Honour, Badge of Honour of the Danish Reserve Officers Asscn, Medal of Merit of the Home Guard, Commdr, Grand Cross, Royal Swedish Order of the Northern Star, Jordanian Mil. Order of Merit of the First Degree, Commdr, Cross with the Star of Merit of the Repub. of Poland, Commdr, Légion d'honneur, Ordre nat. du Mérite. *Address:* Rovsing A/S, Dyregaardsvej 2, 2740 Skovlunde, Denmark (office). *Telephone:* 44-20-08-00 (office). *Fax:* 44-20-08-01 (office). *E-mail:* info@rovsing.dk (office). *Website:* www.rovsing.dk (office).

HVOROSTOVSKY, Dmitri Alexandrovich; Russian opera singer (baritone); b. 16 Oct. 1962, Krasnoyarsk; m. 1st (divorced), two c.; m. 2nd Florence Illi Hvorostovsky; one s. one d.; ed Krasnoyarsk Inst. of Arts; debut as opera singer 1985; soloist, Krasnoyarsk Opera Theatre 1985–90; winner All-Union Glinka Competition 1987; winner int. competitions in Toulouse 1988, Cardiff 1989; has gained worldwide reputation after his recitals around the world; performances in La Scala, Covent Garden, Metropolitan Opera and Paris Opéra; roles include The Queen of Spades (Opéra de Nice) 1989, (Metropolitan Opera, New York) 1999, Eugene Onegin (La Fenice) 1991, (Châtelet, Paris) 1992, (Covent Garden) 1993, 2005, (Vienna) 2010, Il Barbiere di Siviglia (Berlin State Opera) 1994, San Francisco Opera) 1996, I Puritani (Covent Garden) 1993, La Traviata (Chicago Lyric Opera) 1993, (Covent Garden) 1996, 2012, (Metropolitan Opera, New York) 2003, 2012, (Cagliari) 2004, (San Francisco Opera) 2004, (La Fenice) 2004, (San Carlo, Naples) 2007, I Masnadieri (Covent Garden) 1998, 2002, Rigoletto (Novaya Opera, Moscow) 2000, (Covent Garden) 2005, 2010, Don Giovanni (Geneva and Salzburg) 1999, (Metropolitan Opera, New York) 2002, Don Carlos (Teatro Real, Madrid) 2001, (Zürich Oper) 2003, (Vienna) 2005, (Tokyo and Nagoya) 2012, Don Giovanni and Leporello in the film Don Giovanni Unmasked 2003, Pikovaya Dama (Metropolitan Opera, New York) 1995, (La Scala, Milan) 2005, (Vienna State Opera), War and Peace (Metropolitan Opera) 2003, (Salzburg Festival) 2004, Il Trovatore (Covent Garden) 2003, (Bastille Opera, Paris) 2004, (Metropolitan Opera) 2009, 2011, 2012, (Arena Verona) 2012, Faust (Metropolitan Opera, New York) 2005, Un Ballo in Maschera (Chicago Lyric Opera) 2003, (Covent Garden) 2006, (Metropolitan Opera) 2008; First Prize, USSR Nat. Glinka Competition 1987, Toulouse Int. Competition 1988, BBC Cardiff Singer of the World Competition 1989, State Prize of Russia 1991, People's Artist of Russia 1995, Opera News Award for invaluable contrib. to opera 2011. *Address:* c/o Diane Blackman, President, BR Public Relations 144 East 84th Street, Suite 7G, New York, NY 10028, USA (office). *Telephone:* (212) 249-5125 (office). *E-mail:* dblackman@ brpublicrelations.com (office); elenalvista@mail.ru (home). *Website:* www .brpublicrelations.com (office); www.hvorostovsky.com/en.

HWANG, Robert; Taiwanese computer industry executive; *President and Chief Operating Officer, Wistron Corporation;* ed Tatung Inst. of Tech. Business Admin Exec. Program, Nat. Chengchi Univ.; began career at Sampo and Acer Computers 1980s; managed product devt for mobile product lines for more than ten years at Wistron Corpn, currently Pres. and COO. *Address:* Wistron Corporation, 158 Singshan Road, Neihu, Taipei 11469, Taiwan (office). *Telephone:* (2) 66169999 (office). *Fax:* (2) 66125188 (office). *E-mail:* info@wistron.com (office). *Website:* www .wistron.com (office).

HWANG, Woo-yea, LLD; South Korean lawyer, judge and politician; *Chairman, Saenuri Party;* b. 13 Aug. 1947, Incheon; ed Seoul Nat. Univ.; Judge, Seoul High Court 1974–85; Chief Judge, District Courts, Chuncheon and Jeju 1985–89; fmr Dir of Research, Constitutional Court; Chief Judge, Incheon Inst. of Law 1990–92; mem. Bd of Audit and Inspection 1993–96; mem. Nat. Ass. for Yeonsu Dist, Incheon 1996–2000, 2000–, fmr Chair. Parl. Human Rights Forum; Chair. Korea-Japan Parl. League; mem. Grand Nat. Party (renamed Saenuri Party, New Frontier Party 2012), Leader 2012–. *Address:* Saenuri Party, 14-31, Yeouido-dong, Yeongdeungpo-gu, Seoul 156-768, Republic of Korea (office). *Telephone:* (2) 3786-3000 (office). *Fax:* (2) 3786-3610 (office). *Website:* www.saenuriparty.kr (office); www.hwy.pe.kr.

HWANG, Young-key, MBA; South Korean banker and financial services industry executive; *Senior Adviser, Shin & Kim;* ed London School of Econs, UK; long career with Samsung Corpn, becoming Head of Int. Finance Team 1989–90, Head of Personnel Dept 1993–94, Sr Man Dir and Chief of Staff of Strategic Planning Office, Samsung Life Insurance Co Ltd 1997–99, Pres. and CEO, Samsung Securities Co Ltd 2001–04; Pres. Woora Bank 2004–07; Adviser, Shin & Kim (law firm), Seoul 2007–08; Sr Adviser 2012–; Chair. KB Financial Group Inc. (fmrly Kookmin Bank) 2008–09; Chair and CEO, Cha Hospital Group 2010–12. *Address:* Shin & Kim, 8th Floor, State Tower Namsan, 100 Toegye-ro, Jung-gu, Seoul 100-052, Republic of Korea (office). *Telephone:* (2) 316-4114 (office). *Fax:* (2) 756-6220 (office). *E-mail:* ykhwang@shinkim.com (office). *Website:* www .shinkim.com (office).

HYLAND, J. M(artin) E., DPhil; British mathematician and academic; *Professor of Mathematical Logic, King's College, Cambridge;* b. 1949; ed Univ. of Oxford; currently Prof. in Mathematical Logic and Head of Dept of Pure Math. and Math. Statistics, King's Coll., Cambridge; Pres. British Logic Colloquium; Vice-Pres. Cambridge Philosophical Soc.; mem. Bd of Eds Mathematical Proceedings, Cambridge Philosophical Soc.; mem. Man. Cttee Isaac Newton Inst. for Math. Sciences. *Address:* Department of Pure Mathematics and Mathematical Statistics, King's College, University of Cambridge, Cambridge, CB2 1ST, England (office). *Telephone:* (1223) 337986 (office). *Fax:* (1223) 337986 (office). *E-mail:* j.m.e .hyland@dpmms.cam.ac.uk (office). *Website:* www.dpmms.cam.ac.uk (office); www .statslab.cam.ac.uk (office).

HYLTON, G. Anthony, BA, JD, LLM; Jamaican lawyer and politician; *Minister of Industry, Commerce and Investment;* b. 27 April 1957, Yallahs, St Thomas; m.; two c.; ed Kingston Coll., Morgan State Univ. and Georgetown Univ., USA, Univ. of London, UK; lawyer, Melnicove, Kaufman, Weiner and Smouse, Baltimore 1983–85, with Curtis, Mallet-Prevost, Colt and Mosle, New York 1986–88, with Dickstein, Shapiro and Morin, Washington, DC 1988–89; fmr legal asst to Gen. Counsel, Inter-American Foundation; fmr Dir Jamaica Public Service Co.; mem. Parl. for Western St Thomas 1993–2002; Exec. Dir of Legal and Foreign Affairs, Policy Review Unit, Ministry of Foreign Affairs and Trade 1990–93, Minister of State 1993–2001; Minister of Mining and Energy 2001–02; Amb. and Special Prime Ministerial Envoy 2002–06; Minister of Foreign Affairs and Foreign Trade 2006–07, also mem. of Senate; Minister of Industry, Commerce and Investment 2012–; negotiator at WTO, Cotonou Agreement, Free Trade Area of the Americas and CARICOM; Chair. Inst. of Law and Econs, People's Nat. Party Policy Comm.; Chair. Commercial Div., Coffee Industry Bd; mem. Md and Jamaica Bar Assocns; Nat. Honours from Govt of Benin. *Leisure interests:* dominos, music, writing, debating, sport. *Address:* Ministry of Industry, Commerce and Investment (MITEC), 4 St Lucia Ave, Kingston 5 (office); People's National Party, 89 Old Hope Road, Kingston 6, Jamaica (office). *Telephone:* 968-7116 (ministry) (office); 978-1337 (office). *Fax:* 960-7422 (ministry) (office); 927-4389 (office). *E-mail:*

information@pnpjamaica.com (office). *Website:* www.miic.gov.jm; www .pnpjamaica.com (office).

HYMAN, Timothy, RA; British painter and writer; b. 17 April 1946, Hove; s. of Alan Hyman and Noreen Gypson; m. Judith Ravenscroft 1982; ed Charterhouse and Slade School of Fine Art, London; Curator Narrative Paintings at Arnolfini and ICA Galleries, etc. 1979–80; public collections include Arts Council, Bristol City Art Gallery, British Council Collection, Museum of London, Contemporary Art Soc., British Museum, Govt Art Collection, Los Angeles Co. Museum; Visiting Prof. at Baroda, India, two British Council lecture tours 1981–83; Artist-in-Residence, Lincoln Cathedral 1983–84, Sandown Racecourse 1992, Maggie's Cancer Caring Centres 2011–12; Purchaser for Arts Council Collection 1985; selector, John Moores Prize 1995; Lead Curator Stanley Spencer retrospective exhbn, Tate Gallery, London 2001–; Co-curator British Vision, Museum of Fine Arts, Ghent 2007; Leverhulme Award 1992, Rootstein Hopkins Foundation Award 1995, Wingate Award 1998, Medaglio Beato Angelico, Florence 2005, Nat. Portrait Gallery/BP Travel Award 2007. *Publications:* Hodgkin 1975, Kitaj 1977, Beckmann 1978, Balthus 1980, Narrative Paintings 1979, English Romanesque 1984, Kiff 1986, Domenico Tiepolo 1987, Bhupen Khakhar (monograph) 1998, Bonnard (monograph) 1998, Carnivalesque (catalogue) 2000, Stanley Spencer (catalogue) 2001, Sienese Painting (monograph) 2003; numerous articles on contemporary figurative painting in London Magazine, Artscribe, Times Literary Supplement 1975–. *Leisure interests:* the novels of John Cowper Powys, reading, travel, cinema, walking London. *Address:* 62 Myddelton Square, London, EC1R 1XX, England (home). *Telephone:* (20) 7837-1933 (home).

HYND, Ronald; British choreographer; b. 22 April 1931, London; s. of William John Hens and Alice Louisa Griffiths; m. Annette Page 1957; one d.; ed Holloway Co. School, numerous wartime emergency schools; trained with Marie Rambert 1946; joined Ballet Rambert 1949, Royal Ballet (then known as Sadler's Wells Ballet) 1952 (Prin. Dancer 1959–70); Ballet Dir Bavarian State Opera 1970–73, 1984–86; freelance choreographer; ballets presented by numerous int. ballet cos, including English Nat. Ballet, Royal Sadler's Wells, La Scala Milan, Deutsche Oper Berlin, Vienna State Opera, Houston Ballet, Bavarian State Opera, American Ballet Theater, Australian Ballet, Santiago Ballet, Tokyo Ballet, Canadian Nat. Ballet, Grands Ballets Canadiens, Dutch Nat. Ballet, Northern Ballet, Slovenian Nat. Ballet, South African State Theatre Ballet, Tulsa Ballet Theater, Royal Danish Ballet, Ballet Maggio Musicale, Florence and Pacific Northwest Ballet, Ballet West, USA, Cincinnati Ballet, Bonn Opera, Ballet de Nice Opera, New London Ballet, Hong Kong Ballet, Estonian Nat. Ballet, Joffrey Ballet Chicago, Ballet Nacional de Sodre Montevideo. *Works choreographed include:* Three Act Ballets: Merry Widow 1975 (15 productions), The Nutcracker 1976, Rosalinda 1978 (11 productions), Papillon 1979 (5 productions), Le Diable à Quatre 1984, Coppelia 1985 (5 productions), Ludwig II 1986, The Hunchback of Notre Dame 1988, The Sleeping Beauty 1993; one act ballets include: The Fairy's Kiss 1967, Dvorak Variations 1970, Wendekreise 1971, Mozartiana 1972, Das Telefon 1972, Marco Polo 1975, Sanguine Fan 1976, La Chatte 1978, Les Valses 1981, Seasons 1982, Scherzo Capriccioso 1982, Fanfare 1985, Liaisons Amoureuses 1989, Ballade 1989. *Choreography for:* Galileo (film) 1974, La Traviata (BBC TV) 1974, Amahl and Night Visitors (BBC TV) 1975, ice ballets for John Curry 1977, The Sound of Music 1981, Camelot 1982, Sylvia for Princess Diana's 30th Birthday Banquet 1992, Merry Widow (TV and video in Canada and Australia), Rosalinda (Slovenian TV), Sanguine Fan (BBC TV), Nutcracker (BBC TV). *Leisure interests:* gardens, music, travel. *Address:* Fern Cottage, Upper Somerton, Bury St Edmunds, Suffolk, IP29 4ND, England (home). *Telephone:* (1284) 789284 (home). *Fax:* (1284) 789284 (home). *E-mail:* hyndpage@gmail.com (home).

HYNDE, Chrissie; American singer, songwriter and musician; b. 7 Sept. 1951, Akron, Ohio; one d. with Ray Davies; m. 1st Jim Kerr (divorced); one d.; m. 2nd Lucho Brieva 1999 (divorced 2002); contrib. to New Musical Express; co-founder Chrissie Hynde and the Pretenders 1978–, singer, songwriter and guitarist, new band formed 1983; tours in Britain, Europe and USA; platinum and gold discs in USA; Ivor Novello Award for Outstanding Contrib. to British Music 1999; inducted into Rock & Roll Hall of Fame 2005; Q Award for Classic Songwriter 2013. *Singles include:* Stop Your Sobbing (debut) 1978, Kid 1979, Brass in Pocket 1979, I Go to Sleep 1982, Back on the Chain Gang 1982, Middle of the Road 1984, Thin Line Between Love and Hate, Don't Get Me Wrong 1986, Hymn to Her 1987, Night in my Veins 1994, I'll Stand By You 1994, Human 1999. *Albums include:* Pretenders (debut) 1980, Pretenders II 1981, Extended Play 1981, Learn to Crawl 1985, Get Close 1986, The Singles 1987, Packed! 1990, Last of the Independents 1994, The Isle of View 1995, Viva El Amor 1999, Loose Screw 2002, Break Up the Concrete 2009, Fidelity! (with JP Jones and the Fairground Boys) 2010. *Address:* Quietus Management Limited, 13 Bramley Road, 2nd Floor Phoenix Brewery, London, W10 6SP, England (office). *Telephone:* (20) 3220-0310 (office). *Website:* www .quietusmanagement.co.uk (office); www.chrissiehynde.com; www.pretenders .com.

HYNES, James T., AB, PhD; American chemist and academic; *Distinguished Professor of Chemistry and Biochemistry, University of Colorado;* b. 16 Oct. 1943, Miami Beach, Fla; ed Catholic Univ., Princeton Univ.; NIH Post-Doctoral Fellow, MIT 1969–70; Asst Prof., Univ. of Colorado, Boulder 1971–76, Assoc. Prof. 1976–79, Faculty Foundation Fellow 1978–79, Prof. of Chem. 1979–, Faculty Fellow 1986–87, Research Lecturer, Council on Research and Creative Work 1988, Distinguished Prof. of Chemistry and Biochemistry 2012–; Visiting Assoc. Prof., Univ. of Toronto, Canada 1978–79; Visiting Prof., Univ. of Paris VI, France 1985, 1987, Univ. Autonoma de Barcelona, Spain 1995, Univ. Paris Sud, France 1997; Visiting Sr Research Fellow, Univ. of Oxford, England 1985, Visiting Prof. 1987; Visiting Prof., Ecole Normale Supérieure (ENS), Paris 1997, CNRS Dir of Research, ENS 1999–, now Emer.; American Ed. Progress in Reaction Kinetics and Mechanism 1999–2005; Co-Chair. Editorial Bd ChemPhysChem-A European Journal 1999–; mem. Editorial Bd Journal of Physical Chemistry 1990–98, Journal of Molecular Liquids 1991–, International Journal of Quantum Chemistry 1993–97, Chemical Physics Letters 2003–08, Journal of Chemical Physics 2003–05, 2014–; mem. ACS (Vice Chair. Theoretical Div. 1984, Chair. 1986), French Chemical Soc.; Fellow, American Physical Soc. 2000, American Acad. of Arts and Sciences 2008, NAS 2011, American Chemical Soc. 2013; Pople Lecturer, Carnegie Mellon Univ. 2013; ACS Nobel Laureate Signature Award 1983, Nat.

Science Foundation Creativity Award 1991, Hirschfelder Prize in Theoretical Chemistry 2004, ISI Highly Cited Researcher 2002, ACS Hildebrand Award in Theoretical and Experimental Chem. of Liquids 2005. *Publications:* approximately 300 scientific publications, five books edited. *Address:* Department of Chemistry and Biochemistry, University of Colorado, Campus Box 215, Boulder, CO 80309, USA (office); Département de Chimie, Ecole Normale Superieure, 24 rue Lhomond, 75005 Paris, France (office). *Telephone:* (303) 492-6926 (Boulder) (office); 1-44-32-32-78 (Paris) (office). *Fax:* (303) 492-5894 (Boulder) (office); 1-44-32-33-25 (Paris) (office). *E-mail:* james.hynes@colorado.edu (office); chynes43@gmail.com (office). *Website:* chem.colorado.edu (office); www.chimie.ens.fr/?q=profil/james.hynes (office).

HYNES, Samuel, DFC, PhD, FRSL; American academic and writer; *Woodrow Wilson Professor of Literature Emeritus, Princeton University;* b. 29 Aug. 1924, Chicago; s. of Samuel Lynn and Margaret Hynes (née Turner); m. Elizabeth Igleheart 1944 (died 2008); two d.; ed Univ. of Minnesota, Columbia Univ.; served in USMCR 1943–46, 1952–53; mem. faculty, Swarthmore Coll. 1949–68, Prof. of English Literature 1965–68; Prof. of English, Northwestern Univ., Evanston, Ill. 1968–76; Prof. of English, Princeton Univ. 1976–90, Woodrow Wilson Prof. of Literature 1978–90, Prof. Emer. 1990–; Fulbright Fellow 1953–54; Guggenheim Fellow 1959–60, 1981–82; Bollingen Fellow 1964–65; American Council of Learned Socs Fellow 1969, 1985–86; Nat. Endowment for Humanities Sr Fellow 1973–74, 1977–78; American Acad. of Arts and Letters Award in Literature 2004, Robert F. Kennedy Award 1998. *Publications:* The Pattern of Hardy's Poetry (Explicator Award 1962) 1961, William Golding 1964, The Edwardian Turn of Mind 1968, Edwardian Occasions 1972, The Auden Generation 1976, Flights of Passage: Reflections of a World War Two Aviator 1988, A War Imagined: The First World War and English Culture 1990, The Soldiers' Tale (Robert F. Kennedy Book Award 1998) 1997, The Growing Seasons: An American Boyhood Before the War 2003; Ed.: Further Speculations by T. E. Hulme 1955, The Author's Craft and Other Critical Writings of Arnold Bennett 1968, Romance and Realism 1979, Complete Poetical Works of Thomas Hardy, Vol. I 1982, Vol. II 1984, Vol. III 1985, Vols IV, V 1995, Thomas Hardy 1984, Complete Short Fiction of Joseph Conrad (Vol. I–III) 1992, (Vol. IV) 1993. *Address:* 130 Moore Street, Princeton, NJ 08540 (home); Department of English, 22 McCosh Hall, Princeton University, Princeton, NJ 08544-1006, USA (office). *Website:* web.princeton.edu/sites/english/new_web/index.htm (office).

HYODO, Makoto; Japanese business executive; joined Nipponkoa Insurance Co. Ltd, fmr Chief Dir of Tohoku, later Man. of Iwate Office, later Dir of 5th Sales in Main Office, Man. Exec. Officer 2002–05, Sr Man. Exec. Officer and Vice-Pres. 2005–07, Rep. Dir, Pres. and Sr Exec. Officer Nipponkoa Insurance Co. Ltd 2007–10, Rep. Dir, Chair. and Co-CEO NKSJ Holdings, Inc. (following establishment of jt holding co. by Sompo Japan Insurance Inc. and Nipponkoa Insurance Co. Ltd) 2010–12, Dir 2012–. *Address:* NKSJ Holdings, Inc., 26-1, Nishi-Shinjuku 1-chome, Shinjuku-ku, Tokyo 160-8338, Japan (office). *Telephone:* (3) 3349-3000 (operator) (office); (3) 3349-3111 (office). *Fax:* (3) 3349-4697 (office). *E-mail:* info@nksj-hd.com (office). *Website:* www.nksj-hd.com (office).

HYON, Vice-Marshal Yong-choi; North Korean army officer; mem. Korean Workers' Party (KWP), mem. Cen. Cttee 2010–; Field Commdr in charge of NW Region, Korean People's Army –2012, Chief of Gen. Staff 2012–13; attained rank of Four Star Gen. 2010, Vice-Marshall 2012; Order of Kim Jong-il 2012.

HYSENI, Skënder; Kosovo politician; b. 17 Feb. 1955, Dobratin; m. Drita Hyseni; two s. two d.; ed Dept of English Language and Literature, Univ. of Priština, Bloomberg State Coll., USA, Univ. of Aberdeen, UK; early political career with newly est. Democratic League of Kosova 1989, began working with Kosovo Information Centre 1992 as journalist and interpreter; Co-founder and Ed. Kosova Daily Report; Adviser to Pres. Ibrahim Rugova 1992–2006, to Pres. Fatmir Sejdiu 2006–10; Spokesperson for Kosovo negotiating team that took part in UN-sponsored talks with Serbia, launched in 2006; mem. Kuvendi i Kosovës/Skupština Kosova (Kosovo Ass.) (Parl.), Minister of Culture, Youth and Sports Jan.–April 2008, of Foreign Affairs April 2008–10 (resgnd); mem. Kosovo Democratic League, mem. of Presidency and Chair. Cttee for External Relations; mem. Constitutional Comm. charged with compiling first draft of Constitution of Kosovo. *Address:* c/o Ministry of Foreign Affairs, 10000 Priština, Government Building, Rruga Nënë Terezë, Kosovo.

HYTNER, Sir Nicholas Robert, Kt, MA; British theatre director; *Artistic Director, Royal National Theatre;* b. 7 May 1956, Manchester; s. of Benet A. Hytner and Joyce Myers; ed Manchester Grammar School and Trinity Hall, Cambridge; staff producer, ENO 1978–80; Assoc. Dir Royal Exchange Theatre, Manchester 1985–89; Assoc. Dir Royal Nat. Theatre 1989–97, Artistic Dir 2003–(15); Evening Standard Opera Award 1985, Evening Standard Best Dir Award 1989. *Theatre and opera productions include:* Wagner's Rienzi (ENO) 1983, Tippett's King Priam (Kent Opera) 1984, Handel's Xerxes (ENO) 1985, The Scarlet Pimpernel (Chichester Festival) 1985, As You Like It, Edward II, The Country Wife, Schiller's Don Carlos (Royal Exchange) 1986, Handel's Giulio Cesare (Paris Opera), Measure for Measure (RSC) 1987, Tippett's The Knot Garden (Royal Opera), The Magic Flute (ENO), The Tempest (RSC) 1988, The Marriage of Figaro (Geneva Opera), Joshua Sobol's Ghetto (Nat. Theatre), Miss Saigon (Theatre Royal, Drury Lane) 1989, King Lear (RSC) 1990, The Wind in the Willows (Nat. Theatre) 1990, Volpone (Almeida) 1990, The Madness of George III (Nat. Theatre) 1991, The Recruiting Officer (Nat. Theatre) 1992, Carousel (Nat. Theatre) (Tony Award for Best Dir of a Musical 1994) 1992, The Importance of Being Earnest (Aldwych) 1993, Don Giovanni (Bavarian State Opera) 1994, The Cunning Little Vixen (Paris) 1995, The Cripple of Inishmaan 1997, The Crucible 1997, The Lady in the Van 1999, Cressida 2000, Orpheus Descending 2000, The Winter's Tale (Nat. Theatre) 2001, Mother Clap's Molly House (Nat. Theatre) 2001, Sweet Smell of Success (Broadway) 2002, The History Boys (Nat. Theatre) (Olivier Award for Best Director 2004, Tony Award for Best Director 2006) 2004, Così fan tutte (Glyndebourne) 2006, The Man of Mode (Nat. Theatre) 2007, The Rose Tattoo (Nat. Theatre) 2007, England People Very Nice (Nat. Theatre) 2009, Phèdre (Nat. Theatre) 2009, One Man, Two Guvnors (Nat. Theatre and touring) (Best Play, Evening Standard Theatre Awards 2011) 2011. *Films:* The Madness of King George 1994, The Crucible 1996, The Object of My Affection 1998, Twelfth Night, or What You Will (TV) 1998, Center Stage 2000, The History Boys 2006, Phèdre 2009. *Address:* Royal National Theatre, South Bank, London, SE1 9PX, England (office). *Telephone:* (20) 7452-3333 (office). *E-mail:* info@nationaltheatre.org.uk (office). *Website:* www.nationaltheatre.org.uk (office).

HYUN, Jeong-eun, BA, MA; South Korean business executive; *Chairwoman, Hyundai Group;* b. 26 Jan. 1955, Seoul; m. Chung Mong-hun (died 2003); three c.; ed Ewha Women's Univ. Graduate School, Seoul, Fairleigh Dickinson Univ. Graduate School, NJ, USA; Chair. Hyundai Group and affiliate cos (following death of husband, Hyundai's Chair. and heir apparent) 2003–; mem. Nat. Supporting Cttee, Int. Cttee of Girl Scouts Korea 1983–98, Dir, HQ of Girl Scouts Korea 1998–2007; Commr, Financial Section, Korean Asscn of Women's Univs 1988–91; Commr, Presidential Cttee on Govt Innovation and Decentralization 2005–08, Civil Service Comm. 2006–08, Special Advisory Cttee for Woman Volunteers, Korean Red Cross 1999–; Hon. Consul to Brazil 2011; ranked 36th by The Wall Street Journal amongst Fifty Woman to Watch 2007, ranked by Forbes magazine amongst 100 Most Powerful Women (73rd) 2008, (80th) 2009, ranked 18th by Trade Winds amongst Influential People in the World Shipping Industry 2010, ranked 48th on Financial Times Top 50 Women in World Business list 2011; elected mem. Pinnacle Soc., Fairleigh Dickinson Univ. 2006. *Address:* Hyundai Group, 1-7 Yeonji-dong, Jongno-gu, 110-754 Seoul, Republic of Korea (office). *Telephone:* (2) 3706-5114 (office). *E-mail:* webmaster@hyundaigroup.com (office). *Website:* www.hyundaigroup.com (office).

HYUN, Oh-seok, BA, MA, PhD; South Korean politician; *Deputy Prime Minister and Minister of Strategy and Finance;* ed Seoul Nat. Univ., Univ. of Pennsylvania, USA; Economist, Macroeconomic Adjustment and Growth Div., The World Bank, Washington, DC 1989–91; Dir-Gen., Bureau of Treasury, Bureau of Econ. Policy, Bureau of Budget, Ministry of Finance and Economy 1996–99; Dir-Gen., Nat. Econ. Advisory Council 1999–2000; Dean, Nat. Tax Coll. 2000–01; Pres., Korea Int. Trade Asscn 2002–08; Pres., Korea Devt Inst. 2009–12; Deputy Prime Minister and Minister of Strategy and Finance 2013–; mem. Int. Devt Cooperation Cttee 2005–; mem. Cttee NPSO (Non-governmental Public Serving Org.) Man. 2007, Chair. NPSO Evaluation Bd 2008; Prof., Business School, Korea Advanced Inst. of Science and Tech. 2008–09; mem. Knowledge Advisory Comm., The World Bank 2012–; mem. Saenuri Party (New Frontier Party). *Address:* Ministry of Strategy and Finance, Govt Complex II, 88, Gwanmunro, Gwacheon City, Gyeonggi Prov. 427-725, Republic of Korea (office). *Telephone:* (2) 2150-2450 (office). *Fax:* (2) 503-9070 (office). *E-mail:* fppr@mosf.go.kr (office). *Website:* www.mosf.go.kr (office).

HZAINE, El Hassane, MA, PhD; Moroccan international organization official and academic; *Director-General, Islamic Centre for the Development of Trade;* b. 20 Dec. 1955, Casablanca; ed Univ. Hassan II, Casablanca, The Hague Acad. of Int. Law, Netherlands, Univ. of Strasbourg, France; Prof. of Int. Relations, Univ. Hassan II 1980–2000; Exec. Dir Observatoire Economique et Social du Maghreb (consultative body and think tank on economic integration in N Africa), Casablanca, Morocco 1989–98; Prof. and expert consultant in int. affairs 1991–97; lecturer, Université de Toulouse I, France (Inst. of Political Studies) 1994; several lectures on int. trade (Master's degree), High School of Business (ISCAE), Casablanca; Assoc. Prof. of Int. Econ. Relations and Int. Trade 2000–07; Perm. mem. Secr. of the Trade Negotiating Cttee of the Trade Preferential System among the OIC Member States (TPS-OIC), Islamic Centre for the Devt of Trade, OIC, Casablanca, mem. IDB Task Force on Intra-OIC Trade Expansion 1998–2003, mem. Consultative Group on Enhancing Intra-OIC Trade 2009–11, mem. OIC Consultative Group for Enhancing Intra-OIC Trade (COMCEC, IDB Group-ITFC, ICIEC, Cooperation Office and other OIC insts, including OISA, ICCI, SESRIC and int. insts ITC) 2009–11, mem. working group on development of goods and services and trade finance (cooperation between IDB group, Govt of Malaysia and ICDT), mem. Secr. of the network of Trade Promotion Organs of the OIC, mem. Steering Cttee for the Implementation of the OIC Cotton Action Plan, Observer mem. in ITC's trade capacity building programme of Arab countries (EnAct); Dir of Studies and Training Dept (in charge of TPS/OIC Trade Negotiations and int. cooperation) 1997–2011, Acting Dir-Gen. Islamic Centre for the Devt of Trade, OIC May–June 2000, July–Nov. 2011, Dir-Gen. Nov. 2011–; Honour Medal of the Kingdom of Morocco 1985; Prize for doctorate thesis on African Studies, Council of Economic and Social research in Africa (CODESRIA (Senegal), Distinction granted By HE Dr Ahmad Mohamed Ali, Pres. of IDB Group, Jeddah 2011. *Address:* Islamic Centre for the Development of Trade, Tour des Habous, Avenue des FAR, PO Box 13545, Casablanca 20032, Morocco (office). *Telephone:* (522) 314974 (office). *Fax:* (522) 310110 (office). *E-mail:* icdt@icdt-oic.org (office). *Website:* www.icdt-oic.org (office).

IACOCCA, Lee A.; American business executive; *Chairman, Iacocca Foundation;* b. 15 Oct. 1924, Allentown, Pa; s. of Nicola Iacocca and Antoinette Perrotto; m. 1st Mary McCleary 1956 (died 1983); two d.; m. 2nd Peggy Johnson 1986 (divorced); m. 3rd Darrien Earle 1991; ed Lehigh and Princeton Univs; with Ford Motor Co. 1946; Dist Sales Man., Washington 1956; Ford Div. Truck Marketing Man. 1956; Car Marketing Man. 1957; Vice-Pres. and Gen. Man., Ford Div. 1960–65; Vice-Pres. Car and Truck Group 1965; Exec. Vice-Pres., North American Automotive Operations 1967; Exec. Vice-Pres., Ford Motor Co. and Pres. Ford North American Automotive Operations 1969–70, Pres. Ford Motor Co. 1970–78; Pres., COO Chrysler Corpn 1978–79, Chair. 1979–93, CEO 1979–93, Dir –1993; Prin. Iacocca Pnrs 1994–; Acting Chair. Kro Koo Roo Inc. 1998; Pres. Iacocca Assocs, Los Angeles 1994–; Founding Chair. and CEO EV Global Motors Co.; f. Olivio Premium Products 2000; Fellow, Princeton Univ.; mem. Soc. of Automotive Engineers; Chair. f Presidential Comm. to restore Statue of Liberty 1982–86; mem. Nat. Acad. of Eng 1986–; Founder and Chair. Iacocca Foundation 1984–; Kt, Order of Labour (Italy) 1989; Dr hc (Muhlenberg Coll., Babson Inst.); Detroit's Man of the Year 1982, Jefferson Award 1985. *Publications:* Iacocca, An Autobiography (with William Novak) 1984, Talking Straight 1988, Where Have All the Leaders Gone? 2007. *Address:* Iacocca Foundation, 867 Boylston Street, 6th Floor, Boston, MA 02116, USA (office). *Telephone:* (617) 267-7747 (office). *E-mail:* info@ iacoccafamilyfoundation.org. *Website:* www.iacoccafoundation.org; www .olivioproducts.com (office).

IACOVOU, Georgios Kyriakou, MA, MSc, MA, DIC; Cypriot politician and diplomatist; *Presidential Commissioner;* b. 19 July 1938, Peristeronopigi, Famagusta Dist; s. of Kyriacos Iacovou and Maria Michalopoulou; m. Jennifer Bradley 1963; one s. three d.; ed Greek Gymnasium for Boys, Famagusta, Univ. of London, UK, Univ. of Boston, USA; Eng, Cyprus Building and Road Construction Corpn Ltd 1960–61; Man. Electron Ltd, Nicosia 1961–63; with Operations Research and Finance Depts, British Railways Bd, London 1964–68; Sr Consultant (Man.), Price Waterhouse Assocs, London 1968–72; Dir Cyprus Productivity Centre, Nicosia 1972–76; Dir Special Service for Care and Rehabilitation of Displaced Persons 1974–76; Chief, E African Region, UNHCR, Geneva 1976–79; Amb. to FRG (also accred to Austria and Switzerland) 1979–83; Dir-Gen. Ministry of Foreign Affairs Jan.–Sept. 1983; Perm. Sec., Minister of Foreign Affairs 1983–93, 2003–06; High Commr to UK 2006–07; Presidential Commr 2008–, Adviser to Pres. and his Rep. of Intercommunal Talks; Pres. and CEO Nat. Foundation of Overseas and Repatriated Greeks 1993–97; presidential cand., Cyprus presidential elections 1998; Pres. Cttee of Ministers, Council of Europe 1983; participated in Commonwealth Heads of State and Govt Confs in Delhi 1983, Bahamas 1985, Vancouver 1987, Kuala Lumpur 1989 and non-Aligned Summit, Harare 1986, Belgrade 1989; Chair. Bd Hotel and Catering Inst. 1972–76; Chair. Ministerial Conf. of Non-Aligned Movt, Nicosia 1988; Chair. Ministerial Cttee on Role and Functioning, Non-Aligned Movt; Hon. Citizen, Tsalka, Georgia and City of Sappes, Thrace, Greece; Hon. Prof., Donetsk State Univ., Ukraine; Grosses Verdienstkreuz mit Stern und Schulterband (FRG), Grosses Goldenes Ehrenzeichen (Austria), Grand Cross, Order of Phoenix (Greece), Grand Cross of the Order of Isabella the Catholic (Spain), Grand Cross of the Order of Honour (Greece), Order of the Flag with Sash (Yugoslavia), Order of the Repub. First Class (Egypt), Grand Cross of Infante D. Henrique (Portugal), Decoration of the Cross of St Mark of the First Order of the Patriarchate of Alexandria and All Africa, Decoration of St Catherine's Monastery of Sinai, Order of Xirca Gloh Ir-Republica (Malta), Order of Cedar of Lebanon; Dr hc (State Univ. of Tbilisi, Georgia), (Panteion Univ. Athens), (State Univ. of Marloupol, Ukraine); Meritorious Service Award, Municipality of Peristeri, Athens. *Address:* Presidential Commissioner, Presidential Palace, 1400 Nicosia, Cyprus (office). *Telephone:* (22) 867508 (office). (22) 867404 (office). *Fax:* (22) 867554 (office). *E-mail:* george@iacovou.org (office). giacovou@presidency.gov .cy (office).

IALOMITIANU, Gheorghe; Romanian economist and politician; b. 14 Sept. 1959, Bran, Braşov Co.; m.; one c.; ed Univ. de Vest, Timişoara, Institut Int. d'Admin Publique, Paris, Swedish Nat. Tax Board; Economist, Fabrica de Scule Rasnov (tool mfr) 1983–85; teacher, A Barseanu Scoala Comerciala, Braşov 1983–95; Lecturer, Univ. Transilvania Braşov 1993–97, 2008–10; Dir Gen. DGFP (Public Finance Dept), Braşov 1997–2001, Jt Exec. Dir 2001–08; mem. Camera Deputaţilor (Parl.) for Braşov 2008–, fmr Vice-Pres. Parl. Budget and Finance Cttee; Minister of Public Finance 2010–12; mem. Democratic Liberal Party. *Publications:* 11 books on accounting, finance and taxation, 70 articles in Romanian and foreign specialist publications. *Address:* c/o Ministry of Public Finance, 050741 Bucharest 5, Str. Apolodor 17, Romania.

IALONGO, Giovanni; Italian business executive; *Chairman, Poste Italiane SpA;* Chair. Postel SpA 2007–; Special Commr IPOST (Italian Postal and Telecommunications Services Inst.); Chair. Poste Italiane SpA 2008–. *Address:* Poste Italiane SpA, Viale Europa 190, Rome 00144, Italy (office). *Telephone:* (06) 59587162 (office). *Fax:* (06) 59589100 (office). *E-mail:* info@posteitaliane.it (office). *Website:* www.poste.it (office).

IBARRETXE MARKUARTU, Juan José, BEcons; Spanish politician; b. 15 May 1957, Llodio, Alava; ed Llodio Secondary School, Univ. of the Basque Country; mem. Partido Nacionalista Vaso (PNV); Mayor of Llodio 1983–87; Pres. Alava Prov. Parl. 1986–91; mem. Basque Parl., Chair. Econ. and Budgetary Comm. 1986–90, 1991–94; Vice-Pres. Basque Govt and Minister for Inland Revenue and Public Admin 1995–98, Pres. 1999–2009; fmr mem. Univ. of the Basque Country Social Council. *Address:* Euzko Alderdi Jeltzalea-Partido Nacionalista Vasco, Sabin Etxea, Ibáñez de Bilbao 16, 48001 Bilbao, Spain.

IBBS, Sir (John) Robin, Kt, KBE, MA, DSc, LLD, AM IMechE, FCIB, FRSA, FRSocMed; British banker and business executive; b. 21 April 1926, Birmingham; s. of the late Prof. T. L. Ibbs and of Marjorie Ibbs (née Bell); m. 1st Iris Barbara Hall 1952 (died 2005); one d.; m. 2nd Penelope Ann Buckland 2006; ed West House School, Gresham's School, Upper Canada Coll., Toronto, Univ. of Toronto, Trinity Coll., Cambridge and Lincoln's Inn; Instructor Lt, RN 1947–49; Student Apprentice, C. A. Parsons & Co. Ltd 1949–51; called to Bar by Lincoln's Inn 1952; joined

ICI 1952, held various eng, tech., production, commercial and gen. man. appointments at Head Office, Gen. Chemicals Div. and Metals Div.; Man. Planning Dept, Imperial Metal Industries Ltd 1969–74, Exec. Dir 1972–74, Dir (non-exec.) 1974–76; Gen. Man. Planning, ICI 1974–76, Exec. Dir 1976–80, 1982–88; Dir ICI Americas Inc. 1976–80; Dir ICI Australia Ltd 1982–87; Dir Lloyds Bank PLC 1985–97, Deputy Chair. 1988–93, Chair. 1993–97; Deputy Chair. Lloyds Bank Canada 1989–90; Chair. Lloyds TSB Group PLC 1995–97; Chair. Lloyds Merchant Bank Holdings Ltd 1989–92; mem. Industrial Devt Advisory Bd, Dept of Industry 1978–80, Head, Cen. Policy Review Staff, Cabinet Office 1980–82; mem. Council, Chemical Industries Asscn 1976–80, 1982–88, Vice-Pres. 1983–87, Hon. mem. 1987; mem. Governing Body and Council, British Nat. Cttee, ICC 1976–80, Chair. Finance and Gen. Purposes Cttee 1976–80; mem. Council of CBI 1982–87; mem. Top Salaries Review Body 1983–88; mem. Council, Royal Inst. of Int. Affairs, Chatham House 1983–89; mem. Court, Cranfield Inst. of Tech. 1983–88; Adviser to the Prime Minister on Efficiency and Effectiveness in Govt 1983–88; mem. Advisory Cttee on Business Appointments 1991–98; second mem. Sierra Leone Arms Investigation 1998; Trustee and Deputy Chair. Isaac Newton Trust 1988–99; leader of review of House of Commons services 1990; Chair. Council, Univ. Coll., London 1989–95; Pres. Bankers Club 1994–95; Vice-Pres. Chartered Inst. of Bankers 1993–97; mem. Council Foundation for Science and Tech. 1997–2002; Chair. Salisbury Cathedral Close Preservation Soc. 1998–2009; Hon. Fellow, Univ. Coll., London 1993, Hon. Bencher Lincoln's Inn 1999; Hon. DSc (Bradford) 1986; Hon. LLD (Bath) 1993; British Inst. of Management Special Award 1988. *Leisure interests:* walking, natural history, gardening, social history, music and arts. *Address:* c/o Lloyds Banking Group, 25 Gresham Street, London, EC2V 7HN, England.

IBERS, James Arthur, PhD; American chemist and academic; *Charles E. and Emma H. Morrison Professor of Chemistry, Northwestern University;* b. 9 June 1930, Los Angeles, Calif.; s. of Max Ibers and Esther Ibers (née Imerman); m. Joyce Audrey Henderson 1951; one s. one d.; ed Calif. Inst. of Tech.; NSF Post-doctoral Fellow, Melbourne, Australia 1954–55; chemist, Shell Devt Co. 1955–61, Brookhaven Nat. Lab. 1961–64; mem. Faculty Northwestern Univ. 1964–, Prof. of Chem. 1964–85, Charles E. and Emma H. Morrison Prof. of Chem. 1986–; mem. NAS, American Acad. of Arts and Sciences, ACS, American Crystallographic Asscn; ACS Inorganic Chem. Award 1978, ACS Distinguished Service Award 1992, ACS Pauling Medal 1994, Distinguished Alumni Award, Calif. Inst. of Tech. 1997, American Crystallographic Asscn Buerger Award 2002. *Address:* Department of Chemistry, Tech G147, Northwestern University, Evanston, IL 60208-3113, USA (office). *Telephone:* (847) 491-5449 (office). *Fax:* (847) 491-2976 (office). *E-mail:* ibers@chem.northwestern.edu (office). *Website:* www.chem.northwestern.edu/ ~ibers (office).

IBOBI SINGH, Okram, BA; Indian politician and social worker; *Chief Minister of Manipur;* b. 19 June 1948, Thoubal Athokpam Makha Leikai; s. of Angoubi Singh and Lukamani Devi; m. Landhoni Devi; one s. two d.; mem. Manipur Legis. Ass. 1984–; Chair. Khadi and Village Industries Board 1985–88; fmr Minister of Municipal Admin, Housing and Urban Devt and of Industries, Manipur; Chief Minister of Manipur 2002–; Pres. Manipur Pradesh Congress Cttee 1999–; Sec. Congress Legislature Party. *Leisure interest:* reading. *Address:* Chief Minister's Secretariat, Imphal 795 001, Manipur, India (office). *Telephone:* (385) 2225206 (office); (385) 2221833 (office). *Fax:* (385) 2221398 (office). *E-mail:* cmmani@hub.nic .in (office). *Website:* www.manipur.nic.in (office).

IBRAGIMBEKOV, Maksud Mamed Ibragim ogli; Azerbaijani/Russian writer, scriptwriter and playwright; *Chairman, National Peace Committee of Azerbaijan;* b. 1935, Baku; s. of Mamed Ibragim Ibragimbekov and Fatima Alekper-kyzy Meshadibekova; brother of Rustam Ibragimbekov; m. Anna Yuryebna Ibragimbekova (née Gerulaitis); one s.; ed Baku Polytechnic Inst., High Scenario and Directoral Courses, Moscow; Supt Aztyazhpromstroi 1960–62; freelance scriptwriter, theatre dir 1964–; mem. USSR (now Russian) Union of Writers 1965–; mem. Azerbaijan Parl. 1985–2010; Pres. PEN Club, Azerbaijan 1991–2009; Chair. Nat. Peace Cttee of Azerbaijan 1984–, Nobility Ass. of Azerbaijan 1995–; Amb. for Peace; Order of Labour Red Banner 1981, Order of Glory of Azerbaijan Repub. 1995, Pope of Rome Praise 2002, Order of Independence (Azerbaijan) 2005, Order of Friendship (Russia) 2005, Order of Glory and Honor (Russia) 2010; State Prize of Azerbaijan Repub. 1975, People's Writer of Azerbaijan 1998. *Plays:* Mesozoic Story (Moscow Maly Theatre) 1975, Death of All the Good (Leningrad Theatre of Young Spectator) 1978, Men for Young Woman (Dramatic Theatre) 1992, The Oil Boom is Smiling on Everyone 2002, Restoran Final (Restaurant Final) (Baku Dramatic Theatre) 2006, Rolls Royce of Her Majesty (Baku Dramatic Theatre) 2009. *Films:* 23 films, including Latest Night of Childhood, Djabish-muallim, Who is Going to Travel to Truskavets?, Latest Interview, Etc. 23 films. *Television:* Gold Voyage 1993, The History with Happy End 1998. *Publications:* Who is Going to Travel to Truskavets?, There Was Never a Better Brother, Let Him Stay With Us; novels and prose in magazines and separate editions. *Leisure interests:* travelling, gardening. *Address:* 28 Boyuk Qala Str., 370004 Baku (office); 38 Kutkashenli Str., 370006 Baku, Azerbaijan (home). *Telephone:* (12) 4929843 (office); (12) 4975300 (home). *Fax:* (12) 4928459 (office). *E-mail:* maksud@planet-az.com (office); maksud@azeurotel.com (home).

IBRAGIMBEKOV, Rustam Mamed Ibragimovich; Azerbaijani/Russian screenwriter and writer; b. 5 Feb. 1939, Baku; s. of Mamed Ibragim Ibragimbekov and Fatima Alekper-kyzy Meshadibekova; m. Shokhrat Soltan-kyzy Ibragimbekova; one s., one d.; brother of Maksud Ibragimbekov; ed Azerbaijan State Inst. of Oil and Gas; Chair. Confed. Unions of Cinematographers of CIS and Baltic States; Sec. Union of Cinematographers of Russian Fed.; Chair. Jewish Film Festival in Moscow; Chair. Union of Cinematographers of Azerbaijan, Confederation of Filmmakers' Unions (CFU); Sec., Russian Filmmakers' Union; mem. European Film Acad. Felix, American Acad. of Cinema Oscar; Order for Service to Motherland, Commdr des Arts et des Lettres; USSR State Prize 1981, State Prizes of Russian Fed. 1993, 1998, 1999, 2000, State Prize of Azerbaijan SSR 1980, Comsomol Prize 1979. *Film scripts include:* In This Young Town 1971, White Sun of the Desert 1971, Then I Said No 1974, Heart... Heart 1976, Country House for One Family 1978, Strategy of Risk 1979, Interrogation 1979, Mystery of Vessel Watch 1981, Birthday 1983, In Front of the Closed Door 1985, Save Me, My Talisman 1986, Free Fall, Other Life 1987, Cathedral of Air 1989, Hitchhiking, Taxi-Blues (producer) 1989, Seven Days After Murder, To See Paris and To Die 1990, Duba-Duba (producer) 1990, Urga Territory of Love (producer) 1992, Destroyed Bridges (also producer) 1993, Tired with the Sun 1994, The Man Who Tried (jtly) 1997, Barber of Siberia, Family (also dir and producer) 1998, East–West 1999; Mysteria 2000, Karu süda 2001, Nomad (The Warrior) (also producer) 2005, Proshaj, yuzhny gorod (also producer) 2006, Birds of Paradise 2008, Gagma napiri (adaptation) 2009, Burnt by the Sun 2 2010. *Plays:* 15 plays produced including A Woman Behind a Closed Door, Funeral in California, A House on the Sand, Like a Lion. *Publications:* 10 books and collections of stories including Ultimatum 1983, Woken Up with a Smile 1985, Country House 1988, Selected Stories 1989, Solar Plexus 1996. *Address:* Russian Filmmakers' Union, Moscow 123825, 3 Vasilevskaya St, Russia (office); Lermontova str. 3, Apt. 54, 370006 Baku, Azerbaijan (home). *Telephone:* (495) 250-18-41 (office); (12) 4926313 (home).

IBRAHIM, Abdul Latif, DVM, MSc, PhD; Bangladeshi professor of veterinary physiology; b. 1938; ed East Pakistan Agric. Univ., Univs of Hawaii and California, USA; Lecturer, Faculty of Veterinary Medicine and Animal Science, Univ. of Pertanian, Malaysia 1973, later Prof., Dean 1983–93, now Prof. Emer.; known for research on Newcastle Disease; Fellow, Islamic Acad. of Sciences 1988–; Foundation Fellow, Malaysia Acad. of Sciences; Svon Brohult Award, First Int. Science Award (jtly), Malaysia. *Publications:* over 120 publs on animal science. *Address:* c/o Malaysia Academy of Sciences (Akademi Sains Malaysia), 902-4 Jalan Tun Ismail, 50480 Kuala Lumpur, Malaysia (office).

IBRAHIM, Dato' Seri Encik Anwar bin, BA; Malaysian politician; *Advisor, Parti Keadilan Rakyat (People's Justice Party);* b. 10 Aug. 1947, Penang; m. Dr. Wan Azizah Wan Ismail; six c.; ed Univ. of Malaya; Pres. UMNO Youth Movt 1982–; Vice-Pres. UMNO 1982–; Head UMNO Permatang Pauh Div. 1982–; Deputy Minister, Prime Minister's Dept 1982; Minister of Sport, Youth and Culture 1983, of Agric. 1984–86, of Educ. 1986–91, of Finance 1991–98; Deputy Prime Minister 1993–98; arrested Sept. 1998; sentenced to six years' imprisonment for corruption April 1999; put on trial for sodomy 1999; sentenced to nine years' imprisonment and banned for five years from running for public office after release; sodomy conviction overturned, released from prison Sept. 2004; Visiting Lecturer, Johns Hopkins Univ., Georgetown Univ., USA and Univ. of Oxford, UK 2005–07; Advisor People's Justice Party (Parti Keadilan Rakyat, PKR) 2006–; Chair. Foundation for the Future 2006–; Hon. Pres. AccountAbility 2005–. *Address:* People's Justice (Party Parti Keadilan Rakyat, PKR), 110–3 Jalan Tun Sambanthan, 50470 Kuala Lumpur, Malaysia (office). *Telephone:* (3) 22723220 (office). *Fax:* (3) 22721220 (office). *E-mail:* contact@partikeadilanrakyat.org (office). *Website:* www.keadilanrakyat.org (office); www.anwaribrahim.com (home).

IBRAHIM, Fahad Rashid al-; Kuwaiti business executive and international organization executive; currently Dir-Gen. Inter-Arab Investment Guarantee Corpn. *Address:* Inter-Arab Investment Guarantee Corporation, PO Box 23568, Safat 13096, Kuwait City, Kuwait (office). *Telephone:* 4959000 (office). *Fax:* 4841240 (office). *E-mail:* fahad@iai.org.kw (office). *Website:* (office).

IBRAHIM, Fahmi Said; Comoran lawyer and politician; Minister of External Relations and Cooperation 2010–11. *Address:* c/o Ministry of External Relations and Cooperation, BP 428, Moroni, Comoros (office). *E-mail:* mirex@snpt.km (office). *Website:* www.beit-salam.km (office).

IBRAHIM, Fakhruddin G., LLM; Pakistani lawyer, government official and fmr judge; *Chief Election Commissioner;* b. 12 Feb. 1928, Gujarat, India; ed Sindh Muslim Coll.; fmr Lecturer, Sindh Law Coll.; est. Fakhruddin G Ibrahim and Co. (law firm); Attorney-Gen. 1971–77; Gov. of Sindh 1989–90; fmr Judge Supreme Court, currently Sr Advocate; Interim Minister of Law July–Oct. 1993, Interim Minister of Justice 1996–97; Chief Election Commr 2012–; apptd Chair. Anti-Doping Appeals Cttee 2006; Hon. JD (Sindh Law Coll.) 1960. *Address:* Election Commission of Pakistan, Secretariat, Election House, Constitution Avenue, G-5/2, Islamabad, Pakistan (office). *Telephone:* (51) 9201975 (office). *Fax:* (51) 9205402 (office). *E-mail:* info@ecp.gov.pk (office). *Website:* www.ecp.gov.pk (office).

IBRAHIM, Ibrahim al-, PhD; Qatari economist and academic; *Economic Adviser to the Emir of Qatar;* ed New York Univ., USA; Assoc. Prof. of Business, Econs and Quantitative Methods, Univ. of Hawaii, Honolulu, USA 1970–78; Dir Econ. Dept, Org. of Arab Petroleum Exporting Countries (Kuwait) 1979–86; Sr Economist, Oxford Inst. for Energy Studies, UK 1986–88; Econ. Adviser to Sheikh Hamad Bin Khalifa al-Thani, Emir of Qatar 1988–; Sec. Gen. Gen. Secr. for Devt Planning 2006–11; now also leading Qatar's First Nat. Devt Strategy; Vice-Chair. RasGas Co. Ltd, Chair. Marketing Cttee; Vice-Chair. Qatar Petroleum International and Industrial Bank; mem. Bd of Dirs Qatar Petroleum, Industries Qatar, Qatar Central Bank; Liquefied Natural Gas Visionary Award 2009, ranked by Arabian Business amongst the Power 500: The World's Most Influential Arabs (69th) 2012. *Publications:* has published research internationally in the areas of forecasting, business economics and energy economics. *Address:* RasGas Co. Ltd, PO Box 24200, Doha, Qatar (office). *Telephone:* 44738000 (office). *Fax:* 44833855 (office). *E-mail:* io@rasgas.com (office). *Website:* www.rasgas.com (office).

IBRAHIM, Mohamed (Mo), BSc, MSc, PhD; British (b. Sudanese) telecommunications industry executive; *Founder, Mo Ibrahim Foundation;* b. 1946; ed Univ. of Alexandria, Egypt, Univs of Bradford and Birmingham, UK; worked for Sudan Telecom; Tech. Dir Cellnet (subsidiary of British Telecom) 1983–89, involved in establishing the UK's first mobile telephone network; f. MSI consultancy and software firm 1989, later renamed Celtel) 1998, built co. into one of leading mobile telephone networks in Africa, sold Celtel to Kuwaiti MTC 2005; Founder and mem. Bd of Dirs Mo Ibrahim Foundation, foundation's work includes Ibrahim Index of African Governance and Prize for Achievement in African Leadership; mem. Africa Regional Advisory Bd, London Business School; ranked by Forbes magazine amongst The World's Most Powerful People (71st) 2013. *Address:* Mo Ibrahim Foundation, 3rd Floor North, 35 Portman Square, London, W1H 6LR, England (office). *E-mail:* info@moibrahimfoundation.org (office). *Website:* www.moibrahimfoundation.org (office).

IBRAHIM, Mohamed; Maldivian government official; *President, Elections Commission of Maldives;* headed two state cos before becoming Deputy Minister of Construction and Infrastructure in admin of Maumoon Gayoom; then moved to Interim Election Comm., Chair. interim Election Comm. throughout its period, Pres., Elections Comm. of Maldives 2008–; fmr mem. Dhivehi Rayyithunge Party (DRP—Maldivian People's Party); mem. Maldivian Democratic Party. *Address:* Elections Commission of Maldives, PA Complex, 3rd Floor, Hilaalee Magu, Malé, Maldives (office). *Telephone:* 3324426 (office). *Fax:* 3323997 (office). *E-mail:* info@elections.gov.mv (office). *Website:* www.elections.gov.mv (office).

IBRAHIM, Qasim, (Buruma Qasim); Maldivian politician and business executive; *Leader, Jumhooree Party;* b. 10 Feb. 1952, Malé; s. of Hawwa Ibrahim; m.; four s. four d.; began career as clerk at Govt Hosp., Malé 1969, accountant 1972–73; Man. M/S Alia Furniture Mart 1973; subsequently worked for Crescent (trading org.) 1973; joined outlet of Maldivian Govt Bodu Store (now known as State Trading Org.) 1974; set up own trading business in 1976, registered business as Villa Shipping and Trading Co. Ltd 1986, Villa Shipping (Singapore) Pte Ltd was incorporated in Singapore 1991, opened offices in Frankfurt, Germany 1996, est. Villa Hotels, Tokyo 2001, Villa Hotels, Hong Kong 2002, currently Chair. and Man. Dir Villa Group of Cos; mem. Parl. 1989–; Founding mem. Maldivian Democratic Party 2001; Minister of Finance and Treasury 2005–08, of Home Affairs 2008; Gov. Maldives Monetary Authority –2008; f. Jumhooree Party (Republican Party) 2008, currently Leader; fmr Pres. People's Special Majlis; cand. in presidential election 2013; fmr Pres. South Asian Asscn for Regional Cooperation Chamber of Commerce and Industry; Founder-mem. and fmr Pres. Maldives Nat. Chamber of Commerce and Industry; Founder-mem., Vice-Pres. and mem. Bd Maldives Asscn of Tourism Industry; mem. Bd Maldives Ports Authority; fmr mem. Bd Bank of Maldives. *Address:* Jumhooree Party (Republican Party), M. Chan'beyleege, 4th Floor, Malé (office); Huravee Building, 3rd Floor, Ameer Ahmed Magu, Malé 20-05 (office); Villa Hotels, Villa Building, Ibrahim Hassandidi Magu, PO Box 2073, Malé, Maldives (office); M-Maafannu Villa, Malé (home). *Telephone:* 3309595 (office); 3316161. *Fax:* 3306699 (office); 3314565. *E-mail:* jumhooreepartysg@gmail.com (office); qasim@villa.com.mv (home); info@villahotels.com.mv (office). *Website:* www.jumhooreeparty.org.mv (office); www.villahotels.com (home).

IBRAHIM, Sheikh Walid al-; Saudi Arabian broadcasting executive; *Chairman, Middle East Broadcasting Centre;* ed completed his higher educ. in USA; f. ARA Productions and TV Studios; f. Middle East Broadcasting Corpn (first ind. Pan-Arabic entertainment channel), London, UK 1991, opened Beirut office 2000, moved HQ to Dubai 2002, currently Chair. Middle East Broadcasting Centre; launched Al Arabiya 2003; f. MBC Films 2008; mem. Advisory Bd The Mohammed Bin Rashid School for Communication at the American Univ., Dubai; named by Amwal magazine amongst the top 20 Prominent Gulf Businessmen 2005, ranked by Arabian Business as the 27th most influential Arab among 100 others 2007, Media Man of the Year, 4th MENA Cristal Awards (Lebanon) 2008, Knight Award, Arab League, Innovator of the Year Award, Arabian Business, chosen as the first amongst the top 50 players in MENA's media, marketing and advertising industry 2011, ranked by Gulf News as the world's 66th most influential Arab personality amongst 100 others 2012, ranked by Arabian Business amongst the Power 500: The World's Most Influential Arabs (24th) 2012. *Address:* Middle East Broadcasting Centre, PO Box 76267, Dubai, United Arab Emirates (office). *Telephone:* (4) 3919999 (office). *Fax:* (4) 3919900 (office). *E-mail:* infotv@mbc.ae (office). *Website:* www.mbc.net (office).

IBRAHIM, Yusuf Hasan; Somali politician and diplomatist; *Minister of Foreign Affairs;* fmr Amb.; Minister of Foreign Affairs 2002–04, 2010–. *Address:* Ministry of Foreign Affairs, 1 Villa Somalia, 2525 Mogadishu, Somalia (office). *Telephone:* (5) 424640 (office). *Website:* www.mfa.somaligov.net (office).

IBRAHIMI, Abdul Rauf, BA; Afghan politician; *Speaker, Wolesi Jirga;* b. 1962, Hazrati Amam Saheeb Dist; m.; three s. five d.; ed Kabul Univ.; fought with Hezb-e Islami against Soviets during invasion of Afghanistan in 1980s; Commdr Sherkhan Bandar 1993, later Commdr of Third Southern Border Zone, apptd Commdr of Border Forces 2002; mem. Wolesi Jirga (House of Reps) from Kunduz 2005–, Speaker, Wolesi Jirga 2011–; mem. Emergency Loya Jirga 2002. *Leisure interest:* reading. *Address:* Office of the Speaker, Wolesi Jirga, Kabul, Afghanistan (office). *Telephone:* (70) 5100500 (office). *E-mail:* ibrahimi_999@yahoo.com (office). *Website:* wj.parliament.af/english.aspx (office).

IBRAHIMI, Bedredin, LLB; Macedonian legal administrator and politician; b. 25 Oct. 1952, Mala Recica, nr Tetovo; ed Pristina Univ.; fmr doctor; Sr Officer for Legal Affairs and Sec. of Poloska Kotlina Co., Tetovo Agricultural Complex, Belgrade 1976–81; Officer in charge of Gen. Legal Affairs and Sec. Jelak Tetovo Co., Interpromet Complex 1981–89; with Tekom-Tetovo Trade Co. 1990–96; Sec. of Council, Municipality of Tetovo 1997–98; fmr Gen. Sec. Democratic Party of Albanians (DPA); Deputy Prime Minister of Macedonia 1998–2002, apptd Minister of Labour and Social Welfare 1998. *Address:* c/o Democratic Party of Albanians (Partia Demokratike Shqiptare), Tetovo, Maršal Tito 2, Macedonia (office).

IBRAHIMOVIĆ, Muhamed (Rasim); Bosnia and Herzegovina politician; b. 8 Jan. 1960, Stjepan Polje, Gračanica; m. Alma Ibrahimović; two s.; ed Faculty of Political Sciences, Univ. of Sarajevo; spent three years in Baghdad, Iraq working for several cos from Bosnia and Herzegovina and Slovenia; mem. Party of Democratic Action (Stranka Demokratske Akcije—SDA) 1991–2009, also mem. SDA Bd; Pres. Municipal Council of Gračanica 1991–98, held several positions, including Sec., Municipal Secr. for Defence and Pres. Exec. Cttee 1992–95; mem. Cantonal Cttee, SDA Tuzla Canton 1996–2000; Minister for Relations with Int. and Humanitarian Orgs in first Govt of Tuzla-Podrinje 1994–96; Mayor of Gračanica 1996–2000; Chief of Defence Ministry of Defence, Tuzla Canton Fed. 2000–02; Councillor, Municipal Council of Gračanica 2000–02; mem. Parl., Tuzla Canton 2000–02; elected Deputy to House of Reps, Fed. of Bosnia and Herzegovina 1998, 2002, 2006, 2010, Pres. Comm. for Local Govt, mem. Denationalization and Privatization Cttee, Cttee on Labour and Social Policy, Selection and Appointment Cttee, Speaker, House of Reps 2002–06; unsuccessful cand. for Mayor of Gračanica 2008; Minister of Defence May–Oct. 2012; mem. Governing Bd, Univ. Clinical Center, Tuzla. *Address:* c/o Ministry of Defence, 71000 Sarajevo, Hamdije Kreševljakovića 98, Bosnia and Herzegovina.

IBRAIMOVA, Elmira Sultanovna; Kyrgyzstani diplomatist and economist; *Executive Director, Community Development and Investment Agency (ARIS);* b. 13 April 1962, Frunze (now Bishkek); ed Moscow State Univ.; Perm. Rep. to UN, New York 1999–2002; Exec. Dir Community Devt and Investment Agency, Bishek 2004–; Vice Prime Minister 2008; Coordinator of Interim Govt for Social Affairs 2010; Chair. Accounts Chamber 2012–; Hon. Freeman of Gulchinskiy ayil kenesh of Alay rayon of Osh Oblast 2007; World Women's Summit Foundation Prize 2005. *Address:* Community Development and Investment Agency (ARIS), 102 Bokonbaev Street, Bishkek 720040, Kyrgyzstan (office). *Telephone:* (312) 30-18-05 (office). *Fax:* (312) 62-47-48 (office). *E-mail:* office@aris.kg (office). *Website:* www.aris.kg (office).

IBROW, Salim Aliyow; Somali politician; fmr Sec. of State; Deputy Prime Minister 2004, Minister of Finance 2004–05, of Livestock 2005–07, of Higher Educ. and Culture 2007, and Deputy Prime Minister 2007, Acting Prime Minister Oct.–Nov. 2007, Minister of Justice and Religious Affairs 2007; mem. Transitional Fed. Parl. 2004–. *Address:* Transitional Parliament, Mogadishu, Somalia (office).

IBUKI, Bunmei, BA; Japanese politician; *Speaker, House of Representatives;* b. 9 Jan. 1938, Kyoto; ed Kyoto Univ.; mem. staff, Ministry of Finance from 1960, Dir Treasury Div. 1980, Sec. to Minister of Finance 1982; Sec., Japanese Embassy, London 1965–69; mem. LDP, Deputy Sec.-Gen. 1996, Chair. Public Relations HQ 1999, Research Comm. on the Pension System 1999, Party Org. HQ 2000, Working Group of the Research Comm. on the Tax System 2004, Chair. Shisuikai (Ex-Kamei Ibuki faction) 2005–, Sec.-Gen. 2007–08; mem. House of Reps for Kyoto 1st Dist 1983–96, Kyoto 1st Dist (single-member) 1996–2009, for Kinki PR block 2009–, Chair. Standing Cttee on Educ. 1994, Speaker 2012–; Parl. Vice-Minister of Health 1990; Minister of Labour 1997–98; Minister of State for Disaster Man. 2001, for Nat. Emergency Legislation 2000; Chair. Nat. Public Safety Comm. 2000–01; Minister of Educ., Culture, Sports, Science and Tech. 2006–07, of Finance 2008. *Leisure interests:* go (board game), rakugo, dining tours, tennis, kimono. *Address:* The House of Representatives, 1-7-1 Nagatacho, Chiyoda-ku, Tokyo 100-0014, Japan (office). *Telephone:* (3) 3581-5111 (office). *E-mail:* webmaster@shugiin.go.jp (office). *Website:* www.shugiin.go.jp (office).

ICAHN, Carl Celian, BA; American business executive; *Chairman, Starfire Holding Corporation;* b. 16 Feb. 1936, Queens, New York; m. 1st Liba Icahn (divorced 1999); two c.; m. 2nd Gail Golden 1999; ed Princeton Univ. and New York Univ. School of Medicine; apprentice broker, Dreyfus Corpn, New York 1960–63; Options Man. Tessel, Patrick & Co., New York 1963–64, Gruntal & Co. 1964–68; Chair. and Pres. Icahn & Co., Inc 1968–, Chair. and Pres. Icahn Holding Corpn (now Starfire Holding Corpn) New York 1984–, Chair. ACF Industries Inc. (Starfire subsidiary), St. Charles, Mo. 1984–, American Real Estate Pnrs 1990–, American Property Investors Inc. 1990–, American Railcar Industries 1990–; Chair. Lowestfare.com, LLC 1998, GB Holdings 2000–, XO Communications 2003–; Chair. Trans World Airlines Inc. 1986–99, Manpintour Holdings LLC 1998–2002; Pres. Stratosphere Corpn 1998–; mem. Bd of Dirs ImClone 2006–, Yahoo Inc. 2008–09. *Address:* Starfire Holding Corporation, 767 5th Avenue, 47th Floor, New York, NY 10153-0023 (office); Icahn and Company Inc., 100 South Bedford Road, Mount Kisco, NY 10549-3425, USA (office). *Telephone:* (212) 702-4300 (Starfire); (home).

ICE CUBE; American rap artist and actor; b. (O'Shea Jackson), 15 June 1969, Los Angeles; ed Univ. of Phoenix; formed duo (with Sir Jinx), CIA, then leader of group, HBO; founder mem., N.W.A. 1987–89; formed rap group, Da Lench Mob 1989–; simultaneous solo artist 1989–; collaborated with Public Enemy; began own corpn, producing work by protegée YoYo 1989–; numerous tours; founder mem., Westside Connection 1996–; Founder Cube Vision Productions (film production co.). *Films:* Boyz n the Hood (actor) 1991, Trespass (actor) 1992, The Glass Shield (actor) 1994, Higher Learning (actor) 1995, Friday (actor, writer, exec. prod.) 1995, Dangerous Ground (actor, exec. prod.) 1997, Anaconda (actor) 1997, The Player's Club (actor, writer, exec. prod.) 1998, I Got the Hook Up (actor) 1998, Three Kings (actor) 1999, Thicker Than Water (actor) 1999, Next Friday (actor, writer, exec. prod.) 2000, Ghosts of Mars (actor) 2001, All About the Benjamins (actor, writer, exec. prod.) 2001, Barbershop (actor) 2002, Friday After Next (actor, writer, exec. prod.) 2002, Torque (actor) 2004, Barbershop 2: Back in Business (actor, exec. prod.) 2004, Are We There Yet? (actor, prod.) 2005–, xXx 2: The Next Level (actor) 2005, Are We Done Yet? (actor) 2007, First Sunday (prod.) 2008, The Longshots (prod.) 2008, The Janky Promoters (prod.) 2009, Lottery Ticket (prod.) 2010, 21 Jump Street 2012. *Recordings include:* albums: with N.W.A.: N.W.A. And The Posse 1987, Straight Outta Compton 1989; solo: AmeriKKKa's Most Wanted 1990, Death Certificate 1991, The Predator 1992, Lethal Injection 1993, Bootlegs And B Sides 1994, War And Peace 1998, War And Peace 2: The Peace Disc 2000, Greatest Hits 2001, Laugh Now, Cry Later 2006, Raw Footage 2008, I Am the West 2010; with da Lench Mob: Guerillas In Tha Mist 1992, Planet Of Da Apes 1994; with Westside Connection: Bow Down 1996. *Address:* Cube Vision Productions, 2900 West Olympic Blvd., Santa Monica CA 94404 (office); c/o Capitol Records, 1750 N Vine Street, Hollywood, CA 90028, USA (home). *Telephone:* (310) 255-7100 (Cube Vision) (office). *Fax:* (310) 255-7163 (Cube Vision) (office). *Website:* www.icecubemusic.com; www.icecube.com

ICE-T; American rap artist and actor; b. (Tracey Marrow), 14 Feb. 1959, Newark, NJ; m. Darlene Ortiz; one c.; recording artist 1987–; mem., Body Count 1992–; world-wide tours, numerous television and film appearances; created Rhyme Syndicate Records early 1990s; involved in two youth intervention programmes, Hands Across Watts and South Central Love; Rolling Stone Readers' Poll Best Male Rapper 1992. *Recordings include:* albums: solo: The Pimp Penal Code, Sex, Money, Guns, Rhyme Pays 1987, Power 1988, The Iceberg 1989, O. G. Original Gangster 1991, Home Invasion 1993, VI: Return Of The Real 1996, Seventh Deadly Sin 1999, Ice-T Presents the Westside 2004; with Body Count: Body Count 1992, Born Dead 1994, Violent Demise, The Last Days 1997. *Films:* Breakin' 1984, Breakin' 2: Electric Boogaloo 1984, New Jack City 1991, Ricochet 1991, Trespass 1992, Why Colors? 1992, Who's the Man? 1993, Surviving the Game 1994, Tank Girl 1995, Johnny Mnemonic 1995, Mean Guns 1997, The Deli 1997, Below Utopia 1997, Crazy Six 1998, Urban Menace 1999, Final Voyage 1999, Jacob Two Two Meets the Hooded Fang 1999, Corrupt 1999, The Wrecking Crew 1999, Sonic Impact 1999, Point Doom 1999, Judgment Day 1999, The Heist 1999, Frezno Smooth 1999, Stealth Fighter 2000, Leprechaun in the Hood 2000, Luck of the Draw 2000, The Alternate 2000, Sanity, Aiken's Artifact 2000, Guardian 2000, Gangland 2000, 3000 Miles to Graceland 2001, Deadly Rhapsody 2001, 'R Xmas 2001, Ticker 2001, Out Kold 2001, Ablaze 2001, Tara 2001, Stranded 2001, Kept 2001, Crime Partners 2000, Air Rage 2001, Tracks 2002, Pimpin' 101 2002, On the Edge 2002, Lexie 2004, Copy That 2006, Santorini Blue 2010. *Television:* Players (series) 1997, Exiled (film) 1998, Law & Order: Special Victims Unit (series) 2000–, The Disciples (film) 2000, Ice T's Rap School (series) 2006, The Magic 7 (voice) 2007. *Publications:* The Iceberg/Freedom of Speech... Just Watch What You Say 1989, The Ice Opinion 1994. *Address:* c/o Rhyme Syndicate Management, Warner Bros Records, 75 Rockefeller Plaza, New York, NY 10019-6908, USA (office). *Website:* www.icet.com.

ICHIKAWA, En'o II; Japanese actor; *Founder, Ennosuke Kabuki;* b. (Kinoshi Masahiko), 9 Dec. 1939; s. of Ichikawa Danshiro III (died 1963); grands. of En'o (died 1963); m. Teruyuki Kagawa aka Chuusha Ichikawa; ed Keio Univ.; stage debut aged seven; studied under experimentalist Kabuki actor En'o; took official name Ennosuke III 1963; est. ind. experimental group and spearheaded reformation and modernization of traditional Kabuki theatre; f. 21st Century Kabuki Co.; cr. new style of energetic, fast-paced Kabuki, called Super Kabuki; producer, dir and lead actor in Super Kabuki shows 1986–; teachings, lectures, tours and performances world-wide; became En'o II June 2012. *Address:* Kabuki-za, 4-12-15 Ginza, Chuo-ku, Tokyo, Japan (office).

ICHIKAWA, Yasuo; Japanese politician; b. 6 Feb. 1942, Ishikawa Pref.; ed Mie Univ.; with Ministry of Agric., Forestry and Fisheries 1965–90; mem. Ishikawa Pref. Ass. 1991–96; mem. House of Reps for Ishikawa 1996–2005, mem. Cttee on Agric., Forestry and Fisheries, Cttee on Land, Infrastructure, Transport and Tourism, Cttee on Fundamental Nat. Policies; mem. House of Councillors for Ishikawa 2007–, mem. Cttee on Foreign Affairs and Defence, Cttee on Agric., Forestry and Fisheries, Special Cttee on Disasters; fmr mem. Shinshinto (New Frontier Party), Liberal Party; mem. Democratic Party of Japan (DPJ), Deputy Chair. DPJ Policy Research Cttee, Chair. DPJ Policy Discussion Panel; Minister of Defence 2011–12. *Address:* c/o Ministry of Defence, 5-1, Ichigaya, Honmura-cho, Shinjuku-ku, Tokyo 162-8801, Japan.

ICHIMIYA, Tadao; Japanese business executive; *Representative Director, President and Chief Operating Officer, Yamada Denki Company Ltd;* b. 13 Aug. 1955; ed Soka Univ.; joined Yamada Denki Co. Ltd 1983, has served in various exec. positions including Vice-Pres., Dir of Product Planning, Man. Dir, Chief Dir of Admin, Sr Man. Dir, Deputy Chief Dir of Sales, Chief Dir of Product Admin Business, Chief Dir of IT Business, Exec. Vice-Pres. –1983, Rep. Dir, Pres. and COO 1983–. *Address:* Yamada Denki Co. Ltd, 4-40-11 Hiyoshi-cho, Maebashi 371-0017, Gunma, Japan (office). *Telephone:* (2) 7233-5522 (office). *Fax:* (2) 2 7233-3309 (office); (2) 7233-3568 (office). *E-mail:* info@yamada-denki.jp (office). *Website:* www.yamada-denki.jp (office).

IDA, Yoshinori; Japanese automotive industry executive; *Chairman and Representative Director, Isuzu Motors Limited;* b. 1943; joined Izuzu 1966, Man. Dir responsible for domestic sales, eng, Gen. Motors affairs and portfolio integration, Isuzu Motors Ltd –2000, Rep. Dir, Pres. and COO 2000–07, Chair. and Rep. Dir 2007–. *Address:* Isuzu Motors Ltd, 26-1 Minami 6-chome, Shinagawa-ku, Tokyo 140-8722, Japan (office). *Telephone:* (3) 5471-1141 (office). *Fax:* (3) 5471-1043 (office). *E-mail:* info@isuzu.com (office). *Website:* www.isuzu.com (office).

IDEI, Nobuyuki, BA; Japanese business executive; *CEO, Quantum Leaps Corporation;* b. 1937, Tokyo; m. Teruyo Idei; one d.; ed Waseda Univ., Institut des hautes études internationales, Geneva, Switzerland; joined Sony Corpn 1960, est. Sony of France 1968, fmrly Head of Corp. Communications and Brand Image, Pres. and Rep. Dir Sony Corpn 1995–99, Pres. and CEO 1999–2000, Chair. and CEO 2000–05, Chair. Advisory Bd 2005–; Founder and CEO Quantum Leaps Corpn (man. consulting firm) 2006–; Counsellor, Bank of Japan 1999–2007; mem. Bd of Dirs General Motors 1999–2003, Nestlé SA 2001–, Accenture 2006–, Baidu.com Inc. 2007–, FreeBit Co. Ltd; mem. IT Strategy Council (advisory cttee to Japan's Prime Minister) 2000–05, Chair. July–Nov. 2000; Co-Chair. Admin. Reform, Nippon Keidanren (Japanese Business Fed.) 2002–03, Vice-Chair. 2003–07; Chair. Nat. Conf. on Fostering Beautiful Forests in Japan 2007–. *Leisure interests:* music, cinema, golf, reading. *Address:* Quantum Leaps Corporation, Parkside 6 #502, 9-5-12 Akasaka, Minato-ku, Tokyo 107-0052, Japan (office). *Telephone:* (3) 5785-3968 (office). *Fax:* (3) 5785-3969 (office). *Website:* www.qxl.jp (office).

IDEMITSU, Akira, BEcons; Japanese oil industry executive; b. 5 May 1932, Tokyo; ed Univ. of Tokyo; joined Idemitsu Kosan Co. Ltd April 1961, Gen. Man., Yokohama Br. 1977–79, Deputy Gen. Man., Marketing Dept 1979–81, Dir and Gen. Man. Hokkaido Refinery 1981–83, Gen. Man. Overseas Operations 1983–91, also Man. Dir 1988–91, Pres. Idemitsu Oil Devt Co. Ltd 1991–93, Sr Man. Dir Idemitsu 1993–95, Exec. Vice-Pres. 1995–98, Pres. and Rep. Dir 1998–2002, Chair. and Rep. Dir 2002–09. *Address:* Idemitsu Kosan Co. Ltd, 1-1 Marunouchi 3-chome, Chiyoda-ku, Tokyo, Japan (office). *Telephone:* (3) 3213-3115 (office). *Fax:* (3) 3213-9354 (office). *Website:* www.idemitsu.co.jp (office).

IDJI, Hon. Antoine Kolawolé; Benin politician; b. 31 Dec. 1946, Kétou; Minister of Foreign Affairs and African Integration 1998; Deputy to Nat. Ass., Pres. 2003–07; cand. in presidential election 2006; fmr Chair. African Parliamentarians' Forum for New Partnership for Africa's Devt (NePAD); Gen. Co-ordinator of The Union is the Nation 2010–11. *Address:* c/o Office of the President, Assemblée Nationale, BP 371, Porto-Novo, Benin. *Telephone:* 20212159.

IDLE, Eric, BA; British writer, lyricist and actor; b. 29 March 1943, South Shields, Tyne and Wear, England; m. 1st Lynn Ashley (divorced); one s.; m. 2nd Tania Kosevich; one d.; ed Royal School, Wolverhampton and Pembroke Coll., Cambridge. *Films:* Albert Carter, Q.O.S.O. (writer) 1968, And Now for Something Completely Different (actor, writer) 1971, Monty Python and the Holy Grail (actor, writer, exec. prod.) 1975, Life of Brian (actor, writer) 1979, The Meaning of Life (actor, writer) 1983, Yellowbeard (actor) 1983, European Vacation (actor) 1985, The Transformers: The Movie (voice) 1986, The Adventures of Baron Munchausen (actor) 1988, Nuns on the Run (actor) 1990, Missing Pieces (actor) 1991, Too Much Sun (actor) 1991, Mom and Dad Save the World (actor) 1992, Splitting Heirs (actor, writer, exec. prod.) 1993, Casper (actor) 1995, The Wind in the Willows (actor)

1996, Quest for Camelot (voice) 1998, Rudolph the Red-Nosed Reindeer: The Movie (voice) 1998, The Secret of NIMH 2: Timmy to the Rescue (voice) 1998, Pirates: 3D Show (actor, writer) 1999, Journey into Your Imagination (actor) 1999, Hercules: Zero to Hero (voice) 1999, South Park: Bigger Longer & Uncut (voice) 1999, Dudley Do-Right (actor) 1999, Brightness (actor) 2000, 102 Dalmatians (voice) 2000, Pinocchio (voice) 2002, Hollywood Homicide (actor) 2003, Ella Enchanted (actor) 2004, The Nutcracker and the Mouseking (voice) 2004, Shrek the Third (voice) 2007, Delgo (voice) 2008. *Television:* Alice in Wonderland (actor) 1966, The Frost Report (series, writer) 1966, No, That's Me Over Here! (series, writer) 1967, At Last the 1948 Show (series, actor) 1967, Do Not Adjust Your Set (series, actor and writer) 1967–69, Simply Sheila (writer) 1968, According to Dora (series, writer) 1968, We Have Ways of Making You Laugh (series, actor and writer) 1968, Broaden Your Mind (series, writer) 1968, Hark at Barker (series, writer) 1969, Monty Python's Flying Circus (four series, actor and writer) 1969–74, Euroshow 71 (actor) 1971, The Two Ronnies (series, writer) 1971, The Ronnie Barker Yearbook (writer) 1971, Ronnie Corbett in Bed (writer) 1971, Monty Python's Fliegender Zirkus (actor, writer) 1972, Christmas Box (writer) 1974, Commander Badman (writer) 1974, Rutland Weekend Television (series, actor and writer) 1975, The Rutles (actor, writer, dir) 1978, The Mikado (film, actor) 1987, Nearly Departed (series, actor) 1989, Around the World in 80 Days (series, actor) 1989, Mickey Mouse Works (series, voice) 1999, Suddenly Susan (series, actor) 1999–2000, House of Mouse (series, voice) 2001, The Scream Team (film, actor) 2002, Rutles 2: Can't Buy Me Lunch (writer, dir) 2002, Christmas Vacation 2: Cousin Eddie's Island Adventure (film, actor) 2003, The Simpsons (voice) 2003–07, Super Robot Monkey Team Hyperforce Go! (voice) 2004–05. *Stage productions:* I'm Just Wild About Harry (actor, Edinburgh Festival) 1963, Monty Python Live at the Hollywood Bowl (actor, writer) 1982, The Mikado (actor, ENO) 1987, (actor, Houston Opera House) 1989, Monty Python's Spamalot (writer, The Shubert Theatre, Broadway) 2005. *Compositions:* songs for Monty Python's Flying Circus series 1969, Always Look on the Bright Side of Life.. (for Life of Brian film) 1979, Bruces' Philosophers Song (for Monty Python Live at the Hollywood Bowl) 1982, Sit On My Face (for Monty Python Live at the Hollywood Bowl) 1982, songs for The Meaning of Life film 1983, The Adventures of Baron Munchausen (song, for film) 1988, One Foot in the Grave (TV series theme song) 1990, That's Death (song for video game, Discworld II: Missing Presumed...!?) 1996, songs for Monty Python's Spamalot stage production 2005. *Publications include:* Hello Sailor 1975, The Rutland Dirty Weekend Book 1976, Pass the Butler 1982, Monty Python's Flying Circus: Just the Words (co-author, two vols) 1989, The Fairly Incomplete and Rather Badly Illustrated Monty Python Song Book (co-author) 1994, The Quite Remarkable Adventures of the Owl and the Pussycat (co-author) 1996, The Road to Mars 1998, The "Pythons" Autobiography by the "Pythons" (co-author) 2003, The Greedy Bastard Diary: A Comic Tour of America 2005. *Website:* ericidle.com; pythonline.com.

IDRAC, Anne-Marie André, LenD; French politician, civil servant and business executive; b. 27 July 1951, Saint-Brieuc, Côtes-du-Nord; d. of André Colin and Marguerite Médecin (née Laurent); m. Francis Idrac 1974; four d.; ed Univ. of Paris II, Inst. d'Etudes Politiques de Paris and Ecole Nat. d'Admin; civic admin., Dept of Building and Public Works, Ministry of Equipment, Housing and Transport 1974–77; Chargée de Mission to the Prefect of the Midi-Pyrénées 1977–79; Tech. Councillor in the Cabinets of Marcel Cavaillé (Sec. of State for Housing) and Michel d'Ornano (Minister of the Environment) 1979–81; Deputy Dir for Housing Improvement, Ministry of the Quality of Life 1981–83; Deputy Dir for Finance and Judicial Affairs 1983–87; Chief of Service and Deputy Dir, Dept of Construction, Ministry of Supply 1987–90, Dir-Gen. Public Devt in Cergy-Pontoise 1990–93; Dir of Territorial Transport (DTT) 1993–95; Sec. of State for Transport 1995–97, for External Trade 2008–10; elected Deputy for Yvelines (Union pour la démocratie française—UDF) 1997; Sec.-Gen. Force Démocrate; mem. Regional Council Ile-de-France 1998–2002; Pres. Mouvement Européen France 1999–2002; Vice-Pres., then Sec.-Gen. UDF 2001–02; Pres. and Dir-Gen. Régie Autonome des Transports Parisiens 2002–06; Chair. Soc. Nationale des Chemins de Fer Français (SNCF) 2006–08; Pres. Océanides 2012–; mem. Bd of Dirs Institut Français de Relations Internationales; mem. Advisory Bd Dexia 2002–07, Hautes études commerciales; mem. Orientation Council Asscn En Temps Réel; Chevalier, Ordre nat. du Mérite; Nat. Foundation for Public Enterprise Award 1977, ranked by Fortune magazine amongst 50 Most Powerful Women in Business outside the US (third) 2006, (sixth) 2007, ranked by the Financial Times amongst Top 25 Businesswomen in Europe (22nd) 2007. *Address:* Association Océanides, CESM, place Joffre, Case 08 75700 Paris SP 07, France (office). *E-mail:* association .oceanides@gmail.com (office). *Website:* oceanides-association.org (office).

IDRIS, Kamil E., LLB, BA, MA, PhD; Sudanese diplomatist and lawyer; b. 1945; ed Univ. of Khartoum, Egypt, Ohio Univ., USA, Grad. Inst. of Int. Studies, Switzerland, Inst. of Public Admin, Khartoum; part-time journalist, El-Ayam and El-Sahafa newspapers, Sudan 1971–79; Lecturer, Univ. of Cairo 1976–77, Ohio Univ. 1978, Univ. of Khartoum 1986; Asst Dir Arab Dept, Ministry of Foreign Affairs, Khartoum 1977–78, Asst Dir Research Dept Jan.–June 1978, Deputy Dir Legal Dept July–Dec. 1978; mem. Perm. Mission of Sudan to UN Office, Geneva 1979–82; Vice-Consul of Sudan, Switzerland 1979–82; Sr Program Officer, Devt Cooperation and External Relations Bureau for Africa, WIPO 1982–85, Dir Devt Cooperation and External Relations Bureau for Arab and Cen. and Eastern European Countries 1985–94, Deputy Dir-Gen. WIPO 1994–97, Dir-Gen. 1997–2008 (resgnd); Sec.-Gen. Int. Union for the Protection of New Varieties of Plants (UPOV) 1997–2008; mem. UN Int. Law Comm. (ILC) 1992–96 (Vice-Chair. 45th session 1993), 2000–02; served on numerous cttees of int. orgs including WHO, ILO, ITU, UNHCR, OAU, Group of 77 etc. and Sudanese del. to numerous int. and regional confs; Prof. of Public Int. Law, Univ. of Khartoum; mem. African Jurists Asscn; Hon. Prof. of Laws, Peking Univ., People's Repub. of China 1999; decorations from Sudan 1983, 2002, Egypt 1985, 2000, 2001, Senegal 1998, Russian Fed. 1999, 2000, Saudi Arabia 1999, Slovakia 1999, Syrian Arab Repub. 2000, Portugal 2001, Romania 2001, Mexico 2001, 2005, Repub. of Moldova 2001, Côte d'Ivoire 2002, Poland 2002, Kyrgyzstan 2003, Bulgaria 2003, Italy 2004, Oman 2004; Dr hc (State Univ. of Moldova) 1999), (Franklin Pierce Law Center) 1999, (Fudan Univ., Shanghai) 1999, (Univ. of Nat. and World Economy, Sofia) 2000, (Univ. of Bucharest) 2001, (Hannam Univ., Repub. of Korea) 2001, (Mongolian Univ. of Science and Tech.) 2001), (Matej Bel Univ., Slovakia) 2001,

(Nat. Tech. Univ. of Ukraine) 2002, (Al Eman Al Mahdi Univ., Sudan) 2003, (Indira Gandhi Nat. Open Univ.) 2005), (Latvian Acad. of Sciences) 2005, (Univ. of Al Gezira) 2007; Scholars and Researchers State Gold Medal (Sudan) 1983, Scholars and Researchers Gold Medal, Egyptian Acad. of Scientific Research and Tech. 1985. *Publications include:* State Responsibility in International Law 1977, North-South Insurance Relations: The Unequal Exchange 1984, The Law of Non-navigational Uses of International Water Courses; the ILC's draft articles: An Overview 1995, The Theory of Source and Target in Child Psychology 1996 and articles on law, economics, jurisprudence and aesthetics in newspapers and periodicals.

IDRISOV, Erlan Abilfayizulı; Kazakhstani politician and diplomatist; *Minister of Foreign Affairs;* b. 28 April 1959, Karkalinsk, Karaganda Oblast; m. Nurilla Anarbekovna Idrisova; two s. one d.; ed Moscow Inst. of Int. Relations, Diplomatic Acad., USSR Ministry of Foreign Affairs; rep. for Tyzahpromexport, Pakistan 1981–85; mem. of staff, Ministry of Foreign Affairs, Kazakh SSR 1985–90, trainee USSR Embassy, New Delhi 1991–92, First Sec., Perm. Mission of Kazakhstan to UN, New York 1992–95, Head of American Dept and Amb.-at-Large, Ministry of Foreign Affairs 1995–96, Asst to Pres. on Int. Issues 1996–97, First Deputy Minister of Foreign Affairs 1997–99, 1999–2002, Minister of Foreign Affairs Feb.–Oct. 1999, 2012–; Amb. to UK (also accred to Ireland, Norway and Sweden) 2002–07, to USA (also accred to Brazil) 2007–12. *Leisure interests:* lawn tennis, ice hockey, golf, horse riding, travelling. *Address:* Ministry of Foreign Affairs, 010000 Astana, D. Kunaev kosh. 31, Kazakhstan (office). *Telephone:* (7172) 72-05-18 (office). *Fax:* (7172) 72-05-16 (office). *E-mail:* astana@mfa.kz (office). *Website:* www .mfa.kz (office); www.erlanidrissov.com.

IDURI, Shemuel Sam; Solomon Islands teacher and politician; *Minister for National Unity, Reconciliation and Peace;* b. Boboilangi Village, Malaita; ed Solomon Islands Teacher's Coll., Teacher's Coll., Western Australia; fmr educ. officer; fmr secondary school prin.; mem. Parl. for West Kwara'ae, Malaita Prov. 2006–; Minister for Nat. Unity, Reconciliation and Peace 2006–10 Nov. 2007, 22 Dec. 2007–. *Address:* Ministry of Provincial Government, National Reconciliation and Peace, PO Box 1548, Honiara, Solomon Islands (office). *Telephone:* 28616 (office). *Fax:* 21289 (office).

IEHSI, Ieske K., BA, MPA; Micronesian politician and government official; *General Manager, Pohnpei Ports Authority;* b. 4 Jan. 1955, Pingelap Atoll; m. Merihne John; five c.; ed Univ. of Hawaii, Manoa, Harvard Univ., USA; Asst Chief Clerk, Congress of Micronesia 1977–97, Man., Office of the Attorney-Gen. 1980–81; Special Asst to the Pres. 1981–87, Chief of Staff, Exec. Office of the Pres. 1987–92; Deputy Sec. of the Dept of Foreign Affairs 1997–2001, Sec. of Foreign Affairs 2001–03; Gen. Man. Pohnpei Ports Authority 2003–; mem. Pingelap Council of Traditional Leaders (Benik), holding title of Noahs. *Address:* Pohnpei Ports Authority, PO Box 1150, Kolonia, Pohnpei FM 96941, Federated States of Micronesia (office). *Telephone:* 320-2793 (home). *Fax:* 320-2832 (office). *E-mail:* ieske@mail.fm (office). *Website:* www.ppa.fm (office).

IELEMIA, Apisai, BA; Tuvaluan politician; b. 19 Aug. 1955; m.; one d. one s.; ed USP Suva, Fiji; fmr civil servant; Prime Minister and Minister of Foreign Affairs and Labor 2006–10. *Address:* c/o Ministry of Foreign Affairs and Labour, Vaiaku, Funafuti, Tuvalu (office).

IGARASHI, Mitsuo; Japanese business executive and fmr politician; *Chairman, Okawa Foundation for Information and Telecommunications;* Deputy Minister for Policy Coordination, Ministry of Posts and Telecommunications 1990, Dir-Gen. Telecommunications Bureau then Minister of Telecommunications 1995; Exec. Vice-Pres. KDDI Corpn (telecommunications co.) 2000–03, Chair. 2003–04; Pres. Okawa Foundation for Information and Telecommunications 2005, now Chair.; also currently Adviser, Nomura Research Inst. *Publications:* articles in professional journals on econs. *Address:* Okawa Foundation, Sankyo Hanzomon Palace 301, 1-8-2 Hirakawacho, Chiyoda-ku, Tokyo 102-0093, Japan (office). *Telephone:* (3) 3556-6028 (office). *Fax:* (3) 3288-2280 (office). *E-mail:* okawa-foundation@nifty .com (office). *Website:* www.okawa-foundation.or.jp (office).

IGAŞ, Constantin Traian; Romanian politician; b. 29 Sept. 1968, Cristian, Sibiu Co.; m.; two d.; ed Universitatea de Vest Vasile Goldiş, Arad, Universitatea Aurel Vlaicu, Arad, Nat. Defence Univ. Carol I; Dir Arad Free Youth org. 1990–95; Tech. Dir, SC Astralegno LLC 1996–2000; Admin. SC Costello SRL 2000–04; Vice-Pres. Partidul Democrat (PD) 1998, Pecica Br. Vice-Pres. Perm. Bureau of PD, Arad Co. 2005; Alderman of the City of Pecica, Arad Co. 2000–04; adviser to Arad Co. Council 2004–08; Senator (Partidul Democrat-Liberal—PD-L) 2004–, Chair. PDL Group 2008–; Minister of Admin and the Interior 2010–12. *Address:* c/o Ministry of Administration and the Interior, 010086 Bucharest 1, Piaţa Revoluţiei 1A, Romania. *E-mail:* contact@igas.ro. *Website:* igas.ro.

IGEL, Anders, BSc, MSc; Swedish telecommunications executive; b. 1951, Stockholm; m.; three d.; ed Stockholm School of Econs, Stockholm Royal Inst. of Tech.; began career as radar system devt engineer at Philips Electronics; joined Ericsson 1978, held several positions including Marketing Exec., Head of Ericsson UK 1990–95, Head of Public Networks 1995–97, Head of Infocom Systems 1997–99; Pres. and CEO Esselte 1999–2002; mem. Bd Telia 1999, Pres. and CEO TeliaSonera 2002–07; currently Industrial Adviser, EQT Industrial Network (consultancy); mem. Bd of Dirs Swedbank AB 2006–, Turkcell Iletisim Hizmetleri AS 2006–07. *Address:* c/o EQT Partners AB, PO Box 16409, 103 27 Stockholm, Sweden (office). *Telephone:* (8) 506-55-300 (office). *Fax:* (8) 506-55-319 (office). *Website:* www.eqt.se (office).

IGER, Robert (Bob) A., BA; American business executive; *Chairman and CEO, The Walt Disney Company;* b. 10 Feb. 1951, New York City; m. 1st; one s. one d.; m. 2nd Willow Bay 1995; one s. one d.; ed Ithaca Coll.; studio supervisor, ABC-TV 1974–76, various positions, ABC-TV Sports 1976–85, Vice-Pres. Programme Planning and Devt 1985–87, Vice-Pres. Programme Planning and Acquisition 1987–88, Exec. Vice-Pres. ABC TV Network Group 1988–99, Pres. 1992–94, Pres. ABC Entertainment 1989–92, Exec. Vice-Pres. Capital Cities/ABC Inc., New York 1993–94, Pres. and COO 1994–96, Pres. ABC Inc., New York 1996–99, Chair. ABC Group 1999–2000; Pres. Walt Disney Int. 1999–2000, Pres. and COO The Walt Disney Co., Calif. 2000–05, Pres. and CEO 2005–12, Chair. and CEO 2012–; CEO MarketWatch Inc. 2006–; mem. Bd of Dirs Nat. September 11 Memorial &

Museum, Lincoln Center for the Performing Arts, Inc., Partnership for a New American Economy, US-China Business Council 2011–, Apple Inc. 2011–; apptd by Pres. Obama to the President's Export Council 2010–; mem. American Acad. of Arts and Sciences 2012; Trustee, American Film Inst. Bd; fmr Trustee, Ithaca Coll.; Hon. Chair., Campaign for Ithaca Coll.; Trustees Award, Nat. TV Acad. 2005, MarketWatch CEO of the Year 2006, named by Fortune magazine as one of the 25 Most Powerful People in Business 2006, 2007, named by Forbes magazine as one of the Top Gun CEOs 2009, named by Institutional Investor magazine as one of the Best CEOs 2008–11. *Address:* The Walt Disney Co., 500 South Buena Vista Street, Burbank, CA 91521-9722, USA (office). *Telephone:* (818) 560-1000 (office). *Fax:* (818) 560-1930 (office). *E-mail:* TWDC.Corp.Communications@disney.com (office). *Website:* thewaltdisneycompany.com (office); disney.com (office).

IGGA, James Wani; South Sudanese politician and fmr resistance fighter; *Vice-President;* b. 1949, Krillo, Juba County; ed Cairo Univ. of Econs, Egypt; joined Sudan People's Liberation Army (SPLA, guerrilla army) 1985, becoming Zonal Commdr, Central Equatoria, mem. SPLA High Command, Chair. Sudan People's Liberation Movt Political Affairs Comm. 2000; apptd caretaker Gov., Upper Nile State for transition period to independence of S Sudan 2005; Speaker, Legis. Ass. (Parl.) –2013; Vice-Pres. 2013–. *Address:* Office of the Vice-President, Juba, South Sudan (office).

IGLESIAS, Enrique; Spanish singer and songwriter; b. 8 May 1975, Madrid; s. of Julio Iglesias; sings in English and Spanish; numerous tours; Grammy Award 1997, eight Premios Los Nuestro, Billboard Awards for Artist of the Year, Album of the Year 1997, ASCAP Award for Songwriter of the Year 1998, American Music Award for Favorite Latin Artist 2002, 2008, Billboard Latin Music Award for Best Latin Dance Club Play Track (for Not In Love/No Es Amor) 2005, Top Latin Album (Euphoria) 2011, ASCAP Pop Award for Most Performed Song (Tonight I'm Lovin' You) 2012. *Recordings include:* albums: Enrique Iglesias 1995, Master Pistas 1997, Vivir 1997, Cosas Del Amor 1998, Enrique 1999, Escape 2001, Quizás 2002, 7 2003, Insomniac 2007, Euphoria 2010; singles: Experiencia Religiosa, No Llores Por Mi, Bailamos 1999, Rhythm Divine 1999, Be With You 2000, Solo Me Importas Tu 2000, Sad Eyes 2000, Hero 2001, Don't Turn Off The Lights 2002, Love To See You Cry 2002, Maybe 2002, Addicted 2003, Not In Love 2004. *Address:* c/o Interscope Records, 2220 Colorado Avenue, Santa Monica, CA 90404, USA. *Telephone:* (310) 865-1000. *Website:* www.enriqueiglesias.com.

IGLESIAS, Enrique V.; Uruguayan academic and international organization official; *General Secretary, Ibero-American General Secretariat;* b. 26 July 1931, Asturias, Spain; s. of Isabel García de Iglesias; ed Univ. de la República, Montevideo; held several positions, including Prof. Agregado, Faculty of Political Economy, Prof. of Econ. Policy and Dir Inst. of Econs, Univ. de la República, Montevideo 1952–67; Man. Dir Unión de Bancos del Uruguay 1954; Tech. Dir Nat. Planning Office of Uruguay 1962–66; Pres. (Gov.) Banco Cent. del Uruguay 1966–68; Chair. Council, Latin American Inst. for Econ. and Social Planning, UN 1967–72, Interim Dir-Gen. 1977–78; Head, Advisory Mission on Planning, Govt of Venezuela 1970; Adviser UN Conf. on Human Environment 1971–72; Exec. Sec. Econ. Comm. for Latin America and the Caribbean 1972–85; Minister of External Affairs 1985–88; Pres. IDB 1988–2005; Gen. Sec. Ibero-American Gen. Secr., Madrid, Spain 2005–; Pres. Soc. for Int. Devt; Acting Dir-Gen. Latin American Inst. for Econ. and Social Planning 1973–78; Pres. Third World Forum 1973–76; mem. Steering Cttee, Soc. for Int. Devt 1973–92, Pres. 1989, Selection Cttee, Third World Prize 1979–82; Sec.-Gen. UN Conf. on New and Renewable Sources of Energy Feb.–Aug. 1981; Chair. UN Inter-Agency Group on Devt of Renewable Sources of Energy, Energy Advisory Panel, Brundtland Comm. 1984–86; mem. North-South Round Table on Energy, Club of Rome; Order of Rio Branco; Grand Cross (Brazil); Grand Cross Silver Plaque, Nat. Order of Juan Mora Fernandez (Costa Rica); Commdr Légion d'honneur; Commdr des Arts et des Lettres 1999; Grand Cross of Isabel the Catholic (Spain); numerous other foreign decorations; Hon. LLD (Liverpool) 1987; Hon. PhD (Univ. de Guadalajara, Mexico) 1994, (Candido Mendes Univ., Rio de Janeiro) 1994; Prince of Asturias Award 1982, UNESCO Pablo Picasso Award 1997. *Leisure interests:* music, art. *Address:* Ibero-American General Secretariat, Paseo de Recoletos 8, 28001 Madrid, Spain (office). *Telephone:* (91) 590-19-80 (office). *E-mail:* info@segib.org (office). *Website:* www .segib.org (office).

IGLESIAS (DE LA CUEVA), Julio José; Spanish singer and songwriter; b. 23 Sept. 1943, Madrid; m. Isabel Preysler 1971 (divorced); one d. two s.; pnr Miranda Rijnsburger 1990; three s. two d.; ed Univ. of Cambridge; goalkeeper Real Madrid junior team; professional singer, songwriter 1968–; English language releases 1981–; concerts and television appearances worldwide; hon. mem. Spanish Foreign Legion; winner Spanish Song Festival, Benidorm 1968, Eurovision Song Contest winner 1970, Guinness Book of Records Diamond Disc Award (most records in most languages) 1983, Medaille de Vermeil de la Ville de Paris 1983, Grammy Award for Best Latin Pop Performance 1987. *Compositions include:* La Vida Sigue Igual, Mi Amor, Yo Canto, Alguien El Alamo Al Camino, No Llores. *Recordings include:* albums: Soy 1973, El Amor 1975, A Mis 33 Años 1977, De Niña A Mujer 1981, 1100 Bel Air Lace 1984, Un Hombre Solo 1987, Starry Night 1990, La Carretera 1995, Tango 1996, Corazón Latino 1998, Noche De Cuatro Lunas 2000, Una Donna Puo Cambiar La Vita 2000, Ao Meu Brasil 2000, Divorcio 2003, Romantic Classics 2006; also appears on: Duets (with Frank Sinatra) 1993. *Publication:* Entre el Cielo y el Infierno (autobiog.) 1981. *Address:* Anchor Marketing, 1885 NE 149th Street, Suite G, North Miami, FL 33181, USA (office). *Website:* www.julioiglesias.com (office).

IGLESIAS, María Cristina; Venezuelan politician; *Minister of Labour and Social Security;* Minister of Labour and Social Security 2002–05, 2009–, Minister of Light Industry and Commerce 2006–08; mem. Partido Socialista Unido de Venezuela. *Address:* Ministry of Labour and Social Security, Torre Sur, 5°, Centro Simón Bolívar, Caracas 1919, Venezuela (office). *Telephone:* (212) 481-1368 (office). *Fax:* (212) 483-8914 (office). *Website:* www.mintra.gov.ve (office).

IGNARRO, Louis J.; BS, PhD; American scientist and academic; *Jerome J. Belzer, MD, Distinguished Professor of Pharmacology, Department of Molecular and Medical Pharmacology, School of Medicine, University of California at Los Angeles;* b. 31 May 1941, Brooklyn, NY; m. Sharon E. Ignarro (née Williams); ed Columbia Univ., New York, Univ. of Minnesota; Postdoctoral Fellow, NIH

1966–68; Staff Scientist, Research Dept, Pharmaceutical Div., CIBA-GEIGY Corpn, Ardsley, NY 1968–72; Asst Prof., Dept of Pharmacology, Tulane Univ. School of Medicine, New Orleans 1973, Assoc. Prof. 1973–78, Prof. 1979–85; Prof., Dept of Pharmacology, UCLA School of Medicine 1985–, Prof. and Acting Chair. Dept of Pharmacology 1989–90, Prof. of Pharmacology and Asst Dean for Student Research 1990–93, Jerome J. Belzer, MD, Distinguished Prof. of Pharmacology, Dept of Molecular and Medical Pharmacology 1993–; mem. American Soc. for Pharmacology and Experimental Therapeutics, American Soc. for Biochemistry and Molecular Biology, American Physiological Soc., American Soc. for Cell Biology, American Rheumatism Asscn, American Soc. of Hematology, Soc. for Experimental Biology and Medicine, American Heart Asscn, NAS 1999–, American Acad. of Arts and Sciences 1999–, Inst. of Medicine 2005, American Philosophical Soc. 2007; Founder and Pres. Nitric Oxide Soc. 1996–; Founder and Ed.-in-Chief Nitric Oxide Biology and Chemistry (journal) 1996–; Dr hc (Buenos Aires School of Medicine), 1996, (Napoli School of Medicine) 1999, (Napoli School of Medicine II) 1999, (Univ. of the Republic, Montevideo, Uruguay) 1999, (UniNorte School of Medicine, Paraguay) 2000, (Charles Univ. School of Medicine, Prague) 2000, (Univ. of Bologna School of Medicine) 2000, (Tulane Univ.) 2001, (Univ. of Minnesota) 2002, (Univ. of Athens) 2002, (Univ. of Perugia, Italy) 2004; Roussel UCLA Prize 1994, CIBA Award for Hypertension Research 1995, Nobel Prize for Medicine (jtly) 1998, Basic Research Prize, American Heart Asscn 1998. *Publications:* numerous articles in scientific journals. *Leisure interests:* marathon runner, cyclist. *Address:* Department of Molecular and Medical Pharmacology, David Geffen School of Medicine, UCLA, 23-120 CHS, 650 Charles E. Young Drive, South, Los Angeles, CA 90095-1735, USA (office). *Telephone:* (310) 825-5159 (office); (310) 825-9930 (Lab.) (office). *Fax:* (310) 825-4791 (office). *E-mail:* lignarro@mednet.ucla.edu (office). *Website:* www.nuc.ucla.edu (office); www .ignarro.com (home).

IGNATENKO, Vitaly Nikitich; Russian journalist; *Director-General, ITAR-TASS News Agency;* b. 19 April 1941, Sochi; m. Svetlana Ignatenko; one s.; ed Moscow Univ.; corresp., Deputy Ed.-in-Chief Komsomolskaya Pravda 1963–75; Deputy Dir-Gen. TASS (USSR Telegraph Agency) 1975–78; Deputy Head of Int. Information Section, CPSU Cen. Cttee 1978–86; Ed.-in-Chief Novoe Vremya 1986–90; Asst to fmr Pres. Gorbachev, Head of Press Service 1990–91; Dir-Gen. ITAR-TASS News Agency 1991–; Deputy Chair. Council of Ministers 1995–97; Pres., Chair. of Bd Russian Public TV (ORT) 1998–; Pres. World Asscn of Russian Press; mem. Int. Acad. of Information Science, Russian Fed. Comm. on UNESCO Affairs, Union of Russian Journalists, Union of Russian Cinematographers; Order of the Friendship of Peoples (twice) 1996, Order of Merit to the Fatherland 1999; Lenin Prize 1978, Prize of USSR Journalists' Union 1975. *Publications:* several books and more than 30 film scripts. *Leisure interest:* tennis. *Address:* ITAR-TASS, 125993 Moscow, Tverskoy blvd 10-12, Russia (office). *Telephone:* (495) 202-29-81 (office). *Fax:* (495) 202-54-74 (office). *E-mail:* worldmarket@itar-tass.com (office). *Website:* www.itar-tass.com (office).

IGNATIEFF, Michael, BA, MA, PhD; Canadian writer, historian, academic and fmr politician; b. 12 May 1947, Toronto, Ont.; m. 1st Susan Barrowclough 1977; one s. one d.; m. 2nd Zsuzsana Zsohar; ed Univ. of Toronto, Harvard Univ., USA, Univ. of Cambridge, UK; reporter, Globe and Mail newspaper, Toronto 1966–67; Teaching Fellow, Harvard Univ. 1971–74; Asst Prof., Univ. of British Columbia, Vancouver 1976–78; Sr Research Fellow, King's Coll., Cambridge, UK 1978–84; Visiting Prof., Ecole des Hautes Études, Paris 1985; editorial columnist, The Observer, London 1990–93; corresp. for BBC, The Observer, New Yorker 1984–2000; mem. Int. Comm. on Sovereignty and Intervention; Carr Prof. of Human Rights Practice, Harvard Univ. 2000–05, Dir Carr Center for Human Rights Policy, John F. Kennedy School of Govt 2001–05, Prof. of Practice, John F. Kennedy School of Govt 2012–; MP (Liberal) for Etobicoke-Lakeshore 2006–11; Deputy Leader Liberal Party of Canada 2006–08, interim Leader 2008–09, Leader 2009–11 (resgnd); Fellow, Massey Coll., Univ. of Toronto 2011–, Prof., Munk School of Global Affairs; 11 hon. doctorates; Lionel Gelber Award 1994. *Television:* host of Thinking Aloud (BBC) 1986, Voices (Channel Four) 1986, The Late Show (BBC 2) 1989. *Publications:* A Just Measure of Pain: The Penitentiary in the Industrial Revolution 1978, Wealth and Virtue: The Shaping of Classical Political Economy in the Scottish Enlightenment (co-ed.) 1983, The Needs of Strangers: An Essay on the Philosophy of Human Needs 1984, The Russian Album: A Family Memoir (Royal Soc. of Literature W.H. Heinemann Award (UK), Gov.-Gen. Award (Canada) 1988) 1987, Asya 1991, Scar Tissue (novel) 1993, Blood and Belonging: Journeys into the New Nationalism 1993, Isaiah Berlin: A Life 1998, The Warrior's Honor: Ethnic War and the Modern Conscience 1998, Virtual War: Kosovo and Beyond 2000, The Rights Revolution (Massey Lectures 2000) 2001, Human Rights as Politics and Idolatry (Tanner Lectures) 2001, Charlie Johnson in the Flames 2003, The Lesser Evil: Political Ethics in an Age of Terror 2004, True Patriot Love 2009, Fire and Ashes: Success and Failure in Politics 2013; contribs to New York Times, New Yorker, New York Review of Books. *Address:* Massey College, 4 Devonshire Place, Toronto, ON M5S 2E1, Canada (office).

IGNATIUS, David, AB, Dipl.Econ.; American journalist and novelist; *Associate Editor, The Washington Post;* b. 1950, Cambridge, Mass; m. Dr Eve Ignatius; three d.; ed Harvard Univ., King's Coll., Cambridge, UK; Ed. The Washington Monthly magazine 1975; reporter, The Wall Street Journal 1976–86, assignments included Steelworkers Corresp., Pittsburgh, Senate Corresp., Washington, DC, Middle East Corresp., Chief Diplomatic Corresp.; Ed. Sunday Outlook, The Washington Post 1986–90, Foreign Ed. 1990–93, apptd Asst Man. Business Ed. 1993, Assoc. Ed. 2004–; Exec. Ed. International Herald Tribune 2000–03; columnist, The Washington Post and Washington Post Writers Group 2003–; Chevalier, Légion d'honneur 2010; Frank Knox Fellow, Harvard-Cambridge Univs 1973–75, Edward Weintal Prize for Diplomatic Reporting 1985, Gerald Loeb Award for Commentary 2000, Edward Weintal Certificate 2006, Urbino Press Award 2010, Founder's Award, Int. Cttee for Foreign Journalism 2010. *Film:* Body of Lies. *Publications include:* Agents of Innocence 1987, SIRO 1991, The Bank of Fear 1994, A Firing Offense 1997, The Sun King 1999, Body of Lies 2007, The Increment 2009, Bloodmoney 2011; contribs to The New York Times Magazine, The Atlantic Monthly, Foreign Affairs and The New Republic. *Address:* Washington Post Writers Group, 1150 15th Street NW, Washington, DC 20071, USA (office). *Telephone:* (202) 334-6548 (office). *Fax:* (202) 334-5269 (office). *E-mail:* davidignatius@washpost.com (office). *Website:* www.postwritersgroup.com (office).

IGNATIYEV, Sergei Mikhailovich, CandSci, PhD; Russian economist and banker; *Chairman, Supervisory Board, Sberbank;* b. 10 Jan. 1948, Leningrad (now St Petersburg); m.; ed Moscow M.V. Lomonosov State Univ.; served in armed forces 1967–69; adjuster of hydroelectric equipment, Gidroelektromontazh Enterprise, Leningrad 1969–70; Sr Lecturer, Engels Leningrad Inst. of Soviet Trade 1978–88; Sr Lecturer and Assoc. Prof., Voznesenskii Leningrad Inst. of Finance and Econs 1988–91; Deputy Minister of Econs and Finance 1991–92, of Finance 1992–94, of Econs 1993–96; econ. adviser to Pres. Boris Yeltsin 1996–97; First Deputy Minister of Finance 1997–2002; Deputy Chair. Bank Rossii (Cen. Bank of the Russian Fed.) 1992–93, Chair. 2002–13, Advisor to the Chair. 2013–; Chair. Supervisory Bd Sberbank (Savings Bank of Russian Fed.); Hon. Diploma, Russian Govt 1998; 850th Anniversary of Moscow Medal 1997, several govt awards. *Publications:* numerous articles and more than 20 research papers on econs. *Address:* Sberbank, 117997 Moscow, ul. Vavilova 19, Russia (office). *Telephone:* (495) 974-66-77 (office). *Fax:* (495) 957-57-31 (office). *E-mail:* sbrf@sberbank.ru (office); sberbank@sberbank.ru (office). *Website:* www.sberbank.ru (office).

IGRUNOV, Vyacheslav Vladimirovich; Russian politician; *Director, International Institute for Humanities and Political Studies;* b. 28 Oct. 1948, Chernitsy, Zhytomer region, Ukraine; m.; four c.; ed Odessa State Inst. of Nat. Econs; detained by KGB due to his protest against invasion of Soviet army into Czechoslovakia 1968, participated in dissident movt 1960s, arrested 1975; released after campaign by Andrei Sakharov and Aleksandr Solzhenitsyn in his defence 1977; f. Samizdat Library; mem. staff 20th Century and World (bulletin) 1987; f. ideological Movt Memorial July 1987; f. Moscow Public Information Exchange Bureau M-BIO, newspaper Panorama 1988; Head of Programme Civil Soc. Foundation of Cultural Initiative 1990–92; Head of Analytical Centre in Goscomnats; currently Dir Int. Inst. for Humanities and Political Studies; mem. State Duma (Parl.) 1993–2003; Deputy Chair. public movt Yabloko 1996–2000, mem. faction Yabloko 1993–2003; mem. Expert Bd of Fed. Council (Parl.) 2005–11; Co-founder and Chair. Russian public movement 'Russian Concert' 2011–. *Publications:* Problematics of Social Movements 1972, Informal Political Clubs in Moscow 1989, Economic Reform as One of the Sources of National Clashes 1993, Russia and Ukraine 2001, Common Future 2004, The Shadow Theatre on the Eve of Distemper 2005, Phantoms of Freedom, Equality, and Fraternity 2005, The East is Rising 2006, Nationalism is Exported from the West 2006, The Year Results. A View from Russia 2007, The End of Multi-Ethnicity 2007, Fundamentalistic Liberalism has Ceased to Exist 2008, Iran in the Center of Interests of World Powers in the 21st Century 2009, Chechens and Russians by S. Maksudov (Chief Ed.) 2010, Who Has Won the Elections 2011, The Count-Down for the Regime Has Started 2011, The First Stage of Political Evolution 2012, What If Russia Disappears Tomorrow? 2012. *Leisure interests:* reading history books, writing memoirs and poetry. *Address:* International Institute for Humanities and Political Studies, Tverskaya str. 7, PO Box 82, 1250095 Moscow, Russia (office). *Telephone:* (985) 761-99-61 (office); (916) 860-84-40 (home). *E-mail:* igrunov@igpi.ru (office). *Website:* www.igrunov.ru.

IHAMUOTILA, Jaakko, MSEng; Finnish business executive; b. 15 Nov. 1939, Helsinki; s. of Veikko Artturi Ihamuotila and Anna-Liisa Ihamuotila (née Kouki); m. Tuula Elina Turja 1965; two s. one d.; ed Univ. of Tech., Helsinki; Asst in Reactor Tech. 1963–66, Acting Asst to Prof. of Physics 1964–66; with Canadian Gen. Electric Co. Ltd, Toronto 1966; Imatran Voima Oy 1966–68; Valmet Oy 1968–70, Asst Dir 1970–72, Dir of Planning 1972–73, Man. Dir 1973–79, mem. Bd 1980–82; Pres. Int. Council of Acads. of Eng . and Technological Sciences 2001; mem. Bd Neste Oy 1979, Chair. and Chief Exec. 1980, now retd; Chair. Asko Oy, Silja Oy Ab, Chemical Industry Fed. of Finland; Chair. Millenium Prize Foundation, Finnish Acads of Tech. 2002–08; mem. Supervisory Bd Merita Bank Ltd 1996–2000, MTV Finland 1993–97, Finnish Cultural Foundation a.o.; mem. Bd of Dirs Nordea Bank Finland, Finnair 1984–87, Confed. of Finnish Industry and Employers, Pohjola Insurance Co.; mem. Council Econ. Orgs in Finland, Nat. Bd of Econ. Defence, Council of Univ. of Tech.; Hon. DTech. *Leisure interests:* tennis, outdoor pursuits.

IHAMUOTILA, Timo, MSc(Econ); Finnish business executive; *Chief Financial Officer and Interim President and Chairman of the Nokia Leadership Team, Nokia Corporation;* b. 21 April 1966, Helsinki; m.; three c.; ed Helsinki School of Econs; analyst, Assets and Liability Man., Kansallis Bank 1990–93; with Nokia 1993–96, rejoined 1999, Man., Dealing and Risk Man. 1993–96, Dir, Corp. Finance 1999–2000, Vice-Pres., Finance, and Corp. Treas. 2000–04, Sr Vice-Pres., CDMA Business Unit, Mobile Phones 2004–07, Exec. Vice-Pres., Sales and Portfolio Man., Mobile Phones 2007, Exec. Vice-Pres., Sales, Markets 2008–09, Chief Financial Officer Nokia Corpn 2009–, Interim Pres. 2013–, mem. Nokia Leadership Team 2007–, Chair. 2013–; Vice-Pres. Nordic Derivatives Sales, Citibank plc 1996–99; mem. Bd of Dirs Nokia Solutions and Networks BV, Uponor Corpn, Cen. Chamber of Commerce of Finland. *Leisure interests:* tennis, skiing, reading, spending time with his family. *Address:* Nokia Corporation, Keilalahdentie 4, 00045 Espoo, Finland (office). *Telephone:* (7180) 08000 (office). *Fax:* (7180) 38226 (office). *E-mail:* info@nokia.com (office). *Website:* www.nokia.com (office).

IHSANOĞLU, Ekmeleddin, BSc, MSc, PhD; Turkish academic and international organization official; *Secretary-General, Organization of the Islamic Cooperation;* b. 26 Dec. 1943, Cairo, Egypt; m. Füsun Bilgiç 1971; three s.; ed Ankara Univ.; cataloguer of printed and manuscript books, Dept of Oriental Studies, Cairo Nat. Library 1962–66; Lecturer in Turkish Literature and Language, Ain Shams Univ., Cairo 1966–70, Ankara Univ., Turkey 1971–75; Research Fellow, Univ. of Exeter, UK 1975–77; Lecturer and Assoc. Prof., Faculty of Science, Ankara Univ. 1970–80; Assoc. Prof., İnönü Univ., Malatya, Turkey 1978–80; Dir-Gen. Islamic Conf. Research Centre for Islamic History, Art and Culture, Org. of the Islamic Conf. (now Org. of the Islamic Cooperation), Istanbul 1980–2004, Sec.-Gen. Org. of the Islamic Cooperation, Jeddah, Saudi Arabia 2005–; Sec. Islamic Conf. Org. Int. Comm. for Preservation of Islamic Cultural Heritage, Istanbul 1983–2000 (now defunct); Founder-Chair., Dept of History of Science in Turkey, Univ. of Istanbul 1984–2000; apptd Chair. Turkish Soc. for History of Science, Istanbul 1989; Vice-Chair. Al Furqan Islamic Heritage Foundation, London, UK 1998–; Pres. Int. Union of History and Philosophy of Science/Div. of History of Science 2001; mem. numerous orgs concerned with study of history of science and Islamic civilization, including Acad. Int. d'Histoire des

Sciences, Paris, Cultural Centre of the Atatürk Supreme Council for Culture, Language and History, Ankara, Int. Soc. for History of Arabic and Islamic Sciences and Philosophy, Paris, Royal Acad. of Islamic Civilization Research, Jordan, Middle East and the Balkans, Research Foundation, Istanbul, Acad. of Arabic Language (Jordan, Egypt, Syria), Egyptian History Soc., Cairo, Tunisian Acad. of Sciences, Letters and Arts 'Bait al Hikma', Tunis, Int. Soc. for History of Medicine, Paris; apptd Amb.-at-Large by Govt of Bosnia-Herzegovina 1997; Visiting Prof., Ludwig Maximilians Univ., Munich, Germany 2003; Hon. Consul, The Gambia 1990; Commdr de l'Ordre Nat. du Mérit (Senegal) 2002, Commdr de l'Ordre Nat. du Lion (Senegal) 2006; Dr hc (Mimar Sinan Univ., Istanbul) 1994, (Dowling Coll., New York) 1996, (Azerbaijan Acad. of Sciences) 2000, (Univ. of Sofia) 2001, (Univ. of Sarajevo) 2001, (Univ. of Padova) 2006, (Islamic Univ. of Islamabad) 2007, (Univ. of Exeter) 2007, (Islamic Univ., Uganda) 2008; Distinction of the First Order Medal (Egypt) 1990, Certificate of Honour and Distinction, OIC 1995, Independence Medal of the First Order (Jordan) 1996, Medal of Distinguished State Service (Turkey) 2000, World Prize for Book of the Year (Iran) 2000, UNESCO Avicenna Medal 2004, Medal of Glory (Russia) 2006, Medal of Glory (Azerbaijan) 2006, Int. Acad. of the History of Science Alexandre Koyre Medal 2008. *Publications:* has written, edited and translated several books on Islamic culture and science; over 70 articles and papers. *Leisure interests:* reading and music, sponsoring and collecting Islamic works of art. *Address:* Organization of the Islamic Cooperation, POB 178, Jeddah 21411, Saudi Arabia (office); Türk Bostani Sokak, Dostlar Sitesi 35, Yenikoy 34464 Istanbul, Turkey (home). *Telephone:* (2) 651-5222 (office). *Fax:* (2) 651-2288 (office). *E-mail:* cabinet@oic-oci.org (office). *Website:* www.oic-oci.org (office).

IIJIMA, Masami; Japanese business executive; *Representative Director, President and CEO, Mitsui & Company Limited;* ed Yokohoma Nat. Univ.; has served in a variety of positions at Mitsui & Co. UK Plc and Mitsui & Co. Ltd 1974–, Man. Officer and COO of Iron and Steel Raw Materials and Non-Ferrous Metals Business Unit, Mitsui & Co. Ltd 2006–07, Man. Officer and COO of Mineral and Metal Resources Business Unit 2007–08, Exec. Man. Officer April–June 2008, Rep. Dir and Exec. Man. Officer June–Oct. 2008, Rep. Dir and Sr Exec. Man. Officer Oct. 2008–April 2009, Rep. Dir, Pres. and CEO April 2009–, Chair. Nomination Cttee, mem. Remuneration Cttee and Governance Cttee; mem. Bd of Dirs Companhia Vale do Rio Doce 2008. *Address:* Mitsui & Company Ltd, 2-1 Ohtemachi 1-chome, Chiyoda-ku, Tokyo 100-0004, Japan (office). *Telephone:* (3) 3285-1111 (office). *Fax:* (3) 3285-9819 (office). *E-mail:* info@mitsui.com (office). *Website:* www.mitsui.com (office).

IIJIMA, Sumio, BEng, PhD; Japanese physicist and academic; *Professor, Meijo University;* b. 2 May 1939; ed Univ. of Electro-Communications, Tokyo, Tohoku Univ., Ariz. State Univ., USA; Research Assoc., Research Inst. for Scientific Measurements, Tohoku Univ. 1968–70; Postdoctoral Research Fellow and Research Scientist, Ariz. State Univ., USA 1970–82; Visiting Scholar, Univ. of Cambridge, UK 1979; Researcher, Research Devt Corpn, Japan 1982–87; Prof., Dept of Materials Science and Eng, Meijo Univ., Nagoya 1999–; Sr Research Fellow, NEC Corpn, Ibaraki 1987–; Research Dir, Nanotubulite Project, Int. Cooperative Research Project (ICORP), Japan Science and Tech. Agency Corpn 1998–2002; Dir Research Center for Advanced Carbon Materials, Nat. Inst. of Advanced Science and Tech. (AIST) 2001–; Project Reader, NEDO Advanced Nanocarbon Application Project 2002–06, Carbon Nanotube Capacitator Devt Project 2006–; Research Dir, JST/SORST Iijima Team 2003–08; Dean, Sungkyunkwan Univ. Advanced Inst. of Nanotechnology 2005–; Distinguished Invited Univ. Prof., Nagoya Univ. 2007–; mem. Royal Microscopy Soc., Materials Research Soc., American Crystallographic Asscn, Science Council of Japan, Physical Soc. of Japan, Chemical Soc. of Japan; Foreign Assoc., NAS 2007; Foreign mem. Norwegian Acad. of Science and Letters 2009; Fellow, Japan Soc. for Applied Physics 2007; Hon. Prof., Xi'an Jiaotong Univ. 2005, Peking Univ. 2005, Tsinghua Univ. 2009, Zhejiang Univ. 2010, Southeast Univ. 2010; Hon. mem. Crystallographic Soc. of Japan, Japanese Soc. of Microscopy; Hon. Fellow, American Physical Soc., Royal Microscopy Soc.; Order of Cultural Merits 2009; Dr hc (Antwerp) 2002, (École Polytechnique Fédérale de Lausanne) 2003; Bertram Eugene Warren Diffraction Physics Award 1976, Seto Award 1980, Nishina Memorial Award 1985, Asahi Award 1996, Tsukuba Prize 1998, Agilent Technologies Europhysics Prize 2001, Benjamin Franklin Medal in Physics 2002, American Physical Soc. McGroddy Materials Prize 2002, Japan Acad. Award and Imperial Award 2002, Outstanding Achievement Award, Japan Soc. of Applied Physics 2002, Person of Cultural Merits 2003, Soc. Medal, American Carbon Soc. 2004, Distinguished Scientist Award, Microscopy Soc. of America 2005, John M. Cowley Medal 2006, Gregori Aminoff Prize 2007, Fujiwara Award 2007, Balzan Prize 2007, Plueddemann Award 2008, The Kavli Prize in Nanoscience 2008, The Prince of Asturias Award for Tech. Scientific Research 2008, Economist Innovation Awards 'No Boundaries' 2008. *Achievements:* discovered carbon nanotubes 1991. *Address:* Meijo University, Faculty of Science and Technology, 1-501, Shiogamaguchi, Tenpaku, Nogoya, Aichi 468-8502, Japan (office). *Telephone:* (52) 834-4001 (office). *Fax:* (52) 834-4001 (office). *E-mail:* iijimas@ccmfs.meijo-u.ac.jp (office); c_saito@meijo-u.ac.jp (office). *Website:* nanocarb.meijo-u.ac.jp/jst/iijima.html (office).

IIMURA, Yutaka; Japanese diplomatist; *Special Envoy of the Government of Japan for the Middle East;* b. 16 Oct. 1946; joined Ministry of Foreign Affairs 1969, Dir of Tech. Co-operation 1988, Dir of Press 1990, Asst Dir-Gen., Europe Dept 1997, Dir-Gen. of Econ. Co-operation 1999, Deputy Vice Foreign Minister 2001; Second Sec., Embassy in Moscow 1977, First Sec., Embassy in Paris 1979, First Sec., later Counsellor Embassy in Pasay City, Philippines 1985, Counsellor, later Minister Embassy in Washington, DC 1992, Minister Embassy in Paris 1995, Amb. to Indonesia 2002–06, to France 2006–09, Special Envoy of the Govt of Japan for the Middle East 2009–. *Address:* Ministry of Foreign Affairs, Kasumigaseki 2-2-1, Chiyoda-ku, Tokyo 100-8919, Japan (office). *Telephone:* (3) 3580-3311 (office). *Fax:* (3) 3581-2667 (office). *E-mail:* webmaster@mofa.go.jp (office). *Website:* www.mofa .go.jp (office).

IIPUMBU, Leonard Nangolo; Namibian diplomatist and banker; *CEO, Agricultural Bank of Namibia;* m. Hilma Ndapewa Iipumbu; four c.; Deputy Rep. to Zambia 1980–83, Chief Rep. to Botswana 1984–87, People's Repub. of Congo 1988–89; mem. protocol sub-Cttee for Namibian independence celebrations 1990;

Special Envoy to the Congo 1991, Amb. to France (also accred to Italy, Portugal and Spain) 1992–99, to USA (also accred to Mexico and Brazil) 1999–2004; CEO Agricultural Bank of Namibia 2004–. *Address:* Agricultural Bank of Namibia, 10 Post Street Mall, Private Bag 13208, Windhoek, Namibia (office). *E-mail:* info@agribank.com.na (office). *Website:* www.agribank.com.na (office).

IKAWA, Motomichi, PhD cand.; Japanese banking and finance executive and academic; *Professor, Graduate School of Business, Nihon University;* b. 10 Feb. 1947, Tokyo; m. Yoshiko Ikawa; ed Tokyo Univ., Univ. of California, Berkeley; economist, Balance of Payments Div., OECD, Paris 1976–79; various man. posts at Ministry of Finance, Tokyo 1979–85; Asst Regional Commr, CID, Osaka Taxation Bureau 1985–86; Dir Budget, Personnel and Man. Systems Dept, Asian Devt Bank 1986–89; Asst Vice-Minister of Finance, Int. Affairs 1989–90; Dir Int. Org. Div., Int. Finance Bureau, Ministry of Finance 1990–91, Foreign Exchange and Money Market Div. 1991–92, Devt Policy Div. 1992–93, Co-ordination Div. 1993–94; Man. Dir Co-ordination Dept, Overseas Econ. Co-operation Fund 1994–96; Deputy Dir-Gen. Int. Finance Bureau 1996–97, Sr Deputy Dir-Gen. 1997–98; Exec. Vice-Pres. Multilateral Investment Guarantee Agency, World Bank Group 1998–2004; Prof., Nihon Univ. Grad. School of Business, Tokyo 2004–; mem. Bd of Dirs Transcultural Man. Soc., Japan Platform. *Publications:* Exchange Market Interventions during the Yen Depreciation 1980 1982, IMF Handbook 1990, The Role of the Overseas Economic Co-operation Fund Towards 2010 1994. *Leisure interests:* tennis, golf, hiking. *Address:* Nihon University Graduate School of Business, Kudanminami 4-8-24, Chiyoda-ku, Tokyo 102-8275, Japan (office). *Telephone:* (3) 5275-9440 (office). *Fax:* (3) 5275-8327 (office). *E-mail:* ikawa.motomichi@nihon-u.ac.jp (office). *Website:* www.gsb.nihon-u.ac.jp (office).

IKE, Fumihiko; Japanese automotive industry executive; *Chairman and Representative Director, Honda Motor Co. Ltd;* joined Honda in 1982, positions held include Chief Dir of IT, Risk Man. Officer, Sr Man. Exec. Officer, Chief Dir of Multi-purpose Business, Chief Dir of Asia and Pacific and Chief Dir of Business Admin, Chair. and Rep. Dir, Honda Motor Co. Ltd 2013–. *Address:* Honda Motor Co. Ltd, 2-1-1 Minami-Aoyama, Minato-ku, Tokyo 107-8556, Japan (office). *Telephone:* (3) 3423-1111 (office). *Fax:* (3) 5412-1515 (office). *E-mail:* info@honda.com (office). *Website:* www.honda.com (office); corporate.honda.com (office).

IKEDA, Daisaku; Japanese Buddhist philosopher, peace activist and author; *President, Soka Gakkai International;* b. 2 Jan. 1928, Tokyo; s. of Nenokichi Ikeda and Ichi Ikeda; m. Kaneko Shiraki 1952; two s.; ed Fuji Coll.; Pres. Soka Gakkai 1960–79, Hon. Pres. 1979–, Pres. Soka Gakkai Int. 1975–; Founder Soka Univ., Soka Univ. of America, Soka Women's Coll., Tokyo and Kansai Soka Schools, Soka Kindergartens (Japan, Hong Kong, Singapore, Malaysia, Brazil and S Korea), Makiguchi Foundation for Educ., Inst. of Oriental Philosophy, Ikeda Center for Peace, Learning and Dialogue, Toda Inst. for Global Peace and Policy Research, Tokyo Fuji Art Museum, Min-On Concert Asscn, Victor Hugo House of Literature and Komeito Party; mem. Advisory Bd World Centers of Compassion for Children International, Ireland 2004–; Poet Laureate, World Acad. of Arts and Culture 1981–; World People's Poet, World Poetry Soc. Intercontinental, India 2007–; Foreign mem. Künstlerhaus, Austria 1991–; Brazilian Acad. of Letters 1993–; Hon. Prof., Nat. Univ. of San Marcos 1981, Peking Univ. 1984, Tsinghua Univ. 2010, Nat. Taiwan Normal Univ. 2012, Al-Farabi Kazakh Nat. Univ. 2012 and others; Hon. Senator, European Acad. of Sciences and Arts 1997–; Hon. Adviser, World Fed. of UN Asscns 1999–; Hon. mem. The Club of Rome 1996–, Inst. of Oriental Studies of Russian Acad. of Sciences 1996–, Photographic Soc. of Singapore 1999–, Russian Acad. of Arts 2007–; Hon. Dir, Jao Tsung-I Petite Ecole, Univ. of Hong Kong 2011– and others; Grand Cross, Order of the Sun (Peru) 1984, Grand Cross, Order of May for Merit (Argentina) 1990, Commdr, Nat. Order of Southern Cross (Brazil) 1990, Kt Grand Cross of the Most Noble Order of the Crown (Thailand) 1991, Austrian Cross of Honour for Science and Art, First Class 1992, Kt Grand Cross of Rizal (Philippines) 1996, Grande Officiale, Ordine al Merito (Italy) 2006, Order of Friendship (Russia) 2008, Hwa-Gwan Order of Cultural Merit (Repub. of Korea) 2009, Order of Peace, First Class, Ukrainian Peace Council 2012 and others; Dr hc (Moscow State Univ.) 1975, (Sofia) 1981, (Buenos Aires) 1990, (Univ. of the Philippines) 1991, (Ankara) 1992, (Fed. Univ. of Rio de Janeiro) 1993, (Glasgow) 1994, (Hong Kong) 1996, (Havana) 1996, (Univ. of Ghana) 1996, (Delhi) 1998, (Sydney) 2000, (Morehouse Coll.) 2002, (Univ. of Guadalajara) 2004, (Visva-Bharati Univ.) 2006, (Palermo) 2007, (Univ. Coll. South, Denmark) 2009, (Queen's Univ., Belfast) 2009, (Universitas Indonesia) 2009, (Université Laval) 2010, (George Mason Univ.) 2010, (Univ. of Malaya) 2010, (Univ. of Massachusetts, Boston) 2010, (Pukyong Nat. Univ.) 2011, (Buckingham) 2011, (Guelph) 2012, (KwaZulu-Natal) 2013, (Thammasat) 2013 and others; UN Peace Award 1983, Kenya Oral Literature Award 1986, UNHCR Humanitarian Award 1989, Rosa Parks Humanitarian Award (USA) 1993, Simon Wiesenthal Center Int. Tolerance Award (USA) 1993, Tagore Peace Award, The Asiatic Soc. (India) 1997, Peace Gold Medal, Sydney Peace Foundation 2009, Goethe Medal, Goethe Soc., Weimar 2009 and others. *Publications include:* The Human Revolution Vols I–VI 1972–99, The Living Buddha 1976, Choose Life (with A. Toynbee) 1976 (revised edn 2007), Buddhism: The First Millennium 1977 (revised edn 2009), Songs from My Heart 1978, Glass Children and Other Essays 1979, A Lasting Peace Vols I–II 1981, 1987, Life: An Enigma, a Precious Jewel 1982, Before It Is Too Late (with A. Peccei) 1984 (revised edn 2009), Buddhism and the Cosmos (co-author) 1985, The Flower of Chinese Buddhism 1986, Human Values in a Changing World (with B. Wilson) 1987 (revised edn 2008), Unlocking the Mysteries of Birth and Death 1988 (revised edn 2003), The Snow Country Prince 1990, A Lifelong Quest for Peace (with L. Pauling) 1992 (revised edn 2009), Choose Peace (with J. Galtung) 1995, A New Humanism: The University Addresses of Daisaku Ikeda 1996 (revised edn 2010), The New Human Revolution, Vols I–XXIII (in Japanese) 1995–, The Wisdom of the Lotus Sutra, Vols I–VI 2000–03, For the Sake of Peace 2001, Soka Education 2001, The World is Yours to Change 2002, Choose Hope (with D. Krieger) 2002, Alborada del Pacífico (with P. Aylwin) 2002, On Being Human (with R. Simard and G. Bourgeault) 2002, Global Civilization: A Buddhist–Islamic Dialogue (with M. Tehranian) 2003, Fighting for Peace 2004, Planetary Citizenship (with H. Henderson) 2004, One by One 2004, Moral Lessons of the Twentieth Century (with M. Gorbachev) 2005, Revolutions: To Green the Environment, To Grow the Human Heart (with M. S. Swaminathan) 2005, A Quest for Global Peace (with J. Rotblat) 2006, Dawn after Dark (with R. Huyghe) 2007, A Dialogue between East and West (with R. Díez-Hochleitner) 2008, Embracing the

Future 2008, A Passage to Peace (with N. Yalman) 2008, Search for A New Humanity (with J. Derbolav) 2008, Ode to the Grand Spirit (with C. Aitmatov) 2009, Human Rights in the Twenty-first Century (with A. de Athayde) 2009, Creating Waldens (with R. Bosco and J. Myerson) 2009, The Persistence of Religion (with H. G. Cox) 2009, Dialog Peradaban untuk Toleransi dan Perdamaian (with A. Wahid) (in Indonesian) 2010, Into Full Flower (with E. Boulding) 2010, Discussions on Youth 2010, New Horizons in Eastern Humanism (with W. Tu) 2011, The Inner Philosopher (with L. Marinoff) 2012, America Will Be! Conversations on Hope, Freedom and Democracy (with V. Harding) 2013, Compassionate Light in Asia (with Y. Jin) 2013, José Martí Cuban Apostle: A Dialogue (with C. Vitier) 2013, A Forum for Peace: Daisaku Ikeda's Proposals to the UN 2014 and other writings on Buddhism, civilization, life and peace. *Leisure interests:* poetry, photography. *Address:* 32 Shinano-machi, Shinjuku-ku, Tokyo 160-8583, Japan (office). *Telephone:* (3) 5360-9831 (office). *Fax:* (3) 5360-9885 (office). *E-mail:* contact@sgi.org (office). *Website:* www.sgi.org (office); www.daisakuikeda.org.

IKOUÉBÉ, Basile; Republic of the Congo diplomatist and politician; *Minister of Foreign Affairs and Co-operation;* b. 1 July 1946; m.; six c.; ed Int. Inst. of Public Admin, Paris, Inst. for Political Studies, Bordeaux; apptd Chief Int. Orgs Div., Ministry of Foreign Affairs 1974, Prin. Pvt. Sec. to Minister 1975–77, Sec. to Ministry 1977–79; training assignment in France 1980–82; Diplomatic Adviser to Head of State 1982–92; Minister and Prin. Pvt. Sec. to Head of State 1987–94; Amb.-at-Large 1994–95; Sec. to Ministry of Foreign Affairs and Co-operation 1996–98; Amb. and Perm. Rep. to UN, New York 1998–2007, Pres. UN Security Council 2006; Minister of Foreign Affairs and Co-operation 2007–. *Address:* Ministry of Foreign Affairs and Co-operation, BP 2070, Brazzaville, Republic of the Congo (office). *Telephone:* 22-81-10-89 (office). *Fax:* 22-81-41-61 (office).

IKUTA, Masaharu; Japanese business executive; joined Keio Univ.; joined Mitsui OSK Lines Ltd 1957, mem. Bd of Dirs 1987–2003, Pres. 1994–2000, Chair. 2000–03, Corp. Advisor and Counselor 2007–; Pres. Japan Post (now Japan Post Holdings Co., Ltd) 2003–07; Chair. Business and Industry Advisory Cttee, Japan Fed. of Econ. Orgs (Nippon Keidanren) –2003; fmr Vice-Chair. Japan Asscn of Corp. Execs; mem. Bd of Dirs SourceNext Corpn 2008–, Terumo Corpn, Aeon Co. 2009–; mem. Int. Advisory Council, PSA Corpn Ltd 2002; Hon. Consul of the Repub. of Mauritius 2002–; Blue Ribbon Medal Award 1998. *Address:* c/o Mitsui OSK Lines Ltd, 1-1 Toranomon 2-chome, Minato-ku, Tokyo 105-8688, Japan (office).

ILIA II, Catholicos-Patriarch of All Georgia; Georgian ecclesiastic; b. (Irakli Ghudushauri-Shiolashvili), 4 Dec. 1933, Vladikavkaz, N Ossetian ASSR, Russian SFSR; ed Moscow Theological Seminary, Moscow Theological Acad.; took monastic vows 1957; Father-Superior 1960; Archimandrite 1961; Bishop of Shemokmedi and Vicar to the Georgian Patriarch Ephrem II Aug. 1963; entrusted with Sukhumi and Abkhazia Diocese 1967; Sukhumi-Abkhaz Metropolitanate 1969; Rector Mtskheta Orthodox Theological Seminary 1963–72; awarded Second Panagya 1972; enthroned as Archbishop of Mtskheta-Tbilisi and Catholicos-Patriarch of All Georgia 1977–; Co-Pres. WCC 1978–83; Dr of Theology, American St-Vladimir Theological Acad.; Hon. Academician, Georgian Acad. of Sciences 2003, Int. Acad. for the Promotion of Scientific Research 2007; Order of Friendship of Peoples; Hon. DTheol (St Vladimir's Orthodox Theological Seminary, New York, USA) 1986, (Acad. of Sciences, Crete) 1997, (St Tikhon's Orthodox Theological Seminary, Pa, USA) 1998; holder of highest awards of churches of Georgia, Constantinople, Alexandria, Antioch, Jerusalem, Russia, Czechoslovakia and Poland; David Guramishvili Prize 2008. *Address:* Patriarchate of the Georgian Orthodox Church, 0105 Tbilisi, Erekle II Moedani 1, Georgia. *Telephone:* (32) 99-03-78. *Fax:* (32) 98-71-14. *E-mail:* orthodox@patriarchate.ge. *Website:* www.patriarchate.ge.

ILIĆ, Venceslav; Bosnia and Herzegovina judge; *President of Appellate Division, Supreme Court of the Federation of Bosnia and Herzegovina;* b. 10 Sept. 1937, Sarajevo; s. of Anto Ilić and Ema Ilić (née Uršić); m. Bogdanka Ilić (née Miković); two d.; Dist Court Judge 1972–78; Public Prosecutor 1978–84; Supreme Court Judge 1984–87, 1992–96; Pres. Dist Court 1987–92; apptd Pres. Supreme Court, Fed. of Bosnia and Herzegovina 1996, currently Pres. Appellate Div.; Medallion of the City of Sarajevo. *Publications:* work on educ. of juridical personnel. *Leisure interests:* work for sports orgs, walking in the countryside. *Address:* Appellate Division, Supreme Court of the Federation of Bosnia and Herzegovina, 71000 Sarajevo, Valtera Perića 15, Federation of Bosnia and Herzegovina (office). *Telephone:* (33) 664754 (office).

ILIESCU, Ion; Romanian hydropower engineer and fmr head of state; *Honorary President, Social Democratic Party;* b. 3 March 1930, Oltenița, Ilfov Dist; s. of Alexandru Iliescu; m. Elena (Nina) Șerbănescu 1951; ed Bucharest Polytechnic Inst. and Energy Inst., Moscow, USSR; researcher, Energy Eng Inst., Bucharest 1955; Pres. Union of Student Asscns 1957–60; Alt. mem. Cen. Cttee of RCP 1965–68, mem. 1968–84; First Sec. Cen. Cttee of Union of Communist Youth and Minister for Youth 1967–71; Sec. RCP Cen. Cttee 1971; Vice-Chair. Timiș Co. Council 1971–74; Chair Iași Co. Council 1974–79; accused of "intellectual deviationism" and kept under surveillance; Chair. Nat. Water Council 1979–84; Dir Tech. Publishing House, Bucharest 1984–89; Pres. Nat. Salvation Front 1989–90, Provisional Council for Nat. Unity Feb.–May 1990; Pres. of Romania 1990–96, 2000–04; Senator 1996–2000, 2004–08; fmr Pres. Party of Social Democracy of Romania (merged with SDP to become Social Democratic Party 2001), now Hon. Pres.; Chevalier de la Légion d'honneur and other state decorations; hon. doctorates from numerous univs. *Publications:* Global Problems and Creativity, Revolution and Reform, Romania in Europe and in the World, Where is Romanian Society Going?, Romanian Revolution, Hope Reborn, Integration and Globalisation – A Romanian Vision, Romanian Culture and European Identity, For Sustainable Development, The Great Shock at the End of a Short Century, Fragments of Life and of Lived History; studies on water man. and ecology, political power and social relations. *Leisure interests:* global problems, political and econ. sciences. *Address:* c/o Office of the Former President, Athena str. 11, Bucharest; Molièrestr. 3, Bucharest, Romania (home).

ILIOPOULOS, John, PhD; Greek physicist and academic; *Director, Theoretical Physics Laboratory, École Normale Supérieure;* b. 1940, Kalamata; m.; one s.; ed

École Normale Supérieure, Paris, France; currently Dir Theoretical Physics Lab., École Normale Supérieure, Paris; J.J. Sakurai Prize for Theoretical Particle Physics (co-recipient) 1987, Aristeio Prize (first recipient) 2002, Dirac Medal, Abdus Salam Int. Centre for Theoretical Physics 2007. *Achievements include:* first person to present the Standard Model of particle physics in a single report 1974; also first, along with colleagues Glashow and Maiani, to recognize the critical importance of a fourth quark, later known as the 'Charm quark'. *Publications:* numerous scientific papers in professional journals. *Address:* Laboratoire de Physique Théorique, École Normale Supérieure, École normale supérieure, 45 rue d'Ulm, 75230 Paris Cedex 05, France (office). *Telephone:* 1-44-32-34-22 (office). *Fax:* 1-44-32-20-99 (office). *E-mail:* info@lpt.ens.fr (office). *Website:* www.lpt.ens.fr (office).

ILITCH, Michael (Mike); American business executive; *Chairman, Ilitch Holdings Inc.;* b. (Michael Ilievski), 20 July 1929, Detroit, Mich.; m. Marian Ilitch; four s., three d.; ed Cooley High School; served four years in US Marine Corps; f. Little Caesars Pizza Treat, Garden City, Mich., Co-founder and Chair. Ilitch Holdings Inc. 1999–, cos include Little Caesars Pizza, MotorCity Casino, Olympia Entertainment; Founder, Little Caesars Amateur Hockey Program 1968; Owner, Detroit Red Wings professional ice hockey franchise 1982–; Owner, Detroit Drive football team 1988–92; Owner, Detroit Tigers professional baseball franchise 1992–; Co-founder Ilitch Charities for Children 2000 (renamed Ilitch Charities 2008); inducted into Nat. Hockey Hall of Fame 2003, US Hockey Hall of Fame 2004. *Address:* Ilitch Holdings Inc., 2211 Woodward Avenue, Detroit, MI 48201-3467, USA (office). *Telephone:* (313) 471-6600 (office). *E-mail:* contactus@ilitchholdings.com (office). *Website:* www.ilitchcompanies.com (office); www.littlecaesars.com; detroit.tigers.mlb.com; www.redwings.nhl.com.

İLKER BAŞBUĞ, Gen. Mehmet; Turkish army officer; *Chief of the General Staff;* b. 29 April 1943, Afyon Prov.; m. Sevil Başbuğ; two c.; ed Turkish Mil. Acad., Army Staff Coll., Royal Mil. Acad., Sandhurst, UK, NATO Defense Coll., Rome, Italy; infantry officer 1963, Platoon and Commando Co. Commdr –1970, Deputy Chief of Gen. Staff (Operations Planning Command) 1973, later Instructor, Army Staff Coll.; fmr Chief of Intelligence Div. (Intelligence Plans), Supreme HQ Allied Powers Europe (SHAPE), Mons, Belgium; Chief of Staff of Defence Intelligence (Army Plans and Principles Command), later Commdr, 247th Infantry Regt of 51st Infantry Brigade, rank of Brig. Gen. 1989, rank of Maj. Gen. 1993; fmr Deputy Commdr, Turkish Gendarmerie Public Order Command; Chief of Nat. Mil. Representation (NMR), Mons, Belgium 1993–95; rank of Gen. 2002, Deputy Commdr of Turkish Army 2002–03, Deputy Chief of Gen. Staff 2003–05, Commdr of the First Army 2005–06, Commdr of Turkish Army 2006–08, Chief of the Gen. Staff 2008–; Nishan-ı Imtiaz (Order of Distinction of Pakistan); Turkish Armed Forces Medal of Distinguished Courage and Self-Sacrifice, Turkish Armed Forces Medal of Honour, Golden Medal of the Eagle of the Repub. of Albania 2009. *Address:* Ministry of National Defence, Milli Savunma Bakanlığı, 06100 Ankara, Turkey (office). *Telephone:* (312) 4254596 (office). *Fax:* (312) 4184737 (office). *Website:* www.msb.gov.tr (office).

ILLARIONOV, Andrei (Nikolayevich), PhD; Russian economist; *Senior Fellow, Center for Global Liberty and Prosperity, Cato Institute;* b. 16 Sept. 1961, Leningrad (now St Petersburg); ed Leningrad Univ., Univ. of Birmingham, UK, Georgetown Univ., USA; Asst Researcher, Leningrad State Univ. 1983–90; Head of Sector, St Petersburg Financial and Econ. Inst. 1990–92; Deputy Dir Centre for Econ. Reforms, Russian Govt 1992–93; Adviser to the Prime Minister 1993–94; Dir Inst. of Econ. Analysis 1994–2000, Pres. 2000–; Adviser to Pres. Putin on Econ. Problems 2000–05 (resgnd); Russian Sherpa to G8 2000–05 (resgnd); Sr Fellow, Center for Global Liberty and Prosperity, Cato Inst., Washington, DC 2006–. *Publications:* Russian Economic Reforms: Lost Year 1994, Financial Stabilization in Russia 1995, Russia in a Changing World 1997, Economic Freedom of the World (co-author and co-ed.) 2000; more than 300 articles on Russian econ. and social policy. *Address:* Cato Institute, 1000 Massachusetts Avenue, NW, Washington, DC 20001-5403, USA (office). *Telephone:* (202) 842-0200 (office). *Fax:* (202) 842-3490 (office). *E-mail:* alllarionov@cato.org (office). *Website:* (office).

ILLNEROVÁ, Helena, DSc; Czech physiologist and academic; *Professor Emerita, Institute of Physiology, Academy of Sciences of the Czech Republic;* b. (Helena Lagusova), 28 Dec. 1937, Prague; d. of the late Karel Lagus and Libuše Lagusova; m. Michal Illner; one s. one d.; ed Charles Univ., Prague; researcher, Inst. of Physiology Acad. of Sciences of Czechoslovakia (of Czech Repub. since 1993), Prague 1961–, Vice-Pres. Acad. of Sciences of the Czech Republic, Prague 1993–2001, Pres. 2001–05, currently Prof. Emer., Inst. of Physiology; Pres. Czech Comm. for UNESCO 2006–12, Learned Soc. of the Czech Repub. 2008–10, Comm. for Ethics in Science 2005–13; mem. European Research Advisory Bd 2001–07, Ethics Panel of Czech TV 2005–12, Council for Science of Acad. of Sciences of the Czech Repub. 2005–13, Council for Science of Charles Univ. 2001–14; unsuccessful cand. for the Senate 2008; State Medal for Merits 2005; J.E. Purkyně Prize 1987, Medal of the Slovak Acad. of Sciences 2004, Charles Univ. Gold Medal 2005, Votočkova Medal, Inst. of Chemical Tech. 2005, Award of the Ministry for Educ. 2005, Medal of the Learned Soc. of the Czech Repub. 2007, ASCR Medal of Merit for Science and Humanity 2007, ASCR G.J. Mendel Medal 2013. *Publications:* more than 130 scientific publs. *Leisure interests:* literature, hiking, biking, grandchildren, academic activities. *Address:* Bronzová 2021/23, 155 00 Prague 5 (home); Institute of Physiology, Academy of Sciences, Vídeňská 1083, 142 20 Prague 4, Czech Republic (office). *Telephone:* (2) 41062528 (office); (2) 35512182 (home). *Fax:* (2) 21403525 (office). *E-mail:* illner@biomed.cas.cz (office); illnerova@kav.cas.cz (office). *Website:* www.cas.cz (office); www.helenaillnerova.cz.

ILVES, Toomas Hendrik, MA; Estonian politician, diplomatist, scientist and head of state; *President;* b. 26 Dec. 1953, Stockholm, Sweden; m. 1st Merry Bullock (divorced); one s. one d.; m. 2nd Evelin Int-Lambot 2004; one d.; ed Leonia High School, New Jersey, Columbia Univ., New York, Univ. of Pennsylvania, USA; Research Asst, Dept of Psychology, Columbia Univ. 1974–76, 1979; Asst to Dir and English Teacher, Center for Open Educ., Englewood, New Jersey 1979–81; Arts Admin. and Dir Vancouver Literary Centre, Canada 1981–82; Lecturer in Estonian Literature and Linguistics, Dept of Interdisciplinary Studies, Simon Fraser Univ., Vancouver 1983–84; Research Analyst, Radio Free Europe, Munich, Germany 1984–88, Dir Estonian Service 1988–93; Amb. to USA (also accred to

Canada and Mexico) 1993–96; Minister of Foreign Affairs 1996–98, 1999–2002; Chair. Bd Estonian N Atlantic Trust 1998; Deputy Chair. Moodukad Party, Chair. 1999; mem. Riigikogu (Estonian State Ass.) 2002–04; mem. European Parl. (Estonian Social Democratic Party) 2004–06, Vice-Chair. Cttee on Foreign Affairs, mem. Del. for Relations with the USA, Substitute mem. Cttee on Budgets, Sub-cttee on Security and Defence, Del. to EU-Russia Parl. Cooperation Cttee; Pres. of Estonia 2006–; Pres. Estonian Special Olympics 1997–2004; Bd mem. Tartu Univ. 1996–2003, European Movt Estonia 1999–2004, Estonian Acad. of Arts 2004–06, Trilateral Comm. 2004–06, Friends of Europe (think tank) 2005, Viljandi Co. Municipal Fund, Council on CyberSecurity's Advisory Bd 2013; numerous decorations including Grand Commdr, Légion d'honneur 2001, Third Class, Order of the Seal (Estonia) 2004, Three Star Order of the Repub. (Latvia) 2004, Hon. GCB (UK) 2006, Order of the White Rose of Finland 2007, Grand Cordon of the Supreme Order of the Chrysanthemum of Japan 2007, Order of Isabel the Catholic with collar (Spain) 2007, Collar of the Order of the Nat. Coat of Arms (Estonia) 2008, Grand Cross, Order of the Netherlands Lion 2008, Grand Cordon, Leopold of Belgium 2008, Chain of the Order of the Three Stars (Latvia) 2009, Grand Cross of the Order of Merit (Hungary) 2009, Order of St George (Georgia) 2010, Nat. Order Star of Romania in rank of Collar 2011, Dostyk (Friendship) Star Award I (Kazakhstan) 2011, Grand Collar, Nat. Order of Merit of the Repub. of Malta 2012, Cross of Recognition (Latvia), First Class 2012. *Leisure interests:* reading, cooking, farming. *Address:* Office of the President, A. Weizenbergi 39, Tallinn 15050, Estonia (office). *Telephone:* 631-6202 (office). *Fax:* 631-6250 (office). *E-mail:* vpinfo@vpk.ee (office). *Website:* www.president.ee (office).

ILYUMZHINOV, Kirsan; Russian politician, business executive and inter-national organization official; *President, Fédération Internationale des Échecs, FIDE (World Chess Federation);* b. 5 April 1962, Elista; m.; one s.; ed Moscow State Inst. of Int. Relations; Pres. Repub. of Kalmykiya, S Russia 1993–2010 (youngest leader of any fed. subject of Russian Fed. when first elected); Pres. Fédération Internationale des Echecs (FIDE) 1995–; Honoured Citizen of Elista; Order of Friendship, Order of Nicholas the Wondermaker, Order of Merit – George with a Sword; Gold Medal of Peace for Humanitarian Activity. *Publications include:* The President's Crown of Thorns 1998. *Leisure interest:* chess (chess champion of Kalmykiya as schoolboy). *E-mail:* ki@kalm.ru (office). *Website:* www.fide.com (office); glava.kalm.ru (home).

ILYUSHIN, Viktor Vasilyevich; Russian politician and business executive; *Head, Corporate Interrelations with Regional Authorities of the Russian Feder-ation, Gazprom;* b. 4 June 1947, Nizhny Tagil, Sverdlovsk Oblast; m.; one s. one d.; ed Urals Polytech. Inst., Acad. of Social Science; metalworker Nizhny Tagil metallurgy plant; First Sec. Nizhny Tagil City Komsomol Cttee, then First Sec. Sverdlovsk Regional Komsomol Cttee, Asst to First Sec. Sverdlovsk Regional CPSU Cttee; First Sec. Leninsky Dist CPSU Cttee (Sverdlovsk); counsellor Cen. Cttee Afghanistan People's Democratic Party; Asst to Chair. Russian Supreme Soviet 1990–91; Head, Pres. Yeltsin's Secr. 1991–92; First Asst Pres. of Russian Fed. 1991–96; First Deputy Prime Minister 1996–97; Head, Public Relations and Corp. Interrelations with Regional Authorities of Russian Fed. Admin, Gazprom 1997–98, Head, Corp. Interrelations with Regional Authorities of Russian Fed. Admin 1998–, mem. Man. Cttee; Badge of Honour. *Leisure interests:* tennis, mountain skiing, riding, jazz, cars, computers. *Address:* Gazprom, Nametkina str. 16, 117997 Moscow, Russia (office). *Telephone:* (495) 719-30-01 (office). *Fax:* (495) 719-83-33 (office). *Website:* www.gazprom.ru (office).

IM, Kwon-taek; South Korean film director; b. 2 May 1936, Changsong, Cheollanam-do; ed Sr High School, Kwangju; began career as labourer, Pusan; Production Asst with film Dir Chung Chang-Hwa, Seoul 1956–61; made first feature film 1962, subsequently directed over 100 films; prof. Coll. of Arts, Dongguk Univ. (Seoul) 1998–; mem. Nat. Acad. of Arts Republic of Korea 2002; Hon. DLit (Catholic Univ. of Korea); UNESCO Fellini Gold Medal 2002 for his work as a whole, Hon. Golden Bear Berlin Film Festival 2005; numerous other Korean and int. film festival awards. *Films include:* Dumanganga jal itgeola (Farewell to the Duman River) 1962, Danjang lok (The Prince's Revolt) 1963, Mangbuseog (A Wife Turned to Stone) 1963, Shibjamae seonsaeng (Father of Ten Daughters) 1964, Bisog e Jida (Death of an Informer) 1965, Pungunui gomgaek (Swordsmen) 1967, Cheongsa cholong (The Feudal Tenant) 1967, Tola-on oensonjabi (Return from the Sea) 1968, Mongnyeo (The Waking Woman) 1968, Sibo Ya (Full Moon Night) 1969, Roe Gom (Thunder Sword) 1969, Weolha ui geom (Swords under the Moon) 1970, Bigeom (The Flying Sword) 1970, Yogeom (Swordswoman) 1971, Tuljjae omoni (A Stepmother's Heartache) 1971, Myeong-dong janhoksa (Cruelty on the Streets of Myongdong) 1972, Jung eon (The Testimony) 1973, Jabcho (The Deserted Widow) 1973, Yeonhwa (The Hidden Princess) 1974, Wae geulaess-teunga (Who and Why?) 1975, Anae (The Industri-ous Wife) 1976, Sangnok su (The Evergreen Tree) 1978, Chopko (Genealogy) 1978, Tchak Ko (Pursuit of Death) 1980, Mandala 1981, Angae Maul (Village in the Mist) 1982, Gilsottum 1985, Sibaji (The Surrogate Woman) 1986, Yonsan Ilgi (Diary of King Yongsan) 1987, Adada 1988, Janggunui adeul (Son of the General) 1990, Kae Byok (Fly High Run Far) 1992, Sopyonje 1993 (most honoured Korean film ever: 27 domestic and three international prizes), Taebek sanmaek (Taebak Mountains) 1994, Ch'ukje 1986, Chunhyang 2000, Chihwaseon (Strokes of Fire) (Best Director Award at 2002 Cannes International Film Festival) 2002, Haryu insaeng 2004, Chun nyun hack 2007.

IMAI, Nobuko; Japanese violist; b. 18 March 1943, Tokyo; m. Aart van Bochove 1981; one s. one d.; ed Toho School of Music, Tokyo, Juilliard School and Yale Univ., USA; mem. Vermeer Quartet 1974–79, now mem. Michelangelo String Quartet; soloist with Berlin Philharmonic, London Symphony Orchestra, Royal Philharmonic, the BBC orchestras, Detroit Symphony, Chicago Symphony, Concertgebouw, Montréal Symphony, Boston Symphony, Vienna Symphony, Orchestre de Paris, Stockholm Philharmonic; festival performances include Marlborough, Salzburg, Lockenhaus, Casals, South Bank, Summer Music, Aldeburgh, BBC Proms, Int. Viola Congress (Houston), New York "Y", Festival d'Automne, Paris; conceived Int. Hindemith Viola Festival (London, New York, Tokyo) 1995; Prof. High School of Music, Detmold, Germany 1995–2003; currently teaches at Amsterdam School of the Arts, Conservatory in Geneva; Artistic Adviser, Casals Hall, Tokyo; First Prize Munich, Second Prize Geneva Int. Viola Competitions; Avon Arts Award 1993, Japanese Educ. Minister's Art Prize for

Music 1993, Mobil Japan Art Prize 1995, Suntory Hall Prize 1996. *Leisure interest:* cooking. *Address:* c/o Tivoli & Crescendi Artists, Læderstræde 9, 4, 1202 Copenhagen K, Denmark (office); Amsterdam School of the Arts, Oosterdokskade 151, Postbus 78022, 1070 LP Amsterdam, Netherlands. *Website:* www.ahk.nl.

IMAI, Takashi; Japanese business executive; *Senior Advisor and Honorary Chairman, Nippon Steel & Sumitomo Metal Corporation;* b. 23 Dec. 1929, Kamakura; ed Univ. of Tokyo; joined Fuji Iron & Steel 1952, Man. Raw Materials 1963; Deputy Gen. Man. Fuel and Ferrous Metals, Nippon Steel (formed by merger of Fuji Iron & Steel and Yawata Steel) 1970, Gen. Man. Iron Ore 1973, Man. Dir 1983, Exec. Vice-Pres. 1989, Pres. Nippon Steel Corpn 1992–98, Chair. 1998–2003, Sr Vice-Pres., Chair. Emer. and Exec. Counselor 2003–08, Sr Advisor and Hon. Chair. 2008– (merged with Sumitomo Metal Industries Ltd to become Nippon Steel & Sumitomo Metal Corpn 2012); mem. Bd of Dirs Nippon Telegraph and Telephone 1999–; Outside Dir Japan Securities Finance Co. Ltd 2002–, Nippon Television Network Corpn 2007–. *Address:* Nippon Steel & Sumitomo Metal Corpn, Marunouchi Park Building, 6-1, Marunouchi 2-chome, Chiyoda-ku, Tokyo 100-8071, Japan (office). *Telephone:* (3) 6867-4111 (office). *Fax:* (3) 6867-5607 (office). *E-mail:* info@nssmc.com (office). *Website:* www.nssmc.com (office).

IMAKI, Hisakazu, BS; Japanese automobile industry executive; *Supreme Executive Advisor, Mazda Motor Corporation;* b. 5 Dec. 1942; m.; one s. one d.; ed Himeji Inst. of Tech.; joined Toyo Kogyo Co. Ltd (later renamed Mazda Motor Corpn) 1965, Gen. Man. Admin Group and Advanced Production Eng Group 1988–89, Gen. Man. Painting, Trim and Final Ass. Eng Dept 1989–92, Deputy Gen. Man. Production Eng Div. and Gen. Man. Production Planning Dept 1992–93, Dir, Gen. Man. Production Eng Div. and Gen. Man. Production Planning Dept 1993–96, Dir and Gen. Man. Hiroshima Plant 1996–97, Man.-Dir in charge of Production Eng, Mfg and Business Logistics 1997–99, Sr Man.-Dir 1999–2002, Rep. Dir, Exec. Vice-Pres. and Chief Eng and Mfg Officer in charge of Research & Devt, Production, Quality Assurance and Business Logistics 2002–03, CEO, Pres. and Rep. Dir 2003–06, Chair., Pres., CEO and Rep. Dir 2006–08, Chair. and Rep. Dir 2008–10, Supreme Exec. Advisor 2010–; Person of the Year in Japan, Automotive Researchers and Journalists Conference 2006. *Leisure interests:* basketball, photography, driving. *Address:* Mazda Motor Corpn, 3-1 Shinchi, Fuchu-cho, Aki-gun, Hiroshima 730-8670, Japan (office). *Telephone:* (82) 282-1111 (office). *Fax:* (82) 287-5190 (office). *E-mail:* info@mazda.com (office). *Website:* www.mazda.com (office).

IMAM, Adel; Egyptian actor; *Goodwill Ambassador, United Nations High Commissioner for Refugees;* b. 17 May 1940, Cairo; m. Hala Al Shalaqani; three c.; ed Cairo Univ.; has appeared in over 100 films and nine plays; early success as a comic actor on stage and film, subsequently famous for topical roles, often depicting victims of poverty and injustice, one of most successful actors in Arab world; his play Al -Zaeem (The Leader) has been performed worldwide; apptd UNHCR Goodwill Amb. 2001. *Films include:* Ana Wa Hua Wa Hia (I, He and She) 1964, El Ragol da hai Ganini 1967, Khouroug min el Guana 1967, Karamet Zawgaty 1967, Kayfa Tesrak Millionaire 1968, Helwa wa Shakia 1968, Ana al-Doctor 1968, Afrit Merati 1968, Al-Bahth an Fadiha 1973, Katel ma Katelsh had 1979, Athkiya' Laken Aghbiya' 1980, Ala Bab e l'Wazir 1982, El Harrif (The Street Player) 1983, Al Avokato 1984, Al-Irhabi wal Kabab (Terrorism and Bar-B-Q) 1993, Al-Irhabi (The Terrorist) 1994, Tuyoor Al-Zalam (Birds of Darkness) 1995, Al-Wad Mahrous Beta' Al-Wazir (Mahrous, The Minister's Boy) 1999, Amir El Zalam 2002, Tag Rubah el Danemarkiyyah 2003, Aris Min Geha Amneya 2004, Amarit Ya'koubian 2005, The Yacoubian Building (in trans.) 2006. *Plays include:* Al -Zaeem (The Leader), Shahid ma Shafesh Haga, Bodyguard. *Address:* c/o United Nations High Commissioner for Refugees (UNHCR), CP 2500, 1211 Geneva 2 dépôt, Switzerland.

IMAMI, Arben; Albanian politician; *Minister of Defence;* b. 21 Jan. 1958, Tirana; ed Fine Arts Acad., Tirana, School of Foreign Service, Georgetown Univ., Washington, DC, USA; Minority Leader and Vice-Chair. Democratic Party 1990–92; Founder Democratic Alliance Party 1992, Gen. Sec. 1992–99; mem. Kuvendi Popullor (Parl.) 1991–96, 1997–2005, Co-Chair. Parl. Comm. to Draft New Constitution 1997–98; Minister of State for Legis. Reform and Relations with Parl. 1998–99; Minister of Justice 2000–01; Minister of Local Govt and Decentralization 2001–02; Minister of Defence 2009–; mem. Democratic Party of Albania. *Address:* Ministry of Defence, Bulevardi Dëshmorët e Kombit, Tirana Albania (office). *Telephone:* (4) 2226601 (office). *Fax:* (4) 2228325 (office). *E-mail:* kontakt@mod.gov.al (office). *Website:* www.mod.gov.al (office).

IMAN; American (b. Somali) model and actress; b. (Iman Abdul Majid), 25 July 1955, Mogadishu; d. of Mohamed Abdulmajid and Marian Abdulmajid; m. 2nd Spencer Haywood 1977 (divorced 1987); one d.; m. 3rd David Bowie 1992; one d.; ed Nairobi Univ.; fashion model 1976–90, has modelled for Claude Montana and Thierry Mugler; signed Revlon Polish Ambers contract (first black model to be signed by int. cosmetics co.) 1979; Founder and CEO IMAN Cosmetics, Skincare and Fragrances 1994–; Spokesperson Keep a Child Alive program; Fashion Icon Lifetime Achievement Award, Council of Fashion Designers of America 2010. *Films include:* The Human Factor 1979, Jane Austen in Manhattan 1980, Exposed 1983, Out of Africa 1985, No Way Out 1987, Surrender 1987, In the Heat of the Night 1988, L.A. Story 1991, House Party 2 1991, Star Trek VI: The Undiscovered Country 1991, The Linguini Incident 1991, Exit to Eden 1994, The Deli 1997, Omikron: The Nomad Soul 1999, Project Runway Canada 2007, 2009, The Fashion Show 2010. *Television appearances include:* Miami Vice, The Cosby Show, In the Heat of the Night, Lies of the Twins 1991, Heart of Darkness 1994. *Publications include:* I Am Iman 2001, The Beauty of Color 2005. *Address:* TESS Management, 4th Floor, 9-10 Market Place, London, W1W 8AQ, England (office). *E-mail:* info@tessmanagement.com (office). *Website:* www.tessmanagement.com (office); www.imancosmetics.com.

IMANAKA, Hiroshi, LLD; Japanese professor of law; *Professor Emeritus, Faculty of Law, Hiroshima University;* b. 2 Dec. 1930, Fukuoka City; s. of the late Tsugumaro Imanaka; ed Univs of Hiroshima and Nagoya; Lecturer, Faculty of Educ., Miyazaki Univ. 1960–65; Lecturer, Dept of Gen. Educ., Hiroshima Univ. 1965–67, Assoc. Prof. 1967–78, Prof. of Political Science, Faculty of Integrated Arts and Sciences 1978–81, Faculty of Law 1981–91, Prof. Emer. 1991–; Dean and Prof., Kinjogakuin Univ. 1991–2001, Prof. Emer. 2001–. *Publications include:* Consti-

tutional Law (co-author) 1971, George Lawson's Political Theory of Civil Government 1976, A Study of the History of English Political Thought 1977, Parliamentarism and its Origin in the Era of English Revolution, The English Revolution and the Modern Political Theory of George Lawson 2000. *Address:* 2-6-10 Yoshijima-Higashi, Naka-ku, Hiroshima Shi, Japan (home). *Telephone:* (82) 244-4756 (home). *Fax:* (82) 244-4756 (home). *E-mail:* hiro-imanaka@go7.enjoy.ne.jp.

IMANALIEV, Muratbek Sansyzbayevich; Kyrgyzstani diplomatist; *Secretary-General, Shanghai Cooperation Organisation;* b. 25 Feb. 1956, Frunze (now Bishkek); m.; one s. one d.; ed Moscow State Univ., Leningrad Inst. of Oriental Studies; Second, then First Sec., then Head, Consular Dept, Acting Minister of Foreign Affairs of the Kirghiz SSR 1982–91, Minister for Foreign Affairs 1991–92, 1997–2002; Amb. to China 1993–96; Head of Int. Dept of Presidential Admin 1996–97; Chair. Comm. on Foreign Policy, Ministry of Foreign Affairs and adviser to the Pres. –2009; Sec.-Gen. Shanghai Cooperation Org., Beijing 2010–; Co-founder and Pres. Inst. for Public Policy 2005–09; Assoc. Prof., American Univ.-Central Asia; mem. Justice and Progress Party; Co-founder Jany Bagyt (New Course) movt 2004. *Address:* Office of the Secretary-General, Shanghai Cooperation Organisation, Liangmaqiao Road 41, Chaoyang District, Beijing, People's Republic of China (office). *Telephone:* (10) 65329807 (office). *Fax:* (10) 65329808 (office). *E-mail:* sco@sectsco.org (office). *Website:* www.sectsco.org (office); www.ipp.kg (office).

IMASHEV, Chorobek Imashevich; Kyrgyzstani economist and politician; b. 1963; economist in office of Exec. Dir for Switzerland and in European II Dept, IMF 1993–98; fmr Deputy Minister of Finance and Economy, in charge of int. and devt affairs, including liaison with IMF, World Bank and other institutions; Minister of Finance 2010–11 (resgnd). *Address:* c/o Ministry of Finance, 720040 Bishkek, bul. Erkindik 58, Kyrgyzstan.

IMBERT, Baron (Life Peer), cr. 1999, of New Romney in the County of Kent; **Peter Michael Imbert,** CVO, QPM; British police officer and business executive; b. 27 April 1933, Folkestone, Kent; s. of the late William Henry Imbert and of Frances May Hodge; m. Iris Rosina Dove 1956; one s. two d.; ed Harvey Grammar School, Folkstone; Metropolitan Police 1953–93, Asst Chief Constable, Surrey Constabulary 1976–77, Deputy Chief Constable 1977–79, Chief Constable, Thames Valley Police 1979–85, Deputy Commr Metropolitan Police 1985–87, Commr 1987–93; Metropolitan Police Anti-Terrorist Squad 1973–75; Police negotiator in Balcombe Street (London) IRA Siege Dec. 1975; Sec. Nat. Crime Cttee, ACPO Council 1980–83, Chair. 1983–85; Chair. Vehicle Security Installation Bd 1994–96; Chair. Capital Eye Security Ltd 1997–; Strategic Adviser, Inkerman Group Ltd (int. business risk and intelligence); Dir (non-exec.) Securicor 1993–2000, Camelot Group 1994–2000, Retainagroup 1995–2004; consultant, CDR International 1997–2000; mem. Gen. Advisory Council, BBC 1980–87, Criminal Justice Consultative Cttee 1992–93; Chair. Surrey Co. Cricket Club Youth Trust 1993–96, Vice-Pres. Surrey Co. Cricket Club; currently Pres. Littlestone, Kent, Golf Club; Vice-Pres. Friends of St Thomas' Hosp., Cinq Ports Br., Royal Soc. of St George; mem. Ministerial Advisory Bd on Royal Parks 1993–2000, Public Policy Cttee of Royal Automobile Club 1993–2000; mem. Editorial Advisory Bd and occasional contrib., Professional Security Magazine; Trustee, Help the Aged 1993–95, St Catherine's Foundation Cumberland Lodge, Univ. Coll. Hosp. Charitable Foundation, Metropolitan Police Museum Trust, Police Foundation; DL Greater London 1994–98, Lord Lt of Greater London 1998–2008; mem. (Crossbench) House of Lords 1999–; Hon. DLitt (Reading), Hon. MBA (International Man. Centre). *Leisure interests:* golf, bad bridge, watching good cricket, talking about his grandchildren. *Address:* House of Lords, Westminster, London, SW1A 0PW, England (office). *Telephone:* (20) 7219-3000 (office). *Fax:* (20) 8947-9995 (office). *E-mail:* peterimbert@btinternet.com (office). *Website:* www.parliament.uk/biographies/lords/peter-imbert/26778 (office).

IMBUSCH, George Francis, DSc, PhD, FInstP, FAIP; Irish physicist, academic and university administrator; *Professor Emeritus of Experimental Physics, National University of Ireland, Galway;* b. 7 Oct. 1935, Limerick; s. of George Imbusch and Alice Neville; m. Mary Rita O'Donnell 1961; one s. one d.; ed Christian Brothers' School, Limerick, Univ. Coll., Galway and Stanford Univ., USA; mem. tech. staff, Bell Labs, USA 1964–67; Lecturer in Physics, Univ. Coll. Galway (now Nat. Univ. of Ireland, Galway) 1967–74, Prof. of Experimental Physics 1974–2002, Prof. Emer. 2002–, Head, Dept of Physics 1986–89, Vice-Pres. 1992–98; Science Sec., Royal Irish Acad. 1989–93, Sr Vice-Pres. 2005–08, Hon. Academic Research Officer 2005–08; Visiting Prof., Univ. of Wisconsin 1978, Univ. of Regensburg 1981, Univ. of Utrecht 1988, Univ. of Canterbury, NZ 1995, Univ. of Georgia, USA 1998. *Publications:* Optical Spectroscopy of Inorganic Solids (co-author) 1989; more than 100 scientific papers in journals. *Leisure interests:* painting, reading. *Address:* Room A0204a, Department of Physics, National University of Ireland, Galway, University Road, Galway (office); Forramoyle West, Barna, Co. Galway, Ireland (home). *Telephone:* (91) 492510 (office); (91) 592159 (home). *E-mail:* frank.imbusch@nuigalway.ie (office); g.f.imbusch@nuigalway.ie (office); gfimbusch@eircom.net (home). *Website:* www.nuigalway.ie/physics/research_top.html (office).

IMMELT, Jeffrey R., BA, MBA; American business executive; *Chairman and CEO, General Electric Company;* b. 19 Feb. 1956, Cincinnati, Ohio; s. of Joseph Immelt and Donna Immelt; m. Andrea Allen 1986; one d.; ed Finneytown High School, Dartmouth Coll., Harvard Univ.; joined Gen. Electric Co. 1982, Corp. Marketing Dept 1982, various positions with GE Plastics 1982–89, Vice-Pres. 1992–93, Vice-Pres. GE Appliances 1989–91, Vice-Pres. Worldwide Marketing and Product Man. 1991–93, Vice-Pres. and Gen. Man. GE Plastics Americas 1993–97, Pres. and CEO GE Medical Systems 1997–2001, Pres. and CEO General Electric Co. 2000–01, Chair. and CEO 2001–; Chair. President's Council on Jobs and Competitiveness 2011–; mem. Bd of Dirs Catalyst, Robin Hood, New York City, New York Fed. Reserve Bank; mem. The Business Council; named three times by Barron's as one of the World's Best CEOs, Man of the Year, Financial Times 2003, ranked by Forbes magazine amongst The World's Most Powerful People (13th) 2009, (35th) 2010, (28th) 2011, (24th) 2012, (25th) 2013. *Leisure interest:* golf. *Address:* Board of Directors, General Electric Company, 3135 Easton Turnpike, Fairfield, CT 06828-0001, USA (office). *Telephone:* (203) 373-2652 (Bd) (office);

(203) 373-2211 (office). *Fax:* (203) 373-3131 (office). *E-mail:* directors@corporate.ge.com (office). *Website:* www.ge.com (office).

IMRAN KHAN NIAZI (see KHAN NIAZI, Imran).

IMRAY, Sir Colin Henry, Kt, KBE, CMG, KStJ, MA; British diplomatist (retd); *Vice-President, Royal Over-Seas League;* b. 21 Sept. 1933, Newport, Mon., Wales; s. of Henry Gibbon Imray and Frances Olive Badman; m. Shirley Margaret Matthews 1957; one s. three d.; ed Highgate School, London, Hotchkiss School, Conn., USA and Balliol Coll., Oxford, Royal Coll. of Defence Studies; Second Lt Seaforth Highlanders, Royal W African Frontier Force 1952–54; Asst Prin. Commonwealth Relations Office 1957–58, 1961–63; Third then Second Sec. British High Comm., Canberra 1958–61; First Sec., Nairobi 1963–66; Asst Head Personnel Dept FCO 1966–70; British Trade Commr, Montreal 1970–73; Counsellor, Consul Gen. and Head of Chancery, Islamabad 1973–77; Royal Coll. of Defence Studies 1977–; Commercial Counsellor, Embassy in Tel-Aviv 1977–80; Deputy High Commr, Bombay 1980–84; Asst Under-Sec. of State (Chief Inspector and Deputy Chief Clerk) 1984–85; High Commr to Tanzania 1986–89, to Bangladesh 1989–93; Sec. Gen. Order of St John 1993–97, Dir Overseas Relations 1997–98; mem. Cen. Council Royal Over-Seas League 1998–2005, Exec. Cttee 1999–2005, Chair. 2000–05, Vice-Pres. 2005–; High Steward of Wallingford 2001–; Freeman of the City of London 1994. *Publication:* Remember and Be Glad 2009. *Leisure interests:* walking, gardening. *Address:* Holbrook House, Reading Road, Wallingford, Oxon., OX10 9DT, England (home). *Telephone:* (1491) 833044 (home).

IÑÁRRITU, Alejandro González; Mexican film director and screenwriter; b. 15 Aug. 1963, Mexico City; early career as radio DJ in Mexico City; fmr Head of elevisa (TV production co.); f. Zeta Films (advertising agency and film production co.); Golden Eye Award (for career achievement), Zurich Film Festival 2011. *Films include:* El Timbre (also writer) 1996, Amores perros (also producer) 2000, Powder Keg (also writer) 2001, 11'09"01: September 11 (Mexico segment, also writer and producer) 2002, 21 Grams (also producer) 2003, Nine Lives (exec. producer) 2005, Toro negro (exec. producer) 2005, Babel (Best Dir Cannes Film Festival 2006, Palm Springs Int. Film Festival 2007) (also producer) 2006, Rudo y Cursi (producer), Mother and Child (exec. producer), Biutiful (also producer) 2010. *Address:* c/o Endeavor Agency, 9601 Wilshire Blvd., 10th Floor, Beverly Hills, CA 90212, USA. *Telephone:* (310) 248-2000. *Fax:* (310) 248-2020.

INAZ, Ahmed; Maldivian economist and politician; b. 9 Sept. 1976; ed Nat. Univ. of Singapore, Singapore, Univ. of Westminster, UK; has served in several govt posts, including Minister of State for Econ. Devt, Dir Gen., Ministry of Planning, Trade Policy Coordinator, Ministry of Trade and Econ. Devt; Founding mem. Transparency Maldives (chapter of Transparency International); Visiting Lecturer at various colls 2005–; Minister of Finance and Treasury 2011–12; mem. Maldivian Democratic Party –2012. *Address:* c/o Ministry of Finance and Treasury, Ameenee Magu, Malé 20-379, Maldives.

INBAL, Eliahu; British/Israeli conductor; b. 16 Feb. 1936, Jerusalem, Israel; s. of Jehuda Joseph Inbal and Leah Museri Inbal; m. Helga Fritzsche 1968; two s. one d.; ed Acad. of Music, Jerusalem, Conservatoire Nat. Supérieur, Paris, courses with Franco Ferrara, Hilversum and Sergiu Celebidache, Siena; guest conductor with numerous orchestras including Milan, Rome, Berlin, Munich, Hamburg, Stockholm, Copenhagen, Vienna, Budapest, Amsterdam, London, Paris, Tel-Aviv, New York, Chicago, Toronto and Tokyo from 1963; Chief Conductor HR Radio Symphony Orchestra, Frankfurt 1974–90, Hon. Conductor 1995–; Chief Conductor Teatro La Fenice 1984–87, Music Dir 2007–11; regularly conducted Konzerthaus Berlin Symphony Orchestra 1992–, Chief Conductor 2001–06, Hon. mem. 2006–; Chief Conductor Tokyo Metropolitan Symphony Orchestra 2008–14, Hon. Conductor 2014–; Music Dir Czech Philharmonic Orchestra 2009–12; Hon. Conductor, HR-Sinfonieorchester Frankfurt 1990–, Orchestra Nazionale della RAI, Turin 1995–2001; Officier des Arts et des Lettres 1990, Goldenes Ehrenzeichen, Vienna 2001, Order of Merit (FRG) 2006; First Prize, Int. Conductors' Competition 'G. Cantelli' 1963, Golden Medal for Merit, City of Vienna 2001, Goethe Badge of Honour, City of Frankfurt 2006, numerous prizes for recordings, including Deutscher Schallplattenpreis, Grand Prix du Disque, Prix Caecilia, Symphony Prize of 50th Record Academy Award (Japan) 2012. *Recordings:* numerous recordings, particularly of Mahler, Bruckner, Berlioz and Shostakovich. *Leisure interests:* music reproduction, photography. *Address:* c/o Karsten Witt Music Management, Leuschnerdamm 13, 10999 Berlin, Germany (office). *Telephone:* (30) 214594-0 (office). *E-mail:* info@karstenwitt.com (office). *Website:* www.karstenwitt.com (office).

INDIANA, Robert, BFA; American artist; b. (Robert Clark), 13 Sept. 1928, New Castle, Ind.; ed John Herron School of Art, Indianapolis, Munson-Williams-Proctor Inst., Utica, New York, Art Inst. of Chicago, Skowhegan School of Painting and Sculpture, Univ. of Edinburgh and Edinburgh Coll. of Art, UK; served in USAAF 1946–49; Artist-in-Residence, Center of Contemporary Art, Aspen, Colo 1968; Hon. DFA (Franklin and Marshall Coll., Lancaster, Pa) 1970. *Address:* c/o Simon Salama-Caro, 45 East 80th Street, New York, NY 10021, USA. *Telephone:* (212) 585-3624. *Fax:* (212) 585-3623.

INDIMI, Mohammed; Nigerian business executive; *Chairman and CEO, Oriental Energy Resources Ltd;* b. Aug. 1948, Maiduguri, Borno State; m.; eight c.; f. Oriental Energy Resources Ltd 1990, currently Chair. and CEO; currently also Chair. M & W Pump Nigeria Ltd; Officer, Order of the Federal Repub. (Nigeria); numerous hon. degrees from univs in Nigeria, Ireland, USA. *Address:* Oriental Energy Resources Limited, Plot 397, Muhammadu Buhari Way, Central Business District Area, PMB 5101, Abuja, Nigeria (office). *Telephone:* (9) 4610438 (office). *Fax:* (9) 4610450 (office). *Website:* www.oriental-er.com (office).

INDRAWATI, HE Sri Mulyani, BA, PhD; Indonesian economist, academic and fmr government official; *Managing Director, World Bank Group;* b. 26 Aug. 1962, Tanjungkarang, Lampung; m.; three c.; ed Univ. of Indonesia, Jakarta, Univ. of Illinois at Urbana-Champaign, USA; several positions at Inst. for Econ. and Social Research, Faculty of Econs, Univ. Indonesia (LPEM-FEUI) 1992–2004 including Assoc. Dir Research 1992–93, Assoc. Dir Educ. and Training 1993–95, Dir Program Magister, Planning and Public Policy, Grad. Program Econs 1996–99, Dir 1998–2004; Staff Expert in Policy Analysis, Overseas Training Office 1994–95; adviser, Nat. Econ. Council 1999–2001, Sec.-Gen.; consultant to USAID 2001–;

Visiting Faculty mem., Andrew Young School of Policy Studies, Georgia State Univ. 2001–02; Exec. Dir IMF 2002; Minister of State and Chair. Nat. Devt Planning Agency 2004–05; Minister of Finance and State Enterprises Devt 2005–10 (resgnd), also Acting Co-ordinating Minister for Econ. Affairs 2008–09; Man. Dir responsible for Latin America and Caribbean, Middle East and North Africa and East Asia and Pacific, World Bank Group 2010–; Best Asian Finance Minister, Emerging Market 2006, ranked by Globe Asia amongst Most Influential Indonesian Woman (second) 2006, ranked by Forbes magazine amongst The World's 100 Most Powerful Women (23rd) 2008, (72nd) 2009, (65th) 2011, (72nd) 2012, (55th) 2013. *Publications include:* Potential and Student Savings in DKI Jakarta 1995, Domestic Industry Preparedness for the Free Trade Era 1997, Forget CBS, Get Serious About Reform 1998. *Address:* The World Bank, 1818 H Street NW, Washington, DC 20433, USA (office). *Telephone:* (202) 473-1000 (office). *Fax:* (202) 477-6391 (office). *Website:* web.worldbank.org (office).

INDURÁIN, Miguel; Spanish fmr professional cyclist; b. 16 July 1964, Villava, Navarre; m. Marisa Induráin; one d.; mem. Reynolds team 1984–89, Banesto team 1989–96; five successive wins, Tour de France 1991–95, 1995 winning time, 92 hours, 44 minutes and 59 seconds; Gold Medal, Atlanta Olympics 1996; ranked No. 1 cyclist 1992, 1993; announced retirement Jan. 1997; f. Miguel Induráin Foundation 1998, current Hon. Chair.; fmr mem. Comité Olímpico Español (Spanish Olympic Cttee). *Address:* Villava, Pamplona, Spain.

INDYK, Martin S., BEcons, PhD; American diplomatist and academic; *Senior Fellow, Foreign Policy Studies and Director, Saban Center for Middle East Policy, Brookings Institution;* b. 1 July 1951, London, England; m. Jill Indyk; two c.; ed Sydney Univ., Australian Nat. Univ.; worked as Deputy Dir of current intelligence for Middle East, Austalia intelligence service 1978; Adjunct Prof. Johns Hopkins School of Advanced Int. Studies; Exec. Dir Washington Inst. for Near East Policy 1985; sworn in as US citizen 1993; Special Asst to the Pres. and Sr Dir for Near East and S Asian Affairs, Nat. Security Council; Prin. Adviser to the Pres. and Nat. Security Adviser on Arab–Israeli Issues, Iraq, Iran and S Asia; Sr mem. Warren Christopher's Middle East peace team; Amb. to Israel 1995–97, 2000–01; Asst Sec. for Near Eastern Affairs 1997–2000; Sr Fellow and Dir Saban Center for Middle East Policy, The Brookings Institution 2002–; mem. Int. Inst. for Strategic Studies, Middle East Inst. *Publications:* Innocent Abroad: An Intimate Account of American Peace Diplomacy in the Middle East 2009; numerous articles and contribs to foreign policy journals. *Address:* Saban Center for Middle East Policy, The Brookings Institution, 1775 Massachusetts Avenue, NW, Washington, DC 20036, USA (office). *Telephone:* (202) 797-6462 (office). *Fax:* (202) 797-2481 (office). *E-mail:* SabanCenter@brookings.edu (office). *Website:* www.brookings.edu (office).

ING, Nita; Taiwanese business executive; *Chairman, Taiwan High Speed Rail Corporation;* d. of the late Glyn T. H. Ing; two d.; ed Taipei American School, boarding schools in Mass and New Jersey, UCLA, USA; joined family business Continental Engineering Corpn as personal asst to her father, apptd Pres. 1987, later Chair., currently CEO; Chair. Taiwan Hi-Speed Railway Corpn 1998–; mem. Bd of Dirs Taiwan Mobile; ranked by Fortune magazine amongst 50 Most Powerful Women in Business outside the US (23rd) 2002, (35th) 2003. *Address:* 2190 Broadway Street, Apt 6W, San Francisco, CA 94115, USA; Continental Engineering Corpn, 5, Tun Hua South Road, Sec 2, Taipei, Taiwan (office). *Telephone:* (2) 3701-1000 (office). *Fax:* (2) 8712-8888 (office). *E-mail:* webadmin@mail.cec.com.tw (office). *Website:* www.cec.com.tw; www.thsrc.com.tw (office).

INGE, Baron (Life Peer), cr. 1997, of Richmond in the County of North Yorkshire; **Field Marshal (retd) Peter Anthony Inge,** KG, GCB; British army officer; b. 5 Aug. 1935; s. of Raymond Albert Inge and the late Grace Maud Caroline Inge; m. Letitia Marion Beryl Thornton-Berry 1960; two d.; ed Summer Fields, Wrekin Coll., Royal Mil. Acad., Sandhurst; commissioned, Green Howards 1956, ADC to GOC 4 Div. 1960–61, Adjutant, 1st Green Howards 1963–64, student, Staff Coll. 1966, Ministry of Defence 1967–69, Co. Commdr 1st Green Howards 1969–70, student, Jt Service Staff Coll. 1971, Brigade Maj., 11th Armoured Brigade 1972, Instructor, Staff Coll. 1973–74, CO 1st Green Howards 1974–76, Commdt, Jr Div. Staff Coll. 1977–79, Commdr 4th Armoured Brigade 1980–81, Chief of Staff HQ 1st (BR) Corps 1982–83, GOC NEDIST and Commdr 2nd Infantry Div. 1984–86, Dir-Gen. Logistic Policy (Army) 1986–87, Commdr 1st (BR) Corps 1987–89, Commdr NORTHAG and C-in-C British Army of the Rhine 1989–92, Chief of Gen. Staff 1992–94, of the Defence Staff 1994–97, Constable of HM's Fortress and Palace, The Tower of London 1996–2001; ADC Gen. to the Queen 1991–94, Deputy Lt of N Yorks. 1994; Deputy Chair. Historic Royal Palaces 1997–2007; Chair. King Edward VII Sister Agnes' Hosp. 2004–12; mem. Council Marlborough Coll. 1997–2006; Commr Royal Hosp. Chelsea 1998–2004; Pres. The Pilgrims 2002–; Col The Green Howards 1982–94, Col Commdt Royal Mil. Police 1987–92, Col Commdt Army Physical Training Corps 1988–97; currently Adviser to King and Govt of Bahrain; mem. Bd of Dirs Aegis; mem. of Council IISS; mem. St George's Council, Windsor; Freeman City of London 1994. *Leisure interests:* cricket, walking, music, reading, military history. *Address:* House of Lords, London, SW1A 0PW, England (home). *Telephone:* (20) 7219-8706 (home). *E-mail:* ingep@parliament.uk.

INGELS, Bjarke; Danish architect; *Founder, Bjarke Ingels Group (BIG);* b. 2 Oct. 1974; ed Royal Danish Acad. of Fine Arts, Technica Superior de Arquitectura, Barcelona; worked for Rem Koolhaas, Office for Metropolitan Architecture, Rotterdam 1998–2001; Co-founder (with Julien de Smedt) PLOT (architectural practice), Copenhagen 2001–05; f. Bjarke Ingels Group (BIG) 2006; co-f. KiBiSi (design group) 2009; Visiting Prof., Rice Univ. School of Architecture, Harvard Grad. School of Design, Columbia Univ. Grad. School of Architecture, Planning and Preservation, Yale School of Architecture; numerous awards including Nykredit Architecture Prize 2002, Golden Lion for best concert hall design, Venice Biennale of Architecture (for Stavanger Concert Hall proposal) 2004, European Architecture Prize 2010, Wall Street Journal Innovator of the Year for Architecture 2011, Danish Crown Prince Couple's Culture Award 2011, American Inst. of Architects Honor Award 2012. *Publication:* Yes Is More: An Archicomic on Architectural Evolution 2009. *Address:* BIG CPH, Kløverbladsgade 56, Valby, 2500 Copenhagen, Denmark (office). *Telephone:* 7221-7227 (office). *Fax:* 3512-7227 (office). *E-mail:* big@big.dk (office). *Website:* www.big.dk (office).

INGHAM, Sir Bernard, Kt; British fmr civil servant; b. 21 June 1932, Halifax, Yorks.; s. of Garnet Ingham and Alice Ingham; m. Nancy Hilda Hoyle 1956; one s.;

ed Hebden Bridge Grammar School, Tech. Colls of Todmorden, Halifax and Bradford; reporter, Hebden Bridge Times 1948–52, The Yorkshire Post and Yorkshire Evening Post, Halifax 1952–59; with The Yorkshire Post, Leeds 1959–61, Northern Industrial Corresp. 1961; with The Guardian 1962–67, Labour Staff, London 1965–67; Press and Public Relations Adviser Nat. Bd for Prices and Incomes 1967–68; Chief Information Officer, Dept of Employment and Productivity 1968–72; Dir of Information Dept of Employment 1973; with Dept of Energy 1974–79, Dir of Information 1974–77, Under-Sec. and Head of Energy Conservation Div. 1978–79; Chief Press Sec. to Prime Minister Margaret Thatcher 1979–90, Head, Govt Information Service 1989–90; columnist, Daily Express 1991–98; Chair. Bernard Ingham Communications 1990–2011; Pres. British Franchise Asscn 1994–2012; Vice-Pres. Country Guardian 1991–; Dir (non-exec.) McDonald's Restaurants Ltd 1991–2005 (mem. Advisory Bd 2005–09), Hill and Knowlton 1991–2002; Visiting Fellow and Hon. Dir Applied Policy Science Unit, Univ. of Newcastle-upon-Tyne 1991–2003; mem. Council Univ. of Huddersfield 1994–2000; Visiting Prof., Univ. of Middlesex Business School 1997–2003, Univ. of Surrey 2005–09; Sec., Supporters of Nuclear Energy Sec. 1998–; Dr hc (Buckingham) 1997, (Middx) 1999, (Bradford) 2004. *Publications include:* Kill the Messenger 1991, Yorkshire Millennium 1999, Yorkshire Castles 2001, Yorkshire Villages 2001, The Wages of Spin 2003, Yorkshire Greats 2005. *Leisure interests:* walking, reading, gardening, visiting Yorkshire. *Address:* 9 Monahan Avenue, Purley, Surrey, CR8 3BB, England (home). *Telephone:* (20) 8660-8970 (home). *E-mail:* bernardinghamcom@aol.com (office).

INGLIS, Kenneth Stanley, AO, MA, DPhil; Australian historian, academic and university administrator; *Professor Emeritus of History, Research School of Social Sciences, Australian National University;* b. 7 Oct. 1929, Melbourne; s. of Stanley W. Inglis and Irene Inglis (née Winning); m. 1st Judy Betheras 1952 (deceased 1962); one s. two d.; m. 2nd Amirah Gust 1965; ed Univ. of Melbourne and Univ. of Oxford, UK; Sr Lecturer, Univ. of Adelaide 1956–60, Reader 1960–62; Reader, ANU 1963–65, Prof. 1965–66, Professorial Fellow 1975–76, Prof. of History, Research School of Social Sciences 1977–94, Prof. Emer. 1994–; Prof., Univ. of Papua New Guinea 1967–72, Vice-Chancellor 1972–75; Overseas Visiting Fellow, St John's Coll., Cambridge 1990–91; Hon. DLitt (Melbourne) 1996; Ernest Scott Prize for History 1983–84, 1999, Fellowship of Australian Writers Prize for Literature 1999, NSW Premier's Prize for Australian History 1999; Nat. Centre for Cultural Studies Award 1999. *Publications:* Churches and the Working Classes in Victorian England 1963, The Australian Colonists 1974, This is the ABC: The Australian Broadcasting Comm. 1932–1983, 1983, The Rehearsal 1985, Australians: A Historical Library (11 vols, Gen. Ed.) 1987–88, Nation: The Life of an Independent Journal of Opinion 1958–72 (ed.) 1989, Observing Australia 1959–99 1999, The Stuart Case (revised edn) 2002, Sacred Places: War Memorials in the Australian Landscape (revised edn) 2008. *Address:* Dundas Lane, Albert Park 3206, Australia.

INGOLD, Keith Usherwood, OC, PhD, FRS, FRSC, FCIC; Canadian research chemist and academic; *Distinguished Research Scientist, Steacie Institute for Molecular Sciences, National Research Council Canada;* b. 31 May 1929, Leeds, Yorks., England; s. of Sir Christopher Kelk Ingold and Lady Edith Hilda Usherwood; m. Carmen Cairine Hodgkin 1956; one s. one d.; ed Univ. Coll., London, Univ. of Oxford; Postdoctoral Fellow, Nat. Research Council of Canada 1951–53, Research Officer, Div. of Chem. 1955–90, Head, Hydrocarbon Chem. Section 1965–90, Assoc. Dir 1977–90; Postdoctoral Fellow, Univ. of BC 1953–55; Distinguished Research Scientist, Steacie Inst. for Molecular Sciences, Nat. Research Council 1990–; Adjunct Prof., Dept of Biochemistry, Brunel Univ., UK 1983–94; Adjunct Prof., Dept of Chem. and Biochemistry, Univ. of Guelph, Ont. 1985–89; Adjunct Research Prof., Carleton Univ., Ottawa 1991–; Adjunct Prof., Dept of Chem., Univ. of St Andrews, Scotland 1997–; visiting scientist to numerous univs, numerous lectureships; Sr Carnegie Fellowship, Univ. of St Andrews, Scotland 1977; Fellow, Univ. Coll. London 1987; Vice-Pres. Canadian Soc. for Chem. 1985–87, Pres. 1987–88; mem. ACS; Hon. mem. Sociedad Argentina de Investigaciones en Química Orgánica; Hon. FRSE; Dr hc (Univ. degli Studi di Ancona) 1999; Hon. DSc (Guelph, Ont.) 1985, (St Andrews) 1989, (Carleton Univ.) 1992, (McMaster Univ., Ont.) 1995, (Dalhousie Univ., NS) 1996; Hon. LLD (Mount Allison) 1987; numerous awards, including Chem. Inst. of Canada Medal 1981, Syntex Award in Physical Organic Chem. 1983, RSC Centennial Medal 1982, RSC Henry Marshall Tory Medal 1985, ACS Pauling Award 1988, Alfred Bader Award in Organic Chem., Canadian Soc. for Chem. 1989, Humboldt Research Award 1989, Davy Medal, Royal Soc. 1990, ACS Arthur C. Cope Scholar Award 1992, Izaak Walton Killam Memorial Prize, Canada Council 1992, ACS James Flack Norris Award in Physical Organic Chem. 1993, Angelo Mangini Medal, Italian Chemical Soc. 1997, Canada Gold Medal for Science and Eng, Natural Science and Eng Research Council 1998, Royal Medal A, Royal Soc. 2000, Gold Medal, Professional Inst. of the Public Service of Canada 2009. *Publications include:* Free-Radical Substitution Reactions (with B. P. Roberts) 1971, Nitrogen-centered Radicals, Aminoxyl and Related Radicals (with J. C. Walton) 1994; more than 550 publs in the open scientific literature. *Leisure interests:* skiing, water skiing. *Address:* National Research Council Canada, 100 Sussex Drive, Ottawa, ON K1A 0R6, Canada (office). *Telephone:* (613) 990-0938 (office); (613) 822-1123 (home). *E-mail:* keith.ingold@nrc.ca (office). *Website:* www.nrc-cnrc.gc.ca (office).

INGÓLFSSON, Thorsteinn, CandJur; Icelandic diplomatist; *Permanent Representative to NATO;* b. 9 Dec. 1944, Reykjavik; s. of Ingólfur Thorsteinsson and Helga Gudmundsdóttir; m. 1st Gudrún Valdís Ragnarsdóttir (divorced 1986); one s. one d.; m. 2nd Hólmfrídur Kofoed-Hansen 1994; ed Commercial Coll. of Iceland, Univ. of Iceland; First Sec. (Int. and Political Affairs), Ministry for Foreign Affairs 1971–73, First Sec. and Deputy Chief of Mission, Washington, DC 1973–78; Chief of Div., Ministry of Foreign Affairs 1978–85; Minister Counsellor 1985; Deputy Perm. Rep. to Int. Orgs, Geneva 1985–87, Acting Perm. Rep. Feb.–June 1987; rank of Amb. 1987; Dir Defence Dept, Ministry for Foreign Affairs, 1987–90; Chair. Icelandic-American Defence Council 1987–90; Perm. Under-Sec. for Foreign Affairs 1990–94; Perm. Rep. to N Atlantic Council and WEU 1994–99, to UN, New York 1999–2003; Amb. to Cuba 2001, to Barbados 2002, to Jamaica (with residence in New York) 2003; Exec. Dir for Nordic and Baltic Countries, World Bank Group, Washington, DC 2003–06; Special Envoy of Foreign Minister 2006–08; Amb. and Perm. Rep. to NATO, Brussels 2008–; Grande Croix, Légion d'honneur, Hon. GCMG, numerous other decorations. *Address:* Delegation of Iceland to NATO, Blvd Léopold III 39, 1110 Brussels, Belgium (office). *Telephone:* (2) 707-50-89 (office). *Fax:* (2) 726-45-31 (office). *E-mail:* icedel.nato@mfa.is (office). *Website:* www.iceland.is/iceland-abroad/nato (office).

INGRAHAM, Rt Hon Hubert Alexander, PC; Bahamian lawyer and politician; b. 4 Aug. 1947, Pine Ridge, Grand Bahama; m. Delores Velma Miller; five c.; ed Cooper's Town Public School, Southern Sr School and Govt High School Evening Inst. Nassau; called to the Bar, Bahamas 1972; Sr Pnr, Christie, Ingraham & Co. (law firm); fmr mem. Air Transport Licensing Authority; fmr Chair. Real Property Tax Tribunal; mem. Nat. Gen. Council Progressive Liberal Party (PLP) 1975; Nat. Chair. and mem. Nat. Exec. Cttee PLP 1976; elected to House of Ass. as PLP mem. 1977, 1982, fmr Speaker; Minister of Housing, Nat. Insurance and Social Services 1982–84; Chair. Bahamas Mortgage Corpn 1982; Alt. Del. Conf. of IDB, Uruguay 1983, IMF/IBRD 1979–84; expelled from PLP 1986; elected to Nat. Ass. as ind. 1987; Parl. Leader, Official Opposition 1990–92; Leader, Opposition Free Nat. Movt and of Official Opposition 1990–92, 2002–07; Prime Minister of the Bahamas 1992–2002, 2007–12, also Minister of Finance and Planning 1992–97, of Housing and Local Govt 1995–97 and Trade and Industry 1995–97, of Housing and Social Devt 2001–02, of Finance 2007–12; Dr hc (Buckingham) 2000. *Leisure interests:* reading, swimming, fishing. *Address:* c/o Office of the Prime Minister, Sir Cecil Wallace-Whitfield Centre, West Bay St, PO Box N 3217, Nassau, N.P. Bahamas. *E-mail:* hai@coralwave.com (home).

INGRAM, Christopher (Chris) John; British advertising and marketing executive; b. 9 June 1943; s. of Thomas Frank Ingram and Gladys Agnes Ingram (née Louttid); m. Janet Elizabeth Rye; one s. one d.; ed Woking Grammar School, Surrey; Media Dir KMP Partnership 1969–71; Man. Dir TMD Advertising 1972–75; Founder and Chair. Chris Ingram Assocs. (CIA) Group/Tempus Group PLC 1976–2002; f. Genesis Investments 2002; Chair. Woking Football Club Holdings 2002–; Founding Partner, Ingram 2003, Ingram Enterprise (investment co.); Chair. Centre for Creative Business, London Business School 2005–; Chair. Sports Revolution 2008–; Ernst & Young London Entrepreneur of the Year 2000, Ernst & Young UK Business-to-Business Entrepreneur of the Year 2000. *Leisure interests:* art, theatre, wildlife, travel in cold climates, entrepreneurship, the voluntary sector, Woking Football Club. *Address:* Sports Revolution, 2nd Floor Asta House, 65 Whitfield Street London, W1T 4HE, England (office). *E-mail:* info@sportsrevolution.co.uk (office). *Website:* www.sportsrevolution.co.uk (office); www.ingramenterprise.com (office).

INGRAM, James Charles, AO, BA (Econs), FAIIA; Australian diplomatist and international civil servant; b. 27 Feb. 1928, Warragul, Vic.; s. of James Edward Ingram and Gladys May (née Johnson); m. Odette Koven 1950; one s. two d.; ed De la Salle Coll., Melbourne Univ.; joined Dept of External Affairs 1946; Third Sec., Tel-Aviv 1950; First Sec., Washington, DC 1956; Chargé d'affaires a.i., Brussels 1959; Counsellor, Djakarta 1962, Australian Mission to UN, New York 1964; Asst Sec. External Affairs, Canberra 1967; Amb. to Philippines 1970–73; High Commr to Canada, Jamaica, Barbados, Guyana, Trinidad and Tobago 1973–74; First Asst Sec., Australian Devt Assistance Agency 1975–76; Dir-Gen. Australian Devt Assistance Bureau, Dept of Foreign Affairs 1977–82; Exec. Dir UN WFP 1982–92; Dir Australian Inst. of Int. Affairs 1992–93; Visiting Fellow, Centre for Int. and Public Law, ANU, Canberra 1993–94; Chair. Australian Govt Advisory Cttee on Non-Govt Devt Orgs 1995; mem. Bd of Trustees, Int. Food Policy Research Inst. 1991–98, Crawford Fund for Int. Agric. Research, Melbourne 1994–99 (Chair. 1996–99), Int. Crisis Group, Brussels 1995–99; Chair. Crawford Fund Expert Advisory Panel on Global Food Security 2008, Crawford Fund World Food Crisis Task Force 2008; mem. Governing Council Soc. for Int. Devt 1988–94, Commonwealth Intergovernmental Group on the Emergence of a Global Humanitarian Order, London 1994–95; Chair. UN Asscn of Australia (ACT Div.) 1998–99; mem. Bd Trustees Asia-Pacific Coll. of Diplomacy, ANU 2005–; Fellow, Australian Inst. of Int. Affairs 2010; Alan Shawn Feinstein World Hunger Award, Brown Univ. 1991, Inaugural Food for Life Award, WFP 2000. *Publications:* Bread and Stones: Leadership and the Struggle to Reform the United Nations World Food Programme 2006; contrib. numerous articles to journals and chapters to books. *Leisure interests:* music, reading, gardening, cycling. *Address:* 4 Stokes Street, Manuka, ACT 2603, Australia. *Telephone:* (2) 6295-0446. *E-mail:* jingram@homemail.com.au.

INGRAM, Tamara, OBE, BA; British advertising executive; *Group Executive Vice-President and Executive Managing Director, Grey Group (UK) Limited;* b. 1961; m.; two c.; began career in film production; joined Saatchi & Saatchi 1985, Bd Account Dir 1989–93, Exec. Account Dir 1993–95, Jt CEO 1995–2001, Exec. Chair. 2001–02; Chair. and CEO McCann-Erickson 2002–03; Pres. Added Value, Fusion 5 and Henley Centre (marketing consulting firms of Kantar Div. of WPP Group PLC) 2003–05, CEO Grey London (div. of WPP) 2005–07, also Group Exec. Vice-Pres. and Exec. Man. Dir Grey Group UK (comprising Grey London, Joshua, GCI and MDS Global Consulting) 2005–, Pres. Team P&G (WPP Group's team for Proctor & Gamble Co.) 2004–08; Chair. Visit London Ltd 2002–11; mem. Bd of Dirs Sage Group plc 2004–, London Devt Agency, Council Inst. of Practitioners in Advertising, Marketing Soc., Marketing Group of GB, Women in Advertising and Communications London; Chair. Devt Bd, Royal Court Theatre; Trustee, The Bacon Fellowship. *Address:* Grey Group, The Johnson Building, 77 Hatton Garden, London, EC1N 8JS, England (office). *Telephone:* (20) 3037-3000 (office). *Website:* www.grey.co.uk (office).

INGRAMS, Richard Reid; British journalist; *Editor, The Oldie;* b. 19 Aug. 1937, London; s. of Leonard St Clair and Victoria Ingrams (née Reid); m. Mary Morgan 1962 (divorced 1993); two s. (one deceased) one d.; ed Shrewsbury School, Univ. Coll., Oxford; Co-founder Private Eye 1962, Ed. 1963–86, Chair. 1974–; Founder and Ed. The Oldie 1992–; TV critic, The Spectator 1976–84; columnist, The Observer 1988–90, 1992–2005, The Independent 2005–. *Publications:* Private Eye on London (with Christopher Booker and William Rushton) 1962, Private Eye's Romantic England 1963, Mrs Wilson's Diary (with John Wells) 1965, Mrs Wilson's Second Diary 1966, The Tale of Driver Grope 1968, The Bible for Motorists (with Barry Fantoni) 1970, The Life and Times of Private Eye (ed.) 1971, Harris in Wonderland (as Philip Reid with Andrew Osmond) 1973, Cobbett's Country Book (ed.) 1974, Beachcomber: the works of J. B. Morton (ed.) 1974, The Best of Private Eye 1974, God's Apology 1977, Goldenballs 1979, Romney Marsh (with Fay Godwin) 1980, Dear Bill: The Collected Letters of Denis Thatcher (with John

Wells) 1980, The Other Half 1981, Piper's Places (with John Piper) 1983, Dr Johnson by Mrs Thrale (ed.) 1984, Down the Hatch (with John Wells) 1985, Just the One (with John Wells) 1986, John Stewart Collis: A Memoir 1986, The Best of Dear Bill (with John Wells) 1986, Mud in Your Eye (with John Wells) 1987, The Eye Spy Look-alike Book (ed.) 1988, The Ridgeway 1988, You Might As Well Be Dead 1988, England: An Anthology 1989, No. 10 1989, On and On... Further Letters of Denis Thatcher (with John Wells) 1990, The Oldie Annual (ed.) 1993, The Oldie Annual II (ed.) 1994, Malcolm Muggeridge (ed.) 1995, I Once Met (ed.) 1996, The Oldie Annual III (ed.) 1997, Jesus: Authors Take Sides (anthology) 1999, The Oldie Annual IV (ed.) 1999, The Life and Adventures of William Cobbett (biog.) 2005. *Leisure interests:* music, book selling. *Address:* The Oldie, 65 Newman Street, London, W1T 3EG, England. *Telephone:* (20) 7436-8801. *Fax:* (20) 7436-8804. *E-mail:* editorial@theoldie.co.uk. *Website:* www.theoldie.co.uk.

INGVES, Stefan, MSc, PhD; Swedish central banker; *Governor, Sveriges Riksbank;* b. 1953, Turku, Finland; ed Stockholm School of Econs; Lecturer, Stockholm School of Econs 1976–84; Asst Vice-Pres., Cen. Finance and Fund Man. Div., Svenska Handelsbanken 1984–86; Pres. Sweden Options and Futures Exchange 1987; Under-Sec. for Financial Markets and Insts, Ministry of Finance 1988–92; Dir-Gen. Swedish Bank Support Authority 1993–94; Deputy Gov. Sveriges Riksbank (Swedish Cen. Bank) 1994–98, Gov. 2006–, also Chair. Exec. Bd; Dir Monetary and Financial Systems Dept, IMF 1999–2005, currently Gov. for Sweden; mem. Bd of Dirs BIS; mem. European Cen. Bank Gen. Council; fmr mem. Toronto Int. Leadership Centre for Financial Sector Supervision. *Address:* Sveriges Riksbank, Brunkebergstorg 11, 103 37 Stockholm, Sweden (office). *Telephone:* (8) 787-00-00 (office). *Fax:* (8) 21-05-31 (office). *E-mail:* registratorn@riksbank.se (office). *Website:* www.riksbank.se (office).

INHOFE, James Mountain, BA; American politician; *Senator from Oklahoma;* b. 17 Nov. 1934, Des Moines, Ia; s. of Perry Inhofe and Blanche Mountain; m. Kay Kirkpatrick 1958; two s. two d.; ed Univ. of Tulsa; US Army veteran; mem. Okla House of Reps 1966–68; mem. Okla State Senate 1968–76, Minority Leader 1970–76; Mayor of Tulsa 1978–84; mem. US House of Reps from 1st Dist of Okla 1987–94; Senator from Oklahoma 1995–, mem. Armed Services Cttee, Ranking Mem. Environment and Public Works Cttee (fmr Chair.), mem. Foreign Relations Cttee; Pres. Fly Riverside Inc. 1978, Quaker Life Insurance Co.; Republican; ranked by Human Events magazine as No. 1 amongst the Top 10 Most Outstanding Conservative Senators, ranked by National Journal magazine as the most conservative mem. of the Senate. *Achievement:* became the only mem. of Congress to fly an aeroplane around the world when he recreated American aviator Wiley Post's first solo flight of 1933 around the world. *Address:* 205 Russell Senate Office Building, Washington, DC 20510-0001, USA (office). *Telephone:* (202) 224-4721 (office). *Fax:* (202) 228-0380 (office). *E-mail:* jim-inhofe@inhofe.senate.gov (office). *Website:* inhofe.senate.gov (office).

INNANI, Brij Gopal; Nepalese industrialist and philanthropist; *Chairman and President, Innani Industrial and Trading Organization;* Chair. and Pres. Innani Industrial and Trading Org.; Chair. and Pres. Mahalaxmi Garment Industries Group; Founder, Chair. and Pres. Shri Laxmi Narsingh Dibyadham, Nepal; Chair. Asian Textiles and Garments Council, CACCI; fmr Pres. Garment Asscn of Nepal, Maheswari Soc. of Nepal and of many others; Lifetime mem. Marwadi Soc. of Nepal; Patron and mem. Educ. Trust of Marwadi Soc. of Nepal; mem. London Chamber of Commerce and Industry, Fed. of Nepalese Chambers of Commerce and Industry, Nepal-India Chamber of Commerce and Industry, Nepal-Britain Chamber of Commerce and Industry, Nepal-German Chamber of Commerce and Industry, and of many others; Life and Distinguished mem. Nepal Red Cross Soc.; Suprabala-Gorkha-Dakshina-Bahu (2056 BS), Birendra-Aiswarya Seva Padak, King Birendra Silver Jubilee Medal, King Birendra Silver Jubilee Medal from the Civic Main Cttee, Golden Jubilee Medal of HM the King's Birthday from the Civic Main Cttee; Nat. Personality Award (Rastriya Byaktitva Samman), Hon. Mr Ram Sharan Mahat, Minister of Finance, for 25 years of Excellent Service in the field of Ready-made Garments Industries in Nepal, Mahalaxmi Garment Industries awarded Int. Gold Star for Quality 1997, The Int. Award – Golden America for Quality and Excellence 1999, Letter of Appreciation for securing the first position amongst the top garment exporters, Nepal Chamber of Commerce 2000, and many others. *Publication:* report on 'Solution of the Impact on Garments and Textiles Industries after WTO' to Hon. Prime Minister Sher Bahadur Deuba 2004. *Address:* Innani Organization, V. Narsing Kunj, New Plaza, Putali Sadak, PO Box 4206, Kathmandu, Nepal (office). *Telephone:* (1) 4418126 (office). *Fax:* (1) 4421258 (office). *E-mail:* innaniorg@gmail.com (office); bginnani@gmail.com (home).

INNES OF EDINGIGHT, Sir Malcolm Rognvald, Kt, KCVO, KStJ; b. 25 May 1938, Edinburgh, Scotland; s. of the late Sir Thomas Innes of Learney and of Lady Lucy Buchan; m. Joan Hay 1963; three s.; ed Edinburgh Acad., Univ. of Edinburgh; Falkland Pursuivant Extraordinary 1957; Carrick Pursuivant 1958; Lyon Clerk and Keeper of the Records 1966; Marchmont Herald 1971, Lord Lyon King of Arms 1981–2001; Sec. to Order of the Thistle 1981–2001; Orkney Herald Extraordinary 2001–; mem. Queen's Body Guard for Scotland (Royal Co. of Archers) 1971–; Grand Officer of Merit, Sovereign Mil. Order, Malta. *Leisure interest:* visiting places of historical interest. *Address:* Castleton of Kinnairdy, Bridge of Marnoch, Aberdeenshire, AB54 7RT, Scotland. *Telephone:* (1466) 780866.

INNIS, Roy Emile Alfredo; American human rights organization executive and chemist; *Chairman, Congress of Racial Equality;* b. 6 June 1934, St Croix, Virgin Islands; s. of Alexander Innis and Georgianna Innis; m. Doris Funnye 1965; six s. (two deceased) two d.; ed City Coll., New York; joined US Army 1950, Sergeant 1951, discharged 1952; pharmaceutical research work, Vick Chemical Co., then medical research Montefiore Hosp. until 1967; active in Harlem Chapter of Congress of Racial Equality (CORE) 1963–, Chair. Harlem Educ. Cttee 1964, Chair. Harlem CORE 1965–67, Second Nat. Vice-Chair. 1967–68, Assoc. Nat. Dir CORE Jan.–Sept. 1968, Nat. Dir 1968–70, Nat. Chair. 1982–; Founder Harlem Commonwealth Council, First Exec. Dir 1967–68, now mem. of Bd; Res. Fellow, Metropolitan Applied Research Center 1967–; Co-Publisher The Manhattan Tribune 1968–71; mem. Bd and Steering Cttee Nat. Urban Coalition; mem. of Bd New York Coalition, Haryou Inc., Bd of Dirs New Era Health Educ. and Welfare, Bd of Advisers Pan-African Journal; mem. Editorial Staff Social Policy Magazine; Publr The Correspondent; Co-Chair. Econ. Devt Task Force, New York

Urban Coalition; Founder CORE Community School, South Bronx 1977. *Publications:* The Little Black Book 1971; chapters in: The Endless Crisis, Black Economic Development 1970, Integrating America's Heritage: A Congressional Hearing to Establish A National Commission on Negro History and Culture 1970, Profiles in Black 1976; articles and editorials in Manhattan Tribune, CORE Magazine, Business Weekly, etc. *Leisure interests:* reading, sports, music. *Address:* Congress of Racial Equality, 817 Broadway, 3rd Floor, New York, NY 10003, USA (office). *Telephone:* (212) 598-4000 (office). *Fax:* (212) 598-4141 (office). *E-mail:* rinnis@core-online.org (office). *Website:* www.core-online.org (office).

INOGUCHI, Kuniko, BA, MA, PhD; Japanese academic and politician; b. 3 May 1952, Chiba Pref.; m. Takashi Inoguchi; two d.; ed Sophia Univ., Yale Univ., USA; Assoc. Prof. of Political Science, Faculty of Law, Sophia Univ. 1981–90, Prof. 1990–2006; Visiting Fellow, Center for Int. Affairs, Harvard Univ. 1983–84; Visiting Prof., ANU 1985; Amb. to Conf. on Disarmament, Geneva 2002–04, Head of Japanese Del. 2003–04, Pres. of Conf. 2003, Western Group Co-ordinator 2004; mem. House of Reps 2005–09, Minister of State for Gender Equality and Social Affairs 2005–06; Foreign Policy Adviser to Sec.-Gen. LDP 2006–07, Acting Sec.-Gen., LDP Int. Bureau 2006; mem. House of Councillors (representing Chiba Pref.) 2010–, Chair. Special Cttee on Okinawa and Northern Problems; mem. UN Advisory Bd on Disarmament Issues, New York 2003–06; Co-Chair. Standing Cttee on Mine Clearance, Mine Risk Educ. and Mine Action Technologies, Meeting of States Parties to Convention on Prohibition of Use of Anti-Personnel Mines 2004; mem. Prime Minister's Defence Policy Review Council 1994–95, Prime Minister's Admin. Reform Council 1996–98, Prime Minister's Gender Equity Council 2001–02; mem. Bd Inst. for Democracy and Electoral Assistance (IDEA), Stockholm, Sweden; Exec. mem. Japan Asscn of Gaming and Simulation 1999, Japan Asscn for Int. Relations 2004–, Exec. mem. Science Council of Japan 2005–; Educ. Minister Award 1972, AVON Awards to Women 2003. *Publications include:* An Emerging Post-Hegemonic System: Choices for Japan 1987, War and Peace (Yoshino Sakuzo Prize) 1989, Invitation to Political Science 1989; articles in newspapers, periodicals and professional journals on disarmament matters. *Address:* Office of Kuniko Inoguchi, 2-2-1 Nagata-cho, Chiyoda-ku, Tokyo 100-8962, Japan (office). *Telephone:* (3) 6550-1105 (office). *Fax:* (3) 6551-1105 (office). *Website:* www.kunikoinoguchi.jp (office).

INOKUCHI, Takeo; Japanese insurance industry executive; b. 9 April 1942; joined Taisho Marine & Fire Insurance Co. Ltd (renamed Mitsui Marine & Fire Insurance Co. Ltd 1993) 1965, Gen. Man. of Non-Marine Underwriting Dept 1990–94, apptd Dir 1993, Man.-Dir 1994–96, Pres. 1996–2000, Chair., Pres. and CEO 2000–01; Chair. and CEO Mitsui Sumitomo Insurance Co. Ltd (cr. following merger of Mitsui Marine & Fire Insurance Co. Ltd and Sumitomo Marine & Fire Insurance Co. Ltd 2001) 2001–04; Vice-Chair. Radio Regulatory Council, Ministry of Public Man., Home Affairs, Posts and Telecommunications 2002–; Corp. Auditor, Sanki Engineering Co. Ltd 2003–, Kikkoman Corpn; Deputy Chair. Ind. Admin. Inst. Evaluation Cttee (IAIEC) and Chair. IAIEC Sub-cttee for Japan Int. Cooperation Agency, Ministry of Foreign Affairs 2003–; Vice-Chair. Japan Asscn of Corp. Execs (Keizai Doyukai) 2003–, Chair. Cttee on Fiscal and Admin. Reforms 2003–; Exec. Dir Japan Business Federation (Nippon Keidanren) 1997–, Co-Chair. Cttee on Econ. Policy 2002–; Exec. Councillor Tokyo Chamber of Commerce 1997–; Dir Int. Insurance Soc. Inc. 2002–; Personality of the Year Award, Asia Insurance Industry 2003, inducted into Insurance Hall of Fame, Insurance Soc. 2004. *Address:* c/o Mitsui Sumitomo Insurance Co. Ltd, 27-2 Shinkawa 2-chome, Chuo-ku, Tokyo 104-8252, Japan. *Telephone:* (3) 3297-1111.

INONI, Ephraim, MBA; Cameroonian politician; b. 16 Aug. 1947, Bakingili; s. of Sarah Enjema Elonge; m.; five c.; ed Catholic Teachers' Training Coll., Bonjongo, Higher Elementary Teachers' Training Coll., Mutengene, South Eastern Univ., USA; Head Teacher, Catholic Primary School, Mabanda, Kumba, then Teacher, Sasse Coll.; Asst Prov. Chief of Accounts in the NW, then Asst Prov. Treas., Financial Controller, Douala; Financial Attaché, Embassy in Washington, DC, USA; Dir, Gen. Admin, Ministry of Finance, then Sec. of State; Asst Sec.-Gen. to the Presidency 1992–2004; Prime Minister of Cameroon 2004–09; mem. Bakweri ethnic group. *Address:* c/o Office of the Prime Minister, Yaoundé, Cameroon.

INOUE, Akihisa, PhD; Japanese engineer, academic and fmr university administrator; b. 13 Sept. 1947; ed Grad. School of Eng, Tohoku Univ.; Research Assoc., Inst. for Materials Research, Tohoku Univ. 1976–85, Assoc. Prof. 1985–90, Prof. 1990–, also Prof. of Precision and Intelligence Lab., Tokyo Inst. of Tech. 1997–, Dir Inst. for Materials Research 1995–2001, Deputy Pres. Tohoku Univ. 2002–06, Pres. 2006–12; Visiting Scientist, AT&T Bell Labs, USA 1982–83, 1984, 1986; Visiting Scientist, Swedish Inst. of Metals Research 1985, 1987; Science Adviser to Ministry of Educ., Culture, Sports, Science and Tech. 2001–; more than 50 awards, including ISI Citation Laureate Award 2000, Japan Acad. Prize 2002, Houkou Prize, CONA Award, James C. McGroddy Prize for New Materials 2008, Acta Materialia Gold Medal 2010. *Publications:* Nanocrystalline Alloys, Magnetic and Novel Nanomaterials (co-author) 2004, Materials Science and Engineering of Bulk Metallic Glasses (co-author) 2008, New Functional Materials, Fundamentals of Metallic Glasses and their Applications to Industry 2009. *Address:* c/o Office of the President, Tohoku University, 1-1 Katahira, 2-chome, Aoba-ku, Sendai 980-8577, Japan.

INOUE, Shinya, PhD; American (b. Japanese) biologist and academic; *Distinguished Scientist and Director, Architectural Dynamics in Living Cells Program, Marine Biological Laboratory;* b. 5 Jan. 1921; ed Univ. of Tokyo, Princeton Univ., NJ; Lecturer in Anatomy, Univ. of Washington, Seattle 1951–53; Asst Prof. of Biology, Tokyo Metropolitan Univ. 1953–54; Research Assoc. then Assoc. Prof. in Biology and Instructor in Optics, Univ. of Rochester, NY 1954–59; Prof. and Chair. Dept of Cytology, Dartmouth Medical School, Hanover, NH 1959–66; Prof. of Biology and Dir Program in Biophysical Cytology, Univ. of Pennsylvania 1966–82; Instructor in Chief, Analytical and Quantitative Light Microscopy, Marine Biological Lab. (MBL), Woods Hole, Mass 1979–87, Distinguished Scientist 1986–; mem. NAS 1993; Fellow, AAAS 1971; Hon. Fellow, Royal Microscopical Soc. (UK) 1988; Guggenheim Fellow 1971–72, NIH Merit Award 1982–86, E.B. Wilson Award, American Soc. for Cell Biology 1992, Distinguished Scientist Award, Microscopy Soc. of America 1995, Ernst Abbe Award, New York Microscopical Soc. 1997, Int. Prize for Biology, Japan Soc. for the Promotion of Science 2003. *Publications:* Video Microscopy 1986 (second edn with K. R. Spring

1997); numerous papers in specialist journals. *Address:* Marine Biological Laboratory, 7 MBL Street, Woods Hole, MA 02543, USA (office). *Telephone:* (508) 289-7382 (office). *E-mail:* jmacneil@mbl.edu (office). *Website:* www.mbl.edu/research/resident/lab_arch_dyn.html (office); www.mbl.edu/research/resident/lab_inoue.html (office).

INOUYE, Minoru, BL; Japanese banker; *Adviser, Bank of Tokyo-Mitsubishi UFJ Ltd;* b. 1924, Tokyo; m.; one s.; ed Univ. of Tokyo; joined Bank of Tokyo 1947, Deputy Agent, New York 1964–66, Deputy Gen. Man. Int. Funds and Foreign Exchange Div. 1966–67, Deputy Gen. Man. Planning and Co-ordination Div. 1967–70, Gen. Man. 1970–72, Dir and Gen. Man. London Office 1972–75, Resident Man. Dir for Europe 1975, Man. Dir 1975–79, Sr Man. Dir 1979–80, Deputy Pres. 1980–85, Pres. 1985–90, Adviser 1990, Adviser, Bank of Tokyo-Mitsubishi Ltd 1996–2005, Adviser, Bank of Tokyo-Mitsubishi UFJ Ltd 2006–; Orden Mexicana del Aguila Azteca (Mexico) 1986, Medal of Honour, with Blue Ribbon (Japan) 1989, Ordem Nacional de Cruzeiro do Sul (Brazil) 1989, Chevalier, Légion d'honneur 1990, Order of the Rising Sun, Gold and Silver Star (Japan) 1994. *Leisure interest:* travel. *Address:* The Bank of Tokyo-Mitsubishi UFJ Ltd, 3-2 Nihombashi Hongokucho 1-chome, Chuo-ku, Tokyo 103-0021, Japan (office). *Telephone:* (3) 3240-1111 (office). *Fax:* (3) 3245-9117 (office).

INSANALLY, Samuel Rudolph (Rudy), BA; Guyanese diplomatist and fmr politician; b. 23 Jan. 1936, Georgetown; m. Bonita Insanally; two d.; ed Univ. of London, England, Univ. of Paris, France; teacher of modern languages, Kingston Coll., Jamaica, Queen's Coll., Guyana and Univ. of Guyana 1959–66; Counsellor, Embassy in Washington, DC 1966–69; Chargé d'affaires, Embassy in Venezuela 1970, Amb. 1972–78; Deputy Perm. Rep. to UN, New York 1970–72, Perm. Rep. 1987–2010; Perm. Rep. to EEC 1978–81; Amb. to Belgium (also accred to Sweden, Norway and Austria) 1978–81, to Colombia 1982–86; Head of Political Div. Ministry of Foreign Affairs 1982–86; High Commr to Barbados, Trinidad and Tobago and the Eastern Caribbean 1982–86; Pres. UN Gen. Ass. 1993–94; Chancellor Univ. of Guyana 1994–2001; Minister of Foreign Affairs 2001–08; currently Adviser to Pres. on Foreign Affairs; mem. Bd of Govs Inst. of International Relations, Trinidad and Tobago 1982–86; Gran Cordon, Order of the Liberator (Venezuela) 1973, Cacique Crown of Honour 1980, Grand Cordon, Order of the Rising Sun (Japan) 2009; Golden Arrow of Achievement 1986. *Publications include:* several articles and works on int. relations and diplomacy. *Leisure interests:* reading, listening to classical music. *Address:* Ministry of Foreign Affairs, 254 South Road and Shiv Chanderpaul Drive, Bourda, Georgetown, Guyana (office). *Telephone:* 226-1606 (office). *Fax:* 225-9192 (office). *E-mail:* minfor@guyana.net.gy (office). *Website:* www.minfor.gov.gy (office).

INSEL, Thomas Roland, BA, MD; American neuroscientist, psychiatrist, research institute director and academic; *Director, National Institute of Mental Health;* b. 19 Oct. 1951, Dayton, Ohio; s. of H. Herbert Insel; m. Deborah Silber 1969; ed Boston Univ. Medical School; family moved to Silver Spring, Md 1960; travelled with his wife around the world and worked at a Tuberculosis clinic in Hong Kong and a mission hosp. in Bihar, India 1970; trained in psychiatry at Univ. of California, San Francisco 1976–79; following clinical training, joined Nat. Inst. of Mental Health (NIMH) as a clinical fellow; recruited to Emory Univ. to direct the Yerkes Regional Primate Research Center 1994–99 (resgnd); Head, Center for Behavioral Neuroscience NSF Science and Tech. Center 1999–2002; Dir NIMH 2002–; mem. Inst. of Medicine of NAS; A.E. Bennett Award 1986, Curt Richter Prize 1991, Outstanding Service Award, US Public Health Service 1993, Sachar Prize 2007, Outstanding Alumnus Award, Boston Univ. 2009, Ipsen Prize 2010. *Achievements include:* first to demonstrate that an experimental serotonin reuptake inhibitor (SSRI) antidepressant, clomipramine, was effective in treating obsessive compulsive disorder (OCD); later carried out studies in NIMH Lab. of Brain Evolution and Behavior, Poolesville, Md, investigated social behaviour in animals and the role of oxytocin and vasopressin and their action on brain receptors. *Publications:* New Findings in Obsessive-Compulsive Disorder (ed.) 1984, The Psychobiology of Obsessive-Compulsive Disorder (co-ed.) 1991, Oxytocin in Maternal, Sexual and Social Behaviors (co-ed.) 1992, The Neurobiology of Maternal Behavior (with M. M. Numan) 2011; more than 200 papers in professional journals on studies of oxytocin and vasopressin and their impact on social behaviour. *Address:* National Institute of Mental Health, BG 15K Room 107, MSC 2670, 6001 Executive Boulevard, Bethesda, MD 20892-9663, USA (office). *Telephone:* (301) 443-3673 (office). *Fax:* (301) 443-4279 (office). *E-mail:* ti4g@nih.gov (office); nimhinfo@nih.gov (office). *Website:* www.nimh.nih.gov/about/director (office).

INSLEE, Jay Robert, BA; American lawyer, politician and state governor; *Governor of Washington;* b. 9 Feb. 1951, Seattle, Wash.; s. of Frank E. Inslee and Adele A. Inslee (née Brown); m. Trudi Inslee 1972; three s.; ed Ingraham High School, Univ. of Washington, Seattle, Willamette Univ. Coll. of Law; practised law in Selah, Wash. for ten years; mem. Wash. House of Reps for 14th Dist 1989–93; mem. US House of Reps for 4th Congressional Dist 1993–95, for 1st Congressional Dist 1999–2012, mem. Cttee on Energy and Commerce; Gov. of Washington 2013–; Democrat. *Publication:* Apollo's Fire: Igniting America's Clean Energy Economy (with Bracken Hendricks) 2007. *Leisure interest:* playing basketball (mem. Hoopaholics). *Address:* Office of the Governor, 416 Sid Snyder Avenue SW, Suite 200, PO Box 40002, Olympia, WA 98504-0002, USA (office). *Telephone:* (360) 902-4111 (office). *Fax:* (360) 753-4110 (office). *Website:* www.governor.wa.gov (office).

INSULZA SALINAS, José Miguel, MA; Chilean politician, lawyer and international organization official; *Secretary-General, Organization of American States;* b. 2 June 1943; m. Georgina Núñez Reyes; three c.; ed St George's Coll., Santiago, Law School, Universidad de Chile, Facultad Latinoamericana de Ciencias Sociales and Univ. of Michigan, USA; Prof. of Political Theory, Universidad de Chile, of Political Sciences, Pontificia Universidad Católica de Chile –1973; Political Adviser to Ministry of Foreign Relations, Dir Diplomatic Acad. –1973; researcher, then Dir Instituto de Estudos de Estados Unidos, Centro de Investigación y Docencia Económicas, Mexico 1981–88; Prof., Universidad Autónoma de México 1981–88; Head, Multilateral Econ. Affairs Dept, Ministry of Foreign Relations, Deputy Chair. Int. Co-operation Agency 1990–94; Under-Sec. for Foreign Affairs 1994, Minister 1994–99, Minister Sec.-Gen. Office of the Pres. 1999; Minister of the Interior (Vice-Pres. of the Repub.) 2000–; Sec.-Gen. OAS 2005–; mem. Bd of Dirs Instituto de Fomento de Desarrollo Científico y Tecnológico; mem. Consejo Chileno de Relaciones Internacionales, Consejo de Redacción, Nexos Magazine, Mexico; Corporación de Desarrollo Tecnológico Empresarial, Chilean Asscn of Political Science, Bar Asscn. *Address:* Organization of American States, 17th Street and Constitution Avenue, NW, Washington, DC 20006, USA (office); Ministry of the Interior, Palacio de la Moneda, Santiago, Chile (office). *Telephone:* (2) 690-4000 (Santiago) (office); (202) 458-3000 (Washington) (office). *Fax:* (2) 699-2165 (Santiago) (office). *E-mail:* pi@oas.org (office). *Website:* www.oas.org (office).

INTRILIGATOR, Michael David, SB, MA, PhD; American economist and academic; *Professor Emeritus of Economics, Political Science, and Public Policy, University of California, Los Angeles;* b. 5 Feb. 1938, New York, NY; s. of Allan Intriligator and Sally Intriligator; m. Devrie Shapiro 1963; four s.; ed Massachusetts Inst. of Tech., Yale Univ.; Asst Prof., Dept of Econs, UCLA 1963–66, Assoc. Prof. 1966–72, Prof. 1972–, now Prof. Emer. of Econs, Political Science, and Public Policy, Dir UCLA Inst. of Contemporary Econs 1967, 1969, Prof., Dept of Political Science, UCLA 1981–, Assoc. Dir Center for Int. and Strategic Affairs 1979–82, Dir 1982–92, Vice-Chair. 1991–94, Dir Burkle Center for Int. Relations 2000–02, Prof., Dept of Policy Studies, School of Public Policy and Social Research 1994–, Vice-Chair. 1995–99, Prof., Dept of Public Policy, School of Public Affairs 2004–; Consultant Research Assoc., UCLA Security Studies Project 1967–68, currently co-Dir Marschak Colloquium; Research Assoc., Human Resources Research Center, Univ. of Southern California 1969–81; Lecturer, Div. of Humanities and Social Sciences, California Inst. of Tech. 1969–71; Sr Economist and Consultant, Analytical Assessments Corpn, Marina del Rey, Calif. 1977–81; Co-Dir Center for Int. Studies: Int. Security at UCLA and Univ. of Southern California 1985–86, Dir 1986–91; Co-Dir (with Anatoly A. Gromyko), Project on 'Soviet-US Cooperation for Africa' 1987–; mem. Bd of Dirs California-Russia Trade Asscn, Los Angeles 1989–93, California-Russia Trade Asscn 1992–; mem. Bd of Advisers, California Council on Europe 1991–94; mem. Panel of Experts, Study on Econ. Aspects of Disarmament, UN Inst. for Disarmament Research (UNIDIR), Geneva 1990–92; mem. Int. Advisory Bd Russian Science Foundation, Moscow 1994–; mem. Centre for Econ. Design, Bogazici Univ., Istanbul 1997–2003; reviewer (math. econs), Mathematical Reviews 1975–79; Assoc. Ed. of numerous journals; expert witness before admin. agencies and courts, testifying for govt agencies, corpns and asscns 1976–; Pres. Peace Science Soc. (Int.) 1993; Vice-Chair. Economists Allied for Arms Reduction (ECAAR) 1998–2005, Economists for Peace and Security 2005–; Vice-Pres. Western Econ. Asscn Int. 2006–07, Pres. 2008–09; mem. American Econ. Asscn, American Political Science Asscn, Council on Foreign Relations, New York 1984, Econometric Soc., Economists Allied for Arms Reduction, IISS, London 1983, Int. Political Science Asscn, Int. Studies Asscn, Peace Science Soc. (Int.), Western Econ. Asscn Int.; Founding mem. Pacific Council on Int. Policy 1995–; Foreign mem. Russian Acad. of Sciences 1999; Fellow, Econometric Soc. 1982, AAAS 2001; Woodrow Wilson Fellow, Yale Univ. 1959–60; MIT Fellow 1960–61; Ford Faculty Research Fellow, Stanford Univ. and LSE 1967–68; Sr Fellow, The Gorbachev Foundation of N America, Boston 1998–, The Milken Inst., Santa Monica 1999–; Distinguished Teaching Award, Grad. Student Asscn, UCLA 1966, Warren C. Scoville Distinguished Teaching Award, Dept of Econs, UCLA 1976, 1979, 1982, 1984, invited by Swedish Econ. Asscn and Stockholm Int. Peace Research Inst. to present lecture on 'Non-Armageddon Solutions to the Arms Race' to dels to Conf. on Confidence- and Security-Building Measures and Disarmament in Europe, Stockholm 1984. *Publications include:* Strategy in a Missile War: Targets and Rates of Fire (monograph) 1967, Mathematical Optimization and Economic Theory 1971 (translated into several languages), co-ed. book series Advanced Textbooks in Economics 1972–78, co-ed. book series Handbooks in Economics 1980, co-ed. Handbook of Econometrics, Vol. I 1983, Vol. II 1984, Vol. III 1986, co-ed. Handbook of Mathematical Economics Vol. I 1981, Vol. II 1982, Vol. III 1985, National Security and International Stability (co-ed.) 1983, Strategies for Managing Nuclear Proliferation – Economic and Political Issues (co-ed.) 1983, Non-Armageddon Solutions to the Arms Race (lecture and monograph), Stockholm 1984, Arms Control: Problems and Prospects 1987, Arms Control: The Changing Strategic Environment and the Long-Term Future (monograph) 1989, Accidental Nuclear War (co-ed.) 1990, Economic Aspects of Disarmament: Disarmament as an Investment Process (monograph) 1992, Implications of the Dissolution of the Soviet Union for Accidental/Inadvertent Use of Weapons of Mass Destruction (co-ed.) 1992, Cooperative Models in International Relations Research (co-ed.) 1992, Statistical Sampling in the Medicare Program: Challenging its Use 2001, Eurasia: A New Peace Agenda (co-ed.) 2005, Countering Terrorism and WMD: Creating a Global Anti-Terrorism Network (co-ed.) 2006. *Leisure interests:* travel and art collecting, classical music. *Address:* 140 Foxtail Drive, Santa Monica, CA 90402 (home); Department of Economics, University of California, Los Angeles, CA 90095-1477, USA (office). *Telephone:* (310) 825-4144 (office); (310) 395-7909 (home). *Fax:* (310) 825-9528 (office); (310) 394-8007 (home). *E-mail:* intriligator@econ.ucla.edu (office). *Website:* econweb.sscnet.ucla.edu (office).

INUBUSHI, Yasuo; Japanese metal industry executive; *Advisor, Kobe Steel Ltd (KOBELCO);* b. 10 Feb. 1944, Tokushima; ed Osaka Univ.; joined Kobe Steel (KOBELCO) 1967, worked in Sales Planning and Admin Dept 1969–74, posted to Titan Steel & Wire Co., Canada 1974, also served at Kobe Steel offices New York and Los Angeles, Man. Cold Rolled Sheet Sales Section 1981–90, Gen. Man. Int. Operations Dept, Iron and Steel Div. 1990–99, mem. Bd of Dirs 1996–, Sr Officer 1999–2001, Exec. Officer and Gen. Man. Steel Sales Div. 2001–02, Rep. Dir 2002–, Exec. Vice-Pres. 2002–04, Pres. and CEO 2004–09 (resgnd), Advisor 2009–. *Address:* Kobe Steel Ltd, Shinko Building, 10-26 Wakinohamacho 2-chome, Kobe 651-8585, Japan (office). *Telephone:* (78) 261-5111 (office). *Fax:* (78) 261-4123 (office). *E-mail:* info@kobelco.co.jp (office). *Website:* www.kobelco.co.jp (office).

INZAMAM-UL-HAQ; Pakistani fmr professional cricketer; b. 3 March 1970, Multan, Punjab; right-handed middle order batsman; teams played for: Multan 1985–2004, United Bank Ltd 1988–97, Faisalabad 1996–2001, Rawalpindi 1998–99, Nat. Bank of Pakistan 2001–02, Pakistan 1991–2007 (Capt. 2003–07), Water and Power Devt Authority 2006–07, Yorks. 2007, Hyderabad Heroes (Indian Cricket League—ICL) 2007, Lahore Badshahs (ICL) 2008; First-class debut: 1985/86; Test debut: Pakistan v England, Birmingham 4 June 1992; One-Day Int. (ODI) debut: Pakistan v West Indies, Lahore 22 Nov. 1991; only T20I: England v Pakistan, Bristol 28 Aug. 2006; scored 8,830 runs in 120 tests (highest score 329 against NZ at Lahore 2002) with 25 hundreds; scored 11,739 runs in 378 ODIs (average 39.52) with 10 centuries; scored 16,785 runs in 245 First-class matches with 45 hundreds; Pakistan's second highest-ever run-scorer in tests (behind Javed Miandad Khan); retd from One-Day cricket 2007. *Address:* c/o Pakistan Cricket Board, Gaddafi Stadium, Ferozepur Road, Lahore 54600, Pakistan. *Telephone:* (42) 571-7231. *Website:* www.pcboard.com.pk.

INZKO, Valentin, Jr, DIur; Austrian diplomatist; *High Representative of the International Community in Bosnia and Herzegovina;* b. 22 May 1949, Klagenfurt am Wörthersee, Carinthia; s. of the late Valentin Inzko, Sr; m. Bernarda Fink; one s. one d.; ed attended a Slovene-German bilingual school in Suetschach, Feistritz im Rosental, Univ. of Graz, Diplomatic Acad., Vienna; joined Foreign Service 1974; UNDP Deputy Dir, Ulan Bator, Mongolia 1974–78, Colombo, Sri Lanka 1978–80, Political Section, Dept of Cen., Eastern and Southern Europe, Cen. Asia and Southern Caucasus, Ministry of Foreign Affairs 1981, Press and Culture Attaché, Embassy in Belgrade 1982–86, Counsellor, Del. to First Mission and Deputy Dir UN Disarmament Mission, Austrian Mission to UN, New York, USA 1986–89, Deputy Head of Press and Information Dept, Ministry of Foreign Affairs 1989–90, Cultural Council, Embassy in Prague 1990–96, Founding Dir Austrian Cultural Inst., Prague 1993–96, Founding Head of OSCE Observer Mission in Novi Pazar, Sandzhak, Serbia Oct.–Dec. 1992, Amb. to Bosnia and Herzegovina 1996–99, Head of Dept for Middle, E and S Europe, Cen. Asia and S Caucasus, Ministry of Foreign Affairs 1999–2005, Observer of Montenegrin Parl. Elections 2002, Amb. to Slovenia 2005–09, High Rep. of Int. Community and Special Rep. of EU in Bosnia and Herzegovina 2009–11, High Rep. of Int. Community in Bosnia and Herzegovina 2011–; Hon. Citizen of the City of Sarajevo, Bosnia and Herzegovina 2000; Grand Decoration of Honour in Silver for Services to the Repub. of Austria 2012. *Publications include:* translated essays of Václav Havel, Living in Truth and Power of the Powerless, into Slovene. *Address:* Office of the High Representative, Emerika Bluma 1, 71 000 Sarajevo, Bosnia and Herzegovina (office). *Telephone:* (33) 283500 (office). *Fax:* (33) 283501 (office). *E-mail:* info@ohr.int (office). *Website:* www.ohr.int (office).

IOFFE, Boris Lazarevich, MS; Russian theoretical physicist; *Head of Laboratory, A.I. Alikhanov Institute of Theoretical and Experimental Physics;* b. 6 July 1926, Moscow; s. of Lazar Iof and Pesia Ioffe; m. 1st Svetlana Mikhailova 1957 (divorced 1974); one s.; m. 2nd Nina Libova 1990; ed Moscow Univ.; Jr Scientist, A.I. Alikhanov Inst. of Theoretical and Experimental Physics (ITEP), Moscow 1950–55, Sr Scientist 1955–77, Head of Lab. 1977–, Prof. 1977–, Chair. ITEP Scientific Council 1990–97; Deputy Ed. Moscow Physics Soc. Journal 1991–98; mem. High Energy Physics Scientific Policy Cttee (Russia) 1992–98, Russian Nuclear Soc. –1990; Corresp. mem. USSR (now Russian) Acad. of Sciences 1990; mem. Exec. Cttee United Physical Soc. of Russian Fed. 1998; Fellow, American Physical Soc. 1995; Order of Honour of USSR 1954, 1974; Veteran of Labour Medal 1985, USSR Award for Discovery 1986, 1989, Alexander von Humboldt Award (Germany) 1994, 850 Years of Moscow Medal 1997, Novy Mir Magazine Prize 1999, Acad. of Sciences I.E. Tamm Prize 2008, Pomeranchuk Prize, A.I. Alikhanov Inst. for Theoretical and Experimental Physics 2009. *Publications:* Hard Processes 1984, The Top Secret Assignment 1999, 2001, Without Retouching 2004; 280 articles. *Leisure interests:* mountaineering (especially in Cen. Asia and Far East), skiing. *Address:* A.I. Alikhanov Institute of Theoretical and Experimental Physics, Bolshaya Cheremushkinskaya 25, 117218 Moscow (office); Bolotnikovskaya Street 40, Korp 4, Apt 16, 117209 Moscow, Russia (home). *Telephone:* (499) 123-31-93 (office); (499) 121-44-38 (home). *Fax:* (495) 127-05-43 (office). *E-mail:* ioffe@itep.ru (office). *Website:* www.itep.ru (office).

IOSIFESCU, Marius Vicenţiu Viorel, PhD, DSc; Romanian mathematician and academic; *Director, Institute of Mathematical Statistics and Applied Mathematics and Vice-President, Casa Academiei Romane (Romanian Academy);* b. 12 Aug. 1936, Piteşti; s. of the late Victor Iosifescu and Ecaterina Iosifescu; m. Ştefania Eugenia Zamfirescu 1973; one s.; ed Bucharest Univ.; consultant, Cen. Statistical Bd 1959–62; Asst Prof., Bucharest Polytechnical Inst. 1961–63; Research Mathematician, Inst. of Math. and Centre for Math. Statistics, Romanian Acad., Bucharest 1963–76, Dir 1976–2002, Dir Inst. of Math. Statistics and Applied Math. 2002–, Vice-Pres. Romanian Acad. 2002–; Visiting Prof., Univs of Paris 1974, 1991, 1996, 1998, Mainz 1977–78, Frankfurt am Main 1979–80, Bonn 1981–82, Melbourne 1991, Lille 1997, Bordeaux 1998, 1999; Overseas Fellow, Churchill Coll., Cambridge 1971; mem. Editorial Bds Journal of the Mathematical European Society, Bulletin Mathématique de la Société des Sciences Mathématiques de Roumanie, Mathematica, Revue d'Analyse Numérique et de Théorie de l'Approximation; Deputy Chief Ed. Revue Roumaine de Mathématiques Pures et Appliquées; mem. Int. Statistical Inst., Bernoulli Soc. for Math. Statistics and Probability (mem. Council 1975–79), American Math. Soc., Soc. de Mathématiques Appliquées et Industrielles; Corresp. mem. Romanian Acad. 1991, Titular mem. 2000; Chevalier, Ordre des Palmes académiques 1993; Romanian Acad. Prize 1965, 1972, Bronze Medal, Helsinki Univ. 1975. *Publications include:* Random Processes and Learning (with R. Theodorescu) 1969, Stochastic Processes and Applications in Biology and Medicine, Vol. I Theory, Vol. II Models (with P. Tăutu) 1973, Finite Markov Processes and Their Applications 1980, 2007; Proceedings of Braşov Conference on Probability Theory (ed.) 1971, 1974, 1979, 1982, Dependence with Complete Connections and its Applications (with Ş. Grigorescu) 1982, 1990; Studies in Probability and Related Topics (ed.) 1983, Elements of Stochastic Modelling (with Ş. Grigorescu, G. Oprişan and G. Popescu) 1984, From Real Analysis to Probability: Autobiographical Notes 1986, Metrical Theory of Continued Fractions (with C. Kraaikamp) 2002, Modèles Stochastiques (with N. Limnios and G. Oprisan) 2007, Introduction to Stochastic Models (with N. Limnios and G. Oprisan) 2010, Metrical Theory of Some Continued Fraction Expansions (with G. I. Sebe and D. Lascu) 2011. *Leisure interests:* music, playing violin. *Address:* Institute of Mathematical Statistics and Applied Mathematics, Casa Academiei Romane, Calea 13 Septembrie nr 13, 050711 Bucharest 5 (office); Str. Dr N. Manolescu 9–11, 050583 Bucharest 35, Romania (home). *Telephone:* (21) 3182433 (office); (21) 4103523 (home). *Fax:* (21) 2116608 (office). *E-mail:* miosifes@acad.ro (office). *Website:* www.csm.ro (office).

IOVINE, Jimmy; American record company executive, record producer and film producer; *Chairman, Interscope Records;* b. 11 March 1953, Brooklyn, New York; early career as recording engineer at Record Plant, New York 1973; worked as producer 1977–90, produced first album for Flame 1977, produced Patti Smith's Easter 1978; Co-founder Interscope Records 1989, Co-Chair. Interscope Geffen

A&M Records, Chair. 2001–; Co-founder (with Doug Morris), Chair. and CEO Jimmy and Doug's Farm Club (project comprising a record label, website and cable TV show) 1999–; has worked with Dr Dre, Marilyn Manson, Stevie Nicks, Nine Inch Nails, No Doubt, 2Pac, Tom Petty, The Pretenders, Brian Setzer Orchestra, Patti Smith and U2; Producer of the Year, Rolling Stone Magazine (twice). *Films produced include:* 8 Mile 2002, Get Rich or Die Tryin' 2005. *Address:* Interscope Records, 2220 Colorado Avenue, Santa Monica, CA 90404, USA (office). *Website:* www.interscope.com (office); www.universalmusic.com (office).

IOVV, Vasile, PhD; Moldovan economist and politician; b. 29 Dec. 1942, Corjova, Dubăsari dist.; ed Technologic Inst. of Kiev, Social Science Acad., Moscow; Vice-Pres. then Pres. Balti town exec., fmr inspector, CP of Moldova, First Sec. of Balti Party Cttee then Sec.; fmr Sr Counsellor, CP of USSR; mem. Parl. (CP) 2005–09; fmr Dir Scientific Research and Production, Sugar Industrial Asscn of Moldova; fmr Chief of Commercial-Econ. Office, Embassy of Moldova in Moscow; fmr Minister of Transport and Roads, then First Deputy Prime Minister of Moldova 2002–05, 2005. *Address:* c/o Office of the Council of Ministers, Piaţa Marii Adunări Naţionale 1, 2033 Chişinău, Moldova.

IOZZO, Alfonso; Italian banking executive; ed Univ. of Turin; joined Sanpaolo IMI SpA, Turin 1961, fmr Head, Research Dept, then Foreign Dept and subsequently Deputy Gen. Man., Jt Gen. Man. 1992–95, Gen. Man. Gruppo Bancario Sanpaolo (holding co.) 1995, Gen. Sec., Compagnia di San Paolo 1995–2001, Jt CEO Gruppo Sanpaolo IMI 2001–04, Man. Dir 2004–06 (resgnd); Chair. Banca OPI SpA, Rome 2003–06; Chair. Cassa Depositi e Prestiti 2006–08; mem. Bd of Dirs Natixis SA, Paris 2006–08; Pres. Movimento Federalista Europeo; Pres. A. Spinelli Inst.

IP, Nancy Yuk-Yu, BSc, PhD; Chinese neurobiologist and academic; *Chair Professor of Biochemistry and Director, Molecular Neuroscience Centre, The Hong Kong University of Science and Technology;* b. 30 July , Hong Kong; ed Simmons Coll., Boston and Harvard Medical School, USA; Lab. Head, Lifecodes Corpn, New York, USA 1987–89, Sr Staff Scientist 1989–93; Scientific Consultant, Regeneron Pharmaceuticals Inc., New York 1993–96; Lecturer, Dept of Biology, The Hong Kong Univ. of Science and Tech. 1993–94, Assoc. Prof. 1994–97, Prof. 1998–2000, Dir Biotechnology Research Inst. 1996–2008, Assoc. Dean of Science 1998–2005, Dir Molecular Neuroscience Centre 1999–, Prof., Dept of Biochemistry 2000–05, Head of Dept 2000–09, Chair Prof. 2005–; Fellow, Acad. of Sciences for the Developing World 2004; Hon. Dr of Humane Sciences (Simmons Coll.) 2007; Medal of Honour, Govt of Hong Kong Special Admin. Region 2008; Sr Research Fellowship, Croucher Foundation 1998, Nat. Natural Science Award, Nat. Natural Science Foundation of China 2003, L'Oréal-UNESCO Women in Science Award 2004, Outstanding Women Professionals Award, Hong Kong Women Professionals and Entrepreneurs Asscn 2005, Scientific and Technological Progress Prize, Ho Leung Ho Lee Foundation 2008, Leader of the Year (Research), Sing Tao News Corpn Ltd 2008. *Publications:* more than 190 articles in scientific journals with more than 13,000 SCI citations, holder of 18 patents. *Address:* Department of Biochemistry, The Hong Kong University of Science and Technology, Clear Water Bay, Kowloon, Hong Kong Special Administrative Region, People's Republic of China (office). *Telephone:* 2358-7304 (office). *Fax:* 2358-2765 (office). *E-mail:* boip@ust.hk (office). *Website:* www.ust.hk/bich/facultyprofiles/nancyip.html (office).

IP, Regina, (Lau Suk-yee), BA, MLitt, MSc, MA; Hong Kong politician; *Legislative Councillor and Chairperson, New People's Party;* b. 24 Aug. 1950, Hong Kong; d. of Low Fook Seng; m. (husband deceased); one d.; ed Univ. of Hong Kong, Univ. of Glasgow, UK, Stanford Univ., USA; joined Hong Kong Admin. Service 1975, service in Civil Service Br., Home Affairs Dept, New Territories Admin, City and New Territories Admin, Security Br., Trade Dept, Office of the Chief Sec., Trade and Industry Br.; Dir-Gen. of Industry 1995–96; Dir of Immigration (first woman apptd to head a disciplined service) 1996–98; Dir of Immigration of Hong Kong Special Admin. Region (HKSAR) 1997–98; Sec. for Security (first woman in position) 1998–2002, 2002–03 (resgnd); attended Stanford Univ. 2003–06, then returned to Hong Kong; est. Savantas Policy Inst. (think tank) 2006; apptd mem. Comm. on Strategic Devt 2007; mem. Legis. Council 2008–; Vice-Chair. China Reform Council 2008–; Founder, Legislative Councillor and Chair. New People's Party 2010–; Outstanding Person for Chinese Entrepreneurial Innovation 2008. *Publications:* Four Funerals and One Wedding (autobiog.), Learning English with Regina, Books 1 and 2. *Leisure interests:* movies, Chinese opera, travelling. *Address:* Legislative Council, Room 306, West Wing, Central Government Offices, 11 Ice House Street, Central, Hong Kong Special Administrative Region, People's Republic of China (office). *Telephone:* 31000079 (office); 21159999 (office). *Fax:* 21159688 (office). *E-mail:* regina.ip@savantas.org (office). *Website:* www.reginaip.hk.

IPPEN, Erich P., SB, MS, PhD; American physicist, electrical engineer and academic; *Elihu Thomson Professor of Electrical Engineering, Massachusetts Institute of Technology;* m. Dorothea E. Ippen; two s.; ed Massachusetts Inst. of Tech., Univ. of California, Berkeley; mem. Tech. Staff, Bell Labs 1968–80; joined MIT faculty 1980, currently Prin. Investigator, Research Lab. of Electronics (RLE), Elihu Thomson Prof. of Electrical Eng, Dept of Electrical Eng and Computer Science and Prof. of Physics, one of leaders of RLE's Optics and Quantum Electronics Group; mem. NAS, Nat. Acad. of Eng; Fellow, American Acad. of Arts and Sciences, IEEE, Optical Soc. of America (OSA), American Physical Soc. (APS); OSA R.W. Wood Prize 1981, Edward Longstreth Medal, Franklin Inst. 1982, Morris Leeds Award, IEEE 1983, Humboldt Sr Scientist Award 1986, H. E. Edgerton Award, SPIE 1989, John Scott Award, City of Philadelphia Trusts 1991, Civilian Distinguished Service Medal, USAF 1992, IEEE Quantum Electronics Award 1997, APS Arthur Schawlow Prize 1997, Distinguished Eng Alumnus, Univ. of California, Berkeley 2000, MIT Killian Award 2001, OSA Charles Hard Townes Award 2004, OSA Frederic Ives Medal 2006. *Achievements include:* a founder of field of femtosecond optics. *Publications include:* numerous scientific papers in professional journals on femtosecond science and ultra-highspeed devices to probe ultrafast phenomena in materials. *Address:* Room 36-319, Research Laboratory of Electronics, Massachusetts Institute of Technology, 77 Massachusetts Avenue, Cambridge, MA 02139, USA (office). *Telephone:* (617) 253-8504 (office). *Fax:* (617) 253-9611 (office). *E-mail:* ippen@mit.edu (office). *Website:* www.rle.mit.edu/rleonline/People/ErichP.Ippen .html (office).

IRAN, fmr Empress of (see Pahlavi, Farah Diba).

IRANI, Jamshed Jiji, PhD; Indian business executive; *Director, Tata Sons Limited;* b. 2 June 1936, Nagpur; s. of Jiji D. Irani and Khorshed Irani; m. Daisy Irani 1971; one s. two d.; ed Nagpur Univ., Univ. of Sheffield, UK; worked for British Iron and Steel Research Asscn 1963–67; Tata Iron and Steel Co. Ltd (now Tata Sons Ltd) 1968–, Gen. Man. 1979–81, Deputy Man. Dir 1981–83, Vice-Pres. (Operations) 1983–85, Pres. 1985–88, Jt Man. Dir 1988–92, Man. Dir 1992–97, Dir 1997–; Pres. Indian Inst. of Metals, All India Man. Asscn 1988–89; Nat. Pres. Confed. of Indian Industry 1992–93; Co-chair. Indo-British Partnership 1993–98; Chair. Bd of Govs Xavier Labour Relations Inst., Jamshedpur 1993–03, Bd of Govs Indian Inst. of Man.; mem. Scientific Advisory Cttee to Cabinet, Govt of India, Cen. Advisory Bd of Educ.; Pres. Asian Asscn of Man. Org. 2004–07; Dir (non-exec.) Repro India Ltd 2005–; Chair. (non-exec.) Everonn Skill Development Ltd 2010–11; mem. Council Indian Inst. of Science, Bangalore, Advisory Council of Citigroup India; Trustee, World Wild Fund for Nature (India); Fellow, Inst. of Metals, Inst. of Engineers, All India Man. Asscn, Inst. of Standards Engineers, Indian Acad. of Sciences, Inst. of Industrial Mans; Paul Harris Fellow, Rotary Int. 1977; Melvin Jones Fellow, Lions Int. Foundation 1993; Hon. KBE 1997; Dr hc (Univ. of Sheffield) 1993, Hon. DSc (Banaras Hindu Univ.) 2004; Nat. Metallurgist Award 1974, Platinum Medal, Indian Inst. of Man. 1988, Steel Vision Award, Michael John Memorial Gold Medal 1998, Qimpro Platinum Standard 2000, Juran Quality Medal, Indian Merchants' Chamber 2001, Ernst & Young Lifetime Achievement Award 2001, Padma Bhushan 2007. *Publications include:* numerous tech. papers. *Leisure interests:* philately, photography. *Address:* 7 Beldih Lake, Jamshedpur, 831001, India. *Telephone:* (657) 2431024 (office); (22) 66657565 (office); (22) 66352000 (home); (657) 2431025 (home). *Fax:* (657) 2431818 (office); (22) 66658030 (office); (22) 66352001 (home). *E-mail:* jjirani@tata.com (office). *Website:* www.tata.com (office).

IRANI, Ray R., DSc; American business executive; b. 15 Jan. 1935, Beirut, Lebanon; s. of Rida Irani and Naz Irani; m. Ghada Irani; two s. one d.; ed Univ. of Southern California; Sr Research Leader, Monsanto Co. 1957–67; Assoc. Dir New Products, later Dir of Research, Diamond Shamrock Corpn 1967–73; joined Olin Corpn 1973, Pres. Chemicals Group 1978–80, Dir and Corp. Pres. 1980–83; Exec. Vice-Pres. Occidental Petroleum Corpn, Los Angeles 1983–84, Dir 1984–2013, COO 1984–90, Pres. 1984–96, 2005–07, Chair. and CEO 1990–2011, Exec. Chair. 2011–13; CEO Occidental Chemical Corpn 1983–91, Chair. 1983–94; Chair. Canadian Occidental Petroleum Ltd (now Nexen Inc.), Calgary 1987–99, Hon. Chair. 1999–2000; mem. Bd of Dirs American Petroleum Inst., KB Home 1992–, Lyondell Chemical Co. 2002–, Cedars Bank, Wynn Resorts Ltd, TCW Group; mem. ACS, Scientific Research Soc., American Industrial Research Inst., Council on Foreign Relations, Conf. Bd, US-Saudi Arabian Business Council, World Affairs Council; Trustee, Univ. of Southern California, Chair. USC's Bd Personnel Cttee; Vice-Chair. American Univ. of Beirut; Hon. Fellow, American Inst. of Chemists. *Publications:* Particle Size; numerous papers in field of particle physics. *Address:* c/o Occidental Petroleum Corpn, 10889 Wilshire Blvd, Los Angeles, CA 90024-4201, USA. *E-mail:* info@oxy.com.

IRINEJ, Patriarch; Serbian ecclesiastic; *Patriarch of Serbian Orthodox Church;* b. (Irinej Gavrilovic), 28 Aug. 1930, Vidova, near Čačak; ed Orthodox Seminary, Prizren, Theological Faculty, Belgrade; monk, Rakovica Monastery 1959; Head of monastic school, Ostrog Monastery 1969; Rector, Orthodox Seminary, Prizren 1969; Vicar Bishop of Moravica 1974–75; Bishop of Nis 1975–2010; installed as 45th Patriarch of the Serbian Orthodox Church (Srpska Pravoslavna Crkva), Jan. 2010, also Archbishop of Peć and Metropolitan of Belgrade-Karlovci. *Address:* Serbian Orthodox Church (Srpska Pravoslavna Crkva), 11001 Belgrade, Kralja Petra 5, POB 182, Serbia (office). *Telephone:* (11) 3025-112 (office). *E-mail:* info@spc.rs (office). *Website:* www.spc.rs/eng (office).

IRONS, Jeremy; British actor; b. 19 Sept. 1948, Cowes, Isle of Wight, England; s. of the late Paul Dugan Irons and Barbara Ann Brereton Sharpe; m. 1st (divorced); 2nd Sinead Cusack (q.v.) 1978; two s.; ed Sherborne School, Dorset, Bristol Old Vic Theatre School; TV debut 1968; mem. Gaia Foundation, European Film Acad.; Patron, Prison Phoenix Trust, Archway Foundation; Officier des Arts et des Lettres; European Film Acad. Special Achievement Award 1998. *Stage appearances:* The Real Thing, Broadway (Tony Award) 1984, Rover 1986, The Winter's Tale 1986, Richard II (Stratford) 1986, Embers (Duke of York Theatre, London) 2006, Never So Good (Nat. Theatre) 2008, Impressionism (Broadway) 2009, The Gods Weep (Stratford) 2010. *Films include:* Nijinsky 1980, The French Lieutenant's Woman 1981, Moonlighting 1982, Betrayal 1983, The Wild Duck 1983, Swann in Love 1984, The Mission 1986, A Chorus of Disapproval 1988, Dead Ringers (New York Critics Best Actor Award 1988) 1988, Australia 1989, Danny, The Champion of the World 1989, Reversal of Fortune (Acad. Award 1991, Golden Globe Award for Best Actor 1991) 1990, Zebracka opera 1991, Kafka 1991, Damage 1992, Waterland 1992, M. Butterfly 1993, The House of the Spirits 1993, The Lion King (voice) 1994, Die Hard with a Vengeance 1995, Stealing Beauty 1996, Chinese Box 1997, Lolita 1997, The Man in the Iron Mask 1998, Dungeons and Dragons 2000, The Fourth Angel 2001, The Time Machine 2002, And Now... Ladies and Gentlemen... 2002, Callas Forever 2002, The Merchant of Venice 2004, Being Julia 2004, Kingdom of Heaven 2005, Casanova 2005, Inland Empire 2006, Eragon 2006, Appaloosa 2008, The Pink Panther 2 2009, Margin Call 2011, The Words 2012, Night Train to Lisbon 2013, Beautiful Creatures 2013. *Television includes:* The Pallisers (series) 1974, Notorious Woman (mini-series) 1974, Love for Lydia (mini-series) 1977, Langrishe Go Down 1978, The Voysey Inheritance 1979, Brideshead Revisited 1981, The Captain's Doll 1983, Saturday Night Live (episode 16.16, host) 1991, Tales from Hollywood 1992, Mirad (also dir) 1997, The Great War and the Shaping of the 20th Century (Primetime Emmy Award for Outstanding Voice-Over Performance 1997), Ohio Impromptu 2000, Longitude 2000, Last Call 2002, RSC Meets USA: Working Shakespeare (video) 2002, Comic Relief 2003, Dame Edna Live at the Palace 2003, Elizabeth I (Primetime Emmy Award 2005, Golden Globe Award for Best Supporting Actor in a mini-series 2005, Screen Actors' Guild Award for Outstanding Performance by a Male Actor in a Television Movie 2006) 2005, The Colour of Magic 2008, Georgia O'Keeffe 2009, The Borgias (series) 2011–13, Law & Order: Special Victims Unit (series) 2011, Eco-Hollywood (film) 2011, The Simpsons (series) 2012, The Hollow Crown (mini-series) – Henry IV, Part 1 2012, – Henry IV, Part 2 2012, Life on Fire: Wildlife on

the Volcano's Edge (series, narrator) 2013. *Leisure interests:* skiing, riding, sailing. *Address:* c/o Abi Harris, The Artists Partnership, 101 Finsbury Pavement, London, EC2A 1RS, England (office).

IRVINE, John Maxwell, PhD, CPhys, FInstP, FRAS, FRSA, FRSE, CIMgt, DL; British theoretical physicist and consultant; *Professor of Physics, University of Manchester;* b. 28 Feb. 1939, Edinburgh, Scotland; s. of John MacDonald Irvine and Joan Paterson Irvine; m. Grace Ritchie 1962; one s.; ed George Heriot's School, Edinburgh, Univs of Edinburgh, Manchester, Michigan; Asst Lecturer in Theoretical Physics, Univ. of Manchester 1964–66, Lecturer 1968–73, Sr Lecturer 1973–76, Reader 1976–83, Prof. 1983–91, Dean of Science 1989–91, Prof. of Physics 2001–; Prin. and Vice-Chancellor Univ. of Aberdeen 1991–96; Prin. and Vice-Chancellor Univ. of Birmingham 1996–2001, currently Emeritus Prof.; Chair. Scottish Advisory Group on the Academic Year 1993–96, Cttee of Scottish Univ. Prins 1994–96; Research Assoc., LNS, Cornell Univ., USA 1966–68; Head of Nuclear Theory, Science and Eng Research Council (SERC) Daresbury Lab. 1974–78; Dir Rowett Research Inst. 1992–96, Cobuild Ltd 1996–2001, Barber Trust 1996–2001; mem. Bd Scottish Council Devt and Industry 1991–96, Grampian Enterprise Ltd 1992–96; Council mem. Inst. of Physics 1981–87, 1988–92 (Vice-Pres. 1982–87), European Physical Soc. 1989–92; mem. Nuclear Physics Bd and Chair. Nuclear Structure Cttee, SERC 1984–88; mem. Scottish Econ. Council 1993–96, Council Asscn of Commonwealth Univs 1993–2004 (Chair. 1994–95, Treas. 1998–2004), BT Scottish Advisory Forum 1993–96, British Council (Scotland) 1993–96, Council Cttee of Vice-Chancellors and Prins (now Universities UK) 1995–98, Bd Higher Educ. Quality Cttee 1994–97, Univ. Council for Educational Admin 1995–2001, Univs and Colls Admissions Service (UCAS) 1995–2001, Birmingham Chamber of Commerce and Industry 1996–2001, Public Health Labs Service 1997–2005, Commonwealth Scholarships Comm. 2002–, Educ. Consultancy Service of the British Council 2002–03, Nursing and Midwifery Council 2005–, Oxford Round Table 2002–; Chair. West Midlands Regional Innovation Strategy Group 1996–2001, Jt Information Structure Cttee 1998–2003, Royal Soc. of Edinburgh Inquiry 'Energy Issues for Scotland' 2005–; Specialist Adviser, Cttee on Radioactive Waste Man. 2005; mem. Energy Steering Group, European Acads Science Advisory Council 2005–; Gov. English Speaking Union 1998–2004; Hon. FRCSE 1995; Hon. DSc (William and Mary) 1995, (Aston) 2001; Hon. DEd (Robert Gordon Univ.) 1995; Hon. DUniv (Edin.) 1995, (Birmingham) 2002; Hon. LLD (Aberdeen) 1997. *Publications:* The Basis of Modern Physics 1967, Nuclear Structure Theory 1972, Heavy Nuclei, Superheavy Nuclei and Neutron Stars 1975, Neutron Stars 1978, Nuclear Power: A Very Short Introduction 2011; more than 100 research publs on physics. *Leisure interest:* staying alive. *Address:* 27 Belfield Road, Manchester, M20 6BJ, England (home). *Telephone:* (161) 445-1434 (home). *E-mail:* j.m.irvine@manchester.ac.uk (office). *Website:* www .irvinereports.man.ac.uk.

IRVINE OF LAIRG, Baron (Life Peer), cr. 1987, of Lairg in the District of Sutherland; **Alexander (Derry) Andrew Mackay Irvine,** QC, MA, LLB; British lawyer; b. 23 June 1940; s. of Alexander Irvine and Margaret Christina Irvine; m. 1st Margaret Veitch (divorced 1973); m. 2nd Alison Mary McNair 1974; two s.; ed Inverness Acad., Hutcheson's Boys' Grammar School, Univ. of Glasgow, Christ's Coll., Cambridge; Lecturer, LSE 1965–69; called to the Bar, Inner Temple 1967, Bencher 1985; a Recorder 1985–88; Deputy High Court Judge 1987–97; Shadow Spokesman on Legal Affairs and Home Affairs 1987–92; Shadow Lord Chancellor 1992–97, Lord High Chancellor of GB 1997–2003, Hon. Pres. Legal and Constitutional Affairs Group 2007–; Pres. Magistrates' Asscn; Jt Pres. House of Lords British-American Parl. Group, Commonwealth Parl. Asscn, Inter-Parl. Union; Pres. NI Youth and Family Courts Asscn 1999; Hon. Bencher, Inn of Court of NI 1998; Vice-Patron World Fed. of Mental Health; Trustee Whitechapel Art Gallery 1990–, Hunterian Collection 1997–; Hon. Fellow, LSE; Hon. LLD (Glasgow) 1997, Laurea hc (Siena) 2000. *Leisure interests:* cinema, theatre, art, travel. *Address:* House of Lords, Westminster, London, SW1A 0PW, England. *Telephone:* (20) 7219-1446.

IRVING, Amy; American actress; b. 10 Sept. 1953, Palo Alto, Calif.; m. Steven Spielberg (q.v.) 1985 (divorced); one s.; pnr Bruno Barreto; one s.; ed American Conservatory Theater and London Acad. of Dramatic Art; frequent TV appearances. *Stage appearances include:* Juliet in Romeo and Juliet, Seattle Repertory Theater 1982–83, on Broadway in Amadeus 1981–82, Heartbreak House 1983–84, Three Sisters 1997, off Broadway in The Road to Mecca 1988, The Guys 2002, Celadine 2004, The Waters of March 2008, A Little Night Music 2010. *Films include:* Carrie, The Fury, Voices, Honeysuckle Road, The Competition, Yentl, Mickey and Maude, Rumpelstiltskin, Crossing Delancey, A Show of Force, Benefit of the Doubt, Kleptomania, Acts of Love (also co-exec. producer), I'm Not Rappaport, Carried Away, Deconstructing Harry, One Tough Cop 1998, Blue Ridge Fall 1999, The Confession, The Rage: Carrie 2 1999, Traffic 2000, Bossa Nova 2000, Thirteen Conversations About One Thing 2002, Tuck Everlasting 2002, Hide and Seek 2005, Adam 2009. *Television includes:* Alias (series) 2002–05, Zero Hour (series) 2013.

IRVING, Edward (Ted), CM, ScD, FRS, FRSC; Canadian (b. British) scientist and academic; *Research Scientist Emeritus, Pacific Geoscience Centre;* b. 27 May 1927, Colne, Lancs., England; s. of George E. Irving and Nellie Irving; m. Sheila A. Irwin 1957; two s. two d.; ed Colne Grammar School and Univ. of Cambridge; army service 1945–48; Research Fellow, Fellow and Sr Fellow, ANU 1954–64; Dominion Observatory, Canada 1964–66; Prof. of Geophysics, Univ. of Leeds 1966–67; Research Scientist, Dominion Observatory, later Earth Physics Br. Dept of Energy, Mines and Resources, Ottawa 1967–81; Research Scientist, Pacific Geoscience Centre, North Saanich, BC 1981–92, Research Scientist Emer. 1992–; Adjunct Prof., Carleton Univ., Ottawa 1975–81, Univ. of Vic. 1985–95; Fellow, American Geophysical Union; Fellow, Foreign Assoc. NAS; Distinguished Fellow, Geological Asscn of Canada; Hon. FGS; mem. Order of Canada; Queen's Golden Jubilee Medal 2002, Queen's Diamond Jubilee Medal 2012; Hon. DSc (Carleton Univ.) 1979, (Memorial Univ.) 1986, (Victoria Univ.) 1999. *Publications:* Palaeomagnetism 1964; contribs to learned journals. *Leisure interests:* gardening, carpentry, choral singing. *Address:* Pacific Geoscience Centre, 9860 West Saanich Road, PO Box 6000, North Saanich, BC, V8L 4B2 (office); 9363 Carnoustie Crescent, North Saanich, BC, V8L 5G7, Canada (home). *Telephone:* (250) 656-9645 (home). *Fax:* (250) 363-6565 (office). *E-mail:* stirving@telus.net (home). *Website:* www.pgc.nrcan.gc.ca (office).

IRVING, John Winslow, BA, MFA; American writer; b. 2 March 1942, Exeter, NH; s. of Colin F. N. Irving and Frances Winslow; m. 1st Shyla Leary 1964 (divorced 1981); two s.; m. 2nd Janet Turnbull 1987; one s.; ed Univs of Pittsburgh, Vienna, New Hampshire and Iowa; Asst Prof. of English, Mount Holyoke Coll. 1967–72, 1975–78; Writer-in-Residence, Univ. of Iowa 1972–75; with Bread Loaf Writers' Conf. 1976, Brandeis Univ.; Rockefeller Foundation grantee 1971–72; Nat. Endowment for Arts Fellow 1974–75, Guggenheim Fellow 1976–77; mem. American Acad. of Arts and Letters 2001; O. Henry Award 1981. *Publications:* novels: Setting Free the Bears 1969, The Water-Method Man 1972, The 158-Pound Marriage 1974, The World According to Garp (Nat. Book Award 1980 for paperback fiction 1980) 1978, The Hotel New Hampshire 1981, The Cider House Rules 1985, screenplay (Acad. Award for the best adapted screenplay 2000) 1999, A Prayer for Owen Meany 1989, A Son of the Circus 1994, A Widow for One Year 1998, The Fourth Hand 2001, Until I Find You 2005, Last Night in Twisted River 2009, In One Person 2012; non-fiction: An Introduction to Great Expectations 1986, Trying to Save Piggy Sneed (memoirs, short stories and essays) 1996, An Introduction to A Christmas Carol 1996, My Movie Business (memoir) 1999; contrib. to New York Times Book Review, New Yorker, Rolling Stone, Esquire, Playboy. *Address:* c/o Turnbull Agency, PO Box 757, Dorset, VT 05251, USA (office). *Website:* www.john-irving.com.

IRYANI, Abd al-Karim al-, PhD; Yemeni economist and politician; b. 12 Oct. 1934, Eryan; m.; three s. three d.; ed Univ. of Georgia, Yale Univ., USA; worked in an agricultural project in Yemen 1968–72; Chair. Cen. Planning Org. 1972–76; Minister of Devt 1974–76, of Educ. and Rector San'a Univ. 1976–78; Adviser, Kuwait Fund for Arab Econ. Devt 1978–80; Prime Minister 1980–83; Deputy Prime Minister and Minister of Foreign Affairs 1984–90, 1994–98; Minister of Foreign Affairs 1990–93, of Planning and Devt 1993–94; Prime Minister of Yemen 1998–2001; currently adviser to President Ali Abdullah Saleh; fmr Sec.-Gen. Gen. People's Congress Party; Chair. Council for the Reconstruction of Earthquake Areas 1983–84. *Address:* General People's Congress, San'a, Republic of Yemen (office). *E-mail:* gpc@y.net.ye (office). *Website:* www.almotamar.net (office).

ISA, Dato' Haji Pehin, BA; Brunei politician; b. 1935; ed Univ. of Southampton, UK; trained as barrister in UK; Asst Counsel and Deputy Public Prosecutor, Brunei 1962–65, Asst Attorney-Gen. 1965–68, Deputy Attorney-Gen. 1968–70 fmrly Gen. Adviser to Sultan of Brunei, then Special Adviser, with ministerial rank in Prime Minister's Office 1986–2005; Minister of Home Affairs 1988–95; currently with Ahmad Isa and Pnrs (law firm). *Address:* Ahmad Isa and Partners, Unit 405A/410A, 4th Floor Wisma Jaya, Jalan Pemanca, Bandar Seri Begawan, BS8811, Brunei (office). *E-mail:* ahmisa@brunet.bn (office).

ISAAC, Alan Raymond; New Zealand business executive and sports administrator; *President, International Cricket Council;* b. 20 Jan. 1952, Wellington, North Island; ed Onslow Coll., Victoria Univ. of Wellington; left-handed batsman; represented Wellington through the age groups and for three years captained their second team; mem. New Zealand Cricket Bd for 18 years, Chair. 2008–10; Vice-Pres. Int. Cricket Council (ICC) 2010–12, Pres. 2012–; with KPMG 1971–2006, Chair. –2006; mem. bds several business, health, community and sporting orgs, including New Zealand Red Cross Foundation, New Zealand Community Trust; fmr mem. New Zealand Golf Bd, Bd of Rugby New Zealand 2011 Ltd. *Address:* International Cricket Council, Street 69, Dubai Sports City, Emirates Road, PO Box 500 070, Dubai, United Arab Emirates (office). *Telephone:* (4) 382-8800 (office). *Fax:* (4) 382-8600 (office). *E-mail:* enquiry@icc-cricket.com (office). *Website:* icc-cricket.yahoo.net (office).

ISAAC, Tony; British business executive; *Chairman, Schlumberger Ltd;* Finance Dir, GEC Plessey Telecommunications Ltd 1988–90; Finance Dir, Arjo Wiggins Appleton plc (joined shortly before demerger from BAT Industries plc 1990) 1990–96; Exec. Dir BOC 1994–96, mem. Exec. Man. Bd 1996–2006, Chief Exec. 2000–06; Dir (non-exec.) Schlumberger Ltd 2003–, Chair. 2012–; mem. Bd of Dirs GDF SUEZ Energy International (fmrly International Power plc) 2000–, Chair. Audit Cttee 2011–12; Sr Dir (non-exec.), Hogg Robinson Group, Chair. Audit Cttee, mem. Remuneration Cttee, Nomination Cttee. *Address:* Schlumberger Ltd, 5599 San Felipe, Houston TX 77056, USA (office). *Telephone:* (713) 375-3400 (office). *Fax:* (713) 375-3463 (office). *E-mail:* info@slb.com (office). *Website:* www.slb.com (office).

ISAACS, Sir Jeremy Israel, Kt, MA; British television executive and arts administrator; b. 28 Sept. 1932; s. of Isidore Isaacs and Sara Jacobs; m. 1st Tamara Isaacs (née Weinreich) 1958 (died 1986); one s. one d.; m. 2nd Gillian Widdicombe 1988; ed Glasgow Acad., Merton Coll., Oxford; TV Producer, Granada TV (What the Papers Say, All Our Yesterdays) 1958, Associated Rediffusion (This Week) 1963, BBC TV (Panorama) 1965; Controller of Features, Associated Rediffusion 1967; with Thames TV 1968–78, Producer, The World at War 1974, Cold War 1998; Dir of Programmes 1974–78; special ind. consultant TV series Hollywood, ITV, A Sense of Freedom, ITV, Ireland, a Television Documentary, BBC, Battle for Crete, NZ TV, Cold War, Turner Broadcasting; CEO, Channel Four TV Co. 1981–88; Gen. Dir Royal Opera House 1988–96 (Dir 1985–97); Chief Exec. Jeremy Isaacs Productions 1998–; Gov. BFI 1979–84; Chair. BFI Production Bd 1979–81, Artsworld Channels Ltd 2000–03, Sky Arts; Chair. judging panel, European City of Culture competition 2008; James MacTaggart Memorial Lecturer, Edinburgh TV Festival 1979; Fellow, Royal Television Soc. 1978, BAFTA 1985, BFI 1986; L'Ordre National du Mérite 1992; Hon. DLitt (Strathclyde) 1983, (Bristol) 1988; Dr hc (CNAA) 1987, (RCA) 1988; Hon. LLD (Manchester) 1998; Desmond Davis Award for Outstanding Creative Contrib. to TV 1972; George Polk Memorial Award 1973; Cyril Bennett Award 1982; Lord Willis Award for Distinguished Service to TV 1985. *Publications:* Storm Over Four: A Personal Account 1989, Cold War (co-author) 1999, Never Mind the Moon 1999, Look Me in the Eye: a Life in Television (autobiog.) 2006. *Leisure interests:* books, walks, sleep. *Address:* Jeremy Isaacs Productions Ltd, 8 Shelton Street, London, WC2H 9SR, England. *E-mail:* jip@jip.co.uk (office). *Website:* www.skyarts.co.uk.

ISAACSON, Walter Seff, MA; American journalist and international organization official; *President and CEO, Aspen Institute;* b. 20 May 1952, New Orleans, La; s. of Irwin Isaacson and Betsy Isaacson; m. Cathy Wright 1984; one d.; ed Harvard Univ., Pembroke Coll., Univ. of Oxford; reporter, Sunday Times, London 1976–77, States-Item, New Orleans 1977–78; staff writer, Time magazine, New York 1978–79, political corresp. 1979–81, Assoc. Ed. 1981–84, Sr Ed. 1985–91, Asst Man. Ed. 1991–93, Man. Ed. 1995–2000, Editorial Dir Time Inc. 2000–01; Chair. and CEO CNN Newsgroup 2001–03; Ed. New Media Time, Inc. 1993–96; Pres. and CEO Aspen Inst., Washington, DC 2003–; mem. Council on Foreign Relations, Century Asscn; Overseas Press Club Award, New York 1981, 1984, 1987, Harry Truman Book Prize 1987. *Publications:* Pro and Con 1983, Kissinger: A Biography 1992, The Wise Men (jtly) 1986, Benjamin Franklin: An American Life 2003, Einstein: His Life and Universe (Quill Award for Biography 2007) 2007, American Sketches: Great Leaders, Creative Thinkers and Heroes of a Hurricane 2009, Profiles in Leadership 2010, Steve Jobs 2011. *Address:* The Aspen Institute, Suite 700, One Dupont Circle, NW, Washington, DC 20036-1133, USA (office). *Telephone:* (202) 736-5800 (office). *Fax:* (202) 467-0790 (office). *E-mail:* pat.zindulka@aspeninstitute.org (office). *Website:* www.aspeninstitute.org (office).

ISAAK, Chris, BA; American singer, songwriter and actor; b. 26 June 1956, Stockton, Calif.; singer 1984–; extensive int. tours, festival appearances; Int. Rock Award for Best Male Vocalist of the Year 1991, three MTV Music Video Awards (for Wicked Game) 1991. *Films appearances include:* Married to the Mob 1988, Wild At Heart 1989, The Silence of the Lambs 1991, Twin Peaks: Fire Walk With Me 1992, Little Buddha 1993, Grace of My Heart 1996, That Thing You Do! 1996, Blue Ridge Fall 1999, A Dirty Shame 2004, The Informers 2009. *Television appearances include:* From the Earth to the Moon (mini-series) 1998, The Chris Isaak Show (series) 2001–04, The Chris Isaak Hour 2009–. *Songs contributed to film and television:* Blue Velvet 1986, Married to the Mob 1988, Wild At Heart 1990, La Désenchantée 1990, True Romance 1993, Beautiful Girls 1996, Tin Cup 1996, The Late Late Show with Craig Kilborn (title song) 1999, Eyes Wide Shut 1999, The Family Man 2000. *Recordings include:* albums: Silvertone 1985, Chris Isaak 1987, Heart Shaped World 1989, Wicked Game 1991, San Francisco Days 1993, Forever Blue 1995, Baja Sessions 1996, Speak Of The Devil 1998, Wicked Ways Anthology 1998, Always Got Tonight 2002, Chris Isaak Christmas 2004, Mr Lucky 2009, Live at the Fillmore 2010, Beyond the Sun 2011. *Address:* c/o Reprise Records Inc, Warner Bros., 3300 Warner Boulevard, Burbank, CA 91505-4632, USA (office). *Website:* warnerbrosrecords.com (office); www.chrisisaak.com.

ISABEKOV, Azim Beishembayevich; Kyrgyzstani economist and politician; b. 4 April 1960, Arashan, Chui Oblast; ed Kyrgyz State Univ.; Chief of Staff, Office of Gov. of Chui Oblast Kurmanbek Bakiyev 1997–2000; Head of Admin. Dept, Office of Prime Minister 2001–02; Dir State Fund for Econ. Devt 2002–04; Deputy Chief of Staff, Office of Pres. Kurmanbek Bakiyev 2005–06; Minister of Agric., Water Resources and Mfg Industry June–Dec. 2006; Prime Minister Jan.–March 2007. *Address:* c/o Office of the Prime Minister, Dom Pravitelstva, 720003 Bishkek, Kyrgyzstan.

ISAKOV, Gen. Ismail Isakovich; Kyrgyzstani army officer and government official; b. 1950, Spou-Korgon, Alai Dist., Osh Duban; ed Tashkent Higher Mil. Acad., Frunze Mil. Acad., Moscow, Gen. Staff Mil. Acad., Moscow; Platoon Commdr, then Co. Commdr in southern group of troops, Hungary 1973–78; Deputy Bn Commdr, then Bn Commdr in Ukraine 1978–81; Regimental Chief of Staff, Regimental Commdr, Div. Chief of Staff, Combat Training Deputy Chief of the State Cttee for Defence 1984–94; Chief of the Main Staff 1994–95; First Deputy Minister of Defence 1994–99; Deputy in Legis. Ass. of the Jogorku Kenesh (Parl.) from Alai Dist 2000–05, Chair. Cttee on Nat. Security Issues 2000–05, Dir of Coordinating Cttee for the Resignation of Askar Akaev and for Reforms for the People (political movt) 2003–04; Acting Minister of Defence March–Sept. 2005, Minister of Defence 2005–06 (resgnd), 2007–08, Acting Minister of Defence 2010; Sec., Security Council 2008–10; rank of Gen. (two stars); Medal of Three Degrees for Irreproachable Service, Medal for Combat Merits, Medal for Strengthening of Mil. Cooperation. *Leisure interests:* chess, reading. *Address:* c/o Ministry of Defence, 720001 Bishkek, Logvinenko 261, Kyrgyzstan (office).

ISAKOV, Army-Gen. Vladimir Ilyich; Russian military officer; *Deputy Minister of Defence;* b. 21 July 1950, Voskresenskoye, Kaluga region; ed Moscow Mil. School of Civil Defence, Mil. Acad. of Home Front Transport, Mil. Acad. of Gen. Staff; Platoon Commdr of Civil Defence Forces; served in Group of Soviet Armed Forces in Germany; Deputy Regt Commdr, then Deputy Army Commdr of Home Front.; Deputy Commdr Div. of Home Front, Siberian Mil. Command 1982–84, 40th Army in Afghanistan 1984–86; Deputy Army Commdr, then Head of Home Front, Kiev Mil. Command 1988–89; Head of Gen. Staff of Home Front, W Group of Armed Forces 1989–94; Head of Chair. Mil. Acad. of Gen. Staff 1994; Head of Gen. Staff Armed Forces of Russian Fed. 1996, First Deputy Head of Home Front 1996–97, Head 1997; Chief of Logistics and Deputy Minister of Defence 1997–. *Address:* Ministry of Defence, 105175 Moscow, ul. Myasnitskaya 37, Russia (office). *Telephone:* (495) 293-38-54 (office). *Fax:* (495) 296-84-36 (office). *Website:* www.mil.ru (office).

ISAKSON, Johnny, BBA; American business executive and politician; *Senator from Georgia;* m. Dianne Isakson 1968; three c.; ed Univ. of Georgia; served in Ga Air Nat. Guard 1966–72; began business career with Northside Reality (family-owned real estate co.) 1967, est. Cobb County Office, apptd Pres. 1979; elected to State of Ga House of Reps 1976, Republican Leader in State House 1983–90; Republican nominee for Gov. of Ga 1989; elected to State of Ga Senate 1993, Republican Chair. of Ga Bd of Educ. 1996–99; Ga Chair. for Bob Dole for Pres. Campaign 1996; elected to US House of Reps, Washington, DC 1999, mem. House Transportation Cttee, Educ. Cttee, Co-Chair. Sub-cttee on 21st Century Competitiveness, Deputy Major Whip to House Republican Leadership; Senator from Georgia 2005–; fmr Pres. Realty Alliance; fmr mem. Exec. Cttee, Nat. Assscn of Realtors, Bd of Dirs Ga Chamber of Commerce, Riverside Bank, Advisory Bd SunTrust; teacher, Sunday School, Mount Zion United Methodist Church 1978–2008; an original author of the No Child Left Behind Act; Republican; Best Legislator in America Award, Republican Nat. Cttee 1989. *Address:* 131 Russell Senate Office Building, Washington, DC 20510, USA (office). *Telephone:* (202) 224-3643 (office). *Fax:* (202) 228-0724 (office). *Website:* isakson.senate.gov (office).

ISAMUDDIN, Riduan, (Hambali); Indonesian religious leader; *Leader, Jemaah Islamiah;* b. (Encep Nurjaman), 4 April 1966, Sukamanah, W Java; m. Noral Wizaah Lee; active in opposition to Suharto regime 1970s and 1980s; sought exile in Malaysia 1985; fought as mujahideen guerilla against Soviet occupation, Afghanistan 1988; recruited Muslim supporters to join a jihad (holy war) in order to est. a Pan-Asian Islamic State, Malaysia 1990; believed to have co-f. Jemaah Islamiah (JI—Islamic Community) network with Abu Bakar Bashir with operations throughout SE Asia 1990; returned to Indonesia to recruit supporters 2000; mem. consultative council al-Qaeda; alleged liaison officer between al-Qaeda and radical Islamic groups in SE Asia; allegedly funded numerous mil. terrorist groups fighting jihad, in particular in Maluko Islands 1999; wanted by Govts of Indonesia, Malaysia, Singapore and The Philippines as key suspect for involvement in series of bomb attacks on World Trade Center 1993, Philippine airliner 1994, USS Cole, Yemen 2000, Christian church bombings, Indonesia 2000, Manila bombings 2000, Sept. 11 attacks in USA 2001, Operation Jabril (attempted mass terrorist attacks on US targets in Malaysia, Singapore and Philippines) 2001, Bali nightclub 2002; captured in Thailand by US forces 11 August 2003 and currently in custody.

ISARANGURA, Gen. Thammarak, BSc; Thai government official and military officer; b. 22 July 1938, Roiet Prov.; m. Waneda Isarangura; ed Chulachomklao Royal Mil. Acad.; Commdr Training Directorate of Jt Communications 1964–66, with Radio Station Directorate 1967–72, Asst Chief, Intelligence Section, Seconded to Second Army Area Command Sakon Nakhon 1973–76, Chief, Intelligence Section, Fourth Army Area Command, Nakhonsrithammarat 1982–83, Chief, Intelligence Section, Directorate of Intelligence, Army Operation Centre 1984–88, Commdr of Army Mil. Intelligence 1989–90, Chief of Staff to Deputy Supreme Commdr, Supreme Command Headquarters 1991–95, Commanding Gen. of Armed Forces Security Centre, Supreme Command 1996–97, Special Adviser, Supreme Command Headquarters 1998; Deputy Prime Minister of Thailand 2004; Minister of Defence 2005–06; banned from politics by Constitutional Tribunal 2007; Kt Grand Cordon (Special Class) of the Most Exalted Order of the White Elephant, of the Most Noble Order of the Crown of Thailand. *Address:* c/o Ministry of Defence, Thanon Sanamchai, Bangkok 10200, Thailand (office).

ISĂRESCU, Mugur Constantin, PhD; Romanian economist, central banker and fmr politician; *Governor, Banca Naţională a României (National Bank of Romania);* b. 1 Aug. 1949, Drăgăşani, Vâlcea Co.; s. of Constantin Isărescu and Aritina Isărescu; m. Elena Isărescu; one s. one d.; ed Acad. of Econs; Research Fellow, Inst. for World Econ. 1971–90; Asst Lecturer, Acad. of Econs, Bucharest 1975–89, Prof. 1996–; Prof., Timişoara West Univ. 1994–96; fmrly Prof. of Banking, Coll. of Economic Banking Inst.; First Sec., Embassy in Washington, DC 1990; Gov. Banca Naţională a României (Nat. Bank of Romania) 1990–99, 2001–, IMF Gov. for Romania, World Bank Vice-Gov. for Romania, EBRD Vice-Gov. for Romania; Prime Minister of Romania 1999–2000; Chair. for Romania, Club of Rome; Pres. Central Bank Govs' Club in the Region of the Black Sea, the Balkans and Central Asia; Vice-Pres. Cen. Banks Govs Club; mem. Bd Romanian American Enterprise Fund, Trilateral Comm.; Chair. Romanian Chess Fed. 1995–98; mem. Romanian Acad. (Pres. Econ., Law and Sociological Sciences Section 2006–); Honour Medal, Architects' World Forum. *Publications:* Financial Crisis 1979, Gold, Myth and Reality 1981, Stock Exchange 1982, Recent Developments in Romania 1990, Monetary Policy, Macroeconomic Stability and Banking Reform in Romania 1995, Banking System in Romania: Recent Developments and Prospects 1996, Reform of the Financial System in Romania and European Integration 1996, Monetary Policy After 1989 1997. *Leisure interests:* literature, history. *Address:* Banca Naţională a României, 030031 Bucharest 3, Str. Lipscani 25, Romania (office). *Telephone:* (21) 3124368 (office). *Fax:* (21) 3101630 (office). *E-mail:* mugur.isarescu@bnro.ro (office). *Website:* www.bnro.ro (office).

ISAYEV, Alexander Sergeyevich; Russian biologist and forester; *Professor and Scientific Head of Centre for Ecological Problems and Productivity of Forests, Russian Academy of Sciences;* b. 26 Oct. 1931, Moscow; m. Lidia Pokrovskaya 1953; two d.; ed Leningrad Forestry Acad.; mem. CPSU 1965–91; Deputy Chair. Council for Protection of the Environment and Rational Exploitation of Resources in USSR Supreme Soviet 1979–89; mem. USSR (now Russian) Acad. of Sciences 1984–; Dir V. N. Sukachev Forestry Inst., Krasnoyarsk, Chair. Krasnoyarsk Div., Siberian Dept of USSR Acad. of Sciences 1977–88; Pres. GOSKOMLES (State Comm. on Forestry) 1988–91; Chair. Higher Ecological Council at Russian Fed. Supreme Soviet 1992–93; Prof. and Scientific Head of Centre for Ecological Problems and Productivity of Forests 1991–; Dir Int. Forestry Inst. 1991–; Hon. Diploma (UNEP Programme) 1989; Gold Medal (Int. Union of Forestry Research Orgs.) 1976, Gold Medal (Russian Acad. of Sciences) 1992. *Publications:* eight books, over 310 articles. *Leisure interests:* fishing, hunting. *Address:* Centre for Ecological Problems and Productivity of Forests, Russian Academy of Sciences (CEPL RAS), 117810 Moscow, Profsoyuznaya str. 84/32 (office); 117418 Moscow, Novocheremushkinskaya str. 69, Russia. *Telephone:* (495) 332-2617 (office). *Fax:* (495) 332-2617 (office). *E-mail:* isaev@cepl.rssi.ru (office). *Website:* www.cepl.rssi .ru (office).

ISCHINGER, Wolfgang Friedrich; German diplomatist; *Chairman, Munich Security Conference;* b. 6 April 1946, Beuren, Stuttgart; m. 2nd Jutta Falke-Ischinger; one c., and two c. from previous m.; ed Univ. of Bonn, Univ. of Geneva, Switzerland, Fletcher School of Law and Diplomacy, Harvard Univ. Law School, USA; mem. cabinet staff of UN Sec.-Gen., New York 1973–75; joined Foreign Service 1975, mem. Policy Planning Staff 1977–79; posted to Washington, DC 1979–82; mem. cabinet staff, Minister of Foreign Affairs, Bonn 1982–90, Pvt. Sec. to Minister 1985–87, Dir Cabinet and Parl. Affairs 1987–90; Minister-Counsellor, Head Political Section, Embassy in Paris 1990–93; Dir Policy Planning Staff, Bonn 1993–95, Dir-Gen. for Political Affairs 1995–98, State Sec. 1998–2001, 2000–01; Amb. to USA 2001–06, to UK 2006–08; apptd to represent EU in negotiations on status of Kosovo 2007; Chair. Munich Security Conf. 2008–; Global Head of Govt Relations, Allianz SE, Munich 2008–; mem. High Level German-Russian Strategy Group; mem. Bd of Overseers, Fletcher School of Law and Diplomacy, Alfred Herrhausen Gesellschaft, Frankfurt, Council on Public Policy, AFS Germany (American Field Service), Bd East-West Inst., New York; fmr Chair. Ambs' Advisory Bd, Exec. Council on Diplomacy, Washington, DC. *Publications:* numerous articles on foreign policy, security and arms control policy, European policy issues. *Leisure interests:* skiing, mountaineering, flying. *Address:* Munich Security Conference, Prinzregentenstrasse 7, 80538 Munich, Germany (office). *Telephone:*

(89) 37979490 (office). *Fax:* (89) 379794960 (office). *E-mail:* office@ securityconference.de (office). *Website:* www.securityconference.de (office).

ISDELL, E(dward) Neville, BS; Irish beverage industry executive (retd); b. 8 June 1943, Downpatrick, Co. Down, NI; m. Pamela Anne Gill 1970; one d.; ed Univ. of Cape Town, S Africa, Harvard Business School, USA; joined Coca-Cola Zambia 1966, held positions in S Africa, Australia, The Philippines, Pres. Cen. European Div. 1985–89, Group Pres. for NE Europe, the Middle East and Africa 1989–98, Pres. Greater Europe Group 1995, Chair. Coca-Cola Beverages 1998–2000, CEO Coca-Cola HBC 2000–01, Sr Int. Consultant to CEO, The Coca-Cola Co. 2001–04, Chair. The Coca-Cola Co. 2004–09, CEO 2004–08; Chair. Int. Business Leaders Forum; mem. Bd of Dirs Global Water Challenge, General Motors Corpn; Chair. US-Russia Business Council, Bd of Trustees Int. Business Leaders Forum 2008–11, Atlanta Cttee for Progress; mem. US-Brazil CEO Forum; Hon. DSc (Univ. of Ulster) 2007. *Address:* c/o International Business Leaders Forum, 15–16 Cornwall Terrace, London, NW1 4QP, England.

ISHAYEV, Viktor Ivanovich; Russian politician and government official; b. 5 Feb. 1944, Kemerovo Oblast; m.; two c.; ed Novosibirsk Inst. for Engineers of Waterway Transport; Head of Admin, Khabarovsk Krai 1991–96, Gov. 1996–2009 (re-elected 2000); Deputy of Fed. Council of Fed. Ass. of Russian Fed. 1993–2001; Presidential Rep. to Far Eastern Fed. Okrug 2009–13. *Address:* c/o Office of the Presidential Representative, 603082 Nizhnii Novgorod, Kreml, kor. 1, Russia (office).

ISHI, Hiroyuki; Japanese environmental scientist and academic; *Professor, Public Policy School, Hokkaido University;* ed Univ. of Tokyo; with Asahi Shimbun newspaper 1965–94, positions including Science Writer, New York Bureau Corresp., Science Ed., Sr Staff Writer; undertook field research in 125 countries; apptd Prof., Grad. School of Frontier Sciences, Univ. of Tokyo 1994; fmr Visiting Prof., Int. Research Center for Japanese Studies; Amb. to Zambia 2002; currently Prof., Public Policy School, Hokkaido Univ.; fmr Special Adviser to Exec. Dirs of UNEP and UNDP, to Pres. Japan Int. Co-operation Agency; fmr Chair. Japan Council of Sustainable Devt; fmr mem. Bd Regional Environmental Centre for Cen. and Eastern Europe, Hungary; mem. Selection Cttee, UNEP Sasakawa Environment Prize; FAO A. H. Boerma Award 1986–87. *Publications include:* Crisis of the Global Environment, Acid Rain, The Destruction of the Earth, Undermined Forests. *Address:* Public Policy School, Hokkaido University, Kita 9, Nishi 7, Kita-ku, Sapporo, Japan (office). *Telephone:* (11) 706-3074 (office). *Fax:* (11) 706-4947 (office). *E-mail:* shomu@juris.hokudai.ac.jp (office). *Website:* www .hops.hokudai.ac.jp (office).

ISHIBA, Shigeru; Japanese politician; b. 4 Feb. 1957; s. of Jiro Ishiba; m.; two d.; ed Keio Univ.; began career with Bank of Mitsui 1979; mem. LDP, Chair. Policy Research Council 2009–11; first elected to House of Reps 1986, Parl. Vice-Minister for Agric., Forestry and Fisheries 1992, Chair. Special Cttee on Deregulation 1996, Cttee on Transport 1998; Sr State Sec. for Minister of Agric., Forestry and Fisheries 2000; Sr State Sec. of Defence 2000–01, Sr Vice-Minister for Defence 2001–02, Minister of Defence 2002–04, 2007–08, of Agric., Forestry and Fisheries 2008–09. *Address:* Room 515, Second Members' Office Bldg, House of Representatives, 2-1-2 Nagata-cho, Chiyoda-ku, Tokyo 100-8982, Japan (office). *Telephone:* (3) 3508-7525 (office). *Fax:* (3) 3502-5174 (office). *E-mail:* g00505@shugiin.go.jp (office). *Website:* www.ishiba.com.

ISHIGURO, Denroku, BPharm; Japanese business executive; *Representative Director and President, Alfresa Holdings Corporation;* ed Univ. of Toyama; served as Man. Exec. Officer, later Sr Man. Exec. Officer and Vice-Pres. Alfresa Holdings Corpn –2009, Rep. Dir and Pres. 2009–. *Address:* Alfresa Holdings Corpn, 1-1-3 Otemachi, Chiyoda-ku, Tokyo 100-0004, Japan (office). *Telephone:* (3) 5219-5102 (office). *Fax:* (3) 5219-5103 (office). *E-mail:* info@alfresa.com (office). *Website:* www .alfresa.com (office).

ISHIGURO, Kazuo, OBE, MA, DLitt, FRSL; British writer; b. 8 Nov. 1954, Nagasaki, Japan; s. of Shizuo Ishiguro and Shizuko Ishiguro; m. Lorna Anne Macdougall 1986; one d.; ed Woking Grammar School, Univs of Kent and East Anglia; fmr community worker, Renfrew; writer 1980–; Hon. DLit (Kent) 1990, (East Anglia) 1995, (St Andrews) 2003; Chevalier, Ordre des Arts et des Lettres 1998; Premio Scanno 1995, Premio Mantova 1998. *Publications include:* A Pale View of Hills (RSL Winifred Holtby Prize 1983) 1982, A Profile of Arthur J. Mason (TV play) 1985, An Artist of the Floating World (Whitbread Book of the Year, Fiction Prize 1986) 1986, The Gourmet (TV play) 1987, The Remains of the Day (Booker Prize 1989) 1989, The Unconsoled (Cheltenham Prize 1995) 1995, When We Were Orphans (novel) 2000, The Saddest Music in the World (screenplay, co-author) 2003, Never Let Me Go (novel) (Premio Serono 2006, Corine Int. Book Prize 2006, Casino de Santiago European Novel Prize 2007) 2005, White Countess (screenplay) 2005, Nocturnes: Five Stories of Music and Nightfall 2009. *Address:* c/o Rogers, Coleridge & White Literary Agency, 20 Powis Mews, London, W11 1JN, England (office). *Telephone:* (20) 7221-3717 (office). *Fax:* (20) 7229-9084 (office). *E-mail:* info@rcwlitagency.co.uk (office). *Website:* www.rcwlitagency.co.uk (office).

ISHIHARA, Kunio; Japanese insurance executive; b. 17 Oct. 1943; ed Tokyo Univ.; joined Tokio Marine and Fire Insurance Co. Ltd as underwriter 1966, Dir and Gen. Man. Hokkaido Regional HQ of Tokio Marine 1995–98, Man. Dir and Gen. Man. June–July 1998, Man. Dir and Gen. Man. Hokkaido Div., Tokio Marine July 1998–99, Man. Dir Tokio Marine 1999–2000, Sr Man. Dir Tokio Marine 2000–01, Pres. Tokio Marine 2001–02, Pres. Tokio Marine Holdings, Inc. 2002–04, Pres. Tokio Marine & Nichido (following merger 2004) 2004–07, Chair. Tokio Marine & Nichido 2007–13, Tokio Marine Holdings, Inc. 2007–13; Auditor, Tokyu Corpn 2012–. *Address:* c/o Tokio Marine Nichido Building Shinkan, 1-2-1 Marunouchi, Chiyoda-ku, Tokyo, 100-0005, Japan. *E-mail:* ir@tokiomarinehd .com.

ISHIHARA, Nobuteru; Japanese politician; *Minister of the Environment;* b. 19 April 1957, Kanagawa; s. of Shintaro Ishihara; ed Keio Univ.; political reporter, Nippon TV Network 1981; mem. House of Reps (Parl.) (LDP) 1990–; Minister of State (Admin. Reform, Regulatory Reform) 2001–02; Minister of Land, Infrastructure and Transport 2003–06; Deputy Sec.-Gen. LDP 2006–07, Acting Sec.-Gen. 2008, Chair. Party Org. and Campaign HQ 2009, apptd Sec.-Gen. LDP 2010; Minister of the Environment 2012–, also Minister of State for the Nuclear

Emergency Preparedness. *Address:* Ministry of the Environment, 5 Godochosha, 1-2-2, Kasumigaseki, Chiyoda-ku, Tokyo 100-8975 (office); Liberal-Democratic Party (Jiyu-Minshuto), 1-11-23, Nagata-cho, Chiyoda-ku, Tokyo 100-8910, Japan (office). *Telephone:* (3) 3581-3351 (office); (3) 3581-6211 (office). *Fax:* (3) 3502-0308 (office); (3) 5511-8855 (home). *E-mail:* nobuteru@nobuteru.or.jp (office); koho@ldp .jimin.or.jp (office). *Website:* www.nobuteru.or.jp (office); www.env.go.jp (office); www.jimin.jp (office).

ISHIHARA, Shintaro; Japanese politician and author; b. 30 Sept. 1932, Kobe; brother of the late Yujiro Ishihara; m.; four s.; ed Hitotsubashi Univ.; mem. House of Councillors 1968; mem. House of Reps 1972–95; Minister of State, Dir-Gen. Environment Agency 1976–77; Minister of Transport 1987–88; mem. LDP, cand. in LDP presidential election 1988; left nat. politics 1995; Gov. of Tokyo 1999–2012; apptd mem. Selection Cttee for Akutagawa Prize 1995. *Publications include:* Season of the Sun (Akutagawa Prize for Literature 1956) 1955, The Tree of the Young Man 1959, The Forest of Fossils 1970, The Japan that Can Say No 1989, Undercurrents – Episodes from a Life on the Edge 1990, The State Becomes an Illusion 1999, Victorious Japan (with Soichiro Tahara) 2000. *Leisure interests:* yachting, tennis, scuba diving. *Address:* c/o Tokyo Metropolitan Government, 8-1, Nishi-Shinjuku 2-Chome, Shinjuku-ku, Tokyo 163-8001, Japan.

ISHII, Hajime, MA; Japanese politician; b. 17 Aug. 1934, Kobe; m. Tomoko Sugiguchi 1961; one s.; ed Konan Univ., Stanford Univ. Grad. School, USA; elected mem. House of Reps 1969, House of Councillors 2007–; fmr Parl. Vice-Minister of Transport; Minister of State, Dir-Gen. Nat. Land Agency 1989; Minister of Home Affairs 1994; fmr Chair. LDP Nat. Org. Cttee; fmr Chair. LDP Research Comm. on Foreign Affairs; Vice-Pres. Democratic Party of Japan. *Publications:* The Dream of Young Power, Dacca Hijacking, The Future of Kobe, A Distant Country Getting Closer. *Leisure interests:* golf, saxophone, scuba diving. *Address:* Office of the Vice-President, Democratic Party of Japan, 1-11-1, Nagata-cho, Chiyoda-ku, Tokyo 100-0014, Japan (office). *Telephone:* (03) 3580-1717 (office). *Fax:* (03) 3580-1788 (office). *E-mail:* pin@hajimeishii.net. *Website:* www.dpj.or.jp (office); www.hajimeishii.net (office).

ISHII, Kazuhiro; Japanese architect; b. 1 Feb. 1944, Tokyo; s. of Toshio Ishii and Kyoko Ishii; m. Noriko Nagahama 1988; two d.; ed Univ. of Tokyo and School of Architecture, Yale Univ., USA; f. Kazuhiro Ishii and Assocs 1976; Lecturer, Waseda Univ. 1991–, Univ. of Tokyo 1992–; Japan Inst. of Architecture Prize 1989. *Works include:* Noshima Educational Zone 1970–82, Tanabe Agency Bldg 1983, Gyro-Roof 1987, Sukiya Mura 1989, Kitakyu-shu City Hall 1991. *Publications:* Rebirth of Japanese-style Architecture 1985, Thought on Sukiya 1985, My Architectural Dictionary 1988. *Leisure interests:* golf, music (playing saxophone). *Address:* 4-14-27 Akasaka, Minato-ku, Tokyo 107 (office); 7-5-1-303 Akasaka, Minato-ku, Tokyo 107, Japan (home). *Telephone:* (3) 3505-0765 (office); (3) 3584-0779 (home). *Fax:* (3) 3505-0766 (office). *E-mail:* ishiiarc@blue.ocn.ne.jp (office).

ISHII, Naoko, BA, PhD; Japanese economist and international organization official; *Chairperson and CEO, Global Environment Facility;* ed Univ. of Tokyo; began career at Ministry of Finance 1981, Section Chief, Int. Finance Bureau 1985–87, Deputy Dir, Office of Int. Operations, Nat. Tax Admin 1987–88; Economist, IMF 1992–95; Project Man., Harvard Inst. for Int. Devt, USA 1996–97; Country Programme Coordinator for Vietnam and Mongolia, World Bank 1997–2001, Country Dir for coordination with Multilateral Devt Banks 2002–04, for Bilateral Devt Finance 2004–06, Country Programme Coordinator for Sri Lanka and Maldives 2006–10; Deputy Vice-Minister of Finance 2010–12, Special Adviser to Prime Minister for Global Environmental Affairs –2012; Chair. and CEO Global Environment Facility, Washington, DC 2012–; has taught on subjects of sustainable development and environment at Keio Univ.; Visiting Fellow, Centre for Int. Affairs, Harvard Univ. 1984–85; Okita Memorial Prize 2004, Enjoji Jiro Memorial Prize 2006. *Publications include:* The US-Japan Economic Controversy 1988, The Economics of Macroeconomic Policy Coordination (Suntory Academic Prize) 1990, Empirical Analysis on Modern Economic Growth: Institutions Critical to Sustainable Economic Growth 2003. *Address:* Global Environment Facility Secretariat, 1818 H Street, NW, Mail Stop P4-400, Washington, DC 20433, USA (office). *Telephone:* (202) 473-0508 (office). *Fax:* (202) 522-3240 (office). *E-mail:* secretariat@thegef.org (office). *Website:* www .thegef.org (office).

ISHIKAWA, Hirokazu, BA; Japanese banking and insurance executive; *Adviser, Mitsui Life Insurance Company Ltd;* b. 1942; ed Faculty of Econs, Keio Univ.; joined The Mistui Bank Ltd 1966, Sr Deputy Gen. Man. Europe Div. HQ and Man.-Dir Mitsui Finance Int. Ltd 1989–90, Man.-Dir and Chief Rep. Mitsui Taiyo Kobe Int. Ltd 1990–92, Man.-Dir and Chief Rep. Sakura Finance Int. Ltd 1992, Gen. Man. Europe, Middle E and Africa Div. 1992–94, Gen. Man. Planning Div. 1994–97, apptd Dir 1994, Man.-Dir 1997–99, Man.-Dir and Sr Exec. Officer 1999–2000, Deputy Pres. Sakura Bank Ltd 2000–01; Chair. Mitsui Life Insurance Company Ltd 2002–09, Adviser 2009–; Trustee Hasegawa Int. Scholarship Foundation. *Address:* Mitsui Life Insurance Company Ltd, 1-2-3 Otemachi, Chiyoda-ku, Toyko 100-8123, Japan (office). *Telephone:* (3) 3211-6111 (office). *Fax:* (3) 3215-1580 (office). *Website:* www.mitsui-semei.co.jp (office).

ISHIKAWA, Tadashi; Japanese business executive; *Chairman, Toyota Industries Corporation;* joined Toyoda Automatic Loom Works (later Toyota Industries Corpn) 1968, various man. roles including Corp. Auditor 2003, Exec. Vice-Pres., later Pres., currently Chair. *Address:* Toyota Industries Corpn, 2-1, Toyota-cho, Kariya-shi, Aichi 448-8671, Japan (office). *Telephone:* (566) 222511 (office). *Fax:* (566) 275650 (office). *E-mail:* info@toyota-industries.com (office). *Website:* www .toyota-industries.com (office).

ISHIMARU, Akira, PhD, FIEEE, FInstP; American electrical engineer and academic; *Professor Emeritus, University of Washington, Seattle;* b. 16 March 1928, Fukuoka, Japan; s. of Shigezo Ishimaru and Yumi Ishimaru (née Yamada); m. Yuko Kaneda 1956; two s. two d.; ed Univ. of Tokyo, Univ. of Washington; Asst Prof., Univ. of Washington 1958–61, Assoc. Prof. 1961–65, Prof. of Electrical Eng 1965– Boeing Martin Prof. 1993, also Adjunct Prof. of Applied Math., now Prof. Emer.; Visiting Assoc. Prof., Univ. of Calif., Berkeley 1963–64; Ed. Radio Science 1978–82; mem. Editorial Bd Proc. IEEE 1973–83; mem. Nat. Acad. of Eng 1996–; Founding Ed. Waves in Random and Complex Media 1990–; Fellow, Optical Soc. of America 1982, Acoustical Soc. of America 1997; IEEE Centennial Medal 1984,

Distinguished Achievement Award 1995, 1998, IEEE Heinrich Hertz Medal 1999, URSI John Dellinger Gold Medal 1999, IEEE Third Millennium Medal 2000. *Publications:* Wave Propagation and Scattering in Random Media, Vols 1 and 2 1978, Electromagnetic Wave Propagation, Radiation and Scattering 1991. *Address:* Electrical Engineering Department, Box 352500, University of Washington, Seattle, WA 98195 (office); 2913 165th Place, NE, Bellevue, WA 98008, USA (home). *Telephone:* (206) 543-2169 (office); (425) 885-0018 (home). *Fax:* (206) 543-3842 (office); (425) 881-1622 (home). *E-mail:* ishimaru@ee.washington.edu (office). *Website:* www.ee.washington.edu (office).

ISHIZAKA, Kimishige, MD, PhD; Japanese biomedical research scientist and academic; *President Emeritus, La Jolla Institute for Allergy and Immunology;* b. 12 March 1925, Tokyo; m. Teruko Ishizaka 1949; one s.; ed Univ. of Tokyo; Chief, Dept of Serology, Div. of Immunoserology, Tokyo 1953–62; Prof., Dept of Microbiology, Univ. of Colo Medical School and Chief, Dept of Immunology, Children's Asthma Research Inst. and Hosp., Denver, Colo, USA 1962–70; Assoc. Prof. of Medicine and Microbiology, Johns Hopkins Univ., Baltimore, Md 1970–81, Dir Subdept. of Immunology 1981–88, O'Neill Prof. of Immunology and Medicine 1981–89; Scientific Dir and Head, Div. of Immunobiology, La Jolla Inst. of Allergy and Immunology (LIAI), La Jolla, Calif. 1989–91, Pres. 1991–96, Pres. Emer. 1996–, also LIAI Bd of Dirs as Dir Emer.; Pres. American Asscn of Immunologists 1984–85; mem. NAS 1983–; Emperor's Award 1974, Pioneer of Modern Allergy Award 1982, American Coll. of Physicians Award for Achievement in Medical Science 1985, Distinguished Scientist Award, Japanese Medical Soc. of America 1989, Japan Prize, Science and Tech. Foundation of Japan 2000, and numerous other awards. *Publications:* numerous contribs to scientific journals. *Address:* La Jolla Institute for Allergy and Immunology, 10355 Science Center Drive, San Diego, CA 92121, USA (office). *Telephone:* (858) 558-3500 (office). *Website:* www .liai.org (office).

ISHIZAKA, Koji; Japanese actor; b. (Heikichi Muto), 20 June 1941, Ginza, Tokyo; ed Keio Univ. Faculty of Law; TV debut in Taikouki (drama series), NHK 1965; film debut in Wakai Musume ga Ippai 1966; achieved fame playing role of Kosuke Kindaichi in a series of five detective movies directed by Kon Ichikawa 1976–79; directed and performed in film Chushin-Gura: 47 Assassins 1994; lead actor in Genroku Ryoran (drama series), NHK 1999; currently Co-Host Nademo Kantei Dan (We'll Appraise Anything, TV antique show); regular appearances on TV show Sekai Ururun Taizaiki. *Film appearances include:* Wakai Musume ga Ippai (Young Girls are Everywhere) 1966, Hi mo tsuki mo 1969, Kaze no bojo 1970, The Inaugami Family 1976, Devil's Bouncing Ball Song 1977, Island of Horror 1977, Jo-oh-bachi (Queen Bee) 1978, Death on Hospital Hill 1979, Sasame-yuki (The Makioka Sisters) 1983, Ohan 1984, The Return of Godzilla 1984, The Harp of Burma 1985, Rokumeikan 1986, Eiga jouu (Film Actress) 1987, Taketori Monogatari 1987, Tsuru 1988, Yushun 1988, Tenkawa Densetsu Satsujin Jiken (The Noh Mask Murders) 1991, Last Song 1993, Fusa 1993, Shijushichinin no shikaku (47 Ronin) 1994, Shinsengumi 1999, Urutoraman Kosumosu: First Contact 2001, Kenchô no hoshi 2006, Nihon chinbotsu 2006, Yume jûya 2006, Inugamike no ichizoku 2006, Rasuto gêmu: Saigo no sôkeisen 2008, Suspect X 2008, I Want to Be a Shellfish 2008, King of the Escape 2009, The Unbroken 2009. *Leisure interest:* collecting antiques.

ISHIZU, Shinya, LLB; Japanese business executive; b. 23 Aug. 1938, Tokyo; ed Hitotsubashi Univ.; joined Asahi Glass Co. Ltd April 1962, Gen. Man. Fine Ceramics Div. 1988–90, Fukuoka Sales Office 1990–93, Osaka Sales Office 1993–95, Dir March 1994–, Gen. Man. Corp. Planning Div. 1995–96, Man. Dir 1996–97, Exec. Vice-Pres. 1997–98, Pres. 1998–2003, Chair. 2003–08 (retd); Dir Asahi Glass Foundation. *Address:* c/o Office of the Chairman, Asahi Glass Company Limited, 1–12–1 Yurakucho, Chiyoda-ku, Tokyo 100–8405, Japan.

ISINBAYEVA, Yelena Gadzhievna; Russian pole vaulter; b. 3 June 1982, Volgograd; d. of Gadzhi Gadzhiyevich Isinbayev; ed Volgograd State Acad. of Physical Culture, Donetsk Nat. Tech. Univ.; Sr Lt, Russian Army; gold medal, pole vault, World Youth Games 1999, European Jr Championships 2001, European Under 23 Championships 2003, Olympic Games, Athens 2004, World Indoor Championships 2004, 2006, 2012, World Athletics Championships 2005, 2007, 2013, European Indoor Championships 2005, European Championship 2006, Olympic Games, Beijing 2008; bronze medal, Olympic Games, London 2012; set women's pole vault world record of 5.05m at Olympic Games, Beijing 18 Aug. 2008, IAAF Golden League 2009, World Athletics Final, Greece 2009, Russian Winter Meeting, Moscow 2010, 2011, Pole Vault Stars, Ukraine 2010, 2011; mem. 'Champions for Peace' Club; Distinguished Citizen of Donetsk 2006; IAAF Female Athlete of the Year 2004, 2005, 2008, Women's Track & Field Athlete of the Year 2004–05, Women's European Athlete of the Year 2005, 2008, Laureus Sportswoman of the Year 2007, 2009, Prince of Asturias Award for Sports 2009. *Address:* 3 avenue de Grande Bretagne, 98000 Monte Carlo, Monaco.

ISKANDER, Fazil Abdulovich; Russian/Abkhaz writer; b. 6 March 1929, Sukhumi, Georgian SSR; m.; one s. one d.; ed Maxim Gorky Inst. of Literature, Moscow; first works Publ 1952; USSR People's Deputy 1989–91; Pres. Asscn of Authors and Publrs against Piracy; Head, World of Culture Asscn; Vice-Pres. Russian Acad. of Arts; Academician of RAN, Natural Sciences Dept, Bayerische Akad. der Schönen Künste; Dr hc (Norwich Univ., USA); Malaparti Prize (Italy) 1985, USSR State Prize 1989, State Prize of Russia 1993, A. Sakharov Prize, A. Pushkin Prize (Germany) 1994, Moscow-Penne Prize (Italy) 1996, Triumph Prize (Russia) 1998. *Films include:* Time of Lucky Finds, Crime Kings 1986, A Little Giant of Big Sex, A Night with Stalin. *Plays:* Djamchuch: A Son of a Deer 1986, A Greeting from Zürüpa (The One Who Thinks About Russia) 1999. *Publications include:* Green Rain 1960, Youth of the Sea 1964, Goatibex Constellation 1966, Forbidden Fruit 1966 (English trans. 1972), Summer Forest 1969, Time of Lucky Finds 1970, Tree of Childhood and Other Stories 1970, Sandro from Chegem 1978, Metropol (co-ed.) 1979, Small Giant of the Big Sex 1979, The Path (poems) 1987, Rabbits and Boa Constrictors 1989, School Waltz or the Energy of Shame 1990, Poets and Tsars 1991, Man and His Surroundings 1992, Pshada 1993, Sofichka 1996, The One Who Thinks about Russia and the American 1997, Poet 1998, The Swallow's Nest 2000 and other stories. *Leisure interest:* reading fiction. *Address:* Leningradski prosp. 26, korp. 2, Apt. 67, 125040 Moscow, Russia. *Telephone:* (495) 973-94-53 (office); (495) 212-73-60. *Fax:* (495) 973-94-53 (office).

ISKENDERIAN, Mary Ellen, BS, MBA; American banking executive; *President and CEO, Women's World Banking*; d. of Ara Iskenderian; m. Gregory Owen Lipscomb 1991; ed Yale School of Org. and Man., Georgetown Univ. School of Foreign Service; numerous leadership positions at Int. Finance Corpn (pvt. sector arm of World Bank) including Dir Partnership Devt, Dir Global Financial Markets Portfolio and Dir S Asia Regional Dept –2006; Pres. and CEO Women's World Banking 2006–; Distinguished Citi Fellow in Leadership and Ethics, Leonard N. Stern School of Business, New York Univ. 2009; mem. Bd of Dirs Kashf Microfinance Bank, Pakistan, ASA Foundation, Nat. Bank of Commerce, Tanzania, ShoreCap International; fmr Corp. Dir Banco Caja Social, Confisura SA, Infrastructure Devt Finance Corpn; mem. Advisory Bd Dignity Fund, Kiva; Advisor, Clinton Global Initiative; mem. Women's Leadership Bd of Harvard Univ., Council on Foreign Relations; judge, Financial Times Sustainable Banking Awards; Isabel Benham Award, Women's Bond Club 2009, Women's Finance Award, Inst. of Financial Services, Lucerne Univ., Switzerland 2009. *Address:* Women's World Banking, 8 West 40th Street, 9th Floor, New York, NY 10018, USA (office). *Telephone:* (212) 768-8513 (office). *Fax:* (212) 768-8519 (office). *E-mail:* wwb@swwb.org (office). *Website:* www.swwb.org (office).

ISKROV, Ivan, MSc; Bulgarian central banker; *Governor, Bulgarian National Bank;* b. 26 March 1967, Pirdop; m.; one c.; ed Univ. of Nat. and World Economy, Sofia; Visiting Lecturer, Univ. of Nat. and World Economy, Sofia 1992–93; expert and examiner, Bulgarska Narodna Banka (Bulgarian Nat. Bank) 1993–97, Gov. 2003–; Exec. Dir and mem. Man. Bd DSK Bank 1997–99; Exec. Dir and mem. Man. Bd Rosseksimbank 1999–2001; mem. Parl. 2001–03, held various parl. positions, including Chair. Budget and Finance Comm., mem. European Integration Cttee, Bulgaria-EU Jt Parl. Comm.; mem. Gen. Council of European Cen. Bank, Gen. Bd of European Systemic Risk Bd; Commdr, Order of Leopold (Belgium) 2010. *Publication:* Money, Banks, and Monetary Policy (co-author) 1998. *Address:* Bulgarian National Bank, 1000 Sofia, 1 Knyaz Alexander I Square, Bulgaria (office). *Telephone:* (2) 91459 (switchboard) (office); (2) 91451200 (office). *Fax:* (2) 9802425 (office); (2) 9806493 (office). *E-mail:* governor@bnbank.org (office). *Website:* www.bnb.bg (office).

ISLAM, A. B. Mirza Azizul, BA, MA, PhD; Bangladeshi economist; b. 23 Feb. 1941, Sujanagar, Pabna; m. Nilufar Aziz; one s.; ed Dhaka Univ., Williams Coll. and Boston Univ., USA; Lecturer, Dhaka Univ. 1962–64; joined Civil Service of Pakistan 1964; worked in different capacities in admin. service 1967–82; Econ. Affairs/Sr Econ. Affairs Officer, UN-ESCAP, Bangkok 1982–86, Dir Research and Policy Analysis Div. 1993–2001; Chief of Developing Econs Section, UN Centre on Transnational Corpns, New York 1987–92; consultant to UNCTAD, World Bank and Centre for Policy Dialogue 2002–03; Chair. Bangladesh Securities & Exchange Comm. 2003–06; Chair. Sonali Bank April–Nov. 2006; Hon. Adviser to Caretaker Govt, in charge of Ministry of Finance, of Planning, of Commerce and of Posts and Telecommunications 2007–08, in charge of Ministry of Finance, Ministry of Planning 2008–09; Visiting Prof., BRAC Univ. Business School 2011–. *Publications:* co-authored at least 20 UN publs, including World Invest Report and Economic and Social Survey of Asia and the Pacific; edited books and daily newspapers; numerous articles in refereed journals. *Address:* BRAC University, #UB 635, 66 Mohakhali, Dhaka 1212, Bangladesh (office). *Telephone:* (2) 881-4051 (ext. 4037) (office). *Fax:* (2) 881-3083 (office). *E-mail:* maislam@bracu.ac.bd (office).

ISLAM, Ahmad Shamsul, MSc, PhD; Bangladeshi plant geneticist and academic; *Professor, Brac University;* b. 1 Jan. 1926; ed Presidency Coll., Calcutta, Manchester Univ.; research in genetics, plant breeding and tissue-culture 1955–; postdoctoral research work at Cornell Univ., Univ. of Calif., Davis, USA and Nottingham Univ.,UK; Lecturer, Univ. of Texas, Austin; Prof. of Botany, Dhaka Univ. –1990 (retd); Consultant and Prof., Brac Univ., Dhaka 2003–; Founder Ed. Sind Univ. Research Journal, Pakistan Journal of Botany, Dar-es-Salaam Univ. Scientific Research Journal, Bangladesh Journal of Botany; fmr Pres. Bangladesh Asscn for Plant Tissue Culture; fmr Sec.-Gen. Bangladesh Asscn for the Advancement of Science; mem. Indian and Japanese Socs of Genetic and Plant Breeding; Fellow, Islamic Acad. of Sciences; Ekushey Padak for promoting education 1985-86, President's Gold Medal, Bangladesh Acad of Science 1987. *Publication:* Fundamentals of Genetics (Bongshogati bidyar Moolkatha). *Address:* Brac University, 66 Mohakhali, Dhaka, 1212, Bangladesh (office). *Website:* www .bracu.ac.bd (office).

ISLAM, Atharul; Bangladeshi government official and business executive; Additional Sec., Govt of Bangladesh and fmr Chair. Bangladesh Jute Mills Corpn. *Address:* c/o Bangladesh Jute Mills Corporation, Adamjee Court (Annexe-1), 115-120, Motijheel Commercial Area, Dhaka 1000, Bangladesh. *Telephone:* (2) 9553364. *E-mail:* bjmc@bttb.net.bd; info@bjmc.gov.bd.

ISLAM, Manzurul; Bangladeshi business executive; *Chairman, Islam Group;* s. of the late Al-Haj Jahurul Islam (Founder-Chair. of Islam Group); ed Univ. of London, UK; Chair. Islam Group (businesses include mfg, real estate, eng, construction, manufacturing, land devt, commercial banking, int. trade, cottage and handicrafts, milk and dairy products, information tech., agricultural and poultry products, group water devt, pharmaceutical industry, medical coll. and hosp., nurse training inst.), Chair. Bengal Devt Corpn (unit of Islam Group); Chair. IFIC Bank Ltd; Gold Medal, Int. Fed. of Asia and West Pacific Contractors Asscn 2009, awards for Special Civil Eng Contractor and Award of Honour. *Address:* Navana Pharmaceuticals Ltd, 3/C Purana Paltan, Dhaka 1000, Bangladesh (office). *Telephone:* (2) 9557410 (office). *Fax:* (2) 9569113 (office). *E-mail:* admin@navanapharma.com (office). *Website:* www.navanapharma.com (office).

ISLAM, Nurul, PhD; Bangladeshi economist and academic; *Research Fellow Emeritus, International Food Policy Research Institute;* b. 1 April 1929, Chittagong; s. of Abdur Rahman and Mohsena Begum; m. Rowshan Ara 1957; one s. one d.; ed Univ. of Dhaka and Harvard Univ., USA; Reader in Econs, Dhaka Univ. 1955–60, Prof. 1960–64, Chair., Dept of Econs 1962–64; Dir Pakistan Inst. of Devt Econs, Karachi 1964–70; Visiting Prof., Econ. Devt Inst., World Bank 1967–68; Professorial Research Assoc., Yale Econ. Growth Cen. 1968 and 1971; Dir Bangladesh Inst. of Devt Econs 1971–72; Founder-Dir and Chair. Bangladesh Inst. of Devt Studies, Dhaka 1971–75; Deputy Chair. Bangladesh Planning Comm. (with ministerial status) 1972–75; Asst Dir-Gen., Econ. and Social Policy Research

Inst., FAO, Rome 1977–87; Chair. UN Cttee of Devt Policy 1996–99; mem. Bd of Trustees Int. Rice Research Inst., Manila 1973–77, Exec. Cttee Third World Forum 1974–77, Bd of Govs. Int. Food Policy Research Inst. 1975–87 (Sr Policy Advisor 1987–94, Research Fellow Emer. 1994–), UN Cttee on Devt Planning 1974–77; mem. Editorial Bd The World Economy, London, Research Advisory Cttee, World Bank 1980, Advisory Group, Asian Devt Bank, Manila 1981–82, Advisory Cttee, Inst. of Int. Econ., Washington, DC; consultant for various UN cttees, ESCAP, UNESCO, UNCTAD; Nuffield Foundation Fellow at Univs of London and Cambridge 1958–59; Rockefeller Fellow, Netherlands School of Economics 1959. *Publications include:* A Short-Term Model of Pakistan's Economy: An Econometric Analysis 1964, Studies in Foreign Capital and Economic Development 1960, Studies in Consumer Demand 1965, Studies in Commercial Policy and Economic Growth 1970, Development Planning in Bangladesh – A Study in Political Economy 1977, Development Strategy of Bangladesh 1978, Interdependence of Developed and Developing Countries 1978, Foreign Trade and Economic Controls in Development: The Case of United Pakistan 1980, Aid and Influence: The Case of Bangladesh (co-author) 1981; Agriculture Towards 2000 (co-author) 1981, The Fifth World Food Survey 1985, Agriculture Price Policies 1985, Growth, Poverty and Human Development in Pakistan 1996, The Non-Farm Sector and Rural Development 1997, Development Opportunities in the Non-Farm Sector 2001, Making of a Nation: Bangladesh, An Economist's Tale 2003, Exploration in Development Issues 2003, Looking Outward: Bangladesh in the World Economy 2004, Ethics in Banking 2006, Reducing Rural Poverty in Asia 2006, A Ship Adrift: Governance and Development in Bangladesh (co-author) 2008, The World Economic Crisis and the Lessons for Developing Countries 2010, Role of Experts in Policy Advice: Lessons of Experience 2010, Thoughts on Microfinance and All That 2012. *Leisure interests:* reading political and historical books, movies. *Address:* International Food Policy Research Institute, 2033 K Street, NW, Washington, DC 20006-1002, USA (office). *Telephone:* (202) 862-5619 (office). *Fax:* (202) 467-4439 (office). *E-mail:* n.islam@cgiar.org (office). *Website:* www.ifpri.org (office).

ISLAM, Sayed Ashraful, MA; Bangladeshi politician and business executive; *Minister of Local Government, Rural Development and Co-operatives;* b. 1952, Mymensingh; s. of Syed Nazrul Islam (Acting Pres. during liberation war); one d.; fought during liberation war 1971; involved in politics from student days; went to UK after the killing of his father in prison along with three other nat. leaders in 1975, returned to Bangladesh in 1996; elected MP from Kishoreganj Sadar in seventh nat. elections, re-elected 2001, mem. Parl. Standing Cttee on Foreign Affairs; Gen. Sec. Greater Mymensingh Dist, Chhatra League and Asst Publicity Sec. of Cen. Unit; fmr Acting Gen. Sec. Bangladesh Awami League following arrest of Abdul Jalil, now Spokesman and Gen. Sec.; Minister of Local Govt, Rural Devt and Co-operatives 2010–. *Address:* Ministry of Local Government, Rural Development and Co-operatives, Bangladesh Secretariat, Bhaban 7, Dhaka 1000 (office); Bangladesh Awami League (AL), 23 Bangabandhu Avenue, Dhaka, Bangladesh (office). *Telephone:* (2) 7169179 (Ministry) (office); (2) 9677881 (AL) (office). *Fax:* (2) 8621155 (AL) (office). *E-mail:* info@lgd.gov.bd (office); info@albd.org (office). *Website:* www.lgd.gov.bd (office); www.albd.org (office).

ISLAM, Yusuf, (Cat Stevens); British singer, songwriter and producer; b. (Steven Demetre Georgiou), 21 July 1948, London; m. Fawzia Mubarik Ali 1979; two s. (one deceased) four d.; solo artist as Cat Stevens –1978, then as Yusuf Islam; extensive tours worldwide, numerous television appearances; mem. Musicians' Union; Founder and Chair. Small Kindness (charity); Founder and Chair. Islamia Schools Trust, f. Islamia Primary School, Islamia Girls' Secondary School, Brondesbury Coll. for Boys, London; World Social Award 2003, Gorbachev Foundation Man for Peace Award 2004, ASCAP Award for Songwriter of the Year 2006, Mediterranean Prize for Peace 2007. *Recordings include:* albums: (as Cat Stevens) Matthew And Son 1967, New Masters 1967, World Of Cat Stevens 1970, Mona Bone Jakon 1970, Tea For The Tillerman 1970, Teaser And The Firecat 1971, Very Young and Early Songs 1971, Catch Bull At Four 1972, Foreigner 1973, Buddha And The Chocolate Box 1974, Saturnight (Live in Tokyo) 1974, View From The Top 1974, Numbers 1975, Greatest Hits 1975, Izitso 1977, Back To Earth 1978, Cat's Cradle 1978, Footsteps In The Dark 1984, Classics Vol. 24 – Cat Stevens 1989, Very Best of Cat Stevens 1990, (as Yusuf Islam) The Life Of The Last Prophet 1995, Prayers Of The Last Prophet 1999, I Have No Cannons That Roar 2000, A Is For Allah 2000, Majikat: Earth Tour 1976 2004, An Other Cup (Ivor Novello Award for Outstanding Song Collection 2007) 2006, Roadsinger 2009. *E-mail:* office@yusufislam.com (office). *Website:* www.yusufislam.com.

ISLAM, Lt Gen. Zaheer ul-; Pakistani army officer and intelligence official; *Director-General, Inter-Services Intelligence;* commissioned in Punjab Regt in 55th PMA Long Course 1977; served as DG (C) in Inter-Services Intelligence (ISI) before being promoted as a three-star Gen. and moved to Karachi as Corps Commdr; GOC Murree for some time before coming to ISI; also served as Chief of Staff in Army Strategic Force Command 2004–06; Corps Commdr, V Corps, Karachi –2012; Dir-Gen. ISI 2012–; Hilal-e-Imtiaz (Mil.); ranked by Forbes magazine amongst The World's Most Powerful People (52nd) 2012. *Address:* Inter-Services Intelligence, c/o Ministry of Defence, Pakistan Secretariat, No. II, Rawalpindi 46000, Pakistan (office). *Website:* www.isi.org.pk (office).

ISLAM KAMAL, Shafiul; Bangladeshi business executive; *Chairman and Managing Director, Navana Group;* b. 1949; s. of the late Alhaj Aftabuddin Ahmed; ed early education in science related subjects; joined Islam Group 1968, career in automotive, construction and real estate business, gained experience from involvement in man. of Group's diverse business operations, played role in establishing Navana as leading car co. in Bangladesh, and later, in setting up Aftab Automobiles, responsible for Bengal Devt Corpn (BDC), directly responsible for construction work of BDC in Middle East, oversaw Eastern Housing Limited from 1981, separated from Islam Group with Navana Ltd and Aftab Automobiles Ltd and est. Navana Group 1996, currently Chair. and Man. Dir. *Address:* Navana Ltd/Aftab Automobiles Ltd, 125A Motijheel C/A, Dhaka 1000 (office); Navana Toyota 3S Center, 205–207 Tejgaon Industrial Area, Dhaka 1208, Bangladesh (office). *Telephone:* (2) 9552212 (office); (2) 9884992 (office). *Fax:* (2) 9566324 (office). *E-mail:* info@navana.com (office). *Website:* www.navana.com (office).

ISLAMI, Kastriot, MA, DSc; Albanian politician and physicist; b. 18 Feb. 1952, Tirana; s. of Selman Islami; m.; one s. one d.; ed Univ. of Tirana, Univ. of Paris XI,

Orsay, France; Vice-Dean, Faculty of Natural Sciences, Univ. of Tirana 1987–91; Minister of Educ. 1991; Deputy Speaker (Chair.) of Albanian Parl. 1991–92, Head, Parl. Comm. for Preparation of Draft of Albanian Constitution 1991–96; Minister of State to Prime Minister of Albania 1997–98; Deputy Prime Minister 1998–2002; Minister of Finance 2002–03; Minister of Foreign Affairs 2003–05; Deputy, Kuvendi Popullor (People's Ass.) 2006–; mem. Parl. Ass., Council of Europe, mem. Cttee on Legal Affairs and Human Rights, Cttee on the Honouring of Obligations and Commitments by Member States of the Council of Europe (Monitoring Cttee) 2006–. *Publications include*: The Basis of Quantum Mechanics Vol. I 1989, Vol. II 1990; publs in nat. and int. media. *Address*: Kuvendi Popullor (People's Assembly), Bulevardi Deshmoret e Kombit nr. 4, Tirana (office); Rruga: Dora D'Istria, Pallati R 8-Katesh, Tirana, Albania (home). *Telephone*: (5) 4237413 (office); (5) 4240669 (home). *Fax*: (5) 4227949 (office). *E-mail*: marlind@parlament.al (office); dshtypi@abissnet.com.al; kislami@icc-al.org. *Website*: www.parlament.al (home).

ISMAIL, Abdullahi Sheikh; Somali politician; Minister of Foreign Affairs 2004–07; fmr Chair. Southern Somali Nat. Movt. *Address*: c/o Ministry of Foreign Affairs, 1 Villa Somalia, 2525 Mogadishu, Somalia (office).

ISMAIL, Amat; Chinese politician; b. 1935, Qira, Xinjiang Uygur Autonomous Region; ed CCP Cen. Cttee Cen. Party School (Xinjiang Class); joined CCP 1953; active in People's Commune Movt –1960; Magistrate, Qira Co. (Dist) People's Court 1954–62; Deputy Sec. CCP Cttee, a country admin., Xinjiang 1960; Deputy Head, Publicity Dept, CCP Autonomous Prefectural Cttee, Hotan, Xinjiang Uygur Autonomous Region 1963–65; Deputy Dir Cultural, Educ. and Political Work Dept, CCP Xinjiang Uygur Autonomous Regional Cttee 1966–67, mem. Standing Cttee, CCP Revolutionary Cttee and Head, Group for Regional Cultural, Educational and Health Work 1969–72; Sec. and Head, Org. Dept, CCP Xinjiang Uygur Autonomous Regional Cttee 1972–85; Vice-Chair. CCP Revolutionary Cttee, Xinjiang Uygur Autonomous Region 1972–85; Chair. Xinjiang Uygur Autonomous Regional People's Govt 1972–85; Sec. CCP Cttee, Xinjiang 1974–79; Vice-Chair. Aubnavan Regional Revolutionary Cttee, Xinjiang 1974–79; Political Commissar, Xinjiang Mil. Region 1976–85; First Deputy Dir Party School, Xinjiang 1977–85; Chair. People's Govt, Xinjiang 1979–85; Minister of State Nationalities Affairs Comm. 1985–98; Minister in Charge of State Nat. Ethnic Affairs Comm. 1993–98; State Councillor 1993–2003; Dir China Comm. of Int. Decade for Disaster Reduction 1998–2000, China Comm. for Int. Disaster Reduction 2000–; mem. 10th CCP Cen. Cttee 1972–77, 11th CCP Cen. Cttee 1977–82, 12th CCP Cen. Cttee 1982–87, 13th CCP Cen. Cttee 1987–92, 14th CCP Cen. Cttee 1992–97, 15th CCP Cen. Cttee 1997–2002, 16th CCP Cen. Cttee 2002–07; Vice-Chair. 7th CPPCC Nat. Cttee 1988–93; mem. Standing Cttee of NPC 1978–83, Vice-Chair. 10th Standing Cttee of NPC 2003–08; Pres. China-Turkey Friendship Asscn; Hon. Pres. Chinese Asscn of Ethnic Minorities for External Exchanges. *Address*: The State Council, Zhongnanhai, Beijing, People's Republic of China (office).

ISMAIL, Gameela; Egyptian activist; b. 1966, Champollion, Qasr el-Nil Dist, Cairo; m. Ayman Abd al-Aziz al-Nour (divorced); ed El Gezira language school, Zamalek, American Univ. in Cairo, Cairo Univ.; political activist and advocate for civil and women's rights; started working in public service through a non-govt org., central Cairo 1994; fmr TV presenter; unsuccessful cand. for Shura Council 2001; co-f. Al-Ghad (Tomorrow) Party 2005; unsuccessful parl. cand. (ind.) in Qasr el-Nil Dist Nov. 2010; mem. Nat. Asscn for Change 2010–; co-f. Women for Change. *Address*: Al-Ghad (Tomorrow) Party, Cairo, Egypt. *E-mail*: gameelaismailegypt@gmail.com (office). *Website*: www.elghad.org (office).

ISMAIL, Mustafa Osman, PhD; Sudanese politician; b. 1955, Dongola; joined Ministry of External Relations 1996, Minister of External Relations 1998–2005; currently Presidential Adviser; mem. Nat. Congress Party. *Address*: c/o National Congress Party, Khartoum, Sudan (office).

ISMAT, Riad, PhD; Syrian diplomatist, politician, playwright, short-story writer and critic and stage director; *Research Professor, Northwestern University;* b. 11 July 1947, Damascus; m. Azzah Konbaz; two s. one d.; ed Damascus Univ., studied briefly at Drama Centre, London, UK, Univ. Coll., Cardiff, UK, World Univ.; studied mime with Adam Darius and TV production and direction at the BBC, UK; also apprentice in actor training with Joseph Chaikin, Camille Howard, Jean Shelton and Mark Epstein in USA; Rector, Acad. for Dramatic Arts, Damascus 2000–02; apptd Dir Gen. Syrian State Radio and Television 2003; Vice-Minister of Culture 2004–05; Amb. to Pakistan 2005–10, to Qatar 2010; Minister of Culture 2010–12; Research Prof., Northwestern Univ., USA 2013–; has directed 15 theatrical productions, including interpretations of Shakespeare, Tennessee Williams, Bertolt Brecht, Frank Wedekind and Ariel Dorfman, as well as own version of The Arabian Nights; f. first mime troupe in Damascus; also directed trilogy for Syrian TV; Dr hc (Greenwich Univ., UK) 2007; honouree of Cairo and Damascus int. theatre festivals. *Plays include*: The Game of Love and Revolution, Was Dinner Good My Sister, Mourning Becomes Antigone, Sinbad, Shahryar's Nights, Abla & Antar, Banana Republic, In Search of Zenobia, Mata Hari. *Film*: script for Laila and the Wolves (musical film). *Television*: scripts for seven serials, including Holaco (Golden Award for Best Historical Arabic Serial) 2003. *Publications*: 35 books, including short stories, nine books critiquing Arab and World drama, a book on Nobel Prize laureate Naguib Mahfouz and a book on cinema. *Address*: PO Box 60049, Damascus; c/o Film Organization, Rawda Street, Damascus, Syria.

ISOKALLIO, Kaarlo, MSc; Finnish business executive and writer; b. 13 May 1948, Helsinki; m. Ammi Kristiina; one d.; ed Univ. of Tech., Helsinki; Project Engineer, Wärtsilä Corpn 1972–74; Marketing Dir IBM (Finland) 1974–81; Man. Dir Kabmatik AB, Sweden 1981–83; joined Nokia Corpn 1983, Dept Man. Cables Dept, Machinery Div., 1983–85, Pres. Electronics, Information Systems 1985–86, Pres. Information Systems 1986–88, Exec. Pres. Nokia Data Group 1988–90, Pres. and COO Nokia Corpn 1990–91, Deputy to CEO, Vice-Chair. Group Exec. Bd 1990; mem. Bd of Dirs Oy Lindell Ab 1987, Taloudellinen Tiedotustoimisto 1991; mem. Supervisory Bd Mecrastor Oy 1987, Oy Rastor Ab 1987, Helsinki Univ. Cen. Hosp. Foundation 1991; mem. Bd Econ. Information Bureau 1991, ICL PLC 1991; mem. Tech. Del., Ministry of Trade and Industry 1990; Chair. Bd MTV (Finnish commercial TV) 1991; mem. Acad. for Tech. Sciences 1991; freelance writer and columnist 1996–.

ISOZAKI, Arata; Japanese architect; b. 23 July 1931, Oita City; s. of Soji Isozaki and Tetsu Isozaki; m. Aiko Miyawaki 1974; two s.; ed Univ. of Tokyo; with Kenzo Tange's team 1954–63; Pres. Arata Isozaki and Assocs 1963–; juror, Pritzker Architecture Prize 1979–84, Concours Int. de Parc de la Villette 1982, The Peak Int. Architectural Competition 1983, R. S. Reynolds Memorial Award 1985, The Architectural Competition for the New Nat. Theatre of Japan 1986, competitions for Passenger Terminal Bldg, Kansai Int. Airport 1988, Triangle de la Folie, Paris 1989, Int. Architects' competition, Vienna EXPO '95 1991, Kyoto Station Bldg Renovation Design competition 1991; visiting prof. at numerous univs including Harvard, Yale and Columbia; Hon. Fellow, Acad. Tiberina, AIA, RIBA 1994–; Hon. Academician Royal Acad. of Arts 1994; Hon. mem. Bund Deutscher Architekten (BDA), American Acad. of Arts and Letters 1998; Chevalier Ordre des Arts et des Lettres (France), Grande Ufficiale, Ordine al Merito (Italy) 2007; numerous prizes including RIBA Gold Medal 1983–86, Chicago Architecture Prize 1990, Leon d'Oro, La Biennale di Venezia VI Int. Exhbn of Architecture 1996. *Works include*: Expo '70, Osaka 1966–70, Oita Medical Hall 1959–69, Annex 1970–72, Oita Prefectural Library 1962–66, head office of Fukuoka Mutual Bank 1968–71, Museum of Modern Art, Gunma 1971–74, Kitakyushu City Museum of Art 1972–74, Shuko-sha Bldg, Fukuoka 1974–75, Kamioka Town Hall 1976–78, Gymnasium and Dining Hall, Nippon Electric Glass Co., Otsu 1978–80, Los Angeles Museum of Contemporary Art 1981–86, Tsukuba Centre Bldg 1979–83, Palladium Club, New York 1983–85, Sant Jordi Sports Hall, Barcelona 1983–90, Brooklyn Museum 1986–92, Art Tower, Mito 1986–90, Bond Univ., Australia 1987–89, Hara Museum—ARC 1987–88, Kitakyushu Int. Conf. Center 1987–90, Team Disney Bldg 1987–91, Tokyo Univ. of Art and Design 1986–92, Guggenheim Museum, New York 1991–92, Centre for Advanced Science and Tech., Hyogo 1994–98, Japanese Art and Tech. Centre, Kraków 1990–94, Nagi Museum of Contemporary Art 1991–94, B-Con Plaza (int. conf. centre), Oita 1991–95, Toyonokuni Libraries for Cultural Resources, Oita 1991–95, Kyoto Concert Hall 1991–95, Domus: la casa del hombre, La Coruña, Spain 1993–95, Akiyoshidai Int. Art Village, Yamaguchi 1995–98, Nara Centennial Hall 1992–98, Center of Science and Industry, Columbus, OH 1994–99, Ceramics Park MINO 1996–2002, Yamaguchi Center for Arts and Media 1997–2003, Turin Ice Hockey Stadium 2002–06, Shenzhen Cultural Centre, China 1998–2008, China Cen. Acad. of Fine Arts, Beijing 2003–08. *Publications include*: Kukane 1971, Kenchiku no Kaitai 1975, Shuhō ga 1979, Kenchiku no Shūji 1979, Kenchiku no Seijigaku 1989, Image Game 1990, Arata Isozaki 1960–90, Architecture 1991, Kenchiku to iu Keishiki 1991, GA Architect 6 – Arata Isozaki (Vol. 1) 1991, Arata Isozaki – Works 30 1992, Arata Isozaki – Four Decades of Architecture 1998, GA Architect 15 – Arata Isozaki 2000, UNBUILT 2001, GA Document 77—Arata Isozaki 2004. *Address*: Arata Isozaki and Associates, 6-17 Akasaka 9-chome, Minato-ku, Tokyo 107-0052, Japan (office). *Telephone*: (3) 3405-1526 (office). *Fax*: (3) 3475-5265 (office). *E-mail*: info@isozaki.co.jp (office). *Website*: www.isozaki.co.jp (office).

ISRAEL, Werner, OC, PhD, FRSC, FRS, FInstP; Canadian physicist and academic; *Adjunct Professor of Physics, University of Victoria;* b. 4 Oct. 1931, Berlin, Germany; s. of Arthur Israel and Marie Kappauf; m. Inge Margulies 1958; one s. one d.; ed Univ. of Cape Town, SA and Trinity Coll., Dublin, Ireland; Asst Prof., then Full Prof. of Math., Univ. of Alberta 1958–71, Prof. of Physics 1971–96, Univ. Prof. 1986–96 (retd); Adjunct Prof. of Physics, Univ. of Victoria, BC 1997–; Pres. Int. Soc. of General Relativity and Gravitation 1997–2001; Research Scholar, Dublin Inst. for Advanced Studies 1956–58; Sherman Fairchild Scholar, Calif. Inst. of Tech. 1974–75; Fellow, Canadian Inst. for Advanced Research 1986–; Hon. DSc (Queen's Univ.) 1987, (Univ. of Victoria) 1999; Dr hc (Univ. de Tours) 1994; Izaak Walton Killam Prize 1983, Tomalla Prize (Tomalla Foundation for Gravitational Research, Switzerland) 1996. *Publications*: Relativity, Astrophysics and Cosmology (Ed.) 1973, (Co-Ed. with S.W. Hawking), General Relativity, an Einstein Centenary Survey 1979, 300 Years of Gravitation 1987; numerous papers on black hole theory, general relativity, statistical mechanics. *Leisure interest*: music. *Address*: Department of Physics and Astronomy, University of Victoria, PO Box 3055, Victoria, BC V8W 3P6 (office); Suite 401, 2323 Hamiota Street, Victoria, BC V8R 2N1, Canada (home). *Telephone*: (250) 721-7708 (office). *E-mail*: israel@uvic.ca (office). *Website*: www.phys.uvic.ca (office).

ISRAELACHVILI, Jacob Nissim, BS, PhD, FRS, FAA; Australian/Israeli/American scientist and academic; *Professor of Chemical Engineering and Materials Science and Associate Director, Materials Research Laboratory (MRL), University of California, Santa Barbara;* b. 19 Aug. 1944, Tel-Aviv; s. of Haim Israelachvili and Hela Israelachvili; m. Karin Haglund 1971; two d.; ed Christ's Coll., Univ. of Cambridge; Postdoctoral Research Fellow, Cavendish Lab., Univ. of Cambridge, UK 1971–72; European Molecular Biology Org. Research Fellow, Univ. of Stockholm 1972–74; Professorial Fellow, Inst. of Advanced Studies, ANU, Canberra 1974–86; Prof. of Chemical Eng and Materials Science, Univ. of Calif., Santa Barbara 1986–, also Assoc. Dir Materials Research Lab.; Debye Lecturer, Cornell Univ. 1987; Foreign Assoc. Nat. Acad. of Eng (USA) 1999; Fellow, American Physical Soc. in Biological Physics 2004; mem. NAS 2004–; Pawsey Medal, Australian Acad. of Science 1977, Alpha Chi Sigma Award for Chemical Eng Research, AICHE 1997, Adhesion Soc. Award for Excellence in Adhesion Science 2003, MRS Medal 2004. *Publications*: Intermolecular and Surface Forces 1985; numerous scientific publs on surface forces in liquids and biological membrane structure and interactions. *Leisure interest*: history of science. *Address*: Room 1200–Bldg 570, Department of Chemical Engineering, University of California, Santa Barbara, CA 93106-5080 (office); UCSB, Department of Chemical Engineering, 3357 Engineering II, Santa Barbara, CA 93106-5080; 2233 Foothill Lane, Santa Barbara, CA 93105, USA (home). *Telephone*: (805) 893-8407 (office); (805) 893-8353 (Lab.) (office); (805) 252-5568; (805) 963-9545 (home). *Fax*: (805) 893-7870 (office). *E-mail*: jacob@engineering.ucsb.edu (office). *Website*: www.chemengr.ucsb.edu/people/faculty/israelachvili (office); (office).

ISSAD, Mohand, Docteur en Droit, Professeur Agregé; Algerian lawyer and academic; b. 1939; ed Univ. de Rennes; lawyer specializing in commercial law, Algiers 1965–; Prof. Faculty of Law, Ben-Aknoun Univ. 1969–99; currently Prof. of Int. Law, Univ. of Algiers; apptd by Pres. as Chair. Nat. Comm. for Judicial Reform 2000, Comm. investigating disturbances in Kabylia 2001, Comm. on conditions in Algerian prisons and judicial reform 2002. *Address*: 9 Place des Martyrs, Algiers, Algeria (office). *Telephone*: (21) 71-46-21 (office); (21) 71-46-22 (office); (21) 73-64-99 (home). *Fax:* (21) 71-37-74 (office). *E-mail:* prof.issad@yahoo.fr (office).

ISSAWI, Rafi al-, MD; Iraqi physician and politician; b. Fallujah; ed Baghdad Univ., Basrah Univ.; began career as resident doctor, Al-Ramadi Hosp., Al Anwar 1990–93; served as doctor in Iraqi army 1993–94; fmr Dir of Health, Al-Fallujah Dist; Minister of State for Foreign Affairs 2006–07, Deputy Prime Minister 2007–10, Minister of Finance 2010–13; Leader, Nat. Future Gathering Party; mem. Iraqi Medical Asscn. *Address:* c/o Ministry of Finance, Khulafa St, nr al-Russafi Sq., Baghdad, Iraq (office).

ISSELBACHER, Kurt Julius, MD; American medical scientist, academic and university administrator; *Director Emeritus, Massachusetts General Hospital Cancer Center and Mallinckrodt Distinguished Professor of Medicine, Harvard University;* b. 12 Sept. 1925, Wirges, Germany; s. of Albert Isselbacher and Flori Isselbacher; m. Rhoda Solin 1950; one s. three d.; ed Harvard Univ. and Harvard Medical School; Chief. Gastrointestinal Unit, Mass Gen. Hosp. 1957–88, Chair. Research Cttee 1967, Dir Cancer Center 1987–, now Dir Emer.; Prof. of Medicine, Harvard Medical School 1966–, Mallinckrodt Prof. of Medicine 1972–97, Distinguished Mallinckrodt Prof. 1998–, Chair. Exec. Cttee Medicine Depts 1968–, Chair. Univ. Cancer Cttee 1972–87; mem. Governing Bd Nat. Research Council 1987–90; Ed.-in-Chief Harrison's Principles of Internal Medicine 1991–; mem. NAS (Chair. Food and Nutrition Bd 1983–88, Exec. Cttee and Council 1987–90); Hon. DSc (Northwestern Univ.) 2001; Distinguished Achievement Award, American Gastroenterological Asscn (AGA) 1983, Friedenwald Medal, AGA 1985, John Phillips Memorial Award, American Coll. of Physicians 1989, Bristol-Myers Squibb Award for Distinguished Achievement in Nutrition Research 1991, Kober Medal, Asscn of American Physicians 2001, Jewish Nat. Fund Tree of Life Award 2001. *Leisure interest:* tennis. *Address:* Massachusetts General Hospital, Building 149, 13th Street, Charlestown, MA 02129 (office); 20 Nobscot Road, Newton, MA 02114, USA (home). *Telephone:* (617) 726-5610 (office). *Fax:* (617) 726-5637 (office). *E-mail:* isselbacher@helix.mgh.harvard.edu (office). *Website:* www.massgeneral.org/cancer/research/basic/ccr/faculty/shioda.asp (office).

ISSERLIS, Steven John, CBE; British cellist; b. 19 Dec. 1958, London, England; s. of George Isserlis and the late Cynthia Isserlis; m. Pauline Mara (died 2010); one s.; ed City of London School, Int. Cello Centre, Scotland, Oberlin Coll., Ohio, USA; concerts and recitals world-wide 1977–; exponent of contemporary music as well as authentic period performance; chamber concerts include own 'Shadow of War' series at Wigmore Hall, London 2013; series of recitals with Olli Mustonen and Stephen Hough, and appearances at Verbier and Salzburg Festivals; gives regular children's concerts, 92nd Street Y, New York; Artistic Dir IMS Prussia Cove, Cornwall; writer of children's books about the lives of great composers; Hon. mem. RAM; Piatigorsky Award 1993, Royal Philharmonic Soc. Award 1993, Schumann Prize, Zwickau 2000, Time Out Classical Musician of the Year 2002, Gramophone Hall of Fame 2013. *Recordings:* Brahms Sonatas 2005, Bach Solo Cello Suites (Gramophone Award for Best Instrumental Recording) 2007, Schumann Music for Cello and Piano 2009, Revisions 2010, Lieux Retrouves with Thomas Adès 2012, Dvorak Cello Concertos 2013, Beethoven Cello Sonatas with Robert Levin 2014. *Publications:* transcription of Beethoven Variations in D arranged for violin or cello and piano or harpsichord, Edn of Saint-Saëns pieces for cello and piano, Steven Isserlis's Cello World, Unbeaten Tracks, Why Beethoven Threw the Stew 2001, Why Handel Waggled His Wig 2006. *Leisure interests:* books, films, gossip, e-mail, eating too much, avoiding exercise, wishing I was fitter, wondering why I have so few worthwhile hobbies. *Address:* c/o Alexander Monsey, IMG Artists, The Light Box, 111 Power Road, London, W4 5PY, England (office). *Telephone:* (20) 7957-5800 (office). *Fax:* (20) 7957-5801 (office). *E-mail:* amonsey@imgartists.com (office). *Website:* www.imgartists.com (office); www.stevenisserlis.com (office).

ISSING, Otmar, PhDr; German economist and fmr central banker; *President, Center for Financial Studies, Goethe University, Frankfurt;* b. 27 March 1936, Würzburg; ed Humanistisches Gymnasium, Würzburg, Univ. of Würzburg; Prof. of Econs, Univ. of Erlangen-Nuremberg 1967–73, Univ. of Würzburg 1973–90; mem. Council of Experts for Assessment of Overall Econ. Trends 1988–90; mem. Directorate Deutsche Bundesbank 1990–98; mem. Exec. Bd European Cen. Bank 1998–2006; Pres. Center for Financial Studies, Goethe Univ., Frankfurt 2006–; mem. Acad. of Sciences and Literature, Mainz, Acad. Europaea, Salzburg; Co-founder and Co-ed. of the scientific journal WiSt; mem. Verein für Socialpolitik, American Econ. Asscn, European Acad. of Arts and Sciences, Acad. of Sciences and Literature, Walter Eucken Inst.; mem. High Level Group of EC 2008–09; Int. Advisory Bd, Bocconi Univ. Milan 2009–; Chair. Advisory Group to German Chancellor on New Financial Order 2008–12; Hon. Prof., Univ. of Würzburg 1991–, Univ. of Frankfurt 2007–; Grosses Verdienskreuz des Verdienstordens der Bundesrepublik Deutschland 2006, Officier, Ordre du mérite du Grand-Duché, Luxembourg 2006; Dr hc (Bayreuth) 1996, (Konstanz) 1998, (Frankfurt am Main) 1999; Laurea hc in Int. Econ. integration (Univ. of Pavia) 2010; Int. Prize, Friedrich-August-Hayek Foundation 2003, Ludwig Erhard Preis 2006. *Publications:* Introduction to Monetary Policy (sixth edn) 1996, Introduction to Monetary Theory 1998 (15th edn 2011), Monetary Policy in the Euro Area (co-author) 2001, Imperfect Knowledge and Monetary Policy (co-author) 2005, Der Euro: Geburt – Erfolg – Zukunft (trans. as The Birth of the Euro) 2008, Wie wir den Euro retten und Europa stärken 2012. *Address:* Georg-Sittig-Str. 8, 97074 Würzburg, Germany (office).

ISSOÏBEKA, Pacifique; Republic of the Congo politician; b. Mossaka; Vice-Gov. Banque des États de l'Afrique Centrale 2003–05; Minister of Finance, the Economy and the Budget 2005–09; Alt. Gov. of Repub. of the Congo to World Bank 2005–09. *Address:* c/o Ministry of Finance, the Economy and the Budget, ave de l'Indépendance, croisement ave Foch, BP 2083, Brazzaville, Republic of the Congo (office).

ISSOUFOU, Mahamadou; Niger mining engineer, politician and head of state; *President;* b. 1952, Illéla; Nat. Dir of Mines 1980–85; Sec.-Gen. Mining Co. of Niger (SOMAIR) 1985; Sec.-Gen. Parti nigérien pour la démocratie et le socialisme—Tarayya (PNDS), currently Pres.; mem. Assemblée nationale 1993–99 (Pres. 1995–96); Prime Minister of Niger 1993–94 (resgnd); Chief Economist 1999; presidential cand. 1993, 1996, 1999, 2004; Pres. of Niger 2011–. *Address:* Office of the President, BP 550, Niamey, Niger (office). *Telephone:* 20-72-23-80 (office). *Fax:* 20-72-33-96 (office). *Website:* www.presidence.ne (office).

ITALELI, Sir Iakoba Taeia, GCMG; Tuvaluan politician; *Governor General;* ed Int. Maritime Law Inst., Malta; fmr Attorney Gen.; mem. Fale i Fono (parl.) for Nui constituency 2006–10; Minister of Educ., Sports and Health 2006–10; Gov. Gen. 2010–. *Address:* Office of the Governor General, Private Mail Bag, Vaiaku, Funafuti, Tuvalu (office). *Telephone:* 20715 (office). *Website:* www.tuvaluislands.com/gov_info.htm (office).

ITO, Masao, MD, PhD; Japanese neuroscientist and academic; *Senior Advisor, RIKEN Brain Science Institute;* b. 1928, Nagoya; ed Univ. of Tokyo; Asst Prof., Kumamoto Univ. 1954–57; Asst Prof., Univ. of Tokyo 1957–62, Assoc. Prof. 1963–70, Prof. 1970–90, Dean 1986–89, Prof. Emer. 1990–; Research Scholar and Research Fellow, Sir John Eccles' Lab., ANU 1959–62; Team Leader, Frontier Research Program, Inst. of Physical and Chemical Research (RIKEN) 1989–97, Dir-Gen. 1993–97, Founding Dir RIKEN Brain Science Inst. 1997–2003, Sr Advisor 2003–; Pres. Japanese Physiological Soc. 1978–93, Int. Brain Research Org. 1980–86, Japan Neuroscience Soc. 1982–99, Int. Union of Physiological Sciences 1994–98, Science Council of Japan 1991–97, Human Frontier Science Program 2000–09; mem. Gen. Cttee and Exec. Bd Int. Council for Science (ICSU) 1988–97, Prime Minister's Council for Science and Tech. 1994–97; mem. Japan Acad.; Foreign mem. Royal Swedish Acad. of Sciences, Royal Soc., London, French, Armenian, Russian, Hungarian, Indian, European Acad. of Sciences, NAS; Order of Culture 1996, Chevalier, Légion d'honneur 1998; hon. science degree (Univ. of Southern California) 1995, (Torino Univ.) 1996, (Charles Univ., Prague) 1998; Fujiwara Prize 1981, Academy Prize and Imperial Prize 1986, Robert Dow Neuroscience Award 1993, IPSEN Foundation Award 1993, Person of Cultural Merit 1994, Japan Prize 1996, Gruber Neuroscience Prize, The Peter and Patricia Gruber Foundation (co-recipient) 2006. *Achievements include:* discovered inhibitory action of cerebellar Purkinje cells and characteristic synaptic plasticity, long-term depression in these cells; developed theory that cerebellum is a general learning machine for acquiring not only motor skills but also implicit memory in thought. *Publications:* The Cerebellum as a Neuronal Machine (with J. C. Eccles and J. Szenthgothai) 1967, The Cerebellum and Neural Control 1984; more than 120 scientific papers in professional journals on brain mechanism. *Address:* RIKEN Brain Science Institute, 2-1 Hirosawa, Wako City, Saitama 351-0198, Japan (office). *Telephone:* (48) 467-6984 (office). *Fax:* (48) 467-6975 (office). *E-mail:* ito-BSI@brain.riken.jp (office). *Website:* www.brain.riken.jp/en/m_ito.html (office).

ITO, Masatoshi; Japanese retail executive; *Founder and Honorary Chairman, Ito-Yokado Group;* b. 1925; m.; three c.; ed Yokohama City Univ.; Founder and Hon. Chair. Ito-Yokado Co. Ltd (now Ito-Yokado Group) with Seven-Eleven Japan and Denny's Japan brands. *Address:* Ito-Yokado Co. Ltd, 1-4, Shibakoen 4-chome, Minato-ku, Tokyo 105-8571, Japan (office). *Telephone:* (3) 3459-2111 (office). *Fax:* (3) 3459-6873 (office). *Website:* www.itoyokado.iyg.co.jp (office).

ITO, Takanobu; Japanese automotive industry executive; *President, CEO and Representative Director, Honda Motor Company;* joined Honda Motor Co. in 1978, began career as engineer designing chassis, was in charge of developing frame structure for NSX sports car (went on sale 1990), Exec. Vice-Pres. Honda R&D Americas, Inc. 1998–2000, helped develop first sport-utility vehicle under Acura brand 1998–2000, Dir Honda R&D Co. Ltd 2000–, Sr Man. Dir 2001–03, Man. Dir 2003–04, Pres. and Dir Honda R&D Co. Ltd 2003–04, Motor Sports 2003–04, Gen. Supervisor, Motor Sports 2004–05, Gen. Man. Suzuka Factory of Production Operations 2005–07, Man. Officer 2005–07, COO for Automobile Operations 2007–09, Sr Man. Dir and Head of Core Automaking Operations, Honda Motor Co. 2007–09, Rep. Dir 2007–, Pres. and CEO 2009–. *Address:* Honda Motor Co. Ltd, 2-1-1 Minami-Aoyama, Minato-ku, Tokyo 107-8556, Japan (office). *Telephone:* (3) 3423-1111 (office). *Fax:* (3) 5412-1515 (office). *E-mail:* info@honda.com (office). *Website:* www.honda.com (office); www.honda.co.jp (office); corporate.honda.com (office); world.honda.com (office).

ITO, Tatsuya, LLB; Japanese politician; b. 6 July 1961, Tokyo; ed Faculty of Law, Keio-Gijuku Univ.; Researcher, Matsushita Inst. of Govt and Man. 1984–87; Visiting Researcher, Grad. School of Public Policy and Admin, Calif. State Univ., USA 1987–88; Sec.-Gen. Japan–US Tech. Exchange Programme 1988–93; elected to House of Reps 1993, Dir Cttee on Commerce and Industry 1993–96, Parl. Under-Sec. for Int. Trade and Industry 2000, Dir Cttee on the Environment 2000–01, Dir Cttee on Economy, Trade and Industry 2001–02, Sr Dir Cttee on Economy, Trade and Industry 2002; Acting Dir Science and Tech. Div., LDP 1999–2000, Dir of Economy, Trade and Industry Div. 2000–01, Sec. Admin Reform Promotion HQ 2000–01, Sec.-Gen. Select Comm. on e-Japan Priority Programme 2001–02; Sr Vice Minister for Financial Services 2002–03, Sr Vice Minister for Financial Services and for Econ. and Fiscal Policy 2003–04, Minister of State for Financial Services 2004–05. *Address:* c/o Liberal-Democratic Party (Jiyu-Minshuto), 1-11-23, Nagata-cho, Chiyoda-ku, Tokyo 100-8910, Japan (office).

ITO, Toyo; Japanese architect; *Owner, Toyo Ito & Associates;* b. 1941; ed Tokyo Univ.; began career with Kiyonori Kikutake Architects and Assocs 1965; est. studio Urban Robot (Urbot), Tokyo 1971 (renamed Toyo Ito and Assocs 1979); fmr Guest Prof., Columbia Univ., New York, USA; Hon. Prof., Univ. of N London, UK, Hon. Diploma of the Architectural Asscn 2003; AA Interarch '97 Grand Prix Gold Medal, Union of Bulgarian Architects 1997, Art Encouragement Prize, Ministry of Educ. 1998, Arnold W. Brunner Memorial Prize, American Acad. of Arts and Letters 2000, Gold Prize, Japanese Good Design Award 2001, Golden Lion for Lifetime Achievement Award, Venice Biennale 2002, XX AOI Compasso d'Ore Award 2004, Gold Medal, RIBA 2006, Asahi Prize 2009, Praemium Imperiale 2010, Pritzker Prize 2013. *Architectural works include:* White U 1976, Silver Hut (Architecture Inst. of Japan Award 1986) 1984, A Dwelling for the Tokyo Nomad Woman 1985, Tower of Winds 1986, Egg of Winds 1991, Yatsushiro Municipal Museum (33rd Mainrich Art Award 1992) 1991, Old People's Home, Yatsushiro 1994, Sendai Mediatheque (multi-resource public cultural centre), Sendai 2001, Brugge 2002 Summer Pavilion, Serpentine Gallery, London 2002, Codan Shinonome Canal Court (Block 2) 2003, Matsumoto Performing Arts Centre 2004, VivoCity, Singapore 2006, Tama Art University Library, Tokyo 2007, Za-Koenji Public Theatre 2008, Main Stadium for World Games, Kaohsiung, Taiwan 2009, White O 2009. *Publication:* Toyo Ito Architetto 2001. *Address:* Toyo Ito &

Associates, Architects, Fujiya Building, 1-19-4, Shibuya, Shibuya-ku, Tokyo, 150-0002, Japan (office). *Website:* www.toyo-ito.co.jp (office).

ITOYAMA, Eitaro; Japanese business executive and fmr politician; b. 4 June 1942; s. of Shintaro Sasaki; m.; two c.; ed Nihon Univ.; mem. House of Reps. 1974–90, 1994–96; CEO Shin Nihon Kanko (golf course co.) 1985–; Chair. and Provost Sagami Inst. of Tech. Fujisawa 1981– (renamed Shonan Inst. of Tech. 1990); f. Itoyama Inst. of Politics and Man.; mem. LDP; major shareholder in Japan Airlines International 1998–2006 (currently Special Adviser to CEO), TV Tokyo Corp. *Leisure interests:* golf, tennis, sailing. *Address:* The Itoyama Tower, 7-18 Mita 3-Chome, Minato-ku, Tokyo 108-0073, Japan (office). *E-mail:* info@itoyama.org (office). *Website:* www.itoyama.org (office).

IUE, Satoshi, BEng; Japanese electronics industry executive; *Adviser, Sanyo Electric Company Ltd;* b. 28 Feb. 1930; s. of the late Toshio Iue; ed Doshisha Univ.; joined Sanyo Electric Co. Ltd 1956, Dir 1961–, Man. Dir 1968–72, Exec. Man. Dir 1972–85, Exec. Vice-Pres. 1985–86, Pres. and CEO 1986–92, Chair. and CEO 1992–2005, Exec. Dir and Chair. 2006, now Adviser; Chair. Osaka Symphonic Asscn 1991–, Ashiya Cosmopolitan Asscn 1993–, Kansai New Business Conf. 1996; Vice-Chair. Japan-China Asscn on Economy and Trade 1995–, Osaka Chamber of Commerce and Industry 1995–; Dir Fed. of Econ. Orgs, Kansai Econ. Fed.; Hon. Citizen of Dalian, China 1995, Tarlac, Philippines 1996, Hefei, China 1997; Darjah Dato' Paduka Mahkota Perak, Malaysia; Hon. LLD (Boston Univ. School of Man.) 1990, Hon. DSc (Dalian Univ.) 1995; numerous awards and honours including Nat. Medal of Honor for Philanthropy 1970, Nat. Medal of Honor for Contrib. to Devt of Industry 1992. *Address:* Sanyo Electric Company Limited, 5-5 Keihan-Hondori, 2-chome, Moriguchi City, Osaka 570-8677, Japan (office). *Telephone:* (6) 6991-1181 (office). *Fax:* (6) 6991-6566 (office). *Website:* www.sanyo.co.jp (office).

IUE, Toshimasa, MBA; Japanese electronics industry executive; s. of Satoshi Iue, grands of the late Toshio Iue; ed Konan Univ., Boston Univ., USA; joined Sanyo Electric Co. 1989, Exec. Vice-Pres., also Div. Man. of Group Marketing and CEO Sanyo Consumer Group, Commercial Group, Int. Group, and Components Group 2002–05, Chief Marketing Officer 2003–05, Exec. Dir, Pres. and COO Sanyo Electric Co. 2005–07 (resgnd); mem. Boston Univ. Bd of Trustees 2004–; Boston Univ. Alumni Award for Distinguished Service 2003. *Address:* c/o Sanyo Electric Company, 2-5-5 Keihan-Hondori, Moriguchi 570-8677, Japan (office).

IURES, Marcel; Romanian actor; *Founder and Artistic Director, Theatre ACT;* b. 2 Aug. 1951, Bailesti; ed Inst. of Theatrical Arts and Cinematography; film debut in Vis de ianuarie (January Dream) 1978; comedian Bulandra and Odeon Theatres, Bucharest 1980–94; performed title role in Richard III, Bucharest and London, UK 1994; Founder and Artistic Dir Theatre ACT (ind. theatre), Bucharest 1998–. *Films include:* Vis de ianuarie (January Dream) 1978, Sa mori ranit din dragoste de viata (To Die from Love of Life) 1983, Domnisoara Aurica 1985, Vacanta cea mare (The Great Vacation) 1988, Cei care platesc cu viata (Those Who Pay with Their Lives) 1991, Balanta (The Oak) 1992, Un été inoubliable (An Unforgettable Summer) 1994, Interview with the Vampire 1994, Somnul insulei (Sleep of the Island) 1994, Mission Impossible 1996, The Peacemaker 1997, Faimosul paparazzo (The Famous Paparazzo) 1999, Elite 2000, I Hope 2001, Amen 2002, Hart's War 2002, Dracula the Impaler (voice) 2002, 3 pazeste 2003, Cambridge Spies (TV) 2003, The Tulse Luper Suitcases, Part 2: Vaux to the Sea 2004, The Cave 2005, Isolation 2005, Project W 2005, Goal! 2005, Isolation 2005, Logodnicii din America 2007, Pirates of the Caribbean: At World's End 2007, Youth Without Youth 2007. *Address:* Theatre ACT, Calea Victoriei 126, sector 1, Bucharest, Romania (office). *Telephone:* (1) 3103103 (office). *Fax:* (1) 3103103 (office). *E-mail:* act@teatrulact.ro (office); info@teatrulact.ro (office). *Website:* www.teatrulact.ro (office).

IVANCHENKO, Aleksander Vladimirovich, DJur; Russian lawyer and politician; *Head, Russian Centre for the Studies of Voting Technologies, Central Electoral Commission;* b. 8 Jan. 1954, Krasnodar; m.; one d.; ed Higher School of Ministry of Internal Affairs; worked in Moscow militia forces; Lecturer, Higher School of Ministry of Internal Affairs 1983–88; on staff Supreme Soviet Russian Fed. 1988–93; Deputy Chair. Cen. Electoral Comm. of Russian Fed. 1993–96, Chair. 1996–99, Head, Russian Centre for the Studies of Voting Technologies; Founder and Dir Inst. of Election Tech. Studies 1999–; mem. State Duma/JCP faction 1999–; Chair. Cttee on Fed. Affairs 2000–07. *Publications:* papers and articles on problems of political rights and freedom, on election law. *Leisure interests:* tennis, walks in the countryside. *Address:* Russian Centre for the Studies of Voting Technologies, Central Electoral Commission, 9 B. Cherkasskii per., 109012 Moscow (office); State Duma, Okhotny Ryka 1, 103265 Moscow, Russia. *Telephone:* (495) 606-79-57 (office); (495) 292-97-75. *Fax:* (495) 292-51-40. *Website:* www.cikrf.ru (office).

IVANENKO, Sergei Victorovich, CandEcon; Russian politician and economist; *Deputy Chairman, Yabloko Russian Democratic Party (Rossiisskaya demokraticheskaya partiya 'Yabloko');* b. 12 Jan. 1959, Zestafoni, Georgia; ed Lomonosov Moscow State Univ.; researcher and Asst Prof., Moscow State Univ. 1985–90; Chief Expert State Comm. on Econ. Reform RSFSR Council of Ministers 1994–96; Researcher, Cen. of Econ. and Political Studies 1991–92; mem. State Duma 1993–, Chair. Cttee on Property, Privatisation and Econs 1993–95, mem. Cttee on Ecology 1995–99; currently Deputy Chair. Yabloko Russian Democratic Party (Rossiisskaya demokraticheskaya partiya 'Yabloko'), Chair. Moscow Yabloko; Vice-Pres. Russian Chess Fed. 2003–. *Address:* Yabloko Russian Democratic Party (Rossiisskaya demokraticheskaya partiya 'Yabloko'), 119604 Moscow, per. M. Levshinskii 7/3, Russia (office). *Telephone:* (495) 201-43-79 (office). *Fax:* (495) 292-34-50 (office). *E-mail:* admin@yabloko.ru (office). *Website:* www.yabloko.ru (office).

IVANENKO, Maj.-Gen. Victor Valentinovich; Russian intelligence officer (retd) and business executive; *Chairman, Arctic Trade and Transport Company;* b. 19 Sept. 1947, Koltsovka, Tyumen region; m.; three c.; ed Tyumen State Industrial Inst., Higher KGB Courses; mem. staff KGB, Tyumen region 1970–86, Sr Inspector, Head of Div., Deputy Head of Dept, USSR KGB 1986–91, Chair. RSFSR KGB 1991; Dir-Gen., with rank of Minister, Russian Agency of Fed. Security 1991–1992; Vice-Pres., then First Vice-Pres. YUKOS Jt Stock Oil Co. 1993–98; mem. Bd of Dirs ROSPROM Jt Stock Co. 1996; adviser, Ministry of Taxation and Revenues 1998–99; Vice-Pres. Foundation for Devt of Parliamentarianism in Russia 2000–03; Chair. Arctic Trade and Transportation Co. (ATTC Jt

Stock Co.) 2003–; mem. Supervisory Bd Russia-ASEAN Collaboration Fund; Presidium mem. Nat. Cttee on cooperation with law-enforcement, legislative and law authorities, Independents Civil Society; mem. Foreign and Defence Policy Council; mem. Moscow English Club; Order Red Star, six medals. *E-mail:* kompaszemnoj@gmail.com (office).

IVANIĆ, Mladen, MA, PhD; Bosnia and Herzegovina politician, economist and academic; *Chairman, Party of Democratic Progress of Republika Srpska;* b. 16 Sept. 1958, Sanski Most; m. Gordana Ivanić; one s. one d.; ed Faculties of Econs, Univs of Banja Luka and Belgrade, Univ. of Mannheim, Germany and Univ. of Glasgow, UK; journalist Radio Banja Luka 1981–85; Asst Prof. of Political Economy, Faculty of Econs, Univ. of Banja Luka 1985–88, Docent 1988–, Head of Post-Grad. Study of Reconstruction and Transition (held in conjunction with Univs of Bologna, Sussex and LSE); Teacher Faculty of Econs, Sarajevo 1990–92; Teacher, Faculty of Econs, Srpsko Sarajevo 1992–98; Lecturer, Univ. of Glasgow, UK 1998; mem. Presidency of Yugoslav Repub. of Bosnia and Herzegovina 1988–91; Founder and Chair. Party of Democratic Progress of Republika Srpska 1999–; mem. Govt Econ. Council 1999; Head, Deloitte & Touche Consultancy Office –2001; Prime Minister of Republika Srpska 2001–03; Minister of Foreign Affairs, Council of Ministers of Bosnia and Herzegovina 2003–07 (resgnd); mem. House of Peoples (Parl. Ass. of Bosnia and Herzegovina); mem. Editorial Bd Ideje magazine, Belgrade 1988–91, Aktuelnosti magazine, Banja Luka 1998–99; Del. to OSCE sessions 1991; participant World Forum, Davos, Switzerland 1999, 2000; Pres. Serb Intellectual Forum. *Publications include:* Political Economy, Principles of Political Economy; numerous contribs to newspapers and magazines including Savremenost (Modernity), Pregled (Overview), Ideje (Ideas), Opredjeljenja (Determinations), Lica (Faces), Aktuelnosti (Updates); author or co-author of several programmes for World Bank, UNDP and other int. orgs. *Address:* Partija demokratskog progresa RS, 78000 Banja Luka, ul. Prvog Krajiškog Korpusa 130, Bosnia and Herzegovina (office). *Telephone:* (51) 346210 (office). *Fax:* (51) 300956 (office). *E-mail:* pdp@blic.net (office). *Website:* www.pdpinfo.net (office).

IVANIŠEVIĆ, Goran; Croatian fmr professional tennis player; b. 13 Sept. 1971, Split; s. of Srdjan Ivanišević and Gorana Ivanišević; one d.; won US Open Jr doubles with Nargiso 1987; turned professional 1988; joined Yugoslav Davis Cup squad 1988; semi-finalist, ATP World Championship 1992; bronze medal, men's doubles, Barcelona Olympic Games 1992; runner-up, Wimbledon Championship 1992, 1994, 1998; winner Wimbledon Championship 2001; winner of numerous ATP tournaments, including Kremlin Cup, Moscow 1996; winner of 22 tours singles and nine doubles titles, and over US $19 million prize money; once ranked No. 2 in the world, behind Pete Sampras; retd 2004; now playing on Masters Tennis (sr) tour; Founder and Pres. Children in Need Foundation 1995–; BBC Overseas Sports Personality of the Year Award 2001. *Leisure interests:* football, basketball, reading, music, cinema.

IVANISHVILI, Bidzina; Georgian politician and entrepreneur; b. 18 Feb. 1956, Chorvila; m.; four c.; ed high school in Sachkhere, Tbilisi State Univ., Moscow State Univ. of Railway Eng; formed partnership with Vitalii Malkin to sell computers, later importing push-button telephones into Russia; est. Rossiiskii Kredit Bank 1990; later sold other businesses accumulated during privatization era and invested proceeds in Russian stock market; holds shares in hotels, including Hotel Lux and Russian Doktor Stoletov (chain of pharmacies); Founder of opposition coalition Georgian Dream 2012; Prime Minister 2012–13. *Address:* Georgian Dream—Democratic Georgia (Qartuli Ocneba—Demokratiuli Sakartvelo), 0105 Tbilisi, Erekle II Moedani 3, Georgia (office). *Telephone:* (32) 219-77-11 (office). *E-mail:* info@gd.ge (office). *Website:* gd.ge (office).

IVANOV, Anton Alexandrovich; Russian lawyer and government official; *Chairman, Supreme Commercial Court;* b. 6 July 1965, Gatchina, Leningrad Oblast; ed Leningrad State Univ.; with Faculty of Law, Leningrad State Univ. 1982–87, also worked as Asst Prof., later Assoc. Prof.; Head of Legal Dept Soyuzcontract Corpn 1994–96; Asst Lecturer of Civil Law, St Petersburg State Univ. 1995–97, Sr Lecturer 1999–2004; Head of St Petersburg Dept of Justice, Ministry of Justice 1997–99; Deputy to Dir-Gen. Gasprom-Media OJSC 2004; Chair. Supreme Commercial Court, Moscow 2005–; Chair. of Civil Law and Research Adviser, Faculty of Law, State Univ. 2006; mem. Bd of Dirs Gasprom-Media OJSC, Ekho Moskvy CJSC, TNT-Teleset CJSC, NTV Co. OJSC, Legal Awareness Fund; Chief Ed. Pravovedeniye Journal 1991–94; mem. Council for Codification and Improvement of Civil law, Presidium Russian Lawyers' Asscn, Council for Devt of Financial Market; A.F. Koni Medal. *Publications include:* more than 40 books. *Address:* Supreme Commercial Court, 101000 Moscow, Center, small Hariton'evsk lane 12, Russia (office). *Telephone:* (495) 608-11-97 (office); (495) 608-11-94 (office). *E-mail:* vasrf@arbitr.ru (office). *Website:* www.arbitr.ru (office).

IVANOV, Gjorge; Macedonian political scientist, academic, politician and head of state; *President;* b. 2 May 1960, Valandovo; m. Maja Ivanova; one s.; ed secondary school in Valandovo; activist in League of Socialist Youth of Yugoslavia –1990; Pres. and Supreme Commdr of the Army of Fmr Yugoslav Repub. of Macedonia May 2009–; fmr Visiting Prof. in Greece. *Publications:* (in Macedonian): Civil Society, Democracy in Divided Societies: The Macedonian Model, Current Political Theories (with Lyubomir Frčkoski), Political Theories – Antiquity (with Svetomir Skarik). *Address:* Office of the President, 1000 Skopje, Aco Karamanov 33A, Former Yugoslav Republic of Macedonia (office). *Telephone:* (2) 3253105 (office). *Fax:* (2) 3253105 (office). *E-mail:* president@president.gov.mk (office). *Website:* www.president.gov.mk (office).

IVANOV, Igor Sergeevich, PhD; Russian diplomatist and politician; *President, Russian International Affairs Council;* b. 23 Sept. 1945, Moscow; m.; one d.; ed Maurice Thorez Moscow Inst. of Foreign Languages; Jr researcher Inst. of World Econs and Int. Relations, USSR Acad. of Sciences 1969–73; within diplomatic service, Second, then First Sec., Counsellor, Counsellor-Envoy USSR Embassy, Spain 1973–83; expert First European Dept, Ministry of Foreign Affairs 1983–84; Asst Minister 1984–86; Deputy Chief, then Chief of Dept 1987–91; Amb. to Spain 1991–93; First Deputy Minister of Foreign Affairs 1994–98, Minister of Foreign Affairs 1998–2004; Sec., Security Council of Russia 2004–07; Prof., Moscow State Inst. of Int. Relations (MGIMO) 2007–; Pres. Russian Int. Affairs Council 2013–; Corresp. mem. Russian Acad. of Sciences; Orders For Services to the Fatherland

(2nd, 3rd and 4th Degrees), Order of Honour, Hero of the Russian Fed.; Hon. Dr of Historical Science. *Publications:* New Russian Diplomacy 2001, External Russian Policy in the Epoch of Globalization 2002, Global Security in the Epoch of Globalization: Russia in Global Policy 2003, Russia in the Contemporary World: Responses for the Challenges of the 21st Century 2004; numerous papers and articles. *Address:* Alexander House, 119180 Moscow, Bolshaya Yakimanka Str. 1, Russia (office). *Telephone:* (495) 225-62-83 (office). *Fax:* (495) 225-62-84 (office). *E-mail:* welcome@russiancouncil.ru (office). *Website:* russiancouncil.ru (office).

IVANOV, Ivan Dmitriyevich, DEcon; Russian diplomatist, politician and economist; *Deputy Director, Institute of Europe, Russian Academy of Sciences;* b. 1934, Moscow; m.; two c.; ed Moscow Inst. of Foreign Trade; Head of Div., Inst. of USA and Canada, USSR (now Russian) Acad. of Sciences 1971–76, Deputy Dir, Prof., Inst. of World Econs and Int. Relations 1977–86, Deputy Dir Inst. of Europe, Russian Acad. of Sciences 2001–; Deputy Chair. State Cttee for Foreign Econ. Relations, USSR Ministry of Foreign Affairs, also Chair. USSR State Comm. on Foreign Econ. Orgs 1986–91; Deputy Dir Inst. of Foreign Econ. Research 1991–94; Russian Trade Rep. to Belgium 1994–96, Deputy Perm. Rep. to EU, Brussels 1996–99; Deputy Minister of Foreign Affairs 1999–2001. *Address:* Institute of Europe, Russian Academy of Sciences, 11-3B, Mokhovaya Street, 125993 Moscow, Russia (office). *Telephone:* (495) 203-41-87 (home). *Fax:* (495) 609-92-98 (office). *E-mail:* europe@ieras.ru (office). *Website:* www.ieras.ru (office).

IVANOV, Mikhail Vladimirovich; Russian microbiologist; *Director, Department of Microbial Biogeochemistry and Biogeotechnology, Institute of Microbiology, Russian Academy of Sciences;* b. 6 Dec. 1930; m.; ed Moscow State Univ.; researcher, Inst. of Microbiology, USSR (now Russian) Acad. of Sciences, later Head of Lab. and Deputy Dir Inst. of Biochemistry and Physiology of Plants and Micro-organisms, later Dir Dept of Microbial Biogeochemistry and Biogeotechnology, Inst. of Microbiology 1984–; Ed.-in-Chief Microbiology journal; Corresp. mem. USSR (now Russian) Acad. of Sciences 1981, mem. 1987; research in geochemistry activities of microorganisms and biotechnology, marine microbiology, global ecology and biogeochemistry; S. Vernadsky Prize. *Leisure interest:* coin collecting. *Address:* Department of Microbial Biogeochemistry and Biogeotechnology, Institute of Microbiology, Russian Academy of Sciences, 60-letiya Oktyabrya pr., 7 kor. 2, 117811 Moscow, Russia (office). *Telephone:* (495) 135-11-71 (office); (495) 299-65-30 (home). *E-mail:* ivanov@inmi.host.ru (office). *Website:* www.inmi.ru (office).

IVANOV, Lt-Gen. Sergei Borisovich; Russian politician; *Chief of Staff of the Presidential Administration of Russia;* b. 31 Jan. 1953, Leningrad (now St Petersburg); m. Nataliya Ivanova; two s.; ed Leningrad State Univ., Yu. V. Andropov Inst. at KGB; various posts in KGB including missions abroad 1976–97; Deputy Dir Fed. Service of Security, 1998–2001; Head, Dept of Analysis, Prognosis and Strategic Planning 1998–99; Sec., Security Council of Russian Fed. 1999–2001; Minister of Defence 2001–07, Deputy Chair. of the Govt 2005–07, 2008–11, First Deputy Chair. of the Govt 2007–08; Chief of Staff, Presidential Admin of Russia 2011–; Order for Services to the Fatherland (Second Class) 2003. *Leisure interests:* fishing, reading detective stories in English and Swedish. *Address:* Office of the President, Staraya pl. 4, 103132 Moscow, Russia (office). *Telephone:* (495) 625-35-81 (office). *Fax:* (495) 606-07-66 (office). *E-mail:* president@gov.ru (office). *Website:* www.kremlin.ru (office).

IVANOV, Vadim Tikhonovich, DSc; Russian biochemist; *Director, Shemyakin-Ovchinnikov Institute of Bioorganic Chemistry;* b. 18 Sept. 1937, Pheodossia, Crimea; s. of Tikhon Timofeevitch Ivanov and Lidia Ivanovna Ivanova; m. Raisa Alexandrovna Ivanova (née Osadchaya); one s. one d.; ed Moscow State Univ.; Jr, Sr Researcher, Head of Lab., Deputy Dir, Dir Shemyakin-Ovchinnikov Inst. of Bioorganic Chem., Russian Acad. of Sciences; Corresp. mem. USSR (now Russian) Acad. of Sciences 1976, mem. 1987, mem. Presidium; research in chem. of proteins and peptides, structure and functions of neuropeptides, synthetic vaccines and peptidomics; Einstein Prof., Chinese Acad. of Sciences; several orders of USSR and Russian Fed.; Lenin Prize, USSR State Prize, three Russian Govt Prizes, Ovchinnikov Medal, Lomonosov Gold Medal, Russian Acad. of Sciences 2009. *Publications* include: Membrane Active Complexones 1974, The Way to Protein Synthesis 1982. *Leisure interests:* chess, nature. *Address:* Shemyakin-Ovchinnikov Institute of Bioorganic Chemistry, Russian Academy of Sciences, Miklukho-Maklay str. 16/10, 117997 Moscow, Russia (office). *Telephone:* (495) 330-56-38 (office). *Fax:* (495) 330-56-92 (office). *E-mail:* ivavt@mail.ibch.ru (office); ivavt@ibch.ru (office). *Website:* www.ibch.ru/en/about/history/personalia/1 (office).

IVANOV, Col Viktor Petrovich; Russian government official; *Director, Federal Drug Control Service;* b. 12 May 1950, Novgorod; m.; one s. one d.; ed Leningrad Bonch-Bruyevich Electrical Inst. of Communications; engineer, Scientific-Production co. Mayak 1971–77; employee in nat. security orgs rising to Head of Div., Dept of Fed. Service of Security of St Petersburg and Leningrad region 1977–94, Head of Dept 1998, Deputy Dir, concurrently Head of Dept of Econ. Security 1999–2000; Head of Admin, Office of Mayor of St Petersburg 1994–98; Deputy Head of Admin, Office of the Pres. 2000–04; Adviser to the Pres. 2004–08; Dir Federal Drug Control Service 2008–; participated in mil. operations in Afghanistan 1987–94; Medal for Mil. Service, Order for the Merits to the Motherland (2nd and 4th degree), Order of Honour. *Address:* Federal Drug Control Service of the Russian Federation, 101968 Moscow, Maroseyka st. 12, Russia (office). *Telephone:* (495) 621-43-91 (office). *Website:* fskn.gov.ru/eng.shtml (office).

IVANOV, Vyacheslav Vsevolodovich, DPhil; Russian philologist, translator and academic; *Professor, Slavic Languages and Literatures and Professor, Indo-European Studies Program, Department of Slavic Languages and Literature, University of California, Los Angeles;* b. 21 Aug. 1929, Moscow; s. of Vsevolod Vyacheslavovich Ivanov; m.; one s.; ed Moscow State Univ., Univ. of Vilnius; Dir Library of Foreign Literature, Moscow 1991–94; People's Deputy of the USSR 1989–91; Dir Inst. of World Culture 1990–94; Prof., Dept of Slavic Languages and Literatures, UCLA 1994–; Ed.-in-Chief Baltic and Slavic Studies 1980–, Elementa: Journal of Slavic Studies and Comparative Cultural Semiotics 1992–; mem. Int. Editorial Bd Interdisciplinary Journal of Germanic Linguistics and Semiotic Analysis 1996–; mem. Advisory Bd Eisenstein Center of Cinema Cultural Studies 1993–; mem. Council of Scholars, Library of Congress 1990–, Russian Acad. of Natural Sciences 1991–, Russian PEN Club 1992–, American Acad. of Arts and Sciences 1993–, Russian Acad. of Sciences 2000–; Fellow, Latvian Acad. of Arts

and Sciences 1993–, American Philosophical Soc. 1994–; Foreign Fellow, British Acad. 1977–; Hon. mem. American Linguistics Soc. 1968; Lenin Prize 1988, Best Zvezda Publication, St Petersburg 1995. *Publications:* works on Indo-European linguistics, Slavic and general linguistics, semiotics, including: Indo-European, Praslavic and Anatolian Linguistic Systems 1965, Slavic Linguistic Modelling Systems (with V. Toporov) 1965, Studies in the Field of Slavic Antiquities (with V. Toporov) 1974, Indo-European Language and Indo-Europeans Vols 1-2 (with T. Gamrekelidze) 1984, Balkan Peninsula in the Mediterranean Context 1986, The Ethnolinguistics of the Text 1988, The Category of Passivity in Slavic and Balkan Languages 1989, Novelties in Linguistics 1990, The Hittite Language 2001; ed. works on Balto-slavic spiritual culture. *Address:* Department of Slavic Languages and Literatures and Indo-European Studies Program, UCLA, 2514 Hershey Hall, Box 951502, Los Angeles, CA 90095-1502, USA (office). *Telephone:* (310) 825-6397 (office). *Fax:* (310) 206-5263 (office). *E-mail:* ivanov@ucla.edu (office). *Website:* www.humnet.ucla.edu/humnet/slavic (office).

IVANOVA, Ludmila Nikolayevna, MD; Russian physiologist; *Head of Laboratory, Institute of Cytology and Genetics, Siberian Branch, Russian Academy of Sciences;* b. 10 Feb. 1929, Novosibirsk; ed Novosibirsk Inst. of Medicine; Head of Lab., Inst. of Cytology and Genetics, Siberian br., Russian Acad. of Sciences 1971–; Corresp. mem. Russian Acad. of Sciences 1991, mem. 1997–; main research in the hormonal regulation of water–salt metabolism and kidney function; L.A. Orbeli Award, Russian Acad. of Sciences. *Publications:* contribs to journals include (with N. N. Melidi) Effects of vasopressin on hyaluronate hydrolase activities and water permeability in the frog urinary bladder, in Pflugers-Archiv European Journal of Physiology, Vol. 443, No. 1, 2001; (with others) Effect of an increase in brain serotonin on the osmoregulatory response to a hypo- or hyperosmotic load in wistar and vasopressin-deficient Brattleboro rats, in Neuroendocrinology, Vol. 85, No. 4, 2007, (with others) Reduced Walker 256 carcinosarcoma growth in vasopressin-deficient Brattleboro rats, in Tumor Biology, Vol. 31, No. 3, 2010. *Leisure interests:* music, cookery. *Address:* Institute of Cytology and Genetics, Akademika Lavretyeva prosp. 10, 630090 Novosibirsk 90, Russia (office). *Telephone:* (383) 330-74-74 (office); (383) 330-79-02 (home). *Fax:* (383) 333-12-78 (office). *E-mail:* ludiv@bionet.nsc.ru (office). *Website:* www.bionet.nsc.ru/ICIG (office).

IVANOVIĆ, Predrag, DOec.; Montenegrin academic and government official; b. 10 Oct. 1954, Danilovgrad; m.; three c.; ed Univ. of Montenegro, Podgorica; Research Fellow, Inst. for Social and Econ. Research 1978–; Asst, then Assoc., then full Prof., Univ. of Montenegro Faculty of Econs 1993–, fmr Vice-Dean for Scientific Research and Head of Business Econs Dept, twice elected as Dean of Faculty of Econs, twice elected as Vice-Pres. of the Univ. of Montenegro; Minister of Educ. and Science 2001–03, of Int. Econ. Relations 2003–06; currently Dir Montenegro Investment Promotion Agency (MIPA). *Publications:* several books and research papers. *Address:* Montenegrin Investment Promotion Agency (MIPA), Jovana Tomasevica 2A, 81000 Podgorica, Montenegro (office). *Telephone:* (81) 203141 (office). *E-mail:* info@mipa.co.me (office). *Website:* www.mipa.co.me (office).

IVANOVSKI, Trendafil, PhD, DrIur; Macedonian judge; b. 1946, Badilen, Strumica Municipality; ed Iustinianus Primus Faculty of Law, Skopje; Sec., Legis. Comm., Sobranie (Parl.) 1969–72; Adviser, Nat. Secr. for Legislation and Org. 1972–77; Sec., Municipality of Karpos 1977–82, Sec., City of Skopje 1982–93; State Adviser, Constitutional Court 1993–2003, Judge 2003–, Pres. 2007–10; fmr Sec. and Pres. Macedonian Lawyers Asscn; fmr Pres., Council for Political System of Macedonian Municipalities and Cities; fmr Sec., Nat. Union of Students of Macedonia. *Address:* Constitutional Court (Ustaven Sud na Republika Makedonija), 1000 Skopje, 12 Udarna brig. 2, Macedonia (office). *Telephone:* (2) 3119355 (office). *Fax:* (2) 3119355 (office). *E-mail:* mail@ustavensud.mk (office). *Website:* www.ustavensud.mk (office).

ĪVĀNS, Dainis; Latvian journalist and politician; b. 25 Sept. 1955, Madona; s. of Evalds Ivans and Ilga Ivans; m. Elvira Chrschenovitch 1979; two s. two d.; ed Latvian Univ.; reporter, Latvian TV 1980–85; organized opposition to hydro-electric scheme nr Daugavpils 1986; Ed. School and Family magazine 1986–88; Pres. Latvian People's Front 1988–90; USSR People's Deputy 1989–90; mem. Latvian Supreme Soviet 1990–93, Vice-Chair. 1990–91; Chair. Latvian Social Democratic Workers' Party 2002–05; Gen. Sec. Latvian Comm. of UNESCO 1992–; Sec. Writers Union 1994–; Chair. Riga Council Culture, Art and Religion Cttee 2001–; Deputy Head, Latvian Literature Museum, Riga City Council, Chair. Comm. of Environment; Three Star Order of Repub. of Latvia 1994, Recognition Cross 2008; Best Journalist of the Year, Latvian Journalistic Union 1987. *Television:* several documentary serials on Latvian TV1. *Publications:* six books. *Leisure interests:* Oriental philosophy, literature, fishing. *Address:* Zvaigznu Str. 20, Apt 6, Riga, Latvia (home). *Telephone:* (2) 26554414 (office); (2) 62746441 (home). *E-mail:* dainis.ivans@riga.lv. *Website:* www.riga.lv (office).

IVANTER, Ernest Viktorovich; Russian biologist and academic; *Professor and Chairman, Department of Zoology and Ecology, Petrozavodsk University;* b. 15 Nov. 1935, Moscow; s. of Victor S. Ivanter and Irina F. Riss; m. Tatyana Matusevich 1960; one s. one d.; ed Moscow K. Timiryazev Acad. of Agric.; jr researcher, Kivach Karelian Br. USSR Acad. of Sciences 1958–60; jr researcher, Inst. of Biology, Karelian Br. of USSR Acad. of Sciences 1960–63; Asst, Docent, Prof., Dean Petrozavodsk Univ. 1965–; Chair. Dept of Zoology and Ecology, Petrozavodsk Univ. 1987–; Corresp. mem. USSR (now Russian) Acad. of Sciences 1991; mem. Scientific Council for Biological Fundamentals of Protection and Rational Use of Fauna; mem. US Zoological Soc.; Hon. mem. Finnish Soc. of Teriologues. *Publications* include: Population Ecology of Small Mammals 1975, Adaptive Peculiarities of Mammals 1985, Fauna of Karelia 1988, Statistical Methods for Biologists 1992, Zoogeography 1993, Territorial Ecology of Shrews 2002; numerous articles in scientific journals on ecology, biocenology, morpho-physiology and evolutional ecology of animals. *Leisure interests:* books, sport, tourism. *Address:* Room #327, Petrozavodsk University, Krasnoarmeiskaya str. 31, 185910 Petrozavodsk (office); ul. Anohina la Kv. 5, 185035 Petrozavodsk, Russia (home). *Telephone:* (8142) 78-17-41 (office); (8142) 78-21-08 (home). *Fax:* (8142) 76-38-64 (office). *E-mail:* ivanter@psu.karelia.ru (office). *Website:* www .karelia.ru/psu/Chairs/zool_e.html (office).

IVANY, J. W. George, MA, PhD; Canadian academic and fmr university president; *President Emeritus, University of Saskatchewan;* b. 26 May 1938,

Grand Falls, Newfoundland; s. of Gordon Ivany and Stella Skinner; m. Marsha Gregory 1983; one s. three d.; ed Memorial Univ. of Newfoundland, Columbia Univ., New York and Univ. of Alberta; Head of Science Dept, Prince of Wales Coll., St John's, Newfoundland 1960–63; Grad. Teaching Fellow, Univ. of Alberta 1963–64; Asst Prof. of Elementary Educ. 1965–66; Asst Prof. of Natural Science, Teachers Coll., Columbia Univ. 1966–68, Assoc. Prof. 1968–74, Head, Dept of Science Educ. 1972–74; Visiting Fellow, Inst. of Educ., Univ. of London, UK 1972–73; Dean and Prof., Faculty of Educ., Memorial Univ. of Newfoundland 1974–77; Dean and Prof., Faculty of Educ., Simon Fraser Univ. 1977–84, Vice-Pres. (Academic) 1984–89; Pres. and Vice-Chancellor, Univ. of Sask. 1989–99, Pres. Emer. 1999–; Chair. Bd Nat. Inst. of Nutrition 1995–98; mem. Bd of Dirs Cameco Corpn 1999–, Western Garnet Int., Canada West Foundation; Chair. Bd of Govs Okanagan Univ. Coll., Kelowna, BC 2001–04; Chair. Ivany Comm., Grenfell Coll., Memorial Univ. 2005; Hon. LLD (Memorial Univ. Newfoundland) 1991, (Univ. of Chernivtsi, Ukraine). Publications include: High School Teaching: A Report on Current Practices 1972, Today's Science: A Professional Approach to Teaching Elementary School Science 1975, Who's Afraid of Spiders: Teaching Science in the Elementary School 1988; textbooks; articles in professional journals. Address: c/o Board of Directors, Cameco Corporation, 2121 11th Street West, Saskatoon, Sask., S7M 1J3, Canada.

IVANYAN, Eduard Aleksandrovich, DHist; Russian journalist and political scientist; Editor-in-Chief, USA and Canada: Economics, Politics and Culture, Institute for USA and Canadian Studies, Russian Academy of Sciences; b. 4 June 1931, Tbilisi, Georgia; two d.; ed Moscow State Inst. of Int. Relations; mem. staff, Ministry of Culture 1955–60, UN Sec., Geneva and New York 1961–71; Head of Sector, Prof., Inst. for USA and Canadian Studies, USSR (now Russian) Acad. of Sciences 1971–, Ed.-in-Chief USA and Canada: Economics, Politics and Culture (monthly journal) 1998–; Prof., State Univ. for Humanitarian Sciences 2000–; Order of the Friendship of Nations; Distinguished Scholar of the Russian Fed. 1999. Publications: more than 100 scientific publs, including 25 books on the history of USA, presidential power in USA, Russian (Soviet)-American relations, Russian-American cultural relations, including 'Istoriya SShA.' Uchebnoye posobiye. 2 e izdaniye, pererabotannoye (The History of the USA: A Study Aid, 2nd edn, revised) 2006, U istokov sovetsko-amerikanskikh otnoshenii, fevral 1917 g.-yanvar 1924 g. (Among the Sources of Soviet-American Relations, February 1917 to January 1924) 2006, Reader on US History (ed.) 2005, Inaugural Speeches of US Presidents (ed.) 2001, John F. Kennedy's 'Profiles in Courage' (trans. and ed.) 2005, David Rockefeller's 'Memoirs' (ed. of Russian trans.) 2003, When Muses Speak – History of Russian-American Cultural Relations 2007. Address: USA–Canada Journal, Khlebny per. 2/3, 121814 Moscow, Russia (office). Telephone: (495) 690-46-80 (office). Fax: (495) 609-95-07 (office). E-mail: edivanian@yahoo.com (office). Website: www.iskran.ru (office).

IVASHCHENKO, Valeriy; Ukrainian army officer and politician; b. 30 June 1956, Zaporizhzhya; m.; two c.; ed A.F. Mozhayskiy Mil. Eng Acad., St Petersburg, F.E. Dzerzhinsky Mil. Acad., Moscow; mil. service on Baikonur space port 1978–93; various roles at Armament HQ, Ministry of Defence 1993–95; Head of Admin. Control Group, Ministry of Defence Strategic Nuclear Forces 1995–96, worked in Cabinet Defence Mobilization Agency and Law Enforcement Agency 1996–2000, State Nat. Security Expert, Nat. Security and Defence Council 2000–01, Chief of Dept, State Mil.-Industrial Comm. 2001–03, Head of Mil.-Industrial Policy in Office of the Cabinet of Ministers 2003–05, Deputy Chief of Industrial Policy Agency in Office of the Cabinet of Ministers 2005, Deputy Chief of Security and Defence Policy and Head of Dept of Defence in Office of the Pres. 2005–07, Deputy Minister of Defence 2007–09, Acting Minister of Defence 2009–10; Combat Merit Medal, Order of Danilo Galitskiy. Address: c/o Ministry of Defence, vul. M. Hrushevskoho 30/1, 01021 Kyiv, Ukraine (office).

IVASHENTSOV, Gleb A.; Russian diplomatist; Deputy Director, Russian Centre for APEC Studies; b. 7 June 1945, St Petersburg; s. of Alexandre Ivashentsov and Zinaida Studenikova; m.; one d.; ed Moscow State Inst. of Int. Relations, Diplomatic Acad.; served at Ministry of Foreign Trade and Int. Dept, Cen. Cttee, CP of the Soviet Union 1967–75, First Sec. USSR Embassy in Delhi 1975–81, Counsellor, Head of Section, S Asia Dept, USSR Ministry of Foreign Affairs 1981–83, Head of Section 1985–91, Consul Gen. in Mumbai 1991–95, First Deputy Dir Third Asia Dept, Russian Ministry of Foreign Affairs 1995–97, Amb. to Myanmar 1997–2001, Dir-Gen. Third, Second Asia Dept 2001–05, Amb. to Repub. of Korea 2005–09, Deputy Dir Russian Centre for APEC Studies, Moscow 2010–; Special Research Fellow, China Centre for Contemporary World Studies; Order of Friendship 2003, Khanhwa Medal for Diplomatic Merit (South Korea) 2009. Publications: India 1988, Beyond the Fortifications of 38th Parallel (in Russian and Korean) 2012. Leisure interests: swimming, boating, reading, music. Address: Russian Centre for APEC Studies, 119034 Moscow, Prechistenskaya nab., Russia (office). E-mail: ivagleb1@googlemail.com (office). Website: www.apec-center.ru (office).

IVASHOV, Col-Gen. Leonid Grigoryevich, CandHistSc; Russian business executive and security officer; President, Academy of Geopolitics; b. 1943, m.; ed Tashkent Commdr School, M. Frunze Mil. Acad.; army service 1964, various positions 1964–76; with cen. staff, Ministry of Defence 1976–, Head Admin. Dept 1987–92; Sec. Council of Defence Ministers, CIS Countries 1992–96; Head of Dept, Int. Mil. Co-operation 1996–2001, Head of Staff, Co-ordination of Mil. Co-operation, CIS Countries 1999–2001; Adviser to Minister of Defence 2001–03; mem. Leadership, Great Russia–Eurasian Union electoral bloc, State Duma elections 2003; Chair. Soyuz russkogo naroda (Russian People's Union) 2006–; Vice-Pres. Acad. of Geopolitics 2002–11, now Pres.; Order Red Star; six medals. Website: www.ivashov.ru.

IVE, Sir Jonathan, Kt, KBE, CBE, BA; British designer; Senior Vice-President of Industrial Design, Apple Inc.; b. 1967, London; m. Heather Pegg; two s.; ed Newcastle Polytechnic; Co-founder and Partner, Tangerine (design consultancy), London 1989; Designer, Apple Inc., Cupertino, Calif., USA 1992, Dir of Design 1996, then Vice-Pres. of Industrial Design, now Sr Vice-Pres., designed the iMac 1998, iPod 2001, iPhone 2007, iPad 2010; Dr hc (Northumbria Univ.) 2000; winner of design influence polls by Creative Review, the BBC and Q magazine; RSA student design awards 1988, 1989, RSA Medal for Design Achievement 1999, apptd RSA Designer for Industry 2003, Design Museum Designer of the Year 2003,

RSA Benjamin Franklin Medal 2005, Pres.'s Medal, Royal Acad. of Eng 2005, Pres.'s Award, Design and Art Direction (D&AD) 2005. Address: Apple, 1 Infinite Loop, Cupertino, CA 95014, USA (office). Telephone: (408) 996-1010 (office). Website: www.apple.com (office).

IVENS, Martin Paul; British journalist; Editor, The Sunday Times; b. 29 Aug. 1958, London; s. of the late Michael Ivens; m. Anne McElvoy; two s. one d.; ed St Peter's Coll., Oxford; Deputy Ed. The Sunday Times 1996–2013, Acting Ed. Jan.–Sept. 2013, Ed. Sept. 2013–, also Political Columnist 2007–; fmr mem. Bd of Dirs Social Market Foundation. Address: The Sunday Times, 3 Thomas More Square, London, E98 1RL, England (office). Telephone: (20) 7782-5000 (office). E-mail: newsdesk@sunday-times.co.uk (office). Website: www.sunday-times.co.uk (office).

IVERSEN, Leslie (Les) Lars, CBE, BA, PhD, FRS; British pharmacologist, academic and business executive; Chairman, ACADIA Pharmaceuticals, Inc.; b. 31 Oct. 1937; s. of Svend Iversen and Anna Caia Iversen; m. Susan Diana Iversen (née Kibble) 1961; one s. one d. (one d. deceased); ed Cambridge, Harkness Fellow, USA; with Nat. Inst. of Mental Health and Dept of Neurobiology, Harvard Medical School 1964–66; Locke Research Fellow of Royal Soc., Dept of Pharmacology, Cambridge 1967–71, Dir MRC Neurochemical Pharmacology Unit 1971–82; Exec. Dir Merck, Sharp and Dohme Neuroscience Research Centre 1982–95; Visiting Prof., Dept of Pharmacology, Univ. of Oxford 1995–; Visiting Prof. of Pharmacology, Imperial Coll. School of Medicine 1997–; Prof. of Pharmacology and Dir Wolfson Centre for Age-Related Diseases, King's Coll., London 1999–2004; Interim Chair. Advisory Council on the Misuse of Drugs, UK Home Office 2010, Chair. 2011–; Founder and Dir Panos Therapeutics Ltd (pharmaceutical co.); mem. Bd of Dirs ACADIA Pharmaceuticals, Inc. 1998– (Chair. 2000–), NsGene A/S; mem. Scientific Advisory Bd Lectus Therapeutics Ltd, NeuroTargets Ltd, Neurome, Inc.; Fellow, Trinity Coll., Cambridge 1964–84; Foreign Assoc., NAS 1986. Publications: The Uptake and Storage of Noradrenaline in Sympathetic Nerves (with S. D. Iversen) 1967, Behavioural Pharmacology 1975, The Science of Marijuana 2000, A Very Short Introduction to Drugs 2001, Speed, Ecstasy and Ritalin: The Science of Amphetamines 2006. Leisure interests: reading, gardening. Address: ACADIA Pharmaceuticals, Inc., 3911 Sorrento Valley Blvd, San Diego, CA 92121, USA (office). Telephone: (858) 558-2871 (office). Fax: (858) 558-2872 (office). E-mail: info@acadia-pharm.com (office). Website: www.acadia-pharm.com (office).

IVERSON, Allen; American fmr professional basketball player; b. 7 June 1975, Hampton, Va; m. Tawanna Iverson; two s. two d.; ed Bethel High School, Hampton Univ., Georgetown Univ., Washington, DC; shooting guard; played at Georgetown Univ. 1994–96; selected by Philadelphia 76ers with first overall pick in 1996 Nat. Basketball Asscn (NBA) draft, traded to Denver Nuggets 2006–08, to Detroit Pistons 2008–09, signed with Memphis Grizzlies 2009, signed with Philadelphia 76ers 2009, with Besiktas Cola Turka (Turkey) 2010–11; career scoring average of nearly 28 points per game is third best in NBA history; one of only 30 players to score more than 20,000 career points; scored 40 points in a game for 50th time versus Seattle 19 Feb. 2004; served as a Co-Capt. for Team USA Olympic Games, Athens, Greece 2004, won bronze medal and led team in scoring (13.8 points per game); named to All-Star Team ten times, named Most Valuable Player (MVP) of All-Star Game 2001, 2005; NBA MVP 2001; f. Cross-Over Foundation 2000. Leisure interest: drawing. Website: www.alleniverson.pro; www.crossoverfoundation.org.

IVEY, Susan M., BS, MBA; American tobacco industry executive; b. (Susan Hickok), 31 Oct. 1958, Schenectady, NY; m.; ed Fort Lauderdale High School, Univ. of Florida, Bellarmine Univ.; sales rep., Brown & Williamson Tobacco Corpn (subsidiary of British American Tobacco—BAT) 1981, held various trade and brand positions, including Div. Man. and Brand Dir, Marketing Dir for BAT in China 1994–96, returned to Brown & Williamson in 1999, later Sr Vice-Pres. Marketing and mem. Exec. Cttee, Pres. and CEO Brown & Williamson Tobacco Corpn 2001–04, Pres. and CEO Reynolds American Inc. (following merger with R.J. Reynolds Tobacco Holdings Inc.) 2004–11, Chair. 2006–11, Chair. and CEO R.J. Reynolds Tobacco Co. 2004–08; mem. Exec. Cttee Bellarmine Univ. and Greater Louisville Inc.; Campaign Chair. Greater Metro United Way of Louisville 2003; mem. The Committee of 200 (int. org. of women CEOs, entrepreneurs and business leaders), Women's Leadership Initiative for the United Way of America; mem. Bd Winston-Salem YWCA, Bd Bellarmine Univ., Wake Forest Univ., Univ. of Florida Foundation; mem. Bd of Dirs RR Donnelley 2009–; mem. Advisory Bd of Dirs Wachovia Forsyth Co., Bd of Advisors for Center for Women in Business and Econs at Salem Coll.; ranked by Fortune magazine amongst the 50 Most Powerful Women in Business in the US (36th) 2004, (24th) 2005, (20th) 2006, (24th) 2007, (23rd) 2008, (26th) 2009, (22nd) 2010, ranked by Forbes magazine amongst The World's 100 Most Powerful Women (61st) 2006, (42nd) 2007, (81st) 2008, (59th) 2009, (75th) 2010, ranked 33rd by Financial Times in its Top 50 Women in World Business 2009.

IVORY, James Francis, MFA; American film director; b. 7 June 1928, Berkeley, Calif.; s. of the late Edward Patrick Ivory and Hallie Millicent De Loney; ed Univs of Oregon and Southern California; began to work independently as a film maker 1952; dir, writer and cameraman in first films; co-f. (with the late Ismail Merchant) Merchant Ivory Productions 1962; has collaborated on screenplay of numerous films with author Ruth Prawer Jhabvala; Guggenheim Fellow 1974; BAFTA Fellowship 2002; Commdr des Arts et des Lettres 1995; D. W. Griffith Award (Dirs Guild of America) 1995. Films: documentaries: Venice, Theme and Variations 1957, The Sword and the Flute 1959, The Delhi Way 1964; feature films: The Householder 1963, Shakespeare Wallah 1965, The Guru 1969, Bombay Talkie 1970, Savages 1972, The Wild Party 1975, Roseland 1977, The Europeans 1979, Quartet 1981, Heat and Dust 1983, The Bostonians 1984, A Room with a View 1986, Maurice 1987, Slaves of New York 1989, Mr and Mrs Bridge 1990, Howards End 1992, The Remains of the Day 1993, Jefferson in Paris 1995, Surviving Picasso 1996, A Soldier's Daughter Never Cries 1998, The Golden Bowl 2000, Le Divorce 2003, The White Countess 2005, City of Your Final Destination 2008; TV films: Adventures of a Brown Man in Search of Civilisation 1971, Autobiography of a Princess 1975 (also published as a book 1975), Hullabaloo over Georgie and Bonnie's Pictures 1978, The Five Forty-Eight 1979, Jane Austen in Manhattan 1980. Leisure interest: looking at pictures. Address: Merchant Ivory Productions, 250 West 57th Street, New York, NY 10107 (office); 18 Patroon Street, Claverack,

NY 12513, USA. *Telephone:* (212) 582-8049 (office); (518) 851-7808 (home). *E-mail:* assistant@merchantivory.com (office).

IVRY, Maj.-Gen. (retd) David, BS; Israeli business executive, diplomatist and fmr military officer; *President, Boeing Israel;* b. 20 Sept. 1934, Tel-Aviv; m. Ofra Ivry; three s.; ed Technion-Israel Inst. of Tech., Haifa; Chief Rep. US–Israel Strategic Dialogue 1986–89; Dir-Gen. Ministry of Defence 1986–96, Prin. Asst Minister of Defence for Strategic Affairs 1996–99; Head, Nat. Security Council 1999, Nat. Security Adviser to Head of Nat. Security Council 1999–2000; Amb. to USA 2000–02; Pres. Boeing Israel 2003–; Chair. Elul Asia and Global Outsourcing Services 2002–03; Head of Inter-Ministerial Steering Cttee on Arms Control and Regional Security of the Middle East Peace Process 1992–99; Head of Israeli Del. to Multilateral Working Group on Arms Control and Regional Security 1992–99; mem. Bd of Dirs El-Al 1978–82, Israel Aircraft Industries 1982–92 (Chair. 1983, 1985–86); mem. Bd of Govs Technion, Haifa 1987–; Maj.-Gen., Commdr Israel Air Force 1977–82, Israeli Defence Forces Deputy Chief of Staff 1983–85; USAF Legion of Merit, Distinguished Service Order (Singapore), Kt Commdr's Cross, Order of Merit (FRG); Dr hc (Bar-Ilan, Technion, Haifa); Amitai Distinction Award for Ethical Admin and Conduct, Israel. *Address:* The Boeing Company, The Museum Tower, 4 Berkowitz Street, Tel-Aviv 64238 (office); 6 Hazamir Street, Ramat Hasharon 47226, Israel (home). *Telephone:* (3) 7776100 (office); (3) 5406085 (home). *Fax:* (3) 7776101 (office); (3) 5499183 (home). *E-mail:* david.e.ivry@boeing .com (office). *Website:* www.boeing.com (office).

IWAN, Dafydd, BArch; British politician, singer-composer and record company director; *Director, Sain (Recordiau) Cyf;* b. (Dafydd Iwan Jones), 24 Aug. 1943, Brynaman, Wales; s. of Rev. Gerallt Jones and Elizabeth Jane Jones; m. 1st Marion Thomas 1968 (divorced 1986); two s. one d.; m. 2nd Bethan Jones 1988; two s.; ed Aman Valley Grammar School, Ysgol Ty Tan Domen, Y Bala, Univ. Coll. of Wales, Aberystwyth and Welsh School of Architecture, Cardiff; f. Sain (Recordiau) Cyf (now Wales' leading record co.) 1969, Man. Dir 1984–2006, currently Dir; f. Tai Gwynedd Housing Asscn 1971; Founder-Trustee, Nant Gwrtheyrn Language Centre 1975; Chair. Welsh Language Soc. 1968–71; parl. cand. 1974, 1983, 1984; Chair. Plaid Cymru (Nationalist Party of Wales) 1982–84, Vice-Pres. 1984–95, Pres. 2003–10; Plaid Cymru mem. of Gwynedd Unitary Authority 1995–2008; Chair. Planning and Economic Devt Cttee, Cyngor Gwynedd Council 1995–99, mem. Exec. Cttee responsible for Planning, Highways and Environment 1999–2003, Econ. Devt and Educ. 2003–08; Chair. Gwynedd Econ. Partnership 2008–; Trustee, Portmeirion Foundation, Carers Outreach, Plas Glyn-y-Weddw Gallery; nonconformist lay preacher; has promoted the Welsh language and culture for five decades; Hon. mem. Gorsedd of Bards for services to Welsh language; Hon. Fellow, Univs of Bangor and Aberystwyth for services to Welsh culture and Welsh music 1998; Hon. LLD (Univ. of Wales) 2004; Gold Disc for services to Welsh music. *Music:* composed, sung and recorded more than 250 songs; more than 40 albums and videos 1965–2010; numerous concert tours abroad. *Television:* Yma Mae Ngân, S4C (several series introducing own songs), documentaries on various countries. *Publications:* Dafydd Iwan (autobiog.) 1982, 100 O Ganeuon (collection of songs) 1983, Caneuon Dafydd Iwan (second collection of songs) 1991, Cân Dros Gymru (autobiog.) 2002, Dafydd Iwan: Bywyd mewn lluniau (A Life in Pictures) 2005. *Leisure interests:* composing songs, sketching, reading. *Address:* Sain, Canolfan Sain, Llandwrog, Caernarfon, Gwynedd, LL54 5TG (office); Carrog, Rhos-Bach, Caeathro, Caernarfon, Gwynedd, LL55 2TF, Wales (home). *Telephone:* (1286) 676004 (home); 7984-202922 (mobile). *E-mail:* dafyddiwan@cymru1.net (home); dafydd@sainwales.com (office). *Website:* www .sainwales.com (office); www.dafyddiwan.com (home).

IWASAKI, Yoichi, BS, MS, PhD; Japanese theoretical physicist, fmr university administrator and academic; *Professor Emeritus, University of Tsukuba;* b. 12 Sept. 1941; ed Univ. of Tokyo; Asst, Research Inst. for Fundamental Physics, Kyoto Univ. 1969–72; Postdoctoral Fellow, Dept of Physics, CUNY, USA 1972–75; Asst Prof., Inst. of Physics, Univ. of Tsukuba 1975–76, Assoc. Prof. 1976–77, Prof. 1984–98, Prof. Emer. 1998–, Vice-Pres. (Research) 1998–2004, Pres. Univ. of Tsukuba 2004–09; mem. Inst. for Advanced Study, Princeton, USA 1977; mem. Physical Soc. of Japan; Nishina Memorial Prize, Nishina Memorial Foundation 1994. *Publications:* numerous publs on high-energy physics, in particular large-scale numerical study of quantum chromodynamics and the devt of massively parallel computers for computational physics. *Address:* University of Tsukuba, 1-1-1 Tennodai, Tsukuba-shi, Ibaraki -ken 305-8577, Japan (office). *Telephone:* (29) 853-2111 (office). *Fax:* (29) 853-2059 (office). *Website:* www.tsukuba.ac.jp (office).

IYANDA, (Olufunmilola Aduke) Funmi, BSc; Nigerian television presenter and journalist; *CEO, Ignite Media;* b. 27 July 1971; one d.; ed Herbert Macaulay School, Lagos, Univ. of Ibadan; sports journalist for female Football World Cup 1999, Olympic Games in Sydney 2000, Athens 2004; Man. Dir Funmi Iyanda Productions 2004–08; CEO Ignite Media, Lagos 2008–; participant, ASPEN Inst. Forum for Communications and Society; mem. Nigerian Football Asscn 1995–2003; mem. Bd of Dirs Farafina Trust, Positive Impact Youth Network; Tutu Fellow, African Leadership Inst.; columnist, Tempo Magazine; Nigeria Media Merit Award 2005, Glass Ceiling Breaker Award, Women Writer's Asscn of Nigeria, Jewel of the Future Award, African Cultural Inst., Media Woman of The Year, City People; named Young Global Leader by World Econ. Forum 2011. *Television includes:* Good Morning Nigeria, New Dawn with Funmi 2000–08, Talk with Funmi 2010. *Telephone:* (1) 8940988 (office). *E-mail:* info@ignitemediang.com (office). *Website:* www.ignitemediang.com (office).

IYENGAR, B(ellur) K(rishnamachar) S(undara Raja); Indian yoga teacher and author; *Founder, Ramamani Iyengar Memorial Yoga Institute;* b. 14 Dec. 1918, Bellur, Kolar Dist, Karnataka; s. of Sri Krishnamachar; m. Shrimati Ramamani Iyengar 1943 (died 1973); one s. five d.; introduced to yoga by brother-in-law Guru Sri T. Krishnamacharya in Mysore 1934; gave several demonstrations of yoga and successfully completed a yoga teaching assignment at Dharwar for faculty mems of Karnataka Coll. 1936; yoga instructor, Deccan Gymkhana 1937–40; taught yoga to Shri J. Krishnamurthi 1948–68; introduced by violinist Yehudi Menuhin to the West and made numerous visits worldwide to promote yoga 1954–; developed his own system of yoga which has gained a worldwide following; laid foundation stone for Yoga Inst. in Pune 1973, Hon. Pres. Iyengar Yoga Asscns worldwide; gave lecture-demonstration at Harvard Coll., which inspired creation of monumental sculpture 'After Iyengar' 1976; invited by UK

Dept for Educ. to participate in Festival of India, London 1982; inaugurated Iyengar Yoga Inst., London 1984; first Int. Iyengar Yoga Convention held in San Francisco 1984; invited by Jacques Chirac, Mayor of Paris, to Festival of India in France 1985; conducted yoga classes organized by Govt of UP at Rishikesh 1994, 1995, 1996; has given more than 15,000 demonstrations of yoga and numerous lectures and radio and TV interviews; hundreds of Iyengar Yoga Centres give training in his method of yoga worldwide; involved in social, cultural, educational and health-promotion projects for the poor of India; Hon. Fellow, Int. Council of Ayurveda 1991; Dr hc (Univ. of Pennsylvania) 1988, (Medicina Alternativa Inst.) 2003; Hon. DSc, Mysore Univ. 1996, Hon. DLitt (Tilak Maharashtra Vidyapeeth, Pune) 2002; numerous awards including title of Yogi Raja 1948, Yoganga Shikshaka Chakravati 1962, Yogi Ratna Award 1981, 2002, Vasista Award 1989, Patanjali Award, Govt of Karnataka 1990, Padma Shree 1991, All India Vasistha Award 1991, Purna Swasthya Award, World Fed. of Socs of Holistic Medicine 1991, Vipra Ratna, Karnataka Brahman Mahasabha 1997, title of Arsa-Kula-Sresthah 1998, Jeevan Sadhana Gaurav, Pune Univ., Yoga Dron Award, World Yoga Soc. 1999, Priyadarshni Acad. Award 2000, Rishi Award 2001, Padma Bhushan 2002, included in Time Magazine list of most powerful people in the world 2004, 2005, Industrial Tech. Foundation Award 2004, Indira Gandhi Excellence Award, Indian Solidarity Council, New Delhi 2005, Golden Life Time Achievement Award, Industrial Tech. Foundation, Delhi 2005, Kasba Ganapati Award Puruskar Medal, Pune 2006, Yogiraj of Millennium Award, Inst. of Educ. Research and Devt in asscn with the 'Global Institutes' 2007, Padma Vibhushan 2014. *Achievements include:* Ministry of Fed. Star Registration (USA) announced that a star in the northern hemisphere had been named after Yogacharya B.K.S. Iyengar Aug. 1988. *Publications include:* Light on Yoga 1966, Light on Pranayama 1981, The Art of Yoga 1985, The Tree of Yoga 1988, Light on Astanga Yoga 1999, Astadala Yogamala Vols 1–8 2000–08, Yoga: The Path to Holistic Health 2001, Yog Sarvansathi (in Marathi) 2001, Light on Life 2005, Yaugika Manas 2009, Yoga Sutra Paricaya 2010. *Leisure interests:* listening to music, drama. *Address:* Ramamani Iyengar Memorial Yoga Institute, 1107 B/1 Hare Krishna Mandir Road, Model Colony, Shivaj Nagar, Pune 411 016, Maharashtra, India (office). *Telephone:* (20) 25656134 (office). *E-mail:* info@bksiyengar.com (office). *Website:* www.bksiyengar.com (office).

IZETBEGOVIĆ, Bakir; Bosnia and Herzegovina architect and politician; *Chairman of the State Presidency;* b. 28 June 1956, Sarajevo; s. of the late Bosnian Pres. Alija Izetbegović; m.; one d.; ed Univ. of Sarajevo; consultant with architectural consulting firm 1982–92; Dir Construction Bureau of Sarajevo Canton 1991–2003; mem. Party of Democratic Action (SDA), Chief of SDA Parl. Group, Sarajevo Canton Ass. 2000–02, Chief of SDA Parl. Group, House of Reps, Parl. Ass. of Fed. of Bosnia and Herzegovina 2002–06; Chief of SDA mems, Parl. Ass. of Council of Europe 2006–10; Bosniak mem. of Tripartite State Presidency of Bosnia and Herzegovina 2010–, Chair. March–Nov. 2012, March 2014–; fmr Dir FC Sarajevo, KK Bosna, Merhamet (Muslim humanitarian asscn); mem. Islamic Community Ass. *Address:* Office of the State Presidency, 71000 Sarajevo, Maršala Tita 16, Bosnia and Herzegovina (office). *Telephone:* (33) 567550 (office). *Fax:* (33) 556050 (office). *E-mail:* press@predsjednistvobih.ba (office). *Website:* www .predsjednistvobih.ba (office).

IZMEROV, Nikolay Fedotovich, MD, CandMedSci, PhD; Russian medical official and physician; *Director, Institute of Occupational Health, Russian Academy of Medical Sciences;* b. 19 Dec. 1927, Frunze, Kyrgyzstan; ed Tashkent Medical School and Moscow Cen. Inst. for Advanced Medical Training; worked as doctor in Khavast rural areas, Tashkent Dist; Postgraduate training, Moscow 1952–53; Sr Insp. USSR Ministry of Health 1953–55; Postgraduate training (Municipal Hygiene) 1955–58; doctor in Moscow City Sanitary Epidemiological Station 1956–59; Deputy Dir (Int. Health), Dept of External Relations, USSR Ministry of Health 1960–62; Vice-Minister of Health of RSFSR and Chief Sanitary Insp. 1962–64; Asst Dir-Gen. WHO 1964–71; Dir Inst. of Occupational Health of the USSR (now Russian) Acad. of Medical Sciences 1971–; Corresp. mem. Russian Acad. of Medical Sciences 1980, mem. 1986, Acad.-Sec. Dept of Preventive Medicine 1990–; Order of the Red Banner of Labour (twice), Order of October Revolution, Order for Merit to Home Country (4th Degree) 1997, (3rd Degree) 2002, (2nd Degree) 2007; Merited Scientist of Russia. *Publications:* author or co-author of 23 reference books, monographs, manuals and more than 400 scientific papers in the field of occupational hygiene and industrial ecology etc.; Chief Ed. Russian Encyclopaedia of Occupational Health 2005. *Leisure interest:* theatre, music, art. *Address:* Research Institute of Occupational Health, Russian Academy of Medical Sciences, 31 Prospekt Budennogo, 105275 Moscow, Russia (office). *Telephone:* (495) 365-02-09 (office). *Fax:* (495) 366-05-83 (office). *E-mail:* izmerov@ niimt.ru (office).

IZUMI, Shinya; Japanese politician; b. 1 Aug. 1937, Yoshii, Fukuoka; ed Kyushu Univ.; previously worked as official at transport ministry; mem. House of Councillors (Upper House) 1992–, has held numerous govt posts including Sr State Sec. of Transport, Sr Vice-Minister of Economy, Trade and Industry, Sr Vice-Minister of Land, Infrastructure and Transport; Chair. Nat. Public Safety Comm. and Minister of State for Disaster Man. and Food Safety 2007–08 (resgnd); mem. LDP (Liberal Democratic Party), left party 1993, rejoined 2003. *Address:* Liberal-Democratic Party (LDP), 1-11-23, Nagata-cho, Chiyoda-ku, Tokyo 100-8910, Japan (office). *Telephone:* (3) 3581-6211. *E-mail:* koho@ldp.jimin.or.jp (office). *Website:* www.jimin.jp (office).

IZZO, Lucio; Italian economist, academic and financial services industry executive; b. 5 April 1932, Rome; m. Marga Berg; two d.; ed Univ. of Oxford, UK and Massachusetts Inst. of Tech., USA; worked in Econ. Research Dept, Bank of Italy 1958–60, 1962–63; Rockefeller Fellow, Dept of Econs, MIT 1960–62; Asst Prof. of Econs, Univ. of Siena 1965–67, Assoc. Prof., then Prof. of Econs, Univ. of Siena 1967–74; Visiting Prof. of Econs, LSE 1971–72; Prof. of Econs, Univ. La Sapienza 1974–94; Econ. Adviser to Minister of the Budget 1974–78, to Minister of the Treasury 1980–82; Vice-Pres. and Vice-Chair. EIB 1982–94; mem. Bd of Dirs Efibanca SpA 1995–99, Società Interbancaria di Gestione 1996–98, Stet SpA 1997–99, Telecom Italia SpA 1997–99, Italian Rep. OECD Working Party 3 1973–79; mem. EEC Monetary Cttee 1981–82; mem. American Econ. Asscn, American Finance Asscn, Econometric Soc.; Pres. of Italy's Gold Medal for studies in field of public finance 1978. *E-mail:* lucio@lucioizzo.it. *Website:* www.lucioizzo.it.

JAAFAR ALBAR, Tan Sri Syed Hamid; Malaysian lawyer and politician; *Chairman, Land Public Transport Commission;* b. 15 Jan. 1944, Penang; m. Sharifah Aziah; three s. three d.; ed Monash Univ., Melbourne, Australia, Middle Temple, UK; Magistrate and Pres. of Sessions Court, Kuala Lumpur 1970–72; Head of Legal Dept, Bank Bumiputra Malaysia Bhd (BBMB) 1972, Legal Adviser and later Sr Man. 1972–78, Asst Sec. and Sec. to Man. 1974–79, first Gen. Man. of Bahrain Br. 1979–80, Gen. Man. of London Br., transferred to Kuala Lumpur as Head of Int. Banking Div. (Credit Supervision) 1980–82, Chief Gen. Man. and Sec. of the Bank 1985–86; Sec. Kewangan Bumiputra and Bank Pembangunan Malaysia Bhd 1976–79, Inst. of Bankers 1978–79; Dir and CEO Bumiputra Merchant Bankers 1982–85; Dir Koperasi Usaha Bersatu 1983–88, Kewangan Bumiputra Malaysia Bhd, Bumiputra Lloyds Leasing Bhd, Bumiputra Merchant Bankers, Syarikat Nominee Sdn Bhd, BBMB Properties 1985–86; Advocate and Solicitor-Gen. Pnr, Albar Zulkifly and Yap 1986–90; Chair. Shamelin Holdings 1989–90, Koperasi Shamelin Bhd 1989–90; MP for Kota Tinggi (Johor) 1990; Minister of Justice in Prime Minister's Dept (in charge of oil and gas affairs) 1990–92; Minister of Law and Minister in Prime Minister's Dept 1992–95; Minister of Defence 1995–99, of Foreign Affairs 1999–2008, of Home Affairs and Internal Security 2008–09; Chair. Land Public Transport Comm. 2010–. *Address:* Suruhanjaya Pengangkutan Awam Darat Headquarters, Level 19, 1 Sentral, Jalan Travers, Kuala Lumpur Sentral, 50470 Kuala Lumpur, Malaysia. *Telephone:* 2268-5782 (office). *Website:* www.spad.gov.my (office); www.syedhamidalbar.net.

JA'AFARI, Bashar, BA, PhD; Syrian diplomatist; *Permanent Representative, United Nations;* b. 14 April 1956, Damascus; m.; three c.; ed Damascus Univ., Univ. of Paris V-Sorbonne, Univ. of Sharif Hedayatuallah, Jakarta; joined Ministry of Foreign Affairs 1980, Attaché and Third Sec., Embassy in Paris 1983–88; First Sec. and Counsellor, Perm. Mission to UN, New York 1991–94; Chargé d'affaires a.i., Embassy in Jakarta 1998–2002; Dir Dept of Int. Orgs and Confs, Ministry of Foreign Affairs 2002–04; Amb. and Perm. Rep. to UN, Geneva 2004–06, to UN, New York 2006–. *Address:* Permanent Mission of Syria to the United Nations, 820 Second Avenue, 15th Floor, New York, NY 10017, USA (office). *Telephone:* (212) 661-1313 (office). *Fax:* (212) 983-4439 (office). *E-mail:* exesec.syria@gmail.com (office). *Website:* www.un.int/syria (office).

JAAFARI, Ibrahim al-, MD; Iraqi politician and physician; b. 1947, Karbala; ed Mosul Univ.; after medical school joined Islamic Dawa Party (Hizb ad-Da'wa al-Islamiya), Chief Spokesman 1966, remains leader; moved to Iran when Dawa party in Iraq was outlawed 1980, then to London 1989; fmr mem. Iraq Governing Council; Interim Vice-Pres. of Iraq 2004–05; Prime Minister of Iraq 2005–April 2006; Leader, National Reform Movement 2008–. *Address:* c/o Islamic Dawa Party (Hizb ad-Da'wa al-Islamiya), Baghdad, Iraq (office).

JÄÄTTEENMÄKI, Anneli Tuulikki, LLM; Finnish politician; b. 11 Feb. 1955, Lapua; m. Jorma Melleri 1994; ed Univ. of Helsinki; acting lawyer, Office of the Local Authorities Negotiating Del. 1981–82; Temporary Asst, Ministry for Foreign Affairs 1982, Ministerial Political Adviser 1983–84; Legis. Sec. to Finnish Centre Party Parl. Faction 1986, mem. 1987–, Deputy Party Parl. Faction 1991–94, 1999–2000; mem. Parl. for Vaasa 1987–2003, for Helsinki 2003–; mem. Finnish Del. to the Nordic Council 1987–94; mem. Parl. Cttee for Constitutional Law 1987–99, Legal Affairs Cttee 1987–91, Electors Cttee 1987–91, Parl. Salary Del. 1987–92, Foreign Affairs Cttee 1999–, Parl. Grand Cttee 1999–2003; Deputy mem. Finance Cttee April–Nov. 1991, Defence Cttee April–May 1991, Foreign Affairs Cttee 1991–94; Minister of Justice 1994–95; Parl. Gov. Bank of Finland 1991–92, mem. Supervisory Council Parl. Govs Bank of Finland 1991–94, 1995–2003, Second Deputy mem. Parl. Trustees 1991–93, 1995–99, First Deputy mem. Parl. Trustees Sept.–Nov. 1993, 1999–2000, mem. Trustees 1993–94; mem. and Vice-Chair. Finnish Del. to Parl. Ass. of Council of Europe 1996–2003, Deputy mem. 2003–; mem. Commrs to Govt Guarantee Fund 1996–99; mem. Finnish Del. to WEU Parl. Ass. 1999–2003; Parl. Speaker March–April 2003, Speaker's Council April 2003, Chancellery Comm. Speaker April 2003; Prime Minister of Finland April–June 2003; mem. European Parl. 2004–; mem. Equal Opportunities Comm. 1987–91, Advisory Bd for Prison Affairs 1988–91 (Chair. 1991–94), Helsinki Inst. for Criminal Policy (HEUNI) 1996–; Deputy Chair. Paasikivi Soc. 1994–. *Publications:* Oikeus Voittaa (Justice Wins) 1999, Sillanrakentaja 2002. *Leisure interests:* history, literature, art, sports. *Address:* European Parliament, Rue Wiertz, ASP 096242, 1047 Brussels, Finland (office). *Telephone:* (2) 284-56-14 (office). *Fax:* (2) 284-96-14 (office). *E-mail:* anneli.jaatteenmaki@europarl.europa.eu (office). *Website:* www.annelijaatteenmaki (office).

JABER, Fatima al-, BEng; United Arab Emirates business executive; *Chief Operating Officer, Al Jaber Group;* d. of Obaid al-Jaber; m. 1995; five c.; ed UAE Univ., Al Ain; Asst Under-Sec. for Technical Services, Abu Dhabi Public Works Dept 1988–2005, becoming Asst Under-Sec. for Building Projects Section, Abu Dhabi Municipality; currently Exec. Dir and COO Al Jaber Group (family construction business); Chair. Al Bashayer Investment Co.; Gen. Man. Qaryat Al Beri Resort Devt Co. LLC; mem. Bd of Dirs Abu Dhabi Chamber of Commerce and Industry (first woman) 2009–; Deputy Chair. Abu Dhabi Businesswomen's Council; Arabian Business Businesswoman of the Year 2008, Construction Industry Personality of the Year 2009. *Address:* Al Jaber Group, PO Box 2175, Abu Dhabi, United Arab Emirates (office). *Telephone:* (2) 5554300 (office). *Fax:* (2) 5553370 (office). *E-mail:* aljaber@aje.ae (office). *Website:* www.aljaber.com (office).

JABER, Hessa Sultan al-, BSc, MSc, PhD; Qatar communications industry executive; *Secretary-General, Supreme Council of Information and Communication Technology (ictQATAR);* ed Kuwait Univ., George Washington Univ., USA; fmr IT Adviser for Qtel; fmr Chair. Computer Science Dept, Qatar Univ.; fmr mem. Strategic ICT Cttee; Sec.-Gen. Supreme Council of Information and Communication Tech. (ictQATAR) 2004–; Commr WHO/ITU Comm. and Accountability for Women and Children's Health; mem. Bd of Regents, Qatar Univ.; mem. Bd of Govs American School of Doha, Bloomsbury Qatar Foundation Journals, Qatar Foundation Nat. Research Forum, Qatar Financial Markets Authority, Network of Global Agenda Councils of World Econ. Forum, Global Alliance for Information and Communication Techs and Devt; Nat. Figure of the Year, Ministry of Interior Affairs 2008. *Address:* Supreme Council of Information and Communication Technology (ictQATAR), PO Box 23264, Al Nassr Tower, Post Office Roundabout, Al Corniche Street, Doha, Qatar (office). *Telephone:* 44995333 (office). *Fax:* 44995913 (office). *E-mail:* info@ict.gov.qa (office); communication@ict.gov.qa (office). *Website:* www.ictQATAR.qa/en (office).

JABER, Mohammed bin Issa al-; Saudi Arabian/Austrian business executive; *Chairman and CEO, MBI International;* b. 1959, Jeddah; m. 1978; one s. two d.; f. Jadawel International Construction and Development 1982; f. JJW Hotels & Resorts, Portugal 1989, now owner-operator of more than 60 hotel and leisure resorts in Europe and the Middle East; f. AJWA Group for Agro and Food Industries, Jeddah 1992; currently Chair. and CEO MBI International; Founding sponsor, London Middle East Inst., SOAS; Dir Olive Tree Educational Trust, London; Founder, Chair. and sole Patron, MBI Al Jaber Foundation; UN Spokesperson for Global Forums on Reinventing Govt 2007–; UNESCO Envoy for Educ. Tolerance and Cultures in the Middle East 2005–; Chair. Mediterranean East Peace Forum, Lecce, Italy 2008; Austrian citizen since 2007; Hon. Fellow, SOAS 2002, Corpus Christi Coll., Oxford 2009; Hon. DSc (City Univ., London) 2004; Hon. DLitt (Westminster) 2004; Arab League Educational, Cultural and Scientific Org. Gold Medal 2007, Gold Medal of Honour, Mayor of Vienna, Gold Medal, Islamic Educational, Scientific and Cultural Organization (ISESCO) 2012, ranked by Arabian Business amongst the Power 500: The World's Most Influential Arabs (sixth) 2012. *Address:* MBI & Partners UK Ltd, 78–80 Wigmore Street, London, W1U 2SJ, England (office). *Telephone:* (20) 7935-5859 (office). *E-mail:* info@mbiinternational.com (office). *Website:* www.mbiinternational.com (office); www.mbifoundation.com; www.mbialjaber.com.

JACAMON, Jean-Paul; French business executive; *Senior Adviser, COGNETAS SA;* b. 5 Aug. 1947, Thaon-les-Vosges; m. Colette Jacquier; four c.; ed Ecole Polytechnique de Paris and Ecole des Mines de Paris; mem. staff Ministry of Industry 1975, sr civil servant, French Regional Land Use Planning Comm. (DATAR) –1981; Exec. Asst Groupe Schneider 1981, various positions with Spie Batignolles (electrical eng construction subsidiary) 1983–, Man. of 'Ferrière la Grande' plant, Vice-Pres. Eng and Gen. Contracting Div., Vice-Pres. Electric and Nuclear Power Div. 1988, Vice-Pres. responsible for electrical contracting activities, Chair. and CEO Spie-Trindel (local contracting for electrical and electro-mechanical projects) –1993, COO Spie Batignolles 1993–94; Exec. Vice-Pres. European Div., Schneider Electric 1995, COO 1996–2002, Vice-Chair. 1999–2002; ind. consultant 2002–; Chair. (non-exec.) Bonna Sabla 2003–05, Gardiner 2003–06, CPI 2006–; Dir (non-exec.) AMEC PLC 2002–06, Péchiney 2002–04, Carbonne Lorraine 2003–, Alcan 2004–07; currently Sr Adviser, COGNETAS SA; Chevalier, Ordre nat. du Mérite 1994. *Leisure interests:* golf, bridge. *Address:* Gaipare 4, rue du Général Lanrezac, 75017 Paris (office); 64 route de l'Etang la Ville, 78750 Mareil-Marly, France (home). *Telephone:* 1-56-68-97-83 (office). *Fax:* 1-39-16-89-21 (office). *E-mail:* jp.jacamon@wanadoo.fr (home).

JACK, Ian; British writer and journalist; b. 7 Feb. 1945, Farnworth, Lancs.; s. of Harry Jack and Isabella Jack (née Gillespie); m. 1st 1979; m. 2nd Rosalind Sharpe 1998; one s. one d.; newspaper journalist in Scotland 1960s; variously reporter, feature writer, Foreign Corresp., Sunday Times 1970–86; co-f. Independent on Sunday 1989, Ed. 1991–95; Ed. Granta magazine 1995–2007; currently writes for The Guardian newspaper; Journalist of the Year 1986, Reporter of the Year 1989, Editor of the Year 1992. *Publications:* Before the Oil Ran Out 1987, The Crash that Stopped Britain 2001, The Country Formerly Known as Great Britain 2009; various Granta anthologies. *Address:* The Guardian, Kings Place, 90 York Way, London, N1 9GU, England (office). *Telephone:* (20) 3353-2000 (office). *Fax:* (20) 3353-3193 (office). *E-mail:* ian.jack@guardian.co.uk (office); iangjack@blueyonder.co.uk (home). *Website:* www.guardian.co.uk (office).

JACK, James Julian Bennett, PhD, FRS, FRCP, FMedSci; New Zealand neurophysiologist and academic; b. 25 March 1936, Invercargill; ed Univ. of Otago, Univ. of Oxford, UK; Rhodes Scholarship 1960–63; Foulerton Gift Researcher 1964–68; demonstrator, Univ. Lecturer then Reader, then Prof. of Cellular Neuroscience, Lab. of Physiology (now Dept of Physiology, Anatomy and Genetics), Univ. of Oxford 1968–; Fellow, Univ. Coll., Oxford, Acad. of Medical Sciences 1998, fmr Supernumerary Fellow; Gov. Wellcome Trust 1987– (Deputy Chair. 1994–99); Hon. FRSNZ 1998; Hon. DSc (Univ. of Otago) 1999. *Address:* 24 Claylands Road, Kennington, London, SW8 1NZ, England.

JACKAMAN, Michael Clifford John, MA; British business executive; b. 7 Nov. 1935; s. of Air Commodore Clifford Thomas Jackaman and Lily Margaret Jackaman; m. Valerie Jane Pankhurst 1960; one s. one d.; ed Felsted School, Essex, Jesus Coll., Cambridge; with Yardley Ltd 1959–60, Beecham Foods Ltd 1960–63, John Harvey & Sons Ltd 1963–65, Findus Ltd 1965, Harveys of Bristol 1966–92 (Chair. 1984–93); Marketing Dir Allied Breweries Ltd 1978–80, Deputy Man. Dir 1978–83; Chair. Allied Vintners Ltd 1983–88; Chair. and CEO Hiram Walker-Allied Vintners Ltd 1988–91; Chair. Allied-Lyons (now Allied Domecq) PLC 1991–96; Chair. Grand Appeal, Royal Hosp. for Sick Children, Bristol 1996–; mem. Bd of Dirs Rank Group PLC 1992–97, Kleinwort Benson Group 1994–98, Theatre Royal, Bath 1999–; Hon. DBA (Univ. of West of England). *Leisure interests:* opera, gardening, tennis, walking, oriental antiques, theatre. *Address:* c/o Board of Directors, Theatre Royal Bath, Sawclose, Bath, BA1 1ET, England.

JACKLIN, Anthony (Tony), CBE; British fmr professional golfer; b. 7 July 1944, Scunthorpe; s. of Arthur David Jacklin and Doris Lillian Jacklin; m. Vivien Jacklin 1966 (died 1988); two s. one d.; m. 2nd Astrid May Waagen 1988; one s. one step-s. one step-d.; Lincolnshire Open champion 1961; professional 1962–85, 1988–; won British Asst Professionals' title 1965; won Dunlop Masters 1967, 1973; first British player to win British Open since 1951 1969; US Open champion 1970; first British player to win US Open since 1920 and first since 1900 to hold US and British Open titles simultaneously; Greater Greensboro Open champion, USA 1968, 1972; won Italian Open 1973, German Open 1979, Venezuelan Open 1979, Jersey Open 1981, British Professional Golfers' Asscn (PGA) champion 1982 and 15 major tournaments in various parts of the world; played in eight Ryder Cup matches and four times for England in World Cup; Capt. of 1983 GB and Europe Ryder Cup Team; Capt. of victorious European Ryder Cup team 1985 (first win for Europe since 1957), 1987; BBC TV golf commentator; moved to Sotogrande, Spain from Jersey 1983; Commr of Golf, Las Aves Club, Sotogrande 1983–; Dir of Golf, San Roque Club 1988–; now golf course designer; Hon. Life Pres. British Professional Golfers' Asscn; Hon. Fellow, Birmingham Polytechnic 1989. *Publications:* Golf With Tony Jacklin 1969, The Price of Success 1979, Jacklin's Golfing Secrets (with Peter Dobereiner), The First Forty Years (with Renton Laidlaw) 1985, Your Game and Mine (with Bill Robertson) 1999, Jacklin: The Autobiography 2006. *Address:* Tony Jacklin Golf Academy, 222 Haben Blvd, Palmetto,, FL 34221, USA (office). *Telephone:* (941) 722-4895.

JACKLIN, Bill, MA, RA; British artist and painter; b. (Walter William Burke-Jacklin), 1 Jan. 1943, Hampstead, London, England; s. of Harold Jacklin and Alice Jacklin; m. 1st Lesley Berman 1979 (divorced 1993); m. 2nd Janet Russo 1993; ed Walthamstow School of Art, London and Royal Coll. of Art; teacher at numerous art colls 1967–75; moved to New York 1985; elected to Royal Acad. 1990; Bursary Award, Arts Council, London 1975. *Publications:* numerous Marlborough catalogues 1980–2005. *Leisure interests:* walking, reading. *Address:* c/o Marlborough Fine Art, 6 Albemarle Street, London, W1X 4BY, England. *Telephone:* (401) 848-0774 (Newport, RI, USA) (office). *Website:* www.bjacklin.com.

JACKMAN, Hugh; Australian actor; b. 12 Oct. 1968; m. Deborra-Lee Furness; two c.; ed Univ. of Tech. Sydney, Western Australian Acad. of Performing Arts. *Stage appearances include:* Beauty and the Beast (Australia), Sunset Boulevard (Australia), Oklahoma (UK), The Boy from Oz (Broadway) 2004, A Steady Rain (Broadway) 2009, Hugh Jackman, Back on Broadway 2011. *Films include:* Paperback Hero 1999, Erskineville Kings 1999, X-Men 2000, Someone Like You 2001, Swordfish 2001, Kate and Leopold 2001, X-Men 2 2003, Standing Room Only 2004, Van Helsing 2004, X-Men: The Last Stand 2006, Scoop 2006, The Fountain 2006, The Prestige 2006, Flushed Away (voice) 2006, Happy Feet (voice) 2006, Uncle Jonny 2008, Deception 2008, Australia 2008, X-Men Origins: Wolverine 2009, Snow Flower and the Secret Fan 2011, Butter 2011, Real Steel 2011, Les Misérables (Golden Globe Award for Best Performance by an Actor in a Motion Picture – Comedy or Musical 2013) 2012, Rise of the Guardians (voice) 2012. *Television includes:* Correlli 1995, Snowy River: The McGregor Saga 1996, Hey, Mr Producer! 1998, Halifax F. P. 1998, Oklahoma 1999. *Leisure interests:* piano, guitar, golf, windsurfing. *Address:* c/o Penny Williams Management, Level 2, 181 Glebe Point Road, Glebe, NSW 2037, Australia (office). *Telephone:* (2) 9552-1701 (office). *Fax:* (2) 9660-0434 (office). *Website:* www.pennywilliamsmgt.com.au (office).

JACKSON, Alphonso, BSc, LLB; American fmr government official; *Director, Center for Public Policy, Hampton University;* m. Marcia Jackson; two d.; ed Truman State Univ., Washington Univ. Law School; apptd Dir of Public Safety for City of St Louis 1977; fmr Exec. Dir St Louis Housing Authority; fmr Dir consultant services Laventhol and Howarth; fmr Special Asst to the Chancellor and Asst Prof., Univ. of Missouri; fmr Dir Dept of Public and Assisted Housing, Washington, DC, Chair. DC Redevelopment Land Agency Bd; Pres. and CEO Housing Authority City of Dallas, Tex. 1989–96; Pres. American Electric Power 1996–2001; Deputy Sec. and COO Dept of Housing and Urban Devt 2001–04, Sec. 2004–08 (resgnd); currently Dir Center for Public Policy, Hampton Univ. *Address:* Center for Public Policy, Hampton University, Wigwam Building, Suite 100, Hampton, VA 23668, USA (office). *Telephone:* (757) 727-5426 (office). *Fax:* (757) 728-4913 (office). *Website:* www.hamptonu.edu/cppl/ (office).

JACKSON, Colin Ray, CBE; British fmr professional athlete; b. 18 Feb. 1967, Cardiff; world-class 110m hurdler; holds the 60m world indoor record and 110m outdoor record (as at end of 2003); 110m hurdles achievements include: silver medal European Jr Championships 1985, gold medal World Jr Championships 1986, silver medal Commonwealth Games 1986, silver medal European Cup 1987, bronze medal World Championships 1987, silver medal Olympic Games 1988, silver medal World Cup 1989, gold medal European Cup 1989, 1993, gold medal Commonwealth Games 1990, gold medal World Cup 1992, gold medal (and new world record) World Championships 1993 (silver medal 4x100m relay); achievements (60m hurdles): silver medal World Indoor Championships 1989, 1993, gold medal European Indoor Championships 1989 (silver medal 1987), 1994, gold medals European and Commonwealth Championships 1994, gold medal European Championships 1998, 2002, gold medal World Championships 1999; in world's top ten at 110m each year from 1986–2003; over 70 int. caps (most capped British athlete); 23 major championships medals (13 gold, nine silver, one bronze); retd March 2003; mem. Brecon Athletics Club, UK Int. 1985–; numerous Welsh, UK, European and Commonwealth records; currently commentator BBC Sport; Hon. BA (Aberystwyth) 1994, Hon. BSc (Univ. of Wales) 1999; Athlete of the Decade, French Sporting Council, Hurdler of the Century, German Athletic Asscn (DLV), Athlete of the Year 1993–94, British Athletics Writers, Sportsman of the Year 1994, Sports Writers Asscn. *Address:* c/o MTC (UK) Ltd, 20 York Street, London, W1V 6PU, England; 4 Jackson Close, Rhoose, Vale of Glamorgan, CF62 3DQ, Wales. *Telephone:* (20) 7935-8000 (MTC). *Fax:* (1446) 710642 (home). *Website:* www.mtc-uk.com.

JACKSON, Daryl Sanders, AO, DipArch, BArch, LFRAIA, ARIBA; Australian architect; b. 7 Feb. 1937, Clunes, Victoria; s. of Cecil John Jackson and Doreen May Sanders; m. Kay Parsons 1960; one s. three d.; ed Wesley Coll., Melbourne, Royal Melbourne Inst. of Tech., Univ. of Melbourne; Asst, Edwards, Madigan and Torzillo, Sydney 1959, Don Henry Fulton, Melbourne 1960, Chamberlin, Powell and Bon, London 1961–63, Paul Rudolph, New Haven, Conn. 1963–64, Skidmore, Owings and Merrill, San Francisco 1964; Partner, Daryl Jackson, Evan Walker Architects, Melbourne 1965–79; Dir Daryl Jackson Pty Ltd Architects 1979–; Dir Daryl Jackson, Robin Dyke Pty Ltd (Sydney) 1985–; Assoc. Prof. of Architecture, Melbourne Univ. 1985–, Deakin Univ. 2001–; Pres. Wesley Coll. Council, Melbourne 1993–; Dir Daryl Jackson Alastair Swayn Pty Ltd (Canberra); Dir Daryl Jackson Int. Ltd (London) 1989–; Dir RAIA Victorian Chapter Housing Service 1966–69; mem. RAIA Victorian Chapter Council 1967–77, Victorian Tapestry Workshop Cttee 1975–84, Parl. House Construction Authority, Canberra 1985–89, Victorian Arts Centre Trust 1991, Melbourne Cricket Club 1992– (Vice-Pres. 1997–); Trustee, Nat. Gallery of Vic. 1983–95; Chair. Australian Film Inst.

1990–94, Melbourne Major Events Co. Ltd 1991–; Life Fellow Royal Australia Inst. of Architects; Hon. FAIA; Hon. Diploma and Bronze Medal (Third World Biennale of Architecture, Interarch 85, Sofia) 1985; Royal Australia Inst. of Architects Architecture Awards: Bronze Medal 1970, 1973, 1976, 1978, Press Award 1990, Canberra Medallion 1981, Sir Zehlman Cowen Award 1981, 1984, Robert Haddon Award 1982, Walter Burley Griffin Award for Urban Design, William Wardle Public Architecture Award, Sustainable Architecture Award; ACT Architecture Awards: 1984, 1985, 1987, 1991, Gold Medal 1987, Australian Council Nat. Trusts Heritage Award 1990, Int. Award 1991, MCG Southern Stand 1991, Georges Interior Architectural Award 1998, Masterplanner, Univ. of Melbourne 2000, County Court of Australia Award 2003. *Major works:* YWCA Community Resource Centre, Suva, Fiji 1973, Princes Hill High School, Melbourne 1973, Methodist Ladies' Coll., Library Resource Centre, Melbourne 1973, City Edge Housing Devt, Melbourne 1976, School of Music, Canberra 1976, Asscn for Modern Educ. School, Canberra 1977, Emu Ridge Govt Housing Devt, Canberra 1978, School of Art, Canberra 1980, McLachlan Offices, Canberra 1980, The Walter and Eliza Hall Inst. of Medical Research, Melbourne 1982, Nat. Sports Centre, Swimming Training Hall, Bruce, ACT 1982, Australian Chancery Complex, Riyadh, Saudi Arabia 1987, Hyatt Hotel, Canberra, Bond Univ., Gold Coast 1989, Commercial Union Office Bldg, Melbourne 1990, Melbourne Cricket Ground Southern Stand 1991, 120 Collins Street, Melbourne, Methodist Ladies' Coll. Music School, Kew 1994, Subiaco Oval Redevelopment, Perth 1994, Wesley Coll. Pre-Preparatory School, Prahran 1995, Brisbane Cricket Ground Redevelopment, 'The Gabba' 1995, Royal Melbourne Hosp. 1995, Colonial Stadium, Melbourne 2000, Sydney Conservatorium of Music (with Robin Dyke) 2001, Royal Brisbane Hosp. 2003, Victorian County Court 2003, UN Int. School, Hanoi 2004, Melbourne Cricket Ground Northern Stand Re-Development (with MCGS) 2005, Southern Cross Station Redevelopment (with Grimshaw Architects) 2006. *Publications:* Daryl Jackson Architecture: Drawings and Photos 1984, Daryl Jackson, The Master Architect 1996; numerous articles and papers. *Address:* 35 Little Bourke Street, Melbourne, Vic. 3000, Australia (office). *Telephone:* (3) 9662-3022 (office). *Fax:* (3) 9663-5239 (office). *E-mail:* djackson@jacksonarchitecture.com (office). *Website:* www.jacksonarchitecture.com (office).

JACKSON, Frank Cameron, AO, PhD, FAHA, FASSA, FBA; Australian philosopher and academic; *Distinguished Professor, Australian National University;* b. 31 Aug. 1943, Melbourne, Vic.; s. of Allan C. Jackson and Ann E. Jackson; m. Morag E. Fraser 1966; two d.; ed Univ. of Melbourne, La Trobe Univ.; Prof. of Philosophy, Monash Univ., Vic. 1978–86, 1991; Prof. of Philosophy, ANU 1986–90, 1992–2007, Dir Inst. of Advanced Studies 1998–2001, Deputy Vice-Chancellor (Research) 2001, Distinguished Prof. 2003–, Dir Research School of Social Sciences 2004–07; Fractional Research Prof., La Trobe Univ. 2008–12; Visiting Prof., Princeton Univ., USA 2007–13; Leverhulme Visiting Prof., Univ. of Cambridge, UK 2011; Locke Lecturer, Univ. of Oxford 1995, Blackwell Lecturer, Brown Univ. 2006. *Publications:* Perception 1978, Conditionals 1986, The Philosophy of Mind and Cognition (with David Braddon-Mitchell) 1996, From Metaphysics to Ethics 1998, Mind, Method and Conditionals 1998, Mind, Morality and Explanation (with Philip Pettit and Michael Smith) 2004, Language, Names and Information 2010. *Leisure interests:* reading, tennis. *Address:* School of Philosophy, Coombs Building, Australian National University, Acton, ACT 0200 (office); 33 David Street, O'Connor, ACT 2602, Australia (home). *Telephone:* (2) 6125-2341 (office); (2) 6247-0513 (home). *E-mail:* frank.jackson@anu.edu.au (office); fcjack321@gmail.com (home). *Website:* philosophy.cass.anu.edu.au/profile/frank-jackson (office).

JACKSON, Glenda, CBE; British politician and fmr actress; b. 9 May 1936, Birkenhead, Cheshire; d. of Harry Jackson and Joan Jackson; m. Roy Hodges 1958 (divorced 1976); one s.; ed Royal Acad. of Dramatic Art; fmr mem. Royal Shakespeare Co.; played Queen Elizabeth I in TV series Elizabeth R; Pres., Play Matters (fmrly Toy Libraries Asscn) 1976–; Dir United British Artists 1983–; Labour MP for Hampstead and Highgate 1992–2010, Hampstead and Kilburn 2010–; Parl. Under-Sec. of State, Dept for the Environment and Transport 1997–99; Adviser on Homelessness, GLA 2000–04; Hon. Fellow, Liverpool Polytechnic 1987; Hon. DLitt (Liverpool) 1978; Hon. LLM (Nottingham) 1992. *Plays include:* Marat/Sade, New York and Paris 1965, The Investigation 1965, Hamlet 1965, US 1966, Three Sisters 1967, Collaborators 1973, The Maids 1974, Hedda Gabler 1975, The White Devil 1976, Antony and Cleopatra 1978, Rose 1980, Strange Interlude 1984, Phaedra 1984, 1985, Across from the Garden of Allah 1986, Strange Interlude 1986, The House of Bernarda Alba 1986, Macbeth 1988, Scenes from an Execution 1990, Mermaid 1990, Mother Courage 1990, Mourning Becomes Electra 1991. *Films include:* Marat/Sade 1966, Negatives 1968, Women in Love (Acad. Award 1970) 1969, The Music Lovers 1970, Sunday, Bloody Sunday 1971, The Boy Friend 1971, Mary, Queen of Scots 1971, The Triple Echo 1972, Bequest to the Nation 1972, A Touch of Class (Acad. Award 1974) 1973, The Romantic Englishwoman 1975, The Tempter 1975, The Incredible Sarah 1976, The Abbess of Crewe 1977, Stevie 1977, Hedda 1977, House Calls 1978, The Class of Miss McMichael 1978, Lost and Found 1979, Hopscotch 1980, The Return of the Soldier 1982, Giro City 1982, Summit Conference 1982, Great and Small 1983, And Nothing But the Truth 1984, Turtle Diary 1985, Beyond Therapy 1985, Business as Usual 1986, Salome's Last Dance 1988, The Rainbow 1989, The Secret Life of Sir Arnold Bax 1992. *Leisure interests:* gardening, reading, listening to music. *Address:* House of Commons, London, SW1A 0AA, England. *Telephone:* (20) 7219-4008. *Fax:* (20) 7219-2112. *E-mail:* jacksong@parliament.uk. *Website:* www.glenda-jackson.co.uk.

JACKSON, Janet Damita Jo; American singer and choreographer; b. 16 May 1966, Gary, Ind.; d. of Joseph Jackson and Katherine Jackson; m. 1st James DeBarge 1984 (annulled 1985); m. 2nd Rene Elizondo Jr 1991–2000; m. 3rd Wissam Al Mana 2012; ed Valley Professional School; singing debut at age seven with family singing group, The Jacksons; television actress 1977–81, appearing in series Good Times (CBS), Diff'rent Strokes, Fame, A New Kind of Family; solo recording artist 1982–; worldwide concerts and tours; American Music Awards for Best Female Soul Singer (for Nasty), Best Female Soul Video (for What Have You Done For Me Lately?) 1986, for Best Pop Video (for When I Think of You) 1986, for Best Dance Artist, Best Female Pop Rock Artist and Best Female Soul R&B Artist 1991, for Favourite Pop/Rock Female Artist 2002, MTV Video Vanguard Award 1990, MTV Award for Best Female Video (for If) 1993, Starlight Foundation Humanitarian of the Year Award 1991, Grammy Award for Best R&B Song (for That's the

Way Love Goes) 1993. *Recordings include:* albums: Janet Jackson 1982, Dream Street 1984, Control 1986, Janet Jackson's Rhythm Nation 1989, Rhythm Nation Compilation 1990, Janet 1993, Design of a Decade 1986–96 1995, The Velvet Rope 1997, All For You 2001, Damita Jo 2004, 20 Y.O. 2006, Discipline 2008. *Films include:* Poetic Justice 1993, Nutty Professor II: The Klumps 2000, Why Did I Get Married? 2007, Why Did I Get Married Too? 2010, For Colored Girls 2010. *TV includes:* The Jacksons 1976–77, Good Times 1977–79, A New Kind of Family 1979–80, Diff'rent Strokes 1980–84, Fame 1984–85. *Publication:* True You 2011. *Address:* Johnny Wright, Wright Entertainment Group, 7680 Universal Boulevard, #500, Orlando, FL 32819, USA (office). *Telephone:* (407) 826-9100 (office). *E-mail:* info@wegmusic.com (office). *Website:* www.wegmusic.com (office); www.janet-jackson.com.

JACKSON, Rev. Jesse Louis; American clergyman and civic leader; *President, Rainbow PUSH Coalition;* b. 8 Oct. 1941, Greenville, N Carolina; s. of Charles Henry and Helen Jackson; m. Jacqueline Lavinia Brown 1964; three s. two d. one d. by Karin Stanford; ed Univ. of Illinois, Illinois Agricultural and Tech. Coll., Chicago Theological Seminary; ordained to Ministry Baptist Church 1968; active Black Coalition for United Community Action 1969; Co-Founder Operation Breadbasket S Christian Leadership Conf.; Co-ordinating Council Community Orgs, Chicago 1966, Nat. Dir 1966–77; Founder and Exec. Dir Operation PUSH (People United to Save Humanity), Chicago 1971–96, Pres. Rainbow PUSH Coalition (formed by merger with Rainbow Coalition) 1996–; unsuccessful cand. for Democratic nomination for US Presidency 1983–84, 1987–88; TV Host, Voices of America 1990; Pres. Award Nat. Medical Asscn 1969; Humanitarian Father of the Year Award Nat. Father's Day Cttee 1971. *Address:* Rainbow PUSH Coalition, 930 East 50th Street, Chicago, IL 60615, USA (office). *Telephone:* (773) 373-3366 (office). *Fax:* (773) 373-3571 (office). *E-mail:* jjackson@rainbowpush.org (office). *Website:* www.rainbowpush.org (office).

JACKSON, John B. H.; British barrister and business executive; *Chairman, Oxford Technology VCTs;* ed The Kings School, Canterbury, Queens College; with Philips Electrical Ltd, UK, 1952–80, mem. Bd of Dirs Philips Electronics 1966–94; currently Chair. Oxford Technology VCT, Oxford Technology 2 VCT, Oxford Technology 3 VCT, Oxford Technology 4 VCT; Chair. (non-solicitor) Mishconde Reya; fmr Chair. Xenova Group; mem. Bd of Dirs Instore plc. *Address:* The Oxford Technology VCTs, Magdalen Centre, Oxford Science Park, Oxford, OX4 4GA, England. *Telephone:* (1865) 784466 (office). *Fax:* (1865) 784430 (office). *Website:* www.oxfordtechnology.com (office).

JACKSON, Lisa P., BS, MEng; American fmr government official and business executive; *Environmental Director, Apple, Inc.;* b. 8 Feb. 1962, New Orleans, La; m. Kenny Jackson; two s.; ed Tulane Univ., Princeton Univ.; worked in various roles with US Environmental Protection Agency (EPA), Washington, DC 1986–2002; Asst Commr of Compliance and Enforcement, NJ Dept of Environmental Protection 2002–05, Asst Commr for Land Use Man. 2005–06, Commr of Environmental Protection 2006–08; Chief of Staff to Gov of NJ 2008; Admin. EPA, Washington, DC 2009–13; Environmental Dir Apple, Inc. 2013–. *Leisure interest:* cooking. *Address:* Apple, Inc., 1 Infinite Loop, Cupertino, CA 95014, USA (office). *Telephone:* (408) 996-1010 (office). *Website:* www.apple.com (office).

JACKSON, Margaret Anne, AC, BEcons, MBA, FCA; Australian business executive; b. 17 March 1953, Vic.; d. of Wallace James Jackson and Dorothy Jean Jackson; m. Roger Donazzan 1977; one s. one d.; ed Monash Univ. and Univ. of Melbourne; accountant, Price Waterhouse Co. 1973–77; accountant, Nelson Parkhill BDO 1977–91, Partner 1983–90; Partner KPMG Peat Marwick 1990–92; Chair. Transport Accident Comm. (Vic.) 1993–2001; fmr Deputy Chair. Southcorp Ltd; Dir (non-exec.) Qantas Airways Ltd 1992–2007, Chair. 2000–07, also Chair. Remuneration and Nominations Cttees; Dir Telecom Australia 1983–90, Australian Wool Corp. 1986–89, Int. Wool Secr. 1986–89, Pacific Dunlop 1992–2000, The Broken Hill Pty Co. Ltd 1994–2000, Australia and New Zealand Banking Group Ltd 1994–2008, Billabong International Ltd 2000–; fmr Chair. Malthouse Pty Ltd; Chair. Flexigroup Ltd 2006–; Deputy Chair. People Telecom Ltd; mem. Exec. Cttee Australia Japan Business Co-operation Cttee; Dir Brain Imaging Research Inst.; Chair. Asia Pacific Business Coalition on HIV-AIDS 2006–; Pres. Australian Volunteers Int.; Deputy Chair. Baker Capital Campaign Task Force, Baker Medical Research Inst., St Vincent's Medical Research Inst. 1994–96; Chair. Playbox Theatre Co. Pty Ltd 1998–2000 (Dir 1991–98); mem. Bd of Dirs Australia Foundation for Culture and the Humanities Ltd; mem. Vic. State Council Inst. of Chartered Accountants 1985–93 (Chair. 1989–90), Pharmaceutical Remuneration Benefits Tribunal 1985–90, Foreign Affairs Council, Nat. Council 1988–91, Convocation Cttee Univ. of Melbourne 1988–91, Australian Science and Tech. Council 1990–93, Nat. Health and Medical Research Council 1991, French Australian Industrial Research Steering Cttee 1997–98, Business Council of Australia Chair.'s Panel, The Walter & Eliza Hall Inst. of Medical Research, Melbourne Univ. Business School Asscn; Fellow, Australian Inst. of Co. Dirs, Inst. of Chartered Accountants in Australia; Int. Trustee Carnegie Mellon Univ., S Australia; Patron Salvation Army Capital Appeal for Homeless Youth, Vic.; Hon. LLD (Monash) 2002; Inst. of Chartered Accountants Distinguished Service Award. *Leisure interests:* travelling, bush-walking, fishing, reading, photography, gardening. *Address:* c/o Qantas Airways Ltd, Level 12, Exhibition Street, Melbourne, Vic. 3000, Australia.

JACKSON, Michael, BA; British broadcasting executive; *President of Programming, IAC/InterActiveCorp;* b. 11 Feb. 1958; s. of Ernest Jackson and Margaret Jackson (née Kearsley); ed King's School, Macclesfield, Polytechnic of Central London; Organizer, Channel 4 Group 1979; Producer, The Sixties 1982; ind. producer Beat Productions Ltd 1983–87; Ed. The Late Show, BBC TV (BFI Award) 1988–90; with Late Show Productions 1990–91; Head of Music and Arts BBC TV 1991–93, Controller BBC2 1993–96, Controller BBC1 and BBC Dir of TV 1996–97; CEO Channel 4 1997–2001, Dir of Programmes 1997–98; Chair. Film Four Ltd 1997–2001; Dir (non-exec.) EMI Group 1999–; Pres., CEO USA Entertainment Group 2001–02; Chair. Universal Television Group 2002–2004 (resgnd following merger Universal's merger with NBC 2004); Pres. of Programming, IAC/InterActiveCorp, New York, also Sr Adviser on Content Strategy 2006–; Hon. DLitt (Westminster) 1995. *Programmes produced include:* Whose Town is it Anyway?, Open the Box, The Media Show, The Nelson Mandela Tribute, Tales from Prague (Grierson Documentary Award), Moving Pictures, The American

Late Show (Public Broadcasting Service, USA), Naked Hollywood (BAFTA Best Factual Series Award), Sounds of the Sixties, The Lime Grove Story, TV Hell. *Leisure interests:* reading, walking. *Address:* IAC/InterActiveCorp, 555 West 18th Street, New York, NY 10011, USA (office). *Telephone:* (212) 314-7300 (office). *Website:* www.iac.com (office).

JACKSON, Gen. Sir Michael David (Mike), GCB, CBE, DSO; British military officer (retd) and consultant; *Senior Advisor, PA Consulting Group;* b. 21 March 1944; s. of George Jackson and Ivy Jackson (née Bower); m. Sarah Coombe 1985; two s. one d.; ed Stamford School, Sandhurst Mil. Acad., Univ. of Birmingham; commissioned Intelligence Corps 1963; transferred to Parachute Regt 1970, attended Staff Coll. 1976, Chief of Staff Berlin Infantry Brigade 1977–78, commanded a parachute co., NI 1979–81, mem. Directing Staff, Staff Coll. 1981–83, Commdr 1st Bn Parachute Regt 1984–86; with Sr Defence Staff, Jt Service Defence Coll., Greenwich 1986–88; Services Fellow, Wolfson Coll. Cambridge 1989; Commdr 39 Infantry Brigade, NI 1989–92; Dir-Gen. of Personnel Services, Ministry of Defence (Army) 1992–94; Commdr 3rd Div. 1994–96, Commdr Implementation Force (IFOR) Multinational Div. SW, Bosnia and Herzegovina 1995–96; Dir-Gen. of Devt and Doctrine, Ministry of Defence 1996–97; rank of Lt-Gen. 1997; Commdr Allied Rapid Reaction Force 1997–2000; Commdr Kosovo Force (KFOR) March–Oct. 1999; C-in-C Land Command 2000–03; Chief of the Gen. Staff 2003–06; Sr Advisor, PA Consulting Group 2007–; Dir (non-exec.) Longhorn Mining 2007–, Legion Group 2009–10, Force Select 2010–; Freeman City of London 1988, D.L Wiltshire 2007. *Publication:* Soldier: The Autobiography 2007. *Address:* PA Consulting Group, 123 Buckingham Palace Road, London, SW1W 9SR, England (office). *Telephone:* (20) 7730-9000 (office). *Fax:* (20) 7333-5050 (office). *E-mail:* info@paconsulting.com (office). *Website:* www.paconsulting.com (office).

JACKSON, Michael (Mike) J., BA; American automobile sales executive; *Chairman and CEO, AutoNation Inc.;* b. 7 Feb. 1949, NJ; m. Patricia Jackson; one d.; ed St Joseph's Univ.; Technician Specialist, Mercedes-Benz USA 1974; Man. Partner, Euro Motorcars, Bethesda, Md 1979–90; Sr Vice Pres. of Marketing, Mercedes-Benz USA 1990–97, Pres. 1997, Pres. and CEO 1997–98; mem. Bd Dirs and CEO AutoNation Inc. 1999–, Chair. 2003–; Chair. Museum of Art, Fort Lauderdale; included in Advertising Age Top Marketing 100 (four times), mem. Automotive News All-Star Team of automotive execs (five times), Industry Leader of the Year, Automotive Hall of Fame 2003. *Address:* AutoNation Inc., The Atrium, 110 South East 6th Street, Fort Lauderdale, FL 33301, USA (office). *Telephone:* (954) 769-6000 (office). *Fax:* (954) 769-6537 (office). *E-mail:* info@autonation.com (office). *Website:* www.autonation.com (office).

JACKSON, (Kevin) Paul, BA, FID; British media industry executive and television producer; *CEO, Eyeworks UK;* b. 2 Oct. 1947, London; s. of the late T. Leslie Jackson and Jo Spoonley; m. Judith E. Cain 1981; two d.; ed Gunnersbury Grammar School and Univ. of Exeter; stage man. Marlowe Theatre, Canterbury 1970, Thorndike Theatre, Leatherhead 1971; production work for BBC TV: Two Ronnies, Three of a Kind, Carrott's Lib, The Young Ones, Happy Families 1971–82; freelance Producer and Dir Canon and Ball, Girls on Top 1982–84; Producer and Chair. Paul Jackson Productions: Red Dwarf, Don't Miss Wax, Saturday Live 1984–86; Exec. Producer, Appointments of Dennis Jennings (Acad. Award 'Oscar' for Best Live Action Short 1989); Man. Dir NGTV 1987–91; Dir of Programmes, Carlton TV 1991–93, Man. Dir Carlton TV 1993–94, Carlton UK Productions 1994–96; Controller BBC Entertainment 1997–2000; Man. Dir Granada Australia and CEO Red Heart Productions 2000–03; Dir Granada Int. Production and Entertainment (UK) 2003, CEO Granada America 2003–06; Dir of Comedy and Entertainment, ITV 2006–09; CEO Eyeworks UK 2009–; Visiting Prof., School of English, Exeter Univ.; mem. Exec. Cttee US Comedy Arts Festival; Chair. Timebank (UK charity); Chair. Comic Relief 1987–98; Vice-Chair. Charity Projects 1990–92, Chair. 1992–99; Chair. RTS 1994–96; Stanford Exec. Programme 1993; Fellow, Inst. of Dirs, Royal TV Soc.; Hon. Fellow (Exeter) 1999, Dr hc (Exeter) 2004; BAFTA 1983, 1984. *Leisure interests:* theatre, rugby, travel, food and wine, friends and family. *Address:* Eyeworks UK, 68 Salusbury Road, Queens Park, London, NW6 6NU, England (office). *Telephone:* (20) 7644-0000 (office). *Fax:* (20) 7644-0001 (office). *E-mail:* pjacksonemail@aol.com (office). *Website:* www.eyeworks.tv/countries/uk/overview (office).

JACKSON, Sir Peter, KNZM; New Zealand film director and producer; b. 31 Oct. 1961, Pukerua Bay, North Island. *Films:* Bad Taste 1987, Meet the Feebles 1989, Dead Alive, Heavenly Creatures 1994, The Frighteners 1996, Contact (special effects only), The Lord of the Rings: The Fellowship of the Ring (BAFTA Award for Best Dir) 2001, The Lord of the Rings: The Two Towers 2002, The Lord of the Rings: The Return of the King (Golden Globe Award, Best Dir 2004, Critics' Choice Award, Best Dir 2004, Acad. Award, Best Dir, Best Picture 2004) 2003, King Kong 2005, District 9 2009, The Lovely Bones (also producer) 2009, The Adventures of Tintin: Secret of the Unicorn (producer) 2011, The Hobbit: An Unexpected Journey 2012. *Publication:* Peter Jackson (autobiog., with Brian Sibley) 2005. *Address:* c/o ICM, 8942 Wilshire Boulevard, Beverly Hills, CA 90211, USA.

JACKSON, Peter John, BSc; British business executive; *Chairman, Kingfisher PLC;* b. 16 Jan. 1947, Sheffield; s. of Jack Jackson and Joan Jackson; m. Anne Campbell 1974; two s. one d.; ed Univ. of Leeds; personnel and industrial relations positions at British Steel, Comm. on Industrial Relations, Guthrie Industries 1968–76; Dir Personnel and Employee Relations, Deputy Man. Dir Perkins Engines (Shrewsbury), Perkins Engines Group 1976–87; Personnel Dir British Sugar PLC 1987–88, Deputy Man. Dir 1988–89, Man. Dir 1989–93, Chief Exec. 1994–99; Chief Exec. Associated British Foods PLC 1999–2005 (Dir 1992–2005); Chair. Kingfisher PLC 2006–. *Leisure interests:* garden, Sheffield United. *Address:* Kingfisher PLC, 3 Sheldon Square, Paddington, London, W2 6PX, England (office). *Telephone:* (20) 7372-8008 (office). *Fax:* (20) 7644-1001 (office). *E-mail:* info@kingfisher.co.uk (office). *Website:* www.kingfisher.co.uk (office).

JACKSON, Samuel L(eroy), BA; American film and television actor and film producer; b. 21 Dec. 1948, Washington, DC; s. of Elizabeth Jackson (née Montgomery); m. LaTanya Richardson 1980; one d.; ed Morehouse Coll., Atlanta; Co-founder and mem. Just Us theatre co., Atlanta. *Stage appearances:* Home, A Soldier's Story, Sally/Prince, Colored People's Time, Mother Courage, Spell No. 7, The Mighty Gents, The Piano Lesson, Two Trains Running, Fences. *Films include:*

Together for Days 1972, Ragtime 1981, Eddie Murphy Raw 1987, Coming to America 1988, School Daze 1988, Do The Right Thing 1989, Sea of Love 1989, A Shock to the System 1990, Def by Temptation 1990, Betsy's Wedding 1990, Mo' Better Blues 1990, The Exorcist III 1990, GoodFellas 1990, Return of the Superfly 1990, Jungle Fever (Best Actor Award, Cannes Int. Film Festival, New York Film Critics' Award) 1991, Strictly Business 1991, Juice 1992, White Sands 1992, Patriot Games 1992, Johnny Suede 1992, Jumpin' at the Boneyard 1992, Fathers and Sons 1992, National Lampoon's Loaded Weapon 1 1993, Amos & Andrew 1993, Jurassic Park 1993, True Romance 1993, Hail Caesar 1994, The New Age 1994, Pulp Fiction 1994, Losing Isaiah 1995, Kiss of Death 1995, Die Hard With a Vengeance 1995, Fluke (voice) 1995, The Great White Hype 1996, A Time to Kill 1996, The Long Kiss Goodnight 1996, One Eight Seven 1996, Trees Lounge 1996, Hard Eight 1996, Eve's Bayou (also producer) 1997, Jackie Brown 1997, Out of Sight 1998, The Negotiator 1998, Star Wars Episode I: The Phantom Menace 1999, Deep Blue Sea 1999, Any Given Wednesday (short) 2000, Rules of Engagement 2000, Shaft 2000, Unbreakable 2000, The Caveman's Valentine 2001, The 51st State 2001, The Comeback (short) 2002, Changing Lanes 2002, Star Wars: Episode II - Attack of the Clones 2002, No Good Deed 2002, xXx 2002, Basic 2003, S.W.A.T. 2003, Country of My Skull 2004, Twisted 2004, Kill Bill: Vol. 2 2004, The Incredibles (voice) 2004, Coach Carter (Image Award for Best Actor 2006) 2005, The Adventures of Mr. Incredible (video short) (voice) 2005, xXx 2: The Next Level 2005, Star Wars: Episode III - Revenge of the Sith 2005, The Man 2005, Farce of the Penguins (voice) 2006, Freedomland 2006, Snakes on a Plane 2006, Black Snake Moan 2006, Home of the Brave 2006, Resurrecting the Champ 2007, 1408 2007, Cleaner 2007, Jumper 2008, Gospel Hill 2008, Iron Man (uncredited) 2008, Star Wars: The Clone Wars (voice) 2008, Lakeview Terrace 2008, Soul Men 2008, The Spirit 2008, Inglourious Basterds (voice) (uncredited) 2009, Mother and Child 2009, Astro Boy (voice) 2009, Iron Man 2 2010, Unthinkable 2010, The Other Guys 2010, Quantum Quest: A Cassini Space Odyssey (voice) 2010, Thor (uncredited) 2011, Captain America: The First Avenger 2011, Fury 2012, Meeting Evil 2012, Avengers Assemble 2012, Zambezia (voice) 2012, Django Unchained 2012, Oldboy 2013. *Television includes:* Movin' On (series) 1972, The Trial of the Moke (film) 1978, Uncle Tom's Cabin (film) 1987, Common Ground (film) 1990, Dead and Alive: The Race for Gus Farace (film) 1991, Ghostwriter (series) 1992, Simple Justice (film) 1993, Assault at West Point (film) 1994, Against the Wall (film) 1994, The Proud Family (series) – Seven Days of Kwanzaa (voice) 2001, Freedom: A History of Us (series documentary) 2003, Extras (series) 2005, The Boondocks (series) 2005–10, Honor Deferred (film) 2006, Afro Samurai (mini-series) 2007, Great Performances (series) – Respect Yourself: The Stax Records Story (voice) 2007, Afro Samurai: Resurrection (voice) 2009, The Sunset Limited (film) 2011, The Colbert Report (series) – Carrie Rebora Barratt (uncredited) 2012. *Address:* c/o Toni Howard, ICM, 10250 Constellation Boulevard, Los Angeles, CA 90067, USA (office). *Telephone:* (310) 550-4000 (office). *Website:* www.icmtalent.com (office); samuelljackson.com.

JACKSON-NELSON, Marjorie, AC, CVO, MBE; Australian state official and fmr athlete; b. 13 Sept. 1931, Coffs Harbour, NSW; d. of William Alfred Jackson and Mary Robinson; m. Peter Nelson 1953 (died 1977); one s. two d.; popularly known as 'The Lithgow Flash'; winner gold medal 100m and 200m (world record), Olympic Games 1952; winner four gold medals, Commonwealth Games 1950, three gold medals 1954; broke world sprint records on ten occasions; Man. Women's Section, Australian Commonwealth Games Teams 1982, 1986, 1990; Deputy Chair. Adelaide's bid to host 1998 Commonwealth Games 1990–92; Gen. Team Man. Commonwealth Games (first woman in position) 1994; fmr Pres. S Australia Div., Australian Olympic Fed.; Athletes Liaison Officer, Commonwealth Games 1998; f. Peter Nelson Leukaemia Research Fellowship 1977–; Gov. of S Australia 2001–07; mem. S Australian Olympic Council 1997–, SOCOG 1998–2000; honoured by Australia Post on stamp celebrating Olympic legends 1998; featured on Olympic coin produced by Perth Mint 1999; Bearer, Olympic Flag at Opening Ceremony of Olympic Games, Sydney 2000; Hon. PhD (Charles Sturt Univ., Bathurst, NSW) 2001; Australian Sportsman of the Year 1952, Outstanding Athlete, Helms Foundation, USA 1952, Outstanding Athlete, Int. Amateur Athletics Asscn 1986, nominated by Gov.-Gen. and Prime Minister as one of twenty living mems of 200 Great Australians 1988, named Legend in Australian Sport 1995, Paul Harris Fellow Rotary 1995, inducted into Australian Sporting Hall of Fame 1995, Int. Women's Hall of Fame, New York, USA 2000, Australian Sports Medal 2000, Olympic Order, Beijing 2008.

JACOB, Christian; French politician; b. 4 Dec. 1959, Rozay-en-Brie, Seine-et-Marne; ed Sainte-Maure dans l'Aube School of Agric.; farmer and dairy producer at Vaudoy-en-Brie 1982–; Pres. Young Farmers Local Admin (Département) Centre of Seine-et-Marne 1986–89, Regional Centre for Northern France 1987–90, Nat. Centre 1992; mem. Nat. Social and Econ. Council 1992; elected MEP 1994, Chair. European Parl. Comm. on Agric. and Rural Devt 1994–97; elected Deputy for Seine-et-Marne, Nat. Ass. 1995–2002, 2007–; Mayor of Provins 2001–02, 2006–; Minister-Desig. of Family Affairs, Health and Disabled People 2002–04, of Small and Medium Enterprises, Commerce, Craftsmen, Liberal Professions and Consumption 2004; Minister of the Economy, Finance and Industry 2004–05, of the Civil Service 2005–07; Chair. Rassemblement pour la Repub. (RPR) Fed. of Seine-et-Marne 1998–2000 (mem. Parl. Group 1997–2002); Chair. Union for a Popular Movt (UMP) Fed. of Seine-et-Marne 2002–; mem. Del. to EU 1997; mem. Bd of Dirs SOPEXA (Soc. for the Expansion of Sales of Agricultural and Grocery Products) 1996–. *Publications:* La clé des champs 1994, Le pari du bon sens, un paysan en politique 1999. *Address:* Mairie, place Maréchal Leclerc, 77160 Provins, France. *Telephone:* 1-64-60-38-33 (office). *Fax:* 1-64-00-61-27 (office). *E-mail:* cjacob@ assemblee-nationale.fr (office). *Website:* www.assemblee-nationale.fr (office).

JACOB, Gilles; French film director and producer and film festival director; b. 22 June 1930, Paris; s. of André Jacob; ed Lycée Carnot, Lycée Louis-le-Grand, Paris; Gen. Del. Cannes Film Festival 1978–2000, Pres. 2001–14; apptd Vice-Pres. Supervisory Bd Canal+ 2002; Chair. Louis Delluc Prize 1993–; mem. Bd Sept Cinéma 1992–, Bifi 1996–; directed the collection of La Bibliothèque du cinéma at Hatier 1979–92; mem. Bd of Dirs Films A2 1980–92; Commdr, Ordre nat. du Mérite 1999, Légion d'honneur 2005, des Arts et des Lettres; Grand Officer, Order of Merit of the Italian Repub.; Gold Medal of European Merit, EU 2009. *Screen adaptation:* Ça n'arrive qu'à moi (adaptation) 1985. *Film roles:* Grosse fatigue 1994, Femme Fatale 2002, HH, Hitler à Hollywood 2010. *Films produced or

directed: Le Cinéma dans les yeux (dir and producer) 1987, Liberté (documentary) (producer) 1989, Histories de festival (dir and producer) 2002, Les Marches etc… (une comédie musicale) (documentary short) (dir and producer) 2003, To Each His Own Cinema (producer) 2007, Une journée particulière (documentary) (dir) 2012. *Television:* Épreuves d'artistes (Words in Progress) (documentary) (dir and producer) 2004. *Address:* c/o Association française du festival international du film, 3 rue Amélie, 75007 Paris, France (office). *Telephone:* 1-53-59-61-00 (office). *Fax:* 1-53-59-61-10 (office). *E-mail:* gilles.jacob@festival-cannes.fr (office). *Website:* www.festival-cannes.org (office).

JACOBI, Sir Derek George, Kt, CBE, MA; British actor; b. 22 Oct. 1938, London, England; s. of Alfred George Jacobi and Daisy Gertrude Masters; ed Leyton County High School and St John's Coll., Cambridge; Birmingham Repertory Theatre 1960–63 (first appeared in One Way Pendulum 1961); Nat. Theatre 1963–71; Prospect Theatre Co. 1972, 1974, 1976–78, Artistic Assoc. 1976–91; Old Vic Co. 1978–79; joined RSC April 1982; Vice-Pres., Nat. Youth Theatre 1982–; Artistic Dir Chichester Festival Theatre 1995–96; Hon. Fellow, St John's Coll., Cambridge; Kt 1st Class, Order of the Dannebrog 1989; Variety Club Award 1976, British Acad. Award 1976, Press Guild Award 1976, Royal Television Soc. Award 1976, Hamburg Shakespeare Award 1998, Helen Hayes Tribute for Lifetime Achievement, Annual Helen Hayes Awards 2008. *Plays include:* The Lunatic 1980, Lover and the Poet 1980, The Suicide 1980, Much Ado About Nothing (Tony Award for Best Actor in a Play) 1982–85, Peer Gynt 1982, The Tempest 1982, Cyrano de Bergerac (Critics Circle Theatre Award Best Actor, Laurence Olivier Award for Actor of the Year in a Revival) 1983–85, Breaking the Code 1986, Richard II 1988, Richard III 1989, Kean 1990, Becket 1991, Mad, Bad and Dangerous to Know, Ambassadors 1992, Macbeth 1993, Hadrian VII, Playing the Wife 1995, Uncle Vanya 1996, God Only Knows 2000, Twelfth Night (Laurence Olivier Award for Best Actor) 2009, King Lear 2010–11; Dir Hamlet 1988, 2000. *Films include:* Othello 1965, Interlude 1968, Three Sisters 1970, Blue Blood 1973, The Day of the Jackal 1973, The Odessa File 1974, The Medusa Touch 1978, The Human Factor 1979, Charlotte 1981, The Man Who Went up in Smoke 1981, The Secret of NIMH (voice) 1982, Enigma 1983, Little Dorrit (Evening Standard British Film Award) 1988, Henry V 1989, The Fool 1990, Dead Again 1991, Looking for Richard 1996, Hamlet 1996, Basil 1998, Love is the Devil: Study for a Portrait of Francis Bacon (Edinburgh Int. Film Festival for Best British Performance 1998, Evening Standard Award for Best Actor 1999) 1997, Molokai: The Story of Father Damien 1999, Up at the Villa 2000, Gladiator 2000, The Body 2001, Gosford Park 2001, The Diaries of Vaslav Nijinsky 2001, Revelation 2001, The gathering Storm 2002, Revengers Tragedy 2002, Night's Noontime 2002, Two Men Went to War 2002, Strings 2004, Cloud Cuckoo Land 2004, Bye Bye Blackbird 2005, Underworld Evolution 2005, Nanny McPhee 2005, Project Huxley 2005, Arritmia 2007, The Riddle 2007, Anastezsi 2007, Airlock Or How To Say Goodbye In Space 2007, The Golden Compass 2007, A Bunch of Amateurs 2008, Sidney Turtlebaum 2008, Morris: A Life with Bells On 2009, Adam Resurrected 2009, Charles Dickens' England 2009, The King's Speech 2010, Capture Anthologies: The Dimensions of Self 2011, Ironclad 2011, There Be Dragons 2011, Anonymous 2011, My Week with Marilyn 2011, The Halloween Kid (short) (voice) 2011, Jail Caesar 2012, Cloud Cuckoo Land 2012, The Man Who Tried to Steal an Island (short) (voice) 2013, Effie Gray 2014, Hippie Hippie Shake 2014, Grace of Monaco 2014, Cinderella 2015. *Television includes:* BBC Sunday-Night Play (series) – She Stoops to Conquer 1961, Armchair Theatre (series) – The Fishing Match 1962, Much Ado About Nothing (film) 1967, ITV Playhouse (series) – The Photographer 1968, Man of Straw (mini-series) 1972, Budgie (series) 1972, The Strauss Family (mini-series) 1972, The Rivals of Sherlock Holmes (series) 1973, The Pallisers 1974, Markheim (film) 1974, Affairs of the Heart (series) 1975, I Claudius (BAFTA Award for Best Actor) 1976, Philby, Burgess and Maclean 1977, King Richard the Second (film) 1978, Minder (series) 1979, Hamlet, Prince of Denmark (film) 1980, Tales of the Unexpected (series) 1980–82, The Hunchback of Notre Dame (film) 1982, Inside the Third Reich (film) 1982, Cyrano de Bergerac (film) 1985, Mr Pye (mini-series) 1986, The Secret Garden (film) 1987, David Macaulay: Pyramid (film) 1988, The Tenth Man (film) (Emmy Award for Outstanding Supporting Actor in a Miniseries or a Special 1989) 1988, The American Civil War (mini-series documentary) 1990, The Storyteller: Greek Myths (mini-series) 1991, Screenplay (series) – The Vision Thing 1993, Circle of Deceit (film) 1993, The World of Peter Rabbit and Friends (series) 1994, ABC Weekend Specials (series) – The Secret Garden 1994, Cadfael 1994–98, Witness Against Hitler (film) 1996, Breaking the Code (film) 1996, Great Performances (series) – San Francisco Opera Gala Celebration 1997, Animated Epics: Beowulf (short) (voice) 1998, Flora Britannica (series) 1999, The Wyvern Mystery (film) 2000, Jason and the Argonauts (film) 2000, Frasier (series) (Emmy Award for Outstanding Guest Actor in a Comedy Series) 2001, Randall & Hopkirk (Deceased) (series) 2001, The Jury (mini-series) 2002, The Gathering Storm (film) 2002, Angelina Ballerina: The Show Must Go On (film) 2002, Inquisition (film) 2002, The Dinosaur Hunters (film) 2002, Angelina Ballerina (series) 2003, Henry VIII (film) (voice, uncredited) 2003, Doctor Who: Scream of the Shalka (mini-series) 2003, Mr. Ambassador (film) 2003, London (film) 2004, The Long Firm (series) 2004, Marple: The Murder at the Vicarage (film) 2004, Pinochet in Suburbia (film) 2006, Mist: The Tale of a Sheepdog Puppy (film) 2006, The Old Curiosity Shop (film) 2007, Mist: Sheepdog Tales (series, voice) 2007–09, Diamonds (film) 2009, Masterpiece Classic (series) – The Old Curiosity Shop 2009, Masterpiece Contemporary (series) – Endgame 2009, Margot (film) 2009, Joe Maddison's War (film) 2010, The Borgias (series) 2011, National Theatre Live (series) – King Lear 2011, – 50 Years on Stage 2013, Titanic: Blood and Steel (series) 2012, Last Tango in Halifax (series) 2012–13, Vicious (series) 2013–14, This Is Jinsy (series) 2014. *Leisure interests:* gardening, reading, looking for the next job. *Address:* c/o ICM, 3rd Floor, Marlborough House, 10 Earlham Street, London, WC2H 9LN, England. *Telephone:* (20) 7836-8564. *Website:* www .icmtalent.com.

JACOBOVITS DE SZEGED, Adriaan, MA, LLM; Dutch diplomatist (retd); b. 27 Dec. 1935, Vienna, Austria; s. of Giulio Jacobovits de Szeged and Eveline Tak van Poortvliet; m. Françoise S. Montant 1968; two s.; ed Univ. of Leiden; Master of Netherlands Law; Master of Russian Studies; Ministry of Finance 1963; joined Foreign Service 1964; postings to Embassy in Moscow, Perm. Mission to UN and other int. orgs, Geneva, Embassy, London, Embassy in Nairobi, Perm. Del. to EC, Brussels; Dir Econ. Co-operation, Ministry of Foreign Affairs 1978–82; Dir-Gen.

Political Affairs 1982–86; Perm. Rep. to UN, New York 1986–89; Perm. Rep. to NATO, Brussels 1989–93; Amb. to USA 1993–97; Pres. Int. Comm. for the Protection of the River Rhine 1999–2001; Personal Rep. of the OSCE Chair.-in-Office for Moldova 2002–03; EU Special Rep. for Moldova 2005–07; mem. East Europe Foundation Moldova Bd; Kt, Order of the Netherlands Lion, Grosses Verdienstkreuz mit dem Stern (Germany), Commdr, Légion d'honneur. *Address:* Neuhuyskade 20, 2596 XL The Hague, The Netherlands (home). *E-mail:* ajacobovits@planet.nl (office).

JACOBS, Rt Hon. Sir Francis Geoffrey, KCMG, PC, QC, DPhil; British lawyer and academic; *Professor of Law, King's College, London;* b. 8 June 1939, Cliftonville, Kent; s. of the late Cecil Sigismund Jacobs and Louise Jacobs (née Fischhof); m. 1st Ruth Freeman 1964; m. 2nd Susan Felicity Gordon Cox 1975; two s. three d.; ed City of London School, Christ Church, Oxford and Nuffield Coll., Oxford; Lecturer in Jurisprudence, Univ. of Glasgow 1963–65; Lecturer in Law, LSE 1965–69; Prof. of European Law, King's Coll., London 1974–88, Prof. of Law 2006–, Fellow, King's Coll. 1990; Secr. European Comm. of Human Rights and Legal Directorate, Council of Europe 1969–72; Legal Sec. Court of Justice of the EC 1972–74, Advocate Gen. 1988–2006; Barrister, Middle Temple 1964, QC 1984, Bencher 1990; Gov. Inns of Court School of Law 1996–2001; apptd to Privy Council 2005; Commdr, Ordre de Mérite (Luxembourg) 1983; Hon. LLD (Birmingham) 1996, (Glasgow) 2006, (Kingston) 2012; Hon. DCL (City Univ., London) 1997; Dr hc (Ghent) 2007. *Publications include:* The Sovereignty of Law: The European Way 2007, The Oxford EC Law Library (Gen. Ed.); several books on European law and Yearbook of European Law (Founding Ed.) 1981–88. *Address:* School of Law, King's College, Strand, London, WC2R 2LS (office); Fountain Court Chambers, Temple, London, EC4Y 9DH (office); Wayside, 15 St Alban's Gardens, Teddington, Middx, TW11 8AE, England (home). *E-mail:* francis.jacobs@kcl.ac.uk (office). *Website:* www.kcl.ac.uk/schools/law (office); www.fountaincourt.co.uk/francis-jacobs-qc (office).

JACOBS, Count Jacobs de Hagen; Georges, MEconSc, DJur; Belgian business executive; *Chairman, Delhaize Group;* b. 1940; ed Univ. Catholique de Louvain, Univ. of California, Berkeley, USA; economist IMF, Washington, DC, USA 1966; joined UCB Group 1970, Chair. Exec. Cttee 1987–2004, currently Chair. Bd of Dirs; mem. Bd of Dirs Delhaize Group 2003–, Chair. 2005–; mem. Bd of Dirs Belgacom, Bekaert, SN Brussels Airlines, Générale de Banque, IBM Belgium, Spadel SA, L.I.V. NV (Groupe Carmeuse); Pres. Union of Industrial and Employers' Confeds of Europe (UNICE) 1998–2003; mem. Man. Cttee Fed. of Belgian Cos (also Hon. Chair.); Chair. Belgo-Luxemburg-Polish Chamber of Commerce; mem. Bd American Chamber of Commerce, British Chamber of Commerce in Belgium. *Address:* Delhaize Group, Square Marie Curie 40, 1070 Brussels, Belgium (office). *Telephone:* (2) 412-22-11 (office). *Fax:* (2) 412-22-22 (office). *E-mail:* info@delhaizegroup.com (office). *Website:* www.delhaizegroup.com (office).

JACOBS, Irwin Mark, BEE, MS, PhD; American electrical engineer, computer scientist, business executive and fmr academic; *Founding Chairman and CEO Emeritus, Qualcomm Corporation;* b. New Bedford, Mass; m. Joan Jacobs; ed Cornell Univ., Massachusetts Inst. of Tech.; Asst Prof., then Assoc. Prof. of Electrical Eng, MIT 1959–66; Prof. of Computer Science and Eng, Univ. of California, San Diego 1966–72; Co-founder, Chair. and CEO Linkabit Corpn (merged with M/A-COM 1980), Exec. Vice-Pres. and mem. Bd of Dirs –1985; Founding Chair. and CEO Qualcomm –2005, CEO Emer. 2005–, Chair. –2009; Chair. Bd of Trustees, Salk Inst. 2006, Nat. Acad. of Eng 2008; mem. Nat. Acad. of Eng 1982; Fellow, IEEE 1974, American Acad. of Arts and Sciences 2001, AAAS 2010; Hon. Prof., Beijing Univ. of Posts and Telecom 2005; Dr hc (Technion Israel Inst. of Tech.) 2000, (Univ. of Pennsylvania) 2002, (Univ. of Waterloo) 2005, (San Diego State Univ.) 2006, (Univ. of San Diego) 2007, (Univ. of Massachusetts, Dartmouth) 2008; Hon. PhD (Tel-Aviv Univ.) 2010; Nat. Medal of Tech. Award 1994, IEEE Alexander Graham Bell Medal 1995, Medal of Achievement Award, American Electronics Asscn 1998, inducted into Radio Communication Report Wireless Hall of Fame 2000, Bower Award in Business Leadership, Franklin Inst. 2001, Dr Morris Chang Exemplary Leadership Award, The Fabless Semiconductor Asscn 2003, Dorothy I. Height Chair's Award, Leadership Council on Civil Rights 2004, Lifetime Achievement Award (for 25 years in telecommunications), Financial Times 2005, Wolfson James Clerk Maxwell Award, IEEE/Royal Soc. of Edinburgh (co-recipient) 2007, Robert N. Noyce Award, Semiconductor Industry Asscn 2007, Visionary Award, SDForum 2008, Inaugural Hall of Fame Award, IEEE VTC 2009, inducted into Consumer Electronics Hall of Fame 2009, Lifetime Achievement Award, Ernst and Young 2011, ACE Award's Lifetime Achievement Award, EE Times 2011, Marconi Prize 2011. *Publications:* Principles of Communication Engineering (with Jack Wozencraft) 1965; numerous papers in professional journals; 14 patents. *Address:* c/o Qualcomm, 5775 Morehouse Drive, San Diego, CA 92121, USA.

JACOBS, Kenneth Marc, AB, MBA; American investment banker; *Chairman and CEO, Lazard LLC;* b. 1958; m. Agnes Mentre; ed Univ. of Chicago, Stanford Univ.; with Goldman Sachs 1984–88; joined Lazard 1988, Pnr, 1991–, Head of N America and Deputy Chair. 2002–09, Chair. and CEO 2009–; Trustee, Univ. of Chicago, Brookings Inst. *Address:* Lazard LLC, 30 Rockefeller Plaza, New York, NY 10020-0015, USA (office). *Telephone:* (212) 632-6000 (office). *E-mail:* kenneth.jacobs@lazard.com (office). *Website:* www.lazard.com (office).

JACOBS, Marc; American fashion designer; b. 9 April 1963, New York City; ed High School of Art and Design, New York, Parsons School of Design; f. Jacobs Duffy Designs (with Robert Duffy) 1984; initiated Marc Jacobs design label 1986; Vice-Pres. Women's Design, Perry Ellis 1989; promoted 'grunge' fashion, early 1990s; Artistic Dir Louis Vuitton 1997–; CFDA Perry Ellis Award for New Talent 1987, CFDA Women's Designer of the Year Award 1992, VH1 Women's Designer of the Year Award, CFDA Accessory Designer of the Year, Best New Retail Concept Award, British Fashion Awards 2007. *Address:* 163 Mercer Street, New York, NY 10012, USA (office). *Telephone:* (212) 343-0222 (office). *Fax:* (212) 343-2960 (office). *Website:* www.marcjacobs.com (office).

JACOBS, Peter Alan, BSc; British business executive; b. 22 Feb. 1943, Ayrshire, Scotland; m. Eileen Dorothy Naftalin 1966; two s. one d.; ed Univs of Glasgow and Aston; Production Man. Pedigree Petfoods 1981–83; Sales Dir Mars Confectionery

1983–86; Man. Dir British Sugar PLC 1986–91; Dir S. & W. Berisford PLC 1986–91; CEO British United Provident Asscn 1991–98; Chair. Healthcall 1998–2001; Chair. L. A. Fitness 1999–, W.T. Foods; Chair. Hillsdown Holdings 1998–99, Bank Leumi (UK) 1998–2003, Allied Domecq 1998–2004, Cove Park 2000–, RAF Strike Command 2002–09, abc media 2005–10. *Leisure interests:* tennis, squash, music, theatre, fund-raising. *Address:* 29 Daleham Gardens, London, NW3 5BY, England (home). *E-mail:* jacobs@peatonhouse.co.uk (office).

JACOBS, René, BPhil; Belgian conductor and singer (countertenor); *Artistic Director, Innsbrucker Festwochen der alten Musik;* b. 30 Oct. 1946, Ghent; m. Roubina Saidkhanian; ed Univ. of Ghent, studied singing with Louis Devos in Brussels, Lucie Frateur in The Hague; recitals in Europe, Canada, USA, Japan, Mexico and the Philippines; performances with madrigal ensembles and with early music groups, including the Leonhardt Consort, Il Complesso Barocco, La Petite Bande and groups led by Alan Curtis and Nikolaus Harnoncourt; sings Baroque music and directs his own ensemble, Concerto Vocale; best known in operas by Monteverdi, Cesti, Handel, Gluck and Cavalli; sacred music by Charpentier and Couperin; teacher of performing practice in Baroque singing, Schola Cantorum, Basle; appointments at the Int. Summer School for Early Music, Innsbruck, and the Aston Magna Acad. for Baroque Music, USA; regularly invited as conductor by Brussels La Monnaie, Berlin Staatsoper Unter den Linden and Theater an der Wien; conducted Cavalli's Giasone, La Calisto, Eliogabalo, Gassmann's Opera seria, Handel's Flavio, Agrippina, Rinaldo, Semele, Giulio Cesare, Monteverdi's L'Incoronazione de Poppea, L'Orfeo, Il ritorno d'Ulisse in patria, Madrigals, Graun's Cleopatra e Cesare, Scarlatti's Griselda, Haydn's Il mondo della luna, Orlando Paladino, Conti's Don Chisciotte, Telemann's Orpheus, Der geduldige Sokrates, Keiser's Croesus, Mozart's Nozze di Figaro, Così fan tutte, Don Giovanni, La Clemenza di Tito, Idomeneo, Die Zauberflöte, La Finta Giardiniera; Rossini's Tancredi; Artistic Dir Innsbrucker Festwochen der alten Musik –2009; Dr hc (Univ. of Ghent) 2008; Acad. Charles Cros Prix in Honorem 2001, Deutsche Schallplattenpreis Ehrenurkunde 2004, MIDEM Classical Award for Artist of the Year 2005, Gramophone Award for Musical Personality of the Year 2006, Partituren Dirigent des Jahres 2007, Grammy Awards 2007, Telemannpreis Preis 2008. *Recordings:* Cesti's L'Orontea (from the 1982 Holland Festival), Arias by Monteverdi and Benedetto Ferrari, Motets by Charpentier, Bach's St Matthew Passion, Handel's Admeto and Partenope, Lully's Bourgeois Gentilhomme, Gluck's Orfeo ed Euridice and Echo et Narcisse, Giasone and La Calisto by Cavalli, Handel's Alessandro and Tamerlano, Charpentier's David et Jonathas, Handel's Flavio (Deutsche Schallplattenkritik Jahrespreis 1991), Telemann's Orpheus (Deutsche Schaalplattenkritik Jahrespreis 1998), Scarlatti's Il primo omicidio, Keiser's Croesus, Handel's Giulio Cesare, Handel's Rinaldo (Cannes Classical Award 2004), Mozart's Così fan tutte, Mozart's Le nozze di Figaro (Echo Klassik 2005, MIDEM Classical Music Award for Recording of the Year 2005, Grammy Award for Best Opera 2007) 2004, Handel's Saul (MIDEM Classical Music Award Baroque category 2006, Gramophone Award for Best Baroque Vocal Recording 2006, Echo Klassik 2006) 2005, Haydn's Symphonies Nos 91 & 92 2005, Handel's Messiah 2006, La Clemenza di Tito (Deutsche Schallplattenkritik Jahrespreis 2006, Abendzeitung Stern des Jahres 2006, Classical BRIT Award Critics' Award 2007, Echo Klassik 2007, Openwelt 2007), Mozart's Don Giovanni, Idomeneo 2009, Mozart's The Magic Flute 2010, Handel's Agrippina (BBC Music Magazine Opera Award 2012). *Address:* c/o Double Bande, 2 passage Philippe Auguste, 75011 Paris, France (office). *E-mail:* doublebande@aol.com (office).

JACOBSEN, Eric N., BS, PhD; American chemist and academic; *Sheldon Emery Professor of Chemistry, Harvard University;* b. 22 Feb. 1960, New York, NY; m. Virginia Estevez 1997; three d.; ed New York Univ., Univ. of California, Berkeley; NIH Postdoctoral Fellow, MIT, Cambridge, Mass 1986–88; Asst Prof., Univ. of Illinois, Urbana-Champaign 1988–91, Assoc. Prof. 1991–93; Prof. of Chem., Harvard Univ. 1993–2001, Sheldon Emery Prof. of Chem. 2001–; consultant, Sepracor, Marlboro, Mass 1990–2007, Merck, Rahway, NJ 1994–, Amgen, Thousand Oaks, Calif. 2003–, Daiso Co., Osaka, Japan 2006–, Firmenich, Geneva, Switzerland 2009–; mem. Scientific Advisory Bd PTC Therapeutics, South Plainfield, NJ 2001–, Cubist Pharmaceuticals, Lexington, Mass 2007–; Perm. mem. NIH Medicinal Chem. Study Section 1996–2000, mem. NIH Gen. Medical Sciences Council 2003–07; mem. Editorial Bd Advanced Synthesis and Catalysis, Science of Synthesis; mem. Advisory Editorial Bd Journal of Organic Chemistry, Synthesis, Synlett, Organic Letters, Journal of Combinatorial Chemistry, Journal of Molecular Catalysis, Current Opinion in Drug Discovery & Development, Chemistry: An Asian Journal; Fellow, AAAS 1997; mem. American Acad. of Arts and Sciences 2004, NAS 2008; New York State Regents Scholarship Award 1978–82, George Granger Brown Award 1981, New York Univ. Chem. Alumni Award 1982, Univ. of California Regents Fellowship 1984, 1985, Teaching Award, Univ. of Illinois School of Chemical Sciences 1989, UIUC List of Teachers Ranked as Outstanding by Their Students (five semesters) 1989–93, NSF Presidential Young Investigator Award 1990, Beckman Fellow 1991, Packard Fellowship 1991, Eli Lilly Grantee 1991, Merck Faculty Devt Award 1991, Union Carbide Innovation Award 1992, A.P. Sloan Foundation Fellowship 1992, Camile and Henry Dreyfus Teacher-Scholar Award 1992, Cyanamid Young Faculty Award 1992, Univ. of Illinois Scholar 1992, Pfizer Young Faculty Award for Synthetic Organic Chem. 1993, Zeneca Chem. Award 1993, Arthur C. Cope Scholar 1994, Fluka Prize for 'Reagent of the Year' 1994, Thieme-IUPAC Award in Synthetic Organic Chem. 1996, Harvard Coll. Professorship 1998–2003, Van't Hoff Prize 1998, Piero Pino Prize 1999, Baekeland Award 1999, ACS Award for Creative Work in Organic Synthesis 2001, NIH Merit Award 2002, Phi Beta Kappa Teaching Prize 2003, AIC Chemical Pioneer Award 2004, Mitsui Catalysis Award 2005, Alan R. Day Award 2007, ACS H.C. Brown Award for Synthetic Methods 2008, Yamada-Koga Prize 2008, Aldrich Lectureship, Scripps Research Inst., La Jolla, Calif. 2009, Boeringer-Ingelheim Lectureship, Columbia Univ., New York 2009, Astra-Zeneca Excellence in Chem. Award Keynote Lecturer, Wilmington, Del. 2009, Closs Lecturer, Univ. of Chicago 2009, Janssen Pharmaceutica Prize for Creativity in Organic Synthesis 2010. *Publications:* more than 200 papers in professional journals. *Address:* Department of Chemistry and Chemical Biology, 12 Oxford Street, Cambridge, MA 02138, USA (office). *Telephone:* (617) 496-3688 (office). *Fax:* (617) 496-1880 (office). *E-mail:* jacobsen@chemistry.harvard.edu (office). *Website:* www.chem.harvard.edu/groups/Jacobsen (office).

JACOBSON, Nina; American film industry executive; ed Brown Univ.; began film career as documentary researcher; joined Disney as story analyst in 1987; joined Silver Pictures as Dir of Film Devt 1988; fmr Head of Devt, MacDonald/Parkes Productions; fmr Sr Vice-Pres. of Production, Universal Pictures; fmr Sr Film Exec., DreamWorks SKG; joined Walt Disney in 1998, responsible for developing scripts and overseeing film production for Walt Disney Pictures, Touchstone Pictures and Hollywood Pictures, Pres. Buena Vista Motion Pictures Group –2006; f. Color Force (production co.) 2007, affiliated with Dreamworks SKG; Co-founder (with Bruce Cohen) Out There (collection of gay and lesbian entertainment industry activists) 1995; ranked 94th by Forbes magazine amongst 100 Most Powerful Women 2005. *Films produced include:* Diary of a Wimpy Kid 2010, One Day 2011, The Hunger Games 2012. *Address:* c/o DreamWorks Studios, 100 Universal City Plaza, Building 5125, Universal City, CA 91608, USA (office).

JACOMB, Sir Martin Wakefield, Kt, MA; British banker and business executive; *Chairman, Share PLC;* b. 11 Nov. 1929, Chiddingfold, Surrey; s. of Felise Jacomb and Hilary W. Jacomb; m. Evelyn Heathcoat Amory 1960; two s. one d.; ed Eton Coll. and Worcester Coll. Oxford; practised at the Bar 1955–68; Kleinwort, Benson Ltd 1968–85, Vice-Chair. 1976–85; Dir Hudson's Bay Co., Canada 1971–86; Chair. The Merchants Trust PLC 1974–85, Transatlantic Fund Inc. 1978–85; Dir Christian Salvesen PLC 1974–88, British Gas PLC 1981–88; Deputy Chair. Securities and Investments Bd Ltd 1985–87; a Deputy Chair. Barclays Bank PLC 1985–93; Chair. Barclays de Zoete Wedd 1986–91, British Council 1992–98; Dir Commercial Union Assurance Co. PLC 1984–93 (Deputy Chair. 1988–93); Dir Bank of England 1986–95, Daily Telegraph 1986–95, RTZ Corpn PLC (now Rio Tinto PLC) 1988–2000; Chair. Postel Investment Man. Ltd 1991–95; Dir Marks and Spencer 1991–2000, Canary Wharf Group PLC 1999– (Chair. 2004–11), Minorplanet Systems PLC 2000–04; Deputy Chair. (non-exec.) Delta PLC 1993–94, Chair. 1993–2004; Chair. Prudential Corpn 1995–2000 (Dir 1994–2000), Share PLC 2001–; Dir Royal Opera House Covent Garden Ltd 1987–92, Oxford Playhouse Trust Ltd 1994, Oxford Playhouse Ltd 1994; External mem., Finance Cttee, Oxford University Press 1971–95; Hon. Master of the Bench of the Inner Temple 1987; Trustee, Nat. Heritage Memorial Fund 1982–97; Chancellor Univ. of Buckingham 1998–2010; Hon. Fellow, Worcester Coll. Oxford 1994; Dr hc (Buckingham) 1997, (Oxford) 1997. *Leisure interests:* theatre, family bridge. *Address:* Share PLC, The Share Centre, Oxford House, Oxford Road, Aylesbury, Bucks., HP21 8SZ, England (office). *Telephone:* (1296) 414141 (office). *Fax:* (1296) 414140 (office). *E-mail:* barbara.pierssene@share.co.uk (office). *Website:* www.share.co.uk (office).

JACQUEMARD, Simonne; French novelist, poet and essayist; b. 6 May 1924, Paris; d. of André Jacquemard and Andrée Jacquemard (née Raimondi); m. 2nd Jacques Brosse 1955; ed Inst. Saint-Pierre, Univ. of Paris; teacher of music; collaborator, Laffont-Bompiani Dictionaries; contrib. to Figaro Littéraire, La Table Ronde; travelled in USSR, Egypt, Greece, Italy, N Africa and Spain; Officier Ordre des Arts et des Lettres 1993, Chevalier Légion d'honneur 1999; Prix Renaudot 1962, Grand prix Thyde-Monnier 1984. *Dance:* Sacred dances of India; flamenco dance shows 1982–2000. *Publications include:* Les fascinés 1951, Sable 1952, La leçon des ténèbres 1954, Planant sur les airs 1960, Compagnons insolites 1961, Le veilleur de nuit 1962 (Prix Renaudot 1962), L'orangerie 1963, Les derniers rapaces 1965, Dérive au zénith 1965, Exploration d'un corps 1965, Navigation vers les îles 1967, A l'état sauvage 1967, L'éruption du Krakatoa 1969, La thessalienne 1973, Des roses pour mes chevreuils 1974, Le mariage berbère 1975, Danse de l'orée 1979, Le funambule 1981, Lalla Zahra 1983, La fête en éclats 1985, Les belles échappées 1987, L'huître dans la perle 1993, Le Jardin d'Hérodote 1995, L'Éphèbe couronné de lierre 1995, La Gloire d'Ishwara 1996, Vers l'estuaire ébloui 1996, Trois mystiques grecs 1997, Orphée ou l'initiation mystique (jtly) 1998, L'Oiseau 1963, 1998 (Prix Jacques Lacroix, l'Académie française 1999), Héraclite d'Ephèse 2003, Rituels 2004, Pythagore et l'Harmonie des Sphères 2004. *Leisure interests:* studies on music (with Lucette Descave and Henriette Casadesus) and on bird life and observation of wild animals.

JACQUES, Paula; French author and broadcaster; b. 8 May 1949, Cairo, Egypt; d. of Jacques Abadi and Esther Sasson; m. (divorced 1970); worked as comedienne in Africa; joined Radio France Internationale as reporter, worked on Après-midi de France-Culture, L'Oreille en coin 1975–90; presenter, Nuits-noires France-Inter radio 1997–, Cosmopolitaine 2000–; sometime writer, F Magazine; mem. jury Prix Femina 1996–, Prix des Cinq Continents. *Play:* Zanouba. *Publications:* Lumière de l'oeil 1980, Un baiser froid comme la lune 1983, L'Heritage de Tante Carlotta 1987, Deborah et les anges dissipés (Prix Femina 1991), La Déscente au Paradis (Prix Nice Baie des Anges) 1995, Les femmes avec leur amour 1997, Gilda Stambouli souffre et se plaint... (Prix Europe 1) 2001, Rachel-Rose et l'officier arabe (Prix des Sables d'Olonne) 2006, Kairo Jacobi, juste avant l'oubli 2011. *Address:* France-Inter, 116 avenue du Président Kennedy, 75220 Paris cedex 16, France.

JACQUET, Luc; French filmmaker and writer; b. 5 Dec. 1967, Bourg-en-Bresse; fmr biologist. *Films:* Le congès des pingouins (cinematographer) 1993, Le printemps des phoques de Weddell (Ancre de bronze, Festival Int. du Film Maritime et d'Exploration, Toulon 1996, Coup de coeur du jury, Festival Int. du Film Montagne et Aventure, Autrans 1996) 1996, Le léopard de mer: la part de l'ogre (Palme d'Argent & Prix de la Meilleure Composition Musicale, Festival Mondial de l'Image Sous-Marine, Antibes 1999, Prix pour l'Excellente Qualité des Prises de Vues Sous-marines & Prix pour la Musique, Festival Int. du Film sur la Vie Sauvage, Missoula, Mont., USA 2000, Prix de la Meilleure Réalisation, Ekofilm – Festival Int. du Film de l'Environnement, Prague 2000) 1999, Killer Whales: Up Close and Personal (cinematographer) 2000, Une plage et trop de manchots (Primé au Festival Int. du Film Ornithologique de Ménigoute 2001) 2001, La tique et l'oiseau (Prix Nature et Découvertes, Festival Int. du Film Ornithologique de Ménigoute 2002, Prix du meilleur commentaire, Festival Valvert, Brussels 2002, Prix de la côte Picarde, Festival de l'oiseau d'Abbeville 2002) 2001, Sous le signe du serpent 2004, Antarctique printemps express (Prix Spécial Meilleur son, Festival Vertical de Moscou 2006) 2004, Des manchots et des hommes (Of Penguins and Men) (One Planet Award, Wildlife Film Festival, Toyama 2005, Grand prix du public Festival Grandeur Nature, Val d'Isère 2005, Best Film, Prix Jules Verne du Public, Prix Jules Verne de la Jeunesse, Festival Jules Verne 2005, Grand Prix, Festival de l'oiseau, Abbeville 2005, Ancre d'Argent, Prix des collégiens, Festival Int. du Film Maritime et d'Exploration, Toulon 2005, Edelweiss d'Argent, Festival

du film de montagne de Torello 2005, Prix Adventura Homme et environnement, Mountain Film Festival, Canada 2005) 2004, La marche de l'empereur (The Emperor's Journey, aka March of the Penguins, USA) (Best Film Documentary, Las Vegas Film Critics Soc. Awards 2005, Nat. Board of Review (USA) 2005, Southeastern Film Critics Asscn Awards (USA) 2005, Broadcast Film Critics Asscn Awards (USA) 2006, Golden Trailer Awards (USA) 2006, Camie, Character and Morality in Entertainment Awards (co-recipient) 2006) 2005, Academy Award for Best Documentary, Features 2006, and numerous other awards) 2005, Le renard et l'enfant (The Fox and the Child) 2007. *E-mail:* contact@luc-jacquet.com (office). *Website:* www.luc-jacquet.com (office).

JACQUET, Michel Antoine Paul Marie; French business executive; b. 28 March 1936, Dijon; s. of André Jacquet and Marie-Antoinette Baut; m. 2nd Marie-Agnès Corbière 1976; one s. and one s. one d. by first m.; ed Lycée Rouget de Lisle, Lons-le-Saulnier, Lycée du Parc, Lyons and Ecole Polytechnique; Dir-Gen. Crédit Lyonnais d'Espagne 1971–77; Dir-Gen. Paribas Gabon and Pres. Sogapar 1977–79; Deputy Dir Banque Paribas 1980–84; CEO Paribas New York 1985–88; Pres. Nord-Est and Magnésia 1989–95, Hon. Pres. Nord-Est 1995–; currently Pres. Ledo-Salina; Vice-Chair. Supervisory Bd EDF Partenaires Capital Investissement; mem. Supervisory Bd Poincaré Investissements; mem. Bd of Dirs Lombard Int. Assurance, Texavenir, Renaissance Holdings, Cinq A Sec Holdings, LCIE Landaver;; Croix de valeur militaire, Chevalier Légion d'honneur. *Address:* Ledo-Salina, 46–48 rue Lauriston, 75116 Paris (office); 15 rue Raynouard, 75016 Paris, France (home). *E-mail:* .

JADHAV, Arvind, MA, MBA; Indian civil servant and airline industry executive; *Chairman, Karnataka Urban Infrastructure Development and Finance Corporation Limited;* b. 5 June 1956; ed Kanpur Univ., Indian Inst. of Foreign Trade, Italian Inst. of Foreign Trade, Rome, Curtin Univ., Australia; joined Indian Admin. Service 1978; Asst Commr Land Revenue Man. Div. 1980; Jt Sec. Ministry of Power; Chief Vigilance Officer Gas Authority of India Ltd; Prin. Sec., Infrastructure Devt Dept, Govt of Karnataka –2009; fmr Commr Karnataka Housing Bd; fmr Sec. Energy Dept; fmr Man. Dir Mysore Minerals Ltd; fmr Commr Commerce and Industries Dept; Dir Société Internationale de Télécommunications Aéronautiques, Bangalore Int. Airport Ltd, Nat. Thermal Power Corpn 2003–05, Rural Electrification Corpn Ltd 2002–07, Power Finance Corpn Ltd –2006; played active role in introducing public-pvt. partnership model to develop Bangalore Int. Airport Ltd; Chair. and Man. Dir Nat. Aviation Co. of India Ltd which operates Air India 2009–11; Chair. Karnataka Urban Infrastructure Devt and Finance Corpn Ltd 2012–; Distinguished Fellowship, Golden Peacock Awards 2010. *Address:* Karnataka Urban Infrastructure Development and Finance Corporation Limited, Silver Jubilee Block, II Floor, III Cross, Mission Road, Bangalore, 560 027, India (office). *Telephone:* (80) 22232021 (office). *Fax:* (80) 2223215 (office). *E-mail:* info@kuidfc.com (office). *Website:* www.kuidfc.com (office).

JAEGER, Heinrich Martin, PhD; German physicist and academic; *Director, James Franck Institute, University of Chicago;* b. 15 May 1957, Flensburg; m. Julie Jaeger; one c.; ed Univ. of Kiel, Germany, Univ. of Minnesota, USA; Postdoctoral Fellow, Univ. of Chicago 1987–88, Asst Prof. 1991–96, Assoc. Prof. 1996–2000, Prof. 2000, Dir Materials Research Center 2001–06, Argonne Consortium for Nanoscience Research 2001–, James Franck Inst. 2007–, Chair. Physical Sciences Div. Cttee on Diversity 2005–; Sr Researcher, Centre for Submicron Tech., Delft Univ. of Tech., The Netherlands 1989–91; mem. Tech. Advisory Bd Atomworks 2003–; mem. Scientific Advisory Cttee, Argonne Center for Nanoscale Materials 2003–; mem. Essential Science Task Force, Chicago Museum of Science and Industry 2003–; mem. External Advisory Bd Centro para la Investigación Interdisciplinaria Avanzada en Ciencias de los Materiales, Chile 2004–; Fellow, American Physical Soc. 2002; Fulbright Scholarship 1981–82, Univ. of Minnesota Dissertation Fellowship 1986–87, James Franck Fellowship, Univ. of Chicago 1987–88, David and Lucile Packard Fellowship 1991–96, Alfred P. Sloan Research Fellowship 1992–94, Research Corpn Cottrell Scholarship 1994–96, Outstanding Achievement Award, Univ. of Minnesota 2002, Quantrell Award for Excellence in Undergraduate Teaching. *Publications:* author or co-author of over 130 scientific publs. *Address:* James Franck Institute, Center for Integrative Science, E229, University of Chicago, 929 East 57th Street, Chicago, IL 60637, USA (office). *Telephone:* (773) 702-6074 (office). *Fax:* (773) 834-0471 (office). *E-mail:* h-jaeger@uchicago.edu (office). *Website:* jfi.uchicago.edu (office).

JAEGER, Marc; Luxembourg judge; *President, Court of First Instance of the European Communities;* b. 1954; fmr attaché de justice, Public Attorney's Office; fmr Judge and Vice-Pres. Luxembourg Dist Court; Lecturer, Centre Univ. de Luxembourg; Legal Sec. Court of Justice of the European Communities 1986–; Judge, Court of First Instance 1996–, Pres. 2007–. *Address:* Court of the First Instance of the European Communities, rue du Fort Niedergrünewald, 2925 Luxembourg, Luxembourg (office). *Telephone:* 4303-1 (office). *Fax:* 4303-2100 (office). *Website:* www.curia.eu.int (office).

JAENICKE, Lothar, DPhil, DiplChem; German biochemist; b. 14 Sept. 1923, Berlin; s. of Johannes Jaenicke and Erna Jaenicke (née Buttermilch); m. Dr Doris Heinzel 1949 (died 2005); two s. two d.; ed Univs of Marburg, Tübingen; taught Univ. of Marburg 1946–57, Munich 1957–62, Cologne 1962, apptd. Prof. Cologne Univ. 1963, also Dir Inst. of Biochem. 1988, now Prof. Emer.; Visiting Scientist All India Inst. of Medicine, New Delhi 1961, Univ. of Texas, Austin 1977, 1992, 1994, 1996; Visiting Prof. American Univ. of Beirut 1971, Ain Shams Univ., Cairo 1974, Indian Inst. of Science, Bangalore 1980; mem. Nordrhein-Westfälische Akademie der Wissenschaften, Deutsche Akademie der Naturforscher Leopoldina, American Acad. of Microbiology 2000; Corresp. mem. Bayerische Akad. der Wissenschaften, Academia Europea; Fellow, Wissenschaftskolleg Berlin 1986–87; Hon. mem. Gesellschaft für Biochemie und Molekular Biologie, Gesellschaft der Naturforschung und Ärzte 2000; Paul Ehrlich/Ludwig-Darmstaedter-Preis 1963, Otto Warburg Medal 1979, Richard Kuhn Medal 1984, Lorenz Oken Medal 2000. *Publications:* Profiles in Biochemistry 2007, Profiles in Cell Biology 2010; around 270 original papers on enzymology and biochemical signalling in scientific journals. *Address:* Kaesenstr. 13, 50677 Cologne (home); University of Cologne Institute of Biochemistry, Zülpicherstr. 47, 50674 Cologne, Germany (office). *Telephone:* (221) 4706425 (office); (221) 315725 (home). *Fax:* (221) 4706431 (office).

JAENISCH, Rudolf, MD; German biologist and academic; *Professor of Biology, Whitehead Institute for Biomedical Research, Massachusetts Institute of Technology;* b. 1942, Wölfelsgrund; ed Univ. of Munich; fmr Head of Dept of Tumor Virology, Heinrich Pette Inst., Univ. of Hamburg; currently mem. Whitehead Inst. for Biomedical Research and Prof. of Biology, MIT; Visiting Scientist, Max Planck Inst. for Biochemistry, Munich, Princeton Univ. Fox Chase Cancer Center, Philadelphia, Salk Inst., La Jolla, Calif.; participated in science conf. on human cloning at UN 2004; mem. Science Advisory Bd Genetics Policy Inst., Stemgent; mem. NAS 2003, Inst. of Medicine; Fellow, American Acad. of Arts and Sciences; Boehringer Mannheim Molecular Bioanalytics Prize 1996, first Peter Gruber Foundation Award in Genetics 2001, Robert Koch Prize for Excellence in Scientific Achievement 2002, Brupracher Foundation Cancer Award 2003, Vilcek Prize 2007, Meira and Shaul G. Massry Prize 2008, Cozzarelli Prize, Proceedings of the NAS (PNAS) 2009, Ernst Schering Prize 2009, Pres.'s Nat. Medal of Science for 2010, Wolf Prize in Medicine 2011, J. Allyn Taylor Int. Prize in Medicine 2011, Benjamin Franklin Medal in Life Science 2013. *Achievements include:* recognized as a leader in the field of therapeutic cloning, also known as nuclear transfer; first breakthrough when, along with Beatrice Mintz, showed that foreign DNA could be integrated into DNA of early mouse embryos 1974; created first transgenic animal model, carried out first experiment showing that therapeutic cloning could correct genetic defects in mice. *Publications:* more than 375 research papers in professional journals. *Address:* Room WI 467, Whitehead Institute for Biomedical Research, 9 Cambridge Center, Cambridge, MA 02142-1479, USA (office). *Telephone:* (617) 258-5186 (office); (617) 258-5189 (office). *E-mail:* jaenisch@wi .mit.edu (office); kemske@wi.mit.edu (office). *Website:* biology.mit.edu/people/ rudolf_jaenisch (office); wi.mit.edu/people/faculty/jaenisch (office); www .stemcellsportal.com/stem-cells-articles/featured-labs/1-dr-rudolf-jaenisch-lab .html (office).

JAFFE, Harold W., BA, MD; American epidemiologist and academic; *Associate Director for Science, Centers for Disease Control and Prevention;* b. 26 April 1946, Newton, Mass.; ed Univ. of California, Berkeley, Univ. of California, Los Angeles; Jr doctor at UCLA Hosp. 1971–74; Clinical Research Investigator, Venereal Disease Control Div., Centers for Disease Control (CDC), Atlanta 1974–77, 1980–81, Epidemic Intelligence Service Officer for AIDS Activity 1981–83, f. (with James W. Curran and others) Kaposi's Sarcoma-Opportunistic Infections Task Force, Center for Infectious Diseases to study causes of immune-deficiency disease in homosexual men 1981, Chief, Epidemiology Br. of AIDS Programme, CDC 1983–, Dir Div. AIDS, STD and TB Laboratory Research –2001, Acting Dir Nat. Center for HIV, STD, and TB Prevention (NCHSTP) 2001, Dir 2002–03; Fellow, St Cross College, Prof. of Public Health and Chair. Dept of Public Health, Univ. of Oxford, UK 2004–10; Assoc. Dir for Science, CDC, Atlanta 2010–; Fellow in Infectious Diseases, Univ. of Chicago 1977–80; Visiting Prof., Chester Beatty Labs, Inst. of Cancer Research and Dept of Medicine, Hammersmith Hosp., London, 1988–90; Clinical Instructor of Medicine, Emory Univ. School of Medicine, Atlanta; Assoc. Ed. American Journal of Epidemiology; mem. Editorial Bd AIDS journal; mem. Inst. of Medicine, NAS 2006–, Infectious Diseases Soc. of America; Commendation Medal for work on HIV/AIDS, US Public Health Service 1984, Meritorious Service Medal 1986, Distinguished Service Medal 1992. *Publications:* book chapters and over 90 articles in scientific journals, including Epidemiologic Aspects of the Current Outbreak of Kaposi's Sarcoma and Opportunistic Infections, in New England Journal of Medicine Jan. 1982, The Epidemiology of AIDS: Current Status and Future Prospects, in Science Sept. 1985 (co-author), HIV Infection and AIDS in the United States, in Science Feb. 1989 (co-author). *Address:* Centers for Disease Control and Prevention, 1600 Clifton Road, Atlanta, GA 30333, USA (office). *E-mail:* cdcinfo@cdc.gov (office). *Website:* www.cdc.gov (office).

JAFFE, Stanley Richard, BEcons; American film producer and director; b. 31 July 1940, New Rochelle, New York; s. of Leo Jaffe and Dora Bressler; m. Melinda Long; two s. two d.; ed Wharton School, Univ. of Pennsylvania; with Seven Arts Assoc. Corpn 1962–67, exec. Asst to Pres. 1964; Dir East Coast Programming, Seven Arts TV 1963–64, Dir Programming 1965–67; Exec. Vice-Pres., Chief Corp. Officer, Paramount Pictures Corpn 1969–70, Pres. Corpn also Pres. Paramount TV 1970–71; Pres. Jaffilms Inc. 1971; Exec. Vice-Pres. Worldwide Production, Columbia Pictures Corpn 1965–76; Pres. and COO Paramount Communications, New York 1991–94; Gov., Pres., COO New York Knicks 1991–94; Gov. New York Rangers 1991–94; Owner, Jaffilms LLC 1994–. *Films include:* The Professionals 1963, Goodbye Columbus 1968, Bad Company 1971, Man on A Swing 1973, Bad News Bears 1974, Kramer vs Kramer 1979, Taps 1981, Without a Trace 1983, Racing with the Moon 1984, Firstborn 1984, Fatal Attraction 1987, The Accused 1988, Black Rain 1989, School Ties 1992, The Firm 1993, Madeleine 1998, I Dreamed of Africa 2000, Four Feathers 2002. *Address:* 2 Sackett Landing, Rye, NY 10580-4315; Jaffilms LLC, 152 West 57th St, New York, NY 10019-3386, USA.

JAFFRELOT, Christophe, PhD; French political scientist and academic; *Director, Centre d'Études et de Recherches Internationales;* ed Institut d'études politiques, Univ. Paris I – Sorbonne, Institut nat. des langues et civilisations orientales; Lecturer in South Asian Politics, Institut d'études politiques, Univ. Paris I – Sorbonne and Institut nat. des langues et civilisations orientales; Dir Centre d'études et de recherches internationales (CERI); Alliance Visiting Prof., Columbia Univ. 2009; Ed. Critique internationale. *Publications:* The Hindu Nationalist Movement and Indian Politics 1996, L'Inde contemporaine de 1950 à nos jours (ed.) 1997, La démocratie en Inde – Religion, caste et politique 1998, BJP – The Compulsions of Politics (co-ed.) 1998, Le Pakistan, carrefour de tensions régionales (ed.) 1999, Démocraties d'ailleurs: démocraties et démocratisations hors d'Occident (ed.) 2000, Le Pakistan (ed.) 2000, Dr Ambedkar 2000, Inde: La Démocratie par la caste 2005. *Address:* CERI, 56 rue Jacob, 75006 Paris, France (office). *Telephone:* 1-58-71-70-00 (office). *Fax:* 1-58-71-70-91 (office). *E-mail:* info@ ceri-sciences-po.org (office). *Website:* www.ceri-sciences-po.org (office).

JAGAT, Gurbachan, MA; Indian politician and fmr police officer; b. 1 July 1942; ed Punjab Univ., Chandigarh; joined Indian Police Service 1966; Sr Supt, Amritsar 1978–81; Deputy Insp. Gen. Intelligence/Security Div., Punjab Police Force 1982–90; Man. Dir Punjab Police Housing Corpn 1990–95; Dir-Gen. of Admin 1995–97; Dir-Gen. of Police, Jammu and Kashmir 1997–2000; Dir-Gen. Border Security Force 2000–02; Chair. Union Public Service Comm. 2006–07; Gov. of

Manipur 2008–13, of Nagaland July–Oct. 2009; Indian Police Medal for Meritorious Service 1982, Padma Shri 1987, Pres.'s Police Medal for Distinguished Service 1992, Police Officer of the Year Award (Govt of Jammu and Kashmir) 2001, Pres.'s Police Medal for Distinguished Service 1992, Pashchimi Star, Sangram Medal, Special Duty Medal, Aantrik Seva Suraksha Medal, Operation Rakhshak, Operation Vijay Medals. *Address:* c/o Raj Bhawan, Imphal 795 001, India.

JAGDEO, Bharrat, MEconSc; Guyanese politician and fmr head of state; b. 23 Jan. 1964, Unity Village, East Coast Demerara; ed Moscow State Univ.; mem. People's Progressive Party, elected to Cen. Cttee 1993, later mem. Exec. Cttee; worked as economist in State Planning Secr. 1990–92; Special Adviser to Minister of Finance 1992–93; Jr Minister of Finance 1993; fmrly Dir Guyana Water Authority; Dir Caribbean Devt Bank, Nat. Bank of Industry and Commerce, Gov. for Guyana, World Bank; Sr Finance Minister 1995–99; Prime Minister of Guyana 9–11 Aug. 1999; Pres. of Guyana 1999–2011; Pushkin Medal (Russia), Pravasi Bharatiya Samman Award (India). *Address:* c/o Office of the President, New Garden Street, Bourda, Georgetown, Guyana.

JAGENDORF, André Tridon, PhD; American biologist and academic; *Liberty Hyde Bailey Professor Emeritus of Plant Physiology, College of Agriculture and Life Sciences, Cornell University;* b. 21 Oct. 1926, New York, NY; s. of Moritz A. Jagendorf and Sophie S. Jagendorf; m. Jean Whitenack 1952; one s. two d.; ed Cornell and Yale Univs; Postdoctoral Fellow, UCLA 1951–53; Asst Prof., Johns Hopkins Univ., Baltimore, MD 1953–58, Assoc. Prof. 1958–65, Prof. of Biology 1966; Prof. of Plant Physiology, Cornell Univ., Ithaca, NY 1966–, Liberty Hyde Bailey Prof. of Plant Physiology 1981–96, Prof. Emer. 1997–; Pres. American Soc. of Plant Physiologists; Merck Fellow in Natural Sciences 1951–53; Weizmann Fellow 1962; AAAS Fellow 1964; mem. NAS 1983; Fellow, American Acad. of Arts and Sciences 1972; Distinguished Fellow, American Soc. of Plant Physiologists 2006; Outstanding Young Scientist Award, Md Acad. of Sciences 1961, Kettering Research Award 1963, Charles F. Kettering Award in Photosynthesis, American Soc. of Plant Physiologists 1979, Charles Reid Barnes Life Membership Award, American Soc. of Plant Physiologists 1989, Lifetime Achievement Award, Rebeiz Foundation 2013. *Publications:* more than 160 papers in scientific journals. *Leisure interests:* music, ballet, art, computer solitaire, jigsaw puzzles. *Address:* Plant Biology Department, 412 Mann Library Building, Cornell University, Ithaca, NY 14853 (office); 455 Savage Farm Drive, Ithaca, NY 14850, USA (home). *Telephone:* (607) 255-8940 (office); (607) 255-8826 (lab.) (office). *Fax:* (607) 255-5407 (office); (607) 266-0243 (home). *E-mail:* atj1@cornell.edu (office). *Website:* plantbio.cals.cornell.edu/people/emeritus-faculty (office).

JAGGER, Bianca, MA; British (b. Nicaraguan) artist, film director, human rights activist and environmental campaigner; *Founder and Chairman, Bianca Jagger Human Rights Foundation;* b. 2 May 1950, Managua, Nicaragua; d. of Carlos Perez-Mora and Dora Macias Somassiba; m. Michael (Mick) Jagger 1971 (divorced 1979); one d.; ed Inst. of Political Sciences, Paris and New York Univ.; lecturer on Cen. America at several colls and univs; Co-Founder Iris House, New York; has campaigned for human rights in Cen. America, mem. several US Congressional dels and dels from int. human rights orgs; visited the Fmr Yugoslavia to document alleged human rights violations and testified before Helsinki Comm. on Human Rights and US Congressional Human Rights Caucus; has helped to evacuate children from Bosnia 1993; works to protect rainforests in Honduras, Nicaragua and Brazil and indigenous peoples in Brazil, India and elsewhere; headed AIDS campaign 2001; Founder and Chair. Bianca Jagger Human Rights Foundation 2005–; mem. Exec. Dir's Leadership Council, Amnesty International USA, Advisory Cttee Human Rights Watch America, Bd of Dirs Action Council for Peace in the Balkans, Bd Hispanic Fed., New York; Special Adviser Indigenous Devt International, Cambridge, UK; Council of Europe Goodwill Amb. against the death penalty; Amb. for the Int. Union for Conservation of Nature (IUCN) Plant a Pledge campaign; Hon. DH (Stone Hill Coll., MA) 1983; Hon. Dr of Human Rights (Simmons Coll., Boston) 2008; Hon. LLD (Univ. of East London) 2010; UN Earth Day Int. Award 1994, Humanitarian Award, Hispanic Fed. of New York City 1996, 1996 Woman of the Year, Boys Town, Italy, Abolitionist of the Year Award, Nat. Coalition to Abolish the Death Penalty 1996, Right Livelihood Award 2004. *Films include:* Flesh Color, Success, Cannonball Run, Chud II, The Rutles. *Television includes:* Hotel, Miami Vice, The Colbys. *Publications:* contribs to New York Times, Observer, Guardian; has a blog on the Huffington Post. *Leisure interests:* horse-riding, water-skiing. *Address:* Bianca Jagger Human Rights Foundation, Unit 246, 272 Kensington High Street, London, W8 6ND, England. *Fax:* (20) 7361-0077. *Website:* www.biancajagger.org.

JAGGER, Sir Michael (Mick) Philip, Kt, KBE; British singer, songwriter and actor; b. 26 July 1943, Dartford, Kent; s. of the late Joe Jagger and Eva Jagger; m. 1st Bianca Pérez Morena de Macías 1971 (divorced 1979); one d.; m. 2nd Jerry Hall (q.v.) 1990 (divorced 1999); two s. two d.; one d. by Marsha Hunt; one c. by Luciana Morad; ed London School of Econs, Univ. of London; began singing career with Little Boy Blue and the Blue Boys while at LSE; appeared with Blues Inc. at Ealing Blues Club, singer with Blues Inc. at London Marquee Club 1962; Founder-mem. and lead singer, Rolling Stones 1962–; wrote songs with Keith Richards under pseudonyms Nanker, Phelge until 1965, without pseudonyms 1965–; first own composition to reach No. 1 in UK charts The Last Time 1965; first major UK tour 1964; tours to USA, Europe; fmrly lived in France; Pres. LSE Students' Union 1994–; Nordoff-Robbins Silver Clef 1982, Grammy Lifetime Achievement Award 1986, Ivor Novello Award for Outstanding Contribution to British Music 1991, Golden Globe Award for Best Original Song (for Old Habits Die Hard, with Dave Stewart, for film Alfie) 2005. *Films:* Ned Kelly (actor) 1969, Performance (actor) 1969, Gimme Shelter (actor) 1972, Free Jack (actor) 1991, Freejack (actor) 1992, Bent (actor) 1996, Enigma (producer) 2001, Shine a Light 2007. *Recordings include:* albums: with The Rolling Stones: The Rolling Stones 1964, The Rolling Stones No. 2 1965, Out Of Our Heads 1965, Aftermath 1966, Between The Buttons 1967, Their Satanic Majesties Request 1967, Beggar's Banquet 1968, Let It Bleed 1969, Get Yer Ya-Ya's Out 1969, Sticky Fingers 1971, Exile On Main Street 1972, Goat's Head Soup 1973, It's Only Rock And Roll 1974, Black And Blue 1976, Some Girls 1978, Emotional Rescue 1980, Tattoo You 1981, Still Life 1982, Undercover 1983, Dirty Work 1986, Steel Wheels 1989, Flashpoint 1991, Voodoo Lounge 1994, Stripped 1995, Bridges to Babylon 1997, Forty Licks 2002, Live Licks 2004, A Bigger Bang 2005; solo: She's The Boss 1985, Primitive Cool 1987, Wandering

Spirit 1993, Goddess In The Doorway 2001, The Very Best of 2007. *Publication:* According to the Rolling Stones (autobiog., jtly) 2003. *Telephone:* (20) 8877-3100 (office). *Fax:* (20) 8877-3077 (office). *Website:* www.mickjagger.com.

JAGLAND, Thorbjørn; Norwegian politician and international organization official; *Secretary-General, Council of Europe;* b. 5 Nov. 1950, Drammen; m. Hanne Grotjord 1975; two c.; ed Univ. of Oslo; mem. Buskerud Co. Council 1975–83; Chair. Labour Youth League (AUF), Buskerud Co. 1973–76, Chair. Norwegian Labour Youth League 1977–81, Sec. Labour Party Cttee on Disarmament 1982–, Acting Party Sec. Labour Party 1986–87, Chair. Labour Party Int. Cttee 1986–, Sec. Labour Party Programme Cttee 1986–89, Party Sec. Labour Party 1987–92, Chair. Norwegian Labour Party 1992–2002; mem. Storting for Buskerud Co. 1993–2009, Chair. Labour Party Parl. Group, Chair. Parl. EEA Consultative Cttee 2000–05, Parl. Standing Cttee on Foreign Affairs and Enlarged Foreign Affairs Cttee 2001–05, Pres. Storting 2005–09; Prime Minister 1996–97; Minister of Foreign Affairs 2000–01; Sec.-Gen. Council of Europe 2009–; mem. Norwegian del. for Relations with the European Parl. 1993–96, 1997–2000, Head of del. 2001–05; mem. Norwegian del. to Nordic Council 1993–96, 1997–2000, to NATO Parl. Ass. 2001–05; Head of Norwegian del. at Second Summit of Council of Europe, Strasbourg 1997; Chair. Socialist Int. Finance and Admin Cttee 1987–92, Vice-Pres. Socialist International 1999–2008, Chair. Middle East Cttee 2000–06; Chair. Oslo Center for Peace and Human Rights 2006–, Nobel Norwegian Cttee 2009–; mem. Int. Bd of Govs Peres Center for Peace 1997–; mem. Sharm El-Sheikh Fact-Finding Comm. ('Mitchell Comm.') 2000–01; Commdr, Légion d'honneur 2013. *Publications include:* Min europeiske drøm 1990, Ny solidaritet 1993, Brev 1995, Vår sårbare verden 2002, For det blir for sent (co-author) 1982, Ti tescr om EU og Norge 2003; numerous articles on defence, nat. security and disarmament. *Address:* Office of the Secretary-General, Council of Europe, 67075 Strasbourg Cedex, France (office). *Telephone:* (3) 88-41-20-00 (office). *Fax:* (3) 88-41-27-99 (office). *E-mail:* private.office@coe.int (office). *Website:* www.coe.int (office).

JAGNE, Baboucarr-Blaise Ismaila, MA; Gambian diplomatist; *Head of United Nations Political Affairs Division, African Union;* b. 11 Feb. 1955, Banjul; m.; four c.; ed Univ. of Dakar and Univs of Grenoble and Paris, France; Asst Sec., Foreign Ministry 1980–84, Sec. to Pres. of Gambia, Chair. Islamic Peace Cttee on Iran–Iraq War 1984–88, Sr Asst Sec. for Political Legal Affairs 1986–89, Prin. Asst Sec. 1989–92; Deputy Perm. Sec. for Educ. 1992–93, for Political Affairs 1993–95; Minister of External Affairs 1995–97; Amb. to Saudi Arabia 1997–98; Perm. Rep. to UN, New York 1998–2001; Sec. of State for Foreign Affairs 2001–05; Head of UN Political Affairs Div., African Union HQ, Addis Abba. *Address:* UN Political Affairs Division, African Union, POB 3243, Addis Ababa, Ethiopia (office). *Telephone:* (1) 51-7700 (office). *Fax:* (1) 51-7844 (office). *E-mail:* webmaster@africa-union.org (office). *Website:* www.africa-union.org (office).

JÁGR, Jaromír; Czech professional ice hockey player; b. 15 Feb. 1972, Kladno, Czechoslovakia (now Czech Repub.); s. of Jaromír Jágr; began skating aged three; was playing at highest level of competition in Czechoslovakia aged 16; first Czechoslovakian player drafted by NHL (Nat. Hockey League) without first defecting to West; taken by Pittsburgh Penguins with fifth overall pick in NHL Entry Draft 1990–2001; won five NHL scoring titles with the Penguins 1994–95 to 2000–01, including four in a row 1997–98 to 2000–01; team gold medal (Capt.), Winter Olympics, Nagano 1998; youngest player in NHL history (aged 19) to score a goal in Stanley Cup finals; traded to Washington Capitals 2001–03, to New York Rangers 2003–08, Avangard Omsk (Kontinental Hockey League, Russia) 2008–; played for Kladno, Czech Repub. 2004–05 (during NHL players strike), later for Avangard ice-hockey team, Omsk, Russia; captained Czech Repub. Gold Medal-winning team, World Hockey Championships, Austria 2005; scored 1,400th point 2 March 2006; leading active point scorer among European-born NHL players, second on all-time points list for European players; scored his 600th career NHL goal Nov. 2006; wears no. 68 in honour of Prague Spring rebellion in Czechoslovakia in 1968, also the year in which his grandfather died while in prison; mem. Triple Gold Club (players who have won a Stanley Cup, a World Hockey Championship and an Olympic gold medal), Stanley Cup Winner 1991,1992, NHL All-Rookie Team 1991, Golden Stick Award 1995, 1996, 1999, 2000, 2002, 2005, 2006, Art Ross Trophy (Leading Point Scorer) 1995, 1998, 1999, 2000, 2001, NHL First Team All-Star 1995, 1996, 1998, 1999, 2000, 2001, 2006, NHL Second Team All-Star 1997, ranked 37th on The Hockey News' list of 100 Greatest Hockey Players 1998, Hart Trophy 1999, Lester B. Pearson Award 1999, 2000, 2006, Czech Sportsman of the Year 2005, IIHF World Championship All-Star Team 2005. *Address:* c/o Avangard Omsk, Arena Omsk, Omsk, Russia. *Telephone:* (3812) 302-320. *E-mail:* avangard@omskcity.com. *Website:* www.hawk.ru.

JAGUARIBE GOMES DE MATTOS, Roberto; Brazilian government official and diplomatist; *Ambassador to UK;* b. 27 Dec. 1952, Rio de Janeiro; m. Cinara Maria Fonseca de Lima; ed Pontifical Catholic Univ., Rio de Janeiro; career diplomat since 1979, postings include Perm. Mission to UN, New York 1983–87, Embassy in Montevideo 1987–90, Head, Div. for Intellectual Property and Sensitive Technologies, Ministry of External Relations 1990–93, Head, Intellectual Property Section, Mission to Int. Orgs, Geneva 1993–95; Sec. for Int. Affairs, Ministry of Planning and Budget 1995–98; Dir Gen. for Trade Promotion, Ministry of External Relations 1998–2000; Deputy Head of Mission, Embassy in Washington, DC 2000–03; Sec. for Industrial Tech., Ministry of Devt, Industry and Foreign Trade 2003–05; Under-sec. Gen. for Political Affairs II, Ministry of External Relations 2007–10; Amb. to UK 2010–; Pres. Nat. Inst. of Industrial Property of Brazil 2005–07. *Leisure interests:* football, cookery, sailing, golf and tennis. *Address:* Embassy of Brazil, 14–16 Cockspur Street, London, SW1Y 5BL, England (office). *Telephone:* (20) 7747-4500 (office). *Fax:* (20) 7747-4555 (office). *E-mail:* info.london@itamaraty.gov.br (office). *Website:* www.brazil.org.uk (office).

JAHAN, Ismat, BA, MA; Bangladeshi lawyer and diplomatist; *Ambassador to Belgium, Luxembourg and the European Communities;* b. 1960; m. Prof. Johannes den Heijer; ed Dhaka Univ., Fletcher School, Tufts Univ., with cross-registered course works at Harvard Univ., USA; career diplomat 1982–; fmr Visiting Fellow, School of Foreign Service, Georgetown Univ., Washington, DC; served in various capacities at Ministry of Foreign Affairs as well as missions abroad including Perm. Missions to UN in New York and Geneva, and High Comm. in New Delhi; Dir-Gen. Int. Orgs, UN and Multilateral Econ. Affairs, Ministry of Foreign Affairs –2005; Amb. to the Netherlands 2005–07; Amb. and Perm. Rep. to UN, New York

2007–09; Amb. to Belgium, Luxembourg and the European Communities 2009–; mem. Cttee on Elimination of Discrimination Against Women (CEDAW) 2011–. *Address:* Embassy of Bangladesh, 29–31 rue Jacques Jordaens, 1000 Brussels, Belgium (office). *Telephone:* (2) 640-55-00 (office). *Fax:* (2) 646-59-98 (office). *E-mail:* bdootbrussels@skynet.be (office). *Website:* www.bangladeshembassy.be (office).

JAHANGIR, Asma, BA, BLL; Pakistani lawyer and human rights activist; *Chairman, Human Rights Commission of Pakistan;* b. 27 Jan. 1952, Lahore; d. of Malik Jilani; sister of Hina Jilani; ed Kinnard Coll., Lahore, Univ. of the Punjab; qualified as lawyer 1978; Advocate of the High Court 1982–; Co-founder (with Hina Jilani) and Partner, AGHS Law Assocs (all-women law firm), Lahore 1980–, also Founder and Dir AGHS Legal Aid Cell (first free legal aid centre in Pakistan), Lahore 1984–; Advocate of the Supreme Court 1992–; Founding mem. and Chair. Human Rights Comm. of Pakistan, Lahore 1993–; mem. Women's Action Forum, Punjab Women Lawyers Asscn; mem. Comm. of Enquiry for Women (est. by Govt of Pakistan) 1994–97; UN Special Rapporteur on Extra Judicial, Summary or Arbitrary Executions 1998–2004, Special Rapporteur on Freedom of Religion or Belief 2004–10; Commr Int. Comm. of Jurists, Geneva 1998–; Prof. of Law, Quaid-e-Azam Law Coll., Lahore; Co-chair South Asians for Human Rights 2000–; Council Mem. Minority Rights Group Int. 2002–04; mem. Bd of Dirs UN Research Inst. for Social Devt, Commonwealth Lawyers' Asscn, London 1997–2002, Interights, London 1997–2002, Asia Pacific Forum on Women Law and Devt, Kuala Lumpur 1988–2000; Exec. mem. Int. Crisis Group 2002–; placed under house arrest for 90 days 2007; Hon. LLD (Univ. of St Gallen, Switzerland) 1998, (Queen's Univ., Canada) 1998, (Amherst Coll.) 2003; ABA Int. Human Rights Award 1992, Sitara-I-Imtiaz 1995, King Baudouin Int. Devt Prize 1998, Human Rights Award, Lawyers Cttee for Human Rights 1999, Millennium Peace Prize 2001, Ramon Magsaysay Award for Public Service 2002, Lisl and Leo Eitinger Prize 2002, Four Freedoms Award 2010, Hilal-i-Imtiaz 2010, UNESCO/Bilbao Prize 2010, North-South Prize of the Council of Europe 2012, Polish Foreign Ministry Prize 'Pro Dignitate Humana' 2014. *Achievements include:* led student protest against mil. dictator Ayub Khan 1969; filed a constitutional petition in Supreme Court challenging arrest of her father and questioning legality of Bhutto's govt 1972, won case 1982. *Publications include:* Divine Sanction?: The Hadood Ordinance 1988, Children of a Lesser God: Child Prisoners of Pakistan 1992; numerous pubns on topics ranging from child labour to electoral processes in Pakistan. *Address:* 131-E/1, Gulberg-III, Lahore (office); c/o Human Rights Commission of Pakistan, Aiwan-i-Jahmoor, 107 Tipu Block, New Garden Town, Lahore 54600, Pakistan (office). *Telephone:* (42) 5763234 (office). *Fax:* (42) 5763236 (office). *E-mail:* law@aghs.brain.net.pk (office). *Website:* www2.ohchr.org/ ENGLISH/ISSUES/RELIGION/index.htm (office); www.hrcp-web.org.

JAHANGIRI, Guissou Jeannot, BA; French/Iranian international organization official; *Director, Open Asia France;* b. Iran; ed American Univ., Paris, Ecole des Hautes Etudes en Sciences Sociales, Paris; journalist (responsible for Iran, Cen. Asia and Afghanistan), Courier International 1990–, mem. Bd 1990–; Co-Founder and Dir Open Asia France (fmrly called The Asscn for Research and Information on Cen. Asia), Paris 1994–; Rep. of Human Rights Watch, Helsinki and Tajikistan 1995–96; Consultant to World Bank, Tajikistan 1996; Consultant and NGO Liaison Officer, UN Office for the Coordination of Humanitarian Affairs 1997–98. *Publications include:* articles in professional journals, UN reports. *Address:* Open Asia France, 12 rue Victor Letalle, 75020 Paris, France (office). *Telephone:* 1-47-97-32-97 (office). *Fax:* 1-47-97-32-97 (office). *E-mail:* Jeannot@enpc.fr (office); openasia@asia-mail.com (office). *Website:* oainternational.free.fr (office).

JAHJAGA, Atifete; Kosovo fmr police officer and head of state; *President;* b. 20 April 1975, Gjakovë/Đakovica; m. Astrit Kuçi; ed Univ. of Prishtina, Univ. of Leicester, UK, George C. Marshall European Centre for Security Studies, Germany, Fed. Bureau of Investigation (FBI) Nat. Acad., USA; following Kosovo War, began working as an interpreter for the int. police; completed officer training and was promoted to Maj., then Col, and finally Gen. Maj.; first deployed with border police and then transferred to Training Dept; held position of Deputy Dir of Kosovo Police, and briefly filled in as Acting Gen. Dir 2010; announced as a consensual presidential cand. by Democratic Party of Kosovo, Democratic League of Kosovo and New Kosovo Alliance 6 April 2011; Pres. of Kosovo 7 April 2011–. *Address:* Office of the President, 10000 Prishtina, Rruga Nënë Terezë, Kosovo (office). *Telephone:* (38) 213222 (office). *Fax:* (38) 211651 (office). *E-mail:* fehmi@ president-ksgov.net (office). *Website:* www.president-ksgov.net (office).

JAHN, Helmut, FAIA; German architect; b. 4 Jan. 1940, Nuremberg; s. of Wilhelm Anton Jahn and Karolina Wirth; m. Deborah Lampe 1970; one s.; ed Technische Hochschule, Munich, Illinois Inst. of Tech., USA; with C.F. Murphy Assocs 1967–73, Exec. Vice-Pres. and Dir of Planning and Design 1973; registered architect, NCARB 1975; mem. German Chamber of Architects, State of Hesse 1986; Prin. Murphy/Jahn (Chicago, Ill., USA and Berlin) 1981, Pres. 1982, Pres. and CEO 1983–; Visiting Prof., Harvard Univ., USA 1981, Yale Univ., USA 1983; completed bldgs include libraries, exhbn halls, court bldgs, office and leisure bldgs, univ. bldgs, hotels, apartments and airport terminals in USA, Europe and Far East; Corp. mem. AIA 1975, Fellow 1987; Hon. DFA (St Mary's Coll. Notre Dame, Ind.); Chevalier des Arts et des Lettres, Bundesverdienstkreuz Erster Klasse; numerous professional awards. *Major completed projects include:* Kemper Arena, Kansas City, Mo. 1974, Xerox Centre, Chicago 1980, Argonne Program Support Facility, Argonne, Ill. 1981, 11 Diagonal Street, Johannesburg, SA 1983, James R. Thompson Center, Chicago 1985, 362 West Street, Durban, SA 1986, Park Avenue Tower, NY, USA 1986, United Airlines Terminal One Complex, O'Hare Airport, Chicago 1987, One Liberty Place, Phila, USA 1987, Northwestern Atrium Center, Chicago 1987, Wilshire/Westwood, LA 1988, Bartnett Center, Jacksonville, Fla, USA 1990, Messeturm, Frankfurt 1991, 120 North LaSalle, Chicago 1992, One America Plaza, San Diego, Calif., USA 1992, Mannheimer Lebensversicherung, Mannheim 1992, Hyatt Regency Roissy, Paris, France 1992, Munich Order Center 1993, Hitachi Tower, Singapore 1993, Caltex House, Singapore 1993, Hotel Kempinski, Munich 1994, Pallas, Stuttgart 1994, Kurfürstendamm 70, Berlin 1994, Principal Mutual Life Insurance Co., Des Moines, Ia, USA 1996, RCID Admin Bldg, Orlando, Fla 1997, JC Decaux Bus Shelter 1998, New EU HQ, Belgium, Brussels 1998, Munich Airport Center 1999, Sony Center, Berlin 2000, Airport Köln/Bonn 2000, Ha-Lo HQ, Chicago 2000, Neues Kranzler Eck, Berlin

2000, Kaufhof Galeria, Chemnitz 2002, Shanghai Int. Expo Centre 2002, Bayer AG Konzernzentrale, Leverkusen 2002, Post Tower, Bonn 2003, State Street Village IIT, Chicago 2003, Train Station, Airport Köln/Bonn 2004, Highlight Business Towers, Munich 2004, Mannheimer-2, Mannheim 2005, Suvarnabhumi Airport, Bangkok, Thailand 2006, Merck-Serono HQ, Geneva 2007, Margot & Harold Schiff Residences, Chicago 2007, 600 Fairbanks Court, Chicago 2008, 1999K Street, Washington, DC, USA 2009, Chicago-O'Hare Int. Airport (façade and circulation enhancements) 2009, West Combined Utility Plant/South Campus Chiller Plant, Univ. of Chicago 2009, Hegau Tower, Singen, Germany 2009, Veer Towers, Las Vegas, Nev., USA 2010. *Leisure interests:* sailing, skiing. *Address:* Murphy/Jahn, Inc., Suite 300, 35 East Wacker Drive, Chicago, IL 60601, USA (office). *Telephone:* (312) 427-7300 (home). *Fax:* (312) 332-0274 (office). *Website:* www.murphyjahn .com (office).

JAHN, Martin, MBA; Czech automobile industry executive and fmr government official; b. 20 Jan. 1970, Prague; s. of Vladimír Jahn and Hana Jahn; m. Karolina Jahn; two d.; ed Prague School of Econs, DePaul Univ., Chicago, USA; Dir American Operations, Czechinvest 1996–99, CEO 1999–2004; Deputy Prime Minister, responsible for the Economy 2004–06; joined Skoda, Mlada Boleslav 2006, Man. Dir Volkswagen Group Rus, Moscow Br. 2008–10, Head of World Corp. Sales and Multi-Brand Sales, Volkswagen AG, Wolfsburg 2010–; mem. Bd CMC Celákovice; mem. Czech-American Chamber of Commerce, Czech-Canadian Chamber of Commerce 2000–; Ordre National du Mérite. *Leisure interests:* tennis, squash, skiing, film, literature, music. *Address:* Volkswagen AG, Brieffach 1849, Wolfsburg 38436, Germany (office). *Telephone:* (5361) 90 (office). *Fax:* (5361) 928282 (home). *Website:* www.volkswagen.com (office).

JAHN, Robert George, BSE, MA, PhD; American aerospace scientist and academic; *Dean Emeritus, School of Engineering and Applied Science, Princeton University;* b. 1 April 1930, Kearny, NJ; s. of George Jahn and Minnie Holroyd; m. Catherine Seibert 1953; one s. three d.; ed Princeton Univ.; teaching asst, Princeton Univ. 1953–55; Instructor, Lehigh Univ. Bethlehem, Pa 1955–56, Asst Prof. 1956–58; Asst Prof. of Jet Propulsion, Calif. Inst. of Tech., Pasadena 1958–62; Asst Prof. of Aeronautical Eng, Princeton Univ. 1962–64, Assoc. Prof. 1964–67, Prof. of Aerospace Sciences 1967–2005, Dean, School of Eng and Applied Science 1971–86, now Dean Emer., also Program Dir Princeton Eng Anomalies Research; Pres. Int. Consciousness Research Labs 1996–2001, Chair. 2001–; mem. various NASA research cttees; numerous professional appointments etc.; Fellow, American Physical Soc., AIAA; Hon. ScD (Andhra) 1986; Curtis W. McGraw Award, American Soc. for Eng Educ. 1969, Medal for Outstanding Achievement in Electric Propulsion 2005, Edgar Mitchell Award for Noetic Achievement 2006, AIAA Wyld Propulsion Award 2012. *Publications:* Physics of Electric Propulsion 1968, Margins of Reality (with B. J. Dunne) 1987, Consciousness and the Source of Reality (with B. J. Dunne) 2011, Quirks of the Quantum Mind (with B. J. Dunne) 2012; numerous articles on aerospace science. *Leisure interests:* his dog, sports, music, home crafts. *Address:* Mechanical and Aerospace Engineering Department, School of Engineering/Applied Science, Princeton University, Princeton, NJ 08544-5263 (office); ICRL, Inc., 211 North Harrison Street, Suite C, Princeton, NJ 08540, USA (office). *Telephone:* (609) 921-1007 (office). *E-mail:* rgjahn@ princeton.edu (office). *Website:* www.icrl.org (office).

JAHNÁTEK, L'ubomír, CSc; Slovak academic and politician; b. 16 Sept. 1954, Nitra; m.; two c.; ed Slovak Tech. Univ.; worked for VUSPAL (Plastics Processing and Application Research Inst.) 1978–98; Dir Gen. Production–Tech. Dept, Plastika Nitra a.s. 1992–2003; Strategy Dir Duslo Sala a.s. 2003–05; Lecturer, Faculty of Material Sciences and Tech., Slovak Tech. Univ. 2004–06, Head of Field Div. 2005–06; Minister of the Economy 2006–10. *Address:* c/o Ministry of the Economy, Mierová 19, 827 15 Bratislava, Slovakia (office).

JAIDEE, Thongchai; Thai professional golfer; b. 8 Nov. 1969, Lopburi; m.; two s.; fmr paratrooper, Royal Thai Army; professional golfer 1999–; first major championship played US Open 2001; European Tour wins include Carlsberg Malaysian Open 2004 (first Thai winner on European Tour), 2005, Enjoy Jakarta Indonesia Open 2009, Ballantine's Championship 2009; Asian Tour wins include Kolon Cup Korean Open 2000, Volvo Masters of Asia 2003, 2006, Hana Bank Vietnam Masters, Johnnie Walker Cambodian Open 2008; represented Thailand in World Cup 2007, 2008, 2009; represented Asia in Dynasty Cup 2003, 2005, Royal Trophy 2007, 2008, 2009; invited to play in US Masters Tournament 2006 (first Thai to play in all four major championships); Asian Tour Order of Merit 2001, 2004, 2009, voted Asian Tour Players' Player of the Year 2009. *Address:* c/o Thai Golf Association, Ratchamangla National Stadium 286, Ramkhamhaeng Road, Hua Mark, Bangkapi, Bangkok 10241, Thailand. *E-mail:* secretary@tga.or.th. *Website:* www.tga.or.th (office).

JAIM-ETCHEVERRY, Guillermo, MD; Argentine neurobiologist, academic, foundation executive and fmr university administrator; *President, Fundación Carolina de Argentina;* ed Univ. of Buenos Aires; Prof. and Dir Dept of Cellular Biology and Histology, Faculty of Medicine, Univ. of Buenos Aires –2008, Dean of Faculty 1986–90, Pres. Univ. of Buenos Aires 2002–06; currently Pres. Fundación Carolina de Argentina; Prin. Investigator, CONICET, IBRO/UNESCO, John Simon Guggenheim Memorial Foundation; mem. Nat. Acad. of Educ., Argentina Acad. of Communication Arts and Sciences; Corresp. mem. of Medical Sciences of Córdoba; Hon. Foreign Mem. American Acad. of Arts and Sciences 2004; Chevalier, Ordre des Palmes Académiques 2005; Dr hc (Univ. of Morón) 2009; Bernardo Houssay Prize 1987, Master of Medicine, Nat. Acad. of Medicine, Argentina 2001, Medaille d'Or of the Societe d'Encouragement au Progres 2007, Medallas del Bicentenario 2010. *Publication:* The Educational Tragedy. *E-mail:* info@fundacioncarolina.org.ar. *Website:* www.fundacioncarolina.org.ar.

JAIME, Aguinaldo; Angolan politician; Minister of Finance 1990–92; fmr Pres. Banco Africano de Investimentos; Provincial Gov. 1999–2002; Gov. Nat. Bank of Angola 1999–2002; Deputy Prime Minister of Angola 2002; Dir Agência Nacional para o Investimento Privado (ANIP). *Address:* Agência Nacional para o Investimento Privado (ANIP) Rua Cerqueira Lukoki No. 25, Edificio do Ministerio da Industria, 9º Andar, Luanda, Angola (office). *Telephone:* 222391434 (office). *Fax:* 222332965 (office). *E-mail:* info@investinangola.com (office). *Website:* investinangola.com (office).

JAIN, Anshuman, BA, MBA; Indian business executive; *Co-Chairman of the Management Board and Co-CEO, Deutsche Bank AG;* b. 7 Jan. 1963, Jaipur, Rajasthan; m.; two c.; ed Shri Ram Coll. of Commerce, Univ. of Delhi, Univ. of Massachusetts, Amherst, USA; began career as analyst in derivatives research at Kidder, Peabody & Co. (now part of UBS) 1985–88; joined Merrill Lynch, New York 1988, f. and led first dedicated hedge fund coverage group; joined Deutsche Bank's nascent markets business 1995, mem. Deutsche Bank Group Exec. Cttee 2002–, fmrly Head of Global Markets and Jt Head of Corp. and Investment Bank 2004–10, roles included Head of Fixed Income Sales and Trading, Global Head of Derivatives and Emerging Markets and Global Head of Institutional Client Coverage, mem. Man. Bd Deutsche Bank AG, Head of Corp. and Investment Bank 2010–12, Co-Chair. Man. Bd and Group Exec. Cttee 2012–, Co-CEO 2013–; Dir (non-exec.) Sasol (South Africa); fmr mem. Prime Minister's Working Group on Inward Investment in India; led Deutsche Bank's team advising UK Treasury on financial stability; mem. Financial Services Global Competitiveness Group 2008; Euromoney Magazine Capital Markets Achievement Award 2003, American Indian Foundation's Achievement Award 2005, Risk Magazine Lifetime Achievement Award 2010, NASSCOM Business Leader Award 2010. *Leisure interests:* photography, cricket, golf, active supporter of several wildlife and environmental conservation charities. *Address:* Deutsche Bank AG, Taunusanlage 12, 60262 Frankfurt am Main, Germany (office). *Telephone:* (69) 910-00 (office). *Fax:* (69) 910-34225 (office). *E-mail:* info@db.com (office). *Website:* www.db.com (office).

JAISHANKAR, Subrahmanyam, MA, MPhil, PhD; Indian diplomatist; *Ambassador to USA;* s. of K. Subrahmanyam; m. Kyoko Jaishankar; two s. one d.; joined Foreign Service 1977, worked in various capacities in Embassies in Washington, DC and Moscow 1979–81, Americas Div., Ministry of External Affairs 1981–85, Embassy in Colombo 1988–90, Embassy in Budapest 1990–93; Press Sec. to Pres. of India 1994–95; Deputy Chief of Mission, Embassy in Tokyo 1996–2000, Amb. to Czech Repub. 2000–04, Head of Americas Div., Ministry of External Affairs 2004–07, High Commr to Singapore 2007–09, Amb. to People's Repub. of China 2009–13, to USA 2013–; mem. IISS, London; one of key negotiators of India–USA civilian nuclear co-operation agreement 2005–07. *Address:* Embassy of India, 2107 Massachusetts Avenue NW, Washington, DC 20008, USA (office). *Telephone:* (202) 939-7000 (office). *Fax:* (202) 265-4351 (office). *E-mail:* info2@indiagov.org (office). *Website:* www.indianembassy.org (office).

JAKIČ, Roman; Slovenian politician; *Minister of Defence;* b. 1 May 1967; Vice-Dean, Faculty of Arts, Univ. of Ljubljana 1987–90; Deputy, Chamber of Associated Labour, Ass. of Repub. of Slovenia 1990–92; Pres. Young Liberal Democracy of Slovenia 1991–98; mem. Liberal Democracy of Slovenia, Head of Int. Relations Office 1992–96, Sec.-Gen. 2004–05; Vice-Pres. and Sec.-Gen. Int. Fed. of Liberal Youth 1993–96; Deputy, Nat. Ass. of Slovenia 1996–2000, 2000–04, 2011–; Vice-Chair. Alliance of Liberals and Democrats for Europe, Parl. Ass. of Council of Europe 1998–2004; mem. City Council, Municipality of Ljubljana 1998; mem. European Parl. 2003–04; Minister of Defence 2013–; Dir GALITIJA – Business Consulting, Roman Jakič sp 2005–08; Dir Javni zavod Šport Ljubljana (public inst.) 2008–12; Pres. Slovenia Athletics Fed. 2001–05; mem. Exec. Bd Olympic Cttee of Slovenia 2001–05; mem. Positive Slovenia (PS). *Address:* Ministry of Defence, 1000 Ljubljana, Vojkova cesta 55, Slovenia (office). *Telephone:* (1) 4712211 (office). *Fax:* (1) 4712978 (office). *E-mail:* glavna.pisarna@mors.si (office). *Website:* www.mors.si (office).

JAKIYANOV, Qalimjan, PhD; Kazakhstani engineer and politician; b. 8 May 1963, Kurchumskii Dist, Eastern Kazakhstan Oblast; s. of Badyljan Jakiyanov and Rasch Jakiyanova; m.; two s.; ed Bauman Higher Inst., Moscow, Russia; specialized in rocket and turbine eng; worked at Semipalatinsk Mil. Plant, Br. Head of Komsomol (CP Youth League), dismissed 1989; became leader of ind. youth movt; Publr and Ed. Sodeistviye (Assistance) newspaper 1989–91; Propr Semey coalmine 1990–94; Gov., Semipalatinsk 1994–97; Chair. State Agency for Strategic Resources Control 1997; Akim (Gov.), Pavlodar Oblast 1997–2001 (resgnd); Co-founder and Co-Chair. Democratic Choice of Kazakhstan (DCK) 2001; arrested on charges of abuse of power during tenure as Gov. April 2002, sentenced to seven-year prison term Aug. 2002, released on parole 2006.

JAKSITY, György, BEcons; Hungarian stockbroker and stock exchange executive; b. 1968; m. Kinga Jaksity; two c.; ed Karl Marx Univ. of Econs; Financial Adviser, Ministry of Finance 1989; consultant for several cos including Girozentrale Investment, Ibusz and Fotex, Budapest 1989–92; training with Price Waterhouse 1992; Chair. and Man. Dir Concorde Securities 1993–; Chair. Budapest Stock Exchange 2002–04; f. The Self Reliance Foundation. *Leisure interest:* reading. *Address:* c/o Budapest Stock Exchange, Deak Ferenc u.5, Budapest, 1052, Hungary (office). *Telephone:* (1) 429-6700 (office). *Fax:* (1) 429-6800 (office). *E-mail:* info@bse.hu (office).

JAKUBISKO, Juraj, MFA; Slovak film director, producer, scriptwriter and artist; b. 30 April 1938, Kojšov; m. Horváthová Jakubisko; one s. one d.; ed Prague Film Acad.; films censored by Communist regime late 1970s (Birds, Orphans and Fools, See You in Hell, My Friends); blacklisted and banned from producing films for ten years; retrospective tour of his work in USA, Canada and Europe 1991; mem. Twentieth Century Acad. 1999–; Pribina Cross, Second Class (Slovakia) 2003; more than 80 nat. and int. awards, including Maverick Award for vision in filmmaking, Taos Talking Picture Festival, USA 1998, Award in Recognition of Outstanding Achievement in the Art of the Film, Denver Int. Film Festival, USA 1998, Golden Seal Award of Yugoslavian Cinematheque for outstanding contrib. to world cinema, Belgrade 2000, Best Slovak Director Award in survey of the best Slovak and int. artists of 20th century conducted by Slovak film journalists and critics 2000, Lifetime Achievement Award, Masaryk Acad. of Art, Prague 2001, CFTA Award: Czech Lion for Best Film Poster of the Year 2000, CFTA Award: Czech Lion for Lifetime Artistic Contrib. 2002, Crystal Globe for Outstanding Artistic Contrib. to World Cinema, Karlovy Vary 2007. *Films:* Silence (Brussels Film Acad. Award, Knokke Experimental Film Festival, Belgium), Waiting for Godot (Best Short Film Award, Oberhausen, Simone Dubroilh Award, Mannheim) 1968, Birds, Orphans and Fools (banned 1968, Fipresci Prize 1991), The Bee Millennium (Golden Phoenix Award, Venice Film Festival) 1983, The Feather Fairy 1985, Frankenstein's Aunt 1986, A Rosy Story 1990, See You in Hell, My Friends (originally made in 1968 but banned by political censors) 1991, It's Better to Be Wealthy and Healthy Than Poor and Ill 1992 (re-released 2002), An

Ambiguous Report About the End of the World (also TV series) 1999, Post Coitum 2004, Bathory 2008. *Leisure interests:* painting, golf. *Address:* Jakubisko Film Asscn Ltd, Palác Lucerna, Vodičkova 36, 116 02 Prague 1, Czech Republic (office). *Telephone:* (2) 9623-6353 (office). *Fax:* (2) 9623-6389 (office). *E-mail:* info@jakubiskofilm.com (office). *Website:* www.jakubiskofilm.com (office).

JALADE EKEINDE, Omotola; Nigerian actress, singer and philanthropist; b. 7 Feb. 1978, Lagos; d. of Oluwashola Jalade and Oluwatoyin Jalade (née Amori Oguntade); m. Matthew Ekeinde; four c.; ed Yaba Coll. of Tech.; first acting role in Venom of Justice 1995 (Nollywood film debut); US debut in Hit the Floor (TV drama) 2013; WFP Amb. 2005–; f. Omotola Youth Empowerment Programme (charity); Amnesty Int. campaigner; columnist, OK! Nigeria Magazine; Screen Nation Awards Pan African Best Actress 2012. *Television:* Omotola: The Real Me (reality show) 2012–. *Recordings:* GBA 2005, Me, Myself, and Eyes 2010. *Films:* over 300 film appearances including Mortal Inheritance 1995, Blood Sisters 2003, Games Women Play 2005, My Last Ambition 2009, Ije: The Journey 2010, Ties that Bind 2011, Last Flight to Abuja 2012. *Address:* c/o Africa Magic Entertainment, 271 Oak Avenue, Randburg, South Africa (office). *Website:* www.omotola.tv (office).

JALAL, Masooda; Afghan paediatrician and fmr government official; b. 5 Jan. 1962, Gulbahar, Kapisa Prov.; d. of Alhaj Tellah Mohammad; m.; three c.; ed Gulbahar High School; began medical career as physician at Maiwand Hosp., then served at Kabul Medical Inst. and Ataturk Hosp.; pvt. practice in paediatrics 1988–92; worked for UNHCR then health adviser to WFP 1993–2004; presidential cand. in Afghanistan 2004, 2008; Minister of Women's Affairs 2004–06; documentary film maker 2009–. *Address:* c/o Ministry of Women's Affairs, beside Cinema Zainab, Shar-i-Nau, Kabul, Afghanistan. *E-mail:* spokesman.mowa@gmail.com.

JALAL KHAN, Zubaida, MA; Pakistani politician; b. 31 Aug. 1959, Kuwait; ed Univ. of Balochistan; est. Girls Primary School, Mand, Balochistan 1982; volunteer, Family Planning Asscn of Pakistan 1986–; Del. to World Conf. on Women, People's Repub. of China 1995; Minister of Social Welfare and Women's Affairs 1999–2000, of Educ. 2000–04, of Women's Devt, Social Welfare and Special Educ. 2004–07; travelled to Nepal, Repub. of Korea and Philippines to study primary educ. systems. *Address:* c/o Ministry of Social Welfare and Special Education, opp. Noori Hospital, G-8/4, Islamabad, Pakistan.

JALALI, Ali Ahmad, BA, MA, PSC; Afghan/American academic and fmr government official; *Distinguished Professor, Near East South Asia Center for Strategic Studies (NESA);* b. 1940, Kabul; m.; one s. one d.; ed Afghan Mil. Univ., British Army Staff Coll., Acad. Frunze, Moscow, Naval Postgraduate School, USA; mil. studies in Afghanistan, UK and Turkey; army col, Afghan Armed Forces –1978; Dir Islamic Unity of Afghan Mujahidin and Sr Mil. Commdr during rebellion against Soviet occupation 1980s; obtained US citizenship 1987; Dir, Broadcaster and Head of Pashto and Persian Services, Voice of America (int. radio station), Washington, DC –2003; Minister of Interior Affairs (of Afghan Transitional Authority) 2003–04, (of Afghanistan Govt) 2004–05 (resgnd); currently Distinguished Prof., Near East South Asia Center for Strategic Studies (NESA), Washington, DC, also Researcher, Inst. for Nat. Strategic Studies; seven State Medals and Decorations, including Wazir Akbar Khan and Distinguished Service Medals, Royal Afghan Army, highest State Medal, Islamic Repub. of Afghanistan. *Publications include:* The Other Side of the Mountain (co-author) 1998, three-vol. mil. history of Afghanistan, several other books. *Address:* NESA Center for Strategic Studies, 2100 2nd Street SW, Suite 4308, Washington, DC 20593, USA (office). *Telephone:* (202) 685-3794 (office); (202) 285-4701 (office). *Fax:* (202) 685-4999 (office). *E-mail:* JalaliA@ndu.edu (office). *Website:* nesa-center.org (office).

JALAN, Bimal, PhD; Indian economist and fmr politician; *Chairman, Centre for Development Studies, Trivandrum;* b. 3 July 1941, Calcutta (now Kolkata); ed Univ. of Calcutta, Univs of Cambridge and Oxford, UK; various positions at IMF, World Bank, Pearson Comm. 1964–70; Chief Economist, Industrial Credit and Investment Corpn of India 1970–73; Econ. Adviser, Ministry of Finance and of Industry, India 1973–79; Chief Econ. Adviser, Ministry of Finance 1981–88, Sec. for Banking 1985–88; Dir Econ. Affairs, Commonwealth Secr., London 1979–81; Exec. Dir IMF 1988–90, World Bank 1993–96; fmr Exec. Dir IBRD (India); Gov. Reserve Bank 1997–2003; nominated mem. Rajya Sabha (upper house of Parl.) 2003–09; Chair. Centre for Devt Studies, Trivandrum, Indian Statistical Inst., Indira Gandhi Inst. of Devt Research, Nat. Council of Applied Econ. Research, Inst. of Economic Growth. *Publications include:* Essays in Development Policy 1975, Problems and Policies in Small Economies 1982, India's Economic Crisis: The Way Ahead 1991, The Indian Economy: Problems and Prospects 1993, India's Economic Policy: Preparing for the 21st Century 1997, India's Economy in the New Millennium – Selected Essays 2002, The Future of India: Politics, Economics and Governance 2005, India's Politics: A View from the Backbench 2007, Emerging India 2012. *Address:* 4 Babar Road, New Delhi 110001, India (office). *Telephone:* (11) 41509184 (office). *Fax:* (11) 23711197 (office). *E-mail:* bimaljalan@gmail.com (home). *Website:* www.bimaljalan.com.

JALEEL, Mohamed, MA; Maldivian politician; b. 19 Nov. 1959, Malé; s. of Ahmed Jaleel and Mariyam Waheeda; fmr Minister of State for Finance and Treasury, Minister of Finance and Treasury 2004–05, Minister of Econ. Devt and Trade 2005–08 (resgnd); Vice-Gov., then Gov. Maldives Monetary Authority. *Address:* M. Faamudheyrige, Orchid Magu, Malé, Maldives (home). *Telephone:* 3323888 (home). *Fax:* 3324432 (home).

JALEEL, Maj.-Gen. (retd) Moosa Ali, MSc; Maldivian fmr army officer; b. 26 June 1960, Malé; m. Jazeela Ibrahim; one c.; four c. from previous marriages; ed Singapore Armed Forces Training Inst., Singapore, US Army Infantry School, USA, Royal Marines Commando School, England, Nat. Defence Coll., India, Univ. of Madras, India; fmr Commdr of all front-line infantry units in Maldives Nat. Defence Force (MNDF) including Rapid Reaction Force, Quick Reaction Force III, Quick Reaction Force I, Special Protection Group; fmr Dir-Gen. Maldivian Coast Guard; Vice-Chief, MNDF –2008, Chief of Nat. Defence Force 2008–12; numerous service medals and ribbons including Huravee Ran Medal for Exceptional Bravery, Presidential Medal, Distinguished Service Medal, Royal Marines Commando Badge. *Address:* c/o Maldives National Defence Force Headquarters, Bandaara Koshi, Ameer Ahmed Magu, Malé, Maldives.

JALILI, Saeed, PhD; Iranian government official; *Secretary, Shura-ye Ali-ye Amniyyat-e Melli (Supreme National Security Council);* b. 6 Sept. 1965, Mashhad; m.; one c.; ed Univ. of Science and Industry, Tehran; veteran of the 1980–88 Iran-Iraq war; Dir-Gen. Office of Supreme Leader Ayatollah Ali Khamenei 2001–05; adviser to Pres. Mahmoud Ahmadinejad 2005–; Deputy Foreign Minister for European and American Affairs 2005–07; Sec., Shura-ye Ali-ye Amniyyat-e Melli (Supreme Nat. Security Council) 2007–, role includes being Iran's chief nuclear negotiator; unsuccessful cand. in presidential election 2013. *Address:* Office of the Secretary, Shura-ye Ali-ye Amniyyat-e Melli, Tehran, Iran.

JALLAD, Farid al-; Palestinian lawyer and politician; trained as lawyer; Head of Arab Lawyers' Cttee in the W Bank; apptd to High Judiciary Council by the late Pres. Arafat 2003; Deputy Minister of Justice –2005, Minister of Justice 2005; Pres. Palestinian Bar Asscn; mem. Palestinian Legal Group, Inst. for the Study and Devt of Legal Systems (ISDLS), Calif. *Address:* c/o Ministry of Justice, POB 267, Ramallah, Palestinian Autonomous Areas (office).

JALLOUD, Maj. Abd as-Salam; Libyan politician and army officer; b. 15 Dec. 1944, Mizdah; from the Magariha tribe; ed Secondary School, Sebha, Mil. Acad., Benghazi, also briefly in USA and UK; mem. and Deputy Chair. Revolutionary Command Council 1969–77, Gen. Secr. of Gen. People's Congress 1977–79; Minister of Industry and the Economy, Acting Minister of the Treasury 1970–72; Prime Minister 1972–77; regarded as the 'Deputy Supreme Leader' until 1993, fell out of favour Aug. 1993, placed under house arrest Oct. 1993, passport confiscated and kept under surveillance 1995; reported that he had defected to the rebel forces opposing Gaddafi Aug. 2011. *Address:* c/o General Secretariat of the General People's Congress, Tripoli, Libya.

JALLOW, Hassan Bubacar, LLB, LLM; Gambian lawyer and UN official; *Chief Prosecutor, United Nations Mechanism for International Criminal Tribunals;* b. 14 Aug. 1951, Bansang; ed Univ. of Dar es Salaam, Tanzania, Nigerian Law School, Univ. Coll., London; State Attorney, Attorney-Gen.'s Chamber, Gambia 1976–82, Solicitor-Gen. 1982–84, Attorney-Gen. and Minister of Justice 1984–94, Judge, Supreme Court 1998–2002; Judge, Appeals Chamber, Special Court for Sierra Leone 2002; Prosecutor, UN Int. Criminal Tribunal 1998–, carried out judicial evaluation for Yugoslavia; Chief Prosecutor, Int. Criminal Tribunal for Rwanda (UN-ICTR) 2003–; Chief Prosecutor, UN Mechanism for Int. Criminal Tribunals (MICT) 2012–; legal expert for OAU and Commonwealth; Chair. Commonwealth Governmental Working Group of Experts in Human Rights; worked on drafting and conclusion of African Charter on Human Rights, adopted 1981; Commdr, Nat. Order of the Repub. of The Gambia. *Publications include:* Law, Justice and Governance – Selected Papers 1998, The Law of Evidence in The Gambia 1998, The Law of the African Charter on Human and Peoples' Rights, Introduction to the Zikr of the Tidjanniya Tariqat, Journey for Justice 2012. *Address:* United Nations Mechanism for International Criminal Tribunals, New York, NY 10017, USA (office); Office of the Prosecutor, International Criminal Tribunal for Rwanda (UN-ICTR), Arusha International Conference Centre, PO Box 6016, Arusha, Tanzania (office). *Telephone:* (27) 2504207 (office). *Fax:* (27) 2504000 (office). *E-mail:* jallowh@un.org (office). *Website:* www.unmict.org (office); www.ictr.org (office).

JALOLOV, Abdulkhafiz, DPhil; Uzbekistani politician and philosopher; b. 1 June 1947, Namangan; m. Jalolova Zarifahon; two s. one d.; ed Tashkent State Univ.; mil. service 1969–71; Lecturer of Philosophy, Tashkent Univ. 1971–72; researcher, Philosophy and Law Inst., Uzbekistan Acad. of Sciences 1972–77, Dir 1993–2001; Chair. of Philosophy, State Inst. of Physical Culture 1977–81; Asst Prof., Deputy Dir Social Science Lecturers' Skills Level Raising Inst., Tashkent State Univ. 1981–93; Second Sec. of Gen. Council, People's Democratic Party of Uzbekistan (PDP) 1991–94, First Sec. 1994–2003; unsuccessful PDP cand. in presidential elections 2000. *Publications include:* Mustakillik Mas'uliyati 1996, Istikbol Ufklari 1998, Demokratiya: mashakkatli yuri 2000. *Address:* c/o People's Democratic Party of Uzbekistan, pl. Mustakillik, 5/1, 100029 Tashkent, Uzbekistan (office). *Telephone:* (71) 139-83-11 (office). *Fax:* (71) 133-59-34 (office).

JAMAL, Ahmad; American composer and pianist; b. 2 July 1930, Pittsburgh, Pa; (divorced); one d.; ed pvt. master-classes with Mary Cardwell Dawson and James Miller; George Hudson Orchestra nat. tour 1949; mem. The Four Strings 1949; accompanist to The Caldwells 1950; trio The Three Strings 1950–; numerous concert tours, including with Philip Morris; exclusive Steinway artist 1960s–; appeared on film soundtracks of M*A*S*H 1970, Bridges of Madison County 1995; Duke Ellington Fellow, Yale Univ.; Officier, Ordre des Arts et des Lettres 2007; NEA American Jazz Master, Pittsburgh Mellon Jazz Festival dedication 1994. *Television:* The Sound of Jazz 1962. *Compositions include:* six works for Asai Quartet 1994, New Rhumba, Ahmad's Blues, Night Mist Blues, Extensions, The Awakening, Excerpts From The Blues, Tranquility, Manhattan Reflections. *Recordings include:* Poinciana, But Not For Me (including Bridges of Madison County) 1995, Essence Part 1 (Django D'Or Award, Paris) 1996, Olympia 2000, Live in Baalbeck (DVD) 2003, After Fajr 2005, It's Magic 2008, A Quiet Time 2010, Blue Moon: The New York Session/The Paris Concert 2012, Saturday Morning 2013. *Address:* c/o Ellora Management, PO Box 755, 11 Brook Street, Lakeville, CT 06039, USA (office). *Telephone:* (860) 435-1305 (office). *Fax:* (860) 435-9916 (office). *E-mail:* elloramanagement@aol.com (office); elloradesigns@aol.com. *Website:* www.ahmadjamal.net.

JAMALI, Mir Zafarullah Khan, MA; Pakistani politician; b. 1 Jan. 1944, Rowjhan, Balochistan; s. of Mir Zafarullah Khan Jamali; m.; four s. one d.; ed Murree Royal Coll., Aitchison Coll., Lahore, Punjab Univ.; tribal elder from South West Prov. of Balochistan; joined Pakistan People's Party 1970s; elected mem. Prov. Ass., Balochistan 1977; fmr Minister for Food and Information; Minister for Food and Agric. 1982, for Local Govt, for Water and Power 1985, for Railways 1986; mem. Nat. Ass. 1985–89; Chief Minister for Balochistan 1988–89; apptd Rep. to UN 1991; elected ind. mem. Nat. Ass. 1993–, mem. Cabinet 1997–2004; Senator for Balochistan 1997–2006; Sr mem. Pakistan Muslim League –1999; mem. Pakistan Muslim League–Quaid-e-Azam; Prime Minister of Pakistan 2002–04 (resgnd); fmr mem. Nat. Security Council. *Leisure interest:* hockey. *Address:* c/o Office of the Prime Minister, Constitution Ave, Islamabad, Pakistan.

JAMALOODIN, George (Jorge) R. M.; Curaçao business executive and politician; Minister of Finance (first holder after dissolution of Netherlands

Antilles) 2010–12; mem. Movementu Futuro Kòrsou (MFK); Propr Speedy Kopter. *Address:* c/o Ministry of Finance, Pietermaai 17, Willemstad, Curaçao.

JAMBREK, Peter, MA, PhD; Slovenian judge, legal consultant and author; b. 14 Jan. 1940, Ljubljana; ed Grammar School, Ljubljana, Ljubljana Univ. and Univ. of Chicago, USA; Prof., Dept of Theory of Law and State, Ljubljana; Judge, Constitutional Court of Repub. of Slovenia 1990, Pres. 1991–95; Judge, European Court of Human Rights 1993–99; Dean, Grad. School of Govt and European Affairs, Univ. of Ljubljana 2003; mem. Venice Comm. 2003; Co-founder and Chair. Zbor za republiko (Rally for the Republic) 2004–08; currently ind. consultant and author. *Publications:* Development and Social Change in Yugoslavia: Crises and Perspectives of Building a Nation 1975, Participation as a Human Right and as a Means for the Exercise of Human Rights 1982, Contributions for the Slovenian Constitution 1988, Constitutional Democracy 1992. *Address:* c/o Zbor za republiko, Cankarjeva cesta 10 B, 1000 Ljubljana; Ceste v Megre 4, 64260 Bled, Slovenia (home). *Telephone:* (64) 77449 (home).

JAMES, Clive Vivian Leopold, CBE, AM, FRSL; Australian writer, broadcaster, journalist and poet; b. (Vivian James), 7 Oct. 1939, Kogarah, Sydney, NSW; s. of Albert A. James and Minora M. Darke; m. Prue Shaw; two d.; ed Sydney Technical High School, Sydney Univ. and Pembroke Coll. Cambridge; Asst Ed. Morning Herald, Sydney 1961; Pres. of Footlights at Cambridge, UK; TV critic, The Observer 1972–82, feature writer 1972–; Dir Watchmaker Productions 1994–; as lyricist for Pete Atkin, record albums include Beware of the Beautiful Stranger, Driving Through Mythical America, A King at Nightfall, The Road of Silk, Secret Drinker, Live Libel, The Master of the Revels; also songbook, A First Folio (with Pete Atkin); Patron Burma Campaign UK; Dr hc (Sydney), (East Anglia); Philip Hodgins Memorial Medal for Literature 2003, Orwell Prize for Lifetime Achievement in Journalism 2008. *Television series include:* Cinema, Up Sunday, So It Goes, A Question of Sex, Saturday Night People, Clive James on Television, The Late Clive James, The Late Show with Clive James, Saturday Night Clive, Fame in the 20th Century, Sunday Night Clive, The Clive James Show, Clive James on Safari; numerous TV documentaries including Clive James meets Katharine Hepburn 1986, Clive James meets Jane Fonda, Clive James meets Mel Gibson 1998, Clive James meets the Supermodels 1998, Postcard series 1989–. *Publications:* non-fiction: The Metropolitan Critic 1974, The Fate of Felicity Fark in the Land of the Media 1975, Peregrine Prykke's Pilgrimage through the London Literary World 1976, Britannia Bright's Bewilderment in the Wilderness of Westminster 1976, Visions Before Midnight 1977, At the Pillars of Hercules 1979, First Reactions 1980, The Crystal Bucket 1981, Charles Charming's Challenges on the Pathway to the Throne 1981, From the Land of Shadows 1982, Glued to the Box 1982, Flying Visits 1984, Snakecharmers in Texas 1988, The Dreaming Swimmer 1992, Clive James on Television 1993, Fame 1993, The Speaker in Ground Zero 1999, Even as We Speak (essays) 2000, Reliable Essays 2001, The Meaning of Recognition: New Essays 2001–2005 2005, North Face of Soho 2006, Alone in the Café 2007, Cultural Amnesia 2007, The Revolt of the Pendulum 2009, The Blaze of Obscurity: The TV Years 2009, The Revolt of the Pendulum: Essays 2005–2008 2010, A Point of View 2011; novels: Brilliant Creatures 1983, The Remake 1987, The Silver Castle 1996; autobiography: Unreliable Memoirs 1980, Falling Towards England: Unreliable Memoirs Vol. II 1985, Unreliable Memoirs Vol. III 1990, May Week was in June 1990, Brrm! Brrm! or The Man from Japan or Perfume at Anchorage 1991, Fame in the 20th Century 1993, The Metropolitan Critic 1993; poetry: Fanmail 1977, Poem of the Year 1983, Other Passports: Poems 1958–85 1986, The Book of My Enemy: Collected Verse 1958–2003 2004, Opal Sunset: Selected Poems 1958–2008 2008, Angels Over Elsinore 2008; trans.: The Divine Comedy 2013; contribs to numerous publs including Commentary, Encounter, Listener, London Review of Books, Nation, New Review, New Statesman, New York Review of Books, New Yorker, TLS. *Leisure interest:* dancing the tango. *Address:* c/o United Agents, 12–26 Lexington Street, London, W1F 0LE, England (office). *Telephone:* (20) 3214-0800 (office). *Fax:* (20) 3214-0801 (office). *E-mail:* info@unitedagents.co.uk (office). *Website:* unitedagents.co.uk (office); www.clivejames.com.

JAMES, Deborah Lee, BA; American government official; *Secretary of the Air Force;* b. 1957, New Jersey; ed Duke Univ., Columbia Univ.; Intern, Presidential Man. Program, Washington, DC 1981; Professional staff mem., House of Reps Armed Services Cttee 1983–93; Asst Sec. of Defense for Reserve Affairs, US Dept of Defense 1993–98; Vice-Pres., Int. Operations & Marketing, United Technologies Corpn 1998–2000; Exec. Vice-Pres. and COO, Business Executives for National Security (BENS) 2000–01; Sr Vice-Pres. and Dir, Homeland Security, Science Applications International Corpn (SAIC) 2002, Sr Vice-Pres., C4IT Business Unit 2004–10, Exec. Vice-Pres., Communications & Govt Affairs 2010–13, Pres., Technical & Eng Sector 2013–; Sec., Dept of the Air Force, US Dept of Defense 2013–; mem. US Dept of Defense Advisory Cttee on Women in the Services. *Address:* Office of the Secretary, US Air Force, 1670 Air Force, Pentagon, Washington, DC 20330, USA (office). *Telephone:* (703) 697-6061 (office). *Website:* www.af.mil (office).

JAMES, Edison Chenfil, MSc; Dominican agronomist and politician; b. 18 Oct. 1943, Marigot; s. of David James and Patricia James; m.; one s. two d.; ed North East London Polytechnic, Univ. of Reading, Imperial Coll., Univ. of London, UK; teacher, St Mary's Acad. Sept.–Dec. 1973; agronomist, Ministry of Agric. 1974–76; Farm Improvement Officer, Caribbean Devt Bank (attached to Dominica Agricultural and Industrial Devt Bank) 1976–80, Loans Officer 1976–80; Co-ordinator Coconut Rehabilitation and Devt Project; Chief Exec. (Gen. Man.) Dominica Banana Marketing Corpn 1980–87; Adviser to Bd of Dirs Windward Islands Banana Growers Asscn 1980–87; Man. Dir Agricultural Man. Corpn Ltd 1987–95; Leader Dominica United Workers Party and Parl. Leader of the Opposition 1990–95, 2000–2013; Prime Minister of Dominica 1995–2000, also Minister of Legal and Foreign Affairs and Labour; leading negotiator with several int. aid agencies; served on numerous public service cttees. *Leisure interests:* cricket, football, int. affairs, politics, table tennis. *Address:* c/o Dominica United Workers Party, 37 Cork Street, Roseau, Dominica.

JAMES, Geraldine, OBE; British actress; b. (Geraldine Thomas), 6 July 1950, Maidenhead, Berks., England; d. of Gerald Trevor Thomas and Annabella Doogan Thomas; m. Joseph Sebastian Blatchley 1986; one d.; ed Downe House, Newbury, Drama Centre London Ltd; Royal TV Soc. Award for Best Actress 1978, Venice

Film Festival Award for Best Actress 1989, Drama Desk (New York) Award for Best Actress 1990. *Stage appearances:* repertory, Chester 1972–74, Exeter 1974–75, Coventry 1975, Passion of Dracula 1978, The White Devil 1981, Turning Over 1984, When I was a Girl I used to Scream and Shout 1987, Cymbeline 1988, Merchant of Venice 1989 (and Broadway 1990), Death and the Maiden 1992, Lysistrata 1993, Hedda Gabler 1993, Give Me Your Answer Do 1998, Faith Healer 2001–02, The Cherry Orchard 2003, Home 2004, The UN Inspector 2005, Victory 2009, Hamlet 2009, The Seagull 2011, '13' 2011. *Films include:* Night Cruiser 1978, Bloody Kids 1979, Sweet William 1980, Gandhi 1982, The Storm 1985, The Wolves of Willoughby Chase 1989, The Tall Guy 1989, If Looks Could Kill 1990, Prince of Shadows 1991, Teen Agent 1991, The Bridge 1992, Words on the Window Pane 1994, No Worries 1994, Moll Flanders 1996, The Man Who Knew Too Little 1997, The Luzhin Defence 2000, The Testimony of Taliesin Jones 2000, All Forgotten 2001, Tom & Thomas 2002, An Angel for May 2002, Calendar Girls 2003, The Fever 2004, Sherlock Holmes 2009, Alice in Wonderland 2010, Made in Dagenham 2010, Arthur 2011, Sherlock Holmes: A Game of Shadows 2011, The Girl with the Dragon Tattoo 2011, The Farmer's Wife (short) 2012, Diana 2013, Our Robot Overlords 2014. *Radio:* The Hours 2000, King Lear 2001, Whale Music 2003, Richard III 2003, The Raj Quartet 2004, The Waves 2007, Dombey and Son 2007, Sacred Hearts 2009, The Carhullan Army 2010, Memory of Gold 2012. *Television films include:* Dummy 1977, Time and the Conways 1985 Freedom Fighter 1988, She's Been Away 1989, The Doll's House 1991, Ex 1991, Doggin' Around 1994, The Healer 1994, Over Here 1996, Rebecca 1997, See Saw 1997, Crime and Punishment 2002, An Angel for May 2002, The Hound of the Baskervilles 2002, Hearts of Gold 2003, State of Play 2003, Hans Christian Andersen: My Life as a Fairy Tale 2003, A Harlot's Progress 2006, Northanger Abbey 2007, Caught in a Trap 2008, Phoo Action 2008, Heist 2008, Legacy 2013. *Television series include:* The Sweeney 1976, Crown Court 1978, Play for Today – Who's Who 1979, Love Among the Artists (mini-series) 1979, Shoestring 1979, The History Man 1981, Chains 1982, The Jewel in the Crown (mini-series) 1984, Blott on the Landscape (mini-series) 1985, Echoes (mini-series) 1988, Screen One 1989–92, Stanley and the Women (mini-series) 1991, Inspector Morse 1991, In Suspicious Circumstances 1994, Kavanagh QC 1995, 1997, Band of Gold 1995–97, Gold 1997, Drovers' Gold (mini-series) 1997, Seesaw (mini-series) 1998, The Sins (mini-series) 2000, White Teeth 2002, State of Play (mini-series) 2003, He Knew He Was Right (mini-series) 2004, Little Britain 2004, Agatha Christie: Poirot – After the Funeral 2006, Jane Hall 2006, Ancient Rome: The Rise and Fall of an Empire 2006, The Battle for Rome (mini-series) 2006, The Amazing Mrs Pritchard 2006, The Time of Your Life 2007, Fairy Tales (mini-series) 2008, City of Vice 2008, The Last Enemy (mini-series) 2008, Little Britain USA 2008, Midsomer Murders – Fit for Murder 2011, Planet of the Apemen: Battle for Earth (narrator) 2011, Playhouse Presents – The Other Woman 2012, 13 Steps Down 2012, Utopia (mini-series) 2013–14. *Address:* c/o Julian Belfrage Associates, 3rd Floor, 9 Argyll Street, London, W1F 7TG, England (office). *Telephone:* (20) 7287-8544 (office). *Fax:* (20) 7287-8832 (office). *E-mail:* email@julianbelfrage.co.uk (office).

JAMES, Kirani; Grenadian sprinter; b. 1 Sept. 1992, St George's; ed Univ. of Alabama, USA; took up athletics at the age of twelve; gold medal, 400m Caribbean Free Trade Asscn (CARIFTA) Games, Providenciales 2007; silver medal, 400m World Youth Championships, Ostrava 2007; gold medal, 200m, 400m, CARIFTA Games, Basseterre 2008; silver medal, 400m World Junior Championships, Bydgoszcz 2008; gold medal, 400m Commonwealth Youth Games, Pune 2008; gold medal, 400m, bronze medal, 4×400m relay CARIFTA Games, Vieux Fort 2009; gold medal, 200m, 400m World Youth Championships, Brixen 2009; gold medal, 400m Pan American Junior Championships, Port-of-Spain 2009; gold medal, 200m, 400m CARIFTA, George Town 2010; gold medal, 200m Pan American Junior Championships, Miramar 2010; gold medal, 400m World Championships, Daegu 2011; gold medal, 400m Olympic Games, London 2012; Sportsman of the Year 2009, 2010, Austin Sealy Trophy 2009. *Address:* c/o Grenada Olympic Committee, PO Box 370, Woolwich Road, St. George's, Grenada.

JAMES, LeBron Raymone; American professional basketball player; b. 30 Dec. 1984, Akron, Ohio; s. of Gloria James; two s. with Savannah Brinson; ed St Vincent-St Mary High School, Akron; selected at age 18 with first overall pick in 2003 NBA (Nat. Basketball Asscn) draft by Cleveland Cavaliers, becoming only second high school player taken at the number one draft position 2003–10; signed as free agent with Miami Heat 2010–; played in bronze medal-winning Team USA at Olympic Games, Athens 2004; played in bronze medal-winning US Nat. Team at FIBA World Championships, Japan 2006; played in gold medal-winning US Nat. Team at FIBA Americas Championships, Las Vegas 2007; played in gold medal-winning Team USA at Olympic Games, Beijing 2008, London 2012; youngest player to register a triple-double and youngest player to score 50 points in one game 2004–05; youngest player in NBA history to average at least 30 points per game in a season 2005–06; named as one of three capts for US Men's Basketball Nat. Team for 2006–08; acquired minority stake in Liverpool Football Club 2011; named Ohio's Mr Basketball and selected to the USA Today All-USA First Team (three times) 2001–03, named Gatorade Nat. Boys Basketball Player of the Year 2001–02, Rookie of the Year 2003–04, NBA All-Star 2005, 2006, 2007, 2008, 2009, 2010, 2011, 2012, All-NBA selection First Team: 2006, 2008, 2009, 2010, 2011, 2012, Second Team: 2005, 2007, The Sporting News NBA Co-MVP 2005–06, NBA All-Star Game MVP (Most Valuable Player) 2006, 2008, Best Male Athlete Award, BET Award for Best Male Athlete 2006, 2007, NBA Scoring Champion 2008, NBA MVP (Most Valuable Player) 2009, 2010, 2012, 2013, NBA All-Defensive First Team: 2009, 2010, 2011, 2012, NBA Finals MVP 2012, 2013. *Publication:* Shooting Stars (with Buzz Bissinger) 2009. *Address:* c/o Miami Heat, AmericanAirlines Arena, 601 Biscayne Blvd., Miami, FL 33132, USA. *Telephone:* (786) 777-1000. *Fax:* (786) 777-1615. *Website:* www.nba.com/heat; www.lebronjames.com.

JAMES, Michael Leonard, (Michael Hartland, Ruth Carrington), MBE, FRSA; British government official, writer and broadcaster; *President, Kennaway House Trust;* b. 7 Feb. 1941; m. 1975; two d.; ed Christ's Coll., Cambridge; entered govt service (GCHQ) 1963; Pvt. Sec. to Rt Hon. Jennie Lee, Minister for the Arts 1966–68; DES 1968–71; Planning Unit of Rt Hon Margaret Thatcher, Sec. of State for Educ. and Science 1971–73; Asst Sec. 1973; Deputy Chief Scientific Officer 1974; served in London, Milan, Paris, Tokyo 1973–78; Dir, IAEA Vienna 1978–83; Adviser, Int. Relations to Comm. of the European Union, Brussels 1983–85; Chair. Civil Service Selection Bds 1983–93; Gov. Colyton Grammar School 1985–90,

Sidmouth Community Coll. 1988–2004, Chair. Bd of Govs 1998–2001; Chair. Gen. Medical Council Fitness to Practise Panels 2000–06; Founder and Chair. Kennaway House Trust 2001–11, Pres. 2011–; mem. Immigration Appeal Tribunal 1987–2005, Asylum and Immigration Tribunal 2005–12; feature writer and book reviewer, The Times (thriller critic 1989–90, travel corresp. 1993–), Daily Telegraph (thriller critic 1993–2000), Sunday Times, Guardian; Hon. Fellow, Univ. of Exeter 1985–. *TV and radio include:* Seven Steps to Treason (BBC Radio 4) 1990, Sonja's Report (ITV documentary) 1990, Masterspy: interviews with KGB defector Oleg Gordievsky (BBC Radio 4) 1991. *Publications:* Internationalization to Prevent the Spread of Nuclear Weapons (co-author) 1980; novels as Michael Hartland: Down Among the Dead Men 1983, Seven Steps to Treason (South West Arts Literary Award) 1985, The Third Betrayal 1986, Frontier of Fear 1989, The Year of the Scorpion 1991, The Verdict of Us All (short stories) (co-author) 2006; other: Masters of Crime – Lionel Davidson and Dick Francis 2006; novel as Ruth Carrington: Dead Fish 1998. *Address:* Branscombe, Devon, EX12 3BH, England (home). *E-mail:* michaelhartland@live.co.uk (office).

JAMES, Renée J., BA, MBA; American computer industry executive; *President, Intel Corporation;* ed Univ. of Oregon; joined Intel through co.'s acquisition of Bell Technologies in 1987, served as Chief of Staff to fmr Intel CEO Andy Grove, later Dir and COO Intel Online Services, held product R&D leadership positions and as Chair. of Intel's software subsidiaries, Havok, McAfee and Wind River, Exec. Vice-Pres. and Gen. Man. Software and Services Group –2013, Pres. Intel Corpn and, with CEO, part of Intel's two-person Exec. Office 2013–; Dir (non-exec.) Vodafone Group Plc; Ind. Dir, VMware Inc.; mem. C200. *Address:* Intel Corporation, 2200 Mission College Boulevard, Santa Clara, CA 95052-8119, USA (office). *Telephone:* (408) 765-8080 (office). *Fax:* (408) 765-9904 (office). *E-mail:* info@intel.com (office). *Website:* www.intel.com (office).

JAMES OF HOLLAND PARK, Baroness (Life Peer), cr. 1991, of Southwold in the County of Suffolk; **Phyllis Dorothy (P. D.) James,** OBE, JP, FRSL, FRSA; British author; b. 3 Aug. 1920, Oxford; d. of Sidney Victor James and Dorothy Amelia Hone; m. Ernest Connor Bantry White 1941 (deceased 1964); two d.; ed Cambridge Girls' High School; Admin., Nat. Health Service 1949–68; Prin., Home Office 1968; Police Dept 1968–72; Criminal Policy Dept 1972–79; JP, Willesden 1979–82, Inner London 1984; Chair. Soc. of Authors 1984–86, Pres. 1997–; mem. BBC Gen. Advisory Council 1987–88, Gov. BBC 1988–93; Assoc. Fellow, Downing Coll., Cambridge 1986; mem. Bd of British Council 1988–93, Arts Council; Chair. Arts Council Literary Advisory Panel 1988–92; mem. Detection Club; mem. Church of England Liturgical Comm. 1991–2000; Hon. Fellow, St Hilda's Coll., Oxford 1996, Downing Coll., Cambridge 2000, Girton Coll., Cambridge 2000, Kellogg Coll., Oxford 2006; Hon. Bencher Inner Temple 2009; Hon. DLitt (Buckingham) 1992, (Herts.) 1994, (Glasgow) 1995, (Durham) 1998, (Portsmouth) 1999; Hon. LitD (London) 1993; Dr hc (Essex) 1996; Grand Master Award, Mystery Writers of America 1999. *Publications:* Cover Her Face 1962, A Mind to Murder 1963, Unnatural Causes 1967, Shroud for a Nightingale 1971, The Maul and the Pear Tree (with T. A. Critchley) 1971, An Unsuitable Job for a Woman 1972, The Black Tower 1975, Death of an Expert Witness 1977, Innocent Blood 1980, The Skull Beneath the Skin 1982, A Taste for Death 1986, Devices and Desires 1989, The Children of Men 1992, Original Sin 1994, A Certain Justice 1997, Time To Be in Earnest 1999, Death in Holy Orders 2001, The Murder Room 2003, The Lighthouse 2005, The Private Patient 2008, Talking About Detective Fiction 2009, Death Comes to Pemberley 2011. *Leisure interests:* exploring churches, walking by the sea. *Address:* c/o Greene & Heaton Ltd, 37A Goldhawk Road, London, W12 8QQ, England (office).

JAMIR, Sanayangba Chubatoshi, BA, LLB; Indian politician; *Governor of Odisha;* b. 17 Oct. 1931, Ungma, Nagaland; s. of Shri Senayangba; m. Imkonglemla Jamir 1959; three s. two d.; ed Univ. of Allahabad; Pres. Student Christian Movt 1954–57; mem. Interim Body of Nagaland, then Jt Sec. Naga People's Convention; Vice-Chair. Mokokchung Town Cttee 1959–60; MP 1961–70, MP Rajya Sabha 1987–89; Parl. Sec., Ministry of External Affairs, Govt of India 1961–67; Union Deputy Minister of Railways, of Labour and Rehabilitation, of Community Devt and Co-operation, Food and Agric. 1968–70; elected mem. to Nagaland Legis. Ass. 1971–73, re-elected mem. from Aonglenden Constituency 1974; subsequently apptd Minister of Finance, Revenue and Border Affairs; re-elected 1977 and apptd Deputy Chief Minister in UDF Ministry; Chief Minister of ULP Ministry April 1980; resgnd when NNDP Ministry came to power June 1980; Leader of Opposition Congress (I) in State Legis. Ass. 1980–82; elected from 26 Aonglenden Constituency, Gen. Elections 1982; unanimously elected Leader Congress (I) Legislature Party, Chief Minister Nagaland 1982–86, 1989–92, 1993–2003; Gov. of Goa 2004–08, of Maharashtra 2008–10, also of Gujarat July–Nov. 2009, of Odisha 2013–; Lokshree Award, Inst. of Econ. Studies 1989, Hind Rattan Award, All India Nat. Unity Conf., Rajiv Gandhi Memorial Award, Rajiv Gandhi Birthday Celebration Cttee 1993, Indira Gandhi Smriti Puraskar, West Bengal Journalist Asscn 1994, Rajiv Gandhi Excellence Award 1994, Arch of Asia Award, Nat. Citizens Award 1996, Rashtriya Ekta Puraskar, Cttee for Nat. Integration 1997, Nat. Integration Award, Forum for Unity and Integrity 1998. *Publication:* Reminiscences of Correspondence (co-author). *Leisure interests:* reading, badminton. *Address:* Raj Bhavan, Bhubaneswar, India (office). *Telephone:* (674) 2536111 (office); (674) 2536582 (office). *Fax:* (674) 2404695 (office). *E-mail:* info@rajbhavanorissa.gov.in (office). *Website:* rajbhavanorissa.gov.in (office).

JÄMIŞEV, Bolat Bïdaxmetulı, PhD; Kazakhstani banker and politician; *Minister of Regional Development;* b. 28 June 1957, Almaty, Kazakh SSR, USSR; m. two s.; ed Kazakh Inst. of Agric.; First Vice-Minister of Finance 1999–2001, 2002–03; Vice-Minister of Internal Affairs 2001–02; Deputy Chair. Nat. Bank of Kazakhstan 2003–04; Chair. Agency for Regulation and Oversight of Financial Orgs 2004–06; Deputy Chair. Exec. Bd, Russian-Kazakh Eurasian Devt Bank 2006–07; Minister of Finance 2007–13, of Regional Devt 2013–. *Address:* Ministry of Regional Development, 010000 Astana, Orynbor kosh. 8, Ministrilkter uyi, 10 kireberis, Kazakhstan (office). *Telephone:* (7172) 74-21-78 (office). *E-mail:* kense@mrr.gov.kz (office). *Website:* minregion.gov.kz (office).

JAMMEH, Col Yahya A.J.J.; Gambian head of state and fmr army officer; *President and Minister of Defence, of Agriculture, and of Energy;* b. 25 May 1965, Kanilai Village, Foni Kansala Dist, Western Div.; m. Zineb Yahya-Jammeh (née

Soumah); one d.; ed Gambia High School; joined fmr Gambia Nat. Gendarmerie as pvt. 1984; with Special Intervention Unit, Gambia Nat. Army 1984–86, Sergeant 1986, Escort Training Instructor, Gendarmerie Training School 1986–89, Cadet Officer 1987, commissioned 1989, Second Lt 1989, in charge of Presidential Escort, Presidential Guards 1989–90, CO Mobile Gendarmerie Jan.–June 1991, Mil. Police Unit June–Aug. 1991, Lt 1992, Commdr Gambia Nat. Army Mil. Police Aug.–Nov. 1992, Capt. 1994, Col 1996; became Chair. Armed Forces Provisional Ruling Council, Head of State 1994–; retd from army 1996; elected Pres. of The Gambia 1996–, also Minister of Defence, Agric. and Energy; Chair., Pres. Alliance for Patriotic Reorientation and Construction (APRC) 1996–; Chair. Inter-states Cttee for Control of Drought in the Sahel 1997–2000; 1st Vice-Chair. Org. of the Islamic Conf. 2000–; Grand Commdr, Order of Al-Fatah (Libya) 1995; Order of Distinction (Liberia) 2000; Grand Master of the Repub. of The Gambia 2001; Pan-African Humanitarian Award 1997 and numerous other awards. *Leisure interests:* playing tennis, soccer, hunting, reading, correspondence, driving and riding motorcycles, music, films and animal rearing. *Address:* Office of the President, State House, Banjul, The Gambia (office); Alliance for Patriotic Reorientation and Construction, GAMSTAR Building, Banjul. *Telephone:* 4223811 (office). *Fax:* 4227034 (office). *E-mail:* info@statehouse.gm (office). *Website:* www.statehouse.gm (office); www.jammeh2001.org (office).

JANABIL; Chinese party official; *Chairman, Xinjiang Uygur Autonomous Regional Committee, Chinese People's Political Consultative Conference;* b. April 1934, Habahe (Kaba) Co., Xinjiang Uygur Autonomous Region; s. of Simagul Janabil and Ajikhan Janabil; m. Zubila Janabil 1955; two s. two d.; joined CCP 1953; Vice-Chair. Revolutionary Cttee, Xinjiang Autonomous Region 1975–79; Chair. Revolutionary Cttee and First Sec. CCP Cttee, Ili Autonomous Kazakh Pref. 1975–80; Deputy Sec. CCP Cttee, Xinjiang 1977–83, Sec. 1983–85; Vice-Chair. Xinjiang 1979–83; Deputy Sec. then Sec. CCP 4th Xinjiang Uyghur Autonomous Regional Cttee 1985–; Chair. CPPCC 7th Xinjiang Uygur Autonomous Regional Cttee 1993–; Alt. mem. 10th CCP Cen. Cttee 1972–77, 11th CCP Cen. Cttee 1977–82, 12th CCP Cen. Cttee 1982–87, 13th Cen. Cttee 1987–92, 14th Cen. Cttee 1992–97; mem. 8th CPPCC Nat. Cttee 1993–98, 9th CPPCC Nat. Cttee 1998–2003; Del., 15th CCP Nat. Congress 1997–2002; Pres. Xinjiang Br. Futurology Soc. 1980. *Address:* c/o Xinjiang Autonomous Regional Chinese Communist Party, Urumqi, Xinjiang, People's Republic of China.

JANDA, Krystyna; Polish actress and film and theatre director; b. 18 Dec. 1952, Starachowice; m.; two s. one d.; ed State Higher School of Drama, Warsaw; actress, Atheneum Theatre, Warsaw 1976–88, Powszechny Theatre, Warsaw 1988–; opened Theatre Polonia, Warsaw 2005; acting on TV and performing in cabaret; numerous awards in Poland and abroad; over 50 leading roles in classic and contemporary plays and over 50 leading roles in film and TV; Best Actress 40th Int. Film Festival, San Sebastián, Golden Duck Award 2007. *Films include:* Man of Marble 1976, Without Anaesthetic 1978, The Border 1978, The Conductor 1979, Die Grünen Vögel 1979, Golem 1979, Mephisto 1980, War Between Worlds 1980, Man of Iron 1981, Espion lève toi 1981, Interrogation 1982, Ce fut un bel été 1982, Bella Donna 1983, Gluth 1983, Der Bulle und das Mädchen 1984, Vertige 1985, My Mother's Lovers 1985, Laputa 1986, Short Film About Killing 1987, II Decalogue, V Decalogue 1988, Ownership 1989, Polish Kitchen 1991, Relieved of the Life 1992, As 1995, Pestka (actress and Dir) 1996, Mother's Mother 1996, Unwritten Principles 1997, Last Chapter 1997, David Weissen 1999, Żółtyszalik (Yellow Muffler) 2000, Przedwiośnie 2000, Życie jako śmiertelna choroba prienoszona drogą płciową (Life as a Fatal Sexually Transmitted Disease) 2000. *Stage appearances include:* Bal manekinów 1974, Edukacja Rity 1984, Z życia glist 1984, Biała bluzka 1987, Medea 1988, Shirley Valentine 1990, Kobieta zawied-ziona 1996, Kotka na gorącym blaszanym dachu 1997, Maria Callas – Lekcja śpiewu (Song Lesson) 1997, Harry i ja (Harry and Me) 1998, Opowiadania zebrane (Collected Stories) 2001, Siedem grzechów głównych 2001, Mała Steinberg (Spoonface Steinberg) 2001, Kto się boi Virginii Woolf (Who's Afraid of Virginia Woolf) 2002, Mewa 2003, Czego nie Widać 2003, Janosik albo na Szkle Malowane 2004, Namiętność 2005, Lekcje stepowania 2005. *Plays directed include:* Hedda Gabler 1999, Związek otwarty (Friendship Opened) 2000, Zazdrość (Jealousy) 2001. *TV series:* Mierzejewska 1989, From Time to Time 1999. *Website:* www.krystynajanda.net.

JANDOSOV, Oraz, MEcon; Kazakhstani economist and politician; *Director, RAKURS Center for Economic Analysis;* b. 26 Oct. 1961, Almaty; m. Gulnara Ussubakunova; three c.; ed Lomonosov Moscow State Univ.; Research Assoc., Inst. of Econs, Acad. of Sciences of Kazakhstan 1987–90; Adviser, then Head of Div., Supreme Econ. Council under Pres. of Kazakhstan 1991–92; First Deputy Minister for the Economy and Chair. Nat. Agency on Foreign Investment 1993–94; First Deputy Gov. Bank of Kazakhstan 1994–96, Gov. 1996–98; First Deputy Prime Minister and Chair. State Cttee on Investment 1998–99, Deputy Prime Minister and Minister of Finance Jan.–Oct. 1999; Pres. KEGOC (Kazakhstan Electricity Grid Operating Co.) 1999–2000; Deputy Prime Minister 2000–01 (resgnd following protest by Prime Minister Kasimzhomart Tokayev regarding his membership of Democratic Choice of Kazakhstan (DCK) movt which he co-founded in 2001); Chair. Kazakhstan's Asscn of Financial Insts 2001–02; Asst to Pres. of Kazakhstan on econ. and financial issues Jan.–June 2003; Chair. Agency for Regulation of Natural Monopolies and Protection of Competition 2003–04; Founder and Co-Chair. Ak Zhol (Bright Path) (later Naghyz Ak Zhol—True Bright Path) Democratic Party of Kazakhstan 2002–08; Dir RAKURS Center for Econ. Analysis 2008–; mem. Presidium, Nat. Chamber of Entrepreneurs 2013–; Order of Kurmet. *Leisure interests:* tennis, soccer, skiing. *Address:* RAKURS Centre for Economic Analysis, 97B Dostyk Avenue, Office 7/2, Almaty 050051, Kazakhstan (office). *Telephone:* (727) 264-61-55 (office); (727) 263-02-78 (office). *E-mail:* ojandosov@cear.kz (office). *Website:* www.cear.kz (office).

JANDROKOVIĆ, Gordan; Croatian politician and diplomatist; b. 2 Aug. 1967, Bjelovar; m.; three c.; ed Faculties of Civil Eng and Political Science, Univ. of Zagreb, Diplomatic School, Ministry of Foreign Affairs, The Netherlands Inst. of Int. Relations, Clingendael, Erasmus Universiteit, Rotterdam; pvt. construction co. 1989–94; with Ministry of Foreign Affairs 1994–2000; Man. Stanić Co., Zagreb 2000–02; Gen. Man. Beming Co., Bjelovar 2002–03; mem. Croatian Democratic Union (HDZ) 1992–, Chair. HDZ Cttee for Small and Medium-Size Enterprises 2002–, HDZ Cttee for Bjelovar-Bilogora Co. 2003–, mem. HDZ Presidency 2004–;

mem. Parl. 2003–, Chair. Parl. Cttee for the Economy, Devt and Reconstruction 2003–04, Parl. Foreign Policy Cttee 2004–07, Head of Parl. Del. to Croatia-EU Jt Parl. Cttee 2004–07; Minister of Foreign Affairs and European Integration 2008–11, also Deputy Prime Minister 2010–11; Man. Ed. The Witnesses to History series 1997–2002. *Leisure interests:* tennis, football, reading. *Address:* c/o Ministry of Foreign Affairs and European Integration, 10000 Zagreb, trg Nikole Šubića Zrinskog 7–8, Croatia.

JANEWAY, Richard, AB, MD; American physician, academic and medical school administrator; *Executive Vice-President Emeritus for Health Affairs, Wake Forest University;* b. 12 Feb. 1933, Los Angeles, Calif.; s. of VanZandt Janeway and Grace Ellen Bell Janeway; m. Katherine Esmond Pillsbury 1955; one s. two d.; ed Colgate Univ., Univ. of Pennsylvania School of Medicine; Instructor in Neurology, Bowman Gray School of Medicine of Wake Forest Univ. (now Wake Forest Univ. School of Medicine) 1966–67, Asst Prof. 1967–70, Assoc. Prof. 1970–71, Prof. 1971–, Dean 1971–85, Exec. Dean 1985–94, Vice-Pres. for Health Affairs 1983–90, Exec. Vice-Pres. 1990–97, Univ. Prof. of Medicine and Man. 1997–, Exec. Vice-Pres. Emer. for Health Affairs 1997–; mem. Winston-Salem Foundation Bd 1994–2002 (Chair. 1997–98); Dir Idealliance 1999–; Chair. Asscn of American Medical Colls. 1984–85; mem. Bd of Dirs BB&T Corpn 1995– (Exec. Cttee 2000–, Chair. 2001–), S. Nat. Corpn 1989–95; mem. Nat. Asscn for Biomedical Research 1993–96, Americans for Medical Progress Inc. 1993–97; mem. Bd of Trustees Colgate Univ., 1988–95, Winston-Salem State Univ. 1991–95; mem. Inst. of Medicine of NAS, American Medical Asscn, American Heart Asscn, American Neurological Asscn, Soc. for Neuroscience, Soc. of Medical Admins, American Clinical and Climatological Asscn; Fellow, American Acad. of Neurology; Life Fellow, American Coll. of Physicians; John and Mary R. Markle Scholar in Academic Medicine 1968–73, Distinguished Service mem. Asscn of American Medical Colls 1991, Medallion of Merit, Wake Forest Univ. 2000, Maroon Citation, Colgate Univ. 2004. *Publications:* one monograph, 16 book chapters, 39 original articles, 16 abstracts, nine editorials, eight invited comments, one patent. *Leisure interests:* golf, photography, gardening, travel. *Address:* Wake Forest University, School of Medicine, Medical Center Blvd., Winston-Salem, NC 27157 (office); 2710 Old Town Club Road, Winston-Salem, NC 27106, USA (home). *Telephone:* (336) 716-3840 (office); (336) 727-7537 (home). *Fax:* (336) 773-0082. *E-mail:* djaneway@wfubmc.edu (office); rjaneway@triad.rr.com.

JANG, Ha Sung, PhD; South Korean academic; *Professor of Finance and Dean of the Business School, Korea University;* b. 19 Sept. 1953, Kwangju; ed Wharton School, Univ. of Pennsylvania, USA; joined in pro-democracy protests early 1970s; moved to USA to study for doctorate 1980s; taught finance at Wharton School and Univ. of Houston; returned to S Korea 1990; special adviser to Lazard's Korea Corp. Governance Fund; int. adviser to Chinese Security Regulatory Comm.; currently Prof. and Dean of the Business School, Korea Univ.; Exec. Dir Asian Inst. of Corp. Governance; Chair. Inst. of Dirs in E Asia Network; helped est. Center for Good Corp. Governance 2001; runs advocacy group, People's Solidarity for Participatory Democracy, to attempt to make S Korea's chaebol (large conglomerates) more accountable to minority shareholders, has won several milestone court victories; Int. Corp. Governance Network Excellence in Corp. Governance Award, Financial Analyst Journal Graham and Dodd Award, Maekyung Business Daily Maekyung Economist Award, Korea Univ. Granite Teaching Award, Korea Univ. Business School Prof. of the Year Award. *Publications:* numerous articles in professional journals. *Address:* Korea University Business School, 5 Anam-dong, Seongbuk-Gu, Seoul, 136-701 South Korea (office). *Telephone:* (2) 3290-1929 (office). *E-mail:* jangya@korea.ac.kr (office). *Website:* biz.korea.ac.kr/~jangya (office).

JANG, Gen. Jong-nam; North Korean army officer and government official; *Minister of the People's Armed Forces;* fmr Commdr, First Corps of the Korean People's Army; attained rank of Col-Gen. 2011, Gen. 2012; Minister of the People's Armed Forces 2013–. *Address:* Ministry of the People's Armed Forces, Pyongyang, Democratic People's Republic of Korea (office).

JANG, Seok-hyo, BA, MBA; South Korean business executive; *President and CEO, Korea Gas Corporation (KOGAS);* b. 27 Oct. 1957; ed Jung-Dong High School, Seoul, In-Ha Univ., Univ. of Minnesota, USA; joined Korea Gas Corpn (KOGAS) 1983, Vice-Pres. LNG Purchase Div. 2003-07, Acting Exec. Vice-Pres. Marketing Div. July–Sept. 2007, Exec. Vice-Pres. Marketing Div. 2007–08, Exec. Vice-Pres. Resources Div. 2008–10, Exec. Vice-Pres. Resources Business Div. 2010–11, Pres. and CEO Tong Yeong Tug Co. Ltd 2011–13, Pres. and CEO Korea Gas Corpn 2013-. *Address:* Korea Gas Corporation, 93 Dolmaro, 215 Jeongja-dong, Bundang-gu, Seongnam, Gyeonggi-do, 463-754, South Korea (office). *Telephone:* (31) 710-0114 (office). *Fax:* (31) 710-0117 (office). *E-mail:* kogasmaster@kogas.or.kr (office). *Website:* www.kogas.or.kr (office).

JANICOT, Daniel Claude Emmanuel, LenD; French international official; *Member, Conseil d'Etat;* b. 20 May 1948, Neuilly; s. of François-Xavier Janicot and Antoinette Mauxion; m. 2nd Catherine Lachenal 1991; one s.; two d. from previous marriage; ed Ecole Nat. d'Admin, Inst. d'Etudes Politiques and Faculté de Droit, Paris; Auditeur, Conseil d'Etat 1975–, Deputy Sec.-Gen. 1978–82, Maître des requêtes 1979; Maître de Conférences, Instituts d'Etudes Politiques, Paris and Bordeaux and Ecole Nat. des Ponts et Chaussées; mem. Admin. Council, Public Information Library, Beaubourg 1979; Del.-Gen. American Center 1980–90; Vice-Pres. Bibliothèque Nationale 1981; Maître de séminaire, Ecole Nat. d'Admin 1982–83; Del.-Gen. Union Centrale des Arts Décoratifs 1982–86; Special Adviser Office of Dir-Gen. of UNESCO 1990–91, Dir of Exec. Office of Dir-Gen. 1991–94, Asst Dir-Gen. 1994–99; mem. Conseil d'état 1995–; Chair. Bd, Centre Nat. d'Art Contemporain de Grenoble 1995–; Vice-Chair. Bd, Institut Français de Gestion 1996–; Dir Musée des arts premiers; mem. Bd of Dirs Artcurial Holding SA; Chevalier, Ordre nat. du Mérite, Ordre des Arts et Lettres, Légion d'honneur. *Address:* Conseil d'Etat, 1 place du Palais-Royal, 75100 Paris 01 SP (office); 6 rue Casimir-Périer, 75007 Paris, France (home). *Telephone:* 1-40-20-80-50 (office). *Fax:* 1-40-20-80-08 (office). *E-mail:* webmestre@conseil-etat.fr (office). *Website:* www.conseil-etat.fr (office).

JANION, Maria, PhD; Polish academic; *Lecturer, Institute of Literary Research, Polish Academy of Sciences;* b. 24 Dec. 1926, Mońki; d. of Cyprian Janion and Ludwika Kudryk; ed Łódź Univ., Warsaw Univ.; researcher, Inst. of Literary

Research, Polish Acad. of Sciences (PAN), Warsaw 1946–96, mem. Scientific Bd 1957–, Lecturer, Inst. of Philosophy and Sociology School of Social Research, PAN 1992–, mem. Cttee of Literary Sciences 1996–; Asst, Warsaw Univ. 1951–52, Lecturer 1981–87, apptd. Prof. 1987; researcher, Higher Pedagogic School, Gdańsk 1957–69, Prof. 1963–70; Prof., Inst. of Polish Studies, Gdańsk Univ. 1970–81, 1984–90; Ed.-in-Chief Historia i teoria literatury Studia (series) 1968–78, Biblioteka Romanistyczna (series) 1978–; Ordinary mem. Polish Acad. of Arts and Sciences 1990–; Corresp. mem. PAN 1991, mem. 1998–; mem. jury, Nike Literature Award 1997–, Chair. 2000–; Ordre national du Mérite 2012; Dr hc (Gdańsk Univ.) 1994; Alfred Jurzykowski Foundation Award 1980, Culture Foundation Great Prize for the Year 1998, Chair. of Council of Ministers Award 2001, Kazimierz Wyka Award 2001, Gloria Artis 2007. *Publications include:* Romantism—Studies of Ideas and Style 1969, Gorączka romantyczna (Romantic Fever) 1975, Romantyzm i historia (with M. Żmigrodzka) 1978, Renewing of Meanings 1980, Transgresje (seven-vol. series, also co-ed.) 1981–88, Wobec zła 1989, Życie Pośmiertne Konrada Wallenroda 1990, Kobiety i duch inności (Women and the Spirit of Strangeness) 1996, Płacz generała. Eseje o wojnie 1998, Do Europy tak, ale razem z naszymi umarłymi (To Europe, Yes, but with Our Dead) 2000, Żyjąc tracimy życie. Niepokojące tematy egzystencji 2001, Niesamowita słowiańszczyzna 2006. *Address:* Institute of Literary Research, Polish Academy of Sciences, 00-330 Warsaw, ul. Nowy Świat 72, Poland (office). *Telephone:* (22) 6572764 (office). *Fax:* (22) 8269945 (office). *E-mail:* ibadlit@ibl.waw.pl (office). *Website:* www.ibl.waw.pl (office).

JANKOVIĆ, Jelena; Serbian professional tennis player; b. 28 Feb. 1985, Belgrade, SFR Yugoslavia; d. of Veselin Janković and Snežana Janković; ed French diplomatic school in Belgrade, 'Megatrend' Coll., Belgrade; plays right-handed with two-handed backhand; first played in practice at Tennis Club of Red Star Belgrade Nov. 1994; first tournament: reached semifinals in Nat. Yugoslavian Championship for children up to 10 years old 1995; won on Limon Bowl Tournament in Italy; moved to USA and joined Nick Bolitieri's Acad.; turned professional 2000; Grand Slam winner aged 16, winning Australian Open, Melbourne and becoming No. 1 Jr in the world 2001; also played in finals of US Open and Orange Bowl; played in finals at Virginia tournament 2002, at China Open 2013; in quarter finals at tournament in Stanford 2002; won at Int. Tennis Fed. (ITF) tournament in Dubai 2003, won first Women's Tennis Asscn (WTA) title at tournament in Budapest 2004; WTA titles: Budapest 2004, Auckland 2007, Charleston 2007, Rome 2007, 2008, Birmingham 2007, Beijing 2008, Stuttgart 2008, Moscow 2008, Marbella 2009; doubles titles: Birmingham (with Na Li) 2006; mixed doubles titles: Wimbledon (with Jamie Murray) 2007; first played for Serbia and Montenegro nat. team in Fed. Cup aged 16; first official match for nat. team on tournament in Mursia 2001; undefeated at first Afro-European group of Fed. Cup 2004; only tennis player to represent Serbia and Montenegro at Olympic Games, Athens 2004; partnered Novak Djokovic to play for Serbia in Hopman Cup (exhibition team event sanctioned by ITF) 2008; UNICEF Nat. Amb. for Serbia 2007–; Best Tennis Player in Serbia and Montenegro 2004. *Film:* starred in Jelenin svet (Jelena's World), a documentary about her life 2008. *Leisure interests:* travelling, reading, watching TV. *E-mail:* info@jelenajankovic.net (office); info@jj-jelenajankovic.com (office). *Website:* www.jelenajankovic.net (office); www.jj-jelenajankovic.com (office).

JANKOVIĆ, Zoran, BEcons; Slovenian business executive and politician; *Mayor of Ljubljana;* b. 1 Jan. 1953, Saraorci, Smederevo; m. Mija Janković; two s.; ed Univ. of Ljubljana; Sales Man. Mercator Investa 1979–84, Dir 1984–88; Vice-Pres. Emona SOZD and Acting Gen. Man. Emona VPS 1988–90; f. Electa company 1990, Dir 1990–97; Pres. and CEO Mercator d.d. 1997–2005; Mayor of Ljubljana 2006–11, 2012–; Founder and Pres. Positive Slovenia (Pozitivna Slovenija) 2011–; mem. Državni zbor (Nat. Ass.) 2011–; designated as Prime Minister Jan. 2012, but appointment rejected by parl.; fmr Chair. Supervisory Bd Pokojninska družba A. d.d. (pension fund); mem. Exec. Bd Mans Asscn; mem. Exec. Bd Chamber of Commerce and Industry of Slovenia; Pres. Alumni Club of Faculty of Econs, Univ. of Ljubljana; Pres. Slovenian Handball Fed. 1996–2004, Hon. Pres. 2004–; Hon. Pres. Handball Club Krim Mercator; Hon. Citizen of Chengdu, China 2011; Slovenian Chamber of Commerce's Award for outstanding economic achievement 2001, Manager of the Year, Managers' Asscn 2002, Best Director, Kapital magazine 2003, 2004, 2005, 2006, Foremost Manager Award, Manager magazine 2003, Primus Award for Excellence in Communication, Slovenian Public Relations Soc., Slovenian Chamber of Commerce and Managers' Asscn 2003, Foremost Director, Manager magazine and Kline & Partner 2004, 2005, Best Director as chosen by the readers of Nedeljski dnevnik newspaper 2006, Person of the Year in the field of politics 2006, Best Manager Award, Direkcija for the selection of the best manager in Bosnia and Herzegovina, South East and Central Europe (in Sarajevo) 2009, chosen by French newspaper Libération for its list of 36 individuals from the 27 EU member states that would shape tomorrow's Europe 2008, named by The City Mayors Foundation as its Mayor of the Month Dec. 2011, also among its 25 Best Mayors in the World of 2012. *Address:* Office of the Mayor, 1000 Ljubljana, Mestni trg 1 (office); Pozitivna Slovenija (Positive Slovenia), 1000 Ljubljana, Dalmatinova 2, Slovenia. *Telephone:* (1) 3061288 (office); (5) 9927077. *Fax:* (1) 3061214 (office); (5) 9927077. *E-mail:* zoran.jankovic@ljubljana.si (office); info@pozitivnaslovenija.si. *Website:* www.ljubljana.si/en/municipality/mayor (office); www.pozitivnaslovenija.si.

JANKOWITSCH, Peter, DDL; Austrian lawyer, politician and diplomatist; *Secretary-General, Franco-Austrian Centre for Rapprochement in Europe;* b. 10 July 1933, Vienna; s. of Karl Jankowitsch and Gertrude Jankowitsch (née Ladstaetter); m. 1st Odette Prevor 1962 (divorced); one s.; m. 2nd Silvia Lahner 2001; ed Vienna Univ. and The Hague Acad. of Int. Law; fmr lawyer; joined Foreign Service 1957, worked in Int. Law Dept; Pvt. Sec., Cabinet of Minister of Foreign Affairs 1959–62; posted to London 1962–64; Chargé d'affaires, Dakar, Senegal 1964–66; Head of Office of Bruno Kreisky, Chair. Austrian Socialist Party 1967; Chief of Cabinet of Fed. Chancellor (Kreisky) 1970–72; Perm. Rep. to UN 1972–78; Chair. UN Cttee on Peaceful Uses of Outer Space 1972–91; Vice-Chair. of Bd, Int. Energy Agency 1979–83; Rep. for Austria to UN Security Council 1973–74, Pres. Security Council 1973, Vice-Pres. 29th Gen. Assembly; Vice-Pres. 7th Special Session of Gen. Assembly 1975; mem. UN Security Council Mission to Zambia 1973; Perm. Rep. to OECD 1978–82; Deputy Perm. Under-Sec., Chief of Cabinet, Fed. Ministry of Foreign Affairs 1982–83; Fed. Minister for Foreign Affairs

1986–87; mem. Austrian Nat. Ass. (Nationalrat) 1983–90 (Chair. Foreign Relations Cttee 1987–90), 1992–93; Minister of State for Integration and Devt Cooperation 1990–92; Perm. Rep. to OECD and ESA 1993–98; Chair. OECD Devt Centre 1994–98; Chair. Jt Cttee European Parl.–Austrian Parl.; Sec.-Gen. Franco-Austrian Centre for Rapprochement in Europe 1998–; Int. Sec. Social Democratic Party of Austria 1983–90; Chair. Human Rights Cttee Socialist Int. 1987–97, Vice-Chair. Socialist Int. Cttee on Econ. Affairs 1997–99; Pres. Cttee of Parliamentarians of EFTA 1989–90; mem. Bd Austrian Inst. for Int. Politics, Vienna Inst. for Devt, Int. Acad. of Astronautics 1998; Pres. Austrian Nat. Cttee for Unispace 1999; Chair. Austrian Air and Space Agency 1998–; Pres. Austria-Viet Nam Soc. 1999–, Jerusalem Foundation, Austria 2002–; Assoc. Ed. Acta Astronomica 2003–; Special Envoy Austrian Fed. Govt 2006–09; Vice-Pres. Austrian Foreign Policy and UN Soc. 2008–; mem. Advisory Bd, European Space Policy Inst.; Hon. Pres. Austrian Soc. for European Policy 1996–, Hon. mem. Bd Int. Inst. of Space Law, Hon. Pres. Austria-Namibia Soc. 2008; Commdr, Légion d'honneur and numerous other Austrian and foreign decorations; Allan D. Emil Memorial Award for Int. Cooperation in Astronautics 1981, Social Sciences Award, Int. Acad. of Astronautics 2001. *Publications:* Kreisky's Era in Austrian Foreign Policy (co-ed. with E. Bielka and H. Thalberg) 1982, Red Markings–International (co-ed. with H. Fischer) 1984, The European Integration Process and Neutral Austria 1994, Austria and the Non-Aligned 2002; and papers and articles on Austria and on econ. and political devt of the Third World; contrib. to Wörterbuch des Völkerrechts 1960. *Leisure interests:* history and baroque music. *Address:* Franco-Austrian Centre for Rapprochement in Europe, Salzgries 19, 1010 Vienna (office); Mariahilferstrasse 57–59/12, 1060 Vienna, Austria. *Telephone:* (1) 5338927 (office); (1) 5855227 (home). *Fax:* (1) 5338927-10 (office). *E-mail:* peter.jankowitsch@oefz.at (office); peter.jankowitsch@chello.at (home). *Website:* www.peter-jankowitsch.net (home); www.oefz.at (office).

JANKULOSKA, Gordana, MA; Macedonian lawyer and politician; *Minister of Internal Affairs;* b. 12 Oct. 1975, Ohrid; ed SS Cyril and Methodius Univ., Skopje and Univ. of Kent, UK; early career as lawyer in pvt. law firm 1999–2000; Head of Cabinet, Minister of Finance 2000–02; Gen.-Sec. Internal Macedonian Revolutionary Org.-Democratic Party for Macedonian Nat. Unity (VMRO-DPMNE) 2004–06; Minister of Internal Affairs 2006–; Special Achievement in Law Award, Univ. of Kent, UK 2004. *Address:* Ministry of Internal Affairs, 1000 Skopje, ul. Dimče Mirčev 9, Former Yugoslav Republic of Macedonia (office). *Telephone:* (2) 3117222 (office). *Fax:* (2) 3112468 (office). *E-mail:* kontakt@mvr.gov.mk (office). *Website:* www.mvr.gov.mk (office).

JANNEH, Abdoulie, MA; Gambian UN official; ed Fourah Bay Coll., Sierra Leone, Univs of Nottingham and Bradford, UK, Econ. Devt Inst., World Bank (Project Man.); joined UNDP from Govt of Gambia as Programme Adviser 1979, Adviser, Office to Combat Desertification and Drought (UNSO), Burkina Faso 1979–80, Programme Officer, UNSO, New York 1981–83, Deputy Resident Rep. in Guinea 1984–86, Sierra Leone 1987–89, Deputy Exec. Sec. UN Capital Devt Fund 1990–93, Resident Coordinator and Resident Rep., Niger 1993–96, Ghana 1996–99, reassigned to New York to lead Transition Team 1999, Asst Sec.-Gen. and UNDP Regional Dir for Africa 2000–05, Under-Sec.-Gen. and Exec. Sec. UN Econ. Comm. for Africa, Addis Ababa, Ethiopia 2005–12. *Address:* c/o United Nations Economic Commission for Africa, Africa Hall, PO Box 3001, Addis Ababa, Ethiopia.

JANOWITZ, Gundula; Austrian singer (soprano); b. 2 Aug. 1937, Berlin, Germany; d. of Theodor Janowitz and Else Janowitz (née Neumann); m.; one d.; ed Acad. of Music and Performing Arts, Graz; debut with Vienna State Opera 1960; perm. mem. Deutsche Oper, Berlin 1966; sang with Metropolitan Opera, New York 1967, Salzburg Festival 1968–81, Teatro Colón, Buenos Aires 1970, Munich State Opera 1971, Grand Opera, Paris 73, Covent Garden Opera 1976, La Scala 1978; concerts in maj. cities throughout the world, appearances at Bayreuth, Aix-en-Provence, Glyndebourne, Spoleto, Salzburg, Munich Festivals; Opera Dir at Graz 1990–91; mem. Vienna State Opera, Deutsche Oper, Berlin; mem. Main Prize Jury, BBC Cardiff Singer of the World Competition 2003, 2005, 2007; Hon. Mem. Vienna State Opera, Acad. of Music, Graz, RAM, London. *Leisure interest:* modern literature. *Address:* 3072 Kasten 75, Austria.

JANOWSKI, Marek; German conductor; *Chief Conductor and Artistic Director, Rundfunk Sinfonieorchester Berlin;* b. 18 Feb. 1939, Warsaw, Poland; ed Cologne Musikhochschule and studied in Siena, Italy; fmrly Asst Conductor in Aachen, Cologne and Düsseldorf opera houses; Music Dir, Freiburg and Dortmund Operas 1973–79; Artistic Adviser and Conductor Royal Liverpool Philharmonic Orchestra 1983–86; Music Dir and Chief Conductor Orchestre Philharmonique de Radio France 1984–2000; Chief Conductor Gurzenich-Orchester, Cologne 1986–90; Artistic Dir Monte Carlo Philharmonic Orchestra 1999, Music Dir and Chief Conductor 2000–05; Prin. Conductor and Artistic Dir Dresden Philharmonic Orchestra 2001–03; Chief Conductor and Artistic Dir Rundfunk Sinfonieorchester Berlin 2002–; Artistic and Music Dir Orchestre de la Suisse-Romande, Geneva 2005–12; Endowed Guest Conductor Chair Pittsburgh Symphony Orchestra 2005–; regular guest conductor in Paris, Berlin, Hamburg, Cologne and Munich opera houses; has also conducted at Metropolitan Opera (New York), Chicago, San Francisco (American opera debut 1983), Dresden and Vienna State Operas, Teatro Colón (Buenos Aires), Orange Festival (France) and Théâtre du Châtelet (Paris); has conducted concerts with Berlin Philharmonic, Chicago Symphony, London Symphony Orchestra, Philharmonia, NHK (Tokyo), Dresden Staatskapelle, Boston Symphony Orchestra, Stockholm Philharmonic and BBC Symphony Orchestra. *Recordings include:* Wagner's Der Ring des Nibelungen (with the Dresden Staatskapelle), Weber's Euryanthe, Strauss's Die Schweigsame Frau, Penderecki's The Devils of Loudun, Korngold's Violanta, Hindemith's Die Harmonie der Welt, Bruckner Symphonies No. 4 and No. 6 (with Orchestre Philharmonique de Radio France), Roussel four symphonies (with Orchestre Philharmonique de Radio France) (Diapason D'Or 1996), Weber's Oberon 1997, Strauss's Four Last Songs (Gramophone magazine Editor's Choice Award 2002). *Address:* c/o Jessica Ford, Intermusica Artists' Management Ltd, 36 Graham Street, Crystal Wharf, London, N1 8GJ, England (office); Orchestre de la Suisse Romande, Rue Bovy-Lysberg 2, 1204 Geneva, Switzerland (office). *Telephone:* (20) 7608-9900 (office). *Fax:* (20) 7490-3263 (office). *E-mail:* mail@intermusica.co.uk (office). www.intermusica.co.uk (office); www.osr.ch (office).

JANŠA, Janez; Slovenian politician; *President, Slovenian Democratic Party;* b. (Ivan Janša), 17 Sept. 1958, Ljubljana; one s. one d. with Silva Predalič; m. Urška Bačovnik 2009; one s.; ed Univ. of Ljubljana; intern at Republican Secr. for Defence; apptd Pres. Cttee for Basic People's Defence and Social Self-Protection, Alliance of Socialist Youth of Slovenia 1982; wrote paper critical of conditions within Yugoslav People's Army labelled counter-revolutionary 1983, indicted by mil. prosecutor 1985; served as Minister of Defence in Slovenia 1990–94, 2000; Pres. Slovenian Democratic Party 1993–; Prime Minister 2004–08, 2012–13; Minister of Finance 2012–13; Pres. European Council 2008. *Publications include:* Podružbljanje varnosti in obrambe (The Socialization of Security and Defence) (ed.) 1984, Stane Kavčič, Dnevnik in spomini (The Memoirs of Stane Kavčič) (co-ed. with Igor Bavčar) 1988, Na svoji strani (On One's Own Side) (collection of articles) 1988, Premiki: nastajanje in obramba slovenske države 1988–1992 (The Making of the Slovenian State 1988–1992), The Collapse of Yugoslavia 1994, Okopi: pot slovenske države 1991–1994 (Trenches: The Evolution of the Slovenian State 1991–1994) 1994, Sedem let pozneje (Seven Years Later) 1994, Osem let pozneje (Eight Years Later) (with Ivan Borštner and David Tasić) 1995; hundreds of articles, commentaries, essays and scientific discussions; also several poems and literary compositions. *Leisure interests:* mountaineering, golf, football, skiing, snowboarding. *Address:* Slovenian Democratic Party (Slovenska Demokratska Stranka), 1000 Ljubljana, Trstenjakova 8, Slovenia (office). *Telephone:* (1) 4345450 (office). *Fax:* (1) 4345452 (office). *E-mail:* tajnistvo@sds.si (office). *Website:* www.sds.si (office).

JANSONS, Mariss; Latvian conductor; *Chief Conductor, Royal Concertgebouw Orchestra;* b. 14 Jan. 1943, Riga; s. of Arvid Jansons and Erhaida Jansons; m. Irina Jansons 1967; one d.; ed studied with father, Leningrad Conservatory with N. Rabinovich, Vienna Conservatory with Hans Swarovsky, Salzburg with von Karajan; Prin. Guest Conductor Leningrad (now St Petersburg) Philharmonic Orchestra; Chief Conductor Oslo Philharmonic 1979–2002; Guest Conductor Welsh Symphony Orchestra 1985–88; Salzburg debut with the Vienna Philharmonic 1994; Prin. Guest Conductor London Philharmonic Orchestra –1997; Prof. of Conducting, St Petersburg Conservatory 1995–; Music Dir Pittsburgh Symphony Orchestra 1995, Chief Conductor 1997–2002; Chief Conductor Symphonieorchester des Bayerischen Rundfunks and the Bavarian Radio Choir 2003–; Chief Conductor Royal Concertgebouw Orchestra 2004–; has appeared all over world, with Baltimore Symphony Orchestra, Berlin Philharmonic, Boston Symphony Orchestra, Chicago Symphony Orchestra, Cleveland Orchestra, London Philharmonia Orchestra, New York Philharmonic, Philadelphia Orchestra; winner Herbert von Karajan Competition 1971, Anders Jahre Cultural Prize (Norway), RSFSR People's Artist 1986, Royal Philharmonic Soc. Conductor of the Year Award 2004, Midem Classical Music Award for Artist of the Year 2006, Ernst von Siemens Music Prize 2013; Commdr with Star Royal Norwegian Order of Merit. *Recordings include:* Shostakovich Symphony No. 7 (BBC Music Magazine Orchestral Award 2007) 2006. *Leisure interests:* arts, theatre, films, sports. *Address:* Opus 3 Artists, 470 Park Avenue South, 9th Floor North, New York 10016, USA (office); Royal Concertgebouw Orchestra, Jacob Obrechtstraat 51, 1071 KJ Amsterdam, Netherlands (office). *Telephone:* (212) 584-7500 (office); (20) 3051010 (home). *Fax:* (646) 300-8200 (office); (20) 3051001 (office). *E-mail:* info@opus3artists.com (office); info@concertgebouworkest.nl (office). *Website:* www.opus3artists.com (office); www.concertgebouworkest.nl (office).

JANSSEN, Baron Daniel, IngLic, MBA; Belgian business executive; *Chairman and CEO, Financière de Tubize SA;* b. 15 April 1936, Brussels; s. of Baron Charles-Emmanuel Janssen and Marie-Anne Janssen (née Boël); brother of Paul-Emmanuel Janssen; m. Thérèse Bracht 1970; three s.; ed Univ. of Brussels, Harvard Univ., USA; Asst Sec., Euratom Comm., Brussels 1959–60; Prof., Brussels Univ. 1965–71; Chair. Exec. Cttee UCB 1975–84 (now Hon. Vice-Chair. and Hon. Chair. of Exec. Cttee); CEO Solvay & Cie (now Solvay) SA 1986–2006 (also Chair.); currently Chair. and CEO Financière de Tubize SA, Brussels; Chair. Fed. of Belgian Enterprises 1981–84; mem. Club of Rome 1968–87; mem. Bd of Dirs Brussels Univ. 1969–70, Inst. pour l'Encouragement de la Recherche Scientifique dans l'Industrie et l'Agriculture (IRSIA) 1971–77 (Vice-Chair. 1974–77), Belgian Fed. of Chemical Industries 1972–76 (Chair. 1976–79), Fortis NV 1999–2006; mem. European Cttee for R & D, EEC 1974–79; Grand Cordon of the Order of the Rising Sun (Japan), 2006; Alumni Achievement Award, Harvard Business School. *Leisure interests:* tennis, skiing, shooting. *Address:* Financière de Tubize SA, Allee de la Recherche 60, Brussels 1070, Belgium (office).

JANSSEN, Baron Paul-Emmanuel, LLD; Belgian banker; *Honorary Chair, Générale de Banque;* b. 22 Feb. 1931, Brussels; s. of Baron Charles-Emmanuel Janssen and Marie-Anne Janssen (née Boël); brother of Daniel Janssen; m. Cecilia Löfgren; one s. one d.; ed Univ. Libre de Bruxelles, Harvard Business School, USA; fmr Chair. Générale de Banque SA (now Hon. Chair.), Belgium, Belgian Banking Asscn; fmr Dir Solvay, Solvac, Boël, Atlas Copco, European Banking Fed., Belgian Fed. of Enterprises; Commdr Ordre de la Couronne, Commdr Ordre de Léopold, Officier Légion d'honneur. *Leisure interests:* riding, hunting, forestry, music. *Address:* Le Bonnier, 79 rue Gaston, Bary B, 1310 La Hulpe, Belgium (home). *Telephone:* (2) 653-88-08 (office); (2) 652-03-50 (home). *Fax:* (2) 652-12-29 (office); (2) 652-07-38 (home). *E-mail:* lebonnier@skynet.be (home).

JANSSON, Mats; Swedish business executive; *Chairman, Delhaize Group;* ed Univ. of Örebro; began career with ICA (Swedish food retailer), held positions of increasing responsibility and served as Pres. ICA Detaljhandel and Deputy CEO and Chair. of the Group 1990–94; CEO Catena/Bilia 1994–99; CEO Karl Fazor Oy 1999–2000; CEO Axfood 2000–05; Pres. and CEO Axel Johnson AB 2005–06; Pres. and CEO SAS 2006–10; Chair. Delhaize Group 2012–; Ind. Dir, Danske Bank; fmr Dir Axfood, Mekonomen, Swedish Match, Hufvudstaden. *Address:* Delhaize Group SA, Rue Osseghemstraat 53, 1080 Brussels, Belgium (office). *Telephone:* (2) 412-22-11 (office). *Fax:* (2) 412-22-22 (office). *E-mail:* info@delhaizegroup.com (office). *Website:* www.delhaizegroup.com (office).

JANVIER, Gen. Bernard Louis Antonin; French army officer; b. 16 July 1939, La Voulte-sur-Rhône, Ardèche; s. of Pierre Janvier and Eugénie Bernard; m. Denise Diaz 1963; two s. one d.; ed Lycée de Nice, Coll. d'Orange, Lycée Bugeaud, Algiers, Univ. of Rennes and Ecole Spéciale Militaire de Saint-Cyr; commissioned 2nd Lt 1960; served in Algeria 1962–64, Madagascar and Comoros 1964–67; Co. Commdt 9th Parachute Regt 1968–70; Commdt in charge of trainee officers, Ecole

Spéciale Militaire de Saint-Cyr 1970–72; Bn Chief 1974; training course, Ecole Supérieure de Guerre 1974–76; Lt-Col 1978; Second-in-Command, Bureau of Operations-Instruction 1981; Col 1982; Chef de Corps, 2nd Overseas Parachute Regt 1982–84; Head, Office of Personnel, Chief of Ground Forces 1984–87; Deputy to Gen. Commdt 6th Armoured Div. 1987–89; Brig.-Gen. 1988; Chief Org.-Logistic Div. of Army Chief of Staff 1989–91; Commdt Operation Requin, Port Gentil, Gabon 1991; Commdt Daguet Div. Saudi Arabia and Iraq 1991; Div. Gen. 1991; Commdt 6th Armoured Div. Nîmes 1991–93; Army Chief of Staff, Operational Planning (Emia) 1993–95; Gen. Army Corps 1994; apptd Army Chief of Staff 1995; Dir Centre des hautes études militaires, Inst. des hautes études de la défense nat. 1996–98; Commdt UN Peace Forces in Fmr Yugoslavia 1995–96; Commdr Légion d'honneur, Ordre nat. du Mérite, Legion of Merit (USA) and numerous other decorations; medals from Kuwait and Saudi Arabia. *Leisure interests:* history of Provence, running. *Address:* 6 place de l'Eglise, 83310 Grimaud, France (home).

JANZEN, Daniel Hunt, PhD; American biologist and academic; *Professor of Biology and Thomas G. and Louise E. DiMaura Term Chair, University of Pennsylvania;* b. 18 Jan. 1939, Milwaukee, Wis.; s. of Daniel Hugo Janzen and Floyd Foster Janzen; m. twice (divorced twice); one s. one d. from 1st marriage; ed Univ. of Minnesota and Univ. of California, Berkeley; Asst and Assoc. Prof., Univ. of Kansas 1965–68; Assoc. Prof., Univ. of Chicago 1969–72; Assoc. Prof. and Prof. of Ecology and Evolutionary Biology, Univ. of Michigan 1972–76; Prof. of Biology and Thomas G. and Louise E. DiMaura Term Chair, Univ. of Pennsylvania, Philadelphia 1976–; teacher, Org. for Tropical Studies in Costa Rica 1965–; field research in tropical ecology, supported mainly by grants from NSF, USA 1963; MacArthur Fellow 1989; mem. NAS 1992–; Hon. Fellow, Asscn for Tropical Biology 1992; Dr hc (Univ. of Minnesota) 1996; Gleason Award, American Botanical Soc. 1975, Crafoord Prize, Coevolutionary Ecology, Swedish Royal Acad. of Sciences 1984, Joseph Leidy Medal, Philadelphia Acad. of Natural Sciences 1989, Founder's Council Award of Merit, Field Museum of Natural History 1991, Silver Medal Award, Int. Soc. of Chemical Ecology 1994, Conservation Soc. Award 1995, Kyoto Prize (Basic Sciences) 1997, Albert Einstein World Award for Science 2002. *Publications:* Herbivores (co-ed., with G. A. Rosenthal) 1979, Costa Rican Natural History (ed.) 1983 and over 250 papers in scientific journals. *Leisure interest:* tropical ecology. *Address:* 301 Leidy Laboratories, Department of Biology, University of Pennsylvania, Philadelphia, PA 19104, USA (office); Parque Nacional Santa Rosa, Apdo. 169, Liberia, Guanacaste Province, Costa Rica. *Telephone:* (215) 898-5636 (office). *Fax:* (215) 898-8780 (office). *E-mail:* djanzen@ sas.upenn.edu (office). *Website:* www.bio.upenn.edu/faculty/janzen (office).

JAOUI, Agnès; French actress, screenwriter and director; b. 19 Oct. 1964, Antony, Hauts-de-Seine; d. of Hubert Jaoui and Josiane Jaoui (née Zerah); m. Jean-Pierre Bacri; ed Lycée Henri IV, Paris, Théâtre des Amandiers, Nanterre. *Films:* as actress: Le Faucon (The Hawk) 1983, Hôtel de France 1987, L'Amoureuse 1987, Canti 1991, Cuisine et Dépendances (Kitchen with Apartment) 1993, Un Air de Famille (Family Resemblances) (Lumiere Award: Best Screenplay 1997) 1996, Le Déménagement 1997, On Connaît la Chanson (Same Old Song) (César: Best Supporting Actress 1998) 1997, Le Cousin 1997, La Méthode 1997, On the Run 1999, Une Femme d'Extérieur (Outgoing Woman) 2000, Le Goût des Autres (The Taste of Others) 2000, 24 Heures de la Vie d'une Femme (24 Hours in the Life of a Woman) 2002, Le Rôle de sa Vie 2004, Comme une Image (Look at Me) 2004, La Maison de Nina 2004, Le Rôle de sa vie 2004, La Maison de Nina 2005, Let's Talk About the Rain 2008, Du vent dans mes mollets 2012, Au bout du conte 2013; as screenwriter: Cuisine et Dépendances, Smoking/No Smoking 1993, On Connaît la Chanson, Un Air de Famille; as screenwriter and dir: Le Goût des Autres (Grand Prix des Amériques 2000, César: Best Film and Best Original Adaptation 2001, David di Donatello Award: Best Foreign Film 2001, European Film Award: Best Screenwriter, Lumiere Award: Best Director 2001) 2000, Comme une Image (Bodil Award, Palme D'Or: Best Screen Play 2004, European Film Award: Best Screenwriter 2004) 2004, Parlez-moi de la pluie (Let's Talk About the Rain) 2008, Au bout du conte 2013. *Address:* c/o Zelig, 57, rue Réaumur, 75002 Paris, France (office). *Website:* www.agnes-jaoui.over-blog.com.

JAPAN, H.M. Emperor of (see Akihito).

JAPARIDZE, Tedo, PhD; Georgian politician, diplomatist and international organization official; *Alternate General Director, International Centre for Black Sea Studies;* b. 18 Sept. 1946, Tbilisi; m. Tamar Japaridze; one s.; ed Tbilisi State Univ., Inst. of USA and Canadian Studies, Moscow, Russia; fmr teacher, Dept of Int. Relations and Int. Law, Tbilisi State Univ.; with Ministry of Foreign Affairs 1989–92, positions included Head of Political Dept, Deputy Foreign Minister, First Deputy Foreign Minister, Vice-Chair. Council for UNESCO Affairs 1989–92, Nat. Security Adviser to Head of State 1992–94; Amb. to USA, Canada and Mexico 1995–2002; Sec. Nat. Security Council 2002–03; Minister of Foreign Affairs 2003–04; Hon. Chair. Transcaucasus Foundation and Special Advisor to Washington Strategic Advisors LLC –2004; Sec.-Gen. Org. of the Black Sea Econ. Cooperation, Perm. Int. Secr. 2004–05; Public Policy Scholar, Woodrow Wilson Int. Center for Scholars, USA 2006; Pres. US-Caucasus Inst., Tbilisi 2007; Alt. Gen. Dir Int. Centre for Black Sea Studies, Athens 2007–; mem. Comm. on the Black Sea 2007–10, Comm. of Euro-Atlantic Security Initiative, Carnegie Endowment. *Publications include:* White House: Mechanism of Decision-Making 1985, American Political Institutions: History and Currrent State (co-author) 1987; numerous articles on US domestic and foreign policy, issues of Black Sea regional econ. cooperation, security policy, problems of illicit trafficking in wider Black Sea area. *Address:* International Centre for Black Sea Studies, 4 Xenophontos Str., 10557 Athens, Greece (office). *Telephone:* (210) 3242321 (office); (30) 6930496892 (home). *Fax:* (210) 3242244 (office). *E-mail:* tjaparidze@icbss.org (office). *Website:* www.icbss.org (office).

JAPAROV, Tuvakmammed; Turkmenistani politician and central banker; *Governor, Central Bank of Turkmenistan;* Chair. Supreme Control Chamber of Turkmenistan –2009; Deputy Chair. of the Govt, responsible for Econ. Affairs 2009–11; Gov. Cen. Bank of Turkmenistan (Türkmenistanyň Merkezi Banky) 2011–. *Address:* Türkmenistanyň Merkezi Banky, 744000 Aşgabat, Bitarap Türkmenistan şaýoly 36, Turkmenistan (office). *Telephone:* (12) 38-10-27 (office). *Fax:* (12) 51-08-12 (office). *Website:* www.cbt.tm (office).

JAQSIBEKOV, Ädılbek Ryskeldinulı, CandEconSci; Kazakhstani diplomatist and politician; *Secretary of State;* b. 26 July 1954, Burliy, Komsomol (now Karabalyk) Dist, Qostanay Oblast; ed All-USSR State Inst. of Cinematography, Moscow, Russia, Plekhanov Inst. of Nat. Economy, Moscow; began career in Kazakhstani state system as cinematographer; Dir Tsesna Corpn 1988–95; Deputy to Senate (Parl.) 1995–; First Deputy Akim, Aqmola Oblast 1996, Mayor of Astana 1997–2003; Minister of Industry and Trade 2003–04; Chief of Admin to Pres. of Kazakhstan 2004; First Deputy Chair. People's Democratic Party (Nur Otan) 2008–; Adviser to Pres. of Kazakhstan Jan.–Oct. 2008; Amb. to Russia 2008–09; Minister of Defence 2009–14; Sec. of State 2014–; Head of Football Fed. of Astana City 2000–07, Pres. Football Fed. of Kazakhstan 2007–; Order of Kazakhstan Respublikasynyn Toongysh Presidenti Nursultan Nazarbayev, Order of Barys (Third Degree), Order of Prince Yaroslav the Wise (Third Degree) (Ukraine); State Prize of the Repub. of Kazakhstan 2008. *Publications:* To Light Star: Capital City, This Way Astana Began (memoirs). *Address:* Office of the Government, 010000 Astana, Beibitshilik kosh. 11, Kazakhstan (office). *Telephone:* (7172) 74-54-00 (office). *Fax:* (7172) 32-40-89 (office). *Website:* www.government.kz (office).

JARA, Alejandro; Chilean diplomatist and international organization executive; *Deputy Director-General, World Trade Organization;* b. 1949, Santiago; m. Daniela Benavente; one s. two d.; ed high schools in Rio de Janeiro, Brazil and Santiago, Chile, Universidad de Chile, Law School, Univ. of California, Berkeley, USA (Fulbright Scholarship); joined Foreign Service 1976, specialized in int. econ. relations, served in Del. to GATT, Geneva 1979–84, seconded as Co-ordinator of Trade Policy Affairs to Econ. System for Latin America (SELA), Caracas, Venezuela, Dir for Bilateral Econ. Affairs 1993–94, Dir for Multilateral Econ. Affairs 1994–99, Sr Official to APEC and Deputy Chief Negotiator for the Chile–Canada Free Trade Agreement 1996–97, Chief Negotiator for the Chile–Mexico Free Trade Agreement 1997–98, Dir-Gen. for Int. Econ. 1999–2000, Amb. and Perm. Rep. to WTO, Geneva 2000–05, Chair. WTO Cttee on Trade and Environment 2001, Chair. Special Session of the Council for Trade in Services 2002; Deputy Dir-Gen. WTO 2005–. *Publications:* numerous articles and papers on int. trade. *Address:* World Trade Organization, Centre William Rappard, rue de Lausanne 154, 1211 Geneva, Switzerland (office). *Telephone:* (22) 7395111 (office). *Fax:* (22) 7314206 (office). *E-mail:* enquiries@wto.org (office). *Website:* www.wto .org (office).

JÁRAI, Zsigmond; Hungarian economist and banker; b. 29 Dec. 1951, Biharkeresztes; m. Marianna Kiss; one s. one d.; ed Univ. of Econs, Budapest; banker, State Devt Bank, Hungary 1976–89; Deputy Minister of Finance and Dir of State Bank Supervision 1989–90; Sr Exec. for Eastern Europe, James Capel & Co., London 1990–92; Man. Dir Samuel Montagu Financial Consultant and Securities Co., Budapest 1993–95; Chair. and CEO ABN AMRO (Magyar) Bank (fmrly Hungarian Credit Bank) 1995–98; Chair. Hungarian Stock Exchange 1996–98; Minister of Finance 1998–2000; Pres. Nat. Bank of Hungary 2001–07. *Address:* c/o National Bank of Hungary (Magyar Nemzeti Bank), Szabadság tér 8–9, 1850 Budapest, Hungary.

JARDIM, José M. N.; Curaçao politician; *Minister of Finance;* ed Universidade Nova, Lisbon; Man., Directorate of Finance, Netherlands Antilles –2010; Sec.-Gen., Ministry of Finance and Econ. Devt, Curaçao (following dissolution of Netherlands Antilles) 2010–12, Minister of Finance and of Econ. Devt 2012–13, 2013–. *Address:* Ministry of Finance, Pietermaai 17, Willemstad, Curaçao (office). *Telephone:* (9) 432-8000 (office). *Fax:* (9) 461-3339 (office). *E-mail:* directie .financien@gobiernu.cw (office).

JARDIM GONÇALVES, Jorge Manuel, BCE; Portuguese banker; b. 4 Oct. 1935, Funchal, Madeira Island; ed Univ. of Oporto; military service in the Army Eng Corps 1960–63; engineer in Angola; Lecturer, Eng School of Oporto –1970; joined Banco de Agricultura 1970, later apptd. to Bd of Dirs; worked at Companhia de Gestion de Industrias (subsidiary of Banco Popular Español) 1975–76; Exec. Dir Banco Português do Atlântico 1977, Chair. 1979–85; Chair. Banco Comercial de Macao and Dir Companhia de Seguros de Macao 1979–85; CEO Banco Comercial Português (BCP) 1985–2005, Chair. Sr Bd 1985–2008; Chair. Millenium Banco Comercial Português, SA 1985–2005; Deputy Pres. of Man. Bd Union of Portuguese Banks; mem. Supervisory Bd Eureko BV 1993–2007, Bank Millennium SA 1999–2007; mem. Int. Monetary Conf.; mem. Sr Bd Novabank, Greece. *Address:* c/o Banco Comercial Português, Praça D. João I, 28, 4000-295 Porto, Portugal (office).

JARDINE, Al; American musician (guitar) and singer; b. 3 Sept. 1942, Lima, OH; mem. The Beach Boys 1961–62, 1963–; numerous tours and concerts, festival appearances; band est. Brother Records label 1967; American Music Awards Special Award of Merit 1988, Grammy Lifetime Achievement Award 2001. *Recordings include:* albums: Surfin' Safari 1962, Surfer Girl 1963, Little Deuce Coupe 1963, Shut Down Vol. 2, All Summer Long 1964, Christmas Album 1964, The Beach Boys Today! 1965, Summer Days (and Summer Nights) 1965, Beach Boys Party 1966, Pet Sounds 1966, Smiley Smile 1967, Wild Honey 1968, Friends 1968, 20/20 1969, Sunflower 1970, Surf's Up 1971, Carl and the Passions – So Tough 1972, Holland 1973, The Beach Boys in Concert 1973, Endless Summer 1974, 15 Big Ones 1976, The Beach Boys Love You 1977, M.I.U. 1978, LA (Light Album) 1979, Keepin' The Summer Alive 1980, The Beach Boys 1985, Still Cruisin' 1989, Two Rooms 1991, Summer in Paradise 1992, The Sounds of Summer – The Very Best of The Beach Boys 2003, That's Why God Made the Radio 2012. *Address:* c/o Elliott Lott, Boulder Creek Entertainment Corporation, 4860 San Jacinto Circle W, Fallbrook, CA 92028, USA (office); c/o Capitol Records, 1750 North Vine Street, Hollywood, CA 90028, USA. *Website:* www.thebeachboys.com; www .aljardine.com.

JARISLOWSKY, Stephen A., CC, MBA; Canadian business executive; *Chairman, Jarislowsky, Fraser Limited;* b. Sept. 1925, Berlin, Germany; m. Gail Jarislowsky; four c.; ed Cornell Univ., Univ. of Chicago, Harvard Business School; served in US Army during World War Two, in counter-intelligence in Japan after the war; engineer, Alcan Aluminum, Montreal 1949–52; f. Jarislowsky, Fraser Ltd (investment co.) 1955, Chair. and CEO –2012, Chair. 2012–; Founder and Pres. The Jarislowsky Foundation; Chair. Learning Assocs, Goodfellow Lumber Inc.; mem. Bd of Dirs C. D. Howe Research Inst., Fraser Brothers Ltd, Growth Oil & Gas Investment Fund of Canada Ltd (also Pres.), Slocan Forest Products, Velan

Inc.; Co-founder Canadian Coalition for Good Governance 2002; mem. Advisory Bd McGill Univ. Medical School, Queen's Univ. School of Business; has endowed eleven eponymous univ. chairs in Canada; Grand Officer, Nat. Order of Quebec; Hon. LLD (Queen's Univ., Univ. of Alberta, McMaster Univ., Université Laval, Concordia Univ., Univ. of Windsor, Université de Montréal). *Publications:* The Investment Zoo: Taming the Bulls and the Bears (co-author) 2005. *Address:* Jarislowsky, Fraser Limited, 1010 Sherbrooke Street West, Suite 2005, Montreal, PQ H3A 2R7, Canada (office). *Website:* www.jfl.ca (office).

JARMAN, Sir Brian, Kt, OBE, MA, PhD, FRCP, FMedSci, FRCGP, FFPH; British medical scientist and professor of medicine; *Professor Emeritus, Faculty of Medicine, Imperial College London;* b. 9 July 1933, London; s. of George Ernest Richard Jarman and Fan Elizabeth Jarman (née Felton); m. Marina Jarman; three s.; ed Univ. of Cambridge, Imperial Coll., London; began career as exploration geophysicist with Shell Oil Co., Sahara; worked at St Mary's Hosp. Medical School and Harvard in hosp. posts; pioneered devt of research on socio-economic indicators of health status (Under Privileged Area scores or Jarman Index); Head, Dept of Primary Health Care and Gen. Practice and Head Div. of Primary Care and Population Health Sciences, Imperial Coll. School of Medicine, London –1998, Prof. Emer. of Medicine 1998–, also currently Dir Dr Foster Unit; Pres. BMA 2003–04; currently part-time Sr Fellow, Inst. for Healthcare Improvement, Boston, USA; mem. London Strategic Review Panel to advise Dept of Health 1998; medical mem. Bristol Royal Infirmary Enquiry 1999–2001; fmr mem. Council, Royal Coll. of Physicians; European Ed. Journal Watch (mem. Editorial Bd 1982–2004); frequent participant in nat. and int. advisory work, including mem. Dept of Health's Advisory Cttee on Resource Allocation; Fellow, Royal Coll. of Gen. Practitioners, Faculty of Public Health. *Publications include:* numerous books and articles linking socio-economic variables to health status and quality of medical care. *Address:* 62 Aberdare Gardens, London, NW6 3QD, England (home). *Telephone:* 7786-431691 (mobile) (office). *E-mail:* b.jarman@imperial.ac.uk (office). *Website:* wwwfom.sk.med.ic.ac.uk/medicine/people/b.jarman (office).

JARMUSCH, Jim; American film director and screenwriter; b. 22 Jan. 1953, Akron, OH; ed Medill School of Journalism, Northwestern Univ., Evanston, Ill., Colombia Coll., SC; teaching asst to Nicholas Ray at New York Univ. Graduate Film School 1976–79; has worked on several films as sound recordist, cameraman and actor. *Films:* Permanent Vacation (writer, dir) 1980, You Are Not I (writer) 1981, The New World (dir) 1982, Stranger Than Paradise (writer, dir) (Camera d'Or Award, Cannes Film Festival 1984) 1983, Down By Law (writer, dir) 1986, Coffee and Cigarettes (short film, writer and dir) 1986, Mystery Train (writer, dir) 1989, Coffee and Cigarettes II (short film, writer and dir) 1989, Night on Earth (writer, dir) 1992, Coffee and Cigarettes III (short film, writer and dir) 1993, Dead Man (writer, dir) 1995, Year of the Horse (dir) 1997, Ghost Dog: The Way of the Samurai (writer, dir) 1999, Ten Minutes Older: The Trumpet (writer, dir) 2002, Coffee and Cigarettes (writer, dir) 2003, Broken Flowers 2005, The Limits of Control 2009. *Music videos directed include:* The Lady Don't Mind (Talking Heads) 1985, Sightsee MC! (Big Audio Dynamite) 1987, It's Alright With Me (Tom Waits) 1991, I Don't Wanna Grow Up (Tom Waits) 1992, Dead Man Theme (Neil Young) 1995, Big Time (Neil Young and Crazy Horse) 1996. *Address:* c/o Bart Walker, Creative Artists Agency LLC, 162 5th Avenue, 6th Floor, New York, NY 10010, USA (office). *Telephone:* (212) 277-9000 (office).

JARQUÍN CALDERÓN, Edmundo, MA, JD; Nicaraguan economist and politician; b. Sept. 1946, Ocotal, Nuevo Segovia; ed Universidad Centroamericana, Managua, Universidad de Chile Law School; joined Juventud Demócrata Cristiana 1965; student sec., Christian Democratic Youth of Latin America 1966–67; forced to leave academic studies in Chile following Gen. Augusto Pinochet's coup against Pres. Salvador Allende 1973; Co-founder Unión Democrática de Liberación (UDEL) 1974; Minister for Foreign Cooperation 1981–84, Amb. to Mexico 1984–88, to Spain 1988–90; mem. Parl. for Frente Sandinista de Liberación Nacional (FSLN) and mem. Bd of Dirs Nat. Ass. 1990–92; Co-founder Movimiento Renovador Sandinista—MRS (dissident group that split from FSLN) 1992; specialist in public policy for IDB 1992–2005; unsuccessful cand. for Vice-Pres. (with Herty Lewites) 2006, unsuccessful cand. for Pres. (upon death of Lewites) July 2006, Unidad Nicaragüense por la Esperanza (UNE) cand. for Vice-Pres. 2011. *Address:* Movimiento Renovador Sandinista, De los semáforos del Ministerio de Gobernación, 1/2 cuadra al norte, Managua, Nicaragua (office). *Telephone:* 250-9461 (office). *Fax:* 278-0268 (office). *E-mail:* info@partidomrs.com (office). *Website:* www.partidomrs.com (home).

JARRATT, Sir Alexander Anthony, Kt, CB, DL, BCom; British fmr business executive; b. 19 Jan. 1924, London; s. of Alexander Jarratt and Mary Jarratt; m. (Mary) Philomena Keogh 1946; one s. two d.; ed Royal Liberty Grammar School, Essex and Univ. of Birmingham; mil. service in Fleet Air Arm 1942–46; Asst Prin. Ministry of Power 1949–53, Prin. 1953–54; Treasury 1954–55; Prin. Pvt. Sec. to Minister of Fuel and Power 1955–59; Asst Sec. in Oil Div. of Ministry 1959–63, Under-Sec. in Gas Div. 1963–64; Cabinet Office 1964–65; First Sec., Nat. Bd for Prices and Incomes 1965–68; Deputy Under-Sec. of State, Dept of Employment and Productivity 1968; Deputy Sec., Ministry of Agric. 1970; mem. Bds of IPC and Reed Int. Ltd 1970; Man. Dir IPC 1970–74, Chair. 1974, also of IPC Newspapers 1974; Chair. and CEO Reed Int. Ltd 1974–85; Chair. CBI Econ. Policy Cttee 1972–74, Industrial Soc. 1975–79; mem. Supervisory Bd, Thyssen-Bornemisza 1972–89; Dir (non-exec.) ICI Ltd 1975–91, Smith's Industries 1984–96 (Chair. (non-exec.) 1985–91); Dir and Deputy Chair. Midland Bank 1980–91; Jt Deputy Chair. Prudential Corpn 1987–91, 1992–94 (Dir 1985–94); Chair. Admin. Staff Coll., Henley 1976–89, Centre for Dispute Resolution 1990–2000 (Pres. 2001–); Pres. Advertising Asscn 1979–83; mem. Council CBI, Chair. CBI Employment Policy Cttee 1982–86; Pres. Periodical Publishers Asscn 1983–85; Vice-Pres. Inst. of Marketing 1982; Chancellor Univ. of Birmingham 1983–2002; Gov. Ashridge Man. Coll.; Hon. DSc (Cranfield); Hon. DUniv (Brunel, Essex); Hon. DLL (Birmingham). *Leisure interests:* countryside pursuits, theatre, music, reading. *Address:* Barn Mead, Fryerning, Essex, CM4 0NP, England (home).

JARRAUD, Michel; French international organization executive and meteorologist; *Secretary-General, World Meteorological Organization;* b. 31 Jan. 1952, Châtillon-sur-Indre; m.; two c.; ed Ecole Polytechnique, Ecole de la Météorologie Nationale; researcher, Météo-France 1976–78, Dir Weather Forecasting Dept 1986–89; researcher in numerical weather prediction, European Centre for

Medium-Range Weather Forecasts (ECMWF) 1978–85, Dir Operational Dept 1990–91, Deputy Dir ECMWF 1991–95; Deputy Sec.-Gen. WMO 1995–2003, Sec.-Gen. 2004–; Chair. UN-Water 2012–; mem. Soc. Météorologique de France, Royal Meteorological Soc. (UK), African Meteorological Soc.; Fellow, American Meteorological Soc.; Hon. mem. Chinese Meteorological Soc., Cuban Meteorological Soc.; Commdr, Ordre nat. du Lion (Senegal) 2005, First Class Distinction, Civil Defence of Venezuela 1999; Hon. DSc (Universidad Nacional Agraria 'La Molina', Peru) 2004. *Address:* World Meteorological Organization, 7 bis, avenue de la Paix, CP 2300, 1211 Geneva 2, Switzerland (office). *E-mail:* sgomm@wmo.int (office). *Website:* www.wmo.int (office).

JARRE, Jean Michel André, LèsL; French composer, musician (synthesizer, keyboard) and record producer; b. 24 Aug. 1948, Lyons; s. of Maurice Jarre and France Jarre (née Pejot); m. 2nd Charlotte Rampling (q.v.) 1978; m. 3rd Anne Parillaud 2005; one s. and one d. from previous marriage; ed Lycée Michelet, Université de la Sorbonne, Conservatoire de musique de Paris; composer of electronic music 1968–; int. concerts include shows in China, Europe and USA; shows incorporate state-of-the-art sound and vision tech.; composer for ballet Aor and Opéra de Paris 1971; UNESCO Goodwill Amb. 1993–; spokesperson European Music Industry 1998–, Int. Fed. for Phonographic Industry 1998–2000; Soc. des auteurs, compositeurs et éditeurs de musique Gold Medal 1980, Grand Prix de l'Acad. Charles Cros 1985; Officier, Ordre des Arts et des Lettres, Officer, Legion d'honneur. *Major live performances:* Place de la Concorde, Paris 1979 (record audience of one million); Peking, Shanghai 1981; Rendez-vous Houston (record audience of 1.3 million), Rendez-vous Lyons 1986; Destination Docklands, London 1988; Paris–La Défense: A City in Concert 1990 (2.5 million audience); Europe in Concert 1993; Hong Kong 1994; Eiffel Tower, Paris 1995 (one million audience); Moscow 1997 (record audience of 3.5 million); Electronic Night, Eiffel Tower, Paris 1998; Millennium Concert, Pyramids of Cairo (televised worldwide, estimated 2,000m. viewers) 1999; 2001 Rendez-vous in Space, Okinawa, Japan 2001; Akropolis Athens 2001; Aero, Aalborg, Denmark 2002; Forbidden City and Tiananmen Square, Beijing 2004; Gdansk Shipyard, Poland 2005. *Film scores:* Des Garçons et des filles 1968, Deserted Palace 1972, Les Granges brulées 1973, Die Hamburger Krankheit 1978, music and lyrics for numerous songs. *Recordings include:* albums Oxygène 1976, Equinoxe 1978, Magnetic Fields 1980, The China Concerts (live) 1982, Zoolook (Grand Prix Academie du Disque 1985) 1984, Rendez-vous 1986, Cities in Concert: Houston/Lyons (live) 1987, Revolutions 1988, Jarre Live (Victoire de la Musique Best Instrumental Album 1986) 1989, Waiting for Cousteau 1990, Images (compilation) 1991, Chronologie 1993, Hong Kong (live) 1994, Oxygène 7–13 1997, Odyssey Through 02 (interactive) 1998, Metamorphoses 2000, Aero 2004, Téo & Téa 2007. *Publications:* Concert d'Images 1989, Paris-la-Défense, une ville en concert 1990, Europe in Concert 1994, Paris-Tour Eiffel, Concert pour la Tolérance 1995, The Millennium Concert at the Great Pyramids of Egypt 2000, Akropolis 2001, Jean Michel Jarre à Pékin 2004. *Address:* Fiona Commins, Aero Productions, 8 rue de Lévis, 75017 Paris, France (office). *Telephone:* (1) 44-90-91-70 (office). *Fax:* (1) 44-90-91-77 (office). *E-mail:* contactaero@wanadoo.fr (office). *Website:* www.jeanmicheljarre.com (office).

JARREAU, Al, BS, MS; American singer; b. 12 March 1940, Milwaukee, Wis.; ed Ripon Coll., Univ. of Iowa; solo artist 1975–. *Recordings include:* albums: We Got By 1975, Glow 1976, Look To The Rainbow (Grammy Award for Best Jazz Vocal) 1977, All Fly Home (Grammy Award for Best Jazz Vocal) 1978, This Time 1980, Breakin' Away (Grammy Awards for Best Pop Vocal, for Best Jazz Vocal) 1981, Jarreau 1983, High Crime 1984, Al Jarreau Live In London 1985, L Is For Lover 1986, Heart's Horizon 1988, Heaven And Earth (Grammy Award for Best R&B Male Vocal) 1992, Tenderness 1994, Best Of Al Jarreau 1996, Tomorrow Today 2000, Free Spirit 2002, One Note Samba 2002, All I Got 2002, Accentuate the Positive 2004, Love Songs 2008, Christmas 2008, Here I Am 2008, Live 2012. *Address:* c/o Joe Gordon, 1954 First Street, Suite 270, Highland Park, IL 60035, USA (office). *Telephone:* (847) 716-6336 (office). *E-mail:* bzievers@icmpartners.com (office). *Website:* www.aljarreau.com.

JARRETT, Keith; American pianist and composer; b. 8 May 1945, Allentown, Pa; ed Berklee School of Music; gave first solo concert aged 7, followed by professional appearances; two-hour solo concert of own compositions 1962; led own trio in Boston; worked with Roland Kirk, Tony Scott and others in New York; joined Art Blakey 1965; toured Europe with Charles Lloyd 1966, with Miles Davis 1970–71; soloist and leader of own groups 1969–; Guggenheim Fellowship 1972; Prix du Prés. de la République 1991, Royal Swedish Acad. of Music Polar Prize 2003, Léonie Sonning Music Prize 2004, Jazz Masters Award 2014; Officier, Ordre des Arts et des Lettres. *Recordings include:* albums: Bach's Well-Tempered Klavier, Personal Mountains 1974, Luminessence 1974, Mysteries 1975, Changeless 1987, Nude Ants, The Cure 1990, Bye Bye Black 1991, At the Dear Head Inn 1992, Bridge of Light 1993, At the Blue Note 1994, La Scala 1995, Tokyo '96 1998, The Melody at Night With You 1999, Whisper Not 2000, Inside Out 2001, Always Let Me Go 2002, Selected Recordings 2002, Radiance 2005, The Carnegie Hall Concert 2006, Dmitri Shostakovich: 24 Preludes and Fugues 2006, Jasmine (with Charlie Haden) 2010. *Address:* c/o Vincent Ryan, 135 West 16th Street, New York, NY 10011, USA (office).

JARRETT, Valerie Bowman, BA, JD; American lawyer, business executive, civic leader and government official; *White House Senior Advisor and Assistant to the President for Intergovernmental Affairs and Public Engagement;* b. 14 Nov. 1956, Shiraz, Iran; d. of Dr James E. Bowman; m. Dr William Robert Jarrett 1983 (divorced 1988, died 1991); one d.; ed Northfield Mount Hermon School, Mass, Stanford Univ., Calif., Univ. of Michigan Law School; father ran hosp. for children in Shiraz, Iran; moved with family to London, UK aged five 1962–63, returned to Chicago 1963; began career in Chicago politics working for Mayor Harold Washington as Deputy Corpn Counsel for Finance and Devt 1987, continued to work in Mayor's Office in 1990s, Deputy Chief of Staff for Mayor Richard Daley, Commr Dept of Planning and Devt 1992–95, Chair. Chicago Transit Bd 1995–2003; Exec. Vice-Pres. The Habitat Company (real estate devt and man. co.) 1995–2007, Pres. and CEO 2007–09; mem. Bd Chicago Stock Exchange 2000–07, Chair. 2004–07, Chair. Chicago Stock Exchange Holdings, Inc. 2005–07; Finance Chair. US Senatorial Campaign for Barack Obama 2004, first Treas. of Senator's PAC, the Hopefund, also served as a Sr Advisor to the Obama for America Presidential Campaign; Co-Chair. Obama-Biden Transition Project

2008–09; White House Sr Advisor and Asst to the Pres. for Intergovernmental Affairs and Public Liaison (now Asst to the Pres. for Intergovernmental Affairs and Public Engagement) 2008–, manages White House Office of Public Liaison, Office of Intergovernmental Affairs, and Chairs White House Comm. on Women and Girls; Chair. Bd of Trustees, Univ. of Chicago Medical Center, Vice-Chair. Bd of Trustees, Univ. of Chicago; Vice-Chair. Chicago 2016 Olympic Cttee, Metropolis 2020; mem. Bd of Dirs Fed. Reserve Bank of Chicago 2006–07, USG Corpn, Inc., Chicago, Navigant Consulting, Inc., RREEF America II; Dir Local Initiative Support Corpn, The Joyce Foundation, The Metropolitan Planning Council, Cen. Area Cttee; Trustee, Museum of Science and Industry. *Address:* The White House, 1600 Pennsylvania Avenue, NW, Washington, DC 20500, USA (office). *Telephone:* (202) 456-1111 (office). *Fax:* (202) 456-2461 (office). *E-mail:* info@whitehouse.gov (office). *Website:* www.whitehouse.gov/administration/staff/valerie_jarrett (office).

JARRIN, Gen. (retd) Oswaldo; Ecuadorean government official, academic and fmr army officer; *Ministry of Defense Chair and Professor of National Security Affairs, Center for Hemispheric Defense Studies, National Defense University;* Chair. Jt Chiefs of Staff –2003; fmr Sec. Nat. Security Council; Minister of Nat. Defence 2005–08 (resgnd); currently Ministry of Defense Chair and Prof. of Nat. Security Affairs, Center for Hemispheric Defense Studies, Nat. Defense Univ., Washington, DC. *Address:* Center for Hemispheric Defense Studies, National Defense University, Abraham Lincoln Hall, 260 5th Ave., Bldg. 64, Washington, DC 20319-5066, USA (office). *Telephone:* (202) 685-4670 (office). *Fax:* (202) 685-4674 (office). *Website:* www.ndu.edu/chds (office).

JARUZELSKI, Gen. (retd) Wojciech; Polish politician and army officer (retd); b. 6 July 1923, Kurów, Lublin Prov.; s. of Władysław Jaruzelski and Wanda Jaruzelska; m. Barbara Jaruzelska 1961; one d.; ed Infantry Officers' School and Karol Swierczewski Gen. Staff Acad., Warsaw; served in Polish Armed Forces in USSR and Poland 1943–45; various sr army posts 1945–57; Commdr Armoured Div. 1957–60; Chief of Gen. Political Bd of the Armed Forces 1960–65; Chief of Gen. Staff 1965–68; Minister of Nat. Defence 1968–83; Chair. Council of Ministers 1981–85; First Sec. Cen. Cttee PZPR 1981–89; Brig.-Gen. 1956, Divisional-Gen. 1960, Gen. of Arms 1968, Gen. of Army 1973; mem. PZPR 1948–90, mem. PZPR Cen. Cttee 1964–89, mem. Political Bureau 1971–89; Deputy to Sejm (Parl.) 1961–89; Vice-Pres. Chief Council of Union of Fighters for Freedom and Democracy 1972–88; Chair. Comm. for Econ. Reform 1981–86; Chair. Mil. Council for Nat. Salvation 1981–83; mem. Presidium All-Poland Cttee of Nat. Unity Front 1981–83, Provisional Nat. Council of Patriotic Movt for Nat. Rebirth (PRON) 1982–83, mem. Nat. Council PRON 1983–89; Chair. Country Defence Cttee 1983–90, Supreme Commdr of the Armed Forces of Polish People's Repub. for Wartime 1983–90; Chair. Council of State (Head of State) 1985–89, Pres. of Polish People's Repub. (Polish Repub.) 1989–90; charged with murder of shipyard workers in 1970, 2001; Order of Builders of People's Poland, Order of Banner of Labour (First Class), Kt's Cross of Order of Polonia Restituta, Silver Cross of Virtuti Militari and Cross of Valour, Medals of 30th and 40th Anniversary of People's Poland, Hon. Miner of People's Repub., Order of Lenin 1968, 1983, Commdr's Cross Order of the Crown (Belgium) 1967, Order of the October Revolution (USSR) 1973, Scharnhorst Order (GDR) 1975, Grand Cross Order of Henry the Navigator (Portugal) 1975, Order of the State Banner (Democratic People's Repub. of Korea) 1977, Order of Suche Bator (Mongolia) 1977, Order of the Red Banner (Hungary) 1977, Order of the Red Banner (USSR) 1978, Order of the White Lion (Czechoslovakia) 1979, Order of Klement Gottwald (Czechoslovakia) 1983, Karl Marx Order (GDR) 1983, Order of the Star of the Socialist Repub. (First class with Riband) (Romania) 1983, Order of the Golden Star (Vietnam) 1983, Order of Georgi Dimitrov (Bulgaria) 1983, Order of the Red Battle Banner (Mongolia) 1983, Order of the Banner (First Class with Diamonds) (Hungary) 1983, Order of José Martí (Cuba) 1983, Grand Cross of Order of the Holy Saviour (Greece) 1987, Officier Légion d'honneur 1989. *Publications:* Stan Wojenny: Dlaczego 1993, Różnić się mądrze 2001. *Leisure interests:* history, military affairs. *Address:* Biuro Byłego Prezydenta RP Wojciecha Jaruzelskiego, Al. Jerozolimskie 91, 02-001 Warsaw, Poland (office). *Telephone:* (22) 6289942 (office). *Fax:* (22) 6875773 (office).

JÄRVI, Neeme; Estonian conductor; *Music Director, Orchestre de la Suisse Romande;* b. 7 June 1937, Tallinn; s. of August Järvi and Elss Järvi; m. Liilia Järvi 1961; two s. one d.; ed Tallinn Music School, Leningrad Conservatorium and Leningrad Postgraduate Studium, studied with N. Rabinovich and Y. Mravinsky; Conductor Estonian Radio Symphony Orchestra –1963; Chief Conductor Estonian State Opera House 1963–76, Estonian Nat. Symphony Orchestra 1976–80; emigrated to USA 1980; Prin. Guest Conductor City of Birmingham Symphony Orchestra, UK 1981–83; Chief Conductor Royal Scottish Nat. Orchestra 1984–88, Conductor Laureate for Life 1990–; Prin. Conductor Gothenburg Orchestra, Sweden 1982–2004; Music Dir Detroit Symphony Orchestra, USA 1990–2005, Music Dir Emer. 2006–; Music Dir Emer. New Jersey Symphony Orchestra, USA 2005–09, Conductor Laureate and Artistic Advisor 2009–; Chief Conductor Residentie Orchestra, The Hague 2005–11, Chief Conductor Emer. 2012–; Artistic Dir Estonian Nat. Symphony Orchestra 2011–; Music Dir Orchestre de la Suisse Romande 2012–; guest conductor of many int. symphony orchestras, including New York Philharmonic, Boston, Chicago, Royal Concertgebouw, Philharmonia, London Symphony, London Philharmonic; conducted Eugene Onegin 1979, 1984, Samson and Delilah 1982 and Khovanshchina 1985 at Metropolitan Opera House, New York; has held int. master-classes in summer resort town of Pärnu, Estonia 2000–; Hon. mem. Royal Swedish Acad. of Music, Estonian Composers Union 1989; Hon. Citizen, City of Gothenburg 1987, State of Michigan 1992; Kt Commdr Order of the North Star, Sweden 1990, Sash, Order of Nat. Coat of Arms 1996, Insignia, Coat of Arms, Tallinn 1997; Dr hc (Royal Swedish Acad. of Music) 1988, 1990, (Estonian Music Acad.) 1989, (Aberdeen) 1990, (Gothenburg) 1985, 1991, (Tallinn Music Conservatory), Wayne State Univ., USA) 1994, (Michigan) 1999; First Prize, Young Conductors' Competition, Leningrad 1957, Estonian Soviet Socialist Repub. (ESSR) Honoured Artist 1965, First Prize, Accademia Nazionale di Santa Cecilia Conductors' Competition 1971, ESSR People's Artist 1971, USSR State Prize 1978, Sibelius Soc. Medal 1986, Gramophone Magazine's Artist of the Year 1990, Gold Record, Chandos recording co. 1992, Toblach's Mahler Prize (for recording of Mahler's Third Symphony) 1993, Grand Prix du Disque, Charles Cros Recording Acad. of Paris (for CD of Stravinski's Symphony of Psalms) 1993, Toblach's Mahler Prize (for recording of Mahler's Seventh Symphony with the Hague Orchestra)

2010. *Recordings include:* more than 450 CDs since 1983, including all Prokoviev, Sibelius, Grieg, Nielsen, Dvorak, Shostakovich, Franz Berwald and Stenhammar symphonies as well as recordings of Pärt and Tubin. *Address:* c/o Harrison Parrott, 5–6 Albion Court, Albion Place, London, W6 0QT, England (office). *Telephone:* (20) 7229-9166 (office). *Fax:* (20) 7221-5042 (office). *E-mail:* info@harrisonparrott.co.uk (office). *Website:* www.harrisonparrott.com (office); www.neemejarvi.ee.

JARVIK, Robert Koffler, MD; American physician and business executive; *President and CEO, Jarvik Heart, Inc.;* b. 11 May 1946, Midland, Mich.; s. of Norman Eugene Jarvik and Edythe Jarvik (née Koffler); m. Marilyn vos Savant 1987; one s. one d.; ed Syracuse Univ., New York, Univ. of Bologna, New York Univ., Univ. of Utah; Research Asst, Div. of Artificial Organs, Univ. of Utah 1971–77; Acting Dir Old St Mark's Hosp., Div. of Artificial Organs 1977–78, Asst Dir 1978–82; Asst Research Prof. of Surgery, Univ. of Utah 1979–87; Pres. Symbian Inc., Salt Lake City 1981–87; Pres. and CEO Jarvik Research Inc. (now Jarvik Heart Inc.) 1987–; Ed. (US Section) International Journal of Artificial Organs; mem. American Soc. for Artificial Internal Organs, Int. Soc. for Artificial Organs; Hon. DSc (Syracuse) 1983, (Hahnemann Univ.) 1985; numerous awards includng Inventor of the Year 1983, Outstanding Young Men of America 1983, Gold Heart Award 1983, Par Excellence Award (Univ. of Utah). *Address:* Jarvik Heart, Inc., 333 West 52nd Street, New York, NY 10019, USA (office). *Telephone:* (212) 397-3911 (office). *Fax:* (212) 397-3919 (office). *Website:* www.jarvikheart.com (office).

JASCHINSKI, Siegfried; German banking executive; *First Deputy Chairman of the Administrative Board, DekaBank;* b. 21 Aug. 1954, Leverkusen; ed Universität zu Köln; began banking career with Trinkaus und Burkhardt 1982; joined Deutsche Bank AG, Frankfurt 1986; fmr mem. Bd of Man. Dirs SüdwestLB, Deputy Chair. Landesbank Baden-Württemberg (after merger with SüdwestLB) 2004–05, Chair. 2005–09; First Deputy Chair. Admin. Bd DekaBank 2007–, Deputy Chair. Audit Cttee, Deputy Chair. Gen. Cttee and mem. Presidential Cttee; Chair. Supervisory Bd Rheinland-Pfalz Bank; fmr Chair. Supervisory Bd Rohwedder AG; mem. Supervisory Bd Heidelberger Druckmaschinen AG 2007–, HSBC Trinkaus & Burkhardt AG, AdCapital AG; mem. Supervisory Bd and Chair. Credit and Market Risks Cttee, Baden Württembergische Bank AG; mem. Bd of Supervisory Dirs KfW; mem. Advisory Bd Vorarlberger Landes und Hypothekenbank AG, Baden-Württemberg Int. Agency for Int. Econ. and Scientific Cooperation. *Address:* DekaBank, Deutsche Girozentrale, Mainzer Landstraße 16, 60325 Frankfurt, Germany (office). *Telephone:* (69) 7147-0 (office). *E-mail:* kontakt@dekabank.de (office). *Website:* www.dekabank.de (office).

JASMI, Hussein al-; United Arab Emirates singer; b. (Hussein Jasmi el Naqbi), 25 Aug. 1979; performed with siblings in group Firqat El Khalij; signed with Rotana record label; performed at numerous int. festivals, including Salalah, Oman, Carthage, Tunisia 2006, Gulf Air Bahrain Grand Prix 2010; Al Mawaheb Prize, Dubai 1996, 6th Arab Radio and Television (ART) Award 2008. *Recordings include:* Hussain El Jasmi 2002, Hala Februair 2004, Hussain El Jasmi 2006, Ihtirit Aabar 2007, El Jasmi 2010, Bawada'ak, Wallah Mayiswa, Bahibik Wahachtiny, Bassbour Al Fourgakom, Into Kafo (You are Enough) 2010; theme music for TV shows Ba'ed Al Furaq (After Separating) 2008, Ahil Al Cairo (The People of Cairo) 2010. *Address:* PO Box 2788, Umm Hurair Road, Dubai, UAE. *Telephone:* (4) 3354440. *Fax:* (4) 3354448. *Website:* www.hussainaljassmi.com.

JASON, Sir David, Kt, OBE; British actor; b. (David John White), 2 Feb. 1940, Edmonton, London; s. of Arthur White and Olwyn Jones; partner Myfanwy Talog (died 1995); m. Gill Hinchcliffe 2005; one d.; started acting career in repertory; TV career began as Bert Bradshaw in soap-opera Crossroads 1964; best known for his role voicing Mr. Toad in adaptations of The Wind in the Willows, and for his long-running TV roles as the main characters of Derek 'Del Boy' Trotter on the BBC sit-com, Only Fools and Horses 1981–2003, and as detective Jack Frost on the ITV crime drama, A Touch of Frost 1992–2010; awards include Best Actor Award, BAFTA 1988, Best Light Entertainment Performance, BAFTA 1991, Best TV Comedy Actor Award, BAFTA 1997, BAFTA Fellowship 2003; four British Comedy Awards 1990, 1992, 1997 and Lifetime Achievement Award 2001; six Nat. Television Awards 1997, 2001, 2002 twice, 2003 and Award for Outstanding Drama Performance 2011; topped the poll to find TV's 50 Greatest Stars, as part of ITVs 50th anniversary celebrations 2006. *Theatre includes:* Under Milk Wood 1971, The Rivals 1972, No Sex Please ... We're British! 1972, Darling Mr London (tour) 1975, Charley's Aunt (tour) 1975, The Norman Conquests 1976, The Relapse 1978, Cinderella 1979, The Unvarnished Truth (Mid/Far East tour) 1983, Look No Hans! (tour and West End) 1985. *Films:* Under Milk Wood 1972, White Cargo 1973, Royal Flash 1975, Wombling Free (voice) 1977, The Odd Job 1978, Only Fools and Horses, The Snow Queen (voice) 1995, All the Way Up (dir) 2010. *Television includes:* Crossroads (series) 1966, Softly, Softly: Task Force (series) 1966, Do Not Adjust Your Set (series) 1967–69, Randall and Hopkirk (Deceased) (series) 1969, Canada Goose (film) 1969, Doctor in the House (series) 1970, Hark at Barker (series) 1969–70, Six Dates with Barker (series) 1971, Doctor at Large (series) 1971, His Lordship Entertains (series) 1972, The Top Secret Life of Edgar Briggs 1973–74, Mr Stabbs 1974, Doctor at Sea (series) 1974, It's Only Me – Whoever I Am 1974, Ronnie Barker Shows 1975, Lucky Feller (series) 1975–76, Granville in Open All Hours 1976–85, Blanco in Porridge 1975–77, A Sharp Intake of Breath (series) 1977–81, The Odd Job 1978, The Dick Emery Show 1979, Only Fools and Horses 1981–2003, Dramarama (series) 1984, Porterhouse Blue (series) 1987, Jackanory 1988, Single Voices: The Chemist 1989, Amongst Barbarians 1989, A Bit of a Do (series) 1989, Oh! Mr. Toad (series) 1989–90, Screenplay (series) 1990, Victor & Hugo: Bunglers in Crime (series) 1991, Pa Larkin in The Darling Buds of May 1991–93, A Touch of Frost 1992–2010, The Bullion Boys 1993, Screen One (series) 1993, March in Windy City (film) 1998, All the King's Men (film) 1999, Micawber (series) 2002, The Quest (film) (also dir) 2002, The Second Quest (film) (also dir) 2004, The Final Quest (film) (also dir) 2004, Diamond Geezer (series) 2005–07, Ghostboat (film) 2006, Hogfather (film) 2006, The Colour of Magic (film) 2008, The Green Green Grass 2009, David Jason: The Battle of Britain (presenter, ITV documentary) 2010), Albert's Memorial (film) 2010, Come Rain Come Shine (film) 2010; animation: The Water Babies 1978, Danger Mouse 1981–92, Wind in the Willows 1983, The Wind in the Willows (series) 1984–88, Count Duckula 1988–93, The BFG 1989, Victor and Hugo 1991–92, The Adventures of Dawdle the Donkey 1993, The Snow Queen 1995, Father Christmas and the Missing Reindeer (voice) 1998, Angelmouse (series, narrator) 1999, Muddle Earth (series) 2010. *Publication:* David Jason: In His Element (with Niall Edworthy) 1999, My Life (Autobiography of the Year, Specsavers Nat. Book Award) 2013. *Leisure interests:* diving, flying, motorcycles. *Address:* c/o Richard Stone Partnership, 2 Henrietta Street, London, WC2E 8PS, England.

JASRAJ, Pandit, DMus; Indian musician; b. 28 Jan. 1930, Hissar, Haryana; s. of Pandit Motiram and Krishnabai; m. Madhura Pandit 1962; one s. one d.; studied under elder brother Maniram Pandit; belongs to Mewati Gharana (school of music); has conducted extensive research in Haveli Sangeet and presented the original Pure Haveli Sangeet with its devotional content intact; has est. an Ashram Motiram Sangeet Natale Acad. with main object of propagating Indian classical music by teaching students free of charge; mem. advisory bds of radio and TV; numerous awards and honours, including Rajiv Gandhi Award for professional excellence, Sangeet Natak Akademi Award 1987, Padma Bhushan 1990, Padma Vibhushan 2000, Yudhvir Memorial Award 2003, Swathi Sangeetha Puraskaram 2008, Bharat Muni Samman 2010 and Sangeet Martand. *Recordings include* Inspiration 2000, Haveli Sangeet 2001, Maheshwara Mantra 2002, Darbar 2003, Soul Food 2005, Tapasya 2005, Miyan Tansen 2006, Upasana 2007, Baiju Bawra 2008, Raga Symphony 2009. *Works include:* compositions for opera, ballet and short films etc., including Kan Khani Sunyo Kare, Geet Govindam, Sur, Laya Aur Chhanda, Aath Prahar, Raga Bairagi, Raga Behag. *Publication:* Sangeet Saurabh. *Leisure interests:* teaching, travel, sport. *Address:* c/o Art & Artistes (I) Pvt. Ltd, B-1 Noorie Apartments, Yari Road, Versova, Andheri (W) Mumbai 400 061, India (office). *Telephone:* (22) 26359674 (office). *Fax:* (22) 26395839 (office). *E-mail:* panditjasraj@panditjasraj.com (office). *Website:* www.aaaind.in (office) www .panditjasraj.com (office).

JATUSRIPITAK, Somkid, BA, MBA, PhD; Thai government official and politician; b. 15 July 1953, Bangkok; m. Anurachanee Jatusripitak; ed Thammasart Univ., Nat. Inst. of Devt Admin, Northwestern Univ., USA; early govt positions include Sec. to Minister of Finance, Adviser to Minister of Foreign Affairs, Minister of Commerce, Vice-Pres., Stock Exchange; Minister of Finance 2001, 2002–03, 2004–; Deputy Prime Minister 2001–02, 2003–04, 2005–06; Co-founder Thai Rak Thai party 1998; Co-founder Ruam Jai Thai Chart Pattana (Thais United National Development) 2007; Kt Grand Cross Second Class 1994, First Class 1997. *Address:* c/o Ruam Jai Thai Chart Pattana (Thais United National Development), c/o House of Representatives, Bangkok, Thailand (office).

JAUA MILANO, Elias, Venezuelan sociologist and politician; *Minister of Foreign Affairs;* b. 1969, Caucagua; ed Univ. Central de Venezuela; fmr univ. lecturer; fmr mem. Unión de Jóvenes Revolucionarios/Bandera Roja (resistance movt); Vice-Pres. Comisión Legislativa Nacional (Congresillo) 2000; Sec. of the Presidency 2000–01; Pres. Fondo Intergubernamental para la Descentralización 2003; Minister of Economy 2003–06, of Agric. and Lands 2006–11, Vice-Pres. 2010–12; Minister of Foreign Affairs 2013–; mem. Movimiento Quinta República, Planning Dir 2002–03. *Address:* Ministry of Foreign Affairs, Torre MRE, al lado del Correo de Carmelitas, Avda Urdaneta, Caracas 1010, Venezuela (office). *Telephone:* (212) 806-4400 (office). *Fax:* (212) 861-2505 (office). *E-mail:* web.master@mre.gov.ve (office). *Website:* www.mre.gov.ve (office).

JAUHO, Pekka Antti Olavi; Finnish scientist and consultant; b. 27 April 1923, Oulu; s. of Antti Arvid Jauho and Sylvi Jauho (née Pajari); m. Kyllikki Hakala 1948; one s.; ed Univ. of Helsinki; Chief Mathematician, Insurance Co. Kansa 1951–54; Assoc. Prof., Tech. Univ. of Helsinki 1955–57 (now Helsinki Univ. of Tech.), Prof. of Tech. Physics 1957–70; Dir-Gen. The State Inst. for Tech. Research (Tech. Research Centre of Finland since 1972) 1970–87; consultant to many Finnish and foreign cos; mem. Acad. of Finland, American Nuclear Soc., European Physical Soc., RILEM, Finnish Acad. of Sciences, IVA (Swedish Acad. of Tech. Sciences) and several Finnish socs; Commdr Order of White Rose, Order of Lion (First Class, Finland), Commdr des Palmes académiques, Officier, Légion d'honneur; Hon. Prize of YDIN Power Asscn, Hon. Prize of VILAMO Foundation 1996. *Publications:* about 140 articles. *Leisure interests:* music, tennis. *Address:* Otakaari 1, 02150 Espoo 15 (office); Tuohikuja 9E, 02130 Espoo, Finland (home). *Telephone:* (9) 4513132 (office); (9) 427705 (home). *Fax:* (9) 427705 (home). *E-mail:* pekka.jauho@kolumbus.fi.

JAUMOTTE, Baron André; Belgian university official, civil engineer and mechanical engineer; b. 8 Dec. 1919, Jambes; s. of Jules Jaumotte and Marie Braibant; m. Valentine Demoulin 1946; ed Free Univ. of Brussels; Head, Depts of Applied Mechanics and Aerodynamics, Free Univ. of Brussels 1958–86, Rector 1968–73, Pres. 1974–81; Chair. von Karman Inst. of Fluid Dynamics 1994–2004; Pres. A-VN 1981–2002; mem. Bd UN Univ., Tokyo 1980–86; Hon. Pres. Asscn des Universités partiellement ou entièrement de langue française (AUPELF) 1981–84; mem. Royal Acad., Belgium, Royal Acad. of Overseas Science, European Acad. of Sciences, Letters and Arts, Int. Acad. of Astronautics, Academia Europaea; mem. Nat. Acad. of Air and Space, France; Foreign mem. Acad. des Sciences, Paris 1989, Romanian Acad. 1994; Commdr, Légion d'honneur 1981, Grand Officier, Ordine al Merito della Repubblica Italiana 1973, Commdr, Ordre du Mérite (Gabon), Grand Officier, Ordre de la Couronne (Belgium) 1983, Grand Officier, Ordre de Léopold 1988, Order of the Sacred Treasure, Gold and Silver Stars (Japan); Dr hc (Free Univ. of Brussels, Laval Univ., Québec, Univ. of Cluj, Romania, Tech. Univ., Bucharest). *Publications:* Rocket Propulsion 1967, Choc et Ondes de Choc 1971, 1973, La science au service du pays 1985, Un demi-siècle de nucléaire en Belgique 1994, Mosaïque: Fragments du tout 2000, Turbopumps and Pumping Systems 2008; 300 articles on internal aerodynamics and thermodynamics of turbomachines; report to King Baudouin Foundation. *Leisure interests:* painting and sculpture. *Address:* 33 avenue Jeanne Bte. 17, 1050 Brussels, Belgium (home). *Telephone:* (2) 647-54-13 (home). *E-mail:* andre.jaumotte@ulb.ac.be (office).

JAVADYAN, Arthur; Armenian fmr engineer, banker and central banker; *Chairman, Central Bank of Armenia;* b. 22 April 1964, Yerevan; m.; one d.; ed Yerevan State Agricultural Univ., American Banking Inst., New York, USA, Central Bank of Switzerland Educational Centre; began career as mechanical engineer, Haygyuktntmekenayatsum 1986–89; engineer, Armglavvodstroy (Gen. Water Trust) 1987–89; Specialist, Acting Head of Unit, Head of Unit, mem. Exec. Bd, Yerevan Bank 1989–91; Chair. Exec. Bd, ArmInvestBank CJSC 1991–97, Adviser to the Chair. on Financial Issues 1999–2000; mem. Bd Central Bank of

Armenia 1997–99, 2001–03, Adviser to the Chair. 2000–01, Sept.–Oct. 2003, Deputy Chair. 2003–08, Chair. 2008–; Dir for Armenia, Black Sea Trade and Devt Bank 2008–. *Address:* Office of the Chairman, Central Bank of Armenia, 0010 Yerevan, Vazgen Sarkissian Street 6, Armenia (office). *Telephone:* (10) 58-38-41 (office). *Fax:* (10) 52-38-52 (office). *E-mail:* mcba@cba.am (office). *Website:* www.cba .am (office).

JAVAN, Jafar, BA, MA, PhD; American UN official; *Director, United Nations System Staff College;* b. 1959, Tehran; m.; one d.; ed North Carolina State Univ., American Univ.; Policy Liaison Adviser, Bureau for Devt Policy, UNDP, Washington, DC 2000–03, Chief of the Sub-regional Resource Facility, UNDP, Bratislava 2003–05, Dir Policy Support and Programme Devt, Regional Centre for Europe and the Commonwealth of Ind. States in Bratislava, UNDP 2006–08, Deputy Dir and Head of Programmes, UN System Staff Coll. 2008–12, Dir 2012–. *Address:* United Nations System Staff College, Viale Maestri del Lavoro 10, 10127 Turin, Italy (office). *Telephone:* (011) 6535906 (office). *Fax:* (011) 6535901 (office). *E-mail:* info@unssc.org (office). *Website:* www.unssc.org (office).

JAVED MIANDAD; Pakistani banker and fmr professional cricketer; b. (Mohammad Javed Miandad Khan), 12 June 1957, Karachi, Sind; m. Tahira Saigol 1980; two s. one d.; ed CMS Secondary School, Karachi; right-hand middle-order batsman, leg-break and googly bowler; played for Karachi 1973–76, Sind 1973–76, Sussex 1976–79, Habib Bank 1976–94, Glamorgan 1980–85, Pakistan 1975–93 (Capt. 1980–81, 1992); One-Day Int. (ODI) debut against West Indies at Edgbaston, Birmingham in Cricket World Cup 1975; Test debut against NZ at Lahore 9 Oct. 1976; played in 124 Test matches for Pakistan 1976–94, 34 as Capt., scoring 8,832 runs (average 52.57, highest score 280 not out) including 23 hundreds; played in 233 ODIs, scoring 7,381 runs (average 41.70, highest score 119 not out) including eight hundreds; scored 28,663 First-class runs (average 53.37, highest score 311) including 80 hundreds; toured England 1975, 1979 (World Cup), 1982, 1983 (World Cup), 1987, 1992 (Capt.); holds world record for longest ODI career 11 June 1975–9 March 1996; only cricketer to appear in six World Cup competitions; holds world record for maximum number of consecutive half centuries in ODIs – nine; Pakistan Nat. Team Coach 1998–99, 2000–01, 2003–04; fmr Asst Vice-Pres. Habib Bank of Pakistan; a Wisden Cricketer of the Year 1982, three Pakistani players to have his name in the Hall of Fame at Lords, declared the 44th best Cricketer of all time in ESPN Legend Of Cricket. *Leisure interests:* hockey, soccer, swimming, reading sports books, television, spending time with family. *Address:* c/o National Stadium, National Stadium Road, Karachi, Pakistan. *Website:* www.pcboard.com.pk.

JAVID, Sajid, PC; British politician and fmr banker; *Secretary of State, Department for Culture, Media and Sport;* b. 5 Dec. 1969, Rochdale, Lancs.; m. Laura Javid; one s. three d.; ed Univ. of Exeter; Assoc. and Analyst, Chase Manhattan Bank, New York 1991–94, Vice-Pres. 1994–2000; Partner, JP Morgan Partners LLC 1997–2009; Dir, Deutsche Bank AG 2000–04, Man. Dir 2004–09, Bd mem., Deutsche Bank International Ltd 2007–09; MP for Bromsgrove 2010–, mem. Work and Pensions Select Cttee June–Dec. 2010; Parl. Private Sec. to Minister of State for Further Educ. and Skills 2010–2011, to Chancellor of the Exchequer 2011–12; Econ. Sec. to the Treasury 2012–13, Financial Sec. to the Treasury 2013–14; Sec. of State, Dept for Culture, Media and Sport 2014–; mem. Conservative Party. *Address:* Department for Culture, Media and Sport, 100 Parliament Street, London, SW1A 2BQ, England (office). *Telephone:* (20) 7211-6000 (office). *E-mail:* enquiries@culture.gov.uk (office). *Website:* www.gov.uk/ government/organisations/department-for-culture-media-sport (office); www .sajidjavid.com (office).

JAWAD, Said Tayeb, LLB, MBA; Afghan diplomatist; *Fisher Family Fellow, Future of Diplomacy Project, Belfer Center for Science and International Affairs, John F. Kennedy School of Government, Harvard University;* m. Shamim Jawad; one s.; ed Lycée Istiglal, Kabul Univ., Westfaelische Wilhelms Univ., Germany, Golden Gate Univ., USA; left Afghanistan after Soviet Union invasion 1980, exiled in Germany –1986, moved to USA, worked on Wall Street –1989, moved to San Francisco; Chief of Staff for Afghan Pres. Hamid Karzai, also Pres.'s spokesman, Press Sec. and Dir of Int. Relations 2001–03; Amb. to USA (also accred to Argentina, Bolivia, Brazil, Chile, Colombia, Ecuador, Mexico, Nicaragua, Panama, Uruguay, Venezuela) 2003–10; Diplomat-in-Residence, Future of Diplomacy Project, Belfer Center for Science and International Affairs, John F. Kennedy School of Govt, Harvard Univ. Oct.–Nov. 2010, Fisher Family Fellow 2010–; Diplomat-in-Residence, Paul H. Nitze School of Advanced Int. Studies, Johns Hopkins Univ. 2011–; currently Chair. Foundation for Afghanistan; CEO Capitalize LLC 2010–; Global Political Strategist APCO Worldwide; has worked as writer and commentator on Afghan and int. affairs; Hon. mem. Blackfeet Tribe, Montana 2004; Dr hc (Argosy Univ.) 2007; Loya Jirga Service Medal 2003, Special Award, America Soc. for Civil Engineers 2004, Award of Merit, American Soc. for Engineering Educ. 2007, Global Citizen Award, Roots of Peace 2008. *Address:* Belfer Center for Science and International Affairs, John F. Kennedy School of Government, 79 JFK Street, Cambridge, MA 02138 (office); Capitalize LLC, 1227 25th Street, Suite 700 NW, Washington, DC 20037, USA (office). *Telephone:* (617) 495-1400 (Cambridge) (office); (202) 747-6800 (Washington) (office). *Fax:* (617) 495-8963 (Cambridge) (office); (877) 270-3017 (Washington) (office). *E-mail:* jawad@ ambassadorjawad.com (office); aid@ambassadorjawad.com (office). *Website:* www .belfercenter.org (office); www.capitalizellc.com (office); www.ambassadorjawad .com.

JAWARA, Hon. Alhaji Sir Dawda Kairaba, Kt, FRCVS, DTVM; Gambian politician and fmr head of state; b. 16 May 1924, Barajally; s. of Almamy Jawara and the late Mama Jawara; ed Achimota Coll., Glasgow Univ.; Principal Veterinary Officer, Gambian Civil Service 1957–60; entered politics 1960; Minister of Educ. 1960–61; Premier 1962–65; Prime Minister 1965–70; Pres. of Repub. of The Gambia 1970–94 (overthrown in coup); Vice-Pres. of Confed. of Senegambia 1982; Minister of Defence 1985; Pres. Comité Inter-Etats de Lutte contre la Sécheresse du Sahel; mem. Board Peutinger Coll. (FRG); Hon. GCMG 1974; decorations from Senegal, Mauritania, Lebanon, Grand Master Nat. Order of the Repub. of Gambia 1972; Peutinger Gold Medal 1979. *Leisure interests:* golf, gardening, sailing. *Address:* 15 Birchen Lane, Haywards Heath, West Sussex, RH16 1RY, England (office). *Telephone:* (1444) 456168 (home). *E-mail:* dawda@ kjawara.freeserve.co.uk (home).

JAWED, Sayyed Mohammad Ali; Afghan politician; *Leader, Harakat-i Islami i Afghanistan (Islamic Movement of Afghanistan);* b. 1951, Polebaraq, Mazar-e-Sharif; ed univ. studies in Najaf, Iraq, completed doctorate in religious studies; engaged in Jihad during Soviet invasion of Afghanistan; served as Minister of Planning and Man., Acting Prime Minister, Prime Minister, Minister of Transport; later served as Minister of Transportation, Spokesman of Nat. Communication Front; Leader of MNA representing the people of Balkh Prov.; f. Harakat-i Islami i Afghanistan (Islamic Movt of Afghanistan) during communist regime, Leader 2005–. *Address:* Harakat-i Islami i Afghanistan, Street 4, Qala-i Fathullah, Shar-i-Nau, Kabul, Afghanistan (office). *Telephone:* 79-9343998 (mobile) (office).

JAWORSKI, HE Cardinal Marian, DTheol, DPhil, DPhilR; Ukrainian (b. Polish) ecclesiastic; *Archbishop Emeritus of Lviv;* b. 21 Aug. 1926, Lwów, Poland (now Lviv, Ukraine); ed Theological Acad., Kraków, Catholic Univ. of Lublin, Warsaw Theological Acad.; ordained priest, Kraków 1950; taught for several years at Catholic Theological Acad. of Warsaw and later at Pontifical Theological Faculty of Kraków (First Rector 1981–87); lectured in metaphysics and philosophy of religion at seminaries of various religious orders; consecrated Titular Bishop of Lambaesis and Apostolic Admin. of Lubaczów 1984; Archbishop of Lviv 1991–2008, Archbishop Emer. 2008–; cr. Cardinal (In Pectore) 1998, apptd Cardinal-Priest of S. Sisto 2001; Pres. Ukrainian Episcopal Conf. 1992; Order of Prince Yaroslav the Wise (Fifth Rank) 2004; Dr hc (Bohum) 1985, (Cardinal Stefan Wysyjnski Univ., Warsaw) 2002; Award 'For Great Contributions to Strengthening Peace and International Accord in Ukraine' 2004. *Publications:* three books, 31 monographs, two textbooks, more than 160 scientific articles. *Address:* c/o Metropolis Curia of Archdiocese of Lviv of the Roman Catholic Church, Ploscha Katedralny 1, 79008 Lviv, Ukraine.

JAY, Martin, CBE, BA; British engineering industry executive; *Executive Chairman, Oxsensis Ltd;* b. July 1939; m.; two d. one s.; ed Winchester Coll. and New Coll., Oxford; began career with British Petroleum; Man. Dir and mem. Man. Bd GEC Electronic Components –1989; CEO Vosper Thornycroft PLC (now VT Group PLC) 1989–2002, Chair. (non-exec.) 2002–03; apptd Dir (non-exec.) Invensys PLC Jan. 2003, Chair. July 2003–09; Exec. Chair. Oxsensis Ltd; Trustee Tall Ships Youth Trust. *Address:* Oxsensis Ltd, Rutherford Appleton Laboratory, Harwell Science and Innovation Campus, Didcot, Oxon., OX11 0QX, England (office). *Telephone:* (1235) 778120 (office). *Fax:* (1235) 778276 (office). *E-mail:* contact@oxsensis.com (office). *Website:* www.oxsensis.com (office).

JAY, Peter, MA; British economist, journalist and fmr diplomatist; b. 7 Feb. 1937, London; s. of the late Lord Jay; m. 1st Margaret Ann Callaghan (now Baroness Jay, q.v., d. of the late Lord Callaghan) 1961 (divorced 1986); one s. two d.; one s. by Jane Tustian; m. 2nd Emma Thornton 1986; three s.; ed Winchester Coll. and Christ Church, Oxford; Midshipman and Sub-Lt, RNVR 1956–57; Asst Prin., HM Treasury 1961–64, Pvt. Sec. to Jt Perm. Sec. 1964, Prin. 1964–67; Econs Ed. The Times 1967–77, Assoc. Ed. Times Business News 1969–77; Presenter, Weekend World, ITV 1972–77; The Jay Interview 1975–77; Amb. to USA 1977–79; Consultant, Economist Group 1979–81; Dir The Economist Intelligence Unit (EIU) 1979–83; Columnist,The Times 1980; Dir New Nat. Theatre, Washington, DC 1979–81; Chair. TV-AM 1980–83, TV-AM News 1982–83, Pres. TV-AM 1983; Presenter, A Week in Politics, Channel 4 1983–86; Chief of Staff to Robert Maxwell 1986–89; Econs Ed., BBC 1990–2001; Dir (non-exec.) Bank of England 2003–09; Sr Ed. Consultant, Man. Dir Banking World BPCC, Editor Banking World 1983–86, Supervising Ed. 1986–89; Chair. United Way of GB 1982–83, Feasibility Study 1982–83; Chair. Nat. Council for Voluntary Orgs 1981–86; Visiting Scholar, Brookings Inst., Washington, DC 1979–80; Copland Memorial Lecturer, Australia 1980; Gov. Ditchley Foundation 1982–; Hon. DH (Ohio State Univ.) 1978; Political Broadcaster of Year 1973, Royal TV Soc.'s Male Personality of Year (Pye Award) 1974, Shell Int. TV Award 1974, Wincott Memorial Lecturer 1975. *Publications:* The Budget 1972, Foreign Affairs, America and the World 1979 (contrib.) 1980, The Crisis for Western Political Economy and other essays 1984, Apocalypse 2000 (with Michael Stewart) 1987, Road to Riches, or The Wealth of Man 2000; numerous newspaper and magazine articles. *Leisure interest:* sailing. *Address:* Hensington Farmhouse, Woodstock, Oxon, OX20 1LH, England. *Telephone:* (1993) 811222. *Fax:* (1993) 812861. *E-mail:* peter@jay.prestel.co.uk (office).

JAY OF EWELME, Baron (Life Peer), cr. 2006, of Ewelme in the County of Oxfordshire; **Michael Hastings Jay,** GCMG, MA, MSc; British diplomatist (retd); *Chairman, House of Lords Appointments Commission;* b. 19 June 1946, Shawford, Hants.; s. of the late Alan Jay and of Felicity Vickery; m. Sylvia Mylroie 1975; ed Winchester Coll., Magdalen Coll., Oxford and School of Oriental and African Studies, Univ. of London; Ministry of Overseas Devt 1969–73, 1976–78; UK Del. IMF, IBRD, Washington, DC 1973–75; First Sec. New Delhi 1978–81; FCO 1981–85; Cabinet Office 1985–87; Counsellor, Paris 1987–90; Asst Under-Sec. of State for EC Affairs, FCO 1990–93, Deputy Under-Sec. of State (Dir for EC (now EU) and Econ. Affairs) 1994–96; Amb. to France 1996–2001; Perm. Under-Sec., FCO and Head of Diplomatic Service 2002–06; Personal Rep. to Prime Minister, G8 2005–06; Dir (non-exec.) Associated British Foods 2006–, Crédit Agricole SA 2007–10, Valéo SA 2007–, Candover Investments plc 2008–, Electricité de France (EDF) 2010–; Chair. House of Lords Appointments Comm. 2008–; Vice-Chair. Business for New Europe 2006–; Asscn mem. BUPA 2006–10; Chair. Culham Languages and Sciences (educational charity) 2007–10, Merlin (international medical aid charity) 2007–; mem. Bd Franco-British Chamber of Commerce and Industry, London 2009–11, British Library Advisory Council 2011–; Sr Assoc. mem. St Antony's Coll. Oxford 1996; Hon. Fellow, Magdalen Coll. Oxford. *Address:* House of Lords, Westminster, London, SW1A 0PW, England (office). *Telephone:* (20) 7219-3941 (office). *E-mail:* jaymh@parliament.uk (office).

JAY OF PADDINGTON, Baroness (Life Peer), cr. 1992, of Paddington, in the City of Westminster; **Margaret Ann Jay,** PC, BA; British politician and business executive; *Chair, House of Lords Select Committee on the Constitution;* b. 18 Nov. 1939; d. of the late James Callaghan (Lord Callaghan of Cardiff, Prime Minister 1976–79); m. 1st Peter Jay (q.v.) 1961 (divorced 1986); one s. two d.; m. 2nd Prof. M. W. Adler CBE 1994; ed Somerville Coll., Oxford; began career as producer and journalist with BBC TV 1961–77, producer and reporter, ABC TV and Nat. Public Radio, USA 1979–82, Panorama, BBC TV 1982–86, This Week, Thames TV 1986–88; served as mem. various London Health Authorities 1974–97; Founder-Dir Nat. AIDS Trust 1988–92; apptd Labour Life Peer, House of Lords 1992–; Prin.

Opposition Spokesperson on Health, House of Lords 1995–97, Minister of State, Dept of Health 1997–98, Leader, House of Lords and Minister for Women 1998–2001, currently serves as back-bench Privy Councillor, House of Lords; Dir (non-exec.) London Broadcasting Co. 1992–93, Carlton TV 1995–97, Scottish Power 1996–97; Dir (non-exec.) British Telecommunications (BT) PLC 2001–08, mem. Corp. Social Responsibility Cttee 2008–; Sr Ind. Dir and mem. Int. Advisory Bd, Independent Media Group 2002–; mem. Kensington, Chelsea and Westminster Health Authority 1992–97; Chair. Nat. Asscn Leagues of Hosp. Friends 1994–97; political consultant and Chair. Overseas Devt Inst. 2002–07; Sr Political Consultant, Currie & Brown, Amey Ltd 2002–07; Co-Chair. Iraq Comm. set up by Foreign Policy Centre and Channel 4 TV 2007; Chair. House of Lords Select Cttee on Constitution 2010–; Hon. Fellow, Somerville Coll. Oxford; Dr hc (South Bank Univ.) 1999, (Sunderland Univ.) 2002. *Television:* reporter, contrib. or producer: Panorama (BBC TV) 1982–86, This Week (Thames TV) 1986, The Social History of Medicine (BBC TV) 1991, Hilary Clinton: The Extra President (BBC TV) 1992, Richard Leakey and the new Kenyan Opposition (BBC TV) 1996. *Publication:* Battered – The Story of Child Abuse (co-author) 1986. *Address:* House of Lords, Westminster, London, SW1A 0PW, England (office).

JAY-Z; American rap artist and record producer; b. (Shawn Corey Carter), 4 Dec. 1969, Brooklyn, New York; m. Beyoncé Knowles 2008; one d.; co-founder, Roc-A-Fella Records 1995–, later expanding to include Roc-A-Wear clothing line and film co. (purchased by Universal 2004); collaborations with Puff Daddy, Lil' Kim, Foxy Brown, Notorious BIG, Mary J. Blige, Mariah Carey, Timbaland; numerous live performances; Pres. Def Jam label 2005–08; MTV Video Music Award for Best Rap Video (for Can I Get A. . .) 1999, for Best Video from a Film (for Can I Get A. . .) 1999, Source Awards for Lyricist of the Year 1999, for Best Hip Hop Artist 2001, Billboard Music Award for Rap Artist of the Year 1999, MOBO Award for Best Int. Hip Hop Act 1999, Soul Train Award for Sammy Davis Jr Entertainer of the Year 2001, Grammy Awards for Best Rap Performance by Duo or Group (for Big Pimpin') 2001, (for Swagga Like Us with T.I) 2009, for Best Rap/Sung Collaboration (for Numb/Encore with Linkin Park) 2006, (for Run This Town with Rihanna and Kanye West) 2010, (for Empire State of Mind featuring Alicia Keys) 2011, (for Holy Grail, with Justin Timberlake) 2014, for Best Rap Solo Performance (for D.O.A.) 2010, for Best Rap Song (for Run This Town) 2010, for Best Rap Song (with Alicia Keys) (for Empire State of Mind) 2011, for Best Rap Song by Duo or Group (for On to the Next One featuring Swizz Beatz) 2011, for Rap Performance (for Otis with Kanye West) 2012, for Best Rap Performance, Rap Song (for N****s In Paris), Best Rap/Sung Collaboration (No Church In The Wild) 2013, MOBO Awards for Best Int. Male 2006, Best Hip-Hop Act 2008, Best Int. Act 2010, 2011, Michael Jackson Award for Best Video, Soul Train Awards (for Show Me What You Got) 2007, American Music Award for Favorite Rap/Hip Hop Artist 2009, BRIT Award for Best Int. Male Solo Artist 2010. *Film:* Streets Is Watching (writer and dir) 1998. *Recordings include:* albums: Reasonable Doubt 1996, In My Lifetime Vol. 1 1997, Vol. 2 Hard Knock Life (Grammy Award for Best Rap Album 2001) 1999, Vol. 3 Life And Times Of S. Carter 1999, The Dynasty—Roc La Familia 2000, The Blueprint (Soul Train Award for Album of the Year 2002) 2001, The Best Of Both Worlds (with R. Kelly) 2002, The Blueprint 2: The Gift And The Curse 2002, S Carter Collection 2002, The Black Album 2003, Collision Course (with Linkin Park) 2004, Kingdom Come 2006, American Gangster 2007, The Blueprint 3 (American Music Award for Favorite Rap/Hip Hop Album) 2009, Magna Carta Holy Grail 2013; with Kanye West: Watch the Throne 2011. *Publication:* Decoded 2010. *Address:* Roc-A-Fella Records, 825 Eighth Avenue, New York, NY 10019-7472, USA. *Website:* www .rocafella.com; www.jay-z.com.

JAYAKUMAR, Shunmugam, LLM; Singaporean diplomatist and government official; *Senior Minister for National Security;* b. 12 Aug. 1939, Singapore; m. Dr Lalitha Rajahram 1969; two s. one d.; ed Univ. of Singapore and Yale Univ., USA; Dean, Law Faculty, Univ. of Singapore 1974–80, Prof. of Law; Perm. Rep. of Singapore to UN 1971–74, High Commr to Canada 1971–74; MP 1980–; Minister of State for Law and Home Affairs 1981–84, Minister of Labour 1984–85, of Home Affairs 1985–94, of Foreign Affairs 1994–2004, of Law 1988–2008, Deputy Prime Minister 2004–09; Co-ordinating Minister for Nat. Security 2005–10, Sr Minister 2009–; Hon. Fellow, Singapore Acad. of Law 2008; Public Service Star (BBM) 1980. *Publications:* Constitutional Law Cases from Malaysia and Singapore 1971, Public International Law Cases from Malaysia and Singapore 1974, Constitutional Law (with documentary material) 1976, Pedra Branca: The Road to the World Court 2009 and articles in journals. *Leisure interests:* jogging, golfing, in-line skating, kendo. *Address:* Ministry of Foreign Affairs, MFA Bldg, Tanglin, off Napier Rd, Singapore 248163, Singapore (office). *Telephone:* 63798000 (office). *Fax:* 64747885 (office). *E-mail:* jayakumar_s@mfa.gov.sg (office). *Website:* www.mfa.gov.sg (office).

JAYALALITHAA, Jayaram; Indian politician and fmr film actress; *Chief Minister of Tamil Nadu;* b. (Komalavalli Jayaram), 24 Feb. 1948, Mysore, Karnataka; d. of R. Jayaram and Sandhya Jayaram; ed Bishop Cotton Girls High School, Bangalore, Sacred Heart Matriculation School (known as Church Park) of Presentation Convent, Chennai; film debut in English language film Epistle 1961, Chinnada Gombe (first film, in Kannada) was a major success, first Telugu film Manushulu Mamathalu made her famous, acted opposite Dharmendra in Hindi film Izzat, last film was Nadhiyai Thedi Vandha Kadal 1980, has appeared in more than 100 films altogether; joined All India Anna Dravida Munnetra Kazhagam 1982, Propaganda Sec. 1983, Deputy Leader, elected Legislature Party Leader and Leader of the Opposition 2006–, currently Pres. (Gen. Sec.); elected mem. Rajya Sabha (Parl.) 1984; Chief Minister of Tamil Nadu 1991–96, May–Sept. 2001, 2002–06, 2011–; Hon. DLitt (Univ. of Madras) 1991, (Bharathidasan Univ.) 2003, Hon. DSc (Tamil Nadu Dr MGR Medical Univ.) 1992, (Tamil Nadu Agricultural Univ.) 2003, Hon. LLD (Madurai Kamaraj Univ.) 1993, (Tamil Nadu Dr Ambedkar Law Univ., Chennai) 2005; Kalaimamani Award 1971–72. *Publications:* numerous publs. *Leisure interests:* reading, watching movies. *Address:* Veda Nilayam, 81/36 Poes Garden, Chennai 600 086 (home); All India Anna Dravida Munnetra Kazhagam, 226 Avvai Shanmugam Salai, Roayapettah, Chennai 600 014, India (office). *Telephone:* (44) 28132266 (office); (995) 2176007 (office). *Fax:* (44) 28133510 (office). *E-mail:* aiadmk@vsnl.net (office); bbm@drmgr.org (office); AIADMK@hotmail.com. *Website:* www.admkindia .org (office).

JAYARATNE, D(isanayaka) M(udiyanselage); Sri Lankan politician; *Prime Minister and Minister of Buddha Sasana and Religious Affairs;* b. 6 April 1936; m.; ed Doluwa Maha Vidyalaya, Gampola, Kandy, Univ. of Peradeniya; worked as a teacher at Doluwa Maha Vidyalaya; Postmaster at Doluwa 1960–62; Founding mem. Sri Lanka Freedom Party (SLFP); MP (SLFP) for Gampala 1970–77, for Kandy Dist 1989– (re-elected under the People's Alliance 1994); Minister of Land, Agric. and Forestry 1994–2000, of Agric., Food and Cooperatives 2000–01, of Post and Telecommunications (Upcountry Devt) 2004–05, of Post and Telecommunications (Rural Econ. Devt) 2005–07, of Plantation Industries 2007–10; Prime Minister 2010–, also Minister of Buddha Sasana and Religious Affairs; mem. United Peoples Freedom Alliance. *Address:* Prime Minister's Office, 58 Sir Ernest de Silva Mawatha, Colombo 07 (office); No. 121, Wijerama Road, Colombo 07, Sri Lanka. *Telephone:* (11) 2575317 (office). *Fax:* (11) 2575454 (office). *E-mail:* slpm@pmoffice.gov.lk (office). *Website:* www.pmoffice.gov.lk (office).

JAYASINGHE, Chrysantha Romesh, BA (Hons); Sri Lankan diplomatist; *Secretary, Ministry of Foreign Affairs;* b. 1955; m.; one s. one d.; ed St Thomas's Coll., Mount Lavinia, Univ. of Kelaniya; worked in Ceylon Shipping Corpn as a staff trainee and then as a man. trainee at Lever Brothers (Ceylon) Ltd; joined Foreign Service as Asst Dir UN Div. 1981, assignments in Protocol and South Asia Divs, Ministry of Foreign Affairs, served as Second Sec., Embassy in Bonn, as First Sec., Perm. Mission to UN Office, Geneva, as Counsellor in High Comm. in Dhaka, as Deputy High Commr in New Delhi, Amb. to Belgium and Head of Sri Lankan Del. to European Communities, Brussels (also accred to Portugal and Luxembourg) 2000–05, High Commr to India 2005–09, also accred as Amb. to Afghanistan and Bhutan 2006–09, Sec., Ministry of Foreign Affairs 2009–; Adviser, Sri Lankan Del. to Bd of Govs, Asian Devt Bank 2006. *Leisure interests:* travelling, reading, swimming. *Address:* Ministry of Foreign Affairs, Republic Building, Colombo 1, Sri Lanka (office). *Telephone:* (11) 2438263 (office). *Fax:* (11) 2446091 (office). *E-mail:* sfa@formin.gov.lk (office).

JAYASUNDERA, P. B., BA, MA, PhD; Sri Lankan civil servant, government official and airline industry executive; *Secretary to the Treasury;* ed Univ. of Colombo, Boston Univ. and Williams Coll., USA; held several sr positions in Cen. Bank of Sri Lanka –1980; with civil service since 1980, Econ. Adviser 1990–95, Dir-Gen. Dept of Fiscal Policy and Econ. Affairs 1995–97, Deputy Sec. to the Treasury 1997–99, Sec. to the Treasury 1999–2008, 2009–; Chair. SriLankan Airlines Ltd 2008–09; fmr Chair. Public Enterprises Reform Comm.; fmr Sr Policy Adviser, Ernst & Young; fmr consultant to IMF and World Bank on country assignments; found guilty by Supreme Court of acting with dishonest intent in sale of Lanka Marine Services Ltd shares and of misleading Bd of Investment, ordered to pay Rs 500,000 compensation July 2008. *Address:* Ministry of Finance and Planning, Galle Face Secretariat, Colombo 1, Sri Lanka (office). *Telephone:* (11) 2484500 (office). *Fax:* (11) 2449823 (office). *E-mail:* info@mo.treasury.gov.lk (office). *Website:* www.treasury.gov.lk (office).

JAYASURIYA, Lt-Gen. Jagath, MSc; Sri Lankan army officer; *Commander of the Army;* m. Manjulika Aruna; one s. one d.; ed Royal Coll., Colombo, School of Armour, Pakistan, Armoured Corps Centre and School, India, Sri Lanka Mil. Acad., Diyathalawa, Army Training School, Defence Services Staff Coll., India, Univ. of Madras, India, Defence Resource Man. Inst., Naval Post Grad. School, Calif., USA, Nat. Defence Univ. Course, China; Coll. Prefect, Royal Coll., Colombo, 1977; joined Sri Lanka Army as a Cadet Officer 1978, passed out first in order of merit of Intake-10, commissioned as Second Lt 1980; rank of Lt 1981, Capt. 1984, Maj. 1988, Lt Col 1993, Col 2001, Brig. 2001, Maj. Gen. 2005, currently Lt-Gen.; Troop Leader, 1st Reconnaissance Regt 1980–83, Adjutant 1984–85; apptd Staff Officer Grade 111 in Directorate of Personnel Admin, Army HQ 1985; Squadron Commdr 1st Reconnaissance Regt, Sri Lanka Armoured Corps 1987; Second in Command, 3rd Reconnaissance Regt, Sri Lanka Armoured Corps 1992; CO, 1st Reconnaissance Regt, Sri Lanka Armoured Corps 1994–95; Brigade Maj., 9 Brigade appointment, Jaffna 1990; Chief Instructor, Officers' Study Centre and Staff Officer II (Training), Army Training Centre 1991–92; Staff Officer Grade 1, Armoured Brigade 1992–94; Gen. Staff Officer 1, Jt Operations HQ (JOH), serving all three services and the Police 1995–96; Col Mil. Sec., Army HQ 1996–97; Commdr Armoured Brigade Sept.–Dec. 1997; Commdr 563 Infantry Brigade Jan.–April 1998; Mil. Liaison Officer, Ministry of Defence 1998–2002; Commdt, Sri Lanka Mil. Acad. 2002–04; Dir of Operations, Army HQ 2004–05; GOC 52 Div. 2005–07 Commdr Security Forces HQ, Wanni 2007–09; Commdr of the Army 2009–; int. referee/judge in boxing; Vishishta Seva Vibhushanaya, Uttama Seva Padakkama, Army 50th Anniversary Medal, Long Service Medal and Clasp, 50th Independence Medal, Desha Puthra Sammanaya, North and East Operations Medal, Poorna Bhoomi Padakkama, Riviresa Campaign Service Medal and others. *Achievements include:* capt. of school boxing team, Royal Coll., Colombo, awarded boxing colours 1974, 1976, 1977. *Address:* Army Headquarters, Baladaksha Mawatha, Colombo 03, Sri Lanka (office). *Telephone:* (11) 2432682 (office); (11) 2437079 (office). *E-mail:* info@army.lk (office). *Website:* www.army.lk/commander.php (office).

JAYASURIYA, Sanath Teran; Sri Lankan professional cricketer and politician; b. 30 June 1969, Matara; divorced; left-hand batsman and slow left-arm orthodox spin bowler; played for Sri Lanka 1989–2011 (Capt. 1999–2003), Bloomfield Cricket and Athletic Club 1994–, Colombo Cricket Club, Somerset 2005, MCC 2007, Lancashire 2007, Warwickshire 2008, Mumbai Indians (IPL) 2008–10, Worcestershire 2010, Ruhuna Rhinos 2011, Khulna Royal Bengals 2012, ACC Asian XI; First-class debut: 1988/89; Test debut: NZ v Sri Lanka, Hamilton, NZ 1991, One-Day Int. (ODI) debut: Australia v Sri Lanka, Melbourne, Australia 1989; mem. Sri Lankan team that won World Cup 1996; Test batting: 110 matches, 6,973 runs, highest score 340, average 40.07, 14 centuries, 31 half-centuries; Test bowling: 110 matches, 8,188 balls, 3,366 runs, 98 wickets, 5/34 best bowling in an innings, 9/74 best bowling in a match, 34.34 average; ODIs: 445 matches, 13,430 runs, highest score 189, average 32.36, strike rate 91.21, 323 wickets, average 36.75, economy rate 4.78, best bowling 6/29; holds record for highest test score made by a Sri Lankan: 340 against India 1997; currently has the fastest 50 in ODIs (off 17 balls); became only the fourth batsman to score 10,000 runs in one-day cricket, Indian Oil Cup 2005; first Sri Lankan to play 100 Tests; nicknamed the 'Master Blaster'; MP for Matara Dist (United People's Freedom Alliance) 2010–; Wisden Cricketer of the Year 1997, World Cup Most Valuable Player Award;

stadium named in his honour in Matara. *Television:* contestant on 5th season of Indian celebrity dance show, Jhalak Dikhhla Jaa 2012. *Address:* c/o Sri Lanka Cricket, 35 Maitland Place, Colombo 07; No. 45, Mahamaya Mawatha, Kotuwegoda, Matara, Sri Lanka. *Telephone:* (11) 2681601–4; (11) 2679568. *Fax:* (11) 2697405. *E-mail:* info@srilankacricket.lk. *Website:* www.srilankacricket.lk; content-uk.cricinfo.com/srilanka/content/player/49209.html; www.parliament.lk.

JAYAWARDENA, Amarananda Somasiri, BA, MSc, MPA; Sri Lankan economist, academic, civil servant and banker; b. 3 Aug. 1936, Matale, Sri Lanka; s. of P. de S. Jayawardena and Emaline Weerasinghe; m. Lalitha Subasinghe 1968; one s. one d.; ed Univ. of Ceylon, London School of Econs, UK, Harvard Univ., USA; joined Cen. Bank of Sri Lanka 1958, Gov. and Chair. Monetary Bd 1995–2004 (retd); Visiting Lecturer, Univ. of Vidyodaya, Colombo 1968–75; Gen. Man. Bank of Ceylon 1977, Chair. 1989; Alt. Exec. Dir IMF 1981–86; Sec., Ministry of Industries, Science and Tech. 1989–93, Ministry of Finance and Planning 1994–95. *Radio:* frequent commentator on radio and TV. *Publications:* numerous publs on econs of world tea industry, evaluation of public enterprise performance and econ. aspects of privatization. *Leisure interests:* gardening, reading, the arts. *Address:* c/o Central Bank of Sri Lanka, World Trade Centre, West Tower, Echelon Square, PO Box 590, Colombo 1, Sri Lanka (office).

JAYAWARDENA, D. H. S.; Sri Lankan business executive; *Chairman, Aitken Spence & Company;* Founder-Dir and Chair. Stassen Group; Chair. and CEO Distilleries Co. of Sri Lanka, Lanka Milk Foods (CWE) Ltd, Balangoda Plantations PLC, Madulsima Plantations PLC, Browns Beach Hotels PLC; Chair. Aitken Spence PLC 2003–, Ceylon Petroleum Corpn, Sri Lanka Insurance Corpn, Lanka Bell Pvt. Ltd, Periceyl Pvt. Ltd; fmr Chair. Air Lanka (now Sri Lankan Airlines); mem. Bd of Dirs Hatton Nat. Bank 1988–, Colombo Stock Exchange, Bd of Investments of Sri Lanka; fmr Sr Adviser to Pres. on Int. Trade and Investment; Hon. Consul Gen. for Denmark; Knight Cross of Dannebrog (Denmark) 2010. *Address:* Aitken Spence PLC, Aitken Spence Towers, 305 Vauxhall Street, Colombo 2, Sri Lanka (office). *Telephone:* (11) 2308308 (office). *Fax:* (11) 2445406 (office). *E-mail:* chairman@aitkenspence.lk (office); chairman@ceypetco.gov.lk (office). *Website:* www.aitkenspence.com (office).

JAYAWARDENE, Denagamage Proboth Mahela de Silva, (Mahela Jayawardene); Sri Lankan professional cricketer; *Captain, Sri Lanka National Cricket Team;* b. 27 May 1977, Colombo; s. of Senerath Jayawardene and Sunila Jayawardene; m. Christina Mallika Sirisena; ed Nalanda Coll., Colombo; right-handed batsman; right-arm medium pace bowler; plays for Sinhalese Sports Club 1995–, Sri Lanka 1997– (Capt. 2006, 2012–), Wayamba Elevens 2007–, Derbyshire 2008, Kings XI Punjab 2008–11, Kochi Tuskers Kerala (Capt.) 2011–, Asia XI; First-class debut: 1995/96; Test debut: Sri Lanka v India, Colombo (RPS) 2–6 Aug. 1997; One-Day Int. (ODI) debut: Sri Lanka v Zimbabwe, Colombo (RPS) 24 Jan. 1998; T20I debut: England v Sri Lanka, Southampton 15 June 2006; inaugural ICC Best Capt. of the Year 2006 2007, Capt. of World ODI Team of the Year 2006, Spirit of Cricket Award 2007, Wisden Cricketer of the Year 2007. *Achievements include:* shared world record stand of 624 with Kumar Sangakkara (highest for any wicket in First-class cricket history and first instance of a stand of 600 or more in a First-class or Test match innings) 2006; first Sri-Lankan Capt. to score a Test triple-century, making 374 off 572 deliveries with 43 fours and 1 six, the fourth highest individual score in Test match cricket and the best by a right-hander; with Muttiah Muralitharan ("c Jayawardene b Muralitharan"), part of the most common bowler-fielder combination in history of Test cricket; became ninth player in cricket history, and first Sri Lankan, to score 10,000 Test runs, during second Test of tour in South Africa 2011–12. *Address:* c/o Sri Lanka Cricket, Sinhalese Sports Club, Colombo, Sri Lanka. *E-mail:* info@srilankacricket.lk. *Website:* www.srilankacricket.lk.

JAYSTON, Michael, FGSM; British actor; b. 29 Oct. 1935, Nottingham; s. of Aubrey Jayston and Edna Myfanwy Llewelyn; m. 1st Lynn Farleigh 1965 (divorced 1970); m. 2nd Heather Mary Sneddon (divorced 1977); m. 3rd Elizabeth Ann Smithson 1978; three s. one d.; with the RSC 1965–69, Nat. Theatre 1976–79. *Films include:* A Midsummer Night's Dream 1968, Cromwell 1970, Nicholas and Alexandra 1971, Follow Me! 1972, Alice's Adventures in Wonderland 1972, Craze 1973, A Bequest to the Nation 1973, Tales That Witness Madness 1973, The Homecoming 1973, The Internecine Project 1974, Dominique 1978, Zulu Dawn 1979, From a Far Country 1981, Highlander III: The Sorcerer 1994, Element of Doubt 1996. *TV includes:* The Power Game (series) 1965, The Edwardians (miniseries) 1972, Mr. Rolls and Mr. Royce 1972, Jane Eyre (miniseries) 1973, The Merchant of Venice 1974, The Importance of Being Earnest 1974, Ring Once for Death 1974, Coffin for the Bride 1974, Quiller (series) 1975, She Fell Among Thieves 1978, Gossip from the Forest 1979, Tinker, Tailor, Soldier, Spy (miniseries) 1979, Flesh and Blood (series) 1980, Dust to Dust 1985, Doctor Who (series) 1986, Still Crazy Like a Fox 1987, A Guilty Thing Surprised 1988, Shake Hands Forever 1988, Somewhere to Run 1989, A Bit of a Do (series) 1989, Cluedo (series) 1990, The Darling Buds of May 1993, A Dinner of Herbs (miniseries) 2000, Eastenders 2002, Doctors (series) 2003, The Bill (series) 2000–06, The Royal (series) 2003–07, Foyle's War (series) 2007–08, Emmerdale (series) 2007–08, Albert's Memorial 2009; numerous appearances in series episodes. *Theatre appearances include:* Private Lives 1980, Sound of Music 1981, Way of the World 1984–85, Woman in Mind, Beethoven Readings with Medici String Quartet 1989, Dancing at Lughnasa 1992, Wind in the Willows, Nat. Theatre 1994, Racing Demon, Chichester Prod. in Toronto 1998, Easy Virtue, Chichester 1999. *Leisure interests:* cricket, darts, chess. *Address:* c/o Michael Whitehall Ltd, 125 Gloucester Road, London, SW7 4TE, England. *Telephone:* (20) 7244-8466. *Fax:* (20) 7244-9060.

JAZ, Awad Ahmad al-; Sudanese politician; *Minister of Industry;* Minister of Energy and Mining –2008, of Finance and Nat. Economy 2008–10, of Industry 2010–; mem. Nat. Congress Party. *Address:* Ministry of Industry, PO Box 2184, Khartoum, Sudan (office). *Telephone:* (183) 777830 (office).

JAZAÏRY, Idriss, MA, MEcons, MPA; Algerian international administrator and diplomatist; b. 29 May 1936, Neuilly-sur-Seine, France; four s. one d.; ed Univ. of Oxford, UK, Ecole Nat. d'Admin, Paris, France, Harvard Univ., USA; Chief Econ. and Social Dept Algiers 1963–71; Dir Int. Co-operation, Ministry of Foreign Affairs 1963–71; Adviser to Pres. of Repub. 1971–77; Under-Sec.-Gen. Ministry of Foreign Affairs 1977–79; Amb. to Belgium, Luxembourg and EEC 1979–82; Amb.-at-large specializing in int. econ. affairs, Ministry of Foreign Affairs 1982–84; Pres IFAD Rome 1984–93; Exec. Dir Agency for Co-operation and Research in Devt (ACORD), London 1993–99; Sr Consultant to UNDP 1994–98; Amb. to USA 1999–2004; Special Del. of Pres. of Algeria; mem. Bd of Dirs South Centre, Geneva 2002; Perm. Rep. to UN, Geneva 2004–12; Pres. Bd of Govs African Devt Bank 1971–72; Chair. UN Gen. Ass. Cttee of the Whole on North–South Dialogue 1978–79; organized first World Summit on the Econ. Advancement of Rural Women, Geneva 1992; fmr Pres. Conf. on Disarmament; Grand Officer Order of Merit (Italy), Officer of the Wissam Alaouite (Morocco), Officer of the Order of Merit (Mauritania); Medal of Independence (Jordan); numerous other foreign decorations and awards. *Publication:* The State of World Rural Poverty 1992. *Leisure interests:* jogging, skiing, riding. *Address:* c/o Permanent Mission of Algeria to the United Nations, Route de Lausanne 308, 1293 Bellevue, Switzerland (office).

JAZBEC, Boštjan, BA, MA, PhD; Slovenian economist, academic and central banker; *Governor, Banka Slovenije (Bank of Slovenia);* b. 26 March 1970, Celje; ed Univ. of Ljubljana, Central European Univ., Prague Coll., Czech Repub., Central European Univ., Budapest Coll., Hungary, Inst. for Advanced Studies, Austria; internship at Office of the Chief Economist, EBRD, London, UK Jan.–May 1998, consultancy June–Aug. 2001; consultant, World Bank, Washington, DC July–Aug. 1999, Jan. 2001; mem. Strategic Council, Govt of Slovenia responsible for fiscal issues 2003–04, BIS Working Party on Monetary Policy in Cen. and Eastern Europe 2005–08, European Cen. Bank (ECB) Information Tech. Steering Cttee (EISC), 18-mem. High Level Working Group at ECB 2007–08; mem. Governing Bd, Banka Slovenije (Bank of Slovenia), responsible for Information Tech. Dept and Cash Dept 2003–08, Gov. 2013–; IMF Sr Adviser to Gov. of Cen. Bank of Kosovo, MCM Long-Term Expert 2009–12; IMF Expert, Cen. Bank of Suriname Feb., May–June 2013. *Address:* Banka Slovenije, 1505 Ljubljana, Slovenska 35, Slovenia (office). *Telephone:* (1) 4719005 (office). *Fax:* (1) 2510820 (office). *E-mail:* pr@bsi.si (office). *Website:* www.bsi.si (office).

JAZI, Dali; Tunisian politician; fmr Minister of Higher Educ.; Minister of Nat. Defence 2001–04. *Address:* c/o Ministry of National Defence, boulevard Bab Menara, 1030 Tunis, Tunisia (office).

JEAMBAR, Denis; French journalist and publisher; *Chairman, Institut pratique de journalisme;* mem. staff, Paris-Match 1970–73, Le Point 1973–95 (Ed. 1993–95); Ed. Radio station Europe 1 1995–96; Ed.-in-Chief weekly L'Express 1996–2006; CEO Editions du Seuil 2006–10; Chair. Institut pratique de journalisme 2007–. *Publications:* Sur la route de Flagstaff 1980, George Gershwin 1982, Le PC dans la maison 1984, Dieu s'amuse 1985, Eloge de la trahison (with Yves Roucaute) 1988, Le Poisson pourrit par la tête (with José Frèches) 1992, Le Self-service électoral (with Jean-Marc Lech) 1993, Le Jour ou la girafe s'est assise 1994, La Grande Lessive: anarchie et corruption (with Jean-Marc Lech) 1995, L'Inconnu de Goa 1996, Questions de France 1996, Un Secret d'état 1997, Les Dictateurs à penser et autres donneurs de leçons 2004, Accusé Chirac, levez vous! 2005, Le Défi du monde avec Claude Allègre 2006, Nos enfants nous haïront (with Jacqueline Rémy) 2006. *Leisure interests:* painting, cinema, literature, travel. *Address:* Institut pratique de journalisme, 24, rue Saint-Georges, 75009 Paris, France (office). *Website:* www.ipj.eu (office).

JEAN, Michaëlle, CC, CMM, COM, CD; Canadian (b. Haitian) journalist, broadcaster, documentary film producer, public servant and UN official; *Special Envoy for Haiti, United Nations Educational, Scientific and Cultural Organization (UNESCO);* b. 6 Sept. 1957, Port-au-Prince, Haiti; m. Jean-Daniel Lafond; one d.; ed Univ. of Montréal, Univs of Perugia and Florence and Catholic Univ. of Milan, Italy; fled Haiti 1968, moved to Canada; joined Radio-Canada 1988, reporter, Actuel, Montréal ce soir 1989; Host, Viragos 1991–92, Le Point 1992–95; Host, RDI channel 1995, fmr programmes include Le Monde ce soir, L'Edition quebecoise, Horizons francophones, le Journal RDI, Host, Grands Reportages, Host, The Passionate Eye, Rough Cuts, CBC Newsworld; Gov.-Gen. of Canada 2005–10; Special Envoy for Haiti for UNESCO 2010–; Co-Pres. Michaëlle Jean Foundation, Ottawa 2010–; Chancellor Univ. of Ottawa 2012; Dr hc (Univ. of Ottawa) 2006, (Univ. of Foreigners of Perugia, Italy) 2006, (McGill Univ.) 2006, (York Univ.) 2007, (Univ. of Manitoba) 2007, (Univ. of Alberta) 2008, (Université de Moncton) 2009, (Université Laval) 2009, (Royal Mil. Coll. of Canada) 2010, (Université de Montréal) 2010, (Univ. of Guelph) 2011, (Univ. of Calgary) 2011; Anik Prize for information reporting 1994, Amnesty International Journalism Award 1995, Galaxi Award for best information programme host 2000, UNIFEM Canada Award 2009, Bd of Govs Recognition Achievement Award, Nat. Quality Inst. 2009. *Documentary films:* Tropique Nord 1994, Haiti dans tous nos rêves 1995, L'heure de Cuba 1999. *Address:* Michaëlle Jean Foundation, 143 Séraphin-Marion Street, Ottawa, ON K1N 6N5, Canada (office). *Telephone:* (613) 562-5751 (office). *E-mail:* info@fmjf.ca (office). *Website:* www.fmjf.ca (office).

JEAN BENOÎT GUILLAUME MARIE ROBERT LOUIS ANTOINE ADOLPHE MARC D'AVIANO, HRH, fmr Grand Duke of Luxembourg (Duke of Nassau, Prince of Bourbon-Parma); b. 5 Jan. 1921, Colmar Berg; s. of Felix, Prince of Bourbon-Parma and Prince of Luxembourg and Charlotte, Grand Duchess of Luxembourg; m. Princess Josephine-Charlotte of Belgium 1953 (died 2005); three s. (including HRH Grand Duke Henri) two d.; Lt-Rep. of Grand Duchess 1961–64; became Grand Duke of Luxembourg on abdication of Grand Duchess Charlotte Nov. 1964, abdicated Oct. 2000; Col of the Irish Guards; mem. Int. Olympic Cttee; Chief Scout, Luxembourg Boy Scouts' Asscn; Col Regt Irish Guards 1984–2000; Dr hc (Strasbourg, Miami); numerous decorations. *Leisure interests:* photography and natural history. *Address:* Grand Ducal Palace, 2013 Luxembourg, Luxembourg (office). *Website:* www.gouvernement.lu.

JEAN-MARIE, Marie-Carmelle; Haitian banker, business executive and politician; *Minister of Economy and Finance;* b. 16 July 1956, Vallée de Jacmel; ed Univ. d'État d'Haïti, Univ. Paris II, Assas, France, Inst. Technique de Banques, Inst. Technique de Marchés, Paris, Centre de Formation de la Profession Bancaire, Centre for Latin American Monetary Studies, Mexico; long career with Banque de la République d'Haïti (central bank) 1982–95, positions included Sr Economist, Int. Affairs Dept, Econ. Studies Dept, Training Dept, becoming Asst Dir; co-f. Group Croissance (consultancy) 1995–2001; Sr Adviser to Minister of Economy and Finance 2001; Adviser, Ministry of Educ. 2002–03; Dir, Cuba Br., Caisse d'Epargne 2003; Minister of Economy and Finance 2012–13, 2014–; Chair. Asscn

for Cooperation with Micro-Enterprise; Vice-Chair. Haitian Relief Fund for Women; Dir Total Haïti SA 2002–, SCIOP SA (construction co.), Chambre Franco-Haitienne de Commerce et d'Industrie. *Address:* Ministry of the Economy and Finance, Palais des Ministères, rue Mgr Guilloux, Port-au-Prince, Haiti (office). *Telephone:* 2223-7113 (office). *Fax:* 2223-1247 (office). *E-mail:* mef@mefhaiti.gouv.ht (office). *Website:* www.mefhaiti.gouv.ht (office).

JEANCOURT-GALIGNANI, Antoine; French business executive; b. 12 Jan. 1937, Paris; s. of Paul Jeancourt-Galignani and Germaine Verley; m. 1st Brigitte Auzouy 1961 (divorced 1983); three s. one d.; m. 2nd Hannelore Wagner 1983; one d.; ed Mount St Mary's Coll. Spinkhill, UK, Ecole St Louis de Gonzague, Faculté de Paris, École Nat. d'Admin; Inspecteur de Finances 1965; Asst Sec., Office of Minister of Finance 1968–70, Treasury Dept of Ministry of Finance 1970–71; with Chase Manhattan Bank, New York 1972; Sr then Exec. Vice-Pres. in charge of int. and corp. banking, Crédit Agricole 1973–79; joined Banque Indosuez 1979, Pres. 1980–81, 1982–88, Chair. and CEO 1981–82, 1988–94; Chair. Assurances Générales de France 1994–2001; Chair. Gecina 2001–05; Dir Société Générale, Total 1994–, Euro Disney (Chair. Supervisory Bd 1995–2013), AGF, Kaufman & Broad SA; Officier, Légion d'honneur, Commdr, Ordre nat. du Mérite, Chevalier du Mérite agricole, Croix de la valeur militaire. *Publication:* La Finance Déboussolée 2010. *Address:* 3 avenue Bosquet, 75007 Paris, France. *E-mail:* jeangal@noos.fr.

JEANJEAN, Michel, LLM; French government official; b. May 1951; began career as Attaché in local govt dept 1973–81, Prin. Attaché 1981–82; Head of Commr's Office, St Pierre et Miquelon 1982–83, Head of Admin. Sub-Div., Marquesas Islands, French Polynesia 1983–87, Head of Admin.'s Office, Meurthe-et-Moselle département 1987–88, Deputy Admin. (Sous-préfet), Corte, Corsica 1988–91, Sec.-Gen. Haute-Saône Admin. 1991–93, with Ministry of the Interior, Overseas Possessions and Territorial Collectivities, becoming Head of Territorial Admin. and Political Affairs Dept 1993–96, Sec.-Gen. French Polynesia 1996–99, Sec.-Gen. Hérault Admin. 1999–2001, Deputy Admin. Avesnes-sur-Helpe 2001–05, Deputy Admin. Torcy 2005–10, Chief Admin. (Administrateur Supérieur) Wallis and Futuna 2010–13. *Address:* c/o Bureau de l'Administrateur Supérieur, BP 16, Mata'Utu, Havelu, Hahake, 98600 Uvea, Wallis Islands (office).

JEANMAIRE, (Renée Marcelle) Zizi; French actress, dancer and singer; b. 29 April 1924, Paris; d. of Marcel Jeanmaire; m. Roland Petit 1954; one d.; student, Paris Opera Ballet 1933–40, Dancer 1940–44; with Ballets de Monte-Carlo, Ballets Colonel de Basil, Ballets Roland Petit; Dir (with Roland Petit) Casino de Paris 1969–; leading role in three concerts, Zénith 1995, nine concerts, Opéra Bastille 2000; music hall appearances; Chevalier de la Légion d'honneur, Chevalier des Arts et des Lettres, Officier, Ordre nat. du Mérite. *Films:* Hans Christian Andersen, Anything Goes, Folies Bergère, Charmants Garçons, Black Tights, La Revue, Zizi je t'aime; musical: The Girl in Pink Tights (Broadway). *Leading roles in:* Aubade, Piccoli, Carmen, La Croqueuse de Diamants, Rose des Vents, Cyrano de Bergerac, La Dame dans la Lune, La Symphonie Fantastique 1975, Le loup, La chauve-souris 1979, Hollywood Paradise Show 1985, Java for ever 1988, Marcel et la Belle Excentrique 1992. *Address:* c/o Editions Assouline, 26 rue Danielle Casanova, 75002 Paris, France.

JEANNENEY, Jean-Noël, Agrégé d'Histoire, DèsL; French politician and academic; *Professor Emeritus in Modern History, Institut d'études politiques de Paris (Sciences Po);* b. 2 April 1942, Grenoble; s. of Jean-Marcel Jeanneney and Marie-Laure Jeanneney (née Monod); m. 2nd Annie-Lou Cot 1985; two s.; ed Lycées Champollion and Louis-le-Grand, Ecole normale supérieure, Inst. d'études politiques de Paris, Sorbonne Univ.; Lecturer in Contemporary History, Univ. de Paris X 1969–77, Lecturer 1968; Univ. Prof. in Modern History, Inst. d'études politiques de Paris (Sciences Po) 1977,now Prof. Emer.; Pres., Dir-Gen. Radio-France and Radio-France Int. 1982–86; Pres. Bicentenary of the French Revolution 1988–89; mem. Bd of Dirs, Agence France-Presse 1982–84, Télé-diffusion de France 1982–86, La Sept 1986, Seuil Publs 1987–91, 1993–2002; Chair. Scientific Council, Inst. d'Histoire du Temps Présent 1991–2000; Sec. of State for External Trade 1991–92, for Communication 1992–93; Regional Councillor, Franche-Comté 1992–98; Chair. Advisory Cttee for 'Histoire' (cable TV) 1997–2004; Pres. Europartenaires 1998–, Bibliothèque nationale de France 2002–07, Rendez-vous de l'Histoire de Blois 2003–, Rencontres de la photographie d'Arles 2009–, Jury du Prix du livre d'Histoire du Sénat 2007–; Chevalier, Légion d'honneur, Commdr, Ordre nat. du Mérite; Dr hc (Université Libre de Belgique) 2005. *Play:* L'un de nous deux. *Radio:* Concordance des temps (weekly programme on French culture) 1999–. *Television:* historical films for French TV: Léon Blum ou la fidélité 1973, Eamon de Valera 1975, Le Rhin 1996, Les Grandes Batailles de la République 1996–2006, Senghor entre deux mondes 1998, Histoire des présidentielles 1965–1995 2002, La Drôle de paix 1919–1939 2009, Jean Jaurès 2014. *Publications:* Le Riz et le Rouge, cinq mois en Extrême-Orient 1969, Le Journal politique de Jules Jeanneney 1939–42 1972, François de Wendel en République, l'Argent et le Pouvoir 1976, Leçon d'histoire pour une gauche au pouvoir, La Faillite du Cartel 1924–26 1977, Le Monde de Beuve-Méry ou le métier d'Alceste (co-author) 1979, L'argent caché, milieux d'affaires et pouvoirs politiques dans la France du XXe Siècle 1981, Télévision nouvelle mémoire, les magazines de grand reportage 1959–68 (with others) 1982, Echec à Panurge, l'audiovisuel public au service de la différence 1986, Concordances des temps, chroniques sur l'actualité du passé 1987, Georges Mandel, l'Homme qu'on attendait 1991–2009, L'avenir vient de loin, Essai sur la gauche 1994–2000, Une histoire des médias des origines à nos jours 1996–2012, Le Passé dans le prétoire, l'historien, le juge et le journaliste 1998, L'Echo du siècle, Dictionnaire historique de la radio et de la télévision en France 1999, La République a besoin d'histoire, interventions 2000, L'Histoire va-t-elle plus vite? Variations sur un vertige 2001, Le duel, une passion française 2004–11, Clemenceau, portrait d'un homme libre 2005, Concordance des temps: Dialogues radiophoniques 2005, La Proverbe et l'étamine, lectures historiques et politiques 2007, Concordance des temps, Vol. II 2008, Correspondance de Clemenceau (co-author) 2008, L'un de nous deux, dialogue pour le théâtre 2009, Quand Google défie l'Europe: Plaidoyer pour un sursaut (third edn) 2010, L'Etat blessé 2012, Jours de guerre, 1914–1918 2013, La Grande guerre, si loin, si proche, réflexions sur un Centenaire 2013, L'Histoire, la liberté, l'action, Œuvres 1977–2013, Les Grandes heures de la presse 2013. *Address:* 48 rue Galande, 75005 Paris, France (home). *E-mail:* jean-noel.jeanneney@orange.fr (office).

JEANNIOT, Pierre Jean, OC, CQ, FRAeS; Canadian/French fmr air transport official and international aviation consultant; *Director-General Emeritus, International Air Transport Association;* b. Montpellier, France; m.; two s. one d.; ed Sir George Williams Univ., McGill Univ. and Univ. de Montréal; designer of aircraft and marine instrumentation, Sperry Gyroscope of Canada 1952–55; various positions in research, devt and man., Air Canada 1955–68, Vice-Pres. Computer and Systems Services 1970–76, subsequently held other sr positions in Air Canada, Exec. Vice-Pres. and COO Air Canada 1983, Pres. and CEO 1984–90; contributed to devt of the 'black box'; Vice-Pres. Computers and Communications, Univ. du Québec 1969; Dir-Gen. and CEO IATA, Montreal 1992–2002, Dir-Gen. Emer. 2002–; Chair. Thales Canada, Inc. 2003–09; Dir Bank of Nova Scotia Subsidiary Bds; Dir Jet Airways 2006–09; Chair. Bd Univ. of Québec 1971–77, Chancellor 1996–2009; Pres. and CEO JINMAG Inc.; Founding Chair. Foundation on Antivirals; Chair. Nature Air, Star Navigation Inc.; Sr Aviation Consultant, Gerson Lehrman Group; Chevalier, Légion d'honneur 1991, Independence Medal of First Order (Jordan) 1995; Hon. LLD (Québec) 1988, (Concordia) 1997; Hon. DSc (McGill) 2006; Man. Achievement Award, McGill Univ. 1989, Prix Rogers Demers des Gens de L'Air 1990, Flight Int. Transportation Man of the Year 2002, Québec Hall of Fame 2004, inducted into Canadian Aviation Hall of Fame 2011. *Publications include:* Pierre Jeanniot aux Commandes du Ciel (biography); numerous tech. papers. *Address:* Place du Canada, 1010 de la Gauchetiere West, Suite 960, Montreal, PQ H3B 2N2, Canada (office). *Telephone:* (514) 868-0880 (office); (514) 868-9348 (office). *E-mail:* jeanniotp@jinmag.com (office); goughcooper@jinmag.com (office). *Website:* www.pierrejeanniot.com.

JEANTET, Pierre; French newspaper industry executive; b. 14 May 1947, Neuilly-sur-Seine; ed Université Droit à Paris-II Assas; started career at Agence France-Presse 1972, served as Chief, Econ. Service 1980–82, Asst Sec.-Gen. 1984, Sec.-Gen. 1984–85, Sales Man. 1985–87, Asst Dir-Gen. 1987–90; Chair. Intermonde Presse 1989–91; Dir-Gen. Eurexpansion 1990–93; Dir-Gen. Sud-Ouest press group 1993–2006; Dir-Gen. Le Monde newspaper and Deputy Chair. Le Monde Group 2006–07, Chair. Le Monde Group June–Dec. 2007; Vice-Pres. Syndicat de la Presse Quotidienne Régionale 2001–; Pres. Bd of Trustees Pyrénées Presse 2002–, Charente Libre 2003–, Société des Gratuits de Guyenne et Gascogne 2004–; Chevalier de la Légion d'honneur, Chevalier de la l'Ordre national du Mérite. *Address:* Société des Gratuits de Guyenne et Gascogne, rue Walter Scott, 33600 Pessac, France (office). *Telephone:* 5-57-89-19-00 (office). *Fax:* 5-59-89-19-16 (office). *Website:* www.s3g.fr (office).

JEBREAL, Rula; Palestinian/Italian journalist, broadcaster and author; b. 24 April 1973, Haifa; one d.; ed Univ. of Bologna; fmr newspaper journalist in Italy, Il Resto del Carlino, Il Giorno e La Nazione, Il Messaggero; TV journalist in Italy for 12 years, became first foreign anchorwoman to broadcast evening news bulletin 2000; Media Watch Award (for TV coverage of Iraq War) 2004, Int. Ischia Award for Journalist of the Year 2005. *Television includes:* as presenter: Omnibus (talk show) 2004, as co-presenter: Anno Zero 2006; as writer/producer: Permesso di Soggiorno (documentary on the death penalty) 2008; created own show for Al-Qahira Wai-Nas station, Cairo, Egypt 2009. *Film:* screenplay: Miral 2011. *Publications include:* fiction: Miral 2003, La Sposa di Assuan (The Bride of Aswan) (Winner, Int. Fenice Europa Prize 2007) 2007; non-fiction: Rejected (aka Divieto di Soggiorno) 2007. *Address:* c/o Thomas Colchie, The Colchie Agency, 324 85th Street, Brooklyn, New York, NY 11209 (office); c/o Office of Ari Emanuel, William Morris Endeavor LLC, Beverly Hills, CA 90210, USA (office). *Telephone:* (718) 921-7468 (New York) (office); (310) 248-3064 (Beverly Hills) (office). *E-mail:* colchieagency@gmail.com (office); AEmanuel_Sched@wmeentertainment.com (office). *Website:* www.wma.com (office); rulajebreal.net.

JEENBEKOV, Asilbek Sharipovich; Kyrgyzstani politician; *Chairman (Speaker), Jogorku Kenesh (Supreme Council);* b. 27 Aug. 1963, Biymyrza, Kara Gulja dist, Osh Oblast; ed Kyrgyz Agricultural Inst., Kyrgyz Research Inst. of Agric., Univ. of Econs and Entrepreneurship, Bishkek; worked as agronomist in Uzgen dist, Osh region; Chair. Kyrgyz Agribusiness Asscn 2002–07; mem. Jogorku Kenesh 2007–, Chair. (Speaker) 2011–. *Address:* Jogorku Kenesh (Supreme Council), 720053 Bishkek, Abdymomunov 207, Kyrgyzstan (office). *Telephone:* (312) 61-16-04 (office). *Fax:* (312) 62-50-12 (office). *E-mail:* zs@kenesh.gov.kg (office). *Website:* www.kenesh.kg (office).

JEEVES, Malcolm Alexander, CBE, MA, PhD, FMedSci; British psychologist, academic and writer; *Professor Emeritus of Psychology, University of St Andrews;* b. 16 Nov. 1926, Stamford, Lincs.; s. of Alexander Frederic Thomas Jeeves and Helena May Jeeves (née Hammond); m. Ruth Elisabeth Hartridge 1955; two d.; ed Stamford School, St John's Coll., Cambridge, Harvard Univ., USA; Commd. Royal Lincs. Regt, served with 'Desert Rats' in First Bn Sherwood Foresters, BAOR 1945–48; Research Exhibitioner, St John's Coll., Cambridge 1952; Rotary Foundation Fellow, Harvard Univ. 1953; Lecturer, Univ. of Leeds 1956; Prof. of Psychology, Adelaide Univ. 1959–69, Dean 1962–64; Vice-Prin. Univ. of St Andrews 1981–85, Dir MRC Cognitive Neuroscience Research Group, St Andrews 1984–89, now Prof. Emer. of Psychology; Ed.-in-Chief Neuropsychologia 1990–93; mem. Psychology Cttee SSRC 1972–76, Biology Cttee SERC 1980–84, Science Bd 1985–89, Council 1985–89, Neuroscience and Mental Health Bd, MRC 1985–89, Manpower Sub-cttee, ABRC 1991–93, Council Royal Soc. of Edin. 1984–88, Exec. 1985–87, Vice-Pres. Royal Soc. of Edin. 1990–93, Pres. 1996–99; Pres. Section J, BAAS 1988; Founding Fellow, Acad. of Medical Sciences 1998; Fellow, British Psychological Soc.; Hon. Research Prof., Univ. of St Andrews 1993–; Hon. Sheriff Fife 1986–; Hon. DUniv (Stirling); Hon. DSc (Edin.) 1993, (St Andrews) 2000; Abbie Memorial Lecture, Adelaide Univ. 1981, Cairns Memorial Lecture, 1986, 1987, Burney Student, Cambridge, Kenneth Craik Award, St John's Coll., Cambridge, Gregg Bury Prize, Cambridge, Cairns Medal 1986. *Publications:* Thinking in Structures (with Z. P. Dienes) 1965, The Effects of Structural Relations upon Transfer (with Z. P. Dienes) 1968, The Scientific Enterprise and Christian Faith 1969, Experimental Psychology: An Introduction for Biologists 1974, Psychology and Christianity: The View Both Ways 1976, Analysis of Structural Learning (with G. B. Greer) 1983, Free To Be Different (with R. J. Berry and D. Atkinson) 1984, Behavioural Science: a Christian Perspective 1984, Psychology – Through the Eyes of Faith (with D. G. Myers) 1987, Mind Fields 1994, Callosal Agenesis (co-ed.) 1994, Human Nature at the Millennium 1997, Science, Life and Christian Belief (co-ed.) 1998, From Cells to Souls – and Beyond

(ed. and contrib.) 2004, Human Nature (ed. and contrib.) 2005, Neuroscience, Psychology and Religion (with Warren Brown) 2009; papers on neuropsychology and cognition in scientific journals. *Leisure interests:* music, fly fishing, walking. *Address:* School of Psychology, University of St Andrews, St Andrews, Fife, KY16 9JU (office); 7 Hepburn Gardens, St Andrews, Fife, KY16 9DE, Scotland (home). *Telephone:* (1334) 462072 (office); (1334) 473545 (home). *Fax:* (1334) 477441 (office); (1334) 472539 (home). *E-mail:* maj2@st-andrews.ac.uk (office). *Website:* www.psy.st-andrews.ac.uk (office).

JEEWOOLALL, Sir Ramesh, Kt, LLB; Mauritian lawyer and politician; *Chancellor, University of Mauritius;* b. 20 Dec. 1940; m.; two c.; ed Middle Temple, London, UK; lawyer 1969–71; magistrate 1971–72; Chair. Tea Devt Authority 1976; elected to Legis. Ass. (Labour Party) 1976, Deputy Speaker 1976–79, Speaker 1979–82, 1996–2001; elected to Legis. Ass. (Alliance Party) 1987; Minister of Housing, Lands and Environment 1987–90; Chancellor, Univ. of Mauritius 2006–. *Address:* Office of the Chancellor, University of Mauritius, Reduit, Mauritius (office). *Telephone:* 403-7400 (office). *Fax:* 454-9642 (office). *Website:* www.uom.ac.mu (office).

JEFFERTS SCHORI, Most Rev. Katharine, BSc, MSc, MDiv, PhD; American ecclesiastic; *Presiding Bishop and Primate, The Episcopal Church;* b. 26 March 1954, Pensacola, Fla; m. Richard Schori; one c.; ed Stanford Univ., Oregon State Univ.; qualified oceanographer, worked with Nat. Marine Fisheries Service; ordained priest 1994, served at Church of the Good Samaritan, Corvallis, Ore. with special responsibility for Hispanic congregation; consecrated Bishop of Nevada 2001; elected Presiding Bishop and Primate of Episcopal Church 2006–, also serves as Bishop of the Convocation of American Churches in Europe; Hon. DD (Church Divinity School of the Pacific). *Publications:* A Wing and a Prayer: A Message of Faith and Hope 2007, The Gospel in the Global Village: On the Road with Bishop Katherine 2009, The Heartbeat of God 2010, Gathering at God's Table 2012. *Address:* Office of the Presiding Bishop, 815 Second Avenue, New York, NY 10017, USA (office). *Telephone:* (212) 716-6273 (office). *Fax:* (212) 697-5892 (office). *E-mail:* sjones@episcopalchurch.org (office). *Website:* www.episcopalchurch.org (office).

JEFFERY, Maj.-Gen. (Philip) Michael, AC, AO (Mil.), CVO, MC; Australian company chairman and army officer (retd); *Chairman, Royal Flying Doctor Service of Australia;* b. 12 Dec. 1937, Wiluna, WA; m. Marlena Kerr 1967; three s. one d.; ed Cannington School, E Victoria Park State School, Kent Street High School, Royal Mil. Coll., Duntroon, Canberra; comm. as Lt in Royal Australian Infantry Corps 1958; Platoon Commdr, 17 Nat. Service Training Co., Swanbourne, WA, Reconnaissance Officer, 1 Special Air Service (SAS) Co., Swanbourne 1959; promoted Temporary Capt., 1 SAS Co., Swanbourne 1962; Signal Platoon Commdr, Second Bn, Royal Australian Regt (2 RAR), Malaya 1962; promoted Capt., 2 RAR, Malaya 1962; Signal Platoon Commdr, 3 RAR, Malaya 1963; ADC to Chief of Gen. Staff, Lt-Gen. Sir John Wilton, Army HQ, Canberra, ACT 1964; SAS Regt, Swanbourne 1965; Operations Officer, SAS HQ, Labuan, Borneo 1965; Adjutant, SAS Regt, Swanbourne 1966; promoted Temporary Maj. 1966; Co. Commdr, First Bn, Pacific Islands Regt (1 PIR), Papua New Guinea (PNG); promoted Maj. 1968; Co. Commdr, 8 RAR, Enoggera, Viet Nam (Phuoc Tuy Prov.) and Enoggera 1969–70; Instructor, Battle Wing, Jungle Training Centre, Canungra, Queensland 1971; Student, Royal Mil. Coll. of Science, Schrivenham and British Army Staff Coll., Camberley, UK 1971; Staff Officer, Grade 2 Operations, Directorate of Operations, Army HQ, Canberra 1973; promoted Temporary Lt-Col 1973; Staff Officer Grade 1, Jt Warfare, Directorate of Operations, Army HQ, Canberra; Staff Officer Grade 1, Land Operations, HQ, PNG Defence Force, Port Moresby 1974; promoted Lt-Col 1974; CO Second Bn, Pacific Islands Regt (2 P1R), Wewak, PNG 1975; CO Special Air Service Regt, Swanbourne 1976; Student, Jt Services Staff Coll., Canberra 1978; Mil. Sec.'s Pool of Lt-Cols, Office of the CGS, Canberra 1978; Staff Officer Grade 1, Special Warfare, Operations Br., Army HQ, Canberra 1978; promoted Col and Dir Special Action Forces, Operations Br., Army Office, Canberra 1979; promoted Brig. and Head of Protective Services Co-ordination Centre, Dept of Admin. Services, Canberra 1981; Commdr 1 Brigade, Holsworthy, NSW 1983; Student, Royal Coll. of Defence Studies, UK 1984; promoted Maj. Gen. and Commdr 1 Div., Paddington, NSW 1985; Asst Chief of Gen. Staff, Logistics, Army Office, Canberra 1989; Deputy Chief of Gen. Staff, Army Office, Canberra 1990; Asst Chief of Gen. Staff, Material, Army Office, Canberra, 1991; transferred to Inactive Australian Army Reserve 1993; Gov. of Western Australia 1993–2000; Gov.-Gen. of Commonwealth of Australia 2003–08; Founder and Chair. Future Directions International, Perth, WA 2000–03; currently Chair. Royal Flying Doctor Service of Australia; Citizen of Western Australia 2000, Hon. Life mem. Returned and Services League; KStJ; Grand Companion of the Order of Logohu (Papua New Guinea) 2005; AASM with Bars, Malaysia, Thai/Malay, Borneo and Viet Nam 1945–75, GSM with Bars Borneo and Malay Peninsula 1962, Viet Nam Service Medal, ASM with Bars, Papua New Guinea and South East Asia 1945–75, Australian Centenary Medal, Defence Force Service Medal with four Bars, Nat. Medal with Bar, Papua New Guinea Independence Medal, Mil. Cross and S Vietnamese Cross of Gallantry with Gold Star, S Viet Nam Campaign Medal, Vietnamese Cross of Gallantry Unit Citation, Pingat Jasa Medal Malaysia 2006; Hon. DTech (Curtin Univ.) 2000; Paul Harris Fellow, The Rotary Foundation 1996. *Leisure interests:* golf, cricket, fishing, reading, music. *Address:* PO Box 3162, Manuka, ACT 2603 (office); 18 Hampton Circuit, Yarralumla, ACT 2600, Australia (home). *Telephone:* (2) 6232-6008 (office); (2) 6282-7446 (home). *Fax:* (2) 6295-8716 (office). *E-mail:* wendy.button@pmc.gov.au (office); mikejeffery@netspace.com.au (home).

JEFFORDS, James (Jim) Merrill, BS, LLB; American politician (retd); b. 11 May 1934, Rutland, Vt; s. of Olin M. Jeffords and Marion Hausman; m. Elizabeth Daley (died 2007); one s. one d.; ed Yale and Harvard Univs.; admitted to Vermont Bar 1962; law clerk, Judge Ernest Gibson, Vt District 1962; Pnr Bishop, Crowley & Jeffords 1963–66, Kinney, Carbine & Jeffords 1967–68; mem. Vt Senate 1967–68; Attorney-Gen. State of Vt 1969–73; Pnr, George E. Rice, Jr and James M. Jeffords 1973–74; mem. US House of Reps, Washington, DC 1975–89; Senator from Vermont 1989–2007 (retd), Chair. Environment Cttee 2001–07; Republican –2001, Ind. 2001–07.

JEFFREY, Robin Campbell, BSc, PhD, FREng, FIChemE, FIMechE; British engineer, business executive and fmr academic; b. 19 Feb. 1939, Kirkintilloch, East

Dunbartonshire, Scotland; s. of Robert Jeffrey and Catherine McSporran; m. Barbara Robinson 1962; two s. one d.; ed Kelvinside Acad., Royal Tech. Coll. Glasgow, Pembroke Coll., Cambridge; with Babcock International 1956–79; with South of Scotland Electricity Bd 1979–89, Project Man. Torness AGR Station 1980–88, Chief Engineer, Generation Design and Construction 1988–89; Man. Dir Eng Resources, Scottish Power 1990–92; CEO Scottish Nuclear Ltd 1992–98, Chair. 1995–98; Jt Deputy Chair. British Energy PLC 1995–2001, Chair., CEO 2001–02; fmr Visiting Prof. of Eng, Univ. of Strathclyde; fmr mem. London Transport Bd; Fellow, Royal Acad. of Eng; Canadian Nuclear Assćn's Int. Award 2002. *Address:* Brambles, Spring Copse, Oxford, OX1 5BJ, England (home). *E-mail:* robin.jeffrey1@btinternet.com (office).

JEFFREYS, Sir Alec John, Kt, BA, MA, DPhil, FRCPath, FRS, FLS, FMedSci, CBiol; British geneticist and academic; *Royal Society Wolfson Research Professor, University of Leicester;* b. 9 Jan. 1950, Oxford; s. of Sidney Victor Jeffreys and Joan Jeffreys (née Knight); m. Susan Miles 1971; two d.; ed Luton Grammar School, Luton Sixth Form Coll., Merton Coll., Oxford; European Molecular Biology Org. Postdoctoral Research Fellow, Univ. of Amsterdam 1975–77; Lecturer, Dept of Genetics, Univ. of Leicester 1977–82, Lister Inst. Research Fellow 1982–91, Reader in Genetics 1984–87, Prof. of Genetics 1987–, Royal Soc. Wolfson Research Prof. 1991–; Howard Hughes Int. Research Scholar 1993–97; Inventor of Genetic Fingerprinting; Fellow, Forensic Science Soc. of India 1989–, Int. Inst. of Biotechnology 1990–, Linnean Soc. of London 1994–; Founder Fellow, Acad. of Medical Sciences 1998; Foreign Assoc. NAS 2005; Hon. Freeman (Leicester) 1993; Hon. FRCP 1993, Hon. Fellow (Luton) 1995, (Swansea) 2005, Hon. mem. Dept of Biochemistry, Univ. of Oxford 1997, Int. Soc. for Forensic Haemogenetics 1997, American Acad. of Forensic Sciences 1998, Biochemical Soc. 2003, NAS 2006; Hon. Life mem. Leicestershire Medico-Legal Soc. 1999; Hon. FRSM 2001; Hon. Fellow, Forensic Science Soc. 2005; Hon. DUniv (Open Univ.) 1991; Hon. DSc (St Andrews) 1996, (Strathclyde) 1998, (Hull) 2004, (Oxford) 2004, (Leicester) 2004, (Kingston) 2005, (Liverpool) 2006, (King's Coll., London) 2007, (Teesside) 2007; Hon. DIur (Dundee) 2008; Gibbs Prize in Honours Biochemistry 1972, Colworth Medal for Biochemistry, Biochemical Soc. 1985, Linnean Bicentenary Medal for Zoology 1987, Carter Medal, Clinical Genetics Soc. 1987, 2003, Davy Medal, Royal Soc. 1987, Analytica Prize, German Soc. of Clinical Chemistry 1988, Australia Prize 1998; Midlander of the Year Award, 1988, Achievement of the Year Award, Leicester Publicity Assćn 1989, P. W. Allen Memorial Award, Forensic Science Soc. 1992, Milano Award 1992, Allan Award, American Soc. of Human Genetics 1992, Lloyd of Kilgerran Prize, Foundation for Science and Tech. 1993, Illuminated Address, Bedfordshire Co. Council 1994, Gold Medal for Zoology, Linnean Soc. 1994, Sir Frederick Gowland Hopkins Memorial Medal, Biochemical Soc. 1996, Albert Einstein World of Science Award, World Cultural Council Award, Baly Medal, Royal Coll. of Physicians 1997, Soc. of Chemical Industry Medal 1997, Australia Prize 1998, Sir George Stokes Medal, Royal Soc. of Chem. 2000, Edward Buchner Prize, Soc. for Biochem. and Molecular Biology (Germany) 2001, Nat. Historic Chemical Landmark plaque, Royal Soc. of Chem. 2002, Terence J Green Award, Int. Homicide Investigators Assćn 2003, Howard Steel Medal, British Orthopaedic Assćn 2003, AMP Award for Excellence in Molecular Diagnostics, Assćn for Molecular Pathology, USA 2003, Hon. Medal, Royal Coll. of Surgeons 2004, Daily Mirror Pride of Britain Lifetime Achievement Award 2004, Louis-Jeantet Prize for Medicine, Fondation Louis-Jeantet de Médecine, Switzerland 2004, Royal Medal, Royal Soc. 2004, Induction, Inventors Hall of Fame, Washington, DC 2005, Adelaide Medal, Int. Assćn of Forensic Sciences, Hong Kong 2005, Lasker Prize (for clinical medical research) 2005, Thomson Scientific Laureate Physiology/Medicine, USA 2006, Dr H.P. Heineken Prize for Biochemistry and Biophysics, Royal Netherlands Acad. of Arts and Sciences 2006, Morgan Stanley Great Briton Award 2006, Morgan Stanley Great Briton in Science and Innovation Award 2007, Millennium Laureate, Millennium Foundation, Helsinki 2008, Assćn of Colls Gold Award for Further Educ. Alumni 2008, Croonian Lecturer, The Royal Soc. 2010. *Publications include:* numerous articles on human molecular genetics. *Leisure interests:* walking, swimming, postal history, reading unimproving novels. *Address:* Department of Genetics, Adrian Building, University of Leicester, University Road, Leicester, LE1 7RH, England (office). *Telephone:* (116) 252-3435 (office). *Fax:* (116) 252-3378 (office). *E-mail:* ajj@le.ac .uk (office). *Website:* www.le.ac.uk/ge (office).

JEKER, Robert A.; Swiss business executive; b. 26 Aug. 1935, Basel; m. Vreni Jeker 1967; one s. two d.; ed Univ. of Massachusetts, Amherst, USA; Head of Spalenberg br., Credit Suisse, Basel 1968–72, Head of Credit Suisse, Basel 1972–76, mem. Exec. Bd 1976–83, Pres. 1983–93; Man. Dir Unotec, Anova and Nueva Holdings 1993–96; fmr Chair. Batigroup AG, Basel, MCH Messe Schweiz AG, Basel; fmr Chair., now Vice-Chair. Swiss Steel, Emmenbrücke. *Leisure interests:* sports, concerts, travel. *Address:* Waldrain 2, 4103 Bottmingen, Switzerland (home). *Telephone:* (61) 4013067 (home). *Fax:* (61) 4013075 (home).

JELAŠIĆ, Radovan, MA, MBA; Serbian economist and fmr central banker; b. 19 Feb. 1968, Baja, Hungary; ed Univ. of Belgrade, Univ. of Illinois at Chicago, USA; Regional Man. for Cen. and Eastern Europe and positions in Corp. Banking Dept, Deutsche Bank, Frankfurt, Germany 1995–99; Sr Assoc., McKinsey & Co. Inc., Frankfurt, working on banking projects in Germany, Poland and Bulgaria 1999–2000; Vice-Gov. Nat. Bank of Yugoslavia/Serbia 2000–03, Gov. Narodna banka Srbije (Nat. Bank of Serbia) 2004–10; fmr mem. Bd of Dirs Banking Rehabilitation Agency, Belgrade. *Address:* c/o Narodna banka Srbije, PO Box 1010, Kralja Petra 12, 11000 Belgrade, Serbia (office).

JELIMO, Pamela; Kenyan athlete; b. 5 Dec. 1989; d. of Rodah Jeptoo Keter (fmr 200m and 400m runner); ed Koyo Secondary School, Kapsabet; women's middle distance runner; started running as sprinter aged 13 in 2003; Kenyan High School Champion at 400m and 400m hurdles 2005; finished fifth in 400m race at Kenyan Championships 2007; Gold Medal, African Jr Championships 2007; ran 200m Kenyan nat. jr record (24.68); ran her first 800m race at Kenyan trials for African Championships April 2008 (2:01.02); has been recruited by Kenyan Police, where she trains with Janeth Jepkosgei; at African Championships in Athletics 2008 set new nat. jr record of 1:58.70; won 800m at Hengelo Grand Prix May 2008 (new Jr World Record and Kenyan record of 1:55.76); ran 400m personal best of 52.78 in Nairobi June 2006; won Internationales Stadionfest (ISTAF) Golden League 2008 (set new African record time of 1:54.99); bettered record to 1:54.97 at Int. Assćn of

Athletics Feds (IAAF) Golden League, Paris July 2008; Gold Medal, women's 800m, Olympic Games, Beijing 2008 (record time of 1:54.87); won Gold Medal at World Indoor Championships 2012 in Istanbul; first Kenyan woman to win Olympic gold medal); ran personal best of 1:54.01 at Weltklasse Golden League meeting, Zurich 29 Aug. 2008 (third fastest time ever); coached by Zaid Aziz. *Address:* c/o Kenya Athletics Federation, PO Box 46722, Aerodrome Road, Riadha House, 00100 Nairobi West, Kenya.

JELINEK, Elfriede; Austrian writer, dramatist and poet; b. 20 Oct. 1946, Mürzzuschlag, Styria; m. Gottfried Hüngsberg; ed Vienna Conservatory, Albertsgymnasium, Vienna, Univ. of Vienna; mem. Graz Writers' Assćn; Young Austrian Culture Week Poetry and Prose Prize 1969, Austrian Univ. Students' Poetry Prize 1969, Austrian State Literature Stipendium 1972, City of Stadt Bad Gandersheim Roswitha Memorial Medal 1978, West German Interior Ministry Prize for Film Writing 1979, West German Ministry of Education and Art Appreciation Prize 1983, City of Cologne Heinrich Böll Prize 1986, Province of Styria Literature Prize 1987, City of Vienna Literature Appreciation Prize 1989, City of Aachen Walter Hasenclever Prize 1994, City of Bochum Peter Weiss Prize 1994, Rudolf Alexander Schroder Foundation Bremen Prize for Literature 1996, Georg Büchner Prize 1998, Berlin Theatre Prize 2002, City of Düsseldorf Heinrich Heine Prize 2002, Mülheim and der Ruhr Festival of Theatre Dramatist of the Year 2002, 2004, 2009, 2011, Else Lasker Schüler Prize, Mainz 2003, Lessing Critics' Prize, Wolfenbüttel 2004, Stig Dagerman Prize, Älvkarleby 2004, The Blind War Veterans' Radio Theatre Prize, Berlin 2004, Franz Kafka Prize 2004, Nobel Prize for Literature 2004. *Screenplays:* Die Ausgesperrten (TV) 1982, Malina (from novel by Ingeborg Bachmann) 1991. *Plays include:* Raststätte, Wolken. Heim, Das Werk, Totenauberg: ein Stück, Ein Sportstück, Das Lebewohl, In den Alpen. *Radio:* numerous pieces for radio, including wenn die sonne sinkt ist für manche schon büroschluss (radio play) 1974. *Publications include:* Lisas Schatten (poems) 1967, wir sind lockvögel baby! (novel) 1970, Michael: ein Jugendbuch für die Infantilgesellschaft (novel) 1972, Die Liebhaberinnen (novel, translated as Women as Lovers) 1975, bukolit (novel) 1979, Die Ausgesperrten (novel, translated as Wonderful, Wonderful Times) 1980, ende: gedichte von 1966–1968 1980, Die endlose Unschuldigkeit (essays) 1980, Was geschah, nachdem Nora ihren Mann verlassen hatte oder Stützen der Gesellschaft 1980, Die Klavierspielerin (novel, translated as The Piano Teacher) 1983, Burgtheater 1984, Clara S 1984, Oh Wildnis, oh Schutz vor ihr (non-fiction) 1985, Krankeit oder moderne Frauen 1987, Lust (novel) 1989, Wolken. Heim 1990, Die Kinder der Toten (novel) 1995, Macht nichts: eine kleine Trilogie des Todes 1999, Gier: ein Unterhaltungsroman 2000, Der Tod und das Mädchen I–V: Prinzessinnendramen 2003, Neid: Privatroman (novel) 2007, Die Kontrakte des Kaufmanns. Eine Wirtschaftskomödie (play) 2009; translated works of other writers including Thomas Pynchon, Georges Feydeau, Eugène Labiche, Christopher Marlowe, Oscar Wilde; film scripts and an opera libretto. *Address:* Jupiterweg 40, 1140 Vienna, Austria. *E-mail:* theater@rowohlt.de. *Website:* www.elfriedejelinek.com.

JELINEK, Otto John; Canadian diplomatist, politician and business executive; *Ambassador to Czech Republic;* b. 1940, Prague, Czechoslovakia; m. Leata Mary Bennett 1974; two s.; ed Oakville, Ont., Swiss Alpine Business Coll., Davos, Switzerland; MP 1972–93, apptd Parl. Sec. to Minister of Transport 1979, fmr mem. Caucus Cttee on Trade, Finance, Econ. Affairs, fmr mem. Standing Cttee on Transport and Communications, on External Affairs, fmr mem. Parl. Cttee on Miscellaneous Estimates, Minister of State (Fitness and Amateur Sport) 1984–88, for Multiculturalism 1985–86, of Supply and Services and Receiver Gen. of Canada 1988–89; Acting Minister of Public Works 1988–89, Minister of Nat. Revenue 1989–93; Pres. Jelinek Int. Inc. 1993–97; Chair. Deloitte Czech Repub. 1996–2005, Chair. Deloitte & Touche Central Europe 2002–05; Chairman of Operations in Central & Eastern Europe, Colliers Int. 2007–11; Amb. to the Czech Republic 2013–; mem. Int. Advisory Bd Soho Resources 2005–; fmr mem. Bd of Dirs Hummingbird Communications Ltd, Canbra Foods Ltd; mem. Academic Council of Univ. of Econs Prague; fmr Chair. Canada-Taiwan Friendship Cttee; Hon. Pres. Canada-Czech Republic Chamber of Commerce; mem. Big Brothers' Assćn of Canada, Olympic Club of Canada, Canadian Sports Hall of Fame; Fed. Progressive Conservative Party, Queen's Privy Council. *Achievements include:* fmr pairs figure skating world champion 1962. *Address:* Embassy of Canada to the Czech Republic, Ve struhách 95/2, 160 00 Prague 6, The Czech Republic (office). *Telephone:* 272101800 (office). *Fax:* 272101890 (office). *E-mail:* canada@canada.cz (office). *Website:* www.canada.cz (office).

JELINEK, W. Craig; American business executive; *President and CEO, Costco Wholesale Corporation;* joined Costco Wholesale Corpn 1984, Vice-Pres., Regional Operations Man.—Los Angeles Region 1986–94, Sr Vice-Pres., Operations—Northwest Region 1994–95, COO Northern Div. 1995–2004, Exec. Vice-Pres. and COO Merchandising, Costco Wholesale Corpn 2004–10, mem. Bd of Dirs Costco Wholesale Corpn 2010–, Pres. and COO 2010–12, Pres. and CEO 2012–. *Address:* Costco Wholesale Corporation, 999 Lake Drive, Issaquah, WA 98027, USA (office). *Telephone:* (425) 313-8100 (office). *Fax:* (425) 313-8103 (office). *E-mail:* cjelinek@ costco.com (office). *Website:* www.costco.com (office).

JELUŠIČ, Ljubica, MSc, PhD; Slovenian academic and government official; b. 16 June 1960, Koper, Primorska region; ed Faculty of Sociology, Political Science and Journalism, Royal Mil. Acad., Belgium; has held several academic positions since 1985 at Faculty of Social Sciences, Univ. of Ljubljana including Researcher, Asst, Asst Prof. and Assoc. Prof., Prof. of Defence Studies 2005–; Visiting Lecturer, Univ. of Zagreb, Centre for Civil-Mil. Relations, Belgrade; Deputy Dean, Faculty of Social Sciences, Command and Staff School 1995–97, Chair. Defence Studies Dept 1999–2007; Minister of Defence 2008–11; Leader, Defence Restructuring and Conversion research project, COST Programme of the EC 1996–2001; Exec. Sec., Research Cttee on Armed Forces and Conflict Resolution, Int. Sociological Assćn 2006–08; mem. Editorial Bd Theory and Practice (Teorija in praksa) Magazine, Bulletin of the Slovenian Armed Forces (Bilten Slovenske vojske); reviewer for Security and Peace (Sicherheit und Frieden) magazine; mem. Int. Advisory Cttee, Geneva Centre for Democratic Control of Armed Forces. *Publication:* Legitimacy of the Modern Military 1997. *Address:* c/o Ministry of Defence, 1000 Ljubljana, Vojkova 55, Slovenia (office).

JELVED, Marianne Bruus, EdM; Danish politician and fmr teacher; *Minister of Culture;* b. (Marianne Bruus Hirsbro), 5 Sept. 1943, Charlottenlund; m.; teacher in public schools 1967–89, Royal Danish School of Educ. Studies 1979–87; Deputy Mayor of Gundsø 1982–85; mem. Folketing for North Jutland 1988–; Chair. Social Liberal Party Parl. Group 1988–93, 2001–07 (resgnd), 2011–; Minister of Econ. Affairs 1993–2001, for Nordic Cooperation 1994–2001, 2014–, of Culture 2012–, Minister for Equality and Ecclesiastical Affairs 2014–. *Publication:* BRUD: Radikale vaerdier i en forandret tid (co-author) 1994. *Address:* Ministry of Culture, Nybrogade 2, 1203 Copenhagen K (office); Folketing, Christiansborg, 1240 Copenhagen K, Denmark (office). *Telephone:* 33-12-77-55 (office); 33-37-55-00 (office). *E-mail:* min@kum.dk (office); folketinget@folketinget.dk (office). *Website:* www.folketinget.dk (office); www.radikale.dk.

JEMISON, Mae Carol, MD; American physician, business executive and fmr astronaut; b. 17 Oct. 1956, Decateur, Ala; d. of Charlie Jamison and Dorothy Jamison; ed Morgan Park High School, Chicago, Stanford Univ., Cornell Univ. Medical Coll., Los Angeles County/Univ. of Southern Calif. Medical Center; gen. practitioner, Insurance N America (INA)/Ross Loos Medical Group LA 1982; Area Peace Corps Medical Officer to Sierra Leone and Liberia 1983–85; gen. practitioner, CIGNA Health Plans Calif. 1985–87; astronaut, NASA 1987–93, co-investigator, Bone Cell Research experiment, part of Endeavor space mission 1992; f. The Jemison Group Inc., Houston 1993; Prof. of Environmental Studies Dartmouth Coll. 1995–2002; Founder, Pres. and CEO BioSentient Corpn 1999–; A.D. White Prof.-at-Large, Cornell Univ. 1999–2005; f. The Earth We Share (TEWS) 1994; Founder and Chair. Dorothy Jemison Foundation for Excellence 1994–; elected to NAS Inst. of Medicine 2001; Nat. Science Literary Advocate, Bayer Corpn; Moderator, IEEE-USA Tech. Symposia Space Techs. for Disaster Mitigation and Global Health; Dir Jemison Inst. for Advancing Tech. in Developing Countries; mem. American Medical Asscn, ACS, AAAS; mem. Bd Gen-Probe 2004–, World Sickle Cell Foundation, Scholastic Inc., Valspar Corpn, Texas Gov.'s State Council for Science and Bio Tech. Devt; Hon. mem. Center for Prevention Childhood Malnutrition, Montgomery Fellow, Dartmouth Coll.; Dr hc (Princeton Univ. and others); Essence Award 1988, Gamma Sigma Gamma Woman of the Year Award 1989, Johnson Publs Black Achievement Trailblazers Award 1992, Kilby Science Award 1993, Rachel Carson Award, Nat. Audubon Soc. 2005; mem. Nat. Medical Asscn Hall of Fame, Texas Science Hall of Fame, International Space Hall of Fame. *Television includes:* World of Wonder (Discovery Channel) 1994–95; guest appearances: Star Trek: The Next Generation 1993; as subject: The New Explorers (PBS-TV). *Achievements include:* first African-American woman in space 1992. *Publications:* Find Where the Wind Goes: Moments from My Life 2001. *Address:* PO Box 591455, Houston, TX 77259 USA. *E-mail:* Info@DrMae.com. *Website:* www.drmae.com.

JENČA, Miroslav, DIur; Slovak diplomatist and UN official; *Special Representative of the Secretary-General and Head of Regional Centre for Preventive Diplomacy for Central Asia (UNRCCA), United Nations;* b. 1965, Krompachy; m.; two c.; ed Comenius Univ., Bratislava, Univ. of Econs, Bratislava, Moscow State Inst. of Int. Relations, USSR, Stanford Univ., USA; has held several positions in Ministry of Foreign Affairs, including Head of Div. for Devt Assistance and Cross-border Co-operation and Deputy Political Dir and Dir Dept for EU and NATO countries, has served in overseas missions as Counsellor and Chargé d'affaires, Embassy in Dublin and Press Sec., Embassy in Mexico, also served as Amb. and Perm. Rep. to Political and Security Cttee of EU and as Amb. to Mexico, Venezuela and Columbia, Amb. and Head of Mission to OSCE Centre, Tashkent, Uzbekistan c. 2005, Dir Office of Minister for Foreign Affairs –2008; Special Rep. of UN Sec.-Gen. and Head of UN Regional Centre for Preventive Diplomacy for Cen. Asia (UNRCCA), Ashgabat, Turkmenistan 2008–. *Address:* UN Regional Centre for Preventive Diplomacy for Cen. Asia (UNRCCA), 43 Archabil Shayoly, Ashgabat, Turkmenistan (office). *Telephone:* (12) 481612 (office). *Fax:* (12) 481607 (office). *E-mail:* UNRCCA-DPA@un.org (office). *Website:* www.un.org (office).

JENCKS, Charles Alexander, BA, MA, PhD, FRSE; American architectural historian and designer; b. 21 June 1939, Baltimore; m. Maggie Keswick (deceased); three s. one d.; ed Harvard Univ., Univ. of London, England; studied under Siegfried Giedon and Reyner Banham; with Architectural Asscn 1968–88; Lecturer, UCLA 1974–; has lectured at over forty univs including Univs of Peking, Shanghai, Paris, Tokyo, Milan, Venice, Frankfurt, Montréal, Oslo, Warsaw, Barcelona, Lisbon, Zurich, Vienna, Edinburgh, Columbia, Princeton, Yale and Harvard; producer of furniture designs for Sawaya & Moroni, Milan 1986–; Ed. Consultant Architectural Design and Ed. Academy Editions, London; Trustee and Co-founder, Maggie's Centres; Selection Cttee Venice Biennale 1980; Juror for Phoenix City Hall 1985; Curator Wight Art Centre, Los Angeles and Berlin 1987; mem. RSA, London, Acad. Forum of Royal Acad., London; Sr Fellow, Royal Coll. of Art, London 2005; contrib. to Sunday Times Magazine, Times Literary Supplement, The Observer, The Independent; Architectural works include: Garagia Rotunda, Truro, MA 1976–77, The Elemental House (with Buzz Yudell), Los Angeles, The Thematic House (with Terry Farrell), London 1979–84, The Garden of Six Senses 1998, The Garden of Cosmic Speculation, Scotland 2001, Landform Veda, Scottish Gallery of Modern Art, Edinburgh 2002, Portello Park, Milan 2003; Furniture designs include: 'Architecture in Silver': Tea and Coffee Service, Alessi, Italy 1983, Symbolic Furniture exhbn, Aram Designs, London 1985; other furniture and drawings collected by museums in Japan and Victoria & Albert Museum, London; Dr hc (Univ. of Edinburgh 2005), (Univ. of Glasgow) 2005; Fulbright Scholarship, Univ. of London 1965–67, NARA Gold Medal for Architecture 1992. *Television:* two feature films written for BBC on Le Corbusier and Frank Lloyd Wright. *Publications include:* Meaning in Architecture (co-ed.) 1969, Architecture 2000: Predictions and Methods 1971, Adhocism (co-author) 1972, Modern Movements in Architecture 1973, Le Corbusier and the Tragic View of Architecture 1974, The Language of Post-Modern Architecture 1977, The Daydream Houses of Los Angeles 1978, Bizarre Architecture 1979, Late-Modern Architecture 1980, Signs, Symbols and Architecture (co-author) 1980, Sky-scrapers-Skycities 1980, Architecture Today 1982, Kings of Infinite Space 1983, Towards a Symbolic Architecture 1985, What is Post-Modernism? 1987, Post-Modernism – The New Classicism in Art and Architecture 1987, The Prince, The Architects and New Wave Monarchy 1988, The New Moderns 1990, The Post-Modern Reader (ed.) 1992, The Architecture of the Jumping Universe 1995, Theories and Manifestos of Contemporary Architecture 1997, New Science – New Architecture? 1997, The Chinese Garden (with Maggie Keswick), Le Corbusier and the Architecture of Continual Revolution 2000, The New Paradigm in Architecture

2002, The Garden of Cosmic Speculation 2003, Critical Modernism: Where is Post-Modernism Going? 2007, The Story of Post-Modernism 2011, The Universe in the Landscape 2011. *Address:* Maggie's Centres, 1st Floor, One Waterloo Street, Glasgow G2 6AY, Scotland (office). *Telephone:* (3001) 231801 (office). *E-mail:* enquiries@maggiescentres.org (office); www.charlesjencks.com (office); www.charlesjencks.com.

JENKIN OF KENNINGTON, Baroness (Life Peer), cr. 2011, of Hatfield Peverel in the County of Essex; **Anne Jenkin;** British political activist and charity promoter; d.-in-law of Lord Jenkin of Roding; m. Bernard Jenkin; worked as her husband's sec.; political work for Conservative Party has included co-founding Women2Win, a campaign to get more women Conservatives into Parl.; has raised money for charities, including the Student Partnership Worldwide. *Address:* House of Lords, Westminster, London, SW1A 0PW, England (office). *Telephone:* (20) 7219-5353 (office). *Fax:* (20) 7219-5979 (office). *Website:* www.annejenkin.co.uk.

JENKIN OF RODING, Baron (Life Peer), cr. 1987, of Wanstead and Woodford in Greater London; **(Charles) Patrick (Fleeming) Jenkin,** PC, MA; British politician; *President, Foundation for Science and Technology;* b. 7 Sept. 1926, Edinburgh, Scotland; s. of the late C. O. F. Jenkin and Margaret E. Jenkin (née Sillar); m. Alison Monica Graham 1952; two s. two d.; ed Clifton Coll., Bristol, Jesus Coll., Cambridge; called to the Bar, Middle Temple 1952; Adviser Distillers Co. Ltd 1957–70; Hornsey Borough Council 1960–63; MP for Wanstead and Woodford 1964–87; Opposition Spokesman on Finance, Econs and Trade 1965–66, 1967–70; Financial Sec. to Treasury 1970–72, Chief Sec. 1972–74; Minister for Energy Jan.–March 1974; mem. Shadow Cabinet 1974–79; Opposition Spokesman on Energy 1974–76, on Social Services 1976–79; Sec. of State for Social Services 1979–81, for Industry 1981–83, for the Environment 1983–85; mem. House of Lords Select Cttee on Science and Tech. 1997–2001 (Chair. Sub-Cttee II on Science and Soc. 1999–2000); Dir (non-exec.) Tilbury Contracting Group Ltd 1974–79, Royal Worcs. Co. Ltd 1975–79; Dir Continental and Industrial Trust Ltd 1975–79; Adviser Arthur Andersen 1985–96; Dir Friends Provident Life Office 1986–88, Chair. 1988–98; Chair. Lamco Paper Sales Ltd 1987–93; Dir UK-Japan 2000 Group 1986–99 (Chair. 1986–90); Chair. Crystalate Holdings PLC 1988–90, Target Finland Ltd 1991–96 (Dir 1989–91); Vice-Pres. Local Govt Asscn 1987–, Nat. Asscn of Local Councils 1987–2000, Greater London Area Conservatives 1987–89, Pres. 1989–92; mem. UK Advisory Bd Nat. Econ. Research Assocs. Inc. 1985–98; Dir UK Council for Econ. and Environmental Devt Ltd 1987–2004; Council mem. Guide Dogs for the Blind Asscn 1987–97; Chair. Westfield Coll. Trust 1988–2000; Adviser Sumitomo Trust and Banking Co. Ltd 1989–2010; Pres. British Urban Regeneration Asscn 1990–96; Chair. Forest Healthcare NHS Trust 1991–97; mem. Advisory Bd PPRU, Queen Mary and Westfield Coll. 1991–97 (Fellow 1991–), Supervisory Bd Achmea Holding NV 1991–98; Council mem. Imperial Cancer Research Fund 1991–97 (Deputy Chair. 1994–97); Patron St Clare West Essex Hospice Care Trust 1991–; Jt Pres. MIND (Nat. Asscn of Mental Health) 1991–93, Asscn of London Govt 1995–; Vice-Pres., Nat. Housing Fed. 1991–99; Sr Vice-Pres. World Congress on Urban Growth and Devt 1992–94; Pres. London Boroughs Asscn 1992–95; Adviser Thames Estuary Airport Co. Ltd 1992–; mem. Int. Advisory Bd Marsh & McLennan Cos Inc. (US) 1993–99, Nijenrode Univ., Netherlands 1994–98; Vice-Pres. Foundation for Science and Tech. 1996–97, Chair. 1997–2006, Pres. 2006–; Pres. Asscn for Science Educ. 2002–03; Conservative; Freeman of the City of London; Hon. Freeman, London Borough of Redbridge; Hon. Fellow, Queen Mary Coll., Univ. of London 1991–, Coll. of Optometrists 2003; Hon. FRSE 2001–; Hon. mem. BAAS 2001–; Hon. Patron, Nuclear Inst. 2011–; Hon. Pres. Nat. Skills Acad. Nuclear 2008–; Hon. LLD (Univ. of the South Bank) 1997; Hon. DSc (Univ. of Ulster) 2001. *Leisure interests:* music, gardening, sailing, DIY . *Address:* House of Lords, Westminster, London, SW1A 0PW (office); Foundation for Science and Technology, 10 Carlton House Terrace, London, SW1Y 5AH, England. *Telephone:* (20) 7219-6966 (House of Lords) (office). *Fax:* (20) 7219-0759 (House of Lords) (office). *E-mail:* jenkinp@parliament.uk (office). *Website:* www.parliament.uk/biographies/lords/lord-jenkin-of-roding/1097 (office); www.foundation.org.uk.

JENKINS, Antony, MA, MBA; British banking executive; *Group Chief Executive, Barclays PLC;* b. Stoke-on-Trent, Staffs., England; m.; two c.; ed Univ. of Oxford, Cranfield Inst. of Tech.; joined Barclays 1983, completed Barclays Man. Devt Programme before going on to hold various roles in retail and corp. banking, left group 1989, rejoined bank as Head of Barclaycard 2005–09, mem. Group Exec. Cttee of Barclays PLC 2009–, CEO Barclays Retail and Business Banking (RBB) responsible for retail banking in Barclays Africa and Absa Bank 2009–12, also represented Barclays as non-exec. Dir on Bd of Absa Group Ltd and Absa Bank Ltd (South African banking subsidiaries), Group Chief Exec. Barclays PLC 2012–, Chair. Group Exec. Cttee; with Citigroup, working in London and New York 1989–2005; mem. Bd of Dirs Visa Europe Ltd 2008–11, Inst. of Int. Finance 2013–. *Leisure interests:* running marathons, listening to rock, jazz and classical music. *Address:* Barclays PLC, One Churchill Place, Canary Wharf, London, E14 5HP, England (office). *Telephone:* (20) 7116-1000 (office). *Website:* www.barclays.com (office).

JENKINS, Sir Brian Garton, Kt, GBE, MA, FCA; British fmr business executive and fmr charity administrator; b. 3 Dec. 1935, Beckenham, Kent, England; m. (Elizabeth) Ann Jenkins; one s. one d.; ed Tonbridge, Trinity Coll., Oxford; with RA, Gibraltar 1955–57; Partner, Coopers & Lybrand 1960–95; Chair. Woolwich PLC 1995–2000; Deputy Chair. Barclays PLC 2000–04; Pres. Inst. of Chartered Accountants in England and Wales 1985–86, London Chamber of Commerce and Industry 1996–98, British Computer Soc. 1997–98; Chair. Charities Aid Foundation 1998–2003; Prior of Priory of England and Islands, Order of St John 2004–10 (retd); Lord Mayor of London 1991–92; Hon. Bencher, Inner Temple; Hon. mem. Baltic Exchange; Hon. Fellow Goldsmiths Coll., London; KStJ; Hon. DSc (City Univ.); Hon. DLitt (London Guildhall Univ.). *Publication:* An Audit Approach to Computers 1978.

JENKINS, Charles H., Jr, BA, PhD; American retail executive; *Chairman, Publix Super Markets, Inc.;* b. 1944; m. Dorothy Jenkins; ed Goizueta Business School, Emory Univ. Harvard Univ.; Asst to Real Estate Vice-Pres., Publix Super Markets Inc. 1969–74, Dir 1974–, Vice-Pres. 1974–88, Exec. Vice-Pres. 1988–90, Chair. Exec. Cttee 1990–2000, COO 2000–01, CEO 2001–08, Chair. 2008–; fmr

Pres. Lakeland Chamber of Commerce; fmr mem. Bd of Overseers, Boston Symphony Orchestra; Distinguished Alumni Achievement Award, Goizueta Business School, Emory Univ. *Address:* Publix Super Markets Inc. Corporate Office, 3300 Publix Corporate Parkway, Lakeland, FL 33811, USA (office). *Telephone:* (863) 688-1188 (office). *Fax:* (863) 284-5532 (office). *E-mail:* info@publix.com (office). *Website:* www.publix.com (office).

JENKINS, Rt Rev. David Edward, MA; British ecclesiastic; b. 26 Jan. 1925, London; s. of Lionel C. Jenkins and Dora K. Jenkins (née Page); m. Stella M. Peet 1949; two s. two d.; ed St Dunstan's Coll., Catford, Queen's Coll., Oxford, Lincoln Theological Coll.; Capt. RA 1945–47; priest 1954; Succentor, Birmingham Cathedral 1953–54; Fellow and Chaplain and Praelector in Theology, Queen's Coll., Oxford 1954–69, Hon. Fellow 1990; Dir Humanum Studies, WCC, Geneva 1969–73; Dir William Temple Foundation, Manchester 1973–78; Prof. of Theology, Univ. of Leeds 1979–84, Prof. Emer. 1984–; Bishop of Durham 1984–94; Asst Bishop of Ripon 1994–; Hon. Prof. of Divinity, Univ. of Durham 1994–; Hon. Fellow, Queen's Coll. Oxford, Univ. of Sunderland; Hon. DD (Durham, Aberdeen, Trinity Coll., Toronto, Leeds, Birmingham); Hon. DLit (Teesside); Hon. DCL (Northumbria). *Publications:* The Glory of Man 1967, Living With Questions 1969, What is Man? 1970, The Contradiction of Christianity 1979, God, Miracles and the Church of England 1987, God, Politics and the Future 1988, God, Jesus and Life in the Spirit 1988, Still Living With Questions 1990, Free to Believe (with Rebecca Jenkins) 1991, Market Why and Human Wherefores 2000, The Calling of a Cuckoo 2003. *Leisure interests:* opera and church music, walking, birdwatching, nature and conservation, travel, books. *Address:* Ashbourne, Cotherstone, Barnard Castle, Co. Durham, DL12 9PR, England (home). *Telephone:* (1833) 650804 (home). *Fax:* (1833) 650714 (home).

JENKINS, Roger W., BA, MA; American oil industry executive; *President and CEO, Murphy Oil Corporation;* ed Louisiana State Univ., Tulane Univ.; joined Murphy Oil Corpn 2001, held several positions in Malaysia including man. of development of Kikeh Field, Sr Vice-Pres., North America 2007–09, Exec. Vice-Pres. of Exploration and Production 2009–13, Pres. Murphy Exploration & Production Co. 2009–12, COO Murphy Oil Corpn 2012–13, mem. Bd of Dirs, Pres. and CEO 2013–. *Address:* Murphy Oil Corporation, 200 Peach Street, El Dorado, AR 71730, USA (office). *Telephone:* (870) 862-6411 (office). *Fax:* (870) 864-6373 (office). *E-mail:* info@murphyoilcorp.com (office). *Website:* www.murphyoilcorp.com (office).

JENKINS, Sir Simon David, Kt, BA; British journalist and organization official; *Chairman, The National Trust;* b. 10 June 1943, Birmingham, England; s. of Daniel Jenkins; m. Gayle Hunnicutt 1978; one s. one step-s.; ed Mill Hill School, St John's Coll., Oxford; Hon. DLitt (Univ. of London, City Univ.); Edgar Wallace Prize 1997, Rio Tinto David Watt Memorial Prize 1998; Journalist of the Year, Granada Awards 1988, Columnist of the Year 1993. *Publications:* A City at Risk 1971, Landlords to London 1975, Newspapers: The Power and the Money 1979, The Companion Guide to Outer London 1981, Images of Hampstead 1982, The Battle for the Falklands 1983, With Respect, Ambassador 1985, The Market for Glory 1986, The Selling of Mary Davies and other writings 1993, Against the Grain 1994, Accountable to None: The Tory Nationalization of Britain 1995, England's Thousand Best Churches 1999, England's Thousand Best Houses 2003, Big Bang Localism 2004, Thatcher and Sons 2006, Wales: Churches, Houses, Castles 2008. *Leisure interests:* architecture, history of London. *Address:* The National Trust, 32 Queen Anne's Gate, London, SW1H 9AB, England (office). *Telephone:* (20) 7799-4521 (office). *E-mail:* simon.jenkins@nationaltrust.org.uk (office). *Website:* www.nationaltrust.org.uk (office).

JENNINGS, Hon. Mr Justice John R. R., BA, LLB, QC; Canadian judge; b. 10 July 1937, Toronto; s. of Robert D. Jennings and Mary Rogers; m. Eyton Margaret Embury 1964; two s.; ed Upper Canada Coll., Univ. of Toronto and Osgoode Hall Law School, Toronto; fmr mem. York Co. Legal Aid Area Cttee; mem. and past mem. Council, Medico-Legal Soc.; Chair. Nat. Family Law Section 1974–76; Pres. Co. of York Law Asscn 1976; Chair. Windsor-Essex-Mediation Centre 1981–85; Dir Canadian Bar Insurance Asscn 1987–89; Pres. Advocates' Soc. 1987, Canadian Bar Asscn 1989–90, Canadian Bar Foundation 1989–90, CBANET Inc. 1989–90; Judge, Superior Court of Justice, Ont., Pres. Canadian Superior Courts Judges' Asscn 2001–02; Hon. mem. Law Soc. of England & Wales; Fellow, American Coll. of Trial Lawyers. *Leisure interests:* tennis, travel. *Address:* 70 Montclair Avenue, Apartment 703, Toronto, Ont. M5P 1P7, Canada (home).

JENNINGS, Sir John (Southwood), Kt, CBE, PhD, FRSE, FGS; British business executive; b. 30 March 1937, Oldbury, Worcs.; s. of the late George Southwood Jennings and of Irene Beatrice Jennings (née Bartlett); m. 1st Gloria Ann Griffiths 1961 (divorced 1996); one s. one d.; m. 2nd Linda Elizabeth Baston 1997; ed Oldbury Grammar School, Univs of Birmingham and Edin.; joined Royal Dutch/Shell 1958, held various positions including Gen. Man. and Chief Rep. of Shell cos in Turkey 1976–78, Man. Dir Shell UK Exploration and Production 1979–84, Exploration and Production Co-ordinator, Shell Internationale Petroleum Mij., The Hague 1985–90; Dir The Shell Transport and Trading Co. PLC 1987–2001 (Man. Dir Royal Dutch/Shell Group of Cos. 1987–97, Chair. Shell Transport and Trading Co. 1993–97); Chair. EME (Emerging Market Econs) 2000, Intelligent Energy 2001, Spectron 2002, IdaTech,plc; Dir Det Norske Veritas 1997–2001, Robert Fleming Holdings Ltd 1998–2000, Mitie Group 1998–, Norseman Tectonics 1998–; Vice-Chair. Governing Body London Business School 1993–97 (mem. 1992–97); Vice-Pres. Liverpool School of Tropical Medicine 1991–97; Chancellor Loughborough Univ. 2003–10; mem. Council Royal Inst. of Int. Affairs 1994–97; Adviser, JPMorgan Chase 2000–; Trustee, Univ. of Edinburgh Devt Trust 1996, Exeter Univ. Council 1997–2000, mem. Int. Advisory Bd Toyota Corpn 1997, Bd of Counsellors Bechtel Corpn 1997; Commdr, Ordre Nat. du Mérite (Gabon); Hon. DSc (Edin.) 1991, (Birmingham) 1997. *Leisure interests:* fishing, travel, music, wine. *Address:* c/o Board of Directors, IdaTech plc, 2 Gresham Street, London, EC2V 7QP, EnglandUnited Kingdom.

JENRETTE, Richard Hampton, MBA; American business executive; b. 5 April 1929, Raleigh, NC; s. of Joseph M. Jenrette and Emma Love; ed Univ. of North Carolina and Harvard Grad. School of Business Admin.; with New England Life Insurance Co. 1951–53; with Brown Bros. Harriman & Co. 1957–59; Co-founder Donaldson, Lufkin & Jenrette Inc. (acquired by Credit Suisse Group 2000)

1959–96, Chair. 1986–96; Chair. Equitable Life Assurance Soc. 1987–94, Chair Exec. Cttee 1994–96, Chair. and CEO Equitable Investment Corpn (now Credit Suisse First Boston) 1986–90; mem. Bd of Dirs Blackstone Group LP 2008–; Trustee, Duke Endowment; fmr Trustee The Rockefeller Foundation; Hon. DLitt (Univ. of SC). *Publications:* Adventures With Old Houses 2000. *Website:* www.blackstone.com.

JENSEN, Hans Peter, PhD, DSc; Danish chemist and researcher; b. 11 June 1943, Copenhagen; m. Helle Rønnow Olesen 1965; two s. one d.; ed Univ. of Copenhagen, Chalmers Univ. of Tech., Gothenburg; Asst Prof., Tech. Univ. of Denmark 1969, Assoc. Prof. 1972, Head of Chem. Dept 1980–83, Dean of Chem. Faculty 1983–86, Rector 1986–2001; Deputy Dir Inst. of Food Safety and Nutrition 2001–04; Research Dir Danish Inst. for Food and Veterinary Research 2004–06; Head of Natural Sciences Dept, Roskilde Univ. 2007; currently Prin. Egmont H. Petersens Kollegium, Copenhagen; Research Assoc. Univ. of Oregon 1974–75, Visiting Prof. 1978, 1984; mem. Danish Natural Science Research Council 1984–92, Danish Acad. of Tech. Sciences, Cttee on Higher Educ. and Research (Council of Europe) 1986–2001, Evaluation Group of European Postgrad. Training Programme 1989–93, Cultural Foundation between Denmark and Finland 1989–97, Fulbright Comm. of Denmark 1990–2001; mem. Advisory Forum European Food Safety Authority 2003–, Velux Foundation 2004–14; Chair. Danish Rectors' Conf. 1993–2000; Chair. Asscn of Nordic Univ. Rectors' Confs 1995–2001; mem. Bd of Govs Jt Research Centre of EU 2001–12; Commdr Order of Dannebrog 1999; Dr hc (Shenandoah Univ., USA) 1993, (Helsinki Univ. of Tech.) 1998, (State Univ. of NY) 1998, (Kaunas Univ. of Tech., Lithuania) 2013. *Publications:* General Chemistry (textbook) 1985; articles in professional journals. *Leisure interests:* music, literature. *Address:* Egmont H. Petersens Kollegium, Nørre Allé 75, 2100 Copenhagen; Jagtvej 172, 2100 Copenhagen, Denmark (home). *Telephone:* 35200022 (office); 39653429 (home). *E-mail:* efor@ehp.dk (office). *Website:* www.egmont-kol.dk.

JENSEN, Siv, BEcons; Norwegian politician; *Minister of Finance;* b. 1 June 1969, Oslo; d. of Tore Jensen and Monica Kjelsberg; ed Norwegian School of Econs; began career in Sales Dept, Radio 1 1992–94; mem. City Council, Oslo 1995–99; Deputy mem. Storting (Parl.) 1993–97, mem. Storting for Oslo 1997–, Chair. Finance Cttee 2001–05, mem. Foreign Affairs Cttee 2005–09, Foreign Affairs and Defence Cttee 2009–13; Minister of Finance 2013–; mem. Bd Oslo Progress Party 1992–94, Deputy Chair., Organizational Affairs 1995–96, mem. Progress Party Central Exec. Cttee 1988–99, First Deputy Chair., Progress Party 1999–2006, Leader and Chair. 2006–. *Address:* Ministry of Finance, Akersgt. 40, POB 8008 Dep., 0030 Oslo, Norway (office). *Telephone:* 22-24-90-90 (office). *Fax:* 22-24-95-14 (office). *E-mail:* postmottak@fin.dep.no (office). *Website:* www.regjeringen.no/fin (office).

JENSSEN, Olav Christopher; Norwegian artist; b. 1954, Sortland, Vesteraland; ed Statens Kunstakademi, Oslo; Prof. of Painting, Hochschule fur Bildende Kunst, Hamburg 1996–2003; Prof., Hochschule für Bildende Künste Braunschweig (Braunschweig Univ. of Art) 2007–; official artist, Offshore Northern Seas Int. Conf. 2000; Willy Brandt Award 2001. *Address:* Hochschule für Bildende Künste Braunschweig, Johannes-Selenka-Platz 1, 38118 Braunschweig, Germany.

JENTSCH, Thomas J., PhD, MD; German neuropathologist and academic; *Director, Dept of Physiology and Pathology of Ion Transport, Leibniz Institut für Molekulare Pharmakologie, Berlin;* ed Free Univ., Berlin and Fritz-Haber-Institut, Max-Planck-Gesellschaft; Postdoctoral Researcher, Institut für Klinische Physiologie, Free Univ., Berlin and Whitehead Inst. for Biomedical Research, MIT, USA; Research Group Leader, Zentrum für Molekulare Neurobiologie Hamburg (ZMNH), Hamburg Univ., Prof. and Dir Institute for Molecular Neuropathology, ZMNH 1993–2006, Dir ZMNH 1995–98, 2001–03; Dir, Dept of Physiology and Pathology of Ion Transport, Leibniz Institut für Molekulare Pharmakologie, Berlin 2006–; Prof. Charité, Universitätsmedizin Berlin 2006–; Principal Investigator, NeuroCure Clinical Research Center 2008–; mem. Int. Scientific Advisory Bd, Instituto de Ciencias Biomédicas de la Universidad de Chile; mem. Academia Europaea 2000, European Molecular Biology Org. (EMBO) 2000, Berlin-Brandenburg Acad. of Sciences and Humanities 2001; Wilhelm Vaillant Prize for Biomedical Research 1992, Gottfried Wilhelm Leibniz Prize, Deutsche Forschungsgemeinschaft 1995, Alfred Hauptmann Prize for Research on Epilepsy 1998, Franz Volhard Prize for Research in Nephrology 1998, Zülch Prize, Gertrud-Reemtsma Foundation 1999, Feldberg Prize, Feldberg Foundation for Anglo-German Scientific Exchange 2000, Familie Hansen Prize 2000, Prix Louis-Jeantet de médecine 2000, Ernst Jung Prize for Medicine 2001, Adolf-Fick Prize for Physiology 2004, Homer W. Smith Award for Nephrology 2004. *Publications:* numerous articles in scientific journals. *Address:* Leibniz Institut für Molekulare Pharmakologie, Timoféeff-Ressovsky Haus, Campus Berlin-Buch, Robert Roesslestrasse 10, 13125 Berlin, Germany (office). *Telephone:* (30) 94062961 (office). *Fax:* (30) 94062960 (office). *E-mail:* jentsch@fmp-berlin.de (office). *Website:* www.fmp-berlin.de/jentsch.html (office).

JERANDI, Othman, BA; Tunisian diplomatist and politician; *Minister of Foreign Affairs;* b. Hammam Lif; m. Raja Belarbi Jerandi; three c.; Sec. of Foreign Affairs 1979–81, First Sec., Embassy in Kuwait City 1981–88, Counsellor, Cabinet of Minister of Foreign Affairs 1988–90, Counsellor, Perm. Mission to UN, New York 1990–94, Amb. to Nigeria (also accred to Ghana, Sierra Leone, Liberia) 1994–97, Dir of Political, Econ. and Cooperation Affairs with Africa and African Union 1998–2000, Deputy Perm. Rep., Perm. Mission to UN, New York 2000–02, elected Chair. Comm. on the Status of Women 2002, Amb. to South Korea 2002–05, Dir-Gen. Int. Orgs and Confs 2005–08, Chargé de Mission, Minister of Foreign Affairs 2008–10, Amb. to Jordan 2010–11, Perm. Rep. to UN, New York 2011–13, Minister of Foreign Affairs 2013–. *Address:* Ministry of Foreign Affairs, Avenue de la Ligue des Etats arabes, Nord Hilton, 1030 Tunis, Tunisia. *Telephone:* (71) 847-500. *Fax:* (71) 785-025. *E-mail:* mae@diplomatie.gov.tn. *Website:* www.diplomatie.gov.tn.

JEREMIĆ, Vuk, BA, MPA, PhD; Serbian politician; b. 3 July 1975, Belgrade; s. of Miško Jeremić and Sena Buljubašić; m. Nataša Jeremić; ed Univ. of Cambridge, Imperial Coll., England, Harvard Univ., USA; Co-founder and Financial Man. Org. of Serbian Students Abroad 1997; fmr Financial Analyst, Deutsche Bank, Dresdner Kleinwort Benson Bank and AstraZeneca Pharmaceuticals, London; Adviser to Minister of Telecommunications 2000–03; Adviser to Minister of Defence of Serbia and Montenegro 2003–04; Adviser on Int. Relations and Head,

Office of the Pres. of Serbia 2004–07; Minister of Foreign Affairs 2007–12; Pres. 67th Session of UN Gen. Ass., New York 2012–13; mem. Democratic Party –2013, Pres. Bd of Int. Relations 2004–06, mem. Exec. Bd 2006–13. *Address:* c/o Ministry of Foreign Affairs, 11000 Belgrade, Kneza Miloša 24–26, Serbia. *E-mail:* msp@mfa .rs.

JERIBI, Ghazi, Lic. en Droit; Tunisian lawyer and government official; *Minister of National Defence;* b. 5 Dec. 1955, Tunis; m.; three c.; ed Univ. of Paris, France; served with Admin. Tribunal (part of State Council) 1984–2011, positions included Deputy Adviser 1984–91, Adviser 1991–96, Pres., Educ. Section 1996–99, Pres. of the Chamber 1996–99, State Commr-Gen. 1999–2001, First Pres., Admin. Tribunal 2007–11; teacher, Ecole Nat. d'Admin, Tunis 1988–2013; Lecturer, EPAM Mil. Acad. 1989–96; Lecturer, Judiciary Graduate School 2000–05; expert trainer on competition law, UNCTAD 2005–06; Pres., Competition Council 2001–06; Chair., Comm. on Tax Disputes 1997–2001, High Cttee for Admin. and Financial Control 2011; Minister of Nat. Defence 2014–; Legal Dir, Arab Inst. for Human Rights 1990–92; Vice-Pres. Tunisian Basketball Fed. 1994–96. *Publications:* numerous articles in nat. and int. journals on admin. law and reform, human rights and civil liberties, tax litigation, competition law and sports law. *Leisure interests:* basketball (played for nat. team 1975–85). *Address:* Ministry of National Defence, blvd Bab Menara, 1008 Tunis, Tunisia (office). *Telephone:* (71) 560-240 (office). *Fax:* (71) 561-804 (office). *E-mail:* defnat@defense.tn (office). *Website:* www .defense.tn (office).

JERLAGIĆ, Amer; Bosnia and Herzegovina engineer and politician; *President, Party for Bosnia and Herzegovina;* b. 25 May 1967, Livno; ed Univ. of Sarajevo; several years with Elektroprivreda BiH dd (power transmission co.), including Head of Mostar Section, Elektroprenos Sarajevo 1996–97, Tech. Dir 1997–98, Man., Sarajevo Plant 1998–2000, Dir, Power Distribution, Sarajevo 2004–07, Acting Gen. Man., Elektroprivreda BiH dd 2007–08, Gen. Man. 2008–11; mem. Party for Bosnia and Herzegovina (SBiH), Pres. 2012–. *Address:* Party for Bosnia and Herzegovina (SBiH), 71000 Sarajevo, Fra Grge Martića 2/II, Bosnia (office). *Telephone:* (33) 573470 (office). *Fax:* (33) 475597 (office). *E-mail:* zabih@zabih.ba (office). *Website:* www.zabih.ba (office).

JERUSALEM, Siegfried; German singer (tenor), academic and university administrator; *Rector, Hochschule für Musik Nürnberg-Augsburg;* b. 17 April 1940, Oberhausen; m. 1980; one s. one d.; ed studied violin and piano at Folkwang Hochschule, Essen, studied singing with Hertha Kalcher, Stuttgart; played bassoon in German orchestras, including Stuttgart Radio Symphony Orchestra 1961–77; made singing debut in Zigeunerbaron 1975; debut Bayreuth Festival 1977, Metropolitan Opera, New York 1980, La Scala 1981, Vienna State Opera 1979; sang Loge and Siegfried, Wagner's Ring Cycle, Metropolitan New York 1990, Tristan, Bayreuth 1993, Wagner's Ring Cycle, Vienna 1994, Wagner's Rienzi, Vienna 1997, Tristana, Berlin Staatsoper 2000; Prof., Hochschule für Musik Nürnberg-Augsburg 2000–, Rector 2001–; Order of Merit (Germany) 1997; Grammy Award for Wagner's Ring Cycle 1982, for Rheingold 1991, Bundesverdienstkreuz (1st Class) 1996, Bambi Award 1996. *Leisure interests:* video, tennis, photography, golf. *Address:* Hochschule für Musik Nürnberg-Augsburg, Veilhofstr. 34, 90489 Nürnberg, Germany (office). *Telephone:* (911) 2318443 (office). *Fax:* (911) 2317697 (office). *E-mail:* hfm-rektorat@stadt.nuernberg.de (office). *Website:* www.hfm-n-a.de (office).

JERVIS, Robert, BA, PhD; American political scientist and academic; *Adlai E. Stevenson Professor of International Affairs, Columbia University;* ed Oberlin Coll., Univ. of California, Berkeley; Asst Prof. of Govt, Harvard Univ. 1968–74, Assoc. Prof. 1972–74; Prof. of Political Science, UCLA 1974–80; fmr Prof. Yale Univ., Hebrew Univ.; currently Adlai E. Stevenson Prof. of Int. Affairs and Deputy Chair. Political Science Dept, Columbia Univ., Acting Chair. 2009–10; Vice-Pres. American Political Science Asscn 1988–89, Pres. 1999–2000; Co-ed. Security Studies Series, Cornell Univ. Press; Fellow, AAAS, American Acad. of Arts and Sciences; mem. bd of eight scholarly journals; Career Achievement Award, Security Studies Section, Int. Studies Asscn 1996, Nevitt Sanford Award for Distinguished Professional Contrib. to Political Psychology 1998, Lionel Trilling Award for Best Book by Columbia Faculty Mem. 1998, NAS Award for Behavioral Science Research Relevant to the Prevention of Nuclear War 2006. *Publications:* The Logic of Images in International Relations 1970, Perception and Misperception in International Politics 1976, The Illogic of American Nuclear Strategy 1984, Psychology and Deterrence (co-author) 1985, The Meaning of the Nuclear Revolution (Grawemeyer Award for Ideas Improving World Order 1990) 1989, Systems Effects: Complexity in Political and Social Life 1997, International Politics: Enduring Concepts and Contemporary Issues (co-ed.) 1999, The Origins of Major War (co-ed.) 2000, American Foreign Policy in a New Era 2005; numerous articles in professional journals and chapters in books. *Address:* Department of Political Science, Columbia University, 1333 International Affairs Building, Mail Code 3347, 420 West 118th Street, New York, NY 10027, USA (office). *Telephone:* (212) 854-4610 (office). *Fax:* (212) 864-1686 (office). *E-mail:* rlj1@columbia.edu (office). *Website:* www.columbia.edu/cu/polosci (office).

JERVIS, Simon Swynfen, MA, FSA; British art historian; b. 9 Jan. 1943, Yoxford; s. of the late John Swynfen Jervis and of Diana Parker (née Marriott); m. Fionnuala MacMahon 1969; one s. one d.; ed Downside School, Corpus Christi Coll., Cambridge; with Leicester Museum and Art Gallery 1964–66; Asst Keeper, Furniture Dept, Victoria and Albert Museum, London 1966–75, Deputy Keeper 1975–79, Acting Keeper 1989, Curator 1989–90; Dir Fitzwilliam Museum, Cambridge 1990–95; Dir of Historic Bldgs, Nat. Trust 1995–2002; mem. Council, Soc. of Antiquaries 1986–88 (Pres. 1995–2001), Royal Archaeological Inst. 1987–91, Walpole Soc. 1990–95 (Chair. 2004–); Kelmscott Cttee 2001–; Chair. Nat. Trust Arts Panel 1987–95; Ed. Furniture History Soc. 1987–91, Chair. 1998–; Dir Burlington Magazine 1993–, Trustee 1997–; Guest Scholar, J. Paul Getty Museum 1988–89; Trustee, Royal Collection Trust 1993–2001, Leche Trust 1995–; Sir John Soane's Museum 1999– (Life Trustee 2002–); mem. Reviewing Cttee on the Export of Works of Art; Iris Foundation Award for Outstanding Contributions to the Decorative Arts 2002. *Publications:* Victorian Furniture 1968, Victorian and Edwardian Decorative Art: the Handley Read Collection 1972, Printed Furniture Designs Before 1650 1974, High Victorian Design 1974, The Penguin Dictionary of Design and Designers 1984, Furniture from Austria and Hungary in the Victoria and Albert Museum 1986. *Leisure interests:* churches, tennis. *Address:* 45 Bedford

Gardens, London, W8 7EF, England (office). *Telephone:* (20) 7727-8739 (home). *Fax:* (20) 7727-8739 (home).

JESIH, Boris, PhD; Slovenian artist and poet; b. 8 Aug. 1943, Škofja Loka; s. of Svetoslav Jesih and Kristina Jesih; m. Bojana Žokalj 1970 (divorced 1981); one s. one d.; ed Acad. of Fine Arts, Ljubljana, Berlin; works appear in numerous collections; has published several books of poetry; Ed.-in-Chief Razprave in Gradivo; 10 nat. and 10 int. awards. *Publications include:* The Apple Tree and the Grafts 1979. *Leisure interests:* basketball, fishing. *Address:* Department of Fine Arts Education, University of Ljubljana, Kardeljeva Ploscad 16, 1000 Ljubljana (office). *Telephone:* (1) 589-22-00 (office). *Fax:* (1) 589-22-33 (office). *Website:* www .pef.uni-lj.si (office).

JESSEN-PETERSEN, Søren; Danish UN official and academic; m.; four c.; trained as lawyer and journalist; served in Africa UNHCR 1972–77, Chief of Secr. UNHCR Exec. Cttee 1981–82, Exec. Sec. Second Int. Conf. on Assistance to Refugees in Africa 1983–84, Exec. Sec. Intergovernmental Conf. on Asylum Seekers and Refugees in Europe 1985, opened UNHCR Regional Office for Nordic Countries, Stockholm 1986, served as High Commr's Regional Rep. 1986–89; Special Adviser to UN Under-Sec.-Gen. for Political Affairs 1989; mem. UN Sec.-Gen.'s Task Force on Namibia 1989; Chef de Cabinet of High Commr UNHCR 1990–93, Dir External Relations 1992–94, Dir UNHCR Liaison Office at UN HQ, NY 1994–98, UN Special Envoy to fmr Yugoslavia 1995–96, Asst High Commr UNHCR, Geneva 1998–2001; Chair. MARRI Steering Cttee 2002–04; EU Special Rep. in Skopje 2004; Special Rep. of UN Sec.-Gen. and Head, UN Interim Admin Mission in Kosovo (UNMIK) 2004–06; Dir Washington, DC office, Independent Diplomat (advisory org.) –2010; currently Adjunct Prof. of Int. Relations, School of Advanced International Studies (SAIS), Johns Hopkins Univ., Bologna, Italy, also Adjunct Prof., SAIS Washington; fmr Guest Scholar, United States Institute of Peace. *Address:* Paul H. Nitze School of Advanced International Studies, Johns Hopkins University, 1740 Massachusetts Avenue, NW, Washington, DC 20036, USA. *Website:* www.sais-jhu.edu.

JESZENSZKY, Géza, PhD; Hungarian historian, academic and politician; b. 10 Nov. 1941, Budapest; s. of Zoltán Jeszenszky and Pálma Miskolczy-Simon; m. Edit Héjj; one s. one d.; ed Eötvös Loránd Univ., Budapest; banned from higher educ. for two years 1956–57; subject specialist with Nat. Széchényi Library 1968–76; Sr Lecturer, Budapest Univ. of Econs (now Corvinus Univ. of Budapest) 1976–81, Reader 1981, Dean of the School of Political and Social Sciences 1989–90, Head, Faculty of Int. Relations 1990–91, resumed teaching history and int. relations 2002–; Guest Scholar, Woodrow Wilson Center, USA 1985; Visiting Fulbright Prof., Univ. of California, Santa Barbara, USA 1984–86, UCLA 1986; Helen De Roy Visiting Prof., Univ. of Michigan, USA 1996; Visiting Prof., Coll. of Europe, Warsaw-Natolin, Babes-Bolyai Univ., Cluj-Napoca/Kolozsvár, Romania; Founding mem. Hungarian Democratic Forum 1988–96, Head of Foreign Affairs Cttee 1988–90, mem. Presidency 1990–94; Minister of Foreign Affairs 1990–94; mem. Parl. 1994–98; Pres. Hungarian Atlantic Council 1995–98; Amb. to USA 1998–2002; Pres. Hungarian Carpathian Asscn 2002–; numerous decorations; C.I.E.S. Fulbright Grant 1984–86. *Publications:* Prestige Lost, The Changing Image of Hungary in Great Britain 1894–1918 1986, The Hungarian Question in British Politics 1848–1914 1986, István Tisza: Villain or Tragic Hero? 1987, Lessons of Appeasement 1994, More Bosnias? National and Ethnic Tensions in the Post-Communist World 1997, József Antall, Selected Speeches and Interviews (ed.), Post-Communist Europe and Its National/Ethnic Problems 2009; other studies in Hungarian and English. *Leisure interests:* literature, jazz, skiing, rowing, mountaineering. *Address:* Budapesti Corvinus Egyetem (Corvinus University of Budapest), 1093 Budapest, Fővám tér 8, Hungary (office). *Telephone:* (1) 482-5000 (office). *Fax:* (1) 482-5019 (office). *E-mail:* intoffice@uni-corvinus.hu (office); geza@jeszen.hu (office). *Website:* www.uni-corvinus.hu (office); www .karpategyesulet.hu.

JETER, Carmelita; American track and field athlete; b. 24 Nov. 1979, Los Angeles, Calif.; ed Bishop Montgomery High School, California State Univ., Dominguez Hills; specializes in 100m; silver medal, 60m, US Indoor Track and Field Championships 2007, gold medal, 4×100m relay, World Athletics Championships, Osaka 2007, bronze medal, 100m Osaka 2007, Berlin 2009, gold medal, 100m, 4×100m relay, Daegu 2011, silver medal, 200m, Daegu 2011, silver medal, 100m, London Olympics 2012, bronze medal, 200m London Olympics 2012, bronze medal, World Athletics Championships, Moscow 2013; gold medal, 100m, World Athletics Final, Stuttgart 2007, Thessaloniki 2009; silver medal, 60m, World Indoor Athletics Championships, Doha 2010; winner, Shanghai Golden Grand Prix (10.64s) 2009 (second fastest woman ever in 100m); held three of the top ten times ever run 2011; personal bests: 55m 6.84s, Fresno, Calif. 2008, 60m 7.02s, Albuquerque, NM 2010, 100m 10.64s, Shanghai 2009, 200m 22.20s, Fontvieille, Monaco 2011; mem. Nike Club; coach: John Smith; Women's Jesse Owens Award 2011. *Address:* c/o Chris Layne, Total Sports Management US, Inc., 507 Laurel Avenue, Johnson City, TN 37604, USA. *Telephone:* (423) 282-3888. *Fax:* (423) 282-2996. *E-mail:* office@totalsportsus.com. *Website:* www.totalsportsus.com; www .carmelitajeter.com.

JETER, Derek Sanderson; American professional baseball player; b. 26 June 1974, Pequannock, NJ; s. of Charles Jeter and Dorothy Jeter; ed Kalamazoo Central High School, Mich.; drafted by NY Yankees in first round amateur draft 1992; Major League Baseball debut 29 May 1995; Capt. NY Yankees; Founder and Pres. Turn2 Foundation 1996–; f. Jeter Publishing (imprint of Simon & Schuster) 2013; American Baseball Coaches Asscn High School Player of the Year 1992; American League Rookie of the Year 1996; selected for American League All-Star Team 1998–2002, 2004, 2006–09; Most Valuable Player (MVP) World Series 2000; MVP All-Star Game 2000; Babe Ruth Award 2000; Hank Aaron Award 2006, 2009; Roberto Clemente Award 2009; Sports Illustrated Sportsman of the Year 2009. *Publications:* The Life You Imagine 2001, Game Day: My Life On and Off the Field 2001. *Address:* c/o New York Yankees, Yankee Stadium, East 161st Street and River Avenue, Bronx, New York, NY 10451, USA. *Telephone:* (718) 293-4300. *Fax:* (718) 293-8431. *Website:* derekjeter.mlb.com/players/jeter_derek/index.jsp; newyork.yankees.mlb.com; www.turn2foundation.org.

JETHMALANI, Ram, LLB; Indian lawyer and politician; b. 14 Sept. 1923, Shikharpur, British India (now Pakistan); m. 1st Durga 1941, three c.; m. 2nd Ratna Shehani 1947, one c.; ed S.C. Shahani Law Coll., Karachi; co-f. law firm in Karachi 1940s; relocated to India 1948; part-time Prof., Govt Law Coll., Mumbai 1953; fmrly taught Comparative Law, Wayne State Univ., Detroit, USA; elected mem. Rajya Sabha 1988; Union Minister of Law, Justice and Co. Affairs 1996–98, 1999–2000 (resgnd), Union Minister of Urban Affairs and Employment 1998–99; elected MP (Bharatiya Janata Party) for state of Rajasthan; Chair. Bar Asscn of India 1975–77; fmr Chair. Bar Council of India (four times); fmr mem. International Bar Asscn. *Address:* 2 Akbar Road, New Delhi, 110 011; 41 Advent, 12-A General Jagannath Bhonsale Marg, Mumbai, 400 021, India. *Telephone:* (11) 23792287 (New Delhi); (11) 23794651 (New Delhi); (22) 22024403 (Mumbai). *Fax:* (22) 22024990 (Mumbai). *E-mail:* jetmlni@sansad.nic.in (office).

JETTOU, Driss; Moroccan politician; b. 24 May 1945, El Jadida; m.; four c.; ed Lycée El Khawarizmi de Casablanca, Univ. of Rabat, Cordwainers Coll., London, UK; fmr Pres. Moroccan Fed. of Leather Industries; fmr Vice-Pres. Moroccan Asscn of Exporters; Minister of Trade and Industry 1994–95, of Culture and Foreign Trade 1995–97, of Trade, Industry and Culture 1997–98, of the Interior 1998–2002; Prime Minister of Morocco 2002–07; launched investment fund with Italian pnr Muteo 2008; apptd Pres. Office Cherifien des Phosphates 2002; fmr mem. Gen. Confed. of Moroccan Enterprises; Grande Chevalier, Wissam du Trône. *Address:* c/o Office of the Prime Minister, Palais Royal, Le Méchouar, Rabat, Morocco (office).

JEUNET, Jean-Pierre; French film director; b. 1955, Roanne; worked as telecommunications engineer; dir of TV commercials and short films. *Films:* L'évasion 1978, Le manège (César Award) 1980 (both co-dir with Marc Caro), Le bunker de la dernière rafale 1981, Pas de repos pour Billy Brakko 1984, Foutaises (César Award) 1989, Delicatessen (César Award) 1991, Le cité des enfants perdus 1995, Alien: Resurrection 1997, Le fabuleux destin d'Amélie Poulain (Amélie) (Amanda Award, American Screenwriters Asscn Award, Bafta Film Award, David Lean Award for Direction, Canberra Int. Film Festival Audience Award, Chicago Int. Film Festival Audience Award, Czech Lion, César Award) 2001, Un long dimanche de fiançailles 2004, Micmacs 2009. *Address:* c/o Artmédia, 20 Avenue Rapp, 75007 Paris, France. *Telephone:* 1-43-17-33-00 (office). *Website:* www .jpjeunetlesite.online.fr.

JEWELL, Sally, BS; American (b. British) business executive and government official; *Secretary of the Interior;* b. 1955, England; d. of Peter Roffey and Anne Roffey (née Murphy); m. Warren Jewell; one s. one d.; ed Univ. of Washington; Field Production Engineer, Mobil Oil Corpn, Okla 1978–81; Petroleum Engineer, Rainier Bank, Seattle 1981–87; Exec. Vice-Pres. Security Pacific Bank, Wash. 1987–92; Pres. and CEO, WestOne Bancorp 1992–95; Pres., Commercial Banking, Washington Mutual, Inc. 1996–2000; mem. Bd of Dirs Recreational Equipment, Inc. (REI) 1996–2013, Pres. and COO 2000–05, Pres. and CEO 2005–13; Sec., US Dept of the Interior, Washington, DC 2013–; mem. Bd of Dirs Mountains to Sound Greenway Trust 1991–, Nat. Parks Conservation Asscn, Initiative for Global Devt; CEO of Year, Puget Sound Business Journal 2006, Non-Profit Dir of Year Award, Nat. Asscn of Corp. Dirs 2008, Green Globe Environmental Catalyst Award 2008, Nat. Audubon Soc. Rachel Carson Award for Environmental Conservation 2009. *Address:* Department of the Interior, 1849 C Street, NW, Washington, DC 20240, USA (office). *Telephone:* (202) 208-3100 (office). *Fax:* (202) 208-5048 (office). *E-mail:* feedback@ios.doi.gov (office). *Website:* www.doi.gov (office).

JEWISON, Norman Frederick, BA, CC, DD; Canadian film director; b. 21 July 1926, Toronto; s. of Percy Joseph Jewison and Dorothy Irene Jewison (née Weaver); m. Margaret Dixon 1953; two s. one d.; ed Malvern Collegiate High School, Toronto, Victoria Coll., Univ. of Toronto; stage actor, Toronto; TV actor 1950–52; TV director for CBC 1953–58, CBS 1958–61; film director 1961–; Faculty mem. Inst. for American Studies, Salzburg, Austria 1969; Pres. D'Avoriaz Film Festival 1981–; Dir Centre for Advanced Film Studies 1987–; director TV shows for Harry Belafonte, Andy Williams, Judy Garland and Danny Kaye; mem. Electoral Bd, Dirs Guild of America; mem. Canadian Arts Council; Chair. Canadian Film Centre 2002; Chancellor Victoria Coll., Univ. of Toronto 2004; Hon. LLD (Univ. of Western Ont.) 1974; Acad. of Canada Special Achievement Award 1988, Emmy Award 1960, Golden Globe Award 1966, Best Dir, Berlin Film Festival for Moonstruck 1988, Irving Thalberg Memorial Prize 1999. *Films include:* Forty Pounds of Trouble, The Thrill of It All 1963, Send Me No Flowers 1964 (all for Universal Studios), Art of Love, The Cincinnati Kid 1965, The Russians are Coming (also producer) 1966, In the Heat of the Night (Acad. Award 1967), The Thomas Crown Affair (also producer) 1967, Gaily, Gaily 1968, The Landlord (producer) 1969, Fiddler on the Roof (also producer) 1970, Jesus Christ Superstar (also producer) 1972, Billy Two Hats (producer) 1972, Rollerball 1974, F.I.S.T. (also producer) 1977, And Justice for All 1979, Best Friends 1982, A Soldier's Story 1984, Agnes of God 1985, Moonstruck 1987, In Country 1989, Other People's Money 1991, Only You 1994, Bogus 1996, The Hurricane 1999, Dinner with Friends (tv) 2001, The Statement 2003. *Leisure interests:* skiing, yachting, tennis. *Address:* 18 Gloucester Lane, Toronto, ON M4Y IL5, Canada. *Telephone:* (416) 923-2787 (office). *Fax:* (416) 923-8580 (office).

JEWITT, David C., BSc, MS, PhD; British/American astronomer and academic; *Professor, Department of Earth and Space Sciences and Department of Physics and Astronomy and Director, Institute for Planets and Exoplanets, University of California, Los Angeles;* b. 1958, England; m. Jing Li; ed Univ. Coll., London, California Inst. of Tech.; summer student, Royal Greenwich Observatory, Herstmonceux Castle, Sussex 1978; Anthony Fellowship, California Inst. of Tech. 1979–80, Research Asst 1980–83; Asst Prof., MIT 1983–88; Assoc. Astronomer, Inst. for Astronomy, Univ. of Hawaii 1988–93, Assoc. Prof., Dept of Physics and Astronomy 1988–93, Astronomer, Inst. for Astronomy 1993–2009, Prof., Dept of Physics and Astronomy 1993–2009; Prof., Dept of Earth and Space Sciences, UCLA 2009–, mem. Inst. for Geophysics and Planetary Physics 2009–, Prof., Dept of Physics and Astronomy 2010–, Dir Inst. for Planets and Exoplanets 2011–; Adjunct Prof., Nat. Central Univ., Taiwan 2007; mem. NAS; Foreign mem. Norwegian Acad. of Sciences and Letters 2012; Fellow, American Acad. of Arts and Sciences 2005, AAAS 2005; Hon. Prof., Nat. Astronomical Observatory, Chinese Acad. of Sciences 2006; Regent's Medal for Excellence in Research, Univ. of Hawaii 1994, Hawaii Scientist of the Year, ARCS 1996, Exceptional Scientific Achieve-

ment Medal, NASA 1996, Shaw Prize in Astronomy (co-recipient) 2012, Kavli Prize 2012. *Publications:* numerous papers in professional journals. *Address:* Department of Earth and Space Sciences, 3713 Geology Building, UCLA, 595 Charles Young Drive East, Los Angeles, CA 90095-1567, USA (office). *Telephone:* (310) 825-2521 (office). *E-mail:* jewitt@ucla.edu (office). *Website:* www2.ess.ucla.edu/~jewitt/ David_Jewitt.html (office).

JEWKES, Sir Gordon Wesley, Kt, KCMG; British diplomatist; b. 18 Nov. 1931, Langley Moor, Co. Durham, England; s. of the late Jesse Jewkes; m. 1st Joyce Lyons 1954 (died 2005); two s.; m. 2nd Estelle Heime 2008; ed Barrow Grammar School, Magnus Grammar School, Newark-on-Trent; joined Colonial Office 1948; with army 1950–52; with Gen. Register Office 1950–63, 1965–68; mem. Civil Service Pay Research Unit 1963–65; joined FCO 1968; Commercial Consul, Chicago 1969–72, Consul-Gen. 1982–85; Deputy High Commr, Port of Spain 1972–75; Head of Finance Dept, FCO and Finance Officer of Diplomatic Service 1975–79; Consul-Gen. Cleveland 1979–82; Gov. Falkland Islands, Commr S Georgia and S Sandwich Islands, High Commr British Antarctic Territory 1985–88; Consul-Gen., New York and Dir-Gen. Trade and Investment, USA 1989–91; mem. Bd of Dirs Hogg Group PLC 1992–94, Slough Estates PLC 1992–2002; Exec. Dir The Walpole Cttee 1992–96; mem. Council Univ. of Buckingham 1996–2001, Marshall Aid Commemoration Comm. 1996–99, Salvation Army London Advisory Bd 1996–2001; Hon. DUniv (Buckingham) 2007. *Leisure interests:* music, travel, walking. *Address:* 53 Woodside Avenue, Beaconsfield, Bucks., HP9 1JH, England.

JHA, Paramananda, LLM, MA; Nepalese lawyer and politician; *Vice-President;* b. 20 April 1945, Mauaha, Saptari; s. of the late Madan Jha; m.; two s. two d.; ed Tribhuvan Univ., Kathmandu, Vrije Univ. Brussels, Belgium; joined civil service as Section Officer 1972, becoming Jt Sec., Ministry of Justice 1976; Judge, Kathmandu Dist Court, Zonal and Appellate courts, later Ad Hoc Justice, Supreme Court –2007 (resgnd); mem. Madhesi Jana Adhikar Forum Nepal (Madhesi People's Rights Forum Nepal); Vice-Pres. of Nepal 2008–. *Address:* Office of the Vice President, Kathmandu (office); Boudh Dwar Marg, Kumarigal 446/14, Ward 8, Kathmandu, Nepal (home). *Telephone:* (1) 4228199 (office); (1) 4486118 (home). *Fax:* (1) 4228284 (office); (1) 4486118 (home). *E-mail:* vicepresidentnp@gmail.com (office); Kumarigal 2062@hotmail.com (office).

JHA, Sanjay K., BSc, PhD; British/American computer engineer and business executive; *Co-CEO, Motorola, Inc.;* b. India; ed Univs of Liverpool and Strathclyde, UK; moved to US from UK 1994; held lead design eng roles with Brooktree Corpn, San Diego, and GEC Hirst Research Labs, London, UK; joined Qualcomm as Sr Engineer with VLSI (very large-scale integration) Group 1994–97, Vice-Pres. of Eng 1997–98, Sr Vice-Pres. of Eng 1998–2002, led formation of Qualcomm Technologies & Ventures 2002, managed both tech. investment portfolio and new tech. group as Sr Vice-Pres. and Gen. Man. 2002–03, Exec. Vice-Pres. Qualcomm and Pres. Qualcomm CDMA Technologies (chipset and software div.) 2003–06, COO Qualcomm Inc. 2006–08, oversaw Corp. Research and Devt and Qualcomm Flarion Technologies; joined Motorola, Inc. in 2008, mem. Bd of Dirs and Co-CEO 2008–, also CEO Motorola Mobility. *Address:* Motorola, Inc., 1303 East Algonquin Road, Schaumburg, IL 60196, USA (office). *Telephone:* (847) 576-5000 (office). *Fax:* (847) 576-5372 (office). *E-mail:* info@motorola.com (office). *Website:* www.motorola .com (office).

JI, Chaozhu, BSc; Chinese diplomatist (retired); b. 30 July 1929, Shanxi Prov.; s. of Prof. Chi Kungchuan; m. Wang Xiangtong 1957; two s.; ed Harvard Univ., USA, Tsinghua Univ., Beijing; stenographer and typist at Panmunjom, Korea for Chinese People's Volunteers 1952–54; English interpreter for Mao Zedong, Zhou Enlai and others 1955–73; Counsellor at Liaison Office of China in Washington, DC 1973–75; Deputy Dir Dept for Int. Orgs and Confs, Ministry of Foreign Affairs 1975–79, Deputy Dir of American and Oceanic Affairs 1979–82; Minister-Counsellor of Chinese Embassy in Washington, DC 1982–85; Amb. to Fiji, Kiribati and Vanuatu 1985–87; Amb. to UK 1987–91; UN Under-Sec. for Tech. Co-operation for Devt 1991–92; Under-Sec.-Gen., Dept of Econ. Devt 1992–96 (now Dept for Devt, Support and Man. Services); Vice-Chair. All-China Fed. of Returned Overseas Chinese 1997–2005; Sr Consultant China Inst. of Int. Strategic Studies 1997–; Patron Int. Managers Org. *Publications:* The Man on Mao's Right: From Harvard Yard to Tiananmen Square, My Life Inside China's Foreign Ministry (memoir) 2008. *Leisure interests:* swimming, archaeology, history. *Address:* c/o All–China Federation of Returned Chinese, 112-01 Queens Boulevard, Apartment 18, Huatian Mansion, 26th Floor, Lianhuachi East Road, Haidian District, Beijing 100038, People's Republic of China.

JI, Xiaohui, MBA; Chinese banking executive; *Chairman, Shanghai Pudong Development Bank Company Limited;* fmr Head of Bank-Pudong, Shanghai Br.; fmr Deputy Head of Bank-Shanghai Br.; fmr Head of Bank-Shanghai Br. and Head of Bank-Pudong Br., Industrial and Commercial Bank of China Ltd; Chair. Shanghai Pudong Development Bank Co. Ltd and Party Sec. 2012–; Chair. Shanghai International Group Co. Ltd. *Address:* Shanghai Pudong Development Bank Co. Ltd, 12 Zhongshan Dong Yi Road, Shanghai 200002, People's Republic of China (office). *Telephone:* (21) 6161-8888 (office). *E-mail:* webmaster@spdb.com.cn (office). *Website:* www.spdb.com.cn (office).

JI, Yunshi; Chinese politician; *General Director, State Administration of Foreign Experts Affairs;* b. 26 Sept. 1945, Haimen, Jiangsu Prov.; m. Lu Guohong; one d.; ed Shandong Univ.; sent to do manual labour in Xishan Coal Mine, Suzhou City, Jiangsu Prov. 1970; worker, man. clerk and workshop dir Suzhou Light Industrial Electrical Machinery Plant 1971, Deputy Dir then Dir 1978–80; joined CCP 1975; Deputy Dir then Dir No. 2 Light Industry Bureau, Suzhou City 1980–82 (Deputy Sec. CCP Party Cttee 1980–82); Deputy Sec. then Sec. Jiangsu Prov. Cttee CCP Communist Youth League 1980–82; Sec. CCP Jiangsu City Cttee, Jiangsu Prov. 1984; apptd Vice-Gov. Jiangsu Prov. 1989–93, elected Vice-Gov. 1993–98, acting Gov. 1998–2002; Gov. Hebei Prov. 2002–06; Alt. mem. 15th CCP Cen. Cttee 1997–2002, mem. 16th CCP Cen. Cttee 2002–07; Deputy Sec. CCP Jiangsu Prov. Cttee 2001, mem. Standing Cttee 2001; Gen. Dir State Admin of Foreign Experts Affairs 2006–. *Address:* State Administration of Foreign Experts Affairs, Room 50307, No.1 South Zhongguancun Street, Beijing 100873, People's Republic of China (office).

JIA, Baojun; Chinese steel industry executive; *President, Sinosteel Corporation;* Vice-Pres. Wuhan Iron and Steel Group Corpn, Wuhan Iron and Steel Co. Ltd –2010; Pres. Sinosteel unit, Sinosteel Co. 2010–11; Pres. Sinosteel Corpn 2011–, Deputy Sec. CCP Party Cttee. *Address:* Sinosteel Corpn, Sinosteel International Plaza, 8 Haidian Street, Beijing 100080, People's Republic of China (office). *Telephone:* (10) 62689821 (office); (10) 62686689 (office). *Fax:* (10) 62689800 (office); (10) 62686688 (office). *E-mail:* office@sinosteel.com (office). *Website:* www.sinosteel.com (office).

JIA, Chunwang; Chinese state official; b. 1938, Beijing; ed Tsinghua Univ., Beijing; joined CCP 1962; Sec. CCP Communist Youth League (CYL) and mem. Standing Cttee. CCP Party Cttee, Tsinghua Univ. (in charge of student affairs) 1964; fmr Sec. Beijing Municipal Cttee, CCP CYL; fmr mem. Standing Cttee, CCP CYL; fmr Sec. CCP Haidian Dist Cttee, Beijing; fmr Sec. Comm. for Discipline Inspection, CCP Beijing Municipal Cttee; Minister of State Security 1985–98; Minister of Public Security 1998–2003; mem. Cen. Comm. of Political Science and Law 1991–; ranked Commr-Gen. 1992; apptd First Political Commissar, Chinese People's Armed Police Force 1998; apptd Dir Nat. Narcotics Control Comm. 1999; Vice-Procurator-Gen., Supreme People's Procuratorate 1998–2003, Procurator-Gen. 2003–08; mem. 12th CCP Cen. Cttee 1982–87, 13th Cen. Cttee 1987–92, 14th CCP Cen. Cttee 1992–97, 15th CCP Cen. Cttee 1997–2002, 16th CCP Cen. Cttee 2002–07. *Address:* c/o Chinese Communist Party Central Committee, Quanguo Renmin Daibiao Dahui, Zhongguo Gongchan Dang, 1 Zhongnanhai, Beijing, People's Republic of China (office).

JIA, Pingwa; Chinese writer; b. 21 Feb. 1952, Danfeng Co., Shaanxi Prov.; s. of Jia Yanchun and Zhouzhue; m. 2nd Guo Mei; two c.; ed Dept of Chinese Language, Northwest Univ., Xian; Ed., Shaanxi People's Publishing House 1975–; Chief Ed. magazine Mei Wen (Beautiful Essays); mem. Writers' Asscn 1979–; Chevalier des arts et des lettres (France) 2003; Zhuang Zhongwen Literature Prize 1991, Prize for Nat. Literature (three times), Liu Qing Literature Prize 2006. *Publications:* more than 60 works, including novels Turbulence (Pegasus Prize for Literature) 2003, The Corrupt and Waning, White Night, The Abandoned Capital (Prix Femina Étranger 1997), Neighbours' Wives 2005, Impetuous 2005, Qin Opera 2005, Gaoxing (Happy) 2007, Shaanxi Opera (Mao Dun Literature Prize 2008); short stories and essays; works have been translated into many languages. *Leisure interest:* painting, collecting antiques. *Address:* No. 2 Lian Hu Xiang, Xian City, Shaanxi, People's Republic of China.

JIA, Qinglin; Chinese government official and engineer; b. 1940, Botou, Hebei Prov.; ed Shijiazhuang Industrial Man. School, Hebei Coll. of Eng; joined CCP 1959; technician, Complete Plant Bureau, First Ministry of Machine-Building Industry 1958–62 (Deputy Sec. CCP 1962–69), Policy Research Office of the Gen. Office 1971–73, Chief, Product Man. Bureau, First Ministry of Machine-Building Industry 1973–78; sent to do manual labour, May 7th Cadre School, Fengxin Co., Jiangxi Prov. 1969–71; Gen. Man. China Nat. Machinery and Equipment Import and Export Corpn 1978–83; Dir Taiyuan Heavy Machinery Plant 1983–85 (Sec. CCP Party Cttee 1983–85); Deputy Sec. Standing Cttee, Fujian CCP Prov. Cttee 1986–93, Sec. 1993–96; Head, Org. Dept, CCP Fujian Prov. Cttee 1986–88; Pres. Party School, CCP Fujian Prov. Cttee 1988–90; Sec. Work Cttee of Depts, CCP Fujian Prov. Cttee 1988–90; Deputy Gov. (also Acting Gov.) of Fujian Prov. 1990–91, Gov. 1991–94; Vice-Mayor (also Acting Mayor) of Beijing 1996–97, Mayor 1997–99; Chair. Standing Cttee Fujian Prov. 8th People's Congress 1994–96; Sec. CCP Beijing Municipal Cttee 1997–2002; mem. 14th CCP Cen. Cttee 1992–97, 15th CCP Cen. Cttee 1997–2002 (mem. Politburo 1997–2002), 16th CCP Cen. Cttee 2002–07 (mem. Standing Cttee of the Politburo 2002–07), 17th CCP Cen. Cttee 2007–12 (mem. Standing Cttee of the Politburo 2007–12); Chair. 10th CPPCC Nat. Cttee 2003–08, Chair. 11th CPPCC Nat. Cttee 2008–13. *Address:* c/o Standing Committee, Chinese Communist Party Politburo, Quanguo Renmin Diabiao Dahui, Zhongguo Gongchan Dang, 1 Zhongnanhai, Beijing, People's Republic of China.

JIA, Zhangke; Chinese film director and producer; b. 1970, Fenyang, Shanxi Prov.; ed Shanxi Univ., Beijing Film Acad.; co-f. Xstream Pictures (with Yu Lik-Wai and Chow Keung) 2003; considered leading mem. of 'Sixth Generation' movt of Chinese cinema. *Films:* as dir: Xiao Shan Going Home 1995 (Hong Kong Independent Short Film & Video Award 1997), Du Du 1996, Xiao Wu 1997 (Dragons and Tigers Award, Vancouver Int. Film Festival, Wolfgang Staudt Prize, Berlin Int. Film Festival, Sky Prize, San Francisco Int. Film Festival), Platform 2000, Unknown Pleasures 2002, The World 2004, Still Life 2006 (Lion d'Or, 63rd Venice Int. Film Festival 2006), Our Ten Years 2007, 24 City 2008, I Wish I Knew 2010, A Touch of Sin 2013; as producer: Walking on the Wild Side 2006, Plastic City 2008, Perfect Life 2008. *Address:* XStream Films, Suite 303, Block 7, 6 Zhi Chun Lu, Hai Dian, Beijing 100088, People's Republic of China. *Telephone:* (10) 82350984 (office).

JIA, Zhijie; Chinese party and government official; b. 1935, Fuyu Co., Jilin Prov.; ed in USSR; joined CCP 1960; Dir Lanzhou Petrochemical Machinery Plant; Deputy Sec. Plant CCP Cttee; Deputy Sec. Gansu Prov. CCP Cttee 1983–92; Gov. Gansu Prov. 1986–92; Gov. of Hubei Prov. 1992–94; Sec. CCP Cttee Hubei Prov. 1994–2001; Sec.-in-Chief Hubei Mil. District CCP Cttee 1994; Alt. mem. CCP 13th Cen. Cttee 1987–92, mem. 14th CCP Cen. Cttee 1992–97, 15th CCP Cen. Cttee 1997–2002; Deputy 9th NPC 1998–2003. *Address:* c/o Office of Provincial Governor, 1 Beihuan Road, Wuhan, Hubei Province, People's Republic of China. *Telephone:* (27) 87814585. *Fax:* (27) 87816148.

JIANG, Baolin; Chinese artist; b. 20 Jan. 1942, Penglai Co., Shandong Prov.; s. of the late Jiang Chunfu and Dai Shuzhi; m. Ling Yunhua 1970; one s. one d.; ed Dept of Traditional Chinese Painting, Inst. of Fine Arts, Zhejiang, Cen. Acad. of Fine Arts, Beijing; worked in Cultural House, Fenghua Co. 1967–79; Dir Zhejiang Artists' Gallery 1982–84; Vice-Pres. Zhejiang Landscape Painting Research Inst. 1982–; mem. Council of Zhejiang Br. of Chinese Painters' Asscn 1984–; mem. Bd Zhejiang Painting Acad. 1984–; Visiting Prof., Beijing Cen. Fine Arts Acad. 1996–; Tutor, Acad. of Arts, Tsinghua Univ., Beijing, mem. Council, Cui Zifan Art Foundation Int.; mem. Chinese Artists' Asscn; numerous exhbns 1987–, including Contemporary Chinese Paintings in celebration of Hong Kong's return to China, Beijing, Shanghai, Tianjin 1997; Silver Medal, 9th Nat. Art Exhbn 1999. *Publications:* Collections of Jiang Baolin's Paintings 1984, Jiang Baolin's ink-

wash paintings 1989, Signatur Objekt 15, Jiang Baolin 1991, Jiang Baolin's Paintings (published in France) 1991, A selection of Jiang Baolin's Bird and Flower Paintings 1992, The World of Jiang Baolin's Ink & Wash Painting 1994, The Art World of Jiang Baolin (published in Korea) 1996, Series on Modern Chinese Artists 2000. *Leisure interests:* Beijing Opera, literature, music, gardening. *Address:* 201 Building 11, 2nd District, Nandu Huayuan Wenyi Road, Hangzhou, People's Republic of China. *Telephone:* (571) 8850096. *Fax:* (571) 8850096.

JIANG, Boju; Chinese mathematician and academic; *Professor of Mathematics, Peking University;* b. 4 Sept. 1937, Tianjin City; m. Chuanrong Xu 1968; two d.; ed Peking Univ.; Assoc. Prof. of Math., Peking Univ. 1978–82, Prof. 1983–, Dean School of Math. Sciences 1995–98; mem. Chinese Acad. of Sciences 1980; Fellow, Third World Acad. of Sciences 1985; Nat. Scientific Award of China 1982, 1987, S.S. Chern Mathematics Award 1988, Ho Leung Ho Lee Foundation Math. Prize 1996, L.K. Hua Math. Award 2002. *Address:* Department of Mathematics, Peking University, 5 Yiheyuan Road, Hai Dian, Beijing 100871, People's Republic of China (office). *Telephone:* (10) 62751804 (office). *Fax:* (10) 62751801 (office). *Website:* www.pku.edu.cn (office).

JIANG, Chaoliang, MA; Chinese banking executive; *Executive Chairman and President, Agricultural Bank of China;* ed Southwestern Univ. of Finance and Econs; fmr Gov. Guangzhou Br., People's Bank of China, Shenzhen Br.; Deputy Dir Gen. Banking Div., Dir Shenzhen Div. of State Admin of Foreign Exchange (SAFE), and Gov. Guangdong Br., People's Bank of China and Chief of Guangdong Div. of SAFE 1996–2000; Asst Gov. People's Bank of China 2000–02, mem. Monetary Policy Cttee; Deputy Gov. Hubei Prov. 2002–04; Dir (non-exec.) and Chair. Bank of Communications 2004–08; Exec. Dir and Vice-Chair. China Devt Bank Corpn –2008, Pres. 2008–12; Exec. Dir Agricultural Bank of China Ltd 2011–, Exec. Chair. and Pres. 2012–. *Address:* Agricultural Bank of China, 69 Jianguomen Nei Avenue, Dongcheng District, Beijing 100005, People's Republic of China (office). *Telephone:* (10) 85109619 (office). *Fax:* (10) 85108557 (office). *E-mail:* webmaster@intl.abocn.com (office); ir@abchina.com (office). *Website:* www.abchina.com (office).

JIANG, Chunyun; Chinese party official; b. April 1930, Laixi Co., Shandong Prov.; ed Teachers Training Coll., Laixi Co., Chinese Language and Literature Self-Study Univ.; fmr primary school teacher; Clerk of CCP Maren Dist Cttee, Sec., CCP Laixi Co. Cttee 1946–49; joined CCP 1947; Dir of Gen. Office Laixi Co. CCP Cttee 1949–57; Deputy Section Chief, Qingdao br., China Export Corpn for Local Products 1957–60; with Foreign Trade Bureau, Qingdao City 1957–60; Instructor and Chief Insp. and Deputy Dir of Gen. Office, Propaganda Dept Shandong Prov. CCP Cttee 1960–66; manual work in village in Huimin Co. during Cultural Revolution, sent to cadre school, Qihe Co. 1969; worked under Revolutionary Cttee Shandong Prov. 1970–75; Deputy Dir, Gen. Office, Shandong Prov. CCP Cttee 1975–77, Deputy Sec.-Gen., then Sec.-Gen. 1977–83, Deputy Sec. 1983–84; Sec., Ji'nan Municipal CCP Cttee 1984–87; Acting Gov., Shandong Prov. 1987–88, Gov. 1988–89; Pres. Shandong Prov. Party School 1989–92; First Sec., Shandong Mil. Dist CCP Cttee 1989–94; Sec., CCP Shandong Prov. Cttee 1993–94; Vice-Premier State Council (in charge of agricultural work) 1995–98; Head of State Flood-Control and Drought Relief HQ; mem. 13th CCP Cen. Cttee, 14th CCP Cen. Cttee 1992–97 (mem. Secr. of Politburo 1992–97), 15th CCP Cen. Cttee 1997–2002; Deputy, 7th NPC 1988–93, 8th NPC 1993–98, Vice-Chair. Standing Cttee of 9th NPC 1998–2003; Pres. China Family Planning Asscn 1998–; Prof. (part-time), Shandong Univ.; Hon. Prof., China Agric. Univ. *Address:* Standing Committee of National People's Congress, Beijing, People's Republic of China.

JIANG, Daming; Chinese politician; *Minister of Land and Resources;* b. 1953, Rongcheng City, Shandong Prov.; ed Heilongjiang Univ.; various roles with Production and Construction Corps, Heilongjiang Prov. 1969–77; joined CCP 1976, Clerk, Communist Youth League of China (CYLC) Cen. Cttee Org. Dept 1982–84, Deputy Section Chief 1984–86, Section Chief 1986–87, Deputy Dir 1987–90, Dir 1990–93, Sec., CYLC Cen. Cttee Secr. 1993–98; Vice-Chair. All-China Youth Fed. 1998; mem. 9th CPPCC Nat. Cttee 1998–2003; Deputy Sec., CCP Provincial Cttee, Shandong Prov. 2000–04; Sec., CCP City Cttee, Jinan City 2004–07; Vice-Gov., Shandong Prov. 2007–08, Gov. 2008–13; Minister of Land and Resources 2013–; alt. mem. 16th CCP Cen. Cttee 2002–07, mem. 17th CCP Cen. Cttee 2007–12, 18th CCP Cen. Cttee 2012–. *Address:* Ministry of Land and Resources, 64 Funei Dajie, Xisi, Beijing 100812, People's Republic of China (office). *Telephone:* (10) 66558407 (office). *Fax:* (10) 66127247 (office). *E-mail:* mhwz@mail.mlr.gov.cn (office). *Website:* www.mlr.gov.cn (office).

JIANG, Enzhu; Chinese diplomatist; b. 14 Dec. 1938, Jiangsu Prov.; s. of Jiang Guohua and Yu Wen Guizhen; m. Zhu Manli; one s.; ed Beijing Foreign Languages Univ.; joined Ministry of Foreign Affairs as translator 1964; Attaché, Third and Second Sec., Embassy in London during 1970s; Deputy Dir-Gen., then Dir-Gen. Dept of West European Affairs, Ministry of Foreign Affairs 1984–90, Asst Foreign Minister 1990–91, Vice-Minister 1991–95; Chief Negotiator for People's Repub. of China in Sino-British talks over future of Hong Kong; Deputy Head of Preliminary Working Cttee of Preparatory Cttee of Hong Kong Special Admin. Region; Amb. to UK 1995–97; Dir Hong Kong br., Xinhua News Agency 1997–99; Dir (Minister) Liaison Office of People's Repub. of China to Hong Kong SAR 2000–03; mem. 15th CCP Cen. Cttee 1997–2002; mem. Standing Cttee 9th NPC 1998–2003; Chair. 10th NPC Foreign Affairs Cttee 2003–08. *Address:* c/o Ministry of Foreign Affairs, 225 Chaoyangmen Nan Dajie, Chaoyang Qu, Beijing 100701, People's Republic of China.

JIANG, Gen. Futang; Chinese army officer; *Political Commissar, Shenyang Military Area Command, People's Liberation Army;* b. Oct. 1941, Rongcheng Co., Shandong Prov.; ed Political Acad. of the Chinese PLA; joined PLA 1959, CCP 1960; Dir Political Section, Regt 1969–70; Deputy Div. Political Commissar 1974–76; Dir Army Political Dept 1976–80; Political Commissar, 46th Army, Army (or Ground Force), PLA Services and Arms 1983–85; Dir Political Dept of PLA Jinan Mil. Area Command 1985–93; Deputy Political Commissar and Dir Political Dept of PLA Chengdu Mil. Area Command 1993–95; Political Commissar, PLA Shenyang Mil. Area Command 1995–; rank of Maj.-Gen. 1988–93, Lt-Gen. 1993–2002, Gen. 2002–; mem. 15th CCP Cen. Cttee 1997–2002, 16th CCP Cen. Cttee 2002–07. *Address:* PLA Shenyang Military Area Command, Shenyang City, Liaoning Province, People's Republic of China.

JIANG, Jianqing, MEng, PhD; Chinese banker; *Executive Director and Chairman, Industrial & Commercial Bank of China Limited;* b. Feb. 1953; ed Shanghai Univ. of Finance and Econs, Jiaotong Univ., Shanghai; Dir Shanghai City United Bank (now Bank of Shanghai) 1995–97; Dir Shanghai Br., Industrial and Commercial Bank of China (ICBC) 1997–99, Group Vice-Pres. 1999–2000, Pres. 2000–05, Exec. Dir and Chair. 2005–; Prof. (part-time), Man. Inst., Jiaotong Univ. (also Doctorate Adviser and Researcher); mem. Monetary Policy Comm., People's Bank of China; Alt. mem. 16th CCP Cen. Cttee 2002–07, 17th CCP Cen. Cttee 2007–12, 18th CCP Cen. Cttee 2012–. *Publications:* Analytical View on Foreign Financial Agitation, Thoughts on Financial Agitation, Technical Revolution in American Banking. *Address:* Industrial & Commercial Bank of China Ltd, 55 Fuxingmennan Dajie, Xicheng Qu, Beijing 100140, People's Republic of China (office). *Telephone:* (10) 66106070 (office); (10) 66108608 (office). *Fax:* (10) 66106053 (office); (10) 66106139 (office). *E-mail:* webmaster@icbc.com.cn (office); ir@icbc.com.cn (office). *Website:* www.icbc.com.cn; www.icbc-ltd.com (office).

JIANG, Jiemin; Chinese government official and fmr petroleum industry executive; b. Oct. 1955, Yangxin, Shandong Prov.; ed Party School of CCP Cen. Cttee; Deputy Dir Shengli Petroleum Admin Bureau 1993–94; Sr Exec. Qinghai Petroleum Admin Bureau 1994, Dir 1994–99; Asst to Gen. Man. and Team Leader of Restructuring, China Nat. Petroleum Corpn (CNPC) 1999, Dir and Vice-Pres. PetroChina Co. Ltd 1999–2000, Vice-Chair. and Pres. 2004–07, Chair. 2007–, also Vice-Pres. CNPC 2004–06, Pres. 2006–11, Chair. 2011–13; Chair. and Deputy Sec. Party Cttee, State-owned Assets Supervision and Admin Comm. (SASAC) March–Sept. 2013 (removed from post); Deputy Gov. Qinghai Prov. 2000–04, also mem. Prov. Party Cttee 2000, 2003; Alt. mem. 17th CCP Cen. Cttee 2007–12, mem. 18th CCP Cen. Cttee 2012–. *Address:* c/o State-owned Assets Supervision and Administration Commission, State Council, Beijing 100007, People's Republic of China.

JIANG, Minkuan; Chinese party and state official; b. 1930, Suzhou City, Jiangsu Prov.; ed Shanghai Polytechnic School; joined CCP 1961; fmr technician, workshop dir, factory dir and chief engineer, Southwest China Aluminium Processing Factory 1966–79; Deputy Sec. CCP Cttee, Sichuan Prov. 1982–85; Vice-Gov. Sichuan 1983–85, Gov. 1985–88; Vice-Chair. State Science and Tech. Comm. 1988–90; Dir State Patent Bureau 1988–89; Deputy Dir United Front Work Dept, CCP Cen. Cttee 1990–95, Exec. Deputy Head 1995–98; Vice-Pres. China Asscn of Inventions 1991–2005; Vice-Chair. 7th Exec. Cttee All China Fed. of Industry and Commerce 1993, China Chamber of Commerce 1993–; mem. 12th CCP Cen. Cttee 1982–87, 13th CCP Cen. Cttee 1987–92, 14th Cen. Cttee CCP 1992–97, 15th Cen. Cttee 1997–2002; mem. Standing Cttee 7th to 9th CPPCC Nat. Cttees 1988–2003; Vice-Chair. Science, Educational Culture, Public Health and Physical Culture Cttee, 9th Nat. Cttee of CPPCC 1998–2003. *Address:* c/o China Association of Inventions, PO Box 8020, Beijing 100088, People's Republic of China. *Website:* www.cainet.org.cn.

JIANG, Weixin; Chinese politician; *Minister of Housing and Urban-Rural Construction;* b. 1949, Fuyu County, Heilongjiang Prov.; ed Beijing Univ.; sent to countryside during Cultural Revolution 1968; joined CCP 1969; Deputy Dir, Nat. Devt and Reform Comm. 2003–07; Deputy Minister of Construction 2007–08; Minister of Housing and Urban-Rural Construction 2008–; mem. 17th CCP Cen. Cttee 2007–12. *Address:* Ministry of Housing and Urban-Rural Construction, 9 Sanlihe Lu, Haidian Qu, Beijing 100835, People's Republic of China (office). *Telephone:* (10) 58933575 (office). *E-mail:* cin@mail.cin.gov.cn (office). *Website:* www.mohurd.gov.cn (office).

JIANG, Wen; Chinese actor and film director; b. 1963, Tangshan, Hebei Prov.; m. 1st Sandrine Chenivisse, one d.; m. 2nd Zhou Yun, one s.; ed Cen. Acad. of Drama; joined China Youth Arts Theatre 1984; actor at Cen. Acad. of Drama. *Films include:* Fu rong zhen 1984, Moot doi wong hau 1986, Hong gao liang (Red Sorghum) 1987, Ben ming nian 1990, Da taijian Li Lianying (Li Lianying, the Imperial Eunuch) 1991, Yangguang Canlan de Rizi (In the Heat of the Sun) (dir, actor) 1994, Qin song 1996, Song jia huang chao 1997, The Soong Sisters (Hong Kong Film Award for Best Supporting Actor 1998) 1997, Guizi lai le (Devils on the Doorstep) (dir, producer) (Cannes Film Festival Grand Prix 2000) 2000, Xun qiang (The Missing Gun) (producer) 2002, Tian di ying xiong (Warriors of Heaven and Earth) 2003, Lü cha (Green Tea) 2003, Yi ge mo sheng nu ren de lai xin (A Letter from an Unknown Woman) 2004, Mo li hua kai (Jasmine) 2004, The Sun Also Rises (actor, dir and writer) 2007, Connected 2008, The Founding of a Republic 2009, Let the Bullets Fly (dir) 2010. *Address:* Central Academy of Drama, 39 East Mianhua Lane, Dongcheng District, Beijing 100710, People's Republic of China (office).

JIANG, Xi; Chinese government official; b. (Qing Jong), Jan. 1923, Shanghai; fmr Vice-Minister of Commerce; Pres. China Gen. Commercial 1994–, World Asscn of Chinese Cuisine; currently Sr Adviser Sino-Japan Food Devt Cttee; Hon. Pres., China Cuisine Asscn. *Address:* China Chamber of Commerce, 45 Fuxingmennei Street, Beijing 100801, People's Republic of China. *Telephone:* (10) 66094602 (office); (10) 63467719 (home). *Fax:* (10) 66062700 (office). *E-mail:* wacc@ccas.com.cn (office). *Website:* www.ccas.com.cn.

JIANG, Xinxiong; Chinese party and government official; b. 6 July 1931; ed Nankai Univ., Tianjin; joined CCP 1956; Dir nuclear fuel plant 1979–82; Vice-Minister of Nuclear Industry 1982–83, Minister 1983; Chair. Bd of Dirs, China Isotopes Co. 1983–98; Pres. Nat. Nuclear Corpn 1988–98; Chair. China Atomic Energy Authority 1994–99; Deputy Head Leading Group for Nuclear Power Plants; Vice-Chair Finance and Econ. Cttee of 9th NPC 1998–2003; Pres. China-Canada Friendship Asscn of NPC 1998–2003; Alt. mem. 12th CCP Cen. Cttee 1982–87, 13th CCP Cen. Cttee 1987–92, 14th CCP Cen. Cttee 1992–97. *Address:* c/o Standing Committee of National People's Congress, Beijing, People's Republic of China. *Telephone:* (10) 68533923.

JIANG, Yi-Huah, BA, MA, PhD; Taiwanese academic and government official; *Premier;* b. 18 Nov. 1960; ed Nat. Taiwan Univ., Yale Univ., USA; Asst Research Fellow, Sun Yat-Sen Inst. for Social Sciences and Philosophy, Academia Sinica 1993–95; Assoc. Prof., Dept of Political Science, Nat. Taiwan Univ. 1996–99, Prof. 1999–, Deputy Dean, Coll. of Social Sciences 2003–05, Assoc. Dean, Office of Academic Affairs 2006–08; Visiting Scholar, Darwin Coll., Univ. of Cambridge, UK 2000; Visiting Prof., East Asian Inst., Columbia Univ., USA 2001; Adviser, Ministry of Educ. 2004; Minister of Research, Devt and Evaluation Comm. 2008–09, Minister of the Interior 2009–12; Vice-Premier 2012–13, Premier 2013–.

Address: Executive Yuan, No.1, Sec. 1, Zhongxiao E. Road., Zhongzheng Dist., Taipei 10058, Taiwan (office). *Telephone:* (2) 33566500 (office). *E-mail:* eyemail@eyemail.gio.gov.tw. (office). *Website:* www.ey.gov.tw (office).

JIANG, Yingshi, MA; Chinese business executive; *Chairman of the Board of Supervisors, Shanghai Automotive Industry Corporation (SAIC);* b. Dec. 1949; fmr Party Sec. and Dir Shanghai Municipal Devt and Reform Comm.; currently Chair. Bd of Supervisors, Shanghai Automotive Industry Corpn (SAIC) Group; mem. Nat. Cttee, CPPCC. *Address:* Shanghai Automotive Industry Corporation (SAIC) Ltd, 5/F Building A, 563 Songtao Road, Zhangjiang, High Technology Park, Pu Dong, Shanghai 201203 (office). Shanghai Automotive Industry Corporation (SAIC) Ltd, No. 489, Weihai Road, Shanghai 200041, People's Republic of China (office). *Telephone:* (21) 50803757 (office); (21) 22011688 (office). *Fax:* (21) 50803780 (office); (21) 22011188 (office). *E-mail:* info@saicgroup.com (office). *Website:* www.saicgroup.com (office); www.saicmotor.com (office).

JIANG, Zemin; Chinese fmr head of state; b. 17 Aug. 1926, Yangzhou City, Jiangsu Prov.; ed Jiaotong Univ., Shanghai; joined CCP 1946; worked in Shanghai Yimin No. 1 Foodstuffs Factory, Shanghai Soap Factory, First Ministry of Machine-Bldg Industry; trainee, Stalin Automobile Plant, Moscow, USSR 1955–56; Deputy Chief Power Div., Deputy Chief Power-Engineer, Dir, Power Plant, Changchun No. 1 Auto Works 1957–62; Deputy Dir Shanghai Electric Equipment Research Inst., Dir and Acting Party Sec. Wuhan Thermo-Tech. Machinery Research Inst., Deputy Dir, Dir Foreign Affairs Bureau of First Ministry of Machine-Bldg Industry 1962–80; Vice-Chair. and Sec.-Gen. State Comm. on Admin of Imports and Exports, State Comm. on Admin of Foreign Investment 1980–82; First Vice-Minister Electronics Industry 1982–83, Minister 1983–85; Mayor of Shanghai 1985–88; Deputy Sec., Sec. Shanghai Municipal Party Cttee 1985–89; mem. 12th Nat. Congress CCP Cen. Cttee 1982, Politburo 1st Plenary Session of 13th Cen. Cttee 1987, Gen. Sec. 4th Plenary Session 1989, Chair. Mil. Cttee 5th Plenary Session 1989; mem. Standing Cttee Politburo, Gen. Sec. and Chair. Mil. Cttee 14th and 15th CCP Cen. Cttees 1992–2002; Chair. Cen. Mil. Comm. of CCP Cen. Cttee 1990–2004, Cen. Mil. Comm. of People's Repub. of China 1998–2005; Pres. People's Repub. of China 1993–2003; Hon. Chair. Red Cross Soc. of China; Hon. Pres. Software Industry Asscn, ranked by Forbes magazine amongst The World's Most Powerful People (62nd) 2012. *Address:* Chinese Communist Party, Zhongguo Gongchan Dang, 1 Zhongnanhai, Beijing, People's Republic of China.

JIANG, Zhenghua; Chinese academic, demographer and politician; *Honorary Dean, School of Management, Beijing Normal University;* b. Oct. 1937, Hangzhou City, Zhejiang Prov.; ed Xi'an Jiaotong Univ., Int. Demography Acad., Bombay, India; Lecturer, Auto Control Dept and Dir Population Research Centre, Inst. of Systematic Eng 1958–78; Dir Population and Econs Inst. 1958–78; Prof., Xi'an Jiaotong Univ. 1978–91; Visiting Prof., Univ. of Paris, France, Stanford Univ., USA; Specialist, India Int. Devt Centre 1986; currently Hon. Dean, School of Man., Beijing Normal Univ.; fmr Tech. Adviser, State Census Office; Vice-Minister, State Family Planning Comm. 1991–99; joined Chinese Peasants' and Workers' Democratic Party 1992; Vice-Chair. Cen. Cttee 11th Chinese Peasants' and Workers' Democratic Party (CPWDP) 1992–97, Chair. Cen. Cttee 12th CPWDP 1997–2002; mem. 7th CPPCC Nat. Cttee 1988–93, Standing Cttee 8th CPPCC Nat. Cttee 1993–98 (mem. Sub-cttee of Educ., Science, Culture, Health and Sports 1993–98); Vice-Chair. Standing Cttee of 9th NPC 1998–2003, of 10th NPC 2003–08; mem. Macao Hand-Over Ceremony Govt Del., Macao Special Admin. Region Preparatory Cttee 1999; now Prof. of Systems Eng, Econometrics and Demography; fmr Pres. China Soc. of Tech. and Demography; fmr Vice-Pres. Demographic Inst., Shaanxi Prov.; fmr adviser to and mem. Exec. Council Demography Soc. of China; mem. Council Int. Demography Soc. 1993–; Hon. DSc (Univ. of Minnesota) 2005; Gold Medal, Bombay Int. Demography Acad., India 1981, Outstanding Expert at Nat. Level of China 1985, Nat. Advanced Worker of China 1989, First Class Nat. Science and Tech. Progress Prize 1987. *Publications:* Economic Development Planning Models 1981, Country Report on Population of China 1997, Sustainable Development of China 1999, Population – Systematic and Quantitative Study and its Application (First Class Award, State Scientific and Technological Advancement), Analysis and Planning of Population, Programming Regional Population and Coordination Development of Economy. *Address:* Beijing Normal University, Zhuhai, 18th Jinfeng Road, Tangjiawan, Zhuhai City, Guangdong Province (office); 11 Min Zu Yuan Road, Room 601, Beijing 100029, People's Republic of China (home). *Telephone:* (10) 62357120 (home). *E-mail:* jenjenny@sina.com (office).

JIANG, Zhuping; Chinese engineer and administrator; b. 1937, Yixing Co., Jiangsu Prov.; ed Faculty of Missile Eng, Harbin Mil. Eng Inst.; joined CCP 1960; with Design Inst. of Ministry of Nat. Defence 1963–65; Deputy Dir Design Inst. of Nanchang Aircraft. Mfg Plant 1978–82, Deputy Sec. plant's Party Cttee 1982–84; Sec. Party Cttee of Depts under Ministry of Aeronautics Industry 1984–85; Vice-Gov. of Jiangxi Prov. 1985–88; Deputy Sec. CCP Jiangxi Prov. Cttee 1988–95; Gov. of Hubei Prov. 1995–2001; Sec. CCP Hubei Prov. Cttee 2001; Deputy to 9th NPC 1998–2003, Vice-Chair. NPC Educ., Science, Culture and Health Cttee 2001; mem. 14th CCP Cen. Cttee 1992–97, 15th CCP Cen. Cttee 1997–2002; Deputy Dir Civil Aviation Gen. Admin. of China 1991–95. *Address:* c/o National People's Congress, Tiananmen Square, Beijing, People's Republic of China.

JIANG, Zilong; Chinese writer; b. 2 June 1941, Cang Xian, Hebei; s. of Jiang Junsan and Wei Huanzhang; m. Zhang Qinglian 1968; one s. one d.; worker Tianjin Heavy Machinery Plant 1958; navy conscript 1960–65; apptd Vice-Chair. Chinese Writers' Asscn 1996; Pres. Tianjin Writers' Asscn; Nat. Short Story Prize 1979, Oriental Writer Award, Nat. Asscn of Chinese Writers, USA 2012. *Publications include:* A New Station Master 1965, One Day for the Chief of the Bureau of Electromechanics 1976, Manager Qiao Assumes Office 1979, Developer 1980, Diary of a Plant Secretary 1980, All the Colours of the Rainbow 1983, Yan-Zhao Dirge 1985, Serpent Deity 1986, Jiang Zilong Works Collection (eight vols) 1996, Human Vigour 2000, Ren Qi 2000, Empty Hole 2001, The Empire of Peasants 2008, Popularity 2010, Inanition. *Leisure interests:* swimming, Beijing opera. *Address:* No. 7, Dali Road, Heping District, Tianjin, People's Republic of China (home). *Telephone:* (22) 23306250 (home). *Fax:* (22) 23306250 (home). *E-mail:* jzltj@hotmail.com.

JIAO, Kaihe; Chinese business executive; *President, China North Industries Group Corporation (NORINCO);* fmr Deputy Gen. Man. and Vice-Pres. China North Industries Group Corpn (NORINCO), Pres. 2013–. *Address:* China North Industries Group Corporation, No. 10 Chedaogou, Haidian Dist, Beijing 100089 (office); China North Industries Group Corporation, 46 Sanlihe Road, Beijing 100821, People's Republic of China (office). *Telephone:* (10) 68594210 (office); (10) 68787608 (office). *Fax:* (10) 68594232 (office); (10) 68594555 (office). *E-mail:* webmaster@cngc.com.cn (office). *Website:* www.norincogroup.com.cn (office); www .norinco.com (office); www.cngc.com.cn (office).

JIBRIL, Mahmoud, BA, MA, PhD; Libyan politician and academic; b. 1952, Bani Walid; ed Cairo Univ., Egypt, Univ. of Pittsburgh, USA; taught strategic planning at Univ. of Pittsburgh for several years; taught at Garyounis Univ., Benghazi; ran own co., Gebril for Training and Consultancy; had leading role in drafting of United Arab Training Manual; responsible for organizing and administering the first two Training confs in the Arab world 1987, 1988, later took over man. and admin of leaders' training programmes for sr man. in Arab countries including Bahrain, Egypt, Jordan, Kuwait, Libya, Morocco, Saudi Arabia, Tunisia, UAE, as well as Turkey and UK; Head of Nat. Econ. Devt Bd 2007–10; involved in 'Libya Vision' project aiming at instituting democracy in Libya; Chair. Exec. Bd ('Interim Prime Minister') and Head of Int. Affairs, Nat. Transitional Council of Libya March–Oct. 2011. *Publications:* ten books on strategic planning and decision-making, including Imagery and Ideology in U.S. Policy Toward Libya, 1969–1982 (as Mahmoud G. ElWarfally) 1988. *Address:* c/o The Executive Board, National Transitional Council, Tripoli, Libya. *E-mail:* info@ntclibya.com. *Website:* www .ntclibya.com.

JIČÍNSKÝ, Zdeněk, DJur; Czech politician, academic and jurist; *Chairman, Parliamentary Permanent Commission on the Constitution;* b. 26 Feb. 1929, Ostřešany; m. Nada Jičínská 1961; two s.; ed Charles Univ., Prague; mem. Czech. CP 1951–69; on staff of Inst. of Social Sciences, Cen. Cttee of Czech. CP 1954–60; Prof., Law Faculty, Charles Univ. 1964–70; mem. Scientific Law Council, Charles Univ. 1962–69; mem. Legal Comm., Cen. Cttee of Czech. CP 1964; mem. Expert Comm. of Govt Cttee for Constitutional Regulation of Repub. 1968; Deputy Chair. Czech. Nat. Council 1968; mem. Chamber of Nations, Fed. Ass. of CSSR 1969; forced to leave public life and university 1969; lawyer in insurance co. 1969–77; signed Charter 77; Rep. Civic Forum 1989; Deputy Chair. Fed. Ass. 1989–90, First Deputy Chair. 1990–92; Deputy and mem. Presidium Fed. Ass. 1992–; mem. Civic Movt 1991–92; mem. Czechoslovak Social Democratic Party 1992–; mem. Parl. 1996–2002, 2003–, Deputy Chair. Parl. Constitutional Juridical Cttee 1996–2002; mem. Standing Del. to Inter parl. Union 1996–98, Chair. Parl. Perm. Comm. on the Constitution 2007–; mem. Scientific Law Council Charles Univ. 2006–; political commentator, Právo newspaper (fmrly Rudé Právo) 1992–. *Publications:* Political Ideology of the First Czechoslovak Republic 1961, On the Development of Thinking in Czechoslovakia in the Sixties 1991, Developments in Czechoslovak Parliament since November 1989 1993, The Extinction of Czechoslovakia in 1992 from a Constitutional Viewpoint 1993, Problems of Czech Politics 1994, Charter 77 and Society Governed by the Law 1995, Constitutional and Political Problems of the Czech Republic 1995, The Constitution of the Czech Republic in Political Practice 2007; numerous works on politics, theory of state and law and institutional law. *Leisure interests:* skiing, cycling, jazz. *Address:* Pařísská 12, 110 00 Prague 1, Czech Republic (home). *Telephone:* (2) 22312560 (home). *E-mail:* jicinskyz@psp.cz (office); a2@jicinsky.cz (office). *Website:* www.jicinsky.cz (office).

JIHAD, Abdullah; Maldivian economist, politician and fmr central banker; *Minister of Finance and Treasury;* ed Univ. of Waikato, New Zealand; held several positions in Ministry of Finance, including Minister of State; Gov. Maldives Monetary Authority (first ind. gov.) 2007–08; Minister of Finance and Treasury 2008, 2012–; mem. Civil Service Comm. 2010–12. *Address:* Ministry of Finance and Treasury, Ameenee Magu, Malé 20-379, Maldives (office). *Telephone:* 3328790 (office). *Fax:* 3324432 (office). *E-mail:* admin@finance.gov.mv (office). *Website:* www.finance.gov.mv (office).

JILANI, Hina; Pakistani lawyer and human rights activist; b. 1951; sister of Asma Jahangir; qualified as lawyer 1974; Advocate of the High Court 1981–; co-f. (with Asma Jahangir) AGHS Law Assocs (all-women law firm), Lahore 1981, also co-f. AGHS Legal Aid Cell (first free legal aid centre in Pakistan) 1984; Advocate of the Supreme Court 1992–; Founding mem. Human Rights Comm. of Pakistan, Lahore 1986–, Women's Action Forum; apptd UN Special Rep. on the Situation of Human Rights Defenders 2000–08; involved in UN Center for Human Rights, the Carter Centre, UN Conf. of Women; mem. The Elders 2013–; awards from ABA, Human Rights Watch, Millennium Peace Prize 2001. *Address:* Human Rights Commission of Pakistan, Aiwan-i-Jahmoor, 107 Tipu Block, New Garden Town, Lahore 54600, Pakistan (office). *Telephone:* (42) 5838341 (office). *Fax:* (42) 5883582 (office). *E-mail:* hrcp@hrcp-web.org (office). *Website:* www.hrcp-web.org (office).

JILANI, Jalil Abbas, LLB, MSc; Pakistani diplomatist and government official; *Ambassador to USA;* m. Shaista Jilani; three s.; posted to Embassies in Jeddah 1983–85, London 1985–88; Deputy Sec. in Prime Minister's Secr. 1989–92; for India, Ministry of Foreign Affairs 1992–95, posted to Embassy in Washington, DC 1995–99, Deputy High Commr/Acting High Commr to India 1999–2003, Dir Gen. South Asia and SAARC 2003–07, also served as Govt Spokesman on Foreign Affairs 2005, High Commr to Australia 2007–09, Amb. to Belgium, Luxembourg and EU 2009–12, Minister of Foreign Affairs 2012–13, Amb. to USA 2013–. *Leisure interests:* golf, reading. *Address:* Embassy of Pakistan, 3517 International Court NW, Washington, DC 20008, USA (office). *Telephone:* (202) 243-6500 (ext. 2000 and 2001) (office). *Fax:* (202) 686-1534 (office). *E-mail:* ambassador@ embassyofpakistanusa.org (office). *Website:* www.embassyofpakistanusa.org (office).

JIMENEZ, Joseph, Jr, AB, MBA; American pharmaceuticals industry executive; *CEO, Novartis AG;* b. 27 Dec. 1959; s. of Joseph Jimenez and Catherine Jimenez (née Lucente); m. Denise Lynn Kovach 1987; ed Stanford Univ., Univ. of California, Berkeley; began career as Brand Asst, Hidden Valley Ranch, Clorox Co. 1984–85, Asst Brand Man., New Products 1985–86, Asst Brand Man., Kingsford 1986–87, Brand Man., New Products 1987; joined Hunt-Wesson 1993, various positions including Vice-Pres. Marketing, La Choy/Rosarita Food Co.,

Vice-Pres. and later Sr Vice-Pres. Orville Redenbacher, Pres. Orville Redenbacher/ Swiss Miss Food Co. 1997–98, Pres. Wesson Peter Pan Food Co. 1997–98; Pres. and CEO Heinz North America, H.J. Heinz Co. 1998–2002, Exec. Vice-Pres. 2001–07, Pres. and CEO Heinz Europe 2002–06, Pres. and CEO Heinz Asia, Australia, New Zealand, Latin America, Africa & Middle East 2006–07; Head, Consumer Health Div., Novartis AG 2007, Head, Pharmaceuticals Div. and mem. Exec. Cttee Switzerland 2007–10, CEO Novartis AG 2010–; Dir The Hain Celestial Group Inc. 1999–2004, Blue Nile 2000–, Colgate-Palmolive; Dir (non-exec.) AstraZeneca PLC 2002–07; fmr adviser for Blackstone Group (pvt. equity org.), USA. *Address:* Novartis AG, Lichtstrasse 35, 4056 Basel, Switzerland (office). *Telephone:* (61) 324-11-11 (office). *Fax:* (61) 324-80-01 (office). *E-mail:* info@novartis.com (office). *Website:* www.novartis.com (office).

JIMENEZ, Menardo R., BSc (Com); Philippine business executive; b. 6 Dec. 1932, Manila; s. of the late Marcelo A. Jimenez and Emiliana Rodriguez-Jimenez; m. Carolina L. Gozon 1962; two s. two d.; ed Far Eastern Univ., qualified as certified accountant; worked for Abaca Corpn of Philippines (Abacorp) 1956–70; Pres. and CEO Repub. Broadcasting Inc. (now GMA-Radio TV Arts, GMA-7) –2000; Chair. MA Jimenez Enterprises Inc., Majalco Finance & Investment Corpn, Cable Entertainment Corpn; Pres. Albay-Agro Industrial Devt Corpn, Justitia Realty & Devt Corpn, GMA Marketing & Productions Inc.; Dir many cos; Chair. and Trustee Kapwa Ko Mahal Ko Foundation; Chair. Bd Philippine Constitution Asscn; Chair. Prison Fellowship Philippines Inc.; Gov. Philippine Nat. Red Cross; Dir Philippine Chamber of Commerce and Industry; Dir or Trustee many other bodies; ASNA Award for Business and Entrepreneurship 2010. *Leisure interest:* stamp collection. *Address:* c/o GMA Network Center, EDSA corner Timog Avenue, Diliman, Quezon City, Philippines.

JIMÉNEZ-BELTRÁN, Domingo; Spanish international organization executive; *Adviser to the Prime Minister;* b. 2 April 1944, Zaragoza; s. of Mariano Jiménez and María Gloria Beltrán; m. Elin Solem; one c.; ed High Tech. School of Industrial Engineers and Polytechnic Univ., Madrid; Lecturer, Polytechnic Univ., Madrid 1978–86; Exec. Adviser to Minister for Public Works and Planning 1983–85; Deputy Dir-Gen. for Int. and EU Relations and with Ministry of Public Works and Urban Planning 1985–86; Attaché for Environment and Public Works, Perm. Mission to EU, Brussels 1986–87; Head of Div. Health, Physical Safety and Quality, Consumers Policy Service, EC 1987–91; Dir-Gen. for Environmental Policy, Sec. of State for Environment and Housing, Ministry of Public Works, Transport and Environment 1991–94; Exec. Dir European Environment Agency, Copenhagen 1994–2002; Founder and fmr Dir Observatorio de la Sostenibilidad en España (Spanish Observatory of Sustainability); currently Adviser to the Prime Minister; Nat. Prize on Environment (Spain) 2008, Emisoft Sustainability Prize 2008. *Publications:* Late Lessons From Early Warnings: The Precautionary Principle 1896–2000 (co-author) 2001; author or ed. of various publs and articles. *Address:* c/o Observatorio de la Sostenibilidad en España (OSE), Universidad de Alcalá, Plaza San Diego s/n – Casa Anexa al Rectorado, 2ª planta, 28801 Alcalá de Henares, Madrid; Prime Minister's Chancellery, Complejo de la Moncloa, 28071 Madrid, Spain. *Telephone:* (91) 8854039 (OSE); (91) 3353535 (Chancellery). *E-mail:* juancarlos.ochoa@uah.es. *Website:* www.sostenibilidad-es.org; www.mpr .es.

JIMENEZ MAYOR, Juan; Peruvian lawyer and politician; b. 5 Aug. 1964; ed Pontifical Catholic Univ. of Peru; Prof. of Legal Research, Constitutional Law and Public Man. and Admin of Justice, Pontifical Catholic Univ. of Peru 1994; Prof. Academia de la Magistratura (Judicial Acad.), Lima 2003–; Deputy Minister of Justice 2000–01, Aug.–Dec. 2011, Minister of Justice and Human Rights 2011–12; Pres. Council of Ministers (Prime Minister) 2012–13 (resgnd); mem. Peruvian Asscn of Constitutional Law; Adviser to Peruvian Press Council; Sr Adviser, OAS electoral observation missions to general elections in Guatemala 2007, Paraguay 2008. *Address:* c/o Office of the President of the Council of Ministers, Jirón Carabaya, cuadra 1 s/n, Anexo 1105-1107, Lima, Peru (office).

JIMÉNEZ PUERTO, Milton Danilo; Honduran government official and lawyer; b. 8 Nov. 1961; m. D. Alba María Soto Quezada; ed Universidad Nacional Autónoma de Honduras; joined Partido Liberal de Honduras 1985; fmr Dir Colegio de Abogados Honduras; Co-Dir Consultorio Jurídico Popular; fmr Legal Adviser Cen. Nacional de Trabajadores del Campo; Minister of Foreign Affairs 2006–07 (resgnd). *Address:* Partido Liberal, Col. Miramonte, Teguucigalpa, Honduras (office). *Telephone:* 232-0520 (office). *Fax:* 232-0797 (office). *Website:* www .partidoliberal.net (office).

JIN, Chongji; Chinese historian; b. 13 Dec. 1930, Qingpu, Jiangsu Prov.; ed Fudan Univ.; joined CCP 1948; Lecturer, Admin., Fudan Univ. 1951–65; researcher, Ministry of Culture 1965–73; Deputy Chief Ed., Chief Ed. Cultural Relics Press 1973–81; researcher, Assoc. Exec. Dir, Exec. Dir CCP Cen. Cttee Historical Documents Research Office 1981–; Vice-Dir Cultural and Historical Documents Cttee, CPPCC; Chair. All-China Asscn of Historians. *Publications:* Xinhai Geming de Qian Qian Hou Hou (A History of the 1911 Revolution), Sun Zhongshan he Xinhai Geming (Sun Yat-sen and the 1911 Revolution), Biography of Zhou En-lai (1898–1976), Biography of Mao Zedong (1893–1949). *Leisure interest:* reading. *Address:* Historical Documents Research Office of Chinese Communist Party Central Committee, 1 Maojiawan, Xisi Bei Qian, Beijing 100017 (office); Wanshoulu Jia-15, 7th Zone, 4th Building, 101th Room, Beijing 100036, People's Republic of China (home). *Telephone:* (10) 63095701 (office); (10) 68218172 (home). *Fax:* (10) 63094431 (office).

JIN, Deborah (Debbie) S., AB, PhD; American physicist and academic; *Professor Adjoint, Physics, University of Colorado;* b. 15 Nov. 1968, Palo Alto, Calif.; ed Princeton Univ., Univ. of Chicago; NSF Grad. Fellow, Univ. of Chicago 1990–93, Research Asst 1993–95, Nat. Research Council Research Associateship, NIST-JILA (Nat. Inst. of Standards and Tech.-Jt Inst. for Lab. Astrophysics) 1995–97, Asst Prof. Adjoint, Physics, Univ. of Colorado, Boulder 1997–2004, NIST Physicist 1997–2005, Assoc. Prof. Adjoint, Physics 2004–, Prof., Physics 2007–, NIST Fellow 2005–; mem. NAS 2005, AAAS 2006; Fellow, American Physical Soc. 2003, American Acad. of Arts and Sciences 2007; Allen Goodrich Shenstone Prize, Princeton Univ. 1990, NSF Grad. Fellowship in Physics 1990–93, ONR Young Investigator 1999, Presidential Early Career Award for Scientists and Engineers 2000, NIST Samuel W. Stratton Award 2001, Maria Goeppert-Mayer Award 2002,

NAS Award for Initiatives in Research 2002, John D. and Catherine T. MacArthur Fellowship 2003, Arthur S. Flemming Award (Scientific Category) 2003, Service to America Medal: Science and the Environment 2004, Scientific American 50: Research Leader of the Year 2004, I.I. Rabi Prize, American Physical Soc. 2005, Bonfils-Stanton Foundation Award in Science and Medicine 2006, Benjamin Franklin Medal in Physics 2008, William Proctor Prize for Scientific Achievement, Sigma Xi 2009, Kathryn A. McCarthy Lectureship in Physics, Tufts Univ. 2010, Gold Medal, NIST, Department of Commerce 2011, Laureate for North America, L'Oréal-UNESCO Awards For Women in Science 2013. *Publications:* more than 80 papers in professional journals. *Address:* NIST-JILA, University of Colorado, 440 UCB Boulder, Boulder, CO 80309-0440, USA (office). *Telephone:* (303) 492-0256 (office). *Fax:* (303) 492-8994 (office). *E-mail:* @jilau1.colorado.edu (office). *Website:* jila.colorado.edu/~jin (office).

JIN, Ha, BA, MA, PhD; American/Chinese writer, poet and academic; *Professor, Department of English, Boston University;* b. (Jin Xuefei), 21 Feb. 1956, Jinzhou, China; m. Lisah Bian 1982; one c.; ed Heilongjian Univ., Harbin, Shangdong Univ., Jinan, Brandeis Univ.; Faculty mem. Dept of English, Emory Univ. 1993–2002; Prof., Dept of English, Boston Univ. 2002–; wrote libretto for opera (with Tan Dun), The First Emperor (Metropolitan Opera, New York) 2006; Fellow, American Acad. of Arts and Sciences 2006–; PEN/Hemingway Award 1997, Flannery O'Connor Award 1997, Nat. Book Award 1999, PEN/Faulkner Award 2000, 2005, Asian American Literary Award 2001, Townsend Prize for Fiction 2002. *Publications:* fiction: Ocean of Words: Army Stories 1996, Under the Red Flag 1997, In the Pond 1998, Waiting 1999, The Bridegroom (short stories) 2000, The Crazed 2002, War Trash (novel) 2004, A Free Life 2007, A Good Fall (short stories) 2009; poetry: Between Silences 1990, Facing Shadows 1996, Wreckage 2001; essays: The Writer as Migrant 2008. *Address:* Department of English, College of Arts and Sciences, Boston University, 236 Bay State Road, Boston, MA 02215, USA (office). *Telephone:* (617) 358-2521 (office). *E-mail:* xjin@bu.edu (office). *Website:* www.bu.edu/english (office).

JIN, Nyum; South Korean politician; b. 1940; ed Coll. of Commerce, Seoul Nat. Univ., Washington Univ., Stanford Univ.; with Econ. Planning Bd (EPB); fmr Minister of Labour; fmr Minister of Energy and Resources, of Maritime Affairs and Fisheries; Deputy Prime Minister for Finance and the Economy 2000–02 (resgnd). *Address:* c/o Ministry of Finance and Economy, 1 Jungang-dong, Gwacheon City, Gyeonggi Province, Republic of Korea (office).

JIN, Puqing; Chinese business executive; b. 1950; ed Jinzhou Communist Party School; joined China Railway Construction Corpn Group 1968, Dir 2005–09, Gen. Man., Pres. and Exec. Dir 2007–09 (retd); Deputy Head of 12th Eng Bureau, Ministry of Railways 1993–98, also Chair., Gen. Man. and Deputy Sec., China Railway 12th Bureau Group Co. Ltd CCP Cttee 1998–2005. *Address:* c/o China Railway Construction Corpn, No. 40, Fuxing Road, Beijing, 100855, People's Republic of China. *Telephone:* (10) 51888114. *E-mail:* ir@crcc.cn. *Website:* www.crcc.cn.

JIN, Renqing; Chinese politician; b. July 1944, Suzhou, Jiangsu Prov.; ed Cen. Inst. of Finance and Banking; staff mem. Grain Bureau, Yongsheng Co., Yunnan Prov. 1968–97, Deputy Dir 1977–80; joined CCP 1972; Deputy Dir Financial Office, Yongsheng Co. 1977–80; mem. Standing Cttee CCP Yongsheng Co. Cttee 1980–82 (Vice-Chair. CCP Revolutionary Cttee 1980–82), Deputy Sec. CCP Yongsheng Co. Cttee 1982–83; Deputy Magistrate, Yongsheng Co. (Dist) People's Court 1980–82, Acting Magistrate and Magistrate 1982–83; mem. CCP Lijiang Prefectural Cttee, Yunnan Prov. 1985–91; Deputy Commr Lijiang Prefectural Admin. Office 1985–91; Vice-Gov. Lijiang 1985–91; Vice-Minister of Finance 1991–95; Deputy Sec.-Gen. State Council 1995; apptd Vice-Mayor of Beijing 1995, elected Vice-Mayor 1998; mem. Standing Cttee CCP Beijing Municipal Cttee 1995; Deputy Sec. CCP Beijing Municipal Cttee 1997, Deputy Dir Planning and Construction Cttee 1997; Dir State Tax Bureau 1998–2003; Alt. mem. CCP 15th Cen. Cttee 1997–2002, mem. CCP 16th Cen. Cttee 2002–07; Minister of Finance 2003–07; Hon. Chair. Exec. Cttee All-China Fed. of Industry and Commerce 1996–97. *Address:* c/o Zhongguo Gongchan Dang (Chinese Communist Party), Beijing, People's Republic of China (office).

JIN, Shangyi; Chinese artist; b. 1934, Jiaozuo City, Henan Prov.; ed Cen. Fine Arts Acad., Beijing; known as the forerunner of classicism in Chinese Art; Pres. Cen. Inst. of Fine Arts 1987; Chair. Chinese Artists' Assscn; Vice-Chair. China Fed. of Literary and Art Circles 2001; Guest Lecturer, Art Dept, New York Municipal Univ. 1982. *Works include:* Seeing People Off 1959, The December Meeting 1961, Mao Zedong at the December Conference 1961, Mao Zedong Leads the Red Army on the Long March 1964, Spring of the Rivers 1977, Oil Workers 1978, A Maiden 1981, Tajik Bride 1983, Qu Qiubai 1984, Prayer 1987, Ascending Peak Mushitago, Our Friends are All Over the World, Summer Ranch, Portrait of Sun Yat-Sen. *Address:* c/o Central Institute of Fine Arts, 5 Xiaowei Hutong, East District, Beijing 100730, People's Republic of China (office). *Telephone:* (10) 65254731 (office).

JIN, Xiangwen; Chinese administrator; b. Oct. 1939, Shanghai; ed Wuhan Surveying and Mapping Inst.; joined CCP 1966; Dir State Bureau of Surveying and Mapping 1988–2000. *Address:* c/o State Bureau of Surveying and Mapping, Beijing, People's Republic of China.

JIN, Yong, GBM, OBE; Chinese writer, journalist and newspaper publisher; b. (Louis Cha Liang Yong), 6 Feb. 1924, Haining, Zhejiang Prov.; m. three times; ed Dongwu Law School; writer, Ta Kung Pao newspaper, Shanghai, later Hong Kong; later became film reviewer and screenwriter; first martial arts novel serialised in Xin Wan Bao newspaper, Hong Kong 1955; f. newspaper Ming Bao Daily, Hong Kong; ceased writing novels in 1972; several hon. degrees; Chevalier de la Légion d'Honneur 1992, Commdr de l'Ordre des Arts et des Lettres 2004. *Publications:* (titles translated) Legend of the Book and the Sword 1955, The Sword Stained With Royal Blood (Vol. I Crimson Sabre Saga) 1956, Flying Fox of the Snowy Mountain 1959, The Young Flying Fox, Legend of the Condor Heroes (Vol. I Condor trilogy) 1957, Return of the Condor Heroes (Vol. II Condor trilogy) 1959, Heavenly Sword Dragon Sabre (Vol. III Condor trilogy) 1961, Demi Gods Semi Devils 1963, Way of the Heroes, Requiem of Ling Sing, The Proud Smiling Wanderer 1967, The Duke of Mount Deer (Vol. II Crimson Sabre Saga), The Deer and the Cauldron 1969, Sword of the Yue Maiden 1970. *Address:* c/o The Chinese

University Press, The Chinese University of Hong Kong, Sha Tin, N.T., Hong Kong Special Administrative Region, People's Republic of China (office). *Website:* www.chineseupress.com (office).

JIN, Yongjian; Chinese diplomatist and national organization official; b. 15 Sept. 1934; s. of Jin Zhiying and Bo Canzhang; m. Wang Youping 1955; two s.; ed Beijing Univ. of Foreign Studies; officer, People's Inst. of Foreign Affairs of China 1954–63; Attaché, Embassy in Nairobi 1964–67; officer, African Dept Ministry of Foreign Affairs, Beijing 1967–71, Deputy Dir-Gen., Dir-Gen. 1984–88, Dir-Gen. Dept of Int. Orgs and Confs 1988–90; Third Sec., Second Sec. Embassy in Lagos 1971–76; Second Sec., First Sec. then Counsellor, Perm. Mission to UN, New York, Alt. Rep. to UN Security Council, Rep. to Security Council Special Cttee on Decolonization, UN Council for Namibia 1977–84, Deputy Perm. Rep., Amb. to UN, Deputy Rep. to Security Council 1990–92; Amb. and Perm. Rep. to UN, Geneva, also accred to Other Int. Orgs in Switzerland 1992–96; Under-Sec.-Gen. for Devt Support and Man. Services, UN 1996–97, for Gen. Ass. Affairs and Conf. Services 1997–2001; Pres. UN Asscn of China 2001–07; Adjunct Prof., Nankai Univ. 2005–. *Leisure interests:* walking, Chinese chess, bridge. *Address:* 71 Nanchizi, Beijing 100 006, People's Republic of China (office).

JIN, Zhixin; Chinese business executive; *Vice-Chairman and President, Shanxi Coking Coal Group;* Chair. and Party Sec., Xishan Coal & Electricity (Group) Co. Ltd, Shanxi Xishan Coal and Electricity Share Co. Ltd; currently Vice-Chair. and Pres. Shanxi Coking Coal Group. *Address:* Shanxi Coking Coal Group, 1 Xinjinci Road, Taiyuan 30024, People's Republic of China (office). *Telephone:* (351) 8305000 (office). *Fax:* (351) 8305101 (office). *E-mail:* webmaster@sxcc.com.cn (office). *Website:* en.sxjh.com.cn (office); www.sxcc.com.cn (office).

JINASENA, Deshamanya T. N., BTech (Eng), DLC (Hons), CEng, FIMechE, FIESL; Sri Lankan company director; *Chairman, Jinasena Group of Companies;* b. 13 July 1940, Colombo; ed Loughborough Univ., UK; Chair. Jinasena Group 1965–, Man. Dir 1965–2012, business ventures in hotel industry, agricultural machinery, tyres, garments, pumps, seafood, tractors; Dr hc (Loughborough); Hon. DTech. *Leisure interests:* photography, sailing, motor racing. *Address:* L.M. Jinasena & Co. Ltd, 8/4 Elibank Road, Colombo 5 (office); 9 Gampaha Road, Ekala, Ja Ela, Sri Lanka (home). *Telephone:* (11) 5555310-4 (office); (1) 2232383 (home). *Fax:* (1) 2589207 (office); (1) 2232383 (home). *E-mail:* nihal@l-m-j.com (office); tnjhome@eureka.lk (home). *Website:* www.l-m-j.com (home).

JINDAL, (Piyush) Bobby, ScB, MLitt; American politician; *Governor of Louisiana;* b. 10 June 1971, Baton Rouge, La; s. of Amar Jindal and Raj (Pal) Jindal; m. Supriya Jolly; two s. one d.; ed Baton Rouge Magnet High School, Brown Univ., Providence, RI, Univ. of Oxford, UK (Rhodes Scholar); consultant for McKinsey & Co., Washington, DC 1994–95; Sec., La Dept of Health and Hosps 1996–98; Exec. Dir Nat. Bipartisan Comm. on the Future of Medicare 1998–99; volunteer in Gov. of La Office and State Legislature 1999; Pres. Univ. of Louisiana System 1999–2001; Asst Sec. for Planning and Evaluation of Health and Human Services 2001–03; cand. for Gov. of La 2003; elected to US Congress for La's First Dist 2004, re-elected 2006, mem. House Cttee on Homeland Security, House Cttee on Natural Resources; Gov. of Louisiana 2008–; Chair. Republican Govs Asscn 2012–; mem. Bd of Dirs Our Lady of the Lake Hosp., Baton Rouge 2000–01, Educ. Comm. of States 2000–01, Nat. Conf. Cttee and Justice, Baton Rouge chapter 2000–01; mem. Salvation Army, Baton Rouge 1986–87, Better Business Bureau, Baton Rouge 1987–88, Teach for America, Baton Rouge chapter 1997–98; Republican; named to All-USA First Acad. Team, USA Today 1992, named Louisiana's Most Outstanding Young Man, Jr Chamber of Commerce 1995, Jefferson Award, Nat. Inst. of Public Service 1998, chosen by Scholastic Update magazine as "one of America's top 10 extraordinary young people for the next millennium", India Abroad Person of the Year 2005. *Publications:* Leadership and Crisis 2010; newspaper columns, law review articles and first authorships in several scientific and policy articles that have appeared in the Journal of the American Medical Association, Journal of the Louisiana State Medical Association and Hospital Outlook; several articles published in the New Oxford Review. *Leisure interest:* tennis. *Address:* Office of the Governor, PO Box 94004, Baton Rouge, LA 70804-9004, USA (office). *Telephone:* (225) 342-7015 (office). *Fax:* (225) 342-7099 (office). *E-mail:* info@bobbyjindal.com (office). *Website:* www.gov.state.la.us (office); www.bobbyjindal.com (office).

JINDAL, Naveen, BCom, MBA; Indian business executive and government official; *Executive Vice Chairman and Managing Director, Jindal Steel and Power Ltd;* b. 9 March 1970, Hissar, Haryana; s. of the late O.P. Jindal and of Savitri Devi Jindal; m. Shalu Jindal; one s. one d.; ed Univ. of Delhi, Univ. of Texas, USA; currently Exec. Vice-Chair. and Man. Dir, Jindal Steel and Power Ltd; mem. of Parl. 2004–; Chair. Young Leaders Forum, Fed. of Indian Chamber of Commerce and Industry (FICCI), mem. FICCI Nat. Exec. Cttee; mem. Chhattisgarh State Council, Sports Cttee, Maharaja Agrasen Medical Educ. and Scientific Research Soc., Agroha Medical Coll., Sports Cttee and ITI, Tech. and Vocational Insts; Chancellor OP Jindal Global Univ., Haryana; Pres. Equestrian Asscn of Chhattisgarh; mem. Nat. Rifle Asscn, Parl. Forum on Youth; mem. Cttee on Home Affairs 2004, Consultative Cttee on Ministry of Defence; Student Leader of the Year Award, Univ. of Texas, USA. *Achievements include:* nat. champion and nat. record holder in skeet shooting, participated in South Asian Fed. Games (won silver medal), Pakistan 2004, Open Shooting Championship (gold medal), Singapore 2004, Nat. Shooting Championship (two silver medals), Indore 2004, Nat. Shooting Championship (silver medal), New Delhi 2006, V Sardar Sajjan Singh Sethi Memorial Master Shooting Competition (gold medal) 2007; Capt. Jindal Steel and Power Polo team, won Indian Open (polo) 2003, 2004. *Leisure interests:* polo, horse riding, shooting, reading, yoga. *Address:* Jindal Centre, 12 Bhikaiji Cama Place, New Delhi 110 066 (office); 171, South Avenue, New Delhi 110 011, India (home). *Telephone:* (11) 26188340 (office); (11) 23012253 (home). *Fax:* (11) 26161271 (office); (11) 23012213 (home). *E-mail:* naveen@naveenjindal.com (office); naveen.jindal@sansad.nic.in (office). *Website:* www.naveenjindal.com (office).

JING, Tianliang; Chinese engineer and business executive; b. 1945; s. of Jing Shuping; ed Xi'an Mining Coll.; fmr Deputy Dir-Gen. fmr Ministry of Coal Industry, Ministry of State Energies, China Cen. Coal Distribution Co.; fmr Chair. and Pres. China Nat. Coal Import & Export Corpn Group; fmr Dir-Gen. of Admin

Office of fmr Ministry of Coal Industry; fmr Dir-Gen. of Admin and Foreign Affairs of Nat. Coal Industry Bureau; fmr Pres. China Coal & Energy Corpn; fmr Chair. China Coal & Energy Co. Ltd; Chair. China Metallurgical Group Corpn 2010–13; External Dir Baosteel Group Corpn; mem. 11th Nat. Cttee CPPCC. *Address:* c/o China Metallurgical Group Corporation, 28 Shuguangxili, Chaoyang, Beijing 100028, People's Republic of China (office). *Telephone:* (10) 59869999 (office). *Fax:* (10) 59869988 (office). *E-mail:* mcc@mcc.com.cn (office). *Website:* www.mcc.com.cn (office).

JINGILI, Ali Ahmad Jama; Somali politician; Minister for Information 2007–08, of Foreign Affairs and Int. Co-operation 2008 (resgnd), of Transport 2009, of Foreign Affairs 2009–10. *Address:* c/o Ministry of Foreign Affairs, 1 Villa Somalia, 2525 Mogadishu, Somalia (office).

JIOYEVA, Alla Aleksandrovna; Georgian politician; *Deputy Prime Minister of 'Republic of South Ossetia';* b. 23 Aug. 1949, Staliniri (now Tskhinvali), South Ossetian Autonomous Oblast, Georgian SSR, USSR; ed Secondary School No. 5, Tskhinvali, South Ossetian Pedagogical Inst. but later transferred to Odesa Univ., Ukrainian SSR; returned to Tskhinvali to work as a Russian language and literature teacher in school No. 2, later the school's director until 2002; became a supporter of Eduard Kokoyev (Kokoiti), a candidate in presidential election 2001; Minister of Educ. 2002–08; supports re-unification of South and North Ossetia, involved in intergovernmental group for further integration of the two republics 2006; charged with several offences and placed under house arrest March 2008, detained until April 2010, found guilty by court of fraud and official misconduct but absolved of two other charges, received 24 months' probation and fined 120,000 rubles, appealed to Supreme Court; presidential cand. 2011; received most votes in second round of voting but election annulled by S Ossetian Supreme Court alleging electoral fraud and barred her from running in following one; declared herself Pres.-elect and formed a State Council to serve as the new govt; agreement reached to hold new election in March 2012 and to allow her to contest it Dec. 2011; withdrew from deal Jan. 2012, condemned planned runoff as "illegal"; office raided by police who tried to arrest her Feb. 2012, hospitalized unconscious a day before her inauguration as president, remained in hospital for 45 days and discharged under police guard March 2012; Deputy Prime Minister of 'Republic of South Ossetia' May 2012–. *Address:* Office of the Prime Minister of the 'Republic of South Ossetia', 100001 Tskhinvali, ul. Khetgurova 1, South Ossetia, Georgia (office). *Telephone:* (9974) 45-00-01 (office). *Fax:* (9974) 45-47-63 (office). *E-mail:* ospress@yandex.ru (office).

JIRICNA, Eva Magdalena, CBE, DipArch, RIBA; British architect; *Principal, Eva Jiricna Architects;* b. 3 March 1939, Zlin, Czechoslovakia; d. of the late Josef Jiricny and Eva Jiricna; ed Univ. of Prague, Prague Acad. of Fine Arts; worked with GLC's School Div. 1968; Louis de Soissons Partnership 1969–78, Project Architect; practice with David Hodges 1978; team leader at Richard Rogers Partnership 1982–84; f. own practice 1984, re-formed as Eva Jiricna Architects 1986–; External Examiner for RCA and Schools of Architecture at Leicester, Sheffield, Oxford, Bath, Humberside and Plymouth Univs and for RIBA; Pres. Architectural Assocn, London 2004–05; mem. RIBA Gold Medal Jury 2005–06, RIBA Regional Awards Jury (Chair.) 2005, Design Review panel CABE 2005–07; Adviser, Civic Trust Nat. Awards panel 2005–06; Trustee, London Open House; Hon. RDI (Royal Designers for Industry) 1991; Hon. Fellow, RCA 1990, RSA 1993, Royal Incorporation of Architects in Scotland 1990, RA 1997, AIA 2006; Hon. Prof. of Architecture and Design, Univ. of Applied Arts, Prague 2000; Hon. DTech (Southampton, Brno, Czech Repub.) 2000; Hon. DLitt (Sheffield) 2000; Design Prize, RA 1994. *Television includes:* Tales from Prague, BBC 2, Architecture of the Imagination: Staircases, BBC 2 1990, The Late Show: Czech Modernism 1994, Wideworld, Anglia TV 1997, The Dome: Trouble at the Big Top, BBC 2 1999. *Publications include:* Eva Jiricna: Design in Exile, The Joseph Shops: Eva Jiricna, Staircases, In/Ex Terior: The Works of Eva Jiricna 2005. *Address:* Eva Jiricna Architects, Third Floor, 38 Warren Street, London, W1T 6AE, England (office). *Telephone:* (20) 7554-2400 (office). *Fax:* (20) 7388-8022 (office). *E-mail:* mail@ejal.com (office). *Website:* www.ejal.com (office).

JISCHKE, Martin C., PhD; American engineer and academic administrator; b. 7 Aug. 1941, Chicago, Ill.; m. Patricia Fowler Jischke; one s. one d.; ed Illinois Tech. Inst., Massachusetts Inst. of Tech.; Asst to Transportation Sec. US Dept of Transportation, Washington, DC 1975–76; Dir and Prof., School of Aerospace, Mechanical and Nuclear Eng, Univ. of Okla 1977–81, Dean of Eng Coll. 1981–86, Acting Pres. 1985; Chancellor Mo.-Rolla Univ. 1986–91; Pres. Iowa State Univ. 1991–2000; Pres. Purdue Univ. 2000–07, now Pres. Emeritus; Pres. Assocn of Big Twelve Univs 1994; mem. Bd of Dirs Bankers Trust 1995–, American Council on Educ. 1996–, Nat. Merit Scholarship Corpn 1997–; Founding Pres. Global Consortium of Higher Educ. and Research for Agric. 1999; Fellow, AAAS, AIAA; numerous awards including Centennial Medallion of American Soc. for Eng Educ., Ukraine Medal of Merit, Professional Achievement Award from Ill. Inst. of Tech., Justin Smith Morrill Award from US Dept of Agriculture 2004. *Publications include:* articles in specialist journals. *Leisure interests:* golf, reading, travel. *Address:* c/o School of Aeronautics & Astronautics, Purdue University, 701 West Stadium Avenue, West Lafayette, IN 47907-2045, USA. *E-mail:* mcjischke@purdue.edu. *Website:* www.engineering.purdue.edu/AAE.

JOANNOU, Dakis, BCE, MsCE, DArch; British business executive and art collector; *Chairman, J&P-Avax SA;* b. 30 Dec. 1939, Nicosia, Cyprus; s. of Stelios Joannou and Ellie Joannou; m. Lietta Joannou; two s. two d.; ed Cornell Univ., Columbia Univ., USA, Univ. of Rome, Italy; Chair. J&P-Avax SA, Chair. J&P Group of Cos, J&P (Overseas); Chair. Athenaeum InterContinental Hotel & Touristic Enterprises SA, Yes! Hotels & Restaurants; f. DESTE Foundation for Contemporary Art, Athens 1983, currently Pres.; mem. Int. Dir's Council Solomon R. F. Guggenheim Foundation, New York; mem. Tate Int. Council, Serpentine Council, London, UK; mem. Bd of Trustees, New Museum of Contemporary Art, New York, Cttee on Painting and Sculpture, Museum of Modern Art, New York. *Address:* 9 Fragoklissias Street, 151 25 Marousi (office); DESTE Foundation for Contemporary Art, Filellinon 11 and Em. Pappa Street, Nea Ionia, 142 34, Athens, Greece. *Telephone:* (210) 6185551 (office); (210) 2754846. *Fax:* (210) 6104375 (office); (210) 2754862. *E-mail:* dakis@deste.gr; mpapafloratou@jp-avax.gr (office). *Website:* www.deste.gr; www.jp-avax.gr.

JOAZILE, Jean Rodolphe; Haitian lawyer and politician; b. 15 Sept. 1962, Ferrier; ed Acad. Militaire d'Haiti; fmr officer, Forces Armées d' Haiti; Senator (Nord-Est) 2009–12, Pres. of Sénat May–Dec. 2011; Minister of Nat. Defence 2012–14. *Address:* c/o Ministry of National Defence, Palais des Ministères, rue Mgr Guilloux, Port-au-Prince, Haiti (office).

JOBIM, Nelson Azevedo; Brazilian lawyer and politician; b. 12 April 1946, Santa Maria; ed Universidade Federal do Rio Grande do Sul; practised as lawyer 1969–94; Assoc. Prof. of Law, Universidade Federal de Santa Maria, Universidade de Brasília 1973–87; Pres. Santa Maria section, Bar Asscn 1977–78, Vice-Pres. Rio Grande Do Sul section 1984–86; mem. Partido do Movimento Democrático Brasileiro (PMDB), Leader PMDB in Nat. Ass. 1988; elected mem. of Parl. for Rio Grande do Sul 1987–91, re-elected 1991; Minister of Justice 1995–97, Minister of Defence 2007–11 (resgnd); served as judge and Pres. Supreme Fed. Court. *Address:* c/o Ministry of Defence, Esplanada dos Ministérios, Bloco Q, 70049-900 Brasília, DF, Brazil.

JOČIĆ, Dragan; Serbian lawyer and politician; b. 1960, Belgrade; ed Faculty of Law, Univ. of Belgrade; est. pvt. law practice, Belgrade; founding mem., Democratic Party of Serbia (DSS) 1992, mem. Exec. Bd 1992–, currently Vice-Pres.; elected Deputy to Serbian Parl. 1992–97; mem. Belgrade City Council 2000–; Pres. Parl. Comm. for Defence and Security 2002; Minister of Internal Affairs 2004–08. *Address:* Democratic Party of Serbia (Demokratska stranka Srbije), 11000 Belgrade, Pariska 13, Serbia (office). *Telephone:* (11) 3204719 (office). *Fax:* (11) 3204743 (office). *E-mail:* info@dss.org.yu (office). *Website:* www .dss.org.yu (office).

JODICE, Mimmo; Italian photographer and professor of fine arts; b. 29 March 1934, Naples; m. Angela Jodice; two s. one d.; Prof. Acad. of Fine Arts, Naples 1970–96; first photographic exhbn in Milan (with text of Cesare Zavattini) 1970; exhibited in many major museums including San Francisco Museum of Art, Philadelphia Museum of Art, Museo di Capodimonte, Cleveland Museum of Art, Castello di Rivoli, Turin 1970–; Prix Accad. dei Lincei for Photography 2004. *Publications include:* La Città Invisibile 1990, Mediterranean 1995, Paris 1998, Eden 1998, Isolario Mediterraneo 2000, Anni Settanta 2000, Boston 2001, Mare 2003. *Leisure interest:* classical music. *Address:* Baudoin Lebon Gallery, 38 rue St Croix de la Bretonnerie, 75004 Paris, France (office); Salita Casale 24, 80123 Naples, Italy (office). *Telephone:* (081) 2466144 (office). *Fax:* (081) 2466144 (office). *E-mail:* mimmo.jodice@inwind.it (office).

JOEL, William (Billy) Martin; American singer, songwriter and musician (piano); b. 9 May 1949, Bronx, NY; s. of Howard Joel and Rosalind Nyman; m. 2nd Christie Brinkley 1985 (divorced 1994); one d.; m. 3rd Kate Lee 2004; solo recording artist 1972–; first tour of USSR by American popular music artist 1987; numerous tours, live appearances world-wide; Dr hc (Fairfield Univ.) 1991, (Berklee Coll. of Music) 1993, (Manhattan School of Music) 2008, Hon. DHumLitt (Hofstra Univ.) 1997, Hon. DMus (Long Island Univ.) 2000, Hon. DFA (Syracuse University) 2006; Grammy Awards for Record of the Year (for Just the Way You Are) 1978, for Song of the Year (for Just the Way You Are) 1978, Grammy Legend Award 1990, ASCAP Founders' Award 1997, numerous American Music Awards, including American Music Award of Merit 1999, RIAA Diamond Award 1999, James Smithson Bicentennial Medal of Honor 2000. *Recordings include:* albums: Cold Spring Harbor 1971, Piano Man 1973, Streetlife Serenade 1974, Turnstiles 1976, The Stranger 1977, 52nd Street (Grammy Awards for Album of the Year, for Best Pop Vocal Performance) 1979, Glass Houses (Grammy Award for Best Pop Vocal Performance) 1980, Songs In The Attic 1981, The Nylon Curtain 1982, An Innocent Man 1983, Greatest Hits Volume I & II 1985, The Bridge 1986, Kohuept 1987, Storm Front 1989, River Of Dreams 1993, Greatest Hits Volume III 1997, 2000 Millennium Concert 2000, The Essential Billy Joel 2001, Fantasies and Delusions 2001, Movin Out 2002, My Lives 2005, 12 Gardens Live 2006, The Stranger 2008, The Hits 2010, She's Got A Way 2010, Piano Man 2011. *Publication:* Goodnight My Angel: A Lullabye (juvenile fiction) 2004. *Address:* c/o Columbia Records, Sony BMG Music, 550 Madison Avenue, New York, NY 10022-3211, USA (office). *Website:* www.sonybmg.com (office); www.billyjoel.com.

JOERRES, Jeffrey (Jeff) A., BS; American business executive; *Chairman, President and CEO, Manpower Inc.;* b. ed Marquette Univ., Milwaukee, Wis.; fmr Man. IBM; Vice-Pres. of Sales and Marketing ARI Network Services –1993; Vice-Pres. of Marketing, Manpower Inc. 1993, becoming Sr Vice-Pres. of European Operations, Global Account Man. and Devt, Pres. and CEO 1999–, Chair. 2001–; Dir, Fed. Reserve Bank of Chicago, Johnson Controls Inc., US Council for Int. Business; Co-Chair. NAACP Nat. Convention, Milwaukee 2005, B20 Task Force on Employment 2012, World Econ. Forum on Latin America April 2012, Future Workforce Cttee of the Greater Milwaukee Cttee; Trustee, Cttee for Econ. Devt (CED). *Address:* Manpower Inc., 100 Manpower Place, Milwaukee, WI 53212, USA (office). *Telephone:* (414) 961-1000 (office). *Fax:* (414) 906-7985 (office). *E-mail:* info@manpower.com (office). *Website:* www.manpower.com (office).

JÕERÜÜT, Jaak; Estonian politician and diplomatist; b. 9 Dec. 1947, Tallinn; m.; ed Faculty of Econs, Tallinn Technical Inst.; Ed. Eesti Raamat publishing house 1976–77; Sec. and Deputy Chair. Estonian Writers' Union 1977–89; Deputy Minister, Ministry of Culture 1989–90; mem. Parl. 1990–92, Chair. Standing Cttee on Research, Educ. and Culture; Amb. to Finland 1993–97; Dir-Gen. Protocol Dept, Ministry of Foreign Affairs 1997–98; Amb. to Italy 1998–2002, to Malta 1999–2002, to Cyprus 1999–2004; Inspector-Gen., Ministry of Foreign Affairs 2002–04; Special Adviser to the Govt 2002–03; Perm. Rep. to UN, New York July–Nov. 2004; Minister of Defence 2004–05; Amb. to Latvia 2006–10; mem. Estonian Writers' Union, Estonian PEN. *Address:* c/o Ministry of Foreign Affairs, Islandi Väljak 1, Tallinn 15049, Estonia.

JOFFE, Josef, PhD; German journalist, editor and international relations scholar; *Publisher-Editor, Die Zeit;* b. 15 March 1944, Łódź, Poland; m. Dr Christine Joffe; two d.; ed Swarthmore Coll., Johns Hopkins Univ., Harvard Univ., USA; Foreign and Editorial Page Dir Suddeutsche Zeitung 1985–2000; Publr-Ed. Die Zeit newspaper 2000–; Professorial Lecturer, Johns Hopkins Univ. 1982–84; Adjunct Prof. of Political Science, Stanford Univ. 2004–, Fellow, Inst. for Int. Studies, Stanford 2004, now Sr Fellow; Fellow, Hoover Inst.; Visiting Prof. of Govt, Harvard Univ. 1999–2000, Assoc., Olin Inst. for Strategic Studies; Visiting Lecturer, Princeton Univ., Dartmouth Univ.; Founding Bd mem. The National

Interest 1995–2005, The American Interest; mem. Editorial Bd International Security, Prospect; Order of Merit 1998; hon. degree (Swarthmore Coll.) 2002, (Lewis and Clark Coll.) 2005; Theodor-Wolff-Prize in Journalism (Germany), Ludwig Börne Prize in Essays/Literature (Germany). *Publications include:* The Limited Partnership: Europe, the United States and the Burdens of Alliance 1987, The Great Powers 1998, Überpower: The Imperial Temptation of America 2006, The Myth of America's Decline 2013; numerous articles in scholarly journals and chapters in books. *Address:* Die Zeit, Speersort 1, 20095 Hamburg, Germany (office). *Telephone:* (40) 328-00 (office). *Fax:* (40) 3280-596 (office). *E-mail:* dagmar.gentsch@zeit.de (office). *Website:* www.zeit.de (office).

JOFFE, Roland I.V.; British film director; b. 17 Nov. 1945, London; m. Jane Lapotaire (divorced); one s.; ed Carmel Coll., Berks. and Univ. of Manchester; Prix Italia 1978, Prix de la Presse, Prague 1978, Premio San Fidele 1985. *Films:* The Killing Fields 1984, The Mission 1986, Fat Man and Little Boy 1989, City of Joy 1991, Super Mario Bros (producer only), The Scarlet Letter 1995, Goodbye Lover 1999, Vatel 2000, Captivity 2007, You and I 2010, There Be Dragons 2010, Singularity 2011. *Television includes:* Spongers 1978, No Mama No 1980, United Kingdom 1981, 'Tis Pity She's a Whore 1982, Shadow Makers 1990, The Stars Look Down (series). *Address:* William Morris Agency, 151 South El Camino Drive, Beverly Hills, CA 90212, USA.

JOFFE, Rowan, BA; British film director and screenwriter; b. 1972; s. of Roland Joffe and Jane Lapotaire; ed Westminster School, Oxford Univ. *Theatre:* as writer: Accidental Colour 1998, Emporium 1998, Out of the Mouths 1998, The History of Misfortune 2000, Faithful Dealing 2001. *Television includes:* as writer: Last Resort (Best New British Feature Award, Edinburgh Int. Film Festival) 2000, Gas Attack (Best New British Feature Award, Edinburgh Int. Film Festival) 2001, Turkish Delight 2003, Broadwater Farm 2006, Secret Life 2007; as dir: The Shooting of Thomas Hurndall (BAFTA Award for Best Fiction Dir 2009, Golden Nymph Award, Monte Carlo TV Festival 2009) 2008. *Films:* as writer: 28 Weeks Later 2007, Secret Life (also dir) 2007, The American 2010; as writer and dir: Brighton Rock 2011, Before I Go To Sleep 2012. *Address:* Curtis Brown Group Ltd, 5th Floor, Haymarket House, 28-29 Haymarket, London, SW1Y 4SP, England (office). *Telephone:* (20) 7393-4450 (office). *Fax:* (20) 7393-4401 (office). *E-mail:* camillay@curtisbrown.co.uk (office). *Website:* www.curtisbrown.co.uk/rowan-joffe (office).

JOHANNESEN, Kaj Leo Holm; Faroese politician; *Prime Minister;* b. 28 Aug. 1964, Tórshavn; s. of Leo Hans Johannesen and Karin Holm Johannesen; m. Jórun Bærentsen; three s.; ed Føroya Sjómansskúli (Centre of Maritime Studies); began career in fishing industry, later captaining fishing vessels and freighters; has also worked as car salesman; joined Faroe Seafood 1989, Sales Man., Kósin (fish processing factory) 1995–97; mem. Faroese Unionist Party 1988–, Leader 2004–; mem. Tórshavn City Council 1996–2000; mem. Løgting (Parl.) 2002–, Deputy Chair. Govt Cttee 2003–04, mem. Trade and Industry Cttee 2003–04, Finance Cttee 2004–08, Chair. Foreign Affairs Cttee 2004–08; Prime Minister 2008–. *Achievements include:* fmr goalkeeper for Faroese int. football team, receiving seven caps 1988–94. *Address:* Løgmansskrivstovan (Prime Minister's Office), Tinganes, PO Box 64, 110 Tórshavn, Faroe Islands (office). *Telephone:* 306000 (office). *Fax:* 306015 (office). *E-mail:* info@tinganes.fo (office). *Website:* www.tinganes.fo (office).

JOHANNS, Michael (Mike) Owen, BA, JD; American lawyer and politician; *Senator from Nebraska;* b. 18 June 1950, Osage, Ia; s. of John Robert Johanns and Adeline Lucy Johanns (née Royek); m. 1st Constance J. Weiss 1972 (divorced 1985); one s. one d.; m. 2nd Stephanie Suther 1986; ed St Mary's Coll., Creighton Univ.; law clerk, Neb. State Supreme Court 1974–75; Assoc., Cronin and Hannon (law firm) 1975–76; Pnr, Nelson, Johanns, Morris, Holdeman and Titus, Lincoln, Neb. 1976–91; Commr Lancaster Co., Neb. 1982–86; mem. Lincoln City Council 1989–91, Mayor of Lincoln 1991–98; Gov. of Neb. 1999–2005; Sec., US Dept of Agric., Washington, DC 2005–09; Senator from Neb. 2009–; fmr Chair. Gov.'s Ethanol Coalition; fmr Co-Chair. Govs' Biotechnology Partnership, Gov.s' Public Power Alliance; fmr Vice-Chair. Midwest Govs Asscn; fmr mem. League of Nebraska Municipalities, Midwest Govs Conf., Nat. Govs Assen, Republican Govs Assen, US Conf. of Mayors, Western Govs Assen; Republican. *Address:* 404 Russell Senate Office Building, Washington, DC 20510, USA (office). *Telephone:* (202) 224-4224 (office). *Fax:* (202) 228-0436 (office). *E-mail:* mike_johanns@johanns.senate.gov (office). *Website:* johanns.senate.gov (office).

JÓHANNSSON, Kjartan, CE, PhD; Icelandic politician and diplomatist (retd); b. 19 Dec. 1939, Reykjavik; s. of Jóhann Jóhannsson and Astrid Dahl Thorsteinsson; m. Irma Karlsdóttir 1964; one d.; ed Reykjavik Coll., Tech. Univ. of Stockholm, Sweden, Univ. of Stockholm, Illinois Inst. of Tech., USA; Consulting Eng in Reykjavik 1966–78; Teacher in Faculty of Eng and Science, later Prof. in Faculty for Econs and Business Admin, Univ. of Iceland 1966–78, 1980–89; Chair. Org. for Support of the Elderly, Hafnarfjördur; mem. Bd of Dir Icelandic Aluminium Co. Ltd 1970–75; Chair. Fisheries Bd of Municipal Trawler Co., Hafnarfjördur 1970–74; mem. Municipal Council, Hafnarfjördur 1974–78; mem. Party Council and Exec. Council, Social Democratic Party 1972–89, Vice-Chair. of Social Democratic Party 1974–80, Chair. 1980–84; mem. Althing (Parl.) 1978–89, Speaker of the Lower House 1988–89; Minister of Fisheries 1978–80, also Minister of Commerce 1979–80; Amb. and Perm. Rep. to UN and other int. orgs Geneva 1989–94; Sec.-Gen. EFTA 1994–2001; mem. staff, External Trade Dept, Ministry of Foreign Affairs 2002; Amb. to Belgium, Liechtenstein, Luxembourg and Chief of Mission to the EU 2002–05. *Address:* Vatnsstig 21, 101 Reykjavík, Iceland. *Telephone:* 5342597. *E-mail:* kjartan.johannsson@gmail.com.

JOHANSEN, Hans Christian, DrOec; Danish professor of economic history; b. 27 June 1935, Arhus; s. of Vilhelm Johansen and Clara Andersen; m. Kirstine Madsen 1967; one s. one d.; ed Univ. of Arhus; Danish Foreign Service 1963–64; Sr Lecturer, Univ. of Arhus 1964–70; Prof. of Econ. History, Univ. of Odense 1970–2003; Dir Danish Centre for Demographic Research 1998–2002. *Publications:* books and articles on Danish and int. econ. and social history in the 18th, 19th and 20th centuries. *Address:* Anne Maries Alle 4A, 5250 Odense SV, Denmark (home). *Telephone:* 66-17-21-05 (home). *E-mail:* hcj@hist.sdu.dk (office).

JOHANSEN, Peter, DrPhil; Danish computer scientist and academic; *Professor Emeritus of Computer Science, University of Copenhagen;* b. 29 Jan. 1938, Copenhagen; s. of Paul Johansen and Grethe Johansen (née Smith); m. Jytte

Jepsen 1963; one s. two d.; ed Univ. of Copenhagen; Asst Prof., Tech. Univ. 1964–67; mem. Research Staff, MIT 1967–69; Asst Prof. of Computer Science, Univ. of Copenhagen 1969–74, Prof. 1974–2008, Prof. Emer. 2008–, Dean of Faculty 1988–90; Visiting Prof., Univ. of Manoa, Hawaii 1977–78; mem. Danish Natural Science Research Council 1981–84, Royal Danish Acad. of Sciences 1984–; Kt (First Class), Order of the Dannebrog. *Publications:* An Algebraic Normal Form for Regular Events 1972, The Generating Function of the Number of Subpatterns 1979, Representing Signals by their Toppoints in Scale Space 1986, Inductive Inference of Ultimately Periodic Sequences 1988, On the Classification of Toppoints in Scale Space 1994, On-line string matching with feedback 1995, Adaptive Pattern Recognition 1997, Branch Points in One-dimensional Gaussian Scale Space 2000, Products of Random Matrices 2002. *Address:* Ørnebakken 72, 2840 Holte, Denmark. *E-mail:* peterjo@di.ku.dk.

JOHANSON, Donald Carl, PhD; American vertebrate palaeontologist and academic; *Founding Director, Institute of Human Origins, Arizona State University;* b. 28 June 1943, Chicago, Ill.; s. of Carl Torsten and Sally Eugenia Johanson (née Johnson); m. 1st Chris Boner 1967 (divorced); m. 2nd Susan Whelan 1981 (divorced); one step-s. one step-d.; m. 3rd Lenora Carey 1988 (divorced); one s.; ed Univ. of Illinois, Univ. of Chicago; mem. Dept of Physical Anthropology, Cleveland Museum of Natural History 1972–81, Curator 1974–81; Adjunct Prof. Case Western Reserve Univ. 1982; Prof. of Anthropology, Stanford Univ. 1983–89; Prof. of Anthropology and Dir Inst. of Human Origins, Ariz. State Univ. 1997–2009, Founding Dir Inst. of Human Origins 2009–; host, Nature (series), Public Broadcasting Service TV 1982, host-narrator three-part Nova series In Search of Human Origins 1994; Pres. Inst. of Human Origins, Berkeley 1981–97; Fellow, AAAS, Royal Geographical Soc., California Acad. of Sciences; Hon. DSc (John Carroll) 1979, (The Coll. of Wooster) 1985, (Westfield State Univ.) 2008, (Case Western Reserve) 2009; Fregene Prize 1987, American Book Award 1982, Distinguished Service Award, American Humanist Assen 1983, Golden Plate, American Acad. of Achievement 1976, Professional Achievement Award 1980, Outstanding Achievement Award 1979, Golden Mercury Int. Award 1982, Alumni Achievement Award, Univ. of Illinois 1995, Anthropology in Media Award, American Assen of Anthropologists 1999, Explorers' Club Medal 2010. *Television:* The First Family 1981, Lucy in Disguise 1982, In Search of Human Origins 1994. *Publications:* The Beginnings of Humankind (with M. A. Edey) (American Book Award) 1981, Blueprints: Solving the Mystery of Evolution (with M. A. Edey) 1989, Lucy's Child: The Discovery of a Human Ancestor (with James Shreeve) 1989, Journey from the Dawn (with Kevin O'Farrell) 1990, Ancestors: In Search of Human Origins (with L. E. Johanson and Blake Edgar) 1994, From Lucy to Language (with Blake Edgar) 1997, Ecce Homo (co-ed. with G. Ligabue) 1999, The Skull of Australopithecus afarensis (with W. H. Kimbel and Y. Rak) 2004, Lucy's Legacy: The Quest for Human Origins (with Kate Wong) 2009; many scientific articles, papers and reviews. *Leisure interests:* photography, tennis, fly-fishing, classical music (including opera), golf, cycling. *Address:* Institute of Human Origins, Arizona State University, PO Box 874101, Tempe, AZ 85287, USA (office). *Telephone:* (480) 727-6580 (office). *Fax:* (480) 727-6570 (office). *E-mail:* johanson.iho@asu.edu (office). *Website:* www.becominghuman.org (office); iho.asu.edu (office).

JOHANSSON, Leif, MSc (Eng); Swedish business executive; *Chairman, Telefonaktiebolaget L.M. Ericsson; Chairman, AstraZeneca PLC;* b. 30 Aug. 1951, Gothenburg; s. of the late Lennart Johansson and Inger Johansson; m. Eva Birgitta Fjellman; two s. three d.; ed Chalmers Univ. of Tech.; project consultant, Indevo 1974–76; product developer and Asst to the Pres., Centro-Maskin 1977; Pres. Husqvarna Motorcycles 1979–81; Div. Man., Office Machines, Facit Sweden 1981–82, Pres. Facit 1982–84; Div. Man., AB Electrolux, White Goods 1984–87, Pres. 1987–88, Exec. Vice-Pres. AB Electrolux 1988–91, Pres. 1991–94, Pres. and CEO 1994–97; mem. Bd of Dirs and Pres. AB Volvo and CEO Volvo Group, Gothenburg 1997–2011; Chair. Telefonaktiebolaget L.M. Ericsson 2011–; Chair. AstraZeneca PLC 2012–; mem. Bd of Dirs Bristol-Myers Squibb Co., Svenska Cellulosa AB SCA, Confed. of Swedish Enterprise, Assen of Swedish Eng Industries; Chair. European Round Table of Industrialists; Dir Confed. of Swedish Enterprise; mem. Royal Swedish Acad. of Eng Sciences; Order of the Seraphim 2001, Chevalier, Légion d'honneur 2005; Dr hc (Blekinge Inst. of Tech.) 2006, Hon. MD (Univ. of Gothenborg) 2007; Marcus Wallenberg ASEA Award 1977, Gold Memorial Medal Kungliga Automobilklubben, Royal Swedish Automobile Club 2005, Mekanprisma Award 2009, Large Gold Medal, Royal Swedish Acad. of Eng Sciences 2011. *Address:* Telefonaktiebolaget L.M. Ericsson, Torshamnsgatan 23, Kista, 164 83 Stockholm, Sweden (office); AstraZeneca PLC, 2 Kingdom Street, London, W2 6BD, England (office). *Telephone:* (10) 719-00-00 (Stockholm) (office); (20) 7604-8000 (London) (office). *E-mail:* info@ericsson.com (office); info@astrazeneca.com (office). *Website:* www.ericsson.com (office); www.astrazeneca.com (office).

JOHANSSON, Scarlett; American actress, model and singer; b. 22 Nov. 1984, New York, NY; d. of Karsten Johansson and Melanie Sloan; m. Ryan Reynolds 2008 (divorced 2011); ed Professional Children's School, Manhattan. *Plays:* A View from the Bridge, New York 2010 (Tony Award for Best Performance by a Featured Actress 2010). *Films include:* North 1994, Just Cause 1995, If Lucy Fell 1996, Manny & Lo 1996, Home Alone III 1997, The Horse Whisperer (Hollywood Reporter Young Star Award) 1998, My Brother the Pig 1999, Ghost World (Best Supporting Actress, Toronto Film Critics Assen) 2000, The Man Who Wasn't There 2001, An American Rhapsody 2001, Eight Legged Freaks 2002, Lost in Translation (Countercurrent Prize for Best Actress, Venice Film Festival, Best Actress, BAFTA Awards, Best Actress, Boston Soc. of Film Critics) 2003, Girl with a Pearl Earring 2003, The Perfect Score 2004, A Love Song for Bobby Long 2004, The SpongeBob SquarePants Movie (voice) 2004, In Good Company 2004, Match Point 2005, A Good Woman 2005, The Island 2005, Scoop 2006, The Black Dahlia 2006, The Prestige 2006, The Nanny Diaries 2007, The Other Boleyn Girl 2008, Vicky Cristina Barcelona 2008, The Spirit 2008, He's Just Not That Into You 2009, Iron Man 2 2010, We Bought a Zoo 2011, Avengers Assemble 2012, Hitchcock 2012, Under the Skin 2013, Don Jon's Addiction 2013, Her 2013. *Television includes:* The Client (series) 1995, Robot Chicken (series) 2005–08. *Recordings:* albums: Anywhere I Lay My Head 2008, Break Up (with Pete Yorn) 2009. *Address:* c/o Marcel Pariseau, True Public Relations, 6725 West Sunset Boulevard, Suite 570, Los Angeles, CA 90028, USA.

JOHANSSON-HEDBERG, Birgitta, BA; Swedish psychologist and business executive; *Chairman, Vinnova*; b. 2 March 1947; m. Bo Hedberg 1978 (died 2012); ed Lund Univ.; Chair. AB Lindex 1993–2004; fmr Resident Dir for Scandinavia, Wolters Kluwer; CEO FöreningsSparbanken (Swedbank) (formed by merger of Föreningsbanken AB and Sparbanken Sverige 1997) –2003; Pres. and CEO Svenska Lantmännen (Swedish Farmers' Supply and Crop Marketing Asscn) 2004–06; Chair. Vinnova (Swedish Governmental Agency for Innovation Systems) 2007–; Deputy Chair. A-banan; mem. Bd of Dirs Svea Skog 2002–, Fortum Corpn 2004–, Swedish Financial Supervisory Authority, NAXS Nordic Access Buyout Fund, Forest Co. Ltd 2008–, TeliaSonera AB 1993–2001, Skandia 2004–05; Chair. Univ. of Umeå; mem. Aktiemarknadsnämnden, Swedish Securities Council; ranked by Fortune magazine amongst 50 Most Powerful Women in Business outside the US (32nd) 2002. *Address:* Vinnova, 101 58, Stockholm, Sweden (office). *Telephone:* (8) 473-30-00 (office). *E-mail:* vinnova@vinnova.se (office). *Website:* www.vinnova.se (office).

JOHN, Sir David Glyndwr, Kt, KCMG, MA, MBA; British business executive; *Chairman, Premier Oil PLC;* b. 20 July 1938, Pontypridd; s. of William G. John and Marjorie John; m. Gillian Edwards 1964; one s. one d.; ed Christ's Coll., Cambridge, Columbia Univ., New York and Harvard Univ., USA; trainee man. British Steel; later worked for RTZ and Redland; joined Gray Mackenzie (Inchcape Group) 1981, Chief Exec. 1986; Chief Exec. Inchcape Berhad 1987, Chair. 1990; mem. Bd Inchcape PLC 1988–95; Exec. Chair. Inchcape Toyota Motors 1995, BSI Group 2002–; Chair. (non-exec.) Premier Oil PLC 1998–; Dir (non-exec.) BOC Group PLC 1993– (Chair. (non-exec.) 1996–2002), The St Paul Cos Inc., Minn., USA 1996–2003, Balfour Beatty PLC 2000– (Chair. 2003–), Welsh Devt Agency 2001–02; Dr hc (Univ. of Glamorgan). *Leisure interests:* reading, gardening. *Address:* Premier Oil PLC, 23 Lower Belgrave Street, London, SW1W 0NR, England (office). *Telephone:* (20) 7730-1111 (office). *Fax:* (20) 7730-4696 (office). *E-mail:* premier@premier-oil.com (office). *Website:* www.premier-oil.com (office).

JOHN, Sir Elton Hercules, Kt, CBE; British musician (piano), singer and songwriter; b. (Reginald Kenneth Dwight), 25 March 1947, Pinner, Middx; s. of Stanley Dwight and Sheila Eileen Dwight (née Harris); m. Renata Blauel 1984 (divorced 1988); civil partner David Furnish 2005; two s.; ed Pinner County Grammar School, Royal Acad. of Music, London; began piano lessons 1951; played piano in Northwood Hills Hotel bar 1964; mem. local group Bluesology 1961–67; worked for Mills Music Publrs; began writing songs with Bernie Taupin 1967; solo recording contract with DJM Records 1967; concerts in Los Angeles, USA 1970; formed Rocket Record Co. with Bernie Taupin 1973, first album released 1976; f. publishing co., Big Pig Music 1974; frequent tours in UK, USA, Japan, Australia 1971–76; Vice-Pres. Nat. Youth Theatre of GB 1975–; first int. star to perform concerts in USSR 1979; produced records with Clive Franks for Kiki Dee, Blue, Davey Johnstone's China 1976–77; Chair. Watford Football Club 1976–90, 1997–, Life Pres. 1990–; fmr part-owner Los Angeles Aztecs of the North American Soccer League; occasional columnist, The Guardian; f. Elton John AIDS Foundation 1993, Rocket Pictures; Trustee, Wallace Collection 1999–; Chair. The Old Vic Theatre Trust 2002–; Fellow, British Acad. of Composers and Songwriters 2004–; Officer, Ordre des Arts et des Lettres 1993; Hon. mem. RAM 1997; Dr hc (RAM) 2002; Ivor Novello Awards (for Daniel) 1974, (for Don't Go Breaking My Heart, with Kiki Dee) 1977, (for Song for Guy) 1979, (for Nikita) 1986, (for Sacrifice) 1991, American Music Awards for Favorite Male Artist, Favorite Single 1977, Silver Clef Award 1979, BRIT Awards for Outstanding Contribution to British Music 1986, Best British Male Artist 1991, MTV Special Recognition Trophy 1987, Grammy Awards 1987, 1991, 1998, 2000, Grammy Lifetime Achievement Award 2000, Nat. Acad. of Popular Music Hitmaker Award 1989, Q Magazine Merit Award 1993, Acad. Award for Best Original Song (for Can You Feel the Love Tonight?) 1995, recipient of Kennedy Center Honors 2004, ranked by Billboard magazine as the most successful male solo artist on The Billboard Hot 100 Top All-Time Artists 2008, Brits Icon Award 2013. *Stage productions:* The Lion King (musical) 2001, Billy Elliot (musical) 2005, Lestat (musical, with Bernie Taupin) 2006. *Soundtracks, scores and theatre albums:* Friends 1971, The Lion King 1994, Aida 1998, The Muse 1999, The Road to El Dorado 2000, Billy Elliot 2005, Lestat 2005, Gnomeo & Juliet (exec. producer) 2011. *Films include:* Born to Boogie 1972, Goodbye to Norma Jean 1973, Tommy 1975, To Russia with Elton 1980, The Rainbow 1989, The Lion King (music) 1994, Spice World (as himself) 1997, Desert Flower (producer) 1999, Women Talking Dirty (exec. producer) 1999, The Road to El Dorado (voice) 2000, Bob the Builder: A Christmas to Remember (video) (voice) 2001, The Country Bears (as himself) 2002, Tommy and Quadrophenia Live: The Who (video) 2005, It's a Boy Girl Thing (exec. producer) 2006, Elton John: Me, Myself & I (autobiog. as himself) 2007. *Television includes:* Zomercarroussel (mini-series) 1970, It's Cliff Richard (series) 1970, Russell Harty Plus (TV series) 1974, Great Performances (series) (exec. producer) – Elton John at the Royal Opera House 2003, Him and Us (film) (exec. producer) 2006, Spectacle: Elvis Costello with. . . (series) (exec. producer) 2008–10, David Bowie: The Story of Ziggy Stardust (film) 2012. *Recordings include:* albums: Empty Sky 1969, Elton John 1970, Tumbleweed Connection 1971, Friends (film soundtrack) 1971, 17-11-70 1971, Madman Across the Water 1972, Honky Chateau 1972, Don't Shoot Me, I'm Only the Piano Player 1973, Goodbye Yellow Brick Road 1973, Caribou 1974, Captain Fantastic and the Brown Dirt Cowboy 1975, Rock of the Westies 1975, Here and There 1976, Blue Moves 1976, A Single Man 1978, Victim of Love 1979, Lady Samantha 1980, 21 at 33 1980, The Fox 1981, Jump Up 1982, Too Low for Zero 1983, Breaking Hearts 1984, Ice on Fire 1985, Leather Jackets 1986, Reg Strikes Back 1988, Sleeping with the Past 1989, The One 1992, Made in England 1995, Love Songs 1995, The Big Picture 1997, Aida 1999, El Dorado 2000, Songs from the West Coast 2001, Peachtree Road 2004, The Captain and the Kid 2006, Rocket Man 2007, The Union (with Leon Russell) 2010, Good Morning To The Night (with Pnau) 2012, The Diving Board 2013. *Leisure interests:* football, collecting records, tennis, all sports. *Address:* c/o Sanctuary Artist Management, Sanctuary House, 45–53 Sinclair Road, London, W14 0NS, England (office). *Telephone:* (20) 7602-6351 (office). *Fax:* (20) 7603-5941 (office). *Website:* www.eltonjohn.com.

JOHN, Patrick; Dominican politician and sports administrator; b. 7 Jan. 1937; Leader, Dominica Labour Party 1974–83, Deputy Leader 1983–84; Minister of Communications and Works 1970–73, Deputy Premier and Minister of Finance 1974, Premier of Dominica 1974–78, Prime Minister 1978–79, Minister for Housing, Security and Devt 1978–79; Gen. Sec. Labour Party of Dominica 1985; mem. Parl. July–Nov. 1985; arrested 1981, tried and acquitted May 1982, re-tried Oct. 1985; sentenced to 12 years' imprisonment for conspiracy to overthrow govt; currently Pres. Dominica Football Asscn. *Address:* Dominica Football Association, Patrick John Football House, Bath Estate, PO Box 372, Roseau, Dominica.

JOHN, Radek; Czech journalist, writer, screenwriter and politician; *Chairman, Public Affairs (Věci veřejné) party;* b. 6 Dec. 1954, Prague; s. of Prof. Ctirad John and of the late Bozena Johnová; m. Zlata Adamovská (divorced 2010); one s. one d., and one d. from another relationship; ed Mladý svět (Young World) magazine 1980–93; worked in Filmovém studiu Barrandov as a scriptwriter and for TV 1980s; reporter and then Ed.-in-Chief Na vlastní oči (Own Eyes) public affairs programme, TV Nova 1997–2007, responsible for current affairs programme Snídaně s Novou (Breakfast with Nova), talk show Občanské judo (Civil Judo) and Tabu (Taboo) show; Chair. S & J–Medea Kultur a.s. (later Ora Print) 2002–09; Chair. Public Affairs (Věci veřejné) party 2009–; Deputy Prime Minister and Minister of the Interior 2010–11; Second Prize in category Moderator of Current Affairs Programmes, TýTý poll 1994, First Prize 1995, 1996–2002, 2005, 2006. *Screenplays include:* Jen si tak trochu písknout (Just a Little Whistle), Jako zajíci (Like Rabbits), Sněženky a machři, Bony a klid (Thawing, Bony and Peace), Proč? (Why?), Tankový prapor (Tank Battalion), Ta naše písnička česká II (Our Czech Song II), Prachy dělaj člověka (Money Makin' Man), Sněženky a machři po petadvaceti letech (Thawing After Twenty Years). *Publications:* Džínový svet (novel) 1980, Zacátek letopoctu (with Ivan Pelant) 1984, Memento (novel, translated into ten languages) 1986, Bony a klid 1987, Jak jsem videl Ameriku 1990, Drogy! (with Dr Jiří Presl) 1995. *Address:* Public Affairs (Věci Veřejné), Štefánikova 23/203, 150 00 Prague 5, Czech Republic (office). *Telephone:* 800879709. *E-mail:* info@veciverejne.cz (office). *Website:* www.veciverejne.cz (office).

JOHN, Sajeev O., BSc, PhD, FRSC; Canadian physicist and academic; *University Professor of Physics and Government of Canada Research Chair, Department of Physics, University of Toronto;* ed Massachusetts Inst. of Tech., Harvard Univ.; Natural Sciences and Eng Research Council of Canada Post-doctoral Fellow, Univ. of Pennsylvania 1984–86; Asst Prof. of Physics, Princeton Univ. 1986–89; joined Dept of Physics, Univ. of Toronto 1989, Univ. Prof. of Physics and Govt of Canada Research Chair, Dept of Physics 2001–; fmr Prin. Investigator, Photonics Research Ontario; lab. consultant, Corp. Research Science Labs, Exxon Research and Eng 1985–89; lab. consultant, Bell Communications Research, Red Bank, NJ 1989; mem. Max-Planck Soc. (Germany); Fellow, Canadian Inst. for Advanced Research, American Physical Soc., Optical Soc. of America; C.V. Raman Chair Professorship, Govt of India 2007; Herzberg Medal 1996, McLean Sr Fellowship, Univ. of Toronto 1996–, Steacie Prize in Science and Eng, Nat. Research Council of Canada 1997, Killam Fellowship, Canada Council for the Arts 1998–2000, Guggenheim Fellowship 2000–01, Japan Soc. for the Promotion of Science Fellowship, Humboldt Sr Scientist Award (Germany) 2000, King Faisal Int. Prize for Science (co-recipient) 2001, first ever winner of Premier's Platinum Medal for Science and Medicine 2002, Rutherford Medal, Royal Soc. of Canada (co-recipient) 2004, IEEE LEOS Int. Quantum Electronics Award 2007, Brockhouse Medal for Condensed Matter and Materials Physics, Canadian Asscn of Physicists 2007. *Achievement:* co-invented concept of photonic band gap materials 1987. *Address:* Department of Physics, Room MP1002, University of Toronto, 60 St George Street, Toronto, ON M5S 1A7, Canada (office). *Telephone:* (416) 978-3459 (office). *Fax:* (416) 978-2537 (office). *E-mail:* john@physics.utoronto.ca (office). *Website:* www.physics.utoronto.ca/~john (office).

JOHNOVÁ, Adriena; Czech painter; b. 6 Aug. 1926, Prague; d. of the late Václav Simota and Milena Simota; m. Jiří John 1923 (died 1972); one s.; ed Univ. of Industrial Arts; Grand Prix for Graphics, Ljubljana 1979, Grand Prix Int. for Drawings, Wrocław, Gottfried von Herder Prize, Vienna, Medal of Merit, Prague 1997. *Leisure interests:* human relations, literature, music, nature. *Address:* Na Podkovce 14, 140 00 Prague 4; Nad Královskou oborou 15, 170 00 Prague 7, Czech Republic. *Telephone:* (2) 41430393.

JOHNS, Andrew; Australian professional rugby league player (retd); b. 19 May 1974, Cessnock, NSW; halfback/hooker; player for Newcastle Knights 1994–2007, New South Wales 1995–2007, Australia 1995–2007; 212 appearances (62 as Capt.), 75 tries, 1,952 points, for Newcastle Knights, 21 appearances for New South Wales in State of Origin fixtures, 23 tests for Australia (apptd capt. in 2002); mem. of Australia's World Cup winning teams 1995 (named Player of the Tournament and Man of the Match in final) and 2000; winner Rugby League World Golden Boot Award 1999, 2001; winner Nat. Rugby League Player of the Year award three times; captained Newcastle Knights to Premiership title 1997, 2001. *Leisure interests:* surfing, horse racing. *Address:* The Fordham Company, POB 820, Woollahra, NSW 1350, Australia (office). *Telephone:* (02) 93329111 (office).

JOHNS, Anthony (Tony) Hearle, PhD, FAHA; Australian/British professor of Islamic studies; *Professor Emeritus and Visiting Fellow, Research School of Asian and Pacific Studies, Australian National University;* b. 28 Aug. 1928, Wimbledon, London; s. of the late Frank Charles Johns and of Ivy Doris Kathleen Johns (née Hearle); m. Yohanni Bey 1956; four s. one d.; ed St Boniface's Coll., Plymouth, and School of Oriental and African Studies, Univ. of London; Lecturer at Ford Foundation-sponsored Training Project, Indonesia 1954–58; Sr Lecturer in Indonesian Languages and Literatures, ANU 1958–63, Prof. 1963, now Prof. Emer., Chair. and Head of Dept 1963–83, Dean Faculty of Asian Studies 1963–64, 1965–67, 1975–79, 1988–91, Head of Southeast Asia Centre 1983–88, Visiting Fellow, Research School Pacific and Asian Studies 1994–96, 1997–2000, 2005–; Adjunct Prof., Australian Catholic Univ.; Visiting Prof., Dept of Religious Studies and Dept of Middle East and Islamic Studies, Univ. of Toronto 1989; Special Foreign Visiting Prof. in Islamic Studies, Chiba Univ., Tokyo 1991; Visiting Scholar, Oxford Centre for Hebrew and Jewish Studies, UK 1993–94; Fellow, Inst. for Advanced Studies, Hebrew Univ. of Jerusalem 1984–85; Univ. of London Sr Studentship 1953–54; Rhuvon Guest Prize in Islamic Studies, SOAS 1953–54, Centenary Medal for Service to Australian Soc. and the Humanities 2003. *Publications:* The Gift Addressed to the Spirit of the Prophet 1965, A Road with No End (trans. and Ed.) 1968, Cultural Options and the Role of Tradition 1981, Islam in Asia II Southeast and East Asia (Ed. and contrib. with R. Israeli) 1984, Reflections on the Dynamics and Spirituality of Sūrat al-Furqān in Literary

Structures of Religious Meaning in the Qur'an (contrib.) 2000, Islam in World Politics (Ed. and contrib. with Nelly Lahoud) 2005. *Leisure interests:* music, literature. *Address:* 70 Duffy Street, Ainslie, Canberra, ACT 2602, Australia (home). *Telephone:* (2) 6249-6574 (home). *E-mail:* ah_yjohns@netspeed.com.au (home).

JOHNS, Jasper; American painter; b. 15 May 1930, Augusta; s. of Jasper Johns, Sr and Jean Riley; ed Univ. of South Carolina; works in following collections: Tate Gallery, London, Museum of Modern Art, New York, Albright-Knox Art Gallery, Buffalo, NY, Museum Ludwig, Cologne, Hirshhorn Museum and Sculpture Garden, Washington, DC, Whitney Museum of American Art, Stedelijk Museum, Amsterdam, Moderna Museet, Stockholm, Dallas Museum of Fine Arts, Art Inst. of Chicago, Baltimore Museum of Art, Kunstmuseum Basel, Cleveland Museum of Art, Nat. Gallery of Art, Washington, DC, San Francisco Museum of Modern Art, Va Museum of Fine Arts, Walker Art Center, Minneapolis; mem. American Acad. of Arts and Letters; Hon. RA (London); Prize, Pittsburgh Int. 1958, Wolf Foundation Prize 1986, Gold Medal (American Acad. and Inst. of Arts and Letters) 1986, Int. Prize, Venice Biennale 1988, Nat. Medal of Arts 1990, Officier, Ordre des Arts et Lettres 1990, Praemium Imperiale Award (Japan) 1993, Presidential Medal of Freedom 2010. *Address:* PO Box 642, Sharon, CT 06069, USA.

JOHNS, Air Chief Marshal Sir Richard Edward, Kt, GCB, KCVO, CBE, FRAeS; British air force officer; b. 28 July 1939, Horsham, Sussex, England; s. of the late Lt Col Herbert Edward Johns and Marjory Harley Johns (née Everett); m. Elizabeth Naomi Anne Manning 1965; one s. two d.; ed Portsmouth Grammar School, RAF Coll., Cranwell; commissioned 1959; Night Fighter/Fighter Reconnaissance Squadrons, UK, Cyprus, Aden 1960–67; Flying Instructor 1968–71, Flying Instructor to HRH the Prince of Wales 1970–71; Officer Commanding 3 (Fighter) Squadron (Harrier) 1975–77; Dir Air Staff Briefing 1979–81; Station Commdr and Harrier Force Commdr, RAF Gütersloh 1982–84; ADC to HM The Queen 1983–84; at Royal Coll. of Defence Studies 1985; Sr Air Staff Officer, HQ RAF, Germany 1985–88; Sr Air Staff Officer HQ Strike Command 1989–91; Air Officer Commdg No. 1 Group 1991–93; Chief of Staff, Deputy C-in-C Strike Command and UK Air Forces 1993–94; Air Officer Commdg in Chief Strike Command 1994; C-in-C Allied Forces NW Europe 1994–97; Chief of Air Staff and Air ADC to HM The Queen 1997–2000; Constable and Gov. of Windsor Castle 2000–08; Pres. Windsor Festival 2001–08, Windsor and Eton Choral Soc. 2001–08, Royal Windsor Rose and Horticultural Soc. 2000–08; Nat. Pres. Hearing Dogs for Deaf People 2002–; Vice-Pres. The Wiltshire Historical Mil. Soc. 2009–; Chair. Bd of Trustees, RAF Museum 2000–06; Gov. Portsmouth Grammar School 1996–2009, Dauntsey's School 2009–; mem. Council St George's House 2000–08; Trustee, The Prince Philip Trust Fund 2000–08, Foundation of the Coll. of St George 2007–, The Overlord Embroidery Trust 2009–; Patron Labrador Life Line Trust 2001–; Freeman of the City of London 1999; Liveryman, Guild of Air Pilots & Air Navigators 1999–; Hon. Air Cdre, RAF Regt 2000–13; Hon. Col, 73 Engineer Regt (V) 1994–2001. *Leisure interests:* military history, rugby, cricket, equitation. *Address:* Dolphin House, Warminster Road, Chitterne, Wilts., BA12 0LH, England. *Telephone:* (1985) 850039. *E-mail:* rej76@waitrose.com.

JOHNSEN, Sigbjørn; Norwegian politician; b. 1 Oct. 1950, Lillehammer; m. Helle Laier Johnsen; three c.; ed Norwegian School of Man.; Deputy Rep. for Hedmark Co., Storting (Parl.) 1973–; Vice-Pres. Norwegian Labour League of Youth (AUF) 1975–77; Deputy Chair. Equal Status Council 1976–83; Minister of Finance 1990–96, 2009–13; Del. to Council of Europe's Parl. Ass. 1985–; Gov., Hedmark Co. 1997–2009; mem. Storting (Parl.) Standing Cttee on Justice 1976–77, on Local Govt and the Environment 1977–80, on Finance 1981 (Deputy Chair. 1986–), Nat. Council for Open-Air Recreation 1984–. *Address:* c/o Ministry of Finance, Akersgt. 40, PO Box 8008 Dep., 0030 Oslo, Norway (office).

JOHNSON, Abigail (Abby) Pierrepont, BA, MBA; American business executive; *President, Fidelity Personal Workplace and Institutional Services, Fidelity Management & Research Corporation;* b. 19 Dec. 1961, Boston, Mass; d. of Edward C. (Ned) Johnson III; m. Christopher J. McKown 1988; two c.; ed Buckingham Browne & Nichols School, Hobart Coll., William Smith Coll., Harvard Business School; with Booz Allen Hamilton 1984–86; joined her father's co., Fidelity Management & Research Corpn (better known as Fidelity Investments, f. by her grandfather in 1946), Boston, as an analyst and equity portfolio man. 1988–97, Assoc. Dir Investment Div. 1997–2001, Pres. 2001–05, currently Pres., Fidelity Personal Workplace and Institutional Services; mem. Bd of Dirs Securities Industry and Financial Markets Asscn; mem. Cttee on Capital Markets Regulation; ranked by Fortune magazine amongst the 50 Most Powerful Women in Business in the US (eighth) 2004–05, (18th) 2006, (30th) 2007, (28th) 2008–09, (21st) 2010, (18th) 2011, (ninth) 2012, ranked by Forbes magazine amongst The World's 100 Most Powerful Women (15th) 2004, (37th) 2005, (59th) 2010, (70th) 2011, (57th) 2012, (60th) 2013. *Address:* FMR Corpn, 82 Devonshire Street, Boston, MA 02109, USA (office). *Telephone:* (617) 563-7000 (office). *Fax:* (617) 476-6150 (office). *Website:* www.fidelity.com (office).

JOHNSON, Rt Hon. Alan Arthur; British politician; b. 17 May 1950, Paddington, London; orphaned aged 12 and brought up by older sister; m. 1st Judith Cox 1968 (divorced); one s. two d.; m. 2nd Laura Jane Patient 1991; one s.; ed Sloane Grammar School, Chelsea (now part of Pimlico Acad.); postman, London 1968, Slough 1969; elected to Br. Cttee Union of Communication Workers 1973, apptd Chair. Slough Br. 1976, elected to Nat. Exec. Council 1981, became full-time Officer 1987, elected (youngest ever) Gen. Sec. 1992, apptd Jt Gen. Sec. after merger of Union of Communication Workers and Nat. Communication Union 1995; mem. Gen. Council and Nat. Exec. Cttee of TUC; fmr Dir Unity Trust Bank; MP for Kingston-upon-Hull West and Hessle 1997–; mem. Trade and Industry Select Cttee; apptd Parl. Pvt. Sec. to Financial Sec. to Treasury 1997, to Paymaster Gen. 1998; Minister for Competitiveness, Dept of Trade and Industry 1999–2001, Minister of State for Employment Relations and Regions 2001, Industry added to Portfolio 2002; Minister of State for Lifelong Learning, Higher and Further Educ., Dept for Educ. and Skills 2003–04; Sec. of State for Work and Pensions 2004–05, for Productivity, Energy and Industry 2005–06, for Educ. and Skills 2006–07, for Health 2007–09, for the Home Dept 2009–10; unsuccessful cand. for Deputy Leader of Labour Party 2007; Shadow Home Sec. May–Oct. 2010, Shadow Chancellor of the Exchequer 2010–11; Labour. *Publication:* This Boy (memoir)

2013. *Address:* House of Commons, Westminster, London, SW1A 0AA (office); Goodwin Resource Centre, Icehouse Road, Hull, HU3 2HQ, England (office). *Telephone:* (1482) 219211 (Hull) (office). *Fax:* (1482) 219211 (Hull) (office). *E-mail:* johnsona@parliament.uk (office). *Website:* www.alanjohnson.org (office).

JOHNSON, (Alexander) Boris (de Pfeffel); British politician and journalist; *Mayor of London;* b. 19 June 1964, New York City, NY, USA; s. of Stanley Patrick Johnson and Charlotte Fawcett; m. 1st Allegra Mostyn-Owen; m. 2nd Marina Wheeler 1993; two s. two d.; ed Eton Coll. and Balliol Coll., Oxford; journalist with The Times 1987–88; EC Corresp., The Daily Telegraph 1989–94, Asst Ed. and Chief Political Columnist 1994–99, currently columnist; Ed. The Spectator 1999–2005; MP (Conservative) for Henley 2001–08; Vice-Chair. Conservative Party 2003–04; Shadow Minister for the Arts 2004, for Higher Educ. 2005–07; Mayor of London 2008–; What the Papers Say Award for Columnist of the Year 2006. *Television includes:* Have I Got News for You 1998, 2004, 2006, The Dream of Rome 2006, Who Do You Think You Are? 2008, After Rome 2008. *Publications:* Friends, Voters, Countrymen 2001, Seventy-Two Virgins (novel) 2004, The Dream of Rome 2006, The British 2007, Life in the Fast Lane: The Johnson Guide to Cars 2007, Johnson's Life of London 2011. *Address:* The Mayor's Office, Greater London Authority, City Hall, The Queen's Walk, London, SE1 2AA, England (office). *Telephone:* (20) 7983-4100 (office). *Fax:* (20) 7983-4057 (office). *E-mail:* mayor@london.gov.uk (office). *Website:* www.london.gov.uk (office).

JOHNSON, Allen; American athlete (retd); b. 1 March 1971, Washington, DC; one d.; ed Lake Braddock High School, Burke, Va and Univ. of North Carolina; sprint hurdler; 110m hurdles personal best 12.92 seconds (Brussels, Belgium Aug. 1996); winner: World Championships 110m hurdles 1995, 1997, 2001, 2003, US Indoor Championships 60m hurdles 1995, 2002, 2003, World Indoor Championships 60m hurdles 1995, 2003, US Championships 100m hurdles 1996, 1997, 2000, 2001, 2002, 2003, World Championships 4×400m 1997 (with US team), Olympic Games 110m hurdles 2001, Nat. Indoor Championships 60m 2002, 2003; runner-up: World Cup 110m hurdles 1994, 2002, World Cup 4×100m 1996 (with US team), International Amateur Athletics Federation Grand Final 110m 1995, 2001; 4th: Olympic Games 110m hurdles 2000; eight runs of under 13 seconds in 110m hurdles; North American record holder 110m hurdles; coached by Curtis Frye; retd 2010; Jesse Owens Award 1997. *Address:* c/o HSInternational, Inc., 2600 Michelson Drive, Suite 680, Irvine, CA 92612, USA (office).

JOHNSON, Ben, MA, RCA; British artist; b. 24 Aug. 1946, Llandudno, Wales; s. of Harold Johnson and Ivy Lloyd Jones; m. Sheila Kellehar 1976; two s.; ed Royal Coll. of Art, London; has exhibited internationally since 1969; has undertaken direct comms from Centre Pompidou, Paris and Nat. Museums, Liverpool; work represented in public and corp. collections at Boymans van Beuningen Museum, Rotterdam, British Council, London, Tate Gallery, London, Contemporary Arts Soc., London, RIBA, London, City Art Gallery, Glasgow, Whitworth Gallery, Manchester, Centre Pompidou, Paris, Victoria & Albert Museum, London, Deutsche Bank, British Petroleum, Guildhall Art Gallery, Corpn of London, Special Admin. Regional Govt of Hong Kong, New Convention & Exhbn Centre, Hong Kong, Regional Services Council Museum, Hong Kong, British Museum, London, Walker Art Gallery, Liverpool, Museum of Liverpool; Hon. FRIBA. *Publications:* Cityscape: Ben Johnson's Liverpool, Ben Johnson: Foster in View. *Leisure interests:* architecture, cities. *Address:* c/o Alan Cristea Gallery, 31 Cork Street, London W1S 3NU (office); 4 St Peter's Wharf, Chiswick Mall, London, W6 9UD, England (office). *Telephone:* (20) 7439-1866 (office); (20) 8563-8768 (office). *E-mail:* info@alancristea.com (office); benjohnson@benjohnsonartist.com (office). *Website:* www.alancristea.com (office); www.benjohnsonartist.com (office).

JOHNSON, Betsey Lee, BA; American fashion designer; b. 10 Aug. 1942, Hartford, Conn.; d. of John Herman Johnson and Lena Virginia Johnson; m. 1st John Cale 1966; one d.; m. 2nd Jeffrey Olivier 1981; ed Pratt Inst., Syracuse Univ.; Editorial Asst, Mademoiselle magazine 1964–65; Partner and co-owner Betsey, Bunky & Nini, New York 1969–; shops in New York, LA, San Francisco, Coconut Grove, Fla, Venice, Calif., Boston, Chicago, Seattle; Prin. Designer for Paraphernalia 1965–69; designer, Alvin Duskin Co., San Francisco 1970; Head Designer, Alley Cat by Betsey Johnson (div. of LeDamor, Inc.) 1970–74; freelance designer for Jr Womens' div., Butterick Pattern Co. 1971, Betsey Johnson's Kids Children's Wear (div. of Shutterbug Inc.) 1974–77, Betsey Johnson for Jeanette Maternities, Inc. 1974–75; designer for Gant Shirtmakers Inc. (women's clothing) 1974–75, Tric-Trac by Betsey Johnson (women's knitwear) 1974–76, Butterick's Home Sewing Catalog 1975– (children's wear); Head Designer, Jr sportswear co.; designed for Star Ferry by Betsey Johnson and Michael Miles (children's wear) 1975–77; owner and Head Designer B.J., Inc. (designer wholesale co.), New York 1978; Pres. and Treas. B.J. Vines, New York; opened Betsey Johnson store, New York 1979; mem. Council of Fashion Designers, American Women's Forum; Hon. Chair. Fashion Targets Breast Cancer initiative; Merit Award, Mademoiselle magazine 1970, Coty Award 1971, two Tommy Print Awards 1971. *Address:* Betsey Johnson, 498 7th Avenue, 21st Floor, New York, NY 10018-6798; 110 East 9th Street, Suite A889, Los Angeles, CA 90079, USA. *Telephone:* (212) 244-0843. *Website:* pr@betseyjohnson.com; www.betseyjohnson.com.

JOHNSON, Brian Frederick Gilbert, PhD, FRS, FRSC, FRSE; British chemist and academic; b. 11 Sept. 1938; s. of Frank Johnson and Mona Johnson; m. Christine Draper 1962; two d.; ed Northampton Grammar School, Univ. of Nottingham; Reader in Chem., Univ. of Cambridge 1978–90, Fellow Fitzwilliam Coll. 1970–90, Hon. Fellow 1990–, Master 1999–2005; Crum Brown Prof. of Inorganic Chem., Univ. of Edin. 1991–95; Prof. of Inorganic Chem., Univ. of Cambridge 1995–2005; Tilden Lecturer, RSC; Corday Morgan Medal, RSC, Frankland Medal and Prize, RSC. *Publications:* Transition Metal Clusters 1982, over 1,000 academic papers and review articles. *Leisure interests:* walking, painting, riding, gardening. *Address:* c/o Fitzwilliam College, Cambridge, CB3 0DG, England (home).

JOHNSON, Charles Richard, BS, MA, PhD; American author and academic; *Professor Emeritus, Department of English, University of Washington, Seattle;* b. 23 April 1948, Evanston, Ill.; m. Joan New 1970; one s. one d.; ed Southern Illinois Univ., State Univ. of NY, Stoneybrook; fmr cartoonist and filmmaker; Lecturer, Univ. of Washington, Seattle 1975–79, Assoc. Prof. of English 1979–82, Prof. 1982, then Pollock Endowed Prof. of English, now Prof. Emer.; Co-Dir Twin Tigers (martial arts studio). *Publications include:* novels: Faith and the Good Thing 1974, Oxherding Tale 1982, Middle Passage (Nat. Book Award 1990) 1990; The Sorcerer's Apprentice (short stories); Being and Race: Black Writing Since 1970 1988, The Middle Passage 1990, All This and Moonlight 1990, In Search of a Voice (with Ron Chernow) 1991; Black Humor, Half-Past Nation Time (drawings); Booker, Charlie Smith and the Fritter Tree (broadcast plays); numerous reviews, essays and short stories. *Address:* University of Washington, Department of English, PDL A-406, Seattle, WA 98105, USA (office). *E-mail:* chasjohn@u .washington.edu. *Website:* depts.washington.edu/engl (office).

JOHNSON, David T., BEcons; American diplomatist; *Assistant Secretary for the Bureau of International Narcotics and Law Enforcement Affairs;* b. Georgia; m. Scarlett M. Swan; two d. one s.; ed Emory Univ., Canadian National Defence Coll.; early career as Asst Nat. Trust Examiner, US Treasury Dept; joined Foreign Service 1977, Vice-Consul, Consulate-Gen., Ciudad Juárez, Mexico 1978–79, Econ. Officer, Embassy in Berlin 1981–83, Deputy Dir State Dept Operations Center 1987–89, at Consul-Gen. in Vancouver 1990–93, Deputy Spokesman, State Dept, Dir State Dept Press Office 1993–95; Deputy Press Sec. for Foreign Affairs at the White House and Spokesman for Nat. Sec. Council 1995–97; Chief (with rank of Amb.), Perm. Mission to OSCE 1998, Minister and Deputy Chief of Mission, Embassy in London 2003–07; Asst Sec. of State for Bureau of Int. Narcotics and Law Enforcement Affairs 2007–. *Address:* Bureau of International Narcotics and Law Enforcement Affairs, Department of State, 2201 C St, NW, Washington, DC 20520, USA (office). *Telephone:* (202) 647-4000 (office). *Fax:* (202) 647-6738 (office). *Website:* www.state.gov/p/inl/index.htm (office).

JOHNSON, Dwayne Douglas, (The Rock); American actor and professional wrestler; b. 2 May 1972, Hayward, Calif.; s. of Rocky Johnson and Ata Johnson (née Maivia); m. Dany Garcia 1997 (separated 2007); one d.; ed Pres. William McKinley High School, Honolulu, Hawaii, Freedom High School, Bethlehem, Pa, Univ. of Miami; lived briefly in Auckland, NZ with his mother's family; mem. Univ. of Miami's nat. championship football team 1991; later played for the Calgary Stampeders in Canadian Football League; gained widespread recognition as a wrestler in World Wrestling Fed. (WWF) 1996–2004, originally billed as 'Rocky Maivia' and then as 'The Rock', later role as a villain as part of the Nation of Domination 1997, won WWF Championship 1998; won 16 championships in WWF/E, including nine World Heavyweight Championships (WWF/E Championship seven times and WCW/World Championship twice), two WWF Intercontinental Championships and five times as co-holder of WWF Tag Team Championships; sixth WWF/E Triple Crown Champion; winner of 2000 Royal Rumble; appears for World Wrestling Entertainment, Inc.; ring names: Flex Kavana, Rocky Maivia, The Rock, Dwayne 'The Rock' Johnson. *Films include:* WWF Slammy Awards 1997 (video) 1997, Survivor Series (video) 1998, WWF Judgment Day (video) 1998, WWF Mayhem in Manchester (video) 1998, The Rock – The People's Champ (video) 2000, The Mummy Returns 2001, Longshot 2001, The Scorpion King 2002, WWE Global Warning Tour: Melbourne (video) 2002, WWE: Brock Lesnar: Here Comes the Pain (video) 2003, Welcome to the Jungle 2003, WWE: The Stone Cold Truth (video) 2004, Walking Tall 2004, Be Cool 2005, WWE $250,000 Raw Diva Search (video) 2005, Doom 2005, Southland Tales 2006, WWE: McMahon (video) 2006, Gridiron Gang 2006, Reno 911!: Miami (uncredited) 2007, The Game Plan 2007, Disaster! A Major Motion Picture Ride... Starring You! (short) (uncredited) 2008, Get Smart 2008, Race to Witch Mountain 2009, Planet 51 (voice) 2009, Tooth Fairy 2010, Why Did I Get Married Too? (uncredited) 2010, The Other Guys 2010, You Again (uncredited) 2010, Faster 2010, Fast & Furious 5 2011, Journey 2: The Mysterious Island 2012, Snitch 2013, Empire State 2013, G.I. Joe: Retaliation 2013, Pain & Gain 2013, Fast & Furious 6 2013. *Television includes:* WWF Raw Is War (series) 1997–, WWF SmackDown! (series) 1999–, DAG (series) 2000, Royal Rumble (film) 2002, King of the Ring (film) 2002, Cory in the House (series) 2007, Saturday Night Live (series) 2010, Family Guy (series) 2010, Hannah Montana (series) 2007, Cubed (series) 2010, Transformers Prime (series) 2010, Clash Time (series) 2011–12, Royal Rumble (film) 2013. *Publication:* The Rock Says... (autobiog., co-written with Joe Layden) 2000. *Address:* c/o WME Entertainment, 9601 Wilshire Boulevard, Beverley Hills, CA 90210-5213, USA (office); c/o The Rock Foundation, 2525 Ponce de Leon Blvd, Fifth Floor, Coral Gables, FL 33134, USA. *Website:* www.dwaynetherockjohnson.net.

JOHNSON, Earvin, Jr. (Magic); American fmr professional basketball player and business executive; *Chairman and CEO, Johnson Development Corporation;* b. 14 Aug. 1959, Lansing, Mich.; s. of Earvin Johnson and Christine Johnson; m. Cookie Kelly; one s.; ed Lansing Everett High School, Mich. State Univ.; led Mich. State Univ. to NCAA Men's Basketball Championship 1979; drafted by Los Angeles Lakers Nat. Basketball Asscn (NBA) first overall 1979, played 1979–91 (retd after announcing he was HIV-positive); Vice-Pres., co-owner Los Angeles Lakers 1994–, Head Coach 1994, resumed playing career Feb. 1996, retd July 1996; Chair. Johnson Devt Corpn 1993–, Magic Johnson Entertainment 1997–; presenter TV show The Magic Hour 1998; mem. NBA All-Star Team 1980, 1982–89, mem. LA Lakers NBA championship teams 1980, 1982, 1985, 1987, 1988 (Finals Most Valuable Player 1980, 1982, 1987), US Olympic team 1992 (Gold Medal); NBA Most Valuable Player 1987, 1989, 1990; fmr mem. Nat. Aids Asscn, rejoined 1993; commentator NBC-TV 1995–96; f. Magic Johnson Foundation 1991; Player of the Year (Sporting News) 1987, J. Walter Kennedy Citizenship Award 1992, voted One of 50 Greatest Players in NBA History 1996, elected Naismith Memorial Basketball Hall of Fame 2002. *Publications:* Magic 1983, What You Can Do to Avoid AIDS 1992, My Life (autobiog.) 1992, When the Game was Ours (with Larry Bird and Jackie MacMullan) 2009. *Address:* Johnson Development Corporation, 9100 Wilshire Blvd., Suite 710 East, Beverly Hills, CA 90212, USA (office). *Telephone:* (310) 247-1994 (office). *Fax:* (310) 247-0733 (office). *Website:* www .magicjohnson.org (office); www.johnsondevelopmentcorp.com (office).

JOHNSON, Edward C. (Ned), III, BA; American financial services executive; *Chairman and CEO, Fidelity Investments;* m.; three c.; ed Harvard Univ.; research analyst, Fidelity Management & Research (FMR) Co. 1957, Man. Trend Fund 1960, Pres. FMR Corpn 1972, currently Chair. and CEO Fidelity Investments. *Address:* Fidelity Investments, 82 Devonshire Street, Boston, MA 02109, USA (office). *Telephone:* (617) 563-7000 (office). *Fax:* (617) 476-3876 (office). *Website:* www.fidelity.com (office).

JOHNSON, F(rederick) Ross, OC, BComm, MBA; Canadian business executive; b. 13 Dec. 1931, Winnipeg, Man.; s. of Frederick H. Johnson and Caroline Green; m. Laurie A. Graumann 1979; two s. (from previous marriage); ed Univs of Manitoba and Toronto; Vice-Pres. of Merchandising, T. Eaton Co. (Canada) 1965–66; Exec. Vice-Pres. and COO, GSW Ltd 1966–71; Pres. and CEO, Standard Brands Ltd, Canada 1971–74; Sr Vice-Pres. 1974–75, Pres. 1975–76, Chair. and CEO 1977–81; Pres. and COO Nabisco Brands Inc. 1981–83, Vice-Pres. and CEO 1984–85, Chief Exec. RJR Nabisco 1987–89 (after takeover of Nabisco by Reynolds), Pres. and COO R. J. Reynolds Industries 1985–87, Pres. and CEO 1987–89; Chair. and CEO RJM Group Inc. (investment advisory firm) 1989–; mem. Bd of Dirs AuthentiDate 2003–09, Chair. 2005–09; fmr Dir American Express, Power Corpn of Canada, Wosk's Ltd, Vancouver, Bank of Nova Scotia, Toronto; mem. Advisory Council, Columbia Univ., New York; Trustee, Econ. Club of New York (fmr Chair.); Chair. Multiple Sclerosis Soc., New York; mem. Int. Advisory Council, Power Corpn of Canada; Dr hc (St Francis Xavier Univ., Antigonish, NS) 1978, (Univ. of Newfoundland) 1980. *Leisure interests:* golf, skiing, tennis. *Address:* RJM Group, 200 Galleria Parkway, Suite 970, Atlanta, GA 30339, USA. *Telephone:* (770) 852-5000.

JOHNSON, Gabriel Ampah, DD'État; Togolese biologist, academic and university administrator; *Professor and Chair of Biology, National University of Côte d'Ivoire;* b. 13 Oct. 1930, Aneho; s. of William K. A. Johnson and Rebecca A. Ekue-Hettah; m. Louise Chipan 1962; three s. three d.; ed Univ. of Poitiers, France; Teaching Asst, Univ. of Poitiers –1956; Research Fellow, CNRS, France 1958–60; Deputy Dir of Educ., Togo 1959-60; Asst Prof., Nat. Univ. of Côte d'Ivoire, Abidjan 1961–64, Assoc. Prof. 1965–66, Prof., Chair. of Biology 1966–; Asst Dean, Faculty of Science 1963–68, Founding Dir Nat. Centre for Social Services 1964–68; Founding Rector, Univ. du Bénin, Lomé, Togo 1970–86; currently Rector and Chancellor, Togolese Univs; Dir of Higher Educ., Togo 1970–75; Pres. Nat. Planning Comm. of Togo 1973; Pres. Asscn of African Univs 1977–80; mem. Exec. Bd UNESCO 1997–; mem. Bd of Admin., Asscn of Partially or Fully French-Speaking Univs 1975–, Pan African Inst. for Devt 1977–, Int. Cttee of Bioethics 2001, Admin. Council Int. Fund for the Promotion of Culture (UNESCO) 2003; mem. Cen. Cttee Togo People's Rally (ruling party) 1976–; Founding Pres. Africa Club for an Integrated Devt 1980–; mem. Zoological Soc. of France 1956, Biological Soc. of France 1962, Endocrinological Soc. of France 1966, French Nat. Acad. of Pharmacy 2003; Hon. Vice-Pres. Gold Mercury Int. 1983; Chevalier, Ordre nat. de la Côte d'Ivoire 1966; Officier Légion d'honneur 1971; Commdr Order of Cruzeiro do Sul (Brazil) 1976; Commdr Order of Merit (France) 1983; Commdr, Ordre des Palmes Académiques, (France) 1986; Commdr, Ordre du Mono (Togo) 2000; Dr hc Sherbrooke, (Canada) 1979, (Lille) 1983, (Bordeaux) 1986; Medal of Honour, Univ. of São Paulo, Brazil 1980; Gold Mercury Int. Award 1982, Gold Medal of Honour, Univ. of Benin. *Publications:* several articles in scientific journals. *Leisure interests:* reading, classical and modern music, swimming, farming (cattle breeding). *Address:* BP 7098, Lomé, Togo. *Telephone:* (22) 21-52-41 (office); (22) 21-53-65 (home). *Fax:* (22) 21-52-41 (office); (22) 21-53-65 (home). *E-mail:* gampahjohnson@yahoo.fr.

JOHNSON, Gary Earl, BA; American business executive and politician; b. 1 Jan. 1953, Minot, ND; s. of Earl W. Johnson and Lorraine B. Bostow; m. Dee Sims 1976 (divorced 2005, died 2006); one s. one d.; pnr Kate Prusack 2009; ed Univ. of New Mexico; Pres. and CEO Big J Enterprises, Albuquerque 1976–99; Gov. of New Mexico 1995–2003; cand. for Libertarian Party nomination for presidential election 2012; mem. Bd of Dirs Entrepreneurship Studies programme, Univ. of NM 1993–95, Albuquerque Chamber of Commerce 1993–95; f. Our America Initiative 2009; Libertarian; Entrepreneur of the Year 1995. *Leisure interests:* rock and mountain-climbing (climbed Mount Everest May 2003), skiing, flying, athletics (participated in several Ironman Triathlons). *Address:* Our America Initiative, 731 East South Temple, Salt Lake City, UT 84102, USA (office). *Telephone:* (801) 303-7922 (office). *Website:* ouramericainitiative.com (office); www .garyjohnson2012.com (office).

JOHNSON, Graham Rhodes, OBE, FRAM, FGSM; British pianist; b. 10 July 1950, Bulawayo, Rhodesia (now Zimbabwe); s. of the late John Edward Donald Johnson and of Violet May Johnson; ed Hamilton High School, Bulawayo, Rhodesia, Royal Acad. of Music, London; Artistic Adviser, accompanist Alte Oper Festival, Frankfurt 1981–82; Prof. of Accompaniment, Guildhall School of Music 1986–; Song Adviser, Wigmore Hall 1992–; Artistic Dir The Songmakers' Almanac; writer and presenter of BBC Radio 3 series on Poulenc, BBC TV series on Schubert 1978, Liszt 1986; concert debut, Wigmore Hall 1972; has accompanied numerous singers including Dame Elisabeth Schwarzkopf, Jessye Norman, Victoria de los Angeles, Dame Janet Baker, Sir Peter Pears, Dame Felicity Lott, Ann Murray, Matthias Goerne, Christine Schäfer, Dorothea Roeschmann, François Le Roux; has appeared at festivals in Edinburgh, Munich, Hohenems, Salzburg, Bath, Hong Kong, Bermuda; Chair. Jury Wigmore Hall Int. Singing Competition 1997, 1999, 2001; mem. Royal Swedish Acad. of Music 2000; numerous recordings; Chevalier, Ordre des Arts et des Lettres 2002; Gramophone Award 1989, 1996, 1997, Royal Philharmonic Prize for Instrumentalist 1998, Wigmore Hall Medal 2013. *Publications:* contrib. to The Britten Companion 1984, Gerald Moore: The Unashamed Accompanist, The Spanish Song Companion 1992, The Songmakers' Almanac Reflections and Commentaries 1996, A French Song Companion 2000, Gabriel Fauré: The Songs and Their Poets 2009, Franz Schubert: The Complete Songs 2013, articles and reviews. *Leisure interests:* dining out, book collecting. *Address:* 83 Fordwych Road, London, NW2 3TL, England. *Telephone:* (20) 8452-5193. *Fax:* (20) 8452-5081 (home).

JOHNSON, Hilde Frafjord, MA, PhD, KrF; Norwegian UN official and fmr politician; *Special Representative of Secretary-General and Head of Mission in Republic of South Sudan (UNMISS), United Nations;* b. 29 Aug. 1963, Arusha, Tanzania; ed Univ. of Oslo; started career as journalist for Stavanger Aftenblad 1982, Folkets Framtid 1987; Chair. Christian Democratic Party Rogaland (CDP) 1988–89; Political Adviser to Kjell Magne Bondevik 1988–91, Minister of Foreign Affairs 1989–90; Alt. mem. of Parl. 1989–93, mem. of Parl. 1993–2001; Exec. Officer, UN Summit on Environment and Devt, Ministry of Foreign Affairs 1992–93; Minister of Int. Devt and Human Rights 1997–2000, Minister of Int. Devt 2001–05; Sr Adviser to Pres. of ADB 2006–07; Co-Chair. Global Coalition for Africa; Deputy Exec. Dir UNICEF 2007–11; Special Rep. of Sec.-Gen. and Head of

UN Mission in Repub. of South Sudan, Juba 2011–; Chair. Sudan Cttee IGAD Partners Forum 1998–2000, 2001; initiator and mem. Utstein 4, 1998–2000, 2001; Order of the Two Niles First Class (Sudan); Commitment to Devt Award, Foreign Policy and Centre for Global Devt 2003. *Publication:* Waging Peace in Sudan 2011. *Address:* United Nations Mission in South Sudan, Juba, South Sudan (office); United Nations Mission in Republic of South Sudan (UNMISS), Department of Peacekeeping, United Nations, New York, NY 10017, USA (office). *Telephone:* (212) 963-8077 (New York) (office). *Fax:* (212) 963-9222 (New York) (office). *Website:* www.un.org/en/peacekeeping/missions/unmiss (office).

JOHNSON, Hugh Eric Allan, OBE, MA; British writer, editor and broadcaster; b. 10 March 1939, London; s. of the late Guy F. Johnson CBE and Grace Kittel; m. Judith Eve Grinling 1965; one s. two d.; ed Rayburn School, King's Coll., Cambridge; feature writer, Condé Nast Magazines 1960–63; Wine Corresp., Sunday Times 1962–67, Travel Ed. 1967; Ed. Wine and Food Magazine 1963–65; Ed. Queen Magazine 1968–70; Wine Ed., Gourmet Magazine 1971–72, Cuisine Magazine, New York 1983–84; Chair. Winestar Productions Ltd 1984–2009, The Hugh Johnson Collection Ltd, The Movie Business; Pres. Sunday Times Wine Club 1973–, Circle of Wine Writers 1997–2007; Founder-mem. Tree Council 1974; Founder The Plantsman (quarterly) 1979; Dir Château Latour 1986–2001; Editorial Consultant, The Garden (Royal Horticultural Soc. Journal) 1975–2005; columnist, Tradescant's Diary 1975–; Sec. Wine and Food Soc. 1962–63; Gardening Corresp., New York Times 1986–87; Pres. Metropolitan Public Gardens Asscn 2011; Vice-Pres. Int. Dendrology Soc. 2010–; Hon. Chair. Wine Japan 1989–93; Hon. Pres. Int. Wine and Food Soc. 2004–08, Wine & Spirit Educ. Trust 2009–11; Fellow Commoner, King's Coll. Cambridge 2001; Hon. Freeman of the Vintner's Co. 2003; Chevalier, Ordre nat. du Mérite 2003; Dr hc (Acad. du Vin de Bordeaux) 1987, (Essex) 1998; André Simon Prize 1967, 1989, 2005, Glenfiddich Award 1972, 1986, 1990, Marqués de Cáceres Award 1984, Wines and Vines Trophy 1982, Grand Prix de la Communication de la Vigne et du Vin 1992, 1993, Decanter Magazine Man of the Year 1995, Von Rumor Award, Gastronomische Akad., Germany 1998, Gold Veitch Memorial Medal, Royal Horticultural Soc. 2000. *Television includes:* Wine – A User's Guide (series) 1986, Vintage – A History of Wine (series) 1989, Return Voyage 1992. *Publications:* Wine 1966, Frank Schoonmaker's Encyclopaedia of Wine (ed. of English edn) 1967, The World Atlas of Wine 1971 (sixth edn with Jancis Robinson 2007), The International Book of Trees 1973, The California Wine Book (with Bob Thompson) 1976, Understanding Wine (Sainsbury Guide) 1976, Hugh Johnson's Pocket Wine Book (annually since 1977), The Principles of Gardening 1979 (revised edn with new title, Hugh Johnson's Gardening Companion 1996), Hugh Johnson's Wine Companion 1983 (sixth edn with Stephen Brook 2009), How to Handle a Wine (video) 1984, Hugh Johnson's Cellar Book 1986, The Atlas of German Wines 1986, How to Enjoy Your Wine 1985, The Wine Atlas of France (with Hubrecht Duijker) 1987, The Story of Wine 1989, The Art and Science of Wine (with James Halliday) 1992, Hugh Johnson on Gardening: The Best of Tradescant's Diary 1993, Tuscany and Its Wines 2000, Wine: A Life Uncorked 2005, Hugh Johnson in the Garden 2009, Trees: A Lifetime's Journey through Forests, Woods and Gardens (Garden Media Guild Reference Book of the Year 2011) 2010, Wine Journal 2011. *Leisure interests:* travel, trees, gardening, pictures. *Address:* 73 St James's Street, London, SW1A 1PH; Saling Hall, Great Saling, Essex, CM7 5DT, England. *Telephone:* (1371) 850243. *Website:* www.salinghall.com; www.tradsdiary.com.

JOHNSON, Adm. (retd) Jay L.; American naval officer (retd) and business executive; *Chairman and CEO, General Dynamics Corporation;* b. 5 June 1946, Great Falls, Mont.; ed US Naval Acad., Annapolis, Md; commissioned as Ensign, USN 1968, fmr Adm., USN, Chief of Naval Operations 1996–2000; Sr Vice-Pres. Dominion Energy, Inc. 2000–02, Exec. Vice-Pres., Dominion Resources, Inc. 2002–08, Pres. and CEO Dominion Delivery 2002–07, CEO Dominion Virginia Power 2007–08; mem. Bd of Dirs General Dynamics Corpn 2003–, Vice-Chair. 2008–09, Pres. and CEO 2009–10, Chair. and CEO 2010–. *Address:* General Dynamics Corpn, 2941 Fairview Park Drive, Suite 100, Falls Church, VA 22042-4513, USA (office). *Telephone:* (703) 876-3000 (office). *Fax:* (703) 876-3125 (office). *E-mail:* info@gendyn.com (office). *Website:* www.gendyn.com (office).

JOHNSON, Jeh Charles, BA, JD; American lawyer and government official; *Secretary of Homeland Security;* b. 11 Sept. 1957; s. of Jeh Vincent Johnson and Norma Johnson (née Edelin); m. Susan M. DiMarco; ed Morehouse Coll., Columbia Univ. Law School; Litigation Assoc., Sullivan & Cromwell, New York 1982–84; Assoc., Paul, Weiss, Rifkind, Wharton & Garrison, New York 1984–88, 1992–93, Partner 1994–98, 2001–09; Asst US Attorney (Southern Dist), US Dept of Justice 1989–91, Gen. Counsel, Air Force Dept 1998–2001; Foreign Policy Adviser, Barack Obama's Presidential Campaign 2007–08; Gen. Counsel, US Dept of Defense 2009–12; Sec. of Homeland Security 2013–; Adjunct Lecturer in Law, Columbia Univ. Law School 1995–97; mem. New York Bar Assccn 1983, DC Bar Assccn 1999; Fellow, American Coll. of Trial Lawyers; mem. Council on Foreign Relations; Democrat. *Address:* Department of Homeland Security 1600 Pennsylvania Avenue, NW, Washington, DC 20528, USA (office). *Telephone:* (202) 282-8000 (office). *E-mail:* john.minnick@dhs.gov (office). *Website:* www.dhs.gov (office).

JOHNSON, John D., BBA; American business executive; b. Rhame, ND; ed Black Hills State Univ.; grew up in Spearfish, SDak; began his career with fmr Harvest States as feed consultant in GTA Feeds Div. 1976, then Regional Sales Man., then Dir of Sales and Marketing, then Gen. Man. GTA Feeds, Group Vice-Pres. Harvest States Farm Marketing & Supply for Harvest States Cooperatives 1992–95, Pres. and CEO Harvest States 1995–98, Pres. and Gen. Man. CHS (following merger of Cenex and Harvest States June 1998) 1998–2000, Pres. and CEO CHS 2000–10 (retd); mem. Bd of Dirs Ventura Foods, LLC, CF Industries, Nat. Council of Farmer Cooperatives, Greater Twin Cities United Way; CEO Communicator of the Year, Cooperative Communicators Asscn 2003. *Address:* c/o CHS, PO Box 64089, St Paul, MN 55164-0089; c/o CHS, 5500 Cenex Drive, Inver Grove Heights, MN 55077, USA.

JOHNSON, Linton Kwesi, BA; British poet and writer; b. 24 Aug. 1952, Chapeltown, Jamaica; ed Goldsmiths Coll., London; family emigrated to London 1963; involved in Black Panther movement, London; wrote for NME and Melody Maker in 1970s and 1980s; regular TV/radio apppearances as an authority on reggae; C. Day-Lewis Fellowship 1977, Assoc. Fellow, Warwick Univ. 1985; Founder LKJ Records and LKJ Music Publishers; Trustee, George Padmore Inst.;

Hon. Fellow, Wolverhampton Polytechnic 1987, Goldsmiths Coll., London 2002; Hon. Visiting Prof., Middlesex Univ. 2004; Italian literary awards 1990, 1998, Silver Musgrave Medal Inst. of Jamaica 2005. *Recordings include:* Dread Beat An' Blood, Forces of Victory, More Time, LKJ Live in Paris. *Publications:* Voices of the Living and the Dead 1974, Dread Beat an' Blood 1975, Inglan is a Bitch 1980, Tings an' Times: Selected Poems 1991, Mi Revalueshanary Fren: Selected Poems 2002; contrib. to recordings, television. *Address:* PO Box 623, Herne Hill, London, SE24 0LS, England (office). *Telephone:* (20) 7738-7647 (office). *Fax:* (20) 7738-7647 (office). *E-mail:* info@lkjrecords.com (office). *Website:* www.lkjrecords.com (office).

JOHNSON, Luke; British television executive; s. of Paul Johnson; m.; three c.; ed Univ. of Oxford; started career with BMP (advertising firm); media analyst, Kleinwort Benson Securities; fmr Chair. PizzaExpress PLC –1999; Chair. Signature Restaurants PLC 1999–2005; Chair. Channel Four Television Corpn 2004–10; currently Chair. Risk Capital Partners Ltd (private equity firm); part owner and Chair. Superbrands, Giraffe Restaurants, Patisserie Valerie, Baker and Spice; prin. owner GRA (greyhound tracks) 2005–; Chair. Royal Society of Arts 2008–, StageOne; Gov. Univ. of the Arts, London 2000–06; Co-founder Inst. of Entrepreneurs 2010; columnist, Financial Times. *Address:* Risk Capital Partners, Ltd, 9 Grafton Mews, London, W1T 5HZ, England (office). *E-mail:* luke@lukejohnson.org (office). *Website:* www.lukejohnson.org (office).

JOHNSON, Manuel H., Jr; American economist, academic and fmr government official; *Chairman and Senior Partner, Johnson Smick International;* b. 10 Feb. 1949, Troy, Alabama; s. of Manuel Holman Johnson, Sr and Ethel Lorraine Jordan; m. Mary Lois Wilkerson 1972; two s.; ed Troy State Univ., Florida State Univ., George Mason Univ.; Asst Sec. of US Treasury for Econ. Policy, Washington, DC 1982–86; mem. Fed. Reserve Bd 1985–90, Vice-Chair. 1986–90; Dir Centre for Global Market Studies, George Mason Univ. 1990–94; Co-Chair. and Sr Partner, Johnson Smick International (financial market advisory firm), Washington, DC 1990–; Chair. Financial Accounting Foundation 1997–2004; Founder and Co-Chair. Group of Seven Council; mem. Bd of Dirs NVR, Inc. 1993–, Morgan Stanley Funds, Evergreen Energy, Inc; Distinguished Alumni Award, Coll. of Social Sciences, Fla State Univ. 2003. *Publications:* co-author: Political Economy of Federal Government Growth 1980, Better Government at Half Price 1981, Deregulating Labor Relations 1981. *Address:* Johnson Smick International, 888 16th St, NW, Suite 740, Washington, DC 20066, USA (office). *Telephone:* (202) 861-0770 (office).

JOHNSON, Martin Osborne, CBE; British rugby manager and fmr professional rugby union player; b. 9 March 1970, Solihull, West Midlands; m. Kay Johnson; joined Leicester Football Club (known as Leicester Tigers) 1989, won Premiership honours 1994–95, 1998–99, 1999–2000, 2000–01, 2001–02, retd (362 caps) 2005; toured Australia with England Schoolboys side 1990; int. debut, England versus France 1993; replacement with British and Irish Lions tour of NZ 1993, losing Test series 2–1; part of England team that won Grand Slam 1995; captained British and Irish Lions on SA tour 1997, winning Test series 2–1; apptd Capt. England team in Six Nations Championships 2000; captained Lions tour to Australia 2001, losing Test series 2–1, first player ever to captain two British Lions tours; won Heineken Cup (with Leicester) 2001, 2002; 84 caps (39 as Capt.); captained England to Grand Slam and World Cup wins in 2003; retd from int. rugby after 2003 World Cup Jan. 2004; Man. England nat. team 2008–11 (resgnd), won Six Nations 2011. *Publication:* Agony and Ecstasy, Martin Johnson: The Autobiography (British Book Awards Sports Book of the Year 2004). *Leisure interest:* San Francisco 49ers. *Address:* c/o Rugby Football Union, Rugby House, Rugby Road, Twickenham, Middlesex TW1 1DS, England.

JOHNSON, Michael; American fmr professional athlete; b. 13 Sept. 1967, Dallas; m. Kerry Doyen 1998; one s.; ed Baylor Univ.; world champion 200m. 1991, 400m and 4×400m 1993, 200m, 400m and 4×400m (world record) 1995; 400m 1997, 400m (world record) and 4×400m . 1999; Olympic champion 4×400m (world record) 1992, 200m, 400m 1996, world record holder 400m (indoors) 44.63 seconds 1995, 4×400m (outdoors) 2:55.74 1992, 2:54.29 1993; undefeated at 400m from 1989–97; first man to be ranked World No. one at 200m and 400m simultaneously 1990, 1991, 1994, 1995; Olympic champion 200m (world record), 400m, Atlanta 1996; Olympic Champion 400m and 4×400m, Sydney 2000; announced retirement 2001; currently TV commentator; f. Ultimate Performance (sports man. co.); f. Michael Johnson Performance Centers (trains youngsters in sports); Jesse Owens Award (three times), Track and Field US Athlete of the Year (four times), Asscn of American Univs (AAU)/Sullivan Award 1996. *Publications:* Slaying The Dragon (autobiog.) 1996, Michael Johnson: Sprinter Deluxe. *Leisure interest:* piano. *Address:* Ultimate Performance, 40 Tall Trail, Missouri City, TX (office); Michael Johnson Performance Centers, 6051 Alma Drive, McKinney, TX 75070, USA (office). *Website:* www.upsportmanagement.com (office); www .michaeljohnsonperformance.com (office).

JOHNSON, Paul, DPhil, FRHistS; British economist, academic and university administrator; *Vice-Chancellor, University of Western Australia;* ed Univ. of Oxford; expert adviser on pension reform and econs of demographic change to World Bank, UN Research Inst. for Social Devt, UK Govt, House of Lords; Deputy Dir LSE 2005–08; Vice-Chancellor La Trobe Univ., Vic. 2008–12; Vice-Chancellor Univ. of Western Australia 2012–; Dir, UniSuper (Australian higher educ. superannuation fund), mem. Investment Cttee; mem. Advisory Council, Australian Research Council; fmr mem. Research Grants Bd of Econ. and Social Research Council, Council of Econ. History Soc., Governing Bd of Pensions Policy Inst.; Fellow, Acad. of Social Sciences 2001. *Publications:* numerous papers in professional journals on econ. and social devt of Britain since 1850 and econ. impact of population ageing. *Address:* Office of the Vice-Chancellor, University of Western Australia, 35 Stirling Highway, Crawley, WA 6009, Australia (office). *Telephone:* (8) 6488-2808 (office). *Fax:* (8) 6488-1013 (office). *E-mail:* paul.johnson@uwa.edu .au (office). *Website:* www.uwa.edu.au (office).

JOHNSON, Peggy, BS; American electronics engineer and business executive; *Executive Vice-President and President of Global Market Development, Qualcomm Technologies, Inc.;* ed San Diego State Univ.; worked as engineer for General Electric's Mil. Electronics Div.; joined Qualcomm as software engineer within Qualcomm Wireless Business Solutions 1990, later Vice-Pres. of Tech., joined Qualcomm Consumer Products as Vice-Pres. of Business Devt 1997, later Vice-

Pres. of Sales, served as Pres. of Qualcomm Internet Services and MediaFLO Technologies, later served as Exec. Vice-Pres. of Americas and India, currently Exec. Vice-Pres. and Pres. of Global Market Devt, Qualcomm Technologies, Inc., oversees Qualcomm Labs (wholly owned subsidiary), mem. Qualcomm's Exec. Cttee; recognized by several orgs, including 100 Women Leaders in STEM 2012, Pinnacle Awards, Athena 2011, Most Influential Women in Wireless Awards, Fierce Wireless 2011. *Address:* Qualcomm Technologies, Inc., 5775 Morehouse Drive, San Diego, CA 92121, USA (office). *Telephone:* (858) 587-1121 (office). *E-mail:* info@qualcomm.com (office). *Website:* www.qualcomm.com (office).

JOHNSON, Pierre Marc, BA, LLL, MD, FRSC; Canadian lawyer, physician and politician; *Of Counsel, Heenan Blaikie LLP;* b. 5 July 1946, Montréal, Québec; s. of the late Daniel Johnson and Reine Johnson (née Gagné); one s. one d. from first m.; partner Hélène de Kovachich; ed Collège Jean-Brébeuf, Montreal, Univ. of Montreal and Univ. of Sherbrooke; called to Québec Bar 1971; admitted Québec Coll. of Physicians and Surgeons 1976; elected to Québec Nat. Ass. 1976; mem. Nat. Exec. Council, Parti Québécois 1977–79, Pres. Parti Québécois 1985–87; Minister of Labour and Manpower, Québec 1977–80, of Consumer Affairs, Cooperatives and Financial Insts 1980–81, of Social Affairs 1981–84, of Justice, Attorney-Gen. and Minister Responsible for Canadian Intergovernmental Affairs 1984–85; Premier of Québec Oct.–Dec. 1985; Leader of Opposition, Québec Nat. Ass. 1985–87; Sr Counsel, Heenan Blaikie LLP (law firm), Montreal 1996–; Chair. Quartier de la Santé (health dist corpn) 2006–13; mem. Bd of Dirs Black Rock Metals, Muse Entertainment, Groupe Rozon; Chair. Foresight Cttee, Institut Véolia Environnment; fmr Dir, ACE Aviation Holdings Corpn, Air Canada, Holcim (Canada), Médicago Inc., Union for Conservation of Nature (Geneva), SNC lavalin, Unimedia; Advisor to UN Secrs on int. environmental conventions, to NAEC; Chief Negociator and Advisor, Québec Govt on softwood lumber negociatons with USA and Canada-EU Comprehensive Econ. and Trade Agreement; Grand Officier, Ordre nat. du Québec; Grand Croix, Ordre de la Pléiade; Hon. PhD (Lyon). *Publication:* The Environment and NAFTA: implementing and understanding New Continental Law 1995. *Leisure interests:* swimming, travelling, music, cooking, wine tasting. *Address:* Heenan Blaikie LLP, 1250 René-Lévesque Blvd West, Suite 2500, Montréal, PQ H3B 4Y1, Canada (office). *Telephone:* (514) 846-2200 (office). *Fax:* (514) 921-1200 (office). *E-mail:* pjohnson@heenan.ca (office). *Website:* www.heenanblaikie.com (home).

JOHNSON, Richard Keith; British actor and producer; b. Upminster, Essex; s. of Keith Holcombe Johnson and Frances Louisa Olive Johnson (née Tweed); m. 1st Sheila Ann Sweet 1957 (divorced); one s. one d.; m. 2nd Kim Novak 1965 (divorced); m. 3rd Marie-Louise Nordlund 1982 (divorced); one s. one d.; m. 4th Lynne Gurney 2004; ed Parkfield School, Felsted School, Royal Acad. of Dramatic Art (RADA); Nat. Theatre Player, Assoc. Artist RSC; first stage appearance in Hamlet, Opera House, Manchester 1944; Founder, Chair. and CEO United British Artists 1982–90; mem. Council British Acad. Film and Television Arts 1976–78, Council Royal Acad. of Dramatic Art 2001–; Best Actor Guild of Broadcasting Writers 1992. *Plays:* major parts include Marius Tertius (The First Victoria) 1950, Pierre (The Madwoman of Chaillot) 1951, Demetrius (A Midsummer Night's Dream) 1951, George Phillips (After My Fashion) 1952, Beauchamp, Earl of Warwick (The Lark) 1955, Laertes (Hamlet) 1955, Jack Absolute (The Rivals) 1956, Lord Plynlimmon (Plaintiff in a Pretty Hat) 1956, Orlando (As You Like It), Mark Antony (Julius Caesar), Leonatus (Cymbeline), Ferdinand (The Tempest), Romeo (Romeo and Juliet), Sir Andrew Aguecheek (Twelfth Night), title-role in Pericles, Don Juan (Much Ado About Nothing) 1957–58, Ferdinand (The Tempest) 1957, Romeo (Romeo and Juliet), Sir Andrew Aguecheek (Twelfth Night), Moscow and Leningrad 1959, The Prince (Ondine), Grandier (The Devils), RSC 1960–62, Charles (Blithe Spirit), Pinchwife (The Country Wife), Pilate (The Passion), title-role in The Guardsman all at Nat. Theatre 1975–78; UK tour, Death Trap 1982, An Inspector Calls 1992, The Rivals 1994, Long Day's Journey Into Night 1996, Uncle Vanya 1996, Staying On 1997, To Kill a Mockingbird 1997, Plenty 1999, The Seagull (RSC) 2000, Tales From Hollywood 2001, Gates of Gold 2002, Mrs Warren's Profession 2003–04. *Films:* Never so Few 1959, The Haunting 1963, The Pumpkin Eater 1964, Operation Crossbow 1965, Khartoum 1966, Deadlier Than the Male 1966, Oedipus the King 1967, Hennessy 1975, Turtle Diary 1984, Treasure Island 1989, Milk 1998, Lara Croft: Tomb Raider 2001, Scoop 2006, Two Families 2007, Jump! 2008, The Boy in the Striped Pyjamas 2008,. *TV films:* Man for All Seasons 1988, Voice of the Heart 1988, The Camomile Lawn, Anglo-Saxon Attitudes 1992, Heavy Weather 1995, The Echo 1998, The Whistle Blower 2000, Whatever Love Means 2005, Wallis & Edward 2005, The Raven (voice) 2007; leading roles in productions including Rembrandt, Antony and Cleopatra, Hamlet (Claudius), The Member for Chelsea (Sir Charles Dilke), Cymbeline, MI-5 2008, Inspector Lewis 2010, The Other Child 2011, The Bleak Old Shop of Stuff 2011. *Productions include:* The Biko Inquest, Serjeant Musgrave's Dance, The Playboy of the Western World, Old Times, Turtle Diary, Castaway, The Lonely Passion of Judith Hearne, Tales From Hollywood 2001, Hock and Soda Water 2001, Gates of Gold 2002. *Publication:* Hennessy 1974. *Leisure interests:* photography, music, travel, cooking, gardening. *Address:* c/o Nicola van Gelder, Conway van Gelder, Third Floor, 8/12 Broadwick Street, London, W1F 8HW, England (office).

JOHNSON, Robert L., MA; American business executive; *Chairman, RLJ Companies;* b. 1946, Hickory, Miss.; m. Sheila Johnson; two c.; ed Univ. of Illinois, Woodrow Wilson School, Princeton Univ.; held early positions at Washington, DC Urban League and Corpn for Public Broadcasting; Press Sec. to Hon. Walter E. Fauntroy, Congressional Del. from DC 1973–76; Vice-Pres. of Govt Relations, Nat. Cable & Telecommunications Asscn 1976–79; Founder, Chair. and CEO Black Entertainment TV (BET) 1980–2005 (since 1998 a subsidiary of Viacom), est. BET Pictures and BET Arabesque 1998, BET Interactive 2000; currently Chair. RLJ Cos,; owns a dozen US hotels and a number of lottery licences on Antigua, Anguilla and St Kitts; majority owner of Charlotte (NC) Bobcats professional basketball team 2004–10; mem. Bd of Dirs KB Home, Lowe's Companies, Inc., Strayer Education, Business Council, Smithsonian Inst.'s National Museum of African American History and Culture; mem. Deutsche Bank Advisory Cttee; mem. Bd of Govs Rock and Roll Hall of Fame, Cleveland, Brookings Inst., NBA Board of Govs; Broadcasting & Cable Magazine Hall of Fame Award 1997, Cable & Telecommunications Asscn for Marketing (CTAM) Grand Tam Award, Cablevision magazine 20/20 Vision Award, National Association for the Advancement of Colored People (NAACP) Image Award, Nat. Women's Caucus Good Guys Award, Princeton Nat.

Distinguished Alumni Award, Nat. Cable & Telecommunications Pres.'s Award. *Address:* RLJ Companies, 3 Bethesda Metro Center, Suite 1000, Bethesda, MD 20814, USA (office). *Telephone:* (301) 280-7700 (office). *Fax:* (301) 280-7750 (office). *Website:* www.rljcompanies.com (office).

JOHNSON, Ronald (Ron) Harold, BSB-Accounting; American business executive and politician; *Senator from Wisconsin;* b. 8 April 1955, Mankato, Minn.; s. of Dale Robert Johnson and Jeanette Elizabeth Johnson (née Thisius); m. Jane Curler 1977; three c.; ed Univ. of Minnesota; first job as a dishwasher in a Walgreens grill aged 15, rose through the ranks as a soda jerk, fry cook, and finally night manager by the age of 16; began working as an accountant at Jostens (high school and college class ring supplier); moved to Oshkosh to start a business, PACUR, LLC (polyester and plastics manufacturer), with his brother-in-law 1979, bought out the co. 1997, currently CEO; Senator from Wisconsin 2011–, mem. Cttee on the Budget, Cttee on Appropriations, Cttee on Homeland Security and Governmental Affairs, Special Cttee on Aging; Republican. *Address:* 386 Russell Senate Office Building, Washington, DC 20510, USA (office). *Telephone:* (202) 224-5323 (office). *Website:* ronjohnson.senate.gov (office).

JOHNSON, Stephen L., BA, MS; American scientist and fmr government official; b. 21 March 1951, Washington, DC; ed Taylor Univ., George Washington Univ.; fmr Dir of Operations Hazelton Labs Corpn, Litton Bionetics Inc.; fmr positions at US Environmental Protection Agency (EPA) include Dir Field Operations Div., Office of Pesticide Programs (OPP), Deputy Dir Hazard Evaluation Div., OPP, Exec. Sec. Scientific Advisory Panel for the Fed. Insecticide, Fungicide and Rodenticide Act, Deputy Dir OPP 1997–99, Acting Deputy Asst Admin. 1999–2000, Deputy Asst Admin. 2000, Prin. Deputy Asst Admin., Acting Asst Admin. Office of Prevention, Pesticides and Toxic Substances 2001, Asst Admin. 2001–03, Acting Deputy Admin. EPA 2003–04, Deputy Admin. 2004–05, Acting Admin. Jan.–May 2005, Admin. 2005–09; Presidential Rank Award 1997, 2001, EPA Excellence in Man. Award, Vice-Pres.'s Hammer Award, seven bronze medals, one silver medal. *Address:* c/o Environmental Protection Agency, Ariel Rios Building, 1200 Pennsylvania Avenue, NW, Washington, DC 20460, USA.

JOHNSON, Suzanne M. Nora, BA, JD; American lawyer and business executive; ed Univ. of Southern Calif. and Harvard Law School; attorney with Simpson Thacher & Bartlett; served as law clerk on US Court of Appeals –1985; joined Goldman Sachs in 1985, Pnr 1992, Head of Global Healthcare Business in Investment Banking Div. 1994–2002, Head of Global Investment Research Div. 2002–07, Chair. Global Markets Inst. April 2004–07, Vice-Chair. Goldman Sachs Group, Inc. Nov. 2004–07; mem. Bd Carnegie Inst. of Washington, Univ. of Southern Calif., RAND Health, Technoserve, Women's World Banking; Trustee Brookings Inst., Council for Excellence in Govt; ranked 34th by Forbes magazine amongst 100 Most Powerful Women 2006. *Address:* 365 North Rockingham Ave, Los Angeles, CA 90049, USA (office).

JOHNSON, Thomas S., AB, MBA; American banking executive; *Chairman, The Phoenix Companies;* b. 19 Nov. 1940, Racine, Wis.; s. of H. Norman Johnson and Jane Agnes McAvoy; m. Margaret Ann Werner 1970; two s. one d.; ed Trinity Coll., Harvard; Head of Graduate Business Program and Instructor in Finance and Control, Ateneo de Manila Univ. 1964–66; Special Asst to Controller, Dept of Defense 1966–69; with Chemical Bank and Chemical Banking Corpn 1969–89, Exec. Vice-Pres. 1979, Sr Exec. Vice-Pres. 1981, Pres. 1983–89; Pres. Corp. and Mfrs Hanover Trust Co. 1989–91, Olympia and York Devts Ltd 1992–; Chair., Pres. and CEO GreenPoint Financial Corpn, GreenPoint Savings Bank, Flushing, NY 1993–2004, now mem. Bd of Dirs North Fork Bankcorporation Inc. (acquired GreenPoint 2004); Chair. Union Theological Seminary, Harvard Business School Club of Greater New York; Bank Capital Market Asscn's Cttee for Competitive Securities Market; Dir Bond Club of New York Inc.; Vice-Pres. and Bd mem. Cancer Research Inst. of America; mem. Bd of Dirs Alleghany Corpn, R.R. Donnelley & Sons Co., The Phoenix Cos Inc. (Chair. 2009–); mem. Council on Foreign Relations, Financial Execs Inst., Asscn of Reserve City Bankers, The Group of Thirty; Trustee Trinity Coll.; mem. Business Cttee, Museum of Modern Art, Consultative Group on Int. Econ. and Monetary Affairs. *Address:* Phoenix Companies, One American Row, Hartford, CT 06102, USA (home). *Telephone:* (860) 403-5000 (office).

JOHNSON, Timothy (Tim) Peter, MA, JD; American lawyer and politician; *Senator from South Dakota;* b. 28 Dec. 1946, Canton, SDak; s. of Vandal Johnson and Ruth Ljostveit; m. Barbara Brooks 1969; two s. one d.; ed Univ. of South Dakota and Michigan State Univ.; called to the Bar, SDak 1975, US Dist Court, SDak 1976; fiscal analyst, Legis. Fiscal Agency, Lansing, Mich. 1971–72; pvt. practice, Vermillion, SDak 1975–86; mem. SDak House of Reps 1978–82, SDak Senate 1982–86; mem. US House of Reps, Washington, DC 1987–97, Regional Deputy Whip 1991–94; Senator from South Dakota 1997–, Chair. Banking, Housing and Urban Affairs Cttee, mem. Appropriations Cttee, Energy and Natural Resources Cttee, Indian Affairs Cttee; Democrat; Outstanding Citizen Award, Vermillion Jaycees 1979, first recipient of the Billie Sutton Award for Legislative Achievement, South Dakota Democratic Party 1983, nat. awards from Nat. Farmers Union, Disabled American Veterans, Mothers Against Drunk Driving. *Address:* 136 Hart Senate Office Building, Washington, DC 20510-0001, USA (office). *Telephone:* (202) 224-5842 (office). *Fax:* (202) 228-5765 (office). *Website:* johnson.senate.gov (office).

JOHNSON, Wesley Momo, MBA, CPA; Liberian politician and diplomatist; b. 27 May 1944, Monrovia; m. Isabella Cassell Johnson; eight c.; ed Monrovia Coll., St Francis Coll., Brooklyn, NY, Long Island Univ., NY, USA; represented Liberia in 100m and 200m sprints at Summer Olympic Games, Tokyo 1964; Baptist Licentiate and Deacon, Zion Grove Baptist Church, Brewerville; fmr Auditor, Old Colony Newport Nat. Bank, Providence, RI, USA; Auditor, Treasury Dept of Liberia (now Ministry of Finance) 1968–72; Sr Bookkeeper (Class-I) and Brokerage Man., Skyline Shipping Co. 1972–77; Founding mem. and Vice-Chair. Progressive Alliance of Liberia 1973, Progressive People's Party 1980; Founding mem. United People's Party 1984, Chair. 1999–; fmr Amb. to Egypt, Consul Gen. to New York 1981; mem. Interim Legis. Ass. 1990–94, Chair. House Standing Cttee on Banking and Currency, Cttee on Ways, Means, Finance and Maritime Affairs, Co-Chair. Cttee on Rules, Cttee on Order and Executive, Sec.-Gen. Liberian Parl. Union; Vice-Chair. Nat. Transitional Govt 2003–07; Amb. to UK 2007–13; led Liberian del. to several int. confs including 36th Gen. Ass. of UN (Chair. Cttee on Disarmament) 1981, African Pacific Caribbean Comm., Rosenberg 1992, mem. del. to Inter-Parl. Union, New Delhi, India; Partner, Nimley & Assocs, CPA Inc.; Lecturer, Univ. of Liberia, United Methodist Univ., AME Zion Univ. Coll.; mem. numerous accounting firms and financial insts, including Liberian Certified Public Accountants, Inst. of Certified Internal Auditors, Inc., Atlanta, Ga, American Banking Asscn, RI, MBA Executive, New York, USA. *Leisure interests:* playing soccer, athletics, reading, teaching, hard work. *Address:* Ministry of Foreign Affairs, Mamba Point, PO Box 10-9002, 1000 Monrovia 10, Liberia (office). *Telephone:* 226763 (office). *Website:* www.mofa.gov.lr (office).

JOHNSON, W(illiam) Bruce, BA, MBA, JD; American business executive; *President and CEO, Sears Hometown and Outlet Stores, Inc.;* ed Duke Univ.; spent 16 years at Colgate-Palmolive Co. in various roles; worked as a man. consultant at Booz Allen & Hamilton and at Arthur Andersen & Co. –1998; Dir, Org. and Systems, Carrefour SA 1998–2003; Sr Vice-Pres., Supply Chain and Operations, Kmart 2003, Exec. Vice-Pres., Supply Chain and Operations for combined co. following merger with Sears, Chair. 2005–06, took on store operations 2006–08, Pres. and Interim CEO Sears Holdings Corpn 2008–11, mem. Bd of Dirs 2010–, Exec. Vice-Pres. Off-Mall Businesses and Supply Chain Feb.–Sept. 2011, Exec. Vice-Pres. Off-Mall Businesses Sept. 2011–12, mem. Bd of Dirs, Pres. and CEO Sears Hometown and Outlet Stores, Inc. 2012–. *Address:* Sears Hometown and Outlet Stores, 5500 Trillium Blvd, Suite 501, Hoffman Estates, IL 60192, USA (office). *Telephone:* (847) 286-7000 (office). *E-mail:* info@shos.com (office). *Website:* www.shos.com (office).

JOHNSON-LAIRD, Philip Nicholas, PhD, FRS, FBA; British/American psychologist and academic; *Visiting Scholar, Psychology, New York University;* b. 12 Oct. 1936, Leeds, Yorks., England, UK; s. of Eric Johnson-Laird and Dorothy Johnson-Laird (née Blackett); m. Maureen Mary Sullivan 1959; one s. one d.; ed Culford School, Univ. Coll., London; left school aged 15 and worked as quantity surveyor and in other jobs before univ.; Asst Lecturer, Dept of Psychology, Univ. Coll., London 1966, Lecturer 1967–73, Fellow, 1994–; Visiting mem. Inst. for Advanced Study, Princeton, NJ, USA 1971–72; Reader in Experimental Psychology, Univ. of Sussex 1973, Prof. 1978–82; Asst Dir MRC Applied Psychology Unit, Cambridge 1982–89; Fellow, Darwin Coll. Cambridge 1984–89; Visiting Fellow, Cognitive Science, Stanford Univ., USA 1980, Visiting Prof. of Psychology 1985; Visiting Prof. of Psychology, Princeton Univ., USA 1986, Prof. 1989–94, Stuart Prof. of Psychology 1994–2012, Prof. Emer. 2012–; Visiting Scholar, Psychology, New York Univ. 2012–; mem. NAS, American Philosophical Soc.; Dr hc (Gothenburg) 1983; Laurea hc (Padua) 1997, (Palermo) 2005, (Univ. Ca' Foscari, Venice) 2008; Hon. DSc (Univ. of Dublin Trinity Coll.) 2000, (Sussex) 2007; Hon. DPsych (Universidad Nacional de Educación a Distancia, Madrid) 2000, (Ghent) 2002; Rosa Morison Memorial Medal and James Sully Scholarship, Univ. Coll. London, Spearman Medal, British Psychological Soc. 1974, Pres.'s Award 1985, Medaglia d'Onore, Univ. of Florence 1989, Fyssen Foundation Int. Prize 2003, Mind and Brain Prize, Univ. of Turin 2004, William James Fellow, Asscn of Psychological Science 2010. *Publications:* Thinking and Reasoning (co-ed.) 1968, Psychology of Reasoning (with P. C. Wason) 1972, Language and Perception (with G. A. Miller) 1976, Thinking (co-ed.) 1977, Mental Models 1983, The Computer and the Mind 1988, Deduction (with R. M. J. Byrne) 1992, Human and Machine Thinking 1993, How We Reason 2006; numerous articles in psychological journals; reviews. *Leisure interests:* arts, composing music, talking and arguing. *Address:* Department of Psychology, New York University, 6 Washington Place, New York, NY 10003, USA (office). *E-mail:* pjl303@nyu.edu (office); phil@princeton.edu (office). *Website:* www .psych.nyu.edu/psychology.html (office); mentalmodels.princeton.edu (office).

JOHNSON-SIRLEAF, Ellen, BBA, MPA; Liberian politician and head of state; *President;* b. 29 Oct. 1938; four s.; ed Coll. of West Africa, Monrovia, Madison Business Coll., Madison, Wis., Univ. of Colorado and Harvard Univ., USA; Asst Minister of Finance 1972–78, Deputy Minister of Finance 1979–80; Sr Loan Officer, IBRD, Washington, DC 1973–77, 1980–81; sentenced to ten years' imprisonment for speech that was critical of mil. ruler Samuel Doe; briefly detained twice in Liberia before fleeing country; fmr Pres. Liberian Bank for Devt Investment; Vice-Pres. Citibank Regional Office for Africa, Nairobi 1982–85; Vice-Pres. and mem. Bd Dirs Equator Holders, Hong Kong Equator Bank Ltd, Washington, DC –1992; Asst Admin. UNDP and Dir Regional Bureau for Africa 1992–97; Chair. and CEO Kormah Investment and Devt Corpn; Leader Unity Party (UP), Presidential Cand. 1997; charged with treason by Taylor regime and forced into political exile; Chair. Open Soc. Inst. West Africa (part of Soros Foundation Network); External Adviser, UN Econ. Comm. for Africa; mem. Advisory Bd Modern Africa Growth and Investment Co.; Sr Adviser and W/Cen. Africa Rep. of Modern Africa Fund Mans; Founder Measuagoon (Liberian nongovernmental org.); rep. Liberia on bds of IMF, IBRD and African Devt Bank; selected by OAU to investigate Rwanda genocide 1999; elected Pres. of Liberia (world's first elected black female pres. and Africa's first elected female head of state) 2005–; Chair. Comm. on Good Governance (Liberia) 2004–05; Founding mem. Int. Inst. for Women in Political Leadership; mem. Bd Dirs Synergos Inst. 1988–99; Distinguished Fellow, Claus M. Halle Inst. for Global Learning, Emory Univ. 2006; Grand Commdr, Star of Africa Redemption of Liberia; Commdr de l'Ordre du Togo; Franklin Delano Roosevelt Freedom of Speech Award 1988, Ralph Bunche Int. Leadership Award, Common Ground Award 2006, Laureate of the Africa Prize for Leadership for the Sustainable End of Hunger 2006, ranked by Forbes magazine amongst the The World's 100 Most Powerful Women (51st) 2006, (100th) 2007, (66th) 2008, (67th) 2009, (86th) 2010, (62nd) 2011, (82nd) 2012, (87th) 2013, Bishop John T. Walker Distinguished Humanitarian Service Award, Africare 2007, Nobel Peace Prize (jtly) for "non-violent struggle for the safety of women and for women's rights to full participation in peace-building work" 2011. *Publications:* From Disaster to Development 1991, The Outlook for Commercial Bank Lending to Sub-Saharan Africa 1992, Women, War and Peace: The Independent Experts' Assessment on the Impact of Armed Conflict on Women and Women's Role in Peace-building (co-author) (project of UNIFEM) 2002, This Child Will be Great: Memoir of a Remarkable Life by Africa's First Woman President 2009. *Address:* Executive Mansion, PO Box 10-9001, Capitol Hill, 1000 Monrovia 10, Liberia (office).

JOHNSSON, Anders B., LLM; Swedish international organization official; b. 1948, Lund; m.; three c.; ed Univs of Lund and New York; mem. staff UNHCR, posts in Honduras, Pakistan, Sudan and Viet Nam, then Prin. Legal Adviser to High Commr, Geneva 1976–91; Under-Sec.-Gen. IPU 1991–94, Deputy Sec.-Gen. and Legal Adviser 1994–98, Sec.-Gen. 1998–June 2014. *Address:* c/o Inter-Parliamentary Union, CP 330, 1218 Le Grand-Saconnex/ Geneva, Switzerland.

JOHNSSON, Finn, BSc, MBA; Swedish business executive; *Chairman, Ovako Steel;* b. 1946, Gothenburg; worked for Machine Div., Swedish Match, fmr Pres. Swedish Match Europe and Swedish Match Asia; fmr Pres. Arenco Machine Co., USA; fmr Pres. Tarkett AB; fmr Exec. Vice-Pres. Stora AB; fmr Pres. Industri AB Euroc; Deputy Chief Exec. and COO United Distillers, UK –1998; Pres. and CEO Mölnlycke Health Care AB –2005, Chair. 2005–10; mem. Bd of Dirs AB Volvo 1998–2010, Chair. 2004–10, also Chair. Remuneration Cttee; Chair. Ovako Steel 2010–; Chair. Luvata oy (fmrly Outokumpu Copper Products Oy), Thomas Concrete Group AB, Thomas Concrete Industries Inc., MVI Ltd, KappAhl Holding AB, Region Väst Handelsbanken, City Airline AB, Thomas Concrete Group, KappAhl AB, Handelsbanken Western Sweden Region, Bilisten I Sverige AB, Maersk Medical A and S, Kalmar Industries AB, EFG European Furniture Group AB, Geveko AB 2004–, DSV Miljø A/S 2012–; Chair. Supervisory Bd Unomedical Holding A/s; mem. Bd of Dirs Guinness 1994–, Skanska AB 1998–2011, AB IndustriVärden 2000–, Bilisten, Facile AB, Unomedical Holding A/s 2003–, Geodis Wilson, Industrivärden 2000–, Perstorp AB, Indutrade; Dr hc (Gothenburg). *Address:* Ovako AB, Box 5013, 194 05 Upplands Väsby, Sweden (office). *Telephone:* (8) 6221300 (office). *Fax:* (8) 6221328 (office). *E-mail:* finn.johnsson@ovako.com (office). *Website:* www.ovako.com (office).

JOHNSTON, David Albert Lloyd, BJuris; Australian lawyer and politician; *Minister of Defence;* b. 14 Feb. 1956, Perth; m. Toni Hodge; three c.; ed Univ. of Western Australia; worked for 20 years as barrister and solicitor, Kalgoorlie and Perth; mem. Senate for W Australia 2001–; Minister for Justice and Customs March–Dec. 2007, Minister of Defence 2013–; mem. Liberal Party of Australia. *Leisure interests:* cycling, sailing. *Address:* Department of Defence, Russell Offices, Russell Drive, Campbell, Canberra, ACT 2600, Australia (office). *Telephone:* (2) 6265-9111 (office). *E-mail:* public.enquiries@defence.gov.au (office). *Website:* www .defence.gov.au (office); www.senatorjohnston.com.au.

JOHNSTON, David Lloyd, CC, LLB; Canadian legal scholar and university administrator; *Governor-General of Canada;* b. 28 June 1941, Sudbury, Ont.; s. of Lloyd Johnston and Dorothy Stonehouse; m. Sharon Downey 1964; five d.; ed Sault Collegiate Inst., Sault Ste. Marie, Ont., Harvard Univ., Univ. of Cambridge and Queen's Univ., Kingston, Asst Prof., Faculty of Law, Queen's Univ., Kingston 1966–68; Asst Prof. Faculty of Law, Univ. of Toronto 1968–69, Assoc. Prof. 1969–72, Prof. 1972–74; Dean and Prof., Faculty of Law, Univ. of W Ont. 1974–79; Prof. of Law, McGill Univ. 1979–, Prin. and Vice-Chancellor 1979–94; Pres. and mem. Bd of Governors, Univ. of Waterloo 1999–; Gov.-Gen. of Canada 2010–; Pres. Harvard Univ. Bd of Overseers 1997–98; recipient of 12 hon. degrees. *Publications:* Computers and the Law 1968, Canadian Securities Regulation 1977, The Law of Business Associations (with R. Forbes) 1979, Canadian Companies and the Stock Exchange 1980, If Québec Goes: The Real Cost of Separation (with Marcel Côté) 1995, Getting Canada On Line: Understanding the Information Highway (co-author) 1995, Cyberlaw 1997, Communications Law of Canada 1999; numerous articles in academic journals. *Leisure interests:* jogging, skiing. *Address:* University of Waterloo, 200 University Avenue W, Waterloo, Ont., N2L 3G1 (office); R. R. #1, St Clements, Ont., N0B 2M0, Canada (home). *Telephone:* (519) 888-4400 (office); (519) 699-4877 (home). *Fax:* (519) 888-6337 (office). *E-mail:* president@ waterloo.ca (office). *Website:* www.uwaterloo.ca (office).

JOHNSTON, Hon. Donald James, PC, OC, QC, BA, BCL; Canadian politician, lawyer, international civil servant, consultant and academic; *Chairman, McCall MacBain Foundation;* b. 26 June 1936, Cumberland, Ont.; s. of Wilbur Austin Johnston and Florence Jean Moffat Tucker; m. Heather Bell Maclaren; four d.; ed McGill Univ. and Univ. of Grenoble; joined Stikeman, Elliott (int. law firm) 1961; subsequent f. own law firm, Johnston, Heenan & Blaikie, Montreal 1973, Counsel, Heenan, Blaikie 1988–96, Heenan Blaikie LLP 2006–; taught fiscal law at McGill Univ. 1963–76; MP 1978–88; Pres. Treasury Bd 1980–82; Minister for Econ. Devt and Minister of State for Science and Tech. 1982–83; Minister of State for Econ. Devt and Tech. 1983–84; Minister of Justice and Attorney-Gen. June–Sept. 1984; elected Pres. Liberal Party of Canada 1990, re-elected 1992; Sec.-Gen. OECD 1996–2006; Chair. McCall MacBain Foundation, Geneva 2006–; Chair. Int. Risk Governance Council (IRGC), Geneva 2006–09; Visiting Prof., Yonsei Univ., Seoul, S Korea 2006–09; Grand Cordon, Order of the Rising Sun (Japan) 2006, Commdr's Cross with Star, Order of Merit (Hungary) 2006, Order of the White Double Cross (Slovakia) 2006, Grand Croix, Ordre de Léopold II (Belgium) 2007, Officier, Légion d'honneur 2012; four Hon. LLD degrees in econs and law; Gold Medallist, McGill Univ. 1958. *Films:* As Exec. Producer: Seizure 1974. *Publications:* Up the Hill (political memoirs) 1986; several books and numerous articles on taxation, law and public affairs in professional journals. *Leisure interests:* tennis, piano, writing. *Address:* Heenan Blaikie LLP, 1250 René-Lévesque Blvd West, Suite 2500, Montreal, PQ H3B 4Y1, Canada (office); 537 Courser Road, Glensutton, PQ D0E 2K0 (home). *Telephone:* (514) 846-2280 (office); (450) 538-5124 (home). *Fax:* (514) 921-1280 (office); (450) 538-0304 (home). *E-mail:* djohnston@heenan.ca (office); donaldjames.johnston@gmail.com (home). *Website:* www.heenanblaikie.com (office).

JOHNSTON, Jennifer; Irish writer; b. 12 Jan. 1930, Dublin; d. of Denis Johnston and Shelah Richards; m. 1st Ian Smyth; two s. two d.; m. 2nd David Gilliland; ed Park House School, Dublin, Trinity Coll., Dublin; Hon. Fellow Trinity Coll., Dublin; Hon. DLitt (New Univ. of Ulster, Queen's Univ., Belfast, Trinity Coll., Dublin, Nat. Univ. of Ireland); Whitbread Prize 1980, Giles Cooper Award 1989, Premio Giuseppe Acerbi 2003. *Plays:* The Porch, The Invisible Man, The Desert Lullaby, Moonlight and Music; several radio and TV programmes. *Publications:* novels: The Captains and the Kings 1972, The Gates 1973, How Many Miles to Babylon? 1974, Shadows on Our Skin 1977, The Old Jest 1979, The Christmas Tree 1981, The Railway Station Man 1985, The Invisible Man 1986, Fool's Sanctuary 1988, The Invisible Worm 1992, The Illusionist 1995, Two Moons 1998, The Gingerbread Woman 2000, This is Not a Novel 2003, Grace and Truth 2005, Foolish Mortals 2008, Truth or Fiction 2009, Shadowstory 2011; plays include: The

Porch 1986, The Invisible Man 1986, The Desert Lullaby 1996. *Leisure interests:* reading, theatre, cinema. *Address:* Brook Hall, Culmore Road, Derry, BT48 8JE, Northern Ireland (home). *Telephone:* (28) 7135-1297 (home).

JOHNSTON, J(ohn) Bennett; American consultant and fmr politician; *CEO, Johnston & Associates LLC;* b. 10 June 1932, Shreveport, La; s. of J. Bennett Johnston; m. Mary Gunn; two s. two d.; ed Byrd High School, Washington and Lee Univ., US Mil. Acad. and La State Univ. Law School; mil. service in Judge Advocate Gen. Corps La; State Senator 1968–72; Senator from La 1972–96; Chair. Democratic Senatorial Campaign Cttee 1975–76; mem. Senate Cttee on Energy and Natural Resources, on Appropriations, Senate Budget Cttee, mem. Senate Bldg Cttee; CEO Johnston & Assocs LLC 1996–; co-Chair. American Iranian Council; mem. Bd of Dirs Freeport-McMoRan Copper & Gold, Inc., Chevron, Nexant, Fundacion Amistad, US China Business Council; Vice-Pres. US Pacific Econ. Cooperation Council; Democrat; Hon. DIur (Louisiana State Univ., Tulane Univ., Centenary Coll., Univ. of Louisiana, Southern Univ., Xavier Univ., Louisiana Tech. Univ.). *Leisure interest:* tennis. *Address:* Johnston & Associates LLC, 1330 Connecticut Avenue, NW, Washington, DC, 20036, USA. *Telephone:* (202) 659-8400 (office). *Fax:* (202) 659-1340 (office).

JOHNSTON, Lawrence (Larry) R., BBA; American retail executive; ed Stetson Univ., Deland, Fla; began career as Man. Trainee, Gen. Electric Co. 1972, various man. positions 1979–84, Merchandising Man., Washington, DC 1984, later Regional Man., Cleveland, Corp. Vice-Pres. 1989, Vice-Pres. Sales and Distribution, GE Appliances, Pres. and CEO GE Medical Systems Europe 1997–99, Sr Vice-Pres. 1999–2001, Pres. and CEO GE Appliances 1999–2001; Chair., CEO and Pres. Albertson's Inc. 2001–06; mem. Bd of Dirs Home Depot Inc.; fmr mem. Bd of Dirs World Food Forum, Paris, Food Marketing Inst., Washington, DC. *Address:* 1770 West State Street, Boise, ID 83702, USA (office).

JOHNSTON, Ronald John, OBE, MA, PhD, FBA; British geographer and academic; *Professor of Geography, University of Bristol;* b. 30 March 1941, Swindon, Wilts., England; s. of Henry Louis Johnston and Phyllis Joyce Johnston (née Liddiard); m. Rita Brennan 1963; one s. one d.; ed The Commonweal Co. Secondary Grammar School, Swindon, Univ. of Manchester, Monash Univ., Australia; Teaching Fellow, then Lecturer, Dept of Geography, Monash Univ. 1964–66; Lecturer then Reader, Dept of Geography, Univ. of Canterbury, NZ 1967–74; Prof. of Geography, Univ. of Sheffield 1974–92, Pro-Vice-Chancellor for Academic Affairs 1989–92; Vice-Chancellor Univ. of Essex 1992–95; Prof. of Geography, Univ. of Bristol 1995–; Ed. New Zealand Geographer 1969–74, Proceedings of the British Acad. 2007–; Co-Ed. Environment and Planning 1979–2005, Progress in Human Geography 1979–2007; Hon. DUniv (Essex) 1996; Hon. LLD (Monash) 1999; Hon. DLitt (Sheffield) 2002; Hon. DLH (Bath) 2005; Murchison Award, Royal Geographical Soc. (RGS) 1984, RGS Victoria Medal 1990, Hons Award for Distinguished Contribs, Asscn of American Geographers 1991, Prix Vautrin Lud 1999, Lifetime Achievement Award, Asscn of American Geographers 2010, Political Communicator of the Year Award, Political Studies Asscn 2011. *Publications:* author or co-author of more than 50 books, including Geography and Geographers, Philosophy and Human Geography, City and Society, The Geography of English Politics, A Nation Dividing?, Bell-ringing: The English Art of Change-Ringing, An Atlas of Bells; ed. or co-ed. of more than 40 books, including Geography and the Urban Environment (six vols), The Dictionary of Human Geography; author or co-author of more than 900 articles in academic journals and book chapters. *Leisure interests:* bell-ringing, walking. *Address:* School of Geographical Sciences, University of Bristol, Bristol, BS8 1SS, England (office). *Telephone:* (117) 928-9116 (office). *Fax:* (117) 928-7878 (office). *E-mail:* r.johnston@bris.ac.uk (office). *Website:* www.bris.ac.uk/geography (office).

JOHNSTONE, D(onald) Bruce, Jr, PhD; American university administrator and academic; *Distinguished Service Professor of Higher and Comparative Education Emeritus and Director, International Comparative Finance and Accessibility Project, University at Buffalo;* b. 13 Jan. 1941, Minneapolis, Minn.; s. of Donald Bruce Johnstone and Florence Elliott Johnstone; m. Gail Eberhardt 1965; one s. one d.; ed Harvard Univ. and Univ. of Minnesota; Admin. Asst to Senator Walter F. Mondale (q.v.) 1969–71; Project Specialist, Ford Foundation 1971–72; Exec. Asst to Pres. and Vice-Pres., Univ. of Pennsylvania 1972–77, Adjunct Assoc. Prof. of Educ. 1976–79, Vice-Pres. for Admin. 1977–79; Pres. State Univ. Coll., Buffalo 1979–88; Chancellor State Univ. of New York 1988–94; Univ. Prof. of Higher and Comparative Educ., Univ. at Buffalo 1994–2006, now Distinguished Service Prof. Emer. and Dir Int. Comparative Finance and Accessibility Project, International Comparative Scholar Leader, Fulbright New Century Scholars Program 2006–07; Dr hc (D'Youville Coll.) 1995, (Towson State Univ.) 1995, (Calif. State Univ.) 1997; Golden Quill Award, Nat. Asscn of Student Financial Aid Admins. *Publications:* Financing Higher Education: Cost-Sharing In International Perspective; other works on the econs and man. of higher educ. in domestic and int. perspectives. *Leisure interests:* writing, wilderness canoeing, wildflower botany. *Address:* 428E Baldy Hall, University at Buffalo, Buffalo, NY 12246 (office); 284 Rivermist Drive, Buffalo, NY 14202, USA (home). *Telephone:* (716) 645-1078 (office). *Fax:* (716) 645-2481 (office). *E-mail:* dbj@buffalo.edu (office). *Website:* gse.buffalo.edu/about/directory/faculty/2031 (office).

JOHOR, HRH The Sultan of; Sultan Ibrahim Ismail ibni al-Marhum Sultan Mahmud Iskandar; Malaysian ruler; *Sultan of Johor;* b. 22 Nov. 1958, Johor Bahru; s. of the late Tuanku Mahmood Iskandar ibni al-Marhum Sultan Ismail and of Hajjah Kalsom binti Abdullah (née Josephine Ruby Trevorrow); m. Raja Zarith Sofiah al-Marhum 1982; five s. one d.; ed Sekolah Agama Bukit Zaharah, Sekolah Agama Air Molek, Johor Bahru (religious schools), Trinity Grammar School, Australia, Kota Tinggi army training centre, Fort Benning and Fort Bragg army bases, USA; fmr Deputy Commdr, Johor Mil. Force; named Tengku Makota (Crown Prince) 1981–2010, Regent 1984–89; installed as Sultan of Johor 23 Jan. 2010–; f. Kembara Mahkota Johor (annual royal motorcycle tour event) 2001. *Leisure interests:* polo, tennis, wind-surfing, shooting, motoring. *Address:* Istana Besar, 8000 Johor Bahru, Johor, Malaysia (office).

JOJIMA, Koriki, BA; Japanese politician; b. (Masamitsu Jojima), 1 Jan. 1947, Yanagawa, Fukuoka; ed Faculty of Agric., Univ. of Tokyo; Pres. Ajinomoto Workers' Union for 25 years; fmr Head of Japan Food Industry Workers' Union Council; then served as mem. Council, Japan Productivity Centre for Socio-Econ.

Devt; Founding mem. Democratic Party of Japan (DPJ); first elected to Parl. as mem. House of Reps for Kanagawa No. 10 1996–, Chair. DPJ Diet Affairs Cttee; fmr mem. Cttee on Fundamental Nat. Policies; Minister of Finance Oct.–Dec. 2012. *Address:* Democratic Party of Japan, 1-11-1 Nagata-cho, Chiyoda-ku, Tokyo 100-0014, Japan (office). *Telephone:* (3) 3595-9988 (office). *Fax:* (3) 3595-7318 (office). *Website:* www.dpj.or.jp (office); www.jojima.net.

JOKLIK, Wolfgang Karl (Bill), DPhil; American microbiologist and academic; *James B. Duke Distinguished Professor Emeritus, Department of Molecular Genetics and Microbiology, Duke University;* b. 16 Nov. 1926, Vienna, Austria; s. of Karl F. Joklik and Helene Joklik (née Giessl); m. 1st Judith V. Nicholas 1955 (died 1975); one s. one d.; m. 2nd Patricia H. Downey 1977; ed Sydney Univ. and Univ. of Oxford; Research Fellow, ANU 1954–56, Fellow 1957–62; Assoc. Prof. of Cell Biology, Albert Einstein Coll. of Medicine, New York 1962–65, Siegfried Ullman Prof. 1966–68; Prof. and Chair. Dept of Microbiology and Immunology, Duke Univ. 1968–92 (Chair. Emer. 1993–96), James B. Duke Distinguished Prof. 1972–96, James B. Duke Distinguished Prof. Emer. 1996–; Pres. Virology Div. American Soc. for Microbiology 1966–69; Chair. Virology Study Section NIH 1973–75; Pres. American Medical School Microbiology Chairs' Asscn 1979, American Soc. for Virology 1982–83; Ed.-in-Chief Virology 1975–93, Microbiological Reviews 1991–95; Assoc. Ed. Journal of Biological Chem. 1978–88; mem. NAS, mem. NAS Inst. of Medicine; Humboldt Prize 1986, ICN Int. Prize in Virology 1992, Distinguished Faculty Award, Duke Univ. Medical Center Alumni Asscn 2005. *Publications:* contrib. to and sr ed. specialist books, including Zinsser Microbiology, Principles of Animal Virology, The Reoviridae; more than 200 articles in specialist journals. *Leisure interests:* travel, photography, music, golf, tennis and squash. *Address:* Department of Molecular Genetics and Microbiology, Box 3020, Duke University Medical Center, Durham, NC 27710, USA. *Website:* mgm.duke .edu (office).

JOLIE, Angelina; American actress and philanthropist; b. 4 June 1975, Los Angeles, Calif.; d. of Jon Voight (q.v.) and the late Marcheline Bertrand; m. 1st Jonny Lee Miller 1996 (divorced 1999); m. 2nd Billy Bob Thornton 2000 (divorced 2003); one s. two d. (with Brad Pitt) two adopted s. one adopted d.; ed Lee Strasberg Inst., New York Univ.; apptd Goodwill Amb. by UNHCR 2001–; mem. Council on Foreign Relations 2007–; UN Global Humanitarian Action Award 2005, ranked by Forbes magazine amongst The World's 100 Most Powerful Women (21st) 2010, (29th) 2011, (66th) 2012, (37th) 2013, Jean Hersholt Humanitarian Award 2013. *Films include:* Lookin' to Get Out 1982, Cyborg II: Glass Shadow 1995, Hackers 1995, Foxfire 1996, Mojave Moon 1996, Love is All There Is 1996, True Women 1997, George Wallace (Golden Globe) 1997, Playing God 1997, Hell's Kitchen 1998, Gia (Golden Globe 1999, Screen Actors Guild Award 1999) 1998, Playing by Heart 1999, Girl, Interrupted (Acad. Award for Best Supporting Actress 2000) 1999, Lara Croft: Tomb Raider 2001, Original Sin 2001, Life or Something Like It 2002, Lara Croft Tomb Raider: Cradle of Life 2003, Beyond Borders 2003, Taking Lives 2004, Shark Tale (voice) 2004, Sky Captain and the World of Tomorrow 2004, Alexander 2004, Mr & Mrs Smith 2005, The Good Shepherd 2006, A Mighty Heart 2007, Beowulf (voice) 2007, Kung Fu Panda (voice) 2008, Wanted 2008, Changeling 2008, Salt 2010, The Tourist 2010, Kung Fu Panda 2 (voice) 2011; as dir: In the Land of Blood and Honey (also writer) 2011. *Address:* c/o Geyer Kosinski, Media Talent Group, 9200 Sunset Blvd, Suite 810, West Hollywood, CA 90069 (office); c/o Richard Bauman & Associates, Suite 473, 5757 Wilshire Blvd, Los Angeles, CA 90036, USA (office). *Telephone:* (310) 275-7900 (Media Talent Group) (office). *Fax:* (310) 275-7910 (Media Talent Group) (office).

JOLIOT, Pierre Adrien, DèsSc; French scientist and academic; *Honorary Professor, Collège de France;* b. 12 March 1932, Paris; s. of Frédéric Joliot and Irène Joliot (née Curie); m. Anne Gricouroff 1961; two s.; ed Faculté des Sciences de Paris; researcher, CNRS 1954–81, Dir of Research 1974–; Prof., Collège de France 1981–2002, Hon. Prof. 2002–; Chef de Service, Institut de Biologie Physico-Chimique 1975–94, Admin. 1994–97; Dir Dept of Biology, Ecole Normale Supérieure 1987–92; Scientific Adviser to Prime Minister 1985–86; Pres. Science Ethics Cttee, CNRS 1998–2001; mem. Comité nat. d'évaluation de la recherche, CNER, 1989–92; mem. de l'Institut (Acad. des Sciences, Paris) 1982; mem. NAS, Academia Europaea, Acad. Européenne des Sciences, des Arts et des Lettres; Grand Officier, Légion d'honneur, Commdr, Ordre nat. du Mérite; Prix André Policard-Lacassagne 1968, Charles F. Kettering Award for excellence in photosynthesis 1970, Prix du Commissariat à l'Energie Atomique 1980, CNRS Gold Medal 1982. *Publications:* La recherche passionnément 2001, scientific works on bioenergetics and photosynthesis. *Leisure interests:* tennis, sailing, skiing. *Address:* Institut de Biologie Physico-Chimique, 13, rue Pierre et Marie Curie, 75005 Paris (office); 16 rue de la Glacière, 75013 Paris, France (home). *Telephone:* 1-58-41-50-44 (office); 1-43-37-22-56 (home). *E-mail:* pjoliot@ibpc.fr (office).

JOLLY, Baroness (Life Peer), cr. 2010, of Congdon's Shop in the County of Cornwall; **Rt Hon. Judith Jolly;** British teacher and politician; b. West Cornwall; m.; two s.; maths teacher 1974–97; Chief of Staff to Lord Teverson, MEP for Cornwall and West Plymouth 1997–99; various positions with Liberal Democrats 1984–, Chair. Devon and Cornwall Regional Exec. 2007–10; unsuccessful Parl. cand. for Plymouth Devonport in Gen. Election 2005; apptd to House of Lords 2010, Whip 2013–; Chair. Digital Services Cornwall CIC 2009–; Pres. Soc. of Chiropodists and Podiatrists 2013–. *Address:* House of Lords, Westminster, London, SW1A 0PW, England (office). *Telephone:* (20) 7219-1286 (office). *E-mail:* jollyj@ parliament.uk (office).

JOLLY, Robert Dudley, MNZM, BVSc, PhD, DSc, FRSNZ; New Zealand veterinary pathologist and academic; *Research Fellow and Professor Emeritus, Massey University;* b. 1 Oct. 1930, Hamilton, North Island; s. of Thomas D. Jolly and Violet Mills; m. Aline C. Edwards 1958; two s. two d.; ed King's Coll., Auckland, Univ. of Auckland, Univ. of Sydney, Australia; mixed veterinary practice, Rotorua 1955–59; Teaching Fellow, Univ. of Sydney 1960–63; Assoc. Prof., Univ. of Guelph, Canada 1963–65; Sr Lecturer, Massey Univ. 1965–68, Reader 1968–85, Prof. in Veterinary Pathology and Public Health 1985–96, Research Fellow and Prof. Emer. 1997–; Hon. mem. American Coll. of Veterinary Pathologists; Hon. Fellow, Australian Coll. of Veterinary Science; Hon. Fellow, Royal Coll. of Pathologists of Australasia; mem. NZ Order of Merit 2005; Hector Medal 1996. *Publications:* more than 170 publs in scientific books and journals. *Leisure interest:* gardening. *Address:* 97 Summerset Village, 180 Ruapehu Drive,

Palmerston North 4410 (home); Institute of Veterinary, Animal and Biomedical Science, Massey University, Palmerston North, New Zealand (office). *Telephone:* (6) 356-9099 (office); (6) 354-5852 (home). *E-mail:* r.d.jolly@massey.ac.nz (office). *Website:* ivabs.massey.ac.nz (office).

JOLY, Alain; French business executive; b. 18 April 1938, Nantes; s. of Albert Joly and Yvonne Poyet Rolin; m. Marie-Hélène Capbern-Gasqueton 1966; two s. one d.; ed Lycée Louis Le Grand, Paris and Ecole Polytechnique Paris; engineer, L'Air Liquide 1962–67, Dir of Operations, Canadian Liquid Air 1967–73, Dir Corp. Planning, Soc. L'Air Liquide 1973–76, Regional Man. 1976–78, Gen. Sec. 1978–81, Vice-Pres. 1981, Dir 1982, Chair. and CEO 1995, Chair. Supervisory Bd 2001, now mem. Bd of Dirs; mem. Bd of Dirs BNP Paribas, Lafarge Coppée (now Lafarge) 1993–, Banque Nat. de Paris 1995–; mem. Int. Council, JP Morgan; Croix de la Valeur Militaire, Officier, Légion d'honneur. *Leisure interests:* sailing, golf. *Address:* L'Air Liquide SA, 75 Quai d'Orsay, 75321 Paris cedex 7, France. *Telephone:* 1-40-62-55-55. *Website:* www.airliquide.com.

JOLY, Eva, DenD; Norwegian/French judge and politician; b. (Gro Eva Farseth), 5 Dec. 1945, Oslo; m. Paschal Joly (died 2001); one s. one d.; moved to Paris at 18 to work as au pair; legal counsellor in a psychiatric hosp.; apptd regional judge, Orleans 1981, Asst to Public Prosecutor 1981–83; High Court Judge, Evry 1983–89, then First Examining Judge; legal specialist, Interministerial Cttee for Industrial Reconstruction, Ministry of Finance, Paris 1989, Deputy Sec.-Gen. –1993; investigating magistrate for financial affairs, Palais de Justice, Paris 1993, led to conviction of Bernard Tapie 1994, Roland Dumas 1998, forty exec. mem. of Elf Aquitaine including Chair. Lok Le Floch-Prigent 1995–2002, employees of Pechiney, Crédit Lyonnaise and other high-ranking politicians and businessmen; returned to Norway as special adviser to Norwegian Ministry of Justice with mandate to help strengthen Norway's work internationally against corruption and money laundering Oslo 2002–05; Special Adviser Norwatch (monitored Norwegian businesses in developing countries) 2005; Special Adviser to Iceland's Minister of Justice (assisting in investigation into bank crisis in Iceland) 2009; mem. European Parl. (Greens/European Free Alliance) 2009–; unsuccessful cand. (Europe Ecologie Les Verts) for Pres. of France 2012; Transparency Int. Integrity Award 2001, European of the Year, Reader's Digest 2002. *Publication:* Notre Affaire à Tous (This Concerns All of Us) (autobiog.) 2000, Is This the World We Want To Live In? 2003, Justice Under Siege: One Woman's Battle Against a European Oil Giant (memoir) 2006. *Address:* European Parliament, Bât. Altiero Spinelli 08H353 60, rue Wiertz, 1047 Brusells, Belgium (office); Europe Ecologie Les Verts, 247 rue du Faubourg Saint-Martin, 75010 Paris, France. *Telephone:* (2) 284-53-76 (office). *Fax:* (2) 284-93-76 (office).

JOLY, Hubert; French business executive; *President and CEO, Best Buy Company Inc.;* ed École des Hautes Études Commerciales de Paris, Institut d'Études Politiques de Paris; with McKinsey & Co. Inc., worked in firm's Paris, New York and San Francisco offices 1983–96; drove turnaround of EDS (now part of Hewlett-Packard) in France 1996–99, briefly Chief Information Officer, Vivendi Universal, led restructuring and growth of Vivendi's video game's business (now part of Activision Blizzard) 1999–2001, later oversaw integration of Universal and Vivendi's media assets in USA, then part of team that led restructuring of Vivendi 2002–04; led transformation of Carlson Wagonlit Travel (CWT) 2003–07, CEO Carlson (parent co.), Minneapolis 2008–12; mem. Bd of Dirs, Pres. and CEO Best Buy Co. Inc. 2012–; mem. Bd of Dirs Ralph Lauren Corpn; chaired Travel Facilitation Sub-Cttee of US Dept of Commerce Travel and Tourism Advisory Bd; mem. Bd of Overseers Carlson School of Management, Bd of Trustees Minneapolis Inst. of Arts, Exec. Cttee Minnesota Business Partnership; fmr mem. Exec. Cttee World Travel and Tourism Council; Chevalier, Ordre nat. du Mérite; elected a Global Leader for Tomorrow by the World Econ. Forum, Davos 1997–99. *Address:* Best Buy Company Inc., 7601 Penn Avenue South, Richfield, MN 55423, USA (office). *Telephone:* (612) 291-1000 (office). *Fax:* (612) 292-4001 (office). *E-mail:* info@bestbuy.com (office). *Website:* www.bestbuy.com (office).

JOMAA, Mehdi, DEA; Tunisian engineer and politician; *Prime Minister;* b. Mahdia; five c.; ed Tunis El Manar Univ., Nat. Engineering School, Tunis, HEC Paris, France, Saïd Business School, Oxford, UK; with Hutchinson Group (part of Total Group, operating in aeronautical, defence, automobile, railway, oil and gen. industries) 1988–2012, roles include Head, Paulstra 1990–2003, Tech. Dir, Paulstra & Vibrachoc 2003–04, Tech. Dir, Hutchinson Aerospace Aeronautics and Defence Divs 2004–09, Dir, Hutchinson Aerospace Div., and Dir, six business units in France, USA, India and Tunisia 2009–13; Minister of Industry March–Dec. 2013; Prime Minister 2013–. *Address:* Office of the Prime Minister, place du Gouvernement, La Kasbah, 1030 Tunis, Tunisia (office). *Telephone:* (71) 565-400 (office). *E-mail:* boc@pm.gov.tn (office). *Website:* www.pm.gov.tn (office).

JONAH, Samuel (Sam) Kwesi Esson, MSc, DSc; Ghanaian mining industry executive; *Chairman, Jonah Capital;* b. 19 Nov. 1949, Kibi; m. Belinda Giselle Jonah; three s. two d.; ed Adisadel Coll., Camborne School of Mines, Imperial Coll. of Science and Tech., UK; shovel boy, Obuasi Gold Mine 1969; CEO Ashanti Goldfields Co. Ltd 1986–2004, Exec. Pres. and Dir AngloGold Ashanti (following acquisition) 2004–05, Non-Exec. Pres. and Dir 2005; Chair. Limestone Products Ghana, First Atlantic Merchant Bank Ltd, Equator Exploration Ltd 2005–, Equinox Minerals Ltd 2005–, Jonah Capital 2005–; Dir Lonmin plc, Defiance Mining Corpn, Anglo American Corpn of South Africa, Anglo American Platinum Corpn Ltd; mem. Ghana Investors' Advisory Council, Int. Investment Advisory Council of South Africa, Global Compact Advisory Council; Hon. KBE, Order of the Star of Ghana; Hon. DSc (Camborne School of Mines and Univ. of Exeter) 1966, Hon. DPhil (Ashesi Univ.). *Leisure interests:* fishing, golf. *Address:* 31A Killarney Road, Sandhurst, Sandton 2146 (home); Jonah Capital, 1st Floor, AMB Capital Holdings, 18 Fricker Street, Illovo Boulevard, Johannesburg 2196, South Africa (office). *Telephone:* (11) 215-2282 (office). *Fax:* (11) 268-6868 (office). *E-mail:* sam@jonahcapital.com (office). *Website:* www.jonahcapital.com (office).

JONAS, Sir Peter, Kt, CBE, BA (Hons), LRAM, FRCM, FRNCM, FRSA; British arts administrator, opera company director, academic and lecturer; b. 14 Oct. 1946, London; s. of Walter Adolf and Hilda May Jonas; m. 1st Lucy Hull 1989 (divorced 2000); m. 2nd Barbara Burgdorf 2012; ed Worth School, Univ. of Sussex, Royal Northern Coll. of Music, Manchester, Royal Coll. of Music, London, Eastman School of Music, Univ. of Rochester, USA; Asst to Music Dir, Chicago Symphony Orchestra 1974–76, Artistic Admin. 1976–85; Dir of Artistic Admin., The Orchestral Asscn, Chicago 1977–85; Gen. Dir ENO 1985–93; Staatsintendant (Gen. and Artistic Dir) Bavarian State Opera, Munich 1993–2006 (retd); mem. Bd of Man., Nat. Opera Studio 1985–93, Council, Royal Coll. of Music 1988–95, Council of Man., London Lighthouse 1990–92, Kuratorium Richard Strauss Gesellschaft 1993–, Advisory Bd, Bayerische Vereinsbank 1994–2004, Rundfunkrat (Bd Govs) Bayerische Rundfunk 1999–2006, Supervisory Bd, Berlin State Opera Trust 2004–12, Advisory Bd, Tech. Univ., Munich 2006–12, Governing Bd, Netherlands Opera Amsterdam 2009–, Univ. Council, Univ. of Lucerne 2008–; Visiting Lecturer, St Gallen Univ. 2003–; Lecturer, Univ. of Zurich 2004–, Bavarian Theatre Acad., Univ. of Munich; mem. Bavarian Acad. of Fine Arts 2004; Fellow, Univ. of Sussex 2012; workshop organizer, Wissenschaftzentrum Berlin and Univ. of Zurich; Bayerische Verdienstorden (Germany) 2003, Maximiliansorden (Germany) 2007; Hon. DMus (Sussex) 1993; Queen's Lecturer, Berlin 2001, Bavarian Constitutional Medal 2003, City of Munich Kulturellen Ehrenpreis 2004, Karl Valentin Orden (Germany) 2006. *Publications:* Powerhouse (with M. Elder and D. Pountney) 1993, Eliten und Demokratie 1999. *Leisure interests:* 20th century architecture, cinema, theatre, skiing, mountain hiking, long distance walking, old master paintings, cricket, epic TV series. *Address:* Scheuchzerstrasse 36, 8006 Zurich, Switzerland (home). *Telephone:* (43) 4779871 (office). *Fax:* (43) 4779872 (office). *E-mail:* sirpeterjonas@hispeed.ch (home).

JONATHAN, Goodluck Ebele, BSc, MSc, PhD; Nigerian politician; *President and Commander-in-Chief of the Armed Forces;* b. 20 Nov. 1957, Rivers (now Bayelsa) State; m. Patience Jonathan; ed Univ. of Port Harcourt; Preventative Officer, Dept of Customs and Excise 1975–77; Science Insp. of Educ., Rivers State Ministry of Educ. 1982–83; Lecturer in Biology, Rivers State Coll. of Educ. 1983–93; Asst Dir and Head of Sub–Dept of Environment Protection, Oil Mineral Producing Area Devt Comm. 1993–98; Deputy Gov. Bayelsa State 1999–2007; Vice-Pres. of Nigeria 2007–10, Acting Pres. Feb.–May 2010, Pres. and Commdr-in-Chief of the Armed Forces 2010–, also Minister of Power 2010–14; mem. People's Democratic Party; Fellow, Nigeria Environmental Soc., Inst. of Public Admins, Int. Asscn for Impact Assessment; mem. Science Teachers Asscn of Nigeria, Fisheries Soc. of Nigeria; Inst. of Public Admins Award 2002. *Address:* Office of the Head of State, New Federal Secretariat Complex, Shehu Shagari Way, Central Area District, Abuja, Nigeria (office). *Telephone:* (9) 5233536 (office).

JONES, Alan Stanley, OBE; Australian fmr racing driver; b. 2 Nov. 1946, Melbourne; s. of Stan Jones (fmr Australian champion racing driver); m. Beverly Jones 1971; one adopted s.; ed Xavier Coll., Melbourne; began racing in 1964 in Australia, raced in Britain from 1970; World Champion 1980, runner-up 1979; CanAm Champion 1978; Grand Prix wins: 1977 Austrian (Shadow-Ford), 1979 German (Williams-Ford), 1979 Austrian (Williams-Ford), 1979 Dutch (Williams-Ford), 1979 Canadian (Williams-Ford), 1980 Argentine (Williams-Ford), 1980 French (Williams-Ford), 1980 British (Williams-Ford), 1980 Canadian (Williams-Ford), 1980 US (Williams-Ford), 1981 US (Williams-Ford); announced retirement in 1981; began competng in Australian Touring Car Championships 1990, established own team Pack Leader Racing, 1996, and sold the team in 1997; participated in launch of Australian Motor Sports Acad.; apptd to Bd Australian Grand Prix Corpn 1995; TV commentator. *Leisure interests:* collecting interesting cars, farming in Australia, boating.

JONES, Allen Christopher, RA; British artist; b. 1 Sept. 1937, Southampton, Hants.; s. of William Jones and Madeline Jones; m. 1st Janet Bowen 1964 (divorced 1978); two d.; m. 2nd Deirdre Morrow 1964; ed Hornsey School of Art, Royal Coll. of Art; Sec., Young Contemporaries, London 1961; lived in New York 1964–65; Tamarind Lithography Fellowship, Los Angeles 1966; Guest Prof., Dept of Painting, Univ. of S Florida 1969; Hochschule für Bildende Künste, Hamburg 1968–70, Hochschule der Künste, Berlin 1982–83; Guest Lecturer, Univ. of Calif. 1977; first solo exhbn, London 1963, solo exhbns in UK, USA, Switzerland, Germany, Italy, Australia, Japan, Netherlands, Belgium, Austria, Spain, China, Argentina, Brazil, Czech Repub., Cyprus, Norway, Sweden, Finland, Estonia 1963–; many group exhbns of paintings and graphic work, world-wide 1962–; first travelling retrospective, Europe 1979–80; Welsh Arts Council-sponsored sculpture exhbn 1992; British Council Print Retrospective 1995–98; Commercial Mural Project, Basel 1979; designs for TV and stage in Germany and UK; sculptures commissioned for Liverpool Garden Festival 1984, Cotton's Atrium, Pool of London 1987, Sterling Hotel, Heathrow 1990, Riverside Health Authority, Chelsea and Westminster Hosp., London 1993, Swire Properties, Hong Kong 1997, 2002, Goodwood 1998, GSK World HQ, London 2001–02, Estouteville, Va, USA 2004–05, Yuzi Paradise Sculpture Parks, Guilin and Shanghai, China 2005–06, Chatsworth House 2008; works in many public and pvt. collections in UK and elsewhere, including Tate Gallery, London, Victoria & Albert Museum, London, Museum of 20th Century, Vienna, Stedelijk Museum, Amsterdam, Museum of Modern Art, New York, Hirshhorn Museum, Washington, DC, Chicago Museum of Art, Moderna Museet, Stockholm, Yale Center for British Art, Whitney Museum of American Art, New York; Trustee, British Museum 1990–99, now Trustee Emer.; Hon. Dr of Arts (Southampton) 2007; Prix des Jeunes Artistes, Paris Biennale 1963, Art and Work Award, Wapping Arts Trust 1989, Heitland Foundation Award 1995. *Publications:* Allen Jones Figures 1969, Allen Jones Projects 1971, Waitress 1972, Ways and Means 1977, Sheer Magic (Paintings 1959–79) 1979, UK 1980, Allen Jones (painting and sculpture) 1963–93 1993, Allen Jones Prints 1995, Allen Jones 1997, Allen Jones Sculptures 1965–2002 2002, Allen Jones Works 2006. *Leisure interest:* gardening. *Address:* 41 Charterhouse Square, London, EC1M 6EA, England (home). *Telephone:* (20) 7606-2984 (home). *Fax:* (20) 7600-1204 (home). *E-mail:* dm@allenjonestheartist.com (home).

JONES, Arthur (Alun) Gwynne (see CHALFONT).

JONES, Hon. Barry Owen, AO, MA, LLD, DSc, DLitt, DUniv, FAA, FAHA, FTSE, FASSA, FRSA, FRSN, FRSV, FACE, FAIM; Australian politician, fmr public servant, university lecturer and lawyer; *Professorial Fellow, University of Melbourne;* b. 11 Oct. 1932, Geelong, Vic.; s. of Claud Edward Jones and Ruth Marion Jones (née Black); m. Rosemary Hanbury 1961 (died 2006); ed Melbourne High School, Melbourne Univ.; MP, Victorian Parl. 1972–77, House of Reps 1977–98; Minister for Science 1983–90, for Tech. 1983–84, Minister Assisting the Minister for Industry, Tech. and Commerce 1984–87, Minister for Science, Customs and Small Business 1988–90; Minister Assisting the Prime Minister for

Science and Tech. 1989–90; Visiting Prof., Wollongong Univ. 1991–98, Victoria Univ. of Tech. 1994–; Adjunct Prof., Monash Univ. 1999–; Chair. Port Arthur Historic Site, Tasmania 2000–13, Victorian Schools Innovation Comm. 2001–05; mem. Nat. Comm. for UNESCO 1990–99, Exec. Bd of UNESCO, Paris 1991–95; Chair. House of Reps Cttee on Long Term Strategies 1990–96; Nat. Pres. Australian Labor Party 1992–2000, 2005–06, Vice-Pres. 2004–05, 2006–07; Chair. Australian Film and TV School 1973–75, Australian Film Inst. 1974–80, Vision 2020 Australia 2002–; Deputy Chair. Australian Council for the Arts 1969–73, Australian Constitutional Convention 1997–98; Vice-Pres. World Heritage Cttee, Paris 1995–96, Australia ICOMOS Inc. 1998–2000; mem. Australian Film Devt Corpn 1970–75, Australian Nat. Library Council 1996–98; mem. Bd Australian Stem Cells Centre 2002–08; Visiting Fellow, Trinity Coll., Cambridge, UK 1999–; Vice-Chancellor's Fellow, Univ. of Melbourne 2005–07, Professorial Fellow 2007–; Silver Jubilee Medal 1977, Longford Life Achievement Award, Australian Film Inst. 1986, Redmond Barry Award, Australian Library and Information Asscn 1996, Living Nat. Treasure, Nat. Trust 1997, 1998, John Curtin Medal 2001, Centenary Medal 2003, Research Australia Lifetime Achievement Award 2008, Barry Jones Bay, Antarctica named for him. *Films:* several cameo roles. *Television:* host, Encounter 1968–69. *Publications include:* Macmillan Dictionary of Biography 1981, Sleepers, Wake!: Technology and the Future of Work 1982, Managing Our Opportunities 1984, Living by Our Wits 1986, Dictionary of World Biography 1994 (revised edn and e-book 2013), Coming to the Party (ed.) 2006, A Thinking Reed (autobiog.) 2006. *Leisure interests:* films, music, travel, collecting autographed documents, antique terracottas and Luristan metal work, paintings, reading. *Address:* GPO Box 496, Melbourne, Vic. 3001, Australia (home). *Telephone:* (3) 8344-8628 (office); (418) 399196 (home). *E-mail:* bojones@unimelb .edu.au (office).

JONES, Bill T.; American dancer and choreographer; *Artistic Director, Bill T. Jones/Arnie Zane Dance Company;* b. 15 Feb. 1952, Bunnell, Fla; ed State Univ. of New York, Binghamton; Co-founder American Dance Asylum 1973; Co-founder and Artistic Dir Bill T. Jones/Arnie Zane Dance Co. 1982–; collaborations with Toni Morrison, Max Roach, Jessye Norman, Sir Peter Hall; dir Guthrie Theatre, Minneapolis 1994; Assoc. Choreographer, Lyons Opera Ballet 1995–; MacArthur Foundation Grant; Fellow, American Acad. of Arts and Sciences 2009–; Dr hc (Bard Coll.) 1996; New York Dance and Performance (Bessie) Award (with Arnie Zane) 1986, Bessie Award for D-Man in the Waters 1989, Dorothy B. Chandler Performing Arts Award 1991, Dance Magazine Award 1993, Edin. Festival Critics' Award (presented to Jones/Zane Dance Co.) 1993, Dorothy and Lillian Gish Prize 2003, Harlem Renaissance Award 2005, Samuel H. Scripps American Dance Festival Award for Lifetime Achievement 2005, Wexner Prize 2005, Eileen Harris Norton Fellowship 2007, Kennedy Center Honor 2010. *Dance:* choreographer (with Arnie Zane) Pas de Deux for Two 1974, Across the Street 1975, Whosedebabedoll? Baby Doll 1977, Monkey Run Road 1979, Blauvelt Mountain 1980; Choreographer Negroes for Sale (soloist) 1973, Track Dance 1974, Everybody Works/All Beasts Count 1976, De Sweet Streak to Loveland 1977, The Runner Dreams 1978, Stories, Steps and Stomps 1978, Progresso 1979, Echo 1979, Naming Things Is Only the Intention to Make Things 1979, Floating the Tongue 1979, Sisyphus Act I and II 1980, Open Spaces 1980, Tribeca, Automation, Three Wise Men, Christmas 1980, Secret Pastures 1984, History of Collage 1988, D-Man in the Waters 1989, Dances 1989, Last Supper at Uncle Tom's Cabin/The Promised Land 1991, Love Defined 1991, Aria 1992, Last Night on Earth 1992, Fête 1992, Still/Here 1993 (Edin. Festival 1995), Achilles Loved Patroclus 1993, War Between the States 1993, Still/ Here 1994, We Set Out Early . . . Visibility Was Poor 1997, Out Some Place 1998, The Breathing Show 1999, You Walk? 2000, Fantasy in C Major 2000, The Table Project 2001, Verbum 2002, WORLDWITHOUT/IN 2002, Black Suzanne 2002, WORLD II 2002, There Were. . . 2002, Power/Full 2002, Another Evening 2003, Reading, Mercy and The Artificial Nigger 2003, Mercy 10 x 8 on a Circle 2003, and before. . . 2003, Blind Date 2005, As I Was Saying. . . 2005, Another Evening: I Bow Down 2006, Chapel/Chapter 2006, The Seven (Lucille Lortel Award) 2006, Spring Awakening (Joseph Callaway Award 2006, Tony Award for Best Choreography 2007, Obie Award 2007) 2006; has also choreographed for Alvin Ailey American Dance Theater, Axis Dance Co., Boston Ballet, Lyon Opera Ballet, Berlin Opera Ballet, Dayton Contemporary Dance Co., Diversions Dance Co.; dir and choreographer of operas including: New Year 1990 (Co-Dir BBC TV production), The Mother of Three Sons, Lost in the Stars; theatre productions include Perfect Courage (co-dir), Dream on Monkey Mountain (dir). *Publication:* Last Night on Earth 1995. *Address:* Bill T. Jones/Arnie Zane Dance Company, 27 West 120th Street., Suite 1, New York, NY 10027, USA (office). *Telephone:* (212) 426-6655 (office). *Fax:* (212) 426-5883 (office). *E-mail:* info@billtjones.org (office). *Website:* www.billtjones.org (office).

JONES, Bobby Louis, BS, BEd, MA, PhD; American gospel singer, television broadcaster and lecturer; *Presenter and Producer, The Bobby Jones Gospel Hour;* b. 1938, Henry, TN; m. Ethel Williams Jones; ed Tenn. State Univ. and Vanderbilt Univ., Nashville, Tenn.; teacher, elementary schools in Tenn. and Missouri; textbook consultant for educational publr; Instructor in Reading and Study Skills, Tenn. State Univ. 1974–86; began performing as gospel singer 1970s; Producer and Host Fun City 5 (children's programme), WTBF, Nashville; formed gospel group 'New Life' 1975; cr. first Black Expo, Nashville 1976; signed contract for first TV gospel show (Channel 4) 1976; Producer and Host The Bobby Jones Gospel Hour (BET) 1980–, Bobby Jones World (BET) 1978–84, Video Gospel (BET) 1986–, Bobby Jones Gospel Classics (Word Network) 2001–, Bobby Jones Presents (Word Network) 2001–, Let's Talk Church (BET) 2002–, Bobby Jones Next Generation (The Gospel Channel) 2008–, radio programme The Bobby Jones Gospel Countdown (Sheridan Network); composed and acted in gospel opera 'Make a Joyful Noise' (Gabriel Award, Int. Film Festival Award) 1980; Instructor, Nova Southeastern Univ. 2007–; co-ordinator Exec. Int. Record Label Gospel Artists Retreat; Hon. PhD (Payne Theological Seminary, Wilberforce, Ohio) 1991; Commonwealth Award, Gospel Music Asscn 1990, 352 honours and awards housed at Indiana Univ. *Recordings include:* New Life albums: Sooner or Later 1976, There Is Hope in This World 1978, Caught Up 1979, Tin Gladje 1981, Soul Set Free 1982, Come Together (Dove Award, Gospel Music Asscn) 1984, I'll Never Forget 1990, Bring It to Jesus 1993, Another Time 1996, Just Churchin' (featuring the Nashville Superchoir) 1998, Faith Unscripted 2007, The Ambassador 2007; singles: I'm So Glad I'm Standing Here Today (with Barbara Mandrell, Grammy Award) 1984.

Television includes: Sister Sister (film) 1982. *Plays:* Yes God is Real. *Radio:* The Bobby Jones Gospel Countdown, The Bobby Jones Gospel Radio Show. *Publication:* Touched by God: Stories of Nineteen Gospel Artists 1998, Make a Joyful Noise: My 25 Years in Gospel Music (autobiog.) 2000. *Leisure interests:* TV, basketball, tennis, football. *Address:* c/o Danyelle Haley, PO Box 158947, Nashville, TN 37215, USA (office). *Telephone:* (615) 750-3426 (office). *Fax:* (615) 739-6539 (office). *E-mail:* danyelle19995841@aol.com (office). *Website:* www .bobbyjonesgospel.info.

JONES, Bryn Terfel (see TERFEL, Bryn).

JONES, Carwyn, AM; British/Welsh barrister and politician; *First Minister of Wales;* b. 1967, Swansea; m. Lisa Jones; two c.; ed Univ. of Wales, Aberystwyth, Inns of Court School of Law, London; called to the Bar at Gray's Inn 1989; began career as barrister, Gower Chambers, Swansea, then Temple Chambers, Cardiff; fmr tutor, Cardiff Univ. Law School; fmr mem. Bridgend County Borough Council and Chair., Co. Borough Council Labour Group; mem. Nat. Ass. for Wales (Labour) for Bridgend constituency 1999–, Deputy Sec. 2000, Sec. (later Minister) for Agric. and Rural Devt 2000, also Minister for Ass. Business 2002–03, fmr Open Govt 2002, for the Environment, Planning and the Countryside 2000–07, for Educ., Culture and Welsh Language 2007, Counsel Gen. for Wales and Leader of the House 2007–09, First Minister of Wales 2009–; mem. Labour Party 1987–, Leader, Welsh Labour Party 2009–; mem. Amnesty Int., UNISON, Unite, Fabian Soc.; Wales Year Book Welsh Politician of the Year 2009. *Leisure interests:* sport, reading, travel. *Address:* Office of the First Minister, Welsh Assembly Government, Cathays Park, Cardiff, CF10 3NQ, Wales (office). *Telephone:* (300) 0603300 (office). *Fax:* (300) 0604400 (office). *E-mail:* carwyn.jones@wales.gsi.gov.uk (office). *Website:* wales.gov.uk (office).

JONES, David A., Jr, BA, JD; American health care industry executive; b. Louisville, Ky; s. of David A. Jones, Founder and fmr Chair. Humana Inc.; ed Univ. of Louisville, Yale Univ.; certified public accountant 1954; served in USN 1954–57; mem. Faculty of Econs, Yale Univ. 1958–60; Co-founder Humana Corpn 1961, CEO 1961–97, Dir Humana Inc. (health benefits co. cr. following separation of Humana Corpn into two cos 1993) 1993–, Vice-Chair. 1996–2005, Chair. 2005–10; Chair. and Man. Dir Chrysalis Ventures 1993–; Chair. Hospira; fmr Chair. Healthcare Leadership Council, Nat. Cttee for Quality Health Care; mem. Bd Dirs Abbott Labs, Glenview Trust Co.; mem. The Business Roundtable, Bd American Asscn of Health Plans; Founding Chair. Bd of Visitors, Peter F. Drucker Grad. Man. Centre; Hon. PhD (Chicago Medical School, Univ. of Louisville, Transylvania Univ., Claremont Grad. School); Alumnus of the Year, Univ. of Louisville 2004. *Address:* Humana Inc., 500 West Main Street, Louisville, KY 40202, USA (office). *Telephone:* (502) 580-1000 (office). *Fax:* (502) 580-3677 (office). *E-mail:* info@ humana.com (office). *Website:* www.humana.com (office).

JONES, (David) Huw, MA, FRTS; British broadcasting executive; b. 5 May 1948, Manchester; s. of late Idris Jones and of Olwen Edwards; m. Siân Marylka Miarczynska 1972; one s. one d.; ed Cardiff High School for Boys, Jesus Coll., Oxford; pop singer, recording artist, TV presenter 1968–76; Dir, Gen. Man. Sain Recording Co. 1969–81; Chair. Barcud Cyf (TV Facilities), Caernarfon 1981–93; Man. Dir, Producer Teledu'r Tir Glas Cyf (ind. production co.) 1982–93; first Chair. Teledwyr Annibynnol Cymru (Welsh Ind. Producers) 1984–86; Chief Exec. S4C (Welsh Fourth Channel) 1994–2005; Chair. Skillset Cymru 2002–05; currently Chair. Portmeirion Ltd, Cyfle Cyf; Deputy Chair. Wales Employment and Skills Bd; Vice? Chair. Nant Gwrtheyrn Trust; Dir Sgrin Cyf, SDN Ltd, Skillset Ltd, Nat. Ass. of Wales Broadcasting Co. Ltd, mem. British Screen Advisory Council; Hon. Fellow, Univ. of Wales, Aberystwyth 1997. *Leisure interests:* reading, cycling, walking. *E-mail:* wesb2@wales.gsi.gov.uk (office). *Website:* www.wesb.org.uk (office).

JONES, Rt Hon. David Ian, PC; British politician and solicitor; *Secretary of State for Wales;* b. 22 March 1952, London; s. of Bryn Jones and Elspeth Jones (née Sauvage Willams); m. Sara Jones; two s.; ed Ruabon Grammar School, University Coll. London, Chester Coll. of Law; fmr mem. UCL Conservative Soc.; fmr Sr Partner, David Jones & Co., Llandudno; contested Conwy constituency in Gen. Election 1997, City of Chester 2001; Mem. Welsh Ass. for North Wales 2002–03; MP (Conservative) for Clwyd West 2005–10, for Clwyd West (revised boundary) 2010–, mem. Welsh Affairs Select Cttee 2005–10; Shadow Minister for Wales 2006–10; Parl. Under-Sec. of State, Wales Office 2010–12; Sec. of State for Wales 2012–; Chair. Conwy Conservative Asscn 1998–99; Patron, Chinese Conservative Group. *Leisure interest:* Liverpool Football Club. *Address:* Wales Office, Gwydyr House, Whitehall, London, SW1A 2NP (office); House of Commons, Westminster, London, SW1A 0AA, England (office). *Telephone:* (20) 7270-0540 (Wales Office) (office); (20) 7219-8070 (Westminster) (office). *Fax:* (20) 7270-0568 (Wales Office) (office); (20) 7219-0142 (Westminster) (office). *E-mail:* david.jones@walesoffice.gsi .gov.uk (office); jonesdi@parliament.uk (office). *Website:* www.walesoffice.gov.uk (office); www.parliament.uk/biographies/commons/mr-david-jones/1502 (office); www.davidjones-mp.com.

JONES, Dean Mervyn; Australian sports commentator and fmr professional cricketer; b. 24 March 1961, Coburg, Melbourne, Vic.; m. Jane Jones 1986; one d.; ed Mt Waverley High School, Vic.; right-hand batsman; played for Victoria 1981/ 82–97/98; (Capt. 1993/94–95/96), Durham 1992, Derbyshire (Capt.) 1996–97, resigning mid-way through season and returning home, Australia 1984–92; Test debut: West Indies v Australia, Port of Spain 16–21 March 1984; played in 52 Tests, scoring 3,631 runs (average 46.55, highest score 216) including 11 hundreds; toured England 1989; played in 164 One-Day Ints, scoring 6,068 runs (average 44.61, highest score 145) including seven hundreds; played in 245 First-class matches, scoring 19,188 runs (average 51.85, highest score 324 not out) including 55 hundreds; commentator for TEN Sports –2006; mem. Exec. Cttee and sr commentator for Indian Cricket League 2007–; Wisden Cricketer of the Year 1990. *Publication:* Deano: My Call 1995. *Leisure interests:* golf, baseball, looking after his two Rottweilers. *Address:* Indian Cricket League, Essel Sports Pvt. Ltd, 135 Continental Building, Dr Annie Besant Road, Worli, Mumbai 400018, India (office). *E-mail:* response@iclonline.in (office). *Website:* www.indiancricketleague .in (office).

JONES, Edward Paul, BA, MFA; American writer; b. 5 Oct. 1950, Arlington, Va; ed Holy Cross Coll., Univ. of Virginia; teaches periodically at George Washington

University, Washington, DC; Morgan Writer-in-Residence, Univ. of North Carolina 2010. *Publications:* Lost in the City (short stories) (PEN/Hemingway Award) 1992, The Known World (novel) (Pulitzer Prize for Fiction 2004, Lannan Literary Award, Int. IMPAC Dublin Literary Award 2005) 2003, All Aunt Hagar's Children 2006. *Address:* c/o Department of English, George Washington University, 801 22nd Street, NW, Suite 760, Washington, DC 20052, USA (office).

JONES, Grace; American singer, model and actress; b. 19 May 1952, Spanish-town, Jamaica; d. of Robert and Marjorie P. Jones; one s.; m. Atila Altaunbay 1996 (divorced); moved to New York at age of 12; abandoned Spanish studies at Syracuse Univ. for first stage role, Phila; became fashion model in New York, then Paris; made first album, Portfolio, for Island Records 1977; debut as disco singer New York 1977; opened La Vie en Rose restaurant, New York 1987; Q Idol Award 2008. *Films include:* Gordon's War 1973, Let's Make a Dirty Movie 1976, Colt 38 Special Squad 1976, Army of Lovers or Revolution of the Perverts (documentary) 1979, Deadly Vengeance 1981, Made in France (documentary) 1984, Conan the Destroyer 1984, A View to a Kill 1985, Vamp 1986, Straight to Hell 1987, Siesta 1987, Boomerang 1992, Cyber Bandits 1995, McCinsey's Island 1998, Palmer's Pick Up 1999, No Place Like Home 2006, Falco 2008, Chelsea on the Rocks 2008. *Television:* Stryx 1978, A One Man Show 1982, Pee-wee's Playhouse Christmas Special 1988, Beastmaster 1999, Wolf Girl 2001, Shaka Zulu: The Citadel 2001. *Recordings:* albums: Portfolio 1977, Fame 1978, Muse 1979, Warm Leatherette 1980, Nightclubbing 1981, Living My Life 1982, Island Life 1985, Slave to the Rhythm 1985, Inside Story 1986, Bulletproof Heart 1989, Hurricane 2008. *Address:* Wall of Sound, 338A Ladbroke Grove, London, W10 5AH, England. *E-mail:* info@wallofsound.net; enquiries@theworldofgracejones.com. *Website:* www.wallofsound.net; www.theworldofgracejones.com.

JONES, Dame Gwyneth, DBE, FRCM, ARCM; British/Swiss singer (soprano); b. 7 Nov. 1936, Pontnewynydd, Mon., Wales; d. of the late Edward George Jones and Violet Webster; one d.; ed Royal Coll. of Music, London, Accad. Chigiana, Siena, Zurich Int. Opera Centre; with Zürich Opera House 1962–63; a Prin. Dramatic Soprano, Royal Opera House, Covent Garden 1963–; with Vienna State Opera House 1966–, Deutsche Oper Berlin 1966–, Bavarian State Opera 1967–; guest performances in numerous opera houses throughout the world including La Scala, Milan, Rome Opera, Berlin State Opera, Munich State Opera, Hamburg, Paris, Metropolitan Opera, New York, San Francisco, Los Angeles, Zürich, Geneva, Dallas, Chicago, Teatro Colón, Buenos Aires, Tokyo, Beijing, Hong Kong, Seoul, Bayreuth Festival, Salzburg Festival, Arena di Verona, Edin. Festival and Welsh Nat. Opera; known for many opera roles including title roles in Aida, Madame Butterfly, Norma, Tosca, Elektra, Salome, and Medea, Leonora in Il Trovatore, Desdemona in Otello, Leonore in Fidelio, Senta in The Flying Dutchman, Sieglinde in Die Walküre, Lady Macbeth in Macbeth, Elizabeth in Don Carlos, Donna Anna in Don Giovanni, Eva in Die Meistersinger, Kundry in Parsifal, Isolde in Tristan und Isolde, Helena in Aegyptische Helena (R. Strauss), Färberin in Frau ohne Schatten, Elisabeth/Venus in Tannhäuser, Marschallin and Octavian in Der Rosenkavalier, Brünnhilde in Der Ring des Nibelungen, Ortrud in Lohengrin, Minnie in Fanciulla del West, Erwartung (Schoenberg), La voix humaine (Poulenc), Kabanicha in Katia Kabanowa (Janacek), Kostelnicka Küsterin in Jenůfa (Janacek), Herodias in Salome (Richard Strauss), Klytämnestra in Elektra (Richard Strauss), Queen of Hearts in Alice in Wonderland (Unsuk Chin), Begbick in Mahagonny (Kurt Weill); Pres. Richard Wagner Soc., London 1990; master-classes in UK, Germany, France, Netherlands, Canada and Switzerland; debut as Stage Dir with new production of Der Fliegende Holländer by Richard Wagner at Deutsches Nat. Theater, Weimar; recordings for Decca, DGG, Philips, Chandos, EMI, CBS, Claves, Orfeo; Fellow, Royal Welsh Coll. of Music and Drama 1992; Kammersängerin in Austria and Bavaria; Hon. mem. RAM 1980, Vienna State Opera 1989; Bundesverdienstkreuz (Germany) 1988, Commdr des Arts et des Lettres 1993, Österreichisches Ehrenkreuz für Wissenschaft und Kunst, 1. Klasse 1998; Hon. DMus (Glamorgan) 1995, (Wales) 1998; Shakespeare Prize, Hamburg 1987, Golden Medal of Honour, Vienna 1991, Premio Puccini Award Torre del Lago 2003, Cymry for the World Honour, Wales Millennium Centre, Cardiff 2004. *Film:* Quartet (Anne Langley), directed by Dustin Hoffman. *Television films:* Fidelio, Aida, Flying Dutchman, Leonore, Beethoven 9th Symphony, Elisabeth and Venus in Tannhäuser, Poppea (Monteverdi), Rosenkavalier (R. Strauss), Die Walküre, Siegfried, Götterdämmerung, Die lustige Witwe, Don Carlos, Tristan und Isolde, La voix humaine (Mahagonny), Begbick (Mahagonny), Turandot, Senta (Der fliegende Holländer), Queen of Hearts (Alice in Wonderland). *Address:* PO Box 2000, 8700 Küsnacht, Switzerland.

JONES, Ieuan Wyn, LLB; British politician and lawyer; *Director, Menai Science Park;* b. 22 May 1949, Denbigh, Wales; s. of the late John Jones and of Mair Jones; m. Eirian Llwyd; three c.; ed Liverpool Polytechnic; practised as solicitor 1974–87; MP for Ynys Môn 1987–2001, mem. Nat. Ass. for Wales (AM) for Ynys Môn 1999–13, Deputy First Minister 2007–11; Chair. Plaid Cymru—The Party of Wales 1980–82, 1990–92, Pres. and Leader 2000–03, Leader Ass. Group 2003–06, Leader 2006–12; Dir Menai Science Park 2013–. *Publications:* Europe: The Challenge Facing Wales 1996, Y Llinyn Arian: Thomas Gee (biog.) 1998. *Leisure interests:* history, sport. *Address:* Parc Menai, Bangor, Gwynedd, LL57 4HJ, Wales (office). *Telephone:* (7767) 301810 (office). *E-mail:* info@parcmenai.com (office). *Website:* www.parcmenai.com (office).

JONES, J. Steve, BSc, PhD, FRS; British geneticist and writer; *Professor Emeritus of Human Genetics, University College London;* b. 24 March 1944, Aberystwyth, Wales; m. Norma Percy; ed Wirral Grammar School, studied in Edinburgh and Chicago; Prof. of Human Genetics, Univ. Coll. London (UCL), currently Prof. Emer., Principal Research Assoc., Div. of Biosciences, Faculty of Life Sciences; Pres. Galton Inst.; several visiting professorships, including Harvard Univ., Univ. of Chicago, Univ. of California at Davis, Univ. of Botswana, Fourah Bay Coll., Sierra Leone and Flinders Univ., Adelaide, Australia; Royal Soc. Faraday Medal for public understanding of science 1997, BP Natural World Book Prize 1999, 2000, Inst. of Biology Charter Medal 2002, Irwin Prize for Secularist of the Year, Nat. Secular Soc. 2006. *Radio and television:* gave Reith Lectures on 'The Language of the Genes' 1991, Blue Skies (BBC Radio 3), In the Blood (six-part TV series on human genetics) 1996. *Publications include:* Genetics for Beginners (with B. van Loon) 1991, The Cambridge Encyclopedia of Human Evolution (ed. with R. D. Martin, D. Pilbeam) 1992, The Language of the Genes (Rhone-Poulenc Book

Prize, Yorkshire Post First Book Prize 1994) 1993, In The Blood 1995, Almost like a Whale: The Origin of Species Updated (aka Darwin's Ghost) 1999, Y: The Descent of Men 2002, The Single Helix: A Turn Around the World of Science 2005, Twelve Galton Lectures: A Centenary Selection with Commentaries (co-ed.) 2007, Coral: A Pessimist in Paradise 2007, Darwin's Island 2009. *Address:* Department of Biology, University College London, Gower Street, London, WC1E 6BT (office); Wolfson House, 4 Stephenson Way, London, NW1 2HE, England (office). *Telephone:* (207) 679-7416 (office). *E-mail:* j.s.jones@ucl.ac.uk (office). *Website:* iris.ucl.ac.uk/research/personal/index?upi=JSJON91 (office).

JONES, James Earl; American actor; b. 17 Jan. 1931, Arkabutla, Miss.; s. of Robert Earl Jones and Ruth Williams; m. Cecilia Hart 1982; ed Univ. of Mich.; numerous stage appearances on Broadway and elsewhere include Master Harold . . . And the Boys, Othello, King Lear, Hamlet, Paul Robeson, A Lesson From Aloes, Of Mice and Men, The Iceman Cometh, A Hand is on the Gate, The Cherry Orchard, Danton's Death, Fences; frequent TV appearances; cast as voice of Darth Vader in films Star Wars, The Empire Strikes Back and The Return of the Jedi; Fellow, American Acad. of Arts and Sciences 2009–; Hon. DFA (Princeton, Yale, Mich.); Tony Award for role in stage version and Golden Globe Award for role in screen version of The Great White Hope, Lifetime Achievement Award, Screen Actor's Guild 2008, numerous other awards. *Films include:* Matewan, Gardens of Stone, Soul Man, My Little Girl, The Man, The End of the Road, Dr Strangelove, Conan the Barbarian, The Red Tide, A Piece of the Action, The Last Remake of Beau Geste, The Greatest, The Heretic, The River Niger, Deadly Hero, Claudine, The Great White Hope, The Comedians, Coming to America, Three Fugitives, Field of Dreams, Patriot Games, Sommersby, The Lion King (voice), Clear and Present Danger, Cry the Beloved Country, Lone Star, A Family Thing, Gang Related, Rebound, Summer's End 1998, Undercover Angel 1999, Quest for Atlantis 1999, Our Friend Martin (voice) 1999, On the Q.T. 1999, Finder's Fee 2001, Recess Christmas: A Miracle on Third Street (voice) 2001, 2004: A Light Knight's Odyssey (voice) 2004, Robots (voice) 2005, The Sandlot 2 2005, The Benchwarmers (voice) 2006, Welcome Home, Roscoe Jenkins 2008. *Address:* Horatio Productions, PO Box 610, Pawling, NY 12564-0610, USA.

JONES, Gen. (retd) James L., BSc; American diplomatist and army officer (retd) and government official; *Director-designate, Brent Scowcroft Center on International Security;* b. 19 Dec. 1943, Kansas City, Mo.; m. Diane Jones (née Johnson); four c.; ed Georgetown Univ. School of Foreign Service, Basic and Amphibious Warfare Schools, Quantico, Virginia, Nat. War Coll., Washington, DC; Second Lt, US Marine Corps 1967, Platoon Commdr and Co. Commdr Co. G, 2nd Bn, 3rd Marines, Viet Nam 1967–68, rank of First Lt 1968, Co. Commdr Camp Pendleton, Calif. 1968–70, Marine Barracks, Washington, DC 1970–73, Co. H, 2nd Bn, 9th Marines, 3rd Marine Div., Okinawa 1974–75; served in Officer Assign-ments Section, HQ Marine Corps, Washington, DC 1976–79; rank of Maj. 1977; Marine Corps Liaison Officer to US Senate 1979–84; rank of Lt-Col 1982; Commdr 3rd Bn, 9th Marines, 1st Marine Div., Camp Pendleton 1985–87; Sr Aide to Commdr of Marine Corps 1987–89; rank of Col 1988; Mil. Sec. to Commdt 1989–90; CO 24th Marine Expeditionary Unit, Camp Lejeune, NC 1990–92; rank of Brig.-Gen. 1992; Deputy Dir J-3, US European Command, Stuttgart, Germany 1992–94; Chief of Staff Jt Task Force Provide Promise, Operations in Bosnia and Herzegovina and Macedonia 1992–94; rank of Maj.-Gen. 1994; Commanding Gen. 2nd Marine Div., Marine Forces Atlantic, Camp Lejeune 1994–96; Dir Expeditionary Warfare Div., Office of the Chief of Naval Operations 1996; Deputy Chief of Staff for Plans, Policies and Operations, HQ Marine Corps 1996; rank of Lt-Gen. 1996; Mil. Asst to Sec. of Defense 1997–99; rank of Gen. 1999; 32nd Commdt Marine Corps 1999–2003; Commdr US European Command and 14th Supreme Allied Commdr Europe, NATO 2003–06; Chair. US Ind. Comm. on the Security Forces of Iraq 2007; Pres. and CEO US Chamber of Commerce Inst. for 21st Century Energy 2007–09; apptd by US State Dept to act as Special Envoy for Middle East Security 2007–09; Nat. Security Adviser to the Pres., The White House 2009–10; Dir-designate Brent Scowcroft Center on International Security 2012–; fmr mem. Bd of Dirs Invacare Corpn; numerous decorations; Dr hc (Georgetown Univ.) 2002; Defense Distinguished Service Medal, Silver Star Medal, Legion of Merit with 4 Gold Stars, Bronze Star Medal with Combat V, Combat Action Ribbon and numerous other awards. *Address:* Brent Scowcroft Center on International Security, The Atlantic Council, 1101 15th Street, NW, 11th Floor, Washington, DC 20005, USA. *Telephone:* (202) 463-7226. *Fax:* (202) 463-7241. *Website:* www.acus.org.

JONES, James Robert, LLB; American lawyer and fmr diplomatist; *Chairman, Manatt Jones Global Strategies LLC;* b. 5 May 1939, Muskogee, Okla; s. of Robert Jones and Margaret Wich; m. Olivia Barclay 1968; two s.; ed Univ. of Oklahoma and Georgetown Univ.; Asst to Pres. Johnson, White House, Washington, DC 1965–69; practising lawyer and business consultant, Tulsa, Okla 1969–73; mem. US Congress 1973–87; Partner, Dickstein, Shapiro & Moran (law firm), Washington, DC 1987–89; Chair. and CEO American Stock Exchange, New York 1989–93; Amb. to Mexico 1993–97; Pres. Warnaco Int. 1997–98; Sr Counsel, Manatt, Phelps and Phillips LLP 1998–99; Chair. Manatt Jones Global Strategies LLC 1999–; Steiger Award 1979, Humanitarian Award, Anti Defamation League 1990, Aztec Eagle Award (Mexico) 1997. *Leisure interests:* golf, reading. *Address:* Manatt Jones Global Strategies LLC, One Metro Center, 700 12th Street, NW, Suite 1100, NW, Suite 1100, Washington, DC 20005, USA. *Telephone:* (202) 585-6560. *E-mail:* jjones@manatt.com (office). *Website:* www.manattjones.com (office).

JONES, Rt Rev. James Stuart, BA; British ecclesiastic; *Bishop of Liverpool;* b. 18 Aug. 1948, Glasgow, Scotland; s. of Maj. James Stuart Anthony Jones and Helen Deans Dick Telfer (née McIntyre); m. Sarah Caroline Rosalind Marrow 1980; three d.; ed Univ. of Exeter and Wycliffe Hall, Oxford; Asst Master Sevenoaks School 1971–74; producer, Scripture Union 1975–81; asst curate, Christ Church, Clifton 1982–84, Assoc. Vicar 1984–90; Vicar Emmanuel Church, Croydon 1990–94; Bishop of Hull 1994–98; Bishop of Liverpool 1998–; Hon. DD (Hull) 1999; Hon. DLitt (Univ. of Lincolnshire and Humberside) 2001. *Television:* The Word on the Street 1999. *Publications include:* Following Jesus 1984, Finding God 1987, Why Do People Suffer? 1993, The Power and the Glory 1994, The People of the Blessing 1998, The Moral Leader 2002, Jesus and the Earth 2003. *Leisure interests:* swimming, opera, holidays in France. *Address:* Bishop's Lodge, Woolton Park, Woolton, Liverpool, L25 6DT, England (office). *Telephone:* (151) 421-0831 (office). *Fax:* (151) 428-3055 (office). *E-mail:* bishopslodge@liverpool.anglican.org (office). *Website:* www.liverpool.anglican.org (office).

JONES, Sir Mark, Kt, MA, FSA, FRSE; British museum director; *Director, Victoria and Albert Museum;* b. 5 Feb. 1951; s. of John Ernest Powell-Jones and Ann Paludan; m. Ann Camilla Toulmin 1983; two s. two d.; ed Eton Coll., Worcester Coll., Oxford and Courtauld Inst. of Art; Asst Keeper Dept of Coins and Medals, British Museum 1974–90, Keeper 1990–92; Dir Nat. Museums of Scotland 1992–2001; Dir Victoria and Albert Museum, London 2001–(11); Master, St Cross Coll., Oxford (2011–); Ed. The Medal 1983–94; Chair. Nat. Museum Dirs' Conf.; Pres. Fédération Int. de la Médaille 1994–2000, British Art Medal Soc. 1998–2004 (Sec. 1982–94, currently Vice-Pres.); Vice-Pres. Kensington & Chelsea Decorative & Fine Arts Soc.; co-f. Scottish Cultural Resources Access Network 1994–96, mem. Bd 1996–2006; mem. Royal Mint Advisory Cttee 1994–2004, Arts and Humanities Data Service Steering Cttee 1997–99, Focus Group Nat. Cultural Strategy 1999–2000; Dir, Edin. and Lothians Tourist Bd 1998–2000; mem. Bd Resource (Museums, Libraries and Archives Council) 2000–05; mem. Court and Council, RCA 2001–; Trustee, Nat. Trust 2005–, The Pilgrim Trust 2006–; Gilbert Collection; Patron, Embroiderer's Guild; Hon. Prof., Univ. of Edin. 1997; Chevalier, Ordre des Arts et des Lettres; Hon. DLitt (Royal Holloway) 2002, Hon. Dr of Arts (Abertay Univ., Dundee) 2009. *Publications include:* The Art of the Medal 1977, Impressionist Painting 1979, Contemporary British Medals 1986, Fake?: the Art of Deception (ed.) 1990, Why Fakes Matter (ed.) 1992, Designs on Posterity (ed.) 1994. *Address:* Victoria and Albert Museum, Cromwell Road, South Kensington, London, SW7 2RL, England (office). *E-mail:* mark.jones@vam.ac.uk (office). *Website:* www.vam.ac.uk (office).

JONES, Michael Frederick; British journalist; b. 3 July 1937, Gloucester, Glos., England; s. of Glyn F. Jones and Elizabeth Jones (née Coopey); m. Sheila Dawes 1959; three s.; ed Crypt Grammar School, Gloucester; reporter on prov. newspapers 1956–64; Financial Times 1964–65; Daily Telegraph 1965–67; Business News Asst Ed. The Times 1967–70; Man. Ed. The Asian, Hong Kong 1971; News Ed. Sunday Times 1972, Political Corresp. 1975, Political Ed. 1984, Assoc. Ed. 1990–95, Assoc. Ed. (Politics) 1995–2002; Chair. Parl. Press Gallery, House of Commons 1989–91; Media Adviser, Memorial to the Women of World War II Cttee, London 2004–05; Visiting Fellow, Goldsmith's Coll., Univ. of London 2000–02; currently Research Asst to Baroness Boothroyd, House of Lords. *Publication:* Betty Boothroyd: The Autobiography (collaborated) 2001. *Leisure interest:* researching modern history. *Address:* 43 Hillview Road, Orpington, Kent, BR6 0SE, England. *E-mail:* micjon1937@hotmail.com.

JONES, Monty Patrick, BSc, MSc, PhD; Sierra Leonean plant breeder; *Executive Director, Forum for Agricultural Research in Africa;* b. 5 Feb. 1951, Freetown; m. Geraldine Bamidele Jones; ed Univ. of Sierra Leone, Univ. of Birmingham, UK; began career with West Africa Rice Devt Agency 1975, worked as rice breeder and researcher 1980s, Head of Upland Rice Breeding Program, Côte d'Ivoire 1991; Exec. Dir Forum for Agricultural Research in Africa, Ghana 2002–; mem. Bd AGRA; Grand Officer, Order of the Rokel (Sierra Leone) 2004, Nat. Order of Merit of Cote d'Ivoire; Hon. DSc (Birmingham) 2005, Hon. PhD (Ghent); World Food Prize 2004, World's 100 Most Influential Men 2007. *Achievements include:* made breakthrough in combining Asian and African rice varieties to develop Nerica, a 'New Rice for Africa', uniquely suited to poor African rice farmers 1994. *Publications:* numerous specialist papers, including The Rice Plant and its Environment 1996, Biotechnology Application in Agriculture: Challenges and Opportunities for Africa 2007, A New Green Revolution: An Answer to the Challenge for Africa? 2007, Priorities for Sustainable Agriculture and Food Security 2007. *Address:* FARA Secretariat, PMB CT 173 Cantonments, #12 Anmeda Street, Roman Ridge, Accra, Ghana (office). *Telephone:* (21) 772823 (office), (21) 779421 (office). *Fax:* (21) 773676 (office). *Website:* www.fara-africa.org (office).

JONES, Norah; American singer and pianist; b. (Geetali Norah Jones Shankar), 30 March 1979, New York, NY; d. of the late Ravi Shankar and Sue Jones; ed Booker T. Washington High School for the Performing and Visual Arts, Dallas, North Texas Univ.; mem. Wax Poetic; formed band with Jesse Harris, Lee Alexander and Dan Rieser; solo artist 2001–; also mem. live band, The Little Willies; MOBO Award for Best Jazz Act 2002, VH1 Best Young Female Singer Award 2002, Grammy Awards for Best New Artist, for Record of the Year, for Best Female Pop Vocal Performance (both for Don't Know Why) 2003, BRIT Award for Int. Breakthrough Artist 2003, World Music Awards for Best Female Artist, Best Pop Female Artist 2004, Grammy Awards for Best Female Pop Vocal Performance (for Sunrise), for Record of the Year (for Here We Go Again, with Ray Charles) 2005. *Film appearances:* My Blueberry Nights 2007, Ted 2012. *Recordings include:* albums: solo: Come Away With Me (Grammy Awards for Album of the Year, Best Pop Vocal Album 2003) 2002, Feels Like Home 2004, Not Too Late 2007, The Fall 2009, Little Broken Hearts 2012; with The Little Willies: The Little Willies 2006. *Address:* Macklam Feldman Management, Suite 200, 1505 W Second Avenue, Vancouver, BC V6H 3Y4, Canada (office); c/o Blue Note Records, 304 Park Avenue S, Third Floor, New York, NY 10010, USA (office). *Website:* www.norahjones.com.

JONES, Quincy; American composer, arranger, conductor and musician (trumpet); b. 14 March 1933, Chicago; s. of Quincy Delight and Sarah Jones; m. 2nd Peggy Lipton; two d.; three c. by previous m.; one d. with Nastassja Kinski (q.v.); ed Seattle Univ., Berklee School of Music and Boston Conservatory; musician and arranger, Lionel Hampton Orchestra 1950–53; arranger for orchestras and singers including Frank Sinatra, Dinah Washington, Count Basie, Sarah Vaughan and Peggy Lee; organizer and trumpeter, Dizzy Gillespie Orchestra, Dept of State tour of Near and Middle East and S. America 1956; Music Dir Barclay Disques, Paris; led own European tour 1960; Music Dir Mercury Records 1961, Vice-Pres. 1964; conductor of numerous film scores; composer, actor in film Blues for Trumpet and Koto; producer recordings of Off the Wall 1979 by Michael Jackson (q.v.), Thriller 1982, Bad, videotape Portrait of An Album: Frank Sinatra with Quincy Jones and Orchestra 1986; composer The Oprah Winfrey Show 1989–; producer, Fresh Prince of Bel Air 1990–; Dr hc (Berklee Music Coll.) 1983; (Hebrew Univ.) 1993, (Clark Univ.) 1993; German Jazz Fed. Award, Edison Int. Award (Sweden), Downbeat Critics' Poll Award, Downbeat Readers' Poll Award, Billboard Trendsetters Award 1983, Martell Foundation Humanitarian Award 1986, Nat. Acad. of Songwriters Lifetime Achievement Award 1989, Jean Hersholt Humanitarian Award 1995,

several Grammy Awards, Scopus Award, Producers' Guild of America Award 1999, World Econ. Forum Crystal Award 2000, Marian Anderson Award 2001, Nat. Foundation for Advancement in the Arts Ted Arison Prize 2001, Kennedy Center Honor 2001, BBC Jazz Lifetime Achievement Award 2006, Ivor Novello Special Int. Award 2007. *Recordings include:* albums: Body Heat 1974, The Dude 1981, Back on the Block 1989. *Publication:* The Complete Quincy Jones: My Journey and Passions 2008. *Address:* 10850 Wilshire Blvd, Suite 1200, Los Angeles, CA 90024 (office); Quincy Jones Music Company, 6671 Sunset Blvd, #1574A, Los Angeles, CA 90028, USA (office). *Telephone:* (323) 957-6601 (office). *Fax:* (323) 962-5231 (office). *E-mail:* info@quincyjonesmusic.com (office). *Website:* www.quincyjonesmusic.com (office); www.quincyjones.com (office).

JONES, Randall Todd, Sr; American retail executive; *President, Publix Super Markets;* joined Publix Super Markets 1980, Regional Dir of Retail Operations 1999–2003, Vice-Pres. 2003–05, Sr Vice-Pres. 2005–08, Pres. 2008–. *Address:* Publix Super Markets Corporate Office, PO Box 407, Lakeland, FL 33802-0407 (office); 525 East Christina Blvd, Lakeland, FL 33811, USA. *Telephone:* (863) 688-1188 (office). *Fax:* (863) 284-5532 (office). *E-mail:* info@publix.com (office). *Website:* www.publix.com (office).

JONES, Roy, Jr; American professional boxer; b. 16 Jan. 1969, Pensacola, Fla; three s.; professional career record of 49 wins, three defeats, 38 knock-outs; voted Outstanding Boxer Olympic Games 1988; won IBF (Int. Boxing Fed.) middle-weight crown beating Bernard Hopkins 1993; moved up to super middleweight, won IBF title from James Toney 1994; moved up to light heavyweight div. winning WBC (World Boxing Council) (1997), WBA (World Boxing Asscn) (1998) and IBF (1999) titles; winner WBA heavyweight title 2003 (first fmr middleweight champion since 1897 to win title); winner WBC light heavyweight title 2003, defeated by Glen Johnson losing IBF light heavyweight title 2004, lost to Antonio Tarver losing WBC and WBA light heavyweight title 2004; minor league professional basketball player for five years with the Sarasota Sun Dogs; f. Body Head Entertainment 1998; has appeared in numerous films and TV programmes; currently boxing analyst and commentator for Home Box Office (HBO); Boxing Writers' Asscn of America Fighter of the Decade (for 1990s), The Ring Fighter of the Year 1994, WBC Lifetime Achievement Award 2001. *Leisure interests:* music, basketball, hunting, fishing, raising livestock. *Address:* c/o Home Box Office Inc., 1100 Avenue of the Americas, New York, NY 10036, USA (office). *Telephone:* (212) 512-1000 (office). *Fax:* (212) 512-1182 (office). *Website:* www.hbo.com/boxing (office).

JONES, Stephanie (Steffi) Ann; German/American football executive and fmr professional football player; *Director, German Football Association;* b. 22 Dec. 1972, Frankfurt am Main; ed German Sport Univ., Cologne; defender; youth career: played with SV Bonames 1979–86, SV Dörnigheim FC 1986–88, FC Hochstadt 1988–92; sr career: played with SG Praunheim 1988–91, FSV Frankfurt 1991–92, SG Praunheim 1992–93, TuS Niederkirchen 1993–94, SG Praunheim 1994–95, FSV Frankfurt 1995–96, SC 07 Bad Neuenahr 1998–2000, Washington Freedom 2002–03 (WUSA Founders Cup Champion 2003), 1. FFC Frankfurt 2000–07 (German Championship 2001, 2002, 2003, 2005, German Cup Winner 2001, 2002, 2003, UEFA Women's Cup Winner 2002, 2006); scored nine goals in 111 caps for the German nat. team 1993–2007 (retd), won three consecutive UEFA Women's Championships 1997, 2001, 2005, bronze medal at Summer Olympics, Sydney 2000, part of German squad that won FIFA Women's World Cup 2003, bronze medal, Summer Olympics, Athens 2004; announced retirement from active football to become Pres. of Organizing Cttee of 2011 FIFA Women's World Cup in Germany Dec. 2007; Dir, German Football Association (DFB); FIFA Amb. for Women's Football; UEFA Amb. for Women's Football; Hessian Order of Merit 2006; Georg August Zinn Prize, Hall of Freedom (USA), Deutscher PR-Preis 'Kommunikator des Jahres 2011', Horizont Sportbusiness Award 'Persönlichkeit 2011', Ehren-Preis 11 Freundinnen 2011. *Publication:* Der Kick des Lebens (The Kick of Life) (autobiog.) 2007. *Address:* c/o Sportsfreude, Kirchstraße 104, 65375 Oestrich-Winkel, Germany (office); Deutscher Fußball-Bund, Hermann-Neuberger-Haus, Otto-Fleck-Schneise 6, 60528 Frankfurt am Main, Germany (office). *Telephone:* (6723) 804934 (office); (69) 67880 (office). *Fax:* (6723) 8049339 (office); (69) 6788266 (office). *E-mail:* mail@sportsfreude.com (office); info@dfb.de (office). *Website:* sportsfreude.com/projects/steffi-jones (office); www.dfb.de (office).

JONES, Stephen John Moffat, OBE, BA (Hons); British milliner; *Chairman, Stephen Jones Millinery Ltd;* b. 31 May 1957, West Kirby, Cheshire; s. of Gordon Jones and Margaret Jones; ed Liverpool Coll., St Martin's School of Art; milliner 1980–, collaborating with int. designers including Jean-Paul Gaultier, Comme des Garçons, Claude Montana, John Galliano, Christian Dior (Paris) 1997–; colour creator for Shiseido Cosmetics; licences in Japan for gloves, sunglasses, kimonos, scarves, handkerchiefs, handbags; hats in perm. collections of Victoria and Albert Museum, London, Brooklyn Musuem, New York, Kyoto Costume Inst., Australian Nat. Gallery, Canberra; Hon. Prof., Univ. of the Arts, London; Accessory Designer of the Year 2005, Outstanding Contrib. to Fashion Design 2009, Fashion Star Honoree, New York 2009, Royal Designer for Industry 2009; Chevalier des Chapeaux de Caussade, France 2005. *Dance:* Eternal Light, Ballet Rambert 2009. *Films:* Coco avant Chanel, Sex and the City 2. *Publication:* Hats: An Anthology by Stephen Jones. *Leisure interest:* sculpture. *Address:* Stephen Jones Millinery Ltd, 36 Great Queen Street, London, WC2B 5AA, England (office). *Telephone:* (20) 7242-0770 (office). *Fax:* (20) 7242-0796 (office). *E-mail:* admin@stephenjonesmillinery.com (office). *Website:* www.stephenjonesmillinery.com (office).

JONES, Sir Tom, Kt; British singer; b. (Thomas Jones Woodward), 7 June 1940, Pontypridd, Mid Glamorgan, S Wales; s. of Thomas Woodward and Freda Woodward (née Jones); m. Melinda Trenchard 1956; one s.; fmr bricklayer, factory worker; sang in clubs and dance halls billing himself as Tommy Scott, singing with the Senators and with self-formed group The Playboys; changed his name to Tom Jones, signed contract with Decca as solo artist 1963; first hit record It's Not Unusual 1965; toured USA 1965; appeared in Ed Sullivan Show at Copacabana, New York and in variety show This Is Tom Jones in UK and USA 1969; score for musical play Matador 1987; acted and sang in live performance of Dylan Thomas' Under Milk Wood 1992; performed in Amnesty International 40th Anniversary Special 2001, Pavarotti and Friends 2001, Prince's Trust Party in the Park 2001; mem. Screen Actors Guild, American Fed. of TV and Radio Artists, American Guild of Variety Artists; Hon. Fellow, Welsh Coll. of Music and Drama 1994; voted Britain's Most Popular Male Singer in Melody Maker Poll 1967, 1968, MTV Video Award 1988, BRIT Award for Best British Male Solo Artist 2000, Nordoff-Robbins Music Therapy Silver Clef Award 2001, Q Magazine Merit Prize 2002, BRIT Award for Outstanding Contrib. to Music 2003, Music Industry Trust Award for Outstanding Contrib. to Music 2010. *Films:* The Jerky Boys – The Movie 1995, Mars Attacks! 1996, Agnes Browne 1999, The Emperor's New Groove (voice) 2000. *Television includes:* Beat Room, Top Gear, Thank Your Lucky Stars, Sunday Night at the London Palladium, The Right Time (series) 1992, The Voice 2012–. *Albums:* Along Came Jones 1965, A-Tom-Ic Jones 1966, From The Great 1966, Green Green Grass Of Home 1966, Live At The Talk Of The Town 1967, Delilah 1968, Help Yourself 1968, Tom Jones Live In Las Vegas 1969, This Is Tom Jones 1969, Tom 1970, I Who Have Nothing 1970, Tom Jones Sings She's A Lady 1971, Tom Jones Live At Caesar's Palace, Las Vegas 1971, Close Up 1972, The Body And Soul Of Tom Jones 1973, Somethin' 'Bout You Baby I Like 1974, Memories Don't Leave Like People 1975, Say You'll Stay Until Tomorrow 1977, Rescue Me 1980, Darlin' 1981, Matador: The Musical Life Of El Cordorbes 1987, At This Moment 1989, After Dark 1989, Move Closer 1989, Carrying A Torch 1991, The Lead And How To Swing It 1994, Reload 1999, Mr Jones 2002, Reload 2 2002, 24 Hours 2008, Praise and Blame 2010. *Singles include:* It's Not Unusual 1965, What's New Pussycat 1965, Thunderball 1966, Green Green Grass of Home 1966, Detroit City 1967, Funny Familiar Forgotten Feelings 1967, I'll Never Fall In Love Again 1967, I'm Coming Home 1967, Delilah 1968, Help Yourself 1968, Love Me Tonight 1969, Without Love 1969, Daughter of Darkness 1970, I Who Have Nothing 1970, She's A Lady 1971, Till 1971, The Young New Mexican Puppeteer 1972, Can't Stop Loving You, Letter To Lucille 1973, Somethin' 'Bout You Baby I Like 1974, Say You Stay Until Tomorrow 1976, A Boy From Nowhere 1987, Kiss (with Art of Noise) 1988, All You Need Is Love 1993, If I Only Knew 1994, Burning Down The House (with The Cardigans) 1999, Baby It's Cold Outside (with Cerys Matthews) 1999, Mama Told Me Not To Come (with Stereophonics) 2000, Sex Bomb (with Mousse T) 2000, You Need Love Like I Do (with Heather Small) 2000, Tom Jones International 2002. *Publication:* The Fantasticks (screenplay) 2000. *Leisure interests:* history, music. *Address:* c/o Jennie Harris, Valley Music Ltd, Unit 6, Upper Culham Farm Barns, Upper Culham, Wargrave, Henley on Thames, Oxon., RG10 8NR, England (office); Tom Jones Enterprises LLC, 1801 Avenue of the Stars, Suite 200, Los Angeles, CA 90067, USA (office). *Telephone:* (1491) 845840 (office); (310) 552-0044 (office). *E-mail:* jennieharris@valleymusicuk.com (office); office@tomjones.com (office). *Fax:* (310) 552-0714 (office). *Website:* www.tomjones .com (office).

JONES, Tommy Lee; American actor; b. 15 Sept. 1946, San Saba, Tex.; s. of Clyde L. Jones and Lucille Marie Scott; m. 1st Kimberlea Cloughley 1981; m. 2nd Dawn Laurel 2001; ed Harvard Univ.; Broadway debut in A Patriot for Me; other Broadway appearances include Four in a Garden, Ulysses in Night Town, Fortune and Men's Eyes; Emmy Award for TV role as Gary Gilmon in The Executioner's Song. *Films include:* Love Story 1970, Eliza's Horoscope, Jackson County Jail, Rolling Thunder, The Betsy, Eyes of Laura Mars, Coal Miner's Daughter, Back Roads, Nate and Hayes, River Rat, Black Moon Rising, The Big Town, Stormy Monday, The Package, Firebirds, JFK, Under Siege, House of Cards, The Fugitive, Blue Sky, Heaven and Earth, Natural Born Killers, The Client, Blue Sky, Cobb, Batman Forever, Men In Black 1997, Volcano 1997, Marshals 1997, Small Soldiers (voice) 1998, Rules of Engagement 1999, Double Jeopardy 1999, Space Cowboys 2000, Men in Black II 2002, The Hunted 2003, Man of the House 2005, The Three Burials of Melquiades Estrada (also dir) 2005, A Prairie Home Companion 2006, No Country for Old Men 2007, In the Valley of Elah 2007, Men in Black III 2012, Lincoln 2012. *Television appearances include:* The Amazing Howard Hughes, Lonesome Dove, The Rainmaker, Cat on a Hot Tin Roof, Yuri Nosemko, KGB, April Morning. *Address:* William Morris Agency, One William Morris Place, Beverly Hills, CA 90212, USA (office). *Telephone:* (310) 859-4000 (office). *Fax:* (310) 859-4462 (office). *Website:* www.wma.com (office).

JONES, Vaughan Frederick Randal, DCNZM, BSc, MSc, DèsSc, FRS; New Zealand mathematician and academic; *Professor of Mathematics, University of California, Berkeley;* b. 31 Dec. 1952, Gisborne; m. Martha Weare Jones (née Myers) 1979; one s. two d.; ed Auckland Grammar School, Univ. of Auckland, Univ. of Geneva, Switzerland; fmr Asst Lecturer, Univ. of Auckland; at Ecole de Physique, Geneva 1974–76, Ecoles Mathématiques 1976–79, taught as asst; E. R. Hedrick Asst Prof. of Math., UCLA 1980–81; Asst Prof., Univ. of Pennsylvania 1981–84, Assoc. Prof. 1984–85; Prof., Univ. of California, Berkeley 1985–; mem. American Acad. of Arts and Sciences 1993–, American Math. Soc. (Vice-Pres. 2004–); Foreign mem. Norwegian Royal Soc. of Letters and Sciences 2001–; Hon. mem. London Math. Soc. 2002–; Hon. DSc (Univ. of Auckland) 1992, (Univ. of Wales) 1993; Dr hc (Universite du Littoral, Cote d'Opale) 2002; Univ. Entrance Scholarship 1970, Gilles Scholarship, Phillips Industries Bursary 1970, Swiss Gov. Scholarship 1973, F.W.W. Rhodes Memorial Scholarship, Vacheron Constantin Prize 1980, Guggenheim Fellowship 1986, Fields Medal, Int. Congress of Mathematicians, Kyoto, Japan 1990, New Zealand Gov. Science Medal 1991, Onsager Medal, Trondheim Univ. 2000, Prix Mondial Nessim Habif 2007. *Publications:* numerous articles in math. journals on functional analysis, knot theory and Von Neumann algebras. *Address:* Department of Mathematics, 925 Evans Hall, University of California, Berkeley, CA 94720-3840, USA (office). *Telephone:* (510) 642-4196 (office). *E-mail:* vfr@math.berkeley.edu (office). *Website:* www.math.berkeley.edu (office).

JONES-MORGAN, Judith, LLB, LLM; Saint Vincent and the Grenadines lawyer and government official; *Attorney-General;* b. 7 Sept. 1957, Trinidad and Tobago; d. of Rita Jones; m. Desmond Carlos Richardson Morgan; ed Univ. of E London and Jesus Coll. Cambridge, UK; accounts technician Ministry of Finance and Treasury, Trinidad and Tobago 1976–80; legal clerk, Nat. Energy Corpn, Trinidad and Tobago 1980–84; legal asst, Graham Ritchie & Co., UK 1988–89; pupil barrister Chancery/Commercial Chambers, UK 1991; Crown Counsel in Chambers of Attorney-Gen., Saint Vincent and the Grenadines 1992–93; Sr Crown Counsel 1993–99; registrar, High Court 2000–01, Attorney-Gen. of Saint Vincent and the Grenadines 2001–; mem. Interim Study Programme for Judicial Educators 2000; mem. Bar of England and Wales, Saint Vincent and the Grenadines, Trinidad and Tobago; mem. Hon. Soc. of the Middle Temple, UK; Fellow, Cambridge Commonwealth Soc. 1990; Cambridge Commonwealth Award, Max-

well Law Prize, UKCOSA Essay Competition. *Leisure interests:* politics, drama, public speaking, cricket, jogging, travel. *Address:* Attorney-General's Chambers, New Methodist Church Building, Granby Street, Kingstown (office); PO Box 78, Mount Pleasant, Argyle, Saint Vincent and the Grenadines, West Indies (home). *Telephone:* 457-2807 (office); 458-2010 (home). *Fax:* 457-2898 (office). *E-mail:* att .gen.chambers@vincysurf.com (office); judithmorgan_ag@hotmail.com (home). *Website:* www.legal.gov.vc (office).

JONES OF BIRMINGHAM, Baron (Life Peer), cr. 2007, of Alvechurch and of Bromsgrove in the County of Worcestershire; **Digby Marritt Jones,** LLB, FRSA, CIMgt; British lawyer, business consultant and fmr government official; b. 28 Oct. 1955, Birmingham; s. of Derek Jones and Bernice Jones; m. Patricia Mary Jones; ed Bromsgrove School, Univ. Coll. London; joined Edge & Ellison (corp. law firm) 1978, Pnr 1984, Deputy Sr Pnr 1990, Sr Pnr 1995; joined KPMG as Vice-Chair. Corp. Finance 1998; Dir-Gen. CBI 2000–06; Sr Adviser to Deloitte 2006–07; Sr Adviser, Barclays Capital 2006–07, Ford (Europe) 2006–07, JCB 2006–07, 2009–, Monitise 2009–, Jaguar Land Rover 2009; UK Skills Envoy 2006–07; Minister of State for Trade and Investment, Dept for Business, Enterprise and Regulatory Reform (jtly with FCO) 2007–08, also Labour whip in House of Lords 2007–08; Chair. Triumph Motorcycles Ltd 2009–; Dir (non-exec.) Alba PLC 2003–07; Dir Leicester Tigers 2005–, Königswinter 2003–07; mem. Advisory Bd Commonwealth Educ. Fund 2000–07; fmr Pres. Tourism Alliance 2001–06; Commr Comm. for Racial Equality 2002–07; fmr mem. Nat. Learning and Skills Council 2004–06, Skills Alliance 2002; Companion Inst. of Man. 2000; Chair. HSBC Int. Business Advisory Bd 2009–, Univ. of Birmingham Business School Advisory Bd 2004; Full mem. Aston Reinvestment Trust 2003; Fellow, RSA 2001, Royal Inst. 2002, University Coll. London 2004 (Pres. University Coll. London Campaign 2004–); Hon. Fellow, Cardiff Univ. 2004; Dr hc (Central England) 2002, (Birmingham) 2002, (Manchester), (Inst. of Science and Tech.) 2003, (Hertfordshire) 2004, (Middlesex) 2005, (Sheffield Hallam) 2005, (Warwick) 2006, (Aston) 2006, (Bradford) 2006, (Hull) 2006, (Queens Univ., Belfast) 2006, (Loughborough) 2007, (Nottingham) 2007, (Thames Valley) 2007, (Wolverhampton) 2007,. *Leisure interests:* Aston Villa, theatre, skiing, cycling, rugby, military history. *Address:* House of Lords, Westminster, London, SW1A 0PW (office); 58 Elizabeth Court, 1 Palgrave Gardens, London, NW1 6EJ, England (home). *Telephone:* (20) 7219-3232 (office); 7827-828283 (mobile) (office). *E-mail:* Joanne@digbylordjones.com (office). *Website:* www.digbylordjones.com (office); www.parliament.uk/biographies/lords/ digby-jones/38751 (office).

JONES PARRY, Sir Emyr, GCMG, PhD, FInstP; British diplomatist and university administrator; *President, University of Aberystwyth;* b. 21 Sept. 1947, Carmarthen, Wales; s. of Hugh Jones Parry and Eirwen Jones Parry; m. Lynn Jones Parry; two s.; ed Gwendraeth Grammar School, Univ. Coll., Cardiff, St Catharine's Coll., Cambridge; joined FCO 1973; Deputy Chef du Cabinet of Pres. of European Parl. 1987–89; Head EC Dept (External) FCO 1989–93; Minister, Embassy in Madrid 1993–96; Deputy Political Dir FCO 1996–97; Dir EU, FCO 1997–98; Political Dir, FCO 1998–2001; Perm. Rep. to N Atlantic Council, NATO 2001–03, to UN, New York 2003–07; Pres. Univ. of Aberystwyth 2007–; Chair. All Wales Convention 2007–09, Wales Millennium Centre 2010–, Redress 2008–; Pres. Welsh Centre for Int. Affairs 2011–; various univ. fellowships; Hon. LLD (Wales). *Publications:* various scientific publs, speeches on current int. issues. *Leisure interests:* gardening, theatre, reading, sport. *Address:* Office of the President, Aberystwyth University, Penglais Campus, Aberystwyth, Ceredigion, SY23 3BF, Wales (office). *Telephone:* (1970) 622004 (office). *E-mail:* sjj@aber.ac.uk (home). *Website:* www.aber.ac.uk (office).

JONG, Erica Mann, BA, MA; American writer, poet and journalist; b. 26 March 1942, New York; d. of Seymour Mann and Eda Mann (née Mirsky); m. 1st Michael Werthman 1963 (divorced 1965); m. 2nd Allan Jong 1966 (divorced 1975); m. 3rd Jonathan Fast 1977 (divorced 1983); one d.; m. 4th Kenneth David Burrows 1989; ed Barnard Coll., Columbia Univ.; studied poetry with Mark Strand and Stanley Kunitz; Lecturer in English, City Coll. of New York 1965–66, 1969–70; Poetry Instructor, Poetry Center of the 92nd Street Y 1966–69; Lecturer in English, Overseas Div., Univ. of Maryland, Heidelberg, Germany 1970–72; Bread Loaf Writers Conf., Middlebury, Vt 1970–73; mem. Literature Panel, New York State Council on Arts 1972–74; mem. of Faculty, Salzburg Seminar, Austria 1993; Visiting Writer, Ben Gurion Univ., Beersheva, Israel 1998, Bennington Coll. 1998, Marymount Coll. Writers Workshop Poetry Seminar 2007; Writing Prof., Barnard Coll. 2011–12; Writing Prof., Rancho La Puerta, 2001–; Hon. Fellow, Welsh Coll. of Music and Drama 1994; New York State Council on the Arts Grants 1971, Nat. Endowment of the Arts grant 1973; Hon. PhD (CUNY) 2006; Acad. of American Poets Prize 1971, Poetry magazine Bess Hokin Prize 1971, Poetry Soc. of America Alice Faye di Castagnola Award 1972, Freud Award for Literature, Italy 1975, UN Award for Excellence in Literature 1995, Prix Littéraire de Deauville Film Festival (France) 1998, Fernanda Pivano Award for Literature (Italy) 2009. *Publications include:* poetry: Fruits and Vegetables 1971, Half-Lives 1973, Loveroot 1975, At the Edge of the Body 1979, Ordinary Miracles 1983, Becoming Light: Poems New and Selected 1991, Love Comes First 2009; novels: Fear of Flying 1973, How to Save Your Own Life 1977, Fanny: Being the True History of Fanny Hackabout-Jones 1980, Parachutes and Kisses 1984, Serenissima: A Novel of Venice (aka Shylock's Daughter: A Novel of Love in Venice) 1987, Any Woman's Blues 1990, Inventing Memory: A Novel of Mothers and Daughters 1997, Sappho's Leap 2004; non-fiction: Witches 1981, Megan's Book of Divorce (for children) 1984, The Devil at Large: Erica Jong on Henry Miller 1993, Fear of Fifty: A Midlife Memoir 1994, Composer Zipless: Songs of Abandon from the Erotic Poetry of Erica Jong 1995, What Do Women Want? Bread. Roses. Sex. Power. 1998, Seducing the Demon: Writing for my Life 2006, Love Comes First 2009, Sugar in My Bowl 2011, A Letter to the President 2012. *Leisure interests:* sailing, flying, spending time with family. *Address:* 150 East 68th Street, Apt 27G, New York, NY 10021, USA (office). *Telephone:* (212) 517-2907 (home). *E-mail:* officejongleur@gmail.com. *Website:* www.ericajong.com.

JONSEN, Albert R., MA, PhD, STM; American academic; *Co-Director and Senior Scholar in Residence, Program in Medicine and Human Values, California Pacific Medical Center;* b. 4 April 1931, San Francisco, Calif.; s. of Albert R. Jonsen and Helen C. Sweigert; m. Mary E. Carolan 1976; ed Gonzaga Univ., Spokane, Wash., Santa Clara Univ., Calif. and Yale Univ.; Instructor in Philosophy, Loyola Univ. of

Los Angeles 1956–59; Instructor in Divinity, Yale Univ. 1966–67; Asst. Assoc. Prof. in Philosophy and Theology, Univ. of San Francisco 1968–73, Pres. 1969–72; Prof. of Ethics in Medicine and Chief, Div. of Medical Ethics, Univ. of California, San Francisco 1973–87; Prof. of Ethics in Medicine, Chair. Dept of Medical History and Ethics, Univ. of Washington, Seattle 1987–99, Prof. Emer. 1999–; currently Co-Dir and Sr Scholar in Residence, Program in Medicine and Human Values, California Pacific Medical Center; Commr, US Nat. Comm. for Protection of Human Subjects of Biomedical and Behavioral Research 1974–78; Commr, Pres.'s Comm. for Study of Ethical Problems in Medicine and in Biomedical and Behavioral Research 1979–82; mem. Artificial Heart Assessment Panel, Nat. Heart and Lung Inst. 1972–73, 1984–86; mem. Nat. Bd of Medical Examiners 1985–88; Consultant, American Bd of Internal Medicine 1978–84; mem. Ethics Advisory Bd GERON Corpn 2000–05; mem. NAS Inst. of Medicine, mem. NAS Cttee on AIDS Research; Chair. NRC Cttee on the Social Implications of AIDS 1987–92, Nat. Advisory Bd on Ethics and Reproduction 1992–97; Pres. Soc. for Health and Human Values 1986; Guggenheim Fellowship 1982, 1986–87; Visiting Prof., Yale Univ. 1999–2000, Stanford Univ. School of Medicine 2002, Univ. of Virginia Law School 2002; Nelson Lectureship, Univ. of California, Davis 2010; Davies Award, American Coll. of Physicians 1987, Convocation Medal, American Coll. of Surgeons 1988, Annual Award, Soc. for Health and Humanities 1993, Lifetime Achievement Award, American Soc. for Bioethics and Humanities 1999, Leadership Award, Professional Responsibility in Medicine and Research 2000, Lifetime Achievement Award, Berman Inst. of Bioethics, Johns Hopkins Univ. 2009. *Publications:* Responsibility in Modern Religious Ethics 1968, Ethics of Newborn Intensive Care 1976, Clinical Ethics (with M. Siegler and W. Winslade) 1982, The Abuse of Casuistry (with S. Toulmin) 1986, The Old Ethics and the New Medicine 1990, The Impact of AIDS on American Society (with J. Stryker) 1993, The Birth of Bioethics 1997, A Short History of Medical Ethics 2000, Bioethics Beyond the Headlines 2005. *Leisure interests:* sketching, swimming, walking, music. *Address:* 3400 Laguna Street, Apt 412, San Francisco, CA 94123, USA (home). *Telephone:* (415) 600-1647 (office). *E-mail:* arjonsen@aol.com (office); jonsena@sutterhealth.com (office). *Website:* depts.washington.edu/mhedept/facres/aj_bio.html (office).

JONZE, Spike; American film director, film producer, actor and screenwriter; b. (Adam Spiegel), 1969, Rockville, Md; s. of Arthur Spiegel III and Sandy Granzow; m. Sofia Coppola 1999 (divorced 2003); fmr Ed. Freestylin', Go, BMX Action, Homeboy, Grand Royal magazines; f. Dirt magazine with Andy Jenkins and Mark Lewman 1991; began directing skating films and music videos. *Music videos as director:* California by Wax, Sure Shot by the Beastie Boys, Sabotage by the Beastie Boys, Drop by the Pharcyde, Cannonball by The Breeders, What's Up Fatlip? by Fatlip, Undone (The Sweater Song) by Weezer, Buddy Holly by Weezer (MTV Video Music Award for Best Direction 1995), Feel The Pain by Dinosaur Jr, If I Only Had A Brain by MC 900ft Jesus, Sky's The Limit by The Notorious B.I.G., Crush with Eyeliner by R.E.M., It's Oh So Quiet by Björk, Da Funk by Daft Punk, Praise You by Fatboy Slim, Weapon of Choice by Fatboy Slim, Elektrobank by The Chemical Brothers, Wonderboy by Tenacious D (as Spike Jones). *Films include:* Video Days (dir) 1991, Mi Vida Loca (actor) 1994, How They Get There (dir) 1997, The Game (actor) 1997, Amarillo by Morning (dir) 1998, Being John Malkovich (dir, actor) (New York Film Critics Circle Award for Best First Film, Broadcast Film Critics Asscn Breakthrough Performer, Online Film Critics Soc. Award for Best Debut) 1999, Three Kings (actor) 1999, Torrance Rises (dir, as Richard Coufey) 1999, Human Nature (producer) 2001, Adaptation (dir) (Berlin Film Festival Silver Bear 2003) 2002, Jackass: The Movie (writer, producer) 2002, Yeah Right! (prod.) 2003, Jackass Number Two (producer) 2006, Synecdoche, New York (producer) 2008, Where the Wild Things Are 2009, Her (Golden Globe Award for Best Screenplay, Motion Picture, Academy Award for Best Original Screenplay 2014) 2013. *Television includes:* Jackass (series writer and producer) 2000. *Address:* MJZ, 2201 Carmelina Avenue, Los Angeles, CA 90064, USA (office). *Telephone:* (310) 826-6200 (office). *Fax:* (310) 826-6219 (office).

JOPLING, Jay; British art dealer and gallery owner; *Owner, White Cube gallery;* b. 1963; s. of Lord Jopling, fmr Minister of Agric., Fisheries and Food; m. Sam Taylor-Wood (divorced 2008); two d.; ed Eton Coll., Univ. of Edinburgh; began by selling fire extinguishers before starting to deal in post-war American art; formed friendship with artist Damien Hirst 1991; arranged financing for production of new work; supported small list of artists, including Hirst and Marc Quinn organizing exhbns in warehouses; opened White Cube gallery, St James's, London 1993, gallery moved to larger space in Hoxton 2000 (closed 2012), Mason's Yard gallery located off Duke Street, St James's opened in Sept. 2006, White Cube Bermondsey opened in Oct. 2012, White Cube Hong Kong (first outside UK) opened with a show of Gilbert & George in March 2012, White Cube São Paulo opened with a solo show by Tracey Emin in Dec. 2012; represents young British artists, Damien Hirst, Chapman Brothers, Tracey Emin and Antony Gormley; also represents int. artists, including Gabriel Orozco, Anselm Kiefer, Mona Hatoum and Julie Mehretu. *Address:* White Cube, 144–152 Bermondsey Street, London, SE1 3TQ (office); White Cube, 25–26 Mason's Yard (off Duke Street), St James's, London, SW1Y 6BU, England; White Cube Hong Kong, 50 Connaught Road, Hong Kong Special Administrative Region, People's Republic of China. *Telephone:* (20) 7930-5373 (office); 2592-2000 (Hong Kong). *Fax:* (20) 7749-7480 (office). *E-mail:* enquiries@whitecube.com (office). *Website:* www.whitecube.com (office); www .jayjopling.co.uk.

JOPLING, Baron (Life Peer), cr. 1997, of Ainderby Quernhow in the County of North Yorkshire; **(Thomas) Michael Jopling,** PC, BSc; British politician and farmer; *Member of Parliamentary Assembly, NATO;* b. 10 Dec. 1930, Ripon, Yorks.; s. of Mark Bellerby Jopling; m. Gail Dickinson 1958; two s.; ed Cheltenham Coll. and King's Coll., Durham Univ., Newcastle-upon-Tyne; mem. Thirsk Rural Dist Council 1958–64; Conservative MP for Westmorland 1964–83, Westmorland and Lonsdale 1983–97; Jt Sec. Conservative Parl. Agric. Cttee 1966–70; Parl. Pvt. Sec. to Minister of Agric. 1970–71; an Asst Govt Whip 1971–73; Lord Commr of the Treasury 1973–74; an Opposition Spokesman on Agric. 1974–75, 1976–79; Shadow Minister of Agric. 1975–76; Parl. Sec. to HM Treasury and Chief Whip 1979–83; Minister of Agric., Fisheries and Food 1983–87; mem. Nat. Council, Nat. Farmers' Union 1962–64, UK Exec., Commonwealth Parl. Assen 1974–79, 1987–97, Vice-Chair. 1977–79, Int. Exec. 1988–89; Chair. Select Cttee on Sittings of the House 1991–92; mem. Select Cttee on Agric. 1967–69, on Foreign Affairs 1987–97; mem. Privy Council 1979–; mem. NATO Parl. Ass. 1987–97, 2001–, Chair. Cttee Civilian

Aspects of Security 2011–; Leader UK Del. to Parl. Ass., OSCE 1990–97, mem. 2000–01; mem. Lords Sub-Cttee 'C' European Defence and Security 1999–2003 (Chair. 2000–03), 2010–, mem. Sub-Cttee'F' Home Affairs 2006–10 (Chair. 2007–10); mem. Lords SEL Cttee, Merits of Statutory Instruments 2004–07; Pres. Auto-Cycle Union 1989–2003, Pres. Emer. 2003–; DL Cumbria 1991–97, N Yorks. 1998–2006; Hon. Sec. British American Parl. Group 1987–2001; Hon. DCL (Newcastle) 1992. *Address:* Ainderby Hall, Thirsk, North Yorks., YO7 4HZ, England. *Telephone:* (1845) 567224.

JORDA, Claude Jean Charles; French judge and international official; *Section President, Cour nationale du droit d'asile;* b. 16 Feb. 1938, Bône, Algeria; ed Institut d'Etudes Politiques and School of Law, Univ. of Toulouse, Ecole Nat. de la Magistrature (ENM); called to the Bar, Toulouse 1961; Auditeur de Justice (magistrate in training) 1963–66; Magistrate, Cen. Admin. Services Dept, Ministry of Justice 1966–70, Deputy Dir for Legal Org. and Regulations 1976–78, Dir Legal Services 1982–85; Sec.-Gen. ENM 1970–76; Vice-Pres. Tribunal de Grande Instance, Paris 1978–82; Prosecutor-Gen. Court of Appeals, Bordeaux 1985–92, Paris 1992–94; Judge, Int. Criminal Tribunal for the Fmr Yugoslavia (ICTY) 1994–96, Pres. Trial Chamber I 1995–99, Pres. ICTY 1999–2003; Judge, Int. Criminal Court 2003–07 (resgnd); Section Pres. Cour nationale du droit d'asile 2008–; Hon. Pres. Cour nationale du droit d'asile (fmrly Comm. des recours des réfugiés); Officier, Légion d'honneur 1993, Commdr, Ordre nat. du Mérite 2000, Commdr des Palmes académiques, Commdr du Mérite agricole; Médaille de l'Educ. Surveillée (for services to young people in difficulty and in prison). *Publications include:* Un nouveau statut pour l'accusé dans le procédure du Tribunal pénal international pour l'ex-Yougoslavie (essays) 2000; academic contribs, book chapters and conf. proc., articles on ICTY. *Address:* Cour nationale du droit d'asile, 35 rue Cuvier, 93558 Montreuil, Seine-Saint-Denis (office); 21 rue Boudet, 33000 Bordeaux, France (home). *Telephone:* 6-08-67-97-72 (home). *E-mail:* jordaclaude@hotmail.com (home). *Website:* www.commission -refugies.fr (office).

JORDAN, Michael Jeffery; American business executive and fmr professional basketball player; b. 17 Feb. 1963, Brooklyn, NY; s. of the late James Jordan and of Delores Jordan; m. Juanita Vanoy 1989 (divorced 2006); two s. one d.; ed Univ. of North Carolina; player for Univ. of North Carolina (won NCAA championship 1982); drafted by Nat. Basketball Asscn (NBA) Chicago Bulls in first round 1984, played 1984–93, 1995–98 (NBA Champions 1991, 1992, 1993, 1996, 1997, 1998); mem. US Olympic basketball team 1984, 1992; mem. NBA All-Star team 1985, 1987–93, 1996–98, 2003; played for Birmingham Barons minor league baseball team 1993, Nashville Sounds 1994–95; scored 32,292 points during career (third highest in NBA history), holds record for most points in NBA playoff game with 63, for highest points-scoring average (30.12) and many other records; named world's highest paid athlete, Forbes Magazine 1992; retd from Chicago Bulls 1998; Pres. Basketball Operations, Washington Wizards NBA professional basketball team 1999–2003, came out of retirement to play for Washington Wizards 2001–03; extensive business interests include Michael Jordan's: The Restaurant 1993, Jordan Brand Clothing 1997; f. Jordan Motorsports/Suzuki 2004; part owner Bobcats Basketball Holdings, LLC (NBA's Charlotte Bobcats basketball franchise) 2006–10, majority owner 2010–; Seagram's NBA Player of the Year 1987; Most Valuable Player, NBA All-Star Game 1988, NBA Most Valuable Player 1988, 1991, 1992, 1996, 1998. *Publications:* Rare Air: Michael on Michael (autobiography) 1993, I Can't Accept Not Trying: Michael Jordan on the Pursuit of Excellence, Driven From Within (co-author) 2004. *Address:* Bobcats Basketball Holdings, LLC, 333 East Trade Street, Suite 700, Charlotte, NC 28202; Jordan Brand, c/o Nike World Headquarters, One Bowerman Drive, Beaverton OR, 97005-6453, USA (office). *Telephone:* (704) 424-4120 (Charlotte). *Fax:* (704) 388-8734. *Website:* www.nba.com/bobcats; www.jumpman23.com (office).

JORDAN, Neil Patrick, BA; Irish writer and film director; b. 25 Feb. 1950, Sligo; three s. two d.; ed St Paul's Coll. Raheny, Dublin and Univ. Coll., Dublin; co-f. Irish Writers' Co-operative, Dublin 1974; Dr hc (Univ. Coll. Dublin) 2005; London Evening Standard Most Promising Newcomer Award 1982, Irish Film and TV Awards Lifetime Achievement Award 2003. *Films directed:* Angel 1982, Company of Wolves (London Film Critics' Circle Award 1984) 1984, Mona Lisa 1986, High Spirits 1988, We're No Angels 1989, The Miracle (Evening Standard British Film Award) 1990, The Crying Game (Acad. Award for Best Screenplay 1993, Boston Soc. of Film Critics Award 1992, New York Film Critics Circle Award 1992, Writers Guild of America Award 1992, Los Angeles Film Critics Asscn Award, London Film Critics' Circle Award) (dir), Interview with the Vampire 1995, Michael Collins (Golden Lion, Venice Film Festival 1996) 1995, The Butcher Boy (Silver Bear for Best Dir, Berlin Film Festival 1998) 1997, In Dreams 1999, The End of the Affair (BAFTA for Best Screenplay 2000) 1999, Not I 2000, The Good Thief 2002, Breakfast on Pluto (Best Dir, Best Writer, IFTA 2007) 2005, The Brave One 2007, Ondine 2009, Byzantium 2013. *Television includes:* The Borgias (series) (Gemini Award for Best Int. Drama 2011, Canadian Screen Award for Best Int. Drama 2013) 2011, 2012, 2013. *Publications include:* Night in Tunisia and Other Stories (Guardian Fiction Award 1979) 1976, The Past 1979, The Dream of a Beast 1983, Sunrise with Sea Monster 1994, Nightlines 1995, Shade (novel) 2004, Mistaken 2011. *Leisure interest:* music. *Address:* 6 Sorrento Terrace, Dalkey, Co. Dublin, Ireland.

JORDAN, Mgr Thierry; French ecclesiastic; *Archbishop of Rheims;* b. 31 Aug. 1943, Shanghai, China; ed Lycée Hoche, Grand Séminaire de Versailles, Institut catholique de Paris, Gregorian Univ., Rome, Italy; ordained priest, Versailles 1966; chaplain, Church of Saint-Louis-des-Français, Rome, then Sec. to Cardinal Jean Villot, Vatican 1967–79; curate, Vésinet, Versailles 1980–84; Vicar-Episcopal, Saint-Quentin-en-Yvelines 1984–87; Vicar-Gen. Versailles diocese 1986–88; Bishop of Pontoise (Val-d'Oise) 1988–99; Archbishop of Rheims 1999–; Chair. Comm. épiscopale de la vie consacrée of Conf. of French Bishops 1993–96. *Address:* Archevêché de REIMS, secrétariat et Chancellerie, 3, rue du Cardinal de Lorraine, BP.2729, 51058 Rheims, France (office). *Telephone:* 3-26-47-05-33 (office). *Fax:* 3-26-84-94-66 (office). *Website:* catholique-reims.cef.fr (office).

JORDAN, Thomas J.; Swiss economist, academic and central banker; *Chairman of the Governing Board, Schweizerische Nationalbank;* b. 28 Jan. 1963, Biel; m.; two s.; ed Univ. of Bern, Harvard Univ., USA; Econ. Adviser, Dept I, Schweizerische Nationalbank (SNB, Swiss Nat. Bank, central bank) 1997–99,

Asst Dir Econ. Studies Unit 1999–2002, Head of Research Unit 2002, Dir SNB 2004–, Alt. mem. Governing Bd 2004–07, mem. 2007–, Dir Dept III (Financial Markets, Banking Operations and Information Tech.) 2007–10, Dir Dept II (Financial Stability, Cash, Finance and Risk) 2010–12, Vice-Chair. SNB Governing Bd 2010–12, Chair. 2012–; Lecturer, Univ. of Bern 1998–, Hon. Prof. 2003; Lecturer, Univ. of Zürich 2002–07; Chair. SNB StabFund; Chair. G10 Central Bank Counterfeit Deterrence Group, Int. Center for Monetary and Banking Studies, Geneva; mem. Bd of Dirs BIS, Basel; mem. Steering Cttee Financial Stability Bd, Basel. *Publications:* numerous articles on monetary theory and policy in leading int. journals. *Address:* Office of the Chairman of the Governing Board, Schweizerische Nationalbank, Börsenstr. 15, Postfach 2800, 8022 Zürich, Switzerland (office). *Telephone:* 446313111 (office). *Fax:* 446313911 (office). *E-mail:* snb@snb.ch (office). *Website:* www.snb.ch (office).

JORDAN, Vernon Eulion, Jr; American lawyer and investment banker; *Senior Managing Director, Lazard Freres & Company LLC;* b. 15 Aug. 1935, Atlanta, Ga; s. of Vernon Eulion Jordan and Mary Jordan (née Griggs); m. 1st Shirley M. Yarbrough 1958 (died 1985); one c.; m. 2nd Ann Dibble Cook 1986; ed DePauw Univ., Howard Univ.; mem. Bar, Ga 1960, Ark. 1964; law practice, Atlanta 1960–61; Ga Field Dir Nat. Asscn for the Advancement of Colored People (NAACP) 1961–63; law practice, Pine Bluff, Ark. 1964–65; Dir Voter Educ. Project Southern Regional Council 1964–68; Attorney, Office of Econ. Opportunity, Atlanta 1969; Exec. Dir United Negro Coll. Fund 1970–71; Pres. Nat. Urban League 1972–81; Sr Partner, Akin, Gump, Strauss, Hauer & Feld 1981–2000, of Counsel Akin, Gump, Strauss, Hauer & Feld LLP 2000–; Chair. Clinton Pres. Transition Bd; joined Lazard Freres and Co. LLC 2000, Sr Man. Dir 2000–; mem. Bd Dirs American Express Co. (Sr Advisor), Asbury Automotive Group, Inc., Lazard Ltd, Xerox Corpn (Sr Advisor); mem. Int. Advisory Bd Barrick Gold; mem. American Bar Asscn, Nat. Bar Asscn, Council on Foreign Relations, The Bilderberg Meetings and Bars of Ark., DC, Ga, US Supreme Court; Trustee Howard Univ.; fmr Pres. Econ. Club of Washington, DC; fmr Dir Voter Educ. Project of Southern Regional Council; Presidential appointments have included mem. Pres.'s Cttee for the Points of Light Initiative Foundation, Sec. of State's Advisory Cttee on SA, Advisory Council on Social Security, Presidential Clemency Bd, American Revolution Bicentennial Comm., Nat. Advisory Cttee on Selective Service, Council White House Conf. 'To Fulfill These Rights'; mem. Iraq Study Group, US Inst. of Peace 2006; more than 60 hon. degrees, including Princeton Univ., Harvard Univ. *Publications:* Vernon Can Read! A Memoir 2001, Make It Plain 2008. *Leisure interests:* golf, tennis, yoga. *Address:* Lazard Freres & Co. LLC, 30 Rockefeller Plaza, New York, NY 10112-0002 (office). *Telephone:* (212) 632-6190 (office). *Fax:* (212) 332-1640 (office). *E-mail:* jeannie.adashek@lazard.com (office). *Website:* www.lazard.com (office).

JORDAN, (Zweledinga) Pallo, PhD; South African politician; *Minister of Arts and Culture;* b. 22 May 1942, Kroonstad, OFS; s. of Dr Archibald Jordan and Priscilla Ntantala; m. Carolyn Roth 1972; one d.; ed Athlone High School, Cape Town, Univs of Cape Town and Wisconsin and London School of Econs; joined African Nat. Congress (ANC) 1960; worked full time for ANC in London 1975–77; Head, Radio Freedom, Luanda, Angola 1977–79; in Lusaka, Zambia 1980–90; Mem. ANC Nat. Exec. Cttee (NEC) 1985–, Deputy Sec. of Information 1985, Admin. Sec. of NEC Secr. –1988, Head of Dept. of Information and Publicity 1989–; MP 1994–; Minister of Posts, Telecommunications and Broadcasting 1994–96, of Environmental Affairs and Tourism 1996–99, of Arts and Culture 2004–; Head of Foreign Affairs Cttee 2002–04. *Publications:* articles and papers on South African political questions. *Address:* Ministry of Arts and Culture, Department of Arts and Culture, Nassau Building, Room 7060, 188 Schoeman Street, Pretoria 0002, South Africa (office). *Telephone:* (12) 32440968 (office). *Fax:* (12) 3242687 (office). *E-mail:* andile.xaba@dac.gov.za (office). *Website:* www.dac.gov.za (office).

JORDAN OF BOURNVILLE, Baron (Life Peer), cr. 2000, of Bournville in the County of West Midlands; **William Brian Jordan,** CBE; British trade union official; b. 28 Jan. 1936, Birmingham; s. of Walter Jordan and Alice Jordan; m. Jean Livesey 1958; three d.; ed Secondary Modern School, Birmingham; machine-tool fitter 1961; joined eng union and served as shop steward; convenor of shop stewards, Guest Keen & Nettlefolds 1966, later Dist Pres.; Div. Organizer for West Midlands AUEW 1977; Pres. Amalgamated Eng and Electrical (fmrly Amalgamated and Eng) Union 1986–95; mem. TUC Gen. Council 1986–95 (Chair. Cttee on European Strategy 1988–95); mem. NEDC (Chair. Eng Industry Cttee) 1986–92, Energy Industry Training Bd 1986–91, Council, Industrial Soc. 1987–, Advisory, Conciliation & Arbitration Service (ACAS) 1987–95, Nat. Training Task Force 1989–92, Eng Training Authority 1991–, Foundation for Manufacturing and Industry; Gen. Sec. ICFTU 1994–2002; fmr Pres. European Metalworkers' Fed.; fmr Exec. mem. Int. Metalworkers' Fed.; fmr mem. European Trade Union Confed., Bd Govs BBC, Nat. Advisory Council for Educ. and Training Targets, UK Skills Council; mem. Victim Support Advisory Cttee, Bd English Partnership, Winston Churchill Trust; a Gov. of LSE, Ashridge Man. Coll.; mem. Royal Soc. of Arts; Dr hc (Univ. of Cen. England) 1993, (Univ. of Cranfield) 1995. *Leisure interests:* reading, sports (especially football, Birmingham City Football Club supporter). *Address:* c/o ICFTU, Boulevard Emile Jacqmain 155, 1210 Brussels, Belgium.

JORDANOV, Minco; Macedonian business executive and politician; *Chairman, Makstil AD;* b. 1 July 1944, Stip; ed Univ. of Belgrade; Gen. Man. Rudnici i Zelezarnica Co., Skopje 1983–89; Man. Techometal-Vardar Rep. Office, Moscow 1989–92; Man. Duferko SA 1992–94; mem. Bd of Dirs 1994–2004, also responsible for countries of fmr USSR 1994–97; Chair. Makstil AD 1997–; Deputy Prime Minister in Charge of Econ. Reforms 2004–06; Pres. Man. Bd Nat. Entrepreneurship and Competitiveness Council 2006; Owner, RK Metalurg Skopje (handball team); mem. Social Democratic Alliance of Macedonia. *Address:* Office of the Chairman, Makstil AD, 16 Makedonska brigada, 18, 1000 Skopje, Macedonia (office). *Telephone:* (2) 3287023 (office). *Fax:* (2) 3287076 (office). *E-mail:* info@makstil.com.mk (office). *Website:* www.makstil.com (office).

JØRGENSEN, Anker; Danish politician and trade union official; b. 13 July 1922, Copenhagen; s. of Johannes Jørgensen; m. Ingrid Jørgensen 1948; four c.; ed School for Orphans and evening classes; messenger, shipyard worker, warehouse worker 1936–50; Vice-Pres. Warehouse Workers' Union 1950, Pres. 1958–62; Group Sec. Transport and Gen. Workers' Union 1962–68, Pres. 1968–72; mem.

Folketing (Parl.) 1964–94; mem. Bd of Dirs, Workers' Bank of Denmark 1969–; Prime Minister 1972–73; Parl. Leader, Social Democratic Group 1973–75; Prime Minister 1975–82; Chair. Social Democratic Party, Social Democratic Parl. Group 1972–87; mem. European Cttee Against Racism 1994. *Publication:* Memoirs (Vol. I) 1994. *Address:* Borgbjergsvej 1, 2450 S.V. Copenhagen, Denmark.

JØRGENSEN, Bo Barker, PhD, DSc; Danish biologist and academic; *Professor of Biology, University of Aarhus;* b. 22 Sept. 1946, Copenhagen; s. of Carl C. B. Jørgensen and Vibeke Balsley Smidt; m. Inga M. Vestergaard 1971; two s. one d.; ed Univs of Copenhagen and Arhus; Lecturer, Dept of Ecology and Genetics, Univ. of Arhus 1973–77, Sr Lecturer 1977–87, Prof. 1987–92, Adjunct Prof. 1993–2011, Prof. of Biology 2011–; Dir Max Planck Inst. for Marine Microbiology, Bremen, Germany 1992–2011; Prof., Univ. of Bremen 1993–2011; researcher, Marine Biology Lab., Eilat, Israel 1974, 1978, NASA-ARC, Moffett Field, Calif., USA 1984–85. *Publications:* more than 250 scientific publs in int. journals in the fields of ecology, microbiology and geochemistry. *Address:* Tranebaerkaeret 3, 8220 Brabrand, Denmark (home). *Telephone:* 86-26-31-23 (home). *E-mail:* bo.barker@biology.au.dk (office). *Website:* pure.au.dk/portal/en/bo.barker@biology.au.dk (office).

JØRGENSEN, Sven-Aage, MA; Danish professor of German philology (retd); b. 22 July 1929, Herstedvester; s. of Aage Julius Jørgensen and Emma Lydia Jørgensen (née Eriksen); m. Elli Andresen 1957 (divorced 1985); two s. one d.; ed Birkerød Statsskole, Univ. of Copenhagen, Univ. of Würzburg and Warburg Inst., London; Lecturer, Univ. of Copenhagen 1961, Prof. of German Philology 1968; Research Prof., Univ. of Bielefeld 1980–81; Visiting Prof., Heidelberg 1973, Regensburg 1985, Kiel 1986, Cologne 1990; Visiting Fellow, ANU 1975; mem. Royal Danish Acad. of Sciences and Letters 1986, Akad. der Wissenschaften in Göttingen 1998; Kt, Order of Dannebrog; Alexander von Humboldt Prize 1995, Univ. Gold Medal 1957. *Publications:* J. G. Hamann's Fünf Hirtenbriefe 1962, J. G. Hamann's Sokratische Denkwurdigkeiten und Aesthetica in Nuce 1962, Th. Fontane's Unwiederbringlich 1971, J. G. Hamann 1976, Deutsch-dänische Literaturbeziehungen im 18. Jhdrt. (co-ed.) 1977, Dänische 'guldalderliteratur' und deutsche Klassik (co-ed.) 1982, Tysk et sprog Fire Stater–Fire Kulturer 1989, Wieland's Oberon 1990, Geschichte der deutschen Literatur 1740–1789 (co-author) 1990, Zentrum der Aufklärung: Kopenhagen–Kiel Altona (co-ed.) 1992, Verfilmte Litteratur (co-ed.) 1993, Fortschritt ohne Ende–Ende des Fortschritts? (ed.) 1994, Wieland Epoche-Werk-Wirkung (co-author) 1994, C. M. Wieland's Die Abenteuer des Don Sylvio von Rosalva 2001, Hjertets regnebræt, skyld og skærsild i europæisk litteratur fra Dante til Graham Greene 2012, Querdenker der Aufklärung Studien zu Johann Georg Hamann 2013; numerous articles. *Leisure interests:* jogging, swimming. *Address:* Valby Gade 16, 3200 Helsinge, Denmark. *Telephone:* 33-15-76-04. *E-mail:* sven.aage@get2net.dk.

JORGENSON, Dale W., PhD; American economist and academic; *Samuel W. Morris University Professor, Harvard University;* b. 7 May 1933, Bozeman, Mont.; s. of Emmett B. Jorgenson and Jewell T. Jorgenson; m. Linda Ann Mabus 1971; one s. one d.; ed Reed Coll., Portland, Ore. and Harvard Univ.; Asst Prof. of Econs, Univ. of Calif., Berkeley 1959–61, Assoc. Prof. 1961–63, Prof. 1963–69; Ford Foundation Research Prof. of Econs, Univ. of Chicago 1962–63; Prof. of Econs, Harvard Univ. 1969–80, Frederic Eaton Abbe Prof. of Econs 1980–2002, Samuel W. Morris Univ. Prof. 2002–, Frank William Taussig Research Prof. of Econs 1992–94, Chair. Dept of Econs 1994–97; Dir Program on Tech. and Econ. Policy, Kennedy School of Govt, Harvard Univ. 1984–; mem. Science Advisory Cttee, Gen. Motors Corpn 1996–2002; Visiting Prof. of Econs, Hebrew Univ., Jerusalem 1967, Stanford Univ. 1973; Visiting Prof. of Statistics, Univ. of Oxford, UK 1968; Chair. Section 54, Econ. Sciences, Nat. Acad. of Sciences 2000–03; Founding mem. Bd on Science, Tech. and Econ. Policy, Nat. Research Council 1991–98, Chair. 1998–; Consulting Ed., North-Holland Publishing Co., Amsterdam, Netherlands 1970–2002; Fellow, American Statistical Asscn 1965, AAAS 1982, Econometric Soc. 1984 (Pres. 1987); mem. American Acad. of Arts and Sciences 1969, NAS 1978, American Econ. Asscn (Pres. 2000, Distinguished Fellow 2001), Royal Econ. Soc., Econ. Study Soc., Conf. on Research in Income and Wealth, Int. Asscn for Research in Income and Wealth, American Philosophical Soc. 1998; Foreign mem. Royal Swedish Acad. of Sciences 1989; several fellowships including NSF Sr Postdoctoral Fellowship, Netherlands School of Econs, Rotterdam 1967–68; lectures include Shinzo Koizumi, Keio Univ., Tokyo, Japan 1972, Fisher-Schultz, 3rd World Congress, Econometric Soc. 1975, Frank Paish, Asscn of Univ. Teachers of Econs Conf., UK 1980, Erik Lindahl Lectures, Uppsala Univ. 1987, Inst. Lecture, Inst. of Industrial Econs, Univ. of Toulouse 2001, Astra Zeneca/Ericsson Lecture, Research Inst. of Industrial Econs, Stockholm 2002; Dr hc (Uppsala, Oslo) 1991, (Keio) 2003, (Mannheim) 2004, (Rome) 2006, (Stockholm School of Econs) 2007, (Chinese Univ. of HK) 2007, (Kansai) 2009; John Bates Clark Medal, American Econ. Asscn 1971, Outstanding Contrib. Award, Int. Asscn of Energy Economists 1994. *Publications:* Optimal Replacement Policy (co-author) 1967, Measuring Performance in the Private Economy of the Federal Republic of Germany 1950–1973 (co-author) 1975, Econometric Studies of U.S. Energy Policy (ed.) 1976, Technology and Economic Policy (co-ed. with R. Landau) 1986, Productivity and U.S. Economic Growth (co-author) 1987, Technology and Capital Formation (co-ed. with R. Landau) 1989, General Equilibrium Modeling and Economic Policy Analysis (co-ed.) 1990, Technology and Agricultural Policy (co-ed.) 1990, Tax Reform and the Cost of Capital (with Kun-Young Yun) 1991, Tax Reform and the Cost of Capital: An International Comparison (co-ed. with R. Landau) 1993, Postwar U.S. Economic Growth (Productivity, Vol. 1) 1995, International Comparisons of Economic Growth (Productivity, Vol. 2) 1995, Capital Theory and Investment Behavior (Investment, Vol. 1) 1996, Tax Policy and the Cost of Capital (Investment, Vol. 2) 1996, Improving the Performance of America's Schools: The Role of Inventives (co-author) 1996, Aggregate Consumer Behavior (Welfare, Vol. 1) 1997, Measuring Social Welfare (Welfare, Vol. 2) 1997, Econometric General Equilibrium Modeling (Growth, Vol. 1) 1998, Energy, the Environmental and Economic Growth (Growth, Vol. 2) 1998, Economic Modeling of Producer Behavior (Econometrics, Vol. 1) 2000, Lifting the Burden: Tax Reform, the Cost of Capital and U.S. Economic Growth (Investment, Vol. 3) (with Kun-Young Yun) 2001, Industry-Level Productivity and International Competitiveness Between Canada and the United States (co-ed. with Franck C. Lee) 2001, Economic Growth in the Information Age (Econometrics, Vol. 3) 2002, Measuring and Sustaining the New Economy (co-ed. with C. Wessner) 2002; over 232 papers and contribs to learned journals and collections of essays. *Address:* Department of Economics, 122 Littauer Center, Harvard University, Cambridge, MA 02138-3001 (office); 1010 Memorial Drive, Cambridge, MA 02138, USA (home). *Telephone:* (617) 495-4661 (office); (617) 491-4069 (home). *Fax:* (617) 495-4660 (office); (617) 491-4105 (home). *E-mail:* djorgenson@harvard.edu (office). *Website:* post.economics.harvard.edu/faculty/jorgenson (office).

JORTNER, Joshua, PhD; Israeli chemist and academic; *Professor Emeritus of Chemistry, Tel-Aviv University;* b. 14 March 1933, Tarnow, Poland; s. of Arthur Jortner and Regina Jortner; m. Ruth Sanger 1960; one s. one d.; ed Hebrew Univ. of Jerusalem; Instructor, Dept of Physical Chem., Hebrew Univ. of Jerusalem 1961–62, Sr Lecturer 1963–65; Research Assoc., Univ. of Chicago, USA 1962–64, Prof. 1965–72; Assoc. Prof. of Physical Chem., Tel-Aviv Univ. 1965–66, Prof. 1966–2003, Head of Inst. of Chem. 1966–72, Deputy Rector 1966–69, Vice-Pres. 1970–72, Heinemann Prof. of Chem. 1973–2003, Prof. Emer. 2003–; Visiting Prof. of Chem., H.C. Orsted Inst., Univ. of Copenhagen 1974, 1978; Visiting Prof., Univ. of Calif., Berkeley 1975; Christen Visiting Fellow, St Catherine's Coll., Oxford, UK 1995; Int. Research Chair 'Blaise Pascal', Fondation de l'École Normale Supérieure, France 1998–2000; Vice-Pres. Israeli Acad. of Sciences and Humanities 1980–86, Pres. 1986–95, mem. Council 1996–; Founding Pres. Israel Science Foundation 1996; Vice-Pres. IUPAC 1996–97, Pres. 1998–99, Past Pres. 2000–01; Int. Acad. of Quantum Science Award 1972, Weizmann Prize 1973, Rothschild Prize 1976, Kolthof Prize 1976, Israel Prize in Chem. 1982, Wolf Prize in Chemistry (jtly) 1988, Hon. J. Heyrovsky Gold Medal 1993, August Wilhelm von Hofmann Medal 1995, Joseph O. Hirschfelder Prize in Theoretical Chem. 1999, Maria Sklodowska-Curie Medal 2003, Medal of Israeli Chemical Soc. 2004, EMET Prize 2008. *Publications:* author or ed. of 29 books, including Intramolecular Radiationless Transitions (with M. Bixon) 1968, Energy Gap Law for Radiationless Transitions (with E. Englman) 1970, Electronic Excitations in Condensed Rare Gases (with N. Schwentner and E. E. Koch) 1985, Cluster Size Effects 1992, The Jerusalem Symposia on Quantum Chemistry and Biochemistry (co-ed. with Bernard Pullman) Vols 15–27 1982–93; author or co-author of more than 730 scientific articles in professional journals. *Leisure interest:* science policy. *Address:* School of Chemistry, Tel-Aviv University, Ramat Aviv, 69978 Tel-Aviv, Israel (office). *Telephone:* (3) 6408322 (office); (3) 6406474 (office). *Fax:* (3) 6415054 (office). *E-mail:* jortner@post.tau.ac.il (office). *Website:* www.tau.ac.il/chemistry/jortner (office).

JORY, Edward John, PhD, FAHA; British/Australian classicist and academic; *Senior Honorary Research Fellow, Department of Classics and Ancient History, University of Western Australia;* b. 20 June 1936, England; s. of E. B. A. Jory; m. Marie McGee 1965; three s.; ed Humphry Davy Grammar School, Penzance and Univ. Coll., London; Lecturer, Dept of Classics and Ancient History, Univ. of Western Australia 1959–65, Sr Lecturer 1966–73, Assoc. Prof. 1974–78, Dean of Faculty of Arts 1976–79, Prof. and Head of Dept 1979–84, 1988–89, Head of Div. of Arts and Architecture 1990–93, Exec. Dean Faculty of Arts 1994–2000, currently Sr Hon. Research Fellow; Visiting Prof., Inst. of Classical Studies, Univ. of London 1990; Alexander von Humboldt Fellow 1974, 1980, Kommission für Alte Geschichte und Epigraphik, Munich 1974, T.B.L. Webster Fellow, Inst. of Classical Studies 2000. *Publications:* contrib. to Corpus Inscriptionum Latinarum 1974, 1989; numerous articles on the Roman theatre. *Leisure interests:* cricket, skin diving, golf. *Address:* Department of Classics and Ancient History, University of Western Australia, Crawley, WA 6009 (office); 36 Marita Road, Nedlands, WA 6009, Australia (home). *Telephone:* (8) 6488-2165 (office); (8) 9386-2714 (home). *Fax:* (8) 9380-1009 (office). *E-mail:* john.jory@uwa.edu.au (office). *Website:* www.classics.uwa.edu.au (office).

JOSEFSSON, Lars-Göran, BEng; Swedish energy industry executive; b. 29 Oct. 1950; m.; four c.; ed secondary school in Ulricehamn, Chalmers Inst. of Tech.; began career as systems engineer at Defence Electronics Div. L.M. Ericsson 1974, several exec. posts until Pres. Chemtronics 1984, Ericsson Radio Systems Head, Radar Div. 1985, Vice-Pres. and head of Surface Sensor Div. 1987, Schrack Telecom AG (later named Ericsson Schrack AG 1994 and Ericsson Austria 1996), Vienna, 1993–97; Pres. and CEO Celsius Corpn 1997–2000; Pres. and CEO Vattenfall AB 2000–10 (retd), Deputy Dir 2008–09, also Chair. Vattenfall Europe AG, Vattenfall Europe Mining AG; mem. Supervisory Bd Bohler-Uddeholm AG, Eskom Holdings Ltd; mem. Royal Swedish Mil. Acad., Royal Swedish Soc. of Naval Sciences. *Leisure interests:* tennis, skiing, hunting.

JOSEPH, Cedric Luckie, MA; Guyanese diplomatist (retd) and historian; b. 14 May 1933, Georgetown; s. of the late Frederick McConnell Joseph and Cassie Edith Joseph (née Austin); m. Dona Avril Barrett 1973; two s.; ed London School of Econs and Univ. Coll. of Wales, Aberystwyth, UK; taught history at a London comprehensive school 1962–66; Lecturer in History, Univ. of the W Indies, Kingston, Jamaica 1966–71; Prin. Asst Sec., Ministry of Foreign Affairs, Guyana 1971–74; Deputy High Commr to Jamaica 1974–76; Counsellor, Embassy in Washington, DC 1976; Deputy Perm. Rep., Perm. Mission of Guyana to the UN, New York 1976–77; High Commr to Zambia (also accred to Angola, Botswana, Mozambique, Tanzania and Zimbabwe) 1977–82, to UK (also accred as Amb. to France, the Netherlands, Yugoslavia and UNESCO) 1982–86; Chair. Commonwealth Cttee on Southern Africa 1983–86; Head of the Presidential Secr. 1986–91; Sec. to Cabinet 1987–91; Sr Amb., Ministry of Foreign Affairs 1991–94; foreign policy analyst/consultant with reference to Guyana's frontiers 1995–; Cacique's Crown of Honour 1983. *Publications include:* Reconstruction of the Caribbean Community 1994, Dependency and Mendicancy 1995, Transition and Guyana 1995, Caribbean Community – Security and Survival 1997, Intervention, Border and Maritime Issues in CARICOM (tech. ed.) 2007, Anglo-American Diplomacy and the Reopening of the Guyana/Venezuela Boundary Controversy 1961–1966 1998 (revised edn 2008), The British West Indies Regiment 1914–1918 2008, Africa and its History, Guyana Review July 2011; several articles in professional journals. *Leisure interests:* the fine arts, reading. *Address:* 332 Republic Park, Peter's Hall, East Bank Demerara, Guyana. *E-mail:* clmdj@networksgy.com.

JOSEPH, Martin, MSc; Trinidad and Tobago politician; b. 1 Oct. 1949, Trinidad; ed Univ. of Maryland, USA; mem. Senate of Trinidad and Tobago; fmr Minister of Public Utilities and the Environment; Minister of Housing –2003, of Nat. Security and Rehabilitation 2003–10. *Address:* c/o Ministry of National Security, Temple Court, 31–33 Abercromby Street, Port of Spain, Trinidad and Tobago (office).

JOSEPH, Robert G., MA, PhD; American academic and diplomatist; *Senior Scholar, National Institute for Public Policy;* b. 1949, Williston, North Dakota; ed US Naval Acad., St. Louis Univ., Univ. of Chicago, Columbia Univ.; joined Foreign Service, held several positions including Commr to Standing Consultative Comm., Amb. to US-Russian Consultative Comm. on Nuclear Testing, Prin. Deputy Asst, Sec. of Defense for Int. Security Policy, Deputy Asst, Sec. for Nuclear Forces and Arms Control Policy; Prof. of Nat. Security Studies and Founder/Dir, Center for Counterproliferation Research, Nat. Defense Univ. 1992–2001; Special Asst to Pres. and Sr Dir for Proliferation Strategy, Counterproliferation and Homeland Defense, Nat. Security Council 2001–05; Under-Sec. for Arms Control and Int. Security 2005–07 (resgnd); Dir of Studies, Nat. Inst. for Public Policy 2004–05, Sr Scholar 2004–; mem. Defense Policy Bd Advisory Cttee 2007; mem. Nat. Security Advisory Council, Center for Security Policy; fmr Research Consultant, Inst. for Foreign Policy Analysis; Ronald Reagan Award for his contribs to US missle defense 2006. *Address:* National Institute for Public Policy, 9302 Lee Highway, Suite 750, Fairfax, VA 22031, USA (office). *E-mail:* Amy.joseph@nipp.org (office). *Website:* www.nipp.org (office).

JOSEPHSON, Brian David, PhD, FRS, FInstP; British physicist and academic; *Professor Emeritus of Physics, University of Cambridge;* b. 4 Jan. 1940, Cardiff, Wales; s. of Abraham Josephson and Mimi Josephson; m. Carol Anne Olivier 1976; one d.; ed Cardiff High School, Univ. of Cambridge; Fellow, Trinity Coll., Cambridge 1962–; Research Asst, Prof., Univ. of Illinois 1965–66; Asst Dir of Research, Univ. of Cambridge 1967–72, Reader in Physics 1972–74, Prof. of Physics 1974–2007, Prof. Emer. 2007–; Hon. mem. IEEE; Foreign Hon. mem. American Acad. of Arts and Sciences; Hon. DSc (Univ. of Wales, Univ. of Exeter); New Scientist Award 1969, Research Corpn Award 1969, Fritz London Award 1970, Hughes Medal Royal Soc. 1972, Guthrie Medal 1972, van der Pol 1972, Elliott Cresson Medal 1972, Holweck Medal 1972, Nobel Prize in Physics (jtly) 1973, Faraday Medal 1982, Sir George Thomson Medal 1984, Computing Anticipatory Systems Award 2000. *Music:* Sweet and Sour Harmony 2007. *Publications include:* Consciousness and the Physical World (co-ed.) 1980, The Paranormal and the Platonic Worlds (in Japanese) 1997; research papers on superconductivity, critical phenomena, theory of intelligence, science and mysticism. *Leisure interests:* walking, ice skating, photography, astronomy. *Address:* Cavendish Laboratory, J.J. Thomson Avenue, Cambridge, CB3 0HE, England (office). *Telephone:* (1223) 337254 (office). *Fax:* (1223) 337356 (office). *E-mail:* bdj10@cam.ac.uk (office). *Website:* www.tcm.phy.cam.ac.uk/~bdj10 (office).

JOSHI, Aravind Krishna, BE, DIISc, MS, PhD, FIEEE; American (b. Indian) computer scientist and academic; *Henry Salvatori Professor of Computer and Cognitive Sciences, University of Pennsylvania;* b. 5 Aug. 1929, Poona, India; m. Susan Joshi; two d.; ed Pune Univ., Poona, Indian Inst. of Science, Bangalore, Univ. of Pennsylvania; Research Asst, Indian Inst. of Science, Bangalore 1952; Research Asst, Tata Inst. of Fundamental Research, Bombay 1953; engineer, Radio Corpn of America, Camden, NJ 1954–58; Research Asst, Dept of Linguistics, Univ. of Pennsylvania, Philadelphia 1958–61; Asst Prof. of Electrical Eng 1961–67, Asst Prof. of Linguistics 1964–67, Assoc. Prof. of Electrical Eng and mem. Grad. Group in Linguistics 1967–72, Prof. of Computer and Information Science and mem. Grad. Group in Linguistics 1972–83, Chair. Dept of Computer and Information Science 1972–85, Henry Salvatori Prof. of Computer and Cognitive Sciences with Secondary appointment in Dept of Linguistics, Secondary appointment in Dept of Psychology and Dir Artificial Intelligence Center 1983–, Co-Dir Cognitive Science Program 1979–2002, Co-Dir Inst. for Research in Cognitive Science 1990–2002, Co-Dir NSF Science and Tech. Center for Research in Cognitive Science 1991–2002; Distinguished Visitor, IEEE Computer Group 1970; mem. Inst. for Advanced Study, Princeton, NJ 1971–72; mem. NSF Advisory Panel for Computer Science and Eng 1976–79, NSF Advisory Panel for Dept of Information, Robotics, and Intelligent Systems 1988–; mem. Int. Jt Cttee on Computational Linguistics 1994, Perm. mem. 1995–; Visiting Prof., Univ. of Paris VII, France May–June 1994; mem. Nat. Acad. of Eng 1999–, Asscn for Computing Machinery (mem. Special Interest Group on Theory of Computation, Fellow 1998–), American Math. Soc., Linguistic Soc. of America, Asscn for Computational Linguistics (ACL), mem. Exec. Cttee, Pres. ACL 1975), Cognitive Science Soc.; Founding Fellow, American Asscn for Artificial Intelligence 1990–; Hon. Chair. ACL 2000, Hong Kong 2000; Dr hc (Univ. of Paris VII) 2002, (Charles Univ. Prague) 2013; Guggenheim Fellow 1971–72, Best Paper Award, Nat. Conf. on Artificial Intelligence 1987, Research Excellence Award, Int. Jt Conf. of Artificial Intelligence 1997, ACL Lifetime Achievement Award 2002, David Rumelhart Prize, Cognitive Science Soc. 2003, Benjamin Franklin Medal for Cognitive Science, The Franklin Inst. 2005. *Publications:* Elements of Discourse Understanding (co-ed.) 1981, Special Issue of journal Computational Intelligence (ed.) 1994, Centering on Discourse (co-ed.) 1998, Supertagging (co-ed.) 2007; numerous scientific papers in professional journals. *Address:* University of Pennsylvania, IRCS, Suite 476A, 3401 Walnut Street, Philadelphia, PA 19104-6228 (office); Department of Computer and Information Science, 506 Levine Bldg, 200 S 33rd Street, Philadelphia, PA 19104-6389 (office); 919 South 48th Street, Philadelphia, PA 19143, USA (home). *Telephone:* (215) 898-0359 (IRCS) (office); (215) 898-8540 (Computer and Information Science) (office); (215) 727-0513 (home). *Fax:* (215) 573-9247 (IRCS) (office); (215) 898-0587 (Computer and Information Science) (office). *E-mail:* joshi@cis.upenn.edu (office). *Website:* www.cis.upenn.edu/~joshi (office).

JOSHI, Banwari Lal; Indian diplomatist, politician and fmr police officer; *Governor of Uttar Pradesh;* b. 27 March 1936, Choti Khatu, Rajasthan; ed Scottish Church Coll., Kolkata, Univ. Law Coll., Kolkata; began career with police service 1957, worked with Intelligence Bureau on subjects including Interpol, counterfeiting, narcotics, industrial security, UN correctional work and juvenile delinquency; worked in Prime Minister's office with Lal Bahadur Shastri and then with Indira Gandhi for over four years, and with Ministry of External Affairs as First Sec. in High Comms of India in Islamabad and London and as Head of Chancery, Embassy in Washington, DC; took voluntary retirement from IPS in 1991 and became involved in social work; also worked as adviser in a large industrial group; moved to USA in 1993, becoming dir with two cos and also Exec. Dir Foundation for Excellence, Inc., Calif.; returned to India in 2000; apptd mem. Rajasthan State Human Rights Comm., with rank of High Court Judge, for four years; Lt Gov. of Delhi 2004–07; Gov. of Meghalaya April–Aug. 2007, of Uttarakhand 2007–09, of

Uttar Pradesh 2009–. *Address:* Office of the Governor, Raj Bhavan, Lucknow 227 132, Uttar Pradesh, India (office). *Telephone:* (522) 2236992 (office). *Fax:* (522) 2625995 (office). *Website:* hgovup@up.nic.in (office).

JOSHI, C.P., BA, MA, PhD; Indian politician; b. 29 July 1950, Nathdwara, Rajastan; ed M.B. Coll., Udaipur, Mohanlal Sukhadia Univ., Udaipur; fmr Lecturer, M.B. Coll.; fmr Prof. of Psychology, Mohanlal Sukhadia Univ., Udaipur; elected MLA from Nathdwara Ass. 1980, 1985, 1998, 2003; currently MP for Bhilwara constituency; Union Minister for Rural Devt 2009–11, Minister for Road Transport and Highways 2011–13, Minister of Railways Sept.–Oct. 2012, May–June 2013, Gen. Sec. and responsible for Assam, Bihar, West Bengal and Andaman Nicobar Islands, Indian Nat. Congress 2013–; Pres. Rajasthan Pradesh Congress Cttee 2003. *Address:* Indian National Congress, 24 Akbar Road, New Delhi 110 011, India (office). *Telephone:* (11) 23019080. *Fax:* (11) 23017047. *E-mail:* aicc@congress.org.in. *Website:* www.aicc.org.in.

JOSHI, Adm. Devendra Kumar; Indian naval officer; b. 4 July 1954; s. of Hira Ballabh Joshi and Hansa Joshi; m. Chitra Joshi; two d.; ed Nat. Defence Coll., Coll. of Naval Warfare, Mumbai, Naval War Coll., USA; commissioned into Exec. Br., Indian Navy 1974; Defence Adviser, High Comm. in Singapore 1996–99; has served as Deputy Chief of Naval Staff, C-in-C Andaman and Nicobar Island Command, Flag Officer Commdg Eastern Fleet of Indian Navy, Chief of Integrated Defence Staff to Chair. of Chiefs of Staff Cttee; Flag Officer C-in-C, Western Naval Command 2011–12, Chief of Naval Staff 2012–14; Hon. ADC to Pres. 2010; Param Vishist Seva Medal, Ati Vishist Seva Medal, Yudh Seva Medal, Nau Sena Medal, Vishist Seva Medal. *Address:* c/o Integrated Headquarters of Ministry of Defence (Navy), South Block, New Delhi 110 011, India.

JOSIPOVIĆ, Ivo, MA, PhD; Croatian composer, lawyer, academic, politician and head of state; *President;* b. 28 Aug. 1957, Zagreb; m. Tatjana Klepac; one d.; ed Univ. of Zagreb, Music Acad., Zagreb; co-f. Hrvatski pravni centar (Croatian Law Centre) 1994–; musical debut with two children's songs 1978; compositions performed in nearly all European countries, USA, Canada and Japan (European Broadcasting Union concert transmitted over 30 stations world-wide); recordings for radio and TV stations; performances at European festivals; Dir of Music, Zagreb Biennale 1981–; Docent, Music Acad., Univ. of Zagreb 1992–; Prof. for Criminal Procedure Law, Univ. of Zagreb; has represented Croatia at Int. Court of Justice (ICJ) and Int. Criminal Tribunal for fmr Yugoslavia (ICTY); mem. League of Communists of Croatia 1980 (later renamed Social Democratic Party of Croatia, SDP); mem. Sabor (Parl.) 2003–10; SDP presidential cand. 2009; Pres. of Croatia 2010– (inaugurated 18 Feb.). *Compositions include:* Variations for piano, Play of the Golden Pearls for piano, Enypion for harp solo, Quartetto rusticano for string quartet, Per fiati for wind quintet, Passacaglia for string orchestra, Samba da camera for 13 strings, Diptych for large orchestra, Epicurus' Garden for symphony orchestra, Man and Death for soloists, choir and orchestra, Pro musica for accordion orchestra, The Most Beautiful Flower for voice and instrumental ensemble, Drmeš for Penderecki for folk orchestra, Thousands of Lotuses for choir and instrumental ensemble, Jubilus for piano solo, Elegaic Song for violin and piano, Dreams for voice and string orchestra. *Address:* Office of the President, 10000 Pantovčak 241, Zagreb, Croatia (office). *Telephone:* (1) 4565191 (office). *Fax:* (1) 4565299 (office). *E-mail:* ured@predsjednik.hr (office). *Website:* www.predsjednik.hr (office).

JOSPIN, Lionel Robert; French politician; b. 12 July 1937, Meudon, Hauts-de-Seine; s. of Robert Jospin and Mireille Dandieu; m. 2nd Sylviane Agacinski 1994; one s. one d. (from previous m.), one step-s.; ed Institut d'études politiques de Paris, École nat. d'admin; Sec. Ministry of Foreign Affairs 1965–70; Prof., Econ. Inst. universitaire de tech. de Paris-Sceaux, also attached to Univ. de Paris XI 1970–81; Nat. Sec. Socialist Party, mem. Steering Cttee 1973–75, spokesman on Third World Affairs 1975–79, Int. Relations 1979–81, First Sec. 1981–88, Head 1995–97; Councillor for Paris (18E arrondissement) 1977–86; Socialist Deputy to Nat. Ass. for Paris (27E circ.) 1981–86, for Haute-Garonne 1986–88; mem. Gen. Council Haute-Garonne 1988–; Conseiller régional, Midi-Pyrénées 1992–98; Minister of State, Nat. Educ., Research and Sport May–June 1988; Minister of State, Nat. Educ., of Youth and Sport 1988–91, Minister of Nat. Educ. 1991–92; presidential cand. 1995, 2002; Prime Minister of France 1997–2002; Grand Officier, Légion d'honneur 2008; Trombinoscope Politician of the Year 1997. *Publications:* L'Invention du Possible 1991, 1995–2000: Propositions pour la France 1995, Le Temps de répondre 2002, Le Monde comme je le vois 2005, L'impasse 2007, Lionel raconte Jospin 2010, Le mal napoléonier 2014. *Leisure interests:* tennis. *Address:* c/o Parti Socialiste, 10 rue de Solférino, 75333 Paris, Cédex 07, France.

JOSS, Robert L., PhD; American business executive, academic and university administrator; ed Univ. of Washington, Stanford Univ.; Deputy to Asst Sec. for Econ. Policy, US Treasury Dept, Washington, DC 1968–71; joined Wells Fargo Bank 1971, Vice-Chair. 1987–93, Dir Wells Fargo and Co. 1999; CEO and Man. Dir Westpac Banking Corpn, Sydney, Australia 1993–99; Philip H. Knight Prof. and Dean, Grad. School of Business, Stanford Univ. 1999–2009, now Prof. and Dean Emer.; mem. Bd of Dirs Citigroup 2009–, Bechtel Group 2009–, Makena Capital Management 2006–, SRI International 2013–, CM Capital; Sloan Fellow, Stanford Business School 1965–66; White House Fellow 1968–69; Dr hc (William F. Miller School of Management, Konkuk Univ., Korea) 2009; Meritorious Service Award, US Treasury Dept 1971, Centenary Medal, Commonwealth of Australia 2001. *Address:* Graduate School of Business, Stanford University, 450 Serra Mall, Stanford, CA 94305, USA (office). *Telephone:* (650) 723-3951 (office). *E-mail:* rjoss@gsb.stanford.edu (office). *Website:* www.gsb.stanford.edu/academicareas/finance.html (office).

JOSSELIN, Charles, LenD; French economist and politician; b. 31 March 1938, Pleslin-Trigavou; s. of Charles Josselin and Marie Hamoniaux; m. 2nd Evelyne Besnard 1987; four c.; fmr attaché, financial secr., Banque de l'Union Parisienne, economist, Soc. centrale pour l'équipement du territoire; Parti Socialiste (PS) Nat. Ass. Deputy for 2nd Côtes d'Armor Constituency (Dinan) 1973–78, 1981–97 1; Minister of State for Transport 1985–86, for the Sea 1992–93; Sec. of State attached to Minister of Foreign Affairs, with responsibility for Co-operation 1997, for Co-operation and Francophonie 1997–98, Deputy Minister for Co-operation and Francophonie 1998–2002, Minister of State 1998–2002; Mayor of Pleslin-Trigavou 1977–97; mem. European Parl. 1979–81; Chair. Nat. Council for

Regional Economies and Productivity 1982–86, Nat. Ass.'s EC Select Cttee 1981–85, 1988–92, Vice-Chair. EU Select Cttee 1993–; Chair. Parl. Study Group on int. aid orgs; mem. Côtes d'Armor Gen. Council for Ploubalay canton 1973–, Chair. 1976–97, Vice-Chair. 1997–; mem. Nat. Council for Town and Country Planning, Local Finance Cttee, EU Cttee of the Regions; Vice-Pres. High Comm. Int. Co-operation 2003–08; Chair. Cités Unies France (twin city org.) 2004–; Senator representing Côtes d'Armor 2006–. *Address:* Conseil général des Côtes-d'Armor, 9 rue du Parc, 22000 Saint-Brieuc, France. *E-mail:* josselincharles@cg22.fr (home).

JOUAHRI, Abdellatif; Moroccan economist, central banker and fmr politician; *Governor, Bank Al-Maghrib;* b. 10 June 1939, Fès; various managerial positions with Bank Al-Maghrib (central bank) 1962–78, Gov. 2003–; Minister Del. to Prime Minister in charge of Public Sector Reform 1978; Minister of Finance 1981–86; CEO Banque Marocaine du Commerce Extérieur SA (BMCE) 1986–95; Chair. Groupement Professionnel des Banques du Maroc 1986–95; CEO Caisse Inter-professionnelle Marocaine de Retraite (CIMR, non-profit pension org.) 2002–03; Chancellor Univ. Al-Akhawayn, Ifrane; fmr Chair. Ubac Curaçao NV; Chair. Supervisory Cttee Caisse de Dépôt et de Gestion Morocco; Vice-Chair. Maroc Lear; Dir Fonds Hassan II, Banca UBAE, Union de Banques Arabes et Françaises; Dir British Arab Commercial Bank Ltd 2003–10; mem. Steering Cttee Institut Royal des Études Stratégiques. *Address:* Office of the Governor, Bank Al-Maghrib, 277 ave Muhammad V, BP 445, Rabat, Morocco (office). *Telephone:* (53) 7702626 (office). *Fax:* (53) 7706667 (office). *E-mail:* webmaster@bkam.ma (office). *Website:* www.bkam.ma (office).

JOUANNEAU, Daniel, LLM; French diplomatist; b. 15 Sept. 1946, Vendôme (Loir-et-Cher); m.; one d.; ed French Inst. of Political Studies, École nationale d'admin (French Nat. School of Public Admin); worked in Legal Adviser's Office, Ministry of Foreign Affairs 1971–74; First Sec. in Egypt 1974–76; Office of Econ. and Financial Affairs (multilateral commercial matters) 1976–80; Consul Gen., Salisbury, Rhodesia 1980; Chargé d'affaires, Zimbabwe 1980–81; Asst-Dir for Western Europe, then European Correspondent 1981–85, Ministry of Foreign Affairs; Chief of Mission (ODA), Guinea 1985–87; Consul Gen., Québec, Canada 1987–89; Chief of European-Union Dept 1989–90; Amb. to Mozambique, non-resident Amb. in Lesotho and Swaziland 1990–93; Chief of Protocol 1993–97; Amb. to Lebanon 1997–2000; Inspector Gen. of Foreign Affairs 2000–04; Amb. to Canada 2004–08, to Pakistan 2008–11. *Address:* c/o Embassy of France, Diplomatic Enclave 1, Ramna 5, Islamabad, Pakistan (office).

JOUANNO, Chantal; French politician; b. 12 Aug. 1969, Vernon (Eure); d. of Jean-Louis Paul and Françoise Paul; m. Hervé Jouanno 1996; three c.; ed Ecole nationale d'administration, Université Paris 1 Panthéon-Sorbonne, Institut d'Études Politiques, Paris; began career as Export Asst, Citroën 1988; with Accounts Dept, Banque Internationale pour l'Afrique Occidentale 1989–90; with Ministry of Labour and Employment 1992, Ministry of the Interior 1999; Head of Cabinet, Préfet of Vienne and Poitou-Charentes 1999–2001; Head of Cabinet for Man. Dir, Coframi (software co.) 2001; Adviser to Minister of Interior (Nicolas Sarkozy) 2002–06, becoming Councillor responsible for Sustainable Devt; Pres. Agence de l'environnement et de la maîtrise de l'énergie (Ademe) 2008–09; Sec. of State for Ecology 2009–10; Minister of Sport 2010–11; Regional councillor, Ile-de-France 2010–; Senator of Paris 2011–; mem. Union pour un Mouvement Populaire (UMP); mem. Sporting Int. de karaté. *Achievements include:* fmr nat. karate champion (12 nat. titles). *Address:* Le Senat, 15, rue de Vaugirard, 75291640 Paris Cedex 06, France (office). *Telephone:* 1-42-34-20-00 (office). *Website:* www.senat.fr (office).

JOUHAUD, Fabrice; French journalist and newspaper editor; *Editor-in-Chief, L'Équipe;* ed Université Paris X Nanterre, Centre de Formation des Journalistes, Institut d'études politiques de Paris (Sciences Po); Dir Centre de Formation des Journalistes 2004–07; Assoc. Ed., Axel Springer AG March–July 2007; Deputy Dir of Information, M6 Metropole Television 2007–08; News Ed., L'Équipe sports newspaper 2008–09, Man. Ed. 2009–13, Ed.-in-Chief 2013–. *Address:* L'Équipe, 4 cours de l'Ile-Seguin, 92102 Boulogne-Billancourt, France (office). *Telephone:* 1-40-93-20-20 (office). *E-mail:* webmaster@lequipe.fr (office). *Website:* lequipe.fr (office).

JOULWAN, Gen. (retd) George Alfred, BS, MA; American army officer (retd); b. 16 Nov. 1939, Pottsville, Pa; m. Karen E. Jones; three d.; ed US Mil. Acad. West Point, Loyola Univ., Chicago, US Army War Coll., Washington, DC; served in Viet Nam as Co. Commdr and Operations Officer, 1st Bn, 26th Infantry, 1st Infantry Div. and as Brigade Operations Officer and Deputy Div. Operations Officer, 101st Airborne Div. (Air Assault); Aide-de-Camp to Vice-Chief of Staff, US Army; Special Asst to the Pres. 1973–74, to Supreme Allied Commdr, Europe 1974–75; Bn Commdr, US Army, Europe 1975–77; Dir Political and Economic Studies, US Army War Coll., Pa 1978–79; Commdr 2nd Brigade, 3rd Infantry Div. (Mechan-ized), US Army, Europe 1979–81, Chief of Staff 1981–82; Exec. Officer to Chair., Jt Chiefs of Staff, Washington, DC 1982–85; Dir Force Requirements (Combat Support Systems), Office of Deputy Chief of Staff for Operations and Plans, Washington, DC 1985–86; Deputy Chief of Staff for Operations, US Army, Europe and Seventh Army 1986–88, Commdg Gen., 3rd Armored Div. 1988–89, V Corps, 1989–90; C-in-C US Southern Command, Quarry Heights, Panama 1990–93, US European Command, Stuttgart/Vaihingen, Germany 1993–97; Supreme Allied Commdr, Europe, SHAPE, Belgium 1993–97 (retd); Pres. One Team Inc. 2002–05; Adjunct Prof., Nat. Defense Univ. 2000–05; mem. Bd of Dirs General Dynamics Corpn 1998–, Beagle Holdings Inc. 2002–, Alion Science and Technology Corpn 2002–, Remington Arms Co. Inc. 2007–; mem. Int. Advisory Bd Garda World Security Corpn 2008–; Hon. Col 26th Infantry Regiment Asscn; numerous decorations including Defense Distinguished Service Medal (with Oak Leaf Cluster), Defense Superior Service Medal, Silver Star (with Oak Leaf Cluster); numerous orders including Légion d'honneur, Hessian Order of Merit (Germany). *Telephone:* (703) 486-8173 (office). *Fax:* (703) 486-8176 (office).

JOURDA, Françoise Hélène; French architect and academic; b. 26 Nov. 1955, Lyon; teacher at various schools in Europe including Ecole d'Architecture de Lyon 1979–83, Ecole d'Architecture de Saint Etienne 1985–89, Ecole d'Architecture d'Oslo, Norway 1990, Cen. London Polytechnic, UK, Univ. of Minnesota, USA 1992, Tech. Univ. of Kassel, Germany 1998; Prof. Inst. of Spatial Design, Vienna Univ. of Tech. 1999–; mem. Acad. of Architecture (France), Acad. of Arts (Germany), Nat. Comm. on Historical Monuments; Co-founder Jourda &

Perraudin Architectural Agency (now Jourda Architectes); Hon. mem. German Acad. of Architecture; Chevalier, Legion d'honneur, Ordre nat. du Mérite, des Arts et des Lettres. *Architectural works include:* Acad. of the Ministry of the Interior, Herne Sodigen 1993, Palace of Justice, Melun 1994, Greenhouse, Potsdam 1995, European Hosp., Lyon 1998, Décathlon Store, Hannover 1999, French Pavilion for Expo 2000, Lille Police station 2001, office block, Vienna 2003, Commercial Centre, Athens 2004. *Address:* Jourda Architectes Paris, 4 cité de Paradis, 75010 Paris, France (office); Institute of Spatial and Sustainable Design, Vienna University of Technology, Karlsplatz 13, 1040 Vienna, Austria (office). *Telephone:* 1-55-28-82-20 (Paris) (office). *Fax:* 1-55-28-85-18 (Paris) (office). *E-mail:* archi@jourda-architectes .com (office); fhjourda@nerim.com (office). *Website:* www.jourda-architectes.com (office).

JOUSSEN, Friedrich; German engineer and business executive; *CEO, TUI AG;* b. 19 April 1963, Duisburg; ed RWTH Aachen Univ.; gained professional experience in Portland, Ore., USA and joined Mannesmann AG in Düsseldorf 1988, one of the first managers of newly founded Mannesmann Mobilfunk GmbH, held various man. positions in Group Strategy, Innovation Man. and Marketing, Marketing Dir, Mannesmann Mobilfunk GmbH 1997–2000 (group acquired by Vodafone), Head of Global Product Man., Vodafone Group, Newbury, UK, returned to Germany as COO Vodafone Deutschland 2003–05, CEO Vodafone Germany 2005–12, mem. Bd of Dirs Vodafone Ventures, mem. CEO Council and Strategy Bd of Vodafone Group; mem. Exec. Bd TUI AG 2012–, CEO 2013–. *Address:* TUI AG, Postfach 610209, 30602 Hanover (office); TUI AG, Karl-Wiechert-Allee 4, 30625 Hanover, Germany (office). *Telephone:* (511) 56600 (office). *Fax:* (511) 5661901 (office). *E-mail:* info@tui-group.com (office). *Website:* www.tui-group.com (office).

JOVANOVIĆ, Čedomir (Čeda); Serbian politician; *President, Liberal Democratic Party;* b. 13 April 1971, Belgrade, SR Serbia, SFR Yugoslavia; s. of Jovica Jovanović and Milena Mršić; m. Jelena Savić 2003; ed Ninth Belgrade Gymnasium, Third Econs High School, Faculty of Dramatic Arts, Arts Univ., Belgrade; worked as journalist while student; leader of student protests in Belgrade during winter of 1996/97, formed the Student Political Club (Studentski politički klub—SPK) with fellow univ. students; joined the Democratic Party (DS) 1998–2005, Vice-Pres. 2001–05; elected to Serbian Parl. 2000 on list of Democratic Opposition of Serbia (DOS), also held post of DOS parl. caucus leader –2003; Deputy Prime Minister of Serbia 2003–04; Founder and first Pres. Liberal Democratic Party (Liberalno-demokratska partija—LDP) 2005–; unsuccessful cand. in presidential election 2008. *Address:* Liberal Democratic Party (Liberalno-demokratska partija), 11000 Belgrade, Simina 41, Serbia (office). *Telephone:* 11 3208300 (office). *Fax:* (11) 3208301 (office). *E-mail:* predsednik@ldp.rs (office). *Website:* www.ldp.rs (office).

JOVANOVIĆ, Živadin; Serbian politician and diplomatist; *President, Belgrade Forum for the World of Equals;* b. 14 Nov. 1938, Oparic, Rekovač Dist; ed Belgrade Univ.; legal adviser, Novi Beograd Dist Council 1961–64; with Ministry of Foreign Affairs 1964–, diplomatic service in Toronto, Canada 1966–70, Nairobi, Kenya 1974–78; Yugoslavian Amb. to Angola 1988–93; Asst to Minister of Foreign Affairs 1994–97; mem. Narosna Skuptina of Serbia (Parl.) 1997–; Deputy Chair. Socialist Party of Serbia 1997–, Acting Pres. 2001; Minister of Foreign Affairs of Yugoslavia 1998–2000; Founder and Pres. Belgrade Forum for World of Equals 1999–; numerous Nat. and foreign decorations. *Publications include:* Abolishment of the State 2003, National Minorities 2004, Intellectuals and Society 2005, Foreign Policy 2006, Critical Analyses of the Serbian Constitution 2007. *Address:* Socialist Party of Serbia, bul. Lenjina 6, 11000 Belgrade (office); Ilijê Garasanina 8, St 6, 11000 Belgrade, Serbia (home). *Telephone:* (11) 2455822 (office); (11) 2452071 (office); (11) 3237074 (office). *Fax:* (11) 2445421 (office). *E-mail:* bedforum@gmail .com (office); jovanovici@beotel.yu (home). *Website:* www.bedforum.com (office).

JOVIĆ, Ivo Miro; Bosnia and Herzegovina politician; b. 15 July 1950, Trebizat, Capljina; s. of Mio Jović and Mara Bukovac; m. Lucija; three c.; ed Sarajevo Dept of History; fmr teacher in Ilijas and Kiseljak; fmr Dir adult educ. center, Kiseljak; fmr Prin. secondary school, Kiseljak; Deputy Minister of Educ., Science, Culture and Sport, Canton of Middle Bosnia 1997–99; Deputy Minister of Educ., Science, Culture and Sport of Bosnia and Herzegovina Fed. 1999–2001; mem. House of Reps 2002–05; Mem. of the Presidency June 2005–06, Chair. June 2005–Feb. 2006; mem. Hrvatska Demokratska Zajednica Bosne i Hercegovine (Croatian Democratic Union of Bosnia and Herzegovina). *Address:* c/o Hrvatska Demokratska Zajednica Bosne i Hercegovine (Croatian Democratic Union of Bosnia and Herzegovina), 88000 Mostar, Kneza Domagoja bb, Bosnia and Herzegovina (office).

JOVIČIĆ, Radislav; Bosnia and Herzegovina police official and politician; *Minister of Internal Affairs of Republika Srpska;* b. 1971, Ugljevik; m.; one c.; ed Police Coll. and Faculty of Security Studies, Belgrade, postgraduate studies at Faculty of Security and Protection, Univ. Sinergija; 20 years' experience working in the police, served as Commdr of the Special Police Squad, as Deputy Head for Internal Control at Special Police, Commdr of the Police Unit for VIP Protection, Head of Admin for Protection of Persons and Objects of Republika Srpska Ministry of Internal Affairs; also served as Deputy Commdr of Special Support Unit and Head of Operational Support Unit with State Investigation and Protection Agency; Chief of Security Dept, Univ. of Banja Luka; Consultant for Information and Investigation Protection 2012–; Minister of Internal Affairs of Republika Srpska 2012–. *Address:* Ministry of Internal Affairs of Republika Srpska, 78000 Banja Luka, Desanke Maksimović 4, Bosnia and Herzegovina (office). *Telephone:* (51) 338478 (office). *Fax:* (51) 338844 (office). *E-mail:* mup@mup.vladars.net (office). *Website:* www.mup.vladars.net (office).

JOWELL, Rt Hon. Dame Tessa Jane Helen Douglas, DBE, PC, MA; British politician; b. 17 Sept. 1947, Marylebone, London, England; d. of Kenneth Palmer and Rosemary Palmer; m. 1st Roger Jowell 1970 (divorced 1978); m. 2nd David Mills 1979; one s. one d. and one step-s. two step-d.; ed St Margaret's School, Aberdeen, Univs of Aberdeen and Edinburgh; childcare officer, social worker, community care Dir; Asst Dir MIND 1974–86; Dir Community Care Special Action Project 1987–90, Joseph Rowntree Foundation Community Care Programme 1990–92; mem. Labour Party 1969–; Councillor, London Borough of Camden 1971–86; MP for Dulwich 1992–97, for Dulwich and W Norwood 1997–; Opposition Whip, responsible for Trade and Industry 1994–95, Opposition Spokeswoman on Women 1995–96, on Health 1996–97; Minister of State for Public Health 1997–99,

for Employment 1999–2001; Minister for Women, House of Commons 1998–2001; Sec. of State for Culture, Media and Sport 2001–07; Minister for the Olympics 2005–10, for London 2007–08, 2009–10, Paymaster Gen. 2007–10, Minister for the Cabinet Office 2009–10; Shadow Minister for London and the Olympics 2010–12, Shadow Minister for the Cabinet Office Jan.–Oct. 2011; Chair. Social Services Cttee, Housing Man. Cttee, Staff Cttee, Asscn of Metropolitan Authorities 1978–86; mem. Mental Health Act Comm. 1985–90, Health Select Cttee 1992–94; Gov. Nat. Inst. of Social Work 1985–97; Visiting Fellow, Nuffield Coll., Oxford. *Publications:* numerous papers on social policy and community care. *Address:* House of Commons, Westminster, London, SW1A 0AA, England (office). *Telephone:* (20) 7219-3409 (office). *Fax:* (20) 7219-2702 (office). *E-mail:* jowellt@ parliament.uk (office). *Website:* www.parliament.uk/biographies/commons/dame--tessa-jowell/159 (office); www.tessajowell.net (office).

JOXE, Pierre Daniel, LenD; French lawyer; b. 28 Nov. 1934, Paris; s. of Louis Joxe and Françoise-Hélène Halevy; m. 4th Laurence Fradin; two s. two d. from previous m.; ed Lycée Henri IV, Faculté de droit and Ecole Nat. d'Admin; mil. service 1958–60; auditor, later Counsellor Cour des Comptes; mem. Exec. Bureau and Exec. Cttee, Socialist Party 1971–93; Deputy for Saône and Loire 1973, 1978, 1981, 1986, 1988; Minister of Industry and Admin May–June 1981, of the Interior, Decentralization and Admin July 1984 and March 1986, of the Interior 1988–91, of Defence 1991–93; First Pres. Cour des Comptes (audit court) 1993–2001; mem. Conseil Constitutionnel 2001–10; mem. European Parl. 1977–79; Pres. Regional Council, Burgundy 1979–82, Socialist Parl. Group 1981–84, 1986–88; Hon. KBE; Commdr, Ordre nat. du Mérite. *Publications:* Parti socialiste 1973, Atlas du Socialisme 1973, L'édit de Nantes (Literary Prize, Droits de l'homme) 1998, A propos de la France 1998, Pourquoi Mitterrand 2006, Cas de conscience (Jean Zay Literary Prize) 2010, Pas de Quartier? 2012, Soif de justice 2014. *Address:* 39 quai de l'Horloge, 75100 Paris, France (office).

JOYA, Malalai; Afghan politician and writer; b. 25 April 1978, Farah Prov.; family fled to Iran and Pakistan 1982, returned to Afghanistan and, under Taliban rule, began home-based secret classes for young girls and women deprived of educ. under the Taliban 1998; moved to Farah and f. Malalai Health Clinic and Orphanage 2002; elected to Constitutional Loya Jirga from Farah Prov. 2003 (made worldwide news headlines by denouncing the warlords in the assembly 17 Dec. 2003); mem. Parl. for Farah Prov. 2005–07 (suspended from parl. on the grounds that she had insulted fellow reps in a TV interview 21 May 2007, suspension being appealed, supported by Human Rights Watch); a fmr Dir Org. for Promoting Afghan Women's Capabilities; Hon. Citizen of Commune of Provincia di Arezzo 2007, Comune di Bucine 2007, Comune di Supino 2007; Malalai of Maiwand Award 2004, Int. Women of the Year Award, Valle d'Aosta Prov. of Italy 2004, Gwangju Award for Human Rights, May 18th Foundation, S Korea 2006, Women of Peace Award 2006, Women's Peacepower Foundation 2006, named amongst 1000 Women for the Nobel Peace Prize 2005, named by World Econ. Forum amongst 250 Young Global Leaders for 2007, certificate of honour from Mayor of Berkeley, Calif. 2007, 14th Angel Award, The Angel Festival 2007, Golden Fleur-de-Lis (Giglio d'Oro) Award, Town Council of Toscana Region of Italy 2007, Mare Nostrum Award, Commune of Palazzo in Viareggio, Italy 2007, Juan Maria Bandres Award for Human Rights and solidarity with the refugees 2008, Anna Politkovskaya Award 2008, Int. Anti-Discrimination Award 2009 and others. *Publications:* Raising My Voice 2009, A Woman Among Warlords: The Extraordinary Story of the Afghan Woman Who Dares to Speak Out (autobiography, translated into 13 languages) 2009. *Telephone:* (799) 9544358 (office). *E-mail:* mj@malalaijoya.com (home). *Website:* www.malalaijoya.com

JOYNER-KERSEE, Jacqueline, BA; American fmr athlete; b. 3 March 1962, East St Louis, Ill.; d. of Alfred Joyner and the late Mary Joyner; m. Bobby Kersee 1986; ed Univ. of California, Los Angeles; specialized in heptathlon; coached by husband; world record heptathlon scores: 7,158 points, Houston, 1986; 7,215 points, USA Olympic trial, Indianapolis 1988 (still world record as at Dec. 2003); 7,291 points, Seoul 1988; 7,044 points (gold medal), Olympic Games, Barcelona 1992; three Olympic gold medals, four world championships; long jump: gold medal, World Championships 1987, gold medal, Olympic Games, Seoul 1988, bronze medal, Olympic Games, Barcelona 1992, bronze medal, Olympic Games, Atlanta 1996; winner IAAF Mobil Grand Prix 1994; Chair. St Louis Sports Comm. 1996–; played basketball for Richmond Rage, American Basketball League 1996; business interests include Gold Medal Rehab (sports medicine); CEO Elite International Sports Marketing; f. Jackie Joyner-Kersee Gold Medal Scholarship program (now Jackie Joyner-Kersee Youth Foundation) 1988; Co-founder Athletes for Hope (charity) 2007; mem. Bd of Dirs USA Track & Field 2013–; Hon. DHL (Spellman Coll.) 1998, (Howard Univ.) 1999, (George Washington Univ.) 1999; numerous honours including Associated Press Female Athlete of the Year 1988, first woman to win Sporting News Man of the Year Award, Jim Thorpe Award 1993, Jackie Robinson Robie Award 1994, Jesse Owens Humanitarian Award 1999, World Women and Sport Trophy for the Americas, IOC 2007; recognised by Sports Illustrated as the greatest female athlete of the 20th century. *Publication:* A Kind of Grace (autobiog.) 1997. *Address:* c/o Chicago Sports and Entertainment Partners, 3818 North Troy Street, Suite 100, Chicago, IL 60618, USA. *Website:* jackiejoynerkersee.com

JOYON, Francis; French yachtsman; b. 28 May 1956, Hanches, Eure-et-Loire; m. Virginie Joyon; two s.; worked at Glénans Nautical Centre, working as boat-builder, later sailing instructor; first major race 1988 Route of Discovery (finished in third place); other races include 1989 Round Europe Race, 1990 Route du Rhum, 1992 OSTAR, Route du Cafe, 2000 Europe 1 Newman Star race (first major win, on board Eure et Loir), 2000 Transat (winner), 2001 Fastnet Race (winner); became fastest world non-stop solo yachtsman 2004; solo North Transatlantic record 2005; set new solo round-the-world record on board IDEC II 2008. *Address:* c/o Les Glénans, Quai Louis Blériot, 75016 Paris, France (office). *Website:* www.trimaran -idec.com.

JU, Gen. Sang-song; North Korean army officer and politician; *Minister of People's Security;* career in Korean People's Armed Forces; attained rank of Gen. 1997; commdr of army unit stationed on border with S Korea 2000; cand. mem. Korean Worker's Party 1970–90, full mem. 1990–; mem. Supreme People's Parl. 1990–98; Minister of People's Security and mem. Nat. Defence Comm. 2004–.

Address: Ministry of Defence, Pyongyang, Democratic People's Republic of Korea (office).

JU MING; Taiwanese sculptor; b. (Ju Chuan-tai), 20 Jan. 1938, Miaoli Tunghsiao; s. of Lee-chi Chu and Ai Wang; m. Chen Fu-mei 1961; apprenticeship with Master Chin-chuan Lee 1953–57; trained in modern sculpture by Yu Yu Yang 1968–76; moved to USA and made debut in int. arena 1981; produced two series: Taichi Series in wood and bronze and Living World Series in wood, bronze, sponge and stainless steel; f. Ju Ming Museum, Taipai; Hon. Dr of Art (Fu Jen Catholic Univ.) 2003; Sculpture Award Chinese Sculptors and Artists Asscn 1976, Nat. Culture Award, Repub. of China Nat. Culture Foundation 1976, Award for Ten Outstanding Young People 1987, Achievement Award of Fok Ying Tung, Hong Kong 1998, The Second Enku Award Japan 2002, Fukuoka Asian Culture Prize, Art and Cultures Prize 2007. *Publications:* Juming Sculptures – The Living World 1, 2, 3, Juming – Mixed Media, Juming – Oil Paintings, Juming Sculpture 1976–1993, Taichi in Wood, Ju Ming Wood Sculptures – Buffalo, Ju Ming Paintings, Ju Ming On Art, Carving for Humanity (biog.), Secret Garden of Ju Ming, Ju Ming. *Leisure interest:* tai-chi. *Address:* Juming Museum, 208 No. 2 She-shi-hu, Chin-shan, Taipei (office); 111 No. 28, Lane 460, Sec. 2, Chih-shan Road, Taipei, Taiwan (home). *Telephone:* (2) 24989940 (office); (2) 28412011 (home). *Fax:* (2) 24988529 (office); (2) 28413000 (home). *E-mail:* rese1502@juming.org.tw (office); www .juming.org.tw (office).

JUAN, Alexis Raymond, LLD; French banking executive; *Honorary Chairman, Komercni Banka;* b. 11 June 1943, Sidi Bel Abbes, Algeria; ed Political Studies Inst., Grenoble; joined Société Générale 1968, various man. roles including positions with subsidiary cos in Tokyo 1973–76, Athens 1980–84, Seoul as Dir Korean French Banking Corpn 1978–80, Deputy CEO Société Générale, UK Div., London 1984–87, various man. roles with Société Générale in France 1987–98, mem. Bd of Dirs Comm. 1998, Chair. Komercni Banka, Prague, Czech Repub. 2001–05, Hon. Chair. 2005–; mem. Bd of Dirs Orco Property Group SA 2009–. *Address:* c/o Komercni Banka, Na Prikope 33, 11047 Prague 1, Czech Republic (office).

JUAN CARLOS I, HM The King of Spain; b. 5 Jan. 1938, Rome, Italy; s. of the late HRH Don Juan de Borbón y Battenberg, Count of Barcelona and of the late HRH María de las Mercedes de Borbón y Orleans and grandson of King Alfonso XIII and Queen Victoria Eugenia of Spain; m. Princess Sophia, d. of the late King Paul of the Hellenes and of Queen Frederica, 1962; one s., HRH Prince Felipe, The Prince of Asturias, b. Jan. 1968; two daughters, Princess Elena, Princess Cristina; ed privately in Fribourg, Switzerland, Madrid, San Sebastián, Inst. of San Isidro, Madrid, Colegio del Carmen, Gen. Mil. Acad., Zaragoza and Univ. of Madrid; spent childhood in Rome, Lausanne, Estoril and Madrid; commissioned into the three armed forces and undertook training in each of them 1957–59; studied the org. and activities of various govt ministries; named by Gen. Franco as future King of Spain 1969, inaugurated as King of Spain 22 Nov. 1975, named as Capt.-Gen. of the Armed Forces Nov. 1975; Foreign mem. Acad. des sciences morales et politiques, Assoc. mem. 1988; Dr hc (Strasbourg) 1979, (Madrid), (Harvard) 1984, (Sorbonne) 1985, (Oxford) 1986, (Trinity Coll., Dublin) 1986, (Bologna) 1988, (Cambridge) 1988, (Coimbra) 1989, (Tokyo, Bogotá, Limerick, Tufts, Chile) 1990, (Toronto) 1991, (Jerusalem) 1993; Charlemagne Prize 1982, Bolívar Prize (UNESCO) 1983, Gold Medal Order 1985, Candenhove Kalergi Prize, Switzerland 1986, Nansen Medal 1987, Humanitarian Award Elie Wiesel, USA 1991, shared Houphouët Boigny Peace Prize (UNESCO) 1995, Franklin D. Roosevelt Four Freedoms Award 1995. *Address:* Palacio de la Zarzuela, 28071 Madrid, Spain. *Website:* www.casareal.es.

JUANGROONGRUANGKIT, Somporn; Thai business executive; *President, Thai Summit Group;* b. 1951; widowed; five c.; Pres. Thai Summit Group 2002–, Thai Summit Autoparts Industries Co. Ltd; Dir Thai Summit Grand Estate Co.; Founder Pattana Golf and Sports Resort. *Address:* Thai Summit Group, 4/3 Moo 1, Bangna-Trad HWY, KM.16 Bangchalong, Bangplee District, Samuthprakarn 10549, Thailand (office). *Telephone:* (2) 337-0022 (office). *Fax:* (2) 325-8015 (office). *Website:* www.thaisummit.co.th (office).

JUANTORENA, Alberto; Cuban sports administrator, politician and fmr athlete; b. 3 Dec. 1950, Santiago; m.; five c.; moved to Havana to train under Polish coach Zygmunt Zabierzowski 1971; gold 400m (45.36) Dominica Cen. American Games 1974; gold 800m (1:43.50), gold 400m (44.26) Montreal Olympic Games 1976; gold 800m (1:44.01), gold 400m (45.36) Dusseldorf World Cup 1977; gold 400m (44.27), gold 800m (1:47.78) Columbia Cen. American Games 1978; fmr Vice-Minister of Sports for Cuba, Vice-Pres. Cuban Olympic Cttee, Vice-Pres. for Latinamerica UNESCO, Sr Vice-Pres. Cuban Olympic Cttee; mem. Council IAAF; Track & Field News Athlete of the Year 1976, 1977; Olympic Order. *Address:* c/o Cubadeportes S.A., Calle 20 No. 710 e/ 7ma y 9na, Miramar, Playa, Havana, Cuba (office).

JUBEIR, Adel bin Ahmed al-, BA, MA; Saudi Arabian diplomatist; *Ambassador to USA;* b. 1 Feb. 1962, Riyadh; ed schools in Germany, Yemen, Lebanon and USA, Univ. of North Texas and Georgetown Univ., USA; served in Jt Information Bureau in Dhahran during Operation Desert Shield/Desert Storm 1990–91; fmr Special Asst to Amb., Embassy in Washington, DC; fmr Dir Saudi Arabian Information and Congressional Affairs Office; Foreign Affairs Advisor, Crown Prince's Court 2000–05; Advisor, Royal Court 2005–07; Amb. to USA 2007–; mem. numerous int. dels; fmr Co-Sec. US-Saudi Strategic Dialogue; Visiting Diplomatic Fellow, Council of Foreign Relations, New York 1994–95; has lectured at univs and academic insts in USA and has appeared frequently in the media; Hon. DHumLitt (North Texas) 2006. *Address:* Embassy of Saudi Arabia, 601 New Hampshire Avenue NW, Washington, DC 20037, USA (office). *Telephone:* (202) 342-3800 (office). *Fax:* (202) 944-5983 (office); (202) 944-6750 (office); (202) 944-3113 (office). *E-mail:* info@saudiembassy.net (office). *Website:* www.saudiembassy.net (office).

JUDD, Ashley; American actress; b. 19 April 1968, Granada Hills, Calif.; d. of Naomi Judd; half-sister of Wynonna Judd; m. Dario Franchitti 2001. *Films include:* Kuffs 1992, Ruby in Paradise 1993, Natural Born Killers (scenes deleted) 1994, Smoke 1995, Heat 1995, The Passion of Darkly Noon 1995, A Time to Kill 1996, Normal Life 1996, The Locusts (A Secret Sin, UK) 1997, Kiss the Girls 1997, Simon Birch 1998, Eye of the Beholder 1999, Double Jeopardy 1999, Our Friend, Martin (video, voice) 1999, Dexterity 2000, Where the Heart Is 2000, Someone Like

You (aka Animal Attraction, UK) 2001, High Crimes 2002, Divine Secrets of the Ya-Ya Sisterhood 2002, Frida 2002, The Husband I Bought 2003, The Blackout Murders 2003, Just One of Those Things 2003, Twisted 2004, De-Lovely 2004, Come Early Morning 2006, Bug 2006, Helen 2009, Crossing Over 2009, Tooth Fairy 2010. *Television includes:* Sisters (series) 1991–94, Till Death Us Do Part 1992, Naomi and Wynonna: Love Can Build a Bridge 1995, Norman Jean and Marilyn 1996, The Ryan Interview 2000. *Address:* 11766 Wilshire Blvd, Suite 1610, Los Angeles, CA 00025-6565; William Morris Endeavor, One William Morris Place, Beverly Hills, CA 90212, USA. *Telephone:* (310) 859-4000. *Fax:* (310) 859-4462. *Website:* www.wma.com.

JUDEH, Nasser, BSc; Jordanian government official and politician; *Minister of Foreign Affairs;* ed Georgetown Univ., USA; Pvt. Sec. and Press Sec. to HRH Prince Hassan 1985–92; Dir Jordan Information Bureau, London 1992–94; Dir Jordan TV Corpn 1994–98, Dir-Gen. 1998; Minister of Information 1998–99, Official Govt Spokesman 1998–99, 2005–07; Chair. Bd of Information and Communication Expertise 1999–2005; Minister of State for Media Affairs and Communication 2007; Minister of Foreign Affairs 2009–; media adviser to Royal Jordanian Airlines 2003; Grand Cordon of the Order of Al Kawkab, Grand Cordon of the Order of Al- Istiklal, Officier, Légion d'honneur, Grand Officer, Order of Orange-Nassau (The Netherlands). *Leisure interests:* underwater sports, hunting, reading, tennis. *Address:* Ministry of Foreign Affairs, POB 35217, Amman 11180, Jordan (office). *Telephone:* (6) 5735150 (office). *Fax:* (6) 5735163 (office). *E-mail:* inquiry@mfa.gov.jo (office). *Website:* www.mfa.gov.jo (office).

JUDGE, Lady Barbara Singer Thomas, CBE, BA, JD; American/British lawyer and business executive; *Chairman, Pension Protection Fund;* b. 28 Dec. 1946, New York; m. 1st Allen L. Thomas, one s.; m. 2nd Sir Paul Judge; ed Univ. of Pennsylvania, New York Univ. School of Law; began career as corporate lawyer in New York; joined Kaye, Scholer, Fierman, Hays and Handler (law firm) 1973, later becoming Partner; mem. Securities and Exchange Comm., Washington, DC 1980–83; Dir Samuel Montagu & Co. (merchant bank) 1983–87; Sr Vice-Pres. Bankers Trust International Banking, New York 1987; Exec. Dir News International 1993; f. Private Equity Investor PLC, London 2000; Dir (non-exec.) UK Atomic Energy Authority 2002, Chair. 2004–10, Chair. Emer. 2010–; Chair. Pension Protection Fund 2010–, Hyperion Power Generation; Chair. Energy Inst., Univ. Coll., London, SOAS, London 2006–, Advisory Bd London Middle East Inst.; Deputy Chair. UK Financial Reporting Council 2004–07; Visiting Fellow, Saïd Business School, Univ. of Oxford; Dir (non-exec.) Statoil ASA (Norway), NV Bekaert SA (Belgium), Magna International Inc. (Canada); Public mem. Int. Ethics Standards Bd for Accountants 2007–10; mem. TEPCO Nuclear Reform Monitoring Cttee, Tokyo 2012–; Deputy Chair. 2013–; Trustee, Royal Acad. of Arts. *Address:* Pension Protection Fund, Knollys House, 17 Addiscombe Road, Croydon, CR0 6SR, England (office). *Telephone:* (845) 600 2541 (office). *Fax:* (20) 8633-4910 (office). *E-mail:* information@ppf.gsi.gov.uk (office). *Website:* www .pensionprotectionfund.org.uk (office).

JUDGE, Sir Paul, Kt, MA, MBA; British business executive; *Chairman, Schroder Income Growth Fund PLC;* b. 25 April 1949, London; s. of Rupert Cyril Judge and Betty Rosa Muriel Judge (née Daniels); m. Barbara Judge; two s.; ed St Dunstan's Coll., Trinity Coll., Cambridge, Wharton Business School, Univ. of Pennsylvania, USA; joined Cadbury Schweppes 1973, various positions in Overseas Group finance dept 1973–78, Group Deputy Finance Dir 1978, Man. Dir Cadbury Schweppes Kenya 1980–82, Cadbury Typhoo 1982–84, Group Planning Dir and mem. Exec. Cttee 1984–85, led buyout of Cadbury Schweppes food cos to form Premier Brands 1985; apptd mem. Milk Marketing Bd and Chair. of Food for Britain, UK Govt 1989; Dir-Gen. Conservative Party 1992–95; Ministerial Adviser, Cabinet Office 1995–96; Chair. Schroder Income Growth Fund PLC; Dir ENRC plc, UK Accreditation Service, Tempur Pedic International Inc. (Kentucky), Standard Bank Group Ltd (Johannesburg), Abraaj Capital (Dubai); mem. Advisory Bd Barclays Pvt. Bank 2001–10; Dir Boddington Group PLC 1989–93, Grosvenor Devt Capital PLC 1989–93, WPP Group PLC 1991–97; Chair. Royal Soc. for Arts, Manufactures and Commerce 2003–06, Marketing Standards Bd 2001–10, Govs of St Dunstan's Coll. 2001–, British-N American Cttee 2001–, Teachers TV 2005–08, British-Serbian Chamber of Commerce 2010–; Deputy Chair. American Man. Asscn; Pres. Chartered Man. Inst. 2004–05, Asscn of MBAs 1997–, Chartered Inst. of Marketing; Vice-Pres. Marketing Council 2000–06; mem. Council of the Higher Educ. Funding Council for England 2008–10, Council of the Crown Agents; Special Adviser, Chatham House; Registrar Imperial Soc. of Kts Batchelor; mem. Togolese Pres.'s Int. Advisory Council; Trustee Emer., The Cambridge Foundation; Master Worshipful Co. of Marketers 2005–06; Key Benefactor, Judge Business School, Univ. of Cambridge; Alderman, City of London; Hon. LLD (Cantab.), Hon. DSc (City), Hon. DLitt (Westminster). *Leisure interests:* photography, travel. *Address:* 152 Grosvenor Road, London, SW1V 3JL, England (office). *Telephone:* (20) 7834-9041 (office). *E-mail:* paul@paulrjudge.com. *Website:* www.paulrjudge.com.

JUGNAUTH, Rt Hon. Sir Aneerood, KCMG, PC, QC; Mauritian politician, lawyer and fmr head of state; b. 29 March 1930, Palma; m. Sarojni Devi Ballah; one s. one d.; ed Church of England School, Palma, Regent Coll., Quakre, Borneo, Lincoln's Inn, London; called to Bar 1954; won seat on Legis. Ass., Mauritius 1963; Minister of State and Devt 1965–67, of Labour 1967; Dist Magistrate 1967; Crown Counsel and Sr Crown Counsel 1971; co-founder and Pres. Mouvement Militant Mauricien with Paul Bérenger (q.v.) Dec. 1971–; Leader of Opposition 1976; Prime Minister of Mauritius 1982–95, other portfolios include Minister of Finance 1983–84, of Defence and Internal Security and Reform Insts, of Information, Internal and External Communications and the Outer Islands, of Justice; Prime Minister and Minister of Defence and Home Affairs and of External Communications 2000–03; Pres. 2003–12 (resgnd); Order of the Rising Sun (Japan) 1988, Grand Officier, Légion d'honneur 1990; Hon. DCL (Mauritius) 1985, Hon. LLD (Madras) 2001, Dr hc (Aix-en-Provence) 1985. *Leisure interests:* football, reading. *Address:* La Caverne No. 1, Vacoas, Mauritius (home).

JUGNAUTH, Pravind Kumar, LLB; Mauritian politician and barrister; b. 25 Dec. 1961; m.; three c.; ed Univ. of Buckingham, UK; joined Mouvement Socialiste Militant 1987, Deputy Leader 1999–2003, Leader 2003–; Councillor, Municipality of Vacoas/Phoenix 1996; mem. Parl. for Constituency No 11 (Vieux Grand Port and Rose Belle); Minister of Agric., Food, Trade and Natural Resources 2000–03,

Deputy Prime Minister and Minister of Finance Sept.–Dec. 2003, Deputy Prime Minister and Minister of Finance and Econ. Devt Dec. 2003–05, 2010–11. *Address:* Mouvement Socialiste Militant, 1st Floor, Sun Trust Building, Edith Cavell Street, Port Louis (office); La Caverne No 1, Vacoas, Mauritius (home). *Telephone:* 212-8787 (office). *Fax:* 212-9334 (office). *E-mail:* info@msmparty.org (office). *Website:* www.msmparty.org (office).

JUGNOT, Gérard; French actor, writer, director and producer; b. 4 May 1951, Paris; one s. with Cécile Magna; Chevalier de la Légion d'honneur 2004. *Films include:* L'an 01 (The Year 01) 1973, Salut l'artiste (Hail the Artist) (uncredited)) 1973, Que la fête commence… (Let Joy Reign Supreme) (uncredited) 1974, Les valseuses (Getting It Up) 1974, Le bol d'air (also writer) 1975, C'est pas parce qu'on a rien à dire qu'il faut fermer sa gueule (also writer) 1975, Vous ne l'emporterez pas au paradis 1975, Pas de problème! (No Problem!) 1975, Calmos (Cool, Calm and Collected) 1976, Oublie-moi, Mandoline (Forget Me, Mandoline) 1976, Le juge et l'assassin (The Judge and the Assassin) (uncredited) 1976, Le locataire (The Tenant) 1976, On aura tout vu (The Bottom Line) 1976, Dracula père et fils (Dracula and Son) 1976, Monsieur Klein 1976, Le jouet (The Toy) 1976, Le chasseur de chez Maxim's (Maxim's Porter) 1976, Casanova & Co. (aka Some Like It Cool, USA), Herbie Goes to Monte Carlo 1977, Des enfants gâtés (Spoiled Children) 1977, Vous n'aurez pas l'Alsace et la Lorraine (You Won't Have Alsace-Lorraine 1977, La septième compagnie au clair de lune (The Seventh Company Outdoors) 1977, Les petits câlins (The Little Wheedlers) 1978, Pauline et l'ordinateur 1978, Les bronzés (French Fried Vacation, USA) (also writer) 1978, Les héros n'ont pas froid aux oreilles (Heroes Are Not Wet Behind the Ears, USA) (also writer) 1979, Un si joli village… (The Investigation) 1979, le coup de sirocco 1979, Les bronzés font du ski (also writer) 1979, Retour en force (Return in Bond) 1980, Le coup du parapluie (Umbrella Coup) 1980, Les Charlots contre Dracula 1980, Pourquoi pas nous? 1981, Pour 100 briques t'as plus rien… (For 200 Grand, You Get Nothing Now) 1980, Le Père Noël est une ordure (also writer) 1982, Le quart d'heure américain (also writer) 1982, La fiancée qui venait du froid 1983, Papy fait de la résistance 1983, Le garde du corps 1984, Pinot simple flic (also writer and dir) 1984, Just the Way You Are 1984, Tranches de vie (Slices of Life) 1985, Les rois du gag 1985, Scout toujours… (also writer and dir) 1985, Nuit d'ivresse 1986, Le beauf 1987, Tandem 1987, Tant qu'il y aura des femmes (uncredited) 1987, Sans peur et sans reproche (Without Fear or Blame) (also writer and dir) 1988, Les cigognes n'en font qu'à leur tête 1989, Les 1001 nuits (1001 Nights, aka Scheherazade, UK) 1990, Les secrets professionnels du Dr Apfelglück 1991, Une époque formidable… (Wonderful Times) (also writer and dir) 1991, Les clés du paradis (The Keys to Paradise) 1991, Voyage à Rome 1992, Grosse fatigue (Dead Tired) 1994, Casque bleu (Blue Helmet) (also writer and dir) 1994, Les faussaires (The Impostors) 1994, 3,000 scénarios contre le virus (3,000 Scenarios to Combat a Virus) (dir segment 'La pharmacie') 1994, Fantôme avec chauffeur 1996, Fallait pas!… (also writer and dir) 1996, Marthe 1997, Au bain… Mari! 1999, Trafic d'influence (Influence Peddling) 1999, L'ami du jardin 1999, Meilleur espoir féminin (Most Promising Young Actress) (also writer and dir) 2000, Oui, mais… (Yes, But…) 2001, Monsieur Batignole (also writer, dir and producer) 2002, Le raid (The Race) 2002, Les clefs de bagnole (The Car Keys) 2003, Les choristes (Chorists) (also dir and assoc. producer) 2004, The Magic Roundabout (voice) 2005, Boudu (also dir and co-producer) 2005, Il ne faut jurer… de rien! 2005, Les bronzés amis pour la vie (also writer) 2006, Les brigades du tigre 2006, L'île aux trésors 2007, L'auberge rouge 2007, Ça se soigne? 2008, Faubourg 36 2008, Musée haut, musée bas 2008, Envoyés très spéciaux 2009, La siciliana ribelle 2009, Rose et noir 2009. *Television includes:* Pierrot mon ami (Pierrot My Friend) 1979, Merci Bernard (series) 1982, L'adieu aux as (mini-series) 1982, Le Père Noël est une ordure (also writer) 1985, Restauratec 2002, Volpone 2003, Trois petites filles 2004.

JUHÁSZ, Ferenc; Hungarian politician; b. 6 Jan. 1960, Nyíregyháza; m.; two c.; ed Lajos Kossuth Vocational School, György Bessenyei Teachers' Training Coll., Nyíregyháza, Coll. of Finance and Public Accountancy, Univ. of Pécs; Head of Co. Office, HSP (Magyar Szocialista Párt—MSZP) 1991–94; elected mem. of Parl. 1994, mem. Defence Cttee 1994–96, Vice-Chair. 1996–98; apptd Vice-Chair. Defence Cttee on Legislation, Chair. Control Comm. 1998; Head, Working Group of HSP faction for Defence and Nat. Security 1998–2002, Deputy Head of faction for Parl. 1999–2000; Deputy Chair. HSP 2000–; Minister of Nat. Defence 2002–06. *Address:* Hungarian Socialist Party, Köztársaság tér 26, 1081 Budapest, Hungary (office). *Telephone:* (1) 210-0046 (office). *Fax:* (1) 210-0081 (office). *E-mail:* info@mszp.hu (office); ferenc.juhasz@mszp.hu. *Website:* www.mszp.hu; www .juhaszferenc.hu.

JUILLET, Alain; French intelligence officer and fmr business executive; b. 1943; ed Centre de perfectionnement des affaires, Institut des hautes études de défense nationale, Paris, Stanford Univ., USA; fmr employee, Pernod-Ricard, Jacobs-Suchard, Union Laitière Normande, France Champignon; Chief Exec. French Operations, Marks & Spencer Ltd –2001; Head of Information, Direction Générale de la Sécurité Extérieure (DGSE) 2002–03, Sr Officer responsible for econ. intelligence, Secrétariat général de la défense nationale (SGDN) 2004.

JUKNEVIČIENÉ, Rasa; Lithuanian physician and politician; b. 26 Jan. 1958, Panevėžio raj. Tiltagalių km; m. Zenonas Juknevičius; ed Kaunas Medical Inst.; paediatrician, Cen. Hosp., Poswolu 1984–90; mem. Supreme Council, Reconstituent Seimas 1990–92; Deputy in Seimas 1996–, Vice-Pres. Parl. Del. to NATO Parl. Ass. 1999–2000, mem. Comm. for NATO Affairs 2004–08 (Deputy Chair. 2005–08); Minister of Nat. Defence 2008–12; mem. and Deputy Leader Homeland Union—Lithuanian Christian Democrats (Tėvynės Sąjunga); Lithuanian Grand Duke Gediminas Order of the Commdr's Cross of Lithuania's 10th Anniversary of Independence. *Leisure interests:* reading, growing flowers. *Address:* Homeland Union—Lithuanian Christian Democrats, L. Stuokos-Gucevičiaus g. 11, Vilnius 01122, Lithuania (office). *Telephone:* (5) 212-1657 (office). *Fax:* (5) 278-4722 (office). *E-mail:* sekretoriatas@tsajunga.lt (office). *Website:* www.tsajunga.lt (office).

JULIEN, Michael Frederick, FCA, FCT; British business executive and accountant (retd); b. 22 March 1938, London, England; s. of the late Robert A. F. Julien and Olive R. Evans; m. Ellen Martinsen 1963; one s. two d.; ed St Edward's School, Oxford; Chartered Accountant (Hons Intermediate); Price Waterhouse & Co. 1958–67; other commercial appointments 1967–76; Group Finance Dir BICC (now Balfour Beatty PLC) 1976–83; Exec. Dir Finance and Planning, Midland Bank (now HSBC Bank PLC) 1983–86; Man. Dir Finance and Admin. Guinness PLC (now Diageo PLC) 1987–88, Dir (non-exec.) 1988–97; Group Chief Exec. Storehouse PLC (now Mothercare PLC) 1988–92; Chair. Owners Abroad PLC (now First Choice Holidays PLC) 1993–97; Dir Medeva PLC 1993–98; fmr Deputy Chair. Oxford Professional Training Ltd. *Leisure interests:* family, travel, computing (including video editing). *Website:* www.julienco.com.

JULIET, Charles; French poet, playwright and novelist; b. 30 Sept. 1934, Jujurieux (Ain); ed school in Aix-en-Provence, studies in Lyon. *Publications:* Au long de la spirale 1975, Pages de pierre 1977, La Plus Fragile 1977, Croissances 1978, Pages de journal 1978, Vers la rencontre 1980, Reviens à la solitude 1983, Convergences 1984, La lente montée 1984, Lettre suit 1985, La Soif 1987, Tes yeux blessés 1987, Entretien (with Pierre Soulages) 1987, Accords 1987, La vie affleure 1989, Tant de chemins 1989, L'Année de l'éveil 1989, Affûts 1990, Dans la lumière des saisons 1991), Le Don de présence 1992, Bribes pour un double 1992, Ce pays du silence 1992, Jean Reverzy 1992, L'Inattendu 1992, Tu avives 1993, Telluriennes 1993, Cette flamme claire 1994, Ce chemin 1994, Carnets de Saorge 1994, Entretien (with Raoul Ubac) 1994, Accueils – Journal 4 1982–1988 1994, Ce foyer secret 1995, Césire, n°4 1995, En amont 1995, Giacometti 1995, Failles 1995, Lambeaux 1995, A voix basse 1997), Lueur après labour – Journal 3 1968–1981 1997, Traversée de nuit – Journal 2 1965–1968 1997, Creuser 1998, La Mue 1998, Ferveur 1998, Fouilles 1998, L'Autre Chemin 1998, Rencontres (with Bram van Velde) 1998, La Traversée 1999, Ecarte la nuit 1999, Rencontres (with Samuel Beckett) 1999, Chez François Dilasser 1999, Attente en automne 1999, Galet 2000, Un lourd destin 2000, Ténèbres en terre froide – Journal 1 1957–1964 2000), La Vague 2001, Invite le vent 2002, Une joie secrète 2002, Eclats 2002, Te rejoindre 2002, L'Incessant 2002, L'Autre Faim 2003, Notules 2005, Ces bruits du monde extérieur 2005, Les Autoportraits de Jean-Michel Marchetti 2005, Au pays du long nuage blanc 2005, T.R.U.P.H.E.M.U.S 2006, L'opulence de la nuit 2006, D'une rive à l'autre 2006, Un jour 2006, L'absente 2007, Etty Hillesum, la fille qui ne savait pas prier 2007, Conversations with Samuel Beckett and Bram Van Velde (co-author) 2009. *Address:* c/o Dalkey Archive Press, Dutch House, 307–308 High Holborn, London, WC1V 7LL, England. *E-mail:* contact@dalkeyarchive.com. *Website:* www.dalkeyarchive.com.

JULIUS, Anthony Robert, MA, PhD; British lawyer; *Deputy Chairman, Mishcon de Reya;* b. 16 July 1956; s. of Morris Julius and Myrna Julius; m. 1st Judith Bernie 1979 (divorced 1998); two s. two d.; m. 2nd Dina Rabinovitch 1999 (died 2007); one s.; m. 3rd Katarina Lester 2009; one s.; ed City of London School, Jesus Coll., Cambridge, Univ. Coll. London; articled Victor Mishcon & Co., qualified 1981, partner Mishcon de Reya 1984–, (Head of Litigation 1987–98), Consultant 1998–, currently also Deputy Chair.; Solicitor Advocate 1999; Teacher (part–time), Law Faculty, Univ. Coll. London 1995–97; Dir Inst. of Jewish Policy Research (reporting on Holocaust Denial Legislation) 1995–97 (Deputy Chair. Research Bd 1995–97); f., Trustee and Chair. Diana, Princess of Wales Memorial Trust, Vice-Pres. 1997–2003; Chair. Man. Bd Centre for Cultural Analysis, Theory and History, Univ. of Leeds 2001–06; Chair. London Consortium 2005–10. *Publications:* T. S. Eliot, Anti-Semitism and Literary Form 1995, Art Crimes (chapter in Law and Literature) 1999, Idolising Pictures 2000, Transgressions 2002, Trials of the Diaspora 2010. *Leisure interest:* cooking. *Address:* Mishcon de Reya, Summit House, 12 Red Lion Square, London, WC1R 4QD, England (office). *Telephone:* (20) 7440-7000 (office). *Fax:* (20) 7404-8171 (office). *E-mail:* anthony .julius@mishcon.com (office). *Website:* www.mishcon.com (office).

JULIUS, David, BS, PhD; American physiologist and academic; *Professor and Chairman, Department of Physiology, School of Medicine, University of California, San Francisco;* ed Univ. of California, Berkeley, Massachusetts Inst. of Tech.; Undergraduate Research Asst, Dept of Biology, MIT 1975–77; Visiting Research Assoc., Dept of Biochemistry, Univ. of Bordeaux, France, Summer 1976; Grad. Student, Dept of Biochemistry, Univ. of California, Berkeley 1977–84; Postdoctoral Fellow, Inst. of Cancer Research, Columbia Univ., New York 1984–89; Asst Prof., Dept of Cellular and Molecular Pharmacology, Univ. of California, San Francisco 1989–96, Assoc. Prof. 1996–99, Prof. 1999–2006, Prof. and Chair. Dept of Physiology 2006–; mem. NAS 2004, American Acad. of Arts and Sciences 2005; Eloranta Research Fellow, MIT 1976, Grad. Studies Award, Univ. of California 1981, Jane Coffin Childs Postdoctoral Fellow 1984, March of Dimes Basil O'Connor Research Award 1990, PEW Scholars Award in the Biomedical Sciences 1990, NSF Presidential Young Investigator Award 1990, McKnight Neuroscience Foundation Scholars Award 1990, Numa Memorial Lecturer, Kyoto Univ., Japan 1996, McKnight Neuroscience Foundation Investigator Award 1997, Syntex Prize in Receptor Pharmacology 1997, Sir Lewis Thomas Pain Lecturer, Univ. Coll. London 1997, Presidential Lecturer, Soc. for Neuroscience 1998, Sandler Award in Basic Science, UCSF 1998, Brook Byers Award in Basic Science, Univ. of California, San Francisco 1998, Louis S. Harris Distinguished Lecturer, Medical Coll. of Virginia 1999, S.W. Kuffler Lecturer, Dept of Neurobiology, Harvard Medical School 2000, First Perl-UNC Neuroscience Prize 2001, Jacob Javits Award NIH/Nat. Inst. of Neurological Disorders and Stroke 2003, Yngve Zoterman Prize, Physiological Soc., Stockholm, Sweden 2003, Frederick W.L. Kerr Basic Research Award, American Pain Soc. 2006, K.L. Zulch Prize for Basic Neurological Research, Max Planck Soc. (co-recipient) 2006, Edward M. Scolnick Prize in Neuroscience, McGovern Inst. for Brain Research, MIT 2007, W. Alden Spencer Award, Columbia Univ. Center for Neurobiology and Behavior (co-recipient) 2007, Inaugural Julius Axelrod Prize, Soc. for Neuroscience (co-recipient) 2007, Unilever Science Prize 2007, Passano Award 2010, Shaw Prize in Life Sciences and Medicine (co-recipient) 2010, Prince of Asturias Award in Tech. and Scientific Research 2010. *Publications:* more than 100 papers in professional journals. *Address:* Department of Physiology, University of California, San Francisco, Mail Code 2140, Genentech Hall, Room N-272E, 600 16th Street, San Francisco, CA 94158-2140, USA (office). *Telephone:* (415) 476-0431 (office); (415) 476-0432 (lab.) (office). *Fax:* (415) 502-8644 (office). *E-mail:* david.julius@ucsf.edu (office). *Website:* profiles.ucsf.edu/david.julius (office); physio.ucsf.edu/julius (office).

JULIUS, Dame DeAnne Shirley, DCMG, CBE, PhD; American/British economist; b. 14 April 1949; d. of Marvin Julius; m. Ian A. Harvey 1976; one s. one d.; ed Iowa State Univ. and Univ. of California, Davis; Econ. Adviser for Energy, World Bank 1975–82; Man. Dir Logan Assocs, Inc. 1983–86; Dir of Econs, Royal Inst. of Int. Affairs (RIIA), Chatham House), London 1986–89, Chair. RIIA 2003–12; Chief

Economist, Shell International Petroleum Co., London 1989–93, British Airways 1993–97; Founder-mem. Monetary Policy Cttee, Bank of England 1997–2001, Dir Bank of England Court 2001–04; Chair. British Airways Pension Investment Man. Ltd 1995–97; Dir (non-exec.) Lloyds TSB 2001–07, BP (British Petroleum) 2001–, Serco Group 2001–, Roche 2002–, Jones Lang LaSalle 2008–, Deloitte (UK); Dr hc (Warwick) 2000, (South Bank) 2001, (Bath) 2002, (Birmingham) 2006. *Publications include:* The Economics of Natural Gas 1990, Global Companies and Public Policy: The Growing Challenge of Foreign Direct Investment 1990, Is Manufacturing Still Special in the New World Order? (co-author) (Amex Bank Prize) 1993; numerous articles on int. econs. *Leisure interests:* skiing, windsurfing, bonsai. *Address:* c/o Chatham House, 10 St James's Square, London, SW1Y 4LE, England.

JULLIEN, François, DèsSc; French academic; *Professor of Philosophy, University de Paris VII-Denis Diderot;* b. 2 June 1951, Embrun, Hautes-Alpes; s. of Raymond Jullien and Marie Cler; m. Odile Sournies 1974; one s. two d.; ed Ecole normale supérieure, Univs of Peking and Shanghai, China, Univ. Paris-Sorbonne; Head French Sinology Unit, Hong Kong 1978–81; Resident Maison franco-japonaise, Tokyo 1985–87; Sr Lecturer, Univ. de Paris VIII-Saint-Denis 1981–87, Prof. 1987–90; Prof. Univ. de Paris VII-Denis Diderot 1990–, Dir l'UFR Asie orientale 1990–2000; Pres. Asscn française des études chinoises 1988–90; Pres. Collège Int. de philosophie 1995–98; Dir Oriental collection, Presses Univ. de France (PUF), Dir Inst. de la Pensée Contemporaine, des collections Orientales et Libelles, currently Dir Agenda de la Pensée Contemporaine, PUF, Dir Centre Marcel Granet; sr mem. Inst. Universitaire de France 2001–; mem. Editorial Cttee Critique journal. *Publications:* Fleurs du matin cueillies le soir 1976, Sous le dais fleuri 1978 (both translations of the Chinese texts of Lu Xun), La Valeur allusive 1985, Procès ou création 1989, Eloge de la fadeur 1991, La Propension des choses 1992, Figures de l'immanence 1993, Le Détour et l'accès 1995, Fonder la morale 1995, Traité de l'efficacité 1997, Un sage est sans idée ou l'autre de la philosophie 1998, De l'essence ou du nu 2000, Penser d'un dehors (la Chine) 2000, Du "temps": éléments d'une philosophie du vivre 2001, La Grande image n'a pas de forme 2003 (trans. into Vietnamese, Italian, Castillian, German), L'Ombre au tableau 2004, Nourrir sa vie, à l'écart du bonheur 2005, Conférence sur l'efficacité 2005. *Address:* Université Paris VII-Denis Diderot, 2 place Jussieu, 75251 Paris Cedex 05 (office); 8 rue Tournefort, 75005 Paris, France (home). *Telephone:* 1-44-27-82-95 (office).

JUMAGULOV, Apas; Kyrgyzstani diplomatist, politician and business executive; b. Sept. 1934, Arashan; s. of Jumagul Jumagulov; ed Moscow Inst. of the Petrochemical and Gas Industry; began working as geologist in state oil industry; actively participated in activities of local CP br.; Chief Engineer, Kyrgyzneft (state oil and gas co.)–1973; apptd Head of Industry and Transportation Dept, Cen. Cttee of CP of Kyrgyz SSR 1973; later took on several other admin. posts at regional and nat. levels; Head of Govt of Kyrgyzia 1986–91; nominated himself as a cand. in presidential elections 1990; Admin. Head of his native region of Chui Oblast 1990–93; Prime Minister 1993–98 (retd); Amb. to Germany 1998–2003, also accred to Holy See and Scandinavian countries 1999–2003; withdrew from politics and became intermediary and consultant; Chair. Moscow br. of Postnoff co. 2003–; entered leadership ranks of Eurasian Movt 2004–; Amb. to Russian Fed. 2005–07; Order of Merit (Germany) 2003. *Address:* c/o Ministry of Foreign Affairs, 720040 Bishkek, bul. Erkindik 57, Kyrgyzstan.

JUN, Ho-suck, MA; South Korean automobile industry executive; *President and CEO, Hyundai Mobis;* ed Grad. School of Cranfield Univ., UK; fmr Vice-Pres. Hyundai Motor Co. Ltd, Pres. and CEO Hyundai Mobis 2011–, Pres. and CEO Hyundai Motor Group 2011–, CEO Beijing Mobis Transmission Co. Ltd. *Address:* Hyundai Mobis, 679-4 Seoul International Tower, Seoul 135-977, South Korea (office). *Telephone:* (2) 20185114 (office). *Fax:* (2) 20186000 (office). *E-mail:* info@mobis.co.kr (office). *Website:* www.mobis.co.kr (office).

JUNCKER, Jean-Claude, LLM; Luxembourg politician; b. 9 Dec. 1954, Redange-sur-Attert; s. of Jos Juncker and Marguerite Hecker; m. Christiane Frising 1979; ed Univ. of Strasbourg; Parl. Sec. to Christian Social Party 1979–82; Sec. of State for Labour and Social Affairs 1982–84; mem. Chamber of Deputies 1984–; Minister of Labour, Minister in charge of Budget 1984–89; Minister of Labour, of Finance 1989–94; Prime Minister of Luxembourg 1995–2013, also Minister of State, of Finance and the Treasury, of Labour and Employment 1995–99, of State and of Finance 1999–2009, Minister of the Treasury 2009–13; Chair. Christian Social Party 1990–95; Chair. Social Affairs and Budget Councils 1985; Gov. IBRD 1989–95, fmr Gov. IMF, EBRD; elected first Perm. Pres. Eurogroup 2005; Foreign Assoc. mem. Acad. of Ethics and Political Science, Inst. of France 2007–; Hon. Citizen of Trier 2003, Hon. Senator, European Acad. of Sciences and Arts 2009; Grand Officier, Légion d'honneur 2002; Dr hc (Münster) 2001, (Bucharest) 2003, (Demokritos Univ. of Thrace) 2004, (Robert Schuman Univ., Strasbourg) 2007, (Pittsburgh) 2008, (Sophia Univ., Tokyo) 2010, (Medizinische Universität, Innsbruck) 2011, (Athens) 2011; Int. Karlspreis, Aachen 2006. *Leisure interest:* reading. *Address:* Chamber of Deputies, Hôtel de la Chambre des Députés, 19 rue du Marché-aux-Herbes, 1728 Luxembourg, Luxembourg (office). *Telephone:* 466-966-1 (office). *Fax:* 22-02-301 (office). *E-mail:* info@chd.lu (office). *Website:* www.chd.lu (office).

JUNG, Andrea, BA; American retail executive; *Chairman and CEO, Avon Products Inc.;* b. (Zhong Binxian), 18 Sept. 1958, Toronto, Canada; eldest child of Chinese immigrants; m. 2nd Michael Gould (divorced); one adopted s. one d. from previous m.; ed Princeton Univ.; grew up in Wellesley, Mass; joined man. trainee programme at Bloomingdale's 1979; fmr Sr Vice-Pres. Gen. Merchandising, I. Magnin, San Francisco; Exec. Vice-Pres. Neiman Marcus –1994; consultant for Avon Products 1993, Pres. Product Marketing Group Marketing, Avon US 1994–96, Sr Vice-Pres. Global Marketing, Avon Products Inc. 1996–97, mem. Bd of Dirs 1998–, Pres. and COO 1998–2000, CEO 1999–, Chair. 2001–; Chair. The Cosmetic, Toiletry and Fragrance Asscn (first woman) 2001–05; mem. Bd of Dirs Gen. Electric Co. 1998–, Princeton Univ., Fashion Inst. of Tech., Fragrance Foundation, Cosmetic Exec. Women, Sales Corpn Donna Karan Int., Catalyst, Apple 2008–; mem. Int. Advisory Council, Salomon Smith Barney; Trustee New York Presbyterian Hosp.; ranked by Fortune magazine amongst 50 Most Powerful Women in Business in the US 1998–2001, (fifth) 2002, (third) 2003–04, (fifth) 2005, (seventh) 2006, (ninth) 2007, (sixth) 2008, (fifth) 2009–10, (sixth) 2011, named by Ladies Home Journal as one of the 30 Most Powerful Women in America 2001, named by BusinessWeek magazine as one of Best Managers of the Year 2003,

ranked by Forbes magazine amongst The World's 100 Most Powerful Women (61st) 2004, (35th) 2005, (37th) 2006, (30th) 2007, (19th) 2008, (25th) 2009, (57th) 2010, (64th) 2011, named by Newsweek magazine as one of 10 Prominent People to Watch in 2005 2004, ranked third by The Wall Street Journal amongst its 50 Women to Watch in Business 2005, Clinton Global Citizen Award for the corp. sector 2010. *Leisure interest:* playing the piano. *Address:* Avon Products Inc. Headquarters, 1345 Avenue of the Americas, New York, NY 10105-0302, USA (office). *Telephone:* (800) 367-2866 (office). *Website:* www.avoncompany.com (office).

JUNG, Franz Josef, DJur; German lawyer and politician; b. 5 March 1949, Erbach, Rheingau-Taunus Dist, Hesse; m.; three c.; ed Rheingau School, Geisenheim, Univ. of Mainz; legal training at Wiesbaden Dist Court 1974–76; solicitor in Eltville 1976–; public notary 1983–; mem. Dist Ass. of Rheingau-Taunus 1972–87; mem. Nat. Exec., CDU German Youth Union 1973–93, Vice-Chair. 1981–83; elected to Hessen State Parl. (Landtag), Wiesbaden 1983–2005; Hessian State Minister for Fed. and European Affairs and Head of Hessian State Chancellory 1999–2000; Gen. Sec. of CDU in Hessen 1987–91, CDU Parl. Sec., Hessen Landtag 1987–99; CDU Parl. Whip in Hessen Landtag 2003–05; mem. CDU Nat. Exec. Cttee 1998–; elected to Fed. Parl. (Bundestag), Berlin 2005–; Federal Minister of Defence 2005–09, of Labour and Social Affairs Oct.–Nov. 2009 (resgnd); Chair. Producers' Asscn Research Inst. of Geisenheim 1999, Friends of ZDF TV 2002; mem. Rheingau Music Festival Cttee 1989–, ZDF TV Advisory Bd 1999, Eintracht Frankfurt e.V. Man. Bd 1999, Eintracht Frankfurt AG Supervisory Bd 2003–05. *Address:* Bundestag (Federal Assembly) Platz der Republik 1, 11011 Berlin, Germany (office). *Telephone:* (30) 22775447 (office). *Fax:* (30) 22776447 (office). *E-mail:* franz-josef.jung@bundestag.de. *Website:* www.bundestag.de (office); www.franz-josef-jung.de (office).

JUNG, Man-won, BA, MBA; South Korean energy industry executive; *Vice-Chairman, SK Telecom Company, Ltd;* ed Yonsei Univ., New York Univ., USA; served in Korean Ministry of Energy and Resources 1980–94; consultant, SKC Chemical Business Group (fmrly Yukong Oxichemical) 1994–96, Vice-Pres. Man. and Planning Office 1996–2000, Vice-Pres. SK Customer Service Devt Div. 2000–01, Vice-Pres. Wireless Internet Business Div. Group and Finance Business Div., SK Telecom 2001–02, Pres. SK Global Energy Sales Group and Head SK Global Normalization Process Task Force 2002–03, Pres. and CEO SK Networks 2003–08, Pres. and CEO SK Telecom 2009–10, Vice-Chair. 2010–. *Address:* SK Telecom Company, Ltd, 11 Eulijiro, 2-ga, Jung-gu, Seoul 100-999, Republic of Korea (office). *Telephone:* (2) 6100-2114 (office). *Fax:* (2) 6100-7827 (office). *Website:* www.sktelecom.com (office).

JUNG, Roland Tadeusz, BChir, MA, MB, MD, FRCP, FRCPE; British physician; b. 1948, Glasgow; m.; one d.; ed Pembroke Coll., Cambridge, St Thomas' Hosp. Medical School, London; MRC Clinical Scientist, Dunn Nutrition Unit, Cambridge 1977–80; Sr Registrar, Royal Postgrad. Medical School, London 1980–82; Consultant Physician, Ninewells Hosp. and Medical School, Dundee 1982–91, Clinical Dir of Medicine 1991–94; Dir Tayside Research & Devt NHS Consortium, Dundee 1997–2000; Chair. Scottish Hosp. Endowments Research Trust 2000–01; Chief Scientist, Scottish Exec. Health Dept 2001–07 (retd); mem. Innogen Centre Advisory Cttee; Sr Distinction Advisor, Eastern Region for Scottish Advisory Cttee for Distinction Award 2004; Card Medal, Asscn of Physicians of GB and Ireland 1987. *Publications:* Endocrine Problems in Oncology 1984, Colour Atlas of Obesity 1990. *Leisure interest:* gardening, walking, reading, visiting gardens. *Address:* c/o Innogen Centre Advisory Committee, ESRC Innogen Centre, Technology Faculty, Development Policy and Practice Group, The Open University, Walton Hall, Milton Keynes, MK7 6AA, England.

JUNG, Yeon-joo, BBA; South Korean business executive; *President and CEO, Samsung C&T Corporation;* ed Dong-guk Univ., Advanced Man. Program, Stanford Univ., USA; fmr Vice-Pres., later Exec. Vice-Pres. and Chief Financial Officer, Samsung SDI Co. Ltd, Dir, Samsung Engineering Co. Ltd, Pres. and CEO –2010, fmr Dir of Finance and Accounting Div., Samsung C&T Corpn, mem. Bd of Dirs 2010–, Pres. and CEO Samsung C&T Corpn 2011–. *Address:* Samsung C&T Corporation, 310 Taepyeong-Ro 1 Ga, Jung-Gu, Seoul, Republic of Korea (office). *Telephone:* (2) 2145-2114 (office). *Fax:* (2) 2145-3114 (office). *E-mail:* info@samsungcorp.com (office). *Website:* www.samsungcorp.com (office).

JÜNGEL, Eberhard Klaus, DTheol; German professor of theology and philosophy; b. 5 Dec. 1934, Magdeburg; s. of Kurt Jüngel and Margarete Jüngel (née Rothemann); ed Humboldtschule, Magdeburg, Katechetisches Oberseminar, Naumburg/Saale, Kirchliche Hochschule, Berlin and Univs of Zürich and Basel, Switzerland; asst, Kirchliche Hochschule (Sprachenkonvikt), East Berlin 1959–61, Lecturer in New Testament 1961–63, Lecturer in Systematic Theology 1963–66; ordained priest of the Evangelical Church 1962; Prof. of Systematic Theology and History of Dogma, Univ. of Zürich 1966–69; Prof. of Systematic Theology and Philosophy of Religion and Dir Inst. für Hermeneutik, Univ. of Tübingen 1969–2003, Dean, Faculty of Evangelical Theology 1970–72, 1992–94; Ephorus Evangelisches Stift, Tübingen 1987–2005; Guest Prof. of Systematic Theology, Univ. of Halle-Wittenberg 1990–93, Univ. of Berlin 1994, 1999–2000; various appointments within Evangelical Church, etc.; mem. Heidelberg and Norwegian Acads, Academia Scientiarum et Artium Europaea, Salzburg, Akad. der Wissenschaften, Göttingen; Fellow, Inst. for Advanced Study, Berlin; Officier, Ordre pour le Mérite 1992, Grosses Verdienstkreuz mit Stern des Verdienstordens 1994, Verdienstmedaille des Landes Baden-Württemberg; Hon. DD (Aberdeen) 1985; Dr hc (Greifswald) 2000, (Basel) 2000; Karl Barth Prize 1986. *Publications:* more than 20 books including Paulus und Jesus 1962, Gottes Sein ist im Werden 1965, Unterwegs zur Sache 1972, Gott als Geheimnis der Welt 1977, Entsprechungen 1980, Glauben und Verstehen, Zum Theologiebegriff Rudolf Bultmanns 1985, Wertlose Wahrheit. Zur Identität und Relevanz des christlichen Glaubens 1990, Das Evangelium von der Rechtfertigung des Gottlosen als Zentrum des Glaubens 1998, Indikative der Gnade-Imperative der Freiheit 2000, Ed. Religion in Geschichte und Gegenwart and seven vols of sermons. *Address:* c/o Institut für Hermeneutik, Liebermeisterstrasse 12, 72076 Tübingen (office); Schwabstrasse 51, 72074 Tübingen, Germany (home).

JUNGERIUS, Pieter Dirk, DSc; Dutch professor of geography; *Professor, Institute for Biodiversity and Ecosystem Dynamics, University of Amsterdam;* b.

10 June 1933, Rÿnsburg; ed Gymnasium B, Leiden and Univ. of Amsterdam; Asst Univ. of Amsterdam 1955–59; Scientific Officer, Soil Survey of England and Wales 1959–63; on secondment to Soil and Land Use Survey, Ghana 1959, Ministry of Agric. E Nigeria 1960–63; Sr Lecturer in Physical Geography, Univ. of Amsterdam 1963–70; seasonal staff mem. Ministry of Mines and Tech. Surveys, Canada 1965–67; Prof., Inst. for Biodiversity and Ecosystem Dynamics, Univ. of Amsterdam 1970–; mem. Royal Netherlands Acad. of Sciences 1987. *Publications:* Soil Evidence of Tree Line Fluctuations, Alberta, Canada 1969, Quarternary Landscape Developments, Río Magdalena, Colombia 1976, Soils and Geomorphology 1985, Perception and Use of the Physical Environment in Peasant Societies 1986, Dunes of the European Coast: Geomorphology, Hydrology, Soils. *Address:* Institute for Biodiversity and Ecosystem Dynamics (IBED), POSTBUS 94248, 1090 GE Amsterdam, Netherlands (office). *Telephone:* (20) 5257451 (office). *Fax:* (20) 5257832 (office). *E-mail:* P.D.Jungerius@uva.nl (office). *Website:* www.science .uva.nl/ibed/home.cfm (office).

JUNIPER, Tony, BSc, MSc; British environmental campaigner, ecologist and environmental writer; b. 24 Sept. 1960, Oxford; s. of the late Austin Wilfred Juniper and Constance Margaret Elliston; m. Sue Sparkes; three c.; ed Univ. of Bristol, Univ. Coll. London; began career with Birdlife Int. (conservation network); joined Friends of the Earth 1990, fmr campaigns and policy Dir, Dir Ilisu Dam campaign, Vice-Chair. Friends of the Earth International 2000–08, Exec. Dir Friends of the Earth, England, Wales and NI 2003–08; Founding Bd mem. Stop Climate Chaos 2005–; Special Adviser to Prince of Wales' Rainforest Project; Sr Assoc., Univ. of Cambridge Programme for Industry; sits on several advisory panels. *Publications:* Deserts of Trees: The Environmental and Social Impacts of Large-scale Tropical Reforestation in Response to Global Climate Change (co-author) 1992, Whose Hand on the Chainsaw? UK Government Policy and the Tropical Rainforests (co-author) 1992, Wildlife Bill 1995, Threatened Planet 1996, Parrots: A Guide to Parrots of the World (Juniper and Parr) (McColvin Medal for Outstanding Work of Reference, Library Asscn 1999) 1998, Spix's Macaw: The Race to Save the World's Rarest Bird 2002, How Many Light Bulbs Does It Take to Change A Planet? 2007, Saving Planet Earth 2007, Harmony: A New Way of Looking at the World (with HRH The Prince of Wales and Ian Skelly) 2010. *Leisure interests:* natural history, fishing, walking, writing. *Address:* c/o Friends of the Earth, 26–28 Underwood Street, London, N1 7JQ, England (office). *Website:* www .tonyjuniper.com.

JUPPÉ, Alain Marie; French politician; b. 15 Aug. 1945, Mont-de-Marsan, Landes; s. of Robert Juppé and Marie Juppé (née Darroze); m. 1st Christine Leblond 1965; one s. one d.; m. 2nd Isabelle Legrand-Bodin 1993; one d.; ed Lycée Louis-le-Grand, Paris, Ecole normale supérieure, Inst. d'études politiques, Paris and Ecole Nat. d'Admin; Insp. of Finance 1972; Office of Prime Minister Jacques Chirac (q.v.) June–Aug. 1976; tech. adviser, Office of Minister of Cooperation 1976–78; Nat. del. of RPR 1976–78, Nat. Sec. of RPR with responsibility for econ. and social recovery 1984–88, Sec.-Gen. 1988–95, Acting Pres. 1994–95, Pres. 1995–97; tech. adviser, Office of Mayor of Paris (Jacques Chirac) 1978; Dir-Gen. with responsibility for finance and econ. affairs, Commune de Paris 1980; Councillor, 18th arrondissement, Paris 1983–95; Second Asst to Mayor of Paris in charge of budget and financial affairs 1983–95; Deputy to Nat. Ass. from Paris 1988–97, from Gironde 1997–; Mayor of Bordeaux 1995–2001, 2001–04, 2006–; mem. European Parl. 1984–86, 1989–93; Deputy to Minister of Economy, Finance and Privatization with responsibility for budget 1986–88; Minister of Foreign Affairs 1993–95; Prime Minister of France 1995–97; convicted of mishandling public funds 2004, received 18-month suspended jail sentence (later reduced on appeal); Pres. Union pour la majorité presidentielle (UMP) 2002–04 (resgnd); Minister of State for Ecology and Sustainable Devt May–June 2007; Minister of Defence and Veterans' Affairs 2010–11, of Foreign and European Affairs 2011–12; Grand Officier, Légion d'honneur 2009, Grand Cross of Merit, Sovereign Order of Malta. *Publications:* La Tentation de Venise 1993, Entre Nous 1996, Montesquieu, Le moderne 1999, Entre quatre z'yeux (with Serge July) France mon pays – Lettres d'un voyageur 2006, Je ne mangerai plus de cerises en hiver 2009. *Address:* c/o Ministry of Foreign Affairs, 37 quai d'Orsay, 75351 Paris Cedex 07, France. *Website:* www.al1jup.com.

JURGENSEN, William G. (Jerry), BCom, MBA; American insurance industry executive; m. Patty Jurgensen; two c.; ed Creighton Univ., Omaha, Neb.; 17 years with Norwest Corpn, various man. positions including Pres. and CEO, Norwest Investment Services and later Exec. Vice-Pres., Corp. Banking; Man. First Chicago NBD Corpn –1998, Exec. Vice-Pres. Bank One Corpn (following merger) 1998–2000; CEO Nationwide Mutual Insurance Co. 2000–09; mem. Bd Dirs Achieve, Inc., ConAgra Foods, Inc., The Scotts Miracle-Gro Co.; Dir Greater Columbus Chamber of Commerce, Law Enforcement Foundation of Ohio, Nation-wide Children's Hosp.; Chair. Gov.'s Comm. on Teaching Success 2001–03; Chair. 2002 Campaign for United Way of Cen. Ohio; Co-Chair. Ohio Gov.'s Public-Pvt. Collaborative Comm.; mem. Columbus Downtown Devt Corpn, Ohio Business Roundtable, Financial Services Roundtable, Columbus Partnership, Ohio State Univ. Hosp., Business Higher Educ. Forum; Trustee, Loyola Univ., Newberry Library. *Address:* c/o Office of the Chairman, The Scotts Miracle-Gro Co., 14111 Scottslawn Road, Marysville, OH 43041, USA (office). *Telephone:* (937) 644-0011 (office). *Fax:* (937) 644-7614 (office). *E-mail:* info@scotts.com (office). *Website:* www .scotts.com (office).

JURKOVIĆ, Pero, PhD; Croatian economist, academic and fmr central banker; b. 4 June 1936, Brštanica, Neum, Bosnia and Herzegovina; ed Univs of Sarajevo, Skopje and Zagreb; chief accountant in construction materials industry, Neretva, Čapljina 1956–57; Officer for Planning, Municipality of Čapljina 1960–61, Chief Officer for Agric. 1961–63; Dir Inst. of Economy, Mostar 1963–67; Assoc. to Adviser, Econ. Inst., Zagreb, also Assoc. Prof., Foreign Trade School and Faculties of Econs Zagreb and Mostar 1967–80; Prof., Faculty of Econs, Zagreb 1980–92; Gov. Nat. Bank of Croatia 1992–96; apptd Chief Econ. Adviser to Pres. of Croatia 1997; currently lectures at Univ. of Zagreb Grad. School of Econs and Business; mem. Int. Inst. for Financing, Saarbrücken, Int. Asscn of Economists; Guest Lecturer, Univs of Rotterdam, London, Lexington and Florida; B. Adžija and M. Mirkovic awards. *Publications:* more than 150 publs including System of Public Financing (with Ksente Bogoev) 1977, Introduction to the Theory of Economic Policy 1984, Fundamentals of the

Economics of Public Services 1987, Commercial Finances 1987, Fiscal Policy 1989. *Address:* University of Zagreb Graduate School of Economics and Business, Room 101, Trg. J.F. Kennedy 6, 10000 Zagreb, Croatia (office). *Telephone:* (1) 238-3199 (office). *Fax:* (1) 233-5633 (office). *E-mail:* pero.jurkovic@ efzg.hr (office). *Website:* www.efzg.hr (office).

JUROWSKI, Vladimir; Russian conductor; *Principal Conductor, London Philharmonic Orchestra;* b. 4 April 1972, Moscow; ed Music Acad., Berlin and Dresden, Germany; Chief Conductor, Sibelius Orchestra, Berlin 1993–96; Founder and Conductor, United Berlin ensemble, performing modern music; int. debut conducting May Night by Rimsky-Korsakov, Wexford Festival 1995; fmr Prin. Guest Conductor, Orchestra Sinfonica Verdi, Milan; Prin. Guest Conductor, Teatro Comunale, Bologna 2001; Music Dir, Glyndebourne Festival Opera 2001–07, Glyndebourne Opera 2001–13; Prin. Guest Conductor, London Philharmonic Orchestra 2003–06, Prin. Conductor 2007–; Prin. Guest Conductor, Russian Nat. Orchestra 2006–09; Prin. Artist, Orchestra of the Age of Enlight-enment; Artistic Dir, Russian State Academic Symphony Orchestra 2011–; has conducted in major venues world-wide, including Metropolitan Opera (New York), Opera Bastille (Paris), Komische Oper (Berlin), Teatro Comunale (Bologna), Teatro Real (Madrid), Royal Opera House (London), and with Chicago Symphony, Philadelphia, Berlin Philharmonic, Mahler Chamber Orchestras, Chamber Orchestra of Europe, Tonhalle-orchester Zurich, Gewandhausorchester Leipzig and Staatskapelle Dresden; Royal Philharmonic Soc. Conductor Award 2007. *Recordings include:* Stravinsky's The Rake's Progress (with London Philharmonic Orchestra and Glyndebourne Chorus), Complete Symphonies of Brahms (with London Philharmonic Orchestra); DVD releases: La Cerentola, Gianni Schicchi, Die Fledermaus, Don Giovanni (Glyndebourne Festival Opera), Hansel und Gretel (Metropolitan Opera of New York). *Address:* c/o IMG Artists, The Light Box, 111 Power Road, London, W4 5PY, England (office); London Philharmonic Orchestra, 89 Albert Embankment, London, SE1 7TP, England (office). *Telephone:* (20) 7957-5800 (office). *Fax:* (20) 7957-5801 (office). *E-mail:* nmathias@imgartists.com (office). *Website:* www.imgartists.com (office); www.lpo .co.uk (office).

JURŠĖNAS, Česlovas, Lithuanian journalist, editor and politician; b. 18 May 1938, Panižiškėje village, Švenčioniai Co. (now Ignalina Dist); m. Jadvyga Juršenas; one s.; ed Ignalina Secondary School, Vilnius Univ., Higher Party School, Leningrad (now St Petersburg); awarded journalist diploma 1960, worked as journalist for 15 years, first in editorial offices of weekly newspaper Statyba (Construction) and daily newspaper Tiesa (Truth), int. reviewer at Lithuania Radio and Television from 1964, Ed.-in-Chief TV Information broadcasts, later edited TV programme Atgimimo Banga (Wave of Revival) and other broadcasts; worked at Cen. Cttee and Council of Ministers of Lithuanian CP 1973–78; Head of editorial office of Vakarinės Naujienos (Evening News) 1978–83; first Press Officer for Govt of Lithuania 1989; with others, signed Act on the Re-establishment of the State of the Repub. of Lithuania 11 March 1990; stood for elections as ind. cand. of LCP, worked in Comm. on State Re-establishment and the Constitution, elected to Supreme Council – Reconstituent Seimas 1990–92, elected Deputy Elder of the Parl. 1992, mem. Seimas (Parl.) for Ignalina-Švenčioniai single-member constitu-ency No. 53 1992–, Deputy Chair. 6th Seimas, later Chair., Deputy Chair. 8th Seimas 2000–02, First Deputy Chair. 2002–04, July–Nov. 2004, Acting Chair. Seimas April–July 2004, Speaker of the Seimas 2008; mem. Council of Švenčioniai Dist 1997–2000; active participant in separation of LCP from CPSU and ind. reorganization of LCP; mem. Presidium of LDLP Council 1990–, Chair. of party 1996–2001, First Deputy Chair. Lithuanian Social Democratic Party (LSDP— Lietuvos Socialdemokratų Partija) following unification of Social Democrats (SDPL) and LDLP 2001–; mem. Journalists' Union of Lithuania; mem. Editorial Science Council of the Lithuanian General Encyclopaedia and the Courts Council; Pres. Lithuanian Chess Fed.; Citizen of Honour of the Švenčioniai Dist; Grand Cross of the Order of Vytautas the Great 2004; Dr hc (Univ. of Lithuania); Gold Medal, Ignalina Secondary School. *Publications:* has published several books on politics and world affairs. *Leisure interests:* playing chess, collecting writings and caricatures of famous contemporary politicians. *Address:* Seimas, 01109 Vilnius, Gedimino pr. 53, Lithuania (office). *Telephone:* (5) 239-6626 (office). *Fax:* (5) 239-6077 (office). *E-mail:* Ceslovas.Jursenas@lrs.lt (office); cejurs@lrs.lt (office). *Website:* www.lrs.lt (office).

JUSKO, Marián, DPhil; Slovak fmr central banker and business executive; b. 24 March 1956, Prešov; m.; one c.; ed Univ. of Econs, Bratislava; Lecturer, Univ. of Econs, Bratislava 1979–90, Adviser, Slovak Nat. Council 1990; Head of Banking Analyses and Prognoses, State Bank of Czechoslovakia 1991; Deputy Minister, Ministry of Admin. and Privatization of Nat. Property of Slovak Repub.; Chair. Nat. Property Fund 1991–92; mem. man. team State Bank of Czechoslovakia for Slovakia, Bratislava 1992; Vice-Gov. Nat. Bank of Slovakia 1993–99, Gov. 1999–2004; Chair. Slovnaft, a.s. 2005–09; Pres. Republic Union of Employers, Slovakia 2007–; mem. Academic Bd Univ. of Econs, Bratislava 2000–, Comenius Univ., Bratislava 2002–. *Address:* c/o Slovnaft a.s., Vlčie hrdlo 1, 824 12 Bratislava, Slovakia (office).

JUSYS, Oskaras, BA, MA, DPhil; Lithuanian diplomatist and civil servant; *Director, United Nations, International Organizations and Human Rights Department, Ministry of Foreign Affairs;* b. 13 Jan. 1954, Anyksciai Region; m. Roma Jusys; one s.; ed Vilnius Univ. Law School, M. Lomonosov Univ. Law School, Moscow, Columbia Univ. Law School; Sr Lecturer, Faculty of Law, Vilnius Univ. 1981–1985, Assoc. Prof. 1986–90; Scientific Scholarship, IREX Exchange Programme, Law School, Columbia Univ., New York, USA 1985–86; Dir Legal Dept, Ministry of Foreign Affairs 1990–92, Counsellor to Minister of Foreign Affairs 1993–94; Amb., Perm. Rep. of Lithuania to UN 1994–2000; Deputy Minister of Foreign Affairs 2000–01; Perm. Rep. to EU 2001–05; at Ministry of Foreign Affairs 2005–09; Amb. to UK 2009–12; Dir UN, Int. Orgs and Human Rights Dept, Ministry of Foreign Affairs 2012–; Dir Lithuanian Br. of US law firm McDermott, Will & Emery 1993–94. *Leisure interests:* jazz, basketball. *Address:* Ministry of Foreign Affairs, J. Tumo-Vaižganto g. 2, 01511 Vilnius, Lithuania (office). *Telephone:* (5) 236-2444 (office). *Fax:* (5) 231-3090 (office). *E-mail:* urm@ urm.lt (office). *Website:* www.urm.lt (office).

JUVENALY, Metropolitan (Vladimir Poyarkov); Russian ecclesiastic; b. 22 Sept. 1935, Yaroslavl; ed Leningrad Seminary, Moscow Theological Acad.;

hieromonk 1960; Sec. Dept of Foreign Relations, Moscow Patriarchy 1960; teacher, Moscow Seminary 1961–62; Ed. Golos Pravoslavia (magazine) 1962–63; Dean Russian Orthodox Church in West Berlin 1962–63; ordained as archimandrite 1963; Chief Russian Holy Mission in Jerusalem 1963–64; Deputy Chair. Dept of Foreign Relations, Moscow Patriarchy 1964–72, Chair. 1972–81; consecrated Bishop 1965; Bishop of Zaraisk, Vicar of Moscow Diocese 1965–69; Bishop of Tula and Belev, Archbishop, Metropolitan 1969–77; Perm. mem. Holy Synod 1972–; Metropolitan of Krutitsy and Kolomna 1977–; Chair. Synodal Comm. on Canonization of Saints; Hon. Citizen of Moscow region, Podolsk, Kolomna, Dmitrov; Hon. mem. Leningrad (now St Petersburg) Theological Seminary 1973–, Moscow Theological Seminary 1974–; Order of Peoples' Friendship 1985, Order of Honour 2000, Order of Services to the Fatherland (IV) 2006 and (III) 2010, numerous other state and church decorations. *Publications:* numerous articles in Journal of Moscow Patriarchate. *Address:* Moscow Diocese, 119435 Moscow, Novodevichy Proezd 1/1, Russia (home). *Telephone:* (495) 246-08-81 (home).

JUWAILI, Col Osama al-; Libyan politician and fmr army officer; b. 1961; ed Tripoli Mil. Acad.; Lecturer, Tripoli Mil. Acad. –1987; resgnd from army (rank of Capt.) 1992; fmr Head of Vocational Guidance Centre, Yifrin (part of Ministry of Workforce and Training); defected to anti-Gaddafi forces during 2011 uprising; Head of Military Council, Zintan 2011; Minister of Defence 2011–12. *Address:* c/o Ministry of Defence, Tripoli, Libya (office).

JYOTI, Roop, MBA MPA; Nepalese business executive and fmr politician; *Vice-Chairman, Jyoti Group;* b. Sept. 1948; s. of the late Shri Maniharsha Jyoti; ed Indian Inst. of Tech., Bombay, Harvard Univ.; qualified as chemical engineer; exec. positions at several Jyoti Group enterprises (family-owned), then Vice-Chair. (following death of his father); fmrly Nat. Adviser to Resident Rep. of UNDP in Nepal; mem. Tariff Bd, Govt of Nepal; Minister of Finance 2005–06; mem. Senate, TribhuvanUniv.;mem.Trust of Nepal Vipassana Centre. *Address:* Jyoti Group, Jyoti Bhawan, Kantipath, Kathmandu, Nepal (office). *E-mail:* info@jyotigroup.org (office). *Website:* www.jyotigroup.org (office).

JYRÄNKI, Antero, DIur; Finnish professor of constitutional law; *Professor Emeritus, University of Turku;* b. 9 Aug. 1933, Hamina; two s. one d.; ed Univ. of Helsinki; Assoc. Prof. of Public Law, Univ. of Tampere 1966–70; Gen. Sec. to the Pres. of the Repub. 1970–73; Sr Research Fellow, Acad. of Finland 1974–77; Vice-Chair., Comm. on the Revision of the Constitution 1970–74; Assoc. Prof. of Public Law, Univ. of Tampere 1977–79; Prof. of Constitutional and Int. Law, Univ. of Turku 1980–98, Dean, Law Faculty 1981–83, 1991–93; Research Prof., Acad. of Finland 1983–87; Pres. Finnish Asscn of Constitutional Law 1982–88; mem. Council of the Int. Asscn of Constitutional Law 1983–95, mem. Exec. Cttee 1993–2004; mem. Admin. Bd Finnish Broadcasting Corpn 1983–99, Finnish Acad. of Science 1987–; Perm. Expert for the Constitutional Comm. of Parl. 1982–; Expert for the Comm. on the Revision of the Constitution 1996–97; Commdr of the Finnish Lion 1995. *Publications include:* Sotavoiman ylin päällikkyys (The Commander-in-Chief of the Armed Forces) 1967, Yleisradio ja sananvapaus (The Freedom of Expression and Broadcasting) 1969, Perustuslaki ja yhteiskunnan muutos (The Constitution and the Change of Society) 1973, Presidentti (The President of the Republic) 1978, Lakien laki (The Law of the Laws) 1989, Kolme vuotta linnassa (Three Years in the Presidential Castle) 1990, Valta ja vapaus (Power and Freedom) 1994 (revised edn 2003), Uusi perustuslakimme (Our New Constitution) 2000, Kansanedustuslaitos ja valtiosääntö 1906–2005 (Parliament and the Constitution 1906–2005) 2006, Presidentti-instituutio aikamme Euro-opassa (Presidency of the Republic in Contemporary Europe) 2009. *Leisure interests:* languages, literature, problems of mass communication. *Address:* Faculty of Law, Room 315, University of Turku, 20014 Turku, Finland (office). *Telephone:* (2) 3335522 (office). *E-mail:* antero.jyranki@utu.fi (office). *Website:* www.law.utu.fi/english (home).

KÄÄRIÄINEN, Seppo, PhD; Finnish politician; b. 29 March 1948, Ilisalmi, Kirma; m. Pirjo Terttu Tuulikki (née Kolehmainen) 1975; one s.; Party Sec., Finnish Centre Party 1980–90, Chair. Party Parl. Group 1991–93, Vice-Pres. 1994–2000; mem. Suomen Eduskunta (Parl.) 1987–, mem. Foreign Affairs Cttee 1987–93, 1999–2000, Finance Cttee 1990–91, 1999–2003, Vice-Chair. Commerce Cttee 1995–99, Chair. Defence Cttee 2003; Minister of Trade and Industry 1993–95; Minister, Ministry for Foreign Affairs 1993–95; Minister of Defence 2004–07; First Deputy Speaker, Eduskunta 2007–; Chair. Del. to Jt Comm. of European Parl. and Eduskunta 1993; Pres. Bd of Dirs Itä-Suomen Ammattitaito Ry 2003–; Vice-Pres. Bd of Dirs Finnvera Oy 1999–2003. *Publications:* Suomen oma tie (Finland's Own Way) 1986, Haastaja (The Contender) 1989, The Strategic Choices of the Centre Party 1964–2001 2002. *Leisure interests:* walking, marathons. *Address:* Suomen Eduskunta, Mannerheimintie 30, 00102 Helsinki, Finland (office). *Telephone:* (9) 4321 (office). *Fax:* (9) 4322274 (office). *E-mail:* eduskunta@eduskunta.fi (office). *Website:* www.eduskunta.fi (office).

KAAS, Patricia; French singer; b. 5 Dec. 1966, Stiring Wendel, nr Forbach; teadance and night-club appearances aged 13; first single, Jalouse aged 17; first major success with Mademoiselle Chante le Blues; toured Viet Nam and Cambodia 1994; tours world-wide; six Victoires de la Musique, two World Music Awards; de Gaulle-Adenauer Prize 2001, Goldene Europa Award for Best International Artist 2002, Zolotoy Gramophon Award for Best Song and International Artist 2008. *Recordings include:* albums: Mademoiselle Chante 1988, Scène de Vie 1990, Carnet de Scène (live) 1991, Je Te Dis Vous 1993, Tour de Charme (live) 1994, Café noir 1996, Dans Ma Chair 1997, Rendez-vous 1998, Le mot de passe 1999, Patricia Kaas Live 2000, Rien ne s'arrête 2001, Piano bar 2002, Sexe fort 2004, Toute la Musique 2005, Kabaret 2008, Kaas chante Piaf 2012. *Publications:* Patricia Kaas – Tour de Charme 1994. *Address:* Attitude, 71 rue Robespierre, 93100 Montreuil, France. *Website:* www.patriciakaas.net; www.kabaretkaas.com/kabaret.

KABA, Sidiki; Senegalese lawyer, international organization official and politician; *Minister of Justice;* human rights lawyer associated with cases in Senegal, Chad, Côte d'Ivoire, Guinea; Pres. Nat. Org. for Human Rights, Senegal; Vice-Pres. Int. Fed. of the League for Human Rights, Paris, Pres. 2001–07, now Pres. of Honour; Minister of Justice 2013–. *Address:* Ministry of Justice, Bldg Administratif, 7e étage, ave Léopold Sédar Senghor, BP 4030, Dakar, Senegal (office). *Telephone:* 33-849-7000 (office). *Fax:* 33-823-2727 (office). *E-mail:* justice@justice .gouv.sn (office). *Website:* www.justice.gouv.sn (office).

KABAKOV, Alexander Abramovich; Russian writer and journalist; b. 22 Oct. 1943, Novosibirsk; m.; one d.; ed Dniepropetrovsk Univ.; engineer, space rocket production co. 1965–70; journalist, Gudok 1972–88; columnist, then Deputy Ed.-in-Chief Moscow News 1988–97; special corresp., Commersant Publishing 1997–2000, apptd Departmental Ed. 2000; columnist, New Media Publishing Group 2002–; apptd Chief Ed. journal Sak Voyazh; Chair. jury for Russian Booker Prize 2006; first literary publ. 1975; Golden Calf Award 1980, Moscow Journalists' Union Prize 1989, Best Pens of Russia Award 1999, Short Story of the Year Award 1999. *Publications include:* Cheap Novel 1982, Cafe Yunost 1984, Oil, Comma, Canvas 1986, Approach of Kristapovich (trilogy) 1985, Obviously False Fabrications (collection of short stories) 1989, No Return 1988, The Story-Teller 1991, Imposter 1992, The Last Hero (novel) 1995, Selected Prose 1997, The Imposter 1997, One Day from the Life of a Fool 1998, The Arrival Hall 1999, Youth Café 2000, The Journey of an Extrapolator 2000, The Tardy Visitor 2001, Qualified as Escape 2001, Survivor 2003, Nothing's Lost (Apollon Grigoryev Prize 2005, Big Book Prize 2006) 2004, Moscow Tales (Prose of the Year Prize 2005, Ivan Bunin Prize 2006) 2005, The Role of a Cut Glass in Family Life 2008, A Runaway (Book of the Year) 2009, Aksenov (with Evgeny Popov) 2011. *Leisure interest:* jazz. *Address:* c/o Natalia Tsarkova, Moskovskaya oblast, gorod Pushkino, mkr. Serebrianka, d. 48, k.1, kv.118, 141202, Russia (office). *Telephone:* (915) 197-45-70 (office). *E-mail:* post.nat@mail.ru (office). *Website:* www.elkost.com (office).

KABARITI, Abdul Karim A., BA; Jordanian banking executive and fmr politician; *Chairman and CEO, Jordan Kuwait Bank;* b. 15 Dec. 1949, Amman; m.; two c.; ed St Edward's Univ., Austin, Tex., USA, American Univ. of Beirut, Lebanon; licensed financial adviser, New York –1986; proprietor of a money exchange co.; mem. bd of dirs of many cos; mem. House of Reps for Governorate of Ma'an 1989–93, 1993–95, Minister of Tourism 1989–92, of Labour 1992–93, of Foreign Affairs 1995–96, Prime Minister, Minister of Defence and of Foreign Affairs 1996–97; currently Chair. and CEO Jordan Kuwait Bank; mem. Bd of Dirs Burgan Bank; fmr Chair. Foreign Relations Cttee of House of Reps; fmr Head, Royal Court; Chair. Bd Social Security Corpn 1992–93; Chair. Bd Vocational Training Corpn 1992–93. *Leisure interests:* water skiing, music. *Address:* Jordan Kuwait Bank, POB 9776, Amman 11194, Jordan (office). *Telephone:* (6) 5629400 (office). *Fax:* (6) 5687452 (office). *E-mail:* webmaster@jkbank.com.jo (office). *Website:* www.jordan-kuwait-bank.com (office).

KABBAJ, Omar; Moroccan government official; *Adviser to HM the King of Morocco;* b. 15 Aug. 1942, Rabat; s. of Ahmed Kabbaj and Khadija Moulato; m. Saida Lebbar; four s.; ed Ecole Supérieure de Commerce et d'Admin des Entreprises de Toulouse, France; Exec. Asst BRPM 1963–66; Dir Gen. SUNAT 1970–74; Special Adviser to Office of Ministry of Commerce, Industry, Mines and Shipping 1974–77; Dir Gen. Sunac 1974–79; Chief of Staff of Minister of Finance 1977–79; mem. Exec. Bd World Bank 1979–80, IMF 1980–93; Minister of Econ. Affairs 1993–95; Exec. Pres. and Chair. Bd of Dirs African Devt Bank and African Devt Fund 1995–2005, now Hon. Pres.; Adviser to HM the King of Morocco, Royal Cabinet 2006–; mem. Bd of Dirs Agence Française de developpement; mem. Advisory Bd of Sec.-Gen. of UN on Water and Sanitation; fmr mem. UN Comm. on HIV/AIDS and Governance in Africa; Kt of the Order of the Throne of Morocco, Grand Officer of the Nat. Order of Tunisia, Officer of the Nat. Order of Burkina Faso. *Publication:* The Challenge of African Development 2003. *Leisure interest:* golf. *Address:* Royal Cabinet, Dar al Makhzen, Rabat, Morocco (office). *Telephone:* (537) 207710 (office). *Fax:* (537) 767680 (office). *E-mail:* omarkabbaj@yahoo.com (home).

KABBARAH, Mohammad Bashar, PhD; Syrian economist and fmr central banker; b. 1944, Damascus; s. of M. Jamil and Hikmat Kouatly; m. 1968; three c.; ed American Univ. Washington, DC, Western Illinois Univ. and American Univ. of Beirut; Section Head, Office of Gen. Studies, The Presidency 1973–74; Economist, Econ. Bureau, The Presidency 1974–77, Sr Economist 1977–82; Adviser/Dir Econ. Bureau of Pres. of Syria 1982–95; Gov. Cen. Bank of Syria 1995–2004, Arab Monetary Fund; Chief Ed. The Syrian Economic Journal 1975–84; Alt. Gov. IMF; Alt. Exec. Dir Arab Fund for Econ. and Social Devt, Programme for Financing Arab Trade; mem. Syrian Higher Planning Bd; Washington-Lincoln Honor Award 1968, Hall of Nations Award 1969–70, Union of Arab Banks Award 1996. *Publications:* more than 20 papers and articles in professional journals and contribs. to The Arabic Encyclopedia. *Leisure interests:* historical reading, antiquities, agronomy, sports. *Address:* c/o Central Bank of Syria, PO Box 2254, At-Tajrida al-Mughrabia Square, Damascus, Syria.

KABER, Saddek Omar Ali el-, MS, MBA; Libyan central banker; *Governor and Chair, Central Bank of Libya;* ed Univ. of Hartford, USA; Gov. and Chair. Central Bank of Libya 2011–; Chair. Arab Banking Corpn, Bahrain 2011–, also Chair. Exec. Cttee and Risk Cttee; Sr Lecturer, Higher Inst. of Admin. Sciences and Finance, Tripoli. *Address:* Office of the Governor, Central Bank of Libya, POB 1103, Sharia al-Malik Seoud, Tripoli, Libya (office). *Telephone:* (21) 3333591 (office). *Fax:* (21) 4441488 (office). *E-mail:* info@cbl.gov.ly (office). *Website:* www.cbl .gov.ly (office).

KABERUKA, Donald, MPhil, PhD; Rwandan economist, politician and international organization official; *Executive President and Chairman, African Development Bank;* ed Tanzania, Glasgow Univ., LSE; early career in banking industry; fmr State Minister for Budget and Planning; Minister of Finance and Econ. Planning 1997–2005; Exec. Pres. and Chair. African Devt Bank 2005–; Chair. Bd of Govs Africa Trade Insurance Agency 2003–; Chair. Nat. Africa Peer Review Comm. 2004–; Chair. PTA Bank (East, Central and Southern Africa devt bank) 2001-02; Vice-Chair. Nat. AIDS Comm. 2002–03. *Address:* African Development Bank, rue Joseph Anoma, 01 BP 1387, Abidjan 01, Côte d'Ivoire (office). *Telephone:* 20-20-44-44 (office). *Fax:* 20-20-49-59 (office). *E-mail:* afdb@afdb.org (office). *Website:* www.afdb.org (office).

KABILA KABANGE, Maj.-Gen. Joseph, BA; Democratic Republic of the Congo army officer and head of state; *President;* b. 4 June 1970, Sud-Kivu Prov.; s. of the late Laurent-Désiré Kabila; m. Olive Lembe; one d.; ed Nat. Defence Univ., People's Repub. of China; Deputy Chair. Jt Chiefs of Staff, Congolese Armed Forces 1998–2000, Army Chief of Staff 2000–01; Pres. Democratic Repub. of the Congo 2001–, fmrly Minister of Defence; Dr hc (Hankuk Univ., S Korea). *Address:* Office of the President, Hôtel du Conseil Exécutif, ave de Lemera, Kinshasa-Gombé, Democratic Republic of the Congo (office). *Telephone:* (12) 30892 (office). *E-mail:* pr@presidentrdc.cd (office). *Website:* www.presidentrdc.cd (office).

KABIRI, Muhiddin; Tajikistani politician; *Chairman, Islamic Rebirth Party of Tajikistan;* b. (Muhiddin Kabirov), 1966, Fayzobod dist; m.; five c.; ed Tajik Nat. Univ., San'a Univ., Yemen, Diplomatic Acad., Moscow; aide to Chair., Islamic Rebirth Party of Tajikistan 1997–2000, Deputy Chair. 2000–04, First Deputy Chair. 2004–06, Chair. 2006–; mem. Majlisi Namoyandagon (Ass. of Reps) 2005–, mem. Cttee on Science, Educ., Culture and Youth Police. *Address:* Islamic Rebirth Party of Tajikistan, 734000 Dushanbe, pos. Kalinina, Kuchai Tukhagul 55, Tajikistan (office). *Telephone:* (372) 27-25-30 (office). *Fax:* (372) 27-53-93 (office).

KABORÉ, Roch Marc-Christian; Burkinabè politician; *President, Assemblée nationale;* b. 25 April 1957, Ouagadougou; ed Univ. of Dijon, France; Minister of State in charge of Relations with Insts 1990–94; Prime Minister of Burkina Faso 1994–96; Special Adviser to the Pres. 1996–97; mem. Assemblée nationale 1997–, Pres. 2002–; mem. Org. pour la démocratie populaire/Mouvement du travail (ODP/MT), First Vice-Pres., then Pres. Congrès pour la démocratie et le progrès (CDP) (f. 1996 as successor to ODP/MT) 1996–. *Leisure interests:* reading, music, agropastoral activities, sponsor of Rail Club du Kadiaogo (First Div. football team). *Address:* Office of the President, Assemblée nationale, 01 BP 6482, Ouagadougou 01 (office); Congrès pour la démocratie et le progrès, 1146 avenue Dr Kwamé N'Krumah, 01 BP 1605, Ouagadougou 01, Burkina Faso (office). *Telephone:* 50-31-46-84 (Assemblée nationale) (office); 50-31-50-18 (office). *Fax:* 50-31-45-90 (Assemblée nationale) (office); 50-31-43-93 (office). *E-mail:* contact@cdp-burkina .org (office). *Website:* www.cdp-burkina.org (office).

KABUI, Frank Ofagioro, GCMG, CSI, OBE, LLB, Grad. Dipl. in Int. Law; Solomon Islands judge (retd) and government official; *Governor General;* b. 20 April 1946, Manakwai, Malaita; s. of Michael Frank Kabui and Nammah Angialatha; m. 1st Meeanni Kabui; three s. one d.; m. 2nd Lady Grace Delight Kabui; one s. one d.; ed Univ. of Papua New Guinea, Australian Nat. Univ., Canberra; Attorney Gen. 1980–94; High Court Judge 1998–2006 (retd); Chair. Law Reform Comm. 1994–2009; Gov. Gen. 2009–; Chancellor Univ. of the South Pacific, Suva, Fiji 2011–12; mem. Solomon Islands Bar Asscn (fmr Pres.); Cross of Solomon Islands. *Leisure interests:* current affairs, lawn tennis, squash, table tennis, darts, watching TV. *Address:* Office of the Governor General, Government House, PO Box 252, Honiara, Solomon Islands (office). *Telephone:* 21777 (office); 21778 (office). *Fax:* 22533 (office).

KAC, Eduardo, BA, MFA, PhD; Brazilian/American artist and writer; *Professor of Art and Technology, School of Art, Art Institute of Chicago;* b. 1962, Rio de Janeiro, Brazil; ed Pontifícia Universidade Católica do Rio de Janeiro, School of the Art Institute of Chicago, Univ. of Wales, UK; pioneer of holopoetry, telepresence art, biotelematics, transgenic art; moved to Chicago 1989; Prof. of Art and Tech., School of Art, Art Inst. of Chicago 1997–; mem. Editorial Bd Leonardo (journal); Shearwater Foundation Holography Award 1995, Leonardo Award for Excellence 1998, award for telepresence work Uirapuru, InterCommunication Centre Biennale, Tokyo 1999. *Publications:* New Media Poetry: Poetic Innovation and New Technologies (anthology) 1996; Luz & Letra, Ensaios de arte, literatura e comunicação 2004; Telepresence and Bio Art: Networking Humans, Rabbits and Robots 2005, Signs of Life: Bio Art and Beyond 2007; articles in periodicals.

Address: Art and Technology Department, School of the Art Institute of Chicago, 37 South Wabash Avenue, Chicago, IL 60603, USA (office). *Telephone:* (312) 899-5100 (office). *E-mail:* ekac@artic.edu (office). *Website:* www.ekac.org (office).

KACZMAREK, Janusz; Polish lawyer and politician; b. 25 Dec. 1961, Gdynia; m.; two s.; ed Univ. of Gdańsk; started legal training in Dist Prosecutor's Office, Elbląg 1985–88, in Gdańsk 1988; Dist Prosecutor, Gdynia 1993–2000; Regional Prosecutor, Gdańsk 2000–01; Deputy Prosecutor Gen. 2001; Deputy Dir Preparatory Proceedings Dept, Nat. Prosecutor's Office 2001–03; Appellate Prosecutor, Gdańsk 2003–05; Head, Nat. Prosecutor's Office 2005–07; Minister of Internal Affairs and Admin Feb.–Aug. 2007; lecturer on material criminal law to public prosecutor's trainees 1992–; Chair. Editorial Bd Prokuratura i Prawo, Kwartalnik Apelacji Gdańskiej, Kwartalnik Krajowego Centrum Szkolenia Kadr Sadów Powszechnych i Prokuratury; co-organizer Razem przeciw przemocy (Together Against Violence) program; mem. Law and Justice (PiS) (Prawo i Sprawiedliwość); arrested Polish anti-corruption agency Aug. 2007. *Publications:* author of numerous book and articles on law. *Address:* Prawo i Sprawiedliwość, ul. Nowogrodzka 84/86, 02-018 Warsaw, Poland (office). *Telephone:* (22) 6215035 (office). *Fax:* (22) 6216767 (office). *E-mail:* biuro@pis.org.pl (office). *Website:* www.pis.org.pl (office).

KACZYŃSKI, Jarosław Aleksander, DJur; Polish politician and lawyer; *President, Law and Justice;* b. 18 June 1949, Warsaw; s. of Rajmund Kaczyński and Jadwiga Kaczyńska; identical twin brother of the late Pres. of Poland, Lech Kaczyński (died 2010); ed Warsaw Univ.; Asst, Sr Asst in Inst. of Science and Higher Educ. 1971–76; collaborator, Workers' Defence Cttee (KOR) 1976–80; scientific worker, Białystok br. of Warsaw Univ. 1977–81; ed. Głos (independent magazine) 1980–82; warehouseman 1982; mem. Solidarity Trade Union 1980–90; Sec. Nat. Exec. Comm. of Solidarity 1986–87; took part in Round Table talks in Comm. for Political Reforms Feb.–April 1989; Ed.-in-Chief Tygodnik Solidarność (weekly) 1989–90; Deputy to Senate 1989–91; Dir Office of Pres. and Minister of State 1990–92; Deputy to Sejm (Parl.) 1991–93, 1997–, mem. Ethics Comm. 2001–; Founder and Chair. Centre Alliance 1990–98; Co-founder with his late brother and mem. Main Bd Law and Justice (PiS) 2001–, Pres. Law and Justice Parl. Club 2001–03, Pres. PiS and Chair. Main Bd 2003–; Prime Minister 2006–07; Acting Minister of Agric. Sept.–Oct. 2006, July 2007; Acting Minister of Sport and Tourism July 2007; Leader of the Opposition 2007–; unsuccessful cand. in presidential election 2010; mem. Helsinki Comm. in Poland 1982–89. *Film:* starred, with his brother, in Polish film The Two Who Stole the Moon (O dwóch takich, co ukradli księżyc) 1962. *Leisure interests:* animals (especially cats), reading, history of Poland. *Address:* Law and Justice (Prawo i Sprawiedliwość—PiS), 02-018 Warsaw, ul. Nowogrodzka 84/86 (office); Sejm RP, 00-902 Warsaw, ul. Wiejska 4/6/8, Poland. *Telephone:* (22) 6215035 (office). *Fax:* (22) 6216767 (office). *E-mail:* biuro@pis.org.pl (office). *Website:* www.pis.org.pl (office); www.jaroslawkaczynski.info.

KADAGA, Rt Hon. Rebecca Alitwala, LLB, MA; Ugandan lawyer and politician; *Speaker of Parliament;* b. 24 May 1956, Kamuli; ed Namasagali Coll., Makerere Univ., Kampala, Univ. of Zimbabwe, Harare; Diploma in Legal Practice, Law Devt Centre, Kampala, Diploma in Women's Law, Univ. of Zimbabwe, Harare; in pvt. law practice 1984–88; MP (Nat. Resistance Movt Party) for Kamuli Dist Women's Constituency, Busoga sub-region 1989–, Deputy Speaker of Parl. 2001–11, Speaker (first woman) 2011–, Chair. Appointments Cttee, Parl. Comm., Business Cttee; Minister of State for Regional Cooperation (Africa and the Middle East) 1996–98; Minister of State for Communication and Aviation 1998–99; Minister for Parl. Affairs 1999–2000; Chair. Univ. Council for Mbarara Univ. 1993–96; Sec. Gen. East African Women Parliamentarians Asscn 1996. *Leisure interests:* reading, art, travel. *Address:* Public Relations Office, Parliament of Uganda, PO Box 7178, Parliamentary Avenue, Kampala, Uganda (office). *Telephone:* (41) 4377180 (office). *E-mail:* info@parliament.go.ug (office). *Website:* www.parliament.go.ug (office).

KADAGIDZE, Giorgi, MPA; Georgian economist and central banker; *Chairman and Governor, National Bank of Georgia;* b. 10 April 1980, Tbilisi; ed European School of Man., Preston Univ., Georgia Inst. of Public Affairs, USA; Auditor, later Sr Auditor and Audit Man., UBC International (audit and consulting firm) 2000–03; Head of Credit Dept, People's Bank of Georgia (now Liberty Bank) 2003–04; Head of Financial Div., later Head of Financial Service and of Municipal Financial Service, Tbilisi Municipality Jan.–July 2005; Head of Bank and Non-Bank Depository Insts Supervisory Dept, Nat. Bank of Georgia (central bank) 2005–06, Chair. and Gov. 2009–; Head of Econ. Dept, Office of Prosecutor-Gen. 2006–07; Head, Financial Monitoring Service of Georgia 2007–08; Head, Georgian Financial Supervisory Agency 2008–09; Alt. Gov. EBRD. *Address:* Office of the Governor, National Bank of Georgia, 0105 Tbilisi, Leonidze 3–5, Georgia (office). *Telephone:* (32) 244-25-44 (office). *Fax:* (32) 244-25-77 (office). *E-mail:* info@nbg.gov.ge (office). *Website:* www.nbg.gov.ge (office).

KADAKIN, Alexander Mikhailovich; Russian diplomatist; *Ambassador to India;* b. 22 July 1949, Kishinev, Moldova; ed Moscow Inst. of Int. Relations; translator Special Construction Bureau Vibpribor, Kishinev 1966–67; joined diplomatic service 1971; with USSR Embassy, India 1972, Attaché 1972–75, Third Sec. 1975–78; Second Sec. Secr., First Deputy to USSR Minister of Foreign Affairs 1978–80, First Sec., Secr. 1980–83, Asst 1983–86, Asst to Deputy Minister 1986–88, Asst First Deputy Minister 1988–89; Minister-Counsellor USSR Embassy, India 1989–91; First Deputy Head of Dept USSR Ministry of Foreign Affairs 1991; Counsellor Embassy, India 1991–93; Amb. to Nepal 1993–97; mem. Collegium, Dir of Linguistic Support Dept, Ministry of Foreign Affairs 1997–99; Amb. to India 1999–2004, 2009–, to Sweden 2004–09; Asst Prof., Dept of Indian Studies, Moscow State Inst. of Int. Relations 1979–85. *Address:* Embassy of Russia, Shanti Path, Chanakyapuri, New Delhi 110 021, India (office). *Telephone:* (11) 26873799 (office). *Fax:* (11) 26876823 (office). *E-mail:* emb@rusembassy.in (office). *Website:* www.india.mid.ru (office).

KADANNIKOV, Vladimir Vasilievich; Russian politician and business executive; b. 3 Sept. 1941, Gorky (now Nizhny Novgorod); m.; two d.; ed Gorky Polytech. Inst.; fitter, foreman, then area man., Gorky Automotive Plant 1959–67; Deputy Workshop Man., Volga Automotive Works 1967–76; Deputy Dir-Gen. PO AvtoVAZ in charge of production 1976–86, First Deputy Dir-Gen., then Dir R&D Centre 1986–88, Dir-Gen. PO AvtoVAZ 1988–93, Pres. and Dir-Gen. joint stock co.

AvtoVAZ Inc. 1993–96; First Deputy Prime Minister of Russia Jan.–Aug. 1996; Chair. AvtoVAZ Inc. 1996–2005 (resgnd), GM-AvtoVAZ –2005; Chair. Council for Industrial Policy; mem. Presidential Consultative Council; mem. Int. Eng Acad., Russian Eng Acad.; fmr People's Deputy of the USSR; Hon. Prof., Samara State Univ.; Hero of Socialist Labour. *Publications:* book chapters and scientific articles on cold sheet stamping by stretch forming. *Leisure interests:* reading, basketball. *Address:* Yuzhnoe Shosse 36, 445633 Togliatti, Russia.

KADANOFF, Leo Philip, PhD; American physicist and academic; *John D. MacArthur Distinguished Service Professor Emeritus, University of Chicago;* b. 14 Jan. 1937, New York; s. of Abraham Kadanoff and Celia Kadanoff (née Kibrick); m. Ruth Ditzian 1979; four d.; ed Harvard Univ.; postdoctoral research at Bohr Inst. for Theoretical Studies, Copenhagen, Denmark 1960–62; Asst Prof. of Physics, Univ. of Ill. 1962–63, Assoc. Prof. 1963, Prof. 1965–69; Visiting Prof., Univ. of Cambridge, UK 1965; Univ. Prof. of Physics, Brown Univ. 1969–78, Prof. of Eng 1971–78; Prof. of Physics, Univ. of Chicago 1978–82, John D. MacArthur Distinguished Service Prof. of Physics and Math. 1982–, now Prof. Emer.; Alfred P. Sloan Foundation Fellow 1962–67; mem. Editorial Bd Annals of Physics 1982–, Nuclear Physics 1980–; mem. NAS 1978 American Philosophical Soc. 1997; Fellow American Acad. of Arts and Sciences, American Physical Soc.; Ryerson Lectureship, Univ. of Chicago 2000; Buckley Prize, American Physical Soc. 1977, Onsager Prize, American Physical Soc. 1998; Wolf Foundation Award 1980, Elliott Cresson Medal, Franklin Inst. 1986, IUPAP Boltzmann Medal 1989, Quantrell Award, Univ. of Chicago 1990, Centennial Medal, Harvard Univ. 1990, Grande Médaille d'or, Acad. des Sciences de l'Inst. de France 1998, Nat. Medal of Science 2000. *Publications:* Quantum Statistical Mechanics (with G. Baym) 1962, From Order to Chaos: Essays Critical Chaotic and Otherwise 1993, Statistical Physics: Statics, Dynamics and Renormalization 2000. *Address:* 5421 South Cornell Avenue, Chicago, IL 60615 (home); James Franck Institute, University of Chicago, 5640 South Ellis Avenue, Chicago, IL 60637, USA (office). *Telephone:* (773) 702-7189 (office). *Fax:* (773) 702-2172 (office). *E-mail:* l-kadanoff@uchicago.edu (office); leop@uchicago.edu (office). *Website:* jfi.uchicago.edu/~leop (office).

KÁDÁR, Béla, PhD, DSc; Hungarian politician, economist and academic; *Life Honorary Chair, Hungarian Association of Economists;* b. 21 March 1934, Pécs; s. of Lajos Kádár and Teréz Schmidt; m. Patricia Derzső; one s.; ed Budapest Univ. of Economy; worked for Int. Econ. Dept, Nat. Bank of Hungary, Elektro-impex Foreign Trading Co.; fmr dept head and research man., Business and Market Research Inst.; with Hungarian Acad. of Sciences Research Inst. of World Economy 1965–88; Lecturer, Eötvös Loránd Univ. of Budapest; Visiting Prof., Santiago de Chile and San Marcos Univ. of Lima; Dir Econ. Planning Inst. 1988–90; Minister of Int. Econ. Relations 1990–94; mem. Parl. 1994–98, Chair. Cttee on Budget and Finances; Vice-Chair. Hungarian Asscn of Economists 1990–2000, Chair. 2002–08, Life Hon. Chair. 2008–; Univ. Prof. 1998–2012; Pres. Hungarian Export-Import Bank 1998–99; Vice-Pres. Hungarian Soc. of Foreign Affairs 1998–; Amb. to OECD 1999–2003; mem. Monetary Council of Hungarian Nat. Bank 1999–2009; Chair. Hungarian Group in Trilateral Comm. 1999–; Academician, Hungarian Acad. of Sciences; Dr hc (San Marcos Univ., Lima) 1970, (Budapest) 1999, (Miskolc) 2008; Grand Prix, Hungarian Acad. of Sciences 1984, Econ. Policy Club (Bonn) Prize for Social Market Econs 1993. *Publications:* author of eight books and more than 400 papers. *Leisure interests:* music, literature. *Address:* Mártonhegyi u. 38/B, Budapest 1124, Hungary. *Telephone:* (1) 355-7987. *Fax:* (1) 355-7987.

KADARÉ, Ismail; Albanian writer; b. 28 Jan. 1936, Gjirokastër; s. of Halit Kadaré; m. Elena Gushi 1963; two d.; ed Univ. of Tirana and Gorky Inst., Moscow; full-time writer since 1963; works translated into more than 30 languages; sought political asylum in Paris 1990; mem. Albanian Acad.; Corresponding, then Assoc. Foreign mem. Acad. des sciences morales et politiques; mem. Acad. of Arts, Berlin, Acad. Mallarmé; Dr hc (Grenoble III) 1992, (St Etienne) 1997, (South East European Univ.) 2005; Prix Mondial Cino del Duca 1992, Int. Booker Prize 2005, Premio Príncipe de Asturias, Spain 2009. *Plays:* Mauvaise saison pour Olymp. *Publications:* fiction: Gjenerali i ushtërisë së vdekur (trans. as The General of the Dead Army) 1963, Kështjella (trans. as The Castle, later as The Siege) 1970, Kronikë në gur (trans. as Chronicle in Stone) 1971, The Great Winter (novel, in trans.) 1973, Ura më tri harque (trans. as The Three-Arched Bridge) 1978, The Twilight (in trans.) 1978, The Niche of Shame (in trans.) 1978, Kush e solli doruntinen (trans. as Who Brought Back Doruntine?) 1980, Prilli i thyer (trans. as Broken April) 1980, Nëpunësi I pallatit të ëndrrave (trans. as The Palace of Dreams) 1980, Nje dosje per Homerin (trans. as The H Dossier) 1980, Koncert në fund të dimrit (trans. as The Concert) 1985, Eschyle or The Eternal Loser (in trans.) 1988, Albanian Spring (in trans.) 1991, Le Monstre (in trans.) 1991, Piramida (trans. as The Pyramid) 1992, La Grande muraille 1993, Le Firman aveugle 1993, Clair de Lune 1993, L'Ombre 1994, L'Aigle 1996, Spiritus 1996, Oeuvres 1993–97 (12 vols) 1997, Temps barbares, de l'Albanie au Kosovo 1999, Il a fallu ce deuil pour se retrouver 2000, Froides fleurs d'avril (trans. as Spring Flowers, Spring Frost) 2000, L'envol du migrateur 2001, Vie, jeu et mort de Lul Mazrek 2002, La fille d'Agamemnon 2003, Le successeur 2003, L'Accident 2010; six vols of poetry 1954–80, criticism, essays. *Address:* 63 blvd Saint-Michel, 75005 Paris (home); c/o Librairie Arthème Fayard, 75 rue des Saints Pères, 75006 Paris, France (office). *Telephone:* 1-43-29-16-20 (home).

KADDOUMI, Farouk (Abu Lutef); Palestinian politician; *President of the Executive Committee, Fatah (The Palestine National Liberation Movement);* b. 1931, Qalqilyah; ed Cairo Univ.; moved to Nablus during Arab–Israeli War 1948; worked for Arab–American Petroleum Co. (ARAMCO), Saudi Arabia early 1950s; joined Baath Party, Egypt 1954; joined Fatah in UAE 1960; with Ministry of Health, Kuwait 1965–66; expelled from Kuwait for anti-governmental activities connected with Palestinian Liberation Org. (PLO) 1966; became key figure in PLO 1969, apptd Head of Political Dept, Damascus, Syria 1973; participated in activities of Said al-Muraghi (Aba Musa) Group 1980s; opposed signing of Oslo Peace Accords with Israel 1993; apptd Dir of Palestinian Econ. Council for Reconstruction and Devt (PEDCAR) by Yasser Arafat; Pres. Exec. Cttee, Palestine Nat. Liberation Movt (al-Fatah) 2004–. *Address:* Fatah (The Palestine National Liberation Movement), Palestinian Autonomous Areas (office). *Website:* www.fateh.net (office).

KADEER, Rebiya; Chinese (Uyghur) human rights activist; *President, World Uyghur Congress;* b. 15 June 1947, Altay, East Turkistan; m. 1st 1965; m. 2nd Prof. Sidik Rouzi 1981; 11 c.; moved to Aksu, Xinjiang 1965; opened launderette 1976; moved to Ürümqi 1981; leased a market in local business dist, converted it into dept store that specialized in Uyghur ethnic costumes; engaged in cross-border trade, following collapse of Soviet Union, business included dept stores, real estate, timber, scrap iron, factories and other enterprises; est. trading co. operating in China, Russia and Kazakhstan; active philanthropist within community, most notably through 1,000 Families Mothers Project (charity to help Uyghur women start their own local businesses); del., eighth session of CPPCC 1993; Rep. to UN Fourth World Conf. for Women, Beijing 1995; fmr Vice-Chair. Xinjiang Autonomous Region Fed. of Industry and Commerce, Xinjiang Asscn of Women Entrepreneurs; removed from Nat. People's Consultative Conf. and passport revoked after she criticized the Chinese Govt; detained on charges of leaking state secrets Aug. 1999, convicted in Ürümqi Intermediate People's Court of endangering state security March 2000, spent two years in solitary confinement; released early on medical grounds into US custody March 2005, flew to USA March 2005; Pres. World Uyghur Congress 2006–, Bd of Uyghur American Asscn; Dir Int. Uyghur Human Rights and Democracy Foundation; Rafto Prize for Human Rights 2004. *Publication:* Dragon Fighter (autobiography) 2009. *Address:* World Uyghur Congress, PO Box 310312, 80103 Munich, Germany (office). *Telephone:* (89) 54321999 (office). *Fax:* (89) 54349789 (office). *E-mail:* contact@uyghurcongress.org (office); duq@uyghurcongress.org (office). *Website:* www.uyghurcongress.org (office).

KADOMATSU, Masahiro; Japanese business executive; *Chairman and CEO, Asahi Glass Company;* b. 29 Oct. 1942, Tokyo; ed Keio Univ.; joined Asahi Glass Co. 1965, numerous man. positions 1965–98 including Gen. Man. Sales, Gen. Man. Electronic Products Div. 1998–2000, Man. Dir and Gen. Man., Display Glass 2000–02, Sr Exec. Officer and Pres. Display Co. 2002–03, Sr Exec. Vice Pres. and Pres. Display Co. 2003–04, CEO and Pres. Asahi Glass Co. 2004–07, Chair. and CEO 2007–; Counsellor, Energy Conservation Centre, Japan, Int. Centre for the Study of East Asian Devt; Commdr, Order of the Crown of Belgium 2010. *Address:* Asahi Glass Company, 1-12-1 Yuraku-cho, Chiyoda-ku, Tokyo 100-8405, Japan (office). *Telephone:* (3) 3218-5096 (office). *Website:* www.agc.co.jp (office).

KADOORIE, Hon. Sir Michael, Kt; Hong Kong business executive; *Chairman, CLP Holdings Limited;* b. 1941, Hong Kong; s. of the late Lawrence, Lord Kadoorie and of Muriel Gubbay; m.; three c.; ed Institut Le Rosey, Switzerland; family roots in business in the Far East go back to his grandfather, who made a fortune in Shanghai, mostly lost in 1949, and later, in Hong Kong through finance, real estate and utilities; Chair. CLP Group, Hong Kong (electricity provider); Chair. Hong Kong & Shanghai Hotels, owners and operators of Peninsula Hotel Group; controls and is a mem. Bd of Dirs Metrojet Ltd, Heliservices (Hong Kong) Ltd; mem. Bd of Dirs Sir Elly Kadoorie & Sons Ltd, Hutchison Whampoa Ltd; Alternate Dir Hong Kong Aircraft Engineering Co. Ltd 1989–; Founder CLP Research Inst. (subsidiary of CLP Holdings); fmr mem. Council of Univ. of Hong Kong; Trustee, Kadoorie Charitable Foundation; Grand Bauhinia Star; Officier, Légion d'honneur; Commdr, Order of Léopold II (Belgium); Hon. LLD (Univ. of Hong Kong) 2004. *Leisure interests:* photography, helicopter pilot, collecting classic cars. *Address:* CLP Holdings, 147 Argyle Street, Kowloon, Hong Kong Special Administrative Region, People's Republic of China (office). *Telephone:* 2678-8111 (office). *Fax:* 2760-4448 (office). *E-mail:* clp_info@clp.com.hk (office). *Website:* www.clpgroup.com (office).

KADUMA, Ibrahim Mohamed, BSc (Econs), BPhil; Tanzanian economist and politician; *Chancellor, Mzumbe University;* b. 1937, Mtwango Njombe, Iringa Region; s. of the late Mohamed Maleva Kaduma and of Mwanaidza Kaduma; m. Happiness Y. Mgonja 1969; four s. one d.; ed Makerere Univ. Coll. Uganda and Univ. of York, UK; Accounts Clerk, the Treasury 1959–61, Accounts Asst 1961, Asst Accountant 1962–65, Economist 1965–66, Dir of External Finance and Technical Co-operation 1967–69, Deputy Sec. Treasury 1969–70; Prin. Sec., Ministry of Communications, Transport and Labour, 1970–72, Treasury 1972–73; Dir Inst. of Devt Studies, Univ. of Dar es Salaam 1973–75, Centre on Integrated Rural Devt for Africa 1982–85; Minister for Foreign Affairs 1975–77, of Trade 1980–81, of Communications and Transport 1981–82; Vice-Chancellor Univ. of Dar es Salaam 1977–80; fmr Gen. Man. Tanzania Sisal Devt Bd; currently Chancellor Mzube Univ.; mem. Bd of Dirs National Investments Company Ltd; Arts Research Prize, Makerere Univ., Uganda 1964–65. *Leisure interests:* tennis, squash, gardening, dairy farming. *Address:* Office of the Chancellor, Mzumbe University, PO Box 1, Mzumbe, Tanzania (office). *Telephone:* (23) 2604380 (office). *Fax:* (23) 2604382 (office). *E-mail:* mu@mzumbe.ac.tz (office). *Website:* www.mzumbe.ac.tz (office).

KADYROV, Ramzan Akhmatovich; Russian government official; *President of the Chechen Republic;* b. 5 Oct. 1976, Tsenteroi, Checheno-Ingush ASSR (now Chechen Repub.), Russian SFSR, USSR; s. of the late Pres. Akhmad Kadyrov; m.; seven c.; fmr Commdr of 'Kadyrovtsy' militia (Presidential security service); fmr Head of Security, Chechen Repub.; First Deputy Chair. of Govt, Chechen Repub. 2004–05, Acting Chair. of Govt 2005–06, Chair. of Govt 2006–07, Pres. 2007–; Chair. Ramzan boxing club, Terek Grozny football club; escaped assassination attempt Oct. 2009; Pres. Chechen League KVN; Hon. mem. Russian Acad. of Natural Sciences 2006; Hon. Citizen of the Chechen Repub.; Honoured Worker of Physical Culture; Honoured Builder of the Chechen Repub.; Hon. Pres. Movt of Afghan Veterans of the Southern Fed. Dist; Medal 'For Distinction in the Protection of Public Order' 2002, 2004, Order of Courage 2003, Hero of the Russian Fed. 2004, Order of Merit for the Fatherland (Fourth Class) 2006, Certificate of Merit of the State Duma of the Russian Fed. 2009, Medal 'For Services to conduct national census', Zhukov Medal (twice), Medal 'In Commemoration of the 850th Anniversary of Moscow', Medal 'In Commemoration of the 300th Anniversary of Saint Petersburg', Military Merit (Grade 2), Ministry of Defence; Order of Akhmad Kadyrov 2005, Caucasus Service Medal, Defender of the Chechen Repub. 2006, Order 'For the development of parliamentarism in the Chechen Republic' 2007; Medal 'Astana 10 years' (Kazakhstan) 2008; Man of the Year in the Chechen Repub. 2004, Laureate of the 'Russian of the Year' in the nomination 'For the sake of life on Earth' 2007, Aksakal Award 2008. *Leisure interests:* football, horses, collecting sports cars and Chechen daggers. *Address:* Office of the President of the Republic, 364000 Chechen Republic, Groznyi, ul. Garazhnaya 10A, Russia (office). *Telephone:* (8712) 22-20-01 (office); (8712) 22-20-09 (office). *Fax:* (8712) 22-20-14 (office). *E-mail:* secretariat_chr@mail.ru (office). *Website:* www.chechnya.gov.ru (office); www.ramzan-kadyrov.ru.

KADYSHEVSKY, Vladimir G.; Russian physicist; *Scientific Leader, Joint Institute for Nuclear Research;* b. 5 May 1937, Moscow; widowed; one d.; ed Moscow State Univ.; Jr, then Sr Researcher, Head of Sector, then Dir Lab. of Theoretical Physics, Jt Inst. for Nuclear Research 1987–92, Dir Jt Inst. for Nuclear Research 1992–2005, Scientific Leader 2006–; mem. Presidium of Russian Acad. of Sciences (RAS), Corresp. mem. RAS 1991–2000, mem. 2000–; Hon. Citizen of Moscow Region 2001; N.M. Krylov Prize 1990 and N.N. Bogolubov Prize 2001 from Acad. of Sciences of Ukraine, Gold Medal, Int. Asscn of Acads of Sciences 2002, Gold Medal, Inst. of European Integration 2003. *Publications include:* numerous scientific papers on particle physics, quantum field theory, math. physics, and group theoretical and geometrical methods in field theory. *Leisure interests:* art, cinema, theatre, music. *Address:* Joint Institute for Nuclear Research, 6 Joliot-Curie str., 141980 Dubna, Moscow region (office); 2 Vekslera str., 141980 Dubna, Moscow region, Russia (home). *Telephone:* (495) 632-78-67 (office); (09621) 6-22-43 (office); (09621) 6-22-16 (home). *Fax:* (495) 632-78-80 (office); (09621) 6-58-92 (office). *E-mail:* kadyshev@jinr.ru (office). *Website:* www.jinr.ru (office).

KAESER, Joe, Dipl.-Betriebswirt; German business executive; *President and CEO, Siemens AG;* b. 23 June 1957, Arnbruck, Regen, Bavaria; joined Components Group, Discrete Components Div., Siemens AG 1980, later Head of Business Admin Semiconductor Plant, Regensburg, Finance Dir, Semiconductors Group, Head of Accounting & Product Planning, Siemens Semiconductors, Malacca, Malaysia 1987–88, Head of Business Admin Projects, Semiconductors Group, Discrete Semiconductors Div., Siemens AG 1988–90, Head of Business Admin, Opto Semiconductors Div. 1990–95, Head of Business Admin, Siemens Microelectronics Inc., San José, Calif., USA 1995–99, Exec. Vice-Pres. and Chief Financial Officer (CFO), Siemens AG, responsible for Corp. Finance, Accounting Unit, Controlling and Taxes 1999–2001, mem. Group Exec. Man., Information and Communication Mobile Group 2001–04, Chief Strategy Officer 2004–06, mem. Man. Bd and CFO 2006–13, Pres. and CEO 2013–; mem. Bd Allianz Deutschland AG, Nokia Siemens Networks, Bosch Siemens Hausgeräte GmbH (Chair.), NXP Semiconductors NV. *Address:* Siemens AG, Wittelsbacherplatz 2, 80333 Munich, Germany (office). *Telephone:* (89) 63600 (office). *Fax:* (89) 63652000 (office). *E-mail:* contact@siemens.com (office). *Website:* www.siemens.com (office).

KAFELNIKOV, Yevgeny Aleksandrovich; Russian fmr professional tennis player; b. 18 Feb. 1974, Sochi; m. two d.; ed Krasnodar Pedagogical Inst.; ATP professional 1992; won ATP tournaments including Milan, St Petersburg, Gstaad, Long Island; won French Open (singles and doubles) 1996; won Moscow Kremlin Cup 1997, 1999; won Australian Open 1999; mem. Russian Fed. Davis Cup Championship Team 1993, winner (with Russian team) 2002; runner-up World Championship, Hanover 1997; highest ATP rating 1st (May 1999); Olympic champion (singles), Sydney 2000; winner of 26 singles titles and 27 doubles titles; retd 2004. *Leisure interests:* fishing, flying, golf. *Address:* c/o All-Russian Tennis Association, Luzhnetskaya nab. 8, 119871 Moscow, Russia. *Website:* yevgenykafelnikov.com.

KAFRAWY, Hassaballah Mohamed El-, BEng; Egyptian politician; b. 22 Nov. 1930, Kafr Saad Area, Damietta Governorate; s. of Mohamed El-Kafrawy; m. Elham Fouad 1961; three s.; ed Alexandria Univ.; with southern region of High Dam electricity lines until 1966; Chair. Canal Gen. Contracting Co.; Vice-Pres. exec. organ for reconstruction of Suez Canal region 1974, Pres. 1975; Gov. of Damietta 1976; Deputy Minister for Reconstruction, then Minister of Devt, Housing and Land Reclamation 1977–86; supervised planning of satellite cities and public utilities of Sadat, Ramadan 10, October 6, May 15, Cairo Sanitary Project, Damietta Port etc.; Minister of Devt, New Communities, Housing and Public Utilities 1986–93; mem. Egyptian People's Ass. 1979–93; Chair. and CEO El rehab Saudi-Egyptian Group of cos 1997; Pres. Egyptian Eng Asscn 1990; Chair. New Communities Authority; Perm. mem. and fmr Vice-Chair. World Asscn of the Major Metropolises (Metropolis); mem. Egyptian Specialized Nat. Councils, Egyptian Acad. for Scientific Research and Tech. (Chair. New Communities Research Council Acad.), Gen. Authority for Investment and Free Zones; Pres. or fmr Pres. Egyptian Engineers Syndicate, Univ. Councils of Alexandria, Helwan and Mansoura, Cairo Univ. Centre for Devt and Technological Planning Research; Egyptian Order of Merit (First Class) 1964, 1975, 1980, Medal for Championship of Labour (USSR) 1964, Order of Merit (First Class) (France) 1983, Order of the Nile (Kiladat El Nil) (highest state honour) 1994; UN Habitat Prize for Housing 1992. *Address:* No. 20, Alhamd Building, El-Kafrawy Road, District 2/Section 5, 6th of October City, Egypt. *Telephone:* (2) 38369851. *Fax:* (2) 38369853. *E-mail:* kafegy@yahoo.com; mkafrawi@gmail.com.

KAGAME, Maj.-Gen. Paul; Rwandan politician, army officer and head of state; *President;* b. 1957; m.; four c.; ed Fort Leavenworth, USA; escaped to Uganda with family from anti-Tutsi persecution 1960; joined Ugandan Rebel Army 1982, Chief of Intelligence Ugandan Army 1986; formed rebel army of Rwandan exiles 1990, Leader campaign in Rwanda 1990–94, helped broker cease-fire 1993; Vice-Pres. and Minister of Nat. Defence 1994–2000, Pres. of Rwanda April 2000–; Head Rwandan Patriotic Front Party (FPR) 2000; Young Presidents' Org. 2003, Africa Gender Award 2007. *Leisure interests:* tennis, reading. *Address:* Office of the President, BP 15, Kigali, Rwanda (office). *Telephone:* (590) 62007 (office). *Fax:* 752431 (office). *E-mail:* pkagame@gov.rw (office). *Website:* www.gov.rw (office).

KAGAN, Elena, MPh, JD; American lawyer, academic and government official; *Associate Justice, Supreme Court;* b. 28 April 1960, New York City; d. of Robert Kagan and Gloria Gittelman; ed Hunter Coll. High School, Princeton Univ., Worcester Coll., Oxford, UK, Harvard Law School; law clerk for Judge Abner Mikva, US Court of Appeals, DC Circuit 1986–87, for Justice Thurgood Marshall, US Supreme Court 1987–88; Assoc., Williams & Connolly (law firm), Washington, DC 1989–91; Asst Prof., Univ. of Chicago Law School 1991–95, Tenured Prof. of Law 1995; Assoc. Counsel to the Pres., The White House 1995–96, Deputy Asst to Pres. for Domestic Policy and Deputy Dir of Domestic Policy Council 1997–99; Visiting Prof., Harvard Law School 1999–2001, Prof. of Law 2001–03, Charles Hamilton Houston Prof. of Law 2003–09, Dean of Faculty of Law 2003–09; Solicitor

Gen. of the US, Dept of Justice, Washington, DC 2009–10; Assoc. Justice, US Supreme Court 2010–; ranked by Forbes magazine amongst The World's 100 Most Powerful Women (25th) 2010. *Publications:* contribs to journals including Harvard Law Review, Supreme Court Review, Univ. of Chicago Law Review, Texas Law Review, Law and Social Inquiry. *Address:* Supreme Court of the United States, 1 First Street, NE, Washington, DC 20543, USA (office). *Telephone:* (202) 479-3000 (office); (202) 479-3011 (Clerk's Office) (office); (202) 479-3211 (Public Information Office) (office). *E-mail:* info@supremecourt.gov (office). *Website:* www .supremecourt.gov (office).

KAGAN, Henri B., PhD; French chemist and academic; *Professor Emeritus, Université Paris-Sud 11;* b. 15 Dec. 1930, Boulogne-sur-Seine; s. of Alexandre Kagan and Adeline Celmiker; m. Claude Vignon 1960; three d.; ed Sorbonne, École Nat. Supérieure de Chimie, Paris; Research Assoc., Collège de France 1962–67; Visiting Researcher, Univ. of Texas, Austin, USA 1965, Visiting Prof. 1980; Asst Prof., Université Paris-Sud 11, Orsay 1967–73, Prof. 1973–99, Prof. Emer. 1999–; Prof., Institut Universitaire de France 1993–99; mem. Acad. des Sciences 1991–; Foreign mem. Polish Acad. of Sciences 1994–; Visiting Prof. at several int. univs including Fort Collins, Colo, USA 1976, Uppsala, Sweden 1998, Weizmann Inst., Israel 1988; JSPS, Japan 1977, 2001–03; Hon. Fellow, Chemical Research Soc. of India 2000; Hon. FRSC 2003; Chevalier, Ordre nat. du Mérite 1996, Légion d'honneur 2002; Dr hc (Bucharest) 1999, (Basilicata) 2004, (Montréal) 2008; numerous awards including French Chemical Soc. Le Bel Award 1967, Cahours Award, Acad. des Sciences 1968, Prelog Medal, ETH, Zurich 1990, Chaire Francqui, Louvain 1994, August-Wilhelm von Hofmann Medal 1991, Yamada Prize 1998, Nagoya Medal for Organic Chem. 1998, Tetrahedron Prize 1999, Wolf Prize in Chem. 2001, Grand Prix de la Fondation de la Maison de la Chimie 2002, Ryoji Noyori Prize 2002, Bower Award and Prize for Achievement in Science, Franklin Inst. 2005, Horst-Pracejus Prize 2007. *Publications:* books include Stéréochimie organique 1975; more than 300 scientific articles 1955–2005. *Leisure interest:* history. *Address:* Equipe de Catalyse Moléculaire-ICMMO – Bât 420, Université Paris-Sud 11, 15 rue Georges Clemenceau, 91405 Orsay Cedex (office); 10 rue Georges Clemenceau, 91400 Orsay, France (home). *Telephone:* 1-69-15-78-95 (office). *Fax:* 1-69-15-46-80 (office). *E-mail:* henri.kagan@u-psud.fr (office). *Website:* www.icmo.u-psud.fr/Labos/LCM/cv/hkagan.php (office).

KAGARLITSKY, Boris Yuliyevich, PhD; Russian journalist and writer; *Director, Institute of Globalization Studies and Social Movements;* b. 1958, Moscow; ed State Inst. of Theatrical Art; Ed. Leviy povorot (samizdat journal) 1978–82; Co-ordinator Moscow People's Front 1988; Deputy, Moscow city Soviet (prov. Parl.) 1990–93; Founding mem. Party of Labour 1992; fmr adviser to Chair., Fed. of Ind. Trade Unions of Russia; Sr Research Fellow, Inst. of Comparative Political Studies, Russian Acad. of Sciences 1994–2002; Dir Inst. of Globalization Studies 2003–07, Inst. of Globalization Studies and Social Movts 2007–; columnist, The Moscow Times, ZNet. *Publications:* The Thinking Reed (Deutscher Memorial Prize) 1988, The Dialectic of Hope 1989, Farewell Perestroika: A Soviet Chronicle 1990, Disintegration of the Monolith 1993, Square Wheels: How Russian Democracy Got Derailed 1994, The Mirage of Modernisation 1995, Restoration in Russia 1995, New Realism, New Barbarism: Socialist Theory in the Era of Globalization 1999, The Twilight of Globalization: Property, State and Capitalism 1999, The Return of Radicalism: Reshaping the Left Institutions 2000, Russia under Yeltsin and Putin: Neo-liberal Autocracy 2002, The Politics of Empire: Globalisation in Crisis (co–ed.) 2004; contribs Novaya Gazeta, The Progressive, Red Pepper, Green Left Weekly. *Address:* Institute of Globalization Studies and Social Movements, Gazetny per. 5, Moscow, Russia (office). *E-mail:* kagarlitsky@narod.ru. *Website:* kagarlitsky.narod.ru (office); www.iprog.ru (office).

KAGERMANN, Henning, PhD; German software industry executive; *Chairman of the Executive Board and CEO, SAP AG;* b. 1948; Lecturer in Theoretical Physics and Computer Science, Tech. Univ. of Braunschweig and Univ. of Mannheim 1982–92; joined SAP (business-application software co.) AG 1982, apptd to Exec. Bd 1991, Co-Chair. 1998–2002, Co-Chair. and CEO 2002–03, Chair. and CEO 2003–; mem. Supervisory Bd Deutsche Bank AG, Daimler-Chrysler Services AG, Münchener Rückversicherungs-Gesellschaft AG; Trustee Tech. Univ. of Munich. *Address:* SAP AG, Neuroffstrasse 16, 69190 Walldorf, Germany (office). *Telephone:* (6227) 747474 (office). *Fax:* (6227) 757575 (office). *E-mail:* info.germany@sap.com (office). *Website:* www.sap.com (office).

KAGEYAMA, Mahito; Japanese business executive; *Executive Vice-President, Toyota Tsusho Corporation;* b. 28 Jan. 1949; joined Sanwa Bank Ltd (later UFJ Bank Ltd) 1972, Exec. Officer 1999–2002, Sr Exec. Officer 2002–03 (resgnd); Sr Advisor, Tomen Corpn Feb.–June 2003, Pres. June 2003–2006, Exec. Vice-Pres. Toyota Tsusho Corp. (after merger of Tomen with Toyota Tsusho Corp.) 2006–. *Address:* Toyota Tsusho Corporation, 9-8, Meieki, 4-chome, Nakamura-ku, Nagoya 450-8575, Japan (office). *Telephone:* (52) 584-5000 (office). *Fax:* (52) 584-5663 (office). *Website:* www.toyota-tsusho.com (office).

KAHIN, Dahir Riyale; Somali politician; mem. United Peoples' Democratic Party; fmr Gov. Awdal Prov; Vice-Pres. self-proclaimed Repub. of Somaliland (NW Somalia)–2002, Pres. 2002–10. *Address:* c/o Office of the President of the Republic of Somaliland, Hargeysa, Somalia (office). *Website:* www.somalilandgov.com.

KAHN, C. Ronald, BA, MD, MS; American medical scientist and academic; *Senior Investigator and Head of the Section on Obesity and Hormone Action, Mary K. Iacocca Professor of Medicine and Vice Chairman of the Board, Elliott P. Joslin Diabetes Center, Harvard Medical School;* b. Louisville, Ky; ed Univ. of Louisville; Intern and Resident, Barnes Hosp., Ward Medicine Saint Louis, Mo. 1968–70; Clinical Assoc. and Sr Clinical Assoc., Clinical Endocrinology Br., Nat. Insts of Arthritis, Metabolism and Digestive Diseases, NIH, Bethesda, Md 1970–73, Diabetes Br. 1973–78 (Chief of Section on Cellular and Molecular Physiology 1979–81), Admitting and Attending Physician, Clinical Center 1972–81; Visiting Scientist, Centre de Moleculaire, CNRS, Gif-Sur-Yvette, France 1979–80; Adjunct Prof. of Genetics, George Washington Univ., Washington, DC 1980–81; Clinical Assoc. Prof. of Medicine, Uniformed Services Univ. of Health Sciences, Bethesda 1981; Assoc. Prof. of Medicine, Harvard Univ. Medical School Boston, Mass 1981–84, Prof. of Medicine 1984–, Mary K. Iacocca Prof. of Medicine 1986–, also Sr Investigator and Head, Section on Obesity and Hormone Action, Dir Elliot P. Joslin Research Lab., Joslin Diabetes Center, Boston 1981–, Sr Staff, Joslin Clinic

1985–, Exec. Vice-Pres. and Dir Joslin Diabetes Center 1997–2000, Pres. 2000, now Vice-Chair.; Assoc. Staff, Dept of Endocrinology and Internal Medicine, New England Deaconess Hosp., Boston 1981–85, Active Staff 1986–; Physician, Brigham and Women's Hosp., Boston 1981–91, Chief, Div. of Diabetes and Metabolism, Dept of Medicine 1981–92, Sr Physician 1992–, Sr Consultant in Diabetes and Metabolism 1993–; Prof. in Endocrinology and Metabolism, The Hosp. of the Good Samaritan, Los Angeles, CA 1985; Visiting Prof., Royal Postgraduate Hosp., London, UK 1985; Overseas Visiting Prof., Royal Melbourne Hosp., Melbourne, Australia 1985; Roerig Visiting Professorship in Diabetes, Univ. of Colorado Health Sciences Center, Denver, Colo 1990; Visiting Scientist, Dana Farber Cancer Inst., Dept of Cellular and Molecular Biology, Boston 1990–91; Visiting Research Scientist, Brandeis Univ., Waltham, Mass 1998–99; Exec. Ed. Trends in Endocrinology and Metabolism 1989–90; Consulting Ed. The Journal of Clinical Investigation 1992–; Assoc. Ed. Diabetes 1996–; mem. Editorial Bd Diabetes and Metabolism Reviews 1984–, Receptor 1989–, Trends in Endocrinology and Metabolism 1991–, Journal of Receptor Research 1992–, Proceedings of the Association of American Physicians 1997–, American Journal of Medicine 1998–; mem. Advisory Bd Endocrine Reviews 2001–; mem. American Fed. for Clinical Research 1972–, The Endocrine Soc. 1975– (mem. Council 1990–93), American Diabetes Assccn (ADA) 1976–, American Soc. for Clinical Investigation 1979– (Pres. 1988–89), American Soc. of Biological Chem. 1982–, Asscn of American Physicians 1983–, Nat. Council of American Soc. for Clinical Investigation 1985–, NAS 1999–, NAS Insts of Medicine 1999–; Fellow, American Acad. of Arts and Sciences 1991–, AAAS 1994–; Alumni Fellow, Univ. of Louisville 1993–; Hon. DSc (Louisville) 1984, (Université de Paris Pierre et Marie Curie) 1990; Hon. MA (Louisville) 1984; David Rumbough Memorial Award for Scientific Achievement, Juvenile Diabetes Foundation 1977, ADA Eli Lilly Award for Research 1981, Award for Outstanding Clinical Research Under Age 40, American Fed. for Clinical Research 1983, Pfizer Biomedical Research Award 1986, Cristobal Diaz Award, Int. Diabetes Foundation 1988, Top 100 Most-Cited Scientists for 1973–84 and 1981–88, The Scientist 1990, ADA Banting Medal for Distinguished Scientific Achievement 1993, Distinguished Scientist Award, Clinical Ligand Assay Soc. 1997, ADA Albert Renold Award 1998, Dorothy Hodgkin Award, British Diabetes Asscn 1999, Int. Soc. of Endocrinology Award, CCISE 2000, Fred Conrad Koch Award, The Endocrine Soc. 2000, and other awards. *Publications:* more than 440 articles in medical and scientific journals. *Address:* Kahn Lab, Harvard Medical School, Joslin Diabetes Center, One Joslin Place, Room 705, Boston, MA 02215, USA (office). *Telephone:* (617) 732-2635 (office). *Fax:* (617) 732-2540 (office). *E-mail:* c.ronald.kahn@joslin.harvard.edu (office). *Website:* www.joslin.org (office).

KAHN, Eugene (Gene) S.; American retail executive; *CEO, Claire's Stores Inc.;* b. 1950; ed City Coll. of NY; began retail career at Gimbel's 1971; joined The May Dept Stores Co. 1990, Pres. and CEO G. Fox Div. 1990–92, Pres. and CEO Filene Div. 1992–96, apptd to Bd of Dirs 1996, Vice-Chair. 1996–97, Exec. Vice-Chair. 1997–98, Pres. and CEO 1998–2001, Chair. and CEO 2001–05; CEO Claire's Stores Inc. 2005–, also mem. Bd of Dirs; fmr Treas., Mary Inst. and St Louis Country Day School; fmr mem. Bd of Trustees, Wash. Univ. at St Louis. *Address:* Claire's Stores, Inc. 3 S.W. 129th Avenue, Pembroke Pines, FL 33027, USA (office). *Telephone:* (954) 433-3900 (office). *Fax:* (954) 433-3999 (office). *Website:* www .clairestores.com (office).

KAHN, Jacob Meyer, BA (Law), MBA; South African business executive; b. 29 June 1939, Pretoria; m. Lynette Sandra Asher 1968; two d.; ed Univ. of Pretoria; apptd Dir South African Breweries Ltd 1981, Group Man. Dir 1983, Exec. Chair. 1990, Group Chair. 1999; Chair. SABMiller plc 1999–2012; Chief Exec. South African Police Service 1997–99; Co-founder AfroCentric Investment Corpn Ltd 2006–; fmr Pres. SA Foundation; Prof. Extraordinaire 1989; Hon. DComm (Univ. of Pretoria) 1990; Marketing Man of the Year 1987, Business Man of the Year 1990, Award for Business Excellence 1991, South African Police Star of Excellence for Outstanding Service 2000. *Leisure interests:* reading, golf. *Address:* Afro-Centric Investment Corporation Limited, 37 Conrad Road, Florida North, Roodepoort, Johannesburg 1709 (office); 4 East Road, Morningside, Sandton, Johannesburg, South Africa (home). *Telephone:* (11) 7836061 (home). *Fax:* (11) 7836061 (home). *Website:* www.afrocentric.za.com (office).

KAHN, Robert Elliot (Bob), BEE, MA, PhD; American computer scientist and electrical engineer; *Chairman, President and CEO, Corporation for National Research Initiatives;* b. 23 Dec. 1938, Brooklyn, NY; s. of Lawrence Kahn and Beatrice Pauline Kahn (née Tashker); ed City Coll. of New York, Princeton Univ.; fmr mem. Tech. Staff, Bell Labs; later Asst Prof. of Electrical Eng, MIT; joined US Defense Advanced Research Projects Agency 1972, later Dir Information Processing Techniques Office; f. Corpn for Nat. Research Initiatives (CNRI) 1986, currently Chair., Pres. and CEO; mem. Bd of Dirs Qualcomm; mem. Nat. Acad. of Eng; Fellow, IEEE, AAAI, Asscn for Computing Machinery (ACM) 2001, Computer History Museum 2006; Hon. Fellow, Soc. for Tech. Communication 2006, Univ. Coll. London; Dr hc (Princeton, Pavia, ETH Zurich, Maryland, George Mason, Central Florida, Pisa, St Petersburg Nat. Research Univ. of Information Technologies, Mechanics and Optics); AFIPS Harry Goode Memorial Award, Marconi Award, ACM SIGCOMM Award, ACM Pres.'s Award, ACM Software Systems Award, IEEE Koji Kobayashi Computer and Communications Award, IEEE Alexander Graham Bell Medal, IEEE Third Millennium Medal, Computerworld/Smithsonian Award, ASIS Special Award, Computing Research Bd Public Service Award, Sec. of Defense Civilian Service Award (twice), Nat. Medal of Tech. 1997, Charles Stark Draper Prize, Nat. Acad. of Eng 2001, Prince of Asturias Award 2002, Digital ID World Award 2003, A.M. Turing Award, Asscn for Computing Machinery 2004, Townsend Harris Medal, Alumni Asscn of the City Coll. of New York 2005, Presidential Medal of Freedom 2005, C & C Prize, Tokyo, Japan 2005, inducted into Nat. Inventors Hall of Fame 2006, Japan Prize (co-recipient) 2008, Harold Pender Award, Univ. of Pennsylvania 2010, inducted into Internet Hall of Fame 2012, Queen Elizabeth Prize for Eng (co-recipient) 2013. *Achievements include:* co-inventor of TCP/IP protocols, Knowbot programs, originated concept of architecture networking. *Address:* Corporation for National Research Initiatives, 1895 Preston White Drive, Suite 100, Reston, VA 20191-5434, USA (office). *Telephone:* (703) 620-8990 (office). *Fax:* (703) 620-0913 (office). *E-mail:* web-comments@cnri.reston.va.us (office). *Website:* www.cnri.reston.va.us (office).

KAHNEMAN, Daniel, PhD; Israeli/American psychologist and academic; *Eugene Higgins Professor of Psychology and Professor of Public Affairs, Woodrow Wilson School, Princeton University;* b. 1934, Tel-Aviv; m. Anne Treisman; ed The Hebrew Univ., Jerusalem, Univ. of California, Berkeley; Lecturer in Psychology, The Hebrew Univ. 1961–66, Sr Lecturer 1966–70, Assoc. Prof. 1970–73, Prof. 1973–78; Lecturer in Psychology, Harvard Univ. 1966–67; Prof. of Psychology, Univ. of British Columbia, Canada 1978–86; Prof. of Psychology, Univ. of Calif., Berkeley 1986–94; Eugene Higgins Prof. of Psychology, Princeton Univ. 1993–, Prof. of Public Affairs, Woodrow Wilson School 1993–; Visiting Scientist, Univ. of Michigan 1965–66, Applied Psychological Research Unit, Cambridge, UK 1968–69; Fellow, Centre for Cognitive Studies 1966–67, Centre for Advanced Studies in the Behavioural Sciences 1977–78, Centre for Rationality, The Hebrew Univ. 2000–; Assoc. Fellow, Canadian Inst. for Advanced Research 1984–86; Visiting Scholar, Russell Sage Foundation 1991–92; Fellow, American Acad. of Arts and Sciences, Econometric Soc., American Psychological Asscn, American Psychological Soc., Canadian Psychological Asscn; mem. NAS, Soc. of Experimental Psychologists, Psychonomic Soc., Soc. for Econ. Science, Soc. for Judgement and Decision Making (Pres. 1992–93); mem. Ed. Bd Journal of Behavioral Decision Making, Journal of Risk and Uncertainty, Thinking and Reasoning, Economics and Philosophy; Hon. DrSc (Univ. of Pennsylvania Contrib.) 2001; Distinguished Scientific Contrib. Award, American Psychological Soc. 1982, Distinguished Scientific Contrib. Award, Soc. of Consumer Psychology 1992, Warren Medal, Soc. of Experimental Psychologists 1995, Hilgard Award for Lifetime Contrib. to General Psychology 1995, Nobel Prize for Econ. Sciences 2002. *Achievements include:* pioneered integration of research about decision-making into field of econs. *Publications include:* Attention and Effort 1973, Human Engineering of Decisions in Ethics in an Age of Uncertainty 1980, Well-Being: Foundations of Hedonic Psychology (co-ed.) 1999, Choices, Values and Frames (co-ed.) 2000, Heuristics and Biases: The Psychology of Intuitive Judgement (co-ed.) 2002; author or co-author of over 120 articles in professional journals and chapters in books. *Address:* 332 Wallace Hall, Woodrow Wilson School, Princeton University, Princeton, NJ 08544-1013, USA (office). *Telephone:* (609) 258-2280 (office). *Fax:* (609) 258-5974 (office). *E-mail:* kahneman@princeton.edu (office). *Website:* www.wws.princeton.edu (office).

KAIFU, Toshiki; Japanese politician; b. 2 Jan. 1931, Nagoya City; m. Sachiyo Kaifu; ed Waseda Univ.; elected to House of Reps (LDP) 1960 and served 16 terms –2009; Parl. Vice-Minister of Labour; Chair. Steering Cttee of House of Reps; various posts in admin. of the late Takeo Miki 1974–76, including Deputy Chief Cabinet Sec. 1974–76, Chair. of Diet Policy Cttee of Liberal Democratic Party (LDP); Minister of Educ. 1976–77, 1985–86; Prime Minister of Japan 1989–91 (resgnd); Leader New Frontier Party (opposition coalition) 1994–95; currently Chair. 21st Century World Expo Promotion Parliamentary League. *Address:* ; c/o Liberal-Democratic Party, 1-11-23, Nagata-cho, Chiyoda-ku, Tokyo 100-8910, Japan.

KAIN, Karen, CC; Canadian ballet dancer and arts administrator; *Artistic Director, National Ballet of Canada;* b. 28 March 1951, Hamilton, Ont.; d. of Charles A. Kain and Winifred Mary Kelly; m. Ross Petty 1983; ed Nat. Ballet School; joined Nat. Ballet of Canada 1969, Prin. 1970, Artistic Assoc. 1999–2005, Artistic Dir 2005–; has danced most of major roles in repertoire, appeared as Giselle with Bolshoi Ballet on USSR tour, Aurora in the Sleeping Beauty with London Festival Ballet in UK and Australia, in Swan Lake with Vienna State Opera Ballet; toured Japan and Korea with Ballet national de Marseille 1981; cr. roles of Chosen Maiden in The Rite of Spring for Nat. Ballet 1979, Giuletta in Tales of Hoffman for Ballet national de Marseille 1982, the Bride in The Seven Daggers/ Los Siete Puñales and roles in Glen Tetley's Alice 1986, La Ronde 1987, Daphnis and Chlöe 1988, Tagore 1989, Musings 1991, James Kudelka's The Actress 1994; appeared in CBC-TV productions of Giselle, La Fille Mal Gardée, The Merry Widow, Alice, La Ronde; Pres. The Dancer's Transition Centre; Officier des Arts et Lettres; hon. degrees from York, McMaster and Trent Univs; Silver Medal, Second Int. Ballet Competition, Moscow 1973, Int. Emmy Award for Karen Kain: Dancing in the Moment, Gov.-Gen.'s Award for Lifetime Achievement in the Performing Arts, Barbara Hamilton Memorial Award 2007, Distinguished Artist Award, Int. Soc. for the Performing Arts 2011. *Publication:* Movement Never Lies (autobiog.) 1994. *Address:* The Walter Carsen Centre for The National Ballet of Canada, 470 Queens Quay West, Toronto, ON M5V 3K4, Canada (office). *Telephone:* (416) 345-9686 (office). *Fax:* (416) 345-8323 (office). *E-mail:* info@national.ballet.ca (office). *Website:* www.national.ballet.ca (office).

KAINE, Timothy (Tim) Michael, BA (Econ); American politician; *Senator from Virginia;* b. 26 Feb. 1958, St Paul, Minn.; s. of Albert A. Kaine and Mary Kathleen Kaine (née Burns); m. Anne Holton 1984; two s. one d.; ed Rockhurst High School, Kansas City, Mo., Univ. of Missouri, Columbia, Harvard Law School; Coro Foundation Fellow, Kansas City 1978; worked as missionary in Honduras; admitted to the Virginia Bar; clerked for Judge R. Lanier Anderson on the 11th Circuit Court of Appeals; practised law in Richmond for 17 years; taught legal ethics at Univ. of Richmond Law School for six years; mem. City Council of Richmond, Va, Mayor of Richmond 1998–2001; Lt Gov. and Pres. of the Senate of Va 2002–06; Gov. of Va 2006–10; Chair. Democratic Nat. Cttee 2009–11; Senator from Virginia 2013–; Democrat. *Leisure interests:* camping, hiking, cycling, canoeing. *Address:* United States Senate, Washington, DC 20510, USA (office). *Telephone:* (202) 224-3121 (switchboard) (office). *Website:* www.senate.gov (office).

KAISER, Karl, PhD; German/American political scientist and academic; *Adjunct Professor of Public Policy, John F. Kennedy School of Government and Director, Program on Transatlantic Relations, Weatherhead Center for International Affairs, Harvard University;* b. 8 Dec. 1934, Siegen, North Rhine-Westphalia, Germany; s. of Walther Kaiser and Martha Müller; m. Deborah Strong 1967; two s. one d.; ed Univs of Cologne, Bonn and Grenoble and Nuffield Coll., Oxford, UK; Lecturer, Harvard Univ., USA 1963–67, Univ. of Bonn 1968–69, Johns Hopkins Univ. Bologna Center, Italy 1968–69; Prof. of Political Science, Univ. of the Saarland 1969–74, Univ. of Cologne 1974–91, Univ. of Bonn 1991–2000; Otto-Wolf Dir Research Inst. of German Council on Foreign Relations, Bonn and Berlin 1973–2003; Ralph I. Straus Visiting Prof., John F. Kennedy School of Govt, Harvard Univ., now Adjunct Prof. of Public Policy and Dir Program on Transat- lantic Relations, Weatherhead Center for Int. Affairs; Visiting Prof., European Univ. Inst., Florence, Hebrew Univ., Jerusalem; mem. German Council of

Environmental Advisors; mem. Bd Foreign Policy, Internationale Politik, Asian-Pacific Review, Russia in Global Affairs; mem. Advisory Bd American-Jewish Cttee, Berlin; mem. Bd Fed. Acad. of Security Policy, Berlin; mem. American Philosophical Soc. 2007; Hon. CBE 1989, Officier, Légion d'honneur 1991, Bundesverdienstkreuz, Erster Klasse 1999, Großes Verdienstkreuz 2009, Polish Order of Merit (First Class) 2002; Dr hc (Russian Acad. of Sciences); Prix Adolphe Bentinck 1973, NATO Atlantic Award 1986. *Publications:* EEC and Free Trade Area 1963, German Foreign Policy in Transition 1968, Europe and the USA 1973, New Tasks for Security Policy 1977, Reconciling Energy Needs and Proliferation 1978, Western Security: What Has Changed, What Can be Done? 1981, Atomic Energy Without Nuclear Weapons 1982, German–French Security Policy 1986, British–German Co-operation 1987, Space and International Politics 1987, Germany's Unification, The International Aspects 1991, Germany and the Iraq Conflict 1992, Foreign Policies of the New Republics in Eastern Europe 1994, Germany's New Foreign Policy, Vol. 1 1994, Vol. 2 1995, Vol. 3 1996, The Foreign Policies of the New Democracies in Central and Eastern Europe 1994, Acting for Europe, German-French Co-operation in a Changing World 1995, World Politics in a New Era 1996, Interests and Strategies 1996, Institutions and Resources 1998, The Future of German Foreign Policy 1999, Russia and the West 1999, Germany's New Foreign Policy 2001, Shaping a New International Financial System 2002. *Leisure interests:* music, sailing. *Address:* Kennedy School of Government, Mailbox 40, 79 JFK Street, Cambridge, MA 02138-5801, USA (office). *Telephone:* (617) 495-1899 (office). *Fax:* (617) 495-8292 (office). *E-mail:* karl_kaiser@hks.harvard.edu (office). *Website:* www.hks.harvard.edu (office).

KAISER, Michael M., BA, SM; American arts administrator; *President, John F. Kennedy Center for Performing Arts;* ed Brandeis Univ. and Sloan School of Man., MIT; Founder and Dir Michael M. Kaiser Assocs (consultancy) 1981–85, Kaiser/ Engler (arts man. consultancy) 1994, Pres. 1994–95; Exec. Dir Alvin Ailey Dance Theater Foundation 1991–93, American Ballet Theatre 1995–98, Royal Opera House, London 1998–2000; Pres. John F. Kennedy Center for Performing Arts, Washington DC 2001–; Adjunct Prof. of Business Admin., Rockhurst Coll., Kan. 1985–86; Adjunct Prof. of Arts Admin., New York Univ.; US Del. to Advisory Comm. on Arts Funding Policies of S African Govt 1994–95; Visiting Prof. of Arts Admin., Univ. of Witwatersrand 1995; Assoc. Dir State Ballet of Mo. 1985–87, Pierpoint Morgan Library 1987–89; mem. Bd of Dirs New York Foundation for the Arts; fmr Dir Washington Opera, Ensemble Studio Theater, PS 122; Order of the Mexican Eagle 2006; Dance Magazine Award 2001, Capezio Award 2002, Helen Hayes Washington Post Award for Innovative Leadership in the Theater Community 2003, St Petersburg 300 Medal 2004, Washingtonian of the Year 2004, US Dept of State Citation 2005, Blacks in Dance Award 2005, Award for Cultural Exchange (China) 2005, Impresario of the Year by Musical America 2006, George Peabody Medal for Outstanding Contribs to Music in America 2009. *Publications:* Understanding the Competition: A Practical Guide to Competitive Analysis 1981, Developing Industry Strategies: A Practical Guide to Industry Analysis 1983, Strategic Planning in the Arts: A Practical Guide 1995, The Art of the Turnaround 2008. *Address:* John F. Kennedy Center for Performing Arts, 2700 F Street, NW, Washington, DC 20566, USA (office). *Telephone:* (202) 416-8000 (office). *Website:* www.kennedy-center.org (office).

KAIWA, Makoto; Japanese business executive; *Representative Director and President, Tohoku Electric Power Company Inc.;* Exec. Dir Yurtec Corpn 2005–; Exec. Vice-Pres. and Dir Tohoku Electric Power Co. Inc. –2010, Rep. Dir and Pres. 2010-. *Address:* Tohoku Electric Power Company Inc., 7-1 Honcho 1-chome, Aoba-ku, Sendai, Miyagi 980-8550, Japan (office). *Telephone:* (2) 2225-2111 (office). *Fax:* (2) 2225-2500 (office). *Website:* www.tohoku-epco.co.jp (office).

KAJANTIE, Keijo Olavi, PhD; Finnish physicist and academic (retd); b. 31 Jan. 1940, Hämeenlinna; m. Riitta Erkiö 1963; one s. one d.; ed Univ. of Helsinki; mil. service 1957–58; Visiting Scientist, CERN, Geneva 1966–67, 1969–70, 1995–98; Assoc. Prof. of Physics, Univ. of Helsinki 1970–72, Prof. 1973–2008 (retd), fmr Head of Theoretical Physics Div.; Visiting Prof., Univ. of Wis., Madison 1975; Research Prof., Acad. of Finland 1985–90; Sr Scientist 2002–03. *Publications:* more than 180 publs in the field of elementary particle physics. *Address:* Department of Physics, PO Box 64, 00014 University of Helsinki, Helsinki (office); Liisankatu 1D 26, 00170 Helsinki, Finland (home). *Telephone:* (9) 19150530 (office); (9) 1352232 (home). *E-mail:* keijo.kajantie@helsinki.fi (office). *Website:* www.helsinki.fi/~kajantie (office); theory.physics.helsinki.fi/~qftgroup (office).

KAJIYAMA, Tisato, PhD, DEng; Japanese polymer chemist, academic and university administrator; ed Univ. of Massachusetts, USA, Kyushu Univ.; Prof., Dept of Applied Chem., Faculty of Eng, Kyushu Univ., Pres. Kyushu Univ. and Head, Kyushu Univ. User Science Inst. 2001–10. *Publications include:* New Developments in Construction and Functions of Organic Thin Films 1996, Polymer Science and Industrial Research in the Fast-Changing Age: 7th SPSJ Int. Polymer Conference (ed.) 2000, Macromolecular Symposia 159: Polymer Science and Industrial Research (ed.); numerous scientific papers in professional journals on polymer chemistry.

KAJORNPRASART, Maj.-Gen. Sanan; Thai politician and fmr military officer; b. 7 Sept. 1944, Phichit; ed Chulachomklao Royal Mil. Acad.; aide-de-camp to Gen. Chalard Hiranyasiri; involved in attempted coup 1981; mem. Parl. (Democrat Party) for Phichit 1983, 1986, 1988; Deputy Communications Minister 1986; Minister of Agric. and Co-operatives 1989, of Industry 1992–94, of the Interior 1997–2000; Deputy Prime Minister 1990–91, 1997–2000, 2008–11; Sec.-Gen. Democrat Party 1988–2000; Leader, Mahachon Party 2005–07; mem. Chart Thai Pattana (Thai Nation Devt) Party 2008–. *Address:* Chart Thai Pattana, 37/157 Moo 11, Sansab, Minburi, Bangkok, Thailand (office).

KAKÁ; Brazilian/Italian professional footballer; b. (Ricardo Izecson dos Santos Leite), 22 April 1982, Brasilia; s. of Bosco Izecson Pereira Leite and Simone Cristina Santos Leite; m. Caroline Celico 2005; one s.; attacking midfielder; began career playing for local club Alphaville aged eight; signed first professional contract with São Paulo FC aged 15, sr team debut Jan. 2001, scored 12 goals in 27 appearances, also led São Paulo to first and only Torneio Rio-São Paulo championship, scored 10 goals in 22 matches 2002, led team to Super Campeonato Paulista title 2002, made 58 appearances for São Paulo, scoring 23 times; signed by AC Milan, Italy for 8.5 million euros ($12 million) 2003, added Champions League title for first time when AC Milan defeated Liverpool 2007, won Club World Cup title, UEFA Super Cup, FIFA Club World Cup and the Seria A title 2007; debuted with Brazilian nat. team in friendly against Bolivia Jan. 2002; mem. FIFA World Cup-winning squad 2002; Capt. of Brazil for CONCACAF Gold Cup tournament 2003, started in his first FIFA World Cup finals in Germany 2006, participated in FIFA Confederations Cup in S Africa 2009, winner of Golden Ball as player of the tournament, has made 73 appearances and scored 26 goals for Brazil–2009; signed by Real Madrid, Spain for 65 million euros ($100 million) 2009; Amb. Against Hunger for UN World Food Programme (youngest ever) 2004–; mem. Atletas de Cristo (Athletes of Christ); attained Italian citizenship 2007; Revista Placar Bola de Ouro 2002, Campeonato Brasileiro Bola de Prata (best player by position) 2002, CONCACAF Gold Cup Best XI 2003, Serie A Best New Player 2003, Serie A Foreign Footballer of the Year 2004, 2006, 2007, Serie A Footballer of the Year 2004, 2007, UEFA Champions League Bronze Top Scorer 2005–06, UEFA Champions League Best Midfielder 2005, UEFA Team of the Year 2006, 2007, FIFPro World XI 2006, 2007, 2008, Pallone d'Argento 2006–07, UEFA Champions League Top Scorer 2006–07, UEFA Champions League Best Forward 2006–07, UEFA Club Footballer of the Year 2006–07, FIFPro World Player of the Year 2007, Ballon d'Or 2007, FIFA Club World Cup Golden Ball 2007, Toyota Award 2007, FIFA World Player of the Year 2007, Onze d'Or 2007, IFFHS World's Best Playmaker 2007, IAAF Latin Sportsman of the Year 2007, Time 100 2008, 2009, Maracanã Hall Of Fame 2008, Samba d'Or: 2008, FIFA Team of the Year 2008, FIFA Confederations Cup Golden Ball 2009, FIFA Confederations Cup Best XI 2009. *Leisure interests:* favourite music is gospel, favourite book is the Bible. *Address:* c/o FC Real Madrid, Estadio Santiago Bernabeu, Paseo de la Castellana 104, Madrid, Spain. *Website:* www.realmadrid.com.

KAKAR, Sudhir, BE, Dipl.Kfm, PhD; Indian psychoanalyst, author and academic; *Adjunct Professor, INSEAD;* b. 1938, Nainital, Uttarakhand; m. Katharina Kakar; two c.; ed Gujarat Univ., Univ. of Mannheim, Germany, Sigmund Freud Inst., Frankfurt; Lecturer in Gen. Educ., Faculty of Arts and Sciences, Harvard Univ. 1966–67; Asst Prof., Indian Inst. of Man., Ahmedabad 1968–71; Visiting Lecturer, Sigmund Freud Inst., Frankfurt 1972; Visiting Prof. of Behavioural Sciences, Univ. of Econs, Vienna 1974–75; Prof. and Chair. Dept of Humanities and Social Sciences, Indian Inst. of Tech., New Delhi 1976–77; Visiting Prof., Dept of Psychology, Coll. and School of Divinity, Univ. of Chicago 1989–93; Adjunct Prof., INSEAD, Fontainbleau, France 1994–; Research Fellow, Program for Applied Psychoanalysis, Grad. School of Business Admin, Harvard Univ. 1967–78; Sr Fellow, Center for Study of Developing Socs, New Delhi 1980–90; Sr Fellow, Center for Study of World Religions, Harvard Univ. 2001–02; Fellow, Insts of Advanced Study, Princeton and Berlin; mem. Int. Psychoanalytical Asscn, New York Acad. of Sciences, Indian Psychological Soc.; Karolyi Foundation Award for Young Writers 1963, Boyer Prize for Psychological Anthropology, American Anthropological Asscn Award 1987, Goethe Medal of Goethe Institut Germany 1998, Abraham Kardiner Award, Columbia Univ. 2002, Distinguished Service Award of Indo-American Psychiatric Asscn 2007. *Publications include:* non-fiction: Fredrick Taylor: A Study in Personality and Innovation 1970, Conflict and Choice: Indian Youth in a Changing Society (co-author) 1971, The Inner World: A Psychoanalytic Study of Childhood and Society in India 1978, Shamans, Mystics and Doctors 1982, Tales of Love, Sex and Danger (co-author) 1986, Intimate Relations: Exploring Indian Sexuality 1989, The Analyst and the Mystic 1991, The Colours of Violence 1995, The Indian Psyche 1996, Culture and Psyche: Selected Essays 1996, The Indians: Portrait of a People (co-author) 2007, Mad and Divine: Spirit and Psyche in the Modern World 2008; fiction: novels: The Ascetic of Desire 1998, Ecstasy 2001, Mira and the Mahatma 2004, The Crimson Throne 2010; as ed.: Indian Love Stories 1999; as trans.: Kamasutra: A New Translation (co-author) 2002. *Address:* INSEAD, Boulevard de Constance, 77305 Fontaine-bleau, France (office); Pulwaddo Pequeno, Benaulim, Salcete, Goa, 403716, India (home). *Telephone:* (1) 60-72-43-68 (office). *Fax:* (1) 60-74-55-00/01 (office). *E-mail:* sudhir.kakar@insead.edu (home); sudhir_kakar@rediffmail.com. *Website:* www .insead.edu/facultyresearch/faculty/profiles/skakar (office); www.sudhirkakar .com (home).

KAKARAYA, Sir Pato, KBE, CMG, CBE; Papua New Guinea government official; b. 16 May 1939, Sambakmanda village, Enga Prov.; m. Immambu Kakaraya; four c.; adviser, Waso Ltd 1967–71; with Wabag Native Trading Co. 1971–72; MP for Wapenamanda 1972–87; Minister for Youth, Recreation and Women's Affairs 1977–78, for Environment and Conservation 1978–80; f. Peoples Democratic Movt; Gov.-Gen. of Papua New Guinea 2004; unsuccessful cand. for Gov.-Gen. Jan. 2011; currently Chair., Community Negotiation Cttee, Wapen; Nat. Patron, PNG Christian Community Services. *Address:* c/o Chairman, PNG Christian Community Services, POB 4699, Boroko NCD, Port Moresby (office); PO Box 787, Boroko NCD, Port Moresby, Papua New Guinea (home). *Telephone:* 76867210 (home); 73363231 (home). *E-mail:* mkakaraya@gmail.com (home).

KAKLAMANIS, Apostolos; Greek politician and lawyer; b. 7 Sept. 1936, Lefkas; s. of Christos Kaklamanis and Evageloula Kaklamanis; m. Athina-Anna Gavera 1972; one s. one d.; ed Univ. of Athens; Gen. Sec. Ministry of Welfare 1964–65; political prisoner during colonels' dictatorship; Founding mem. Pasok and mem. Cen. Cttee and Exec. Cttee; mem. Vouli (Parl.) for Athens B 1974–; Minister of Labour 1981–82, of Educ. and Religious Affairs 1982–86, of Justice 1986–87, Minister in charge of the Prime Minister's Office 1987–88, Minister of Health, Welfare and Social Services 1988–89, of Labour 1989–90; Speaker of Parl. 1993–2004. *Address:* Vouli, Parliament Bldg, Syntagma Square, 100 21 Athens (office); Solomou 58, 106 82 Athens, Greece (office). *Telephone:* (210) 3608640 (office); (210) 3708200 (office). *Fax:* (210) 3708210 (office). *E-mail:* apkaklamanis@ parliament.gr (office); ak@apkaklamanis.gr (office). *Website:* www.parliament.gr (office); www.apkaklamanis.gr (office).

KALADZE, Kakha; Georgian politician and fmr professional football player; *Deputy Prime Minister and Minister of Energy and Natural Resources;* b. 27 Feb. 1978, Samtredia, Imereti Prov.; m. Anouki Kaladze; one s.; began football career 1993, centre back, left back; played for: Dinamo Tbilisi 1993–98 (won Georgian League 1993/94, 1994/95, 1995/96, 1996/97, 1997/98, Georgian Cup 1994, 1995, 1996, 1997), Dynamo Kyiv 1998–2001 (won Ukrainian Premier League 1998/99, 1999/2000, 2000/01, Ukrainian Cup 1998, 1999, 2000), AC Milan 2001–10 (won Serie A 2003/04, Coppa Italia 2002/03, Italian Supercup 2004, UEFA Champions

League 2003, 2007, UEFA Super Cup 2003, 2007, FIFA Club World Cup 2007), Genoa 2010–12; played for Georgia U-17 team 1993–94, Georgia U-19 team 1995, Georgia U-21 team 1995–96, Georgia Nat. Team 1996–2011, Capt. 50 times in 84 appearances, announced retirement Dec. 2011; Owner Kala Capital, Kala Foundation; Amb. for SOS Children's Villages; mem. Georgian Dream-Democratic Georgia (Qartuli Ocneba) party 2012–; mem. Parl. 2012–; Deputy Prime Minister and Minister of Energy and Natural Resources Oct. 2012–; voted Georgian Footballer of the Year 2001–03, 2006, 2011. *Address:* Ministry of Energy and Natural Resources, 0105 Tbilisi, Gulua 6, Georgia (office). *Telephone:* (32) 235-78-00 (office). *Fax:* (32) 235-78-28 (office). *E-mail:* mail@menr.gov.ge (office). *Website:* www.minenergy.gov.ge (office).

KALAM, Aavul Pakkiri Jainulabidin Abdul, PhD; Indian nuclear scientist, university administrator and fmr head of state; *Chancellor, Indian Institute of Space Science and Technology;* b. 15 Oct. 1931, Dhanushkodi, Rameswaram Dist; ed Madras Inst. of Tech.; mem. staff Space Dept 1960s and 1970s, later Defence Lab., Hyderabad; launched India's first satellite 1980, masterminded integrated guided missile devt and nuclear programmes, developed Agni, Trishul and Prithvi missiles, responsible for carrying out underground nuclear tests 1998; fmr Cabinet Minister and Prin. Scientific Adviser to Govt 1999–2001; Chair. Tech. Information, Forecasting and Assessment Council; head of an agricultural devt agency; Pres. of India 2002–07; currently Chancellor, Indian Inst. of Space Science and Tech., Thiruvanthapuram; Prof., Anna Univ. 2001–; Dr hc (Univ. of Wolverhampton) 2007; Padma Bhusan 1981, Padma Vibhushan 1990, Prof. Y Nayudamma Memorial Gold Medal 1996, GM Modi Award for Science 1996, HK Firodia Award 1996, Bharat Ratna 1997, Indira Gandhi Award for Nat. Integration 1997, Veer Savarkar Award 1998, Ramanujan Award, Alwars Research Centre, Chennai 2000, Hoover Medal 2009. *Publications include:* Yenudaya Prayana (Tamil poems), Wings of Fire (bestselling autobiog.) 1999, Eternal Quest (children's novel), Ignited Minds: Unleashing the Power Within India 2001, India 2020: A Vision for the New Millennium 2003, India-my-dream 2004, Envisioning an Empowered Nation: Technology for Societal Transformation 2004, Guiding Souls: Dialogues on the Purpose of Life 2005, Children Ask Kalam. *Leisure interest:* music. *Address:* Office of the Chancellor, Indian Institute of Space Science and Technology, Thiruvananthapuram (office); 10 Rajaji Marg, New Delhi, India (home). *Telephone:* (471) 2564808 (office). *Fax:* (471) 2564806 (office). *E-mail:* ao@ iist.ac.in (office). *Website:* www.iist.ac.in/IIST (office).

KALAMANOV, Vladimir Avdashevich, DrHist; Russian government official; b. 1951, Moscow; ed Moscow State Inst. of Int. Relations; Head of Dept Ministry of Problems with Nationalities; Plenipotentiary Rep. of Pres. in Repubs. of N Ossetia and of Ingushetia 1997–99; Dir Fed. Migration Service of Russian Fed. 1999–2002; Special Rep. of Pres. to supervise observance of human rights and freedom in Chechen Repub. 2000; Perm. Rep. of Russian Fed. to UNESCO, Paris 2002–09, now with Int. Sustainable Energy Devt Centre under the Auspices of UNESCO (ISEDC), Moscow. *Address:* International Sustainable Energy Development Centre under the Auspices of UNESCO, Slavyanskaya sq. 4/2, Moscow, Russia (office). *Telephone:* (495) 625-46-03 (office). *E-mail:* info@isedc.com (office). *Website:* www.isedc.com (office).

KALANTARI, Issa, PhD; Iranian scientist and agriculturalist; *Director, Farmers' House;* b. 1952, Marand; s. of Mohammad Hussein Kalantari and Kobra Kalantari (née Esfandi); m. 1982; one s. one d.; ed Univ. of Urmiya, Univ. Nebraska and Iowa State Univ., USA; Dir Farmers' House (agricultural union) 1981–; Head of Agricultural Extension Org. 1982, Plant and Seed Improvement Research Inst. 1983, Deputy Minister for Agricultural Research, Educ. and Extension 1983–85, Man. Dir and Head of Bd of Dirs Moghan Stock-farming and Agro-Industry Complex, Ministry of Agric. 1985–88; Minister of Agric. 1988–2001; Pres. World Food Council 1991–95. *Publications:* A Policy for Reforming Nutrition Patterns: Nutrition Physiology and Foodstuff Economics 1997; series of articles in journal Agricultural Economics and Development. *Leisure interests:* reading, sport. *Address:* Farmers' House, 21, 33rd Street, JahanAra Avenue, Tehran (office); 5, Morshed, Sheidai Street, Gholhak, Tehran, Iran (home). *Telephone:* (21) 886390612 (office); 22001057 (home). *Fax:* (21) 88639060 (office). *E-mail:* issakalantari@gmail.com (home).

KALASHNIKOV, Sergey Vyacheslavovich, DPsych; Russian politician; b. 3 July 1951, Akmolinsk, Kazakh SSR; m. Natalia Kalashnikova; three c.; ed Leningrad State Univ., Inst. of Psychology, USSR (now Russian) Acad. of Sciences, Acad. of Nat. Econs USSR Council of Ministers, Russian Diplomatic Acad.; Head, Social-Psychological service of the Research Inst., USSR Ministry of Defence Industry, concurrently Chair. Inst. of Advanced Studies, USSR Ministry of Oil and Chemical Industry, Dir Intermanager State Enterprise 1979–91; Chair. Euro-pean-Asian Bank; concurrently Dir-Gen. Asscn of Defence against Unemployment and Poverty, Chair. Cttee on Labour and Social Policy in the State Duma, Deputy of the Duma, Chair. Perm. Cttee on Social Policy, Interparliamentary Ass. of CIS 1993–98; Minister of Labour and Social Devt 1998–2000; Deputy Sec.-Gen. Union of Russia and Belarus 2000–03; Head, Dept of Social Devt, Office of the Govt 2003–; Pres. Russian Fed. of the Sports Lover, Russian Asscn of Professional Golf; Chair. Nat. Council for Political and Social Reform; Co-Chair. Int. Forum 'World Experience and the Russian Economy'; mem. Bd Moscow English Club, Jury All-Russian Competition 'Best Russian Firms'; mem. Int. Acad. of Informatics, Russian Acad. of Science; Order of Friendship; Badge of Excellence for Border Services, Distinguished Worker of the Russian Ministry of Labour, Laureate, Nat. Peter the Great Prize. *Publications:* more than 50 works including two mono-graphs and textbook Social Psychology of Management. *Address:* Office of the Government, Krasnopresnenskaya nab. 2, 103274 Moscow, Russia (office). *Tele-phone:* (495) 205-57-35 (office). *Fax:* (495) 205-42-19 (office). *Website:* www .government.ru (office).

KALBFELL, Karl-Heinz; German automotive industry executive; b. 29 Dec. 1949; ed FH Druck Univ.; fmr boxer; responsible for advertising at Eriba/Hymer, camper and caravan builder 1975–77; Head of Marketing, BMW GmbH 1977, Man. 1988, Sr Vice-Pres. BMW Group Marketing, Dir Rolls-Royce Project 2001, Dir (non-exec.) 2003, Chair. and CEO Rolls-Royce Motor Cars June–Oct. 2004; Head, Alfa Romeo Jan.–Sept. 2005, CEO Maserati SpA 2005–06 (resgnd), Chair. Fiat Polo Sportivo planning comm. *Address:* c/o Maserati SpA, Viale Ciro Menotti 322, 41100 Modena, Italy (office).

KALETSKY, Anatole, MA; British journalist; *Chairman, Institute for New Economic Thinking*; b. 1 June 1952, Moscow, Russia; s. of Jacob Kaletsky and Esther Kaletsky; m. Fiona Murphy 1985; two s. one d.; ed Melbourne High School, Australia, Westminster City School and King's Coll., Cambridge, UK and Harvard Univ., USA; Hon. Sr Scholar, King's Coll., Cambridge 1973–74; Kennedy Scholar, Harvard Univ., USA 1974–76; financial writer, The Economist 1976–79; leader writer, Financial Times 1979–81, Washington Corresp. 1981–83, Int. Econs Corresp. 1984–86, Chief, New York Bureau 1986–90, Moscow Assignment 1990; Econs Ed. The Times 1990–96, Assoc. Ed. and econ. commentator 1992, Ed.-at-Large and Prin. Econ. Commentator –2012; with Reuters news agency 2012–; Chair. Inst. for New Economic Thinking 2012–; Dir Kaletsky Econ. Consulting 1997–; mem. Advisory Bd UK Know-How Fund for E Europe and fmr Soviet Union 1991, Royal Econs Soc. 1999–; Specialist Writer of the Year, British Press Awards 1980, 1992, Press Awards Commentator of the Year 1995, What the Papers Say 1996, Financial Journalist of the Year, Wincott Foundation Award 1997. *Publications:* The Costs of Default 1985, In the Shadow of Debt 1992, Capitalism 4.0 2010. *Leisure interests:* playing the violin, cinema, family life. *Address:* Institute for New Economic Thinking, 570 Lexington Avenue, 39th Floor, New York, NY 10022, USA (office). *Telephone:* (212) 444-9612 (office). *E-mail:* info@ineteconomics.org (office). *Website:* www.ineteconomics.org (office); blogs.reuters.com/anatole-kaletsky (office).

KALEYFAANU, Thalhath Ibrahim; Maldivian military officer and government official; joined Nat. Security Service 1989, First Lt, Nat. Defence Force –2006; Minister of Defence and Nat. Security 2011–12. *Address:* c/o Ministry of Defence and National Security, Ameer Ahmed Magu, Malé 20-126, Maldives.

KALFIN, Ivailo Georgiev, MSc; Bulgarian politician; b. 30 May 1964, Sofia; m.; one d.; ed French Language School, Sofia, Univ. of Nat. and World Economy, Sofia, Business Univ., Vienna, Austria, Univ. of Loughborough, UK, Coll. of Europe, Bruges, Belgium; scholarship student under Chevening program, UK and German Marshall Fund, USA; taught Finance at Int. Univ., Sofia; worked for Machinoexport as well as in pvt. sector in the field of foreign trade, finance and consulting; mem. Municipal Council of Bulgarian Socialist Party (BSP), Supreme Council of BSP, Political Council of the Bulgarian Euroleft; Spokesperson for pre-election coalition 'Together for Bulgaria' 1996; mem. Parl. for Sofia (Parl. Group of the Democratic Left) 1994–97, 2000–01, 2005–, mem. Foreign Policy Cttee, Budgeting and Finance Cttee, Deputy Chair. Bulgarian-EU Jt Parl. Cttee; Sec. for Econ. Affairs to the Pres. 2002–05; Deputy Prime Minister and Minister of Foreign Affairs 2005–09; mem. European Parl. (Group of the Progressive Alliance of Socialists and Democrats) 2009–; Bulgarian Socialist Party cand. in presidential election 2011; Founder Social Democrats Political Movt; Man. and Sr Partner in consulting cos 1990–94, 1997–2000; Sr Prof., Univ., Sofia 2000–; observer of elections in Kosovo as mem. OSCE Missions 2001, 2003; mem. Advisory Bd Bulgarian Nat. Bank 2004–, Bulgaria Beyond the Facts Early Warning System implemented by UNDP and USAID; Founding mem. Bulgarian Macroeconomics Asscn; mem. Bd Dirs Inst. for Econs and Int. Relations; recipient of nat. honours from several European countries. *Publications:* Factors of Economic Growth in Bulgaria (co-author) 2000, Bulgaria 2010: Economic Challenges (report to Pres. of Bulgaria) (co-author) 2005; numerous articles in Bulgaria and in int. trade journals on EU and macroeconomic issues. *Address:* European Parliament, 60 Rue Wiertz, ASP 14G146, 1047 Brussels, Belgium (office). *Telephone:* (2) 284-54-89 (office). *Fax:* (2) 284-94-89 (office). *E-mail:* ivailo.kalfin@europarl.europa.eu (office). *Website:* www.europarl.europa.eu/meps/en/96807/IVAILO_KALFIN.html (office); www.kalfin.eu (home).

KALHOR, Kayhan; Iranian musician (kamancheh) and composer; b. 23 Nov. 1963, Tehran; ed Carleton Univ., Canada; began musical studies under Master Ahmad Mohajer at age of seven; played with Nat. Orchestra of Radio and Television of Iran 1976–81; collaborated with Shayda Ensemble, Chavosh Cultural Centre (Iranian arts org.) 1980; virtuoso on kamancheh (traditional Persian bowed string instrument); specializes in classical Persian music, in particular that of Khorason and Kordesta; has collaborated on many int. projects including the Silk Road Ensemble with cellist Yo-Yo Ma; has toured the world as soloist with various ensembles and orchestras including New York Philharmonic and Orchestre Nat. de Lyon; co-founder Dastan 1991, Ghazal Ensemble 1997. *Compositions include:* Blue as the Turquoise Night of Neyshabur, Silent City, Mountains are Far Away. *Albums include:* Eastern Apertures 1995, Scattering Stars like Dust 1998, Through Eternity: Homage to Molavi 1999, Caravan 2000, Moonrise over the Silk Road 2000, Night Silence Desert 2000, Without You 2002, Rain 2003, In the Mirror of the Sky 2004, Faryad 2005, Wind 2006, Silent City 2008, Provenance 2010, I Will Not Stand Alone 2011; contrib. to Yo-Yo Ma and Silk Road Ensemble albums: When Strangers Meet 2001, Beyond the Sky 2004, New Impossibilities 2007. *E-mail:* isArtsNY@gmail.com (office). *Website:* kayhankalhor.net (office).

KALICHSTEIN, Joseph, MSc; American/Israeli pianist; b. 15 Jan. 1946, Tel-Aviv; s. of Isaac Kalichstein and Mali Kalichstein; m. Rowain (née Schultz) Kalichstein; two c.; ed Juilliard School, New York; New York debut 1967; European debut 1970; appearances with all the world's leading orchestras; engagements include Nat. Symphony Orchestra, Washington, DC, Cincinnati Symphony, US tour with Jerusalem Symphony and Lawrence Foster, and return tours to Japan and Scandinavia; mem. Piano Faculty of Juilliard School 1985–; First Prize, Leventritt Int. Competition 1969, Edward Stevermann Memorial Prize 1969. *Leisure interests:* reading, chess. *Address:* Opus 3 Artists, 470 Park Avenue South, 9th Floor North, New York, NY 10016, USA (office); Harrison Parrott, 5–6 Albion Court, London, W6 0QT, England (office). *Telephone:* (212) 584-7500 (office); (20) 7229-9166 (office). *Fax:* (646) 300-8200 (office); (20) 7221-5042 (office). *E-mail:* info@opus3artists.com (office); info@harrisonparrott.co.uk (office). *Website:* www.opus3artists.com (office); www.harrisonparrott.com (office).

KALILOMBE, Rt Rev. Patrick-Augustine, STL, SSL, PhD; Malawi ecclesiastic and lecturer; *Bishop Emeritus of Lilongwe*; b. 28 Aug. 1933, Dedza; s. of Pierre Kalilombe and Helena Mzifei; ed Kasina Seminary, Kachebere Theological Coll., Gregorian Univ., Rome, Graduate Theological Union, Berkeley, USA; trained as White Father, Algeria and Tunisia 1954–58; ordained priest 1958; teacher and Rector, Kachebere Major Seminary 1964–72; Bishop of Lilongwe 1972–79 (resgnd), now Bishop Emer.; Fellow and Lecturer in Third World Theologies, Selly Oak Colls, Univ. of Birmingham, UK 1982–86, Dir Centre for Black and White

Christian Partnership, Selly Oak Colls 1985, Sr Lecturer, Third World Theologies 1982–87; Sr Lecturer, Chancellor Coll., Univ. of Malawi Zomba 1998–2007; work with Malawi Bible Soc. 2007–; Vice-Pres. East African Episcopal Confs 1974–76, Ecumenical Asscn of Third World Theologians 1976–78, Ecumenical Asscn of African Theologians 1985; Cttee mem. Symposium of Episcopal Confs of Africa and Madagascar 1974–76; mem. Council, Malawi Univ. 1974–76. *Publications:* Christ's Church in Lilongwe 1973, From Outstations to Small Christian Communities 1983, Doing Theology at the Grassroots 2000. *Address:* c/o Diocese of Lilongwe, PO Box 33, Lilongwe, Malawi.

KALIMBETOVA, Tajikan B.; Kyrgyzstani politician; b. 1964; Deputy Minister of Finance –2007, also head of financial intelligence service 2005–07, Minister of Finance 2007–09, Chair. Iran-Kyrgyzstan Jt Econ. Comm.; Deputy Chair. EurAsian Group 2006–07; Chair. Social Fund 2007–09; Deputy Prime Minister 2009. *Address:* c/o Office of the Prime Minister, 720003 Bishkek, Dom Pravitelstva, Kyrgyzstan.

KALIŇÁK, Robert; Slovak lawyer and politician; *Deputy Prime Minister and Minister of the Interior;* b. 11 May 1971, Bratislava; ed Faculty of Law, Comenius Univ., Bratislava; Man. ACE Press (legal publrs) 1991; Asst, Commercial Law Office 1992–95; Articled Clerk, Maríková and Pnrs (law firm), Bratislava 1995–99; Attorney, MKKT (law firm) 1999–2002; mem. Národná rada Slovenskej republiky (Nat. Council of the Slovak Repub.) 2002–06, Chair. Cttee for Defence and Security 2002–04, Special Supervision Cttee of Nat. Security Office 2004–06; mem. Regional Council of Bratislava 2005–; Deputy Prime Minister and Minister of the Interior 2006–10, 2012–; Vice-Chair. SMER—Social Democracy; mem. Slovak Bar Asscn. *Address:* Ministry of the Interior, Pribinova 2, 812 72 Bratislava, Slovakia (office). *Telephone:* (2) 5094-1111 (office). *Fax:* (2) 5094-4397 (office). *E-mail:* tokmv@minv.sk (office); robert_kalinak@nrsr.sk (office). *Website:* www.minv.sk (office).

KALINOWSKI, Jarosław; Polish politician; b. 12 April 1962, Wyszków; m. Aleksandra Kalinowska; three s. two d.; ed Warsaw Agricultural Univ., Inst. of Law Sciences of the Polish Acad. of Sciences; owner of farm in Jackowo Górne; mem. Union of Rural Youth 1981–89; Admin. Somianka village 1990–97; Deputy to Sejm (Parl.) 1993–2009, Deputy Speaker 2005–09; Deputy Prime Minister and Minister of Agric. and Food Economy (later Rural Devt) 1997, 2001–03; mem. European Parl. 2009–; mem. and fmr Pres. Polish People's Party (Polskie Stronnictwo Ludowe—PSL) 1997–, Chair. PSL Parl. Club 2000–, Chair. Caucus 2000–01; cand. in Polish presidential election 2000; Deputy to Local Ass. of the Voivodship of Mazovia 1998–2000. *Leisure interests:* culture and folk music. *Address:* ul. Kopernika 36/40 p. 407, 00-924 Warsaw, Poland (office). *Telephone:* (22) 6206755 (office). *Fax:* (22) 6206755 (office). *E-mail:* eurobiuro.warszawa@kalinowski.pl. *Website:* www.kalinowski.pl.

KALLA, Yusuf, BEcons; Indonesian politician and business executive; b. 15 May 1942, Watampone, South Sulawesi; ed Hassanudin Univ., Makassar (fmrly Ujungpandang), South Sulawesi; began career as Chair. Advisory Council of Indonesian Chamber of Commerce and Industry (KADIN) at prov. level (South Sulawesi) and Coordinator of KADIN for Eastern Indonesia; Rep. of South Sulawesi in Peoples' Consultative Ass.; served in House of Reps for four consecutive terms (including chair. of communication forum for reps at regional level); apptd Chief of Nat. Logistics Agency (Bulog) 1999–2000; Minister of Trade and Industry 1999–2000 (forced to resign by Pres. Wahid on suspicion of corruption); Coordinating Minister for People's Welfare 2001–04; Vice-Pres. of Indonesia 2004–09; mem. Partai Golongan Karya (Golkar), Pres. and Chair. 2004–; Chair. PT Makassar Mina Usaha, PT Kalla Inti Karsa and NV Hadji Kalla Trading Co. *Address:* Partai Golongan Karya (Golkar), Jalan Anggrek Nellimurni, Jakarta 11480, Indonesia. *Telephone:* (21) 5302222. *Fax:* (21) 5303380. *E-mail:* info@golkar.or.id. *Website:* www.golkar.or.id.

KALLAS, Siim; Estonian banker, politician and international organization official; *Commissioner for Transport and Vice-President, European Commission;* b. 2 Oct. 1948, Tallinn; s. of Udo Kallas and Rita Kallas; m. Kristi Kartus 1972; one s. one d.; ed Tartu State Univ.; Chief Specialist, Ministry of Finance, Estonian SSR 1975–79; Gen. Man. Estonian Savings Banks 1979–86; Deputy Ed. Rahva Hääl 1986–89; Chair. Asscn of Estonian Trade Unions 1989–91; Pres. Eesti Pank (Bank of Estonia) 1991–95; Founder and Chair., Estonian Reform Party (Eesti Reformierakond) 1994–2004; elected to Riigikogu (Parl.) 1995–99, also mem. Parl. Nat. Defence Cttee and Parl. Foreign Affairs Cttee 2003–04; Minister of Foreign Affairs 1995–96, of Finance 1999–2002; Prime Minister of Estonia 2002–03; Visiting Prof., Tartu State Univ.; EU Commr without Portfolio 2004, Vice-Pres. for Admin. Affairs, Audit and Anti-Fraud 2004–10, Commr for Transport and Vice-Pres. EC 2010–; Cross of the Order of Merit (Germany) 2000, Grand Officier, Légion d'honneur 2001, Order of the Nat. Coat of Arms 2003; chosen as one of 100 Great Estonians of the 20th Century 2002. *Leisure interests:* history, reading, opera, tennis, cycling. *Address:* Commissioner for Transport, European Commission, 200 Rue de la Loi, 1049 Brussels, Belgium (office). *Telephone:* (2) 298-87-62 (direct line) (office); (2) 298-87-63 (office); (2) 299-11-11 (switchboard) (office). *Fax:* (2) 298-84-92 (office). *E-mail:* siim.kallas@ec.europa.eu (office); cab-kallas-web-feedback@ec.europa.eu (office). *Website:* ec.europa.eu/commission_2010-2014/kallas (office).

KALLASVUO, Olli-Pekka, LLM; Finnish telecommunications executive; *Chairman, Nokia Siemens Networks;* b. 13 July 1953, Lavia; ed Univ. of Helsinki; fmrly with Union Bank of Finland; Corp. Counsel Nokia 1980, Asst Vice-Pres. Legal Dept 1987, Asst Vice-Pres. Finance 1988–90, mem. Group Exec. Bd 1990–, Sr Vice-Pres. Finance 1990–91, Exec. Vice-Pres. and Chief Financial Officer Nokia 1992–96, 1999–2003, Corp. Exec. Vice-Pres. Nokia Americas 1997–98, Exec. Vice-Pres. and Gen. Man. of Mobile Phones 2004–05, Pres. and COO Nokia 2005–06, Pres. and CEO 2006–10, mem. Bd Dirs 2007–; Chair. Nokia Siemens Networks 2007–, NAVTEQ Corpn; mem. Bd Confed. of Finnish Industries (EK) 2009–; mem. European Round Table of Industrialists, Council of the EU-Russia Industrialists' Round Table; Hon. LLD (Helsinki). *Leisure interests:* golf, tennis, reading political history. *Address:* Nokia Siemens Networks, PO Box 1, 02022 Nokia Siemens Networks (office); Nokia Siemens Networks, Karaportti 3, 02610 Espoo, Finland (office). *Telephone:* (71) 400-4000 (office). *E-mail:* info@

nokiasiemensnetworks.com (office). *Website:* www.nokiasiemensnetworks.com (office).

KALLIO, Heikki Olavi, LLM, PhD; Finnish historian, writer and fmr organization official; *Legal Adviser, Academy of Finland;* b. 9 June 1937, Turku; m. 1st Liisa Toivonen 1961 (divorced 1995); three s. one d.; m. 2nd Anneli Hämäläinen 1997; ed Helsinki Univ., Tallinn Univ. (Estonia); Chief Admin. Officer, Univ. of Turku 1963–71; Admin. Dir Acad. of Finland 1971–72, Exec. Vice-Pres. (Admin.) 1973–2002, currently Legal Adviser; Admin. Dir State Tech. Research Centre 1973; historian and writer 2002–; Dr hc (Tallinn); Finnish Order of White Cross, Kt 1st Class, Hungarian Order of Merit, Kt Commdr, Ordo Supremus Militaris Templi Hierosolymitani, Kt Grand Cross, Medal of Honour, Merited Service of the State of Finland, Cross of Merit, Finnish Physical Culture and Sports. *Publications:* Finnish–Estonian Scientific Relations with Special Focus on the Occupation Years 1940–91. *Leisure interests:* sailing, navigation, safety and security at sea, historiography. *Address:* Meritullinkatu YBG5, 00710 Helsinki, Finland (home). *Telephone:* (40) 5569755 (home). *E-mail:* heikki.kallio@pp1.inet.fi (home).

KALLIOMÄKI, Antti Tapana; Finnish politician; b. 8 Jan. 1947, Siikainen; m. Helena Marjatta Kalliomäki 1969; two s.; physical training teacher, Hämeenkylä Upper Comprehensive School 1973–91; Project Man. Finnish Sports Asscn 1981–83; mem. Vantaa City Council 1984–2000; Chair. Vantaa Municipal Org. 1988–92; mem. Suomen Eduskunta (Parl.) 1983–, Chair. SDP Parl. Group 1991–95, 1999–2003, Vice-Chair. Cttee for the Future 1993–95, mem. Parl. Cttee on Defence Policy 1986–87, Cttee on Sports 1988–90, Parl. Advisory Bd on Defence Policy 1989–91; Chair. Parl. Security Policy Monitoring Group 2002–03; mem. SDP Party Cttee/Party Exec. 1990–2002; Vice-Chair. European SDP 2001–; Sec. to Prime Minister 1986–87; Minister of Trade and Industry 1995–99; Deputy Prime Minister and Minister of Finance 2003–05; Minister of Educ. 2005–07; mem. Parl. Supervisory Council, Bank of Finland 1987–91, Admin. Council, Finnish Broadcasting Co. (YLE) 2001–03 (Vice-Chair. 2002–03); Chair. Supervisory Bd Neste 1994–95. *Address:* Suomen Eduskunta, Mannerheimintie 30, 00102 Helsinki, Finland (office). *Telephone:* (9) 4323052 (office). *Fax:* (9) 4322274 (office). *E-mail:* antti.kalliomaki@eduskunta.fi (office). *Website:* www.eduskunta.fi (office); www .anttikalliomaki.net (home).

KALLIS, Jacques Henry; South African professional cricketer; b. 16 Oct. 1975, Pinelands, Cape Town, Cape Prov.; ed Wynberg Boys' High School; all-rounder; right-handed batsman and right-arm fast-medium bowler; teams played for various age-group teams (Western Prov. Under-13, Under-19, S Africa Schools, Under-17, Under-19, Under-24), Western Prov./Cape Cobras 1993–, Middx 1997, Glamorgan 1999, South Africa 1995–2013, Royal Challengers Bangalore 2008–10, Kolkata Knight Riders 2011–; First-class debut: 1993/94; Test debut: S Africa v England, Durban 14 Dec. 1995; One-Day Int. (ODI) debut: S Africa v England, Cape Town 9 Jan. 1996; T20I debut: S Africa v NZ, Johannesburg 21 Oct. 2005; played in 166 Tests and scored 13,289 runs, average 55.37, 45 centuries, 58 half-centuries, highest score 224, took 292 wickets, average 32.65; ODIs: 325 matches, 11,574 runs, average 44.86, 273 wickets; First-class: 257 matches, 19,695 runs, average 54.10, 62 centuries, 97 half-centuries, 427 wickets; in 2004 became first batsman since Sir Donald Bradman to hit five centuries in consecutive test innings; selected for World XI team 2005; ranked World No. 1 Batsman for first time Jan. 2005; became the fourth player and first South African to score 13,000 Test runs, in first Test against NZ 2 Jan. 2013; first and only player in cricket history to achieve 10,000 runs and take 200 wickets in both Tests and ODIs, now more than 11,000 runs and 250 wickets; retd from Test and First-class cricket Dec. 2013; Founder Jacques Kallis Scholarship Foundation 2006; South Africa Cricketer of the Year 1999, 2000, 2004, Int. Cricket Council (ICC) Player of the Year 2005, Sir Garfield Sobers Trophy 2004, ICC Test Player of the Year 2005, named by Wisden as Leading Cricketer in the World for his performances in 2007 and 2008, a Wisden Cricketer of the Year 2013. *Leisure interest:* golf. *Address:* c/o United Cricket Board of South Africa, Gauteng, South Africa; c/o Dave Rundle (office). *Telephone:* (11) 8802810. *E-mail:* proteas@cricket.co.za; rms@mweb.co.za (office). *Website:* www.cricket.co.za; www.kallis.co.za.

KALLSBERG, Anfinn; Faroese politician; b. 19 Nov. 1947; s. of Gunnar Kallsberg and Katrina Kallsberg; with J. F. Kjølbro 1964–74; self-employed bookkeeper, Vidareidi 1974–96; Mayor of Vidareidi 1974–80; mem. Faroese Rep. Council 1980–, Chair. 1991–93, Chair. Finance Cttee 1989–91, 2004–, mem. Foreign Affairs Cttee 2004; Prime Minister and Minister of Constitutional Affairs, Foreign Affairs and Municipal Affairs 1998–2004; one of two reps of Faroe Islands in Danish Folketing (Parl.) 2005–; mem. Nordic Council 1991, 1994–98; mem. Man. Cttee Klaksvik Hosp. 1991–96; mem. Fólkaflokkurin (People's Party). *Address:* FO-750, Vidareidi; c/o Fólkaflokkurin (People's Party), Jónas Broncksgøta 29, 100 Tórshavn, Faroe Islands. *Telephone:* 451032. *Fax:* 451032. *E-mail:* anfinn.kallsberg@ft.dk; folkaflokkurin@logting.fo. *Website:* www.kallsberg.fo; folkaflokkurin.fo.

KÁLMÁN, Rudolf Emil, SciB, SciM, SciD; Hungarian/American mathematician and academic; *Professor Emeritus, Eidgenössische Technische Hochschule (ETH) Zürich;* b. 19 May 1930, Budapest; m. Constantina Stavrou; one s. one d.; ed Massachusetts Inst. of Tech., Columbia Univ.; Research Mathematician, Research Inst. for Advanced Study, Baltimore, Md 1958–64; Prof., Stanford Univ., Calif. 1964–71; Grad. Research Prof. and Dir Center for Math. System Theory, Univ. of Florida, Gainesville 1971–92; Chair. for Math. System Theory, ETH Zürich 1973–; mem. NAS, Nat. Acad. of Eng, American Acad. of Arts and Sciences; Foreign mem. Hungarian, French and Russian Acads of Science; numerous hon. doctorates; IEEE Medal of Honor 1974, IEEE Centennial Medal 1984, Inamori Foundation Kyoto Prize in High Tech. 1985, American Math. Soc. Steele Prize 1987, Richard E. Bellman Control Heritage Award 1997, Nat. Acad. of Eng Charles Stark Draper Prize 2008, Nat. Medal of Science 2008. *Achievements include:* inventor of Kalman filter, optical digital technique used in control systems and avionics. *Publications:* more than 50 technical articles. *Address:* ETH Zürich, ETH Zentrum, Weinbergstrasse 94, 8092 Zürich, Switzerland (office). *E-mail:* rudolf.kalman@math.ethz.ch (office). *Website:* www.math.ethz.ch (office).

KALMÁR, Stefan; German gallery curator; *Director, Artists Space;* oversaw programming at Kunstverein München 2006–10, organized exhbns including The Secret Public: The Last Days of the British Underground 1978–1988 and a Liam Gillick retrospective, in collaboration with Witte de With, Kunsthalle Zurich and the Museum of Contemporary Art, Chicago; took over as Dir non-profit Artists Space, New York 2010–; aided in establishment and programming of Ludlow 38, a satellite space of the Goethe-Institut in New York. *Publication:* large book project documenting his curatorial approach in Munich. *Address:* Artists Space, 38 Greene Street, 3rd Floor, New York, NY 10013, USA (office). *Telephone:* (212) 226-3970 (office). *Fax:* (212) 966-1434 (office). *E-mail:* info@artistsspace.org (office). *Website:* www.artistsspace.org (office).

KALMS, Baron (Life Peer), cr. 2004, of Edgware in the London Borough of Barnet; **(Harold) Stanley Kalms;** British business executive; b. 21 Nov. 1931; s. of Charles Kalms and Cissie Kalms; m. Pamela Jimack 1954; three s.; ed Christ's Coll., Finchley; began career with Dixons 1948 working in father's photographic store; opened 16 shops; Dixons Photographic floated 1962, Man. Dir 1962–72, Chair. Dixons Group PLC (now DSG Int. PLC) 1972–2002, Pres. 2002, now Life Pres.; Dir British Gas 1987–97; Chair. (non-exec.) Volvere PLC; Chair. King's Healthcare NHS Trust 1993–96; Dir Centre for Policy Studies 1991– (Treas. 1993–98), Business for Sterling 1998–; Treas. Conservative Party 2001–03; Founder and sponsor Dixons Bradford City Tech. Coll.; Visiting Prof., Business School, Univ. of N London 1991; fmr Visiting Prof., Univ. of London Business School; Gov. Nat. Inst. of Econ. and Social Research 1995; Trustee, Econ. Educ. Trust; Hon. Fellow, London Business School 1995; Hon. DLitt (CNAA) 1991, Hon. DUniv (N London) 1994, Hon. DEcon (Richmond) 1996. *Leisure interests:* ballet, communal activities, opera. *Address:* House of Lords, London, SW1A 0PW, England. *Telephone:* (20) 7219-5353.

KALNIETE, Sandra, MA; Latvian politician and diplomatist; b. 22 Dec. 1952, Togur, Tomsk Oblast, Russia; m. (divorced); ed Latvian Acad. of Art, Univ. of Leeds, UK and Univ. of Geneva, Switzerland; Sec.-Gen. Latvian Artists' Union 1987–88; f. Latvian Popular Front 1988, Sec.-Gen., Deputy Chair. Co-ordinating Council 1988–90; Chief of Protocol Dept, Deputy Foreign Minister, Ministry of Foreign Affairs 1990–93, Minister of Foreign Affairs 2002–04; Amb. to UN, Geneva, Switzerland 1993–97, to France 1997–2000, to UNESCO 2000–02; EU Commr without Portfolio May–Nov. 2004; mem. Saeima (Parl.) (New Era—Jaunais laiks) 2006–09; left New Era party and joined newly founded Civic Union (Pilsoniskā savienība—PS) party, Chair. Civic Union 2008–10; mem. European Parl. (Group of the European People's Party (Christian Democrats)) 2009–, Vice-Chair. Del. for relations with Japan, mem. Cttee on the Internal Market and Consumer Protection, Substitute mem. Cttee on Agric. and Rural Devt, Cttee on Women's Rights and Gender Equality, Del. to the EU-Turkey Jt Parl. Cttee; Patron, Prix Europa 2005; Commdr, Order of the Three Stars 1995, Commdr, Légion d'honneur 2001, Commdr des Palmes académiques 2002, Commdr, Order of Grand Cross of Grand Duke Gediminas (Lithuania) 2004, Commdr, Grand Cross of Recognition 2005; Latvian Cabinet Ministers' Award, Ethics and Culture Award (Switzerland) 2007, Gold Medal for services to Europe (Luxembourg) 2009, Medal of the Baltic Ass. 2009. *Publications:* Latviesu tekstilmaksla (Latvian Textile Art) 1989, Es lauzu, tu lauzi, mes lauzam. Vini luza (I Broke, You Broke, We Broke. They Fell Apart) 2000, Ar balles kurpem Sibirijas sniegos (With Dancing Shoes in Siberian Snows) 2001. *Address:* Civic Union (Pilsoniskā savienība), Aspazijas bulvāris 24, Rīga 1050, Latvia (office); European Parliament, 60 Rue Wiertz, ASP 10E253, 1047 Brussels, Belgium (office). *Telephone:* 6732-3325 (Rīga) (office); (2) 284-52-04 (Brussels). *Fax:* 6732-3315 (Rīga) (office); (2) 284-92-04 (Brussels) (office). *E-mail:* sandra.kalniete@europarl.europa.eu (office); birojs@pilsoniska -savieniba.lv (office). *Website:* www.europarl.europa.eu (home); pilsoniska -savieniba.lv (office).

KALORKOTI, Panayiotis, BA, MA; British artist; b. 11 April 1957, Cyprus; one s.; ed Univ. of Newcastle-upon-Tyne, RCA, Koninklijke Akad. voor Kunst en Vormgeving, 's-Hertogenbosch; Artist in Residence, Leeds Playhouse 1985, Cleveland Co. 1992, The Grizedale Soc., Cumbria 1994; Bartlett Fellow in Visual Arts, Univ. of Newcastle-upon-Tyne 1988; commissioned by Imperial War Museum, London 1988, Nat. Garden Festival, Gateshead 1989–90; now part-time tutor and visiting lecturer at various art depts; Granada Prize for Northern Young Contemporaries, Whitworth Art Gallery, Manchester 1983. *Publications include:* Kalorkoti 1988, A Retrospective of Etchings and Screenprints 1990, A Retrospective View 1985–91 1992, Etchings and Drawings 1992, Retrospective (Etchings 1983–93) 1994, Reflections of Grizedale (Acrylics, Watercolours, Etchings) 1995, An Exhibition of Acrylics, Watercolours and Etchings 1997, Heads, Faces and Figures 1998. *Leisure interests:* music, films, malt whisky, travel. *E-mail:* kalorkoti@googlemail.com. *Website:* www.kalorkoti.com.

KALOUSEK, Miroslav; Czech politician; *Vice-President, Traditions, Responsibility, Prosperity 09 (TOP 09) party;* b. 17 Dec. 1960, Tábor; m. Radka Kalousková; two c.; ed Inst. of Chemical Tech., Prague; Head of Investment, Mitas Praha (tyre mfrs) 1985–90; Econ. Adviser to Vice-Chair. of Czech Govt 1990–92, Dir Dept of Advisers 1992–93, Govt Rep. on Advisory Cttee, Deputy Chair. 1991–92; mem. Parl. (Christian Democratic Union–Czechoslovak People's Party, KDU-ČSL) 1993–, Chair. Parl. Budget Cttee 2002–05, Vice-Chair. 2006–; Deputy Minister of Defence 1998–, Minister of Finance 2007–09, 2010–13, Chair. EU's Ecofin Council Jan.–May 2009; Chair. KDU-ČSL 2003–06, left party 2009; Co-founder, with Karel Schwarzenberg (q.v.), Tradition Responsibility Prosperity 09 (TOP 09) party June 2009, First Vice-Pres. Nov. 2009–; mem. Bd of Dirs West-Bohemian Brewery 1992–94, Land Fund of the Czech Repub. 1994–96. *Address:* Traditions, Responsibility, Prosperity 09 (TOP 09) party, Michnův palác, budova č. 2, Újezd 450/40, Malá Strana, 118 00 Prague 1, Czech Republic (office). *Telephone:* 255790999 (office). *Fax:* 255790899 (office). *E-mail:* info@top09.cz (office). *Website:* www.top09.cz; www.miroslav-kalousek.cz.

KALPOKAS, Donald Masike'Vanua; Ni-Vanuatu politician and diplomatist; *Permanent Representative, United Nations;* ed Univ. of South Pacific; fmr Minister of Educ. and Judicial Services; Pres. Vanuaaku Pati –2001, now Hon. Pres.; Prime Minister of Vanuatu Sept.–Dec. 1991, 1998–99, also Minister of Comprehensive Reform Programme 1998–99, the Public Service, of Foreign Affairs and Acting Minister of Agric., Forestry and Fisheries, Deputy Prime Minister and Minister of Educ. 1996–97, –2004; unsuccessful presidential cand. 2004; Amb. and Perm. Rep. to UN, New York 2007–. *Address:* Permanent Mission of Vanuatu to the United Nations, 800 Second Avenue, Suite 400B, New York, NY 10017, USA (office).

Telephone: (212) 661-4303 (office). *Fax:* (212) 422-3427 (office); (212) 661-5544 (office). *E-mail:* vanunmis@aol.com (office).

KALTENBORN, Monisha, LLM; Austrian (b. Indian) motorsport executive; *CEO, Sauber Motorsport AG;* b. (Monisha Narang), 10 May 1971, Dehradun, India; m. Jens Kaltenborn; two c.; ed Univ. of Vienna, London School of Econs, UK; Research Asst, UNIDO, Vienna 1995; Researcher, UN Comm. for Int. Trade Law, Vienna 1995; worked at Gleiss Lutz (law firm), Stuttgart and Wolf & Theis (law firm), Vienna 1996–97; worked at Fritz Kaiser Group 1998–99; Co-owner and Head of Legal Dept, Sauber Group 2000–, mem. Bd of Man. 2001–; CEO Sauber Motorsport AG 2010–; involved in Fédération Internationale de l'Automobile's Comm. for Women and Motorsport. *Leisure interests:* yoga, tennis, opera. *Address:* Sauber Motorsport AG, Wildbachstrasse 9, 8340 Hinwil, Switzerland (office). *Telephone:* (44) 937-90-00 (office). *Fax:* (44) 937-90-01 (office). *E-mail:* info@sauber -motorsport.com (office). *Website:* www.sauber-motorsport.com (office).

KALTONGA, Bakoa; Ni-Vanuatu politician; First Political Adviser, Ministry of Infrastructure and Public Utilities –2008; mem. Parl. for Rural Efate constituency 2008–June 2009, Aug. 2009–; Minister of Foreign Affairs and External Trade 2008–09, of Justice and Women's Affairs 2009–10, of Finance and Economic Man. April–May 2011; mem. Vanuaaku Pati (Our Land Party). *Address:* c/o Ministry of Finance and Economic Management, Port Vila, PMB 9058, Port Vila, Vanuatu (office).

KALUGIN, Maj.-Gen. Oleg Danilovich; Russian/American intelligence officer and politician; b. 6 Sept. 1934, Leningrad; m.; two d.; ed Leningrad Univ., Columbia Univ.; on staff of KGB 1958–89; corresp., Soviet Radio, New York 1959–65; Second, then First Sec., Embassy in Washington, DC 1965–70; Chief, Dept of External Intelligence Service, KGB 1973–80; First Deputy Chief of KGB for City of Leningrad and Leningrad Region 1980–87; returned to Moscow 1987, forced to retire for participation in democratic movt and criticism of KGB 1989, deprived of all decorations and titles by order of Pres. Gorbachev 1990; prosecuted, all charges lifted at end of 1991; USSR People's Deputy 1990–91; gave evidence on activities of KGB in courts and mass media; consultant, Information Service Agency; mem. Fed. Democratic Movt 1995–; has lived in USA 1996–; sentenced in absentia by Russian court to 15 years' imprisonment for treason after disclosing Russian agents in USA 2001; mem. Advisory Bd Dirs, Int. Spy Museum, Washington, DC; acquired US citizenship 2003; Man. Dir Cannistraro Assocs (security consulting firm) 1998–; numerous decorations. *Publications:* The First Directorate: My 32 Years in Intelligence and Espionage Against the West (autobiog.) 1994; numerous articles. *Leisure interests:* hunting, fishing, swimming. *Address:* c/o Cannistraro Associates, PO Box 854, McLean, VA 22101, USA (office). *Telephone:* (202) 257-1621 (office). *Fax:* (703) 506-4620 (office). *Website:* intelligencebrief.net (office).

KALUMBA, Katele, PhD; Zambian politician; m. Lumba Kalumba; ed Univ. of Zambia, Washington Univ., USA, Univ. of Toronto, Canada; fmr health consultant to govts and int. orgs; Minister of Health 1991–98, of Home Affairs and of Tourism 1998–99, of Finance and Econ. Devt 1999–2002, of Foreign Affairs 2002 (resgnd) mem. Nat. Ass. (Movt for Multi-party Democracy—MMD) 2002–; Nat. Sec., MMD –2011. *Address:* c/o Movement for Multi-party Democracy, POB 30708, Lusaka, Zambia (office).

KALVĪTIS, Aigars, MSc; Latvian politician; b. 27 June 1966, Rīga; m.; three s.; ed Univ. of Wisconsin, USA, Latvian Univ. of Agric., Univ. Coll. Cork, Ireland; milkman and tractor driver, Alamnas Bruk AB, Sweden 1990–91; Dir Agro Biznesa Centrs 1992–94; Chair. Bd Zemgales piens 1994; Chair. Comm. of the Cen. Union of Latvian Dairying 1994–98; mem. Saeima (Parl.) 1998–99, 2002–04, mem. Budget and Finance (Taxation) Cttee, Public Expenditure and Audit Cttee; Minister of Agric. 1999–2000, of Econs 2000–02; Prime Minister 2004–07 (resgnd) mem. People's Party (Tautas partija), Chair. of Parl. Group 2002–04. *Leisure interest:* ice hockey. *Address:* Saeima, Jekaba str. 11, Rīga 1811, Latvia (office). *Telephone:* 67087222 (office). *Fax:* 67087100 (office). *E-mail:* tautpart@saeima.lv. *Website:* www.saeima.lv (office); www.tautaspartija.lv.

KALYAGIN, Aleksander Aleksandrovich; Russian actor; b. 25 May 1942, Malmysh, Kirov Region; m. Glushenko Yevgeniya Konstantinovna; one s. one d.; ed Shchukin Higher School of Theatre Art; actor Taganka Theatre and Yermolova Theatre in Moscow 1966–71; Moscow Art Theatre 1971–93; master classes in Russia and in Europe; Chair. Union of Theatre Workers of Russia 1996–; f. and Artistic Dir Et Cetera Theatre in Moscow 1992–; People's Artist of Russia 1983, State Prize 1981, 1983. *Roles in productions:* Dark Lady of the Sonnets by G. B. Shaw, Don Quixote by A. Morfov after Cervantes, Old New Year by M. Roshchin, Notes of the Lunatic and Marriage by Gogol, Galileo by Brecht, Tartuffe by Molière, several plays by A. Gelman, M. Shatrov, A. Galin and other contemporary dramatists; in cinema since 1967. *Films include:* Untimely Man 1973, One's Own Among Strangers 1974, Slave of Love 1976, Interrogation 1979, Aesop 1982, Prokhindiada or Run on the Spot 1985, How Are You Doing, Crucians? 1992, Moi Ivan, toi Abraham 1993, Deti chugunnykh bogov 1993, Prokhindiada 2 1994, Foto 2003. *Television:* Bednaya Nastya (series) 2003. *Leisure interests:* collecting art books, museums. *Address:* Union of Theatre Workers, 10333 Moscow, Strastnoy blvd 10 (office); 123100 Moscow, 1905 Goda str., 3 Apt 91, Russia (home). *Telephone:* (495) 209-28-46 (office); (495) 205-26-54 (home). *Fax:* (495) 230-22-58 (office). *E-mail:* stdrf@rc.ru.

KALYUZHNY, Victor Ivanovich; Russian engineer, diplomat, politician and business executive; b. 18 April 1947, Birsk, Bashkiria; ed Ufa Inst. of Oil; Mgr, then Deputy Head Tomskneft Co. 1970–78, First Deputy Dir.-Gen. 1993–97; Chief Engineer Dept of Oil and Gas Vasyuganneft Co., Strezhevoy; Sec. CP Cttee Strezhevoyneft Co. 1980–84, later Deputy Dir; Second Sec. Strezhevoy Town CP Exec. Cttee 1984–86; Deputy Dir USSR Ministry of Oil Industry 1986; Chief Engineer, then Dir Priobneft Co., Nizhevartovsk Tumen 1986–90; Dir Vietsovpetro, Vu Tan, Viet Nam 1990–93; First Vice-Pres. Vostochnaya Neftyanaya Komapniya, Tomsk 1997–98; First Deputy Minister of Fuel and Power Industry 1998–99, Minister 1999–2000; Special Rep. of Pres. for Caspian Sea with rank of Deputy Minister of Foreign Affairs 2000–; Amb. to Latvia 2004–07 (retd); mem. Bd of Dirs Eurasia Drilling Co. 2009–. *Address:* c/o Board of Directors, Eurasia Drilling Company, c/o Burovaya Kompaniya Eurasia, Moscow 119071, 15 A,

Leninsky prospect, Russia. *E-mail:* mail@eurasiadrilling.com. *Website:* www .eurasiadrilling.com.

KAMAL, Fida M.; Bangladeshi barrister; ed Univ. of Dhaka, Punjab Univ., Pakistan, Inner Temple, London, UK; called to the Bar 1979, enrolled as lawyer of High Court 1979, of Appellate Div. 1986; ex-officio Chair. Bangladesh Bar Council; Additional Attorney-Gen. 2002–07, Acting Attorney-Gen. Jan.–Feb. 2007, Attorney-Gen. 2007–08. *Address:* c/o Office of the Attorney-General, Supreme Court Building, Ramna, Dhaka 1000, Bangladesh (office).

KAMAL, Riad Burhan, BSc, MSc; Palestinian civil engineer and business executive; *CEO, Arabtec Holding PJSC;* ed Imperial Coll. London, UK; began career in London 1966, worked on construction projects in UK, Jordan and Spain for Tarmac Ltd and Sir Robert McAlpine Ltd; moved to Dubai 1974, f. Arab Technical Construction (Arabtec Construction) 1975, CEO Arabtec Construction Co. PJSC 2004–09, mem. Bd of Dirs and CEO Arabtec Holding PJSC 2008–, currently Chair. of projects including Burj Dubai, Burj Al Arab (Dubai), Okhta Centre Tower (St Petersburg); Founder and Deputy Chair. DEPA Interiors; Dir, Arab Bank, Amman, Turkland Bank, Istanbul, Arabia Insurance Co., Beirut, Depa United Co., Satellite Inter-Active Systems; Dir and mem. Advisory Bd Gulf Capital; mem. Advisory Bd for MENA Region (Private Wealth Management), Deutsche Bank – Swiss; mem. Bd of Trustees, American Univ. of Beirut; Deputy Chair. Welfare Asscn, Geneva; mem. World Presidents' Org.; ITP Lifetime Achievement Award 2009, ranked by Arabian Business amongst the Power 500: The World's Most Influential Arabs (49th) 2012. *Address:* Arabtec Holding PJSC, PO Box 721 22, Dubai, United Arab Emirates (office). *Telephone:* (4) 3400700 (office). *Fax:* (4) 3404004 (office). *E-mail:* info@arabtecuae.com (office). *Website:* www.arabtecholding.com (office).

KAMAL, Yousuf bin Hussein, BBA; Qatari government official; b. 1948; ed Cairo Univ.; previous positions in Ministry of Finance include Asst Deputy Dir, Deputy Dir, Gen. Dir, Deputy Minister, Minister of Finance (later renamed Economy and Finance) 1998–2013, also Acting Minister of Economy and Trade 2006; fmr Deputy Head, Bd of Dirs Qatar Petroleum; fmr mem. Bd of Dirs Qatar Cen. Bank, Q-Tel; fmr Head, Bd of Dirs Ras Laffan LNG. *Address:* c/o Ministry of Economy and Finance, POB 83, Doha, Qatar (office).

KAMALI, Norma, BFA; American fashion designer; b. 27 June 1945, New York; d. of Sam Arraez and Estelle Galib; m. M. H. Kamali (divorced); ed Fashion Inst. of Tech., New York; ind. fashion designer, New York 1965–; opened first shop in East 53rd Street 1968, moving to Madison Avenue 1974; retitled business OMO (On My Own) and moved to 56th Street 1978; second boutique opened Spring Street, New York 1986; OMO Home opened 1988; collaboration with Bloomingdale's on production of exclusive collections 1988–; OMO Tokyo opened 1990; Coty American Fashion Critics' Winnie Award 1981, 1982, Outstanding Women's Fashion Designer of the Year Award, Council of Fashion Designers of America 1982, Coty Hall of Fame Award 1983, American Success Award 1989, Pencil Award 1999, Fashion Outreach Style Award 1999, Business Outreach Award, Manhattan Chamber of Commerce 2001, Entrepreneur Award, The Fashion Group 2002, inducted Fashion Walk of Fame 2002, Bd of Dirs Special Tribute Award, Council of Fashion Designers of America 2006. *Address:* OMO Norma Kamali, 11 West 56th Street, New York, NY 10019, USA. *Website:* www.normakamalicollection.com.

KAMALUDHEEN, Abdullah, BSc; Maldivian politician; b. 12 July 1954; m.; five c.; ed Majeediyya School and Almeda Univ., USA; clerk, Ministry of Foreign Affairs 1972; Admin. Sec., Office of the Pres. 1972–76; Under-Sec., Port Comm. and Public Works Dept, Ministry of Finance 1976–77, Dir 1977–82; Dir Dept of Tourism and Foreign Investment, Office of the Pres. 1978, Dir Dept of Public Works and Labour 1982–89, Dir Islamic Centre 1984–93; Minister of Public Works and Labour 1989–93; Chair. and Man. Dir Maldives Ports Authority 1990–93; Chair. Bank of Maldives Ltd 1990–93, Maldives Electricity Board 1991–93; Exec. Dir, Maldives National Ship Man. Ltd 1991–93; mem. Parl. 1992–; mem. Constitutional Ass. 1995–; Minister of Human Resources, Employment and Labour 1998–2003, of Fisheries, Agric. and Marine Resources 2003–07, of Home Affairs 2007–08. *Address:* c/o Ministry of Home Affairs, Huravee Building, 3rd Floor, Ameer Ahmed Magu, Malé 20-05, Maldives. *Telephone:* 3323820. *E-mail:* minhah@dhivenhinet .net.mv.

KAMANDA, Kama Sywor, DipHumLit, BJ, BA, LèsL, HD; Democratic Republic of the Congo writer, poet, novelist, playwright and essayist and lecturer; b. 11 Nov. 1952, Luebo; s. of the late Malaba Kamenga and Kony Ngalula; ed Journalism School, Kinshasa, Univ. of Kinshasa, Univ. of Liège, Belgium; political leader; freelance journalist; lecturer at various univs, schools, etc.; literary critic for several newspapers; mem. French Soc. of Men of Letters, Conseil Int. d'Etudes Francophones, Belgian Soc. of Authors, Composers and Editors (SABAM), Maison de la poésie (MAPI – Dakar, Senegal); SCAM; Acad. française Paul Verlaine Award 1987, Acad. française Théophile Gautier Award 1993, Louise Labé Award 1990, Black African Asscn of French-Speaking Writers Award 1991, Acad. Inst. of Paris Special Poetry Award 1992, Silver Jasmine for Poetic Originality 1992, Gen. Council Agen Special Prize for French-Speaking Countries 1992, Greek Poets and Writers Asscn Melina Mercouri Award 1999, Int. Poets Acad. India Poet of the Millennium Award 2000, Joal Fadiouth hon. citation, Senegal 2000, Int. Soc. of Greek Writers Poetry Award 2002, Int. Council for French Studies Maurice-Cagnon Exceptional Contribution Honour Certificate 2005, World Acad. of Letters Master Diploma for Specialty Honors in Writing, USA 2006, United Cultural Convention Int. Peace Prize, USA 2006, Golden Medal Youth Book (Czech Repub.) 2008, Heredia Award, French Acad. 2009. *Publications:* Les Contes des veillées africaines 1967, Chants de brumes 1986, Les Résignations 1986, Éclipse d'étoiles 1987, Les Contes du griot Vol. 1 1988, Vol. 2: La Nuit des griots 1991, Vol. 3: Les Contes des veillées africaines 1998, La Somme du néant 1989, L'Exil des songes 1992, Les Myriades des temps vécus 1992, Les Vents de l'épreuve 1993, Quand dans l'âme les mers s'agitent 1994, Lointaines sont les rives du destin 1994, L'Étreinte des mots 1995, Œuvre poétique 1999, Les Contes du crépuscule 2000, Le Sang des solitudes 2002, Contes (édition illustrée) 2003, Contes (œuvres complètes) 2004, La Traversée des mirages 2006, La Joueuse de Kora 2006, Contes africains (Grund) 2006, Au-delà de Dieu, au-delà des chimères 2007, Oeuvre poétique (édition intégrale) 2008. *Leisure interests:* travel, reading. *Address:* 18 Am Moul, 7418 Buschdorf, Luxembourg (office). *Telephone:*

26610948 (office); (621) 301611 (mobile) (office). *E-mail:* kamanda@pt.lu (office). *Website:* www.kamanda.jp (office); webplaza.pt.lu/public/kamanda (office); www .kamanda.net.

KAMANDA WA KAMANDA, Gérard, LenD; Democratic Republic of the Congo politician, administrator and lawyer; b. 10 Dec. 1940, Kikwit; s. of Raphaël Kamanda and Germaine Kukikidika; two s. one d.; ed Coll. St Ignace de Kiniati, Coll. Notre Dame de Mbansa Boma, Univ. Lovanium, Kinshasa; lawyer, Court of Appeal 1964; Legal Adviser, Fédération congolaise des travailleurs 1964–65; Prof., Inst. Nat. d'Etudes Politiques 1965–66; Legal Adviser to Presidency of Repub. 1965–66, Sec.-Gen. 1966–67; Prin. Adviser with responsibility for legal, admin., political and diplomatic affairs to Presidency of Repub.; Dir de Cabinet to Sec.-Gen. of OAU 1967–72, Asst Sec.-Gen. 1972–78; Perm. Rep. to UN 1979–82; State Commr for Foreign Affairs and Int. Co-operation 1982–83, for Justice 1983–84; Deputy Sec.-Gen. MPR 1987; f. Mouvement populaire de la revolution (MPR) 1997; Assoc. mem. Office Nat. de la Recherche Scientifique et du Développement; Vice-Pres. Zairian section, Soc. Africaine de la Culture; del. to several int. confs; Deputy Prime Minister 1994–97, in charge of Institutional Reforms, Justice and Keeper of the Seals 1994–96, of Interior 1996–97, of Minister of Scientific Research 1997–2004; unsuccessful cand. (Nationalist Common Front) for Pres. of Democratic Repub. of Congo 2006. *Publications:* Essai-critique du système de la criminalité d'emprunt 1964, Négritude face au devenir de l'Afrique 1967, L'université aujourd'hui en Afrique 1969, L'intégration juridique et le développement harmonieux des nations africaines 1969, L'incidence de la culture audiovisuelle sur le phénomène du pouvoir 1970, Les organisations africaines Vol. I: L'OUA ou la croisade de l'unité africaine 1970, Vol. II: 1970, Le défi africain: une puissance économique qui s'ignore 1976, L'enracinement: culture et progrès 1976. *Address:* c/o Ministry of Scientific Research, Kinshasa, Democratic Republic of the Congo (office).

KAMANZI, Stanislas; Rwandan diplomatist; Perm. Rep. to UN, New York 2003–06; Minister of Infrastructure 2006–08, of Natural Resources 2008, currently Minister of Lands, the Environment, Forestry and Mines. *Address:* Ministry of Lands, the Environment, Forestry and Mines, BP 3052, Kigali, Rwanda (office). *Telephone:* 250582628 (office). *Fax:* 250582629 (office). *E-mail:* info@minirena.gov .rw (office). *Website:* www.minirena.gov.rw (office).

KAMARA, Samura Matthew Wilson; Sierra Leonean economist, central banker and government official; *Minister of Foreign Affairs and International Co-operation;* b. 15 Dec. 1963, Kamalo, Bombali Dist; Minister of Finance 1996; fmr Exec., IMF, Washington, DC; Gov. Bank of Sierra Leone (central bank) 2007–09; fmr Financial Sec., Ministry of Finance, Minister of Finance 2009–12; Minister of Foreign Affairs and Int. Cooperation 2013–. *Address:* Ministry of Foreign Affairs and International Co-operation, Gloucester Street, Freetown, Sierra Leone (office). *Telephone:* (22) 223260 (office). *Fax:* (22) 225615 (office). *E-mail:* mfaicsl@yahoo .com (office).

KAMAT, Digambar V., BSc; Indian politician; b. 8 March 1954, Margao, Goa; s. of Vasant Kamat; m. Asha Kamat; two c.; Councillor, Margao Municipal Council 1985–90; mem. Legis. Ass. of State of Goa 1994–, mem. Cttee on Govt Assurances 1995–96, 1996–97, 1997–98, 1999–2000 (fmr Chair.), Select Cttee on Bill No. 29 of Goa Advocates Welfare Fund Bill 1995, Business Advisory Cttee 1996–97, House Cttee to study Model Rent Control Legislation, Panel of Presiding Mems 1997–98, Cttee on Public Undertakings, Chair. Public Accounts Cttee 1999–2000; Minister for Power, Protocol, and Art and Culture 1999; mem. Town and Country Planning Bd; Minister for Power, Urban Devt and Mines 2002; Chief Minister of Goa 2007–12; Chair. Produce Market Cttee 1979–91; mem. Southern Planning and Devt Authority 1986–89; mem. Exec. Cttee Nat. Council of State Agricultural Marketing Bd, New Delhi 1992–94; Vice-Chair. Nat. Council of State Agricultural Marketing Bds 1994–96; mem. State Consumer Protection Council 1993–96; Founder-mem. Damodar Educ. Soc.; Sec. Model Educ. Soc.; mem. Advisory Cttee for Parshuram Girijan Samaj; Treas., Margao Cricket Club 1973; Pres. Swimming Fed. of India, Sparkling Stars Asscn, Margao 1973–74; Founder-Pres. Rotary Club of Margao 1973, Samrat Club; mem. Goa, Daman and Diu State Council of Sports 1976–78; Vice-Pres. Goa Badminton Asscn 1980–83, Pres. 1999–2000; Trustee, Margao Ambulance Trust; Hon. Sec., Goa Badminton Asscn; Nat. Council of State Agricultural Marketing Bds Award 1994–96, Bakshi Jivabadada Kerkar State Award, Govt of Goa. *Leisure interests:* reading, playing badminton, swimming, cricket. *Address:* Sanrit Apartments, 1st Floor, nr Masjid, Malbhat, Margao, India (home). *Telephone:* (832) 2730432 (home).

KAMATA, Michisada; Japanese energy industy executive; *Chairman, Kyushu Electric Power Company Inc.;* joined Kyushu Electric Power Co. Inc. 1958, served as Man. Dir., Vice-Pres. and Pres., Chair. 2003–; Vice-Chairman Kyushu Tourism Promotion Org.; Chair. Kyushu-Yamaguchi Econ. Fed.; Vice-Chair. Fed. of Electric Power Cos 2001–03; Dir Japan Nuclear Fuel Ltd, Kyushu-Yamaguchi Econ. Fed. (Kyukeiren), Japan Productivity Center for Socio-Econ. Devt (JPC-SED), Energy Conservation Center of Japan; Trustee, Int. Center for the Study of E Asian Devt (ICSEAD). *Address:* Kyushu Electric Power Company Incorporated, 1–82 Watanabe Dori 2-chome, Chuo-ku, Fukuoka 810–8720, Japan (office). *Telephone:* (92) 761–3031 (office). *Fax:* (92) 733–1435 (office). *Website:* www .kyuden.co.jp (office).

KAMATH, Kundapur Vaman, BSc, MBA; Indian banker and business executive; *Non-Executive Chairman, Industrial Credit and Investment Corporation of India (ICICI) Bank Ltd; Chairman, Infosys Limited;* b. 2 Dec. 1947, Mangalore, Karnataka; m.; one s. one d.; ed Karnataka Regional Eng Coll. (now Nat. Inst. of Tech., Karnataka), Indian Inst. of Man., Ahmedabad; mem. of staff, Industrial Credit and Investment Corpn of India (ICICI) Bank Ltd 1971–88, CEO and Man. Dir 1996–2009, Chair. (non-exec.) 2009–; Adviser, Asian Devt Bank, Manila 1988–96; Dir Infosys Ltd 2009–, Chair. 2011–; mem. Man. Cttee, Associated Chambers of Commerce and Industry; mem. Nat. Council Confed. of Indian Industry; mem. Governing Bd Indian Inst. of Man., Ahmedabad, Indian School of Business, Nat. Inst. of Bank Man., Manipal Acad. of Higher Educ.; mem. Bd of Dirs Inst. of Int. Finance, Infosys Technologies; mem. Bd of Govs Indian Inst. of Man., Ahmedabad; Dr hc (Banaras Hindu Univ.); Asian Business Leader of the Year, CNBC 2001, Businessman of the Year, Business India magazine 2005, Outstanding Business Leader of the Year, CNBC-TV18 2006, Banker of the Year, Business

Standard 2006, Businessman of the Year, Forbes Asia 2007, Economic Times Business Leader of the Year 2007, Padma Bhushan 2008, Lifetime Achievement Award, Financial Express 2008, NDTV Profit Business Leadership Award 2008. *Address:* ICICI Bank Ltd, ICICI Bank Towers, Bandra-Kurla Complex, Mumbai 400 051, India (office). *Telephone:* (22) 26531414 (office). *Fax:* (22) 26531167 (office). *E-mail:* info@icicibank.com (office). *Website:* www.icicibank.com (office).

KAMATH, Madhav Vittal, BSc; Indian journalist and broadcasting executive; *Honorary Director, Manipal Institute of Communications, Manipal University;* b. 7 Sept. 1921, Udupi; ed St Xavier's Coll., Mumbai; worked for five years as chemist; changed careers and became reporter, then special adviser, then Ed. Free Press Journal, Mumbai 1946–54; Foreign Corresp. Times of India reporting from Germany and France, Ed. Sunday Times 1967–69, US Corresp., Times of India, Washington, DC 1969–78; Ed. Illustrated Weekly 1978–81; columnist in numerous newspapers and magazines 1981–; mem. Bd of Dirs Prasar Bharati (Broadcasting Corpn of India) 2002, Chair. 2003–09; fmr Dir Manipal Inst. of Communications, Manipal Univ., now Hon. Dir; fmr Chair. Vigyan Prasar; Hon. DLit (Mangalore Univ.) 2007; Padma Bhushan 2004. *Publications include:* over 45 books including The United States and India 1776–1976 1976, Philosophy of Death and Dying 1978, The Other Face of India 1988, A Banking Odyssey: The Canara Bank Story 1991, Ganesh Vasudeo Mavalankar 1992, Management Kurien-Style: The Story of the White Revolution, Points and Lines, Charat RAM: A Biography 1994, Journalist's Handbook 1995, Gandhi's Coolie: Life and Times of Ramkrishna Bajaj 1995, Professional Journalism 1996, Some of Us are Lucky 1996, Milkman from Anand: The Story of Verghese Kurien 1996, Sai Baba of Shirdi: A Unique Saint (co-author) 2005, A Reporter at Large (autobiog.), Collection of Articles on Politics, Media and Literature 2009. *Leisure interests:* reading, cooking. *Address:* c/o Manipal Institute of Communications, Manipal University, Manipal 576 104 (office); Kalyanpur House, 3rd Road, Near Railway Station, Kar, Mumbai, India (home). *Telephone:* (820) 2922080 (office); (22) 26483418 (home). *E-mail:* mv .kamath@manipal.edu (office). *Website:* www.manipal.edu (office).

KAMEI, Shizuka; Japanese politician; Parl. Vice-Minister of Transport, Minister 1994–95, of Construction 1996; mem. House of Reps for Hiroshima 1977–; Chair. LDP Nat. Org. Cttee and Acting Chair. LDP Policy Research Council; Minister of State for Financial Services and for Postal Reform 2009–10. *Address:* c/o Cabinet Office, 1-6-1, Nagata-cho, Chiyoda-ku, Tokyo 100-8914, Japan (office). *Telephone:* (3) 5253-2111 (office). *Website:* www.cao.go.jp (office); www.kamei-shizuka.net.

KAMEL, Sheikh Saleh Abdullah, BA, MBA; Saudi Arabian business executive; *Chairman, ART (Arab Radio and Television);* m.; ed King Abdulaziz Univ.; est. business based on contracts with Saudi Arabian Govt; est. real-estate devts in Buhairat, Tunisia and Durat al-Arous, Jeddah; f. MBC (Middle Eastern Broadcasting Center) and ART (Arab Radio and TV); majority owner and Chief Exec. Dallah al Baraka Group, Chair. and Man. Dir Al Baraka Banking Group, Chair. Al Baraka Investment and Devt; Deputy Chair. Al Jazira Bank; mem. Bd Al Baraka Investment and Devt Co., Savola, Jeddah Chamber of Commerce and Industry, Saudi Research and Publishing Ltd. *Address:* Dallah al Baraka Group, Dallah Tower, Palestine Street, Jeddah 21452 (office); PO Box 430, Jeddah 21411, Saudia Arabia (office). *Telephone:* (2) 671-0000 (Dallah al Baraka) (office); (2) 667-3316 (office). *Fax:* (2) 617-0347 (Dallah al Baraka) (office); (2) 671-7056 (office). *Website:* www.albaraka.com (office).

KAMEN, Dean; American inventor, physicist and engineer; *President, DEKA Research and Development Corporation;* ed Worcester Polytechnic Inst.; while undergrad. invented wearable infusion pump; f. AutoSyringe Inc. 1976; developed first portable pump to dispense insulin 1978; est. Science Enrichment Encounters (SEE) museum 1985; developed portable dialysis machine 1993; created the Segway Human Transporter (motorized, low-energy scooter) 2001; mem. Nat. Acad. of Eng; Owner and Pres. DEKA Research and Devt Corpn 1992–; f. US FIRST (For Inspiration and Recognition of Science and Tech.) Foundation 1989; Hon. DSc (Rensselaer Polytechnic Inst.), (Worcester Polytechnic Inst.); Engineer of the Year (Design News Magazine) 1994, Hoover Medal 1995, NH Business Leader of the Year 1996, Heinz Award in Tech., the Economy and Employment 1998, Nat. Medal of Tech. 2000, Lemelson-MIT Prize 2002; inducted into Nat. Inventors Hall of Fame 2005. *Achievements include:* holds more than 100 US patents. *Address:* DEKA Research and Development Corporation, Technology Center, 340 Commercial Street, Manchester, NH 03101, USA (office). *Telephone:* (603) 669-5139 (office). *Fax:* (603) 624-0573 (office). *E-mail:* contactdeka@ dekaresearch.com (office). *Website:* www.dekaresearch.com (office); www.usfirst .org.

KAMIJO, Kiyofumi, BSc; Japanese business executive; *Chairman, Tokyu Corporation;* ed Waseda Univ.; joined Tokyu Corpn 1958, Vice-Pres.–June 2001, Pres. and CEO June 2001–05, Chair. 2005–; Dir Tokyu Land Corpn, Japan-Fiji Friendship Soc. *Address:* Tokyu Corporation, 5–6 Nanpeidai-cho, Shibuya-ku, Tokyo 150–8511, Japan (office). *Telephone:* (3) 3477–6111 (office). *Fax:* (3) 3462–1690 (office). *Website:* www.tokyu.co.jp (office).

KAMIKAWA, Yoko, MPA; Japanese politician; *Deputy Minister of Internal Affairs and Communications;* b. 1 March 1953, Shizuoka; two c.; ed Coll. of Arts and Sciences, Tokyo Univ., John F. Kennedy School of Govt, Harvard Univ., USA; Researcher, Mitsubishi Research Inst. 1977; est. policy consultancy 1977; served on policymaking staff of US Senator Max Baucus; joined LDP 1997; elected to House of Reps 2000, as LDP representative for Shizuoka Pref., currently Head of First District; Dir of Women's Affairs Div., LDP 2000, Parl. Sec. for Internal Affairs and Communication 2005; Deputy Minister of Internal Affairs and Communications 2005–06, 2013–; Minister of State for Gender Equality, Population and Social Affairs 2007–08 (resgnd). *Address:* Liberal-Democratic Party (LDP), 18–10 Shichkien-cho, Aoi-ku, Shizuoka, 420-0035 (office); 780–1 Oya, Suruga-ku, Shizuoka, Japan (home). *Telephone:* (54) 251-8424 (office); (54) 281-1000 (home). *Fax:* (54) 251-8425 (office); (54) 283-7743 (home). *E-mail:* yoko@kamikawayoko.net (office). *Website:* www.kamikawayoko.net (office); www.jimin.jp (office).

KAMILOV, Abdulaziz Xafizovich, PhD; Uzbekistani diplomatist and politician; *Minister of Foreign Affairs;* b. 16 Nov. 1947, Yangiyul; m.; one s.; ed Moscow Inst. of Oriental Languages; served at Diplomatic Acad., USSR Ministry of Foreign Affairs; joined USSR diplomatic service 1972, Attaché, USSR Embassy in Beirut 1973–76, Second Sec., Damascus 1980–84, mem. Div. of Near East, USSR Ministry of Foreign Affairs 1984–88; Sr Researcher, Inst. of World Econs and Int. Affairs, USSR Acad. of Sciences 1988–91; Counsellor, Uzbekistan Embassy in Moscow 1991–92; Deputy Chair. Security Service of Uzbekistan Repub. 1992–94; First Deputy Minister of Foreign Affairs Jan.–Aug. 1994, 2010–12, Minister of Foreign Affairs 1994–2003, 2012–, Amb. to USA (also accred to Canada and Brazil) 2003–10; First Deputy Minister of Foreign Affairs 2010–12. *Address:* Ministry of Foreign Affairs, 100029 Tashkent, O'zbekiston shoh ko'ch. 9, Uzbekistan (office). *Telephone:* (71) 233-64-75 (office). *Fax:* (71) 239-15-17 (office). *E-mail:* info@tiv.uz (office). *Website:* www.mfa.uz (office).

KAMINOW, Ivan P., BSEE, MSE, AM, PhD; American electrical engineer, computer scientist and academic; b. New Jersey; ed Passaic High School, Union Coll., Univ. of California, Los Angeles, Harvard Univ.; carried out research on microwave antenna arrays at Hughes Aircraft Co. 1952–54; worked at Bell Labs, Murray Hill, NJ 1954–96, mostly in lightwave research, later Head of Photonic Networks and Components Research Dept; served as IEEE Congressional Fellow on staffs of US House Science Cttee and Congressional Research Service (Science Policy Research Div.), Library of Congress 1996–97; returned to Lucent Bell Labs as part-time consultant 1997–99; est. Kaminow Lightwave Technology to provide consulting services to various tech. cos and to patent and litigation law firms; Sr Science Advisor, Optical Soc. of America, Washington, DC 1999; Hughes Fellow, UCLA; Bell Labs Fellow, Harvard Univ.; Visiting Prof., Princeton Univ., Univ. of California, Berkeley, Columbia Univ., Univ. of Tokyo, Kwangju Univ., South Korea; Adjunct Prof. in Electrical Eng and Computer Sciences, Univ. of California, Berkeley 2004–12 (retd); mem. Nat. Acad. of Eng; Diplomate of American Bd of Laser Surgery; Fellow, New York Acad. of Medicine; Life Fellow, IEEE; Bell Labs Distinguished Mem. of Tech. Staff Award, IEEE Quantum Electronics Award, Charles Townes Award, Optical Soc. of America, John Tyndall Award, IEEE/ LEOS/Optical Soc. of America, IEEE Third Millennium Medal, Alumni Gold Medal, Union Coll., Frederic Ives Medal/Quinn Prize, Optical Society of Soc. 2011, IEEE Photonics Award 2012. *Publications:* has written or co-edited five books, including Optical Fiber Telecommunications IV A&B (co-ed.) 2002, Optical Fiber Telecommunications V A&B (co-ed.) 2008; more than 240 papers in professional journals; 47 patents. *Address:* c/o Electrical Engineering and Computer Sciences, College of Engineering, Berkeley, CA 94720-1776, USA.

KAMINSKI, Janusz, BA; Polish cinematographer and film director; b. 27 June 1959, Ziembice; m. Holly Hunter (q.v.) 1995; ed Columbia Coll., Chicago, American Film Inst., Washington, DC; mem. American Soc. of Cinematographers. *Films include:* All the Love in the World 1990, The Rain Killer 1990, The Terror Within II 1990, Grim Prairie Tales 1990, Pyrates 1991, Killer Instinct 1991, Cool as Ice 1991, Mad Dog Coll 1992, Trouble Bound 1993, The Adventures of Huck Finn (dir of photography) 1993, Schindler's List (Acad. Award for Best Cinematographer 1994) 1993, Little Giants 1994, Tall Tale 1995, How to Make an American Quilt 1995, Jerry Maguire 1996, Amistad 1997, The Lost World: Jurassic Park 1997, Saving Private Ryan 1998, Lost Souls 2000, AI: Artificial Intelligence 2001, Minority Report 2002 (dir of photography), Catch Me If You Can 2002, The Terminal 2004, Jumbo Girl 2004, War of the Worlds 2005, Munich 2005, Mission Zero (dir of photography) 2007, Le Scaphandre et le Papillon (Prize Vulcain de l'Artiste-Technicien, Cannes Film Festival 2007) 2007. *Address:* 1223 Wilshire Boulevard, #645 Santa Monica, CA 90403, USA (office).

KAMIŃSKI, Marek; Polish explorer; b. 24 March 1964, Gdańsk; s. of Zdzisław Kamiński and Maria Kamińska; Founder, Game San SA and Marek Kamiński Foundation; mem. The Explorers Club 1996–; Hon. mem. Polar Research Cttee Polish Acad. of Sciences; Kt's Cross Order of Polonia Restituta; Finalist, World Young Business Achiever 1994, Man of the Year 1995, Życie Warszawy daily, Gold Medal for Outstanding Achievments in Sport, Chopin Award, Super Kolos Award 2004, Caritas Reward, Pope John Paul II 2005. *Expeditions to:* Mexico, Guatemala, crossing of Spitsbergen, crossing of Greenland (twice); attempted solo crossing of Antarctica; first man who reached alone both North and South Poles in the same year 1995; climbed Mount Vinson (Antarctica) 1998; crossed Gibson Desert 1999; sailed yacht across the Atlantic (twice); participated in expedition to sources of the Amazon 2000 and North Pole expedition 2001, 2002. *Publications:* Not Only a Pole 1996, My Poles: Diaries from Expeditions 1990–98 (Artus Award for the Best Book of the Year) 1998, My Expeditions 2001, Razem na biegun (Together to the Pole) 2005. *Leisure interests:* travelling to the coldest places in the world, sailing, philosophy. *Address:* c/o Marek Kamiński Foundation, ul. Grunwaldzka 212, 80-266 Gdańsk, Poland. *Telephone:* (58) 5544522. *Fax:* (58) 5523315. *E-mail:* mkaminski@gamasan.pl (office). *Website:* www.kaminski.pl (home).

KAMMENOS, Panos; Greek economist and politician; *Leader, Independent Greeks;* b. 12 May 1965, Athens; m. Eleni Tzouli; five c.; ed Univ. of Lyon Business Admin School of Mans, Switzerland; mem. Parl. (New Democracy) for Second Dist of Athens 1993–2012, (Independent Greeks) 2012–; apptd Deputy Minister of Mercantile Marine, Aegean and Island Policy 2007; has served as mediator and official observer at elections in foreign countries; Co-founder and Leader, Independent Greeks party 2012–; Grand Cross of Merit, Czech Patriarchate, Medal of Honour, Patriarchate of Jerusalem; Chevalier, Ordre nat. du Mérite. *Address:* Independent Greeks (Anexartitoi Ellines), 2 Charokopu Avenue, Kallithea, 176 71 Athens, Greece (office). *Telephone:* (210) 9545000 (office). *E-mail:* info@anexartitoiellines.gr (office). *Website:* anexartitoiellines.gr (office).

KAMOSHITA, Ichirō, MD; Japanese physician and politician; b. 16 Jan. 1949, Adachi, Tokyo; ed Nihon Univ.; Dir Hibiya Kokusai Clinic 1981–88; Head Dir Kamoshita-gakuen Acad., Educational Corpn 1988–93, Aojuji-kai, Healthcare Corpn 1993; mem. House of Reps (originally for Japan New Party; joined LDP 1997) 1993–, has served as dir of numerous parl. cttees including Judicial Affairs 1996, 1998, Election Law 1998, Finance 1998, Audit and Oversight 1998, 2006, Political Ethics and Election Law 1999, Health and Welfare 2000, Health, Labour and Welfare 2002–06; Sr Vice-Minister of Health, Labour and Welfare 2002–03, Minister of the Environment 2007–08, Minister in Charge of Global Environmental Problems 2007–08. *Address:* Liberal-Democratic Party (LDP), 1-11-23, Nagatacho, Chiyoda-ku, Tokyo 100-8910, Japan (office). *Telephone:* (3) 3581-6211 (office). *E-mail:* koho@ldp.jimin.or.jp (office). *Website:* www.jimin.jp (office).

KAMP, Henricus (Henk) Gregorius Jozeph; Dutch politician; *Minister of Social Affairs and Employment;* b. 23 July 1952, Hengelo; ed Tax and Customs

Admin Centre, Utrecht; worked as investigator Fiscal Information and Investigation Service 1980–86; mem. Borculo Municipal Council 1976–94, alderman 1986–94; mem. Gelderland Provincial Council 1987–94; mem. House of Reps 1994–; apptd Minister of Housing, Planning and Environment 2002; Minister of Defence 2003–06, Minister of Social Affairs and Employment 2010–. *Address:* Ministry of Social Affairs and Employment, Anna van Hannoverstraat 4, POB 90801, 2509 LV The Hague, Netherlands. *Telephone:* (70) 3334444 (office). *Fax:* (70) 3334033 (office). *Website:* www.rijksoverheid.nl/ministeries/szw (office).

KAMPFNER, John, BA (Hons); British writer and journalist; *Adviser, Freedom of Expression and Culture, Google Inc.;* b. 27 Dec. 1962, Singapore; s. of Fred Kampfner and Elizabeth Kampfner (née Andrews); m. Lucy Ash; two d.; ed Westminster School, London, The Queen's Coll., Oxford; fmr foreign corresp. with Reuters and Daily Telegraph; Chief Political Corresp., Financial Times mid-1990s; fmr political commentator, Today programme (BBC Radio 4); Political Ed. New Statesman 2002–05, Ed. 2005–08; CEO Index on Censorship 2008–12, Trustee 2012–; Chair. Turner Contemporary 2008–; mem. Council, King's Coll. London 2012–; Adviser, Freedom of Expression and Culture, Google Inc. 2012–, Global Network Initiative 2012–; regular appearances on radio and TV; British Soc. of Magazine Eds. Ed. of the Year Award for Current Affairs Magazines 2006. *Television documentary films:* (all for BBC) Israel Undercover 2002, The Ugly War: Children of Vengeance (Foreign Press Asscn Award for Film of the Year and Journalist of the Year) 2002, War Spin 2003, Robin Cook: The Lost Leader (profile) 2003, Clare Short: The Conscientious Objector (profile) 2003, Who Runs Britain (series) 2004. *Publications:* Inside Yeltsin's Russia: Corruption, Conflict, Capitalism 1995, Robin Cook 1999, Blair's Wars 2003, Freedom for Sale 2009; contrib. to The Times, Sunday Times, Observer, Independent, Guardian, Financial Times, Daily Telegraph, Daily Mail, Mail on Sunday, Evening Standard, Washington Post, Los Angeles Times, Time, Newsweek, Prospect, New Statesman, Spectator. *Leisure interests:* tennis, soccer, skiing, fine art, music. *E-mail:* john@jkampfner .net (office). *Website:* www.jkampfner.net.

KAMPRAD, Ingvar; Swedish home furnishings industry executive; *Special Adviser, Ikano Group;* b. 30 March 1926, Småland; m. Margaretha Kamprad (died 2011); three s.; f. IKEA home furnishings co. 1943, Sr Adviser, Ikano Group (est. as ind. group of Kamprad family cos in 1988); est. Stichting Ingka Foundation, Leiden, Netherlands 1982; currently resides near near Lausanne, Switzerland. *Publication:* The History of IKEA 1998. *Address:* Ikano Group, POB 229, 2012 Luxembourg. *E-mail:* info@ikanogroup.com. *Website:* www.ikanogroup.com; www .ikea.com.

KAMU, Okko; Finnish conductor and violinist; b. 7 March 1946, Helsinki; m. Anna Aminoff; ed Sibelius Acad.; leader, Suhonen Quartet 1964; began professional career with Helsinki Philharmonic Orchestra 1965; subsequently appointed leader, Finnish Nat. Opera Orchestra 1966–69, Third Conductor 1967; guest conductor, Swedish Royal Opera, Stockholm 1969; Chief Conductor, Finnish Radio Symphony Orchestra 1971–77; Music Dir Oslo Philharmonic 1975–79, Helsinki Philharmonic 1981–89; Prin. Conductor, Netherlands Radio Symphony 1983–86; Prin. Guest Conductor, City of Birmingham Symphony Orchestra 1985–88; Prin. Conductor, Sjaelland Symphony Orchestra, Copenhagen 1988–94; Music Dir Stockholm Sinfonietta 1989–93; Prin. Conductor Helsingborg Symphony Orchestra 1991–2000; First Guest Conductor, Singapore Symphony Orchestra 1995–2001; Music Dir Finnish Nat. Opera, Helsinki 1996–2000; Prin. Guest Conductor Lausanne Chamber Orchestra 1999–2002; Principal Conductor, Lahti Symphony Orchestra 2011–; Artistic Dir, Int. Sibelius Festival 2011–; conducted world premières of Sallinen's operas The Red Line, The King Goes Forth to France, Palace and King Lear; numerous engagements with orchestras and opera houses worldwide; mem. Royal Swedish Acad. of Music 1996; First Prize, First Int. Karajan Conductor Competition, Berlin 1969. *Recordings include:* Sibelius: La Tempête, Le Barde, Tapiola, with Orchestre symphonique de Lahti (Diapason d'Or de l'année 2011). *Leisure interests:* golf, gastronomy. *Address:* Lahti Symphony Orchestra, Sibelius Hall, Ankkurikatu 7, 15140 Lahti, Finland (office). *Telephone:* (3) 8144451 (office). *Fax:* (3) 8144451 (office). *Website:* www.sinfonialahti.fi (office).

KAMUNANWIRE, Perezi Karukubiro, PhD; Ugandan academic and diplomatist; b. 25 July 1937, Mbarara; m.; two c.; ed Columbia Univ., New York, USA; Chair. Uganda People's Congress Youth League 1958–63; Pres. and Chair. Pan-African Students' Org. in the Americas 1965–70; Prof., CUNY, USA 1974–86, fmr Prof., Black Studies Program; Amb. to Austria (also accred to FRG and the Holy See) and Perm. Rep. to Int. Orgs in Vienna 1986–88, Perm. Rep. to UN, New York 1988–95, Chair. UN Gen. Ass. Special Political Cttee 1990–95; Adjunct Prof., Center for Conflict Man. and Organizational Research, Sophia Univ., Bulgaria 2003–06; Amb. to USA 2006–13. *Publications:* A Study Guide to Uganda (co-ed.) 1970; numerous articles in the field of int. relations. *Address:* Ministry of Foreign Affairs, PO Box 7048, 2A/B Apollo Kaggwa Road, Kampala, Uganda (office). *Telephone:* (41) 4345661 (office). *Fax:* (41) 4258722 (office). *E-mail:* info@mofa.go .ug (office). *Website:* www.mofa.go.ug (office).

KAMYNIN, Mikhail Leonidovich; Russian diplomatist; *Ambassador to Cuba;* b. 13 Aug. 1956, Moscow; m.; one d. one s.; ed Moscow Inst. of Int. Relations, Diplomatic Acad. of Ministry of Foreign Affairs; various positions at Embassy in Mexico 1978–82, 1987–91; Press Sec., Ministry of Foreign Affairs 1991–92; Counsellor, Embassy in Spain 1992–97; Asst Dir of Press and Information, Ministry of Foreign Affairs 1997–99; Minister Counsellor, Embassy in Havana 1999–2002; Asst Dir European Affairs, Ministry of Foreign Affairs 2002; Amb. to Spain 2002–05; Dir of Information and Press Dept, Ministry of Foreign Affairs 2005–08; Amb. to Cuba (also accred to Bahamas) 2008–; mem. Russian Union of Journalists. *Address:* Embassy of Russia, Avenida 5, No 6402, entre 62 y 66, Miramar, Havana, Cuba (office). *Telephone:* (7) 204-2686 (office). *Fax:* (7) 204-1038 (office). *E-mail:* embrusia@newmail.cu (office). *Website:* www.cuba.mid.ru (office).

KAN, Naoto; Japanese politician; *President, Democratic Party of Japan;* b. 10 Oct. 1946, Ube City, Yamaguchi Pref.; m.; two s.; ed Tokyo Inst. of Tech.; fmr patent attorney; Rep. for Tokyo's 7th Dist (multi-mem.) as mem. Socialist Democratic Fed. 1980–96, for 18th Dist 1996–; Minister of Health and Welfare Jan.–Nov. 1996; mem. House of Reps; mem. New Party Sakigake (NPS), now Sakigake; Founder-mem. Democratic Party of Japan 1996, Leader 1996–97, 1997–98, Pres. 1998–99, Sec.-Gen. 2000–02, Pres. 2002–04 (resgnd), Acting Pres. 2006–08, Pres. 2010–;

Deputy Prime Minister and Minister of State for Nat. Strategy, for Econ. and Fiscal Policy, and for Science and Tech. Policy 2009–10; Minister of Finance Jan.–June 2010; Prime Minister 2010–11 (resgnd); ranked 27th by Forbes magazine amongst The World's Most Powerful People 2010. *Publication:* Dai-jin (Minister). *Leisure interest:* playing Go. *Address:* The Democratic Party of Japan, 1-11-1 Nagata-cho, Chiyoda-ku, Tokyo 100-0014, Japan (office). *Telephone:* (3) 3595-9988 (office). *Fax:* (3) 3595-7318 (office). *Website:* www.dpj.or.jp/english/ (office).

KAN, Yuet Wai, MD, DSc, FRCP, FRS; American (b. Hong Kong) physician, investigator and academic; *Louis K. Diamond Professor of Hematology, Departments of Laboratory Medicine and Medicine, University of California, San Francisco;* b. 11 June 1936, Hong Kong; s. of Tong Po Kan and Lai Wai Li; m. Alvera Lorraine Limauro 1964; two d.; ed Wah Yan Coll., Hong Kong and Univ. of Hong Kong Medical School; Asst Prof. of Pediatrics, Harvard Medical School 1970–72; Assoc. Prof., Dept of Medicine, Univ. of California, San Francisco 1972–77, Prof., Depts of Lab. Medicine, Medicine 1977–, Louis K. Diamond Prof. of Hematology 1991–, Investigator, Howard Hughes Medical Inst. 1976–2003; Dir and Hon. Prof., Inst. of Molecular Biology, Univ. of Hong Kong 1991–94; Pres. American Soc. of Hematology 1990, Soc. of Chinese Bioscientists in America 1998–99; Chair. Shaw Prize in Life Science and Medicine Selection Cttee 2006–, American Asscn of Cancer Research Foundation 2011–; mem. Research Grants Council, Hong Kong 1990–94, NIH Blood Diseases and Resources Advisory Cttee 1985–89, Nat. Inst. of Digestive and Kidney Disease Advisory Council, NIH 1991–95, Scientific Advisory Bd, St Jude's Children's Hosp. 1994–97, Scientific Advisory Bd and Exec. Cttee, Qiu Shi Foundation on Science and Tech., Hong Kong 1994–, Nat. Heart, Lung & Blood Inst. 1995–96; Trustee, Croucher Foundation 1992–2011, Chair. 1997–2011; mem. NAS, Academia Sinica; Assoc. Fellow, Third World Acad. of Sciences; Foreign mem. Chinese Acad. of Sciences; Hon. MD (Univ. of Cagliari, Sardinia, Italy) 1981; Hon. DSc (Chinese Univ. of Hong Kong) 1981, (Univ. of Hong Kong) 1987, (Open Univ. of Hong Kong) 1998; Damashek Award, American Soc. of Hematology 1979, Stratton Lecture Award, Int. Soc. of Hematology 1980, George Thorn Award, Howard Hughes Medical Inst. 1980, Gairdner Foundation Int. Award 1984, Allan Award, American Soc. of Human Genetics 1984, Lita Annenberg Hazen Award for Excellence in Clinical Research 1984, Waterford Award in Biomedical Sciences 1987, NIH Merit Award 1987, American Coll. of Physicians Award 1988, Sanremo Int. Award for Genetic Research 1989, Warren Alpert Foundation Prize 1989, Albert Lasker Clinical Medical Research Award 1991, Christopher Columbus Discovery Award in Biomedical Research 1992, City of Medicine Award 1992, Cotlove Award, Acad. of Clinical Lab. Physicians and Scientists 1993, Merit Award, Fed. of Chinese Canadians Educ. Foundation 1994, Helmut Horten Research Award 1995, Shaw Prize in Life Science and Medicine, Hong Kong 2004, Lifetime Achievement Award, Soc. of Chinese Bioscientists in America 2006, Ernest Beutler Orize and Lecture A, American Soc. of Hematology 2009, Karl Landsteiner Prize and Lecturer, American Asscn of Blood Banks 2011. *Publications:* chapters in numerous books and more than 290 articles in scientific journals. *Address:* HSW 901E, 513 Parnassus Avenue, San Francisco, CA 94143-0793, USA (office). *Telephone:* (415) 476-5841 (office). *Fax:* (415) 476-2956 (office). *E-mail:* yw.kan@ucsf.edu (office).

KAN-DAPAAH, Albert; Ghanaian politician and chartered accountant; b. 14 March 1953, Maase-Boaman, Ashanti Region; ed Acherensua Secondary School, Inst. of Professional Studies, North East London Polytechnic and Emile Woolf Coll. of Accountancy, UK; Audit Sr with Pannel Kerr Forster, transferred to Monrovia, Liberia and London, UK offices 1978–86; Head of Audit, Social Security and Nat. Insurance Trust Jan.–Sept. 1987; Dir of Audit, Electricity Co. of Ghana 1987, later Dir of Finance for six years; Pnr, Kwesie, Kan-Dapaah & Baah Co., Accra; Man. Consultant Kan-Dapaah and Assocs; fmr part-time Lecturer in Auditing, School of Admin, Univ. of Ghana, Inst. of Professional Studies; Pres. Inst. of Chartered Accountants (Ghana) 1996; Vice-Pres. Asscn of Accountancy Bodies in West Africa 1996; mem. Bd of Dirs SSB Consumer Credit Ltd 1987–95; Alt. Bd mem. Kabel Metal Ghana Ltd 1987–95, New Times Corpn 1987–95; Ashanti Regional Rep. on Nat. Council of the New Patriotic Party, mem. Finance and Econ. Affairs Cttee 1992–96; mem. Parl. for Afigya Sekyere West 1997–; Minister for Energy 2000–03, for Communications and Tech. 2003–07, for Interior 2006–07, of Defence 2007–09; mem. Ghana Inst. of Chartered Accountants; Fellow, Chartered Asscn of Certified Accountants (UK). *Address:* c/o New Patriotic Party, C912/2 Duade Street, Kokomlemle, POB 3456, Accra, Ghana (office). *Telephone:* (21) 227951 (office). *Fax:* (21) 224418 (office). *E-mail:* npp@africanonline.com.gh (office).

KANAAN, Taher Hamdi, PhD; Jordanian business consultant and organization official; *Managing Director, Jordan Center for Policy Research and Dialogue;* b. 1 March 1935, Nablus, Palestine; s. of Hamdi and Najiah (née Quttainah) Kanaan; m. Ilham Kahwaji 1960; three s.; ed American Univ. of Beirut, Trinity Coll., Cambridge, UK; Econ. Adviser, Ministry of Planning, Iraq 1964–65; Dir of Programmes at Arab Fund for Econ. and Social Devt, Kuwait 1973–76; Consultant in Industrial Devt, Ministry of Planning, Morocco 1977–78; Chief External Financing and Devt, UNCTAD, Geneva 1979–83; Dir and Econ. Adviser Arab Fund 1983–85; Minister of Occupied Territories Affairs 1985, of Planning 1986–89, Deputy Prime Minister for Devt 1998–99; Gen. Man. Industrial Devt Bank of Jordan 1989–92; mem. Bd of Higher Educ., Jordan; mem. Bd of Govs World Bank, Arab Fund for Econ. and Social Devt 1985–89; mem. Exec. Bd Arab Center for Research and Policy Studies, Doha; mem. Bd of Trustees Center for Arab Unity Studies, Beirut, Econ. Research Forum, Cairo, Arab Anti-Corruption Org.; Man. Dir Jordan Center for Policy Research and Dialogue, Amman 2003–; mem. Advisory Group Arab Human Devt Report. *Leisure interests:* swimming, music, history, philosophy, surfing the Internet. *Address:* Jordan Center for Policy Research and Dialogue, PO Box 830825, Zahran, Amman 11183, Jordan (office). *Telephone:* (6) 5923676 (office). *Fax:* (6) 5923368 (office). *E-mail:* info@jcpprd.org (office); taher.kanaan@gmail.com (home). *Website:* www.jcpprd.org (office).

KANAI, Tsutomu, BS, PhD; Japanese electronics industry executive; *Chairman Emeritus, Hitachi Ltd;* b. 1930, Kyoto; ed Univ. of Tokyo; trained as mechanical engineer; joined Hitachi Ltd 1958, worked on devt of nuclear reactors in Cen. Research Lab., sr positions include Exec. Man.-Dir and Group Exec. Power Group 1985–87, Sr Exec. Man.-Dir 1987–89, Exec. Vice-Pres. and Dir 1989–91, Pres. and Rep. Dir 1991–99, Chair. and Rep. Dir 1999–2005, now Chair. Emer.; Singapore

Honorary Citizen Award 2005. *Address:* c/o Hitachi Ltd, 4-6 Kanda-Surugadai, Chiyoda-ku, Tokyo 101-8010, Japan (office).

KANANIN, Roman Grigorevich; Russian architect; b. 19 June 1935, Moscow; s. of Grigoriy Kananin and Maria Kananin; m. 1959; one d.; ed Moscow Architectural Inst.; Head of Atelier No. 3. of Public Jt Stock Co. Mosproject 1972–; mem. Russian Acad. of Architecture and Bldg Sciences 2005–; Lenin Prize 1984, Honoured Builder of Moscow 1999, People's Architect 2005. *Works include:* Patrice Lumumba Univ. (now Univ. of People's Friendship), Moscow (with others) 1969–73, residential blocks on Lenin Prospekt, Moscow 1965–70, multi-storey brick residential complex, Noviye Cheremushky 1973–84, memorial complex to war veterans in Novorossiysk 1982, various monuments in Moscow and Magnitogorsk, including monument to Gerzen and Ogarev, Vorobyevy Hils, Moscow, Palace of Youth, Moscow 1978, IRIS Pulman Hotel and apartments, Moscow 1991, Parus Business Centre, Tverskaya-Yamskaya St, Moscow 1994, exclusive multi-storey residential bldgs, Krasnoproletarskaya str., vl. 7 1999, Dolgorukovskaya str., vl. 24–30 2001, B. Gruzinskaya str., vl. 37 2001, residential complexes, Petrovsko-Razumkovsky proezd, B Academicheskaya St, Moscow. *Leisure interests:* sport, travelling. *Address:* Joint-Stock Company Mosproject, 13/14, 1-st Brestkaya str., GSP, 125190 Moscow, Russia. *Telephone:* (495) 209-61-22; (495) 250-46-99. *Fax:* (495) 209-50-02.

KANAPLYOU, Uladzimir; Belarusian politician; *Chairman, Palata Predstaviteley (House of Representatives);* Deputy Chair. Palata Predstaviteley 2000–04, Chair. 2004–. *Address:* Palata Predstaviteley, 220010 Minsk, vul. Savetskaya 11, Belarus (office). *Telephone:* (17) 227-25-14 (office). *Fax:* (17) 222-31-78 (office). *E-mail:* admin@gov.house.by (office). *Website:* house.gov.by (office).

KANAWA, Dame Kiri Te (see TE KANAWA, Dame Kiri).

KANBUR, Ravi, MA, DPhil; British economist and academic; *T.H. Lee Professor of World Affairs, International Professor of Applied Economics and Management and Professor of Economics, Cornell University;* b. 28 Aug. 1954, Dharwar, India; s. of Prof. M. G. Kanbur and M. M. Kanbur; m. Margaret S. Grieco 1979; ed King Edward VI Camp Hill School, Birmingham, Gonville & Caius Coll., Cambridge, Merton and Worcester Colls, Oxford; Prize Fellow, Nuffield Coll. Oxford 1978–79; Fellow in Econs, Clare Coll. Cambridge 1979–83; Prof. of Econs, Univ. of Essex 1983–85; Visiting Prof., Princeton Univ. 1985–87; Prof. of Econs and Dir Devt Econs Research Centre, Univ. of Warwick 1987–89, Hon. Prof. 1994; Sr Adviser and Ed. World Bank Economic Review and World Bank Research Observer, IBRD, Washington, DC 1989–92; World Bank Resident Rep. in Ghana 1992–94, World Bank Chief Economist for Africa 1994–96, Prin. Adviser to Sr Vice-Pres. and Chief Economist 1996–97; T. H. Lee Prof. of World Affairs, Int. Prof. of Applied Econs and Man. and Prof. of Econs, Cornell Univ., Ithaca, NY 1997–; Research Fellow, Center for Econ. Policy Research, London 1983–; V.K.R.V. Chair Prof., Inst. for Social and Econ. Change, Bangalore 2004–05; Academic Visitor, Univ. of Edinburgh 2000–, Univ. of Cambridge 2002–03, 2004–, Univ. of Birmingham 2010–; Sr Visiting Fellow, Nat. Council of Applied Econ. Research, Delhi 2009–; Hon. Prof., Univ. of Warwick; American Agricultural Econs Asscn Research Award (co-recipient with L. Haddad) 1991. *Publications:* articles in learned journals. *Address:* 221 Warren Hall, Cornell University, Ithaca, NY 14853-7801, USA (office). *Telephone:* (607) 255-7966 (office). *Fax:* (607) 255-9984 (office). *E-mail:* sk145@cornell.edu (office). *Website:* kanbur.dyson.cornell.edu (office).

KANCHELI, Giya (Georgy); Georgian composer; b. 10 Aug. 1935, Tbilisi; s. of Alexander Kancheli and Agnessa Kancheli; m. Valentina Djikia; one s. one d.; ed Tbilisi State Conservatory, studied composition with I. Tuskiya; worked as a freelance composer following graduation from 1963; hailed as a member of the 'Soviet avant-garde' 1960s, subsequently dedicated himself to developing a personal musical style based on simple formulas occurring in the music of different epochs, ancient folk songs and in popular music; later collaborated with dir Robert Sturua who inspired him to write music for films and several plays; Prof., Tbilisi Conservatory 1970–90; Dir of Music, Rustaveli Theatre, Tbilisi 1971–91, wrote incidental music for many of Sturua's productions, including his opera 'Music for the Living' 1984 (re-staged for Deutsches Nat. Theater, Weimar 1999), for Brecht's The Caucasian Chalk Circle, Shakespeare's Richard III, Hamlet and King Lear, Sophocles' Oedipus and Beckett's Waiting for Godot; best known as a composer of symphonic and other large-scale works; Fourth Symphony, 'In Memoria di Michelangelo', received its US premiere with the Philadelphia Orchestra, Yury Temirkanov conducting 1978; left Georgia with his family 1991, first went to Berlin and received a grant from German Academic Exchange Service; commissions and frequent performances in Europe and USA with Jansug Kakhidze, Dennis Russell Davies, Kim Kashkashian, Gidon Kremer, Yuri Bashmet, Mstislav Rostropovich and the Kronos Quartet; Composer-in-Residence, Royal Flemish Philharmonic Orchestra, Antwerp 1995–96; USSR State Prize 1976, USSR People's Artist 1988, State Prize of Georgia 1982, Nika Prize for film music 1987, Triumph Prize Moscow 1998, Wolf Foundation Prize in the Arts (Music) 2008, Lifetime Achievement Award, Istanbul 2012. *Compositions include:* symphonies: First 1967, Second 1970, Third 1973, Fourth (In Memoria di Michelangelo) 1975, Fifth 1977, Sixth (In Memory of Parents) 1980, Seventh (Epilogue) 1986; other symphonic works: Mourned by the Wind for orchestra and viola 1989, Lament (in memory of Luigi Nono), for violin, soprano and orchestra 1995; opera: Music for the Living 1984; chamber works: Life Without Christmas 1989–90 (cycle of four works for chamber ensembles), Magnum Ignotum, for wind ensemble and tape 1994, Exil, for soprano, small ensemble and tape 1994, Dixi for mixed choir and symphony orchestra 2009, Chiaroscuro for soloist (violin/viola) and orchestra 2010, Lingering for symphony orchestra 2012, Angels of Sorrow 2013. *Address:* Tovstonogov str. 6, 0162 Tbilisi, Georgia (home). *E-mail:* mail@kancheli.de (office).

KANDARIAN, Steven A., BA, MBA, JD; American business executive; *Chairman, President and CEO, MetLife Inc.;* ed Clark Univ., Harvard Business School, Georgetown Univ. Law Center; began career as investment banker with Rotan Mosle, Inc., Houston, Tex.; Man. Dir Lee Capital Holdings, Boston 1984–90; Founder and Pres. Eagle Capital Holdings 1990–93; Founder and Man. Dir Orion Partners, LP 1993–2001; Exec. Dir Pension Benefit Guaranty Corpn 2001–04; joined MetLife as Exec. Vice-Pres. and Chief Investment Officer 2005–11, mem. Bd of Dirs, Pres. and CEO MetLife Inc. 2011–, Chair. 2012–; mem. Bd of Dirs Damon

Runyon Cancer Research Foundation; mem. Economic Club of New York. *Address:* MetLife Inc., 2701 Queens Plaza North, Long Island City, NY 11101-4015, USA (office). *Telephone:* (212) 578-2211 (office). *Fax:* (212) 578-3320 (office). *E-mail:* info@metlife.com (office). *Website:* www.metlife.com (office).

KANDBORG, Lt.-Gen. Ole Larson; Danish army officer (retd) and consultant; b. 16 May 1941, nr Skanderborg; m. Lis Kandborg; two c.; ed Viborg, Army Officers' Acad., Copenhagen, Canadian Forces' Staff Coll., Toronto, Canada, NATO Defence Coll., Rome, Italy; nat. service with Prince's Life Regt, Viborg, Sergeant, Lt; First Lt, Capt. of mechanized infantry Bn 1966–72; Instructor, Danish Combat Arms School 1974–77; Staff Officer, HQ of the UN Peace-keeping Force in Cyprus 1977–78; Co. Commdr, Skive, G3 of Mechanized Brigade 1978–82; at Faculty of Danish Defence Coll. 1982–84; Instructor, annual Nordic UN Staff Officers' Course (Sweden), Chief Instructor; Lt-Col, Commdr of 1st Tank Bn, Jutland Dragoon Regt, Holstebro 1984–85; Public Information Adviser and Deputy to Chief of Defence, Defence HQ, Copenhagen 1986–89, Deputy Chief of Staff for Plans and Policy 1992; Col, Commdr 2nd New Zealand Brigade, Vordingborg 1989–90; Maj.-Gen., Commdr Jutland Div., Fredericia 1990–92; Commdr of Danish Operational Command based in Århus and Kamp 1993–96; Danish Mil. Rep. to NATO Mil. Cttee April–Sept. 1996, Dir Int. Mil. Staff, NATO 1996–2001 (retd); currently Mil. Adviser on strategic and NATO matters, DCS Group; Commdr, Order of Dannebrog, Mil. Good Service Medal, Reserve Officers' Asscn's Good Service Medal, Commdr 1st Degree, Order of the Swedish North Star, Legion of Merit (Degree of Commdr); UN Medal 7. *Address:* c/o DCS Group, Virkelyst 10, 9400 Noerresundby, Denmark (office).

KANDEL, Eric Richard, BA, MD; American psychiatrist, biochemist and academic; *Professor of Neuroscience, Columbia University;* b. 7 Nov. 1929, Vienna, Austria; m. 1956; two c.; ed Harvard Coll., New York Univ.; New York Univ. (NYU) School of Medicine 1956; Resident in Psychiatry, Harvard Medical School 1960–64, staff psychiatrist 1964–65; Assoc. Prof. of Physiology, NYU 1965–74; Prof. of Physiology and Psychiatry, Columbia Univ. 1974–, Prof. of Biochemistry 1992, now Prof. of Neuroscience; Sr Investigator, Howard Hughes Medical Inst. 1983–; mem. NAS, American Acad. of Arts and Sciences, Soc. of Neurosciences (Pres. 1980–81), Int. Brain Research Org., New York Acad. of Sciences; numerous awards and prizes including Nat. Medal of Science 1988, Warren Triennial Prize 1992, Harvey Prize 1993, Mayor Award for Excellence in Science and Tech. 1994, New York Acad. of Medicine Award 1996, Wolf Foundation Prize in Medicine 1999, Heineken Prize 2000, Nobel Prize for Medicine (jt recipient) 2000. *Publications:* In Search of Memory (Los Angeles Times Book Prize for Science and Technology) 2006; numerous articles in academic journals. *Address:* Howard Hughes Medical Institute, Columbia University, 1051 Riverside Drive, New York, NY 10032, USA (office). *Telephone:* (212) 543-5204 (office). *Fax:* (212) 543-5474 (office). *E-mail:* erk5@columbia.edu (office). *Website:* www.excalibur.cpmc.columbia.edu (office).

KANDODO, Ken Edward, BEcons, MBA; Malawi politician; fmr positions include auditor and foreign investment adviser, KPMG, UK and Mozambique, financial consultant for UNICEF, Gen. Man., Blantyre Print and Packaging Ltd; fmr Head, Nat. Food Reserve Agency; MP for Kasungu Central 2009–; Minister of Finance 2009–11, also Gov. of Malawi to Eastern and Southern African Trade and Devt Bank; mem. Democratic Progressive Party. *Address:* c/o Ministry of Finance, Capital Hill, POB 30049, Lilongwe 3, Malawi (office).

KANE, Amadou; Senegalese banker and politician; b. 1954, Thiès; m.; three c.; ed Univ. Paris I–Sorbonne, Univ. Paris IX–Dauphine, France; began career as credit analyst, Africa and Latin America Div., Union de Banques Arabes et Françaises SA, Neuilly, Paris; Dir, Financial Insts and Industry Dept, West African Devt Bank, Lomé 1990–94, Head, Financial Operations Dept 1994–95; joined BNP Paribas 1995, Dir, Banque Internationale pour le Commerce et l'Industrie (BICI) 1995, Gen. Man. 1996, Man. Dir Banque Internationale pour le Commerce et l'Industrie du Sénégal (BICIS) 1996–2006, 2010–12, Head of Africa within BNP Paribas Retail Banking, Emerging Markets and Overseas Territories Dept 2006–10; Minister of the Economy and Finance 2012–13; Pres. Asscn professionnelle de banques et établissements financiers du Sénégal 1998–2004; Vice-Pres. Conseil national du patronat du Sénégal 2002; Dir Banque régionale d'investissement de la Banque Centrale des États de l'Afrique de l'Ouest (BCEAO) 2004–; Ordre Nat. du Lion de la République Sénégalaise 1997, Chevalier, Légion d'honneur 2007. *Publications:* contribs to numerous journals including Jeune Afrique, le Monde diplomatique, Banque, Journal de l'économie africaine. *Address:* c/o Ministry of the Economy and Finance, ave Carde, Bâtiment CEPOD, Dakar, Senegal.

KANEKO, Hisashi, MSc; Japanese business executive and foundation executive; *President, NEC Foundation of America;* b. 19 Nov. 1933, Tokyo; s. of Shozo Kaneko and Toshi Kaneko; m. Mokoto Washino; three c.; ed Tokyo Univ., Univ. of Calif., Berkeley; joined NEC Corpn 1956, Pres. NEC America 1989–91, NEC Corpn 1994–99 (resgnd), Counselor 1999–; currently Pres. and mem. Bd of Dirs NEC Foundation of America. *Address:* NEC Foundation of America, 2950 Express Drive South, Suite 102, Islandia, NY 11749-1412, USA (office). *Telephone:* (631) 232-2212 (office). *Website:* www.necfoundation.org (office).

KANEKO, Isao; Japanese airline industry executive; *Senior Adviser, Japan Airlines Corporation;* b. 1 March 1938; m.; one d.; ed Tokyo Univ.; joined Japan Airlines (JAL) 1960, worked in Int. Cargo Dept then joined Industrial Relations Dept; posted to American Region HQ, New York 1968–72; Deputy Vice Pres. Industrial Relations 1985–95, mem. Bd of Dirs 1991–; Man. Dir and Sr Vice Pres., Human Resources 1995–97, Sr Man. Dir and Sr Vice Pres., Human Resources 1997–98, Pres. JAL 1998–2002, Pres. and CEO Japan Airlines and concurrently Pres. and CEO Japan Airlines System Corpn 2002–04, Chair. and CEO Japan Airlines Corpn (JAL Group holding co.) and concurrently Chair. Japan Airlines Int. and Japan Airlines Domestic System 2004–05, Sr Adviser 2005–; Chair. Japan-Asia Exchange Cttee, Keiza Doyukai (Japan Asscn of Corp. Execs). *Address:* Japan Airlines Corporation, 2-4-11, Higashi-Shinagawa, Shinagawa-ku, Tokyo 140-8605, Japan. *Telephone:* (3) 5769-6098. *Website:* www.jal.co.jp.

KANEKO, Ryotaro; Japanese insurance industry executive; b. 20 June 1941; Man. Dir Meiji Life Insurance Co. 1994–97, Sr Man. Dir 1997–98, Pres. 1998–2004, Pres. and Dir Meiji Yasuda Life Insurance Co. (following merger with Yasuda Mutual Life) 2004–05 (resgnd); Dir Mitsubishi Tokyo Financial Group 2003–05. *Address:* c/o Meiji Yasuda Life Insurance Company, 19–1 Nishi-Shinjuku, Shinjuku-ku, Tokyo 169-8701, Japan (office).

KANERVA, Ilkka Armas Mikael, MPolSc; Finnish politician; b. 28 Jan. 1948, Lokalahti; mem. Turku City Council 1972–; Party Man., Nat. Coalition Party 1972–93 (mem. Exec. Cttee 1975–93), Chair. Nat. Coalition Party Youth League 1972–76; mem. Suomen Eduskunta (Parl.) 1975–, mem. Foreign Affairs Cttee 1979-1987, 1995–99, Chair. Parl. Supervisory Bd, Bank of Finland 1995–99, Chair. Defence Cttee 1999–2003, Deputy Speaker 2003–07; Minister of State (attached to Office of the Council of State) 1987–90, Minister at the Ministry of Finance 1989–91, 1991, Minister of Transport and Communications 1990–91, of Labour 1991–94, of Foreign Affairs 2007–08 (resgnd); Chair. Comm. of State Guarantee Fund 1996–; Chair. Supervisory Bd, Veikkaus Oy (Nat. Lottery Co.) 1996–; Pres. Finnish Athletics Fed.; Pres. Helsinki 2005 World Championships Organising Cttee; Council mem. Int. Asscn of Athletics Fed. 2003–. *Address:* c/o Kansallinen Kokoomus (Kok) (National Coalition Party), Pohjoinen Rautatiekatu 21b, 00100 Helsinki, Finland. *Telephone:* (20) 7488488. *Fax:* (20) 7488505. *E-mail:* jori .arvonen@kokoomus.fi. *Website:* www.kokoomus.fi; www.ilkkakanerva.net.

KANG, Chang-oh; South Korean business executive; Sr Man.-Dir and Gen. Superintendent, Pohang Works, Pohang Iron & Steel Corpn (POSCO) 1988, apptd Dir 1995, Sr Exec. Vice-Pres. and Chief Financial Officer 2002–03, Pres. and Rep. Dir 2003–06. *Address:* c/o POSCO, POSCO Centre 892, Daechi-dong, Kangnam-ku, Seoul 135–777, Republic of Korea. *Telephone:* (2) 3457-0114. *Fax:* (2) 3457-1999. *Website:* www.posco.com.

KANG, Chung-won, BA, MA; South Korean banking executive; b. 19 Dec. 1950; ed Dartmouth Coll., Fletcher School of Law and Diplomacy, Tufts Univ., USA; held numerous exec. positions for Citibank including in New York 1979, in Repub. of Korea 1979–83; with Bankers Trust Group, Seoul 1983–92, Chief Rep. Bankers Trust Securities Corpn 1992–96, Chief Country Officer, Korea Bankers Trust Group 1996–99; Chief Country Officer, Deutsche Bank Group, Korea 1999–2000; Pres. and CEO Seoul Bank 2000–02; Adviser, Kim & Chang (law firm) 2003–04, World Bank Group 2003–04; Pres. and CEO Kookmin Bank 2004–10; Vice-Chairman and CEO KB Financial Holding Inc. 2009–10; Dir (non-exec.) LG Investment & Securities Co. 2003–04. *Address:* c/o Kookmin Bank, 9-1, 2-ga, Namdaemoon-ro, Jung-gu, Seoul 100-703, Republic of Korea (office).

KANG, Dong-suk; American violinist; b. 28 April 1954, Seoul, Repub. of Korea; m. Martine Schittenhelm; one s. one d.; ed Juilliard School, New York and Curtis Inst. Philadelphia (under Ivan Galamian); went to New York to study 1967; won San Francisco Symphony Foundation Competition and Merriweather Post Competition, Washington, DC 1971; winner at other competitons including Queen Elisabeth, Brussels, Montréal, and Carl Flesch, London; has appeared with maj. orchestras throughout USA, UK, Europe and Far East and at music festivals around the world including BBC Promenade concerts (debut 1987). *Recordings include:* complete repertoire for violin and orchestra by Sibelius, Nielsen Violin Concerto, Elgar Violin Concerto, Bruch Violin Concerto, Walton Violin Concerto. *Address:* 17 rue du Lieutenant Heitz, 94300 Vincennes, France (office).

KANG, Gum-sil; South Korean civil rights lawyer and politician; b. 1957; ed Seoul Nat. Univ.; admitted to Bar 1981; served as judge 1983–96 (under S Korean mil. rule, defied common practice of jailing student activists by releasing them on bail); led group of judges advocating reform of outdated legal system 1994; attorney 1996–; Vice-Pres. Lawyers for a Democratic Soc. (Minbyun) 2000–; Minister of Justice (first woman) 2003–04; Chief Attorney, Horizon Law Group, Seoul –2006; unsuccessful cand. for Mayor of Seoul (Uri Party) 2006. *Leisure interests:* amateur singer and dancer. *Address:* Uri Party, National Assembly, 1 Yeouido-dong, Yeongdeungpo-gu, Seoul 150-701, Republic of Korea (office).

KANG, Man-soo; South Korean civil servant and politician; b. 1945, Hapcheon, S Gyeongsang Prov.; began career at Ministry of Finance 1970, Vice-Minister of Finance 1997–98 (resgnd over Asian financial crisis); econ. affairs adviser to Pres. Lee for several years, Head of Econ. Affairs Sub-cttee on Lee's Transition Cttee –2008; Pres. Seoul Devt Inst. during Lee's tenure as Mayor of Seoul; co-ordinated Lee's economy-related pledges during presidential campaign; Minister of Strategy and Finance 2008–09. *Address:* c/o Ministry of Strategy and Finance, Government Complex II, 88 Gwanmunro, Gwacheon City, Gyeonggi Province, 427-725, South Korea (office).

KANG, Sok-ju; North Korean politician; *Vice-Premier;* b. 4 Aug. 1939, Pyongwan, S Pyongan Prov.; First Vice-Minister, Admin. Council, Ministry of Foreign Affairs 1986–87, First Vice-Minister of Foreign Affairs 1987–2010, Vice-Premier 2010–; del. to UN following N Korean accession to UN 1991, Head of Del. to negotiations with USA 1993, attended meeting of Kim Il Sung and US Pres. Jimmy Carter 1994, signed nuclear agreement with USA, Geneva 1994, accompanied Kim Jong Il to Russia 2001, to summit with Japanese Prime Minister Junichiro Koizumi 2002; mem. Cen. Cttee Korean Workers' Party 1991–. *Address:* Ministry of Foreign Affairs, Pyongyang, Democratic People's Republic of Korea (office).

KANG, Sung-mo (Steve), BS, MS, PhD; South Korean electrical engineer, academic and university administrator; *President, Korea Advanced Institute of Science and Technology;* ed Fairleigh Dickinson Univ., State Univ. of New York, Buffalo, Univ. of California, Berkeley, USA; Asst Prof., Rutgers Univ.,1975–77, Visiting Faculty mem. 1977–84; mem. Tech. Staff, AT&T Bell Labs, Murray Hill, NJ 1977–82, Supervisor, AT&T Bell Labs 1982–85; Humboldt Visiting Prof., Univ. of Karlsruhe, Germany 1997, Tech. Univ. of Munich, Germany 1998; Visiting Prof., Swiss Fed. Inst. of Tech. (EPFL), Lausanne 1989, 2012, Honoured Visiting Prof. 2006; Research Assoc. Prof., Co-ordinated Science Lab., Univ. of Illinois, Urbana-Champaign 1985–89, Assoc. Prof., Electrical and Computer Eng 1985–89, Research Prof., Co-ordinated Science Lab. 1989–2000, Prof. of Electrical and Computer Eng 1989–2000, Research Prof., Beckman Inst. 1990–2000, Prof. of Computer Science 1990–2000, Founding Dir Center for ASIC Research and Devt 1993–96, Head, Dept of EEC 1995–2000; Prof. Highest Step, Electrical Eng, Univ. of California, Santa Cruz 2001–03, Dean, Baskin School of Eng 2001–07, Prof. Above-Scale, Electrical Eng 2004–07, SOE Distinguished Chair Prof. 2011–13; Chaired Visiting Prof., Korean Advanced Inst. of Science and Tech. (KAIST) 2003–05, Pres. KAIST 2013–; Prof. Above-Scale of Eng and Chancellor Univ. of California, Merced 2007–11, Chancellor Emer. 2011–13; Assoc., Center for

Advanced Study, UIUC 1991–92; Founding Ed.-in-Chief, IEEE Transactions on VLSI Systems 1992–94; Pres. Silicon Valley Eng Council 2002–03; Chair. IEEE Circuits and Systems Soc. Industrial Pioneer Award Subcommittee 2012, Cttee of Creative Economy, Presidential Advisory Council on Science and Tech. 2013–; mem. Int. Review Bd Western Asscn of Schools and Colls 2012–; External Assessor, Dean of Eng Search, Hong Kong Polytechnic Univ. 2012; Foreign mem. Nat. Acad. of Eng of Korea 1997; mem. Korean Acad. of Science and Tech. 2010; Fellow, IEEE 1990, AAAS 1997, Asscn of Computing Machinery 2000; Myril B. Reed Best Paper Award 1979, Exceptional Contrib. Award, AT&T Bell Labs 1984, Best Paper Award, Int. Conf. on Computer Design 1987, Meritorious Service Award and Distinguished Service Award, IEEE Computer Soc. 1990, IEEE Darlington Best Journal Paper Award 1993, Nat. Science Council Distinguished Lecturer (Repub. of China) 1993, SRC Inventor Recognition Award 1993, 1996, 2002, Meritorious Service Award, IEEE Circuits and Systems Soc. 1994, also Distinguished Lecturer 1994–97, Charles Marshall Sr Univ. Scholar, Univ. of Illinois 1995, Alexander von Humboldt Award for Sr US Scientists 1996, IEEE Leon K. Kirchmayer Grad. Teaching Tech. Field Award 1996, IEEE CAS Soc. Tech. Achievement Award 1997, Korea Broadcasting System Award in Industrial Tech. 1998, SRC Tech. Excellence Award 1999, IEEE CAS Golden Jubilee Medal 1999, IEEE Millennium Medal 2000, Outstanding Alumni Award in Electrical Eng, Univ. of California, Berkeley 2001, Low Power Design Contest Award, Int. Symposium on Low Power Electronics and Design 2001, Meritorious Service Award, Univ. of Illinois, Urbana-Champaign ECE Alumni Asscn 2001, Distinguished Lecturer, IEEE Solid-State Circuits Soc. 2002–05, Chancellor's Stellar Service Award, Univ. of California, Santa Cruz 2003, Distinguished Lecturer, IEEE Circuits and Systems Soc. 2003–05, IEEE Mac E. Van Valkenburg Award, IEEE Circuits and Systems Soc. 2005, Chang-Lin Tien Educ. Leadership Award 2007, Outstanding Leadership Appreciation and Recognition Award, Univ. of California, Santa Cruz 2007, Gandhi, King, Ikeda Community Builder Award, Morehouse Coll. 2007, Cultural Amb. Award, APA-FIVE 2007, Distinguished Yonsei Alumni Award 2008, Korean-American Leadership Award 2008, ISQED Quality Award 2008, inducted into Silicon Valley Eng Hall of Fame 2009, Deockmyeong Eng Award, Korean Acad. of Science and Tech. 2010, Pride of Korea Award, Korean Press Asscn of Northern California 2010, Soc. of Pinnacle Award, Fairleigh Dickinson Univ. 2013. *Publications:* co-author: Hot-Carrier Reliability of MOS VLSI Circuits 1993, Design Automation for Timing-Driven Layout Synthesis 1993, Physical Design for Multichip Modules 1994, Modeling of Electrical Overstress in Integrated Circuits 1994, Computer-Aided Design of Optoelectronic Integrated Circuits and Systems 1996, Electrothermal Analysis of VLSI Systems 2000, CMOS Digital Integrated Circuits: Analysis and Design, CMOS Digital Integrated Circuits: Analysis and Design (fourth edn) 2014; co-editor: Series in Advances in Design and Analysis of VLSI Systems; chapter editor: Computer-Aided Design and Optimization, The Circuits and Filters Handbook 1995, VLSI and ASIC, VLSI Handbook 1999; section editor: The Circuits and Filters Handbook, Section VII, Computer-Aided Design and Optimization 2003; 16 US patents, several book chapters and numerous papers in professional journals. *Address:* Korea Advanced Institute of Science and Technology, 291 Daehak-ro (373-1 Guseong-dong), Yuseong-gu, Daejeon, 305-701, South Korea (office). *Telephone:* (42) 350-2114 (office). *Fax:* (42) 350-2210 (office). *Website:* www.kaist .edu (office).

KANG, Young-joong; South Korean business executive; *Chairman, Daekyo Group;* b. 1950; m.; two c.; ed Konkuk Univ., Yonsei Univ.; f. Jong Am Learning Inst. for Children (after-school education co.) 1975, now Daekyo Co. Ltd, Chair. Daekyo Culture Foundation 1992, Chair. Daekyo Group 2001–; Founder and Chair. World Youth and Culture Foundation 2007–, Bong-Ahm Educational Foundation 2008–; Pres. Korea Badminton Asscn 2003–09, Asia Badminton Confed. 2003–05, Badminton World Fed. 2005–13, Korea Scout Asscn 2008–12; Hon. PhD (Konkuk) 2000, (Korea Nat. Sport Univ.) 2004; Man of Merit Recognition from Pres. of Korea 1995, Ok Kwan Jang (cultural medal) from Ministry of Culture and Tourism 2004, Korea Man. Asscn Business Leader of Korea Award 2005, Kiggi Medal, Scout Asscn of Japan 2012. *Address:* Daekyo Co. Ltd, 446-3, Bangbae-dong, Seocho-gu, Seoul 137-060, South Korea (office). *Telephone:* (2) 829-1114 (office). *Fax:* (2) 829-0647 (office). *Website:* www.daekyo .co.kr (office); youngjoongkang.com.

KANG, Yu-sig, BS; South Korean business executive; *Vice-Chairman and Co-CEO, LG Corporation;* ed Chongju High School, Coll. of Business Admin, Seoul Nat. Univ.; joined LG Chem 1972, Sr Man. Dir LG Semicon 1995–96, Vice-Pres. 1996–97, Vice-Pres. LG Chair.'s Office 1997–98, Vice-Pres. LG EOCR 1998–99, Pres. and Head of LG EOCR 1999–2002, COO LG Corpn 2002–03, mem. Bd of Dirs and Chair. LG Electronics Inc., Head of LG Exec. Office for Corp. Restructuring 2002–08, CEO LG Corpn 2003–08, Vice-Chair. and Co-CEO LG Corpn 2009–. *Address:* LG Corporation, LG Twin Towers, 20 Youido-dong, Youngdungpo-gu, Seoul 150-721, Republic of Korea (office). *Telephone:* (2) 3773-1114 (office). *Fax:* (2) 3773-7813 (office). *E-mail:* info@lgcorp.com (office). *Website:* www.lgcorp.com (office); www.lg.com (office).

KANG, Yukun, BA; Chinese economist and business executive; *Chairman of the Board of Supervisors, Industrial Bank Company Limited;* served as Deputy Man. Credit Dept, Industrial Bank Co. Ltd, fmr Vice-Pres., Putian Br. and Vice-Pres. and Pres. Fuzhou Br., mem. Bd of Dirs and Vice-Pres. Industrial Bank Co. Ltd 2007–, Chair. Bd of Supervisors 2012–. *Address:* Industrial Bank Co. Ltd, 154 Hudong Road, Fuzhou 350003, People's Republic of China (office). *Telephone:* (591) 87839338 (office). *Fax:* (591) 87841932 (office). *E-mail:* webmaster@cib.com.cn (office). *Website:* www.cib.com.cn (office).

KANGAS, Edward A. (Ed), BA, MBA, CPA; American accountant and health care industry executive; *Chairman, Tenet Healthcare Corporation;* b. 22 May 1944; ed Univ. of Kansas; began career as staff accountant at Touche Ross 1967, Pnr 1975, Man.-Dir 1985–89, Man. Pnr, Deloitte Touche USA (following merger of Deloitte Haskins & Sells and Touche Ross 1989) 1989–94, Chair. and CEO Deloitte Touche Tohmatsu (DTT) 1989–2000, Consultant 2000–03; Chair. Tenet Healthcare Corpn 2003–; mem. Bd of Dirs Hovnavian Enterprises Inc., Electronic Data Systems Corpn (EDS), Eclipsys Corpn; Chair. Nat. Multiple Sclerosis Soc. 2000–; mem. Policy Cttee, Cttee for Econ. Devt (also Trustee); mem. Bd of Advisers Univ. of Kansas Business School, now Emer. Bd mem.; mem. Bd of Overseers Wharton School, Univ. of Pa, Bd of Trustees, Univ. of Kansas Endowment Foundation; CPA in New York and Conn.; Distinguished Alumni Award, Univ. of Kansas School of Business 2000. *Address:* Tenet Healthcare Corporation, 3820 State Street, Santa Barbara, CA 93105, USA (office). *Telephone:* (805) 563-7000 (office). *Fax:* (805) 563-7070 (office). *Website:* www.tenethealth.com (office).

KANI, John; South African actor; b. 1943; fmrly worked on a car ass. line; began acting in amateur production; many stage tours abroad and appearances in S. Africa particularly at Market Theatre, Johannesburg; appeared in Sizwe Banzi is Dead, Royal Court Theatre, London 1973, Nat. Theatre, London 2007, Waiting for Godot, Miss Julie, Othello 1987; fmr Exec. Trustee, Market Theatre, Foundation, currently mem. Exec. Council; Dr hc (Cape Town) 2006; Tony Award for Broadway performance in Athol Fugard's Sizwe Banzi is Dead, Hiroshima Foundation for Peace & Culture Award 2000. *Films:* Marigolds in August 1980, Gräset sjunger 1981, Saturday Night at the Palace 1987, An African Dream 1987, Options 1988, A Dry White Season 1989, The Native Who Caused All the Trouble 1989, Sarafina! 1992, Soweto Green 1995, The Ghost and the Darkness 1996, Kini and Adams 1997, The Tichborne Claimant 1998, Final Solution 2001, Nothing But The Truth (Fleur de Cap Award for Best Actor and Best New South African Play, Olive Schreiner Prize 2005) 2002. *Address:* The Market Theatre, PO Box 8656, Johannesburg, 2000 South Africa (office). *Telephone:* (11) 8321641 (office). *Website:* www.markettheatre.co.za (office).

KANN, Peter Robert; American journalist, publisher and business executive; b. 13 Dec. 1942, New York; s. of Robert Kann and Marie Kann (née Breuer); m. 1st Francesca Mayer 1969 (died 1983); m. 2nd Karen House 1984; one s. three d.; ed Harvard Univ.; joined Wall Street Journal 1964, worked as journalist in New York 1964–67, in Viet Nam 1967–68, in Hong Kong 1968–75, Publr and Ed. Wall Street Journal Asian Edn 1976–79, Assoc. Publr 1979–88, Exec. Vice-Pres. Dow Jones & Co. 1986, Pres. int. and magazine groups 1986–89, mem. Bd of Dirs 1987, Pres. Dow Jones & Co., New York 1989–91, Publr and Editorial Dir The Wall Street Journal 1989–2002, CEO Dow Jones & Co. 1991–2006, Chair. 1991–2007 (retd); mem. Adjunct Faculty Columbia Univ. Grad. School of Journalism; Chair. Bd Far Eastern Econ. Review 1987–89; Trustee, Asia Soc. 1989–94 (now Trustee Emer.), Inst. for Advanced Study, Princeton 1990–, Aspen Inst. 1994–98; mem. Council on Foreign Relations, Pulitzer Prize Bd 1987–96; Pulitzer Prize for int. reporting 1972 for his coverage of the 1971 India-Pakistan War. *Address:* c/o Columbia University Graduate School of Journalism, 2950 Broadway (at 116th Street), New York, NY 10027; 58 Cleveland Lane, Princeton, NJ 08540, USA. *E-mail:* prk2106@columbia .edu.

KANNAN, Madhu, BE, MSc, MBA; Indian business executive and fmr stock exchange official; *Group Head for Business Development, Tata Sons;* b. Chennai; m. Shubha Srinivasan Kannan; one d.; ed Birla Inst. of Tech. & Science, Vanderbilt Univ., USA; joined New York Stock Exchange (now NYSE Euronext) 1997, Account Man. 2001–02, Man. Dir, Asia-Pacific 2002–05, then Special Asst to Head of Int., the Vice-Pres. Global Corp. Client Group; Man. Dir, Corp Strategy Group, Bank of America-Merrill Lynch, New York 2008–09; CEO and Man. Dir Bombay Stock Exchange 2009–12; Group Head, Business Development, Tata Sons 2012–; fmr mem. Bd of Dirs Central Depository Services (India) Ltd, BOI Shareholding Ltd, Indian Clearing Corpn Ltd; named among Young Global Leaders, World Econ. Forum 2007. *Address:* Tata Sons, Bombay House, 24, Homi Mody Street, Mumbai 400 001, India (office). *Telephone:* (22) 66658282 (office). *Website:* www.tata.com (office).

KANOO, Mishal Hamed, MBA; Bahraini business executive; *Deputy Chairman and CEO, Kanoo Group;* b. 1969; ed Univ. of St Thomas, Tex., USA, American Univ. of Sharjah; began career as auditor for Arthur Andersen, Dubai; Deputy Chair. and CEO Kanoo Group 1997–; Prof. (part-time), American Univ. of Sharjah School of Business Admin; columnist, Money Works magazine; ranked by Arabian Business amongst the Power 500: The World's Most Influential Arabs (146th) 2011, (91st) 2012. *Address:* Kanoo Group, PO Box 290, Dubai, United Arab Emirates (office). *Telephone:* (4) 3933633 (office). *Fax:* (4) 3933636 (office). *E-mail:* guest@mishalkanoo.com; info@kanoogroup.com (office). *Website:* www .kanoogroup.com (office); www.mishalkanoo.com.

KANTHA, Ashok K.; Indian diplomatist; *Ambassador to the People's Republic of China;* b. 14 May 1955; m. Sharmila Kantha; one s.; ed Patna Univ.; briefly worked as an exec. with State Bank of India; joined Indian Foreign Service 1977, studied Chinese Language at Nanyang Univ., Singapore 1979–81, Special Asst to Chair., Policy Planning Cttee mid-1980s, worked in different capacities at Missions in Singapore, China and USA and in Ministry of External Affairs, New Delhi dealing with India's relations with China, Pakistan, Afghanistan and Iran –1997, Deputy Chief of Mission, Embassy in Kathmandu 1997–2000, Consul Gen. to Hong Kong and Macao 2000–03, Head of East Asia Div., Ministry of External Affairs 2003–07, High Commr to Malaysia 2007–09, to Sri Lanka 2009–13, Sec. (East), Ministry of External Affairs 2013–14; Amb. to People's Republic of China 2014–. *Address:* Embassy of India, 5 Liang Ma Qiao Bei Jie, Chao Yang Qu, Beijing 100060, People's Republic of China (office). *Telephone:* (10) 65321908 (office). *Fax:* (10) 65324684 (office). *E-mail:* hoc@indianembassy.org.cn (office). *Website:* www .indianembassy.org.cn (office).

KANTOR, Mickey; American corporate lawyer; *Partner, Mayer Brown LLP;* b. 1939; m. 1st (died 1978); m. 2nd 1982; one s. (died 1988); three living c.; ed Vanderbilt Univ., Georgetown Univ. Law School; served in USN; began career as lawyer protecting rights of migrant farm workers; Dir acting for Legal Rights 1971; Staff Coordinator, Sargent Shriver 1972; partner, Los Angeles law firm 1993; mem. Bd of Legal Services Corpn in Carter Admin; mem. Comm. investigating LA Riots 1992; Chair. Clinton Presidential Campaign 1992; US Trade Rep. 1993–97; Sec. of Commerce 1996–97; Partner, Mayer Brown LLP 1997–; mem. Int. Advisory Bd Fleishman-Hillard, Bd of Visitors, Georgetown Univ. Law Center; Chief Negotiator, NAFTA, Uruguay Round, Free Trade Areas of America, APEC, ING USA, CB Richard Ellis Group; Order of Southern Cross (Brazil); Distinguished Public Service Medal, Center for Study of Presidency, Albert Schweitzer Humanitarianism Award, Eagle & Badge Award, Los Angeles Civic Medal 2012. *Address:* Mayer Brown LLP, 350 South Grand Avenue, 25th Floor, Los Angeles, CA 90071, USA (office). *Telephone:* (213) 229-9579 (office). *Fax:* (213) 625-0248 (office). *E-mail:* mkantor@mayerbrown.com (office). *Website:* www.mayerbrown .com (office).

KANWAR, Asha Singh, BA, MA, MPhil, DPhil; Indian educationalist and academic; *President and CEO, Commonwealth of Learning;* b. 27 Sept. 1951, Darjeeling; ed Panjab Univ., Univ. of Sussex, UK; Reader, Indira Gandhi Nat. Open Univ. (IGNOU) 1988–92, apptd Prof. 1992, Dir School of Humanities 1996–99, apptd Pro-Vice Chancellor IGNOU 1999; fmr consultant in open and distance learning at UNESCO Regional Office for Educ. in Africa (BREDA), Dakar, Senegal; Educ. Specialist, Higher Educ. Commonwealth of Learning 2003–06, Vice-Pres. 2006–12, Programme Dir 2007–12, Pres. and CEO 2012–; Fulbright Fellow for post-doctoral research, Iowa State Univ., later invited to teach; Visiting Fellow, Univ. of Leiden, Univ. of Toronto, Open Univ. of Hong Kong; Fellow, NTI, Kaduna, Nigeria; Hon. Prof., Tianjin Open Univ., People's Repub. of China; Dr hc (Kota Open Univ., India); several awards and fellowships, including scholarship to Univ. of Sussex, Prize of Excellence, Int. Council for Open and Distance Educ. 2009, Award for Empowerment, NOUN, Nigeria, ICDE Prize for Excellence (Norway). *Publications include:* several books, research papers and articles on gender studies, especially the impact of distance education on the lives of Asian women. *Address:* Commonwealth of Learning, 1055 West Hastings Street, Suite 1200, Vancouver, BC V6E 2E9, Canada (office). *Telephone:* (604) 775-8200 (office). *Fax:* (604) 775-8210 (office). *E-mail:* akanwar@col.org (office). *Website:* www.col .org (office).

KANZAKI, Takenori, LLB; Japanese politician; b. 15 July 1943, Tien-Tsin, (Tianjin), People's Repub. of China; ed Tokyo Univ.; public prosecutor 1968–76; lawyer 1982–; mem. House of Reps; mem. Komeito party (now New Komeito party), Chair. Foreign Affairs Cttee, Chief Rep. 1998–2006, now Standing Adviser; Chair. Diet Policy Cttee; Minister of Posts and Telecommunications 1993–94. *Publication:* Prohibition of Profit Granting (co-author). *Leisure interests:* shogi (Japanese chess), reading, travelling, theatre. *Address:* New Komeito Headquarters, 17 Minami-Motomachi, Shinjuku-ku, Tokyo 160-0012 (office); Room No. 201, No. 6 Green Building, 2-12-7 Hakata-Ekimae, Hakata-ku, Fukuoka-shi 812, Fukuoka Prefecture, Japan (home). *Telephone:* (3) 3353-0111 (office); (3) 3581-5111. *Fax:* (3) 3353-9746 (office); (3) 3503-2388. *Website:* www.komei.or.jp (office); www.kanzakitakenori.org.

KAO, Charles K., CBE, PhD, FRS, FREng; American (b. Chinese) electrical engineer and academic (retd); b. (Kao Kuen), 4 Nov. 1933, Shanghai, China; s. of the late Chun-Hsian and Tsing-Fong King; m. May-Wan Wong 1959; one s. one d.; ed Univ. of London; engineer, Standard Telephones and Cables Ltd, UK 1957–60, Research Scientist/Research Man., Standard Telecommunications Labs Ltd/ITT Cen. European Lab., Essex, UK 1960–70; Chair. Dept of Electronics, Chinese Univ. of Hong Kong 1970–74; Chief Scientist and Dir of Eng, Electro-Optical Products Div., ITT, Roanoke, Va 1974–81, Vice-Pres. and Dir of Eng 1981–88; Exec. Scientist and Corp. Dir of Research, ITT Advanced Tech. Centre, Conn. 1983–87; Vice-Chancellor The Chinese Univ. of Hong Kong 1987–96; Chair. and CEO Transtech Services Ltd 1996–2001, ITX Services Ltd 2000–04; Hon. CBE 1993; Hon. DSc (Chinese Univ. of Hong Kong) 1985, (Sussex) 1990, (Durham) 1994, (Hull) 1998, (Yale) 1999, (Princeton) 2002, (Toronto) 2005; Dr hc (Soka) 1991; Hon. DEng (Glasgow) 1992; Hon. Dr of Telecommunications Eng (Padova, Italy) 1996; numerous awards and prizes including IEEE Alexander Graham Bell Medal 1985, Marconi Int. 1985, IEEE Faraday Medal (UK) 1989, Japan Prize 1996, Charles Stark Draper Prize, Nat. Acad. of Eng (USA) 1999, Asian of the Century in Science and Tech., Asiaweek (magazine) 1999, Nobel Prize in Physics (with Willard Boyle and George Smith) 2009. *Achievements include:* discovered how to transmit light over long distances with fiber-optic cables 1966. *Publications:* Optical Fiber Technology II 1981, Optical Fiber Systems: Technology, Design and Applications 1982, Optical Fibre 1988, A Choice Fulfilled – The Business of High Technology 1991. *Leisure interests:* tennis, hiking, pottery-making. *Address:* c/o S. K. Yee Foundation, Unit 1708, Office Tower, Convention Plaza, 1 Harbour Road, Wan Chai, Hong Kong Special Administrative Region, People's Republic of China (office). *Telephone:* 26037643 (office). *Fax:* 26037663 (office). *E-mail:* ckao@ie.cuhk .edu.hk (home).

KAO, Chin-Yen; Taiwanese business executive; *Chairman, UNI–President Enterprises Corporation;* b. 24 May 1929, Taiwan; m. Lai-Kwan Kao; one d.; ed Tainan Co. Tienchow Elementary School; Sales Man. Tainan Fabric Corpn 1957–67; f. Pres. Enterprises Group (now UNI-Pres. Enterprises Corpn) 1968, Vice-Chair., Pres. and CEO 1989, now Chair.; Chair. Pres. Enterprises Chain Store Corpn 1986–; Chair. Ztong Yee Industrial Co. Ltd 1977–, Ton Yi Industrial Corpn 1979–, ScinoPharm Taiwan Ltd; Chair. Bd of Trustees Southern Taiwan Univ. of Tech.; mem. Cen. Standing Cttee, Kuomintang 1994–; Chair. Taiwan Industrial Mfrs Asscn 1999; Hon. PhD (Lincoln) 1983. *Address:* UNI–President Enterprises Corporation, 301 Jhongjheng Road, Yongkang City, Tainan County 710, Taiwan (office). *Telephone:* (6) 2532121 (office). *Fax:* (6) 2532661 (office). *Website:* www.uni-president.biz (office).

KAO, Gen. Hua-chu, BA; Taiwanese army officer and government official; b. 2 Oct. 1942; ed Repub. of China Military Acad. (ROCMA), Ministry of Nat. Defence (MND) Army Infantry School, Armed Forces Univ.; Company Commdr, 6th Bn, 26th Infantry Div., Repub. of China Army 1971–72, Bn Commdr, 852nd Brigade, 284th Infantry Div. 1978–79, Brigade Commdr, 678th Brigade, 226th Infantry Div. 1985–87, Instructor-Gen., Mil. Training Dept and Commdr, Cadet Training Command 1987–90, Exec. Dir of Training and Educ., Army Infantry Training Commanding and Infantry School, MND 1990, Div. Commdr, 127th Infantry Div. 1990–92, Chief of Staff, 10th Army Corps Commanding HQ 1992–93, Chief of Staff for Intelligence, Gen. Army HQ 1993–94, Commanding Gen., Chengkungling Training Center 1996–98, Deputy Chief of Gen. Staff for Logistics, MND 1998–99, Commanding Gen., 10th Army Corps 1999–2000, Deputy Commander-in-Chief, Gen. Army HQ 2000–03, Dir Gen., Jt Operations Training and Doctrine Office, MND 2003, Commanding Gen., Combined Logistics Command 2003–04; Minister, Veterans Affairs Comm. 2004–07, 2008–09, Minister of Nat. Defence 2009–13. *Address:* c/o Ministry of National Defence, 2/F, 164 Po Ai Rd, Taipei 10048, Taiwan.

KAPADIA, Sarosh Homi, BA (Hons), LLB; Indian judge; b. 29 Sept. 1947, Mumbai; m. Shahnaz Kapadia; two s.; began career as a class IV employee; later

became a law clerk with lawyer's office in Mumbai; joined Gagrat & Co. (law firm) as a clerk; later worked for labour lawyer Feroze Damania; advocate, Bombay High Court 1974–91, appeared as counsel for Dept in income tax matters, Additional Judge 1991–93, Perm. Judge 1993–2003, Judge of the Special Court (Trial of Offences Relating to Transaction in Securities) 1999–2003; Chief Justice of Uttaranchal High Court Aug.–Dec. 2003; Judge of the Supreme Court 2003–, Chief Justice of India 2010–12 (retd). *Leisure interests:* economics, public finance, theoretical physics, Hindu and Buddhist philosophies. *Address:* c/o Supreme Court of India, Tilak Marg, New Delhi 110 001, India (office). *E-mail:* supremecourt@nic .in.

KAPAMBWE, Lazarous, BSc; Zambian diplomatist and UN official; b. 31 Dec. 1959; m.; ed Univ. of Zambia, Nairobi Univ., Kenya, New York Univ.; Exec. Officer, Directorate of Int. Orgs and Research Dept, Ministry for Foreign Affairs 1981–85, Prin. in Research Dept 1985–87; Prin. in Cabinet Office and speech writer for Prime Minister of Zambia 1987; Counsellor for Political Affairs, Perm. Mission to UN, New York 1987–88; Counsellor and Deputy Chief of Mission, Embassy in Washington, DC 1988–93, Embassy in Bonn 1993–96; Dir for European Affairs, Ministry for Foreign Affairs June–Aug. 1996, Dir for Africa and OAU Affairs 1996–2000, Deputy Perm. Sec. responsible for Asia, Africa and the Middle East 2000–02, Perm. Sec. 2002–03; Amb. to Ethiopia and African Union 2003–07; Amb. and Perm. Rep. to UN, New York 2007–11; Pres. Econ. and Social Council, UN 2011–12. *Address:* Ministry of Foreign Affairs and Tourism, POB RW50069, Lusaka, Zambia (office). *Telephone:* (21) 1252718 (office). *Fax:* (21) 1222440 (office).

KAPARTIS, Costas, MA; Cypriot labour relations official; b. 28 Sept. 1933, Nicosia; m. Anna Kapartis; three c.; ed Webster and Cornell Univs, USA; various positions in Ministry of Labour and Social Insurance 1957–65; Dir-Gen. Cyprus Employers' Fed. 1965–75; Exec. Sec. Int. Org. of Employers 1975, Deputy Sec.-Gen. 1980–90, Sec.-Gen. 1990–2001. *Address:* 9 chemin A. Pasteur, 1209 Geneva, Switzerland (home).

KAPIL DEV; Indian business executive, sports administrator and fmr professional cricketer; *Chairman, Executive Board, Indian Cricket League;* b. (Kapildev Ramlal Nikhanj), 6 Jan. 1959, Chandigarh; s. of Ram Lal Nikhanj and Raj Kumari Lajwanti; m. Romi Dev; one d.; ed D.A.V. School, Punjab Univ.; right-hand middle-order batsman, right-arm fast-medium bowler; played for Haryana 1975/76–91/92, Northamptonshire 1981–83, Worcestershire 1984–85; played in 131 Tests for India 1978/79–93/94, 34 as Capt., scoring 5,248 runs (average 31.05, highest score 163) including eight hundreds and taking record 434 wickets (average 29.64), best bowling (innings) 9/83, (match) 11/146; youngest to take 100 Test wickets (21 years 25 days); hit four successive balls for six against England, Lord's 1990; played in 225 One-Day Ints, scoring 3,783 runs (average 23.79, highest score 175 not out) and taking 253 wickets; scored 11,356 runs (18 hundreds) and took 835 wickets in first-class cricket; toured England 1979, 1982, 1983 (World Cup), 1986, 1990; only person to take 400 wickets and score more than 5,000 runs in Test cricket; Indian Nat. Coach 1999–2000; Founding mem. and Acad. mem. Laureus World Sports Foundation 2000; Chair. Nat. Cricket Acad. 2006–07; Chair. Exec. Bd breakaway Indian Cricket League 2007–; Owner Kapil's Eleven restaurants in Chandigarh and Patna, Kaptain's Retreat Hotel, Chandigarh; est. Dev Musco Lighting Pvt. Ltd in partnership with Musco Lighting to install floodlights in major stadia and sports venues in India; commissioned as Lt Col in Indian Territorial Army 2008–; Arjuna Award 1979–80, Padma Shri 1982, Wisden Cricketer of the Year 1983, Padma Bhushan 1991, Electrolux Kelvinator Wisden Indian Cricketer of the Century 2002, inducted into ICC Cricket Hall of Fame 2010. *Films:* cameo appearances in Iqbal, Chain Khuli ki Main Khuli and Mujhse Shadi Karogi. *Publications:* By God's Decree (autobiography) 1985, Cricket My Style (autobiography) 1987, Kapil Dev: Triumph of the Spirit 1995, Straight from the Heart (autobiography) 2004. *Leisure interests:* hunting, riding, dancing, playing golf. *Address:* Dev Musco Lighting Pvt. Ltd, B-41, Greater Kailash-1, New Delhi 110 048 (office); Indian Cricket League, Essel Sports Pvt. Ltd, 135 Continental Building, Dr Annie Besant Road, Worli, Mumbai 400 018; 39 Sunder Nagar, New Delhi 110 003, India. *Telephone:* (11) 41431166 (office); (11) 44698333 (New Delhi). *Fax:* (11) 41431406 (office); (11) 3719776 (New Delhi). *E-mail:* kapildev58@yahoo.co.in (office); response@iclonline.in. *Website:* www.musco.com/reps/in/india.html (office); www .indiancricketleague.in; www.kapildev.asia.

KAPLAN, Jonathan Stewart; American film writer, film director, television producer and television director; b. 25 Nov. 1947, Paris, France; s. of Sol Kaplan and Frances Heflin; m. Julie Selzer 1987 (divorced 2001); one d.; ed Univ. of Chicago, New York Univ.; mem. tech. staff, Bill Graham's Fillmore East, New York 1969–71; appeared in The Dark at the Top of the Stairs, Broadway 1956–57; Best Male Vocal Concept Video, Billboard 1986. *Films:* Night Call Nurses 1972, Student Teachers 1973, The Slams 1973, Truck Turner 1974, White Line Fever 1974, Mr Billion 1976, Over the Edge 1978, 11th Victim 1979, Muscle Beach 1980, Gentleman Bandit 1981, White Orchid 1982, Heart Like a Wheel 1983, Project X 1986, The Accused 1987, Immediate Family 1989, Love Field 1990, Unlawful Entry 1992, Bad Girls 1994, Rebel Highway 1994, Picture Windows 1995, Fallen Angels 1996, Brokedown Palace 1999. *Video films:* directed 15 music videos for John Mellencamp, two for Rod Stewart (q.v.), one for Barbra Streisand (q.v.) and one for Paula Abdul (q.v.). *TV includes:* JAG (writer) 1995, ER (producer/dir) 1999–2005, The Court (Dir) 2002, Inconceivable (Dir) 2005, Crossing Jordan (Dir) 2005, Law & Order (Dir) 2005–06, Without a Trace (Dir) 2006–07. *Address:* Industry Entertainment, 953 Carillo Drive, Suite 300, Los Angeles, CA 90048, USA (office).

KAPLINSKI, Jaan; Estonian poet, writer, linguist and translator (retd); b. 22 Jan. 1941, Tartu (Dorpat); s. of Jerzy Kaplinski and Nora Raudsepp; m. Tiia Toomet 1969; four s. two d.; ed Univ. of Tartu; mem. Riigikogu (State Ass.) 1992–95; Lecturer in History of Western Civilization, Univ. of Tartu; columnist at various Estonian and Scandinavian newspapers; has written around 900 poems, 20 stories and some plays; mem. Universal Acad. of Cultures, Estonian Writers' Union, European Acad. of Poetry, Finnish Literature Soc.; IV Class Order of Nat. Coat of Arms 1997, Chevalier, Légion d'honneur 2000, Kt, Order of the Lion of Finland 2003; Dr hc; received Estonian awards, Baltic Ass. Prize for Literature 1997, Prix Max Jacob Etranger 2003. *Publications include:* poetry: Ma vaatasin päikese aknasse 1976, Uute kivide kasvamine 1977, The New Heaven & Earth of Jaan Kaplinski 1981, Raske on kergeks saada 1982, Tule tagasi helmemänd 1984,

Õhtu toob tagasi kõik 1985, Käoraamat: Luulet 1956–80 1986, The Wandering Border 1987, The Same Sea in Us All 1990, Sjunger näktergalen än i Dorpat?: En brevväxling 1990, I Am The Spring in Tartu and other poems in English 1991, Non-Existent Frontier 1995, Võimaluste võimalikkus 1997, Öölinnud, öömõtted yölintuja, yöajatuksia: Luuletusi 1995–97 1998, Evening Brings Everything Back 2004, Selected Poems 2011; novel: Seesama jõgi 2007 (English trans. The Same Sea 2009). *Leisure interests:* gardening, forestry, astronomy, photography. *Address:* c/o Bloodaxe Books Ltd, Highgreen, Tarset, Northumberland, NE48 1RP, England (office); Nisu 33-9, 50407 Tartu, Estonia. *E-mail:* editor@bloodaxebooks.com (office); jaan.kaplinski@gmail.com. *Telephone:* (7) 425755. *Website:* jaan.kaplinski.com; jaankaplinski.blogspot.com.

KAPOOR, Anil; Indian actor and producer; b. 24 Dec. 1959, Tilak Nagar, Mumbai; s. of Surinder Kapoor and Nirmal Kapoor; m. Sunita Kapoor (née Bhambhani) 1984; one s., two d.; ed Our Lady of Perpetual Succour High School, Chembur, St. Xaviers Coll.; Nata Kalaratna by Govt of Andhra Pradesh 1997, Avadh Samman by Govt of UP 2002; Performer with All-Round Comic Excellence, Vodafone Comedy Honors 2008, Special Award, Stardust Award 2009. *Films include:* Hamare Tumhare 1979, Ex Baar Kaho 1980, Vamsa Vriksham 1980, Hum Paanch 1981, Shakti 1982, Pallavi Anu Pallavi 1983, Woh Saat Din 1983, Mashaal (Filmfare Best Supporting Actor Award) 1984, Andar Baahar 1984, Laila 1984, Love Marriage 1984, Saaheb 1985, Yudh 1985, Mohabbat 1985, Meri Jung 1985, Kahan Kahan Se Guzar 1986, Pyaar Ka Sindoor 1986, Chameli Ki Shaadi 1986, Aap Ke Saath 1986, Janbaaz 1986, Pyar Kiya Hai Pyar Karenge 1986, Karma 1986, Insaaf Ki Awaaz 1986, Itihaas 1987, Mr India 1987, Hifazat 1987, Thikana 1987, Kasam 1988, Ram-Avtar 1988, Vijay 1988, Sone Pe Suhaaga 1988, Tezaab (Filmfare Best Actor Award) 1988, Inteqam 1988, Ram Lakhan 1989, Joshilay 1989, Eeshwar 1989, Rakhwala 1989, Abhimanyu 1989, Aag Se Khelenge 1989, Kala Bazaar 1989, Parinda 1989, Awaargi 1990, Kishen Kanhaiya 1990, Ghar Ho Ta Aisa 1990, Jeevan Ek Sangharsh 1990, Amba 1990, Jamai Raja 1990, Jigarwala 1991, Benaam Badsha 1991, Pratikar 1991, Lamhe 1991, Beta (Filmfare Best Actor Award) 1992, Zindagi Ek Jua 1992, Humlaa 1992, Khel 1992, Heer Ranjha 1992, Apradhi 1992, Roop Ki Rani Choron Ka Raja 1993, Guru Deev 1993, Laadla 1994, Andaz 1994, 1942: A Love Story 1994, Mr. Azaad 1994, Trimurti 1995, Rajkumar 1996, Loafer 1996, Mr. Bechara 1996, Virasat (Filmfare Critics Award for Best Performance, Star Screen Award Best Actor) 1997, Deewana Mastana 1997, Kabhi Na Kabhi 1998, Gharwali Baharwali 1998, Jhooth Bole Kauwa Kaate 1998, Hum Aapke Dil Mein Rehte Hain 1999, Biwi No. 1 (Best Comedian Award, Int. Indian Film Acad. Awards) 1999, Mann 1999, Taal (Filmfare Best Supporting Actor Award, Best Supporting Actor Award, Int. Indian Film Acad. Awards, Star Screen Award Best Supporting Actor, Zee Cine Award, Best Actor in a Supporting Role–Male) 1999, Bulandi 2000, Pukar (National Film Award for Best Actor, Bollywood Movie Award for Most Sensational Actor) 2000, Hamara Dil Aapke Paas Hai 2000, Karobaar 2000, Lajja 2001, Nayak 2001, Badhaai Ho Badhaai 2002, Om Jai Jagadish 2002, Rishtey 2002, Armaan 2003, Calcutta Mail 2003, Musafir 2004, Bewafaa 2004, My Wife's Murder 2005, No Entry 2005, Chocolate 2005, Humko Deewana Kar Gaye 2006, Darna Zaroori Hai 2006, Salaam-e-Ishq: A Tribute to Love 2007, Welcome (Best Role as a Comedian, German Public Bollywood Awards) 2007, My Name is Anthony Gonsalves 2008, Black & White 2008, Race 2008, Tashan (Best Actor in a Negative Role Award, Stardust Awards) 2008, Slumdog Millionaire (Screen Actors Guild Award for Outstanding Performance by a Cast in a Motion Picture) 2008, Yuvvraaj 2008; as producer: Badhaai Ho Badhaai 2002, My Wife's Murder 2005, Gandhi, My Father (Hottest Film Producer Award, Stardust Awards) 2007. *Address:* c/o 31 Shrinagar, Presidency Society, 7th Road, JVPD Scheme, Mumbai 400 049, India (office). *Telephone:* (22) 6209997.

KAPOOR, Sir Anish, Kt, CBE, MA, RA; British sculptor; b. 12 March 1954, Bombay, India; s. of Rear-Adm. Kapoor and Mrs D. C. Kapoor; m. Susanne Spicale 1995; one d. one s.; ed Hornsey Coll. of Art, Chelsea Coll. of Art and Design, London; has lived in London since early 1970s; Royal Academician 1999; Guest Artistic Dir, Brighton Festival 2009; Hon. Fellow, London Inst. 1997, Univ. of Leeds 1997, Univ. of Wolverhampton 1999; Hon. FRIBA 2001; Commdr, Ordre des Arts et des Lettres 2011; Hon. DLitt (Leeds) 1993; Premio Duemila, Venice Biennale 1990, Turner Prize, Tate Gallery, London 1991, Premium Imperiale 2011, Padma Bhushan 2012. *Address:* c/o Lisson Gallery, 67 Lisson Street, London, NW1 5DA, England. *Telephone:* (20) 7724-2739. *Fax:* (20) 7724-7124. *Website:* www.anishkapoor.com.

KAPOOR, Gen. Deepak, MA, MSc, MBA; Indian army officer (retd); b. 12 March 1948, Delhi; m. Kirti Kapoor; one s. one d.; ed Sainik School, Kunjpara, Defence Services Staff Coll., Wellington, Nat. Defence Coll., New Delhi, Indira Gandhi Nat. Open Univ., New Delhi; commissioned into Regt of Artillery 1967; veteran of Indo-Pak War in eastern theatre (Bangladesh) 1971; Chief Operations Officer for UNOSOM II (UN Operation in Somalia – Phase 2) 1994–95; commanded 161 Infantry Brigade in Uri, Jammu and Kashmir, 22nd Mountain Div. (as part of a Strike Corps during Operation Parakram) 2001–02; Chief of Staff of 4 Corps in Tezpur (involved in counter-insurgency operations in Assam); promoted to Lt-Gen.; commanded 33 Corps at Siliguri, West Bengal, commanded Army Training Command (ARTRAC) in Shimla, Commdr Northern Army; apptd Hon. ADC to Pres. of India; Sr Col Commdt Regt of Artillery; Vice-Chief of Army –2007, Chief of Army Staff 2007–10; Chair. Chiefs of Staff Cttee 2009–10; Hon. Col of Brigade of the Guards 2008–; Hon. Life Col Commdt, Regt of Artillery; Vishisht Seva Medal 1996, Sena Medal 1998, Ati Vishisht Seva Medal 2006, Param Vishisht Seva Medal 2007. *Publication:* India's China Concern (essay), Strategic Analysis, Vol. 36, No. 4 July–Aug. 2012. *Leisure interest:* golf. *E-mail:* gendkapoor@gmail.com (office).

KAPOOR, Kareena; Indian film actress; b. 21 Sept. 1980, Mumbai, Maharashtra; d. of Randhir Kapoor and Babita Kapoor (née Shivdasani); younger sister of Karisma Kapoor; m. Saif Ali Khan 2012; ed Welham Girls' Boarding School, Mithibai Coll., Mumbai, Harvard Univ., USA, Govt Law Coll., Churchgate, Mumbai, Kishore Namit Kapoor Acting School; Style Diva of the Year Award, Int. Indian Film Acad. 2004, Marco Ricci Soc. Young Achiever Award 2004, Rajiv Gandhi Young Achiever Award 2005, Smita Patil Memorial Award 2006, Future Group Global Indian TV Honours, Global Achievement Award 2008, Vocational Excellence Award, Rotary Int. 2009, India Today Woman Award 2009, among the 10 recipients of IIFA-FICCI Frames Award for Most Powerful Entertainers of the Decade 2009, GQ Excellence Award 2009, Geetanjali Glamour Icon of the Year

2011, Superstar Unique Ada (Female), Airtel Superstar Awards 2011. *Films include:* Refugee (Filmfare Best Female Debut Award 2001, Zee Cine Award 2001, Bollywood Movie Award 2001, Sansui Award 2001) 2000, Mujhe Kucch Kehna Hai 2001, Yaadein 2001, Asoka 2001, Ajnabee 2001, Kabhi Khushi Kabhie Gham 2001, Mujhse Dosti Karoge! 2002, Jeena Sirf Merre Liye 2002, Talaash: The Hunt Begins 2003, Khushi 2003, Main Prem Ki Diwani Hoon (Anandalok Puraskar Award 2004) 2003, LOC: Kargil 2003, Chameli (Filmfare Special Performance Award 2004, Stardust Award 2004, Bollywood Movie Award 2004, Sansui Award 2004) 2003, Yuva 2004, Dev (Filmfare Critics' Award for Best Actress 2005) 2004, Fida 2004, Aitraaz 2004, Hulchul 2004, Bewafaa 2005, Kyon Ki 2005, Dosti: Friends Forever 2005, 36 China Town 2006, Chup Chup Ke 2006, Omkara (Filmfare Critics' Award for Best Actress 2007, Star Screen Award 2007, Stardust Award 2007) 2006, Don 2006, Jab We Met (Filmfare Best Actress Award 2008, Star Screen Award 2008, Int. Indian Film Acad. Award 2008, Zee Cine Award 2008, Stardust Award 2008, Apsara Film and Television Producers Guild Award 2008, HT Café Film Award 2007, Reader's Choice Award 2008, Planet Bollywood People's Choice Award 2008, Annual Central European Bollywood Award 2008, Li'l Star Award 2008) 2007, Tashan 2008, Roadside Romeo (voice) 2008, Golmaal Returns 2008, Kambakkht Ishq 2009, Main Aur Mrs Khanna 2009, Kurbaan (Star Screen Award 2010, Stardust Award 2010) 2009, 3 Idiots (Star Screen Award 2010, Stardust Award 2010) 2009, Milenge Milenge 2010, We Are Family (Filmfare Award for Best Supporting Actress) 2010, Golmaal 3 2010, Bodyguard (Most Entertaining Female Actor in a Romantic Role, Big Star Entertainment Awards)2011, Ra One 2011, Ek Main Aur Ek Tu 2012, Agent Vinod 2012, Heroine 2012, Talaash: The Answer Lies Within (Most Entertaining Female Actor in a Thriller, Big Star Entertainment Awards, Editor's Choice for Best Actress Stardust Awards) 2012, Satyagraha 2013, Gori Tere Pyaar Mein 2013. *Address:* 2-B/110/1201, Excellency, 4th Cross Road, Lokhandwala Complex, Andheri (West), Mumbai 400 058, India.

KAPOOR, Shashi; Indian actor and producer; b. (Balbir Raj Kapoor), 18 March 1938, Calcutta (now Kolkata); s. of Prithviraj Kapoor; m. Jennifer Kendal 1958 (died 1984); two s. one d.; part of Prithviraj Kapoor's touring repertory theatre co. Prithvi Theatres; then joined Shakespeareana Co. 1955 and toured India, Pakistan and Malaysia; Padma Bhushan 2011; Nat. Film Award for Best Actor, New Delhi Times 1986, Nat. Film Award for Best Actor Special Jury Award for Muhafiz 1994, Lifetime Achievement Award, Pune Int. Film Festival 2009, Filmfare Lifetime Achievement Award 2010. *Film roles in:* Meena 1944, Tadbir 1945, Renuka 1947, Bhakta Dhruva 1947, Bhakta Gopalbhaiya 1948, Bhakta Bilwamangal 1948, Aag 1948, Patanga 1949, Veer Babruwahan 1950, Samadhi 1950, Ram Darshan 1950, Aawara 1951, Sanskar 1952, Mordhwaj 1952, Dana Paani 1953, Dharmputra 1961, Char Diwari 1961, Prem Patra 1962, Mehendi Lagi Mere Hath 1962, Yeh Dil Kisko Doon 1963, Jab Se Tumhe Dekha Hai 1963, Holiday in Bombay 1963, The Householder 1963, Benazir 1964, Waqt 1965, Mohabbat Isko Kahete Hain 1965, Jab Jab Phool Khile (BFJA Award 1965) 1965, Shakespeare-Wallah 1965, Pyaar Kiye Jaa 1966, Neend Hamari Khwab Tumhare 1966, Biradari 1966, Dil Ne Pukara 1967, Aamne Samne 1967, Pretty Polly 1967, Juaari 1968, Haseena Maan Jayegi 1968, Raja Saab 1969, Pyar Ka Mausam 1969, Kanyadaan 1969, Jahan Pyar Mile 1969, Ek Shriman Ek Shrimati 1969, Suhana Safar 1970, Rootha Na Karo 1970, My Love 1970, Abhinetri 1970, Bombay Talkie 1970, Sharmeelee 1971, Patanga 1971, Janwar Aur Insaan 1972, Siddhartha 1972, Naina 1973, Aa Gale Lag Jaa 1973, Roti Kapada Aur Makaan 1974, Paap Aur Punya 1974, Mr. Romeo 1974, Jeevan Sangram 1974, Insaniyat 1974, Chor Machaye Shor 1974, Salaakhen 1975, Prem Kahani 1975, Deewaar (Filmfare Award 1975) 1975, Chori Mera Kaam 1975, Anari 1975, Shankar Dada 1976, Naach Utha Sansar 1976, Koi Jeeta Koi Haara 1976, Jai Bajrang Bali 1976, Deewangee 1976, Aap Beeti 1976, Kabhi Kabhie: Love Is Life (1976, Fakira 1976, Hira Aur Patthar 1977, Farishta Ya Qatil 1977, Doosra Aadmi 1977, Chor Sipahi 1977, Chakkar Pe Chakkar 1977, Immaan Dharam 1977, Mukti 1977, Rahuketu 1978, Rahuketu 1978, Phaansi 1978, Muqaddar 1978, Junoon 1978, Heeralal Pannalal 1978, Atithee 1978, Apna Khoon 1978, Amar Shakti 1978, Aahuti 1978, Satyam Shivam Sundaram: Love Sublime 1978, Trishul 1978, Do Musafir 1978, Ahsaas 1979, Gautam Govinda 1979, Kaala Patthar 1979, Duniya Meri Jeb Mein 1979, Suhaag 1979, Swayamvar 1980, Kalyug 1980, Ganga Aur Suraj 1980, Kali Ghata 1980, Do Aur Do Paanch 1980, Neeyat 1980, Shaan 1980, Maan Gaye Ustad 1981, Krodhi 1981, Bezubaan 1981, Kranti 1981, Silsila 1981, Baseraa 1981, Ek Aur Ek Gyarah 1981, Vijeta 1982, Namak Halaal 1982, Vakil Babu 1982, Heat and Dust 1983, Door-desh 1983, Ghungroo 1983, Bandhan Kuchchey Dhaagon Ka 1983, Yaadon Ki Zanjeer 1984, Utsav 1984, Pakhandi 1984, Ghar Ek Mandir 1984, Zameen Aasmaan 1984, Bhawani Junction 1985, Bepanaah 1985, Alag Alag 1985, Swati 1986, New Delhi Times (BFJA Film Award 1986) 1986, Maa Beti 1986, Ek Main Aur Ek Tu 1986, Aurat 1986, Abodh 1986, Ilzaam 1986, Pyaar Ki Jeet 1987, Naam O Nishan 1987, Ijaazat 1987, Anjaam 1987, Sindoor 1987, Sammy and Rosie Get Laid 1987, Hum To Chale Pardes 1988, The Deceivers 1988, Meri Zabaan 1989, Jaaydaad 1989, Clerk 1989, Farz Ki Jung 1989, Gair Kanooni 1989, Touhean 1989, Oonch Neech Beech 1989, Raeeszada 1990, Akayla 1991, In Custody 1993, Aag Ka Toofan 1993, Vivekananda 1994, Gulliver's Travels (TV) 1996, Jinnah 1998, Side Streets 1998. *Films produced or directed:* produced: Junoon 1978 (Nat. Award), Kalyug 1980, 36 Chowringhee Lane 1981, Vijeta 1982, Utsav 1984; directed Ajooba 1992. *Address:* Prithvi House, 26 Janki Kutir, Juhu Church Road, Mumbai 400 049, India (home); Film Walas, Janki Kutir, Juhu Church Road, Mumbai 400 049 (office). *Telephone:* (22) 6142922 (office). *E-mail:* mail@film-valas.com (office). *Website:* film-valas.com (office).

KAPOR, Mitchell David, BA; American computer industry executive; *President and Chairman, Open Source Applications Foundation;* b. 1950, New York; m. Freada Kapor Klein; ed Campus-Free Coll., Yale Univ., Massachusetts Inst. of Tech.; early career as disc jockey with WHCN-FM, Hartford, Conn.; teacher of transcendental meditation, Cambridge, Mass, Fairfield, Iowa; entry level computer programmer in Cambridge; mental health counsellor, New England Memorial Hosp., Stoneham, Mass; ind. software consultant 1978, co-developed Tiny Troll program; Product Man. Personal Software Inc.; Publr VisiCalc software, designer and programer of VisiPlot and VisiTrend; f. Lotus Devt Corpn 1982, Pres. then Chair. and CEO 1982–86; Chair. and CEO ON Tech. 1987–90; Co-founder and Chair. Electronic Frontier Foundation 1990–94; Chair. Mass Comm. on Computer Tech. and Law 1992–93; Adjunct Prof., MIT Media Lab. 1994–96; Pnr, Accel Pnrs 1999–2001; Founder and Chair. Open Source Applications Foundation 2001–;

Lecturer, Univ. of Calif., Berkeley 2005–06, Adjunct Prof., School of Information 2006–; mem. Computer Science and Tech. Bd, Nat. Information Infrastructure Advisory Council; Founding investor, UUNET and Real Networks; Chair. Bd Linden Research; fmr mem. Bd of Dirs Groove Networks, Ximian, Reactivity; Trustee, Kapor Family Foundation 1984–98; f. Mitchell Kapor Foundation 1997; Founding Chair. Mozilla Foundation 2003; Trustee, Level Playing Field Inst. *Publications:* numerous articles on impact of personal computing and networks on society information infrastructure policy, intellectual property issues, anti-trust in the digital era. *Address:* Open Source Applications Foundation, 543 Howard Street, Suite 500, San Francisco, CA 94105, USA (office). *Telephone:* (415) 946-3016 (office). *Fax:* (415) 946-3001 (office). *E-mail:* mitch@kapor.com. *Website:* www .osafoundation.org (office); www.kapor.com (office).

KAPPES, Stephen R., BS, MS; American government official; *Deputy Director of Operations, Central Intelligence Agency;* b. 22 Aug. 1951, Cincinnati; m. Kathleen Kappes (née Morgan); two c.; ed Athens High School, Ohio Univ., Ohio State Univ.; served as Officer in US Marine Corps 1976–81; worked at CIA 1981–2004, 2006–, various positions including Chief of Counterintelligence Center, Assoc. Deputy Dir for Operations for Counterintelligence, Asst Deputy Dir of Operations 2002–04, Deputy Dir of Operations 2004, 2006–; Exec. Vice-Pres. for Global Strategy, ArmorGroup Int. 2005–06, COO 2006. *Address:* Central Intelligence Agency, Office of Public Affairs, Washington, DC 20505, USA (office). *Telephone:* (703) 482-0623 (office). *Fax:* (703) 482-1739 (office). *Website:* www.cia.gov (office).

KAPSE, Ramchandra Ganesh, LLB, MA; Indian government official; b. 1 Dec. 1933, Nasik, Maharashtra; ed Univ. of Bombay; fmr Head, Dept of Marathi Literature, D. G. Ruparel Coll., Mumbai; mem. Bharatiya Jan Sangh 1955–; mem. Kalyan Municipality 1962–74; mem. Maharashtra Legis. Ass. 1978–89, Leader Bharatiya Janata Group 1985–89; Chair. CIDCO, Maharashtra 1979–80; mem. Lok Sabha 1989–96, Rajya Sabha 1996–98; Lt Gov. of Andaman and Nicobar Islands 2004–06 (resgnd); Chair. Standing Cttee on Food, Civil Supplies and Consumer Protection 1998–99, Railway Passengers Services Cttee; Pres. Pragati Pratishthan non-governmental org.; Founder-Sec. Rambhau Mhalgi Prabodhini; Hon. Advisor, Bureau of Parl. Studies and Training 1998–. *Address:* c/o Office of the Lieutenant-Governor, Administration of the Andaman and Nicobar Islands, Raj Nivas, Port Blair 744 101, India (office).

KAPUR, Shekhar, CA; Indian film director; b. 6 Dec. 1945, Lahore, Pakistan; s. of Kulbhushan Kapur and Sheel Kanta; m. Suchitra Krishnamurthy; one d.; ed St Stephen's Coll., Delhi; early career with multinational oil co.; moved to GB 1970 and worked as accountant and man. consultant; appeared in several Hindi TV serials including Udaan; f. Virgin Comics; Padma Shri 2000. *Films include:* as actor: Ishq Ishq Ishq 1974, Jaan Hazir Hai 1975, Toote Khilone 1978, Jeena Yahan 1979, Bhula Na Dena 1981, Agni Pareeksha 1981, Bindiya Chamkegi 1984, Falak 1988, Gawahi 1989,Drishti 1990, Nazar 1991, Saatwan Aasman 1992; as dir: Masoom (Filmfare Award 1983) 1983, Mr India 1987, Bandit Queen (Filmfare Award 1995, 1997) 1994, Dil Se Dushmani 1998, Elizabeth (Int. Award 1998, National Board of Review) 1998, The Four Feathers 2002, The Guru (exec. producer) 2002, Elizabeth: The Golden Age 2007. *Television includes:* Tahqiqat (series) 1994. *Address:* 42 New Sital Apartments, A. B. Nair Road, Juhu, Mumbai 400 449, India (home). *Telephone:* (22) 6204988 (home). *Website:* www .shekharkapur.com.

KAPUTIN, Sir John, CMG; Papua New Guinea politician and international organization official; b. (John Rumet), 11 July 1941; s. of the late Daniel ToKaputin and Rellie Iakirara; ed Rockhampton Boys Grammar School, Queensland, Australia, Univ. of Hawaii, USA; trained as teacher and bureaucrat 1960s; mem. House of Ass. (Rabaul constituency) 1972–2002; mem. Constitutional Planning Cttee that developed PNG Constitution 1972; Minister for Justice 1973–74, for Nat. Planning and Devt 1978–80, for Finance and Planning 1980–82, for Minerals and Energy 1985–88, for Foreign Affairs 1992–94, 1999–2000, for Mining and Petroleum 1994; Deputy Speaker 1975–77; Chair. Bipartisan Cttee on Bougainville Crisis 1988–90, Special State Negotiator for Bougainville 1998; Co-Pres. African, Caribbean and Pacific (ACP) Group of States-EU Jt Ass., Brussels, Belgium 1995–97, Sec.-Gen. ACP Secr. 2005–10; Special Ministerial Envoy for Int. Financial Insts, responsible for negotiations with IMF, World Bank, EU and Asian Devt Bank 2000–02; led ACP Ministerial Missions to Burundi, Rwanda, Equatorial Guinea, Togo, Fiji and Solomon Islands; Hon. Pres. ACP/EU Jt Parl. Ass. 1997; Togolese Medal of Freedom and Liberty, Govt of Repub. of Togo. *Address:* c/o Secretariat of the African, Caribbean and Pacific Group of States, Avenue Georges Henri 451, 1200 Brussels, Belgium. *Telephone:* (2) 743-06-00. *E-mail:* info@acp.int.

KAPUYA, Hon. Juma Athumani, BSc MSc PhD; Tanzanian academic and politician; *Minister of Labour, Employment and Youth Development;* b. 22 June 1945; ed Tabora Boys' Secondary School, Univ. of Dar es Salaam; Tutorial Asst, Univ. of Dar es Salaam 1971–74, Asst Lecturer 1974–76, Lecturer 1976–78, Sr Lecturer 1978–83, Assoc. Prof. 1983–87, Prof. 1987–95; adviser, Tanganyika Youth League (Univ. of Dar es Salaam) 1971–77, Chama Cha Mapinduzi (CCM) Youth 1977–82; Leader, CCM, Univ. of Dar es Salaam 1983–95; mem. Parl. (CCM) for Urambo Magharibi; Minister of Defence and Nat. Service 2006–08; Minister of Labour, Employment and Youth Devt 2008–; Dir Tobacco Authority, Sugar Authority; Dir and Rep. OTTU, Univ. of Dar es Salaam, Inst. of Adult Educ. *Address:* Ministry of Labour, Employment and Youth Development, POB 1422, Dar es Salaam, Tanzania (office). *Telephone:* (22) 2120419 (office). *Fax:* (22) 2113082 (office).

KARA-MURZA, Alexei Alexeyevich, Dr rer. pol, DPhil; Russian academic and politician; b. 1956; ed Moscow State Univ.; Dir Cen. for Theoretical Studies of Russian Reforms, Inst. of Philosophy, Russian Acad. of Sciences; Co-Pres. Moscow Foundation of Freedom and Human Rights (now Moscow Liberal Fund) 1992–; worked as scientific researcher; Head of Dept of Social and Political Philosophy, Russian Acad. of Sciences 1995–; also currently Prof. of Practical Philosophy, Higher School of Econs, Nat. Research Univ.; Deputy Chair. Union of Rightist Forces party 2000–; mem. Council of Trustees Obshchaya Gazeta (weekly); Ed.-in-Chief Pravoe Delo newspaper. *Publications:* scientific publs on modern philosophy and politology. *Address:* Centre for Theoretical Studies of Russian Reforms, Russian Academy of Sciences, 119842 Moscow, Volkhonka str. 14 Bldg 5, Russia (office).

KARABAYEV, Ednan Oskonovich, PhD; Kyrgyzstani academic and government official; b. 17 Jan. 1953, Talas; ed Kyrgyz State Univ., Inst. of History of Kyrgyz SSR Acad. of Sciences; early career as history teacher, Frunze (now Bishkek); Minister of Foreign Affairs 1992–93, 2007–09; Head Int. Relations Dept, Kyrgyz-Russian Slavic Univ. 1994–2007, also fmr Dean; Adviser to Pres. 2000; Pres. UNA of Kyrgyzstan; mem. Cyril-Mefody Acad. of Slavic Enlightenment; Honoured Worker of Educ. in Kyrgyz Repub. *Publications:* more than 200 scientific and other articles and contribs to monographs. *Address:* c/o Ministry of Foreign Affairs, 720040 Bishkek, bul. Erkindik 57, Kyrgyzstan. *Telephone:* (312) 62-05-45. *E-mail:* gendep@mfa.gov.kg.

KARADJORDJEVIC, HRH Crown Prince Alexander (see ALEXANDER KARADJORDJEVIC, HRH Crown Prince).

KARADŽIĆ, Radovan; Serbian psychiatrist, poet and fmr political leader; b. 19 June 1945, Petnjica, nr Savnik, Montenegro; s. of Vuk Karadžić; m. Lilijana Zelen Karadžić; one s. one d.; ed Univ. of Sarajevo, Columbia Univ., USA; moved to Sarajevo, Bosnia and Herzegovina in 1960; worked in state hosps, including Koševo Hosp. (specialized in neuroses and depression); team psychologist for Red Star Belgrade football club 1983; with Unis Co.; Co.-founder and Pres. Serbian Democratic Party 1989; leader of self-declared Republika Srpska (in Bosnia and Herzegovina), Pres. 1992–96 (resgnd); attended ceasefire talks in London Aug. 1992, Geneva Jan. 1993, after outbreak of hostilities; named as war crimes suspect by UN Tribunal for the Fmr Yugoslavia April 1995; int. arrest warrant issued for him July 1996; formally charged with genocide and crimes against humanity by Int. War Crimes Tribunal for Fmr Yugoslavia 1995; in hiding 1996–2008; arrested in Belgrade 21 July 2008, brought before Belgrade's War Crimes Court, had been working at pvt. clinic in Belgrade specializing in alternative medicine and psychology; on trial since Jan. 2009 at Int. Criminal Tribunal for the Fmr Yugoslavia at The Hague, Netherlands, accused on two counts of genocide and other war crimes; Order of St Dionysus of Xanthe (First Rank); Risto Ratković Prize for Literature, Mikhail Sholokhov Prize for Poetry, Russian Writers' Union 1994. *Publications include:* Slavic Guest (poems) (main literary award of Montenegro 1993), There Are Miracles, There Are No Miracles (poems for children), Miraculous Chronicles of the Night (novel), Under the Left Tit of the Century (poems) 2005. *Leisure interest:* composes music.

KARAGANOV, Sergei Aleksandrovich, DHist; Russian defence and foreign affairs specialist; *Chairman of the Presidium, Council of Foreign and Defence Policy, Russian Academy of Sciences;* b. 12 Sept. 1952, Moscow; m.; one d.; ed Moscow State Univ., postgraduate study in USA; Jr Fellow, Sr Fellow, Head of Section, USA and Canada Studies Inst. 1978–88; Research Fellow, Perm. Mission of USSR at UN 1976–77; Head of Dept, Deputy Dir Inst. of Europe of Russian Acad. of Sciences 1988–; mem. Foreign Policy Council, Ministry of Foreign Affairs of Russia 1991; Founder and Chair. of the Presidium, Council of Foreign and Defence Policy, Russian Acad. of Sciences 1991–; mem. Presidential Council of Russia 1992–99; Adviser to Presidential Admin.; mem. Consulting Council to Security Council of Russia 1993–; mem. Consultative Council of Fed. 1996–; Chair. Dept on World Politics, State Univ. Higher School of Econs 2002–, Dean, School of Int. Econs and Foreign Affairs 2006–; Chair. Editorial Bd Russia in Global Affairs magazine 2002–; mem. Pres.'s Public Council for Assisting the Devt of Civil Society and Human Rights 2004–, Ministry of Defence Public Council 2006–; mem. IISS, London. *Publications:* 18 books and brochures, including Russia: State of Reforms 1993, Security of the Future Europe (ed.; in Russian) 1993, Harmonization: the Evolution of U.S. and Russian Defense Policies (co-ed. with F. Ikle; also published in Russian) 1993, Where Russia Goes? Foreign and Defense Policy in the New Era 1994, Damage Limitation or Crisis? Russia and the World (co-ed. with Robert D. Blackwill) 1994, Wither Western Aid to Russia (ed. and dir of the study; also published in Russian) 1994, Russia's Economic Role in Europe. Report of the Commission for the Greater Europe, Vol. II (co-authored with O. Lambsdorf; also published in Russian) 1995, Geopolitics Change in Europe, Policies of the West and Russia's Alternatives (ed. and head of the study) 1995, Towards a New Democratic Commonwealth (co-authored with Graham Allison and Karl Kaiser) 1996, Russian-American Relations on the Threshold of Two Centuries (co-author) 2000, Strategy for Russia: Agenda for the President-2000 (ed.; in Russian) 2000, Strategy for Russia: Ten Years of CFDP (ed.) 2002; more than 350 articles in Russian on econs of foreign policy, arms control, nat. security strategy, Russian foreign and defence policies. *Leisure interests:* athletics, literature, cooking. *Address:* Mokhovaya Street 11-3B, 125993 Moscow (office); Chernyahovskogo, 9/5 Apt 387, 125139 Moscow, Russia (home). *Telephone:* (495) 692-84-72 (office); (495) 152-99-82 (home). *Fax:* (495) 609-92-98 (office). *E-mail:* cfdp@online.ru (office); cfdp@mail.ru (home). *Website:* www.svop.ru.

KARAGEORGHIS, Vassos, PhD, FSA, FRSA; Cypriot archaeologist and academic; b. 29 April 1929, Trikomo; s. of George Karageorghis and Panagiota Karageorghis; m. Jacqueline Girard 1953; one s. one d.; ed Pancyprian Gymnasium, Nicosia, Univ. Coll. and Inst. of Archaeology, Univ. of London; Asst Curator, Cyprus Museum 1952–60, Curator 1960–63, Acting Dir, Dept of Antiquities, Cyprus 1963–64, Dir 1964–89; Dir Archaeological Research Unit, Prof. of Archaeology, Univ. of Cyprus 1992–96; excavations at Salamis 1952–73, Akhera and Pendayia 1960, Kition 1962–81, Maa-Palaeokastro, Pyla-Kokkinokremos 1979–87, Former. Emer. 2004–; Dir d'Etudes, Ecole Pratique des Hautes Etudes, Sorbonne, Paris 1983–84; Adjunct. Prof. of Classical Archaeology, State Univ. of New York, Albany 1973–; Geddes-Harrower Prof. of Classical Art and Archaeology, Univ. of Aberdeen 1975; Visiting Mellon Prof., Inst. for Advanced Study, Princeton 1989–90; adviser to the Pres. of Cyprus on cultural heritage 1989–92; mem. Council, Anastasios G. Leventis Foundation (Dir 1996–2010), Cultural Foundation of the Bank of Cyprus; mem. Royal Swedish Acad., Accad. dei Lincei, Acad. des Inscriptions et Belles Lettres, German Archaeological Inst., Acad. of Athens; Corresp. mem. Austrian Acad. of Sciences, Royal Acad. of Spain 1997; Hon. mem. Soc. for Promotion of Hellenic Studies, Archaeological Inst. of America, Council of Greek Archaeological Soc., ICOMOS 2005; Visiting Fellow, Merton Coll., Oxford 1979, 1988, Sr Research Fellow 1980, Hon. Fellow 1990; Visiting Fellow, All Souls Coll., Oxford 1982; Visiting Scholar Harvard Univ. 1997–; Fellow, Royal Soc. of Humanistic Studies, Lund, Univ. Coll., London; Corresp. Fellow, British Acad.; mem. Nat. Olympic Cttee Greece 1998; Hon. Fellow, Soc. of Antiquaries, London; Hon. Citizen of Plovdiv (Bulgaria) 2003; Order of Merit (1st

Class), FRG 1980, Commdr, Royal Order of Polar Star (Sweden) 1990, Commdr, des Arts et des Lettres 1990, Commdr, Order of Merit (Italy) 1990, Austrian Decoration for Arts and Sciences 1997, Officier, Légion d'honneur 1998, Commdr of the Order of Honour (Greece) 2008; Dr hc (Lyon, Göteborg, Athens, Birmingham, Toulouse, Brock, Brussels, Oxford, Dublin, Mariupolis—Ukraine); Prix de la Soc. des Études Grecques, Sorbonne 1966, R. B. Bennett Commonwealth Prize 1978, Onassis Prize 'Olympia' 1991, Premio Internazionale 'I Cavalli d'Oro di San Marco' 1996, Award for Excellence in Science and Arts, Govt of Cyprus 1998, G. Maraslis Medal (Odessa) 2003. *Publications include:* Treasures in the Cyprus Museum 1962, Corpus Vasorum Antiquorum 1963, 1965, Nouveaux documents pour l'étude du bronze récent à Chypre 1964, Sculptures from Salamis, Vol. I 1964, Vol. II 1966, Excavations in the Necropolis of Salamis, Vol. I 1967, Vol. II 1970, Vol. III 1973, Vol. IV 1978, Salamis in Cyprus 1969, Altägäis und Altkypros (with H. G. Buchholz) 1971, Kition, Mycenaean and Phoenician discoveries in Cyprus 1976, The Civilization of Prehistoric Cyprus 1976, Vases et figurines de l'Age du Bronze (with Jean des Gagniers) 1976, Hala Sultan Tekké I (with P. Aström, D. M. Bailey) 1976, Two Cypriot sanctuaries of the end of the Cypro-Archaic period 1977, Mycenaean Pictorial Vase Painting (with Emily Vermeule) 1981, Cyprus from the Stone Age to the Romans 1982, Cyprus at the close of the Late Bronze Age (co-ed. with J. D. Muhly) 1984, Archaeology in Cyprus 1960–85 (ed.) 1985, La Nécropole d'Amathonte III: Les Terres Cuites 1987, Blacks in Ancient Cypriot Art 1988, The End of the Late Bronze Age in Cyprus 1990, Tombs at Palaepaphos 1990, Les anciens Chypriotes: entre orient et occident 1990, The Coroplastic Art of Ancient Cyprus (Vols I-VI), Cyprus in the Eleventh Century BC (ed.) 1994, The Evolution of the Economy of Cyprus from the Prehistoric Period to the Present Day (co-ed. with D. Michaelides) 1996, The Potters' Art of Ancient Cyprus (with Y. Olenik) 1997, Greek Gods and Heroes in Ancient Cyprus 1998, Cypriot Archaeology Today: Achievements and Perspectives 1998, Excavating at Salamis in Cyprus, 1952–74 1999, Ancient Cypriot Art in the Severis Collection 1999, Ancient Art from Cyprus. The Cesnola Collection (with J. R. Mertens, M. E. Rose), Ancient Cypriot Art in Copenhagen. The Collections of the Nat. Museum of Denmark and the New York Carlsberg Glyptotek (with Bodil Bundgaard Rasmussen et al.), Defensive Settlements of the Aegean and Eastern Mediterranean after c. 1200 B.C. (with Christine Morris), Italy and Cyprus in Antiquity, 1500-450 B.C. (with L. Bonfante), Early Cyprus, Crossroads of the Mediterranean, Ancient Cypriote Art in the National Archaeological Museum Athens, The Cyprus Collections in the Medelhausmuseet (with S. Houby-Nielsen et al.), Ancient Cypriot Art in Russian Museums (with A. Bukina et al.), Early Cyprus: Crossroads of the Mediterranean, Aspects of Everyday Life in Ancient Cyprus: Iconographic Representations 2006, and more than 380 articles in Greek, German, American, English and French journals. *Leisure interests:* gardening, photography. *Address:* 16 Kastorias Street, Nicosia 1055, Cyprus. *Telephone:* (2) 2755249. *Fax:* (2) 2755249. *E-mail:* vassoskarageorghis@cytanet.com.cy (office).

KARAKI, Khaled A. Al-, BA, MA, PhD; Jordanian university administrator, academic and government official; b. 1946, Karak; ed Univ. of Jordan, Univ. of Cambridge, UK; fmr faculty mem. Dept of Arabic, Univ. of Jordan, then Asst Dean of Faculty of Arts, then Dean of Student Affairs, currently Pres. Univ. of Jordan; Pres. Jerash Private Univ. 2001; Minister of Culture and Youth, of Culture and Information, of Culture and Higher Educ. in successive cabinets 1989–91; Deputy Prime Minister and Minister of Information 1995–96; Deputy Prime Minister and Minister of Educ. 2010–11; Adviser to HM the late King Hussein of Jordan; fmr Chief of the Royal Court; fmr Chair. Jordan Press Foundation (Al-Rai Newspaper); Pres. Jordanian Writers' Asscn 1985–90; mem. or Chair. numerous high-ranking cttees, asscns and councils, including Arab Asscn for Comparative Literature, Al-Albait Foundation, Higher Cttee for Declaring Amman Capital for Arab Culture, Cttee for Preserving the Arabic Language, Jordan Acad. for Arabic, amongst others; specialist in Arabic language, literature and culture; numerous grants and awards. *Publications:* more than 20 books and numerous articles. *Address:* c/o Ministry of Education, POB 1646, Amman 11118, Jordan (office).

KARAMANLIS, Konstantinos (Kostas) Alexandrou, MA, PhD; Greek politician and lawyer; b. 14 Sept. 1956, Athens; m. Natasha Pazaitis 1998; twin s. one d.; ed Athens Univ. Law School, Deree Coll., Fletcher School of Law and Diplomacy, Tufts Univ., USA; served in Greek Navy 1977–79; Lecturer in Political Science, Diplomatic History and Corp. Law, Deree Coll.; mem. Parl. (New Democracy Party) for Thessaloniki 1989–2004, for Larissa 2004–; Pres. Nea Demokratia (New Democracy Party) 1997–2009; Leader of the Opposition 1997–2004; Vice-Pres. European People's Party 1999–2006; Prime Minister of Greece 2004–09; Minister of Culture 2004–06; Vice-Pres. Int. Democratic Union 2002–; Chair. European Democrat Union Party Leaders Conf. 2003. *Publications:* Eleftherios Venizelos and Greek Foreign Relations 1928–32 1986, Spirit and Era of Gorbachev 1987. *Address:* New Democracy Party (Nea Demokratia), Odos Rhigillis 18, 106 74 Athens, Greece (office). *Telephone:* (210) 7418000 (office). *Fax:* (210) 7418119 (office). *E-mail:* ir@nd.gr (office). *Website:* www.nd.gr (office).

KARAMANOV, Alemdar Sabitovich; Ukrainian/Crimean Tatar composer; b. 10 Sept. 1934, Simferopol; ed Moscow State Conservatory (pupil of S. Bogatyrev and D. Kabalevsky); author of numerous symphonic compositions including 24 symphonies 1954–94, vocal-orchestral compositions of secular and religious character, including Requiem 1991, Mysteria of Khersones 1993, 3 piano concertos, 2 violin concertos, Nat. Anthem of Crimea Repub. 1992, chamber ensembles, piano music, choruses and vocal compositions; most of his music not performed up to late 1980s. *Address:* Voykova str. 2, Apt. 4, Simferopol, Crimea, Ukraine (home).

KARAMARKO, Tomislav; Croatian politician; *President, Croatian Democratic Union;* b. 25 May 1959, Zadar; m. Enisa Muftić 1993 (died 2011); two c.; ed Univ. of Zagreb; archivist, Nat. Archives of Croatia 1987–88; Head, Office of the Prime Minister 1991–92, Cabinet Chief 1992–93; Chief of Police Admin, Zagreb 1993–96; Deputy Minister of the Interior 1996–98; Nat. Security Adviser to Pres. of Croatia 2000; Head, Office for Nat. Security 2000–02; Head, Counter-Intelligence Agency 2004–06; Dir Intelligence-Security Agency 2006–08; Minister of the Interior 2008–11; mem. Croatian Democratic Union (Hrvatska demokratska zajednica—HDZ) 1989–, Pres. 2012–; Leader of the Opposition 2012–. *Address:* Croatian Democratic Union (Hrvatska demokratska zajednica—HDZ), 10000 Zagreb, trg

Žrtava fašizma 4, Croatia (office). *Telephone:* (1) 4553000 (office). *Fax:* (1) 4552600 (office). *E-mail:* hdz@hdz.hr (office). *Website:* www.hdz.hr (office).

KARAMI, Omar; Lebanese lawyer and politician; b. 7 Sept. 1934, An Nouri; s. of the late Abdul Hamid Karami; brother of Rashid Karami; elected mem. Parl. 1991; fmr Minister of Educ. and the Arts; Prime Minister of Lebanon 1990–92 (resgnd), Oct. 2004–Feb. 2005 (resgnd). *Address:* c/o Majlis Alnwab, Beirut, Lebanon (office).

KARANNAGODA, Adm. Wasantha, MBA, PhD; Sri Lankan diplomatist, civil servant and fmr naval officer; *Ambassador to Japan;* ed Ananda Coll., Colombo, Univ. of Colombo, Quai-i-Azam Univ., Islamabad, Pakistan, Univ. of Kelaniya, Nat. Defence Coll., Pakistan, Royal Naval Staff Coll., UK, Asia-Pacific Center for Security Studies, Hawaii, Near East-South Asia Center for Strategic Studies at Nat. Defense Univ., Washington, DC, USA; Flag Lt for Adm. Basil Gunasekara (Commdr of Navy) early 1980s; long naval career as navigator until final duty on board SLNS Wickrama as Commdr, 7th Surveillance Command Squadron 1992; held many sr commands, including four Operational Naval Commands on seven occasions – Northern, Eastern and Western Commands (twice each) and North Cen. once, for total period spanning six years; first ever Dir-Gen. (Operations), Naval HQ, Dir Naval Projects and Plans, Dir Naval Personnel and Training, Commdt of Naval and Maritime Acad., Deputy Area Commdr (West), Deputy Area Commdr (North) and Deputy Area Commdr (East); Commdr of Sri Lankan Navy 2005–09; awarded rank of Adm. after Eelam War IV and demise of LTTE (Tamil Tigers) (first officer thus promoted whilst in the service); Nat. Security Adviser to the Pres. 2009–11; Sec., Ministry of Highways 2009–10; Amb. to Japan 2011–; mem. Royal Inst. of Navigation, UK, Nautical Inst., UK; Rana Sura Padakkama for gallantry, Vishista Seva Vibhushanaya, Uttama Seva Padakkama, North and East Operational Medal, Clasp I and Clasp II and several other service and campaign medals, including Repub. of Sri Lanka Armed Services Medal, Sri Lanka Navy 50th Anniversary Medal, Commemoration Medal, Sri Lanka Armed Services Long Service Medal, Pres.'s Inauguration Medal 1978, 50th Anniversary of Independence Commemoration Medal, Purna Bhumi Padakkama, Operation 'Reviresa' Campaign Medal, Commdr of the Navy's Commendation Badge (five stars), Surface Warfare Badge. *Leisure interest:* golf. *Address:* Embassy of Sri Lanka, 2-1-54, Takanawa, Minato-ku, Tokyo 108-0074, Japan (office). *Telephone:* (3) 3440-6913 (office). *Fax:* (3) 3440-6914 (office). *E-mail:* tokyojp@lankaembassy.jp (office). *Website:* www.lankaembassy.jp (office).

KARAOSMANOGLU, Attila, PhD; Turkish economist; b. 20 Sept. 1932, Manisa; s. of Ibrahim Ethem Karaosmanoglu and Fatma Eda Karaosmanoglu; m. Sukriye Ozyet 1960; one s.; ed Univs of Ankara and Istanbul, Harvard and New York Univs, USA; mem. Faculty, Middle East Tech. Univ. and Ankara Univ. 1954–63; Head, Econ. Planning Dept, State Planning Org. of Turkey 1960–62; Adviser, Fed. of Turkish Trade Unions and consultant to Turkish Scientific and Tech. Research Council 1963–65; Consultant, Directorate for Scientific Affairs, OECD 1965–66; Economist, then Sr Economist, World Bank 1966–71, Chief Economist 1973–75, Dir of Devt Policy 1975–79, Dir of Europe, Middle East and N Africa Region Country Programmes 1979–82, Vice-Pres. E Asia and Pacific Region 1983–87, Asia Region 1987–91 Man. Dir World Bank 1991–95 (retd); Deputy Prime Minister in Charge of Econ. Affairs and Chair. High Planning Council, Turkish Govt 1971; mem. Exec. Bd Is Bank, Turkey 1972; Chief Adviser, Istanbul Chamber of Industry 1995–; mem. Bd Scientific and Technological Research Council of Turkey 1995–; Alt., Bank of Turkey 1996–; Chair. Bd Nat. Inst. of Metrology 1997–. *Publications:* Towards Full Employment and Price Stability (OECD publ., co-author) 1977, Poverty and Prosperity – The Two Realities of Asian Development 1989, Diversity and Consensus – The Emergence of an Asian Development Paradigm 1991. *Address:* c/o Istanbul Chamber of Industry, Meşrutiyet Cad. No: 62, Istanbul, Turkey.

KARASHEV, Aaly Azimovich; Kyrgyzstani politician; b. 30 Oct. 1968, Osh Oblast; ed Kyrgyz Agricultural Inst.; worked in Admin of the Pres. 1998–2006, becoming Head of Dept; Gov., Osh Oblast 2007–09; Deputy Prime Minister and Chief of Govt Apparatus 2009–12, Acting Prime Minister 1–5 Sept. 2012. *Address:* c/o Office of the Prime Minister, 720003 Bishkek, Dom Pravitelstva, Kyrgyzstan (office). *Telephone:* (312) 66-12-20 (office). *Fax:* (312) 66-66-58 (office). *E-mail:* pmoffice@mail.gov.kg (office). *Website:* www.government.gov.kg (office).

KARASIN, Grigory Borisovich; Russian diplomatist; *Deputy Minister of Foreign Affairs;* b. 23 Aug. 1949, Moscow; m.; two d.; ed Moscow Inst. of Oriental Languages, Moscow State Univ.; diplomatic service since 1972; translator, attaché USSR Embassy, Senegal 1972–76; attaché First African Div., USSR Ministry of Foreign Affairs 1976–77; sec. to Deputy Minister of Foreign Affairs 1977–79; Second, First Sec. Embassy, Australia 1979–85; First Sec., Counsellor Second European Div. Ministry of Foreign Affairs 1985–88; Counsellor USSR Embassy, UK 1988–92; Head of Dept of Africa, Ministry of Foreign Affairs of Russia 1992–93, Head. Dept of Information and Press 1993–96; Deputy Minister of Foreign Affairs 1996–2000; Amb. to UK 2000–05; Deputy Minister of Foreign Affairs 2005–. *Address:* Ministry of Foreign Affairs, 119200 Moscow, Smolenskaya-Sennaya pl. 32/34, Russia (office). *Telephone:* (495) 244-16-06 (office). *Fax:* (495) 230-21-30 (office). *E-mail:* ministry@mid.ru (office). *Website:* www.mid.ru (office).

KARAT, Prakash, BA, MSc, PhD; Indian politician; *General Secretary of the Communist Party of India—Marxist;* b. 7 March 1948, Letpadan, Myanmar; m. Brinda Karat 1975; ed Madras Christian Coll., Univ. of Edinburgh, UK; at Jawaharlal Nehru Univ., New Delhi 1970, Pres. Students' Union 1972–73; worked as aide to A.K. Gopalan (leader of Communist Party of India—Marxist, CPI(M)) 1971–73; Co-founder Students Fed. of India, Pres. 1974–79; Sec., Delhi State Cttee, CPI(M) 1982–85, elected to Cen. Cttee 1985, mem. Politbureau 1992, Gen. Sec. CPI(M) 2005–; Man. Dir Leftword Books. *Publications include:* Language, Nationality and Politics in India 1972, A World To Win – Essays on The Communist Manifesto (ed) 1999, Across Time and Continents: A Tribute to Victor Kiernan (ed) 2003, Subordinate Ally: The Nuclear Deal and India-US Strategic Relations 2008. *Address:* Communist Party of India (Marxist), Central Committee, A.K. Gopalan Bhawan, 27-29, Bhai Vir Singh Marg, New Delhi 110 001, India (office). *Telephone:* (11) 23344918 (office). *Fax:* (11) 23747483 (office). *E-mail:* cc@cpim.org (office). *Website:* www.cpim.org (office).

KARATZAFERIS, Georgios; Greek politician, journalist and media executive; *Leader, Popular Orthodox Rally (Laikos Orthodoxos Synagermos—LAOS);* b. 11

Aug. 1947, Athens; ed London School of Journalism, UK; producer of radio broadcasts aged 15, TV producer aged 22; f. R.TV.P.R. AE advertising agency 1977; columnist for Nea Poreia political newsletter early 1980s; cr. TV Press Video Review 1983; set up radio and TV stations Radio City and TeleAsty (initially known as TeleCity) 1990; Ed. Alpha Ena newspaper 2000; also contributed to daily newspapers including Eleftheros, Apogevmatini and Eleftheros Typos; f. Acad. of Communications Studies, Athens 2005; mem. Vouli (Parl.) for Athens (New Democracy, expelled from party 2000, with LAOS 2000–) 1993–2012, responsibilities included chairmanship of Parl. Watchdog Cttee, Public Order Cttee and the Press and Mass Media Cttee 1993–2000, mem. Cttee on Public Admin and Cttee on Foreign Affairs 1993–2004, Nat. Communications' Confidentiality Protection Cttee 1999, Vice-Chair. Greco-Spanish Friendship Asscn 1999; Founder and Pres. Popular Orthodox Rally (Laikos Orthodoxos Synagermos—LAOS) 2000–; mem. European Parl. 2004–07, Vice-Pres. Independence and Democracy group; elected as a Prefectural Councillor as Head of the Me Kathari Kardia (With Clean Heart) party 2002; Adenauer Foundation scholarship 1983. *Publications:* six books in Greek, including The Model of Democracy, The Woman of Today, Liani Supports the Allagi (Change), Struggles and Agonies of the 1990–2000 Decade, Biographies of Saints. *Address:* Popular Orthodox Rally (Laikos Orthodoxos Synagermos), Leoforos Kallirrois 52, 117 45 Athens, Greece (office). *Telephone:* (210) 7522700 (office). *Fax:* (210) 7522704 (office). *E-mail:* pr@laos.gr (office). *Website:* www.laos .gr (office); www.karatzaferis.gr.

KARDASHEV, Nikolai Semenovich; Russian astronomer; *Director, Astro Space Centre, Lebedev Physical Institute, Russian Academy of Sciences;* b. 25 April 1932; m.; one d.; ed Moscow State Univ.; lab.; sr lab., jr, sr researcher State Astronomical Inst. 1955–67; head of lab., Deputy Dir Inst. of Space Studies USSR Acad. of Sciences 1967–90; Dir Astro Space Cen., Lebedev Physical Inst., USSR Acad. of Sciences 1990–; corresp. mem. USSR (now Russian) Acad. of Sciences 1976, mem. 1994; research in radiophysics, radioastronomy, radio radiation of galaxies and quasars; USSR State Prize. *Publications include:* Pulsars and nonthermal Radio Sources 1970, Strategy and Future Projects 1977; numerous articles in scientific journals. *Address:* Astro Space Centre, Lebedev Physical Institute, Russian Academy of Sciences, 117997 Moscow, Profsoyuznaya str. 84/32, Russia (office). *Telephone:* (495) 333-21-89 (office). *E-mail:* nkardash@asc.rssi.ru (office). *Website:* www.asc.rssi.ru (office).

KAREKIN II, His Holiness (Ktritch Narssisian); Armenian ecclesiastic; *Supreme Patriarch and Catholicos of All Armenians;* b. 16 Aug. 1951, Etchmiadzin; ed Kevorkian Theological Seminary, Univ. of Vienna, Univ. of Bonn; Asst Dean, Kevorkian Theological Seminary; ordained priest 1972; pastor in Germany 1975; Asst to Vicar-Gen. of Araratian Patriarchal Diocese 1980, Vicar-Gen., Bishop 1983, later Archbishop; mem. Supreme Spiritual Council of Catholicosate of All Armenians 1990–; Supreme Patriarch and Catholicos of All Armenians 1999–; f. Vazkenian Seminary, Sevan 1989, Christian Educ. Centre 1990; Dr hc (Artsakh); Kawkab Medal (First Class) Jordan 2000, Bethlehem 2000 Award (Palestinian Nat. Authority) 2000, Star of Romania 2000;. *Address:* Residence of the Catholicosate of all Armenians, Vagharshapat, Monastery of St Etchmiadzin, Armenia (office). *Telephone:* (10) 28-57-37 (office). *Fax:* (10) 15-10-77 (office). *E-mail:* holysee@etchmiadzin.am (office). *Website:* www.holyetchmiadzin .am (office).

KARELIN, Col Aleksander Aleksandrovich; Russian politician and fmr professional wrestler; b. 19 Sept. 1967, Novosibirsk; m. Olga Karelina; two s. one d.; ed Novosibirsk Pedagogical Inst., Motor-Transport Tech. Coll., Omsk Inst. of Physical Culture, Lesgaft Acad. of Physical Culture; Greco-Roman wrestler, turned professional 1978; unbeaten for 12 years until the Sydney Olympics; world champion (nine times), European champion (12 times); Olympic champion 1988, 1992, 1996; Olympic silver medallist, Sydney 2000, then retd; mem. of team Dynamo; Specialist, Fed. Tax Police Service 1995–99, Col of the Tax Police 1995; Co-founder and Co-leader Yedinstvo; Chair. Interregional Co-ordinating Council, Unity (Yedinstvo) party in Siberian Fed. Dist; mem. State Duma 1999–, Deputy Chair. Cttee for Int. Affairs 2003–; currently mem. Supreme Council, United Russia party; USSR Merited Master of Sports, Hero of Russia 1997. *Leisure interests:* poetry, literature, classical music. *Address:* State Duma, Yedinstvo Faction, Okhotny Ryad 1, 103265 Moscow, Russia (office). *Telephone:* (495) 292-56-97 (office). *Website:* www.karelin.ru.

KARIBZHANOV, Zhanybek Salimovich; Kazakhstani agronomist, economist, diplomatist and government official; b. 23 Nov. 1948, Aybas village of Sherbakulsky rayon, Omsk region, Russia; ed Omsk Agricultural Inst.; Head of Lab. and Sr Scientific Officer, All-Union Research and Design Tech. Inst. Cybernetics, Moscow 1979–82; Chief Economist, Zarya kommunizma (state farm), October rayon, Turgaysky region and Dir Panfilov state farm, Oktyabrski rayon 1982–87; Chief of Cen. Admin of Social and Econ. Devt Planning of Agric., State Agro-Industrial Cttee of Kazakh SSR, Alma-Ata 1987–89; Head, Agrarian Dept of Cen. Cttee, CP of Kazakhstan 1989–92; Head, Kokchetav regional admin 1992–93; Deputy Prime Minister and Chair. State Cttee on State Property 1993–94; Minister of Agric. 1994–96; Deputy Prime Minister 1996–97; Akim, Akmolinsk region July–Dec. 1997; Deputy Prime-Minister and Minister of Agric. 1997–99; Adviser to the Pres. of Kazakhstan 1999–2001; Amb. to People's Repub. of China 2001–07; Akim, Eastern Kazakhstan Oblast Admin. Jan.–May 2008. *Address:* c/o Eastern Kazakhstan Oblast Administration, 070000 Eastern Kazakhstan obl., Ust-Kamenogorsk, ul. M. Gorkogo, Kazakhstan.

KARIM, Ahmed Tariq; Bangladeshi diplomatist; *High Commissioner to India;* ed Notre Dame Coll., Dhaka, Dhaka Univ., Univ. of Maryland, USA; Lecturer in English, Notre Dame Coll., Dhaka 1965–66; joined Pakistan (later Bangladesh) Foreign Service 1967, served in various capacities at Missions in Iran 1969–72, Germany 1975–78, Thailand 1979–80, UK 1980–82, High Commr to India 1984–88, Deputy Chief of Mission, Embassy in Beijing 1989–91, Amb. to Iran (also accred to Lebanon) 1991–95, Additional Foreign Sec. with responsibility for South Asian region 1995–97, High Commr to S Africa (also accred to Botswana, Namibia and Lesotho with consular jurisdiction in Zambia and Zimbabwe) 1997–98, Amb. to USA 2001–02, High Commr to India 2009–; Sr Adviser, Center for Institutional Reform and the Informal Sector (IRIS), Univ. of Maryland 2002–05; Vice-Pres. Bangladesh Enterprise Inst. (pvt. think-tank) 2009–; mem. Adjunct Faculty, Univ. of Maryland 2007, 2008, Elliott School of Int. Affairs,

George Washington Univ., Washington, DC 2008, Virginia International Univ. 2007, 2008; Life mem. Bangladesh Inst. of Law and Int. Affairs. *Address:* High Commission of Bangladesh, EP-39 Dr S. Radhakrishnan Marg, Chanakyapuri, New Delhi 110 021, India (office). *Telephone:* (11) 24121389 (office). *Fax:* (11) 26878953 (office). *E-mail:* bdhcdelhi@gmail.com (office). *Website:* www.bhcdelhi .org (office).

KARIM, Bachtiar; Indonesian business executive; *President Director, PT Musim Mas;* b. 1957; s. of Anwar Karim; m.; four c.; joined family firm Musim Mas (palm oil processing co.), Medan, currently Pres. Dir PT Musim Mas; mem. Exec. Bd Round Table for Sustainable Palm Oil. *Address:* PT Musim Mas, Jl KL Yos Sudarso KM 7, 8 Tanjung Mulia, Medan 20241, North Sumatra, Indonesia (office). *Telephone:* (61) 6615511 (office). *Fax:* (61) 6617386 (office). *Website:* www .musimmas.com (office).

KARIM, Mohammad Fazlul, LLB; Bangladeshi judge; b. 30 Sept. 1943, Suchakradandi village, Chittagong; s. of the Al-haj Ahmed Kabir and Sunia Ara Begum; ed Univ. of Dhaka; enrolled as Advocate of Dist Court, Chittagong 1965, in High Court Div. 1970, in Appellate Div. 1979; Sec. to Supreme Court Bar Asscn 1982; mem. Bangladesh Bar Council 1992; Additional Judge of High Court Div. of Supreme Court 1992–94, Regular Judge 1994–2001, Sr-most Judge of Appellate Div. of Supreme Court 2001–10, Chief Justice of Bangladesh 2010–11; Chair. Judicial Service Pay Comm.; mem. Delhi-based Asia Pacific Advisory Forum on Judicial Educ. on Gender Equality Issue; fmr Chair. Court Admin and Court Man. Scheme of Capacity Building Project; fmr mem. Scheme for Mediation and Alternative Dispute Resolution under the aid programme of USIS; participated in Conf. on Prison Reform in SE Asia, Kathmandu Nepal 1996, confs on Judicial Educ. on Gender Equality Issue held in India, Pakistan, Sri Lanka and Nepal 1998–2006, in SAARC Law Conf., Dhaka; visited various courts and insts to observe case man., court admin and alternative dispute resolution in UK and USA 2002. *Address:* c/o Supreme Court of Bangladesh, Ramna, Dhaka 1000, Bangladesh.

KARIMI, Gen. Sher Mohammad; Afghan army officer; *Chief of Staff of the Afghan National Army;* b. 11 Nov. 1945, Khost Prov.; s. of Mohammad Karim; ed Royal Mil. Acad. Sandhurst, UK, Egyptian Commando School, US Army Ranger and Special Forces schools, Indian Defence Coll.; arrested and held as a prisoner after invasion by Soviet Army 1978, forced into exile in Pakistan, returned to Afghanistan 2001; served in Afghanistan Army Commando Brigade, as ADC and Army Dir of Recruiting and Training, served as Deputy Chief of Staff then Chief of Operations of the Gen. Staff, Ministry of Defence, then Chief of Operations, Afghan Nat. Army –2010, Chief of Staff of the Afghan Nat. Army 2010–; US Bronze Star Medal; NESA Alumnus Award. *Achievements include:* first Afghan to graduate from Royal Mil. Acad., Sandhurst. *Address:* Ministry of Defence, Shash Darak, Kabul, Afghanistan (office). *Telephone:* (20) 2100466 (office). *Website:* www .mod.gov.af (office).

KARIMOV, Dzhamshed Khilolovich, DEcon; Tajikistani politician; b. 4 Aug. 1940, Dushanbe; m.; two c.; ed Moscow Technological Inst. of Light Industry; researcher, Cen. Research Inst. of Econs and Math., USSR Acad. of Sciences; Asst Chair of Econ. of Industry Tajik State Univ., Jr researcher, Head of Div. of Optimal Planning Inst. of Econ., Tajik Acad. of Sciences 1962–72, Deputy Dir, Dir Research Inst. of Econ. and Econ.-Math. Methods of Planning, State Planning Cttee, Tajik SSR 1972–81; Corresp. mem. Tajik Acad. of Sciences; Deputy Chair. State Planning Cttee 1981–88; Deputy Chair. Council of Ministers, State Planning Cttee 1988–89; First Sec. Dushanbe City Cttee of CP Tajikistan 1989–91; USSR People's Deputy 1989–92; Deputy, First Deputy Chair. Council of Ministers Tajik Repub. 1991–92; represented Repub. of Tajikistan in Russia 1992–93; Chief Adviser on Econ. to Pres. Sept.–Nov. 1994; Prime Minister of Tajikistan 1994–96 (forced to resign after bloodless coup); Adviser to Pres. Rakhmonov 1996–97; apptd Amb. to People's Repub. China 1997. *Address:* c/o Ministry of Foreign Affairs, Rudaki prosp. 42, 734051 Dushanbe, Tajikistan.

KARIMOV, Islam Abduganiyevich, CandEconSc; Uzbekistani politician and head of state; *President;* b. 30 Jan. 1938, Samarqand, Uzbek SSR, USSR; m. 1st Natalia Petrovna Kuchmi (divorced late 1960s); one s.; m. 2nd Tatyana Akbarovna Karimova; two d.; ed Cen. Asian Polytechnic Inst. and Tashkent Econs Inst.; mem. CPSU 1964–91; Engineer, then Leading Engineer-Constructor in Tashkent aviation construction factory 1960–66; Chief Specialist, Head of Dept, First Deputy Chair. State Planning Cttee 1966–83, Chair. 1986; Minister of Finance, Deputy Chair. of Council of Ministers, Uzbek SSR 1983–86; First Sec., Qashqadaryo Viloyat Party Cttee 1986–89; First Sec., Uzbek SSR CP Cen. Cttee 1989–91; USSR People's Deputy 1989–91; mem. Cen. Cttee CPSU and Politburo 1990–91; Pres. of Uzbek SSR 1990; Chair. People's Democratic Party of Uzbekistan 1991–96; Pres. of Uzbekistan 1991– (elected by Supreme Soviet 24 March 1990, term of office extended by popular referendum 27 March 1995, re-elected 9 Jan. 2000 and 23 Dec. 2007); concurrently Chair. Cabinet of Ministers; mem. Acad. of Sciences of Uzbekistan; Hon. Chair. Fund of Friendship of Cen. Asia and Kazakhstan; Hon. DEcon; Dr hc and from nine foreign univs and acads; Mustaqillik (Independence) Award, Amir Temur Award, Borobudur Gold Medal, UNESCO 2006. *Publications:* Uzbekistan: Its Own Model of Renovation and Progress 1992, Uzbekistan – A State with a Great Future 1992, On the Priorities of the Economic Policy of Uzbekistan 1993, Uzbek Model of Deepening Economic Reforms 1995, Uzbekistan's Way of Restoration and Progress, To Complete the Noble Cause, Stability and Reforms 1996, Uzbekistan on the Threshold of the Twenty-First Century 1997, Uzbekistan Striving Towards the 21st Century 1999, The Spiritual Path of Renewal 2000. *Leisure interest:* tennis. *Address:* Office of the President, 100163 Tashkent, O'zbekiston shoh ko'ch. 43, Uzbekistan (office). *Telephone:* (71) 239-54-04 (office). *Fax:* (71) 239-53-25 (office). *E-mail:* presidents_office@press-service.uz (office). *Website:* www.press-service.uz.

KARIMOVA, Gulnora Islamovna; Uzbekistani business executive, diplomatist, fashion designer and singer; b. 8 July 1972, Farg'ona; d. of Pres. of Uzbekistan, Islam Karimov and Tatyana Akbarovna Karimova; m. Mansur Maqsudi (divorced); one s. one d.; ed Tashkent State Univ., Univ. of World Economy and Diplomacy, Tashkent, Univ. of Information and Tech., Tashkent, New York, Univ., Fashion Inst. of Tech., Harvard Grad. School of Arts and Sciences, USA; early academic career at Dept of Int. Studies, Univ. of World Economy and Diplomacy,

Tashkent; fmrly with Perm. Mission to UN, New York; returned to Uzbekistan and developed business interests in mobile cellular telephone operator and numerous industrial cos; consultant and adviser to Minister of Foreign Affairs; Minister-Counsellor, Embassy of Uzbekistan, Moscow 2003–08; Deputy Minister of Foreign Affairs, responsible for Cultural and Humanitarian Co-operation 2008; Amb. and Perm. Rep. to UN Office and other Int. Orgs, Geneva 2008–11; Amb. to Spain 2010–12; Chair. Forum of Culture and Arts Foundation of Uzbekistan; mem. Cercle Diplomatique de Genève; designed jewellery collection GULI for Swiss co. Chopard 2009; presented fashion lines under name Guli at New York Fashion Week 2010 and Cipriani, New York 2011; est. Forum of Socially Responsible Citizens of Uzbekistan 2012; left Switzerland after her immunity was lifted by a court 2013; announced by Swiss Prosecutor's Office that it had extended a money laundering investigation to include her March 2014; Pushkin Gold Medal for outstanding contrib. to the arts and culture 2009, IOC Sport – Inspiring Young People Trophy for activities in the area of sport, education and culture among youth 2010, Silk Road and Humanitarian Cooperation Award, Shanghai Cooperation Org. 2012. *Film screenplay:* The Theft of the White Cocoon (story about the origin of the famed Central Asian silk) 2012. *Music includes:* Round Run (single) 2012, various remixes by DJ White Shadow, Razor N. Guido and Max Fadeev; released self-titled debut album 2012; released a duet with French actor Gérard Depardieu 2012. *Publications:* Categories of Competitiveness of Countries with Transitional Economies: The Example of Uzbekistan 1998, Problems of Security in Central Asia: The Conditions, Tendency and Prospect of Development 2001. *Leisure interests:* jewellery and accessory designer, singer, poet. *Address:* Forum of Culture and Arts Foundation of Uzbekistan, 100057 Tashkent, O'zbekistan shoh ko'ch. 80, Uzbekistan. *E-mail:* fonduz@mail.ru. *Website:* www.fondforum.uz; www.googoosha.uz; gulnarakarimova.com; www.gulicollections.com.

KARIMULLAH, Adm. Shahid; Pakistani naval officer (retd); ed Nat. Defence Coll., US War Coll.; joined navy operations br. 1965, Pakistan Fleet Commdr, apptd Admiral 2002, Chief of Naval Staff 2002–05; Amb. to Saudi Arabia 2005–09; mem. Nat. Security Council; Sitara-i-Jurrat, Sitara-i-Imtiaz (mil.), Hilal-i-Imtiaz (mil.), Medal of Merit of the Turkish Armed Forces 2003. *Address:* c/o Ministry of Foreign Affairs, Constitution Ave, Islamabad, Pakistan.

KARIN, Michael, BSc, PhD; American pharmacologist and academic; *Distinguished Professor of Pharmacology and Pathology, School of Medicine, University of California, San Diego;* ed Tel-Aviv Univ., Israel, Univ. of California, Los Angeles; mem. Faculty, Univ. of California, San Diego 1987–, currently Distinguished Prof. of Pharmacology and Pathology, School of Medicine; an American Cancer Soc. Research Prof. 1999–; Co-founder Signal Pharmaceutical (currently Celgene), fmr mem. Scientific Advisory Bd; fmr mem. Nat. Advisory Council for Environmental Health Sciences; mem. NAS 2005; Assoc. mem. European Molecular Biology Org. 2007; Harvey Prize, Technion, Israel 2010. *Publications:* more than 300 papers in professional journals; 30 patents or pending patent applications. *Address:* Department of Pharmacology, University of California, San Diego, 9500 Gilman Drive, La Jolla, CA 92093-0636, USA (office). *Telephone:* (858) 534-1361 (office). *Fax:* (858) 534-8158 (office). *E-mail:* karinoffice@ucsd.edu (office). *Website:* pharmacology.ucsd.edu/faculty/karin.html (office); molpath.ucsd.edu/faculty/Karin.shtml (office); biomedsci.ucsd.edu/faculty/faculty_descrip.aspx?id=7 (office).

KARINA, Anna; French actress; b. (Hanne Karen Blarke Bayer), 22 Sept. 1940, Fredriksburg, Solbjerg, Denmark; d. of Carl Johann Bayer and of Elva Helvig Frederiksen; m. 1st Jean-Luc Godard (q.v.) (divorced); m. 2nd Pierre-Antoine Fabre 1968 (divorced); m. 3rd Daniel Georges Duval 1978; Prix Orange. *Films include:* She'll Have To Go 1961, Une femme est une femme 1961, Vivre sa vie 1962, Le petit soldat 1963, Bande à part 1964, Alphaville 1965, Made in the USA 1966, La religieuse 1968, The Magus 1968, Before Winter Comes 1968, Laughter in the Dark 1969, Justine 1969, The Salzburg Connection 1972, Living Together 1974, L'assassin musicien 1975, Les oeufs brouillés 1976, Boulette chinoise 1977, L'ami de Vincent 1983, Ave Maria 1984, Dernier été à Tanger 1987, Cayenne Palace 1987, L'Oeuvre au noir 1988, Last Song 1989, L'Homme qui voulait être coupable 1990, Une Histoire d'amour 2000, The Truth About Charlie 2002, Moi César 2003, Victoria 2008. *Album:* Une histoire d'amour 2000. *Publications:* Golden City 1983, On n'achète pas le soleil (novel) 1988. *Address:* c/o Ammédia, 20 avenue Rapp, 75007 Paris; Orban éditions, 76 rue Bonaparte, 75006 Paris, France.

KARIYAWASAM, Prasad, BSc (Hons); Sri Lankan diplomatist; *High Commissioner to India;* b. 21 March 1954, Galle; m. Kanthi Kariyawasam; ed Univ. of Peradeniya; joined Foreign Service 1981, diplomatic assignments include missions in Geneva, Riyadh, Washington, DC, New Delhi, New York; fmr Deputy High Commr in India 1998–2001; Perm. Rep. to UN, Geneva 2001–03, Consul Gen. to Switzerland 2001, Perm. Rep. to Conf. on Disarmament, Personal Rep. to Head of State to Group of 15 2001–03, Amb. and Perm. Rep. to UN, New York 2005–08, High Commr to India 2009–; fmr mem. UN Panel of Experts on Small Arms, Group of Governmental Experts on Relationship between Disarmament and Devt; Vice-Chair. Main Cttee, World Conf. on Racism, UN Comm. on Human Rights, Durban, S Africa 2001; Leader, Sri Lanka Del. to Conf. on Disarmament, Geneva 2001–03; Special Coordinator for Improved Functioning, Conf. on Disarmament 2001, 2002; Del. to Ad Hoc Cttee on Int. Terrorism 2001–03; Chair. Global System of Trade Preferences Cttee of Participants, UNCTAD, UNCTAD Expert Group on Market Access Issues in Mode 4 (Movement of Natural Persons to Supply Services) 2002–03; mem. UN Cttee on Protection of Rights of All Migrant Workers and Members of Their Families 2003–; Chair. Chairpersons of Human Rights, Treaty Bodies and Inter-Cttee Meetings 2004; Vice-Chair. ECOSOC of the UN, New York 2006–07; mem. Advisory Bd Int. Comm. on Nuclear non-proliferation and Disarmament 2008–09. *Address:* Sri Lankan High Commission, 27 Kautilya Marg, Chanakyapuri, New Delhi 110 021, India (office). *Telephone:* (11) 23010201 (office). *Fax:* (11) 23793604 (office). *E-mail:* prasad.kariyawasam@formin.gov.lk (office); lankacomnd@mea.gov.lk (office); lankacomnd@gmail.com (office). *Website:* www.slhcindia.org (office).

KARKARIA, Bachi J.; Indian editor; *Consulting Editor, The Times of India;* m.; two s.; ed Loreto Coll., Calcutta, Calcutta Univ.; began career at Illustrated Weekly of India 1969; Asst Ed. The Statesman, Calcutta (first woman) 1980; Group Editorial Dir, Mid Day Multimedia Ltd 2000–02; Ed. Sunday Times of India 1998–2000, Resident Ed. The Times of India 2003, in charge of Delhi section, then Nat. Metro Ed., now Consulting Ed., columnist and blogger; mem. Int. Women's Media Foundation; mem. Bd World Editors Forum 2002–, India AIDS Initiative of Bill and Melinda Gates Foundation; Jefferson Fellow, East West Center, Honolulu; mem. Professional Women's Advisory Bd, American Biographical Inst.; Media India Award (for human interest stories) 1992, Mary Morgan-Hewitt Award for Lifetime Achievement 1994. *Publications include:* Dare to Dream: The Life of M.S. Oberoi 2007, To a Grand Design. *Address:* The Times of India, 7 Bahadur Shah Zafar Marg, New Delhi 110 002, India (office). *Telephone:* (11) 23492049 (office). *Fax:* (11) 23351606 (office). *E-mail:* bachi.karkaria@timesgroup.com (office). *Website:* blogs.timesofindia.indiatimes.com/erratica (office).

KARKI, Bharat Bahadur, BA, MA, LLB, LLM, PhD; Nepalese professor of business law and government official; *Ad-Hoc Judge of Supreme Court;* b. 18 Aug. 1950, Khotang Dist; ed Univ. of Delhi, India; has been teaching law since late 1970s; mem. Legal Adviser's Forum, Kathmandu; fmr Head of Dept of Law and Dean of Law Faculty, Tribhuvan Univ., Kathmandu; Attorney Gen. 2009–10 (resgnd); Ad-Hoc Judge of Supreme Court 2010–. *Address:* Supreme Court, Ramashah Path, Kathmandu, Nepal (office). *E-mail:* info@supremecourt.gov.np (office). *Website:* www.supremecourt.gov.np (office).

KARLE, Isabella Helen, PhD; American physicist and academic; *Physicist, Naval Research Laboratory;* b. 2 Dec. 1921, Detroit, Mich.; d. of Zygmunt A. Lugoski and Elizabeth Lugoski (née Graczyk); m. Jerome Karle 1942; three d.; ed Univ. of Michigan; Assoc. Chemist, Univ. of Chicago 1944; Instructor in Chem., Univ. of Mich. 1944–46; physicist, Naval Research Lab., Washington, DC 1946–; mem. NAS, American Crystallographic Asscn, ACS, American Physical Soc., American Biophysical Soc., American Peptide Soc., American Philosophical Soc.; Hon. DSc (Michigan) 1976, (Wayne State) 1979, (Maryland) 1986, (Athens) 1997, (Pennsylvania) 1999, (Harvard) 2001, (Jagiellonian Univ., Kraków) 2002; Hon. DHumLitt (Georgetown) 1984; Women in Science and Eng Lifetime Achievement Award 1986, Swedish Royal Acad. of Sciences Gregori Aminoff Prize 1988, Bijvoet Medal, Univ. of Utrecht, Netherlands 1990, Franklin Inst. Bower Award in Science 1993, NAS Chemical Sciences Award 1995, Nat. Medal of Science, Pres.'s Award, USA 1995, Merrifield Award, American Peptide Soc. 2007, and other awards and honours. *Publications:* over 350 scientific articles, chapters and reviews. *Leisure interests:* swimming, ice skating, needlework. *Address:* 6304 Lakeview Drive, Falls Church, VA 22041, USA (home).

KARLIC, HE Cardinal Estanislao Esteban, DTheol; Argentine ecclesiastic (retd); b. 7 Feb. 1926, Oliva; ed Pontifical Gregorian Univ.; ordained priest 1954; Auxiliary Bishop of Córdoba and Titular Bishop of Castrum 1977–83; Coadjutor Archbishop of Paraná 1983–86; Archbishop of Paraná 1986–2003 (retd), Archbishop Emer. 2003–; cr. Cardinal 2007, Cardinal-Priest of Beata Maria Vergine Addolorata a piazza Buenos Aires 2007–; fmr Pres. Exec. Comm. of Episcopal Conf. of Argentina; fmr mem. Special Council for America of Gen. Secr. of Synod of Bishops, served as Co-Sec.; mem. comm. appointed by Pope John Paul II to write the Catechism of the Roman Catholic Church 1986–92. *Address:* c/o Archdiocese of Paraná, Monte Caseros 77, 3100 Paraná [Entre Rios], Argentina.

KARLOV, Nikolai Vasilyevich; Russian physicist; *Chief Research Fellow, Institute of General Physics, Russian Academy of Sciences;* b. 15 Oct. 1929, Leningrad; m.; one s. one d.; ed Moscow State Univ.; worker in aviation plant, Moscow 1943–47; Jr, then Sr Researcher, then Head of Sector, Lebedev Physical Insts, USSR Acad. of Sciences 1955–83, Head of Sector, then Head of Div. Inst. of Gen. Physics 1983–87, now Chief Research Fellow; Rector Moscow Inst. of Physics and Tech. 1987–97; USSR People's Deputy 1989–91; Chair. Higher Attestation Cttee 1992–98; Corresp. mem. Russian Acad. of Sciences 1984, Adviser 1999–; mem. American Physical Soc.; Order of Friendship 1995; USSR State Prize 1976. *Publications:* 15 scientific books including Intense Resonant Interactions in Quantum Electronics (with V. M. Akulin) 1992, Lectures on Quantum Electronics 1993, Oscillations, Waves, Structures (with N. A. Kirichenko) 2001, Initial Chapters on Quantum Mechanics (with N. A. Kirichenko) 2004; more than 300 articles in scientific journals. *Leisure interests:* history of Russia, old Russian literature, foreign languages. *Address:* Moscow Institute of Physics and Technology, Institutsky per. 9, 141700 Dolgoprudny, Moscow (office); Acad. Zelinsky str. 3818135, 119334 Moscow, Russia (home). *Telephone:* (495) 408-81-54 (office); (495) 135-13-86 (home). *Fax:* (495) 408-81-54 (office); (495) 135-13-86 (home). *E-mail:* nkarlov@mfti.ru (office). *Website:* www.gpi.ru (office).

KARLSSON, Jan O., BA; Swedish politician, international organization official and fmr civil servant; b. 1 June 1939, Stockholm; m.; two c.; ed Univ. of Stockholm; Admin. Officer, Head of Section, Ministry of Agric. 1962–68; Political Adviser, Cabinet Office 1968–73, Co-ordinating Adviser 1990–91; Sec. to City Commr, Stockholm City Council 1973–77; Deputy Sec. to Presidium, Nordic Council 1977–82; Under-Sec. of State to Minister for Nordic Co-operation 1982–85; Under-Sec. of State, Ministry of Finance 1985–88; Chair. Comm. on Metropolitan Problems 1988–90; Prime Minister's Personal Rep. on Nordic Co-operation in connection with membership of European Environment Agency and EU 1991–92; Negotiator and Adviser, SDP 1992–94; Dir-Gen. Ministry for Foreign Affairs 1994; joined European Court of Auditors 1995, Pres. 1999–2001 (resgnd); Minister for Devt Co-operation, Migration and Asylum Policy 2002–03; Acting Minister for Foreign Affairs and Minister (Devt Co-operation, Migration and Asylum Policy), Ministry of Foreign Affairs 11 Sept.–9 Oct. 2003; Co-Chair. Global Comm. on Int. Migration 2004–05, Chair. Financial Irregularity Panel 2004–; Sr Adviser, Global Utmaning (think tank) 2008–; Special Adviser to EU Commr Siim Kallas, Brussels, 2009–; mem. editorial staff, TIDEN periodical 1974–82, Ed.-in-Chief 1978–82; mem. Bd Nordic Investment Bank 1983–89, Nat. Pharmacy Corpn 1986–91; Chair. Bd Swedish Nat. Housing Finance Corpn 1986–89; Chair. OECD Project Group on Housing, Social Integration and Liveable Environments in Cities 1991–93; fmr mem. Bd Stockholm Philharmonic. *Address:* Office of Vice-President Siim Kallas, European Commission, 200 Rue de la Loi Berlaymont B, 1049 Brussels, Belgium (office). *Telephone:* (2) 299-11-11 (office). *Fax:* (2) 298-84-92 (office). *Website:* ec.europa.eu/commission_2010-2014/kallas/index_en.htm (office).

KARLSTRÖM, Johan, MSc (Eng); Swedish construction industry executive; *President and CEO, Skanska AB;* b. 1957; ed Royal Inst. of Tech., Stockholm, Advanced Man. Program, Harvard Univ., USA; joined Skanska 1983, began career as Regional Man., Skanska Northern Sweden, later Exec. Vice-Pres. Skanska, Nordic region, Exec. Vice-Pres. Skanska USA –2008, Pres. and CEO Skanska AB 2008–; fmr Pres. BPA (now Bravida). *Address:* Skanska AB, Klarabergsviadukten 90, 111 91 Stockholm, Sweden (office). *Telephone:* (8) 753-88-00 (office). *Fax:* (8) 755-12-56 (office). *E-mail:* info@skanska.com (office). *Website:* www.skanska.com (office).

KARMAN, Tawakul; Yemeni journalist, human rights activist and politician; *Leader, Women Journalists Without Chains;* b. 7 Feb. 1979, Mekhlaf, Ta'izz Prov.; d. of Abdel Salam Karman; m. Mohammed al-Nahmi; three c.; ed Univ. of Science and Tech., Sana'a, Sana'a Univ.; Founder and Leader Women Journalists Without Chains (human rights org.) 2005–; sr mem. in leading Islamist opposition party, Al-Islah; jailed several times for her activism during 'Arab Spring' 2011, led a series of protests calling for the departure of Pres. Ali Abdullah Saleh; Nobel Peace Prize (jtly, first Arab woman and second Muslim woman) for "non-violent struggle for the safety of women and for women's rights to full participation in peace-building work" 2011, selected as first place of the Foreign Policy top 100 global thinkers of 2011, ranked by Arabian Business amongst the Power 500: The World's Most Influential Arabs (13th) 2012. *Address:* Women Journalists Without Chains, PO Box, Daeery Street behind Old University Post Office, Sana'a 12702, Yemen (office). *Telephone:* (1) 210543 (office). *Fax:* (1) 210523 (office). *E-mail:* info@womenpress.org (office); withoutchains@gmail.com (office). *Website:* womenpress.org (office).

THE KARMAPA, (Urgyen Trinley Dorje); Tibetan Buddhist leader; b. 1985; Living Buddha of the White Sect, Tibet; Seventeenth Incarnation; enthroned 1992; now living in exile in Dharamsala, India.

KARMAZIN, Melvin (Mel) Alan, BS; American media executive; *President and CEO, Sirius Satellite Radio Inc.;* b. 24 Aug. 1943, New York; m. Sharon Karmazin (divorced 1994); one s. one d.; ed Pace Univ.; stage man. CBS Radio 1960–70, Chair., CEO CBS Station Group 1996–, now Pres., COO CBS Corpn; Vice-Pres., Gen. Man. Metromedia Inc. 1970–81; Pres. Infinity Broadcasting Corpn 1981–96, CEO 1988–96; Pres., COO Viacom Inc. 2000–04 (resgnd); Pres. and CEO Sirius Satellite Radio Inc. 2004–; fmr mem. Bd of Dirs Westwood One, Blockbuster, New York Stock Exchange; Vice-Chair. Bd of Trustees, Museum of TV and Radio; numerous awards including Nat. Assen of Broadcasters Nat. Radio Award and IRTS Gold Medal Award; inducted into Broadcasting Hall of Fame. *Address:* Sirius Satellite Radio Inc., 1221 Avenue of the Americas, 36th Floor, New York, NY 10020, USA (office). *Telephone:* (212) 584-5100 (office). *Fax:* (212) 584-5200 (office). *Website:* www.siriusradio.com (office).

KARMI, Ram, RIBA; Israeli architect; b. 13 Sept. 1931, Jerusalem; m. Rivka Edery; three s. three d.; ed Architectural Assen School, London, UK; joined father's architectural office in partnership Karmi-Meltzer-Karmi 1956–67; est. (with sister) office of Karmi Assoc. Architects 1967–92, est. br. offices Tel-Aviv, New York 1972; Chief Architect, Ministry of Housing 1975–79; Pnr, Karmi Architects & Co., Tel-Aviv 1979–92; various teaching posts at Faculty of Architecture and Town Planning, Technion 1964, Assoc. Prof. 1987–94; Visiting Prof., Princeton Univ. 1969, MIT 1972, 1983, Columbia Univ. 1969–70; projects include univ. bldgs (Faculty of Humanities, Hebrew Univ., Mt Scopus), schools, hotels (Holyland Compound, Jerusalem), pvt. homes, large housing projects (Gilo, Jerusalem), public bldgs (Museum of Children of the Holocaust, Supreme Court, Jerusalem, Habima Theater, renovation Tel-Aviv), Ben Gurion Airport (main terminal, landside and industrial complexes) 2000 and industrial complexes; won competition for Prime Minister's Office Bldg 1996; mem. Israel Inst. of Architects and Engineers, Architectural Assen, London; Rokach Prize for El Al Bldg, Tel-Aviv 1965, Rechter Prize for Negev Center–Combined Commercial Center and Housing, Beer Sheba 1967, Reinholds Prize for Commercial Center and Housing, Beer Sheba 1969, Rokach Prize for Residential Bldgs, Be'eri Street, Tel-Aviv 1970, Assen of Architects and Engineers in Israel Prize for Supreme Court Bldg (with Ada Karmi-Melamede) 1998, Rechter Prize for Yad Layeled Museum, Kibbutz Lohamei Hagetaot 1999, Israel Prize for Architecture 2002. *Publications:* numerous articles in professional journals. *Address:* c/o Ada Karmi-Melamede Architects, 17 Kaplan Street, Tel-Aviv 64734 (office); 2 Yehoshua Ben-Noon Street, Herzeliya Pituah, Israel (home). *Telephone:* (3) 6912112 (office); (9) 9586767 (home). *Fax:* (3) 6913508 (office). *E-mail:* ada@akmp.co.il (office). *Website:* adakarmimelamede.com (office).

KARMOKOV, Khachim Mukhamedovich, DEcon; Russian economist and politician; b. 2 May 1941, Zayukovo, Kabardin-Balkar Autonomous Repub.; m.; one d.; ed Kabardin-Balkar State Univ., Moscow Inst. for Eng and Econs; Eng and managerial posts in construction industry 1963–67, 1978–81; teacher, docent Kabardin-Balkar State Univ. 1967–78; Financial Dir Trust Kabbalpromstroi 1981–90; Deputy Chair. Council of Ministers, Kabardin-Balkar Repub. 1990–91; Chair. Supreme Soviet Kabardin-Balkar Repub. 1991–93; Chair. Accounts Chamber of Russian Fed. 1994; mem. State Duma Russian Fed. 1993–95; Rep. of Kabardino-Balkan Repub. in Council of Fed. 2001–; mem. Russian Acad. of Natural Sciences, Int. Acad. of Informatization. *Leisure interest:* hunting.

KARMOUL, Akram Jamil, PhD; Jordanian business executive and consultant; *Chairman and Managing Director, Rawda Company for Info, Tech and E-Commerce;* b. 13 Aug. 1939, W Bank; m. Huda Abu-Errub 1964; two s. two d.; ed Assiut Univ., Univ. of Strathclyde and Imperial Coll., London, UK; geologist, geophysicist and mining engineer 1961–72; Dir Industry, later Dir Science and Tech. Ministry of Planning 1972–80; Dir Gen. of Industry Ministry of Industry and Trade 1980–87; Dir, Man. Industrial, Commercial and Agric. Co. 1987; Exec. Dir and Asst Man. Dalla-Al-Baraka Saudi Group, Jeddah 1988–89; Dir of Industry Dept UN-ECWA Comm. for W Asia 1989–93; Gen. Man. United Textile Group 1995; Assoc. Consultant, Arab Consulting Centre and Assignments UNDP 1996; currently Chair. and Man. Dir Rawda Co. for Info, Tech and E-Ccommerce; mem. Arab Knowledge Man. Soc.; Science Award for Outstanding Persons. *Publications:* numerous works on mineral wealth and industrial tech. of Jordan, public enterprises. *Leisure interests:* reading, swimming. *Address:* Rawda Company for Info, Tech and E-Commerce, PO Box 960555, Amman, Jordan (office). *Telephone:* (6) 5660155 (office). *Fax:* (6) 5660366 (office). *E-mail:* info@e-ritt.com (office).

KARNAD, Girish, MA; Indian playwright, filmmaker and actor; b. 19 May 1938, Matheran; s. of Raghunath Karnad and Krishnabai Karnad; m. Saraswathy Ganapathy 1980; one s. one d.; ed Karnatak Coll., Dharwad, Magdalene Coll., Univ. of Oxford; Rhodes Scholar, Oxford 1960–63; Pres. Oxford Union Soc. 1963; Asst Man. Oxford Univ. Press, Madras 1963–69, Man. 1969–70; Homi Bhabha Fellow 1970–72; Dir Film & TV Inst. of India, Pune 1974–75; Pres. Karnataka Nataka Acad. 1976–78; Visiting Prof. and Fulbright Scholar-in-Residence, Univ. of Chicago 1987–88; Indian Co-Chair., Media Cttee, Indo-US Subcomm. 1984–93; Chair. Sangeet Natak Akademi (Nat. Acad. of Performing Arts) 1988–93; Dir The Nehru Centre, London 2000; World Theatre Amb., Int. Theatre Inst. of UNESCO 2008; Fellow, Sangeet Natak Acad. 1994; Hon. DLitt (Univ. of Karnataka) 1994, (Univ. of Vidyasagar, Midnapur) 2010, (Univ. of Ravenshaw, Bhubaneshwar) 2011; Dr hc (Univ. of Southern Calif.) 2011; several awards for film work; Govt of Mysore Rajyotsava Award 1970, Sangeet Natak Acad. (Nat. Acad. of Performing Arts) Award 1972, Padma Shri 1974, Karnataka Nataka Acad. Award 1984, Nandikar, Calcutta Award 1989, Padma Bhushan 1992, Booksellers and Publishers Asscn of South India Award 1992, Bharatiya Jnanpith Award 1999, Sahitya Acad. Award 1994, Gubbi Veeranna Award 1996–97. *Plays include:* Yayati (Mysore State Award 1962) 1961, Tughlaq 1964, Hayavadana (Kamaladevi Award Bharatiya Natya Sangh 1972) 1971, Anjumallige 1976, Nagamandala 1988, Taledanda (Writer of the Year Award 1990, B.H. Sridhar Award 1992, Karnataka Sahitya Acad. Award 1992, Sahitya Acad. Award 1994) 1990, Agni Mattu Male 1995, Tipu Sultan Kanda Kanasu 2000, Bali 2002, Broken Images 2005, Flowers 2008, Wedding Album 2009. *Films include:* Samskara (President's Gold Medal 1970) 1970, Vamsha Vriksha (Nat. Award 1972, Mysore State Award 1972) 1971, Kaadu (President's Silver Medal 1974) 1973, Tabbaliyu Neenade Magane 1977, Swami (Best Bengal Film Journalists' Asscn Award 1978) 1977, Ondanondu Kaaladalli (Nat. Award 1978) 1978, Utsav 1984, Cheluvi 1992, Kanooru Heggadithi 1999, Iqbal (as actor) 2005, Dor (as actor) 2006, 8 x 10 Tasveer (as actor) 2009, Life Goes On (as actor) 2009. *Radio:* Ma Nishada 1986, The Dreams of Tipu Sultan 1997. *Television:* Antaraal 1996, Swarajnama 1997, Kanooru Ki Thakurani 1999, wrote and presented The Bhagavad Gita for BBC Two 2002. *Address:* 697, 15th Cross, JP Nagar Phase II, Bangalore 560 078, India (home). *Telephone:* (80) 26590463 (home). *Fax:* (80) 26590019 (home). *E-mail:* karnad .girish@gmail.com (home).

KARNIK, Kiran, BSc, MBA; Indian business executive; b. March 1947; ed Bombay Univ., Indian Inst. of Man.; various positions at Indian Space Research Org. including Dir Devt and Educational Communication Unit 1983–91; Dir Consortium for Educational Communication 1991–95; worked briefly at UN, New York and Vienna; Man. Dir Discovery Networks India 1995–2001; Pres. Nat. Asscn of Software and Service Cos (NASSCOM) 2001–07, currently Trustee; fmr Chair. Satyam Computer Services; mem. Bd of Dirs ExlService Holdings Inc.; mem. numerous govt cttees including Prasar Bharati Review Cttee; Frank Malina Medal for Space Education, Int. Astronautical Fed. 1998. *Address:* R/O Q-2A, Hauz Khas Enclave, New Delhi 110 016, India (home).

KARP, Richard Manning, AB, SM, PhD; American computer scientist and academic; *Senior Research Scientist, International Computer Science Institute;* b. 3 Jan. 1935, Boston, Mass; s. of Abraham Karp and Rose Karp; ed Harvard Univ.; Researcher, IBM Thomas J. Watson Research Center 1959–68; Prof. of Computer Science, Math. and Operations Research, Univ. of California, Berkeley 1968–94, 1999–; Research Scientist, Int. Computer Science Inst. 1988–95, Sr Research Scientist 1999–; Prof., Univ. of Washington 1995–99; mem. NAS, Nat. Acad. of Eng, American Philosophical Soc., French Acad. of Sciences; Fellow, American Acad. of Arts and Sciences, AAAS, Asscn for Computing Machinery, Inst. for Operations Research and Man. Science; eight hon. degrees; numerous awards including Turing Award 1985, Nat. Medal of Science 1996, Israel Inst. of Tech. Harvey Prize 1998, Benjamin Franklin Medal in Computer and Cognitive Science 2004, Kyoto Prize, Inamori Foundation (co-recipient) 2008. *Achievements include:* co-developer with Jack Edmonds of Edmonds-Karp algorithm 1971. *Address:* 621 Soda Hall, Electrical Engineer and Computer Sciences, College of Engineer, University of California, Berkeley, CA 94720 (office); International Computer Science Institute, 1947 Center Street, Suite 600, Berkeley, CA 94704, USA (office). *Telephone:* (510) 642-5799 (office); (510) 666-2900 (office). *Fax:* (510) 666-2956 (office). *E-mail:* karp@cs.berkeley.edu; karp@icsi.berkeley.edu (office). *Website:* www.eecs.berkeley.edu/Faculty/Homepages/karp.html (office).

KARPLUS, Martin, PhD; American/Austrian chemist and academic; *Theodore William Richards Professor Emeritus of Chemistry, Harvard University;* b. 15 March 1930, Vienna, Austria; s. of Hans Karplus and Isabella Karplus; m. Marci Hazard 1981; one s. two d.; ed Harvard Univ. and California Inst. of Tech.; NSF Postdoctoral Fellow, Math. Inst., Oxford, UK; Asst Prof., Dept of Chem., Univ. of Illinois 1955–59, Assoc. Prof. 1960; Prof. of Chem., Columbia Univ. 1960–66; Prof. of Chem., Harvard Univ. 1966–, Theodore William Richards Prof. of Chem. 1979–99, Theodore William Richards Research Prof. 1999–2007, Prof. Emer. 2007–; Visiting Prof., Univ. of Paris 1972–73, 1980–81 (Prof. 1974–75), Collège de France 1980–81, 1987–88; Professeur Associé, Univ. Louis Pasteur 1992, 1994–95; Prof. Conventionné, Univ. de Strasbourg 1995–; Eastman Prof., Univ. of Oxford 1999–2000; mem. European Acad. of Arts, Sciences and Humanities, NAS, American Acad. of Arts and Sciences, Int. Acad. of Quantum Molecular Science; Foreign mem. Netherlands Acad. of Arts and Science, Royal Soc. (UK); Dr hc (Sherbrooke) 1998, Ehrendoktorat (Zürich) 2006; Joseph O. Hirschfelder Prize in Theoretical Chem., Univ. of Wisconsin 1995, ACS Harrison Howe Award, Rochester Section 1967, Award for Outstanding Contrib. to Quantum Biology, Int. Soc. of Quantum Biology 1979, Distinguished Alumni Award, California Inst. of Tech. 1986, Irving Langmuir Award, American Physical Soc. 1987, Nat. Lecturer, Biophysical Soc. 1991, ACS Theoretical Chem. Award (first recipient) 1993, Anfinsen Award, Protein Soc. 2001, Pauling Award, Northwest Section ACS 2004, David Weaver Lecturer in Biophysics ad Computational Biology (first recipient) 2007, Lifetime Achievement Award in Theoretical Biophysics, Int. Asscn of Schools and Insts of Admin 2008, G.N. Ramachandran Award Lecturer, Indian Biophysical Soc. 2009, Russell Varian Prize 2010, Antonio Feltrinelli Int. Prize for Chem., Accad. Nazionale dei Lincei 2011, Nobel Prize in Chem. (shared with Michael Levitt and Arieh Warshel) 2013. *Publications include:* Atoms and Molecules (with R. N. Porter) 1970, A Theoretical Perspective of Dynamics, Structure and Thermodynamics (with C. L. Brooks III and B. M. Pettitt) 1988, A Guide to Biomolecular Simulations (with O. M. Becker) 2006, Images from the 50's 2011; more than 800 articles in the field of theoretical chem. and biophysics.

Address: Department of Chemistry and Chemical Biology, Harvard University, 12 Oxford Street, Cambridge, MA 02138, USA (office); Laboratoire de Chimie Biophysique, ISIS, Université de Strasbourg, 67000 Strasbourg, France (office). *Telephone:* (617) 495-4076 (office). *Fax:* (617) 496-3204 (office). *Website:* www.chem .harvard.edu/research/faculty/martin_karplus.php (office).

KARPOV, Anatolii Yevgenievich, DEcon; Russian chess player; b. 23 May 1951, Zlatoust; s. of Yevgeniy Stepanovich Karpov and Nina Karpov; m. 1st Irina Karpov; one s.; m. 2nd Natalia Bulanova; one d.; ed Leningrad Univ.; mem. CPSU 1980–91; USSR Candidate Master 1962, Master 1966; European Jr Champion 1967, 1968, World Jr Champion 1969; Int. Master 1969, Int. Grandmaster 1970; USSR Champion 1976, 1983, 1988; world champion 1975–85; became world champion when the holder Bobby Fischer refused to defend the title and he retained his title against Viktor Korchnoi in 1978 and in 1981; defended against Garry Kasparov (q.v.) in Moscow Sept. 1984; the match later adjourned due to the illness of both players; lost to the same player in 1985; unsuccessfully challenged Kasparov 1986, 1987, 1990; won World Championship title under FIDE after split in chess orgs 1993, 1996, 1998; has won more tournaments than any other player (over 160); first player to become a millionaire from playing chess; People's Deputy of USSR 1989–91; Pres. Soviet Peace Fund (now Int. Asscn of Peace Funds) 1982–; Pres. Chernobyl-Aid org. 1989–; UNICEF Amb. for Russia and E Europe 1998–; Chair. Council of Dirs Fed. Industrial Bank, Moscow; mem. Soviet (now Russian) UNESCO Affairs Comm.; mem. Bd Int. Chess Fed.; Ed.-in-Chief Chess Review 64 (magazine) 1980–91; Winner of Oscar Chess Prize 1973–77, 1979–81, 1984, 1994, Fontany di Roma Prize for humanitarian achievements 1996; Hon. Texan, Hon. Citizen of Tula, Zlatoust, Orsk and other cities in Russia, Belarus and Ukraine. *Publications:* Chess is My Life 1980, Karpov Teaches Chess 1987, Karpov on Karpov 1991, How to Play Chess and 47 other books. *Leisure interest:* philately. *Address:* International Peace Fund, Prechistenka 10, Moscow, Russia. *Telephone:* (495) 202-41-71; (495) 202-42-36.

KARRUBI, Mahdi; Iranian cleric and politician; *Secretary-General, Hezb-e Etemad-e Melli (National Confidence Party);* b. 1937, Aligoudarz, Lorestan; mem. Majles (Parl.) and Speaker 1989–92, 2000–04; unsuccessful cand. for Pres. 2005; Founder and Sec.-Gen. Hezb-e Etemad-e Melli (Nat. Confidence Party—NCP) 2005–; mem. Asscn of Militant Clerics –2005 (fmr Sec.-Gen.), Expediency Discernment Council of the System –2005 (resgnd); f. Etemad-e Melli (daily newspaper) 2006. *Address:* Hezb-e Etemad-e Melli (National Confidence Party—NCP), Tehran, Iran (office). *Telephone:* (21) 88373306 (office). *E-mail:* Ravabet_Omomi@Etemademelli.ir (office). *Website:* www.etemademelli.ir (office).

KARSENTI, René, MS, MBA, PhD; French international finance official; *Executive President, International Capital Market Association;* b. 27 Jan. 1950, Tlemcen, Algeria; s. of Leon Karsenti and Mireille Benhaim; m. Hélène Dayan 1978; two d.; ed ESCIL, Lyons; Paris Business School and Sorbonne, Paris; researcher in finance and econs, Univ. of Calif. Berkeley 1973; investment analyst/ portfolio man. Caisse des Dépôts, Paris 1975–79; Finance Officer, World Bank (IBRD), Washington, DC 1979–83, Financial Adviser 1983–85, Div. Chief 1985–87, Sr Man. Finance Dept, Treasury 1987–89; Treas., Dir Financial Policy Dept, Int. Finance Corp, World Bank Group, Washington, DC 1989–91; Treas. EBRD 1991–95; Dir-Gen. Finance, European Investment Bank 1995–2006; Exec. Pres. and mem. Bd of Dirs International Capital Market Asscn, Zürich and London 2006–; Chair. Euro Debt Market Asscn 2004–; mem. Man. Selection Cttee, French Pensions Reserve Fund (FRR) and Strategic Cttee, Agence France Trésor (French Ministry of Finance); mem. Investment Advisory Cttee, FAO, Rome; mem. Bd of Dirs International Finance Facility for Immunisation (IFFIm), Chair. 2012–; Chevalier Légion d'honneur. *Publications:* Research in Pharmaceutical Industry 1977; various financial lectures and articles on int. finance, capital markets and European Monetary Union. *Leisure interests:* swimming, antiques, opera. *Address:* International Capital Market Association, Talacker 29, 8001 Zurich, Switzerland (office). *Telephone:* 443634222 (office). *Fax:* 443637772 (office). *E-mail:* rene .karsenti@icmagroup.org (office). *Website:* www.icmagroup.org (office).

KARTAREDJASA, Butet; Indonesian actor and artist; b. 1961, Yogyakarta; s. of Bagong Kussudiardja; m.; three c.; ed Sekolah Menengah Seni Rupa (Sr High School of Fine Art), Yogyakarta, Institut Seni Indonesia (Yogyakarta Inst. of the Arts); began acting with Theatre of Kita-kita 1978; f. theatre group Teater Gandrik 1985; has appeared in several soap operas including Oom Pasikom, Badut Pasti Berlalu; awards include Tokoh Seni from PWI Yogya, art awards from Pemda Daerah Istimewa Yogyakarta. *Films:* Petualangan Sherina (Sherina's Adventure) 1999, Banyu Biru (Blue Water) 2004, Koper 2006, Maskot (Mascot) 2006, Anak-Anak Borobudur 2007, Drupadi 2008, Capres (Calo Presiden) 2009. *Theatre includes:* Benggol Maling 1998, Raja Rimba Jadi Pawang 1999, Iblis Nganggur 1999, Guru Ngambeg 2000, Mayat Terhormat 2003, Matinya Toekang Kritik 2006, Sarimin 2007, Presiden Guyonan 2008. *Publications:* Presiden Guyonan (Joke President) 2008. *Leisure interest:* collecting art. *Address:* c/o Teater Gandrik, Concert Hall Taman Budaya, Yogyakarta Ndalem Tejokusuman, Jl. KH Wahid Hasyim, Yogyakarta, Indonesia (office).

KARTASHKIN, Vladimir Alekseevich, DJur; Russian politician; *Editor-in-Chief, International Lawyer Magazine;* b. 4 March 1934; m. Elena Kovanova 1991; one s. one d.; ed Moscow State Univ.; Chief Scientific Researcher, Inst. of State and Law 1957–63, Chief Researcher, Prof. 1985–; with Div. of Human Rights UN 1969–73; consultant, UN Dir-Gen. on Juridical Problems 1979–85; Chair. Comm. on Human Rights, Russian Presidency 1996–2002; Prof., Int. Inst. of Human Rights, Strasbourg, Cornell Univ., Santa-Clair Univ., Univ. of Peoples' Friendship, Moscow; Ed.-in-Chief International Lawyer Magazine 2003–; mem. UN Human Rights Council Advisory Cttee 2008; Meritorious Lawyer of Russia. *Publications:* over 200 books and articles including Human Rights in International and State Law. *Leisure interests:* tennis, swimming. *Address:* Institute of State and Law, Russian Academy of Sciences, Znemaenka str. 10, 119841, Moscow, Russia (office). *Telephone:* (495) 291-34-90 (office); (495) 242-37-63 (home). *E-mail:* kartashkin@ comtv.ru (office).

KARTHIKEYAN, Kumar Ram Narain; Indian motor racing driver; b. 14 Jan. 1977, Coimbatore; s. of G.R. Karthikeyan; m. Pavarna Karthikeyan; ed Elf-Winfield School, France; won British Formula Ford Winter Series 1994, Formula Asia Championship 1996, Formula 3 Madras Grand Prix 1999, British Formula Three Championship 1998, 2000, Korea Super Prix 2000, Superfund Word Series 2003, World Series by Nissan 2004; raced in Telefonica World Series 2002, Australian Grand Prix 2005, US Grand Prix 2005, Japanese Grand Prix 2005, Chinese Grand Prix 2005, A1GP World Championship 2009, 24 Hours of Le Mans and Le Mans Series, Kolles Audi R10 TDI 2009, Nat. Asscn for Stock Car Auto Racing Inc. (NASCAR) World Truck Series 2010, Superleague Formula Series Dutch Squad PSV Eindhoven 2010; Williams F1 test driver 2006, 2007; est. NK Racing Acad.; Padma Shri Award 2010. *Telephone:* 9244225266 (mobile). *Fax:* (42) 22574868 (office). *E-mail:* yohann@narainracing.com (office). *Website:* www .narainracing.com (office).

KARTI, Ali Ahmed; Sudanese politician; *Minister of Foreign Affairs;* fmr head of Popular Defence Force (paramilitary force); fmr Deputy Minister of Foreign Affairs, Minister of Foreign Affairs 2010–; mem. Nat. Congress Party. *Address:* Ministry of Foreign Affairs, POB 873, Khartoum, Sudan (office). *Telephone:* (183) 773101 (office). *Fax:* (183) 772941 (office). *E-mail:* ministry@mfa.gov.sd (office). *Website:* www.sudanmfa.com (office).

KARTOMI, Margaret Joy, AM, BA, BMus, DrPhil, FAHA; Australian musicologist and professor of music; *Professor of Music, School of Music, Monash University;* b. 24 Nov. 1940, Adelaide; d. of George Hutchesson and Edna Hutchesson; m. Hidris Kartomi 1961; one d.; ed Univ. of Adelaide, Humboldt Univ.; Lecturer, Music Dept, Monash Univ. 1969–70, Sr Lecturer 1971–73, Reader 1974–88, Prof. of Music 1989–, Head of Music School 1989–2001, currently Coordinator of Research and Ethnomusicology; Dir Inst. of Contemporary Asian Studies, Monash Univ. 1989–91; Dir Monash-ANZ Centre for International Briefing 1988–90, Monash Asia Inst. 1988–90; Dir-at-large International Musicology Soc. 1993–; mem. Nat. Cttee Musicological Soc. of Australia (Nat. Pres. 1978–92), American Musicological Soc., International Council for Traditional Music, Council Soc. for Ethnomusicology; Visiting Prof., Univ. of California, Berkeley 1986–87; Dir Symposium of International Musicological Soc., Melbourne 1988, 2004; Program Chair. and Chair. E. Wachsmann Prize Cttee 2005–06; mem. Editorial Bd Journal of Musicological Research, Ethnomusicology Forum, Wacana Seni, Musicology Australia 2008–; conferred with title Ratu Berlian Sangun Anggun (Very Beautiful Queen Jewel) by Gov. and Elders' Council of Sumatran Prov. of Lampung 2011; Alexander Clarke Prize for Pianoforte Performance 1960, Dr Ruby Davy Prize for Musical Composition 1961, Fed. German Record Critics' Prize 1983, 1998, 2007, Australian Centenary Medal 2001, presented with a Festschrift in the Journal of Musicological Research Vol. 24, Nos 3–4 in honour of her 65th birthday 2005. *Publications include:* On Concepts and Classifications of Musical Instruments 1990, The Gamelan Digul and the Prison Camp Musician Who Built It: An Australian Link with the Indonesian Revolution 2003; author or ed. of 12 other books; numerous articles and 300 articles in the New Grove Dictionary of Musical Instruments 1989. *Leisure interests:* tennis, badminton, concerts, theatre. *Address:* School of Music, Monash University, Wellington Road, Clayton, Vic. 3168, Australia (office). *Telephone:* (3) 9905-3238 (office). *Fax:* (3) 9905-3241 (office). *E-mail:* margaret.kartomi@arts.monash.edu.au (office). *Website:* www.arts.monash.edu.au/music/staff/mkartomi.php (office).

KARUME, Amani Abeid; Tanzanian accountant and politician; b. 1 Nov. 1948, Zanzibar; s. of the late Abeid Amani Karume; m. Shadya Amani Karume; six c.; ed Lumumba Coll. Zanzibar; accountant, Zanzibar Treasury 1969–70, Chief Accountant 1970–71, Prin. Sec., Ministery of Finance 1971–74, Prin. Sec., Ministry of Planning 1974–78, Prin. Sec., Ministry of Communications and Transport 1978–80, Zanzibar; Pvt. Business Consultant Rep., GEC. of UK, Zanzibar 1980–90; mem. House of Reps 1990–2000, served as Minister of Trade and Industries and Minister of Communications and Transport; Pres. and Chair. Supreme Revolutionary Council of Zanzibar 2000–10, also Minister of Finance and Econ. Planning; mem. Chama Cha Mapunduzi (Revolutionary Party of Tanzania); mem. Bd of Dirs East African Harbours Corpn –1973. *Address:* c/o Office of the President, State House, PO Box 9120, Zanzibar, Tanzania (office).

KARUNANIDHI, Muthuvel 'Kalaignar'; Indian playwright and politician; *President, Dravida Munnetra Kazhagam;* b. (Dakshinamurthy Karunanidhi), 3 June 1924, Thirukkuvalai, Tamil Nadu; s. of Muthuvel Karunanidhi and Anjugam Ammaiyar Karunanidhi; four s. two d.; ed Thiruvarur Bd High School; journalist and stage and screen playwright in Tamil, acting in his own plays staged to collect party funds; has written over 35 films-plays, including screen version of Tamil classic Silappadhikaram, stage plays and short stories; started first student wing of Dravidian movt called Tamilnadu Tamil Manavar Mandram; Founder-mem. Dravida Munnetra Kazhagam Legis. Party (DMK) 1949, Treas. 1961, Deputy Leader 1962–67, Pres. 1969–; Founder-mem. Tamil Nadu Legis. Ass. 1957–; led Kallakkudi Agitation and was imprisoned for six months; State Minister of Public Works 1967–69; Chief Minister of Tamil Nadu (Madras) 1969–76 (presidential rule imposed), 1989–90, 1996–2001, 2006–11; arrested on corruption charges 2001, then released; fmr Ed.-in-Charge Kudiarasu; Thamizha Vell (Patron of Tamil), Asscn of Research Scholars in Tamil 1971; Ed. DMK Murasoli (Tamil daily organ), Kudiyarasu; Founder Mutharam (journal), State Govt News Reel, Arau Studio, Tamil Arasu (govt journal); Hon. DLitt (Annamalai Univ., Tamil Nadu) 1971, (Madurai Kamaraj Univ.) 2006; Friend of the Muslim Community (Yaaran-E-Millath), Tamil Nadu Muslim Makkal Katchi 2007. *Plays:* writer: Manimagudam, Ore Ratham, Palaniappan, Thooku Medai, Kagithapoo, Naane Arivali, Vellikizhamai, Udhayasooriyan, Silapathikaram. *Publications:* Thenpandi Singham (Raja Rajan Award) and more than 100 books of prose and poetry; also screenplays. *Leisure interests:* reading, writing, discussion. *Address:* Dravida Munnetra Kazhagam, Anna Arivalayam, Teynampet, Chennai 600 018 (office); New No. 15, Old No. 18, 4th Street, Gopalapuram, Chennai 600 086, India (home). *Telephone:* (44) 28115225 (home).

KARVE, Priyadarshini, MSc, PhD; Indian scientist and business executive; *Founder-Director, Samuchit Enviro Tech Pvt. Ltd;* b. 3 Dec. 1971; d. of Anand Karve; ed Univ. of Pune; Prin. Investigator, Dept of Science and Tech., Govt of India 1997–99; Lecturer, Sinhgad Coll. of Eng 1999–2001, Smt. Kashibai Navale Coll. of Eng 2001–; Sec., Organising Cttee Int. Conf. on Biomass-based Fuels and Cooking Systems, Pune 2000; Consultant, Sunind Systems Pvt. Ltd; Resource Person, Second Planning and Tech. Advisory Meeting, Asia Regional Cookstove Program, Nepal 2002; Founder-Dir Samuchit Enviro Tech Pvt. Ltd; co-ordinated project 'Commercialisation of Improved Biomass Fuels and Cooking Devices in

India–Pilot Project' funded by Household Energy and Health Programme of Shell Foundation in state of Maharashtra with help of 10 local NGOs 2003–05, scaled-up project 2006–; mem. Third World Org. of Women in Science 1998–, Indian Asscn of Physics Teachers 2001–, Engineers for Tech. and Humanitarian Opportunities of Service 2004–, Indian Soc. for Tech. Educ.; Fellow, World Tech. Network 2005–; Hon. mem. editorial team Shaikshanik Sandarbh 1999–; Hon. consultant Appropriate Rural Tech. Inst. Pune 1999–2002; Prof. Yashwantrao Kelkar Youth Award 2002, World Tech. Award in Environment, The World Tech. Network 2005. *Achievements include:* developed technique for converting agro-waste into char briquettes using environment-friendly process and scaled it up for economically feasible rural tech.; also involved in various R&D activities to develop cleaner wood-burning stoves and other energy appliances for rural households. *Publication:* Oorjechya Shodhat (autobiography). *Address:* Appropriate Rural Technology Institute, c/o Samuchit Enviro Tech Pvt. Ltd, Flat No. 6, Ekta Park Co-op Housing Society, Behind Nirmitee Showroom, Law College Road, Pune 411004 (office); 6, Koyna Apartments, S.No.133, Kothrud, Pune 411 038, India (home). *Telephone:* (20) 25460138 (office); 9822558743. *Fax:* (20) 25460138 (office). *E-mail:* pkarve@arti-india.org (office); priyadarshini.karve@gmail.com. *Website:* www.arti-india.org (office).

KARVINEN, Jouko, MSc (Eng); Finnish business executive; *CEO, Stora Enso Oyj;* b. 31 Aug. 1957, Helsinki; m.; two c.; ed Tampere Univ. of Tech.; various positions in Traction Div., Stromberg OY 1982–87, Man. Advanced Devt Allen-Bradley Stromberg Inc., Wis., USA 1987–88; Profit Centre Man. LV AC Drives 1988–90; Vice-Pres. Power Electronics Div., ABB Drives OY 1990–93, Vice-Pres. Business Unit Drives Products & Systems, Zürich 1993–98, Sr Vice-Pres. Business Area Automation Power Products 1998–2000, Exec. Vice-Pres. ABB Group Ltd 2000–02, also Head of Automation Tech. Products Div. and mem. Group Exec. Cttee 2000–02; CEO Medical Systems Div., Royal Philips Electronics, Boston, USA 2002–06, also Sr Vice-Pres. and mem. Group Man. Cttee 2002–06, CEO Philips Medical Systems Div., Amsterdam 2006, also Exec. Vice-Pres. and mem. Bd of Man. 2006; mem. Bd Dirs and CEO Stora Enso Oyj 2007–. *Address:* Stora Enso Oyj, Kanavaranta 1, PO Box 309, 00101 Helsinki, Finland (office). *Telephone:* (20) 46131 (office). *Fax:* (20) 4621471 (office). *E-mail:* info@storaenso.com (office). *Website:* www.storaenso.com (office).

KARZAI, Hamid, MA; Afghan politician and head of state; *President;* b. 24 Dec. 1954, Karz, Qandahar; s. of the late Abdul-Ahad Karzai, Chief of Popolzai tribe, assassinated in Quetta 1999; m. Zeenat Karzai 1999; one s.; ed Habibia High School, Simla Univ., India; Dir of Information, Nat. Liberation Front 1985–86, Deputy Dir, Political Office 1986–89; Dir Foreign Relations Dept, Office of Interim Pres. 1989–91; fmr official rep. of deposed Afghan king, Zahir Shah; Deputy Foreign Minister 1992–96; went into exile 1996–2001; Chief of Popolzai tribe, S Afghanistan 1999–; served as consultant to Union Oil Co. of Calif. (UNOCAL), USA; mem. Del. to Future of Afghanistan Govt Talks, Bonn, Germany Nov. 2001; Chair. Afghan Interim Authority Dec. 2001–June 2002; Pres. of Transitional Authority (elected by Loya Jirga) June 2002–Nov. 2004, elected Pres. of Afghanistan Nov. 2004–; Hon. KCMG 2003; Hon. DLitt (Himachal Univ.) 2003, Hon. DLit (Nebraska Univ.) 2005, Hon. DJur (Georgetown Univ.) 2006; Int. Rescue Cttee Freedom Award 2002, American Bar Assocn Asia Rule of Law Award 2003, Int. Republican Inst. Freedom Award 2003, Philadelphia Liberty Medal 2004, Int. Der Steiger Award 2007. *Address:* Office of the President, Gul Khana Palace, Presidential Palace, Kabul, Afghanistan (office). *E-mail:* president@afghanistangov.org (office). *Website:* www.president.gov.af (office).

KASAI, Yoshiyuki, MEconSc; Japanese transport industry executive; *Chairman, Central Japan Railway Company (JR Central);* ed Faculty of Law, Univ. of Tokyo, Univ. of Wisconsin, USA; joined Japanese Nat. Railways (JNR) 1963, becoming Deputy Dir-Gen. –1987, apptd Pres. and Rep. Dir Central Japan Railway Company (JR Central) (following JNR privatization) 1987, Chair. 2004–; Visiting Prof., Research Center for Advanced Science and Tech., Univ. of Tokyo; Univ. of Wis. Distinguished Alumnus Award 1999. *Publications:* Japanese National Railways: Its Break-up and Privatization 2003. *Address:* Central Japan Railway Company, 1-1-4 Meiki, Nakamura-ku, Nagoya 450-6101, Japan (office). *Telephone:* (5) 2564-2413 (office). *Fax:* (5) 2587-1300 (office). (5) 5255-6780 (office). *Website:* www.jr-central.co.jp (office).

KASAL, Jan; Czech politician; *Vice-Chairman, Poslanecká sněmovna (Chamber of Deputies);* b. 6 Nov. 1951, Nove Město na Moravě; m. Jaroslava Ranecká; three c.; ed Czech Tech. Univ.; ind. research worker in hydraulic systems 1975–90; mem. Czechoslovak People's Party 1986–89; First Vice-Chair. Christian Democratic Union–Czechoslovak People's Party 1992–99, 2001–06, Chair. 1999–2001; mem. Poslanecká sněmovna (Chamber of Deputies) 1990–, Vice-Chair. Poslanecká sněmovna 1990–98, 2002–; Pres. European Acad. for Democracy 1993–. *Leisure interests:* history, literature, music. *Address:* Poslanecká sněmovna (Chamber of Deputies), Parliament Buildings, Sněmovní 4, 118 26 Prague 1, Czech Republic (office). *Telephone:* (2) 57172095 (office). *Fax:* (2) 57173637 (office). *E-mail:* kasal@psp.cz (office). *Website:* www.psp.cz (office).

KASASBEH, Hamad al-, PhD; Jordanian economist and politician; b. 1956, Karak; ed Columbia Univ., USA; Econ. Researcher and Adviser, Cen. Bank of Jordan –1996; Gen. Man. Cities and Villages Devt Bank 1996–99; Sec.-Gen. Accounting Bureau 1999–2003, Sec.-Gen., Ministry of Finance 2003–07, Minister of Finance 2007–11; fmr Lecturer, Univ. of Jordan; Chair. Jordanian Free Zones Corpn; Dir Royal Jordanian Airline. *Publications:* 14 publs in the field of finance. *Address:* c/o Ministry of Finance, POB 85, Amman 11118, Jordan (office).

KASATKINA, Natalya Dmitriyevna; Russian ballet dancer and choreographer; b. 7 June 1934, Moscow; d. of Dmitriy A. Kasatkin and Anna A. Kardashova; m. Vladimir Vasilyov 1956; one s.; ed Bolshoi Theatre Ballet School; with Bolshoi Theatre Ballet Company 1954–76, main roles including Frigia (Spartacus), Fate (Carmen), The Possessed (The Rite of Spring); Choreographer (with V. Vasilyov) of Vanina Vannini 1962, Geologists 1964, The Rite of Spring 1965, Tristan and Isolde 1967, Preludes and Fugues 1968, Our Yard 1970, The Creation of the World 1971, Romeo and Juliet 1972, Prozrienie 1974, Gayane 1977, Mayakovsky (opera) 1981, Adam and Eve (film ballet) 1982, The Magic Cloak 1982, The Mischiefs of Terpsichore 1984, Blue Roses for a Ballerina (film ballet) 1985, Pushkin 1986, The Faces of Love 1987, Petersburg's Twilights 1987, The Fairy's Kiss 1989, Don

Quixote (film ballet) 1990, Sleeping Beauty 2004; Artistic Dir (with V. Vasilyov), Moscow Classical Ballet Theatre 1977–; wrote libretto and produced operas Peter I 1975, Così fan Tutte (with V. Vasilyov) 1978; choreographed (with V. Vasolyov) Spartacus (Khachaturian) 2002; State Prize of USSR 1976, People's Actress of RSFSR 1984. *Television:* Ballet Ballet, Bolshoi Legends. *Leisure interests:* drawing, cooking. *Address:* Moscow Classical Ballet Theatre, 125040, Moscow, Leningradskiy prospect, 25, Russia. *E-mail:* info@classicalballet.ru. *Website:* www.classicalballet.ru.

KASBAR, Michael J.; American business executive; *President and CEO, World Fuel Services Corporation;* ed State Univ. of New York, Plattsburgh; began career in energy industry with KPI (marine fuel brokerage co. in New York); f. Gray Bunkering Services to buy marine fuel and lubricants for a large in-house shipping fleet while providing brokerage services 1983; co-f., with Paul Stebbins, Trans-Tec Services, Inc. (global marine fuel services co.), acquired by World Fuel 1995, Dir and CEO of marine segment, Pres. and COO World Fuel Services Corpn 2002–12, mem. Bd of Dirs, Pres. and CEO 2012–. *Address:* World Fuel Services Corporation, 9800 NW 41st Street, Suite 400, Miami, FL 33178, USA (office). *Telephone:* (305) 428-8000 (office). *E-mail:* info@wfscorp.com (office). *Website:* www.wfscorp.com (office).

KASDAN, Lawrence Edward, BA, MA; American film director, screenwriter and producer; b. 14 Jan. 1949, Miami Beach, Fla; s. of Clarence Norman Kasdan and Sylvia Sarah Kasdan (née Landau); m. Meg Goldman 1971; two s.; ed Univ. of Michigan; copywriter W. B. Doner and Co. (advertising co.), Detroit 1972–75, Doyle, Dane Berbach, LA 1975–77; freelance screenwriter 1977–80; film dir and screenwriter, LA 1980–; mem. Writers Guild, American West, Dirs Guild, American West; Clio awards for Advertising, Writers Guild Award for The Big Chill 1983, Distinguished Screenwriter Award, Austin Film Festival 2001, Laurel Award for Screen Writing Achievement, Writers Guild of America 2006. *Films include:* The Empire Strikes Back (co-writer) 1980, Continental Divide (writer) 1981, Raiders of the Lost Ark (writer) 1981, Body Heat (writer and dir) 1981, Return of the Jedi (co-screenwriter) 1982, The Big Chill (writer, dir and exec. producer) 1983, Silverado (writer, dir and producer) 1985, Cross My Heart (producer) 1987, The Accidental Tourist (screenplay, dir and producer) 1989, Immediate Family (exec. producer) 1989, I Love You to Death (dir) 1989, Grand Canyon (dir and writer, Golden Bear, Berlin Film Festival 1992) 1991, Jumpin' at the Boneyard (exec. producer) 1992, The Bodyguard (writer and producer) 1992, Wyatt Earp (dir, co-producer, writer) 1994, French Kiss (dir) 1995, Home Fries (producer) 1998, Mumford (writer and dir) 1999, Dreamcatcher (screenplay and dir) 2003, Darling Companion 2012. *Address:* c/o CAA, 2000 Avenue of the Stars, Los Angeles, CA 90067, USA.

KASEL, Jean-Jacques, DenD; Luxembourg diplomatist; *Maréchal and Chef de Cabinet at the Court of the Grand Duke of Luxembourg;* b. 17 Jan. 1946, Luxembourg; m. Jacqueline Vandervorst; one s., two d.; ed Inst. d'Etudes Politiques, Paris; joined Foreign Ministry 1973, Embassy in Paris (also Deputy Perm. Rep. to OECD) 1976–79; Pvt. Sec. to Gaston Thorn 1979–81; Dir for Budget and Staff Regulation, Gen. Secr. EC Council 1981–84; Chargé, Special Missions, Perm. Mission of Luxembourg to EC 1984–86; Dir Political and Cultural Affairs, Foreign Ministry 1986–89; Amb. to Greece (resident in Luxembourg) 1989; Perm. Rep. to EU 1991–98, Chair. Perm. Reps Cttee of Council of Ministers of EU 1997–98; Amb. to Belgium 1998; Perm. Rep. to NATO 1998–2003; Maréchal at the Court of Grand Duke of Luxembourg and Chef de Cabinet 2007–; Grand-Croix, Ordre Civil et Militaire d'Adolphe de Nassau, Grand Officier, Ordre de la Couronne de Chêne, Officier, Ordre de Mérite, Grand Croix, Ordre de la Couronne (Belgium), Grand Croix, Ordre de Léopold II (Belgium), Grand Croix, Ordre du Phoenix (Greece), Grand Croix, Ordre de Mérite (Italy), Grand Croix, Ordre de Danebrog (Denmark), Grand Croix, Ordre Infant Henrique (Portugal), Grand Croix, Ordre Nat. (Romania), Grand Officier Mérite (Austria), Grand Officier Mérite (Sweden), Grand Officier Mérite (Norway), Grand Officier Faucon (Iceland), Grand Officier Mérite (Germany), Commdr, Ordre nat. du Mérite, Commdr, Ordre de Mérite (Spain). *Leisure interests:* horseriding, tennis, skiing, cycling, gardening, the press. *Address:* Palais Grand-Ducal, Luxembourg, Luxembourg (office).

KASER, Michael Charles, MA, DLitt; British economist; b. 2 May 1926, London; s. of Joseph Kaser and Mabel Blunden; m. Elizabeth Anne Mary Piggford 1954; four s. one d.; ed King's Coll., Cambridge; with Econs Section Ministry of Works, London 1946–47; HM Foreign Service 1947–51, Second Sec., Moscow 1949; UN Econ. Comm. for Europe, Geneva 1951–63; Lecturer in Soviet Econs, Univ. of Oxford 1963–72, Chair. Faculty Bd 1974–76; Gov. Plater Coll., Oxford 1968–95, Gov. Emer. 1995–; Visiting Prof. of Econs, Univ. of Mich., USA 1966; Visiting Lecturer, European Inst. of Business Admin, Fontainebleau 1959–82, 1988–92, Univ. of Cambridge 1967–68, 1977–78, 1978–79; Reader in Econs and Professorial Fellow, St Antony's Coll., Oxford 1972–93, Sub-Warden 1986–87, Reader Emer. 1993–; Dir Inst. of Russian, Soviet and E European Studies, Univ. of Oxford 1988–93; Assoc. Fellow, Templeton Coll., Oxford 1983–; Visiting Faculty mem. Henley Man. Coll. 1987–2002; mem. Centre for Euro-Asian Studies, Univ. of Reading 1997–; Vice-Chair. Social Science Research Council Int. Activities Cttee 1980–84; Chair. Co-ordinating Council, Area Studies Asscns 1986–88 (mem. 1980–93, 1995), Wilton Park Academic Council, FCO 1986–92 (mem. 1985–2001); Pres. British Asscn of Slavonic and E European Studies 1988–91, Vice-Pres. 1991–93; Prin. Charlemagne Inst., Edin. 1993–94, Hon. Fellow, Divinity Faculty, Univ. of Edin. 1993–96; mem. Int. Social Science Council, UNESCO 1980–91, Council of Royal Inst. of Int. Affairs 1979–85, 1986–92, Royal Econ. Soc. 1975–86, 1987–90, Council School of Slavonic and East European Studies 1981–87, Cttee Nat. Asscn for Soviet and E European Studies 1965–88, Steering Cttee Königswinter Anglo-German Confs 1969–90, Exec. Cttee Int. Econ. Asscn 1974–83, 1986–2009 (Gen. Ed.), also various editorial bds, Anglo-Soviet, British-Mongolian, Anglo-Polish, British-Bulgarian, British-Yugoslav (Chair.), Canada-UK, British-Romanian and UK-Uzbek Round Tables; Sec. British Nat. Cttee of AIESEE 1988–93; Chair. Council, the Keston Inst., Oxford 1994–2002; Trustee, Foundation of King George VI and Queen Elizabeth, St Catharine's 1987–2006 (Chair. Academic Consultative Cttee 1987–2002), Sir Heinz Koeppler Trust 1987–2001 (Chair. 1992–2001); mem. Higher Educ. Funding Council for England Advisory Bd on E European Studies 1995–2000; Hon. Prof., Inst. for German

Studies, Univ. of Birmingham 1994–; Kt Order of St Gregory the Great 1990, Order of Naim Frashëri (Albania) 1995, Kt Order of Merit (Poland) 1999; Dr hc (Birmingham) 1996. *Publications include:* Comecon: Integration Problems of the Planned Economies 1965, Planning in East Europe (with J. Zielinski) 1970, Soviet Economics 1970, Health Care in the Soviet Union and Eastern Europe 1976, Planning and Market Relations (with R. Portes) 1971, The New Economic Systems of Eastern Europe (co-author) 1975, The Soviet Union since the Fall of Khrushchev (with A. H. Brown) 1975, Soviet Policy for the 1980s (with A. H. Brown) 1982, Economic History of Eastern Europe, Vols I–III (with E. A. Radice) 1985–86, Early Steps in Comparing East-West Economies (with E. A. G. Robinson) 1991, Reforms in Foreign Economic Relations of Eastern Europe and the Soviet Union 1991, The Macroeconomics of Transition in Eastern Europe (with D. Morris) 1992, The Central Asian Economies after Independence (with S. Mehrotra) 1992, 1996, Cambridge Encyclopedia of Russia and the Former Soviet Union (co-author) 1994, Privatization in the CIS 1996, The Economies of Kazakstan and Uzbekistan 1997, The Prudential Management of Hydrocarbon Revenues in Resource-Rich Transition Economies (co-author) 2006; articles in econ. and Slavic journals. *Address:* 31 Capel Close, Oxford, OX2 7LA, England (home). *Telephone:* (1865) 515581 (home). *Fax:* (1865) 515581 (home). *E-mail:* michael.kaser@economics.ox.ac.uk (office).

KASHAF, Maulvi Qiamuddin; Afghan religious leader; b. 1945; Interim Supreme Court Justice 2005–06; Acting Head, The High Council of Ulema and Clergy of Afghanistan and a Deputy Chair. of the Peace Jirga June 2010. *Address:* The High Council of Ulema and Clergy of Afghanistan, Kabul, Afghanistan (office).

KASHIO, Kazuo; Japanese business executive; *President and CEO, Casio Computer Company Ltd;* b. 9 Jan. 1929, Tokyo; ed Nihon Univ.; Corp. Officer, Casio Computer Co. Ltd, Tokyo, currently Pres. and CEO. *Address:* Casio Computer Co. Ltd, 1-6-2, Hon-machi, Shibuya-ku, Tokyo 151-8543, Japan (office). *Telephone:* (3) 5334-4111 (office). *Website:* world.casio.com (office).

KASIBWE, Speciosa Wandira, MD, ChB; Ugandan physician, politician, government official and UN official; *Special Envoy of the Secretary-General for HIV/AIDS in Africa, United Nations;* b. 1 July 1955, Iganga Dist; ed Makerere Univ., Kampala; mem. Nat. Resistance Movt (NRM); MP for Kigulu S Iganga Dist; Deputy Minister for Industry 1989–91; fmr Minister for Gender and Community Devt; fmr Minister of Agric., Animal Industry and Fisheries; Vice-Pres. of Uganda 1994–2003 (resgnd to attend Harvard Univ. School of Public Health, USA); Chair. Microfinance Support Centre Ltd, Uganda 2008–; Special Envoy of the UN Sec.-Gen. for HIV/AIDS in Africa 2013–; Co-founder Concave International Ltd. (agricultural co-op consulting co.); fmr Chair. African Women's Cttee on Peace and Devt; mem. Bd of Dirs African Science Acad. Devt Initiative; Chair. Sr Women's Advisory Group on the Environment; mem. Uganda Women Entrepreneurs Asscn, Uganda Women Doctors Asscn, UN Comm. on the Status of Women 2006; fmr Co-Chair. Study Panel on Agricultural Productivity in Africa, InterAcademy Council; mem. Global Bd, Hunger Project. *Address:* UNAIDS Secretariat, 20 Avenue Appia, 1211, Geneva 27, Switzerland (office). *Telephone:* 227913666 (office). *Fax:* 227914187 (office). *Website:* www.unaids.org (office).

KASICH, John Richard, BA; American politician, television presenter and state governor; *Governor of Ohio;* b. 13 May 1952, McKees Rocks, Pa; m. 1st Mary Lee Griffith 1975 (divorced 1980); m. 2nd Karen Waldbillig 1997; twin d.; ed Ohio State Univ.; Admin. Asst to Rep. Buz Lukens, Ohio State Senate 1975–77; mem. Dist 15, Ohio State Legislature 1979–82; mem. 98th–104th Congress from 12th Ohio Dist, Washington, DC 1983–2001, mem. Nat. Security Cttee, mem. House Budget Cttee (Chair. 1995–2001); Man. Dir, Investment Banking Div., Lehman Brothers, Columbus, Ohio 2001–08; fmr mem. Bd of Dirs of several corpns, including Invacare Corpn and Norvax Inc., Chicago; Chair. New Century Project, Columbus 2001–; Gov. of Ohio 2011–; fmr host, Fox News current affairs TV show, Heartland with John Kasich, also guest hosted The O'Reilly Factor, also frequently appeared as a guest host and analyst on Hannity & Colmes (now Hannity); Guest Lecturer, Fisher Coll. of Business, Ohio State Univ.; fmr Guest Fellow, George Bush School of Govt and Public Service, Texas A&M Univ., Annenberg School for Communication, Univ. of Pennsylvania; Republican; Hon. Chair. Recharge Ohio 2008–. *Publications:* Courage is Contagious: Ordinary People Doing Extraordinary Things to Change the Face of America 1998, Stand for Something: The Battle for America's Soul 2006, Every Other Monday: Twenty Years of Life, Lunch, Faith and Friendship 2010. *Address:* Office of the Governor, Riffe Center, 30th Floor, 77 South High Street, Columbus, OH 43215-6117 (office); Washington Office of the Governor, State of Ohio, 444 North Capitol Street, Suite 546, Washington, DC 20001, USA (office). *Telephone:* (614) 466-3555 (Columbus) (office); (202) 624-5844 (DC) (office). *Fax:* (614) 466-9354 (Columbus) (office); (202) 624-5847 (DC) (office). *Website:* governor.ohio.gov (office); www.kasichforohio.com.

KAŠICKÝ, František; Slovak government official and diplomatist; *Permanent Representative, North Atlantic Treaty Organization;* b. 18 Nov. 1968, Gelnica, Czechoslovakia; m.; two c.; ed Mil. Pedagogical Acad., Bratislava, Akad. der Bundeswehr für Information und Kommunikation, Strausberg, Germany; Sr Officer for Social Man., Ministry of Defence 1991–93; Ed. Specialist, OBRANA (mil. newspaper) 1993–98, also Press Sec. for Minister of Defence; Asst Sec. of State, Ministry of Defence 1998–2000; Defence Ministry Spokesman, Office Dir and Dir of Communications Dept 2001–03; Dir Mil. Defence Intelligence 2003–04; Sec. Parl. Cttee of Nat. Council for Defence and Security, Special Control Cttee of Nat. Council for Control of Activities of Nat. Security Authority, Cttee of Nat. Council for Control of Information Tech. 2004–06; Minister of Defence 2006–08 (resgnd); Amb. and Perm. Rep. to NATO, Brussels 2008–; mem. Direction-Social Democracy (Smer-Sociálna demokracia). *Address:* Permanent Representation of Slovakia to NATO, Blvd Léopold III, 1110 Brussels, Belgium (office). *Telephone:* (2) 707-27-35 (office). *Fax:* (2) 707-27-42 (office). *E-mail:* nato.brussel@mzv.sk (office). *Website:* www.natobrusel.mfa.sk (office).

KASIM, Marwan al-, PhD; Jordanian politician; b. 12 May 1938, Amman; ed Eastern Michigan Univ., Columbia Univ. and Georgetown Univ., USA; joined Ministry of Foreign Affairs 1962, Consul-Gen., New York 1964–65, Deputy Dir of Protocol 1966, Political Officer, Embassy in Beirut 1967–68, Embassy in Washington, DC 1968–72; Sec. to Crown Prince Hassan 1972–75; Dir-Gen. Royal Hashemite Court 1975–76, Chief 1988; Minister of State 1976; Minister of Supply 1977–79; Minister of State for Foreign Affairs 1979–80, Minister of Foreign Affairs

1980–83; Deputy Prime Minister and Minister of Foreign Affairs 1988–90; Jordanian, Syrian, Mexican, Lebanese, Chinese and Italian decorations. *Address:* c/o Ministry of Foreign Affairs, Amman, Jordan.

KASIRER, Nicholas, FRSC, BCL, LLB, DEA, BA; Canadian professor of law and university administrator; *Judge, Court of Appeal;* ed Univ. of Toronto, McGill Univ., Univ. Paris I, France; law clerk to Hon. Jean Beetz, Supreme Court of Canada, Ottawa 1987–88; Asst Prof., Faculty of Law, McGill Univ., Montréal 1989–94, Assoc Prof. 1994–2000, Prof. 2000–02, James McGill Prof. 2002–09, Dean, Faculty of Law 2003–09, Dir Québec Research Centre for Pvt. and Comparative Law 1996–2003; Judge, Court of Appeal 2009–; mem. Editorial Bd Canadian Journal of Law and Society, The Philanthropist, The Estates and Trusts Reports, Canadian Legal Education Annual Review; mem. Québec Bar; American Soc. of Comparative Law, Hessel Yntema Award in Comparative Law; Prix de la Fondation du Barreau, Law Students' Asscn John W. Durnford Teaching Excellence Award, McGill Alumni Asscn David Johnston Medal. *Address:* Office of the Court of Appeal, Édifice Ernest-Cormier 100, Notre-Dame Street East, Montréal, PQ H2Y 4B6, Canada (office). *Telephone:* (514) 393-2022 (office). *Fax:* (514) 393-2022 (office). *E-mail:* courdappel@justice.gouv.qc.ca (office). *Website:* www.tribunaux.qc.ca/c-appel/english (office).

KASIT, Piromya, BSc, MSc; Thai diplomatist and politician; b. 15 Dec. 1944, Bangkok; m. Chintana Piromya (née Wajanabukka); one s. (died 1994) one d.; ed Chulalongkorn Univ., Georgetown Univ., Inst. of Social Studies, The Hague, Nat. Defence Coll.; Third Sec., Dept of Int. Orgs, Ministry of Foreign Affairs 1968, News Analysis Div., Dept of Information 1969–72, SEATO Div., Dept of Int. Orgs 1972–75; Third, then Second Sec., Embassy in Brussels and Perm. Mission to EU 1975–79; Second Sec., Int. Econ. Affairs Div., Dept of Econ. Affairs, Ministry of Foreign Affairs, then First Sec., Office of the Dir-Gen. 1979–81, Dir Econ. Information Div. 1983–84, Deputy Dir-Gen. 1985–88, Dir Commerce and Industry Div., ASEAN Dept 1981–83, Dir Policy and Planning Div., Office of the Perm. Sec., Dir-Gen. Dept of Int. Orgs 1988–91; Amb. to USSR (also accred to Mongolia) 1991, to Russian Fed. 1991–93, to Indonesia (also accred to Papua New Guinea) 1994–96, to Germany 1997–2001, to Japan 2001–04, to USA 2004–08; Minister of Foreign Affairs 2008–11; Commdr (Fourth Class), Most Exalted Order of the White Elephant 1974, Kt Commdr (Second Class) 1987, Kt Grand Cross (First Class) 1991, Kt Grand Cordon (Special Class) 1999, Commdr (Third Class) Most Noble Order of the Crown of Thailand 1977, Kt Commdr (Second Class) 1982, Kt Grand Cross (First Class) 1988, Kt Grand Cordon (Special Class) 1994, Grand Cross of the Order of Merit (Germany) 2001, Grand Cordon of the Order of the Rising Sun (Japan) 2004; Chakrabarti Mala Medal 1993. *Address:* c/o Ministry of Foreign Affairs, Thanon Sri Ayudhya, Bangkok 10400, Thailand (office).

KASKARELIS, Vassilis, BSc, LLB; Greek diplomatist and foundation executive; *Senior Advisor and Member, Executive Management Team, Stavros Niarchos Foundation;* b. 26 Nov. 1948, Athens; m. Anna Kaskarelis; two s.; ed Univ. of Thessalonoki, Univ. of Athens; joined Greek Foreign Service 1974, Embassy Attaché, Ministry of Foreign Affairs 1974–76, Third Sec., Embassy in Ankara 1976–79, Consul in Venice 1979–84, First Sec. in Nicosia 1984–87, Head of Mil. Mission in Berlin 1987–90, Consul-Gen. in Greece 1990–91, Deputy Dir Turkish Desk, Ministry of Foreign Affairs 1991–93, Minister Plenipotentiary, Head of Cabinet of Sec.-Gen. 1993–95, Deputy Perm. Rep. to UN, New York 1995–2000, Perm. Rep. to NATO, Brussels 2000–04, Perm. Rep. to EU, Brussels 2004–09, Amb. to USA 2009–12, Sec.-Gen., Ministry of Foreign Affairs 2012–13; Sr Advisor and mem. Exec. Man. Team, Stavros Niarchos Foundation, Athens 2013–; Chevalier, Ordre nat. du Mérite 1975, Grand Commdr, Order of the Phoenix (Greece) 1996, Grand Cross, Order of the Phoenix 2005, Grand-Cross of the Order of the Cedar of Lebanon; Diplomat of the Year, World Affairs Council 2011. *Address:* Stavros Niarchos Foundation, 86A Vasilissis Sofias Avenue, 115 28 Athens, Greece (office). *E-mail:* info@snf.org (office); brp.kaskarelis@rp-grece.be (office). *Website:* www.snf.org (office).

KASMIN, John; British art dealer; *Managing Director, Kasmin Ltd;* b. 24 Sept. 1934, London; s. of David Kosminsky and Vera d'Olszewski; m. Jane Nicholson 1959 (divorced 1975); two s.; ed Magdalen Coll. School, Oxford; worked for Gallery One, Soho, London 1956–58; Dir New London Gallery@Marlborough Fine Art, Bond St 1960–61; f. Kasmin Gallery, Man. Dir Kasmin Ltd 1961–, Knoedler Kasmin Ltd 1977–92. *Leisure interests:* reading, walking on hills and in museums and art galleries, collecting early postcards. *Address:* Kasmin Ltd, 34 Warwick Avenue, London, W9 2PT, England. *Fax:* (20) 7289-0746.

KASOULIDES, Ioannis; Cypriot physician and politician; *Minister of Foreign Affairs;* b. 10 Aug. 1948, Nicosia; m. Emy Droushiotou; one d.; ed Univ. of Lyon, France; physician and medical lecturer, London 1975–81; returned to practice medicine in Nicosia 1981; held various posts in Democratic Rally (DISY) party 1981–89, Chair. DISY Youth Movt 1990–93, mem. DISY Political Bureau 1993; Deputy for Nicosia, House of Reps 1991–93; Govt spokesman 1993–97; Minister of Foreign Affairs 1997–2003, 2013–; Founder and consultant, DDK Strategy and Public Affairs Ltd 2003; MEP 2004–13, Vice-Chair. European People Party parl. Group, responsible for Foreign Affairs; unsuccessful cand. (DISY) for Pres. of Cyprus 2008; Commdr Order of the Phoenix (Greece), Order of Merit (Greece), Order of Xirka (Malta), Order of the Cedar (Lebanon), Order of the Knights of the Holy Sepulchre; Palestinian Bethlehem Award 2000, Athens Municipality Highest Distinction Award. *Publication:* Cyprus – EU: The Accession as I Witnessed It. *Address:* Ministry of Foreign Affairs, Presidential Palace Avenue, 1447, Nicosia, Cyprus (office). *Telephone:* 22401000. *Fax:* 22661881. *E-mail:* minforeign1@mfa .gov.cy. *Website:* www.mfa.gov.cy.

KASPAROV, Garry Kimovich; Russian/Armenian fmr chess player and political activist; *Leader, United Civil Front;* b. (Garry Weinstein), 13 April 1963, Baku, Azerbaijan SSR; s. of the late Kim Weinstein and of Klara Kasparova; m. 1st Maria Arapova (divorced); one d.; m. 2nd Yulia Vovk 1996; one s.; ed Azerbaijan Pedagogical Inst. of Foreign Languages; started playing chess in 1967; Azerbaijan Champion 1976; USSR Jr Champion 1976; Int. Master 1978, Int. Grandmaster 1980; World Jr Champion 1980; won USSR Championship 1981, subsequently replacing Anatolii Karpov (q.v.) at top of world ranking list; won match against Viktor Korchnoi, challenged Karpov for World Title in Moscow Sept. 1985, the match being adjourned; won rescheduled match to become the youngest-ever world champion in 1985; successfully defended his title against Karpov 1986, 1987, 1990; series of promotional matches in London Feb. 1987; won Times World Championship against Nigel Short 1993; stripped of title by World Chess Fed. 1993; winner Oscar Chess Prize 1982–83, 1985–89, World Chess Cup 1989; highest-ever chess rating of over 2800 1992–; f. Professional Chess Asscn (PCA) 1993; won PCA World Championship against V. Anand 1995, lost title against V. Kramnik 2000; won match against Deep Blue computer 1996, lost 1997; defeated in four-game match of rapid chess against Karpov, New York 2002; retd from professional chess 2005; Deputy Leader Democratic Party of Russia 1990–91; f. The Kasparov Foundation, Moscow; actively promotes use of chess in schools as an educational subject; f. Kasparov Int. Chess Acad.; Founder and Leader United Civil Front 2005–; Order of Red Banner of Labour; ranked 25th in The Daily Telegraph's list of 100 greatest living geniuses 2007. *Publications:* World Chess Championship Match: Moscow, 1985 1986, The Test of Time (Russian Chess) 1986, Child of Change (with Donald Trelford) 1987, London-Leningrad Championship Games 1987, Unlimited Challenge 1990, The Sicilian Scheveningen 1991, The Queen's Indian Defence: Kasparov System 1991, Kasparov Versus Karpov, 1990 1991, Kasparov on the King's Indian 1993, Garry Kasparov's Chess Challenge 1996, Lessons in Chess 1997, Kasparov Against the World: The Story of the Greatest Online Challenge 2000, My Great Predecessors Part I 2003, My Great Predecessors Part II 2003, My First Chess Book 2004, Great Predecessors Part III 2004, Great Predecessors Part IV 2004, Great Predecessors Part V 2006, How Life Imitates Chess 2007, Garry Kasparov on Modern Chess, Part 1: Revolution in the 70s 2007, Kasparov on Modern Chess, Part 2: Kasparov vs Karpov 1975–1985 2008, Kasparov on Modern Chess, Part 3: Kasparov vs Karpov 1986–1987 2009, Kasparov on Modern Chess, Part 4: Kasparov vs Karpov 1988–2009 2010. *Leisure interests:* history (new chronology), politics, computers, literature, walking, weight training, swimming, rowing, most sports. *Address:* United Civil Front (Obyedinennyi Grazhdanskii Front), 119002 Moscow, Gagarinskii per. 26/12, Russia (home). *Telephone:* (499) 241-16-92 (office), (499) 241-82-80 (home). *Fax:* (499) 241-16-92 (office), (499) 241-95-96 (home). *E-mail:* maiavia@dol.ru (office). *Website:* www.rufront.ru (office).

KASPER, HE Cardinal Walter Josef, DTheol; German ecclesiastic and Catholic theologian; *President, Pontifical Council for Promoting Christian Unity;* b. 5 March 1933, Heidenheim/Brenz; s. of Josef Kasper and Theresia Bacher; ed Univs of Tübingen and Munich; ordained priest 1957; Prof. of Dogmatic Theology, Univ. of Münster 1964–70, Univ. of Tübingen 1970–89; Bishop of Rottenburg-Stuttgart 1989–99; Chair. Comm. for World Church Affairs 1991–99, Comm. for Doctrine of Faith, German Bishops Conf. 1996–99; Special Sec. Synod of Bishops 1985; mem. Heidelberger Akad. der Wissenschaften, Academia Scientiarum et Artium Europaea; mem. Congregation for the Doctrine of Faith, Pontifical Council for Culture 1998; Sec. Pontifical Council for Promoting Christian Unity 1999, Pres. 2001–; cr. Cardinal (Cardinal-Deacon of Ognissanti in Via Appia Nuova) 2001; Hon. Prof. (Eberhard-Karls Univ., Tübingen) 2001; Bundesverdienstkreuz; Dr hc (Catholic Univ. of America, Washington, DC) 1990, (St Mary's Seminary and Univ., Baltimore) 1991, (Marc Bloch Univ., Strasbourg 2000; Landesverdienstmedaille. *Publications:* Die Tradition in der Römischen Schule 1962, Das Absolute in der Geschichte 1965, Glaube und Geschichte 1970, Einführung in den Glauben 1972 (An Introduction to Christian Faith 1980), Jesus der Christus 1974, Der Gott Jesu Christi 1982, Theologie und Kirche 1987 (Theology and Church 1989), The Christian Understanding of Freedom and the History of Freedom in the Modern Era 1988, Wahrheit und Freiheit in der Erklärung über die Religionsfreiheit des II. Vatikanischen Konzils 1988, Lexikon für Theologie und Kirche 1993–2001, Theologie und Kirche II 1999. *Leisure interest:* climbing. *Address:* Pontificio Consiglio per l'Unita dei Cristiani, Via dell'Erba 1, 00193, Città del Vaticano, Rome, Italy. *Fax:* (06) 69885365 (office). *E-mail:* office@christianunity.va. *Website:* www.vaticano.va.

KASPSZYK, Jacek; Polish conductor; *Music Director, Polish National Radio Symphony Orchestra;* b. 1952; ed Acad. of Music, Warsaw; conducting debut at age 14; debut Warsaw Nat. Opera 1975; Prin. Guest Conductor Deutsche Oper am Rhein, Düsseldorf 1976–77; Prin. Conductor Polish Nat. Radio Symphony Orchestra, Katowice 1978–80, Music Dir 1980–82, 2009–; debut Berlin Philharmonic and New York 1978, London (with Philharmonia) 1982; conducted French Nat., Stockholm Philharmonic, Bavarian Radio Symphony, Rotterdam, Czech Philharmonic Orchestras; conducted Detroit Opera and San Diego Symphony Orchestra 1982; concerts at La Scala, Milan 1982; Australian tour with Chamber Orchestra of Europe 1983; conducted UK orchestras 1982–; debut Henry Wood Promenade Concerts 1984; Prin. Conductor and Artistic Adviser North Netherlands Orchestra 1991–95; Prin. Guest Conductor English Sinfonia 1992–; has toured with the Yomiuri Nippon Symphony and performed with Tokyo and Hong Kong Philarmonics, New Zealand, San Diego, Cincinnati, Winnipeg, Calgary Symphonies, and Detroit Opera; Prin. Guest Conductor Polish Philharmonic 1996–; Artistic and Musical Dir Polish National Opera, Warsaw 1998–2005, Artistic and Gen. Dir 2005–; III Prize, Karajan Competition 1977. *Music:* operas conducted include: Queen of Spades (Düsseldorf) 1977, Haunted Manor (Detroit) 1982, A Midsummer Night's Dream (Lyon) 1983, Eugene Onegin (Bordeaux) 1985, The Magic Flute (Opéra Comique, Paris and Stockholm) 1986, Seven Deadly Sins (Lyon) 1987, Die Fledermaus (Scottish Opera), Flying Dutchman (Opera North, UK) 1988, Barber of Seville (English Nat. Opera) 1992, Der Rosenkavalier (Warsaw) 1997, Don Giovanni (Warsaw) 1999, The Nutcracker (Zürich) 2000; many productions and recordings with Teatr Wielki, Warsaw, including performances in Luxembourg, Lvov, Beijing, Paphos, Japan (tour) and Bolshoi Theatre in Moscow; recordings with London Symphony Orchestra, London Philharmonic Orchestra, Royal Philharmonic, Philharmonic Orchestras, Warsaw Symphony Orchestra; several other recordings. *Address:* c/o The Music Partnership Limited, New Broad Street House, New Broad Street, London EC2M 1NH, England (office); National Polish Radio Symphony Orchestra, 40-032, Katowice, Plac Sejmu Slaskiego 2, Poland (office). *Telephone:* (20) 7840-9590 (office), (32) 2518903 (office). *Fax:* (20) 7735-7505 (office), (32) 2571384 (office). *E-mail:* office@musicpartnership.co.uk (office); nospr@nospr.org.pl (office). *Website:* www .musicpartnership.co.uk (office); www.nospr.org.pl (office).

KASRASHVILI, Makvala; Georgian singer (soprano); *Artistic Director, Bolshoi Theatre Opera;* b. 13 March 1948, Kutaisi; d. of Nina Nanikashvili and Filimon Kasrashvili; m. (divorced); ed Tbilisi Conservatory; joined Bolshoi Co., Moscow 1968, Artistic Dir Bolshoi Theatre Opera Dept 2000–; has performed internation-

ally, including Covent Garden, London, Metropolitan Opera, New York, Verona, Vienna State Opera; Grand Prix, Montreal Vocal Competition 1973, Merited Artist of Russian Fed. 1975, People's Artist of Georgian SSR 1980, Zakhar Paliashvili Georgian SSR State Prize 1983, People's Artist of the USSR 1986, State Prize of Russia 1998. *Roles include:* Lisa, Tatyana, Maria, Tosca, Lauretta, Donna Anna, Leonora, Aida, Turandot, Amelia. *Leisure interest:* car driving. *Address:* Bolshoi Theatre, Teatralnaya Pl. 1, Moscow, Russia. *Telephone:* (495) 200-58-00 (home). *Website:* www.bolshoi.ru (office).

KASRIEL, Bernard L. M.; French business executive; *Managing Partner, LBO France;* b. 1946; three c.; ed Ecole Polytechnique, Institut Européen d'Admin des Affaires (INSEAD), Fontainebleau, Harvard Univ., USA; several man. positions with industrial cos 1970–77; joined Lafarge SA 1977, with Sanitaryware Div. 1977–81, Group Exec. Vice-Pres. 1982–87, Sr Exec. Vice-Pres. 1987–89, seconded as Pres. and COO Nat. Gypsum, Dallas, Tex. 1987–89, Group Man.-Dir 1989–95, Vice-Chair. and COO 1995–2003, CEO 2003–06, Vice-Chair. 2006; Man. Pnr, LBO France (pvt. equity fund) 2006–; mem. Bd of Dirs Lafarge SA, L'Oréal, Arkema, Nucor Corpn, Sonoco Products Co. 1995–; Chevalier de la Légion d'honneur 1996. *Leisure interests:* tennis. *Address:* LBO France, 148 rue de l'Université, 75007 Paris, France (office). *Telephone:* 1-40-62-77-67 (office). *Fax:* 1-40-62-75-55 (office). *E-mail:* elizabeth.oreilly@lbofrance.com (office). *Website:* www.lbofrance.com (office).

KASSEM, Abdul-Rauf al-, DArch; Syrian architect and politician; b. 1932, Damascus; ed Damascus Univ. School of Arts, Istanbul Univ., Turkey and Geneva Univ., Switzerland; teacher of architecture, School of Fine Arts Damascus, Dean 1964–70, Head, Architecture Dept, School of Civil Engineering, Damascus Univ. 1970–77, Rector 1977–79; concurrently engineer 1964–77; Gov. of Damascus 1979–80; elected mem. Baath party Regional Command Dec. 1979, Cen. Command of Progressive Nat. Front April 1980; Prime Minister 1980–87; mem. Higher Council for Town Planning 1968; mem. Nat. Union of Architects' Perm. Comm. on Town Planning 1975; Hon. Prof., Geneva Univ. 1975. *Address:* c/o Office of the Prime Minister, Damascus, Syria.

KASSOMA, António Paulo; Angolan politician; *Speaker, Assembléia Nacional;* b. 6 June 1951, Luanda; s. of Paulo Kassoma and Laurinda Katuta; mil. techniques instructor 1975; Tech. Dir Base Central de Reparações 1976–78; Vice Minister of Defence for Armament and Technique 1978–79, of Transports and Communication 1988–89; Minister of Territory Admin 1991–92; Sr Officer, Angolan Armed Forces 2001; mem. People's Movt for Liberation of Angola (MPLA) 2003–; Gov. Huambo Prov. 2004–08; Prime Minister of Angola 2008–10 (post abolished by new constitution); Speaker, Assembléia Nacional (parl.) 2010–. *Address:* Assembléia Nacional, CP 1204, Luanda, Angola (office). *Telephone:* 222334021 (office). *Fax:* 222331118 (office). *E-mail:* assembleianacional@parlamento.ebonet.net (office). *Website:* www.parlamento.ao (office).

KASTANIDIS, Haris; Greek lawyer and politician; *Chairman Parliamentary Group, Social Agreement;* b. 11 March 1956, Thessaloniki; m. Elisavet Symeonidou; two d.; ed Law School of the Aristotle Univ. of Thessaloniki, postgraduate studies in Criminal Law; mem. Panhellenic Socialist Movt (PASOK) 1974–2012, mem. Cen. Cttee 1984–2012; mem. Parl. 1981–, Parl. Spokesman for PASOK 2004–07; Deputy Minister for the Interior and Public Order 1985–86, of Nat. Educ. and Religious Affairs Sept.–Nov. 1988, for the Interior 18–29 Nov. 1988, Minister for the Interior, Public Admin and Decentralization 1995–96, for Transport and Communications 1996–97, for Macedonia and Thrace 2003–04, for Justice, Transparency and Human Rights 2009–11, of the Interior, Decentralization and e-Governance June–Nov. 2011; expelled from PASOK parl. group for voting against Greece's loan deal with its foreign creditors 2012; Co-founder, with Louka Katseli (q.v.), Social Agreement party 2012–, Chair. Social Agreement parl. group 2012–. *E-mail:* info@koinonikisymfonia.gr (office). *Website:* www .koinonikisymfonia.gr (office); kastanidisharis.gr.

KASTEN, Robert (Bob) Walter, Jr., BA; American fmr politician; *President, Kasten & Company;* b. 19 June 1942, Milwaukee, Wis.; s. of Robert W. Kasten and Mary Kasten (née Ogden); m. Eva J. Nimmons 1986; one d.; ed Univ. of Arizona and Columbia Univ., New York; with Genesco, Nashville, Tenn. 1966–68; Dir and Vice-Pres. Gilbert Shoe Co., Thiensville, Wis. 1968–75; mem. Wis. State Senate 1972–75, mem. Jt Finance Cttee 1973–75, Chair. Jt Survey Cttee on Tax Exemptions 1973–80; Designee, Eagleton Inst. of Politics 1973; mem. US House of Reps from Wis. 9th Dist 1975–79, mem. Govt Operations Cttee, Small Businesses Cttee, Appropriations, Budget, Commerce, Science and Transportation Cttee; Alt. del. Republican Nat. Convention 1972, del. 1976, Co-Chair. 1988; Senator from Wis. 1980–93; Founder and Pres. Kasten & Co (consulting firm), Washington, DC 1993–; Sr Assoc., Center for Strategic and Int. Studies, Washington, DC 1993–. *Address:* Kasten & Co., 1629 K Street, NW, Washington, DC 20006, USA. *Telephone:* (202) 223-9151 (office). *E-mail:* kastenco@aol.com (office).

KASTNER, Marc A., MS, PhD; American (b. Canadian) physicist and academic; *Donner Professor of Science and Dean, School of Science, Massachusetts Institute of Technology;* b. 20 Nov. 1945, Toronto; m.; two d.; ed Univ. of Chicago; Research Fellow, Harvard Univ. 1972–73; Asst Prof. of Physics, MIT 1973–77, Assoc. Prof. 1977–83, Head, Dept of Physics, Div. of Atomic Condensed Matter and Plasma Physics 1983–87, Prof. of Physics 1983–89, Asst Dir MIT Consortium for Superconducting Electronics 1989–92, Donner Prof. of Science 1989–, Head, Dept of Physics 1998–2007, Dean of School of Science 2007–; Dir NSF Materials Research Science and Eng Center, Center for Materials Science and Eng 1993–98; Dir Brookhaven Science Associates 2000–; mem. Nat. Research Council Solid State Sciences Cttee 1995–2001; Fellow, Hertz Foundation, American Physical Soc., AAAS; American Physical Soc. Oliver E. Buckley Prize 2000. *Address:* Massachusetts Institute of Technology, 77 Massachusetts Avenue, Bldg 6-123, Cambridge, MA 02139, USA (office). *Telephone:* (617) 253-8900 (office). *Fax:* (617) 253-8554 (office). *E-mail:* mkastner@mit.edu (office). *Website:* web.mit.edu/kastner-group (office).

KASURI, Khurshid Mehmoud, BA, DPhil; Pakistani politician; b. 1941, Lahore; s. of Mahmud Ali Kasuri; ed Punjab Univ., Univs of Cambridge and Oxford, UK; fmr Sec.-Gen. Tehrik-e-Istiqlal; first Sec.-Gen. People's Democratic Alliance 1990–93; Fed. Minister for Parl. Affairs, Interim Govt 1991–93; mem. Pakistan

Muslim League 1997–; mem. Nat. Ass. 1997–; Minister of Foreign Affairs 2002–07, also of Law, Justice and Human Rights 2002–04; cand. in parl. elections 2008; mem. Nat. Security Council. *Address:* c/o Ministry of Foreign Affairs, Constitution Avenue, Islamabad, Pakistan. *Telephone:* (51) 9210335.

KASYANOV, Mikhail Mikhailovich; Russian politician; *Leader, Russian People's Democratic Union;* b. 8 Dec. 1957, Solntsevo, Moscow Oblast; ed Moscow Inst. of Automobile Transport; held sr positions at RSFSR State Planning Comm., then Ministry of Econs 1981–90; Chief of Section for Foreign Econ. Relations, Russian State Cttee for Econs 1990–91; Head, Dept for Foreign Econ. Relations, Ministry of Finance 1991–93, Head, Dept of Overseas Credits 1993–95, Deputy Minister of Finance 1995–99, First Deputy Minister, then Minister 1999–2000; main negotiator with Western financial orgs on questions of Russian liabilities; Deputy Man. for Russian Fed., EBRD 1999; First Deputy Prime Minister Jan. 2000, Acting Chair. of Govt, then Chair. of Govt (Prime Minister) 2000–04; mem. Presidium of Russian Govt 1999–2004, Security Council 1999–2004; f. MK-Analytics (consultancy) 2005; currently Leader, Russian People's Democratic Union; barred by Cen. Election Comm. of Russia from being cand. in presidential election on grounds of alleged forged signatures in support of him 2008; Co-Chair. Republican Party of Russia—Party of People's Freedom (RPR-PARNAS) 2012–. *Address:* Russian People's Democratic Union (Rossiiskii narodno-demokraticheski soyuz), 117279 Moscow, ul. Profsoyuznaya 93, korp. 4, Russia (office). *Telephone:* (495) 429-61-70 (office). *Fax:* (495) 429-63-10 (office). *E-mail:* newtypeparty@mail .ru (office). *Website:* nardemsoyuz.ru (office); kasyanov.ru.

KATAINEN, Jyrki, MScS; Finnish politician; *Prime Minister;* b. 14 Oct. 1971, Siilinjärvi; m. Mervi Katainen; two c.; mem. Siilinjärvi Municipal Council 1993–; Vice-Chair. Regional Council of Pohjois-Savo 1994–95; mem. Parl. (Finnish Nat. Coalition Party—Kokoomus) 1999–, Vice-Chair. Kokoomus Youth League 1994–95, Vice-Chair. Kokoomus 2001–04, Chair. 2004–; Chair. Cttee for the Future 2003–; mem. Finnish Del. to W European Union Parl. Ass. 2004–; Deputy mem. Finnish Del. to OSCE Parl. Ass. 2003–; mem. Admin. Bd Finnish Broadcasting Corpn 2003–; Deputy Prime Minister and Minister of Finance 2007–11; Prime Minister 2011–; named among World Econ. Forum's Global Leaders for Tomorrow 2003. *Address:* Prime Minister's Office, Snellmaninkatu 1a, POB 23, 00023 Helsinki, Finland (office). *Telephone:* (9) 16001 (office). *Fax:* (9) 16022165 (office). *E-mail:* info@vnk.fi (office). *Website:* www.vnk.fi (office); www .jyrkikatainen.fi.

KATANANDOV, Sergey Leonidovich; Russian politician; b. 21 April 1955, Petrozavodsk; m.; two s.; ed Petrozavodsk State Univ., NW Acad. of State and Municipal Service; worked as Head of Sector, Sr Engineer, Petrozavodskstroi 1977–91; mem. Petrozavodsk City Exec. Cttee, Chair. City Soviet 1991–98, Mayor of Petrozavodsk 1994–98; elected Chair. Karelian Govt 1998–2002; Pres., Repub. of Karelia 2002–10 (resgnd); Merited Worker of Nat. Economy of Repub. of Karelia 1995, Order of Honour of Russian Fed. 2000, Medal of Merits 2004. *Publications include:* articles in Russian and Finnish journals and newspapers. *Leisure interests:* fishing, hunting, swimming, reading. *Address:* c/o Government of Karelia, Lenina prosp. 19, Petrozavodsk 185020, Karelia (office); Andropova av. 30, Petrozavodsk, Karelia, Russia.

KATAYAMA, Mikio; Japanese business executive; *Chairman, Sharp Corporation;* b. 1958; ed Univ. of Tokyo; joined Sharp Corpn 1981, Group Gen. Man. Liquid Crystal Display (LCD) Div. 2002, Dir 2003–, Exec. Dir 2005–, Corp. Sr Exec. Dir for LCD Business –2006, Pres. Sharp Corpn 2006–07, Pres. and COO 2007–12, Chair. 2012–. *Address:* Sharp Corpn, 22-22 Nagaike-cho, Abeno-ku, Osaka 545-8522, Japan (office). *Telephone:* (6) 6621-1221 (office). *Fax:* (6) 6627-1759 (office). *E-mail:* info@sharp.co.jp (office). *Website:* sharp-world.com (office); www.sharp.co .jp (office).

KATAYAMA, Yoshihiro; Japanese lawyer and government official; b. 29 Aug. 1951, Okayama Pref.; m. (deceased); four s. two d.; ed Univ. of Tokyo; Prof. of Local Admin, Keio Univ. 2007; worked several years with Ministry of Home Affairs; Gov. Tottori Pref. 1999–2007; mem. Govt Revitalization Unit 2009–; Minister of Internal Affairs and Communications and Minister of State for Promotion of Local Sovereignty and for Regional Revitalization 2010–11 (only non-Diet member of Cabinet). *Address:* c/o Ministry of Internal Affairs and Communications, 2-1-2, Kasumigaseki, Chiyoda-ku, Tokyo 100-8926, Japan (office).

KATEHI, Linda P. B., BS, MS, PhD; American engineer, academic and university administrator; *Chancellor, University of California, Davis;* b. 1954, Greece; ed Nat. Tech. Univ. of Athens, Greece, Univ. of California, Los Angeles; Lecturer, Nat. Tech. Univ., Greece 1977–78; Research Engineer, Dept of Defence, Naval Research Lab., GETEN, Greece 1978–79; Grad. Student Research Asst, UCLA 1979–84; Asst Prof. of Electrical Eng, Univ. of Michigan 1984–89, Assoc. Prof. of Electrical Eng and Computer Science 1989–94, Prof. 1994–2002, Assoc. Dir of Grad. Program, Coll. of Eng 1994–95, Assoc. Dean for Grad. Educ. 1998–99, Assoc. Dean for Academic Affairs 1999–2002; John A. Edwardson Dean of Eng, Prof. of Electrical and Computer Eng, Purdue Univ., West Lafayette, Ind. 2002–06; Prof. of Electrical and Computer Eng, Univ. of Illinois 2006–09, also Provost and Vice-Chancellor for Academic Affairs and Prof. in Gender and Women's Studies programme; Chancellor, Univ. of California, Davis 2009–; Chair. Pres.'s Cttee for Nat. Medal of Tech. 2007–10; Vice-Chair. Eng Dean's Council, American Asscn of Eng Educ. 2005–06; mem. Bd of Dirs Consortium on Institutional Collaboration 2006, AAAS 2007–, Cyprus Inst. 2008–, BACEI 2010–, Business Higher Educ. Forum, 2010–; mem. Exec. Cttee Coll. of Eng, Iowa State Univ. 1995–98, mem. Eng Advisory Cttee 2003–06; mem. NASA Council of Deans 2004–; mem. Advisory Cttee, Harvard Radcliff Coll. 2006–10, American Acad. of Arts and Sciences Cttee on Fed. Support of Research 2007–, NAS Cttee for Sensors and Communication Systems for Special Operation Forces 2008–10, Nat. Security Higher Educ. Cttee 2010–, NASA Aerospace Tech. Advisory Cttee; mem. Nat. Acad. of Eng 2006–, Int. Union of Radio Science, Int. Soc. of Hybrid Microelectronics, Advanced Computational Electromagnetics Soc., American Soc. of Eng Educ., IEEE Antennas and Propagation Soc., IEEE Microwave Theory and Techniques Soc.; Fellow, AAAS 2007–; IEEE Fellow 1995; Amelia Earhart Fellowship Award, Zonta International 1982–83, 1983–84, Presidential Young Investigator Award, NSF 1987, URSI Booker Award 1987, Research Excellence Award, Univ. of Michigan 1993, Faculty Recognition Award, Univ. of Michigan 1994, Humboldt Research Award 1994,

Third Millennium Medal, IEEE Microwave Theory and Techniques Soc. 2000, Distinguished Educator Award 2002, Leading Light Award for Women in High Tech 2004, UCLA Eng Alumnus of the Year Award 2006. *Achievements include:* holds more than 15 patents. *Address:* Office of the Chancellor, 5th Floor, Mrak Hall, University of California, One Shields Avenue, Davis, CA 95616, USA (office). *Telephone:* (530) 752-2067 (office). *Fax:* (530) 752-2400 (office). *E-mail:* katehi@ ucdavis.edu (office); chancellor@ucdavis.edu (office). *Website:* chancellor.ucdavis .edu (office).

KATEN, Karen L., BA, MBA; American pharmaceutical industry executive (retd); b. Kansas City, Mo.; ed Univ. of Chicago; work in sales at office supply co.; joined Pfizer in 1974, Vice-Pres. Marketing 1983–86, Vice-Pres. and Dir of Operations 1986–91, Vice-Pres. and Gen. Man. 1991–93, Exec. Vice-Pres. Pfizer Pharmaceuticals Group 1993, Pres. Pfizer US Pharmaceuticals 1995–2002, Sr Vice-Pres. 1999–2001, mem. Pfizer Leadership Team, Exec. Vice-Pres. Pfizer Inc. and Pres. Pfizer Global Pharmaceuticals 2001–05, Pres. Pfizer Human Health and Vice-Chair. Pfizer Inc. 2005–07 (retd), Chair. Pfizer Foundation 2006–08; Sr Advisor, Essex Woodlands Health Ventures 2007–; mem. Bd of Dirs Harris Corporation, The Home Depot 2007–, Catamaran Corp., and Air Liquide, Catalyst; Chair. RAND Corpn Health Bd of Advisors; apptd to US-Japan Pvt. Sector/Govt Comm. and Nat. Infrastructure Cttee; mem. ARMGO Pharmaceutical Board; Trustee, Economic Club of New York, Univ. of Chicago; ranked by Fortune magazine amongst 50 Most Powerful Women in Business in the US 1998–2001, (seventh) 2002, (sixth) 2003, (10th) 2004, (ninth) 2005, ranked by Business Week magazine's annually amongst 25 Top Executives, 11 separate Woman of the Year or similar awards from civic groups, nat. asscns and univs, Hallene Lecturer, Univ. of Illinois 2004, Dolan Lecturer, Fairfield Univ., Conn. 2004. *Address:* Essex Woodlands, 280 Park Avenue, 27th Floor East, New York, NY 10017, USA (office). *Website:* www.essexwoodlands.com (office).

KATES, Robert William, PhD; American geographer, academic and editor; b. 31 Jan. 1929, Brooklyn, New York; s. of Simon J. Kates and Helen G. Brener; m. Eleanor C. Hackman 1948; one s. two d.; ed Univ. of Chicago; Asst Prof., Grad. School of Geography, Clark Univ. 1962–65, Assoc. Prof. 1965–67, Prof. 1968–92, Univ. Prof. 1974–80, Univ. Prof. and Dir Alan Shawn Feinstein World Hunger Program 1986–92, Prof. Emer., Watson Inst. for Int. Studies 1992–; Visiting Research Scholar, Belfer Center for Science and Int. Affairs, Harvard Univ., now Sr Research Fellow; Exec. Ed. Environment Magazine; Dir Bureau of Resource Assessment and Land Use Planning, Univ. Coll., Dar es Salaam 1967–68; Hon. Research Prof., Univ. of Dar es Salaam 1970–71; Fellow, Woodrow Wilson Int. Center for Scholars 1979; mem. Asscn of American Geographers (Pres. 1993–94); Co-Convener, Initiative on Science and Tech. for Sustainability; mem. NAS, AAAS. *Publications include:* Risk Assessment of Environmental Hazard 1978, The Environment as Hazard (with Ian Burton and Gilbert F. White) 1978; co-ed. of 18 books; monographs and articles on environmental topics. *Address:* Initiative on Science and Technology for Sustainability, 33 Popple Point, Trenton, ME 04605, USA. *Telephone:* (207) 667-5450. *Fax:* (207) 664-0375. *E-mail:* rwkates@verizon .net. *Website:* rwkates.org.

KATHER, Lt-Gen. (retd) Roland; German army officer (retd); m. Christiane Kather; ed Gen. Staff Course of Spanish Army, Madrid, Spain; commissioned in German Army Armoured Reconnaissance Corps 1968; served in various regimental appointments in Panzeraufklärungsbataillon 6, Eutin, followed by Gen. Staff training at Führungsakademie der Bundeswehr, Hamburg 1979–81; served as Chief G 4 with Panzerbrigade 18, Neumünster; served in German Army Staff, Ministry of Defence, Bonn 1984–87; Plans Officer of G 3 Div., SHAPE, Mons, Belgium 1987–91; assumed command of Panzeraufklärungsbataillon 6, Eutin; Exec. Officer for Chief of Staff of Armed Forces Staff, Ministry of Defence 1991–95; Chief of Staff, HQ 7, Panzerdivision/Army Dist Command III, Düsseldorf 1995–97, deployed to Trogir, Croatia as Chief of Staff, German Contingent, Implementation Force (IFOR); Deputy Dir Armed Forces Jt Operations Centre, Ministry of Defence 1997–99; Commdr Panzerbrigade 42, Potsdam 1999–2001, deployed to Balkans as Commdr Multinational Brigade South, Prizren, Kosovo; Chief of Staff, HQ German Army Operational Command, Koblenz 2001–03; commanded 13 Panzergrenadierdivision, Leipzig 2003–06; Commdr Kosovo Force (KFOR) 2006–07; Commdr Allied Land Component Command, Heidelberg 2007–10; Mil. Rep. to NATO, Brussels 2010–11, to EU 2010–11. *Leisure interests:* politics, contemporary history, outdoor activities, especially mountain biking. *E-mail:* roland.kather@t -online.de.

KATHRADA, Ahmed, BA; South African fmr politician; b. 21 Aug. 1929, Schweizer Reneke; joined Young Communist League 1941; first imprisoned for participation in Passive Resistance 1946, subsequently imprisoned several times during 1950s and 1960s; first banned in 1954, accused in treason trial 1956–61, placed under house arrest Oct. 1962; sentenced to life imprisonment, Rivonia Trial 1964, unconditionally released 1989; rep. SA in World Fed. of Democratic Youth 1951–52; involved in Defiance Campaign 1952, Congress of People's Campaign 1955; Sec. first Free Mandela Cttee 1962; mem. African Nat. Congress (ANC) Del. to Talks about Talks with South African Govt 1990, Nat. Exec. Cttee ANC 1991–99, Internal Leadership Cttee of ANC, Head of Public Relations Dept; MP Govt of Nat. Unity 1994–99; Parl. Counsellor in Office of Pres. 1994–99; Chair. Robben Island Museum Council –2006; Chair. Ex-Political Prisoners Cttee; Fellow, Mayibuye Centre, Univ. of Western Cape; Patron, Trauma Centre, Cape Town; Presidential Order for Meritorious Service, Class 1 (Gold); Dr hc (University of Massachusetts) 2000, (University of Durban-Westville) 2002, (University of Missouri) 2004, (Michigan State University) 2005; Isithwalandwe, ANC Merit Award, Pravasi Bharatiya Samman (India) 2005. *Publications:* Letters from Robben Island 1999, Memoirs 2004, A Free Mind: Ahmed Kathrada's Notebook from Robben Island 2005. *Address:* c/o Ahmed Kathrada Foundation, PO Box 10621, Lenasia, 1820, South Africa.

KATIN, Peter Roy, FRAM, ARCM; British pianist and teacher; b. 14 Nov. 1930, London, England; s. of the late Jerrold Katin and Gertrude Katin; m. Eva Zweig 1954; two s.; ed Henry Thornton School, Royal Acad. of Music, Westminster Abbey; London debut, Wigmore Hall 1948; extensive concert tours in UK, Europe, Africa, Canada, USA and Far East; special interest in Chopin; Prof., RAM 1956–60, Univ. of Western Ontario 1978–84, Royal Coll. of Music, London 1992–2001; Founder Katin Centre for Advanced Piano Studies 1991, Katin Trio 1997; Pres. Camerata of

London 1994–; Hon. DMus (De Montfort) 1994; Eric Brough Memorial Prize 1944, Chopin Arts Award (New York) 1977. *Leisure interests:* writing, recording, theatre, reading, photography. *Address:* 41 First Avenue, Bexhill-on-Sea, East Sussex, TN40 2PL, England. *Telephone:* (1424) 211167. *Fax:* (1424) 211167. *E-mail:* peter.katin@btinternet.com. *Website:* www.peterkatin.com.

KATNIĆ, Milorad, MEconSc, PhD; Montenegrin politician; b. 12 Dec. 1977, Podgorica; ed Univ. of Montenegro; began career as researcher, later analyst at Inst. for Strategic Studies and Prognoses, Podgorica; Deputy Minister of Finance 2004–10, Alt. Gov. of Montenegro to World Bank 2007, Minister of Finance 2010–12; mem. Admin. Bd Council of Europe Devt Bank 2007; fmr Lecturer, Faculty of International Econs, Finance and Business, Univ. Donja Gorica; mem. Democratic Party of Socialists of Montenegro (Demokratska Partija Socijalista Crne Gore) (DPS); Bd mem. Union of Economists of Montenegro, Center for Young Scientists of the Montenegrin Acad. of Arts and Science. *Publications include:* numerous working and scientific papers in the area of economic growth, financial crisis, tax systems and public spending. *Address:* Democratic Party of Socialists of Montenegro (DPS), 81000 Podgorica, Jovana Tomaševića bb, Montenegro (office). *Telephone:* (20) 242971 (office). *Fax:* (20) 246356 (office). *E-mail:* portparol@dps.me (office). *Website:* www.dps.me (office).

KATO, Kazuyasu, BS, MS; Japanese business executive; *Consultant, Kirin Holdings Company Ltd;* b. 24 Nov. 1944; ed Keio Univ., Massachusetts Inst. of Tech. Sloan School of Man., USA; joined Kirin Brewery Co. Ltd 1968, Vice-Pres. Kirin USA, Inc. 1986–90, Pres. 1990–93, Man. of Sales Dept, Tokyo Sales Head Office March–Nov. 1993, Deputy Gen. Man. Tokyo Regional Head Office 1993–97, Gen. Man. Hokkaido Regional Head Office 1997–2000, Dir of Kirin Holdings Co. Ltd 2000–, Gen. Man. Kyushu Regional Head Office 2000–01, Gen. Man. Domestic Alcohol Sales Dept 2001–02, Deputy Gen. Man. Domestic Alcohol Div. and Gen. Man. Domestic Alcohol Sales Dept 2002–03, Sr Exec. Officer and Gen. Man. Domestic Alcohol Div. 2003–04, Man. Dir, Sr Exec. and Gen. Man. 2004–06, Pres. and COO Kirin Brewery Co. Ltd 2006–07, Pres. and CEO March–July 2007, Pres. and CEO Kirin Holdings Co. Ltd July 2007–10, Chair. 2010–12, Consultant 2012–. *Address:* Kirin Holdings Co. Ltd, 10-1 Shinkawa 2-chome, Chuo-ku, Tokyo 104-8288, Japan (office). *Telephone:* (3) 5541-5321 (office). *Fax:* (3) 5540-3547 (office). *E-mail:* info@kirin.co.jp (office). *Website:* www.kirinholdings.co.jp (office).

KATO, Ryozo; Japanese diplomatist and sports administrator; *Commissioner, Nippon Professional Baseball;* b. 1941, Saitama Pref.; m. Hanayo Kato; three c.; ed Univ. of Tokyo; joined Ministry of Foreign Affairs 1965, Dir Security Affairs Div. 1981–84, Dir Treaties Div. 1984–87, with Internal Affairs and Communications Div. 1990–92, Deputy Dir N American Affairs Bureau 1992–94, Dir-Gen. Asian Affairs Bureau 1995–97, Dir-Gen. Foreign Policy Bureau 1997–99, Minister, Washington, DC 1987, Consul-Gen., San Francisco 1994, Deputy Minister for Foreign Affairs 1999–2001, Amb. to USA 2001–08; Commr of Nippon Professional Baseball 2008–;*Website:* www.npb.or.jp/eng (office).

KATO, Shigeya; Japanese business executive; *Chairman and Representative Director, Showa Shell Sekiyu K.K.;* b. 2 Aug. 1947; joined Shell Sekiyu K.K. 1970 (acquired by Showa Oil Co. Ltd to form Showa Shell Sekiyu K.K. 1985), Gen. Man. Change Promotion Centre 1998–99, Exec. Officer/Gen. Man. Change Promotion Centre 1999–2001, Dir 2001–03, Man. Dir 2003–05, Sr Man. Dir 2005–06, Vice-Chair. and Rep. Dir Showa Shell Sekiyu K.K. 2006–09, Chair. and Rep. Dir 2009–. *Address:* Showa Shell Sekiyu K.K., Daiba Frontier Building, 2-3-2, Daiba, Minato-ku, Tokyo 135-8074, Japan (office). *Telephone:* (3) 5531-5591 (office). *Fax:* (3) 5531-5598 (office). *E-mail:* info@showa-shell.co.jp (office). *Website:* www.showa-shell.co.jp (office).

KATO, Susumu; Japanese business executive; *Chairman, Sumitomo Corporation;* b. 21 May 1947, Kyoto; ed Kobe Univ.; joined Sumitomo Corpn 1970, Asst Man. Sumitomo Corpn of America, LA 1979–85, Asst Man., Rolled Steel Import-Export Dept 1985–89, Man. Sumitomo Corpn of America, Detroit 1989–96, Deputy Gen. Man. Steel Sheets Int. Trade Dept 1996–97, Gen. Man. 1997–99, Corp. Officer and Deputy Gen. Man., Iron and Steel Div. 1999–2000, Man., Personnel and Gen. Affairs Div. 2000–03, mem. Bd of Dirs 2000–, also Gen. Man. Corp. Planning and Co-ordination 2001–03, Man. Exec. Officer 2003–05, Sr Man. Exec. Officer 2005–07, Pres. and CEO Sumitomo Corpn of America, NY 2005–07, also Gen. Man. for the Americas 2005–07, Exec. Vice-Pres. Sumitomo Corpn, Tokyo 2007, Pres. and CEO 2007–12, Chair. 2012–. *Address:* Sumitomo Corpn, 8-11 Harumi 1-chome, Chuo-ku, Tokyo 104-8610, Japan (office). *Telephone:* (3) 5166-5000 (office). *Fax:* (3) 5166-6292 (office). *E-mail:* info@sumitomocorp.co.jp (office). *Website:* www.sumitomocorp.co.jp (office).

KATO, Susumu, PhD; Japanese physicist and academic; *Professor Emeritus of Atmospheric Physics, Kyoto University;* b. 27 Aug. 1928, Saitama; s. of Nimpei Kato and Minoru Kato; m. Kyoko Kojo; ed Kyoto Univ.; Lecturer, Faculty of Eng, Kyoto Univ. 1955–61, Asst Prof., Ionosphere Research Lab. 1961–62, Assoc. Prof. 1964–67, Prof. 1967–81, Dir and Prof., Radio Atmospheric Science Centre 1981–92, Prof. Emer. of Atmospheric Physics 1992–; Research Officer, Upper Atmosphere Section, CSIRO, NSW, Australia 1962–64; Visiting Scientist, High Altitude Observatory, Nat. Center for Atmospheric Research, Colo 1967–68, 1973–74; Visiting Prof., Dept of Meteorology, UCLA 1973–74, Bandung Inst. of Tech., Indonesia 1994–97; Vice-Chair. Japan-Indonesia Science and Tech. Forum 1992–96; AGU Fellow 1991; Foreign Assoc. Nat. Acad. of Eng, USA 1995–; Fellow, Int. Inst. for Advanced Studies 1998; Tanakadate Prize 1959, Yamaji Science Prize 1974, Appleton Prize 1987, Hasegawa Prize 1987, Fujiwara Prize 1989, Japan Acad. Award 1989. *Publications:* Dynamics of the Upper Atmosphere 1980, Dinamika Atmosfer 1998; over 100 scientific papers on atmospheric tidal theory, observation of atmospheric waves by MST radar. *Leisure interests:* reading, music, jogging, swimming, Japanese calligraphy. *Address:* 22-15 Fujimidai, Otsu, Shiga Prefecture, 520-0846, Japan (home). *Telephone:* (77) 534-1177 (home). *Fax:* (77) 533-4013 (home). *E-mail:* kato@rish.kyoto-u.ac.jp (office).

KATOCH, Chandresh Kumari; Indian politician; *Minister of Culture;* b. 1 Feb. 1944, Jodhpur, Rajasthan; d. of the late Hanumant Singhji and Krishana Kumari; m. Aditya Katoch 1968; one s.; ed Jodhpur Univ., Rajasthan; mem. Himachal Pradesh Legis. Ass. 1972–77, 1982–84, 2003–07, various roles with Govt of Himachal Pradesh including Deputy Minister 1977, Minister of State for Tourism 1984, Cabinet Minister 2003–04; elected to 8th Lok Sabha (lower house of Parl.)

1984, re-elected to 15th Lok Sabha for Jodhpur constituency 2009–; elected to Rajya Sabha (upper house of Parl.) 1996, Deputy Chief Whip, Congress Party in Rajya Sabha 1998–99; Pres. All-India Mahila Congress 1999–2003; Union Cabinet Minister of Culture 2012–. *Leisure interests:* reading, listening to music, looking after animals, horse riding, tennis. *Address:* Ministry of Culture, 'C' Wing, Shastri Bhavan, Dr Rajendra Prasad Road, New Delhi 110 001, India (office). *Telephone:* (11) 23386995 (office). *Fax:* (11) 23384093 (office). *E-mail:* pvtsecymoc@gmail.com (office). *Website:* indiaculture.gov.in (office).

KATOH, Nobuaki; Japanese business executive; *President and CEO, DENSO Corporation;* ed Keio Univ., Tokyo; joined DENSO Corpn in 1971, served as Gen. Man. Air-Conditioning Planning and Gen. Planning Depts, Man. Officer 2004–05, Pres. DENSO's European HQ 2005–07, Sr Man. Dir responsible for Corp. Center and Thermal Systems Business Group 2007–08, Pres. and CEO DENSO Corpn 2008–. *Address:* DENSO Corpn, 1-1 Showa-cho, Kariya, Aichi 448-8661, Japan (office). *Telephone:* (556) 25-5511 (office). *Fax:* (566) 25-4509 (office). *E-mail:* info@globaldenso.com (office). *Website:* www.globaldenso.com (office).

KATONA, Béla, PhD; Hungarian engineer, economist and politician; b. 9 Feb. 1944, Budapest; ed József Attila High School, Budapest, Tech. Univ. of Budapest, Karl Marx Univ. of Econs; mem. Országgyülés (Nat. Ass.) 1990–2010, Deputy Leader Parl. Group 1990–94, 2000–09, Speaker of Országgyülés 2009–10; Vice-Pres. Hungarian Socialist Party (Magyar Szocialista Párt—MSZP) 1996–98; Minister without portfolio in charge of civil secret services 1994–95; mem. Hungarian Acad. of Eng 2011–. *E-mail:* drkatonabela@gmail.com (office); bela.katona@mszp.hu (office).

KATONA, Tamás; Hungarian diplomat, politician and historian; *Chairman, Manfred Wörner Foundation;* b. 2 Feb. 1932, Budapest; s. of Tibor Katona and Magdolna Halász; m. Klára Barta; one s. two d.; ed Archiepiscopal High School (Rákóczianum), Budapest, Eötvös Loránd Univ., Budapest; head of public libraries 1954–61; Ed. Magyar Helikon Publishing House and Európa Publishing House 1961–86; Lecturer in 19th-century Hungarian History, Eötvös Coll. 1980–85, József Attila Univ. of Szeged 1986–90; mem. Parl. 1990–98; Sec. of State for Foreign Affairs 1990–92; Sec. of State, Prime Minister's Office 1992–94; First Vice-Pres. IPU, Hungary; Mayor, Castle Dist, Budapest 1994–98; Prof., Károli Gáspár Protestant Univ. 1998–2000; Amb. to Poland 2000–03; Chair. Hungarian Scout Asscn 1994–98, Manfred Wörner Foundation 1998–; Scientific Adviser, Inst. of History, Hungarian Acad. of Sciences 2003–; Ed. serial publs Bibliotheca Historica and Pro Memoria (pocket library of history and cultural history); Grand Officer, Order of Merit (Poland), Grand Officer, Order of Merit of the Sovereign Order of St John, Hungarian Defence Cross (First Class), Medal of Merit of the 1956 Revolution. *Publications:* Az aradi vértanúk (The Martyrs of Arad) 1979, 1983, 1991, 2003, A korona kilenc évszázada (Nine Centuries of the Crown) 1979, A tatárjárás emlékezete (The Mongol Invasion) 1981, 1987, Budavár bevételének emlékezete, 1849 (Capture of Fort Buda in 1849) 1991, Csány László erdélyi fökormánybiztos (László Csány High Commissioner of Transylvania) 1991. *Leisure interests:* tennis, music. *Address:* Fortuna-utca 13, 1014 Budapest, Hungary (home). *Telephone:* (1) 201-13-65 (home). *Fax:* (1) 225-32-93 (home). *E-mail:* fortunau13@hotmail.com (home).

KATORI, Hidetoshi, BA, MA, PhD, DEng; Japanese physicist and academic; *Chief Scientist, Quantum Metrology Laboratory, Rikagaku Kenkyūjo (RIKEN);* b. 27 Sept. 1964, Tokyo; ed Univ. of Tokyo; Research Assoc., Dept of Applied Physics, Univ. of Tokyo 1991, Assoc. Prof., Eng Research Inst. 1999–2010, Prof., Dept of Applied Physics, Grad. School of Eng 2010–; Research Dir, ERATO Katori Innovative Space-Time Project, Japan Science and Tech. Agency 2010–; Chief Scientist, Quantum Metrology Lab., Rikagaku Kenkyūjo (RIKEN) 2011–; Visiting Scientist, Max-Planck Inst. of Quantum Optics, Germany 1994; Prize of French Soc. of Chronometry 2005, Prize of Japan Soc. for the Promotion of Science 2005, Julius Springer Prize for Applied Physics 2005, European Time and Frequency Award, Soc. Française de Chronométrie 2005, Rabi Award, IEEE Int. Frequency Control Symposium 2008, Philipp Franz von Siebold Award, Alexander von Humboldt Foundation, Berlin, German 2011. *Publications:* numerous scientific papers in professional journals. *Address:* Department of Applied Physics, Graduate School of Engineering, University of Tokyo, 7-3-1 Hongo, Bunkyo-ku, Tokyo 113-8656, Japan (office). *Telephone:* (3) 5841-6800 (office). *Fax:* (3) 5841-8760 (office). *E-mail:* katori@amo.t.u-tokyo.ac.jp (office). *Website:* www.amo.t.u-tokyo.ac.jp (office).

KATRENKO, Vladimir Semenovich, DEcon; Russian politician; b. 11 Nov. 1956, Mineralnye Vody, Stavropol Krai; m.; two d., one s.; ed Mineralnye Vody Railway-Tech. Inst. no.4, Rostov Inst. of Railway Engineers, All-Union Corresp. Legal Inst.; worked as carpenter; served in army 1976–78; trained as electrical mechanic, qualified as engineer mechanic; driver Soviet Auto Transport, Mineralnye Vody, manager of convoys, apptd Gen. Dir 1988, 1996, Sec. Communist Party Cttee; elected to State Duma 1993, 1999, 2003, First Deputy Chair. 2004–07, First Deputy Head of United Russian faction, currently Auditor, Accounts Chamber of the Russian Federation; mem. Cttee for Ethnic Affairs, head of Comm. on North Caucasus, Head of Specialized Cttee for Energy, Transport and Communications 2008; head of state admin, Mineralnye Vody 1996–99; fmr deputy head Govt of Stavropol Krai province, Sec. Political Council; mem. Gen. Council United Russia party; Hon. Transport Worker of Russian Fed. 1994, Award for Services to the Devt of Physical Culture and Sport 1998, Esteemed Railwayman 2003, Friendship Order 2003. *Leisure interests:* playing guitar, poetry, arts, mini-football. *Address:* Accounts Chamber of the Russian Federation, 119991 Moscow, Zubovskaya street, 2, Russia (office). *Telephone:* (495) 986-05-09 (office). *Fax:* (495) 986-09-52 (office). *E-mail:* www.ach.gov.ru/en (office).

KATSAV, Moshe; Israeli politician and fmr head of state; b. 5 Dec. 1945, Iran; m. Gila Katsav; four s. one d.; ed Hebrew Univ. of Jerusalem; reporter for Yediot Aharonot (newspaper) 1966–68; Mayor of Kiryat Malachi 1969, 1974–81; mem. Knesset 1977–85; mem. Interior and Educ. Cttees 1977–81; Deputy Minister of Housing and Construction 1981–84; Minister of Labour and Social Affairs 1984–88, of Transportation 1988–92; mem. Cttee on Defence 1988–92, 1996–99; Chair. Likud faction in the Knesset, Parl. Cttee of Chinese–Israeli Friendship League 1992–96; Deputy Prime Minister 1996–99, also Minister of Tourism, for Israeli Arab Affairs; Pres. of Israel 2000–07 (resgnd); Chair. Cttee for Nat. Events

1996–99; mem. Foreign Affairs and Defence Cttee 1999–2000; mem. Bd of Trustees Ben-Gurion Univ. 1978; convicted of several counts of rape and sexual harassment 2010, sentenced to seven years in prison Nov. 2011; Dr hc (Univ. of Nebraska) 1998, (George Washington Univ.) 2001, (Hartford Univ., Conn.) 2001, (Yeshivah Univ., NY) 2002, (Bar Ilan Univ., Israel) 2003, (China Agricultural Univ., Beijing) 2003, (Sorbonne, Paris) 2004, (ELTE Univ. of Budapest) 2004; Bene Merito Medal of the Acad. of Science of Austria 2004.

KATSELI, Loukia-Tarsitsa (Louka), BA, MPA, MA, PhD; Greek economist, academic and politician; *President, Social Agreement;* b. 20 April 1952, Athens; d. of Aleka Katseli (actress); m. Gerasimos Arsenis; one s. one d.; ed Smith Coll., Mass and Princeton Univ., USA; Asst Prof., then Assoc. Prof., Yale Univ., USA 1977–85, Fellow, Saybrook Coll. 1979–85; Visiting Prof., Birkbeck Coll., London, UK 1986, Athens Univ. of Econs 1986–87; Prof., Dept of Econs, Nat. Univ. of Athens 1987–, Chair. 1997–2001; mem. Panhellenic Socialist Movt (PASOK) 1976–2011 (expelled), 2011–12 (expelled from parl. group for voting against Greece's loan deal with its foreign creditors); Scientific Dir Centre of Planning and Econ. Research (KEPE) 1982–86; mem. Council of Econ. Advisers 1982–84, Nat. Advisory Council for Research and Tech. 1997–2000; mem. and Vice-Chair. UN Cttee on Devt Planning 1998–99; Special Econ. Advisor to fmr Prime Minister Andreas Papandreou 1993–96; mem. numerous int. and European initiatives, including EU Cttee on Econ. and Monetary Affairs, 'Committee of Wise Men' Review of the Social Charter of Europe; Head of Devt Centre, OECD, Paris 2003–07; mem. Vouli (Parl.) for Athens B 2007–; Minister for the Economy, Competitiveness and Shipping 2009–10, of Labour and Social Protection 2010–11; Co-founder Social Agreement party with Haris Kastanidis (q.v.), Pres. 2012–; Sidney Cohen Prize for Econs, Smith Coll. 1971, Concilium Faculty Research Award, Summer 1979, Award for Best New Teacher, Yale Univ. 1980, scholarship from German Marshall Fund 1982–84. *Publications:* more than 40 books and articles in int. journals on int. and macroeconomic policy, especially in devt cooperation and migration policy. *Address:* 23 Sina str., 106 80 Athens, Greece. *Telephone:* (210) 3644260. *Fax:* (210) 3603558. *E-mail:* louka.katseli@parliament.gr (office); info@koinonikisymfonia.gr (office). *Website:* www.koinonikisymfonia.gr (office); loukakatseli.gr.

KATSONGA, Davies Chester, BA, MBA; Malawi politician; b. 6 Aug. 1955, Mwanza; m.; two s.; ed Schiller Int. Univ., Inst. of Marketing, South-Bank Univ., London, UK; MP for Mwanza Cen. Constituency 1999–; Minister of Mines, Natural Resources and Environmental Affairs, then Speaker of Parl. 1999–2004; Minister of Natural Resources 2004–05, of Foreign Affairs 2005–06, of Defence 2006–07, for Presidential and Parl. Affairs 2007–08, of Labour and Vocational Training 2008; mem. Democratic Progressive Party 2005–. *Leisure interests:* playing and watching soccer, reading political autobiographies, travel, angling, carpentry, environmental affairs and computers. *Address:* c/o Ministry of Labour, Private Bag 344, Capital City, Lilongwe 3, Malawi (office).

KATSUMATA, Nobuo; Japanese business executive; b. 1943; m. Fusae Katsumata; joined Marubeni Corpn 1966, various man. positions, mem. Bd of Dirs 1996–, fmr Chief Dir of Paper Pulp, Sr Man. Dir –2003, Pres. and CEO 2003–08, Chair. 2008–13; Chair. Japan Foreign Trade Council, Inc.; Dir, Hitachi America Ltd, Sapporo Holdings Ltd 2009–; Outside Dir, Yokogawa Electric Corpn 2009–, Hitachi Ltd 2011–; Commdr of the Lion of Finland 2003. *Leisure interest:* sailing. *Address:* c/o Marubeni Corpn, 42 Ohtemachi 1-chome, Chiyoda-ku, Tokyo 100-8088, Japan. *E-mail:* info@marubeni.com.

KATSUMATA, Tsunehisa; Japanese energy industry executive; b. 1940; ed Univ. of Tokyo; joined Tokyo Electric Power Co., Inc. (TEPCO) as grad. trainee, held various man. positions, including Man., Corp. Planning Dept, Exec. Vice-Pres. for Corp. Planning –2002, Pres. 2002–08, Chair. 2008–12; Vice-Chair. Bd of Councillors, Nippon-Keidanren; Dir Japan Nuclear Fuels Ltd, Japan Productivity Center for Socio-Econ. Devt, Japan Investor Relations Asscn; mem. Bd Dirs KDDI Corp.; Chair. Fed. of Electric Power Cos of Japan. *Leisure interests:* reading, Go (traditional Japanese strategy game). *Address:* c/o Tokyo Electric Power Co., Inc., 1-1-3 Uchisaiwai-cho, Chiyoda-ku, Tokyo 100-8560, Japan.

KATTAN, Naïm, OC, FRSC; Canadian writer; b. 26 Aug. 1928, Baghdad, Iraq; s. of Nessim Kattan and Hela Kattan; m. Gaetane Laniel 1961; one s.; ed Univ. of Baghdad, Univ. of Paris (Sorbonne), France; newspaper corresp. in Near East and Europe, broadcaster throughout Europe; emigrated to Canada 1954; Int. Politics Ed. for Nouveau Journal 1961–62; fmr teacher at Laval Univ.; fmr Sec. Cercle Juif de langue française de Montreal; freelance journalist and broadcaster; Prof., Univ. of Québec, Montreal; Assoc. Dir Canada Council; Pres. RSC; mem. Acad. Canadienne-Française; Chevalier, Légion d'honneur, Officier des Arts et des Lettres. Chevalier, Ordre nat. du Québec; Dr hc (Middlebury Coll.), (Concordia). *Play:* Avant le ceremonie 2009. *Publications:* novels: Adieu Babylone 1975, Les Fruits arrachés 1981, La Fiancée promise 1983, La Fortune du passager 1989, La Célébration 1997, L'Anniversaire 2000; (essays) Le Réel et le théâtral 1970, Ecrivains des Amériques, Tomes I-III, Le Repos et l'Oubli 1987, Le Père 1990, Farida 1991, La Reconciliation 1992, A. M. Klein 1994, La Distraction 1994, Culture: Alibi ou liberté 1996, Idoles et images 1996, Figures bibliques 1997, L'Amour reconnu 1999, Le Silence des adieux 1999, Le gardien de mon frère 2003, La Parole et le lieu 2004, Les Villes de naissance, L'Ecrivain migrant, Farewell Babylon: Coming of Age in Jewish Baghdad 2007; numerous short stories and criticisms. *Address:* 2463 rue Sainte Famille No. 2114, Montreal, PQ, H2X 2K7, Canada. *Telephone:* (514) 499-2836. *Fax:* (514) 499-9954. *E-mail:* kattan.naim@uqam.ca. *Website:* www.uqam.ca.

KATUARI, Eddy William; Indonesian business executive; *CEO, Wings Group;* b. 1951, Surabaya; s. of Johannes Ferdinand Katuari; m.; four c.; worked with family business Wings Group (consumer goods mfr), took over following death of father 2004; Commr PT Petrocentral, Unggul Indah Investama, PT Wiranusa Grahatama; Dir Albright & Wilson (Australia) Ltd, United Austindo Chemicals Pte Ltd. *Address:* Wings Group, Kawasan Perluasan Utara, PT JIEP, Jalan Tipar Cakung Kav F 5-7, Jakarta 13910, Indonesia (office). *Telephone:* (21) 4602696 (office). *Fax:* (21) 4603494 (office). *Website:* www.wingscorp.com (office).

KATUWAL, Gen. Rukmangad, BA, MA; Nepalese army officer retd); b. 12 Dec. 1948, Okahldhunga Dist; s. of Khadgadhoj Katawal; m. Uma Katawal; one s. one d.; ed Tribhuwan Univ., Quaid-i-Azam Univ., Indian Nat. Defence Acad., Indian

Mil. Acad., Special Forces Course, USA, Army Command and Staff Coll., Camberley, UK, Sr Command Course, India, Nat. Defence Univ., Islamabad, Pakistan; commissioned into Shree Shreenath Bn (Infantry) of Nepalese Army 1969; Instructor, Nepalese Army School 1973; served in UN Emergency Force (UNEF) in Suez Canal area 1973; commanded Ind. Co.– Shree Kalidhoj Co. (currently a bn) 1976–77; held several key staff appointments before serving as Liaison Officer of Nepalese Govt to Brigade of Gurkhas of British Army and Govt of Hong Kong 1983–86; Chief Mil. Personnel Officer, UN Interim Force in Lebanon (UNIFIL) 1988–90; took over command of Shree Pashupati Prashad Bn 1990; served in Research and Devt Wing, Army HQ; apptd Commdt of Nepalese Mil. Acad. 1993; promoted to Brig.-Gen. 1996, holds distinction of having commanded three consecutive Brigades, two Infantry and one Special Forces; apptd Dir of Mil. Intelligence 1999; promoted to Maj.-Gen. 2001; took over as Adjutant Gen. of Nepalese Army 2001; apptd as first Co-coordinator of Nat. Security Council Secr. 2001; commanded the then Western Div. on combat operations at peak of counterinsurgency 2003–04; promoted to Lt-Gen. 2004; Chief of Gen. Staff 2004–06; 'Col Commdt' of Mother Unit, Shree Pashupati Prashad Bn; promoted to Gen. 2006; Deputy Chief of Army Staff –Aug. 2006, Acting Chief of Army Staff Aug.–Sept. 2006, Chief of Army Staff (first commoner officer) Sept. 2006–09 (retd); has been at odds with Maoist Govt on several issues, leading to his brief sacking by Prime Minister Prachanda 3 May 2009, ordered by Pres. of Nepal to continue his service, resulting in Prime Minister's resignation and a general collapse of the govt; has participated widely in nat. and int. confs and seminars at sr level, including Multilateral Planner's Conf. in Romania and Int. Symposium Course on Asian Pacific Security in China; Birendra Prajatantra Bhaskar (Second Class); numerous other decorations and medals; Distinguished Int. Honour Grad., US Special Forces Course, earned the Gideon in US Ranger Course. *Leisure interests:* athletics, keen sportsman, especially fond of basketball, racquet games and golf, travel, reading, hiking, riding, social work, writing songs in Nepalese folk, patriotic and popular song disciplines. *Address:* c/o Office of the Chief of Army Staff, Ministry of Defence, Singha Durbar, Kathmandu, Nepal (office).

KATZ, Daryl, LLB; Canadian lawyer and business executive; *Chairman and CEO, Katz Group;* b. 1962, Edmonton; s. of Barry Katz; m.; two c.; ed Univ. of Alberta Law School; fmr lawyer; Founder, Katz Group, group of pharmacy cos that includes Rexall, Guardian IDA, Medicine Shop and Pharm Plus drugstore chains, Chair. and CEO 1996–; Owner, Edmonton Oilers (professional ice hockey team). *Address:* Katz Group, Suite 1702 Bell Tower, 10104 103rd Avenue, Edmonton, Alberta T5J 0H8, Canada (office). *Telephone:* (780) 990-0505 (office). *Fax:* (780) 702-0647 (office). *E-mail:* esilverman@katzgroup.ca (office). *Website:* www.katzgroup.ca (office).

KATZ, Michael, AB, MD, FAAP; American (b. Polish) paediatrician and academic; *Senior Adviser, Transdisciplinary Research, March of Dimes Foundation;* b. (Michal Katz), 13 Feb. 1928, Lwów, Poland; s. of Edward Katz and Rita Gluzman; m. Robin J. Roy 1986; one s.; ed Medical Univ., Łódź, Poland, Univ. of Pennsylvania, State Univ. of New York, Brooklyn, Columbia Univ. School of Public Health; Intern, UCLA Medical Center 1956–57; Resident, Presbyterian Hosp. New York 1960–62, Dir Pediatric Service 1977–92; Hon. Lecturer in Paediatrics, Makerere Univ. Coll., Kampala, Uganda 1963–64; Instructor in Pediatrics, Columbia Univ. 1964–65, Prof. in Tropical Medicine, School of Public Health 1971–92, Prof. Emer. 1992–, Prof. of Pediatrics, Coll. of Physicians and Surgeons 1972–77, Reuben S. Carpentier Prof. and Chair. Dept of Pediatrics 1977–92, Prof. Emer. 1992–; Asst Prof. of Pediatrics, Univ. of Pennsylvania 1966–71; Sr Vice-Pres. for Research and Global Programs, March of Dimes Foundation 1992–2011, Sr Adviser, Transdisciplinary Research 2011–; Pres. World Alliance of Orgs for the Prevention of Birth Defects 1995–2008; Assoc. mem. Wistar Inst., Philadelphia 1965–71; Consultant, WHO regional offices, Guatemala, Venezuela, Egypt, Yemen; mem. US Del. to 32nd World Health Ass., Geneva 1979; Consultant, UNICEF, New York and Tokyo; mem. numerous medical socs including Inst. of Medicine of NAS; Fellow, American Acad. of Pediatrics, AAAS, IDSA; Hon. DMedSc (Medical Univ. of Łódź, Poland) 2009; Jurzykowski Foundation Award in Medicine 1983, Alexander von Humboldt Foundation Sr US Scientist Award 1987. *Publications:* contribs to numerous journals and medical works. *Leisure interest:* music. *Address:* 200 East 57th Street, New York, NY 10022 (home); March of Dimes Foundation, 1275 Mamaroneck Avenue, White Plains, NY 10605, USA (office). *Telephone:* (914) 997-4555 (office). *Fax:* (914) 997-4560 (office). *E-mail:* mkatz@marchofdimes.com (office); robinroy@optonline.net (home). *Website:* www.marchofdimes.com (office).

KATZ, Samuel (Sam) Lawrence, BA, MD; American paediatrician, vaccinologist and academic; *Wilbert C. Davison Professor Emeritus, Department of Pediatrics, Medical Center, Duke University School of Medicine;* b. 29 May 1927, Manchester, NH; s. of Morris Katz and Ethel Lawrence Katz; m. 1st Betsy Jane Cohan 1950 (divorced 1971); four s. (one s. deceased) three d.; m. 2nd Catherine Minock Wilfert 1971; two step-d.; ed Dartmouth Coll. and Harvard Medical School; hosp. appointments, Boston, Mass 1952–56; Exchange Registrar, Paediatric Unit, St Mary's Hosp. Medical School, London, UK 1956; Research Fellow in Pediatrics, Harvard Medical School at Research Div. of Infectious Diseases, Children's Hosp. Medical Center, Boston 1956–58, Research Assoc. 1958–68; Pediatrician-in-Chief, Beth Israel Hosp., Boston 1958–61, Visiting Pediatrician 1961–68; Assoc. Physician, Children's Hosp. Medical Center 1958–63, Sr Assoc. in Medicine 1963–68, Chief, Newborn Div. 1961–67; Instructor in Pediatrics, Harvard Medical School, Boston 1958–59, Assoc. 1959–63, Tutor in Medical Sciences 1961–63, Asst Prof. of Pediatrics 1963–68; Co-Dir Combined Beth Israel Hosp.-Children's Hosp. Medical Center, Infectious Disease Career Training Program 1967–68; Prof. and Chair. Dept of Pediatrics, Duke Univ. School of Medicine, Durham, NC 1968–90, Wilbert C. Davison Prof. of Pediatrics 1972–97, Wilbert C. Davison Prof. Emer. 1997–, Chair. Emer. 1990–; prin. activities involve research on children's vaccines and on pediatric AIDS; mem. Bd of Dirs Georgetown Univ. 1987–93, Hawkins Foundation 1988–2006, Burroughs Wellcome Fund 1991–99 (Chair. 1995–99); mem. Scientific Advisory Bd, St Jude Children's Research Hosp. 1977–85; Consultant, NIH AIDS Exec. Cttee 1986–89, mem. NIH Pediatric AIDS Exec. Cttee 1994–97; mem. Editorial Bd Pediatric Infectious Diseases Report; fmr mem. Editorial Bd Annual Review in Medicine, Postgraduate Medicine, Reviews of Infectious Diseases, Current Problems in Pediatrics, Ped Sat (TV Educ.); Chair. Bd of Trustees, Int. Vaccine Inst., Seoul, S Korea 2004–08; Co-Chair. Indo-US Vaccine

Action Program 1999–2004; mem. Soc. for Pediatric Research, American Soc. for Microbiology, American Asscn of Immunologists, American Public Health Asscn, American Soc. for Clinical Investigation, American Pediatric Soc., American Epidemiological Soc., American Soc. for Virology, American Fed. for Clinical Research, Inst. of Medicine; Fellow, American Acad. of Pediatrics, Infectious Diseases Soc. of America, AAAS; Hon. DSc (Georgetown Univ.) 1996, (Dartmouth Coll.) 1998; Presidential Medal of Dartmouth Coll. for Leadership and Achievement 1991, Distinguished Physician Award, Pediatric Infectious Diseases Soc. 1991, Bristol Award and Soc. Citation, Infectious Diseases Soc. of America 1993, Needleman Medal and Award, American Public Health Asscn 1997, Howland Award, American Pediatric Soc. 2000, Gold Medal, Sabin Vaccine Inst. 2003, Founders Medal, Duke Univ. 2004 and other awards. *Publications:* numerous articles in scientific journals, textbooks of paediatrics and infectious diseases. *Leisure interests:* jazz drumming (Joe Butterfield Dixieland Jazz Concert 1994–2003), cycling, reading, opera. *Address:* Duke University Medical Center, Box 2925, Durham, NC 27710, USA (office). *Telephone:* (919) 668-4852 (office); (919) 968-0008 (home). *Fax:* (919) 668-4859 (office); (919) 968-0447 (home). *E-mail:* katz0004@mc.duke.edu (office); slkatz@mindspring.com (home). *Website:* www.mc.duke.edu (office).

KATZENBERG, Jeffrey; American film industry executive; *CEO, DreamWorks Animation SKG; b.* 21 Dec. 1950; m. Marilyn Siegal; one s. one d.; Asst to Chair., CEO Paramount Pictures, New York 1975–77; Exec. Dir Marketing, Paramount TV, Calif. 1977, Vice-Pres. Programming 1977–78; Vice-Pres. feature production, Paramount Pictures 1978–80, Sr Vice-Pres. production, motion picture div. 1980–82, Pres. production, motion pictures and TV 1982–94; Chair. Walt Disney Studios, Burbank, Calif. –1994; Co-founder and Prin. DreamWorks SKG 1995–2005, CEO DreamWorks Animation SKG 1994–. *Address:* DreamWorks Animation SKG, 1000 Flower Street, Glendale, CA 91201, USA (office). *Telephone:* (818) 695-5000 (office). *Fax:* (818) 695-9944 (office). *Website:* www.dreamworksanimation.com (office).

KAUFMAN, Charles (Charlie) Stuart; American screenwriter; *b.* Nov. 1958, West Hartford, Conn.; m. Denise Kaufman; two c.; ed Boston Univ., New York Univ.; worked in newspaper circulation dept, The Star Tribune, Minneapolis, Minn. 1986–90; contrib. to National Lampoon 1991; began scriptwriting 1991; cr. short films shown on Late Night with David Letterman TV show 1990s; writer of 30 episodes for TV shows 1991–96; Producer, Misery Loves Company (TV series) 1995. *Screenplays include:* films: Being John Malkovich 1999, Human Nature 2001, Adaptation (Best Screenplay, Broadcast Film Critics Asscn, Chicago Film Critics Asscn, Nat. Bd of Review, Toronto Film Critics Asscn) 2002, Confessions of a Dangerous Mind 2002, Eternal Sunshine of the Spotless Mind (Nat. Bd of Review Best Original Screenplay Award 2004, BAFTA Award 2005, Writers' Guild of America Award for Best Original Screenplay 2005, Acad. Award for Best Original Screenplay 2005) 2004, Synecdoche, New York (also dir) 2008; TV: Get A Life 1991–92, The Edge 1992–93, The Trouble with Larry 1993, Ned and Stacey 1996–97, The Dana Carvey Show 1996. *Leisure interest:* reading. *Address:* William Morris Endeavor Entertainment, 9601 Wilshire Blvd., 3rd Floor, Beverly Hills, CA 90210-5213, USA (office).

KAUFMAN, Sir Gerald Bernard, Kt, PC, MA, MP; British politician; *b.* 21 June 1930; s. of Louis Kaufman and Jane Kaufman; ed Leeds Grammar School and Queen's Coll., Oxford; Asst Gen. Sec. Fabian Soc. 1954–55; political staff, Daily Mirror 1955–64; Political Corresp., New Statesman 1964–65; Parl. Press Liaison, Labour Party 1965–70; MP for Manchester, Ardwick 1970–83, for Manchester, Gorton 1983–; Under-Sec. of State for the Environment 1974–75, for Industry 1975; Minister of State, Dept of Industry 1975–79; mem. Parl. Cttee of Labour Party 1980–92; Opposition Spokesman for Environment 1980–83, Home Affairs 1983–87; Shadow Foreign Sec. 1987–92; Chair. House of Commons Nat. Heritage Select Cttee 1992–97, Culture, Media and Sport Select Cttee 1997–2005, All-Party Parliamentary Dance Group 2006–; currently Chair. All-Party Parliamentary Opera Group; mem. Labour Party Nat. Exec. Cttee 1991–92; mem. Royal Comm. on House of Lords Reform 1999; Chair. Booker Prize Judges 1999; Hillal-e-Pakistan 1999. *Publications:* How to Live under Labour (co-author) 1964, To Build the Promised Land 1973, How to Be a Minister 1980 (revised edn 1997), Renewal: Labour's Britain in the 1980s 1983, My Life in the Silver Screen 1985, Inside the Promised Land 1986, Meet Me in St Louis 1994. *Leisure interests:* cinema, opera, records, theatre, concerts, travel. *Address:* House of Commons, Westminster, London, SW1A 0AA (office); 87 Charlbert Court, Eamont Street, London, NW8 7DA, England (home). *Telephone:* (20) 7219-5145 (office). *Fax:* (20) 7219-6825 (office).

KAUFMAN, Henry, BA, MS, PhD; American banker and investment manager; *President, Henry Kaufman & Company Inc.; b.* 20 Oct. 1927, Wenings, Germany; s. of Gustav Kaufman and Hilda Kaufman (née Rosenthal); m. Elaine Reinheimer 1957; three s.; ed New York and Columbia Univs; emigrated to USA in 1937; Asst Chief Economist, Research Dept, Fed. Reserve Bank of New York 1957–61; with Salomon Bros., New York 1962–88, Gen. Pnr 1967–88, mem. Exec. Cttee 1972–88, Man. Dir 1981–88, also Chief Economist, in charge Bond Market Research, Industry and Stock Research and Bond Portfolio Analysis Research Depts.; f. Henry Kaufman & Co. Inc., New York 1988–; Pres. Money Marketeers, New York Univ. 1964–65; fmr Dir Lehman Bros., Statue of Liberty-Ellis Island Foundation, Inc., W.R. Berkley Corpn, Federal Home Loan Mortgage Corpn; Trustee, New York Univ., Whitney Museum of American Art, Hudson Inst.; mem. Bd of Govs, Tel-Aviv Univ.; mem. American Econ. Asscn, American Finance Asscn, Conf. of Business Economists, Econ. Club, New York (also Dir), UN Asscn (also Dir), Council on Foreign Relations; mem. Int. Advisory Cttee, Federal Reserve Bank of New York, Advisory Cttee to Investment Cttee for the IMF Staff Retirement Plan; Trustee Inst. of Int. Educ. 1982–2003, Chair. 1989–2003, Chair. Emer. 2003–; George S. Eccles Prize for excellence in economic writing, Columbia Business School 1987. *Publication:* Interest Rates, the Markets and the New Financial World 1986, On Money and Markets, A Wall Street Memoir 2000. *Address:* Henry Kaufman & Co., 590 Madison Avenue, New York, NY 10022, USA (office). *Telephone:* (212) 758-7100 (office).

KAUFMAN, Philip; American screenwriter and film director; *b.* 23 Oct. 1936, Chicago, Ill.; s. of Nathan Kaufman and Betty Kaufman; m. Rose Kaufman; one s.; ed Univ. of Chicago and Harvard Law School; fmr teacher in Italy. *Films:* Goldstein (co-screenplay, co-dir and co-producer) (Prix de la Nouvelle Critique, Cannes 1964), Fearless Frank 1965, The Great Northfield Minnesota Raid 1971, The White Dawn (dir) 1973, Invasion of the Body Snatchers (dir) 1977, The Wanderers (co-screenplay and dir) 1979, The Right Stuff (dir and screenplay) (winner of four Acad. Awards) 1983, The Unbearable Lightness of Being (dir and co-screenplay) (Orson Welles Award for Best Filmmaker-Writer/Dir 1988, Nat. Soc. of Film Critics Award for Best Dir 1988) 1988, Henry & June (dir and co-scriptwriter) 1990, Rising Sun (dir and co-screenplay) 1993, China: The Wild East (narrator and exec. producer) 1995, Quills 2000, Twisted 2004, Hemingway and Gellhorn 2012.

KAUFMANN, Jonas; German singer (tenor); *b.* 10 July 1969, Munich; m. Margarete Joswig; three c.; ed Munich Hochschule für Musik, masterclasses with Hans Hotter and James King; first engagement, Saarbrücken Opera 1994–96; Così fan tutte in Milan (last production of Giorgio Strehler) 1997; Salzburg Festival debut as Dr Faust (Busoni) 1999; debut at Zurich Opera in Mozart's Die Zauberflöte 2000; US debut at Lyric Opera in Chicago 2001; debut at Royal Opera House, Covent Garden, London in Puccini's La Rondine 2004; debut at the Metropolitan Opera, New York in Verdi's La Traviata 2006; La Traviata in Zurich, Paris and at La Scala, Milan 2007; Tosca in London, Manon in Chicago, Fidelio in Paris 2008; Lohengrin in Munich, Don Carlo in London 2009; Werther in Paris and Bayreuth Festival debut in Lohengrin 2010; role debut as Siegmund in Die Walküre at the Met 2011; Don Carlo in Munich, Carmen and Ariadne auf Naxos at the Salzburg Festival, Lohengrin at La Scala 2012; Parsifal at the Met 2013; numerous recital performances at leading int. venues including the Met 2011 (first solo recital at the Met since Pavarotti in 1994); best known for playing Don José in Carmen, Cavaradossi in Tosca, title role in Don Carlos and Siegmund in Die Walküre; Bayerische Europamedaille 2012; prizewinner, Meistersinger Competition, Nuremberg 1993, Musical American Vocalist of the Year 2012, Int. Opera Awards Foundation Best Male Singer and Readers' Award 2013. *Recordings include:* Strauss Lieder (Gramophone Award for Best Solo Vocal Recording) 2007, Romantic Arias by Mozart, Schubert, Beethoven and Wagner (Grand Prix du Disque, Diapason d'or, Qobus/Classica: Le meilleur disque) 2008, Madame Butterfly (Gramophone Award) 2009, Sehnsucht (Prix Caecilia, ECHO Klassik Award for Best Vocalist of the Year 2010, Orphée d'or 'Wolfgang Wagner' 2010) 2009, Die schöne Müllerin (Diapason d'or) 2010, Verismo Arias (Diapason d'or 2010, Gramophone Award for Best Recital Recording 2011) 2011, Werther (DVD) (Diapason d'or) 2011, Fidelio (ECHO Klassik for Best Opera Recording of the Year) 2012, Der Ring des Nibelungen (DVD) (Grammy Award for Best Opera Recording) 2013, The Verdi Album 2013, Wagner Arias (Gramophone Award for Best Vocal Recording) 2013, Schubert: Winterreise 2014. *Address:* c/o Zemsky/Green Artists Management, 104 West 73rd Street, Suite 1, New York, NY 10023, USA (office). *Telephone:* (212) 579-6700 (office). *Fax:* (212) 579-4723 (office). *Website:* www.zemskygreen.com (office); www.jonaskaufmann.com.

KAUFMANN-BRÄNDLIR, Irene, Dr oec. publ.; Swiss business executive; *Chairman, Coop; b.* 1955; currently Chair. Coop; mem. Bd of Dirs Coop Immobilien AG, Bern (Chairwoman), Bank Coop AG, Basel, Bell Holding AG, Basel, Coop Mineraloel AG, Allschwil, Dipl. Ing. Fust AG, Oberbüren, Transgourmet Holding SE, Cologne; mem. Bd ETH Zurich Foundation, Juventus Schools, Zurich. *Address:* Coop, Thiersteinerallee 14, 4002 Basel, Switzerland (office). *Telephone:* (61) 336-66-66 (office). *E-mail:* info@coop.ch (office). *Website:* www.coop.ch (office).

KAUL, Hans-Peter, JD; German judge and diplomatist; *Judge and Second Vice-President, International Criminal Court; b.* 25 July 1943; m.; four c.; ed Int. Peace Acad., Vienna, Austria, Max Planck Inst., Heidelberg, Acad. of Int. Law, The Hague, The Netherlands, Ecole Nat. d'Admin, Paris, France, Univs of Heidelberg and Lausanne; mil. service in German army 1963–67, attained rank Capt.; Consul and Press Attaché, Embassy in Oslo, Norway 1977–80; with Office for UN Affairs, Fed. Foreign Office, Bonn 1980–84; Press Counsellor and Spokesman, Embassy in Tel-Aviv, Israel 1984–86; Political Counsellor, Embassy in Washington, USA 1986–90; Deputy Dir, Office of Nr Eastern Affairs, Fed. Foreign Office, Bonn 1990–93; First Counsellor, Perm. Mission to UN, NY 1993–96; Dir Office for Public Int. Law, Fed. Foreign Office, Bonn and Berlin 1996–2002; Amb. and Commr of Fed. Foreign Office for Int. Criminal Court (ICC) 2002–03; Judge, ICC 2003–, Pres. Pre-Trial Div. 2004–09, Second Vice-Pres. ICC 2009–; Head of German Dels to Preparatory Cttee for ICC Rome 1996–98, 1999–2002; mem. Nat. Advisory Cttee of German Red Cross Soc. on Int. Humanitarian Law 1996–; mem. German Soc. for Int. Law, German Soc. for the UN, German Soc. for Foreign Policy, Int. Criminal Law Network. *Publications:* chapters in books, country reports, articles in professional journals in German, English, Spanish, Portuguese and Arabic languages. *Address:* International Criminal Court, PO Box 19519, 2500 CM The Hague, The Netherlands (office); Buchsweildrstr. 16, 14195, Berlin, Germany (office). *Telephone:* (70) 515-8237 (office); 84418040 (home). *Fax:* (70) 515-8789 (office). *E-mail:* hanspeter.kaul@icc-cpi.int (office). *Website:* www.icc-cpi.int (office).

KAUNDA, Kenneth David; Zambian fmr politician and fmr head of state; *b.* (Buchizya), 28 April 1924, Lubwa; m. Betty Banda 1946; six s. (two s. deceased) two d. one adopted s.; ed Lubwa Training School and Munali Secondary School; schoolteacher at Lubwa Training School 1943, Headmaster 1944–47; Sec. Chinsali Young Men's Farming Asscn 1947; welfare officer, Chingola Copper Mine 1948; school teaching 1948–49; Founder-Sec. Lubwa branch, African Nat. Congress (ANC) 1950, district organizer 1951, prov. organizer 1952, Sec.-Gen. for N Rhodesia 1953; imprisoned for possession of prohibited literature Jan.–Feb. 1954; broke away from ANC to form Zambia African Nat. Congress 1958; imprisoned for political offences May 1959–Jan. 1960; Pres. United Nat. Independence Party 1960–92, 1995–2000; Minister of Local Govt and Social Welfare, N Rhodesia 1962–64; Prime Minister of N Rhodesia Jan.–Oct. 1964; Pres. Pan-African Freedom Movt for East, Central and South Africa (PAFMECSA) 1963; First Pres. of Zambia 1964–91 and Minister of Defence 1964–70, 1973–78; Head of Sub-Cttee for Defence and Security 1973–78; Minister of Foreign Affairs 1969–70, also of Trade, Industry, Mines and State Participation 1969–73; Chair. Mining and Industrial Devt Corpn of Zambia 1970; Chair. Org. of African Unity (OAU) 1970–71, 1987–88, Non-Aligned Nations Conf. 1970–73, fmr Chair. ZIMCO; Chancellor, Univ. of Zambia 1966–91, Copperbelt Univ. 1988; f. Peace Foundation 1992; charged with 'misprison of treason' over alleged involvement in attempted coup d'état 1997; freed after six months of house arrest after charges dropped June 1998; deprived of citizenship March 1999; citizenship restored by Supreme Court 2000; Founder and Chair. Kenneth Kaunda Children of Africa Foundation 2000–; Freeman of the Municipality of Chipata 1994; Order of the Collar of the Nile, Kt of the Collar of the Order of Pius XII, Order of the Queen of Sheba; Hon. LLD (Fordham, Dublin, Windsor (Canada), Wales, Sussex, York and Chile Univs); Dr hc (Humboldt State Univ., Calif.) 1980; Jawaharlal Nehru Award for Int. Understanding, Quaide Azam Human Rights Inst. Prize (Pakistan) 1976; honoured for his Keynote Address on Conflict Resolution in Africa and for Distinguished Leadership of African People for Over Half A Century, African Studies Coalition, Calif. State Univ., Sacramento 1995, WANGO Universal Peace Award 2004, Ubuntu Award, Nat. Heritage Council of South Africa 2007. *Publications:* Black Government 1961, Zambia Shall Be Free 1962, A Humanist in Africa (with Colin Morris) 1966, Humanism in Zambia and a Guide to its Implementation 1967, Humanism Part II 1977, Letter to my Children 1977, Kaunda On Violence 1980. *Address:* Office of the First President of the Republic of Zambia, 21 A Serval Road, PO E 501, Lusaka, Zambia. *Telephone:* (1) 260327 (office); (1) 260323 (home). *Fax:* (1) 220805 (office); (1) 220805 (home).

KAUR, Prabhjot; Indian poet and politician; b. (Matia), 6 July 1924, Langaryal; d. of Nidhan Singh Sachar and Rajinder Kaur; m. Col Narenderpal Singh 1948; two d.; ed Khalsa Coll. for Women, Lahore and Punjab Univ.; first collected poems published 1943 (aged 16); represented India at numerous int. literary confs; mem. Legis. Council, Punjab 1966; Ed. Vikendrit; mem. Sahitya Akademi (Nat. Acad. of Letters), Exec. Bd 1978; mem. Cen. Comm. for UNESCO, Nat. Writers Cttee of India; Fellow Emer., Govt of India; Sahitya Shiromani 1964, Rajya Kavi (Poet Laureate) conferred by Punjab Govt 1964, Sahitya Akademi Award 1964, Golden Laurel Leaves, United Poets Int., Philippines 1967, Padma Shri 1967, Grand Prix de la Rose de la France 1968, Most Distinguished Order of Poetry, World Poetry Soc. Intercontinental, USA 1974; Woman of the Year, UPLI, Philippines 1975, Sewa Sifti Award 1980, NIF Cultural Award 1982, Josh Kenya Award 1982, Delhi State Award 1983, Safdar Hashmi Award. *Television:* Ishak Shara Kee Nata (musical play). *Publications include:* 50 books, including: poetry: Supne Sadhran 1949, Do Rang 1951, Pankheru 1956, Lala (in Persian) 1958, Bankapasi 1958, Pabbi 1962, Khari 1967, Plateau (French) 1968, Wad-darshi Sheesha 1972, Madhiantar 1974, Chandra Yug 1978, Dreams Die Young 1979, Shadows and Light (Bulgarian) 1980, Him Hans 1982, Samrup 1982, Ishq Shara Ki Nata 1983, Shadows (English and Danish) 1985, Charam Serma, Men Tapu Mukhatab Han–Manas Man the Gagan Mokla (collected poems in four vols); short stories: Kinke 1952, Aman de Na 1956, Zindgi de Kujh Pal 1982, Main Amanat Naheen (Hindi), Kuntith, Casket (English); autobiog.: Jeena vi ek Ada Hai (two vols). *Leisure interests:* reading, travel. *Address:* D-203, Defence Colony, New Delhi 110 024, India (home). *Telephone:* (11) 4622756 (home).

KAURISMÄKI, Aki; Finnish filmmaker; b. 4 April 1957; co-founder film production co-operative Filmtotal; Man. Dir and Jt owner (with brother Mika Kaurismäki) film production co. Villealfa; jtly runs distribution co. Senso Film. *Films:* (Co-writer and Asst Dir) The Liar 1980, The Worthless 1982, The Clan: Tale of the Frogs 1984, Rosso 1985; (Co-Dir) The Saimaa Gesture 1981; (Dir) Crime and Punishment 1985, Calamari Union (Special Award, Hong Kong Int. Film Festival) 1985, Shadows in Paradise (Jussi Award for Best Finnish Film) 1986, Hamlet 1987, Ariel 1988, Leningrad Cowboys Go Home 1989, The Match Factory Girl 1989, I Hired a Contract Killer 1990, La Vie Bohème, Leningrad Cowboys Meet Moses 1993, Take Care of Your Scarf, Tatiana 1995, Drifting Clouds 1996, The Man Without a Past (Cannes Film Festival Best Actress Award 2002) 2002, Ten Minutes Older: The Trumpet (segment) (also producer, writer, editor) 2002, Visions of Europe (also writer, producer) 2004, Laitakaupungin valot (Lights in the Dark) 2006. *Rock videos:* Rock'y VI, Thru', The Wire, LA Woman 1986. *Address:* c/o The Finnish Film Foundation, K.13, Kanavakatu 24, SF-00160 Helsinki, Finland.

KAUSAR, Syed Masood, BA, LLB; Pakistani lawyer and politician; b. 2 May 1938, Kohat, Khyber-Pakhtoonkhwa Prov.; ed Islamia Coll., Peshawar Univ.; called to the Bar, Lincoln's Inn, UK 1968; elected Pres. Peshawar High Court Bar Asscn 1984; Speaker, Prov. Ass. of Khyber-Pakhtoonkhwa (previously North-West Frontier Prov.) 1988–90, Leader of Opposition 1990–93; Senator from Khyber-Pakhtoonkhwa Prov. 1994–2000, mem. Senate Standing Cttees on Petroleum and Natural Resources, Interior, Narcotics Control and States and Frontier Regions and Law, Justice and Parliamentary Affairs, mem. Functional Cttee on Less Developed Areas; Gov. Khyber Pakhtoonkhwa 2011–13; mem. Pakistan People's Party (mem. Cen. Exec. Cttee); elected Pres. Peshawar High Court Bar Asscn 1984; Hon. Visiting Prof. of Law, Univ. Law Coll., Peshawar. *Address:* 11 Sahibzada Abdul Qayyum Khan Road, Peshawar, Pakistan (home). *Telephone:* (21) 271405 (home). *E-mail:* ppp@comsats.net.pk (office). *Website:* www.ppp.org.pk (office).

KAVAN, Jan Michael, CH, BSc; Czech politician and journalist; b. 17 Oct. 1946, London, England; s. of Pavel Kavan and Rosemary Kavanová (née Edwards); m. Lenka Mázlová 1991 (divorced 2005); three s. three d.; ed Charles Univ., Prague, London School of Econs, Univ. of Reading and St Antony's Coll., Oxford, UK; politician and journalist, Charles Univ., Prague 1963–68; Ed. East European Reporter, London 1985–90; Dir Palach Press Ltd, London 1974–90, Deputy Dir Jan Palach Information and Research Trust 1982–90; Vice-Pres. East European Cultural Foundation, London 1985–90; mem. Parl. Fed. Ass. of Czech Repub. 1990–92, mem. Foreign Affairs Cttee; mem. Czech Social Democratic (CSSD) Party 1993–, mem. Foreign Affairs Comm. 1994–98, CSSD Spokesman on Foreign Affairs 1996–98, elected to Presidium of Cen. Exec. Cttee 1997–99; Chair. Helsinki Citizens' Ass. in Czech Rep. 1990–95, Policy Centre for the Promotion of Democracy, Prague 1992–98; Senator, Parl. of Czech Repub. 1996–2000; Minister of Foreign Affairs 1998–2002, Deputy Prime Minister 1999–2002; Deputy Chair. Cen. and East European Cttee of the Socialist International 1997–98, State Security Council 1999–2002; Chair. Council for Intelligence Activities 1999–2002; Pres. UN Gen. Ass. 2002–03; mem. Parl. 2002–06, Deputy Chair. Foreign Affairs Cttee 2004–06, Deputy Leader of Parl. Group of Soc. Democratic Party (CSSD) 2004–06, mem. Presidium of Party of European Socialists (PES) 2006; foreign policy adviser to Pres. of Chamber of Deputies 2007–10; Visiting Prof. of Politics and History, Adelphi Univ., New York 1993–94; Karl Loewenstein Fellow in Politics and Jurisprudence, Amherst Coll., Mass 1994; lectured at Columbia and

Stanford Univs, Wellesley Coll., Harvard Center for European Studies; taught at London Adult Educ. Inst. for 15 years; Pres. 57th Session UN Gen. Ass. 2002–03; Hon. Prof., Faculty of Int. Relations, Mongolia State Univ. 1999; Hon. Fellow, LSE 2001; Companion of Honour 2003, Int. Order of Merit 2003; Hon. DHumLitt (Adelphi) 2001; TGM Medal of Honour 2001. *Publications:* Czechoslovak Socialist Opposition 1976, Voices of Czechoslovak Socialists 1977, Voices from Prague 1983, Justice with a Muzzle 1996, McCarthyism Has a New Name: Lustration 2000, Transition to Democracy in Eastern Europe and Russia 2002, Diplomacy 2008; several book chapters and more than 150 articles. *Leisure interests:* int. politics, good literature, film, theatre. *Address:* Klausova 13C, Prague 5, 155 00, Czech Republic. *Telephone:* 72-4210790 (mobile). *E-mail:* kavanjm@seznam.cz; kavanjan17@gmail.com.

KAVANAGH, Dan (see Barnes, Julian Patrick).

KAVÁNEK, Pavel; Czech banker; *Chairman and CEO, ČSOB Group;* m.; two d.; ed Prague School of Econs, Georgetown Univ., USA; staff mem., Foreign Exchange Dept, Československá Obchodní Banka (now ČSOB Group) 1972–76, Chief Dealer 1977–90, mem. Bd of Dirs 1990–93, Chair. and CEO 1993–; with Zivnostenská Banka, London, UK 1976–77; Vice-Pres. Asscn of Banks, Prague; Pew Econ. Freedom Fellowship, Georgetown Univ. 1992, MasterCard Banker of the Year 2007. *Address:* Office of the Chairman, ČSOB Group, Na Příkope 14, 11520 Prague 1, Czech Republic (office). *Telephone:* (26) 1351000 (office). *Fax:* (22) 4225282 (office). *E-mail:* pkavanek@csob.cz (home). *Website:* www.csob.cz (office).

KAVINDELE, Enoch Percy; Zambian politician and business executive; Vice-Pres. Movt for Multi-Party Democracy; Minister of Health –2001; Vice-Pres. of Zambia 2001–03; fmr mem. Nat. Assembly for Kabompo West; Chair. North-Western Railways Co. 2006–. *Address:* c/o Movement for Multi-party Democracy, POB 30708, Lusaka, Zambia (office).

KAWABATA, Tatsuo, MS; Japanese politician; b. 24 Jan. 1945, Ōmihachiman, Shiga Pref.; ed Kyoto Univ.; started career as researcher, Toray Industries Inc.; mem. House of Reps for Shiga at-large constituency 1986–96, for Shiga No 1 Dist 1996–2005, 2009–; Chair. House of Reps Cttee on Rules and Admin; fmr mem. Democratic Socialist Party, Shinshinto (New Frontier Party); mem. Democratic Party of Japan 1998–; Minister of Educ., Culture, Sports, Science and Tech. 2009–10, Minister of State for Science and Tech. Policy 2010, Minister for Internal Affairs and Communications and for Regional Revitalization, Minister of State for Okinawa and Northern Territories' Affairs and for Promotion of Local Sovereignty 2011–12. *Address:* c/o Ministry of Internal Affairs and Communications, 2-1-2, Kasumigaseki, Chiyoda-ku, Tokyo 100-8926, Japan (office). *Website:* www.kawa-bata.net.

KAWADA, Kenji; Japanese banking executive; fmr Exec. Officer, Resona Holdings Inc., Dir, Pres. and Rep. Exec. Officer 2003, Pres. and Rep. Dir Saitama Resona Bank Ltd –2009. *Address:* c/o Saitama Resona Bank Ltd, 4-1 Tokiwa 7-chome, Saitama-shi, Saitama City, Japan.

KAWAGUCHI, Fumio; Japanese energy industry executive; *Honorary Advisor, Chubu Electric Power Co., Inc.;* b. 8 Sept. 1940; Aichi Pref.; ed Waseda Univ. School of Commerce; joined Chubu Electric Power Co., Inc. 1964, Man. Nagoya Office 1999, Man. Dir 1999–2001, Pres. 2001–06, Chair. and Rep. Dir 2006–10, Hon. Advisor 2010–; Chair. Chubu Econ. Fed., Chubu Industrial Advancement Center; mem. Bd of Councillors, Japan Co-operation Center for the Middle East; Hon. Consul of FRG in Nagoya 2007. *Address:* Chubu Electric Power Co., Inc., 1 Higashi-shincho, Higashi-ku, Nagoya 461-8680, Japan (office). *Telephone:* (52) 951-8211 (office). *Fax:* (52) 962-4624 (office). *E-mail:* info@chuden.co.jp (office). *Website:* www.chuden.co.jp (office); www.chukeiren.or.jp (office).

KAWAGUCHI, Yoriko, BA, MPh; Japanese economist and politician; b. 14 Jan. 1941, Tokyo; m.; two c.; ed Univ. of Tokyo, Yale Univ., USA; at Ministry of Int. Trade and Industry 1965–76, 1979–90, Dir-Gen. Global Environmental Affairs 1992–93; economist, IBRD (World Bank), Washington, DC, USA 1976–78; Minister, Embassy in Washington, DC 1991–92; Man. Dir Suntory Ltd 1993–2000; Minister of the Environment 2000–02, of Foreign Affairs 2002–04; Special Adviser to the Prime Minister responsible for Foreign Affairs 2004–05; mem. House of Councillors (LDP) 2005–, Chair. Cttee on Environment; Chair. Okinawa Promotion Cttee; Acting Chair. Research Comm. on Foreign Affairs and Econ. Partnership; Deputy Dir Environment Div., Policy Research Council, LDP; Co-Chair. Int. Cttee on Nuclear Non-Proliferation and Disarmament; mem. Foundation Bd of Forum of Young Global Leaders, World Econ. Forum; Councillor Int. Cttee, Parliamentarians for Global Action; mem. Hon. Advisory Cttee, UN Univ.; Vice-Chair. GLOBE Japan, GLOBE Int.; mem. Pres.'s Council of Int. Activities; mem. Bd of Trustees, US-Japan Foundation; Band, Order of the Aztec Eagle (Mexico) 2003, Extraordinary Grand Cross, Nat. Order of Merit (Paraguay) 2004; Dr hc (Nat. Univ. of Mongolia) 2004; Wilbur Cross Medal (Yale Univ.) 2008, Star of Jerusalem from Mahmoud Abbas, Pres. Palestinian Nat. Authority 2010, Anniversary Medal for a major contrib. to global security promotion and non-proliferation regime by Kadyzhanov, Dir Gen. Nat. Nuclear Centre (Kazakhstan) 2011. *Address:* Room 308, Saingiin-kaikan, 2-1-1 Nagata-cho, Chiyoda-ku, Tokyo 100-8962, Japan (office). *Telephone:* (3) 6550-0308 (office). *Fax:* (3) 6551-0308 (office). *E-mail:* yoriko_kawaguchi3@sangiin.go.jp (office). *Website:* www.yoriko-kawaguchi.jp (office).

KAWAI, Masanori; Japanese freight company executive; *President, Representative Director and CEO, Nippon Express Company;* joined Nippon Express Co. 1966, has held numerous exec. positions including Deputy Chief Operating Officer and Exec. Vice-Pres. –2005, Pres., Rep. Dir and CEO 2005–. *Address:* Nippon Express Company Ltd, 1-9-3, Higashi Shimbashi, Minato-ku, Tokyo 105-8322, Japan (office). *Telephone:* (3) 6251-1111 (office). *Website:* www.nittsu.co.jp (office).

KAWAKUBO, Rei; Japanese couturier; b. 1942, Toyko; m. Adrian Joffe; ed Keio Univ., Tokyo; joined Asahikasei 1964; freelance designer 1966; est. Comme des Garçons Label 1969, Founder and Pres. Comme des Garçons Co. Ltd,Tokyo 1973–; opened first overseas Comme des Garçons Boutique in Paris 1982; opened Dover Street Market, first London store October 2004; joined Fed. Française de la Couture 1982; Japan Comme des Garçons Collection presented twice a year, Tokyo; 395 outlets in Japan, five Comme des Garçons shops and 550 outlets outside Japan; currently has 11 lines of clothing, one line of furniture and a perfume; f. Six magazine 1988; cr. costumes and stage design for Merce Cunningham's Scenario 1997; mem. Chambre Syndicale du Pret-a-Porter; Chevalier, Ordre des Arts et des Lettres; Dr hc (RCA, London) 1997; Mainichi Newspaper Fashion Award 1983, 1988, Excellence in Design Award, Harvard Univ. 2000. *Address:* Comme des Garçons Co. Ltd, 5-11-5 Minamiaoyama, Minato-ku, Tokyo 107, Japan (office). *Telephone:* (3) 3407-2480 (office). *Fax:* (3) 5485-2439 (office). *Website:* www.comme-des-garcons.com (office).

KAWAMATA, Tadashi, MFA; Japanese visual artist; *Professor, Ecole Nationale Superieure des Beaux-Arts, Paris;* b. 1953, Hokkaido; ed Tokyo Nat. Univ. of Fine Art and Music; works exhibited at Venice Biennale 1982, Int. Youth Triennale of Drawing, Nuremberg 1983, Documenta 8 1987, São Paulo Biennale 1987, Tyne Int. Exhbn for Contemporary Art, Newcastle-upon-Tyne and Gateshead, UK 1990; apartment projects: Takara House Room 205, Tokyo 1982, Slip in Tokorozawa 1983, Tetra House N-3 W-26, Sapporo 1983; construction site projects: Spui Project, The Hague 1986, La Maison des Squatters, Grenoble 1987, Nove de Julho Cacapave, São Paulo 1987, Fukuroi Project 1988; urban projects: P.S.1 Project, New York 1985, Destroyed Church, Kassel 1987, Toronto Project at Colonial Tavern Park, Toronto 1989, Project at Begijnhof St Elisabeth, Kortrijk, Belgium 1989–90, Documente 9 1992, Biennale d'Art Contemporain, Lyon 1993, Münster Skulptor Projekt 1997, 11th Biennale of Sydney 1989, Echigo Tsumari Art Triennial 2000, 4th Shanghai Biennale 2002, Busan Biennale 2002, Bienal de Valencia 2003; Prof., Tokyo Univ. of Fine Art and Music 1999–2005; Prof., École Nationale Superieure des Beaux-Arts, Paris 2006–; mem. Program Advisory Cttee Space Shower TV 2002–05; Dir Yokohama Triennale 2005; Asian Cultural Council Fellowship Grant (worked in New York 1984–86); Grand Prix Int. Youth Triennale 1983. *Address:* c/o Annely Juda Fine Art, 4th Floor, 23 Dering Street, London, W1S 1AW, England; c/o Kamel Mennour, 47 rue Saint André des Arts, 75006 Paris, France. *Website:* www.tk-onthetable.com; www.cafetalk.net.

KAWAMURA, Takashi; Japanese business executive; *Chairman and Representative Executive Officer, Hitachi Ltd;* ed Tokyo Univ.; joined Hitachi Ltd 1962, Div. Man. Thermal Power Eng Div., Power Group 1987–92, Gen. Man. Hitachi Works 1992–95, Group Exec., Electric Utility Sales Operations Group 1995–97, Exec. Man. Dir and Group Exec., Power Group 1997–99, Exec. Vice-Pres., Hitachi Ltd 1999–, Chair. and Rep. Exec. Officer, Hitachi Software Eng Co. Ltd (subsidiary of Hitachi Ltd) 2003–07, Dir, Hitachi Ltd 2003–07, Chair. Hitachi Plant Technologies Ltd (fmrly Hitachi Plant Eng & Construction Co. Ltd) 2005–, Chair. Hitachi Maxell Ltd 2007–, Chair., Pres. and CEO Hitachi Ltd 2009–10 (Chair. Nominating Cttee, Compensation Cttee), Chair. and Rep. Exec. Officer 2010–, Pres. and CEO Babcock-Hitachi K.K.; mem. Bd of Dirs Babcock-Hitachi K.K., Hitachi America Ltd, Hitachi China Ltd; fmr Auditor, Ines Corpn. *Address:* Hitachi Ltd, 6-6 Marunouchi 1-chome, Chiyoda-ku, Tokyo 100-8280, Japan (office). *Telephone:* (3) 3258-1111 (office). *Fax:* (3) 3258-2375 (office). *E-mail:* service@cm.hbi.co.jp (office). *Website:* www.hitachi.com (office).

KAWAR, Karim Tawfik, BSc; Jordanian business executive and fmr diplomatist; *President, Kawar Group;* b. 14 June 1966, Amman; m. Luma Kawar; one s. two d.; ed Boston Coll., USA; founding mem. several business asscns and non-governmental orgs, including Jordan American Business Asscn, Young Entrepreneurs Asscn, Jordanian Intellectual Property Asscn; est. computer co. and headed an umbrella group encompassing 10 information systems and software cos; apptd to Econ. Consultative Council by King Abdullah II 1999; Head of REACH Initiative (led team of 40 Jordanian information tech. professionals to launch the IT industry in Jordan) 1999; Amb. to USA (also accred to Mexico) 2002–07; fmr Network Coordinator UN Information and Communication Technologies Task Force–Arab Regional Network; fmr Chair. Information Tech. Asscn of Jordan (INTAJ); Vice-Chair. Jordan River Foundation; mem. Young Presidents Org.; Pres. Kawar Group 2007–; Eisenhower Fellow 2000; named Global Leader for Tomorrow by World Econ. Forum. *Address:* Kawar Group, PO Box 222, Amman 11118, Jordan (office). *Telephone:* (6) 5609500 (office). *Fax:* (6) 5698322 (office). *E-mail:* president@kawar.com.jo (office). *Website:* www.kawar.com (office).

KAWARA, Tsutomu; Japanese politician; fmr mem. House of Reps; fmr Deputy Chief Cabinet Sec.; fmr Dir.-Gen. Defence Agency; fmr Construction Minister; Dir.-Gen. Defence Agency 1987–88, 1999–2000. *Address:* c/o Defence Agency, 9-7-45, Akasaka, Minato-ku, Tokyo 107-8513, Japan (office).

KAWASAKI, Jiro; Japanese politician; b. 15 Nov. 1947, Mie; s. of Hideji Kawasaki; ed Keio Univ.; with Matsushita Electric Industrial Co. 1973–80; mem. House of Reps for Mie dist 1980–, Parl. Vice-Minister, Ministry of Posts and Telecommunications 1990, Minister of Transport 1998–99, of Hokkaido Devt Agency 1999, of Economy, Trade and Industry 2004–05, of Health, Labour and Welfare 2005–06; fmr Head, Public Relations Dept of LDP. *Leisure interests:* reading, tennis. *Address:* c/o Liberal-Democratic Party—LDP (Jiyu-Minshuto), 1-11-23, Nagata-cho, Chiyoda-ku, Tokyo 100-8910, Japan. *Telephone:* (3) 3581-6211. *E-mail:* koho@ldp.jimin.or.jp. *Website:* www.jimin.jp.

KAWASE, Naomi; Japanese film director, screenwriter and writer; b. 30 May 1969, Nara; m. Takenori Sento 1997 (divorced 2000); one s.; ed Osaka School of Photography (now School of Visual Arts, Osaka); spent four years as lecturer at Osaka School of Photography before releasing Embracing 1992; retrospective organized for the 1st Infinity Film Festival in Alba, Italy and for Jeu de Paume hosted by Petit Palais in Paris 2002, also for RED/CAT, Los Angeles 2005. *Films include:* I Focus on That Which Interests Me (short) 1988, The Concretization of These Things Flying around Me (short) 1988, My J-W-F (short) 1988, Papa's Icecream (short) 1988, My Solo Family (short) 1989, Presently (short) 1989, A Small Largeness (short) 1989, The Girl's Daily Bread (short) 1990, Like Happiness (short) 1991, Embracing (documentary short) 1992, White Moon 1993, Katatsumori (documentary short) 1994, See Heaven (documentary short) 1995, Memory of the Wind (short) 1995, This World (short) 1996, Hi wa katabuki (documentary) 1996, Moe no suzaku (youngest winner of la Caméra d'Or Award (Best New Dir) at Cannes Film Festival 1997) 1997, The Weald (Special Mention Prize at Vision du Reel 1999) 1997, Kaleidoscope 1999, Hotaru (Firefly) (FIPRESCI Prize and CICAE Prize, Locarno Int. Film Festival 2000, Best Achievement in Cinematography and Directing and Leading Actress Award (Yuko Nakamura), Buenos Aires Int. Film Festival 2001) 2000, Sky, Wind, Fire, Water, Earth (documentary) 2001, Shara 2003, Letter from a Yellow Cherry Blossom (documentary) 2003, Shadow

(documentary short) 2004, Tarachime (documentary short) (Special Prize, Yamagata Int. Film Festival 2007) 2006, Mogari no mori (The Mourning Forest) (Grand Prix, Cannes Film Festival 2007) 2007, Nanayo 2008, In Between Days (documentary short) 2009, Visitors (segment 'Koma') 2009, Genpin (documentary) 2010, Hanezu no tsuki 2011. *Publications include:* novels: Moe no Suzaku, Hotaru; articles for various publs. *Address:* Kumie Inc., 2F Art Fukuzumi Building, 45 Takama-cho, Nara-shi, Nara 630-8241, Japan (office). *Telephone:* (742) 27-2216 (office). *Fax:* (742) 26-1830 (office). *E-mail:* info@kawasenaomi.com. *Website:* www.kawasenaomi.com.

KAWATABA, Tatsuo; Japanese engineer and politician; *Minister of Education, Culture, Sports, Science and Technology;* b. 24 Jan. 1945, Omihachiman, Shiga Pref.; ed Kyoto Univ.; began career as engineer, Toray Industries Inc. Research Inst., became involved in trade union activities, later Regional Head of union in Shiga Dist; mem. House of Reps for Shiga-1 constituency 1986–; fmr mem. Democratic Socialist Party, fmr mem. Shinshinto (New Frontier Party); mem. Democratic Party of Japan 1998–, fmr Vice-Pres. and Chair. Cttee on Audits and Admin Oversight; Minister of Educ., Culture, Sports, Science and Tech. 2009–. *Address:* Ministry of Educ., Culture, Sports, Science and Technology, 3-2-2, Kasumigaseki, Chiyoda-ku, Tokyo 100-8959, Japan (office). *Telephone:* (3) 5253-4111 (office). *Fax:* (3) 3595-2017 (office). *Website:* www.mext.go.jp (office).

KAY, Alan, MS, PhD; American computer scientist and academic; *President, Viewpoints Research Institute;* ed Univs of Colorado and Utah; fmr professional jazz guitarist, composer and theatrical designer; worked for Univ. of Utah Advanced Research Project Agency (ARPA) research team that designed or developed 3D-graphics, the FLEX machine (an early interactive object-oriented personal computer), the Dynabook (notebook-sized laptop computer for children), and participated in original design of the ARPANet (later became the Internet) late 1960s; Co-founder Xerox Palo Alto Research Center (PARC) early 1970s; fmr Chief Scientist, Atari; fmr Fellow, Apple Computer; fmr Vice-Pres. Research and Devt, The Walt Disney Co.; Founder and Pres. Viewpoints Research Inst., Inc., Glendale, Calif. 2001–; Sr Fellow, Hewlett-Packard Co. 2002–; Sr Scientist, Div. of Information Tech., Univ. of Wis. 2005–; currently Adjunct Prof., UCLA; Visiting Prof., Kyoto Univ., Japan 2005; Fellow, American Acad. of Arts and Sciences, Nat. Acad. of Eng (NAE), Royal Soc. of Arts (UK), Computer Museum History Center; Dr hc (Kungl Tekniska Hoegskolan, Stockholm, Columbia Coll., Chicago); A.M. Turing Award, Asscn of Computing Machinery (ACM), Kyoto Prize, Inamori Foundation, ACM Software Systems Award, ACM Outstanding Educator Award, J-D Warnier Prix d'lnformatique, NEC C&C Prize 2001, Funai Prize, ZeroOne Award, Univ. of Berlin, inducted into Utah Information Tech. Asscn Hall of Fame 2003, NAE Charles Stark Draper Prize 2004. *Publications:* numerous articles in scientific journals. *Leisure interest:* classical pipe organist. *Address:* Viewpoints Research Institute, Inc., 1209 Grand Central Avenue, Glendale, CA 91201, USA (office). *Telephone:* (818) 332-3001 (office). *Fax:* (818) 244-9761 (office). *E-mail:* kim.rose@vpri.org (office). *Website:* www.viewpointsresearch.org (office).

KAY, John Anderson, CBE, FBA, FRSE; British economist; b. 3 Aug. 1948, Edinburgh, Scotland; s. of the late James Kay and Allison Kay; m. 1st Deborah Freeman 1986 (divorced 1995); m. 2nd Mika Oldham 2009; ed Royal High School, Edinburgh, Univ. of Edinburgh and Nuffield Coll., Oxford; Fellow, St John's Coll. Oxford 1970–; Lecturer in Econs, Univ. of Oxford 1971–79; Research Dir Inst. for Fiscal Studies 1979–82, Dir 1982–86; Dir Centre for Business Strategy, London Business School 1986–91; Chair. London Econs 1986–96; Dir Said Business School, Univ. of Oxford 1997–99, Undervalued Assets Trust PLC 1994–2005; Dir (non-exec.) Halifax Bldg Soc. 1991–97, Foreign & Colonial Special Utilities Investment Trust PLC 1993–2003, Value and Income Trust PLC 1994–, Halifax PLC 1997–2000, Clear Capital Ltd 2004–08, Law Debenture Corpn 2004–, Scottish Mortgage Investment Trust PLC 2008–; mem. Corp. Governance Advisory Bd, Norges Bank Investment Management 2013–; Hon. DLitt (Heriot-Watt) 2008. *Publications:* The British Tax System 1979, Foundations of Corporate Success 1993, Why Firms Succeed 1995, The Business of Economics 1996, The Truth about Markets 2003, Everlasting Light Bulbs 2004, Culture and Prosperity 2005, The Hare and the Tortoise 2006, The Long and the Short of It 2009, Obliquity 2010; co-author: Concentration in Modern Industry, The Reform of Social Security, The Economic Analysis of Accounting Profitability; articles in scholarly journals. *Leisure interests:* walking, travel. *Address:* The Erasmus Press Ltd, PO Box 4026, London, W1A 6NZ, England (office). *Telephone:* (20) 7224-8797 (office). *E-mail:* johnkay@johnkay.com (office). *Website:* www.johnkay.com.

KAYANI, Gen. Ashfaq Pervez; Pakistani fmr army officer; b. April 1952, Jehlum; m.; one s. one d.; ed Mil. Coll., Jhelum, Command and Staff Coll., Quetta, Command and Gen. Staff Coll., Fort Leavenworth, USA, Nat. Defence Coll., Islamabad; commissioned in Baloch Regt 1971, commanded infantry bn, infantry brigade, infantry div. and corps; Deputy Mil. Sec. for Benazir Bhutto 1988–89; fmr Dir-Gen. of Mil. Operations; Corps Commdr of Rawalpindi 2003–04; Dir-Gen. Inter-Services Intelligence 2004–07; chosen to carry out investigations of two assassination attempts on Gen. Pervaiz Musharraf; Vice-Chief of Army Staff (also promoted to four-star Gen.) Oct.–Nov. 2007, Chief of Army Staff 2007–13 (retd); Pres. Pakistan Golf Fed. 2004–; ranked by Forbes magazine amongst The World's Most Powerful People (29th) 2010, (34th) 2011, (28th) 2012. *Leisure interest:* golf. *Address:* c/o Ministry of Defence, Pakistan Secretariat, No. II, Rawalpindi 46000, Pakistan.

KAYE, Carol; American musician (electric bass guitar, guitar); b. 24 March 1935, Everett, Wash.; one s. two d.; teacher of guitar 1949–, electric bass 1969–; on the road, big band 1954–55; played bebop jazz, night clubs 1956–61; special records, studio guitarist 1957–66; studio electric bassist 1963–; invented 16th note bass recording styles; over 10,000 sessions; television credits, playing bass include M.A.S.H, Mission Impossible, Hawaii 5-O, Brady Bunch, Soap; film credits, playing bass include Thomas Crown Affair, Heat of the Night, Valley of the Dolls, Shaft (theme); columnist, Bassics Magazine; mem. Musicians' Union; Women in Music Award 2000, Lifetime Achievement Award, Duquesne Univ. Pittsburgh Jazz Soc. 2000, Los Angeles Composers–Arrangers Award 2004, Lifetime Achievement Award, Bass Player Magazine 2008. *Television:* First Lady of Bass TV (documentary). *Recordings include:* albums: Carol Kaye: Bass, Thumbs Up, Carol Kaye Guitars '65; credits on guitar include: Zippity Doo Dah, Batman Theme, Birds and Bees, The Beat Goes On, You've Lost That Lovin Feelin, La

Bamba; credits on bass guitar include: Way We Were, Feelin' Alright, Good Vibrations, Help Me Rhonda, Wouldn't It Be Nice, Can't Help Myself, Heat of Night, I Don't Need No Doctor, Little Green Apples, Baby Love, River Deep Mountain High, Something Stupid, This is My Song, Mission Impossible, Pet Sounds, Smile. *Publications:* writer, composer of over 30 tutorials; How to Play the Electric Bass, Jazz Improvisation for Bass. *Leisure interests:* reading, teaching. *Address:* 25852 McBean Parkway, Suite 200, Valencia, CA 91355, USA (office). *Telephone:* (661) 288-6551 (office). *E-mail:* carol@carolkaye.com. *Website:* www .carolkaye.com.

KAYE, Harvey Jordan, PhD; American academic and writer; *Ben & Joyce Rosenberg Professor of Democracy and Justice Studies and Director, Center for History and Social Change, University of Wisconsin-Green Bay;* b. 9 Oct. 1949, Englewood, NJ; s. of Murray N. Kaye and Frances Kaye; m. Lorna Stewart 1973; two d.; ed Paramus High School, Rutgers Univ., Univ. of Mexico, Univ. of London, UK and Louisiana State Univ.; Asst Prof. of Interdisciplinary Studies, St Cloud Univ., Minn. 1977–78; Asst Prof. of Social Change and Devt, Univ. of Wis., Green Bay 1978–83, Assoc. Prof. 1983–86, Head of Dept 1985–88, Prof. 1986–, Ben & Joyce Rosenberg Prof. of Social Change and Devt 1990–2010, Ben and Joyce Rosenberg Prof. of Democracy and Justice Studies 2010–, Dir Center for History and Social Change 1991–; Visiting Fellow, Univ. of Birmingham, UK 1987; mem. Editorial Bd Marxist Perspectives 1978–80, The Wisconsin Sociologist, Wis. Sociological Asscn 1985–87, Rethinking History 1996–; Consulting Ed., Verso Publishers, London 1988–94, NYU Press 1996–; Series Ed., American Radicals (Routledge) 1992–98; columnist, Times Higher Educational Supplement 1994–2001, Tikkun magazine 1996–97, Index on Censorship 1996–, The Guardian Unlimited 2007–08, New Deal 2.0 2010–, Huffington Post 2010–; mem. Exec. Bd, Center for Democratic Values 1996–2000, Scholars, Artists and Writers for Social Justice 1997–2000; mem. American Historical Asscn, American Sociological Asscn, Org. of American Historians, PEN; Nat. Endowment for the Humanities Fellowship 2002–03; Historical Adviser, Remix America 2008–10, Thomas Paine documentary, Four Freedoms Park Project; Founders' Award for Scholarship 1985, Isaac Deutscher Memorial Prize 1993, Best Book for the Teen Age, New York Public Library 2001, Best Book 2006, Wisconsin Library Asscn. *Publications:* The British Marxist Historians 1984, The Powers of the Past 1991, The Education of Desire 1992, Why do Ruling Classes Fear History? 1996, Thomas Paine 2000, Are We Good Citizens? 2001, Thomas Paine and the Promise of America 2005; as editor: History, Classes and Nation-States 1988, The Face of the Crowd: Studies in Revolution, Ideology and Popular Protest 1988, Poets, Politics and the People 1989, E. P. Thompson: Critical Perspectives (with K. McClelland) 1990, The American Radical (with M. Buhle and P. Buhle) 1994, Imperialism and its Contradictions 1995, Ideology and Popular Protest 1995; numerous articles on history and historians; contrib. to on-line websites and magazines, including Next New Deal, Huffington Post, Salon. *Leisure interests:* politics, friendship and conversation. *Address:* Democracy and Justice Studies Department, University of Wisconsin-Green Bay, 2420 Nicolet Drive, Green Bay, WI 54311, USA (office). *Telephone:* (920) 465-2355 (office); (920) 465-2755 (office). *Fax:* (920) 465-2791 (office). *E-mail:* kayeh@uwgb.edu (office).

KAYMER, Martin; German professional golfer; b. 28 Dec. 1984, Düsseldorf; turned professional 2005; plays mainly on European Tour; winner Abu Dhabi Golf Championship 2008, 2010, BMW Int. Open 2008, Open de France ALSTOM 2009, Barclays Scottish Open 2009, KLM Open 2010, Alfred Dunhill Links Championship 2010, Abu Dhabi HSBC Golf Championship 2011, WGC-HSBC Champions 2011; results in major championships: tied for sixth at PGA Championship 2009, tied for eighth at US Open 2010, tied for seventh at British Open 2010, won PGA Championship 2010 (only the second German to win a major championship, after Bernhard Langer); mem. World Cup team representing Germany 2007, 2008, 2009, winning Ryder Cup team representing Europe 2010, 2012; ranked No. 1 in World (after his runner-up finish to Luke Donald at WGC-Accenture Match Play Championship) Feb.–April 2011; Sir Henry Cotton Rookie of the Year Award (first German) 2007, European Tour Players' Player of the Year for 2010. *Address:* c/o Sportyard AB, Sveavägen 166, 21st Floor, 113 46 Stockholm, Sweden (office). *Telephone:* (8) 410-269-40 (office). *Fax:* (8) 34-87-62 (office). *E-mail:* info@sportyard .com (office); presse@martinkaymer.com. *Website:* www.sportyard.com (office); www.martinkaymer.com.

KAYODE, Prince Adetokunbo Adeyinka, LLB, FCIA; Nigerian lawyer and politician; b. 31 Oct. 1958, Ikare-Akoko, Ondo State; m. Funmilayo Kayode; two s. two d.; ed Univ. of Lagos; called to Nigerian Bar 1982; f. Kayode & Co. (legal practice) 1990; fmr Minister of Justice and Attorney-Gen.; Minister of Culture and Tourism 2007, of Labour and Productivity 2007–10, of Defence 2010–11; mem. Nigerian Bar Asscn, Chair. Abuja Br. 1988–90, mem. Nat. Exec. Cttee and Third Nat. Vice-Pres., Chair. Human Rights Cttee; mem. Fed. Judicial Service Comm., Council of Legal Educ., Presidential Ad hoc Cttee on Democracy and Good Governance; fmr legal counsel to Fed. Govt, Ind. Nat. Electoral Comm., etc.; mem. numerous int. asscns including Commonwealth Lawyers Asscn, Swiss Arbitration Asscn, London Court of Int. Arbitration, Abuja Arbitration Forum, Centre for Sports Arbitration; mem. People's Democratic Party; Sr Advocate of Nigeria (SAN). *Address:* c/o Ministry of Defence, Ship House, Central Area, Abuja, Nigeria (office).

KAZAKBAYEV, Ruslan Aitbaevich; Kyrgyzstani diplomatist and politician; b. 18 May 1967, Beisheke village, Talas Oblast, Kyrgyz SSR, USSR; ed Frunze Polytechnical Inst., Frunze (now Bishkek), Faculty of Law, Jusup Balasagyn Kyrgyz Nat. Inst., Diplomatic Acad. of the Ministry of Foreign Affairs of the Kyrgyz Repub.; Acad. of Sciences of the Kyrgyz Repub. 1992–94; joined Foreign Service, Ministry of Foreign Affairs 1995, Third Sec., then Second Sec., Consular Dept 1995–96, Vice-Consul, Consulate Gen., Istanbul 1996–99, returned to Bishkek and served in several positions including Adviser, Head of Dept and Deputy Chief, Consular Dept 1999–2005, Consul Gen. in Istanbul 2005–09, First Deputy Minister of Foreign Affairs 2009, Minister of Foreign Affairs 2010–12; rank of Amb. 2007; Hon. Prof., I. Razzakov Kyrgyz Tech. Univ. 2003, M. Kashgari Kyrgyz-Kuwaiti Univ. 2008; Diploma, Govt of the Kyrgyz Repub. 2005, 2007. *Address:* c/o Ministry of Foreign Affairs, 720040 Bishkek, bul. Erkindik 57, Kyrgyzstan. *E-mail:* gendep@mfa.gov.kg.

KAZAMIAS, Kikis, MEcons; Cypriot economist and politician; b. 27 Aug. 1951, Lefkonoiko, Famagusta Dist; m. Rodoula Koliandri; three c.; ed Hochschule für Ökonomie, Berlin; has held numerous exec. positions in various cos, including import man. 1977–84, man. of family co. 1984–97, Dir Gen. Co-Operative Consumer Soc. of Limassol 1997–2003, Pres. Investment Group of the Co-Operative Consumer Socs 'Lefkoniko' 1999–2003; mem. House of Reps (Progressive Party of the Working People—AKEL) 1991, re-elected 1996, mem. Financial and Budgetary Parl. Cttee 1991–2001, Communications and Public Works Cttee 1991–94, Jt Cttee of Cyprus Parl. with EU 1996–2001; elected mem. AKEL Cen. Cttee; elected Mayor of Famagusta 2001, also First Vice-Pres. Union of Cyprus Municipalities; Minister of Communications and Works 2003–04 (resgnd); mem. European Court of Auditors 2004–10; Minister of Finance 2011–12. *Address:* c/o Ministry of Finance, Cnr M. Karaolis Street and G. Afxentiou Street, 1439 Nicosia, Cyprus (office).

KAZANNIK, Aleksei Ivanovich, DIur; Russian lawyer; b. 26 July 1941, Perepis, Chernigov Region; m.; two s.; ed Irkutsk Univ.; teacher, Irkutsk Univ. 1975–79; Prof., Head of Chair, Omsk Univ. 1979–89, 1994–; forbidden to give public lectures because of criticism of Soviet invasion of Afghanistan; USSR People's Deputy 1989–91; fmr mem. USSR Supreme Soviet; active participant Movt Democratic Russia; mem. Interregional Group of Deputies; mem. Cttee on ecology problems and rational use of natural resources, USSR Supreme Soviet; mem. Pres.'s Council 1993–94; Prosecutor-Gen. of Russia 1993–94 (resgnd); Founder and Chair. Party of People's Conscience 1995; Chair. Cttee on problems of nationalities, religions and public orgs of Omsk Region 1996; Deputy Gov. Omsk Region 1999; currently Prof. of Law, Omsk State Univ. *Publications:* legal aspects of regional problems of nature preservation, numerous articles on ecology, law, pamphlets. *Address:* Omsk State University, Mira Prosp. 55A, 644077 Omsk, Russia. *E-mail:* eshish@ univer.omsk.ru.

KAZANTSEV, Col-Gen. Victor Germanovich; Russian army officer; b. 22 Feb. 1946, Kokhanovo, Vitebsk Region, Belarus; m. Tamara Valentinovna Kazantseva; ed Leningrad Higher School of Gen. Army, M. Frunze Mil. Acad., Mil. Acad. of Gen. Staff; officer in Caucasian, Middle-Asian, Turkestan, Baikal Mil. Commands, Cen. Army Group in Czechoslovakia, First Deputy Commdr of Army N Caucasian Mil. Command; Chief of Staff to Commdr of troops N Caucasian Mil. Command 1996–97, Commdr 1997–99; Commdr group of Fed. forces in N Caucasus 1999–2000; Rep. of Pres. to S Fed. Dist 2000–04; Hero of Russia for operations in Dagestan and Chechnya 1999.

KAZARNOVSKAYA, Ljuba (Lubov); Russian singer (soprano); *Chairman, Russian Music Society (RMPO);* b. 18 July 1960, Moscow; m.; one c.; ed Moscow Conservatory with Irina Arkhipova and Elena Shumilova, N. Malysheva; debut, La Scala Milan 1989 in Verdi's Requiem under R. Muti; has sung at the Bolshoi, Moscow as Nedda, Mimi and Lida in La Battaglia di Legnano; tour of Italy with the Maily Theatre, Leningrad 1984; Kirov Theatre, Leningrad from 1986 as Leonora (La Forza del Destino and Trovatore), Marina, Violetta, Marguerite, Donna Anna and Tchaikovsky's Iolanta; Paris Opéra and Covent Garden 1987, as Tatiana with the Kirov Co.; Salzburg Festival 1989, in the Verdi Requiem, conducted by Karajan; Zürich Opera 1989–90, as Amelia Boccanegra and the Trovatore Leonora; Cologne Opera 1989–90, as Manon Lescaut and Amelia; Covent Garden 1990, as Desdemona; Metropolitan Opera as Tatjana in Eugene Onegin under Levine, Desdemona in Otello, Nedda in Pagliacci 1991–95; debut in Strauss' Salome 1995; new productions of Clemenza di Tito and Il Trovatore at San Francisco Opera and at Lyric Chicago, Tosca in Houston, Berlin and Vienna; recitals at the major music festivals; sang Pauline in Prokofiev's The Gambler at La Scala and in Paris 1996–97; Aithra in Strauss' Aegyptische Helena under Thielemann with the Royal Opera at the Festival Hall 1998; Massenet and Puccini premiere at the Bolshoi Theatre, Moscow and afterwards at opera festivals in Italy, Sweden, Germany and USA; personal television music show 'Glimpse of Love' 2000; concert and oratorio appearances, song recitals with works by Brahms, Wolf, de Falla, Dvořák and Rachmaninov; film and opera projects; recital tours in Europe and Asia; int. masterclasses in Russia and Europe; mem. Russian Opera Forum; Chair. Russian Music Soc. (RMPO); Pres., Ljuba Kazarnovskaya Foundation; Chair. and Artistic Dir, Nat. Verdi Museum, Busetto, Italy; Founder and Artistic Dir, Summer Acad. of Music, Slovenia; annual masterclasses at Chengdu Conservatory, People's Repub. of China; Chair. Jury, Renato Bruson Int. Vocal Competition (global internet vocal competition); The Voice of the Year (Russia) 2001. *Radio:* weekly programme 'Vocalissimo', Radio Orpheus. *Recordings include:* Shostakovich's 12th Symphony, Prokofiev's The Gambler, Tchaikovsky's The Complete Songs Op 103 (five vols), The Great Singers of Russia (video) 1901–99, Gypsy Love (recital programme), Glimpse of Love (DVD). *Leisure interests:* music, literature, sports. *Address:* Arbat 35, Moscow 121002, Russia (home). *Telephone:* (495) 248-09-44 (home). *Fax:* (495) 248-09-44 (home). *E-mail:* fond_kl@mail.ru (home). *Website:* www.kazarnovskaya.ru.

KAZHEGELDIN, Akezhan Magzhan-Uly; Kazakhstani economist and politician; b. 27 March 1952, Georgiyevka, Semipalatinsk Region; m. Bykova Natalia Kazhegeldina; one s. one d.; ed Kazakh State Univ., Moscow Inst. of Oriental Studies; Chair. Regional Exec. Cttee of Semipalatinsk 1983; Dir Ore-enriching Factory, Deputy Gov. Admin. of Semipalatinsk Region 1991–94; Pres. Kazakhstan Union of Industrialists and Entrepreneurs 1992–; apptd First Deputy Prime Minister of Kazakhstan 1994, Prime Minister 1994–97; Adviser to Pres. Nazarbayev May–Oct. 1998; disbarred from presidential election in 1998; f. Republican People's Party of Kazakhstan 1998, Chair. Bd 1998–2001; mem. Politburo Bd United Democratic Party 2001; in opposition to Pres. Nazarbayev 1999–, now lives abroad, sentenced to 10 years imprisonment in absentia 1999. *Publications include:* six books including Kazakhstan in the Conditions of Reforms, Problems of State Regulation in the Conditions of Socio-Economic Transformation, Socio-Economic Problems of Development of Kazakhstan in the Conditions of Reforms 1999, Opposition to Middle Ages 2000. *Address:* c/o Republican Independent Political Club Association (Assotsiatsiya Respublianskogo Nezavisimogo Politicheskogo Kluba), ul. Zhestoksan 12/514–515, 480050, Almaty, Kazakhstan.

KAŽIMÍR, Peter; Slovak business executive and politician; *Deputy Prime Minister and Minister of Finance;* b. 28 June 1968, Košice; ed Univ. of Economics, Bratislava; assistant tax adviser, Shubert and Partners 1993–95; mem. Bd of Dirs

VIVANT a.s. 1995–2006, PARTA-GAS a.s. 1999–2006; Chair. Supervisory Bd Sceptrum a.s. Brno 1997–2006, Nat. Nuclear Fund 2006–10; mem. Supervisory Bd DDP Credit Suisse Life and Pensions 2001–06; State Sec., Ministry of Finance 2006–10; mem. Nat. Council of the Slovak Repub. 2010–12, Vice-Chair. Finance and Budget Cttee; Vice-Chair. SMER-SD 2010–; Deputy Prime Minister and Minister of Finance 2012–. *Address:* Ministry of Finance, Štefanovičova 5, PO Box 82, 817 82 Bratislava, Slovakia (office). *Telephone:* (2) 5958-1111 (office). *Fax:* (2) 5249-8042 (office). *E-mail:* podatelna@mfsr.sk (office). *Website:* www.finance.gov .sk (office).

KAZMIN, Andrei Ilyich, PhD; Russian banker; b. 25 June 1958, Moscow; m.; ed Moscow Inst. of Finance; Economist, State Bank of the USSR 1982–83; Asst Prof., then Deputy Dean Faculty of Credit, Moscow Inst. of Finance 1983–88; Sr Researcher USSR (now Russian) Acad. of Sciences 1988–91; Sr Research Fellow Alexander von Humboldt Foundation, Inst. for Int. Politics and Security, Ebenhausen, Germany 1991–93; training at Austrian Nat. Bank, Bundesbank, German Fed. Ministry of Finance and Inst. of German Research Centres 1991–93; Adviser to Minister of Finance 1993; Deputy Minister of Finance, Russian Fed. 1993–96; Chair. and CEO Sberbank (Savings Bank of Russian Fed.) 1996–2007; CEO Pochta Rossii (Russian Post) 2007–09; Vice-Pres. World Savings Banks Inst. 2000–; mem. Supervisory Bd Vneshtorgbank, JSC Agency for Housing Mortgage Lending; mem. Asscn of Russian Banks, Russian Union of Industrialists and Entrepreneurs (RSPP), Bd of Trustees, Finance and Devt Foundation; Order of Honour 2002; Banker of the Year 2008. *Publications:* more than 40 publs. *Leisure interest:* theatre, literature, sports. *Address:* c/o Pochta Rossii, Varshavskoye shossye 37, 131000 Moscow, Russia. *Telephone:* (495) 956-20-67. *E-mail:* Client@ russianpost.ru. *Website:* www.russianpost.ru.

KAZULIN, Alyaksandr, PhD; Belarusian mathematician, university rector and politician; b. 25 Nov. 1955, Minsk, Byelorussian SSR, USSR; m. Iryna Kazulina (died 2008); two d.; ed Belarusian State Univ.; mil. service in Soviet Navy as Marine 1974–76; Lecturer and Instructor, Youth Communist League (Komsomol); Dean, Belarusian State Univ. 1980–88, Rector 1996–2003; Dept Chief, then First Deputy Minister, Educ. Ministry 1988–96; Minister of Educ. 1998–2001; f. People's Will political movt 2005; joined Belarusian Social-Democratic Party, March 2005, elected Chair. Assembly (Hramada)—Belarusian Social-Democratic Party following merger of parties in April 2005; sentenced to five-and-a-half years' imprisonment on charges of hooliganism and inciting mass disorder July 2006, granted early release following pressure by US Govt 16 Aug. 2008. *Address:* 220049 Minsk, str. Knorina 3, Belarus (office). *Telephone:* (17) 287-30-00 (office). *Fax:* (17) 287-30-00 (office). *E-mail:* bsdp_minsk_ck@tut.by (office); raisa_mikhailovskaia@yahoo .com (office). *Website:* www.bsdp.org (office).

KE, Bingsheng, BS, MA, PhD; Chinese agricultural economist and university administrator; *President, China Agricultural University;* ed Univ. of Hohenheim, Germany, Peking Univ., China Agric. Univ.; economist with Ministry of Agric., becoming Dir Centre for Rural Economy Studies 1997–2007; Prof., China Agricultural Univ., also fmr Deputy Dean, Grad. School, Dean Coll. of Econs and Man., Vice-Pres. China Agric. Univ., Pres. 2008–; adviser to Chinese Govt on agricultural policy issues. *Publications:* China's Grain Market and Policy 1995. *Address:* Office of the President, China Agricultural University, 17 Qinghua Donglu, Haidian District, Beijing 100083, People's Republic of China (office). *Telephone:* (10) 6273 6482 (office). *Fax:* (10) 6273 7704 (office). *E-mail:* cauie@cau .edu.cn (office). *Website:* www.cau.edu.cn (office).

KEACH, Stacy; American actor and director; b. 2 June 1941, Savannah, Ga; s. of Walter Edmund Keach and Dora Stacy; m. Malgossia Tomassi 1986; two d.; stage debut in Joseph Papp's production of Hamlet, Cen. Park 1964; other stage appearances include A Long Day's Journey into Night, Macbird (Vernon Rice Drama Desk Award), Indians, Deathtrap, Hughie, Barnum, Cyrano de Bergerac, Peer Gynt, Henry IV (Parts I & II), Idiot's Delight, The King and I 1989, Love Letters 1990–93, Richard III 1991, Stieglitz Loves O'Keefe 1995; Dir Incident at Vichy and Six Characters in Search of an Author for TV; mem. Artists Cttee Kennedy Center Honors 1986–; Hon. Chair. American Cleft Palate Foundation 1995–; recipient of three Obie Awards, Pasadena Playhouse Alumni Man of the Year 1995, Pacific Pioneers Broadcasters' Asscn Diamond Circle Award 1996. *Films include:* The Heart is a Lonely Hunter, End of the Road, The Travelling Executioner, Brewster McCloud, Doc, Judge Roy Bean, The New Centurions, Fat City, The Killer Inside Me, Conduct Unbecoming, Luther, Street People, The Squeeze, Gray Lady Down, The Ninth Configuration, The Long Riders, Road Games, Butterfly, Up in Smoke, Nice Dreams, That Championship Season, The Lover, False Identity, The Forgotten Milena, John Carpenter's Escape from LA 1996, Prey of the Jaguar 1996, The Truth Configuration 1998, American History X 1998, Icebreaker 1999, Unshackled 2000, Militia 2000, Mercy Streets 2000, Sunstorm 2001, When Eagles Strike 2003, Jesus, Mary and Joey 2003, Caught in the Headlights 2004, Galaxy Hunter 2004, El Padrino 2004, The Hollow 2004, Man with the Screaming Brain 2005, Keep Your Distance 2005, Come Early Morning 2006, Jesus, Mary and Joey 2006, Death Row 2006, W. 2008, Chicago Overcoat 2009, The Portal 2009, The Boxer 2009, The Bourne Legacy 2012. *Television includes:* Mike Hammer, Private Eye (series) 1997, The Courage to Love 2000, Titus (series) 2000, Lightning: Fire From the Sky 2001, Rods! (series) 2002, The Santa Trap 2002, Miracle Dogs 2003, Frozen Impact 2003, Desolation Canyon 2006, Fatal Contact: Bird Flu in America 2006, Washington the Warrior (voice, miniseries) 2006, Blackbeard (miniseries) 2006, Prison Break (series) 2005–07. *Publication:* Keach, Go Home! 1996 (autobiog.). *Address:* William Morris Agency, 1 William Morris Place, Beverly Hills, CA 90212; c/o Palmer & Associates, #950, 23852 Pacific Coast Highway, Malibu, CA 90265, USA (office).

KEAN, Thomas H., MA; American academic administrator and fmr politician; b. 21 April 1935, New York; m. Deborah Bye; two s. one d.; ed Princeton Univ., Columbia Univ. Teachers Coll.; fmr teacher of history and Govt; mem. NJ Ass. 1967–77, Speaker 1972, Minority Leader 1974; Acting Gov. of NJ 1973, Gov. 1982–90; Pres. Drew Univ., Madison, NJ 1990–2005 (retd); mem. White House Conf. on Youth 1970–71; fmr Chair. Carnegie Corpn of New York, Educate America, Nat. Environmental Educ. and Training Foundation; Chair. Newark Alliance, Nat. Campaign to Prevent Teen Pregnancy, Nat. Comm. on Terrorist Attacks upon the US (9-11 Comm.) 2002–04; mem. Bd Robert Wood Johnson Foundation, Nat. Council World Wildlife Fund; regular columnist, The Star

Ledger. *Publications include:* The Politics of Inclusion, Without Precedent: The Inside Story of the 9/11 Commission (with Lee H. Hamilton) 2006. *Address:* PO Box 332, Far Hills, NJ 07931, USA.

KEANE, Fergal Patrick, OBE; Irish journalist and broadcaster; b. 6 Jan. 1961; s. of the late Eamon Brendan Keane and of Mary Hasset; m. Anne Frances Flaherty 1986; one s.; ed Terenure Coll., Dublin and Presentation Coll., Cork; trainee reporter with Limerick Leader 1979–82; reporter Irish Press Group, Dublin 1982–84, Radio Telefis Eireann, Belfast 1986–89 (Dublin 1984–86); NI Corresp. BBC Radio 1989–91, South Africa Corresp. 1991–94, Asia Corresp. 1994–97, Special Corresp. Radio 4 1997–; presenter, Fergal Keane's Forgotten Britain (BBC) 2000; columnist The Independent newspaper; Hon. DLitt (Strathclyde) 2001, (Staffs.) 2002; James Cameron Prize 1996, Bayeux Prize for war reporting 1999; Reporter of the Year Sony Silver Award 1992 and Sony Gold Award 1993, Int. Reporter of the Year 1993, Amnesty Int. Press Awards, RTS Journalist of the Year 1994, BAFTA Award 1997. *Publications:* Irish Politics Now 1987, The Bondage of Fear 1994, Season of Blood: A Rwandan Journey 1995, Letter to Daniel 1996, Letters Home 1999, A Stranger's Eye 2000, There will be Sunlight Later: A Memoir of War 2004, All of These People (memoir) 2005, Road of Bones 2010. *Leisure interests:* fishing, golf, poetry. *Address:* BBC Radio, Broadcasting House, Portland Place, London, W1A 1AA, England. *Website:* www.bbc.co.uk/radio4/ presenters/fergal_keane.shtml.

KEANEY, Thomas, BSc, MA, PhD; American defence analyst, research institute director and academic; *Associate Director, Strategic Studies Program and Senior Adjunct Professor of Strategic Studies, The Phillip Merrill Center for Strategic Studies, Paul H. Nitze School of Advanced International Studies, Johns Hopkins University;* b. 14 June 1940, Boston, Mass; ed USAF Acad., Colo, Univ. of Michigan; fmr Prof. of Mil. Strategy, Nat. War Coll.; several positions with USAF including Air Staff planner, Forward Air Controller, B-52 Squadron Commdr; Assoc. Prof. of History, USAF Acad.; Exec. Dir Foreign Policy Inst. 1998–2007; Assoc. Dir Strategic Studies Program and Sr Adjunct Prof. of Strategic Studies, The Phillip Merrill Center for Strategic Studies, Paul H. Nitze School of Advanced International Studies, Johns Hopkins Univ. 2004–. *Publications include:* Revolution in Warfare? Air Power in the Persian Gulf 1995, US Allies in a Changing World 2000, The Armed Forces in the Contemporary Middle East (co-ed.) 2001, War in Iraq, Planning and Execution (co-ed.) 2007, Understanding Counterinsurgency Warfare (co-ed.) 2010. *Address:* Merrill Center for Strategic Studies, Paul H. Nitze School of Advanced International Studies, Johns Hopkins University, The Rome Building, 1619 Massachusetts Avenue NW, Washington, DC 20036, USA (office). *Telephone:* (202) 663-5886 (office). *Fax:* (202) 663-5782 (office). *E-mail:* tkeaney@jhu.edu (office). *Website:* www.sais-jhu.edu/centers/merrill (office).

KEARNEY, Gerardine (Ged), BEd; Australian nurse and trade union executive; *President, Australian Council of Trade Unions;* b. Richmond, Melbourne, Vic.; m.; four c.; registered nurse 1985, also served as nursing educator, including as Man. Clinical Nursing Educ. Dept at Austin Health; elected official with Australian Nursing Fed. 1997–2010, also served as Asst Fed. Sec., Fed. Pres. and Pres. Victorian Br., Fed. Sec. 2008–10; Pres. Australian Council of Trade Unions 2010–; mem. Bd of Dirs HESTA Super Fund. *Address:* Australian Council of Trade Unions, 365 Queen Street, Melbourne, Vic. 3000, Australia (office). *Telephone:* (3) 9664-7333 (office). *Fax:* (3) 9600-0859 (office). *E-mail:* info@actu.asn.au (office). *Website:* www.actu.asn.au (office).

KEAT CHHON, PhD; Cambodian politician; *Senior Minister and Minister of the Economy and Finance;* b. 11 Aug. 1934, Kratie Prov.; m. Lay Neari; one s. one d.; ed Charles Stuart Univ., Australia; naval architect, marine engineer and nuclear engineer; fmr Gov. Bank of Cambodia; elected mem. of Parl.; currently Sr Minister, Minister of the Economy and Finance and Sr Minister in charge of Rehabilitation and Devt; Coordinator Working Group for Govt Pvt. Sector Forum; Vice Chair. Council for the Devt of Cambodia; Co-founder and Vice-Chair. Cambodian Inst. for Cooperation and Peace, Phnom-Penh; Commdr Légion d'honneur, Grand Cross Order of Sowathara (Cambodia), Grand Cross Order of Kingdom of Cambodia; Dr hc (Univ. of Cambodia) 2005. *Publications:* Cambodia's Economic Development: Policies, Strategies and Implementation 1999. *Address:* Ministry of the Economy and Finance, 60 rue 92, Phnom-Penh, Cambodia (office). *Telephone:* (23) 723164 (office). *Fax:* (23) 723164 (office). *E-mail:* mef@mef.gov.kh (office). *Website:* www .mef.gov.kh (office).

KEATING, Francis (Frank) Anthony, II, JD; American lawyer and fmr politician; *President and CEO, American Council of Life Insurers;* b. 10 Feb. 1944, St Louis, Mo.; s. of Anthony Francis Keating and Anne Martin; m. Catherine Dunn Heller 1972; one s. two d.; ed Georgetown Univ., Univ. of Oklahoma; called to the Bar, Okla 1969; Special Agent with FBI 1969–71; Asst Dist Attorney, Tulsa Co. 1971–72; mem. Okla House of Reps 1972–74, Okla Senate 1974–81; attorney, Northern Dist, Okla 1981–84; Asst Sec., US Treasury Dept, Washington, DC 1985–88, Assoc. Attorney-Gen., US Dept of Justice 1988–89, Gen. Counsel and Acting Deputy Sec., US Dept of Housing and Urban Devt 1989–93; attorney in pvt. practice, Tulsa 1993–95; Gov. of Okla 1995–2003; Pres. and CEO American Council of Life Insurers 2003–; mem. Okla Bar Asscn; mem. Bd Dirs Nat. Archives Foundation, Mt Vernon; Pres. Fed. City Council; hon. degrees from Marymount Univ., Groves Coll., Univ. of Tulsa, LaRoche Coll., Regentes Univ.; Order of Malta, Fed. Asscn. *Publications:* for children: Will Rogers (Spur Award, Western Writers of America 2003), Theodore (Int. Children's Book Award for Non-fiction 2007). *Address:* American Council of Life Insurers, 101 Constitution Avenue, NW, Washington, DC 20001-2133, USA (office). *Telephone:* (202) 624-2000 (office). *Fax:* (202) 572-4840 (office). *E-mail:* Media@acli.com (office). *Website:* www.acli.com (office).

KEATING, Michael, BA, MA, PhD, FRSE, AcSS; Canadian/British/Irish political scientist and academic; *Chair in Scottish Politics, University of Aberdeen;* b. 2 Feb. 1950, Hartlepool, Cleveland, England; s. of Michael Joseph Keating and Margaret Watson Keating; m. Patricia Ann Keating; one s.; ed Univ. of Oxford, Council for Nat. Academic Awards, Inst. of Linguists; grad. student and part-time Lecturer in Politics and Econs, Glasgow Coll. of Tech. 1972–75; Sr Research Officer in Govt, Univ. of Essex 1975–76; Lecturer in Politics, North Straffordshire Polytechnic 1976–79; Sr Lecturer in Politics, Univ. of Strathclyde 1979–88; Prof. of Political

Science, Univ. of Western Ontario, Canada 1988–99; Chair in Scottish Politics, Univ. of Aberdeen 1999–; Prof. of Political and Social Sciences, European Univ. Inst., Florence, Italy 2000–10, Head of Dept 2004–07; Visiting Prof. of Political Science, Virginia Polytechnic Inst. and State Univ., USA 1987–88, Univ. of Sunderland 1995–2000; Visiting Prof. of Govt, Univ. of Strathclyde 1988–99; Visiting Prof., Institut d'Etudes Politiques, Paris 1991, Univ. of Santiago de Compostela, Spain 1992, Univ. of the Basque Country, Norwegian Nobel Inst.; Scholar in Residence, Rockefeller Foundation Center, Bellagio, Italy 1997; Norman Chester Sr Visiting Research Fellow, Nuffield Coll. Oxford 1998; Visiting Fellow, Schuman Centre, European Univ. Inst. 1999, McQuarie Univ., Sydney, Australia 2005; Econ. and Social Research Council Professorial Fellow 2010–(13); Founder and Co-Dir European Consortium for Political Research Standing Group on Regionalism; Jt Ed. Regional and Federal Studies; mem. Editorial Bd Environment and Planning, Government and Policy, Space and Polity, Modern and Contemporary France, Spanish Cultural Studies, Regional Studies, Politique et Sociétés. *Publications include:* State and Regional Nationalism: Territorial Politics and the European State 1988, Comparative Urban Politics: Power and the City in the United States, Canada, Britain and France 1991, The Politics of Modern Europe: The State and Political Authority in the Major Democracies 1993, The European Union and the Regions (co-ed.) 1995, Nations Against the State: The New Politics of Nationalism in Quebec, Catalonia and Scotland 1996, The New Regionalism in Western Europe: Territorial Restructuring and Political Change 1998, Paradiplomacy in Action: The External Activities of Subnational Governments 1999, The Government of Scotland 2005, Methodologies and Approaches in the Social Sciences (co-ed.) 2008, The Independence of Scotland 2009. *Address:* School of Social Sciences, University of Aberdeen, Dunbar Street, Aberdeen, AB24 3EN, Scotland (office). *Telephone:* (1224) 272770 (office); (131) 556-0962 (office); 7758-329876 (mobile); (1224) 272726 (office). *Fax:* (1224) 272552 (office). *E-mail:* m.keating@abdn.ac.uk (office). *Website:* www.abdn.ac.uk/socsci (office).

KEATING, Hon. Paul John; Australian politician; b. 18 Jan. 1944, Sydney; s. of Matthew Keating and Min Keating; m. Anna Van Iersel 1975; one s. three d.; ed De La Salle Coll., Bankstown; Research Officer, Federated Municipal and Shire Council Employees' Union of Australia 1967; mem. House of Reps for Fed. Seat of Blaxland 1969–96; Minister for N Australia Oct.–Nov. 1975; Opposition Spokesman on Agric. Jan.–March 1976, on Minerals and Energy 1976–83, on Treasury Matters Jan.–March 1983; Fed. Treas. 1983–91; Leader, Australian Labor Party 1991–96; Deputy Prime Minister 1990–91, Prime Minister of Australia 1991–96; Hon. LLD (Keio Univ., Tokyo) 1995, (Nat. Univ. of Singapore) 1999, (Univ. NSW) 2003, Hon. DLit (Macquarie Univ.) 2012. *Publications include:* Engagement: Australia Faces the Asia Pacific 2000, After Words: The Post-Prime Ministerial Speeches 2011. *Leisure interests:* classical music, architecture, swimming, fine arts. *Address:* PO Box 1265, Potts Point, 1335 NSW, Australia. *Telephone:* (2) 9358 5466 (office). *Fax:* (2) 9358 5477 (office). *Website:* www.keating.org.au (office).

KEATING, Roland "Roly" Francis Kester; British broadcasting executive and library administrator; *Chief Executive, British Library;* b. 1961; joined BBC as trainee 1983, Series Ed. Bookmark 1992–97, Head of Programming for UKTV 1997–2001, Controller of Digital Channels 1999–2001, Controller of Arts Commissioning 2000–01, Controller of BBC 4 2001–04, of BBC 2 2004–08, Dir of Archive Content 2008–12; Chief Exec., British Library 2012–; BAFTA Award for Best Arts Programme (Bookmark) 1993, Broadcast Channel of the Year (BBC 2) 2007. *Address:* British Library, 96 Euston Rd, London, NW1 2DB, England (office). *Website:* www.bl.uk/ (office).

KEATING, Ronan; Irish singer, songwriter and actor; b. (Ronan Patrick John Keating), 3 March 1977, Dublin; s. of Gerry Keating and the late Marie Keating; m. Yvonne Keating (divorced 2013); one s. two d.; mem. Boyzone 1993–2001, 2007–; tours: Hotfest Tour 1995, Said And Done Tour 1995, Did you have a big buzz feelin Tour 1996, A Different Beat Tour 1997, Where We Belong Tour 1998, Boyzone... Greatest Hits Tour 1999–2000, Boyzone Back Again Tour 2008, Better Tour 2009, Brother Tour 2011, BZ20 tour 2013; solo artist 1999–; UN Goodwill Amb.; BMI European Song Writing Award, Ivor Novello Award. *Television:* hosted Miss World Competition, Eurovision Song Contest and MTV Europe Awards; judge on X Factor in Australia for four seasons. *Films:* (as actor) Postman Pat: The Movie 2014, Goddess 2014. *Recordings include:* albums: with Boyzone: Said and Done 1994, A Different Beat 1996, Where We Belong 1998, By Request 1999, Back Again... No Matter What 2008, Brother 2010, BZ20; solo: Ronan 2000, Destination 2002, Turn It On 2003, Bring You Home 2006, Songs for My Mother 2009, Winter Songs 2009, Duet 2010, When Ronan Met Burt 2011. *Publications include:* No Matter What 2000, Life is a Rollercoaster 2000. *Address:* c/o MP Music Services Ltd, 123 Winston Road, London, N16 9LL, England (office). *E-mail:* info@mpmusicservices.co.uk (office). *Website:* www.mpmusicservices.co.uk (office); boyzonenetwork.com; www.ronankeating.com.

KEATON, Diane; American actress; b. 5 Jan. 1946, Calif.; student Neighbourhood Playhouse, New York; New York stage appearances in Hair 1968, Play It Again Sam 1971, The Primary English Class 1976; f. Blue Relief Productions (film production co.). *Films include:* Lovers and Other Strangers 1970, Play It Again Sam 1972, The Godfather 1972, Sleeper 1973, The Godfather Part 2 1974, Love and Death 1975, I Will-I Will–For Now 1975, Harry and Walter Go To New York 1976, Annie Hall (Acad. Award for Best Actress and other awards) 1977, Looking for Mr. Goodbar 1977, Interiors 1978, Manhattan 1979, Reds 1981, Shoot the Moon 1982, Mrs Soffel 1985, Crimes of the Heart 1986, Trial and Error 1986, Radio Days 1987, Heaven (Dir) 1987, Baby Boom 1988, The Good Mother 1988, The Lemon Sisters 1989, Running Mates 1989, The Godfather III, Wildflower (Dir) 1992, Secret Society (Dir), Manhattan Murder Mystery 1993, Unsung Heroes (Dir) 1995, Father of the Bride 2 1995, Marvin's Room, The First Wives Club 1996, The Only Thrill 1997, The Other Sister 1999, Hanging Up (also Dir) 2000, Town and Country 2001, Plan B 2001, Sister Mary Explains It All 2001, Wildflower 2002, Something's Gotta Give (Golden Globe Award, Best Actress Musical or Comedy 2004) 2003, The Family Stone 2005, Because I Said So 2007, Mama's Boy 2007, Mad Money 2008, Morning Glory 2010, Darling Companion 2012, The Big Wedding 2013. *Publications:* Reservations, Still Life (Ed.), Then Again (autobiog.) 2011. *Address:* Blue Relief Productions, 301 North Canyon Drive, Suite 205, Beverly Hills, CA 90210; c/o The Gersh Agency, 232 North Canyon Drive, Suite 201, Beverly Hills, CA 90210, USA. *Telephone:* (310) 275-7900 (Blue Relief).

KEATON, Michael; American actor; b. 9 Sept. 1951, Pittsburgh, Pa; m. Caroline MacWilliams (divorced); one s.; ed Kent State Univ.; with comedy group, Second City, LA. *Films:* Night Shift 1982, Mr Mom 1983, Johnny Dangerously 1984, Touch and Go 1986, Gung Ho 1986, The Squeeze 1987, Beetlejuice 1988, Clean and Sober 1988, The Dream Team 1989, Batman 1989, Pacific Heights 1990, One Good Cop 1991, Batman Returns 1992, Much Ado About Nothing 1992, My Life, The Paper 1994, Speechless 1994, Multiplicity 1996, Jackie Brown 1997, Desperate Measures 1998, Out of Sight 1998, Jack Frost 1999, Shot at Glory 2000, Quicksand 2001, First Daughter 2004, White Noise 2005, Game 6 2005, Herbie Fully Loaded 2005, Cars (voice) 2006, The Last Time 2006, The Merry Gentleman (also dir) 2009. *Television appearances include:* All in the Family, Maude, Mary Tyler Moore Show, Working Stiffs, Report to Murphy, Roosevelt and Truman (TV film), Body Shots (producer) 1999, Live from Baghdad 2002. *Address:* c/o ICM Management, 8942 Wilshire Boulevard, Beverly Hills, CA 90211, USA.

KEAVENEY, Raymond, MA; Irish gallery director and art historian; *Director, National Gallery of Ireland;* b. 1947, Carlanstown, Co. Meath; ed Franciscan Coll., Gormanston, University Coll. Dublin; worked and studied abroad 1975–78; Curator, Nat. Gallery of Ireland, Dublin 1979–81, Asst Dir 1981–88, Dir 1988–; specializes in Italian art and Old Master drawings. *Publications:* Master European Drawings 1983, Views of Rome 1988. *Address:* National Gallery of Ireland, Merrion Square West, Dublin 2, Ireland. *Telephone:* (1) 6615133 (office), (1) 6615133. *Fax:* (1) 6615372. *E-mail:* rkeaveney@ngi.ie (office). *Website:* www .nationalgallery.ie (office).

KEBEKOV, Aliaskhab Alibulatovich, (Ali Abu-Mukhammad); Russian (Avar) rebel leader; *Emir, Caucasus Emirate;* b. 1 Jan. 1972, Sovetsky Dist, Dagestan, Russian SFSR, USSR (now the Shamilsky Dist of Dagestan); joined Vilayat Dagestan wing of terrorist org. Caucasus Emirate, Supreme Qadi of the Sharia Court 2010–; closest associate of, and deputy to, Doku Umarov, head of underground Dagestan Ibragimhahila Daudova (Amir Salih), before his death; included in list of existing Russian terrorists and extremists; recognized as extremist by Soviet Dist Court of Repub. of Dagestan April 2012; rejected proposal by other emirs of the group that he should succeed Umarov, acceded to demands and accepted appointment as Emir of Caucasus Emirate March 2014–.

KEBICH, Vyacheslau Frantsavich; Belarusian politician; b. 10 June 1936, Konyushevshchina, Minsk Dist; s. of Frants Karlovich Kebich and Tatyana Vasilyevna Kebicha; m. Yelena Kebicha 1970; one s. one d.; ed Belarus Polytechnic Inst., Higher Party School; mem. CPSU 1962–91, Cen. Cttee 1980–91; engineer, man. in Minsk 1973–80; party official 1980–85; Deputy Chair. Council of Ministers, Chair. State Planning Cttee 1985–90; USSR People's Deputy 1989–91; Chair. Council of Ministers (Prime Minister) of Byelorussia (now Belarus) 1990–94; unsuccessful Presidential cand. 1994; Chair. Belarus Trade and Finance Union 1994–; mem. Supreme Soviet (Parl.) 1980–96, MP 1996; Corresp. mem. Int. Eng Acad.; Belarus State Prize. *Leisure interest:* fishing.

KECHICHE, Abdellatif; Tunisian actor, screenwriter and director; b. 7 Dec. 1960, Tunis; stage acting debut in Sans titre by Garcia Lorca 1978; followed by Un balcon sur les Andes by Eduardo Manet, Nat. Odeon Theatre; film debut in Le thé à la menthe; directing debut with La faute à Voltaire 2000. *Films include:* as actor: Le thé à la menthe 1984, Les innocents (The Innocents) 1987, Bezness (Acting Prize, Festival du Film Francophone de Namur 1992, Acting Prize, Festival de Damas 1993) 1992, Un vampire au paradis (A Vampire in Paradise) 1992, La boîte magique (The Magic Box) 2002, Sorry, Haters 2005; as dir: La faute à Voltaire (Blame It on Voltaire) (Golden Lion, Venice Film Festival 2000, Distribution Prize, Munich Int Film Festival 2002) 2000, L'esquive (Special Jury Prize, Istanbul Int. Film Festival 2004, César Award for Best Film, Best Dir, Best Screenplay 2005) 2003, La Graine et le mulet (Couscous) (Special Jury Prize, Venice Film Festival 2007, César Award for Best Film, Best Dir, Best Screenplay 2008, Prix Louis Delluc) 2007, Black Venus 2010, Blue is the Warmest Colour (Palme d'Or, Cannes Film Festival 2013, British Independent Film Award for Best Int. Independent Film 2013) 2013.

KEDAH, HM The Sultan of; Tuanku Haji Abdul Halim Mu'adzam Shah ibni al-Marhum Sultan Badlishah, GCB, KStJ, DK, DKH, DKM, DMN, DUK, DK (Kelantan), DK (Pahang), DK (Selangor), DK (Perlis), DK (Johore), DK (Trengganu), DP (Sarawak), SPMK, SSDK, DHMS; *Yang di-Pertuan Agong (Supreme Head of State);* b. 28 Nov. 1927, Alor Setar; m. Tuanku Bahiyah binti Al-Marhum Tuanku Abdul Rahman, d. of 1st Yang di Pertuan Agong of Malaya, 1956; three d.; ed Sultan Abdul Hamid Coll., Alor Setar and Wadham Coll., Oxford; Raja Muda (Heir to Throne of Kedah) 1949, Regent of Kedah 1957, Sultan 1958–; Timbalan Yang di-Pertuan Agong (Deputy Supreme Head of State) 1965–70, 2006–11, Yang di-Pertuan Agong (Supreme Head of State) 1970–75, 2011–; Col Commdt Malaysian Reconnaissance Corps 1966; Col-in-Chief, Royal Malay Regt 1972–; C-in-C of the Malaysian Armed Forces; Marshal of the Royal Malaysian Air Force; Field Marshal of the Malaysian Army; Adm. of the Fleet of the Royal Malaysian Navy; Collar of the Order of the Chrysanthemum (Japan) 1970, Collar of the Star of Mahaputra, First Class (Indonesia) 1970, Collar of the Order of Pahlavi (Iran) 1971, Kt of the Most Auspicious Order of the Rajamitrabhorn (Thailand) 1973, Grand Cross, Order of Charles III (with Collar) (Spain) 1974, Nishan-e-Pakistan, First Class (Pakistan) 1974. *Leisure interests:* golf, billiards, photography, tennis. *Address:* Istana Anak Bukit, Alor Setar, Kedah, Darul Aman, Malaysia (office). *Website:* www.parlimen.gov.my/yang-di-pertuan-agong .html?uweb=yg (office).

KEDIKILWE, Ponatshego, MA; Botswana politician; *Vice-President and Minister of Minerals, Energy and Water Affairs;* b. 4 Aug. 1938, Sefhophe; ed Univ. of Connecticut, Syracuse Univ.; joined Govt 1970; Prin. Finance Officer, Finance Ministry 1974–76; Sec. for Financial Affairs 1976; Perm. Sec., Ministry of Works, Transport and Communications 1977–79; Dir Public Service Man., Office of the Pres. 1979–84; mem. Parl. 1984–; Deputy Minister of Finance 1984; Minister of Presidential Affairs and Public Admin 1985–89, 1994–98, of Commerce and Industry 1989–94, of Finance and Devt Planning 1998, of Educ. 1999–2000, of Minerals, Energy and Water Affairs 2007–; Vice-Pres. 2012–; fmr Chair. Botswana Democratic Party; Presidential Order of Honour 1992. *Leisure interests:* soccer, ranching, debating, gardening, speech writing, traditional music, folklore and poetry. *Address:* Ministry of Minerals, Energy and Water Affairs, Khama Cres.,

Private Bag 0018, Gaborone, Botswana (office). *Telephone:* 3656600 (office). *Fax:* 3972738 (office). *Website:* www.mmewr.gov.bw (office).

KEEFFE, Barrie Colin Noel; British dramatist, novelist, director and university tutor; *Patron, Writing for Performance, Ruskin College Oxford;* b. 31 Oct. 1945, London; s. of the late Edward Thomas Keeffe and Constance Beatrice Keeffe (née Marsh); m. 1st Sarah Dee (Truman) 1969 (divorced 1975); m. 2nd Verity Eileen Bargate 1981 (died 1981); two step-s.; m. 3rd Julia Lindsay 1983 (divorced 1991); m. 4th Jacky Stoller 2013; ed East Ham Grammar School, West Ham Coll., Nat. Council for Training of Journalists; fmr actor with Nat. Youth Theatre, journalist; has written plays for theatre, TV and radio; fmr Resident Writer, Shaw Theatre, London, RSC; Assoc. Writer, Theatre Royal, Stratford East, also mem. Bd; Assoc. Soho Theatre Co.; Writers' Mentor, Nat. Theatre 1999–2002; Tutor, City Univ., London 2001–05; Bye-Fellow, Christ's Coll., Cambridge 2003; Resident Writer, Kingston Univ. 2010–12; Patron Writing for Performance, Ruskin Coll., Oxford 2010–; tutor, Collaldra School and Writers' Retreat, Venice, Italy; UN Amb., 50th Anniversary Year 1995; Dir Newbell Production Ltd 2012–; mem. Soc. des auteurs et compositeurs dramatiques; Hon. DLitt (Warwick) 2010; French Critics' Prix Révélation 1978, Thames TV Playwright Award 1979, Giles Cooper Award Best Radio Plays, Mystery Writers of America Edgar Allan Poe Award 1982. *Theatre plays include:* Only a Game 1973, A Sight of Glory 1975, Scribes 1975, Here Comes the Sun 1976, Gimme Shelter 1977, A Mad World My Masters 1977, Barbarians 1977, Frozen Assets 1978, Sus 1979, Heaven Scent 1979, Bastard Angel 1980, She's So Modern 1980, Black Lear 1980, Chorus Girls 1981, Better Times 1985, King of England 1988, My Girl 1989, Not Fade Away 1990, Wild Justice 1990, I Only Want to Be With You 1995, Shadows on The Sun 2001, Still Killing Time 2005. *Plays directed include:* A Certain Vincent, A Gentle Spirit, Talking of Chekov (Amsterdam and London), My Girl (London and Bombay), The Gary Oldman Fan Club (London). *Film:* The Long Good Friday (screenplay) 1980, Sus (screenplay) 2010. *Television plays include:* Substitute 1972, Not Quite Cricket 1977, Gotcha 1977, Nipper 1977, Champions 1978, Hanging Around 1978, Waterloo Sunset 1979, No Excuses (series) 1983, King 1984. *Radio plays include:* Good Old Uncle Jack 1975, Pigeon Skyline 1975, Self- Portrait 1977, Paradise 1990, On the Eve of the Millennium 1999, Tales 2000, Feng Shui and Me 2000, The Five of Us 2002. *Television:* Substitute, Gotcha, Not Quite Cricket, Hanging Around, Champions, Nipper, Waterloo Sunset, King, No Excuses (series). *Publications:* novels: Gadabout 1969, No Excuses 1983; screenplay: The Long Good Friday 1998; Barrie Keeffe Plays I 2001. *Leisure interests:* playing tennis, watching soccer. *Address:* c/o The Agency, 24 Pottery Lane, Holland Park, London, W11 4LZ, England (office); 33 Brookfield, Highgate West Hill, London, N6 6AT, England (home). *Telephone:* (20) 7727-1346 (office); (20) 8340-9309 (office). *Fax:* (20) 8340-9309 (office). *E-mail:* barriekeeffe@aol.com (office).

KEEGAN, Kevin Joseph, OBE; British professional football manager, fmr professional footballer and business executive; b. 14 Feb. 1951, Armthorpe, Doncaster; s. of the late Joseph Keegan; m. Jean Woodhouse 1974; two s.; forward; youth player for Enfield House YC, Scunthorpe United 1967–68; sr player for Scunthorpe United 1968–71, Liverpool 1971–77 (won League Championship 1972/ 73, 1975/76, 1976/77, FA Cup 1974, European Cup 1977, UEFA Cup 1973, 1976, FA Charity Shield 1974, 1976), SV Hamburg 1977–80 (Bundesliga 1978/79), Southampton 1980–82, Newcastle United (also Capt.) 1982–84 (won Kirin Cup 1983; retd); scored 274 goals in approx. 800 appearances; capped for England 63 times (31 as Capt.), scoring 21 goals 1972–82, Capt. 1976–82; Man. Newcastle United 1992–97 (won Football League First Div. 1992/93), 2008, Fulham 1998–99 (won Football League Second Div. 1998/99), Manchester City 2001–05 (won Football League First Div. 2001/02); Man. England nat. team 1999–2000; f. Soccer Circus (interactive football training games), Glasgow 2006; Footballer of the Year 1976, European Footballer of the Year 1978, 1979, Southampton FC Player of the Season 1981/82, inducted into inaugural English Football Hall of Fame 2002, named eighth on Liverpool FC list of 100 Players who shook the Kop, Football Writers' Asscn Footballer of the Year 1976, Professional Footballers' Asscn Players' Player of the Year 1982, Premier League Man. of the Month Nov. 1993, Aug. 1994, Feb. 1995, Aug. 1995, Sept. 1995. *Publications:* Kevin Keegan 1978, Against the World: Playing for England 1979, Kevin Keegan: My Autobiography 1997. *Address:* Soccer Circus, Xscape, Kings Inch Road, Renfrew, Glasgow, PA4 8XU, Scotland (office). *Telephone:* (141) 885-1222. *E-mail:* info@soccercircus.com. *Website:* www.soccercircus.com.

KEEGAN, Robert (Bob) J., BS, MBA; American business executive; b. 27 July 1947, New York; m. Lynn Keegan; two c.; ed LeMoyne Coll., Syracuse, NY, Univ. of Rochester, NY; joined Eastman Kodak Co. 1972, various man. positions in Distribution and Marketing Depts, Rochester, NY, Gen. Man. Kodak NZ 1986–87, Dir of Finance, Rochester 1987–90, Gen. Man. Kodak Spain 1990–91, Gen. Man. of Consumer Imaging, Kodak Europe, Middle E and Africa 1991–93, Corp. Vice-Pres. 1993–95, Pres. Kodak Professional and Corp. Vice-Pres. July–Oct. 1997, Pres. of Consumer Imaging and Sr Vice-Pres. 1997–2000, Exec. Vice-Pres. 2000–03; Exec. Vice-Pres. and Global Strategy Officer, Avery Dennison Corpn 1995–97; mem. Bd of Dirs and COO Goodyear Tire & Rubber Co. 2000–02, Pres. and CEO Jan. 2003–April 2010, Chair. July 2003–Oct. 2010. *Address:* c/o Goodyear Tire & Rubber Company, 1144 East Market Street, Akron, OH 44316-0001, USA. *E-mail:* info@ goodyear.com.

KEEL, Alton G., Jr, BS, PhD; American diplomatist, civil servant, engineer, banker and business executive; *Chairman and Managing Director, Atlantic Partners, LLC;* b. 8 Sept. , Newport News, Va; s. of Alton G. Keel and Ella Kennedy; m. 1st Franmarie Kennedy-Keel 1982 (divorced); one d.; m. 2nd Lynn Matti Keel (divorced); ed Univ. of Virginia, Univ. of California, Berkeley, postdoctoral studies; Facility Man. Naval Weapons Center 1971–77; Sr Official Senate Armed Services Cttee, US Senate 1977–81; Asst Sec., US Air Force for Research, Devt and Logistics, The Pentagon, Washington, DC 1981–82; Assoc. Dir Nat. Security and Int. Affairs, Exec. Office of the Pres. 1982–86; Exec. Dir and Pres. Comm. on Space Shuttle Challenger Accident 1986; Acting Asst to the Pres. for Nat. Security Affairs 1986; Amb. and Perm. Rep. to NATO 1987–89; Pres. and Man. Dir Carlyle International, The Carlyle Group 1992–94; Chair. Carlyle SEAG 1994–95, Chair. and Man. Dir Atlantic Partners, LLC (pvt. investment group), Washington, DC 1992–; Chair. and CEO Land-5 Corpn 1999–2002; mem. Dean's Advisory Bd, Univ. of Virginia 1996–2006, Trustee, Eng School 2009–; CEO InoStor Corpn 2002–05;

mem. Bd and Exec. Cttee Piedmont Environmental Council 2004–; Sec. Piedmont Environmental Council 2011–; Nat. Congressional Science Fellow, AIAA 1977; Young Scientist Award 1974, Air Force Decoration for Exceptional Civilian Service 1982, NASA Group Achievement Award 1987, Distinguished Alumnus Award, Univ. of Virginia 1987. *Publications:* numerous scientific and tech. articles, foreign policy and nat. security publs. *Leisure interests:* running, golf, sailing, physical fitness. *Address:* Fairhill Farm, 2891 South River Road, Stanardsville, VA 22973, USA. *Telephone:* (434) 990-9501. *Fax:* (434) 990-9503. *E-mail:* fairhillfarm@ fairhillfarmusa.com. *Website:* www.fairhillfarmusa.com.

KEELER, HE Cardinal William Henry, DCL; American ecclesiastic (retd); b. 4 March 1931, San Antonio, Tex.; s. of Thomas L. Keeler and Margaret T. Keeler (née Conway); ed Lebanon Catholic High School, Pa, St Charles Seminary, Overbrook, Phila, Pontifical Gregorian Univ., Rome, Italy; ordained priest 1955; Asst Pastor, Our Lady of Good Counsel Church, Marysville 1956–58, 1961–64, Pastor 1964; Sec. Diocesan Tribunal 1956–58; Sec. to Bishop Leech during Second Vatican Council, Rome 1962–65; apptd Peritus or 'Special Advisor' to the Council by Pope John XXIII, served on staff of Council Digest (daily communication service sponsored by US Bishops), named Papal Chamberlain (with title of Mgr) by Pope Paul VI 1965; Vice-Chancellor Harrisburg Diocese 1965–69, Chancellor 1969, later Vicar Gen.; apptd Auxiliary Bishop of Harrisburg and Titular Bishop of Ulcinium (Dulcigno) 1979; Admin. Diocese of Harrisburg 1983; Bishop of Harrisburg 1983–89; Chair. Nat. Conf. of Catholic Bishops (NCCB)'s Cttee for Ecumenical and Interreligious Affairs 1984–87, Vice-Pres. NCCB 1989–92, Pres. 1992–95; Archbishop of Baltimore 1989–2007 (retd); cr. Cardinal (Titular Church of St Mary of the Angels) 1994; Pres. American Div. Catholic Near East Welfare Asscn, Cathedral Foundation; Chair. Black and Native American Missions Bd of Catholic Charities; mem. Bd Basilica of the Nat. Shrine of the Immaculate Conception, Washington, DC, Mount St Mary's Coll.; Publr The Catholic Review; mem. Bd of Trustees Catholic Univ. 1989–93, Advisory Panel for Father Michael McGivney Fund for New Initiatives in Catholic Educ. 1993, Pontifical Council for Promoting Christian Unity 1994; named Prelate of Honor by Pope Paul VI 1970; hon. degrees from Lebanon Valley Coll., Mount St Mary's Coll., Gettysburg Coll., Susquehanna Univ., Gannon Univ., Pa 1993, Loyola Coll., Baltimore, St Mary's Coll. of Minnesota, Shippensburg State Univ., Pa, Elizabethtown Coll., Pa, Univ. of Notre Dame, Ateneo Univ., The Philippines, Coll. of Notre Dame of Maryland, Franciscan Univ., Steubenville, OH, Viterbo Univ., Wis. *Address:* 408 North Charles Street, Baltimore, MD 21201, USA (home). *Fax:* (410) 727-8234 (home).

KÉFI, Muhammad Mouldi; Tunisian diplomatist and politician; b. 10 Feb. 1946, Kef; m.; four c.; ed Univ. of Strasbourg, France; joined Ministry of Foreign Affairs 1967, has held numerous positions including Head of Central and S America Dept 1978, Head of Diplomatic Protocol Dept 1980, Deputy Dir American Dept 1989, Chef de Cabinet to Minister of Foreign Affairs 1994, Special Adviser to Cabinet of Minister of Foreign Affairs 1999, Dir Gen. of Political Affairs and Cooperation for Americas and Asia Dept 2006, diplomatic attachments at embassies in Prague, London and Berlin, Amb. to Nigeria 1990–94, to Russia 1996–99, to Indonesia 2002–05; Minister of Foreign Affairs Feb.–Dec. 2011. *Address:* c/o Ministry of Foreign Affairs, ave de la Ligue des états arabes, 1030 Tunis, Tunisia.

KEIB, Abdurrahim al-, BS (Hons), MS, PhD; Libyan politician, electrical engineer and academic; b. Tripoli; ed Univ. of Tripoli, Univ. of Southern California and North Carolina State Univ., USA; Asst Prof. of Electrical Eng., Univ. of Alabama, USA 1985–96, Prof. of Electrical Eng 1996–2011; also taught at Univ. of Tripoli, North Carolina State Univ., American Univ. of Sharjah, UAE 1999–2001, Petroleum Inst., UAE (Chair. Electrical Eng Dept) 2007–09; Dir Div. of Electrical, Electronics, and Computer Eng, American Univ. of Sharjah 1999–2001; Interim Prime Minister of Libya 24 Nov. 2011–12 Sept. 2012; work on Emissions Constrained Dispatch and VoltlVar compensation on primary distribution feeders has been implemented by several cos in USA; consultant to several industries, including Alabama Power Co. and Southern Co. Services; experienced with ABET (fmrly Accreditation Bd for Eng and Tech.) accreditation and curriculum design, trained to serve as an ABET evaluator, served as Chair. of Assessment Cttee, Univ. of Alabama; mem. Bd of Dirs Arab Science and Tech. Foundation 2001–07; mem. Science and Tech. Panel, Islamic Development Bank; Assoc. Ed. IEEE/PES Power Engineering Letters 1992–2000, World Science and Engineering Academy and Society Transactions on Power Systems; mem. Editorial Advisory Bd Korean Inst. of Electrical Engineers/Soc. of Power Eng, Advisory Bd International Journal of Innovations in Energy Systems and Power; Sr mem. IEEE; NSF Eng Research Initiation Award 1989–90, T. Morris Hackney Endowed Faculty Leadership Award, Coll. of Eng, Univ. of Alabama 1997, 1998, Excellence in Service Award, American Univ. of Sharjah 2001, Outstanding Electrical and Computer Eng Instructor Award, Univ. of Alabama 1999, Certificate of Appreciation, Pres. of IEEE/PES issued by Energy Devt and Power Generation Cttee of IEEE Power and Energy Soc. 2009, Outstanding Engineer of the Year Award, IEEE/PES UAE Chapter 2009. *Publications:* one book chapter and numerous papers and research reports in scientific and engineering journals on power system economics, planning, operation and control. *Address:* c/o Executive Board, National Transitional Council, Tripoli, Libya (office). *E-mail:* info@ntclibya.com (office). *Website:* www.ntclibya.com (office).

KEILLOR, Garrison Edward, BA; American author and broadcaster; b. (Gary Edward Keillor), 7 Aug. 1942, Anoka, Minn.; s. of John P. Keillor and Grace R. Keillor (née Denham); m. 1st Mary Guntzel (divorced 1976, died 1998); one s.; m. 2nd Ulla Skaerved (divorced); m. 3rd Jenny Lind Nilsson; one d.; ed Anoka High School and Univ. of Minnesota; journalist 1962–63; radio announcer and presenter 1969–73; creator and host, A Prairie Home Companion radio show 1974–87, 1993–; host, American Radio Co. 1989–93; staff writer, The New Yorker 1987–92; George Foster Peabody Award 1980, Ace Award for best musical host (A Prairie Home Companion) 1988, Best Music and Entertainment Host Awards 1988, 1989, American Acad. and Institute of Arts and Letters Medal 1990, Music Broadcast Communications Radio Hall of Fame 1994, Nat. Humanities Medal 1999, John Steinbeck Award 2007. *Film:* A Prairie Home Companion 2006. *Publications:* Happy to Be Here 1982, Lake Wobegon Days (Grammy Award for best non-musical recording 1987) 1985, Leaving Home 1987, We Are Still Married: Stories and Letters 1989, WLT: A Radio Romance 1991, Wobegon Boy The Book of Guys 1993, Cat, You Better Come Home (children's book) 1995, The Old Man Who Loved

Cheese 1996, The Sandy Bottom Orchestra 1996, Wobegon Boy 1997, ME by Jimmy (Big Boy) Valente as told to Garrison Keillor 1999, Lake Wobegon Summer 1956 2001, Love Me 2004, Pontoon 2007, Liberty: A Lake Wobegon Novel 2008, Pilgrims: A Lake Wobegon Romance 2010, Good Poems, American Places 2011, Guy Noir and the Straight Skinny 2012; contrib. to newspapers and magazines. *Address:* A Prairie Home Companion, Minnesota Public Radio, 480 Cedar Street, St Paul, MN 55101, USA (office). *Website:* prairiehome.publicradio.org (office).

KEINÄNEN, Eino, MPolSc; Finnish fmr civil servant and business executive; b. 17 Nov. 1939; ed Univ. of Helsinki; credit official, Kansallis-Osake-Pankki 1962–64; Head of Section, Finnish State Computer Centre and Planning Organ for State Accounting 1965–68; various posts, Budget Dept, Ministry of Finance 1969–85, Head Budget Dept 1985–87, Perm. Under-Sec. 1987–89, Perm. State Sec. 1989–95; Gen. Man. and mem. Bd Postipankki Ltd 1995–96, Chair. and Chief Exec. 1996–2000; Chair. Leonia Plc 1997–2000; fmr Chair. State Pension Fund; mem. Bd of Dirs Finnish State Treasury 1985–89, Finnish Tourist Bd 1985–89, Finnish Foreign Trade Asscn 1985–89, Cen. Statistical Office of Finland 1985–89; mem. Investment Fund of Finland 1985–89; Vice-Pres. Supervisory Bd Finnish Export Credit Ltd 1987, Finnish Fund for Industrial Devt Co-operation Ltd (Finnfund) 1994; Pres. Bd of Dirs State Computer Centre 1988; mem. Supervisory Bd Slot Machine Asscn 1989, Regional Devt Fund of Finland Ltd 1989, Finnish Grain Bd 1989; mem. Bd of Admin Alko Ltd 1989; Pres. Supervisory Bd Finnish Ice-Hockey Asscn 1989.

KEINO, Kipchoge A. (Kip); Kenyan fmr athlete; b. 1940, Kipsamo; m. Phyllis Keino; fmr physical training instructor in police force; began int. running career in 1962; set two world records at 3000m and 5000m 1964; winner 1500m and 5000m, African Games 1964, 1965; winner one mile and three miles, Commonwealth Games 1966; gold medallist 1500m, silver medallist 5000m, Olympic Games, Mexico City 1968; gold medallist 3000m steeplechase, silver medallist 1500m, Olympic Games, Munich 1972; retd from int. running 1973; Pres. Kenyan Olympic Cttee; mem. IOC; helped establish high-altitude training as a technique to improve running time at any altitude; helped coach Kenyan track-and-field teams; ran in London Marathon for Oxfam 2002; f. Kip Keino Foundation, acquired a farm in Kenya (with wife Phyllis), est. Kip Keino School and orphanage on farm land; apptd by Athletics Kenya to lead investigation into country's poor performance at World Championships 2003 and to find a new head coach for Kenya's Olympic team Sept. 2003–; Laureus World Sports Acad. 'Sport for Good' Award. *Address:* Kip Keino School, Eldoret, Kenya; Kip Keino Foundation Inc., 14 Redwood Lane, B-101, Ithaca, NY 14850, USA. *Website:* www.kipkeinotraining.org.

KEÏTA, Ibrahim Boubacar, (IBK), DEA, MA; Malian politician and head of state; *President;* b. 29 Jan. 1945, Koutiala; m. Aminata Maiga; ed Lycée Janson-de-Sailly, Paris, Lycée Askia-Mohamed, Bamako, Univ. of Dakar, Univ. of Paris 1, Institut d'Histoire des Relations Internationales Contemporaines; led research at CNRS following graduation; taught Third World political systems at Univ. of Paris 1; returned to Mali 1986; Prin. Tech. Adviser to EU for European Devt Fund, then within Terre des Hommes France (Dir for West Africa) mid-1980s; mem. Asscn of African Students in France; Sec.-Gen. Comité de Défense des Libertés Démocratiques au Mali, Paris; underground participant in Malian democratic movt from 1986, helped bring about the 1991 revolution, ending 23 years of dictatorship; Founder-mem. Alliance pour la démocratie au Mali (Adema), Pres. 1994–2000; Deputy Campaign Dir for Alpha Oumar Konare who was elected Pres. 1992; Spokesman and Diplomatic Adviser to Pres. Konare 1992; Amb. to Côte d'Ivoire 1993 (also accred to Niger and Gabon); Minister of Foreign Affairs 1993–94; Prime Minister of Mali 1994–2000; left Adema following disagreements within the party 2000; Founder and Pres. Rassemblement pour le Mali party 2001–; unsuccessful cand. in presidential elections 2002, 2007, 2012 (elections not held because of coup d'état); Pres. of Mali 2013–; mem. Assemblée nationale 2002–, Pres. 2002–07; Vice-Pres. Socialist International; also presided over the African Parl. Union; Commdr de la Légion d'honneur, Grand Officier, Ordre Nat. du Mali. *Leisure interest:* reading. *Address:* Office of the President, BP 1463, Koulouba, Bamako, Mali (office). *Telephone:* 2022-2572 (office). *Fax:* 2023-0026 (office). *Website:* www .koulouba.pr.ml (office).

KEITA, Modibo, DScS; Malian academic and psychologist; *Managing Director, Cabinet d'Etudes Keita-Kala Saba;* b. 13 Jan. 1953, Bamako; m.; three s.; ed Tübingen Univ., Germany; Prof. of Higher Educ., Ecole normale supérieure de Bamako 1984–86; Founder and Man. Dir Cabinet d'Etudes pour l'Education et le Développement 1987– (renamed Cabinet d'Etudes Keita-Kala Saba 1997); Dir Boutique de Gestion, d'Echanges et de Conseils – Promotion de l'Artisanat 1993–94; Co-ordinator of Urban Waste Expertise Programme in W Africa 1996–, Making Decentralization Work/Mali 2001. *Publications:* numerous articles in magazines. *Leisure interests:* art, culture, sport. *Address:* Cek-Kala Saba, BP 9014, Bamako (office); 868 Rue Faladié Sema, Porte 66, Bamako, Mali (home). *Telephone:* 220-94-12 (office); 220-12-60 (home). *Fax:* 220-94-13 (office). *E-mail:* cek@afribone.net.ml (office); mokesn@yahoo.fr (home). *Website:* www.cek.com.ml (office).

KEITA, Salif; Malian singer; b. 25 Aug. 1949, Djoliba; began musical career in Bamako 1967; joined govt-sponsored group Super Rail Band; moved to Paris to begin solo career as a singer 1984; performances at festivals, tours of Japan, Australia, Canada, USA, Africa (including South Africa); annual European tour including summer festivals; Chevalier, Ordre des Arts et des Lettres, Chevalier, Order of the Nation (Mali), Nat. Order of Guinea 1977; Grammy Award. *Recordings include:* albums: Soro 1987, Ko-Yan 1989, Destiny of a Noble Outcast 1991, Amen 1991, L'Enfant Lion 1992, Mansa of Mali 1994, Folon 1995, Rail Band 1996, Seydou Bathili 1997, Papa 1999, Sosie 2001, Compilation 1969–80 2001, Moffou 2002, Salif Keita: The Lost Album (with Kante Manfila) 2005, M'Bemba 2005, La Différence 2010. *Address:* c/o Universal Jazz France, 22 rue des Fossés St Jacques, 75005 Paris, France (office). *E-mail:* lau.bizot@wanadoo.fr (office). *Website:* salifkeita.artistes.universalmusic.fr.

KEITEL, Hans-Peter, DrIng; German business executive; b. 1947, Kusel; m.; three c.; ed Stuttgart Technical Univ., Tech. Univ. of Munich; with Alfred Kunz & Co. Contractors, Munich 1971–72; with Burkhardt KG, Consulting Engineers, Munich 1973–75; various sr and man. positions with Lahmeyer Int. (consulting engineers) 1975–87; tech. consultant to banking consortium involved in Channel

Tunnel project 1986–87; joined Hochtief AG, Essen 1988, Dir and Head of Int. Business 1988–90, mem. Man. Bd 1990–92, CEO and Head of Construction Service Europe 1992–99, Chair. and CEO 1999–2007, now mem. Supervisory Bd; Pres. Fed. of the German Construction Industry 2005–08; Vice-Pres. Bundesverband der Deutschen Industrie eV (Fed. of German Industry) 2005–08, Pres. 2009–12; fmr mem. Supervisory Bd Commerzbank AG, National-Bank AG, ThyssenKrupp AG 2010–; Trustee, RAG-Stiftung; Verdienstorden des Landes Nordrhein-Westfalen 2004, Verdienstkreuz 1. Klasse der Bundesrepublik Deutschland 2011. *Address:* c/o Bundesverband der Deutschen Industrie eV (Federation of German Industry), Breite Str. 29, 10178 Berlin, Germany.

KEITEL, Harvey, BFA; American actor and producer; b. 13 May 1939, Brooklyn, NY; s. of Harry Keitel and Miriam Keitel (née Klein); partner Lorraine Bracco 1982–93; one d.; one s. with Lisa Karmazin; m. Daphna Kastner 2001; one s.; ed Abraham Lincoln High School, The Actors Studio, New School Univ.; served in US Marine Corps; starred in Martin Scorsese's student film Who's That Knocking at My Door?; stage appearances in Death of a Salesman, Hurlyburly; co-Pres. The Actors Studio; f. The Goatsingers (production co.). *Films include:* Mean Streets 1973, Alice Doesn't Live Here Anymore 1974, That's the Way of the World 1975, Taxi Driver 1976, Buffalo Bill and the Indians 1976, The Duellists 1978, Fingers 1978, Blue Collar 1978, Eagle's Wing 1979, Deathwatch 1980, Saturn 3 1980, The Border 1982, Exposed 1983, La Nuit de Varennes 1982, Falling in Love 1984, Knight of the Dragon 1985, Wise Guys 1986, The Men's Club 1986, The Pick-up Artist 1987, The Last Temptation of Christ 1988, The January Man 1989, The Two Jakes 1990, Thelma & Louise 1991, Bugsy 1991, Reservoir Dogs 1992, Bad Lieutenant 1992, Young Americans 1993, Dangerous Game 1993, The Piano 1993, Rising Sun 1993, Monkey Trouble 1994, Clockers 1995, Pulp Fiction 1994, Smoke 1995, Ulysses' Gaze 1995, Blue in the Face 1995, Head Above Water 1996, Somebody to Love 1996, City of Industry 1997, Cop Land 1997, Simpatico 1999, U-571 2000, Prince of Central Park 2000, Little Nicky 2000, Viper 2000, Holy Smoke 2000, Nailed 2001, Taking Sides 2001, The Grey Zone 2001, Nowhere 2002, Ginostra 2002, Red Dragon 2002, Beeper 2002, Crime Spree 2003, The Galindez File 2003, Who Killed the Idea? (short) 2003, Dreaming of Julia 2003, Chasing the Elephant (short) 2003, Puerto Vallarta Squeeze 2003, National Treasure 2004, The Bridge of San Luis Rey 2004, Shadows in the Sun 2005, Be Cool 2005, The Shadow Dancer 2005, One Last Dance 2006, A Crime 2006, The Stone Merchant 2006, Arthur et les Minimoys (voice) 2006, My Sexiest Year 2007, National Treasure: Book of Secrets 2007, The Ministers 2009, Inglourious Basterds (voice, uncredited) 2009, Wrong Turn at Tahoe 2009, A Beginner's Guide to Endings 2010, Little Fockers 2010, The Last Godfather 2010, Death in Paradise 2012, Moonrise Kingdom 2012, Gandhi of the Month 2012, The Congress 2013, A Farewell to Fools 2013. *Television includes:* Fail Safe (film) 2000, Saturday Night Live (series) – Robert De Niro/Norah Jones (uncredited) 2002, The Path to 9/11 (film) 2006, Life on Mars (series) 2008–09, Fatal Honeymoon (film) 2012. *Address:* c/o WME Entertainment, 9601 Wilshire Boulevard, Beverley Hills, CA 90210-5213, USA; The Goatsingers, 179 Franklin Street, 6th Floor, New York, NY 10013, USA. *Telephone:* (310) 285-9000; (212) 966-3045. *Fax:* (310) 285-9010; (212) 966-4362. *Website:* www.wma.com.

KEITH, Rt Hon. Sir Kenneth James, Kt, KBE, PC, LLB, LLM, QC; New Zealand judge; *Judge, International Court of Justice;* b. 19 Nov. 1937, Auckland; s. of Patrick James Keith and Amy Irene Keith (née Witheridge); m. Jocelyn Margaret Buckett 1961; two s. two d.; ed Auckland Grammar School, Univ. of Auckland, Victoria Univ. of Wellington, Harvard Law School; with Dept of External Affairs, Wellington 1960–62; with Law Faculty, Vic. Univ. 1962–64, 1966–91, Prof. 1973–91, Dean 1977–81; UN Secr. Office of Legal Affairs 1968–70; with NZ Inst. of Int. Affairs 1971–73; Judge, Courts of Appeal of Samoa 1982–, Cook Islands 1982–, Niue 1995–, NZ 1996–2003; Judge, Supreme Court of Fiji 2003–05, Supreme Court of NZ 2004–05, Int. Court of Justice 2006–; mem. NZ Law Comm. 1986–91, Pres. 1991–96; mem. NZ Nat. Group of Perm. Court of Arbitration 1985–2006, Panel of Arbitrators, Int. Centre for Settlement of Investment Disputes 1994–2012, Inst. of Int. Law 2003–; Pres. NZ Inst. of Int. Affairs 2000–06; Hon. Bencher, Inner Temple, London, UK; Commemoration Medal 1990; Hon. LLD (Auckland) 2001, (Victoria) 2004. *Publications:* Advisory Jurisdiction of the International Court 1971, Essays on Human Rights (ed.) 1968; numerous Law Comm. publs and papers on constitutional and int. law in legal journals. *Leisure interests:* family, walking, reading. *Address:* International Court of Justice, Peace Palace, Carnegieplein 2, 2517 KJ, The Hague, Netherlands (office); 11 Salamanca Road, Kelburn, Wellington, New Zealand (home). *Telephone:* (70) 302-2483 (office); (4) 472-6664 (home). *Fax:* (70) 364-9928 (office); (4) 472-6664 (home). *E-mail:* k.keith@icj-cij.org (office). *Website:* www.icj-cij.org (office).

KEITH, Dame Penelope Anne Constance, DBE, CBE, OBE, DL; British actress; b. (Penelope Anne Constance Hatfield), 2 April 1940, Sutton, Surrey, England; d. of Frederick Hatfield and Constance Mary Keith; m. Rodney Timson 1978; ed Annecy Convent, Seaford, Sussex, Convent Bayeux, Normandy, Webber Douglas School, London; first professional appearance, Civic Theatre, Chesterfield 1959; repertory, Lincoln, Salisbury, Manchester 1960–63, Cheltenham 1967; RSC, Stratford 1963, Aldwych 1965; Pres. Actors Benevolent Fund 1990–; Gov. Queen Elizabeth's Foundation for the Disabled 1989–, Guildford School of Acting 1991–; Trustee Yvonne Arnaud Theatre 1992–; High Sheriff of Surrey 2002; Best Light Entertainment Performance (British Acad. of Film and TV Arts) 1976, Best Actress 1977, Show Business Personality (Variety Club of GB) 1976, BBC TV Personality 1979, Comedy Performance of the Year (Soc. of West End. Theatre) 1976, Female TV Personality, T.V. Times Awards 1976–78, BBC TV Personality of the Year 1978–79, TV Female Personality (Daily Express) 1979–82. *Stage appearances include:* Suddenly at Home 1971, The Norman Conquests 1974, Donkey's Years 1976, The Apple Cart 1977, The Millionairess 1978, Moving 1980, Hobson's Choice, Captain Brassbound's Conversion 1982, Hay Fever 1983, The Dragon's Tail 1985, Miranda 1987, The Deep Blue Sea 1988, Dear Charles 1990, The Merry Wives of Windsor 1990, The Importance of Being Earnest 1991, On Approval 1992, Relatively Speaking 1992, Glyn and It 1994, Monsieur Amilcar 1995, Mrs Warren's Profession 1997, Good Grief 1998, Star Quality 2001. *Films include:* Every Home Should Have One 1970, Take a Girl Like You 1970, Rentadick 1972, Penny Gold 1973, Ghost Story 1974, Priest of Love 1981. *Radio includes:* Agatha Raison series. *Television includes:* Kate (series) 1970, The Good

Life 1974–78, Private Lives 1976, The Norman Conquests 1977, Much Ado About Nothing 1978, The Hound of the Baskervilles 1978, To the Manor Born 1979–81, 2007, Spider's Web 1982, On Approval 1982, Waters of the Moon 1983, Sweet Sixteen (series) 1983, Tickle on the Tum (series) 1984, Moving (series) 1985, Executive Stress (series) 1986–88, Growing Places 1989, No Job for a Lady (series) 1990–92, Law and Disorder (series) 1994, Next of Kin (series) 1995–96, Coming Home 1998, Margery and Gladys 2003, The Secret Show (series) 2006, Death Comes to Pemberley (mini-series) 2013. *Leisure interest:* gardening.

KEJRIWAL, Arvind; Indian politician; *Chief Minister of Delhi;* b. 16 June 1968, Haryana; s. of Gobind Ram Kejriwal and Gita Devi; m. Sunita Kejriwal; one s. one d.; ed Indian Inst. of Tech., Kharagpur; began career with Tata Steel, Jamshedpur 1989–92; joined Indian Revenue Service 1995, Jt Commr, Income Tax Dept –2006; co-f. Parivartan (Change, NGO), Delhi 2000; f. Public Cause Research Foundation (self-governance NGO) 2006; f. Aam Aadmi Party (AAP) 2012; Chief Minister of Delhi 2013–; CNN-IBN Indian of the Year (Public Service) 2006, Ramon Magsaysay Award for Emergent Leadership 2006, CNN-IBN Indian of the Year (Politics) 2013. *Publication:* Swaraj 2012. *Address:* Office of the Chief Minister, AB-17, Mathura Road, New Delhi 110 001, India (office). *Telephone:* (11) 23392020 (office). *Fax:* (11) 23392111 (office). *E-mail:* cmdelhi@ren02.nic.in (office). *Website:* delhi.gov.in (office); www.arvindkejriwal.net.in (office).

KEKE, Kieren Aedogan, MD; Nauruan physician and politician; b. 27 June 1971, Yaren; s. of Ludwig Keke; mem. Parl. for Yaren (fmr Speaker); mem. Naoero Amo (Nauru First) party; Minister of Health and Transport –2007 (resgnd), led breakaway opposition faction following vote of no-confidence in Prime Minister Nov. 2007, Minister of Foreign Affairs and Trade, Transport and Telecommunications Nov. 2007–11, of Foreign Affairs and Trade 2012–13; fmr Pres. Nat. Youth Council for Nauru. *Address:* Naoero Amo, c/o Parliament House, Yaren, Nauru (office). *Telephone:* 444-3133 (office). *E-mail:* visionary@naoeroamo.com (office). *Website:* www.naurugov.nr (office).

KEKILBAYEV, Abish Kekilbayevich, (Abish Tagan); Kazakhstani politician and writer; b. 6 Dec. 1939, Ondy, Mangystau Region; s. of Kekilbay Kokimov and Aysaule Kokimova; m. Klara Zhumabaeva; four c.; ed Kazakh State Univ.; schoolteacher of Kazakh language; worked for newspapers Kazakh Adebieti and Leninshil Zhas; Ed.-in-Chief Studio Kazakhfilm; CP official in Alma-Ata; Deputy Minister of Culture Kazakh SSR; Sec. Man. Cttee Kazakh Writers' Union; Chair. Presidium of Kazakh Soc. for Protection of Monuments of History and Culture 1962–89; Chair. Cttee on Nat. Policy, Language and Culture Devt, Kazakhstan Supreme Soviet 1991–93; Ed.-in-Chief Egemen Kazakhstan (newspaper) 1992–93; State Counsellor 1993–94; Chair. Supreme Council of Repub. 1994–95; State Counsellor to Pres. of Repub. 1995–; Deputy to Majlis (Parl.) 1995–; State Sec. Rep. of Kazakhstan 1996–2002; Senator (Parl.) 2002–. *Publications:* author of novels, short stories, critical reviews, translations. *Address:* House of Parliament, Abai Ave 33, 010000 Astana (office); 14 Magistralnaya 1, Apt 98, 473000 Astana, Kazakhstan (home). *Telephone:* (7172) 15-35-20 (office). *Fax:* (7172) 32-69-55 (office). *E-mail:* sarsenova@parlam.kz.

KELAM, Tunne; Estonian politician and historian; b. 10 July 1936, Taheva, Valgamaa Region; m. Mari-Ann Kelam; one d.; ed Univ. of Tartu; Sr Researcher, Central State Archives 1959–65; Sr Academic Ed., Estonian Soviet Encyclopedia 1965–75; Sr Bibliographer, Fr. R. Kreutzwald Nat. Library 1976–79; labourer, Ranna collective farm 1979–87; mem. Cttee of Estonia 1990–92, Chair. (perm. directorial organ of the Congress of Estonia) 1990–92; mem. Riigikogu (Parl.) 1992–2004, Deputy Speaker 1992–2003, Chair. European Affairs Cttee 1997–2003; mem. European Parl. 2004–, mem. Bureau of European People's Party group, Cttee of Foreign Affairs, Sub-cttee of Security and Defence, Parl. Del. for relations with USA; mem. Exec., Estonian Nat. Independence Party 1989–93, Chair. of party 1993–95; Chair. Isamaaliit Party 2002–05; mem. Exec., Isamaa ja Res Publica Union 2006; mem. Congress of Estonia (transitional parl. ass.) 1990–92; mem. Constitutional Ass. 1991–92; presidential cand. 1996; mem. Parl. Ass. of the Council of Europe (PACE) 1992–2000, Head of Estonian Parl. del. to PACE 1992–95, Vice-Pres. PACE 1994–95, rapporteur on Ukraine for the Monitoring Cttee of PACE 1996–2000; Head of Estonian del., Inter-Parl. Union 1992–95; mem. Convention on the Future of Europe 2002–03; Chief Elder of the Estonian Scouting Asscn 1996–2007; mem. Exec., Human Rights Inst. 1996–2009, Kistler-Ritso Fund (occupation museum) 1998–2009; Hon. Citizen of Maryland, USA, Hon. Pres. Estonian Scout Asscn 1996–; Officier, Ordre nat. du Mérite, Badge of the Order of the Nat. Coat of Arms (Second Class) 2001, I Class Order of the Nat. Coat of Arms 2006; Paul Harris Fellowship, Rotary Int. Award, Estonian Newspapers' Union Award 1996, Baltic Ass. Award, Robert Schuman Medal 2006. *Publications:* Tunne Kelam (autobiog.) 1999, Estonian Way to Freedom, Tallinn 2002; numerous articles and trans from English, French, Polish, German, Italian and Russian. *Address:* ASP 10E146, European Parliament, Bâtiment Altiero Spinelli, 60 rue Wiertz, 1047 Brussels, Belgium (office). *Telephone:* (2) 284-72-79 (office). *Fax:* (2) 284-92-79 (office). *E-mail:* tunne.kelam@europarl.europa.eu (office); tunne.kelam@irl.ee. *Website:* www.kelam.ee.

KELANTAN, HRH Former Sultan of; Tuanku Ismail Petra ibni al-Marhum Sultan Yahaya Petra, DK, SPMK, SJMK, SPKK, SPSK, DMN, SMN, DK of Negri Sembilan, Selangor, Johor, Kedah, Perak, Trengganu and Perlis, DKMB of Brunei, DPSS of Sarawak, DP of Sarawak; b. 11 Nov. 1949, Kota Bharu, Kelantan; s. of the late al-Marhum Tengku Yahaya Petra Ibni al-Marhum Sultan Ibrahim and al-Marhum Tengku Zainab binti Tengku Mohamed Petra; m. 1st Tengku Anis Binti Tengku Abdul Hamid 1968; three s. one d.; m. 2nd Elia Suhana binti Ahmad 2007 (divorced 2010); installed as Heir Apparent with the title of Tengku Mahkota 11 Nov. 1967; Attaché, State Secr. and Kota Bharu Land Office 1968; served as Regent during the absence of his father from the state 6–25 July 1974, 12 July–28 Aug. 1975, 21 Sept. 1975–29 March 1979; succeeded as Sultan of Kelantan on the death of his father 29 March 1979; crowned at Istana Balai Besar, Kota Bharu 30 March 1980; formally deposed in favour of his eldest son by the Kelantan Royal Succession Council of State on the grounds of incapacity after failing to fully recover from a debilitating stroke 13 Sept. 2010; thereafter styled Duli Yang Maha Mulia Sultan Ismail Petra (instead of Kebawah Duli Yang Maha Mulia Sultan Kelantan); Maj., Territorial Army 1974, promoted to Hon. Lt-Col 1976, Hon. Col 1988, Hon. Maj.-Gen., Col-in-Chief of the Royal Artillery Regt 1997, and of Royal Intelligence Corps; Patron Royal Kelantan Club –1992; mem. The Conf. of Rulers,

Malaysia; Hon. DPhil (Univ. of Malaysia Sabah) 2007. *Website:* www.kelantan.gov .my.

KELANTAN, HRH Sultan Muhammad V; Tengku Muhammad Faris Petra ibni Sultan Ismail Petra; *Timbalan Yang di-Pertuan Agong (Deputy Supreme Head of State);* b. 6 Oct. 1969, Kota Bharu, Kelantan; s. of Tuanku Ismail Petra ibni al-Marhum Sultan Yahaya Petra and Tengku Anis Binti Tengku Abdul Hamid; m. Tengku Zubaidah Tengku Norudin (divorced); ed Oakham School, Rutland, St Cross Coll., Oxford, Oxford Centre for Islamic Studies, UK; named Tengku Mahkota (Crown Prince) Oct. 1985, apptd as Regent after his father suffered a stroke May 2009, proclaimed Ruler due to indisposition of father 13 Sept. 2010; Timbalan Yang di-Pertuan Agong (Deputy Supreme Head of State) 2011–; Hon. Commdr, 506 Territorial Army Regt with rank of Brig.-Gen. *Address:* Palace of the Sultan, 09 Kota Bharu, Kelantan, Malaysia (office). *Website:* www .kelantan.gov.my (office).

KELCHE, Gen. Jean-Pierre; French army officer; *Le Grand Chancelier de la Légion d'honneur;* b. 19 Jan. 1942, Macon; m.; two c.; ed Mil. Acad., Saint Cyr; served in Côte d'Ivoire, then Djibouti 1971–73, Jr Staff Course, Staff Coll., then with French Caribbean and Guiana Territorial Command 1979–81; Commdr 5th Combined Bn, Djibouti 1985–87; Staff Officer, Doctrine and Devt Div., rank of Brig.-Gen. 1991; Deputy Commdr 5th Armoured Div., Landau, Germany 1991; Chief Plans, Programmes and Evaluation Div., Gen. Staff 1992–95; Chief of Prime Minister's Mil. Cabinet 1995–96; Vice-Chief of Defence Staff 1996–98, Chief of Defence Staff, rank of Gen. 1998–2002; Le Grand Chancelier de la Légion d'honneur 2004–; Commdr, Légion d'honneur, Officier, Ordre nat. du Mérite. *Address:* c/o Le Musée national de la Légion d'honneur, 2, rue de la Légion d'honneur, 75007 Paris; Palais de Salm, 64 rue de Lille, Paris, France (office). *Website:* www.legiondhonneur.fr.

KELDIBEKOV, Akhmatbek, CandEconSci; Kyrgyzstani politician and engineer; b. 15 June 1966, Sufi-Kurgan village, Alai Dist, Osh Oblast, Kyrgyz SSR, USSR; m.; two s. two d.; ed Voronezh Polytechnical Inst., Russian FSFR, Inst. of Retraining and Higher Qualifications of Cadres at Kyrgyz Nat. Univ.; served in Soviet Army in Kutaisi, Georgian SSR 1984–86; worker at 'Pravda' Soviet farm, Alai Dist 1986; 'Impuls' Academic Research Centre, Acad. of Sciences of the Kyrgyz SSR 1990–92, Deputy Dir for Gen. Questions, Inst. of Machine Construction, Acad. of Sciences of the Repub. of Kyrgyzstan 1992–93; Sr Specialist, Dept of Devt of Brs of Industry, Ministry of the Economy and Finance 1993–94; Sr Specialist, Dept of Financing of Industry, Ministry of Finance 1994–95, Chief of Dept of Financing of Transport and Communications 1995–98, Head of Man. of the Economy and Financing of Productive Infrastructure 1998–2001; Deputy Minister of Finance 2001–02; Chair. Social Fund of the Kyrgyz Repub. 2002–05; Deputy in Jogorku Kenesh (Parl.), Chair. Cttee on Budget and Finances 2005–07, Chair. (Speaker) 2010–11; Chair. State Cttee for Taxes and Duties 2008–09, State Tax Service 2009–10; Leader of nationalist Ata-Jurt (Fatherland) party; Deputy, Interparliamentary Ass. of Eurasian Econ. Community (EURASEC) May 2011; State Councillor of the Second Class; Col of the Tax Service; Gen.-Lt Merited Economist of the Kyrgyz Repub.; 'Dank' Medal 2011. *Address:* Jogorku Kenesh (Supreme Council), 720053 Bishkek, Abdymomunov 207, Kyrgyzstan (office). *Telephone:* (312) 61-16-04 (office). *Fax:* (312) 62-50-12 (office). *E-mail:* zs@kenesh.gov.kg (office). *Website:* www.kenesh.kg (office).

KELDYSH, Leonid Veniaminovich, DrPhysMathSc; Russian physicist and academic; *Adviser, Russian Academy of Sciences;* b. 7 April 1931, Moscow; s. of Benjamin L. Granovskii and Lyudmila V. Keldysh; m. Galina S. Krasnikova 1983 (deceased); one s.; ed Moscow State Univ., P.N. Lebedev Physics Inst., Russian Acad. of Sciences; Jr then Sr Researcher, Head of Sector, Head of Dept, Lebedev Physical Inst., USSR (now Russian) Acad. of Sciences 1954–89, Dir 1989–93, Sr Researcher 1993–2011, Adviser 2011–; Prof., Moscow State Univ. 1965–; Prof., Dept of Physics, Texas A&M Univ. 2005–; Röntgen Prof., Univ. of Würzburg 1997; Pres. Physical Soc. of Russian Fed. 1998–; Corresp. mem. USSR (now Russian) Acad. of Sciences 1968, Full mem. 1976, Academic Sec. Dept of Gen. Physics 1991–96; fmr Visiting Miller Prof., Miller Inst., Univ. of California, Berkeley; Ed. Solid State Communications, Fyzika i Tekhnika Poluprovodnikov; Ed.-in-Chief Uspekhi Fizicheskikh Nauk; main research on quantum many body theory, solid state theory, physics of semiconductors, interaction of electromagnetic radiation with matter; Foreign Assoc. NAS (USA) 1995–; Lomonosov Prize, USSR Acad. of Sciences 1965, Hewlett-Packard Prize, European Physics Soc. 1975, Lenin Prize 1976, A.V. Humboldt Research Award 1994, Triumph Prize (Russian Fed.) 2001, S.I. Vavilov Gold Medal, Russian Acad. of Sciences 2006, Rusnano Prize 2009, Eugene Feenberg Medal 2011. *Publications:* Ionization in the Field of the Strong Electromagnetic Wave 1964, Diagram Technique for Nonequilibrium Processes 1964, Coherent Exciton States 1972, Electron-Hole Drops in Semiconductors 1976; numerous articles in scientific journals 1957–. *Address:* P.N. Lebedev Physical Institute, 119991 Moscow, Leninski Prospect 53, V-333, Russia (office). *Telephone:* (499) 135-30-33 (office). *E-mail:* keldysh@lpi.ru (office). *Website:* www.lebedev.ru (office).

KELEMEN, Hunor; Romanian politician and writer; *President, Democratic Alliance of Hungarians in Romania (RMDSz);* b. 18 Oct. 1967, Cârța; m. Eva Czezar 2012; ed Univ. of Agricultural Sciences and Veterinary Medicine, Cluj-Napoca, Babeş-Bolyai Univ., Cluj-Napoca; Sec. of State from Democratic Alliance of Hungarians in Romania (RMDSz) in Ministry of Culture 1997–2000; elected to Chamber of Deputies (Lower House of Romanian Parl.) on RMDSz list 2000– (re-elected 2004, 2008); unsuccessful cand. in presidential election 2009; Minister of Culture 2009–12; currently Pres. RMDSz; Hungarian language writer; Commdr, Order of the Star of Romania 2000, Commdr's Cross, Order of Merit (Hungary) 2008. *Address:* Democratic Alliance of Hungarians in Romania (Uniunea Democrată Maghiară din România/Romániai Magyar Demokrata Szövetség), 011995 Bucharest, Alexandru Puskin str. 5, Romania (office). *Telephone:* (21) 3144356 (office); 722-303493 (mobile). *E-mail:* kelemenhunor@rmdsz.ro (office); internationalsecretary@rmdsz.ro (office). *Website:* www.udmr.ro (office); www .rmdsz.ro (office); www.kelemenhunor.ro; www.dahr.ro (office).

KELETI, György; Hungarian politician and army officer; b. 18 May 1946, Losonc; m. Erzsébet Petrik; three c.; ed Toldy Ferenc Secondary School, Budapest, Zalka Máté Mil. Tech. Coll., Zrinyi Miklós War Coll.; co. commdr, then later deputy commdr of a bn in Vác Dist 1969–74; posts in Ministry of Defence 1980; Press Spokesman, Ministry of Defence 1977; mem. Hungarian Socialist Workers' Party (MSZMP) 1969–89; mem. Oroszlány org. of HSP (MSZP) 1992–, mem. nat. presidium of party 1996–2003; mem. Parl. for Constituency 3, Kisbér, Komárom-Esztergom Co. 1992–, Chair. Nat. Security Cttee 1998–2002, Defence Cttee 2002–, Deputy Parl. Group Leader 2004–, mem. Cttee on Standing Orders 2004–; Minister of Defence 1994–98; Chair. Regional Asscn of Komárom-Esztergom Co. 1998, Chair. Election Cttee at 7th Congress 2000; rank of Col in army reserve; Order of Star (with swords), Silver Cross of Merit. *Address:* Hungarian National Assembly, Kossuth tér 1-3, PO Box 1357, 1055 Budapest, Pf.: 2, Hungary (office). *Telephone:* (1) 441-4000 (office). *E-mail:* gyorgy.keleti@parlament.hu (office). *Website:* www.parlament.hu (office).

KELL, Georg; German financial analyst and UN official; *Executive Director, United Nations Global Compact;* ed Tech. Univ. of Berlin; extensive experience as financial analyst in Africa and Asia; began UN career with UNCTAD in Geneva 1987–90, joined New York office of UNCTAD 1990, Head of New York Office 1993–97, Sr Officer in Exec. Office of UN Sec.-Gen. Kofi Annan 1997–2000, Exec. Dir UN Global Compact 2000–. *Address:* Global Compact Office, UN Headquarters, First Avenue at 46th Street, New York, NY 10017, USA (office). *E-mail:* wynhoven@un.org (office). *Website:* www.unglobalcompact.org (office).

KELLENBERGER, Jakob, DPhil; Swiss diplomatist and international organization official; b. 19 Oct. 1944, Heiden; m. Elisabeth Kellenberger-Jossi 1973; two d.; ed Univ. of Zürich, with stays at Univs of Tours, Granada; joined Swiss diplomatic service 1974, diplomatic postings in Madrid, Brussels and London; Head of Office in Charge of European Integration, Berne 1984–92, Minister 1984, Amb. 1988, State Sec. Fed. Dept of Foreign Affairs 1992–99; Pres. International Cttee of the Red Cross 2000–12; Dr hc (Basle Univ.) 2003. *Address:* c/o International Committee of the Red Cross, 19 avenue de la Paix, 1202 Geneva, Switzerland.

KELLER, Bill, BA; American newspaper editor; b. 18 Jan. 1949; s. of George M. Keller, fmr Chair. and Chief Exec. Chevron Corpn; m. Emma Gilbey 1999; one s. two d.; ed Junípero Serra High School, San Mateo, Calif., Pomona Coll., Wharton School, Univ. of Pennsylvania; reporter, The Portland Oregonian 1970–79, Congressional Quarterly Weekly Report, Washington, DC 1980–82, The Dallas Times Herald 1982–84; domestic corresp., The New York Times 1984–86, Russian Corresp., Moscow 1986–88, Bureau Chief 1988–91, Bureau Chief, Johannesburg, SA 1992–95, Foreign Ed., New York 1995–97, Man. Ed. 1997–2001, Op-Ed. Columnist and Sr Writer 2001–03, Exec. Ed. 2003–11, columnist 2011–; Trustee, Pomona Coll.; Pulitzer Prize for coverage of the USSR 1989, ranked by Forbes magazine amongst The World's Most Powerful People (51st) 2009, (50th) 2010. *Publication:* Tree Shaker: the Story of Nelson Mandela 2008. *Address:* The New York Times, 620 Eighth Avenue, New York, NY 10018, USA (office). *Telephone:* (212) 556-1234 (office). *Website:* www.nytimes.com (office).

KELLER, Evelyn Fox, PhD; American historian, philosopher of science and academic; *Professor of History and Philosophy of Science Emerita, Massachusetts Institute of Technology;* b. 20 March 1936, New York, NY; d. of Albert Fox and Ray Fox; m. Joseph B. Keller 1964 (divorced); one s. one d.; ed Radcliffe Coll., Brandeis and Harvard Univs; Asst Research Scientist, New York Univ. 1963–66, Assoc. Prof. 1970–72; Assoc. Prof., State Univ. of New York, Purchase 1972–82; Prof. of Math. and Humanities, Northwestern Univ. 1982–88; Prof., Univ. of California, Berkeley 1988–92; Visiting Fellow, later Scholar, MIT 1979–84, Visiting Prof. 1985–86, Prof. of History and Philosophy of Science 1992–2009, Prof. Emer. 2009–; mem. Inst. of Advanced Studies, Princeton 1987–88; Pres. West Coast History of Science Soc. 1990–91; Dr hc (Mount Holyoke Coll.) 1991, (Univ. of Amsterdam) 1993, (Simmons Coll.) 1995, (Rensslaer Polytechnic Inst.) 1995, (Tech. Univ. of Luleå, Sweden) 1996, (New School Univ.) 2000, (Allegheny Coll.) 2000, (Wesleyan Univ.) 2001, (Dartmouth Coll.) 2007; MacArthur Fellow 1992–97, Guggenheim Fellowship 2000–01, Moore Scholar, California Inst. Tech. 2002, Winton Chair, Univ. of Minnesota 2002–05, Dibner Fellow 2003, Radcliffe Inst. Fellow 2005, Rothschild Lecturer, Harvard Univ. 2005, Plenary Speaker, Int. History of Science Congress, Beijing 2005; numerous awards, including Mina Shaughnessey Award 1981–82, Radcliffe Grad. Soc. Medal 1985, Medal of the Italian Senate 2001, Chaire Blaise Pascal 2005–07; inducted into AAAS Science Hall of Fame 2011. *Publications include:* A Feeling for the Organism 1983, Reflections on Gender and Science 1985, Secrets of Life, Secrets of Death 1992, Keywords in Evolutionary Biology (ed.) 1994, Refiguring Life 1995, Feminism and Science (co-author) 1996, The Century of the Gene 2000, Making Sense of Life 2002, The Mirage of a Space between Nature and Nurture 2010. *Address:* Massachusetts Institute of Technology, E51-171, 77 Massachusetts Avenue, Cambridge, MA 02139, USA (office). *Telephone:* (617) 324-2095 (office). *Fax:* (617) 253-8118 (office). *E-mail:* efkeller@mit.edu (office). *Website:* web.mit.edu.sts (office).

KELLER, Joseph Bishop, PhD; American mathematician and academic; *Professor Emeritus of Mathematics and Mechanical Engineering, Stanford University;* b. 31 July 1923, Paterson, NJ; s. of Isaac Keller and Sally Bishop; m. Evelyn Fox 1963 (divorced 1976); one s. one d.; ed New York Univ.; ed New York Univ.; Prof. of Math. Courant Inst. of Math. Sciences, New York Univ. 1948–79, Chair. Dept of Math., Univ. Coll. of Arts and Sciences and Graduate School of Eng and Sciences 1967–73; Prof. of Math. and Mechanical Eng, Stanford Univ. 1979– now Prof. Emer.; Research Assoc. Woods Hole Oceanographic Inst. 1965–; mem. NAS; Foreign mem. Royal Soc.; Hon. Prof. of Math. Sciences (Univ. of Cambridge) 1990; Hon. DTech (Tech. Univ. of Denmark) 1979, Hon. DSc (Northwestern Univ.) 1988, (Crete) 1993, (New Jersey Inst. Tech.) 1995, (Carlos Tercero de Madrid) 1995, (New York Univ.) 2002, (Univ. Notre Dame) 2005; Nemmers Prize 1996, shared Wolf Prize 1997, Nat. Medal of Science 1988, NAS Award in Applied Math. and Numerical Analysis 1995, numerous awards and lectureships. *Publications:* over 400 articles in professional journals. *Leisure interests:* hiking, skiing. *Address:* 382-G, Department of Mathematics, 450 Serra Mall, Stanford University, Stanford, CA 94305 (office); 820 Sonoma Terrace, Stanford, CA 94305, USA (home). *Telephone:* (650) 723-0851 (office). *Fax:* (650) 725-4066 (office). *E-mail:* keller@math.stanford.edu (office). *Website:* math.stanford.edu/~keller (office).

KELLER, Samuel; Swiss museum director and foundation executive; *Director, Fondation Beyeler;* joined Art Basel 1994, Dir 2000–07, currently Chair. Advisory Bd, launched sister fair Art Basel Miami Beach 2002; Dir Fondation Beyeler, Riehen 2008–; Young Global Leader, World Econ. Forum 2005; Medal of Honour, City of Miami Beach 2007, Swiss Inst. Award, New York 2010. *Address:* Fondation Beyeler, Baselstrasse 101, 4125 Riehen, Switzerland (office). *Telephone:* (61) 6459700 (office). *Fax:* (61) 6459719 (office). *E-mail:* info@fondationbeyeler.ch (office). *Website:* www.fondationbeyeler.ch (office).

KELLER, Thomas A.; American chef; b. 1955, Southern Calif.; fmr chef, La Reserve and Restaurant Raphael, New York; served an estagiere apprentice in France in restaurants of Guy Savoy, Michael Pasquet, Gerard Besson, also Taillevant, Le Toit de Passey, Chiberta and Le Pre Catalan; est. restaurant Rakel, New York; Exec. Chef, Checkers Hotel, Los Angeles; acquired The French Laundry, Yountville, Calif. 1994, currently Chef and Owner; Founder and Owner EVO Inc. (retail line of olive oils and vinegar); spokesperson for Calif. Milk Advisory Bd 1997–98; Owner Bouchon 1998, Bouchon Bakery 2003, Per Se 2004, Bouchon at the Venetian 2004, Ad Hoc 2007; Dr hc (Johnson and Wales Univ.) 2003; Ivy Award, Restaurants and Insts 1996; named Best American Chef: Calif., James Beard Foundation 1996; Oustanding Chef: America 1997; World's Best Chef, Wedgewood 2002. *Publications include:* The French Laundry 2004, Bouchon 2004, Under Pressure 2008, Ad Hoc at Home: Family-style Recipes 2009. *Address:* c/o Stefanie Cangiano, PR Consulting, 403 Hudson Street, 6th Floor, New York, NY 10013, USA (office). *Telephone:* (212) 228-8181 (office). *Fax:* (212) 228-8787 (office). *E-mail:* tkpress@prconsulting.net (office). *Website:* www.frenchlaundry.com.com.

KELLNER, Lawrence W. (Larry), BS; American business executive; m. Susan Kellner; four c.; ed Univ. of South Carolina; Exec. Vice-Pres. and Chief Financial Officer American Savings Bank –1995; Sr Vice-Pres. and Chief Financial Officer Continental Airlines Inc. 1995–96, Exec. Vice-Pres. and Chief Financial Officer 1996–2001, Dir 2001–, Pres. 2001–04, COO 2003–04, Chair. and CEO 2004–; mem. or fmr mem. Bd of Dirs Marriott International, Air Transport Asscn, Greater Houston Partnership, Methodist Hosp., Cen. Houston Inc., Spring Br. Educ. Foundation; mem. Nat. Exec. Bd Boy Scouts of America; mem. Advisory Bd March of Dimes, Teach for America; mem. Devt Bd Univ. of Texas Health Science Center; Univ. of South Carolina Distinguished Alumni Award 1998. *Address:* 10915 Pifer Way, Houston, TX 77024, USA.

KELLY, Alfred F., Jr., MBA; American financial services industry executive; *President, American Express Company;* m. Margaret P. Kelly; two s. three d.; ed Iona Coll.; Asst Prof., Iona Coll. 1980–85; fmr Head of Information Systems, Exec. Office of the Pres., The White House; fmrly with Information Systems and Strategic and Financial Planning Dept, PepsiCo; joined Strategic Planning Dept, American Express Co. 1987, Vice-Pres. of Technologies 1988, Exec. Vice-Pres. and Gen. Man., Consumer Marketing 1997–98, Pres. Consumer Card Services Group 1998–2000, Group Pres., Consumer, Small Business and Merchant Services 2000–07, Pres. 2007–; Chair. Wall Street Charity Golf Classic; mem. Bd of Dirs The Hershey Co. 2005–07 (resgnd), Concern Worldwide USA, Carvel Children's Rehabilitation Center; Trustee, Iona Coll., NY-Presbyterian Hosp.; mem. Council on Foreign Relations. *Address:* American Express Company, World Financial Center, 200 Vesey Street, New York NY 10285, USA (office). *Telephone:* (212) 640-2000 (office). *Fax:* (212) 640-2428 (office). *Website:* www.americanexpress.com (office).

KELLY, Edmund (Ted) F., BA; American (b. Northern Irish) insurance industry executive; b. 1946, Co. Armagh, Northern Ireland; ed Queen's Univ., Belfast, Massachusetts Inst. of Tech.; served in a variety of positions with Aetna Life and Casualty Co. 1974–92, including as its Group Exec.; Pres. and COO Liberty Mutual Insurance Co. 1992–98, Pres. and CEO Liberty Mutual Holding Co. Inc. 1998–2010, Chair. and CEO 2000–11, Chair. 2011–13, Chair. Liberty Mutual Agency Corpn, Chair. Liberty Financial Cos Inc. 2000–13, also Chair. Employers Insurance Co. of Wausau (EICOW, subsidiary of Liberty Mutual); Pres. and COO Mellon Financial Corpn 1992–98, CEO 1998–; mem. Bd of Dirs EICOW 1998–, Segue Software Inc. 2000–04, EMC Corpn 2007–, The Bank of New York Mellon Corpn 2007–; fmr Chair. Alliance of American Insurers Inc.; Dir, Financial Services Roundtable; Dir, Initiative for a Competitive Inner City, Citizens Financial Group Inc., American Insurers, RBS Citizens, N.A.; Ind. Dir, Mellon Financial Corpn 2004–; Trustee Assoc., Boston Coll.; mem. Bd Govs Property Casualty Insurers Asscn of America; Chair. Boston Symphony Orchestra Inc. 2011–; mem. Bd United Way of Massachusetts Bay, American Red Cross of Massachusetts Bay, Boston Pvt. Industry Council, American Ireland Fund, The Massachusetts Mentoring Partnership; Pres. Boston Minuteman Council, Boy Scouts of America; also serves on various other community and educ. bds; held asst professorships in math. depts at Univ. of New Brunswick and Univ. of Missouri at St Louis; mem. American Acad. of Actuaries; Fellow, Soc. of Actuaries. *Address:* c/o Liberty Mutual Holding Co. Inc., 175 Berkeley Street, Boston, MA 02116, USA. *E-mail:* info@libertymutual.com.

KELLY, Ellsworth; American painter and sculptor; b. 31 May 1923, Newburgh, NY; ed Pratt Inst., Boston Museum Fine Arts School, Ecole des Beaux Arts, France; mil. service 1943–45; works exhibited at Salon de Réalités Nouvelles, Paris 1950, 1951, Carnegie Int. 1958, 1961, 1964, 1967, São Paulo Biennale 1961, Tokyo Int. 1963, Documenta III and IV, Germany 1964, 1968, Venice Biennale 1966, Guggenheim Int. 1967, Corcoran Annual, Washington, DC 1979, etc.; works in numerous perm. collections including Museum of Modern Art, Whitney Museum, Carnegie Inst., Chicago Art Inst., Guggenheim Museum, Tate Gallery, London, Musée d'Art Moderne, Paris, Stedelijk Museum, Amsterdam; mem. Nat. Inst. of Arts and Letters; Chevalier Ordre des Arts et des Lettres 1993; Mayor of Barcelona Medal 1993, Nat. Medal of Arts 2012, numerous other awards and prizes. *Address:* c/o Matthew Marks Gallery, 523 West 24th Street, New York, NY 10011, USA. *E-mail:* info@matthewmarks.com. *Website:* www.matthewmarks.com.

KELLY, Gail P., HigherDipEd, BA, MBA; South African banking executive; *Managing Director and CEO, Westpac Banking Corporation;* b. 25 April 1956, Pretoria; m. Allan Kelly 1977; ed Univ. of Cape Town, Charles Sturt Univ., Australia; worked as a teacher in Rhodesia and SA; began banking career with Nedcor Bank, Head of Human Resources 1990–97; joined Commonwealth Bank, Sydney, Australia as Gen. Man. of Strategic Marketing 1997, becoming Head, Customer Service Div.; CEO St George Bank 2002–07 (merged with Westpac

2008), Man. Dir and CEO Westpac Banking Corpn (only woman CEO of a top 20 Australian co.) 2008–, also Dir, Westpac New Zealand Ltd; mem. Bd Dirs Melbourne Business School Ltd; Hon. DBus; Best Financial Services Exec., Australian Banking & Finance magazine 2003, 2004, ranked by Fortune magazine amongst the 50 Most Powerful Women in Business outside the USA (28th) 2007, (second) 2008–12, ranked by Forbes magazine amongst The World's 100 Most Powerful Women (11th) 2008, (18th) 2009, (eighth) 2010, (32nd) 2011, (60th) 2012, (62nd) 2013. *Address:* Westpac Banking Corpn, Level 20, Westpac Place, 275 Kent Street, Sydney, NSW 2000, Australia (office). *Telephone:* (2) 8253-0390 (office). *Fax:* (2) 8253-1888 (office). *E-mail:* info@westpac.com.au (office). *Website:* www .westpac.com.au (office).

KELLY, James A., BS, MBA; American fmr government official; *Senior Advisor and CSIS Distinguished Alumni, Center for Strategic and International Studies;* m. Audrey Pool Kelly; two c.; ed Harvard Univ., US Naval Acad., Nat. War Coll.; served in USN 1959–83, retd from active duty as Capt., Supply Corps; Deputy Asst Sec. of Defence for Int. Security Affairs (East Asia and Pacific), Pentagon 1983–86; Special Asst for Nat. Security Affairs to Pres. Ronald Reagan and Sr Dir of Asian Affairs, Nat. Security Council 1986–89; Pres. EAP Assocs Inc. (int. business consultants), Honolulu 1989–94; Pres. The Pacific Forum, Center for Strategic and Int. Studies, Honolulu 1994–2001; Asst Sec. of State for East Asian and Pacific Affairs 2001–05; currently Sr Advisor, Center for Strategic and Int. Studies. *Address:* c/o Center for Strategic and International Studies, 1800 K Street, NW, Suite 400, Washington, DC 20006, USA (office). *Website:* www.csis.org (office).

KELLY, Jim; American journalist; b. 15 Dec. 1953, Brooklyn, New York; m. Lisa Henricksson; one s.; ed Princeton Univ.; joined Time magazine 1977, as writer in Nation section, Foreign Ed. early 1990s, Deputy Man. Ed. 1996–2000, Man. Ed. 2001–06, Man. Ed. Time Inc. 2006–09, consultant to Time Inc. 2009–; Ed. Corporate Welfare series 1998, Visions 21 series 1999–2000; mem. Bd of Visitors Columbia Univ. Grad. School of Journalism. *Address:* Time Inc., Time-Life Building, Rockefeller Center, 1271 Avenue of the Americas, New York, NY 10020-1393, USA (office). *Telephone:* (212) 522-1212 (office). *Fax:* (212) 522-0323 (office). *Website:* www.time.com (office).

KELLY, John Hubert, BA; American diplomatist; *Ambassador-in-Residence, Center for International Strategy, Technology and Policy, Sam Nunn School of International Affairs, Georgia Institute of Technology;* b. 20 July 1939, Fond du Lac, Wis.; m. Helena Marita Ajo; one s. one d.; ed Emory Univ., Atlanta; Second Sec. US Embassy, Ankara 1966–67; American Consul, Songkhla, Thailand 1969–71; First Sec. US Embassy, Paris 1976–80; Deputy Exec. Sec., Dept of State, Washington DC 1980–81, Sr Deputy Asst Sec. of State for Public Affairs 1982–83, Prin. Deputy Asst Sec. of State for European Affairs 1983–85; Amb. to Lebanon 1986–88, to Finland 1991–94; Prin. Deputy Dir of Policy Planning Staff 1988–89; Asst Sec. for Near Eastern and SE Asian Affairs 1989–93; Man. Dir Int. Equity Partners, Atlanta 1995–98; Pres. John Kelly Consulting Inc. 1999–; Dir Finnish-American Chamber of Commerce 1998, American Int. Petroleum Co. 1999; Trustee, Lebanese American Univ. 1997; Amb.-in-Residence, Sam Nunn School for Int. Affairs, Georgia Inst. of Tech. 1999–; mem. Council on Foreign Relations, American-Turkish Council, Middle East Inst., Southern Center for Int. Studies. *Address:* Sam Nunn School of International Affairs, Georgia Tech, 781 Marietta Street, NW, Atlanta, GA 30332-1610; John Kelly Consulting, Inc., 1808 Over Lake Drive SE, Suite D, Conyers, GA 30013, USA (office). *Telephone:* (770) 918-9957 (office). *Fax:* (770) 483-3090 (office). *Website:* www.cistp.gatech.edu.

KELLY, John Philip, BA, CMG, LVO, MBE; British diplomatist; *Vice-President, Victoria League for Commonwealth Friendship;* b. 25 June 1941, Tuam, Co. Galway, Ireland; s. of William Kelly and Norah Kelly (née Roche); m. Jennifer Anne Buckler 1964; one s.; ed Oatlands Coll., Dublin, Open Univ.; joined HM Diplomatic Service 1959; worked at Embassies in Kinshasa (fmrly Léopoldville) 1962–65, Cairo 1965–67, Bonn 1967–70; with FCO 1970–73, 1986–89, 1994–96; with High Comm. Canberra 1973–76, Consulate-Gen. Antwerp 1977–78; with Dept of Trade 1980–82; Rep. to Grenada 1982–86; Deputy Gov. of Bermuda 1989–94; Gov. Turks and Caicos Islands 1996–2000; Chair. Victoria League for Commonwealth Friendship 2002–07, Vice-Pres. *Leisure interests:* family, Rotary International, cruise lecturing, golf, reading, walking. *Address:* The Laurels, 56 Garden Lane, Royston, Herts., SG8 9EH, England (home). *Telephone:* (1763) 245128 (home). *E-mail:* johnandjenniferkelly@btinternet.com (home).

KELLY, Michael Joseph, BS, MS, MA, PhD, ScD (Cantab.), CEng, CPhys, FRS, FREng, FInstP, FIET; New Zealand/British engineer, physicist and academic; *Prince Philip Professor of Technology, University of Cambridge;* b. 14 May 1949, New Plymouth, NZ; m.; one d.; ed Victoria Univ. of Wellington, Univ. of Cambridge; Visiting Fellow, Dept of Physics, Victoria Univ. of Wellington 1974; Research Fellow in Physics, Trinity Hall, Cambridge 1974–77, Staff Fellow in Theoretical Physics 1977–81, Staff Fellow in Physics 1989–92; Prof. of Physics and Electronics, Dept of Physics, Univ. of Surrey 1992–2002, Head of Dept of Electronic and Electrical Eng 1996–97, Head of School of Electronic Eng, Information Tech. and Math. 1997–2001, Dir Centre for Solid State Electronics 2000, mem. Senate, Univ. of Surrey 1996, Council, Univ. of Surrey 1997, Planning and Resources Cttee 1997; Prince Philip Prof. of Tech., Dept of Eng, Univ. of Cambridge 2002–, also Professorial Fellow, Trinity Hall, Exec. Dir Cambridge-MIT Inst. 2003–05; Chief Scientific Adviser to Dept of Communities and Local Govt 2006–09; Visiting Researcher, KFA-IFF, Julich, FRG 1975; IBM Research Fellow, Dept of Physics, Univ. of California, Berkeley 1975–76; SRC Advanced Fellow, Cavendish Lab., Cambridge 1977–81, Visiting Fellow 1988–92, Royal Soc./Science and Eng Research Council Industrial Fellow 1989–91; Visiting Fellow, Max Planck Institut für Festkorperforschung, Stuttgart, FRG 1980; mem. research staff, GEC Hirst Research Centre 1981–92, Man. Superlattice Research Group 1984–90, Coordinator GEC Superlattice Research 1984–1992, Man. EEC, Dept of Trade and Industry, Ministry of Defence and GEC Research Contracts 1984–92; Dir (non-exec.) Laird plc 2006–; mem. Council of the Royal Soc. 2001–02, Scientific Assessment Panel, Univ. of East Anglia Climatic Research Unit 2010, Tech. Advisory Group, Renewable Energy Foundation, Advisory Bd, Inst. of Electronics, Communications and Information Tech.; Assoc. Ed. International Journal of Electronics 1996–98; mem. American Inst. of Physics, IEEE; Fellow, Inst. of Physics (Vice-Pres. 2001–05), Inst. of Eng and Tech.; Hon. Fellow, Royal Soc. of NZ 1999; mem. Academia Europaea 2009; GEC Publs Prizewinner 1986, 1987, 1988,

Paterson Medal and Prize, Inst. of Physics 1989, Nelson Gold Medal, GEC 1991, Silver Medal, Royal Acad. of Eng 1999, Hughes Medal, Royal Soc. 2006. *Publications:* The Physics and Fabrication of Microstructures and Microdevices (co-ed.) 1986, Technology Foresight Panel Report #8 on 'IT and Electronics' (co-author) 1995, Low Dimensional Semiconductors 1995, Advanced Materials in the Market Place (co-ed.) 1995, The Current Status of Semiconductor Tunnelling Devices (co-ed.) 1996; more than 210 papers and review articles, book chapters etc. in refereed journals, and in conf. proceedings etc.; 13 patents on semiconductor devices (seven patents still active). *Address:* Centre of Advanced Phatonics and Electronics, Department of Engineering, University of Cambridge, 9 J.J. Thomson Avenue, Cambridge, CB3 0FA, England (office). *Telephone:* (1223) 748303 (office). *Fax:* (1223) 748334 (office). *E-mail:* mjk1@cam.ac.uk (office). *Website:* www.eng .cam.ac.uk (office).

KELLY, Most Rev. Patrick Altham, STL, PhL; British ecclesiastic; *Archbishop of Liverpool and Metropolitan of the Northern Province;* b. 23 Nov. 1938, Morecambe; s. of John Kelly and Mary Kelly (née Altham); ed Preston Catholic Coll., Venerable English Coll., Rome; Asst Priest, Lancaster Cathedral 1964–66; Prof. of Dogmatic Theology, Oscott Coll., Birmingham 1966–79, Rector 1979–84; Bishop of Salford 1984–96; Archbishop of Liverpool, Metropolitan of the Northern Prov. 1996–. *Address:* Archbishop's House, Lowood, Carnatic Road, Mossley Hill, Liverpool, L18 8BY, England. *Telephone:* (151) 724-6398. *Fax:* (151) 724-6405. *E-mail:* archbishop.liverpool@rcaolp.co.uk (office). *Website:* www.archdiocese-of -liverpool.co.uk (office).

KELLY, Roslyn Joan (Ros), AO, BA; Australian fmr politician; *Executive Director, Environmental Resources Management;* b. 25 Jan. 1948, Sydney, NSW; d. of M. Raw and P. Raw; m. David Morgan; one s. one d.; ed Univ. of Sydney; high-school teacher, NSW and ACT 1969–74; consultant and mem. ACT Consumer Affairs Council 1974–79; mem. ACT Legal Aid Comm. 1976–79; fmr mem. ACT Legis. Ass.; mem. Fed. Parl. 1980–95; Sec. Fed. Labor Party Parl. Caucus 1981–87; Minister for Defence, Science and Personnel 1987–89, for Telecommunications and Aviation Support 1989–90, for Sport, the Environment and Territories 1990–94, for the Arts 1990–93, Assisting the Prime Minister for the Status of Women 1993–94; mem. Int. Advisory Council Normandy Mining Ltd 1995–2001; Group Exec. Dames & Moore 1995–2001; Exec. Dir Environmental Resources Management (consulting firm) 2001–; Dir (non-exec.) Theiss Pty Ltd 1998–, Thiess Environmental Services 1998–, External Sustainable Devt Advisory Group, The Rescue Helicopter Service; Chair. NSW Premiers Environmental Mining Awards 1999–, Minerals Council of Australia's External Advisory Group on Sustainability, Nat. Breast Cancer Foundation of Australia 2005–; mem. Advisory Council Sustainable Minerals Inst., Int. Council of Normandy Minerals, Nat. Advisory Council Greenfleet; Trustee, Worldwide Fund for Nature. *Leisure interests:* reading, films, aerobics. *Address:* National Breast Cancer Foundation, GPO Box 4126, Level 3, 18–20 York Street, Sydney, NSW 2000 (office); Environmental Resources Management, Building C, 33 Saunders Street, Pyrmont, NSW 2009, Australia. *E-mail:* info@nbcf.org.au (office); rkelly3@bigpond.net.au (home).

KELLY, Rt Hon. Ruth Maria, BA, MSc; British journalist, economist, business executive and fmr politician; *Global Head of Client Strategy, Global Asset Management, HSBC Holdings plc;* b. 9 May 1968, Limavady, Northern Ireland; d. of Bernard James Kelly and Gertrude Anne Kelly; m. Derek John Gadd 1996; one s. three d.; ed Sutton High School, Westminster School, Queen's Coll., Oxford, London School of Econs; econs writer, The Guardian newspaper 1990–94; economist, Bank of England 1994–97, Deputy Head of Inflation Report Div. 1994–96, Man. Financial Stability 1996–97; MP (Labour) Bolton W 1997–2010; Parl. Pvt. Sec. to Nicholas Brown MP 1998–2001; Econ. Sec. to HM Treasury 2001–02; Financial Sec. to HM Treasury 2002–04; Minister of State, Cabinet Office 2004; Sec. of State for Educ. and Skills 2004–06; for Communities and Local Govt 2006–07, for Transport 2007–08 (resgnd); Minister for Women 2006–07; Global Head of Client Strategy, Global Asset Man., HSBC Holdings plc 2010–; elected to Royal Econ. Soc. Council 1999–2001; mem. House of Commons Treasury Select Cttee 1997–98; mem. Fabian Soc., Council of Man. Nat. Inst. for Econ. and Social Research 1998–2001, Gov. 2001–; Hon. Fellow, Queen's Coll., Oxford; Minister to Watch, Zurich/Spectator Party Awards 2001. *Publications include:* Taxing the Spectator 1993, Hedging Your Futures (co-author) 1994, The Wrecker's Lamp (co-author) 1994, The Case for Universal Payment (chapter in Time Off with the Children: Paying for Parental Leave) 1999, Europe (chapter in Beyond 2000: Long-Term Policies for Labour) 1999, Reforming the Working Family Tax Credit: How An Integrated Child Credit Could Work for Children and Families 2000; chapters in New Gender Agenda 2000, The Progressive Century 2001. *Leisure interests:* family. *Address:* HSBC Holdings plc, 8 Canada Square, London, E14 5HQ, England (office). *Website:* www.hsbc.com (office).

KELMAN, James; British writer; b. 9 June 1946, Glasgow; m. Marie Connors; two d.; ed Greenfield Public School, Govan; Spirit of Scotland Award. *Plays:* Hardie and Baird, The Last Days 1991, One, Two – Hey (R and B musical, toured 1994). *Radio:* The Art of the Big Bass Drum (play, BBC Radio 3) 1998. *Publications include:* novels: The Bus Conductor Hines 1984, A Chancer 1985, A Disaffection (James Tait Black Memorial Prize) 1989, How Late It Was, How Late (Booker Prize) 1994, Translated Accounts 2001, You Have to be Careful in the Land of the Free 2004, Kieron Smith, Boy (Saltire Soc's Book of the Year 2008, Scottish Mortgage Investment Trust Book of the Year 2009) 2008, Mo Said She Was Quirky (Saltire Book of the Year award 2012) 2012; short stories: An Old Pub Near the Angel 1973, Short Tales from the Nightshift 1978, Not Not While the Giro 1983, Lean Tales 1985, Greyhound for Breakfast (Cheltenham Prize) 1987, The Burn (Scottish Arts Council Book Award) 1991, Busted Scotch 1997, The Good Times (Scottish Writer of the Year Award) 1998, If It is Your Life 2010; plays: The Busker 1985, In the Night 1988; other: And the Judges Said (essays) 2002. *Address:* c/o Gill Coleridge, Rogers, Coleridge and White Ltd, 20 Powis Mews, London, W11 1JN, England (office). *Telephone:* (20) 7221-3717 (office). *E-mail:* info@rcwlitagency.com (office). *Website:* www.rcwlitagency.com (office).

KELNER, Simon; British newspaper editor; *Editor-in-Chief, The Independent and The Independent on Sunday;* b. 9 Dec. 1957, Manchester; ed Bury Grammar School, Preston Polytechnic; Trainee Reporter, Neath Guardian 1976–79; Sports Reporter, Extel 1979–80; Sports Ed., Kent Evening Post 1980–83; Asst Sports Ed., The Observer 1983–86; Deputy Sports Ed., The Independent 1986–89; Sports Ed.,

Sunday Corresp. 1989–90; Sports Ed., The Observer 1990–93; Sports Ed., The Independent on Sunday 1993–95, Night Ed., The Independent 1995, Features Ed. 1995–96; Ed. Night and Day Magazine, Mail on Sunday 1996–98; Ed., The Independent 1998–2008, 2010–, The Independent on Sunday 1998–2008, Ed.-in-Chief 2008–, Man. Dir 2008–10, Ed.-in-Chief The Independent May 2010– and i Oct. 2010–; Hon. Fellowship, Univ. of Cen. Lancashire; Ed. of the Year, What the Papers Say Awards 1999, 2003, Newspaper Ed. of the Year, What the Papers Say Awards 2004, Edgar Wallace Award 2000, 2004, Newspaper of the Year, British Press Awards 2004, GQ Editor of the Year 2004, 2010, Media Achiever of the Year, Campaign Media Awards 2004, Marketeer of the Year, Marketing Week Effectiveness Awards 2004, Editorial Intelligence Comment Award 2010. *Publications:* To Jerusalem and Back 1996. *Address:* The Independent, 2 Derry Street, London, W8 5HF, England (office). *Telephone:* (20) 7005-2300 (office). *Fax:* (20) 7005-3859 (office). *E-mail:* s.kelner@independent.co.uk (office). *Website:* www.independent.co.uk (office).

KELTOŠOVÁ, Olga, BSc; Slovak politician; *Mayor of Lamač, Bratislava;* b. (Olga Suchalová), 27 Feb. 1943, Pezinok; m. (divorced); one s. one d.; ed Komenský Univ. Bratislava; collaborated with various students' magazines later banned in 1968; worked as translator and interpreter 1970–89; Press Sec. Democratic Party 1989; Deputy Chair. to Nat. Council 1990–92; expelled from Democratic Party 1991, joined Movt for Democratic Slovakia (now Political Party for Democratic Slovakia) 1991; Minister of Labour, Social Affairs and Family Matters 1992–94, 1995–98; Chair. Co-ordination Cttee for Issues of Handicapped 1995, Co-ordinating Body for Problems of Women 1996; elected mem. Parl. 1998; Mayor of Lamač, Bratislava 2006–; A. Hlinka Order 1998. *Leisure interests:* classical ballet, gardening. *Address:* Miestny úrad Lamač, Heyrovského 2, 841 03 Bratislava (office). *Telephone:* (2) 6478-0065 (office). *Fax:* (2) 6478-0689 (office). *E-mail:* starostka@lamac.sk (office). *Website:* www.lamac.sk (office).

KEMAKEZA, Sir Allan, KBE; Solomon Islands politician; b. 1951, Panueli village, Central Prov.; joined Royal Solomon Islands Police Force 1972, apptd Asst Superintendent 1988; mem. Nat. Parl. representing Savo/Russels, Cen. Islands Prov. 1989–2010, Deputy Speaker 2006–07; Minister for Housing and Govt Service, Solomon Islands 1989–1993; Minister for Forests, Environment and Conservation 1995–96; Deputy Prime Minister 2000–01; Minister for Nat. Unity, Reconciliation and Peace 2000–01; Prime Minister 2001–06 (resgnd); Minister for Forestry 2007; served five months in prison in 2009 after being convicted of demanding money with menace, intimidation and larceny while Prime Minister; mem. People's Alliance Party. *Address:* c/o People's Alliance Party, Honiara, Solomon Islands (office).

KEMAL, Yaşar; Turkish writer and journalist; b. (Kemal Sadık Gökçel), 1926, Adana; m. 1st Thilda Serrero 1952 (deceased); one s.; m. 2nd Ayse Semiha Baban 2002; self-educated; mem. Académie Universelle des Cultures, Paris; Commdr, Légion d'honneur 1984; Dr hc (Strasbourg) 1991, (Akdeniz Univ., Antalya) 1991, (Mediterranean Univ.) 1992, (Free Univ., Berlin) 1998, (Bilkent Univ.) 2002; Prix Mondial Cino del Duca 1982, VIII Premi Internacional Catalunya, Barcelona 1996, Hellman-Hammett Award, New York 1996, Peace Prize of German Book Trade 1997, Prix Nonino, Percoto, Italy 1997, Stig Dagerman Prize, Sweden 1997, Norwegian Authors Union Prize 1997, Prix Ecureuil de littérature étrangère, Bordeaux 1998, Z. Homer Poetry Award 2003, Soranos Prize (Thessalonika, Greece) 2003, Turkish Publisher's Asscn Lifetime Achievement Award 2003. *Publications:* (in English) Memed, My Hawk 1961, The Wind from the Plain 1963, Anatolian Tales 1968, They Burn the Thistles 1973, Iron Earth, Copper Sky 1974, The Legend of Ararat 1975, The Legend of the Thousand Bulls 1976, The Undying Grass 1977, The Lords of Akchasaz (Part I), Murder in the Ironsmiths' Market 1979, The Saga of a Seagull 1981, The Sea-Crossed Fisherman 1985, The Birds Have Also Gone 1987, To Crush the Serpent 1991, Salman the Solitary 1997, The Story of an Island Vols I–IV 1998; novels, short stories, plays and essays in Turkish. *Leisure interest:* folklore. *Address:* P.K. 14, Basinköy, Istanbul, Turkey. *Website:* www.yasarkemal.net.

KEMLER, Rudolf; Austrian business executive; *Chairman of the Supervisory Board, OMV Group;* b. 9 May 1956; m.; two c.; Man., WBG Betriebswirtschaft Beratungsgesellschaft mbH 1984–89; mem. Bd of Dirs and Sr Vice-Pres. for Banking and Insurance, Nixdorf Computer GmbH, Vienna 1989–90, Dir at Siemens Nixdorf Informationssysteme GmbH, Vienna 1990–92, Exec. Vice-Pres., Siemens Nixdorf Informationssysteme AG, Munich 1992–95, Head of Computer Systems Div., Siemens Nixdorf for the region Austria and SE Europe, Vienna 1995–98; Sr Vice-Pres. and Chief Information Officer, GE Capital Corpn, Stamford, Conn., USA 1998–2000; CEO stage1 Beteiligung-Management AG, Vienna 2000–02; CEO T-Systems Austria and Region Man. for Cen. and Eastern Europe 2002–08; Gen. Man. HP Austria 2008–12; mem. Bd of Dirs Österreichische Industrieholding AG (ÖIAG) 2012–; Chair. Supervisory Bd OMV AG, Telekom Austria AG, Österreichische Post AG. *Address:* OMV AG, Trabrennstrasse 6–8, 1020 Vienna, Austria (office). *Telephone:* (1) 40440-21950 (office). *Fax:* (1) 40440-27900 (office). *E-mail:* gerhard.roiss@omv.com (office). *Website:* www.omv.com (office).

KEMMER, Michael; German banking executive; *Chairman of the Board of Management, Bavaria BayernLB;* b. 30 April 1957, Nördlingen; ed Ludwig-Maximilians Univ., Munich; Bank Officer, Bayerische Vereinsbank 1977–79, Cen. Accounts Div. 1988–94; Research Asst, Univ. of Munich 1984–87; Head, Main Finance Dept, DG Bank, Frankfurt 1994–96; Head, Cen. Div., Group Accounts, Bayerische Vereinsbank (now Bayerische Hypo- und Vereinsbank AG) 1996–2003, Head, Accounts and Taxes Div. 2003; mem. Bd of Man. and Chief Risk Officer HVB Group 2003–05; Chief Financial Officer Bavaria BayernLB 2006–08, Chair. Bd of Man. 2008–. *Address:* Bavaria BayernLB, Brienner Strasse, 80333 Munich, Germany (office). *Telephone:* (89) 2171-01 (office). *E-mail:* presse@bayernlb.de (office). *Website:* www.bayernlb.de (office).

KÉMOULARIA, Claude de; French international administrator, diplomatist and banker; *Executive Vice-President, Institut d'Etudes Politiques Mediterraneennes- Club de Monaco;* b. 30 March 1922, Paris; s. of Joseph de Kémoularia and Marguerite Eichenlaub; m. Chantal Julia de Kémoularia 1951; one d. two s.; ed Lycée de Fontainbleau, Faculté de Droit, Univ. de Paris and Ecole Libre des Sciences Politiques; Personal Asst to Minister of Interior 1944–45; sr Adviser,

Office of Gov.-Gen., French Zone of Occupied Germany 1946–47; Parliamentary Sec. to Minister of Finance 1948; Parl. Sec. to Chair. CEO Pres. Paul Reynaud 1948–56; Personal Asst to Sec.-Gen. of UN, Dag Hammarskjöld 1957–61, in charge of World Refugee Year 1960; Dir European Information Services of UN 1961; entered pvt. business 1962; Dir Forges de Chatillon-Commentry 1962–64, Paribas North America 1979–82, S. G. Warburg 1980–82; Sr Consultant to Administrator, UN Devt Programme 1964–80; Dir of Cabinet and Pvt. Adviser to Prince Rainier of Monaco 1965–67; adviser Chair. CEO Pres. int. operations (Banque de Paris et des Pays-Bas) 1968–82; Hon. Chair. Soc. Néo-Calédonienne de Dévt. et Participations, Soc. Gabonaise de Participations; Amb. to Netherlands 1982–84; Perm. Rep. to UN 1984–87; UN Goodwill Amb. for Population Matters 1987–92, Vice-Chair. SGS Holding France 1994–2004; Dir Société générale de surveillance 1987–94, Aerospaitiale, Nina Ricci, Eurocopter; mem. Bd Bank Dhofar Al Omani Al-Fransi, Oman 1975–98, Baiduri Bank Berhad, Brunei 1991–, Bank of Sharjah, UAE; Pres. Paribas Netherlands 1988–92, Hon. Pres. 1992; Pres. Advisory Cttee Revue politique et parlementaire 1989–; Admin., Institut d'Etudes Politiques Mediterranéennes (IEPM) 1999, Co-founder and Vice Pres. IEPM-Club de Monaco 2000–; Hon. Pres. French UN Asscn; Chair. Friends of the French Repub. Asscn; Pres. French Omani Business Club, Qatari French Business Club (French section); mem. Nat. Council, Mouvement Européen, American Club of Paris, France-Amérique, France-Grande Bretagne; Officier, Légion d'honneur, Commdr des Arts et Lettres, Grand Officier, Orange Nassau and other decorations. *Leisure interest:* international affairs. *Address:* Club de Monaco, 73 Champs Elysées, 75008 Paris (office); 41 boulevard du Commandant Charcot, 92200 Neuilly-sur-Seine, France (home). *Telephone:* 1-56-43-36-10 (office); 1-47-22-90-90 (home). *Fax:* 1-56-43-36-11 (office). *E-mail:* iepm@wanadoo.fr (office).

KEMP, Martin John, MA, DLitt, FBA, FRSA, FRSE; British art historian, academic, author and exhibition curator; *Professor Emeritus, University of Oxford;* b. 5 March 1942, Windsor, Berks., England; s. of Frederick Maurice Kemp and Violet Anne Kemp (née Tull); m. Jill Lightfoot 1966 (divorced 2003); one s. one d.; ed Windsor Grammar School, Downing Coll., Cambridge and Courtauld Inst. of Art, London; Lecturer in History of Western Art, Dalhousie Univ., NS, Canada 1965–66; Lecturer in History of Fine Art, Univ. of Glasgow 1966–81; Prof. of Fine Arts, Univ. of St Andrews 1981–90; Prof. of History, Royal Scottish Acad. 1985–; Prof. of History and Theory of Art, Univ. of St Andrews 1990–95; Prof. of History of Art, Univ. of Oxford 1995, now Emer. Prof. and Head of Dept; Fellow Trinity Coll. Oxford 1995–; Provost St Leonard's Coll., Univ. of St Andrews 1991–95; mem. Inst. for Advanced Study, Princeton, NJ, USA 1984–85; Slade Prof., Univ. of Cambridge 1987–88; Benjamin Sonenberg Visiting Prof., Inst. of Fine Arts, New York Univ. 1988; Wiley Visiting Prof., Univ. of North Carolina, Chapel Hill 1993; British Acad. Wolfson Research Prof. 1993–98; Visiting mem. Getty Center, Los Angeles 2002; Mellon Sr Fellow, Canadian Centre for Architecture, Montreal 2004; Lila Wallace-Reader's Digest Visiting Prof., I Tatti, Harvard Univ. 2010; Page-Barbour Lecturer, Univ. of Virginia 2012; Joseph Janson-La Palme Visiting Lecturer, Dept of Art and Archeology, Princeton Univ. 2013; regular columnist on Science in Culture in Nature 1997–2010; Pres. Leonardo da Vinci Soc. 1988–97; Chair. Asscn of Art Historians 1989–92; mem. Exec. Scottish Museums Council 1990–95; Dir and Chair. Graeme Murray Gallery 1990–92; Dir Wallace Kemp/Artakt 2001; mem. Bd Interalia 1992–, Bd Museum Training Inst. 1993–98, Council British Soc. for the History of Science 1994–97; mem. Visual Arts Advisory Panel, Arts Council of England 1996–; Trustee, Nat. Galleries of Scotland 1982–87, Victoria and Albert Museum, London 1986–89, British Museum 1995–, Ashmolean Museum 1995–, Wilhelmina Barns-Graham Trust 2000–12; Fellow, Royal Soc. of Sciences, Uppsala 1995; Hon. mem. American Acad. of Arts and Sciences 1996–; Hon. Fellow, Downing Coll., Cambridge 1999, Trinity Coll., Oxford 2008; Hon. DLitt (Heriot Watt) 1995, (Uppsala) 2009, (Glyndwr, Wales) 2009; Mitchell Prize 1981, Armand Hammer Prize for Leonardo Studies 1992, Pres.'s Prize, Italian Asscn of America 1992. *Publications:* Leonardo da Vinci: The Marvellous Works of Nature and Man 1981, Leonardo da Vinci (co-author) 1989, Leonardo on Painting (co-author) 1989, The Science of Art: Optical Themes in Western Art from Brunelleschi to Seurat 1990, Behind the Picture: Art and Evidence in the Italian Renaissance 1997, Immagine e Verità 1999, The Oxford History of Western Art (ed.) 2000, Spectacular Bodies (with Marina Wallace) 2000, Visualizations: The Nature Book of Science and Art 2001, Leonardo 2004, Leonardo da Vinci: Experience, Experiment and Design 2006, Seen/Unseen 2006, The Human Animal 2007, Leonardo da Vinci: La Bella Principessa 2010, Leonardo da Vinci. I disegni di Leonardo da Vinci e della sua cerchia (with Juliana Barone) 2010, Christ to Coke: How Image Becomes Icon 2011, Madonna of the Yarnwinder (with Thereza Wells) 2011, The Chapel of Trinity College, Oxford 2013. *Leisure interests:* sport, music. *Address:* Trinity College, Oxford, OX1 3BH, England (home). *Telephone:* (1993) 811364 (office). *E-mail:* martin.kemp@trinity.ox.ac.uk (office). *Website:* www.martinjkemp.com.

KEMP-WELCH, Sir John, Kt, FRSA, CCMI; British fmr stock broker; b. 31 March 1936, Hertford; s. of Peter Kemp-Welch and Peggy Kemp-Welch; m. Diana Leishman 1964; one s. three d.; ed Winchester Coll.; Hoare & Co. 1954–58; Cazenove & Co. 1959–94, Jt Sr Partner 1980–94; Dir Savoy Hotel PLC 1985–98; Dir London Stock Exchange 1991–2000, Chair. 1994–2000; Chair. Scottish Eastern Investment Trust 1994–99, Claridge's Hotel 1995–97; Deputy Chair. Financial Reporting Council 1994–2000; Vice-Chair. Fed. of European Stock Exchanges 1996–98; Dir Royal and Sun Alliance Insurance Group PLC 1994–99, British Invisibles 1994–98, Securities and Futures Authority 1994–97, ProShare 1995–97, Accountancy Foundation 2000–, HSBC Holdings 2000–06; mem. Guild of Int. Bankers 2004–; Vice-Pres. Reed's School; Gov. The Ditchley Foundation 1980–2012; Trustee, King's Medical Research Trust (Chair. 1991–2006), Dulverton Trust 1994– (Vice-Chair. 2001–), Farmington Trust 2002–; Hon. Fellow, Chartered Securities Inst.; Hon. DBA (London Guildhall Univ.) 1998. *Leisure interests:* the hills of Perthshire, Impressionist paintings, champagne.

KEMPSTON DARKES, (Vera) Maureen, OC, BA, LLB; Canadian lawyer and automotive industry executive; b. 31 July 1948, Toronto, Ont.; m. Lawrence J. Darkes; ed Victoria Coll., Univ. of Toronto and Univ. of Toronto Law School; called to Bar of Toronto; mem. Legal Staff, General Motors (GM) of Canada Ltd 1975–79, Asst Counsel 1979, Head of Tax Staff 1980–84, Gen. Dir Public Affairs 1987, Vice-Pres. of Corp. Affairs and mem. Bd of Dirs 1991, Gen. Counsel and Sec. 1992, Pres. (first woman) and Gen. Man. 1994–2001, Vice-Pres. GM Corpn (one of only two female vice-pres) 1994–2001, Pres. GM Latin America, Africa and the Middle East and mem. GM Automotive Strategy Bd and Group Vice-Pres. 2002–09 (retd); mem. Legal Staff, General Motors Corpn, Detroit, Mich., USA 1979–80, mem. staff, Treas.'s Office, New York 1985–87, Vice-Pres. 1994–2001; mem. Bd of Dirs Hughes Aircraft of Canada, CAMI Automotive, CN Rail, Brascan Ltd, Thomson Corpn, Nat. Quality Inst., Nat. Research Council, Vehicle Mfrs Asscn, Ont. Govt Educ. Quality and Accountability Bd, Ont. Minister of Health's Women's Health Council; apptd to Free Trade Agreement Automotive Select Panel 1989, Transportation Equipment Sectoral Advisory Group on Int. Trade 1994; mem. Arts and Science Advisory Bd Univ. of Toronto, Bd of Govs Univ. of Waterloo, Business School Advisory Cttee Univ. of Western Ontario, Bd of Dirs Women's Coll. Hosp. Foundation, Chancellor's Council of Victoria Coll., Bd New Directions, Council of Advisory Govs for the YMCA of Greater Toronto; fmr Co-Chair. BC Cancer Foundation's Millennium Campaign; Order of Ontario 1997, Officer, Order of Ontario 2000; Hon. DComm (St Mary's Univ.) 1995; Hon. LLD Univ. of Toronto) 1996, (Univ. of Victoria, McMaster Univ., Dalhousie Univ., Wilfrid Laurier Univ., Law Soc. of Upper Canada); Women's Automotive Asscn Int. Professional Achievement Award 1997, ABA Margaret Brent Women Lawyers of Achievement Award 1998, Automotive Hall of Fame Distinguished Service Citation 1999, Gov. Gen.'s Awards in Commemoration of the Persons Case 2006, ranked by Fortune magazine amongst the 50 Most Powerful Women in Business outside the US (seventh) 2002, (sixth) 2003, (12th) 2008–09, ranked by Latin Business Chronicle as one of Latin America's 100 Most Powerful Businesspeople 2009.

KEMPTHORNE, Dirk Arthur, BS; American government official and fmr politician; b. 29 Oct. 1951, San Diego, Calif.; s. of James Henry Kempthorne and Maxine Jesse Kempthorne (née Gustason); m. Patricia Jean Merrill 1977; one s. one d.; ed Univ. of Idaho; Exec. Asst to Dir Idaho Dept Lands, Boise 1975–78; Exec. Vice-Pres. Idaho Home Builders' Asscn 1978–81; Campaign Man., Batt for Gov., Boise 1981–82; Idaho Public Affairs Man. FMC Corpn, Boise 1983–86; Mayor of Boise 1986–93; Senator from Idaho 1993–99; Gov. of Idaho 1999–2006; US Sec. of Interior 2006–09; Chair. US Conf. of Mayors Standing Cttee on Energy and Environment 1991–93, mem. Advisory Bd 1991–93; Sec. Nat. Conf. of Republican Mayors and Municipal Elected Officials 1991–93; mem. Bd of Dirs Parents and Youth Against Drug Abuse 1987–; Republican; numerous awards. Address: c/o Department of the Interior, 1849 C Street, NW, Washington DC 20240, USA.

KENDAL, Felicity, CBE; British actress; b. 25 Sept. 1946, Olton, Warwicks., England; d. of Geoffrey Kendal and Laura Kendal; m. 1st Drewe Henley (divorced 1979); one s.; m. 2nd Michael Rudman 1983 (divorced 1991); one s.; ed six convents in India; first appeared on stage 1947, at age nine months in A Midsummer Night's Dream; grew up touring India and Far East with parents' theatre co., playing pageboys at age eight and Puck at age nine, graduating to roles such as Viola in Twelfth Night, Jessica in The Merchant of Venice and Ophelia in Hamlet; returned to England 1965; Variety Club Most Promising Newcomer 1974, Variety Club Best Actress 1979, Clarence Derwent Award 1980, Variety Club Woman of the Year, Best Actress 1984, Evening Standard Best Actress Award 1989, Variety Club Best Actress Award 2000. Stage roles include: London debut as Carla in Minor Murder, Savoy Theatre 1967, Katherine in Henry V, Lika in The Promise, Leicester 1968, Amaryllis in Back to Methuselah, Nat. Theatre, Hermia in A Midsummer Night's Dream, Hero in Much Ado About Nothing, Regent's Park, London 1970, Anne Danby in Kean, Oxford 1970, London 1971; Romeo and Juliet, 'Tis Pity She's a Whore and The Three Arrows 1972; The Norman Conquests, London 1974, Viktosha in Once Upon a Time, Bristol 1976, Arms and The Man, Greenwich 1978, Mara in Clouds, London 1978; Constanza Mozart in Amadeus, Desdemona in Othello; On the Razzle 1981, The Second Mrs. Tanqueray, The Real Thing 1982, Jumpers 1985, Made in Bangkok 1986, Hapgood 1988, Ivanov 1989, Much Ado About Nothing 1989, Hidden Laughter 1990, Tartuffe 1991, Heartbreak House 1992, Arcadia 1992, An Absolute Turkey 1994, Indian Ink 1995, Mind Millie for Me 1996, The Seagull 1997, Waste 1997, Alarms and Excursions 1998, Fallen Angels 2000, Humble Boy 2002, Happy Days 2003, Amy's View 2006, The Vortex 2008, The Last Cigarette 2009 and Wyndham's Theatre 2013, Chin Chin 2013. Films include: Shakespeare-Wallah 1965, Valentino 1976, We're Back! A Dinosaur's Story (voice) 1993, Parting Shots 1998. Television includes: Love Story (series) 1966, The Wednesday Play – The Mayfly and the Frog 1966, ITV Play of the Week (series) – Person Unknown 1967, Half Hour Story (series) – Gone, and Never Called Me Mother 1967, Boy Meets Girl (series) – Love with a Few Hairs 1967, Thirty-Minute Theatre (series) – Come Death 1967, Man in a Suitcase (series) – Blind Spot 1968, The Tenant of Wildfell Hall (series) 1968–69, The Woodlanders (series) 1970, Crime of Passion (play) 1971, Jason King (series) 1972, The Dolly Dialogues (series) 1973, Dolly (series) 1973, The Good Life 1975–78, Edward the Seventh (series) 1975, Murder (series) – A Variety of Passion 1976, ITV Sunday Night Drama – Now Is Too Late 1976, – Clouds of Glory: William and Dorothy 1978, – Clouds of Glory: The Rime of the Ancient Mariner 1978, Do You Remember? (series) – Home and Beauty 1978, Wings of Song (film) 1978, The Marriage Counsellor (film) 1978, Twelfth Night 1979, Solo 1981–82, On the Razzle (film) 1983, The Mistress 1985–87, Favourite Things (BBC) 1986, The Camomile Lawn 1992, Shakespeare: The Animated Tales (series) – Romeo and Juliet (narrator) 1992, Honey for Tea (series) 1994, The World of Peter Rabbit and Friends (series) (voice) 1995, How Proust Can Change Your Life (film) 2000, Rosemary & Thyme 2003–06, The Secret Show (series) – It's a Hamster World 2007, Doctor Who (series) – The Unicorn and the Wasp 2008, Strictly Come Dancing 2010, Shakespeare, India & Felicity Kendal 2012. Publication: White Cargo (memoirs) 1998. Address: c/o Dallas Smith, United Agents, 12–26 Lexington Street, London, W1F 0LE, England (office). Telephone: (20) 3214-0800 (office). Fax: (20) 3214-0801 (office). E-mail: info@unitedagents.co.uk (office). Website: www.unitedagents.co.uk (office).

KENDALL, David William, FCA; British business executive; b. 8 May 1935; s. of William Jack Kendall and Alma May Kendall; m. 1st Delphine Hitchcock 1960 (divorced); one s. one d.; m. 2nd Elisabeth Rollison 1973; one s. one d.; ed Enfield Grammar School, Southend High School; with Elles Reeve & Co. 1955–62, Shell-Mex & BP Ltd 1963–68; Finance Dir Irish Shell & BP Ltd 1969–70; Crude Oil Sales Man. British Petroleum Co. Ltd 1971–72, Man. Bulk Trading Div. 1973–74, mem. Org. Planning Cttee 1975; Gen. Man. BP NZ Ltd 1976–79, Man. Dir and CEO 1980–82; Chair. BP South West Pacific 1979–82; Finance and Planning Dir BP Oil

Ltd 1982–85, Man. Dir and CEO 1985–88; Dir BP Chemicals Int. 1985–88, BP Oil Int. 1985–88, BP Detergents Int. 1985–88; Deputy Chair. British Coal Corpn 1989–90; Chair. Ruberoid PLC 1993–2000, Whitecroft PLC 1993–1999, Meyer Int. PLC 1994–95, Celtic Energy Ltd 1994–2003, Wagon PLC 1997–2005, G-T-P Group Ltd 2006–11; Dir STC PLC 1988–90, Danka Business Systems PLC 1993–2000 (Chair. 1998–2000), Gowrings 1993–2004, South Wales Electricity PLC 1993–96; Dir (non-exec.) Bunzl PLC 1988–90 (Chair. 1990–93), Blagden Industries PLC 1993–94 (Chair. 1994–2000), British Standards Inst. 2000–05; Pres. UK Petrol-eum Industries Asscn 1987–88, Oil Industries Club 1988. Leisure interests: golf, music. Address: 41 Albion Street, London, W2 2AU, England. Telephone: (20) 7258-1955.

KENEALLY, Kristina Kerscher, BA, MA; Australian (b. American) politician and organization official; CEO, Basketball Australia; b. 1969, USA; m. Ben Keneally 1996; two s.; ed Univ. of Dayton, Ohio, USA; emigrated to Australia 1994; NSW Youth Coordinator, Soc. of St Vincent de Paul 1995–2003; mem. NSW Legis. Ass. for Heffron constituency 2003–12, NSW Minister for Ageing and Disability Services 2007–08, for Planning 2008–09, also Minister for Redfern Waterloo 2008–12; Premier NSW 2009–11; mem. Australian Labor Party (ALP), Leader ALP in NSW 2009–11; CEO Basketball Australia 2012–. Address: Basketball Australia, PO Box 7141, Alexandria NSW 2015, Australia (office). Telephone: (2) 8396-5522 (office). Fax: (2) 8396-5501 (office). E-mail: ceo@basketball.net.au (office). Website: www.basketball.net.au (office).

KENEALLY, Thomas Michael, AO, FRSL; Australian writer; b. 7 Oct. 1935, Sydney; s. of Edmund Thomas and Elsie Margaret Keneally; m. Judith Mary Martin 1965; two d.; ed St Patrick's Coll., Strathfield, NSW; Lecturer in Drama, Univ. of New England, Armidale, NSW 1968–70; Visiting Prof. Univ. of Calif., Irvine 1985, Prof. Dept of English and Comparative Literature 1991–95; Berg Prof. Dept of English, New York Univ. 1988; Pres. Nat. Book Council of Australia –1987; Chair. Australian Soc. of Authors 1987–90, Pres. 1990–; mem. Literary Arts Bd 1985–; mem. Australia-China Council; mem. American Acad. of Arts and Sciences; Founding Chair. Australian Republican Movt 1991–93; Hon. DLit (Univ. of Queensland), (Nat. Univ. of Ireland) 1994; Hon. DLitt (Fairleigh Dickenson Univ., USA) 1996, (Rollins Coll., USA) 1996; Royal Soc. of Literature Prize, Los Angeles Times Fiction Prize 1983, Peggy V. Helmerich Distinguished Author Award 2007, Special Award, New South Wales Premier's Literary Awards 2008. Publications: The Place at Whitton 1964, The Fear 1965, Bring Larks and Heroes 1967, Three Cheers for the Paraclete 1968, The Survivor 1969, A Dutiful Daughter 1970, The Chant of Jimmie Blacksmith 1972, Blood Red, Sister Rose 1974, Gossip from the Forest 1975, Moses and the Lawgiver 1975, Season in Purgatory 1976, A Victim of the Aurora 1977, Ned Kelly and the City of Bees 1978, Passenger 1978, Confederates 1979, Schindler's Ark (Booker Prize) 1982, Outback 1983, The Cut-Rate Kingdom 1984, A Family Madness 1985, Australia: Beyond the Dreamtime (contrib.) 1987, The Playmaker 1987, Towards Asmara 1989, Flying Hero Class 1991, Now and in Time to Be: Ireland and the Irish 1992, Woman of the Inner Sea 1992, The Place Where Souls Are Born: A Journey into the American Southwest 1992, Jacko: The Great Intruder 1993, The Utility Player – The Story of Des Hassler (non-fiction) 1993, Our Republic (non-fiction) 1993, A River Town 1995, Homebush Boy: A Memoir 1995, The Great Shame: And the Triumph of the Irish in the English-Speaking World 1998, Bettany's Book 2000, An American Scoundrel: The Life of the Notorious Civil War General Dan Sickles (non-fiction) 2002, An Angel in Australia 2002, Abraham Lincoln (biog.) 2003, The Office of Innocence 2003, The Tyrant's Novel 2004, The Commonwealth of Thieves: The Story of the Founding of Australia (non-fiction) 2006, The Widow and Her Hero 2007, Searching for Schindler: A Memoir 2008, The People's Train 2009, Three Famines 2011, The Daughters of Mars 2012. Leisure interest: cross-country skiing, swimming, hiking. Address: Curtis Brown (Australia) Pty Ltd, PO Box 19, Paddington, NSW 2021, Australia (office).

KENEN, Peter B., BA, MA, PhD; American economist and academic; Walker Professor of Economics and International Finance Emeritus, Princeton University; b. 30 Nov. 1932, Cleveland, Ohio; m. Regina Horowitz; four c.; ed Columbia Univ., London School of Econs, UK, Harvard Univ.; Instructor in Econs, Columbia Univ. 1957–58, Asst Prof. 1958–61, Assoc. Prof. 1961–64, Prof. 1964–71, Chair. Dept of Econs 1967–69, Provost, Columbia Univ. 1969–70, Adviser to Pres. of the Univ. 1970–71, Wesley Clair Mitchell Research Prof. 1971; Walker Prof. of Econs and Int. Finance, Princeton Univ. 1971–2004, Prof. Emer. 2004–, Dir of Int. Finance Section, Princeton Univ. 1971–99; Instructor, George Washington Univ. Summer 1957; Assoc. Prof., Univ. of California, Berkeley Summer 1963; Visiting Prof., Hebrew Univ., Jerusalem; Winter 1967; Visiting Prof., Stockholm School of Econs Spring 1967; Visiting Prof., Tel-Aviv Univ. Spring 1977; Ford Visiting Research Prof., Univ. of California, Berkeley 1980; Professorial Fellow, Reserve Bank of Australia, and Visiting Research Prof., ANU 1983–84; Visiting Research Fellow, Royal Inst. of Int. Affairs and Centre for Econ. Policy Research 1987–88; Houblon-Norman Research Fellow, Bank of England 1991–92; Visiting Scholar, Research Dept, IMF 1992; Visiting Scholar, Centre for Econ. Performance, LSE 2000, 2003; Forum Fellow, World Econ. Forum 2000; Visiting Scholar, Reserve Bank of New Zealand 2002; Adjunct Sr Fellow, Council on Foreign Relations 2005–08; mem. Presidential Task Force on Foreign Econ. Policy 1960, Review Cttee on Balance of Payments Statistics 1963–64, UN Group of Experts on Payments Arrangements for Developing Countries 1966, New York State Advisory Cttee to US Civil Rights Comm. 1970–71, Advisory Cttee on Presentation of the Balance of Payments Statistics, Office of Man. and Budget 1974–76, Advisory Cttee on Reform of the Int. Monetary System, US Treasury 1978–82, Econ. Advisory Panel, Fed. Reserve Bank of New York 1990–95; Consultant, Council of Econ. Advisers 1961, US Treasury 1961–68, 1978–80, 1995–96, 1998–99, Bureau of the Budget 1964–68, Bd of Govs Fed. Reserve System 1968–69, UN Conf. on Trade and Devt 1972, IMF 1990, 1992, 1999; Pres. Eastern Econ. Asscn 2000–01; mem. American Econ. Asscn, Royal Econ. Soc., Council on Foreign Relations; mem. Emer. Group of Thirty Consultative Group on Int. Econ. and Monetary Affairs, Inc. (G-30), Washington, DC; Assoc. Ed. of International Economics 1977–80; mem. Editorial Bd Political Science Quarterly 1963–71, Journal of Money, Credit, and Banking 1969–70, International Journal of Finance & Economics 1996–; mem. Bd of Eds Journal of Economic Literature 1969–71, Review of International Econom-ics 1994–96; mem. Editorial Advisory Bd The International Economy 1988–, International Finance 1997–; mem. Bd of Review American Society of International Law 1978–82; mem. Visiting Cttee to Harvard Econs Dept 1978–82, to Columbia Econs Dept 1985–89; mem. Advisory Bd Inst. for Int. Econs 1981–, Overseas Devt Council 1983–90; Woodrow Wilson Fellow 1954–55; Earhart Foundation Fellow 1955–56; Ford Foundation and Social Science Research Council (SSRC) Dissertation Fellow 1956–57; Ford Foundation Faculty Research Fellow 1962–63; SSRC Faculty Research Fellow 1966–67; Fellow, Center for Advanced Study in the Behavioral Sciences 1971–72; John Simon Guggenheim Fellow 1975–76; German Marshall Fund Fellow 1987–88; Houblon-Norman Fellowship, Bank of England 1991–92; Professorial Fellow, Victoria Univ. of Wellington and Reserve Bank of New Zealand 2002; Univ. Medal for Excellence, Columbia Univ. 1977. *Publications:* books: British Monetary Policy and the Balance of Payments 1951–57 (David A. Wells Prize, Harvard Univ. 1958–59) 1960, Giant among Nations: Problems in United States Foreign Economic Policy 1960 (reprinted with Postscript 1963), Money, Debt, and Economic Activity (with A. G. Hart) 1961 (Japanese and Spanish translations, fourth edn with A. Entine and A. G. Hart 1969), International Economics (with R. Lubitz) 1964 (Dutch, Italian, Japanese, Portuguese, Spanish and Swedish translations, third edn 1971), A Model of the U.S. Balance of Payments (in association with D. P. Dungan and D. L. Warner) 1978, Asset Markets, Exchange Rates, and Economic Integration (with P. R. Allen) 1980 (Parts I–III reprinted as Asset Markets and Exchange Rates: Modeling an Open Economy 1983), Essays in International Economics 1980, The International Economy 1985 (fourth edn 2000), Exchange Rates and Policy Coordination 1989, Exchange Rates and the Monetary System: Selected Essays of Peter B. Kenen 1994, Economic and Monetary Union in Europe: Moving beyond Maastricht 1995, The International Financial Architecture: What's New? What's Missing? 2001, Regional Monetary Integration (with Ellen E. Meade) 2007; monographs: United States Commercial Policy: A Program for the 1960s 1961, The Reserve-Asset Preferences of Central Banks and Stability of the Gold-Exchange Standard. Princeton Studies in International Finance, 10 1963, Capital Mobility and Financial Integration: A Survey. Princeton Studies in International Finance, 39 1976, Exchange Rates, Domestic Prices, and the Adjustment Process: A Survey of Recent Evidence. Occasional Paper 1 (with C. Pack) 1980, The Role of the Dollar as an International Currency. Occasional Paper 13 1983, Financing, Adjustment, and the International Monetary Fund 1986, Managing Exchange Rates. The Chatham House Papers 1988 (US edn 1989), EMU after Maastricht 1992, The Evolving Corporation: Global Imperatives and National Responses (with M. V. N. Whitman and others) 1999, International Economic and Financial Cooperation: New Issues, New Actors, New Responses (with Jeffrey Shafer, Nigel Wicks and Charles Wyplosz) 2004, Reform of the International Monetary Fund. Council Special Report 29 2007; ed.: Trade, Growth, and the Balance of Payments: Essays in Honor of Gottfried Haberler (with R. E. Caves and H. G. Johnson) 1965, The Open Economy (with R. C. Lawrence) 1968, International Trade and Finance: Frontiers for Research 1975, The International Monetary System under Flexible Exchange Rates: Essays in Honor of Robert Triffin (with R. Cooper, J. De Macedo and J. Van Ypersele) 1981, The Global Repercussions of U.S. Monetary and Fiscal Policy (with S. A. Hewlett and H. Kaufman) 1984, Handbook of International Economics, Vols I and II (with R. W. Jones) 1984, 1985, The International Monetary System: Highlights from Fifty Years of Princeton's Essays in International Finance 1993, Managing the World Economy: Fifty Years after Bretton Woods 1994, The International Monetary System: Essays in Memory of Rinaldo Ossola (with F. Papadia and F. Saccomanni) 1994, Understanding Interdependence: The Macroeconomics of the Open Economy 1995, Reforming the International Monetary and Financial System (with A. K. Swoboda) 2000; numerous articles in scholarly journals, many reprinted in two vols: Essays in International Economics and Exchange Rates and the Monetary System. *Address:* Department of Economics, 113 Fisher Hall, Princeton University, Princeton, NJ 08544-1021, USA (office). *Telephone:* (609) 258-4051 (office). *Fax:* (609) 258-6419 (office). *E-mail:* pbkenen@princeton.edu (office). *Website:* www.princeton.edu/~pbkenen (office).

KENILOREA, Rt Hon. Sir Peter, KBE, PC, DipEd; Solomon Islands politician; *Speaker, National Parliament;* b. 23 May 1943, Takataka, Malaita; m. Margaret Kwanairara 1971; eight c.; ed Teachers' Coll. in New Zealand; Schoolmaster, King George VI Secondary School 1968–70; Asst Sec. Finance 1971; Admin. Officer, Dist admin. 1971–73; Lands Officer 1973–74; Deputy Sec. to Cabinet and to Chief Minister 1974–75; District Commr, Eastern Solomons 1975–76; mem. Legis. Ass. 1976–78; MP for East Are-Are 1976–; f. United Democratic Party 1980, Pres. 1989–; Chief Minister of the Solomon Islands 1976–78; Prime Minister of the Solomon Islands 1978–81, 1984–86; Deputy Prime Minister 1986–89, Minister of Foreign Affairs 1988–89, of Foreign Affairs and Trade Relations 1990; Speaker of Nat. Parl. 2001–; Ombudsman 1996–; Dir S Pacific Forum Fisheries Agency 1991–94; Co-Chair. Peace Negotiation and Chair. Peace Monitoring Council 2000–; Order of Brilliant Star with Special Grand Cordon (China Taiwan) 1985; Queen's Silver Jubilee Medal 1977, Solomon Islands Ind. Medal 1978. *Publications:* numerous articles for political and scientific publs. *Leisure interests:* reading, sports. *Address:* Rara Village, East Are'Are, Malaita Province (home); National Parliament, POB G19, Honiara (office); PO Box 1674, Honiara, Solomon Islands. *Telephone:* 21751 (office). *Fax:* 23866 (office). *Website:* www.parliament .gov.sb.

KENNARD, Olga, OBE, ScD, FRS; British research scientist; *Trustee, British Museum;* b. 23 March 1924, Budapest, Hungary; d. of Joir Weisz and Catherina Weisz; m. 1st David Kennard 1948 (divorced 1961); two d.; m. 2nd Sir Arnold Burgen (q.v.) 1993; ed schools in Hungary, Prince Henry VIII Grammar School, Evesham and Newnham Coll. Cambridge; Research Asst, Cavendish Lab., Cambridge 1944–48; MRC Scientific Staff, London 1948–61; MRC External Scientific Staff, Univ. of Cambridge 1961–89; Dir Cambridge Crystallographic Data Centre 1965–97; MRC Special Appt. 1969–89; Visiting Prof., Univ. of London 1988–90; mem. Academia Europaea, Council, Royal Soc. 1995–97; Trustee of British Museum 2004; Hon. LLD Univ. of Cambridge 2003; Royal Soc. of Chem. Prize for Structural Chem. 1980. *Publications:* about 200 papers in scientific journals and books on X-ray crystallography, molecular biology, information technology; 20 scientific reference books. *Leisure interests:* swimming, music, modern architecture and design. *Address:* Keelson, 8A Hills Avenue, Cambridge, CB1 7XA, England. *Telephone:* (1223) 415381.

KENNARD, William E.; American business executive, lawyer, fmr diplomatist and fmr government official; *Senior Advisor, Grain Management LLC;* b. 19 Jan. 1957, Los Angeles, Calif.; s. of Robert A. Kennard and Helen Z. King; m. Deborah D. Kennedy 1984; one s.; ed Stanford Univ., Yale Law School; fmrly with Nat. Asscn of Broadcasters; fmr Pnr and mem. Bd Dirs Verner, Liipfert, Bernhard, McPherson and Hand law firm; Gen. Counsel to Fed. Communications Comm. 1993–97, Chair. 1997–2001; Man. Dir Global Telecommunications and Media Investment Strategy, The Carlyle Group LLC 2001–09; Amb. to EU, Brussels 2009–13; Sr Advisor, Grain Management LLC 2013–; mem. Bd of Dirs MetLife; Dr hc (Howard Univ.), (Gallaudet Univ.), (Long Island Univ.). *Address:* Grain Management, LLC, 1900 K Street, NW, Suite 1130, Washington, DC 20006, USA (office). *Telephone:* (202) 779-9043 (office). *Website:* graingc.com (office).

KENNEDY, A(lison) L(ouise), BA (Hons); British writer, entertainer and academic; b. 22 Oct. 1965, Dundee, Scotland; d. of Robert Alan Kennedy and Edwardene Mildred Price; ed Univ. of Warwick; community arts worker for Clydebank & Dist 1988–89; writer 1988–; Writer-in-Residence, Hamilton & East Kilbride Social Work Dept 1989–91, for Project Ability, Arts & Special Needs 1989–95, Copenhagen Univ. 1995; book reviewer for The Scotsman, Glasgow Herald, BBC, STV, The Telegraph 1990–; Ed. New Writing Scotland 1993–95; part-time Lecturer, St Andrews Univ. 2002–07; Assoc. Prof., Creative Writing Programme, Univ. of Warwick 2007–12; columnist, The Guardian; stand-up comedian, reviewer, performer 2005–; radio presenter 2009–; Hon. DLit (Glasgow), (St Andrews); Somerset Maugham Award, Encore Award, SAC Book Award (four times), Saltire Scottish Book of the Year Award, Best of Young British Novelists (twice), Lannan Literary Award for Fiction 2007, Austrian State Prize for European Literature, Eifel Literature Prize. *Plays:* The Audition (Fringe First Award) 1993, Delicate (performance piece for Motionhouse dance co.) 1995, True (performance project for Fierce Productions and Tramway Theatre) 1998. *Film:* Stella Does Tricks (writer) 1996. *Radio:* Born a Fox (BBC Radio 4 drama) 2002, Like an Angel (BBC Radio 4 drama) 2004, Confessions of a Medium (BBC Radio drama) 2010, Blood Empire (SWR, Germany, drama) 2010, That I Should Rise 2012, Love Love Love Like The Beatles (BBC Radio 4) 2012. *Television:* Ghostdancing (BBC drama/documentary, writer and presenter) 1995, Dice (series I and II, with John Burnside, CBC TV). *Publications:* Night Geometry and the Garscadden Trains 1991, Looking for the Possible Dance 1993, Now That You're Back 1994, So I Am Glad 1995, Tea and Biscuits 1996, Original Bliss 1997, The Life and Death of Colonel Blimp 1997, Everything You Need 1999, On Bullfighting 1999, Indelible Acts 2002, Paradise 2004, Day (Saltire Scottish Book of the Year Award 2007, Costa Book of the Year Award 2007) 2007, What Becomes 2009, The Blue Book 2011. *Leisure interest:* sleeping. *Address:* c/o Antony Harwood Ltd, 103 Walton Street, Oxford, OX2 6EB, England (office). *Telephone:* (1865) 559615 (office). *Fax:* (1865) 554173 (office); (1865) 310660 (office). *E-mail:* mail@ antonyharwood.com (office); info@a-l-kennedy.co.uk (office). *Website:* www .antonyharwood.com (office); www.a-l-kennedy.co.uk (office).

KENNEDY, Anthony M., BA, LLB; American lawyer and judge; *Associate Justice, Supreme Court;* b. 23 July 1936, Sacramento, Calif.; s. of Anthony J. Kennedy and Gladys Kennedy; m. Mary Davis; two s. one d.; ed Stanford Univ., LSE and Harvard Univ. Law School; mem. Calif. Bar 1962, US Tax Court Bar 1971; Assoc., Thelen, Marrin, Johnson & Bridges (law firm), San Francisco 1961–63; sole practice, Sacramento 1963–67; Pnr, Evans, Jackson & Kennedy (law firm) 1967–75; Prof. of Constitutional Law, McGeorge School of Law, Univ. of Pacific 1965; Judge US Court of Appeals, 9th Circuit, Sacramento 1976–88; Judge, Supreme Court of USA, Washington, DC 1988–. *Address:* United States Supreme Court, One First Street, NE, Washington, DC 20543, USA (office). *Telephone:* (202) 479-3211 (office). *Website:* www.supremecourtus.gov (office).

KENNEDY, Caroline Bouvier, JD; American lawyer and diplomatist; *Ambassador to Japan;* b. 27 Nov. 1957, New York, NY; d. of the late John F. Kennedy (Pres. of USA) and Jacqueline Bouvier Kennedy; m. Edwin Arthur Schlossberg 1986; one s. two d.; ed Radcliffe Coll., Columbia Univ. Law School; Research Asst, Film and TV Dept, Metropolitan Museum of Art 1980; Dir, Office of Strategic Partnerships, New York City Dept of Educ. 2002–04; Nat. Co-Chair. Pres. Barack Obama's 2012 re-election campaign; Amb. to Japan 2013–; Pres. Kennedy Library Foundation; mem. New York and Washington DC bar asscns. *Publications include:* with Ellen Alderman: In Our Defense: The Bill of Rights in Action 1991, The Right to Privacy 1995; A Family Christmas 2007. *Address:* US Embassy, 1-10-5, Akasaka, Minato-ku, Tokyo, 107-8420, Japan (office). *Telephone:* (3) 3224-5000 (office). *Fax:* (3) 3505-1862 (office). *Website:* tokyo.usembassy.gov (office).

KENNEDY, Rt Hon. Charles Peter, PC, MA; British politician, journalist and broadcaster; *President, European Movement;* b. 25 Nov. 1959, Inverness, Scotland; s. of Ian Kennedy and Mary McVarish MacEachen; m. Sarah Gurling 2002; one s.; ed Lochaber High School, Fort William and Univ. of Glasgow; journalist, BBC Highland, Inverness 1982; Fulbright Scholar and Assoc. Instr, Dept of Speech Communication, Indiana Univ. Bloomington Campus 1982–83; MP for Ross, Cromarty and Skye 1983–97, for Ross, Skye and Inverness W 1997–2005, for Ross, Skye and Lochaber 2005–, mem. Standards and Privileges Select Cttee 1997–99, Works of Art Select Cttee 2011–; mem. Social Democratic Party 1983–88, Liberal Democrats 1988– (Spokesperson on Trade and Industry 1988–89, on Health 1989–92, on Europe and East–West relations 1992–97, on Agric. and Rural Affairs 1997–99); Pres. Liberal Democrats 1990–94, Leader 1999–2006 (resgnd); Pres. European Movt 2008–; Vice-Pres. Liberal International 2006–; Visiting Parl. Fellow, St Antony's Coll., Oxford; Rector Univ. of Glasgow 2008–; Dr hc (Glasgow) 2002. *Publication:* The Future of Politics 2000. *Address:* House of Commons, Westminster, London, SW1A 0AA, England (office); 5 MacGregor's Court, Dingwall, IV15 9HS, Scotland. *Telephone:* (20) 7219-0356 (office); (1349) 862152 (constituency). *Fax:* (20) 7219-4881 (office). *E-mail:* charles@highlandlibdems.org .uk (office); kennedyc@parliament.uk (office). *Website:* www.parliament.uk/ biographies/commons/charles-kennedy/25680 (office); www.highlandlibdems.org .uk/People/Charles-Kennedy-MP.aspx (office); www.euromove.org.uk; www .charleskennedy.org.uk (office).

KENNEDY, Donald, MA, PhD; American biologist, academic, editor and fmr university administrator; *President Emeritus, Stanford University;* b. 18 Aug. 1931, New York; s. of William D. Kennedy and Barbara (Bean) Kennedy; m. 1st Barbara J. Dewey 1953; two d.; m. 2nd Robin Beth Wiseman 1987; two step-s.; ed

Harvard Univ.; Asst Prof., Syracuse Univ. 1956–59, Assoc. Prof. 1959–60; Asst Prof., Stanford Univ. 1960–62, Assoc. Prof. 1962–65, Prof. 1965–77, Chair. Dept of Biological Sciences 1965–72, Benjamin Crocker Prof. of Human Biology 1974–77, Vice-Pres. and Provost 1979–80, Pres. 1980–92, Pres. Emer. and Bing Prof. of Environmental Science Emer. 1992–; Sr Consultant, Office of Science and Tech. Policy, Exec. Office of the Pres. 1976–77; Commr of Food and Drug Admin. 1977–79; Ed.-in-Chief Science Magazine 2000–08; Fellow, American Acad. of Arts and Sciences; mem. NAS; Hon. DSc (Columbia Univ., Williams Coll., Michigan, Rochester, Ariz., Whitman Coll., Coll. of William and Mary); Dinkelspiel Award 1976, Wonderfest's Carl Sagan Prize 2010. *Publications include:* The Biology of Organisms (with W. M. Telfer) 1965, Academic Duty 1997, U.S. Policy and the Global Environment 2000; over 60 articles in scientific journals. *Leisure interests:* skiing, fly fishing, natural history. *Address:* Stanford University, Encina Hall E401, Stanford, CA 94305 (office); 532 Channing Avenue, #302, Palo Alto, CA 94301, USA (home). *Telephone:* (650) 725-9888 (office). *Fax:* (650) 725-1992 (office). *E-mail:* kennedyd@stanford.edu (office). *Website:* fsi.stanford.edu/people/donaldkennedy (office).

KENNEDY, (George) Michael (Sinclair), CBE, MA, CRNCM; British journalist and music critic; b. 19 Feb. 1926, Chorlton-cum-Hardy, Manchester; s. of Hew G. Kennedy and Marian F. Kennedy; m. 1st Eslyn Durdle 1947 (died 1999); m. 2nd Joyce Bourne 1999; ed Berkhamsted School; staff music critic, The Daily Telegraph 1941–50, Northern Music Critic 1950–60, Northern Ed. 1960–86, Jt Chief Music Critic 1986–89; Chief Music Critic, The Sunday Telegraph 1989–2005; now a freelance writer on music; Gov. Royal Northern Coll. of Music 1972–2006; Hon. mem. Royal Manchester Coll. of Music 1971, Royal Philharmonic Soc. 2006; Hon. MA (Manchester) 1975; Hon. MusD (Manchester) 2003. *Publications:* The Hallé Tradition: A Century of Music 1960, The Works of Ralph Vaughan Williams 1964, Portrait of Elgar 1968, Elgar: Orchestral Music 1969, Portrait of Manchester 1970, History of the Royal Manchester College of Music 1971, Barbirolli: Conductor Laureate 1971, Mahler 1974, The Autobiography of Charles Hallé, with Correspondence and Diaries (ed.) 1976, Richard Strauss 1976, Britten 1980, Concise Oxford Dictionary of Music (ed.) 1980, The Hallé 1858–1983 1983, Strauss: Tone Poems 1984, Oxford Dictionary of Music (ed.) 1985, Adrian Boult 1987, Portrait of Walton 1989, Music Enriches All: The First 21 Years of the Royal Northern College of Music, Manchester 1994, Richard Strauss: Man, Musician, Enigma (French critics prize for musical biog. 2003) 1999, The Life of Elgar 2004, Buxton: an English Festival 2004; contrib. to newspapers and magazines, including Gramophone, Listener, Musical Times, Music and Letters, The Sunday Telegraph, BBC Music Magazine. *Leisure interest:* cricket. *Address:* The Bungalow, 62 Edilom Road, Manchester, M8 4HZ, England (home). *Telephone:* (161) 740-4528 (home). *E-mail:* majkennedy@bungalow62.fsnet.co.uk.

KENNEDY, Geraldine; Irish journalist; b. 7 Sept. 1951, Tramore, Co. Waterford; d. of James Kennedy and Nora McGrath; m. David J. Hegarty; two d.; ed Convent S.H.M., Ferrybank, Waterford; Political Corresp. The Sunday Tribune 1980–82, The Sunday Press 1982–87; mem. Dáil Eireann (Irish Parl.) 1987–89; Public Affairs Corresp. The Irish Times 1990–93, Political Corresp. 1993–99, Political Ed. 1999–2002, Duty Ed. 2000–02, Ed. 2002–11, Dir Irish Times Ltd 2002–11; Hon. mem., Royal Irish Acad.; Hon. DUniv (Queen's Univ., Belfast) 2005, Hon. DPhil (Dublin Inst. of Tech.) 2007, Hon. DIur (Univ. Coll., Dublin) 2008; Journalist of the Year 1994. *Leisure interests:* travel, reading, food. *Address:* c/o The Irish Times, PO Box 74, 24–28 Tara Street, Dublin 2, Ireland (office).

KENNEDY, James C., BBA; American publishing and media executive; *Chairman and CEO, Cox Enterprises Inc.;* b. 1947, Honolulu; m.; ed Univ. of Denver; with Atlanta Newspapers 1976–79; Pres. Grand Junction Newspapers 1979–80, Publr Grand Junction Daily Sentinel 1980–85; Vice-Pres. Newspaper Div. Cox Enterprises Inc. 1985–86, Exec. Vice-Pres. then Pres. 1986–87, COO then Chair. 1987–; Chair. and CEO Cox Enterprises Inc. 1988–, also Chair. Cox Communications and Cox Radio. *Cycling achievements:* past Masters Nat., Pan American and World Champion in 3000 meter pursuit; served as capt. of four-man team that won Race Across AMerica (RAAM) 1992, setting world record. *Address:* Cox Enterprises Inc., 6205 Peachtree Dunwoody Road, Atlanta, GA 30328 (office); 1601 W Peachtree Street NE, Atlanta, GA 30309, USA (home). *Telephone:* (678) 645-0000 (office). *Fax:* (678) 645-1079 (office). *Website:* www.coxenterprises.com (office).

KENNEDY, Nigel Paul, ARCM; British violinist; b. 28 Dec. 1956, Brighton; s. of John Kennedy and Scylla Stoner; m. Agnieska Kennedy; one s.; ed Yehudi Menuhin School, Juilliard School of Performing Arts, New York; debut playing Mendelssohn's Violin Concerto at the Royal Festival Hall with the London Philharmonic Orchestra under Riccardo Muti 1977; subsequently chosen by the BBC as the subject of a five-year documentary on the devt of a soloist; other important debuts include with the Berlin Philharmonic 1980, New York 1985; has made appearances at all the leading UK festivals and in Europe at Stresa, Lucerne, Gstaad, Berlin and Lockenhaus; tours to Australia, Austria, Canada, Denmark, Germany, Hong Kong, India, Ireland, Italy, Japan, Republic of Korea, New Zealand, Norway, Poland, Spain, Switzerland, Turkey and the USA; has given concerts in the field of jazz with Stephane Grappelli, including at the Edinburgh Festival and Carnegie Hall; runs his own jazz group; five-year sabbatical 1992–97; Artistic Dir, Polish Chamber Orchestra 2002–; Sr Vice-Pres. Aston Villa Football Club 1990–; Hon. DLitt (Bath) 1991; Golden Rose of Montreux 1990, Variety Club Showbusiness Personality of the Year 1991, BRIT Award for Outstanding Contribution to British Music 2000, Male Artist of the Year 2001, Echo Klassik Award for Instrumentalist of the Year 2008. *Television:* Coming Along Nicely (BBC documentary on his early career) 1973–78. *Recordings include:* Strad Jazz 1984, Elgar Sonata with Peter Pettinger 1985, Elgar's Violin Concerto with the London Philharmonic and Vernon Handley (Gramophone magazine Record of the Year, BPI Award for Best Classical Album of the Year) 1985, Vivaldi's Four Seasons, Bartók Solo Sonata and Mainly Black (arrangement of Ellington's Black Brown and Beige Suite), Sibelius Violin Concerto with the City of Birmingham Symphony Orchestra conducted by Sir Simon Rattle, Walton's Violin Concerto with the Royal Philharmonic Orchestra and André Previn, Bruch and Mendelssohn concertos with the English Chamber Orchestra conducted by Jeffrey Tate, Kafka (Kennedy's compositions), Tchaïkovsky's Chausson Poème with the London Philharmonic Orchestra 1988, Brahms Violin Concerto with the London

Philharmonic under Klaus Tennstedt 1991, Beethoven Violin Concerto with the NDR-Sinfonieorchester and Klaus Tennstedt 1992, chamber works by Debussy and Ravel, Berg's Violin Concerto, Vaughan Williams' The Lark Ascending with Sir Simon Rattle and the CBSO, works by Fritz Kreisler 1998, The Kennedy Experience, chamber works by Bach, Ravel and Kodaly (with Lynn Harrell) 1999, Classic Kennedy with the English Chamber Orchestra 1999, Bach's Concerto for Two Violins in D Minor, Concerto for Oboe and Violin in D Minor and the A Minor and E Major violin concertos the Berlin Philharmonic 2000, Nigel Kennedy Plays Bach 2006, Inner Thoughts 2006, Blue Note Sessions 2006, Polish Spirit 2007, Beethoven and Mozart Violin Concertos 2008, A Very Nice Album 2008, Shhh! 2010. *Publication:* Always Playing 1991. *Leisure interests:* cricket, golf, football. *Address:* c/o John Stanley, Kennedy, 90–96 Brewery Road, London, N7 9NT, England. *Website:* www.kennedyjazz.com.

KENNEDY, Patrick J.; Irish business executive; *Chairman of the Executive Board, SHV Holdings NV;* b. 22 Sept. 1953, Galway; joined Calor Gas Ltd (subsidiary of SHV Energy NV) 1982, becoming man. of various SHV cos in Eastern Europe, UK and Brazil, including Probugas, Slovakia 1993–94, Pamgas 1994–96, Dir Supergasbras Distribuidora de Gás, Brazil 1996–98, Dir Calor Gas Ltd 1998–2000, Chair. SHV Gas 2000–01, mem. Exec. Bd SHV Holdings 2001–, Chair. 2006–. *Address:* SHV Holdings NV, Rijnkade 1, 3511 LC Utrecht, Netherlands (office). *Telephone:* (30) 233-88-33 (office). *Fax:* (30) 233-83-04 (office). *E-mail:* info@shv.nl (office). *Website:* www.shv.nl (office).

KENNEDY, Rt Hon. Sir Paul (Joseph Morrow), PC, MA, LLB; British judge (retd); *Member and President, Court of Appeal of Gibraltar;* b. 12 June 1935, Sheffield, Yorks.; m. Virginia Devlin 1965; two s. two d.; ed Ampleforth Coll., York, Gonville & Caius Coll., Cambridge; called to Bar Gray's Inn 1960, Bencher 1982, Treas. 2002; Recorder of Crown Court 1972–83; QC 1973; Judge, High Court of Justice, Queen's Bench Div. (QBD) 1983–92, Vice-Pres. QBD 1997–2002; Presiding Judge, NE Circuit 1985–89; Lord Justice of Appeal 1992–2005 (retd). Chair. Criminal Cttee Judicial Studies Bd 1993–96; mem. Sentencing Guidelines Council –2005, Court of Appeal of Gibraltar 2006– (Pres. 2011–); Interception of Communications Commr 2006–12; Hon. Fellow, Gonville & Caius Coll. Cambridge 1998; Hon. LLD (Sheffield) 2000. *Leisure interests:* family, walking, occasional golf. *Address:* c/o Court of Appeal Civil Division, The Royal Courts of Justice, Strand, London, WC2A 2LL, England.

KENNEDY, Paul Michael, CBE, MA, DPhil, FRHistS, FBA; British historian and academic; *J. Richardson Dilworth Professor of History and Co-Director, International Security Studies, Yale University;* b. 17 June 1945, Wallsend; s. of John Patrick Kennedy and Margaret (née Hennessy) Kennedy; m. 1st Catherine Urwin 1967 (died 1998); three s.; m. 2nd Cynthia Farrar 2001; ed St Cuthbert's Grammar School, Newcastle-upon-Tyne, Univ. of Newcastle and Oxford Univ.; Research Asst to Sir Basil Liddell Hart 1966–70; Lecturer, Reader and Prof., Univ. of East Anglia 1970–83; J. Richardson Dilworth Prof. of History, Yale Univ. 1983–, Dir Int. Security Studies 1988 (now Co-Dir), also Distinguished Fellow of Brady-Johnson Program in Grand Strategy; Visiting Fellow, Inst. for Advanced Study, Princeton 1978–79; Fellow, Alexander von Humboldt Foundation, American Philosophical Soc., American Acad. of Arts and Sciences; Hon. DHL (New Haven, Alfred, Long Island, Connecticut); Hon. DLitt (Newcastle, East Anglia); Hon. LLD (Ohio); Hon. MA (Yale, Union, Quinnipiac); Dr hc (Leuven). *Publications:* The Samoan Tangle 1974, The Rise and Fall of British Naval Mastery 1976, The Rise of the Anglo-German Antagonism 1980, The Realities Behind Diplomacy 1981, Strategy and Diplomacy 1983, The Rise and Fall of the Great Powers 1988, Grand Strategy in War and Peace 1991, Preparing for the Twenty-First Century 1993, Pivotal States: A New Framework for US Policy in the Developing World (ed.) 1998, The Parliament of Man: The United Nations and the Quest for World Government 2006, Engineers of Victory: The Problem Solvers Who Turned The Tide in the Second World War 2013. *Leisure interests:* soccer, hill-walking, old churches. *Address:* Department of History, Yale Univ., PO Box 208353, New Haven, CT 06520-8353, USA (office). *Telephone:* (203) 432-6242 (office). *Fax:* (203) 432-6250 (office). *E-mail:* paul.kennedy@yale.edu (office). *Website:* www.yale.edu/iss (office).

KENNEDY, William Joseph, BA; American author and academic; *Professor of Creative Writing and Director, New York State Writers' Institute, University at Albany, State University of New York;* b. 16 Jan. 1928, Albany, New York; s. of William J. Kennedy and Mary E. McDonald; m. Ana Segarra 1957; one s. two d.; ed Siena Coll., New York; Asst Sports Ed. and columnist, Glens Falls Post Star, New York 1949–50; reporter, Albany Times-Union, New York 1952–56, special writer 1963–70; Asst Man. Ed. and columnist, P.R. World Journal, San Juan 1956; reporter, Miami Herald 1957; corresp., Time-Life Publs, Puerto Rico 1957–59; reporter, Knight Newspapers 1957–59; Founding Man. Ed. San Juan Star 1959–61; Lecturer, State Univ. of New York, Albany 1974–82, Prof. of English 1983–; Visiting Prof., Cornell Univ. 1982–83; Exec. Dir and Founder, NY State Writers' Inst. 1983–; Nat. Endowment for Arts Fellow 1981, MacArthur Foundation Fellow 1983; several hon. degrees; Gov. of New York Arts Award 1984, Creative Arts Award, Brandeis Univ. 1986. *Publications include:* The Ink Truck 1969, Legs 1975, Billy Phelan's Greatest Game 1978, Ironweed (Pulitzer Prize and Nat. Book Critics Circle Award 1984) 1983, O Albany! (non-fiction) 1983, Charlie Malarkey and the Belly Button Machine (children's book) 1986, Quinn's Book 1988, Very Old Bones 1992, Riding the Yellow Trolley Car 1993, Charlie Malarkey and the Singing Moose (children's book) 1994, The Flaming Corsage 1996, Grand View (play) 1996, Roscoe 2002, Chango's Beads and Two-Tone Shoes 2011; film scripts, The Cotton Club 1984, Ironweed 1987; also short stories, articles in professional journals. *Address:* Department of English, University at Albany, State University of New York, Humanities 333, 1400 Washington Avenue, Albany, NY 12222; New York State Writers Institute, New Library, LE 320, University at Albany, State University of New York, Albany, NY 12222, USA (office). *Telephone:* (518) 442-4055 (office). *Fax:* (518) 442-4599 (office). *E-mail:* writers@uamail.albany .edu (office). *Website:* www.albany.edu/writers-inst (office); www.albany.edu/english (office).

KENNEDY OF THE SHAWS, Baroness (Life Peer) cr. 1997, of Cathcart in the City of Glasgow; **Helena Ann Kennedy,** QC, FRSA; British lawyer; b. 12 May 1950, Glasgow, Scotland; d. of Joshua Kennedy and Mary Jones; pnr (Roger) Iain Mitchell 1978–84; one s.; m. Dr Iain L. Hutchison 1986; one s. one d.; ed Holyrood

Secondary School, Glasgow and Council of Legal Educ.; called to the Bar, Gray's Inn 1972; mem. Bar Council 1990–93; mem. CIBA Comm. into Child Sexual Abuse 1981–83; mem. Bd City Limits Magazine 1982–84, New Statesman 1990–96, Counsel Magazine 1990–93; mem. Council, Howard League for Penal Reform 1989–, Chair. Comm. of Inquiry into Violence in Penal Insts for Young People (report 1995); Commr BAFTA inquiry into future of BBC 1990, Hamlyn Nat. Comm. on Educ. 1991–; Visiting lecturer, British Postgrad. Medical Fed. 1991–; Adviser, Mannheim Inst. on Criminology, LSE 1992–; Leader of inquiry into health, environmental and safety aspects of Atomic Weapons Establishment, Aldermaston (report 1994); Chancellor, Oxford Brookes Univ. 1994–2001; Chair. British Council 1998–2004, Human Genetics Comm. 2000–; author of official report (Learning Works) for Further Educ. Funding Council on widening participation in further educ. 1997; Pres. School of Oriental and African Studies, London Univ. 2002–; mem. Advisory Bd, Int. Centre for Prison Studies 1998; Chair. London Int. Festival of Theatre, Standing Cttee for Youth Justice 1992–97; Chair. Charter 88 1992–97; Pres. London Marriage Guidance Council, Birth Control Campaign, Nat. Children's Bureau, Hillcroft Coll.; Vice-Pres. Haldane Soc., Nat. Ass. of Women; mem. British Council's Law Advisory Cttee Advisory Bd for Study of Women and Gender, Warwick Univ., Int. Bar Asscn's Task Force on Terrorism; presenter of various programmes on radio and TV and creator of BBC drama series Blind Justice 1988; Patron, Liberty; mem. Acad. de Cultures Internationales; Hon. Fellow, Inst. of Advanced Legal Studies, Univ. of London 1997; Hon. mem. Council, Nat. Soc. for Prevention of Cruelty to Children; 18 hon. LLD from British and Irish univs; Women's Network Award 1992, UK Woman of Europe Award 1995; Campaigning and Influencing Award, Nat. Fed. of Women's Insts 1996, Times Newspaper Lifetime Achievement Award in the Law (jtly) 1997; Spectator Magazine's Parl. Campaigner of the Year 2000. *Publications:* The Bar on Trial (jtly) 1978, Child Abuse within the Family (jtly) 1984, Balancing Acts (jtly) 1989, Eve was Framed 1992, Just Law: the Changing Face of Justice and Why it Matters to Us All 2004; articles on legal matters, civil liberties and women. *Leisure interests:* theatre, spending time with family and friends. *Address:* House of Lords, London, SW1A 0PW, England (office). *Telephone:* (20) 7219-5353 (office); (1708) 379482 (home). *Fax:* (20) 7219-5979 (office); (1708) 379482 (home). *E-mail:* info@ helenakennedy.co.uk (home). *Website:* www.parliament.uk (office); www .helenakennedy.co.uk (home).

KENNETT, B(rian) L. N., PhD, ScD, FRS, FAA; British/Australian seismologist and academic; *Distinguished Professor of Seismology, Australian National University;* ed Univ. of Cambridge; Research Fellow, Emmanuel Coll. Cambridge 1972–76, Sr Research Asst, Dept of Geodesy and Geophysics 1975–76, Asst Lecturer, Dept of Applied Math. and Theoretical Physics 1976–79, Lecturer 1979–84; Professorial Fellow and Group Leader, Seismology Group, Research School of Earth Sciences, ANU, Australia 1984–91, Prof. 1991–, Pro-Vice-Chancellor and Chair. Inst. of Advanced Studies 1994–97, 2001–03, Deputy Dir Australian Nat. Seismic Imaging Resource (ANSIR) 1997–2002, Dir ANSIR Nat. Research Facility for Earth Sounding 2002–, Coordinator Earth Physics, Research School of Earth Sciences 2002–06, Distinguished Prof. of Seismology, ANU 2005–, Dir Research School of Earth Sciences 2006–10; Lindemann Trust Fellow, Visiting Asst Research Geophysicist, Univ. of California, San Diego, USA 1974–75; fmr Pres. Int. Asscn of Seismology and Physics of the Earth's Interior; Assoc., Royal Astronomical Soc. 1996–; Fellow, American Geophysical Union 1988–; numerous awards, including Commonwealth of Australia Centenary Medal, Australian Acad. of Sciences Jaeger Medal for Australian Earth Sciences 2005, Geological Soc. of London Murchison Medal 2006, European Geosciences Union Gutenberg Medal 2007, Royal Astronomical Soc. Gold Medal for Geophysics 2008, Flinder Medal and Lecture, Australian Acad. of Sciences 2011. *Publications:* Seismic Wave Propagation in Stratified Media 1983, The Seismic Wavefield: Introduction and Theoretical Development 2001, The Seismic Wavefield: Interpretation of Seismograms on Regional and Global Scales 2002, Geophysical Continua: Deformation in the Earth's Interior (co-author); more than 250 articles in scientific journals. *Address:* Research School of Earth Sciences, Australian National University, Canberra, ACT 0200, Australia (office). *Telephone:* (2) 6125-4621 (office). *Fax:* (2) 6257-2737 (office). *E-mail:* brian.kennett@anu.edu.au (office). *Website:* rses.anu.edu.au/ ~brian (office).

KENNEY, Edward John, MA, FBA; British academic; *Professor Emeritus of Latin, University of Cambridge;* b. 29 Feb. 1924, London; s. of George Kenney and Emmie Carlina Elfrida Schwenke; m. Gwyneth Anne Harris; ed Christ's Hosp. and Trinity Coll. Cambridge; served in Royal Signals, UK and India 1943–46; Asst Lecturer, Univ. of Leeds 1951–52; Research Fellow, Trinity Coll., Cambridge 1952–53, Fellow of Peterhouse 1953–91, Asst Lecturer in Classics, Univ. of Cambridge 1955–60, Lecturer 1960–70, Reader in Latin Literature and Textual Criticism 1970–74, Kennedy Prof. of Latin 1974–82, Prof. Emer. 1982–; Jt Ed. Classical Quarterly 1959–65; Jt Ed. Cambridge Greek and Latin Classics 1970–; Pres. Jt Assccn of Classical Teachers 1977–79, Classical Asscn 1982–83, Horatian Soc. 2003–07; Treas. and Chair. Council of Almoners, Christ's Hosp. 1984–86; Foreign mem. Royal Netherlands Acad. of Arts and Sciences. *Publications:* P. Ovidi Nasonis Amores, etc. 1961 (second edn 1995), Lucretius, de Rerum Natura III 1971 (second edn 2014), The Classical Text 1974 (Italian trans. 1995), The Cambridge History of Classical Literature, Vol. II, Latin Literature (ed. and contrib.) 1982, The Ploughman's Lunch (Moretum) 1984, Ovid, Metamorphoses– Introduction and Notes 1986, Ovid, The Love Poems – Introduction and Notes 1990, Apuleius, Cupid & Psyche 1990, Ovid, Sorrows of an Exile (Tristia) – Introduction and Notes 1992, Ovid, Heroides xvi–xxi 1996, Apuleius, The Golden Ass –Trans. with Introduction and Notes 1998, Ovidio, Metamorfosi VII–IX 2011; numerous articles and reviews. *Leisure interests:* discursive reading, listening to the wireless. *Address:* Peterhouse, Cambridge, CB2 1RD (office); 4 Belvoir Terrace, Trumpington Road, Cambridge, CB2 7AA, England (home).

KENNEY, The Hon. Jason; Canadian politician; *Minister of Employment and Social Development;* b. 30 May 1968, Oakville, Ont.; fmr Exec. Dir Sask. Taxpayers Asscn and Pres. Canadian Taxpayers Fed.; fmr mem. Sask. Liberal Party, mem. Reform Party of Canada 1997–2000, Canadian Alliance 2000–03, Conservative Party of Canada 2003–; mem. Parl. for Calgary Southeast 1997–; served in Shadow Cabinet 1997–2005, positions included Deputy House Leader for the Official Opposition, critic for Canada–US relations, for Nat. Revenue and for Finance; Minister for Citizenship, Immigration and Multiculturalism 2008–13, Minister of Employment and Social Devt 2013–. *Address:* Conservative Party of Canada, 130 Albert Street, Suite 1204, Ottawa, ON K1P 5G4, Canada (office). *Telephone:* (613) 755-2000 (office). *Fax:* (613) 755-2001 (office). *Website:* www.conservative.ca (office).

KENNICUTT, Robert C., Jr, BS, MS, PhD, FRS; American astronomer and academic; *Head of School of the Physical Sciences and Plumian Professor of Astronomy and Experimental Philosophy, University of Cambridge;* b. 4 Sept. 1951, Baltimore, Md; m. Norma Kennicutt 1976 (divorced); one d.; ed Rensselaer Polytechnic Inst., Univ. of Washington; Carnegie Postdoctoral Fellow, Hale Observatories, Pasadena, Calif. 1978–80; Adjunct Research Fellow, California Inst. of Tech. 1978–80; Asst Prof., Dept of Astronomy, Univ. of Minnesota 1980–85, Assoc. Prof. 1985–88; Assoc. Prof. and Astronomer, Steward Observatory, Univ. of Arizona 1988–92, Deputy Head, Dept of Astronomy 1991–98, Prof. and Astronomer, Steward Observatory 1992–2006; Beatrice M. Tinsley Centennial Prof., Univ. of Texas 1994; Adriaan Blaauw Prof., Univ. of Groningen, The Netherlands 2001; Plumian Prof. of Astronomy and Experimental Philosophy, Univ. of Cambridge 2005–, Dir Inst. of Astronomy 2008–11, Head of School of the Physical Sciences 2012–; Professorial Fellow, Churchill Coll. 2007–; Visiting Fellow, Leiden Observatory, Univ. of Leiden 1982; Ed.-in-Chief The Astrophysical Journal 1999–2006; mem. Int. Advisory Cttee, Chinese Journal of Astronomy and Astrophysics 2002–08, Astrophysics Series Editorial Bd, Cambridge University Press 2007–; Chair., Herschel Space Observatory Users' Group 2009–; mem. or chair. numerous cttees and bds, including Science Oversight Cttee, NASA Next Generation Space Telescope Study 1996–98, Spitzer Legacy Science Working Group 2001–, NSF Nat. Virtual Observatory Advisory Cttee 2002–06, Space Telescope Science Inst. Dir Search Cttee 2004–05, Gemini Observatory Visiting Cttee 2004, Wissenschaftlicher Beirat, Astrophyikalishe Institut, Potsdam 2006–, Int. Advisory Bd Netherlands Research School for Astronomy 2007–, Nat. Radio Astronomy Observatory Visiting Cttee 2008–, NRC/NAS Astronomy 2010 Decadal Survey Cttee 2008–10, NAS Section 12 Nominating Cttee 2008–11, RAS Awards Cttee 2008–10, STFC Groundbased Astronomy Facilities Review Panel 2009, AAS Russell Lectureship Prize Cttee 2010–12; numerous lectureships including Dept of Astrophysical Sciences, Princeton Univ. 1990, Canary Islands Winter School in Astronomy 1991, 26th Saas Fee Advanced Course 1996, Les Houches Summer School 1996, Intelligence Agents Group Advanced School on Star Formation, Sao Paulo, Brazil 1998, Dept of Astronomy, Univ. of Wisconsin 2002, Faculty, 9th Vatican Summer School in Observational Astronomy and Astrophysics 2002–03; mem. NAS 2006, American Astronomical Soc. (Vice-Pres. 1998–2001), Int. Astronomical Union, Astronomical Soc. of the Pacific; Fellow, American Acad. of Arts and Sciences 2001; Carnegie Fellowship 1978–80, Alfred P. Sloan Fellowship 1983–87, Gruber Cosmology Prize (with Freedman and Mould) 2009, Dannie Heineman Prize in Astrophysics 2007. *Publications:* as co-author: Galaxies: Interactions and Induced Star Formation 1998, Hubble's Science Legacy: Future Optical/Ultraviolet Astronomy from Space 2002; numerous contribs to science journals. *Address:* Institute of Astronomy, University of Cambridge, Hoyle Building, Room 49, Madingley Road, Cambridge, CB3 0HA, England (office). *Telephone:* (1223) 765844 (office). *Fax:* (1223) 339910 (office). *E-mail:* robk@ast .cam.ac.uk (office). *Website:* www.ast.cam.ac.uk/~robk (office).

KENNY, Sir Anthony John Patrick, Kt, DPhil, FBA; British philosopher and academic; b. 16 March 1931, Liverpool, England; s. of John Kenny and Margaret Kenny (née Jones); m. Nancy Caroline Gayley 1966; two s.; ed Gregorian Univ., Rome, Italy, St Benet's Hall, Oxford; ordained Catholic priest, Rome 1955; curate, Liverpool 1959–63; returned to lay state 1963; Asst Lecturer, Univ. of Liverpool 1961–63; Lecturer in Philosophy, Exeter and Trinity Colls, Oxford 1963–64; Tutor in Philosophy, Balliol Coll., Oxford 1964, Fellow 1964–78, Sr Tutor 1971–72, 1976–77, Master 1978–89; Warden Rhodes House 1989–99; Professorial Fellow, St John's Coll., Oxford 1989–99; Pro-Vice-Chancellor, Univ. of Oxford 1984–99, Pro-Vice Chancellor for Devt 1999–2001; Wilde Lecturer in Natural and Comparative Religion, Oxford 1969–72; Jt Gifford Lecturer, Univ. of Edinburgh 1972–73; Stanton Lecturer, Univ. of Cambridge 1980–83; Speaker's Lecturer in Biblical Studies, Univ. of Oxford 1980–83; Visiting Prof., Stanford, Cornell and Rockefeller Univs and Univs of Chicago, Washington and Michigan; Vice-Pres. British Acad. 1986–88, Pres. 1989–93; Chair. Bd British Library 1993–96 (mem. Bd 1991–96); Pres. Royal Inst. of Philosophy 2005–09; Del. and mem. of Finance Cttee, Oxford Univ. Press 1986–93; Ed. The Oxford Magazine 1972–93; mem. Royal Norwegian Acad. 1993–, American Philosophical Soc. 1994–, American Acad. of Arts and Sciences 2003–; Hon. Bencher, Lincoln's Inn 1999; Hon. DLitt (Bristol) 1982, (Denison Univ.) 1986, (Liverpool) 1988, (Glasgow) 1990, (Lafayette) 1990, (Trinity Coll., Dublin) 1992, (Hull) 1993, (Belfast) 1994; Hon. DCL (Oxford) 1987; Hon. DLit (London) 2002; Hon. DD (Liverpool Hope) 2010; Aquinas Medal 1996. *Publications:* Action, Emotion and Will 1963, Responsa Alumnorum of English College, Rome (two vols) 1963, Descartes 1968, The Five Ways 1969, Wittgenstein 1973, The Anatomy of the Soul 1974, Will, Freedom and Power 1975, Aristotelian Ethics 1978, Freewill and Responsibility 1978, The God of the Philosophers 1979, Aristotle's Theory of the Will 1979, Aquinas 1980, The Computation of Style 1982, Faith and Reason 1983, Thomas More 1983, The Legacy of Wittgenstein 1984, A Path from Rome 1985, The Logic of Deterrence 1985, The Ivory Tower 1985, Wyclif – Past Master 1985, Wyclif's De Universalibus 1985, Rationalism, Empiricism and Idealism 1986, Wyclif in His Times 1986, The Road to Hillsborough 1986, Reason and Religion (essays) 1987, The Heritage of Wisdom 1987, God and Two Poets 1988, The Metaphysics of Mind 1989, Mountains 1991, What is Faith? 1992, Aristotle on the Perfect Life 1992, Aquinas on Mind 1992, The Oxford Illustrated History of Western Philosophy (ed.) 1994, Frege 1995, A Life in Oxford 1997, A Brief History of Western Philosophy 1998, Essays on the Aristotelian Tradition 2001, Aquinas on Being 2002, The Unknown God 2003, A New History of Western Philosophy (one vol.) 2003, A New History of Western Philosophy Vol. 1: Ancient Philosophy 2004, Vol. 2: Medieval Philosophy 2005, Arthur Hugh Clough: A Poet's Life 2005, What I Believe 2006, Life, Liberty and the Pursuit of Utility (with C. Kenny) 2006, The Rise of Modern Philosophy 2006, Philosophy in the Modern World 2007, Can Oxford Be Improved? (with R. Kenny) 2007, From Empedocles to Wittgenstein: Historical Essays in Philosophy 2008, Aristotle, Eudemian Ethics (ed. and trans.) 2011 Aristotle Poetics (ed. and trans.) 2013. *Address:* 1A Larkins Lane, Headington, Oxford, OX3 9DW, England. *Telephone:* (1865) 764174. *E-mail:* anthonyjpkenny@gmail.com.

KENNY, Gen. Sir Brian (Leslie Graham), Kt, GCB, CBE; British army officer (retd); b. 18 June 1934; s. of late Brig. James W. Kenny, CBE and Aileen A. G. Swan; m. Diana C. J. Mathew 1958; two s.; ed Canford School; commissioned into 4th Hussars (later Queen's Royal Irish Hussars) 1954; served British Army of the Rhine (BAOR), Aden, Malaya, Borneo and Cyprus; pilot's course 1961; Ministry of Defence 1966–68; Instructor Staff Coll. 1971–73; CO Queen's Royal Irish Hussars (QRIH), BAOR and UN, Cyprus 1974–76; Col G.S. 4 Armoured Div. 1977–78; Command, 12 Armoured Brigade (Task Force D) 1979–80; Royal Coll. of Defence Studies 1981; Commdr 1st Armoured Div. 1982–83; Dir Army Staff Duties, Ministry of Defence 1983–85; Command, 1st British Corps 1985–87; C-in-C BAOR and Commdr NATO's Northern Army Group 1987–89; Deputy Supreme Allied Commdr Europe 1990–93; Col Commandant RAVC 1983–95; Col QRIH 1985–93; Col Commandant RAC 1988–93; Gov. Royal Hosp. Chelsea 1993–99, Gov. Canford School 1988–; Chair. ABF 1993–99; Dir (non-exec.) Dorset Ambulance Trust 2000–; Bath King of Arms 1999–2009. *Leisure interests:* theatre, cricket, tennis, golf, shooting, racing. *Address:* c/o Lloyds Bank, Camberley, Surrey, GU15 3SE, England (office).

KENNY, Enda; Irish politician; *Taoiseach (Prime Minister);* b. 24 April 1951, Castlebar, Co. Mayo; s. of the late Henry Kenny; m. Fionnuala O'Kelly; two s. one d.; ed St Patrick's Coll. of Educ., Dublin, Univ. Coll. Galway; began career as primary school teacher; mem. Dáil Eireann (Fine Gael) for Mayo 1975–; Minister of State, Dept of Educ. and Labour 1986–87; Minister for Tourism and Trade 1994–97; Taoiseach (Prime Minister) 2011–, Acting Defence Minister 2014; mem. Fine Gael, Pres. and Leader 2002–; Vice-Pres. European People's Party. *Leisure interests:* hill walking, cycling, golf, mountain climbing (has climbed Kilimanjaro for charity). *Address:* Department of the Taoiseach, Government Bldgs, Upper Merrion Street, 1008 Dublin 2, Ireland (office). *Telephone:* (1) 6194000 (office). *Fax:* (1) 6194297 (office). *E-mail:* webmaster@taoiseach.gov.ie (office). *Website:* www .taoiseach.gov.ie (office).

KENT, Bruce Eric, PhD; Australian historian and academic; *Distinguished Fellow, National Europe Centre, Australian National University;* b. 15 Feb. 1932, Melbourne, Vic.; s. of Rev. Eric Deacon Kent and Beatrice Maude Kent; m. Ann Elizabeth Garland 1966; two s.; ed Geelong Grammar School, Melbourne Univ., Univ. of Oxford, UK, Australian Nat. Univ.; Tutor in History, Univ. of Melbourne 1954–55; Lecturer in History, ANU 1962–70, Sr Lecturer 1970–90, Reader 1990–, Acting Head of History Dept 1984, Visiting Fellow, Dept of Econ. History 1998, now Distinguished Fellow, Nat. Europe Centre; Fulbright Visiting Fellow, Hoover Inst., Stanford Univ. and History Dept, Princeton Univ., USA 1970; Visiting Lecturer, East China Normal Univ., Shanghai 1975–76; Pres. Australian Asscn of European Historians 1984–86; Visiting Fellow, Center of Int. Studies, Princeton Univ., USA, 1996; Victorian Rhodes Scholar 1955. *Publication:* The Spoils of War: The Politics, Economics and Diplomacy of Reparations, 1918–1932 1989. *Leisure interests:* violin, cricket, surfing. *Address:* 4/3 Tasmania Circle, Forrest, ACT 2603 (home); National Europe Centre, 1 Liversidge Street, Building 67C, Australian National University, Canberra, ACT 0200, Australia (office). *Telephone:* (2) 6273-1019 (home); (2) 6260-6222 (home); (2) 6125-6697 (office). *Fax:* (2) 6125-5792 (office). *E-mail:* bruce.kent@anu.edu.au (office). *Website:* www.anu.edu.au/NEC (office).

KENT, HRH The Duke of (Prince Edward George Nicholas Paul Patrick), Earl of St Andrew's, Baron Downpatrick, KG, GCMG, GCVO, ADC; b. 9 Oct. 1935; s. of the late Duke of Kent (fourth s. of King George V) and Princess Marina (d. of the late Prince Nicholas of Greece); m. Katherine Worsley 1961; two s. (George, Earl of St Andrew's and Lord Nicholas Windsor) one d. (Lady Helen Windsor); ed Eton Coll. and Le Rosey, Switzerland; Second Lt, Royal Scots Greys 1955; attended Army Staff Course 1966, later on staff, GOC Eastern Command, Hounslow, Major 1967; Lt-Col Royal Scots Dragoon Guards 1972, Maj. Gen. 1983, Deputy Col-in-Chief 1993–; rank of Field Marshal 1993; Ministry of Defence 1972–76; Chair. Nat. Electronics Council 1977–; Vice-Chair. British Overseas Trade Bd 1976–; Pres. All-England Lawn Tennis Club 1969–, Commonwealth War Graves Comm., RNLI 1969–, Football Asscn 1971–, Automobile Asscn 1973–, RAF Benevolent Fund 1974–, Scout Assn 1975–, Royal Inst. of Great Britain 1976–, Business and Technicians Educ. Council 1984–, Eng Council 1989–, British Menswear Guild 1989–; Hon. Pres. Royal Geographical Soc. 1969–; Dir Vickers; Chancellor Univ. of Surrey 1977–; Patron Inst. of Export 1977–, Kent Opera 1978–, The London Philharmonic 1980–, Anglo-Jordanian Soc. 1982–, The Hanover Band 1992–, Anglo-German Asscn 1994; as Queen's Special Rep. has visited Sierra Leone 1961, Uganda 1962, The Gambia 1965, Guyana and Barbados 1966, Tonga 1967; ADC to HM The Queen 1967; Grand Master of the United Grand Lodge of England 1967–; Col-in-Chief Royal Regt of Fusiliers 1969–, Devonshire and Dorset Regt 1978–, Lorne Scots Regt 1978–; Col Scots Guards 1974; Hon. DCL (Durham), Hon. LLD (Leeds), DUniv (York);Colonel-in-Chief, The Royal Regiment of Fusiliers 1969, Colonel, Scots Guards 1974, Colonel-in-Chief, The Devonshire and Dorset Regiment 1977, Colonel-in-Chief, The Lorne Scots (Peel, Dufferin and Hamilton Regiment) 1977, Hon. Air Vice Marshal, Royal Air Force 1985, Colonel-in-Chief, The Royal Scots Dragoon Guards 1994, Honorary Air Commodore, RAF Leuchars 1993, Hon. Air Chief Marshal, RAF 1996; King George VI and Queen Elizabeth Coronation Medal 1937, Queen Elizabeth II Coronation Medal 1953, Queen Elizabeth II Golden Jubilee Medal 2002; The Order of St George and St Constantine, 1st class (Greece), The Most Illustrious Order of Tri Shakti Patta, 1st class (Nepal) 1960, Knight Grand Band, the Order of the Star of Africa (Liberia) 1962, Grand Cordon, the Order of the Renaissance (Jordan) 1966, Grand Cross, the Order of St Olav (Norway) 1988, Grand Cross, the Order of Merit of the Republic of Poland (Poland) 1999. *Leisure interests:* skiing, shooting, photography, opera. *Address:* York House, St James's Palace, London, SW1A 1BQ, England.

KENT, Jonathan; theatre and opera director; b. 1951, Cape Town, SA; ed Cen. School of Speech and Drama, London; began career as actor, Glasgow Citizens 1970s; Jt Artistic Dir (with Ian McDiarmid) The Almeida Theatre, London 1990–2002; freelance dir 2002–. *Plays include:* as Artistic Dir, Almeida Theatre: When We Dead Awaken 1990, All for Love 1991, The Rules of the Game 1992, Medea (also West End, Broadway) 1992, Chatsky 1993, The Showman 1993, The School for Wives 1993, The Life of Galileo 1994, Gangster No. 1 1995, Tartuffe 1996, Ivanov (also Moscow) 1997, The Government Inspector 1997, Naked (also West End) 1998, Phèdre 1998, Britannicus (West End, New York) 1998, The

Tempest 2000, Hamlet (also Broadway), Richard II 2000, Coriolanus (also New York, Tokyo) 2000, Plenty (West End), 2000, Lulu (also Washington) 2001, Platonov 2001, Faith Healer 2001, King Lear 2002; other plays as dir: Le Cid (Nat. Theatre) 1994, Mother Courage and Her Children (Nat. Theatre) 1995, Hamlet 1995, (Japan) 2003, Man of La Mancha (Broadway) 2002, The Paris Letter (New York) 2003, Hecuba (Donmar) 2004, The False Servant 2004, As You Desire Me (West End) 2005, Faith Healer (Dublin and Broadway) 2006, The Country Wife (Theatre Royal Haymarket) 2007, The Sea (Theatre Royal Haymarket) 2008, Marguerite 2008 (Theatre Royal Haymarket) 2008, Oedipus (Nat. Theatre) 2008, A Month in the Country (Chichester Festival) 2010, The Emperor and Galilean (Nat. Theatre) 2011, Sweeney Todd (Chichester, Adelphi) 2011–12. *Operas directed include:* Katya Kabanová (Santa Fe) 2003, The Tempest 2005, Child of Our Time (Santa Fe) 2005, Lucio Silla (Santa Fe) 2005, Tosca (ROH) 2006, Turn of the Screw (Glyndebourne) 2006, The Marriage of Figaro (Santa Fe) 2008, Elektra (Mariinsky St. Petersburg) 2008, The Fairy Queen (Glyndebourne, Paris, New York) 2009, Don Giovanni (Glyndebourne) 2010, The Flying Dutchman (ENO) 2011, Die Frau ohne Schatten (Mariinsky St. Petersburg) 2011. *Address:* c/o St John Donald, United Agents, 12–26 Lexington Street, London, W1F 0LE, England (office). *Telephone:* (20) 3214-0800 (office). *Fax:* (20) 3214-0801 (office). *E-mail:* info@unitedagents.co.uk (office). *Website:* www.unitedagents.co.uk (office).

KENT, Muhtar A., BSc, MSc; Turkish/American business executive; *Chairman and CEO, Coca-Cola Company;* b. 1952, New York City; m. Defne Kent; two c.; ed Univ. of Hull, London City Univ., UK; joined Coca-Cola Co., Atlanta, Ga 1978, Gen. Man. Coca-Cola Turkey and Cen. Asia 1985–89, Pres. East Cen. Europe Div. and Sr Vice-Pres. Coca-Cola Int. 1989–95, Man. Dir Coca-Cola Amatil-Europe 1995–98, Pres. and CEO Efes Beverage Group (majority owner of Turkish bottler Coca-Cola Icecek) 1999–2005, Pres. and COO Coca-Cola N Asia, Eurasia and Middle East Group 2005–06, Pres. Coca-Cola International Jan.–Dec. 2006, Pres. and COO Coca-Cola Co., Atlanta 2006–08, Pres. and CEO 2008–09, Chair. and CEO 2009–; Chair. Int. Business Council of the World Econ. Forum; past Chair. US-China Business Council; Chair. Emer. US ASEAN Business Council, mem. Eminent Persons Group for ASEAN; Co-Chair. Bipartisan Policy Center's CEO Council on Health and Innovation; immediate past Co-Chair. The Consumer Goods Forum; mem. Bd of Dirs 3M, Special Olympics International, Ronald McDonald House Charities, Catalyst, Emory Univ.; mem. Business Roundtable; Fellow, Foreign Policy Asscn; Hon. LLD (Oglethorpe Univ., Atlanta), Hon. DEcon (Univ. of Hull). *Address:* The Coca-Cola Co., 1 Coca-Cola Plaza, Atlanta, GA 30313-2499, USA (office). *Telephone:* (404) 676-2121 (office). *Fax:* (404) 676-6792 (office). *E-mail:* info@thecoca-colacompany.com (office). *Website:* www.thecoca -colacompany.com (office).

KENT, The Hon. Peter, PC; Canadian broadcaster and politician; b. 27 July 1943, Sussex, England; s. of Parker Kent; m. Cilla Kent; one d.; began career as radio journalist in early 1960s; joined CFCN-TV, Calgary 1965; spent several years as freelance foreign corresp. correspondent, later Anchor, CBC News programme The National 1976–78; Founding producer, corresp. and co-host The Journal, CBC 1982–84; European corresp., NBC in late 1980s; MP for Thornhill (Ont.) 2008–; Minister of the Environment 2011–13; mem. Bd ParticipACTION, Ontario Cabinet of Canadian Museum for Human Rights, Honest Reporting Canada, The Accessible Channel; mem. Conservative Party of Canada; Robert F. Kennedy Journalism Award 1991, Radio-Television News Dirs Asscn of Canada Pres.'s Award 2006. *Website:* www.peterkent.ca.

KENTRIDGE, Sir Sydney, Kt, KCMG, QC, MA; British lawyer; b. 5 Nov. 1922, Johannesburg, South Africa; s. of Morris Kentridge and May Kentridge; m. Felicia Geffen 1952; two s. two d.; ed King Edward VII School, Johannesburg, Univ. of the Witwatersrand and Exeter Coll., Oxford; war service with S African forces 1942–46; Advocate, SA 1949, Sr Counsel 1965; called to Bar, Lincoln's Inn, London 1977, Bencher 1986; Queen's Counsel, England 1984; Judge, Court of Appeal, Jersey and Guernsey 1988–92; mem. Court of Appeal, Botswana 1981–89, Constitutional Court, SA 1995–97; Roberts Lecturer, Univ. of Pa 1979; Hon. Fellow American Coll. of Trial Lawyers 1998; Hon. Fellow Exeter Coll., Oxford 1986; Hon. mem. Bar Asscn New York City 2001; Hon. LLD (Leicester) 1985, (Cape Town) 1987, (Natal) 1989, (London) 1995, (Sussex) 1997, (Witwatersrand) 2000, (Buckingham) 2009; Order of the Baobab (Gold), S Africa; Granville Clark Prize, USA 1978. *Publications:* Free Country: Selected Lectures and Talks 2012. *Leisure interests:* opera, theatre. *Address:* 7–8 Essex Street, London, WC2R 3LD, England. *Telephone:* (20) 7379-3550. *Fax:* (20) 7379-3558.

KENTRIDGE, William, BA; South African artist; b. 1955, Johannesburg; ed King Edward VII School, Houghton, Johannesburg, Univ. of the Witwatersrand, diploma in Fine Arts from Johannesburg Art Foundation, studied mime and theatre at École Internationale de Théâtre Jacques Lecoq, Paris, France; best known for his animated films, constructed by filming a drawing, making erasures and changes, and filming it again; drawings later displayed along with the films as finished pieces of art; Founder mem. Junction Avenue Theatre Co., Johannesburg 1975–91; worked on TV films and series as art dir 1980s; cr. 20 to 30 monotypes, which soon became known as the 'Pit' series 1979; executed about 50 small-format etchings, the 'Domestic Scenes' 1980; cr. first animated film, Johannesburg, 2nd Greatest City After Paris, in series Drawings for Projection 1989; staged first theatre project in conjunction with Handspring Puppet Co. 1992; animations deal with political and social themes from a personal viewpoint, often including self-portrait in his works; series of nine short films introduces two characters, Soho Eckstein and Felix Teitlebaum who depict an emotional and political struggle that reflects the lives of many South Africans in the pre-democracy era; co-f. Free Film-makers Co-Operative, Johannesburg 1985; staged first opera, Return of Ulysses, Brussels, Belgium 1998; apptd a film-maker by Stereoscope 1999; staged Il ritorno d'Ulisse in patria (Monteverdi), Die Zauberflöte (Mozart) and The Nose (Shostakovich); also made a short show with French composer François Sarhan called Telegrams from the Nose; Red Ribbon Award for Short Fiction 1982, Market Theatre Award for New Vision exhbn 1986, AA Vita Award, Cassirer Fine Art 1986, Standard Bank Young Artist Award 1987, Woyzeck on the Highveld Awards for production, set design and direction 1992, Loerie Award Memo 1994, Five Themes exhibit included in TIME 100 2009, Five Themes exhibit awarded First Place in AICA (Int. Asscn of Art Critics Awards) Best Monographic Museum Show Nationally category 2009. *Films:* Johannesburg: 2nd Greatest City After Paris

1989, Monument 1990, Mine 1991, Sobriety, Obesity & growing old 1991, Felix in Exile 1994, History of the Main Complaint 1996, Ubu Tells the Truth 1996–97, Weighing and Waiting 1998, Stereoscope 1999, Medicine Chest 2001, Automatic Writing 2003, films shown at Cannes Film Festival 2004. *Address:* c/o Robert Brown Gallery, 2219 California Street, NW, #32, Washington, DC 20008, USA. *Telephone:* (202) 483-0722. *E-mail:* info@robertbrowngallery.com. *Website:* www .robertbrowngallery.com.

KENWORTHY, Duncan, OBE, MA, FRSA; British film producer; *Managing Director, Toledo Productions Ltd;* b. 9 Sept. 1949; s. of Bernard Ian Kenworthy and Edna Muriel Kenworthy (née Calligan); ed Rydal School North Wales, Christ's Coll., Cambridge, Annenberg School, Univ. of Pennsylvania, USA; Children's Television Workshop, New York 1973–76; Consulting Producer, Arabic Sesame Street, Kuwait 1977–79; Producer and Exec., Jim Henson Productions, London 1979–95; Producer and Man. Dir Toledo Productions Ltd 1995–; Dir DNA Films Ltd 1997–2008; mem. Council of Man., BAFTA 1996–2006, Chair. BAFTA Film Cttee 2002–04, Chair. BAFTA 2004–06, Vice-Pres. BAFTA 2009–; Chair. British Council Film Advisory Cttee 1999–2008, Dir Film Council 1999–2003, mem. Film Policy Review Group 1997–99; Gov. Nat. Film and TV School 2001–; mem. UK-China Forum 2000–01, Shanghai Film Festival Jury 2006; British Producer of the Year, London Film Critics 1994. *Films include:* The Dark Crystal (assoc producer) 1980, Four Weddings and a Funeral (Best Film, and Lloyds Bank Peoples' Choice Award, BAFTA 1994, Best Foreign Film, Cesar Award 1994) 1994, Lawn Dogs 1997, Notting Hill (BAFTA Orange Audience Award 2000) 1999, The Parole Officer 2001, Heartlands (exec. producer) 2002, Love Actually 2003, The Eagle 2011. *Television includes:* Fraggle Rock (Emmy Award for Outstanding Children's Programming 1983) 1982, The Storyteller (BAFTA Award for Best Children's Programme 1989) 1986–88; Living with Dinosaurs (Emmy Award for Best Children's Programme 1990) 1988, Monster Maker 1988, Greek Myths (BAFTA for Best Children's Fictional Programme 1991) 1990, Gulliver's Travels (Emmy Award for Outstanding Mini-series 1996) 1996. *Address:* Toledo Productions Ltd, Suite 44, 10 Richmond Mews, London, W1D 3DD, England (office). *Telephone:* (20) 7851-6677 (office). *Fax:* (20) 7437-7740 (office). *E-mail:* info@toledoproductions .com (office).

KENWRIGHT, Bill, CBE; British theatre producer; b. 4 Sept. 1945; s. of Albert Kenwright and Hope Kenwright (née Jones); ed Liverpool Inst.; actor 1964–70; theatre producer 1970–; Vice-Chair. Everton Football Club; Dr hc (Liverpool John Moores) 1994. *Films directed include:* Stepping Out, Don't Go Breaking My Heart 1999. *Plays directed include:* Joseph and The Amazing Technicolor Dreamcoat 1979, The Business of Murder 1981, A Streetcar Named Desire 1984, Stepping Out 1984, Blood Brothers 1988, Shirley Valentine 1989, Travels With My Aunt 1993, Piaf 1993, Lysistrata 1993, Medea 1993, Pygmalion 1997, A Doll's House, An Ideal Husband, The Chairs 2000, Ghosts, The Female Odd Couple. *Leisure interest:* football. *Address:* Bill Kenwright Ltd, 106 Harrow Road, London, W2 1RR, England (office). *Telephone:* (20) 7446-6200 (office). *Fax:* (20) 7446-6222 (office). *Website:* www.kenwright.com (office).

KENYATTA, Uhuru; Kenyan politician and head of state; *President and Commander-in-Chief of the Armed Forces;* b. 1961; s. of the late fmr Pres. Jomo Kenyatta; Chair. Kenya Tourism Bd 1999; nominated MP by Pres. Daniel arap Moi (q.v.); apptd Minister of Local Govt 2001; Vice-Chair. Kenya African Nat. Union (KANU) 2002, then Acting Pres., Pres. 2005–06, 2007–; named heir apparent by Pres. Moi July 2002, failed to be elected in presidential elections Dec. 2002; Deputy Prime Minister 2008–13, also Minister of Trade 2008–09, Minister of Finance 2009–12 (resgnd); Pres. of Kenya and C-in-C of the Armed Forces 2013–. *Address:* Office of the President, Harambee House, Harambee Avenue, POB 62345, 00200 Nairobi, Kenya (office). *Telephone:* (20) 2227411 (office). *E-mail:* president@ statehousekenya.go.ke (office). *Website:* www.statehousekenya.go.ke (office).

KENYON, Sir Nicholas Roger, Kt, CBE, BA; British arts administrator; *Managing Director, Barbican Centre;* b. 23 Feb. 1951, Altrincham, Cheshire; s. of Thomas Kenyon and Kathleen Holmes; m. Marie-Ghislaine Latham-Koenig 1976; three s. one d.; ed Balliol Coll., Oxford; music critic, The New Yorker 1979–82, The Times 1982–85, The Observer 1985–92; Music Ed. The Listener 1982–87; Ed. Early Music 1983–92; programme adviser, Mozart Now Festival, South Bank, London 1991; Controller, BBC Radio 3 1992–98, Dir BBC Proms 1996–2007, Controller BBC Millennium Programmes 1998–2000, BBC Live Events and TV Classical Music 2000–07; Man. Dir Barbican Centre, London 2007–; mem. Bd ENO 2005–; Gov. Wellington School; Royal Philharmonic Soc. Awards for Fairest Isle (BBC Radio 3) 1996 and Sounding the Century 2000. *Publications:* The BBC Symphony Orchestra 1930–80 1981, Simon Rattle: The Making of a Conductor (revised edn as Simon Rattle: From Birmingham to Berlin 2001), Authenticity and Early Music (ed.) 1988, The Viking Opera Guide (co-ed.) 1993, The Penguin Opera Guide (co-ed.) 1995, Musical Lives (ed.) 2001, The BBC Proms Guide to Great Concertos (ed.) 2003, The BBC Proms Pocket Guide to Great Symphonies (ed.) 2003, The Faber Pocket Guide to Mozart 2005, The Faber Pocket Guide to Bach 2011. *Address:* Barbican Centre, Silk Street, London, EC2Y 8DS, England (office). *Telephone:* (20) 7382-7005 (office). *E-mail:* nkenyon@barbican.org.uk (office). *Website:* www.barbican.org.uk (office).

KENZO, Takada; Japanese fashion designer; b. (Kenzo Takada), 1940, Kyoto; ed Bunka Fashion Coll., Tokyo; after graduating designed patterns for a Tokyo magazine; moved to Paris 1964; created own freelance collections and sold designs to Louis Féraud 1964–70; opened boutique Jungle Jap, Paris 1970; noted for translating traditional designs into original contemporary garments and for ready-to-wear knitwear; Head of Kenzo fashion house until retirement in 1999; cr. Yume label 2002. *Film:* Yume, Yume no Ato (dir and writer) 1981. *Address:* c/o KENZO, 1 rue de Pont Neuf, 75001 Paris, France (office).

KEOHANE, Nannerl, PhD; American academic and fmr university president; *Senior Scholar in the Woodrow Wilson School and University Center for Human Values, Princeton University;* b. 18 Sept. 1940, Blytheville, Ark.; d. of James Arthur Overholser and Grace Overholser (née McSpadden); m. 1st Patrick Henry, III 1962 (divorced 1969); m. 2nd Robert O. Keohane 1970; three s. one d.; ed Wellesley Coll., St Anne's Coll., Oxford, UK, Yale Univ.; mem. Faculty, Swarthmore Coll. 1967–73, Stanford Univ. 1973–81, Fellow, Center for Advanced Study in the Behavioral Sciences, Stanford Univ. 1978–79, 1987–88, 2004–05

(mem. Bd of Trustees 1991–97, 2004–11, Vice-Chair. 2008–11); Pres. and Prof. of Political Science, Wellesley Coll. 1981–93, Duke Univ. 1993–2004; Laurance S. Rockefeller Distinguished Visiting Prof. of Public Affairs in the Woodrow Wilson School and the Univ. Center for Human Values, Princeton Univ. 2004–13, Sr Scholar 2013–; mem. Harvard Corpn (Pres. and Fellows of Harvard Coll.) and Fellow, Harvard Coll. 2005–; mem. Bd of Dirs IBM 1986–2004, Bd of Trustees, The Colonial Williamsburg Foundation 1988–2001, The Nat. Humanities Center 1993–2004; mem. MIT Corpn 1992–97, Doris Duke Charitable Foundation 1996– (Chair. 2007–10), Overseers Cttee to Visit the John F. Kennedy School of Govt 1996–2004 (Chair. 2001–03); Fellow, American Acad. of Arts and Sciences, American Philosophical Soc.; Hon. Fellow, St Anne's Coll., Oxford; Dr hc from several univs and colleges; Marshall Scholar 1961–63, Wilbur Cross Medal, Yale Univ., Nat. Women's Hall of Fame 1995, Golden Plate Award, American Acad. of Achievement 1998, Marshall Medal, Clark Kerr Medal, Univ. of California, Berkeley 2006. *Leisure interests:* travel, theatre, music, art, grandchildren, hiking, cycling. *Address:* Woodrow Wilson School, 429 Robertson Hall, Princeton University, Princeton, NJ 08544-1013, USA (office). *Telephone:* (609) 258-8974 (office). *Fax:* (609) 258-0390 (office). *E-mail:* nkeohane@princeton.edu (office). *Website:* wws.princeton.edu (office).

KEOHANE, Robert Owen, BA, MA, PhD; American political scientist and academic; *Professor of International Affairs, Woodrow Wilson School, Princeton University;* b. 3 Oct. 1941, Chicago, Ill.; s. of Robert Emmet Keohane and Marie Irene Keohane (née Pieters); m. Nannerl Overholser 1970; three s. one d.; ed Shimer Coll., Illinois, Harvard Univ.; Fellow, Harvard Univ., Woodrow Wilson School of Public and Int. Affairs, Princeton Univ. 1961–62; mem. Woodrow Wilson Award Cttee 1982, Chair. Nominating Cttee 1990–91, Chair. Minority Identification Project 1990–92; Instructor, then Assoc. Prof., Swarthmore Coll. 1965–73; Assoc. Prof., then Prof., Stanford Univ. 1973–81; Ed. Int. Org. 1974–80, mem. Bd Eds 1968–77, 1982–88, 1992–97, 1998–, Chair. 1986–87; Prof., Brandeis Univ. 1981–85; Pres. Int. Studies Asscn 1988–89, Chair. Nominations Cttee 1985; Prof., then Stanfield Prof. of Int. Peace, Harvard Univ. 1985–96, Chair. Dept of Govt 1988–92; James B. Duke Prof. of Political Science, Duke Univ. –2004; Prof. of Int. Affairs, Woodrow Wilson School, Princeton Univ. 2004–; Sherill Lecturer, Yale Univ. Law School 1996; Pres. American Political Science Asscn 1999–2000; mem. NAS 2005; Frank Kenan Fellow, Nat. Endowment for the Humanities 1995–96; Harold Lasswell Fellow, American Acad. of Political and Social Science 2007–08; Fellow, American Acad. of Arts and Sciences 1983–, Center for Advanced Study in Behavioral Sciences 1977–78, 1987–88, 2004–05; Bell Research Fellow, German Marshall Fund 1977–78; Fellow, Council on Foreign Relations 1967–69, Guggenheim Foundation 1992–93, Sr Foreign Policy Fellow, Social Science Research Council 1986–88; Bellagio Resident Fellow 1993; Hon. PhD (Univ. of Arhus, Denmark) 1988; Grawemeyer Award for Ideas Improving World Order 1989, First Mentorship Award, Soc. for Women in Int. Political Economy 1997, Skytte Prize, Johan Skytte Foundation, Uppsala, Sweden 2005. *Publications include:* After Hegemony: Cooperation and Discord in the World Political Economy 1984, Neorealism and Its Critics 1986, International Institutions and State Power: Essays in International Relations Theory 1989, Power and Interdependence in a Partially Globalized World 2002; (as co-author): Power and Interdependence: World Politics in Transition 1977, Institutions for the Earth: Sources of Effective International Environmental Protection 1993, After the Cold War: State Strategies and International Institutions in Europe, 1989–91 1993, Designing Social Inquiry: Scientific Inference in Qualitative Research 1994, Humanitarian Intervention: Ethical, Legal, and Political Dilemmas 2003, The Regime Complex for Climate Change 2010; (as co-ed.): Transnational Relations and World Politics 1972, The New European Community: Decision-Making and Institutional Change 1991, Ideas and Foreign Policy 1993, From Local Commons to Global Interdependence 1994, Institutions for Environmental Aid: Pitfalls and Promises 1996, Internationalization and Domestic Politics 1996, Imperfect Unions: Security Institutions Across Time and Space 1999, Exploration and Contestation in the Study of World Politics 1998, Legalization and World Politics 2000. *Address:* Woodrow Wilson School, 408 Robertson Hall, Princeton University, Princeton, NJ 08544-1013, USA (office). *Telephone:* (609) 258-1856 (office). *Fax:* (609) 258-0390 (office). *E-mail:* rkeohane@princeton.edu (office). *Website:* www.princeton.edu/ ~rkeohane (office).

KEOUGH, Donald (Don) Raymond, BS; American business executive; *Chairman, Allen & Company Inc.;* b. 4 Sept. 1926, Maurice, Ia; s. of Leo H. Keough and Veronica Keough (née Henkels); m. Marilyn Mulhall 1949; three s. three d.; ed Creighton Univ.; with Butter-Nut Foods Co., Omaha 1950–61, Duncan Foods Co., Houston 1961–67; Vice-Pres. and Dir Marketing Foods Div., The Coca-Cola Co., Atlanta, Ga 1967–71, Pres. 1971–73; Exec. Vice-Pres. Coca-Cola USA 1973–74, Pres. 1974–76; Exec. Vice-Pres. The Coca-Cola Co., Atlanta, Ga 1976–79, Sr Exec. Vice-Pres. 1980–81, Pres., COO and Dir 1981–93; Chair. Bd of Dirs Coca-Cola Enterprises Inc., Atlanta, Ga 1986–93, Adviser to Bd 1993–98; returned as mem. Bd 2004; Chair. Bd Allen & Co., Inc. (investment firm) 1993–, Convera 2002–; mem. Bd of Dirs Berkshire Hathaway Inc., IAC/InterActiveCorp; fmr Chair. Bd of Trustees, Univ. of Notre Dame, now Chair. Emer.; Fellow, American Acad. of Arts and Sciences 2002; Laetare Medal, Univ. of Notre Dame 1993; Dr hc (Univ. of Notre Dame), (Creighton Univ.), (Emory Univ.), (Trinity Coll. Dublin, Ireland), (lark Univ.). *Address:* Allen & Company Inc., 711 5th Avenue, 9th Floor, New York, NY 10022, USA (office). *Telephone:* (212) 832-8000 (office). *Fax:* (212) 832-8023 (office).

KERAVNOS, Makis, MSc; Cypriot banker and fmr government official; *CEO, Hellenic Bank Public Co. Ltd;* b. 1951, Larnaka; m. Niki Keravnos; three c.; ed Pancyprian Gymnasium of Kykkos, Nat. and Kapodistrian Univ. of Athens, Pantion Univ., Brooks Univ., Oxford, UK; various sr exec. positions in private cos; various positions Human Resources Devt Authority including Sr Officer; apptd Minister of Labour 2003; Minister of Finance 2004–05 (resgnd); CEO Hellenic Bank Public Co. Ltd 2005–; founding mem. and Pres. Pancyprian Asscn of Economists; mem. Bd of Dirs Cyprus Asscn of Quality; Vice-Pres Cyprus Inst. of Political Research and European Affairs. *Address:* Hellenic Bank Public Co. Ltd, Digeni Akrita Avenue 92, PO Box 24747, 1394 Nicosia, Cyprus (office). *Telephone:* (22) 860000 (office). *Website:* www.hellenicbank.com (office).

KÉRÉKOU, Brig.-Gen. Mathieu (Ahmed); Benin politician and army officer; b. 2 Sept. 1933, Natitingou; ed Saint-Raphael Mil. School, France; served French Army until 1961; joined Dahomey Army 1961; Aide-de-camp to Pres. Maga 1961–63; took part in mil. coup d'état which removed Pres. Christophe Soglo 1967; Chair. Mil. Revolutionary Council 1967–68; continued studies at French mil. schools 1968–70; Commdr Ouidah Paratroop Unit and Deputy Chief of Staff 1970–72; leader of the mil. coup d'état which ousted Pres. Ahomadegbe Oct. 1972; Pres. and Head of Mil. Revolutionary Govt, Minister of Nat. Defence 1972–91, fmr Minister of Planning, of Co-ordination of Foreign Aid, Information and Nat. Orientation; Pres. of Benin 1996–2006; Chair. Cen. Cttee Parti de la révolution populaire du Bénin. *Leisure interests:* cycling, football. *Address:* c/o Présidence de la république, PO Box 1288, Cotonou, Benin.

KERESZTESI, János; Hungarian business executive; *CEO, FreeSoft Nyrt.;* b. 1958; m.; two c.; began career with SZAMALK; later with Digital Equipment Hungary; Pnr Relationships Man. and later Indirect Sales Man., Oracle Hungary 1995–99; Operations Man., Sun Microsystems Hungary 1999–2004; CEO FreeSoft Nyrt. 2004–; mem. Bd, Asscn of IT Cos 2005–; Asscn of IT Cos IT Man. of the Year 2001. *Address:* FreeSoft Nyrt., Neumann Janos u. 1/C, Iunfopark Budapest, 1117 Budapest, Hungary (office). *Telephone:* (61) 371-2910 (office). *Fax:* (61) 371-2911 (office). *E-mail:* fs.inf@freesoft.hu (office). *Website:* www.freesoft.hu (office).

KERGIN, Michael Frederick, BA, MA (Econs); Canadian government official, academic and fmr diplomatist; *Premier of Ontario's Special Adviser on Border Issues;* b. Canadian Mil. Hosp., Bramshott, UK; m. Margarita Fuentes Kergin; three s.; ed Univ. of Toronto, Magdalen Coll. Oxford, UK; joined Dept of Foreign Affairs and Int. Trade (fmrly Dept. of External Affairs) as Foreign Services Officer 1967, positions include Sr Dept Asst to Sec. of State for External Affairs 1984–86, Asst Deputy Minister responsible for Political and Int. Security Affairs 1994–96, and for the Americas and Security and Intelligence Affairs 1996–98; Amb. to Cuba 1986–89, to USA 2000–05; Premier of Ont.'s Special Adviser on Border Issues 2005–; currently Adjunct Prof., Faculty of Political Studies, Univ. of Ottawa, also Sr Fellow, Grad. School of Public and Int. Affairs; Sr Adviser, Bennett Jones LLP; Visiting Scholar, Western Michigan Univ., Kalamazoo 2006–07; Foreign Policy Adviser to the Prime Minister and Asst Sec. to the Cabinet for Foreign and Defence Policy 1998–2000; mem. Del. to Inter-American Devt Bank; fmr Embassy Minister, Washington, DC, USA, Santiago, Chile and Yaoundé, Cameroon; fmr Deputy Head of Mission to UN, New York; mem. Univ. of Toronto President's Advisory Council. *Address:* Bennett Jones LLP, Suite 1900 World Exchange Plaza, 45 O'Connor Street, Ottawa, ON K1P 1A4 (office); 55, Laurier Avenue East, Desmarais Building, Room 11129a, University of Ottawa, Ottawa, ON K1N 6N5, Canada. *Telephone:* (613) 683-2306 (Bennett Jones) (office). *E-mail:* kerginm@bennettjones.com (office); Michael.Kergin@uottawa.ca (office). *Website:* www .bennettjones.com (office).

KERIM, Srgjan, PhD; Macedonian diplomatist, politician and academic; *Secretary-General's Special Envoy for Climate Change, United Nations;* b. 12 Dec. 1948, Skopje; m.; three c.; ed Belgrade Univ., fmr Yugoslavia; Asst then Prof. of Int. Econ. Relations, Belgrade Univ. 1972–91; Visiting Prof., Univ. of Hamburg, Germany and New York Univ., USA 1972–91; mem. Presidency of Youth Fed. of Yugoslavia, also Chair. Foreign Policy Cttee 1976–78; Minister for Foreign Econ. Relations 1986–89; Asst Minister and Spokesman, Ministry of Foreign Affairs 1989–91; Vice-Pres. Copechim–France Co., Paris 1992–94; Amb. to Germany 1994–2000, to Liechtenstein and Switzerland 1995–2000; Minister of Foreign Affairs 2000–01; Perm. Rep. to UN, New York 2001–04, Pres. 62nd Session UN Gen. Ass. 2007–08, UN Sec.-Gen.'s Special Envoy for Climate Change 2008–; Gen. Man. Media Print Macedonia (part of WAZ Media Group) and Gen. Man. for South-Eastern Europe, WAZ Media Group 2003; Chair. Politika Newspapers and magazines, Belgrade 2004; Pres. Macedonian-German Econ. Asscn 2003–06, Hon. Pres. 2006; UN Millennium Devt Goals Award 2008. *Publications:* nine books and more than 100 scientific works on int. politics, int. economic and youth issues. *Address:* United Nations, New York, NY 10017, USA (office). *Telephone:* (212) 963-1234 (office). *Fax:* (212) 963-4879 (office). *Website:* www.un.org (office).

KERIMOV, Makhmud; Azerbaijani physicist and academic; *President, Azerbaijan National Academy of Sciences;* b. 18 Oct. 1948, Yerevan, Armenia; m.; two c.; ed Baku State Univ.; mem. of staff, Inst. of Physics, Azerbaijan Nat. Acad. of Sciences 1979–, Prof. 2000–, mem. 2001, Pres. 2001–; mem. Int. Eco-Energy Acad. *Publications:* over 119 scientific papers and patents on chemical physics, radiation physics, chem. of condensed matter, electron spin resonance spectroscopy, environmental studies. *Address:* Azerbaijan National Academy of Sciences, Istiglaiyyat str. 10, 370001 Baku, Azerbaijan (office). *Telephone:* (12) 492-35-29 (office); (12) 493-19-03 (home). *Fax:* (12) 492-56-99 (office). *E-mail:* president@aas .ab.az (office). *Website:* www.science.az (office).

KERIN, John Charles, AM, BA, BEcons; Australian politician; b. 21 Nov. 1937, Bowral, NSW; s. of the late Joseph Sydney Kerin and Mary Louise Kerin (née Fuller); m. 1st Barbara Elizabeth Large (divorced 1981); one d.; m. 2nd June Rae Verrier 1983; ed Univ. of New England, Australian Nat. Univ.; Econs Research Officer in wool marketing, Bureau of Agricultural Econs 1971, 1975–78; MP for Macarthur 1972–75, for Werriwa 1978–93; Minister for Primary Industry 1983–87, for Primary Industries and Energy 1987–91, Treas. for Trade and Overseas Devt 1991–93; resgnd from Parl. 1993; Chair. Australian Meat and Livestock Corpn 1994–97; Dir Coal Mines Australia Ltd 1994–2001; Chair. Biologic Int. Ltd 1996–98; Adjunct Prof., ANU 2013; fmr Deputy Chancellor Univ. of Western Sydney, now mem. Bd of Trustees and Chair. Macarthur Council of the Univ.; Chair. NewSouth Wales Forestry Comm.; Bd mem. CSIRO 2008–; Fellow, Australian Inst. of Agricultural Science and Tech., Australian Acad. of Tech. Sciences and Eng, Australian Rural Leadership Foundation; fmr mem. Australian Labor Party (resgnd 2011); Dr hc (New England) 1992, (Western Sydney) 1995, (Tasmania) 2001. *Leisure interests:* opera, bush-walking, classical music, reading. *Address:* PO Box 3, Garran, ACT 2605, Australia (home). *Telephone:* (6) 285-2480 (home). *Fax:* (6) 282-5778 (home). *E-mail:* kerrier1@bigpond.net.au (home).

KERKELING, Hans-Peter (Hape); German writer, actor, television broadcaster, director and comedian; b. 9 Dec. 1964, Recklinghausen; ed Marie Curie Gymnasium, Recklinghausen; at secondary school, formed band Gesundfutter with fellow students and released a record, Hawaii; began career as a comedian on radio, working for various German broadcasting cos, including WDR and BR; breakthrough role in TV comedy show Känguru playing character of a boy called Hannilein 1984; guest appearances and sketches on Radio Bremen show Extratour; started up own comedy TV show Total Normal (satirical spoof on prime-time TV shows) along with pianist Achim Hagemann 1989; show won several TV prizes; directed, starred and co-wrote script of first film Kein Pardon 1992; moved to ind. TV sector with show Cheese 1992; worked again for ARD presenting show Warmumsherz (Heartwarming) late 1990s; returned to success with show Darüber lacht die Welt (What Makes the World Laugh) 1999; also presented yearly fundraising gala for German AIDS fund Deutsche AIDS-Hilfe; presented Großer Deutsch-Test (nat. test show for German grammar and spelling) 2004, 2005, Großer Deutschlandtest (test show about people's knowledge of Germany) 2004, live TV show Let's Dance (German version of Strictly Come Dancing/Dancing with the Stars) with Nazan Eckes 2006; presenter Hape trifft! on RTL 2005–; host, Goldene Kamera 2010–; Verdienstkreuz (North Rhine-Westphalia) 2006, Royal Spanish Order of Merit Illustrissime 2011; Golden Camera, Golden Rose of Montreux, Adolf Grimme Prize, Tele-star, Golden Gong, Europa 1991–93, Peter Frankenfeld Prize 2002, Deutscher Fernsehpreis (German TV Prize) in category of Best Entertainment Presenter 2003, 2004, Bayerischer Fernsehpreis 2004, Comedy Prize 2004, Golden Camera for Best TV Entertainer 2005, Comedy Prize for Best Comedian 2005, 2006, named in survey by Kabel 1 amongst top ten favourite faces on German TV 2005, Adolf-Grimme Honour Award 2007, GQ Man of the Year 2008, Steiger Award, Bavarian Television Award 2009, Karl-Valentin-Orden 2010, Medienpreis für Sprachkultur 2010, Sparte Fernse-hen, Gesellschaft für deutsche Sprache 2011, Goldene Schallplatte 2× Platin für Wieder auf Tour – Live (CD), ROMY-Fernsehpreis Deutscher Comedypreis 2012, Golden Camera – Leserwahl (Best Comedian) 2012. *Films:* Großstadtrevier: Dame in Not 1989, Vorwärts 1990, Kein Pardon 1992, Alles wegen Paul (producer) 2001, Samba in Mettmann 2004, Kung Fu Panda 2008, Ein Mann, ein Fjord! 2008, Horst Schlämmer – Isch kandidiere! 2009, Kung Fu Panda 2 2011. *Television:* comedy: Kerkelings Kindersrunde 1984, Känguru 1985–86, Total Normal 1989, Cheese 1994, Warmumsherz 1995, Zappenduster 1997, Gisbert 1998, Darüber lacht die Welt 1998, Hape's halbe Stunde 2001; presenter: Eurovision Song Contest 1989–91, German TV Awards 2001, Stars in the Manege 2001, Golden Europa Awards 2002, AIDS Gala 2002, 2003, Die 70-er Show 2003, 2004, Der grosse Deutschtest 2004, 2005, Hape trifft 2005; films: Club Las Piranjas (NDR TV) 1995, Willi und die Windzors (NDR TV) 1996, Die Oma ist tot (NDR TV) 1997. *Recordings include:* Hawaii 1984, Hannilein & Co 1986, Erwarten Se nix 1990, Das ganze Leben ist ein Quiz 1991, Hurz (film soundtrack) 1991, Vorsicht Telefon 1993, Der kleine Vampir (film soundtrack) 1993, Sportreporter Rap 1993, Helsinki is Hell 1999, Junge, Junge 2000, Das Ding muss rein 2000, Die 70 min. Show 2003, Tanze Sambe mit mir 2004, Schätzelein 2006, Meine letzte Zigarette 2006; album: Ariola 1984. *Publications:* Hannilein & Co. 1992, Kein Pardon 1993, Cheese 1994, Ich bin dann mal weg 2006, Weisse Bescheid?! 2007. *Telephone:* (30) 32765822 (office). *Fax:* (30) 32765823 (office). *E-mail:* elke@medienbuero-krueger.de (office); hape@medienbuero-krueger.de (office). *Address:* Büro Hape Kerkeling, Postfach 20 02 57, 13512 Berlin, Germany (home). *Website:* www.hapekerkeling.de.

KERKORIAN, Kirk; American business executive; *Co-Chairman, President and CEO, Tracinda Corporation;* b. 6 June 1917, Fresno, Calif.; m. 1st Hilda Schmidt 1942 (divorced 1951); m. 2nd Jane Hardy 1954 (divorced); two d.; m. 3rd Lisa Bonder 1998 (divorced 1998); one d.; commercial airline pilot 1940; Capt. Transport Command, RAF 1942–44; f. LA Air Services (later Trans Int. Airlines Group) 1948, Int. Leisure Corpn 1968; CEO MGM Inc. 1973–74, Chair. Exec. Cttee, Vice-Chair. MGM 1974–79, controlling stockholder MGM/UA Communications Co. and MGM Mirage; Chair.-Dir., Pres. CEO Tracinda Corpn 1979–; majority shareholder MGM Grand casino, fmr minority shareholder, DaimlerChrysler AG. *Address:* Tracinda Corporation, 150 Rodeo Drive, Suite 250, Beverly Hills, CA 90212, USA (office). *Telephone:* (310) 271-0638 (office). *Fax:* (310) 271-3416 (office). *Website:* www.mgmmirage.com (office).

KERNAN, Gen. William F., MA; American army officer (retd) and business executive; *Senior Vice President and General Manager, International Group, MPRI Inc.;* b. Fort Sam Houston, Tex.; m. Marianne Purnell; one s.; ed US Army Command and Gen. Staff Coll., US Army War Coll.; commissioned Infantry Officer 1968; commanded two Airborne Cos, two Ranger Cos, an Airborne Infantry Battalion, the 75th Ranger Regt; exchange officer 3rd Battalion, Parachute Regt, UK; Asst Div. Commdr (Manoeuvre) 7th Infantry Div.; Dir Plans, Policy and Assessments, J5, US Special Operations Command; Commdr 101st Airborne Div. (Air Assault), XVIII Airborne Corps and Fort Bragg; combat tours Viet Nam, Grenada, Panama; rank of Gen. 2000; Supreme Allied Commdr, Atlantic (SACLANT) and C-in-C US Jt Forces Command, Norfolk, Va 2000–02; Sr Vice Pres. and Gen. Man. Int. Group, MPRI Inc., Alexandria, Va 2002–; Legion of Merit (with 3 oak leaf clusters), Kt Commdr's Cross of the Order of Merit of the Fed. Repub. of Germany 2003; Defense Distinguished Service Medal, Distinguished Service Medal (with oak leaf cluster), Bronze Star Medal (with V device), Bronze Star Medal (with oak leaf cluster), Purple Heart, Meritorious Service Medal (with 3 oak leaf clusters), Air Medal and other mil. medals and badges; Outstanding Achievement Award, North Carolina Tech. Asscn 2006. *Address:* MPRI Inc., International Group, 1201 East Abingdon Drive, Suite 425, Alexandria, VA 22314, USA (office). *Telephone:* (703) 684-0853 (office). *Website:* www.mpri.com/main/internationalgroup.html (office).

KERR, David J., CBE, MA, MD, DSc, FRCP (Glas & Lon); British professor of pharmacology; *Rhodes Professor of Clinical Pharmacology and Cancer Therapeutics, University of Oxford;* b. 1956, Glasgow; ed Univ. of Glasgow; Prof. of Clinical Oncology, Univ. of Birmingham 1992–94, also Dir, Clinical Trials Unit; Clinical Dir, Regional Cancer Task Force for W Midlands 1994; Rhodes Prof. of Clinical Pharmacology and Cancer Therapeutics, Univ. of Oxford 2001–; Pres.-elect European Soc. of Medical Oncology 2008–09; Founding Commr for Health Improvement, Nat. Health Service; Chair. Nat. Cancer Services Collaborative; Ed.-in-Chief Annals of Oncology 2000–; mem. editorial bd several journals including Nature Clinical Practice Oncology; Chief Research Adviser, Sidra Medical and Research Center, Doha, Qatar 2009; Dir Qatar Biomedical Research Inst.; mem. Supreme Council of Health, Qatar 2009–; Fellow, Corpus Christi Coll., Oxford, Acad. of Medical Sciences 2000; Hon. Fellow, Royal Coll. of Gen. Practitioners 2007; numerous awards including European School of Oncology

Int. Award for outstanding contribution to chemotherapy research 1987, NHS Nye Bevan Award for Innovation 2000, European Soc. of Medical Oncology Award for distinguished contribution to cancer therapy and research in Europe 2006, Fulton Lecture, Univ. of Glasgow 2007. *Publications:* more than 350 articles in peer-reviewed journals. *Address:* Department of Clinical Pharmacology, University of Oxford, Old Road Campus Research Building, Old Road Campus, off Roosevelt Drive, Oxford, OX3 7DQ, England (office). *Telephone:* (1865) 617024 (office). *Fax:* (1865) 617100 (office). *E-mail:* admin@clinpharm.ox.ac.uk (office). *Website:* www.clinpharm.ox.ac.uk (office).

KERR, David Nicol Sharp, CBE, MSc, FRCP, FRCPE; British physician and academic; b. 27 Dec. 1927, London; s. of William Kerr and Elsie Ransted; m. (Mary) Eleanor Jones 1960; two s. one d.; ed George Watson's Boys' School and Univs of Edinburgh and Wisconsin; Surgeon-Lt RNVR 1953–55; Surgeon Lt-Commdr RNR 1993–95; Prof. of Medicine, Univ. of Newcastle-upon-Tyne 1968–83; Dean, Royal Postgrad. Medical School 1984–91; Prof. of Renal Medicine, Univ. of London 1986–93, Prof. Emer. 1993–; medical adviser and Trustee, Nat. Kidney Research Fund 1999–2003, Chair. 2000–03, Vice-Pres. 2003–; Postgraduate Medical Adviser, North Thames Regional Health Authority, later Nat. Health Service (NHS) Exec. N Thames Regional Office 1991–97; Medical Awards Admin. Commonwealth Scholarships Comm. 1993–98; Ed. Journal of Royal Coll. of Physicians 1994–98; mem. Council, British Heart Foundation 1991–97; Hon. consultant renal physician, Hammersmith Hosp.; numerous awards including Volhard Medal (German Medical Foundation), Distinguished Overseas Medal (Nat. Kidney Foundation of USA). *Publications:* Oxford Textbook of Clinical Nephrology (ed.); other books, book sections and articles in professional journals. *Leisure interests:* walking, theatre, opera, church. *Address:* 22 Carbery Avenue, London, W3 9AL, England (home). *Telephone:* (20) 8992-3231 (home). *Fax:* (20) 8992-3231. *E-mail:* DNSKerr@aol.com (home).

KERR, Philip Ballantyne, LLM; British writer; b. 22 Feb. 1956, Edinburgh, Scotland; s. of William Kerr and Ann Brodie; m. Jane Thynne 1991; two s. one d.; ed Northampton Grammar School and Univ. of Birmingham; film critic, New Statesman. *Play:* Bluesbreakers 2002. *Publications include:* adult fiction: March Violets (Prix du Roman d'Aventures 1993, Prix Mystère de la Critique 1994) 1989, The Pale Criminal 1990, The Penguin Book of Lies (ed.) 1990, A German Requiem 1991, A Philosophical Investigation (Deutsche Krimi Prize 1995) 1992, The Penguin Book of Fights, Feuds, and Heartfelt Hatreds: An Anthology of Antipathy (ed.) 1992, Dead Meat 1993, Gridiron (aka The Grid) (Deutsche Krimi Prize 1997) 1993, Esau 1996, A Five-Year Plan 1997, The Second Angel 1998, The Shot 1999, Dark Matter 2002, The One from the Other 2007, A Quiet Flame 2008, If the Dead Rise Not (CWA Ellis Peters Historical Award) 2009, Field Grey 2010, Prague Fatale, A Man without Breath 2013; juvenile fiction (as P. B. Kerr): Children of the Lamp series: The Akhenaten Adventure 2004, The Blue Djinn of Babylon 2005, The Cobra King of Kathmandu 2006, The Day of the Djinn Warriors 2007, The Eye of the Forest 2009, The Five Fakirs of Faizabad 2010, The Grave Robbers of Genghis Khan 2011. *Leisure interest:* cinema. *Address:* c/o AP Watt at United Agents LLP, 12–26 Lexington Street, London, W1F 0LE, England (office). *Telephone:* (20) 3214-0800 (office). *Fax:* (20) 3214-0801 (office). *E-mail:* info@unitedagents.co.uk (office), pbk@pbkerr.com (office). *Website:* www.apwatt.co.uk (office); www.pbkerr.com.

KERR OF KINLOCHARD, Baron (Life Peer), cr. 2004, of Kinlochard in Perth and Kinross; **John Olav Kerr,** GCMG, BA, LLD, FRSE; British business executive, parliamentarian, fmr diplomatist and fmr international public servant; *Deputy Chairman, Scottish Power;* b. 22 Feb. 1942, Grantown-on-Spey, Scotland; s. of the late Dr J. D. O. Kerr and Mrs Kerr; m. Elizabeth Kalaugher 1965; two s. three d.; ed Glasgow Acad. and Pembroke Coll., Oxford; entered diplomatic service 1966; served in Moscow and Rawalpindi; Pvt. Sec. to Perm. Under-Sec. FCO 1974–79; Head DM1 Div. HM Treasury 1979–81; Prin. Pvt. Sec. to Chancellor of Exchequer 1981–84; Head of Chancery, Washington, DC 1984–87; Asst Under-Sec. of State, FCO 1987–90; Amb. and Perm. Rep. to EC (now EU), Brussels 1990–95; Amb. to USA 1995–97; Perm. Under-Sec. of State and Head of HM Diplomatic Service 1997–2002; Sec.-Gen. European Convention 2002–03; mem. House of Lords 2004–, mem. EU Select Cttee 2006–10; mem. Bd of Dirs Shell Transport and Trading 2002–05, Deputy Chair. and Sr Ind. Non-exec. Dir Royal Dutch Shell plc 2005–12; Dir (non-exec.) Scottish American Investment Co. 2002–, Rio Tinto Ltd 2003–, Rio Tinto plc 2003–, Scottish Power 2007– (Deputy Chair. 2012–); Trustee, Rhodes Trust, Oxford 1997–2010, Nat. Gallery, London 2002–10, Carnegie Trust for the Univs of Scotland 2005–; Chair. Court and Council, Imperial Coll. London 2006–11, Centre for European Reform 2009–; Vice-Pres. European Policy Centre; Council mem. Business for New Europe; Pres. UK-Korea Forum 2007–14; Pres. St Andrews Clinics for Children; Hon. Fellow Pembroke Coll., Oxford 1992, Fellow Imperial Coll., London 2012; Hon. LLD (St Andrews) 1996, (Glasgow) 1999, (Aston) 2010. *Publications:* various articles on int. affairs and EU issues. *Address:* House of Lords, Westminster, London, SW1A 0PW, England (office). *Telephone:* (20) 7219-5353 (office).

KERREY, J. Robert (Bob), BS; American university administrator and fmr politician; *President, The New School;* b. 27 Aug. 1943, Lincoln, Neb.; s. of James Kerrey and Elinor Kerrey; m. 1st; one s. one d.; m. 2nd Sarah Paley 2001; one s.; ed Univ. of Nebraska; served in USN in Viet Nam 1966–69; Owner and Founder of Grandmother's Skillet Restaurant outlets in Omaha and Lincoln, Neb. 1972–75; Owner and Founder of fitness enterprises, including Sun Valley Bowl and Prairie Life Fitness Center, Lincoln; Gov. of Neb. 1983–87; Pnr, Printon, Kane & Co. (law firm), Lincoln 1987; Senator from Neb. 1989–2001; Pres. The New School (fmrly New School Univ.), New York 2001–; mem. Nat. Comm. on Terrorist Attacks Upon the US (9/11 Comm.) 2004; Democrat; Dr hc (New York Law School); Medal of Honor; Bronze Star; Purple Heart; Robert L. Haig Award for Distinguished Public Service, New York State Bar Asscn, Distinguished Nebraskan Award. *Publications:* When I Was a Young Man: A Memoir 2002. *Address:* The New School, Johnson and Kaplan Building, 66 W 12th Street, New York, NY 10011, USA (office). *Telephone:* (212) 229-5600. *Website:* www.newschool.edu/admin/pres/index.html.

KERRY, John Forbes, JD; American lawyer and politician; *Secretary of State;* b. 11 Dec. 1943, Aurora, Colo; s. of Richard J. Kerry and Rosemary Kerry (née Forbes); m. 1st Julia S. Thorne 1970; two d.; m. 2nd Teresa Heinz Kerry 1995; three s.; ed Yale Univ. and Boston Coll.; served in USN 1966–70; called to the Bar, Mass 1976; Nat. Co-ordinator, Vietnam Veterans Against The War 1969–71; Asst Dist Attorney, Middlesex Co., Mass 1976–79; Pnr, Kerry & Sragow (law firm), Boston 1979–82; Lt-Gov. of Mass 1982–84; Senator from Mass 1985–2013; unsuccessful Democratic cand. for US Pres. 2004; Sec. of State 2013–; awarded Bronze Star, Silver Star, three Purple Hearts. *Publications include:* The New Soldier 1971, The New War: The Web of Crime That Threatens America's Security 1997, This Moment on Earth (with Teresa Heinz Kerry) 2007. *Address:* Department of State, 2201 C Street, NW, Washington, DC 20520, USA (office). *Telephone:* (202) 647-4000 (office). *Fax:* (202) 647-6738 (office). *Website:* www.state.gov (office).

KERTÉSZ, Imre; Hungarian writer and translator; b. 9 Nov. 1929, Budapest; m. 2nd Magda Kertész; deported to Auschwitz, then Buchenwald during World War II 1944; worked for newspaper Világosság, Budapest 1948–51 (dismissed when it adopted CP line); mil. service 1951–53; ind. writer and trans. of German authors such as Nietzsche, Schnitzler, Freud, Roth, Wittgenstein and Canetti 1953–; has also written theatre musicals; works have been translated into German, Spanish, French, English, Czech, Russian, Swedish and Hebrew; Brandenburg Literary Prize 1995, Leipzig Book Prize for European Understanding 1997, WELT-Literaturpreis 2000, Ehrenpreis der Robert-Bosch-Stiftung 2001, Hans-Sahl-Preis 2002, Nobel Prize in Literature 2002. *Publications include:* Sorstalanság (trans. as Fatelessness) (Jewish Quarterly Wingate Literary Prize 2006) (made into film 2005) 1975, A nyomkeresö (The Pathfinder) 1977, Detektívtörténet (Detective Story) 1977, A kudarc (Fiasco) 1988, Kaddis a meg nem születetett gyermekért (Kaddish for a Child Not Born 1997) 1990, Az angol labogó (The English Flag) 1991, Gályanapló (Galley Diary) 1992, A Holocaust mint kultúra (The Holocaust as Culture) 1993, Jegyzökönyv 1993, Valaki más: a változás kró'nikája (I, Another: Chronicle of a Metamorphosis) 1997, A gondolatnyi csend, amig kivégzöoztag újratölt (Moment of Silence While the Execution Squad Reloads) 1998, A számüzött nyelv (The Exiled Language) 2001, Felszámolás: regény (Liquidation) 2003, K. dosszié (File "K.") 2006, Európa nyomasztó öröksége (Europe's Depressing Heritage) 2008.

KERTZER, David I., PhD; American historian, anthropologist, writer and academic; *Professor of Anthropology and Italian Studies, Brown University;* b. 20 Feb. 1948, New York City; s. of Morris Kertzer and Julia Hoffman Kertzer; m. Susan; one d. one s.; ed Brown Univ., Brandeis Univ.; Asst Prof. of Anthropology, Bowdoin Coll. 1973–79, Assoc. Prof. 1979–84, Prof. 1984–89, William R. Kenan, Jr Prof. 1989–92, Chair. Dept of Sociology and Anthropology 1979–81, 1984–86, 1987–88, 1992; Paul Dupee, Jr Univ. Prof. of Social Science, Brown Univ. 1992–, also Prof. of Anthropology 1992–, of History 1992–2001, of Italian Studies 2001–, Provost Brown Univ. 2006–11; Fulbright Sr Lecturer, Univ. of Catania 1978; Professore a contratto, Univ. of Bologna 1987; Visiting Fellow, Trinity Coll., Cambridge, UK 1991; Visiting Scholar, Posthumous Inst. and Univ. of Amsterdam 1994; Visiting Dir of Studies, Ecole des Hautes Etudes en Sciences Sociales, Paris 1994; Prof. of Educ., American Acad. of Rome 1999; Fulbright Chair, Univ. of Bologna 2000; Visiting Prof., Ecole Normale Superieure, Paris 2002; guest lecturer at over 40 univs world-wide; Co-founder and Co-ed. Journal of Modern Italian Studies 1994–; Ed. Book Series: New Perspectives in Anthropological and Social Demography 1996–2007; Pres. Soc. for the Anthropology of Europe 1994–96; mem. Editorial Bd Social Science History 1987–96, 2001–04, Journal of Family History 1990–, Continuity and Change 1996–2000, Int. Studies Review 1998–2002; mem. Jury Lynton History Prize 2000–01; mem. Exec. Bd American Anthropological Asscn 1995–96, NIH Population Review Cttee 1996–99, Nat. Research Council Cttee on Population 1999–2005, German Marshall Fund Advisory Bd 2000–02; Vice-Pres. Social Science History Asscn 2005–06, Pres. 2006–07; Fellow, American Acad. of Arts and Sciences 2005–; Fellowship Center for Advanced Studies, Stanford 1982–83, Guggenheim Fellowship 1986, Nat. Endowment for the Humanities Fellowship 1995, Rockefeller Foundation Fellowship, Bellagio, Italy 2000. *Publications include:* Comrades and Christians: Religion and Political Struggle in Communist Italy 1980, Famiglia Contadina e Urbanizzazione 1981, Family Life in Central Italy 1880–1910: Sharecropping, Wage Labour and Coresidence (Helen and Howard R. Marraro Prize in Italian History 1985) 1984, Ritual, Politics and Power 1988, Family, Political Economy and Demographic Change (Helen and Howard R. Marraro Prize in Italian History 1990) 1989, Sacrificed for Honor: Italian Infant Abandonment and the Politics of Reproductive Control 1993, Politics and Symbols: The Italian Communist Party and the Fall of Communism 1996, The Kidnapping of Edgardo Mortara (Nat. Jewish Book Award 1997, Best Books of the Year, Publishers Weekly, Toronto Globe and Mail) 1997; stage version 'Edgard Mine' by Alfred Uhry premiered 2002) 1997, The Popes Against the Jews (UK edn The Unholy War 2002) 2001, Prisoner of the Vatican 2004, Amalia's Tale 2008; contrib. to numerous nat. and state newspapers, contrib., ed. or co-ed. of numerous books, author of over 60 journal articles and 50 academic papers. *Address:* Department of Anthropology, Brown University, Box 1921, 128 Hope Street, Providence, RI 02912, USA (office). *Telephone:* (401) 863-3251 (office). *Fax:* (401) 863-7588 (office). *E-mail:* David_Kertzer@brown.edu (office). *Website:* www.brown.edu/Departments/Anthropology/people/facultypage.php?id=10173 (office); www.davidkertzer.com (office).

KERZNER, Solomon (Sol); South African business executive; *Chairman and CEO, Kerzner International Resorts Inc.;* b. 23 Aug. 1935, Johannesburg; s. of Morris Kerzner; two s. three d.; ed Athlons High School, Univ. of Witwatersrand; Founder and CEO Southern Sun Hotels 1969–83; CEO Sun Int. Hotels (now Kerzner Int. Resorts Inc.) 1983–87, Chair. and CEO 1993–, Pres. 1993–2003; Chair. World Leisure Group 1989–94; Inst. of Marketing Man. Marketing Award of the Year 1978–80, Jewish Businessman of the Year 1993, elected US Gaming Hall of Fame, Lifetime Achievement Award by FEDHASA, South Africa's major tourism agency. *Achievements include:* represented Univ. of Witwatersrand for boxing and wrestling 1954–55. *Address:* Kerzner International Resorts, Inc., The Crown Building, 730 Fifth Avenue, Fifth Floor, New York, NY 10019, USA (office). *Telephone:* (212) 659-5184 (office). *Fax:* (212) 659-5201 (office). *E-mail:* MediaRelations@Kerzner.com (office). *Website:* www.kerzner.com (office).

KESHTMAND, Sultan Ali; Afghan politician; b. 1935; ed univ.; mem. of Hazara ethnic minority; Founder-mem. People's Democratic Party of Afghanistan (PDPA) and mem. Cen. Cttee 1965; with Parcham faction when PDPA split 1967; Minister of Planning April–Aug. 1978; tried on charges of conspiracy and sentenced to death

1978; sentence commuted by Pres. Amin. Oct. 1978; fmr Vice-Pres. of Revolutionary Council; Deputy Prime Minister and Minister of Planning after Soviet intervention 1979–81; Prime Minister of Afghanistan and Chair. Council of Ministers 1981–88, 1989–90; First Vice-Pres. 1990–91.

KESSEL MARTÍNEZ, Georgina Yamilet, BA, PhD; Mexican economist and government official; *Director General, Banco Nacional de Obras y Servicios Públicos SNC (Banobras);* ed Instituto Tecnológico Autónomo de México (ITAM), Columbia Univ., USA; full-time Prof., ITAM for more than nine years, Head of Dept of Econs 1994; fmr Dir-Gen. of Sectoral Econ. Analysis, Petróleos Mexicanos (PEMEX), Univ. –2011; apptd first Pres. Energy Regulating Comm. 1994; fmr Dir Investment Unit, Finance and Public Credit Unit; Dir Gen. Casa de Moneda de México (Mexican Mint) 2002–06; Sec. of Energy 2006–11; Dir Gen. Banco Nacional de Obras y Servicios Públicos SNC (Banobras) 2011–; Premio al mérito profesional, ITAM alumni 2005. *Publications:* El sur también existe (with Santiago Levy and Enrique Dávila), Los peligros del Plan Puebla-Panamá, Lo negociado del Tratado de Libre Comercio (compiler). *Address:* Banobras, Avenida Javier Barros Sierra no. 515, Colonia Lomas de Santa Fe, Delegación Alvaro Obregón, c.p., 01219 México, DF, Mexico (office). *Telephone:* (55) 5270-1200 (office). *E-mail:* info@banobras.gob.mx (office). *Website:* www.banobras.gob.mx (office).

KESSLER, Denis, PhD; French economist and business executive; *Chairman and Chief Executive, SCOR;* b. 1952; ed Ecole des Hautes Etudes Commerciales (HEC Paris), Univ. of Paris; Univ. Prof. of Econ. Sciences, holds the 'agrégation' in Social Sciences and the 'agrégation' in Econs; Chair. Fédération Française des Socs d'Assurances (Asscn of French Insurers) 1990–97, 1998–2002; mem. Conseil Nat. des Assurances 1990–97, 1998–2002, Presidential Council 1990–96, 1998–2001; Vice-Pres. Comité Européen des Assurances 1996–98, 2001–02; Sr Exec. Vice-Pres. and mem. Exec. Cttee of the AXA Group 1997–98; mem. Exec. Cttee Mouvement des Entreprises de France (MEDEF) 1991–94, Exec. Vice-Chair. 1995–98, First Exec. Vice-Chair. 1998–2002; Chair. and chief Exec. SCOR 2002–; Chair. Le Siècle 2008–10, Reinsurance Advisory Bd 2009–10, Global Reinsurance Forum 2009–11, Le Cercle de l'Orchestre de Paris; mem. Conseil Nat. du Patronat Français –1998, Conseil Economique et social 1993–2010; mem. Bd Geneva Asscn, Bd of le Siècle, Global Reinsurance Forum, Reinsurance Advisory Bd, Comm. Economique de la Nation, Fondation pour la Recherche Médicale 2006–12; Global Counsellor, Conference Bd; hon. degrees from Moscow Acad. of Finance and HEC Montréal; elected to Insurance Hall of Fame of the Int. Insurance Soc. 2014. *Address:* 5 avenue Kléber, 75795 Paris cedex 16, France (office). *Telephone:* 1-58-44-70-00 (office). *Fax:* 1-58-44-85-42 (office). *E-mail:* info@scor.com (office). *Website:* www .scor.com (office).

KESSLER, Heinz, Dr rer. pol; Austrian banking executive; *President of the Supervisory Board, Erste Group Bank AG;* b. 19 Aug. 1938, Vienna; m.; three c.; ed Vöcklabruck High School, Univ. of Vienna; joined Nettingsdorfer Papierfabrik AG 1964, apptd mem. Man. Bd 1974, Chair. Man. Bd 1982–2003, Chair. Supervisory Bd 2003–; mem. Supervisory Bd Erste Bank der österreichischen Sparkassen AG 1998–, Deputy Chair. May–Sept. 2003, Chair. 2003–; Chair. Reform-Werke Bauer & Co. GmbH, Reform-Werke Bauer & Co. Holding AG; Deputy Chair. Austria Versicherungsverein auf Gegenseitigkeit Privatstiftung, Duropack AG, Rath AG, UNIQA Versicherungen AG; mem. Die Erste österreichische Spar-Casse Privatstiftung. *Address:* Erste Bank der österreichischen Sparkassen AG, Graben 21, 1010 Vienna, Austria (office). *Telephone:* (50) 100-10100 (office). *Fax:* (50) 100-13112 (office). *E-mail:* investor.relations@erstebank.at (office). *Website:* www .erstebank.com (office).

KESSLER, Ronald, BA, MA, PhD; American sociologist and academic; *Professor of Health Care Policy, Harvard Medical School;* b. 26 April 1947, Bristol, Pa; m. Vicki Shahly; two s. two d.; ed Temple Univ., New York Univ., New York Univ.; Pre-doctoral Fellow, Health Service Research, Montefiore Hosp., Bronx, New York 1972–74; Research Assoc., New York State Psychiatric Inst. 1975–76; Research Assoc., Center for Policy Research 1976–77; Postdoctoral Fellow, Dept of Psychiatry, Univ. of Wis. 1977–79; Asst Prof., Dept of Sociology, Univ. of Mich. 1979–81, Assoc. Prof., Dept of Sociology and Assoc. Research Scientist, Survey Research Center 1981–88, Prof., Dept of Sociology and Program Dir Survey Research Center 1988–96; Prof., Dept of Health Care Policy, Harvard Medical School 1996–; mem. Editorial Bd Journal of Health and Social Behavior 1978–81, 1992–94, Public Opinion Quarterly 1981–84, American Sociological Review 1982–85, 1989–92, Sociological Methods and Research 1983–, Psychological Medicine 1994–, Women's Health: Research on Gender, Behavior, and Policy 1994–, Psychological Methods 1996–, Journal of Evaluation in Clinical Practice 1997–, International Journal of Methods in Psychiatric Research 1998–, Health Services Research 1998–, Journal of Affective Disorders 2003–, Culture, Medicine and Psychiatry 2003–, Archives of General Psychiatry 2003–, Psychiatry and Clinical Neurosciences 2004–, Journal of Health & Productivity 2006–; mem. Scientific Advisory Bd Anxiety Disorders Asscn of America 2000–05, Nat. Depressive and Manic-Depressive Asscn 2001–, Nat. Alliance for the Mentally Ill Scientific Council 2003–; mem. Medical Advisory Bd Jed Foundation 2005–; mem. Inst. of Medicine 1999, American Sociological Asscn, American Public Health Asscn, Sociological Research Asscn, Society of Behavioral Medicine Research; Fellow, American Psychopathological Asscn; Hon. Fellow, American Psychiatric Asscn 1999; Research Scientist Devt Award, Nat. Inst. of Mental Health (NIMH) 1984–94, NIMH MERIT Award 1987–97, NIMH Research Scientist Award 1995–99, Paul Hoch Award, American Psychopathological Asscn 1997, Rema Lapouse Mental Health Epidemiology Award, American Public Health Asscn 1997, Presidential Citation, American Psychological Asscn 2005. *Publications:* Linear Panel Analysis: Models of Quantitative Change (co-author) 1981, Television and Aggression: A Panel Study (co-author) 1982, Methodological Issues in AIDS Behavioral Research (co-ed.) 1993, Measuring Stress: A Guide for Health and Social Scientists (co-ed.) 1995, How Healthy Are We?: A National Study of WellBeing at Midlife (co-ed.) 2003, Health and Work Productivity: Making the Business Case for Quality Health Care (co-ed.) 2006; numerous articles in medical journals. *Address:* Department of Health Care Policy, Harvard Medical School, 180 Longwood Avenue, Boston, MA 02115-5899, USA (office). *Telephone:* (617) 630-8043 (home); (617) 432-3587 (office). *Fax:* (617) 432-3588 (office). *E-mail:* kessler@hcp.med .harvard.edu (office). *Website:* www.hcp.med.harvard.edu (office).

KESTENBAUM, Baron (Life Peer), cr. 2011, of Foxcote in the County of Somerset; **Jonathan Kestenbaum,** BA, MBA; British business executive; *Chief Executive, National Endowment for Science, Technology and the Arts;* b. Japan; ed London School of Econs, Univ. of Cambridge, Cass Business School, London, Cabinet Office Top Man. programme, Strategic Agility programme at Harvard Business School, USA; family moved back to UK when aged four; helped expand large family commodity trading business (ring dealing mem. London Metal Exchange); spent five years living in Israel, Fellow attached to Hebrew Univ.'s School of Educ.; returned to UK 1990; Chief Exec., Office of the Chief Rabbi, Jonathan Sacks; fmr Chief of Staff to Sir Ronald Cohen, Chair. Apax Partners (pvt. equity firm), jtly est. The Portland Trust (Founding Chief Exec.); Chief Exec. Nat. Endowment for Science, Tech. and the Arts –2010; mem. Bd The Design Council, RSC, Tech. Strategy Bd, Innovation Group Advisory Bd at Imperial Coll. London; fmr Chair. (non-exec.) Quest (investigative accounting firm); mem. Bd of Dirs Profero (digital marketing co.); fmr mem. faculty, Cass Business School; Chair. Manchester Science Panel; fmr Commr, Manchester Ind. Econ. Review; Chair. and Chief Exec. Five Arrows Ltd (investment co.) 2011–; trustee of several charitable foundations; Hon. DTech (Plymouth). *Address:* National Endowment for Science, Technology and the Arts, 1 Plough Place, London, EC4A 1DE (office); House of Lords, Westminster, London, SW1A 0PW, England. *Telephone:* (20) 7438-2500 (office); (20) 7219-5353. *Fax:* (20) 7438-2501 (office); (20) 7219-5979. *E-mail:* information@nesta.org.uk (office). *Website:* www.nesta.org.uk (office).

KESWICK, Ben, MBA; British business executive; *Managing Director, Jardine Matheson Holdings Ltd;* b. 1972; s. of Simon Lindley Keswick and Emma Keswick (née Chetwode); ed Institut Européen d'Admin des Affaires (INSEAD), France; joined Jardine Matheson Group 1998, several exec. positions including Finance Dir and CEO Jardine Pacific 2003–07, Group Man. Dir Jardine Cycle & Carriage 2007–12, joined Bd of Jardine Matheson Holdings Ltd 2007, Man. Dir 2012–, Chair. and Man. Dir Jardine Matheson Ltd 2012–, Chair. Jardine Cycle & Carriage; Commr, Astra, United Tractors; Man. Dir Dairy Farm, Hongkong Land, Jardine Strategic, Mandarin Oriental; Dir, Jardine Pacific, Jardine Motors. *Address:* Jardine Matheson Holdings Ltd, 48th Floor, Jardine House, GPO Box 70, Hong Kong Special Administrative Region, People's Republic of China (office). *Telephone:* 2843-8288 (office). *E-mail:* jml@jardines.com (office). *Website:* www .jardines.com (office).

KESWICK, Sir Henry Neville Lindley, Kt; British business executive; *Chairman, Jardine Matheson Holdings Ltd;* b. 29 Sept. 1938; s. of the late Sir William Keswick and Mary Lindley; brother of Sir (John) Chippendale Keswick and of Simon Lindley Keswick (q.v.); m. Lady Tessa Reay 1985; ed Eton Coll., Trinity Coll., Cambridge; Nat. Service 1956–58; joined Matheson & Co. 1961, Chair. 1975–, mem. Bd of Dirs Jardine Matheson Holdings Ltd, Hong Kong 1967–, Chair. 1972–75, 1989–, Jardine Strategic Holdings 1989– (Dir 1988–); Dir Sun Alliance and London Insurance PLC 1975–96, Sun Alliance Group PLC 1989, Deputy Chair. 1993–96, Dir Royal and Sun Alliance Insurance Group PLC 1996–2000; mem. Bd of Dirs Robert Fleming Holdings Ltd 1975–2000, Rothmans Int. 1988–94, Hongkong Land Co. 1988–, Mandarin Oriental Int. 1988–, Dairy Farm Int. Holdings 1988–, The Daily Telegraph 1990–2001, Hong Kong Land, Mandarin Oriental, Rothschilds Continuation Holdings; Chair. Hong Kong Asscn 1988–2001, now Vice-Chair.; mem. 21st Century Trust 1987–97; Propr The Spectator 1975–81; Trustee, Nat. Portrait Gallery 1982–2001 (Chair. 1994–2001); mem. The Tablet Trust (charity). *Leisure interest:* country pursuits. *Address:* Jardine Matheson Holdings Ltd, 48th Floor, Jardine House, GPO Box 70, Hong Kong Special Administrative Region, People's Republic of China (office); Matheson & Co. Ltd, 3 Lombard Street, London, EC3V 9AQ, England (office). *Telephone:* 2843-8288 (Hong Kong) (office), (20) 7816-8100 (London) (office). *Fax:* (20) 7623-5024 (London) (office). *E-mail:* jml@jardines.com (office); enquiries@matheson.co.uk (office). *Website:* www.jardines.com (office); www.matheson.co.uk (office).

KESWICK, Sir (John) Chippendale (Chips) Lindley, Kt; British merchant banker; b. 2 Feb. 1940; s. of the late Sir William Keswick and of Mary Lindley; brother of Henry N. L. Keswick and Simon L. Keswick; m. Lady Sarah Ramsay 1966; three s.; ed Eton Coll., Univ. of Aix-Marseilles; with Glyn Mills & Co. 1961–65; Jt Vice-Chair. Hambros PLC 1986, Jt Deputy Chair. 1990–97, Group Chief Exec. 1995–97; Chair. Hambros Bank Ltd 1986–95, Chair. (non-exec.) 1995–98, Chair. Hambros PLC 1997–98; Sr Banking and Capital Markets Adviser Société Générale 1998–; mem. Bd of Dirs Persimmon PLC 1984–, De Beers 1993–, Bank of England 1993–2000, Edin. Investment Trust PLC 1992–, IMI PLC 1994–, Anglo American Corpn of S Africa Ltd 1995; Vice-Counsellor Cancer Research Campaign 1992–; Sr Ind. Dir Investec 2002–; Hon. Treas. Children's Country Holidays Fund; mem. Queen's Body Guard for Scotland, Royal Co. of Archers 1976–. *Leisure interests:* bridge, country pursuits. *Address:* c/o Board of Directors, Investec Limited, 100 Grayston Drive, 2nd Floor, Sandown Sandton, Gauteng 2196, South Africa; 17 Charterhouse Street, London, EC1N 6RA (office). *Telephone:* (20) 7430-3553 (office). *Fax:* (20) 7430-8670 (office).

KESWICK, Simon Lindley, FRSA; British business executive; *Chairman, Hongkong Land Holdings Ltd;* b. 20 May 1942; s. of the late Sir William Keswick and of Mary Lindley; brother of Henry Neville Lindley Keswick and Sir John Chippendale Lindley Keswick (q.v.); m. Emma Chetwode 1971; two s. two d.; ed Eton Coll. and Trinity Coll., Cambridge; Dir Fleetways Holdings Ltd, Australia 1970–72, Greenfriar Investment Co. 1979–82; Dir Matheson & Co. Ltd 1978–82, Chair. Jardine Matheson Insurance Brokers 1978–82, Dir Jardine Matheson & Co. Ltd, Hong Kong 1972–, Man. Dir 1982, Chair. 1983–89, Jardine Matheson Holdings Ltd 1984–89 (Dir 1972–), Jardine Strategic Holdings Ltd 1987–89, (Dir 1987–), Jardine Int. Motor Holdings 1990–97; Chair. Hongkong Land Holdings Ltd 1983–, Hongkong & Shanghai Banking Corpn 1983–88, Mandarin Oriental Int. Ltd 1984–, Dairy Farm Int. Holdings Ltd 1984–, Fleming Mercantile Investment Trust 1990– (Dir 1988–), Trafalgar House PLC 1993–96; Dir Hanson PLC 1991–, Jardine Lloyd Thomson Group PLC 2001–; Dir (non-exec.) Wellcome 1995–; Trustee, British Museum 1989–. *Leisure interests:* country pursuits, Tottenham Hotspur Football Club. *Address:* Rockcliffe, Upper Slaughter, Cheltenham, Glos., GL54 2JW, England (home); May Tower 1, 5–7 May Road, Hong Kong Special Administrative Region (home); Hongkong Land Ltd, 8th Floor, One Exchange Square, Central, Hong Kong Special Administrative Region, People's Republic of China (office). *Telephone:* (1451) 30648 (England) (home); 2842-8428 (Hong Kong) (office). *Fax:* 2845-9226 (Hong Kong) (office). *E-mail:* gpobox@hkland.com (office). *Website:* www.hkland.com (office).

KESWICK, Hon. Lady Tessa; British administrator and fmr civil servant; *Deputy Chairman, Centre for Policy Studies;* b. (Annabel Therese Fraser), 15 Oct. 1942, Beauly, Scotland; d. of 15th Lord Lovat and Rosamund Broughton; m. 1st Lord Reay 1964 (divorced 1978); two s. one d.; m. 2nd Henry Keswick (q.v.) 1985; ed Sacred Heart Convent, Woldingham, Surrey; Conservative Councillor, Royal Borough of Kensington and Chelsea 1982–86; Conservative cand. for Inverness 1987; special policy adviser to Rt Hon. Kenneth Clarke (q.v.) at Dept of Health 1989, Dept of Educ., Home Office, Treasury –1995; Dir Centre for Policy Studies 1995–2004, Deputy Chair. 2004–; Fellow, King's Coll. London. *Leisure interests:* art, music, breeding horses. *E-mail:* tessa@cps.org.uk (office). *Website:* www.cps.org.uk (office).

KETO, Aila Inkeri, AO, PhD; Australian conservationist and academic; *President, Australian Rainforest Conservation Society Inc.;* b. 14 March 1943, Tully, Qld; d. of Kauko Keto and Ingrid Keto; m. Dr Keith Scott; one s.; ed Univ. of Queensland; Adjunct Prof., School of Agronomy and Horticulture, Univ. of Queensland 2002–11; helped develop Centre for Native Floriculture at Univ. of Queensland Gatton; Co-founder and Pres. Rainforest Conservation Soc. (now Australian Rainforest Conservation Soc. Inc.) 1982–; helped negotiate SE Queensland Forests Agreement with Queensland Govt, conservation groups and Queensland Timber Bd 1999; negotiated Delbessie Agreement with Queensland Govt and AgForce Queensland 2007; collaborated with Queensland Govt on SE Queensland Conservation Initiative; Hon. Life mem. Australian Conservation Foundation 1990, The Wilderness Soc., Int. Union for Conservation of Nature; Hon. DSc (Queensland) 2003; BHP Bicentennial Award for the Pursuit of Excellence (Environment), Advance Australia Foundation Award, UNEP Global 500 Roll of Honour 1988, Avon Spirit of Achievement Award, World Class Achievers, Telecom Australia, Golden Gecko Award, Gold Coast and Hinterland Environment Council 1990, Special Award for Outstanding Environmental Achievement, Sunshine Coast Environment Council 1990, Fred M. Parkard Int. Parks Merit Award, Int. Union for Conversation of Nature 1992, Queenslander of the Year Award 2000, Premier's Millennium Award for Excellence 2000, Centenary Medal 2003, selected as a Queensland Great 2005, Volvo Environment Prize (co-recipient) 2005, Queensland Champion of Conservation, Queensland Conservation 2009. *Achievements include:* work led to protection of more than 1.5 million hectares of Queensland's rainforest; helped achieve closure of rainforest timber industry in North Queensland 1987, and subsequent end of all rainforest-logging on Queensland public land 1994; negotiated Springbrook Rescue programme 2006, Delbessie Agreement 2008. *Publications:* numerous publs in scientific journals. *Address:* Australian Rainforest Conservation Society, PO Box 2111, Milton, Qld 4064, Australia (office). *Telephone:* (7) 3368-1318 (office). *Fax:* (7) 3368-3938 (office). *E-mail:* aila.keto@rainforest.org.au (office). *Website:* www.rainforest.org.au (office).

KETTERLE, Wolfgang, MSc, PhD; German physicist and academic; *John D. MacArthur Professor of Physics, Massachusetts Institute of Technology;* b. 21 Oct. 1957, Heidelberg; m.; five c.; ed Univ. of Heidelberg, Tech. Univ. of Munich, Univ. of Munich, Max-Planck Inst. for Quantum Optics, Garching; Research Asst, Max-Planck Inst. for Quantum Optics, Garching 1982–85, Staff Scientist 1985–88; Research Scientist, Dept of Physical Chem., Univ. of Heidelberg 1989–90; Research Assoc., Dept of Physics, MIT, Mass, USA 1990–93, Asst Prof. of Physics 1993–97, Prof. of Physics 1997–98, John D. MacArthur Prof. of Physics 1998–; Fellow, American Physical Soc. 1997, American Acad. of Arts and Sciences 1999, Inst. of Physics 2002, Optical Soc. of America 2006; mem. German Physical Soc., Optical Soc. of America, European Acad. of Sciences and Arts 2002, Acad. of Sciences in Heidelberg 2002, Bavarian Acad. of Sciences 2003, German Acad. of Natural Scientists Leopoldina 2005; Foreign Assoc., NAS 2002; Officier, Légion d'honneur 2002, Medal of Merit of the State of Baden-Würtemburg (Germany) 2002, Kt Commdr's Cross (Badge and Star), Order of Merit (Germany) 2002; Michael and Philip Platzman Award, MIT 1994, David and Lucille Packard Fellowship 1996, Gustav-Hertz Prize, German Physical Soc. 1997, Rabi Prize, American Physical Soc. 1997, Discover Magazine Award for Tech. Innovation 1998, Fritz London Prize 1999, Dannie-Heineman Prize, German Acad. of Sciences 1999, Benjamin Franklin Medal in Physics (jt recipient) 2000, Nobel Prize in Physics (jt recipient) 2001, Killian Award, MIT 2004. *Address:* 80 Clifton Street, Belmont, MA 02478 (home); Massachusetts Institute of Technology, Room 26–243, 77 Massachusetts Avenue, Cambridge, MA 02139, USA (office). *Telephone:* (617) 489-2421 (home); (617) 253-6815 (office). *Fax:* (617) 253-4876 (office). *E-mail:* ketterle@mit.edu (office). *Website:* cua.mit.edu/ketterle_group (home).

KEUTCHA, Jean; Cameroonian politician, civil servant and diplomatist; b. June 1923, Bangangté; m.; three c.; ed École supérieure d'agriculture de Yaoundé; Chef de Cabinet, Minister of State with Special Responsibilities 1957, subsequently Chef de Cabinet, Sec. of State with responsibility for Information, Posts and Telecommunications; Asst to Chief of Bamiléké Region 1959; Sub-Prefect, Bafoussam 1960; Prefect of Mifi, subsequently of Menoua 1962–64; Sec. of State for Public Works 1964, subsequently Sec. of State for Rural Devt and Sec. of State for Educ.; Minister of Foreign Affairs 1971–72, 1975–80, of Agric. 1972–75; Amb. to EEC 1984–85, to People's Repub. of China 1985–88; fmr Pres. Caisse nationale de réassurances (CNR); currently Amb.-at-Large; Commdr, Ordre Camerounais de la Valeur, Grand Officier, Légion d'honneur, Grand Officier de l'Ordre Nat. Gabonais. *Publication:* Le Guide pratique pour la taille du Cafétier Arabica. *Address:* c/o Caisse nationale de réassurances, avenue Foch, BP 4180, Yaoundé, Cameroon.

KÉVÉS, György; Hungarian architect; *President, Kévés Architects Inc.;* b. 20 March 1935, Osi; s. of Sándor Kévés and Ványi Piroska; m. Éva Földvári 1966; ed Tech. Univ., Budapest; designer for firms, Agroterv and Eliti, Budapest 1959–61, Iparterv, Budapest 1961–69, Studio 'R' 1983–; private practice with Éva Földvári 1966–; teacher, Faculty of Architecture, Tech. Univ., Budapest 1966–73; Sr Architect and Prof., Architectural Masterschool, Budapest 1974–; with Káva Architects 1987–, Kévés Architects Inc.; organizes confs and exhbns Masterschool, including exhbns of post-modern architecture and Mario Bottá's works 1980–; organized lectures by Rob Krier and Mario Bottá, Hungary 1980; Visiting Lecturer, Washington Univ., St Louis, USA 1981; Ybl Prize, Hungarian State

Prize, several first prizes in architecture competitions. *Major works include:* Orczy Forum City Centre, Budapest. *Publications include:* Architecture of the 70s, Architecture of the 20th century; numerous articles in architectural magazines. *Leisure interest:* all kinds of art. *Address:* Kévés és Épitésztársai Rt., Melinda u. 21, 1121 Budapest, Hungary (office). *Telephone:* (1) 275-6002 (office). *Fax:* (1) 395-7623 (office). *E-mail:* kava21@axelero.hu (office). *Website:* www.kevesrt.com/en (office).

KEY, John, BComm; New Zealand politician; *Prime Minister;* b. 9 Aug. 1961, Auckland; m. Bronagh Key; two c.; ed Burnside High School, Univ. of Canterbury; early career as investment banker in mid-1980s, then worked in Singapore, London and Sydney for Merrill Lynch in 1990s; mem. Foreign Exchange Cttee Fed. Reserve Bank of New York 1999–2001; returned to NZ 2001; MP (Nat. Party) for Helensville 2002–, Nat. Party Deputy Finance Spokesman 2002–04, Finance Spokesman 2004–06, Leader 2006–; Prime Minister 2008–. *Address:* Parliament Buildings, Molesworth Street, Wellington 6011, New Zealand (office). *Telephone:* (4) 817-6800 (office). *Fax:* (4) 472-2075 (office). *E-mail:* j.key@ministers.govt.nz (office); john.key@parliament.govt.nz (office). *Website:* www.national.org.nz (office); www.johnkey.co.nz.

KEYS, Alicia; American singer, songwriter and musician (piano); b. (Alicia Augello Cook), 25 Jan. 1981, New York; m. Kasseem Dean (aka Swizz Beatz) 2010; one s.; ed Professional Performing Arts School, Manhattan; classically trained pianist; solo artist; numerous live appearances, festivals; collaborations with Angie Stone, Jimmy Cozier, Jermaine Paul, Jack White, John Mayer, Jay-Z, Usher; numerous awards including: Grammy Awards for Best New Artist 2001, for Song of the Year, Best Female R&B Vocal Performance, Best R&B Song (all for Fallin') 2001, for Best R&B Song (for You Don't Know My Name) 2005, for Best Female R&B Vocal Performance (for No One) 2008, (for Superwoman) 2009, for Best Rap Song (with Jay-Z) (for Empire State of Mind) 2011, Billboard Music Awards for Female Artist of the Year 2001, 2004, for Female New Artist of the Year 2001, for New R&B/Hip-Hop Artist of the Year 2001, American Music Award Favorite New Artist, Pop/Rock, Favourite New Artist, Soul/R&B 2002, MTV Award Best R&B Act 2002, American Music Award for Best Female Soul/R&B Artist 2004, Source Hip Hop Music Award for Female Artist of the Year 2004, MTV Award for Best R&B Video 2005, Lady of Soul Award for Best R&B/Soul or Rap Song (for If I Ain't Got You) 2005, MTV Europe Music Award for Best R&B 2005, Image Awards for Top Female Musical Artist, for Best Song, for Best Video (for Unbreakable) 2006, World Music Award for Best R&B Act 2008. *Recordings include:* albums: Songs In A Minor (Grammy Award for Best R&B Album 2001, MOBO Award for Best Album 2002) 2001, The Diary of Alicia Keys (Grammy Award for Best R&B Album 2005) 2003, Unplugged 2005, As I Am (American Music Awards for Best Album, Pop/Rock 2008, for Best Album, Soul/R&B 2008) 2007, The Element of Freedom 2009, Girl on Fire (Grammy Award for Best R&B Album 2014) 2012. *Films:* Smokin' Aces 2006, The Nanny Diaries 2007, The Secret Life of Bees 2008. *Address:* William Morris Agency, 1325 Avenue of the Americas, New York, NY 10019, USA (office). *Telephone:* (212) 586-5100 (office). *Fax:* (212) 246-3583 (office). *Website:* www.wma.com (office); www.aliciakeys.net.

KEZERASHVILI, Davit; Georgian politician and government official; b. 22 Sept. 1978, Tbilisi; m.; two s.; ed Ivane Javakhishvili Tbilisi State Univ.; Sr Inspector, Penitentiary Dept, Ministry of Justice April–Sept. 2001; Head of Information and Analysis Div., Dept of Informatics, Ministry of Justice 2001–02; Asst to Chair. Tbilisi City Council 2002–04; Head of Finance Police, Ministry of Finance 2004–06; Minister of Defence 2006–08. *Address:* c/o Ministry of Defence, 0112 Tbilisi, Gen. Kvinitadze 20, Georgia.

KHABADZE, Archil, BEcons; Georgian business executive and politician; *Chairman of the Government, Autonomous Republic of Adjara;* b. 11 March 1981, Batumi, Adjara ASSR, Georgian SSR, USSR; ed Batumi Shota Rustaveli State Univ., Agrarian Univ. of Georgia, Tbilisi; Credit Man., Jt Stock Co. (JSC) Georgian Maritime Bank, Batumi 2002–04; Credit Man., JSC Intellect Bank, Batumi 2004–05, Head of Credit Div. 2005–06; Credit Man., JSC Bank Cartu, Batumi March–Dec. 2006, Head of Credit Div. 2006–08, Batumi Br. Dir 2008–12; Chair. of the Govt, Autonomous Repub. of Adjara 2012–. *Address:* Office of the Chairman of the Government, Autonomous Republic of Adjara, 9 Gamsakhurdia Str., Batumi 6010, Georgia (office). *Telephone:* (422) 272006 (office). *Fax:* (422) 277300 (office). *E-mail:* archil.khabadze@ajara.gov.ge (office). *Website:* www.ajara.gov.ge (office).

KHACHATRIAN, Vardan; Armenian politician; b. 6 April 1959, Jermuk City; m.; two c.; ed Yerevan Polytech. Inst., Moscow Supreme Tech. Univ.; engineer Mineral Waters of Armenia Industrial Union 1980–83, Yerevan Polytech. Inst. 1983–85; Sr Engineer in Tech. Div., Div. Head, then Head of Production Tech. Div., Industrial Bakery Union of Armenia 1985–90; Workshop Head in Zovk Production Unit, then Dir Zovk Factory, Food Ministry of ASSR 1990–92; mem. Privatization Cttee, Repub. of Armenia 1992–95; mem. Nat. Ass. and Deputy Head Standing Cttee for Finance, Credit, Fiscal and Econ. Affairs 1995–98, Head Standing Cttee 1999–2000; Head of Finance, Budgetary Dept, Ministry of Defence 1998–99; Minister of Finance and the Economy 2000–08; mem. Yerevan—The Heritage Party –2009, currently mem. Social Democrat Hunchakian Party. *Address:* c/o Ministry of Finance and the Economy, Melik-Adamian St 1, 375010 Yerevan, Armenia.

KHADDAM, Abd al-Halim; Syrian lawyer and politician; *Leader, National Salvation Front in Syria;* b. 15 Sept. 1932, Baniyas; early career as lawyer in Damascus 1954–64; Govt of Damascus 1967–69; Minister of the Economy and Foreign Trade 1969–70; Deputy Prime Minister and Minister of Foreign Affairs 1970–84; mem. Regional Command, Baath Party 1971–84; Vice-Pres. for Political and Foreign Affairs 1984–2005 (resgnd); moved to Paris 2005; charged with treason by Syrian Parl. and expelled from Baath Party, announced govt-in-exile 2006; Founding Ass. Mem. and Leader, Nat. Salvation Front in Syria (opposition group); *Website:* www.free-syria.com.

KHADER, Naser, MA; Danish politician; b. 1 July 1963, Damascus, Syria; s. of Ahmed Khader and Sada Abu Khader; ed univs of Copenhagen, Arhus, Odense; worked as Arabic interpreter and trans. 1983–98; trans. and consultant, Radio Denmark 1989–97; consultant for DAB (housing soc.) 1996–97; mem. Social Liberal Party 1984–2007, mem. Cen. Bd 1996–2007; mem. Parl. for Western

Copenhagen 1994–99, Eastern Copenhagen 2000–11; City Councillor 1997–2000; Founder and Leader Ny Alliance (New Alliance) party 2007; mem. Konservative Folkeparti 2009–; UNICEF Amb. 2000–; Danish Authors' Asscn Award for Peace and Int. Understanding 1998, Cultural Award, Union of Commercial and Clerical Employees 1998, AFS-Interkultur Intercultural Award 1999, Modermål-Selskabets, Native Language Asscn Award 2000, Junior Chamber's Award for The Outstanding Young Person of 2001, Heiberg Award 2002, Life Award (Lifeforum, a Danish business Asscn) 2006, Free Speech Award (JyllandsPosten newspaper) 2006, Int. Award, Comité Laïcité République, France 2007. *Publications:* Ære og Skam (Honour and Shame) 1996, khader.dk (with Jakob Kvist) 2000, Modsætninger Mødes (Opposites Unite) (with Bent Melchior) 2003, Tro mod Tro (Belief Against Belief) (with Kathrine Lillø, 2005. *Address:* c/o Konservative Folkeparti, Nyhavn 4, 1051 Copenhagen K, Denmark (office). *E-mail:* naser@khader.dk (office). *Website:* www.khader.dk (office).

KHADJIEV, Salambek Naibovich, DChemSc; Russian/Chechen professor of chemistry and politician; b. 7 Jan. 1941, Shali, Chechen Repub.; m.; one s. two d.; ed Grozny Oil Inst., Moscow Univ.; Sr Researcher and Hon. Dir Inst. of Oil 1983–87; Dir Scientific Production Union Grozneftekhim 1987-91; USSR People's Deputy 1989-91; Minister of Petroleum Refining and Petrochemicals, USSR 1991; Chair. Democratic Reforms Movt in Chechen Rep. 1991–93, Prime Minister of Chechen Rep. (apptd by Russian govt) March–Oct. 1995; Chair. State Cttee of Industrial Policy, Russian Fed. 1995–96, Vice-Pres. Asscn of Financial and Industrial Groups 1996; Chair. Ecotec-oil Co. Moscow; Corresp. mem. Russian Acad. of Sciences 1990–, currently with A.V. Topchiev Inst. of Petrochemical Synthesis, Moscow; Co-chair. Bd of Trustees Fund for Humanitarian Assistance to the Chechen Repub.; Ed.-in-Chief Petroleum Chemistry magazine; Chair. Scientific Bd of Petrochemistry, Russian Acad. of Sciences; Fellow, Islamic Acad. of Sciences in Amman; Labour Veteran 1988, Hon. Oil-Chemist of the USSR 1990, Honoured Worker of Science & Technology, Chechen Repub., Honoured Worker of Ministry of Fuel & Energy of Russia 2001. *Publications:* Cracking of Oil – Fractions over Zeolite Catalysts; more than 250 scientific publs and more than 120 inventions. *Address:* 107113 Moscow, Apartment 47, House 3, Malenkovskaja Street; A.V. Topchiev Institute of Petrochemical Synthesis, Russian Academy of Sciences, 29 Leninsky Prospekt, Moscow 117912, Russia (office). *Telephone:* (495) 236-41-29 (office). *Fax:* (495) 236-12-62 (office). *E-mail:* ecotek@dol.ru (office); khadzhiev@ips.ac.ru (office). *Website:* www.ips.ac.ru (office).

KHADKA, Purna Bahadur; Nepalese politician; b. 1955; Nepali Congress Dist Pres. 1988–91; elected to House of Reps 1991, 1994, 1999; Minister of Youth, Sports and Culture 1998–99, of Information and Communication and Industry 1999; Minister of Industry, Commerce and Supplies; Minister of Home Affairs 2004–05; mem. Nepali Congress Party. *Address:* Nepali Congress Party, B. P. Smriti Bhavan, B. P. Nagar, Sanepa, Lalitpur, Nepal (office). *Telephone:* (1) 5555263 (office). *Fax:* (1) 5555188 (office). *E-mail:* ncparty@wlink.com.np (office). *Website:* www.nepalicongress.org (office).

KHADURI, Nodar, CandEconSci; Georgian economist, academic and politician; *Minister of Finance;* b. 29 Aug. 1970, Tbilisi; Lecturer, Faculty of Econs and Business (Macroeconomics), Ivane Javakhishvili Tbilisi State Univ. 1999–2006, Full Prof. 2006–, Founder and first Dean of Student Self Govt 1993–94, mem. Bd, Faculty of Econs 1994–96, 2003–05, Deputy Dean, Faculty of Econs 2004–05; Asst to Minister of Econs 1996–97, in charge of managing state finances and coordinating strategic units of the Ministry of Finance 1997–98, in charge of coordinating activities of Strategic Units of Ministry of Econs 1999–2000; Head of Tax and Revenue Cttee, Parl. of Georgia 2000–03; Asst to Minister and managed state finances, Ministry of Finance 2003–04; consulted Parl. of Georgia in econ. and legis. issues as nat. consultant of project implemented by UNDP 2004–08; fmr Head of Financial Admin of Shida Kartli; Minister of Finance 2012–; mem. Editorial Bd Economics and Business, Business and Law, Taxes, New Economist, Economist, The Caucasus and Globalization (Sweden); Founder Debate Club of Macroecomics Policy; has also taught at other educational insts, including CSB and Georgian Inst. of Public Affairs; invited lecturer abroad, especially at St Petersburg State Univ., Russia; f. Asscn of Young Economists of Georgia 1989, mem. Bd of Dirs and Advisory Council; f. The Centre for Econ. Problems Research, Chair. 2008–; mem. oikos Tbilisi Advisory Council. *Publications include:* two monographs and a textbook; more than 70 research papers on macroeconomics, economics of the public sector, macroeconomics policy, economics of Georgia and macroeconomics of post-Soviet transitional period. *Address:* Ministry of Finance, 0114 Tbilisi, V. Gorgasali Str. 16, Georgia (office). *Telephone:* (32) 26-14-44 (office). *Fax:* (32) 45-74-55 (office). *E-mail:* minister@mof.ge (office). *Website:* www.mof.ge (office).

KHAIRI, Haziq-ul-, BA, MA, LLB; Pakistani judge and writer; b. 5 Nov. 1931, Delhi, India; s. of the late Raziq-ul-Khairi, Ed. of Ismat; ed Anglo-Arabic Higher Secondary School, Darya Ganj Delhi and in Karachi, Univ. of Karachi; migrated with family upon partition of India; apptd Judge of Sindh High Court, Prov. Ombudsman (Sindh); fmr mem. Council of Islamic Ideology; Chief Justice Fed. Shari'a Court of Pakistan –2009; Chair. Thinker's Forum (Hamdard Shura), Karachi; ex-officio mem. Nat. Judicial Policy Making Cttee, Law and Justice Comm., Advisory Bd Al-Mizan Foundation, Admin Cttee of Al-Mizan Foundation, Bd of Govs, Bd of Trustees, Council of Trustees and Selection Bd Int. Islamic Univ., Islamabad; Chief Patron SAARC Health, Pakistan; mem. Syndicate, Baqai Medical Univ.; Pres., Cen. and West Asian Studies, Univ. of Karachi; mem. Human Rights Comm. of Pakistan; Pres. Anglo-Arabic School and Coll. Old Boys Asscn; Trustee, Transparency International (Pakistan). *Address:* c/o Federal Shari'a Court, Islamabad, Pakistan.

KHAKAMADA, Irina Mutzuovna, DEcon; Russian politician; b. 13 April 1955, Moscow; m. 3rd Vladimir Sirotinsky; three c.; ed Peoples' Friendship Univ. of Russia, Moscow State Univ.; mem. Research Inst. State Planning Cttee 1981–85; teacher, Tech. Inst. of Automobile Factory 1985–89; Sr Expert, Russian Stock Exchange of Raw Materials 1990; mem. Party of Econ. Freedom 1992, Sec.-Gen. and Co-Chair. 1992–94; Pres. Liberal Women's Foundation 1994; mem. State Duma 1993–97, 1999–2003, Head of Right Forces faction, Deputy Chair. 2000–; Leader, pre-election union Obshcheye Delo 1995; Chair. State Cttee for Support of Small Enterprises 1997–98; Founder and Co-leader pre-election union Pravoye Delo, transformed later into Union of Right Forces party 1999, Co-Chair. 2000–04

(resgnd); cand. for Pres. of Russian Fed. 2004 (ind.); Woman of the Year 2002. *Publications:* The Maiden Name, Peculiarities of National Politics; and numerous articles. *E-mail:* irina@hakamada.ru.

KHAKHAR, Devang V., BTech, PhD; Indian chemical engineer, academic and research institute director; *Director, Indian Institute of Technology Bombay;* ed Indian Inst. of Tech. (IIT), Delhi, Univ. of Massachusetts, Amherst, USA; with Dept of Chemical Eng, IIT Bombay 1987–, Prof.-in-Charge, Continuing Educ. Programme 2001–02, Head of Dept of Chemical Eng 2002–04, Dean of Faculty Affairs 2005–, Dir IIT Bombay 2009–; Fellow, Indian Nat. Acad. of Eng 2001, Indian Nat. Science Acad. 2002, Indian Acad. of Sciences 1996; Amar Dyechem Award, Indian Inst. of Chemical Engineers 1993, Shanti Swarup Bhatnagar Prize, Eng Sciences, Council for Scientific and Industrial Research 1997, Swarnajayanti Fellowship, Dept of Science and Tech. 1998, N. R. Kamath Memorial Lecture, IPI 1999, Herdillia Award, Indian Inst. of Chemical Engineers 1999. Millennium Gold Medal, Indian Science Congress 2000, Excellence in Teaching Award, IIT Bombay 2001, MRSI Medal Lecture 2003, H. H. Mathur Award for Applied Sciences, IIT Bombay 2005, Indira Manudhane Best PG Teacher Award, Chemical Eng Dept, IIT Bombay 2005. *Publications:* more than 150 papers in professional journals on dynamics of particulate systems, polymerization of rigid molecules and fluid mixing. *Address:* Indian Institute of Technology Bombay Powai, Mumbai 400076, Maharashtra, India (office). *Telephone:* (22) 2576-7212 (office); (22) 2576-4148 (office). *Fax:* (22) 2572-6895 (office). *E-mail:* khakhar@che.iitb.ac.in (office). *Website:* www.iitb.ac.in (office). www.che.iitb.ac.in/online/faculty/devang-v-khakhar (office).

KHALAF, Rima, BA, PhD; Jordanian international organization official; *Under-Secretary-General and Executive Secretary, United Nations Economic and Social Commission for Western Asia;* b. 1953; m. Hani K. Hunaidi; two c.; ed American Univ. of Beirut, Portland State Univ., USA; Lecturer, Dept of Econs, Portland State Univ. 1979; Dir-Gen. Jordan Export Devt and Commercial Centres Corpn 1990–93; Dir-Gen. for Investment Promotion Dept, Amman 1990–93; Minister for Industry and Trade 1993–95, for Planning 1995–98; Senator 1997–2000; Deputy Prime Minister 1999–2000; Asst Sec.-Gen. and Dir of Regional Bureau for Arab States, UNDP 2000–06; Under-Sec.-Gen. and Exec. Sec., UN Econ. and Social Comm. for Western Asia 2010–; Chair. Advisory Bd UN Global Democracy Fund 2006–07; Dir Center for Global Devt; CEO Mohammed bin Rashid Al Maktoum Foundation 2008–09; mem. Bd of Dirs AMIDEAST, Carnegie Middle East Advisory Council, IMF Middle East Advisory Group; mem. Bd of Trustees, American Univ. of Beirut, Nat. Center for Human Rights, Higher Educ. Council; mem. Econ. Consultative Council; participated in High-Level Comm. for Modernisation of World Bank Group Governance 2008–09; Grand Codon of the Order of Al-Kawkab Al-Urduni (Jordan) 1995; Hon. DHumLitt (American Univ. of Cairo) 2009; League of Arab States Award 2005, Prince Claus Award, King Hussein Leadership Prize 2009, listed among top fifty people who shaped the decade by Financial Times newspaper 2009. *Address:* United Nations Economic and Social Commission for Western Asia, PO Box 11-8575, Riad el-Solh Square, Beirut, Lebanon (office). *Telephone:* (1) 981301 (office). *Fax:* (1) 981510 (office). *Website:* www.escwa.un.org (office).

KHALATNIKOV, Isaac Markovich, DPhysMathSc; Russian theoretical physicist and academic; *Honorary Director, L.D. Landau Institute of Theoretical Physics, Russian Academy of Sciences;* b. 17 Oct. 1919, Dniepropetrovsk; two d.; ed Dniepropetrovsk State Univ.; Jr Researcher, Sr Researcher, Head of Div., Inst. of Physical Problems, USSR Acad. of Sciences 1945–65, Dir L.D. Landau Inst. of Theoretical Physics, USSR (now Russian) Acad. of Sciences 1965–92, Hon. Dir 1992–, Adviser Russian Acad. of Sciences 1993–; Prof., Moscow Inst. of Physics and Tech. 1954–; Prof., Tel-Aviv Univ. School of Physics and Astronomy 1993–2003; Corresp. mem. USSR Acad. of Sciences 1972, mem. 1984; Foreign mem. Royal Soc. 1994; Hon. Pres. Landau Network Centro Volta, Como, Italy 1995; USSR State Prize 1953, Landau Prize in Physics 1976, Alexander von Humboldt Award 1989, Kiwani Club Int. Prize 1999, Blaise Pascal Medal, European Acad. of Sciences 2005. *Publications:* more than 200 papers on solid state physics, relativistic cosmology, quantum field theory. *Leisure interest:* chess. *Address:* Landau Institute of Theoretical Physics, 119334 Moscow, Kosygina str. 2, Russia (office). *Telephone:* (495) 137-32-44 (office); (495) 702-93-17 (office); (496) 522-10-41 (home). *Fax:* (495) 938-20-77 (office). *E-mail:* khalat@itp.ac.ru (office).

KHALED; Algerian singer, musician (keyboard, accordion) and songwriter; b. (Khaled Hadj Brahim), 29 Feb. 1960, Wahran; mem. The Five Stars; first recording aged 14 as Cheb Khaled; first hit Trigue Al Lissi (The Way To School) 1975; lyrics censored in Algeria until 1983; performed at Bobigny Festival in France 1986, relocated to Paris 1990; first int. rai hit Didi 1992; collaborations with Chaba Zahouania, Rachid Taha and Faudel; apptd Goodwill Amb. of FAO 2003; performed at Opening Ceremony, World Cup (Fédération Internationale de Football Asscn) 2010; crowned 'King of Rai' at the first rai festival Oran 1985, BBC Radio 3 World Music Award for Middle East/North Africa region 2005, Antonio Carlos-Jobim Award, Montreal Int. Jazz Festival 2005, Empowering Award 2006, Mediterranean Prize for Creativity 2009, Big Apple Music Award 2009, NME Award 2009. *Recordings include:* albums: Moule El Kouchi 1985, Rai King of Algeria 1985, Fuir Mais Ou? 1991, Khaled 1992, N'ssi N'ssi (César Award for Best Soundtrack) 1993, Sahra 1996, Kenza 1997, Les Monstres Sacrés du Rai, Ya Taleb (with Chaba Zahouania), Best Of The Early Years 2002, Ya Rayi 2004, Liberté 2009. *Address:* c/o AZ/Universal Music France, 20, rue des Fossés St-Jacques, 75005 Paris, France. *Website:* khaled-lesite.artistes.universalmusic.fr.

KHALED, Mohamed Sidiya Ould Mohamed; Mauritanian politician; Dir-Gen. of the Treasury –2004; Minister of Finance 2004–07. *Address:* c/o Ministry of Finance, BP 181, Nouakchott, Mauritania (office).

KHALID, Mansour, LLD; Sudanese diplomatist and lawyer; *Minister of Foreign Trade;* b. 13 Dec. 1931, Omdurman; s. of Khalid Mohammed and Sara Sawi; ed Univs of Khartoum, Pennsylvania, USA and Paris, France; began his career as attorney, Khartoum 1957–59; Legal Officer, UN, New York 1962–63; Deputy UN Resident Rep., Algeria 1964–65; with Bureau of Relations with Member States, UNESCO, Paris 1965–69; Visiting Prof. of Int. Law, Univ. of Colo 1968, Univ. of Khartoum 1982; Minister of Youth and Social Affairs, Sudan 1969–71; Chair. Del. of Sudan to UN Gen. Ass., Special Consultant and Personal Rep. of UNESCO Dir-

Gen. for UNRWA fund-raising mission 1970; Perm. Rep. to UN, New York 1971, Pres. UN Security Council; Minister of Foreign Affairs 1971–75, of Educ. 1975–77, of Foreign Affairs Feb.–Sept. 1977; Asst to Pres. for Co-ordination and Foreign Affairs 1976, Asst to Pres. for Co-ordination 1977; fmr mem. Political Bureau and Asst Sec.-Gen., Sudan Socialist Union 1978; resgnd from all political posts July 1978 but remained mem. of Gen. Congress of the Sudan Socialist Union; Chair. Bureau of Trilateral Co-operation, Khartoum 1978–80; Personal Rep. for Exec. Dir of UNEP Anti-desertification Programme 1981–82; UN Special Consultant on Co-ordination of UN Information System 1982; Chair. Univ. Devt Cttee, Univ. of Khartoum 1982; Fellow, Woodrow Wilson Center, Smithsonian Inst. 1978–80; financial and investment consultant 1980–; adviser to Pres. Omar Al Bashir –2007; Minister of Foreign Trade 2007–; Loyal Son of Sudan and numerous foreign decorations. *Publications include:* Private Law in Sudan 1970, The Nile Basin, Present and Future 1971, Solution of the Southern Problem and its African Implications 1972, The Decision-Making Process in Foreign Policy 1973, Sudan Experiment with Unity 1973, A Dialogue with the Sudanese Intellectuals, Nimeiri and the Revolution of Dis-May 1985, 1985, The Government They Deserve: The Role of the Elite in Sudan's Political Evolution 1990, War and Prospects of Peace in Sudan 2003. *Leisure interests:* music, gardening. *Address:* Ministry of Foreign Trade, Khartoum (office); PO Box 2930, Khartoum, Sudan (home). *Telephone:* (183) 772793 (office). *Fax:* (183) 773950 (office).

KHALIFA, HE Sheikh Abdullah bin Khalid al-; Bahraini government official; s. of HE Sheikh Isa bin Salman al-Khalifa; Pres. of Historical Documents Centre, Govt of Bahrain; Minister of Justice and Islamic Affairs 2001–06, Deputy Prime Minister 2002–06; Pres. Bahrain Red Crescent Soc.; Hon. Pres. Wisdom Home Soc.; Man.-Dir Lightspeed Communications Co., Manama. *Publications:* Bahrain Through the Ages 1993; articles in journals including Al Watheeqa. *Leisure interests:* historical documents, sports. *Address:* c/o Ministry of Islamic Affairs, POB 450, Diplomatic Area, Manama, Bahrain (office).

KHALIFA, Sheikh Ali bin Khalifa al-; Bahraini politician; *Deputy Prime Minister;* s. of Sheikh Khalifa Bin Salman Al Khalifa; m.; four c.; Asst Under-Sec. for Immigration and Passports 1983–93; Minister of Transportation 1993–; Deputy Prime Minister 2005–; fmr Chair. Bahrain Telecommunications Co.; fmr Chair. Gulf Air Co. GSC, Bahrain Airport Services Co.; mem. Bahrain Econ. Devt Bd 2002–. *Address:* c/o Office of the Prime Minister, PO Box 1000, Government House, Government Road, Manama, Bahrain.

KHALIFA, HM Sheikh Hamad bin Isa al-, (King of Bahrain); b. 28 Jan. 1950, Bahrain; s. of the late Sheikh Isa bin Salman al-Khalifa; m. 1st Sheikha Sabeeka bint Ibrahim al-Khalifa 1968; three s. (including HRH Sheikh Salman bin Hamad bin Isa al-Khalifa) one d.; m. 2nd Sheia bint Hassan al-Khrayyesh al-Ajmi; two s.; m. 3rd a daughter of Shaikh Faisal bin Muhammad bin Shuraim al-Marri; one s. two d.; m. a daughter of Jabor al-Naimi; one s. two d.; ed Secondary School, Manama, Bahrain, Leys School, Cambridge Univ., Mons Officer Cadet School, Aldershot, England and US Army Command and Gen. Staff Coll., Fort Leavenworth, Kan., USA; formed Bahrain Defence Force 1968, C-in-C 1968–, also C-in-C Nat. Guard, raised Defence Air Wing 1978; mem. State Admin. Council 1970–71; Minister of Defence 1971–88; Deputy Pres. Family Council of Al-Khalifa 1974–; succeeded as Ruler on the death of his father March 1999; introduced constitutional monarchical system and assumed title of King Feb. 2002; created Historical Documents Centre 1976; Founder-mem. and Pres. Bahrain High Council for Youth and Sports 1975–; initiated Al-Areen Wildlife Parks Reserve 1976; f. Salman Falcon Centre 1977, Amiri Stud, Bahrain 1977; f. Bahrain Equestrian and Horse Racing Asscn, Pres. 1977–; f. Bahrain Centre for Studies and Research 1989; Hon. Fellow, Royal Coll. of Surgeons of Ireland 2006; Hon. mem. Helicopter Club of GB; Freedom of the City of Kansas, USA 1971; Grand Cordon of the Order of the Star of Jordan 1967, Al-Rafidain of Iraq (1st Class) 1968, Order of the Two Rivers, 1st class (Iraq) 1969, Nat. Defence of Kuwait (1st Class) 1970, Order of Muhammad (Morocco) 1970, Grand Cordon of the Supreme Order of the Renaissance (Jordan) 1972, Collar of the Order of the Republic (Egypt) 1973, Qiladat Gumhooreeya of Egypt (1st Class) 1974, The Taj of Iran (1st Class) 1973 (revoked), Collar of Abdulaziz al Saud (Saudi Arabia) 1976, Star of the Republic of Indonesia (1st Class) 1977, Order of the Repub. of Mauritania (1st Class) 1978, El-Fateh Al-Adheem of Libya (1st Class) 1979, Hon. KCMG (UK) 1979, Grand Conqueror of Libya 1979, Grand Croix, Ordre nat. du Mérite de la République française (1st Class) 1980, Kt Grand Cross, Order of Isabel la Católica of Spain (1st Class) 1981, Kuwait Liberation 1994, Order of Zayed of the UAE 2005, Order of the Repub. of the Yemen (1st Class) 2010, Grand Cross, Order of the Dannebrog (Denmark) 2011; US Army Certificate of Honour 1972. *Leisure interests:* horse riding, golf, study of ancient history and prehistory of Bahrain, water skiing, swimming, fishing, falconry, shooting, football, tennis. *Address:* PO Box 555, Ritala Palace, Manama, Bahrain. *Website:* www.bahrainembassy.org.

KHALIFA, Sheikha Haya Rashed al-, LLB; Bahraini lawyer, international organization executive and diplomatist; b. 18 Oct. 1952; ed Univ. of Kuwait, Univ. of Paris I (Panthéon-Sorbonne), France, Alexandria Univ. and Ain Shams Univ., Egypt; admitted as a lawyer to both Court of Cassation and Constitutional Court of Bahrain 1979; one of the first two women to practise law in Bahrain; fmr counsel at Bahraini Ministry of State for Legal Affairs as well as a sr attorney at a major Bahraini law firm; Prin. and Founding Partner, Haya Rashed Al Khalifa Law Firm; has held many sr positions, including Vice-Chair. Arbitration and Dispute Resolution Cttee Int. Bar Asscn 1997–99; Amb. to France (also accred to Belgium, Switzerland and Spain) 2000–04; Perm. Rep. to UNESCO 2000–04; Legal Adviser to Royal Court of Bahrain; Pres. 61st Session UN Gen. Ass. 2006–07; Rep. of Bahrain to ICC Int. Court of Arbitration; fmr Vice-Pres. Bahrain Bar Soc.; fmr mem. WIPO Arbitration Centre Consultative Cttee, Supreme Council of Culture, Art and Literature; mem. Bahrain Bar Asscn, Child Devt Soc., Arab Women's Legal Network; Bath for Peace Award. *Address:* Haya Rashed Al Khalifa, Attorneys at Law & Legal Consultants, First Floor, Bahrain Development Bank Building, PO Box 1188, Diplomatic Area, Manama, Bahrain. *Telephone:* (17) 537771. *Fax:* (17) 531117. *E-mail:* h.alkhalifa@hraklf.com (home). *Website:* www .hraklf.com/l1.htm.

KHALIFA, Sheikh Isa bin Ali al-; Bahraini government official; *Chairman, Gulf Petrochemicals Industries Co.;* fmr Minister of Oil, currently Adviser to Prime Minister for Industrial and Oil Affairs and Chair. Gulf Petrochemicals Industries

Co. *Address:* Office of the Chairman, Gulf Petrochemicals Industries Co., PO Box 26730, Manama, Bahrain (office). *Telephone:* 17731777 (office). *Fax:* 17731047 (office). *E-mail:* gpic@gpic.com (office). *Website:* www.gpic.com (office).

KHALIFA, Sheikh Khalid bin Ahmed al-, BSc; Bahraini diplomatist and politician; *Minister of Foreign Affairs;* b. 4 April 1960; m. Shaikha Wesal bint Mohamed Al Khalifa; ed Islamic Scientific Coll., Amman, Jordan, Univ. of Texas, USA; served at Embassy in Washington, DC 1985–94; Chief Liaison Officer, Office of Deputy Prime Minister of Foreign Affairs 1995–2000; Amb. to UK 2001–05 (also accred to Netherlands 2002–05, to Ireland 2002–05, to Norway 2002–05, to Sweden 2003–05); Minister of Foreign Affairs 2005–; Bahrain Medal 2001. *Leisure interests:* history, politics, social affairs, literature, travel. *Address:* Ministry of Foreign Affairs, POB 547, Government House, Government Road, Manama, Bahrain (office). *Telephone:* 17227555 (office). *Fax:* 17212603 (office). *Website:* www.mofa.gov.bh.

KHALIFA, Field Marshal Khalifa bin Ahmed al-; Bahraini army officer and government official; *Commander-in-Chief, Bahrain Defence Force;* b. 20 June 1945, Muharraq; ed Royal Mil. Acad., Sandhurst, UK; platoon commdr; training co. commdr; infantry co. commdr; bn second in command; battalion commdr; fmr Chief of Staff, Bahrain Defence Force; Minister of Defence 1988–06; currently C-in-C Bahrain Defence Force. *Address:* Ministry of Defence, PO Box 245, West Rifaa, Bahrain. *Telephone:* 17653333 (office). *Fax:* 17663923 (office).

KHALIFA, Sheikh Khalifa bin Sulman al-; Bahraini politician; *Prime Minister;* b. 1935; s. of the late Sheikh Sulman and brother of the ruler, Sheikh Isa; Dir of Finance and Pres. of Electricity Bd 1961; Pres. Council of Admin 1966–70; Pres. State Council 1970–73, Prime Minister 1973–; fmr Chair. Bahrain Monetary Agency; UN Special Citation of the Habitat Scroll of Honour Award 2006. *Address:* Office of the Prime Minister, PO Box 1000, Government House, Government Road, Manama, Bahrain. *Telephone:* 17253361. *Fax:* 17533033.

KHALIFA, Sheikh Mohammed bin Abdulla al-; Bahraini politician; Minister of State for Defence Affairs 2006–. *Address:* c/o Office of the Prime Minister, PO Box 1000, Government House, Government Road, Manama, Bahrain.

KHALIFA, Sheikh Muhammad bin Mubarak bin Hamad al-, BA; Bahraini government official; *Deputy Prime Minister;* b. 1935; s. of Sheikh Mubarak bin Hamad al-Khalifa; m.; two c.; ed American Univ. of Beirut, Lebanon, Univ. of Oxford and Univ. of London, UK; attended Bahrain Courts as cand. for the bench, Dir of Information 1962; Head of Political Bureau 1968 (now Dept of Foreign Affairs); State Council 1970; Minister of Foreign Affairs 1971–2005; currently Deputy Prime Minister with additional responsibilities for ministerial cttees. *Address:* c/o Office of the Prime Minister, POB 1000, Government House, Government Road, Manama, Bahrain.

KHALIFA, Sahar, BA, MA, PhD; Palestinian writer and feminist; b. 1941, Nablus; m. 1959 (divorced); two d.; ed Rosary Coll. and Bir Zeit Univ., Univ. of North Carolina and Univ. of Iowa, USA; moved to USA to study; Teaching Asst Dept of English and Women Studies Dept, Univ. of Iowa 1984–87; returned to Nablus 1988; Gen. Man. Women and Family Affairs Center, Nablus 1988–2003, Gen. Man. Women's Affairs Center, Gaza City 1991–94; Ed. Women's Affairs Journal 1989–95; Fulbright Scholar 1980–82. *Publications include:* novels (in trans.): We Are Not Your Slave Girls Anymore 1974, Wild Thorns 1975, The Sunflower 1980, Memoirs of an Unrealistic Woman 1986, The Door of the Courtyard 1990, The Inheritance 1996, The Image, the Icon, and the Covenant (Naguib Mahfouz Medal for Literature 2006) 2002, Hot Spring 2004, Roots and Branches 2009. *Address:* PO Box 1257, 11953 Amman, Jordan. *E-mail:* Khalifeh@ next.jo.

KHALIFA, HRH Sheikh Salman bin Hamad bin Isa al-, BPA, MA; Bahraini government official; *Crown Prince and Deputy Commander in Chief, Bahrain Army;* b. 21 Oct. 1969, Rifa'a, British Bahrain; s. of HM Sheikh Hamad bin Isa al-Khalifa, King of Bahrain; m. Hala bint D'aij al-Khalifa; two s. two d.; ed American Univ., Washington, DC, USA, Univ. of Cambridge, UK; Vice-Chair. Bd of Trustees, Bahrain Centre for Studies and Research 1992–95, Chair. 1995–99; Under-Sec. for Defence 1995–99, Crown Prince and C-in-C Bahrain Defence Force 1999–2008; Deputy C-in-C Bahrain Army 2008–; Chair. Supreme Council of Youth and Sport; CEO Econ. Devt Bd. *Address:* Ministry of Defence, PO Box 245, West Rifa'a (office); Crown Prince Court, PO Box 29091, Bahrain (office). *Telephone:* 17662100. *Fax:* 17661200.

KHALIFE, Marcel; Lebanese musician (oud) and composer; b. 10 June 1950, Amchit, Mount Lebanon; ed National Acad. of Music, Beirut; Lecturer, Lebanese Nat. Higher Conservatory of Music, Beirut 1970–75; f. Al Mayadeen Ensemble 1976, extensive int. tours performing songs based on poetry by Mahmoud Darwish; co-f. Qatar Philharmonic Orchestra, Music Dir and resident composer 2008–; appearances at numerous int. festivals including Baalbeck, Beit Eddine (Lebanon), Antakya, Carthage, El Hammamat (Tunisia), Timgad (Algeria), Jarash (Jordan), Arles (France), Krems, Linz (Austria), Bremen (Germany), Re:Orient Club (Sweden), Pavia (Italy), world music festivals in San Francisco, New York, Cleveland (USA), Int. Festival of Carthage; several awards including Jerusalem Medal, Beirut 1981, Palestine Award for Music 1999, named UNESCO Artist for Peace 2005, Charles Cros Award (world music category), Paris 2008, Intellectual Merit and Achievement Medal, Fez, Morocco 2008. *Compositions include:* The Symphony of Return, Sharq, Concerto Al Andalus (suite for oud and orchestra), Mouda'aba (Caress), Diwan Al Oud, Jadal Oud Duo, Oud Quartet, Al Samaa, Taqasimn (duo for oud and double bass), Sharq (choral symphonic composition), Arabian Concerto. *Recordings include:* more than 20 albums and DVDs including Promises of the Storm 1976, Rain Songs 1977, Where from Do I Enter the Homeland? 1978, Weddings 1979, At the Borders 1979, Stripped Bare 1980, Happiness 1981, The Bridge 1983, Collections – 3 Albums 1984, Dreamy Sunrise 1984, Ahmad Al Arabi 1984, Peace Be With You 1989, Ode to a Homeland 1990, Arabic Coffeepot 1995, Jadal Oud Duo 1996, Magic Carpet 1998, Concerto Al Andalus 2002, Caress 2004, Voyageur 2004, Taqasim 2007, Sharq 2007. *Publications:* Al Samaa 1981, Anthology of Studying the Oud 1982, Arabic Music-Theory and Practice 1984, Jadal Oud Duo 1996, OUD 1997, Andalusian Suite for Oud and Orchestra 2002. *E-mail:* general@marcelkhalife.com (office). *Website:* www .marcelkhalife.com (office).

KHALIL, Ali Hassan, Lic.en droit; Lebanese lawyer and politician; *Minister of State for Finance;* b. 15 July 1964, Khiyam; m. Samia Saleh Haider; four s.; ed Lebanese Univ.; began work as lawyer 1992; mem. Majlis al-Nuab (Nat. Ass.) for Marjeyoun/Hasbaya 1996–; Minister of Agric. 2003–04, of Public Health 2011–14, of Finance 2014–; Pres. Alumni Assen of Faculty of Law and Political Sciences, Lebanese Univ., Lebanese Youth Union; mem. Amal Movt. *Address:* Ministry of Finance, MOF Bldg, place Riad el-Solh, Beirut, Lebanon (office). *Telephone:* (1) 981001 (office). *Fax:* (1) 981059 (office). *E-mail:* infocenter@finance.gov.lb (office). *Website:* www.finance.gov.lb (office).

KHALIL, Idriss, PhD; Moroccan mathematician and academic; b. 20 Dec. 1936, El Jadida; m.; two c.; ed Rabat Univ., Univs of Bordeaux, Nancy and Paris, France; Asst Lecturer, Univ. of Bordeaux 1963–65; Asst Lecturer, then Sr Lecturer, then Prof., Univ. Mohammed V, Rabat Univ. 1966–; Jr Lecturer, Univ. of Nancy 1968–70; Research Asst, CNRS 1968–72; Lecturer, Bielefeld Univ. 1973; Dean, Faculty of Sciences, Univ. Mohammed V, Rabat Univ. 1974–85; Prof., Univ. of Nancy, MIT, Ecole Polytechnique, Paris and Paris-Sud Univ. 1979–85; fmr Minister of Educ. and Higher Educ.; Ed. Afrika Mathematika 1979; Founder-mem. Math. Africa Union 1976, African Assen for the Advancement of Science and Tech.; Corresp. mem. Int. Assen for Peace (PUGWASH) 1979; mem. Royal Acad. of Morocco 1982, Int. Assen of French-Speaking Communities; Founding Fellow, Islamic Acad. of Sciences; Chevalier des Palmes académiques 1979, Ordre nat. du Mérite 1982, Ordre du Trône (Morocco) 1982. *Address:* c/o Academy of the Kingdom of Morocco, Charia Imam Malik, Km 10, B.P. 1380, Rabat; Université Mohammed V, BP 554, 3 rue Michlifen, Agdal, Rabat, Morocco (office). *E-mail:* alacademia@iam.net.ma.

KHALILI, Abdul Karim; Afghan politician; *Second Vice-President;* b. Wardak Prov.; mem Nasr (resistance group) 1978, Dir Nasr Central Office, Tehran 1981; mem. Islamic Coalition Council of Afghanistan 1987, later becoming Speaker; fmr Minister of Finance; Leader Hizb-i Wahadat i Islami (Unity Party), an alliance of anti-Taliban fighters from Hazara ethnic minority, located in Bamian prov., 1994; driven out of Cen. Afghanistan by Taliban 1998; Leader Bamian prov. 2001; apptd Vice-Pres. Transitional Authority 2002, elected Second Vice-Pres. 2004–. *Address:* c/o Office of the President, Gul Khana Palace, Presidential Palace, Kabul, Afghanistan (office). *Website:* www.president.gov.af (office).

KHALILOV, Erkin Khamdamovich, DJur, CandJur; Uzbekistani politician; b. 1955, Buxoro; m.; three s.; ed Tashkent State Univ.; engineer, Research-Production Unit Cybernetics 1977–79; Jr, then Sr Researcher, Head of Div. Inst. of Philosophy and Law Uzbek Acad. of Sciences, 1979–90; Deputy, then Chair. Cttee on Law, Deputy Chair. (Speaker) Supreme Soviet (Oliy Majlis) 1990–93, Acting Chair. 1993–95, Chair. 1995–1999, re-elected 2000, Speaker Qoqunchilik palatasi Kengashi (Legis. Chamber) 2005–08; Order Mehnat Shuhrati 1999. *Publications:* about 100 articles on law and politics. *Leisure interests:* lawn tennis, football. *Address:* c/o Qoqunchilik palatasi Kengashi, Oliy Majlis, 100008 Tashkent, Xalqlar Do'stligi shoh ko'ch. 1, Uzbekistan (office). *Telephone:* (71) 139-87-07 (office); (71) 139-41-51 (office). *Website:* www.parliament.gov.uz (office).

KHALILZAD, Zalmay, BA, MA, PhD; American (b. Afghan) consultant and fmr diplomatist; *Chairman and CEO, Khalilzad Associates LLC;* b. 22 March 1951, Mazar-i-Sharif, Afghanistan; s. of Khalilullah Khalilzad; m. Cheryl Benard; two s.; ed American Univ. of Beirut, Lebanon, Univ. of Chicago; Asst Prof. of Political Science, School of Int. and Public Affairs, Columbia Univ. 1979–85; received Council on Foreign Relations fellowship to join US State Dept 1984, Special Advisor on Afghanistan to Under-Sec. of State 1985–89, Under-Sec. of Defence for Policy Planning 1990–92; Defence Analyst, RAND Corpn 1993–2000; headed Bush-Cheney transition team for US Dept of Defense, also served as Counselor to Sec. of Defense, also Special Asst to Pres. and Sr Dir for Southwest Asia, Near East, and North African Affairs, Nat. Security Council 2001; Special Envoy to Kabul, Afghanistan 2002, to Iraqi Nat. Congress, Iraqi Opposition 2003; Amb. to Afghanistan 2003–05, to Iraq 2005–07; Perm. Rep. to UN, New York 2007–09; currently Chair. and CEO Khalilzad Assocs LLC, Washington, DC; Counselor, Center for Strategic and Int. Studies; mem. Bd of Dirs Nat. Endowment for Democracy, America Abroad Media, RAND Corpn Middle East Studies Center, American Univ. of Iraq, Suleymania, American Univ. of Afghanistan; King Ghazi Ammanullah Medal, Afghanistan, Defense Dept Medal for Outstanding Public Service (twice). *Publications include:* The Government of God: Iran's Islamic Republic (with Cheryl Benard) 1984, Sources of Conflict in the 21st Century: Strategic Flashpoints and US Strategy 1998, Strategic Appraisal: United States Air and Space Power in the 21st Century (with Jeremy Shapiro) 2002; numerous articles in journals and books. *Address:* Khalilzad Associates LLC, 1001 Pennsylvania Ave, NW, Suite 600, Washington, DC , 20004, USA (office). *Telephone:* (202) 393-7145 (office). *Fax:* (202) 393-7149 (office). *Website:* www .khalilzadassociates.com (office).

KHAM, Sai Mauk; Myanma physician and politician; *Vice-President;* b. 1950, Muse, Shan State; ed Univ. of Medicine, Mandalay; trained as physician; fmr Chair. Shan Literature and Culture Assen; elected to House of Reps for Shan State constituency-3 2010; Vice-Pres., Repub. of the Union of Myanmar 2011–; mem. Union Solidarity and Devt Party (USDP). *Address:* Office of the Vice-President, Yangon, Myanmar (office).

KHAMA, Lt-Gen. (Seretse Khama) Ian; Botswana politician and head of state; *President;* b. 27 Feb. 1953, Surrey, UK; s. of the late Sir Seretse Khama, Pres. of Botswana 1966–80 and Lady Ruth Khama; ed White Stone school, Bulawayo, Zimbabwe, Waterford school, Swaziland, Sandhurst, UK; joined Police Mobile Unit 1973; Deputy Commdr Botswana Defence Force 1977–89, Commdr 1989–98; Kgosi eKgolo (traditional ruler) of Bangwato 1979–; Minister of Presidential Affairs and Public Admin March–July 1998; elected mem. Nat. Ass. 1998; Vice-Pres. of Botswana 1998–2008, Pres. 2008–. *Address:* Office of the President, Private Bag 001, Gaborone, Botswana (office). *Telephone:* 3950825 (office). *Fax:* 3950858 (office). *E-mail:* op.registry@gov.bw (office). *Website:* www.gov.bw/en/ Ministries–Authorities/Ministries/State-President/Office-of-the-President/About -the-Office-of-the-President/; www.iankhama.com.

KHAMENEI, Ayatollah Sayyed Ali Hoseini; Iranian politician and religious leader; *Wali Faqih (Supreme Religious Leader);* b. 17 July 1939, Mashad, Khorassan; s. of the late Ayatullah Sayyid Jawad Husaini Khamenei; m. 1964;

four s. one d.; ed Qom; studied in Islamic seminary of Najaf 1957, in Islamic seminary of Qom 1958–64, returned to Mashad 1964; joined Revolutionary Movt of Imam Khomeini 1962; imprisoned six times 1964–78, once exiled in 1978; Co-founder Islamic Republican Party 1979, Sec.-Gen. and Pres. Cen. Cttee 1980–87; Sec. of Defence, Supervisor of Islamic Revolutionary Guards, Leader of the Friday Congregational Prayer, Tehran Rep. in Consultative Ass. 1980; Imam Khomeini's Rep. in High Security Council 1981; Pres. of Iran 1981–89; mem. Revolutionary Council until its dissolution Nov. 1979; survived assassination attempt June 1981; Pres. Expedience Council 1988; Wali Faqih (Supreme Religious Leader) 1989–; ranked by Forbes magazine amongst The World's Most Powerful People (40th) 2009, (26th) 2010–11, (21st) 2012, (23rd) 2013. *Leisure interests:* reading, art, literature. *Address:* Office of the Wali Faqih, Shoahada Street, Qom, Iran. *E-mail:* info@leader.ir; istiftaa@wilayah.org. *Website:* www.leader.ir.

KHAMITOV, Rustem Zakievitch; Russian engineer and politician; m.; two c.; ed Moscow Higher Technical Coll.; began career at Ufa engine plant, later at Ufa Aviation Inst.; Head of Aviation Lab., later Head of Research and Production Dept, All-Union Scientific and Research Inst. for Construction of Trunk Pipelines, Ufa 1986; Deputy, Supreme Council of Bashkir Autonomous Soviet Repub. 1990; Dir Bashkortostan Inst. of Applied Ecology and Nature Man. 1993–94; Dir Bashkorto-stan Ministry of Environment Protection 1994–96, Bashkortostan Minister of Emergency Situations and Ecological Security 1996–99; mem. Bashkortostan Security Council 1996–99; Head, Dept of Emergencies Prevention, Russian Fed. 1999; Chief Fed. Inspector for Bashkortostan, Dept of Russian Pres., Volga Fed. Dist 2000, becoming Acting Deputy Plenipotentiary of Russian Pres. in Volga Fed. Dist; Head of Inter-regional Inspectorate on Tax-Payers, Russian Ministry of Taxes and Duties 2003–04; Dir Fed. Water Resources Agency 2004–09; Deputy Pres. RUSHYDRO (jt stock co.) 2009–10; Pres. Repub. of Bashkortostan 2010–, also Prime Minister 2012–; Order of Gratitude of Pres. of Russian Fed.; Hon. Diploma of Repub. of Bashkortostan 1999, Hon. Diploma of Russian Fed. 2004 . *Publications:* more than 100 scientific publications. *Leisure interests:* books, music, Alpine ski, speleology, river rafting. *Address:* Administration of President of Republic of Bashkortostan, 450101 Ufa, Tukaev Street 46, Bashkortostan, Russia (office). *Telephone:* (347) 250-15-66 (office). *Fax:* (347) 250-02-81 (office). *E-mail:* aprb@presidentrb.ru (office). *Website:* www.bashkortostan.ru (office).

KHAMTAY, Gen. Siphandone; Laotian army officer, politician and fmr head of state; b. 8 Feb. 1924, Houa Khong Village, Champassak Prov.; m.; five c.; mil. officer 1947–48, rep. of Lao Itsala 1948, mem. Front Cen. Cttee 1950–52, Chair. Control Cttee 1952–54; Gen. Staff mem. Pathet Lao 1955–56, Head Cen. Cttee 1957–59, propaganda and training officer 1959–60, mem. Cen. Cttee 1957, C-in-C 1960, mem. Politburo 1972–2006; mem. Phak Pasason Pativat Lao (Lao People's Revolutionary Party—LPRP) 1972, Leader 1992–2006, Adviser 2006–; mem. Secr. LPRP 1982; Deputy Prime Minister and Minister of Nat. Defence 1975–91; Prime Minister of Laos 1991–98; fmr Supreme Commdr Lao People's Army; Pres. of Laos 1998–2006.

KHAN, Aamir Hussain; Indian actor; b. 14 March 1965, Mumbai; s. of Tahir Hussain and Zeenat Hussain; m. 1st Reena Khan (divorced); one s. one d.; m. 2nd Kiran Rao; one s.; ed Bombay Scottish and N. M. Coll.; Padma Shri 2003, Indian of the Year in Cinema NDTV 2009, Indian of the Year in Entertainment Award, CNN-IBN 2009, Raj Kapoor Smriti Vishesh Gaurav Puraskar, Govt of Maharastra 2009, Padma Bhushan 2010. *Films include:* Yaadon Ki Baaraat 1973, Daulat Ki Jang, Holi 1984, Parampara 1993, Dil Hai Ki Manta Nahin 1991, Qayamat Se Qayamat Tak (Filmfare Best Male Debut Award) 1988, Raakh (Nat. Film Award) 1989, Jawani Zindabad 1990, Love Love Love 1989, Hum Hain Rahi Pyar Ke 1993, Jo Jeeta Wohi Sikander 1992, Baazi 1995, Dil 1990, Rangeela (Bengal Film Journalists' Assen Awards) 1995, Akele Hum Akele Tum (Best Actor, Bengal Film Journalists' Assen Awards) 1995, Deewana Mujhsa Nahin 1990, Raja Hindustani (Filmfare Award, Star Screen Award) 1996, Ishq 1997, Ghulam 1998, Sarfarosh (Zee Cine Award) 1999, Mann 1999, 1947 Earth 1999, Mela 1999, Lagaan (Nat. Film Award, Filmfare Award, Int. Indian Film Acad. Award, Bengal Film Journalists' Assen Award, Zee Cine Award) 2001, Dil Chahta Hai 2001, The Rising Ballad of Mangal Pandey 2005, Rang De Basanti (Filmfare Critics Award) 2006, Fanaa 2006, Taare Zameen Par (Nat. Film Award, Filmfare Best Dir Award, Star Screen Award, Zee Cine Best Dir Award) 2007, Ghajini 2008, 3 Idiots 2009, Talaash 2012. *Television:* Satyamev Jayte (host, co-producer) 2012. *Address:* 11 Bella Vista Apartments, Pali Hill, Bandra (West), Mumbai 400 050, India. *Telephone:* (22) 6463744; (22) 6463930. *Website:* www.aamirkhan.com.

KHAN, Abdul Qadeer, PhD; Pakistani nuclear scientist; b. 1 April 1936, Bhopal, British India; s. of Dr Abdul Ghafoor Khan; m. Henny Qadeer Khan; two d.; ed Univ. of Karachi, Catholic Univ. of Leuven, Belgium; mem. of staff, Physical Dynamics Research Lab., Amsterdam 1972–76; est. Eng Research Labs (now Dr A.Q. Khan Research Labs), Kahuta 1976, Chair. –2001 (retd); Pres.'s Special Science and Tech. Adviser with Ministerial Rank 2001–04; under house arrest 2004–09; f. Tehreek-e-Tahaffuz-e-Pakistan (political party) 2012, participated in gen. elections 2013, dissolved Sept. 2013; Patron-in-Chief Dr A.Q. Khan Inst. of Tech. and Man.; Hilal-e-Imtiaz 1989, Nishan-e-Imtiaz 1996, 1999. *Publications include:* Advances in Physical Metallurgy 1972, Topics in Metallurgy (co-author) 1972, Metallurgical Thermodynamics and Kinetics 1983, Dr. A. Q. Khan on Science and Education (co-author) 1997. *Address:* Dr A.Q. Khan Institute of Technology and Management, ICCTS Plaza 81, F-7/G-7 Markaz, Blue Area, Islamabad, Pakistan (office). *Telephone:* (51) 9268141 (office). *Fax:* (51) 9268156 (office). *E-mail:* stcd@comsats.net.pk (office). *Website:* www.krl.com.pk (office).

KHAN, Agha Rafiq Ahmed, LLB; Pakistani lawyer and judge; *Chief Justice, Federal Shariat Court;* b. 23 Aug. 1949, Garhi Yasin; s. of the late Agha Mohammad Anwar Khan; ed Sindh Univ., Int. Islamic Univ., Islamabad; enrolled as mem. Sindh Bar Council 1972; joined Sindh Judicial Services as Civil Judge and First Class Magistrate 1973, Sr Civil Judge and Asst Sessions Judge 1978, Additional Dist and Sessions Judge 1983, Additional Sec., Sindh Ass. 1985, Sec., Sindh Ass. 1985, Dir Legal Services 1989–90, Dist and Sessions Judge 1990, Judge, Sindh Labour Court No. 1, Karachi 1991, Law Sec., Sindh 1994–95, Judge, Sindh High Court 1996, 2007–09, Dist and Sessions Judge, Karachi South and Malir –2007, Fed. Sec., Law and Justice Division, Govt of Pakistan 2008–09, Chief Justice Fed. Shariat Court 2009–. *Address:* Federal Shariat Court, Constitution Avenue, G-5/2, Islamabad, Pakistan (office). *Telephone:* (51) 9203446 (office).

E-mail: cj@federalshariatcourt.gov.pk (office). *Website:* www.federalshariatcourt .gov.pk (office).

KHAN, Makhdoom Ali, LLM; Pakistani lawyer; ed Univ. of Karachi, Univ. of Cambridge and London School of Econs, UK; enrolled as Advocate, High Court of Sindh 1977; barrister, England and Wales, Society of Lincoln's Inn 1978; enrolled as Advocate, Supreme Court of Pakistan 1989, Sr Advocate 2001–; Lecturer in Law, Univ. of Keele, UK 1979–80; Prof. of Law, Univ. of Karachi, Sindh Muslim Govt Law Coll. 1980–88; Attorney-Gen. for Pakistan 2001–07 (resgnd); Chair. Pakistan Bar Council 2001–07; fmr Chair. Pakistan Electronic Media and Regulatory Authority, Pakistan Telecommunications Authority; fmr mem. Law and Justice Comm. of Pakistan. *Address:* Supreme Court of Pakistan, Constitution Avenue, Islamabad (office). *Telephone:* (51) 9220581 (office). *Fax:* (51) 9213452 (office). *Website:* www.supremecourt.gov.pk (office).

KHAN, Amjad Ali; Indian musician (sarod) and composer; b. (Masoom Ali Khan), 9 Oct. 1945, Gwalior, Madhya Pradesh; s. of the late Hafiz Ali Khan and Rahat Jahan Begum; m. Subhalakshmi Barooah 1976; two s.; ed Modern School, New Delhi; numerous concert performances and festival appearances worldwide; mem. World Arts Council, Geneva; Founder-Pres. Ustad Hafiz Ali Khan Memorial Soc. (promotion of Indian classical music and dance); Visiting Prof., Univ. of York, UK 1995, Univ. of Pa, Univ. of NM; Nat. Amb. for UNICEF 1996; Commdr, Ordre des Arts et des Lettres 2003; Hon. Citizen of Nashville, Tenn. 1997, of Houston, Tex. 1997, of Mass, of Atlanta, Ga 2002, City of Tulsa, Okla, City of Albuquerque, NM 2007; Dr hc (Univ. of York) 1997, (Delhi Univ.) 1998, (Rabindra Bharati Univ.) 2007, (Jivaji Univ., Gwalior) 2002, (Vishva Bharati Univ.) 2001; Hon. DLitt, Jamia Milia Islamia Univ. 2007; Sarod Samrat, Prayag Sangeet Samiti, Allahabad 1960, UNESCO Award 1970, Gandi UNESCO Medal, Int. Music Forum 1970, 1975, Padma Shri 1975, Special Honour, Sahitya Kala Parishad, Delhi 1977, Kala Ratna, Sangeet Kala Sangam, Bhopal 1980, Musician of Musicians, Bhartiya Vidhya Bhavan, Nagpur 1983, Amjad Ali Khan Day (Mass.) 1984, Shiromani Award 1986, Kala Saraswati, Andhra Ratna Andhra Pradesh Kalavedika 1987, Acad. Nat. Award (Tirupathi) 1987, Smitsmriti Award 1988, Raja Ram Mohan Roy Teacher's Award 1988, Sangit Natak Acad. Award 1989, Tansen Award, Nat. Cultural Org., New Delhi 1989, Vijaya Ratna Award, India Int. Friendship Soc., New Delhi 1990, Padma Bhusan 1991, Rajiv Gandhi Excellence Award 1992, Sarod Samrat 1993, Sangam Award 1993, Jawahar Lal Nehru Excellence Award 1994, Gandhi Medal, UNESCO 1995, Crystal Award, World Econ. Forum 1997, Padma Vibhushan 2001, Shankar Dev Award 2001, Fukuoka Cultural Grand Prize (Japan) 2004, USA-India Business Council 30th Anniversary Honour 2005. *Compositions include:* many ragas; music for Kathak ballets Shan E. Mughal, Shahajahan Ka Khwab, Ganesh; orchestral compositions Ekta Se Shanti, Ekta Ki Shakti, Tribute to Hong Kong (for Hong Kong Philharmonic Orchestra). *Radio includes:* promenade concert, BBC 1995. *Recordings include:* Tribute to Germany 1992, Inde Du Nord 1993, Sarod Ghar 1997, Evening Raga 2001, Amjad Ali Khan (with Amaan Ali Khan and Ayaan Ali Khan) 2002, Guftagoo 2002, Sadaayen 2002, Music from the 13th Century 2004, Ru Ba Ru 2005, Moksha 2005, Potrait of a Legend 2006, My Inspirations 2006, Romancing the Rains 2007, Breaking Barriers 2007, Yaara 2007, Remembering Mahatma Gandhi, Hope, Ancient Sounds (with Rahim AlHaj), Sarod Symphony 2010. *Leisure interests:* music, light reading, long walks. *Address:* 3 Sadhna Enclave, Panchsheel Park, New Delhi 110 017, India; 25 Hillhouse Lane, Old Brooksville, NY 11545-2503, USA. *Telephone:* (11) 6017062 (India) (office); (516) 671-1615 (USA). *Fax:* (11) 6018011 (India). *E-mail:* music@ sarod.com. *Website:* www.sarod.com (office).

KHAN, Asfandyar Wali, BA; Pakistani politician; *President, Awami National Party;* b. 19 Feb. 1949, Charsadda, North-West Frontier Prov. (now Khyber Pakhtunkhwa); s. of Khan Abdul Wali Khan and Taj Bibi; grandson of Khan Abdul Ghaffar Khan, 'Badshah Khan' (King of Khans, founder of non-violent Pashtun political movt, Khudai Khidmatgar (Servants of God) in undivided India); one s.; ed Aitchison Coll., Lahore, Univ. of Peshawar; joined opposition to Ayub Khan as student activist; imprisoned by govt of Zulfiqar Ali Bhutto and convicted as part of Hyderabad tribunal for 15 years 1975, released 1978, stayed away from electoral politics until 1990; Leader of Pakhtun Student Fed. prior to being elected to prov. ass. 1990; elected to Nat. Ass. 1993, re-elected 1997, 2008; Pres. Awami Nat. Party 1999–2002 (resgnd), 2003, 2006, 2011–; elected to Senate 2003. *Address:* Awami National Party, Bacha Khan Markaz, Pajagi Road, Peshawar, Pakistan (office). *Telephone:* (91) 2246851 (office). *Fax:* (91) 2252406 (office). *E-mail:* president@ awaminationalparty.org (office). *Website:* www.awaminationalparty.org (office). www.anp.org.pk (office).

KHAN, Sardar Attiq Ahmed, MA; Pakistani politician and writer; b. 1 Jan. 1955, Ghaziabad, Tehsil Dheerkot, Bagh Dist; s. of Sardar Abdul Qayyum Khan; ed Madina Univ., Saudi Arabia; fmr Chair. youth and student wing All Jammu and Kashmir Muslim Conf., later Chief Organizer, All Jammu and Kashmir Muslim Conf., Pres. 2002–06; elected mem. Legis. Ass. three times; Prime Minister of Azad Jammu and Kashmir 2006–09, 2010–11. *Address:* c/o Prime Minister Secretariat, Muzaffarabad, Azad Kashmir; All Jammu and Kashmir Muslim Conference, POB 184, Satellite Town, Rawalpindi 46300, Pakistan.

KHAN, Hameed Ahmed, PhD; Pakistani physicist and academic; b. 1 May 1942, Rangoon, Burma; ed Punjab Univ., Univ. of Birmingham, UK; joined Pakistan Atomic Energy Comm. (PAEC) 1965; helped to commission country's first research reactor; on staff of teaching and research faculties, Univ. of Birmingham –1974; Chief Scientist, Pakistan Atomic Energy Commission 1965–72, Sr Scientific Officer 1972–77, Principal Scientific Officer 1977–86, Chief Scientific Officer 1986–94, Head, Radiation Physics Div. 1992–94, Assoc. Dir 1994–96; Visiting Prof. Bahauddin Zakarayia Univ., Multan 1994; Dir–Gen. Pakistan Institute of Nuclear Science and Technology (PINSTECH) 1996–2000; Exec.–Dir COMSATS (Comm. on Science and Tech. for Sustainable Devt in the South) 2000–08, currently Adviser, COMSATS Inst. for Information Tech.; fmr Chief Ed. Nucleus; Fellow Islamic Acad. of Sciences, Pakistan Acad. of Sciences, Alexander von Humboldt (AVH), Philips University; First Prize in Physics (Nat. Book Foundation of Pakistan) 1991, 1992, 1993, Khawarizmi Prize (Iranian Research Org. for Science and Tech.) 1993, Prize in Tech. (Third World Network of Scientific Orgs) 1998, Sitara-i-Imtiaz Award, Int. ISESCO Science Prize 2006. *Address:* COMSATS Institute for Information Technology, Plot #30, Sector H8, Islamabad, Pakistan

(office). *Telephone:* (51) 9235381 (office). *E-mail:* drhakhan@comsats.net.pk (office).

KHAN, Rear Adm. Hasan Ali; Bangladeshi naval officer; b. 11 Feb. 1950, Hat-Lakshmipur, Gaibandha; m. Afsana Khan; two d.; ed Defence Service Command and Staff Coll., Nat. Defence Coll., Mirpur; Officer Cadet Navy 1969, mem. Exec. Br. 1972, has commanded several ships, fmr positions include Asst Chief of Naval Staff, Naval Sec., Naval Admin. Authority Dhaka –2005, Chief of Naval Staff 2005–07. *Address:* c/o Ministry of Defence, Gonobhaban Complex, Sher-i-Bangla Nagar, Dhaka 1207, Bangladesh. *Telephone:* (2) 8116955. *E-mail:* modgob@bttb .net.bd.

KHAN, Imran (see KHAN NIAZI, Imran).

KHAN, Irene Zubaida; Bangladeshi international organization executive; b. 24 Dec. 1956, Dhaka; one d.; ed Victoria Univ. of Manchester, UK and Harvard Law School, USA; joined Office of UNHCR 1980, adviser to local project offices, worked in Pakistan, SE Asia, UK, Ireland and numerous crisis deployments 1980–90, Sr Exec. Officer to Sadako Ogata 1991–95, Chief of Comm. in India 1995, Head of Documentation and Research Centre 1998–99, Head of Comm. in Fmr Yugoslav Repub. of Macedonia 1999, Deputy Dir Dept for Int. Legal Protection; Sec.-Gen. Amnesty Int. 2001–09; Consulting Ed., Daily Star 2010–; mem. Bd of Dirs Mary Robinson Foundation - Climate Justice; Chancellor, Univ. of Salford 2009–; Dr hc (Ferris Univ.) 2005, (Ghent Univ.) 2007; Pilkington Woman of the Year 2002, Sydney Peace Prize 2006, Ford Foundation Fellowship. *Publication:* The Unheard Truth: Poverty and Human Rights 2009. *Address:* Office of the Chancellor, University of Salford, The Crescent, Salford, M5 4WT, England (office). *Website:* www.salford.ac.uk (office).

KHAN, Ishratul Ebad; Pakistani government administrator; *Governor of Sindh;* b. 2 March 1963; ed Dow Medical Coll., Karachi; Minister of Housing and Town Planning, Sindh Provincial Govt 1990; 10 years of political exile in London; Gov. of Sindh Prov. 2002–11 (resgnd), resumed office as Gov. of Sindh July 2011. *Address:* Office of the Governor of Sindh, Karachi, Pakistan (office). *Telephone:* (21) 9201201-3 (office). *E-mail:* governor@governorsindh.gov.pk (office). *Website:* www .sindh.gov.pk (office).

KHAN, Jemima; British writer and charity fund-raiser; *Associate Editor, New Statesman;* b. 30 Jan. 1974, London; d. of Sir James Goldsmith and Lady Annabel Vane Tempest Stewart; m. Imran Khan 1995 (divorced 2004); two s.; ed Bristol Univ.; moved to Lahore, Pakistan with husband Imran Khan 1995; developed own brand of tomato ketchup; Jemima Khan Designs (fashion label) 1996–2001; campaigner to improve literacy levels in Pakistan; UK Special Rep. UNICEF 2001–; Assoc. Ed. New Statesman magazine 2011–; European Ed.-at-Large, Vanity Fair magazine; f. Jemima Khan Afghan Refugee Appeal 2001; reporter and news presenter, Channel 5, Bangladesh 2002–04; fund-raiser, Shaukat Khanum Memorial Cancer Hosp.; Rover People's Award for Best Dressed Female Celebrity, British Fashion Awards 2001. *Address:* New Statesman, 7th Floor, John Carpenter House, 7 Carmelite Street, Blackfriars, London, EC4Y 0AN, England (office). *Website:* www.newstatesman.com.

KHAN, K. Rahman, BCom, FCA; Indian accountant and politician; *Minister of Minority Affairs;* b. 5 April 1939, Krishnarajpet, Mandya Dist, Karnataka; s. of the late K. Khasim Khan and Shrimati Khairunnisa; m. Ayesha Rahman; three s. two d.; ed Mysore Univ.; mem. Karnataka Legis. Council 1978–90, Chair. 1982–84, Chair. Karnataka State Minorities Comm. (with rank of Cabinet Minister) 1993–94; elected to Rajya Sabha (upper house of Parl.) 1994, re-elected 2000, 2004, 2012, Deputy Leader, Indian Nat. Congress party in Rajya Sabha 2000–04, Deputy Chair. Rajya Sabha 2004–06, 2006–12; Minister of State in Ministry of Chemicals and Fertilizers 2004; Union Cabinet Minister of Minority Affairs 2012–; Regional Rep. to Exec. Cttee of CPA 2005–06, 2006–; mem. Central Muslim Asscn of Karnataka, later Pres.; mem. numerous parl. dels to int. bodies including European Parl., Strasbourg 2005, several visits to CPA and Ass. of the IPU. *Leisure interests:* music, badminton. *Address:* Ministry of Minority Affairs, 11th Floor, Paryavaran Bhavan, CGO Complex, Lodhi Road, New Delhi 110 003, India (office). *Telephone:* (11) 24364271 (office). *Fax:* (11) 23017999 (office). *E-mail:* vm@ nic.in (office). *Website:* minorityaffairs.gov.in (office).

KHAN, Mohammad Younus; Pakistani professional cricketer; b. 29 Nov. 1977, Mardan, North-West Frontier Prov.; m. Amna Khan 2007; one s.; right-handed batsman; occasional right-arm medium leg-break bowler; plays for Habib Bank Limited 1999–2007, Pakistan 2000– (Capt. 2005, 2006, 2009), Notts. 2005, Peshawar Cricket Asscn 1998–2005, Yorks. 2007, Rajasthan Royals 2008, S Australia 2008–, Surrey 2010; First-class debut: 1998/99; Test debut: Pakistan v Sri Lanka, Rawalpindi 26 Feb.–1 March 2000; One-Day Int. (ODI) debut: Pakistan v Sri Lanka, Karachi 13 Feb. 2000; T20I debut: England v Pakistan, Bristol 28 Aug. 2006; announced retirement from Twenty20 cricket after leading Pakistan to ICC (Int. Cricket Council) World Twenty20 title by beating Sri Lanka at Lord's 2009; banned indefinitely from Test cricket by Pakistan Cricket Bd, along with Mohammad Yousuf, for "infighting" during tour of Australia March 2010, ban lifted June 2010; mem. Pakistan team that lost to India in semifinals of ICC Cricket World Cup 2011; topped ICC's Test Batting Rankings after an innings of 313 in first Test as Capt. Feb. 2009. *Achievements include:* only the third Pakistani player to score 300 or more runs in an innings; second fastest Pakistani in terms of innings (87) to reach 4,000 Test runs, behind Javed Miandad. *Leisure interest:* fishing. *Address:* c/o South Australian Cricket Association, ABN: 94 694 912 780, Adelaide Oval, War Memorial Drive, North Adelaide, South Australia 5006, Australia. *Telephone:* (8) 8300-3800. *Fax:* (8) 8231-4346. *E-mail:* sacareception@ saca.com.au. *Website:* www.cricketsa.com.au.

KHAN, Gen. Mohammed Ismail; Afghan politician; *Minister of Water and Energy;* b. 1954, Herat; ed Kabul Mil. Coll.; served as officer in Afghan army; fmr Mujahidin Commdr during Soviet occupation; joined Jamiat-i Islami (Islamic Soc.) 1979; led uprising and liberated Herat from Soviet control; Gov. of Herat 1993–97, 2001–04; taken prisoner by Taliban following re-occupation of Herat 1997, escaped in 2000; Mil. Commdr Herat –2003; Minister of Water and Energy 2004–; mem. Northern Alliance. *Address:* Ministry of Water and Energy, Darulaman Wat, Kabul, Afghanistan (office). *Telephone:* (75) 2004813 (office).

KHAN, Rahat; Bangladeshi writer and editor; *Editor, Dainik Ittefaq;* b. 1940, Kishoregonj; ed Univ. of Dhaka; taught for eight years in colls including Nasirabad Coll. of Mymensingh, Jagannath Coll. of Dhaka, Commerce Coll. of Chittagong; apptd Asst Ed. Dainik Ittefaq (daily) 1969, now Ed.; Ekushe Padak 1996; Bangla Acad. Award 1973, Suhrid Literary Award 1975, Sufi Motahar Hossain Award 1979, Mahbubullah Zebunnesa Trust Award 1979, Abul Mansur Memorial Award 1980, Humayun Qadir Memorial Award 1982, Shuhrid Literary Award 1975, Trayi Literary Award 1988, Cetana Literary Award 1989. *Publications include:* short story collections: Onischito Lokaloy (Uncertain Human Habitation) 1972, Ontohin Jatra (The Eternal Journey) 1975, Bhalo Monder Taka (Money for Good and Evil) 1981, Apel Songbad (News of the Apple) 1983, and others; novels: Omol Dhobol Chakuri (Milk-White Service) 1982, Ek Priyodorshini (A Beautiful Woman) 1983, Chayadompoti (A Shadow Couple) 1984, Sangharsha (Clash) 1984, Shahar (The City) 1984, Hey Onanter Pakhi (O, Bird of Infinity) 1989, Modhyomather Khelowar (The Forward Footballer) 1991, Akhanksha (Desire), Kayekjan (A Few Persons), Ognidaho (Conflagration), Hey Maton Bongo (O, Mother Bangla). *Address:* Dainik Ittefaq, 1 Ramkrishna Mission Road, Dhaka, Bangladesh (office). *Telephone:* (2) 7122660 (office). *Fax:* (2) 7122651-3 (office). *E-mail:* rahat.khan@ittefaq.com (office); *Website:* www.ittefaq.com (office); ittefaq.com.bd (office).

KHAN, Raja Muhammad Farooq Haider; Pakistani politician; b. 14 Jan. 1955; s. of the late Raja Muhammad Haider Khan and Mohterma Saeeda Khan; ed Abbotabad Public School, Govt Coll., Lahore; mem. Azad Jammu & Kashmir (AJ&K) Legis. Ass. 1985–, held portfolio of Sr Minister as well as Minister of Educ. (re-elected and served as a Minister 1991, re-elected and held portfolio of Chair. Public Accounts Cttee 2006); Chair. Prime Minister's Inspection Comm. 2001–03; Pres. Muslim Conf. Dist Muzaffarabad, AJ&K 1986–90; Chair. Cen. Parl. Bd of Muslim Conf., AJ&K 1989–2001; Gen. Sec. Muslim Conf., AJ&K 1997–2001; Special Asst to Prime Minister of AJ&K 2003–06; Sr Deputy Pres. Muslim Conf. 2004–06, Pres. 2009–; Prime Minister of Azad Kashmir 2009–10 (resgnd). *Address:* c/o Prime Minister Secretariat, Muzaffarabad, Azad Kashmir (office); Kashmir House, F-5, Islamabad, Pakistan (office). *Website:* www.ajk.gov.pk (office).

KHAN, Raja Zulqarnain, BA; Pakistani politician; b. 15 March 1936, Gujrat; s. of the late Khan Bahadur Raja Muhammad Afzal Khan (fmr Gov. and Minister); ed New Delhi Modern High School, Aitcheson Coll., Lahore, Govt Coll., Lahore; Co-founder Jammu Kashmir Liberation League 1960; Minister in cabinet of Pres. Maj.-Gen. Abdul Rehman of Azad Jammu Kashmir (AJK) 1969; elected mem. AJK Legis. Ass. from Samani constituency (then in Mirpur Dist, now in Bhimbher Dist) 1975, elected mem. AJK Legis. Ass. from Bhimbher constituency 1985; Minister for Finance, Planning and Devt, Health and Revenue 1985–91, for Finance and Planning and Devt 1991–96; elected mem. Jammu and Kashmir Council 1996–2001; adviser to Chair. AJK Council and to the Prime Minister; cand. of All Jammu Kashmir Muslim Conf. in presidential elections Aug. 2006; Pres. Azad Jammu and Kashmir 2006–11. *Address:* c/o Office of the President, Azad Jammu and Kashmir Government, Muzaffarabad, Pakistan (office).

KHAN, Salman; Indian actor; b. 27 Dec. 1965, Indore, MP; s. of Salim Khan and Salma Khan; ed St Stanislaus High School; early career as a model; f. Being Human Foundation; TV presenter for 10 Ka Dum and Bigg Boss; ranked seventh best-looking man by People magazine 2004, Rajiv Gandhi Award 2007, Int. Indian Film Acad. (IIFA) Award for Habitat Humanity Ambassadorship 2010. *Films include:* Biwi Ho To Aisi 1988, Maine Pyar Kiya 1989, Baaghi: A Rebel for Love 1990, Saajan 1991, Jaagruti 1992, Dil Tera Aashiq 1993, Andaz Apna Apna 1994, Hum Aapke Hain Kaun 1994, Karan Arjun 1995, Khamoshi: The Musical 1996, Judwaa 1997, Pyaar Kiya To Darna Kya 1998, Kuch Kuch Hota Hai (Filmfare Best Supporting Actor 1999) 1998, Hum Dil De Chuke Sanam 1999, Dulhan Hum Le Jayenge 2000, Chori Chori Chupke Chupke 2001, Hum Tumhare Hain Sanam 2001, Tere Naam 2003, Mujhse Shaadi Karogi 2004, Phir Milenge 2004, Lucky: No Time for Love 2005, Jaan-E-Mann 2006, Partner 2007, Marigold: An Adventure In India 2007, Yuvvraaj 2008, Wanted (IIFA Best Actor 2010) 2009, Dabangg 2010, Ready 2011, Bodyguard 2011, Ek Tha Tiger 2012, Dabangg 2 2012. *Television:* as presenter: 10 Ka Dum 2008–09, Bigg Boss 2010–. *Leisure interests:* travelling, exercising, painting. *Address:* 3 Galaxy Apartments, BJ Road, Bandra, Mumbai 400 050, India (home). *Telephone:* 9821014288 (mobile).

KHAN, Sardar Mahtab Ahmad, LLB; Pakistani lawyer and politician; *Governor of Khyber Pakhtoonkhwa;* b. 15 Dec. 1952, Abbottabad; s. of Sardar Muhammad Nawaz Khan; ed Union Council, Dewal, Murree Sir Sayyad School, Rawalpindi; Prov. Minister of Health, Khyber Pakhtoonkhwa 1986–88; Chief Minister of Khyber Pakhtunkhwa 1997–99; imprisoned following mil. coup 1999–2002; mem. Senate of Pakistan 2003–08; Minister of Railways 2008; mem. Nat. Ass. for NA-17 Abbottabad-I 2008–13; mem. Khyber Pakhtunkhwa Prov. Ass. 2013–14; Gov. of Khyber Pakhtunkhwa 2014–; mem. Pakistan Muslim League Nawaz. *Address:* Office of the Governor, Peshawar, Khyber Pakhtoonkhwa, Pakistan (office). *Telephone:* (91) 9211716 (office). *E-mail:* info@khyberpakhtunkhwa.gov.pk (office). *Website:* www.khyberpakhtunkhwa.gov.pk (office).

KHAN, Sardar Mohammed Yaqoob; Pakistani business executive and politician; *President of Azad Jammu and Kashmir;* b. 26 Feb. 1953, Ali Sojal, Poonch Dist; s. of Sardar Gull Mohammed Khan; fmr Officer, Punjabi Pakhtoon Itehad Party, Karachi; fmr Sr Vice-Pres. Tehreek Amel Party, Azad Jammu and Kashmir; mem. Azad Jammu and Kashmir Legis. Ass. 2001, 2006, fmr Leader of the House; State Minister for Health, Population Welfare and Hydro-electric Bd, Housing and Planning 2001–06, 2009; Prime Minister of Azad Jammu and Kashmir 2009–11; Pres. of Azad Jammu and Kashmir 2011–; mem. Pakistan People's Party. *Address:* Office of the President, Muzaffarabad, Azad Kashmir, Pakistan (office). *Telephone:* 920400 (office). *Website:* www.ajk.gov.pk (office).

KHAN, Shah Rukh; Indian film actor and producer; b. 2 Nov. 1965, New Delhi; s. of the late Mir Taj Mohammed Khan and Fatima Begum; m. Gauri Chibber Khan 1991; one s. one d.; ed St Columba's High School, New Delhi, Hansraj Coll., Jamia Miliya Islamiya, New Delhi; TV debut in role of Abhimanyu in war drama series Fauji (Soldier) 1988; film debut in Deewana 1992; Co-f. Dreamz Unlimited production co. 1999; Co-Founder and Co-owner Red Chillies Entertainments production co. 2002–; Founder Kolkatta Knight Riders cricket team, Indian Premier League 2008–; Goodwill Amb. for South Korea 2013–; Ordre des Arts et des Lettres 2007, Darjah Mulia Seri Melaka, Malacca, Malaysia 2008; Dr hc (Univ. of Bedfordshire) 2009; Best Indian Citizen Award 1997, Jade Magazine Award for Sexiest Man in Asia 2001, Rajiv Gandhi Award for Excellence in the Field of Entertainment 2002, named by Time Magazine one of their 20 Asian Heroes under 40 2004, British Asian Guild Award 2004, MSN Search Personality of the Year Award 2004, Sabse Tez Personality of the Year Award 2004, Chhoton Ka Funda Award 2004, 'F-Awards' for Excellence in Indian Fashion Celebrity Model of the Year 2004, Pepsi Sabsey Favourite Star Kaun Award Favourite Hero 2004, Asian Guild Awards Bollywood Star of the Decade 2004, Padma Shri Award, Govt of India 2005, awarded the title 'Hammer-e-Hind' by Hindi newspaper DeshBakht 2006, HT Café Film Awards Best Actor Award 2007, CNBC-TV18's Entertainment Business Leader Award 2007, named amongst the 500 Most Influential Muslims, Georgetown Univ., USA 2009, Int. Indian Film Acad. (IIFA) Star of the Decade 2009, Global Entertainment and Media Personality Award, Fed. of Indian Chambers of Commerce and Industry Frames 2010 Excellence Awards, Most Popular Actor Award, Zee Aflam 2010, 'Cinematic Icon', GQ Men of the Year Awards 2011, L'Etoile d'Or by King of Morocco 2011, 'Creative Entrepreneur of the Year', NDTV Business Leadership Awards, Life Time Achievement Award, Asianet Film Awards 2012, BrandLaureate Legendary Award 2012, Wissame Al Kafaa Al Fikria, Morocco 2012, Chevalier Sivaji Award, Star Vijay Awards 2013, numerous Filmfare Awards, Rupa Cinegoers Awards, Star Screen Videocon Awards, Sansui Viewers Choice Movie Awards, Zee Cine Awards, People's Choice Movie Awards, (IIFA) Awards, Zee Gold Bollywood Awards, AFJA Awards, Aashirwad Award, Disney Kids Channel Award, MTV Immies Indian Music Excellence Award, Sports World Film Award. *Films include:* Deewana (Crazy) (Filmfare Best Debut Award) 1992, Raju Ban Gaya Gentleman 1992, Maya 1992, Chamatkar 1992, Dil Aashna Hai (The Heart Knows the Truth) 1992, King Uncle 1993, Kabhi Haan Kabhi Naa (Sometimes Yes, Sometimes No) (Filmfare Critics Award for Best Performance) 1993, Darr (Fear) 1993, Baazigar (Filmfare Best Actor Award) 1993, Anjaam (Filmfare Best Villain Award) 1994, Zamaana Deewana 1995, Trimurti 1995, Ram Jaane 1995, Oh Darling Yeh Hai India 1995, Karan Arjun 1995, Guddu 1995, Dilwale Dulhania Le Jayenge (Lovers Will Walk off with the Bride), (Filmfare Best Actor Award) 1995, English Babu Desi Mem 1996, Chaahat 1996, Army 1996, Dushman Duniya Ka 1996, Pardes 1997, Gudgudee 1997, Koyla 1997, Yes Boss 1997, Dil To Pagal Hai (The Heart is Crazy) (Filmfare Best Actor Award) 1997, Duplicate 1998, Dil Se (From the Heart) 1998, Kuch Kuch Hota Hai (Something is Happening) (Filmfare Best Actor Award) 1998, Baadshah 1999, Phir Bhi Dil Hai Hindustani 2000, Hey Ram 2000, Josh 2000, Har Dil Jo Pyar Karega 2000, Mohabbatein (Love Stories) (Filmfare Critics Award for Best Performance) 2000, Gaja Gamini 2000, One 2 Ka 4 2001, Asoka 2001, Kabhi Khushi Kabhie Gham (Sometimes Happy, Sometimes Sad) 2001, Devdas (Filmfare Best Actor Award, IIFA Best Actor Award) 2002, Hum Tumhare Hain Sanam 2002, Shakti: The Power 2002, Saathiya 2002, Chalte Chalte 2003, Kal Ho Naa Ho (Tomorrow May Never Come) 2003, Yeh Lamhe Judaai Ke 2004, Main Hoon Na 2004, Veer-Zaara (Global Indian Film Awards Best Actor Award, IIFA Best Actor Award) 2004, Swades (Our Country) (Filmfare Best Actor Award) 2004, Silsiilay 2005, Paheli 2005, Kabhi Alvida Naa Kehna (Never Say Goodbye) 2006, Don – The Chase Begins Again 2006, Khazan 2006, Chak De India (IIFA Best Actor Award, Nokia 14th Annual Star Screen Best Actor Award, Annual Central European Bollywood Award, V Shantaram Award) 2007, Om Shanti Om 2007, Rab Ne Bana Di Jodi (Apsara Best Actor Award) 2008, Billu Barber 2009, My Name is Khan 2010, Ra.One 2011, Don 2: The Chase Continues 2011, Jab Tak Hai Jaan (Lions Favourite Actor in a Leading Role 2013) 2012, Chennai Express (OK Screen Award for Best Popular Actor 2014) 2013. *Achievements include:* moon crater renamed in his honour as 'Crater S.R.Khan' 2009. *Television includes:* Fauji (series) 1988, Dil Darya 1988, In Which Annie Gives It Those Ones 1989, Circus (series) 1989, Idiot (mini-series) 1991, Kaun Banega Crorepati 2007, Kya Aap Paanchvi Pass Se Tez Hain? 2008. *Leisure interests:* computer games, hi-tech gadgets, acting. *Address:* Red Chillies Entertainment Private Ltd, Plot No 612, Junction of Rama Krishna Mission Road and 15th Road, Santacruz (West), Mumbai 400 054, India (office). *Telephone:* (22) 66699400 (office). *Fax:* (22) 66699599 (office). *E-mail:* info@redchillies.com (office); dreamzandfilms@hotmail.com (office). *Website:* www.redchillies.com (office).

KHAN, Shaukatullah; Pakistani politician and engineer; s. of Bismillah Khan; ed Cadet Coll. Kohat, Univ. of Eng and Tech., Taxila; mem. Nat. Ass. (Pakistan People's Party) from NA-43 (Nawagai, Bajaur Agency) constituency; Fed. Minister for States and Frontier Region –2013; Gov. of Khyber Pakhtoonkhwa 2013–14; mem. Tribal Chamber of Commerce and Industry, All Pakistan Marbles Industry Asscn. *Address:* c/o Governor House, Peshawar, Khyber Pakhtoonkhwa, Pakistan (office).

KHAN, Sikander Mustafa, MSc; Pakistani business executive; *Chairman, Millat Group of Companies;* ed NED Eng Coll., Karachi, Imperial Coll. of Science and Tech., London, Univ. of Newcastle upon Tyne; Man. Dir and CEO Millat Tractors Ltd 1985, Chair. 1991, arranged financial package and structured deal that lead to employee buyout of nationalized Millat Tractors Ltd from Govt 1992, currently Chair. Millat Group of Cos, also Chair. Bolan Castings Limited & Millat Equipment Ltd, Millat Industrial Products (subsidiaries); Chair. Pakistan Business Council 2013–; Pres. Pakistan Foundry Asscn; Vice-Pres. Lahore Chamber of Commerce & Industry 1997–98; mem. Bd of Dirs Habib Bank Ltd; mem. and Hon. Sec., Pakistan Chapter, Inst. of Mechanical Engineers. *Address:* Millat Group of Companies, 83-A, E/1, 4th Floor Main Boulevard, Gulberg, Lahore, Pakistan (office). *E-mail:* smkhan@millat.com.pk (office). *Website:* www.millatgroup.net (office).

KHAN, Zaffar Ahmad; Pakistani engineer and business executive; ed Peshawar Univ., one-year training programme in Japan, Advanced Man. Program, Univ. of Hawaii, short courses at INSEAD, Paris and Harvard Business School, USA; joined Esso Pakistan Fertilizer Co. (later known as Exxon Chemical) 1969, was transferred overseas to serve Exxon Chemical in Hong Kong, USA and Singapore 1973–82, Vice-Pres. Marketing and Dir of Exxon Chemical Pakistan Ltd 1982, held various posts in all divs including Marketing, Manufacturing, Finance and Corp. Services 1982–91, played role in the first employee-led buyout in corp. history of Pakistan which resulted in Engro Chemical Pakistan Ltd 1991, Pres. and CEO 1997–2004; Chair. Pakistan Int. Airlines Corpn 2007–08; Chair., mem. or fmr mem. various pvt. and public sector bds, including Engro Asahi, Engro Vopak,

United Bank, Sui Southern Gas Co., PTML (Ufone), PTCL, Pakistan Steel, Unilever Pakistan, Karachi Stock Exchange, Nat. Commodity Exchange, Pakistan Inst. of Corp. Governance, Acumen Fund, State Bank of Pakistan; Pres. Overseas Chamber of Commerce and Industry; has also served on numerous advisory cttees of Govt of Pakistan, including Econ. Advisory Bd, Pay and Pension Cttee, Cttee that developed Nat. Environment Quality Standards; mem. Pakistan Centre for Philanthropy; Chair. fund-raising cttee of Agha Khan Univ.; Sitara-e-Imtiaz. *Address:* c/o Pakistan International Airlines Corporation, Head Office, Jinnah International Airport, Karachi 75200, Pakistan. *Telephone:* 111-786-786; (21) 457-2011. *E-mail:* info@piac.com.pk.

KHAN HOTI, Amir Haider; Pakistani politician and government official; b. 1971, Mardan; s. of Muhammad Azam Khan Hoti; grand s. of Khan Abdul Wali Khan, nephew of Asfandiyar Wali Khan, Pres. of Awami Nat. Party, of Begum Naseem Wali Khan, grand s. of Amir Muhammad Khan; ed Atchison Coll., Lahore, Working Edwards Coll.; began political career from platform of Awami Nat. Party; mem. provincial assembly of Khyber-Pakhtoonkhwa from PF-23 Mardan constituency 2008–; Chief Minister of NW Frontier Prov. (renamed Khyber Pakhtoonkhwa April 2010) 2008–13. *Address:* c/o Office of the Chief Minister, Khyber Pakhtoonkhwa, Peshawar, Pakistan (office).

KHAN MOHAMMADI, Gen. Bismillah; Afghan military officer and government official; *Minister of Defence;* fought with Northern Alliance against Taliban; fmr Deputy Minister of Defence, Chief of Staff, Ministry of Defence; fmr Chief Commdr Kabul garrison; Chief of Gen. Staff, Afghanistan Nat. Army 2002–10; Minister of Interior Affairs 2010–12, of Defence 2012–. *Address:* Ministry of Defence, Shash Darak, Kabul, Afghanistan (office). *Telephone:* (20) 2100451 (office). *Fax:* (20) 2104172 (office). *Website:* www.mod.gov.af (office).

KHAN NIAZI, Imran; Pakistani politician and fmr professional cricketer; *Chairman, Tehreek-e-Insaf;* b. 25 Nov. 1952, Lahore, Punjab; s. of Ikramullah Khan Niazi and Shaukat Khanum; m. Jemima Goldsmith 1995 (divorced 2004); two s.; ed Aitchison Coll. and Cathedral School, Lahore, Worcester Royal Grammar School and Keble Coll. Oxford, UK; right-arm fast bowler, middle-order right-hand batsman; played for Lahore 1969–71, Worcs. 1971–76, Univ. of Oxford 1973–75 (Capt. 1974), Dawood 1975–76, PIA 1975–81, Sussex 1977–88, NSW 1984–85; played in 88 Test matches for Pakistan 1971–92, 48 as Capt., scoring 3,807 runs (average 37.69, highest score 136) and taking 362 wickets (average 22.81), best bowling (innings) 8/58, (match) 14/116; played in 175 One-Day Ints, 139 as Capt. (including 1992 World Cup victory), scoring 3,709 runs (average 33.41, highest score 102 not out) and taking 182 wickets (average 26.61), best bowling (innings) 6/14; toured England 1971, 1974, 1975 (World Cup), 1979 (World Cup), 1982, 1983 (World Cup), 1987; scored 17,771 First-class runs and took 1,287 First-class wickets; second player to score a century and take 10 wickets in a Test 1983; third player to score over 3,000 Test runs and take 300 wickets; Special Rep. for Sports, UNICEF 1989; Ed.-in-Chief Cricket Life 1989–90; f. Imran Khan Cancer Hosp. Appeal 1991–; f. Tehreek-e-Insaf (Movt for Justice) 1996, Chair. 1996–; Chancellor Univ. of Bradford 2005–, Patron of Born in Bradford research project; mem. Nat. Ass. for Mianwali 2002–07; helped establish Shaukat Khanum Memorial Cancer Hosp. & Research Centre 1996, Mianwali's Namal Coll. 2008; cricket commentator on Asian and British sports networks, including BBC Urdu and Star TV network; columnist for sify.com for India-Pakistan Test series 2005; Hon. Fellow, Keble Coll. Oxford 1988; Wisden Cricketer of the Year 1983, Hilal-e-Imtiaz 1992, Pres.'s Pride of Performance Award 1983, featured in Univ. of Oxford's Hall of Fame, The Cricket Society Wetherall Award 1976, 1980, Sussex Cricket Society Player of the Year 1985, Indian Cricket Cricketer of the Year 1990, currently placed No. 8 on all-time list of ESPN Legends of Cricket, Lifetime Achievement Award, Asian Jewel Awards, London 2004, Humanitarian Award, Asian Sports Awards, Kuala Lumpur 2007, one of several veteran Asian cricketers presented with special Silver Jubilee Awards at inaugural Asian Cricket Council Award Ceremony, Karachi 2008, one of 55 cricketers inducted into ICC (Int. Cricket Council) Hall of Fame 2009. *Film appearance:* Kidnap 2008. *Television:* commentator on TEN Sports' special live show, Straight Drive 2004. *Publications:* Imran: The Autobiography of Imran Khan 1983, Imran Khan's Cricket Skills 1989, Indus Journey: A Personal View of Pakistan 1990, All-Round View (autobiography) 1992, Warrior Race A Journey Through the Land of the Tribal Pathans 1993; writes syndicated newspaper column. *Leisure interests:* shooting, films, music. *Address:* Tehreek-e-Insaf, Central Secretariat, H-07, Parliament Lodges, Islamabad, Pakistan (office). *Telephone:* (51) 2270744 (office). *Fax:* (51) 2873893 (office). *E-mail:* info@insaf.org .pk (office). *Website:* www.insaf.org.pk (office).

KHAN WILLIAMS, Mehr, MA; Pakistani UN official and international organization official; *Chairman, International Service for Human Rights;* b. 1945, India; m.; one c.; ed Univ. of Karachi; fmrly with Univ. of Karachi, United Press Int., Associated Press of Pakistan, World Bank, Washington, DC; joined UN 1976, Deputy Dir UNICEF Programme Funding Office, Dir UNICEF Div. of Communication 1989–96, Acting Dir UN Information Centre, Sydney, Dir UNICEF Innocenti Research Centre, Florence 1998–2000, Regional Dir East Asia and the Pacific, UNICEF Bangkok –2004, Special Adviser to Exec. Dir of UNICEF 2004, 2006–, Deputy High Commr for Human Rights, UN 2004–06; fmr Chair. Jt UN Information Cttee; currently Chair. International Service for Human Rights; fmr Trustee, TV Trust for the Environment, London. *Address:* Office of the Chairman, International Service for Human Rights, Rue de Varembé 1, PO Box 16, 1211 Geneva 20 CIC, Switzerland (office). *Telephone:* 229197100 (office). *Fax:* 229197125 (office). *E-mail:* ishr@ishrny.org (office). *Website:* www.ishr.ch (office).

KHANAL, Jhala Nath; Nepalese politician; *Chairman, Communist Party of Nepal (Unified Marxist-Leninist—UML);* ed Tribhuvan Univ.; fmr mem. Communist Party of Nepal (Marxist-Leninist); mem. Standing Cttee Communist Party of Nepal (Unified Marxist-Leninist—UML), managed foreign relations wing of party, Gen. Sec. 1982–86, 2008–09, Chair. 2009–; Prime Minister Feb.–Aug. 2011 (resgnd); one of ministers during interim govt following restoration of democracy in Nepal 1990; Minister of Information and Communications 1997; participant in first regional political party conf., Bangkok, Thailand 2002. *Address:* Communist Party of Nepal (UML), PO Box 5471, Madan Nagar, Balkhu, Kathmandu, Nepal (office). *Telephone:* (1) 278081 (office). *Fax:* (1) 278084 (office). *E-mail:* uml@ntc.net .np (office). *Website:* www.cpnuml.org (office).

KHANDOGIY, Volodymyr Dmytrovych; Ukrainian diplomatist and government official; *Ambassador to UK;* b. 21 Feb. 1953, Cherkasy; m. Natalia Shevchenko; one s. one d.; ed T.G. Shevchenko Kyiv State Univ.; attaché, Third Sec., Ministry of Foreign Affairs 1976–79; attaché, Perm. Mission to UN, New York 1979–83; Second Sec., Dept of Int. Orgs, Ministry of Foreign Affairs 1983–85, First Sec., Secr. Gen. 1985–88; First Sec., Perm. Mission to UN, New York 1988–92, Deputy Perm. Rep., then Acting Perm. Rep. 1992–94; Head of Dept of Int. Orgs, Ministry of Foreign Affairs 1994–95; Deputy Minister of Foreign Affairs and Chair. Nat. Comm. for UNESCO 1995–98; Rep. to UNESCO Exec. Council 1996–98; Amb. to Canada 1998–2000, to the Netherlands 2000–02, to Belgium (also accred to Luxembourg) and Head of Perm. Mission to NATO 2000–05; Rep. to ICAO 1998–2000, to OPCW 2000–02; Dir Dept for NATO, Ministry of Foreign Affairs 2005–06; Deputy Minister for Foreign Affairs 2006–07, First Deputy Minister for Foreign Affairs 2007–09, Acting Minister of Foreign Affairs March–Oct. 2009, First Deputy Minister for Foreign Affairs and Chair. Nat. Comm. for UNESCO 2010, Amb. to UK 2010–, Perm. Rep. to IMO, London 2010–; Order of Merits (2nd and 3rd Degrees), Grand Cross, Order of Leopold II (Belgium), Order of the Three Stars (Latvia), Commdr's Cross, Order of Merit (Poland). *Address:* Embassy of Ukraine, 60 Holland Park, London, W11 3SJ, England (office). *Telephone:* (20) 7727-6312 (office). *Fax:* (20) 7792-1708 (office). *E-mail:* vkhandogiy@mail.ru (home); emb_gb@mfa.gov.ua (office); mve@ukremb.org.uk (office). *Website:* www .mfa.gov.ua/uk (office).

KHANDURI, Maj. Gen. Bhuwan Chandra, BSc, BE; Indian engineer and army officer (retd), politician and management consultant; b. 1 Oct. 1934, Dehradun, Uttarakhand; s. of the late Shri Jai Ballabh Khanduri and of Durga Devi Khanduri; m. Aruna Khanduri 1964; one s. one d.; ed Allahabad Univ., Coll. of Mil. Eng, Pune, Inst. of Engineers, New Delhi and Inst. of Defence Man., Secunderabad; served in Corps of Engineers, Indian Army 1954–1990; mem. Parl. (Garhwal constituency, Uttarakhand) 1991–96, 1998–; mem. Bharatiya Janata Party, Chief Whip, Parl. Party 1991–96, 1998–99, 2004, mem. Nat. Sec. 1992–97, 2000–, Vice-Pres. Uttar Pradesh State 1996–97; Minister of State (with ind. charge) for Roads, Transport and Highways 2000–03, Minister with Cabinet rank 2003–04; Chief Minister of Uttarakhand 2007–09 (resgnd), 2011–12; mem. Cttee on Public Accounts 1998–99, on Rules, Business Advisory 1998–99, 1999–2000, 2004, on Home Affairs 1998–99, 1999–2000 and Convenor of sub-Cttee on Personnel Policy of Cen. Para-Mil. Forces, Consultative Cttee, Ministry of Defence, Cttee on Public Undertakings 1999–2001, on Ethics; Chair. Cttee on Finance 2004; mem. Cttee on Gen. Purposes, Consultative Cttee Ministry of Petroleum and Natural Gas; Patron, Parvatiya Sanskriti Parishad, Dehradun 1990–93, Chandra Ballabh Trust; Founder and Pres. Poorva Sainik Seva Parishad, Uttar Pradesh 1992–2000, Uttarakhand Pradesh Sangarsh Samsiti 1994–96; mem. Wild Life Soc. of India 1990–2000, G.B. Pant Himalaya Environment and Devt Cttee 1998–2000; Ati Vishisht Seva Medal for Distinguished Service in the Indian Army 1982. *Leisure interests:* sports, reading. *Address:* Jai Durga Niwas, 12 Vikas Marg, Pauri Garhwal, 246 001 (home); Vidhan Bhawan, Haridwar Road, Dehradun 248 001, India. *Telephone:* (1368) 222600 (home).

KHANFAR, Wadah; Palestinian journalist and broadcasting executive; b. Jinin; ed Univ. of Jordan; joined Al-Jazeera 1999, fmr corresp., Africa Bureau, New Delhi, war corresp., Afghanistan 2001–02, Baghdad Bureau Chief 2003, Man. Dir Al-Jazeera 2003–06, Dir-Gen. Al-Jazeera Satellite Network 2006–11 (resgnd); ranked 13th by arabianbusiness.com in Power 100 list of The World's Most Powerful Arabs 2010, ranked 54th by Forbes magazine amongst The World's Most Powerful People 2009. *Address:* c/o Al-Jazeera Satellite Network, PO Box 23123, Doha, Qatar.

KHANH, Emmanuelle, (pseudonym of Renée Nguyen); French fashion designer; b. 12 Sept. 1937, Paris; m. Manh Khanh Nguyen 1957; one s. one d.; fmr fashion model for various Paris houses including Balenciaga and Givenchy 1957–63; designer of jr sportswear for Cacharel, Paris 1962–67; est. own co., launching Missoni knitwear and other products, Paris 1970; f. own label, specializing in embroidered clothes, accessories 1971; Chevalier des Arts et des Lettres 1986. *Leisure interest:* music. *Address:* Emanuelle Khanh, 36 rue du Faubourg Saint-Honoré, 75008 Paris, France (office). *Telephone:* 1-42-68-01-77 (office). *Fax:* 1-42-66-95-82 (office). *Website:* www.emmanuellekhanhparis.com/en.

KHANNA, Tejendra, MSc, MA; Indian business executive and civil servant; b. 16 Dec. 1938; ed Patna Univ., Univ. of California, Berkeley, USA; joined Indian Admin. Service 1961; Prin. Sec. to Chief Minister of Punjab; Sec. of Science, Tech. and Environment, of Food Supplies and of Labour Employment 1970s; fmr Man. Dir for Punjab, State Industrial Devt Corpn; Sec. to Govt of Punjab for Irrigation, Power and Public Works 1983–86, Financial Commr for Revenue 1986–89; Chief Controller of Imports and Exports, Ministry of Commerce, Govt of India 1989–91; Chief Sec. to Govt of Punjab, Head of Civil Service, Chief Co-ordinator of Govt Programmes 1991–92; Sec. for Food, Govt of India 1992–93, for Commerce 1993–96; Prin. Civil Service Co-ordinator of Bilateral, Multilateral and Regional Trade Relations 1993–96; Lt-Gov. and Admin. Nat. Capital Territory of Delhi 1997–98, 2007–13; Chair. Ranbaxy Laboratories Ltd 1999–2007; Trustee, Popular First; mem. Indian Inst. of Public Admin 1978–, Indo-German Consultative Group 1999–; mem. Advisory Bd Standard Chartered Bank, UK 1999–2003; Life mem. Bhartiya Vidya Bhawan. *Address:* c/o Office of the Lieutenant-Governor, National Capital Territory of Delhi, Raj Niwas, Delhi 110 054, India.

KHAR, Hina Rabbani, BSc, MSc; Pakistani economist and politician; b. 19 Jan. 1977, Multan City; d. of Ghulam Rabbani Khar; ed Lahore Univ. of Man. Sciences, Univ. of Massachusetts, USA; mem. Nat. Ass. for NA-177 Muzaffargarh II constituency 2002–; fmr Parl. Sec. for Econ. Affairs and Statistics (first woman to present budget speech to parl. 2009); Minister of State for Foreign Affairs (first woman) Feb.–July 2011; Minister of Foreign Affairs (first woman) 2011–13; fmr mem. Pakistan Muslim League (PML-Q), currently mem. Pakistan People's Party; mem. Young Parliamentarians Forum (YPF); Owner, Polo Lounge, Lahore. *Leisure interests:* riding, reading, travelling. *Address:* Pakistan Peoples Party, 8, St 19, F-8/2, Islamabad, Pakistan. *E-mail:* ppp@comsats.net.pk. *Website:* www.ppp .org.pk.

KHARAFI, Bader Nasser al-; Kuwaiti business executive; *Vice-President, Kharafi Group;* s. of the late Nasser al-Kharafi; Vice-Pres. Mohammed Abdul-mohsen Al-Kharafi & Sons Co. WLL (Kharafi Group) 2011–; Gen. Man. Al Khair National for Stocks and Real Estate Co.; Vice Chair. UNIEXPO; Dir Zain (telecoms co.), Gulf Bank, Coca-Cola Kuwait; ranked by Arabian Business amongst the Power 500: The World's Most Influential Arabs (26th) 2012, (66th) 2013. *Address:* Kharafi Group, Shuwaikh Industrial Area, PO Box 886 Safat, 13009 Kuwait City, Kuwait (office). *Telephone:* 24813622 (office). *Fax:* 24811861 (office). *E-mail:* hazmi@makharafi.net (office). *Website:* www.makharafi.net (office).

KHARAFI, Faiza al-, BSc, MSc, PhD; Kuwaiti chemist and academic; *Professor of Chemistry, Kuwait University;* b. 1946; m. Ali Mohamed Thanian El-Ghanem; five s.; ed Al Merkab High School, Ain Shams Univ., Egypt, Kuwait Univ.; worked in Dept of Chem., Kuwait Univ. 1975–81, Chair. of Dept 1984–86, Dean of Faculty of Science 1986–89, Prof. of Chem. 1987–, Rector (first female) Kuwait Univ. 1993–2002, f. Corrosion and Electrochemistry Research Lab. 1967; organized Kuwait-France Chem. Symposium 2009; Vice-Pres. Acad. of Sciences for the Developing World 2010– (renamed TWAS, The World Acad. of Sciences 2012); mem. Bd, United Nations Univ. 1998, Kuwait Foundation for the Advancement of Science; helped found the American Bilingual School in Kuwait; named by Forbes magazine as one of The 100 Most Powerful Women – Women To Watch In The Middle East 2005, Kuwait Prize in Applied Sciences 2006, named by the Council for Gulf Relations as Top Gulf Woman of the Year 2008, L'Oréal-UNESCO Women in Science Award (Africa and Arab States) 2011. *Address:* Chemistry Department, Faculty of Science, Kuwait University, PO Box 5969, Safat 13060, Kuwait (office). *Telephone:* 24985544 (office). *E-mail:* chesc@kuc01.kuniv.edu.kw (office). *Website:* www.kuniv.com (office).

KHARE, Atul, MB, BS, MA, MBA, FRSA; Indian diplomatist and UN official; b. 14 Aug. 1959; m. Vandna Khare; ed All India Inst. of Medical Sciences, Univ. of Southern Queensland, Australia, Indian Defence School of Languages; mem. of staff, Foreign Service 1984–2006, postings include Deputy High Commr to Mauritius, Counsellor at Perm. Mission to UN, New York and Chargé d'affaires, Embassy in Senegal (also accred to Mali, Mauritania, The Gambia, Guinea-Bissau and Cape Verde), also held posts as Chef de Cabinet of Foreign Sec. of India and Dir UN Div.; Chief of Staff, UN Mission of Support in East Timor (UNMISET) 2002–04, Deputy Special Rep. of Sec.-Gen. for East Timor, UN 2004–05, Special Rep. of Sec.-Gen. for Timor-Leste and Head of UN Integrated Mission in Timor-Leste (UNMIT) 2006–10, Asst Sec.-Gen. for Peacekeeping Operations 2010, Head of UN Change Man. Team 2011–12; Dir Nehru Centre and Minister (Culture) of Indian High Comm., London 2005–06. *Address:* c/o Office of the Secretary-General, United Nations, New York, NY 10017, USA.

KHARGE, Mallikarjun, BA, LLB; Indian lawyer and politician; *Minister of Railways;* b. 21 July 1942, Varavatti, Bhalki Taluk, Bidar Dist, Karnataka; s. of Mapanna Kharge and Saibavva Kharge; m. Radhabai Kharge; three s. two d.; ed Govt Coll., Gulbarga, Karnataka Univ.; mem. Karnataka State Ass. from Gurmitkal constituency 1972–2009, Deputy Leader of the Opposition 1985–94, Leader, Congress Legis. Party and Leader of Opposition, Karnataka 1996–99, 2008–09; Chair. Leather Devt Corpn 1973; Minister of State for Primary and Secondary Educ., Govt of Karnataka 1976–78, for Rural Devt and Panchayati Raj 1979, Minister for Revenue 1980–83, for Revenue, Rural Devt and Panchayati Raj 1990–92, for Co-operation, Medium and Large Industries 1992–94, for Revenue 1980, for Home, Infrastructure Devt and Minor Irrigation 1999–2004, for Transport and Water Resources 2004–06; mem. 15th Lok Sabha (lower house of Parl.) for Gulbarga constituency 2009–; Union Cabinet Minister of Labour and Employment 2009–13, Minister of Railways 2013–; Vice-Pres. Karnataka Pradesh Congress Cttee 1999, Pres. 2005; Founder-Chair. Siddharth Vihar Trust. *Address:* Ministry of Railways, Rail Bhavan, Raisina Road, New Delhi 110 001, India (office). *Telephone:* (11) 23385227 (office). *Fax:* (11) 23382068 (office). *E-mail:* secyrb@rb.railnet.gov.in (office). *Website:* www.indianrailways.gov.in (office).

KHARITONOV, Mark Sergeyevich; Russian writer; b. 31 Aug. 1937, Zhitomir, Ukraine; m. Galina Edelman; one s. two d.; ed Moscow Pedagogical Inst.; early career as teacher in secondary school; fmr exec. sec. of newspaper, of publishing house 1960–69; freelance writer 1969–; trans. Kafka, Stefan Zweig, Elias Canetti, Herman Hesse, Thomas Mann and others; works banned in official press until 1988; Prix du Meilleur Livre Etranger Essai (France) 1997. *Publications include:* Prokor Menshutin 1971 (published 1988), Provincial Philosophy 1977 (published 1993), Two Ivans 1980 (published 1988), Lines of Fate or Milashevich's Trunk 1985 (published 1992, first Booker Russian Novel Prize 1992), Storozh 1994, The Voices 1994, Return from Nowhere 1995, Seasons of Life 1998, A Mode of Existence 1998, The Approach 1998, Amores Novi 1999, The Conveyor 2000, A Professor of Lie 2002, Stenography of the Beginning of the Century 2003, Playing with Yourself 2004, Catcher of the Clouds 2008, Lessons of Happiness 2009, Stenography of the End of the Century 2011, Knot of Life 2011, See More 2012, Write, My Friend (correspondence with Boris Khazanov) 2013. *Address:* 129128 Moscow, Bazhova str. 15, corp. 1, Apartment 182, Russia (home). *Telephone:* (499) 187-56-92 (home). *Fax:* (499) 187-56-92 (home). *E-mail:* mkharitonov@mail.ru.

KHARITONOV, Col Nikolai Mikhailovich; Russian politician; b. 31 Oct. 1948, Rezino, Novosibirsk Region; m.; four d.; ed Novosibirsk Inst. of Agric., Acad. of Nat. Econs; agronomist in sovkhoz (state farm), Novosibirsk Region 1972–76, Dir of sovkhoz 1976–94; Deputy, Novosibirsk Regional Exec. Cttee; RSFSR People's Deputy, mem. Cttee on Agrarian Problems, Supreme Soviet Russian Fed. 1990–93, mem. Agrarian Union 1990; mem. State Duma 1993–2003, Leader, Agrarian Group (later Agrarian-Industrial Group) 1994–2003, re-elected to Duma as ind. cand. 2003–; Deputy Chair. Agrarian Party of Russia 1993–2000; mem. Parl. Ass. of European Council; unsuccessful cand. for Pres. of Russian Fed. (Communist Party) 2004. *Leisure interest:* sports. *Address:* State Duma, 103265 Moscow, Okhotnyi ryad 1, Russia (office). *Telephone:* (495) 292-83-10 (office). *Fax:* (495) 292-94-64 (office). *E-mail:* www@duma.ru (office). *Website:* www.duma.ru (office).

KHARKAVETS, Andrey Mikhailovich; Belarusian politician; *Minister of Finance;* First Deputy Minister of Finance 2006–08, Minister of Finance 2008–. *Address:* Ministry of Finance, vul. Savetskaya 7, 220048 Minsk, Belarus (office). *Telephone:* (17) 227-27-26 (office). *Fax:* (17) 222-45-93 (office). *E-mail:* minfin@minfin.gov.by (office). *Website:* www.minfin.gov.by (office).

KHARRAZI, Kamal, PhD; Iranian diplomatist and fmr academic; *Chairman, Strategic Council on Foreign Relations;* b. 1 Dec. 1944, Tehran; s. of Mehdi

Kharrazi and Kobra Kharrazi; m. Mansoureh Kharrazi; two c.; ed Tehran Univ., Univ. of Houston, USA; Teaching Fellow, Univ. of Houston 1975–76; Man. of Planning and Programming, Nat. Iranian TV 1979; Man. Dir Centre for Intellectual Devt of Children and Young Adults 1979–81; Deputy Foreign Minister for Political Affairs 1979–80, Minister of Foreign Affairs 1997–2005; Chair., Strategic Council on Foreign Relations 2006–; Man. Dir Islamic Repub. News Agency 1980–89; mem. Supreme Defence Council, Head War Information HQ 1980–89; Prof. of Man. and Psychology, Tehran Univ. 1983–89; Perm. Rep. to UN, New York 1989–97; Founding mem. Islamic Research Inst., London; mem. American Asscn of Univ. Profs. *Publications:* numerous textbooks and journal articles on psychology and foreign affairs. *Leisure interest:* mountain climbing. *Address:* Kashani Alley 1, Keshvardust Street, Jomhuri Avenue, Tehran, Iran (office). *Telephone:* (21) 64413131 (office); (21) 64413178 (office). *Fax:* (21) 66466270 (office). *E-mail:* kharrazi@imam-khamenei.ir (office). *Website:* www.leader.ir.

KHASAWNEH, Awn Shawkat al-, MA, LLM; Jordanian judge and government official; b. 22 Feb. 1950, Amman; ed Islamic Educational Coll. of Amman, Queens' Coll., Cambridge, England; entered diplomatic service 1975; with Perm. Mission to UN 1976–80, later as First Sec.; with Ministry of Foreign Affairs 1980–90, Head of Legal Dept 1985–90; Legal Adviser to Crown Prince 1990–95, Adviser to the King 1995, Chief of the Royal Hashemite Court 1996–98; Judge, Int. Court of Justice 2000–11, Vice-Pres. 2006–09; Prime Minister and Minister of Defence 2011–12; mem. Arab Int. Law Comm. 1982–89; mem. Subcommission on Prevention of Discrimination and Protection of Minorities (Chair. 1993), Comm. on Human Rights 1984–93, Special Rapporteur of Comm. on Human Rights on the human rights dimensions of forcible population transfer; mem. Int. Law Comm. 1986–; mem. Royal Jordanian Comm. on Legislative and Admin. Reform 1994–96; mem. Bd of Eds Palestine Yearbook of International Law; mem. Int. Law Asscn (Chair. Cttee on Islamic Law and Int. Law 2003–), Council of the Centre of Islamic and Middle Eastern Law, SOAS; Hon. Fellow, Queens' Coll.; Istiqlal Order (First Class) 1993, Kawkab Order (First Class) 1996, Nahda Order (First Class) 1996, Grand Officier, Légion d'honneur 1997. *Address:* c/o Prime Ministry of Jordan, POB 80, Amman 11180, Jordan.

KHASBULATOV, Ruslan Imranovich; Chechen politician, economist and academic; *Head of Department of World Economy, Plekhanov University of Economics;* b. 22 Nov. 1942, Grozny; s. of Imran Khasbulatov and Govzan Khasbulatova; m.; one s. one d.; ed Kazakh State Univ., Moscow State Univ.; instructor, Cen. Cttee of Comsomol 1970–72, Head of Information Sector Inst. of Social Sciences, USSR Acad. of Sciences 1972–74, Head of Sector, Research Inst. of Higher Educ. 1974–79, Lecturer, Prof., Head of Dept of World Economy, Plekhanov Inst. (now Univ.) of Econs 1979–90, 1992–, Head of Scientific Centre, World Economy Evolution 2009–; Deputy of Supreme Soviet in Russia 1990–93, First Vice-Chair., then Acting Chair. Supreme Soviet 1990–91, Chair. 1991–93; Chair. Interparl. Ass. of CIS 1992–93; charged with fraud and imprisoned Sept.–Oct. 1993, released by State Duma Feb. 1994; one of the leaders of opposition to Pres. Dudayev-Mashadof in Chechen crisis 1991–96 and to mil. policy of Kremlin; Corresp. mem. Russian Acad. of Sciences 1991. *Publications:* Bureaucracy and Socialism 1989, Russia: Time of Change 1991, International Economic Relations (two vols) 1991, Power 1992, The Struggle for Russia 1993, Les Ombres au-dessus de la Maison Blanche (France) 1993, Great Russian Tragedy (two vols) 1994, World Economy 1994, World Economy (two vols) 2001, Crisis of Commonwealth of Independent States and Positive Experience of European Union 2002, The Great American Tragedy and What Should the World Do to Prevent Terrorism? 2001–02, The Kremlin and Russian–Chechen War (five vols): Vol. 1 Exploded Life 2002, Vol. 2 Power: Sword and Guile 2002, Vol. 3 Thoughts of War and Peace 2002, Vol. 4 A Big Strategic Game 2003, Vol. 5 Aliens 2003, Which Policy is Needed for Russia from the Point of View of the World Scientific Community? 2004, Fairy Tales About Reforms 2004, The Principle of Optimum in the Economic System and Social Functions of the State 2005, States and Revolutions 2005, The World Economy and International Economic Relations, Vols 1 and 2 2006. *Leisure interests:* fishing, hunting, playing chess. *Address:* Plekhanov Academy of Economics, Stremyanny per. 36, 117997 Moscow (office); Granatniy per. 10/35, Moscow, Russia (home). *Telephone:* (495) 958-50-15 (office); (495) 697-53-92 (home). *Fax:* (495) 958-46-22 (office). *E-mail:* hasbulatov@rea.ru (home).

KHASIS, Lev Aronovich, PhD; Russian retail executive; *Senior Vice-President and Director of Leveraging, Wal-Mart Stores Inc.;* b. 5 June 1966, Kuybyshev (now Samara); m. Olga Khasis; ed Kuybyshev Aviation Inst., Financial Acad. of Govt of Russian Fed., Faculty of Law, Univ. of Ministry of the Interior; Head, Dept of Int. Affairs, Kuybyshev Aviation Inst. 1989–90; Gen. Dir JSC Samarsky Trading House 1991–93; Gen. Man., Samara Br., Avtovazbank 1993–94; Pres. and Chair. Bd of Dirs, OJSC Aviacor Corpn 1995–99; Vice-Pres. OJSC Alfa-Bank 1996–98; Founder, Daily Store Chain, Moscow; CEO X5 Retail Group NV 2006–11, Dir of Network and mem. Man. Bd 2006–11; Sr Vice Pres. and Dir of Leveraging, Wal-Mart Stores Inc. 2011–; Chair. Supervisory Bd Perekrestok Group of Cos 2002–06, Trade House GUM 2003–04; Dir OAO Transaero Airlines 2005–, CTC Media Inc. 2009–10; Chair. Russian Asscn of Cos of Retail Trade 2008–11. *Address:* Wal-Mart Stores Inc., 702 SW 8th Street, Bentonville, AR 72716-8611, USA (office). *Telephone:* (479) 273-4000 (office). *Website:* walmartstores.com (office).

KHATAMI, Hojatoleslam Sayed Muhammad, BPhil; Iranian cleric, politician and fmr head of state; b. 1943, Ardkan, Yazd; s. of Ayatollah Seyyed Rooh Allah Khatami (religious scholar); m. 1974; one s. two d.; ed Qom and Isfahan seminaries and Univ. of Tehran; Man. Islamic Centre, Hamburg; mem. for Ardakan and Meibod, first Islamic Consultative Ass. (Parl.); rep. of Imam Khomeini and Dir Kayhan newspaper; fmr Ministerr of Culture and Islamic Guidance; Cultural Deputy HQ of C-in-C and Head Defence Publicity Cttee; fmr Minister of Culture and Islamic Guidance; fmr Adviser to Pres. Rafsanjani and Pres. Nat. Library of Iran; fmr mem. High Council of Cultural Revolution; Pres. of Iran 1997–2006; apptd mem. UN group Alliance of Civilizations 2005–; Founder and Head, Int. Center of Dialogue Among Cultures and Civilizations 2004–; f. Baran Foundation; numerous hon. degrees; Global Dialogue Prize 2009. *Publications:* Fear of Wave, From World of City to World City, Faith and Thought Trapped by Selfishness; and numerous articles and speeches. *Website:* www.khatami.ir; www.dialogue.ir; www.baranfoundation.ir.

KHATIB, Abd al-Ilah al-; Jordanian politician and international organization official; *Secretary-General's Special Envoy to Libya, United Nations;* b. 1953, Salt; ed School of Advanced Int. Studies, Johns Hopkins Univ., Washington, DC, American Univ., Panteios School of Political Science, Greece; Admin. Officer, Embassy in Athens 1976–81; mem. Bd of Dirs Arabic Affairs Council, Amman; mem. Del. to UN Gen. Ass. 1982–92; attaché Dept of Int. Org., Ministry of Foreign Affairs 1982–1992, Dir of Special Bureau 1988–93; Second Sec., Embassy in Washington, DC 1984–88; Co-ordinator Jordanian Team for Peace Negotiations 1988–93; Asst for Investment Middle East Insurance Co. 1994–95; Gen. Man. Jordan Cement Factories Co. Ltd 1996–98; Minister of Tourism 1995–96, of Foreign Affairs 1998–2002, 2005–07; UN Sec.-Gen.'s Special Envoy to Libya 2011–. *Address:* Office of the Special Envoy to Libya, United Nations, New York, NY 10017, USA (office). *Telephone:* (212) 963-1234 (office). *Fax:* (212) 963-4879 (office). *Website:* www.un.org/sg (office).

KHATIB, Hisham, PhD; Jordanian energy and environmental consultant and fmr politician; b. 5 Jan. 1936, Acre, Palestine; s. of Mohamed Khatib and Fahima Khatib; m. Maha Khatib 1968; two s. one d.; ed Univ. of Cairo, Egypt, Univs of Birmingham and London, UK; Chief Engineer, Jerusalem Electricity Co. 1965–73; Deputy Dir-Gen. Jordanian Electricity Authority 1974–76, Dir-Gen. 1980–84; Sr Energy Expert, Arab Fund, Kuwait 1976–80; Minister of Energy and Mineral Resources 1984–89; Vice-Chair. World Energy Council 1989–92; int. energy consultant 1990–93; Minister of Water and Irrigation 1993–94, of Planning 1994–95; Chair. Int. Cttee for Developing Countries World Energy Council 1992–95; int. consultant 1995–; Chair. Jordan Electricity Regulatory Comm. 2005–09; int. consultant on energy and its environmental issues; Life Fellow, IEEE; Fellow, Inst. of Eng and Tech. (IET), World Fed. of Scientists-PMP (Energy); Hon. Vice-Chair. World Energy Council, PMP (Energy) World Fed. of Scientists; decorations from Jordan, Sweden, Italy, Indonesia, Austria and the Vatican; Achievement Medal, IET (UK) 1998, Global Energy Award, World Energy Council Rome 2007. *Publications:* Economics of Reliability 1978, Financial and Economic Evaluation of Projects 1997, Palestine and Egypt Under the Ottomans: Paintings, Books, Photographs, Maps and Manuscripts 2003, Economic Evaluation of Projects in the Electricity Supply Industry 2003; numerous articles in professional journals. *Leisure interest:* collecting 19th-century Jerusalem and Holy Land artefacts and rare books and paintings. *Address:* PO Box 410, Amman 11831, Jordan. *Telephone:* (6) 5815316. *Fax:* (6) 5851401. *E-mail:* khatiblive@umniahlive.net.

KHATIWADA, Pradeep Kumar, BA (Econ), MSc, MEd; Nepalese diplomatist; b. 15 Feb. 1950, Kathmandu; s. of the late Shri Gopinath Khatiwada; m. Sarita Upraity; ed Univ. of Berlin, Germany; career diplomat, joined Civil Service 1975, First Sec., Embassy in New Delhi 1986–90, Counsellor and Chargé d'affaires a.i., Washington, DC 1993–94, Counsellor and Deputy Chief of Mission, Bonn and Berlin 1998–2002, Minister and Deputy Chief of Mission, Embassy in New Delhi 2003–05; Jt Sec., Ministry of Foreign Affairs 2006–07; Amb. to Bangladesh 2007–11; Long Service Medal, Govt of Nepal. *Publication:* Nepal-India Relations – Democracy in the Making of Mutual Trust (with Dr Dinesh Bhattarai) 1993. *Address:* 21/472 Kalikasthan, Dillibazar, Kathmandu, Nepal. *E-mail:* pradeepji@aol.com.

KHATIWADA, Yuba Raj, BA, MA, MPA, PhD; Nepalese economist and central banker; *Governor and Chairman, Nepal Rastra Bank (Central Bank);* b. 14 Aug. 1956, Jhapa; m.; three c.; ed Tribhuvan Univ., Delhi School of Econs, Univ. of Delhi, India; Asst Lecturer, Tribhuvan Univ. 1982–83; intermittently a Visiting Faculty mem., Tribhuvan and Kathmandu Univs 1992–2001; Asst Research Officer, Nepal Rastra Bank 1983–91, Research Officer 1991–94, Econ. Adviser 1994–99, Head of Econ. Research Dept 1999–2002, Exec. Dir Office of the Gov. 2002–06, Gov. and Chair. 2010–, Chair. Man. Cttee; Sr Economist, UNDP Regional Centre, Colombo, Sri Lanka 2006–09; mem. Bd of Dirs Rastriya Banijya Bank 1995, Nepal Telecommunication Corpn 1997, Nepal Industrial Devt Corpn 1999–; mem. Task Force for the Study of 'Nepal's Members to GATT and Its Implication for the Nepalese Economy', Ministry of Commerce March–July 1995, Revenue Consultative Cttee, Ministry of Finance 1999–; Coordinator, Macroeconomic Section, Task Force for Drafting Ninth Plan, Nat. Planning Comm. 1997, Adviser for drafting Approach Paper of the Ninth Plan 1997, mem. Nat. Planning Comm. 2002–05, currently Vice-Chair.; Pres. Man. Asscn of Nepal 1999–; Regional Mem. for Nepal, Bd of Int. Centre for Integrated Mountain Devt 2009–; attended numerous nat. and int. training programmes and seminars on issues related to devt and planning techniques; Mahendra Bidhya Bhusan, HM King Birendra Bir Bikram Shah Dev 1994, Suprabal Gorakha Dakshin Bahu, HM King Birendra Bir Bikram Shah Dev 2001, Letter of Commendation, Fed. of Nepalese Chambers of Commerce and Industry for Outstanding Contrib. to Econ. Studies and Promotion of Good Man. Practices in Nepal 2001. *Publications:* An Econometric Analysis of the Determinants of Inflation in Nepal 1981, Some Aspects of Monetary Policy in Nepal 1994; numerous published articles. *Address:* Office of the Governor, Nepal Rastra Bank, Central Office, PO Box 73, Baluwatar, Kathmandu, Nepal (office). *Telephone:* (1) 4410386 (office). *Fax:* (1) 4410159 (office). *E-mail:* ofg@nrb.org.np (office). *Website:* www.nrb.org.np (office).

KHATTAK, Pervez Khan; Pakistani politician; *Chief Minister of Khyber Pakhtoonkhwa;* b. 1 Jan. 1950, Nowshera; s. of Hastim Khan Khattak; three s. two d.; ed Aitchison Coll., Lahore, Gordon Coll., Rawalpindi; started political career as mem. dist council 1983; elected five times as mem. Khyber Pakhtoonkhwa (KP) Prov. Ass. for Constituency PK-13 Nowshera 2008–; fmr KP Minister of Industries and of Irrigation; mem. Nat. Ass. from Constituency NA-5 2013–; Chief Minister of Khyber Pakhtoonkhwa 2013–; mem. Pakistan Tehreek-e-Insaf, currently Sec.-Gen. *Address:* Office of the Chief Minister, Peshawar, Khyber Pakhtoonkhwa, Pakistan (office). *Telephone:* 9213574 (office). *E-mail:* info@khyberpakhtunkhwa.gov.pk (office). *Website:* www.khyberpakhtunkhwa.gov.pk (office).

KHATTAK, Vice-Adm. (retd) Taj Muhammad, MSc; Pakistani naval officer; b. 20 Feb. 1948, Sahiwal; s. of Karra Khan Khattak and Gul Begum; m. Nasim Khattak; two s.; ed Cadet Coll., Hassan Abdal; joined Pakistan Navy 1965, fought during Indo-Pak War 1971 (POW in India for two years), appointments include Flag Officer of Sea Training, Additional Sec./Dir-Gen. Ports and Shipping Wing, Ministry of Communications, Commdr Pakistan Fleet, Deputy Chief of Naval Staff

(Projects), Deputy Chief of Naval Staff (Material), Chief of Staff, Naval HQ, Islamabad; apptd Rear Adm. 1997, Vice-Adm. 2002; Chair. Port Qasim Authority (on secondment), Karachi 2002–04; currently columnist; Sword of Honour 1969, Sitara-e-Jurrat (Gallantry Award) 1971, Sitara-e-Imtiaz 1996, Hilal-e-Imtiaz 2001. *Publications include:* Amphibious Threat to Pakistan, Indian Nuclear Threat. *Leisure interests:* reading, golf. *Address:* 12 B/1 3rd Gizri Street, DHA, Phave-IV Karachi 75020, Pakistan (home). *Telephone:* (21) 5898332 (home). *E-mail:* taj khattak@ymail.com (home).

KHATUN, Sahara, BA, LLB; Bangladeshi politician; b. 1 March 1943, Dhaka; mem. Awami League, currently Legal Sec.; mem. Jatiya Sangsad (Parl.) for Dhaka-18 constituency; Minister of Home Affairs 2009–12; Founder and Pres. Bangladesh Awami Ainjibi Parishad (advocacy group); Gen. Sec. Bangladesh Mahila Samity (women's asscn); mem. Int. Women Lawyers' Asscn, Int. Women's Alliance. *Address:* c/o Ministry of Home Affairs, Bangladesh Secretariat, School Bldg, 2nd and 3rd Floors, Dhaka, Bangladesh (office).

KHAVIN, Vladimir Yosifovich; Russian architect; b. 29 July 1931, Moscow; s. of Yosif Efimovich Khavin and Sophya Danilovna Khavina; m. Nadezhda Ermakova; one s.; ed Moscow Architectural Inst.; Head of Workshop no. 12 of Mosproekt-1; teacher, Moscow Inst. of Architecture 1976–; Corresp. mem. Int. Acad. of Architecture 1999; Lenin Prize 1984, Honoured Architect of Russia 1988. *Works include:* Circus Bldg on Vernadsky St, Moscow 1963–71, October Square 1972, Intourist Hotel Complex by Kakhovskaya Metro Station 1980, Monument to Frunze, Frunze 1965, The Rear to the Front Monument, Magnitogorsk 1972–79, memorial complex To the Heroes of the Civil War and the Great Patriotic War, Novorosiysk 1982, Moscow town-building exhbn, Brestskaya St 1985, Palace of Youth on Komsomolskaya Avenue, Moscow 1988, new residential Dist Yushnoye Buruvo 1990–, reconstruction of Cheryomushkinski Dist, Moscow 1990–, Russian Jt-Stock Co. complex GASPROM 1995, apt houses, Namyotkina str. 1997. *Leisure interest:* painting. *Address:* Glavmosarchitektura, 103001 Moscow, Triumfalnaya Square 1 (office); 123056 Moscow, Novocheryomushkinskaya str. 71/82, Apt 259, Russia (home). *Telephone:* (495) 251-61-72 (office); (495) 719-97-16 (home). *Fax:* (495) 251-61-72.

KHAYANKHYARVAA, Damdingiin; Mongolian civil engineer and politician; *Minister of Finance;* b. 1960, Zavkhan Prov.; ed Moscow Inst. of Man.; economist, Construction Industry Asscn, Darkhan city 1986–89, Head of Section 1990; Instructor with Mongolian People's Revolutionary Party (MPRP) Cttee of Darkhan city 1989–90; Econ. Adviser and Vice-Chair. of People's Deputies Khural (regional ass.), Darkhan city 1990–91; Economist and Deputy Dir, Darkhan city Metallurgical Plant 1991–93; Head of Dept, Gov.'s Office, Darkhan-Uul Prov. 1993–2000, Gov. of Darkhan-Uul Prov. 2000–08; mem. Mongolian Great Khural (Parl.) for Dharkan-Uul 19 constituency 2008–, mem. Parl. Cttee on Safety and Foreign Policy; Minister of Finance 2012–; mem. Mongolian People's Party (fmrly Mongolian People's Revolutionary Party). *Address:* Ministry of Finance, Government Bldg 2, Negdsen Ündestnii Gudamj 5/1, Chingeltei District, Ulan Bator, Mongolia (office). *Telephone:* (11) 264891 (office). *Fax:* (11) 264891 (office). *E-mail:* support@mof.gov.mn (office). *Website:* www.mof.gov.mn (office).

KHAYIL, Ashour ben; Libyan government official and fmr diplomatist; b. Sept. 1939, Derna; ed Coll. of Business and Econs, Univ. of Libya; began career with Office of Accounts and Auditing 1963; joined Diplomatic Service 1964, Assoc. Under-Sec., Ministry of Foreign Affairs 1964–67, Under-Sec./Sec. Libyan People's Bureau (embassy), Rome 1967–71, Chief of Staff and Head of Confidential Dept 1971–74, First Sec. and Adviser, Perm. Mission to UN, New York 1974–78, Admin. Dir for UN Affairs, Ministry of Foreign Affairs 1977–80, for Technical Cooperation 1980–81, Sec., Libyan People's Bureau (Amb.), Repub. of Korea 1981–84 (resgnd following shooting of British police officer from Libyan embassy in London); joined opposition and moved to USA and later Canada; fmr Deputy Sec.-Gen. Nat. Libyan Alliance; Chair. Nat. Conf. of Libyan Opposition 2005–08, Pres. Follow-Up Body for Nat. Conf. of Libyan Opposition 2008–11; returned to Libya following overthrow of Mu'ammar Gaddafi 2011; Minister of Foreign Affairs 2011–12. *Address:* c/o Ministry of Foreign Affairs, Tripoli, Libya (office).

KHAYOYEV, Izatullo; Tajikistani politician and economist; b. 22 June 1936, Khodzhaikhok, Kulyab Dist, Tajik SSR; m. several s.; ed Tajik Univ., Higher Party School; mem. CPSU 1961–91; worked in financial insts 1954–61; Head of Dept, Ministry of Agric. 1961–63; Chair. of collective farm 1963–65; Sr posts in state and CP insts 1966–78; Minister of Meat and Dairy Industry, Tajik SSR 1978–83; First Sec. Kulyab Dist 1983–86; Deputy, USSR Supreme Soviet 1984–89; cand. mem. CPSU Cen. Cttee 1986–91; Chair. Council of Ministers, Tajik SSR 1986–90, Vice-Pres. Tajik SSR 1990–91; Prime Minister 1991–92; Minister of Foreign Econ. Relations 1992–94; Head of Staff of Pres. Rakhmonov 1994–96; in pvt. business 1999–; orders and medals of USSR and Repub. of Tajikistan. *Leisure interests:* saddle-horse riding, reading fiction, science fiction and literature. *Address:* Prospect Rudaki, 1 proezd k. 75/2, Dushanbe, Tajikistan (home). *Telephone:* 24-75-35 (home).

KHAYRULLOYEV, Saidullo Khayrulloyevich; Tajikistani politician; b. 10 Aug. 1945, Garm Dist; ed Tashkent Higher CPSU School, Tajik Inst. of Agric.; Engineer, Chief Engineer, then Head of Div. Garm irrigation system 1969–75; Chair. Exec. Cttee Garm Regional Soviet of People's Deputies 1975–77, Chair. Regional Soviet 1979–85; First Sec., Soviet region CP of Tajikistan 1985–88; Sec. Ktalon Regional CP Cttee 1988–90; Deputy Prime Minister of Tajikistan 1991–92; Minister of Environmental Protection, then Minister of Nature Protection 1992–94; Chair. Govt Cttee on Precious Metals 1994–95, Govt Cttee on Land Construction and Land Reform 1999–2000; Pres. Majlisi Namoyandagon (Ass. of Reps) 2000–10; Merited Worker of Tajikistan, Order of Nishoni Fakhri. *Address:* c/o Majlisi Oli, Majlisi Namoyandagon, 734051 Dushanbe, Xiyoboni Rudaki 42, Tajikistan (office).

KHAZANOV, Gennady Viktorovich; Russian comedian and actor; b. 1945, Moscow; m. Zlata Khazanov; one d.; ed State High School of Circus and Variety Actors; worked in radio equipment factory; debut as actor Moscow Univ. Students' Theatre Nash Dom; compere L. Utyosov Orchestra; on professional stage since 1969 in solo productions, first production Trifles of Life 1981; variety programmes Evident and Unbelievable 1987, Little Tragedies 1987, Selected 1988; leading role Gamblers of XXI Century Moscow Art Theatre; leading role in film Little Giant of

Large Sex; performed in America, Australia, Israel, Germany, Canada; Artistic Dir Variety Theatre Mono 1991–96; Dir, then Artistic Dir Moscow State Estrada Theatre 1997–; First Prize All-Union Competition of Variety Artists; State Prize 1995. *Address:* Moscow State Estrada Theatre, 109072 Moscow, Bersenevskaya Nab. 20/2, Russia. *Telephone:* (495) 230-18-68. *Website:* www.teatr-estrada.ru; www.hazanov.ru.

KHEIFETS, Leonid; Russian stage director; b. 4 May 1934, Minsk, Belarus; ed Belarus Polytech. Inst., Moscow State Inst. of Theatre Arts; stage dir, Moscow Theatre of the Soviet Army 1963–71, chief stage dir 1988–94; stage dir, Moscow Maly Theatre 1971–88; teacher, then Prof., Russian Acad. of Theatre Arts (GITIS) 1980–; State Prize of the Russian Federation 1991. *Plays:* The One Who Made Miracle 1962, My Poor Marat 1965, The Death of Ivan the Terrible 1966, Masters of Time (Moscow Theatre of the Soviet Army) 1967, Wedding of Krechinsky 1971, Before the Sunset 1973, King Lear 1979, Retro (with Galin, Moscow Maly Theatre) 1981, Western Tribune (Sovremennik Theatre) 1983, Cherry Garden, Rudin (on TV), Antigona in New York (Moscow Theatre of the Modern Play) 1995, Running Stranger (Moscow Mossoviet Theatre) 1996. *Address:* Russian Academy of Theatre Arts, 103888 Moscow, 6, Maly Kislovsky pereulok, Russia. *Telephone:* (495) 691-9192. *Fax:* (495) 690-0597. *E-mail:* info@gitis.net. *Website:* www.gitis.net.

KHELAIFI, Nasser Ghanim al-; Qatari sports executive and fmr professional tennis player; *President, Paris Saint-Germain Football Club;* b. 12 Nov. 1973; ed Univ. of Qatar Coll. of Man. and Econs; began career as tennis player, turned professional 1992, retd 2003; mem. of Qatar Davis Cup team, played 43 ties 1992–2002; Dir Al Jazeera Sports (now beIN Sports); led buyout of Paris Saint-Germain (PSG) Football Club 2011, becoming Pres. (first non-French Pres.); Pres. Qatar Tennis Fed.; Vice-Pres. Asian Tennis Fed. *Address:* Paris Saint-Germain Football Club, 24 Rue du Commandant Guilbaud, 75016 Paris, France (office). *Telephone:* (1) 47-43-72-72 (office). *Website:* www.psg.fr (office).

KHELEF, Abdelaziz, Licence in Econ. Sciences, High Diploma in Econ. Sciences; Algerian economist and banker; *Director-General, Arab Bank for Economic Development in Africa (Banque arabe pour le développement économique en Afrique—BADEA);* ed in Algeria and Paris, France; has held numerous high-ranking positions in Algerian Govt, including Minister of Commerce, Minister of Finance, State Sec. in charge of Maghreb Affairs, Amb. to Tunisia and Sec.-Gen. of the Presidency; joined Islamic Devt Bank (IDB) in 1994 where he held several high-ranking positions, including Advisor to Pres. and IDB Regional Dir for Northern and Western Africa; Dir-Gen. Arab Bank for Econ. Devt in Africa (Banque arabe pour le développement économique en Afrique—BADEA) 2006–. *Address:* Arab Bank for Economic Development in Africa, Sayed Abd ar-Rahman el-Mahdi Street, PO Box 2640, Khartoum 11111, Sudan (office). *Telephone:* (1) 83773646 (office). *Fax:* (1) 83770600 (office). *E-mail:* badea@badea.org (office). *Website:* www.badea.org (office).

KHELIL, Chakib, PhD; Algerian engineer, economist and government official; b. 8 Aug. 1939, Oujda, Morocco; m.; two c.; ed Texas A&M Univ., USA; engineer with Shell and Phillips Petroleum, Okla and with McCord and Assocs, Dallas; returned to Algeria as Head of Petroleum Eng Dept Sonatrach 1971, also Pres. Alcore (jt venture between Sonatrach and Corelab); Chair. Valhyd Group (oil recovery co.) 1973–76, also Tech. Adviser to Pres. of Algeria; with World Bank 1980–99 (retd), positions included petroleum projects in Africa, Latin America and Asia, then Head of Energy Unit for Latin America then Petroleum Adviser; Minister of Energy and Mines 1999–10; Pres. OPEC 2001, 2008; Chair. African Energy Comm. 2001; Pres. Org. of Arab Petroleum Exporting Countries 2002, Asscn of African Petroleum Producers 2004; Medal of the Order of the Sun of Peru 2002. *Address:* c/o Ministry of Energy and Mining, BP 677, Tower A, Val d'Hydra, Alger-Gare, Algiers, Algeria (office).

KHENE, Abd-El Rahman, MD; Algerian government official, international organization official and fmr physician; b. 6 March 1931, Collo; m. 1955; three s. one d.; ed Univ. of Algiers; served as officer in Nat. Liberation Army until Algerian independence 1962; mem. Nat. Council Algerian Revolution (CNRA) 1957–60; Sec. of State, provisional Govt (GPRA) 1958–60; Gen. Controller Nat. Liberation Front 1960–61; Head of Finance Dept, GPRA 1961–62; Pres. Algerian-French tech. org. for exploiting wealth of Sahara sub-soil 1965–66; Pres. Electricité et Gaz d'Algérie July–Oct. 1964; mem. Bd of Dirs Nat. Petroleum Research and Exploitation Co. 1965–66; Minister of Public Works and Pres. Algerian-French Industrial Co-operation Org. 1966–70; physician in Cardiology Dept, Univ. Hosp. of Algiers 1970–73; Sec.-Gen. OPEC 1973–74; Exec. Dir UNIDO 1975–85; Founding mem. and Bd mem. Worldwatch Inst., currently mem. Emer. *Address:* 42 chemin B. Brahimi, El Biar, Algiers, Algeria (home). *Telephone:* (21) 924483 (home). *E-mail:* laminekhene@yahoo.fr.

KHER, Anupam; Indian actor; b. 7 March 1955, Shimla; s. of Pushkar Nath Kher and Dulari Kher; m. 1st Madhumalati (divorced); m. 2nd Kirron Kher; one s.; ed Nat. School of Drama, Delhi; fmr Chair. Indian Film Certification Bd; Dir Nat. School of Drama 2001–04; Founder and Chair. Anupam Kher Foundation 2008–; co-f. (with Satish Kaushik) Karol Bagh Productions (production co.) 2007; Actor of the Decade Award, Millennium Honours 2000, Real Life Hero Award, Zee Gold Bollywood Awards 2001, Padma Shri 2004, Divya Himachal Award 2005. *Films include:* Saaransh (Filmfare Award) 1984, Utsav 1984, Hum Naujawan 1985, Wafadaar 1985, Arjun 1985, Aitbaar 1985, Kala Dhanda Goray Log 1986, Karma 1986, Samundar 1986, Raosaheb 1986, Allah Rakha 1986, Uttar Dakshin 1987, Zevar 1987, Sansar 1987, Dozakh 1987, Zakhmi Aurat 1988, Agnee 1988, Vijay (Filmfare Award) 1988, Kabzaa 1988, Ghar Mein Ram Gali Mein Shyam 1988, Bees Saal Baad 1988, Ladaai 1989, Zakhm 1989, Ram Lakhan (Filmfare Award) 1989, Parinda 1989, Nigahen 1989, Main Tera Dushman 1989, Mahadev 1989, Aakhri Gulam 1989, Daddy (Nat. Film Award 1990, Filmfare Critics Award) 1989, Krodh 1990, Dil 1990, Jeevan Ek Sangharsh 1990, Aaj Ka Arjun 1990, Hum 1991, Saudagar 1991, Lamhe (Filmfare Award) 1991, Khel (Filmfare Award) 1991, Haque 1991, Dil Hai Ki Manta Nahin 1991, Sarphira 1992, Umar Pachpan Ki Dil Bachpan Ka 1992, Heer Ranjha 1992, Beta 1992, Apradhi 1992, Phoolan Hasina Ramkali 1993, Dil Ki Baazi 1993, Izzat Ki Roti 1993, Kasam Teri Kasam 1993, Shreeman Aashiq 1993, Parampara 1993, Meri Jaan 1993, 1942 A Love Story (Star Screen Award) 1993, Baali Umar Ko Salaam 1994, Saajan Ka Ghar 1994, Insaniyat 1994, Darr (Filmfare Award) 1994, Janam Kundli 1995, Dilwale

Dulhania Le Jayenge (Filmfare Award) 1995, Raghuveer 1995, Oh Darling! Yeh Hai India 1995, Dushmani 1995, Dil Ka Doctor 1995, Prem Granth 1996, Shohrat 1996, Maahir 1996, Mr Bechara 1996, Vishwasghaat 1996, Shastra 1996, Nirbhay 1996, Chaahat 1996, Zor 1997, Agni Chakra 1997, Ziddi 1997, Judwaa 1997, Hazaar Chaurasi Ki Maa 1998, Keemat 1998, Salaakhen 1998, Aunty No. 1 1998, Jab Pyaar Kisise Hota Hai 1998, Puraido 1998, Hum Aapke Dil Mein Rehte Hain 1999, Sooryavansham 1999, Haseena Maan Jaayegi (Star Screen Award) 1999, Jhooth Bole Kauwe Kaate 1999, Refugee 2000, Dhadkan 2000, Hamara Dil Aapke Paas Hai 2000, Dhaai Akshar Prem Ke 2000, Aaghaaz 2000, Mohabbatein 2000, Jodi No. 1 2001, Kyo Kii 2001, Bend it Like Beckham 2002, Yeh Hai Jalwa 2002, Jaal: The Trap 2003, Banana Brothers 2003, Shart: The Challenge 2004, Bride and Prejudice 2004, Maine Gandhi Ko Nahin Mara (Nat. Film Award 2006, Best Actor Award, Karachi Int. Film Festival 2005, Riverside Int. Film Festival, California 2006) 2005, Jaan-E-Mann 2006, Hope and a Little Sugar 2006, Khosla Ka Ghosla (GIFA Award, Bollywood Movie Award) 2006, It's a Mismatch 2006, Shakalaka Boom Boom 2007, Gandhi Park 2007, Jaane Bhi Do Yaaron 2007, Buddha Mar Gaya 2007, Se, jie 2007, Apna Asmaan 2007, Kuch Khatta Kuch Meetha 2007, A Wednesday! 2008, Dil Bole Hadippa! 2009, Wake Up Sid 2009, Mr Bhatti on Chutti 2010, Apartment: Rent at Your Own Risk 2010, Badmaa$h Company 2010, You Will Meet a Tall Dark Stranger 2010, Lamhaa: The Untold Story of Kashmir 2010, Dabangg 2010, Nakshatra 2010, Jaane Bhi Do Yaaron 2011, Yamla Pagla Deewana 2011, Zokkomon 2011, The Lion of Judah 2011, Aagaah: The Warning 2011, Chatur Singh Two Star 2011, Sahi Dhandhe Galat Bande 2011, Pranayam 2011, Breakaway 2011, Buddha in a Traffic Jam 2011, Chaar Din Ki Chandni 2012, Mudhalvar Mahatma 2012, Chhodo Kal Ki Baatein 2012, Hum Hai Raahi CAR Ke 2012, Midnight's Children 2012, Silver Linings Playbook 2012, Jab Tak Hai Jaan 2012, Zamaanat 2012, Shobhna's Seven Nights 2013. *Television:* host, Say Na Something to Anupam Uncle, Sawaal Dus Crore Ka. *Address:* Anupam Kher Foundation, D53/1137, Azad Nagar, Veera Desai Road, Andheri (West), Mumbai 400 058, India (office). *Telephone:* (22) 65271917 (office); (22) 65261231 (office); 91-67233342 (mobile) (office); 98-33236290 (mobile) (office). *E-mail:* contact@anupamkherfoundation.org (office). *Website:* www .anupamkherfoundation.org (office).

KHER, Bharti, BA; Indian artist; b. 1969, London, England; m. Subodh Gupta; two c.; ed Middlesex Polytechnic, London, Newcastle Polytechnic; grew up and educated in England, moved to New Delhi aged 23; works include sculpture, paintings, installations and photographs; Sanskriti Award 2003, ARKEN Museum of Art Prize (Denmark) 2010. *Works include:* Hungry Dogs Eat Dirty Pudding 2004, Arione 2004, Arione's Sister 2006, The Skin Speaks a Language Not Its Own 2006, An Absence of Assignable Cause 2007, Solarum Series 2007, The Nemesis of Nations 2008, The Waq Tree 2009, Indra's Net 2010, Reveal the Secrets that You Seek 2011, The Hot Winds that Blow from the West 2011, Western Route to China 2013. *Publications include:* Parasol Unit Foundation for Contemporary art, London 2012 (exhibition catalogue), Bharti Kher Blind eyes open, Galerie Perrotin, Hong Kong 2012. *Address:* c/o Hauser & Wirth, 23 Savile Row, London, W1S 2ET, England (office). *Telephone:* (20) 7287-2300 (office). *Fax:* (20) 7287-6600 (office). *Website:* www.hauserwirth.com (office).

KHETRAN, Shahjahan, MPolSci; Pakistani financial services industry executive, government official and fmr diplomatist; *Managing Director, Pakistan Tourism Development Corporation;* ed Govt Coll. Univ., Lahore, Univ. of the Punjab; First Econ. Minister, Embassy in Riyadh 1995–97; spent several years working in capital markets of Pakistan; Founder-mem. Islamabad Stock Exchange; Chair. Intellectual Property Org. of Pakistan 2009–11; Man. Dir Pakistan Tourism Devt Corpn 2011–. *Address:* Pakistan Tourism Development Corporation, Head Office, 78 Margalla Road, F-6/2, Islamabad 44000, Pakistan (office). *Telephone:* (51) 9215123 (office). *Fax:* (51) 9211509 (office). *E-mail:* mdptdc@comsats.net.pk (office); info@tourism.gov.pk (office). *Website:* www .tourism.gov.pk (office).

KHIATI, Mostéfa, PhD; Algerian professor of medicine and academic administrator; *President, FOREM (Fondation pour la Promotion de la Santé et le Développement de la Recherche);* ed Algerian Medical Inst.; fmr Head, Dept of Pediatrics, El-Harrach Hosp.; Chef de service de pédiatrie, Hôpital Zmirli 1989–99, Hôpital Belfort 1999–; Pres. Nat. Foundation for Health Progress and Medical Research Devt in Algeria 1990–; Président du Conseil Médical de l'hôpital Belfort 2003–; mem. Medical Soc. of Algeria, Algerian Soc. of Pediatrics 1983–86, Int. Asscn of Pediatrics; Pres. FOREM (Fondation pour la Promotion de la Santé et le Développement de la Recherche) 1990–; fmr consultant, Ministry of Health; Fellow, Islamic Acad. of Sciences; Dr hc (Univ. de Tiaret) 2002 Shoman Award for Clinical Sciences 1984, Maghrebian Medicine Award 1986, Chadli Benjedid Award 1989, Union of Arab Physicians Award, Prix Maghrébin de Médecine et du Président de la République Tunisienne (Tunis) 1997, Humanitarian prize, XIIe World congress, Wadem (Lyon, France) 2001. *Publications:* 12 medical textbooks; Algérie: l'enfance blessée, les enfants de Bentalha racontent 2002. *Address:* 41, Cité du 20 Août, Oued Errouman, 16 403 El Achour, Algeria (office). *Telephone:* (61) 50-70-95 (office). *Fax:* (21) 52-25-94 (office). *E-mail:* mkhiati@voila.fr. *Website:* www.forem.dz (office).

KHIEU, Samphan; Cambodian politician; b. 1932, Svay Rieng Prov.; m. Khieu Ponnary; ed Univ. of Paris; f. French-language journal, Observer, Cambodia; Deputy Nat. Ass. in Prince Sihanouk's party, Sangkum Reastr Nyum (Popular Socialist Community); served as Sec. of State for Commerce; left Phnom Penh to join Khmer Rouge 1967; Minister of Defence in Royal Govt of Nat. Union of Cambodia (GRUNC) 1970–76, Deputy Prime Minister 1970–76 (in exile 1970–75, in Phnom Penh 1975–76); mem. Politburo Nat. United Front of Cambodia (FUNC) 1970–79; C-in-C Khmer Rouge High Command 1973–79; Pres. of State Presidium (Head of State) 1976–79; Prime Minister of the Khmer Rouge opposition Govt fighting Vietnamese forces 1979–91; Vice-Pres. of Govt of Democratic Kampuchea (in exile) June 1982–91 (responsibility for Foreign Affairs); Pres. Khmer Rouge 1985–91, returned to Cambodia Nov. 1991; apptd 'Prime Minister' of illegal Provisional Govt of Nat. Unity (fmrly Khmer Rouge) 1994; Chair. Party of Democratic Kampuchea; Pres. and founder Nat. Solidarity Party May 1997; mem. Supreme Nat. Council 1991–97; Vice-Pres. in charge of Foreign Affairs, Nat. Govt of Cambodia 1991; Chair. Cambodian Nat. Union Party (CNUP) 1993–97;

surrended to govt Dec. 1997; arrested Nov. 2007; charged with genocide by UN-backed tribunal Dec. 2009.

KHIN NYUNT, Lt-Gen.; Myanma politician and army officer; b. 1940, Kyauktan; m. Khin Win Shwe; one d. two s.; Chief of Military Intelligence 1984–2003; Prime Minister of Myanmar 2003–04; mem. Mil. Council; sentenced to 44 years (suspended) in jail on eight charges including corruption and bribery 2005.

KHLAIFAT, Awad, PhD; Jordanian politician, university administrator and academic; *Deputy Prime Minister and Minister of the Interior;* b. 1945; Pres. Muta Univ. 1989–91; Senator in the Upper House for several terms, Chair. Media, Cultural and Educational Affairs Cttee, Legal Affairs Cttee; Minister in several govts and with several ministerial portfolios; Deputy Prime Minister and Minister of the Interior 2012–; mem. Arab Thought Forum, Jordanian Writers Asscn. *Address:* Ministry of the Interior, PO Box 100, Amman 11101, Jordan (office). *Telephone:* (6) 5691141 (office); (6) 5931500 (home). *Fax:* (6) 5606908 (office); (6) 5689313 (office). *E-mail:* info@moi.gov.jo (office). *Website:* www.moi.gov.jo (office).

KHLOPONIN, Aleksandr Gennadyevich; Russian politician and business-man; *Deputy Chairman of the Government and Presidential Representative in the North Caucasus Federal Okrug;* b. 6 March 1965, Colombo, Ceylon (now Sri Lanka); m.; one d.; ed Moscow Inst. of Finance; army service 1983–85; with Vneshtorgbank 1989–92; Deputy, First Deputy Chair., Chair., Pres., Commercial Bank Int. Financial Co. 1992–; Acting Deputy Chair., mem. Bd of Dirs then Dir-Gen. Norilsky Nikel 1996–2001; mem. Advisory Council, Fed. Comm. 1997–; mem. Bd of Dirs Kolskaya Mine Co., Murmansk 1998–; Gov. Taimyr (Dalgano-Nenets) Autonomous Okrug 2001–02; Gov. Krasnoyarsk Krai 2002–10; Deputy Chair. of the Govt and Presidential Rep. to N Caucasus Fed. Okrug 2010–; Order of Honour 1998; named Person of the Year by Expert magazine (Russian business weekly) 2002. *Address:* Office of the Government, 103274 Moscow, Krasnopresnenskaya nab. 2 (office); Office of the Presidential Representative to the North Caucasus Federal Okrug, 357500 Stavropol Krai, Pyatigorsk, ul. Krasnoarmeiskaya 10, Russia. *Telephone:* (495) 605-46-50 (office); (8793) 39-44-75. *Fax:* (495) 605-84-48 (office). *E-mail:* pr_hloponina@aprf.gov.ru (office). *Website:* www.government.ru (office); www.skfo.gov.ru.

KHODAKOV, Aleksander Georgyevich; Russian diplomatist; *Director, Secretary to Policy Making Organs, Organisation for the Prohibition of Chemical Weapons;* b. 8 March 1952, Moscow; m.; two s.; ed Moscow State Inst. of Int. Relations, Algiers Univ., Algeria; worked in USSR Embassy, Gabon 1974–79; Legal and Treaty Dept, Ministry of Foreign Affairs 1980–85, Deputy Dir Legal Dept 1992–94, Dir 1994–97; First Sec., then Second Sec. Perm. Mission of USSR to UN, New York 1985–91; Perm. Rep. to Org. for banning Chemical Armaments, The Hague; Amb. to the Netherlands 1997–2003; Dir Office of Special Projects, Org. for the Prohibition of Chemical Weapons 2004–05, Dir, Sec. to Policy-Making Organs 2005–. *Address:* Organisation for the Prohibition of Chemical Weapons, Johan de Wittlaan 32, 2517 JR, The Hague, Netherlands (office). *Telephone:* (70) 4163300 (office). *Fax:* (70) 306353 (office). *Website:* www.opcw.org (office).

KHODJAMYRAT, Annagurbanov; Turkmenistani government official; *Minister of Internal Affairs;* b. 1959, Akhal velayat; ed Turkmen State Univ.; Head, Police Dept of Aşgabat 2004–07; Deputy Minister of Internal Affairs Jan.–April 2007, Minister of Internal Affairs April 2007–. *Address:* Ministry of Internal Affairs, 744000 Aşgabat, pr. 2076 85, Turkmenistan (office). *Telephone:* (12) 35-59-23 (office).

KHODORKOVSKII, Mikhail Borisovich; Russian business executive; b. 26 June 1963, Moscow; m. 1st Yelena Khodorkovskaya; one s.; m. 2nd Inna Khodorkovskaya; two s. one d.; ed Moscow Mendeleyev Inst. of Chemistry and Tech., G. V. Plekhanov Inst. of Nat. Econs; Head of Centre of Interfield Research Programmes (NTTM), USSR State Cttee for Science and Tech. (now Menatep Asscn) 1986–93; Chair. Menatep Bank 1993–; Chair. Commercial Innovation Bank of Scientific Progress 1989–90; Econ. Counsellor to Chair. of Russian Council of Ministers 1990–91; Deputy Minister of Fuel and Energy Industry 1991; Chair. Rosprom (Federal Agency for Industry) 1995–96; Vice-Pres. YUKOS Asscn 1996, Chair. United Bd Rosprom-YUKOS Co. 1997–2000, Chair. Exec. Cttee OAO NK YUKOS, Man. Cttee YUKOS-Moscow 2000–03, CEO YUKOS –2003; Owner, Moskovskiye Novosti newspaper 2003–; charged with fraud and tax evasion Oct. 2003, convicted May 2005 and sentenced to nine years in prison, sentence later reduced to eight years, moved into prison camp No. 13 in Krasnokamensk, Zabaykalsky Krai Oct. 2005; new trial began in Moscow on fresh charges on embezzlement and money laundering March 2009, found guilty of the charges laid against him in 2009 Dec. 2010, sentenced to 14 years in prison (including sentence from first trial) 30 Dec. 2010, appealed conviction to European Court of Human Rights, court ruled that he failed to prove his prosecution was politically motivated but that Russia committed serious violations of his rights during his arrest and pre-trial detention May 2011, declared a prisoner of conscience by Amnesty International May 2011, a review of his sentence ordered by Pres. Medvedev March 2012, prison sentence reduced by two years by a Moscow court (due to be released in 2014) Dec. 2012, pardoned by Pres. Putin and released from jail Dec. 2013; granted visa to travel to Switzerland Jan. 2014. *Address:* 105215 Moscow, a/ya 'Press-Tsentr', Russia. *Telephone:* (495) 773-44-66 (for calls in Russia); (20) 7823-4608 (London, for calls from outside Russia). *Website:* www.khodorkovsky.com.

KHOO, Eric; Singaporean filmmaker; b. 27 March 1965; dir, producer, writer and cinematographer of short films; fmr Head Filmmaker, Zhao Wei Films (production co.); Co-founded (with Infinite Frameworks) Gorylah (production co.) 2009; mem. Bd of Dirs Tisch School of the Arts Asia, New York Univ., Singapore 2007–; Chevalier, Ordre des arts et des letters 2008; Young Artist Award for Film, Nat. Arts Council 1997, Singapore Youth Awards 1999. *Films directed include:* Barbie Dogs Joe 1990, Hope and Requiem 1991, August 1991, The Punk Rocker and... 1992, The Watchman 1993, Symphony 92.4 FM 1993, Pain (also Ed. and Cinematographer) 1994, Mee Pok Man (Fukuoka and Pusan Prizes) 1995, Shier lou (Twelve Stories: Fed. of Int. Film Critics Award, UOB Young Cinema Award, Singapore Int. Festival, Golden Maile Award for Best Picture, Hawaii Int. Film Festival) 1997, Home VDO 2000, One Leg Kicking 2001, Be With Me (also writer) 2005, Digital Sam in Sam Saek 2006: Talk to Her 2006, My Magic (also writer) 2008. *Films produced include:* Pain 1994, Liang Po Po 1999, Stories About Love

2000, One Leg Kicking 2001, 15 2003, Zombie Dogs 2004, 4:30 2005. *Television:* as exec. producer: Drive 1998, Seventh Month 2004. *Publications:* One Fine Day (graphic novel) 2005. *Address:* Zhao Wei Films, 22 Scotts Road, No. 01–28, Singapore 228221 (office). *Telephone:* 67357124 (office). *Fax:* 67351181 (office). *E-mail:* info@zhaowei.com (office). *Website:* www.zhaowei.com (office); www.erickhoo.com.

KHOO-OEI, Mavis; Singaporean business executive; *Chairman and Managing Director, Goodwood Park Hotel Limited;* b. (Khoo Bee Geok), d. of the late Khoo Teck Puat; m. Humphrey Oei (deceased); ed Nat. Univ. of Singapore; an heir to banking and hotel fortune of her father; Chair. and Man. Dir Goodwood Park Hotel; involved with running Khoo Teck Puat Foundation; mem. Bd of Dirs Khoo Teck Puat Hosp., Yishun; Founder and Governing Dir Humphrey Oei Foundation. *Address:* Goodwood Park Hotel, 22 Scotts Road, Singapore 228221 (office). *Telephone:* 67377411 (office). *Fax:* 67328558 (office). *E-mail:* enquiries@goodwoodparkhotel.com (office). *Website:* www.goodwoodparkhotel.com (office).

KHOROSHKOVSKY, Valeriy Ivanovych; Ukrainian economist, politician, business executive and media executive; b. 1 Jan. 1969, Kyiv; m. Olena Khoroshkovska; two s. one d.; ed Taras Shevchenko Kyiv State Univ.; Asst to Prime Minister of Ukraine 1997–98; mem. Verkhovna Rada (Parl.) for Crimea 1998–2002; Deputy Head, later First Deputy Head, Pres. of Ukraine's Admin and Chief of Gen. Office of Internal Policy June–Dec. 2002; Minister of Economy and European Integration 2002–04; Prof., Financial Law Dept, State Tax Service of Ukraine Nat. Acad. 2004–05; Vice-Pres. Evraz Holding LLC (steel co.) 2004–06, Pres. 2006; Chair. Ukrainian Ind. TV-Corpn (Inter TV) 2005–06; Owner, UA Inter Media Group Ltd –2013; First Deputy Sec., Nat. Security and Defence Council of Ukraine 2006–07, First Deputy Head and Head of Anti-terrorist Centre 2009–10, Head, Security Service of Ukraine 2010–12; Head, State Customs Service of Ukraine 2007–09; Minister of Finance Jan.–Feb. 2012; First Deputy Prime Minister Feb.–Dec. 2012; Honoured Economist of Ukraine 2008. *Address:* 01601 Kyiv, A. Vorovskogo Str. 22, Ukraine (office). *Telephone:* (44) 484-47-77 (office). *Fax:* (44) 484-47-75 (office).

KHOSA, Muhammad Latif Khan, LLB; Pakistani lawyer and politician; *Governor of Punjab;* b. 25 July 1946; ed Punjab Univ.; Sr Advocate, High Courts and Supreme Court of Pakistan; Chair. Khosa Law Chambers, Lahore; Pres. Punjab Univ. Law Coll. Student Union 1965–66; Senator (Pakistan People's Party) 2003–09; Attorney Gen. 2008–09; Minister-in-Charge, Ministry of Information Tech. –2010, also Adviser to Prime Minister on Information Tech.; Gov. of Punjab 2011–; fmr Chair. Exec. Cttee, Appeals Cttee; Pres. Multan High Court Bar Asscn 1981–82, 1987–88, 1995–96; mem. Pakistan Bar Council 1995–2000, 2000–05, Chair. Exec. Cttee 1995–96, Appeal Cttee Punjab-1 1996–2000, mem. Tribunal Council 1995–2000. *Address:* Khosa Law Chambers, 1 Turner Road, Lahore, Pakistan. *Telephone:* (42) 37312192. *Website:* www.khosas.com.

KHOSLA, Ashok, BA, MA, AM, PhD; Indian scientist, environmentalist, academic and international organization official; *President, International Union for Conservation of Nature (IUCN);* b. 31 March 1940, Kashmir; m.; ed St Lawrence Coll., Kent, Peterhouse, Univ. of Cambridge, UK, Harvard Univ., USA; Faculty mem., Harvard Univ. 1963–70; man. various businesses in USA 1965–70; Dir Office of Environmental Planning, Govt of India, New Delhi 1972–76; Dir Infoterra, UNEP, Nairobi, Kenya 1976–82; Chair. and CEO various social enterprises in India 1985–; Founder and Chair. Development Alternatives, New Delhi 1983–; Special Adviser to Brundtland Comm. (WCED); mem. evaluation teams for GEF pilot phase, World Bank's 25 Years of Environmental Programmes and Sec.-Gen.'s Task Force to Restructure the Environmental Activities of the UN; Chair. NGO Forum at Earth Summit, Rio de Janeiro 1992; has served on bds of several environment and conservation orgs, including Int. Union for Conservation of Nature (IUCN), Worldwide Fund for Nature, Centre for Our Common Future, Int. Inst. for Sustainable Devt, Stockholm Environment Inst., Zero Emissions Research and Initiatives, Alliance for a New Humanity, EnergyGlobe, EXPO 2000, Earth Council, Television Trust for the Environment, Toyota Environmental Awards, Int. Inst. for Environment and Devt, Nat. Environmental Council, Nat. Inst. of Design, Environmental Planning and Coordination Org., Planet2025; first elected Councillor to IUCN, representing Govt of India, at Kinshasa Gen. Ass. 1975, UNEP Rep. at Council 1978, participated in Council as Deputy Chair. and later as Chair. Comm. on Environmental, Econ. and Social Policy (then CEP, later CESP), re-elected Regional Councillor 1988, 1990, Pres. IUCN 2008–; Pres. Club of Rome 2006–, Tech. and Action for Rural Advancement, TARAhaat.com, Decentralised Energy Systems India Pvt. Ltd; mem. Int. Advisory Council, Criteria CaixaCorp, Barcelona 2008–; Chair. Int. Council for Science/Scientific Cttee on Problems of the Environment Programme on Environmental Information 1984–87, IUCN Comm. on Environmental Planning, Nat. Advisory Cttee on Environmental Education, Govt of India, Indian Environment Congress, New Delhi; consultant and advisor, UNEP, Nairobi, UNDP, World Comm. on Environment and Devt, Geneva, World Bank, Global Environment Facility, UNU, Int. Devt Research Centre, Int. Council of Scientific Unions, World Resources Inst., Royal Swedish Acad. of Sciences, East-West Centre, MacArthur Foundation, Ministry of Environment, Govt of India, Ministry of Science and Tech., Ministry of Rural Devt, Planning Comm.; mem. UNEP Governing Council 1972–76, Nat. Security Advisory Bd, Science Advisory Council to Cabinet, Nat. Environment Council, Delhi Urban Art Comm., Indo-UK Roundtable for Strategic Advice to Prime Ministers; Order of the Golden Ark (Netherlands) 1999, Stockholm Challenge Award 2001, UN Sasakawa Environment Prize 2002, Schwab Foundation Award for Outstanding Social Entrepreneur 2004. *Achievements include:* with Prof. Roger Revelle, designed and taught Nat Sci 118, 'Population, Resources and the Environment', Harvard Univ. (first university course on the environment) 1965. *Publications include:* The Survival Equation (co-ed with Roger Revelle, Houghton Mifflin) 1970, contrib. to numerous articles on environmental issues. *Address:* Development Alternatives, B-32 Tara Crescent, New Delhi 110 016 (office); 22 Olof Palme Marg, New Delhi 110 057 India (home); International Union for Conservation of Nature, rue Mauverney 28, Gland 1196, Switzerland (office). *Telephone:* (22) 999-0000 (Switzerland) (office); (11) 55428858 (New Delhi) (office); (11) 26149809 (home). *Fax:* (11) 26866031 (New Delhi) (office); (11) 26142213 (home). *E-mail:* akhosla@devalt.org (office); akhosla@gmail.com (home). *Website:* www.devalt.org (office); www.khosla.in.

KHOSLA, Pradeep K., BEng, MS, PhD; Indian/American electrical engineer, computer scientist, academic and university administrator; *Chancellor, University of California, San Diego;* ed Indian Inst. of Tech., Carnegie Mellon Univ.; Asst Prof., Carnegie Mellon Univ. 1986–90, Assoc. Prof. 1990–94, Prof. 1994–2012, Defense Advanced Research Projects Agency (DARPA) Program Man., Software and Intelligent Systems Tech. Office, Defense Sciences Office and Tactical Tech. Office 1994–96, apptd Philip and Marsha Dowd Prof. 1998, Univ. Prof. 2008, Dean, Coll. of Eng 2004–12, Founding Dir Carnegie Mellon CyLab, Inst. for Complex Engineered Systems; Distinguished Prof., Dept of Electrical and Computer Eng and Dept of Computer Science and Eng and Chancellor Univ. of California, San Diego 2012–; mem. Advisory Bd Rady Children's Hosp. Health Center, La Jolla Playhouse, Cecil and Ida M. Green Foundation for Earth Sciences, Sanford Consortium for Regenerative Medicine; mem. Visiting Cttee on Advanced Tech. for NIST; Chair. Jury for Infosys Foundation Prize in Eng and Computer Science; fmr mem. Strategy Review Bd, Ministry of Science and Tech., Taiwan, Council of Deans of the Aeronautics Advisory Cttee, NASA, Nat. Research Council Bd on Manufacturing and Eng Design, Pennsylvania Treasury Advisory Bd, Sr Advisory Group for DARPA Program on Jt Unmanned Combat Air Systems; mem. Nat. Acad. of Eng, American Soc. for Eng Educ.; Fellow, IEEE, ASME, AAAS, American Asscn of Artificial Intelligence, Indian Acad. of Eng; Hon. Fellow, Indian Acad. of Science; George Westinghouse Award for Educ. 1999, Academic of the Year Award, SiliconIndia 2000, Light of India Award 2012, ASME Lifetime Achievement Award 2012, W. Wallace McDowell Award, IEEE Computer Soc. 2012. *Publications:* three books and more than 350 journal articles and conf. and book contribs. *Address:* Office of the Chancellor, University of California, San Diego, 9500 Gilman Drive #0005, La Jolla, CA 92093-0005, USA (office). *Telephone:* (858) 534-3135 (office). *Fax:* (858) 534-6523 (office). *E-mail:* chancellor@ucsd.edu (office). *Website:* chancellor.ucsd.edu (office).

KHOSLA, Vinod, BTech, MSc, MBA; Indian/American investment industry executive; *Owner, Khosla Ventures;* b. 28 Jan. 1955, Pune, India; m. Neeru Khosla; one s. three d.; ed Indian Inst. of Tech., Delhi, Carnegie Mellon Univ., Stanford Univ. Grad. School of Business; started soy milk co. to service people in India who did not have refrigerators 1975; came to USA to study; one of three founders of Daisy Systems (first significant computer aided design system for electrical engineers) 1980; started Sun Microsystems to build workstations for software developers 1982; pioneered 'open systems' and RISC processors, left co. 1985; Gen. Partner, Kleiner, Perkins, Caufield & Byers (venture capital firm) 1986–; f. Khosla Ventures 2004; Co-founder The Indus Entrepreneurs; assists or serves on bds of eASIC (programmable ASIC platform), Infinera (optical communications), Kovio (printed electronics), Skyblue (internet PC), Spatial Photonics (Micromirror displays), Xsigo (datacentre switch), Grameen Foundation, MetricStream, moka5, Ausra, Zettacore, iSkoot, among others; Charter mem. TiE (not-for-profit global network of entrepreneurs and professionals); Founding Bd mem. Indian School of Business; Hon. Chair. DonorsChoose San Francisco Bay Area Advisory Bd. *Address:* Khosla Ventures, 3000 Sand Hill Road, Building 3, Suite 170, Menlo Park, CA 94025, USA (office). *Telephone:* (650) 376-8500 (office). *Fax:* (650) 926-9590 (office). *E-mail:* kv@khoslaventures.com (office). *Website:* www .khoslaventures.com (office).

KHOSROKHAVAR, Farhad; Iranian/French sociologist and academic; *Professor of Sociology and Director of Studies, Ecole des Hautes Etudes en Sciences Sociales (EHESS);* b. 21 March 1948, Tehran; Asst Prof., Bou Ali Univ. Hamadan, Iran 1977–79; Assoc. Prof., Center for Science Policy, Ministry of Culture and Higher Educ., Iran, 1979–90; Rockefeller Fellow 1990–91; Assoc. Prof. of Sociology, Ecole des Hautes Etudes en Sciences Sociales–Cadis (EHESS), Paris 1991–98, Prof. of Sociology 1998–, currently also Dir of Studies; Visiting Scholar, Yale Univ. 2008, Harvard Univ. 2009. *Publications include:* La Foulard et la République (with Françoise Gaspard) 1995, Sous le voile islamique (with Chala Chafiq) 1995, Anthropologie de la révolution iranienne 1997, L'islam des jeunes 1997, L'Iran, comment sortir d'une révolution religieuse? (with Oliver Roy) 1999, La recherche de soi, dialogues sur le sujet (with Alain Touraine) 2000, L'Instance du sacré 2001, Les Nouveaux martyrs d'Allah (trans. with additional chapter as Suicide Bombers: Allah's New Martyrs 2005) 2002, L'Islam en prison 2004, Muslims in Prison (with James A. Beckford and Danièle Joly) 2005, Avoir vingt ans dans le pays des ayatollahs (with Amir Nikpey) 2009, Jihadism Worldwide 2009. *Address:* EHESS– Paris, 54 boulevard Raspail, 75006 Paris, France (office). *Telephone:* 1-49-54-25-63 (office). *E-mail:* cavard@ehess.fr (office). *Website:* www.ehess.fr (office).

KHOTINENKO, Vladimir I.; Russian film director and producer, actor, script-writer and artist; b. 20 Jan. 1952, Slavgorod, Altai territory; m.; one d.; ed Sverdlovsk Inst. of Architecture; constructor at Pavlodar tractor production factory 1969–70; artist, Sverdlovsk film studio 1978–82; freelance 1982–; All-Union Film Festival Prize 1988, Kinoshok Prizes 1992, 1993, Nika Prizes for Best Film 1993, for Best Film Director 1993. *Films:* Races with Pursuit (production designer) 1979, The Smoke of the Home Country (production designer) 1980, Kinfolk (as actor) 1981, Vot takaya muzyka (production designer) 1981, Kazachya zastava (actor, production designer) 1982, Alone and Unarmed (dir) 1984, V strelyayushchej glushi (dir) 1986, Mirror for a Hero (dir) 1987, Who is the Singer Married To? (actor) 1988, Vagon lit (dir) 1989, The Swarm (dir, writer) 1990, Patriotic Comedy (dir, writer) 1992, Makarov (dir, producer) 1993, A Muslim (dir, producer) 1995, The Arrival of a Train (dir, producer) 1995, Road (producer, actor, dir) 1996, 72 metra (dir, writer) 2004, Vecherniy zvon (dir) 2004, 1612: Khroniki smutnogo vremeni 2007, The Priest 2009. *Television:* Po tu storonu volkov (dir, mini series) 2002, Gibel imperii (mini series) 2005. *Address:* Fadeyeva str. 6, apt 269, Moscow 125047, Russia (office). *Telephone:* (495) 250-47-38 (office).

KHOUNA, Cheikh el Avia Ould Mohamed; Mauritanian politician; b. 1956; mem. Democratic and Social Republican Party (replaced by Republican Party for Democracy and Renewal—RPDR 2005); fmr Minister of Fisheries and Marine Economy; Minister of Foreign Affairs 1998, 2008; Prime Minister of Mauritania 1996–97, 1998–2003. *Address:* Republican Party for Democracy and Renewal (RPDR), ZRB, Tevragh Zeina, Nouakchott, Mauritania (office). *Telephone:* 529-18-36 (office). *Fax:* 529-18-00 (office). *E-mail:* info@prdr.mr (office). *Website:* www.prdr .mr (office).

KHOURI, Elie, MBA; Lebanese/French marketing executive; *CEO, Middle East and North Africa, Omnicom Media Group;* b. 1965, Beirut; m. Mylene Khouri 2002;

three d.; ed American Univ. of Beirut; began career as currency dealer with financial trading co.; joined Impact BBDO, Cyprus 1988, becoming Assoc. Man. Dir 1988–2000; joined Lintas/Gulf Advertising, Paris 1991; Account Dir BBDO, Dubai 1992, also worked in client services at BBDO in Beirut and Cyprus, Co-Man. Impact BBDO, Beirut 1996–2000; co-f. Omnicom Group (OMG) Middle East 2002, later Man. Dir Omnicom Media Direction (OMD) formed out of media depts of three of Omnicom's global advertising agencies (BBDO, DDB and TBWA), Regional Man. Dir, Middle East and N Africa (MENA), OMD 2001–05, CEO MENA, Omnicom Media Group 2006–; mem. Bd START (non-profit org.); named by Arabian Business magazine in the Top 50 Most Influential Arabs for three consecutive years, Media and Marketing CEO of the Year, CEO Middle East magazine 2008, named by CEO Middle East magazine as one of the most admired CEOs in the GCC 2010, ranked second in Communicate magazine's inaugural list of the 50 Most Powerful People in Media 2011, ranked by Arabian Business amongst the Power 500: The World's Most Influential Arabs (17th) 2010, (31st) 2011, (27th) 2012, (23rd) 2013. *Address:* Omnicom Media Group, PO Box 19791, Dubai, United Arab Emirates (office). *Telephone:* (4) 3904323 (office). *E-mail:* Elie .Khouri@omnicommediagroup.com (office). *Website:* www.omnicommediagroup .com (office).

KHOURY, Elias; Lebanese novelist and literary critic; b. 1948, Ashrafiyyeh, nr Beirut; ed Lebanese Univ., Beirut, Univ. of Paris, France; with PLO Research Centre, Beirut 1973–79; Publr Su'un filastiniya (Palestinian Affairs) journal 1976–79; Editorial Dir Al-Karmel 1981–82; Ed. culture section of As-Safir journal 1983–90, Al-Mulhaq cultural supplement of an-Nahar daily newspaper 1992–2009; Dir Masrah Beyrut theatre 1993–98; Global Distinguished Prof. of Middle Eastern and Islamic Studies, New York Univ. 2004–05; fmr Prof., Columbia Univ., Lebanese Univ., American Univ. of Beirut, Lebanese American Univ.; Lettre Ulysses Award 2005. *Publications include:* An 'ilaqat al-da'irah (novel) 1975, Al-Jabal al-Saghir (novel) 1977, Dirasat fi naqd al-shi'r (criticism) 1979, Abwab al-Madinah (novel) 1981, Al-wujuh al-baida' (novel, trans. as White Masks 2010) 1981, Al-dhakira al-mafquda (criticism) 1982, Al-mubtada' wa'l-khabar (short stories) 1984, Tajribat al-ba'th 'an ufq (criticism) 1984, Zaman al-ihtilal (criticism) 1985, Rahlat Gandhi al-Saghir (novel) 1989, Mamlakat al-Ghuraba (novel) 1993, Majma' al-Asrar (novel) 1994, Bab al-Shams (novel, trans. as Gate of the Sun 2006) (Palestine Prize 1998) 1998, Ra'ihat al-Sabun (novel) 2000, Yalo (novel) 2002, Ka'anaha Nae'ma (novel) 2007, Sinalkul 2012. *Address:* c/o An-Nahar (The Day), Immeuble An-Nahar, place des Martyrs, Marfa', Beirut 2014 5401, Lebanon. *Telephone:* (1) 994888. *Fax:* (1) 996777. *E-mail:* webmaster@ annahar.com.lb. *Website:* www.annaharonline.com.

KHOURY, Said T., BA; Lebanese business executive; *Chairman, Consolidated Contractors Company;* b. Safad, Palestine; m.; ed American Univ., Beirut; moved to Lebanon following Arab-Israeli war 1948; Co-founder (with cousin Hasib Sabbagh) Consolidated Contractors Co. (construction co.) 1952, collaborated with the Bechtel Group in projects in 40 countries, especially the Middle East and North Africa; Chair. Palestinian Businessmen's Asscn; Gov. Arab Monetary Fund; major shareholder in Arab Palestinian Investment Co. *Address:* Consolidated Contract-ors Company, PO Box 61092, Amaroussion, 15110 Athens, Greece (office). *Telephone:* (210) 6182000 (office). *Fax:* (210) 6199224 (office). *E-mail:* info@ccc.gr (office). *Website:* www.ccc.gr (office).

KHOURY-GHATA, Vénus, Licence en lettres; Lebanese/French novelist and poet; b. 1937, Bsherre; m. 1st (divorced); three c.; m. 2nd Jean Ghata (died 1981); one d.; ed in Lebanon; fmr journalist; moved to France 1973; fmr contrib. and trans., Europe magazine; Pres. Prix des Cinq Continents, Prix Yvon Goll, Prix France Liban; mem. selection cttee, Prix Mallarmé, Prix Max-Pol-Fouchet, Prix Max-Jacob; frequent radio broadcaster; has written 23 books of poetry, 22 novels; Officier, Ordre nat. du Mérite 2003, Officier, Légion d'honneur 2010; Prix Nice-Baie de Anges 2003, Grand Prix Guillevic de Poésie de Saint-Malo 2010, Grand Prix Doha, Qatar 2010, Prix Concourt de Poesie 2011. *Publications:* poetry includes: (first collection) 1966, Les Ombres et leurs cris (Prix Guillaume-Apollinaire) 1980, Monologue du mort (Prix Mallarmé) 1987, Fable pour un peuple d'argile (Grand Prix de la Société des gens de lettres) 1992, Anthologie person-elle 1997, Elle dit 1999, Here There Was Once a Country (anthology in trans.) 2001, La Compassion des pierres 2001, She Says (trans.) 2003, Quelle est la nuit parmi les nuits 2007, Les obscurcis (Grand Prix de Poésie, Acad. Française 2009) 2008, A quoi sert la neige – Poèmes pour enfants 2008, Où vont les arbres? (Prix Fondation Micheloud 2012) 2011; novels include: Vacarme pour une lune morte 1983, Bayarmine 1990, Mortemaison 1992, La maitresse du notable (Liberatturpreis) 1992, La Maestra 1994, Les Fiancées du Cap Ténès 1995, Une maison au bord des larmes (trans. as A House on the Edge of Tears 2006) 1998, Privilège des morts 2001, Le Moine, l'ottoman et la femme du grand argentier 2003, La Maison aux orties 2006, Sept pierres pour la femme adultère 2007, La Fille qui marchait dans le désert 2010; contrib. in trans. to Ambit, Banipal: A Journal of Modern Arab Literature, Columbia, Field, Contemporary Poetry and Poetics, Gobshite Quarterly, Jacket, Luna, The Manhattan Review, Metre, The New Yorker, Poetry, Shenandoah, Verse, Poetry London. *Address:* 16 avenue Raphael, 75016 Paris, France (home). *Telephone:* 1-45-04-06-37 (home). *Fax:* 1-45-04-06-37 (home).

KHRISTENKO, Viktor Borisovich, BSc, DEcon; Russian politician; *Chairman, Collegium of the Eurasian Economic Commission;* b. 28 Aug. 1957, Chelyabinsk; m. 2nd Tatyana Golikova; three c.; ed Chelyabinsk Polytechnical Inst. and Acad. of Nat. Economy; sr teacher and Lecturer, Faculty of the Econs of Machine Construction, Chelyabinsk Polytechnical Inst. 1979–90; Chair. Perm. Comm., First Deputy Chair. Econs Cttee, Chair. Property Man. Cttee, Chelyabinsk City Exec. Cttee 1990–91; Deputy Head Admin of Chelyabinsk Oblast 1991–94, First Deputy Head 1994–96; Plenipotentiary Rep. of the Pres. of the Russian Fed. in Chelyabinsk Oblast 1997; Deputy Minister of Finances, Russian Fed. June 1997, First Deputy Minister 1998; mem. Presidium May–Aug. 1998; Deputy Chair. of Govt April–Sept. 1998, 2000, First Deputy Chair. 1999, 2000–04, Acting Chair. 24 Feb.–5 March 2004; Minister of Industry and Energy (later Minister of Industry and Trade) 2004–12; Special Presidential Envoy for Integration with CIS 2004–; Chair. Comm. on Chechnya 2000, on Housing Policy 2001, on Reform of the Electrical Energy Sector 2001; Chair. Collegium of the Eurasian Econ. Comm. 2012–; Gratitude of the Pres. of the Russian Fed., Order of Friendship (Second

Class) (Kazakhstan) 2002, Order of Merit for the Fatherland (Fourth Class) 2006, (Third Class) 2007, Grand Officer, Order of Merit of the Italian Repub. 2009, Order of the Holy Prince Daniel of Moscow (First Class) (Russian Orthodox Church) 2010; Diploma of the Russian Fed. Govt. *Address:* c/o Ministry of Industry and Trade, 109074 Moscow, Kitaigorodskii proyezd 7, Russia (office). *Telephone:* (495) 539-21-87 (office). *Fax:* (495) 539-21-72 (office). *E-mail:* info_admin@minprom.gov .ru (office). *Website:* www.minpromtorg.gov.ru (office).

KHRUSHCHOV, Nikolai Grigoryevich; Russian biologist; *Director, Koltsov Institute of Biology of Development, Russian Academy of Sciences;* b. 23 June 1932; m.; one d.; ed 2nd Moscow Inst. of Medicine; Jr, then Sr Researcher, Head of Div. Deputy Dir, currently Dir Koltsov Inst. of Biology of Devt USSR (now Russian) Acad. of Sciences; corresp. mem. Russian Acad. of Sciences 1979, mem. 1990, mem. Presidium 1994, Academician Sec., Dept of Gen. Biology; Mechnikov Prize. *Publications:* main scientific research and numerous scientific publs on problems of biology of devt of tissue and cellular systems. *Address:* Koltsov Institute of Biology of Development, Russian Academy of Sciences, 117808 Moscow, Vavilova str. 26, Russia (office). *Telephone:* (495) 938-16-91 (office); (495) 938-51-90 (Acad.) (office).

KHRZHANOVSKY, Andrei Yurevich; Russian filmmaker, director, producer, scriptwriter and teacher; *Artistic Director, School-Studio 'SHAR';* b. 30 Nov. 1939, Moscow; s. of Yuriy Borisovich Khrzhanovsky and Vera Mihayilovna Khrzhanovsky; m. Mariya Newman 1972; one s.; ed VGIK (workshop of L. Kuleshov); worked with 'Soyuzmultfilm' from 1962; currently Artistic Dir and Chair. Bd Higher Refresher Animation School-Studio 'Shar'; Prof., VGIK; Hon. Artist of Russia; State Prize 1986, 1999, Prizes of Russian Acad. of Cinema 1995, 1998, 2004. *Films include:* Once upon a time there lived a man by the name of Kozyavin 1966, The Glass Harmonica 1968, The Cupboard 1971, The Butterfly 1972, In the World of Fables 1973, A Wonderful Day 1975, The House that Jack Built 1976, I Fly to You in Memory (trilogy of films based on Pushkin's doodles) 1977, 1981, 1982, The King's Sandwich 1985, The School of Fine Arts (Part 1 – A Landscape with Juniper 1987, Part 2 – The Return 1990), The Lion with the Grey Beard 1994, Oleg Kagan: Life after Life (documentary) 1996, The Long Journey (based on Federico Fellini's drawings) 1997, The Dreams about MKHAT (documentary) 1999, Studys about Pushkin, Lullaby for Cricket 1999, Pushkin Take-off 2002, I Love You 2002, A Cat and a Half (based on Joseph Brodsky's drawings) 2002, A Room and a Half (about the life and poetry of Joseph Brodsky) 2008. *Publications:* Der ambivalente Charme des Surrealismus: Die Ost, Frankfurt am Main 2002 (Subversionen des Surrealen un mittel, und osteuropäishen Film), The Pupil of the Wizard: V.S. Meierhold and Erast Garin (ed and contrib.) 2004. *E-mail:* harmonic47@gmail.com (home). *Website:* www.sharstudio.com (office).

KHUBLARYAN, Martin Gaykovich, PhD; Russian hydrologist and academic; b. 5 March 1935; m. Servenik A. Gabrielyan 1968; two d.; ed Armenian Inst. of Agric., Erevan; Sr Researcher, Head of Lab., Deputy Dir Inst. of Water Problems, USSR Acad. of Sciences 1968–88, Dir 1988–2003, Adviser Russian Acad. of Sciences 2003–; Corresp. mem. USSR (now Russian) Acad. of Sciences 1984, mem. and Adviser 1994; mem. American Soc. of Hydrology; Ed.-in-Chief Water Resources Journal; Russian Acad. of Sciences Award for Terrestrial Waters Sciences. *Publications include:* Chemical substance transport in soil and its effect on groundwater quality 1989, Water Streams: Models of flow and quality surface water 1991, The Caspian Sea Phenomenon 1995, The Application of Non-linear Models to the Analysis of Water Level Fluctuations in Reservoirs 1996; numerous other publs on hydromechanics, hydrology and hydrogeology. *Leisure interests:* classical music, chess, museums, literature. *Address:* Proffsouznaya str. 43-1-84, 117420 Moscow, Russia (home). *Telephone:* (495) 331-32-60 (home).

KHUDAIBERDYEV, Narmankhonmadi Dzhurayevich; Uzbekistani politician; b. 1928; ed Uzbek Agricultural Inst.; mem. CPSU 1948–91; dept head, sec. of a regional Uzbek Komsomol Cttee; Lecturer, Asst Prof. Agric. Inst., Samarkand 1943–54; leading CPSU and state posts 1954–; Sec. Bukhara Dist Cttee of Uzbek CP, Head Agric. Dept of Cen. Cttee of Uzbek CP; Second Sec. Bukhara Dist Cttee 1956–60; Deputy to Supreme Soviet of Uzbek SSR 1959–63, 1967; mem. Cen. Cttee of Uzbek CP 1960; Deputy Chair. Council of Ministers of Uzbek SSR 1960–61; First Sec. Surkhan-Darya Dist Cttee of Uzbek CP 1961–62; Prime Minister of Uzbekistan 1971–85; cand. mem. Cen. Cttee of CPSU 1961–66, mem. 1971; mem. Foreign Affairs Comm. of Soviet of the Union, USSR Supreme Soviet 1962–66; Sec. and mem. Presidium of the Cen. Cttee of the Uzbek CP 1962–65, Chair. Agric. Bureau 1962–64; Chair. Council of Ministers of Uzbek SSR 1971–84; mem. Politburo of Cen. Cttee of Uzbek CP 1971–84; sentenced to nine years in a labour camp for bribery Sept. 1989, released 1992.

KHUDAINATOV, Eduard; Russian business executive; *Deputy Chairman of the Management Board and First Vice-President, Rosneft Oil Company;* b. 1960; ed Tyumen State Univ., Int. Acad. of Business, Moscow; Head of Evikhon, Evikhon-2 and Yuganskpromfinco 1993–96; Deputy Head of Nefteyugansk Admin, First Deputy Head of Nefteyugansk region and Head of Poikovsky settlement Admin 1996; Fed. Insp. in Nenets Autonomous Dist of Admin of the Authorized Rep. of the Russian Pres. in Northwestern Fed. Dist 2000–03; Gen. Dir OJSC Severneftegazprom 2003–08; Vice-Pres. Rosneft Oil Co. 2008–09, First Vice-Pres., responsible for production and capital construction projects 2009–, Chair. Man. Bd and Pres. 2010–12, Deputy Chair. Man. Bd and First Vice-Pres. 2012–, CEO TNK-BP (following acquisition by Rosneft) 2013–. *Address:* Rosneft Oil Co., Moscow 115998, 26/1, Sofiyskaya Embankment, 1, GSP-8, Russia (office). *Telephone:* (495) 777-44-22 (office). *Fax:* (495) 777-44-44 (office). *E-mail:* postman@rosneft.ru (office). *Website:* www.rosneft.ru (office).

KHUDONAZAROV, Davlatnazar; Tajikistani film director and politician; b. 13 March 1944; ed All-Union Inst. of Cinematography; film dir and cameraman in documentary cinema 1965–77; debut in feature film The First Morning of Youth 1979; Chair. Confed. of Cinema Unions 1990–; USSR People's Deputy, mem. of Supreme Soviet 1989–91; mem. Inter-regional Deputies' Group; cand. for Pres. of Tajikistan 1991; moved to Moscow after civil war 1992; adviser, Social and Political Union Focus 1999–; Rudaki State Prize of Tajikistan 1972, Distinguished Contributor to Tajik Culture 1977, Badge of Honor and other awards. *Films include:* Dzura Sarkor, Tale about Rustam, Rustam and Sokhrab, One Life is not Enough, Tale about Siyavush, A Brook Ringing in Melted Snow (Prize of All-Union

Film Festival 1983). *Address:* Confederation of Cinema Unions, 123825 Moscow, Vasilyevskaya str. 13, Russia. *Telephone:* (495) 250-41-14 (office).

KHUDYAKOV, Konstantin Pavlovich; Russian film director; b. 13 Oct. 1938, Moscow; m. Irina Mikhailovna Ivanova; one s.; ed All-Union Inst. of Cinematography; film Dir 1970–; with Mosfilm Studio 1970–; mem. Union of Cinematographers 1975; Prof., Head of Studio Higher Courses of Film Dirs; Prof. All-Union Inst. of Cinematography 1995–; Chair. State Attestation Comm. of Russian Inst. of Cinematography 1998–; Crystal Box for Pages of Life 1971, Prize Moscow Film Festival for Who Will Pay for Luck 1980, Grand Prix Barcelona Film Festival 1986, Golden Tulip Prize Istanbul Film Festival 1986, Prize of the 1st Washington Film Festival 1986, Prize of the Royal Acad. of Cinema (Stockholm) for Success 1986, Prize of European Community for From Evening to Noon (TV), 1983, Prize of the Jerusalem Film Festival for Mother of Jesus 1988. *Films include:* Pages of Life, To Live Your Own Way, Ivatsov, Petrov, Sidorov, Success, From Evening to Noon, Death in Cinema, Contender, Mother of Jesus, Without the Return Address, Michel, The Shadows of Fabergé, On, ona i ya 2007. *Televsions productions:* Presence, Behind the Stone Wall, The Sun of the Wall, Such a Long Short Life, Girl without Dowry, Game, Tango for Two Voices, Impostors. *Leisure interests:* avant-garde and jazz music. *Address:* 1812 Iear str. 3, Apt 40, 121293 Moscow, Russia (home). *Telephone:* (495) 148-33-37 (home).

KHUGAYEV, Rostislav Erastovich; Georgian (South Ossetian) politician; b. 17 Dec. 1951, Mirtgadjin, Dzau dist, South Ossetian Autonomous Oblast, Georgian SSR, USSR; ed Kuibyshev Civil Eng Inst.; lived for many years in Samara, Russia; leader of the local Ossetian émigré community; Owner and Head of Amond group of construction cos; Gen. Dir Southern Directorate (Ministry of Regional Devt subdivision working on the restoration of South Ossetia) 2009–11, moving to the Far East Dec. 2011, First Deputy Gen. Dir of financial oversight admin of Far Eastern Directorate, Ministry of Regional Devt 2011–12; Acting Prime Minister of 'Republic of South Ossetia' April–May 2012, Prime Minister May 2012–Jan. 2014; Ind. *Address:* c/o Office of the Prime Minister of the 'Republic of South Ossetia', 100001 Tskhinvali, ul. Khetgurova 1, South Ossetia, Georgia.

KHURSHID, Ahmed, MA, LLB, PhD; Pakistani economist; *Chairman, Institute of Policy Studies;* b. 22 March 1932, Delhi, India; Chair. Inst. of Policy Studies, Islamabad 1979–; Vice-Pres. Islamic Research Acad. 1979–; Fed. Minister of Planning Devt and Statistics 1978–79, mem. Hiira Cttee 1978–83; Senator 1985–97, 2003–; Chair. Islamic Foundation, UK 1978–, Int. Inst. of Islamic Econs, Int. Islamic Univ. 1983–87; mem. Bd Trustees, Islamic Centre, Nigeria 1976–, Bd Trustees, Int. Islamic Univ., Islamabad 1980–, Foundation Council, Royal Acad. for Islamic Civilization, Jordan 1987–; Islamic Devt Bank Award 1988, King Faisal Int. Prize for Services to Islam 1990, La-Riba Prize in Islamic Finance, American Finance House 1998. *Address:* Institute of Policy Studies, Nasr Chambers, Block-19, Markaz F-7, Islamabad 44000, Pakistan (office). *Telephone:* (51) 2650971 (office). *Fax:* (51) 2650704 (office). *E-mail:* khurshid@ips.net.pk (office). *Website:* www.ips.org.pk (office).

KHURSHID, Salman, BA, BCL, MA; Indian politician, lawyer and author; *Minister of External Affairs;* b. 1 Jan. 1953, Aligarh, Uttar Pradesh; s. of Khurshed Alam Khan; m. Louise Khurshid; ed St Xavier's High School, Patna, Bihar, St Stephen's Coll., New Delhi, St Edmund Hall, Oxford, UK; fmr Lecturer in Law, Trinity Coll., Oxford; Officer on Special Duty in Office of Prime Minister Mrs Indira Gandhi early 1980s; MP (Indian Nat. Congress) for Farrukhabad constituency 1991–96, for Farrukhabad Lok Sabha constituency 2009–; Deputy Minister of Commerce 1991–93, Minister of State for External Affairs 1993–96, Union Minister of State (with Ind. Charges) of Corp. Affairs and Minority Affairs 2009–11, Minister of Law and Justice 2011–12, of External Affairs 2012–; fmr Pres. Uttar Pradesh Congress Cttee, Delhi Public School Soc., Dr Zakir Hussain Study Circle. *Publications include:* At Home in India: A Restatement of Indian Muslims 1987, Beyond Terrorism: New Hope for Kashmir 1995; as ed.: The Contemporary Conservative: Selected Writings of Dhiren Bhagat 1990; plays: Sons of Babur: A Play in Search of India 2008. *Address:* Ministry of External Affairs, South Block, New Delhi 110 011 (office); 80 Sukhdev Vihar, Main Mathura Road, New Delhi, 110 025, India. *Telephone:* (11) 23011127 (office); (11) 26936655. *Fax:* (11) 23013254 (office); (11) 26849022. *E-mail:* sk_tipu@yahoo.com; sk_tipu_in@yahoo.com. *Website:* www.mea.gov.in (office); www.salmankhurshid .com.

KHUSH, Gurdev Singh, PhD, FRS; Indian agronomist and academic; *Adjunct Professor, College of Agricultural and Environmental Sciences, University of California, Davis;* b. 22 Aug. 1935, Jalandhar, Punjab; s. of Kartar Singh and Pritam Kaur; m. Harwant Kaur Grewal 1961; one s. three d.; ed Punjab Agricultural Univ., Chandigarh, Univ. of California, Davis, USA; Research Asst, Univ. of Calif., Davis 1957–60, Asst Geneticist 1960–67, currently Adjunct Prof., Coll. of Agricultural and Environmental Sciences; Plant Breeder, Int. Rice Research Inst., Manila, Philippines, 1967–72, Head of Plant Breeding, Genetics and Biochem. Div. 1972–2002; Fellow, Russian Acad. of Sciences, Chinese Acad. of Agricultural Sciences; mem. Indian Nat. Science Acad., Third World Acad. of Sciences, NAS (USA); Dr hc (Ohio State Univ.), (Univ. of Cambridge) 2000, (Guru Nanak Dev Univ.) 2007; Borlaug Award 1977, Japan Prize 1987, Int. Agronomy Award 1989, World Food Prize 1996, Rank Prize 1998, Wolf Prize for Agriculture 2000, Padma Shri 2000, China Int. Scientific and Tech. Cooperation Award 2001, Golden Sickle Award, Govt of Thailand 2007, Mahathir Science Award 2008, Award of Distinction, Univ. of California, Davis 2009. *Achievements include:* noted for his role in developing high-yielding varieties of rice, which led to doubling of world rice production between 1966 and 1990. *Publications:* Cytogenetics of Aneuploids 1974, Plant Breeding Lectures 1984, Host Plant Resistance to Insects 1995; 152 research papers and 40 book chapters. *Leisure interests:* world history, human rights. *Address:* College of Agricultural and Environmental Sciences, University of California, 150 Mrak Hall, One Shields Avenue, Davis, CA 95616-8571 (office); 39399 Blackhawk Place, Davis, CA 95616-7008, USA (office). *Telephone:* (530) 750-2440 (office). *E-mail:* gurdev@khush.org. *Website:* caes .ucdavis.edu (office).

KHUWEITER, Abd al-Aziz al-Abdallah al-, PhD; Saudi Arabian politician; *Minister of State and Cabinet Member;* b. 1927, Onaizah; s. of Abdullah Khuweiter and Moodi al-Khuweiter; m. Fatima al-Khuweiter 1963; one s. three d.; Vice-

Rector King Saud Univ.; Auditor-Gen.; fmr Minister of Health; Minister of Educ. 1987–95, Minister of State and Cabinet Member 1995–; King Abdulaziz Order of Merit (Second Class), Republican Order, Sudan (First Class). *Publications include:* Uthman Ibn Bishr, Fi Turuk al Bahth, Tarikh Shafi Ibn Ali (ed.), Al-Malik al-Zahir Baybars (in Arabic and English), Al-Rawd al Zahir (ed.), Min Hatab al-Layl, Ayy-Bunaay, Qiraah Fi Diwan al-Sha'ir Muh. Uthaymin, Ayy Bonayy (five vols), Itlala Ala Al-Turath, Yowman Wa Malik (two vols), Mal'al-Sallah min Thamar al-Majallah (three vols), Hadeeth al-Rokbatain, Iamhat Min Tareekh al-Ta'leem, Dam'aton Harra, Wasmon Ala Adim al-Zarman (17 vols), Rasd Leseyaha al-Fikr, Nazz al-Yara ', Al-Salamo' Alykum. *Leisure interests:* reading, writing. *Address:* Council of Ministers, Qasar al-Yamamah (office); POB 539, Riyadh 11421, Saudi Arabia (home). *Telephone:* (1) 4882404 (office); (1) 4910033 (home). *Fax:* (1) 4930466 (office); (1) 4882622 (office); (1) 4930466 (home). *E-mail:* aa.khuwater@ hotmail.com (office).

KHVOSTOV, Mikhail Mikhaylovich; Belarusian diplomatist; *Permanent Representative, United Nations, Geneva;* b. 27 June 1949, Vytebsk Region; m. Galina Khvostova; one s. one d.; ed Minsk Inst. of Foreign Languages, Belarusian State Univ.; with Ministry of Foreign Affairs 1982–91; Sr Diplomatic Officer, Perm. Mission of Belarus to UN, New York 1991–92, at Embassy in Washington, DC 1992–93; Head, State Protocol Dept, Legal Dept, Ministry of Foreign Affairs 1993–94, Deputy Minister of Foreign Affairs 1994–97; Amb. to Canada 1997–2000; Asst to Pres. for Foreign Policy Issues Aug.–Nov. 2000; Deputy Prime Minister and Minister of Foreign Affairs 2000–01, Minister of Foreign Affairs 2001–03; Amb. to USA 2003–09 (also accred to Mexico 2004–09); Amb. and Perm. Rep. to UN and other Int. Orgs, Geneva 2009–; Pres. Conf. on Disarmament 2010; mem. Perm. Court of Arbitration, The Hague, Netherlands. *Address:* Permanent Mission of Belarus to the United Nations, 15 avenue de la Paix, 1211 Geneva 20, Switzerland (office). *Telephone:* (22) 7482450 (office). *Fax:* (22) 7482451 (office). *E-mail:* mission .belarus@ties.itu.int (office). *Website:* geneva.mfa.gov.by (office); www.unog.ch (office).

KIAROSTAMI, Abbas, BA; Iranian film director, producer, writer and photographer; b. 22 June 1940, Tehran; m. (divorced); two s.; ed Tehran Coll. of Fine Arts; worked as designer and illustrator (commercials, film credit titles and children's books); involved in establishment of film making Dept at Inst. for Intellectual Devt of Children and Young Adults (Kanoon); ind. film maker from early 1990s; more than 50 int. prizes including special prize of the Pasolini Foundation 1995, UNESCO Fellini Medal 1997, Lifetime Achievemt Award, Yerevan Int. Film Festival 2005. *Films directed:* Nan va kouchek (Bread and Alley, short) (debut production of Kanoon film Dept) 1970, Zangu-e tafrih (Breaktime) 1972, Tajrobeh (The Experience) 1973, Mossafer (The Traveller) 1974, Man ham mitoumam (So Can I, short) 1975, Do rah-e hal baraye yek massaleh (Two Solutions for One Problem, short) 1975, Lebasi bara-ye arusi (A Wedding Suit) 1976, Rang-ha (Colours, short) 1976, Bozorgdasht-e mo'allem (Tribute to the Teachers, documentary) 1977, Az oghat-e faraghat-e khod chegouneh estefadeh konim: Rang-zanie (How to Make Use of Leisure Time: Painting, short) 1977, Gozarech (The Report) 1977, Rah-e hal (Solution, short) 1978, Ghazieh-e shekl-e aval, ghazieh-e shekl-e douuom (First Case, Second Case) 1979, Dandan-dard (Toothache, short) 1979, Beh tartib ya bedoun-e tartib (Orderly or Disorderly, short) 1981, Hamsorayan (The Chorus, short) 1982, Hamshahri (Fellow Citizen) 1983, Avali-ha (First-Graders, documentary) 1984, Khaneh-je doost kojast? (Where Is the Friend's House?, first film of the 'Koker trilogy') 1987, Mashq-e shab (Homework, documentary) 1989, Namay-eh nazdik (Close-Up, documentary) 1990, Zendegi va digar hich (And Life Goes On..., second film of the 'Koker trilogy') (aka Va zendegi edemah darad—Life and Nothing More) (Cannes Film Festival Rossellini Prize) 1991, Zir-e darakhtan-e zeyton (Through the Olive Trees, final film of the 'Koker trilogy') 1994, Tavalod-e noor (Plus Dinner for One, short) 1996, Ta'am-e gilas (The Taste of Cherry) (Cannes Film Festival Palme d'Or) 1997, Bad mara khahad bourd (The Wind Will Carry Us) (Venice Film Festival Grand Jury Prize) 1999, ABC Africa (documentary) 2001, Ta'ziyeh 2002, 10 (also writer) 2002, Five (also writer) 2003, Ten Minutes Older (short) 2003, 10 on Ten (also writer) 2004, Tickets (with others, also writer) 2004, Kargaran mashghoole karand (also writer) 2006, Roads of Kiarostami (also writer) 2006, Kojast jaye residan (also writer) 2007, Certified Copy (also writer) 2010, Like Someone in Love (also writer) 2012. *Film screenplays:* The Key 1987, The Journey 1995, Badkonak-e sefid (The White Balloon) (Cannes Film Festival Caméra d'Or) 1995, Istgah-e matrouk (The Deserted Station) 2002, Talaye sorgh (Crimson Gold) 2003. *Publications:* Walking with the Wind: Poems 2001. *Address:* c/o Zeitgeist Films Ltd, 247 Center Street, Second Floor, New York, NY 10013, USA.

KIBAKI, Mwai, BA, BSc (Econs); Kenyan politician and fmr head of state; b. 15 Nov. 1931, Gatuyaini, Othaya Div., Nyeri Dist, Cen. Prov.; s. of the late Kibaki Githinji and Teresia Wanjiku; m. M. Lucy Muthoni; three s. one d.; ed Mang'u High School, Makerere Univ., London School of Econs, UK; Lecturer in Econs, Makerere Univ. Coll. 1959–60; Nat. Exec. Officer, Kenya African Nat. Union (KANU) 1960–64; elected by Legis. Council as one of Kenya's nine reps in E African Legis. Ass. of E African Common Services Org. 1962; mem. House of Reps for Nairobi Doonholm 1963–78; Parl. Sec. to Treasury 1963–65; Asst Minister of Econ. Planning and Devt 1964–66; Minister for Commerce and Industry 1965–69, of Finance 1969–70, of Finance and Econ. Planning 1970–78, of Finance 1978–82, of Home Affairs 1978–88, of Health 1988–91; Vice-Pres. of Kenya 1978–88; Vice-Pres. KANU 1978–88; Pres. Democratic Party 1991–2002; Leader of the Official Opposition 1998–2002; Pres. of Kenya and C-in-C of the Armed Forces Dec. 2002–13; mem. Party of Nat. Unity—PNU (coalition of several parties); Chief, Order of the Golden Heart; Hon. DrIng (Nairobi), Hon. DLitt (Jomo Kenyatta Univ. of Science and Tech.); Gandhi-King Award for Non-Violence 2003, FDI Personality of the Year Award 2004. *Leisure interests:* reading, golf. *Address:* c/o Party of National Unity, Lenana Road, opp. CVS Plaza, POB 5751, 00100 Nairobi, Kenya.

KIBEDI, Wanume, LLB; Ugandan lawyer and politician; *Chairman, Immigration and Citizenship Board;* b. 3 Aug. 1941, Busesa; s. of Mr and Mrs E. M. Kibedi; m. Elizabeth Kibedi (née Amin) 1970; one d.; ed Busoga Coll. and Univ. of London; articled with Waterhouse and Co., London 1961–66, admitted solicitor 1966; Asst Admin-Gen, Ministry of Justice 1968–69; Pnr, Binaisa and Co. (advocates) 1969–70; Minister of Foreign Affairs 1971–73 (resgnd); fled in exile to UK;

Lecturer, Coll. of Law, Lancaster 1974; f. Kibedi and Co. Solicitors, London 1975; Perm. Rep. to the UN, New York 1986–89; returned to London; Chair. Immigration and Citizenship Bd 2010–. *Leisure interests:* chess, tennis, reading. *Address:* Immigration and Citizenship Board, c/o Ministry of Internal Affairs, Plot 75 Jinja Rd, POB 7191, Kampala, Uganda (office).

KIBEDI VARGA, Aron, PhD; Dutch/Hungarian academic and poet; *Professor of French Literature, Vrije Universiteit;* b. 4 Feb. 1930, Szeged, Hungary; m. 1st T. Spreij 1954; m. 2nd K. Agh 1964; m. 3rd S. Bertho 1991; four s. one d.; ed Univ. of Amsterdam, Leiden Univ., Univ. of Paris (Sorbonne), France; Lecturer in French Literature, Vrije Universiteit, Amsterdam 1954–66, currently Prof.; Prof. of French Literature, Univ. of Amsterdam 1966–95; Visiting Prof., Univ. of Iowa, USA 1971, Yale Univ., USA 1975, Princeton Univ., USA 1980, Rabat Univ., Morocco 1985, Coll. de France 1992, Isparta Univ., Turkey 2006; mem. Cttee Int. Soc. for the History of Rhetoric 1979–83; Pres. Int. Asscn Word and Image Studies 1987–93; mem. Royal Netherlands Acad. of Sciences 1981–; mem. Hungarian Acad. of Sciences 1990–; Officer, Nederlandse Leeuw 1993, Officer, Merit of Hungarian Repub. 2006; Dr hc (Pécs) 1994. *Publications include:* Les Constantes du Poème 1963, Rhétorique et Littérature 1970, Théorie de la Littérature (ed.) 1981, Discours récit, image 1989, Les Poétiques du classicisme (ed.) 1990, Le Classicisme 1998, Szavak, világok 1998, Noé könyvei 1999, Amszterdami krónika 2000, Es felébred aminek neve van 2002, A jelen 2003; poetry (in Hungarian): Kint és Bent 1963, Téged 1975, Szépen 1991, Hántani, fosztani 2000, Oldás 2004, Történések 2008. *Address:* Burgunder Strasse 19, 79104 Freiburg im Breisgau, Germany. *Telephone:* (67) 11371862.

KIBIROV, Timur Yuryevich; Russian poet; b. (Zapoyev), 15 Feb. 1955, Shepetovka, Ukraine; m. Yelena Ivanovna Borisova; one d.; ed Krupskaya Moscow Regional Pedagogical Inst.; Jr Researcher, All-Union Research Inst. of Arts 1981–93; Ed. Tsikady (publr) 1993–; first poems published in Yunost and Continent 1989; Pushkin Prize (Germany) 1993, Prize of Druzhba Narodov (magazine) 1993. *Publications:* collections of poetry: Calendar 1990, Verses about Love 1993; Sentiments 1994; verses in leading literary journals. *Address:* Ostrovityanova str. 34, korp. 1, Apt. 289, Moscow, Russia (home). *Telephone:* (495) 420-6175 (home).

KIBRICK, Anne, EdD, RN; American nurse and academic; *Professor Emerita of Nursing, College of Nursing, University of Massachusetts;* b. 1 June 1919, Palmer, Mass; d. of Martin Karlon and Christine Grigas Karlon; m. Sidney Kibrick 1949; one s. one d.; ed Boston Univ., Columbia Univ., Harvard Univ.; Head Nurse, Worcs. Hahnemann Hosp. 1941–43; Staff Nurse, Children's Hosp. Medical Center, Boston 1943–45; Educ. Dir, Charles V. Chapin Hosp., Providence, RI 1945–47; Asst Educ. Dir, Veterans Admin. Hosp. 1948–49; Asst Prof., Simmons Coll., Boston 1949–55; Dir Grad. Programs in Nursing, Boston Univ. 1958–63, Prof. and Dean 1963–70; Dir Grad. Programs in Nursing, Boston Coll. 1970–74; Chair. School of Nursing, Boston State Coll. 1974–82; Dean Coll. of Nursing, Univ. of Massachusetts, Boston 1982–88, Prof. 1988–93, Prof. Emer. 1993–, now mem. Advisory Council; Consultant Nat. Student Nurses Asscn 1985–88; Consultant, Hadassah Medical Org., Israel, Cumberland Coll. of Health Sciences, NSW, Australia, Menonfia Univ., Shebin El-Kam, Egypt; Fellow, American Acad. of Nursing 1973–; mem. Inst. of Medicine, NAS 1972–, Brookline Town Meeting 1995–2000; Charter mem. Nat. Acads of Practice 1985–; mem. Bd of Dirs Post-Grad. Medical Inst., Mass Medical Soc. 1983–96, Exec. Cttee 1988–96; Dir Landy-Kaplan Nurses Council 1992– (Treas. 1994–98); Hon. DHL (St Joseph's Coll.); Mary Adelaide Nutting Award, Distinguished Service Award and Isabel Stewart Award, Nat. League for Nursing, Service Award, Nat. Hadassah Org. and other awards; Chancellor's Medal, Univ. of Massachusetts, Boston 1992, Hall of Fame, Nursing, Teacher's Coll., Univ. of Columbia 1999, Living Legend, Massachusetts Nurses Asscn, Massachusetts Nurses Asscn Award 2006. *Publications:* Explorations in Nursing Research (with H. Wechsler) 1979; numerous professional articles. *Leisure interests:* reading, travel. *Address:* 130 Seminary Avenue, #312, Auburndale, MA 02466, USA (home). *Telephone:* (617) 969-3225 (home).

KIBSGAARD, Paal, MSc; Norwegian petroleum engineer and business executive; *CEO, Schlumberger Ltd;* ed Norwegian Inst. of Tech., Trondheim; began career working for ExxonMobil 1992, working in Norway and Australia; joined Schlumberger as Reservoir Engineer in Saudi Arabia 1997, held various field positions in technical sales and customer support including Geomarket Man. for the Caspian Geomarket, Atyrau, Kazakhstan, Wireline Marketing Man. in Scandinavia, Stavanger, also held a variety of global man. positions, including Vice-Pres. of Eng, Manufacturing and Sustaining, Wireline Open Hole Business Devt Man., Paris –2003, Pres. of Schlumberger Drilling & Measurements, Schlumberger Oilfield Services – Technologies (OFS) 2003–06, Vice-Pres. of Personnel, Schlumberger Ltd 2006–07, Group Pres. of Reservoir Characterization 2009–10, COO Schlumberger Ltd 2010–11, mem. Bd of Dirs and CEO 2011–. *Address:* Schlumberger Ltd, 5599 San Felipe, Houston TX 77056, USA (office). *Telephone:* (713) 375-3400 (office). *Fax:* (713) 375-3463 (office). *E-mail:* info@slb .com (office). *Website:* www.slb.com (office).

KICILLOF, Axel, PhD; Argentine economist, academic and politician; *Minister of Economy and Public Finance;* b. 25 Sept. 1971, Buenos Aires; m. Soledad Quereilhac; two c.; ed Univ. of Buenos Aires; fmr leader, La Cámpora (political youth org.); Lecturer in Econs, Univ. of Buenos Aires 1996, Adjunct Prof. 2005–, Deputy Dir Centre for Devt Planning Studies (CEPLAD), Inst. of Econ. Research 2006–10; Chief Financial Officer, Aerolíneas Argentinas 2009–11, Deputy Gen. Man. 2011; Asst Researcher, CONICET (Nat. Scientific and Technical Research Council) 2010; Dir (govt rep.) Siderar (steel producer) 2011; Sec. for Econ. Policy and Devt Planning, Ministry of Economy 2011, Deputy Minister of Economy 2012–13, Minister of Economy and Public Finance 2013–. *Address:* Ministry of Economy and Public Finance, Hipólito Yrigoyen 250, C1086AAB Buenos Aires, Argentina (office). *Telephone:* (11) 4349-5000 (office). *E-mail:* ciudadano@mecon .gov.ar (office). *Website:* www.mecon.gov.ar (office).

KIDD, Hon. Sir Douglas Lorimer (Doug), Kt, KNZM, LLB; New Zealand politician and lawyer; b. 12 Sept. 1941, Levin; s. of Lorimer Edward Revington Kidd and Jessie Jean Kidd (née Mottershead); m. Jane Stafford Richardson 1964; one s. two d.; ed Horowhenua Coll., Victoria Univ., Wellington; Partner, Wisheart Macnab & Partners (law firm) 1964–78; fmr part-time mussel farmer, Marlborough Sounds; Nat. Party MP for Marlborough/Kaikoura 1978–99; Minister of State-Owned Enterprises and Assoc. Minister of Finance 1990–91; Minister of Fisheries 1990–96, of Maori Affairs 1991–93, of Energy, of Labour and for Accident Rehabilitation and Compensation Insurance 1993–96; Speaker of House of Reps and Chair. of Parl. Service Comm. 1996–99; fmr Foundation Pres. Marlborough Forest Owners' Assocn; Nat. Party List MP 1999–2002, Opposition Spokesman on Fisheries, Chair. Regulations Review Select Cttee, mem. Privileges and Maori Affairs Select Cttee 1999–2002, Appropriations Review Cttee; mem. Waitangi Tribunal 2004–; Hon. Col of Canterbury, Nelson, Marlborough, West Coast Regt 1997–2003; Commemoration Medal 1990, Chief of Gen. Staff's Commendation for Outstanding Service to NZ Army 1999, NZ Defence Service Medal (Territorial). *Leisure interests:* fishing, walking, reading, travel. *Address:* 6 Elgin Way, Wellington 6035, New Zealand (home). *Website:* www.waitangitribunal.govt.nz (office).

KIDDER, C. Robert, BS, MS; American business executive; b. 1944; m.; c.; ed Univ. of Michigan, Iowa State Univ.; served as officer in US Navy Civil Engineer Corps; worked as gen. man. consultant with McKinsey & Co., Chicago, Ill.; Vice-Pres. Planning and Devt, Dart Industries, Los Angeles, Calif. –1980; Vice-Pres. Finance and Admin, Duracell Europe 1980–81, Vice-Pres. Sales and Marketing, Duracell USA 1981–82, Pres. Duracell USA 1982–84, CEO Duracell Inc. 1984–91, Chair. and CEO Duracell International, Inc. 1991–94; Chair. and CEO Borden, Inc. 1995–2001, Chair. Borden Chemical, Inc. (following merger with Borden Chemical) 2001–03, Founding Pnr, Borden Capital Man. Partners 1996–2003; Prin. and Pnr, Stonehenge Partners, Inc. (pvt. investment firm) 2004–06; Chair. and CEO 3Stone Advisors LLC (pvt. investment firm) 2006–; Chair. Chrysler Group LLC (following Chapter 11 bankruptcy restructuring of Chrysler LLC and global alliance with Fiat SpA) 2009–11; mem. Bd of Dirs Morgan Stanley, Merck, Microvi Biotech Inc.; fmr mem. Bd of Dirs Electronic Data Systems Corpn, General Signal Corpn, McKinsey and Co. Inc.; mem. Bd of Trustees Columbus Children's Hosp.; Pres. Wexner Center Foundation; mem. Bd Ohio Univ.

KIDJO, Angélique, Benin singer and songwriter; b. 14 July 1960, Cotonou; d. of Frank Kidjo and Yvonne Kidjo; m. Jean Hébrail 1987; one d.; ed in Cotonou; began performing in her mother's theatre co. aged six; joined Kidjo Brothers Band, Alafia, Pili Pili and later Parakou; moved to Paris, France 1983; solo artist 1986–; numerous tours and live appearances; collaborations with Carlos Santana, Manu Dibango, Branford Marsalis, Alicia Keys, Peter Gabriel, Joss Stone, Bono, John Legend; UNICEF Int. Goodwill Amb. 2002–; f. Batonga Foundation (non-profit org. which promotes education for girls) 2007; Commdr, Nat. Order of Merit 2008, Officier des Arts et des Lettres 2009; Hon. DMus (Berklee Coll.) 2010; African Musician of the Year 1991, Best African Singer, Kora Awards 1997, MOBO Award for Best World Music Act 2002, Antonio Carlos Jobim Award 2007, NAACP Image Award for Outstanding World Music Album 2008, Grammy Award for Best Contemporary World Music Album 2008, Medal of the Presidency of Italian Repub. 2008, Premio Tenco 2009, UN Champion of The Earth Award 2011, Prix Miroir des Musiques et Folklore du Monde, Quebec 2012, Trophée des Arts, Institut Français 2012, Keep A Child Alive Humanitarian Award 2012, Songlines Music Award 2013. *Recordings include:* albums: Pretty 1980, Ninive, Ewa Kadjo 1985, Parakou 1989, Logozo 1991, Ayé 1994, Fifa 1996, Oremi 1998, Black Ivory Soul 2002, Oyaya! 2004, Djin Djin (Grammy Award for Best Contemporary World Music Album 2008) 2007, Oyo 2010, Spirit Rising 2012, Eve 2014. *Publication:* Spirit Rising: My Life, My Music (autobiography) 2014. *Address:* c/o Redlight Management, 44 Wall Street, 22nd Floor, New York, NY 10005, USA (office). *E-mail:* kevin@redlightmanagement.com (office). *Website:* www.kidjo.com.

KIDMAN, Dame Fiona Judith, DNZM, OBE; New Zealand writer; b. 26 March 1940, Hawera; d. of Hugh Eric Eakin and Flora Cameron Eakin (née Small); m. Ian Kidman 1960; one s. one d.; ed small rural schools in the north of New Zealand; Founding Sec./Organizer, New Zealand Book Council 1972–75, Pres. 1992–95, Pres. of Honour 1997–; Sec. New Zealand Centre, PEN 1972–76, Pres. 1981–83; f. Writers in Schools, Words on Wheels (touring writing co.), Writers Visiting Prisons, Randell Cottage Writers Trust (Trustee); Deputy Chair. French Cultural Trust; Pres. of Honour, NZ Book Council, NZ Poetry Soc.; mem. Cttee, Lauris Edmond Memorial Prize for Poetry; Trustee, Randell Cottage Writers Trust; Patron NZ Poetry Soc., Waipu Old Pupils Alumni; more than 60 radio and 20 TV credits; Chevalier des Arts et des Lettres 2009, Légion d'honneur 2009, Dame Companion, NZ Order of Merit; numerous literary prizes, including New Zealand Book Awards (fiction category), Queen Elizabeth II Arts Council Award for Achievement, Victoria Univ. Writers' Fellow, A. W. Reed Award for Lifetime Achievement 2001, Meridian Energy Katherine Mansfield Fellow 2006, Creative New Zealand Michael King Fellowship 2008, Prime Minister's Award for Literature (Fiction) 2010. *Publications include:* A Breed of Women 1979, Mandarin Summer 1981, Mrs. Dixon and Friend (short stories) 1982, Paddy's Puzzle 1983, The Book of Secrets 1986, Unsuitable Friends (short stories) 1988, True Stars 1990, Wakeful Nights (poems selected and new) 1991, The Foreign Woman (short stories) 1994, Palm Prints (autobiographical essays) 1995, Ricochet Baby 1996, The House Within 1997, The Best of Fiona Kidman's Short Stories 1998, New Zealand Love Stories; An Oxford Anthology (ed.) 1999, A Needle in the Heart (short stories) 2002, Songs from the Violet Café (novel) 2003, Captive Wife 2004, The Best New Zealand Fiction Vols 1, 2 and 3 (ed.) 2004, 2005, 2006, At the End of Darwin Road: A Memoir 2008, Beside the Dark Pool: A Memoir 2009, Where Your Left Hand Rests (poems) 2010, The Trouble with Fire (short stories) 2011, The Infinite Air (novel) 2013. *Leisure interests:* theatre, film, family pursuits. *Address:* c/o Harriet Allan, Random House NZ Ltd, Private Bag 102950, North Shore Mail Centre, Auckland, New Zealand (office). *Telephone:* (9) 444-7197 (office). *E-mail:* admin@randomhouse.co.nz (office); fiona@fionakidman.co.nz (office). *Website:* www.fionakidman.co.nz.

KIDMAN, Nicole, AC; Australian actress; b. 20 June 1967, Hawaii, USA; d. of Dr Antony Kidman and Janelle Glenny; m. 1st Tom Cruise 1990 (divorced 2001); one adopted s. one adopted d.; m. 2nd Keith Urban 2006; one d.; ed St Martin's Youth Theatre, Melbourne, Australian Theatre for Young People, Sydney and Philip Street Theatre; acting debut in Australian film aged 14; Australian Film Inst. Best Actress Award for role in TV mini-series Bangkok Hilton; voted Best Actress of Year in Australia for role in Flirting, Dead Calm 1989, Days of Thunder 1990, Far and Away My Voice Broke, Flirting, Dead Calm 1989, Days of Thunder 1990, Far and Away

1992, Billy Bathgate 1992, Malice 1993, My Life 1993, Batman Forever 1995, To Die For 1995, Portrait of a Lady 1996, The Peacemaker 1997, Eyes Wide Shut 1998, Practical Magic 1999, Moulin Rouge (Golden Globe for Best Actress in a Musical) 2001, The Others 2001, Birthday Girl 2001, The Hours (Golden Globe for Best Dramatic Actress 2003, BAFTA Award for Best Actress in a Leading Role 2003, Acad. Award for Best Actress 2003) 2002, Cold Mountain 2003, The Human Stain 2003, Dogville 2003, The Stepford Wives 2004, Birth 2004, The Interpreter 2005, Bewitched 2005, Fur: An Imaginary Portrait of Diane Arbus 2006, Happy Feet (voice) 2006, I Have Never Forgotten You (voice) 2007, The Invasion 2007, Margot at the Wedding 2007, The Golden Compass 2007, Australia 2008, Nine 2009, Rabbit Hole 2010. *Play:* The Blue Room 1998–99. *Address:* PMK Public Relations, 1775 Broadway, Suite 701, New York, NY 10019, USA (office).

KIDWA, Nasser al-; Palestinian diplomatist and UN official; *Deputy Joint Special Representative of the UN and the League of Arab States for Syria;* b. 1953; ed Cairo Univ.; mem. Fatah 1969–, mem. PLO Cen. Council 1981–86, 1999–; mem. Palestine Nat. Council 1975–; Amb. and Perm. Observer to UN, New York 1991–2005; Chair. Yasser Arafat Foundation, Cairo 2008–; Minister of Foreign Affairs, Palestinian Authority 2005; Deputy Joint Special Rep. of the UN and the League of Arab States for Syria 2012–. *Address:* Office of the Secretary-General, Department of Political Affairs, United Nations, New York, NY 10017, USA (office). *Telephone:* (212) 963-1234 (office). *Fax:* (212) 963-4879 (office). *Website:* www.un.org/Depts/dpa (office).

KIDWAI, Akhlaq R., BA, MS, PhD; Indian politician, academic and scientist; *Chairman, Zaheer Science Foundation;* b. 1 July 1920, Baragaon, Barabanki Dist, UP; s. of the late Shri Ashfaq-ur-Rahman Kidwai and Smt. Nasimunnisa; m. Jadmila Kidwai (deceased); two s. four d.; ed Jamia Millia Islamia, New Delhi, Univ. of Illinois and Cornell Univ., USA; research and devt chemist, Cipla Labs, Bombay 1941–45; Prof. and Head of Dept of Chem., Dean Faculty of Science, Aligarh Muslim Univ. 1951–67, Dir, Dept of Research Plant Products, Chancellor 1983–92; Chair. Union Public Service Comm. 1967–79; Gov. of Bihar 1979–85, 1993–98, of W Bengal 1998–99, of Haryana 2004–09, also of Rajasthan 2007; Chair. Dr Ambedkar Centre for Biomedical Research, Univ. of Delhi 1998–2003; Nat. Chair. Inst. of Marketing and Devt 2000–; Chair. Bombay Mercantile Cooperative Bank 1999–2003; mem. Rajya Sabha (Upper House of Parl.) 2000–04; mem. numerous cttees including Nat. Cttee on Science and Tech. 1968–75, Perspective Science and Tech. Plan Cttee, Dept of Science and Tech. and the Planning Comm., Council and Governing Body of Indian Council of Agricultural Research 1970–73, Bd of Council of Scientific and Industrial Research; mem. and Patron Delhi Public School Soc. 1968–; Pres. Vocational Educ. Soc. for Women 1985–; Chair. Zaheer Science Foundation 2012–; mem. AAAS; Hon. Fellow, Inst. of Engineers, India; Dr hc (Vidhya Vajaspati, Inst. of Tibetan Studies, Sarnath) 1997, Padma Vibhushan Award 2011. *Publications:* more than 40 research papers in organic chem. and biochemistry. *Leisure interests:* gardening, sports. *Address:* Zaheer Science Foundation, 4 Udyan Marg, New Delhi 110 001 (office); 196 Zakir Bagh, Okhla Road, New Delhi 110 025, India (home). *Telephone:* (11) 26936938 (office). *Fax:* (11) 23745697 (office). *E-mail:* zsfindia@yahoo.com (office). *Website:* www.zsfindia.com (office).

KIDWAI, Naina Lal, BA, MBA, CA; Indian chartered accountant and banker; *Country Head and Group General Manager, HSBC (India);* b. 1957; m. Rashid Kidwai; two c.; ed Univ. of Delhi, Harvard Business School, USA; began career at ANZ Grindlay's Bank 1982–94; Vice-Chair. and Head of Investment Banking, JM Morgan Stanley 1994–2002; Exec. Vice-Chair. and Man. Dir HSBC Securities and Capital Markets (India) Pvt. Ltd 2002–, Deputy CEO HSBC (India) 2004–06, CEO 2006–2009, Country Head and Group Gen. Man. 2009–; Chair. Capital Market Cttee, Fed. of Indian Chambers of Commerce and Industry; Chair. Govt of India Science and Tech. Bd, Governing Body of Nat. Council of Applied Econ. Research, Econ. Policy and Reforms Council for the State of Rajasthan, Governing Body of Lady Shri Ram Coll. for Women, Delhi Univ., Governing Council of India Habitat Centre; Dir Int. Bd of Digital Pnrs Foundation, USA, SEWA (non-profit org. for self-employment of underprivileged women); mem. Bd of Dirs Nestlé India Ltd 2006–, Nestlé South Asia 2006–, Nat. Science and Tech. Entrepreneurship Devt, Nat. Integration Council, Indo-German Consultative Group, Chamber of Industry and Commerce, Nat. Council of Confed. of Indian Industries, Nat. Exec. Cttee, Fed. of Indian Chambers of Commerce and Industry, Grassroots Trading Network for Women; mem. Indian Advisory Council of City of London; mem. Advisory Bd IIM Ahmedabad, IIT Mumbai; mem. Global Bd of Dean's Advisers, Harvard Business School; mem. India Advisory Bd John Hopkins School of Advanced Int. Studies USA; adviser, Nat. Entrepreneurship Network; ranked third by Fortune magazine in first ever listing of The World's Top Women in Business in Asia 2000, ranked by Fortune magazine amongst 50 Most Powerful Women in Business outside the US 2001, (50th) 2002, (47th) 2003, (41st) 2006, (38th) 2007, (41st) 2011, (40th) 2012, honoured by Time Magazine as one of their 15 Global Influentials 2002, ranked 34th by The Wall Street Journal in list of World's Top 50 Businesswomen 2004, and 12th in its Global Listing of Women to Watch 2006, recipient of several Awards for Business in India, Padma Shri 2007. *Achievements include:* first Indian woman grad. of Harvard Business School 1982. *Leisure interests:* listening to Indian and Western classical music, wildlife tours. *Address:* HSBC Securities and Capital Markets (India) Pvt. Ltd, New Delhi, India (office). *Telephone:* (22) 22681247 (office). *Fax:* (22) 22631984 (office). *Website:* www.hsbc.co.in (office).

KIEBER, Walter, DJur; Liechtenstein lawyer and politician; b. 20 Feb. 1931, Feldkirch, Austria; s. of Alfons Kieber and Elisabeth Kieber; m. Selma Ritter 1959; one s. one d.; ed Grammar School in Bregenz, Austria, Univ. of Innsbruck; lawyer in Vaduz 1955–59, 1981–; entered civil service as Head of Govt Legal Office 1959; Chief of Presidential Office 1965; Sec.-Gen. of Govt 1969, Deputy Head of Govt 1970–74, Head of Govt 1974–78, Deputy Head of Govt 1978–80; Pres. Liechtenstein Bar Assen 1993–; mem. Fortschrittliche Bürgerpartei (Progressive Citizens' Party); Grand Cross, Liechtenstein Order of Merit, Grosses Goldenes Ehrenzeichen am Bande für Verdienste um die Republik Österreich (Austria). *Address:* c/o Fortschrittliche Bürgerpartei (Progressive Citizens' Party), Aeulestr. 56, Postfach 1213, 9490 Vaduz; Landstrasse 22, 9494 Schaan, Liechtenstein (home).

KIEBER-BECK, Rita; Liechtenstein politician; b. 27 Dec. 1958, Nenzing, Austria; m. Manfred Kieber; ed Oberstufenrealgymnasium, Feldkirch, Univ. of Fribourg, Switzerland, Univ. of Innsbruck, Austria, Chulalongkorn Univ. of

Bangkok and Chiang Mai, Thailand; Instructor in German, Business, Political Science and Econs, Commercial Business School, Buchs, Switzerland 1979–81; full-time instructor, Realschule (Upper School) Balzers 1982–90; with Liechtenstein Inst., Bendern 1990–94, Man. Dir 1991–94; Man. Dir Adiuvaris Treuunternehmen reg. (Fiducary), Triesen 1993, 2001; Consulting mem. Parl. Group of Progressive Citizens' Party (Fortschritte Bürgerpartei, FBP) 1997–2000, mem. Presidency 1997–, Chair. Educ. Working Group 1997–, mem. Man. Presidency and Financial Adviser 2000–01; Deputy Prime Minister with responsibility for Educ., Justice, Transport and Telecommunications 2001–05; Minister of Foreign Affairs, Cultural Affairs and Family and Equal Opportunity 2005–09; CEO and Man. Trustee, Rita Kieber-Beck Trust 2010–; Hon. Consul of Austria in Liechtenstein 2013–; Pres. Liechtenstein Upper School Teachers' Asscn 1988–90; mem. Educational Comm., Upper Schools, Liechtenstein 1984–88, Adult Educ. Comm. 1992–98; Großes Goldenes Ehrenzeichen am Bande für Verdienste um die Republik Österreich 2004. *Address:* Rita Kieber-Beck Trust, Franz-Josef-Oehri-Strasse 6, 9493 Mauren, Liechtenstein (office). *E-mail:* office@kieber-beck.li (office). *Website:* www.kieber-beck.li/en (office).

KIEFER, Anselm; German artist; b. 8 March 1945, Donaueschingen; m.; three c.; ed Univ. of Freiburg and Freiburg Acad., Karlsruhe Acad.; first one-man exhbn, Galerie am Kaiserplatz, Karlsruhe 1969; first one-man exhbn in USA, Marian Goodman Gallery, New York; retrospective exhbns Städtische Kunsthalle, Düsseldorf, Musée d'Art Moderne, Paris and Israel Museum, Jerusalem 1984, Stedelijk Museum, Amsterdam 1986, US tour 1987–89; first group exhbn, Deutscher Künstlerbund, Kunstverein, Hanover 1969; has also exhibited Kunstverein, Frankfurt 1976, Kassel Documenta 1977, 1982, 1987, Biennale de Paris 1977, Venice Biennale 1980, White Cube, London 2005, 2006, Royal Acad., London 2007; other group exhbns include Expressions: New Art from Germany, touring exhbn USA 1983–84, touring exhbn Moscow and Leningrad 1983, 1984 Museum of Modern Art survey of int. art, Fifth Biennale of Sydney, Australia 1984; works in many pvt collections including Saatchi Collection, London and in many public galleries including Art Inst. of Chicago, Museum of Modern Art, Phila Museum of Art, Hirshhorn Museum, Washington, DC, LA Museum of Contemporary Art and San Francisco Museum of Modern Art, Praemium Imperiale 1999; Wolf Foundation Prize 1990. *Publication:* A Book by Anselm Kiefer 1988. *Address:* c/o Gagosian Gallery, 555 West 24th Street, New York, NY 10011, USA.

KIELHOLZ, Walter B., BA; Swiss banking executive; *Independent Non-Executive Chairman, Suisse Reinsurance (Swiss Re);* b. 25 Feb. 1951, Zurich; m. Daphne Kielholz-Pestalozzi; ed Univ. of St Gallen; began career with Gen. Reinsurance Corpn, Zurich 1976 with assignments in USA, UK and Italy, Head of European Marketing –1986; opened art gallery and picture framing business with his wife 1983; Head of Client Relations, Multinational Services Dept, Credit Suisse 1986–89, mem. Bd Dirs 1999–, Chair. Audit Cttee 1999–2002, Chair. Credit Suisse Group 2003–09, also Chair. Chairman's and Governance Cttee; joined Swiss Re, Zurich 1989, apptd mem. Exec. Bd 1993, CEO 1997–2002, mem. Bd of Dirs 1998–, Chair. Audit Cttee 1999–2002, Exec. Vice-Chair. Swiss Re 2003–07, Vice-Chair. 2007–09, Chair. (ind. non-exec.) 2009–; Chair. Supervisory Bd Avenir Suisse (think tank); mem. Int. Business Leader Advisory Council (advisory group to the Mayor of Shanghai) 1998–2005, 2009–, Int. Asscn for the Study of Insurance Econs, Int. Monetary Conf. (Pres. 2006–07), Bd Inst. of Int. Finance, European Financial Roundtable 2004–, Center for Strategic and Int. Studies 2005–, Int. Advisory Panel of the Monetary Authority of Singapore 2009–; mem. Bd Dirs Geneva Asscn 1999–, economiesuisse 2003–; Chair. Zürcher Kunstgesellschaft; mem. Soc. of Zurich Friends of the Arts, Lucerne Festival Foundation Board; inducted by mems of Int. Insurance Soc. into Insurance Hall of Fame 2005. *Leisure interests:* sailing, skiing, tennis, golf, reading, opera, concerts, art. *Address:* Swiss Reinsurance Co., Mythenquai 50/60, 8022 Zürich, Switzerland (office). *Telephone:* (43) 285-21-21 (office). *Fax:* (43) 285-29-99 (office). *E-mail:* info@swissre.com (office). *Website:* www.swissre.com (office).

KIELY, Leo, BEcons, MBA; American brewing industry executive; *CEO, MillerCoors;* b. 16 Jan. 1947; ed Harvard Univ., Wharton School of Business, Univ. of Pa; Brand Asst and Asst Brand Man., Procter & Gamble, Cincinnati 1971–73; various posts at Wilson Sporting Goods Co. including Vice-Pres. of Marketing and Sr Business Man., Chicago 1973–79; Pres. Ventura Coastal Corpn (div. of Seven-Up) 1979–82; Vice-Pres. Brand Man., Frito-Lay Inc. 1982–83, Vice-Pres. Marketing 1983–84, Marketing and Sales 1984–89, Sr Vice-Pres. Field Operations 1989–91, served as Vice-Pres. and Gen. Man., Cen. Div., Div. Pres. 1991–93; joined Coors Brewing Co. 1993, mem. Bd of Dirs 1998–, Pres. and CEO Molson Coors Brewing Co. (after merger of Coors and Molson cos) 2005–07, CEO MillerCoors (after merger of SABMiller and Molson Coors US operations) 2007–; mem. Bd of Dirs Nat. Asscn of Mfrs, SEI Center for Advanced Studies, Wharton School of Finance, Denver Center for the Performing Arts; mem. Foundation Bd Metropolitan State Coll.; Chair. Mile High United Way, Denver; Nat. Trustee Boys and Girls Clubs of America. *Address:* Molson Coors Brewing Company, 1225 17th Street, Denver, CO 80202, USA (office). *Telephone:* (303) 279-6565 (office). *Fax:* (303) 277-5415 (office). *E-mail:* consumers@coors.com (office). *Website:* www.molsoncoors.com (office).

KIEP, Walther Leisler; German politician, business executive, consultant and author; b. 5 Jan. 1926, Hamburg; s. of Louis Leisler Kiep and Eugenie vom Rath; m. Charlotte ter Meer 1950; three s. (one deceased) two d.; ed Hamburg, Istanbul, Frankfurt; with Ford Motor Co., then Insurance Co. of North America 1948–55, joined Gradmann and Holler 1954, Man. Pnr 1968–98; mem. Advisory Council of Deutsche Bank 1972–2001; mem. CDU 1961–, mem. Bundestag 1965–76, 1980–82; fmr Chair. Parl. Cttee on Foreign Aid, Treas., mem. Exec. Cttee 1971–92; Lower Saxony Minister for Econs and Finance 1976–80, concurrently Special Envoy for Turkish aid; Deputy to Leader of Opposition 1988–92; Chair. Atlantik-Brücke Berlin 1984–2000, Hon. Chair. 2004–; mem. Int. European Advisory Bd Fuji-Wolfensohn, New York 1989–98; Chair. Zeneca GmbH, Plankstadt 1993–98; Chair. Int. Advisory Bd, Marsh & McLennan New York 1993–2000; Chair. Supervisory Bd IABG, Ottobrunn 1994–2000; Pres. European Business School, Oestrich-Winkel 1994–2000; mem. Int. Advisory Bd, Columbia Univ., New York 1997–, Int. Advisory Bd, Fuji Bank Ltd, Tokyo 1999–2002; Bundesverdienstkreuz mit Stern und Schulterband, Grosses Verdienstkreuz des Niedersächsischen Verdienstordens; Hon. CBE; Dr hc. *Publications:* Goodbye Amerika – Was Dann?

1972, A New Challenge for Western Europe 1974, Was bleibt ist grosse Zuversicht 1999, Brücken meines Lebens 2006, Bridge Builder 2012. *Leisure interest:* history. *Address:* Westerbachstrasse 23C, 61476 Kronberg im Taunus, Germany (office). *Telephone:* (6173) 7027674 (office). *Fax:* (6173) 7027685 (office). *E-mail:* kiep_consultant@t-online.de (office).

KIERES, Leon; Polish politician and professor of law; *President, Institute of National Remembrance;* b. 26 May 1948, Kolonia Zielona; s. of Józef Kieres and Helena Kieres; m. Anna Kieres; one s. one d.; ed Wrocław Univ.; Jr Librarian, Wrocław Univ. 1970, Research Asst 1971–73, Sr Asst 1973–75, Lecturer in Law 1975–85, Asst Prof. 1985–91, Extraordinary Prof. 1991–96, Ordinary Prof., Faculty of Law and Admin. 1996–; councillor, Wrocław Town Council 1990–98; Pres. Self-governmental Council of Wrocław Voivodship 1990–98; mem. Local Govt Council at the Chancellory of the Pres. 1994; Vice-Pres. Congress of Local and Regional Authorities of Council of Europe 1995, mem. Parl. Ass. 1998–2000, involved in Council of Europe mission in Bosnia and Herzegovina 1998; Senator (Wrocław Voivodship), Vice-Pres. Senate Local Govt and Public Admin. Cttee, mem. Foreign Affairs and European Integration Cttee; Pres. int. group of local govt observers in Croatia 1997; councillor, Dolnoslaskie Voivodship Council, Pres. Culture, Science and Educ. Cttee 1998–2002; Pres. Inst. of Nat. Remembrance 2000–05, The Club of Rome 2000; Vice-Pres. Polish-German Co-operation Foundation 1993; mem. Polish Teachers' Asscn 1970–80, NSZZ Solidarnosc 1980–2000, Cttee on Legal Sciences, Polish Acad. of Sciences 2003–, Warsaw Scientific Asscn 2003, Regional Studies Asscn 2003; Bronze Cross of Merit 1978; Kt's Cross, Order of Polonia Restituta 1996; St Silvester Order of the Pope 1998; Walerian Panka Award 1997, St George Medal 2002, 'Lumen Gentium' Medal, Lublin Archdiocese 2004, Lawyer of the Year Award, Gazeta Pranna 2004. *Publications include:* Zalecenia RWPG w sprawie koordynacji narodowych planów gospodarczych i ich realizacja w PRL (Recomendations of Council for Mutual Economic Aid on Coordination of National Economic Schemes and Their Realization in Poland) 1978, Zagraniczne przedsiebiorstwo socjalistyczne w Polsce (Foreign Socialist Enterprises in Poland) 1986, Struktura Centralnego aparatu gospodarczego i jego funkcje (Structure of Central Economic Machinery and its Functions, ed.) 1989, Tworzenie i funkcjonowanie spółek: zagadnienia cywilnoprawne i administracyjne (Establishment and Functioning of Companies: Civil and Administrative Law Issues, ed.) 1989, Region samorzadowy (Local-governmental Region) 1991, Podejmowanie dzialalnosci gospodarczej przez inwestorów zagranicznych (Foreign Investors' Establishment) 1993, Prawo administracyjne (Administrative Law, co-author), Administracyjne prawo gospodarcze (Administrative Economic Law, co-author) 2003; over 40 scientific publs and numerous articles in nat. and foreign magazines on public admin. law, econ. law and law of local govt. *Leisure interests:* supporting football teams, watching good films. *Address:* ul. Obornicka 34 m. 15, 51-113 Wrocław, Poland (home).

KIIR MAYARDIT, Salva; South Sudanese politician, fmr military leader and head of state; *President of South Sudan;* b. 1951; joined Anyanya separatist movt during First Sudanese Civil War, early 1960s, later becoming an officer, joined regular army after peace settlement 1972; with Army of Sudan 1972–83, attaining rank of Capt.; Founding mem. Sudan People's Liberation Movt (SPLM) 1983, later Deputy Party Leader, Chief of Staff Sudan People's Liberation Army (mil. wing of SPLM) 1999, Chair. SPLM (after death of John Garang) 2005, Commdr-in-Chief SPLA 2005–; Vice-Pres. of Southern Sudan 2005, Pres. 2005–11, also First Vice-Pres. of Sudan 2005–11; sworn in as first Pres. of South Sudan following independence July 2011. *Address:* Office of the President, Juba, South Sudan (office). *E-mail:* webmaster@splmtoday.com (office). *Website:* www.splmtoday.com (office).

KIKABIDZE, Vakhtang Konstantinovich; Georgian actor and singer; b. 19 July 1938, Tbilisi; s. of Konstantin Kikabidze and Manana Bagrationi; m. Irene Kebadze 1964; one s.; soloist and leader of Georgian pop group Orera 1966–; film debut in 1967 with Meeting in the Hills; solo career since 1988; USSR State Prize 1978, People's Artist of Georgian SSR 1980, Order of Honour, special award (Georgia) 1994, Order of Konstantine (Russia) 1997, Order of St Nicholaus 1998, Golden Gramophone Prize 1998, Leonid Utesov Prize for Achievement in field of Music 2000. *Films include:* Meeting in the Hills 1967, Don't Grieve 1968, I'm a Detective 1969, The Stone of the First Water 1970, Pen-name Lukach, The Melodies of Verikysky Block 1973, Lost Expedition 1973, Completely Gone 1972, Mimino 1978, TASS is Authorized to Inform, Hi! Friend (TV film) 1981, To Your Health Dear (dir, scriptwriter, actor) 1983, Man and all the Others (scriptwriter, producer, actor) 1985, Fortuna (actor) 2000. *Music:* albums: My Years, My Wealth 1994, Larisa Ivanovna Please! 1995, Letter to Friend 1996, Tango of Love 1999, Greatest Hits 2000. *Leisure interest:* fishing. *Address:* S. Chikovani Street 20, Apt. 38, 380015 Tbilisi, Georgia. *Telephone:* (32) 98-90-14 (home). *Website:* www.buba.diaspora.ru.

KIKOIN, Konstantin Abramovich, PhD, DrSci; Israeli (b. Russian) theoretical physicist, academic, poet and essayist; *Professor, School of Physics and Astronomy, Tel-Aviv University;* b. 9 Aug. 1945, Kalinin (now Tver), Russian SFSR, USSR; s. of Abraham Kikoin and Ekaterina Sosenkova; m. Larisa Markina 1969; one s. one d.; ed Ural State Univ. (Sverdlovsk/Ekaterinburg), Physical-Tech. Inst. Moscow; Jr Scientific Researcher, Inst. of Optical-Physical Measurements, Moscow 1971–74; Sr Scientific Researcher I.V. Kurchatov Inst. of Atomic Energy, Moscow 1974–85, Leading Scientific Researcher and Vice-Head of Solid State Theory Dept 1985–96; Research Fellow, Dept of Physics, Ben Gurion Univ. of the Negev, Israel 1997–2006; Prof., School of Physics and Astronomy, Tel-Aviv Univ. 2006–; Deputy Chair. Exec. Bd Moscow Physical Soc. 1989–96, Assoc. Ed. Journal of Moscow Physical Soc. 1990–96, Journal of Experimental and Theoretical Physics 1991–; Rep. of American Inst. of Physics in Moscow 1992–94; mem. Expert Council of Supreme Attestation Cttee 1994–96; mem. Israeli Federation of Writers' Unions 2008–; Kapitza Fellowship, Royal Soc. (UK) 1995. *Publications:* three monographs, seven reviews and more than 150 papers in scientific journals, two books of collected verses. *Leisure interest:* translating poetry from Russian into English. *Address:* School of Physics and Astronomy, Tel-Aviv University, Tel-Aviv 69978, Israel (office). *E-mail:* konstk@post.tau.ac.il (office). *Website:* www.tau.ac.il (office).

KIKWETE, Lt-Col Jakaya Mrisho; Tanzanian politician and head of state; *President;* b. 7 Oct. 1950, Msonga, Bagamoyo Dist; m. Salma Kikwete; ed Tengeru School, Kibaha Secondary School, Babati Secondary School, Univ. of Dar es

Salaam; after graduation joined Tanzania African Nat. Union (now Chama Cha Mapinduzi (CCM) party); seconded to Tanzania People's Defence Forces as Chief Political Instructor at Monduli Cen. Mil. Acad.; commissioned as Lt and retd Col 1992; Deputy Minister, Ministries of Finance, of Water and Livestock Devt, of Energy and Minerals 1987–90, Minister 1990–94; Chair. Council of Ministers of the E African Community; Minister of Foreign Affairs and Int. Co-operation 1995–2005; Pres. of Tanzania 2005–; Chair. African Union Ass. 2008–09; Patron Tanzania Nat. Basketball Asscn. *Address:* Office of the President, State House, PO Box 9120, Dar es Salaam, Tanzania (office). *Telephone:* (22) 2116679 (office). *Fax:* (22) 2113425 (office). *Website:* www.tanzania.go.tz/poffice (office).

KILGUS, Martin A., MA, PhD; German journalist; *Editor, SWR Public Radio, Television & Internet;* b. 15 March 1963, Stuttgart; s. of Alfred Kilgus and Charlotte-Pauline Hofmann; ed Wirtemberg-Gymnasium, Stuttgart, Univ. of Stuttgart and The American Univ., Washington, DC, USA; trainee, NBC Radio; joined Dept for Ethnic Broadcasting, SDR Radio & TV, Stuttgart 1989; worked as ed. for migrants' audio broadcasts 1991; now Ed. with SWR (fmrly SDR) Radio, TV & Internet; Chair. Int. Educ. Information Exchange, Stuttgart 1996–2004; Vice-Chair. German Asscn for UN BW; mem. Bd Stiftung Geissstrasse Stuttgart, Konrad-Adenauer-Foundation; special field of research and activity include Digital Audio Broadcasting (DAB) and multi-lingual broadcasts, European integration and int. migration; Caritas Prize for Journalism. *Leisure interests:* arts, literature, cooking, snowboarding. *Address:* SWR Public Radio, TV & Internet, Neckarstrasse 230, 70190 Stuttgart, Germany (office). *Telephone:* (711) 9292648 (office). *Fax:* (711) 929182648 (office). *E-mail:* martin.kilgus@swr.de (office). *Website:* www.swr.de/international (office).

KILLEEN, Tony, TD; Irish politician; b. 9 June 1952, Co. Clare; m. Lily O'Keeffe; five s.; ed St Flannans Coll., Ennis, Co. Clare, Mary Immaculate Coll., Limerick; fmr teacher; mem. Clare Co. Council 1985–97 (Vice-Chair. 1987–89, Chair. 1989–91); mem. Dáil Éireann (Parl.) for Clare constituency 1992–2011, Chair. Jt Oireachtas Cttee on Educ. and Science 2002–04; Minister of State at Dept of Enterprise, Trade and Employment, Minister for Labour Affairs 2004–07, Minister of State at Dept of Communications, Energy and Natural Resources and Dept of Environment, Heritage and Local Govt 2007–08, Minister of State at Dept of Agric., Fisheries and Food 2008–10, Minister of Defence 2010–11; mem. Fianna Fáil. *Address:* c/o Department of Defence, Parkgate, Infirmary Rd, Dublin 7, Ireland (office). *Website:* www.tonykilleen.ie.

KILLIP, Christopher David; British photographer; *Professor of Visual Studies, Harvard University;* b. 11 July 1946, Isle of Man; s. of Allen Killip and Mary Quirk; one s.; ed Douglas High School for Boys; photography in Isle of Man 1969–71; Prof. of Visual Studies, Harvard Univ. 1991–; ACGB Photography Awards 1973–74, Northern Arts Photography Fellow 1975–76, ACGB Bursary Award 1977, Henri Cartier-Bresson Award, Paris 1989. *Publications:* Isle of Man 1980, In Flagrante 1988, Fifty-five 2001, Pirelli Work 2006, Here Comes Everybody 2009, Seacoal 2011, Arbeit (Work) 2012. *Address:* Harvard University, 24 Quincy Street, Cambridge, MA 02138, USA. *Website:* www.chriskillip.com.

KILLY, Jean-Claude; French business executive, sports administrator and fmr Olympic skier; b. 30 Aug. 1943, St-Cloud, Seine-et-Oise; s. of Robert Killy and Madeleine de Ridder; m. Danièlle Gaubert 1973 (died 1987); one d., two step-c.; ed Ecole de Val-d'Isère, Lycées in Chambéry, Grenoble, Saint-Jean-de-Maurienne, Bourg-Saint-Maurice; French champion 1964, 1965, 1966; won three gold medals at Winter Olympics, Grenoble, France 1968; retd from competitive skiing 1968 but returned in 1972 to become professional world champion in 1973; customs officer 1965–68; Publicity Agent, Gen. Motors 1968; Marketing Consultant (concerning skiing information) United Air Lines 1969; settled in Geneva 1969 and moved into the sports clothing business with co. Veleeda-Killy; Tech. Adviser Dynamic 1981; mem. Exec. Bd Alpine Cttee of Int. Skiing Fed. 1977–94; Pres. World Sport Marketing (now Amaury Sport Org.) 1992–2000, Société du Tour de France 1992–2001; fmr Chair. Coca-Cola France, mem. Admin Bd Coca-Cola 1993, Coca-Cola Enterprises 1997; mem. Int. Olympic Cttee 1995–2013, Co-Pres. Winter Olympics, Albertville 1992, Vice-Chair. Coordination Comm. for 2002 Winter Olympic Games in Salt Lake City 1996–2002, Chair. Co-ordination Comm. for 2006 Winter Olympic Games in Turin 2000–06, Coordination Comm. for 2014 Winter Olympic Games in Sochi 2007–14; mem. Bd of Dirs Rolex SA; mem. Organizing Cttee for 2009 Alpine FIS Ski World Championships 2002–07 (resgnd); Commdr, Légion d'honneur; IOC Olympic Order; Export Oscar 1982. *Film:* Snow Job 1972. *Publications:* Skiez avec Killy 1969, Le Ski 1978. *Leisure interests:* flying, reading, cycling, walking, swimming, snowboarding. *Address:* Killy, 21 rue du pré Faucon, 74940 Annecy le Vieux, France; CIO, Château de Vidy, 1007 Lausanne; 13 chemin Bellefontaine, 1223 Cologny -GE, Switzerland. *Website:* www.killy.com.

KILMAN, Sato; Ni-Vanuatu politician; *President, People's Progressive Party;* b. 30 Dec. 1957; joined British Police Force in Vanuatu as Corporal 1977, apptd Commdr of Vanuatu Mobile Force (VMP) 1984, Asst Commr 1986, Commr of Police 1992–93; pursued business interests, SK Logging Co. 1993; Minister for the Comprehensive Reform Program 1999–2001, for Agric. 2002; MP for Lakatoro, Malekula Island 2004–07, 2008–; Deputy Prime Minister and Minister of Foreign Affairs 2004–07; Leader of the Opposition 2009–10; Deputy Prime Minister and Minister of Trade and Industry 2009–10, Prime Minister 2010–13 (resgnd), Minister for Public Service 2010–13; currently Pres. People's Progressive Party. *Address:* People's Progressive Party, Port Vila, Vanuatu (office).

KILMER, Val Edward; American actor; b. 31 Dec. 1959, Los Angeles; m. Joanne Whalley (q.v.) 1988 (divorced 1996); one d.; ed Hollywood's Professional School, Juilliard; began career in theatre then film debut in 1984; f. Blessed Films (production co.). *Films include:* Top Secret 1984, Real Genius 1985, Top Gun 1986, Willow 1988, Kill Me Again 1989, The Doors 1991, Thunderheart 1991, True Romance 1993, The Real McCoy 1993, Tombstone 1993, Wings of Courage 1995, Batman Forever 1995, Heat 1995, The Saint 1996, The Island of Dr. Moreau 1996, The Ghost and the Darkness 1996, Dead Girl 1996, Joe the King 1999, At First Sight 1999, Planet Red 1999, Pollock 2000, Salton Sea 2002, Run for the Money 2002, Masked and Anonymous 2003, Wonderland 2003, Spartan 2004, Blind Horizon 2004, Mindhunters 2004, Alexander 2004, Kiss, Kiss, Bang, Bang 2005, Moscow Zero 2006, 10th & Wolf 2006, Played 2006, Summer Love 2006, Deja Vu 2006, The Ten Commandments: The Musical 2006, Felon 2008, Streets of Blood 2009, Hardwired 2009, Bad Lieutenant: Port of Call New Orleans 2009, The Traveler 2010, MacGruber 2010. *Stage appearances include:* Electra and Orestes, Henry IV Part One 1981, As You Like It 1982, Slab Boys (Broadway debut) 1983, Hamlet 1988, 'Tis Pity She's A Whore 1992, The Postman Always Rings Twice (Playhouse Theatre, London) 2005. *Address:* c/o William Morris Agency, 1 William Morris Place, Beverly Hills, CA 90212, USA. *Telephone:* (310) 859-4000. *Fax:* (310) 859-4462. *Website:* www.wma.com; www.valkilmer.org (office).

KILPATRICK, Helen, CB; British accountant and civil servant; *Governor of the Cayman Islands;* one s. one d.; Grad. Trainee (Finance), Greater London Council 1982–85, Group Auditor 1985–86; Group Accountant (Housing), London Borough of Tower Hamlets 1986–87, Chief Accountant (Technical) 1987–88; Asst Borough Treasurer, London Borough of Greenwich 1988–89, Controller of Financial Services 1989–95; Deputy Chief Exec. and Dir of Resources, W Sussex County Council 1985–2000, also Treas., Sussex Police Authority; Dir Gen. for Finance and Corp. Services, Home Office 2005–13, also acting Home Office Perm. Sec. and Accounting Officer 2012–13; Gov. of Cayman Islands 2013–. *Address:* Office of the Governor, Government Administration Building, 133 Elgin Avenue, George Town, Grand Cayman KY1-9000, Cayman Islands (office). *Telephone:* 244-2401 (office). *Fax:* 945-4131 (office). *E-mail:* staffoff@candw.ky (office). *Website:* www .ukincayman.fco.gov.uk (office).

KILPIÄ, Maj.-Gen. Juha; Finnish army officer and UN official; *Head of Mission and Chief of Staff, United Nations Truce Supervision Organization (UNTSO);* b. 1953; m.; one d.; ed Finnish War Coll., NATO School, Germany, NATO Defense Coll., Italy; commissioned in Army Command Finland 1977; served in several other posts in UN peacekeeping missions including Chief of Operations UN Interim Force in Lebanon (UNIFIL) 1991, UN Disengagement Observer Force (UNDOF) 1993; Battalion Commdr NATO Operations Joint Endeavour (IFOR)/Operation Joint Forge (SFOR) 1996–97; Commdr Multinational Task Force in EU operation 2004–05; Mil. Rep. to EU and NATO, Brussels 2007–09; Chief of Staff, Army Command 2009–11; Head of Mission and Chief of Staff UN Truce Supervision Org. (UNTSO) 2011–. *Address:* United Nations Truce Supervision Organization, Department of Peace-keeping Operations, Room S-3727-B, United Nations, New York, NY 10017, USA (office). *Telephone:* (212) 963-8077 (office). *Fax:* (212) 963-9222 (office). *Website:* www.un.org/en/peacekeeping/missions/untso (office).

KIM, Anatoly Andreyevich; Russian writer; b. 15 June 1939, S Kazakhstan; ed Literary Inst., Moscow; freelance writer 1973–; Prof. of Russian Language and Literature, Inst. of Journalism, Moscow; lecturer in S Korea 1991–95. *Publications include:* more than 20 books including novels: Gatherers of Herbs 1976, Litis 1980, Squirrel 1984, Forest-Father 1989, Onlyrya 1995, Mushroom Picking with Bach's Music 1997, The Wall 1998, Twins 2000; numerous short stories; film scripts: My Sister Lucy, Revenge, To Go Out of the Forest. *Address:* Akademika Pavlova str. 36, apt. 112, 121552 Moscow, Russia (home). *Telephone:* (495) 140-15-31 (home).

KIM, Choong-soo, BA, PhD; South Korean economist, government official, diplomatist and central banker; *Governor, Bank of Korea;* b. 6 June 1947; ed Seoul Nat. Univ., Univ. of Pennsylvania, USA; Research Asst, Korea Devt Inst. 1973–76, Dir, Office of Research Planning & Coordination 1988–91, Dir, Econ. Information and Educ. Center 1991–93, Pres. 2002–05; Research Assoc., Wharton Econometric Forecasting Associates Inc., USA 1976–79; Sr Research Assoc., Center for Human Resource Research, Ohio State Univ. 1979–88; Sec. to Pres. for Econ. Affairs, Office of Pres. of Repub. of Korea 1993–95, Sr Sec. to Pres. for Econ. Affairs Feb.–June 2008; Minister and Head of OECD Office, Embassy in Paris 1995–97; Asst Minister and Special Adviser to Deputy Prime Minister, Ministry of Finance and Economy Mar.–Aug. 1997; Pres., Korea Inst. of Public Finance 1997–98; Dean, Graduate School of Pan-Pacific Int. Studies, Kyung Hee Univ. 1998; Pres., Hallym Univ. 2007–08; Amb. and Perm. Rep. to OECD, Paris 2008; Gov. Bank of Korea (central bank) 2010–; Chair. BIS Asian Consultative Council 2012–. *Address:* Office of the Governor, Bank of Korea, 110, 3-ga, Namdaemun-no, Jung-gu, Seoul 100-794, South Korea (office). *Telephone:* (2) 759-4114 (office). *Fax:* (2) 759-4060 (office). *E-mail:* bokdplp@bok.or.kr (office). *Website:* www.bok.or.kr (office).

KIM, Dong-jin, BS, PhD; South Korean automotive industry executive; *President and CEO, Hyundai Star Commercial Vehicle Systems, Inc.;* b. 4 Dec. 1950; m.; two c.; ed Seoul Nat. Univ., Finlay Eng Coll., USA; research engineer, Korea Inst. of Science and Tech. 1972; sr research engineer, Agency for Defence Devt 1973–78; Man. Hyundai Heavy Industries Co. Ltd 1978–79, Sr Exec. Vice-Pres. Hyundai Precision & Industry Co. Ltd 1979–98, Pres. and CEO Hyundai Space & Aircraft Co. Ltd 1998–99, apptd Pres. Hyundai Motor Co. 2000, later Vice-Chair. and Co-CEO, Dir, Pres. and CEO Hyundai Star Commercial Vehicle Systems, Inc.; Pres. and CEO e-HD.com Inc. 2000–; CEO Cas; Chair. Korea Geospatial Information and Tech. Asscn 1999–; Order of Nat. Security Merit (Samil-Jang) 1985; Prize of Devotion Merit, Seoul Nat. Univ. School of Eng 1998. *Address:* Hyundai Motor Company, 231 Yangjae-dong, Seocho-gu, Seoul 137-938, Republic of Korea (office). *Telephone:* (2) 3464-1114 (office). *Fax:* (2) 3463-3484 (office). *Website:* worldwide .hyundai.com (office).

KIM, Gen. Dong-shin, BA, MS; South Korean politician and army officer (retd); b. 13 March 1941, Kwangju City; ed Seoul Nat. Univ., Korean Mil. Acad. and Hannam Univ.; Regimental Commdr, Army of Repub. of Korea 1983; apptd Chief, Foreign Policy Div., Ministry of Nat. Defence 1984; Deputy Dir of Strategic Planning, Jt Chief of Staff 1989–90; Commanding Gen. 51st Infantry Div. 1990–92; Dir of Force Planning 1992–93; Commanding Gen. Capital Corps, 3rd Army 1993–94; Chief Dir of Operations, Jt Chiefs of Staff 1995–96; Deputy C-in-C, Repub. of Korea–US Combined Forces Command 1996–98; Army Chief of Staff 1998–99; Adviser, Nat. Security Cttee 2000; Minister of Nat. Defence 2001–02; Visiting Scholar, RAND Center for Asia Pacific Policy 2002–03; Silver Star Medal 1972, Order of Nat. Security Merit (Samil Medal 1983, Gukson Medal 1993, Tangil Medal 1997), Order of Mil. Merit 1991, US Army Meritorious Service Medal 1999, Legion of Merit 2001. *Address:* c/o Ministry of National Defence 1, 3-ga, Yonsan-don, Yongsan-gu, Seoul, Republic of Korea (office).

KIM, Gye-kwan; North Korean politician and diplomatist; *First Vice-Minister, Ministry of Foreign Affairs;* b. 1943; participated in Pyongyang-Washington negotiations and Geneva talks as working-level rep. of N Korea; travelled widely in Europe before 1993; served as Amb.-at-Large and maintained ties with socialist

1122   **www.worldwhoswho.com**

parties in Western Europe; designated Deputy Negotiator in first nuclear talks with USA, later Chief Negotiator; head of del. to four-party talks between N Korea and S Korea, China and USA to address Korean peninsula issues; Vice-Minister, Ministry of Foreign Affairs –2010, First Vice-Minister 2010–. *Address:* Ministry of Foreign Affairs, Pyongyang, Democratic People's Republic of Korea (office).

KIM, Hak-su, BA, MA, PhD; South Korean international civil servant, economist and academic; *Distinguished Visiting Professor, Graduate School of International Studies, Yonsei University;* b. 27 Feb. 1938, Wonju, Kangwon; ed Yonsei Univ., Univ. of Edinburgh, UK, Univ. of S Carolina, USA; economist, Cen. Bank 1960; Sec. to Minister of Commerce and Industry 1969; London Rep., Bank of Korea 1971–73; Exec. Dir Daewoo Corpn 1977, later Pres.; Chief Planning Officer, Chief Tech. Advisor UN Dept for Tech. Co-operation and Devt 1980s; Sr Research Fellow, Korea Inst. for Int. Econ. Policy 1989–93; Pres. Hanil Banking Inst. 1993–95; Sec.-Gen. of the Colombo Plan, Sri Lanka 1995–99; Korean Amb. for Int. Econ. Affairs 1999; UN Under-Sec.-Gen. and Exec. Sec. UN ESCAP 2000–07 (appointment renewed 2005); Distinguished Visiting Prof., Grad. School of Int. Studies, Yonsei Univ., Seoul 2007–. *Leisure interests:* classical music, trekking, walking. *Address:* Graduate School of International Studies, Yonsei University, 134 Sinchon-dong Seodamun-gu, Seoul 120-749 (office); 319-1601 Hanyong Apt, Bundang, Kyunggi, Republic of Korea (home). *Telephone:* (2) 2123-6297 (office); (2) 656-7556 (home). *E-mail:* magkim16@hotmail.com (office). *Website:* gsis.yonsei.ac .kr (office).

KIM, Hwang-sik, LLB; South Korean lawyer and politician; b. 9 Aug. 1948, Jangseong; ed Seoul Nat. Univ., Philipps-Universität Marburg, Germany; Judge, Seoul Dist Civil Court, Seoul Dist Criminal Court, Seoul High Court 1974–89, Sr Judge, Jeonju Dist Court 1989–96, Sr Judiciary Research Officer, Supreme Court 1997–2000, Chief Judge, Gwangju Dist Court 2004–05, Justice, Supreme Court 2005–08; Vice Minister, Nat. Court Admin 2005; Chair. Bd of Audit and Inspection 2008–10; Sec.-Gen. Asian Org. of Supreme Audit Insts 2009–10; Prime Minister 2010–13. *Address:* c/o Office of the Prime Minister, 55, Sejong-no, Jongno-gu, Seoul 110-760, Republic of Korea.

KIM, Vice-Marshal Il-chol; North Korean politician (retd); b. 1928, Pyongyang; ed Mangyongdae Revolutionary School, Navy Acad., USSR; apptd Commdr East Sea Fleet 1970; mem. Party Cen. Cttee 1980–; Deputy in Supreme People's Ass. 1982; apptd Commdr of Navy 1982; rank of Lt-Gen. 1982, Col-Gen. 1985, Gen. 1992, Vice-Marshal 1997; First Minister of the People's Armed Forces 1997–98, Minister 1998–2010; Vice-Chair. Nat. Defence Comm. 1998–2010; Kim Il Sung medal 1982, Nat. Flag Order, Nat. Hero title 1995. *Address:* c/o Office of the Minister, Ministry of the People's Armed Forces, Pyongyang, Democratic People's Republic of Korea (office).

KIM, Gen. (retd) Jang-soo; South Korean army officer and government official; b. 1948, Gwangju; m. Park Hyo-sook; one s. one d.; ed Korea Mil. Acad., Yonsei Univ.; served in several key posts in Army including Deputy Commdr Korea-US Combined Forces Command and Chief Operations and Strategy Dir Jt Chiefs of Staff; Army Chief of Staff 2005–06; Minister of Nat. Defence 2006–08; mem. Nat. Ass. (Saenuri Party) 2008–12; Chief, Nat. Security Office 2013–. *Address:* Office of the President, Chong Wa Dae (The Blue House), 1, Sejong-no, Jongno-gu, Seoul, Republic of Korea (office).

KIM, Ji-woon; South Korean filmmaker and screenwriter; b. 6 July 1964, Seoul. *Films:* Choyonghan kajok (The Quiet Family, writer, dir) 1998, Banchikwang (The Foul King, writer, dir) 2000, Coming Out (writer, dir) 2001, Saam gaang (Three, segment 'Memories', dir, writer) 2002, Janghwa, Hongryeon (A Tale of Two Sisters, writer, dir) 2003, Dalkomhan insaeng (A Bittersweet Life, writer, dir) 2005, The Good, the Bad, the Weird 2008, I Saw the Devil 2010,.

KIM, Jim Yong, AB, MD, PhD; American (b. South Korean) physician, university administrator and international organization official; *President, World Bank Group;* b. 1959, Seoul, South Korea; m. Younsook Lim; two c.; ed Brown Univ., Harvard Univ.; Founding Trustee, Partners in Health (Harvard-affiliated nonprofit org.) 1987, currently mem. Bd of Dirs; apptd by WHO to help lead int. response to drug-resistant tuberculosis by establishing pilot MDR TB treatment programmes and organizing effective delivery systems for antibiotics 1999; Lecturer in Social Medicine, Dept of Social Medicine, Harvard Medical School 1993–95, Instructor in Social Medicine 1995–2000, Asst Prof. of Medical Anthropology 2000–03, Asst Prof. of Medicine, Dept of Medicine 2002–03, Assoc. Prof. of Social Medicine and Assoc. Prof. of Medicine 2003–05, Assoc. Clinical Prof. of Medicine and Assoc. Clinical Prof. of Social Medicine 2005–06, François-Xavier Bagnoud Prof. of Health and Human Rights, Harvard School of Public Health 2005–09, Prof. of Medicine and Prof. of Social Medicine, Harvard Medical School 2006–09; Co-Chief Div. of Social Medicine and Health Inequalities, Brigham and Women's Hosp., Boston 2002–03; Sr Advisor to Dir-Gen. WHO 2003–06, Dir Dept of HIV/AIDS 2004–06; Pres. Dartmouth Coll. 2009–12; Pres. World Bank Group, Washington, DC 2012–; mem. American Anthropological Asscn 1984–, Soc. for Medical Anthropology 1986–, Soc. for Latin American Anthropology 1996–, Int. Union Against Tuberculosis and Lung Disease 1997–, Critical Anthropology of Health Working Group 1999–, Inst. of Medicine of NAS 2004–, American Acad. of Arts and Sciences 2010–; John D. and Catherine T. MacArthur Foundation Genius Fellowship 2003, Treatment Action Group "Research in Action" Award 2007, William Rogers Award for Service to Soc., Brown Univ. Alumni Asscn 2008, Distinguished Leadership Award, Korean American Coalition 2008, ranked by Forbes magazine amongst The World's Most Powerful People (45th) 2012, (50th) 2013. *Publication:* Dying for Growth: Global Inequality and the Health of the Poor (co-ed.). *Address:* World Bank Group, 1818 H Street NW, Washington, DC 20433, USA (office). *Telephone:* (202) 473-1000 (office). *Fax:* (202) 477-6391 (office). *Website:* www.worldbank.org (office).

KIM, Jin-pyo, MA; South Korean politician; b. 4 May 1947, Suwon, Gyeonggi Prov.; ed Gyeongbok High School, Seoul Nat. Univ., Univ. of Wisconsin, USA; Dir Consumption Tax Bureau, Ministry of Finance 1983, Dir Tax Policy Section 1988, Dir-Gen. Tax Systems Bureau 1993, Dir-Gen. Foreign Trade Affairs Bureau 1995, Asst Minister, Taxations, Ministry of Finance and Economy 1999, Vice Minister of Finance and Economy 2001; Sr Presidential Sec. for Policy and Planning Jan.–June 2002; Minister of Govt Policy Co-ordination 2002–03; Deputy Prime Minister and Minister of Finance 2003–04; mem. Nat. Ass. 2004–; Deputy Prime Minister

and Minister of Educ. and Human Resources Devt –2006; Hon. Dr Public Admin (Univ. of the Cumberlands, Williamsburg, USA). *Publication:* Looking on the Bright Side: Korean Economy 2004. *Address:* c/o Ministry of Education and Human Resources Development, 77, 1-ga, Sejong-no, Jongno-gu, Seoul 110-760, Republic of Korea (office). *E-mail:* jp311@assembly.go.kr (office).

KIM, Vice-Marshal Jong Gak; North Korean army officer and politician; b. 1941, Jungsan County, South Phyongan Prov.; ed Kim Il-sung Mil. Univ.; joined Korean People's Army (KPA) Aug. 1959, attained rank of Col-Gen. 1992, Gen. 2002, Vice-Marshal 2012, First Deputy Dir KPA Gen. Political Bureau 2007–; mem. Korean Workers' Party (KWP), alt. mem. KWP Cen. Cttee 1991, alt. mem. Politburo and mem. Cen. Mil. Comm. 2010–; Vice-Minister of People's Armed Forces 1992, Minister April–Nov. 2012; mem. Supreme People's Ass. (Parl.) 1998–; mem. Nat. Defence Comm. 2009–13. *Address:* c/o Ministry of People's Armed Forces, Pyongyang, Democratic People's Republic of Korea (office).

KIM, Brig.-Gen. (retd) Jong-pil; South Korean politician; b. 7 Jan. 1926, Puyo; m. Park Young Ok (niece of the late Pres. Park Chung Hee); one s. one d.; ed High School, Gyeongju, Seoul Nat. Univ. and Korean Military Acad.; served in Korean war; Dir Korean Cen. Intelligence Agency 1961–63; mem. Nat. Assembly 1963–68, 1971–80; Chair. Democratic Republican Party 1963–68; Sr Adviser to Pres. 1970; Vice-Pres. Democratic Republican Party 1971, Pres. 1979–80 (banned from political activity 1980); Pres. New Democratic Republican Party 1987; Jt Pres. Democratic Liberal Party (DLP) 1990–93, Chair. 1993; Hon. Chair. United Liberal Democrats, Pres. 2000–04 (retd); Prime Minister 1971–75, 1998–2000; mem. Spanish Nat. Acad., Korean Acad.; Hon. LLD (Long Island Univ., NY) 1964, (Chungang Univ., Seoul) 1966, (Fairleigh Dickinson Univ.) 1968; Hon. DHumLitt (Westminster Coll., Fulton, Mo.) 1966; Hon. PhD (Hongik Univ.) 1974; numerous awards from Korean and foreign govts. *Leisure interests:* painting, music. *Address:* 340-38, Shindang 4-dong, Jung-gu, Seoul, Republic of Korea (home). *Telephone:* (2) 783-7061-2 (home). *Fax:* (2) 782-9185 (home).

KIM, Jong-sik, BEng, MEng; South Korean business executive; *President and Chief Operating Officer, LG Display Company Ltd;* ed Yeungnam Univ., Kyungpook Nat. Univ.; fmr Head of Display Production and Head of Quality Control and Procurement, LG Electronics Co. Ltd, Head of Module Centre LG.Philips LCD 2006–07, Exec. Vice-Pres. LG Display Co. Ltd 2006–07, Chief Production Officer 2007–10, COO 2010–, Pres. 2011–; Pres. and CEO Hana Information and System Co. Ltd at Hana Bank; Ind. Dir STX Corpn. *Address:* LG Display Company Ltd, 65-228 Hangang-ro 3-ga, Seoul 140-716, Republic of Korea (office). *Telephone:* (2) 3777-1010 (office). *E-mail:* info@lgdisplay.com (office). *Website:* www.lgdisplay.com (office).

KIM, Marshall Jong-un; North Korean politician and army officer; *Supreme Leader;* b. 8 Jan. 1984, Pyongyang; s. of the late Kim Jong-il and Koh Young-hee; m. Ri Sol-ju; one d.; ed Int. School of Berne, Switzerland (disputed), Kim Il-sung Univ.; rank of Daejang (four-star Gen.) in Korean People's Army (KPA) 2010, rank of Marshall 2012, Supreme Commdr of KPA Dec. 2011–; Vice-Chair. Cen. Mil. Comm. of Korean Workers' Party (KWP) Sept. 2010–, First Sec. KWP 2012–; declared Supreme Leader, Democratic People's Repub. of Korea (following death of his father) Dec. 2011–, Chair. Nat. Defence Comm. 2012–; ranked by Forbes magazine amongst The World's Most Powerful People (44th) 2012, (46th) 2013. *Leisure interests:* skiing, basketball. *Address:* Central Military Commission of the Korean Workers' Party, Pyongyang, Democratic People's Republic of Korea (office).

KIM, Joong-kyum, BS; South Korean business executive; ed Korea Univ.; fmr Pres. Hyundai Engineering & Construction; Pres. and CEO Korea Electric Power Corpn (KEPCO) 2011–12; Chair. Korea Atomic Industrial Forum, Organizing Cttee World Energy Congress, Daegu 2013. *Address:* c/o Korea Electric Power Corporation, 411 Yeongdong-daero, Gangnam-gu, Seoul 135-791, Republic of Korea. *E-mail:* info@kepco.co.kr.

KIM, Jung-ju, MA; South Korean business executive; *Founder and CEO, Nexon Corporation;* b. 1968; m.; two c.; ed Korea Advanced Inst. of Science and Tech.; Founder and CEO Nexon Corpn (online gaming co.) 1994–, also CEO NXC Corpn; Dir GS HomeShopping. *Address:* Nexon Corporation, Minerva Bldg 2/F, 694-25 Yeoksam-dong, Gangnam-gu, Seoul 135-080, Republic of Korea (office). *Telephone:* (2) 2019-8600 (office). *Website:* company.nexon.com (office).

KIM, Jung-tae, BSc; South Korean banker; ed Seoul Nat. Univ.; began career with Daehan Merchant Bank 1969; with Daeshin Securities 1975; Exec. Dir Dongwon Securities 1982, Dir of Venture Capital 1991, Vice-Pres. –1997, CEO 1997–98; Vice-Chair., Pres. and CEO Housing and Commercial Bank 1998–2001, Pres. and CEO Kookmin Bank (est. after merger of Housing and Commercial Bank with Kookmin) 2001–04. *Address:* c/o Kookmin Bank, 9-1 Namdaemunro 2-ga, Jung-gu, Seoul, Republic of Korea (office).

KIM, Jung-won; South Korean business executive; *Chairman, Hanhyo Development Company Ltd;* b. 3 March 1948; ed Kyungnam Sr High School, Guilford Coll., New York; joined Hanil Synthetic Fiber Ind. Co. Ltd 1972, Exec. Man. Dir 1974, Vice-Pres. 1975, Pres. 1979–; Pres. Hanhyo Co. Ltd 1977, Chair. 1984–; Pres. Hanhyo Devt Co. Ltd 1978, Chair. 1984–; Pres. Kyungnam Woollen Textile Co. Ltd 1979; First Chair. Hanhyo Acad. 1982; Pres. Korean Amateur Volleyball Asscn 1983, Vice-Pres. Asian Volleyball Asscn 1983; awarded Saemaul Decoration 1974; First Hon. Consul Kingdom of the Netherlands 1985. *Address:* Kukje-ICC Corpn, C.P.O. Box 747, Seoul, Republic of Korea.

KIM, Gen. (retd) Kwan-jin; South Korean politician and fmr army officer; *Minister of National Defence;* b. 27 Aug. 1949, Jeonju; m.; three d.; ed German Army Office Acad., Korea Mil. Acad., Seoul; commissioned as Infantry Second Lt 1972, becoming Bn Commdr and Div. G-3, 15th Infantry Div. 1983–88, Commdr, 26th Mechanics Brigade, Capital Mechanics Div. 1990–92, Chief of Mil. Strategy, J-5 Directorate, Jt Chiefs of Staff 1992–93, Asst to Pres. for Nat. Defence, Office of the Presidential Secr. 1994–96, Sec. Gen. Staff, Army HQ 1996–98, Chief of Strategic Planning, Army HQ 1998–99, Commdg Gen., 35th Infantry Div. 1999–2000, Deputy Chief of Staff, Planning and Man., Army HQ 2000–02, Commdg Gen., 2nd Corps 2002–04, Chief Dir of Operations, Jt Chiefs of Staff 2004–05, Commdg Gen., 3rd Repub. of Korea Army 2005–06, Chair. of Jt Chiefs of Staff 2006–08; Minister of Nat. Defence 2010–. *Address:* Ministry of National

Defence, 1, 3-ga, Yeongsan-dong, Yeongsan-gu, Seoul 140-701, Republic of Korea (office). *Telephone:* (2) 795-0071 (office). *Fax:* (2) 703-3109 (office). *E-mail:* cyber@ mnd.go.kr (office). *Website:* www.mnd.go.kr (office).

KIM, Gen. Kyok-sik; North Korean army officer and government official; *Chief of General Staff, People's Army;* b. 1943; ed Kim Il-sung Mil. Acad., Mangyongdae-guyok; Mil. Attaché, Embassy in Damascus in 1970s; Deputy, Supreme People's Ass. (Parl.) 1990–; Commdr II Army Corps 1994–2007, Chief of Korean People's Army Gen. Staff 2007–09, Commdr IV Army Corps 2009–11; Alt. mem. Cen. Cttee Korean Workers' Party 1990–91, 2010–, Full mem. 1991–2010; mem. Kim Il-sung Funeral Cttee 1994, O Jin-u Funeral Cttee 1995; Vice-Minister of People's Armed Forces 2011–12, Minister 2012–13; Chief of Gen. Staff 2013–; attained rank of Col-Gen. 1992, Gen. 1997. *Address:* Office of the Chief of General Staff, People's Army, Pyongyang, Democratic Republic of Korea (office).

KIM, Mahn-je, DEcon; South Korean politician and economist; b. 3 Dec. 1934, Sonsan; ed Univs of Denver and Missouri, USA; Assoc. Prof., Sogang Univ., Seoul 1965–70, Prof. 1982–; mem. Legis. Ass. 1980–; Minister of Finance 1983–86; Deputy Prime Minister and Minister of Econ. Planning 1986–88; Pres. Korean Devt Inst. 1971–82, Korean Int. Econ. Inst. (KIEI) 1981, KorAm Bank 1983–84; apptd. CEO Pohang Iron & Steel Co. 1994, Chair. 1996–98, sentenced by Seoul District Court to 30 million won in fines on embezzlement charges 1999; Sr Policy Researcher, Policy Research Inst. of Democratic Justice Party 1982; mem. Monetary Bd 1975, Econ. Planning Bd Advisory Cttee 1982; mem. Bd of Dirs Korea Forum for Progress, East-West Center Foundation. *Address:* c/o East-West Center, 1601 East-West Road, Honolulu, HI 96848, USA.

KIM, Man-bok; South Korean fmr government official; b. 1946, Busan; ed Seoul Nat. Univ., Konkuk Univ.; joined Agency for Nat. Security Planning (now Nat. Intelligence Service) 1974; Councillor, Embassy in Washington, DC 1993–96; fmr Chief, Information Man. Bureau, Nat. Security Council; Chief Office of Planning and Coordination –April 2006, Deputy Dir overseeing overseas operations April–Nov. 2006, Nat. Intelligence Security Chief Nov. 2006–08, resgnd after being accused of leaking classified inter-Korean documents to media. *Address:* c/o National Intelligence Service, Central Government Complex, 77-6 Sejongno, Jongno-gu, Seoul, Republic of Korea (office).

KIM, Oi-hyun, PhD; South Korean business executive; *Vice-Chairman and Co-CEO, Hyundai Heavy Industries Company Ltd;* b. 1 May 1954; ed Seoul Nat. Univ., Univ. of Ulsan; Sr Exec. Vice-Pres. and COO Shipbuilding Div., Hyundai Heavy Industries Co. Ltd –2011, Vice-Pres. and Co-CEO 2011–, Vice-Chair. and Dir 2011–. *Address:* Hyundai Heavy Industries Co. Ltd, 1, Jeonha-dong, Dong-gu, Gyeonsang nam-do, Ulsan 682-792, Republic of Korea (office). *Telephone:* (52) 202-2114 (office). *Fax:* (52) 202-3470 (office). *E-mail:* ir@hhi.co.kr (office); webzine@hhi .co.kr (office). *Website:* www.hhi.co.kr (office).

KIM, Rak-hui; North Korean politician; *Vice-Premier;* b. 18 March 1946; ed Kim Chaek Univ. of Tech.; Gen. Man. Ponghwa Agricultural Cooperative 1953, Chair. 1962; elected Deputy to 3rd Supreme People's Ass. (SPA) 1962, 4th SPA 1967, 5th SPA 1972, 6th SPA 1977, 11th SPA 2003, 12th SPA 2009; elected mem. Korean Workers' Party (KWP) Cen. Cttee 1970–, Alt. mem. 1980, currently Alt. mem. KWP Cen. Cttee Political Bureau; Chair. Kaesong Municipal People's Cttee 1984, South Pyongan Rural Man. Cttee 1990 (Advisory Chair. 1997); mem. Kim Il-sung Funeral Cttee 1994, O Jin U Funeral Cttee 1995; Chief Sec., South Hwanghae KWP Prov. Cttee 2005; Vice-Premier 2010–. *Address:* Office of the Premier, Pyongyang, Democratic People's Republic of Korea (office).

KIM, Seung-youn; South Korean business executive; *Chairman and CEO, Hanwha Chemical Corporation;* m.; three c.; Owner, Hanwha Eagles Professional Baseball Club 1981–; Chair. The Kyunghyang Shinmun (daily newspaper) 1986–97, Bank of Athens, Greece 1993–97, Hanwha Bank Hungary Ltd 1995–2001, Korea Life Insurance Co. Ltd 2002–05; Chair. and CEO Hanwha Chemical Corpn 2008–; mem. Bd of Dirs Overseas Contracts, Pacific Construction Co. Ltd 1977–78 (Pres. 1978–80), Korea Int. Trade Asscn 1977–78; Chair. Korea Certification Asscn for Quality and Environmental Man. 1993–97, Korea-US Exchange Council 1997–, Devt Cttee, Univ. for Peace 2000, 2004–06; Chair. Ad Hoc Cttee on Corp. Restructuring, Fed. of Korean Industries 1999–2000, Cttee on Int. Co-operation 2000–04; Vice-Chair., Admin. HQ, Korea Explosives Group 1980–81, Korea Man. Asscn 1981–, Fed. of Korean Industries 1985–, Korea Employers' Fed. 1990–, Korea-Japan Co-operation Foundation for Industry and Tech. 1996–; Pres. Korea Amateur Boxing Fed. 1980–81, 1982–96, Asian Amateur Boxing Asscn 1982–97, Gen. Asscn of the Asian Sports Feds 1983–98; Vice-Pres. Korean Olympic Cttee 1981–97 (Adviser 2006–), Korea Sports Council 1992–98; Chair. Bd of Trustees, SungKongHoe (Anglican Communion and Church) Univ. 1996–2000; Dir, Korean Union of Youth 1981–, Korean Asscn of UN 1986– (Chair. 2006–07, 2008–), Korea Bang Jung Hwan Foundation 2000–03; mem. Advisory Cttee, Korea-Japan Co-operation Council 1997–2003, World Bd of Govs, United Service Orgs Inc. 1998–; Amb. for Int. Economy and Trade and Special Envoy of the Pres. of Repub. of Korea 2002–03; Amb. for Int. Exchange and Co-operation 2003–04; Chair. Foundation for Better Boxing, Int. Boxing Asscn 2009–; Hon. Consul Gen. of Greece in Korea 1984–93, 2007–; Hon. Pres. Gen. Asscn of the Asian Sports Feds 1991–; Hon. Chair. Korea-Israel Chamber of Commerce 1994–, Korea-Greece Friendship Asscn 2009–; Grand Business Founder Award, Korean Acad. of Business Historians 2009. *Address:* Hanwha Chemical Corpn, Hanwha Building, 1 Changgyo-dong, Chung-ku, Seoul 100-797, Republic of Korea (office). *Telephone:* (2) 729-2700 (office); (2) 729-1114 (office). *Fax:* (2) 729-1762 (office). *E-mail:* hanwhacorp@hanwha.co.kr (office); webhcc@hanwha.co.kr (office). *Website:* english.hanwhacorp.co.kr (office); www.hanwha.co.kr (office).

KIM, Soo-bong, BS, MS, PhD; South Korean particle physicist and academic; *Associate Professor of Physics, Seoul National University;* ed Seoul National Univ., Univ. of Pennsylvania; Research Asst Fellow, Dept of Physics, Univ. of Pennsylvania 1985–89, Postdoctoral Fellow 1989–90; Postdoctoral Fellow, Dept of Physics, Univ. of Michigan 1990–92, Research Investigator 1992–96; Research Asst Prof., Dept of Physics, Boston Univ. 1996–98; Asst Prof., Dept of Physics, Seoul National Univ. 1998–2002, Assoc. Prof. 2002–; COE Visiting Prof., High Energy Accelerator Research Org. (KEK) 1997–98; Visiting Scientist, Fermi National Accelerator Lab. 2002–03; Fellow, Korean Physical Soc. 1998–; mem. Int. Advisory Cttee, Int. Conference on Physics in Collision 1999–, IEEE NSS/MIC CIP

2000–; LG Fellowship 2001; Rossi Prize (as member of Kamiokande-II), High Energy Astrophysics Division, American Astronomical Soc. 1989. *Publications:* numerous articles in scientific journals. *Address:* Gwanak Campus, Bldg 27, Room 203A, Department of Physics, Seoul National University, Shilim-dong, Kwanak-ku, Seoul 151-742, Republic of Korea (office). *Telephone:* (2) 880-5755 (office). *Fax:* (2) 884-3002 (office). *E-mail:* sbkim@phya.snu.ac.kr (office). *Website:* physics.snu .ac.kr/~sbkim (office).

KIM, Ssang-su, BA, BS; South Korean business executive; *President, ACE Technologies Corporation;* b. 2 Jan. 1945, Gimcheon, N Gyeongsang Prov.; m. Shin Kyung-sook; two d. one s.; ed Seongui High School, Coll. of Eng. and Science, Hanyang Univ.; joined LG Electronics (fmrly named Goldstar) as engineer 1969, various sr positions include Factory Head in Refrigerator Div., Pres. of Living System Co., and Pres. of Digital Appliance Co. –2000, Vice-Chair. and CEO 2003–08; Pres. and CEO Korea Electric Power Corpn (KEPCO) 2008–11; Pres. ACE Technologies Corpn 2011–; named The Star of Asia, US Business Week 2003. *Leisure interests:* mountain-climbing, golf, reading. *Address:* ACE Technologies Corpn, 451–3 Nonhyeon-dong, Namdong-gu, Incheon 405-849, Republic of Korea (office). *Telephone:* (32) 458-1050 (office). *Fax:* (32) 458-1929 (office). *E-mail:* webmaster@aceteq.co.kr (office). *Website:* www.acetech.co.kr (office).

KIM, Suk-joon, BA; South Korean business executive; *Chairman and Co-CEO, SsangYong Engineering and Construction Co;* b. 9 April 1955, Gyeongsang Prov.; m.; two s. one d.; ed Korea Univ., Seoul; mil. service Repub. of Korea Marine Corps 1972–75; planning office SsangYong Corpn 1977–79, NY and LA br. offices SsangYong (USA) Inc. 1979–82, Dir Planning and Project Man. Div. SsangYong Eng and Construction Co. Ltd 1982–83, CEO 1983–95, Pres. 1983–92, Chair. 1992–95, Chair. and Co-CEO 2010–, Vice-Chair. SsangYong Business Group (later SsangYong Corpn) 1991–93, 1994–95, CEO 1991–93, 1994, Chair. 1995, Chair., CEO SsangYong Motor Co. 1994–95, Chair., CEO SsangYong Cement Industrial Co. 1995; Co-Chair. Korean Party Korea-France High-Level Businessmens' Club, Korean Party Korea-Singapore Econ. Co-operation Cttee; Vice-Chair. Korea-Japan Econ. Asscn, Fed. of Korean Industries, Korean Employers' Fed.; mem. Korea Chamber of Commerce and Industries; Dir Bd of Trustees Kookmin Univ.; Baden-Powell World Fellow, World Scout Foundation; Order of Industrial Service Merit Gold Tower 1991. *Address:* SsangYong Engineering and Construction Co., 9/ f Daihanjedang Bldg., 7 - 23 Shincheon-Dong, Songpa-Gu, Seoul 138-240, Republic of Korea (office). *Telephone:* (2) 3433-7114 (office). *Fax:* (2) 3433-7111 (office).

KIM, Suk-soo; South Korean lawyer, politician and judge; b. 20 Nov. 1932; ed Yonsei Univ., Seoul; admitted to Korean Bar 1958; Judge Advocate, Repub. of Korea Army HQ 1960–63; judge, Masan Br., Court of Pusan Dist Court 1963–67, Pusan Dist Court 1967–69, Incheon Br., Court of Seoul Civil and Criminal Dist Court 1969–70, Seoul Criminal Dist Court 1970–71, Seoul High Court 1971–73; Research Judge, Supreme Court 1973–74; Presiding Judge, Pusan Dist Court 1974–77, Sungbook Br., Court of Seoul Dist Court 1977–79, Seoul Civil Dist Court 1979–80; Chief Judge, Incheon Br., Court of Suwon Dist Court 1980–81; Presiding Judge, Seoul High Court and Chief Judge Nambu Br., Seoul Dist Court 1981–83; Sr Presiding Judge, Seoul High Court 1983–86; Chief Judge, Pusan Dist Court 1986–88; Vice-Minister of Court Admin 1988–91; Supreme Court Justice 1991–97; Chair. Nat. Election Comm. 1993–97; Chair. Judicial Officers' Ethics Cttee of Supreme Court 1997–2001; Chair. Korea Press Ethics Comm. 2000–02; Chair. Govt Public Service Ethics Cttee 2002; Prime Minister of Repub. of Korea 2002–03; Auditor Bd of Dirs Yonsei Univ. Foundation 1997–2002; Dir Samsung Electronics Co. 1999–2001, Yonsei Law Promotion Foundation 2002; Order of Service Merit (Blue Stripes) 1997; Hon. PhD (Yonsei Univ.) 1997. *Address:* c/o Office of the Prime Minister, 77 Sejong-no, Jongno-gu, Seoul, Republic of Korea (office).

KIM, Sun-dong, MBA; South Korean petroleum industry executive; *Chairman, S-Oil Corporation;* b. 1942; ed Seoul Nat. Univ.; with Korea Oil Corpn 1963–74; Man. SsangYong Cement Industrial Co. Ltd 1974–76, Dir SsangYong Corpn 1978–80; Man. Dir S-Oil Corpn 1980–84, Exec. Dir 1984–87, Vice-Pres. 1987–91, Pres. and CEO 1991–98, Vice-Chair. and CEO 1998–2000, Chair. and CEO 2000–07, Chair. 2007–; mem. Korea Petroleum Asscn (Chair. 1997). *Address:* S-Oil Corporation, PO Box 758, 60 Yoido-dong, Yeongdungpo-gu, Seoul 150-607, Republic of Korea (office). *Telephone:* (2) 3772-5151 (office). *Fax:* (2) 783-7993 (office). *Website:* www.s-oil.com (office).

KIM, Sung-hwan, BEcons; South Korean diplomatist and politician; b. 13 April 1953; m.; two d.; ed Seoul Nat. Univ., Univ. of London, UK; joined Ministry of Foreign Affairs (MOFA) 1977, becoming Vice-Consul, Consulate Gen. in Honolulu, USA 1980, Asst Sec., Office of the Pres. 1987, First Sec., Embassy in New Delhi 1988–90, First Sec., Embassy in Moscow 1990–94, Dir E Europe Div., European Affairs Bureau, MOFA 1994–95, Aide to Minister of Foreign Affairs 1995–96, Counsellor, Embassy in Washington, DC 1996–2000, Deputy Dir-Gen., N American Affairs Bureau, Ministry of Foreign Affairs and Trade (MOFAT) 2000, Sr Aide to Minister 2000, Dir-Gen., N American Affairs Bureau 2001–02 Amb. to Uzbekistan 2002–05, Deputy Minister for Planning and Man., MOFAT 2005–06, Amb. to Austria and Perm. Rep. to Int. Orgs. in Vienna 2006–08, Vice Minister of Foreign Affairs and Trade March–June 2008, Sr Sec. to Pres. for Foreign Affairs and Nat. Security 2008–10, Minister of Foreign Affairs and Trade 2010–13. *Address:* Saenuri Party, 14-31, Yeouido-dong, Yeongdeungpo-gu, Seoul, 156-768, Republic of Korea. *Telephone:* (2) 3786-3000. *Fax:* (2) 3786-3610. *Website:* www .saenuriparty.kr.

KIM, Gen. Tae-young, BA; South Korean army officer and government official; b. 1949, Seoul; m. Lee Beom-sook; one s. one d.; ed Repub. of Korea Mil. Acad., Sogang Univ., West German Mil. Acad.; commissioned as Second Lt 1973; Commdr 26th Artillery Bn 1984; Exec. Asst to Chair. of Jt Chiefs of Staff 1989–91; Commdr Artillery Regt, 8th Infantry Div. 1991–93; Vice Commdr 56th Infantry Div. 1993–95; Chief of Strategic Planning Jt Chiefs of Staff 1995–96; Exec. Defence Asst to Blue House (Office of Pres.) 1996–97; Commdr 6th Artillery Brigade 1997–98; Exec. Asst to Minister of Nat. Defence 1998–2000; Commdr 23rd Infantry Div. 2000–02; Deputy Chief of Staff for Planning and Man., Repub. of Korea Army HQ 2002–03; Dir-Gen. Policy Planning Bureau, Ministry of Nat. Defence 2003–04; Commanding Gen. Capital Defence Command 2004–05; Chief Dir for Operations, Jt Chiefs of Staff 2005–06; Commanding Gen. 1st Repub. of Korea Army 2006; Chair. Jt Chiefs of Staff 2008; Minister of Nat. Defence 2009–10 (resgnd); fmr

Prof., Korean Mil. Acad. *Leisure interests:* running marathons, swimming, playing tennis. *Address:* c/o Ministry of National Defence, 1, 3-ga, Yeongsan-dong, Yeongsan-gu, Seoul 140-701, Republic of Korea.

KIM, Taek-jin, MSc; South Korean computer engineer and business executive; *Chairman, President and CEO, NCSoft Corporation;* m. Yoon Song-yee; one c.; ed Seoul Nat. Univ.; co-author of Hangul (Korean-language word-processing program) while at Univ. 1989; cr. Hanmesoft (computer software) 1989; staff mem. Research and Devt Centre, Hyundai Electronics Industries Co. (now Hynix) 1991–92, Head of Devt Team for Shinbiro (S Korea's first internet service provider), 1994; cr. Lineage (online fantasy computer game) 1997, expanded to Taiwan markets 2000, has signed up five million users –2002; Founder, Chair., Pres. and CEO NCSoft Corpn 1997–, est. subsidiaries and jt ventures in USA, Japan, Hong Kong and China; Regional Dir Microsoft Corpn 1998; Man of the Year, Computer Reporters Asscn 1989, New Venture Age Leader, Naeway Economic Daily 2000, Industrial Medal, Soft Expo/Digital Contents Fair 2001, Best Contrib. to Cultural Industry, Ministry of Culture and Tourism 2001. *Address:* NCSoft Corpn, 157-33 Oksan Bldg., Samsung-dong, Gangnam-gu, Seoul 135-090, Republic of Korea (office). *Telephone:* (2) 2186-3300 (office). *Website:* www .ncsoft.co.kr (office).

KIM, V. Narry, BA, MS, DPhil; South Korean biologist and academic; *Director, Centre for RNA Research, Institute for Basic Science, Seoul National University;* b. 1969; ed Seoul Nat. Univ., Univ. of Oxford, UK; Postdoctoral Fellow, Howard Hughes Medical Inst., Univ. of Pennsylvania, USA 1999–2001; Research Asst Prof., Seoul Nat. Univ. (SNU) 2001–04, Asst Prof. 2004–08, Assoc. Prof. 2008–13, Prof. 2013–, SNU Distinguished Fellow 2010–, Dir Centre for RNA Research, Inst. for Basic Science 2012–; mem. Editorial Bd, Cell 2010, EMBO Journal 2011–, Genes & Development 2012–; mem. European Molecular Biology Org. 2012; Laureate for Asia Pacific, L'Oréal-UNESCO Awards for Women in Science 2008, ranked 13th as author of High-Impact Papers in Molecular Biology & Genetics (2002–06) 2008, Ho-Am Laureate, Medicine 2009, Nat. Honour Scientist, Ministry of Educ., Science and Tech. 2010, Korea Best Scientist Award, Korean Fed. of Science and Tech. Socs 2013. *Publications:* numerous papers in professional journals. *Address:* Lab of RNomics (Narry Kim Lab), Building 504, Room 509, School of Biological Sciences, Seoul National University, 599 Gwanangno, Gwanak-gu, Seoul 151-742, South Korea (office). *Telephone:* (2) 880-9120 (office); (2) 887-1343 (Lab.) (office). *Fax:* (2) 887-0244 (office). *E-mail:* narrykim@snu.ac.kr (office). *Website:* www.narrykim.org/en (office).

KIM, Vladimir, MBA, PhD; Kazakhstani mining industry executive; *Executive Chairman, Kazakhmys PLC;* b. 1961; m.; three c.; ed Alma-Ata Architectural Inst.; joined Kazakhmys Group 1995, apptd Man. Dir and CEO JSC Zhezkazgantsvet-met 1995, Chair. Bd of Dirs Kazakhmys PLC 2000–, currently also Exec. Chair. *Address:* Kazakhmys PLC, 6th & 7th Floor, Cardinal Place, 100 Victoria Street, London, SW1E 5JL, England (office). *Telephone:* (20) 7901-7800 (office). *Fax:* (20) 7901-7859 (office). *Website:* www.kazakhmys.com (office).

KIM, Wan-su; North Korean government official; *Vice Chairman, Supreme People's Assembly;* Deputy Minister of Finance –2004; Pres. Cen. Bank of Democratic People's Repub. of Korea 2004–09; Vice Chairman, Choe Ko In Min Hoe Ui (Supreme People's Ass.) 2009–. *Address:* Choe Ko In Min Hoe Ui, Pyongyang, Democratic People's Republic of Korea (office).

KIM, Woo-choong, BA; South Korean business executive; b. 19 Dec. 1936, Daegu; s. of Yong-ha Kim and In-hang Chun; m. Hrrja Chung 1964; four c.; ed Kyunggi High School, Seoul, Yonsei Univ.; with Econ. Devt Council; with Hansung Industrial Co. Ltd, Dir –1967 (resgnd); Founder, Daewoo Industrial Co. Ltd (textile co.) 1967, Chair. Daewoo Group, includes Daewoo Shipbldg & Heavy Machinery Ltd, Daewoo Motor Co.; Founder, Daewoo Foundation 1978; under investigation for fraud and fled 1999, returned to South Korea and arrested 2005, convicted of charges including embezzlement and accounting fraud, sentenced to 10 years in jail 2006, granted amnesty 2007; Commdr, Légion d'honneur 1996; Dr hc (Yonsei Univ., Korea Univ., George Washington Univ., USA, Univ. of South Carolina, Russian Econ. Acad., Univ. Santiago de Cali/Univ. del Valle, Colombia; numerous honours and awards including Int. Business Award, Int. Chamber of Commerce 1984. *Publications:* It's Big World and There's Lots To Be Done 1989, Every Street is Paved With Gold: The Road to Real Success.

KIM, Vice-Marshall Yong-chun; North Korean army official; b. 1936; Assoc. mem. Workers' Party Cen. Cttee (WPCC) –1980, Deputy Chief of Dept, WPCC 1980–83; rank of Gen. 1992, Vice Marshall 1995; Chief of Staff, North Korean People's Party 1995–07; mem. Nat. Defence Comm. 1998–, Vice-Chair. 2007–, also Minister of the People's Armed Forces 2009–12. *Address:* National Defence Commission, Pyongyang, People's Republic of Korea (office).

KIM, Yong-dae; North Korean government official; *Chairman, Central Committee, Korean Social Democratic Party;* Chair., Cen. Cttee, Korean Social Democratic Party (Joson Sahoeminjudang); Vice-Pres. Supreme People's Ass. (Parl.) 2009–. *Address:* Korean Social Democratic Party, Pyongyang, Democratic People's Republic of Korea (office). *Telephone:* (2) 5591323 (office). *Fax:* (2) 3814410 (office).

KIM, Yong-il; North Korean politician; b. 2 May 1944; ed Rajin Univ. of Marine Transport; served in army 1961–70; various positions in Ministry of Land and Marine Transport 1980–94, including Instructor and Deputy Dir, Minister for Marine and Land Transport 1994–2007; Premier 2007–2010. *Address:* c/o Office of the Premier, Pyongyang, Democratic People's Republic of Korea (office).

KIM, Yong-nam; North Korean politician; *President, Presidium of the Supreme People's Assembly;* b. 1925, North Hamgyong prov.; ed Kim Il Sung Univ., Moscow Univ.; mem. Cen. Cttee Workers' Party of Korea (WPK) 1970, Political Commissar 1977, mem. Political Bureau 1980–; Vice-Premier and Minister of Foreign Affairs 1983–98; Del. to Supreme People's Ass.; apptd Pres. Presidium of the Supreme People's Ass. 1998, re-elected 2014–. *Address:* Choe ko in min hoe ui (Supreme People's Assembly), Pyongyang, Democratic People's Republic of Korea (office).

KIM, Young-sam, BA; South Korean politician and fmr head of state; b. 20 Dec. 1927, Koje-gun, South Gyeongsang Prov.; s. of Kim Hong-jo and Late Park Bu-ryon; m. Sohn Myoung-Soon; two s. three d.; ed Kyongnam High School, Busan and Seoul Nat. Univ.; mem. Nat. Ass. 1954–79; Founder-mem. Democratic Party 1955;

re-elected Pres. New Democratic Party 1974, 1979; expelled from Nat. Ass. for opposition to regime of Pres. Park. 1979; arrested under martial law 1980–81; banned from political activity Nov. 1980; again under house arrest 1982–83; staged 23-day hunger strike demanding democracy May–June 1983; Co-Chair. Council for Promotion of Democracy 1984; played leading role in org. of New Korea Democratic Party (absorbing Democratic Korea Party) which won large number of seats in 1985 election; political ban lifted May 1985; Presidential Cand. 1987 elections; Founder-Pres. Reunification Democracy Party 1987–90; Exec. Chair. Democratic Liberal Party (DLP) 1990–97, Pres. 1992–97; Pres. of Repub. of Korea 1992–97; Dr hc (Towson State Univ., Baltimore) 1974; Martin Luther King Peace Prize 1995. *Publications:* There is No Hill We Can Depend On, Politics is Long and Political Power is Short, Standard-Bearer in his Forties, My Truth and My Country's Truth 1984, My Resolution 1987, Democratization, the Way of Salvation of my Country 1987, New Korea 2000. *Leisure interests:* calligraphy, mountain climbing, jogging, swimming. *Address:* 7-6 Sangdo 1-dong, Dongjak-gu, Seoul, Republic of Korea.

KIM, Young-se, BFA, MA, PhD; South Korean industrial designer and business executive; *CEO, INNODESIGN;* b. 1950, Seoul; ed Seoul Nat. Univ. and Univ. of Illinois, USA; began career as designer at Mel Boldt and Assocs., Chicago and Hari and Assocs., Skokie, Ill.; fmr Design Consultant, DuPont; Asst Prof. of Industrial Design, Univ. of Illinois 1980–82; Founder and CEO INNODESIGN Inc., Palo Alto, Calif. 1986, INNODESIGN Korea 1999, INNODESIGN China 2004; Silver Medal, Industrial Design Excellence Awards 2005, Grand Prix, Korea Industrial Design Awards, winner of Gold, Silver and Bronze Industrial Design Awards. *Publications:* Innovator, The Trendsetter 1999, Design A to Z 2000, A Napkin Worth 12 Hundred Millions 2001, Design, Start from Love! 2001; regular contributor to The Economist. *Address:* INNODESIGN, 577 College Avenue, Palo Alto, CA 94306, USA (office); INNO Tower, 11–13F 61-3, Nonhyun-dong, Gangnam-gu, Seoul, South Korea (office); Beijing Lufthansa Center, C401 50 Liangmaqiao Road, Chaoyang District, Beijing 100016, People's Republic of China (office). *Telephone:* (650) 493-4666 (Palo Alto) (office); (2) 344-56481 (Seoul) (office); (10) 64639490 (Beijing) (office). *Fax:* (650) 493-6198 (Palo Alto) (office); (2) 344-75465 (Seoul) (office); (10) 64639489 (Beijing) (office). *E-mail:* paloalto@innodesign.com (office). *Website:* global.innodesign.com (office).

KIM, Young-tae; South Korean business executive; *CEO and President of Banking & Insurance, National Agricultural Co-operative Federation;* Vice-Pres. of Industrial Relations and Human Resources, SK Holdings Co. Ltd –2011, Pres. and Co-CEO SK Holdings Co. Ltd 2011–13; CEO and Pres. of Banking & Insurance, Nat. Agricultural Co-operative Fed. *Address:* National Agricultural Co-operative Federation, Saemunangil 91, Chung-gu, Seoul 110-110, Republic of Korea (office).

KIM, Yu-na; South Korean figure skater; b. 5 Sept. 1990, Bucheon, Gyeonggi Prov.; ed Korea Univ., Seoul; started figure skating aged seven; sr int. debut 2006; took part in torch relay for Winter Olympic Games, Turin, Italy 2006, but was too young to participate in actual competition; moved to Canada to train under Brian Orser 2007; ranked first in the world by Int. Skating Union (ISU) March 2010; current record holder for ladies in the short programme, the free skating and the combined total under the ISU Judging System; first female skater to surpass the 150-point free skating mark and the 200-point total mark under the ISU Judging System. *Medals include:* Gold Medal, S Korean Championships 2003, 2004, 2005, 2006, 2013, ISU Jr Grand Prix, Hungary 2004, Bulgaria 2005, Slovakia 2005, Gold Medal, World Jr Championships 2006, Trophée Eric Bompard 2006, 2009, ISU Grand Prix Cup of China 2007, 2008, Gold Medal, ISU Grand Prix Final 2007, 2008, 2010, ISU Grand Prix Skate America 2008, 2009, Four Continents Champion 2009, Gold Medal, World Championships 2009, 2013, Gold Medal, Winter Olympic Games, Vancouver, Canada 2010. *Television:* host of Kim Yu-na's Kiss and Cry (SBS) 2011. *Address:* Korea Skating Union, Room No. 412, Olympic Center, 88 Bangyee-Dong, Songpa-ku, Seoul 138-749, Republic of Korea (office). *Telephone:* (2) 422-61-65 (office). *Fax:* (2) 423-80-97 (office). *E-mail:* skating@sports.or.kr (office). *Website:* skating.or.kr (office); www.yunakim.com (office).

KIMBALL, Warren Forbes, PhD; American historian and academic; *Robert Treat Professor Emeritus of History, Rutgers University;* b. 24 Dec. 1935, Brooklyn, New York; s. of Cyril S. Kimball and Carolyn F. Kimball; m. Jacqueline Sue Nelson 1959; one s. two d.; ed Villanova Univ. and Georgetown Univ.; served in USNR 1958–65; Instructor, US Naval Acad. 1961–65; Asst Prof., Georgetown Univ. 1965–67, Univ. of Georgia 1967–70; Assoc. Prof., Rutgers Univ. 1970–85, Prof. II 1985–93, Robert Treat Prof. of History 1993, now Prof. Emer.; Pitt Prof. of American History, Corpus Christi, Cambridge, UK 1988–89; Mark A. Clark Distinguished Visiting Prof. of History, The Citadel 2002–04; Historian, US Tennis Asscn 2005–; Farrow Award for Churchill Scholarship, Int. Churchill Soc. 1999, Arthur Link Prize, Soc. for Historians of American Foreign Relations 2001. *Publications:* 'The Most Unsordid Act': Lend-Lease, 1939–1941 1969, Swords or Ploughshares? The Morgenthau Plan 1976, Churchill and Roosevelt: The Complete Correspondence (3 Vols) 1984, The Juggler: Franklin Roosevelt as Wartime Statesman 1991, Forged in War: Roosevelt, Churchill and the Second World War 1997. *Address:* Department of History, 175 University Avenue, Rutgers University, Newark, NJ 07102-1814 (office); 2540 Otter Lane, John's Island, SC 29455, USA (home). *Telephone:* (843) 768-3879 (home). *E-mail:* wkimball@andromeda.rutgers.edu (office). *Website:* andromeda.rutgers.edu/~history (office).

KIMMEL, James (Jimmy) Christian; American comedian, actor, television presenter and television producer; b. 13 Nov. 1967, Brooklyn, New York; s. of James Kimmel and Joan Kimmel (née Iacono); m. 1st Gina Kimmel 1988 (divorced); two c.; m. 2nd Molly McNearney 2013; ed Univ. of Nevada-Las Vegas, Arizona State Univ.; first radio job as morning drive co-host, The Me and Him Show (KZOK-FM, Seattle) 1989; began TV career on game show Win Ben Stein's Money 1997; host, White House Correspondents' Dinner 2012, 64th Primetime Emmy Awards 2012; Writers Guild Award for Best Comedy/Variety-(Including Talk) Series (co-recipient) 2012. *Television includes:* host and creator of Jimmy Kimmel Live! (ABC late-night talk show) 2003–; host, writer The Man Show (TV series) 1999–2003, host, writer, exec. producer Crank Yankers (voice) 2002–07, writer, exec. producer The Andy Milonakis Show 2005–07, co-host, Win Ben Stein's Money (Daytime Emmy for Outstanding Game Show Host 1999) 2001–02; exec. producer: (TV films) Big Night of Stars 2008, Alligator Boots 2009, Ace in the

Hole 2009, (TV series) The Adam Carolla Project 2005. *Films include:* as actor: Down To You 2000, Road Trip (voice) 2000, Garfield (voice) 2004, Channel 101 (TV film) 2006, The Smurfs 2 (voice) 2013. *Address:* c/o Jimmy Kimmel Live, 6834 Hollywood Boulevard, Los Angeles, CA 90028, USA (office). *Website:* abc.go.com/shows/jimmy-kimmel-live (office).

KIMUNYA, Amos Muhinga, BA, CPA,; Kenyan accountant and politician; *Minister of Transport;* b. 6 March 1962, Embu; ed Univ. of Nairobi; early career as accountant; mem. Parl. for Kipipiri, Minister for Lands and Settlement 2003–06, of Finance 2006–08 (resgnd), of Trade 2009–12, of Transport 2012–; Chair. Inst. of Certified Accountants of Kenya 1999–2001; mem. Nat. Rainbow Coalition. *Address:* Ministry of Transport, Transcom House, Ngong Rd, POB 52692, 00200 Nairobi, Kenya (office). *Telephone:* (20) 2729200 (office). *Fax:* (20) 2730330 (office). *E-mail:* ps@transport.go.ke (office). *Website:* www.transport.go.ke (office).

KIMURA, Hiroshi; Japanese business executive; *Chairman, Japan Tobacco Inc.;* b. 23 April 1953, Yamaguchi Prov.; ed Kyoto Univ.; early career with Japan Tobacco Inc. and Salt Public Corpn, fmr Exec. Vice-Pres. and Asst to CEO JT International Holding BV (subsidiary of Japan Tobacco Inc.), Dir of Business Planning and Head, Overseas Operations, Japan Tobacco Inc. 1999–2006, mem. Bd of Dirs 2005–, Rep. Dir, Pres. and CEO 2006–12, Chair. 2012–. *Address:* Japan Tobacco Inc., 2-1, Toranomon 2-chome, Minato-ku, Tokyo, 105-8422, Japan (office). *Telephone:* (3) 3582-3111 (office). *Fax:* (3) 5572-1441 (office). *E-mail:* info@jti.com (office). *Website:* www.jti.com (office).

KIMURA, Yaichi; Japanese oil industry executive; *Representative Director and Chairman, Cosmo Oil Company Ltd;* b. 1940; joined Daikyo Oil Co. 1963, Gen. Man. Corp. Planning Dept, Cosmo Oil Co. Ltd (after merger of Daikyo Oil, Maruzen Oil and Cosmo Oil) 1988–90, Gen. Man. Finance Dept 1990–94, mem. Bd of Dirs 1993–, Dir-Gen. Corp. Planning Dept 1994–96, Man. Dir 1996–98, Sr Man. Dir 1998–2001, Exec. Vice-Pres. 2001–04, Rep. Dir, Pres. and CEO 2004–12, Rep. Dir and Chair. 2012–. *Address:* Cosmo Oil Co. Ltd, 1-1-1, Shibaura, Minato-ku, Tokyo 105-8528, Japan (office). *Telephone:* (3) 3798-3211 (office). *Fax:* (3) 3798-3841 (office). *E-mail:* info@cosmo-oil.co.jp (office). *Website:* www.cosmo-oil.co.jp (office).

KIMURA, Yasushi; Japanese oil company executive; *Chairman and Representative Director, JX Holdings, Inc.;* ed Keio Univ.; fmr Exec. Dir Energy Solution Div. and Sr Vice-Pres. Nippon Oil Corpn, fmr Gen. Man. Specialities Business Co-ordination Dept, the Lubricants and Kyushu Br. Office, Pres. JX Nippon Oil & Energy Corpn 2010–, also Pres. JX Nippon Oil & Energy (Australia) Pty Ltd, mem. Bd of Dirs JX Holdings, Inc. 2010–, Chair. and Rep. Dir 2012–; mem. Bd of Dirs Japan Oil Transportation Co Ltd 2010–. *Address:* JX Holdings, Inc., 2-6-3, Otemachi, Chiyoda-ku, Tokyo 100-0004, Japan (office). *Telephone:* (3) 3502-1131 (office). *Fax:* (3) 3502-9352 (office). *E-mail:* info@hd.jx-group.co.jp (office). *Website:* www.hd.jx-group.co.jp (office).

KINAKH, Col Anatoliy Kyryllovych; Ukrainian politician; *Chairman, Party of Industrialists and Entrepreneurs;* b. 4 Aug. 1954, Bratuşani, Moldovan SSR; m. Marina Volodymyrivna Kinakh 1960; three d.; ed Leningrad (now St Petersburg) Vessel Construction Inst.; worked on vessel construction and in vessel repair plants in Tallinn and Nikolayev 1978–90; elected to Mykolayiv Oblast Parl. 1990; mem. Comm. on Econ. Reform and Nat. Econ. Man. 1990; Presidential Rep. in Mykolayiv Oblast, then Head of Mykolayiv Regional Admin. 1992–94; Head, Mykolayiv Regional Council of People's Deputies 1994–95; mem. Political Council People's Democratic Party of Ukraine, Deputy Chair. 1996; Deputy Prime Minister of Ukraine in charge of Industrial Policy 1995–96; Presidential Adviser on Industrial Policy, then Pres. Ukrainian Union of Businessmen 1996–97; First Deputy Head, Council of Int. Congress of Businessmen 1997–; mem. Higher Econ. Council at Ukrainian Presidency, Head of Co-ordination Council on Privatization of Industrial Enterprises of Strategic Importance 1997–; mem. Nat. Council of Ukraine on Quality Issues 1997–2001; Head, Verkhovna Rada Cttee on Industrial Policy 1998–2001; Chair. Nat. Cttee of Int. Trade Chamber 1998–2001; First Deputy Prime Minister of Ukraine Aug.–Dec. 1999, Jan.–Sept. 2005; Prime Minister of Ukraine 2001–02; mem. Parl. 2002–; presidential cand. 2004; Chair. Nat. Security and Defence Council 2005–06; Minister of the Economy 2007; currently Chair. Party of Industrialists and Entrepreneurs of Ukraine; mem. Acad. of Cybernetics; Hon. Prof., Mykolaiv Govt Humanitarian Univ. *Leisure interest:* classical music. *Address:* Party of Industrialists and Entrepreneurs, 01203 Kyiv, vul. Sh. Rustaveli 11, Ukraine (office). *Telephone:* (44) 590-17-44 (office). *Fax:* (44) 590-17-44 (office). *E-mail:* info@uspp.org.ua (office). *Website:* www.pppu.info (office); www.kinakh.com.ua.

KINCAID, Jamaica, PhD; Antigua and Barbuda writer and academic; *Josephine Olp Weeks Chair and Professor of Literature, Claremont McKenna College;* b. (Elaine Potter Richardson), 25 May 1949, St John's; d. of Annie Richardson; m. Allen Shawn; one s. one d.; staff writer, The New Yorker 1976; currently Josephine Olp Weeks Chair and Prof. of Literature, Claremont McKenna Coll.; fmr Visiting Lecturer on African and African American Studies and on English and American Literature and Language, Harvard Univ.; mem. American Acad. of Arts and Letters 2004–; Fellow, American Acad. of Arts and Sciences 2009–; Dr hc (Williams Coll.) 1991, (Long Island Coll.) 1991, (Amherst Coll.) 1995, (Bard Coll.) 1997, (Middlebury Coll.) 1998, (Tufts Univ.) 2011; Lila Wallace–Reader's Digest Fund Annual Writer's Award 1992, Anifield-Wolf Book Award 1997, Prix Femina Étranger 2000. *Publications include:* At the Bottom of the River (short stories; American Acad. and Inst. of Arts and Letters Morton Dauwen Zabel Award 1985) 1983, Annie John (novel) 1985, A Small Place (non-fiction) 1988, Lucy (novel) 1990, The Autobiography of My Mother 1995, My Brother 1997, My Favorite Plant 1998, Poetics of Place (with Lynn Geesaman) 1998, My Garden (non-fiction) 1999, Talk Stories 2001, Mr Potter 2002, Among Flowers: A Walk in the Himalaya 2005, See Now Then 2013. *Leisure interest:* gardening. *Address:* Literature Department, Claremont McKenna College, 500 East Ninth Street, Claremont, CA 91711, USA (office). *Telephone:* (909) 607-3228 (office). *E-mail:* jamaica.kincaid@cmc.edu (office). *Website:* www.cmc.edu/lit (office).

KINCSES, Veronika; Hungarian singer (soprano); d. of György Kincses and Etelka Angyal; m. József Vajda; one s.; ed Liszt Ferenc Music Acad. Budapest and Accademia Santa Cecilia, Rome; soloist, State Opera, Budapest; song-recitals, also oratorio performances; guest performances in USA, Argentina, Venezuela, Hong

Kong, Singapore etc. 1997–98; operatic roles include Madame Butterfly, Mimi in La Bohème, Manon Lescaut, Liu in Turandot, Le Villi (Puccini), Contessa in Le Nozze di Figaro, Fiordiligi in Così fan Tutte, Vitellia in La Clemenza di Tito, Elvira in Don Giovanni, Amelia in Simone Boccanegra, Leonora in La Forza del destino, Micaela in Carmen, Marguerita in Faust, Silvana in Fiamma–Respighi, Eva in Meistersinger von Nürnberg, Adriana in Adriana Lecouvreur, Tosca, Judit in Bluebeard's Castle; Prof., Univ. of Pécs 2002–; winner, Dvořák Int. Singing Competition, Prague 1971, Liszt Prize, Kossuth Prize (Hungary), Prix de l'Acad. du Disque, Paris (four times). *Recordings include:* Die Königin von Saba, Haydn's Der Apotheker and La Fedeltà Premiata, Songs by Bellini, Liszt's Hungarian Coronation Mass, Madame Butterfly, Orfeo ed Euridice, La Bohème (also DVD), Suor Angelica, Le Nozze di Figaro, etc. *Leisure interest:* teaching singers. *Address:* International Management of the Hungarian State Opera, Andrássy ut 22, 1061 Budapest, Hungary (office); Robert Lombardo Associates, 61 West 62nd Street, New York, NY 10023, USA (office).

KIND, Dieter Hans, FIEEE; German electrical engineer; *Professor Emeritus, Technical University, Braunschweig;* b. 5 Oct. 1929, Reichenberg, Bohemia (now Liberec, Czech Repub.); s. of Hans Kind and Gerta Kind; m. Waltraud Wagner 1954; three c.; ed Tech. Univ., Munich; Prof. and Dir High-Voltage Inst., Technical Univ., Braunschweig 1962–75, Prof. Emer. 1975–; Pres. Physikalisch-Technische Bundesanstalt, Braunschweig and Berlin 1975–95, Comité Int. des Poids et Mesures, Sèvres/Paris 1975–95; Ehrenring VDE 1988, Dong-Baeg Medal (Korea) 1988, Orden do Mérito Científico (Brazil) 1995, Grosses Bundesverdienstkreuz; Hon. DrIng (Tech. Univ., Munich). *Publications include:* An Introduction to High-Voltage Experimental Technique 1978, High-Voltage Insulation Technology 1985, Herausforderung Metrologie 2002, Naturforscher und Gestalter der Technik 2006; about 50 scientific articles. *Leisure interests:* sport, literature. *Address:* Knapp-strasse 4, 38116 Braunschweig, Germany (home). *Telephone:* (531) 511497 (home). *Fax:* (531) 5160239 (home). *E-mail:* dieterkind@t-online.de.

KINDELAN MESA, Mario Cesar; Cuban boxer; b. 10 Aug. 1971, Holgu; m.; ed Physical Culture and Sport, ISCFM Fasardo, Havana; began boxing aged 14 years, competed as lightweight; trained by Julian R. Gonzalez since 1990; won Pan-American Games 1999, 2003; gold medals World Championships 1999, 2001, 2003; gold medals Olympic Games 2000 (Sydney), 2004 (Athens); undefeated since winning Pan-American Games in 1999; retd after winning second Olympic gold medal 2004, returned to fight Amir Khan in a professional fight 2005 (lost on points), again retd; Best Boxer in Cuba 1999, Russell Cup for Best Boxer at World Championships 2001, Cuban Sportsman of the Year 2001. *Address:* c/o Comité Olímpico Cubano, Zona Postal 4, Calle 13, No. 601, Vedado, Havana, CP 10400, Cuba.

KINDLE, Fred, MBA; Liechtenstein/Swiss business executive; *Partner, Clayton, Dubilier & Rice LLC;* b. 25 March 1959; ed Swiss Fed. Inst. of Tech., Northwestern Univ., USA; Marketing Project Man. Hilti AG, Liechtenstein 1984–86; Assoc. and Engagement Man. McKinsey & Co. (New York and Zurich) 1988–92; Head, Mass Transfer Dept Sulzer Chemtech AG, Switzerland 1992–96, Head, Product Div. 1996–99, CEO Sulzer Industries 1999–2001, CEO Sulzer Ltd 2001–04; CEO ABB Ltd 2005–08, also fmr Pres.; Partner, Clayton, Dubilier & Rice LLC 2008–, Chair. Exova Ltd. 2008–, BCA Group 2010–; mem. Bd of Dirs VZ Holding Ltd 2002–, Zurich Financial Services and Zurich Insurance Company Ltd 2006– (Vice-Chair. 2013–), Stadler Rail AG 2008–; mem. Swiss American Chamber of Commerce. *Address:* Clayton, Dubilier & Rice LLP, Cleveland House, 33 King Street, London, SW1Y 6RJ, England (office). *Website:* www.cdr-inc.com (office).

KINDLER, Jeffrey B., BA, JD; American lawyer and business executive; b. 13 May 1955, Montclair, New Jersey; m. Sharon Sullivan; one s. one d.; ed Tufts Univ., Harvard Law School; worked at Fed. Communications Comm.; served as law clerk to US Supreme Court Justice William J. Brennan, Jr and to Judge David L. Bazelon, US Court of Appeals, DC Circuit; fmr Pnr, Williams & Connolly (law firm), Washington, DC; fmr Vice-Pres. and Sr Counsel, Litigation and Legal Policy, General Electric Co.; Sr Vice-Pres. and Gen. Counsel, McDonald's Corpn 1996–97, Exec. Vice-Pres. for Corp. Relations and Gen. Counsel 1997–2001; Chair. and CEO Boston Market Corpn –2002, Pres. Partner Brands –2002; Sr Vice-Pres. and Gen. Counsel, Pfizer Inc. 2002–04, Exec. Vice-Pres. and Gen. Counsel 2004–05, Vice-Chair. and Gen. Counsel 2005–06, CEO 2006–10 (resgnd), Chair. 2006–10, also Chair. Exec. Cttee and mem. Pfizer Exec. Leadership Team 2006–10; mem. Bd of Dirs Ronald McDonald House Charities, US-Japan Business Council, US Chamber of Commerce, Manhattan Theater Club, New York Philharmonic, Partnership for New York City, Fed. Reserve Bank of New York –2010; mem. Bd of Trustees Tufts Univ.; numerous awards including Stephen E. Banner Award, Lawyers Div. of UJA Fed. of New York 2002. *Address:* c/o Pfizer Inc., 235 East 42nd Street, New York, NY 10017-5755, USA.

KINELEV, Vladimir Georgiyevich, DTechSc; Russian politician; *Director, Institute for Information Technologies in Education, United Nations Educational, Scientific and Cultural Organization (UNESCO);* b. 28 Jan. 1945, Ust-Kalmanka, Altay Region; m.; one d.; ed Bauman Higher Tech. School; worked Cen. Bureau of Experimental Machine-Construction, Asst, Prof., Pro-rector Bauman Higher Tech. School; First Deputy Chair. State Cttee on Science and Higher School 1990–91; Chair. Cttee on Higher School Ministry of Science, Higher School and Tech. Policy of Russian Fed., concurrently First Deputy Minister 1992–93; Chair. State Cttee on Higher Educ. 1993–96; Deputy Chair. Russian Govt 1996; Minister of Gen. and Professional Educ. 1996–98; Dir UNESCO Inst. for Information Technologies in Educ. (IITE) 1998–; Academician, Russian Acad. of Educ., Russian Eng Acad.; Prize of USSR Govt 1990, State Prize of Russia 1997; Order of Honour, Russian Fed. 1995. *Publications:* The Objective Necessity 1995, Education and Culture in the History of Civilization 1998. *Address:* UNESCO Institute for Information Technologies in Education, Kedrova str. 8, 117292 Moscow, Russia (office). *Telephone:* (495) 129-19-98 (office). *Fax:* (495) 718-07-66 (office). *E-mail:* kinelev@iite.ru (office). *Website:* www.iite.ru.

KING, Angus Stanley, Jr, BA, JD; American lawyer, broadcaster and politician; *Senator from Maine;* b. 31 March 1944; m. Mary J. Herman; four s. one d.; ed Dartmouth Coll. and Univ. of Pennsylvania; called to the Bar, Maine 1969; staff attorney, Pine Tree Legal Assistance, Skowhegan, Me 1969–72; Chief Counsel, Office of Senator William D. Hathaway, US Senate Subcttee on Alcoholism and

Narcotics, Washington, DC 1972–75; fmr Pnr, Smith, Lloyd & King (law firm), Brunswick, Me; Gov. of Maine 1995–2003; Distinguished Lecturer, Bowdoin Coll. 2004–, also Bates Coll.; Of Counsel, Bernstein, Shur, Sawyer & Nelson PA, Portland 2004–; Vice-Chair. Medicaid Advisory Comm., US Dept of Health and Human Services 2005–; Senator from Maine 2013–, caucuses with the Democrats; TV host Maine Watch 1977–96; Vice-Pres. and Gen. Counsel Swift River/Hafslund Co. 1983; Prin. Independence Wind; Founder and Pres. Northeast Energy Man. Inc. 1989–94; mem. Bd of Dirs Public Broadcasting Service 2008–, Savings Bank of Maine 2010–; Trustee, The Nature Conservancy in Maine; Independent; Hon. LLD (Bowdoin Coll.) 2007; John Bernotavich Award 2005. *Address:* United States Senate, Washington, DC 20510 (office); Bernstein, Shur, Sawyer & Nelson PA, 100 Middle Street, PO Box 9729, Portland, ME 04104, USA. *Telephone:* (202) 224-3121 (Senate switchboard) (office); (207) 774-1200 (Portland). *Fax:* (207) 774-1127 (Portland). *E-mail:* aking3@bowdoin.edu (office). *Website:* www.senate.gov (office); www.bernsteinshur.com.

KING, Anthony Stephen, DPhil; Canadian political scientist and academic; *Professor of Government, University of Essex;* b. 7 Nov. 1934, Toronto, Ont.; s. of the late Harold King and Marjorie King; m. 1st Vera Korte 1965 (died 1971); m. 2nd Jan Reece 1980; ed Queen's Univ., Kingston, Ont., Magdalen and Nuffield Colls, Oxford; Fellow, Magdalen Coll., Oxford 1961–65; Sr Lecturer, Univ. of Essex 1966–68, Reader 1968–69, Prof. of Govt 1969–; Visiting Prof., Univ. of Wis. 1967, Princeton Univ. 1984; Fellow, Center for Advanced Study in Behavioral Sciences, Stanford Univ., Calif. 1977–78; elections commentator for BBC, various periodicals; mem. Cttee on Standards in Public Life 1994–98, Royal Comm. on House of Lords Reform 1999; Chair. RSA Comm. on Illegal Drugs, Communities and Public Policy 2005–07; mem. Academia Europaea 1998; Hon. Foreign mem. American Acad. of Arts and Sciences 1993, Hon. Life Fellow, RSA. *Publications:* The British General Election of 1964 (co-author) 1965, The British General Election of 1966 (co-author) 1966, British Politics: People, Parties and Parliament (ed.) 1966, The British Prime Minister (ed.) 1969, Westminster and Beyond (co-author) 1973, British Members of Parliament: A Self-portrait 1974, Why is Britain Becoming Harder to Govern? (ed.) 1976, Britain Says Yes: The 1975 Referendum on the Common Market 1977, The New American Political System (ed.) 1978, Both Ends of the Avenue: the Presidency of the Executive Branch and Congress in the 1980s (ed.) 1983, Britain at the Polls 1992 (ed.) 1992, SDP: The Birth, Life and Death of the Social Democratic Party (co-author) 1995, Running Scared: Why America's Politicians Campaign Too Much and Govern Too Little 1997, New Labour Triumphs: Britain at the Polls (ed.) 1997, British Political Opinion 1937–2000 (ed.) 2001, Does the United Kingdom Still Have a Constitution? 2001, Britain at the Polls 2001 (ed.) 2001, Leaders' Personalities and the Outcomes of Democratic Elections (ed.) 2002, Britain at the Polls 2005 (ed.) 2006, The British Constitution 2007; numerous papers in British and American journals. *Leisure interests:* holidays, music, theatre, walking. *Address:* Room 5.022, Department of Government, University of Essex, Wivenhoe Park, Colchester, Essex, CO4 3SQ (office); The Mill House, Lane Road, Wakes Colne, Colchester, Essex, CO6 2BP, England (home). *Telephone:* (1206) 873393 (office); (1787) 222497 (home). *Fax:* (1787) 224221 (home). *Website:* www.essex.ac.uk/government (office).

KING, (Riley B.) B. B.; American singer and musician (guitar); b. 16 Sept. 1925, Itta Bena, Miss.; began teaching himself guitar 1945; later studied Schillinger System; fmr disc jockey and singer, Memphis, Tenn. radio stations; cut his first record in 1949, Miss Martha King; numerous int. appearances; Co-Chair. Foundation for Advancement of Inmate Rehabilitation and Recreation 1972–; toured USSR 1979; performance at closing ceremonies, Summer Olympics, Atlanta, Ga 1996; Hon. LHD (Tougaloo Coll. Miss.) 1973, Hon. DMus (Yale) 1977; Grammy Lifetime Achievement Award 1987, Kennedy Center Honors 1995, Living Legend Award, Trumpet Awards 1997, Royal Swedish Acad. of Music Polar Music Prize 2004, Presidential Medal of Freedom 2006. *Films include:* When We Were Kings 1996, Blues Brothers 2000 1998. *Recordings include:* albums: Completely Well 1970, The Incredible Soul of B. B. King 1970, Indianola Mississippi Seeds 1970, Live In Cook County Jail 1971, Live At The Regal 1971, B. B. King In London 1971, LA Midnight 1972, Guess Who 1972, The Best Of... 1973, To Know You Is To Love You 1973, Friends 1974, Lucille Talks Back 1975, King Size 1977, Midnight Believer 1978, Take It Home 1979, Now Appearing At Ole Miss 1980, There Must Be A Better World Somewhere 1982, Love Me Tender 1982, Blues 'n' Jazz 1984, Six Silver Strings 1986, Live At San Quentin 1991, Blues Summit (Grammy Award for Best Traditional Blues Album) 1993, Lucille and Friends 1995, Live in Japan 1999, Makin' Love Is Good For You 2000, A Christmas Celebration of Hope 2001, Anthology 2001, Reflections 2003, 80 (Grammy Award for Best Traditional Blues Album 2006) 2005, One Kind Favor (Grammy Award for Best Traditional Blues Album 2009) 2008. *Address:* Lieberman Management, 1414 Avenue of the Americas, Suite 202, New York, NY 10019, USA (office). *Telephone:* (212) 421-2021 (office). *Website:* www.liebermangt.com (office); www.bbking.com.

KING, Billie Jean; American fmr tennis player; *Chair, USA Tennis High Performance Committee, United States Tennis Association;* b. 22 Nov. 1943, Long Beach, Calif.; d. of Willard J. Moffitt; m. Larry King 1965 (divorced); ed Los Angeles State Univ.; amateur player 1958–67, turned professional 1967; Australian champion 1968; Italian champion 1970; French champion 1972; Wimbledon champion 1966, 1967, 1968, 1972, 1973, 1975; US Open champion 1967, 1971, 1972, 1974; FRG champion 1971; South African champion 1966, 1967, 1969; won record 20 Wimbledon titles (six singles, 10 doubles, four mixed) and played more than 100 matches; had won 1,046 singles victories by 1984; sports commentator, ABC-TV 1975–78; f. Women's Tennis Asscn 1973; Publisher, Women Sports 1974–; Commr, US Tennis Team 1981–; CEO World TeamTennis 1985–; Capt. US Fed. Cup Team 1995–2004; Chair US Tennis Asscn (USTA) Tennis High Performance Cttee 2005–; Women's Olympic Tennis Coach 1996, 2000; Consultant, Virginia Slims Championship Series; nat. amb. for AIM children's charity; Top Woman Athlete of the Year Award 1973; Lifetime Achievement Award, March of Dimes 1994, Sarah Palfrey Danzig Award 1995, Flo Hyman Award 1997, Presidential Medal of Freedom 2009. *Achievements:* US Tennis Asscn (USTA) opened the Billie Jean King National Tennis Center 2006. *Publications:* Tennis to Win 1970, Billie Jean (with Kim Chapin) 1974, We Have Come a Long Way: The Story of Women's Tennis 1988. *Leisure interests:* ballet, movies. *Address:* USA Tennis High Performance Program, Home Depot Center, 18400 Avalon Boulevard, Suite 600,

Carson, CA 90746, USA (office). *Website:* www.highperformance.usta.com/home/default.sps (office).

KING, Sir David Anthony, Kt, BSc, MA, PhD, ScD, FRS, FRSC, FInstP; British academic and research scientist; *Director of Research, Department of Chemistry, University of Cambridge;* b. 12 Aug. 1939, Durban, South Africa; s. of Arnold King and Patricia Vardy; m. Jane Lichtenstein 1983; three s. one d.; ed St John's Coll., Johannesburg, Univ. of Witwatersrand, Johannesburg, Imperial Coll. London; Lecturer in Chemical Physics, Univ. of East Anglia 1966–74; Brunner Prof. of Physical Chem., Univ. of Liverpool 1974–88, Head, Dept of Inorganic, Physical and Industrial Chem. 1983–88; 1920 Prof. of Physical Chem., Dept of Chem., Univ. of Cambridge 1988, Head, Dept of Chem. 1993–2000, now Dir of Research, Dept of Chem.; Fellow, St John's Coll. 1988–95; Queen's Coll. 2001–, Master of Downing Coll. 1995–2000; Chief Scientific Adviser to UK Govt and Head, Office of Science and Tech. 2000–07; Dir Smith School of Enterprise and the Environment, Univ. of Oxford 2008–12; Ed. Chemical Physics Letters 1990–2001; Pres. Asscn of Univ. Teachers 1976–77; Chair. British Vacuum Council 1982–85; mem. Comité de Direction, Centre Cinétique et Physique, Nancy 1974–81, Research Awards Advisory Cttee Leverhulme Trust 1980–91 (Chair. 1995–2001), Direction Cttee (Beirat) Fritz Haber Inst., Berlin 1981–93; Chair. European Science Foundation Programme 'Gas–Surface Interactions' 1991–96, Kettle's Yard Gallery, Cambridge 1989–2001; Sr Scientific Adviser to UBS; Pres. BAAS; Assoc. Fellow, Third World Acad. of Sciences 2000; Foreign mem. American Acad. of Arts and Sciences 2002; Hon. Fellow, Indian Acad. of Sciences, Downing Coll., Univ. of Cardiff 2001; Hon. Prof., Qingdao Univ., People's Repub. of China; Hon. Life Fellow, Royal Soc. of Arts 2006; Hon. DSc (Liverpool) 2001, (East Anglia) 2001, (Stockholm) 2003, (Genoa) 2002, (Leicester) 2002, Cardiff (2002), (Witwatersrand) 2003, (St Andrews) 2003, (York) 2004, (Oxford Brookes) 2007; Shell Scholar 1963–66, RSC Awards, Surface Chem. 1978, RSC Tilden Lecturer 1988, Medal for Research, British Vacuum Council 1991, Liverside Lectureship and Medal 1997–98, Royal Soc. Rumford Medal 2003. *Publications:* The Chemical Physics of Solid Surfaces and Heterogeneous Catalysis (seven vols) (co-ed. with D. P. Woodruff) 1980–94, The Hot Topic: How to Tackle Global Warming and Still Keep the Lights On (with Gabrielle Walker) 2008, Energy, Transport & the Environment (jtly) 2012; over 450 original publs in scientific literature. *Leisure interests:* photography, art, philosophy. *Address:* Department of Chemistry, University of Cambridge, Lensfield Road, Cambridge, CB2 1EN (office); 20 Glisson Road, Cambridge, CB1 2EW, England (home). *Telephone:* (1223) 336338 (office); (1223) 315629 (home). *Fax:* (1223) 762829 (office). *E-mail:* dak10@cam.ac.uk (office). *Website:* www.ch.cam.ac.uk (office).

KING, Don; American boxing promoter; b. 20 Aug. 1931, Cleveland; s. of Clarence King and Hattie King; m. Henrietta King; two s. one d.; convicted of manslaughter and justifiable homicide; boxing promoter 1972–; Owner, Don King Productions Inc. 1974–; fighters promoted include: Muhammad Ali (q.v.), Sugar Ray Leonard (q.v.), Mike Tyson (q.v.), Ken Norton, Joe Frazier, Larry Holmes (q.v.), Roberto Durán (q.v.), Tim Witherspoon, George Foreman (q.v.), Evander Holyfield (q.v.); f. Don King Foundation and actively supports other charities including The Martin Luther King Jr Foundation; Int. Boxing Hall of Fame 1997. *Address:* c/o Don King Productions Inc., 501 Fairway Drive, Deerfield Beach, FL 33441, USA (office). *E-mail:* info@donking.com. *Website:* www.donking.com.

KING, Gayle; American journalist, editor, television presenter and actress; *Co-Host, CBS This Morning;* b. 28 Dec. 1954, Chevy Chase, Md; m. William G. Bumpus 1983 (divorced 1993); one s. one d.; ed Univ. of Maryland; spent several years of her childhood in Ankara, Turkey before returning with her family to the USA; worked at several TV stations from 1976, including WDAF-TV, Kansas City, Mo., WJZ-TV, Baltimore, Md and WTOP-TV, Washington, DC; worked as TV news anchor for CBS affiliate WFSB-TV, Hartford, Conn. 1981–99; briefly co-hosted with Robin Wagner NBC daytime talk show Cover to Cover 1991; own syndicated talk show, The Gayle King Show 1997; Ed., O, The Oprah Magazine, CBS News & Hearst 1999, now Ed.-at-Large; also worked as a special corresp. for The Oprah Winfrey Show and Good Morning America; began hosting The Gayle King Show on XM Satellite Radio 2006; hosted The Gayle King Show (live, weekday TV interview programme) on OWN: The Oprah Winfrey Network 2011–12; Co-host, with Charlie Rose and Norah O'Donnell, CBS This Morning 2012–; three Emmy Awards, American Women in Radio & Television Gracie Award for Outstanding Radio Talk Show 2008, Individual Achievement Award for Host-Entertainment/Information 2010, New York Women in Communications' Matrix Award 2010. *Film roles:* A Little Bit of Lipstick 2000, The Manchurian Candidate 2004. *Address:* CBS News, 555 West 57th Street, New York, NY 10019, USA (office). *Telephone:* (212) 975-4114 (office). *Website:* www.cbsnews.com (office).

KING, Ian; British business executive; *Chief Executive, BAE Systems plc;* m.; one s.; began career as grad. entrant at Marconi 1976, worked in manufacturing at co.'s defence electronics manufacturing operations in Scotland and Portsmouth 1976–86, Finance Dir, Marconi Defence Systems 1986–92, Finance Dir, Marconi Electronic Systems 1992–98, apptd non-exec. Dir Canadian Marconi Co. and Dir Marconi's two Anglo/French jt ventures in Space and Sonar, first Chief Exec. Alenia Marconi Systems (jt venture between Marconi and Finmeccanica of Italy formed in Dec. 1998), Group Strategy and Planning Dir responsible for initial Strategic Business Plan for BAE Systems (following merger of British Aerospace and Marconi Nov. 1999) 1999–2001, Group Man. Dir for Customer Solutions & Support 2001–07, mem. Bd of Dirs and COO, UK and Rest of the World, BAE Systems plc 2007–, Chief Exec. 2008–; Dir (non-exec.) Rotork plc. *Leisure interests:* ball sports, especially golf, football and cricket, lifetime supporter of Portsmouth Football Club. *Address:* BAE Systems plc, 6 Carlton Gardens, London, SW1Y 5AD, England (office). *Telephone:* (1252) 373232 (office). *Fax:* (1252) 383000 (office). *E-mail:* webmasterplc@baesystems.com (office). *Website:* www.baesystems.com (office).

KING, Ivan Robert, PhD; American astronomer and academic; *Research Professor, Astronomy Department, University of Washington;* b. 25 June 1927, New York, NY; s. of Myram King and Anne King; m. 1st Alice Greene 1952 (divorced 1982); two s. two d.; m. 2nd Judith Ann Schultz 2002; ed Woodmere Acad., Hamilton Coll., Harvard Univ.; served in USNR 1952–54; Methods Analyst, US Dept of Defence 1952–56; Asst Prof., then Assoc. Prof., Univ. of Illinois 1956–64; Assoc. Prof. of Astronomy, Univ. of California, Berkeley 1964–66, Prof.

1966–93, Prof. Emer. 1993–, Chair. Astronomy Dept 1967–70; Research Prof., Astronomy Dept, Univ. of Washington 2002–; Pres. American Astronomical Soc. 1978–80; mem. AAAS, Fellow, Chair. Astronomy Section 1973; mem. NAS, American Acad. of Arts & Sciences; Hon. Laurea (Univ. of Padua) 2002; Hon. ScD (Hamilton Coll.) 2005; Sec. of the Navy Commendation, USN 1954, George Darwin Lecturer, Royal Astronomical Soc. 1978. *Publications:* The Universe Unfolding 1976, The Milky Way as a Galaxy 1990; more than 200 articles in scientific journals. *Address:* Astronomy Department, University of Washington, Physics-Astronomy Bldg, B372, 3910 15th Avenue NE, Seattle, WA 98195, USA (office). *E-mail:* king@astro.washington.edu (office). *Website:* www.astro.washington.edu/king (office).

KING, Justin Matthew, CBE; British retail executive; b. 17 May 1961, Stepney, London, England; m. Claire Simmons 1990; ed Tudor Grange Grammar School (later Comprehensive School), Solihull, Solihull Sixth Form Coll., Univ. of Bath; following graduation, worked for Mars, became production shift man. on Galaxy chocolate; joined PepsiCo 1989, based in Middle East; moved to Grand Metropolitan 1990, as Man. Dir helped launch Häagen-Dazs ice-cream in UK; held various sr positions at Asda Hypermarkets in trading and human resources divs, including Retail Man. Dir 1994–2001; Dir of Food, Marks & Spencer plc 2001–04; CEO J Sainsbury plc 2004–14, also Chair. Operating Bd; Dir (non-exec.) Staples, Inc. 2007–; mem. Bd London Organising Cttee of the Olympic Games and Paralympic Games 2009–13; mem. Prime Minister's Business Advisory Group 2010–12; mem. Pres.'s Cttee, Confed. of British Industry; Patron of Skillsmart Retail; Visiting Fellow, Centre for Corporate Reputation, Univ. of Oxford; Amb. for The Scout Asscn. *Address:* c/o J Sainsbury plc, 33 Holborn, London, EC1N 2HT, England.

KING, Larry; American broadcaster; b. (Lawrence Harvey Zeiger), 19 Nov. 1933, Brooklyn; s. of Eddie Zeiger and Jennie Zeiger; m. 1st Frida Miller 1952; m. 2nd Alene Akins 1961 (divorced 1963, remarried 1967, divorced 1971); one d.; m. 3rd Mickey Sutphin 1993 (divorced 1993); m. 4th Sharon Lepore 1976 (divorced 1984); m. 5th Julia Alexander 1989, (divorced 1992); one s.; m. 6th Shawn Southwick 1997; two c.; disc jockey with various radio stations, Miami, Fla 1957–71; freelance writer and broadcaster 1972–75; radio personality, Station WIOD, Miami 1975–78; writer, entertainment sections of Miami Herald for seven years; host, The Larry King Show (radio talk show) 1978–94, WLA-TV Let's Talk, Washington, DC; host Larry King Live (TV) 1985–2010; host Larry King Now (web series 2012–; columnist, USA Today, Sporting News; f. Larry King Cardiac Foundation; Dr hc (George Washington Univ.), (New England Inst. of Tech.), (Brooklyn Coll.), (Pratt Inst.); Talk Show Host of the Year, Nat. Asscn of Radio Talk Show Hosts 1993, Scopus Award, American Friends of Hebrew Univ. 1994, Golden Plate Award, American Acad. of Achievement 1996, Mahoney Award, Harvard Univ. 2000, March of Dimes' Franklin Delano Roosevelt Award 2000. *Films:* appeared as himself in films Ghostbusters 1984, Lost in America 1985, Crazy People 1990, Exorcist III 1990, Dave 1993, Spin 1995, Open Season 1996, Contact 1997, The Jackal 1997, Primary Colors 1998, Bulworth 1998, Enemy of the State 1998, The Kid 2000, The Contender 2000, America's Sweethearts 2001, John Q 2002, Marilyn's Man 2004, Shrek 2 (voice) 2004, The Stepford Wives 2004, Mr 3000 2004, Shrek the Third (voice) 2007. *Publications:* Mr King, You're Having a Heart Attack (with B. D. Colen) 1989, Larry King: Tell Me More, When You're from Brooklyn, Everything Else is Tokyo 1992, On the Line (jtly) 1993, Daddy Day, Daughter Day (jtly) 1997, My Remarkable Journey (with Cal Fussman) 2009. *Address:* c/o CNN Larry King Live, 820 1st Street, NE, Washington, DC 20002, USA (office).

KING, Mary Elizabeth, MBE; British horse rider; b. 8 June 1961, Newark-on-Trent, Notts.; d. of the late Lt-Commdr M. D. H. Thomson; m. David King 1995; one s. one d.; ed Manor House School, Honiton, King's Grammar School, Ottery St Mary, Evendine Court (Cordon Bleu); team gold medals 1991, 1994, 1995, 1997, 2007; rep. GB in Equestrian Eventing Team at Olympic Games in Barcelona 1992, Atlanta 1996, Sydney 2000, Athens 2004, Beijing 2008, London 2012; Team Silver Medal, Athens 2004, London 2012, Team Bronze Medal, Beijing 2008; British Open champion 1991, 1992, 1996, 2007; winner Badminton Horse Trials 1992, 2000, Burghley Horse Trials 1996; broke her neck in 2001, but made full recovery; mem. winning GBI team at Burghley Horse Trials 2001; fmr Watch Leader on 'Sir Winston Churchill' tall ship; Team Silver Medal, World Equestrian Games 2006; Team Gold and Individual Silver at European Championships, Italy 2007. *Publications:* Mary Thomson's Eventing Year 1993, All the King's Horses 1997, William and Mary 1998, Mary King: The Autobiography 2009. *Leisure interests:* tennis, snow and water skiing. *Address:* Thorn House, Salcombe Regis, Sidmouth, Devon, EX10 0JH, England (office). *Telephone:* (1395) 515842 (office). *Fax:* (1392) 258846 (office).

KING, Maurice Athelstan, QC, LLB; Barbadian lawyer, politician and diplomatist; b. 1 Jan. 1936; s. of James Cliviston King and Caroline Constance King; m. Patricia A. Williams; one s. one d.; ed Harrison Coll., Barbados, Univ. of Manchester and Gray's Inn, London; lawyer in pvt. practice 1960–; Chair. Natural Gas Corpn 1964–76; mem. Barbados Senate 1967–75; Gen. Sec. Democratic Labour Party 1968–69; Amb. to USA and Perm. Rep. to OAS Jan.–Sept. 1976; mem. Parl. 1981–; Attorney-Gen. and Minister of Legal Affairs 1986–91, Attorney-Gen. 1991–94 and Minister of Foreign Affairs 1991–93, of Justice and CARICOM Affairs 1993–94. *Leisure interests:* music, tennis, reading, swimming. *Address:* Radstan Court, Chapman Street, St Michael, Barbados (office). *Telephone:* 426-0847 (office). *Fax:* 426-0849 (office).

KING, Sir Mervyn Allister, Kt, GBE, BA, FBA; British economist, academic and central banker; b. 30 March 1948; s. of Eric Frank King and Kathleen Alice Passingham; ed Wolverhampton Grammar School, King's Coll., Cambridge, Harvard Univ. (Kennedy Scholar), USA; Jr Research Officer, Dept of Applied Econs, Univ. of Cambridge, mem. Cambridge Growth Project 1969–73, Research Officer 1972–76, Lecturer, Faculty of Econs 1976–77; Esmée Fairbairn Prof. of Investment, Univ. of Birmingham 1977–84; Prof. of Econs, LSE 1984–95, f. Financial Markets Group; Dir (non-exec.) Bank of England 1990–91, Exec. Dir and Chief Economist 1991–98, Deputy Gov. (Monetary Policy) 1998–2003, Gov. 2003–13; Pres. Inst. of Fiscal Studies 1999–2003; Research Officer, Kennedy School at Harvard Univ., USA 1971–72, Visiting Prof. of Econs 1982–; Visiting Prof. of Econs MIT 1983–84, LSE 1996–; Visiting Fellow, Nuffield Coll. Oxford 2002–03; Chair. OECD's Working Party 3 (WP3) Cttee 2001–03; Co-Dir LSE Financial Markets Group 1987–91; Man. Ed. Review of Economic Studies 1978–83;

Founding mem. Monetary Policy Cttee 1997; mem. City Capital Markets Cttee 1989–91; Bd mem. The Securities Asscn 1987–89; mem. Council and Exec. Cttee Royal Econ. Soc. 1981–86, 1992–97; mem. Council, European Econ. Asscn (Pres. 1993); Research Assoc., Nat. Bureau of Econ. Research; Assoc. mem. Inst. of Fiscal and Monetary Policy, Ministry of Finance, Japan 1986–91; mem. Group of Thirty Consultative Group on Int. Econ. and Monetary Affairs, Inc. (G-30), Washington, DC 1997–, Advisory Council of the London Symphony Orchestra 2001; mem. Cttee All England Lawn Tennis and Croquet Club; Patron, Worcester Co. Cricket Club; Trustee, Nat. Gallery; mem. Acad. Europaea 1992; Fellow, Econometric Soc. 1982; Hon. Sr Scholarship and Richards Prize, King's Coll. Cambridge 1969; Hon. Fellow, St John's Coll., Cambridge 1997, King's Coll. Cambridge 2004; Foreign Hon. Mem. American Acad. of Arts and Sciences 2000; Hon. Life Mem. Inst. for Fiscal Studies 2006; Dr hc (London Guildhall Univ.) 2001, (Birmingham) 2002, (City Univ., London) 2002, (LSE) 2003, (Wolverhampton) 2003, (Edin.) 2005, (Helsinki) 2006, (Cambridge) 2006; Wrenbury Scholarship, Univ. of Cambridge 1969, Stevenson Prize, Univ. of Cambridge 1970, Kennedy Scholarship and Harkness Fellowship 1971, Medal of Univ. of Helsinki 1982. *Publications:* Public Policy and the Corporation 1977, The British Tax System (with J. A. Kay), Indexing for Inflation (co-ed. with T. Liesner) 1975, The Taxation of Income from Capital Growth (co-author) 1984; numerous articles in various journals. *Address:* c/o Bank of England, Threadneedle Street, London, EC2R 8AH, England.

KING, Phillip, CBE, MA (Cantab.); British sculptor; *Professor Emeritus, Royal College of Art*; b. 1 May 1934, Tunis, Tunisia; s. of the late Thomas J. King and Gabrielle Liautard; m. 1st Lilian Odelle 1957 (divorced 1987); one s. (deceased); m. 2nd Judith Corbalis 1991; ed Mill Hill School, Christ's Coll., Cambridge, St Martin's School of Art, London; Asst to Henry Moore 1957–59; taught at St Martin's School of Art 1959–74; Prof. of Sculpture, Royal Coll. of Art 1980–90, Prof. Emer. 1991–; Prof. of Sculpture, RA 1990–99, Pres. 1999–2004; Trustee, Tate Gallery 1967–69; mem. Art Panel, Arts Council 1977–79; Hon. Fellow, Christ Coll., Cambridge 2002–; 1st Prize Int. Sculpture exhbn, Piestany (Czechoslovakia) 1968. *Leisure interest:* holidays in Corsica close to both land and sea. *Address:* c/o Royal College of Art, Kensington Gore, London, SW7 2EU, England.

KING, Stephen Edwin, (Richard Bachman, John Swithen), BS; American writer and screenwriter; b. 21 Sept. 1947, Portland, Me; s. of Donald Edwin King and Nellie Ruth King (née Pillsbury); m. Tabitha J. Spruce 1971; two s. one d.; ed Univ. of Maine; teacher of English, Hampden Acad., Me 1971–73; Writer-in-Residence, Univ. of Maine, Orono 1978–79; mem. Authors' Guild of America, Screen Artists' Guild, Screen Writers of America, Writers' Guild; Medal for Distinguished Contribution to American Letters, Nat. Book Foundation 2003, World Fantasy Award for Life Achievement 2004, Canadian Booksellers Asscn Lifetime Achievement Award 2007, Grand Master Award, Mystery Writers of America 2007. *Television:* Kingdom Hospital. *Publications:* novels: Carrie 1974, Salem's Lot 1975, The Shining 1976, The Stand 1978, The Dead Zone 1979, Firestarter 1980, Cujo 1981, Different Seasons 1982, The Dark Tower I: The Gunslinger 1982, Christine 1983, Pet Cemetery 1983, The Talisman (with Peter Straub) 1984, It 1986, The Eyes of the Dragon 1987, Misery 1987, The Dark Tower II: The Drawing of the Three 1987, Tommyknockers 1987, The Dark Half 1989, The Dark Tower III: The Waste Lands 1991, Needful Things 1991, Gerald's Game 1992, Dolores Claiborne 1992, Insomnia 1994, Rose Madder 1995, Desperation 1996, The Green Mile (serial novel) 1996, The Dark Tower IV: Wizard and Glass 1997, Bag of Bones 1997, The Girl Who Loved Tom Gordon 1999, Hearts in Atlantis 1999, Riding the Bullet 2000, The Plant (serial novel) 2000, Dreamcatcher 2001, Black House (with Peter Straub) 2001, From a Buick 8 2002, The Dark Tower: The Gunslinger: Revised and Expanded Edition 2003, The Dark Tower V: Wolves of the Calla 2003, The Dark Tower VI: Song of Susannah 2004, The Dark Tower VII: The Dark Tower 2004, The Colorado Kid 2005, Cell 2006, Lisey's Story 2006, Blaze 2007, Duma Key 2008, Under the Dome 2009, Full Dark, No Stars (e-book) 2010, 11/22/63 2011, It: The 25th Anniversary Special Edition 2011, The Dark Tower: The Wind Through the Keyhole 2012, A Face in the Crowd (e-book) 2012, Doctor Sleep 2013, Joyland 2013; other: Night Shift (short stories) 1978, Danse Macabre (non-fiction) 1980, Different Seasons (short stories) 1982, Creepshow (comic book) 1982, Cycle of the Werewolf (illustrated novel) 1984, Skeleton Crew (short stories) 1985, Four Past Midnight (short stories) 1990, Nightmares and Dreamscapes (short stories) 1993, Head Down (story) 1993, Six Stories (short stories) 1997, Storm of the Century (screenplay) 1999, On Writing: A Memoir of the Craft (revised edn as Secret Windows) 2000, Everything's Eventual: 14 Dark Tales (short stories) 2002, Faithful (non-fiction, with Stewart O'Nan) 2005, Just After Sunset (short stories) 2008, Blockade Billy (novella) 2010, Full Dark, No Stars (short stories) 2010, 11/22/63 2011, numerous short stories, screenplays and television plays; as Richard Bachman: Rage 1977, The Long Walk 1979, Roadwork 1981, The Running Man 1982, Thinner 1984, The Regulators 1996, Blaze 2007. *Address:* 49 Florida Avenue, Bangor, ME 04401, USA (office). *Website:* www.stephenking.com (office).

KING, Stephenson; Saint Lucia politician; b. 13 Nov. 1958; m. Rosella Nestor 2008; MP for Castries North 2006–; Minister for Health and Labour Relations 2006–07, of Finance (including Int. Financial Services), External Affairs, Home Affairs and Nat. Security 2007–11, Prime Minister 2007–11; mem. United Workers Party. *Address:* c/o Office of the Prime Minister, Greaham Louisy Administrative Bldg, 5th Floor, Waterfront, Castries, Saint Lucia (office).

KING AKERELE, Olu Banke (Bankie), BA, MA; Liberian politician; b. 11 May 1946, granddaughter of fmr Liberian Pres. Charles D. B. King; ed Univ. of Ibadan, Nigeria, Brandeis Univ., Northeastern Univ., Colombia Univ., USA; Sr Planning Officer, Ministry of Planning and Econ. Affairs 1968–69, Deputy Dir Nat. Social Security and Welfare Corpn 1975–80; Deputy Dir UNIFEM 1982–89, Deputy Resident Rep. of UN in Senegal 1989–91, UNDP Rep. in Mauritius and the Seychelles 1991–94, Man. Dir Country Strategy and Program Devt Div., UNIDO 1994–96, Chief, E and Cen. Africa Div. Regional Bureau for Africa, UNDP 1996–97, Country Programme Advisor UNDP Africa 1998, UNDP Resident Rep. and Resident Co-ordinator UN System Operational activities for Devt in Zambia 1998–2003, Programme Co-ordinator UNDP-UNESCO Project Foundations for Africa's Future Leadership, UNESCO's Regional Officer for Educ. in Africa, 2006; Minister of Commerce and Industry 2006–07, of Foreign Affairs 2007–10; Order Distinguished Services, Second Div. (Zambia); Liberian Business Asscn Award.

Address: c/o Ministry of Foreign Affairs, Mamba Point, PO Box 10-9002, 1000 Monrovia 10, Liberia.

KING-HELE, Desmond George, MA, FRS; British writer and scientist; b. 3 Nov. 1927, Seaford, Sussex; s. of late S. G. King-Hele and Mrs B. King-Hele; m. Marie Newman 1954 (separated 1992); two d.; ed Epsom Coll. and Trinity Coll., Cambridge; Royal Aircraft Establishment, Farnborough 1948–88 (research on earth's gravity field and upper atmosphere by analysis of satellite orbits), Deputy Chief Scientific Officer, Space Dept 1968–88; mem. Int. Acad. of Astronautics 1961–; Chair. British Nat. Cttee for the History of Science, Medicine and Tech. 1985–89, History of Science Grants Cttee 1990–93; Ed. Notes and Records of the Royal Soc. 1989–96; Bakerian Lecturer, Royal Soc. 1974, Wilkins Lecturer, Royal Soc. 1997; Hon. DSc (Univ. of Aston) 1979, Hon. DUniv (Univ. of Surrey) 1986; Soc. of Authors' Medical History Prize 1999; Eddington Medal, Royal Astronomical Soc. 1971, Chree Medal, Inst. of Physics 1971, Nordberg Medal, Int. Cttee on Space Research 1990. *Radio:* dramas: A Mind of Universal Sympathy 1973, The Lunaticks 1978. *Publications:* Shelley: His Thought and Work 1960, Satellites and Scientific Research 1960, Erasmus Darwin 1963, Theory of Satellite Orbits in an Atmosphere 1964, Observing Earth Satellites 1966, Essential Writings of Erasmus Darwin 1968, The End of the Twentieth Century? 1970, Poems and Trixies 1972, Doctor of Revolution 1977, Letters of Erasmus Darwin 1981, Animal Spirits 1983, Erasmus Darwin and the Romantic Poets 1986, Satellite Orbits in an Atmosphere 1987, The R.A.E. Table of Earth Satellites 1957–1989, 1990, A Tapestry of Orbits 1992, John Herschel 1992, Erasmus Darwin: A Life of Unequalled Achievement 1999, Antic and Romantic 2000, Charles Darwin's The Life of Erasmus Darwin 2002, The Collected Letters of Erasmus Darwin 2006, The Shorter Poems of Erasmus Darwin (with Stuart Harris) 2012; more than 400 scientific or literary papers in various learned journals. *Leisure interests:* playing tennis, savouring the beauties of nature, writing verse. *Address:* 7 Hilltops Court, 65 North Lane, Buriton, Hants., GU31 5RS, England (home). *Telephone:* (1730) 261646 (home).

KING OF BOW, Baroness (Life Peer), cr. 2011, of Bow in the London Borough of Tower Hamlets; **Oona Tamsyn King,** BA (Hons); British broadcaster, journalist, writer and fmr politician; *Head of Diversity, Channel 4 Television;* b. 22 Oct. 1967, Sheffield, S Yorks.; d. of Preston King and Murreil Hazel Sterns; niece of Tom Stoppard and Miriam Stoppard; m. Tiberio Santomarco 1994; one s. one d. (both adopted); ed Haverstock Comprehensive Secondary School, London, Univ. of York, Univ. of California, Berkeley, USA; worked as trade union organizer for GMB Southern Region representing low-paid workers; spent five years as a researcher at European Parl. in Brussels and Strasbourg; worked as political asst to Glyn Ford MEP, Labour Party Leader in European Parl., and later Glenys Kinnock MEP; MP for Bethnal Green & Bow 1997–2005, Parl. Pvt. Sec. to Cabinet Minister for Trade & Industry, apptd to Int. Devt Select Cttee, Urban Affairs Select Cttee; Sr Policy Adviser on Equalities and Diversity and Faith to Prime Minister Gordon Brown 2008; Founding Chair. All-Party Parl. Group on Genocide Prevention, House of Commons; Chair. Inst. for Community Cohesion (iCoCo), Rich Mix Cultural Foundation; fmr Chair. All-Party Group on Business Services; fmr Vice-Chair. British Council, London Labour MPs; fmr Treas. Friends of Islam; Head of Diversity, Channel 4 TV 2009–; unsuccessfully challenged Ken Livingstone for Labour nomination for 2012 Mayor of London election 2010; writes for several newspapers, including the Guardian, New Statesman, Sunday Telegraph and the Observer; presenter of radio and TV documentaries; has presented parts of Open Univ. W100 course (Introduction to Law); Assoc. Fellow, Chatham House (Royal Inst. of Int. Affairs). *Television:* appearances on This Week, The Daily Politics Show, The All Star Talent Show and Have I Got News For You; hosted BBC documentary American Prophet on Martin Luther King Jr and the deep South. *Publication:* The Oona King Diaries: House Music 2007. *Leisure interests:* cinema, dance music (especially house music), cooking, history, walking in Mile End Park. *Address:* Head of Diversity, Channel 4 Enquiries, PO Box 1058, Belfast, BT1 9DU, Northern Ireland (office); House of Lords, Westminster, London, SW1A 0PW, England. *Telephone:* 0845-076-0191 (from within UK) (office); (20) 7219-3000; (7583) 006923 (mobile). *Fax:* (20) 7219-5979. *E-mail:* info@oonaking.com. *Website:* www.channel4.com (office); www.oonaking.com.

KING OF BRIDGWATER, Baron (Life Peer), cr. 2001, of Bridgwater in the County of Somerset; **Thomas (Tom) Jeremy King,** PC, CH, MA; British politician; b. 13 June 1933, Glasgow; s. of John H. King and Mollie King; m. Elizabeth J. Tilney 1960; one s. one d.; ed Rugby School and Emmanuel Coll., Cambridge; in packaging and printing industry 1958–70; MP for Bridgwater 1970–2001; Parl. Pvt. Sec. to Rt Hon Christopher Chataway 1970–74; Shadow Spokesman for Energy 1976–79; Minister for Local Govt 1979–83; Sec. of State for the Environment Jan.–June 1983 for Transport June–Oct. 1983, for Employment 1983–85, for NI 1985–89, for Defence 1989–92; Chair. Intelligence and Security Cttee 1994–2001; Chair. London Int. Exhbn Centre (Excel London) 1994–2007, Dir 2007–; Dir (non-exec.) Electra Investment Trust 1992–2008; mem. Nolan Cttee on Standards in Public Life 1994–97; Conservative. *Leisure interests:* cricket, skiing, forestry. *Address:* House of Lords, Westminster, London, SW1A 0PW, England (office).

KINGA, Dasho Sonam, BA, MA, PhD; Bhutanese politician; *Chairperson, National Council;* b. 6 June 1973, Galing, Shongphu, Trashigan; ed Sherubtse Coll., Kyoto Univ., Japan, Lestor B. Pearson Coll., Canada; Ed. Bhutan Observer; Sr Program Officer, Save the Children US, Thimphu; Sr Research Officer, Centre for Bhutan Studies (govt think-tank), Thimphu; Publication Officer, CAPSD, Ministry of Educ.; mem. Nat. Film and TV Review Bd 1999–2003; mem. Bd of Dirs BBSC-Nat. Radio Television 2002–04; MP for Trashigang in the Nat. Council (Parl.) 2007–; Chair. House Cttee, fmr Chair. Good Governance Cttee, Deputy Chair. Nat. Council 2009–13, Chair. 2013–; Visiting Research Fellowship, Inst. of Developing Economies (Japan) 2001; scholarship for academic excellence, Canadian Int. Devt Agency 1991, First Place, Royal Civil Service Examination 1997, Red Scarf by HM the King 2012. *Publications include:* Gaylong Sumdar Tashi (trans. of 18th century autobiographical poem from Dzongkha to English) 1998, Changes in Bhutanese Social Structure: Impact of 50 Years of Reforms 1952–2002, Flying Rocks, Speaking Statues: Writings on Bhutanese History, Myth and Culture 2004, Polity, Kingship and Democracy: A Biography of the Bhutanese State 2009; numerous articles published in Bhutan and abroad. *Address:* National

Council Secretariat, Langjophakha, PO Box 200, Thimphu, Bhutan (office). *Telephone:* (2) 336616 (office). *Fax:* (2) 325543 (office). *E-mail:* skinga@ nationalcouncil.bt (office). *Website:* www.nationalcouncil.bt (office).

KINGMAN, Sir John Frank Charles, Kt, ScD, CStat, FRS; British mathematician, statistician and academic; b. 28 Aug. 1939, Beckenham; s. of the late Frank E. T. Kingman and Maud Elsie Kingman (née Harley); m. Valerie Cromwell 1964; one s. one d.; ed Christ's Coll., Finchley, London, Pembroke Coll., Cambridge; Asst Lecturer in Math., Univ. of Cambridge 1962–64, Lecturer 1964–65; Reader in Math. and Statistics, Univ. of Sussex 1965–66, Prof. 1966–69; Prof. of Math., Univ. of Oxford 1969–85; Chair. Science and Eng Research Council 1981–85; Vice-Chancellor Univ. of Bristol 1985–2001; N M Rothschild Professorship of Mathematical Sciences and Dir Isaac Newton Inst. for Mathematical Sciences, Univ. of Cambridge 2001–06; mem. council British Tech. Group 1984–92; mem. Bd British Council 1986–91; Pres. London Math. Society 1990–92; Chair. Statistics Comm. 2000–03; Hon. Fellow, St Anne's Coll., Oxford, Pembroke Coll., Cambridge; Hon. Senator Univ. of Hannover; Officier des Palmes académiques; Hon. DSc (Sussex) 1983, (Southampton) 1985, Hon. LLD (Bristol) 1989, (Queen's Univ., Univ.) 1999. *Publications:* Introduction to Measure and Probability (with S. J. Taylor) 1966, The Algebra of Queues 1966, Regenerative Phenomena 1972, Mathematics of Genetic Diversity 1980, Poisson Processes 1993. *Address:* c/o Isaac Newton Institute for Mathematical Sciences, 20 Clarkson Road, Cambridge, CB3 0EH, England (office).

KINGSLEY, Sir Ben; British actor; b. (Krishna Bhanji), 31 Dec. 1943, Scarborough; s. of Rahimtulla Harji Bhanji and Anna Leina Mary Bhanji; m. Daniela Barbosa de Carneiro 2007; three s. one d. from previous relationships; ed Manchester Grammar School; with RSC 1970–80; Nat. Theatre 1977–78; Assoc. Artist, RSC; Hon. MA (Salford Univ.), Hon. DLitt (Sussex), (Hull); Padma Shri (Govt of India) 1985. *Stage appearances include:* A Midsummer Night's Dream, Occupations, The Tempest, Hamlet (title role), The Merry Wives of Windsor, Baal, Nicholas Nickleby, Volpone, The Cherry Orchard, The Country Wife, Judgement, Statements After An Arrest, Othello (title role), Caracol in Melons, Waiting for Godot. *Television appearances include:* The Love School 1974, Kean, Silas Marner, The Train 1987, Murderous Amongst Us 1988, Sweeney Todd 1998, Anne Frank (Screen Actors' Guild Award for Best Actor 2002) 2001, several plays. *Films include:* Gandhi (two Hollywood Golden Globe Awards 1982, New York Film Critics' Award, two BAFTA Awards, Acad. Award, Los Angeles Film Critics' Award 1983), Betrayal 1982, Harem 1985, Turtle Diary 1985, Without A Clue 1988, Testimony 1988, Pascali's Island 1988, Bugsy 1991, Sneakers 1992, Innocent Moves 1992, Dave 1992, Schindler's List 1993, Death and the Maiden 1994, Species 1995, Twelfth Night 1996, The Assignment 1998, Weapons of Mass Destruction 1998, The Confession 1999, Parting Shots 1999, Spooky House 2000, What Planet Are You From? 2000, Rules of Engagement 2000, Sexy Beast (Best Actor, British Ind. Film Awards 2001) 2000, The Triumph of Love 2001, A.I. (voice) 2001, Tuck Everlasting 2002, House of Sand and Fog 2003, Thunderbirds 2004, Suspect Zero 2004, A Sound of Thunder 2005, Oliver Twist 2005, Lucky Number Slevin 2005, BloodRayne 2005, I Have Never Forgotten You: The Life and Legacy of Simon Wiesenthal 2006, You Kill Me 2007, The Last Legion 2007, The Ten Commandments (voice) 2007, Elegy 2007, The Wackness 2007, Transsiberian 2008, War, Inc. 2008, The Love Guru 2008, Fifty Dead Men Walking 2008, Shutter Island 2010, 1001 Inventions and the Library of Secrets 2010, Prince of Persia 2010, The Dictator 2012, Iron Man 3 2013. *Address:* c/o ICM, 76 Oxford Street, London, WIN 0AX, England. *Telephone:* (20) 7636-6565. *Fax:* (20) 7323-0101.

KINGSMILL, Baroness (Life Peer), cr. 2006, of Holland Park in the London Borough of Kensington and Chelsea; **Denise Patricia Byrne Kingsmill,** CBE; British lawyer; b. 24 April 1947, New Zealand; d. of Patrick Henry Byrne and Hester Jean Byrne; m. David Gordon Kingsmill 1970 (divorced 2002); one s. one d.; ed Girton Coll., Cambridge; admitted as solicitor 1980; with ICI Fibres then Int. Wool Secr. 1968–75; Robin Thompson & Partners 1979–82; Russell Jones & Walker 1982–85; Denise Kingsmill & Co. 1985–90; Partner, D.J. Freeman 1990–93; consultant, Denton Hall 1994–2000; Chair. Optimum Health Services NHS Trust 1992–99; Deputy Chair. Competition Comm. (fmrly Monopolies and Mergers Comm.) 1997–2003; apptd Head Ind. Review into Women's Employment and Pay, Dept of Trade and Industry 2001, Chair. Accounting For People Task Force –2003; Sr Adviser, Royal Bank of Scotland 2004–08; Chair. Sadler's Wells 2003–04; Deputy Chair. MFI Furniture Group 1999–2001; mem. Bd of Dirs British Airways 2004–10; Dir (non-exec.) Korn/Ferry International Ltd (executive recruiting firm), Horizon plc (IT), E.On AG Supervisory Bd; Ind. Dir (non-exec.)/ Bd mem. International Consolidated Airlines Group SA (formed by merger of British Airways and Iberia), Betfair plc (gambling products and services); mem. Microsoft European Policy Council, PWC Advisory Bd (also Deputy Chair.); mem. Bd of Dirs Home Office, Rainbow UK 1993–94, Norwich and Peterborough Building Soc. 1997–2001; fmr mem. Bd of Dirs MFI Furniture Group, Telewest Communications, Manpower UK; Trustee, Design Museum 2000–10; mem. Devt Cttee, Judge Inst., Cambridge Univ. Business School 2001–06; mem. Gov. Coll. of Law 1992–2001; fmr Pro-Chancellor Brunel Univ.; mem. (Labour) House of Lords 2006–; columnist, Management Today; Hon. Fellow, Univ. of Wales, Cardiff 2000; Hon. LLD (Brunel) 2001, (Stirling) 2003; Hon. DSc (Cranfield) 2007. *Publications:* Women's Employment and Pay Review 2001. *Leisure interests:* fly-fishing, walking. *Address:* House of Lords, Westminster, London, SW1A 0PW, England (office). *Telephone:* (20) 7219-4537 (office). *Website:* www.parliament.uk/ biographies/lords/denise-kingsmill/54155 (office).

KINGSOLVER, Barbara, MS; American writer; b. 8 April 1955, Annapolis, Md; m. Steven Hopp; two d.; ed DePauw Univ., Univ. of Arizona; scientific writer, Office of Arid Land Studies, Univ. of Ariz. 1981–85; freelance journalist 1985–87, novelist 1987–; book reviewer, New York Times 1988–, Los Angeles Times 1989–, San Francisco Chronicle, The Nation, The Progressive, The Washington Post, Women's Review of Books and others; Woodrow Wilson Foundation/Lila Wallace Fellowship 1992; est. The Bellwether Prize for Fiction: In Support of a Literature of Social Change 1997; Hon. LittD (DePauw) 1994; Nat. Writers Union Andrea Egan Award 1998, Arizona Civil Liberties Union Award 1998, Nat. Humanities Medal 2000, Best American Science and Nature Writing 2001, Gov.'s Nat. Award in the Arts, Kentucky 2002, John P. McGovern Award for the Family 2002, Physicians for Social Responsibility Nat. Award 2002, Duke LEAF Award for Lifetime Environmental Achievement in the Fine Arts 2011, Richard C. Holbrooke Distinguished Achievement Award 2011. *Publications:* The Bean Trees (Enoch Pratt Library Youth-to-Youth Books Award) 1988, Holding the Line 1989, Homeland and Other Stories 1989, Animal Dreams (Edward Abbey Award for Ecofiction, PEN/USA West Fiction Award) 1990, Another America 1992, Pigs in Heaven (Mountains and Plains Booksellers Award for Fiction, Los Angeles Times Fiction Prize) 1993, High Tide in Tucson 1995, The Poisonwood Bible (Village Voice Best Books 1998, New York Times Top Ten Books 1998, Los Angeles Times Best Books for 1998, Independence Publisher Brilliance Audio 1999, Booksense Prize 1999, Nat. Book Award (SA) 2000) 1998, Prodigal Summer 2000, Small Wonder 2002, Last Stand 2002, Animal, Vegetable, Miracle: Our Year of Seasonal Eating (American Booksellers Book of the Year Award, James Beard Foundation Award) 2007, The Lacuna (Orange Prize for Fiction 2010) 2009, Flight Behavior: A Novel 2012. *Leisure interests:* human rights, environmental conservation, natural history, farming. *Address:* PO Box 160, Meadowview, VA 24361 (office); Frances Goldin Literary Agency, 57 East 11th Street, #5B, New York, NY 10003; c/o Harper Collins, 10 East 53rd Street, New York, NY 10022, USA. *Website:* www.kingsolver.com.

KINGSTON, Arthur Edward, PhD, FRAS, FInstP, MRIA; British physicist and academic; *Professor Emeritus, Queen's University Belfast;* b. 18 Feb. 1936, Armagh, Northern Ireland; s. of Arthur Kingston and Henrietta Duff; m. Helen McCann 1962; one s. one d.; ed Royal School Armagh and Queen's Univ. Belfast; Research Fellow, Queen's Univ. 1959–60, Sr Research Fellow 1960–61; Asst Lecturer, Liverpool Univ. 1961–62, Lecturer 1962–63; Visiting Fellow, Univ. of Colorado, USA 1963–64; Lecturer, Queen's Univ. 1964–68, Sr Lecturer 1968–71, Reader 1971–83, Prof. of Theoretical Atomic Physics 1983–2000, Dean, Faculty of Science 1989–94, Provost for Science and Agric. 1994–98, Prof. Emer. 2000–; NASA Public Service Award. *Publications:* more than 260 papers in atomic physics and astrophysics. *Leisure interests:* gardening, reading. *Address:* Department of Applied Mathematics and Theoretical Physics, David Bates Building, The Queen's University of Belfast, University Road, Belfast, BT7 1NN (office); 25 Cadogan Park, Belfast, BT9 6HH, Northern Ireland (home). *Telephone:* (28) 9097-6040 (office); (28) 9066-9658 (home). *Fax:* (28) 9097-6061 (office). *E-mail:* a.kingston@qub.ac.uk (office). *Website:* www.qub.ac.uk/mp/amtp (office).

KINGSTON, Maxine Hong, BA; American author and academic; *Professor Emerita, Department of English, University of California, Berkeley;* b. 27 Oct. 1940, Stockton, Calif.; d. of Tom and Ying Lan Hong (née Chew); m. Earl Kingston 1962; one s.; ed Univ. of California, Berkeley; taught English, Sunset High School, Hayward, Calif. 1965–66, Kahuku High School, Hawaii 1967, Kahaluu Drop-In School 1968, Kailua High School 1969, Honolulu Business Coll. 1969, Mid-Pacific Inst., Honolulu 1970–77; Prof. of English, Visiting Writer, Univ. of Hawaii, Honolulu 1977; Thelma McCandless Distinguished Prof., Eastern Mich. Univ., Ypsilanti 1986; Chancellor's Distinguished Prof., Univ. of California, Berkeley 1990–, now Prof. Emer.; Mademoiselle Magazine Award 1977, Anisfield-Wolf Book Award 1978, Stockton (Calif.) Arts Comm. Award 1981, Hawaii Award for Literature 1982, NEA Writing Fellow 1980, Guggenheim Fellow 1981, named Living Treasure of Hawaii 1980, American Acad. and Inst. Award in Literature 1990, Nat. Humanities Medal 1997, Fred Cody Lifetime Achievement Award 1998, John Dos Passos Prize 1998, Ka Palapola Po'okela Award 1999, Commonwealth Club Silver Medal 2001, California State Library Gold Medal 2002, Spirituality and Health Book Award, KPFA Peace Award 2005, Red Hen Press Lifetime Achievement Award 2006, Los Angeles Times Book Festival Lifetime Achievement Award 2007, Nat. Book Foundation Medal for Distinguished ContribS to American Letters 2008. *Publications:* The Woman Warrior: Memoirs of a Girlhood Among Ghosts (Nat. Book Critics Circle Award for non-fiction) 1976, China Men (Nat. Book Award) 1981, Hawaii One Summer (Ka Palapola Po'okela Award 1999) 1987, Through The Black Curtain 1988, Tripmaster Monkey – His Fake Books (PEN USA West Award in Fiction) 1989, The Literature of California (ed.) 2001, To Be The Poet 2002; The Fifth Book of Peace 2004, Veterans of War, Veterans of Peace (ed., Northern California Book Award 2007, Pacific Justice and Reconciliation Center Peace Book Award) 2006, I Love a Broad Margin to My Life 2011; short stories, articles and poems. *Leisure interests:* roller-blading, gardening. *Address:* Department of English, University of California, 413 Wheeler Hall, Berkeley, CA 94720, USA (office). *Telephone:* (510) 643-5127 (office). *E-mail:* yinglan@berkeley.edu (office). *Website:* english.berkeley.edu (office).

KINIGI, Sylvie; Burundian civil servant, politician and UN official; b. 1952; m. (died 1993); five c.; ed Burundi Univ.; fmr exec. officer of structural adjustment programme; Prime Minister of Burundi 1993–94; fmr mem. Union pour le progrès nat. (UPRONA); fmr Sr Political Adviser and Coordinator of Programs, Special Rep. of the UN Sec.-Gen. to the Great Lakes Region in Africa; currently with Burundi Women Access Trust. *Address:* Burundi Women Access Trust, c/o Women Land Access Trusts, PO Box 18968-00100, Nairobi, Kenya. *Telephone:* 77790274. *E-mail:* skinigi@yahoo.com.

KINKEL, Klaus, LLD; German politician and lawyer; b. 17 Dec. 1936, Metzingen; s. of Ludwig Kinkel and Charlotte Klaus; m. Ursula Vogel 1961; one s. three d.; ed Bonn, Cologne, Tübingen Univs; lawyer 1962–70; Personal Aide to Hans Dietrich Genscher (q.v.) 1970–79; State Sec. Justice Ministry 1982–83, 1987–91, Justice Minister 1991–92; Minister of Foreign Affairs 1992–98; Fed. Vice-Chancellor 1992–99; Head of External Intelligence Service 1983–87; mem. Bundestag (Parl.) 1994–2002, Chair. Free Democratic Party 1993–95; Sr Adviser, Lehman Brothers Europe 2003–; mem. Advisory Bd EnBW Energie Baden-Wuerttemberg AG; mem. Int. Advisory Cttee, Robert Bosch GMBH. *Leisure interests:* jogging, tennis. *Address:* c/o Lehman Brothers, Rathenauplatz 1, 60313 Frankfurt, Germany (office). *Telephone:* (69) 153070 (office). *Fax:* (69) 153076599 (office). *Website:* www.lehman.com.

KINNEAR, Greg; American actor; b. 17 June 1963, Logansport, Ind.; s. of Edward Kinnear and Suzanne Kinnear; m. Helen Labdon 1999; ed Univ. of Ariz.; began career as marketing asst, Empire Entertainment, Los Angeles; worked as reporter for MTV; creator, co-exec. producer and host Best of the Worst TV show 1990–91; host Talk Soup TV show 1991–95, Later with Greg Kinnear 1994; Male Discovery of the Year, Golden Apple Awards 1996. *Television:* host: Best of the Worst, Talk Soup (Daytime Emmy Award (jtly) 1995), Later with Greg Kinnear; actor: Murder in Mississippi 1990, Dillinger 1991, Based on an Untrue Story 1993, Dinner with Friends 2001. *Films:* Blankman 1994, Sabrina (Most Promising Actor, Chicago Film Critics Asscn Awards 1996) 1995, Dear God 1996, A Smile Like Yours 1997, As Good as It Gets (Best Supporting Actor, NBR Awards 1997, Southeastern Film Critics Asscn Awards 1998, Golden Satellite Awards 1998) 1997, You've Got Mail (Best Supporting Actor in Comedy/Romance, Blockbuster Entertainment Awards 1999) 1998, Mystery Men 1999, What Planet Are You From? 2000, Nurse Betty 2000, Loser 2000, The Gift 2000, Someone Like You 2001, We Were Soldiers 2002, Stuck On You 2003, Godsend 2004, Robots (voice) 2005, Bad News Bears 2005, The Matador 2005, Fast Food Nation 2006, Little Miss Sunshine 2006, Invincible 2006, Unknown 2006, Feast of Love 2007, Baby Mama 2008, Ghost Town 2008, Flash of Genius 2008, Green Zone 2009. *Address:* Creative Artists Agency, 2000 Avenue of the Stars, Los Angeles, CA 90067, USA (office). *Telephone:* (424) 288-2000 (office). *Fax:* (424) 288-2900 (office). *Website:* www.caa.com (office).

KINNELL, Galway, MA; American writer and academic; b. 1 Feb. 1927, Providence, RI; s. of James S. Kinnell and Elizabeth Mills; m. 1st Inés Delgado de Torres 1965; (divorced) one s. two d.; m. 2nd Barbara K. Bristol 1997; ed Princeton Univ. and Univ. of Rochester; Guggenheim Fellow 1963–64, 1974–75, MacArthur Fellow 1984; Dir Writing Programme, New York Univ. 1981–84, Samuel F. B. Morse Prof. of Arts and Sciences 1985–92, Erich Maria Remarque Prof. of Creative Writing 1992–2005; fmr Chancellor, Acad. of American Poets; named Vt State Poet 1989–93; mem. Nat. Inst., Acad. of Arts and Letters; Award of Nat. Inst. of Arts and Letters 1962, Cecil Hemley Poetry Prize 1969, Medal of Merit 1975, Pulitzer Prize 1983, Nat. Book Award 1983, Frost Medal 2001, Wallace Stevens Award 2010. *Publications:* poetry: What a Kingdom it Was 1960, Flower Herding on Mount Monadnock 1963, Body Rags 1966, The Book of Nightmares 1971, The Avenue Bearing the Initial of Christ into the New World 1974, Mortal Acts, Mortal Words 1980, Selected Poems 1982, The Past 1985, Imperfect Thirst 1994; novel: Black Light 1966; children's story: How the Alligator Missed Breakfast 1982; trans.: The Poems of François Villon 1965, On the Motion and Immobility of Douve by Yves Bonnefoy 1968, The Lackawanna Elegy by Yvan Goll 1970, The Essential Rilke; interviews: Walking Down the Stairs 1977. *Address:* 1218 Town Road 16, Sheffield, VT 05866, USA (home).

KINNEY, Catherine R.; American securities industry executive; b. 1952; m.; ed Iona Coll., Harvard Graduate School of Business; joined New York Stock Exchange (NYSE) 1974, responsible for trading-floor operations and tech. 1986–95, Group Exec. Vice-Pres. 1995–2002, Pres., Co-COO, Exec. Vice-Chair. and mem. Bd of Dirs 2002–06, Pres. and Co-COO NYSE Group (after merger of NYSE and Archipelago) 2006–07, Pres. and Co-COO NYSE Euronext Inc., Paris (after acquisition of Euronext by NYSE) 2007, Group Exec. Vice-Pres. and Head of Global Listings 2007–09, also mem. Man. Bd; mem. Economic Club of New York; mem. Bd of Dirs MSCI Inc. 2009–, MetLife, Inc. 2002–04, 2009–, NetSuite, Inc. 2009–, New York City Ballet, Sharegift USA; Trustee, Catholic Charities of New York; Woman of the Year (Financial Women's Asscn) 2001, ranked by the Financial Times amongst Top 25 Businesswomen in Europe (18th) 2007.

KINNOCK, Baron (Life Peer), cr. 2005, of Bedwellty; **Neil Gordon Kinnock,** PC, BA; British politician; b. 28 March 1942, Tredegar, S Wales; s. of Gordon Kinnock and Mary Howells; m. Glenys Elizabeth Parry 1967; one s. one d.; ed Lewis School, Pengam, Univ. Coll., Cardiff; Pres. Univ. Coll., Cardiff Students' Union 1965–66; Tutor Organizer in Industrial and Trade Union Studies, Workers' Educational Asscn 1966–70; MP for Bedwellty 1970–83, for Islwyn 1983–95; mem. Welsh Hosp. Bd 1969–71; Parl. Pvt. Sec. to Sec. of State for Employment 1974–75; mem. Gen. Advisory Council BBC 1976–80; mem. Nat. Exec. Cttee, Labour Party 1978–94 (Chair. 1987–88); Leader of Labour Party 1983–92; Leader of the Opposition 1983–92; EU Commr with responsibility for Transport 1995–99, Vice-Pres. European Comm. 1999–2004; Chair. British Council 2004–09; Chair. Advisory Bd Heads of the Valleys Int. Motor Racing Circuit 2011–; Pres. Cardiff Univ. 1998–2009; Dir (non-exec.) Data Research Services 2005–12; mem. Bd of Trustees, RAND Europe 2010–; Hon. LLD (Wales) 1992, Alexis de Tocqueville Prize 2003. *Publications:* Wales and the Common Market 1971, Making Our Way 1986, Thorns and Roses 1992; contribs to newspapers, periodicals and books including The Future of Social Democracy 1999. *Leisure interests:* male voice choral music, opera, theatre, reading, grandchildren, rugby, soccer, cricket. *Address:* House of Lords, London, SW1A 0PW, England (office). *Telephone:* (20) 7219-8304 (office). *Fax:* (20) 7219-4599 (office). *E-mail:* kinnockn@parliament.uk (office).

KINSCH, Joseph, MSc; Luxembourg business executive; b. 2 May 1933, Esch-sur-Alzette; m. Ruth Lauxen; two s.; began career with Arbed, Burbach, Saar, Germany 1961, moved to Luxembourg HQ 1962, Dir of Accounting and Finance 1977–79, Head of Steel Processing Firms 1979–85, Group Chief Financial Officer 1985–92, apptd mem. Bd of Man. 1985, Pres. and CEO 1992–93, Chair. and CEO 1993–1998, Chair. 1998–2002, Chair. Arcelor SA (following merger of Arbed, Aceralia and Usinor and now Arcelor-Mittal) 2002–07, apptd Chair. ArcelorMittal Foundation; Hon. Pres. Union of Luxembourg Enterprises, Chamber of Commerce of the Grand-Duchy of Luxembourg; Hon. Consul of Brazil in Luxembourg; Grand Officer of the Oak Crown, Officer of the Crown, Civil and Mil. Order of Adolph of Nassau, Grand Cross of Civil Merit (Spain), Grand Officer of the Order of Leopold II (Belgium), Grand Officer of the Order of Merit (Portugal), Officier, Légion d'honneur, Grand Cross of the Order of Merit of the FRG, Commdr, Cruzeiro do Sul (Brazil), Commdr, Order of the Polar Star (Sweden), Order of Industrial Merit (South Korea); Dr hc (Sacred Heart Univ., Luxembourg) 2004. *Leisure interests:* art, golf, reading.

KINSELLA, John; Australian poet, writer, editor and publisher; b. 1963, Perth, WA; ed Univ. of Western Australia; Writer-in-Residence, Churchill Coll., Cambridge 1997; Ed. Salt literary journal; Publr and Ed. Folio (Salt) Publishing; Richard L. Thomas Prof. of Creative Writing, Kenyon Coll., USA 2001, then Prof. of English; Adjunct Prof., Edith Cowan University, Western Australia, and Prin. of the Landscape and Language Centre; Consultant Ed. Westerly (journal); Int. Ed. The Kenyon Review; Fellow, Churchill Coll., Cambridge; Western Australia Premier's Award for Poetry 1993, Harri Jones Memorial Prize for Poetry, Adelaide Festival John Bray Poetry Award 1996, Sr Fellowships Literature Bd of the Australia Council, Young Australian Creative Fellowship, Grace Leven Poetry Prize, The Age Poetry Book of the Year. *Publications:* poetry: The Frozen Sea 1983, Night Parrots 1989, The Book of Two Faces 1989, Poems 1991, Ultramarine 1992, Eschatologies 1991, Full Fathom Five 1993, Syzygy (with Anthony Lawrence) 1992, Eschatologies 1991, Full Fathom Five 1993, Syzygy

1993, Erratum/Frame(d) 1995, Intensities of Blue (with Tracy Ryan) 1995, The Silo: A Pastoral Symphony 1995, The Radnoti Poems 1996, The Undertow: New and Selected Poems 1996, Lightning Tree 1996, Graphology (ed.) 1997, Poems: 1980–1994 1997, voice-overs (with Susan Schultz) 1997, The Hunt 1998, Kangaroo Virus (with Ron Sims) 1998, Sheep Dip 1998, Pine (with Keston Sutherland) 1998, alterity: poems without tom raworth 1998, The Benefaction (ed.) 1999, Fenland Pastorals 1999, Visitants 1999, Counter-Pastorals 1999, Wheatlands 2000, Zone 2000, Zoo (with Coral Hull) 2000, The Hierarchy of Sheep 2001, Auto 2001, Speed Factory (with Bernard Cohen, McKenzie Wark and Terri-ann White) 2002, Rivers (with Peter Porter and Sean O'Brien) 2002, Outside the Panopticon 2002, Lightning Tree 2003, Peripheral Light: New and Selected Poems (Western Australian Premier's Book Award for Poetry 2004) 2003, Four Australian Poets (with others) 2003, Doppler Effect 2004, The New Arcadia 2005, Shades of the Sublime and Beautiful 2008, Armour 2011; prose: Genre (novel) 1997, Grappling Eros (short stories) 1998, Crop Circles (play in verse) 1998, Paydirt (play), The Wasps (play), From Poetry to Politics and Back Again 2000, Divinations: Four Plays 2003, Peter Porter in Conversation with John Kinsella (with Peter Porter) 2003. *Address:* Salt Publishing Ltd, PO Box 937, Great Wilbraham, Cambridge, CB21 5JX, England (office). *Telephone:* (1223) 882220 (office). *Fax:* (1223) 882260 (office). *Website:* www.saltpublishing.com (office); www.johnkinsella.org.

KINSELLA, Hon. Noël A., BA, LPh, STL, PhD, STD; Canadian human rights advocate, public servant, politician and academic; *Speaker of the Senate;* b. 28 Nov. 1939, Saint John, NB; m. Ann Kinsella (née Conley); ed Univ. Coll., Dublin, Ireland, St Thomas Aquinas Univ. and Pontifical Lateran Univ., Rome, Italy; spent 42 years as Faculty mem. St Thomas Univ., Fredericton, NB where he taught psychology, philosophy and human rights; Assoc. Under-Sec. of State of Canada –1990; Senator 1990–; Opposition Whip 1994–99, Deputy Leader of the Opposition 1999–2004, Leader of the Opposition 2004–06, Speaker of the Senate 2006–, Chair. Internal Economy Cttee 2013–, fmr mem. several Senate Standing Cttees, including Human Rights, Social Affairs, Science and Tech., and Nat. Finance; Chair. New Brunswick Human Rights Comm. 1967–88; licensed mem. Coll. of Psychologists of New Brunswick; fmr Pres. Canadian Human Rights Foundation; mem. Advisory Council, Canadian Museum for Human Rights; mem. Bd of Govs St Thomas Univ.; Hon. Capt. (Navy); Kt, Order of Malta 1984, Order of St John 2011; Queen's Diamond Jubilee Medal 2012, Grand Cross 1st Class, Order of Merit (Germany) 2013; Dr hc (Dominican Univ. Coll., Ottawa) 2006, Hon. LLD (St Thomas Univ.) 2007, Hon. DLit (Univ. Coll. Dublin) 2011. *Publications* include: three books, several monographs and more than 50 articles on psychology and human rights. *Address:* Office of the Speaker of the Senate, 280-F Centre Block, Parliament Buildings, Ottawa, ON K1A 0A4, Canada (office). *Telephone:* (613) 992-4416 (office). *Fax:* (613) 992-9772 (office). *E-mail:* noel.kinsella@sen.parl.gc.ca (office). *Website:* www.sen.parl.gc.ca/nkinsella (office).

KINSELLA, Thomas; Irish poet; b. 4 May 1928, Dublin; s. of John Paul Kinsella and Agnes Casserly Kinsella; m. Eleanor Walsh 1955; one s. two d.; with Irish Civil Service 1946–65, resgnd as Asst Prin. Officer, Dept of Finance 1965; Artist-in-Residence, Southern Illinois Univ. 1965–67, Prof. of English 1967–70; Prof. of English, Temple Univ., Philadelphia 1970–90; Dir Dolmen Press Ltd, Cuala Press Ltd, Dublin; f. Peppercanister (pvt. publishing co.) Dublin 1972; mem. Irish Acad. of Letters 1965–; Guggenheim Fellowship 1968–69, 1971–72; Hon. Sr Fellow, School of English, Univ. Coll. Dublin 2003; Hon. DLitt (Nat. Univ. of Ireland) 1985, (Turin) 2005; Guinness Poetry Award 1958, Irish Arts Council Triennial Book Award 1960, Denis Devlin Memorial Award 1966, 1969, 1992, First European Poetry Award 2001, Freedom of City of Dublin 2007, Ulysses Medal, Univ. Coll. Dublin 2008. *Publications* include: Poems 1956, Another September (poems) 1958, Downstream (poems) 1962, Nightwalker and Other Poems 1966, The Táin (trans.) 1969, Notes from the Land of the Dead (poems) 1972, Butcher's Dozen (poem) 1972, New Poems 1973, Selected Poems 1956–1968 1973, Selected Poems of Austin Clarke 1976, Song of the Night and Other Poems 1978, The Messenger (poem) 1978, Fifteen Dead (poems) 1979, One and Other Poems 1979, Poems 1956–1973, Peppercanister Poems 1972–1978 1979, Poems of the Dispossessed 1600–1900 (with 100 translations from the Irish) (co-ed.) 1981, Ireland's Musical Heritage: Sean O'Riada's Radio Talks on Irish Traditional Music (ed.) 1981, Songs of the Psyche (poems) 1985, Her Vertical Smile (poem) 1985, The New Oxford Book of Irish Verse (including all new trans from the Irish) (ed.) 1986, St Catherine's Clock (poem) 1987, Out of Ireland (poems) 1987, Blood and Family (collected poems from 1978) 1988, Poems from Centre City 1990, Personal Places (poems) 1990, One Fond Embrace (poem) 1990, Madonna and other Poems 1991, Butcher's Dozen (anniversary reissue) 1992, From Centre City (collected poems from 1990) 1994, The Dual Tradition: An Essay on Poetry and Politics in Ireland 1995, Collected Poems 1956–94, The Pen Shop (poem) 1997, The Familiar (poems) 1999, Godhead (poems) 1999, Citizen of the World (poems) 2001, Marginal Economy (poems) 2006, Readings in Poetry (essays) 2006, A Dublin Documentary 2006, Man of War (poems) 2007, Belief and Unbelief (poems) 2007, Prose Occasions 1951–2006 2009, Fat Master (poems) 2012, Love Joy Peace (poems) 2012. *Leisure interests:* history, publishing.

KINSELLA, William Patrick, OC, BA, MFA; Canadian writer and poet; b. 25 May 1935, Edmonton, Alberta; s. of John M. Kinsella and Olive M. Elliot; m. 1st Myrna Salls 1957; m. 2nd Mildred Heming 1965; m. 3rd Ann Knight 1978; m. 4th Barbara L. Turner 1999, three d.; ed Eastwood High School, Edmonton, Univ. of Victoria, Univ. of Iowa, USA; Houghton Mifflin Literary Fellowship 1982; Order of BC 2005; Hon. DLitt. (Univ. of Victoria) 1991; Books in Canada First Novel Award 1982; Canadian Authors' Asscn Award for Fiction 1982; Writers Guild Alberta Award for Fiction 1982, 1983; Vancouver Award for Writing 1987; Stephen Leacock Award for Humour 1987; Canadian Booksellers Asscn Author of the Year 1987. *Publications:* stories: Dance Me Outside 1977, Scars 1978, Shoeless Joe Jackson Comes to Iowa 1980, Born Indian 1981, The Moccasin Telegraph 1983, The Thrill of the Grass 1984, The Alligator Report 1985, The Fencepost Chronicles 1986, Five Stories 1987, Red Wolf, Red Wolf 1987, The Further Adventures of Slugger McBatt (reissued as Go the Distance 1995) 1988, The Miss Hobbema Pageant 1988, Dixon Cornbelt League 1993, Brother Frank's Gospel Hour 1994, The Secret of the Northern Lights 1998, The Silas Stories 1998, Japanese Baseball 2000; novels: Shoeless Joe 1982, The Iowa Baseball Confederacy 1986, Box Socials 1991, The Winter Helen Dropped By 1995, If Wishes Were Horses 1996, Magic Time 1998; other works: The Ballad of the Public Trustee 1982, The Rainbow

Warehouse (poetry, with Ann Knight) 1989, Two Spirits Soar: The Art of Allen Sapp 1990, Even at This Distance (poetry, with Ann Knight) 1993. *Leisure interests:* baseball, sumo wrestling, Scrabble. *Address:* #201, 14881 Marine Drive, White Rock, BC V4B 1C2, Canada (office); PO Box 3067, Sumas, WA 98295, USA.

KINSKI, Nastassja; German actress; b. (Nastassja Nakszynski), 24 Jan. 1961, W Berlin; d. of the late Klaus Kinski and of Ruth Brigitte Kinski; m. Ibrahim Moussa 1984 (divorced 1992); one s. one d.; one d. by Quincy Jones; film début in Falsche Bewegung 1975; Bundespreis 1983. *Films include:* Stay As You Are 1978, Tess 1978, One From The Heart 1982, Cat People 1982, Moon In The Gutter 1983, Spring Symphony 1983, Unfaithfully Yours 1984, The Hotel New Hampshire 1984, Maria's Lovers 1984, Paris, Texas 1984, Revolution 1985, Harem, Torrents of Spring 1989, On a Moonlit Night 1989, Magdalene 1989, The King's Future 1989, The Secret, Night Sun 1991, Faraway, So Close!, Terminal Velocity 1994, One Night Stand 1997, Little Boy Blue 1997, Father's Day 1997, Somebody is Waiting 1997, Sunshine 1998, Your Friends and Neighbors 1999, The Magic of Marciano 1999, The Intruder 1999, Town and Country 1999, The Lost 1999, The Claim 2000, The Day the World Ended 2001, An American Rhapsody 2001, Say Nothing 2001, Diary of a Sex Addict 2001, Beyond the City Limits 2001, .com for Murder 2002, Paradise Found 2003, A ton image 2004, Inland Empire 2006.

KINSLEY, Michael, BA, JD; American journalist; b. 9 March 1951, Detroit, Mich.; m. Patty Stonesifer; ed Cranbrook Kingswood School, Mich., Harvard Univ., Magdalen Coll., Oxford, UK and George Washington Univ.; journalist, The New Republic (magazine), Ed. 1978–95, writing 'TRB from Washington' column; editorial posts at Washington Monthly, Harper's, The Economist; Co-host Crossfire TV program (CNN) 1989–95; Founding Ed. Slate online magazine 1995–2002, columnist 2002–04; Editorial and Opinion Ed. Los Angeles Times 2004–05; columnist Time magazine 2006–09, Politico 2009–; fmr columnist Wall Street Journal, The Times (London), Washington Post; contrib. to New Yorker, Reader's Digest, Condé Nast Traveler, Vanity Fair; American Ed. Guardian Unlimited (London) 2006; Columbia Journalism Review Editor of the Year 1999. *Publications:* Please Don't Remain Calm: Provocations and Commentaries 2008, Creative Capitalism (ed) 2009. *Address:* c/o Politico, 1100 Wilson Boulevard, Suite 601, Arlington, VA 22209, USA. *Telephone:* (703) 647-7999. *Website:* www.politico .com.

KINZLER, Kenneth W., PhD; American oncologist and academic; *Professor of Oncology, Johns Hopkins Oncology Center, Johns Hopkins University School of Medicine;* b. 30 Jan. 1962, Philadelphia, Pa; ed Philadelphia Coll. of Pharmacy and Science and Johns Hopkins Univ. School of Medicine (JHUSM), Baltimore, Md; Postdoctoral Fellow in Oncology, JHUSM 1988–90, Asst Prof. 1990–94, Assoc. Prof. and Co-Dir Molecular Genetics Lab. 1994–99, Prof. of Oncology 1999–, also Prof. of Oncology, McKusick-Nathans Inst. of Genetic Medicine, Johns Hopkins Univ.; mem. Scientific Advisory Bd Morphotek, Inc; Alumni Award for Highest Average in Toxicology Curriculum, PCPS 1983, David Israel Macht Award for Excellence in Research, JHUSM 1988, Sandoz Award for Superior Academic Achievement and Contribution to Health Care, JHUSM 1988, Postdoctoral Award in Basic Science, JHUSM 1990, Young Alumnus Award, PCPS 1993, Merit Award, Nat. Cancer Inst. 2002. *Achievements* include: co-inventor of morphogenics, broad-based proprietary platform technology that regulates the ability of host organisms to repair mutations that occur during DNA replication. *Publications:* more than 220 articles in scientific journals. *Address:* Johns Hopkins Oncology Center, Room 588, Cancer Research Building, 1650 Orleans Street, Baltimore, MD 21231, USA (office). *Telephone:* (410) 955-2928 (office). *Fax:* (410) 955-0548 (office). *E-mail:* kinzlke@welch.jhu.edu (office); kinzlke@jhmi.edu (office). *Website:* www .hopkinsmedicine.org/pharmacology/research/kinzler.html (office).

KIPCHOGE, Eliud; Kenyan athlete; b. 5 Nov. 1984, Kapsisiywa, nr Kapsabet, Nandi Dist, Rift Valley Prov.; ed Kaptel Secondary School; distance runner; based in Nijmegen, Netherlands during track season; began racing in local cross-country events 2001; won jr race in nat. cross country trials 2002 and selection to nat. team; won 5,000m at trials for World Jr Championship, but did not travel to event due to illness; won jr nat. cross country trials and world event in Lausanne 2003; broke world jr 5,000m record, Oslo 2003; Gold Medal, 5,000m, World Championships, Paris 2003 (championship record time); won nat. cross country trials 2004, 2005 over 12 kilometres; won Kenya's 2004 Olympic Trials at 5,000m; Bronze Medal, 5,000m, Olympic Games, Athens 2004, World Indoor Championships, Moscow 2006; Silver Medal, 5,000m, World Championships, Osaka 2007, Olympic Games, Beijing 2008; Men's 3,000m Best Year Performance 2004–05, Head of State's Commendation 2006. *Address:* Athletics Kenya, Riadha House, PO Box 46722, 00100 Nairobi, Kenya. *E-mail:* athleticskenya@gt.co.ke.

KIPKETER, Wilson; Kenyan/Danish professional athlete; b. 12 Dec. 1972, Kapchemoiywo, Kenya; m. Pernille Kipketer 2000; ed St Patrick's High School, Iten, Kenya; world outdoor record-holder for 800m (1 minute 41.11 seconds) 1997 and indoor record (1 minute 42.67 seconds) 1997; set new world indoor record for 1000m (2 minutes 14.96 seconds), Birmingham, UK 2000; coached by Slawomir Nowak; resident in Denmark since 1990, qualified to compete for Denmark May 1995; gold medal, World Championships 1995, 1997, 1999; gold medal, World Indoor Championships 1997; Olympic silver medal 800m, Sydney 2000; European champion 800m, Munich 2002; silver medal, World Indoor Championships 2003; unbeaten over 800m for 33 races in 1996–97; retd 2005; currently Amb., Int. Asscn of Athletics Feds, also Head of Int. Devt; mem. Champions for Peace club. *Address:* c/o International Association of Athletics Federations, 17 rue Princesse Florestine, BP 359, 98007, Monaco. *E-mail:* info@iaaf.org.

KIPPENHAHN, Rudolf; German astronomer; b. 24 May 1926, Bärringen, Czechoslovakia; s. of Rudolf Kippenhahn and Alma Belz; m. Johanna Rasper 1955; three d.; ed Graslitz and St Joachimsthal Schools, Univs of Halle and Erlangen; Scientific Asst, Bamberg Observatory 1951–57; staff mem., Max-Planck-Inst. für Physik and Astrophysik, Inst. für Astrophysik 1957–65, mem. of Directorate 1963, Dir 1975–91, now Prof. Emer.; Visiting Prof., Caltech, Pasadena and Princeton Univ. 1961–62; Prof., Univ. Observatory, Göttingen 1965–75; Visiting Prof., UCLA 1968, Ohio State Univ. 1979, Univ. Observatory, Hamburg 1986–87; Assoc. mem. Royal Astronomical Soc., London; mem. Bayerische Akademie der Wissenschaften, Munich; Corresp. mem. Austrian Acad. of Sciences; Hon. Prof., Univ. of Munich 1975–; Verdienstkreuz (1st Class) (FRG); Carus-Medal, Leopoldina, Halle, Carus

Prize, City of Schweinfurt, Lorenz-Oken-Medal, Gesellschaft Deutscher Naturforscher und Ärzte, Eddington Medal, Royal Astronomical Soc. 2005. *Publications:* One Hundred Billion Suns: The Birth, Life and Death of the Stars 1983, Licht vom Rande der Welt 1984, Light from the Depth of Time 1987, Unheimliche Welten 1987, Stellar Structure and Evolution 1990, Der Stern von dem wir Leben 1990, Abenteuer Weltall 1991, Discovering the Secrets of the Sun 1994; and numerous articles in astronomical and astrophysical journals. *Address:* Rautenbreite 2, 37077 Göttingen, Germany. *Telephone:* (551) 24714. *Fax:* (551) 22902.

KIRALY, Charles Frederick (Karch); American professional volleyball player (retd); b. 3 Nov. 1960, Jackson, Mich.; s. of Lazlo Kiraly; m. Janna Miller; two s.; ed Univ. of California, Los Angeles; led UCLA to Nat. Collegiate Athletic Asscn (NCAA) championships 1979, 1981, 1982; played on nat. team, winning gold medals, Olympic Games 1984, 1988, world championship titles 1982, 1986; won inaugural gold medal for Olympic beach volleyball (with Kent Steffes) 1996; record for most pro beach titles (148); f. Karch Kiraly Volleyball Acad., Karch Kiraly Scholarship Fund; Asst Coach of US Women's Nat. Volleyball Team 2009–; Fédération Internationale de Volleyball (FIVB) Player of the Century; Asscn of Volleyball Professionals (AVP) Sportsman of the Year 1995, 1997, 1998, AVP Most Valuable Player 1990, 1992, 1993, 1994, 1995, 1998, inducted into Volleyball Hall of Fame 2001, California Sports Hall of Fame 2010. *Publications include:* co-author (with Byron Shewman) Beach Volleyball, The Sand Man (autobiog.). *Address:* c/o USA Volleyball Headquarters, 715 South Circle Drive, Colorado Springs, CO 80910, USA.

KIRANA, Kusnan; Indonesian airline executive; *Chairman, Lion Air;* b. 1959, brother of Rusdi Kirana; m.; two c.; began career as travel agent; co-f. (with brother) PT Lion Mentari Airlines (Lion Air) 2000, currently Chair. *Address:* PT Lion Mentari Airlines, Jl. Gajah Mada No. 7, Jakarta, Indonesia (office). *Telephone:* (21) 6326039 (office). *Fax:* (21) 6348744 (office). *E-mail:* info@lionair .co.id (office). *Website:* www2.lionair.co.id (office).

KIRANA, Rusdi; Indonesian airline executive; *President, Lion Air;* b. 1963, brother of Kusnan Kirana; m.; three c.; began career as travel agent; co-f. (with brother) PT Lion Mentari Airlines (Lion Air) 2000, currently Pres. *Address:* PT Lion Mentari Airlines, Jl. Gajah Mada No. 7, Jakarta, Indonesia (office). *Telephone:* (21) 6326039 (office). *Fax:* (21) 6348744 (office). *E-mail:* info@lionair .co.id (office). *Website:* www2.lionair.co.id (office).

KIRANANDANA, Khunying Suchada, BComm, PhD; Thai university professor; *Professor Emeritus and Chairperson of the University Council, Chulalongkorn University;* b. Bangkok; m. Thienchay Kiranandana; two s.; ed Chulalongkorn Univ., Bangkok, Harvard Univ., USA; several positions in Faculty of Commerce and Accountancy, Chulalongkorn Univ. 1979–99, Grad. School 1999–2004, Pres. Chulalongkorn Univ. 2004–08, now Prof. Emer., Chair. Univ. Council 2012–; mem. Sasin Advisory Bd 2004–08; mem. Test of English as a Foreign Language (TOEFL) Policy Council 1997–2000; Dir Kasikornbank PLC 2000–, Serm Suk Public Co. Ltd 2008–; Chair. Phufa Shop Operations Cttee 2001–; mem. Thai Red Cross Soc. Cttee 2006–, Nat. Legislature Council 2006–08; Kt, Grand Cordon (Special Class), Most Exalted Order of the White Elephant, Kt, Grand Cordon, Most Noble Order of the Crown of Thailand, Most Illustrious Order (Fourth Class) of Chula Chom Klao; Hon. DBA. *Publications:* Inferential Statistics, an Introduction 1982, Theory of Sample Surveys 1995, Statistical Information Technology: Data in Information Systems 1998, Statistics in Everyday Life 2004. *Leisure interest:* reading. *Address:* Office of the University Council, Chulalongkorn University, 254 Phyathai Road, Patumwan, Bangkok 10330, Thailand (office). *Telephone:* (2) 218-3305 (office). *Fax:* (2) 218-3309 (office). *E-mail:* suchada.ki@chula.ac.th (office). *Website:* www.chula .ac.th (office).

KIRBY, Anthony John, PhD, FRS, FRSC; British chemist, academic and research scientist; *Professor Emeritus of Bio-organic Chemistry, University of Cambridge;* b. 18 Aug. 1935, Welwyn Garden City, Herts.; s. of Samuel A. Kirby and Gladys R. Kirby (née Welch); m. Sara Nieweg 1962; one s. two d.; ed Eton Coll., Gonville and Caius Coll., Cambridge; Fellow, Gonville and Caius Coll. 1962–; Demonstrator, Lecturer in Organic Chem., Univ. of Cambridge 1968–85, Tutor 1967–75, Reader 1985–95, Prof. of Bio-organic Chem. 1995–2002, Prof. Emer. 2002–, Dir of Studies in Natural Sciences, Gonville and Caius Coll. Cambridge 1968–96; NATO Research Fellow, Brandeis Univ., Mass, USA 1963–64; Coordinator European Network on Artificial Nucleases 2000–04; Hon. DPhil (Turku) 2006; RSC Award in Organic Reaction Mechanisms 1983, RSC Tilden Lecturer 1987, RSC Ingold Lecturer 1996, Marin Drinov Medal, Bulgarian Acad. of Sciences 2003. *Publications:* The Organic Chemistry of Phosphorus (with S. G. Warren) 1967, Stereoelectronic Effects at Oxygen 1983, Stereoelectronic Effects 1996; more than 300 articles on mechanistic bio-organic chemistry. *Address:* University Chemical Laboratory, Cambridge, CB2 1EW (office); 87 Holbrook Road, Cambridge, CB1 2SX, England (home). *Telephone:* (1223) 336370 (office); (1223) 210403 (home). *Fax:* (1223) 336362 (office). *E-mail:* ajk1@cam.ac.uk (office). *Website:* www.ch.cam.ac.uk/staff/ajk.html (office).

KIRBY, Hon. Michael Donald, AC, CMG, BA, BEcons, LLM; Australian jurist; b. 18 March 1939, Sydney, NSW; s. of the late Donald Kirby and Jean Kirby (née Knowles); partner Johan van Vloten 1969; ed Fort Street Boys' High School and Univ. of Sydney; Fellow, Senate, Univ. of Sydney 1964–69; mem. NSW Bar Council 1974; Deputy Pres., Australian Conciliation & Arbitration Comm. 1975–83; Chair. Australian Law Reform Comm. 1975–84, OECD Expert Group on Privacy and Int. Data Flows 1978–80, Cttee of Counsellors, Human and People's Rights UNESCO 1985, UNESCO Expert Group on the Rights of Peoples 1989; mem. Admin. Review Council of Australia 1976–84; mem. Council, Univ. of Newcastle, NSW 1977–83, Deputy Chancellor 1978–83; mem. Australian Nat. Comm. for UNESCO 1980–84 (Hon. mem. 1997–2007), Australian Inst. of Multicultural Affairs 1979–83; Judge, Fed. Court of Australia 1983–84; mem. Exec. CSIRO 1983–86; Chancellor, Macquarie Univ., Sydney 1984–93; Pres. Court of Appeal, Supreme Court of NSW 1984–96; Acting Chief Justice of NSW 1988, 1990, 1993, 1995; Admin. (Acting Gov.) NSW 1991; Justice, High Court of Australia 1996–2009; Acting Chief Justice of Australia 2007–08; Commr WHO Global Comm. on AIDS 1989–91; mem. Int. Comm. of Jurists, Geneva 1985–99, mem. Exec. Cttee 1989–95, Chair. 1992–95, Pres. 1995–98, Pres. Australian Section 1989–96; Special Rep. of Sec.-Gen. of UN on Human Rights for Cambodia 1993–96; Pres. Court of Appeal of

Solomon Islands 1995–96; Pres. Australian Acad. of Forensic Sciences 1987–89; mem. Ethics Cttee of Human Genome Org. 1995–2003; mem. Perm. Tribunal of Peoples' Session on Tibet 1992; Trustee, AIDS Trust of Australia 1987–93; mem. UNESCO Jury for Prize for Teaching of Human Rights 1994–96, UNESCO Int. Bioethics Cttee 1996–2006; Rapporteur, UNAIDS Global Panel on HIV/AIDS and Human Rights 2003–, Int. Group on Judicial Integrity (UNHCR) 2004–; Co-Chair. Expert Group on Bioethics and Human Rights, High Commr of Human Rights 2002–; Chair. Group of Experts, UNESCO IBC drafting of Declaration of Universal Norms in Bioethics 2004–05; mem. Judicial Reference Group, High Commr for Human Rights 2007–; mem. Advisory Bd Int. Human Rights Inst., De Paul Univ., Chicago, USA; Pres. Inst. of Arbitrators and Mediators 2009–; Dir Australian Centre for Int. Commercial Arbitration 2010–; mem. Arbitration Panel CSID (World Bank) 2010–; mem. UNDP Global Comm. on HIV and Law 2010–12, Eminent Persons Group on Future of the Commonwealth of Nations 2010–11; Chair. Commonwealth Expert Group on Rule of Law 2011; Chair, UN Comm. of Inquiry on Democratic People's Repub. of Korea 2013–; Commr UNAIDS/Lancet Comm. on AIDS To Sustainable Health 2013–; Ed. in Chief, The Laws of Australia 2009–; Hon. Fellow, New Zealand Research Foundation, Australian Acad. of Social Sciences 1996, Acad. of Social Sciences in Australia 2004, Australian Acad. of Humanities 2006, Hon. Bencher, Inner Temple (London) 2006, Hon. mem. American Law Inst. 2000, Soc. of Legal Scholars (UK) 2007; numerous hon. doctorates; Loewenthal Medal, Sydney Univ., Australian Human Rights Medal 1991, Laureate, UNESCO Prize for Human Rights Educ. 1998, Centenary Medal 2003, Australian Privacy Medal 2010, Int. Privacy Champion Award, EPIC 2010, Gruber Justice Prize 2010. *Publications include:* Industrial Index to Australian Labour Law 1978, 1984, Reform the Law 1983, The Judges 1984, A Touch of Healing 1986 (co-ed.), Through the World's Eye 2000, Judicial Activism (Hamlyn Lectures 2003) 2004, A Private Life 2011, What would Gandhi Do? 2013. *Leisure interest:* work. *Address:* Level 7, 195 Macquarie Street, Sydney, NSW 2000, Australia (home). *Telephone:* (9) 231-5800 (office). *Fax:* (9) 231-5811 (office). *E-mail:* mail@michaelkirby.com.au (office). *Website:* www.michaelkirby.com.au.

KIRBY, Peter Maxwell, MA, MBA; Australian business executive; *Chairman, DuluxGroup Ltd;* b. 2 Aug. 1947, South Africa; s. of Robert Maxwell Kirby and May Kirby; m. Erica Anne Ebden; one s.; ed Rhodes Univ., Natal Univ., Univ. of Manchester, UK, Univ. of the Witwatersrand, Harvard Business School, USA; Man. Dir Dulux Paints 1991–92; CEO ICI Paints Asia Pacific 1992–95, Chair. and CEO ICI Paints 1995–98, Exec. Bd Dir ICI PLC, Chair. DuluxGroup Ltd 2010–; Man. Dir and CEO CSR Ltd 1998–2003; Chair. Medibank Private Ltd 2004–08; mem. Bd of Dirs Macquarie Bank Ltd 2003–; Centenary Medal 2003. *Leisure interests:* classic sports cars, boating. *Address:* Macquarie Group Ltd, 1 Martin Place, Sydney, NSW 2000, Australia (office). *Telephone:* (2) 8232-3333 (office). *Fax:* (2) 8232-4330 (office). *Website:* www.macquarie.com.au (office).

KIRBY, Ronald Hubert, BArch; Zambian architect and urban designer; b. 3 Jan. 1936, Lusaka, N Rhodesia; s. of Hubert Rowland Kirby and May Elizabeth Kirby (née Hinds); m. Davina Anne Roderick 1985; one d.; ed Muir Coll., Uitenhage, Univ. of Cape Town, Univ. of Witwatersrand; external examiner, Univs of Cape Town and Pretoria 1985; Chair. Transvaal Prov. Inst. of Architecture PR and Press Communication 1985–87; Prof. of Architecture and Head of Dept Univ. of Witwatersrand 1991–94; Dir Zambia Nat. Housing Authority 1991–92; mem. South Africa Council of Architects Educational Inspection Comm. to Univ. of Witwatersrand 1985–, Transvaal Prov. Inst. of Architecture Commn. 1983–87; fmr Pres. Zambia Inst. of Architecture; Zambia Inst. of Architecture Industrial Award 1964, Commercial Awards 1964, 1968, Civic Award 1968, Institutional Awards 1971, 1973, 1983, Inst. of S African Architecture Awards of Merit 1983, 1987, RIBA Bronze Medal, Rhodesia 1963, Habitation Space Int. Award 1981. *Publications:* numerous articles in professional journals. *Address:* PO Box 337, Melville, 2109 Johannesburg, South Africa. *Telephone:* (271) 482-2323. *Fax:* (271) 482-1218. *E-mail:* plandesign@icon.co.za (office).

KIRCHHOFF, Frank, Dr rer. nat et med. hab.; German virologist and academic; *University Professor of Virology and Director, Institute of Molecular Virology, University of Ulm;* b. 24 April 1961, Bückeburg; ed Gymnasium Adolfinum, Bückeburg, Univ. of Göttingen; Postdoctoral Fellow, Harvard Medical School 1991–94; Head of Research Group, Inst. for Clinical and Molecular Virology, Univ. of Erlangen-Nuremberg 1994–99, Lecturer 1997–99, Research Asst Prof. (C2) 1999–2001; Univ. Prof. (C3) of Virology, Faculty of Medicine, Univ. of Ulm 2001–, Dir Inst. for Molecular Virology 2009–; Professorship, Imperial Coll. London 2007; Professorships at Univs of Giessen, Basel and Göttingen 2008; mem. Comm. GfV for Univ. Affairs and Int. Relations, Scientific Advisory Bd, ViroPharmaceuticals GmbH, Hanover; mem. Editorial Bd, Journal of Virology, Retrovirology, Advances in Virology, Cell 2009–, Nat. AIDS Advisory Council 2012; mem. German Nat. Acad. of Sciences Leopoldina, Soc. for Virology, American Soc. for Microbiology; Nachwuchsförderpreis, German Primate Centre 1990, German AIDS Research Award, Soc. for Infectious Diseases 1995, Thiersch Prize, Medical Faculty of Univ. Erlangen-Nuremberg 1998, Research Award, BUPA Foundation (co-recipient) 1999, Foundation Award, Univ. of Ulm 2002, German AIDS Prize, German AIDS Soc. 2003, AIDS Research Award, Heinz-Ansmann Foundation 2006, AIDS Research Award, Hector Foundation 2007, Innovation Award, German Univ. Hosps 2007, Merckle Research Prize 2007, Research Award, GlaxoSmithKline Foundation for Clinical Research 2008, Gottfried Wilhelm Leibniz Prize 2009, Advanced Grant, European Research Council 2012, Ernst Schering Prize 2013. *Publications:* numerous papers in professional journals. *Address:* Albert-Einstein-Allee 11, 89081 Ulm, Germany (office). *Telephone:* (731) 50023344 (office). *Fax:* (731) 50023389 (office). *E-mail:* frank.kirchhoff@uni-ulm.de (office). *Website:* www .uni-ulm.de/en/fakultaeten/medicine.html (office).

KIRCHNER, Alfred; German theatre director; b. 22 May 1937, Göppingen; s. of Julius Kirchner and Alice Kirchner (née Bonatz); two d.; ed Max Reinhardt Schule, Berlin; Chief Producer, Staatstheater, Stuttgart 1972–79; mem. Bd of Dirs and Chief Producer, Schauspielhaus, Bochum 1979–86, Burgtheater, Vienna 1986–89; Gen. Dir Staatliche Schauspielbühnen, Berlin 1990–97; guest producer at Residenztheater, Munich, Hamburg Schauspielhaus, Hamburg State Opera, Frankfurt Opera, Holland Festival, Brussels Opera, Vienna State Opera, Santa Fé Opera, etc.; has directed operas by Udo Zimmermann, Bernd Alois Zimmermann, Hans Zender, Hans Werner Henze, Mozart, Verdi, Mussorgsky,

Tchaikovsky; Dir Der Ring des Niebelungen, Bayreuth 1994–98, La Bohème, Frankfurt 1998, Rosenkavalier, Leipzig 1998, Rigoletto, Leipzig 1999, Peter Grimes, Strasbourg 1999, Manon Lescaut, Frankfurt 1999.

KIRCHSCHLAGER, Angelika; Austrian singer (mezzo-soprano); b. 1965, Salzburg; m.; one s.; ed Musisches Gymnasium, Salzburg and Vienna Music Acad.; studied with Walter Berry in Vienna 1984; first performance in Die Zauberflöte, Vienna Kammeroper; concert performances in Austria, France, Germany, Italy, Czech Repub., Denmark, USA and Japan; recitals in London, Edinburgh, Amsterdam, Cologne, Frankfurt, Hohenems, Graz, Bilbao and in Scandinavia; role of Composer in Jonathan Miller production of Ariadne auf Naxos, Lausanne Opera 1998–99; sang with London Symphony Orchestra, New York Chamber Orchestra and Vienna Symphony Orchestra 1999–2000; feature broadcasts on Austrian Nat. Radio and TV (ORF); participated in film production about Hugo Wolf in role of Frieda Zerny 1992; operatic roles include appearances in Le nozze de Figaro (Schloss Schönbrunn, Vienna), Der Rosenkavalier (Geneva), Hänsel und Gretel (Graz), The Merry Widow (Vienna), Palestrina (Vienna), Don Giovanni (Ravenna and Milan), Les Contes d'Hoffmann (Paris), Ariadne auf Naxos (London), Die Dreigroschenoper (London and Paris) 2009, Die Fledermaus (Vienna) 2010–11, Pelleas et Melisande (Helsinki) 2012; currently Prof., Mozarteum in Salzburg, Univ. of Graz; awarded the title Kammersängerin (Govt of Austria) 2007; three prizes, Int. Belvedere Competition, Vienna 1991. *Recordings include:* album of lieder by Alma Mahler, Gustav Mahler and Erich Wolfgang Korngold (solo debut) 1997; featured on recording of Mendelssohn with Claudio Abbado and Berlin Philharmonic; When Night Falls (solo recital) 1999, Handel Arias 2006, Bach Arias 2008, Hugo Wolf Songs 2009, Schumann Songs 2010, Brahms Songs Vol. 1 2010, Liszt Songs Vol. 1, Vol. 2 (BBC Music Magazine Vocal Award 2013). *Website:* www.askonasholt.co.uk/artists/singers/mezzo-soprano/angelika-kirchschlager.

KIRIENKO, Sergey Vladilenovich; Russian economist, politician, government official and energy industry executive; *Head, State Atomic Energy Corporation (Rosatom)*; b. 26 July 1962, Sukhumi; m. Maria Kirienko; one s. two d.; ed Inst. of Naval Engineers, Gorky (now Nizhy Novgorod), Acad. of Nat. Econ., Moscow; served in Soviet arm 1984–86; worked as Master in Krasnoe Sormovo shipbuilding facility, Nizhny Novgorod; elected Sec. of regional Komsomol org. 1986, then Sec., Krasnoye Sormovo Komsomol Cttee, First Sec., Gorky regional Komsomol Cttee, mem. All-Union Leninist Communist Youth League (Komsomol) Cen. Cttee; Founder and Chair. Garantia Bank, Nizhy Novgorod 1993–96; Pres. NorSea Oil Co., Nizhy Novgorod 1996–97; First Deputy, Ministry of Fuel and Energy May–Oct. 1997, also apptd Deputy Chair. Governmental Comm. for Coordination of Implementation of Production-Sharing Agreements (between fed. exec. bodies and regional authorities), Head Interdepartmental Comm. for ind. entities' access to Gazprom's gas transportation network, also became mem. panel of state reps in Transneft; Minister of Fuel and Energy 1997–98; Prime Minister, Russian Fed. April–Aug. 1998; Founder and Co-Chair. Novaya Sila party 1998; mem. State Duma representing Right Force Alliance 1999–2000, Leader Parl. faction Union of Right Forces; Presidential Rep. Volga Fed. Dist 2000–05; Chair. State Comm. on Chemical Weapons Destruction 2001–05; Head, Fed. Agency for Atomic Energy 2005–08; Head, State Atomic Energy Corpn (Rosatom) 2007–. *Address:* c/o RosEnergoAtom, 119017 Moscow, Bolshaya Ordynka, 24/26, Russia (office). *Telephone:* (495) 239-2422 (office). *Fax:* (495) 239-4603 (office). *E-mail:* npp@rosatom.ru (office). *Website:* www.rosatom.com/en (office).

KIRILL I, His Holiness Patriarch, Cand. Theol.; Russian ecclesiastic; *Patriarch of Moscow and All Russia;* b. (Vladimir Mikhailovich Gundyayev), 20 Nov. 1946, Leningrad (now St Petersburg); s. of Mikhail Gundyayev; ed Leningrad Theological Acad.; ordained as Hierodeacon 1969, Hieromonk 1969; Prof. of Dogmatic Theology and Aide to Insp., Leningrad Theological Acad. 1970; Personal Sec. to Metropolitan Nikodim, Leningrad 1970; ordained Archimandrite 1971; Rector, Leningrad Acad. and Seminary 1974; consecrated Bishop of Vyborg 1976, Archbishop 1977; Archbishop (later Metropolitan), Smolensk and Vyazma 1984–89, Archbishop, Smolensk and Kaliningrad 1989–91, Metropolitan, Smolensk and Kaliningrad 1991–2009; Patriarch of Moscow and All Russia 2009–; Deputy Chair. Dept for External Church Relations, Moscow Patriarchate 1978–89, Chair. 1989–; Perm. mem. Holy Synod 1989–; Co-Chair. World Conf. of Religions for Peace 2006–; fmr Russian Orthodox Church Rep. to WCC, mem. WCC Cen. Cttee and Exec. Cttee 1975–; fmr Man. Patriarch's parishes, Finland; Hon. Citizen, Lukoyanovskogo Dist of Nizhny Novgorod Region 2000, Smolensk 2003, Rizskoe Vyazemsky Dist of Smolensk Region 2004, Kaliningrad Region of the Neman 2006, Vyazemsky Dist of Smolensk Region 2006, Kaliningrad 2006, Khoroshevo-Mnevniki North-Western Admin. Dist of Moscow 2006, Smolensk Region 2009, Kaliningrad Region 2009, Kemerovo Region 2010, Repub. of Mordovia 2011; decorated by the Churches of Alexandria, Antioch, Jerusalem, Georgia, Serbia, Bulgaria, Greece, Poland, the Czech Lands and Slovakia, America and Finland; awarded Russian Orthodox Church Orders of St Vladimir Equal-to-the-Apostles, St Alexis the Metropolitan of Moscow, St Daniel of Moscow, St Sergius of Radonezh and St Innocent the Metropolitan of Moscow; several state decorations, including Order of the Friendship of Nations 1988, Order of Friendship 1996, Order for Services for the Motherland (Third Class) 2000, (Second Class) 2006; Order 'Honour' (Azerbaijan) 2010, Medal '65th Anniversary of Victory in the Great Patriotic War' (Transnistria) 2010, Order of the Repub. (Moldova) 2011; Hon. DTheol (Theological Acad., Budapest) 1987. *Television:* host of weekly programme, ORT/Channel One 1994–. *Publication:* co-authored book on judo and sambo and their relationship to Orthodox Christianity. *Address:* Danilov Monastery DECR, MP, 115191 Moscow, ul. Danilovskii Val 22, Russia (office). *Telephone:* (495) 633-8428 (office). *Fax:* (495) 633-8428 (office). *E-mail:* cs@mospatr.ru (office). *Website:* www.mospat.ru/en/the_patriarch (office).

KIRK, David Edward, MBE, MB, ChB; New Zealand media executive and fmr rugby union player; *CEO, Fairfax Media Ltd;* b. 5 Oct. 1961, Wellington; ed Wanganui Collegiate School, Univ. of Otago, Univ. of Oxford, UK; played prov. rugby for Otago, toured with New Zealand Colts and first toured with All Blacks in 1983, refused to join rebel "Cavaliers" team on moral grounds when planned 1986 All Black tour to SA was cancelled, captained so-called "Baby Blacks", was made capt. of NZ team in inaugural Rugby World Cup in 1987 and led team to victory over France in final, retd from competitive rugby aged 25 and took up Rhodes Scholarship at Worcester Coll., Oxford 1987; returned to NZ becoming coach of Wellington NPC team 1993, media commentator 1994; worked as staffer for Prime Minister Jim Bolger and as man. consultant McKinsey & Co.; CEO Fairfax Media Ltd (publr of The Sydney Morning Herald, The Age and The Australian Financial Review in Australia, and The Dominion Post and The Christchurch Press in NZ) 2005–. *Address:* Fairfax Media Ltd, Level 19, Darling Park, Sussex Street, Sydney, NSW 2000, Australia (office). *Telephone:* (2) 9282-3046 (office). *Fax:* (2) 9282-3065 (office). *E-mail:* info@fxj.com.au (office). *Website:* www.fxj.com.au (office).

KIRK, Kent Sand; Danish fishing captain, politician and business executive; b. 29 Aug. 1948, Esbjerg; s. of Sand Kirk and Brynhild Kirk; m. Ruth Henriksen 1971; three s. one d.; Master's certificate, capt. of fishing boat 1971; Gen. Man. K. and K. Kirk Ltd 1973; Chair. Bd Fishermen's Asscn, Esbjerg 1975; mem. Bd Danish Deep Sea Fishing Fed., Danish Fishermen's Producers' Org., Esbjerg Harbour Council 1976; mem. European Parl. 1979–84; mem. Folketing 1984–98; Minister for Fisheries 1989–93; mem. Bd Danish Conservative Party 1980–84; Vice-Pres. European Democratic Group 1981–83; Pnr, Esvagt Ltd (stand-by vessels) 1981–; Chair. Bd Int. School, Esbjerg 1982. *Leisure interests:* skiing, reading. *Address:* Esvagt AS, Adgangsvejen 1, 6700 Esbjerg, Denmark. *E-mail:* mail@esvagt.dk. *Website:* /www.esvagt.dk.

KIRK, Mark Steven, BA, MS, JD; American naval officer, lawyer and politician; *Senator from Illinois;* b. 15 Sept. 1959, Champaign, Ill.; s. of Francis Gabriel Kirk and Judith Ann Kirk (née Brady); m. Kimberly Vertolli 2001 (divorced 2009); ed New Trier High School, Blackburn Coll., Universidad Nacional Autónoma de México, Cornell Univ., London School of Econs, UK, Georgetown Univ. Law Center; commissioned as intelligence officer in US Naval Reserve 1989, holds rank of Commdr; admitted to Bar of Ill. 1992, DC 1993; Parl. aide to Julian Critchley, MP, London 1982–83; worked on staff of John Porter, fmr Rep. from Illinois 10th Congressional Dist 1984–90; campaigner, Porter for Congress, Northern Ill. 1984–90; Organizer, Bush/Quayle Campaign, Northern Ill. 1988, Dole for President 1988, various states; officer, World Bank, Washington, DC 1990; Special Asst to Asst Sec. of State for Inter-American Affairs 1991–93; attorney, Baker & McKenzie LLP 1993–95; named as Counsel to US House Int. Relations Cttee 1995–99; mem. US House of Reps for 10th Congressional Dist of Ill. 2001–10, mem. Appropriations Cttee, House Iran Working Group, Founder and Co-Chair. House US-China Working Group, Co-Chair. Congressional Caucus on Armenian Issues, Albanian Issues Caucus in ex-Yugoslavia, mem. GOP Tuesday Group; Senator from Illinois 2010–, mem. Appropriations Cttee, Banking, Housing and Urban Affairs Cttee, Health, Educ., Labor and Pensions, Special Cttee on Aging; mem. Bd of Dirs Population Resource Center, Princeton, NJ; mem. Navy League, Naval Reserve Asscn, New Trier Republican Org.; Republican; Navy and Marine Corps Commendation Medal, Navy Achievement Medal, Nat. Defense Service Medal, Global War on Terror Service Medal, Jt Meritorious Unit Award, Navy Unit Commendation, Navy Meritorious Unit Commendation; Kellogg Fellow, Chicago 1980, Council of Jewish Fed. Award, Washington 1988. *Publications:* contrib. of articles to various newspapers. *Leisure interests:* backpacking, skydiving. *Address:* 524 Hart Senate Office Building, United States Senate, Washington, DC 20510, USA (office). *Telephone:* (202) 224-2854 (office). *Fax:* (202) 228-4611 (office). *Website:* kirk.senate.gov (office).

KIRK, Paul Grattan, Jr, AB, LLB; American political official and lawyer; b. 18 Jan. 1938, Newton, Mass.; s. of Paul G. Kirk and Josephine Kirk (née O'Connell); m. Gail Loudermilk 1974; ed Harvard Univ.; Pnr, Sullivan & Worcester LLP (law firm), Boston and Washington, DC 1977–90, Counsel 1990, now Retd Pnr; Chair. Kirk & Assocs Inc. 1990–; Special Asst to Senator Edward Kennedy; Nat. Political Dir Kennedy for Pres. Cttee 1980; Treas. Democratic Nat. Cttee 1983–85, Chair. 1985–89; Interim Senator from Mass Sept. 2009–Jan. 2010; Visiting Lecturer, Mass. Continuing Legal Educ. Program, New England Law Inst., J. F. Kennedy Inst. of Politics, Harvard Univ.; Chair., Bd of Dirs J. F. Kennedy Library Foundation 1992–2009, Nominating Cttee Harvard Bd of Overseers 1993, Nat. Democratic Inst. for Int. Affairs 1992–2001; mem. Bd of Dirs ITT Corpn 1989–97, Bradley Real Estate Inc. 1992–99, The Hartford Life Insurance Co. 1995–2000, The Hartford Financial Services Group 1995–2009, 2010–, Rayonier Corpn 1993–2011, Cedar Shopping Centers Inc. 2006–; mem. Bd of Trustees, Stonehill Coll. 1984–2002, St Sebastian's School 1992–2008; Co-Chair. Comm. on Pres. Debates 1987–2009; Chair. Visiting Comm. on Harvard Athletics 2000–; Hon. LLD (Stonehill Coll.) 2002, (Southern New England School of Law) 2003; W. Averell Harriman Democracy Award 1988, Univ. of Mass Distinguished Achievement Award 2010; Hubert Humphrey Public Leadership Award 2010. *Leisure interest:* athletics. *Address:* Sullivan & Worcester LLP, One Post Office Square, Suite 2400, Boston, MA 02109, USA (office). *Telephone:* (617) 338-2987 (office). *Fax:* (617) 338-2880 (office). *E-mail:* pkirk@sandw.com (office). *Website:* www.sandw.com (office).

KIRK, Ronald, BA, JD; American lawyer, government official and fmr politician; *United States Trade Representative;* b. 27 June 1954, Austin, Tex.; m. Matrice Kirk; two d.; ed Austin Coll., Univ. of Texas; Legis. Asst to US Senator Lloyd Bentsen, Washington, DC 1981–83; Asst City Attorney for Intergovernmental Relations and Chief Lobbyist, City of Dallas, Tex. 1983–89; shareholder, Johnson & Gibbs P.C. (law firm) Dallas 1990–94; Pnr, Gardere Wynne Sewell LLP (law firm) 1994–2004; Sec. of State, State of Texas 1994–95; Mayor of Dallas 1995–2001; Pnr, Vinson & Elkins LLP, Dallas 2005–09; US Trade Rep., Washington, DC 2009–; mem. ABA, Nat. Bar Asscn, Tex. State Bar, JL Turner Legal Asscn, Austin Coll. Alumni Asscn, Univ. of Texas Alumni Asscn (Pres.-elect 2008–09); Democrat; Hon. LHD (Austin Coll.) 2006; CB Bunkley Community Service Award, JL Turner Legal Asscn 1994, Woodrow Wilson Center Award 2000, Jurisprudence Award, Anti-Defamation League 2004, Justinian Award, Dallas Lawyers Auxiliary 2008; named one of The 50 Most Influential Minority Lawyers in America by The National Law Journal 2008. *Address:* Office of the United States Trade Representative, Winder Bldg, 600 17th St, NW, Washington, DC 20508, USA. *Telephone:* (202) 395-3230. *Fax:* (202) 395-4549. *E-mail:* contactustr@ustr.eop.gov. *Website:* www.ustr.gov.

KIRKBY, Dame (Carolyn) Emma, DBE, OBE, MA; British singer (soprano); b. 26 Feb. 1949, Camberley, Surrey; d. of the late Capt. Geoffrey Kirkby and of Beatrice Daphne Kirkby; one s. with Anthony Rooley; ed Sherborne School for Girls and Somerville Coll., Oxford and pvt singing lessons with Jessica Cash; specialist singer of renaissance, baroque and classical repertoire; debut London concert 1974; full-time professional singer 1975–; since mid-1970s involved in revival of performances with period instruments and the attempt to recreate the sounds the composers would have heard; performances at the Proms from 1977; freelance work with many groups and orchestras in the UK and Germany, including Consort of Musicke, Taverner Players, Acad. of Ancient Music, London Baroque, Florilegium, Freiburger Barockorchester, Fretwork, Orchestra of the Age of Enlightenment, Concerto Copenhagen, Purcell Quartet; appearances at festivals, including Bruges, Utrecht, Luzern, Mosel, Rheingau, Passau, Schleswig-Holstein, Saintes, Beaune, Ottawa, Elora, Tanglewood, Mostly Mozart (New York) and many others; Hon. DLitt (Salford) 1985; Hon. DMus (Bath) 1994, (Sheffield) 2000, (Oxford) 2008, (Newcastle) 2010; Hon. FGSM; Hon. FRAM; Hon. Fellow, Royal Coll. of Music, Trinity Coll. of Music; Handel Prize, Halle, Germany 1997, Classic FM Artist of the Year 1999. *Television:* subject of South Bank Show (ITV) 2008. *Recordings include:* Complete songs of John Dowland 1976–77, Messiah (Handel) 1979, 1988, Madrigals by Monteverdi, Wert, Scarlatti and other Italians, Schütz, Grabbe, Wilbye, Ward and other English composers, Monteverdi Vespers, Mass in B Minor (Bach), Handel's Athalia, Joshua, Judas Maccabaeus, Sequences by Hildegarde of Bingen (Hyperion), Arie Antiche and Songs of Maurice Greene, Dido and Aeneas, Handel's German Arias, Italian Cantatas, Songs by Arne and Handel, Stabat Mater (Pergolesi), Haydn's Creation, Mozart Motets, Mozart Concert Arias, Vivaldi Opera Arias, Handel Opera Arias, Christmas Music with Westminster Abbey Choir, Christmas Music with London Baroque, with Bell'Arte Salzburg, Bach Cantatas with Freiburger Barockorchester and with Purcell Quartet, Byrd Consort Songs with Fretwork, Handel: Sacred Contatas, Handel Gloria 2001, Lute song recitals with Anthony Rooley and with Jakob Lindberg, Bingen: A Feather On The Breath Of God 2010, Emma Kirkby - A Portrait 2011. *Address:* c/o Consort of Musicke, 13 Pages Lane, London, N10 1PU, England (office). *Telephone:* (20) 8444-6565 (office). *Fax:* (20) 8444-1008 (office). *E-mail:* consort@musicke.net (office). *Website:* www.emmakirkby.com.

KIRKILAS, Gediminas; Lithuanian politician; *Deputy Chairman, Lithuanian Social Democratic Party (Lietuvos Socialdemokratų Partija);* b. 30 Aug. 1951, Vilnius; m. Liudmila Kirkilienė; one s. one d.; ed Vilnius Teachers' Training Coll., Vilnius Higher School of Politics, Vilnius Univ.; interior restorer, Monument Restoration Trust 1972–78; worked within CP 1982–90; Asst to First Sec. of Cen. Cttee of Lithuanian CP, later to Deputy of Supreme Council–Reconstituted Seimas (Parl.), Repub. of Lithuania 1989–92; Ed. and Publr Golos Litvy (The Voice of Lithuania) daily newspaper 1991–95; mem. Seimas 1992–; fmr Chair. Cttee on Nat. Security and Defence, Cttee on Foreign Affairs, Deputy Chair. Cttee on European Affairs, Head of Seimas Del. to NATO Parl. Ass.; Elder Group of Lithuanian Social Democratic Labour Party 1993–96; head, Presidential working group to develop nat. security strategy 1993–96; Special Rep. of Pres. for matters related to transportation between Lithuania and Kaliningrad region of Russian Fed. 2002; given rank of Amb. 2003; Minister of Nat. Defence and mem. Cttee on Nat. Security and Defence 2004–06; Prime Minister of Lithuania 2006–08; acting Sec. of Ind. Cen. Cttee of Lithuanian CP 1990; elected Deputy Chair. Constitutive Ass. of Lithuanian Democratic Labour Party (LDLP) 1990, first Asst to the Sec. 1991–96, temporary Chair. 1993, mem. Presidium 1996–2001; following absorption of LLDP in 2001, Deputy Chair. Lithuanian Social Democratic Party (Lietuvos Socialdemokratų Partija) 2001–07, 2009–, Chair. 2007–09; Cross of Officer of the Lithuanian Grand Duke Vytautas, Order of the Cross of Vytis, Commdr Cross of the Repub. of Poland, Grand Cross of Portugal. *Publications:* Political Commentary for the Period 1995, numerous articles on policy and public life. *Leisure interests:* fishing, tennis, philosophy, literature, arts, cycling, pipe smoking. *Address:* Lietuvos Socialdemokratų Partija, Barboros Radvilaites g. 1, Vilnius 01124, Lithuania (office). *Telephone:* (5) 261-3907 (office). *Fax:* (5) 261-5420 (office). *E-mail:* info@lsdp.lt (office). *Website:* www.lsdp.lt (office); www.kirkilas.eu.

KIRKLAND, Gelsey; American ballet dancer and ballet teacher; b. 29 Dec. 1952, Bethlehem, Pa; m. Greg Lawrence; ed School of American Ballet; youngest mem. of New York Ballet at age 15 in 1968, Soloist 1969–72, Prin. Dancer 1972–74; with American Ballet Theater 1974–81, 1982–84, teacher, coach American Ballet Theatre 1992; Guest Dancer, Royal Ballet, London 1980–86, Stuttgart Ballet 1980; Co-founder and Co-Artistic Dir Gelsey Kirkland Acad. of Classical Ballet 2010–; fmr mem. Guest Faculty, Broadway Dance Center, New York. *Ballets include:* Firebird, The Goldberg Variations, Scherzo fantastique, An Evening's Waltzes, The Leaves are Fading, Hamlet, The Tiller in the Field, Four Bagatelles, Stravinsky Symphony in C, Song of the Nightingale Connotations, Romeo and Juliet and others. *Publications:* Dancing on My Grave (autobiog.) 1987, The Shape of Love (with Greg Lawrence) 1990, The Little Ballerina and Her Dancing Horse 1993. *Address:* Gelsey Kirkland Academy of Classical Ballet, 355 Broadway, Second Floor, New York, NY 10013, USA (office). *Telephone:* (212) 600-0047 (office). *Website:* www.gelseykirklandballet.org (office).

KIRKWOOD, Thomas (Tom) Burton Loram, CBE, BA, MSc, PhD, FMedSci; British medical scientist and academic; *Professor of Medicine and Head, Department of Gerontology, Institute for Ageing and Health, University of Newcastle-upon-Tyne;* b. 6 July 1951; s. of the late Kenneth Kirkwood and of Deborah Burton Kirkwood (née Collings); m. 1st Betty Rosamund Bartlett 1973 (divorced 1975); one s. one d.; m. 2nd Jane Louise Buttomley 1995; ed Dragon School, Oxford, Magdalen Coll. School, Oxford, St Catharine's Coll., Cambridge, Worcester Coll., Oxford; initially qualified as a mathematician; developed 'disposable soma' theory of ageing; Scientist, Nat. Inst. for Biological Standards and Control, London 1973–79, Staff Scientist 1979–81; Staff Scientist, Computing Lab., MRC Nat. Inst. for Medical Research, London 1981–87, Sr Staff Scientist 1987–88, Head, Lab. of Math. Biology 1988–93; Prof. of Biological Gerontology, Univ. of Manchester 1993–99 (first in GB); Prof. of Medicine and Head of Dept of Gerontology, Univ. of Newcastle-upon-Tyne 1999–; Chair. British Soc. for Research on Ageing 1992–99; Dir Jt Centre on Ageing, Univs of Manchester and Newcastle upon Tyne 1996–; Gov. Research Advisory Council, Research into Ageing 1998–2001, Chair. 1999–2000; Chair. Foresight Task Force on Health Care of Older People 1999–2001; mem. WHO Expert Advisory Panel on Biological Standardization 1985–, UK Human Genome Mapping Project Cttee 1991–93, Basic Scis Interest Group, Wellcome Trust 1992–97, Bio tech. and Biological Sciences Research Council 2001–; Co-Ed. Mechanisms of Ageing and Devt 2000–; Pres. Int. Biometric Soc. (British Region) 1998–2000; Fellow, Inst. for Advanced Study, Budapest 1997; Heinz Karger Prize 1983, Fritz Verzár Medal 1996, British Geriatrics Soc. Dhole-

Eddlestone Prize 2001, Royal Inst. Henry Dale Prize 2002. *Radio:* BBC Reith Lectures 2001. *Publications:* (jtly): Accuracy in Molecular Processes: Its Control and Relevance to Living Systems 1986, Time of Our Lives: The Science of Human Ageing 1999, Sex and Longevity: Sexuality, Gender, Reproduction, Parenthood 2001; (with C. E. Finch): Chance, Development and Aging 2000, The End of Age 2001; numerous scientific articles in learned journals. *Leisure interests:* gardening, hill-walking, running, pottery. *Address:* Newcastle University, Institute for Ageing and Health, Henry Wellcome Laboratory for Biogerontology Research, Newcastle General Hospital, Newcastle-upon-Tyne, NE4 6BE (office); Roughlees, Ewesley, Morpeth, Northumberland, NE61 4PH, England (home). *Telephone:* (191) 256-3319 (office). *Fax:* (191) 256-3445 (office). *E-mail:* tom.kirkwood@ncl.ac .uk (office). *Website:* www.ncl.ac.uk/medi/research/gerontology (office).

KIRMANI, Tariq, MBA; Pakistani business executive; *Chairman, UBL Fund Managers Ltd;* ed Inst. of Business Admin, Karachi; spent seven years working in USA, UAE and Australia; served in oil sector in various marketing, operations and finance man. positions, first Pakistani to be elected a co. dir of a multinational oil co. 1991; Deputy Man. Dir (Marketing) Pakistan State Oil 1999–2001, Man. Dir 2001–05; Chair. and CEO Pakistan Int. Airlines 2005–07 (resgnd); Chair. UBL Fund Managers Ltd, Karachi 2010–; mem. Bd of Dirs NBP, Asia Care Health and Life Insurance Co., Marie Adelaide Leprosy Centre, Pakistan Sports Trust, Nat. Acad. of Performing Arts, Professional Education Foundation; Chair. Oil Cos Advisory Cttee 2001–; Vice-Chair. Pakistan Advertisers Soc.; mem. Selection Bd Inst. of Business Admin; mem. Corp. Governance Cttee Karachi Stock Exchange; Pres. Pakistan Hockey Fed. 2005–06. *Address:* Office of the Chairman, UBL Fund Managers Ltd, 8th Floor, Executive Tower, Dolmen City, Block 4, Clifton, Karachi, Pakistan (office). *Telephone:* (21) 35290080 (office). *Fax:* (21) 35290070 (office). *E-mail:* info@UBLfunds.com (home). *Website:* www.ublfunds.com (office).

KIRPICHNIKOV, Mikhail Petrovich, DBiolSc; Russian politician, scientist and academic; *Dean, Faculty of Biology, Lomonosov Moscow State University;* b. 9 Nov. 1945, Moscow; m.; one d.; ed Moscow Inst. of Physics and Tech.; with Inst. of Molecular Biology 1972–89; Deputy Head, Head of Div., USSR Cttee on Science and Tech. 1989–91; Head of Div., Head of Dept, Ministry of Science and Tech. Policy 1991–93; Head, Div. of Science, Educ., High School and Tech., Russian Govt 1993–94, Head, Dept of Science and Educ. 1994–98; First Deputy Minister of Science and Tech. July–Sept. 1998, Minister 1998–2001; Prof. and Head, Protein Eng Lab., Inst. of Bio-organic Chemistry, Russian Acad. of Sciences 2000–; Pro-Rector and Head, Innovation Policy and Innovation Project Management Dept, Lomonosov Moscow State Univ. 2004–06, Dean, Faculty of Biology 2006–; Pres. Higher Attestation Comm. of Russian Fed. 2006–; mem. Russian Acad. of Sciences 1997–; Order of Honour 1998, Order of Friendship 2006; State Award in Science and Tech. 1999, Certificate of Merit, Govt of Russian Fed. 1995. *Publications:* several books and more than 300 articles and papers on biology. *Address:* Faculty of Biology, Lomonosov Moscow State University, GSP-2, Leninskie Gory 1/12, Moscow 119992 (office); Institute of Bio-organic Chemistry, Mirlukho-Maklaya str. 16/10, GSP-7 Moscow 117871, Russia (office). *Telephone:* (495) 939-27-76 (office). *E-mail:* kirpichnikov@inbox.ru (office).

KIRPICHNIKOV, Valery Aleksandrovich; Russian politician; b. 29 June 1946, Rostov-on-Don; m.; two c.; ed Leningrad Polytech. Inst.; Lt in air defence forces 1969–71; engineer, sr engineer, Deputy Head of lab., S. Vavilov State Inst. of Optics, Leningrad Region br. 1971–81; Chief Engineer, Research Inst. of Complex Tests 1981–88; Deputy Chair., Chair., Exec. Cttee Sosnovy Bor Town Soviet 1988–92; RSFSR Peoples' Deputy 1990, mem. Supreme Soviet 1990–93; mem. State Duma 1993–98; Deputy Gov. Leningrad Region 1996–98; Pres. Union of Russian Towns 1993–98; Minister of Regional Policy of Russian Fed. 1998–99; First Deputy Minister of Fed., Nat. and Migration Policy 2000–01; f. Russian Union of Local Self-Man. *Publications:* scientific works, patents.

KIRSCH, Philippe, QC, LLM; Canadian judge and fmr diplomatist; b. 1 April 1947, Quebec; ed Stanislas Coll., Montreal, Univ. of Montreal, Acad. of Int. Law, The Hague, The Netherlands, Int. Peace Acad., Vienna, Austria; called to the Bar, Quebec 1970; apptd QC 1988; joined diplomatic service, assignments with Bureau of Legal Affairs and US Div., Dept of Foreign Affairs and Int. Trade, Ottawa, with Embassy in Peru, Perm. Mission to the UN, New York –1985; Dir Legal Operations Div., Dept of External Affairs, Ottawa 1983–88; Amb. and Deputy Perm. Rep. to UN, New York 1988–92; Deputy Legal Adviser and Dir-Gen., Bureau of Legal Affairs, Dept of Foreign Affairs and Int. Trade 1992–94, Asst Deputy Minister for Legal and Consular Affairs 1994–96, Legal Adviser 1994–99; Amb. to Sweden 1999–2003; Judge, Appeals Div., Int. Criminal Court (ICC), The Hague 2003–09, first Pres. ICC 2006–09; Amb. and Agent of Canada in legal disputes 1985–86, 1995–98, 1999–2003; Chair. Preparatory Comm. for ICC 1999–2002; Rep. of Canada to various int. orgs and confs; Chair. UN Legal Ad Hoc Cttees 1993–94, 1997–99; mem. Perm. Court of Arbitration 1995–99; Robert S. Litvack Human Rights Memorial Award 1999, Minister of Foreign Affairs Award for Foreign Policy Excellence 1999, William J. Butler Human Rights Medal 2001. *Publications:* chapters in books, articles in professional journals. *Address:* c/o International Criminal Court, PO Box 19519, 2500 CM The Hague, The Netherlands. *Telephone:* (70) 515-8515. *E-mail:* otp.informationdesk@icc-cpi.int.

KIRSCH, Wolfgang; German banking executive; *CEO, DZ Bank AG;* b. 19 March 1955, Bensberg; m.; two c.; ed Univ. of Cologne; banking apprenticeship at Deutsche Bank 1975–77, Corp. Customers Man. and Authorised Officer, Deutsche Bank, Düsseldorf 1981–88, Gen. Man. Deutsche Bank, Viersen 1988–93, Deputy Man. and Head of Corp. Customers Business, Deutsche Bank, Düsseldorf 1993–96, Deputy Head of Credit Line Man. for Corp. Customers Business Germany, Deutsche Bank, Frankfurt am Main 1996–98, Gen. Man. and Chief Country Officer, Deutsche Bank, Singapore 1998–2000, Man. Dir and Sr Credit Exec. of the Corporates and Real Estate Div. and CIB Corp. and Investment Bank Div., Deutsche Bank, Frankfurt am Main 2000–02; mem. Bd of Man. Dirs and Dir Risk Man. and Int. Business Devt, Deutsche Zentral-Genossenschaftsbank (DZ Bank) AG 2002–05, Deputy Chair. 2005–06, CEO 2006–, also Chair. Supervisory Bd of R + V Versicherung AG, Bausparkasse Schwäbisch Hall AG, Union Asset Man. Holding AG; mem. Supervisory Bd Südzucker AG; Chair. Steering Cttee Unico Banking Group. *Address:* Deutsche Zentral-Genossenschaftsbank AG, Platz der Republik, 60265 Frankfurt am Main, Germany (office). *Telephone:* (69) 7447-01 (office). *Fax:* (69) 7447-1685 (office). *E-mail:* mail@dzbank.de (office). *Website:* www .dzbank.de (office).

KIRSCHNER, Marc W., PhD; American cell biologist and academic; *Professor and Chairman, Department of Systems Biology, Harvard Medical School;* ed Northwestern Univ., Univ. of California, Berkeley; postdoctoral research at Univ. of California, Berkeley and Univ. of Oxford, UK; Asst Prof. of Biochemical Sciences, Princeton Univ. 1972; Assoc. Prof. of Biochemical Sciences, Princeton Univ. 1976–78, Prof. of Biochemical Sciences 1978; Prof. of Biochemistry and Biophysics, Univ. of California, San Francisco 1978–93; Carl W. Walter Prof. and Chair. Dept of Cell Biology, Harvard Medical School 1993–2003, Founder and Chair. Dept of Systems Biology 2003–, Co-Founder Inst. for Chem. and Cell Biology, Harvard Univ. 1999; mem. NAS, American Acad. of Arts and Sciences; Foreign mem. Royal Soc. 1999–, Academia Europaea; William C. Rose Award, American Soc. for Biochemistry and Molecular Biology 2001, Gairdner Foundation Int. Award (Canada) 2001, E.B. Wilson Medal, American Soc. for Cell Biology 2003, Dickson Prize for Science, Carnegie Mellon Univ. 2004. *Publication:* Cells, Embryos and Evolution (with John C. Gerhart) 1997, The Plausibility of Life: Resolving Darwin's Dilemma (with John C. Gerhart) 2005. *Address:* Department of Systems Biology, Harvard Medical School, 200 Longwood Avenue, Boston, MA 02115, USA (office). *Telephone:* (617) 432-2250 (office). *Fax:* (617) 432-0420 (office). *E-mail:* marc@hms.harvard.edu (office). *Website:* sysbio.med.harvard.edu/faculty/ kirschner (office); (office).

KIRSH, Nathan (Natie), BA; South African business executive; *Founder, Kirsh Holding Group;* b. 6 Jan. 1932, Potchefstroom; m. Frances Herr; one s. two d.; ed Univ. of Witwatersrand; est. first business venture, corn milling business, in Swaziland 1958, expanded into wholesale food distribution in S Africa; f. Kirsh Holding Group, currently Chair. Kirsh Group of Cos (interests include property holdings in Australia, S Africa, UK and USA); group cos include interests in Swazi Plaza Properties, Crest JMT Leather, Holmes Place (fitness chain), Kitec Industries (pipe maker), Abacus Property Group Ltd; property portfolio includes Tower 42 (fmrly Nat West Tower), London; Propr Jetro Holdings Inc. (operates Jetro Cash and Carry stores and Restaurant Depot warehouses in New York City); Dir Magal Security Systems, Israel 1984–; Trustee Eurona Foundation; Hon. DrIur (Univ. of Swaziland) 1994. *Address:* Kirsh Holding Group, 4th Floor, Liqhaga House, Nkoseluhlaza Street, Manzini, Swaziland (office). *Telephone:* 5052693 (office). *Fax:* 5052001 (office). *E-mail:* info@swaki.co.sz (office). *Website:* www.swaki.co.sz (office).

KIRST, Michael W., MPA, PhD; American academic; *Professor Emeritus of Education and Business Administration, Stanford University;* b. 1 Aug. 1939, West Reading, Pa; s. of Russell Kirst and Marian Kirst (née Weile); m. Wendy Burdsall 1975; one s. one d.; ed Dartmouth Coll., Harvard Univ.; Assoc. Dir President's Comm. on White House Fellows. Nat. Advisory Council on Educ. of Disadvantaged Children 1966; Dir Program Planning and Evaluation, Bureau of Elementary and Secondary Educ., Office of Educ. 1967; Staff Dir Senate Sub-cttee on Manpower, Employment and Poverty 1968; Prof. of Educ. and Business Admin., Stanford Univ. 1968, now Prof. Emer., also affiliated with Stanford Center on Adolescence; Pres. California State Bd of Educ. 1977–81; Chair. Bd of International Comparative Studies in Educ., NAS 1994–; Dir Policy Analysis for California Educ.; Dir Consortium for Policy Research in Educ.; mem. Nat. Acad. of Educ., USA, International Acad. of Educ. and numerous other educ. bds, cttees, etc. *Publications include:* Schools in Conflict: Political Turbulence in American Education (with F. Wirt) 1992, Contemporary Issues in Education: Perspectives from Australia and USA (with G. Hancock and D. Grossman) 1983, Who Controls Our Schools: American Values in Conflict 1984, Political Dynamics of American Education 2001, From High School to College 2004. *Address:* School of Education, Stanford University, 485 Lasuen Mall, Stanford, CA 94305-3096, USA (office). *Telephone:* (650) 723-4412 (office). *Fax:* (650) 725-7412 (office). *E-mail:* mwk@ stanford.edu (office). *Website:* www.michaelwkirst.com.

KIRWAN, William E., PhD; American university administrator, academic and mathematician; *Chancellor, University System of Maryland;* b. 14 April 1938, Louisville, Ky; s. of Albert Dennis Kirwan and Elizabeth H. Kirwan; m. Patricia Harper 1960; one s. one d.; ed Univ. of Kentucky, Rutgers Univ.; Asst Instructor, Rutgers Univ. 1963–64; Asst Prof., Dept of Math., Univ. of Maryland 1964–68; Visiting Lecturer, Royal Holloway Coll., Univ. of London, UK 1966–67; Assoc. Prof., Dept of Math., Univ. of Md at Coll. Park 1968–72, Prof. 1972–, Chair. Dept of Math. 1977–81, Vice-Chancellor for Academic Affairs 1981–88, Acting Chancellor 1982, Vice-Pres. for Academic Affairs and Provost 1988–89, Acting Pres. 1988–89, Pres. 1989–98; Pres. Ohio State Univ. 1998–2002; Chancellor Univ. System of Md 2002–; Chair. Nat. Asscn of State Univs and Land Grant Colls 1995–; mem. Knight Comm. on Intercollegiate Athletics (Co-Chair 2007–), American Math. Soc., Math. Asscn of America; American Acad. of Arts and Sciences 2002–; mem. Editorial Bd Journal of Diversity in Higher Education 2007–; Ed. Proceedings of the American Mathematical Society 1979–85; NDEA Fellow 1960–63; NSF Grants 1965–82; mem. Bd Dirs Council for Higher Educ. Accreditation; Greater Baltimore Cttee, Econ. Alliance of Greater Baltimore, Md Business Roundtable for Educ., Wendy's Int; Officier, Order of Leopold II, Belgium 1989; Hall of Distinguished Alumni, Univ. of Kentucky, Md House of Dels Speaker's Medallion 2007. *Publications:* Advances in Complex Analysis (co-ed. with L. Zalcman) 1976; numerous published research articles and seminar talks. *Leisure interests:* classical music, tennis. *Address:* Office of the Chancellor, University System of Maryland, 3300 Metzerott Road, Adelphi, MD 20783-1690, USA (office). *Telephone:* (301) 445-1901 (office). *Fax:* (301) 445-1931 (office). *E-mail:* bkirwan@usmd.edu (office). *Website:* www.usmd .edu/usm/chancellor (office).

KISELEV, Anatoly Ivanovich; Russian aviation engineer; b. 29 April 1938, Moscow; m.; one s. one d.; ed Moscow Inst. of Aviation Tech.; fmr electrician, Moscow Khrunichev Machine Construction Factory, then Eng, tester, head of lab., head of workshop, Deputy Dir 1956–72, Dir 1975–93, involved in merger of Moscow Khrunichev Machine Construction Factory and Salut Construction Bureau, Dir M.V. Khrunichev State Space Scientific Production Cen. 1993; Deputy Head, then First Chief of Dept USSR Ministry of Gen. Machine Construction 1972–75; Dir-Gen. Russian-American Lokhid-Khrunichev (Int. Launch Services) 1994–2001, mem. Bd Dirs 2001–; Order for Service to Motherland,; Lenin Prize, Hero of Socialist Labour. *Address:* M.V. Khrunichev State Space Scientific Production Center, 121087 Moscow, Novozavodskaya str. 18, Russia (office). *Telephone:* (495) 145-88-54 (office). *Fax:* (495) 142-59-00 (home). *Website:* www.khrunichev.ru.

KISELEV, Oleg Vladimirovich, CandTechSci; Russian politician and engineer; *Chairman, Renaissance Capital;* b. 1 June 1953, Divnoye, Stavropol territory; m.; one s.; ed Moscow State Inst. of Construction; teacher Inst. of Steel and Alloys 1981–86; Deputy Dir Inst. of Chem. Physics USSR (now Russian) Acad. of Sciences 1986–88; Founder and Head Alfa-Eco co-operative, then Jt Venture Alfa-Eco, then Alfa production-finance co. including Alfa Bank and other affiliates 1988–91; Founder, Pres. and Chair. Bd Dirs Mosexpo Co. 1991–; co-f. IMPEX Bank 1993, Pres. and Chair. Bd Dirs 1993–2001; mem. Bd Dirs Russian Bank of Reconstruction and Devt 2001–; Man. Dir, Chair. Bd Metalloinvest (holding co.) 2001–; Chair. Bd of Dirs Renaissance Capital 2004–; Vice-Pres. Russian Union of Industrialists & Entrepreneurs; mem. Int. Asscn of Business Dirs 1989–; Chair. Council on Foreign Econ. Relations, Ministry of Foreign Affairs 1992; mem. Govt Union on Business 1993–94, Pres. Council 1994, Bd Dirs Russian-American Foundation of Support of Business 1994–, Public Council on Foreign and Defence Policy, Bd Asscn of Russian Banks 1999–. *Address:* Metalloinvest Co., Yefremova str. 12a, 119048 Moscow, Russia (office). *Telephone:* (495) 245-72-10 (office).

KISELEV, Yevgenii Alekseyevich; Russian broadcast journalist; b. 15 June 1956, Moscow; s. of Aleksei Kiselev and Anna Kiselev; m. Masha Shakhova 1974; one s.; ed Inst. of Asian and African Studies, Moscow State Univ.; teacher of Persian (Farsi) language, Higher School of KGB 1981–84; corresp., Radio Moscow Middle Eastern Dept 1984–86; TV journalist 1987–; regular host '120 Minutes' breakfast show 1987–90, staff corresp. news div. Gosteleradio (fmr USSR State Cttee for TV and radio broadcasting) 1989–90; made series of documentaries on everyday life in Israel 1989, 1990; joined newly founded Russian TV 1991, anchorman 'Vesti' late-night news programme; joined Ostankino State TV co. 1992; started 'Itogi' weekly news and current affairs programme 1992, on TNT station 2001–; Co-Founder and Vice-Pres. NTV independent broadcasting co. 1993–2000, Gen. Dir 2000–01; Co-founder, NTV-Plus Co. (direct satellite broadcasting) 1996; Gen. Dir TV-6 Independent Broadcasting Co. 2001–02; Ed.-in-Chief TVS Broadcasting 2002–2003; Ed.-in-Chief Moskovskiye Novosti (Moscow News) newspaper Oct. 2003–2005 (resgnd); currently radio programme presenter for Ekho Moskvy (Radio Echo of Moscow) 2005–; mem. Acad. of Russian TV; Journalist of the Year, Moscow Journalistic Union 1993, included on list of 100 most influential people in Russia, publ monthly by Nezavisimaya Gazeta 1993–; Int. Press Freedom Award, Cttee to Protect Journalists, New York 1995. *Leisure interest:* playing tennis. *Address:* Ekho Moskvy, 119019, Moscow, ul. Novyi Arbat 11, Russia (office). *Telephone:* (495) 695-92-29 (office). *Fax:* (495) 695-91-02 (office). *E-mail:* echo@echo.msk.ru (office). *Website:* echo.msk.ru (office).

KISHIDA, Fumio; Japanese politician; *Minister of Foreign Affairs;* b. 29 July 1957; mem. House of Reps representing Hiroshima Pref. First Dist 1993–; fmr Vice-Minister for Construction, fmr Sr Vice-Minister of Educ.; Minister of State for Okinawa and Northern Territories Affairs, Quality-of-Life Policy, Science and Tech. Policy, Challenge Again, and Regulatory Reform 2007–08 (resgnd); Minister of Foreign Affairs 2012–; mem. LDP (Liberal Democratic Party). *Address:* Ministry of Foreign Affairs, 2-2-1, Kasumigaseki, Chiyoda-ku, Tokyo 100-8919 (office); Jiyu-Minshuto (Liberal Democratic Party), 1-11-23, Nagata-cho, Chiyoda-ku, Tokyo 100-8910, Japan (office). *Telephone:* (3) 3580-3311 (office); (3) 3581-6211 (office). *Fax:* (3) 3581-2667 (office). *E-mail:* webmaster@mofa.go.jp (office); koho@ldp.jimin .or.jp (office). *Website:* www.mofa.go.jp (office); www.jimin.jp (office); www.kantei .go.jp (office).

KISHIDA, Katsuhiko; Japanese business executive; *Chairman and Representative Director, Yamaha Corporation;* b. 19 Nov. 1941; joined Nippon Gakki Co. Ltd (now Yamaha Corpn) 1966, Gen. Man. Piano Div. 1992, Dir 1994, Man. Dir 1998, Sr Man. Dir 2000, Chair. and Rep. Dir 2004–. *Address:* Yamaha Corporation, 10-1 hakazawa-cho, Hamamatsu, Shizuoka 430-8650, Japan (office). *Telephone:* (5) 3460-2800 (office). *Fax:* (5) 3460-2802 (office). *Website:* www.global.yamaha.com (office).

KISHIMOTO, Tadamitsu, MD, PhD; Japanese immunologist, academic and fmr university president; *Visiting Professor, Laboratory of Immune Regulation, Immunology Frontier Research Center, Osaka University;* b. 7 May 1939, Osaka; s. of Tadanobu Kishimoto and Yasuko Kishimoto; ed Osaka Univ. Medical School; Research Fellow, Dept of Medicine, Johns Hopkins Univ. School of Medicine, USA 1970–73, Asst Prof. 1973–74; Asst Prof., Dept of Medicine III, Osaka Univ. Medical School 1974–79, Prof. and Chair. 1991–98, Prof., Dept of Pathology and Medicine 1979–83, Prof., Inst. for Molecular and Cellular Biology 1983–91, Dean, Osaka Univ. Medical School 1995–97, Pres. Osaka Univ. 1997–2003, now Visiting Prof., Lab. of Immune Regulation, Immunology Frontier Research Center; Clemens von Pirquet Distinguished Prof., Medicine and Immunology, Univ. California, Davis, USA 2004; Chair. Seventh Int. Congress on AIDS in Asia and the Pacific 2005, 14th Int. Congress of Immunology 2010; mem. Council for Science and Tech. Policy, Cabinet Office 2004–06; fmr Pres. Int. Immunopharmacology Soc., Int. Cytokine Soc., Japanese Immunology Soc.; mem. Japan Acad. 1995, Deutsche Akad. der Naturforscher Leopoldina 2005; Foreign Assoc., NAS 1991; Foreign Assoc. mem. Inst. of Medicine, NAS 1997; Hon. Citizen, Tondabayashi City 1992; Hon. Prof., Fourth Mil. Medical Univ., Xi'an, People's Repub. of China 2002; Hon. mem. American Asscn of Immunologists 1992, American Soc. of Hematology 1997, Int. Asscn of Dental Research 2001, World Innovation Foundation 2002; Order of Culture (conferred by Emperor) 1998, Royal Decoration (Thailand) 2012; Hon. DSc (Mahidol Univ.) 2003; Dr hc (Universidad Technologica de Santiago) 2001; Behring-Kitasato Prize 1982, Osaka Science Prize 1983, Erwin von Bälz Prize 1986, Takeda Prize 1988, Asahi Prize 1988, Prize of the Japanese Medical Asscn 1990, Person of Cultural Merits, Japan 1990, Scientific Achievement Award, Int. Asscn of Allergology and Clinical Immunology 1991, Imperial Prize, Japan Acad. 1992, Sandoz Prize for Immunology, Int. Union of Immunology Soc. 1992, Avery-Landsteiner Prize, German Immunology Soc. 1996, Donald Seldin Award, Int. Soc. of Nephrology 1999, ISI Citation Laureate Award 2000, Robert Koch Gold Medal 2003, Honorary Lifetime Achievement Award, Int. Cytokine Soc. 2006, Seventh Int. Award, Japan Rheumatism Foundation 2008, Crafoord Prize, Royal Swedish Acad. of Sciences (co-recipient) 2009, Japan Prize (co-recipient) 2011. *Achievements include:* has made fundamental contribs to the understanding of cytokine functions through a series of studies on IL-6, its receptor system and transcription factors; developed anti-IL6 receptor therapy for several immune disorders, including Castleman's disease, rheumatoid arthritis and juvenile idiopathic arthritis. *Address:* Laboratory of Immune Regulation, Immunology Frontier Research Center, Osaka University, 1-3 Yamadaoka, Suita, Osaka 565-0871 (office); 3-5-31, Nankano-cho, Tondabayashi City, Osaka, Japan (home). *Telephone:* (6) 6879-4956 (office); (7) 2124-0532 (home). *Fax:* (6) 6879-4958 (office). *E-mail:* kishimot@ifrec.osaka-u.ac.jp (office). *Website:* www.ifrec.osaka-u.ac.jp/jpn/laboratory/immuneregulation (office).

KISHLANSKY, Mark Alan, PhD, FRHistS; American historian and academic; *Frank Baird, Jr Professor of History, Harvard University;* b. 10 Nov. 1948, Brooklyn, NY; s. of Morris Kishlansky and Charlotte Katz; m. Jeanne Thiel 1975; two s.; ed Commack High School, State Univ. of New York at Stony Brook and Brown Univ.; Prof. of History, Univ. of Chicago 1975–91, Northwestern Univ. 1983; Prof. of History, Harvard Univ. 1991–97, Frank Baird, Jr Prof. of History 1997–; Mellon Visiting Prof. of History, California Inst. of Tech. 1990; mem. Cttee on Social Thought 1990–91; various research awards and other distinctions. *Publications:* The Rise of the New Model Army 1979, Parliamentary Selection: Social and Political Choice in Early Modern England, Early Modern Europe: The Crisis of Authority (co-ed. with C. M. Gray and E. Cochrane) 1987, Civilization in the West (with P. Geary and P. O'Brien) 1991, Sources of the West (ed.) 1991, Societies and Cultures in World Civilizations (with P. Geary, P. O'Brien, R. B. Worg) 1995, A Monarchy Transformed 1996. *Leisure interests:* Shakespeare, baseball, comedy. *Address:* Department of History, Robinson M-01, Harvard University, Cambridge, MA 02138, USA (office). *Telephone:* (617) 496-3427 (office). *Fax:* (617) 496-3425 (office). *E-mail:* mkishlan@fas.harvard.edu (office). *Website:* www.courses.fas.harvard.edu/~history (office).

KISKA, Andrej; Slovak business executive, politician and head of state; *President;* b. 2 Feb. 1963, Poprad; m. Martina Kisková; four c.; ed Slovak Tech. Univ., Bratislava; began career as designer, Naftoprojekt, Poprad; worked in USA in construction and gas stations 1990–91; f. financial services cos Triangle Group International 1992, TatraCredit 1996, Quatro 1999; f. Dobrý Anjel (Good Angel, non-profit org.), Chair. 2006–13; Pres. of Slovakia 2014–; Trend Magazine Man. of the Year 2006; Krištálové krídlo (Crystal Wing award for philanthropy) 2011. *Address:* Office of the President, Hodžovo nám. 1, POB 128, 810 00 Bratislava, Slovakia (office). *Telephone:* (2) 5788-8173 (office). *Fax:* (2) 5788-8105 (office). *E-mail:* informacie@prezident.sk (office). *Website:* www.prezident.sk (office); www.andrejkiska.sk.

KISLYAK, Sergey Ivanovich; Russian diplomatist; *Ambassador to USA;* b. 1950; m.; one d.; ed Moscow State Inst. of Eng and Tech., USSR Acad. of Foreign Trade; joined Ministry of Foreign Affairs 1977, Second Sec., Perm. Mission to UN, New York 1981–85, First Sec., Counsellor of Embassy in Washington, DC 1985–89, Deputy Dir Dept of Int. Orgs, Ministry of Foreign Affairs 1989–91, Deputy Dir Dept of Int. Scientific and Tech. Cooperation 1991–93, Dir 1993–95, Dir Dept of Security and Disarmament 1995–98, Amb. to Belgium, concurrently Perm. Rep. to NATO, Brussels 1998–2003, Deputy Minister of Foreign Affairs 2003–08, Amb. to USA and Perm. Observer, OAS, Washington, DC 2008–; fmr mem. Coll. of Ministry of Foreign Affairs. *Address:* Embassy of the Russian Federation, 2650 Wisconsin Avenue NW, Washington, DC 20007, USA (office). *Telephone:* (202) 298-5700 (office). *Fax:* (202) 298-5735 (office). *E-mail:* russianembassy@mindspring.com (office); rusembus@erols.com (office). *Website:* www.russianembassy.org (office).

KISSIN, Evgeny Igorevich; Russian pianist; b. 10 Oct. 1971, Moscow; s. of Igor Kissin and Emilia Kissin; ed Moscow Gnessin Music School, studied piano with Anna Kantor; debut playing Mozart's D-minor concerto aged 10; appeared with Moscow Philharmonic, playing Chopin concertos 1984; tour of Japan with the Moscow Virtuosi; debut in Western Europe with the Berlin Radio orchestra 1987; British debut at the Lichfield Festival with the BBC Philharmonic 1987; London Symphony Orchestra concert 1988; concerts with the Royal Philharmonic and Yuri Temirkanov 1990; promenade concert debut with the BBC Symphony, playing Tchaikovsky's First Concerto 1990; US debut with the New York Philharmonic and a solo recital at Carnegie Hall 1990; subsequent US tour included Tanglewood 1991; Grammy Award ceremony and performances with the Chicago Symphony and Philadelphia Orchestra 1991–92; performed with the Boston Symphony; London recital debut and concert with the Philharmonia 1992–93; Prokofiev Concertos with the Berlin Philharmonic 1992–93; played Chopin and Schumann at the Royal Festival Hall, London 1997; first pianist to perform a recital at the London Proms 1997; Chopin's First Concerto at the London Proms with the Bavarian State Orchestra 1999; first concerto soloist to play in the Proms Opening concert 2000; 10th anniversary tour of recitals in the USA, including Carnegie Hall 2000–01; appearances with the Warsaw Philharmonic, Philharmonia Orchestra, Bavarian Staatskapelle, Chicago Symphony, Boston Symphony, Metropolitan Opera, Bayerische Rundfunk, and the Leipzig Gewandhaus 1999–2001; Brahms' Concerto No. 2 in B flat major at the London Proms 2002; Hon. mem. Royal Acad. of Music; Hon. DMus (Manhattan School of Music) 2001, Dr hc (Hebrew Univ. of Jerusalem) 2010; Diapason d'Or (France), Grand Prix Nobel Academie de Disque (France), Edison Klassiek Award (Netherlands) 1990, Chigiana Acad. Musician of the Year (Sienna) 1991, Musical America's Instrumentalist of the Year 1995, Triumph Award for outstanding contribution to Russia's culture 1997, Echo Award (Germany) 2002, Shostakovich Award (Moscow) 2003, Herbert von Karajan Award 2005, Arturo Benedetti Michelangeli Award 2007, Distinguished Artistic Leadership Award, Atlantic Council 2008. *Recordings include:* Tchaikovsky Concerto No.1 with Berlin Philharmonic conducted by Herbert von Karajan; live recording of Chopin Conertos with Moscow Philharmonic conducted by Dmitri Kitaenko 1984, Rachmaninov 2nd Concerto and Etudes Tableaux with the London Symphony conducted by Gergiev, Rachmaninov Concerto No. 3, Chopin Vols I and II live recital from Carnegie Hall, Prokofiev Piano Concertos 1 and 3 with Berlin Philharmonic conducted by Claudio Abbado, Haydn and Schubert Sonatas 1995, Beethoven: Moonlight Sonata, Franck: Prelude, Choral et Fugue, Brahms: Paganini Variations 1998, Chopin: 4 Ballades, Berceuse op 57, Barcarolle op 60, Scherzo No. 4 op 54 1999, Chopin recital including 24 Preludes Op. 28, Sonata No, 2 and Polonaise in A-flat, Brahms 2003, Scriabin, Medtner, Stravinsky (Grammy Award for Best Instrumental Soloist Performance, without orchestra 2006) 2005,

Schubert: Piano Music for Four Hands (with James Levine) 2006, Schumann's Piano Concerto and Mozart's Piano Concerto No. 24 2007, Beethoven's Complete Piano Concertos 2008, Prokofiev Piano Concertos Nos. 2 and 3 (Grammy Award for Best Instrumental Soloist Performance with Orchestra 2010) 2009, Mozart Piano Concertos Nos. 20 and 27 2010. *Leisure interests:* friends, reading, theatre, walking. *Address:* c/o EMI Classics, 27 Wrights Lane, London, W8 5SW, England (office). *Telephone:* (20) 7795-7000 (office). *Website:* www.emimusic.com (office); www.kissinmusic.com.

KISSINGER, Henry Alfred, MA, PhD; American academic, international consultant and fmr government official; *Chairman, Kissinger Associates;* b. 27 May 1923, Fuerth, Germany; s. of Louis Kissinger and Paula Stern; m. 1st Anne Fleisher 1949 (divorced 1964); one s. one d.; m. 2nd Nancy Maginnes 1974; ed George Washington High School, Harvard Coll., Harvard Univ.; went to USA 1938; naturalized US Citizen 1943; US Army 1943–46; Dir Study Group on Nuclear Weapons and Foreign Policy, Council of Foreign Relations 1955–56; Dir Special Studies Project, Rockefeller Brothers Fund 1956–58; Consultant, Weapons System Evaluation Group, Joint Chiefs of Staff 1956–60, Nat. Security Council 1961–63, US Arms Control and Disarmament Agency 1961–69, Dept of State 1965–68 and to various other bodies; Faculty mem. Harvard Univ. 1954–69; Dept of Govt and Center for Int. Affairs; faculty Harvard Univ. Center for Int. Affairs 1960–69; Dir Harvard Int. Seminar 1951–69, Harvard Defense Studies Program 1958–69, Asst to Pres. of USA for Nat. Security Affairs 1969–75; Sec. of State 1973–77; prominent in American negotiations for the Viet Nam settlement of Jan. 1973 and in the negotiations for a Middle East ceasefire 1973, 1974; Trustee, Center for Strategic and Int. Studies 1977–; Chair. Kissinger Assocs Inc. (Kissinger McLarty Assocs Inc. 1999–2008) 1982–; mem. Pres.'s Foreign Intelligence Advisory Bd 1984–90; Chair. Nat. Bipartisan Comm. on Cen. America 1983–84; fmr Chair. US Comm. investigating Sept. 11 attacks; Counsellor to J. P. Morgan Chase Bank and mem. of its Int. Advisory Council; Hon. Gov. Foreign Policy Asscn; Sr Fellow, Aspen Inst., syndicated columnist LA Times 1984–; Adviser to Bd of Dirs American Express, Forstmann Little & Co., Dir Emer. Freeport McMoran Copper and Gold Inc., Conti Group Cos Ltd, The TCW Group, US Olympic Cttee, Int. Rescue Cttee; Chair. American Int. Group, Int. Advisory Bd; mem. Exec. Cttee Trilateral Comm.; Chair. Eisenhower Exchange Fellowships; Chancellor The Coll. of William and Mary; Hon. Chair. World Cup USA 1994; Woodrow Wilson Book Prize 1958, American Inst. for Public Service Award 1973, Nobel Peace Prize 1973, American Legion Distinguished Service Medal 1974, Wateler Peace Prize 1974, Presidential Medal of Freedom 1977, Medal of Liberty 1986, Hon. KCMG 1995, and many other awards and prizes. *Publications:* Nuclear Weapons and Foreign Policy 1956, A World Restored: Castlereagh, Metternich and the Restoration of Peace 1812–22 1957, The Necessity for Choice: Prospects of American Foreign Policy 1961, The Troubled Partnership: A Reappraisal of the Atlantic Alliance 1965, American Foreign Policy (3 essays) 1969, White House Years 1979, For the Record 1981, Years of Upheaval 1982, Observations: Selected Speeches and Essays 1982–84 1985, Diplomacy 1994, Years of Renewal 1999, Does America Need a Foreign Policy? 2001, Ending the Vietnam War 2003, Crisis 2003; and numerous articles on US foreign policy, international affairs and diplomatic history. *Address:* 350 Park Avenue, New York, NY 10022; Suite 400, 1800 K Street, NW, Washington, DC 20006, USA. *Telephone:* (212) 759-7919 (NY); (202) 822-8182 (DC). *Website:* www.kmaglobal.com.

KITAGAWA, Kazuo, LLB; Japanese lawyer and politician; b. 2 March 1953; ed Faculty of Law, Soka Univ.; practised law 1981–90; licensed tax accountant 2000; mem. House of Reps for Osaka Constituency 1990–, Dir Standing Cttee on Audit 1990–93, on Security 1990–93, on Finance 1994–96, on Budget 1998–99, Nat. Basic Policies 2000; Parl. Vice-Minister for Finance 1993–94; Chair. Standing Cttee on Science and Tech. 1999–2000, New Komeito Policy Research Council 2000–03; Minister of Land, Infrastructure and Transport 2004–06. *Address:* c/o Liberal-Democratic Party—LDP (Jiyu-Minshuto), 1-11-23, Nagata-cho, Chiyoda-ku, Tokyo 100-8910, Japan. *Telephone:* (3) 3581-6211. *E-mail:* koho@ldp.jimin.or.jp. *Website:* www.jimin.jp.

KITAJIMA, Kosuke; Japanese swimmer; b. 22 Sept. 1982, Tokyo; ed Nippon Sport Science Univ., Tokyo; fourth place in 100m breaststroke, Olympic Games, Sydney 2000; broke oldest swimming world record (200m breaststroke) at Asian Games 2002; gold medal, 100m and 200m breaststroke (set two world records), World Championships (long course), Barcelona 2003, 100m and 200m breaststroke, Olympic Games, Athens 2004, 200m breaststroke, World Championships (long course), Melbourne 2007, 100m (world record time of 58.91) and 200m breaststroke, Olympic Games, Beijing 2008, Pan Pacific Championships 2010; silver medal, 100m breaststroke, FINA World Championships (short course), Moscow 2002, 100m breaststroke, World Championships (long course), Melbourne 2007, 200m breaststroke, World Championships (long course), Shanghai 2011, 4×100m medley relay, Olympic Games, London 2012; bronze medal, 100m breaststroke, World Championships, Fukuoka 2001, 4×100m medley relay, World Championships, Barcelona 2003, 4×100m medley relay, Olympic Games, Athens 2004, 4×100m medley relay, Olympic Games, Beijing 2008, 4×100m medley relay, World Championships (long course), Barcelona 2013; set world record time of 2:07.51 for 200m breaststroke June 2008; Medal with Purple Ribbon; Most Valuable Player, Asian Games 2002, Tokyo Medal of Honour, World Pacific Rim Swimmer of the Year 2003, 2007. *Leisure interests:* fashion, driving. *Address:* c/o IMPRINT, 2-16-9-7F, Higashi, Shibuya-ku, Tokyo 150-0011, Japan (office). *Telephone:* (3) 6690-0305 (office). *Fax:* (3) 6849-4248 (office). *E-mail:* info@imprint.jp (office). *Website:* www.imprint.jp (office); www.kitajima-kosuke.com.

KITAJIMA, Yoshitoshi; Japanese business executive; *Chairman, President and CEO, Dai Nippon Printing Company Ltd;* joined The Fuji Bank Ltd 1958; joined Dai Nippon Printing Co. Ltd 1963, CEO 1970–, Chair. and Pres. 1979–; Pres. DNP IMS America Corpn 1979–; Dir Hokkaido Coca-Cola Bottling Co. Ltd 1971–, Rep. Dir and Pres. 1980–, Chair. 2007–; mem. Bd of Dirs TV Asahi Corpn, The Japan Forum; Corp. Auditor, Dai-ichi Mutual Life Insurance Co.; mem. EU-Japan Fest Cttee, Advisory Cttee Asia Pacific Univ.; Kt of the Dannebrog (Denmark), Commdr, Légion d'honneur 2007. *Address:* Dai Nippon Printing Company Ltd, 1-1 Ichigaya Kagacho1-chome, Shinjuku-ku, Tokyo 162-8001, Japan (office). *Telephone:* (3) 3266-2111 (office). *Fax:* (3) 5225-8239 (office). *E-mail:* info@dnp.co.jp (office). *Website:* www.dnp.co.jp (office).

KITAMURA, Hiroshi, KBE; Japanese diplomatist and university administrator; b. 20 Jan. 1929, Osaka; m. Sachiko Kitamura 1953; two d.; ed Univ. of Tokyo, Fletcher School of Law and Diplomacy, Tufts Univ., Mass., USA; joined Foreign Affairs Ministry 1953, served in Washington, DC, New York, Delhi; First Sec., Embassy in London 1963–66; with Mission to OECD, Paris 1971–74; Exec. Asst to Prime Minister 1974–76; Deputy Dir-Gen. American Affairs Bureau 1977–79, Dir-Gen. 1982–84, Deputy Vice-Minister of Foreign Affairs 1984–87, Deputy Minister 1987–88; Consul-Gen. San Francisco 1979–82, Amb. to Canada 1988–90, to the UK 1991–94; Corp. Adviser, Mitsubishi Corpn 1994–99; Pres. Shumei Univ. 1998–2001; Prime Minister's Personal Rep. to Venice Summit 1987, Toronto Summit 1988; Fellow, Center for Int. Affairs, Harvard Univ. 1970; Chair. Japan–British Soc. 1994–2003; Gold and Silver Star, Order of the Rising Sun 1999; Hon. LLD (Northumbria) 1993. *Publications include:* Psychological Dimensions of US–Japanese Relations 1971, Between Friends (co-author) 1985, The UK Seen through an Ambassador's Eyes (in Japanese), Diplomacy and Food (in Japanese), An Ambassador and his Lhasa Apso (in Japanese). *Leisure interests:* Japanese classical music, food and wine, golf. *Address:* 1-15-6 Jingumae, Shibuya-ku, Tokyo, Japan (office). *Telephone:* (3) 3470-4630 (home). *Fax:* (3) 3470-4830 (home).

KITAMURA, Norio; Japanese business executive; b. 1942; ed Kagoshima Univ.; joined Toyota Motor Corpn, Pres. Toyota Motor Italia SpA 1996–2005, Chair. and CEO 2005–06; joined Japan Post Service Co. Ltd 2006, Chair. and CEO (following privatization Oct. 2007) 2007–10, CEO Japan Post Holdings Co. Ltd (Japan Post Group) 2007–10. *Address:* c/o Japan Post Service Co. Ltd, 1-3-2 Kasumigaseki, Chiyoda-ku, Tokyo 100-8798, Japan.

KITAMURA, So; Japanese playwright; b. 5 July 1952, Ohtsu-shi; m. Konomi Kitamura; one d.; Leader, Project Navi 1986–2003; Dir Shiga Prefecture Center for Creation of Art for Citizens, Kusatsu 2006–07; Kishida Gikyoku-sho 1984, Kinoleuni-ya engeki-sho 1989. *Films:* Tokiwa-so no seishun 1996, The Angel's Egg 2006. *Publications:* plays include: Hogiuta, So-Ko Gingatetsudo no yoru; novels include: Kaijin nijumenso den (Shincho sha), Seido no majin (Shincho sha), Kenji (Kadokawa). *Leisure interest:* movies.

KITANO, Takeshi; Japanese film director, actor, comedian and screenwriter; b. 18 Jan. 1947, Tokyo; ed Meiji Univ. *Films:* Makoto-chan (actor) 1980, Danpu wataridori (actor) 1981, Manon (actor) 1981, Sukkari... sono ki de! (actor) 1981, Merry Christmas, Mr. Lawrence (actor) 1983, Jukkai no mosquito (actor) 1983, Kanashii kibun de joke (actor) 1985, Yasha (actor) 1985, Komikku zasshi nanka iranai! (actor) 1986, Anego (actor) 1988, Sono otoko, kyobo ni tsuki (writer, director, actor) 1989, Hoshi tsugu mono (actor) 1990, 3-4x jugatsu (writer, director, actor) 1990, Ano natsu, ichiban shizukana umi (writer, director) 1991, Sakana kara daiokishin! (actor) 1992, Erotikkuna kankei (actor) 1992, Sonatine (writer, director, actor) 1993, Kyôto tanjô (writer, actor) 1993, Minnâ-yatteruka! (writer, director, actor) 1995, Johnny Mnemonic (actor) 1995, Gonin (actor) 1995, Kidzu ritan (writer, director) 1996, Hana-bi (writer, director, actor) (Venice Film Festival Golden Lion) 1997, Tokyo Eyes (actor) 1998, Kikujiro no natsu (writer, director, actor) 1999, Gohatto (actor) 1999, Brother (writer, director, actor) 2000, Batoru rowairau (Battle Royale) (actor) 2000, Dolls (writer, director) 2002, Asakusa Kid (writer) 2002, Battle Royale II (actor) 2003, Zatôichi (writer, director, actor) (Venice Film Festival Silver Lion) 2003, Izô: Kaosu mataha fujôri no kijin (actor) 2004, Chi to hone 2004, Takeshis' 2005, Gegege no Kitano 2007, Achilles and the Tortoise 2008, Outrage 2010. *Leisure interest:* writing. *Address:* Office Kitano Inc., Tokyo, Japan. *E-mail:* office@office-kitano.co.jp. *Website:* www.office-kitano.co.jp.

KITARO; Japanese musician; b. (Takahashi Masanori), 1953, Toyohashi; self-taught electric guitar player; began music career during school studies; founding mem. rock band The Far East Family Band –1976; abandoned rock for new age music and released first solo album Astral Voyage 1978; composed musical score for TV documentary series Silk Road 1980; signed with Geffen Records 1986; first live tour of N America leading to sales of two million albums in US 1987; featured as key artist and composer in Japan's Millennium celebration event; composed soundtrack for Chinese drama The Soong Sisters 2002; performs annual televised concerts from mountain location at his Japanese home and studio base in Nagano Pref. *Albums include:* Astral Voyage 1978, Millennia 1978, Ten Kai Astral Trip 1978, Full Moon Story 1979, Ki 1979, Oasis 1979, Silk Road Suite (Vols 1–4) 1980–83, Ten Huang 1980, Queen of Millennia 1982, India 1983, Tenjiku 1983, Tenku 1986, Silver Cloud 1986, Toward the West 1986, The Light of the Spirit 1987, Kojiki 1990, Kitaro Live in America 1991, Dream 1992, Mandala 1994, Peace on Earth 1996, Cirque Ingenieux 1998, Heaven and Earth 1997, Gaia 1998, Thinking of You 1999, Ancient 2001, An Ancient Journey 2002, Mizuniinorite 2002, The Soong Sisters 2002, Sacred Journey of Ku-Kai 2003, Shikoku 88 Kasho 2004, Impressions Of The West Lake 2009. *Address:* c/o Domo Records Inc., 11340 West Olympic Boulevard, Suite 270, Los Angeles, CA 90064, USA. *Website:* domo.com/kitaro (office).

KITAYAMA, Teisuke, BA; Japanese banking executive; *Chairman and Representative Director, Sumitomo Mitsui Banking Corporation;* b. 26 Oct. 1946; ed Univ. of Tokyo; joined Mitsui Bank 1969, Gen. Man. Yokohama-Ekimae Br., Sakura Bank (fmrly Mitsui Taiyo Kobe Bank) 1992–95, Gen. Rep. in Thailand and Gen. Man. of Bangkok Br. 1995–97, Dir and Gen. Man. Planning Div. 1997–2000, Man. Dir 2000, Man. Dir Sumitomo Mitsui Banking Corpn (formed by merger of Sakura Bank and Sumitomo Bank) 2001–02, Sr Man. Dir 2002–03, Sr Man. Dir Sumitomo Mitsui Financial Group, Inc. (holding co. of Sumitomo Mitsui Banking Corpn) 2003–04, Deputy Pres. 2004–05, Pres. and Rep. Dir 2005–11, currently Chair. and Rep. Dir Sumitomo Mitsui Banking Corpn. *Address:* Sumitomo Mitsui Banking Corporation, 1-2, Yurakucho 1-Chome, Chiyoda-ku, Tokyo 100-0006, Japan (office). *Telephone:* (3) 5512-3411 (office). *Fax:* (3) 5512-4429 (office). *E-mail:* info@smbc.co.gp (office). *Website:* www.smbc.co.jp (office); www.smbcgroup.com (office).

KITAYENKO, Dmitriy Georgievich; Russian conductor; b. 18 Aug. 1940, Leningrad; ed Leningrad Conservatory, postgraduate study at Moscow Conservatory under Khazanov and Ginzburg; further study at Acad. of Music, Vienna; teacher at Moscow Conservatory 1969, Prof. 1986–90; Conductor, Nemirovich-Danchenko Theatre 1969, Prin. Conductor 1970–76; Chief Conductor, Moscow Philharmonic 1976–89; Music Dir Frankfurt Radio Orchestra 1990–95; Perm. Conductor and Music Adviser, Bergen Philharmonic Orchestra 1990–98; Con-

ductor, Bern Symphony Orchestra 1994–2004; Prin. Conductor, KBS Symphony Orchestra, Seoul 1999–2004; USSR People's Artist 1984; RSFSR State Prize 1988. *Address:* Chalet Kalimor, 1652 Botterens, Switzerland (home).

KITAZAWA, Toshimi; Japanese politician; b. 6 March 1938, Nagano; ed Waseda Univ., Tokyo; started political career as Sec. to MP; mem. Nagano Prefectural Ass. 1975–92; mem. House of Councillors for Nagano constituency 1992–, mem. Parl. Land and Transport Cttee, Fundamental Nat. Policies Cttee; mem. LDP –1993; mem. Shinshinto (New Frontier Party) 1993–98; mem. Democratic Party of Japan 1998–, fmr Vice-Pres. and Chair. Foreign Policy and Defence Cttee; Minister of Defence 2009–11. *Address:* c/o Ministry of Defence, 5-1, Ichigaya, Honmura-cho, Shinjuku-ku, Tokyo 162-8801, Japan.

KITBUNCHU, HE Cardinal Michael Michai; Thai ecclesiastic; b. 25 Jan. 1929, Samphran, Nakhon Pathom; ordained priest, Bangkok 1959; Archbishop of Bangkok 1973–2009 (retd); elevated to Cardinal, apptd Cardinal-Priest of S. Lorenzo in Panisperna 1983. *Address:* c/o Archdiocese of Bangkok, 51 Catholic Mission, Charoenkrung 40, Bangrak, Bangkok 10500, Thailand.

KITE, Thomas (Tom) O., Jr; American professional golfer; b. 9 Dec. 1949, Austin, Tex.; m. Christy Kite; two s. one d.; ed Univ. of Texas; won Walker Cup 1971; professional golfer, PGA 1972–2000; won Ryder Cup 1979, 1981, 1983, 1985, 1987, 1989, 1993, European Open 1980, US Open, Pebble Beach, Calif. 1992; LA Open 1993; 14 US PGA Tour wins; apptd Capt. US team for 1997 Ryder Cup, Valderrama, Spain; joined Sr PGA Tour 2000, wins include The Countryside Tradition 2000, MasterCard Championship 2002; currently plays on Champions Tour; spokesman for Chrysler Jr Golf Scholarship program; f. Tom Kite Design (golf course design co.); Bob Jones Award 1979, Player of the Year (Golf Writers) 1981, 1989, Vardon Trophy 1981, 1982, PGA Player of the Year 1989, elected to World Golf Hall of Fame 2004. *Leisure interest:* landscaping. *Address:* c/o PGA Tour, 112 Tpc Boulevard Ponte Vedra Beach, FL 32082, USA. *Telephone:* (512) 983-5483. *E-mail:* info@tomkitedesign.com.

KITONGA, Nzamba; Kenyan senior counsel and judge; *President, Court of Justice, Common Market for Eastern and Southern Africa (COMESA);* b. 1956; fmr Chair. Law Soc. of Kenya; fmr Pres. and Chair. East African Law Soc.; fmr Vice-Chair. Goldenberg Comm. of Inquiry; Judge of Appellate Div., Common Market for Eastern and Southern Africa (COMESA) Court of Justice 2005–, Pres. Court of Justice 2005–. *Address:* COMESA Secretariat, Ben Bella Road, PO Box 30051, 101101 Lusaka, Zambia (office). *Telephone:* (1) 229725 (office). *Fax:* (1) 225107 (office). *E-mail:* comesa@comesa.int (office). *Website:* www.comesa.int (office).

KITSIKIS, Dimitri, MA, PhD, FRSC; Canadian/French/Greek poet, historian and academic; *Professor Emeritus, Department of History, University of Ottawa;* b. 2 June 1935, Athens, Greece; s. of the late Nikolas Kitsikis and Beata Kitsikis (née Petychakis); m. 1st Anne Hubbard 1955 (divorced 1973); one s. one d.; m. 2nd Ada Nikolaros 1975; one s. one d.; ed American Coll. Athens, Ecole des Roches, Normandy, Lycée Lakanal and Lycée Carnot, Paris and Sorbonne, Paris; Research Assoc. Grad. Inst. of Int. Studies, Geneva 1960–62, Centre for Int. Relations, Nat. Foundation of Political Science, Paris 1962–65, Nat. Centre for Scientific Research, Paris 1965–70; Assoc. Prof. of History of Int. Relations, Univ. of Ottawa 1970–83, Prof. 1983–96, Prof. Emer. 1996–; Sr Research Scholar, Nat. Centre of Social Research, Athens 1972–74; Founder, Ed. Intermediate Region (journal) 1996–; adviser to Govts of Greece and Turkey; numerous visiting professorships, including at Univ. of Bogazici, Istanbul, Univ. of Bilkent, Ankara, Univ. of Gediz, Izmir, Sun Yat-Sen Univ., Guangzhou, and other appointments; Founder and Hon. Pres. Dimitri Kitsikis Public Foundation and Library, Athens 2008–; Study of Ataturk's Principles Award, Bogazici Univ. 1981, First Prize in Poetry, Abdi Ipekçi Peace and Friendship Prize 1992, Homo Hellenicus Award, Hellenic Evergetes Soc. 2010. *Publications include:* 37 books, including Propaganda and Pressure in International Politics 1963, The Role of the Experts at the Paris Peace Conference of 1919 1972, A Comparative History of Greece and Turkey in the 20th Century 1978, History of the Greek-Turkish Area 1981, The Ottoman Empire 1985, The Third Ideology and Orthodoxy 1990, The Old Calendarists 1995, Turkish-Greek Empire 1996, The Byzantine Model of Government 2001, J.-J. Rousseau and the French Origins of Fascism 2006, Bektashism and Alevism 2006, A Comparative History of Greece and China 2007, The Rise of National-Bolshevism in the Balkans 2008, National Bolshevism 2010; co-author of 43 other books; six vols of poetry, including Omphalos 1977, L'Orocc dans l'age de Kali 1985, Le Paradis Perdu sur les Barricades 1993, two vols of poetry and painting; hundreds of scholarly articles. *Leisure interests:* art, science fiction, study of languages. *Address:* Department of History, University of Ottawa, Ottawa, ON K1N 6N5 (office); 2104 Benjamin Avenue, Ottawa, ON K2A 1P4, Canada (home); 29 Travlantoni, Zographou, Athens 15772, Greece (home); Dimitri Kitsikis Foundation, Hagiou Ioannou Theologou 22, Zographou, Athens 15772 (office). *Telephone:* (613) 562-5735 (Ottawa) (office); (210) 778-0225 (Athens) (office); (613) 729-9814 (Ottawa) (home); (210) 7777-6937 (Athens) (home); (27310) 83096 (Pikoulianika, Greece) (home); 1-40-31-32-34 (Paris) (home); (613) 842-9175 (Ottawa) (home). *Fax:* (613) 562-5995 (Ottawa) (office). *E-mail:* dimitri.kitsikis@uottawa.ca (office). *Website:* www.idkf.gr (office).

KITTEL, Charles, PhD; American physicist, academic and writer; *Professor Emeritus, Department of Physics, University of California, Berkeley;* b. 18 July 1916, New York; s. of George Paul Kittel and Helen Kittel; m. Muriel Agnes Lister 1938; two s. one d.; ed Massachusetts Inst. of Tech., Univ. of Cambridge, UK and Univ. of Wisconsin; Prof. of Physics, Univ. of California, Berkeley 1951–78, Prof. Emer. 1978–; mem. NAS, American Acad. of Arts and Sciences; Buckley Prize for Solid State Physics 1957, Berkeley Distinguished Teaching Award 1970, Oersted Medal, American Asscn of Physics Teachers 1972. *Publications include:* Quantum Theory of Solids 1963, Thermal Physics 1980, Introduction to Solid State Physics 1996, Elementary Statistical Physics 2004. *Leisure interests:* friends, wine. *Address:* Department of Physics, University of California, 559 Birge, Berkeley, CA 94720-7300, USA (office). *Telephone:* (510) 643-9473 (office). *E-mail:* kittel@berkeley.edu (office). *Website:* www.physics.berkeley.edu (office).

KITTELMANN, Udo; German arts administrator and writer; *Director, Nationalgalerie, Berlin;* b. 15 March 1958, Düsseldorf; began career as optician; became ind. exhbn curator for several orgs including Städtische Galerie im Lenbachhaus, Munich, Kunsthalle, Innsbruck, Austria, Salzburg Kunstverein, Austria 1987–93;

Artistic Dir Kunstverein Ludwigsburg 1993–94; Dir Cologne Kunstverein 1994–2001; Commr of German Pavilion at 49th Venice Biennale 2001; Dir Museum für Moderne Kunst (MMK), Frankfurt 2002–08; Dir Nationalgalerie, Staatliche Museen zu Berlin (State Museums in Berlin) 2008–, responsible for the Alte Nationalgalerie (Old Nat. Galley), Neue Nationalgalerie (New Nat. Gallery) and the Hamburger Bahnhof, Museum für Gegenwart – Berlin (Museum for Contemporary Art), as well as the Berggruen Museum, Sammlung Scharf-Gerstenberg (Scharf-Gerstenberg Collection) and Friedrichswerdersche Kirche; curated Russian Pavilion at 55th Venice Biennale 2013. *Publications include:* Jonathan Borofsky: Dedicated to the Audience 1994, Rirkrit Tiravanija: Untitled 1996, Obsession (co-author) 1999, Gregor Schneider: Totes Haus, Biennale di Venezia 2001, World's Best New Art: Unreal Projects (co-author) 2007, Michel Majerus: If We Are Dead, So It Is 2008, Luc Tuymans: Ende 2009. *Address:* Nationalgalerie, Staatliche Museen zu Berlin, Genthiner Strasse 38, 10785 Berlin, Germany (office). *Telephone:* (30) 266-42-2201 (office). *Fax:* (30) 266-42-2202 (office). *Website:* www.smb.museum/smb (office).

KITTIKHOUN, Alounkèo; Laotian diplomatist; *Assistant Minister of Foreign Affairs;* b. 10 Oct. 1951, Pakse, Champasark; m. Dr Kongpadith Kittikhoun; two s.; ed Royal Inst. of Law and Admin, Vientiane, Univ. of Paris I (Panthéon-Sorbonne), Int. Inst. of Public Admin, Paris, France; joined Foreign Ministry 1977; Second Sec., then First Sec. and Counsellor, Perm. Mission to UN 1980–90, Perm. Rep. 1993–2007; Chair. Landlocked Developing Countries Group at the UN 1999–2003 and of numerous other UN bodies and cttees; Deputy Dir Dept of Int. Orgs, Foreign Ministry 1990–92, Dir 1992–93; Assistant Minister of Foreign Affairs 2007–. *Leisure interests:* golf, reading, eating, relaxing with family. *Address:* Ministry of Foreign Affairs, rue That Luang 01004, Ban Phonxay, Vientiane, Laos (office). *Telephone:* (21) 413148 (office). *Fax:* (21) 414009 (office). *E-mail:* cabinet@mofa.gov .la (office); alkktk@hotmail.com (home). *Website:* www.mofa.gov.la (office).

KITUYI, Mukhisa, BA, MPhil, PhD; Kenyan academic, politician and UN official; *Secretary-General, United Nations Conference on Trade and Development (UNCTAD);* b. 20 Oct. 1956, Bungoma Dist; s. of Jamin Kituyi and Joinah Mukasa Kituyi; m. Ling Merete (née Andersen); three s. one d.; ed Makerere Univ., Uganda, Univ. of Bergen, Norway; Researcher, Business and Econ. Research Centre, Nairobi 1982–83, Christian Michelsens Inst., Norway 1986–88; Programme Officer, Norwegian Agency for International Devt 1989–90; Programme Dir African Centre for Tech. Studies 1990–92; Exec. Dir Forum for Restoration of Democracy in Kenya 1992; MP for Kimilili constituency 1992–2007, served as Chief Opposition Whip and Chair. Defence and Foreign Affairs Cttee; Minister for Trade and Industry 2003–08, served as Chair. COMESA Council of Ministers, African Trade Ministers' Council, Council of Ministers of African, Caribbean and Pacific Group of States; Exec. Dir Kenya Inst. of Governance (think–tank), Nairobi 2008–; Under-Sec.-Gen., UN Sept. 2013–; Sec.-Gen. UNCTAD Sept. 2013–; Fellow (non-resident), Africa Growth Initiative, Brookings Inst. 2011–; Resident Scholar 2011; columnist, Sunday Nation. *Address:* United Nations Conference on Trade and Development (UNCTAD), Palais des Nations, 8–14, Avenue de la Paix, 1211 Geneva 10, Switzerland. *Telephone:* 229171234. *Fax:* 229170057. *E-mail:* sgo@ unctad.org. *Website:* unctad.org.

KITZHABER, John Albert, BS, MD; American physician, academic, politician and state governor; *Governor of Oregon;* b. 5 March 1947, Colfax, Wash.; s. of Albert Raymond Kitzhaber and Annabel Reed Kitzhaber (née Wetzel); m. 1st Sharon LaCroix 1995 (divorced 2003); one s.; partner Cylvia Hayes 2003–; ed South Eugene High School, Dartmouth Coll., Univ. of Oregon Medical School (now Oregon Health & Science Univ.); intern, Gen. Rose Memorial Hosp., Denver, Colo 1976–77; Emergency Physician, Mercy Hosp., Roseburg, Ore. 1974–75; mem. Ore. House of Reps 1979–81, Ore. Senate 1981–85, Pres. 1985, 1987, 1989, 1991; Gov. of Oregon 1995–2003, 2011–; Pres. Estes Park Inst., Englewood, Colo 2003–, The Kitzhaber Center, Lewis and Clark Law School 2005–; Assoc. Prof., Oregon Health & Science Univ. 1989–95, now also Dir Center for Evidence Based Policy; endowed Chair on Health Care Policy, The Foundation for Medical Excellence 2003–, first recipient John Kitzhaber, MD Chair on Health Care Policy 2011–; Founder Archimedes Movt 2006–; mem. American Coll. of Emergency Physicians, Inst. of Medicine, Douglas Co. Medical Soc., Physicians for Social Responsibility, American Council of Young Political Leaders, Oregon Trout; Democrat; Neuberger Award, Oregon Environmental Council 1987, Dr Nathan Davis Award, American Medical Asscn 1992. *Address:* Office of the Governor, Room 160, State Capitol Building, 900 Court Street NE, Salem, OR 97301-4047 (office); The Foundation for Medical Excellence, Suite 860, 1 SW Columbia Street, Portland, OR 97258, USA. *Telephone:* (503) 378-4582 (office); (503) 373-1027 (office); (503) 222-1960. *Fax:* (503) 378-6827 (office); (503) 378-8970 (office); (503) 796-0699. *E-mail:* info@tfme .org. *Website:* governor.oregon.gov (office); www.johnkitzhaber.com.

KITZINGER, Sheila Helena Elizabeth, MBE, MLitt; British birth educator, writer, social anthropologist and lecturer; b. 29 March 1929, Taunton, Somerset, England; d. of Alex Webster and Clare Webster; m. Uwe Kitzinger 1952; five d.; ed Bishop Fox's Girls' School, Taunton, Ruskin Coll. and St Hugh's Coll., Oxford; Research Asst, Dept of Anthropology, Univ. of Edinburgh 1952–53; Course Team Chair., Open Univ. 1981–83; Man. Cttee Midwives' Information and Resource Service 1985–87, Editorial Cttee 1987–; Chair. Steering Cttee Int. Homebirth Movt; mem. Bd Int. Caesarean Awareness Network; Consultant, Int. Childbirth Educ. Asscn; Adviser, Baby Milk Coalition, Maternity Alliance; Patron of the Seattle School of Midwifery; Dir Birth Crisis Network; frequent appearances internationally on TV and film productions on midwifery educational and health-care activism, internationally; campaigner on behalf of mothers and babies behind bars and midwifery and home birth in Eastern Europe; Hon. Prof., Thames Valley Univ. 1993–; Hon. Pres. Birth Companions; Joost de Blank Award for Research 1971–73. *Publications:* The Experience of Childbirth 1962, Education and Counselling for Childbirth 1977, Women as Mothers 1978, The Place of Birth (co-ed. with John Davis) 1978, Birth at Home 1979, The Good Birth Guide 1979, The Experience of Breastfeeding 1979, Pregnancy and Childbirth 1980, Some Women's Experience of Episiotomy (with Rhiannon Walters) 1981, 1983, Episiotomy: physical and emotional aspects 1981, The New Good Birth Guide 1983, Women's Experience of Sex 1983, Episiotomy and the Second Stage of Labor 1984, Being Born 1986, Celebration of Birth 1987, Freedom and Choice in Childbirth 1987, Some Women's Experiences of Epidurals 1987, Giving Birth: How

It Really Feels 1987, The Midwife Challenge (ed.) 1988, The Crying Baby 1989, Breastfeeding Your Baby 1989, Talking with Children about Things that Matter (with Celia Kitzinger) 1989, Pregnancy Day by Day (with Vicky Bailey) 1990, Homebirth and Other Alternatives to Hospital 1991, Ourselves as Mothers 1993, Birth over Thirty-Five 1994 (revised edn 2011), The Year after Childbirth 1994, The New Pregnancy and Childbirth 1997 (revised edn 2008), Becoming a Grandmother 1997, Breastfeeding 1998, Rediscovering Birth 2000 (revised edn 2011), Midwifery Guidelines on Water Birth (with Ethel Burns) 2000, Birth Your Way: Choosing Birth at Home or in a Birth Centre 2002 (revised edn 2011), Pregnancy and Childbirth: Choices and Challenges 2003, The New Experience of Childbirth 2004, The Politics of Birth 2005, Understanding Your Crying Baby 2005, Birth Crisis 2006, Birth and Sex 2012; regular contrib. of Letter From Europe, in Birth: Issues in Perinatal Care. *Leisure interest:* painting. *Address:* The Manor, Standlake, Oxon., OX29 7RH, England. *Telephone:* (1865) 300266. *E-mail:* sheila@sheilakitzinger.com. *Website:* www.sheilakitzinger.com.

KITZINGER, Uwe, CBE, MA, MLitt; British academic; *Patron, Asylum Welcome;* b. 12 April 1928, Nuremberg, Germany; s. of the late Dr G. Kitzinger and Lucy Kitzinger; m. Sheila Helena Elizabeth Webster 1952; five d.; ed Watford Grammar School, Balliol and New Colls, Oxford; Foundation Scholar, New Coll., Oxford 1947; Pres. of Oxford Union 1950; Econ. Section, Council of Europe 1951–58; Research Fellow, Nuffield Coll., Oxford 1956–62, Official Fellow and Investment Bursar 1962–76, Emer. Fellow 1976–; Dean, European Inst. of Business Admin. (INSEAD), Fontainebleau 1976–80; Dir Oxford Centre for Man. Studies 1980–84; first Pres. Templeton Coll., Oxford 1984–91; Founding Ed., Journal of Common Market Studies 1962–; Visiting Prof. Univ. of West Indies 1964–65; Visiting Prof. of Govt and Assoc., Centre for Int. Affairs, Harvard 1969–70; Visiting Prof., Univ. of Paris VIII 1970–73; Adviser to the late Lord Soames (Vice-Pres. Comm. of the European Communities), Brussels 1973–75; Sr Research Fellow, Atlantic Council 1993–; Visiting Scholar, Harvard Univ. 1993–2003; Founding Chair. Cttee on Atlantic Studies 1967–70, Major Projects Asscn 1981–86; Pres. Int. Asscn of Macro-Eng Socs 1987–2003, Féd. Britannique des Alliances Françaises 1998–2004; Council mem. European Movt 1974–76, Royal Inst. of Int. Affairs 1976–85, Oxfam 1981–84, Fondation Jean Monnet 1990–; Chair. Oxfordshire Radio Ltd 1988, GARIWO, Sarajevo 2001–12; co-f. Lentils for Dubrovnik 1991; Trustee, Ourtree Charitable Trust 1994–; Patron, Asylum Welcome 2004–; Hon. Fellow, Templeton Coll. 2001, Green Templeton Coll. 2008; Order of the Morning Star (Croatia) 1997; Hon. LLD 1986. *Publications:* German Electoral Politics 1960, The Challenge of the Common Market 1961, The Politics and Economics of European Integration 1963, Britain, Europe and Beyond 1964, Commitment and Identity 1968, The Second Try 1968, Diplomacy and Persuasion 1973, Europe's Wider Horizons 1975, The 1975 Referendum (with David Butler) 1976, Macro-Engineering and the Earth (co-ed. with Ernst Frankel) 1998; broadcasts, pamphlets and articles in the European University Inst. Historical Archives, Florence. *Leisure interest:* cruising under sail (ketch Anne of Cleves). *Address:* Standlake Manor, Standlake nr Witney, Oxon., OX29 7RH, England (home); La Rivière, 11100 Bages d'Aude, France. *Telephone:* (1865) 300438 (England) (office); (1865) 300266 (England) (home); (4) 68-41-70-13 (France) (home). *E-mail:* uwe_kitzinger@yahoo.com (office); uwek@ymail.com (home). *Website:* www.eui.eu/ HAEU/pdfinv/inv-uwkns.pdf.

KIVEJINJA, Kirunda; Ugandan politician; mem. Parl. (Nat. Resistance Movt— NRM) for Bugweri –2007; Minister of Transport and Communications –1999 (resgnd), Minister in charge of the Presidency 2003, Third Deputy Prime Minister and Minister of Information and Nat. Guidance 2006–09; Minister of Internal Affairs 2009–11; Dir of External Affairs, NRM Secr. 1999–2003. *Address:* c/o Ministry of Internal Affairs, Plot 75 Jinja Road, POB 7191 Kampala, Uganda (office).

KIVINIEMI, Mari Johanna; Finnish politician; b. 27 Sept. 1968, Seinäjoki; m. Juha Mikael Louhivuori; two c.; ed Univ. of Helsinki; mem. Suomen Keskusta (Kesk–Finnish Centre Party), Vice-Chair. for S Ostrobothnia Region 1994–2000, Party Vice-Chair. 2003–08, Chair. 2010–; mem. Suomen Eduskunta (Parl.) for Vaasa Co. 1995–99, for Helsinki 2007–; Special Adviser to Prime Minister Matti Vanhanen 2004–05; mem. Helsinki City Council 2005–; Minister for Foreign Trade and Devt 2005–06, Minister of Public Admin and Local Govt 2007–10; Prime Minister 2010–11. *Address:* c/o Prime Minister's Office, Snellmaninkatu 1a, POB 23, 00023, Helsinki, Finland. *Website:* www.marikiviniemi.com.

KIVRIKOGLU, Gen. Huseyin; Turkish army officer; b. Dec. 1934, Bozuyuk, Bilecik; m.; one s.; ed Isiklar Mil. School, Army Acad., Army War Coll., Armed Forces Coll., NATO Defence Coll., Rome, Italy; served as platoon and battery commdr in various artillery units 1957–65, Staff Officer 9th Infantry Div. in Sarikamis 1967–70; Planning Officer, Allied Forces S Europe Operations Div., Italy 1979–72; Instructor, Army War Coll. 1972–73; Section Chief of Gen. Staff and Br. Chief of Land Forces Command; Commdr of Cadet Regt, Army Acad., Ankara 1978–80; rank of Brig.-Gen. 1980; Chief of Operations Centre, Supreme HQ Allied Powers in Europe (SHAPE), Belgium 1980–83; CO 3rd and 11th Brigades 1983–84; rank of Maj. Gen. 1984; Chief of Staff NATO Allied Land Forces SE Europe (CLSE), Izmir 1984–86; CO 9th Infantry Div. 1986–88; rank of Lt-Gen. 1988; Asst Chief of Staff, Gen. Staff HQ; CO 5th Corps and Under-Sec. Ministry of Nat. Defence 1990–93; promoted to Four Star 1993; Commdr CLSE 1993–96, First Army, Istanbul 1996–97, Land Forces 1997–98; C-in-C Armed Forces and Chief of Gen. Staff 1998–2002; Armed Forces Distinguished Service Medal, Grand Cross and Golden Honour Medal (Turkey), Star of Romania, Order of Merit (USA), Order of Distinction Medal (Pakistan); numerous Army Acad. Badges, NATO Service Badge, Commdr Armed Forces Identification Badge. *Address:* c/o Ministry of National Defence, Milli Savunma Bakanligi, 06100 Ankara, Turkey (office).

KIWANUKA, Maria, BCom, MBA; Ugandan economist, business executive and politician; *Minister of Finance and Economic Planning;* b. 12 May 1955, Kampala; d. of Alistaluko Sekagya Nsibirwa Kiwana and Margaret Ndibalekera Lubega Kiwana; m. Mohan Kiwanuka; three c.; ed Makerere Univ., London Business School, UK; economist and financial analyst for E Asia and Southern Africa regions, World Bank Group 1980–90; worked for family businesses in private sector; fmr Man. Dir Radio One and Radio Two; Minister of Finance and Economic Planning 2011–; mem. Bd of Dirs Aga Khan Foundation (East Africa), Nabagereka Devt Trust, Nkumba Univ., Uganda Devt Bank, Stanbic Bank Uganda Ltd.

Address: Ministry of Finance, Planning and Economic Development, Appollo Kaggwa Rd, Plot 2-12, POB 8147, Kampala, Uganda (office). *Telephone:* (41) 4707000 (office). *E-mail:* webmaster@finance.go.ug (office); mkiwanuka@parliament.go.ug (office). *Website:* www.finance.go.ug (office).

KIYONGA, Crispus, MD; Ugandan physician and politician; *Minister of Defence;* b. Kasese; ed Johns Hopkins Univ., USA; mem. Parl. for Bukonzo West; posts have included Minister for Cooperatives and Marketing 1986, Minister of Finance 1986–92, Minister of Health –2001, Minister without Portfolio, Nat. Political Commissar, Nat. Resistance Movt 2001–06, Minister of Defence 2006–; apptd Chair Transitional Working Group for Establishment of Global AIDS and Health Fund by UN Sec.-Gen. 2001. *Address:* Ministry of Defence, Bombo, POB 7069, Kampala, Uganda (office). *Telephone:* (41) 2270331 (office). *Fax:* (41) 2245911 (office). *E-mail:* spokesman@defenceuganda.mil.ug (office). *Website:* www.defenceuganda.mil.ug (office).

KJAERSGAARD, Pia; Danish politician; *Chairwoman, Danish People's Party;* b. 23 Feb. 1947, Copenhagen; d. of Poul Kjærsgaard and Inge Munch Jensen; m. Henrik Thorup; two c.; ed Gentofte Folkeskole, Copenhagen School of Commerce; office asst for insurance and advertising co. 1963–67; home care asst 1978–84; mem. Folketing (Parl.) for Progress Party in Copenhagen Co. constituency 1984–87, in Funen Co. constituency 1987–95, for Danish People's Party in Funen Co. constituency 1995–98, in Copenhagen Co. constituency 1998–2007, in Zealand Greater constituency 2007–; Leader of Fremskridtspartiet (Progress Party) 1985–94; mem. Ministry of Justice's Road Safety Comm. 1986–87; Chair. Parl.'s Health Cttee 1988–91; mem. Council of Reps Danmarks Nationalbank 1989–96; mem. Nordic Council 1990–94, 1998–2000, Vice-Chair. Liberal Group 1990–94; Del. to 49th, 54th and 57th UN Gen. Ass., New York 1995, 2000, 2003; mem. Defence Comm. of 1997 1997–98; Progress Party cand. in Ryvang Nomination Dist 1979–81, in Ballerup and Gladsaxe Nomination Dist 1981–84, in Hvidovre Nomination Dist 1983–84, in Middelfart Nomination Dist 1984–95; Co-founder and Chair. Danish People's Party 1995–; Danish People's Party cand. in Hellerup and Gentofte Nomination Dists 1997–2000, in Glostrup Nomination Dist 1997–2007, in Kalundborg Nomination Dist 2007–; Deputy Chair. Council of Foreign Affairs; mem. Bd Political Foreign Affairs and OSCE; mem. Comm. of the Intelligence Service, Political-Econ. Bd; mem. Justice Comm.; mem. Man. Cttee Danish-Taiwanese Asscn; Kt (First Class), Order of the Dannebrog 2002; Kosan Prize 1986, Politician of the Year 1989, Golden Post Horn, Dansk Postordre Forening (Danish Mail-Order Asscn) 1992, Medal of Honour, Friends of Overseas Chinese Asscn 1999, Special Medal of Diplomacy (Taiwan) 2003, named Politician of the Year by Landsforeningen for Erhvervsinteresser (Nat. Asscn of Business Interests), Medal of Brilliant Star (Taiwan) 2008. *Publications:* ... Men Udsigten er god (... But the View is Good) 1998, Digteren og Partiformanden (co-author) 2006. *Leisure interests:* gardening, music, physical fitness. *Address:* Kaermindevej 31, 2820 Gentofte (home); Dansk Folkeparti, Christiansborg, 1240 Copenhagen K, Denmark (office). *Telephone:* 33-37-51-07 (office). *Fax:* 33-37-51-91 (office). *E-mail:* dfkala@ft.dk (office). *Website:* www.ft.dk (office).

KJELLÉN, Bo, MPolSc; Swedish diplomatist and environment campaigner; *Senior Research Fellow, Stockholm Environment Institute;* b. 8 Feb. 1933, Stockholm; s. of John Kjellen and Elsa Kjellen; m. 1st Margareta Lindblom 1959 (died 1978); m. 2nd Gia Boyd 1980; four c.; ed Univ. of Stockholm; entered Foreign Service 1957, posted to Rio de Janeiro, Brussels, Stockholm 1959–69; Prin. Pvt. Sec. to Sec.-Gen., OECD 1969–72; Deputy Head of Mission Del. to EEC, Brussels 1972–74; Amb. to Viet Nam 1974–77; Head Multilateral Dept for Devt Co-operation, Ministry of Foreign Affairs 1977–81; Under-Sec. Admin. and Personnel 1981–85; Amb. to OECD and UNESCO 1985–91; Chief Negotiator, Ministry of Environment 1991–98; Negotiator Climate Convention 1991–2001; Chair. Swedish Research Council for Environment, Agricultural Sciences and Spatial Planning 2001–04; Visiting Fellow, Tyndall Centre, Univ. of E Anglia 2003, 2005; Sr Research Fellow, Stockholm Environment Inst. 2005–; Hon. DSc (Cranfield, UK) 1997; Hon. PhD (Gothenburg) 1999; Hon. DLaw (Stockholm) 2011; Hon. DTech (Mälardalen Univ., Sweden) 2005; Elizabeth Haub Prize for Environmental Diplomacy 1999, GEF Award for Environmental Leadership 1999. *Publications include:* A New Diplomacy for Sustainable Development: The Challenge of Global Change 2008; several articles in academic publs and in the press on environment and sustainable devt. *Address:* Stockholm Environment Institute, Kräftriket 2 B, 10691 Stockholm, Sweden (office). *Telephone:* (8) 674-74-00 (office); (18) 71-03-07 (home). *E-mail:* bo.kjellen@sei.se (office). *Website:* www.sei.se (office).

KJØNSTAD, Asbjørn, DJur; Norwegian legal scholar and academic; *Professor of Social Law, University of Oslo;* b. 6 Feb. 1943, Levanger; s. of the late Arne Kjønstad and of Nelly Stavern Kjønstad; m. 1st Lise-Lena Stubberød 1971–81 (divorced); one d.; m. 2nd Ayala Orkan 1995 (divorced 2002); m. 3rd Ingeborg Marie Helgeland 2009; Legal Adviser, Nat. Insurance Admin. 1970–72; Research Fellow, Univ. of Oslo 1972–78, Prof. of Pvt. Law 1978–84, Head, Inst. of Pvt. Law 1983–84, Prof. of Social Law 1985–, Dean of Faculty of Law 1986–88, mem. Bd of Univ. of Oslo 1986–88, 1999–2001; Chair. Royal Comm. on Social Security Law 1982–90; Chair. Governmental Comm. on Co-ordination of Pension Schemes 1991–95, on Transfer of Pension Rights 1999–2000, on Industrial Injuries Compensation 2001–04; Guest Scholar, Boston Univ., USA 1995–96; Guest Prof., Leuven Univ., Belgium 1997; Vice-Pres. European Inst. of Social Security 1993–97; mem. Bd Nat. Council on Tobacco and Health 1972–93, 1997–2003, Head of Research Project on Tobacco Products Liability 1998–2000; Ed. Student Law Journal 1969, Norwegian Journal of Law 1991–2000, Tort Law Journal 2004–; mem. Norwegian Acad. of Science 1987–; Hon. JuD (Lund Univ., Sweden) 1996, (Copenhagen) 2012; Hon. Prize Smokefree 2004, Health Dir Karl Evang's Prize 2007. *Publications:* 40 scientific books and reports and some 300 articles on social security law, medical law, tort law, constitutional law and human rights, including: Social Security and Compensation for Personal Injuries 1977, The Industrial Injuries Insurance 1979, Constitutional Protection of Social Security 1984, Medical Law 1987, Norwegian Social Law 1987, A Simplified National Insurance Act 1990, The National Insurance Disablement Pension 1992, Health Priority and Patient's Rights (co-ed.) 1992, Law, Power and Poverty (co-ed.) 1997, Introduction to Social Security Law 1998, European Social Security Law (co-ed.) 1999, Social Services and the Rule of Law (co-author) 2000, Welfare Law (Vol. I, co-author) 2000, Confidentiality About Children 2001, Welfare Law II – Social

Services (co-author and co-ed.) 2003, Law and Poverty (co-author and co-ed.) 2003, The Development of Tort Law 2003, Duty of Confidentiality about Children (third edn) 2009, Introduction to Social Security Law (third edn) 2009, Twelve Main Principles in Norwegian Health Law 2010, Theory Formation in Social Law 2010, Academic Freedom and Academic Manners 2010, The Right to Primary Healthcare 2011, The Rights to Specialized Healthcare 2011, Old Age Pension 2012, The Development of Patients' Rights in Norway 2012, Welfare Law I – Fundamental Rights, the Rule of Law and Coercion (fifth edn) with Syse) 2012, Welfare Law II – Child Care and Social Law (fourth edn) (co-author with Syse and co-ed.) 2012. *Leisure interests:* outdoor exercise, skiing, jogging, mountain walking. *Address:* University of Oslo, Karl Johans gate 47, PO Box 6706, 0130 Oslo (office); Lillevannsveien 37C, 0788 Oslo, Norway (home). *Telephone:* 22-85-94-80 (office); 22-13-80-75 (home). *Fax:* 22-85-94-20 (office); 22-49-64-51 (home). *E-mail:* asbjorn.kjonstad@jus.uio.no (office). *Website:* www.jus.uio.no (office).

KLACKENBERG, Dag, LLB, MBA; Swedish business executive; *Managing Director, Svensk Handel (Swedish Trade Federation);* b. 5 Jan. 1948, Stockholm; s. of Gunnar Klackenberg and Brita Klackenberg; m.; two c.; ed Stockholm School of Econs, Stockholm Univ.; trainee, Ministry of Foreign Affairs 1974, becoming Dir-Gen. for Admin. Affairs 1993–2001; Chair. Vattenfall AB 2001–08; Man. Dir Svensk Handel (Swedish Trade Fed.) 2001–; Chair. Swedish Booksellers' Fed. 1986–, Vattenfall AB 2001–08, Handelsbanken Regionbank Mellansverige 2003–07, Ersta Sköndal Univ. Coll. 2006–, Swedish Foreign Trade Asscn 2006–, Svensk Byggtjänst 2007–, Swedish Export Credits Guarantee Bd 2008–; mem. Bd Atrium Ljungberg Gruppen AB 2004–. *Address:* Svensk Handel, Regeringsgatan 60, 103 29 Stockholm, Sweden (office). *Telephone:* (10) 4718500 (office). *Fax:* (10) 4718665 (office). *E-mail:* dag.klackenbergv@svenskhandel.se (office). *Website:* www.svenskhandel.se (office).

KLAFTER, Joseph, BSc, MSc, PhD; Israeli chemist, academic and university administrator; *President, Tel-Aviv University;* b. 1945, Tel-Aviv; ed Bar-Ilan Univ., Tel-Aviv Univ.; post-doctoral studies in chemistry, MIT, USA; with Research and Eng Div., Exxon 1980–87; joined Raymond and Beverly Sackler School of Chem., Tel-Aviv Univ. 1987, Full Prof. 1989–, Gordon Chair in Chem. 1998–2003, Chair. Dept of Physical Chem. 1990–92, 1998–2002, Heineman Chair of Physical Chem. 2003–, Pres. Tel-Aviv Univ. 2009–; mem. Academic Bd, Israel Science Foundation 1996–2002, Chair. 2002–; Fellow, American Physical Soc.; mem. American Acad. of Arts and Sciences 2011; Dr hc (Wrocław Univ. of Tech.); numerous awards including Alexander von Humboldt Foundation Prize 1996, Weizmann Prize for Sciences 1999, Rothschild Prize in Chem. 2004, Israel Chemical Soc. Prize 2005. *Publications:* around 400 scientific articles; ed 18 books. *Address:* Office of the President, Tel-Aviv University, PO Box 39040, Tel-Aviv 69978, Israel (office). *Telephone:* 3-6408111 (office). *E-mail:* klafter@post.tau.ac.il (office). *Website:* www.tau.ac.il/president/ (office).

KLAG, Michael J., BS, MD, MPH, FACP; American epidemiologist and academic; *Dean, Bloomberg School of Public Health, Johns Hopkins University;* ed Juanita Coll., Univ. of Pennsylvania, Johns Hopkins School of Hygiene and Public Health; Asst Clinical Prof., State Univ. of New York Upstate Medical Center 1982–84; Surgeon, Commissioned Corps, US Public Health Service 1982–84; joined Johns Hopkins Hosp. staff 1987, Dir Clinical Track, Preventative Medicine Residency, Johns Hopkins Univ. School of Hygiene and Public Health 1987–88, Instructor of Medicine, Jt Appointment in Epidemiology and Health Policy and Man., Johns Hopkins Univ. School of Medicine 1987–88, Asst Prof. of Medicine 1988–92, Assoc. Prof. 1992–97, Prof. 1998, Acting Dir Div. of Gen. Internal Medicine, Dept of Medicine, Johns Hopkins Univ. School of Medicine 1994–96, Dir 1996–2002, Assoc. Dir for Gen. Medicine 1996–2001, Interim Dir Dept of Medicine 2000–01, Vice Dean for Clinical Investigation 2001–05 Interim Dir Welch Center for Prevention, Epidemiology and Clinical Research, Johns Hopkins Medical Insts 1996–97 Interim Physician-in-Chief, Johns Hopkins Hosp. 2000–01, Dean, Johns Hopkins Bloomberg School of Public Health 2005–; Dir Precursors Study 1988–; Fellow, American Coll. of Physicians; mem. American Heart Asscn; David M. Levine Excellence in Mentoring Award 2003, Champion of Public Health Award 2004. *Publications:* more than 120 articles. *Address:* Johns Hopkins Bloomberg School of Public Health, 615 North Wolfe Street, Baltimore, MD 21205, USA (office). *Telephone:* (410) 955-3540 (office). *Fax:* (410) 955-0121 (office). *E-mail:* mklag@jhsph.edu (office). *Website:* faculty.jhsph.edu (office).

KLAMMER, Franz; Austrian fmr skier; b. 3 Dec. 1953, Mooswald; m.; two d.; 26 World Cup race wins, including downhill titles 1975, 1976, 1977, 1978, 1983; gold medal, downhill race, Winter Olympics 1976; retd from skiing 1985; took up car racing; won European Championship Touring Car race, Nurburgring, Germany; f. Franz Klammer Foundation; UN Goodwill Amb.; mem. Laureus World Sports Acad. *Leisure interests:* golf. *Address:* Franz Klammer Foundation, Singerstrasse 27/17, 1010 Vienna, Austria (home). *Telephone:* 699-100-25-735 (home). *Fax:* (1) 479-90-55 (home). *E-mail:* charity@franzklammerfoundation.com (home). *Website:* www.franzklammerfoundation.com (home).

KLARESKOG, Lars, MD, PhD; Swedish medical scientist and academic; *Professor of Reumatology and Centre for Molecular Medicine, Karolinska Institute;* b. 1945; ed Uppsala Univ.; Research Fellow in Experimental Rheumatology, Swedish Medical Research Council 1979–82; Assoc. Prof. in Immunology, Uppsala Univ. 1982–83 Clinical Fellow in Rheumatology and Internal Medicine (and part-time research), Uppsala Univ. Hosp. 1983–90, Prof. of Clinical Immunology and Chair. Dept of Clinical Immunology 1990–93, Prof. of Rheumatology and Chair. Rheumatology Clinic and Rheumatology Research Unit, Karolinska Inst. and Karolinska Hosp. 1993–, Chair. Dept of Medicine, Karolinska Inst./Karolinska Hosp. 1993–99, Chair. Centre for Pharmaco-epidemiology 2005–, Dir Centre for Molecular Medicine 2008–, mem. Nobel Ass. 1995– (Chair. 2011), mem. Nobel Cttee 1995–97, 2009–; Visiting Scientist, Harvard Medical School 2004; Visiting Prof., Dept of Medicine, Univ. of Colorado, Denver, USA 2006; Visiting Prof. and Physician-in-Chief pro tempore, Hosp. for Special Surgery, Cornell Univ., USA 2007, Heraklion, Greece 2009; Visiting Prof., Imperial Coll., London (Kennedy Inst. Rheumatology) 2010; Pres. European Rheumatology Congress, Stockholm 2002; Chair. European Standing Cttee for Investigative Rheumatology 2006–08; mem. Editorial Bd, Arthritis & Rheumatism – 2005), Annals of Rheumatic Diseases, Arthritis Research and Therapy, Current Opinion in Rheumatology, Rheumatology, Nature: Clinical Practice in Rheumatology; Jaan van Bremer Medal, Dutch

Rheumatology Soc. Int. Prize for Rheumatology Research 2004, Haasinga Lecturer, Deutsche RheumaForschungsZentrum, Berlin/Charité 2004, First Wyeth Rheumatology Prize, Swedish Soc. for Rheumatology 2004, European League against Rheumatism Annual Meeting State of the Art Lecturer 2007, Int. Carol Nachman Prize for Rheumatoloy Research 2008, American Coll. of Rheumatology Annual Meeting State of the Art Lecturer on Rheumatoid Arthritis 2008, Söderberg Prize, Swedish Soc. for Medicine 2009–10, Sr Investigator grant, European Research Council 2010–14, Crafoord Prize, Royal Swedish Acad. of Sciences (co-recipient) 2013. *Publications:* numerous papers in professional journals. *Address:* Rheumatology Unit, Department of Medicine (Solna), Building D2:02, Karolinska University Hospital, Eugeniahemmet T2, Stockholm, 171 76, Sweden (office). *Telephone:* (8) 517-793-04 (office). *E-mail:* lars.klareskog@ki.se (office). *Website:* ki.se (office).

KLAS, Eri; Estonian conductor; *Chief Conductor, Kolobov Novaya Opera Theatre;* b. 7 June 1939, Tallinn; s. of Eduard Klas and Anna Klas; m.; one d.; ed Tallinn State Conservatory, studied at Leningrad State Conservatory with Nikolai Rabinovich; percussionist, Estonian State Symphony Orchestra 1959–65; Asst Conductor to Boris Khaikin Bolshoi Theatre, Moscow 1969–72; Conductor Orchestra of Estonian Radio 1964–70; Conductor Nat. Opera Theatre Estonia 1965–94, Music Dir 1975–94, Laureate Conductor 1994–; conducted more than 100 symphony orchestras in 40 different countries; Music Dir Royal Opera, Stockholm 1985–89; Prin. Guest Conductor Finnish Nat. Opera 1990–; Chief Conductor Århus Symphony Orchestra, Denmark 1991–96; Prof., Sibelius Acad. Helsinki 1994–; Music Dir Orchestra of Netherlands Radio Symphony Orchestra 1996–2003; Artistic Dir and Prin. Conductor Tampere Philharmonic Orchestra 1998–2006, Conductor Laureate 2006–; Musical Adviser, Israel Sinfonietta 1999–; Chief Conductor, Kolobov Novaya Opera Theatre, Moscow 2006–; Chair. Bd Estonia Nat. Cultural Foundation 1991–; conducted at the Nobel Prize Ceremonial Concert in Stockholm 1989; Order of Nordstjernen (Sweden), Order of the Finnish Lion, Order of the White Star (Estonia); Dr hc (Estonian Acad. of Music) 1994. *Repertoire includes:* more than 50 operas, operettas, musicals and ballets. *Address:* The Kolobov Novaya Opera Theatre, 127006 Moscow, 3/2 Karetny Ryad, Russia (office). *Telephone:* (495) 694-08-68 (office). *E-mail:* info@novayaopera.ru (office). *Website:* www.novayaopera.freeland.ru (office).

KLASSEN, Cindy; Canadian speed skater; b. 12 Aug. 1979, Winnipeg, Man.; ed Mennonite Brethren Collegiate Inst., Winnipeg; began sports career as ice hockey player; played for Canadian Nat. Youth Team; switched to speed skating when she failed to be selected for Winter Olympics in 1998; bronze medal, 3000m, Winter Olympics, Salt Lake City 2002; World All-round Champion 2003; missed 2003–04 season due to serious injury; gold medal, 1500m and 3000m, World Single Distance Championships 2005; silver medal, World All-round Championships 2005; gold medal, 1500m, Winter Olympics, Turin 2006, silver medal, 1000m and Team Pursuit, bronze medal, 3000m and 5000m; World All-round Champion 2006; holder of world records at 1000m, 1500m and 3000m distances; Canada's all-time most decorated Olympian (five gold and one bronze medals); named flag-bearer for closing ceremony of Winter Olympics at Turin 2006, Lou Marsh Award as Canadian Athlete of the Year, Toronto Star 2006, Bobbie Rosenfeld Award as Canadian Female Athlete of the Year 2005, 2006. *Address:* c/o Landmark Sport Group, 1 City Centre Drive, Suite 605, Mississauga, ON L5B 1M2, Canada. *E-mail:* admin@landmarksport.com. *Website:* www.cindyklassen.com.

KLATTEN, Susanne, BSc, MBA; German business executive; b. 28 April 1962, Bad Homburg; d. of the late Herbert Quandt and the late Johanna Quandt; m. Jan Klatten; three c.; ed Univ. of Buckingham, UK, Int. Inst. for Man. Devt, Lausanne, Switzerland; trained as advertising exec.; man. asst Burda GmbH 1989–90; work experience in USA 1991; inherited share of BMW Group and majority of shares of Altana AG; Owner, SKion GmbH; mem. Bd of Dirs BMW Group 1997–, Byk Gulden Lomberg GmbH; Deputy Chair. Supervisory Bd SGL Carbon 2012–13, Chair. 2013–; Deputy Chair. Supervisory Bd Altana AG; Chair. Bd of Counsellors Herbert Quandt Foundation, Bad Homburg; ranked by Forbes magazine amongst 100 Most Powerful Women (41st) 2004, (71st) 2005. *Address:* SKion GmbH, Herbert-Quandt-Haus, Seedammweg 55, 61352 Bad Homburg, Germany (office). *Telephone:* (6172) 404531 (office). *E-mail:* info@skion.de (office). *Website:* www .skion.de (office).

KLAUS, Václav, PhD; Czech politician, economist and fmr head of state; b. 19 June 1941, Prague; s. of Václav Klaus and Marie Klausová; m. Livia Klausová 1968; two s.; ed Prague School of Econs, Cornell Univ., Czech Acad. of Sciences; researcher, Inst. of Econs Czechoslovak Acad. of Sciences –1970; various positions Czechoslovak State Bank 1971–86; Head, Dept of Macroeconomic Policy, Inst. of Forecasting, Acad. of Sciences 1987–; f. Civic Forum Movt (Chair. 1990–91); Minister of Finance 1989–92; Chair. Civic Democratic Party 1991–2002; Deputy Prime Minister 1991–92; last Prime Minister of the Czech Socialist Repub. from July 1992 until the dissolution of Czechoslovakia in Jan. 1993; Prime Minister of the Czech Repub. 1993–97; Chair. State Defence Council 1993–97; Chair. Govt Cttee for Integration of Czech Repub. in NATO 1997; Chair. Chamber of Deputies 1998–2002; Pres. of Czech Repub. 2003–13; serves as a Nat. Centre for Policy Analysis Distinguished Leader; mem. Scientific Council, Palacký Univ., Olomouc 1997–; Distinguished Sr Fellow, Cato Inst. 2013; known as a vocal critic of the notion of anthropogenic global warming; Hon. Prof., Univ. Guadalajara 1993; Hon. Chair. ODS (Civic Democratic Party) 2002–08; Kt Grand Cross, Order of the White Lion 2003, Kt Grand Cross, Order of Tomáš Garrigue Masaryk 2003, Kt Grand Cross, Order of Isabella the Catholic (Spain) 2004, Order of the White Eagle (Poland) 2007, Saxon Merit Cross 2008, Grand Cross, Order of Vytautas the Great (Lithuania) 2009, Grand Star of the Decoration for Services to the Repub. of Austria 2009, Order of the White Double Cross (Slovakia) 2013; Hon. DHumLitt (Suffolk Univ.) 1991, Dr hc (Rochester Inst. of Tech.) 1991, (Univ. Francisco Marroquín, Guatemala) 1993, (Jacksonville, USA) 1995, (Buckingham, UK) 1996, (Prague School of Econs) 1994, (Belgrano Univ., Argentina) 1994, (Tufts Univ., USA) 1994, (Univ. of Aix-Marseilles) 1994, (Tech. Univ. of Ostrava) 1997, (Toronto, Canada) 1997, (Arizona) 1997, (Dallas) 1999, (Chicago) 1999; Schumpeter Prize for Econs, Freedom Award (New York) 1990, Max Schmidheiny Freedom Prize, St Gallen 1992, Ludwig Erhard Prize, Germany 1993, Poeutinger Collegium Prize 1993, Hermann Lindrath Prize (Hanover) 1993, Konrad Adenauer Prize (Prague) 1993, Club of Europe Award 1994, Prix Transition (Fondation du Forum

Universal) 1994, Adam Smith Award (Libertas, Copenhagen) 1995, Int. Democracy Medal (Center for Democracy, Washington, DC) 1995, Transatlantic Leadership Award (European Inst., Washington, DC) 1995, Prognos Award (Prognos Forum, Basel) 1995, James Madison Award (James Madison Inst., Jacksonville, USA) 1995, Karel Engliš Prize (Universitas Masarykiana Foundation, Brno) 1995, European Prize for Craftsmanship, Germany 1996, Goldwater Medal for Econ. Freedom, Phoenix, USA 1997, Bernhard Harms Medal (Kiel Inst. of World Econs) 1999, Medal of Pushkin 2007. *Publications include:* A Road to Market Economy 1991, Tomorrow's Challenge 1991, Economic Theory and Economic Reform 1991, Why am I a Conservative? 1992, Dismantling Socialism: A Road to Market Economy II 1993, The Year–How much is it in the History of the Country? 1993, The Czech Way 1994, Rebirth of a Country: Five Years After 1994, Counting Down to One 1995, Between the Past and the Future: Philosophical Reflections and Essays 1996, The Defence of Forgotten Ideas 1997, Tak pravil Václav Klaus (So Said Václav Klaus, conversations with J. Klusáková), Why I Am Not a Social Democrat 1998, Země, kde se již dva roky nevládne (The Land that has not been Governed for 2 years) 1999, Cesta z pasti (The Way Out of the Trap) 1999, From the Opposition Treaty to the Tolerance Patent 2000, Evropa pohledem politika a pohledem ekonoma (Europe, The View of the Politician and the View of the Economist) 2001, Conversations with Václav Klaus 2001, Klaus v Bruselu (Klaus in Brussels) 2001, On the Road to Democracy–The Czech Republic From Communism to Free Society 2005, Modrá, nikoli zelená planeta (Blue Planet in Green Shackles) 2007; numerous articles. *Leisure interests:* tennis, skiing, basketball, volleyball, jazz, music, reading fiction. *E-mail:* webmaster@klaus.cz. *Website:* www.klaus.cz.

KLEBANOV, Ilya Iosifovich; Russian politician; b. 7 May 1951, Leningrad; m. Yevgenya Yakovlevna Klebanova; one s. one d.; ed M.I. Kalinin Leningrad Polytechnical Inst.; eng electrophysicist, Electron Scientific Production Unit 1974–77; engineer, then Sr Master, Head of Construction Bureau, later Head of Div. Leningrad Optical-Mechanical Complex (LOMO) 1977–92, Dir-Gen. 1992–97; First Vice-Gov. St Petersburg 1997–98; Deputy Chair. of Russian Govt 1999–2002, Minister of Industry, Science and Tech. (Minpromnauki) 2001–03; Presidential Envoy to the Northwestern Fed. Okrug (Dist) 2003–11; mem. Russian Security Council 2003–. *Leisure interests:* classical music, reading, mushroom-picking. *Address:* c/o Office of the Plenipotentiary Representative of the President, 199004 St Petersburg, Vasilyevskii ostrov, 3-ya liniya 12, Russia.

KLEIN, Calvin Richard; American fashion designer; b. 19 Nov. 1942, Bronx, New York; s. of Leo Klein and Flore Klein (née Stern); m. 1st Jayne Centre 1964 (divorced 1974); one d.; m. 2nd Kelly Rector 1986 (divorced 2006); ed Fashion Inst. of Tech., New York and High School of Art and Design; started fashion business 1968; Pres./Designer Calvin Klein Ltd 1968–2002 (co. sold to Phillips-Van Heusen Corpn); Consultant, Fashion Inst. of Tech. 1975–; mem. Council of Fashion Designers; Coty Award 1973, 1974, 1975; Coty Hall of Fame, FIT Pres.'s Award, Outstanding Design Council of Fashion Designers of America (four womenswear, two menswear). *Address:* Calvin Klein Studio, LLC, 545 West 25th Street, 18th Floor, New York, NY 10001-5501, USA. *Website:* www.calvinklein.com.

KLEIN, George, MD, DSc, PhD; Swedish tumour biologist; *Research Group Leader, Microbiology and Tumour Biology Centre, Karolinksa Institute;* b. 28 July 1925, Budapest, Hungary; s. of Henrik Klein and Ilona Engel; m. Eva Fischer 1947; one s. two d.; ed medical schools at Pécs, Szeged and Budapest, Hungary and Stockholm, Sweden; Instructor Histology, Budapest Univ. 1945, Pathology 1946; Research Fellow, Karolinska Inst. 1947–49, Asst Prof. of Cell Research 1951–57; Prof. of Tumour Biology and Head of the Dept for Tumour Biology, Karolinska Inst. Med. School, Stockholm 1957–93, Research Group Leader, Microbiology and Tumour Biology Centre, Karolinksa Inst. 1993–; Guest Investigator, Inst. for Cancer Research, Philadelphia, Pa 1950; Visiting Prof., Stanford Univ. 1961; Fogarty Scholar, NIH 1972; Dunham Lecturer, Harvard Medical School 1966; Visiting Prof., Hebrew Univ., Jerusalem 1973–93; Harvey Lecturer 1973; Donald Wae Waddel Lecturer, Univ. of Arizona 1991; mem. Scientific Advisory Council of Swedish Medical Bd, Royal Swedish Acad. of Sciences; mem. Bioethics Cttee, UNESCO; Corresp. mem. American Asscn of Cancer Research; Foreign Assoc. NAS; Fellow, New York Acad. of Science; Ed. Advances in Cancer Research; Hon. mem. American Asscn of Immunologists, of Cancer Research, French Soc. of Immunology, Hungarian Acad. of Sciences, American Acad. of Arts and Sciences; Hon. DSc (Univ. of Chicago) 1966, (Univ. of Neb.) 1991; Hon. MD (Univ. of Debrecen) 1988; Hon. PhD (Hebrew Univ., Jerusalem) 1989, (Tel-Aviv Univ.) 1994, (Osaka Univ.) 2001; Bertha Goldblatt Teplitz Award (jtly) 1960, Rabbi Shai Shacknai Prize in Tumour Immunology 1972, Bertner Award 1973, Award of American Cancer Soc. 1973, Prize of Danish Pathological Soc., Harvey Prize 1975, Prize of Cancer Research Inst. 1975, Gairdner Prize 1976, Behring Prize 1977, Annual Award Virus Cancer Program 1977, Gen. Motors Sloan Prize for Cancer Research, Björkén Award of Uppsala Univ. 1979, Award of the Santa Chiara Acad., Italy, 1979, Erik Fernström Prize (with Eva Klein) 1983, Anniversary Prize of the Swedish Med. Asscn 1983, Letterstedt Prize, Royal Swedish Acad. of Sciences 1989, Doblong Prize, Swedish Acad. of Literature 1990, Lisl and Leo Eitinger Prize, Oslo Univ. 1990, Robert Koch Gold Medal 1998, Lifetime Achievement Award, Inst. of Human Virology 1998, Brupbacher Foundation Prize, Zürich 1999, Paracelsus Medal 2001, Wick R. Williams Memorial Lecture Award 2001, Ingemar Hedenius Prize 2002, G.J. Mendel Hon. Medal for Merit in the Biological Sciences 2005, IARC Medal of Honour 2006, Herbert J. Block Memorial Lectureship Award, Ohio State Univ. 2008, Biomedicum medaljen, Helsinfors, Finland 2009, KI:s Jubileumsmedalj 2010, Royal Award of the Swedish Royal Acad. 2010 Distinguished Prof. Award, Karolinska Inst. 2010. *Publications include:* more than 1,385 papers in fields of experimental cell research and cancer research; The Atheist and the Holy City 1990, Hack i häl på Minerva (with Lars Gyllensten) 1993, Pietà 1993, Live Now 1997, Korpens Blick 1998, Så jag kan svara döden, när den kommer 2001, Skapelsens fullkomlighet och livets tragik 2005, Péters Europa (with Eva Dickson and Egon Fenyö) 2005, Meteorer 2008. *Address:* MTC, Karolinska Institutet, Box 280, 171 77 Stockholm (office); Kottlavagen 10, 181 61 Lidingo, Sweden (home). *Telephone:* (8) 524-867-30 (office). *Fax:* (8) 33-04-98 (office). *E-mail:* georg.klein@ki.se (office). *Website:* ki.se/ki/jsp/polopoly.jsp?d=23385&a=26107&l=en (office).

KLEIN, Maj.-Gen. Jacques Paul; American air force officer (retd) and international organization official; m. Dr Margrete Siebert Klein; two c.; fmr Air Force Officer (retd as Maj.-Gen.); joined Foreign Service in Operations Center of Exec. Secr. of Sec. of State 1971; Consular Officer, Consulate-Gen., Bremen; Political Officer, Office of Southern European Affairs, Dept of State; Counsellor Officer, Berlin; Political Officer, Embassy in Bonn; Man. Analysis Officer, Office of Dir-Gen. of Foreign Service; seconded to Dept of Defense as Adviser on Int. Affairs to Sec. of Air Force with rank of Deputy Asst Sec.; Dir Office of Strategic Tech. Matters, Bureau of Politico-Mil. Affairs, Dept of State; Asst Deputy Under-Sec. of Air Force for Int. Affairs, Dept of Defense 1989–90; Prin. Adviser to Dir-Gen. Foreign Service 1990–93; Political Adviser to C-in-C, US European Command, Stuttgart 1993–96; Prin. Deputy High Rep., Bosnia and Herzegovina 1997–99; UN Transitional Admin. for Eastern Slavonia, Baranja and Western Sirmium, rank of Under-Sec.-Gen. 1996–97; Special Rep. of Sec.-Gen. to Bosnia and Herzegovina, rank of Under-Sec.-Gen. 1999–2003; UN Special Rep. for Liberia 2003–05; Visiting Lecturer in Int. Affairs and Frederick Schultz Visiting Prof. of Public and Int. Affairs, Woodrow Wilson School, Princeton Univ. 2005–06 (retd); currently Expert, Woodrow Wilson International Center for Scholars; mem. Cosmos Club and Army and Navy Clubs of Washington, DC, Acad. d'Alsace, Council on Foreign Relations; Grand Officer, Order of the Crown (Belgium), Grand Cross of Merit (Germany), Order of King Dmitar Zvonimir with Sash and Morning Star (Croatia), Commdr, Aeronautical Order of Merit (Brazil), Commdr, Order of the Lion (Senegal), Officier, Légion d'honneur, Kt Great Band of the Humane Order of African Redemption (Nat. Transitional Govt of Liberia); Air Force Distinguished Service Medal, Legion of Merit (with oak leaf cluster), Bronze Star, Distinguished Honor Award, Dept of State, Defense Medal for Outstanding Public Service, Dept of the Air Force Award for Exceptional and Meritorious Civilian Service. *Address:* Woodrow Wilson International Center for Scholars, Ronald Reagan Building and International Trade Center One Woodrow Wilson Plaza, 1300 Pennsylvania Avenue, NW, Washington, DC 20004-3027, USA. *Website:* www.wilsoncenter.org.

KLEIN, Jonathan David; British/South African business executive; *Co-founder and CEO, Getty Images Inc.;* b. 13 May 1960, South Africa; m. Deborah Klein; three s.; with Hambros Bank Ltd, London 1983–93, Dir 1989–93; co-f. Getty Investment Holdings 1993–95; Jt Chair. Getty Communications PLC 1995–96, CEO and Dir 1996–98; Co-founder, CEO and Dir Getty Images 1998–; mem. Bd of Dirs Getty Investments LLC, Real Networks Inc., The Global Business Coalition on HIV/AIDS, Friends of the Global Fight against AIDS, Tuberculosis and Malaria; Trustee, Groton School; Int. Center of Photography Trustee's Award (with Mark Getty) 2006. *Leisure interests:* skiing, tennis, reading, world traveller. *Address:* Getty Images Inc., 75 Varick Street, 5th Floor, New York, NY 10013, USA (office). *Telephone:* (646) 613-3960 Asst); (646) 613-3622 (office). *Fax:* (646) 613-4402 (office). *E-mail:* abby.loewenstein@gettyimages.com (office); jonathan.klein@gettyimages.com (office). *Website:* www.gettyimages.com (office).

KLEIN, Michael L., BSc, PhD, FRS, FRSC, FInstP; British chemist, materials scientist and academic; *Laura H. Carnell Professor of Science, Department of Chemistry, Temple University;* b. 13 March 1940, London, England; m. Brenda M. Woodman; two d.; ed Univ. of Bristol; Ciba-Geigy Fellow, Univ. of Genoa, Italy 1964–65; ICI Fellow, Univ. of Bristol, Dept of Theoretical Chem. 1965–67; Research Assoc., Physics Dept, Rutgers Univ., USA 1967–68; Assoc. Research Officer, Nat. Research Council of Canada, Chem. Div., Ottawa, Canada 1968–74, Sr Research Officer 1974–85, Prin. Research Officer 1985–87; Adjunct Prof. of Physics, Univ. of Waterloo, Ont., Canada 1977–83; Prof. of Chem., McMaster Univ., Ont. 1977–88; Visiting Prof., Univ. of Amsterdam, Netherlands 1985; Néel Visiting Prof., École Normale Supérieure, Lyon, France 1988; William Smith Prof. of Chem., Univ. of Pennsylvania 1991–93, Hepburn Prof. of Physical Science 1993–2009, Dir Lab. for Research on the Structure of Matter 1993–2009, also Dir Penn Center for Molecular Modelling 1994–2009; Laura H. Carnell Prof. of Science, Dept of Chem., Temple Univ. 2009–; Dir Temple Inst. for Computational Molecular Science 2009–, Dean, Temple Coll. of Science and Tech. 2012–; mem. Editorial Bd several journals, including Journal of Physics Condensed Matter 1993–97, Molecular Physics 1993–99, Computational Materials Science 1993–, Journal of Chemical Physics 2003–, Chemical Physics Letters 2003–, Proceedings of the National Academy of Sciences 2009–; mem. RSC (Faraday Div.), ACS 1998–, American Physical Soc. 1999–, American Acad. of Arts and Sciences 2003–, TWAS – The World Acad. of Sciences 2004–, NAS 2009–; Fellow, American Physical Soc. 1991; Hon. Fellow, Chemical Inst. of Canada 1979–, Indian Acad. of Sciences 2005–, Mongolian Acad. Sciences 2008, Chemical Research Soc. of India 2008–; Hon. Fellow, Trinity Coll. Cambridge 2013; Guggenheim Foundation Fellow 1989–90, Alexander von Humboldt Award, Max Planck Inst., Stuttgart 1996, Linnett Lecturer, Univ. of Cambridge 1998, ACS Phila Section Award 1998, American Physical Soc. Aneesur Rahman Prize 1999, CECAM Prize for Computational Science, European Physical Soc. 2004, CNR Rao Award, Chemical Research Soc. of India 2006, Peter Debye Award in Physical Chemistry, ACS 2008, Hinshelwood Lecturer, Univ. of Oxford 2008, RSC S. F. Boys – A Rahman Award 2011. *Publications:* four books and more than 630 papers. *Address:* Department of Chemistry, Temple University, Bio-Life Building, Suite 113, 1900 North 12th Street, Philadelphia, PA 19122, USA (office). *Telephone:* (215) 204-4212 (office). *E-mail:* mike.klein@temple.edu (office). *Website:* www.temple.edu/cst/icms (office).

KLEIN, Naomi; Canadian writer, journalist and social critic; b. 1970, Montréal; syndicated columnist for The Nation, The Guardian, UK; contributing editor, Harper's; reporter, Rolling Stone; contrib. to numerous publs including The New York Times, The Washington Post, Newsweek, The Los Angeles Times, The Globe and Mail, El Pais, L'Espresso, The New Statesman; guest lecturer at Harvard Univ., Yale Univ., McGill Univ., New York Univ.; Puffin Foundation Writing Fellow, The Nation Inst.; fmr Miliband Fellow, London School of Economics; Dr hc (University of King's College, Nova Scotia); Canadian Nat. Business Book Award 2001, Le Prix Médiations, France 2001, Ms. Magazine's Women of the Year Award 2001, James Aronson Award for Social Justice Journalism (for reporting from Iraq for Harper's) 2004. *Publications:* No Logo: Taking Aim at the Brand Bullies (translated into 22 languages) 2000, Fences and Windows: Dispatches from the Front Lines of the Globalization Debate 2002, The Shock Doctrine: The Rise of Disaster Capitalism (Warwick Prize for Writing 2009) 2007. *E-mail:* klp123@gmail .com (office). *Website:* www.naomiklein.org.

KLEIN, Peter Wolfgang, PhD; Dutch historian and academic; b. 10 Dec. 1931, Vienna, Austria; ed Netherlands School of Econs, Rotterdam; Asst Prof. of Econ. History 1959–65; Reader in Social History 1965–67; Prof. of Econ. and Social History, Erasmus Univ., Rotterdam 1969–85, Part-time Prof. of Econ. History 1969–74, Vice-Chancellor 1974–75, Dean Faculty of Econs 1977–78, Head History Dept 1979–81; Prof. of Early Modern History, State Univ. Leiden 1985–, Head of History Dept 1986–88; Pres. Dutch Historical Soc. 1987; mem. State Cttee for Nat. History 1981, Bd State Inst. for History Second World War 1972–89, Scientific Cttee Inst. of Econ. History Francesco Datini 1986, Cttee Int. Asscn of Econ. History 1985, Royal Netherlands Acad. of Arts and Sciences 1979 (Chair. Arts Dept); Founding mem. Academia Europaea. *Publication:* Dr Trippen in de 17e. eeuw 1965. *Address:* Oude Herengracht 24, Leiden, Netherlands (home).

KLEINBERG, Jon M., AB, SM, PhD; American computer scientist and academic; *Professor of Computer Science, Cornell University;* ed Cornell Univ., Massachusetts Inst. of Tech.; researcher, IBM Theory and Computation Group 1995, Computer Science Principles and Methodologies Group 1996–97, mem. Visiting Faculty Program, IBM Almaden Research Center 1998–; mem. faculty, Dept of Computer Science, Cornell Univ. 1996–, currently Prof. of Computer Science; mem. Nat. Acad. of Eng, American Acad. of Arts and Sciences; NSF Career Award, Office of Naval Research Young Investigator Award, MacArthur Foundation Fellowship, Packard Foundation Fellowship, Sloan Foundation Fellowship, grants from NSF, Faculty of the Year Award, Cornell Univ. Asscn of Computer Science Undergraduates 2002, Nevanlinna Prize 2006. *Achievements include:* devised the HITS algorithm for ranking Web pages. *Publications:* Algorithm Design (co-author) 2005, Networks, Crowds, and Markets: Reasoning About a Highly Connected World (co-author) 2010; numerous scientific papers in professional journals. *Address:* Department of Computer Science, Upson Hall, Cornell University, Ithaca, NY 14853, USA (office). *Telephone:* (607) 255-3600 (office); (607) 255-5331 (office). *Fax:* (607) 255-7316 (office). *E-mail:* kleinber@cs.cornell.edu (office). *Website:* www.cs.cornell.edu/home/kleinber (office).

KLEINFELD, Klaus, Dr rer. pol, Dipl.-Kfm; German business executive; *Chairman and CEO, Alcoa Inc.;* b. 6 Nov. 1957, Bremen; m.; several c.; ed Georg-August Univ., Göttingen, Univ. of Würzburg; Researcher Inst. of Foundation for Empirical Social Research, Nuremberg 1982–86; Product Man. Pharmaceuticals Div., Ciba-Geigy AG, Basel 1986–87; joined Corp. Sales and Marketing Siemens AG, Advertising and Design Man. 1987, Corp. Strategies Man. 1988–94, Head, Corp. Projects 1994–95, Head, Siemens Corp. Consulting 1995–98, Head, Angiography, Fluoroscopic and Radiographic Systems Div. 1998–2000, mem. Group Exec. Man., Medical Solutions Group, COO Siemens Corpn, USA 2001–02, CEO 2002–04, mem. Man. Bd Siemens AG 2002–07, mem. Corp. Exec. Cttee 2004–07, Deputy Chair. Man. Bd 2004, Pres. and CEO 2005–07; mem. Bd of Dirs Alcoa Inc. 2003–, Pres. and COO 2007–08, Pres. and CEO 2008–10, Chair. and CEO 2010–; mem. Supervisory Bd Bayer AG; Chair. US-Russia Business Council 2009–; mem. Bd of Trustees Brookings Inst. 2010–. *Publication:* Corporate Identity und strategische Unternehmensführung 1994. *Leisure interests:* skiing, tennis, the arts, running marathons. *Address:* Alcoa Inc., 390 Park Avenue, New York, NY 10022 (office); Alcoa Corporate Center, 201 Isabella Street, Pittsburgh, PA 15212-5858 USA (office). *Telephone:* (212) 836-2600 (New York) (office); (412) 553-4545 (Pittsburgh) (office). *Fax:* (212) 836-2815 (New York) (office); (412) 553-4498 (Pittsburgh) (office). *E-mail:* info@alcoa.com (office). *Website:* www.alcoa.com (office).

KLEINROCK, Leonard, BEE, MS, PhD; American computer scientist and academic; *Professor of Computer Science, Henry Samueli School of Engineering and Applied Science, Unversity of California, Los Angeles;* b. 13 June 1934, New York; ed Bronx High School of Science, City Coll. of New York, Massachusetts Inst. of Tech.; Prof. of Computer Science, Henry Samueli School of Eng and Applied Science, UCLA 1963–, Chair. Dept 1991–95, currently Distinguished Prof. of Computer Science; Co-founder and first Pres. Linkabit Corpn; Co-founder Nomadix, Inc.; Founder and Chair. TTI/Vanguard (advanced tech. forum org.); mem. Nat. Acad. of Eng, American Acad. of Arts and Sciences; Fellow, IEEE, Asscn for Computing Machinery, INFORMS (Inst. For Operations Research and The Man. Sciences), Int. Electrotechnical Comm.; Founding mem. Computer Science and Telecommunications Bd of Nat. Research Council; hon. doctorates from around the world; Guggenheim Fellow, L.M. Ericsson Prize, NAE Charles Stark Draper Prize, Marconi Int. Fellowship Award, Okawa Prize, IEEE Internet Millennium Award, ORSA Lanchester Prize, ACM SIGCOMM Award, NEC Computer and Communications Award, Sigma Xi Monie A. Ferst Award, Townsend Harris Medal and Electrical Eng Award, City Coll. of New York, UCLA Outstanding Faculty Mem. Award, UCLA Distinguished Teaching Award, UCLA Faculty Research Lecturer, INFORMS Pres.'s Award, ICC Prize Paper Award, IEEE Leonard G. Abraham Prize Paper Award, IEEE Harry M. Goode Award, listed by Los Angeles Times amongst "50 People Who Most Influenced Business This Century" 1999, listed by Atlantic Monthly amongst 33 most influential living Americans Dec. 2006, Nat. Medal of Science 2007, Dan David Prize 2010. *Achievements include:* known as a "father of the Internet"; developed math. theory of packet switching networks, tech. underpinning the Internet, while a grad. student at MIT 1960–62; wrote first paper and published first book on the subject; also directed transmission of first message ever sent over Internet. *Publications:* six books and more than 250 papers in professional journals on packet switching networks, packet radio networks, local area networks, broadband networks, gigabit networks, nomadic computing, performance evaluation and peer-to-peer networks. *Address:* Computer Science Department, Unversity of California, Los Angeles, 3732G Boelter Hall, Los Angeles, CA 90095, USA (office). *Telephone:* (310) 825-2543 (office). *Fax:* (310) 825-7578 (office). *E-mail:* lk@cs.ucla .edu (office). *Website:* www.lk.cs.ucla.edu (office); www.engineer.ucla.edu (office).

KLEISTERLEE, Gerard Johannes, MA; Dutch business executive; *Chairman, Vodafone Group plc;* b. (Gerhard Johannes Kleisterlee), 28 Sept. 1946, Germany; ed Eindhoven Tech. Univ., Netherlands; joined Royal Philips Electronics in 1974, several manufacturing and business man. positions in various divs and regions, apptd Exec. Vice-Pres. Royal Philips Electronics and mem. Bd of Man. 2000, COO Philips 2000–01, Chair. Bd of Man., Pres. and CEO Royal Philips Electronics 2001–11; Dir (non-exec.) Vodafone Group plc April 2011–, Chair. July 2011–; mem. Supervisory Bd De Nederlandsche Bank NV 2006–12, Daimler AG 2009–; Dir (non-exec.), Supervisory Bd and mem. Audit Comm., Royal Dutch Shell 2010–; mem. Bd of Dirs Dell Inc. 2010–; mem. European Table of Industrialists 2001–11 (Vice-Chair. 2010–11); mem. Asia Business Council 2002–; Chair. Foundation of the Cancer Centre, Amsterdam 2001–12, Supervisory Bd of Eindhoven Tech. Univ. 2001–09; mem. Exec. Cttee IMD Business School, Lausanne 2007–11 (Chair. 2008–11); Dr hc (Catholic Univ. of Leuven) 2005. *Leisure interests:* music, reading about history. *Address:* Office of the Chairman, Vodafone Group plc, 25 Park Lane, London, W1K 1RA, England (office). *Telephone:* (1635) 33251 (Newbury) (office). *Fax:* (1635) 45713 (Newbury) (office). *E-mail:* info@vodafone.com (office). *Website:* www.vodafone.com (office).

KLEMPERER, Paul David, BA, MBA, PhD, FBA; British economist and academic; *Edgeworth Professor of Economics, University of Oxford;* b. 15 Aug. 1956; s. of the late Hugh G. Klemperer and Ruth Jordan; m. Margaret Meyer 1989; two s. one d.; ed King Edward's School, Birmingham, Peterhouse, Cambridge, Stanford Univ., USA; Consultant, Andersen Consulting (now Accenture) 1978–80; Harkness Fellow of Commonwealth Fund 1980–82; Lecturer in Operations Research and Math. Econs, Univ. of Oxford 1985–90, Reader in Econs 1990–95, Edgeworth Prof. of Econs 1995–, John Thomson Fellow and Tutor, St Catherine's Coll. 1985–95, Fellow, Nuffield Coll. 1995–; Visiting Lecturer, MIT 1987, Univ. of Calif., Berkeley 1991, 1993, Stanford Univ. 1991, 1993, Yale Univ. 1994, Princeton Univ. 1998; consultant to Dept of Trade and Industry 1997–2000, US Fed. Trade Comm. 1999–2001, Dept for Energy, Transport and the Regions 2000–01, Dept for the Environment, Food and Rural Affairs 2001–02 and pvt. cos; mem. UK Competition Comm. 2001–05; Ed. RAND Journal of Economics 1993–99; Assoc. or mem. Editorial Bd Oxford Economic Papers 1986–, Review of Economic Studies 1989–97, Journal of Industrial Economics 1989–96, International Journal of Industrial Organization 1993–2000, European Economic Review 1997–2001, Review of Economic Design 1997–2000, Economic Policy 1998–99, Economic Journal 2000–04, Frontiers in Economics 2000–, Journal of Economic Analysis and Policy 2001–, Journal of Competition Law and Economics 2004–; mem. Council, Royal Econ. Soc. 2001–, Econometric Soc. 2001– (Fellow 1994), European Econ. Asscn 2002–; Hon. Fellow, ELSE 2001–, Foreign Hon. mem. American Acad. of Arts and Sciences 2005–. *Publications:* The Economic Theory of Auctions 1999, Auctions: Theory and Practice 2004; articles in econs journals. *Address:* Nuffield College, Oxford, OX1 1NF, England (office). *Telephone:* (1865) 278588 (office). *E-mail:* paul.klemperer@economics.ox.ac.uk (office). *Website:* www.economics.ox .ac.uk/index.php/staff/klemperer (office); www.paulklemperer.org (home).

KLEMPERER, William (Bill), PhD; American chemist and academic; *Professor Emeritus of Chemistry, Harvard University;* b. 6 Oct. 1927, New York, NY; s. of Paul Klemperer and Margit Klemperer (née Freund); m. Elizabeth Cole 1949; one s. two d.; ed New Rochelle High School, NY, Harvard Univ. and Univ. of California, Berkeley; USN Air Corps 1944–46; Instructor, Berkeley Feb.–June 1954; Instructor, Dept of Chem. and Chemical Biology, Harvard Univ. 1954–57, Asst Prof. 1957–61, Assoc. Prof. 1961–65, Research Prof. 1965–2011, Prof. Emer. 2011–; Asst Dir NSF (for math. and physical sciences) 1979–81; mem. ACS, American Physical Soc. (APS), NAS, American Acad. of Arts and Sciences; several memorial lectures; Hon. Citizen of Toulouse, France 2000; Hon. DSc (Univ. of Chicago) 1996; Wetherill Medal, Franklin Inst., ACS Irving Langmuir Award, APS Earle Plyler Award, NSF Distinguished Service Medal, Bomem Michelson Award, Coblentz Soc., Remsen Award, Maryland Section of ACS, ACS Peter Debye Award in Physical Chem., Faraday Medal, Royal Soc. of Chem., ACS E. Bright Wilson Award in Spectroscopy 2001, Ionnes Marcus Marci Medal, Prague 2004. *Address:* 53 Shattuck Road, Watertown, MA 02472 (home); Department of Chemistry and Chemical Biology, Harvard University, 12 Oxford Street, Cambridge, MA 02138, USA (office). *Telephone:* (617) 924-5775 (home); (617) 495-4094 (office). *Fax:* (617) 496-5175 (office). *E-mail:* billk@otto.harvard.edu (office). *Website:* www.chem .harvard.edu/research/faculty/william_klemperer.php (office).

KLEOPAS, Myrna Y.; Cypriot lawyer, diplomatist and UN official; *Rapporteur, Committee against Torture, United Nations Office of the High Commissioner for Human Rights;* b. 23 Aug. 1944; m. Yiangos P. Kleopas; practiced as lawyer 1971–79; Legal Adviser for Human Rights, Ministry of Foreign Affairs 1977–79; joined Foreign Service 1979, worked in Political Affairs Div. 1979–80, 1986–90, Dir 1996–97; Counsellor and Consul Gen., High Comm. in London 1980–86; Dir Office of Perm. Sec., Ministry of Foreign Affairs 1990–93; Amb. to China (also accred to Japan, Pakistan, Mongolia, Philippines) 1993–96, to Italy (also accred to Switzerland, Malta, San Marino) 1997–2000; High Commr to UK 2000–04 (retd); currently Rapporteur, UN Cttee against Torture, Convention against Torture and Other Cruel, Inhuman or Degrading Treatment or Punishment. *Address:* Committee against Torture, Office of the United Nations High Commissioner for Human Rights, Palais des Nations, 1211 Geneva 10, Switzerland (office). *Website:* www2 .ohchr.org/english/bodies/cat (office).

KLEPPE, Johan; Norwegian politician and veterinary surgeon; b. 29 Sept. 1928, Bjørnskinn, Andøya; s. of Jon Kleppe and Alvhild Caroliussen Kleppe; m. Inger Johansen 1961; one s. one d.; ed Veterinary Coll. of Norway; veterinary surgeon 1954–63, Dist veterinary surgeon, Andøy 1963–76, Supervisory veterinary surgeon 1966–76; Regional Veterinary Officer of N Norway 1976–94; mem. Bjørnskinn Municipal Council 1956–64; Deputy Mayor of Andøy 1964–66, Mayor 1966–68, 1975–78, mem. Exec. Cttee Andøy Municipality 1964–78; Deputy mem. of Parl. 1967; Parl. Under-Sec. of State, Ministry of Agric. 1968–69; Liberal mem. of Parl. for Nordland 1969–73, mem. Bd of Liberal Parl. faction 1969–73; mem. Liberal Party's Cttee on Oil Policy and EC Cttee, mem. Prin. Planning Cttee; Minister of Defence 1972–73; mem. Liberal Nat. Exec. 1966–72; Leader, Norwegian del., FAO confs, Rome and Malta 1969; Norwegian Del., UN Gen. Ass., New York 1971; fmr Bd mem. Nordland Co. Liberal Asscn; fmr Chair. Students Liberal Asscn, Oslo and Bjørnskinn and Andøy Liberal Asscn; Chair. of Bd, Directorate of State Forests 1969–77, Chair. Nat. Council on Sheep-breeding 1969–82; Chair. of Bd Nordlandsbanken A/S, 8480 Andenes 1974–90, State Veterinary Lab. for Northern Norway 1976–91, Vesteraalen Intermunicipal Planning Office 1978–88; Vice-Chair. Cttee Norwegian Veterinary Asscn 1981–84, Chair. 1984–91; Chair. of Bd Andøyposten a/s 1981–90, Troms Population Acad. Assgn 1987–94; mem. Bd Norwegian Nat. Programme for Sea Ranching 1990–94. *Address:* 8484 Risøyhamn, Norway (office). *Telephone:* 76-14-76-30

(office); 90-83-99-86 (home). *Fax:* 76-14-76-30 (office). *E-mail:* johankleppe@ hotmail.com (home).

KLEPPNER, Daniel, PhD; American physicist and academic; *Lester Wolfe Professor Emeritus of Physics, Massachusetts Institute of Technology;* ed Williams Coll., Williamstown, Mass, Univ. of Cambridge, UK, Harvard Univ.; Fulbright Fellow, Univ. of Cambridge 1953–55; NSF Postdoctoral Fellow 1959–60; Alfred E. Sloan Foundation Fellow 1962–64; Asst Prof. of Physics, Harvard Univ. 1962–66; Assoc. Prof. of Physics, MIT 1966–73, Prof. of Physics 1974, Head, Div. of Atomic, Plasma Condensed Matter Physics, Dept of Physics 1976–79, Lester Wolfe Prof. of Physics and Assoc. Dir Research Lab. of Electronics (RLE) 1987–2000 (now Prof. Emer.), Dir NSF MIT-Harvard Center for Ultracold Atoms 2000–, Prin. Investigator, RLE Atomic, Molecular and Optical Physics Group; mem. NAS; Fellow, American Physical Soc. (APS), AAAS, American Acad. of Arts and Sciences; APS Davisson-Germer Prize 1985, APS Julius Edgar Lilienfeld Prize 1990, William F. Meggers Award, Optical Soc. of America 1990, James Rhyne Killian, Jr Faculty Achievement Award, MIT, Oersted Award, American Asscn of Physics Teachers, Wolf Prize for Physics, Wolf Foundation (Israel) 2005. *Publications:* numerous articles in scientific journals. *Address:* Room 26-237, 77 Massachusetts Avenue, Massachusetts Institute of Technology, Cambridge, MA 02139-4307, USA (office). *Telephone:* (617) 253-6811 (office). *Fax:* (617) 253-4876 (office). *E-mail:* Kleppner@ mit.edu (office). *Website:* www.rle.mit.edu (office).

KLERIDES, Takis; Cypriot accountant, business consultant and fmr government official; *Chairman, Tufton Oceanic Finance Group;* b. 21 Aug. 1951, Nicosia; m. Nancy Hak 1976; one s. one d.; ed Birmingham Polytechnic, UK; joined KPMG Cyprus 1977, Pnr 1983–97, Sr Pnr 1997–; Minister of Finance 1999–2003, also apptd a Gov. of the IMF and EBRD 1999–2003; pvt. business consultant 2003–; mem. Monopolies Comm. 1998–99, Cyprus Olympic Cttee 1996–99; Chair. Cyprus Basketball Fed. 1988–98; Chair. Tufton Oceanic Finance Group; mem. Bd of Dirs Logicom Public Ltd; Fellow, Chartered Asscn of Certified Accountants; mem. Inst. of Certified Public Accountants of Cyprus (mem. Council 1991–99). *Leisure interest:* sports. *Address:* Tufton Oceanic Finance Group, 3 Thalia Street, PO Box 51309, 3504 Limassol, Cyprus (office). *Telephone:* 25840300 (office). *Fax:* 25575895 (office). *Website:* www.tuftonoceanic.com (office).

KLESSE, William (Bill) R., BS, MBA; American business executive; *Chairman and CEO, Valero Energy Corporation;* ed Univ. of Dayton, West Texas A&M Univ.; numerous exec. positions with Valero Energy Corpn and its predecessors for almost 40 years including Vice-Pres. of Logistics and Strategy 1982–84, then Dir of Corporate Devt, Sr Vice-Pres., Exec. Vice-Pres., Exec. Vice-Pres. Ultramar Diamond Shamrock (refining operations) 1996–99, Exec. Vice-Pres. of Operations and Chair. Shamrock Logistics LLC 1999–2001, Exec. Vice-Pres. of Refining and Commercial Operations (after merger of Ultramar Diamond Shamrock and Valero) 2001–03, Exec. Vice-Pres. and COO Valero Energy Corpn 2003–06, CEO and Vice-Chair. 2006–07, Chair. and CEO 2007–. *Address:* Valero Corporate Headquarters, PO Box 696000, One Valero Way, San Antonio, TX 78269-6000, USA (office). *Telephone:* (210) 345-2000 (office). *Fax:* (210) 345-2646 (office). *E-mail:* info@valero.com (office). *Website:* www.valero.com (office).

KLEY, Karl-Ludwig, PhD; German lawyer and business executive; *Chairman of the Executive Board and General Partner, Merck KGaA;* b. 11 June 1951, Munich; ed Ludwig-Maximilians Univ., Munich; completed industrial business apprenticeship at Siemens AG then trained as lawyer in Hamburg and Johannesburg; joined Bayer AG as Asst to Chair. of Man. Bd 1982, then Chief Financial Officer, Japan 1987–91, then numerous exec. positions in Pharmaceuticals Div. including Head, Pharmaceuticals, Italy 1994–97, then Head Corp. Finance and Investor Relations 1998; Chief Financial Officer and mem. Exec. Bd Lufthansa AG 1998–2008; Vice-Chair. Exec. Bd Merck KGaA 2006–07, Chair. Exec. Bd 2007–, also mem. Exec. Bd E. Merck OHG; mem. Supervisory Bd Bertelsmann AG, WestLB AG; fmr mem. Supervisory Bd Vattenfall Europe AG, MAN AG; mem. Presidential Council of German Chemical Industry Asscn (VCI); Hon. Prof., Otto Beisheim School of Man. 2006. *Address:* Merck KGaA, Frankfurter Str. 250, 64293 Darmstadt, Germany. *Telephone:* (6151) 720. *Fax:* (6151) 722000. *Website:* www .merck.de.

KLEY, Max Dietrich; German business executive; b. 1940, Berlin; m.; three c.; ed Univs of Munich and Heidelberg; joined Legal Dept, BASF AG 1969, Head of Tax Dept 1977–82, CEO Gewerkschaft Auguste Vic., Marl 1982–87, Pres. Energy and Coal Div. 1987–90, mem. Bd of Exec. Dirs 1990–2003, Deputy Chair. 1999–2003, mem. Supervisory Bd BASF SE 2003–; Chair. Supervisory Bd Infineon Technologies AG 2002–10, Interim CEO March–Aug. 2004; Chair. Supervisory Bd SGL Group 2004–13; mem. Supervisory Bd HeidelbergCement AG (fmrly Heidelberger Zement AG) 2004–; Chair. Industrial Energy and Power Asscn 1991–97; mem. Bd of Trustees Accounting Standards Cttee Foundation 2003–; Hon. Pres. Deutsches Aktieninstitut. *Address:* c/o Supervisory Board, BASF SE, 67056 Ludwigshafen, Germany (office).

KLIBI, Chedli, BA; Tunisian politician and international official; b. 6 Sept. 1925, Tunis; s. of Hassouna Klibi and Habiba Bannani; m. Kalthoum Lasram 1956; one s. two d.; ed Sadiki Coll., Tunis, Sorbonne, Paris; successively high school teacher, Lecturer, Univ. of Tunis and journalist 1951–57; Dir-Gen. Tunisian Radio and TV 1958–61; Minister of Information and Cultural Affairs 1961–64, 1969–73, of Cultural Affairs 1976–78, of Information Sept. 1978; Minister, Dir Cabinet of Pres. 1974–76; Sec.-Gen. League of Arab States 1979–90; Mayor of Carthage 1963–90; currently mem. Tunisian Senat; mem. Political Bureau and Cen. Cttee, Neo Destour (Parti Socialiste Destourien); mem. Cairo Arabic Language Acad.; Grand Officier, Légion de Honneur 1972, Grand Cordon, Order of Independence and Order of Repub. (Tunisia) and several foreign decorations. *Publications include:* The Arabs and the Palestinian Question, Islam and Modernity, Culture is a Civilisational Challenge, Orient–Occident, la paix violente. *Leisure interest:* reading. *Address:* 9 rue Ibn Kaldoun, Carthage, Tunisia (home). *Telephone:* (71) 734-535 (home). *Fax:* (71) 734-820 (home).

KLICH, Bogdan Adam, MA; Polish physician, politician and academic; b. 6 May 1960, Kraków; ed Bartholomew Nowodworski High School, Kraków, Kraków Medical Acad., Jagiellonian Univ.; interned during martial law set by the communist regime 1981; physician, Kraków Medical Acad. 1986; Adviser to Chief Negotiator of Poland with EU 1989–99; doctoral studies, Dept of Historical

Philosophy 1991–95; mem. Parl. 2001–04, Vice-Chair. Cttee on Foreign Affairs, mem. Cttee on Nat. Defence; Deputy Minister of Nat. Defence 1999–2000; Observer to European Parl. 2003–04; Polish Rep. and mem. Policy Cttee of Parl. Ass. of Council of Europe 2001–04; mem. European Parl. (Group of European People's Party (Christian Democrats) and European Democrats) 2004–07, Chair. Del. for Relations with Belarus 2004–07, mem. Cttee on Foreign Affairs, Human Rights, Common Security and Defence Policy 2004–07, Conf. of Del. Chairmen 2004–07; Minister of Nat. Defence 2007–11; Lecturer, Centre for European Studies, Jagiellonian Univ.; f. Inst. for Strategic Studies, Kraków; Order of Merit for Defence of Lithuania, Gold Medal of Merit, Ministry of Foreign Affairs, Slovakia. *Address:* Centre for European Studies, Jagiellonian University, ul. Garbarska 7A 31-131 Kraków, Poland (office). *Telephone:* (12) 4296207 (office). *Fax:* (12) 4296195 (office). *E-mail:* biuro@klich.pl (office); office@ces.uj.edu.pl (office). *Website:* www.ces.uj.edu.pl (office).

KLÍMA, Ivan, MA; Czech author and dramatist; b. 14 Sept. 1931, Prague; s. of Vilém Klíma and Marta Klíma; m. Helena Malá-Klímová 1958; one s. one d.; ed Charles Univ., Prague; Ed. Československoslovensky spisovatel (publishing house) 1958–63; Ed. Literárni noviny 1963–67, Literárni Listy 1968, Listy 1968–69; Visiting Prof., Univ. of Michigan, Ann Arbor, USA 1969–70, Univ. of California, Berkeley, USA 1998; freelance author publishing abroad 1970–89; columnist, Lidove Noviny newspaper; mem. Council, Czech Writers 1989–, Ed.'s Council, Lidové noviny 1996–97; Exec. Pres. Czech PEN Centre 1990–93, Deputy Pres. 1993–; Hostovský Award, New York 1985, George Theiner Prize (UK) 1993, Franz Kafka Prize 2002, Medal for Outstanding Service to the Czech Repub. 2002, Karel Capek Prize 2010. *Publications:* Ship Named Hope 1968, A Summer Affair 1972, My Merry Mornings (short stories) 1979, My First Loves (short stories) 1985, Love and Garbage 1987, Judge on Trial 1987, My Golden Trades (short stories) 1992, The Island of Dead Kings 1992, The Spirit of Prague (essays) 1994, Waiting for the Dark, Waiting for the Light 1996, The Ultimate Intimacy (novel) 1997, No Saints or Angels 1999, Between Security and Insecurity: Prospects for Tomorrow 2000, Lovers for a Day: New and Collected Stories on Love 2000, Karel Capek: Life and Work 2002, The Premier and the Angel (in Czech) 2004; plays: The Castle 1964, The Master 1967, The Sweetshop Myriam 1968, President and the Angel, Klara and Two Men 1968, Bridegroom for Marcela 1968, The Games 1975, Kafka and Felice 1986, My Crazy Century 2009; contribs to magazines. *Leisure interests:* tennis, gathering mushrooms. *Address:* Na Dubiné 5, 14700 Prague 4, Czech Republic. *Telephone:* 73-7788981 (mobile).

KLIMA, Viktor; Austrian politician and business executive; *Chief Representative, South American Operations and President, Volkswagen Argentina;* b. 4 June 1947, Vienna; s. of Viktor Klima and Anna Varga; m. Sonja Holzinger 1995; one s. one d.; ed Vienna Tech. Univ., Univ. of Vienna; worked at Inst. for Automation and Scientific Business Consultancy; joined staff of Österreichische Mineralöl-Verwaltungs AG (ÖMV) 1970, Head Organizational Div. 1980–85, Dir Cen. Personnel Office and group's Prokuriet (holder of a gen. power of attorney) 1986, mem. Man. Bd with responsibility for finance, control, accountancy and acquisitions (subsequently also chemical div.) 1990–92; Minister of Public Economy and Transport 1992–96, of Finance 1996–97, Fed. Chancellor of Austria 1997–2000; Chief Rep., South America Operations and Pres. Volkswagen Argentina 2000–; fmr mem. several supervisory and advisory bds, Governing Bd Fed. of Public Economy and Utility Enterprises; fmr Chair. Fed. Econ. Chamber's Petroleum Industry Labour Law Cttee, Cttee on Public and Utility Enterprises. *Address:* Volkswagen Argentina S.A., Avda. Henry Ford y Delcasse, 1617 General Pacheco, Buenos Aires, Argentina (office). *Telephone:* (11) 4317-9000 (office). *Fax:* (11) 4317-9001 (office). *Website:* www.volkswagen.com.ar (office).

KLIMMT, Reinhard; German politician and historian; b. 16 Aug. 1942; elected mem. of Landtag 1975; Chair. SPD Landtag Party, mem. SPD Party Exec., Chair. Media Comm. of SPD Party Exec. –1998; Minister-Pres. of Saarland 1998–99; Minister of Regional Planning, Urban Devt, Construction and Transport 1999–2000; consultant to Bd of Deutsche Bahn AG 2002–. *Publication:* überall und irgendwo: Aus der Welt der Bücher 2006. *Address:* c/o Board of Directors, Deutsche Bahn Aktiengesellschaft, Potsdamer Platz 2, 10785 Berlin, Germany. *Telephone:* (30) 297-0. *Fax:* (30) 297-6-19-19. *Website:* www.db.de.

KLIMOV, Dmitri Mikhailovich; Russian mechanical engineer; *Councillor, Institute for Problems in Mechanics, Russian Academy of Sciences;* b. 13 July 1933; m.; ed Moscow State Univ.; Researcher, Research Inst. of Applied Mechanics. 1958–67; Deputy Dir Inst. for Problems in Mechanics, USSR (now Russian) Acad. of Sciences 1967–89, Dir 1989, now Councillor, Corresp. mem. USSR (now Russian) Acad. of Sciences 1981, mem. 1992, Academician-Sec. Div. for Problems of Machine Engineering, Mechanics and Control Processes 1996–; Deputy Chair. Scientific Council on Problems of Man. of Navigation Movt; USSR State Prize 1976, Russian State Prize 1994. *Publications:* Inertial Navigation on the Sea 1984, Applied Methods in Oscillations Theory 1988, Methods of Computer Algebra in Problems of Mechanics 1989; numerous articles. *Leisure interest:* chess. *Address:* Institute for Problems in Mechanics, 119526 Moscow, Vernadskogo prosp. 101, block 1, Russia (office). *Telephone:* (495) 434-46-10 (office); (495) 938-14-04 (Academy). *Fax:* (495) 938-20-48 (office). *E-mail:* ipm@ipmnet.ru (office). *Website:* www.ipmnet.ru (office).

KLIMOVSKI, Savo, LLD, PhD; Macedonian politician and academic; b. 1947, Skopje; m. Radmila Klimovski; one s. one d.; ed Skopje Univ., Ljubljana Univ.; Lecturer, Asst Prof., Prof., Dean of Law Faculty, Pres., St Cyril and Methodius Univ., Skopje; mem. Exec. Council, Macedonian Ass. 1986–90; Pres. Macedonian Cttee for Educ., Culture and Physical Culture; f. Democratic Alternative (political party) 1998; mem. Govt Coalition For Changes; Speaker, Ass. of Repub. of Macedonia 1998–2000, Pres. Cttee for Constitutional Issues, Council for Interethnic Relations; Pres. Repub. of Macedonia Nov.–Dec. 1999. *Publications:* Constitutional and Political System, Politics and Institutions, Political Philosophy, Parliamentary Law. *Address:* c/o Democratic Alternative (DA) (Demokratska Alternativa), 1000 Skopje, ul. Dame Gruev 7; Bul. 'Patizanski odredi' nr. 3/II-19, Skopje (home); Sobranje, Oktomyri blvd 11, 91000 Skopje, Macedonia. *E-mail:* klimovski@eccf.ukim.edu.mk. *Website:* www.klimovski.com.mk (home).

KLIMUK, Col-Gen. Piotr Ilyich, DTechSc; Russian cosmonaut; b. 10 July 1942, Komarovka, Brest Region; m. Lilia Vladimirovna Klimuk; one s.; ed Chernigov

Higher Mil. Aviation School, Air Force Acad., Lenin Mil. Political Acad.; three space flights (Soyuz 13, Soyuz 18, Soyuz 30) 1973–78; Deputy Head, then Head of Political Dept Yuriy Gagarin Centre for Cosmonauts Training 1978–91, Head of Centre 1991–2003 (retd); USSR People's Deputy 1989–91; Hero of Soviet Union 1973, 1975; Tsiolkovsky Gold Medal, USSR State Prize 1978, 1981, Gold Medal (Polish Acad. of Sciences); Order of Fatherland of the 2nd class 2002. *Publications:* Next to the Stars, Attacking Weightlessness. *Address:* c/o Yuriy Gagarin Centre for Cosmonauts Training, Zvezdny Gorodok, Moscow, Russia.

KLINE, Kevin Delaney, BA; American actor and director; b. 24 Oct. 1947, St Louis; s. of Robert J. Kline and Peggy Kirk; m. Phoebe Cates 1989; one s. one d.; ed Indiana Univ. and Juilliard School Drama Div. New York; founding mem. The Acting Co. New York 1972–76; Obie Award for sustained achievement, Will Award for classical theatre; Joseph Papp Award 1990, John Houseman Award 1993, Gotham Award 1997. *Films include:* Sophie's Choice 1982, Pirates of Penzance 1983, The Big Chill 1983, Silverado 1985, Violets are Blue 1985, Cry Freedom 1987, A Fish Called Wanda (Acad. Award for Best Supporting Actor 1989) 1988, The January Man 1989, I Love You to Death 1989, Soapdish 1991, Grand Canyon 1991, Consenting Adults 1992, Chaplin 1992, Dave 1993, Princess Caraboo 1994, French Kiss 1995, The Hunchback of Notre Dame (voice) 1996, Fierce Creatures 1996, The Ice Storm 1997, In and Out 1997, A Midsummer Night's Dream 1999, Wild Wild West 1999, The Road to El Dorado (voice) 2000, The Anniversary Party 2001, Life as a House 2001, Orange County 2002, The Emperor's Club 2002, The Hunchback of Notre Dame II (voice) 2002, De-Lovely 2004, Pink Panther 2006, A Prairie Home Companion 2006, As You Like It 2006, Trade 2007, Definitely, Maybe 2008, The Extra Man 2010, The Conspirator 2010, Darling Companion 2012. *Theatre:* Broadway appearances in On the Twentieth Century 1978 (Tony Award 1978), Loose Ends 1979, Pirates of Penzance 1980 (Tony Award 1980), Arms and the Man 1985; off-Broadway appearances in Richard III 1983, Henry V 1984, Hamlet (also Dir) 1986, 1990, Much Ado About Nothing 1988, Measure for Measure 1995, The Seagull 2001, Cyrano de Bergerac 2008, Darling Companion 2012. *Television includes:* Freedom: A History of Us (series) 2003, As You Like It (Outstanding Performance by a Male Actor in a Television Movie or Miniseries 2008) 2007. *Address:* c/o William Morris Agency, 1325 Avenue of the Americas, New York, NY 10019, USA.

KLINE, Lowry F., BA, JD; American lawyer and beverage industry executive; b. 1941, Louden, Tenn.; m. Jane Kline; three c.; ed Univ. of Tennessee; Pnr, Miller & Martin (law firm) 1970–95; Gen. Counsel, Johnston Coca-Cola Bottling Group 1981–91; Sr Vice-Pres. and Gen. Counsel, Coca-Cola Enterprises Inc. (bottler) 1996–97, Exec. Vice-Pres. and Gen. Counsel, 1997–99, Exec. Vice-Pres. and Chief Admin. Officer 1999–2000, Dir 2000–, Vice-Chair. 2000–02, CEO 2001–04, 2005–06, Chair. 2002–08; mem. Bd of Dirs The Dixie Group, Inc., Jackson Furniture Industries; fmr Pres. Chattanooga Bar Asscn, Tenn. Bd of Law Examiners; fmr Chair. Tenn. Bar Foundation. *Address:* Coca-Cola Enterprises Inc., POB 723040, Atlanta, GA 31139-0040, USA (office). *Telephone:* (770) 989-3000 (office). *Fax:* (770) 989-3788 (office). *Website:* www.cokecce.com (office).

KLINSMANN, Jürgen; German football coach, fmr professional footballer and business executive; b. 30 July 1964, Göppingen; m. Debbie Chin 1995; one s. one d.; striker; youth player for TB Gingen 1972–74, SC Geislingen an der Steige 1974–78, Stuttgarter Kickers 1978–81; sr career with Stuttgarter Kickers 1981–84, VfB Stuttgart 1984–89 (79 goals), Inter Milan 1989–92 (won UEFA Cup 1991, Supercoppa Italiana 1989), AS Monaco 1992–94, Tottenham Hotspur 1994–95, Bayern Munich 1995–97 (won UEFA Cup 1996, Bundesliga 1997), Sampdoria 1997–98, Tottenham Hotspur (on loan) 1997–98, Orange County Blue Star 2003; won 108 caps for West Germany/Germany and scored 47 goals, mem. winning team, World Cup 1990, European Championship 1996, Capt. nat. team 1994–98, Head Coach 2004–06; Int. Amb. for FIFA World Cup, Germany 2006; Head Coach, FC Bayern Munich 2008–09; fmr Tech. Advisor, Los Angeles Galaxy (Major League Soccer); worked for RTL as 2010 FIFA World Cup Moderator; Head Coach, US men's nat. football team 2011–; f. AGAPEDIA (children's care charity); Vice-Pres. SoccerSolutions (sports marketing and business devt consultancy); Int. Spokesman, Mastercard; West German Footballer of the Year 1988, German Footballer of the Year 1994, Football Writers' Asscn Footballer of the Year 1995, German Football Manager of the Year 2006. *Leisure interests:* travel, cinema, music, languages, family. *Address:* US Soccer Federation, 1801 South Prairie Avenue, Chicago, IL 60616 (office); Soccer Solutions LLC, 744 SW Regency Place, Portland, OR 97225, USA (office). *Telephone:* (312) 808-1300 (US Soccer Federation) (office); (503) 297-0844 (Soccer Solutions) (office). *Fax:* (312) 808-1301 (US Soccer Federation) (office); (503) 297-0749 (Soccer Solutions) (office). *E-mail:* mick@soccersolutions.com (office). *Website:* www.ussoccer.com (office); www.soccersolutions.com (office).

KLOBUCHAR, Amy, BA, JD; American lawyer and politician; *Senator from Minnesota;* b. 25 May 1960, Plymouth, Minn.; d. of Jim Klobuchar and Rose Klobuchar; m. John Bessler 1993; one d.; ed Yale Univ. and Univ. of Chicago Law School; practised law in Minn. and worked closely with fmr Vice-Pres. Walter Mondale; Assoc. Pnr, Dorsey & Whitney LLP (law firm) 1985–93; Pnr, Gray Plant Mooty LLP 1993–98; Attorney and Chief Prosecutor, Hennepin Co., Minn. 1998–2007; Senator from Minnesota 2007–, mem. Cttee on Agric., Nutrition and Forestry, Cttee on Environment and Public Works, Cttee on Commerce, Science and Transportation, US Congress Jt Econ. Cttee; Pres. Minnesota Co. Attorneys Asscn 2002–03; Democrat; '40 Under 40' Award, CityBusiness, named by Minnesota Lawyer magazine "Lawyer of the Year" 2001. *Publication:* Uncovering the Dome. *Address:* 302 Hart Senate Office Building, Washington, DC 20510, USA (office). *Telephone:* (202) 224-3244 (office). *Fax:* (202) 228-2186 (office). *Website:* klobuchar.senate.gov (office); www.amyklobuchar.com (office).

KLOPPERS, Marius, BE (Chem.), MBA, PhD; South African engineer and mining industry executive; b. 26 Aug. 1962; m. Carin Kloppers; three c.; ed Univ. of Pretoria, Massachusetts Inst. of Tech., USA, Institut Européen d'Admin des Affaires (INSEAD), France; early career with Sasol Ltd, S Africa; fmr man. consultant with McKinsey & Co., Netherlands; joined Billiton (BHP Billiton after 2001) 1993, held several man. positions including Gen. Man. Hillside Aluminium, COO Aluminium, CEO Samancor Manganese, Group Exec. Billiton plc, Chief Marketing Officer, apptd Chief Commercial Officer, BHP Billiton Group 2003, mem. Bd of Dirs BHP Billiton Ltd and BHP Billiton Plc 2006–13, Group Pres. Nonferrous Materials Group –2007, Exec. Dir BHP Billiton, also CEO BHP Billiton 2007–13, Chair. Group Man. Cttee; Deputy Chair. Int. Council on Mining and Metals 2008–11, Chair. 2011–. *Address:* c/o BHP Billiton Ltd, BHP Billiton Centre, 180 Lonsdale Street, Melbourne, Vic. 3000, Australia. *E-mail:* webmaster@bhpbilliton.com.

KLOSE, Hans-Ulrich; German lawyer and politician; *Senior Adviser, Bosch-Stiftung;* b. 14 June 1937, Breslau; m. Anne Steinbeck-Klose; two s. two d.; ed gymnasium in Bielefeld High School, Clinton, Iowa USA and Univs of Freiburg and Hamburg; fmr lawyer in Hamburg; mem. Social Democratic Party (SPD) 1964–; mem. Public Services and Transport Workers' Union 1968; mem. Hamburgische Bürgerschaft 1970, Chair. SPD Parl. Group 1972; Senator of the Interior 1973; Mayor of Hamburg 1974–81 (resgnd); mem. (Constituency 18, Hamburg-Harburg) Bundestag 1983–2013, Chair. SPD Parl. Party 1991–94, Vice-Pres. Bundestag 1994–98, Chair. Foreign Affairs Cttee 1998–2002, Vice-Chair. 2002–13; Chair. German-American Parl. Group 2003–13; Treas. SPD 1987–91; Sr Adviser, Bosch-Stiftung; Hon. Citizen of Lima 1981; Int. Statesmanship Award, US Asscn of Former Members of Congress 2013. *Publications:* Das Altern der Gesellschaft 1993, Altern hat Zukunft 1993, Charade (poems) 1997, Charade 2 (poems) 1999, Zeitschreiben (poems) 2007. *Leisure interests:* early American cultures, art and antiques, painting, literature. *Address:* Heylstrasse 29, 10825 Berlin, Germany (office). *E-mail:* ulriklose@t-online.de (office).

KLOSSA, Guillaume, MSc, MPA; French business executive, government official and journalist; *President, EuropaNova;* ed Institut d'Études politiques, Paris, London School of Econs and Political Science, UK, Ecole des hautes Études commerciales, Paris; fmr Dir in charge of consulting and digital activities for Bureau Veritas group in Europe; fmr Vice-Pres. and mem. Exec. Cttee at McDonald's France; adviser to French presidency of EU 2007–08, to reflection group for future of Europe at European Council 2009–10; European columnist for Metro International 2004–10; Pres. EuropaNova (European think-tank based in Paris and Brussels); Founder 40under40 (European young leaders programme); currently Head of the Mission 'Innovation et production en Europe', Directorate-Gen. for Competition, Consumption and Fraud Prevention, Ministry of Economy, Industry and Employment; contrib. to Forbes magazine 2011–. *Publication:* Europe, la dernière chance? (with Jean-François Jamet) 2011. *Address:* EuropaNova, 18/20 place de la Madeleine, 75008 Paris, France (office). *Telephone:* 1-43-42-40-90 (office). *E-mail:* thomas@europanova.eu (office). *Website:* www.europanova.eu (office); www.40under40.eu; www.guillaume-klossa.eu.

KLOSTER, Einar, BA; Norwegian business executive; b. 22 Sept. 1937, Oslo; s. of Knut Utstein Kloster and Ingeborg Kloster (née Ihlen); m. Elizabeth Blake (née Haüan) 1961; two d.; ed Dartmouth Coll. and Harvard Univ., USA; Marketing Man. Philips Norway 1961–68, Philips Head Office, Netherlands 1968–70; Marketing Dir Philips Japan 1970–74; CEO Philips East Africa 1974–77, Philips Norway 1978–82, Philips Brazil 1982–85; Exec. Vice-Pres. North American Philips Corpn 1985–86, Pres. 1989; Chair. and CEO Kloster Cruise Ltd 1986–88, Pres. and CEO 1989–2004; Chair. Norsk Hydro 1997–2001. *Leisure interests:* golf, tennis, skiing. *Address:* PO Box 1365, Vika, 0114 Oslo, Norway (office). *Telephone:* 22-40-31-30 (office). *Fax:* 22-40-31-31 (office). *E-mail:* einar.kloster@online.no (office).

KLÜFT, Carolina Evelyn, (Carro); Swedish athlete; b. 2 Feb. 1983, Boras; d. of Johnny Klüft and Ingalill Klüft; m. Patrik Klüft 2007; ed Växjö Katedralskola, Växjö Univ.; heptathlete; took up athletics in 1995, int. debut in Santiago 2000; gold medals: European Jr Championships 2000, 2002, World Jr Championships 2000, European Championships, Munich 2002 (broke her own world junior record), Gothenburg 2006, European Indoor Championships, Madrid 2005, Birmingham 2007, World Championships, Paris 2003 (became third athlete to score over 7,000 points), Helsinki 2005, Osaka 2007 and Olympic Games, Athens 2004; also won gold medal at the pentathlon at World Indoor Championships, Birmingham 2003, bronze medal at Long Jump at World Indoor Championships, Budapest 2004; mem. IFK Växjö club; European Athletic Asscn Athlete of the Year 2003, 2006, Swedish Sports Fed. Sportswoman of the Year 2003, Svenska Dagbladet Gold Medal 2003. *Leisure interests:* friends and family. *Address:* Norgatan 24, 352 31 Växjö, Sweden (office). *Telephone:* (470) 70-35-32 (office). *Fax:* (470) 70-35-39 (office). *E-mail:* johnny.kluft@euroaccident.com (office). *Website:* www.rf.se.

KLUG, Sir Aaron, Kt, OM, ScD, FRS; British biochemist and academic; *Group Leader, Division of Structural Studies, Medical Research Council Laboratory of Molecular Biology, Cambridge;* b. 11 Aug. 1926; s. of Lazar Klug and Bella Silin; m. Liebe Bobrow 1948; two s. (one deceased); ed Durban High School and Univs of the Witwatersrand, Cape Town and Cambridge; Jr Lecturer 1947–48; Research Student, Cavendish Lab., Univ. of Cambridge 1949–52, Rouse-Ball Research Studentship, Trinity Coll., Cambridge 1949–52, Colloid Science Dept, Cambridge 1953; Nuffield Research Fellow, Birkbeck Coll., London 1954–57; Dir Virus Structure Research Group, Birkbeck Coll. 1958–61; mem. of staff and Group Leader, MRC Lab. of Molecular Biology, Cambridge 1962–, Jt Head, Div. of Structural Studies 1978–86, Dir 1986–96; Pres. Royal Soc. 1995–2000; Fellow of Peterhouse 1962–93; Foreign Assoc. NAS; Foreign mem. Max Planck Gesellschaft 1984, Acad. des Sciences, Paris 1989, Japan Acad. 1999; Foreign Hon. mem. American Acad. of Arts and Sciences; Hon. Fellow, Trinity Coll., Cambridge, Royal Coll. of Physicians 1987, Royal Coll. of Pathologists 1991, Peterhouse, Cambridge 1993–, Birkbeck Coll. 1994; Hon. Prof., Univ. of Cambridge 1989; Hon. DSc (Chicago) 1978, (Columbia) 1978, (Witwatersrand 1984), (Hull) 1985, (Jerusalem) 1985, (St Andrews) 1987, (Western Ont.) 1991, (Warwick) 1994, (Cape Town) 1997, (London) 1999, (Oxford) 2001; Hon. Dr Fil. (Stockholm) 1980; Hon. LittD (Cantab.) 1998; Hon. DLitt (Cambridge) 1998; Dr hc (Strasbourg) 1998, (Stirling) 1998; Heineken Prize, Royal Netherlands Acad. of Science 1979, Louisa Gross Horwitz Prize, Columbia Univ. 1981, Nobel Prize for Chem. 1982, Copley Medal, Royal Soc. 1985, Harden Medal, Biochemical Soc. 1985, Baly Medal, Royal Coll. of Physicians 1987; William Bate Hardy Prize, Cambridge Philosophical Soc. 1996, Croonian Prize Lecture, Royal Soc. 2007. *Publications:* articles in scientific journals. *Leisure interests:* reading, ancient history. *Address:* MRC Laboratory of Molecular Biology, Hills Road, Cambridge, CB2 0QH, England (office). *Telephone:* (1223) 248011 (office). *E-mail:* akl@mrc-lmb.cam.ac.uk (office). *Website:* www2.mrc-lmb.cam.ac.uk/research/structuralstudies/aaronklug (office).

KLUG, Gerald Rudolf, Mag.Iur; Austrian politician and fmr trade union official; *Federal Minister of Defence and Sports;* b. 13 Nov. 1968, Graz; ed Acad. for Social Studies, Mödling Chamber of Labour, Karl-Franzens-Univ., Graz; began career as skilled worker (lathe operator), Siemens Mobility Co. 1987–90; mem. Pro-Ge (trade union) 1984–, Sec. 1990–; Lay Judge, Graz Court of Appeal 2000–; mem. Ind. Financial Tribunal of Graz Regional Financial Directorate 2001–11; Substitute mem., Gen. Ass. of Styria Prov. Health Insurance Fund 2004–05; mem. Directorate, Styria Prov. Employment Office 2003–05; mem. Bundesrat (Parl.) (Sozialdemokratische Partei Österreichs (SPÖ—Social Democratic Party of Austria) 2005–13, SPÖ Chief Whip 2010–13; Fed. Minister of Defence and Sports 2013–. *Address:* Federal Ministry of Defence, Rossauer Lände 1, 1090 Vienna, Austria (office). *Telephone:* (1) 502-01-0 (office). *Fax:* (1) 502-01-10-17-041 (office). *E-mail:* presse@bmlvs.gv.at (office). *Website:* www.bmlv.gv.at (office).

KLUGE, Jürgen, Dr rer. nat, MPhys; German physicist, business executive and consultant; *Senior Advisor, Bank of America Merrill Lynch;* b. 2 Sept. 1953, Hagen; ed Univs of Cologne and Essen; with McKinsey & Co., Düsseldorf 1984–2009, German Office Man. 1999–2006; Chair. Man. Bd Franz Haniel & Cie. GmbH and Group Human Resources Man. 2010–12; Chair. Supervisory Bd Celesio AG 2010–12, Metro AG 2010–11; Vice-Chair. TAKKT AG 2010–12; Consultant, Kluge & Partner, Düsseldorf 2012–; Sr Advisor, Bank of America Merrill Lynch 2012–; mem. Supervisory Bd SMS Holding GmbH; Hon. Prof. of Mechanical Eng, Darmstadt Tech. Univ. 2004–. *Address:* Kluge & Partner, Unternehmensberater Consulting, Advice and Projects Kaiser-Wilhelm-Ring 10, 40545 Düsseldorf, Germany (office). *Telephone:* (211) 15949400 (office). *Fax:* (211) 15949402 (office). *E-mail:* info@juergen-kluge.com (office). *Website:* www.juergen-kluge.com (office).

KLUM, Heidi, (Heidi Samuel); German/American model, fashion designer, actress, television presenter and artist and singer; b. 1 June 1973, Bergisch Gladbach, North Rhine-Westphalia, West Germany; d. of Günther Klum and Erna Klum; m. 1st Ric Pipino 1997 (divorced 2002); one d. with Flavio Briatore; m. 2nd British singer Seal (divorced 2012) 2005; two s. one d.; won nat. modelling contest Model 92 1992, offered modelling contract with Metropolitan Models New York; has appeared on cover of fashion magazines, including Vogue, ELLE and Marie Claire; became known after appearing on cover of Sports Illustrated Swimsuit Issue and for work with Victoria's Secret 1997–2010; hosted Victoria's Secret Fashion Shows 2002, 2006, 2007, 2009; signed to IMG Models, New York; designer of several clothing lines, fragrances and make-up; became new face and creative adviser for European cosmetics brand Astor 2010; host, judge and exec. producer of reality show Project Runway on Bravo US cable TV channel 2004; host, judge and co-producer of Germany's Next Topmodel (German version of int. reality TV show) on German station ProSieben 2006–; became Barbie's official amb. for doll's 50th anniversary 2009; naturalized American citizen 2008; named by Forbes magazine on list of the World's 15 Top-Earning Supermodels (third) 2007, (second) 2008, (second) 2009, Peabody Award 2008, ranked 4th by Peoplestar.co.uk Celebrity Magazine on list of The World's Most Beautiful Women 2010, ranked by Forbes magazine amongst The World's 100 Most Powerful Women (39th) 2010. *Films include:* 54 1998, Blow Dry 2001, Ella Enchanted 2004, The Life and Death of Peter Sellers 2004, The Devil Wears Prada 2006, Perfect Stranger 2007. *Music includes:* debut single Wonderland 2006. *Music videos include:* Jamiroquai's video Love Foolosophy, Kelis's Young, Fresh 'n' New 2001, video for Seal's song Secret 2010. *Television includes:* appeared in episodes of Malcolm in the Middle and Cursed; guest-starred as herself in I Get That a Lot, Spin City, Sex and the City, CSI: Miami, How I Met Your Mother, Yes, Dear, Ugly Betty, and Desperate Housewives. *Address:* IMG Models, 304 Park Avenue South, New York, NY 10010, USA (office). *Telephone:* (212) 253-8884 (office). *Fax:* (212) 253-8883 (office). *E-mail:* info@imgmodels.com (office). *Website:* www.imgmodels.com (office); www.heidiklum.com.

KLUZA, Stanisław, PhD; Polish economist and government official; *Chairman, Komisji Nadzoru Finansowego (Polish Financial Supervision Authority);* b. 2 June 1972, Warsaw; m.; ed Warsaw School of Econs, Washington Univ., St Louis, USA, Univ. of Glasgow, UK; early positions included working at Higher School of Int. Commerce and Finance (GSBE-HSICF and Computerland shop; worked at Unilever Polska 1994–98, McKinsey & Co. 1998–99; Head, Econ. Analysis Team, Office for Strategic Planning, Bank Gospodarki Żymnościowej SA (BGŻ) 2002–03, Chief Economist and Adviser to Pres. of Man. Bd 2003–06; Second Sec. of State and Deputy Minister of Finance May–July 2006, Minister of Finance July–Sept. 2006; Chair. Komisji Nadzoru Finansowego (Polish Financial Supervision Authority) 2006–; Asst Prof., Inst. of Statistics and Demography, Warsaw School of Econs; mem. Supervisory Bd, Siersza Power Generation Plant; mem. Soc. of Polish Economists, Hon. Council of Experts of AISEC Poland, Club 01; Fulbright Scholar, Dekaban-Liddle Scholar; Prime Minister's Award for Doctoral Thesis, Foundation for Polish Science Award. *Publications:* numerous articles in professional publications. *Address:* Komisji Nadzoru Finansowego, Plac Powstańców, Warszawy 1, 00-950 Warsaw, Poland (office). *Telephone:* (22) 3326600 (office). *Fax:* (22) 3326793 (office). *Website:* www.knf.gov.pl (office).

KLYCHKO, Vitaliy Volodymyrovych, CandSci, MA, PhD; Ukrainian professional boxer and politician; *World Boxing Council Heavyweight Champion Emeritus; Leader, Ukrainian Democratic Alliance for Reform;* b. 19 July 1971, Bilovodske, Kyrgyz SSR, USSR; s. of the late Volodymyr Rodionovich Klychko; m. Nataliya Yegorova 1996; two s. one d.; ed Pereyaslav-Khmelnitsky State Pedagogical Univ., Taras Shevchenko Nat. Univ. of Kyiv, Nat. Acad. of Public Admin of Pres. of Ukraine; lived in different parts of the Soviet Union until his family moved to Ukraine 1984; began boxing aged 14; two-time world amateur kickboxing champion and four-time professional kickboxing champion, three-time Ukrainian boxing champion, champion of First World Mil. Championship, silver medallist at World Amateur Boxing Championship; professional boxer 1996–2013, WBO Inter-Continental Heavyweight Champion May–Oct. 1998, EBU Heavyweight Champion 1998–99, 2000–02, WBO Heavyweight Champion 1999–2000, WBA Inter-Continental Heavyweight Champion 2001–03, The Ring Heavyweight Champion 2004–05, WBC Heavyweight Champion 2004–05, Champion Emer. 2005–08, Champion 2008–13, Champion Emer. 2013–; co-f. (with brother Volodymyr) Klitschko Brothers Foundation 2003; began political career 2006, ran simultaneously for Verkhovna Rada (Parl.) and Kyiv City Council as Head of Pora-PRP Bloc (union of PORA and Reform and Order parties); became bloc group leader at Kyiv City Council, group renamed UDAR of Vitaliy Klychko group 2011; Leader Ukrainian Democratic Alliance for Reform (Ukrainsky Demokratychny Alyans za Reformy—UDAR) 2010–; mem. Verkhovna Rada (Parl.) 2012–, Leader of party group UDAR of Vitaliy Klychko; a leading figure in the Euromaidan protests 2013–14; cand. in presidential election 2014; agreed to carry charitable work for UNESCO 2002; Hero of Ukraine, Bundesverdienstkreuz 2010; named by World Boxing Council as the best puncher in the history of heavyweight boxing, rated by Ring Magazine as the No. 9 pound-for-pound boxer in the world 2012. *Leisure interests:* diving, music, chess. *Address:* Ukrainian Democratic Alliance for Reform, 01008 Kyiv, vul. Hrushevskoho 3, Ukraine (office). *Telephone:* (44) 481-22-29 (office). *E-mail:* press.klichko@gmail.com (office). *Website:* klichko.org (office).

KLYUYEV, Andriy Petrovych, PhD; Ukrainian politician and fmr mining engineer; b. 12 Sept. 1964, Donetsk; m. Zhanna Klyuyeva; three s.; ed Donetsk Polytechnic Inst. (now Donetsk Nat. Tech. Univ.); underground mine worker at Zasyadko coalmine, Donetsk 1983–86; Deputy Head of Mine Transport Dept, Bilorichenska coalmine (Voroshylovgrad Coal) 1986; fmr Eng Dir Shelf Group; fmr Pres. Promcomservice Jt Stock Co.; Dir-Gen. Ukrpidshypnyk Jt Stock Co. 1991–94; Deputy Chair. Donetsk Regional Council 1994–96, 1998, mem. Donetsk City Council 1996–2002, First Deputy Mayor of Donetsk 1996; mem. Verkhovna Rada (Supreme Council, Parl.) 2002–06, 2006–; mem. Party of the Regions, First Deputy Chair. 2001–08, Sec. of Political Council 2003–08, Deputy Chair. 2008–; Deputy Prime Minister of Ukraine 2003–04, 2006–10, First Deputy Prime Minister and Minister of Econ. Devt and Trade 2010–12; Sec. Nat. Security and Defence Council of Ukraine 2012–14; Head of Presidential Admin Jan.–Feb. 2014 (resgnd); wanted, along with other politicians and sr army officers, for his alleged involvement in mass murder March 2014; assets frozen by EU; Order for Service of the 1st Grade 1999, 2nd Grade 2004, Diploma of Honour of the Verkhovna Rada of Ukraine 2005; ranked as seventh most influential person in Ukraine by the Korrespondent 2011. *Publications:* author of 18 scientific and tech. inventions in the mining sector. *Address:* c/o National Security and Defence Council of Ukraine, 01601 Kyiv, vul. Komandarma Kameneva 8, Ukraine.

KNAIFEL, Alexander Aronovich; Russian composer; b. 28 Nov. 1943, Tashkent; s. of Aron Iosifovich Knaifel and Muza Veniaminovna Shapiro-Knaifel; m. Tatiana Ivanovna Melentieva 1965; one d.; ed Moscow and Leningrad Conservatoires; freelance composer; mem. Composers' Union 1968–, Cinematographers' Union 1987–; Order of Friendship 2004; DAAD Honoured Grant-Aided Composer, Berlin 1993, Honoured Art Worker of Russia 1996. *Compositions include:* Sonata on a Fairy Tale 1961, A Sling 1962, Diada 1962, Burlesca 1963, Non stop 1963, Marching and Dancing Two-voice Textures 1963, A Toast to Robert Burns 1963, Ostinati 1964, An Angel and Five Poems by Mikhail Lermontov 1964, Piano: musique militaire 1964, A Plain-air-fugue, a Fugue-interior 1964, An Anthem to Foolishness 1964, Turno a turno 1964, In via 1964, In Memory of Samuil Marshak 1964, Those Seeking the City to Come 1964–65, Passacaglia 1965, The Canterville Ghost 1965, Canterville 1965–66, Disarmament 1966, 150 000 000 1966, Lamento 1967, Salve! 1967, Petrograd Sparrows 1967, A Little White One and a Little Black One 1968, Monodia 1968, Medea 1968, Argumentum de jure 1969, Jeanne 1970–78, Baby Songs in Sleep 1972, A prima vista 1972, Appelli 1972, Status nascendi 1973–75, Two Times Two 1975, Vampampet 1975, Ainana 1978, FFPh 1978–2004, Rafferty Jazz Chorus 1980, Vera (Faith) 1980, A Call 1980, Solaris 1980, Da (Yes) 1980, A Silly Horse 1981, Accidental 1982, Nika 1983–84, Churiki 1984, Epitaphs 1984, God 1985, Agnus Dei 1985, A Kholop's Wings (A Serf's Wings) 1986, Through the Rainbow of Involuntary Tears 1987–88, Litania 1988, Notturno 1988, Shramy Marsha (Scars of Marching) 1988, Voznosheniye (The Holy Oblation) 1991, Svete Tikhiy (O Gladsome Light) 1991, Once Again on the Hypothesis 1992, Ionus – postludia 1992, Scalae Iacobis 1992, Chapter Eight 1992–93, Cantus 1993, Maranatha 1993, Butterfly 1993, In Air Clear and Unseen 1994, Alice in Wonderland 1994–2002, Amicta sole 1995, Blazhenstva 1996, Bliss 1997, With the White on the White 1997–98, Lux aeterna 1997, This Child 1997, The Tabernacle 1998, A Snowflake on a Spiderthread 1998, A Day 1999, Small Blue Feathers 2001, Petia i Dolg (Folk) 2001, A Fairy Tale of a Fisherman and a Little Fish 2002, Lukomoriye 2002–03, Confession 2003, Birth 2003, The Cherubimic Hymn 2004, Gee! 2004, Chalice 2004, Old Photos 2004, The Little Beads for Njua 2004, Of the Pope and of His Workman Balda 2004, O Spirit of Truth 2005, Tzarevna (A Tzar's Daughter) 2005, Bridge 2006–08, O Master of My Days 2007, A Mad Tea-Party 2007, For Tatianka and Annushka 2007, E.F. 2008, The Spire of Bujan 2010; incidental music for 40 films. *Publications:* Musique militaire 1974, Diada (Two Pieces) 1975, Classical Suite 1976, The Canterville Ghost 1977, Five Poems by Mikhail Lermontov 1978, Lamento 1979, The Petrograd Sparrows 1981, A Silly Horse 1985, Medea 1989, Vera (Faith) 1990, Passacaglia 1990, Da (Yes) 1991, O Comforter 1997, Bliss 1997. *Leisure interests:* photography, shooting video films. *Address:* Skobelevski pr. 5, Apt 130, 194214 St Petersburg, Russia. *Telephone:* (812) 293-82-68. *Fax:* (812) 293-53-97. *E-mail:* knaifel@hotmail.com (office), knaifel@mail.ru (home). *Website:* www.ceo.spb.ru/rus/music/knaifel.a.a.

KNAPP, Charles, MA, PhD; American economist, academic, fmr university administrator and fmr government official; *Distinguished Public Service Fellow, Institute of Higher Education, University of Georgia;* b. 13 Aug. 1946, Ames, Ia; s. of Albert B. Knapp and Anne Marie Knapp; m. Lynne Vickers Knapp 1967; one d.; ed Iowa State Univ. and Univ. of Wisconsin; Asst Prof. of Econs, Univ. of Texas, Austin 1972–76; Special Asst to US Sec. of Labor 1976–79; Deputy Asst Sec. of Labor for Employment Training 1979–81; Visiting Faculty, George Washington Univ. 1981–82; Sr Vice-Pres., Tulane Univ. 1982–85, Exec. Vice-Pres. 1985–87; Pres. and Prof. of Econs, Univ. of Georgia 1987–97, Pres. Emer. 2004–, Distinguished Public Service Fellow, Inst. of Higher Educ. 2005–; fmr Pres. Aspen Inst. 1997–99; Sr Fellow, Asscn of Governing Bds of Univs and Colls 1999–2000; Partner, Heidrick & Struggles Int. Inc., Atlanta 2000; Dir Aflac, Inc. *Publications:* A Human Capital Approach to the Burden of the Military Draft 1973, Earnings and Individual Variations in Postschool Human Investment 1976, Employment Discrimination 1978. *Address:* Institute of Higher Education, Meigs Hall, University of Georgia, Athens, Athens, GA 30602, USA (office). *Telephone:* (706) 542-0620 (office). *E-mail:* cknapp@uga.edu (office). *Website:* www.uga.edu/ihe/knapp.html (office).

KNAPP, Oscar, PhD; Swiss economist and diplomatist; *Head of Market Division, State Secretariat for International Financial Affairs;* b. 14 Aug. 1948, Grisons; m. Elisabeth Knapp; ed Univs of St Gallen and Geneva; fmr Head of Financial, Econ. and Trade Div., Embassy in Washington, DC; Amb. to Brazil 1996–2000; Exec. mem. State Secr. of Econ. Affairs, mem. Bd of Dirs and Head, Econ. Devt Co-operation Office 2003–06; Amb. to Austria 2006–10; Head of Market Div., State Secr. for Int. Financial Affairs 2010–. *Leisure interests:* skiing, golf, mountains. *Address:* Bundesgasse 3, 3003 Bern, Switzerland (office). *Telephone:* (31) 3223211 (office). *E-mail:* oscar.knapp@sif.admin.ch (office). *Website:* www.sif.admin.ch (office).

KNAUSGÅRD, Karl Ove; Norwegian author; b. 6 Dec. 1968, Oslo; m.; three c.; ed Univ. of Bergen; consultant, new Norwegian trans. of The Bible; wrote six autobiographical novels under series title Min kamp (My Struggle) 2009–11; Southern Norway Literature Prize 2005, 2010, NRK P2 Listeners' Prize 2009, Morgenbladet Book of the Year Prize 2010, Gyldendal Prize 2011. *Publications include:* novels: Ute av verden (Out of the World) (Norwegian Critics Prize for Literature 2004) 1998, En tid for alt (A Time to Every Purpose Under Heaven) 2004, Min kamp 1 (My Struggle Vol. 1) (Brage Prize 2009) 2009, Min kamp 2 (My Struggle Vol. 2) 2009, Min kamp 3 (My Struggle Vol. 3) 2009, Min kamp 4 (My Struggle Vol. 4) 2010, Min kamp 5 (My Struggle Vol. 5) 2010, Min kamp 6 (My Struggle Vol. 6) 2011. *Address:* c/o Aschehoug Agency, Sehesteds gate 3, PO Box 363, Sentrum, 0102 Oslo, Norway; c/o Forlaget Oktober AS, PO Box 6848, St. Olavs plass, 0130 Oslo, Norway (office). *E-mail:* epost@aschehougaency.no; oktober@oktober.no (office). *Website:* www.aschehougagency.no; oktober.no/nor/In-English (office). *Telephone:* (23) 35-46-20 (office). *Fax:* (23) 35-46-21 (office).

KŇAŽKO, Milan; Slovak politician, actor and broadcast industry executive; b. 28 Aug. 1945, Horné Plachtince, Velký Krtíš Dist; m. Eugenia Kňažková; three s.; ed Acad. of Performing Arts, Bratislava, Univ. of Nancy, France; mem. Theatre on the Promenade (drama co.), Bratislava 1970–71; actor, New Theatre, Bratislava 1971–85; mem. Slovak Nat. Theatre Drama Co. Bratislava, 1985–; Co-founder, Public Against Violence (political movt) Nov. 1989, rally speaker 1989–90; adviser to Pres. of Czechoslovakia 1989–90; Deputy Fed. Ass. 1990–92; Minister for Foreign Affairs, Govt of Slovak Repub. 1990–91; mem. and Vice-Chair. Movt for Democratic Slovakia 1991–93 (resgnd); Deputy Prime Minister, Slovak Repub. 1992–93, Minister for Foreign Affairs 1992–93; cand. in presidential election 2014; apptd Minister of Culture 1998; Chair. Govt Council of Slovak Repub. for Ethnic Groups 1992–93; Chair. Alliance of Democrats 1993–94, Ind. Deputies Club 1993–; First Deputy Chair. Democratic Union of Slovakia 1994–2000; Vice-Chair. Slovak Democratic and Christian Union (SDCHU) 2000–; Dir Gen. Televízia JOJ (pvt. TV network) 2003–07; numerous roles on stage, in film, on TV, on radio; Merited Artist Award 1986 (returned award 1989). *Film roles include:* Nevesta hôl (The Bride of the Mountains, UK) 1972, Kohút nezaspieva 1986, Svet nic neví 1987, Maria Stuarda (TV) 1988, Dobrí holubi se vracejí 1988, Omyly tradicnej moralky (TV) 1989, Dlouhá míle (TV mini-series) 1989, Devet kruhu pekla 1989, Svedek umírajícího casu 1990, Poslední motýl (The Last Butterfly) 1991, Bel ami (TV) 2005. *Leisure interests:* family, sport, culture, theatre, golf. *Address:* c/o Televízia JOJ, PO Box 33, 830 07 Bratislava 37, Slovakia (office).

KNEALE, (Robert) Bryan (Charles), RA, RWA, FRBS; British sculptor; b. 19 June 1930, Douglas, Isle of Man; s. of the late William Kneale and Lilian Kewley; m. Doreen Lister 1956 (died 1998); one s. (deceased) one d.; ed Douglas High School, Douglas School of Art, Isle of Man, Royal Acad. Schools; Tutor, RCA Sculpture School 1964, Fellow, RCA 1972, Sr Tutor 1980–85, Head of Dept of Sculpture 1985–90, Prof. of Drawing 1990–95, Sr Fellow 1995; Head of Sculpture School, Hornsey 1967; Assoc. Lecturer, Chelsea School of Art 1970; Master of Sculpture RA 1982–85, Prof. 1985–90; mem. Fine Art Panels, Nat. Council for Art Design 1964–71, Arts Council 1971–73, CNAA 1974–82; Chair. Air and Space 1972–73; organized Sculpture '72, RA 1972, Battersea Park Silver Jubilee Sculpture 1977, Sade Exhbn, Cork 1982, Sculpture for Westminster Cathedral 1999; comms include Bronze Doors, Portsmouth Cathedral 1999, sculpture for Villa Marina Douglas and Nobles Hosp., Isle of Man 2004, Capt. Quilliam Memorial, Castletown, Isle of Man 2005, Illiam Dhone Memorial, Malew Church, Isle of Man 2006; Rome Prize 1949, Leverhulme Award 1952, Young Artist Competition Prize 1955, Arts Council Purchase Award 1978. *Address:* 10A Muswell Road, London, N10 2BG, England. *Telephone:* (20) 8444-7617. *E-mail:* bryan.kneale@googlemail.com (home).

KNELL, Gary Evan, BA, JD; American lawyer and business executive; *President and CEO, National Geographic Society;* b. 27 Feb. 1954, Sacramento, Calif.; m. Kim Larson 1981; four c.; ed Grant High School, Univ. of California, Los Angeles, Loyola Univ. School of Law; worked in Calif. State Legislature and Gov.'s Office; fmr Counsel to US Senate Judiciary and Governmental Affairs Cttees; Sr Vice-Pres. and Gen. Counsel, WNET/Channel 13, New York 1981–89; fmr Man. Dir Manager Media International (print and multimedia publishing co. in Bangkok, Hong Kong and Singapore); joined Sesame Workshop (fmrly Children's Television Workshop), producer of Sesame Street, Dragon Tales, Sagwa etc. 1989, COO 1998–2000, Chief Exec. 2000–11, responsibilities included Noggin (educational cable and online jt venture with Nickelodeon), publishing partnership with Time, Inc., and Sesame Street co-productions in S Africa, India, NI and Egypt; Pres. and CEO NPR (fmrly Nat. Public Radio) 2011–13; Pres. and CEO National Geographic Society 2013–; mem. Bd of Dirs Heidrick & Struggles 2007–, AARP Services, Inc., Jacob Burns Film Center, Save the Children; mem. Bd of Trustees Nat. Video Resources, Bd of Govs American Center for Children and Media, Advisory Bd Columbia Univ.'s electronic learning venture, Fathom, Music Educators Nat. Conf., Alexandria, Va, Center on Public Diplomacy, Univ. of Southern California; mem. Council on Foreign Relations, US Nat. Comm. for UNESCO; adviser, WFUV, public radio at Fordham Univ., Annenberg School of Communications at Univ. of Southern California, Common Sense Media; participant, Aspen Inst. Forum on Communications and Society, Columbia Univ. American Ass.; Gordon Grand Fellow, Yale Univ., Guest Lecturer, Harvard Univ., Duke Univ., Carnegie Mellon Univ., Commencement Speaker, Johns Hopkins Univ., UCLA, Univ. of Texas. *Address:* National Geographic Society, 1145 17th Street, NW, Washington, DC 20036-4688, USA (office). *E-mail:* askngs@nationalgeographic.com (office). *Website:* www.nationalgeographic.com (office).

KNIAZEV, Alexander A.; Russian cellist; b. 21 April 1961, Moscow; s. of Alexandre S. Schwarzmann and Ludmila P. Kniazeva; m. (deceased); ed Moscow State Conservatory, Nyzhny-Novgorod State Conservatory; Prof., Moscow State Conservatory 1995–; masterclasses in France, Spain, Republic of Korea, Philippines; concerts 1978–, in Russia, UK, France, Germany, Italy, Spain, Belgium, Austria, USA, South Africa, South America, South Korea, Japan and elsewhere; performed with partners V. Afanasyev, S. Milstein, E. Leonskaya, B. Engerer, Kun Woo Oark, V. Spivakov, V. Tretyakov, M. Brunello, Yu. Bashmet, Yu. Milkis; First Prize Nat. Competition, Vilnius, Lithuania 1977, Third Prize G. Cassado Int. Competition, Florence, Italy 1979, First Prize Int. Chamber Music Competition, Trapani, Italy 1987, Second Prize Tchaikovsky Int. Competition, Moscow, Russia 1990, First Prize Unisa Int. Competition, Pretoria, S Africa. *Leisure interest:* chess. *Address:* Moscow 107078, Skornyzhny per. 1, apt 58, Russia (home).

KNIGHT, Andrew Stephen Bower, MA; British editor and business executive; *Chairman, J. Rothschild Capital Management;* b. 1 Nov. 1939; s. of M. W. B. Knight and S. E. F. Knight; m. 1st Victoria Catherine Brittain 1966 (divorced); one s.; m. 2nd Begum Sabiha Rumani Malik 1975 (divorced 1991); two d.; m. 3rd Marita Georgina Phillips Crawley 2006; ed Ampleforth Coll., York, Balliol Coll., Oxford; Ed. The Economist 1974–86; Chief Exec. Daily Telegraph 1986–89, Ed.-in-Chief 1987–89; Chair. News Int. PLC 1990–94, Chair. Times Newspapers 2012–; Chair. Ballet Rambert 1984–87; Chair. Times Newspaper Holdings 1990–94; Dir News Corpn 1991–2012; Dir Rothschild Investment Trust CP 1996–2008, Chair. J. Rothschild Capital Management 2008–; Chair. Shipston Home Nursing 1996–2006; Chair. Jerwood Charity 2003–06; mem. Advisory Bd Center for Econ. Policy Research, Stanford Univ., USA 1981–; Gov. mem. Council of Man. Ditchley Foundation 1982–; Founder-Trustee Spinal Muscular Atrophy Trust; now farms in Warwicks. and Dannevirke, NZ. *Address:* J. Rothschild Capital Management Ltd, 27 St James's Place, London, SW1A 1NR (office); Compton Scorpion Manor, Shipston-on-Stour, Warwicks., CV36 4PJ, England (home).

KNIGHT, Gladys Maria; American singer; b. 28 May 1944, Atlanta, Ga; d. of Merald Knight and Elizabeth Knight (née Woods); m. 2nd Barry Hankerson 1974 (divorced 1979); one s. and two c. (from previous marriage); tours with Morris Brown Choir 1950–53; formed Gladys Knight and The Pips 1953–89; mem. Lloyd Terry Jazz Ltd 1959–61; numerous tours and live appearances, TV and film appearances; solo artist 1989–; four Grammy Awards, American Music Awards 1984, 1988. *Film and TV appearances:* Pipe Dreams 1976, Charlie & Co. (series) 1985, Desperado (TV film) 1987, An Enemy Among Us (TV film) 1987, Twenty Bucks 1993, Hollywood Homicide 2003, Unbeatable Harold 2005. *Recordings include:* albums: Letter Full of Tears 1961, Gladys Knight and The Pips 1964, Everybody Needs Love 1967, Feelin' Bluesy 1968, Silk & Soul 1968, Nitty Gritty 1969, All in a Knight's Work 1970, If I Were Your Woman 1971, Standing Ovation 1971, All I Need Is Time 1973, Imagination 1973, Help Me Make It Through The Night 1973, It Hurt Me So Bad 1973, Neither One Of Us 1973, Claudine (OST) 1974, I Feel A Song 1974, Knight Time 1974, 2nd Anniversary 1975, A Little Knight Music 1975, Bless This House 1976, Pipe Dreams 1976, Love Is Always On Your Mind 1977, Still Together 1977, Miss Gladys Knight 1978, The One And Only 1978, Gladys Knight 1979, Memories 1979, About Love 1980, Midnight Train To Georgia 1980, That Special Time of Year 1980, Teen Anguish 1981, Touch 1980, Visions 1983, Life 1985, All Our Love 1988, Christmas Album 1989, Good Woman 1991, Just For You 1994, Many Different Roads 1998, At Last 2000, Christmas Celebrations 2002, The Best Thing That Ever Happened To Me 2003, One Voice 2005, Before Me 2006. *Address:* c/o WME, 9601 Wilshire Blvd, Beverly Hills, CA 90210, USA (office). *Telephone:* (310) 285-9000 (office). *Fax:* (310) 285-9010 (office). *Website:* www.wma.com (office); www.gladysknight.com.

KNIGHT, Keith Desmond St. Aubyn, BA, QC; Jamaican lawyer and politician; b. Brompton, St Elizabeth; m.; two c.; ed Howard Univ. and Univ. of Pittsburgh, USA; admitted to Bar, Grays Inn, London, UK 1973, admitted to Inner Bar as QC 1995; entered elective politics 1989, MP for E Cen. St Catherine; Minister of Nat. Security and Justice 1989–2001, of Foreign Affairs and Foreign Trade 2001–06; Council Pres. UN Security Council Meeting concerning Afghanistan 2001; Co-founder and Sr Pnr, Knight, Junor & Samuels, Kingston (law firm) 2006–; Exec. mem. People's Nat. Party; mem. Advocate Asscn, Jamaican Bar Asscn; Founder-Pres. Jamaica Nat. Asscn; fmr Pres. Caribbean Asscn of Students. *Address:* Upstairs Bog Walk Post Office, St. Catherine, Jamaica (office). *Telephone:* 985-1192 (office). *Fax:* 985-1192 (home).

KNIGHT, Malcolm D., MSc, PhD; Canadian economist; b. Windsor, Ont.; m.; three d.; ed Univ. of Toronto and London School of Econs, UK; teacher of econs, Univ. of Toronto and LSE 1971–75; joined Research Dept, IMF 1975, served successively as economist in Financial Studies Div., Chief of External Adjustment Issues, Asst Dir of Research Dept for Developing Country Studies, Deputy Dir of Middle East Dept, Monetary and Exchange Affairs Dept, European Dept; fmrly COO Bank of Canada, Sr Deputy Gov. 1999–2003, mem. Bd of Dirs; Gen. Man. BIS 2003–09; fmrly Adjunct Prof., Centre for Canadian Studies, Johns Hopkins Univ. School of Advanced Int. Studies, Virginia Polytechnic and State Univ.; Academic Visitor, Centre for Labour Econs, LSE 1985–86; mem. Editorial Bd IMF Staff Papers 1987–97; Trustee, Int. Accounting Standards Cttee Foundation, Per Jacobsson Foundation; mem. Bd of Patrons European Asscn for Banking and Financial History, Johns Hopkins Univ. Soc. of Scholars. *Publications:* numerous publs in fields of macroeconomics, int. finance and banking. *Address:* c/o Bank for International Settlements, Centralbahnplatz 2, 4002 Basel, Switzerland. *Telephone:* (61) 280-80-80.

KNIGHT, Sir Peter L., Kt, PhD, FRS, FInstP; British physicist and academic; *Professor Emeritus and Senior Research Investigator, Physics Department, Imperial College London;* ed Univ. of Sussex; Research Assoc., Joe Eberly group, Dept of Physics and Astronomy, Univ. of Rochester and at Physics Dept and SLAC, Stanford Univ., USA 1972–74; SRC Research Fellow, Univ. of Sussex 1974–76; Visiting Scientist, Johns Hopkins Univ., USA 1976; Jubilee Research Fellow, Royal Holloway Coll., London 1976–78, SERC Advanced Fellowship 1978–83, transferred to Imperial Coll. London 1978–79, Lecturer, Imperial Coll. London 1983–87, Reader 1987–88, Prof. 1988, now Prof. Emer., fmr mem. Imperial Coll. Man. Bd and Council, Prof. of Quantum Optics, Head of Physics Dept 2001–05, Prin. Faculty of Natural Sciences –2008, Deputy Rector (Research) –2010, Sr

Research Investigator, Physics Dept 2010–; Sr Fellow in Residence, Kavli Royal Soc. Int. Centre, Chicheley Hall; Visiting Prof., Univ. of Louvain-la-Neuve; Humboldt Research Award Holder, Univ. of Konstanz; Visiting Scholar, Univ. of Texas, Univ. of Rochester; Pres. Inst. of Physics 2011–13; Past-Pres. Optical Soc. of America (OSA), mem. Bd of Dirs for seven years, Dir OSA Foundation; Co-ordinator SERC Nonlinear Optics Initiative, Past-Chair. EPS Quantum Electronics and Optics Div.; Ed. Journal of Modern Optics 1987–2006, Contemporary Physics; Chair. Defence Scientific Advisory Council, Ministry of Defence –2010, remains a Govt science adviser; Council mem. Science and Tech. Facilities Council –2012; Chief Scientific Adviser, UK Nat. Physical Lab. –2005; Chair. University Research Fellowships Ai Panel 2010–13; mem. Council of Royal Soc. 2005–07, mem. Audit Cttee and Chair. Hooke Cttee responsible for scientific meetings; Fellow, OSA; numerous prizes and awards, including the Thomas Young Medal and Glazebrook Medal of Inst. of Physics, OSA Frederic Ives Medal/Quinn Prize 2008, Royal Medal, Royal Soc. *Publications:* numerous papers in professional journals. *Address:* Quantum Optics and Laser Science Group, Department of Physics, 6M02 Huxley, Huxley Building, Imperial College, South Kensington Campus, London, SW7 2AZ, England (office). *Telephone:* (20) 7594-7727 (office). *E-mail:* p.knight@imperial.ac.uk (office). *Website:* www.lsr.ph.imperial.ac.uk/~plk (office).

KNIGHT, Philip H(ampson), MBA; American business executive; *Chairman, Nike Inc.;* b. 24 Feb. 1938, Portland, Ore.; s. of William W. Knight and Lota Hatfield; m. Penelope Parks 1968; two s.; ed Univ. of Oregon, Stanford Univ.; First Lt, US Army 1959–60; certified public accountant, Price Waterhouse and Coopers & Lybrand –1968; Asst Prof. of Business Admin, Portland State Univ. –1968; Co-founder and Pres. Nike Inc., Beaverton, Ore. 1968–83, 1984–90, 2000–04, Chair. 1969–; Dir US-Asian Business Council, Wash.; mem. American Inst. of Certified Public Accountants; Oregon Businessman of the Year 1982. *Leisure interests:* sports, reading, movies. *Address:* Nike Inc., 1 Bowerman Drive, Beaverton, OR 97005, USA (office). *Telephone:* (503) 671-3598 (office). *Fax:* (503) 644-6655 (office). *E-mail:* lisa.mckillips@nike.com (office). *Website:* www.nike.com (office).

KNÍŽÁK, Milan; Czech multimedia artist, writer, art theorist and musician; *Director-General, National Gallery, Prague;* b. 19 April 1940, Plzeň; s. of Karel Knížák and Emilie Knížáková; m. 1st Soňa Švecová 1967; m., 2nd Jarka Charvátová 1970; m., 3rd Marie Geislerová 1975; ed Acad. of Fine Arts, Charles Univ., Prague; f. Aktual group; prosecuted and imprisoned on numerous occasions 1957–89 mostly for his art activities; in USA (at invitation of Fluxus group of artists) 1968–70; Rector Acad. of Fine Arts, Prague 1990–97; Dir Gen. Nat. Gallery Prague 1999–; mem. Czech TV Council 2001–03; DAAD Berlin, Barkenhoff Worpswede, Germany, Schloss Bleckede, Germany, Schloss Solitude, Germany, 5th Inter-Triennale Wrocław, Poland; Medal 1st Degree, Ministry for Educ. and Physical Training 1997, Medal of Merit 2010. *Films:* Stone Ceremony, Material Events, Kill Yourself and Fly. *Albums:* Broken Music 1979, Obřad hořící mysli (The Rite of a Burning Mind) 1992, Navrhuju krysy (I Propose the Rats) 2002. *Plays:* Also in my Belly Grows a Tree, Heads. *Radio Play:* Adamits. *Television:* Kill Yourself and Fly (a film about M. Knížák) 1991. *Publications:* Zeremonien 1971, Action as a Life Style 1986, Neo Knížák 1991, Nový ráj (New Paradise) 1996, Bez důvodu (Without Reason) 1996, Jeden z možných postojů, jak být s uměním (One Way to Exist with Art) 1998, Skutečnost, že jsem se narodil, beru jako výzvu (The Fact I was Born I Take as a Challenge) 1999, Tady ve Skotsku (Here in Scotland) (with J. Lancaster) 2000, Básně 1974–2001 (Poems 1974–2001) 2001, Vedle umění (Close to the Arts) 2002, and many others. *Leisure interests:* collecting old marionettes and scientific research on them. *Address:* Národní galerie v Praze, Palác Kinských, Staroměstské náměstí 12, 11015 Prague 1 (office); AVU, U Akademie 4, 17000 Prague 7, Czech Republic. *Telephone:* (22) 2329331 (office); (602) 321208 (home). *Fax:* (22) 2324641 (office); (22) 4919782 (home). *E-mail:* genreditel@ngprague.cz (office). *Website:* www.ngprague.cz (office); www.avu.cz (office).

KNOBLOCH, Bernd, BBA, LLB; German business executive; b. 20 Nov. 1951, Munich; ed Ludwig-Maximilians-Universität, Munich; admitted to German Bar 1979; mem. Bd of Man. Dirs Eurohypo AG 1992–, Deputy Chair. of Man. Bd, Eurohypo AG (cr. following merger of Deutsche Hypo AG, Rheinhypo AG and Eurohypo AG 2002) 2002–04, Chair. of Man. Bd 2004–08; mem. Bd of Man. Dirs Commerzbank AG 2006–08; mem. Supervisory Bd, Hypo Real Estate Holding AG 2008–; mem. Städel Admin, Frankfurt 2005; mem. Bd, Hertie Foundation, Josef Schörghuber Foundation 2009–12, Citycon 2012–. *Address:* Opernplatz 6, 60313 Frankfurt-am-Main (office); Frauenlobstrasse 60A, 60487 Frankfurt-am-Main, Germany (home). *Telephone:* (69) 77062001 (office); (69) 77075555 (home). *Fax:* (69) 77062015 (office). *E-mail:* bernd.knobloch@palatium.com (office). *Website:* www.palatium.com (office).

KNOLL, József, MD, PhD, DSc; Hungarian pharmacologist; *Professor Emeritus of Pharmacology, Semmelweis University;* b. 30 May 1925, Kassa, Hungary (now Kosice, Slovakia); s. of Jakab Knoll and Blanka Deutscher; m. Dr Berta Knoll; one d.; ed Gymnasium, Budapest, Faculty of Medicine, Pázmány Péter Univ. (later Univ. of Medicine, Budapest, later Semmelweis Univ. of Medicine, later Semmelweis Univ.); Asst Lecturer Univ. Pharmacological Inst.; Lecturer Medical Univ. 1958, Prof. and Head 1962–95, Vice-Rector 1964–70; currently Prof. Emer., Dept of Pharmacology and Pharmacotherapy, Semmelweis Univ.; Gen. Sec. Hungarian Pharmacological Soc. 1962–67, Pres. 1967–83, Hon. Pres. 1984–; Chair. Nat. Drug Admin. Cttee and Drug Research Cttee of the Acad. of Sciences; Vice-Pres. Medical Sciences Section, Hungarian Acad. of Sciences 1967–76; Councillor, Int. Union of Pharmacological Sciences 1981–84, First Vice-Pres. 1984–87; mem. editorial bd of numerous int. pharmacological periodicals; Corresp. mem. Hungarian Acad. of Sciences 1970, Full mem. 1979; mem. German Acad. of Sciences (earlier Leopoldina Acad. of Natural Sciences) 1974; Foreign mem. Polish Acad. of Arts and Sciences 1995; Hon. mem. Pharmacological Socs of Poland 1980, Czechoslovakia 1985, Bulgaria, 1985, Austrian Parkinson Soc. 1986; Hon. FRSM 1990; Middlecross Order with the Star (Hungary) 2010; Dr hc (Medizinische Akad., Magdeburg) 1984, (Bologna Univ.) 1989; Award of Hungarian Acad. of Sciences 1961, 1964, Semmelweis Prize 1981, Issekutz Prize 1982, Nat. Prize of Hungary 1985, Festschrift: Neuropharmacology 85, Dedicated to Prof. Knoll on the occasion of his 60th birthday (eds K. Kelemen, K. Magyar & E. S. Vizi) 1985, Award for Distinguished Service in European Pharmacology 1999, Festschrift: Milestones in Monoamine Oxidase Research: Discovery of (-)deprenyl. Dedicated to Prof. Knoll on the occasion of his 75th birthday (eds K. Magyar & E. S. Vizi) 2000, Arany János Award, Hungarian Acad. of Sciences 2000, Award for Outstanding Contribs to Anti-Ageing Medicine 2001, Széchenyi Prize (renamed Nat. Prize of Hungary) 2003, Hungarian Award for Achievements in Drug Research 2008. *Achievements include:* developed L-deprenyl (Selegiline), a drug used world-wide. *Publications:* Theory of Active Reflexes 1969, Handbook of Pharmacology (nine edns since 1965), The Brain and Its Self 2005, How Selegiline ((-)-Deprenyl) Slows Brain Aging (e-book) 2012; more than 800 papers in int. trade journals; 53 patents. *Leisure interest:* visual arts. *Address:* Semmelweis University, Faculty of General Medicine, Department of Pharmacology and Pharmacotherapy, Budapest 1089, Nagyvárad tér 4, Hungary (office). *Telephone:* (1) 210-4405 (office); (1) 329-3805 (home). *Fax:* (1) 210-4405 (office). *E-mail:* jozsefknoll@hotmail.com (office). *Website:* semmelweispharma.com (office).

KNOLL, Wolfgang, PhD; German scientist and academic; *Scientific Managing Director, Austrian Institute of Technology;* b. 1949, Schwäbisch Hall; ed Tech. Univ. of Karlsruhe, Univ. of Konstanz; Postdoctoral Fellow, Univ. of Konstanz 1976–77, Univ. of Ulm 1977–80, Fellow, IBM Research Lab., San José, Calif., USA 1980–81; Visiting Scientist, Institut Laue-Langevin, Grenoble, France 1981; Asst Prof., Tech. Univ. of Munich 1981–86; Visiting Scientist, IBM Research Lab., San José, Calif. 1985; received Habilitation from Tech. Univ. of Munich 1986; Young Investigator/Assoc. Prof., Max Planck Inst. for Polymer Research, Mainz 1986–91, Dir 1993–2008; Visiting Scientist, Optical Sciences Center, Tucson, Ariz., USA 1988, Dept of Chem. and Nuclear Eng, Univ. of California, Santa Barbara 1990; Visiting Prof., Univ. of Erlangen 1990–91; Head of Lab. for Exotic Nano-Materials, Frontier Research Program, RIKEN Inst., Japan 1991–99; Consulting Prof., Dept of Chemical Eng, Stanford Univ., Calif. 1992–; Prof. (by Courtesy), Chem. Dept, Univ. of Florida, Gainesville 1998–; Adjunct Prof., Hanyang Univ., S Korea 1999–; Temasek Prof., Nat. Univ. of Singapore 1999–2003; Visiting Prin. Scientist, Inst. of Materials Research and Eng, Singapore 2004–; Scientific Man. Dir AIT Austrian Inst. of Tech., Vienna 2008–; mem. Exec. Cttee Biomaterials Interfaces Group implementing biofunctional surface science into the AVS Teaching courses at Stanford Univ., Univ. of Leuwen, Belgium, Hanyang Univ., S Korea, Univ. of Florida, Gainesville, Nat. Univ. of Singapore, Univ. of Venice, Italy, Univ. of Mainz, Germany; mem. editorial bds of several int. journals; has organized several int. confs on biointerfaces and nanotechnology; Corresp. mem. Austrian Acad. of Sciences 1999; Hon. Prof., Univ. of Natural Resources and Applied Life Sciences, Vienna 2009–; Heisenbergstipendium, Deutsche Forschungsgemeinschaft 1986, Merck Centennial Lecturer, Univ. of Iowa, Ames 1988, Heinrich Welker Award, Siemens/Univ. of Erlangen 1990, Eugen and Ilse Seibold Prize, Deutsche Forschungsgemeinschaft 2003, Wilhelm Exner Medal, Austrian Asscn for SME (Oesterreichischer Gewerbeverein—OGV) (jtly) 2008. *Publications:* numerous papers in professional journals on aspects of the structure/order-property/function relationships of polymeric/organic systems, in particular, in thin films and at functionalized surfaces. *Address:* AIT Austrian Institute of Technology GmbH, Donau-City-Straße 1, 1220 Vienna, Austria (office). *Telephone:* (505) 50-0 (office). *E-mail:* office@ait.ac.at (office). *Website:* www.ait.ac.at (office).

KNOPFLER, Mark, OBE, BA; British musician (guitar), singer, songwriter and record producer; b. 12 Aug. 1949, Glasgow, Scotland; s. of late Erwin Knopfler and of Louisa Knopfler; brother of David Knopfler; m. Lourdes Salomone 1983; two s.; ed Leeds Univ.; fmr music journalist Yorkshire Evening Post; fmr mem. bands, Brewer's Droop, Cafe Racers; f. mem., Dire Straits 1977–88, 1991–95; group toured world-wide; first-ever CD single, Brothers In Arms 1985; formed own ad hoc band, Notting Hillbillies 1989; solo artist 1984–, guest on numerous albums by other artists; Hon. DMus (Leeds) 1995; Ivor Novello Awards for Outstanding British Lyric 1983, Best Film Theme 1984, Outstanding Contribution to British Music 1989, Lifetime Achievement Award 2012, Nordoff-Robbins Silver Clef Award for Outstanding Services to British Music 1985, Grammy Awards for Best Country Performance (with Chet Atkins) 1986, 1991, for Best Surround Sound Album (for Brothers in Arms) 2006, Music Producers Guild Award for Best Studio (British Grove Studios) 2009. *Film music composition:* Local Hero 1983, Cal 1984, Comfort and Joy 1984, Alchemy Live (television) 1984, The Princess Bride 1987, Last Exit to Brooklyn 1989, Tishina 1991, Wag the Dog 1998, Hooves of Fire (television) 1999, Metroland 1999, A Shot at Glory 2001, songs for numerous other films. *Recordings include:* albums: with Dire Straits: Dire Straits 1978, Communiqué 1979, Making Movies 1980, Love Over Gold 1982, Extendedanceplay 1983, Alchemy: Dire Straits Live 1984, Brothers In Arms 1985, Money For Nothing 1988, On Every Street 1991, On The Night 1993, Live at the BBC 1995, Sultans of Swing 1998; solo: Comfort and Joy 1984, Neck and Neck (with Chet Atkins) 1990, Golden Heart 1996, Sailing To Philadelphia 2000, The Ragpicker's Dream 2002, Shangri-La 2004, All the Roadrunning (with Emmylou Harris) 2006, Kill to get Crimson 2007, Get Lucky 2009, Privateering 2012; with Notting Hillbillies: Missing... Presumed Having a Good Time 1990. *Address:* c/o Paul Crockford Management, Latimer House, 272 Latimer Road, London W10 6QY, England (office). *E-mail:* help@markknopfler.com (office). *Website:* www.markknopfler.com.

KNOT, Klaas Henderikus Willem, BEcons, DEcon; Dutch economist and central banker; *President, De Nederlandsche Bank NV;* b. 14 April 1967, Onderdendam; m.; two c.; ed Univ. of Groningen; joined De Nederlandsche Bank NV (DNB, central bank) 1995, becoming Sr Economist 1995–98, Head of Banking and Supervisory Strategies Dept 1999–2002, with Pensions and Insurance Supervisory Authority 2003–04, Dir DNB Supervisory Policy Div. 2004–09, Pres. DNB 2011–, also mem. Governing Council and Gen. Council, European Central Bank; Economist, European Dept, IMF, Washington, DC 1998–99; Dir of Financial Markets and Deputy Treas.-Gen., Ministry of Finance 2009–11; Prof. of Econs of Central Banking, Univ. of Groningen 2005–; mem. Bd of Dirs Bank for Int. Settlements; Chair. Koning Willem I Foundation, N.G. Pierson Foundation. *Publications:* numerous articles in leading int. journals in monetary and financial econs. *Address:* Office of the President, De Nederlandsche Bank NV, Westeinde 1, POB 98, 1000 AB Amsterdam, Netherlands (office). *Telephone:* (20) 5242411 (office). *Fax:* (20) 5242500 (office). *E-mail:* info@dnb.nl (office). *Website:* www.dnb .nl (office).

KNOTT, John Frederick, OBE, BMet, PhD, ScD, FRS, FREng, FRSA; British materials scientist and academic; *Professor of Metallurgy and Materials, Univer-* sity of Birmingham; ed Univs of Sheffield and Cambridge; Feeney Prof. of Materials and Metallurgy, Univ. of Birmingham, also Head of School of Metallurgy and Materials –1995, Dean 1995, now Prof. of Metallurgy and Materials; Pres. Int. Congress on Fracture 1993–97; Past Pres. Birmingham Metallurgical Asscn; Ed. Materials Science and Technology 2003–; mem. Governing Body and Fellow, Churchill Coll., Cambridge; Fellow, Royal Acad. of Eng 1988, Inst. of Materials, Welding Inst.; mem. Rolls-Royce Materials, Mfg and Structures Advisory Bd 1989– (Chair. 2002–); mem. Technical Advisory Group on Structural Integrity 1988– (Deputy Chair. 2000–); mem. TWI Research Bd 1988–, Graphite Technical Advisory Cttee 2003–, Research Programmes Group (Ministry of Defence) 2003–, Defence Nuclear Safety Cttee 2006–; Foreign mem. Acad. of Sciences of Ukraine, Japan Inst. of Metals 2005; Foreign Assoc. Nat. Acad. of Eng 2003; Foreign Fellow, Indian Nat. Acad. of Eng 2006; Hon. Prof., Beijing Univ. of Aeronautics and Astronautics, Xi'an Jiatong Univ., People's Repub. of China; Hon. DEng (Univ. of Glasgow) 2004; Inst. of Metals Lecturer 2005, Robert Franklin Mehl Award 2005, Leverhulme Medal, Royal Soc. 2005, Brooker Medal, Welding Inst. 2008. *Publications:* numerous scientific articles in professional journals on the quantitative scientific understanding of fracture processes in metals and alloys and its eng applications. *Address:* Department of Metallurgy and Materials, School of Engineering, Elms Road, Edgbaston, Birmingham, B15 2TT (office); 5 Mildmay Close, Stratford-upon-Avon, Warwicks., CV37 9FR, England (home). *Telephone:* (121) 414-6729 (office); (1789) 261977 (home). *Fax:* (121) 414-7468 (office). *E-mail:* J.F.Knott@bham.ac.uk (office). *Website:* www.eng.bham.ac.uk/metallurgy (office).

KNOWLES, Anthony (Tony) Carroll, BA; American fmr politician; b. 1 Jan. 1943, Tulsa, Okla; m. Susan Morris; two s. one d.; ed Yale Univ.; served in US Army, Vietnam 1961–65; Owner and Man. restaurants The Works, Anchorage 1968, Downtown Deli, Anchorage 1978; Mayor of Anchorage 1981–87; Gov. of Alaska 1994–2002; unsuccessful cand. for US Senate 2004, for Gov. of Alaska 2006; mem. Citizen's Cttee for Planned Growth and Devt of Anchorage 1972, Borough Ass., Anchorage 1975–79; fmr mem. Bd of Dirs KAKM TV Station, Anchorage Chamber of Commerce; Child Advocate of the Year, American Child Welfare League 1999. *Address:* c/o Office of the Governor, PO Box 110001, Juneau, AK 99811, USA.

KNOWLES, Beyoncé (see BEYONCÉ).

KNOWLING, Robert E., Jr, BA, MBA; American computer engineer and business executive; *Chairman, Eagles Landing Partners;* b. 1955, Ind.; m.; four c.; ed Wabash Coll., Kellogg Graduate School of Man., Northwestern Univ.; staff mem. Indiana Bell 1970s, Head of Eng Devt Team, Ameritech 1992, later Vice-Pres. Network Operations; Exec. Vice-Pres. of Operations and Techs US West; Pres. and CEO Covad Communications, Calif. 1998–2001; Chair. and CEO Information Access Technologies Inc. 2001–03; CEO New York Leadership Acad., New York City Bd of Educ. 2003–05; CEO Vercuity Solutions, Inc. (later Telewares Inc.) 2005–09; Chair. Eagles Landing Partners (strategic man. consulting firm) 2009–; Consultant, Grupo Salinas 2009–11; mem. Bd of Dirs Ariba Inc., Heidrick & Struggles Int., Roper Industries, Inc. 2008–; mem. Advisory Bd Ontologent, Inc., Northwestern Univ. Kellogg Graduate School of Man., Univ. of Mich. Graduate School of Business; Wall Street Project's Reginald Lewis Trailblazers Award 1999. *Leisure interest:* YMCA volunteer. *Address:* c/o Board of Directors, Ariba Inc., 807 11th Avenue, Sunnyvale, CA 94089, USA.

KNOX, Selby Albert Richard, PhD, DSc; British chemist and academic (retd); b. 24 Sept. 1944, Newcastle-upon-Tyne, England; s. of George H. Knox and Elsie Knox; m. Julie D. Edwards 1979; one s. two d.; ed Rutherford Grammar School, Newcastle-upon-Tyne and Univ. of Bristol; Research Fellow, UCLA 1970–71; Lecturer, Univ. of Bristol 1972–83, Reader 1983–90, Prof. of Inorganic Chem. 1990–96, Head, Dept of Chem. 1992–2001, Head, Inorganic and Materials Chem. 2001–04, Alfred Capper Pass Prof. of Chem. 1996–2004, Pro-Vice-Chancellor 2004–08; Corday-Morgan Medal and Prize 1980, RSC Award for Chem. of Noble Metals and Their Compounds 1986, RSC Tilden Lecturer 1992–93. *Publications:* more than 160 scientific papers on organometallic chem. *Leisure interests:* fly fishing, sailing, skiing, golf.

KNUDSEN, Eric Ingvald, BA, MA, PhD; American neuroscientist and academic; *Professor of Neurobiology, School of Medicine, Stanford University;* ed Univ. of California, Santa Barbara, George August Univ., Göttingen, Germany, Woods Hole Marine Biological Lab., Univ. of California, San Diego; Postdoctoral Research Fellow, California Inst. of Tech. 1976–79; Asst Prof., Dept of Neurobiology, Stanford Univ. School of Medicine 1979–85, Assoc. Prof. 1985–88, Prof. 1988–, Assoc. Chair. Dept of Neurobiology 1997–2000, Chair. 2001–05, Chair. Stanford Medical Student Scholars Program 1986–90, mem. Cttee on Courses and Curriculum 1994–96, mem. School of Medicine Appointments and Promotions Cttee 1995–98, Dir Neurosciences Grad. Program 1998–2000, mem. Research Planning Cttee Medical School Strategic Planning 2001–02, Exec. Cttee Neuroscience Inst. 2001–; Assoc. Ed. Journal of Neuroscience 1986–88, Journal of Neurophysiology 1986–89; mem. Editorial Cttee Annual Review of Neuroscience 1988–92; Co-organizer Int. Meeting: Advances in Auditory Neuroscience, San Francisco; mem. Satellite of the IUPS 1986, NSF Advisory Panel: Sensory Physiology and Perception 1986; Councillor, Int. Soc. for Neuroethology 2002–; mem. Core research network on early experience and brain development, MacArthur Foundation 2002–, Nat. Scientific Council on the Developing Child 2003–; mem. NAS 2002–; Fellow, American Acad. of Arts and Sciences 1996–; AAAS Newcomb Cleveland Prize 1978, Young Investigator Award, Soc. for Neuroscience 1984, NAS Troland Research Award 1988, Claude Pepper Award, Nat. Inst. of Deafness and Communicative Disorders 1991, Edward C. and Amy H. Sewall Professorship, Stanford Univ. School of Medicine 1995, Givaudan-Roure Award, Asscn for Chemoreception Sciences 1996, W. Alden Spencer Award, Coll. of Physicians and Surgeons, Columbia Univ. 2002, Kuffler Lecturer, Harvard Medical School 2004, Gruber Neuroscience Prize, The Peter and Patricia Gruber Foundation 2005. *Publications:* more than 70 scientific papers, book chapters and reviews on the mechanisms of attention, learning and strategies of information processing in the central auditory system of developing and adult barn owls, using neurophysiological, pharmacological, anatomical and behavioural techniques. *Address:* Stanford University School of Medicine, 300 Pasteur Drive, Stanford, CA 94305, USA (office). *Telephone:* (650) 723-5492 (office). *E-mail:* eknudsen@stanford .edu (office). *Website:* med.stanford.edu/profiles/Eric_Knudsen (office).

KNUDSON, Alfred G., Jr, MD, PhD; American geneticist, physician and academic; *Distinguished Scientist, Fox Chase Cancer Center;* b. 9 Aug. 1952, Los Angeles, Calif.; m. Anna T. Meadows MD; ed Calif. Inst. of Tech., Columbia Univ., New York; intern, Huntington Memorial Hosp., Pasadena, Calif. 1947–48; Asst Resident in Pediatrics, New York Hosp. 1948–49; Resident in Pediatrics, Los Angeles Childrens' Hosp., 1949–50, Research Fellow 1950–51; Pediatrician (1st Lt, MC, USAR) USAH Fort Riley, Kansas 1951–53; on staff, City of Hope Medical Center 1956–66, Chair. Dept of Pediatrics 1956–62, Chair. Dept of Biology 1962–66; Assoc. Dean for Basic Sciences, State Univ. of New York at Stony Brook 1966–69; Prof. of Biology and Pediatrics, M.D. Anderson Hospital and Tumor Inst., Houston, Texas 1969–76, Assoc. Dir (Educ.) 1969–70; Dean and Prof. of Medical Genetics, Univ. of Texas Grad. School of Biomedical Sciences, Health Science Center, 1970–76, Prof. of Pediatrics, Medical School, 1972–76; Sr mem. Scientific Research Staff, Fox Chase Cancer Center 1976–, Dir Inst. for Cancer Research 1976–83, Pres. Fox Chase Cancer Center 1980–82, Leader, Molecular Oncology Program 1989–98, Fox Chase Distinguished Scientist and Sr Adviser to Pres. 1992–; Special Adviser to Dir Nat. Cancer Inst. and Acting Dir Human Genetics Program, Div. of Cancer Epidemiology and Genetics 1995–98; mem. NAS, American Philosophical Soc., American Acad. of Arts and Sciences, Asscn of American Physicians, American Soc. of Human Genetics (Pres. 1978), AAAS (Fellow 1987–), American Pediatric Soc., American Asscn for Cancer Research, Int. Soc. of Pediatric Oncology; Guggenheim Fellowship 1953–54, Nat. Foundation – March of Dimes Fellowship 1954–56, Charles S. Mott Prize, General Motors Cancer Research Foundation 1988, Medal of Honor, American Cancer Soc. 1989, Founders' Award, Chemical Industry Inst. for Toxicology 1990, Janeway Medal, American Radium Soc. 1990, Katharine Berkan Judd Award, Memorial Sloan-Kettering Cancer Center 1990, William Allan Memorial Award, American Soc. of Human Genetics 1991, Bertner Award, M.D. Anderson Cancer Center 1995, Charles Rodolphe Brupbacher Foundation Award (Switzerland) 1995; Robert J. and Claire Pasarow Foundation Award 1996, Selikoff Cancer Award, Ramazzini Inst. for Occupational and Environmental Health Research 1996, Durham City of Medicine Award 1996, Strang Award, Strang Cancer Prevention Center, New York 1996; Gairdner Foundation Int. Award 1997, IBM-Princess Takamatsu Cancer Research Fund Lectureship and Award, Tokyo 1997, Karnofsky Memorial Lecture Award, American Soc. of Clinical Oncology 1997, Trondheim Millennium Lecturer (Norway) 1997, Albert Lasker Award for Clinical Medical Research (jtly) 1998, Distinguished Career Award, American Soc. of Hematology/Oncology, Int. John Scott Award, City of Philadelphia 1999, Lila Gruber Memorial Cancer Research Award, American Acad. of Dermatology 2000, Pediatric Oncology Lectureship, American Soc. of Clinical Oncology 2002, Kyoto Prize in Basic Science 2004, Bristol-Myers Squibb Award in Cancer Research 2005. *Publications:* Genetics and Disease 1965; contrib. numerous articles to scientific and medical journals. *Leisure interests:* travel, tennis, reading. *Address:* Fox Chase Cancer Center, 7701 Burholme Avenue, Philadelphia, PA 19111, USA (office). *Telephone:* (215) 728-3642 (office). *Fax:* (215) 214-1623 (office). *E-mail:* AG_Knudson@fccc.edu (office). *Website:* www.fccc.edu (office).

KNUSSEN, (Stuart) Oliver, CBE; British composer and conductor; b. 12 June 1952, Glasgow; s. of Stuart Knussen and Ethelyn Jane Alexander; m. Susan Freedman 1972; one d.; ed Watford Field School, Watford Boys Grammar School, Purcell School; pvt. composition study with John Lambert 1963–68; conducted first performance of his First Symphony with London Symphony Orchestra 1968; Fellowships to Berkshire Music Center, Tanglewood, USA 1970, 1971, 1973; Caird Travelling Scholarship 1971; Head of Contemporary Music Activities, Tanglewood Music Center 1986–93; Co-Artistic Dir, Aldeburgh Festival 1983–98; Music Dir, London Sinfonietta 1998–2002, Conductor Laureate 2002–; Artist in Association, BBC Symphony Orchestra 2009–, Artist in Association, Birmingham Contemporary Music Group; Hon. mem. American Acad. of Arts and Letters 1994, Royal Philharmonic Soc. 2002; Dr hc (Royal Scottish Acad. of Music and Drama) 2002; Countess of Munster Awards 1964, 1965, 1967; Peter Stuyvesant Foundation Award 1965; Watney-Sargent Award for Young Conductors 1969; Arts Council Bursaries 1979, 1981; winner, first Park Lane Group Composer Award 1982, Michael Ludwig Nemmers Prize in Musical Composition 2006, Royal Philharmonic Soc. Award for Best Conductor 2010. *Compositions include:* operas: Where the Wild Things Are 1979–81, Higglety Pigglety Pop! 1984–85; symphonies: Symphony in one movement 1969, No. 2 (soprano and small orchestra) 1970–71, No. 3 1973–79; concertos: Horn Concerto 1994, Violin Concerto 2002; other: Requiem (Songs for Sue), for soprano and ensemble 2005–06; other works for chamber ensemble and for voice and ensemble, for orchestra and for piano. *Leisure interests:* cinema, record collecting, whale watching. *Address:* Harrison Parrott, 5–6 Albion Court, London, W6 0QT, England (office); c/o Faber Music Ltd, 74–77 Great Russell Street, London, WC1B 3DA, England (office). *Telephone:* (20) 7229-9166 (office). *Fax:* (20) 7221-5042 (office). *E-mail:* info@harrisonparrott.co.uk (office). *Website:* www .harrisonparrott.com (office); www.fabermusic.com (office).

KNUTH, Donald Ervin, MS, PhD; American computer scientist and academic; *Professor Emeritus of The Art of Computer Programming, Stanford University;* b. 10 Jan. 1938, Milwaukee, Wis.; s. of Ervin Henry Knuth and Louise Marie Knuth (née Bohning); m. Nancy Jill Carter 1961; one s. one d.; ed Case Inst. of Tech., California Inst. of Tech.; Asst Prof. of Math., Calif. Inst. of Tech. 1963–66, Assoc. Prof. 1966–68; Prof. of Computer Science, Stanford Univ. 1968–77, Fletcher Jones Prof. of Computer Science 1977–89, Prof. of.The Art of Computer Programming 1990–93, Prof. Emer. 1993–; mem. American Acad. of Arts and Sciences, NAS, Nat. Acad. of Eng, American Philosophical Soc.; Foreign mem. French, Norwegian, Bavarian, Russian Science Acads, Royal Soc. of London; 34 hon. degrees, including Paris 1986, Oxford 1988, St Petersburg 1992, Harvard 2003; Nat. Medal of Science 1979, Steele Prize, American Math. Soc. 1986, Franklin Medal, Franklin Inst. of Philadelphia 1988, Harvey Prize, Israel Inst. of Tech. 1995, John Von Neumann Medal, IEEE 1995, Kyoto Prize 1996, BBVA Award 2011 and numerous other awards. *Publications:* The Art of Computer Programming (Vol. 1) 1968, (Vol. 2) 1969, (Vol. 3) 1973, (Vol. 4A) 2011, Surreal Numbers 1974, Mariages Stables 1976, Computers and Typesetting (five Vols) 1986, Concrete Mathematics 1988, 3:16 Bible Texts Illuminated 1990, Literate Programming 1992, The Stanford GraphBase 1993, Selected Papers on Computer Science 1996, Digital Typography 1999, MMIXware 1999, Selected Papers on Analysis of Algorithms 2000, Things a

Computer Scientist Rarely Talks About 2001, Selected Papers on Computer Languages 2003, Selected Papers on Discrete Mathematics 2003, Selected Papers on Design of Algorithms 2010, Selected Papers on Fun and Games 2011, Companion to the Papers of Donald Knuth 2011. *Leisure interests:* piano and organ playing, browsing in libraries. *Address:* Computer Science Department, Gates 477, Stanford University, Stanford, CA 94305, USA (office). *Telephone:* (650) 723-4367 (office). *Website:* www-cs-faculty.stanford.edu/~uno (office).

KO, Un; South Korean novelist, essayist, critic and poet; *Poet-in-Residence and Professor, Dankook University;* b. (Ko Un-Tae), 10 April 1933, Kunsan; s. of Ko Geun-Shik and Choi Jeom-Rye; m. Lee Sang-wha 1983; one d.; teacher of Korean language and art, Kunsan Middle School 1950; served as Buddhist monk 1952–62; Sec.-Gen. Asscn of Writers for Practical Freedom 1974; arrested many times for political activities and served several prison terms; Resident Prof., Grad. School, Kyonggi Univ., Seoul 1994–98, Poet–in–Residence and Prof., Dankook Univ. 2008–; Pres. Asscn of Korean Artists 1989–90, Asscn of Writers for Nat. Literature 1992–94, Co-Pres. Nat. Trust of Korea 2000; Chair. South and North Korea Writers' Conf. 2004; Visiting Research Scholar, Yenching Inst., Harvard Univ., USA 1999, Visiting Prof., Univ. California at Berkeley; Silver Order of Merit in Culture 2002, Bjornson Order for Literature (Norway) 2005; Dr hc (Dankook Univ.) 2010; Korean Literature Prize 1974, 1987, Manhae Prize in Literature 1989, Joong-Ang Prize for Literature 1991, Daesan Prize for Literature 1994, Manhae Grand Prize 1998, Buddhist Literature Prize 1999, Danjae Prize 2004, Unification Award 2005, Cikada Prize (Sweden) 2006, Young-Rang Poetry Award 2007, Yusim Literature Prize 2008, Lifetime Achievement Award, Griffin Fund for Excellence in Poetry (Canada) 2008, Korea Acad. of Arts Award 2008. *Publications include:* Maninbo (Ten Thousand Lives) (poetry) 30 vols., has written numerous books of poetry, novels, non-fiction, literary criticism, travel books, biographies, translation; I, Ko Un (autobiography, three vols.) 1993, My Bronze Period (autobiography) 1995. *Address:* 173 Changmikol, Daerimdongsan Ansong, Kyonggi-do, 456–820, Republic of Korea. *Telephone:* (31) 618-1783. *Fax:* (31) 618-1781. *E-mail:* koun_poet@yahoo.co.kr. *Website:* www.koun.co.kr.

KOBALIA, Vera; Georgian politician; b. 24 Aug. 1981, Sokhumi, Abkhazia; d. of Otari Kobalia; ed Kilby George's High School, Vancouver and British Columbia Inst. of Tech., Canada; emigrated with family to Canada 1996; Researcher, Canadian Soc. for Int. Health, Ottawa 2001–02; Producer, Global TV–Destination Funny Entertainment 2004–06; Marketing and Sales Man., Boston International 2007–08; Partner, European Breads Bakery, Vancouver 2008–10; returned to Georgia to work for Coalition for Justice (non-govt org. assisting displaced people) 2010; Minister of the Economy and Sustainable Devt 2010–12. *Address:* c/o Ministry of the Economy and Sustainable Development, 0108 Tbilisi, Chanturia 12, Georgia. *E-mail:* ministry@economy.ge.

KOBAYASHI, Akiko, PhD; Japanese chemist and academic; *Professor Emeritus, University of Tokyo;* b. 1943, Tokyo; ed Univ. of Tokyo; Research Assoc., Univ. of Tokyo 1972–93, Assoc. Prof., Dept of Chem. 1993–99, apptd Prof., Research Centre for Spectrochemistry, Grad. School of Science 1999, now Prof. Emer.; currently Prof. at Nihon Univ.; L'OREAL-UNESCO Award for Women in Science (Asia-Pacific) 2009. *Achievements include:* first person to design and create single-component molecular metals. *Publications:* numerous papers in professional journals. *Address:* Research Centre for Spectrochemistry, Graduate School of Science, University of Tokyo, Hongo 7-3-1, Bunkyo-ku, Tokyo 113-0033, Japan (office). *Telephone:* (3) 5841-4417 (office). *Fax:* (3) 5841-4417 (office). *Website:* www .chem.s.u-tokyo.ac.jp (office).

KOBAYASHI, Eizo; Japanese business executive; *Chairman, ITOCHU Corporation;* joined ITOCHU Corpn 1972, various sr positions including mem. Exec. Bd 2000, COO of Information Tech. and Telecommunications Div. 2001–02, Man. Dir and Chief Information Officer 2002–03, Sr Man. Dir 2003–04, Pres. and CEO 2004–10, Chair. 2010–; Vice-Chair. Japan Foreign Council Inc.; Exec. Dir Bank of Japan 2004–. *Address:* ITOCHU Corporation, 5-1 Kita-Aoyama 2-chome, Minato-ku, Tokyo 107-8077, Japan (office). *Telephone:* (3) 3497-2121 (office). *Fax:* (3) 3497-4141 (office). *E-mail:* info@itochu.co.jp (office). *Website:* www.itochu.co.jp (office).

KOBAYASHI, Izumi; Japanese banking executive and international organization official; *President and Rep. Dir Merrill Lynch Japan;* joined Seikei Univ.; joined Merrill Lynch Japan, Tokyo 1985, held several global exec. roles, Pres. and Rep. Dir Merrill Lynch Japan –2008, also served as Dir of Operations and Chief Admin. Officer; Exec. Vice-Pres. Multilateral Investment Guarantee Agency (MIGA), World Bank Group, New York, USA Nov. 2008–July 2013; mem. Bd of Dirs Keizai Doyukai (Japanese Asscn of Corp. Execs); Business Woman of the Year Award, Veuve Clicquot 2004, featured in the Wall Street Journal's '50 Women to Watch' Oct. 2005. *Address:* c/o Multilateral Investment Guarantee Agency, World Bank Group, 1818 H Street, NW, Washington, DC 20433, USA.

KOBAYASHI, Ken; Japanese business executive; *President and CEO, Mitsubishi Corporation;* b. 14 Feb. 1949, Tokyo; ed Faculty of Law, Tokyo Univ.; joined Mitsubishi Corpn (Ship Sales Dept), Tokyo 1971–80, Mitsubishi Corpn London Br., UK 1980–85, Ship and Rolling Stock Dept, Tokyo 1985–89, Ship and Industrial Project Dept 1989–98, Gen. Man. Ship and Industrial Project Dept 1998–2001, Gen. Man. Mitsubishi Corpn Singapore Br. 2001–03, Sr Vice-Pres., Mitsubishi Corpn and Gen. Man. Mitsubishi Corpn Singapore Br. 2003–04, Sr Vice-Pres., Div. COO, Plant Project Div., Tokyo 2004–06, Sr Vice-Pres., Div. COO, Ship, Aerospace and Transportation Systems Div. 2006–07, Exec. Vice-Pres. and Group CEO, Industrial Finance, Logistics and Devt Group April–June 2007, mem. Bd, Exec. Vice-Pres. and Group CEO, Industrial Finance, Logistics and Devt Group June 2007–08, Exec. Vice-Pres. Mitsubishi Corpn 2008–10, Sr Exec. Vice-Pres. April–June 2010, Pres. and CEO 2010–. *Address:* Mitsubishi Corporation, Mitsubishi Shoji Building, 3-1, Marunouchi 2-chome, Chiyoda-ku, Tokyo 100-8086, Japan (office). *Telephone:* (3) 3210-2121 (office). *Fax:* (3) 3210-8583 (office). *E-mail:* info@ mitsubishicorp.com (office). *Website:* www.mitsubishicorp.com (office).

KOBAYASHI, Makoto, PhD; Japanese physicist and academic; *Professor Emeritus, High Energy Accelerator Research Organization (KEK);* b. 7 April 1944, Nagoya; ed Nagoya Univ.; Research Assoc., Kyoto Univ. 1972–79; Asst Prof., Nat. Lab. of High Energy Physics 1979–89, Prof. 1989–97, Head of Physics Div. II 1989–97; Prof., Inst. of Particle and Nuclear Science, High Energy Accelerator Research Org. (KEK) 1997–2006, Prof. Emer. 2006–, Dir Inst. of Particle and

Nuclear Science 2003–06; Nishina Memorial Prize 1979, J.J.Sakurai Prize (American Physical Soc.) 1985, Japan Acad. Prize 1985, Asahi Prize 1995, Chunichi Cultural Prize 1995, Person of Cultural Merit Award 2001, Nobel Prize in Physics (jt recipient) 2008. *Address:* High Energy Accelerator Research Organization, 1-1 Oho, Tsukuba, Ibaraki 305-0801, Japan (office). *Website:* www .kek.jp (office).

KOBAYASHI, Shu, PhD; Japanese chemist and academic; *Professor, Graduate School of Pharmaceutical Sciences, University of Tokyo;* ed Univ. of Tokyo; Asst Prof., Science Univ. of Tokyo 1987–91, Lecturer, Dept of Applied Chem., Faculty of Science 1991–92, Assoc. Prof. 1992–98, Special Promoted Researcher 1997; Prof., Grad. School of Pharmaceutical Sciences, Univ. of Tokyo 1998–; Visiting Prof., Université Louis Pasteur, Strasbourg, France 1993, Kyoto Univ. 1995, Nijmegen Univ., Netherlands 1996, Philipps-Universität Marburg, Germany 1997; CREST Investigator, Japan Science and Tech. Agency, 1997–2001, SORST Investigator 2002–04, ERATO Investigator 2003–; Assoc. Ed. Journal of Combinatorial Chemistry 1999–, Advanced Synthesis and Catalysis 2000–; mem. Editorial Advisory Bd Molecules Online 1997–2000, Synthesis 1999–, Chemical Reviews 2000–; Expert Analyst, CHEMTRACTS-Organic Chemistry 1999–; Chemical Soc. of Japan Award for Young Chemists 1991, Teijin Award in Synthetic Organic Chem. 1992, New Chem. Inst. Research Award 1992, Nissan Science Foundation for Younger Generation Award 1993, Ciba-Geigy Research Foundation Award 1994, Kurata Research Foundation Award 1995, first Springer Award in Organometallic Chem. 1997, Bio-Mega/Boehringer Ingelheim Lecturer 1999, Merck-SFC Lectureship 1999, Wyeth-Ayerst Lectureship 1999, Novartis Chem. Lectureship 2000, MIT/Wyeth-Ayerst Lectureship 2000, Nagoya Lectureship 2000, Roche Lectureship 2001, NPS Distinguished Lecturer 2001, IBM Science Award 2001, Organic Reactions Lecturer 2002, Nagoya Silver Medal 2002, Novo-Nortis Lectureship 2003, Manchester-Merck Lecturer 2004, Mitsui Chemical Catalysis Science Award 2005, JSPS Prize 205, Arthur C. Cope Scholar Award 2006, Howard Memorial Lecturer 2006. *Publications:* numerous articles in scientific journals on devt of new synthetic methods, novel catalysts, organic synthesis in water, solid-phase organic synthesis, total synthesis of biologically interesting compounds and organometallic chem. *Address:* Department of Chemistry, School of Science, University of Tokyo, Hongo, Bunkyo-ku, Tokyo 113-0033, Japan (office). *Telephone:* (3) 5841-4790 (office). *Fax:* (3) 5684-0634 (office). *E-mail:* admin@tokyo.jst.go.jp (office). *Website:* www.jst.go.jp/EN (office); utsc2.chem.s.u -tokyo.ac.jp/%7Esynorg/index_E.html (office).

KOBAYASHI, Takashi; Japanese particle physicist and academic; currently Assoc. Prof., Neutrino Group, 4th Physics Div., Inst. for Particle and Nuclear Studies, High Energy Accelerator Research Org. (KEK), Tsukuba; Spokesman, T2K collaboration. *Publications:* numerous articles in scientific journals on neutrino physics. *Address:* The 4th Physics Division, Institute for Particle and Nuclear Studies, High Energy Accelerator Research Organization (KEK), 1-1 Oho, Tsukuba 305-0801, Japan (office). *Telephone:* (29) 864-5414 (office); (29) 864-5200 ext. 4669 (KEK local cell phone) (office). *Fax:* (29) 864-7831 (office). *E-mail:* takashi .kobayashi@kek.jp (office). *Website:* jnusrv01.kek.jp/~kobayasi (office).

KOBAYASHI, Yoshimitsu, MSc, PhD; Japanese business executive; *Representative Director, President and CEO, Mitsubishi Chemical Holdings Corporation;* b. 18 Nov. 1946, Yamanashi; ed Univ. of Tokyo, Hebrew Univ., Jerusalem; joined Mitsubishi Chemical Industry Ltd (later Mitsubishi Chemical Corpn), Tokyo 1974, Gen. Man. Information Storage Products Dept, Pres. Mitsubishi Kagaku Media 1996, CEO 2001–03, Exec. Officer, Chief Tech. Officer and Man. Exec. Officer, Mitsubishi Chemical Corpn, Man. Exec. Officer and Chief Tech. Officer –2007, Rep. Dir, Pres. and CEO 2007–, Pres. Mitsubishi Chemical Group Science and Tech. Research Center Inc. 2005–06, mem. Bd Dirs and Rep. Dir, Mitsubishi Chemical Holdings Corpn 2006–, Pres. and CEO 2007–, Chair. Mitsubishi Kagaku Inst. of Life Sciences 2006, Rep. Dir, Pres. and CEO 2007–. *Address:* Mitsubishi Chemical Holdings Corporation, 14-1 Shiba 4-chome, Minato-ku, Tokyo 108-0014, Japan (office). *Telephone:* (3) 6414-4870 (office). *Fax:* (3) 6414-3745 (office). *E-mail:* info@mitsubishichem-hd.co.jp (office). *Website:* www.mitsubishichem-hd.co.jp (office).

KOBAYASHI, Yotaro, BA, MBA; Japanese business executive and international organization official; b. 25 April 1933, UK; s. of Setsutaro Kobayashi; ed Keio Univ., Wharton School of Finance and Commerce, Univ. of Pennsylvania, USA; joined Fuji Photo Film Co. Ltd (now FUJIFILM Corpn) 1958, transferred to Fuji Xerox 1963, mem. Bd of Dirs 1968, promoted to Gen. Man. of Planning and Exec. Gen. Man. of Sales, Exec. Vice-Pres. 1976–78, Pres. and CEO 1978–92, Chair. and CEO 1992–99, Chair. 1999–2006, Chief Corp. Adviser 2006–09; mem. Bd of Dirs Xerox Corpn 1987, Sony Corpn, Nippon Telegraph and Telephone Corpn, Callaway Golf Co., American Productivity and Quality Center; Chair. Cttee of Foreign-Affiliated Corpns, Japan Fed. of Econ. Orgs (now Japan Business Fed. or Nippon Keidanren) 1986; served on Japanese Govt's Third Provisional Council for the Promotion of Admin. Reform 1990s; Chair. Japan-US Business Council 1990s, Japan Asscn of Corp. Execs 1999–2003 (Lifetime Trustee 2003–), Co-Chair. World Econ. Forum (Davos Forum), New York 2002; Co-founder and Chair. Aspen Inst. Japan 1998–; involved in New 21st Century Cttee for Japan-China Friendship, Co-Chair. 2003–08; currently Pacific Asia Chair. Trilateral Comm.; mem. World Premier Int. Research Centre Initiative, Ministry of Educ., Culture, Sports, Science and Tech.; Chair., Japan Folk Crafts Museum, Int. Univ. of Japan; mem. Bd of Trustees Keio Univ.; Insignia of Commdr First Class, Royal Order of the Polar Star (Sweden) 1995, Royal Norwegian Order of Merit 1997; Hon. DHumLitt (St Peter's Coll., NJ); Dr hc (Xi'an Jiaotong Univ.) 2001, Hon. DSc (Mapua Inst. of Tech., Manila) 2003; first recipient of Morton H. Meyerson Award for Distinguished Service to Higher Educ. and Int. Understanding, Univ. of Texas, Austin 1988, Medal with Blue Ribbon, Govt of Japan 1991. *Address:* Secretariat of Trilateral Commission – The Pacific Asian Group, Japan Center for International Exchange, 4-9-17 Minami-Azabu, Minato-ku, Tokyo 106, Japan (office). *Telephone:* (3) 3446-7781 (office). *Fax:* (3) 3443-7580 (office). *E-mail:* info@jcie.or.jp (office). *Website:* www.trilateral.org (office); www.jcie.or.jp (office).

KÖBBEN, André J. F., PhD; Dutch professor of cultural anthropology and administrator; b. 3 April 1925, 's-Hertogenbosch; m. Agatha H. van Vessem 1953; one s. two d.; ed Municipal Gymnasium and Univ. of Amsterdam; Prof. of Cultural Anthropology, Univ. of Amsterdam 1955–76; Visiting Prof., Univ. of Pittsburgh

1972; Cleveringa Prof., Univ. of Leiden 1980–81; Prof., Erasmus Univ. 1981–90; Dir Centre for the Study of Social Conflicts 1976–90; Curl Bequest Prize, Royal Anthropological Inst. 1952; mem. Royal Netherlands Acad. of Science 1975; Hon. mem. Anthropological Soc. 1986. *Publications include:* Le Planteur noir 1956, Van primitieven tot medeburgers 1964, Why exceptions? The logic of cross-cultural analysis 1967, Why Slavery? 1997, De Onwelkome Boodschap (The Unwelcome Message) 1999, Goldhagen Versus Browning 2002, Het Gevecht met de Engel (The Struggle with the Angel) 2003, De tijdgeest en andere ongemakken (The Spirit of the Age and other inconveniences) 2008, and many others. *Address:* Libellenveld 2, 2318 VG Leiden, Netherlands. *Telephone:* (71) 5215369 (home). *E-mail:* ajfkobben@planet.nl (home).

KOBEH GONZÁLEZ, Roberto; Mexican engineer, public servant and international organization official; *President, Council, International Civil Aviation Organization (ICAO);* ed Nat. Polytechnic Inst. of Mexico; fmr Prof. of Aeronautical Electronics, Nat. Polytechnic Inst.; 40 years of experience as public servant in Mexican Govt, occupying various posts in Civil Aeronautics Directorate, including Deputy Dir-Gen. for Admin and Air Transport, Dir-Gen. Air Navigation Services of Mexico (SENEAM) 1978–97; Rep. of Mexico on Council of ICAO, serving as First Vice-Pres., Chair. Finance Cttee, and as mem. Air Transport and Unlawful Interference Cttees 1998–2006, Pres. Council 2006–; Emilio Carranza Medal, Award for Extraordinary Service, Fed. Aviation Admin (USA), honoured by Cen. American Corpn of Aerial Navigation Services for his contrib. to devt of aviation in Cen. America. *Address:* International Civil Aviation Organization, External Relations and Public Information Office, 999 University Street, Montréal, PQ H3C 5H7, Canada (office). *Telephone:* (514) 954-8220 (office); (514) 954-8221 (office). *Fax:* (514) 954-6376 (office). *E-mail:* icaohq@icao.int (office). *Website:* www .icao.int (office).

KOBIA, Rev. Samuel, MA, DD; Kenyan ecclesiastic and international organization official; b. 20 March 1947, Miathene, Meru; m. Ruth Kobia; two d. two s.; ed St Paul's United Theological Coll., Nairobi, McCormick Theological Seminary, Indianapolis, Ind., Christian Theological Seminary, Massachusetts Inst. of Tech., USA; ordained minister in Methodist Church, Kenya; Exec. Sec. for Urban Rural Mission, WCC 1978–84, Chair. Frontier Internship in Mission Int. Coordination Cttee 1981–85, Vice-Moderator Comm. to Combat Racism 1984–91, Exec. Dir Justice, Peace and Creation Unit 1993–99, Dir Cluster on Issues and Themes 1999–2002, Dir and Special Rep. for Africa 2002–04, Gen.-Sec. WCC 2003–10; Dir Church Devt Activities, Nat. Council of Churches Kenya (NCCK), 1984–87, Gen.-Sec. NCCK 1987–93; helped est. Zimbabwe Christian Council 1980–81; Co-founder Nairobi Peace Group 1987, Fellowship of Councils of Churches in E and S Africa (FOCCESA) 1991; Chair. Peace Talks for Sudan 1991; Chair. Kenya Nat. Election Monitoring Unit 1992; Fellow, Centre for the Values in Public Life, Divinity School, Harvard Univ., USA 2000; Chancellor St Paul's Univ., Limuru, Kenya 2007–; Hon. Prof., Univ. of Buenos Aires, Argentina 2004; Nat. Ecumenical Award (Kenya) 2007. *Publications include:* Origins of Squatting and Community Organization in Nairobi 1985, Together in Hope 1990, The Quest for Democracy in Africa 1993, The Courage to Hope 2003. *Address:* c/o World Council of Churches, PO Box 2100, 150 Route de Ferney, 1211 Geneva, Switzerland (office). *Telephone:* (22) 791-6111 (office). *Fax:* (22) 791-0361 (office). *Website:* www.oikoumene.org (office).

KOBIERACKI, Adam; Polish diplomatist; *Director, Conflict Prevention Centre, Organization for Security and Co-operation in Europe;* b. 1 June 1957, Warsaw; m.; two c.; ed Warsaw Univ., Faculty of Journalism and Political Sciences, Moscow State Inst. of Int. Relations, USSR; served in Polish Ministry of Foreign Affairs 1982–2003, Dept of Studies and Programming (security and arms control issues) 1982–89, expert in Polish Mission to the UN, Vienna 1985–86, mem. Polish Del. to the Mutual and Balanced Force Reductions Talks, Vienna 1986, to the CSCE Vienna Follow-up Meeting and Conventional Forces in Europe (CFE) Mandate Talks 1986–87, mem. and Deputy Head of Polish Del. to the CFE negotiation in Vienna 1989–90, with Dept of European Insts 1989–91, in Polish Mission to the UN (and IAEA) and the OSCE in Vienna, Counsellor and Deputy Head 1993–96, Minister Counsellor and Deputy Head of Mission and of Polish Del. to the Jt Consultative Group 1996–97, Amb. and Head of the Perm. Mission of Poland to the IAEA, UN Office and the Int. Orgs in Vienna, Head of the Mission of Poland to OSCE, Head of the Polish Del. to the Jt Consultative Group (CFE Treaty) 1997–2000, Dir Dept for European Security Policy, Ministry of Foreign Affairs 2000–01, Dir Security Policy Dept 2001–03; Asst Sec. Gen. for Operations, NATO, Brussels 2003–07; Dir Conflict Prevention Centre, OSCE 2011–; Chief Polish negotiator at CFE adaptation talks, Vienna 1997–99; Chair. Working Group at, and Deputy Head of the Polish Del. to, the First CFE Treaty Review Conf., Vienna May 1996; Head of Polish Del. to Second CFE Treaty Review Conf., Vienna May 2001. *Publications:* contrib. to: Miedzy równowaga sil a bezpieczenstwem kooperatywnym w Europie (adaptacja rezimu CFE do nowego srodowiska miedzynarodowego) (Between the Balance of Power and Co-operative Security in Europe – The Adaptation of the CFE Regime to New International Environment) (Z. Lachowski and J. M. Nowak) 1999, Polska polityka bezpieczenstwa 1989–2000 (co-ed. R. Kuzniar) 2001, WN Scholar (Polish Security Policy 1989–2000). *Address:* Conflict Prevention Centre, OSCE Secretariat, Wallnerstrasse 6, 1010 Vienna, Austria (office). *Telephone:* (1) 514-36-6122 (office). *Fax:* (1) 514-36-6996 (office). *E-mail:* pm-cpc@osce.org (office). *Website:* www.osce.org (office).

KOBILKA, Brian Kent, MD; American molecular biologist and academic; *Professor and Chair of Molecular and Cellular Physiology, School of Medicine, Stanford University;* b. 30 May 1955, Little Falls, Minn.; s. of Franklyn A. Kobilka and Betty L. Kobilka (née Faust); m. Tong Sun Thian; two c.; ed Univ. of Minnesota-Duluth, Yale Univ.; Postdoctoral Research Fellow, Lefkowitz Lab., Duke Univ. 1984–89, Asst Prof., Duke Univ. School of Medicine 1988–89; Howard Hughes Medical Inst. Investigator 1987–2003; joined Dept of Molecular and Cellular Physiology, Stanford Univ. School of Medicine 1989, Prof. of Molecular and Cellular Physiology 2000–, also Chair of Molecular and Cellular Physiology and Helene Irwin Fagan Chair in Cardiology; Co-founder ConfometRx (biotechnology co.); mem. NAS 2011; American Soc. for Pharmacology and Experimental Therapeutics John J. Abel Award in Pharmacology 1994, Nobel Prize in Chem. (jtly with Robert Lefkowitz) 2012. *Publications:* more than 140 publs. *Address:* Department of Molecular and Cellular Physiology and Medicine, 157 Beckman

Center, 279 Campus Drive, Stanford, CA 94305-5345, USA (office). *Telephone:* (650) 723-7069 (office). *Fax:* (650) 498 5092 (office). *E-mail:* kobilka@stanford.edu (office). *Website:* med.stanford.edu/profiles/Brian_Kobilka (office); med.stanford.edu/kobilkalab/brian.html (office).

KOBLER, Martin; German diplomatist and UN official; *Special Representative of the Secretary General and Head, United Nations Organization Stabilization Mission in the Democratic Republic of the Congo (MONUSCO);* b. 1953, Stuttgart; m.; three c.; ed Pajajaran Univ., Indonesia; served as legal practitioner 1980–83; entered foreign service 1983, Deputy Head, Balkan Task Force, Foreign Ministry 1997–98; Chief of Cabinet to fmr German Foreign Minister Joschka Fischer 2000–03, fmr Dir-Gen. for Culture and Communication, Ministry of Foreign Affairs; fmr Amb. to Egypt and Iraq 2003–07; Electoral Observer with UN missions in Haiti, Nicaragua and Cambodia, Deputy Special Rep. (Political) for Afghanistan 2010–11, Special Rep. of UN Sec.-Gen. for Iraq and Head, UN Assistance Mission for Iraq (UNAMI) 2011–13, Special Rep. of UN Sec.-Gen. for Democratic Repub. of Congo and Head, UN Stabilization Mission in DRC (MONUSCO). 2013–. *Address:* UN Organization Stabilization Mission in the Democratic Republic of the Congo (MONUSCO), 12 Av. des Aviateurs, Kinshasa (office); UN Organization Stabilization Mission in the Democratic Republic of the Congo (MONUSCO), BP 8811, Kinshasa, Democratic Republic of the Congo (office). *Telephone:* (81) 8906000 (office). *Fax:* (81) 89056208 (office). *Website:* www.monuc.unmissions.org (office).

KOBZON, Iosif Davydovich, DPhil; Russian singer and politician; b. 11 Sept. 1937, Chasov Yar, Ukraine; m. Nelly Kobzon; one s. one d.; ed Moscow Gnessin Pedagogical Inst. of Music; army service 1956–59, soloist, Ensemble of Dance and Song of Caucasian Mil. command 1957–59; soloist, All-Union Radio and TV Co. 1959–62; soloist, Moskonzert 1962–89; Artistic Dir and Chair. Vocal and Variety Show Faculty Gnessin Inst. (now Acad.) of Music 1989–, Prof. 1992; soloist and Artistic Dir Concert Co. Moskva; retd from concert activity 1997; Pres. Jt Stock Co. Moscovit 1990–97; USSR People's Deputy 1989–92; mem. State Duma (Parl.) 1997–98 (suspended membership), 1999–2003, re-elected (Yedinaya Rossiya faction) 2003–, Deputy Chair. Comm. on Culture 1999–2003, Chair. 2005–07; Order of Courage 2002, Order of Friendship 2003; People's Artist of USSR, Russia, Ukraine, Checheno-Ingushetia and Dagestan Autonomous Repub.; USSR State Prize 1984. *Address:* State Duma, 103265 Moscow, Okhotny ryad 1, Russia (office). *Telephone:* (495) 292-17-53 (office). *Fax:* (495) 292-73-85 (office). *Website:* www .iosifkobzon.ru (home).

KOÇ, Mustafa Vehbi, BA; Turkish business executive; *Chairman, Koç Holding AŞ;* b. 29 Oct. 1960, Istanbul; s. of Rahmi M. Koç; m. Caroline N. Koç; two d.; ed George Washington Univ., USA; Chair. Koç Holding AŞ, Istanbul; Chair. TÜSIAD High Advisory Council; fmr Chair. Turkish-American Business Council; Vice-Chair. Bd Turkish Industrialists and Businessmen's Asscn, American-Turkish Council; mem. Istanbul Chamber of Industry, Foreign Econ. Relations Bd, Young Presidents' Org., JP Morgan Int. Council 2004–, Rolls-Royce Int. Advisory Bd, Nat. Bank of Kuwait Int. Advisory Council, Bd of Vehbi Koç Foundation, Bd of Trustees of Educational Volunteers Foundation; Hon. Consul-Gen. of Finland in Istanbul; Grande Ufficiale (Italy); Hadrian Award, World Monuments Fund 2008. *Address:* Koç Holding AŞ, Nakkastepe, Azizbey Sok. No. 1, Kuzguncuk, 34674 Istanbul, Turkey (office). *Telephone:* (216) 5310272 (office). *Fax:* (216) 3414519 (office). *E-mail:* stephenk@koc.com.tr (office). *Website:* www.koc.com.tr (office).

KOÇ, Rahmi M., BA; Turkish business executive; *Honorary Chairman, Koç Holding AŞ;* b. 1930, Ankara; divorced; three s.; ed Johns Hopkins Univ., USA; joined family business Koç Group 1958 working for Otokoç Co., Ankara, Chair. Exec. Cttee Koç Holding AŞ 1970–75, Deputy Chair. Bd of Man. 1975–80, Chair. Man. Cttee 1980, Chair. Koç Holding AŞ 1984–2003, now mem. Bd and Hon. Chair.; Pres. Rotary Club in Turkey 1976–77, Turkish Greek Business Council 1992–99, ICC 1995–96; fmr Co-Chair. Business Advisory Council for South East Europe (BAC SEE); Founder and Chair. Rahmi M. Koç Museum and Cultural Foundation, Istanbul; Chair. Bd of Trustees, Koç Univ., Bd of Vehbi Koç Foundation American Hosp.; Vice-Chair. Bd of Trustees, Vehbi Koç Foundation; Founding mem. The Turkish Marine and Environment Protection Assen (TURMEPA), now Hon. Chair.; mem. Advisory Bd Turkish Employers Assen, Int. Advisory Bd Council on Foreign Relations, New York, Int. Advisory Bd Allianz AG; fmr mem. JP Morgan Int. Council; Hon. Pres. Advisory Bd Turkish Industrialists' and Businessmen's Assen; Hon. Trustee, Metropolitan Museum of Art, New York City; Hon. Fellow, Foreign Policy Assen; Grosses Verdienstkreuz (Germany) 1982, Order of High Merit of the Italian Repub. 2001; Dr hc (Johns Hopkins) 1998, (Anadolu Üniversitesi) 1998, (Ege Üniversitesi) 1999, (Bilkent Üniversitesi) 1999, (Ovidius Univ., Romania) 2001, (Adnan Menderes Univ., Aydın) 2008; Outstanding Service Award, Pres. of Turkey 1997, Hadrian Award, World Monuments Fund 2007. *Address:* Koç Holding AŞ, Nakkastepe Aziz Bey Sok. 1, Kuzguncuk, 34674 Istanbul, Turkey (office). *Telephone:* (216) 5310000 (office). *Fax:* (216) 5310099 (office). *E-mail:* info@koc.com.tr (office). *Website:* www .koc.com.tr (office); www.rmk-museum.org.tr (office).

KOČÁRNÍK, Ivan, CSc; Czech politician and business executive; b. 29 Nov. 1944, Třebonín, Kutna Hora Dist; m.; two d., one s.; ed Prague Inst. of Econs; worked at Research Inst. of Financial and Credit System until 1985; Dir Research Dept, Fed. Ministry of Finance 1985–89; Deputy Minister of Finance of Czechoslovakia 1990; mem. Civic Democratic Party; Vice-Premier and Minister of Finance of Czech Repub. 1992–97; Chair. Council of Econ. and Social Agreement 1992–97; Chair. Bd Czech Insurance Co. 1997–2001, Chair. Supervisory Bd 2000–07; Vice-Chair. of Supervisory Bd Unipetrol 2006; Chair. Supervisory Bd Czech Airlines (ČSA) 2007–09; Adviser to Minister of Finance 2010–; Central European magazine Best Minister of Finance in 1994 1995. *Leisure interests:* tennis, skiing, hiking, music. *Address:* Letenská 15, 118 00 Prague 1, Czech Republic (office). *Telephone:* (2) 57041111 (office). *Fax:* (2) 57042788 (office). *E-mail:* podatelna@mfcr.cz (office). *Website:* www.mfcr.cz (office).

KOCH, Charles de Ganahl; American engineer, business executive and political activist; *Chairman and CEO, Koch Industries, Inc.;* b. 1 Nov. 1935, Wichita, Kan.; s. of Fred C. Koch and Mary Robinson; brother of David Hamilton Koch; m. Liz Koch; two c.; ed Massachusetts Inst. of Tech.; engineer, Arthur D. Little, Inc., Cambridge, Mass 1959–61; Vice-Pres. Koch Engineering Co., Inc. 1961–63, Pres. 1963–71, Koch Industries, Inc. 1966–74, Chair. and CEO 1967–; mem. The

MIT Corpn 1977–82; supported brother, David H. Koch as Libertarian Party's cand. for Vice-Pres. 1980; funds Charles G. Koch Summer Fellow Program through Inst. for Humane Studies; Hon. Life mem. Washburn Law School Assen; Hon. DSc (George Mason Univ.), Hon. LLD (Babson Coll.), Hon. DComm (Washburn Univ.); numerous awards including Distinguished Citizen Award, Kansas State Univ., inducted into Kansas Oil and Gas Hall of Fame, inducted into Wichita and Kansas Business Halls of Fame, Wichita State Univ. Entrepreneur in Residence, Uncommon Citizen Award, Wichita Chamber of Commerce, Recognition Award, Wichita State Univ., Distinguished Service Citation, Univ. of Kansas, Gov.'s Arts Patrons Award, Kansas Arts Comm. 1999, Dirs' Award for Global Vision in Energy, New York Mercantile Exchange 1999, Herman W. Lay Memorial Award, Assen of Pvt. Enterprise Educ., Entrepreneurial Leadership Award, Nat. Foundation for Teaching Entrepreneurship, Adam Smith Award, American Legis. Exchange Council, Spirit of Justice Award, The Heritage Foundation, Free Enterprise Award, Council for Nat. Policy, Nat. Distinguished Service Award, The Tax Foundation 2000, Pres.'s Medal, Wichita State Univ., 2004, ranked, with brother David, by Forbes magazine amongst The World's Most Powerful People (jt 54th) 2010, (jt 45th) 2011, (jt 41st) 2012, (jt 31st) 2013. *Publication:* The Science of Success: How Market-Based Management Built the World's Largest Private Company 2007. *Address:* Koch Industries, Inc., PO Box 2256, Wichita, KS 67201-2256 (office); Koch Industries, Inc., 4111 East 37th Street North, Wichita, KS 67220, USA (office). *Telephone:* (316) 828-5500 (office). *Fax:* (316) 828-5739 (office). *E-mail:* info@kochind.com (office). *Website:* www.kochind.com (office).

KOCH, David Hamilton; American chemical engineer and business executive; *Executive Vice-President, Koch Industries, Inc.;* b. 3 May 1940, Wichita, Kan.; s. of Fred C. Koch and Mary Robinson; brother of Charles de Ganahl Koch; m. Julia M. Flesher Koch; three c.; ed Deerfield Acad. prep school, Mass, Massachusetts Inst. of Tech.; began career as research engineer and process design engineer for Amicon Corpn, Cambridge, Mass; later worked for Arthur D. Little, Inc., Cambridge, Mass, Halcon International, Inc. and its affiliate, Scientific Design Co., New York City; joined Koch Industries 1970, currently Co-owner (with brother Charles), mem. Bd of Dirs and Exec. Vice-Pres. Koch Industries, Inc., also Chair. and CEO Koch Chemical Technology Group, LLC (wholly owned subsidiary); f. David H. Koch Charitable Foundation 2000; ran on Libertarian ticket for Vice-Pres. against Carter–Mondale and Reagan–Bush 1980; Founder, fmr Chair. and donated to the free-market Citizens for a Sound Economy 1984 (separated into Americans for Prosperity Foundation and FreedomWorks 2004, continues as Chair. Americans for Prosperity Foundation); mem. Bd Cato Inst., Reason Foundation; presidential appointment to Nat. Cancer Advisory Bd of Nat. Cancer Inst. 2005; mem. Bd of Dirs The Economic Club of New York, Rockefeller Univ., American Museum of Natural History, Aspen Inst., Inst. of Human Origins, Cato Inst., The Reason Foundation; mem. Bd of Trustees, Allen-Stevenson School, New York, Metropolitan Museum of Art, Memorial Sloan-Kettering Cancer Center, Hosp. for Special Surgery, New York, House Ear Inst., Los Angeles, Johns Hopkins Univ., Baltimore, Prostate Cancer Foundation, Los Angeles, Smithsonian Nat. Museum of Natural History, Washington, DC, Educational Broadcasting Corpn, Channel 13, New York; Chair. Bd of Trustees, Americans for Prosperity Foundation, Washington, DC; Vice-Chair. American Ballet Theatre, New York; Gov., New York-Presbyterian Hosp.; Life mem. MIT Corpn; mem. Bd of Visitors, M.D. Anderson Cancer Center, Houston; mem. Bd of Assocs, Whitehead Inst., Cambridge, Mass; mem. Bd of Overseers, WGBH, Channel 2, Boston; mem. James Madison Council, Library of Congress, Washington, DC; first and only Lifetime Trustee, Koch Center for Math., Science and Tech., Deerfield Acad.; Hon. mem. Bd of Trustees, Cold Spring Harbor Lab., NY; Hon. DHumLitt (Cambridge Coll.); Entrepreneurial Leadership Award, Nat. Foundation for Teaching Entrepreneurship, Manhattan Republican Party's Business Statesman of the Year Award 2002, Corp. Citizens Award, Woodrow Wilson Int. Center for Scholars 2004, David Koch Center for Applied Research in Genitourinary Cancers est. at M.D. Anderson Cancer Center, Houston, Tex., David H. Koch Dinosaur Wing est. at American Museum of Natural History, Washington, DC 2006, David H. Koch Cancer Research Center est. at Johns Hopkins Univ.'s East Baltimore medical campus 2006, David H. Koch Inst. for Integrative Cancer Research est. at MIT 2007, New York State Theater at Lincoln Center for the Performing Arts renamed the David H. Koch Theater 2008, David H. Koch Hall of Human Origins est. at Nat. Museum of Natural History 2010, Double Helix Medal for Corp. Leadership, Cold Spring Harbor Lab., ranked, with brother Charles, by Forbes magazine amongst The World's Most Powerful People (jt 54th) 2010, (jt 45th) 2011, (jt 41st) 2012, (jt 31st) 2013. *Achievements include:* est. an MIT record in basketball by scoring an average of 21 points per game over three years, and held MIT's single-game scoring record of 41 points from 1962, when he was team capt., until broken by Jimmy Bartolotta 2009. *Address:* Koch Industries, Inc., PO Box 2256, Wichita, KS 67201-2256 (office); Koch Industries, Inc., 4111 East 37th Street North, Wichita, KS 67220, USA (office). *Telephone:* (316) 828-5500 (office). *Fax:* (316) 828-5739 (office). *E-mail:* info@kochind.com (office). *Website:* www.kochind.com (office).

KOCH, HE Cardinal Kurt, ThD; Swiss ecclesiastic; *President of the Pontifical Council for Promoting Christian Unity;* b. 15 March 1950, Emmenbrücke, canton of Lucerne; ed Ludwig-Maximilians Univ., Munich, Germany, Univ. of Lucerne; ordained priest, Diocese of Basel 1982; Bishop of Basel 1995–2010, Bishop Emer. 2010–; Pres. Swiss Episcopal Conf. 2007–10; mem. Swiss Council of Religions; Pres. of the Pontifical Council for Promoting Christian Unity 2010–13, 2013–; Archbishop (Personal Title) 2010–; mem. Congregation for the Doctrine of the Faith 2010–; cr. Cardinal (Cardinal-Deacon of Nostra Signora del Sacro Cuore) 2010; participated in Papal Conclave 2013. *Address:* Pontifical Council for Promoting Christian Unity, Via dell'Erba 1, 00193 Rome, Italy (office). *Telephone:* (06) 69883072 (office), (06) 69884271 (office). *Fax:* (06) 69885365 (office). *Website:* www.vatican.va/roman_curia/pontifical_councils/chrstuni (office).

KOCH, Olaf; German business executive; *Chairman of the Management Board and Chief Human Resources Officer, METRO AG;* b. 1 June 1970, Bad Soden am Taunus; m.; three c.; ed Univ. of Co-operative Educ., Stuttgart; Man., Finance Process and Systems, Daimler Benz AG 1994–95; Founder and CEO IT-Networks GmbH 1996–98; Sr Man., Corp. War Room, DaimlerChrysler AG 1998–99, Dir, Corp. e-Business Strategy and Corp. War Room, DaimlerChrysler AG 1999–2000, Vice-Pres., Corp. e-Business 2000–02, mem. Bd of Man., Mercedes Car Group, responsible for Finance, Controlling and Strategy 2002–07; Man. Dir Operations,

Permira Beteiligungsberatung GmbH 2007–09; mem. Bd of Man. METRO AG and Chief Financial Officer, responsible for Accounting, Finance Governance Centre, Planning and Controlling, Tax, Treasury, Del Credere/Collection (MIAG), Insurance (MIB) 2009–11, further responsible for CIO-Office, Information Man. and Information Tech. 2010–11, responsible for Galeria Kaufhof in Bd of Man. of METRO AG 2010–11, Chair. Man. Bd and Chief Human Resources Officer, METRO AG 2012–, responsible for Communications, Corp. Office, CSR, Investor Relations, Internal Audit, Legal Affairs & Compliance, Projects and M&A, Public Affairs as well as Strategy, Chair. Galeria Kaufhof GmbH, mem. Advisory Bd Media-Saturn-Holding GmbH, Chair. Shareholders' Cttee, METRO Properties GmbH & Co. KG, mem. Bd of Dirs MGB Metro Group Buying HK Ltd, Hong Kong. *Address:* METRO AG, Schlüterstrasse 1, 40235 Düsseldorf, Germany (office). *Telephone:* (211) 6886-0 (office). *E-mail:* kontakt@metro.de (office). *Website:* www .metrogroup.de (office).

KOCH, Roland; German lawyer and politician; b. 24 March 1958; m.; two c.; ed Johann Wolfgang Goethe-Universität, Frankfurt am Main; co-f. Junge Union, youth org. of Christian Democratic Party (CDU) 1972, Deputy Nat. Chair. 1983–87; Town Councillor Eschborn 1997–94; Chair. CDU Main-Taunus Dist 1979–1990; mem. State Parl., Hessen 1987–2010; Fed. State Chair. CDU Hessen 1998–2010; Minister-Pres. Hessen 1999–2010 (resgnd); Pres. Bundesrat 1999; Fed. Vice-Chair. of CDU 2006–10; mem. Weißer Ring charitable org.; initiator, Darmstadt Manifesto for promotion of arts and culture; EWS Award, European Econ. Affairs Council 2005. *Publications:* Chancengesellschaft 1996, Vision 21 1998, Aktive Bürgergesellschaft 1998, Die Zukunft der Bürgergesellschaft, Gemeinsam Chancen nutzen 2001. *Leisure interests:* cooking, art museums, tennis. *Address:* Georg-August-Zinn Str. 1, 65183 Wiesbaden, Germany (home). *Website:* www .roland-koch.de.

KOCHARIAN, Robert S.; Armenian politician and fmr head of state; b. 31 Aug. 1954, Stepanakert (Xankändi), Nagornyi Karabakh Autonomous Oblast, Azerbaijan SSR, USSR; s. of Sedrack S. Kocharian and Emma A. Ohanian; m. Bella L. Kocharian; two s. one d.; ed Yerevan Polytechnic Inst.; served in Soviet Army 1972–74; worked in different enterprises in Stepanakert and Moscow 1975–76; engineer and electrotechnician, Electro-Tech. plant, Stepanakert 1981–87; various positions at Municipal Cttee, Stepanakert town Cttee of the Komsomol Union, including post of Asst Sec. 1981–85; concurrently sec. factory CP Cttee 1987–89; Co-founder Karabakh Movt 1988; Deputy to Armenian Supreme Council 1989–94; left CP 1989; after proclamation of 'Repub. of Nagornyi Karabakh' in Azerbaijan 2 Sept. 1991 and Referendum 10 Dec. 1991 elected to Supreme Council 'Nagornyi Karabakh Repub.', Chair. State Cttee of Defence and Leader of Repub. 1992–94; apptd First Pres. of 'Nagornyi Karabakh Repub.' by Supreme Council 1994–97; Prime Minister 1997–98; Pres. of Armenia 1998–2008. *Leisure interests:* basketball, jazz. *Address:* c/o Office of the President, 0077 Yerevan, Marshal Baghramian Avenue 26, Armenia.

KOCHERGIN, Eduard Stepanovich; Russian theatrical designer; b. 22 Sept. 1937, Leningrad; s. of Stepan Kochergin and Bronislava (née Odinets) Kochergina; m. Inna Gabai 1962; one s.; ed Leningrad Theatre Art Inst., theatre production faculty (pupil of N. Akimov and T. Bruni); chief set-designer in various Leningrad theatres 1960–; chief set-designer at Gorky (now Tovstonogov) Bolshoi Drama Theatre 1972; worked as set-designer, Maly Drama Theatre and in Japan, USA, Poland, Germany, Finland, Canada, France; Prof. Y.I. Repin Inst. of Painting 1983–; mem. Russian Acad. of Fine Arts 1991; Fatherland's Decoration of Merit (3rd and 4th Order), State Prize 1974, 1978; three Golden and two Silver awards, int. exhbns theatre design Novisad 1975, 1978, Prague 1975, 1979, 1987, Ind. Public Triumph Award 2008; Honoured Artist of Russia. *Publications:* Angel's Doll 2003, Baptised by Crosses 2009. *Leisure interest:* research in Russian pre-Christian culture and symbolism. *Address:* Tovstonogov Bolshoi Drama Theatre, Fontanka 65, 191023 St Petersburg, Russia. *Telephone:* (812) 352-89-33 (office); (812) 351-23-79 (home). *Fax:* (812) 110-47-10.

KOCHHAR, Chanda D., MA, MBA; Indian banker and accountant; *CEO and Managing Director, ICICI Bank Ltd;* b. 17 Nov. 1961, Jodhpur, Rajasthan; m.; one s. one d.; ed Jai Hind Coll., Mumbai, Inst. of Cost and Works Accountants of India, Jamnalal Bajaj Inst. of Man. Studies, Mumbai; joined Project Appraisal Div., ICICI 1984, handled projects in various industries and was actively involved in bank's computerization initiatives, deputed to newly formed ICICI Bank as a part of core group for setting up and conceptualizing strategic direction for the bank 1993, served as first Head of Credit 1993–96 returned to ICICI to become part of initiatives such as infrastructure lending, structured products group and major clients group 1996–2000, Man. Dir ICICI Home Finance Ltd and ICICI Personal Financial Services 2000–01, Exec. Dir ICICI Bank Ltd 2001–06, Deputy Man. Dir 2006–07, Jt Man. Dir 2007–09, CEO and Man. Dir 2009–, also Chair. ICICI Bank Canada Ltd, ICICI Bank UK PLC, ICICI Securities Ltd, ICICI Lombard Gen. Insurance Co. Ltd; mem. Bd of Dirs Oil and Natural Gas Corpn Ltd 2008–09; J.N. Bose Gold Medal in Cost Accountancy and Wockhardt Gold Medal for Excellence in Man. Studies, Jamnalal Bajaj Inst. of Man. Studies, Retail Banker of the Year in Asia 2004, Economic Times Award for Corporate Excellence as the Businesswoman of the Year 2005, ranked by Fortune magazine amongst the 50 Most Powerful Women in Business outside the US (47th) 2005, (37th) 2006, (33rd) 2007, (25th) 2008, (15th) 2009, (tenth) 2010, (fifth) 2011–12, Teacher's Achievement Award, Beam Global Spirits & Wine 2007, ranked by Forbes magazine amongst The World's 100 Most Powerful Women (20th) 2009, (92nd) 2010, (43rd) 2011, (59th) 2012, (65th) 2013, FLO Women of Excellence Award 2009. *Leisure interest:* designing saris. *Address:* ICICI Bank Ltd, ICICI Bank Towers, Bandra-Kurla Complex, Mumbai 400 051, India (office). *Telephone:* (22) 26531414 (office); (22) 26536157 (office). *Fax:* (22) 26531167 (office); (22) 26531175 (office). *Website:* www .icicibank.com (office).

KOCIJANČIČ, Andreja; Slovenian physician and university administrator; *President, Council of Slovenian Quality Assurance Agency for Higher Education (NAKVIS);* b. 1942; m. Janez Kocijančič; one s. one d.; ed Univ. of Ljubljana; worked at Mil. Medical Acad. 1969–71; Asst Prof., Faculty of Medicine, Univ. of Ljubljana 1978–84, Assoc. Prof. 1984–89, Prof. of Medicine 1989–1995, Sr Counselor for Health 1995, Pres. Comm. for Postgraduate and Doctoral Studies 1995–2003, Rector Univ. of Ljubljana 2005–09; Deputy Dir Internal Zaloška Clinic, Clinical Centre Ljubljana 1982–87; Pres. Yugoslavia Endocrinology Asscn

1972–76; Vice-Pres. Council for Higher Educ. of the Repub. of Slovenia 1998–2002; Pres. 2002–04; Vice-Pres. Medical Chamber of Slovenia 2004–08; Pres. Council of Slovenian Quality Assurance Agency for Higher Education (NAKVIS) 2013–; Chair. Health Council of Slovenia 1982–86; mem. Exec. Cttee Int. Soc. of Endocrinology 1979–89; mem. Cen. Cttee European Fed. of Endocrine Socs 1987–95; mem. Bd of Dirs European Foundation for Osteoporosis 1995–2000. *Address:* Council of Slovenian Quality Assurance Agency for Higher Education (NAKVIS), Slovenska 9, 1000 Ljubljana, Slovenia (office). *Telephone:* (1) 4005771 (office). *E-mail:* info@nakvis.si (office). *Website:* test.nakvis.si (office).

KOCK, Manfred; German ecclesiastic; b. 14 Sept. 1936, Burgsteinfurt; s. of Walter Kock and Erika Braunschweig; m. Gisela Stephany 1960; two s. one d.; ed Univs of Bethel, Münster and Tübingen; pastor, Recklinghausen 1962–70, Cologne 1970–97; Chair. Evangelical Church in the Rhineland 1997–2003 (resgnd), Council of the Evangelical Church in Germany (EKD) 1997–2003 (resgnd). *Address:* c/o Evangelical Church in Germany, Herrenhäuser Str. 12, 30419 Hanover, Germany (office).

KOCSIS, Zoltán; Hungarian pianist, conductor and composer; *General Music Director, Hungarian National Philharmonic Orchestra;* b. 30 May 1952, Budapest; s. of Ottó Kocsis and Mária Mátyás; m. 1st Adrienne Hauser 1986; one s. one d.; m. 2nd Erika Tóth 1997; one s. one d.; ed Budapest Music Acad. (under Pál Kadosa); appeared with Berlin Philharmonic Orchestra and performed in Germany, USSR, Austria and Czechoslovakia 1971; toured USA together with Dezsö Ranki and Budapest Symphony Orchestra (under George Lehel) 1971; recitals in Netherlands, Paris, London and Ireland 1972; concerts in Norway, with Svyatoslav Richter in France and Austria, with Claudio Abbado and London Symphony Orchestra and at BBC Promenade Concerts in London and Festival Estival, Paris 1977, Edinburgh Festival 1978, Verbier Festival, Ferrara Festival, La Roque d'Anthéron Festival, with New York Philharmonic, Chicago Symphony, Atlanta Symphony and Minnesota orchestras; Asst Prof., Music Acad. Budapest 1976–79, Prof. 1979–; Producer of Archive Section of Hungaroton (record co.); Co-founder and Artistic Co-Dir Budapest Festival Orchestra 1983–96; Gen. Music Dir Hungarian Nat. Philharmonic Orchestra 1997–; Chevalier, Ordre des Arts et des Lettres 2002; First Prize, Beethoven Piano Competition, Hungarian Radio and Television 1970, Liszt Prize 1973, Kossuth Prize 1978, 2005, Cæcilia Award (Belgium) 1981, Merited Artist's Title 1984, Mumm Award, Ovation magazine (USA) 1988, Bartók-Pásztory Award 1988, 2004, Lifetime Achievement Award, MIDEM, Cannes 2004, Classical Internet Award 2004, Prima Primissima Award 2007. *Compositions:* completion of Schoenberg's Moses & Aron (Third Act) 2008, Little Christmas – Variations on a Hungarian Folk Song for choir and orchestra 2010. *Recordings include:* Debussy Solo Piano Works (Gramophone Award for Best Instrumental Recording 1990), Bartók Violin Sonatas Nos 1& 2 (as pianist) (Gramophone Award for Best Chamber Recording 2013). *Publications:* Miscellaneous Publications, Arrangements for Piano and 2 Pianos, Violoncello, Clarinet etc.; orchestrations from the originals of Liszt, Debussy, Rachmaninov, Bartók, Kodály, completion of Ravel's Le Tombeau de Couperin (Fugue, Toccata) and Bartók's Village Scenes. *Leisure interest:* photography. *Address:* Hungarian National Philharmonic Orchestra, Komor Marcell u. 1, 1095 Budapest, Hungary (office). *Telephone:* (1) 4116620 (office). *Fax:* (1) 4116624 (office). *E-mail:* kocsis.z@ filharmonikusok.hu (office). *Website:* www.filharmonikusok.hu (office).

KODA, Madhu; Indian politician and social worker; b. 6 Jan. 1971, Patahatu village, W Singhbhoom Dist, Jharkhand; s. of Rasika Koda and Kuni Kui Koda; m. Geeta Koda 2004; ed Zilla school, Chaibasa, correspondence course with Utkal Univ., Orissa; began political career as activist with All Jharkhand Students Union early 1990s, later associated with Rashtriya Swayamsevak Sangh; elected to Jharkhand Legis. Ass. (Bharatiya Janata Party—BJP) for Jagannathpur constituency 2000, elected as ind. mem. for W Singhbhoom Dist 2005; Panchayati Raj Minister, Jharkhand 2000–03, Minister for Mines and Geology 2005–06; led rebellion that toppled BJP-led coalition govt of Arjun Munda Sept. 2006; Chief Minister of Jharkhand 2006–08 (resgnd). *Leisure interests:* cricket, football.

KODEŠ, Jan, DiplIng; Czech fmr tennis player and Jan Jaromir Kodeš; b. 1 March 1946, Prague; s. of Jan Kodeš and Vlasta Richterová-Kodešová; m. 1st Lenka Rösslerová-Kodešová 1967 (divorced 1988); one s. one d.; m. 2nd Martina Schlonzová; one d.; ed Univ. of Econs, Prague; first Czech national to win a Grand Slam title; Wimbledon Singles Champion 1973, French Open Singles Champion 1970, 1971, runner-up US Championships 1971, 1973, Italian Championships 1970, 1971, 1972; mem. Czechoslovak Davis Cup Team 1964–80, including 1975 (runners-up), 1980 (winners), non-playing Capt. 1982–87; Czechoslovak No. 1 player 1966–77; Bd mem. Czechoslovak Tennis Asscn 1982–98; mem. ETA Men's Cttee 1990–93; mem. ITF Davis Cup European Cttee 1997–98; Founder and Tournament Dir Czech Open, Prague 1987–98; Pres. Czech Tennis Asscn 1994–98; Dir Czechoslovak Tennis Centre 1986–92; mem. ITF/ITHF Golden Achievement Award Cttee 2006–, ITHF Enshrinee Nominating Cttee 2008–; part-owner and CEO Prague CZ Fashion sro 1994–2003; Meritorious Master of Sports 1971, State Decoration for Outstanding Work 1973, ITF Award for Services to the Game 1988, Int. Tennis Hall of Fame 1990, Czech Sport Legend (Emil Zatopek Award) 2011, ITF DC Committment Award 20122, Czech Fair Play Award 2012, USTA-IC Bill Johnston Trophy 2013. *Publications:* Tennis Was My Life (in Czech) 2006, A Journey to Glory from Behind the Iron Curtain 2010. *Leisure interests:* football, other sports, stamp and coin collecting, films, history, travelling, tennis game consulting. *Address:* Jan Kodes – PRO-TENNIS JK Consulting, Na Bérance 20, Prague 6, 160 00 Czech Republic (office). *Telephone:* (2) 33321536 (office); (2) 33321536 (home). *E-mail:* jan@kodes-tennis.com (office). *Website:* www.kodes -tennis.com (office).

KODJO, Edem; Togolese politician and administrator; b. 23 May 1938, Sokodé; m. 1962; two s. two d.; ed Coll. St Joseph, Univ. of Rennes, Ecole Nat. d'Admin, Paris, France; worked as admin. for Office de Radiodiffusion-Télévision Française (ORTF) 1964–67; returned to Togo 1967; Sec.-Gen., Ministry of Finance, Economy and Planning 1967–72; Admin., Banque Centrale des Etats de l'Afrique de l'Ouest 1967–76, Pres. of Admin. Council 1973–76; Dir-Gen. Soc. Nat. d'Investissement 1972–73; Minister of Finance and Economy 1973–76, of Foreign Affairs 1976–77, of Foreign Affairs and Co-operation 1977–78; Sec.-Gen. of the OAU 1978–84; Assoc. Prof. Sorbonne, Paris 1985–90; Prime Minister of Togo 1994–96, 2005–06; Founder and Chair. Pan-African Inst. of Int. Relations (IPRI); Ed. Afrique 2000; mem.

Rassemblement du Peuple Togolaise (RPT), RPT Political Bureau (Sec.-Gen. 1967–71); Leader Togolese Union for Democracy (UTD) –1999, Pres. Convergence patriotique panafricaine 1999–2003, then merger with several other parties to form Coalition des forces démocrates (CFD), currently acting Chair.; mem. Club of Rome; Gov. for Togo, IMF 1973–76; fmr Chair. OAU Council of Ministers, Afro-Arab Perm. Comm. on Co-operation, OAU Cttee of Ten; Commdr, Ordre du Mono, Togo, Officier, Légion d'honneur; Dr hc (Univ. of Bordeaux I); Univ. of Sorbonne Medal. *Address:* Coalition des forces démocrates, Lomé, Togo (office).

KODJO, Messan Abgéyomé; Togolese politician; *President, Organisation pour bâtir dans l'union un Togo solidaire;* b. 12 Oct. 1954, Tokpli, Yoto Pref.; m.; ed Higher School of Sciences and Tech., Univ. of Benin, Univ. of Poitiers, France; fmr Sales Man. SONACOM; Minister for Youth, Sports and Culture 1988–91, for Territorial Admin and Security 1992; organized Constitutional Referendum; Gen. Man. Port Authority of Lomé 1993–99; elected Deputy 1999; Prime Minister of Togo 2000–02; Pres. Organisation pour bâtir dans l'union un Togo solidaire (OBUTS) 2008–, cand. for Pres. of Togo 2010. *Address:* Organisation pour bâtir dans l'union un Togo solidaire, Quartier Djidjole, 686 rue 19 Tosti, Lomé, Togo (office). *Telephone:* 226-93-41 (office). *Website:* www.obuts.org (office).

KOEDA, Itaru, BEng; Japanese motor industry executive; *Co-Chairman, Nissan Motor Co. Ltd;* b. 25 Aug. 1941; ed Univ. of Tokyo; joined Nissan Motor Co. Ltd 1965, becoming Gen. Man. of several corp. depts, fmr Vice-Pres. and Dir Nissan UK, mem. Bd of Dirs Nissan Motor Co. Ltd 1993–, Exec. Vice-Pres. –2003, Exec. Vice-Pres. and Co-Chair. 2003–; mem. Bd of Dirs Renault SA 2003–; Chair. Japan Automobile Mfrs Asscn 2004–06; Chair. Japan-Mexico Econ. Cttee, Keidanren (Japan Business Fed.). *Address:* Nissan Motor Co. Ltd, 17-1 Ginza 6 chome Chuo-Ku, Tokyo 104 8023, Japan (office). *Telephone:* (3) 3543-5523 (office). *Fax:* (3) 5565-2228 (office). *Website:* www.nissan.co.jp (office).

KOENDERS, Albert (Bert) Gerard, BA, MA; Dutch politician and UN official; *Special Representative of the Secretary-General and Head, United Nations Multidimensional Integrated Stabilization Mission in Mali (MINUSMA);* b. 28 May 1958, Arnhem; ed Free Univ., Johns Hopkins Univ., USA; personal asst to mems of House of Reps, Coordinating Foreign Policy Asst for Labour Party 1983–92; Adjunct Prof. of Int. Relations, Webster Univ., Leiden 1984–87; part-time consultant and European Dir of Parliamentarians for Global Action, New York 1987; European staff mem. and Political Adviser to Special Rep. of UN Sec.-Gen. working in Mozambique, South Africa and Mexico 1993–94; Prin. Admin., Policy Planning Staff, Directorate-Gen. for External Relations, Conflict Prevention and EU Enlargement, EC, Brussels –1997; mem. House of Reps 1997–2007; Minister for Devt Cooperation 2007–10; Special Rep. of the Sec.-Gen. and Head of the UN Operation in Côte d'Ivoire (UNOCI) 2011–13; Co-Chair. and negotiator, BUSAN Working Group on Aid Effectiveness; Special Rep. of the Sec.-Gen. and Head, UN Multidimensional Integrated Stabilization Mission in Mali (MINUSMA) 2013–; Visiting Prof. for Conflict Man., Johns Hopkins Univ., Bologna 2000–02; f. Parl. Network on World Bank/IMF 2000–07; Chair. Supervisory Bd, Rutgers World Population Foundation 2011–; fmr Pres. NATO Parliamentary Ass.; fmr Deputy Chair. Netherlands Atlantic Asscn; mem. French-Dutch Cooperation Council; mem. Governing Council, Soc. for International Development; mem. Supervisory Council, Inst. for Multiparty Democracy. *Address:* United Nations Multidimensional Integrated Stabilization Mission in Mali (MINUSMA), Department of Peacekeeping Operations, United Nations, New York, NY 10017, USA (office). *Telephone:* (212) 963-1234 (office). *Fax:* (212) 963-4879 (office). *Website:* www.un.org/en/peacekeeping/missions/minusma (office).

KOENIGS, Tom, MBA; German politician and fmr UN official; b. 25 Jan. 1944, Frankfurt am Main; m.; three c.; ed Univ. of Berlin; co-f. (with Joschka Fischer) first Ministry for Environmental Protection of Hessen Fed. Region 1985; Head of Environmental Protection Dept, City of Frankfurt 1989–, Treas. for Frankfurt 1993–97; Co-Founder and Deputy Pres. Alliance for the Climate (int. NGO) 1990–99; Deputy Special Rep. for Civil Admin, UN Interim Admin Mission in Kosovo (UNMIK) 1999–2002; Special Rep. of the Sec.-Gen. and Head, UN Verification Mission in Guatemala (MINUGUA) 2002–05; Commr for Human Rights Policy and Humanitarian Aid, Ministry of Foreign Affairs 2005; Special Rep. of the Sec.-Gen. for Afghanistan and Head, UN Assistance Mission in Afghanistan (UNAMA) 2006–07; mem. Exec. Bd UNICEF Germany 2008; mem. Bundestag (Bündnis 90/Die Grünen—Alliance 90/Greens) 2009–. *Address:* Deutscher Bundestag, Platz der Republik 1, 11011 Berlin (office); Constituency Office, Liebigstraße 83, 35392 Gießen, Germany. *Telephone:* (30) 22773335 (office). *Fax:* (30) 22776147 (office). *E-mail:* tom.koenigs@bundestag.de (office). *Website:* www.tomkoenigs.de (office).

KOEPP, David; American screenwriter; b. 9 June 1963, Pewaukee, Wis. *Film screenplays:* Apartment Zero 1989, Bad Influence 1990 (with Martin Donovan), Toy Soldiers (with Daniel Petrie, Jr) 1991, Death Becomes Her (with Martin Donovan) 1992, Jurassic Park (with Michael Crichton) 1993, Carlito's Way 1993, The Paper (with Stephen Koepp) 1994, The Shadow 1994, Suspicious 1994, Mission: Impossible 1996, Lost World: Jurassic Park 1997, Snake Eyes 1998, Stir of Echos 1999, Panic Room 2002, Spider-Man 2002, Secret Window 2004, War of the Worlds 2005, Zathura: A Space Adventure 2005, Ghost Town (also dir) 2008, Indiana Jones and the Kingdom of the Crystal Skull 2008, Angels & Demons (with Akiva Goldsman) 2009. *Address:* c/o Creative Artists Agency, 2000 Avenue of the Stars, Los Angeles, CA 90067, USA (office). *Telephone:* (424) 288-2000 (office). *Fax:* (424) 288-2900 (office). *E-mail:* info@caa.com (office). *Website:* www.caa.com (office).

KOERFER, Rolf; German lawyer and business executive; *Chairman of the Supervisory Board, Continental AG;* m.; three c.; fmr Pnr, Oppenhoff & Rädler law firm, Shearman & Sterling LLP law firm; currently Pnr, Allen & Overy LLP int. law firm; mem. Corp. Law Cttee Bundesrechtsanwaltskammer (German fed. chamber of lawyers); Chair. Supervisory Bd GLOBALE Rückversicherungs AG, Continental AG 2009–. *Address:* Continental AG, Vahrenwalder Straße 9, 30165 Hanover, Germany (office). *Telephone:* (511) 938-01 (office). *E-mail:* info@conti-online.com (office). *Website:* www.conti-online.com (office).

KOFFI KOFFI, Paul; Côte d'Ivoire statistician, academic and politician; *Minister-delegate to the President in charge of Defence;* b. 26 Jan. 1957, M'Bahiakro; m.; one c.; ed Ecole Nat. Supérieure de Statistique et d'Economie

Appliquée, Abidjan, Int. School of Man., Paris, St John's Univ., New York; Lecturer, Ecole Nat. Supérieure des Postes et Télécommunications, Abidjan 1986–89; Lecturer in Statistics and Employment Policy, Ecole Nat. d'Admin, Abidjan 1985–89; Lecturer in Accounting, Ecole Nat. Supérieure de Statistique et d'Economie Appliquée, Abidjan 1984–89; Head of Research Dept, Ministry of Employment 1983–84, Deputy Dir of Human Resource Planning Feb.–Dec. 1984, Dir of Employment 1985–89; Sr Technical Adviser responsible for Population Planning, UN Population Fund, Conakry, Guinea 1989–94, Antananarivo, Madagascar 1995–97; Technical Adviser to Minister of Economy and Finance, responsible for monitoring econ. and financial programmes 1997–98, Deputy Chief of Staff to Minister of Economy and Finance 1998–2000, Econ. Adviser to Prime Minister 2000–03, Special Adviser to Prime Minister for financial and econ. matters and poverty reduction 2003–07, Deputy Chief of Staff to Prime Minister, responsible for crisis resolution programme 2007; Minister-Del. to Pres. in charge of Defence 2012–; Chevalier du mérite ivoirienne 2003. *Publications:* Houphouët et les mutations politiques en Côte d'Ivoire 1980-1993, Le défi du développement en Côte d'Ivoire 2008. *Leisure interests:* reading, cinema, football. *Address:* Ministry of Defence, Camp Galliéni, côté Bibliothèque Nationale, BP V241, Abidjan, Côte d'Ivoire (office). *Fax:* 20-22-41-75 (office).

KOFFIGOH, Joseph Kokou; Togolese politician; *President, Coordination nationale des forces nouvelles;* b. 1948, Kpele Dafo; m.; three s. one d.; ed Univs of Abidjan and Poitiers, France; called to the Bar, Poitiers, France; joined Viale Chambers, Togo; f. Togo Bar Asscn 1980, Pres. 1990; founder mem. Observatoire panafricain de la démocratie (OPAD) 1991, Ligue togolaise des droits de l'homme 1990; founder mem. and Vice-Pres. FAR (Asscn for reform); Vice-Pres. Nat. Sovereign Conf.; Prime Minister of Togo 1991–94, also Minister of Defence, Minister of Foreign Affairs and Co-operation 1999–2001; apptd Minister of Regional Integration responsible for relations with Parl. 2001; Pres. Coordination nat. des forces nouvelles. *Leisure interests:* lawn tennis, basketball, shadow-boxing. *Address:* Coordination nationale des forces nouvelles, Lomé, Togo (office).

KOFLER, Georg; German (b. Italian) business executive; *Founder and Vice-Chairman of the Supervisory Board, Kofler Energies AG;* b. 26 April 1957, Brunico, Italy; m. José Kofler; two s.; ed Univ. of Vienna; fmrly mem. staff, Österreichischer Rundfunk (Austrian state broadcasting co.); with Eureka TV 1987–89; Co-founder (with Gerhard Ackermans and Thomas Kirch) and Chair. Pro 7 TV network 1989–2000; CEO KirchPayTV (now Premiere Fernsehen GmbH and Company KG), Munich 2002–07; f. Kofler Energies AG, Munich 2008, now Vice-Chair. Supervisory Bd. *Address:* Kofler Energies AG, Zimmerstraße 23, 10969 Berlin, Germany (home). *Telephone:* (89) 5390690 (office). *Fax:* (89) 53906969 (office). *E-mail:* info@koflerenergies.com (office). *Website:* www.koflerenergies.com (office).

KOGA, Nobuyuki; Japanese business executive; *Chairman, Nomura Holdings, Inc.;* b. 22 Aug. 1950, Fukuoka; ed Faculty of Law, Univ. of Tokyo; joined Nomura Securities Co. Ltd 1974, held numerous exec. positions including Gen. Man. of Personnel Dept, Gen. Man. of Corp. Planning Dept, Dir 1995–99, Man. Dir Nomura Holdings, Inc. 1999–2000, Exec. Vice-Pres. and COO 2000–03, Pres. and CEO 2003–08 (also of subsidiary Nomura Securities Co. Ltd, Chair. 2008–), Chair. 2011–; Exec. Officer, Olympus Corpn. *Address:* Nomura Holdings, Inc., 1-9-1, Nihonbashi, Chuo-ku, Tokyo 103-8645, Japan (office). *Telephone:* (3) 3211-1811 (office). *E-mail:* info@nomura.co.jp (office). *Website:* www.nomura.co.jp (office).

KOGAI, Masamichi; Japanese automotive industry executive; *Representative Director, President and CEO, Mazda Motor Corporation;* fmr Pres. AutoAlliance (Thailand) Co. Ltd; fmr Gen. Man. Hofu Plant, Mazda Motor Corpn, later Man. Exec. Officer and Gen. Man. Production Eng Div., Mazda Motor Corpn, Dir and Sr Man. Exec. Officer –2013, Rep. Dir, Pres. and CEO 2013–. *Address:* Mazda Motor Corpn, 3-1 Shinchi, Fuchu-cho, Aki-gun, Hiroshima 730-8670, Japan (office). *Telephone:* (82) 282-1111 (office). *Fax:* (82) 287-5190 (office). *E-mail:* info@mazda .com (office). *Website:* www.mazda.com (office).

KOGAN, Pavel; Russian violinist and conductor; *Music Director and Chief Conductor, Moscow State Symphony Orchestra;* b. 6 June 1952, Moscow; s. of Leonid Kogan and Elizaveta Gilels; m. (divorced); one s.; ed Moscow Conservatory, studied conducting in Leningrad with I. Mussin and in Moscow with Leo Ginzburg; has performed as soloist and conductor in major concert halls of Europe, USA and Asia with leading orchestras; Conductor Bolshoi Theatre 1986–87; Music Dir Zagreb Philharmonic Orchestra 1987–90; Music Dir and Chief Conductor Moscow State Symphony Orchestra 1989–; Prin. Guest Conductor, Utah Symphony Orchestra, USA 1997–2005; mem. Russian Acad. of Arts; Peoples' Artist of Russia 1994, Order of Friendship of the Russian Fed. 2002, Order of Merit of Russia 2007; First Prize, Jean Sibelius Int. Violin Competition 1970, State Prize of the Russian Fed. 1997. *Recordings:* numerous works with the Moscow State Symphony Orchestra and other ensembles. *Address:* 105082 Moscow, Spartakovskaya sq., 1/2 (office); 125009 Moscow, Brusov per. 8-10, Apt 8, Russia (home). *Telephone:* (499) 763-35-36 (office); (495) 692-13-95 (home). *Fax:* (499) 763-35-37 (office). *E-mail:* a.mizikaeva@msso-kogan.ru (office); info@msso-kogan.ru (office). *Website:* www .msso-kogan.ru (office).

KOGAN, Richard Jay, MBA; American business executive; *Principal, Kogan Group LLC;* b. 6 June 1941, New York, NY; s. of Benjamin Kogan and Ida Kogan; m. Susan Linda Scher 1965; ed City Coll. of City Univ. of New York and Stern School of Business, New York Univ.; fmr Pres. US Pharmaceuticals Div., Ciba-Geigy Corpn; Exec. Vice-Pres. Pharmaceutical Operations, Schering-Plough Corpn 1982–86, Pres. and COO 1986–95, CEO 1996–2003 (retd); currently Prin. Kogan Group LLC; mem. Bd Dirs Colgate-Palmolive Co., Bank of New York Co. Inc., St Barnabas Medical Center and Corpn; mem. Council on Foreign Relations; Trustee, New York Univ. *Address:* Kogan Group LLC, Suite 415, 51 JFK Parkway, Short Hills, NJ 07078-2702, USA (office). *Telephone:* (973) 379-6560 (office). *Fax:* (973) 379-7050 (office). *E-mail:* RJK@RJKogan.com (office). *Website:* www .thekogangroupllc.com (office).

KOH, Harold Hongju, AB, BA, MA, JD; American lawyer, academic, university administrator and fmr government official; *Dean and Gerard C. and Bernice Latrobe Smith Professor of International Law, Yale University Law School;* b. 8 Dec. 1954, Boston; m. Mary-Christy Fisher; one s. one d.; ed Harvard Univ., Magdalen Coll., Oxford Univ., UK, Harvard Law School; Teaching Fellow, First-Year Legal Methods Program, Harvard Law School (Contracts and Civil Procedure) 1978–79; Clerk to Judge Malcolm Richard Wilkey, DC Circuit Court 1980–81; Clerk to Justice Harry A. Blackmun, US Supreme Court 1981–82; Assoc., Covington & Burling (pvt. law firm), Washington, DC 1982–83; Adjunct Asst Professorial Lecturer in Law, George Washington Univ. Nat. Law Center 1982–85; Attorney-Advisor, Office of Legal Counsel, US Dept of Justice 1983–85; Assoc. Prof., Yale Law School 1985–90, Prof. 1990–93, Gerard C. and Bernice Latrobe Smith Prof. of Int. Law 1993–, Dir Orville H. Schell, Jr. Center for Int. Human Rights 1993–98, Dean, Yale Law School 2004–; Asst Sec. of State for Democracy, Human Rights and Labor, US State Dept 1998–2001; Visiting Prof. of Int. Law, Faculty of Law, Univ. of Toronto 1990, 2002; Visiting Prof., Hague Acad. of Int. Law 1993; Visiting Fellow, All Souls College and Waynflete Lecturer, Magdalen Coll., Oxford Univ. 1996–97; fmr Ed. American Journal of International Law, Foundation Press Casebook Series; Fellow, American Acad. of Arts and Sciences; mem. Bd Harvard Univ., Brookings Inst., Nat. Democratic Inst., Human Rights First, Human Rights in China; Hon. Fellow, Magdalen Coll., Oxford; Dr hc (CUNY Law School); Asian American Bar Asscn of New York's Outstanding Lawyer of the Year Award 1997, Wolfgang Friedmann Award, Columbia Law School 2003, Louis B. Sohn Award, American Bar Asscn. *Publications:* has written more than 80 articles and authored or co-authored eight books including National Security Constitution (Richard E. Neustadt Award from American Political Science Asscn as best book on American Presidency 1991) 1990, Transnational Legal Problems (with H. Steiner and D. Vagts) 1994, International Business Transactions in United States Courts 1998, Deliberative Democracy and Human Rights (with Ronald C. Slye 1999. *Address:* Office of the Dean, Yale Law School, PO Box 208215, New Haven, CT 06520, USA (office). *Telephone:* (203) 432-1660 (office). *Fax:* (203) 432-7117 (office). *E-mail:* harold.koh@yale.edu (office). *Website:* www.law.yale.edu/about/officeofthedean.asp (home).

KOH, Tommy Thong Bee, LLD; Singaporean diplomatist and law professor; *Ambassador-at-Large, Ministry of Foreign Affairs;* b. 12 Nov. 1937, Singapore; s. of Koh Han Kok and Tsai Ying; m. Siew Aing 1967; two s.; ed Univ. of Singapore, Harvard Univ., USA and Univ. of Cambridge, UK; Asst Lecturer, Univ. of Singapore 1962–64, Lecturer 1964–71, Sub-Dean, Faculty of Law, Univ. of Singapore 1965–67, Vice-Dean 1967–68, Assoc. Prof. of Law and Dean, Faculty of Law 1971–74, currently Prof. of Law; Perm. Rep. of Singapore to UN 1968–71, concurrently High Commr to Canada 1969–71; Perm. Rep. to UN, (also accred to Canada and Mexico) 1974–84; Amb. to USA 1984–90; Amb.-at-Large, Ministry of Foreign Affairs 1990–; Dir Inst. of Policy Studies 1990–97; Exec. Dir Asia–Europe Foundation 1997–2000; Pres. Third UN Law of the Sea Conf. (Chair. Singapore Del. to Conf.) 1981–82; Chair. Preparatory Cttee, Chair. Main Cttee UN Conf. on Environment and Devt 1990–92; UN Sec.-Gen.'s Special Envoy to Russian Fed., Latvia, Lithuania and Estonia Aug.–Sept. 1993; Chair. Nat. Arts Council 1991–96; Chair. Nat. Heritage Bd 2002–; Commdr Order of the Golden Ark, The Netherlands 1993, Grand Cross of Order of Bernardo O'Higgins, Chile 1997; Hon. LLD (Yale) 1984; Adrian Clarke Memorial Medal 1961, Leow Chia Heng Prize 1961, Public Service Star 1971, Meritorious Service Medal 1979, Wolfgang Friedman Award 1984, Jackson H. Ralston Prize 1985, Annual Award of the Asia Soc., New York, 1985, Int. Service Award, Fletcher School of Law and Diplomacy, Tufts Univ., USA 1987, Jit Trainor Award for Distinction in Diplomacy, Georgetown Univ., USA 1987, Distinguished Service Order Award 1990, Elizabeth Haub Prize, Univ. of Brussels and Int. Council on Environmental Law 1997, Fok Ying Tung Southeast Asia Prize, Hong Kong 1998. *Publications:* United States and East Asia: Conflict and Cooperation 1995, The Quest for World Order: Perspectives of a Pragmatic Idealist 1998. *Leisure interests:* sport, reading, music. *Address:* Ministry of Foreign Affairs, MFA Bldg, Tanglin, off Napier Road, Singapore 248163 (office). *Telephone:* 63798000 (office). *Fax:* 64747885 (office). *E-mail:* mfa@mfa.gov.sg (office). *Website:* www.mfa.gov.sg (office).

KOHÁK, Erazim, BA, MA, PhD; Czech philosopher, academic and author; *Senior Scholar, Centre for Global Studies, Philosophy Institute, Academy of Science of Czech Republic;* b. 21 May 1933, Prague; s. of Dr Miloslav Kohák and Dr Zdislava Koháková; m. 3rd Dorothy Koháková; three d. from 1st m.; ed Yale Univ.; exiled with parents to USA 1948; Lecturer, Boston Univ. 1960–72, Prof. 1972–90, Prof. Emer. 1995–; returned to Czechoslovakia 1990; Prof. Ordinarius, Inst. of Philosophy and Religious Studies, Charles Univ., Prague 1990–2001, Prof. Emer. 2000–; currently Sr Scholar Centre for Global Studies, Philosophy Inst., Acad. of Science of Czech Repub.; mem. American Philosophical Asscn, Husserl Circle, Ethical Panel, Nat. Public TV 2005–; mem. Czech TV Council 2001–05; Medal of Merit (Czech Repub.) 1998; Scientia et Humanitate Optimi Meritis, Acad. of Science of Czech Repub. 2009; Hlávka Medal, Czechoslavak Acad. of Science 1992, Great Gold Medal, Charles Univ. 1994, Josef Vavroušek Prize for Ecology 1997. *Publications:* The Victors and the Vanquished 1973, Na vlastní kui 1973, Národ v nás 1978, Idea and Experience 1978, The Embers and the Stars 1984, Oheň a hvězdy (trans. by Milan Šimečka) 1985, Krize rozumu a přirozený svět 1986, Jan Patočka: His Thought and Writings (Jan Patočka: Mšlení a dílo) 1989, Dopisy přes oceán (Letters Across the Ocean) 1992, Jan Patočka: filosofický ivotopis (trans. by Josef Moural) 1993, P.S.: Psové 1993, Praské přednášky: ivot v pravě a moderní skepse (Life in Truth and Modern Scepsis) 1992, Clovek, dobro a zlo 1993, Hesla Erazima Koháka 1995, Průvodce po demokracii 1997, Pravda a pestrost 1997, Zelená svatozář: Přednášky z ekologické etiky 1998, Hesla mladých svišťů 1999, The Green Halo: Bird's Eye View of Ecological Ethics (trans. from the Czech by the author) 2000, Erazim Kohák, Poutník po hvezdách 2001, Orbis bene vivendi (Vybral a uspořádal Roman Šantora) 2001, P.S. Psové 2002, Dary noci 2003, Erazim Kohák: Zorným úhlem filosofa 2004, Svoboda, svědomí, soužití 2004, Buď Bohu sláva za vše kropenaté 2005, Hearth and Horizon: Ethnic Identity and Global Humanity in Czech Philosophy 2008, Domov a dálava: Kulturní totonost a obecné lidství v českém myšlení 2009, Oheň a hvězdy 2010; numerous articles in professional and popular journals. *Leisure interests:* hiking, railways, ecology. *Address:* Philosophy Institute AVČR, Jilská 1, 110 00 Prague 1 (office); Babákova 2200, 148 00 Prague 414, Czech Republic (home). *Telephone:* 736-467144 (mobile) (office); (2) 72935568 (home). *E-mail:* kohak.e@ecn.cz (home); kohak@flu.cas.cz (office).

KOHL, Herbert H. (Herb), BA, MBA; American retail executive and politician; b. 7 Feb. 1935, Milwaukee, Wis.; ed Univ. of Wisconsin-Madison, Harvard Business School; served in Army Reserve 1958–64; worked in family-owned Kohl's grocery and dept stores, Pres. 1970–79; Chair. Wis. Democratic Party 1975–77;

acquired Milwaukee Bucks professional basketball team 1985; Pres. Herb Kohl Investments; Senator from Wisconsin 1988–2013 (retd), Chair. Special Cttee on Aging, mem. Appropriations Cttee, Judiciary Cttee, Agric. Appropriations Sub-cttee, Judiciary Sub-cttee on Antitrust, Business Rights and Competition; f. Herb Kohl Educational Foundation Achievement Award Program 1990; Owner Milwaukee Bucks Nat. Basketball Asscn team; Democrat; Food Research and Action Center Distinguished Service Award, Wis. Farm Bureau Fed. Distinguished Service to Agric. Award, Best of Congress Award, Working Mother Magazine and Corporate Voices for Working Families 2010. *Address:* c/o 330 Hart Senate Office Building, Washington, DC 20510. *Website:* bucks.com.

KÖHLER, Horst, Dr rer. pol; German banker, politician and fmr head of state; b. 22 Feb. 1943, Skierbieszow, Poland; m.; two c.; ed Univ. of Tübingen; began career as scientific research asst, Inst. for Applied Econ. Research, Univ. of Tübingen, 1969–76; held various positions in Germany's Ministries of Econs and Finance 1976–89; Sec. of State, Ministry of Finance, Bonn 1990–93; Pres. Deutsche Sparkassen- und Giroverband, Bonn 1993–98; Deputy German Gov. IBRD and EBRD, Pres. EBRD 1998–2000; Pres. European Asscn of Savings Banks 1994–97; Man. Dir IMF 2000–04; Fed. Pres. of Germany 2004–10 (resgnd); Hon. Prof., Univ. of Tübingen 2003; Commdr de l'Ordre Grand-ducal de la Couronne de Chêne 1994; Officier, Légion d'honneur 1995, Sonderstufe des Grossen Verdienstkreuzes der Bundesrepublik Deutschland 2004; Verdienstmedaille des Landes Baden-Württemberg 2002. *Address:* c/o Office of the Federal President, Bundespräsidialamt, Referat Z1, 11010 Berlin, Germany (office).

KOHLHAUSSEN, Martin; German business executive; b. 6 Nov. 1935, Marburg/Lahn; m.; three c.; ed Univs of Frankfurt am Main, Freiburg and Marburg; bank training, Deutsche Bank, Frankfurt am Main; Man. Lloyds Bank, Frankfurt am Main 1974–76; Man. Tokyo Br. Westdeutsche Landesbank Girozentrale 1976–78, New York Br. 1979–81; mem. Bd Man. Dirs Commerzbank AG 1982–2001, Chair. Exec. Cttee 1991–2001, Chair. Supervisory Bd 2001–10; fmr Chair. Supervisory Bd Hochtief AG, Heraeus Holding GmbH; Pres. Int. Monetary Conf. 1999, 2000; Pres. Bundesverband Deutscher Banken 1997–2000; mem. Supervisory Bd ThyssenKrupp AG, Intermediate Capital Group, Nat. Pensions Reserve Fund, Schering AG, Verlagsgruppe Georg von Holtzbrinck GmbH; mem. Bd of Dirs Bayer AG 1992–, Intermediate Capital Group 2004–; Hon. Dr rer. pol (Technische Univ., Chemnitz) 1998. *Address:* c/o Commerzbank AG, Kaiserplatz, 60311 Frankfurt am Main, Germany.

KOHN, Walter, BA, MA, PhD; American physicist, chemist and academic; *Research Professor of Physics and Chemistry, University of California, Santa Barbara;* b. 9 March 1923, Vienna, Austria; s. of Salomon Kohn and Gusti Rappaport; m. 1st Lois Mary Adams 1948 (divorced); three d.; m. 2nd Mara Schiff 1978; ed Harvard Univ. and Univ. of Toronto, Canada; served with Canadian Infantry 1944–45; Instructor Harvard Univ. 1948–50; Asst Prof., Assoc. Prof., then Prof., Carnegie Mellon Inst. of Tech. 1950–60; Prof. Univ. of Calif. at San Diego 1960–79, Chair. Dept of Physics 1961–63, Dir Inst. for Theoretical Physics 1979–84; Prof. of Physics, Univ. of Calif. at Santa Barbara 1984–91, Prof. Emer. and Research Prof. 1991–, Research Prof. of Physics and Chem.; mem. revision cttee reactor div. NIST, Md 1994–; Visiting Prof., Univs of Mich. and Pa 1957–58, Imperial Coll. of Science and Tech., London 1960; Nat. Research Council Fellow, Inst. of Theoretical Physics, Copenhagen 1951–52; Guggenheim Fellow and Visiting Prof., Ecole Normale Supérieure, Paris 1963–64; NSF Sr Postdoctoral Fellow, Univ. of Paris 1967; Councillor-at-Large, American Physical Soc. 1968–72; Visiting Prof., Hebrew Univ., Jerusalem 1970 and Univs of Washington, Paris, Copenhagen, ETH, Zürich; mem. Bd of Govs Weizmann Inst. 1996–; mem. Int. Acad. of Quantum Molecular Sciences, NAS; Foreign mem. Royal Soc.; Fellow, American Acad. of Arts and Sciences, AAAS; Hon. LLD (Toronto) 1967, Hon. DSc (Univ. of Paris) 1980, (Queen's Univ., Canada) 1986, Hon. DPhil (Brandeis Univ.) 1981, (Hebrew Univ. of Jerusalem) 1981; Oliver E. Buckley Prize in Solid State Physics 1960, Davisson-Germer Prize in Surface Physics 1977, Nat. Medal of Science 1988, Feenberg Medal 1991, Nobel Prize in Chem. (jt winner) 1998, Neils Bohr/UNESCO Gold Medal 1998. *Publications:* 205 scientific articles in professional journals 1945–2005. *Leisure interests:* music, reading, sports. *Address:* Department of Physics, University of California, Santa Barbara, CA 93106 (office); 236 La Vista Grande, Santa Barbara, CA 93103, USA (home). *Telephone:* (805) 893-3061 (office), (805) 962-1489 (home). *Fax:* (805) 893-5816 (office), (805) 962-1489 (home). *E-mail:* kohn@physics.ucsb.edu (office). *Website:* www.physics.ucsb.edu/~kohn (office).

KOHONA, Palitha T. B., LLB, LLM, PhD; Sri Lankan/Australian lawyer and diplomatist; *Permanent Representative, United Nations;* b. Matale, Sri Lanka; ed St Thomas Coll., Mount Lavinia, Sri Lanka, Univ. of Sri Lanka, Australian Nat. Univ., Univ. of Cambridge, UK; attorney-at-law, Supreme Court of Sri Lanka; with Dept of Foreign Affairs and Trade (FAT) of Australia, led Australian del. to UNCTAD Trade and Devt Bd 1988, assigned to Uruguay Round negotiating team of Australia, in charge of Institutional Mechanisms, posted to Australian Perm. Mission, Geneva 1989, chaired UN negotiating group that developed the compliance mechanism under Montreal Protocol to Convention on Ozone Layer, mem. UN Working Group on liability mechanism under Basel Convention on Hazardous Wastes, Head of Trade and Investment Section, FAT –1995, Chief of UN Treaty Section, New York 1995–2006; initiated Annual UN Treaty Event, est. treaty training programme, oversaw computerization and on-line presentation of UN Treaty Database, oversaw preparation of UN Treaty Handbook; returned to Sri Lanka 2006; Sec.-Gen. Secr. for Coordinating the Peace Process (SCOPP) 2006–07, participated in two rounds of peace negotiations with Liberation Tigers of Tamil Eelam in Geneva and led del. to a round organized in Oslo 2006; Perm. Sec., Ministry of Foreign Affairs 2007–09; Amb. and Perm. Rep. to UN, New York 2009–; mem. del. to UN Gen. Ass. 2006, 2008; has led official-level dels to several countries on bilateral matters, Leader of UN legal del. to North Korea at invitation of DPRK Govt 2005; Adviser, Sustainable Devt and Co-Chair. UN Working Group on Marine Biological Diversity Beyond Nat. Jurisdiction, mem. UN Advisory Panel on the Shirley Amerasinghe Prize on the Law of the Sea; Adviser, Helping Hands; Patron Renewable Energy and Int. Law, Making Art Everywhere; two merit prizes on results of First Examination in Law, Univ. of Sri Lanka, UN 21 Pin 1996, Global Citizen, Orphans International (USA). *Publications include:* The Regulation of International Trade through Law, more than 60 publs on treaty law, the environment, climate change, biological diversity, non-governmental orgs, trade and the environment, terrorism. *Leisure interests:* cricket, grass hockey, travel, music. *Address:* Permanent Mission of Sri Lanka to the United Nations, 630 Third Avenue, 20th Floor, New York, NY 10017, USA (office). *Telephone:* (212) 986-7040 (office). *Fax:* (212) 986-1838 (office). *E-mail:* mail@slmission.com (office). *Website:* www.slmission.com (office).

KOHONEN, Teuvo Kalevi, DEng, FIEEE; Finnish physicist, computer scientist and academic; *Professor, Department of Information and Computer Science, Helsinki University of Technology;* b. 11 July 1934, Lauritsala; s. of Väinö Kohonen and Tyyne E. Koivunen; m. Elvi Anneli Trast 1959; two s. two d.; ed Helsinki Univ. of Tech.; Teaching Asst in Physics, Helsinki Univ. of Tech. 1957–59, Asst Prof. in Physics 1963–65, Prof. of Tech. Physics 1965–93; currently Prof., Dept of Information and Computer Science, Aalto Univ.; Research Assoc., Finnish Atomic Energy Comm. 1959–62; Visiting Prof., Univ. of Washington, Seattle 1968–69; Research Prof., Acad. of Finland 1975–78, 1980–99, Prof. Emer. 1999–; Pres. European Neural Network Soc. 1991–92; Vice-Chair. Int. Asscn for Pattern Recognition 1982–84; mem. Acad. Scientiarum et Artium Europaea, Académie Européenne des Sciences, des Arts et des Lettres, Finnish Acad. of Sciences, Finnish Acad. of Eng Sciences; Commdr, Order of Lion of Finland, Kt, Order of White Rose of Finland; Dr hc (Univ. of York, Abo Akademi, Univ. of Dortmund); Emil Aaltonen Prize 1983, Cultural Prize, Finnish Commercial TV (MTV) 1984, IEEE Neural Networks Pioneer Award 1991, Int. Neural Network Soc. Lifetime Achievement Award 1992, Finnish Cultural Foundation Prize 1994, Tech. Achievement Award, IEEE Signal Processing Soc. 1995, King-Sun Fu Prize, Int. Asscn for Pattern Recognition 1996, Centennial Prize, Finnish Asscn of Grad. Engineers (TEK) 1996, Medal of Finnish Acad. of Eng Sciences 1997, SEFI Leonardo da Vinci Medal, European Soc. for Eng Educ. 1998, Jubilee Prize Finnish Foundation of Tech. 1999, Italgas Prize 1999, Caianiello Int. Award 2000, Third Millennium Medal, IEEE Signal Processing Soc. 2000, Academician 2000, IEEE Frank Rosenblatt Award 2008. *Publications:* Digital Circuits and Devices 1972, Associative Memory: A System Theoretical Approach 1977, Content-Addressable Memories 1982, Self-Organization and Associative Memory 1984, Self-Organizing Maps (Springer Series in Information Sciences, Vol. 30) 1995. *Leisure interests:* philosophy of music, literature. *Address:* Department of Information and Computer Science, Aalto University, PO Box 15400, 00076 Aalto (office); Mellstenintie 9 C 2, 02170 Espoo, Finland (home). *Telephone:* (9) 4702-3268 (office). *E-mail:* teuvo.kohonen@tkk.fi (office). *Website:* www.cis.hut.fi/teuvo (office).

KOHOUT, Jan; Czech diplomatist and politician; b. 29 March 1961, Pilsen; m. (divorced); one s. one d.; ed Charles Univ., Prague; mil. service 1984–85; researcher, Inst. of Int. Relations, Prague 1985–90; Desk Officer, Int. Orgs Dept, Ministry of Foreign Affairs 1990–92, Dir UN Dept 1993–95; Deputy Head, Perm. Mission to UN, OSCE and other orgs, Vienna 1995–2000; Deputy Dir EU and Western Europe Dept, Ministry of Foreign Affairs 2000–01, apptd Political Dir 2001, apptd Deputy Minister 2002; Perm. Rep. to EU 2004–08; Deputy Minister of Foreign Affairs 2008–09; Deputy Prime Minister and Minister of Foreign Affairs 2009–10; Minister of Foreign Affairs 2013–14; mem. Czech Social Democratic Party. *Address:* c/o Ministry of Foreign Affairs, Loretánské nám. 101/5, 118 00 Prague 1, Czech Republic. *E-mail:* epodatelna@mzv.cz.

KOIKE, Yuriko, BA; Japanese politician and fmr broadcaster; b. 15 July 1952; ed Faculty of Sociology, Kwansei Gakuin Univ., Cairo Univ. and American Univ. of Cairo, Egypt; began career as interpreter and translator of Arabic 1977; Sec.-Gen. Japan–Arab Asscn 1977–78, 1990–92; interviewer and coordinator, Nippon TV Special Col Qadaffi and Yasser Arafat 1978; Anchor, Current Issues, Nippon TV 1979–88; Anchor, World Business Satellite and Top Business Execs, TV Tokyo 1988–90; elected to House of Councillors (Japan New Party) 1998; mem. House of Reps (now LDP) for Tokyo 10th District 1993–, Vice-Minister Man. and Coordination Agency 1992–94, Chair. Standing Cttee on Science and Tech. 1997–98, mem. Standing Cttee on Trade and Industry 1998–99, Dir Standing Cttee on Finance 1998–2000, mem. Standing Cttee on Health and Welfare 2000–03; Vice-Pres. Japan New Party 1994; Founding mem. New Frontier Party 1994, Asst to Sec.-Gen. 1995–96, Dir Public Relations Bureau 1996–97; Founding mem. Liberal Party 1998, mem. Cttee on Public Relations 1999–2000; Vice-Chair. Policy Planning Cttee, Conservative Party 2000–03; Minister of Environment 2003–06; Minister of State for Okinawa and Northern Territories Affairs 2004–06, in Charge of Global Environmental Problems 2005–06; Adviser to Prime Minister on Nat. Security 2006–07; Minister of Defence (first woman) June–Aug. 2007; Visiting Prof., Chuo Univ. Grad. School 2009–. *Address:* House of Representatives, 1-7-1 Nagata-cho, Chiyoda-ku, Tokyo 100-0014, Japan (office). *E-mail:* koike@yuriko.or.jp. *Website:* www.yuriko.or.jp.

KOIRALA, Anuradha, BA; Nepalese activist and organization official; *Founding Chairperson, Maiti Nepal;* b. 14 April 1949; d. of the late Col Pratap Singh Gurung and Laxmi Gurung; one s.; ed St Xavier's Coll., Kolkata, India; fmr schoolteacher; Founder and Chair. Maiti Nepal (Mother's Home – shelter, educational facility, hospice and lobbying org. to fight domestic abuse, rape, child prostitution, child labour and trafficking of girls for sex trade) 1993–; Asst Minister for Women, Children and Social Welfare 2002–03; Distinguished Social Worker Award, Nepal 1997–98, 1999, Noted Social Worker Award, Nepal 1997–98, 100 Heroines Award 1998, Best Social Worker of the Year Award, Social Welfare Council, Nepal 1998–99, 2000, Prabal Gorkha Dakshin Bahu Medal, Nepal 1999–2000, Everest Foundation Nepal Felicitation 2000, Best Social Worker, Women's Asscn Nepal 2000, Int. Children's Award 2002, Trishaktipatta 2002, Birendra Aiswarya Padak 2002. *Leisure interests:* singing, dancing. *Address:* Maiti Nepal Central Office, 83–Maiti Marg, Pingalsthan, Gaushala, Nepal (office). *Telephone:* (1) 4492904 (office); (1) 4478401 (home). *Fax:* (1) 4489978 (office). *E-mail:* anuradha@maitinepal.org (office). *Website:* www.maitinepal.org (office).

KOIRALA, Shanker Prasad, LLB, MEcon, MA; Nepalese civil servant and government official; *Minister of Finance;* ed Tribhuvan Univ., Kathmandu, Centre for Research and Communications, Manila, Philippines; Section Officer, Ministry of Industry 1986–91, Section Officer, Ministry of Finance, 1991–94, Asst Dir, Asian Devt Bank, Manila 1994–96, Jt Sec., Ministry of Commerce 1996–97, Jt Sec., Ministry of Culture, Tourism and Civil Aviation 1997–2007, Sec., Ministry of Information and Communication 2007–08, Sec., Ministry of Water Resources 2008, Sec., Ministry of Energy 2010–11, Sec., Ministry of Industry 2011–12, Sec.,

Election Comm. 2012–13; Minister of Finance, Industry, and Commerce and Supplies 2013–. *Albums include:* Dhadkan Bhitra (solo music) 2005, Prahar (joint music album) 2007, Upamaa (Upahar – 2) (solo music) 2008. *Publications include:* Taankiko Ghans (anthology of Nepali poems) 2002, Dhadkan Bhitra (anthology of lyrics) 2005, Nirbastra Nagarimaa (anthology of poems) 2008. *Address:* Ministry of Finance, Singha Durbar, Kathmandu, Nepal (office). *Telephone:* (1) 4211809 (office). *Fax:* (1) 4211831 (office). *E-mail:* spk@mof.gov.np (office); spk228@hotmail.com. *Website:* www.mof.gov.np (office).

KOIRALA, Sujata, BA, MA; Nepalese politician; b. 9 Feb. 1954, Biratnagar, Morang Dist; d. of Girija Prasad Koirala, Pres. Nepali Congress Party and fmr Prime Minister (PM), and the late Sushma Koirala; m.; one s. one d.; ed Coll., Univ.; mem. Cen. Working Cttee, Nepali Congress Party, Head of Int. Relations Dept; Minister at Prime Minister's Office 2007–08; Deputy Prime Minister and Minister of Foreign Affairs 2009–11; mem. Nepalese dels under leadership of Prime Minister Girija Prasad Koirala at Sixth and 15th South Asian Asscn for Regional Cooperation Summits, Colombo 1991, 2008; mem. Nepalese dels in state, official and goodwill visits of Prime Minister Girija Prasad Koirala to India 1991, 2006, 2009, China 1992, 2002, Israel 1993, Finland 1993, Tibet Autonomous Region of China 1993, Japan 1998; mem. Nepalese del. to 10th Summit of Non-Aligned Movt, Jakarta 1992, 11th Summit, Durban 1998, to UN Human Rights Summit, Vienna 1993, UN Millennium Summit, New York 2000; lobbied in USA, India and Europe for restoration of parl. and protection of democracy in Nepal following Royal takeover 2005; led del. of Nepali Congress Int. Relations Dept to India 2008, 2009, to China 2008; Founder-Pres. Sushma Koirala Memorial Trust, Kathmandu, Sushma Koirala Memorial Plastic Reconstructive Surgery Hosp., Kathmandu, Sushma Koirala Memorial CMA/ANM Campus, Kathmandu and Nepalgunj. *Leisure interests:* painting, listening to classical music, reading, social work, philanthropic activities. *Address:* c/o Ministry of Foreign Affairs, Narayan-hiti, Kathmandu, Nepal.

KOIRALA, Sushil; Nepalese politician; *Prime Minister;* b. 1939; s. of Bodh Prasad Koirala and Kuminidi Koirala; brother/cousin of fmr Prime Ministers Girija Prasad Koirala and Bisheshwar Prasad Koirala; mem. Pratinidhi Sabha (House of Reps) 1999–; Gen. Sec. Nepali Congress Party 1996–98, Vice-Pres. 1998, Acting Pres. 2009–10, Pres. 2010–13; Prime Minister of Nepal 2014–. *Address:* Office of the Prime Minister and Council of Ministers, Singha Durbar, POB 23312, Kathmandu (home); Nepali Congress Party, B.P. Smriti Bhavan, B.P. Nagar, Sanepa, Lalitpur, Nepal (office). *Telephone:* (1) 5555263 (office); (1) 5555189 (office). *Fax:* (1) 5555188 (office). *E-mail:* ncparty@wlink.com.np (office). *Website:* www.nepalicongress.org (office).

KOIVISTO, Mauno Henrik, PhD; Finnish politician and fmr head of state; b. 25 Nov. 1923, Turku; s. of Juho Koivisto and Hymni Sofia Koivisto (née Eskola); m. Taimi Tellervo Kankaanranta 1952; one d.; ed Turku Univ.; Man. Dir Helsinki Workers' Savings Bank 1959–67; Gov. Bank of Finland 1968–82, Gov. for Finland IBRD 1966–69, IMF 1970–79; Minister of Finance 1966–67; Prime Minister 1968–70, 1979–82; Minister of Finance and Deputy Prime Minister Feb.–Sept. 1972; Pres. of Finland 1982–94; Chair. Bd of Postipankki 1970–82, Mortgage Bank of Finland Ltd 1971–82, Bd of Admin. of Co-operative Soc. ELANTO 1966–82; mem. Bd of Admin., Co-operative Union KK 1964–82. *Publications:* Sosiaaliset suhteet Turun satamassa (doctoral thesis) 1956, Landmarks: Finland in the World 1985, Foreign Policy Standpoints 1982–92: Finland and Europe 1992, Witness to History 1997; 11 books on econs and social politics. *Leisure interest:* volleyball. *Address:* c/o Presidential Palace, Mariankatu 2, 00170 Helsinki, Finland.

KOIVULEHTO, Jorma Juhani, PhD; Finnish professor of Germanic philology; *Professor Emeritus, University of Helsinki;* b. 12 Oct. 1934, Tampere; m. Marja-Liisa Pakarinen 1963; one s. one d.; ed Univ. of Helsinki and German Dialect Research Centre of Marburg/Lahn, Fed. Repub. of Germany; Assoc. Prof. of Germanic Philology, Univ. of Helsinki 1973–83, Prof. 1983–98, Prof. Emer. 1998–; Research Prof., Acad. of Finland 1988–93; mem. Finnish Acad. of Sciences; Corresp. mem. Akad. der Wissenschaften, Gottingen, Österreichische Akad. der Wissenschaften; Hon. mem. Finno-Ugrian Soc. (Helsinki) 1997–. *Publications include:* 'Jäten' in deutschen Mundarten 1971, Idg. Laryngale und die finnisch-ugrische Evidenz 1988, Uralische Evidenz für die Laryngaltheorie 1991, Indogermanisch-Uralisch: Lehnbeziehungen oder (auch) Urverwandtschaft? 1994, Verba mutuata 1999, Finno-Ugric Reflexes of North-West Indo-European and Early Stages of Indo-Iranian 2000, The Earliest Contacts Between Indo-European and Uralic Speakers in the Light of Lexical Loans 2001, Frühe Kontakte zwischen Uralisch und Indogermanisch im nordwestindogermanischen Raum 2003. *Address:* Sallatunturintie 1 D 24, 00970 Helsinki, Finland (home).

KOIZUMI, Junichiro; Japanese fmr politician; b. 8 Jan. 1942, s. of Junya Koizumi; m. Kayoko Miyamoto 1978 (divorced 1982); three s.; mem. House of Reps from Kanagawa 1972–2006; fmr Parl. Vice-Minister of Finance and of Health and Welfare; Minister of Posts and Telecommunications 1992–93; Chair. House of Reps Finance Cttee; mem. Mitsuzuka Faction of LDP; Minister of Health and Welfare 1996–98, Prime Minister of Japan 2001–06; Pres. Jiyu Minshuto (Liberal-Democratic Party) 2001–06. *Address:* c/o Jiya Minshuto, 1-11-23, Nogata-che, Chiyoda-ku, Tokyo 100-8910, Japan (office).

KOIZUMI, Mitsuomi; Japanese business executive; *President and CEO, Japan Tobacco Inc.;* served successively as Sr Vice-Pres. and Head of Human Resources Group, Japan Tobacco Inc., Head of Tobacco Business Planning Div., Tobacco Business, Chief Marketing and Sales Officer, Tobacco Business and Exec. Vice-Pres. Japan Tobacco Inc., Dir 2007–, Exec. Deputy Pres. 2009–12, Pres. and CEO 2012–. *Address:* Japan Tobacco Inc., 2-1, Toranomon 2-chome, Minato-ku, Tokyo, 105-8422, Japan (office). *Telephone:* (3) 3582-3111 (office). *Fax:* (3) 5572-1441 (office). *E-mail:* info@jti.com (office). *Website:* www.jti.com (office).

KOJIMA, Yorihiko, BS; Japanese business executive; *Chairman, Mitsubishi Corporation;* b. 15 Oct. 1941, Tokyo; s. of Kazuo Kojima and Sakae Kojima; ed Tokyo Metropolitan Hibiya High School, Univ. of Tokyo; joined Mitsubishi Corpn (Heavy Machinery Dept) 1965, assigned to heavy machinery section of machinery group, worked at Olayan Saudi Holdings Co. Ltd, Al-Khobar, Saudi Arabia 1978–80, with Heavy Machinery Dept, Tokyo 1980–85, with Mitsubishi International Corpn, New York, USA 1985–92, Gen. Man. Corp. Planning Office, Tokyo 1992–95, mem. Bd of Dirs Mitsubishi Corpn 1995–, Dir Corporate, Mitsubishi

Corpn 1996–97, Man. Dir, Coordination 1997–98, Man. Dir, Admin 1998–2000, Man. Dir and Group CEO New Business Initiative Group 2000–01, Exec. Vice-Pres. and Group CEO 2001, Sr Exec. Vice-Pres. and Group CEO 2001–04, Pres. and CEO Mitsubishi Corpn 2004–10, Chair. Mitsubishi Corpn 2010–; mem. Japan Asscn of Corp. Execs (Keizai Doyukai), Vice-Chair. 2003–08. *Address:* Mitsubishi Corporation, Mitsubishi Shoji Building, 3-1, Marunouchi 2-chome, Chiyoda-ku, Tokyo 100-8086, Japan (office). *Telephone:* (3) 3210-2121 (office). *Fax:* (3) 3210-8583 (office). *E-mail:* info@mitsubishicorp.com (office). *Website:* www
.mitsubishicorp.com (office).

KOK, Willem (Wim); Dutch fmr politician; b. 29 Sept. 1938, Bergambacht; m.; three c.; ed Nijenrode Business School; Asst Int. Officer Netherlands Fed. of Trade Unions (Construction Sectors) 1961–67, Sec. 1967–69; Sec. Netherlands Fed. of Trade Unions (NVV) 1969–73, Chair. (later renamed Fed. of Netherlands Trade Unions, FNV) 1973–85; Chair. European Trade Union Confed. 1979–82; mem. Parl. 1986–2002, Party Leader Labour Party 1986–2002; Deputy Prime Minister and Minister of Finance 1989–94; Prime Minister of the Netherlands and Minister for Gen. Affairs 1994–2002; apptd Deputy Chair. Socialist Int. 1989; Vice-Chair. De Nederlandsche Bank; Adviser to European Comm.; mem. Supervisory Bd KLM 2003–, Royal Dutch/Shell, ING 2003–, TPG 2003–; mem. Club of Madrid, Pres. 2009–. *Address:* Dijsselhofplantsoen 12, 1077 BL, Amsterdam, Netherlands (home).

KÓKA, János, PhD; Hungarian business executive and fmr politician; *Chairman and CEO, Cellum Global Inc.;* b. 5 July 1972, Budapest; m.; two c.; ed Esztergom Pelbárt Timisoara Franciscan High School, Faculty of Gen. Medicine, Semmelweis Univ. of Medical Sciences; CEO Elender Computer Ltd (Elender Computer Kft.) 1996–2004 (and CEO of legal successors of co.); Chair. and CEO Cellum Global Inc. 2011–; European Deputy Pres. PSINet Inc. 1999–2001; Pres. Asscn of Information Tech. Enterprises 2003–; Chair. Information Tech. Program, Cttee of the Office for Nat. Research, Devt and Tech. 2004–; Minister of Economy and Transport 2004–08; mem. Parl. 2006–; mem. Szabad Demokraták Szövetsége (SzDSz—Alliance of Free Democrats), Chair. 2007–08, Leader of SzDSz Parl. Group 2007–10; IT Manager of Year Award 2000. *Leisure interests:* aviation, sailing, travel. *Address:* Cellum Global Inc., 2040 Budaörs, Távíró köz 4, Hungary (office). *Telephone:* (23) 814633 (office). *Fax:* (23) 814634 (office). *E-mail:* contact@cellum
.com (office). *Website:* www.cellum.com (office).

KOKH, Alfred Reingoldovich, CandEconSci; Russian economist, media executive, writer and fmr government official; b. 28 Feb. 1961, Zyryanovsk, Kazakhstan; m.; two d.; ed Leningrad Inst. of Finance and Econs; fmr Sr Researcher, Prometey Inst.; Asst, Leningrad Polytech. Inst. 1987–90; Chair. Sestroretsk Dist Exec. Cttee, Leningrad 1990–91; Deputy Dir Cttee on Man. of State Property of St Petersburg 1991–93; First Deputy Chair. State Cttee on Property in Russian Fed. 1993–96, Chair. 1996–97; Vice-Chair. Russian Fed. Govt responsible for Privatization and Budget 1997 (resgnd); Chair. Bd of Dirs Montes Auri Investment Co. 1997–; Dir-Gen. Gasprom-Media 1998–2001 (resgnd), with NTV Broadcasting 2001–03; mem. Exec. Cttee Union of Rightist Forces (SPS) party, led SPS parl. election campaign 2003; Contributing Ed. Medved magazine. *Publications:* History of Privatization in Russia (with A. Chubais and M. Boyko) 1997, Sale of Soviet Empire 1998, A Crate of Vodka (co-author) 2006. *Address:* Medved, c/o Forward Media Group, 123022 Moscow, ul. Rochdelskaya, 15, p. 10, Russia. *Telephone:* (495) 620-08-00. *Fax:* (495) 620-08-01. *Website:* medved-magazine.ru

KOKJE, Vishnu Sadashiv, LLB, MA; Indian lawyer and government official; b. 6 Sept. 1939, Dahi village, Tehsil Kukshi Dist, Dhar, Madhya Pradesh (MP); m. Leena Vishnu Kokje; two d.; ed secondary educ. in Dhar MP, Holkar Coll., Indore, MP, Govt Arts and Commerce Coll., Indore, Christian Coll., Indore; practised in various legal fields, including civil law, labour and industrial law, co. matters and constitutional writs 1964–90; appeared before several Enquiry Comms and in election petitions; apptd Judge of MP High Court 1990; Pres. MP State Consumer Disputes Redressal Comm. 1992–94; Admin. Judge, Rajasthan High Court 1998–2001, Acting Chief Justice of Rajasthan High Court 2001; Sr Advocate, Supreme Court of India 2002–03; Gov. of Himachal Pradesh 2003–08. *Leisure interests:* reading, travelling, long motor drives, computers and Internet surfing, badminton and cricket. *Address:* c/o Raj Bhawan, Shimla, Himachal Pradesh (office); 201 Park Residency, 24 Bapna Compound, Race Course Road No. 2, Indore 452 003, Madhya Pradesh, India (home).

KOKOSHIN, Andrei Afanasievich, DHisSc; Russian political scientist, politician and academic; *Professor and Dean of School of World Politics, Lomonosov Moscow State University;* b. 26 Oct. 1945, Moscow; m.; two d.; ed Bauman Moscow Higher Tech. Univ.; scientific researcher, Head of Dept, Deputy Dir, Inst. of USA and Canada, Acad. of Sciences 1974–92; First Deputy Minister of Defence 1992–97; Chair. Interagency Cttee on Defence Security, Security Council of the Russian Fed. 1993–97; mem. Govt Council on Industrial Policy 1993–97; Sec., Council of Defence of Russian Fed. 1993–97; fmr Chief Military Inspector of Russian Fed.; Sec., Security Council of Russian Fed. 1997–98; mem. State Duma 1999– (mem. Otechestvo–All Russia faction –2003, United Russia faction 2003–, Deputy Chair. United Russia faction 2008–), Vice-Chair. Cttee on Industry, Construction and High Technologies 1999–2003, Chair. Cttee on CIS and Compatriot Affairs 2003–07; mem. Russian Acad. of Sciences 1987 (Acting Vice-Pres. 1998–99, Dir Inst. of Int. Security 2000–), Academician-Sec. of Social Sciences Section 2009–; mem. Russian Acad. of Social Sciences 1993, Russian Acad. of Artillery and Rocket Science and Eng 1993–, Russian Acad. of Natural Sciences; Chair. Bd High Tech. Foundation/Gorbachev Project 2001, Russian Public Bd for Educ. Devt 2001; mem. Scientific Advisory Council, Inst. for Int. Studies, Stanford Univ., USA 2000–, Gen. Council United Russia Party 2001–, Bd Dirs Nuclear Threat Initiative 2001–, Bd of Trustees Russian–American Business Council 2002, Nat. Anticorruption Comm. 2002; Dean, School of World Politics, Prof., Lomonosov Moscow State Univ. (MGU) 2003–; Hon. Chair. Russian Rugby Football League 1992–; Services for the Fatherland, Mark of Honour, Military Comradeship 1987, 1997, 2000, 2005. *Publications:* 25 books (including six as co-author) on nat. security, int. affairs, Russian nat. industrial policy and econs including Forecasting and Foreign Policy 1975, The USA in the System of International Relations in the 1980s 1984, Weapons in Space: Security Dilemma 1986, National Industrial Policy of Russia 1992, Soviet Strategic Thought 1918–1991 1999, The National Industrial Policy and the National Security of Russia (jtly) 2001, Deterrence in the Second Nuclear

Age (jtly) 2001, Types and Categories of Nuclear Conflicts in the XXI Century 2003, Strategic Governance 2003, Sociology and Politology of the Military Strategy 2006, Technocrats, Neotechnocrats and Technocracy 2008, On Strategic Stability in the Past and in the Future 2009; more than 150 articles and papers. *Address:* State Duma, Okhotny Ryad 1, 103265 Moscow, Russia. *Telephone:* (495) 692-69-65 (office); (495) 938-18-92 (office). *Fax:* (495) 692-84-53 (office); (495) 938-18-93 (office). *E-mail:* kokoshin@duma.gov.ru (office).

KOKOYEV (KOKOITI), Eduard Dzhabeyevich; Georgian politician; b. 31 Oct. 1964, Tskhinvali, S Ossetian Autonomous Oblast, Georgian SSR; fmr mem. Russian nat. wrestling team; First Sec. Tskhinvali Br. of Komsomol 1989–92; business activities, Moscow 1992–2001; 'Rep.' of 'Repub. of South Ossetia', Moscow 1997–99; Pres., 'Repub. of South Ossetia' 2001–11; mem. Kleta Partia party. *Address:* c/o Office of the President of the 'Republic of South Ossetia', 100001 Tskhinvali, ul. Khetgurova 1, South Ossetia, Georgia.

KOKUBU, Fumia; Japanese business executive; *President and CEO, Marubeni Corporation;* joined Marubeni Corpn 1975, Corp. Vice-Pres. 2005–08, mem. Bd of Dirs 2008–, Man. Exec. Officer 2008–10, Pres. and CEO Marubeni America Corpn and Marubeni Canada Ltd, Sr Man. Exec. Officer and Regional Chief Exec. Officer for the Americas 2010–12, Chief Information Officer, Sr Exec. Vice-Pres. and COO of Global Strategy and Co-ordination Dept, Information Strategy Dept, and Research Inst. 2012–13, Pres. and CEO 2013–; Outside Statutory Auditor, Inpex Corpn. *Address:* Marubeni Corpn, 42 Ohtemachi 1-chome, Chiyoda-ku, Tokyo 100-8088, Japan (office). *Telephone:* (3) 3282-2111 (office). *Fax:* (3) 3282-4241 (office). *E-mail:* info@marubeni.com (office). *Website:* www.marubeni.com (office).

KOLA, Jukka, MSc, LicSc, MSc, PhD; Finnish agricultural scientist, academic and university administrator; *Rector, University of Helsinki;* ed Univ. of Arkansas, USA, Univ. of Helsinki, Univ. of Illinois, USA; Researcher/Sr Researcher, Agricultural Econs Research Inst., Helsinki 1986–92; Acting Prof., Agricultural Policy, Dept of Econs and Man., Univ. of Helsinki 1992–99, Docent, Agricultural Policy 1994, Prof. 1999–, Head of Dept of Econs and Man. 2001–03, Dean, Faculty of Agric. and Forestry 2004–06, 2007–09, Vice-Rector, Univ. of Helsinki 2010–13, Rector 2013–; Insp. of student org. Wiipurilainen osakunta 2010–; mem. European Asscn of Agricultural Economists, American Agricultural Economists Asscn, Int. Asscn of Agricultural Economists, Int. Food and Agribusiness Man. Asscn, Nordic Asscn of Agricultural Scientists, Scientific Agricultural Soc. of Finland, The CAP Forum, Univ. of Reading, UK; Fulbright Scholarship, Univ. of Illinois 1989–90, Award for the best scientific article published by a younger Nordic agricultural economist in int. peer-review scientific journals 1991–94, Nordic Asscn of Agricultural Scientists, Section IX (agricultural economics), NJF-Congress 1995, Eino Kaila Award 1999, Annual Award for the Best Teacher of Univ. of Helsinki, Teacher of the Year Award 1994, 1995, 1996, 1997, Co-operative Special Award, Pellervo-Seura, in association with UN Int. Year of Co-operatives 2012. *Publications:* numerous papers in professional journals on agricultural, food and rural economics and policy, international trade and development, new political economy, welfare economics and supply and demand analysis. *Address:* Office of the Rector, University of Helsinki, PO Box 33, Yliopistonkatu 4, Helsinki 00014, Finland (office). *Telephone:* (9) 191-22211 (office). *E-mail:* jukka.kola@helsinki.fi (office). *Website:* www.helsinki.fi/administration/rector (office).

KOLAGHASSI, Ali Hassan; Saudi Arabian business executive; currently Vice-Chair. and CEO, Saraya Holdings Ltd, also Chair. Saraya Aqaba, Saraya Bandar Jissah, Saraya Abdali (subsidiaries); Vice-Pres. Saudi Oger; Chair. Saraya Real Estate Middle East and N Africa Fund, Saraya Skies, Oger Abu Dhabi, Oger Jordan, MDI (Millennium Devt Int.), Rubicon; Dir Saudi Oger Telecom, MEDGULF-Jordan (Mediterranean and Gulf Insurance and Reinsurance Co.), Saudi Med Investment Co., AB Capital; mem. Bd of Trustees, King Hussein Cancer Foundation; Real Estate Industry Champion, Young Arab Leaders Org. 2005. *Address:* Saraya Holdings Ltd, Um Uthainah Al-Janoubi, Al-Koufeh Street, Amman, Jordan (office). *Telephone:* (6) 5505444 (office). *Fax:* (6) 5561738 (office). *E-mail:* info@sarayaholdings.com (office). *Website:* www.sarayaholdings.com (office).

KOLDING, Eivind, LLM; Danish lawyer and business executive; *Partner, A.P. Møller – Maersk Group;* b. 1959; ed Copenhagen Univ.; admitted to the Bar 1986; lawyer, Corp. Secr., A.P. Møller, Copenhagen 1989, later Sr Vice-Pres. and Head of Secr., Man. Dir Maersk Hong Kong Ltd 1996–98, Chief Financial Officer, A.P. Møller – Maersk Group 1998–2006, mem. Exec. Bd and Pnr, A.P. Møller – Maersk and Co-CEO Container Business, A.P. Moller – Maersk Group 2006–, CEO Maersk Line 2007–; mem. Bd of Dirs Danske Bank 2001–, later Vice-Chair., currently Chair.; Vice-Chair. Danmarks Skibskredit (Denmark Ship Finance); Chair. Safmarine Container Lines NV; mem. Bd of Dirs Maersk China Ltd, Maersk Inc., Maersk BV, The Maersk Co. Ltd, London, Dansk Supermarked. *Address:* A.P. Møller, Esplanaden 50, 1098 Copenhagen K, Denmark (office). *Telephone:* 3363-3363 (office). *Fax:* 3363-4108 (office). *E-mail:* grphrhqhrd@maersk.com (office). *Website:* www.apmoller.com (office); www.maersk.com (office).

KOLESNIKOV, Lt.-Gen. Vladimir Ilyich; Russian lawyer, government official and politician; b. 1938; m.; two c.; ed Rostov State Univ., Acad. of Ministry of Internal Affairs; worked as investigator, Deputy Head, Dept of Criminal Investigation; Deputy Head, Dept of Internal Affairs; Head, Main Dept of Criminal Investigation 1991–; First Deputy Minister of Internal Affairs 1999–2000; Adviser to Prosecutor Gen. of Russia 2000, Deputy Prosecutor Gen. 2002–06; Deputy Minister of Justice 2006; mem. State Duma 2007–, Deputy Chair. Cttee on Security.

KOLEV, Gen. (retd) Nikola; Bulgarian government official and fmr air force commander; *Head of the Office to the President of the Republic;* b. 9 Aug. 1951, Karadzhalovo, Plovdiv Region; m. Velichka Koleva; two d.; ed Electrical Eng Tech. School, Plovdiv, Air Force Acad., G.S. Rakovski Nat. War Coll., Gen. Staff Coll., Moscow, Russia, Defence Language Inst., San Antonio, USA; Asst Chief of Staff for Plans, 19th Fighter Air Regiment HQ 1975–76; Asst Chief Operations Dept, 10th Mixed Air Corps HQ 1976–78; Chief of Staff, 19th Fighter Air Regt 1982–85; Sr Asst Chief of Operations Dept, Air Defence and Air Force HQ 1985–88; Chief of Staff, 1st Air Defence Div. 1990–92; Mil. Adviser for Air Force and Air Defence to Pres. of Bulgaria 1992–96; First Deputy Chief of Air Force HQ 1996–98; Deputy Chief of Gen. Staff for Resources 1998–2000, for Operations 2000–02; Chief of Gen.

Staff, Bulgarian Armed Forces 2002–06; Head of Office to Pres. of Repub. 2006–; mem. NATO Mil. Cttee 2002–06; apptd Maj.-Gen. 1996, Lt-Gen. 1997, Gen. 2002; eight medals and awards presented by Ministry of Defence. *Address:* Office of the President, 1123 Sofia, bul. Dondukov 2, Bulgaria (office). *Telephone:* (2) 923-93-33 (office). *E-mail:* press@president.bg (office). *Website:* www.president.bg (office).

KOLGA, Margus, BA, MA; Estonian diplomatist and government official; *Permanent Representative, United Nations;* b. 1966, Tallinn; m. Maarja Maasikas; three c.; ed Tartu Univ.; Deputy Sec.-Gen., Ministry of Defence 1996–2003 (resgnd); Sr Research Fellow, Baltic Defence Coll. 2003–07; Acting Co-Chair. Defence and Mil. Terminology Comm. and mem. Mil. Educ. Bd 2004–06; Academic Dir, State Defence Course 2006–07; Dir Gen. First Political Dept (Security Policy and Int. Orgs), Ministry of Foreign Affairs 2007–10; Amb. and Perm. Rep. to UN, New York 2010–. *Address:* Permanent Mission of Estonia to the United Nations, 3 Dag Hammarskjöld Plaza, 305 East 47th Street, Unit 6B, New York, NY 10017, USA (office). *Telephone:* (212) 883-0640 (office). *Fax:* (212) 514-0099 (office). *E-mail:* mission.newyork@mfa.ee (office). *Website:* www.un.estemb.org (office).

KOLLER, Arnold, Dr iur, Lic oec; Swiss politician and academic; b. 29 Aug. 1933, Appenzell; m. Erica Brauder 1972; two c.; ed Univ. of St Gallen, Freiburg Univ., Univ. of Berkeley, USA; fmr Univ. Prof. of Law, Univ. of St Gallen; mem. Swiss Parl. 1971–85; Pres. Nat. Council 1984–85; mem. Bundesrat (Fed. Council) 1986–99, Head of Fed. Mil. (Defence) Dept 1986–89; Head Fed. Dept of Justice and Police 1989–99; Pres. of Switzerland 1990, 1997; Pres. Int. Conf. on Federalism 2002; Chair. Forum of Feds, Fellow; Dr hc (Bern) 2002. *Publications:* Grundfragen einer Typuslehre im Gesellschaftsrecht 1967, Die unmittelbare Anwendbarkeit völkerrechtlicher Verträge und des EWG-Vertrags 1971, Für eine starke und solidarische Schweiz 1999, Zur Entstehung der neuen Bundesverfassung 2002. *Leisure interests:* skiing, tennis. *Address:* Steinegg, Gschwendes 8, 9050 Appenzell, Switzerland (home). *Telephone:* (71) 7872290 (home). *Fax:* (71) 7875590 (home). *E-mail:* arnold.koller@bluemail.ch (home). *Website:* www.forumfed.org (office).

KOLLER, Daphne, BSc, MSc, PhD; Israeli/American computer scientist and academic; *Professor of Computer Science, Stanford University;* b. Jerusalem, Israel; m. Dan Avida; ed Hebrew Univ. of Jerusalem, Stanford Univ.; Postdoctoral Researcher, Computer Science Div., Univ. of California, Berkeley 1993–95; Asst Prof., Dept of Computer Science, Stanford Univ. 1995–2001, Assoc. Prof. 2001–06, Arthur G. Villard Fellow for Undergraduate Teaching 2004–, Prof. 2006–; Co-Founder Coursera (educational technology co.) 2012; Fellow, American Assen for Artificial Intelligence 2004; Rothschild Grad. Fellowship 1989–90, Univ. of California Pres.'s Postdoctoral Fellowship 1993–95, Arthur L. Samuel Award for best thesis in the Computer Science Dept, Stanford Univ. 1994, Sloan Foundation Research Fellowship 1996, Office of Naval Research Young Investigator Award 1999, Presidential Early Career Award for Scientists and Engineers 1999, IJCAI Computers and Thought Award 2001, MacArthur Foundation Fellowship 2004, World Tech. Award in Information Tech. (Software), The World Tech. Network 2004, ACM/Infosys Award 2007. *Publications:* numerous scientific papers in professional journals. *Leisure interests:* reading, listening to music, hiking, travelling to exotic locations with her husband. *Address:* Room 142, Gates Building 1A, Computer Science Department, Stanford University, Stanford, CA 94305-9010, USA (office). *Telephone:* (650) 723-6598 (office). *Fax:* (650) 723-6598 (office). *E-mail:* koller@cs.stanford.edu (office). *Website:* ai.stanford.edu/~koller/bio .html (office).

KOLLEY, Hon. Abdou, MEconSc; Gambian economist and politician; *Minister of Trade, Regional Integration and Employment;* b. 1 Jan. 1970, Kembujeh; ed Univ. Jean Monnet, France (Advanced Diploma in French Language); Economist, Dept of State for Finance and Econ. Affairs 1997–2000; Sr Economist, later Prin. Economist and Dir, Gambia Divestiture Agency 2000–04; Econs Analyst, Strategic Policy Unit, UNDP, Banjul 2004–07; Minister for Trade, Employment and Industry 2007–09, Minister of Finance and Econ. Affairs 2009–10, 2010–11, 2012–13, of Trade, Regional Integration and Employment March–July 2010, 2011–12, 2013–; fmr mem. Nat. Planning Comm. (now defunct); Insignia of Officer of Nat. Order of the Repub. of The Gambia 2010; Partner to the Private Sector Award, Gambia Chamber of Commerce and Industry 2009. *Publications include:* articles in Economic Watch magazine 2001, 2002, Cash Budgeting and PRSP/ Poverty Reduction Strategies: A Review of Case Studies and Lessons for The Gambia (unpublished) 2005. *Leisure interests:* gardening, reading, public lectures. *Address:* Ministry of Trade, Regional Integration and Employment, Central Bank Building, Independence Drive, Banjul, The Gambia (office). *Telephone:* 4228868 (office). *Fax:* 4227756 (office). *E-mail:* info@motie.gov.gm (office); abdoukolley@ hotmail.com. *Website:* www.motie.gov.gm (office).

KOLLO, René; German singer (tenor); b. 20 Nov. 1937, Berlin; s. of the late Willi Kollodzieyski and of Marie-Louise Kollodzieyski; m. 1st Dorthe Larsen 1967; one d.; m. 2nd Beatrice Bouquet 1982; began career with Staatstheater, Brunswick 1965; First Tenor, Deutsche Oper am Rhein 1967–71; Dir Metropol Theater, Berlin 1996–97; guest appearances with numerous leading opera cos and at annual Bayreuth Wagner Festival; Bundesverdienstkreuz Goldene Kamera Award, Hörzu 2000. *Performances include:* The Flying Dutchman 1969, 1970, Lohengrin 1971, Die Meistersinger von Nürnberg 1973, 1974, Parsifal 1975, Siegfried 1976, 1977, Tristan (Zürich) 1980, (Bayreuth) 1981. *Publication:* Imre Fabian im Gespräch mit René Kollo 1982. *Leisure interests:* sailing, tennis, flying. *Address:* c/o Pran Event GmbH, Ralf Sesselberg, An der Brücke 18, 26180 Rastede, Germany (office). *Telephone:* (4) 402-8687 (office). *Website:* www.kollo.com.

KOLOBOV, Yuriy Volodymyrovych; Ukrainian economist, banker and politician; *Minister of Finance;* b. 8 April 1973, Pavlograd, Dnipropetrovsk Region; m.; one s. one d.; ed V. Karazin Kharkiv State Univ., Kyiv Higher School of Finance, Int. Business Inst.; Head of interbank foreign exchange transactions and Deputy Dir, Kharkiv Br., PrivatBank 1995–2000; First Deputy Dir, Kyiv Br., Credit Dnepr Bank 2000–01; Deputy Chair. Bd TAS-Investbank CJSC 2001–02; Dir of Treasury, State Savings Bank of Ukraine (OshchadBank) 2003–08, Adviser to Chair. 2009–10; Chair. BTA Bank JSC June–Dec. 2008; mem. Bd and First Deputy Chair. State Export-Import Bank of Ukraine JSC 2010–12; First Deputy Chair. Nat. Bank of Ukraine 2012; Minister of Finance 2012–. *Address:* Ministry of Finance, 01008 Kyiv, vul. M. Hrushevskoho 12/2, Ukraine (office). *Telephone:* (44) 253-54-28

(office). *Fax:* (44) 425-90-26 (office). *E-mail:* infomf@minfin.gov.ua (office). *Website:* www.minfin.gov.ua (office).

KOŁODKO, Grzegorz Witold, PhD; Polish economist, academic, author and politician; *Founding Director and Professor, Transformation, Integration and Globalization Economic Research;* b. 28 Jan. 1949, Tczew; m.; two d.; ed Kozminski Univ., Warsaw; Prof., Warsaw School of Econs 1972–2001, Dir Inst. of Finance 1989–94; Prof. of Econs, Kozminski Univ. (ALK), Warsaw 2000–; fmr consultant, World Inst. for Devt Econs Research of UN, Helsinki; IMF and World Bank expert 1991–92, 1999–2000; First Deputy Prime Minister 1994–97, 2002–03; Minister of Finance 1994–97, 2002–03; Founding Dir and Prof., Transformation, Integration and Globalization Econ. Research (TIGER) 2000–; Visiting Prof., Yale Univ., UCLA; John C. Evans Prof. in European Studies, Univ. of Rochester, NY 1998–2004; Visiting Prof. Universita di Trento, Italy 2007–, Moscow School of Econs, Lomonosov Univ. 2005–; Hon. Prof., Indian Inst. of Finance 2004, Tianjin Univ., China 2005, Moscow Acad. of Econs and Law 2005, Guizhou Finance and Econs Univ., Guiyang, People's Repub. of China 2009; Commdr's Medal, Order of Polonia Restituta 1997; Dr hc (Univ. of Lvov) 2003, (Univ. of Chengdu) 2004, (Finance Acad., Moscow) 2009, (Univ. of Debrecen) 2009; numerous prizes and awards including Polish Broadcasting Award 1985, Man of the Year Award 1994, Polish TV Best Politician Award 1997, Award of Minister for Science 2002. *Publications include:* more than 400 publs in 26 languages on econ. theory and policy, including books in English: Strategy for Poland 1994, The Polish Alternative: Old Myths, Hard Facts and New Strategies in Successful Transformation of the Polish Economy 1997, From Shock to Therapy: The Political Economy of Postsocialist Transformations 2000, Post-Communist Transition: The Thorny Road 2000, Globalization and Transformation: Illusions and Reality 2001, Globalization and Catching-up in Transition Economies 2001, Emerging Market Economies: Globalization and Development 2003, Globalization and Social Stress 2005, The Polish Miracle: Lessons for Emerging Markets 2005, The World Economy and Great Post-Communist Change 2006, 20 Years of Transformation: Achievements, Problems, Prospects 2010, Truth, Errors, and Lies: Politics and Economics in a Volatile World 2011. *Leisure interests:* contemporary literature, ancient civilizations, nature, sport, marathon runner (best time 3:38), travelling (explored 160 countries), nature. *Address:* Transformation, Integration and Globalization Economic Research (TIGER), 59 Jagiellonska Street, 03-301 Warsaw, Poland (office). *Telephone:* (22) 5192108 (office). *Fax:* (22) 5192265 (office). *E-mail:* kolodko@tiger.edu.pl (office). *Website:* www.tiger.edu.pl (office); www .kolodko.net.

KOLOKOLTSEV, Lt Gen. Vladimir Alexandrovich, DJur; Russian police officer and government official; *Minister of Internal Affairs;* b. 11 May 1961, Nizhnii Lomov, Penza Oblast, Russian SFSR, USSR; m.; one s. one d.; ed Political Coll. of VLKSM (All-Union Lenin Young Communist League) MVD of the USSR; began career in police unit on guard at foreign diplomatic missions in Moscow from 1982, apptd platoon commdr of separate patrol bn of Gagarinskii Dist Exec. Cttee, Moscow 1984; entered Higher Political Coll. of Ministry of the Interior, studied at Faculty of Jurisprudence, graduated 1989; returned to police service as detective of Criminal Investigation Unit of Kuntshevskii Dist Exec. Cttee, Moscow, apptd Deputy Chief of Police Station No. 20 in Moscow, later Chief of Police Station No. 8, assigned to Criminal Investigation Dept of Moscow Police Dept HQ as Sr Detective of the Second Unit 1992, apptd Chief of Police Station No. 108 in Moscow 1993–95, Chief of Criminal Investigation Div. in cen. Dist Police Dept 1995–97; worked in Ministry of the Interior and as Chief of Regional Unit No. 4, Dept on Organized Crime Prevention 1997–99, Chief of Regional Operational Search Bureau, Dept on Organized Crime Prevention for southeastern admin. region of Moscow 1999–2001, Chief of Unit No. 3, Operational Search Bureau, Ministry of the Interior for Cen. Fed. Region of Russia 2001, later apptd Deputy Chief of this Operational Search Bureau, Chief of Police Dept in Orel region 2007–09, Deputy Chief of Criminal Investigation Dept, Ministry of the Interior April–Sept. 2009, Moscow Police Commr 2009–12, rank of Militsiya Lt-Gen. 2010, rank of Police Lt-Gen. 2011; Minister of Internal Affairs 2012–; Honoured Officer of Internal Affairs Authorities, several state and departmental awards. *Address:* Ministry of Internal Affairs, 119049 Moscow, ul. Zhitnaya 16, Russia (office). *Telephone:* (495) 667-72-64 (office). *Fax:* (495) 667-57-33 (office). *E-mail:* mvd12@mvdrf.ru (office). *Website:* www.mvd.ru (office).

KOLOMOISKY, Igor; Ukrainian/Israeli business executive; b. 13 Feb. 1963, Dnipropetrovsk; ed Dnipropetrovsk Metallurgical Inst.; currently Co-owner Privat Dnepropetrovsk business group; Co-f. Sentosa Ltd (oil supplier) 1991, currently mem. Bd of Dirs; Co-founder PrivatBank 1992 Chair. 1997–, mem. Supervisory Bd Ukrnafta oil and gas co. 2003–, mem. Bd of Dirs Central European Media Enterprises (CME), owns numerous other cos in other industries; apptd Gov. Dnipropetrovsk region 2014. *Address:* . *Website:* www.privatbank.ua (office).

KOLPAKOVA, Irina; Russian ballerina (retd) and ballet teacher; b. 22 May 1933, Leningrad (now St Petersburg); m. Vladilen Semenov 1955; one d.; ed Leningrad Choreographic School, Leningrad Conservatory; Prima Ballerina, Kirov Theatre of Opera and Ballet, Leningrad (now Mariinsky Theatre, St Petersburg) 1957–91; Ballet Mistress, American Ballet Theatre 1990–; fmr Ballet Master, Ballet Internationale, Indianapolis Ind. 1997, then Asst Artistic Dir; Prof., Vaganova Acad. of Russian Ballet, St Petersburg 1995–; Artistic Advisor and Perm. Guest Faculty, Central Wisconsin School of Ballet; Order of Lenin 1967; People's Artist of the USSR 1965, Grand Prix de Ballet, Paris 1966, USSR State Prize 1980, Hero of Socialist Labour 1983. *Main ballet roles:* Aurora (Sleeping Beauty), Juliet (Romeo and Juliet), Desdemona (Othello), Tao Khao (The Red Poppy), Maria (Fountain of Bakhchisarai), title roles in Giselle, Cinderella, Raymonda and La Sylphide, Chopiniana (Les Sylphides), Kitri (Don Quixote), Natalie Pushkin (Pushkin), Eve (Creation of the World); cr. role of Katerina (The Stone Flower) and Shirin (Legend of Love). *Television:* main roles: The Lady (The Lady and the Hooligan), Woman (The House by the Roadside), Aurora (Sleeping Beauty), Raymonda (Raymonda). *Address:* American Ballet Theatre, 890 Broadway, New York, NY 10003, USA. *Website:* www.abt.org; www.cwschoolofballet.com.

KOLTAI, Ralph, CBE FRSA; British stage designer; b. 31 July 1924, Berlin, Germany; s. of Alfred Koltai and Charlotte Koltai (née Weinstein); m. Annena Stubbs 1954 (divorced 1976); ed Cen. School of Art and Design, London; served in Royal Army Service Corps and with British Intelligence 1945–47; Assoc. Designer

RSC 1963–66, 1976–; Head, Dept of Theatre Design, Cen. School of Art and Design 1965–72; elected Royal Designer for Industry, Royal Soc. of the Arts 1984; Opera Dir The Flying Dutchman, Hong Kong Arts Festival 1987 and La Traviata 1990; over 200 productions of opera, drama and dance throughout Europe, the USA, Canada and Australia; Fellow, Acad. of Performing Arts, Hong Kong 1994, London Inst., Rose Bruford Coll. Art 1999; Hon. Fellow, London Inst. 1996; Dr hc (Liverpool Inst. for Performing Arts) 2007; Royal Design for Industry, London Drama Critics' Award (for As You Like It) 1967, Gold Medal (Prague Quadriennale) 1975, Soc. of West End Theatres Designer of the Year (for Brand) 1978, Golden Triga (Prague) 1979, 1991, 2003, London Drama Critics' Award (for The Love Girl and The Innocent) 1981, Designer of the Year Award (for Cyrano de Bergerac) 1989, Silver Medal, Prague (for Othello) 1987, Distinguished Service to Theater, US Inst. of Theater Tech. 1993. Designs include: musical Metropolis 1989 (London), The Planets (Royal Ballet) 1990, The Makropulos Affair (Norwegian Opera) 1992, My Fair Lady (New York) 1993, La Traviata (Stockholm) 1993, Hair (London) 1993, Othello (Essen) 1994, (Tokyo) 1995, Madame Butterfly (Tokyo) 1995, Twelfth Night (Copenhagen) 1996, Carmen (Royal Albert Hall, London) 1997, Simon Boccanegra (Wales) 1997, Timon of Athens (Chicago) 1997, Nabucco (Festival Orange, France) 1998, Suddenly Last Summer (also Dir, Nottingham Playhouse) 1998, Dalibor (Edin. Festival) 1998, A Midsummer Night's Dream (Copenhagen 1998), Don Giovanni (St Petersburg) 1999, Genoveva (Edin. Festival) 2000, Katya Kabanova (La Fenice, Venice) 2003. Publication: Ralph Koltai: Designer for the Stage 1997. Leisure interest: wildlife photography. Address: c/o Rachel Daniels, Berlin Associates, 7 Tyers Gate, London SE1 3HX; Suite 118, 78 Marylebone High Street, London, W1U 5AP, England. Telephone: (20) 7836-1112. Fax: (20) 7836-1112. Website: www.ralphkoltai.com.

KOLYADA, Nikolai Vladimirovich; Russian actor, writer and playwright; b. 4 Dec. 1957, Presnogorkovka, Kustanai region, Kazakhstan; ed Sverdlovsk Higher School of Theatre Arts; actor, Sverdlovsk Drama theatre 1972–77; mem. USSR Writers Union 1989–; teacher, Yekaterinburg Inst. of Theatre Arts 1998–; Ed.-in-Chief Ural Journal 1999–; Sverdlovsk Komsomol Cttee Prize 1978, Teatralnaya Zhizn (magazine) Prize 1988, Schloss Solitude Academy Award, Stuttgart, Germany 1992. Plays: Forfeits, Our Unsociable Sea or A Fool's Vessels, Rajab Lashkaldak, Parents' Day, Slingshot, Chicken, Polonaise, Mannequin, A Tale About the Dead Tsarina, Persian Lilac, Chicken Blindness. Publications: Plays for Beloved Theatre 1994. Address: Ural Journal, Malysheva str. 24, 620219 GSP 352, Yekaterinburg, Russia.

KOM, Mangte Chungneijang Mary; Indian boxer and police officer; Superintendent of Police (Sports), Manipur; b. 1 March 1983; d. of Mangte Tonpa Kom and Mangte Akham Kom; m. K. Onkholer (Onler) 2005; ed Loktak Christian Mission School, St Xavier School, Adimjati School; Sub-Insp., Manipur Police 2005, Insp. 2008, Deputy Supt 2010–; Supt of Police (Sports) 2012–; East Open Boxing Championship (gold medal) 2000, World Women Boxing Championship (silver medal), Pennsylvania, USA 2001, Women Nat. Boxing Championship (gold medal), Chennai 2001, Sr Women Nat. Boxing Championship (gold medal), New Delhi 2001, Witch Cup Boxing Championship (gold medal), Hungary 2002, World Women Boxing Championship (gold medal), Turkey 2002, Nat. Games (gold medal), Hyderabad 2002, Nat. Women Sports Meet (gold medal), New Delhi 2002, Asian Women Boxing Championship (gold medal), India 2003, Sr Women Nat. Boxing Championship, (gold medal) Aizawl 2003, (gold medal) Assam 2004, (gold medal) Kerala 2004, World Women Boxing Tournament (gold medal), Norway 2004, Asian Women Boxing Championship (gold medal), Taiwan 2005, World Women Boxing Championship (gold medal), Russia 2005, Nat. Sr Women Boxing Championship (gold medal), Jamshedpur 2005, Asian Cadet Boxing Championship (gold medal), Viet Nam 2006, Vijle Women Box Tournament (gold medal), Denmark 2006, World Women Boxing Championship (gold medal), India 2006, Asian Women Boxing Championship (silver medal), India 2008, World Women Boxing Championship (gold medal), China 2008, Indo- Sweden Dual Match Boxing Tournament (gold medal), Sweden 2009, Indoor Asian Games (gold medal), Vietnam 2009, Asian Women's Boxing Championship (gold medal), Kazakhstan 2010, AIBA Women World Boxing Championship (gold medal), Barbados 2010, India Police Meet (gold medal), Pune 2010, 16th Asian Games (Bronze Medal), Guangzhou, China 2010, 12th Sr Nat. Women Boxing Championship (gold medal), Bhopal, India 2011, Asia Cup (gold medal), Haikou China 2011, 6th Asian Women's Boxing Championship (gold medal), Mongolia 2012, Olympic Games (bronze medal), London 2012; Dr hc (Mangalayatan Univ.); Arjuna Award 2004, Padma Shri 2006, NETV People's Choice Awards 2006, People of the Year- Limca Book of Records 2007, CNN-IBN 'Real Heroes' Award 2008, Pepsi MTV Youth Icon 2008, 'Magnificent Mary', AIBA 2008, Sports Women of the year, Sahara India Pariwar 2008–09, Rajiv Gandhi Khel Ratna 2009, Amb. for Women's Boxing, Int. Boxing Asscn 2009, Param Poojaniya Shri Guruji Puruskar 2009, North East Excellence Award 2009, YFLO Women Achiever, FCCI Ladies Org. 2009–10, Sports Person of the year, Northeast, Assam Sports Journalist Asscn 2010, Sports Women of the year 2010–2011, Sahara India Pariwar, Spirit of Sports Award, NDTV India 2012, Tribal Achievers' Award, Ministry of Tribal Affairs 2012, GoI, Karmavir Purushkar Award, ICONGO 2012, Padma Bhushan (Sports) 2013. Address: c/o Infinity Optimal Solutions Pvt. Ltd., F-301 A, Ground Floor, Lado Sarai, New Delhi 110 030, India (office); Mary Kom Regional Boxing Foundation, National Games Village Langol, A-112, Zone-II, Imphal 795 004 (office); Samulamlan, Moirang 795 133, India (home). Telephone: (11) 41416161 (office); (38) 52411789 (home); 9856157822 (mobile). Fax: (11) 41416160 (office). E-mail: admin@iosindia.com (office); mcmary.kom@gmail.com; kcmarykom@yahoo.co.in. Website: www.iosindia.com (office); www.marykom.com.

KOMBO-YAYA, Dieudonné; Central African Republic politician; fmr Deputy Dir Org. for African Unity, fmr Sr Political Officer, Africa Union Comm.; Minister of Foreign and Francophone Affairs and Regional Integration 2008–09; UN Conseiller during presidential election in Benin 2011. Address: c/o Ministry of Foreign and Francophone Affairs and Regional Integration, Bangui, The Central African Republic (office).

KOMISARJEVSKY, Christopher, BS, MBA; American public relations executive; Member, International Advisory Council, APCO Worldwide; b. 16 Feb. 1945, New Haven, Conn.; m. Reina Komisarjevsky;; ed Union Coll., Univ. of Freiburg, Univ. of Connecticut School of Business, Wharton School; Capt. US Army

(helicopter pilot) 1967–72, combat service in Viet Nam, 1st Cavalry Div. 1969–70; Sr Vice-Pres. Hill & Knowlton 1974–85, Deputy Man. Dir Hill & Knowlton Int. 1985–86, COO 1986–87, Pres. and CEO of Europe/Middle East/ Africa operations 1987–88, Exec. Vice-Pres. and Man. Dir Corp. and Financial Counselling Office, USA 1990–91, Exec. Vice-Pres. and Gen. Man., New York and Eastern USA, 1991–93; Pres. and CEO Carl Byoir and Assocs 1988–90; Pres. and CEO Gavin Anderson & Co. 1993–95; Pres. and CEO Burson Marsteller, USA 1995–98, Pres. and CEO Burson Marsteller (Worldwide) 1998–2004 (retd); ad interim Harold Burson Faculty Chair Boston Univ. Coll. of Communication 2006; with APCO Worldwide, New York, mem. APCO Worldwide Int. Advisory Council and Sr Counselor 2006–; Trustee, EQ Advisors Trust; mem. Univ. of Miami Rosenstiel School, Asscn for the Help of Retarded Children; mem. Arthur Page Soc.; lectured on communications and business in Spain, Switzerland and New York; Ellis Island Medal of Honor 1996. Publications: Peanut Butter & Jelly Management 2000 (with Reina Komisarjevsky); numerous articles on public relations topics. Address: APCO Worldwide, 51 Madison Avenue, Suite 2510, New York, NY 10100, USA (office). Telephone: (212) 300-1800. Fax: (212) 300-1819. Website: www.apcoworldwide.com.

KOMIYAMA, Hiroshi, MEng, PhD; Japanese chemical engineer, university administrator and academic; Chairman, Mitsubishi Research Institute, Inc.; b. 15 Dec. 1944, Tochigi Pref., Tokyo; ed Toyama High School, Tokyo, Univ. of Tokyo; mem. staff, Univ. of Tokyo 1972–, Lecturer 1977–81, Asst Prof. 1981–88, Prof., Dept of Chemical System Eng 1988–2005, Dean, School of Eng 2000–02, Vice-Pres. Univ. of Tokyo 2003–04, Exec. Vice-Pres. 2004–05, Pres. 2005–09, Pres. Emer. 2009–; Chair. Mitsubishi Research Inst. 2009–; f. Platinum Network 2010; mem. Bd of Dirs Global Green Growth Inst. 2011–; mem. Bd of Govs Okinawa Inst. of Science and Tech.; Adviser, KAITEKI Inst.; Councillor, Asahi Glass Foundation; Pres. Soc. of Chemical Engineers of Japan 2002–03; Best Paper of the Year, Soc. of Chemical Engineers of Japan 1979, Best Research of the Year 1992, Society Award of the Year 2003. Publications: Technology to Sustain the Earth 1999, Answering to the Issues of Global Warming 1999, Structuring the Knowledge 2004; numerous scientific papers in professional journals. Address: Office of the Chairman, Mitsubishi Research Institute, Inc., 10-3, Nagatacho 2-Chome, Chiyoda-Ku, Tokyo 100-8141, Japan (office). Website: www.mri.co.jp (office).

KOMLÓS, Péter; Hungarian violinist and academic; Professor of Violin, Liszt Ferenc Academy of Music; b. 25 Oct. 1935, Budapest; s. of László Komlós and Franciska Graf; m. 1st Edit Fehér 1960, two s.; m. 2nd Zsuzsa Árki 1984, one s.; ed Budapest Music Acad.; f. Komlós String Quartet 1957; First Violinist, Budapest Opera Orchestra 1960; Leader, Bartók String Quartet 1963–; Prof. of Violin, Liszt Ferenc Acad. of Music, Budapest 1981–; first prize Int. String Quartet Competition, Liège 1964, Liszt Prize 1965, Gramophone Record Prize of Germany 1969, Kossuth Prize 1970, 1997, Eminent Artist Title 1980, UNESCO Music Council Plaque 1981; Order of Merit, Middle Cross of Repub. of Hungary 1995. Performances: extensive concert tours to USSR, Scandinavia, Italy, Austria, German Democratic Repub. Czechoslovakia 1958–64, USA, Canada, NZ and Australia 1970, including Human Rights Day concert, UN HQ New York, Japan, Spain and Portugal 1971, Far East, USA and Europe 1973; performed at music festivals of Ascona, Edin., Adelaide, Spoleto, Menton, Schwetzingen, Lucerne, Aix-en-Provence. Recordings: recordings of Beethoven's string quartets for Hungaroton, Budapest and of Bartók's string quartets for Erato, Paris. Leisure interest: watching sports. Address: 2083 Solymár, Sport-u. 6, Hungary. Telephone: (6) 26-360-697. Fax: (6) 26-360-772. E-mail: stradivari@axelero.hu (office). Website: www .lfze.hu (office).

KOMORI, Shigetaka, BEcons; Japanese business executive; Chairman and CEO, Fujifilm Holdings Corporation; ed Univ. of Tokyo; joined Fuji Photo Film Co. Ltd 1963, held various sr positions in Graphic Arts and Printing Div., Industrial Products Dept and Corp. Planning Office, Head of Fuji Photo Film Europe GmbH, Düsseldorf, Dir Fuji Photo Film Co. Ltd 1995, Man.-Dir 1999, Pres. 2000–03, Rep. Dir, Pres. and CEO Fujifilm Holdings Corpn 2003–12, Chair. and CEO 2012–; Pres. Photo-Sensitized Materials Mfrs Asscn, Japan-German Soc., Japan-Netherlands Soc.; Chair. Japan Asscn of Graphic Arts Suppliers and Mfrs; Grand Cross of the Order of Merit (Germany) 2006; Medal with Blue Ribbon by HM the Emperor of Japan 2004, Leadership Award, Int. Imaging Industry Asscn (I3A) 2004, inducted into Photo Marketing Asscn Int. Hall of Fame 2006. Address: Fujifilm Holdings Corpn, 26–30 Nishiazabu 2-chome, Minato-ku, Tokyo 106-8620, Japan (office). Telephone: (3) 3406-2111 (office). Fax: (3) 3406-2173 (office). E-mail: info@fujifilm.com (office). Website: www.fujifilm.com (office).

KOMOROWSKI, Bronisław Maria; Polish politician and head of state; President; b. 4 June 1952, Oborniki Śląskie, nr Wrocław; s. of the late Count Zygmunt Leon Komorowski and of Jadwiga Komorowska (née Szalkowska); m. Anna Dembowska 1977; two s. three d.; ed Cyprian Kamil Norwid High School, Univ. of Warsaw; belonged to 75th Mazovian Scout Team in Pruszków, scout instructor in 208 WDHiZ scout team, Mokotów; Ed. Słowo Powszechne 1977–80; acted as underground publr at Polish People's Repub. (PRL), co-operated with Antoni Macierewicz in monthly publ. Voice; sentenced with activists of Movt for Defence of Human and Civic Rights to one month's imprisonment for organizing demonstration of 11 Nov. 1979 1980; worked in Centre of Social Investigations of NSZZ 'Solidarity' 1980–81; a signatory of founder's declaration of Clubs in the Service of Independence 27 Sept. 1981; internee during 1980s; taught in Lower Seminar in Niepokalanów 1981–89; Man. Minister Aleksander Hall's office 1989–90; Civil Vice-Minister of Nat. Defence in govts of Tadeusz Mazowiecki, Jan Krzysztof Bielecki and Hanna Suchocka 1990–93; connected to Democratic Union and Freedom Union in early 1990s, Gen. Sec. of these parties 1993–95; elected to Parl. for Democratic Union 1991, 1993; co-f. Conservative People's Circle 1997, joined with newly created Conservative People's Party and Solidarity Electoral Action (AWS); won parl. mandate as cand. of AWS 1997, Chair. Parl. Cttee of Nat. Defence 1997–2000; Minister of Nat. Defence 2000–01; became mem. of Civic Platform 2001; re-elected to Sejm 2001, 2005; mem. Nat. Civic Platform Bd 2001–; Deputy Chair. Parl. Cttee of Nat. Defence and mem. Parl. Cttee of Foreign Matters, Vice-Marshal of the Sejm 2005–07, Marshal 2007–10; Acting Pres. of Poland (following death of Pres. Kaczyński in a plane crash) April–July 2010, elected Pres. 4 July 2010, assumed office Aug. 2010–; Order of the White Eagle, Grand Cross of the Order of Polonia Restituta, Royal Order of the Seraphim

(Sweden) 2011, Collar of the Order of Prince Henry (Portugal) 2012, Collar Grand Cross, Order of Merit of the Italian Repub. (Italy) 2012, Grand Officer, Order of Saint Charles (Monaco) 2012, Grand Croix, Légion d'honneur 2012, Order of the Three Stars (Latvia) 2012, Kt Grand Cross, Grand Order of King Tomislav (Croatia) 2013; Dr hc (Mykolas Romeris Univ., Vilnius, Lithuania) 2008. *Address:* Chancellery of the President, 00-902 Warsaw, ul. Wiejska 10, Poland (office). *Telephone:* (22) 6252900 (office). *Fax:* (22) 6952238 (office). *E-mail:* listy@prezydent .pl (office). *Website:* www.prezydent.pl (office).

KOMŠIĆ, Željko; Bosnia and Herzegovina lawyer and politician; *Member of the State Presidency;* b. 20 Jan. 1964, Sarajevo; m. Sabina Komšić; one d.; ed Univ. of Sarajevo, Edmund A. Walsh School of Foreign Service, Georgetown Univ., USA; served in Army of Repub. of Bosnia and Herzegovina during Bosnian War; embarked on political career during which he served as Deputy Mayor of Sarajevo, twice as Head of Municipal Govt of Novo Sarajevo 2000–06, and Amb. to Fed. Repub. of Yugoslavia 2001–02; mem. Social Democratic Party of Bosnia and Herzegovina (SDP BiH) 1997–2012, Vice-Pres 2006–12; Croat mem. State Presidency 2006–, Chair. (Pres. of Bosnia and Herzegovina) 2007–08, 2009–10, 2011–12, 2013–14; Golden Lily, Bosnian Govt. *Address:* Office of the State Presidency, 71000 Sarajevo, Maršala Tita 16, Bosnia and Herzegovina (office). *Telephone:* (33) 567550 (office). *Fax:* (33) 556050 (office). *E-mail:* press@ predsjednistvobih.ba (office); info@zeljkokomsic.ba. *Website:* www .predsjednistvobih.ba (office); www.zeljkokomsic.ba.

KONARÉ, Alpha Oumar, PhD; Malian international organization official and fmr head of state; b. 2 Feb. 1946, Kayes; m. Adame Ba Konaré; four c.; ed Ecole nat. supérieure, Univ. of Warsaw, Poland; fmr teacher; Dir Inst. for Human Sciences, Bamako 1974, Historic and Ethnographic Div., Ministry of Culture 1975–78; Minister for Youth, Sports and Culture 1978–80 (resgnd); Research Fellow, Institut supérieur de formation et de recherche appliquée, Bamako 1980–89; consultant, UNESCO and UNDP 1981–92; f. Jamana, a cultural co-operative 1983; f. daily Les Echos, monthly for young people, Grin Grin and news service on tape cassettes for rural population 1989; Pres. of Mali 1992–2002; Chair. African Union Comm. 2003–08; mem. ADEMA-PASJ party, Club of Madrid. *Publications:* Le Concept du pouvoir en Afrique, Bibliographie archéologique du Mali, Les grandes dates du Mali (with Adam Ba), Sikasso Tata, Les Constitutions du Mali, Les Partis politiques au Mali. *Address:* c/o Office of the Secretary-General of the Government, BP 14, Koulouba, Bamako, Mali.

KONATÉ, Gen. Sékouba; Guinean politician; b. 1966, Kissidougou; m.; four c.; joined Guinean Army 1985, Lt 1993–2000, Capt. 2000–06, Commdr 2006–08, Lt Col 2008–09, Gen. 2009–; Commdr, Macenta Parachute Detachment 2000–06; Deputy Commdr Guekedou Ind. Batallion 2007–08; Commdr Autonomous Air Transport Battalion (BATA) 2008–09; Minister at the Presidency, in charge of Nat. Defence 2009; Interim Pres. of Guinea 2009–10. *Address:* c/o Office of the President BP 1000, Boulbinet, Conakry, Guinea.

KONDIĆ, Novak, MBA, PhD; Bosnia and Herzegovina economist, academic and fmr government official; *Professor of Economics, University of Banja Luka;* b. 20 July 1952, Stratinska, Banja Luka; s. of Vlado Kondić and Gospa Kondić; m. Nevenka Predragović 1980; two s.; ed Univ. of Banja Luka; Head of Co. Accountancy Dept, Serbian Devt Bank, Banja Luka 1977–86, Head of Inspectorate Control and Information Analysis 1986–90, Dir Municipal Admin. of Public Revenues 1990–92, mem. Municipal Exec. Bd 1990–92; Deputy Dir-Gen. Payment Transaction Services for Repub. of Srpska 1992–95, for Banja Luka 1997; Minister of Finance, Repub. of Srpska 1995–97, 1998–2000; Rep. of Bosnia and Herzegovina to IMF 1998; Exec. Dir Razvojna Banka, Gen. Dir 2004–06; currently Prof. of Econs, Univ. of Banja Luka; Medal for Mil. Valour. *Leisure interests:* beekeeping, gardening, vineyard cultivation, fruit farming. *Address:* Faculty of Economics, University of Banja Luka, Trg srpskih vladara 2, 78000 Banja Luka, Bosnia and Herzegovina (office). *Telephone:* (51) 218-997 (office). *Fax:* (51) 315-694 (office). *E-mail:* info@unibl.rs (office). *Website:* unibl.org (office).

KONDO, Seiichi, BA; Japanese government official and diplomatist; *Ambassador to Denmark;* m.; one d.; ed Univ. of Tokyo, St Catherine's Coll., Oxford, UK; seconded by Foreign Ministry to Ministry of Int. Trade and Industry 1977–80, to Int. Energy Agency, OECD 1980–83; Deputy Dir OECD Desk, Foreign Ministry 1983–86, Deputy Head Korea Desk 1986–87, Chef de Cabinet, Vice-Minister of Foreign Affairs 1987–88, Dir Int. Press Div. 1988–90; Head of Chancery, Manila 1990–92; Counsellor for Public Affairs, Washington, DC 1992–95, Minister 1996; Head Co-ordination and Logistics Office for G8 Summits, Asia-Pacific Econ. Co-operation and Asia-Europe Meeting 1996–97; Deputy Dir-Gen. Econ. Affairs Bureau 1998–99; Deputy Sec.-Gen. OECD 1999–2003; Dir-Gen. for Public Diplomacy, Ministry of Foreign Affairs 2003–06; Amb. and Perm. Del. of Japan to UNESCO, Paris 2006–08; Amb. to Denmark 2008–; Chevalier, Légion d'honneur. *Publications:* Image of Japan in the American Media 1994, The Distorted Image of Japan – The Perception Game Inside The Beltway 1997; many articles in Japanese and English-language magazines. *Leisure interests:* reading, music, tennis, golf, horse riding. *Address:* Embassy of Japan, Pilestræde 61, 1112 Copenhagen K, Denmark (office); 1-11-16 Kamiosaki, Shinagawa-ku, Tokyo 141-0021, Japan (home). *Telephone:* 33-11-33-44 (office). *Fax:* 33-11-33-77 (office). *E-mail:* amb@embjapan.dk (office). *Website:* www.dk.emb-japan.go.jp (office).

KONDO, Shiro; Japanese business executive; *Representative Director and Chairman, Ricoh Company Limited;* b. 1950; joined Ricoh Co. Ltd 1973, Deputy Gen. Man. Imaging System Business Group 2000, Sr Vice-Pres. 2000–02, Exec. Vice-Pres. 2002–07, Man. Dir 2003, Dir 2005–07, Rep. Dir 2007–, Pres. and CEO 2007–13, Chair. 2013–; mem. Bd of Dirs Sindo Ricoh Co. Ltd. *Address:* Ricoh Company Ltd, 8-13-1 Ginza, Chuo-ku, Tokyo 104-8222, Japan (office). *Telephone:* (3) 6278-2111 (office). *Fax:* (3) 3543-9329 (office). *E-mail:* www-admin@ricoh.co.jp (office). *Website:* www.ricoh.com (office).

KONDRUSEVIC, Tadeusz Ignatyevich, DTheol; Russian ecclesiastic; *Titular Archbishop of Hippo Diarrhytus and Apostolic Administrator for Catholics of the Latin Rite in Northern European Russia;* b. 3 Jan. 1946; ed Vilnius Polytech. Inst., Kaunas Ecclesiastical Seminary; with St Therese Church, Ostra Brama Church, Vilnius 1981–87; Dean Cathedral of God's mother–Angels' Tsarina, Grodno 1988–89; Titular Bishop and Apostle Admin. of Minsk, First Bishop of Belarus Catholics 1989; currently Titular Archbishop of Hippo Diarrhytus and Apostolic Admin. for Catholics of the Latin Rite in Northern European Russia, Moscow. *Address:* Church of St Ludovic, 101000 Moscow, M. Lubyanka str. 12, Russia (office). *Telephone:* (495) 925-20-34 (office).

KONÉ, Tiémoko Meyliet; Côte d'Ivoirian economist, politician and central banker; *Governor, Banque Centrale des Etats de l'Afrique de l'Ouest;* b. 1949, Ferkessédougou; m.; five c.; ed Banque Centrale des Etats de l'Afrique de l'Ouest Centre d'Application Technique et Professionnel, Dakar, Senegal; joined Banque Centrale des Etats de l'Afrique de l'Ouest (BCEAO) 1975, positions include Asst to Nat. Dir for Côte d'Ivoire, Central Dir for Issue and Financial Operations, BCEAO HQ, Dakar, mem. Econ. Analysis Cttee, Nat. Dir for Côte d'Ivoire and Alt. Gov. at IMF 1991–98, Controller-Gen., in charge of Supervision of Operations and Inspection, Internal Audit, Control and Risk Prevention, Special Adviser and mem. BCEAO Govt, Adviser to Gov. and Dir Dept of Gen. Admin and Training, BCEAO Gov. 2011–; Head of cabinet of Côte d'Ivoire Prime Minister Guillaume Soro, with rank of Minister 2007–10; Special Adviser to Côte d'Ivoire Pres. Alassane Ouattara, in charge of Econ. and Monetary Affairs 2010–11; Minister of Construction, Urban Affairs and Habitat 2011. *Address:* Office of the Governor, Banque Centrale des Etats de l'Afrique de l'Ouest, rue Branly, BP 120, Lomé, Togo (office). *Telephone:* 22-21-25-12 (office). *Fax:* 22-21-76-02 (office). *E-mail:* ocourrier@lome.bceao.int (office). *Website:* www.bceao.int (office).

KONG, Dan, MA; Chinese economist and business executive; *Chairman, CITIC International Financial Holdings Limited;* b. May 1947, Beijing; ed Grad. School of China Acad. of Social Sciences; Vice-Pres., later Pres., later Vice-Chair. China Everbright Group –2000, later Chair.; Vice-Chair. and Pres. China International Trust & Investment Corpn (CITIC) 2000–06, Chair. CITIC Group 2006–10, Chair. CITIC International Financial Holdings Ltd 2001–, fmrly Chair. China CITIC Bank Corpn Ltd and CITIC Resources Holdings Ltd, fmrly Dir (non-exec.) China CITIC Bank International Ltd. *Address:* CITIC International Financial Holdings Ltd, Suites 2701–9, 27th Floor, CITIC Tower, 1 Tim Mei Avenue, Central, Hong Kong Special Administrative Region, People's Republic of China (office). *Telephone:* 3607-3000 (office). *Fax:* 2525-3303 (office). *E-mail:* info@citicifh.com (office). *Website:* www.citicifh.com (office).

KONG, Jiesheng; Chinese writer; b. 1952, Guangzhou City, Guangdong Prov.; Vice-Chair. Guangzhou Br. of Writers' Asscn 1985; travelled to USA and co-f. literary magazine; joined Editorial bd of Today magazine 1990. *Publications:* My Marriage 1978, On the Other side of the Stream 1979, A Life and Death Ordeal 1981, The Southern Bank 1982, The Big Jungle 1984, Story Investigations 1985. *Address:* Guangzhou Branch of Writers' Association, Guangzhou City, Guangdong Province, People's Republic of China.

KONG, Quan; Chinese diplomatist; b. 1955, Beijing; m.; one d.; served at Embassy in Brussels 1977–82, Attaché, Western Europe Dept, Ministry of Foreign Affairs 1982–84, Third, then Second Sec. 1985–95, Counsellor 1995–96, Counsellor, then Minister-Counsellor, Embassy in Paris 1996–99, Asst Dir-Gen. 1999–2000, Dir-Gen. of Communications 2001–06, Dir-Gen. Western Europe Dept 2006, Vice-Minister for Foreign Affairs 2006–08, Amb. to France 2008–14; mem. Perm. Cttee CCP, Tanggu Dist, Tianjin 2000–01. *Address:* c/o Ministry of Foreign Affairs, 2 Chao Yang Men Nan Dajie, Chao Yang Qu, Beijing 100701, The People's Republic of China (office).

KONG NYUON, Gen. John; South Sudanese politician; b. Jonglei, Upper Nile; several years' mil. service with Sudan People's Liberation Army; fmr adviser on security affairs to Pres. of S Sudan; Minister of Defence and Veteran Affairs (first holder following independence 9 July 2011) 2011–13. *Address:* c/o Ministry of Defence and Veteran Affairs, Juba, South Sudan.

KONGANTIYEV, Moldomusa Tashbolotovich, LLB; Kyrgyzstani police officer and politician; b. 31 March 1958, Maili-Sai town, Osh Oblast; ed Kyrgyz State Univ.; joined Militsia (police force) as Asst, Ministry of Internal Affairs Unit, Mailisaisky Town Exec. Cttee 1979–85; mem. Road Traffic Inspectorate and Detective, Criminal Search Dept and Theft of Social Property Dept, Ministry of Internal Affairs Unit, Uzgen Dist Exec. Cttee 1985–88; Detective, Theft of Social Property Dept, Ministry of Internal Affairs Unit, Kara-Suy Dist Exec. Cttee 1988–90; Sr Detective, Theft of Social Property Dept, Ministry of Internal Affairs Unit, Bazar-Korgon Dist Exec. Cttee 1990–91; Head, Econ. Crime Dept, also Deputy Head, Ministry of Internal Affairs Unit, Jalal-Abad City 1991–95; with Directorate of Internal Affairs, Jalal-Abad Oblast 1995–99; Head, Dept of Inter-Regional Man., Ministry of Internal Affairs, Osh and Jalal-Abad Oblasts 1999–2000; Deputy Head with responsibility for Mans, Ministry of Internal Affairs, Suzak Dist, Jalal-Abad Oblast 2000–01; Head, Ministry of Internal Affairs Transport Dept, Jalal-Abad 2001–04; Head, Ministry of Internal Affairs Rail Transport Office 2004–05; Head, Directorate of Internal Affairs, Bishkek City 2005; Deputy Minister of Internal Affairs 2005; Head, Chief Admin of Internal Affairs, Bishkek 2005–08; Minister of Internal Affairs 2008–10; Militsia rank of Gen.-Maj. *Address:* c/o Ministry of Internal Affairs, 720040 Bishkek, Frunze 469, Kyrgyzstan (office).

KONGO-DOUDOU, Toussaint; Central African Republic government official and fmr international organization official; *Minister of Foreign Affairs, African Integration and the Francophonie;* ed Univ. of Wisconsin, USA; served several years with UN including as Chief of Communications and Public Information, UN Stabilization Mission in Haiti (MINUSTAH) in early 2000s, later Dir Centre d'Information des Nations-Unies (CINU), Dakar, Senegal; Minister of Foreign Affairs, African Integration and the Francophonie 2014–. *Address:* Ministry of Foreign Affairs, African Integration and the Francophonie, Bangui, Central African Republic (office).

KONIDARIS, Ioannis (John), DrIur; Greek professor of law; *Professor of Ecclesiastical Law, University of Athens;* b. 10 Sept. 1948, Chios; s. of Marinos Konidaris and Ioanna Konidaris; m. Ersi Mantakas 1975, one d.; ed Univs of Athens, Thessaloniki and Munich; mil. service 1971–73; mem. Bar Asscn of Athens 1974–; Asst Faculty of Law, Univ. of Frankfurt, Germany 1978–81; Lecturer in Ecclesiastical Law 1985; mem. Editorial Bd of official journal of Bar Asscn of Athens 1985–2006; Prof. of Ecclesiastical Law, Univ. of Athens 1985–; Research Scholarship, Max Planck Inst. for European History of Law, Frankfurt am Main 1989–90; Dir Research Centre for the History of Greek Law, Acad. of Athens

1994–2000, Ed. the Centre's Yearbook (Vol. 31) 1995, (Vol. 32) 1996, (Vol. 33) 1997, (Vol. 34) 1998; columnist on ecclesiastical issues, BHMA newspaper 1992–; adviser on religious subjects to Minister of Foreign Affairs 1996–99, 2001; Sec.-Gen. for Religious Affairs, Ministry of Nat. Educ. and Religious Affairs 2001–04; Founder and Ed. Nomokanonika 2002–. *Publications include:* Monastic Property Law Between 9th and 12th Centuries 1979, Legal Aspects of Monastery 'Typika' 1984, 2003, Legal Theory and Praxis concerning Jehovah's Witnesses in Greece 1987, 1988, 1991, 2005, Law 1700/1987 and the Recent Crisis Between the Orthodox Church and the Greek State 1988, 1991, Issues of Byzantine and Ecclesiastical Law Vol. I 1990, Church and State in Greece 1993, The Conflict Between Law and Canon and the Establishment of Harmony Between Them 1994, Ekklesiastika Atakta 1999, Basic Legislation of State-Church Relations 1999, 2006, A Manual of Ecclesiastical Law 2000 (second edn 2011), Regulations of the Church of Greece 2001, Regulations of the Monasteries of the Church of Greece (two vols) 2002, Mount Athos Avaton 2003, Issues of Byzantine and Ecclesiastical Law Vol. II 2008, Regulations of the Church of Greece, of the Church of Crete, of Mount Athos and of the Church of Cyprus 2012, Particular Ecclesiastical Regimes in Greek Territory (Ecumenical Patriarchate-Dodecanese, Mount Athos, Crete) 2013; numerous articles on ecclesiastical law and history of law, especially Byzantine law. *Address:* University of Athens, 45 Akadimias Street, 10672 Athens (office); 107 Asklipiou Street, 11472 Athens (pvt. office) (office); 20 Bizaniou Street, 15237 Filothei/Athens, Greece (home). *Telephone:* (210) 3688607 (office); (210) 3630391 (pvt. office) (office); (210) 6742896 (home). *Fax:* (210) 3630391 (pvt. office) (office). *E-mail:* imkonidaris@law.uoa.gr (office). *Website:* www.law.uoa.gr (office).

KÖNIG, Johann; German gallery owner; *Owner, Johann König Gallery, Berlin;* b. 1981; s. of Kasper König and Edda Köchl-König; f. own gallery located in fmr industrial bldg, Martin-Gropius-Bau 2002 and New Nat. Gallery since 2006, and in fmr church of St Agnes since 2013, currently represents around 20 int. artists, both young emerging and established, including Micol Assaël, Henning Bohl, Manuel Graf, Tue Greenfort, Katharina Grosse, Jeppe Hein, Nathan Hylden, Annette Kelm, Manfred Kuttner, Alicja Kwade, Lisa Lapinski, Helen Marten, Justin Matherly, Michaela Meise, Natascha Sadr Haghighian, Michael Sailstorfer, Tatiana Trouvé, Corinne Wasmuht, Johannes Wohnseifer, Jordan Wolfson and David Zink Yi; programme includes a variety of media, including sculpture, video, sound, painting, printmaking, photography and performance; alternates solo exhbns with curated group shows and a performance-lecture series; participates in several int. art fairs, including Art Basel, Frieze Art Fair, London, FIAC, Paris and Art Basel Miami Beach; has placed works in both private and public collections, including Museum of Modern Art, New York and the Guggenheim Foundation. *Address:* Johann König, Dessauer Straße 6–7, 10963 Berlin, Germany (office). *Telephone:* (30) 26103080 (office). *Fax:* (30) 261030811 (office). *E-mail:* info@johannkoenig.de (office). *Website:* www.johannkoenig.de (office).

KÖNIG, Kasper; German curator; b. (Rudolf Hans König), 1943, Mettingen, Westphalia; m. Barbara Weiss; began career as curator, Claes Oldenburg Exhbn, Moderna Museet, Stockholm, Sweden 1966; Chair. Kunst und Öffentlichkeit (Art and the Public Realm), Kunstakademie Düsseldorf 1985–88; Prof., Städelschule Frankfurt 1988–2001, Dir 1989–2001; Founding Dir Portikus Exhbn Hall, Frankfurt; Dir Ludwig Museum, Cologne 2001–12. *Exhibitions curated include:* sculpture projects, Münster 1977, Westkunst, Cologne Fair 1981, von hier aus, Düsseldorf Fair 1984, Der zerbrochene Spiegel, Vienna and Hamburg 1993, In-Between Architecture, Hanover EXPO 2000, Manifesta 10, St Petersburg, Russia 2014. *Address:* Kurfürstenstraße 13, 10785 Berlin, Germany (office). *E-mail:* office@kasperkoenig.com (office).

KONISHI, Masakazu (Mark), PhD; American (b. Japanese) neurobiologist and academic; *Bing Professor of Behavioral Biology, California Institute of Technology;* b. 17 Feb. 1933, Kyoto, Japan; ed Hokkaido Univ., Univ. of California, Berkeley; held posts at Univ. of Tubingen and Max-Planck Inst., Germany, Univ. of Wisconsin and Princeton Univ., USA; Prof. of Biology, Calif. Inst. of Tech. 1975–80, Bing Prof. of Behavioral Biology 1980–; Coues Award 1983, Dana Award 1992, inaugural Edward M. Scolnick Prize in Neuroscience Research, McGovern Inst. 2004, Gruber Prize for Neuroscience 2005, and numerous other awards. *Publications include:* The Harvey Lectures: Series 86, 1992 (The Harvey Lectures) (co-author) 1994; numerous articles in scientific journals. *Address:* Division of Biology, 156-29, California Institute of Technology, 1200 East California Boulevard, Pasadena, CA 91125, USA (office). *Telephone:* (626) 395-4951 (office). *Fax:* (626) 449-0756 (office). *E-mail:* konishim@caltech.edu (office). *Website:* biology.caltech.edu/Members/Konishi (office).

KONJANOVSKI, Zoran, BA; Macedonian engineer and politician; *Minister of Defence;* b. 3 March 1967, Bitola; m. Jasmina Konjanovska; two s.; ed Univ. of 'Ss Cyril and Methodius', Skopje; mechanical engineer, JP Streevo, Bitola 1999–2005; mem. Vnatresno-Makedonska Revolucionerna Organizacija-Demokratska Partija za Makedonsko Nacionalno Edinstvo (VMRO-DPMNE) 1993–, mem. Exec. Cttee 2005–; Pres. Municipal Council of Bitola 2005–06; mem. Nat. Ass. 2006–; Minister of Local Self-Govt 2006–07, of Defence 2008–; Dir Gen. REK (Bitola Br.) 2007–08. *Address:* Ministry of Defence, Orce Nikolov bb, Skopje 1000, Former Yugoslav Republic of Macedonia (office). *Telephone:* (2) 3282042 (office). *Fax:* (2) 3282042 (office). *E-mail:* info@morm.gov.mk (office). *Website:* www.morm.gov.mk (office).

KONJEVIĆ, Raško, BA, MA; Montenegrin economist and politician; *Minister of Internal Affairs;* b. 12 April 1979; ed Econs Faculty, Univ. of Montenegro, Podgorica, European Integration School; worked as journalist on daily magazine Vijesti 2000–03; Co-founder and Public Relations Man., Centre for Democratic Transition 2001–04; attended numerous specialized courses in economic science and security, organized by DCAF, as well as in public relations in co-operation with Nat. Democratic Inst., Washington, DC, USA; worked in Office of the Parl. of Montenegro 2003–06; Assoc., 'Introduction in Management', Montenegro Business School 2005–12; Assoc. Prof., School of Econs, Univ. of the Mediterranean 2006–11; mem. Social Democratic Party of Montenegro (SDP) (Socijaldemokratska Partija Crne Gore) Presidency 2007–, Vice-Pres. SDP 2009–12; Chief of Cabinet of Pres. of Parl. 2006–08; mem. Parl. 2009–12, Leader of SDP Parl. Group, mem. Security and Defence Cttee, Economy, Finances and Budget Cttee, Int. Co-operation and European Integration Cttee, EU-Montenegro Stabilization and Asscn Parl. Cttee; Pres. Capital City Ass. 2010–11; Minister of the Interior 2012–; mem. Bd of Dirs Budvanska rivijera 2007–11. *Address:* Ministry of Internal Affairs, 81000

Podgorica, bul. Svetog Petra Cetinjskog 22, Montenegro (office). *Telephone:* (20) 241590 (office). *Fax:* (20) 246779 (office). *E-mail:* kabinet@mup.gov.me (office). *Website:* www.mup.gov.me (office).

KONNEH, Amara Mohamed, BSc, MPA; Liberian politician; *Minister of Finance;* b. Balla Bassa, Gbamah Dist; s. of Majumah Konneh and Mamadee Konneh; m. Hawah Konneh; four c.; ed Monrovia Coll., Drexel Univ., Pennsylvania State Univ., John F. Kennedy School of Govt, Harvard Univ., USA; refugee in Guinea aged 18; Educ. Coordinator for Liberian and Sierra Leonean refugee schools, Guinea Forest Region 1991–93; worked for more than 10 years with devt foundations and as policy, financial systems analyst and project man. with Vanguard Group of Investment Cos, USA; returned to Liberia, becoming Deputy Chief of Staff to Pres. Ellen Johnson-Sirleaf for Policy and Communications –2008; Minister of Planning and Econ. Affairs 2008, of Finance 2012–, serves as Alt. Gov., African Devt Bank and World Bank; Chair. Mano River Union Ministerial Council. *Address:* Ministry of Finance, Broad Street, POB 10-9013, 1000 Monrovia 10s, Liberia (office). *Telephone:* 47510680 (mobile) (office). *Website:* www.mof.gov.lr (office).

KONO, Masaharu; Japanese diplomatist; m.; ed Faculty of Law, Univ. of Tokyo; joined Ministry of Foreign Affairs 1973, has held various positions including Chief of First Div. of N America Dept, Minister, Embassy in London, Embassy in Washington, DC, Deputy Dir-Gen. Asia Dept, Deputy Dir-Gen. N America and the Department of Foreign Policy Planning, Consul Gen. in Los Angeles; Asst Sec. of the Cabinet 1991–93; Dir-Gen. for Sub-Saharan Africa 2003–05; Dir-Gen. Dept of Foreign Policy Planning 2005–07; Deputy Foreign Minister 2007–09; Amb. to Russia (also accred to Belarus and Armenia) 2009–11. *Address:* c/o Embassy of Japan, 125009 Moscow, Kalashnyi per. 12, Russia.

KONO, Yohei; Japanese politician; b. 15 Jan. 1937; s. of Ichiro Kono; ed Waseda Univ., Stanford Univ.; began career with Marubeni Co.; mem. House of Reps from Kanagawa; fmr Parl. Vice-Minister of Educ., Dir-Gen. Science and Tech. Agency; Chief Cabinet Sec. (State Minister) 1992–93; Chair. LDP Research Comm. on Foreign Affairs, Pres. 1993–99; Deputy Prime Minister and Minister of Foreign Affairs 1994–96, Minister of Foreign Affairs 1999–2001; Speaker, House of Reps 2003–09; left LDP to co-found New Liberal Club (now defunct) 1976–86; mem. Miyazawa faction of LDP; Pres. Japan Asscn of Athletics Federations 1999–. *Address:* Liberal Democratic Party (Jiyu-Minshuto), 1-11-23, Nagata-cho, Chiyoda-ku, Tokyo 100-8910, Japan. *Telephone:* (3) 3581-6211. *E-mail:* koho@ldp .jimin.or.jp (office). *Website:* www.jimin.jp (office); www.jaaf.or.jp/fan.

KONOÉ, Tadateru, BA; Japanese international organization official; *President, International Federation of Red Cross and Red Crescent Societies;* b. 8 May 1939, brother of fmr Prime Minister Morihiro Hosokawa; m. Yasuko Konoe 1966; one s.; ed Gakushuin Univ., Tokyo, London School of Econs, UK; joined Japanese Red Cross Soc. as volunteer 1964, Dir Int. Dept 1964–72, Dir-Gen. Int. Dept 1976–81, Dir Social Dept 1985–88, Dir-Gen. 1988, Vice-Pres. Japanese Red Cross Soc. 1991–2005, Pres. 2005–; seconded to Secr., Int. Fed. of Red Cross and Red Crescent Socs (IFRC), Geneva, Switzerland 1972, becoming officer, IFRC Disaster Preparedness Bureau 1972–75, Dir 1981–85, mem. IFRC Finance Comm. 1985–93, 2003–, mem. Standing Comm. 1995–2003, mem. Governing Bd 2001–05, Vice Pres. IFRC 2005–09, Pres. 2009–; Councillor, Japan Cttee for UNICEF; Adviser, Japan Campaign to Ban Landmines, Japan Center for Conflict Prevention. *Address:* International Federation of Red Cross and Red Crescent Societies, 17 Chemin des Créts, Petit-Saconnex, CP 372, 1211 Geneva 19, Switzerland (office). *Telephone:* (22) 7304333 (office). *Fax:* (22) 7330395 (office). *E-mail:* secretariat@ifrc.org (office). *Website:* www.ifrc.org (office); tadateru-konoe.com.

KONOVALOV, Aleksander Nikolayevich, MD; Russian neurosurgeon; *Director, N. N. Burdenko Institute of Neurosurgery, Russian Academy of Medical Sciences;* b. 12 Dec. 1933, Moscow; s. of Nikolai Konovalov and Ekaterina Konovalova; m. Inna Konovalova 1957, one s.; ed First Moscow Medical Inst.; intern, researcher, Deputy Dir N. N. Burdenko Research Inst. of Neurosurgery 1957–75, Dir 1975–; mem. Russian Acad. of Medical Sciences 1992, Russian Acad. of Sciences 2000; Pres. Asscn of Neurosurgeons of Russia 2003–; conducted unique operation on separation of the heads of Siamese twins 1989; Ed.-in-Chief Voprosi Neurochirurgii; Orden Druzba Narodov; USSR and Russian Fed. State Prizes. *Publications:* more than 215 works on problems of surgery. *Leisure interests:* tennis, skiing. *Address:* N. N. Burdenko Institute of Neurosurgery, 16 4th Tverskaya Yamskaya str, 125047 Moscow (office); Novoslobodskaya str. 57/65, Apt. 33, 127057 Moscow, Russia (home). *Telephone:* (495) 251-65-26 (office); (499) 978-76-18 (home). *Fax:* (495) 250-93-51 (office); (495) 975-22-28. *E-mail:* akonovalov@nsi.ru (office). *Website:* www.nsi.ru (office).

KONOVALOV, Aleksandr Vladimirovich, PhD; Russian lawyer and government official; *Minister of Justice;* b. 19 June 1968, Leningrad (now St Petersburg); ed Law Faculty, Leningrad State Univ.; served in USSR Army 1986–88; joined St Petersburg Prosecutor's Office 1992, positions included Asst to Prosecutor of Vyborg Dist 1992, Investigator, Vyborg Dist Office 1992–94, Prosecutor, Fed. Security Law Enforcement Supervision Dept 1994–97, Deputy Prosecutor of Moskovskii Dist 1997–98, Prosecutor of Moskovskii Dist 1998–2001, First Deputy Prosecutor, St Petersburg 2001–05; Prosecutor, Repub. of Bashkortostan 2005; Presidential Envoy to Volga Fed. Dist 2005–08; Minister of Justice 2008–; fmr mem. Security Council of Russian Fed. *Address:* Ministry of Justice, 119991 Moscow, ul. Zhitnaya 14, Russia (office). *Telephone:* (495) 955-59-99 (office). *Fax:* (495) 955-57-79 (office); (495) 916-29-03 (office). *E-mail:* pst@minjust.ru (office); pr@minjust.ru (office). *Website:* www.minjust.ru (office).

KONRÁD, György; Hungarian novelist and essayist; b. 2 April 1933, Berettyóújfalu, nr Debrecen; s. of József Konrád and Róza Klein; m. Judit Lakner; three s. two d.; ed Debrecen Reform Coll., Madách Gymnasium, Budapest, Eötvös Loránd Univ., Budapest; teacher at general gymnasium in Csepel; Ed. Életképek 1956; social worker, Budapest 7th Dist Council 1959–65; Ed. Magyar Helikon 1960–66; urban sociologist on staff of City Planning Research Inst. 1965–73; full-time writer 1973–; Pres. Akad. der Künste Berlin-Brandenburg 1997; Visiting Prof. of Comparative Literature, Colorado Springs Coll. 1988; Corresp. mem. Bayerische Akad., Munich; fmr Pres. Int. PEN; Herder Prize, Vienna-Hamburg 1984, Charles Veillon European Essay, Zürich 1985, Fredfonden Peace Foundation, Copenhagen 1986, Fed. Critics' Prize for Novel of the Year (FRG) 1986,

Maecenas Prize 1989, Manès-Sperber Prize 1990, Kossuth Prize, Friedens-Preis des Deutschen Buchhandels 1991, Karlspreis zu Aachen 2001; numerous scholarships. *Publications include:* novels: A látogató (The Case Worker) 1969, A városlapító (The City Builder) 1977, A cinkos (The Loser) 1982, Kerti mulatság (Feast in the Garden) (Vol. 1 of trilogy Agenda) 1989, Kóóra (Stone Dial) (Vol. 2 of Agenda) 1995; essays: Új lakótelepek szociológiai problémái 1969, Az értelmiség utja az osztályhatalomhoz (The Intellectuals on the Road to Class Power) 1978, Az autonómia kisértése (The Temptation of Autonomy) 1980, Antipolitics 1986, Esszék 91–93 (Essays 1991–93) 1993, The Melancholy of Rebirth 1995, Várakozás (Expectation) 1995, Aramló leltár 1996, Láthatatlan hang (The Invisible Voice: Meditations on Jewish Themes) 2000. *Address:* Torockó utca 3, 1026 Budapest, Hungary. *Telephone:* (1) 560-425.

KONROTE, Maj.-Gen. Jioji (George); Fijian politician, diplomatist and retd army officer; *Minister of State for Immigration and Ex-Servicemen;* served in Fijian Armed Forces; Force Commdr UNFIL Peace-keeping Force, Lebanon 1999; Perm. Sec. for Home Affairs 2001; High Commr to Australia 2001–06; mem. Parl. representing Rotuman Communal Constituency 2006–; Minister of State for Immigration and Ex-Servicemen 2006–. *Address:* Office of the Minister of State for Immigration and Ex-Servicemen, New Wing, Govt Bldgs, PO Box 2349, Suva, Fiji (office). *Telephone:* 3211754 (office). *Fax:* 3300346 (office). *E-mail:* infohomaff@ govnet.gov.fj (office). *Website:* www.parliament.gov.fj (office).

KONSTANTINOV, Boris A., Dr Med.; Russian cardiac surgeon; *Director, Scientific Centre of Surgery, Russian Academy of Medical Sciences;* b. Moscow; m.; three s.; ed Moscow Sechenov Med. Inst.; head of division, Research Centre for Surgery (now Scientific Centre of Surgery), Russian Acad. of Medical Sciences 1968–88, Dir 1988–; mem. Presidium Pirogov Assoc. of Surgeons, Inst. Soc. of Cardiovascular Surgeons, European Acad. of Cardiac Surgeons, Russian Acad. of Medical Sciences; two State Prizes; two Orders of Friendship of People. *Publications include:* over 300 scientific papers on heart transplants and eight monographs, including Diseases in Early Age Children 1970, Physiological and Clinical Fundamentals of Surgical Cardiology 1981. *Address:* Scientific Centre of Surgery, Russian Academy of Medical Sciences, Moscow 119879, Abrikosovsky per. 2, Russia (office). *Telephone:* (495) 246-95-63 (office). *E-mail:* admin@med.ru (office). *Website:* www.med.ru (office).

KONTSEVICH, Maxim, PhD; Russian/French mathematician and academic; *Resident Professor, Institut des Hautes Études Scientifiques;* b. 25 Aug. 1964, Khimki, Russia; ed Moscow Univ. and Univ. of Bonn, Germany; began research at Inst. for Problems of Information Processing, Russian Acad. of Sciences, Moscow; held positions at Univ. of Bonn –1994 and Harvard Univ. and Inst. for Advanced Studies, Princeton, USA; Prof., Univ. of California, Berkeley 1993–95; Resident Prof., Institut des Hautes Études Scientifiques, Bures-sur-Yvette, France 1995–; Visiting Prof., Rutgers Univ., NJ, USA 1997–2002, Univ. of Miami, USA 2007–; mem. Editorial Bd, Compositio Mathematica 1994–, International Mathematical Research Notices 1994–, Publications Mathematiques IHES 1996–, Selecta Mathematica (New Series) 1996–, Letters in Mathematical Physics 1999–, Journal of Noncommutative Geometry 2007–, Communications in Number Theory and Physics 2007–; mem. Academia Europaea 2000, Acad. des sciences 2002; Chevalier, Légion d'honneur 2004; Otto Hahn Prize, Max-Planck Gesellschaft, Bonn 1992, Prix de la mairie de Paris 1992, Prix Iagolnitzer, Int. Asscn of Math. Physics 1997, Fields Medal, 23th Int. Congress of Mathematicians, Berlin (jtly) 1998, Crafoord Prize (jtly) 2008, Shaw Prize 2012, Fundamental Physics Prize 2012. *Publications:* more than 50 articles in math. journals on various problems in geometry and algebra, often related to string theory and quantum field theory. *Address:* Institut des Hautes Études Scientifiques, 35 route de Chartres, 91440 Bures-sur-Yvette, France (office). *Telephone:* 1-60-92-66-00 (office). *Fax:* 1-60-92-66-09 (office). *E-mail:* maxim@ihes.fr (office). *Website:* www.ihes.fr/~maxim (office).

KONUK, Nejat; Turkish-Cypriot politician, lawyer and writer; b. 1928, Nicosia; ed Turkish Lycée, Cyprus and Law Faculty of Ankara Univ., Turkey; Legal Adviser in Turkish Civil Service, Turkey; Sec.-Gen. and Acting Dir-Gen. of Turkish Communal Chamber, Cyprus; Under-Sec. to Rauf Denktaş 1968–69; Minister of Justice and Internal Affairs, Turkish Cypriot Admin. 1969–75; mem. for Nicosia, Turkish Communal Chamber, Constituent Ass., Turkish Cypriot Leg. Ass. 1970–; Co-founder Nat. Unity Party 1975, Leader 1976–78; Prime Minister 'Turkish Federated State of Cyprus' 1976–78; Leader of the Democratic People's Party 1979–82 (resgnd); Pres. Legis. Ass. 'Turkish Federated State of Cyprus' July–Dec. 1981, 1982–83; Prime Minister 'Turkish Repub. of N Cyprus' 1983–85. *Publications:* essays on literature, various papers on Cyprus, political articles 1953–77. *Leisure interests:* reading, swimming. *Address:* Kumsal, Lefkoşa, (Nicosia), Mersin 10, Turkey.

KONUMA, Michiji, DS; Japanese physicist and academic; *Trustee, Kanagawa Dental College;* b. 25 Jan. 1931, Tokyo; s. of Haruo Konuma and Taka Konuma; m. Masae Shinohara 1960; one s. one d.; ed Musashi High School and Univ. of Tokyo; Research Assoc. Univ. of Tokyo 1958–67 (leave of absence 1963–67); Research Fellow, Consiglio Nazionale Ricerche, Italy and Visiting Prof. Scuola Normale Superiore, Pisa 1963–65; Visiting Prof., Catholic Univ. of Louvain, Belgium 1965–67; Assoc. Prof., Kyoto Univ. 1967–83; Prof., Keio Univ. 1983–96, Prof. Emer. 1996–; Prof. and Dean, Faculty of Environmental and Information Studies, Musashi Inst. of Tech., Yokohama 1996–2001, Adviser 2001–03, Prof. Emer. 2005–; Trustee, Kanagawa Dental Coll. 2009–; Visiting Prof., Univ. of the Air 1992–2001; Visiting Researcher, Int. Peace Research Inst., Meiji Gakuin Univ., Tokyo 2004–; Chair. Special Cttee of Nuclear Physics, Science Council of Japan 1969–72; Assoc. Ed. Progress of Theoretical Physics 1976–84; Ed. Bulletin of the Physical Society of Japan 1986–87; mem. Physics Action Council, UNESCO 1994–96; Pres. Physical Soc. of Japan 1987–88, 1991–92, Asscn of Asia Pacific Physical Socs 1994–97 (Special Adviser 2001–07); mem. Council, Pugwash Confs on Science and World Affairs 1992–2002; Dir Tokyu Foundation for Better Environment 2001–; Councillor, Shimonaka Memorial Foundation 2006–08, Dir 2008–; other professional appointments; Hon. mem. Roland Eötvös Physical Soc., Hungary 1997, Hungarian Acad. of Sciences 1998; Soryushi Medal for Distinguished Service 2004. *Publications:* numerous books and articles on theoretical particle physics, history of modern physics, physics educ. and 'Science and Society'.

Address: 200-9 Kudencho, Sakaeku, Yokohama 247-0014, Japan. *Telephone:* (45) 891-8386. *Fax:* (45) 891-8386. *E-mail:* mkonuma254@m4.dion.ne.jp.

KONWAR, Devanand, BA, MA, LLB; Indian lawyer and politician; *Governor of Tripura;* s. of the late Padma Kant Konwar; m. Neeva Konwar; ed Cotton Coll., Guwahati, Delhi Univ., Guwahati Univ.; student leader, Nat. Congress Party 1955, various party posts including Gen. Sec. and Vice-Pres. Assam Pradesh Congress Cttee 1982–90; elected to Assam State Ass. 1983, Minister, State Govt of Assam 1991, 2001; fmr Lecturer, English Dept, Cotton Coll., Guwahati, Assam; Marketing Man. American Standard Vacuum Oil Co. (later ESSO-Standard Oil Co.), Mumbai 1961–68; Founding Prin., Guwahati Coll. 1968; called to Guwahati High Court Bar 1969; Advocate, Supreme Court of India 1969–91, also served as Govt Advocate for states of Assam, Tripura, Arunachal Pradesh and Mizoram; elected to Lok Sabha (parl.) for Congress (I) 1978; Gov. Bihar State 2009–13, also of W Bengal Dec. 2009–Jan. 2010, of Tripura 2013–. *Address:* Office of the Governor, Raj Bhavan, Pushpavant Palace, Agartala 799 001, India (office). *Telephone:* (381) 2224091 (office). *Fax:* (381) 2224350 (office). *E-mail:* govtrp@trp.nic.in (office).

KONYUKHOV, Fedor Filippovich; Russian explorer and artist; b. 12 Dec. 1951, Chkalovo, Zaporizhye Region, USSR (now Ukraine); m. Irina Konyukhov; two s. one d.; ed Odessa Navigation Coll., Leningrad Arctic Coll., Kronstadt Marine Higher School, Bobruysk School of Arts; completed solo expedition to North Pole 1989; f. School of Travellers 1991; Head, Lab. for Remote Training under Extreme Conditions, Modern Humanitarian Acad., Moscow 1998–; Plenipotentiary Rep. of UNEP (UN programme on Environmental Protection) 1997–; mem. Russian Union of Artists 1983–, Moscow Union of Artists, Graphic Arts section 1996–, Union of Journalists of Russian Fed., Union of Writers of Russian Fed.; Hon. Citizen Terni, Italy 1991, Taipei, Taiwan 1995, Nakhodka, Russia 1996; Hon. Academician of Russian Arts Acad.; Order of Friendship of Peoples, UNESCO Order; Merited Master of Sports of Russia 1989, Gold Medal of the Russian Arts Acad. *Expeditions include:* North Geographical Pole (3 times), South Geographical Pole, Pole of considerable inaccessibility in Arctic Ocean, Mt. Everest (Alpinists pole), Cape Horn (Yachtsmen pole); within program Seven Summits of the World climbed highest mountains on each continent: Elbrus (Europe/Russia) 1992, Everest (Asia) 1992, Winson Massif (Antarctica) 1996, Aconcagua (South America) 1996, Kilimanjaro (Africa) 1997, Mt. Kosciusko (Australia) 1997, Mt. McKinley (North America) 1997. *Address:* Tourism and Sports Union of Russia, Studeniy proyezd 7, 129282 Moscow, Russia. *Telephone:* (495) 478-63-02 (office). *E-mail:* oscar75@ yandex.ru. *Website:* www.konyukhov.ru/eng.

KOO, Bon-joon, BS, MBA; South Korean business executive; *Vice-Chairman and CEO, LG Electronics;* b. 1951, grandson of In-hwoi Koo, Founder of Lucky GoldStar (now LG); ed Seoul Nat. Univ., Univ. of Chicago Booth School of Business, USA; worked at GoldStar/LG Electronics in a range of business areas including planning and strategy 1986–95, held various exec. roles overseeing semiconductors, PCs, IT and chemicals, cr. and led jt venture LG.Philips LCD (became LG Display 2008) 1999–2004, Vice-Chair. and CEO LG International –2010, Vice-Chair. and CEO LG Electronics 2010–, also Head of Business Innovation Office; Jt Rep. Dir Koninklijke Philips Electronics NV –2007; Gen. Man. LG Twins (Korea Baseball Org.) 1990–. *Address:* LG Electronics, LG Twin Towers, 20 Yoido-dong, Youngdungpo-gu, Seoul, 150-721, Republic of Korea (office). *Telephone:* (2) 3773-1114 (office). *Fax:* (2) 3773-7813 (office). *E-mail:* info@ lg.com (office). *Website:* www.lg.com (office).

KOO, Bon-moo; South Korean business executive; *Chairman and Co-CEO, LG Corporation;* b. 10 Feb. 1945, Kyongsangnam-do Chinju; m.; three c.; ed Yonsei Univ., Ashland Univ., Cleveland State Univ., USA; served in various man. roles at Lucky Co., Ltd 1975–80 including Gen. Man. Export Man. 1979, Gen. Man. 1979–81, Goldstar Electronics Co. Ltd 1981, Dir 1981–85, Man. Dir 1985, Exec. Dir Planning and Man. Office, Lucky Goldstar 1985–89, Vice Pres. Planning and Man. Office 1989, Vice Chair. 1989–95, Chair. Overseas Business Devt Cttee 1993, Vice-Chair. and CEO Goldstar Electronics Co., Ltd 1993, Chair. and CEO LG Corpn (fmrly Lucky Goldstar Group) 1995–2008, Chair. and Co-CEO 2009–, Chair. and CEO LG Chemical Ltd 1998–, LG Electronics Inc. 1998–; CEO LG Evergreen Foundation 1997; Vice-Chair. Fed. of Korean Industries 1989, Chair. Tax Revision Cttee 1999; Owner, LG Twins professional baseball team 1990–. *Leisure interests:* golf, birdwatching. *Address:* LG Corporation, LG Twin Towers, 20 Yoido-dong, Youngdungpo-gu, Seoul 150-721, Republic of Korea (office). *Telephone:* (2) 3773-1114 (office). *Fax:* (2) 3773-7813 (office). *E-mail:* info@lgcorp.com (office). *Website:* www.lgcorp.com (office); www.lg.com (office); www.koobonmoo.pe.kr.

KOO, John, BEcons; South Korean electronics industry executive; *Chairman and CEO, LS Group;* b. 11 Dec. 1946, Jinjoo, Namdo Prov.; ed Kyonggi High School, Princeton Univ., USA; joined LG Int. 1973, Import Section 1973–76, Man., Machinery and Electronics Div. 1976–79, Gen. Man. Hong Kong Office 1979–81, Singapore Office 1982–83, Chief, Singapore Office 1983–87, joined LG Electronics Co. Ltd (fmrly Goldstar Co. Ltd) 1987, Man. Dir Overseas Operations Div. 1987–88, Sr Man. Dir Overseas Operations Div. 1988–91, Vice-Pres. 1991–95, CEO 1994–2003, Pres. 1995–99, Vice-Chair. 1999–2003, Chair. LG Cable Ltd (now LS Cable) 2004–08, Chair. and CEO LS Group 2008–; Chair. Electronic Industries Asscn of Korea (EIAK), Industrial Design Cttee of Fed. of Korean Industries, Electronic Display Industrial Research Asscn; Chair. Zenith Electronics Corpn; Vice-Chair. Korea Industrial Tech. Asscn; mem. Korea Inst. for Industrial Econs and Trade; Iron Tower Order of Industrial Service Merit 1985, Gold Tower Order of Industrial Service Merit 1995. *Address:* Office of the Chairman, LS Group, LS Tower, Hogye-dong, Dongan-gu, Anyang-si, Gyeonggi-do, 431-848, Republic of Korea (office). *Telephone:* (2) 2034-4867 (office). *Website:* www.lsholdings.com/eng (office); www.johnkoo.pe.kr.

KOOGLE, Timothy (Tim) A., BS, MS, DEng; American engineer and business executive; *Chairman, Method Products Inc.;* b. 1952; m. (divorced); ed Univ. of Virginia, Stanford Univ.; several years with Motorola Inc. holding various exec. positions; Pres. Intermec Corpn 1990–95, also Corp. Vice-Pres. Western Atlas Inc. (parent co.); CEO Corpn 1992–99, Chair., CEO Yahoo! Inc. 1995–2001, Vice-Chair. 2001–2003; CEO Friendster 2004; Founder and CEO Serendipity Land Holdings LLC (pvt land development co.), developer of El Banco resort, Punta de Mita, Mexico; Chair. Method Products, Inc., San Francisco; Founder and Man. Dir The Koogle Foundation; mem. Bd of Dirs Room to Read 2010–, Thomas Weisel Pnrs

Group LLC 2006–10; fmr Chair. Bd of Dirs AIM. *Leisure interests:* vintage guitars, cars. *Address:* Office of the Chairman, Method Products Inc., 637 Commercial Street, San Francisco, CA 94111, USA (office). *Telephone:* (415) 931-3947 (office).

KOOLHAAS, Remment (Rem); Dutch architect and academic; *Professor in Practice, Department of Architecture, Graduate School of Design, Harvard University;* b. 1944; ed Architectural Assen, London, UK, Cornell Univ., USA; fmr journalist, Haagse Post, Amsterdam; Co-founder and Prin., Office of Metropolitan Architecture (OMA) 1975–; Prof. of Architecture, Technical Univ., Delft 1988–89; Prof. of Architecture, Rice Univ., Houston, Tex. 1991–92; Arthur Rotch Adjunct Prof. of Architecture, Grad. School of Design, Harvard Univ. 1990–95, Prof. in Practice and Urban Design 1995–, oversees Project on the City; Visiting Scholar, The Getty Center, LA 1993; f. Grosztstadt Foundation; Chevalier, Légion d'honneur 2001; Progressive Architecture Award (jtly) 1974, Le Moniteur, Prix d'Architecture 1991, Antonio Gaudi Prize 1992, Pritzker Prize 2000, Praemium Imperiale 2003, Royal Gold Medal (RIBA) 2004, European Union Prize for Contemporary Architecture 2005, Golden Lion for Lifetime Achievement, Venice Biennale 2010. *Major works include:* China Central Television, Beijing, Milstein Hall, Cornell Univ., Rothschild Bank, London, Wyly Theatre, Dallas, Prada Transformer, Seoul, Serpentine Gallery Pavilion, London, Zeche Zollverein Historical Museum and masterplan, Essen, Seoul Nat. Univ., Museum of Art Casa da Música, Porto Prada Epicenter, Los Angeles Seattle Central Library, Leeum Samsung Museum of Art, Seoul, Netherlands Embassy, Berlin, IIT Campus Center, Chicago. *Exhibitions include:* The Sparkling Metropolis, Guggenheim Museum 1978, OMA 1972–88, ArchitecturMuseum, Basel 1988, OMA: The First Decade, Boymans Museum, Rotterdam 1989, OMA, Museum of Modern Art, New York 1994, Light Construction, Museum of Modern Art, New York 1995. *Publications:* Project Japan: An Oral History of Metabolism, Al Manakh, Al Manakh II, Harvard Design School Guide to Shopping, Great Leap Forward, Delirious New York: A Retroactive Manifesto for Manhattan. *Address:* OMA/AMO Rotterdam, Heer Bokelweg 149, 3032 AD Rotterdam (office); Harvard University Graduate School of Design, 48 Quincy Street, Cambridge, MA 02138, USA (office). *Telephone:* (10) 2438200 (Rotterdam) (office); (617) 495-1000 (Harvard) (office). *Fax:* (10) 2438202 (Rotterdam) (office). *E-mail:* office@oma.com (office); jinaba@gsd.harvard.edu (office). *Website:* www.oma.nl (office); www.gsd.harvard.edu (office).

KOOMPIROCHANA, Vikrom, BA, MA, PhD; Thai diplomatist (retd) and business executive; *Chairman, Dragon One PCL;* m. Sasin Monvoisin; ed Chulalongkorn Univ., Michigan State Univ., USA; Lecturer in History, Faculty of Arts, Chulalongkorn Univ. –1973; joined Ministry of Foreign Affairs in 1973, Amb. to Singapore 1991–95, to Malaysia 1996, to New Zealand 1997–99, Deputy Perm. Sec., Ministry of Foreign Affairs 2000–01, Amb. to Italy 2002, to UK 2003–06 (retd); Chair. Dragon One PLC 2006–; Chair. Audit Cttee, Oishi Group of Cos; Adviser to TCC Holding Co. Ltd, TCC Land Co. Ltd; Hon. Adviser, British Chamber of Commerce Thailand. *Address:* Dragon One PLC, Room 1103, 11th Floor, Q House Lumpini, 1, South Sathon Road, Thung Maha Mek, Sathon, Bangkok 10120, Thailand (office).

KOONS, Jeff; American artist; b. 21 Jan. 1955, York, Pa; m. 1st Ilona Staller (née La Cicciolina) 1991 (divorced 1994); one s.; m. 2nd Justine Wheeler; one s.; ed School of the Art Inst. of Chicago, Maryland Inst. Coll. of Art; fmr commodities broker, New York; Fellow, American Acad. of Arts and Sciences 2005. *Website:* www.jeffkoons.com.

KOONTZ, Dean Ray, (David Axton, Brian Coffey, Deanna Dwyer, K. R. Dwyer, John Hill, Leigh Nichols, Anthony North, Richard Paige, Owen West), BS; American writer; b. 9 July 1945, Everett, PA; s. of Raymond Koontz and Florence Logue; m. Gerda Ann Cerra 1966; ed Shippensburg Univ.; fmr teacher of English; freelance author 1969–; work includes novels, short stories, science fiction/fantasy, social commentary/phenomena and journalism; Hon. DLitt (Shippensburg) 1989. *Publications include:* Star Quest 1968, The Fall of the Dream Machine 1969, Fear That Man 1969, Anti-Man 1970, Beastchild 1970, Dark of the Woods 1970, The Dark Symphony 1970, Hell's Gate 1970, The Crimson Witch 1971, A Darkness in My Soul 1972, The Flesh in the Furnace 1972, Starblood 1972, Time Thieves 1972, Warlock 1972, A Werewolf Among Us 1973, Hanging On 1973, The Haunted Earth 1973, Demon Seed 1973, Strike Deep 1974, After the Last Race 1974, Nightmare Journey 1975, The Long Sleep 1975, Night Chills 1976, The Voice of the Night 1980, Whispers 1980, The Funhouse 1980, The Eyes of Darkness 1981, The Mask 1981, House of Thunder 1982, Phantoms 1983, Darkness Comes 1984, Twilight 1984, The Door to December 1985, Strangers 1986, Shadow Fires 1987, Watchers 1987, Twilight Eyes 1987, Oddkins 1988, Servants of Twilight 1988, Lightning 1988, Midnight 1989, The Bad Place 1990, Cold Fire 1991, Hideaway 1992, Dragon Tears 1992, Winter Moon 1993, The House of Thunder 1993, Dark Rivers of the Heart 1994, Mr Murder 1994, Fun House 1994, Strange Highways 1994, Icebound 1995, Intensity 1995, The Key to Midnight 1995, Ticktock 1996, Santa's Twin 1996, Sole Survivor 1996, Fear Nothing 1997, Seize the Night 1998, False Memory 1999, From the Corner of his Eye 2001, One Door Away From Heaven 2001, By the Light of the Moon 2002, The Face 2003, Odd Thomas 2003, Life Expectancy 2004, Frankenstein Book 1: Prodigal Son (with Kevin J. Anderson) 2004, Frankenstein Book 2: City of Night (with Ed Gorman) 2005, Forever Odd 2005, The Husband 2006, Brother Odd 2006, The Good Guy 2007, The Darkest Evening of the Year 2007, Odd Hours 2008, Bliss to You 2008, In Odd We Trust 2008, Shadowfires 2008, The Bad Place 2008, Your Heart Belongs to Me 2008, Relentless 2009, Frankenstein Book 3: Dead and Alive 2009, Breathless 2009, A Big Little Life 2009, Frankenstein Book 4: Lost Souls 2010, Odd is On Our Side 2010, Darkness Under the Sun 2010, What the Night Knows 2011, Frankenstein Book 5: The Dead Town 2011, The Moonlit Mind 2011, 77 Shadow Street 2011, House of Odd 2012, Odd Apocalypse 2012, Odd Interlude #1–#3 2012. *Address:* POB 9529, Newport Beach, CA 92658, USA (office). *E-mail:* dean@deankoontz.com (office). *Website:* www.deankoontz.com.

KOOPMAN, Antonius (Ton) Gerhardus Michael; Dutch musician, academic and conductor; *Professor of Harpsichord, Royal Conservatory, The Hague;* b. 2 Oct. 1944, Zwolle; m. Christine H. H. Mathot 1975; three d.; ed Amsterdam Conservatory and Univ. of Amsterdam; Prof. of Harpsichord, Royal Conservatory, The Hague; f. Amsterdam Baroque Orchestra 1979, Amsterdam Baroque Choir 1992; appears on concert platforms around the world and on radio and TV; has made over

200 recordings of harpsichord and organ works by Bach, Handel, others; f. Antoine Marchand record label (sub-label of Challenge Classics); Hon. mem. RAM, London; Dr hc (Utrecht) 2000; winner of several prizes. *Publications:* Interpretation of Baroque Music 1985 and a small book about J. S. Bach 1985; The Harpsichord in Dutch Paintings (co-), The World of the Bach Cantatas (co-ed with Christoph Wolff) 1996. *Leisure interests:* art and culture of the Renaissance and Baroque period. *Address:* Meerweg 23, 1405 BC Bussum, Netherlands. *Telephone:* (35) 6913676. *Fax:* (35) 6939752. *E-mail:* ton.koopman@wxs.nl (office). *Website:* www.tonkoopman.com (office).

KOOPMANS, Lense; Dutch banking executive; b. 17 June 1943; Prof. Emer., Univ. of Groningen; mem. Bd of Dirs Rabobank Nederland 1996–2002, mem. Supervisory Bd 2002–13, Chair. 2007–13; Chair. Stichting TBI; Chair. Supervisory Bd Burgfonds BV –2004, Siers Groep BV, Arriva Nederland BV, TSS BV; Vice-Chair. Supervisory Bd KIWA NV; mem. Bd Dirs Stichting Administratiekantoor Unilever NV; mem. Supervisory Bd, Eureko BV 2005–09, NOM NV 2009–; Chair. Bd of Supervision Fries Museum en Princessehof; Vice-Chair. Bd of Supervision, Univ. Medical Centre, Groningen; mem. Bd of Supervision Stichting TNO. *Address:* c/o Rabobank Group, Postbus 17100, Croeselaan 18, 3500 HG Utrecht, Netherlands. *E-mail:* info@rabobank.com.

KÖÖRNA, Arno, PhD; Estonian economist and academic; *Professor Emeritus, Eurouniversity, Tallinn;* b. 2 Feb. 1926, Tartu; s. of Artur Köörna and Anna Köörna; m. Eha Lind 1946; two c.; ed Univ. of Tartu; Lecturer, Tartu Univ. 1953–65, Prof. 1971; Scientific Dir Inst. of Econs, Estonian Acad. of Sciences 1965–66, Dir 1966–73; Prof., Eurouniversity, Tallinn, Prof. Emer. 2005–; Corresp. mem. Estonian Acad. of Sciences 1972, mem. 1975; Chief Scientific Sec., Presidium of Estonian Acad. of Sciences 1973–82, Vice-Pres. 1978–82, Pres. 1990–94. *Publications:* Science in Estonia 1993, Introduction to the Theory of Innovation 1997, In the Service of Prometheus 2002. *Address:* Kapi 9-22, 10136 Tallinn, Estonia. *E-mail:* arno.koorna@mail.ee.

KOOSER, Theodore (Ted), BS, MA; American poet and writer; b. 25 April 1939, Ames, Ia; m. 1st Diana Tresslar 1962 (divorced 1969); one s.; m. 2nd Kathleen Rutledge 1977; ed Iowa State Univ., Univ. of Nebraska; Underwriter, Bankers Life Nebraska 1965–73; part-time instructor in creative writing 1970–, Sr Underwriter, Lincoln Benefit Life 1973–84, Vice-Pres. 1984–98; currently Prof., Univ. of Neb., Lincoln; Ed. and Publr, Windflower Press; Poet Laureate of the USA 2004–06; John H. Vreeland Award for Creative Writing 1964, Prairier Schooner Prizes in Poetry 1976, 1978, NEA Literary Fellowships 1976, 1984, Columbia Magazine Stanley Kunitz Poetry Prize 1984, Governor's Arts Award 1988, Mayor's Arts Award 1989, Poetry Northwest Richard Hugo Prize 1994, Nebraska Arts Council Merit Award 2000, Pushcart Prize, James Boatwright Prize. *Publications include:* Official Entry Blank 1969, Grass County 1971, A Local Habitation and a Name 1974, Shooting a Farmhouse: So This is Nebraska 1975, Not Coming to be Barked At 1976, Voyages to the Inland Sea (with Harley Elliott) 1976, Hatcher 1978, Old Marriage and New 1978, Cottonwood County (with William Kloefkorn) 1979, Windflower Home Almanac of Poetry (ed.) 1980, Sure Signs: New and Selected Poems (Soc. of Midland Authors Poetry Prize) 1980, One World at a Time 1985, As Far as I Can See: Contemporary Writers of the Middle Plains (ed.) 1989, Etudes 1992, Weather Central 1994, A Book of Things 1995, A Decade of Ted Kooser Valentines 1996, Riding with Colonel Carter 1999, Winter Morning Walks: 100 Postcards to Jim Harrison (Nebraska Book Award for poetry 2001) 2000, Braided Creek: A Conversation in Poetry (with Jim Harrison) 2003, Local Wonders: Seasons in the Bohemian Alps (Friends of American Writers Chicago Award, ForeWord Magazine Gold Award for Autobiography, Nebraska Book Award for Nonfiction 2003) 2002, Delights and Shadows (Pulitzer Prize for Poetry 2005) 2004, The Poetry Home Repair Manual 2004, Flying at Night: Poems 1965–1985 2005, Valentines 2008, House Held Up by Trees 2012; contrib. to The American Poetry Review, Antioch Review, Cream City Review, The Hudson Review, Kansas Quarterly, The Kenyon Review, Midwest Quarterly, The New Yorker, Poetry Northwest, Poetry, Prairie Schooner, Shenandoah, Tailwind. *Website:* www.blueflowerarts.com (office); www.tedkooser.net (home). *Address:* 1820 Branched Oak Road, Garland, NE 68360-9303, USA (home). *E-mail:* kr84428@windstream.net (home).

KOPELSON, Arnold, BS, JD; American film producer; *Co-Chairman and CEO, Kopelson Entertainment;* b. 14 Feb. 1935, New York; m. Anne Kopelson; ed New York Univ., New York Law School; with Anne Kopelson exec. producer, producer, packager, developer and distributor of over 100 films; Co-Chair. and CEO Kopelson Entertainment; mem. Bd of Dirs CBS Corpn 2007–; Variety Showbiz Expo Hall of Fame 1986, NATO/ShoWest Producer of the Year 1994, Cinema Expo Int. Lifetime Achievement in Film-making Award, Nat. Assen of Theater Owners Producer of the Year Award, Publicists Guild of America Motion Picture Showmanship Award, New York Law School Distinguished Alumnus Award for Lifetime Achievement. *Television:* series: The Fugitive 2000, Thieves 2001. *Films produced:* Lost and Found (exec. producer) 1979, The Legacy (exec. producer) 1979, Night of the Juggler (exec. producer) 1980, Foolin' Around 1980, Final Assignment (exec. producer) 1980, Dirty Tricks (exec. producer) 1981, Platoon 1986 (Acad. Award for Best Picture), Warlock (exec. producer and int. distributor) 1989, Triumph of the Spirit 1989, Fire Birds (exec. producer) 1990, Out for Justice 1991, Falling Down 1993, The Fugitive 1993, Outbreak 1995, Seven 1995, Eraser 1996, Murder at 1600 1997, Mad City 1997, The Devil's Advocate 1997, U.S. Marshals 1998, Perfect Murder 1998, Don't Say a Word 2001, Joe Somebody 2001, Twisted 2004. *TV film:* Past Tense. *Address:* Kopelson Entertainment, 15335 Morrison Street, #375, Sherman Oaks, CA 91403-1587, USA (office). *Telephone:* (818) 817-2610 (office).

KOPETZ, Hermann, PhD; Austrian physicist and academic; *Professor of Real-Time Systems, Vienna University of Technology;* ed Univ. of Vienna; fmr man. of computer process control dept at Voest Alpine, Linz; Prof. of Computer Process Control, Tech. Univ. of Berlin 1978–82; Prof. of Real-Time Systems, Vienna Univ. of Tech. 1982–; Dir Max Planck Inst., Saarbrücken, Germany 1993; Visiting Prof., Univ. of California, Irvine and Santa Barbara several times; organizer of numerous int. confs; Chair. IEEE Tech. Cttee on Fault-Tolerant Computing 1990–92, Int. Fed. for Information Processing Working Group 10.4 on Dependable Computing and Fault-Tolerance 1996–; Fellow, IEEE 1993; Wilhelm Exner Medal, Austrian Assen for SME (Oesterreichischer Gewerbeverein—OGV) (jtly) 2005.

Achievements include: chief architect of Time-Triggered Protocol (TTP) for distributed fault-tolerant real-time systems, which evolved out of the MARS project at Tech. Univ. of Vienna. *Publications include:* more than 100 papers and patents in the fields of real-time computing, distributed computing and fault tolerance. *Address:* Institut für Technische Informatik, Abteilung für Echtzeitsysteme und Softwaretechnologie, Treitlstraße 3/3/182-1, 1040 Vienna, Austria (office). *Telephone:* (1) 58801-18210 (office). *Fax:* (1) 58801-18299 (office). *E-mail:* hk@vmars.tuwien.ac.at (office). *Website:* www.vmars.tuwien.ac.at (office).

KOPONEN, Harri; Finnish telecommunications industry executive; *CEO and General Manager, Wataniya Telecom;* b. 6 Dec. 1962, Lahti; s. of Onni Koponen and Aili Ikonen; m.; four c.; ed Commercial Coll. of Turku, Helsinki Univ., Helsinki School of Econs; fmr Educ. Officer, Finnish Defence Force; fmr Office Man. Oy Shell AB; fmr Head Telecom Sales, Hewlett-Packard; Global Account Exec., Ericsson, Exec. Vice-Pres. and Gen. Man. Ericsson Consumer Products in Americas, Man. Dir SonyEricsson Americas; Pres. and CEO Sonera, then Deputy CEO TeliaSonera and Head, TeliaSonera International (after merger of Swedish Telia and Sonera) 2002–04; CEO and Gen. Man. Wataniya Telecom, Kuwait 2005–; Defence Cross of Finland; Hon. PhD. *Achievement:* European Champion in American Football 1985. *Leisure interests:* hockey, golf, coaching. *Address:* Wataniya Telecom, PO Box 613, Safat 13007, Kuwait (office). *Telephone:* (965) 805555 (office). *Fax:* (965) 2441967 (office). *E-mail:* harri@wataniya.com (office). *Website:* www.wataniya.com (office).

KOPPEL, Ted, MA; American journalist and broadcaster; b. 8 Feb. 1940, Lancs., England; m. Grace A. Dorney; four c.; ed Syracuse and Stanford Univs; went to USA 1953; news corresp., writer, WMCA, New York 1963; with ABC (American Broadcasting Corpn) News 1963, fmr news corresp. Vietnam; Chief, Miami Bureau, ABC News; Chief, Hong Kong Bureau; diplomatic corresp. Hong Kong Bureau, ABC News, Washington; anchorman, ABC News Nightline 1980–2005, Ed. Man. 1980–2005; Man. Ed., Discovery Channel US 2005–08; corresp. for ABC TV specials including The People of People's China 1973, Kissinger: Action Biography 1974, Second to None 1979, The Koppel Reports 1988–90; co-author with Marvin Kalb, TV special: In the National Interest (Overseas Press Club Award); numerous awards. *Publications:* The Wit and Wisdom of Adlai Stevenson 1985, In The National Interest 1977, Nightline: History In the Making 1996. *Address:* c/o Discovery Channel, Discovery Communications Inc., 1 Discovery Place, Silver Spring, MD 20910, USA (office).

KOPPER, Hilmar; German business executive; b. 13 March 1935, Oslanin, West Prussia; m. Brigitte Seebacher-Brandt 2003; CEO Deutsche Bank AG 1989–97, Chair. Supervisory Bd 1997–99; Chair. Supervisory Bd Daimler-Benz AG (DaimlerChrysler then Daimler AG), Stuttgart 1990–2007; Chair. Supervisory Bd Lincas GmbH, Hamburg; Chair. Supervisory Bd HSH Nordbank AG 2009–13; mem. Supervisory Bd Akzo, Arnhem, Netherlands, Bayer AG, Leverkusen, Deutsche Lufthansa AG, Cologne, Deutsche Bank, Frankfurt, Mannesmann AG, Düsseldorf, Municher Rückversicherungs-Gesellschaft, Munich, VEBA AG, Düsseldorf; Chair. Advisory Bd Brauerei Beck & Co., Bremen, Frowein GmbH & Co. KG, Wuppertal, Leopold Kostal GmbH & Co. KG, Lüdenscheid; mem. Advisory Bd Solvay & Cie SA, Brussels; fmr Deputy Chair. Morgan Grenfell Group PLC, London; Chair. Freunden und Förderern der Johann Wolfgang Goethe-Universität Frankfurt am Main eV 2001–10; Hon. Senator, Johann Wolfgang Goethe-Universität Frankfurt am Main eV 2010– Distinguished Leadership Award, International Management Development Institute 2005. *Leisure interests:* reading, collecting the wrappings that encase citrus fruits in greengrocers' shops.

KOPTEV, Yuri Nikolayevich, Cand Tech Sc; Russian engineer and manager; b. 13 March 1940, Stavropol; m.; two s.; ed Bauman Higher Tech. School; worked as engineer for Lavochkin Science-Tech. Corpn 1965–69; author of a number of spacerocket projects; Sr Engineer, Head of Dept, then Deputy Minister, Ministry of Gen. Machine Construction 1969–91; Vice-Pres. Rosobshchemash Corpn 1991–92; Dir-Gen. Russian Space Agency 1992–99, Russian Aviation and Space Agency 1999–2004; Chair. Tupolev Corpn 1999–; Co-Chair. Space Cttee Russian-American Comm. for Econ. and Tech. Co-operation 1993–; Prof., Bauman Moscow State Tech. Univ.; mem. Tsiolkovsky Acad. of Cosmonautics and Presidium, Cosmonautics Fed. of Russia and Presidium, Int. Acad. of Eng; three state prizes 1997, 1993, 1999, four state awards. *Address:* c/o Russian Aviation and Space Agency, 129857 Moscow, 42 Shchepkina str., Russia (office).

KORALEK, Paul George, CBE, RA, RIBA; British architect (retd); b. 7 April 1933, Vienna, Austria; s. of the late Ernest Koralek and Alice Koralek (née Müller); m. (Audrey) Jennifer Koralek 1956; one s. two d.; ed Aldenham, Architectural Asscn; Partner and Dir Ahrends, Burton & Koralek, Architects (now ABK Architects) 1961–2009 (retd); Fellow, Royal Inst. of the Architects of Ireland; Winner Int. Competition for New Library, Trinity Coll., Dublin 1961, Competition for Nat. Gallery Extension 1982–85, Int. Competition for Devt Plan, Grenoble Univ. 1991, RIBA Architecture Award 1978, 1996, 1999, RIBA Housing Award 1977, Structural Steel Design Award 1976, 1980, 1985, Financial Times Award 1976 (Commendation 1986, 1987), Civic Trust Award 1986, 1992, Royal Inst. of the Architects of Ireland Award 1999. *Buildings include:* new British Embassy, Moscow 1999; Docklands Light Railway Extension Stations; Templeton Coll., Oxford 1969, Nebenzahl House, Jerusalem 1972, Warehouse and Showroom for Habitat, Wallingford 1974, residential bldg for Keble Coll., Oxford 1976, Arts Faculty bldg, Trinity Coll. Dublin 1979, factory for Cummins Engines, Shotts 1983, supermarket, J. Sainsbury, Canterbury 1984, Retail HQ, W.H. Smith, Swindon 1985, 1995, dept store John Lewis, Kingston 1990, St Mary's Hosp., Newport, Isle of Wight 1990, White Cliffs Heritage Centre, Dover 1991, Dublin Dental Hosp. 1998–, Techniquest Science Discovery Centre, Cardiff 1995, Insts of Tech. Tralee, Waterford, Blanchardstown 2002–, Offaly Co. Council HQ 2002, Tipperary N Riding County Offices 2000–, Convent Lands Devt Plan, Dublin 2000–, Trinity Coll. Dublin Arts Faculty extension 2002, Galway Co. Council offices extension, new library and HQ 2002, housing at Newcastle West, Co. Limerick 2004, John Wheatley Coll., Glasgow 2005. *Publications include:* Ahrends, Burton & Koralek 1991, Collaborations – The Architecture of ABK 2002. *Address:* c/o ABK Architects Dublin, 34 Lower Leeson Street, Dublin 2, Ireland (office).

KORASEV, Vladislav Borisovich; Kazakhstani politician; *Secretary, Central Committee, Communist People's Party of Kazakhstan;* b. 16 Nov. 1937, Volodarskoye, Kokshetau Oblast, Kazakh SSR, USSR; ed Omsk Agricultural Institute, Higher Party School of the Central Committee of the Communist Party; joined CP of the Soviet Union 1958; worked as a tractor driver on the Borovsk state farm in Rusayevsk region of Kokshetau Oblast; served in Soviet army for three years; began working as sec. of Borovsk state farm's Komsomol (Communist Youth League) 1959–61, Sec. of Party Cttee at Michurinskiy, Volodarskiy and Chervonnyy state farms 1961–70; Instructor, Oblast Cttee 1968–70; first Sec. Kokshetau Oblast Komsomol 1970–73, first Sec. Leninskiy regional Party Cttee 1973–80; Chair. Kokshetau Oblast Union of Agricultural Workers 1980–90, Kokshetau Oblast Council of Labour Unions 1990–97; Deputy of the Majlis (Parl.) 1999–2004, Sec. Cttee on Int. Affairs, Defence and Security; Sec. Cen. Cttee, Communist People's Party of Kazakhstan (Kazakstan Kommunistik Khalyk Partiyasy) 2004–. *Address:* Communist People's Party of Kazakhstan (Kazakstan Kommunistik Khalyk Partiyasy), 010000 Astana, Karasai batyr 14/7, Kazakhstan (office). *Telephone:* (7172) 24-06-09 (office). *E-mail:* knpkastana@gmail.com (office). *Website:* www.knpk.kz (office); www.parlam.kz/kk/mazhilis (office).

KÖRBER, Hans-Joachim; German retail executive; ed Tech. Univ. of Berlin; Sr Controller, Beverages Div., R.A. Oetker 1974–80; worked for Söhnlein Rheingold 1980–85; mem. Man. Bd, Metro SB-Grossmarkle 1985–91; mem. Exec. Bd, Chair. and CEO, Metro AG 1999–2007; Dir Skandinaviska Enskilda Banken AB 2000–, Sysco Corpn; Dir (non-exec.) Air Berlin PLC 2006–, Esprit Holdings Ltd 2008–; mem. Supervisory Bd Bertelsmann AG 2004; mem. Global Advisory Bd, Egon Zehnder Int.; mem. Bd of Advisors, Palamon Capital Partners 2012–. *Address:* Palamon Capital Partners, Cleveland House, 33 King Street, London, SW1Y 6RJ, England (office). *Telephone:* (20) 7766-2000 (office). *Fax:* (20) 7766-2002 (office). *E-mail:* info@palamon.com (office). *Website:* www.palamon.com (office).

KORDA, Michael Vincent, BA; American publishing executive (retd); *Editor-in-Chief Emeritus, Simon & Schuster Inc.;* b. 8 Oct. 1933, London, England; s. of Vincent Korda and Gertrude Korda (née Musgrove); m. Carolyn Keese 1958; one s.; ed Magdalen Coll., Oxford, UK; served in RAF 1952–54; joined Simon and Schuster, New York 1958– first as Ed., then Sr Ed., Man. Ed., Exec. Ed., Sr Vice-Pres. and Ed.-in-Chief, Ed.-in-Chief Emer. 2005–; mem. Nat. Soc. of Film Critics, American Horse Shows Asscn. *Publications:* Male Chauvinism: How It Works 1973, Power: How to Get It, How to Use It 1975, Success! 1977, Charmed Lives 1979, Worldly Goods 1982, The Fortune 1989, Man to Man: Surviving Prostate Cancer 1997, Another Life, 2000, Making the List 2001, Country Matters 2002, Horse People 2004, Ulysses S. Grant: The Unlikely Hero 2004, Marking Time: Collecting Watches and Thinking about Time 2004, Journey to a Revolution: A Personal Memoir and History of the Hungarian Revolution of 1956 2006, Cat People (with Margaret Korda) 2006, Ike: An American Hero 2007, With Wings Like Eagles 2009, Hero: The Life and Legend of Lawrence of Arabia 2010. *Address:* c/o Simon and Schuster, 1230 Avenue of the Americas, New York, NY 10020, USA.

KORDA, Petr; Czech professional tennis player (retd); b. 23 Jan. 1968, Prague; s. of Petr Korda and Jana Korda; m. Regina Rajchrtová 1992; two d. one s.; coached by his father until aged 18; winner Wimbledon Jr Doubles 1986; turned professional 1987; runner-up French Open 1992; winner Grand Slam Cup 1993; winner Stuttgart Open 1997, Australian Open 1998, Qatar Open 1998; mem. Czechoslovak Davis Cup Team 1988, 1996; lives in Monte Carlo; received one-year ban after testing positive for nandrolone in Wimbledon Championship 1998; retd in 1999 having won 20 professional titles (including 10 singles titles); now plays in Srs Tour; runner-up to Guy Forget 2001; won Honda Challenge 2002; Chair. Bd of Supervisors Karlštejn golf resort, Czech Repub. 2000–. *Leisure interest:* golf. *Address:* c/o Czech Tenisova Asociace, Ostrov Stvanice 38, 170 00 Prague, Czech Republic.

KORDJE, Bedoumra, PhD; Chadian politician and fmr telecommunications engineer; *Minister of Finance and the Budget;* ed Univ. Paul Sabatier, Toulouse, Ecole Nat. Supérieure des Télécommunications, Paris, France; engineer, Posts and Telecommunications Corpn of Chad 1981–82; engineering consultant with pvt. consultancy firm, Abidjan 1982–83; joined ADB 1983 as Telecommunications Expert, becoming Chief Telecommunications Expert –1996, Man., Infrastructure and Industry Div., N Region 1996–2002, Dir, Infrastructure Dept (North, East and South Regions) 2002–05, Dir, Water and Sanitation Dept and African Water Facility 2006–08, Sec.-Gen., ADB 2008–09, Vice Pres., Corp. Services 2009; Minister of Finance and the Budget 2013–. *Address:* Ministry of Finance and the Budget, BP 816, N'Djamena, Chad (office). *Telephone:* 22-52-68-61 (office). *Fax:* 22-52-49-08 (office). *E-mail:* d.dette@intnet.td (office).

KORHONEN, Keijo Tero, PhD; Finnish academic, fmr politician and diplomatist; b. 23 Feb. 1934, Paltamo; s. of Hannes Korhonen and Anna Korhonen (née Laari); m. 1st Anneli Korhonen (née Torkkila) 1958; three s.; m. 2nd Anita Korhonen (née Uggeldahl) 1990; ed Turku Univ.; Prof. of Int. Relations, Univ. of Arizona 1964, currently Assoc Prof. of Political Science; Fellow, Weatherhead Center for Int. Affairs, Harvard Univ. 1969–70; Deputy Dir for Political Affairs, Ministry of Foreign Affairs 1971–74; Prof. of Political History, Univ. of Helsinki 1974–77; Minister of Foreign Affairs 1976–77; Under-Sec. of State for Political Affairs, Ministry of Foreign Affairs 1977–83; Perm. Rep. to UN, New York 1983–88; Special Adviser to Prime Minister 1988–89; Ed.-in-Chief Kainuun Sanomat 1989–94; unsuccessful presidential cand. (ind.) 1994; fmr Deputy Chair. Paasikivi Soc.; mem. Exec. Bd Tucson Cttee on Foreign Relations. *Publications:* four books about Finnish–Soviet and Finnish–Russian relations since 1808; Finland in the Russian Political Thought of the 19th century 1966, An Ambassador's Journal, Urho Kekkonen, the Leader and the Man, The Reverse Side of the Coin 1989, This Country Is Not For Sale 1991, An Accidental Corporal (memoir) 1999. *Leisure interests:* reading, jogging, horse riding. *Address:* Social Science 320, Social Science Building, University of Arizona, Tucson, AZ 85721, USA. *Telephone:* (520) 621-3980 (office). *E-mail:* keijok@email.arizona.edu (office). *Website:* web.arizona.edu/~polisci (office).

KORIKI, Jojima; Japanese politician and fmr union leader; *Minister of Finance;* b. (Jojima Masamitsu), 1 Jan. 1947, Yanagawa City, Fukuoka Pref.; m.; one s. one d.; ed Univ. of Tokyo; with Central Research Lab., Ajinomoto Co. Inc. 1970–96, also becoming Pres., Workers' Union; mem. House of Reps (Parl.) (New Frontier Party, later DPJ) for Kanagawa 10th Dist constituency 1996–; mem. Democratic Party of Japan (DPJ), Chair. Policy Research Council 2010–, Acting Sec.-Gen. 2011, Chair. DPJ Diet Affairs Cttee 2012; Minister of Finance 2012–; fmr Pres. Japan Food Industry Workers' Union Council; Council mem., Japan Productivity Center for Socio-Econ. Devt. *Address:* Ministry of Finance, 3-1-1, Kasumigaseki, Chiyoda-ku, Tokyo 100-8940, Japan (office). *Telephone:* (3) 3581-4111 (office). *Fax:* (3) 5251-2667 (office). *E-mail:* info@mof.go.jp (office). *Website:* www.mof.go.jp (office); www.jojima.net.

KORMILTSEV, Col.-Gen. Nikolai Viktorovich; Russian army officer; b. 14 March 1946, Omsk; ed Omsk Higher Military General Army School, Moscow M.V. Frunze Military Acad., Moscow Military Acad. of General Staff; Commdr of Army corps, Turkestan Mil. Command –1994; Deputy Commdr, then Commdr of Armed Forces, Baikal Mil. Command 1994–98; Commdr of Armed Forces, Siberian Mil. Command 1998–2001; C-in-C Land Armed Forces 2001–04; Deputy Minister of Defence 2001–04. *Address:* c/o Ministry of Defence, Znamenka str. 19, 103160 Moscow, Russia (office).

KORNAI, János, DrSc; Hungarian economist; *Allie S. Freed Professor Emeritus of Economics, Harvard University;* b. 21 Jan. 1928, Budapest; m. Zsuzsa Dániel 1971; two s. one d.; ed Univ. of Budapest; Econ. Ed. 1947–55; Research Assoc. Inst. of Econs, Hungarian Acad. of Sciences 1955–58, Inst. of Textile Industry 1958–63; Sr Research Assoc., Computer Centre, Hungarian Acad. of Sciences 1963–67; Research Prof., Inst. of Econs, Hungarian Acad. of Sciences 1967–; Allie S. Freed Prof. of Econs, Harvard Univ. 1986–2002, Allie S. Freed Prof. Emer. 2002–; Perm. Fellow, Collegium Budapest 1992–2002, Perm. Fellow Emer. 2002–11; Distinguished Research Prof. Central European Univ. 2005–; Prof. Emer., Corvinus Univ., Budapest 2011–; Visiting Prof., LSE 1964, Univ. of Sussex 1966, Stanford Univ. 1968, Yale 1970, Princeton and Stanford 1972–73, Stockholm 1976–77, Geneva 1981, Munich 1983, Princeton 1983–84, Harvard 1984–85; Pres. Hungarian Social Science Asscn 1992, Int. Econ. Asscn 2002–05; mem. Hungarian Acad. of Sciences; Corresp. mem. British Acad.; Foreign mem. Royal Swedish Acad., Finnish Acad., Russian Acad. of Sciences, Bulgarian Acad. of Sciences; Hon. mem. American Acad. of Arts and Sciences 1972, American Econ. Asscn 1976, European Asscn for Comparative Econ. Studies 1996; Hon. Pres. Asscn of New Institutional Economists of Hungary 2004; Hon. Citizen of Budapest 2005; Officier, Légion d'honneur 1997, Order of Merit, Commdr's Cross (Hungary) 2002, Order of Merit, Commdr's Cross with Star (Hungary) 2007, Leontief Medal (Russia) 2010, Grand Cross, Order of Merit (Hungary) 2010; Dr hc (Paris) 1978, (Poznań) 1978, (London) 1990, (Amsterdam), (Budapest) 1992, (Wrocław) 1993, (Turin) 1993, (Debrecen) 2001, (Stockholm) 2001, (Varna) 2003, (Veszprem) 2003, (Pecs) 2003, (Cen. European Univ.) 2004, (Krakow) 2008; Seidman Award 1982, Hungarian State Prize 1983, Humboldt Prize 1983, Széchenyi Prize 1994, Prima Primissima Prize 2005, Lifetime Achievement Award 2008. *Publications:* Overcentralization in Economic Administration 1959, Mathematical Planning of Structural Decisions 1967, Anti-Equilibrium 1971, Rush versus Harmonic Growth 1972, Economics of Shortage 1980, Non-Price Control 1981, Growth, Shortage and Efficiency 1982, Contradictions and Dilemmas 1985, The Road to a Free Economy 1990, Vision and Reality 1990, The Socialist System 1992, Highways and Byways 1995, Struggle and Hope 1997, Welfare, Choice and Solidarity in Transition (with K. Eggleston) 2001, By Force of Thought: Irregular Memoirs of an Intellectual Journey 2006, From Socialism to Capitalism 2008. *Address:* Corvinus University of Budapest, Fővám tér 8, 1093 Budapest, Hungary (office). *Telephone:* (1) 482-5375 (office). *Fax:* (1) 482-5536 (office). *E-mail:* janos.kornai@uni-corvinus.hu (office). *Website:* www.kornai-janos.hu.

KORNBERG, Sir Hans (Leo), Kt, MA, PhD, DSc, ScD, FRS, FRSA, FIBiol; British/American biochemist and academic; *University Professor and Professor of Biology, Boston University;* b. 14 Jan. 1928, Herford, Germany; s. of Max Kornberg and Margarete Kornberg (née Silberbach); m. 1st Monica M. King 1956 (died 1989); twin s. two d.; m. 2nd Donna Haber 1991; ed Queen Elizabeth Grammar School, Wakefield, England and Univs of Sheffield, Oxford and Cambridge; John Stokes Research Fellow, Univ. of Sheffield 1952–53; mem. MRC Cell Metabolism Research Unit, Univ. of Oxford 1955–61; Lecturer in Biochemistry, Worcester Coll., Oxford 1958–61; Prof. of Biochemistry, Univ. of Leicester 1961–75; Sir William Dunn Prof. of Biochemistry, Univ. of Cambridge 1975–95; Univ. Prof. and Prof. of Biology, Boston Univ., USA 1995–; Fellow, Christ's Coll., Cambridge 1975–, Master 1982–95; mem. SRC 1967–72, Chair. Science Bd 1969–72; Chair. Royal Comm. on Environmental Pollution 1976–81; mem. Agric. and Food Research Council 1980–84; Chair. Advisory Cttee on Genetic Modification 1986–95; Chair. Jt Policy Group Agric. and Environment 1986–89; mem. Bd NIREX 1986–95; Pres. Int. Union of Biochemistry and Molecular Biology 1991–94, The Biochemical Soc. 1990–95 (Hon. mem. 2001–); mem. Advisory Council for Applied Research and Devt 1982–85, Scientific Advisory Cttee, Inst. for Molecular Biology and Medicine, Monash Univ. 1987–; Commonwealth Fund Fellow, Yale Univ. and Public Health Research Inst., New York 1953–55; Vice-Pres. Inst. of Biology 1969–72; Vice-Chair. European Molecular Biological Org. 1978–81; Pres. BAAS 1984–85 (Hon. mem. 2003–); Pres. Asscn for Science Educ. 1991–92; Man. Trustee, Nuffield Foundation 1973–93; Gov. Wellcome Trust 1990–95; mem. Council, Imperial Soc. of Kts Bachelor 2005–; mem. German Acad. of Sciences Leopoldina 1982; Foreign Assoc. NAS 1986; mem. Academia Europaea 1988; Foreign mem. American Acad. of Arts and Sciences 1987, American Philosophical Soc. 1993, Accad. Nazionale dei Lincei 1997; Fellow, American Acad. of Microbiology 1992; Hon. mem. Soc. for Biological Chem., USA 1972, Japanese Biochemistry Soc. 1981; Hon. FRCP 1989; Hon. Fellow, Worcester Coll., Oxford, Brasenose Coll., Oxford, Wolfson Coll., Cambridge; Hon. FIBiol 2004, Hon. Fellow, BAAS 2005; Hon. ScD (Cincinnati) 1974; Hon. DSc (Warwick) 1975, (Leicester) 1979, (Sheffield) 1979, (Bath) 1980, (Strathclyde) 1985, (South Bank) 1994, (Leeds) 1995, (La Trobe) 1997; Hon. DUniv (Essex) 1979; Hon. MD (Leipzig) 1984; Hon. LLD (Dundee) 1999; Colworth Medal, Biochemical Soc. 1963, Leeuwenhoek Lecturer, Royal Soc. 1972, Warburg Medal, German Biochemical Soc. 1973. *Publications:* numerous articles in scientific journals. *Leisure interests:* conversation, cooking. *Address:* Biology Department, Boston University, 5 Cummington Mall, Boston, MA 02215 (office); 134 Sewall Avenue, #2, Brookline, MA 02446, USA (home). *Telephone:* (617) 353-2440 (office); (617) 739-6103 (home). *Fax:* (617) 353-6340 (office). *E-mail:* hlk@bu.edu (office). *Website:* www.bu.edu/biology/people/faculty/kornberg (office).

KORNBERG, Roger D., BS, PhD; American biochemist and academic; *Mrs. George A. Winzer Professor of Medicine, Department of Structural Biology, School of Medicine, Stanford University;* b. 24 April 1947, St Louis, Mo.; s. of the late Arthur Kornberg (winner of Nobel Prize in Medicine 1959) and Sylvy Kornberg; m. Yahli Lorch; two s. one d.; ed Harvard Univ., Stanford Univ.; Postdoctoral Fellow and mem. of scientific staff, Lab. of Molecular Biology, Univ. of Cambridge, UK 1972–75; Asst Prof., Dept of Biological Chem., Harvard Medical School 1976–78; Prof., Dept of Structural Biology, School of Medicine, Stanford Univ. 1978–, now Mrs. George A. Winzer Prof. of Medicine, Dept Chair. 1984–92; Visiting Prof., Hebrew Univ. of Jerusalem 1986–; Ed. Annual Reviews of Biochemistry; mem. NAS, American Acad. of Arts and Sciences; Assoc. mem. European Molecular Biology Org.; Foreign mem. Royal Soc., London; Hon. mem. Japanese Biochemical Soc.; Dr hc (Hebrew Univ. of Jerusalem) 2001, (Univ. of Umeå) 2003, (Univ. of Regensburg) 2008, (Bar-Ilan Univ.) 2009; Eli Lilly Award 1981, Passano Award 1982, Harvey Prize 1987, Ciba-Drew Award 1990, Gairdner Int. Award (co-winner with Robert Roeder) 2000, Welch Award 2001, Gran Prix, French Acad. of Sciences 2002, Sloan Award 2005, Louisa Gross Horwitz Prize, Columbia Univ. 2006, Dickson Prize in Medicine, Univ. of Pittsburgh 2006, Nobel Prize in Chem. 2006, Aharon Katzir-Katchalsky Award, Int. Union for Pure and Applied Biophysics 2008, Ahmed Zewail Prize, Wayne State Univ. 2008, Pauling Legacy Award 2010. *Address:* Stanford University Medical School, Department of Structural Biology, Fairchild Building, 1st Floor, 299 Campus Drive, Stanford, CA 94305-5126, USA (office). *Telephone:* (650) 723-6988 (office); (650) 725-5390 (office). *E-mail:* kornberg@stanford.edu (office). *Website:* kornberg.stanford.edu (office).

KORNUKOV, Col.-Gen. Anatoly Mikhailovich; Russian army officer (retd); *Adviser, Ministry of Defence;* b. 10 Jan. 1942, Stakhanovo, Lugansk Region; m.; one s. one d.; ed Chernigov Higher Mil. Aviation School, Zhukov Mil. Acad., Mil. Gen. Staff Acad.; Commdr of fighter squadron, Aviation Regt of Fighter Div. in Far E; qualified as Mil. Pilot-Sniper; Commdr Anti-Aircraft Defence Forces of Moscow Command 1991–97; C-in-C Mil. Aircraft Forces of Russian Fed. 1998–2002 (resgnd); adviser to Ministry of Defence 2002–. *Leisure interests:* nature, music. *Address:* c/o Ministry of Defence, 105175 Moscow, ul. Myasnitskaya 37, Russia (office). *Telephone:* (495) 696-71-71 (office). *Website:* www.mil.ru (office).

KOROLEV, Mikhail Antonovich, DEconSc; Russian statistician; *Member of the Public Council on Statistics, Rosstat;* b. 12 Sept. 1931, Almaty, Kazakh SSR, USSR; s. of A. I. Korolev and T. A. Ivanova; m. Letalina Koroleva 1957; one d.; ed Moscow Plekhanov Inst. of Nat. Econ.; Asst Dean, Dept Head, Moscow Inst. of Econs and Statistics 1954–66, Rector 1966–72, Prof. 1967–; Deputy, First Deputy Dir Cen. Statistics Bd of USSR 1972–85, Dir 1985–87; Pres. USSR State Cttee on Statistics 1987–89; Adviser to Prime Minister of USSR 1991; Pres. Interstate Statistical Cttee of CIS 1992–2009, Vice-Pres. 2010–12; cand. mem. CPSU Cen. Cttee 1986–90; Deputy to USSR Supreme Soviet 1986–89; Chair. Statistical Comm. of UN 1979–81, Vice-Chair. 1976–79, 1989–91; mem. Int. Statistical Inst.; Academician Int. Informatization Acad.; Hon. Scientist of the Russian Fed.; Hon. Statistician of several countries; numerous orders and medals; name 'Korolev Mikhail Antonovich' given to star in the constellation Sagittarius. *Publications:* 20 books, numerous articles. *Leisure interests:* chess, art, tennis, poetry. *E-mail:* korolev1209@mail.ru (office). *Website:* mikhailkorolev.narod.ru.

KOROLOGOS, Tom Chris, BA, MS; American journalist, business executive and diplomatist (retd); b. 1933, Salt Lake City, Utah; s. of Chris T. Korologos and Irene M. Kolendrianos; m. 1st Joy G. Korologos (died 1997); one s. two d.; m. 2nd Ann McLaughlin; ed Univ. of Utah and Columbia Univ. Grad. School of Journalism (Grantland Rice Fellowship and Pulitzer Fellowship); officer, USAF 1956–57; journalist, New York Herald Tribune, Long Island Press, Salt Lake Tribune, Associated Press; Co-founder, Pres. and Chair. Exec. Cttee, Timmons & Co., Washington DC 1975–2003; Dir Congressional Relations for Pres. Reagan's transition 1980–81, for Nat. Bipartisan (Kissinger) Comm. for Cen. America; Sr Advisor to Senator Bob Dole during his 1996 presidential campaign; mem. Bush-Cheney transition team 2001; served in the Nixon and Ford Admins as Deputy Asst to Pres. for Legis. Affairs (Senate); served for nine years under Senator Wallace F. Bennett (Republican, Utah) as his Chief of Staff in the Senate; served as a Sr Staff mem. in US Congress, as an asst to two Pres in the White House; Sr Counselor with Coalition Provisional Authority, Baghdad, Iraq May–Dec. 2003; Amb. to Belgium 2004–07; fmr mem. US Advisory Comm. on Public Diplomacy; fmr charter mem. Broadcasting Bd of Govs with jurisdiction over all non-mil. US Govt radio and TV broadcasting overseas; Republican. *Address:* c/o US Department of State, 2201 C Street NW, Washington, DC 20520, USA.

KOROMA, Abdul G.; Sierra Leonean diplomatist and lawyer; ed King's Coll., London, UK, Kiev State Univ., USSR (now Ukraine); barrister and Hon. Bencher (Lincoln's Inn) and legal practitioner, High Court of Sierra Leone; joined Sierra Leone Govt service 1964, Int. Div., Ministry of External Affairs 1969; del. to UN Gen. Ass.; mem. Int. Law Comm. (Chair. 43rd Session); mem. of dels to 3rd UN Conf. on the Law of the Sea, UN Conf. on Succession of States in Respect of Treaties, UN Comm. on Int. Trade Law, Special Cttee on the Review of the UN Charter and on the Strengthening of the Role of the Org. Cttee on the Peaceful Uses of Outer Space; Vice-Chair. UN Charter Cttee 1978; Chair. UN Special Cttee of 24 on Self-Determination of Peoples; Deputy Perm. Rep. of Sierra Leone to the UN 1978–81, Perm. Rep. 1981–85; fmr Amb. to S Korea, to Cuba and to EEC and Perm. Del. to UNESCO; Amb. to France, Belgium, Netherlands, Luxembourg and to Ethiopia and OAU 1988; Perm. Rep. to UN –1994; Judge, Int. Court of Justice 1994–2012; fmr High Commr in Zambia, Tanzania and Kenya; Chair. UN 6th Cttee (Legal), UN Int. Law Comm.; Vice-Pres. African Soc. of Int. and Comparative Law, African Soc. of Int. Law; Pres. Henry Dunant Centre for Humanitarian Dialogue, Geneva; mem. Int. Planning Council of Int. Ocean Inst., Cttee of Experts on the Application of Conventions and Recommendations, ILO, Geneva, Institut de droit international; del. to numerous int. confs; Visiting Prof., Univ. of Bangalore, India; lecturer at numerous univs, including Stockholm, Cambridge, Columbia, Zurich, Louvain; mem. American Soc. of Int. Law, Inst. of Int. Law; Insignia of Commdr of Rokel 1991, Order of Grand Officer of Repub. of Sierra Leone 2007; Hon. LLD; Prize for the Promotion, Dissemination and Teaching of Int. Humanitarian Law, Int. Inst. of Humanitarian Law 2005. *Publications:* numerous articles on int. law. *Leisure interests:* reading, music, sports. *Address:* c/o International

Court of Justice, Peace Palace, Carnegieplein, 2517 KJ The Hague, Netherlands (office).

KOROMA, Ernest Bai; Sierra Leonean politician and head of state; *President;* b. 23 Oct. 1953, Makeni, Bombali Dist; m. Sia Koroma; two c.; ed Univ. of Sierra Leone; began career as teacher, St Francis Secondary School, Makeni; joined Sierra Leone Nat. Insurance Co. 1978; joined Reliance Insurance Trust Corpn 1985, Man. Dir 1988–2002; represented All People's Congress (APC) in presidential and parl. elections 2002, lost presidential vote but elected to parl. representing Bombali Dist; Leader APC 2002–, temporarily stripped of leadership due to internal party dispute 2005; Pres. of Sierra Leone 2007–; Fellow, West African Insurance Inst.; Assoc. Inst. of Risk Man., UK; mem. Inst. of Dirs, UK. *Address:* All-People's Congress, 137h Fourah Bay Road, Freetown, Sierra Leone (office). *E-mail:* info@new-apc.org (office); info@statehouse-sl.org. *Website:* apcparty.org (office); www.statehouse.gov.sl.

KOROMA, Momodu, MSc; Sierra Leonean politician; b. 12 Sept. 1956; m.; five c.; ed Njala Univ. Coll., Univ. of Nairobi, Kenya, Univ. of Reading, UK, Int. Centre for Theoretical Physics, Trieste, Italy; govt minister 1996–, fmr Minister of Presidential Affairs; Minister of Foreign Affairs and Int. Co-operation 2002–07; mem. Sierra Leone Peoples Party (SLPP), unsuccessful cand. for Vice-Pres. of Sierra Leone 2007. *Leisure interests:* tennis, sight-seeing. *Address:* c/o Sierra Leone People's Party, 15 Wallace Johnson St, Freetown (office); MQ8 Spur Road, Wilberforce, Freetown, Sierra Leone (home). *Telephone:* (22) 2256341 (office); (22) 232873 (home). *E-mail:* info@slpp.ws (office); graceful@sierratel.se (home). *Website:* www.slpp.ws (office).

KOROTCHENYA, Ivan Mikhailovich; Belarusian politician; ed Minsk Agric. Acad.; worked as chief agronomist, then Chair. of collective farm; fmr Chair. Regional Union of Collective Farms then Chair. Viley Dist Soviet of People's Deputies; Deputy Belarus Supreme Soviet, mem. Accord faction 1994–96; mem. Presidium; Chair. Comm. on Problems of Glasnost, Mass Media and Human Rights 1990–92; elected coordinator of Workgroup at Council of Leaders of States and Leaders of Govts CIS Countries after disintegration of USSR 1992–98; Deputy Exec. Sec. CIS Secr. 1998–2001. *Address:* Secretariat of Russia and Belarus Union, Kirova str. 17, 220050 Minsk, Belarus (office).

KOROTEEV, Anatoly Sazonovich, DTechSc; Russian physicist; *General Director, SSC Keldysh Research Centre;* b. 22 July 1936, Moscow Region; s. of Sazon Z. Koroteev and Maria P. Koroteeva; m.; one s.; ed Moscow Aviation Inst.; engineer, Sr Engineer, Head of Div., First Deputy Dir Research Inst. of Thermal Processes (now SSC Keldysh Research Centre) 1959–88, Dir 1988–; Corresp. mem. USSR (now Russian) Acad. of Sciences 1990, Academician 1994; Pres. Russian Acad. of Cosmonautics (named after K. Tsiolkovsky) 2005–11; mem. Int. Acad. of Astronautics, NAS; Order for Service to Fatherland Rank IV 1996, Rank III 2006; Order of Alexander Nevsky 2013; USSR State Prize 1982, Russian Acad. of Science Prize 2001, Russian Fed. Govt Prize in Science and Tech. 2001, 2012, State Prize of Russian Fed. 2002, Russian Pres.'s Prize 2005, Russian Fed. Honoured Scientist. *Publications:* Low-Temperature Plasma Generators 1966, Generator for Low-Temperature Plasma 1969, Applied Dynamics of Thermal Plasma 1975, Electric-arc Plasmotrons 1980, Plasmatrons: Structures, Characteristics, Calculation 1993, Electron-Beam Plasma 1993, Nuclear Rocket Engines 2001, Rocket Engines and Power Systems on the Basis of Nuclear Reactor 2002, Seventy Years at the Forefront of Rocket-Space Technics 2003, Gasdynamic and Thermophysical Processes in Solid Rocket Propulsion 2004, Manned Flight to Mars 2007, Advanced Energetics Technologies on Earth and in Space 2008; numerous articles on propulsion and power systems of rocket and space complexes, generation and diagnostics of low-temperature plasma, creation of electric arc plasma generators and derivation of concentrated pulse electron flows in dense environments. *Leisure interests:* history, skiing. *Address:* SSC Keldysh Research Centre, Onezhskaya str. 8, 125438 Moscow, Russia (office). *Telephone:* (495) 456-46-08 (office). *Fax:* (495) 456-82-28 (office). *E-mail:* kerc@elnet.msk.ru (office); kerc@comcor.ru (office). *Website:* www.kerc.msk.ru (home).

KOROTYCH, Vitaliy Alekseyevich; Russian/Ukrainian physician, writer and poet; *Editor, Boulevard magazine;* b. 26 May 1936, Kiev; s. of Aleksey Korotych and Zoa Korotych; m. Zinaida Korotych 1958; two s.; ed Kiev Medical Inst.; physician 1959–66; Ed. Ukrainian literary journal Ranok 1966–77; Ed.-in-Chief Vsesvit magazine 1978–86; Ed.-in-Chief Ogonyok weekly magazine 1986–91; Sec. of Ukrainian Writers' Union 1966–69; mem. USSR Writers' Union 1981–90; USSR People's Deputy 1989–91; Prof. Boston Univ., USA 1991–98, returned to Moscow; ed. Boulevard magazine and others 1998–; several Russian, Ukrainian, Polish and Bulgarian decorations and medals including two USSR State Prizes, A. Tolstoy Prize 1982, Int. Julius Fuchik Prize 1984, Wiental Prize, Georgetown Univ. (USA) 1987, Int. Ed. of the year, W P Revue (USA) 1989, Johann Wolfgang von Goethe Medallion, European Acad. of Natural Sciences 2006, Moscow Writers' Union Prize 2007. *Publications include:* Golden Hands 1961, The Smell of Heaven 1962, Cornflower Street 1963, O Canada! 1966, Poetry 1967, Metronome (novel) 1982, The Face of Enmity (novel) 1984, Memory, Bread and Love 1986, Le Visage de la haine (travel essays) 1988, Glasnost und Perestroika 1990, The Waiting Room (memoirs, Vol. I) 1991, On My Behalf (memoirs, Vol. II) 2000, Selected Poems 2005, Selected Essays 2005; many translations from English into Ukrainian and other Slavonic languages. *Address:* Trifonovskaya str. 11, Apt. 256, 127018 Moscow, Russia (home). *Telephone:* (495) 689-03-84 (home); (496) 462-67-44 (home). *Fax:* (495) 689-03-84 (home). *E-mail:* vkorotich@yandex.ru (home); vak1137@mail.ru (home).

KORS, Michael; American fashion designer; b. 9 Aug. 1959, Mineola, NY; s. of Karl Anderson and Joan L. Kors; pnr Lance LePere; ed Fashion Inst. of Tech.; early career designing for Lothar's boutique, New York; f. Kors Co. (now Michael Kors Inc.) 1981, Pres. 1981–; launched accessories line 2001; launched Michael fragrance for women 2000, Island fragrance for men 2005 (FiFi Award for Best Bath and Body Collection 2006), Very Hollywood Michael Kors (fragrance franchise) 2009; Dupont American Original Award 1983, Elle/Cadillac Fashion Award for Excellence 1995, New York Award 1999, CFDA Award for Womenswear Designer of the Year 1999, CFDA Menswear Award 2003, Oliver R. Grace Award for Distinguished Service in Advancing Cancer Research, Cancer Research Inst. 2010, Geoffrey Beene Lifetime Achievement Award, Council of Fashion Designers

of America 2010, Fragrance Foundation FiFi Award for Lifetime Achievement 2010. *Publications:* articles in Vogue, The New York Times and other newspapers and magazines. *Leisure interests:* theatre, film, travel. *Address:* Corporate Headquarters, Michael Kors Inc., 11 West 42nd Street, New York, NY 10036, USA. *Website:* www.michaelkors.com.

KORTHALS ALTES, Frederik; Dutch lawyer and politician; *Chairman, Advisory Council on International Affairs;* b. 15 May 1931, Amsterdam; s. of Everhardus Joannes Korthals Altes and Mary s'Jacob; m. Henny Matthijssen; ed Leiden Univ.; practised as solicitor 1958–82; mem. First Chamber, States-Gen. 1981–82, 1991–2001; Minister of Justice 1982–89; Chair. Volkspartij voor Vrijheid en Democratie (VVD) 1975–81, Floor Leader in First Chamber, States-Gen. 1995–97, Pres. 1997–2001; Chair. Advisory Council on Int. Affairs 2002–; Pnr, Nauta Dutilh (law firm) 1990–96; Hon. Minister of State 2001–; Grand Officier, Légion d'honneur 1984, Grosses Verdienstkreuz des Verdienstordens 1985, Commdr, Order of Orange-Nassau, Grand Cross Ordem do Mérito 1989, Grand Cross Ordre nat. du Mérite, Grand Cross of Sacred Treasure (Japan) 2000; Prof. E.M. Meijers Medal of Law Faculty (Leiden) 1988, Nat. Police Award 1990. *Address:* Advisory Council on International Affairs, Bezuidenhoutseweg 67, Room 9E19, PO Box 20061, 2500 EB, The Hague, (office); Oudorpweg 9, 3062 RB, Rotterdam, Netherlands (home). *Telephone:* (70) 3485325 (office); (10) 4526163 (home); 653-301424 (mobile) (home). *Fax:* (70) 3486256 (office); (10) 4529491 (home). *E-mail:* aiv@minbuza.nl (office); fka@planet.nl (home). *Website:* www.aiv-advies.nl (office).

KORTLANDT, Frederik H. H., BA, MA, PhD; Dutch academic; *Professor of Descriptive and Comparative Linguistics, University of Leiden;* b. 19 June 1946, Utrecht; ed Univ. of Amsterdam; Asst Prof. of Slavic Linguistics, Univ. of Amsterdam 1969–72; Assoc. Prof. of Balto-Slavic Languages, Univ. of Leiden 1972–74, Prof. 1974–; Prof. of Descriptive and Comparative Linguistics 1985–; mem. Royal Netherlands Acad. 1986–; Spinoza Prize 1997. *Publications:* Modelling the Phoneme 1972, Slavic Accentuation 1975; numerous articles on linguistics and Slavic, Baltic, Germanic, Celtic, Armenian, Japanese and other languages. *Leisure interest:* classical music. *Address:* Faculty of Letters, PO Box 9515, 2300 RA Leiden (office); Cobetstraat 24, 2313 KC Leiden, Netherlands (home). *Telephone:* (71) 527-2501 (office). *Fax:* (71) 527-7569 (office). *E-mail:* f.kortlandt@hum.leidenuniv.nl (office). *Website:* www.kortlandt.nl (office).

KORTÜM, Franz-Josef; German business executive; *Chairman of the Management Board, Webasto AG;* b. 18 Aug. 1950, Billerbeck, Coesfeld; m.; three c.; ed studies in Münster and Regensburg; employed in family car retailing co. Billerbeck 1975; car sales exec., Bielefeld subsidiary of Daimler-Benz AG 1976; Head, Passenger Car Field Sales, Used Vehicle Sales and Truck Sales, Berlin subsidiary of Daimler-Benz AG 1979; Asst to Dir of Sales Org. Germany, Daimler-Benz AG, Stuttgart-Untertürkheim 1985; Dir Saarbrücken subsidiary of Daimler-Benz AG 1987; Dir Cen. Admin. Daimler-Benz AG 1989; Man. Dir Mercedes-Benz-owned co. Rheinische Kraftwagengesellschaft (RKW), Bonn 1990; Man. Dir Webasto AG 1994, CEO 1999, currently Chair. Man. Bd; mem. Man. Bd Audi AG 1992, Chair. 1993–95. *Address:* Webasto AG, Kraillinger Strasse 5, Stockdorf 82131, Germany (office). *Telephone:* (49) 8985794 (office). *Website:* www.webasto.com (office).

KORTUN, Vasif; Turkish gallery curator, writer and teacher; b. 6 Nov. 1958; Founding Dir Museum of Center for Curatorial Studies, Bard Coll., USA 1994–97, Proje 4L, Istanbul Museum of Contemporary Art 2001–03, Platform Garanti Contemporary Art Center, Istanbul 2001–; Co-Curator Tirana Biennial, Second Ceramics Biennial, Albisola 2003, (with ManRay Hsu) Taipei Biennial 2008, among other biennial projects; Chief Curator and Director Third Int. Istanbul Biennial 1992; Co-Dir, with Charles Esche, Ninth Int. Istanbul Biennial 2005; curated Turkish pavilions for São Paulo Biennial 1994, 1998, Venice Biennale 2007; has undertaken numerous ind. curatorial projects including exhbn of works by Cengiz Çekil at Rampa, Istanbul 2010, The Columns Held Us Up at Artists Space, New York 2009, UAE Pavilion for the Venice Biennale 2011; Ed. annual contemporary art magazine RG (in Turkish); currently Dir of Research and Programs, SALT, Istanbul; mem. Bush Global Advisory Cttee of Walker Art Center, Foundation for Arts Initiatives 2009–, Tate Turner Prize Selection Cttee 2011; mem. Bd Int. Foundation Manifesta 2000–02, CIMAM 2010–; mem. Jury of The Querini Stampalia Foundation-Furla for Art Prize, Venice 2002; Ninth Annual Award for Curatorial Excellence, Center for Curatorial Studies, Bard Coll. 2006. *Publications:* Jahresring 51: Szene Turkei: Abseits aber Tor (with Erden Kosova) 2004; has written extensively on contemporary art and the cultural situation in Turkey for int. periodicals and publs, including Mars, NU, Flash Art, Art Asia Pacific, Art Journal, New Art Examiner, Contemporary, Crudelia, Art Fan. *Address:* SALT Beyoğlu, İstiklal Caddesi 136, Beyoğlu, 34430 Istanbul, Turkey (office). *Telephone:* (212) 3774200 (office). *Fax:* (212) 2921667 (office). *E-mail:* salt@saltonline.org (office). *Website:* www.saltonline.org (office); vasif-kortun-eng.blogspot.com (office).

KORZENIOWSKI, Robert Marek, (Korzeń); Polish sports coach, manager and fmr athlete; *President, Sportowa Polska Foundation;* b. 30 July 1968, Lubaczów; m. Magdalena Kłys; two d.; ed Acad. of Physical Educ., Katowice; gold medal, 20km walk, Olympic Games, Atlanta 1996, 20km walk and 50km walk, Sydney 2000, 50km walk, Athens 2004; winner 20km walk, European Cup, La Coruña 1996; gold medal, 50km walk, World Championships, Athens 1997, Edmonton 2001, Paris 2003; gold medal, 50km walk, European Championships 1998, Munich 2002; Sport and Fair Play Amb. to European Council, Strasbourg 1997–; Creator and first Man. dedicated sports channel on Polish public TV 2006–09; Pres. Sportowa Polska Foundation; organizer Int. Asscn of Athletics Feds race-walking meeting 'Na Rynek marsz!' in Kraków 1997–; Hon. Citizen of Athens 2000; Officer's Cross, Order of Polonia Restituta 2000, Commdr's Cross 2004; Gold Medal for Outstanding Achievement in Sport 1996, 'Give a Hand' Ronald McDonald Foundation Award. *Television:* Talks in Walk (two reportages with Hicham El Gerouj and Seghey Bubka), Dancing with the Stars (TVN). *Publication:* I o to chodzi (biog.). *Leisure interests:* books, cinema, cooking, history, politics. *Address:* Robert Korzeniowski, ul. Żytnia 18 A, 01-014 Warsaw, Poland (office). *Telephone:* (883) 989588 (mobile) (office). *Fax:* (22) 427-50-83 (office). *E-mail:* andrzej@korzeniowski.pl (office); info@korzeniowski.pl (office). *Website:* www.korzeniowski.pl.

KORZHAKOV, Lt-Gen. (retd) Aleksander Vasilyevich; Russian army officer (retd) and politician; b. 31 Jan. 1950, Moscow; m.; two d.; ed All-Union Inst. of Law;

mem. Dept 9 State Security Cttee 1970–89; personal bodyguard of First Sec. Moscow CPSU Cttee Boris Yeltsin 1986–87; Founder and Chief of Security Service of Russian Supreme Soviet 1990–91; Head of Security Service of Pres. of Russia 1991–96, Deputy Chief, Main Admin. of Bodyguards 1992–96 (discharged); mem. State Duma (Parl.) 1997–; joined Otechestvo-All Russia faction 2000. *Publication:* Boris Yeltsin: From Dawn to Dusk (memoirs) 1997. *Leisure interest:* tennis. *Address:* State Duma, 103009 Moscow, Okhotny Ryad 1, Russia. *Telephone:* (495) 292-87-78. *Fax:* (495) 292-87-78.

KORZHOVA, Natalya Artemovna; Kazakhstani politician; b. 8 April 1958, Sarkand; ed Alma-Ata (Almaty) Inst. of Nat. Economy; numerous positions at Ministry of Finance 1979–, including Deputy Minister of Finance 1999–2002, Vice-Minister, then First Deputy Minister of Econs and Budgetary Planning 2002–06, Minister of Finance 2006–07; mem. Cttee on Human Rights; Pres. Female Football and Mini-Football Fed. of Repub. of Kazakhstan. *Publications:* numerous articles in specialist publications and periodicals. *Address:* Ministry of Finance, 010000 Astana, pl. Respubliki 60, Kazakhstan (office).

KOSAI, Akio, BA; Japanese business executive; b. 19 April 1931, Okayama; ed Univ. of Tokyo; joined Sumitomo Chemical Co., Ltd 1954, Dir and Gen. Man. Industrial Chemicals and Fertilizers Div. 1983; Pres. Petrochemical Corpn of Singapore (Pte) Ltd 1984–87; Man. Dir Sumitomo Chemical Co., Ltd 1987–91, Sr Man. Dir 1991–93, Pres. 1993–2000, Chair. 2000–05, Counsellor 2005–11; Deputy Chair. Nippon-Keidanren (Japan Business Fed.) and Chair. Japanese Cttee of East Asia Businessmen's Conf.; mem. Int. Advisory Council, Econ. Devt Bd (EDB) Singapore; mem. Bd of Dirs Sumitomo Bakelite Co. Ltd, Sumitomo Life Insurance Co., Inabata and Co. Ltd. *Address:* c/o Sumitomo Chemical Co. Ltd, 2-27-1, Shinkawa, Chuo-ku, Tokyo, 104-8260, Japan. *E-mail:* info@sumitomo-chem.co.jp.

KOSCIUSKO-MORIZET, Nathalie, MBA; French politician; b. 14 May 1973, Paris; d. of François Kosciusko-Morizet and Bénédicte Treuille; ed École nationale du génie rural, des eaux et des forêts (ENGREF), Collège des ingénieurs, Paris; Adviser, Ministry of Economy, Finance and Industry 1997–99, Man. Foreign Econ. Relations Div. 1999–2001; Head of Mission of Strategic Dir Alstom (multinational conglomerate) 2001–02; mem. Assemblée nationale (Parl.) for Essonne 2002–10; Tech. Adviser to Prime Minister on Ecology and Sustainable Devt 2002; Regional Councillor, Île-de-France 2004–10; Sec. of State for Ecology 2007–09, for Prospective Devt of the Digital Economy 2009–10, Minister for Ecology, Sustainable Devt, Transport and Housing 2010–12; spokeswoman for Nicolas Sarkozy's presidential campaign 2012; Municipal Councillor and Mayor of Longjumeau (Essonne) 2008–; mem. and Vice-Pres. Agglomeration Community Council 2008–; mem. Union pour un Mouvement Populaire (UMP). *Address:* c/o Ministry for Ecology, Sustainable Development and Energy, Grande Arche, Tour Pascal A et B, 92055 La Défense Cedex, France.

KOSHIBA, Masatoshi, PhD; Japanese physicist and academic; *Professor Emeritus, Department of Physics, University of Tokyo;* b. 19 Sept. 1926, Toyohashi City, Aichi Pref.; ed Univ. of Tokyo, Univ. of Rochester, New York, USA; Prof., Dept of Physics, Univ. of Tokyo 1970–87, now Prof. Emer., Sr Counselor Int. Centre for Elementary Particle Physics 1987–; Prof., Tokai Univ. 1987–97; Chair., Heisel Foundation for Basic Science 2003–; Grosse Verdienstkreuz (Germany) 1985, Order of Culture 1988, Order of Cultural Merit 1997; Nishina Prize, Nishina Foundation 1987, Ashai Prize, Ashai Press 1988, 1999, Acad. Award, Acad. of Japan 1989, Fujuwara Science Foundation 1997, Wolf Prize, Govt of Israel 2000, Nobel Prize in Physics 2002. *Achievements include:* pioneer of neutrino-astronomy and cosmic-ray physics; led path-breaking experiments Kamiokande and Super-Kamiokande (massive detectors capturing neutrinos from the Sun and a distant supernova explosion 1987). *Address:* Heisel Foundation for Basic Science, Marunouchi Building, 11th Floor, Room 1109A, 2-4-1 Marunouchi, Chiyoda, Tokyo 100-6311 (office); International Centre for Elementary Particle Physics, University of Tokyo, 7-3-1 Hongo, Bunkyo-ku, Tokyo 113-0033, Japan (office). *Telephone:* (3) 3815-8384 (office). *Fax:* (3) 3814-8806 (office). *E-mail:* office@hfbs.or.jp (office). *Website:* www.hfbs.or.jp (office); www.icepp.s.u-tokyo.ac.jp (office).

KOSHIRO, Matsumoto, IX; Japanese actor; b. (Teruaki Fujima), 1942; s. of the late Koshiro VIII; m.; one s.; debut in Kabuki (Japanese traditional theatre) when child; as child acted under name Kintaro, as young man Somegoro Ichikawa; became Koshiro IX 1980. *Plays include:* Kanjincho (and many other Kabuki plays), Man of La Mancha (included ten-week run on Broadway), The King and I (including six-month run in West End), Half a Sixpence, Sweeney Todd, Fiddler on the Roof, Amadeus (Salieri). *Address:* c/o Kabukiza Theatre, No. 12–15 Ginza 4 chome, Chuo-ku, Tokyo 104, Japan.

KOSHMAN, Col.-Gen. Nikolai Pavlovich; Russian politician; b. 5 April 1944, Mironovka; s. of Pavel Porfirievich Koshman and Maria Fiedoseevna Koshman; m.; two s.; ed Mil. Acad. of Home Front and Transport; numerous posts from Commdr of team to Commdr of corps, railway armed forces 1973–91, Deputy Commdr 1991–95; mem. of Mission of Plenipotentiary Rep. of Russian Pres. to Chechen Repub.; Chair. Govt of Chechen Repub. 1996, Plenipotentiary Rep. of Russian Govt in Chechen Repub. with rank of Deputy Prime Minister 1999–2000; Deputy Minister of Transport, Russian Fed. 1997–; Head Fed. Service of Special Construction Rosspetsstroy 1997–98; Adviser to the Pres. of the Russian Fed. 2001–02; Deputy Minister of Communications Jan.–Oct. 2002; Chair. State Cttee of Construction 2002–. *Publication:* Restoration of the Economy and Social Sphere of the Chechen Republic 1999. *Leisure interests:* theatre, sports (football, tennis), hunting, travelling. *Address:* Gosstroi Rosii, Stroiteley str. 8, korp. 2, 117987 Moscow (office); A. Zelynsky str. 6-37, 117534 Moscow, Russia (home). *Telephone:* (495) 930-17-55 (office); (495) 137-74-85 (home). *Fax:* (495) 939-27-02 (office).

KOSICE, Gyula; Argentine artist, poet and writer; b. (Fernando Fallik), 26 April 1924, Košice, Czechoslovakia (now Slovakia); s. of Joseph F. Fallik and Eta Fallik (née Berger); m. Haydée Itzkovitz 1947; two d.; ed Acad. of Arts, Buenos Aires; born to Hungarian family, came to Argentina aged four; pioneer of kinetic and luminance art; studied drawing and modelling at free academies; Co-founder Arturo magazine 1944; first articulated and movable sculpture Röyi 1944; Co-founder Arte Concreto Invención (Concrete Art Invention) 1945; Founder Movt of Madí Art 1946; cr. luminance structures with neon gas used for the first time 1946; exhbn of Madí Art representing Argentina, Salón des Réalités Nouvelles, Paris 1948; creator of the hydraulic sculpture, uses water as an essential element of his

work 1949; creator of the Hydrospatial City described in Arturo magazine; has constructed monumental sculptures, hydrospatial routes, hydromurals, etc.; works held in museums and private collections in Argentina, the rest of Latin America, USA, Europe and Asia; Hon. Citizen of Buenos Aires 1997, Hon. Citizen of Košice 2011; Chevalier des Arts et des Lettres 1989; numerous awards including Silver Pen, PEN Int. (Argentina section) 1983, First Municipal Essay Prize, Buenos Aires 1986, Distinción de Honor, Premio EUDEBA 30th anniversary, Buenos Aires 1988, Lifetime Achievement Award in the Arts, Nat. Arts Foundation, Buenos Aires 1995, Belt of Honour, Asscn of Argentine Writers 1997, Premio Cultura Nación, Buenos Aires 2007, ORT Tribute, Retrovisort 2009. *Publications:* Invención 1945, Madí Manifesto 1946, Golse-Se (poems) 1952, Peso y Medida de Alberto Hidalgo 1953, Antología Madí 1955, Geocultura de la Europa de Hoy 1959, Poème hydraulique 1960, Arte Hidrocinético (Faja de Honor, Sociedad Argentina de Escritores) 1968, La Ciudad Hidroespacial 1972, Arte y Arquitectura del Agua 1974, Arte Madí (Best Art Book, Asscn of Art Critics) 1982, Obra Poética 1984, Entrevisiones 1984, Teoría sobre el Arte 1987, Arte y Filosofía Porvenirista 1996, Madí grafias 2001, Autobiography 2010, 500 Places to Live (Hydrospatial City) 2010. *Leisure interests:* writing books on art, creating works of art. *Address:* Humahuaca 4662, Buenos Aires (office); República de la India 3135 6° A, 1425 Buenos Aires, Argentina (home). *Telephone:* (11) 4867-1240 (office); (11) 4801-8615 (home). *Fax:* (11) 4801-8615 (home). *E-mail:* gyula@kosice.com.ar (home). *Website:* www.kosice.com.ar (office).

KOSKINEN, John A.; American business executive; ed Duke Univ., Yale Law School, Univ. of Cambridge, UK; worked as a sr exec. of the Palmieri Co., including as Pres. and CEO; Deputy Dir for Man., US Office of Man. and Budget, Washington, DC 1994–97; chaired the Washington, DC Host Cttee for the 1994 World Cup; Asst to the US Pres. and Chair. of the Pres.'s Council on Year 2000 Conversion 1998–2000; Deputy Mayor and City Admin. of Washington, DC 2000–03; Pres. US Soccer Foundation 2004–08; Chair. (non-exec.) Freddie Mac (Fed. Home Loan Mortgage Corpn) Sept. 2008–March 2009, Aug. 2009–11, Interim CEO March–Aug. 2009, mem. Bd of Dirs 2008–12; mem. Bd of Dirs AES Corpn, American Capital Ltd, DC Education Compact; fmr Chair. Duke Univ. Bd of Trustees. *Address:* c/o Freddie Mac, 8200 Jones Branch Drive, McLean, VA 22102-3110, USA. *E-mail:* info@freddiemac.com.

KOSOR, Jadranka, LLB; Croatian politician and fmr journalist; b. 1 July 1953, Pakrac; one s.; ed high school in Pakrac, Faculty of Law, Univ. of Zagreb; worked as journalist for Večernji list and Radio Zagreb 1972, radio journalist covering war topics for Croatian Radio and briefly for BBC 1991–95; mem. Parl. 1995–; apptd Vice Pres. of Parl. 1995; mem. Croatian Democratic Union (HDZ) 1995–2013, Vice-Pres. 1995–98, Deputy Pres. 2000–09, Pres. 2009–12; Ind. 2013–; Minister of Family, Veterans' Affairs and Intergenerational Solidarity 2003–09, Deputy Prime Minister of Croatia 2004–09, Prime Minister 2009–11; Leader of the Opposition 2011–12; presidential cand. 2005; Hon. Pres. Asscn of Croatian War Veteran Invalids, Asscn of Missing Persons from the Croatian War of Independence; Hon. Vice-Pres. Deaf and Blind Asscn 'Dodir'; Hon. mem. Asscn of Parents of Deceased War Veterans; Zlatno pero Award Croatian Journalists Asscn, EC Award for Humanitarian Work, Europski krug Award of Croatian European House, Lifetime Achievement Award Ivan Sibl Croatian Nat. TV. *Publications:* two books related to the Croatian War of Independence, two books of poetry, including Koraci 1971, one children's book. *Leisure interests:* music, dancing, reading. *Address:* Croatian Parliament, 10000 Zagreb, trg sv. Marka 6, Croatia (office). *Telephone:* (1) 4553000 (office). *Fax:* (1) 4552600 (office). *E-mail:* jadranka.kosor@ymail.com (office). *Website:* jadrankakosor.eu.

KOSOVAN, Col.-Gen. Alexander Davydovich; Russian construction engineer and army officer; *Head of Department of Urban Development of Moscow;* b. 26 Oct. 1941, Akhtyrskaya, Krasnodar Territory, Russia; m.; one s. one d.; ed Novosibirsk Inst. of Eng and Construction; head of construction group, chief engineer, Deputy Head Dept of Eng Construction, Ministry of Defence 1966–84; Chief Eng, Deputy Head Construction Dept Volga Mil. Command 1984–88; Deputy Commdr Caucasus Mil. Command on construction and quartering of forces 1988–92; First Deputy Head of Dept on Construction and Quartering of Forces, Russian Ministry of Defence 1992–97, Deputy Minister of Defence in charge of military construction and housing 1997–2003; First Deputy Head Dept of City Construction Policy Making, Devt and Reconstruction of Moscow –2008, Head of Dept of Urban Devt of Moscow 2008–; Order for Service to Motherland in Armed Forces 1989, Order of Labour Red Banner 1990, Hon. Builder of Russia, Hon. Builder of Moscow, other Govt decorations. *Publications:* numerous articles on problems of mil. construction, text-books and methodical manuals for univ. and mil. schools. *Leisure interest:* fishing. *Address:* Department of Urban Development of Moscow, Moscow, 103864, 5, Nikitsky Lane, Russia (office). *Telephone:* (495) 956-64-63 (office). *Fax:* (495) 956-81-89 (office). *Website:* www.dgs.mos.ru (office).

KOSSOWSKI, Marek, BE; Polish business executive; b. 1952; ed Silesian Univ.; with Wytwórnia Sprzętu Komunikacyjnego "PZE-Kalisz" (production plant) 1971–72; clerk, Silesian Univ., Katowice 1975–76; mem. Man. Bd, then Vice-Chair., Socialist Union of Polish Students, Katowice 1976–80; Man., Regional Cttee, Polish United Workers' Party (PZPR), Katowice 1980–83; at Office of Council of Ministers, becoming Vice-Dir of Chair.'s Office 1983–86; Dir Minister's Cabinet, Ministry of Mining and Energy 1986–87; Deputy Dir-Gen., Warsaw Br., Coal Community 1988–90; Br. Dir and Mem. Man. Bd Państwowa Agencja Węgla Kamiennego SA (Govt Coal Agency) 1990–93; Dir Polski Bank Inwestycyjny SA, Warsaw 1993–94; Advisor to Pres. of Man. Bd, TUiR Warta SA (insurance co.) 1994–95, also Vice-Pres., Man. Bd Warta Vita SA; mem. Man. Bd Powszechny Bank Kredytowy SA 1995–99; Pres. Man. Bd PBK Nieruchomości SA 1999–2000; Dir, Przedsiębiorstwo Obsługi Cudzoziemców Dipservice (real estate co.) 2000–01; Under-Sec. of State, Ministry of the Economy, Labour and Social Policy 2001–03; Pres., Man. Bd, PGNiG 2003–06 (resgnd); currently Chair. EnercoNet SP.

KOSTABI, Kalev Marki (Mark); American artist and composer; b. 27 Nov. 1960, Los Angeles; ed Calif. State Univ., Fullerton; involved in East Village art movt, New York 1984; f. Kostabi World (studio, gallery, offices) 1988; retrospective exhbns, Mitsukoshi Museum, Tokyo 1992, Art Museum of Estonia, Tallinn 1998; represented in various perm. collections including Museum of Modern Art, New York, Metropolitan Museum of Art, New York, Guggenheim Museum, New York, Brooklyn Museum, Corcoran Gallery of Art, Washington, DC, Groninger Museum;

has designed album covers including Guns 'n' Roses, Use Your Illusion, The Ramones' Adios Amigos; has also designed a Swatch watch, limited-edn vases, computer accessories; produces weekly cable TV show Inside Kostabi. *Albums:* I Did It Steinway 1998, Songs for Sumera 2003, New Alliance 2006. *Publications include:* Sadness Because the Video Rental Store Was Closed, Kostabi: The Early Years, Conversations With Kostabi, The Rhythm of Inspiration. *Address:* Kostabi World, 514 West 24th Street, New York, NY 10011, USA (office). *Telephone:* (212) 334-7442 (office). *E-mail:* kostabiworld@yahoo.com (office). *Website:* kostabi.com.

KOSTADINOVA, Stefka; Bulgarian high jumper (retd), government official and national organization official; *President, Bulgarian Olympic Committee;* b. 15 March 1965, Plovdiv; m. Nikolay Petrov (divorced 1999); one s.; ed Plovdiv Sports School; initially concentrated on gymnastics and swimming, later transferred to athletics; four-time European Indoor Champion: Athens 1985, Lievenne 1987, Budapest 1988, Paris 1994; European Outdoor Champion, Stuttgart 1986; set world high jump record (2.09m, still unbeaten Sept. 2005), Rome 1987; World Outdoor Champion 1987, 1995; won Silver Medal, Olympic Games, Seoul, S Korea 1988, Gold Medal, Olympic Games, Atlanta, Ga, USA 1996; five world indoor championship titles: Paris 1985, Indianapolis 1987, Budapest 1989, Toronto 1993, Paris 1997; has set altogether seven world records: three outdoors and four indoors, and has jumped over 2.00m more than 100 times, an achievement unequalled by any other athlete in the women's high jump; 1997 outdoor season curtailed due to foot injury requiring two operations, retd 1999; Vice-Pres. Bulgarian Athletics Fed. 1999–2005, Pres. 2005–; Deputy Minister of Sport and Youth 2003–; voted Sportsperson of the Year in Bulgaria 1985, 1987, 1995, 1996, voted Sportsperson of the Year in the Balkans five times, included by IAAF in the Top 10 of the Twentieth Century Female Athletes. *Address:* Bulgarian Olympic Committee, Sofia 1040, Angel Kanchev str. 4, Bulgaria (office). *Telephone:* (2) 987-56-95 (office). *Fax:* (2) 987-03-79 (office). *E-mail:* boc@bgolympic.org (office). *Website:* www.bgolympic.org (office).

KOSTELIĆ, Janica; Croatian professional skier; b. 5 Jan. 1982, Zagreb; d. of Ante Kostelić and Marica Kostelić; ed high school in Zagreb; began skiing aged three; competed at top level since age 15; competed for first time in World Cup race at Cortina d'Ampezzo, Italy 1998; competed in Olympics Games, Nagano, Japan 1998; severely damaged right knee aged 17 (at St Moritz Dec. 1999) whilst leading World Cup standings; returned to competition and won Overall World Cup title (First in Slalom and Combined), Are 2001; Gold Medals in Combined, Slalom, Giant Slalom at Winter Olympic Games, Salt Lake City, UT, USA 2002, Silver Medal at Super-G (first alpine skier to win four Olympic medals at the same Winter Games) 2002; won Slalom and Overall World Cups 2003; diagnosed with hyperthyroidism Oct. 2003; career interrupted by knee injury early 2004; third major comeback late 2004; won Slalom at Aspen, Colo Nov. 2004, Santa Caterina and San Sicario, Italy 2005; five victories in FIS World Cup in all five disciplines (Downhill, Combined, Giant Slalom, Super-G and Slalom) 2005; Gold Medal in Combined, Winter Olympic Games, Torino 2006, Silver Medal in Super-G 2006; brother Ivica Kostelić won Gold Medal in Slalom, Winter Olympics 2002; numerous nat. and int. sport awards, including Eurosport Award as World's Best Athlete 2006, Laureus Sportswoman of the Year 2006. *Leisure interests:* scuba diving, photography, music. *Address:* c/o Croatian Ski Association, Trg Krešimira Cosića 11, 10000 Zagreb, Croatia. *Telephone:* (1) 3093-009. *Fax:* (1) 3093-008. *E-mail:* janica@croski.hr. *Website:* www.janica.hr.

KOSTELKA, Lt-Gen. Miroslav; Czech politician, diplomatist and army officer (retd); b. 31 Jan. 1951, Františkovy Lázně; m.; one s. two d.; ed Mil. Acad. of Brno, NATO Defence Coll., Rome, Italy; began mil. career as bn commdr; Deputy Chief of Nat. Rear Anti-Aircraft Defences 1987–92; Chief of Staff of Main Rear Service 1992–93; Inspector, Czech Repub. Army Logistics 1994–98; Mil. Attaché, Embassy in Ottawa, Canada 1998–2002; Deputy Chief of Gen. Staff 2002–03; Minister of Defence 2003–04; Dir Prime Minister Section 2004–05; Amb. to Russia 2005–10; Ordre nat. du Mérite; Hon. Memorial Badge for services in IFOR, UN Peace Service Medal, Medal of Army of Czech Repub., Přemysl Otakar II Hon. Memorial Badge. *Address:* Ministry of Foreign Affairs, Loretánské nám. 101/5, 118 00 Prague 1, Czech Republic (office). *Telephone:* (2) 2418-1111 (office); (2) 2418-2565 (office). *Fax:* (2) 2418-2041 (office). *E-mail:* podatelna@mzv.cz (office). *Website:* www.mzv.cz (office).

KOSTIĆ, Branko, PhD; Montenegrin politician and academic; *Professor of Economy, University of Montenegro;* b. 1939, Rvaši, Montenegro; s. of Vlado Kostić and Veúka Kostić (née Vukotić; m. Milica Kostić (née Pejović); two d.; ed Belgrade Univ.; joined CP 1957; Pres. Cen. Cttee of Montenegrin Youth 1963–69; Vice-Exec. and Gen. Exec. of Aluminium Combine, Titograd 1969–79; Prof. of Economy, Univ. of Montenegro 1979–; Vice-Pres. Montenegrin Govt 1986–89; Pres. of Presidency of Montenegro 1989–90; mem. Yugoslav Collective Presidency, Vice-Pres. 1991–92; Decoration, Work Achievements with Golden Wreath; Decoration, Mil. Achievements with Silver Swords; several honours and awards. *Publications include:* Aluminium and Technical Progress 1981, 1991: To be Remembered 1996, Memoirs 2005; several publs, articles and scientific papers. *Leisure interests:* reading, writing, viniculture, gardening. *Address:* University of Montenegro, Cetinjski, put b.b., 81000 Podgorica (office); Moskovska 16, 81000 Podgorica, Montenegro (home). *Telephone:* (81) 245-014 (office); (81) 244-096 (home). *Fax:* (81) 244-096 (home). *E-mail:* majak@cg.yu (home).

KOSTIN, Andrey Leonidovich, PhD; Russian banking executive; *Chairman of the Management Board and President, VTB Bank;* b. 1956, Moscow; m.; one s.; ed Lomonosov Moscow State Univ.; various positions with Ministry of Foreign Affairs 1979–92, including USSR Consulate Gen. in Australia 1979–82, Embassy in UK 1985–90; joined Russian Investment and Finance Co. 1992; Sr Exec. and Deputy Head of Foreign Investment Dept, Imperial Bank 1993–95; First Deputy Chair., Nat. Reserve Bank (NRB) 1995–96; Exec. Chair. Vnesheconombank (Bank for Foreign Econ. Affairs) 1996–2002; Chair. Man. Bd and Pres. VTB Bank 2002–; Orders of Merit for the Fatherland III, IVth Degree, Medal of Honour, Chevalier, Ordre nat. du Mérite. *Leisure interests:* painting, football, Alpine skiing. *Address:* VTB Bank, Federation Tower West 12, Presnenskaya emb. 123100 Moscow, Russia (office). *Telephone:* (495) 739-77-39 (office). *Fax:* (495) 783-19-09 (office). *E-mail:* info@vtb.ru (office). *Website:* www.vtb.ru (office).

KOSTOV, Ivan Yordanov; Bulgarian economist and politician; *Chairman, Demokrati za silna Balgariya (Democrats for a Strong Bulgaria);* b. 23 Dec. 1949; m.; two d.; ed Karl Marx Higher Inst. of Econs, Sofia and Kliment Ohridski Univ., Sofia; Asst Prof., Karl Marx Higher Inst. of Econs 1974; Sr Asst Prof., Scientific Communism Dept, V. Iyich Lenin Higher Inst. of Mechanical and Electrical Eng, Sofia (now Tech. Univ.) 1979, Asst Prof. 1991; elected Deputy (Union of Democratic Forces—UDF) to 7th Grand Nat. Ass., Chair. Econ. Affairs Cttee 1990, Deputy to 36th Nat. Ass. 1991, 37th Ass. 1993, Deputy Floor Leader of UDF Parl. Group 1993, Deputy to 38th Ass. 1997, 39th Ass. 2001; Minister of Finance 1990–92; Chair. and Pres. Union of Democratic Forces (SDS) 1993; Prime Minister of Bulgaria 1997–2001; led group of deputies who split from UDF to form new parl. group (United Democratic Forces) and, later, Founder and Chair. Demokrati za silna Balgarija (Democrats for a Strong Bulgaria) 2004–. *Address:* Demokrati za silna Balgariya (Democrats for a Strong Bulgaria), 1000 Sofia, bul. Vitosha 18, Bulgaria (office). *Telephone:* (2) 980-53-34 (office). *Fax:* (2) 987-17-51 (office). *E-mail:* mediacentre@dsb.bg (office). *Website:* www.dsb.bg (office).

KOŠTUNICA, Vojislav, LLB, PhD; Serbian lawyer and politician; *Leader, Democratic Party of Serbia (Demokratska stranka Srbije);* b. 24 March 1944, Belgrade; s. of Jovan Koštunica and Radmila Arandjelovic; m. Dr Zorica Radović; ed Univ. of Belgrade; Lecturer in Law, Belgrade Univ. 1970–74; expelled for opposition to univ. admin. 1974; Sr Researcher, Inst. of Philosophy and Social Theories in Belgrade; took part in opposition movt from 1980s; Founder-mem. Democratic Party; left party in 1992 to form Demokratska stranka Srbije (Democratic Party of Serbia), now Chair.; remained outside mainstream politics until nominated by opposition parties to stand as a cand. against Slobodan Milošević; Pres. of the Fed. Repub. of Yugoslavia 2000–03; Prime Minister of Serbia 2004–08. *Publications include:* Political System of Capitalism and Opposition 1978, Party Pluralism or Monism (co-author) 1983, Between Force and the Law 2000, Freedom Endangered 2002, The Defence of Kosovo: Why Serbia and Not the European Union. *Address:* Demokratska stranka Srbije, 11000 Belgrade, Pariska 13, Serbia (office). *Telephone:* (11) 3204719 (office). *Fax:* (11) 3204743 (office). *E-mail:* info@dss.rs (office). *Website:* www.dss.rs (office).

KOSTYUK, Valery V., Dr Tech.; Russian mechanical engineer; *Chief Scientific Secretary of the Presidium, Russian Academy of Sciences;* b. 26 Aug. 1940, Zaporozhye, Ukraine; ed Chelyabinsk State Polytech. Inst.; engineer, Chelyabinsk Polytechnic Inst. 1962–63; Jr, then Sr Researcher and Prof., Moscow Aviation Inst. 1963–78; Chief of Research Dept, USSR Ministry of Secondary Educ. 1978–79, Deputy Dir-Gen. of Scientific Div. 1979–84; Head of Div., USSR State Planning Comm. 1984–91; Vice-Pres., then Pres. Asscn of Int. Co-operation 1993–96; First Deputy Chair. State Cttee on Science and Tech. 1996–97; First Deputy Minister of Sciences and Tech. 1997–99; mem. Russian Acad. of Sciences, Corresp. mem. 1991–97, Chief Scientific Sec. of the Presidium 2001–; mem. Russian Acad. of Eng and Tech.; USSR State Prize 1985. *Publications include:* numerous scientific papers on energy, thermal exchange and hydrodynamics in energy, cryogenics, rocket-space installations and nuclear reactors. *Address:* Russian Academy of Sciences, Moscow 119991, Leninsky prosp. 14, Russia (office). *Website:* www.ras.ru (office).

KOSUMI, Bajram, DPhil; Kosovo politician and academic; *Professor, University of Priština;* b. 20 March 1960, Tuxhec, Kamenicë; m.; four c.; ed Univ. of Priština; student movt leader, Priština 1981; sentenced to 10 years for opposing communist govt of Yugoslavia; journalist 1991–93; mem. Alliance for Future of Kosova (AAK), Pres. Parl. Party 1994–96, Vice-Pres. AAK 2000–02; Minister of Public Information, Interim Govt of Kosovo 1999; mem. Ass. of Kosovo 2001–04, 2004–07, 2007–; Minister for Environment and Spatial Planning of Kosovo 2004–05; Prime Minister of Kosovo 2005–06 (resgnd); Prof., Univ. of Priština. *Publications:* A Concept on Sub-Policy 1995, Vocabulary of Barbarians 2000, A Concept on the New Political Thought 2001, Lyric of Fishta 2004, Literature from Prison 2006, A Decisive Year 2006. *Leisure interest:* mountain hiking. *Address:* Street Sylejman Vokshi H A, 9A Priština (home); c/o Government Building, Assembly of Republic of Kosovo, Mother Teresa Street, N.N., Priština, Kosovo (office). *E-mail:* bajram .kosumi@ks-gov.net (office); lamippk@yahoo.com (home).

KOSUTH, Joseph; American artist; b. 31 Jan. 1945, Toledo, Ohio; two d.; ed Toledo Museum School of Design, privately under the Belgian painter Line Bloom Draper, Cleveland Inst. of Art, School of Visual Arts, New York; pioneer of conceptual art and installation art during 1960s; moved to New York 1965; f. Museum of Normal Art, New York 1967; Prof., School of Visual Arts, New York 1967–85, Hochschule für Bildende Künste, Hamburg, Germany 1988–90, Staatliche Akad. der Bildende Künste, Stuttgart 1991–97, Kunstakademie Munich 2001–06, currently at Inst. Universitario di Architettura, Venice, Italy; Visiting and Guest Lecturer, Yale Univ., Cornell Univ., New York Univ., Duke Univ., UCLA, Cal Arts, Cooper Union, Pratt Inst., The Musuem of Modern Art, Art Inst. of Chicago, Royal Academy, Copenhagen, Ashmolean Museum, Oxford, of Rome, Berliln Kunstakademie, RCA, London, Glasgow School of Art, Hayward Gallery, London, Sorbonne, Paris, Sigmund Freud Museum, Vienna; co-ed. The Fox magazine 1975–76; art ed. Marxist Perspectives 1977–78; Chevalier des Arts et Lettres 1993, Decoration of Honour in Gold (Austria) 2003; Dr hc (Bologna, Italy); Cassandra Foundation Grant 1968, Brandeis Univ. Creative Art Award 1990, Frederick R. Weisman Art Foundation Award 1991, Venice Biennale Menzione d'Onore 1993, 3 franc postage stamp issued in honour of his work in Figeac (France) 1999. *Publication:* Art After Philosophy and After (collected writings) 1991, Purloined (novel) 2001, Guide to Contemporary Art Special Edn 2003. *Address:* 591 Broadway, New York, NY 10012 (home); c/o Sean Kelly, 528 East 29th Street, New York, NY 10001, USA (office). *Telephone:* (212) 219-8984 (New York) (home); (6) 68809621 (Rome) (home).

KOTAITE, Assad, LLD; Lebanese lawyer and international aviation official (retd); b. 6 Nov. 1924, Hasbaya; s. of Adib Kotaite and Kamle Abousamra; m. Monique Ayoub 1983; ed French Univ., Beirut, Univ. of Paris and Acad. of Int. Law, The Hague; Head of Legal and Int. Affairs, Directorate of Civil Aviation, Lebanon 1953–56; Rep. of Lebanon, Council of ICAO 1956–70; Sec.-Gen. ICAO 1970–76, Pres. Council 1976–2006 (retd); Pres. Int. Court of Aviation and Space Arbitration, Paris 1995–; many decorations from academic insts and foreign states. *Address:* 5955 Wilderton Avenue, Apt O4A, Montreal, PQ, H3S 2V1, Canada (home).

KOTAK, Uday, BCom, MMS; Indian business executive; *Executive Vice-Chairman and Managing Director, Kotak Mahindra Bank;* b. 15 March 1959; s. of Suresh Kotak and Indira Kotak; m.; two c.; ed Sydenham Coll. and Jamnalal Bajaj Inst. of Man. Studies, Bombay Univ.; Exec. Vice-Chair. and Man. Dir Kotak Mahindra Bank (fmrly Kotak Mahindra Finance Ltd) 2002–; Chair. Kotak Securities Ltd; Chair. and Dir Kotak Mahindra Primus Ltd; Dir of various subsidiary cos including Kotak Securities Ltd, Kotak Mahindra Asset Man. Co Ltd, Kotak Mahindra Capital Co Ltd, OM Kotak Mahindra Life Insurance Co Ltd; mem. Bd of Dirs Bajaj Hindustan Ltd, Dabur India Ltd, Ford Credit Kotak Mahindra Ltd, Kotak Forex Brokerage Ltd, Mahindra & Mahindra Financial Services Ltd, Hutchison Max Telecom Pvt. Ltd, Business Standard Ltd, Indiacar.com Pvt. Ltd, Blue Star Ltd –2002; mem. Advisory Cttee Nat. Stock Exchange of India Ltd; mem. Exec. Bd Indian School of Business; mem. Bd of Govs. Indian Council for Research on Int. Econ. Relations; Governing mem. Mahindra United World Coll. of India; named Global Leader of Tomorrow by the World Econ. Forum 1996, Centre for Org. Devt V. Krishnamurthy Award for Excellence 2007. *Leisure interests:* plays sitar, cricket. *Address:* Kotak Mahindra Bank, 36–38A, Nariman Bhavan, 227 Nariman Point, Mumbai 400 021, India (office). *Telephone:* (22) 66384444 (office). *Fax:* (22) 66384455 (office). *Website:* www.kotak.com (office).

KOTANKO, Christoph, PhD; Austrian editor; *Editor-in-Chief, Kurier;* b. 27 July 1953, Braunau am Inn; m. Ingrid Kotanko; one d.; ed Gymnasium, Braunau, studied Romance languages and journalism in Vienna and Paris; Domestic Ed., Wochenpresse 1979–86, Ed. news magazine profile 1986–88; Head of Domestic Policy and commentator for daily newspaper Kurier, with a special focus on European and security policy 1988–97, Deputy Ed.-in-Chief 1997–2003, Exec. Ed.-in-Chief 2003–05, Ed.-in-Chief 2005–; Goldenes Verdienstzeichen der Republik Österreich (für EU-Berichterstattung), Officier, Ordre nat. du Mérite 2005; Kurt-Vorhofer Prize 1999. *Address:* Kurier, Lindengasse 48–52, 1072 Vienna, Austria (office). *Telephone:* (1) 521-00 (office). *Fax:* (1) 521-00-22-57 (office). *E-mail:* leser@kurier.at (office). *Website:* www.kurier.at (office).

KOTCHEFF, Ted; Canadian film and stage director; b. 7 April 1931, Toronto; m. Laifun Chung; two c.; ed Univ. of Toronto; with CBC Television 1952–57; joined ABC-TV, London 1957; f. Panoptica Productions in Canada with wife Laifun Chung 1996. *Films include:* Life At The Top 1965, Two Gentlemen Sharing 1968, Wake In Fright 1971, The Apprenticeship of Duddy Kravitz (in Canada) 1973–74, Fun with Dick and Jane 1977, Who is Killing the Great Chefs of Europe? 1978, North Dallas Forty (dir and writer) 1979, First Blood, Split Image, 1982–83, Uncommon Valour 1984, Joshua, Then and Now 1985, Switching Channels 1988, Weekend at Bernie's 1989, Winter People (dir) 1989, Folks! (actor) 1992, The Shooter 1995,. *Plays include:* Play With A Tiger, Maggie May, The Au Pair Man, Have You Any Dirty Washing, Mother Dear?. *Television includes:* The Human Voice 1966, Of Mice And Men 1968, Edna The Inebriate Woman 1971, What Are Families for? 1993, Love on the Run 1994, Family of Cops 1995, A Husband, a Wife and a Lover 1996, Borrowed Hearts 1997, Buddy Faro (series) 1998, Crime in Connecticut: The Story of Alex Kelly 1999, Law & Order: Special Victims Unit (exec. producer) 2000–05.

KOTENEV, Vladimir V.; Russian diplomatist and business executive; *Managing Director, GAZPROM Germania GmbH;* b. 1957, Moscow; m. Maria S. Koteneva; two c.; ed Moscow State Univ.; joined Foreign Service 1979, served in various positions, including Cen. Apparatus, Ministry of Foreign Affairs, becoming Adviser and Deputy Dir, Secr. of Minister of Foreign Affairs, postings abroad include Cultural Attaché, Embassy in Vienna, Amb. to Switzerland, Chargé d'affaires a.i., Embassy in Berne 1999–2001, Dir Dept for Consular Services, Ministry of Foreign Affairs 2001–04, Amb. to Germany 2004–10; Man. Dir GAZPROM Germania GmbH 2010–. *Address:* GAZPROM Germania GmbH, Corporate Communication, Markgrafenstraße 23, 10117 Berlin, Germany (office). *Telephone:* (30) 20195-0 (office). *Fax:* (30) 20195-313 (office). *E-mail:* info@gazprom-germania.de (office). *Website:* www.gazprom-germania.de (office).

KOTENKOV, Maj.-Gen. Aleksander Alekseyevich; Russian politician; *Representative of the President, Federation Council;* b. 23 Sept. 1952, Krasnodar Territory; m.; one s.; ed Rostov-on-Don Inst. of Agric. Machine Construction, Mil.-Political Acad. by corresp.; engineer Rostov Don Factory Rubin 1974–75; army service 1975–90; People's Deputy Russian Fed. 1990–93; Deputy Chair. Cttee Supreme Soviet on Defence and Security 1991; Deputy Head, Head State Law Dept, Russian Presidency, 1992–93; Head Provincial Admin, Martial Law Zone, N Ossetia and Ingushetia 1993–95; Deputy Minister of Nat. Policy 1995–96; mem. State Duma (Parl.) 1993–96; Rep. of President in State Duma 1996–2004, in Fed. Council 2004–. *Address:* c/o Office of the President, Staraya pl. 4, 103132 Moscow, Russia (office). *Telephone:* (495) 925-35-81 (office). *Fax:* (495) 206-07-66 (office). *E-mail:* president@gov.ru (office). *Website:* www.kremlin.ru (office).

KOTEREC, Miloš, MSc, MBA; Slovak politician, diplomatist and UN official; *State Secretary, Ministry of Defence;* b. 11 Oct. 1962, Partizánske; m. (divorced); two c.; ed Faculty of Electrotechnical Eng and Informatics, Slovak Tech. Univ., Bratislava, Faculty of Law, Commenius Univ., Bratislava; Asst Lecturer, Faculty of Electrotechnical Eng and Informatics, Slovak Tech. Univ., Bratislava 1989–93; began career in civil service 1993, promoted to Chief of UN Section, Dept of the UN and Other Int. Orgs, Ministry of Foreign Affairs, Second Sec., Perm. Mission to UN, New York 1995–98, First Sec. and Acting Deputy Chief of Mission 1998–99, served in Dept for the OSCE, Disarmament and Council of Europe, Ministry of Foreign Affairs 1999–2000, Dir 2000–01, apptd Counsellor, Mission of Slovakia to NATO, Brussels 2001, Deputy Perm. Rep. 2001–04, Amb. and Perm. Rep. to UN, New York 2009–12, apptd Chair of First Cttee (Disarmament and International Security), UN 2010, Sr Vice-Pres. UN ECOSOC 2011–12, Pres. 2012–13; State Sec., Ministry of Defence 2012–; mem. European Parl. 2004–09. *Address:* Ministry of Defence, Kutuzovova 8, 832 47 Bratislava, Slovakia (office). *Telephone:* 960-311-740 (office). *Fax:* 960-312-642 (office). *E-mail:* press@mod.gov.sk (office). *Website:* www.mosr.sk (office).

KOTLER, Philip, MA, PhD; American professor of marketing; *S.C. Johnson & Son Distinguished Professor of International Marketing, Kellogg School of Management, Northwestern University;* b. 27 May 1931; s. of Maurice Kotler and Betty Kotler; three d.; ed Univ. of Chicago, Massachusetts Inst. of Tech.; post-doctoral research in math., Harvard Univ., in behavioural science, Univ. of

Chicago; currently S.C. Johnson & Son Distinguished Prof. of Int. Marketing, Kellogg School of Man., Northwestern Univ., Evanston, IL; consultant for IBM, Gen. Electric, AT&T, Honeywell, Bank of America, Merck; fmr Chair. Coll. of Marketing, Inst. of Man. Sciences; fmr Dir American Marketing Asscn (AMA), MAC Group; fmr mem. Yankelovivh Advisory Bd; currently mem. Bd of Govs School of Art Inst., Chicago, Advisory Bd Drucker Foundation; fmr Trustee, Marketing Science Inst.; Hon. PhD (Stockholm Univ., Univ. of Zürich, Athens Univ. of Econs and Business, DePaul Univ., Kraków School of Business and Econs, HEC–Paris, Vienna Univ. of Econs and Business Admin, Budapest Univ. of Econ. Science and Public Admin, Catholic Univ. of Santo Domingo); Paul Converse Award, AMA 1978, Distinguished Marketing Educator Award, AMA 1985, Award for Marketing Excellence, European Asscn of Marketing Consultants and Sales Trainers, Annual Charles Coolidge Parlin Marketing Research Award 1989, Marketer of the Year, Sales and Marketing Execs Int. 1995, Marketing Educator of the Year, Acad. of Marketing Science 2002. *Publications include:* Marketing Management: Analysis, Planning, Implementation and Control 1967, Principles of Marketing, Marketing Models, Strategic Marketing for Non-Profit Organizations, The New Competition, High Visibility, Social Marketing, Marketing Places, Marketing for Congregations, Marketing for Hospitality and Tourism, The Marketing of Nations, Kotler on Marketing, Marketing Insights from A to Z 2003; over 100 articles in professional journals. *Address:* Kellogg School of Management, Northwestern University, 2001 Sheridan Road, Evanston, IL 60208, USA (office). *Telephone:* (847) 491-3522 (office). *Fax:* (847) 491-2498 (office). *E-mail:* kelloggmedia@kellogg.northwestern.edu (office). *Website:* www.kellogg.northwestern.edu (office).

KOTLYAKOV, Vladimir Mikhailovich, DrGeogSc; Russian geographer and glaciologist; *Director, Institute of Geography, Russian Academy of Sciences;* b. 6 Nov. 1931, Lobnya, Moscow Region; m. Valentina Alexeevna Bazanova; two s.; ed Moscow State Univ.; Jr Researcher, Sr Researcher, Head of Glaciology Dept, Inst. of Geography USSR (now Russian) Acad. of Sciences 1954–86, Dir 1986–; Corresp. mem., Russian Acad. of Sciences 1976, mem. 1991–; Vice-Pres. Russian Geographical Soc. 1980–2000, Hon. Pres. 2000–; People's Deputy of USSR 1989–91; mem. Academia Europaea, Earth Council 1993–2000, French Acad. of Sciences 2002–, Georgian Acad. of Sciences 1996–; Hon. mem. American, Mexican, Italian, Estonian and Georgian Geographical Socs, Int. Glaciological Soc.; Litke Gold Medal, Russian Geographical Soc. 1985, Przhevalsky Gold Medal, Russian Geographical Soc. 1995, State Prize of Russian Fed. 2002, Russian Ind. Prize 'Triumph' 2004, Berg Gold Medal, Russian Acad. of Sciences 2005, Nobel Peace Prize 2007, Great Gold Medal, Russian Geographical Soc. 2004, Konstantin Medal, Russian Geographical Soc. 2011, Demidoff Prize 2012, Schmidt Prize, Russian Acad. of Sciences 2013. *Publications include:* Snow Cover of Antarctica 1961, Snow Cover of the Earth and Glaciers 1968, Glaciology Dictionary 1984, Elsevier's Dictionary of Glaciology 1990, World of Snow and Ice 1994, Science, Society, Environment 1997, World Atlas of Snow and Ice Resources 1997; Collection of Selected Works: Glaciology of Antarctica (Vol. 1) 2000, Snow Cover and Glaciers of the Earth (Vol. 2) 2004, Geography in the Changing World (Vol. 3) 2001, Ice, Love and Hypothesis (Vol. 4) 2001, In the World of Snow and Ice (Vol. 5) 2002, Science is a Life (Vol. 6) 2003, Elsevier's Dictionary of Geography 2007, Dictionary of Tourism, Culture and Travel 2013. *Leisure interest:* travelling. *Address:* Institute of Geography, Russian Academy of Sciences, Staromonetny per. 29, 119017 Moscow (office); Profsoyuznaya str. 43-1-80, 117420 Moscow, Russia (home). *Telephone:* (495) 959-00-32 (office); (495) 957-08-34 (home). *Fax:* (495) 959-00-33 (office). *E-mail:* vladkot6@gmail.com; vladkot4@gmail.com. *Website:* www.igras.com (office).

KOTROMANOVIĆ, Ante, MBA; Croatian politician and fmr army officer; *Minister of Defence;* b. 8 May 1968, Potravlje, Sinj; m.; one d.; ed Croatian Mil. Acad., Ban Josip Jelacic War Coll., Univ. of Zagreb; Company Commdr, Special Forces of the Croatian Armed Forces Gen. Staff 1991–92, Bn Commdr, Sinj Training Centre 1992–93, Commdr, Sinj Operations Group and 126th Sinj Brigade 1993–96, Commdr, 4th Guard Brigade Split 1996–2001, Chief of Staff of Dubrovnik Mil. Dist 2001–02, retd (rank of Col) 2002; columnist, Vecernji List (daily newspaper) 2004–05; Dir Demining Co. Zdrug Ltd 2005–06; mem. Man. Bd Urbaniko Ltd 2006–07; mem. Sabor (Parl.) 2007–11, Chair. Veterans' Cttee 2007–11; Minister of Defence 2011–; mem. Social Democratic Party of Croatia (Socijaldemokratska partija Hrvatske) 2007–; Order of Duke Domagoj, Order of Nikola Subic Zrinski, Order of Count Jelacic; Medal for Exceptional Ventures, Memorial of Homeland War, Memorial of Homeland Gratitude. *Address:* Ministry of Defence, 10000 Zagreb, Sarajevska cesta 7, Croatia (office). *Telephone:* (1) 4832404 (office). *Fax:* (1) 4613310 (office). *E-mail:* infor@morh.hr (office). *Website:* www.morh.hr (office).

KÖTSCHAU, Gabriele, DrIur; German barrister, politician and international organization official; b. (Gabriele Bögelsack), 1950, Berlin; m.; two c.; ed Free Univ. of Berlin, Christian-Albrechts Univ. of Kiel; practised as lawyer in Flensburg; joined SPD 1972, Chair. SPD, Schleswig-Flensburg Dist 1994–2000; mem. Schleswig-Holstein Parl. 1988–2005, Adjunct mem. Bd SPD Parl. Group 1992–96, also Chair. Interior and Legal Affairs Cttee, Second Vice-Pres. Parl. 1996–2005; Dir Gen. of the Secr., Council of the Baltic Sea States 2005–10; Bundesverdienstkreuz. *Publications:* numerous lectures and articles on Baltic Sea cooperation and Eastern Europe. *Address:* c/o Council of the Baltic Sea States, Strömsborg, PO Box 2010, Stockholm 103 11, Sweden.

KOTSCHERGA, Anatoly Ivanovich; Ukrainian singer (bass); b. 9 July 1947, Vinnitsa; s. of Ivan Kotscherga and Maria Kotscherga; m. Lina Kotscherga 1985; one d.; ed Kiev Conservatoire and studied at La Scala, Milan; soloist, Shevchenko Opera and Ballet, Kiev 1972–, also Vienna State Opera 1990–; Glinka Prize 1971, Tchaikovsky Prize 1974, USSR People's Artist 1983. *Major roles include:* Boris Godunov, Galitsky (Borodin's Prince Igor), Don Basilio (Barber of Seville), Mephistopheles (Gounod's Faust), Don Carlos (Verdi), Don Giovanni (Mozart), Khovanshchina (Mussorgsky), Dosiphey (Khovanshchina), Nilakanta (Lakmé), USSR People's Artist 1983. *Leisure interest:* tennis. *Address:* Michael Lewin International Artists' Management, c/o EUROARTISTS Künstlermanagement GmbH (Geschäftsführerin: Elisabetta Hartl), Gluckgasse 1/1, 1010 Vienna, Austria; Gogolevskaho 37, Korp. 2, Apt. 47, Kiev 254053, Ukraine. *E-mail:* office@lewin-management.com.

KOTTO, Yaphet Fredrick; American actor; b. 15 Nov. 1944, Harlem, New York; s. of Yaphet Mangobell Kotto and Gladys M. Kotto; m. Antoinette Pettyjohn 1975; six c. *Films include*: Nothing But a Man 1963, Liberation of Lord Byron Jones 1964, Across 110th Street 1973, Live and Let Die 1974, Report to the Commissioner 1974, Sharks Treasure 1974, Monkey Hustle 1975, Drum 1976, Blue Collar 1977, Alien 1978, Brubaker 1979, Hey Good Looking 1982, Fighting Back 1982, Star Chamber 1983, Warning Sign 1985, Terminal Entry 1986, Eye of the Tiger 1986, PrettyKill 1987, The Running Man 1987, Midnight Run 1988, Nightmare of the Devil (also dir), Terminal Entry 1986, Jigsaw Murders 1988, A Whisper to a Scream 1989, Ministry of Vengeance 1989, Tripwire 1990, Hangfire 1991, Freddy's Dead 1991, Almost Blue 1992, Extreme Justice 1993, Intent to Kill 1993, The Puppet Masters 1994, Dead Badge 1995, Out-of-Sync 1995, Two If By Sea 1996. *Theatre includes*: Great White Hope, Blood Knot, Black Monday, In White America, A Good Place to Raise a Boy, Fences (London) 1990. *Television includes*: Raid on Entebbe 1977, Rage 1980, Women of San Quentin 1983, In Self Defense 1987, Badge of the Assassin, Harem, Desperado, Perry Mason, Prime Target, After the Shock, Chrome Soldiers, It's Nothing Personal, Extreme Justice, The American Clock, Deadline For Murder, Homicide: Life on the Street (series) 1993–99, The Defenders: Payback 1997, Homicide: The Movie 2000, The Ride 2000, Stiletto Dance 2001. *Address*: 480 N. Westlake Boulevard, Malibu, CA 90265, USA (office).

KOUCHNER, Bernard, (Bernard Gridaine), KBE, DenM; French politician, physician and screenwriter; b. 1 Nov. 1939, Avignon; m. 1st Evelyne Pisier, two s. one d.; m. 2nd Christine Ockrent (q.v.), one s.; gastro-enterologist, Hôpital Cochin, Paris; Co-founder and Pres. Médecins sans Frontières 1971–79; Founder, Médecins du Monde 1980; has organized and undertaken numerous humanitarian missions world-wide since 1968; Sec. of State, Ministry of Social Affairs and Employment May 1988; Sec. of State responsible for Humanitarian Action, Office of Prime Minister 1988–91, Ministry of Foreign Affairs 1991–92; Minister of Health and Humanitarian Action 1992–93, 1997–99, Minister Del., Ministry of Health 2001–02; Minister of Foreign and European Affairs 2007–10; mem. European Parl. 1994–97; UN Chief Admin., Kosovo 1999–2001; Founder, Foundation for Humanitarian Action 1993–; radio broadcaster RTL 2 1995; Founder, Malades sans Frontières 2003; fmr Prof. of Public Health and Devt, CNAM; Dr hc (Durham, Pristina, Sarajevo, Ben Gurion, Erasmus Rotterdam); Dag Hammarskjöld Prize 1979, Louis Weiss Prize (European Parl.) 1979, Athinai Prize (Alexander Onassis Foundation) 1981, Prix Europa 1984, Nobel Peace Prize (with Médecins sans Frontières) 1999, Prix de la Tolerance 2003. *Television*: as Bernard Gridaine has written scripts for series including Médecins de Nuit, Hotel de Police, Bonjour Maitre. *Publications*: La France Sauvage, Les Voraces, L'Ile de Lumière, Charité Business, Le Devoir d'Ingérence (co-author) 1988, Les Nouvelles Solidarités 1989, Le Malheur des Autres 1991, Dieu et les Hommes (co-author) 1993, Vingt idées pour l'an 2000 1995, Ce que je crois 1995, La dictature médicale 1995, le Premier qui dit la Verité 2002, Les Guerres de la Paix 2004, Quand tu sera Président (co-author) 2004. *Address*: c/o Ministry of Foreign Affairs, 37 quai d'Orsay, 75351 Paris Cedex 07, France (office).

KOUDELKA, Josef; French (b. Czechslovakian) photographer; b. 10 Jan. 1938, Boskovice; ed Technical Univ. of Prague; aeronautical engineer, Prague and Bratislava 1961–67; specialized in photography 1967–; extensive travel throughout Europe documenting lives of gypsies; exhibited in Prague 1961, 1967, MOMA, New York 1975, Amsterdam 1978, Stockholm 1980, Hayward Gallery, London 1984 etc. mem. Magnum Photos Inc. 1971–; mem. Union of Czechoslovakian artists 1965–; Chevalier des Arts et Lettres 1992; Prix Nadar 1978, Grand Prix Nat. de la Photographie (France) 1987, Hugo Erhurth Prize 1989, Prix Romanes 1989, Henri Cartier-Bresson Award 1991, Century Medal of the Royal Photographic Soc., UK, Medal of Merit 2002, and others. *Publications*: Gypsies 1975, Photopoche Josef Koudelka 1984, Exils 1 1988, Mission Photographique Transmanche 1989, Prague 1990, Z. Fotografickeho Dila 1958–1990 1990, Divaldo Za Branou 1965–1970 1993, Black Triangle 1994, Wales Reconnaissance 1998, Chaos 1999, Lime Stone 2001, Teatro del Tempo 2003. *Address*: c/o Magnum Photos, 19 rue Hégesippe Moneau, 75018 Paris, France.

KOULIBALY, Mamadou, PhD; Côte d'Ivoirian economist, academic and politician; *President of National Assembly;* b. 21 April 1957, Azaguié, Agboville; m.; three c.; Prof. of Econ. Science, Univ. of Abidjan; Minister of Economy and Finance 2000–01; Pres. of Nat. Ass. 2001–; acting Pres. Ivorian Popular Front (FPI) 2011–. *Address*: Assemblée Nationale, 01 BP 1381, Abidjan 01, Côte d'Ivoire (office). *Telephone*: 20-21-60-69 (office). *Fax*: 20-22-20-87 (office).

KOUMI, Margaret (Maggie); British journalist; b. 15 July 1942; d. of the late Yiasoumis Koumi and Melexidia Paraskeva; m. Ramon Sola 1980; ed Buckingham Gate, London; sec. Thomas Cook 1957–60; sub-ed., feature and fiction writer Visual Features Ltd 1960–66; sub-ed. TV World 1966–67; Production Ed. 19 Magazine 1967–69, Ed. 1969–86, concurrently Ed. Hair Magazine; Man. Ed. Practical Parenting, Practical Health, Practical Hair and Beauty 1986–87; Jt Ed. Hello! 1988–93, Ed. 1993–2001, Consultant Ed. 2001–; Jt Ed. of the Year Award 1991. *Publications*: Beauty Care 1981, Clarides – Within The Image 2004. *Leisure interests*: reading, travel, exploring markets.

KOUMURA, Masahiko, LLB; Japanese politician; b. Ehime; m.; two s. one d.; ed Chuo Univ.; Parl. Vice-Minister Defence Agency 1987, for Finance 1989, for Foreign Affairs 1996; Minister of State, Dir-Gen. Econ. Planning Agency 1994–95; mem. House of Reps for Yamaguchi 1980–, Chair. Special Cttee on Disasters 1991, on Agric., Forestry and Fisheries 1991, on Prevention of Int. Terrorism and Japan's Cooperation and Support 2003, on Humanitarian Assistance for Reconstruction in Iraq 2003; Deputy Sec.-Gen. LDP, Dir Nat. Defence Div. 1991, Chair. Special Cttee on External Econ. Cooperation 2002; Minister of Foreign Affairs 1999, 2007–08, of Justice 2000–01, of Defence 2007; Pres. Japan-China Friendship Parliamentarians' Union. *Address*: Liberal-Democratic Party (LDP), 1-11-23, Nagata-cho, Chiyoda-ku, Tokyo 100-8910, Japan (office). *Telephone*: (3) 3581-6211 (office). *E-mail*: koho@ldp.jimin.or.jp (office). *Website*: www.jimin.jp (office).

KOUPAKI, Pascal Irénée, MA; Benin politician; *Prime Minister;* b. 1951; ed Université Nationale du Benin, Université de Paris I, France, Centre de Formation Banque Centrale des Etats de l'Afrique de l'Ouest, Dakar, Senegal; various positions with Centre de Formation Banque Centrale des Etats de l'Afrique de l'Ouest, including Dir and Asst Gov., Dakar 1979–90, Dir of Research Dept 1998–2006; Deputy Head of Cabinet of Prime Minister of Côte d'Ivoire 1990–94; with IMF 1994–96; Head of Cabinet of Prime Minister of Benin Adrien Houngbédjiego 1996–98; Minister of Devt, Economy and Finance 2006–07, Minister of State for Planning, Devt, Evaluation of Public Policy and Coordination of Govt 2007–10; Prime Minister of Benin, responsible for Co-ordination of Govt Action, Evaluation of Public Policy, Denationalization and Social Dialogue 2011–; Leader, Union for the Devt of the New Benin (Union pour le Développement du Benin Nouveau). *Address*: Office of the Prime Minister, Cotonou, Benin (office).

KOURULA, Erkki, LLL, LLM, PhD; Finnish lawyer, diplomatist and judge; *Judge, Appeals Division, International Criminal Court;* b. 12 June 1948, Lappee; m. Dr Pirkko Kourula; two c.; ed Univ. of Helsinki, Univ. of Oxford, UK; research posts at Univs of Oxford and Helsinki, Acad. of Finland, UN, Geneva 1972–82, 1984–85; Dist Judge 1979; Prof. of Int. Law, Univ. of Lapland, Rovaniemi 1982–83; Counsellor and Legal Adviser, Ministry of Foreign Affairs 1986–89, Dir Int. Law Div. 1989–91; Minister Counsellor and Legal Adviser, Perm. Mission to UN, New York 1991–95; Amb., Deputy Dir Gen. for Legal Affairs, Ministry of Foreign Affairs 1995–98, Dir Gen. for Legal Affairs 2002–03; Amb., Perm. Rep. to Council of Europe, Strasbourg 1998–2002; Judge, Appeals Div., Int. Criminal Court (ICC), The Hague 2003–; Head Del. to Preparatory Cttee for ICC 1994–98; Agent of Finland to European Courts of Justice and Human Rights; mem. Del. to UN Gen. Ass. 1986–90, 1995–97; mem., chair. or del. to numerous int. orgs, cttees and confs. *Publications include*: The Identification and Characteristics of Regional Arrangements for the Purpose of the United Nations Charter (doctoral thesis); contribs to publs and articles on activities of UN and ICC. *Address*: International Criminal Court, PO Box 19519, 2500 CM The Hague, The Netherlands (office). *Telephone*: (70) 515-8072 (office). *Fax*: (70) 515-8789 (office). *E-mail*: erkki.kourula@icc-cpi.int (office). *Website*: icc-cpi.int (office).

KÕUTS, Vice Adm. Tarmo; Estonian naval officer; b. 27 Nov. 1953, Saaremaa Island; m. Velina Kõuts; one s.; ed Tallinn Maritime Coll., Kaliningrad Tech. Inst., Nat. Defence Acad., Finland; held positions successively as officer, capt. and capt.-instructor on various ships, Estonian Shipping Co. 1973–90; Rector, Estonian Maritime Acad. 1990–93; Dir-Gen. Estonian Border Guard 1993–99; Commdr of Estonian Defence Forces 2000–06 (resgnd); mem. Riigikogu (State Ass.) 2007–, mem. Union of Pro Patria and Res Publica (IRL—Isamaa ja Res Publica Liit); Pres. Estonian Shooting Union; Order of the Cross of Eagle (2nd Class) 1998, Royal Norwegian Order of Merit 2002, Grand Cross Order of Prince Henry the Navigator (Portugal) 2003, Order of the National Coat of Arms (2nd Class) 2005, Commdr Grand Cross of Order of Viesturs (Latvia) 2005, Distinguished Service Decoration Estonian Defence Forces. *Leisure interests*: hunting, fishing, sailing. *Address*: Riigikogu (State Assembly) Lossi plats 1a, Tallinn 15165, Estonia (office). *Telephone*: 631-6331 (office). *Fax*: 631-6334 (office). *E-mail*: riigikogu@riigikogu.ee (office). *Website*: www.riigikogu.ee (office).

KOUVELIS, Fotis-Fanourios (Fotis); Greek lawyer and politician; *President, Democratic Left;* b. 3 Sept. 1948, Volos; m. Photeine Pallas; two d.; ed Univ. of Athens; mem. Lambrakis Youth; Founding mem. CP of Greece (Interior) (KKE Interior), mem. Cen. Cttee 1975–86; Founding mem. Greek Left party 1987, Gen. Sec. 1989–92; mem. Synaspismós 1992–2010; Pres. Democratic Left (Dimokratiki Aristera—DIMAR) (f. by fmr mems of Coalition of the Left of Movements and Ecology 2010) 2010–; mem. of the Vouli (Parl.) 1989–93, 1996–; Minister for Justice July–Oct. 1989; Municipal Councillor, Municipality of Athens 2002–04; mem. Bd Athens Bar Asscn 1975–, Chair. 1987–89; Chair. Rehabilitation Centre for Torture Victims 1991–94; mem. Peace Movements and Human Rights. *Address*: Democratic Left (Dimokratiki Aristera), Kriezotou 4, 106 71 Athens, Greece (office). *Telephone*: (210) 3820790 (office). *Fax*: (210) 3834831 (office). *E-mail*: info@dimokratikiaristera.gr (office). *Website*: www.dimokratikiaristera.gr (office); www.kouvelis.gr.

KOUYATÉ, Lansana; Guinean international organization official, diplomatist and politician; b. 1950, Koba; m.; three c.; joined Foreign Service 1983, Counsellor, Embassy in Cote d'Ivoire 1983–85, Head of Africa and OAU Dept, Ministry of Foreign Affairs 1985–87, Amb. to Egypt, Sudan, Turkey, Jordan, Syria and Lebanon 1987–92, Perm. Rep. to UN, New York 1992–97, Vice-Pres. ECOSOC 1992–93, Sec. Gen's Special Rep. to Somalia 1993–94, Under-Sec.-Gen. in charge of Political Affairs for Africa, Western Asia and Middle East, UN Security Council 1994–97; Exec. Sec. Econ. Community of W African States (ECOWAS) 1997–2002; Perm. Rep. to Int. Org. of Francophone Countries 2002–07; Prime Minister of Guinea 2007–08; cand. in presidential election 2010; Commdr, Légion d'honneur, Commdr of the Mono Order (Togo), African Star (Liberia). *Publications include*: International Funding of State-owned Companies in Guinea: Problems and Prospects, The End of the Cold War and its Impact on Third-World Countries. *Address*: c/o Office of the Prime Miinister, National Assembly, Palais du Peuple, BP 414, Conakry, Guinea (office).

KOVÁČ, Michal; Slovak politician, economist and banker; b. 5 Aug. 1930, Lubiša, E Slovakia; m. Emília Kováčová; two c.; ed Commercial Acad., Bratislava Univ. of Econs; Asst Lecturer, Bratislava Univ. of Econs 1954; joined staff State Bank of Czechoslovakia 1956; fmr financial adviser to Nat. Bank of Cuba; Deputy Dir Zivnostenska (trade bank), London 1967–69, recalled, expelled from CP and demoted to bank clerk 1969; researcher, lecturer 1970–78; elected to Fed. Ass. 1990; Minister of Finance, Slovak Repub. 1990, resgnd 1991; re-elected to Fed. Ass., Chair. Czech Fed. Ass. of Czech and Slovak Fed. Rep. June–Dec. 1992; Pres. of Slovak Repub. 1993–98; C-in-C the Armed Forces 1993–98; Chair. M. Kováč and V. Havel Foundation 1993–; fmr mem. Movt for a Democratic Slovakia, Deputy Chair. 1991–93; Grand Cross, Order of Merit (Poland) 1994, White Eagle Order (Poland) 1997, numerous Slovak decorations including White Double Cross Order, Ľudovít Štúr Order; CEELIA Award, American Bar Asscn 1995, Lions Club Award 1995. *Address*: c/o Office of the President, Hodžovo nám. 1, PO Box 128, 810 00 Bratislava, Slovakia.

KOVACEVICH, Richard (Dick) M., BEng, MEng, MBA; American banking executive; *Chairman, Wells Fargo & Company;* b. 1944; ed Stanford Univ.; Exec. Vice-Pres. Kenner Div., Gen. Mills Inc., Minneapolis 1967–72; Prin. Venture Capital 1972–75; Vice-Pres. Consumer Services Norwest Corpn, Minneapolis 1975, subsequently Sr Vice-Pres. New York banking group, Exec. Vice-Pres., Man.

New York bank div., Exec. Vice-Pres., mem. Policy Cttee, Vice-Chair., COO banking group, Pres., COO, Vice-Chair., Chair. and CEO 1996–98; Pres. and CEO Wells Fargo & Co. (after merger with Norwest Corpn), San Francisco 1999–2005, Chair. and CEO 2005–06, Chair. 2006–; mem. Bd of Dirs Cargill, Inc., Cisco Systems, Inc., Target Corpn; mem. Gov. Arnold Schwarzenegger's California Comm. for Jobs and Econ. Growth; Vice-Pres. and mem. Bd of Govs of San Francisco Symphony; Vice-Chair. and mem. Bd of Trustees of San Francisco Museum of Modern Art. *Leisure interest:* playing basketball. *Address:* Wells Fargo & Co., PO Box 63750, San Francisco, CA 94163 (office); Wells Fargo & Co., 420 Montgomery Street, San Francisco, CA 94104, USA (office). *Telephone:* (800) 869-3557 (office); (866) 878-5865 (office). *Fax:* (415) 677-9075 (office); (626) 312-3515 (office). *E-mail:* BoardCommunications@wellsfargo.com (office). *Website:* www.wellsfargo.com (office).

KOVACEVICH, Stephen; American pianist; b. 17 Oct. 1940, Los Angeles, Calif.; s. of Nicholas Kovacevich and Loreta Kovacevich (née Zuban); ed Berkeley High School, Calif., studied under Lev Shorr and Dame Myra Hess; concert debut as a pianist aged 11; moved to UK to study with Dame Myra Hess 1959; has appeared with leading world orchestras and conductors, including Colin Davis, Hans Graf, Bernard Haitink, Kurt Masur, Simon Rattle and Georg Solti; int. reputation built both on his concert appearances and on his recordings for Philips and EMI; chamber music collaborations with Jacqueline du Pré, Steven Isserlis, Gautier Capuçon, Renaud Capuçon, Kyung-wha Chung, Truls Mørk, Emmanuel Pahud, Anna Larsson, Khatia Buniatishvili, Belcea Quartet, Philippe Graffin, Alina Ibragimova and Martha Argerich; Kimber Award, Calif. 1959, Mozart Prize, London 1962. *Recordings include:* Beethoven's Diabelli Variations 1968, Beethoven's Sonatas No. 3 and No. 5 with Jacqueline du Pré, Brahms' Piano Concerto No. 1 (Gramophone Award) 1993, series of Schubert Sonatas, set of the 32 Beethoven Sonatas 2003, Piano Concertos of Beethoven and Brahms and Bartók's Piano Concerto No. 2 (Edison Award) with Sir Colin Davis, Beethoven's Diabelli Variations (Classic FM Gramophone Ed.'s Choice Award 2009) 2008. *Publication:* Schubert Anthology. *Leisure interests:* tennis, chess, cinema, Indian food. *Address:* c/o Claire Parker-Paphitis, International Classical Artists, Dunstan House, 14A St Cross Street, London, EC1N 8XA, England (office). *Telephone:* (20) 7902-0520 (office). *Fax:* (20) 7404-0150 (office). *E-mail:* info@icartists.co.uk (office). *Website:* www.icartists.co.uk (office).

KOVACIC, Ernst; Austrian violinist and conductor; *Artistic Director, Leopoldinum Orchestra Wrocław;* b. 12 April 1943, Kapfenberg; m. Traude Holzer; four s.; ed Acad. of Music, Univ. of Music, Vienna; teacher Univ. of Music, Vienna 1975–; prizewinner, int. competitions, Geneva 1970, Barcelona 1971, Munich 1972; appears throughout Europe, UK and USA with leading orchestras and has appeared at many festivals including Salzburg, Berlin, Vienna, Bath, Edin., Aldeburgh and London Proms; first performances of works by composers including H. K. Gruber, K. Schwertsik, E. Krenek, F. Cerhe, I. Erod, R. Holloway, B. Furrer, G. F. Haas, N. Osbourne, K. H. Essl, H. Eder; repertoire includes maj. works of baroque, classical and romantic periods and contemporary works; Artistic Dir Vienna Chamber Orchestra 1996–98, Leopoldinum Orchestra Wrocław, Poland 2007–; Pres. Ernst Krenek Privatstiftung; mem. Zebra String Trio. *Address:* Kriehuberpasse 29/5, 1050 Vienna, Austria (home).

KOVÁCS, András; Hungarian film director and scriptwriter; b. 20 June 1925, Kide (now in Romania); m. Gabriella Pongrác; one s. one d.; ed Győrffy Coll. and Acad. of Dramatic and Cinematic Arts; Drama reader, Hungarian Film Studio 1950, Drama Dept Head 1951–57, Film Dir 1960–; Chair. Parl. Curatorium of Public Foundation for Hungarian Film 1996–98; Pres. Fed. of Hungarian Film and TV Artists 1981–86; Balázs B. Prize, Kossuth Prize 1970, Master of the Hungarian Moving Pictures 2004; named Eminent Artist. *Films:* Zápor (Summer Rain) 1960, Pesti háztetők (On the Roofs of Budapest) 1961, Isten őszi csillaga (Autumn Star) 1962, Nehéz emberek (Difficult People) 1964, Hideg napok (Cold Days) 1966, Falak (Walls) 1968, Ecstasy from 7 to 10 1969, Staféta (Relay Race) 1971, A magyar ugaron (Fallow Land) 1973, Bekötött szemmel (Blindfold) 1975, Labirintus (Labyrinth) 1976, A ménesgazda (The Stud Farm) 1978, Októberi vasárnap (A Sunday in October) 1979, Ideiglenes Paradicsom (Temporary Paradise) 1981, Szeretők (An Afternoon Affair) 1983, A vörös grófnő (The Red Countess) 1985, Valahol Magyarországon (Rearguard Struggle) 1987, Az álommenedzser (The Dream Manager) 1994, A Nehéz emberek ma 1996. *TV films:* Menekülés Magyarországra (Flight to Hungary) 1980, György Lukács Portray 1986, Volt egyszer egy egyetem (Once Upon a University) 1995, Utak Vásárhelyről (Roads from Vásárhely) 1996, Két szólamban 2000, Reggeltől hajnalig Válaszúton 2001, Film egy regényről 2002, Egy borértő ember 2003, Polixena and John 2005. *Publication:* scenario and studies: Hideg napok 1967, Felak 1968, A ménesgazda 1979; Egy film forrásvidéke 1972. *Leisure interest:* gardening. *Address:* Magyar jakobinusok tere 2/3, 1122 Budapest, Hungary. *Telephone:* (1) 356-7227.

KOVÁCS, László; Hungarian politician; b. 3 July 1939; m.; one d.; ed Coll. of Politics, Univ. of Econ. Sciences, Petrik Lajos Tech. School; chemical technician, Medicolor, Kobánya Pharmaceutical Works 1957–66; youth and student movt 1966–75; consultant and Deputy Head, Dept for Int. Relations, Hungarian Socialist Workers' Party 1975–86; mem. Parl. 1990–2004, mem. Foreign Affairs Cttee 1990–93 (Chair. 1993–94); mem. Presidium Hungarian Socialist Party (MSZP) 1990–2004, Head of Parl. Faction 1998–2000, Chair. 1998–2004; Deputy Minister of Foreign Affairs 1986–89, State Sec. 1989–90, Minister of Foreign Affairs 1994–98, 2002–04; EU Commr for Taxation and Customs Union 2004–10; Chair.-in-Office OSCE 1995; Vice-Chair. Socialist International 2003–08; Co-Chair. Cen. and East European Cttee 1996–2003; mem. Council of Wise Men of Council of Europe 1997–99. *Address:* c/o Országgyűlés (National Assembly), 1055 Budapest, Kossuth Lajos tér 1–3, Hungary (office).

KOVAL, Col-Gen. Mikhail; Ukrainian army officer and government official; *Interim Minister of Defence;* served as high-ranking official in admin of Ukraine's Border Guards –2014; Interim Minister of Defence March 2014–. *Address:* Ministry of Defence, 01021 Kyiv, vul. M. Hrushevskoho 30/1, Ukraine (office). *Telephone:* (44) 253-11-56 (office). *Fax:* (44) 226-20-15 (office). *E-mail:* webmaster@ mil.gov.ua (office). *Website:* www.mil.gov.ua (office).

KOVALEV, Col-Gen. Nikolai Dmitriyevich; Russian security officer and politician; b. 1949, Moscow; m.; one d.; ed Moscow Inst. of Electronic Machine

Construction; on staff system of state security KGB 1974–; served for 2 years in Afghanistan; staff mem. Dept of Fed. Service of Counterespionage of Moscow and Moscow Region –1994; Deputy Dir Fed. Security Service (FSB) 1994–96; Acting Dir then Dir 1996–98; mem. Security Council of Russia; mem. Comm. on Higher Mil. Titles and Posts, Council on Personnel Policy of Pres. of Russia; mem. State Duma 1999–, mem. Otechestvo-All Russia faction, Chair. Comm. for Struggle Against Corruption 2000–05, Cttee on Veterans' Affairs 2005–. *Address:* State Duma, 103265 Moscow, Okhotny ryad 1, Russia. *Telephone:* (495) 292-89-19 (office). *Fax:* (495) 292-89-24 (office).

KOVALEV, Sergey Adamovich, PhD; Russian politician; b. 2 March 1930, Seredina-Buda, Ukraine; s. of Adam Vasil'evich Kovalev and Valentina Vasilerna Kovaleva; m. 1st Elena Viktorovna Tokareva 1949; m. 2nd Luydmila Uyr'evna Boitsova 1967; one s. two d.; ed Moscow State Univ.; worked as researcher, Moscow Univ.; active participant in movt for human rights since late 1960s; one of assocs of Academician A. Sakharov, one of founders Initiative Group for Human Rights 1969; ed. Samizdat Bulletin Chronicles of Current Events, expelled from Moscow Univ. 1969; arrested on charge of anti-Soviet propaganda 1974, sentenced to seven years' imprisonment and three years in exile 1974; lived in Kalinin, returned to Moscow 1987; mem. Project Group for Human Rights of Int. Foundation for Survival and Devt of Humanity, Engineer Inst. of Problems of Data Transmission USSR Acad. of Sciences 1987–90; People's Deputy of Russian Fed. 1990–93; Chair. Cttee for Human Rights of Supreme Soviet of Russia 1990–93; Co-Chair. Soviet Del. on Moscow Conf. on Human Rights 1991; Chief of Russian Del. to UN Comm. on Human Rights 1992–95; one of founders and leaders of Vybor Rossii; mem. State Duma (Parl.) 1993–95, 1999–; Chair. Pres.'s Cttee on Human Rights 1994–96; Ombudsman of Russian Fed. 1994–95; Kt of Honour of Chkezia 1997; Council of Europe Human Rights Prize 1995, Olof Palme Prize 2004. *Leisure interests:* hunting, fishing. *Address:* State Duma, Okhotny ryad 1, 103009 Moscow, Russia (office). *Telephone:* (495) 292-93-43 (office). *Fax:* (495) 292-94-64 (office). *E-mail:* www@duma.ru (office). *Website:* www.duma.ru (office).

KOVALEVSKY, Jean, DèsSc; French astronomer; *Astronomer, Observatoire de la Côte d'Azur;* b. 18 May 1929, Neuilly-sur-Seine; s. of Jean Kovalevsky and Hélène Pavloff; m. Jeannine Reige 1956 (died 2003); two s. one d.; ed Univ. of Paris and Ecole Normale Supérieure; Research Asst Paris Observatory 1955–59, Yale Univ. 1957–58; Head of Computing and Celestial Mechanics Service, Bureau des Longitudes 1960–71; Exec. Dir Groupe de Recherches de Geodésie Spatiale 1971–78; Founder and first Dir Centre d'Etudes et de Recherches Géodynamiques et Astronomiques 1974–82, 1988–92; astronomer, Observatoire de la Côte d'Azur, Grasse 1986–; Sec. Bureau Int. des Poids et Mesures 1991–97, Pres. 1997–2004; Pres. Bureau Nat. de Métrologie 1995–2005; mem. French Acad. of Sciences, Int. Acad. of Astronautics, Academia Europaea, Acad. of Sciences of Turin, French Acad. of Tech., Scientific Cttee European Space Agency 1979–81; Chevalier, Légion d'honneur, Commdr, Ordre du Mérite. *Publications:* Introduction to Celestial Mechanics 1967, Traité de Géodésie (with J. Levallois), Vol 4 1971, Astrométrie moderne 1990, Modern Astronomy 1995 (reprint 2002), Fundamentals of Astrometry (with P. K. Seidelmann) 2004; about 250 scientific papers. *Leisure interests:* gardening, stamp collection. *Address:* 59 Boulevard Émile Zola, 06130 Grasse (home); Geoazur, Observatoire de la Côte d'Azur, avenue Copernic, 06130 Grasse, France (office). *Telephone:* 4-93-70-60-29 (home); 4-93-40-53-87 (office). *Fax:* 4-93-40-53-33 (office). *E-mail:* jean.kovalevsky@obs-azur.fr (office). *Website:* www.obs-nice.fr (office).

KOVANDA, Karel, MBA, PhD; Czech/British/American diplomatist (retd), consultant and business executive; *Manager, Brussels Representative Office, ČEZ Group;* b. 5 Oct. 1944, Gilsland, Cumbria, UK; s. of Oldřich Kovanda and Ivy Norman; m. Noemi Berová 1993; one s. two d.; ed Prague School of Agric., Massachusetts Inst. of Tech. and Pepperdine Univ., USA; leadership, Czech Nat. Student Union 1968–69; emigrated to USA 1970; lecturer in political science and freelance journalist 1975–80; man. positions in US pvt. sector 1980–90; returned to Czechoslovakia 1990; Czech Ministry of Foreign Affairs 1991–93, Political Dir 1993, Deputy Minister 1997–98; Perm. Rep. of Czech Repub. to UN 1993–97, to UN Security Council 1994–95, to NATO 1998–2005; Deputy Dir Gen. of External Relations, EC 2005–10; Pres. ECOSOC 1997; Gov., Asia-Europe Foundation (Singapore) 2011–13; Man., Brussels Rep. Office, ČEZ Group 2013–; Czech Order of Merit (First Class) 2003; Umurinzi – Campaign Against Genocide Medal (Rwanda) 2010. *Leisure interests:* literature, theatre, travel, stamp collecting. *Address:* Rue du Trône 60, 1050 Brussels, Belgium (office). *Telephone:* (2) 502-00-02 (office). *E-mail:* karel.kovanda01@cez.cz (office); kovankl@gmail.com (home).

KOVÁŘOVÁ, Daniela, JUDr; Czech politician and writer; b. 17 Nov. 1965, Ostrava; m. Martin Kovar; two s.; ed Jízdárenská High School, Ostrava, Univ., Faculty of Law, Univ. of Jan Evangelista Purkyně, Brno; mem. Legal Fees Section, Czech Bar Asscn (CBA) 1997–, Chair. Criminal Law and Defence Section 1999–2005, mem. Bd of Dirs CBA 1999–2002, mem. External Relations Cttee 2005, Chair. Cttee for Training and Educ. 2005–08, Head of Dept of Training and Educ. 2005–; test inspector for bar exams in field of criminal law 2002–; Dir Judicial Acad. 2008–; Minister of Justice 2009–10; Chair. Govt Legis. Council 2009; mem. City Asscn Cttee, Czech Lawyers' Union 2005–07, mem. Czech Lawyers Union, Prague City Asscn 2005–; mem. Science Council, Faculty of Law, Palacký Univ. 2009–; mem. Mensa Czech Repub. 1998–. *Publications:* Legal Fee Regulations (co-author; special edn of Bar Bulletin, CBA) 2006, Legislation on the Legal Profession, Professional Rules and Rulings of the 3rd Congress of the CAB (compilation and editing; special edn of Bar Bulletin, CBA) 2006, Questions on Legal Fees and Related Statutes (co-author; special edn of Bar Bulletin, CBA) 2006, Legal Fees, text with references to literature, judicature and positions of CAB authorities (co-author; special edn of Bar Bulletin, CBA) 2006, Oratory or How To Speak, Negotiate and Communicate Well (co-author) 2008; numerous professional articles and essays. *Address:* c/o Ministry of Justice, Vyšehradská 16, 128 10 Prague 2, Czech Republic (office).

KÖVÉR, László; Hungarian politician; *Chairman (Speaker), Országgyűlés (National Assembly);* b. 29 Dec. 1959, Pápa; s. of the late László Kövér, Sr and of Erzsébet Ábrahám; m. Mária Bekk 1987; three c.; ed Eötvös Loránd Univ.; Founding mem. Fidesz 1988, Pres. 2000–01; participant in Opposition Round Table discussions as well as tripartite political negotiations 1989; mem. Parl. 1990–, Leader of Fidesz Parl. group 1994, Chair. Cttee on Nat. Security for two terms; Minister without Portfolio in charge of Civil Nat. Security Services 1998–2000; Chair. (Speaker), Országgyűlés (Nat. Ass.) 2010–; Acting Pres. of Hungary following resignation of Pál Schmitt 2 April 2012–10 May 2012; mem. Bd Hungarian Asscn of Int. Children's Safety Service 1990– (Pres. 1994–), Hungarian Asscn for Civic Co-operation 1996–2009. *Address:* Office of the Speaker, Országgyűlés, 1055 Budapest, Kossuth Lajos tér 1–3, Hungary (office). *Telephone:* (1) 441-4000 (office). *Fax:* (1) 441-5000 (office). *E-mail:* elnoki.kabinet@parlament .hu (office). *Website:* www.parlament.hu (office).

KOWALCZYK, Most Rev. Archbishop Józef, DCL; Polish ecclesiastic and diplomatist; *Archbishop of Gniezno;* b. 28 Aug. 1938, Jadowniki Mokre; ed Hosianum Higher Ecclesiastic Seminary, Olsztyn, Catholic Univ. of Lublin, Pontifical Gregorian Univ., Rome, Roman Rota Studium; ordained priest 1962; employee, Roman Rota, Congregation for the Discipline of the Sacraments; organizer and Head of Polish Section, State Secr. 1978–89; Titular Archbishop of Heraclea and Apostolic Nuncio in Poland 1989–, Archbishop of Gniezno, Poland 2010–; Hon. mem. Soc. of Polish Canon Lawyers; Dr hc (Agric. Acad., Kraków 1999, Cardinal S. Wyszyński Univ. 2000, Catholic Univ. of Lublin 2001). *Publications:* Dojrzewanie czasu 1998, Na drodze konsekrowanej 1999, Służyć słowu 2000 and ed. of Karol Wojtyła's papers and Polish edition of papal teaching (14 vols). *Address:* Archdiocese of Gniezno, ul. Kanclerza Jana Laskiego 7, 62-200 Gniezno, Poland (office). *Website:* www.archidiecezja.pl (office).

KOWNACKI, Piotr, LLB; Polish civil servant and petroleum industry executive; *Chief of the Chancellery of the President of Poland;* b. 8 Oct. 1954, Warsaw; m. 1976; two d.; ed Univ. of Warsaw; with Inst. of Law Studies, Polish Acad. of Sciences 1979–83; Press Officer Sejm (Parl.) 1983–87; Adjudicating Counsellor, Office of the Constitutional Tribunal 1987–89; Dir Office of Govt Plenipotentiary for Reform of Local Govt Structures 1989–91; Under-Sec. of State in Office of Council of Ministers 1991; Vice-Pres. Supreme Chamber of Control 1991–99, 2001–06; Vice-Pres. Bank Ochrony Srodowiska (Bank for Environmental Protection) 1999–2001; Vice-Pres. for Auditing and Regulation, Deputy CEO and mem. Man. Bd Polski Koncern Naftowy (PKN) Orlen 2006–07, Pres. and CEO Jan.–July 2008; Chair. Supervisory Bd Unipetrol; Sec. of State and Deputy Chief of Chancellery of Pres. of Poland July–Sept. 2008–, Chief of Chancellery Sept. 2008–. *Address:* Chancellery of the President of the Republic of Poland, ul. Wiejska 10, 00-902 Warsaw, Poland (office). *Telephone:* (22) 695-29-00 (office). *Fax:* (22) 695-12-53 (office). *E-mail:* fnowaczynski@prezydent.pl (office). *Website:* www .president.pl (office).

KOYAGIALO NGSASE TE GERENGBO, Louis Alphonse; Democratic Republic of Congo politician; *Governor of Équateur Province;* b. 1947, Yakoma, Équateur Prov.; ed Kinshasa Univ.; Gov. Shaba Prov. (renamed Katanga Prov. 1997) 1986; accused of involvement in the massacre of students at Lubumbashi Univ., May 1990, sentenced to 15 years in prison 1991; Deputy Prime Minister with responsibility for Ministry of Postal Services, Telephones, and Telecommunications 2011–12, Acting Prime Minister March–April 2012; Gov. Équateur Prov. 2013–; mem. Parti lumumbiste unifié (PALU). *Publication:* Massacre de Lubumbashi 2006. *Address:* Office of the Governor, Équateur Province, Mbandaka, Democratic Republic of Congo (office).

KOYAMBOUNOU, Gabriel Jean Edouard; Central African Republic politician; b. Bangui; ed Univ. of Abidjan, École Nat. des Douanes, Françaises, Neuilly-sur-Seine, France; fmr Inspector Gen.; Prime Minister of Cen. African Repub. 1995–96; Minister of State in charge of Communication, Posts and Telecommunications, New Technologies and Francophone Affairs –2003; Second Vice-Pres. Mouvement pour la libération du peuple centrafricain; Pres. Handball Fed.; Grand Officier, Ordre du Merite; Gold Medal in Sport. *Publication:* Mémoire sur le 'Droit Douanier'. *Leisure interest:* handball. *Address:* Mouvement pour la libération du peuple centrafricain, Bangui, Central African Republic (office). *Website:* www .lemlpc.net (office).

KOZACHENKO, Leonid Petrovich; Ukrainian engineer, economist and politician; *President, Ukrainian Agrarian Confederation;* b. 14 May 1955, Veprik, Kiev region; m.; two d.; ed Ukrainian Acad. of Agric., All-Union Acad. of Foreign Trade; worked in agric. enterprises in Fastov region 1972–86, head of collective farm in Fastiv dist 1979; party functionary CP of Ukraine 1986–88; Deputy Head of Dept, Ukrainian Ministry of Agric. 1991–2001, Dir Agroland 2000–01, Deputy Prime Minister of Agric. 2001–02; f. Ukrainian League of Businessmen 1993; Co-f. Ukrainian Asscn of Corn, Nat. Asscn of Stock Exchanges, Ukrainian Asscn for Ecology Protection; Founder and Pres. Ukrainian Agrarian Confed. 1998–; mem. Presidential Comm. on Agric., Presidium Ukrainian Union of Businessmen; mem. Co-ordination Council of Businessmen at Ministry of Agrarian Policy; Charter of Honour of Verkhovna Rada; Merited Worker of Agric. of Ukraine 1998. *Address:* Ukrainian Agrarian Confederation, Saksaganskogo str., 53/80, office 807, Kiev 01033, Ukraine (office). *Telephone:* (44) 284-32-38 (office). *E-mail:* agroconf@ agroconf.org (office). *Website:* www.agroconf.org (office).

KOZAI, Toyoki, BS, MS, PhD; Japanese horticulturist, university administrator and academic; *President, Chiba University;* b. 25 Sept. 1943, Tokyo; ed Chiba Univ., Univ. of Tokyo; Research Asst, Dept of Agricultural Eng, Faculty of Agric., Univ. of Osaka Pref. 1973–77; Assoc. Prof., Dept of Horticulture, Faculty of Horticulture, Chiba Univ. 1977–90, Prof., Dept of Bioproduction Science 1990–2005, Dean Faculty of Horticulture 1999–2005, Pres. Chiba Univ. 2005–; Post-doctoral Fellow, Centre for Agro-Biological Research, Wageningen, Netherlands 1974–75; Visiting Researcher, Dept of Biological and Agricultural Eng, Cook Coll., Rutgers Univ., NJ, USA 1989; Prize for Academic Achievement, Soc. of Agricultural Meteorology of Japan 1982, Prize for Academic Achievement, Japanese Soc. of High Tech. in Agric. 1991, Prize for Academic Achievement, Japanese Soc. of Environment Control in Biology 1992, Prize for Academic Achievement, Japanese Acad. of Agricultural Sciences and Yomiuri Newspaper Co. 1997, Int. Scientific and Technological Award, Kunming City, People's Repub. of China 2002, Friendship Award, State Admin of Foreign Experts Affairs, People's Repub. of China 2002, Medal with Purple Ribbon, Japanese Govt 2002. *Publications:* numerous scientific papers in professional journals. *Address:* Office of the President, Chiba University, 1-33 Yayoi-cho, Inage-ku, Chiba-shi, Chiba 263-8522, Japan (office). *Telephone:* (43) 251-1111 (office). *Fax:* (43) 290-2041 (office). *E-mail:* kokusai@office.chiba-u.jp (office). *Website:* www.chiba-u.jp (office).

KOZAK, Dmitrii Nikolayevich; Russian lawyer and politician; *Deputy Chairman of the Government;* b. 7 Nov. 1958, Kirovohrad Oblast, Ukrainian SSR; m.; two s.; ed Vinnytsia Polytechnical Inst., Ukrainian SSR, Leningrad (now St Petersburg) State Univ.; Asst to Prosecutor of Leningrad; on staff, Asscn of Marine Trade Ports 1985–89; on staff, Exec. Cttee, Leningrad City Council 1990–91; Head of Law Dept Office, St Petersburg 1991–94; Chair. Law Cttee, Admin. St Petersburg; mem. Govt of St Petersburg, mem. Comm. on Human Rights 1994–96; apptd Deputy Gov. St Petersburg 1998, resgnd end of year; pvt. law practice 1998–99; Deputy Head of Admin. of Russian Pres. on Legal Problems May–Aug. 1999; First Deputy Head of Govt of Russian Fed. 1999, Head 1999–2000; Deputy Head of Admin. of Russian Pres. 2000–03, First Deputy Head 2003–04; Head of Govt Admin. March–Sept. 2004; Presidential Rep. in Southern Fed. Okrug 2004–07; Minister of Regional Devt 2007–08; Deputy Chair. of Govt 2008–. *Address:* Office of the Government, 103274 Moscow, Krasnopresnenskaya nab. 2, Russia (office). *Telephone:* (495) 205-57-35 (office). *Fax:* (495) 205-42-19 (office). *Website:* www.government.ru (office).

KOZARIĆ, Kemal, PhD; Bosnia and Herzegovina economist and central banker; *Governor, Central Bank of Bosnia and Herzegovina;* b. 13 Oct. 1956, Sarajevo; ed Univ. of Sarajevo; worked for 15 years in banking with Privredna Banka Sarajevo (now Central Profit Banka DD Sarajevo) as Chief of Br., Asst to Gen. Dir, City Savings Bank, Exec. Dir for Operations, Exec. Dir for Gen. Affairs, Dir, Assets and Investments Dept; Minister of Finance, Sarajevo Canton Govt 1996–2000; Deputy Gov., Central Bank of Bosnia and Herzegovina 2000–05, mem. Governing Bd 2003–, Gov. and Chair. Governing Bd 2005–; Chair. Governing Bd, BH Deposit Insurance Agency 2007–. *Address:* Office of the Governor, Central Bank of Bosnia and Herzegovina, 71000 Sarajevo, Maršala Tita 25, Bosnia and Herzegovina (office). *Telephone:* (33) 278222 (office). *Fax:* (33) 215094 (office). *E-mail:* contact@ cbbh.ba (office). *Website:* www.cbbh.ba (office).

KOŽENÁ, Magdalena; Czech singer (mezzo-soprano); b. 26 May 1973, Brno; m. Sir Simon Rattle 2008; two s.; ed Conservatoire, Brno, Coll. of Performing Arts, Bratislava; guest singer, Janáček Opera, Brno 1991–; debut as soloist, Vienna Volksoper 1996–97; appearances include Bach's B Minor Mass at the Queen Elizabeth Hall, London 2000, Salzburg Festival debut as Zerlina in Don Giovanni 2002, charity concerts following floods in Czech Repub. 2002, Idamante in Idomeneo at Glyndebourne 2003 and Salzburg Festival, Cherubino for Bavarian State Opera, Metropolitan Opera, Dorabella at Salzburg Easter Festival, Berlin, Varvara, Dorabella, Zerlina at Metropolitan Opera, Theatre des Champs Elysees, Covent Garden debut in La Cenerentola 2007; regular broadcasts for Czech radio and TV; tours in Europe, USA, Japan, Venezuela, Taiwan, Hong Kong, S Korea, Canada; roles include Dorabella in Così fan tutte, Isabella in Italiana in Algeri (Rossini), Venus in Dardanus (Rameau), Mercedes in Carmen, Annius in La Clemenza di Tito, Paris in Paride ed Elena, lead in Orfeo ed Eurydice (both Gluck), lead in Hermia (Britten), Poppea in L'Incoronazione di Poppea (Monteverdi), Mélisande (Debussy); Chevalier, Ordre des Arts et des Lettres 2003; First Place in Int. Scheider Competition 1992, First Place in Int. Mozart Competition, Salzburg 1995, Georg Solti Prize (France), Youngster of Arts, Europe 1996, Orphée d'Or, L'Académie du Disque Lyrique (France) 1999, Diapason d'Or (France) 2000, Echo Klassik Best New Artist (Germany) 2000, Gramophone Award (London) 2001, Gramophone Artist of the Year 2004, Person of the Year in Culture (Czech Repub.) 2002, 2003. *Recordings include:* Bach Arias (Harmony Magazine Award 1998), Johann Sebastian Bach Cantatas 2000, G.F. Handel Italian Cantatas 2000, G.F. Handel Messiah 2001, Magdalena Kožená – Le belle imagini (Echo Klassik Award 2002, Gold Record of Universal 2003) 2002, Johann Sebastian Bach Arias (Gold Record of Universal 2003, Platinum Record of Universal 2003) 2003, G.F. Handel – Giulio Cesare 2003, Magdalena Kožená – French Arias (Gramophone Award 2003) 2003, Magdalena Kožená – Songs 2004, Magdalena Kožená – Lamento 2005, Paride ed Elena 2005, La Clemenza di Tito 2006, Enchantment 2006, Mozart Arias 2006, Ah! Mio Cor 2007, Songs My Mother Taught Me 2008, Martinů's Julietta Fragments (Gramophone Award for Best Recital Recording 2009, Echo Klassik Award for Recording of the Year 2010) 2009, Ryba: Czech Christmas Mass 2009, Vivaldi Arias 2009, Des Knaben Wunderhorn 2010, Letter Amorose 2010. *Leisure interests:* philosophy, music, swimming, cycling. *Address:* c/o Central European Music Agency, Polní 6, 639 00 Brno, Czech Republic (office). *Telephone:* (5) 42213053 (office). *Fax:* (5) 42213056 (office). *E-mail:* david@cema-music.com (office). *Website:* www.cema-music.com (office); www.kozena.cz.

KOZHARA, Leonid Oleksandrovych, MA; Ukrainian diplomatist and politician; b. 14 Jan. 1963, Poltava; m.; one s.; ed Kyiv State Univ., Nat. Inst. of State and Law; Lecturer in Constitutional Law, Kyiv State Politology Inst. 1985–90; Sr Adviser to the Secr., Verkhovna Rada (Supreme Council, Parl.) 1990–92; First Sec., Embassy in Washington, DC 1994–97; various positions with Foreign Policy Dept, Admin of the Pres. 1992–94, 1997–2002; Amb. to Sweden 2002–04; Deputy Head, Admin of the Pres. 2004–05, also Head of Foreign Policy Dept, Foreign Policy Adviser to Pres. and Sec., State Council for European and Euro-Atlantic Integration 2004–05; mem. Verkhovna Rada 2006–, Deputy Chair. Int. Relations Cttee 2006–; Foreign Policy Adviser to Pres. 2010–12; Minister of Foreign Affairs 2012–14 (dismissed by parl.); Pres. Centre for Int. and Comparative Studies 2008–. *Address:* c/o Ministry of Foreign Affairs, 01018 Kyiv, pl. Mykhailivska 1, Ukraine. *E-mail:* zsmfa@mfa.gov.ua.

KOZHIN, Vladimir Igorevich; Russian business executive; *Head, Presidential Administrative Directorate;* b. 28 Feb. 1959, Troitsk, Chelyabinsk Region; m. Alla Kozhina; one s.; ed Leningrad Electrotech. Inst.; instructor, Head of Div., Petrograd Dist Comsomol Cttee; then on staff Research-Production Co. Azimuth, Dir-Gen. Russian-Polish Jt Co. Azimuth Int. Ltd 1991–93; Dir-Gen. St Petersburg Asscn of Jt Cos 1993–94; Head NW Cen. Fed. Dept of Currency and Export Control 1994–99, Head 1999–2000; Head, Office of Russian Pres. and Presidential Admin. Directorate 2000–. *Address:* Office of the President, 103132 Moscow, Nikitnikov per. 2, Russia (office). *Telephone:* (495) 606-35-63 (office). *Fax:* (495) 606-30-06 (office). *E-mail:* udprf@gov.ru (office). *Website:* www.udprf.ru (office).

KOZHOKIN, Mikhail Mikhailovich, CandHist; Russian journalist and business executive; *Deputy President and Chairman, Bank VTB24;* b. 23 Feb. 1962, Moscow; ed Moscow State Univ.; Jr Researcher, Researcher, then Sr Researcher, Inst. of USA and Canada, USSR (now Russian) Acad. of Sciences 1988–92, Sr Researcher, Cen. of Econ. and Political Studies, worked with G. Yavlinsky

1992–93; Head of Information Dept ONEXIM Bank 1993–96, Deputy Chair. Exec. Cttee 1996; Asst to First Deputy Chair. of Russian Govt 1996–97, mem. Govt Comm. on Econ. Reform 1997; Ed.-in-Chief, Izvestia (newspaper) 1998–2003 (resgnd); First Vice-Pres. Public Relations Development Company CJSC 2004; Deputy Pres. and Chair. Bank VTB24 (banking services co.), Moscow 2005–; fmr Dir Holding Co. Interros on work with mass media and public relations. *Leisure interests:* travelling, water tourism. *Address:* Bank VTB24, 101000 Moscow, 35 Miasnitskaya Ul., Russia (office). *Telephone:* (495) 777-24-24 (office). *Fax:* (495) 980-46-66 (office). *Website:* www.vtb24.ru (office).

KOZHOKIN, Yevgeny Mikhailovich, DHist; Russian politologist and historian; *Deputy Head, Federal Agency for the Commonwealth of Independent States, Compatriots Living Abroad and International Human Co-operation;* b. 9 April 1954, Moscow; m.; two d.; ed Moscow State Univ.; on staff Inst. of World History, USSR Acad. of Sciences 1984–90; People's Deputy of Russian Fed. 1990–93; Founder and Dir Inst. for Strategic Studies 1994–2009; Deputy Head, Federal Agency for the Commonwealth of Independent States, Compatriots Living Abroad and Int. Human Co-operation 2009–. *Film:* Producer and idea's author for documentary A Lonely Battalion. *Publications:* The French Workers: From the Great French Revolution to the Revolution of 1848 1985, The State and the People: From the Fronde to the Great French Revolution 1989, The History of Poor Capitalism 2005, and more than 100 others. *Leisure interest:* swimming. *Address:* Federal Agency for the Commonwealth of Independent States, Compatriots Living Abroad and International Human Co-operation, 125009 Moscow, 18/9 Vozdvizhenka ul., Russia (office). *Telephone:* (495) 690-12-45 (office). *E-mail:* e.kozhokin@rs.gov.ru (office); kozhokin@yandex.ru (home). *Website:* rs.gov.ru (office).

KOZLÍK, Sergej; Slovak politician; b. 27 July 1950, Bratislava; ed Univ. of Econs; clerk with Price Authority 1974–88; Head of Dept of Industrial Prices, Ministry of Finance 1988–90; Dir Exec. Dept of Antimonopoly Office 1990–92; Sec., Movt for a Democratic Slovakia (became political party 2000) 1992–; Vice-Premier, Govt of Slovakia 1993–94; Minister of Finance of Slovak Repub. 1994–97; Deputy to Nat. Council 1994–; mem. European Parl. (Group of the Alliance of Liberals and Democrats for Europe) 2004–, mem. Cttee on Budgets, Del. to EU-Russia Parl. Co-operation Cttee; Gov. World Bank 1994–98 Alt. Gov. IMF 1994–98. *Address:* European Parliament, Bâtiment Altiero Spinelli, 01E252, 60 rue Wiertz, 1047 Brussels, Belgium (office). *Fax:* (2) 284-92-57 (office). *E-mail:* sergej_kozlik@nrsr.sk (office). *Website:* www.europarl.europa.eu (office).

KOZLOV, Alexey Semenovich; Russian composer, saxophone player and band leader; b. 13 Oct. 1935, Moscow; m. 1st; one s.; m. 2nd Lyalya Adburakhmanovna Absalyamova; ed Moscow Inst. of Architecture, Moscow Music Coll.; researcher, Inst. of Design 1963–76; started playing saxophone in youth clubs 1955; founder and leader of jazz quintet 1959, jazz band of café Molodezhnoye 1961–66; arranger and soloist orchestra VIO-66; teacher Moscow Experimental Studio of Jazz Music 1967–76; Founder and music Dir jazz-rock ensemble Arsenal 1973–, festivals and tours including Delhi and Bombay 1989, Woodstock 1990, Jazz Rally, Düsseldorf 1993, Carnegie Hall 1995, Bonn 1996, with Arsenal, Chamber Soloists of Moscow, the Shostakovich String Quartet, Ars Nova Trio; master classes in towns of Russia and Oklahoma City Univ. 1994; Gen.-Man. Jazz Div., Goskoncert 1995–97; mem. Musical Cttee under Pres. of Russia 1997–; Art Dir Radio Jazz, Moscow 2001–; author of TV programmes, All That Jazz, Improvisation; composer of jazz, film and theatre music; Merited Artist of Russia; his ensemble Arsenal awarded Ovation Prize as the best jazz band in Russia 1995. *Publications:* Rock: Roots and Development 1989, Memoirs—My 20th Century, He-Goat on the Saxophone 2000; numerous articles in music journals. *Address:* Shchepkin str. 25, Apt. 28, 129090 Moscow, Russia (home). *Telephone:* (495) 688-31-56 (home); (916) 183-88-82 (home). *E-mail:* askozlov@mtu-net.ru (home); askozlov1@jandex.ru (home). *Website:* www.musiclab.ru (office); www.arsenalband.com (office).

KOZLOV, Valery Yassilyevich, DrSc; Russian politician; *Vice-President, Russian Academy of Sciences;* b. 1 Jan. 1950, Kostyly, Ryazan Region; ed Moscow State Univ.; Sr Researcher Moscow State Univ. 1972, Deputy Dean, Chief Scientific Sec. –1998; Adviser to Ministry of Gen. and Professional Educ. (later Ministry of Educ.) 1998–99; Deputy Minister 1999–; Corresp. mem. Russian Acad. of Sciences 1997–2000, mem. 2000–; Vice-Pres. 2002–; Founder, Ed.-in-Chief Int. Journal of Regular and Chaotic Dynamics; State Prize of the Russian Fed. 1994. *Address:* Russian Academy of Sciences, Leninsky prosp. 14, GSP-1, 117910 Moscow, Russia (office). *Telephone:* (495) 237-45-32 (office). *Fax:* (495) 954-26-21 (office). *E-mail:* kozlov@pran.ru (office). *Website:* www.pran.ru (office).

KOZLOV, Vladimir; Kazakhstani politician and fmr media executive; *Leader, Alga! (Forward!);* b. 10 Aug. 1960, Aqtöbe; Ed. AKTiVi TV channel 1990–96; later co-founder of first pvt. television channel, Aktau-Lada; worked in advertising and PR sector 1996–98; communications specialist, Mangyshlak Nuclear Power Plant 1998; joined Democratic Choice of Kazakhstan, mem. Political Council 2003, subsequently mem. Presidium of Political Council; est. co-operation with Western politicians and non-governmental orgs 2004; Co-founder Alga! (Forward!) party after Democratic Choice of Kazakhstan party was declared illegal 2005, Leader Alga! 2007–, party denied its right to register despite being the most widely supported opposition party; paid several visits to parls of European countries, including Polish Senate, as well as European Parl. 2006–12; campaigned in European countries against granting Kazakhstan the presidency of OSCE 2009; forbidden from participating in presidential election of 3 April 2011; arrested by staff of Nat. Security Cttee 23 Jan. 2012, went on trial in Mañğistaw Regional Court, Aktaw 16 Aug. 2012, accused of "inciting social hatred", "calling to the overthrow of the constitutional order of the state", and of "creating and managing an organised criminal group with a view to committing one or more crimes, as well as participation in such a group", sentenced to 7½ years' imprisonment in Aqtöbe with confiscation of his property Oct. 2012. *Address:* c/o 150000 Petropavl, ul. 1-ya Zarechnaya 100, zakład karny EC 164/3, Kazakhstan. *E-mail:* kazakhstanfree@gmail.com. *Website:* vladimirkozlov.org.

KOZLOVSKIS, Rihards; Latvian lawyer and politician; *Minister of the Interior;* b. 26 May 1969; ed Rīga Secondary School No. 69, Murjani Sports Gymnasium, Faculty of Law, Univ. of Latvia; teacher of Physical Educ., Latvian Acad. of Sport Educ. 1987–93; Jr Insp., 1st Police Bn, Ministry of the Interior 1991; Insp., Govt Security Agency 1991–93; Sr Insp., Dept for the Protection of Econ. Sovereignty

(VESAD) 1994–96; Lt Col, Deputy Chief of the Security Police 1996–2005; Adviser and Head of Div., Security and Coordination Div. of the NATO Summit Latvia Task Force, Ministry of Defence 2005–07; lawyer, BBF Consulting Ltd 2007–11; Minister of the Interior 2011–; mem. Zatlers' Reform Party (renamed Reform Party April 2012); Order of Viesturs 2006. *Address:* Ministry of the Interior, Čiekurkalna 1, līnija 1, korp. 2, Rīga, 1026, Latvia (office). *Telephone:* 6721-9263 (office). *Fax:* 6722-9686 (office). *E-mail:* kanceleja@iem.gov.lv (office). *Website:* www.iem.gov.lv (office).

KOZOL, Jonathan, BA; American writer; b. 5 Sept. 1936, Boston; s. of Harry L. Kozol and Ruth Massell Kozol; ed Harvard Coll., Magdalen Coll., Oxford, UK; Rhodes Scholar 1958; teacher in Boston area 1964–72; lecturer at numerous univs 1973–2006; Guggenheim Fellow 1972, 1984; Field Foundation Fellow 1973, 1974; Rockefeller Fellow 1978, Sr Fellow 1983; f. Education Action! (non-profit org.); mem. Editorial Bd Greater Good Magazine. *Publications include:* Death At An Early Age (Nat. Book Award 1968) 1967, Free Schools 1972, The Night Is Dark 1975, Children of the Revolution 1978, On Being a Teacher 1979, Prisoners of Silence 1980, Illiterate America 1985, Rachel and Her Children: Homeless Families in America (Robert F. Kennedy Book Award 1989, Conscience in Media Award, American Soc. of Journalists and Authors 1989) 1988, Savage Inequalities: Children in America's Schools (New England Book Award 1992) 1991, Amazing Grace (Anisfield-Wolf Book Award 1996) 1995, Ordinary Resurrections 2000, The Shame of the Nation: The Restoration of Apartheid Schooling in America (Nation Magazine Book Award) 2005, Letters to a Young Teacher 2007, Fire in the Ashes: Twenty-Five Years Among the Poorest Children in America 2012. *Address:* Education Action!, Cambridge Institute for Public Education, 16 Lowell Street, Cambridge, MA 02138, USA (office). *Telephone:* (617) 945-5568 (office). *Fax:* (617) 945-5562 (office). *Telephone:* (978) 462-8557 (home). *E-mail:* jonathankozol@gmail.com; educationactioninfo@gmail.com. *Website:* www.jonathankozol.com.

KOZYREV, Andrey Vladimirovich, CandHist; Russian politician; b. 27 March 1951, Brussels, Belgium; m. 2nd Elena Kozyreva; one d.; ed Moscow State Inst. of Int. Relations; worker, Kommunar factory, Moscow 1968–69; mem. staff, USSR Ministry of Foreign Affairs, various posts, to Head of Sector 1974–86, Head of Dept of Int. Orgs 1986–90; Minister of Foreign Affairs 1991–96; Deputy State Duma (Parl.) 1995–2000; mem. Bd of Dirs, Dir East European Div., ICN Pharmaceuticals 1998–; Lecturer, Moscow Inst. of Int. Relations 1996–. *Publications:* Transfiguration 1995; numerous articles on foreign policy. *Address:* International Office, MGIMO University, 76 Prospect Vernadskogo, 119454 Moscow; ICN Pharmaceuticals, Uscheva str. 24, 119048, Moscow, Russia. *Telephone:* (495) 434-9066 (MGIMO). *E-mail:* umosmgimo@gmail.com.

KPOTSRA, Roland Yao; Togolese politician, diplomatist and civil servant; b. 20 Feb. 1947, Lom; m.; two c.; joined Foreign Ministry as Desk Officer in Admin. Affairs Div. 1974, Dir Treaties and Legal Affairs Div. 1982–88, Dir Admin and Personnel 1987–90; Sec. Perm. Mission to UN, New York 1976–79, Counsellor 1979–, Chargé d'affaires April–Aug. 1980, Perm. Rep. to UN 1996–2002, 2007–09; Chargé de Mission, Ministry of Foreign Affairs and Co-operation 1992–93, Sec.-Gen. 1993–96, Minister of Foreign Affairs and Co-operation 2002–03; First Counsellor Embassy in Brazil 1980–82; Chargé d'affaires in Zimbabwe 1990–91; Leader of Del. to 63rd session of OAU Council of Ministers, 10th Ministerial Conf. of Movt of Non-Aligned Countries 1995; Deputy Head of Del. to OAU 50th Ass.; headed team at int. French-speaking conf. on conflict resolution from African perspective 1995; Lecturer in Diplomatic History, École Nat. d'Admin, Togo; Chevalier, Nat. Order of Merit 1984; Officer, Order of Mono 1996. *Address:* c/o Ministry of Foreign Affairs and Regional Integration, pl. du Monument aux Morts, BP 900, Lomé, Togo.

KRABBÉ, Jeroen Aart; Dutch actor, artist and director; b. 5 Dec. 1944; m. Herma van Geemert; three s.; ed Acad. of Fine Arts and Toneel Drama School, Amsterdam; acted in repertory theatre and formed own acting co. within the Netherlands; Commdr, Order of the Netherlands Lion 1999; Best Actor Award, Madrid, Sorrento, Oxford 1984, Anne Frank Medal 1985, Golden Heart of Rotterdam 1986, Golden Calf Award 1996. *Theatre includes:* The Diary of Anne Frank, Clouds, Relatively Speaking, How the Other Half Lives, Cyrano de Bergerac, Danton's Death, Love's Labours Lost, Sleuth, A Day in the Death of Joe Egg, Sweet Bird of Youth, Love Letters, Amadeus 2005, Vaslav 2014. *Films include:* Soldier of Orange 1977, A Flight of Rainbirds 1981, The Fourth Man 1984, The Shadow of Victory 1985, Turtle Diary, No Mercy 1987, The Living Daylights, A World Apart, Crossing Delancey, Melancholia 1989, The Prince of Tides 1991, Stalin 1991, Kafka 1991, King of the Hill 1991, The Fugitive 1993, Farinelli 1994, Immortal Beloved 1994, The Disappearance of García Lorca 1995, Business for Pleasure 1996, The Honest Courtesan 1996, Cinderella 1997, Left Luggage (directorial debut; Berlin Film Festival award 1998) 1997, Dangerous Beauty 1998, Discovery of Heaven (actor and dir, Rembrandt Best Film Award 2001) 2001, Ocean's Twelve 2004, Deuce Bigalow 2004, Man with a Camera 2004, Snuff 2006, Albert Schweitzer (title role) 2009, Transporter 3 2008, Yankee Go Home 2009, Only Decent People 2012, Tula: the Revolt 2013. *Television includes:* William of Orange (Netherlands), Miami Vice, Dynasty, One for the Dancer, Sweet Weapon, Only Love, Jesus, Stalin (all American TV), Midsomer Murders 2008, Verborgen gebreken (series) 2009, In Therapy (series) 2011, A House for Vincent (series) 2013, The Man with the Hammer (series) 2013; host of talk shows; numerous roles in plays and series. *Publications:* The Economy Cookbook, Jeroen Krabbe: Painter, The Demise of Abraham Reiss: Nine Paintings by Jeroen Krabbe, Dum Vivimus Vivamus: 14 Paintings by Jeroen Krabbe 2013. *Telephone:* (20) 7287-0077 (Jeremy Conway, London) (office). *E-mail:* jermey@conwayvg.com (office). *Address:* Van Eeghenstraat 107, 1071 EZ Amsterdam, The Netherlands.

KRAEHE, Graham J., AO; Australian business executive; *Chairman, Bluescope Steel Ltd;* ed Adelaide Univ.; fmr Man.-Dir Pacifica Ltd and WH Wylie Ltd (now Monroe); Man.-Dir Southcorp Ltd 1994–2001; apptd Dir National Australian Bank Ltd 1997, Chair. 2004–05; mem. Bd of Dirs BHP Steel Ltd (now Bluescope Steel Ltd) 2002–, currently Chair.; mem. Bd of Dirs Brambles Ltd 2000–2004 (resgnd), 2005–, Deputy Chair. 2007–08, Chair. 2008–; mem. Reserve Bank of Australia Bd 2007–11; mem. Bd of Dirs Djerriwarrh Investments Ltd 2002–; mem. Prime Minister's Business Advisory Council 2013–; fmr Nat. Pres. Metal Trade Industry Assen; Chair. Australian Future Directions Forum. *Address:* Bluescope Steel Ltd, Level 11, 120 Collins Street, Melbourne, Vic. 3000, Australia (office). *Telephone:* (3)

9666-4000 (office). *Fax:* (3) 9666-4111 (office). *Website:* www.bluescopesteel.com (office).

KRAFT, Christopher Columbus, Jr., BS; American engineer and space agency administrator (retd); b. 28 Feb. 1924, Phoebus, Va; s. of Christopher Columbus Kraft and Vanda Olivia Kraft (née Suddreth); m. Elizabeth Anne Turnbull 1950; one s. one d.; ed Virginia Polytechnic Inst.; mem. Langley Aeronautical Lab., Nat. Advisory Cttee for Aeronautics 1945; selected to join Space Task Group on Project Mercury 1958; Flight Dir of all Mercury Missions: head of mission operations Gemini program; Dir of Flight Operations, Manned Spacecraft Center 1963–69; elected mem. Nat. Acad. of Eng 1970; Deputy Dir Johnson Space Center 1970–72; Dir NASA Johnson Space Center 1972–82; Fellow, American Inst. of Aeronautics and Astronautics 1966, American Astronautical Soc.; Chevalier, Légion d'honneur 1976; Hon. DEng (Indiana Inst. of Tech.) 1966, (St Louis Univ., Ill.) 1967, (Villanova) 1979; Arthur S. Fleming Award 1963, NASA Outstanding Leadership Award 1963, Spirit of St Louis Medal, American Soc. of Mechanical Engineers 1967, NASA Distinguished Service Medal (twice) 1969, Nat. Civil Service League Career Service Award 1976, W. Randolph Lovelace Award (American Astronautical Soc.) 1977, Daniel and Florence Guggenheim Award (Int. Astronautics Fed.) 1978, AAIA von Karman Lectureship Award 1979, Goddard Memorial Trophy 1979, Roger W. Jones Award 1979, inducted into Virginia Aviation Hall of Fame 1979. *Publications:* Flight: My Life in Mission Control 2001.

KRAFT, Robert Paul, BS, MS, PhD; American astronomer and academic; *Professor Emeritus of Astronomy and Astrophysics and Astronomer Emeritus, UC Observatories / Lick Observatory, University of California, Santa Cruz;* b. 16 June 1927, Seattle, Wash.; s. of Victor P. Kraft and Viola E. Ellis; m. Rosalie A. Reichmuth 1949; two s.; ed Univ. of Washington and Univ. of California at Berkeley; Instructor in mathematics and astronomy, Whittier Coll. 1949–51; Asst Prof. of Astronomy, Indiana Univ. 1956–58; Asst Prof. of Astronomy, Univ. of Chicago 1958–59; mem. staff, Mt Wilson and Palomar Observatories 1960–67; Astronomer and Prof., Lick Observatory 1967–92, Astronomer and Prof. Emer. 1992–, Acting Dir Lick Observatory 1968–70, 1971–73, Dir 1981–91; Dir Univ. of California Observatories 1988–91; Visiting Fellow, Joint Inst. of Laboratory Astrophysics, Univ. of Colo 1970; Pres. American Astronomical Soc. 1974–76; Vice-Pres. Int. Astronomical Union 1982–88, Pres. 1997–2000; mem. NAS, American Acad. of Arts and Sciences; Nat. Science Foundation Fellow 1953–55, Fairchild Scholar, California Inst. of Tech. 1980; Beatrice Tinsley Visiting Prof., Univ. of Texas 1991–92; Henry Norris Russell Lecturer 1995; DSc hc (Ind. Univ.) 1995; Warner Prize, American Astronomical Soc. 1962, Distinguished Alumnus Award, Univ. of Wash. 1995, Bruce Medal 2005. *Publications:* articles in professional journals. *Leisure interests:* music (classical and rock), oenology, duplicate bridge. *Address:* Lick Observatory, University of California, Santa Cruz, CA 95064, USA (office). *Telephone:* (831) 459-3281 (office). *Fax:* (831) 426-3115 (office). *E-mail:* kraft@ucolick.org (office). *Website:* astro.ucsc.edu (office).

KRAFT, Vahur, BA; Estonian banker; *New Country Manager, Nordea Bank Finland Plc (Estonia Branch);* b. 11 March 1961, Tartu; s. of Ulo Kraft and Aime Kraft; m. Anne Kraft 1990; one s.; ed Tartu Univ.; with Eesti Hoiupank (Estonian Savings Bank), rising to Head of Br. 1984–90; Vice-Chair. Bd Dirs Eesti Sotsiaalpank (Estonian Social Bank) 1990–91; Deputy Gov. Eesti Pank (Bank of Estonia) 1991–95, Gov. 1995–2005, Vice-Gov. for Estonia of IMF 1992–95, Gov. 1995–2005; New Country Man. for Nordea Bank Findland Plc (Estonia Br.) 2005–; Chair. Bd of Trustees Tartu Univ. Foundation; Chair. Supervisory Bd Estonian Deposit Guarantee Fund; mem. Supervisory Council, Financial Supervision Authority, Council of the Stabilization Reserves, Bd Centre for Strategic Initiatives; Hon. mem. Tallinn Jr Chamber of Commerce; Order of White Star, Second Class. *Address:* Nordea Bank Finland Plc (Estonia Branch), Hobujaama 4, 15068 Tallinn, Estonia (office). *Telephone:* (2) 628-3200 (office). *Fax:* (2) 628-3201 (office). *E-mail:* tallinn@nordea.com (office). *Website:* www.nordea.ee (office).

KRAGGERUD, Egil, DPhil; Norwegian classical philologist and academic; *Professor Emeritus of Classical Philology, University of Oslo;* b. 7 July 1939, S Høland, Akershus; s. of John Kraggerud and Borghild Westeren; m. Beate Sinding-Larsen 1963; three s. one d.; ed Oslo Katedralskole and Oslo Univ.; Research Fellow, Univ. of Oslo 1965–67, Lecturer in Classics 1967–68, Prof. of Classical Philology 1969–2002, Prof. Emer. 2002–; Ed. Symbolae Osloenses 1972–94; mem. Norwegian Acad. of Science and Letters, Royal Norwegian Soc. of Sciences and Letters, Acad. Europaea; Thorleif Dahl's Literary Award 1992. *Publications:* Aeneisstudien 1968, Horaz und Actium 1984, Aeneiden (seven vols) 1983–89; about 100 articles in int. journals. *Leisure interests:* skiing, concerts. *Address:* Bygdöy allé 13, 0257 Oslo, Norway. *Telephone:* 22-44-27-44. *E-mail:* egil .kraggerud@ifikk.uio.no. *Website:* egil.kraggerud.no.

KRAGULY, Radovan; British artist; b. 10 Sept. 1935, Prijedor, Yugoslavia; s. of Dragoja Kraguly and Mileva Kraguly; ed Acad. of Fine Arts, Belgrade, Cen. School of Arts and Crafts, London; lecturer Cambridge School of Art and Tech. –1965, Manchester Coll. of Art 1965–67, London Coll. of Printing and Design 1967–69, Ecole des Beaux Arts, Mons 1969–78, Parson School of Art and Design 1978–88; represented in perm. and major collections at Museum of Modern Art, Paris, British Museum, Victoria and Albert Museum, Museum of Modern Art, New York, Leicester Univ. Library, Library of Congress, Washington, City Art Gallery, Sarajevo, Art Council of Wales, Cardiff, Power Gallery, Sydney, Prenten Cabinet, Brussels, Nat. Museum and Gallery of Wales, Cardiff, Fond Nat. d'Art Contemporain, Paris, Manchester City Art Gallery, City Art Gallery, Banja Luka, Nat. Library of Wales, Aberystwyth, The Whitworth Art Gallery, Manchester, South London Art Gallery; numerous prizes and awards including Printmaking Prize (Jazu-Zagreb) 1962, Yugoslav Trienale Prize 1967, Grafika Creativa Prize (Helsinki) 1975, Int. Grand Prix Fondation Pierre Cornette de St Cyr (Paris) 1978, Int. Grand Prix, Drawing Biennial (Rijeka) 1980. *Publications include:* La Vache dans l'imaginaire 1989, The Imaginary Cow of Kraguly 1990, Kraguly–Gallery Vera Van Laer 1992, Hathor: Voies Lactées Kraguly 1995, Kraguly Hathor: VLK 1998. *Address:* Llwyngarth Fawr, Comin Coch, Builth Wells, Powys, LD2 3PP, Wales (home); 22 rue Quincampoix, 75004 Paris, France. *Telephone:* (1597) 860340 (Wales) (home); 1-42-74-70-47 (Paris). *Fax:* (1597) 860340 (Wales) (home); 1-42-74-70-47 (Paris). *E-mail:* nenak@free.fr (home).

KRÄHENBÜHL, Pierre, BA; Swiss international organization executive; *Commissioner-General, United Nations Relief and Works Agency for Palestine Refugees in the Near East (UNRWA);* b. 1966; m.; three c.; ed Univ. of Geneva; began a career in journalism and photography, but then began work at Lutheran World Fed.; joined Int. Cttee of Red Cross (ICRC) 1991, first served in field operations as del. in El Salvador and Peru, given managerial responsibilities in Afghanistan 1993–95, and subsequently in Bosnia and Herzegovina, served as Head of Operations for Cen. and South-Eastern Europe in Geneva, personal adviser to Jakob Kellenberger (Pres. ICRC) 2000–02, Dir of Operations 2002–; Commr-Gen. UNRWA 2013–. *Address:* United Nations Relief and Works Agency for Palestine Refugees in the Near East (UNRWA), Bayader Wadi Seer, POB 140157, Amman, 11814, Jordan (office). *Telephone:* (6) 5808100 (office). *Fax:* (6) 5808335 (office). *E-mail:* unrwa -pio@unrwa.org (office). *Website:* www.unrwa.org (office).

KRAJICEK, Richard; Dutch professional tennis player; b. 6 Dec. 1972, Rotterdam; s. of Petr Krajicek and Ludmilla Krajicek; m. Daphne Dekkers 1999; one s. one d.; started playing tennis aged three; turned professional 1989; reached semi-finals Australian Open 1992; Wimbledon Men's Singles Champion 1996; won 20 titles to retirement in June 2003; now competes on Masters Tour; f. Richard Krajicek Foundation 1993; Arthur Ashe Humanitarian of Year Award 2000. *Leisure interests:* basketball, golf. *Address:* c/o Richard Krajicek Foundation, Olympisch Stadion 3, 1076 DE Amsterdam, Netherlands (office). *Telephone:* (20) 6705400 (office). *Fax:* (20) 6705390 (office). *E-mail:* info@krajicek.nl (office). *Website:* www.krajicek.nl (office).

KRALL, Diana; Canadian singer, pianist and composer; b. 16 Nov. 1966, Nanaimo, BC; m. Elvis Costello 2003; twin s.; ed Berklee Coll., Boston; began classical piano aged four; regular tours of North America, Britain, Europe and the Far East. *Film appearance:* De-Lovely 2004. *Recordings include:* albums: Steppin' Out 1993, Only Trust Your Heart 1994, All For You 1995, Love Scenes 1997, When I Look In Your Eyes (Grammy Award Best Jazz Vocal) 1999, The Look Of Love 2001, Heartdrops: Vince Benedetti Meets Diana Krall 2003, The Girl in the Other Room 2004, Christmas Songs 2005, From This Moment On (Juno Award for Vocal Jazz Album Of The Year 2007) 2006, The Very Best Of Diana Krall 2007, Quiet Nights 2009, Glad Rag Doll 2012. *Address:* Macklam/Feldman Management, 1505 West Second Avenue, Suite 200, Vancouver, BC V6H 3Y4, Canada (office). *Telephone:* (604) 734-5945 (office). *Fax:* (604) 732-0922 (office). *E-mail:* management@mfmgt.com (office). *Website:* www.mfmgt.com (office); www .dianakrall.com.

KRALL, Hanna; Polish journalist and writer; b. 20 May 1935, Warsaw; m. Jerzy Szperkowicz; one d.; ed Univ. of Warsaw; reporter, Życie Warszawy 1955–66, Polityka 1966–, corresp. in Moscow 1966–69; corresp., Tygodnik Powszechny, Gazeta Wyborcza; freelance writer early 1980s–; Solidarity Cultural Prize 1985, Prize of Minister of Culture and Art 1989, J. Shocken Literary Prize (Germany), Kulture Foundation Award 1999, Leipzig Book Fair Award 2000, Herder Prize 2005, Ricarda Huch Award (Germany) 2008. *Publications include:* Na wschód od Arbatu (East of the Arbat) 1972, Zdążyć przed Panem Bogiem (Shielding the Flame) 1977, Sześć odcieni bieli (Six Shades of White) 1978, Sublokatorka (The Sub-tenant) 1985, Hipnoza (Hypnosis) 1989, Trudności ze wstawaniem (Difficulties Getting Up) 1990, Taniec na cudzym weselu (Dance at a Stranger's Wedding) 1993, Co się stało z naszą bajką (What's Happened to Our Fairy Tale) 1994, Dowody na istnienie (Proofs of Existence) 1996, Tam już nie ma żadnej rzeki (There is No River There Anymore) 1998, To ty jesteś Daniel (So You Are Daniel) 2001, Wyjątkowo długa linia (Incredible Long Line) 2004, Król kier znów na wylocie (King of Hearts) 2006, Różowe Strusie Pióra (Rosy Ostrich Feathers) 2009 (books translated into over 18 languages). *Address:* Stowarzyszenie Pisarzy Polskich, ul. Krakowskie Przedmieście 87/89, 00-079 Warsaw, Poland (office). *Telephone:* (22) 6433164 (home). *Fax:* (22) 6433164 (home).

KRAMAR, Marjan, BEcons; Slovenian business executive; *President of the Management Board, Nova Ljubljanska Banka d.d.;* ed Univ. of Ljubljana; began career with Helios Domzale 1982; Dir of Planning, Analyses and Business Counselling, Ljubljanska Banka Trbovlje 1983–88; mem. Man. Bd Gradbeno Podjetje SGD Beton 1988–89; Adviser to Slovenian Rep., SFRY Presidency 1989–91; Head of Prime Minister's Cabinet 1991–94; mem. Man. Bd Slovene Export Corpn 1994–2004, Pres. 1998–2004; Pres. Man. Bd Nova Ljubljanska Banka d.d. 2004–; Chair. Supervisory Bd ETI Elektroelement Izlake; fmr Vice-Chair. Supervisory Bd Revoz. *Address:* Nova Ljubljanska Banka d.d., Trg republike 2, 1520 Ljubljana, Slovenia (office). *Telephone:* (1) 4250155 (office). *Fax:* (1) 4250331 (office). *E-mail:* info@nlb.si (office). *Website:* www.nlb.si (office).

KRAMER, Larry D., BA; American writer; b. 25 June 1935, Bridgeport, Conn.; s. of George L. Kramer and Rea Kramer; ed Yale Univ.; Production Exec. Columbia Pictures Corpn, London 1961–65; Asst to Pres. United Artists, New York; producer-screenwriter, Women in Love 1970; Co-founder Gay Men's Health Crisis Inc., New York 1981; Co-founder ACT UP-AIDS Coalition to Unleash Power, New York 1988; Two Obie Awards. *Films:* Here We Go Round the Mulberry Bush (assoc. producer) 1967, Women in Love (screenwriter, producer) 1970. *Publications include:* Faggots 1978, The Normal Heart (play) 1985, Just Say No 1988, The Furniture of Home 1989, The Destiny of Me 1993, The Tragedy of Today's Gays 2005. *Website:* www.actupny.org.

KRAMER, Dame Leonie Judith, AC, DBE, DPhil, FAHA, FACE; Australian academic; *Professor Emerita of Australian Literature, University of Sydney;* b. 1 Oct. 1924; d. of the late A. L. Gibson and G. Gibson; m. Harold Kramer 1952 (deceased); two d.; ed Presbyterian Ladies Coll., Melbourne and Univs of Melbourne and Oxford; Tutor, St Hugh's Coll., Oxford 1949–52; Assoc. Prof. Univ. of NSW 1963–68; Prof. of Australian Literature, Univ. of Sydney, 1968–89, Prof. Emer. 1989–; Deputy Chancellor, Univ. of Sydney 1988–91, Chancellor 1991–2001; Vice-Pres. Australian Assocn for Teaching of English 1967–70; Vice-Pres. Australian Soc. of Authors 1969–71; mem. Nat. Literature Bd of Review 1970–73; mem. Council, Nat. Library of Australia 1975–81; Pres., then Vice-Pres. Australian Council for Educ. Standards 1973–; mem. Univs Comm. 1974–86; Commr Australian Broadcasting Comm. (ABC) 1977–81, Chair. 1982–83, Dir Australia and NZ Banking Group 1983–94, Western Mining Corpn 1984–96, Quadrant Magazine Co. Ltd 1986–99 (Chair. 1988–99); mem. Council Nat. Roads and Motorists' Asscn 1984–95, Council Foundation for Young Australians

1989–2000, Asia Soc. 1991–2000; Nat. Pres. Australia-Britain Soc. 1984–93, Order of Australia Asscn 2001–04; mem. Council ANU 1984–87; mem. Bd of Studies, NSW Dept. of Educ. 1990–2001; Chair. Bd of Dirs Nat. Inst. of Dramatic Art 1987–91, Deputy Chair. 1991–95; Sr Fellow, Inst. of Public Affairs 1988–96; Commr Electricity Comm. (NSW) 1988–95; mem. World Book Encyclopaedia Advisory Bd 1989–99, Int. Advisory Cttee Encyclopaedia Britannica 1991–99, NSW Council of Australian Inst. of Co. Dirs 1992–2001; Chair. Operation Rainbow Australia Ltd 1996–2003; mem. Governing Council Old Testament House, Canberra 1998–2001; Gov. Medical Benefits Fund 2005–; Patron, United World Colleges Australia; Hon. Fellow, St Hugh's Coll. Oxford 1994, St Andrew's Coll., Univ. of Sydney, Hon. Prof. Dept of English (Sydney) 2002, Janet Clarke Hall, Univ. of Melbourne 2005; Hon. DLitt (Tasmania), 1977 (Queensland) 1991, (NSW) 1992, (Sydney) 2009; Hon. LLD (Melbourne) 1983, (ANU) 1984; Hon. MA (Sydney) 1989; Britannica Award 1986. *Publications include:* (as L. J. Gibson): Henry Handel Richardson and Some of Her Sources 1954; (as Leonie Kramer): Australian Poetry 1961 (ed.) 1962, Companion to Australia Felix 1962, Myself When Laura 1966, A Guide to Language and Literature (with Robert D. Eagleson) 1977, A. D. Hope 1979, The Oxford History of Australian Literature (ed.) 1981, The Oxford Anthology of Australian Literature (ed. with Adrian Mitchell) 1985, My Country: Australian Poetry and Short Stories – Two Hundred Years (two vols) 1985, James McAuley: Poetry, Essays etc. (ed.) 1988, David Campbell: Collected Poems (ed.) 1989, Collected Poems of James McAuley 1995. *Leisure interests:* gardening, music. *Address:* A20–John Woolley, Room S365, University of Sydney, Sydney, NSW 2006 (office); 12 Vaucluse Road, Vaucluse, NSW 2030 Australia (home). *Telephone:* (2) 93514164 (office). *Fax:* (2) 93514773 (office). *E-mail:* L.Kramer@staff .unisyd.edu.au (office).

KRAMER, Rich, BS; American business executive; *Chairman, President and CEO, Goodyear Tire & Rubber Company;* b. 30 Oct. 1963, Cleveland, Ohio; m.; four c.; ed John Carroll Univ., Ohio; certified public accountant; fmr Partner with PricewaterhouseCoopers, where he worked for 13 years; joined Goodyear Tire & Rubber Co. as Vice-Pres., Corp. Finance 2000, Vice-Pres., Finance for North American Tire 2002–03, Sr Vice-Pres., Strategic Planning and Restructuring 2003–04, Exec. Vice-Pres. and Chief Financial Officer 2004–07, Pres. North American Tire business unit 2007–10, COO Goodyear Tire & Rubber Co. 2009–10, mem Bd of Dirs Feb. 2010–, Pres. and CEO Goodyear Tire & Rubber Co. April 2010–, Chair. Oct. 2010–; mem Bd of Dirs The Sherwin-Williams Co. *Address:* Goodyear Tire & Rubber Co., 1144 East Market Street, Akron, OH 44316-0001, USA (office). *Telephone:* (330) 796-2121 (office). *Fax:* (330) 796-2222 (office). *E-mail:* info@goodyear.com (office). *Website:* www.goodyear.com (office).

KRAMER, Baroness (Life Peer), cr. 2010, of Richmond Park in the London Borough of Richmond upon Thames; **Susan Veronica Kramer,** BA, MBA; British politician and business executive; *Minister of State for Transport;* b. 22 July 1950, Holborn, London; m. John Kramer (died 2006); two c.; ed St Paul's Girls' School, St Hilda's Coll., Oxford, Univ. of Illinois, USA; Pres. Oxford Union 1971; began career in finance, rose to become a Vice-Pres. of Citibank, Chicago; est. (with her husband) International Capital Partners, (advises on infrastructure projects, primarily in Cen. and Eastern Europe), currently Dir; mem. Women Liberal Democrats Exec. 1997–2000, Liberal Democrat Fed. Exec. 2001–04, Chair. Twickenham and Richmond Liberal Democrats 2001–02; mem. London Regional Exec. 1997–2003; on Liberal Democrat party list for London constituency at European Parliament elections 1999; Liberal Democrat cand. for Mayor of London 2000; MP for Richmond Park, SW London 2005–10, apptd to Treasury Team and joined Treasury Select Cttee 2005; Liberal Democrat Shadow Int. Devt Sec. March–Dec. 2006, Shadow Trade and Industry Sec. 2006–07; Liberal Democrat Amb. to The City of London and Chair. Environmental Taxation Taskforce 2006; Shadow Transport Sec. 2007; Chancellor for the Duchy of Lancaster 2007; Shadow Minister for the Cabinet Office 2007; Families Spokesperson 2007–09; Minister of State for Transport 2013–; Trustee Kingston Trust, Richmond Park Charitable Trust. *Publication:* contributed chapter to the Orange Book, on using market mechanisms to achieve environmental goals 2004; numerous articles. *Address:* Department for Transport, Great Minster House, 33 Horseferry Road, London, SW1P 4DR (office); House of Lords, London, SW1A 0PW, England (office). *Telephone:* (300) 330-3000 (office); (20) 7219-1492 (House of Lords) (office). *E-mail:* kramers@parliament.uk (office). *Website:* www.gov.uk/government/organisations/ department-for-transport (office); www.susankramer.co.uk.

KRAMMER, Peter H., MD; German immunologist and academic; *Speaker, Tumorimmunology Program, German Cancer Research Centre;* b. 2 April 1946, Rheydt; ed Univ. of Freiburg; Internship in Internal Medicine and Pathology, Univ. of Freiburg, Univ. Hosp. and Inst. of Pathology 1971–72, Study mem. Low Molecular Weight Nuclear RNA 1972, Internship in Surgery 1972–73; mem. Basel Inst. for Immunology, Switzerland 1973–75; Assoc., German Cancer Research Centre, Inst. for Immunology and Genetics, Heidelberg 1976, Acting Head, Div. of Immunogenetics 1981–88, Head 1989–, Acting Dir 1990–; mem. Max-Planck Inst. for Immunology, Freiburg 1976; Visiting Prof., Dept of Microbiology, Univ. of Texas Health Science Center at Dallas, Tex., USA 1981; Visiting Scientist, Centre for Molecular Biology, Heidelberg 1984–85; Speaker, Tumorimmunology Program, German Cancer Research Centre, Heidelberg 1993–; mem. German Immunologi- cal Soc. 1973, American Asscn for Cancer Research, European Molecular Biology Org. 1999, APOGENIX Foundation 2000; mem. Medical Faculty, Heidelberg Univ. 1978; mem. Scientific Cttee Health Research Council; mem. Scientific Bd German Cancer Research Centre 1978–83, 1990–94, 1995–97, 1997–2000; mem. Editorial Bd Immunology Letters, Immunobiology, Cell Death and Differentiation, Cancer Research, European Journal of Immunology, Journal of Clinical Investigation, International Journal of Cancer; Order of Merit (FRG) 1991; King Phillip Award for Leukemia Research 1991, Robert Koch Prize 1995, Behring Lecturer 1995, Meyenburg Prize 1996, Heinz-Ansmann Prize 1996, Kitasato-Behring Prize 1996, German Cancer Prize 1996, Cancer Research Award, Wilhelm Warner Foundation 1997, Avery Landsteiner Prize 1998, Theodor Kocher Lecture 2000, Ludwick Hirszfeld Medal, Polish Soc. for Experimental and Clinical Immunology 2000, Ernst-Jung Prize for Medicine 2000, Norman Heatley Lecturer, Univ. of Oxford, UK 2000, Annual MRC Lecturer, SOT Meeting 2001, Genius Biotech Award APOGENIX 2001, Lautenschläger Research Prize 2003. *Publications:* more than 360 articles in medical and scientific journals. *Address:* Tumorimmunology Program, Deutsches Krebsforschungszentrum, Im Neuenheimer Feld 280, 69120

Heidelberg, Germany (office). *Telephone:* (6221) 423718 (office). *Fax:* (6221) 411715 (office). *E-mail:* p.krammer@dkfz.de (office). *Website:* www.sfb405.uni-hd.de/ Krammer.html; www.zmbh.uni-heidelberg.de/mcb/Brochure/Krammer.html (office).

KRAMNIK, Vladimir Borisovich; Russian chess master; b. 25 June 1975, Tuapse, Krasnodar Territory, Russia; m.; started playing chess at age of 4; cand. for Master title 1986; Grandmaster title 1991; World Champion among young people 16–18 years of age, winner World Chess Olympiads Manila 1992, Moscow 1994, Yerevan 1996; winner maj. int. tournaments and matches; since 1995 holds place among the 3 highest-rated players of the world; took part in World Championship 1993; ranked number one world player 1996; won match against Gary Kasparov for World Championship Oct. 2000, won unified world chess championship 2006; winner of Chess Oscar 2000, 2001. *Publication:* Kramnik: My Life and Games (autobiog. with Takov Damsky). *Telephone:* (495) 495-32-72 (Moscow) (home). *Website:* www.kramnik.com.

KRANJEC, Marko, PhD; Slovenian economist, academic and central banker; b. 12 April 1940, Novo mesto; ed Faculty of Econs, Univ. of Ljubljana; fmr Asst Prof., Faculty of Public Admin, Univ. of Ljubljana, Prof. of Public Finance 2002–06; Head, Analysis Dept, Ljubljanska Bank 1968–70; Researcher, Inst. of Int. Econ. Research 1970–76, Research Adviser 1986–90; macroeconomist, OECD, Paris –1984; economist, IBRD (World Bank), Washington, DC 1984–86; first Minister of Finance of ind. Slovenia 1990–91; Vice-Gov. Banka Slovenije (Bank of Slovenia) 1991–97, Gov. 2007–13; Amb. to the EU, Brussels 1997–2002; mem. Governing Council European Cen. Bank, Govt's Strategic Council for Econ. Devt; fmr mem. Supervisory Bd Krka, Novo mesto; Silver Order of Freedom of Repub. of Slovenia 2001. *Address:* Ministry of Foreign Affairs, 1001 Ljubljana, Prešernova 25, Slovenia (office). *Telephone:* (1) 4782231 (office). *Fax:* (1) 4782340 (office). *E-mail:* info.mzz@gov.si (office). *Website:* www.mzz.gov.si (office).

KRANTZ, Judith, BA; American author; b. 9 Jan. 1928, New York City; d. of Jack David Tarcher and Mary Brager; m. Stephen Krantz 1954 (died 2007); two s.; ed Wellesley Coll.; contrib. to Good Housekeeping 1948–54, McCalls 1954–59, Ladies Home Journal 1959–71; Contributing Ed. Cosmopolitan 1971–79. *Publications:* Scruples 1978, Princess Daisy 1980, Mistral's Daughter 1982, I'll Take Manhattan 1986, Till We Meet Again 1988, Dazzle 1990, Scruples Two 1992, Lovers 1994, Spring Collection 1996, The Jewels of Teresa Kant 1998, Sex & Shopping: Confessions of a Nice Jewish Girl 2000. *Address:* c/o Esther Newberg, Inter- national Creative Management Inc., 825 Eighth Avenue, New York, NY 10019, USA (office).

KRARUP, Thorleif, BSc, BComm; Danish business executive; *Chairman, ALK- Abelló A/S;* b. 1952; Chair. Man. Bd Nykredit 1987–91; Group CEO Tryg Nykredit Holding 1991–92; Group CEO Unidanmark 1992–2000; Chair. Exec. Bd Unibank 1992–2000; Deputy CEO Nordic Baltic Holding 2000; Group CEO Nordea 2000–02, Sr Vice-Pres. 2002–2004; Chair. TDC –2006; Chair. Dangaard Telecom A/S 2006; mem. Bd of Dirs ALK-Abelló A/S 2005–, Chair. 2011–; mem. Bd of Dirs Bisca A/S Exiqon A/S (Chair.), Falck A/S (Vice-Chair.), H. Lundbeck A/S, The Lundbeck Foundation. *Address:* ALK-Abelló A/S, Bøge Allé 6, 2970 Hørsholm, Denmark (office). *Website:* www.alk-abello.com (office).

KRASHENINNIKOV, Pavel Vladimirovich, DJur; Russian lawyer and polit- ician; b. 21 June 1964, Polevskoye, Sverdlovsk Region; m. Catherine Krashenin- nikov; one s. one d.; ed Sverdlovsk Inst. of Law; teacher, Sverdlovsk Inst. of Law 1991–93; Lecturer, Moscow State Univ. 1994–; Deputy Head, Chief Dept of Housing Policy, State Cttee on Construction of Russian Fed. 1993–; Head, Dept of Civil and Econ. Law, Ministry of Justice 1993–96; Deputy Chair. State Cttee on Antimonopoly Policy and Support of New Econ. Structures 1996–97; First Deputy Minister of Justice 1997–98, Acting Minister March 1998, Minister 1998–99; Co- ordinator, Pres., Comm. for Counteraction against Political Extremism in Russia 1998–99; mem. State Duma (Union of Right-Wing Forces faction) 1999–2003, Chair. Legis. Cttee 2000–03, re-elected as ind. (later joined Yedinaya Rossiya (United Russia) faction) 2003–, Chair. Cttee for Civil, Criminal, Arbitration and Remedial Legislation; Rector Russian School of Private Law 1999; State Counsellor of Justice, 1st Class 1997; Order of Friendship. *Publications:* Zhilishchnoe pravo 2006, Privatizatsiia zhil'ia: prava grazhdan do i posle privatizatsii 2006, Federal'nyi zakonotvorcheskii protsess 2009; more than 100 articles on private and public law. *Address:* State Duma, Okhotny ryad 1, 103265 Moscow, Russia (office). *Telephone:* (495) 292-92-10 (office). *Fax:* (495) 292-97-82 (office). *Website:* www.duma.gov.ru (office).

KRASIKOV, Anatoly Andreyevich, DHist; Russian journalist and scholar; *Chief Researcher, Institute of Europe, Russian Academy of Sciences;* b. 3 Aug. 1931, Moscow; m.; one d.; ed Moscow Inst. of Int. Relations; on staff USSR Telegraph Agency TASS 1955–92; Deputy Dir-Gen. ITAR-TASS 1978–92; on staff of Pres. Yeltsin, Head of Press, Exec. Sec., Council on Interaction with Religious Orgs of Russian Presidency 1992–96; Chair. Int. Christianity Cttee 1996; Head, Centre for Studies of Problems of Religion and Soc.; Chief Researcher, Inst. of Europe, Russian Acad. of Sciences 1996–; Pres. Russian Chapter, Int. Religious Liberty Asscn 1997–2003, Hon. Pres. Euro-Asia Chapter, 2004–; Public Policy Scholar, Woodrow Wilson Center, Washington, DC 2000; Galina Starovoitova Fellow on Human Rights and Conflict Resolution, Kennan Inst., Washington, DC 2004. *Publications:* Church-State Relations in Russia 1998, Proselytism and Religious Liberty in Russia 1999, The Enigma of Liberty 2001, Russian Orthodoxy: Striving for Monopoly? 2004. *Leisure interests:* music, archives, tourism. *Address:* Institute of Europe, Mokhovaya str. 11, Bldg 3v, 103873 Moscow, Russia (office). *Telephone:* (495) 292-23-04 (office). *Fax:* (495) 200-42-98 (office). *E-mail:* ankras@ok.ru (office). *Website:* www.ieras.ru (office).

KRASIN, Yury Andreyevich, DSc; Russian political scientist and academic; *Head, Department for Analysis of Socio-Political Processes, Institute of Sociology, Russian Academy of Sciences;* b. 7 June 1929, Penza; one d.; ed Philosophical Faculty, Leningrad State Univ.; Lecturer, Asst Prof., Leningrad State Pedagogical Inst. 1952–60; Asst Prof., Inst. of Professional Skill Improvement, Moscow State Univ. 1960–63; Sr Fellow, Inst. of Philosophy USSR (now Russian) Acad. of Sciences 1963; consultant, Int. Div. CP Cen. Cttee; Prof., Moscow Inst. of Professional Skill Improvement at Moscow State Univ. 1963–75; Prof., Head of Dept, Prorector, Acad. of Social Sciences at CPSU Cen. Cttee 1975–87; Rector Inst.

of Social Sciences at CPSU Cen. Cttee 1987–91; Dir-Gen. Foundation of Social and Political Studies 1991–92; Dir Centre of Social Programmes, Int. Foundation of Social, Econ. and Politological Studies 1992–97; Head, Dept for Analysis of Socio-Political Processes, Inst. of Sociology, Russian Acad. of Sciences 1993–; Adviser, Gorbachev Foundation 1997–2011; Prof., Russian State Humanitarian Univ. 2009–; mem. Presidium Acad. of Political Science; mem. Russian Acad. of Natural Sciences; Medal for 'Labour Valour' 1961, Order 'Decoration of Esteem' 1971, Order 'Friendship of Peoples' 1979, Medal 'Veteran of Labour' 1985; Dr hc (Inst. of Sociology, Russian Acad. of Sciences) 2008; Lomonosov Prize of Moscow State Univ. 1968, USSR State Prize 1980, Pitirim Sorokin Silver Medal 2008, George Shahnasarov Medal, Russian Asscn of Political Science 2012. *Publications:* 20 books, including Dialectic of the Revolutionary Process 1972, Capitalism Today: Paradoxes of Development (co-author) 1989, Russia at the Crossroads: Authoritarianism or Democracy 1998, Russia: Quo Vadis? (with A. Galkin) 2003, Public Policy in Russia (ed.) 2005, Social Inequality and Public Policy (ed.) 2007, Metamorphoses of the Russian Reformation – Political Subjects 2009; articles on social movts, democratic reform in Russia, civil, social and political matters. *Leisure interests:* classical music, skiing. *Address:* Institute of Sociology, 117218 Moscow, Krzhizhanovskogo str. 24/35, korp. 5 (office); 121433 Moscow, Malaya Philevskaya str. 44, Apt 11, Russia (home). *Telephone:* (495) 719-09-40 (office); (499) 144-29-83 (home). *E-mail:* krasinyua@mtu-net.ru (home). *Website:* www.spbrc.nw.ru (office).

KRASNIQI, Jakup; Kosovo politician and teacher; *President, Kosovo Assembly;* b. 1 Jan. 1951, Negrofc/Negrovce, Drenas/Glogovac municipality; m.; one s. three d.; ed secondary school in Prishtina, Univ. of Prishtina, Univ. of Kosovo; teacher, schools in Fatos and Arllat 1972–77, in secondary school in Drenas 1976–77, in Arllat and in secondary school in Skënderaj/Srbica 1979–81, in secondary school 'Skënderbeu' in Drenas 1991–94; Chair. Educ. Council, Drenas 1995–98; clandestine political activity 1973–81, political prisoner 1981–91; Deputy of unconstituted Parl. of Kosovo 1992–98; Spokesman, HQ of Kosovo Liberation Army (KLA) 1998–99, mem. of HQ and of Political Directorate; Minister in Ministry for Reconstruction and Devt 1999–2000, in Ministry of Public Services 2002–04; Gen. Sec. Democratic Prosperity Party of Kosovo (PPDK), later Democratic Party of Kosovo (PDK) 1998–2003, re-elected Gen. Sec. 2005, currently Chair. Parl. Group of PDK; Deputy in first Legislation 2001–, Deputy, Second Mandate in Kosovo Ass. 2004, Leader of Parl. Group of PDK, Deputy, Third Mandate 2007–, Pres. Kosovo Ass. 2007–, also Acting Pres. of Kosovo Sept. 2010–Feb. 2011, March–April 2011; mem. Presidency of Democratic League of Kosovo (LDK), Drenas br. 1991–99. *Publications:* books: Kthesa e Madhe – Ushtria Çlirimtare e Kosovës 2006, Kosova in a Historical Context 2007, Një luftë ndryshe për Kosovën (A Different War for Kosova) 2007, Pavarësia si kompromis 2010, Lëvizja për Republikën e Kosovës 1981–1991 sipas shtypit shqiptar 2011; numerous political and scientific articles published in daily papers, periodicals and scientific magazines. *Address:* Kuvendi i Kosovës/Skupština Kosova (Kosovo Assembly), 10000 Prishtina, Rruga Nënë Terezë, Kosovo (office). *Telephone:* (38) 20010004 (office); (38) 211186 (office). *Fax:* (38) 211188 (office). *E-mail:* info@assembly-kosova.org (office). *Website:* www.assembly-kosova.org (office).

KRASTS, Guntars; Latvian economist and politician; b. 16 Oct. 1957, Rīga; m.; three s.; ed Latvian State Univ.; researcher, Inst. of Agric. Econs 1983–91; Chair. Exec. Bd RANG Ltd 1991–95; Minister of Econs 1995–97; Prime Minister of Latvia 1997–98; Vice-Prime Minister for EU Affairs 1998–99; Chair. Saeima (Parl.) Foreign Affairs Cttee 1998–2002, European Affairs Cttee 2002–04; MEP 2004–09, Vice-Chair. Cttee on Econ. and Monetary Affairs; Leader, Libertas Latvia (slate of MEP cands) 2009. *Publications:* numerous publs in Latvia and abroad on econ. and foreign policy issues. *Leisure interests:* swimming, skiing. *Address:* Jēkaba str. 10/12, 1811 Rīga, Latvia.

KRAUSS, Alison; American country and bluegrass singer and musician (fiddle); b. 23 July 1971, Champaign, Ill.; m. Pat Bergeson (divorced 2001); one s.; singer, musician since age 14; lead singer with Union Station 1987–; Int. Bluegrass Music Asscn Awards for Female Vocalist of the Year 1990, 1991, 1993, 1995, Country Music Television Award for Independent Video of the Year (for I've Got That Old Feeling) 1991, Entertainer of the Year 1991, 1995, Country Music Asscn Awards for Female Vocalist of the Year, Single of the Year (for When You Say Nothing At All), Vocal Event of the Year (for Somewhere In The Vicinity Of The Heart, with Shenandoah), and Horizon Award 1995, Grammy Award for Female Country Vocal Performance (for Baby, Now That I've Found You) 1995, Country Music Television Award for Rising Video Star of the Year 1995, GAVIN Americana Artist of the Year 1995, Great British Country Music Award for Int. Female Vocalist of the Year 1996, for Int. Bluegrass Band of the Year 1997, 1998, 1999, 2000, Grammy Awards for Best Country Performance by a Duo or Group (for Looking In The Eyes Of Love), for Best Country Instrumental Performance (for Little Liza Jane) 1997, Gospel Music Asscn Dove Award for Bluegrass Recorded Song of the Year (for Children of the Living God, with Fernando Ortega) 1998, Canadian Country Music Award for Vocal/Instrumental Collaboration (for Get Me Through December, with Natalie MacMaster) 2000, Int. Bluegrass Music Asscn Award for Gospel Recorded Event of the Year (for I'll Fly Away, with Gillian Welch) 2001, Grammy Award for Country Performance by a Duo or Group (for The Lucky One) 2001, Grammy Award for Best Country Instrumental Performance (for Cluck Old Hen) 2003, Country Music Asscn Award for Best Video and Music Event (for Whiskey Lullaby, with Brad Paisley) 2004, Grammy Awards for Best Country Performance by a Duo or Group with Vocal (for Restless, with Union Station), for Best Country Instrumental Performance (for Unionhouse Branch with Union Station) 2006, for Best Pop Collaboration with Vocals (for Gone Gone Gone with Robert Plant) 2008, (for Rich Woman with Robert Plant) 2009, for Record of the Year (for Please Read the Letter with Robert Plant) 2009, for Best Country Collaboration with Vocals (for Killing the Blues with Robert Plant) 2009, CMA Award for Musical Event of the Year (for Gone Gone Gone with Robert Plant) 2008. *Recordings include:* albums: Different Strokes 1985, Too Late to Cry 1987, Two Highways (with Union Station) 1989, I've Got That Old Feeling (Grammy Award for Bluegrass Recording 1990, Int. Bluegrass Music Asscn Award for Album of the Year 1991) 1990, Every Time You Say Goodbye (with Union Station) (Grammy Award for Bluegrass Recording 1992, Int. Bluegrass Music Asscn Award for Album of the Year 1993) 1992, I Know Who Holds Tomorrow (with The Cox Family) (Grammy Award for Southern, Country or Bluegrass Gospel Album) 1994, Now

That I've Found You: A Collection 1995, So Long So Wrong (with Union Station) (GAVIN Americana Album of the Year, Grammy Award for Best Bluegrass Album) 1997, Forget About It 1999, New Favorite (with Union Station) (Grammy Award for Best Bluegrass Album) 2001, Live (with Union Station) (Int. Bluegrass Music Asscn Awards Album of the Year, Grammy Award for Best Bluegrass Album 2003) 2002, Lonely Runs Both Ways (with Union Station) (Grammy Award for Best Country Album 2006) 2004, A Hundred Miles or More 2007, Raising Sand (with Robert Plant) (Grammy Awards for Album of the Year 2009, for Best Contemporary Folk/Americana Album 2009) 2007, Paper Airplane (with Union Station) (Grammy Award for Best Bluegrass Album 2012) 2011. *Address:* D. S. Management, 2814 12th Avenue S, Nashville, TN 37204, USA (office); Union Station Land Inc., PO Box 121711, Nashville, TN 37212, USA. *Website:* www.alisonkrauss.com.

KRAUSZ, Ferenc, DipEng, DrTechn; Hungarian/Austrian physicist and academic; *Director, Max Planck Institute of Quantum Optics;* b. 17 May 1962, Mór, Hungary; m.; two c.; ed Eötvös Loránd Univ., Budapest, Budapest Univ. of Tech., Vienna Univ. of Tech.; Asst Prof., Vienna Univ. of Tech. 1996–98, Prof. of Electrical Eng 1999–2004; Dir Max Planck Inst. of Quantum Optics, Garching, Germany 2003–; Prof. of Physics, also Chair. of Experimental Physics, Ludwig-Maximilians-Univ., Munich 2004–; mem. Austrian Acad. of Sciences 2003–; Dr hc (Tech. Univ. Budapest) 2005; Austrian Physical Soc. Fritz Kohlrausch Award 1994, Federal Ministry of Science and Educ. START Award 1996, Ernst Abbe Foundation Carl Zeiss Award 1998, Federal Ministry of Science and Educ. Wittgenstein Award 2002, Julius Springer Award in Applied Physics (USA) 2003, Gottfried Wilhelm Leibniz Award Deutsche Forschungsgemeinschaft 2006, King Faisal Int. Prize for Science (co-recipient) 2013. *Publications:* one book (ed.), five book chapters and more than 100 papers on ultrashort-pulse laser physics, intense light–matter interactions, nonlinear optics, and atomic, plasma and x-ray physics. *Address:* Max Planck Institute of Quantum Optics, Hans-Kopfermann-Strasse 1, 85748 Garching (office); Lehrstuhl für Experimentalphysik, Department für Physik, Ludwig-Maximilians-University Munich, Am Coulombwall 1, 85748 Garching, Germany (office). *Telephone:* (89) 32905602 (office); (89) 28914013 (office). *Fax:* (89) 32905649 (office); (89) 28914141 (office). *E-mail:* krausz@lmu.de (office); ferenc.krausz@mpq.mpg.de (office); ferenc.krausz@physik.uni-muenchen.de. *Website:* www.attoworld.de (office); www.atto.physik.uni-muenchen.de/personen/professoren/krausz/index.html (office).

KRAUTHAMMER, Charles, MD; American psychiatrist and journalist; b. 13 March 1950, New York; s. of Shulim Krauthammer and Thea Krauthammer; m. Robyn Trethewey; one s.; ed McGill Univ., Balliol Coll. Oxford and Harvard Univs, Medical School; Resident in Psychiatry, Mass. Gen. Hosp., Boston 1975–78; Scientific Adviser, Dept of Health and Human Services, Washington, DC 1978–80; speech writer to Vice-Pres. Walter Mondale (q.v.), Washington, DC 1980–81; Sr Ed. The New Republic, Washington, DC 1981–88, now Contributing Ed.; Contributing Ed. Weekly Standard; fmr essayist, Time Magazine; syndicated columnist, The Washington Post 1984–; commentator, Fox News; mem. Bd of Advisers, The Nat. Interest, Public Interest; mem. President's Council on Bioethics 2002–; Nat. Magazine Award (for essays), American Soc. of Magazine Eds 1984, First Amendment Award, People for the American Way 1985, Pulitzer Prize (for commentary) 1987. *Publications:* Cutting Edges 1985; contribs to psychiatric journals. *Leisure interest:* chess. *Address:* c/o The Washington Post Writers Group, 1150 15th Street, NW, Washington, DC 20071, USA. *Website:* www.washingtonpost.com.

KRAUZE, Andrzej; Polish painter, illustrator and political cartoonist; b. 1947, Warsaw; m. Małgosia Krauze; three s.; ed Acad. of Fine Art, Warsaw; worked as cartoonist for periodicals Szpilki, Kultura, Solidarity Weekly 1970s; moved to London 1981; cartoonist for The Guardian, Sunday Telegraph, The Bookseller, New Society, New Statesman, Rzeczpospolita (Polish daily) and numerous other publs in UK, France and USA. *Address:* c/o Guardian News and Media Ltd, Kings Place, 90 York Way, London, N1 9GU, England (office).

KRAVCHENKO, Adm. Victor Andreyevich; Russian naval officer; b. 5 Dec. 1943, Bogdanovich, Sverdlovsk Region; m.; one d.; ed Higher Mil. Marine School, Mil. Marine Acad., Acad. of the Gen. Staff; served as Sr Asst, submarine Commdr, Head of staff, submarine div. Commdr, First Deputy Head of Staff, Black Sea Fleet 1968–91; First Deputy Commdr, Baltic Fleet 1991–96; Commdr, Black Sea Fleet 1996–98; Head of Gen. Staff, First Deputy C-in-C Russian Navy 1998–2005; Russian Acad. of Natural Sciences Hon. 'For Merits' Award; numerous other awards and decorations. *Address:* c/o General Staff of the Russian Navy, B. Kozlovsky Per. 6, 103175 Moscow, Russia.

KRAVCHUK, Leonid Makarovych, CandEconSc; Ukrainian politician and fmr head of state; b. 10 Jan. 1934, Velykyi Zhytyn (Poland, now in Rivne Oblast, Ukraine); s. of Makar Olexiyovich and Khima Ivanivna Kravchuk; m. Antonina Mikhailivna Kravchuk 1957; one s.; ed Kyiv State Univ. and Acad. of Social Sciences, Moscow; teacher of Political Economy, Chernovitsky Tech. School; party work since 1960, on staff Ukrainian CP Cen. Cttee 1970–; Head, Propaganda Dept 1980–88, Ideology Dept 1988–89, Sec., Cen. Cttee, mem. Politburo 1990; Chair. Ukrainian Supreme Soviet 1990–91; Pres. of Ukraine 1991–94; C-in-C Armed Forces of Ukraine 1991–94; mem. Verkhovna Rada (Parl.) 1994–2006; f. Mutual Understanding Movt 1994; mem. Social Democratic Party; Head, All-Ukrainian Union of Democratic Forces Zlagoda 1999–; Chair. State Cttee for Admin. Reforms 1997–99; Protector Mohyla Acad.-Nat. Univ. of Kyiv 1991; Head, Trusteeship Council, Children and Youth Activity Cen. of Ukraine 1992; Hon. Pres. East European Asscn of Businessmen; Dr hc (La Salle Univ., Phila, USA) 1992. *Publications include:* State and Authorities: Experience of Administrative Reforms 2001, We Have What We Have 2002. *Leisure interests:* chess, books, cinema. *Address:* Verkhovna Rada, 01008 Kyiv, vul. M. Hrushevskoho 5, Ukraine (office). *Telephone:* (44) 255-21-15 (office). *Fax:* (44) 253-32-17 (office). *E-mail:* umz@rada.gov.ua (office). *Website:* www.rada.gov.ua (office).

KRAVIS, Henry R., BA, MBA; American investment banker; *Founding Partner, Kohlberg Kravis Roberts & Co.;* b. 6 Jan. 1944, Tulsa, Okla; s. of the late Raymond Kravis and Bessie Kravis (née Roberts); m. 1st the late Diane Shulman (divorced); two c.; m. 2nd Carolyn Roehm 1985 (divorced 1993); m. 3rd Marie-Josée Drouin 1994; ed Loomis Chaffee School, Claremont McKenna Coll., Columbia Univ.; began career as Vice-Pres. Katy Industries, New York; Pnr, Bear Stearns & Co.,

New York 1969–76; Founding Pnr, Kohlberg Kravis Roberts & Co. (investment bank), New York 1976–, Sr Pnr 1987–; Co-Chair. Bd of Overseers, Columbia Univ. Business School; Vice-Chair. Rockefeller Univ.; Trustee Mount Sinai Medical Center, Metropolitan Musuem of Art; Chair. Emer. WNET, New York (public TV station); mem. Bd of Dirs Partnership for New York City (fmr Co-Chair.), Council on Foreign Relations; Founder and Chair. New York City Investment Fund; Co-founder Republican Leadership Council; mem. Business Council. *Leisure interest:* collecting art. *Address:* Kohlberg Kravis Roberts & Co., 9 West 57th Street, Suite 4200, New York, NY 10019, USA (office). *Telephone:* (212) 750-8300 (office). *Website:* www.kkr.com (office).

KRAVITZ, Lenny; American singer, musician (piano, guitar), songwriter and producer; b. 26 May 1964, New York; m. Lisa Bonet (divorced); actor, as teenager; mem. Calif. Boys Choir and Metropolitan Opera; solo artist 1989–; numerous tours world-wide, TV and live appearances; f. Kravitz Design, Miami 2005; Ordre des Arts et des Lettres 2011; BRIT Award for Best Int. Male 1994, Grammy Awards for Male Rock Vocal Performance 2000, 2001, American Music Award for Favorite Pop/Rock Male Artist 2002. *Recordings include:* albums: Let Love Rule 1989, Mama Said 1991, Are You Gonna Go My Way 1993, Circus 1995, 5 1998, Greatest Hits 2000, Lenny 2001, Baptism 2004, It Is Time For A Love Revolution 2008, Black and White America 2011. *Address:* Kravitz Design Inc, 13 Crosby Street, 5th Floor, New York, NY 10013, USA (office). *Telephone:* (212) 625-1644. *E-mail:* info@kravitzdesign.com. *Website:* www.kravitzdesign.com; www.lennykravitz.com.

KRAWCHECK, Sallie L., BA, MBA; American banker; b. 1965, Charleston, SC; m. Gary Appel; ed Univ. of North Carolina at Chapel Hill, Columbia Business School, New York; worked with Fortune magazine; worked for Salomon Brothers; worked for Donaldson, Lufkin & Jenrette; joined Sanford C. Bernstein stock research firm in 1994, Dir of Research 1998–2001, Chair. and CEO 2001–02; Chair. and CEO Smith Barney (div. of Citigroup) 2002–04, Chief Financial Officer and Head of Strategy 2004–07, Chair. and CEO Global Wealth Man. Div. 2007–08, mem. Man. Cttee Citigroup 2004–08; Pres. Global Wealth and Investment Man., Bank of America Corpn 2009–11, also mem. Exec. Man. Team; mem. Bd of Dirs Dell Inc., Motif Investing Inc. 2012–; mem. Advisory mem. Eurasia Group; mem. The Morehead Foundation's Cen. Selection Cttee; mem. Bd Gold Bullion International, Univ. of North Carolina at Chapel Hill Foundations, Carnegie Hall; recognized by the World Economic Forum as one of its Young Global Leaders, ranked by Fortune magazine amongst the 50 Most Powerful Women in Business in the US (14th) 2003, (seventh) 2004–05, (ninth) 2006, (12th) 2007, (30th) 2009, (24th) 2010, ranked by Forbes magazine amongst The World's 100 Most Powerful Women (48th) 2004, (seventh) 2005, (sixth) 2006, (64th) 2008, (88th) 2009, (44th) 2010, (67th) 2011, CNBC Business Leader of the Future Award 2007. *Address:* Motif Investing, Inc., PO Box 3548, Rancho Cordova, CA 95741, USA (office). *Telephone:* (855) 586-6843 (office). *E-mail:* service@motifinvesting.com (office). *Website:* www.motifinvesting.com (office).

KRAWIEC, Dariusz Jacek; Polish business executive; *President and CEO, PKN Orlen;* ed Poznań Univ. of Econs; with PEKAO SA (bank) 1992; Consultant, Man. Consulting Dept, Ernst & Young SA 1993; Asst, Sr Asst, Man. Asst and Man. in Corp. Finance Dept, Price Waterhouse Sp. z o.o. 1993–97; with Nomura International plc (investment bank), London, UK, responsible for Polish market 1997–2002; Pres. Man. Bd and Gen. Dir Impexmetal SA 1998–2002; Pres. Man. Bd Elektrim SA 2002; Man. Dir Sindicatum Ltd, London 2003–04; Pres. Man. Bd Action SA 2006–08; participant in PKN Orlen Man. Bd Mems' competition for a new term of office Feb. 2008, Vice-Pres. Man. Bd PKN Orlen June–Sept. 2008, Pres. Man. Bd and CEO Sept. 2008–; Chair. Supervisory Bd Unipetrol a.s.; fmr Chair. Supervisory Bd Huta Aluminium 'Konin' SA, Metalexfrance SA, S and I SA, cemarket.com SA; mem. Supervisory Bd Impexmetal SA, Elektrim SA, PTC Sp. z o.o. (ERA GSM), Elektrim Telekomunikacja Sp. z o.o., Elektrim Magadex SA, Elektrim Volt SA, PTE AIG, Polkomtel SA. *Address:* PKN Orlen, 09-411 Plock, ul. Chemikow 7, Poland (office). *Telephone:* (24) 3650000 (office). *Fax:* (24) 3654040 (office). *E-mail:* info@orlen.pl (office). *Website:* www.orlen.pl (office).

KRAYER, Georg F., LLD; Swiss banking executive; *Honorary Chairman, Bank Sarasin & Company Ltd;* b. 30 May 1943, Basel; m. Luise Krayer; two d.; ed Univ. of Basel; joined A. Sarasin & Cie (now Bank Sarasin & Co. Ltd), Basel 1970, vocational training in Paris, France and New York, apptd Pnr 1978, Chair. Bd of Admin 1997–2002, Chair. Bd of Dirs 1997–2008, Hon. Chair. 2008–; mem. Basel Stock Exchange 1978–92, Pres. 1989–92; Vice-Chair.Bâloise Holding AG; Chair. Swiss Bankers Asscn 1992–2003; Hon. Dr rer. pol 2004. *Leisure interest:* rowing. *Address:* Bank Sarasin & Company Ltd, Elisabethenstrasse 62, 4002 Basel, Switzerland (office). *Telephone:* (61) 2777777 (office). *Fax:* (61) 2727610 (office). *E-mail:* georg.krayer@sarasin.ch (office). *Website:* www.sarasin.ch (office).

KREBS, Baron (Life Peer), cr. 2007, of Wytham in the County of Oxfordshire; **John Richard Krebs,** Kt, MA, DPhil, FRS, FMedSci; British zoologist and scientific administrator; *Principal, Jesus College, Oxford;* b. 11 April 1945, Sheffield, Yorks., England; s. of Prof. Sir Hans Adolf Krebs and Margaret Fieldhouse; m. 1st Katharine A. Fullerton 1968 (divorced 2013); two d.; m. 2nd Sarah M. Phibbs 2013; ed City of Oxford High School, Pembroke Coll. Oxford; Departmental Demonstrator in Ornithology, Edward Grey Inst. of Field Orni-thology and Oxford Lecturer in Zoology, Pembroke Coll. Oxford 1969–70, Lecturer in Zoology, Edward Grey Inst. 1976–88, E.P. Abraham Fellow in Zoology, Pembroke Coll. 1981–88, Fellow 1988–2005, Hon. Fellow 2005–; Asst Prof., Inst. of Resource Ecology, Univ. of British Columbia, Vancouver, Canada 1970–73; Lecturer in Zoology, Univ. Coll. of North Wales, Bangor 1973–74; SRC Research Officer, Animal Behaviour Research Group, Dept of Zoology, Oxford 1975–76; Fellow, Wolfson Coll. 1976–81; Royal Soc. Research Prof., Univ. of Oxford 1988–2005, Prin. Jesus Coll. Oxford 2005–; Chief Exec. NERC 1994–2000; Chair. Food Standards Agency 2000–05; Dir Agric. and Food Research Council (AFRC) Unit of Ecology and Behaviour and NERC Unit of Behavioural Ecology 1989–94; Sr Scientific Consultant and Chair. Animals Research Cttee, AFRC 1991–94; External Scientific mem. Max Planck Soc. 1985; Pres. Int. Soc. of Behavioural Ecology 1988–90, Asscn for Study of Animal Behaviour 1992–94; Pres. British Science Asscn (fmrly BAAS) 2012–13; mem. (Crossbench) House of Lords 2007–, Chair. House of Lords Science and Tech. Cttee 2010–14; Chair. UK Science and Tech. Honours Cttee 2008–14, UK Climate Adaptation Cttee 2009–; Trustee, Nuffield Foundation 2007–; mem. Academia Europaea 1995; Foreign mem.

American Philosophical Soc. 2000, American Acad. of Arts and Sciences 2000; Fellow, German Nat. Acad. of Sciences Leopoldina 2013; Hon. Fellow, Univ. of Cardiff 1999, Univ. Wales Inst. Cardiff 2006, Univ. Wales Bangor 2007; Hon. Fellow, German Ornithological Soc. 2003, Salters' Co. 2006, Asscn for Nutrition 2012, British Science Asscn 2012; Hon. FZS 2006; Hon. mem. British Ecological Soc. 1999; Foreign Hon. mem. NAS 2004; Hon. DSc (Sheffield) 1993, (Wales) 1997, (Birmingham) 1997, (Exeter) 1998, (Warwick) 2000, (Cranfield) 2001, (Kent) 2001, (Plymouth) 2001, (South Bank) 2003, (Heriot-Watt) 2002, (Queen's Univ., Belfast) 2002, (Lancaster) 2005, (Guelph) 2006, (Aberdeen) 2010, (Newcastle-upon-Tyne) 2012; Dr hc (Stirling) 2000; Nuffield Foundation Science Fellowship 1981, Scientific Medal, Zoological Soc. 1981, Bicentenary Medal, Linnaean Soc. 1983, Frink Medal, Zoological Soc. 1996, Elliott Coues Award, American Ornithologists' Union 1999, Asscn for Study of Animal Behaviour Medal 2000, Benjamin Ward Richardson Gold Medal, Royal Soc. for Promotion of Health 2002, Wooldridge Medal, British Veterinary Asscn 2004, Croonian Lecture and Medal, Royal Soc., London 2004, Lord Raynor Medal & Lecture, Royal Coll. of Physicians 2005, Award for Outstanding Achievement, Soc. for Food Hygiene Tech. 2005, Harben Gold Medal, Royal Inst. of Public Health 2006. *Publications:* Behavioural Ecology: An Evolutionary Aproach (co-ed.) 1978, 1984, 1991, 1997, An Introduction to Behavioural Ecology (with N. B. Davies) 1981 (revised edn 2012), Foraging Theory: Princeton Monographs in Behaviour and Ecology, No. 4 (with D. W. Stephens) 1987, Foraging Behaviour (co-ed.) 1987, Behavioural and Neural Studies of Learning and Memory (co-ed.) 1991. *Leisure interests:* gardening, music, running, walking, tennis. *Address:* Jesus College, Oxford, OX1 3DW, England (office). *Telephone:* (1865) 279701 (office). *E-mail:* principal@jesus.ox.ac.uk (office). *Website:* www.jesus.ox.ac.uk (office); www.parliament.uk/biographies/lords/lord-krebs/3736.

KREBS, Robert Duncan, MBA; American transport industry executive (retd); b. 2 May 1942, Sacramento, Calif.; s. of Ward C. Krebs and Eleanor B. Krebs (née Duncan); m. Anne Lindstrom 1971; two s. one d.; ed Stanford and Harvard Univs; Asst Gen. Man. S Pacific Transportation Co., Houston 1974–75, Asst Regional Operations Man. 1975–76, Asst Vice-Pres. San Francisco 1967–77, Asst to Pres. 1977–79, Gen. Man. 1979, Vice-Pres. Transportation 1979-80, Operations 1980–82, Pres. 1982–83; Dir and Pres. Santa Fe S Pacific Corpn (now Santa Fe Pacific Corpn) 1983–96, Pres., Chair. and CEO 1988–96, Pres. and CEO Burlington Northern Santa Fe Corpn 1995–2002, Chair. 2000–02; mem. Bd of Dirs Railpower Techs Corpn 2005, Phelps Dodge Corpn –2006, UAL Corpn 2006–, Fort Worth Symphony Orchestra; Vice Chair. Bd of Trustees Ravinia Festival. *Address:* c/o Board of Trustees, Ravinia Festival, 418 Sheridan Road, Highland Park, IL 60035, USA.

KREITZBERG, Peeter, DPhil; Estonian politician and academic; b. 14 Dec. 1948, Parnu; m. (divorced); one s. two d.; ed Tartu State Univ., Lund Univ., Sweden; Head of Students Bureau of Comprehensive Research, Tartu Univ. 1972–74, Lecturer, Sr Teacher, Asst Prof., then Prof. 1977–96; Prof., Tallinn Pedagogical Univ. 1977–; Minister of Culture and Educ. 1995; Deputy Mayor of Tallinn 1996–99; mem. Riigikogu (Parl.) 1999–, Vice-Chair. 2001–05, currently Chair., Cultural Affairs Cttee; mem. British Soc. of Educ. Philosophy; Grand Officier, Ordre nat. du Mérite 2001, Grand Oficial, Ordem do Infante Dom Henrique, Order of the Nat. Coat of Arms, Third Class (Estonia) 2003. *Publications include:* Principles of Classification and Concretising Targets in Education 1987, Legitimisation of Education Aims: Paradigms and Metaphors 1993. *Leisure interest:* fishing. *Address:* Riigikogu, Tompea Castle, Lossi plats 1A, 0100 Tallinn (office); Esku 3, Tallinn, Estonia (home). *Telephone:* (2) 631-64-80 (office); (2) 600-25-90 (home). *Fax:* (2) 631-64-85 (office). *E-mail:* peeter.kreitzberg@riigikogu.ee (office). *Website:* www.riigikogu.ee (office).

KREMENYUK, Victor Aleksandrovich, DHist; Russian civil servant and scholar; *Deputy Director, Institute for USA and Canadian Studies, Russian Academy of Sciences;* b. 13 Dec. 1940, Odessa (now in Ukraine); m. Lyudmila Agapova; one d.; ed Moscow Inst. of Int. Relations; army service 1963–68; with Mezdunarodnaya Zhizn magazine 1968–70; with Inst. for USA and Canadian Studies, USSR (now Russian) Acad. of Sciences 1970–, Deputy Dir 1989–; expert, Cttee on Int. Problems, USSR Supreme Soviet 1989–91; expert, State Duma 1993–; worked on project Process of Int. Negotiations in Int. Inst. of Applied System Analysis Austria, lectures and seminars in USA, Germany, Austria; Chair. Expert Council of Political Sciences 1992–99; mem. Council on Higher Policy at Ministry of Foreign Affairs 1991–96; mem. Scientific Council, Russian Inst. of Strategic Studies 1995–; mem. Council of Social Sciences, Presidium of Russian Acad. of Sciences 1991–; mem. Nat. Geographical Soc., USA, Int. Asscn of Conflictology; mem. Consultative and Observation Councils Salzburg Seminar, Austria, Centre of Applied Studies on Negotiations, Switzerland; mem. Editorial Bds, magazines Econ., Politics and Ideology, Journal of Negotiations, USA 1990–2000, Journal of Peace Studies, USA; Corresp. mem. Russian Acad. of Sciences 2011; Nat. Prize for Science and Tech. (USSR) 1980, CPR Inst. for Dispute Resolution (New York) Book Award 2002, Russian Ministry for Emergencies Award for Risk Analysis. *Publications:* more than 100 articles and 12 scientific monographs; ed. more than 50 scientific works in Russian and English. *Address:* Institute for USA and Canadian Studies, Khlebny per. 2/3, 123995 Moscow, Russia (office). *Telephone:* (495) 691-14-83 (office); (495) 430-07-95 (home). *Fax:* (495) 697-70-17 (office). *E-mail:* vkremenyuk@gmail.com (office). *Website:* www.iskran.ru (office).

KREMER, Gidon; Russian/German violinist; *Artistic Director, Kremerata Baltica;* b. 27 Feb. 1947, Riga, Latvia; ed Riga School of Music, Moscow Conservatory (with David Oistrakh); recitalist and orchestral soloist worldwide 1965–; has played in most major int. festivals including Berlin, Dubrovnik, Helsinki, London, Moscow, Prague, Salzburg, Tokyo and Zürich; has played with most major int. orchestras including Berlin Philharmonic, Boston Symphony, Concertgebouw, LA Philharmonic, New York Philharmonic, Philadelphia, San Francisco Symphony, Vienna Philharmonic, London Philharmonic, Royal Phil-harmonic, Philharmonia, NHK Symphony of Japan and all main Soviet orchestras; has worked with Bernstein, von Karajan, Giulini, Jochum, Previn, Abbado, Levine, Maazel, Muti, Harnoncourt, Mehta and Marriner; f. Kremerata Baltica (chamber orchestra) 1977, Artistic Dir 1977–; f. Lockenhaus Chamber Music Festival 1981; plays a Stradivarius; lives in Germany; prizewinner at Queen

Elisabeth Competition, Brussels, Montreal Competition and Fourth Int. Tchaikovsky Competition (First Prize) 1970, Paganini Prize, Genoa; Grand Prix du Disque and Deutsche Schallplattenpreis. *Recordings:* has made more than 45 records. *Performances:* first performances include Henze, Stockhausen, Schnittke, Pärt, Astor Piazzola. *Address:* Opus 3 Artists, 470 Park Avenue South, 9th Floor North, New York, NY 10016, USA (office); Kremerata Baltica, R. Vagnera iela 4, 1050 Riga, Latvia (office). *Telephone:* (212) 584-7500 (office); 6722-4055 (office). *Fax:* (646) 300-8200 (office); 6721-3072 (office). *E-mail:* info@opus3artists.com (office); kremerata@tvnet.lv (office). *Website:* www.opus3artists.com (office); www.kremerata-baltica.com (office).

KREMP, Herbert, DPhil; German journalist; b. 12 Aug. 1928, Munich; s. of Johann Kremp and Elisabeth Kremp; m. Brigitte Steffal 1956; two d. (one deceased); ed Munich Univ.; reporter, Frankfurter Neue Presse 1956–57; Political Ed. Rheinische Post 1957–59; Dir Political Dept, Der Tag, Berlin 1959–61; Bonn Corresp. Rheinische Post 1961–63; Ed.-in-Chief Rheinische Post 1963–68; Ed.-in-Chief Die Welt 1969–77, Co-Ed. 1981, Co-Publr 1984–87, Chief Corresp. in Beijing 1977–81, Ed.-in-Chief 1981–85, apptd Chief Corresp. in Brussels 1987, Co-Ed., Springer Group newspapers 1984–87, commentator, Die Welt, Berliner Morgenpost, Welt am Sonntag, Bild, B.Z. Berlin, Hamburger Abendblatt; currently associated with Axel Springer publishing house; Bundesverdienstkreuz 1988; Konrad Adenauer Prize 1984, Theodor-Wolff Prize 1978, 2003. *Publications:* Am Ufer der Rubikon: Eine politische Anthropologie, Die Bambusbrücke: Ein asiatisches Tagebuch 1979, Wir brauchen unsere Geschichte 1988. *Address:* c/o Axel Springer Verlag AG, Axel-Springer-Str. 65, 10888 Berlin, Germany.

KRENS, Thomas, MA; American museum director; *Senior Adviser on International Affairs, Solomon R. Guggenheim Foundation;* b. 26 Dec. 1946, New York; ed Williams Coll., State Univ. of New York, Albany and Yale Univ.; Asst Prof. of Art, Williams Coll., Williamstown, Mass. 1972–80, Asst Prof. of History of Art, Grad. Program 1977–80, Adjunct Prof. of Art History 1988–; Dir Williams Coll. Museum of Art 1980–88; consultant, Solomon R. Guggenheim Museum, New York 1986–88, Dir 1988, Dir Guggenheim Museums Worldwide, Dir and Trustee Solomon R. Guggenheim Foundation 1988–2008, Sr Adviser on Int. Affairs 2008–; Dir The Peggy Guggenheim Collection, Venice 1988–; Hon. DHumLitt (State Univ. of NY). *Publications:* Jim Dine Prints: 1970–77 1977, The Prints of Helen Frankenthaler 1980, The Drawing of Robert Morris 1982, Robert Morris: The Mind/Body Problem 1994. *Address:* c/o Solomon R. Guggenheim Museum, 1071 Fifth Avenue, New York, NY 10128-0173, USA (office). *Telephone:* (212) 423-3500 (office). *Website:* www.guggenheim.org (office).

KRENZ, Egon; German politician; b. 1937; ed Teacher Training Inst. Putbus and Cen. Cttee of CPSU Party Univ. Moscow; joined Freie Deutsche Jugend (FDJ) 1953, Socialist Unity Party (SED) and Confed. of Free German Trade Unions 1955; various functions within FDJ and SED 1957–64; Sec. Ernst Thälmann Pioneer Org. 1967–74, Chair. 1971–74; First Sec. FDJ Cen. Council 1974–83; mem. Nat. Council of Nat. Front 1969–; cand. mem. Cen. Cttee of SED 1971–73, mem. 1973–90, Sec. 1989–90, cand. mem. Politburo 1976–83, mem. 1983–90, Gen. Sec. 1989–90; Deputy to Volkskammer 1971–90, mem. Presidium 1971–81, Chair. FDJ Faction 1971–76; mem. Council of State 1981–84, Deputy Chair. 1984–89, Chair. (Head of State) 1989–90; stripped of membership of CP (fmrly SED); now property developer, Berlin; faced charges of manslaughter for killings of persons fleeing over Berlin Wall and other borders 1994; on trial Aug. 1995, sentenced to six and a half years' imprisonment for the deaths of those trying to cross the Berlin Wall Aug. 1997, sentence upheld on appeal Nov. 1999, released Dec. 2003; decorations include Karl Marx Orden, Banner der Arbeit, Verdienstmedaille der DDR.

KRENZ, Jan; Polish conductor and composer; b. 14 July 1926, Włocławek; s. of Otton Krenz and Eleonora Krenz; m. Alina Krenz 1958; one s.; ed Higher School of Music; conducting debut, Łódź Philharmonic Orchestra 1946; Chief Conductor, State Poznań Philharmonic Orchestra 1947–49; Chief Conductor Polish Nat. Radio Symphony Orchestra of Katowice 1953–67; Chief Conductor Danish Radio Orchestra, Copenhagen 1960s; Leader, Grand Opera House Orchestra (Teatr Wielki), Warsaw 1968–73; conducted Berlin Philharmonic, Staatskapelle Dresden, Leningrad Philharmonic and all the major London orchestras; Gen. Dir of Music, Bonn Orchestra 1979–82; frequent collaboration with Yomiuri Nippon Symphony Orchestra; performing only as guest conductor 1983–; Diploma of Ministry of Foreign Affairs 1980; Hon. mem. Asscn of Polish Composers; Hon. Conductor Polish Nat. Radio Symphony Orchestra of Katowice; decorations include Order of Banner of Labour (First Class), Commdr's Cross with Star of Polonia Restituta Order; State Prize 1955, 1972, Prize of Asscn of Polish Composers 1968, Grand Prix du Disque, France 1972, Prize of Polish Artists' and Musicians' Asscn (SPAM) Orfeusz 1974. *Compositions include:* chamber, vocal and symphonic music, orchestral transcriptions of Polish classics, J. S. Bach (including Polyphonic suite on four fragments from Bach's Die Kunst der Fuge) and Szymanowski, film and stage music. *Leisure interest:* painting. *Address:* al. J. Ch. Szucha 16, 00-582 Warsaw, Poland.

KRESAL, Katarina; Slovenian lawyer and politician; *President, Liberal Democracy of Slovenia;* b. 28 Jan. 1973, Ljubljana; ed Bezigrad High School, Faculty of Law, Univ. of Ljubljana; contractual work, Slovenian Chamber of Physiotherapists 1994–96; clerk trainee, High Court in Ljubljana 1996–98; Slovenian State Bar Exam 1999; Sr Clerk, Commercial Disputes Dept, Ljubljana Dist Court 1999–2000; Sr Consultant for Commercial and Corp. Law, Kapitalska družba d.d., Ljubljana 2000–01; mem. advisory bodies of Delo Tiskarna, BTC Terminal and Konstruktor (rep. of Kapitalska družba) 2000–01; Head of Legal Dept, Western Wireless International d.o.o., Ljubljana and mem. Sr Man. Team 2001–03; attorney cand., Attorneys at law Miro Senica in odvetniki, Ljubljana 2003–04, attorney at law 2004–08, Deputy Dir and Dir Econ. and Int. Affairs Dept 2005–08; Pres. Liberal Democracy of Slovenia 2007–; Minister of Internal Affairs 2008–11 (resgnd); mem. advisory bodies of GV Zalozbe and Ius Software; mem. Asscn of Young Lawyers of Slovenia, European Young Bar Asscn. *Publications:* has published articles in foreign publs such as International Financial Review 1000 and The Guide to Mergers and Acquisitions. *Address:* Liberal Democracy of Slovenia (Liberalna demokracija Slovenije), trg Republike 3, 1000 Ljubljana, Slovenia (office). *Telephone:* (1) 4325125 (office). *E-mail:* katarina.kresal@lds.si (office). *Website:* www.lds.si.

KRESS, Victor Melkhiorovich, Dr Econs; Russian politician; b. 16 Nov. 1948, Kostroma Region; m.; two c.; ed Novosibirsk Inst. of Agric., Russian Acad. of Man.; agronomist, agric. enterprises Tomsk Region; Deputy Chair., Agric.-Industrial complex Tomsk Region 1971–87; First Sec. Dist CP Cttee, Tomsk Region 1987–90; Chair. Tomsk Regional Soviet 1990–91, Interregional Asscn Siberian Agreement 1998–2001; Head, Admin. of Tomsk Region 1991–96, Gov. 1996–12; mem. Federal Council of the Federation, representing Tomsk Oblast Admin. 2012–; mem. Council of Russian Fed. 1993–2000; Chair. Interregional Asscn Siberian Agreement; Order of The Sign of Respect (Znak Potcheta) 1986, Order of Merit to Russia of the IV Grade (Za Zaslugi pered Otetchestrom) 1998, Order of Merit for the Fatherland, (second class) 2008, Order of St. Sergius (first class) 2008; Medal for Working Virtue (Za Trudovya Doblest) 1976. *Publications:* Tomsk Region: Today and Tomorrow (4 vols) 1997, Russia's Hard Time: View from the Province 1998, Tomsk Region: at the Crossroads of Centuries 1999, Tomsk Region: Beginning of the 21st Century 2002. *Address:* Federal Council of the Federation, 103426 Moscow, B. Dmitrovka, 26, Russia (office). *Website:* eng.duma.tomsk.ru (office).

KRGOVIĆ, Ljubiša, MA; Montenegrin economist and fmr central banker; b. 1957, Mojkovac; ed secondary school in Berane, Univ. of Montenegro, Belgrade Univ.; researcher, Econs Inst., Univ. of Montenegro 1983–91; Dir Montenegrin Employment Bureau 1991–92; Advisor to the Prime Minister in Govt of Montenegro 1992–94; Vice-Gov. Nat. Bank of Yugoslavia 1995–99; mem. Monetary Council, Nat. Bank of Montenegro 1999–2001; Deputy Prime Minister for financial system and public spending 2000–01; Pres. Montenegro Securities Exchange 2000–02; Pres. of Council, Centralna banka Crne Gore (Cen. Bank of Montenegro) 2001–10. *Address:* c/o Centralna Banka Crne Gore, 81000 Podgorica, bul. Svetog Petra Cetinjskog 7, Montenegro (office).

KRICK, Gerd; German engineer and business executive; *Chairman of the Supervisory Board, Fresenius SE;* b. 8 Oct. 1938, Dresden; mil. service 1960; began career with Continental AG, Hanover 1969; moved to medium-sized enterprise in Munich 1970–75; joined Fresenius AG (now Fresenius SE), Bad Homburg 1975, mem. Bd for Research and Devt and Production and Tech. 1975–81, mem. Man. Bd 1981–91, Dir Medical Systems Div. and Deputy Chair. Man. Bd –1992, Chair. Man. Bd and CEO 1992–2003, Chair. Man. Bd and CEO Fresenius Medical Care AG 1996–97, Chair. Supervisory Bd Fresenius Medical Care AG from 1998 (until transformation of legal form to a KGaA), also Chair. Supervisory Bd Fresenius Medical Care AG & Co. KGaA, Chair. Supervisory Bd Fresenius SE 2003–, mem. Supervisory Bd of Man. 2005–, Fresenius AG, Chair. Fresenius USA Inc. 1989–; mem. Bd of Dirs Gull Laboratories Inc., Adelphi Capital Europe Fund; mem. Advisory Bd HDI Haftpflichtverband der deutschen Industrie V.a.G –2008, Vereinte AG (Vereinte Krankenversicherung AG), Bd of Trustees Donau Universität Krems; Chair. Supervisory Bd Vamed AG (Austria), Fresenius Kabi AG (subsidiaries of Fresenius SE), Fresenius Kabi Austria GmbH –2004; mem. Supervisory Bd Allianz Private Krankenversicherungs-AG –2008; fmr Dir Dresdner Bank Luxembourg SA. *Address:* Fresenius SE, 61346 Bad Homburg (office), Fresenius SE, Else-Kröner-Straße 1, 61352 Bad Homburg, Germany (office). *Telephone:* (6172) 608-0 (office). *E-mail:* pr-fre@fresenius.com (office). *Website:* www.fresenius.com (office); www.fresenius.se (office).

KRIEL, Hermanus Jacobus, BA, LLB; South African politician and lawyer; b. 14 Nov. 1941, Kakamas; s. of Prof. Kriel and Mrs Kriel; one s. two d.; ed Hugenote Hoërskool, Univ. of Stellenbosch; conveyancer and notary 1968; Chair. Cape Div. Council 1976–77; mem. Cape Prov. Council 1977–84, Cape Exec. Cttee 1981–84; MP 1984–89; Minister of Planning, Prov. Affairs and Nat. Housing 1989–91, of Law and Order 1991–94; Premier of Western Cape Provincial Parl. 1994–97; F. C. Erasmus Award, Stella Officii Egregii. *Leisure interests:* golf, reading. *Address:* c/o Private Bag 9043, Cape Town 8000, South Africa.

KRIELE, Martin, DJur, LLM; German legal scholar and academic; *Professor Emeritus of Philosophy and Public Law, University of Cologne;* b. 19 Jan. 1931, Opladen; s. of the late Dr Rudolf Kriele and of Konstanze Henckels; m. 1st Christel Grothues 1960; one s. one d.; m. 2nd Alexa Michalsen; ed Freiburg, Münster, Bonn and Yale Univs, USA; admitted to the Court 1961; Prof. of Philosophy of Law and Public Law, Univ. of Cologne 1967–96, Prof. Emer. 1996–; currently Co-Publr Zeitschrift für Rechtspolitik (journal); Dir Inst. for Political Philosophy and Problems of Legislation 1967; Judge, Constitutional Court of North Rhine-Westphalia 1976–88. *Publications:* Kriterien der Gerechtigkeit 1963, Theorie der Rechtsgewinnung 1967, Einführung in die Staatslehre 1975, Legitimitätsprobleme der Bundesrepublik 1977, Die Menschenrechte zwischen Ost und West 1977, Recht und praktische Vernunft 1979, Befreiung und politische Aufklärung 1980, Nicaragua, das blutende Herz Amerikas 1985, Die Demokratische Weltrevolution 1987, Recht, Vernunft, Wirklichkeit (essays) 1990. *Leisure interest:* music (piano). *Address:* University of Cologne, Seminar für Staatsphilosophie und Rechtspolitik, Albertus-Magnus-Platz 1, 50923 Cologne, Germany (office); Dorf 11, 6900 Möggen, Austria (home). *Telephone:* (221) 4702230 (office); (5573) 3772 (home). *Fax:* (221) 4705010 (office); (5573) 3772 (home).

KRIER, Léon; Luxembourg architect, urban planner and designer; b. 7 April 1946, Luxembourg; ed Univ. of Stuttgart; Asst to James Stirling London 1968–70, 1973–74; project pnr with J. P. Kleihues, Berlin 1971–72; in pvt. practice in London 1974–; Lecturer, Architectural Asscn School, London 1973–76, Royal Coll. of Art, London 1977, Princeton Univ. 1977; Jefferson Prof. of Architecture, Univ. Va Charlottesville 1982; E. Saarinen Prof., Yale Univ. 2001, Davenport Prof. 2004; architectural and urban design adviser to HRH The Prince of Wales; works include numerous city centre and housing re devt plans, schools, univs, public bldgs etc. in UK, Germany, Luxembourg, Spain, Italy, Greece, Sweden, USA, Belgium, St Lucia, France and Portugal; City of Berlin Architecture Prize (with Rob Krier) 1975, Jefferson Medal for Architecture 1985, European Culture Prize 1995, Silver Medal Acad. Française 1997, first recipient of Richard H Driehaus Prize for Classical Architecture 2003. *Projects include:* masterplans for Poundbury 1988, 2004, Novoli, Florence 1993, Città Nuova, Alessandria, Italy 1997, Village Hall Windsor Florida USA 1997, Val d'Europe Brasserie Agape France 2000–03, Hardelot, France 2001, School of Architecture Auditorium Univ. of Miami USA 2001–04, Knokke Heuleburg Masterplan Belgium 2001–04; designs furniture for Giorgetti, Italy 1991–. *Publications include:* Buildings and Projects of James Stirling (ed.) 1974, The Reconstruction of the European City 1978, The City within the City (ed.) 1979, Architecture and Urban Design (ed. by Richard Economakis)

1967–92, Architecture: Choice or Fate 1997 (trans. into 7 languages). *Address:* 37 rue du X Octobre, 7243 Bereldange, Luxembourg.

KRIKALEV, Sergey Konstantinovich; Russian cosmonaut; b. 27 Aug. 1958, Leningrad; m.; one d.; ed Leningrad Mechanical Inst.; engineer Research Production Co. Energia 1981–85, took part in developing new samples of space tech.; Master of Sports in piloting; mem. Cosmonauts' team since 1985; flight engineer Soyuz TM-7 1988, Soyuz TM-12 1991–92, STS-60 (first joint US/Russian Space Shuttle Mission) 1994, STS-88 Endeavour 1998, Expedition-1 2000–01, Commdr Expedition-11 2005; spent 310 days in orbit on Soyuz TM-12 1991–92; Champion of Moscow 1983, Hero of the Soviet Union 1989, Hero of the Russian Fed. 1992, NASA Space Flight Medal 1994, 1998; Order of Lenin, Officier de la Légion d'Honneur. *Address:* Yuriy Gagarin Centre for Cosmonauts Training, Zvezdny Gorodok, Moscow Region, Russia. *Telephone:* (495) 971-86-16.

KRIM, Mathilde, BS, PhD; American medical researcher and organization official; *Founding Chairman, American Foundation for AIDS Research (amfAR);* b. 9 July 1926, Como, Italy; m. Arthur B. Krim (deceased); one d.; ed Univ. of Geneva, Switzerland; research scientist, Weizmann Inst. of Science, Israel 1953–59, Cornell Univ. Medical School 1959–62, Sloan-Kettering Inst. for Cancer Research 1962–81, Dir Interferon Lab. 1981–85; at Dept of Pediatrics, St Luke's Roosevelt Hosp. Center and Columbia Univ. 1986–90; Adjunct Prof. of Public Health and Man., Columbia Univ., New York 1990, now mem. Bd of Overseers; f. AIDS Medical Foundation (renamed American Foundation for AIDS Research 1985) 1983, Chair. 1983–2004, now Founding Chair.; mem. Bd of Dirs Drug Policy Alliance; 16 hon. doctorates including Dr hc (Dartmouth) 2005; Presidential Medal of Freedom 2000, Eleanor Roosevelt Val-Kill Medal 2001, ranked 86th by Forbes magazine amongst 100 Most Powerful Women 2004, and numerous other awards. *Publications:* 76 articles and papers in scientific and medical journals on cellular biology, virology and interferon research. *Leisure interests:* horticulture, zoology, visual arts. *Address:* c/o American Foundation for AIDS Research, 120 Wall Street, 13th Floor, New York, NY 10005-3908, USA. *Website:* www.amfar.org.

KRIPKE, Saul Aaron, BA, LHD; American philosopher, logician and academic; *Distinguished Professor, Graduate Program in Philosophy, City University of New York;* b. 13 Nov. 1940, Bay Shore, NY; s. of Myer Samuel Kripke and Dorothy Kripke; m. Margaret P. Gilbert 1976 (divorced 1998); ed Harvard Univ.; Soc. of Fellows, Harvard Univ. 1963–66, concurrently Lecturer with rank of Asst Prof., Princeton Univ. 1964–66; Lecturer, Harvard Univ. 1966–68; Assoc. Prof., Rockefeller Univ. 1968–72, Prof. 1972–76; McCosh Prof. of Philosophy, Princeton Univ. 1977–98, now Prof. Emer.; currently Distinguished Prof., Grad. Program in Philosophy, CUNY; Fulbright Fellow 1962–63; Guggenheim Fellow 1968–69, 1977–78; Visiting Fellow, All Souls Coll., Oxford, UK 1977–78, 1989–90; Visiting Prof., The Hebrew Univ. 1998–; mem. American Philosophical Soc. 2004–; Fellow, American Acad. of Arts and Sciences; Corresp. Fellow, British Acad.; Hon. DHumLitt (Univ. of Neb. at Omaha) 1977, (Johns Hopkins Univ.) 1997, (Univ. of Haifa) 1998, (Univ. of Penn) 2005; Detur Prize 1960, Charles J. Wister Prize 1962, Howard Behrman Award 1988, Schock Prize in Logic and Philosophy 2001. *Publications:* Naming and Necessity 1980, Wittgenstein on Rules and Private Language 1982; numerous papers in professional journals and anthologies. *Address:* Graduate Program in Philosophy, CUNY Graduate Center, 365 Fifth Avenue, New York, NY 10016, USA (office). *Telephone:* (212) 817-8615 (home). *Website:* web.gc.cuny.edu/Philosophy (office).

KRISHNA, Somanahalli Mallaiah, BA, BL, MCL; Indian lawyer, politician and professor of international law; b. 1 May 1932; s. of S. C. Mallaiah; m. Prema Krishna 1964; two d.; ed Maharaja's Coll. Mysore, Govt Law Coll., Bangalore, Southern Methodist Univ. Dallas, USA, George Washington Univ., USA; Fulbright Scholar, George Washington Univ. Law School, Washington, DC, later taught Int. Law; Prof. of Int. Law, Renukacharya Law Coll., Bangalore 1962–68; mem. Karnataka Legis. Ass. 1962–67, 1989–94, Speaker 1989–92; mem. Lok Sabha (Parl.) 1968–72; mem. Karnataka Legis. Council 1972–77; Minister of Commerce and Industries and Parl. Affairs 1972–77; returned to Parl. 1980; Minister of State for Industry 1983–84, for Finance 1984–85, of External Affairs 2009–12 (resgnd); Deputy Chief Minister of Karnataka 1992–94, Chief Minister 1999–2004; mem. Rajya Sabha 1996–99, 2009–; Gov. of Maharashtra 2004–08 (resgnd); fmr mem. del. to UN, New York 1982; Pres. KPCC 1999–2000; Del. Commonwealth Parl. Seminar, Westminster, UK 1990; Global Alumni Award, Southern Methodist Univ., USA 2010. *Leisure interests:* reading, designing men's clothes, sport. *Address:* c/o Ministry of External Affairs, South Block, Room 144C, New Delhi 110 011, India.

KRISHNAMURTHY, G. V. G., BA, BSc, BL; Indian election commissioner (retd) and lawyer; b. 19 Nov. 1934, Chirala, AP; s. of G.V. Subbarao and G. Rajeswaramma; m. G. Padma 1957; one s. one d.; ed Andhra Univ.; pro-independence student activist and mem. Azad Hindu Fauz Youth League 1945–47; advocate, Andhra Pradesh High Court 1958; lecturer, Law Coll. Osmania Univ. 1958, 1962; Sr Research Officer, Indian Law Inst. 1962–63; advocate, Supreme Court; Deputy Legal Adviser, Comm. of Inquiry, Cabinet Secr. 1972–73; Additional Legal Adviser, Ministry of Law and ex-officio Govt Counsel, Delhi High Court 1973–76, Supreme Court of India 1978–79; Govt Arbitrator 1979–83; Jt Sec. and Legal Adviser 1983–87; Additional Sec. Govt of India 1987–88, Special Sec. 1988–89; Sec. Law Comm. of India 1989–92; Election Commr of India 1993–99; Int. Observer Sri Lanka Pres. Elections 1999, Kazakhstan Parl. Elections 2004; del. to various int. confs etc.; numerous professional appointments and other distinctions; Hon. LLD (Jhansi Univ.) 1996; National Citizen's Award 1990, Great Son of the Soil Award 1996, NRI Gold Int. Award 1996, Glory of India Int. Award 1998, Champion of Indian Democracy Award 2001, Pride of India Int. Award 2002. *Publications include:* Dynamics of Diplomacy 1968, Modern Diplomacy, Dialectics and Dimensions 1980; articles in legal journals. *Leisure interests:* reading, watching nature, cultural activities. *Address:* 1402 Kausumbhi, opp. Delhi Anand Vihar ISBT, Ghaziabad, India. *Telephone:* (120) 2778056 (office); (120) 2778056 (home). *Fax:* (120) 2778056 (office); (120) 2778056 (home).

KRISHNAN, Tan Sri T(atparanandam) Ananda, BA, MBA; Malaysian business executive; *CEO, Usaha Tegas Sendirian Berhad;* b. 1938, Kuala Lumpur; m.; three c.; ed Victoria Inst., Kuala Lumpur, Univ. of Melbourne, Australia, Harvard Univ., USA; f. Exoil Trading; CEO Usaha Tegas Sendirian Berhad (investment and consulting org. with interests in communications, broadcasting, media, leisure, entertainment and energy); cos in which it has an interest include Maxis Communications (took pvt. in leveraged buyout 2007), MEASAT Broadcast Network Systems, Binariang Satellites Systems, Bumi Armada, Objektif Bersatu, Celestial Pictures Ltd, Hong Kong; Man. Usaha Tegas Entertainment Systems; Head of Astro All Asia Networks PLC; developer of Petronas Twin Towers, Kuala Lumpur. *Address:* Usaha Tegas Sendirian Berhad, Level 44, Menara MAXIS, Kuala Lumpur City Centre, 50088 Kuala Lumpur (office); Maxis Communications Berhad, Level 18, Menara Maxis, KLCC Off Jalan Ampang, 50088 Kuala Lumpur, Malaysia. *Telephone:* (3) 23807788 (office); (3) 23307000. *Fax:* (3) 23806677 (office); (3) 23300008. *E-mail:* corpinfo@maxis.com.my. *Website:* www.maxis.com.my.

KRISTAN, Ivan, BA, DJur; Slovenian politician, lawyer and academic; *Professor Emeritus, Faculty of Law, Ljubljana University;* b. 12 June 1930, Arnovo; ed Ljubljana Univ.; worked in trade unions 1956–67; Teacher, Faculty of Law, Ljubljana Univ. 1967–77, Prof. 1977–87, Dean 1983–85, Rector 1985–87, now Prof. Emer.; mem. Cttee for Constitutional Reforms of the Slovenian Repub. 1970–74, 1987–90; mem. Constitutional Court of Yugoslavia 1987–91; Pres. Nat. Council of Slovenian Repub. 1992–98; Pres. of Supervising Cttee, Int. Asscn for Constitutional Law (IACL); mem. Asscn of Fighters for the Liberation of Slovenia. *Publications:* moe than 200 books, articles and scientific papers on legal problems of human rights, federalism, self-determination and sovereignty of nations, including Constitutional Law of Socialist Fed. Repub. of Yugoslavia (co-author). *Address:* c/o Drustvo za ustavno pravo, Subiceva 4, 1000, Ljubljana, Slovenia (office). *E-mail:* ivan.kristan@siol.net.

KRISTEVA, Julia, DèsL; French psychoanalyst and writer; b. 24 June 1941, Silven, Bulgaria; m. Philippe Sollers 1967; one s.; ed Univ. of Sofia and Ecole des Hautes Etudes en Sciences Sociales, Paris, Univ. of Paris VII; researcher in linguistics and French literature, Lab. of Social Anthropology, Ecole des Hautes Etudes en Sciences Sociales 1967–73; Prof., Univ. of Paris VII 1973–99, Prof. classe exceptionelle 1999–; Dir Ecole Doctorale Langue, Littérature, Image, civilisations et sciences humaines; Chargé de mission auprès du Pres. for the handicapped; Visiting Prof., Columbia Univ., New York 1974, Univ. of Toronto 1992; mem. Editorial Bd Telquel 1970–82; mem. Soc. psychanalytique de Paris, American Acad. of Arts and Sciences, Inst. Universitaire de France, British Acad., Acad. universelle des cultures; Chevalier, Ordre des Arts et des Lettres 1987, Chevalier, Légion d'honneur 1997, Officier, Ordre nat. du Mérite 2004, Officier de la Légion d'honneur 2008; Dr hc (Western Ontario, Canada) 1995, (Victoria, Toronto) 1997, (Harvard) 1999, (Univ. Libre de Belgique) 2000, (Bayreuth) 2000, (Toronto) 2000, (Sofia) 2002, (New School, New York) 2003; Prix Henri Hertz Chancellerie des Universités de Paris 1989, Holberg Int. Memorial Prize, Norway 2004, Grande Médaille de Vermeil de la Mairie de Paris 2005, Award of Merit, Bucknell Univ. 2006. *Publications include:* Sémiotike: Recherches pour une sémanalyse 1969, Le Texte du roman, approche sémiologique d'une structure discursive transformationnelle 1970, La Révolution du langage poétique: l'avant-garde à la fin du XIXème siècle, Lautréamont et Mallarmé 1974, Des chinoises 1974, Polylogue 1977, Folle Vérité (with Jean Michel Ribettes) 1979, Pouvoirs de l'horreur: Essai sur l'abjection 1980, Le Langage, cet inconnu 1981, Histoires d'amour 1985, Au commencement était l'amour 1985, Soleil noir, dépression et mélancolie 1987, Etrangers à nous-mêmes (Prix Henri Hertz 1989) 1988, Les Samouraïs 1990, Lettre ouverte à Harlem Désir 1990, Le Vieil homme et les loups 1991, Les Nouvelles maladies de l'âme 1993, Le Temps sensible: Proust et l'expérience littéraire (essay) 1994, Possessions 1996, Sens et non-sens de la révolte 1996, La Révolte intime 1997, L'Avenir d'une révolte 1998, Le Génie féminin, Vol. 1: Hannah Arendt 1999, Vol. 2: Melanie Klein 2000, Colette 2002, Meurtre à Byzance 2004, La Haine et le Pardon: Pouvoirs et limites de la psychanalyse III 2005, Thérèse mon amour 2008, Leur regard perce nos ombres (with Jean Vanier) 2011, Visions capitales: Arts et rituels de la décapitation 2013, Pulsions du temps 2013. *Address:* Université de Paris VII, Grands Moulins, 7th Floor, bureau 777C, 5, rue Thomas Mann, 75013 Paris, France (office). *Telephone:* 1-57-27-65-25 (office). *E-mail:* julia.kristeva@univ-paris-diderot.fr (office). *Website:* www.kristeva.fr.

KRISTIANSEN, Kjeld Kirk, BSc, MBA; Danish business executive; *Vice-Chairman, LEGO Group;* b. 27 Dec. 1947; s. of Godtfred Kirk Christiansen and Edith Kirk Christiansen; grandson of Ole Kirk Christiansen, founder of LEGO; m. Camilla Kirk Christiansen 1974; one s. two d.; ed Århus Business School, IMD International, Lausanne, Switzerland; mem. Bd LEGO Toy Co. 1975–, inherited co. (majority shareholder) 1979, Vice-Chair. LEGO Group 1996–, Pres. and CEO 1979–2004, Chair. and Co-owner (with his three c.) LEGO A/S, Chair. and Co-owner (with sister Gunhild) KIRKBI A/S, Chair. LEGO Foundation, Ole Kirk's Foundation, Edith and Godtfred Kirk Christiansen's Foundation. *Leisure interests:* breeding Danish horses, sports cars. *Address:* LEGO Holding A/S, Aastvej 1, 7190 Billund, Denmark (office). *Telephone:* 79-50-60-70 (office). *Fax:* 75-33-27-25 (office). *Website:* www.lego.com (office).

KRIŠTO, Borjana; Bosnia and Herzegovina politician; b. 13 Aug. 1961, Livno; m.; fmr Vice-Pres. of Parl.; fmr Vice-Pres., Fed. of Bosnia and Herzegovina; Minister of Justice 2003–07; Rep. to Council of Europe 2007–; Pres. Fed. of Bosnia and Herzegovina (first woman) 2007–11; mem. Croatian Democratic Union of Bosnia and Herzegovina. *Address:* c/o Office of the President of the Federation of Bosnia and Herzegovina, 71000 Sarajevo, Alipašina 41, Bosnia and Herzegovina. *E-mail:* borjana@borjanakristo.com. *Website:* www.borjanakristo.com.

KRISTO, Vladimir, CSc, DIur; Albanian politician and judge; *Judge, Constitutional Court;* b. 8 April 1947, Korça; m.; one c.; ed Faculty of Law, Tirana Univ.; Chief of Studies' Dept, Gen. Attorney's Office 1983–92; Deputy Minister of Justice 1992–96, 2005–07; Legal Adviser to Prime Minister of Albania 1996–98; pvt. legal practice 1998–2005; mem. Constitutional Court 2007–, Pres. 2007–10, Judge 2010–; fmr mem. High Council of Justice, Co-ordination and Legal Co-operation Cttee, Council of Europe. *Publications:* numerous articles and academic papers on law and public admin. *Address:* Constitutional Court, Bulevardi Dëshmorët e Kombit, N.26, Tirana, Albania (office). *Telephone:* (4) 228357 (office). *Fax:* (4) 228357 (office). *E-mail:* vkristo@gjk.gov.al (office). *Website:* www.gjk.gov.al (office).

KRISTOFFERSON, Kris, BA, PhD; American country singer, songwriter and actor; b. (Kris Carson), 22 June 1936, Brownsville, TX; m. 1st; one s. one d.; m. 2nd Rita Coolidge 1973 (divorced 1980); one d.; m. 3rd Lisa Meyers 1983; four s., one d.;

ed Pomona Coll. and Univ. of Oxford; Capt. in US Army 1960–65; songwriter 1965–; solo recording artist 1969–; mem. of side project, The Highwaymen (with Willie Nelson, Johnny Cash, Waylon Jennings) 1985–; numerous concerts worldwide; actor 1972–; CMA Song of the Year (for Sunday Morning Coming Down) 1970, Grammy Awards for Best Country Song 1972, Best Country Vocal Performance (with Coolidge) 1973, 1976, Golden Globe for Best Actor 1976, ACM Single of the Year (for Highwayman, with The Highwaymen) 1986, two American Music Awards (with The Highwaymen) 1986, Americana Awards Free Speech Award 2003, Johnny Cash Visionary Award, CMT Music Awards 2007. *Films include:* Cisco Pike 1972, Pat Garrett and Billy the Kid 1973, Blume in Love 1973, Bring Me the Head of Alfredo Garcia 1974, Alice Doesn't Live Here Anymore 1974, The Sailor Who Fell From Grace With The Sea 1976, A Star is Born 1976, Vigilante Force 1976, Semi-Tough 1977, Convoy 1978, Heaven's Gate 1981, Rollover 1981, Welcome Home 1989, Millennium 1989, A Soldier's Daughter Never Cries 1998, Blade 1 1998, Come Dance with Me 1999, Payback 1999, Limbo 1999, Joyriders 1999, Comanche 2000, Planet of the Apes 2001, Chelsea Walls 2001, Wooly Boys 2001, D-Tox 2002, Blade II 2002, Where the Red Fern Grows 2003, Blade III 2003, The Jacket, Lives of the Saints, Where the Red Fern Grows, Dreamer 2005, Gun (voice) 2005, The Wendell Baker Story 2005, Fast Food Nation 2006, Disappearances 2006, Requiem for Billy the Kid (voice) 2006, Room 10 2006, Crossing the Heart 2007, Jump Out Boys 2008, Powder Blue 2009, He's Just Not That Into You 2009, The Last Rites of Ransom Pride 2009. *Television appearances include:* Freedom Road (TV film) 1979, Amerika (series) 1987, Rip 1989, Sandino, Christmas in Connecticut 1992, Tad 1995. *Recordings include:* albums: Kristofferson 1970, The Silver-Tongued Devil and I 1971, Border Lord 1972, Jesus Was a Capricorn 1973, Full Moon (with Rita Coolidge) 1973, Spooky Lady's Sideshow 1974, Who's to Bless and Who's to Blame 1975, Breakaway (with Rita Coolidge) 1975, A Star Is Born (soundtrack) 1977, Surreal Thing 1976, Songs of Kristofferson 1977, Easter Island 1978, Natural Act (with Rita Coolidge) 1979, Shake Hands With The Devil (with Rita Coolidge) 1979, Help Me Make It Through The Night 1980, To The Bone 1981, The Winning Hand 1983, Music From Songwriter (with Willie Nelson) 1984, Highwayman (with The Highwaymen) 1985, Repossessed 1986, Third World Warrior 1990, Highwaymen 2 (with The Highwaymen) 1992, A Moment of Forever 1995, The Austin Sessions 1999, Broken Freedom Song: Live from San Francisco 2003, Repossessed/Third World Warrior 2004, This Old Road 2006, Closer to the Bone 2009, Please Don't Tell Me How the Story Ends 2010. *Address:* c/o Tamara Saviano, Ellis Creative (office); c/o New West Records, 9215 West Olympic Boulevard, Beverly Hills, CA 90212, USA (office). *Telephone:* (615) 400-0388 (office). *E-mail:* tamara@ellis-creative.com (office). *Website:* www.ellis-creative.com (office); www.kriskristofferson.com.

KRISTOPANS, Vilis; Latvian politician; b. 13 June 1954; m.; ed Riga State Tech. Univ.; basketball player, Latvian nat. team 1972–81; sports instructor Sports Cttee, Daugava Cen. Council 1977–83; coach, Head coach, basketball team VEF 1983–89; Chair. co-operative soc. Noster 1990; Dir-Gen. Jt Dardedze 1990–92; Vice-Pres. Interbaltija Ltd 1992–93; Minister of State Revenue 1993–94; Chair. Deutsche-Lettische Bank 1994–95; Minister of Transport Latvian Repub. 1995–98; Prime Minister of Latvia, also Minister of Agric. 1998–99; mem. Parl. (Seimas) 1993–98; mem. Bd Latvijas ceļš (Latvian Way); Pres. Latvian Basketball League 1992–97; mem. Ventspils Free Ports Bd 1994–. *Address:* Latvijas ceļš, Terbatas jela 4-9, 1011 Riga, Latvia (office). *Telephone:* 6708-7111 (office).

KRISTOVSKIS, Ģirts Valdis, LLD; Latvian politician; *Deputy Chairman, Unity;* b. 19 Feb. 1962, Ventspils; m.; two d.; ed Riga Technical Univ., Univ. of Latvia; Sr Engineer, Ventspils Section, Inter-Collective Farm Production and Supplies Enterprise 1984–89; Deputy, Ventspils Council of People's Deputies (city govt) 1989–94; mem. Supreme Council of Latvia (fmr Parl.) 1990–93; Chief of Staff of Nat. Guard 1991–93; mem. Saeima (Parl.) 1993–2003, 2004–10, fmr Vice-Chair. Defence and Internal Affairs Cttee, mem. European Affairs Cttee; Minister of the Interior 1993–94, of Defence 1998–2004, of Foreign Affairs 2010–11; mem. European Parl. 2004–09; mem. Latvijas Tautas fronte (Popular Front of Latvia) 1988–93 (Chair. Ventspils Section 1989–90); mem. Latvijas ceļš (Latvian Way) 1993–98; mem. Tēvzemei un brīvībai/LNNK (For Fatherland and Freedom/LNNK) 1998–2008; Founder Civic Union 2008, Deputy Chair. Unity (founded as a coalition of Civic Union, New Era, and Society for a Different Politics 2010) 2010–; Pres. Track and Field Athletics Union of Latvia 2001–05, Latvian Olympic Cttee; Latvian Defence Ministry Badge of Honour 1994, Mich. Distinguished Service Medal 2000, Three Star Order (Third Class) 2000, Order of the Lithuanian Grand Duke Gediminas (Third Class) 2001, Order of Viesturs 2004, Ministry of Defence Award (Commemorative Medal for Advancing Latvia's Accession to NATO) 2004, Order of the Cross of Terra Mariana, Award of the Pres. of the Repub. of Estonia 2005. *Leisure interests:* basketball, journalism. *Address:* Unity (Vienotība), K. Barona iela 3, Riga 1050, Latvia (office). *Telephone:* 2666-1600 (office). *E-mail:* birojs@vienotiba.lv (office). *Website:* vienotiba.lv (office).

KRIVINE, Alain; French journalist and politician; b. 10 July 1941, Paris; m. Michèle Martinet 1960; two d.; ed Lycée Condorcet and Faculté des Lettres de Paris; mem. Jeunesses communistes 1956, French CP 1958; Leader Union of Student Communists, Paris-Sorbonne Univ. 1964–65; f. Revolutionary Communist Youth 1966 (disbanded by the Govt 1968), Communist League 1969 (dissolved 1973); cand. presidential elections 1969, 1974; journalist, Rouge 1969–; mem. Political Bureau of Ligue Communiste Révolutionnaire 1974–2006; mem. European Parl. 1999–2004; mem. Secretariat UNIFI de la IVe Internationale; mem. Nouveau Parti Anticapitaliste 2009–. *Publications:* La Farce électorale 1969, Questions sur la révolution 1973, Mais si, rebelles et repentis (with Daniel Bensaid) 1988, Ca ta passera avec l'âge 2008. *Address:* Nouveau Parti Anticapitaliste (NPA), 2 rue Richard-Lenoir, 93100 Montreuil, France. *Telephone:* 1-48-70-42-30. *Fax:* 1-48-59-23-28. *E-mail:* alain.krivine17@gmail.com.

KRIVINE, Emmanuel; French violinist and conductor; *Music Director, Orchestre Philharmonique du Luxembourg;* b. 7 May 1947, Grenoble; s. of Henri Krivine and Rejla Krivine (née Weisbrod); one d.; ed Conservatoire Nat. Supérieur de Musique et de Danse, Paris, Conservatoire Royal de Bruxelles; pupil of Henryk Szeryng and Yehudi Menuhin; solo violinist, Paris 1964, Brussels 1965–68; Perm. Guest Conductor Radio-France 1976–83; Dir Lorraine-Metz Regional Orchestra 1981–83; Prin. Guest Conductor Orchestra of Lyon 1983; Artistic Dir French Nat. Youth Orchestra 1983–94; Music Dir Nat. Orchestra of Lyon 1987–2000;

Conductor French Nat. Orchestra 2001–; co-founder and Principal Conductor, La Chambre Philharmonique 2004–; Music Dir Orchestre Philharmonique du Luxembourg 2006–; guest conductor to various int. orchestras including Berlin Philharmonic, Philadelphia Orchestra, Nat. Symphony Orchestra, Washington, London Philharmonic, Mahler Chamber Orchestra, Concertgebouw and Chamber Orchestra of Europe 1977–; Chevalier, Ordre nat. du Mérite, Officier des Arts et Lettres; Ginette-Neveu Medal 1971 and numerous other awards. *Leisure interests:* literature, philosophy. *Address:* c/o Nicholas Mathias, IMG Artists, The Light Box, 111 Power Road, London, W4 5PY, England (office). *Telephone:* (20) 7957-5800 (office). *Fax:* (20) 7957-5801 (office). *E-mail:* nmathias@imgartists.com (office). *Website:* www.imgartists.com (office); www.opl.lu; www.lachambrephilharmonique.com.

KRIVOKAPIĆ, Ranko, MA; Montenegrin lawyer and politician; *President (Speaker), Skupština Crne Gore (Parliament);* b. 17 Aug. 1961, Kotor; two c.; ed Faculty of Law, Belgrade; Founder and longtime Vice-Pres. Social Democratic Party (SDP) of Montenegro (Socijaldemokratska Partija Crne Gore), Pres. 2001–; mem. Skupština Republike Crne Gore (Parl.) 1989–, Pres. SDP Parl. Group 1998–2003, Pres. (Speaker) (within state union of Serbia and Montenegro) 2003–06, (sovereign state of Montenegro) 2006–; mem. Presidency of Union of Reform Forces of Montenegro 1990, Presidency of Party of European Socialists; fmr Head of Montenegrin Del. to Parl. Ass., OSCE. *Address:* Office of the President, Skupština Crne Gore, 81000 Podgorica, bul. Svetog Petra Cetinjskog 10, Montenegro (office). *Telephone:* (20) 244759 (office); (20) 242182 (office). *Fax:* (20) 242192 (office). *E-mail:* predsjednik@skupstina.me (office). *Website:* www.skupstina.me (office).

KRIŽANIČ, Franc, MSc, PhD; Slovenian economist, academic and government official; b. 4 Dec. 1954, Ljubljana; m.; two c.; ed Univ. of Ljubljana; Assoc. Prof., Faculty of Econs, Univ. of Ljubljana 2000–, Dir Law School, Econ. Inst. 2001–08; Pres. Council of Experts, Insurance Supervision Agency 2000–05; mem. Prime Minister's Strategic Council for Econ. Devt 2006–08; Pres. Supervisory Bd Slovenian Red Cross 2007–08; mem. Parl. 2008–11; Minister of Finance 2008–11. *Publications:* The Investment Multiplier in Slovenia 1992, The Slovenian Economy: An Econometric Study of the Periods 1986–1992–1994 1995. *Address:* c/o Ministry of Finance, 1502 Ljubljana, Župančičeva 3, Slovenia.

KROEMER, Herbert, PhD; American scientist and academic; *Professor of Electrical and Computer Engineering, University of California, Santa Barbara;* b. 25 Aug. 1928, Weimar, Germany; ed Univ. of Göttingen; carried out pioneering work in semi-conductor research; Prof. of Electrical and Computer Eng, Univ. of Calif., Santa Barbara 1985–; Nat. Lecturer, IEEE Electron Devices Soc.; mem. NAS, Nat. Acad. of Eng, IEEE, American Physics Soc.; Dr hc (Tech. Univ., Aachen) 1985, (Lund) 1998; J. Erbers Award 1973, Heinrich Welker Medal 1982, Jack Morton Award (IEEE) 1986, Alexander von Humboldt Research Award 1994, Nobel Prize for Physics (jt recipient) 2000. *Publications:* Quantum Mechanics: For Engineering, Materials Science and Applied Physics, Thermal Physics (jt author). *Address:* ECE Department and Materials Department 2205A Engineering Science Building, Electrical and Computer Engineering Department, University of California, Santa Barbara, CA 93106-9560, USA (office). *Telephone:* (805) 893-3078 (office). *Fax:* (805) 893-7990 (office). *E-mail:* kroemer@ece.ucsb.edu (office). *Website:* www.ece.ucsb.edu/Faculty/Kroemer/default.html (office).

KROES, Neelie, MSc (Econs); Dutch economist, politician and international organization official; *Vice-President and Commissioner for the Digital Agenda, European Commission;* b. 19 July 1941, Rotterdam; ed Erasmus Univ., Rotterdam; Asst Prof. of Transport Econs, Erasmus Univ. 1965–71; mem. Rotterdam Municipal Council, Rotterdam Chamber of Commerce 1969–71; mem. Parl. 1971–77; Vice-Minister of Transport, Public Works and Telecommunication 1977–81, Minister of Transport, Public Works and Telecommunication 1982–89; Advisor to EU Commr for Transport 1989–91; Commr for Competition, EC 2004–10, Vice-Pres. and Commr for the Digital Agenda 2010–; Pres. Nijenrode Univ. 1991–2000; Chair. Supervisory Bd MeyerMonitor –2004, Nederlands Luchtvaart Overleg (Dutch Aviation Platform) –2004; mem. Supervisory Bd Cório, Royal P&O Nedlloyd NV, Ballast Nedam, New Skies Satellites, Lucent Technologies BV (Netherlands), Nederlandse Spoorwegen NV (Dutch Railways), Volvo Group, Thales Group –2004; Dir (non-exec.) MM02 plc –2004; mem. Bd of Trustees ProLogis International –2004; Chair. Governing Bd Delta Psychiatrical Hosp., Het Rembrandthuis Foundation, Poets of All Nations, Overlegorgaan Waterbeheer en Noordzee-aangelegenheden; fmr Chair. Nyenrode Fund, Supervisory Bd Port Support International BV, Governing Bd TBS Mental Hosp. De Kijvelanden, Governing Bd Bezinnings Groep Water, Supervisory Bd NIB Capital NV, Supervisory Bd Intis BV, Governing Bd Kunsthal; mem. Governing Bd Nelson Mandela Children Fund Member, Bd Dirs World Cancer Research Fund; fmr mem. Governing Bd Royal Trade Fair (Koninklijke Jaarbeurs), Governing Bd Stichting International Human Resources, Development VNO/NCW, Advisory Bd International Problems (AIV), Supervisory Bd of Dirs Prologis European Properties, Advisory Bd PriceWaterhouseCooper, Supervisory Bd NCM Holding NV, Bd of Dirs Brambles Industries Ltd (Australia), Supervisory Bd McDonald's, Bd of Dirs SC Johnson Wax Euro Bd, Supervisory Bd Digital Equipment BV, Supervisory Bd Groeneveld Transport Efficiency, Raad van Toezicht Veerstichting, Competitiveness Group to Chair. EC, Governing Bd Insurance Authority, Governing Bd Conservation of Nature, High Level Group on the trans-European Network; fmr adviser, Monitor Group, Arcadis (Heidemij/Grabowsky); Kt, Order of the Dutch Lion 1981, Grand Officier, Légion d'honneur 1984, Bundesverdienstkreuz 1985, Grand Officer, Order of Orange Nassau 1989, Bintang Mahaputra Adiprana Order (Indonesia) 1993; Dr hc (Hull) 1989; Woman of the Year in Infrastructure, Int. Road Fed. 1993, ranked by Forbes magazine amongst 100 Most Powerful Women (44th) 2005, (38th) 2006, (59th) 2007, (47th) 2008, (53rd) 2009. *Address:* European Commission, 200 rue de la Loi, 1049 Brussels, Belgium (office). *Telephone:* (2) 299-11-11 (office). *Fax:* (2) 295-01-38 (office). *E-mail:* Neelie.Kroes@cec.eu.int (office). *Website:* ec.europa.eu/comm/commission_barroso/kroes/index_en.html (office).

KROGSGAARD-LARSEN, Povl, PhD, DSc; Danish scientist and academic; *Professor, Department of Drug Design and Pharmacology, University of Copenhagen;* b. 17 May 1941, Frøslev Mors; s. of Niels Saaby and Marie Saaby (née Krogsgaard) Larsen; m. Tove Krogsgaard-Larsen 1964; one s. one d.; ed Danish Univ. of Pharmaceutical Sciences; Asst Prof., Royal Danish School of Pharmacy (later Danish Univ. of Pharmaceutical Sciences, currently part of Univ. of Copenhagen) 1970–75, Assoc. Prof. 1975–86, Prof., Dept of Drug Design and Pharmacology, Faculty of Health and Medical Sciences 1986–, Rector 2001–02; mem. Royal Danish Acad. of Sciences and Letters 1986, Danish Acad. of Natural Sciences 1987, Danish Acad. of Tech. Sciences 1987; mem. Bd Dirs Alfred Beuzon Foundation 1991– (currently Vice-Chair.); mem. Bd Dirs Carlsberg Foundation 1993–2011; mem. Bd Dirs Lundbeck Foundation 2011–, Grete Lundbeck Foundation 2013– (currently Chair.); Chair. Carlsberg A/S 1993–2012, Aūriga A/S 2002–12; Dr hc (Louis Pasteur) (Uppsala); Paul Ehrlich Prize 1989, Lundbeck Foundation Prize 1989, H. C. Ørsted Award 1967, Ole Rømer Award 1983, Astra Award 1991, W. Th. Nauta Award 1996, Pharmaceutical Research Achievement Award 2004, H C. Ørsted Gold Medal 2006, Silver Medal 2011. *Publications:* 450 scientific articles, 80 scientific reviews, eight science books (ed.), one textbook (ed.). *Leisure interests:* history, sport. *Address:* Department of Drug Design and Pharmacology, Faculty of Health and Medical Sciences, University of Copenhagen, 2 Universitetsparken, 2100 Copenhagen (office); 25 Elmevej, Blovstrød, 3450 Allerød, Denmark (home). *Telephone:* 35-33-62-47 (office); 48-17-12-15 (home). *Fax:* 35-30-60-41 (office); 48-17-55-50 (home). *E-mail:* pkl@sund.ku.dk. *Website:* www.dfh.dk/uk (office).

KROHN DEVOLD, Kristin, MSc; Norwegian national organization official and fmr politician; *Secretary General, Den Norske Turistforening (Norwegian Trekking Association);* b. 12 Aug. 1961, Ålesund; d. of Edvard Hans A. Devold and Kristin Hoegh Krohn Devold; single; two c.; ed Univ. of Bergen, Norwegian School of Econs, Univ. of Oslo, Norwegian Nat. Defence Coll.; mem. Oslo City Parl. 1991–93; mem. Stortinget (Parl.) for Oslo 1993–97, 1997–2001, 2001–05, Sec. of the Lagting (Presidium, Stortinget) 1993–97, mem. Standing Cttee on Business and Industry 1993–97, Election Cttee 1997–2001, 2001–05, Working Procedures Cttee 1997–2001, Extended Foreign Affairs Cttee 1997–2001, Chair. Standing Cttee on Justice 1997–2001; Minister of Defence 2001–05; Substitute mem. Del. to Consultation Organ for European Econ. Area Affairs, Brussels 1993–97; Group Sec. Parl. Group, Conservative Party 1987–92, mem. Bd Party 1996, Parl. Steering Cttee 1997–2001; Sec. Gen. Norwegian Trekking Asscn 2006–; mem. Bd Statistics Norway 1989–93, St Hanshaugen Residence for the Elderly and Nursing Home 1991–92, Main Cttee of World Handball Championship 1999, Save the Children Norway 1999–. *Address:* Den Norske Turistforening (Norwegian Trekking Association), Youngstorget 1, 0181 Oslo, Norway (office). *Telephone:* 40-00-18-68 (office). *E-mail:* info@turistforeningen.no (office). *Website:* www.turistforeningen .no (home).

KRÓL, Jan Władysław; Polish politician and economist; *Strategic Advisor, Ernst and Young Poland;* b. 24 June 1950, Mielec; four c.; ed Higher School of Econs, Kraków, Jagiellonian Univ., Kraków; Worker PAX Soc. 1974–81, Inco-Veritas 1982–83, Remo and Rovan cos. 1983–89; mem. Solidarity Independent Self-governing Trade Union (NSZZ Solidarność) 1980–; assoc. Dziekania Political Thought Club 1984–88; deputy Govt Plenipotentiary for Local Govt Reform 1989–90; Deputy to the Sejm (Parl.) 1989–2001, Vice-Leader Trade and Services Comm. 1989–97, Sec. Democratic Union (UD) Parl. Caucus 1989–91, leader Extraordinary Cttee for consideration of bills within the State Enterprise Pact 1991–93, Vice-Marshal of Sejm 1997–2001; (Speaker) Co-Chair. Polish Ass. of Sejms of Poland and Lithuania 1997–2001; co.-f. and mem. ROAD (Democratic Campaign Citizens' Movt) 1990–91; Chair Polish-Canadian Econ. Council 1990; co.-f. and mem. Democratic Union 1991–94; mem. Nat. Polish Bd of the Friends of Lithuania Club 1992; mem. Freedom Union (UW) 1994– (also mem. Nat. Bd); Chair. Programme Bd Foundation for Econ. Educ. 1999–; Deputy Pres., Council of the Bd, Foundation in Support of Local Democracy; currently Strategic Advisor Ernst and Young Poland, Warsaw. *Publications:* Swiadectwo (Evidence) 1989, Przodem do przodu (Face forward) 1993, Z notatnika posła (From Deputy Notebook) 1997, W dialogu (In Dialogue) 1999, Pułapki polskiej demokracji (Polish Democracy Traps) 2001; and numerous articles. *Leisure interests:* tourism, horses. *Address:* Ernst and Young Poland, 39 Sienna Street, 00-121 Warsaw, Poland (office). *Telephone:* (22) 557-79-49 (office). *Fax:* (22) 557-70-01 (office). *E-mail:* fee@ gdnet.pl (office); jan.krol@pl.ey.com (office). *Website:* www.europa.edu.pl (office).

KROL, John A., BS, MSc; American business executive; *Chairman, Delphi Automotive LLP;* b. 16 Oct. 1936, Ware, Mass.; m. Janet Valley; two d.; ed Tufts Univ., Bettis Nuclear Reactor Eng School; commissioned into USN 1959, worked as nuclear engineer Bureau of Ships Naval Reactors Br.; joined E.I. du Pont de Nemours & Company as chemist, Wilmington, Del. 1963, marketing and manufacturing positions with DuPont Fibers 1965–83, Vice-Pres. 1983, Sr Vice-Pres. 1990, Group Vice-Pres., Sr Vice-Pres. DuPont Agric. Products 1986, Vice-Chair. DuPont 1992–97, Chair. 1997–98, Pres. 1995–97, CEO 1995–98 (retd); Chair. Delphi Automotive LLP 2009–; Trustee Tufts Univ., Univ. of Del., Hagley Museum, US Council for Int. Business; mem. Nat. Agricultural Chemists Asscn, American Chemical Soc. Corp. Liaison Bd, Business Roundtable, Business Council; mem. exec. Cttee Del. Business Roundtable, Business/Public Educ. Council. *Leisure interests:* golf, tennis, squash, skiing. *Address:* Delphi Automotive LLP, 5725 Delphi Drive, Troy, MI 48098-2815, USA (office). *Website:* delphi.com (office).

KROLL, Alexander (Alex) S., BA; American advertising executive; *Chairman Emeritus, Young and Rubicam Inc.;* b. 1937, Leechburg, Pa; ed Rutgers Univ.; fmr player, NY Titans, American Football League; with Young & Rubicam, Inc., New York 1962–, copywriter 1962–68, Vice-Pres. 1968–69, Sr Vice-Pres. 1969–70, Exec. Vice-Pres. and Worldwide Creative Dir 1970–75, Pres. and COO 1982, CEO 1985, then Chair. and CEO 1986, also Dir, Chair. Emer. 1994–; Man. Dir Young & Rubicam USA 1975–77, Pres. 1977; Chair. Emer. The Advertising Council; Kodak Life Achievement Award 1985, Nat. Coll. Athletic Asscn Silver Anniversary Award 1987, Coll. Football Hall of Fame 1997. *Address:* c/o Young & Rubicam Brands, 285 Madison Avenue, New York, NY 10017, USA.

KROLL, Lucien; Belgian architect, town planner, critic and writer; b. 17 March 1927, Brussels; m. Simone Marti; two d.; ed Athénée Royal de Huy, Ecole Nat. Supérieure d'Architecture de la Cambre, Institut Supérieur d'Urbanisme de la Cambre, Institut Supérieur and Int. d'Urbanisme Appliqué, Brussels; numerous works in Belgium, France, Italy, Germany, Italy and Rwanda 1953–; Founder mem. Inst. d'Esthétique Industrielle 1956; own architectural practice 1952–; environmental research, Ecolonia, Netherlands; exhbns of work in Brussels,

Hanover, Utrecht, Aubervilliers, Copenhagen, Aarhus, Luxembourg, Boston; organized confs including Habiter?, Brussels 1972; visiting prof. and lecturer on urban ecology at numerous univs world-wide; mem. Acad. française d'Architecture 1985–, BDA; Hon. mem. Bund der Deutschen Architekten; Commdr, Ordre des Arts et des Lettres; Médaille J.-F. Delarue, Acad. française d'Architecture 1980. *Publications:* CAD-Architektur 1985, Architecture of Complexity 1986, Buildings and Projects (also in German and French) 1987, Componenten 1995, Bien vieillir chez soi 1995, Enfin chez soi 1996, Eco, Bio, Psycho about Urban Ecology 1996, Tutto e paesaggio (also in French 2001), Ecologie urbane 2002, Rassegna 'Lucien Kroll'; more than 800 articles on industrial and urban architectural design and comparative architecture. *Address:* Atelier d'Urbanisme, d'Architecture et d'Informatique L. Kroll, Avenue Louis Berlaimont 20, Boîte 9, 1160 Brussels, Belgium (office). *Telephone:* (2) 673-35-39 (office). *Fax:* (2) 673-89-27 (office). *E-mail:* kroll@brutele.be (office). *Website:* homeusers.brutele.be/kroll (office).

KROLL, Sue, BA; American film industry executive; *President of Worldwide Marketing, Warner Bros. Pictures;* ed Glassboro State Univ.; began career in New York working over a seven-year period in various divs of Viacom, including Showtime Networks Inc., The Movie Channel and Viewer's Choice; relocated to Atlanta, Ga to head the Marketing Dept at Turner Network Television (TNT), then Sr Vice-Pres. and Man. Dir TNT and Cartoon Network Europe, then relocated to London, UK; joined Warner Bros. Pictures as Head of Programming and Operations for Warner Bros. International Channels 1994, Sr Vice-Pres. prior to leading the Div. (following Time Warner merger with Turner), Pres. Int. Marketing Div. 2000–07, Pres. Worldwide Marketing, Warner Bros. Pictures 2008–; active in numerous mentoring and volunteering orgs, including Big Brothers Big Sisters of Los Angeles, inaugural mem. Big Brothers Big Sisters' Women in Entertainment Mentorship Program; mem. Exec. Cttee Film Independent, Los Angeles; Sherry Lansing Award, Big Brothers Big Sisters of Los Angeles 2009. *Address:* Warner Bros Pictures, 4000 Warner Boulevard, Building 90, Burbank, CA 91522-0001, USA (office). *Telephone:* (818) 954-6000 (office). *Website:* www.warnerbros.com (office).

KRON, Patrick; French manufacturing executive; *Chairman and CEO, Alstom;* b. 26 Sept. 1953, Paris; ed École Polytechnique, École des Mines, Paris; with Ministry of Industry 1979–84; joined Pechiney Group 1984, various operational roles, Pechiney, Greece 1984–88, various sr financial roles, Paris 1988–93, becoming Pres., Electrometallurgy Div., mem. Exec. Cttee, Pechiney Group 1993–97, Chair. Carbone Lorraine Co. 1993–95, Head, Food and Healthcare Packaging Sector, Pechiney 1995–97, and COO, American Nat. Can Co., Chicago 1995–97; CEO Imerys 1998–2002; mem. Exec. Bd Alstom 2001–, CEO Jan. 2003–, Chair. March 2003–, also Chair. Alstom Resources Man. and Dir Alstom UK Holdings Ltd; mem. Bd of Dirs Asscn Française des Entreprises Privées, Bouygues, Les Arts Florissants; mem. Supervisory Bd Imerys 2003–05 (Dir 2005–06), Vivendi Universal 2005–06; Chevalier, Légion d'honneur 2004, Officier, Ordre nat. du Mérite 2007. *Address:* Alstom, 3 avenue André Malraux, 92309 Levallois-Perret Cedex, France (office). *Telephone:* 1-41-49-20-00 (office). *Fax:* 1-41-49-24-85 (office). *E-mail:* info@alstom.com (office). *Website:* www.alstom.com (office).

KRONKAITIS, Maj.-Gen. (retd) Jonas A., BS, MBA; Lithuanian army officer (retd); m. Rūta Kronkaitis; one s. one d.; ed Univ. of Connecticut, Syracuse Univ., US Army War Coll., US Army Command and Gen. Staff Coll., USA; 27 years mil. service in US Armed Forces; held positions successively as infantry platoon leader, battalion commdr, G-4 of 1st Armoured Div., Instructor in Man. Studies Ordnance School and Centre, served with 4th Armoured Corps, 2nd Armoured Cavalry Regiment and 1st Armoured Div., Germany, with 1st Cavalry Div., Viet Nam, Insp.-Gen. US Army, Jt Project Man. (Army and Navy) Guided Projectiles and Cannon Artillery Weapons Systems; Man.-Gen. Rock Island Arsenal (state-owned armament mfg co.); Dir Dept of Defence Programs, Atlantic Research Corpn (co. mfg rocket motors), USA –1997; Vice-Minister of Defence, Repub. of Lithuania 1997–99; Commdr Lithuanian Armed Forces 1999–2004; apptd Brig.-Gen. 1999, Maj.-Gen. 2001; Co-founder Piliečiu Santalka (civic group) 2006; fmr mem. AIAA, Assoc. of US Army, Lithuanian–American Community, Nat. Security Industrial Asscn, Navy League; fmr Chair. Bd Trustees Baltic Inst.; Legion of Merit; Viet Nam Cross of Gallantry, three Bronze Stars, three Meritorious Service Medals, Army Commendation Medal, Air Medal. *Address:* c/o Ministry of National Defence, Šv. Ignoto 8/29, 2001 Vilnius, Lithuania.

KROPF, Susan J., BA, MBA; American retail executive; ed St John's Univ., New York Univ.; joined Avon Products Inc. 1970, Vice-Pres. Product Devt 1990–92, Sr Vice-Pres. US Marketing 1992–93, Sr Vice-Pres. Global Product Man. 1993–94, Pres. New and Emerging Markets Div. 1994–97, Pres. Avon US 1997–98, COO for N America 1999–2001, Co. Pres. and COO 2001–07 (retd); Trustee, Wallace Foundation; mem. Bd of Dirs MeadWestvaco Corpn 2002–, Sherwin Williams Co. 2003–, Coach, Inc. 2006–, Fragrance Foundation; mem. Cosmetic Exec. Women, Fashion Group Int; YWCA Acad. of Women Achievers Award 1997, Beautiful Apple Award, March of Dimes 2004, Lifetime Achievement Award, Cosmetic Exec. Women 2006. *Address:* The Kroger Co., 1014 Vine Street Cincinnati, OH 45202-1100, USA (office).

KROPIWNICKI, Jerzy Janusz, DEcon; Polish politician and economist; b. 5 July 1945, Częstochowa; m.; one s.; ed Warsaw School of Econs; scientific worker, Łódź Univ. 1968–81 (dismissed); mem. Solidarity Ind. Self-governing Trade Union 1980–, Deputy Chair. Solidarity Łódź Region Br., mem. Solidarity Nat. Comm., co-organizer demonstration under martial law, arrested 13 Dec. 1981, sentenced to 6 years' imprisonment, released under amnesty July 1984; illegal activity 1984–90, co-organizer, Solidarity Regional Exec. Comm., Łódź 1984–86, co-organizer and activist, Working Group of Solidarity Nat. Comm. 1986–90; co-organizer and activist of Pastoral Care of Working People 1985–; lay worker, St Teresa's Roman Catholic Parish Church, Łódź 1986–89; scientific worker, Econ.-Sociological Faculty of Łódź Univ. 1989–; mem. Christian-Nat. Union (ZChN) 1989–, mem. Presidium of ZChN Gen. Bd 1989–93, Vice-Pres. 1991–93, 2000–; Deputy to Sejm (Parl.) 1991–93 and 1997–2001; Minister of Labour and Social Policy 1991–93; Minister-Head of Cen. Office of Planning 1992–93; Minister and Head of Governmental Centre for Strategic Studies 1997–2001; Minister of Regional Devt and Construction 2000–01; Mayor of Łódź 2002–10. *Publications:* numerous articles on econs and four books. *Leisure interests:* mountain hiking, reading (history and science-fiction). *Address:* Christian National Union, ul. Twarda 28, 00-853 Warsaw, Poland.

KROTO, Sir Harold Walter, Kt, BSc, PhD, FRS, FRSC; British scientist and academic; *Francis Eppes Professor of Chemistry, Florida State University;* b. 7 Oct. 1939, Wisbech, Cambs.; s. of Heinz Kroto (fmrly Krotoschiner) and Edith Kroto; m. Margaret Henrietta Hunter 1963; two s.; ed Bolton School, Univ. of Sheffield; Postdoctoral Fellow, Nat. Research Council, Canada 1964–66; Research Scientist, Bell Telephone Labs, NJ, USA 1966–67; Tutorial Fellow, Univ. of Sussex 1967–68, Lecturer 1968–77, Reader 1977–85, Prof. of Chem. 1985–2005, Royal Soc. Research Prof. 1991–2001, Research Prof. Emer. 2001–; Francis Eppes Prof. of Chem., Florida State Univ. 2004–; Visiting Prof., Univ. of British Columbia 1973, Univ. of Southern California 1981, UCLA 1988–92, Univ. of California, Santa Barbara (Distinguished Visiting Prof. 1996–); Chair. Bd Vega Science Trust 1995–; Pres. Royal Soc. of Chem. (RSC) 2002–04; exec. producer of science programmes for network TV; fmr mem. Nat. Advisory Cttee on Cultural and Creative Educ.; Foreign mem. Finnish Acad. of Sciences, Academy of Sciences (Turin) 2005; Foreign Assoc. NAS 2007; Freeman, City of Turin; Hon. Foreign mem. Korean Acad. of Science and Tech. 1997; Hon. Fellow, Royal Microscopical Soc. 1998; Hon. FRSE 1998; Hon. Fellowship, Bolton Inst.; Order of Cherubini (Turin) 2005; 36 hon. degrees, including Univs of Brussels (Univ. Libre), Stockholm, Limburg, Sheffield, Kingston, Sussex, Helsinki, Nottingham, Yokohama City, Sheffield-Hallam, Hertfordshire (returned due to closure of Chem. Dept), Aberdeen, Leicester, Aveiro (Portugal), Bielefeld (Germany), Hull, Manchester Metropolitan, Exeter (returned due to closure of Chem. Dept), Hong Kong City, Gustavus Adolphus Coll. (USA), Univ. Coll. London, Patras (Greece), Dalhousie (Canada), Strathclyde, Manchester, Kraków, Durham, Queen's Belfast, Surrey, Polytechnico (Turin), Beijing, Liverpool; RSC Tilden Lectureship 1981, shared Int. Prize for New Materials, American Physical Soc. 1992, Italgas Prize for Innovation in Chem. 1992, shared Hewlett Packard Europhysics Prize 1994, Nobel Prize in Chem. (co-recipient) for discovery of C_{60}, Buckminsterfullerene 1996, RSC Longstaff Medal 1993, shared Medal for Achievement in Carbon Science, American Carbon Soc. 1997, Ioannes Marcus Marei Medal, Prague 2000, Prix Leonardo Bronze Medal 2001, Copley Medal, Royal Soc. 2004, Erasmus Medal, Academia Europaea, Kavli Lecturer 2008. *Publications:* Molecular Rotation Spectra 1975, 1983; more than 300 papers in chem., chemical physics and astronomy journals. *Leisure interests:* graphic design (winner Sunday Times Book Jacket Design Competition 1964, Möet Hennessy/Louis Vuitton Science pour l'Art Prize 1994), tennis. *Address:* Room 2007 CSL, Department of Chemistry and Biochemistry, The Florida State University, Tallahassee, FL 32306-4390, USA (office); School of Chemistry, Chichester 3 3r341, Physics and Environmental Science, University of Sussex, Brighton, BN1 9QJ, England (office). *Telephone:* (850) 644-8274 (Tallahassee) (office); (1273) 678329 (Brighton) (office). *Fax:* (850) 644-8274 (Tallahassee) (office). *E-mail:* kroto@chem.fsu.edu (office); h.w.kroto@sussex.ac.uk (office). *Website:* www.chem.fsu.edu (office); www.sussex.ac.uk/chemistry (office); www.kroto.info.

KROTOV, Mikhail Valentinovich, Cand. Law; Russian government official; *Plenipotentiary Presidential Representative in the Constitutional Court;* b. 14 March 1963, Leningrad (now St Petersburg); ed A.A. Zhdanov Leningrad State Univ.; with St Petersburg Univ. 1986–2005, positions including Sr Lecturer, Head of Chair of Legal Protection for the Environment, Pro-Rector for Legal and Econ. Matters; First Deputy Gen. Dir Gazprom-Media 2005; Plenipotentiary Presidential Rep. in the Constitutional Court of the Russian Fed. 2005–; Order 'Of Honour', Hon. title 'Deserved Lawyer of the Russian Federation'; Educ. Prize of the Pres. of the Russian Fed. 2001, Educ. Prize of the Govt of the Russian Fed. 2007. *Publications:* Collection of Speeches by the Plenipotentiary Presidential Representative in the Constitutional Court of the Russian Federation 2009, Civil Right 2011. *Address:* The Presidential Executive Office, Staraya Square 4, Moscow 103132, Russia (office). *Telephone:* (495) 606-44-18 (office). *Fax:* (495) 606-30-27 (office). *Website:* archive.kremlin.ru/eng/subj/97793.shtml (office).

KRSTIĆ, Lazar; Serbian politician; *Minister of Finance and the Economy;* b. 1984, Nis; ed Yale Univ., USA; Consultant, later Assoc. Prin., McKinsey & Co., New York –2013; Minister of Finance and the Economy 2013–. *Address:* Ministry of Finance and the Economy, 11000 Belgrade,, Kneza Miloša 20, Serbia (office). *Telephone:* (11) 3642626 (office). *Fax:* (11) 3618961 (office). *E-mail:* kabinet@mfp .gov.rs (office). *Website:* www.mfp.gov.rs (office).

KRUEGER, Alan Bennett, BS, AM, PhD; American economist, academic and government official; *Bendheim Professor of Economics and Public Policy, Woodrow Wilson School of Public and International Affairs, Princeton University;* b. 17 Sept. 1960, Livingston, New Jersey; ed Livingston High School, Cornell Univ., Harvard Univ.; Faculty Research Fellow, Nat. Bureau of Econ. Research 1987–92, Research Assoc. 1992–2009, Dir Program on Children's Econ. Welfare 1993–94; Chief Economist, Dept of Labor, Washington, DC 1994–95; Research Assoc., Princeton Univ. 1987–, Asst Prof. of Econs and Public Affairs, Dept of Econs and Woodrow Wilson School, Princeton Univ. 1987–92, Bendheim Prof. of Econs and Public Policy 1992–, Founding Dir Princeton Univ. Survey Research Center 1993–, Dir Princeton Univ. Industrial Relations Section 2001–06, Acting Dir Fall 1990, Research Assoc., Office of Population Research 1993–, Center for Research on Health and Well-Being 2000–, Faculty Affiliate, Center for Migration and Devt 2001–; Research Assoc., Inst. for Policy Reform, USAID 1993–94; Research Fellow, IZA, Bonn, Germany 2000–; Visiting Scholar, Russell Sage Foundation 2003–04; Chief Economist, Nat. Council on Econ. Educ. 2003–09; Chief Economist, Dept of the Treasury, Washington, DC 2009–10, Asst Sec. for Econ. Policy 2009–10; Chair. Council of Econ. Advisors, The White House 2011–13; consultant to Interagency Taskforce on Health Care Reform 1993; columnist, New York Times Economic Scene 2000–06; mem. Bd of Dirs American Insts for Research 2002–09, MacArthur Foundation 2008–09, 2011–; mem. Bd of Trustees, Russell Sage Foundation 2004–09; mem. Exec. Cttee American Econ. Assn 2005–07, Co-Chair. Cttee on Econ. Statistics 2011–, mem. Cttee on Econ. Educ. 2005–09; mem. Exec. and Supervisory Cttee of CERGE-EI (Center for Econ. Research and Grad. Educ.–Econs Inst.), Charles Univ. 2010–; mem. Panel on Estimation Procedures, Cttee on Nat. Needs for Biomedical and Behavioral Research Personnel, Nat. Research Council 1993–94, Advisory Bd, John Burton's Workers' Compensation Monitor 1993–97, Research Advisory Cttee, Public/Private Ventures 1996–2009, Bd of Overseers, Panel Study of Income Dynamics 1998–2001, Advisory Bd, Milken Inst. Review 1998–, Fed. Econ. Statistics Advisory Cttee 2000–01, Visiting Panel on Research, Educational Testing Service 2001–04, Exec. Cttee, Int. Econ. Assn 2005–07, Econ. Advisory Council for Nat. Urban League 2007–09, Pres. Sarkozy's Comm. on Econ. Performance and Social Progress 2008; Panel mem. Nonmarket Accounts, NAS 2003–04; External mem. Business and Public Policy Dept Quinquennial Review, Wharton School, Univ. of Pennsylvania April 2004; Co-Ed. Economics Letters 1992–94; mem. Bd of Reviewers, Industrial Relations 1992–96; Assoc. Ed. Quarterly Journal of Economics 1992–97; mem. Bd of Reviewing Eds, Science 2001–09; Assoc. Ed. Journal of Economic Perspectives 1992–93, Co-Ed. 1993–94, 1995–96, Ed. 1996–2003; Co-Ed. Journal of the European Economic Association 2003–05; Fellow, Econometric Soc. 1996, Center for Advanced Study in the Behavioral Sciences, Stanford Univ. 1999–2000, American Acad. of Arts and Sciences 2002 (Chair. Membership Cttee Panel II (2) 2007–09), American Acad. of Political and Social Science 2003, Soc. of Labor Economists 2006; mem. Nat. Acad. of Social Insurance 1991; Dr hc (Université Libre de Bruxelles) 2005; Alpern Prize, Cornell Univ. 1983, NBER Olin Fellow in Econs 1989–90, NSF Grant (with Joshua Angrist) 1990, Ford Foundation grant on econ. growth and the environment (with Gene Grossman) 1992, Alfred P. Sloan Research Fellow in Econs 1992–94, Nat. Inst. of Child Health and Devt Grant (with David Card) 1995, grants to establish Princeton Survey Research Center, Mellon Foundation, Teaching Prize, Woodrow Wilson School, Princeton Univ. 1996, David N. Kershaw Prize, Asscn for Public Policy and Man. 1997, Mahalanobis Memorial Medal, Indian Econometric Soc. 2001, IZA Prize (with David Card), Carnegie Scholars Program 2003–04, IZA Prize for Labor Econs (with David Card) 2006, Susan Eaton Outstanding Scholar-Practioner Award, Labor and Employment Relations Asscn 2008, amongst the 50 highest ranked economists in the world according to IDEAS/RePEc; numerous invited lectures. *Achievements include:* developed and applied the method of natural experiments to study the effect of education on earnings, the minimum wage on employment, and other issues, also known for his work on the Environmental Kuznets Curve. *Publications include:* Myth and Measurement: The New Economics of the Minimum Wage (with David Card) 1995, Education Matters: Selected Essays by Alan B. Krueger 2000, The Roaring '90s: Can Full Employment Be Sustained (co-ed.) 2001, Inequality in America: What Role for Human Capital Policies (co-ed.) 2004, The Market Comes to Education in Sweden: An Evaluation of Sweden's Surprising School Reforms (co-author) 2005, What Makes a Terrorist: Economics and the Roots of Terrorism 2007, Measuring the Subjective Well-Being of Nations: National Accounts of Time Use and Well-Being (ed.) 2009; numerous papers in professional journals. *Address:* Woodrow Wilson School of Public and International Affairs, Robertson Hall, Princeton University, Princeton, NJ 08544, USA (office). *E-mail:* akrueger@princeton.edu (office). *Website:* wws.princeton.edu (office).

KRUEGER, Anne Osborn, PhD; American economist, international organization official and academic; *Professor of International Economics, Paul H. Nitze School of Advanced International Studies, Johns Hopkins University;* b. 12 Feb. 1934, Endicott, NY; d. of Leslie A. Osborn and Dora W. Osborn; m. James Henderson 1981; one d.; ed Oberlin Coll. and Univ. of Wisconsin; Asst Prof. of Econs, Univ. of Minnesota 1959–63, Assoc. Prof. 1963–66, Prof. 1966–82; Research Assoc., Nat. Bureau of Econ. Research 1969–82; Vice-Pres. Econs and Research, IBRD 1982–86; Univ. Arts and Sciences Prof. of Econs, Duke Univ. 1987–92; Sr Fellow (non-resident), Brookings Inst. 1988–94; Herald L. and Caroline L. Ritch Prof. of Humanities and Sciences, Stanford Univ. 1993–, Dir Center for Research on Econ. Devt and Policy Reform 1996–2001; First Deputy Man. Dir IMF 2001–06, Acting Man. Dir March–May 2004, Special Adviser to the Man. Dir 2006–; Prof. of Int. Econs, Paul H. Nitze School of Advanced Int. Studies, Johns Hopkins Univ. 2007–; visiting prof. at univs in USA, Denmark, Germany, France, Australia and Sweden; mem. editorial bds of several int. econ. journals; fmr Vice-Pres. American Econ. Asscn, Pres. 1996–97; mem. NAS; Fellow, American Acad. of Arts and Sciences, Econometric Soc.; Hon. Prof., Nat. Acad. of the Economy, Moscow 2004; Dr hc (Hacettepe Univ., Ankara) 1990; Hon. DHumLitt (Georgetown) 1993; Hon. DEcons (Monash Univ., Australia) 1995; Hon. Dr of Business (Melbourne Business School) 2004; Robertson Prize, NAS 1984, Bernhard-Harms Prize, Kiel Inst. 1990; Kenan Enterprise Award, Kenan Charitable Trust 1990, Frank E. Seidman Distinguished Award in Political Economy 1993. *Publications include:* Foreign Trade Regimes and Economic Development: Turkey 1974, The Benefits and Costs of Import Substitution in India: A Microeconomic Study 1975, Trade and Development in Korea (co-ed.) 1975, Growth, Distortions and Patterns of Trade Among Many Countries 1977, The Developmental Role of the Foreign Sector and Aid: Korea 1979, Trade and Employment in Developing Countries (co-ed.) 1981, Exchange Rate Determination 1983, The Political Economy of International Trade (co-ed.) 1989, Aid and Development (co-author) 1989, Perspectives on Trade and Development 1990, Political Economy of Policy Reform in Developing Countries 1993, American Trade Policy 1995, The WTO as an International Institution (ed.) 1998, Struggling with Success: Challenges to the International Economy 2012. *Address:* Bernstein-Offit Building 574, The Paul H. Nitze School of Advanced International Studies, The Johns Hopkins University, 1717 Massachusetts Avenue NW, Washington, DC 20036, USA (office). *Telephone:* (202) 587-3238 (office). *Fax:* (202) 663-5656 (office). *E-mail:* annekrueger@jhu.edu (office). *Website:* www.sais-jhu.edu (office).

KRÜGER, Hardy; German actor and writer; b. 12 April 1928, Berlin; s. of Max Krüger and Auguste Krüger (née Meier); m. 1st Renate Damrow; one d.; m. 2nd Francesca Marazzi; one s. one d.; m. 3rd Anita Park 1978; German repertory theatre 1945–56, entered films in 1943; several awards and prizes. *Films include:* Der Rest ist Schweigen 1959, Blind Date 1959, Taxi pour Tobrouk 1961, Hatari 1961, Les Dimanches de Ville d'Avray 1962, Les Quatre Verités 1962, Le Gros Coup 1963, Le Chant du Monde 1964, Flight of the Phoenix 1965, The Defector 1966, La Grande Sauterelle 1966, The Battle of Neretva 1968, The Secret of Santa Vittoria 1969, Death of A Stranger 1972, Le Solitaire 1973, Barry Lyndon 1974, Paper Tiger 1974, Potato Fritz (Best Actor Award, Cannes) 1975, A Bridge Too Far 1976, L'Autopsie d'un Monster 1976, The Wild Geese 1978. *Publications:* Ein Farm in Afrika 1970, Sawimbulu 1971, Wer stehend stirbt, lebt länger 1973, Diè Schallmauer 1978, Die Frau des Griechen 1980, Junge Unrast 1983, Sibirienfahrt, Tagebuch einer Reise 1985, Frühstück mit Theodore 1990, Weltenbummler, Reisen zu Menschen und Göttern 1992, Weltenbummler, Willkommen auf funf

Kontinenten 1994, Weltenbummler, Glückliche Tage auf dem Blauen Planeten 1996, Wanderjahre 1999, Szenen eines Clowns 2001. *Address:* Maximilianstrasse 23, 80539 Munich, Germany.

KRÜGER, Manfred Paul, DPhil; German writer, academic and editor; *Lecturer, Institute for Spiritual Science and Arts, Nuremberg;* b. 23 Feb. 1938, Köslin; s. of Paul Krüger and Hildegard Krüger; m. Christine Petersen 1962; three s. four d.; ed Oberrealschule Ansbach, Heidelberg Univ., Tübingen Univ.; Asst Prof., Erlangen Univ. 1966–73; Lecturer, Inst. for Spiritual Science and Arts, Nuremberg 1972–; Lecturer, Fachhochschule Ottersberg 1980–2010; Co-Ed. Goetheanum weekly 1984–96. *Publications:* Gérard de Nerval 1966, Wandlungen des Tragischen 1973, Nora Ruhtenberg 1976, Bilder und Gegenbilder 1978, Wortspuren 1980, Denkbilder 1981, Literatur und Geschichte 1982, Mondland 1982, Nah ist er 1983, Meditation 1983, Rosenroman 1985, Meditation und Karma 1988, Anthroposophie und Kunst 1988, Ästhetik der Freiheit 1992, Ichgeburt 1996, Das Ich und seine Masken 1997, Die Verklärung auf dem Berge 2003. *Address:* Rieterstrasse 20, 90419 Nuremberg, Germany (home). *Telephone:* (911) 338678 (home).

KRUGMAN, Paul Robin, PhD; American economist and academic; *Professor of Economics and International Affairs, Princeton University;* b. 28 Feb. 1953, Albany, NY; s. of David Krugman and Anita Krugman; m. Robin Leslie Bergman 1983; ed Yale Univ., Massachusetts Inst. of Tech.; taught at Stanford Univ.; Asst Prof., Yale Univ. 1977–79; Asst Prof., MIT 1979–80, Assoc. Prof. 1980–82, Ford Int. Prof. of Econs 1983–2000; Sr Int. Economist for Pres.'s Council of Econ. Advisers, under Ronald Reagan 1982–83; Op-Ed Columnist, New York Times 1999–; Prof. of Econs and Int. Affairs, Princeton Univ. 2000–; Centenary Prof., LSE, UK; Research Assoc., Nat. Bureau of Econ. Research; mem. Group of Thirty Consultative Group on Int. Econ. and Monetary Affairs, Inc. (G-30), Washington, DC; has served as a consultant to Fed. Reserve Bank of New York, World Bank, IMF, UN, as well as to several countries, including Portugal and the Philippines; Fellow, Econometric Soc.; John Bates Clark Medal, American Econ. Asscn 1991, Nobel Prize for Econs 2008, named by The Washington Monthly as "the most important political columnist in America", named by The Asia Times as "the Mick Jagger of political/economic punditry", named by The Economist as "the most celebrated economist of his generation", Asturias Award from the King of Spain. *Publications:* author, co-author or ed. or more than 23 books, including Market Structure and Foreign Trade (with E. Helpman) 1985, International Economics, Theory and Policy (with M. Obsfeld) 1988, The Age of Diminished Expectations 1990, Rethinking International Trade 1990, Geography and Trade 1991, Currencies and Crises 1992, Peddling Prosperity 1994, The Great Unravelling: From Boom to Bust in Three Short Years (New York Times best-seller) 2003, Microeconomics (with Robin Wells) 2004, Macroeconomics (with Robin Wells) 2005, The Conscience of a Liberal 2007, The Return of Depression Economics and the Crisis of 2008 2009, End This Depression Now! 2012; more than 200 professional journal articles, many of them on int. trade and finance; monthly column, The Dismal Science, for online magazine Slate, columnist for Fortune and has published articles in The New Republic, Foreign Policy, Newsweek and The New York Times Magazine. *Leisure interest:* music. *Address:* Department of Economics, 414 Robertson Hall, Princeton University, Princeton, NJ 08544, USA (office). *E-mail:* pkrugman@princeton.edu (office). *Website:* www.princeton.edu/~pkrugman (office); www.econ.princeton.edu (office); www.krugmanonline.com.

KRUMMACHER, Hans-Henrik, DPhil; German academic; *Professor Emeritus, University of Mainz;* b. 24 Aug. 1931, Essen-Werden; m. Eva Wentscher 1956; one s. four d.; ed Humboldt Univ. Berlin, Univs. of Heidelberg and Tübingen; Archivist, Schiller-Nationalmuseum, Marbach a.N. 1956–58; Asst Prof., Univ. of Cologne 1958–67; Prof. of German Literature, Univ. of Mainz 1967–99, Prof. Emer. 1999–; mem. Akademie der Wissenschaften und der Literatur zu Mainz 1984; Corresp. mem. Österreichische Akad. der Wissenschaften 1993. *Publications:* Das 'als ob' in der Lyrik 1965, Der junge Gryphius und die Tradition 1976; Ed. Eduard Mörike, Werke und Briefe 1967–, Neudrucke deutscher Literaturwerke 1975–, Lyra: Studien zur Theorie und Geschichte der Lyrik vom 16. bis zum 19. Jahrhundert 2013. *Address:* Am Mainzer Weg 10, 55127 Mainz-Drais, Germany (home). *Telephone:* (6131) 477550 (home).

KRUMNOW, Jürgen, Dr rer. pol; German business executive; b. 18 May 1944, Grünberg, Silesia; m. Christiane Krumnow; ed Hamburg Univ.; trainee, Deutsche Bank AG, Bremen 1964–66, Accounting Dept, Frankfurt am Main 1970–74, Exec. Secr. 1974–78, Head, Reutlingen/Tübingen Br. 1978–82, Head, Cen. Accounting and Planning Dept 1982–86, Exec. Man. 1986–88, mem. Exec. Bd 1988–99, Consultant 1999–2004; mem. Supervisory Bd TUI AG 1997–2011, Chair. 2004–11, Chair. Audit Cttee –2004; fmr mem. Supervisory Bd Volkswagen AG, Deutsche Bahn AG, Hapag Lloyd AG, Peek & Cloppenburg KG; Deputy Chair. Lenze Holding; fmr Chair. Deutsches Rechnungslegungs Standards Cttee (DRSC—German Accounting Standards Bd); mem. European Advisory Council, Air Products & Chemicals Inc., Pa, USA. *Address:* c/o TUI AG, Postfach 610209, 30602 Hanover, Germany.

KRUPP, Fred; American lawyer, environmental activist and negotiation official; *President, Environmental Defense Fund;* m. Laurie Krupp; three c.; ed Yale Univ., Univ. of Michigan Law School; spent several years in pvt. law practice in New Haven, Conn. in several firms: Cooper, Whitney, Cochran & Krupp 1984; Pnr, Albis & Krupp 1978–84; Founder and Gen. Counsel, Connecticut Fund for the Environment 1978–84; Pres. Environmental Defense Fund 1984–; mem. Bd H. John Heinz III Center for Science, Econs and the Environment, John F. Kennedy School of Govt Environment Council, Leadership Council of the Yale School of Forestry and Environmental Studies; fmr mem. Pres.'s Advisory Cttee on Trade Policy and Negotiations for both Pres. Bill Clinton and Pres. George W. Bush; helped launch corp. coalition US Climate Action Partnership; Keystone Leadership in Environment Award 1999, Champion Award, Women's Council on Energy and the Environment 2002, among 16 people named America's Best Leaders by US News and World Report 2007. *Achievements include:* won gold medal in FISA World Rowing Championships 2006. *Publication:* Earth: The Sequel: The Race to Reinvent Energy and Stop Global Warming (with Miriam Horn) (New York Times Best Seller) 2008. *Address:* Environmental Defense Fund, 257 Park Avenue South, New York, NY 10010, USA (office). *Telephone:* (212) 505-2100 (office). *Fax:* (212) 505-2375 (office). *E-mail:* info@edf.org (office). *Website:* www.edf.org (office).

KRUPP, Georg; German business executive; b. 15 July 1936; fmr Deputy mem. Bd of Man. Dirs Deutsche Bank; Chair. Supervisory Bd WMF AG, Geislingen, Kunz Holding GmbH & Co. KG, Gschwend; mem. Supervisory Bd IVECO Magirus AG, Ulm, Strabag AG, Cologne, Gerling-Konzern Versicherungs-Beteiligungs AG, Cologne, Rheinmetall AG, Düsseldorf, BHS Tabletop AG, Selb, Bizerba GmbH & Co. KG, Balingen, IVECO NV, Amstelveen, Netherlands. *Address:* WMF AG, Eberhardstrasse, Geislingen 73309, Germany.

KRYLOV, Sergey Borisovich; Russian diplomatist and business executive; b. 26 Oct. 1949, Moscow; m.; two d.; ed Moscow State Inst. of Int. Relations, Diplomatic Acad. of Ministry of Foreign Relations; diplomatic service 1971–; translator, attaché Embassy, Zaire 1971–76; attaché, Third, Second Sec. Second Africa Dept, USSR Ministry of Foreign Affairs 1976–79; First Sec., Counsellor to Minister 1979–86, Asst to Deputy Minister 1986–89; Minister-Counsellor USSR Embassy, Portugal 1990–92; Dir of Dept, Exec. Sec. Ministry of Foreign Affairs of Russia 1992–93; Deputy Minister of Foreign Affairs, Russia 1993–96; Perm. Rep. to UN, New York and other int. orgs, Geneva 1997–98; Amb. to Germany 1998–2004; Head, Int. Relations Office, Sistema Corpn 2004.

KRZAKLEWSKI, Marian, DIng; Polish politician and trade union official; b. 23 Aug. 1950, Kolbuszowa; m.; two s.; ed Silesian Tech. Univ., Gliwice 1975; scientific worker Polish Acad. of Sciences (PAN) and Silesian Tech. Univ., Gliwice 1976–90; mem. Solidarity Trade Union (independent, self-governing union) 1980–; Chair. of Solidarity 1991–2002; mem. ICFTU 1991–; Co-founder and Leader Solidarity Election Action (AWS) 1996–2001; Deputy to Sejm (Parl.) 1997–2001; Chair. Solidarity Election Action Parl. Club 1997–2001; main negotiator and jt architect of parl. and govt coalition Solidarity Election Action–Freedom Union; Co-founder and Chair. Social Movt of Solidarity Election Action (RS AWS) 1997–2000 (merged with three other parties to form Solidarity Electoral Action of the Right 2000); Hon. Chair. Social Movt of Solidarity Election Action (RS AWS) 1999; Man of the Year, Zycie newspaper 1996, Kisiel Prize 1997, Platinum Laurel of Skills 1998. *Publication:* Solidarity's Revival and Polish Politics. *Leisure interests:* family life, tourism, sport, arts, literature. *Address:* Komisja Krajowa NSZZ Solidarnose, ul. Wały Piastowskie 24, 80-855 Gdańsk, Poland. *Telephone:* (58) 308 44 72. *Fax:* (58) 305 90 44.

KRZANIC, Brian Matthew, BS; American business executive; *CEO, Intel Corporation;* b. 9 May 1960; two c.; ed San Jose State Univ.; began career as process engineer at Intel in NM 1982, held plant and manufacturing man. roles at several Intel factories, responsible for implementation of 0.13-micron logic process technology across Intel's global factory network 2001–03, Fab 17 plant manager 1997–2001, oversaw integration of Digital Equipment Corpn's semiconductor manufacturing operations into Intel's manufacturing network, Head of Assembly and Test 2003–07, Head of Fab/Sort Manufacturing 2007–11, Exec. Vice-Pres. and COO Intel Corpn 2012–13, mem. Bd of Dirs and CEO Intel Corpn 2013–; mem. Bd of Dirs Semiconductor Industry Asscn. *Achievements include:* holds one patent for semiconductor processing. *Address:* Intel Corporation, 2200 Mission College Boulevard, Santa Clara, CA 95052-8119, USA (office). *Telephone:* (408) 765-8080 (office). *Fax:* (408) 765-9904 (office). *E-mail:* info@intel.com (office). *Website:* www .intel.com (office).

KRZYZEWSKI, Mike, BS; American basketball coach; *Head Basketball Coach and Executive-in-Residence, Duke University;* b. 13 Feb. 1947, Chicago, Ill.; m.; three d.; ed Weber High School, Chicago, US Mil. Acad., West Point; served as officer in US Army 1969–74; Grad. Asst Coach at Ind. Univ. 1974–75; Coach, US Mil. Acad., West Point 1976–80; Head Coach, Duke Univ. 1980–, has led Duke to Nat. Collegiate Athletic Asscn (NCAA) Championships 1991, 1992, 2001, 2010; Olympic Trials Instructor 1984; coached US team in World Univ. Games 1987, World Championship Games and Goodwill Games 1990; Asst Coach US Gold Medal Team, Olympic Games 1992; Pres. Nat. Asscn of Basketball Coaches (NABC) 1998–99; coach of Team USA 2006 World Championships, 2008 Beijing Olympics; named Nat. Coach of the Year (eight times), ACC Coach of the Year (five times), named NABC Coach of the Decade (1990s) 2000, inducted into Basketball Hall of Fame 2001, named America's Best Coach by Time magazine/CNN 2001. *Publications include:* Leading with the Heart 2001, Beyond Basketball 2006. *Address:* Athletic Department, Duke University, Box 90555, Durham, NC 27708, USA (office). *Telephone:* (919) 613-7505 (office). *E-mail:* gbbrown@duaa.duke.edu (office). *Website:* www.coachk.com (office).

KSEŃ, Jacek, PhD; Polish banking executive; *Chairman, Sygnity SA;* ed Poznan School of Econs, Higher School of Planning and Statistics; Financial Markets Operator, Bank Handlowy –1978; Vice-Dir, Foreign Currency Dept, Polska Kasa Opieka SA, Paris 1978, becoming Head, Foreign Exchange Deals, Head, Foreign Bonds Team 1985–87; Commercial Rep, Bond Dept, Lyonnaise de Banque, Paris 1987–90, also Vice-Dir for Int. Financial Markets 1989–90; Ind. Sr Dealer, Int. Futures Dept, Caisse Nat. Credit Agricole 1990–96, mem. Sr Man. Team 1991–96; Pres. Man. Bd, Wielkopolski Bank Kredytowy (WBK), Poland 1996–2001, Pres. Bank Zachodni WBK (following merger) 2001; mem. Supervisory Bd Sygnity SA 2007–, currently Chair. *Address:* Synity SA, Al. Jerozolimskie 180, 02-486 Warsaw, Poland (office). *Telephone:* (61) 856-40-00 (office). *Fax:* (61) 856-40-11 (office). *E-mail:* jacek.ksen@bzwbk.pl (office). *Website:* www.bzbk.pl (office).

KUBASIK, Christopher E., BA; American business executive; *President and Chief Operating Officer, Lockheed Martin Corporation;* ed Univ. of Maryland, Carnegie Mellon Univ., Defense Acquisition Univ., Fort Belvoir; Partner, Ernst & Young, LLP –1999; joined Lockheed Martin 1999, Chief Financial Officer, Lockheed Martin Corpn 2001–07, Exec. Vice-Pres. Electronic Systems Business Area 2007–09, Pres. and COO 2010–; Chair. Sandia Corpn (operates Sandia Nat. Labs for US Dept of Energy) 2007–10; serves on United Service Orgs (USO) Bd of Govs, Asscn of the United States Army Council of Trustees, Univ. of Maryland College Park Foundation Bd of Trustees. *Address:* Lockheed Martin Corporation, 6801 Rockledge Drive, Bethesda, MD 20817-1877, USA (office). *Telephone:* (301) 897-6000 (office). *Fax:* (301) 897-6704 (office). *E-mail:* info@lockheedmartin.com (office). *Website:* www.lockheedmartin.com (office).

KUBICE, Col Jan; Czech police officer and politician; b. 3 Oct. 1953; one s.; Dir Buildings of Special Importance Protection Service, Fed. Police Corps 1991–92; Dir Protection Service, Police of the Czech Repub. 1993–94, Dir Operative Documentation Unit 1994–95, Dir Organized Crime Detection Unit 1995–2008; Minister of the Interior 2011–13. *Address:* c/o Ministry of the Interior, Nad Štolou 3, PO Box 21, 170 34 Prague 7, Czech Republic. *E-mail:* public@mvcr.cz.

KUBILIUS, Andrius; Lithuanian politician; *Chairman, Homeland Union – Lithuanian Christian Democrats;* b. 8 Dec. 1956, Vilnius; m. Rasa Kubilienė; two s.; ed 22nd secondary school, Vilnius, Vilnius Univ.; lab. technician, Vilnius Univ. 1979–90, then engineer, then scientific research asst; mem. Sajūdis Movt 1988–, Exec. Sec. Sajūdis Council 1990–92; mem. Seimas 1992–, First Vice-Chair. 1996–99, mem. Ass. of Elders 2000–03, 2005–, mem. Cttee on European Affairs 2004–12, Cttee of Devt of Information Society 2004–05, Cttee on Rural Affairs 2005–12, Leader of Opposition 2005–08; Prime Minister 1999–2000, 2008–12; mem. Homeland Union 1993, First Deputy Chair. 2000–03 (party absorbed Lithuanian Rightist Union Nov. 2003), Chair. Homeland Union 2003– (party merged with Lithuanian Union of Political Prisoners and Deportees Feb. 2004, merged with Lithuanian Christian Democrats May 2008); Independence Medal of Lithuania 2000, Commdr's Cross, Order of the Lithuanian Grand Duke Gediminas 2004, Third Class Order of the Cross of St Mary's Land (Estonia) 2007. *Publications include:* Kodėl krepšinis Lietuvoje gražesnis už politiką (Why Basketball is More Fascinating than Politics in Lithuania) 2004, Konservatyvioji bendruomenė (The Conservative Community) 2006. *Address:* Homeland Union—Lithuanian Christian Democrats (Tėvynės Sąjunga—Lietuvos Krikščionys Demokratai), L. Stuokos-Gucevičiaus g. 11, Vilnius 01122, Lithuania (office). *Telephone:* (5) 212-1657 (office). *Fax:* (5) 278-4722 (office). *E-mail:* sekretoriatas@tsajunga.lt (office). *Website:* www.tsajunga.lt (office); www.kubilius.lt.

KUBIŠ, Ján; Slovak diplomatist, government official and UN official; *Special Representative and Head, United Nations Assistance Mission in Afghanistan (UNAMA), United Nations;* b. 12 Nov. 1952, Bratislava; m.; one d.; ed Moscow State Inst. for Int. Affairs; served in Dept of Int. Econ. Orgs, Ministry of Foreign Affairs (Czechoslovakia) 1976–80, Head of Security and Arms Control Section 1985–88, Dir-Gen. Euro-Atlantic Section 1991–92; served in Embassy in Addis Ababa 1980–85; First Sec. Embassy in Moscow 1989–90, Deputy Head and Head of Political Dept 1990–91; Chair. CSCE Cttee of Sr Officials and Amb.-at-Large 1992; Perm. Rep. (for Slovakia), UN Office, GATT and other Int. Orgs, Geneva 1993–94; Chief Negotiator (for Slovakia) for Pact for Stability in Europe 1994; Dir OSCE Conflict Prevention Centre 1994–98; Special Rep. of UN Sec.-Gen. for Tajikistan and Head, UN Mission of Mil. Observers 1998–99; Sec.-Gen. OSCE 1999–2005, Personal Rep. of Chair.-in-Office for Cen. Asia 2000; EU Special Rep. for Cen. Asia 2005–06; Minister of Foreign Affairs 2006–09; Under-Sec.-Gen. and Exec. Sec. UN Econ. Comm. for Europe 2009–12; Special Rep. of UN Sec.-Gen. for Afghanistan and Head, UN Assistance Mission in Afghanistan (UNAMA) 2012–; mem. UN Sec.-Gen. Sr Man. Group; OSCE Medal 1998. *Address:* United Nations Assistance Mission in Afghanistan (UNAMA), PO Box 5858, Grand Central Station, New York, NY 10163-5858, USA (office); United Nations Assistance Mission in Afghanistan (UNAMA), Compound B, Peace Street, Kabul, Afghanistan (office). *E-mail:* spokesman-unama@un.org (office). *Website:* unama.unmissions.org (office).

KUBIV, Stepan Ivanovych; Ukrainian central banker and academic; *Governor, National Bank of Ukraine;* b. 3 July 1962, Mshanets, Zboriv Raion, Ternopil Oblast, Ukrainian SSR, USSR; ed Lviv Polytechnic, Lviv Univ.; Researcher, Ivan Franko Univ., Lviv 1983–88; youth worker and dir, Municipality of Lviv 1988–91; Dir Student Union of Lviv 1991–94; with Western Ukrainian Commercial Bank 1994–2000, Chair. 1997–2000; Chair. JSC Kredobank 2000–08; Assoc. Prof. of Marketing and Logistics, Lviv Polytechnic 2008–; mem. Bank Supervisory Bd, Nat. Bank of Ukraine 2010–12, Gov. Feb. 2014–; mem. Verkhovna Rada (Parl.) 2012–14 (resgnd); commdr in House of Trade Unions, Kyiv, during mass anti-govt protests in Ukraine 2013–14; mem. Nat. Security Council Feb. 2014–. *Address:* Office of the Governor, Natsionalny Bank Ukrainy, 01601 Kyiv, vul. Institutska 9, Ukraine (office). *Telephone:* (44) 253-01-80 (office). *Fax:* (44) 230-20-33 (office). *E-mail:* webmaster@bank.gov.ua (office). *Website:* www.bank.gov.ua (office).

KUBUABOLA, Ratu Inoke; Fijian diplomatist and politician; *Minister for Foreign Affairs, International Co-operation and Civil Aviation;* brother of Ratu Jone Kubuabola; Chair. Cakaudrove Prov. Council 1991–2001; Leader of Fijian Political Party (Soqosoqo ni Vakavulewa ni Taukei, or SVT) following its defeat in 1999 election; MP for Cakaudrove West Fijian Communal Constituency in House of Reps –2001, Leader of Opposition 1999–2000; Minister for Information and Communications in interim Cabinet formed by Laisenia Qarase 2000–01; High Commr to Papua New Guinea 2002–05; Amb. to Japan (also accred to S Korea) 2006–09; Minister for Foreign Affairs, International Co-operation and Civil Aviation 2009–. *Address:* Ministry of Foreign Affairs, International Co-operation and Civil Aviation, Government Buildings, PO Box 2220, Suva, Fiji (office). *Telephone:* 3309631 (office). *Fax:* 3301741 (office). *E-mail:* info@foreignaffairs.gov.fj (office). *Website:* www.foreignaffairs.gov.fj (office).

KUBUABOLA, Ratu Jone; Fijian politician; brother of Ratu Inoke Kubuabola; fmr meteorologost; joined Govt as Planning Officer; Perm. Sec. for Finance 1983; Gov. Reserve Bank of Fiji 1988–2000; elected MP for SW Urban (Fijian Communal) Constituency; Minister for Finance, Nat. Planning and Communications 2000–06; mem. Soqosoqo ni Duavata ni Lewenivanua Party. *Address:* c/o Soqosoqo ni Duavata ni Lewenivanua Party Office, Edinburgh Drive, Suva, Fiji.

KUČAN, Milan; Slovenian politician and lawyer; b. 14 Jan. 1941, Križevci, Prekmurje; m. Štefka Kučan; two d.; ed Ljubljana Univ.; joined Fed. of Communists of Slovenia 1958; mem. Cen. Cttee Fed. of Communists of Slovenia; Chair. Comm. on Educational Problems of Cen. Cttee, Youth Union of Slovenia 1963–65; Chair. Cen. Cttee 1968–69; mem. Cen. Cttee Communist Union of Slovenia 1973–78, Chair. 1986–89; Sec. Republican Conf. of Socialist Alliance of Slovenia 1973–78; Chair. Slovenian Skupščina (Parl.) 1978–86; Pres. of Slovenia 1990–2002; Founder and Chair. Forum 21 group of leaders who discuss Slovenian issues 2004–; mem. Club of Madrid. *Address:* c/o Office of the President, 1000 Ljubljana, Erjavčeva 17, Slovenia (office).

KUČERA, Jan; Czech scientist; Sr Researcher, Nuclear Physics Inst., Acad. of Sciences of Czech Repub., Řež; mem. Nuclear Analytical Methods in the Life Sciences Int. Cttee, Chair. 2002–, Gen. Chair. Fifth Int. Conf., Prague 1993; Hevesy Medal 2006. *Publications:* Nuclear Analytical Methods in the Life Sciences (co-ed.) 1994; numerous scientific papers in professional journals. *Address:*

Nuclear Physics Institute, Academy of Sciences of the Czech Republic, 250 68 Řež, Czech Republic (office). *Telephone:* (2) 66172268 (office). *Fax:* (2) 20941130 (office). *E-mail:* kucera@ujf.cas.cz (office). *Website:* www.ujf.cas.cz (office).

KUCHERENA, Anatoly G., Dr Jur; Russian barrister; *Chairman, Institute of Democracy and Cooperation;* b. 23 Aug. 1961; ed Moscow Inst. of Law; Prof., Chair. Moscow Acad. of Law; f. one of the first Bureaux of Barristers' Argument 1995–; currently Chair. Inst. of Democracy and Cooperation; mem. Moscow Collegium of Barristers, Public Chamber; Head, Civil Soc.(NGO). *Publications include:* Ball of Lawlessness, Diagnosis of a Barrister, Who Profits, One Cannot Do Without Blood; contrib. numerous publications to the press on legal problems. *Address:* Bureau of Barristers' Argument, Prechistenka str. 33/19, Moscow 119031, Russia (office). *Telephone:* (495) 105-05-21 (office).

KUCHMA, Leonid Danylovych, CTechSc; Ukrainian manager, politician and fmr head of state; b. 1938, Chatikine, Chernihiv Oblast; s. of Danylo Prokopovych Kuchma and Paraska Trokhymivna Kuchma; m. Ludmyla Mykolayovna Kuchma; one d.; ed Dnipropetrovsk Nat. Univ.; mem. CPSU 1960–91; engineer, constructor, Chief Constructor Research-Production, Yuzmash eng plant 1960–75, Sec. Party Cttee 1975–82, Deputy Dir-Gen. 1982–86, Dir-Gen. 1986–92; mem. Cen. Cttee CP Ukrainian SSR 1981–91; People's Deputy of Ukraine 1991–94; Prime Minister of Ukraine 1992–93 (resgnd); Chair. Ukrainian Union of Industrialists and Entrepreneurs 1993–94; Pres. of Ukraine 1994–2005; charged by Ukrainian prosecutors with involvement in the murder of journalist Georgiy Gongadze March 2011, prosecutors ordered by district court to drop criminal charges on grounds that evidence linking him to the murder was insufficient Dec. 2011, Higher Special Court for Civil and Criminal Cases turned down appeal by Prosecutor Gen.'s Office and upheld legality of Appeals Court decision in Jan. 2012 to throw out a criminal case against him June 2012; Hon. Citizen of the Donetsk Oblast 2002; Kt Grand Cross with Grand Cordon, Order of Merit of the Italian Repub. 1995, Grand Cross, Order of Vytautas the Great (Lithuania) 1996, Grand Cross, Order of the Lithuanian Grand Duke Gediminas (Lithuania) 1998, Chain of the Order of Prince Henry (Portugal) 1998, Order of the Golden Eagle (Kazakhstan) 1999, Azerbaijani Istiglal Order 1999, Order of St Volodymyr (Gold) 1999, Order 'Bethlehem – 2000' (State of Palestine) 2000, Order of the Repub. (Moldova) 2003, Order of the Ukrainian Orthodox Church (Moscow Patriarchate) of St Ilya of Murom, First Class 2004, Order Laila Utama Dardzha Kerabat, First Class (Brunei) 2004, Order of Merit for the Fatherland, First Class (Russia) 2004; Lenin Prize 1981, State Prize 1993. *Address:* Ukrainian Presidential Fund of Leonid Kuchma Charity Organization, 01024 Kyiv, vul. P. Orlyka 1/15, Ukraine (office). *Telephone:* (44) 465-93-77 (office). *Fax:* (44) 465-93-78 (office). *E-mail:* press@ldk-fund.org.ua (office). *Website:* www.kuchma.org.ua (office).

KÜÇÜK, İrsen, BAgr; Turkish-Cypriot politician; b. 1940, Lefkoşa; m.; two c.; ed Faculty of Agric., Ankara Univ.; elected mem. Parl. 1976, 1998, 2003, 2005, 2009; fmr Minister of Natural Resources and Energy, of Health, of Social Affairs, of Labor; Minister of Agriculture 1998–2004; Prime Minister 2010–13; Sec. Gen. Nat. Unity Party (UBP) 2010–. *Address:* c/o Prime Minister's Office, Selcuklu Rd, Lefkosa Mersin 10, Turkey (office).

KUCZYNSKI, Pedro Pablo, BA, MA, MPA; Peruvian economist, politician and business executive; *Senior Adviser and Partner, Rohatyn Group;* b. 1939, Lima; ed Oxford Univ., UK, Princeton Univ., USA; Loan Officer and Economist Latin America and New Zealand, World Bank 1961–66; Deputy Dir Peruvian Central Bank 1967–69; Sr Economist, IMF 1973–75; Chief Economist, Northern Latin America, World Bank 1971–72, Head of Planning Div. 1972–73; Vice-Pres. Kuhn, Loeb & Co. Int. 1973–75; Chief Economist, Int. Finance Corpn 1975–77; Pres. Halco Mining Co. 1977–80; Minister of Energy and Mines 1980–82; Man. Dir First Boston Corpn then Pres. First Boston Int. 1982–92; Pres. Westfield Capital 1992–94; Co-founder, Pres. and CEO Latin America Enterprise Fund 1994; Minister of Economy and Finance 2001–02, 2004–2005; Prime Minister 2005–06; Founder and Hon. Chair. Aqualimpia (non-profit involved in water projects) 2006–; Sr Adviser and Pnr, Rohatyn Group 2007–; Chair. Supervisory Bd AMG Advanced Metallurgical Group NV 2007–; fmr mem. Bd Tenaris SA, Southern Peru Copper Corpn, current mem. Comm. on Growth and Devt. *Publications:* Peruvian Democracy under Economic Stress 1977. *Address:* Aqualimpia, Calle Andrés Reyes 524 Piso 3, San Isidro, Lima 27, Peru (office). *Telephone:* (1) 2223605 (office). *Website:* www.agualimpia.org (office).

KUDELKA, James Alexander, OC; Canadian choreographer, dancer and fmr ballet company artistic director; b. 10 Sept. 1955, Newmarket, Ont.; s. of John Kudelka and Kathleen Mary Kudelka (née Kellington); ed Nat. Ballet School of Canada; dancer, Nat. Ballet of Canada 1972–81, Artist in Residence 1992–96, Artistic Dir 1996–2005, Resident Choreographer 2005–07; Prin. Dancer, Grand Ballets Canadiens 1981–84, Resident Choreographer 1984–90; Isadora Duncan Dance Award 1988, Dora Mavor Moore Award (for Fifteen Heterosexual Duets) 1991–92, (for The Nutcracker) 1995–96, Jean A. Chalmers Choreographic Award 1993, numerous Canada Council Grants. *Major works:* (for Nat. Ballet of Canada) Washington Square 1977, Pastorale 1990, Musings 1991, The Miraculous Mandarin 1993, Spring Awakening 1994, The Actress 1994, The Nutcracker 1995, The Four Seasons 1997, Swan Lake 1999, The Firebird 2000, The Contract (The Pied Piper) 2002, Chacony 2004, Cinderella 2004, An Italian Straw Hat 2005; (for Grand Ballets Canadiens) In Paradisum 1983, Désir 1991; (for Toronto Dance Theatre) Fifteen Heterosexual Duets 1991; (for Birmingham Royal Ballet, UK) Le Baiser de la fée 1996; (for American Ballet Theater) Cruel World 1994, States of Grace 1995; (for San Francisco Ballet) The Comfort Zone 1989, The End 1992, Terra Firma 1995, Some Women and Men 1998; (for Joffrey Ballet) The Heart of the Matter 1986. *Address:* The Walter Carsen Centre for The National Ballet of Canada, 470 Queens Quay West, Toronto, ON M5V 3K4, Canada (office). *Telephone:* (416) 345-9686 (office). *Fax:* (416) 345-8323 (office). *E-mail:* info@national.ballet.ca (office). *Website:* www.national.ballet.ca (office).

KUDLOW, Lawrence A., BA; American economist, broadcaster and fmr government official; *CEO, Kudlow and Company, LLC;* b. 20 Aug. 1947, Englewood, NJ; s. of Irving Howard and Ruth Kudlow (née Grodnick); m. 1st Susan Cullman 1981, one d.; m. 2nd Judith Pond 1987; ed Univ. of Rochester, Woodrow Wilson School of Public and Int. Affairs, Princeton Univ.; economist, Fed. Reserve Bank of New York 1973–75; Chief Economist and Corporate Vice-Pres. Paine, Webber, Jackson and Curtis, New York 1975–79; Chief Economist and Partner, Bear, Stearns and Co., New York 1979–81; Asst Dir for Econ. Policy, Office of Man. and Budget, Washington, DC 1981–82, Assoc. Dir for Econs and Planning 1982–83; Pres. and CEO Lawrence Kudlow and Assocs, Washington, DC 1983–84; Pres. and CEO Rodman & Renshaw Economics Inc. 1984–86; Chief Economist and Man. Dir Rodman and Renshaw Capital Group Inc. 1984–86; Chief Economist, Bear, Stearns & Co. 1986–94; currently CEO Kudlow and Co. LLC, New York; host, Kudlow and Co. (daily TV current affairs program on CNBC) and Larry Kudlow Show (weekly radio show); columnist and econs Ed. National Review magazine. *Publication:* American Abundance: The New Economic and Moral Prosperity 1998. *Leisure interests:* tennis, golf. *Address:* Kudlow and Company LLC, 1375 Kings Highway East, Suite 260, Fairfield, CT 06824, USA (office). *Telephone:* (203) 228-5050 (office). *Fax:* (203) 228-5040 (office). *E-mail:* svarga@kudlow.com (office). *Website:* www.kudlow.com (office).

KUDO, Yasumi; Japanese shipping industry executive; *President and President Corporate Officer, Nippon Yusen Kabushiki Kaisha (NYK Line);* joined Nippon Yusen Kabushiki Kaisha (NYK Line) 1975, Dir 2004–, has served as Vice-Pres. Corp. Officer, Man. of Automobile Vessel Group, Man. Dir, Corp. Officer and Sr Man. Corp. Officer, Chief Exec. of Global Logistics HQ, Pres. and Rep. Dir Nippon Yusen Kabushiki Kaisha 2009–, Chief Exec. Bulk/Energy Resources Transportation 2010–11, Pres. Corp. Officer 2011–. *Address:* Nippon Yusen Kabushiki Kaisha, 3-2, Marunouchi 2-chome, Chiyoda-ku, Tokyo 100-0005, Japan (office). *Telephone:* (3) 3284-5151 (office). *Fax:* (3) 3284-6359 (office). *E-mail:* info@nyk.com (office). *Website:* www.nyk.com (office).

KUDRIN, Aleksei Leonidovich, CandEcon; Russian politician; b. 12 Oct. 1960, Dobele, Latvian SSR, USSR; m. 1st; one d.; m. 2nd Irina Kudrina; one s.; ed Leningrad (now St Petersburg) State Univ., Inst. of Econs, USSR Acad. of Sciences; worked as a motor mechanic and training asst at engine lab. of Acad. of Procurement and Transportation, Ministry of Defence; on staff Inst. of Social-Econ. Problems, Acad. of Sciences 1983–90; Deputy Chair. Cttee on Econ. Reform, Leningrad City Exec. Bd 1990–91; Chair. Cttee on Finance, St Petersburg Mayor's Office 1992–94; First Deputy Mayor of St Petersburg, Head Dept of Finance, Mayor's Office, St Petersburg 1994–96; Deputy Head of Admin., Head Controlling Dept at Russian Presidency 1996–97; First Deputy Minister of Finance, Russian Fed. 1997–99, concurrently Deputy Man. BRD 1997–99; First Deputy Chair. Unified Power Systems of Russia (state co.) 1999–2000; Deputy Chair. of the Govt 2000–04, 2007–11 (resgnd); Minister of Finance 2000–11 (resgnd); named Finance Minister of the Year by Euromoney magazine 2010. *Leisure interests:* tennis, swimming, listening to music. *Address:* c/o Ministry of Finance, 109097 Moscow, ul. Ilyinka 9, Russia.

KUDROW, Lisa, BSc; American actress; b. 30 July 1963, Encino, Calif.; m. Michael Stern; one c.; ed Vassar Coll. *Television includes:* To the Moon Alice 1990, Murder in High Places 1991, Bob (series) 1992, Friends (series) 1994–2004, The Comeback (series) 2005, Web Therapy 2008–13. *Films include:* L.A. on $5 a Day 1989, Dance with Death 1991, The Unborn 1991, In the Heat of Passion 1992, In the Heat of Passion II: Unfaithful 1994, The Crazysitter 1995, Mother 1996, Romy and Michelle's High School Reunion 1997, Clockwatchers 1997, The Opposite of Sex 1998, Analyze This 1999, Hanging Up 2000, Lucky Numbers 2000, All Over the Guy 2001, Dr. Dolittle 2 (voice) 2001, Analyze That 2002, Bark 2002, Marci X 2003, Happy Endings 2005, Kabluey 2007, P.S. I Love You 2007, Powder Blue 2009, Hotel for Dogs 2009, Paper Man 2009, Bandslam 2009, Love and Other Impossible Pursuits 2009, Easy A 2010. *Address:* c/o PMK/HBH, 700 San Vicente Boulevard, Suite G 910, West Hollywood, CA 90069; POB 36849, Los Angeles, CA 90036-0849, USA (office).

KUDRYAVTSEV, Nikolay, PhD; Russian academic; *Rector, Moscow Institute of Physics and Technology;* b. 8 May 1950, Moscow; ed Moscow Inst. of Physics and Tech.; Asst, Dept of Molecular Physics, Moscow Inst. of Physics and Tech. 1977, Deputy Dean, Faculty of Molecular and Chemical Physics 1978–87, Dean 1987–88, Head of Dept of Molecular Physics 1988, Prof. 1990, Founder mem. Lab Pulse Tech. 1991, Rector, Moscow Inst. of Physics and Tech. 1997–; Dir Gen. JSC Phonon Defense Industry Ministry 1994; mem. Bd of Dirs Schlumberger 2007–; Corresponding mem. Russian Acad. of Sciences, Int. Acad. of Informatization; Laureate Award of the Council of Ministers 2001. *Achievements include:* holds ten patents. *Address:* Moscow Institute of Physics and Technology, 141700 Moscow, Dolgoprudny Institutskiy lane 9, Russia (office). *Telephone:* (495) 408-45-54 (office). *Fax:* (495) 408-42-54 (office). *Website:* www.mipt.ru (office).

KUDYBERDIYEV, Abibilla; Kyrgyzstani politician; *Minister of Defence;* Minister of Defence 2010–11, 2014–. *Address:* Ministry of Defence, 720001 Bishkek, Logvinenko 26, Kyrgyzstan (office). *Telephone:* (312) 66-18-04 (office). *Fax:* (312) 66-19-04 (office). *E-mail:* ud@bishkek.gov.kg (office). *Website:* www.mil.kg (office).

KUEHN, Ronald L., Jr; American energy industry executive; *Chairman, El Paso Corporation;* b. 1935; Pres. and CEO Sonat Inc. 1984–99, also Chair. 1986–99; Chair. (non-exec.), El Paso Corpn 1999–2000, Lead Dir 2002–03, Chair. 2003–, also CEO March–Sept. 2003; business consultant 2001–03; mem. Bd of Dirs AmSouth Bancorporation, Praxair Inc., Dun & Bradstreet Corpn. *Address:* El Paso Corporation, 1001 Louisiana Street, Houston, TX 77002, USA. *Telephone:* (713) 420–2600 (office). *Fax:* (713) 420–6030 (office). *Website:* www.elpaso.com (office).

KUFUOR, John Kofi Agyekum, KCB, MA; Ghanaian lawyer, business executive and fmr head of state; b. 8 Dec. 1938, Kumasi, Ashanti Region; m. Theresa Kufuor; five c.; ed Osei Tutu Boarding School, Prempeh Coll., Kumasi, Lincoln's Inn, London and Exeter Coll., Oxford, UK; called to Bar, Lincoln's Inn 1961; Clerk of Kumasi City Council; Council Rep., Constituent Ass. 1968–69; mem. Parl.; founding mem. Progress Party (PP) 1969, Popular Front Party (PFP) 1979, PFP Spokesman on Foreign Affairs 1979–82, Founding mem. New Patriotic Party (NPP) 1992–; Deputy Minister of Foreign Affairs 1969–72; arrested after mil. coup and imprisoned for 15 months 1972–73; Sec. for Local Govt 1982; returned to law practice; presidential cand. for New Patriotic Party 1996; Pres. of Ghana and C-in-C of Armed Forces 2001–09 (re-elected 2004); Chair. African Union Ass. 2007–08; UN Special Envoy on Climate Change 2013–; Hon. Fellow, Exeter Coll., Oxford, Liverpool John Moores Univ., UK; Grand Cordon of The Most Venerable Order of the Kts of the Pioneers (Liberia) 2008, Order of the Gold Star, World Fed. of Honorary Consuls 2008, Order of the House of Orange, state honours from several

countries, including Italy, Germany and Brazil; Dr hc (Univ. of Cape Coast, Ghana); Chatham House Prize 2008, World Food Prize (co-recipient) 2011. *Leisure interests:* table tennis, reading, soccer, films. *Address:* New Patriotic Party (NPP), C912/2 Duade Street, Kokomlemle, POB 3456, Accra-North, Ghana (office). *Telephone:* (21) 227951 (office). *Fax:* (21) 224418 (office). *E-mail:* npp@africanonline.com.gh (office).

KUHN, Gustav, DPhil; Austrian conductor, director, producer and composer; b. 28 Aug. 1945, Salzburg; s. of Friedrich Kuhn and Hilde Kuhn; m. Andrea Kuhn 1971; one s. one d.; ed Acads of Salzburg and Vienna and Univs of Salzburg and Vienna; advanced conducting studies under Bruno Maderna and Herbert von Karajan; professional conductor in Istanbul (three years), Enschede (Netherlands), Dortmund (prin. conductor) and Vienna; début at Vienna State Opera (Elektra) 1977, Munich Nat. Theatre (Così fan tutte) 1978, Covent Garden, London 1979, Glyndebourne, Munich Opera Festival and Salzburg Festival 1980, Chicago (Fidelio) 1981, Paris Opéra 1982, La Scala, Milan 1984, Arena di Verona (Masked Ball) 1986, Rossini Opera Festival, Pesaro 1987; Gen. Music Dir in Berne, Bonn and Rome; production début in Trieste (Fliegender Holländer) 1986; other projects include Parsifal, Naples 1988, Salome, Rome 1988, Don Carlos (French version) and Don Carlo (Italian) for 250th anniversary Teatro Reggio, Turin 1990; Artistic Dir Neue Stimmen (New Voices), Bertelsmann Foundation 1987–, Macerata Festival, Italy (productions of Così fan tutte and Don Giovanni) 1990/91, Marchigiana Philharmonic Orchestra (Dir-Gen. 2003–), Haydn Orchestra 2003–, Conservatorio di Milano Philharmonic Orchestra 2004; Founder and Pres. Accad. di Montegral 1992, Tyrolean Festival, Erl, Austria 1997–; Producer and Conductor Complete Ring Cycle of Richard Wagner, Tyrolean Festival, Erl 2003, 2004, 2005, 2007; First Prize, Int. Conducting Contest of Austrian TV and Broadcasting Corpn (ORF) 1969, Lilly Lehmann Medal (Mozarteum Foundation), Max Reinhardt Medal (Salzburg), Senator of Honour Award 'Lorenzo il Magnifico' (Florence) 1988. *Publication:* Aus Liebe zur Musik 1993. *Leisure interests:* sailing, motorcycling. *Address:* Winkl 25, 6343 Erl, Austria (office). *Telephone:* (5373) 8181. *Website:* www.tiroler-festspiele.at; www.gustavkuhn.at.

KUHN, Michael, LLB; film producer; ed Univ. of Cambridge; solicitor, Supreme Court 1974; lawyer, Denton, Hall and Burgin, London; legal adviser, Polygram UK, London 1974–78, Gen. Counsel, Polygram Int., London 1983–87, Sr Vice-Pres. 1987–93, Pres. Polygram Filmed Entertainment, Beverly Hills, Calif. 1991–93, fmr Exec. Vice-Pres. Polygram Holding Inc., New York, mem. Man. Bd Polygram NV, Pres. and CEO Polygram Filmed Entertainment, Beverly Hills; f. Qwerty Films, London. *Films produced include:* Red Rock West 1993, Being John Malkovich 1999, Wonderous Oblivion 2003, The Order 2003, Stage Beauty 2004, Kinsey 2004, I Heart Huckabees 2004, The Moguls 2005, Alien Autopsy 2006, Severance 2006, The Duchess 2008. *Address:* Qwerty Films, 42–44 Beak Street, London, W1F 9RH, England (office). *Telephone:* (20) 7440-5920 (office). *Fax:* (20) 7440-5959 (office).

KÜHNE, Gunther Albert Hermann, DrIur, LLM; German legal scholar and academic; *Director Emeritus, Institute for German and International Mining and Energy Law, Technical University, Clausthal;* b. 25 Aug. 1939, Gelsenkirchen; s. of Friedrich Kühne and Gertrud Kühne (née Belgard); m. Elvira Schulz 1992; ed Univ. of Cologne and Columbia Univ., New York; part-time legal adviser to German mining cos 1963–68; Research Asst Bochum Univ. Law School 1967–70; Sr Govt official, Ministry of Econs, Bonn 1971–74; Sr official German del. OECD, Paris 1972–73; Sr Govt official, Ministry of Justice, Bonn 1974–78; Lecturer Private Law, Private Int. and Comparative Law, Bochum Univ. 1971–79; Prof. of Mining and Energy Law, Dir Inst. for German and Int. Mining and Energy Law, Tech. Univ. Clausthal 1978–2007; Visiting Prof. Bergakademie Freiberg 1992, Tel-Aviv Univ. 1993–2003, Nanjing Univ. 2004, 2007; Ordinary mem. Braunschweig Soc. of Sciences 1994; Hon. Prof. of Law, Univ. of Göttingen 1986–. *Publications:* numerous books and articles on aspects of law, including Die Parteiautonomie im internationalen Erbrecht 1973, IPR-Gesetz-Entwurf (Private Int. Law Reform Draft) 1980, Memorandum on the State and Reform of German International Family Law 1980, Wandel und Beharren im Bergrecht (jtly) 1992, Rechtsfragen der Aufsuchung und Gewinnung von in Steinkohleflözen beisitzendem Methangas 1994, Gegenwartsprobleme des Bergrechts (jtly) 1995, Wettbewerb, Bestandsschutz, Umweltschutz (jtly) 1997, Bestandsschutz alten Bergwerkseigentums unter besonderer Berücksichtigung des Art. 14 Grundgesetz 1998, Braunkohlenplanung und bergrechtliche Zulassungsverfahren 1999, Das deutsche Berg- und Energierecht auf dem Wege nach Europa (jtly) 2002, Das neue Energierecht in der Bewährung (co-ed.) 2002, Berg- und Energierecht im Zugriff europäischer Regulierungstendenzen (ed.) 2004, Bergrecht zwischen Tradition und Moderne (co-ed.) 2010, Das deutsche Wirtschaftsrecht unter dem Einfluss des US-amerikanischen Rechts (jtly) 2011. *Leisure interest:* Jewish history (numerous publs). *Address:* Arnold-Sommerfeld-Strasse 6, 38678 Clausthal-Zellerfeld, Germany. *Telephone:* (5323) 723025. *Fax:* (5323) 722507. *E-mail:* gunther.kuehne@iber.tu-clausthal.de (office). *Website:* www.iber.tu-clausthal.de (office).

KÜHNL, Karel, Jr; DIur; Czech politician; b. 12 Sept. 1954, Prague; m. Daniela Kühnlová; one s. one d.; ed Charles Univ., Prague; freelance journalist in Australia 1978–87; ed. Radio Free Europe, Munich 1987–91; Econ. Adviser to Premier 1991–92, to Minister of Economics 1992–93; Amb. to UK 1993–97; MP for Freedom Union Party 1998–, Chair. 1999–2002; Minister of Industry and Trade 1997–98, of Defence 2004–06; Chair. of Freedom Union Club 1999–; Leader, Coalition Freedom Union Party–DEU, KDU–ČSL, ODA (after merger of Freedom Union Party and DEU Dec. 2001). *Leisure interests:* cycling, tennis. *Address:* c/o Ministry of Defence, Tychonova 1, 160 01 Prague 6, Czech Republic (office).

KUHNT, Dietmar, PhD; German business executive; b. 16 Nov. 1937, Wrocław (Breslau); m. 1966; two c.; ed Univs of Cologne and Freiburg; perm. legal adviser, Rheinisch-Westfälisches Elektrizitätswerk AG 1968; mem. Bd of Man. RWE Energie AG 1989, Chair. 1992–94; mem. Bd Man. RWE AG 1992–94, Chair. 1995–2003, mem. Supervisory Bd 2003–06, mem. Exec. Bd RWE Thames Water PLC; mem. Supervisory Bd Hochtief AG –2008, Allianz Versicherungs AG –2008, Dresdner Bank AG –2009, GEA Group AG (fmrly MG Technologies AG) –2011, TUI AG –2011 (Chair. 2009–11), BDO Deutsche Warentreuhand AG, GEA Group AG, Hapag-Lloyd, Hapag-Lloyd Holding AG (fmrly Hapag-Lloyd AG) 2010–, Heidelberger Druckmaschinen AG; mem. Bd of Dirs COMSTAR-United Tele-

Systems –2008. *Address:* c/o TUI AG, Postfach 610209, 30602 Hanover, Germany. *E-mail:* info@tui-group.com.

KUI, Gen. Fulin; Chinese army officer; b. Feb. 1938, Xinbin Co., Liaoning Prov.; joined CCP 1961; joined PLA Infantry School, Qiqihar 1956; served in combat units of Shenyang Mil. Region, successively promoted from platoon commdr to div. chief-of-staff; studied at PLA Mil. Acad. 1982; served as div. commdr then corps chief-of-staff; Deputy Dir and Dir Operation Dept, PLA Gen. Staff HQ 1985, Asst to Chief of Gen. Staff 1992–95, Deputy Chief PLA Gen. Staff 1995; mem. 15th CCP Cen. Cttee 1997–2002; rank of Gen. 2000. *Address:* c/o Ministry of National Defence, Jingshanqian Jie, Beijing, People's Republic of China.

KUIVASHEV, Yevgeny Vladimirovich; Russian government official; *Presidential Representative to the Urals Federal Okrug;* b. 16 March 1971, Khanty-Mansiysk region; m.; one s. one d.; ed Moscow Mil. Inst. of the Russian Border Guard Service, Yale Univ., USA, Tyumen State Univ.; mil. service 1989–91; various positions with Surgutneftegas 1991–97; worked in Pokovsky Town Council, Khanty-Mansiysk region 1997–2000, Head of Admin 2000–05; Lecturer in Law, Tyumen State Univ. 2000–05; Deputy Head, Federal Bailiff Service, Moscow 2005; head of Tobolsk City Admin 2005–07; Head of Tyumen City Admin 2007–11; Deputy Presidential Rep. to Urals Federal Okrug Jan.–Sept. 2011, Presidential Rep. Sept. 2011–. *Address:* Office of the Presidential Representative to the Urals Federal Okrug, 620031, Sverdlovsk obl., Yekaterinburg, pl. Oktyabrskaya 3, Russia (office). *Telephone:* (343) 277-18-96 (office). *E-mail:* support@uralfo.ru (office). *Website:* www.uralfo.ru (office).

KUJAT, Gen. (retd) Harald; German air force officer (retd); b. 1 March 1942, Mielke; m. Sabine Kujat (née Becker); three c.; ed Armed Forces and Command College Hamburg, NATO Defence Coll. Rome, Italy; Instructor in Non-commissioned Officer Training, Fed. Armed Forces, then Platoon Leader, Co. Exec. Officer and Personnel Officer 1959–72; with Fed. Ministry of Defence, positions included ADC to Minister 1972–75, Mil. Asst 1977–78, Armed Forces Staff Br. Chief (Operational Doctrines, AF) 1978–80, Br. Chief (Nuclear and Global Arms Control) 1990–92, Deputy Chief of Staff (Mil. Policy and Strategy) 1995, Dir Policy and Advisory Staff to Minister 1998–2000; 20th Gen. Staff Course (AF), Bundeswehr Command and Staff Coll. 1975–77; Section Chief (A3a), AF Support Command N 1977; Commdr Second Bn AF Training Regt 1985–88; Section Chief, Staff German Mil. Rep., NATO Mil. Cttee, Brussels 1988–90, Dir of Staff and Deputy Mil. Rep. 1992–95, Asst Dir Int. Mil. Staff (Plans and Policy) and Deputy Dir IMS, NATO 1996–98, Chair. NATO Mil. Cttee 2002–05 (retd); currently Chair. Advisory Council, Network Centric Operations Industry Consortium; Dir IFOR Co-ordination Centre (ICC), Supreme HQ Allied Powers in Europe (SHAPE), Belgium 1996; Chief of Staff, Fed. Armed Forces 2000–02; rank of Lt 1968, First Lt 1968, Capt. 1971, Maj. 1974, Lt-Col 1979, Col 1988, Brig.-Gen. 1992, Maj.-Gen. 1995, Lt-Gen. 1998, Gen. 2000; Gold Cross of Honour of the Bundeswehr, Commdr's Cross of the Order of Merit of the FRG, Commdr Ordre Nat. de la Légion d'honneur France, Commdr's Cross of Merit Poland, Order of the Cross of the Eagle 1st class Estonia; Tidal Flood Memorial Medal 1962. *Publications:* numerous works on int. security and military policy. *Leisure interests:* photography, horse riding. *Address:* c/o Advisory Council, Network Centric Operations Industry Consortium, 1209 Orange Street, Wilmington, DE 19801, USA. *Website:* www.ncoic.org.

KUKAN, Eduard, LLD; Slovak politician and diplomatist; b. 26 Dec. 1939, Trnovec nad Váhom, W Slovakia; m.; one s. one d.; ed Moscow Inst. of Int. Relations, Charles Univ., Prague; joined Czechoslovakian Foreign Service 1964, mem. Africa Dept 1964–68, various posts at Embassy in Zambia 1968–73, mem. Secr. of Minister for Foreign Affairs 1973–77, Minister Counsellor, Embassy in USA 1977–81, Head Dept of Sub-Saharan Africa 1981–85, Amb. to Ethiopia 1985–88, Perm. Rep. of Czechoslovakia to UN, New York 1990–93, of Slovakia 1993–94; Deputy to Nat. Council of Slovak Repub. (Parl.) 1994–, Minister of Foreign Affairs March–Dec. 1994, mem. Foreign Relations Cttee 1994–; mem. Exec. Cttee Democratic Union of Slovakia 1994–, Chair. 1997–98; Vice-Chair. Slovak Democratic Coalition (SDK) 1998–; Minister of Foreign Affairs 1998–2006; UN Special Envoy for the Balkans 1999–2001; Rep. to Parl. Ass., Council of Europe 2006–; mem. Advisory Bd Global Panel; Hon. LLD (Upsala Coll., NJ, USA) 1993. *Leisure interests:* tennis, theatre. *Address:* National Council of the Slovak Republic, 812 80 Bratislava, Namestie A. Dubceka 1, Slovakia (office). *Telephone:* (2) 5972-2501 (office). *E-mail:* eduard_kukan@nrsr.sk (office). *Website:* www.nrsr .sk (office).

KUKES, Simon Grigorievich, MSc; American (b. Russian) business executive; b. 1946, Moscow; ed Moscow Chemical-Tech. Inst. (Mendeleyev Inst.), Rice Univ., Houston, Tex.; engineer, Titan Production Co. 1969–70; mem. of staff USSR Acad. of Sciences 1970–77; emigrated from USSR to Tex., USA 1977; Tech. Dir Philips Petroleum 1980s; Tech. Dir then Vice-Pres. in charge of devt in Commonwealth of Ind. States, Amoco 1991–96; Dir Planning and Devt, Yukos (largest oil refinery in Russia) 1996–98, Chair. and CEO Tyumen Oil Co. (TNK), Russia 1998–2003, helped engineer merger between TNK and BP 2002; Chair. and CEO Yukos Corpn 2003–04; CEO CJSC Samara-Nafta (exploration and production co in Volga-Urals) 2005–13 (co. acquired by NK Lukoil OAO 2013); mem. Bd of Dirs Amarin Corpn plc 2005; mem. Council of Energy, Marine Transportation and Public Policy, Columbia Univ.

KULAKOV, Anatoly Vasilyevich, DPhysMathSci; Russian scientist; b. 15 July 1938; m.; one s.; ed Leningrad Polytech. Inst.; researcher, Sr Engineer, Deputy Dean, Leningrad Polytechnic Inst. 1962–79; Scientific Sec., Deputy Chair., First Deputy Chair., Council on Science and Tech., USSR Council of Ministers 1979–90; Dir-Gen. Russian Industrialists and Entrepreneurs Union from 1991; Vice-Pres. Moscow Econ. Union from 1997; mem. Bd Russian Bank of Reconstruction and Devt from 1998; Corresp. mem. USSR (now Russian) Acad. of Sciences 1984; main research in theory of electromagnetic interactions in systems of charged particles, plasma and solids. *Address:* c/o Russian Academy of Sciences, 119991 Moscow, Leninsky prosp. 32A, Russia. *Telephone:* (495) 938-03-09. *Fax:* (495) 954-33-20. *E-mail:* info@ras.ru. *Website:* www.ras.ru.

KULCZYK, Jan, PhD; Polish business executive; *President of the Supervisory Board, Kulczyk Investments;* b. 6 June 1950, Bydgoszcz; m. Grazyna Kulczyk; two c.; ed Adam Mickiewicz Univ., Acad. of Economy, Poznań; researcher, Western Studies Inst., Polish Acad. of Sciences (PAN) 1974–; employee in family business

Kulczyk Aussenhandelgesellschaft, Germany; Founder Interkulpol co. and other cos 1981–91, merged into Kulczyk Holding SA 1991 (now Kulczyk Investments), currently Pres. Supervisory Bd; Pres. Polish Council of Business 1995–97, Vice-Pres. 1997–; Co-founder and Pres. Polish-German Chamber of Industry and Commerce 1995–98, Vice-Pres. 1998–2002, Pres. 2002, now Hon. Chair.; Chair. Green Cross International 2007–, Polish - Ukrainian Chamber of Commerce 2005–07; Co-founder Polish Business Roundtable; Founder EU - Ukraine Commercial Council, Brussels; Pres. Adam Mickiewicz Univ. Council; f. CEED Inst. 2010; mem. Nat. Museum Council, Church Commercial Council, Int. Govs Council, Peres Centre for Peace 2000; Order of Polonia Restituta, Order of Saint Stanisław, Order of Saint Bridget; Golden Medal of Saint Paul Fathers, Kisiel Award. *Address:* Kulczyk Investments, 65, boulevard Grande Duchesse Charlotte, 1331 Luxembourg (office). *Website:* kulczykinvestments.com (office).

KULHÁNEK, Vratislav; Czech economist and engineer; *Chairman of the Supervisory Board, Škoda Auto AS;* b. 20 Nov. 1943, Plzeň; m. Marie Kulhánek 1944; two d.; ed Univs of Prague and Pardubice; Dir Motor Jirkov, České Budějovice 1991–92, Robert Bosch, České Budějovice; Chair. Bd Škoda Auto Mladá Boleslav 1998–, Chair. Supervisory Bd 2004–; Pres. Asscn of Car Industry; Chair. ICC 2001–, CIOD; Dr hc Ing.; Prize of Czech–German Understanding, Germany 2000, Man. for the 21st Century 2000. *Leisure interests:* tennis, cars, golf. *Address:* Škoda Auto A.S., Representative Offices, Masarykovo Nabrezi 28, Prague, 1 (office); Srubec 346, 370 06 České Budějovice, Czech Republic (home). *Telephone:* 221907262 (office). *Fax:* 221907297 (office). *E-mail:* vratislav.kulhanek@skoda -auto.cz (office); kulhanek.cb@volny.cz (home). *Website:* www.skoda-auto.cz (office).

KULICHKOV, Alyaksandr N.; Belarusian politician; fmr Minister of Trade; Head of Property Man. Directorate, Office of the Pres. 2005–. *Address:* c/o Office of the President, vul. K. Marksa 38, Dom Urada, 220016 Minsk, Belarus (office).

KULIK, Gennady Vasilyevich; Russian politician; b. 20 Jan. 1935, Zhekomskoye, Pskov region; m.; one s.; ed Leningrad State Univ.; researcher, Head of Dept, Siberian Div. of All-Union Inst. of Agricultural Econ. 1957–65; First Deputy Head, Novosibirsk Regional Dept of Agric. 1965; Deputy Head, Chief Dept of Planning and Econs, Ministry of Agric. RSFSR 1965–86; First Deputy Chair., RSFSR State Cttee of Agric. and Industry 1986–90; First Deputy Chair., RSFSR Council of Ministers, Minister of Agric. and Food 1990–91; USSR Peoples' Deputy 1990–92; adviser to Dir, Inex-Interexport (Moscow) 1993; mem. Exec. Bd Russian Agrarian Party, Deputy Chair. Russian Agrarian Union; mem. State Duma; Deputy Chair. Cttee on Budget, Taxes, Banks and Finance 1993–98; Deputy Chair. Govt of Russian Fed. 1998–99; mem. State Duma (Parl.) (Otechestvo-All Russia faction, Yedinaya Rossiya faction) 1999–2003, re-elected 2003–, mem. Cttee on Budget and Taxes; Merited Economist of Russia. *Address:* State Duma, Okhotny ryad 1, 103265 Moscow, Russia. *Telephone:* (495) 292-62-23 (office). *Fax:* (495) 292-69-66 (office).

KULIKOV, Army Gen. Anatoly Sergeyevich, DEconSc; Russian politician and military officer; *Deputy Chairman, Committee on Security, State Duma;* b. 4 Sept. 1946, Aigursky Apanasenkovsky, Stavropol Region; m.; two s. one d.; ed Vladikavkaz Mil. Command School, USSR Ministry of Internal Affairs, M. Frunze Mil. Acad., Mil. Acad. of Gen. Staff; numerous mil. postings including Commdr of Internal Troops 1992–95; Head United Grouping of Fed. Troops in Chechen Repub. Jan.–July 1995; Minister of Internal Affairs 1995–98; Deputy Chair. of Russian Govt 1996–98; mem. Security Council of Russian Fed. 1995–98; mem. State Duma (Parl.) 1999–, Deputy Chair., Cttee on Security 2004–; Chair. Cen. Council Ratniki Otechestva (Warriors of the Fatherland) Movt; Chair. Council on Econ. Security, Russian Acad. of Social Sciences; Chair. World Anticriminal and Antiterrorism Forum –2001; mem. Acad. of Mil. Sciences, Acad. of Natural Sciences; Order for Services to the Fatherland (Third Degree), Order for Personal Courage, Order for Service to the Motherland in the Armed Forces of the USSR, 3rd Class, Order of Honour; more than 30 medals. *Publications:* Chechen Node 2000, Heavy Stars 2002; numerous articles in journals and newspapers. *Leisure interests:* hunting, fishing, shooting, woodworking. *Address:* 1 Okhotny ryad, 103265 Moscow, Russia (office). *Telephone:* (495) 692-97-45 (office); (495) 202-15-65 (office); (495) 290-15-66 (office). *Fax:* (495) 692-74-32 (office); (495) 290-46-28 (office). *E-mail:* askulikov@ duma.gov.ru (office).

KULKA, Konstanty Andrzej; Polish violinist; *Professor, Warsaw Academy of Music;* b. 5 March 1947, Gdańsk; m.; two d.; ed Higher State School of Music, Gdańsk; Prof., Acad. of Music, Warsaw 1994–; participant in two music competitions: Paganini Competition, Genoa 1964, Diploma and Special Prize; Music Competition, Munich 1966 (1st Prize); many gramophone, radio and TV recordings; soloist with Nat. Philharmonic Orchestra, Warsaw 1984–; Gold Cross of Merit, Commdr's Cross, Order of Polonia Restituta; Minister of Culture and Arts Prize 1969, 1973, Minister of Foreign Affairs Prize 1977, Pres. of Radio and TV Cttee Prize 1978, Prize Winner, 33rd Grand Prix du Disque Int. Sound Festival, Paris 1981. *Performances:* since 1967 has given some 1,500 concerts all over the world and participates in many int. festivals including Lucerne, Prague, Bordeaux, Berlin, Granada, Barcelona, Brighton; concerts with Berlin Philharmonic Orchestra, Chicago Symphony Orchestra, Minneapolis Orchestra, London Symphony Orchestra, Konzertgebouw Amsterdam Orchestra, English Chamber Orchestra and others. *Recordings include:* Antonio Vivaldi Cztery pory roku (The Four Seasons), Szymanowski: Violin Concertos Nos. 1 & 2 1997, Mozart: Best Of 2000, Karlowicz: Tone Poems/Violin Concerto 2002, Paderewski: Violin & Piano Works 2003, Penderecki: Violin Concertos Nos. 1 & 2 2003. *Leisure interests:* collecting gramophone records, bridge, collecting interesting kitchen recipes. *Address:* Filharmonia Narodowa, ul. Jasna 5, 00-950 Warsaw, Poland. *Telephone:* (605) 194753; (22) 5517203. *E-mail:* konstanty.kulka@wp.pl (office).

KULLMAN, Ellen J., BSc, MA; American business executive; *Chairman and CEO, E. I. du Pont de Nemours and Co. (DuPont);* b. 22 Jan. 1956, Wilmington, Del.; d. of Joseph Jamison and Margaret Jamison; m. Michael Kullman; twin s. one d.; ed Tower Hill School, Wilmington, Tufts Univ., Northwestern Univ.; fmrly with General Electric; Marketing Man. medical imaging business, DuPont 1988, later Business Dir x-ray film business, Global Business Dir electronic imaging, Printing & Publishing, Global Business Dir White Pigment & Mineral Products 1994, Vice-Pres. and Gen. Man. 1995, Head DuPont Safety Resources 1998, Bio-Based

Materials 1999, Group Vice-Pres. and Gen. Man. 2000, Head DuPont Flooring Systems and DuPont Surfaces 2001, Group Vice-Pres. Safety & Protection 2002–06, Exec. Vice-Pres. Safety & Protection, Coatings and Color, Marketing and Sales, and Safety and Sustainability 2006–08, Pres. and Dir Oct.–Dec. 2008, CEO and Dir E. I. du Pont de Nemours and Co. Jan. 2009–, Chair. Dec. 2009–; mem. Bd of Dirs United Technologies Corpn; Co-Chair. Nat. Acad. of Eng Cttee on Changing the Conversation: From Research to Action; mem. US-India CEO Forum, Exec. Cttee The Business Council 2011–12, Exec. Cttee SCI-America; mem. Bd of Trustees Tufts Univ., Bd of Overseers Tufts Univ. School of Eng; Aiming High Award 2004, ranked by Fortune magazine amongst the 50 Most Powerful Women in Business in the US (46th) 2005, (21st) 2006, (25th) 2007, (15th) 2008, (seventh) 2009–10, (fourth) 2011, (fifth) 2012, ranked by Forbes magazine amongst The World's 100 Most Powerful Women (86th) 2008, (seventh) 2009, (18th) 2010, (38th) 2011, (62nd) 2012, (42nd) 2013, Sellinger's Business Leader of the Year. *Address:* E. I. du Pont de Nemours and Co., 1007 Market Street, Wilmington, DE 19898, USA (office). *Telephone:* (302) 774-1000 (office). *Website:* www.dupont.com (office).

KULLMANN FIVE, Karin Cecilie (Kaci) (see FIVE, Karin Cecilie (Kaci) Kullmann).

KULONGOSKI, Theodore Ralph (Ted), BA, JD; American politician, lawyer and judge (retd); b. 5 Nov. 1940, Washington Co., Mo.; m. Mary Oberst; three c.; ed Univ. of Missouri; served in US Marine Corps; fmr truck driver and steelworker; called to Bar of Ore., Mo., US Dist Court, Ore., US Court of Appeals (9th Circuit); Legal Counsel, Oregon House of Reps 1973–74, Rep. from Lane Co. 1974–77; Founding Sr Partner, Kulongoski, Durham, Drummonds & Colombo 1974–87; mem. Ore. State Senate 1978–83; Dir Oregon Dept of Insurance & Finance 1987–91; Deputy Dist Attorney, Multnomah Co. 1992; Attorney Gen., State of Oregon 1993–97; Justice, Oregon Supreme Court 1997–2001; Gov. of Ore. 2003–11; Chair. Juvenile Justice Task Force 1994, Gov.'s Comm. on Organized Crime; mem. Lane Co. Bar Asscn, Missouri Bar Asscn, Oregon State Bar Asscn; Democrat. *Leisure interest:* fly-fishing. *Address:* c/o Office of the Governor, 160 Capitol Building, 900 Court Street NE, Salem, OR 97301-4047, USA.

KULOV, Feliks Sharshenbayevich; Kyrgyzstani politician; *Chairman, Dignity (Ar-Namys);* b. 29 Oct. 1948, Frunze (now Bishkek); m. 1st Nailya Bayaliyeva; two d.; m. 2nd Fatima Kulova; two d.; ed Omsk Higher School of the Ministry of Internal Affairs of the USSR (now Omsk Judicial Inst.), Acad. of the Ministry of Internal Affairs of the USSR, Moscow; police officer in Frunze, operational platoon, Internal Affairs Bd 1966–67; Insp., Dept for Combating Narcotics, Sr Insp. in Dept A, Criminal Investigation Dept, Ministry of Internal Affairs, Kyrgyz SSR 1971–75, Head of Dept 1978–80; Deputy Head of Internal Affairs Bd, Talas Oblast Exec. Cttee 1980–84, Head of Internal Affairs Bd 1984–87; First Deputy Minister of Internal Affairs, Kyrgyz SSR 1987–91; Mil. Commdr in Frunze 1990; mem. of Presidential Council of Kyrgyz SSR 1990–91; unsuccessful cand. for Chair. of Supreme Soviet of Kyrgyz SSR Dec. 1990; resgnd party membership following coup attempt in Moscow 1991; Minister of Internal Affairs, Kyrgyz SSR/Repub. of Kyrgyzstan 1991–92; Vice-Pres. of Kyrgyzstan 1992–93; investigated on charges of corruption 1993; resgnd following scandals surrounding Seabeco Affair 1993; Gov. of Chui Oblast 1993–97; Head of State Admin (Gov.), Chui Oblast 1993–97; Minister of Nat. Security 1997–98; Acting Mayor of Bishkek April–July 1998, Mayor of Bishkek 1998–99; Founding Chair. Dignity (Ar-Namys) Party 1999–; withdrew candidacy at presidential election because of his refusal to take Kyrgyz language test Feb. 2000; arrested on charges of abuse of office as Mayor of Bishkek 22 March 2000, found not guilty and released; cand. for presidential elections Aug. 2000 but candidacy withdrawn by Cen. Electoral Comm. Oct. 2000; sentenced to seven years' imprisonment with confiscation of property, stripped of rank of Gen.-Lt for abuse of office as Minister of Internal Affairs Jan. 2001; elected Chair. of People's Congress of Kyrgyzstan (opposition alliance) Nov. 2001; sentenced to ten years' imprisonment and prohibited from working for the Govt and for organs of local self-admin for a further three years following his release; found guilty on charges of embezzlement of state property while Gov. of Chui Oblast May 2002, freed from prison during 'Tulip Revolution'; named by Jogorku Kenesh (Supreme Council) "Co-ordinator of all Security Institutions", stepped down from this position once order had been restored in Bishkek 24 March 2005, Supreme Court annulled all charges against him April 2005; Acting First Deputy Prime Minister May 2005, Acting Prime Minister Aug. 2005, Prime Minister Sept. 2005–19 Dec. 2006 (resgnd), re-apptd Acting Prime Minister 19 Dec. 2006–29 Jan. 2007; Co-founder and Chair. United Front For A Worthy Future For Kyrgyzstan Feb. 2007–; charged with organizing mass disturbances in April 2007; Head of Directorate for Devt of Small and Light Energy Resources 2008–09, Dir of that Directorate at Cen. Agency for Devt, Investment and Innovation 2009–10; Head of interim Council for Social Security May 2010; Deputy of Jogorku Kenesh 2010–; awarded title of Gen.-Maj. by Pres. of USSR 1991, awarded title of Gen.-Lt by Pres. of Kyrgyzstan 1997; Dank, 1000th anniversary of Manas, Badge of Honour. *Publication:* Na perevale (On the Crossing—memoirs) 2009. *Address:* Dignity (Ar-Namys), 720033 Bishkek, Pushkin 135, Kyrgyzstan (office). *Telephone:* (312) 61-04-07 (office). *E-mail:* ar -namys@mail.kg (office). *Website:* www.ar-namys.org (office).

KULUKUNDIS, Sir Eddie, Kt, OBE, FRSA; British fmr business executive and theatre producer; b. 20 April 1932, London; s. of the late George Elias Kulukundis and Eugenie Diacakis; m. Susan Hampshire 1981; ed Collegiate School, New York, Salisbury School, Conn. and Yale Univ., USA; mem. Baltic Exchange 1959–; mem. Lloyds 1964–95, mem. Council 1983–89; Dir Rethymnis & Kulukundis Ltd 1964–, London & Overseas Freighters 1980–85, 1989–97; Chair. Knightsbridge Theatrical Productions Ltd 1970–2000; Chair. Ambassadors Theatre Group 1992–2009; Trustee, Sports Aid Trust 1986–; mem. Exec. Cttee Royal Shakespeare Theatre 1977–2003, Royal Shakespeare Theatre Trust 1969 (Vice-Chair. 1983–), Gov. Royal Shakespeare Theatre 1977–2003; Vice-Pres. Traverse Theatre Club; Dir Hampstead Theatre Ltd 1969–2004; mem. Bd of Man. Soc. of London Theatre 1973–2003, Hon. Vice-Pres. Soc. of London Theatre 2003–; Vice-Pres. UK Athletics 1998–2003. *London productions include:* (some jtly): Enemy 1969, The Happy Apple, Poor Horace, The Friends, How the Other Half Loves, Tea Party and the Basement (double bill), The Wild Duck 1970, After Haggerty, Hamlet, Charley's Aunt, Straight Up 1971, London Assurance, Journey's End 1972; Small Craft Warnings, A Private Matter, Dandy Dick 1973, The Waltz of the Toreadors, Life

Class, Pygmalion, Play Mas, The Gentle Hook 1974, A Little Night Music, Entertaining Mr Sloane, The Gay Lord Quex, What the Butler Saw, Travesties, Lies, The Seagull, A Month in the Country, A Room with a View, Too True to be Good, The Bed Before Yesterday 1975, Dimetos, Banana Ridge, Wild Oats 1976, Candida, Man and Superman, Once a Catholic 1977, Privates on Parade, Gloo Joo 1978, Bent, Outside Edge, Last of the Red Hot Lovers 1979, Beecham, Born in the Gardens 1980, Tonight at 8.30, Steaming, Arms and the Man 1981, Steafel's Variations 1982, Messiah, Pack of Lies 1983, Of Mice and Men, The Secret Diary of Adrian Mole Aged 13³⁄₄ 1984, Camille 1985, The Cocktail Party 1986, Curtains 1987, Separation, South Pacific, Married Love, Over My Dead Body 1989, Never the Sinner 1990, The King and I, Carmen Jones 1991, Noel & Gertie, Slip of the Tongue, Shades, Annie Get Your Gun, Making it Better 1992, The Prime of Miss Jean Brodie 1994, Neville's Island 1994, The Killing of Sister George 1995. *New York productions include:* (jtly): How the Other Half Loves 1971, Sherlock Holmes, London Assurance 1974, Travesties 1975, The Merchant 1977, Once a Catholic 1979.

KULUMBEGOV, Domenti Sardionovich; Georgian civil servant and politician; *Acting Prime Minister, 'Republic of South Ossetia';* b. 4 Jan. 1955, Thinala, Gori dist, Georgian SSR, USSR; ed South Ossetian State Pedagogical Inst., Modern Humanitarian Acad., North Caucasian Acad. of Public Admin, Rostov-on-Don; worked in trans-shipment base tunnel squad, Tbiltonnelstroy, Tskhinvali 1978–79; Instructor, Head of Group, Head of South Ossetian Regional Cttee of Komsomol of Georgia, Tskhinvali 1980–83; First Sec., Komsomol CC Tskhinvali 1983–85; First Sec., South Ossetian Regional Cttee of Komsomol of Georgia 1985–88; Head of South Ossetian Regional Cttee of CP Party of Georgia, Tskhinvali 1988–91; Chief Insp., Head of Dept, Deputy Dir, First Deputy Head of Migration Service of North Ossetia-Alania Vladikavkaz 1992–2000, Deputy Head of Directorate of Immigration, Ministry of Internal Affairs, RNO-Alania Vladikavkaz 2000–06, Head of Directorate 2006; Head of Dept of Domestic Policy Admin 2006; later Head of North Ossetia-Alania and the Govt of 'Republic of North Ossetia-Alania'; Deputy Prime Minister, 'Republic of South Ossetia' 2009–12, Acting Prime Minister Jan. 2014–; Ind.; Medal 'For Valour'. *Address:* Office of the Prime Minister of the 'Republic of South Ossetia', 100001 Tskhinvali, ul. Khetgurova 1, South Ossetia, Georgia (office). *Telephone:* (9974) 45-00-01 (office). *Fax:* (9974) 45-47-63 (office). *E-mail:* ospress@yandex.ru (office).

KUM, Dongwha, BS, MS, PhD; South Korean scientist, academic and research institute director; *Endowed Chair Research Scientist, Korea Institute of Science and Technology;* b. 15 Dec. 1951, Okcheon; m. Dr Eun-Ae Kim; two d.; ed Seoul Nat. Univ., Stanford Univ., USA; lab. engineer, GM Korea Incheon 1975–78; Postdoctoral Research Fellow, Stanford Univ. 1984–85; mem. staff, Korea Inst. of Science and Tech. (KIST) 1985–, Pres. KIST 2006–09, Endowed Chair Research Scientist 2009–; Council mem., Nat. Science and Tech. Council 2007, 2010; Exec. Vice-Pres., Nat. Acad. of Eng, Korea 2010–; Pres. Korean Inst. of Metals and Materials (KIMM) 2008; mem. American Soc. for Metals 1980–, Materials Research Soc. 1985–, Korea Soc. of Microscopy 1986 (Pres. 2005–06), Minerals, Metals and Materials Soc. 1990–; Lecturer, Korea Advanced Inst. of Science and Tech., Seoul Nat. Univ., Yonsei Univ., Hanyang Univ., Ajou Univ., Ulsan Univ.; Science and Tech. Medal (Doyackjang) 2005; Nat. Scholarship for advanced studies in a foreign country 1978–, Prime Minister's Award 1986, Recognition for Distinguished Tech. Service, Korean Air Force 1996, Accomplishment Award (Seojungsang), KIMM 2002. *Publications:* two books (ed.), 47 scientific papers, 45 presentations in tech. meetings, seven patents, 30 R&D reports. *Address:* Korea Institute of Science and Technology, 39-1 Hawolgok-dong, Wolsong-gil 5, Seongbuk-gu, Seoul 136-791, Republic of Korea (office). *Telephone:* (2) 958-5455 (office). *Fax:* (2) 958-5449 (office). *E-mail:* dwkum@kist.re.kr (office). *Website:* www.kist.re.kr (office).

KUMA, Kengo; Japanese architect and academic; *Principal, Kengo Kuma and Associates;* b. 8 Aug. 1954, Kanagawa; s. of Hiroko Kuma and Toma Kuma; m.; one s.; ed Univ. of Tokyo; Visiting Scholar, Columbia Univ., USA 1985–86; f. Spatial Design Studio 1987; f. Kengo Kuma & Assocs 1990; Visiting Prof. Keio Univ. 1998, Prof. 2001–; AIA Benedictus Award 1997, Architectural Inst. of Japan Award 1997, Int. Stone Architecture Award 2001. *Publications:* 10 Houses 1990, Introduction to Architecture – History and Ideology 1994, Catastrophe of Architectural Desire 1994, Anti Object 2000. *Address:* Kengo Kuma and Associates, 2-24-8 BY-CUBE 2F, Minamiaoyama, Minato-ku, Tokyo 107-0062 (office); 37-7-301 Yaraicho Shinjuku-ku, Tokyo 162-0805, Japan (home). *Telephone:* (3) 3401-7721 (office); (3) 3235-7784 (home). *Fax:* (3) 3401-7778 (office); (3) 3268-0928 (home). *E-mail:* kuma@ba2.so-net.ne.jp (office). *Website:* kkaa.co.jp (office).

KUMACHEVA, Eugenia, MSc, PhD, FRSC; Canadian (b. Russian) chemist and academic; *University Professor of Chemistry, University of Toronto;* ed Inst. of Chemical Tech. (now Tech. Univ.), USSR, Inst. of Physical Chem., USSR (now Russian) Acad. of Sciences; joined Dept of Chem., Moscow State Univ.; Postdoctoral Fellow, Lab. of Prof. Jacob Klein, Weizmann Inst. of Science, Israel 1991–94; joined group of Prof. Mitchel Winnik, Dept of Chem., Univ. of Toronto 1995, Asst Prof. of Chem. 1996–2001, Assoc. Prof. 2001–05, Prof. 2005–13, Univ. Prof. 2013–; sabbatical leave at Harvard Univ., USA 2002; Visiting Prof., Univ. of Oxford, UK 2003, Université Louis Pasteur, Strasbourg, France 2006, Moscow State Univ. 2009, Univ. of Cambridge, UK 2010, Univ. of Bayreuth, Germany 2011; mem. Advisory Bd Max Planck Inst. for Polymer Research, Germany, Waterloo Inst. of Nanotechnology, Advanced Science Inst. (RIKEN), Japan, Brookhaven Nat. Lab., USA, Triangle Materials Science and Engineering Center, USA; Minerva Foundation Fellowship (Germany) 1992, Imperial Coll. Visiting Fellowship (UK) 1994, Premier Research Excellence Award (Canada) 1999, Int. Chorafas Foundation Award 2000, Canada Research Chair in Advanced Polymer Materials/Tier 2 2002, Schlumberger Scholarship, Univ. of Oxford 2003, Clara Benson Award (CSC) 2004, Macromolecular Science and Eng CIC Award 2005, Canada Research Chair in Advanced Polymer Materials/Tier 1 2006, E. Gordon Young Lecturer, Chemical Inst. of Canada 2007, L'ORÉAL-UNESCO Award for Women in Science (N America) 2009, Connaught Innovation Award, Connaught Foundation 2011, Humboldt Research Award, Alexander von Humboldt Foundation (Germany) 2012, Inventor of the Year, Univ. of Toronto 2012. *Publications:* numerous papers in professional journals on studies of self-assembly and non-equilibrium phenomena in polymer systems, especially polymers at surfaces and interfaces, devt of advanced polymer materials, and convection in polymeric liquids. *Address:* Room LM 627, Department of Chemistry, University of Toronto, 80 St George Street, Toronto, ON M5S 3H6, Canada (office). *Telephone:* (416) 978-3576 (office). *Fax:* (416) 978-3576 (office). *E-mail:* ekumache@chem.utoronto.ca (office). *Website:* www.chem.utoronto.ca/staff/EK (office).

KUMAKURA, Sadatake; Japanese pharmaceuticals distribution executive; *Representative Director and Chairman, Medipal Holdings Corporation;* fmr Pres. and CEO Kuraya Sanseido Inc., Rep. Dir, Pres. and CEO Mediceo Paltac Holdings Co. Ltd (name changed to Medipal Holdings Corpn following separation of prescription pharmaceutical wholesale business 2009; Kuraya Sanseido Inc. took over prescription pharmaceutical wholesale business, merged with Senshu Yakuhin Co. Ltd, Ushioda Kuraya Sanseido Inc., Yamahiro Kuraya Sanseido Inc., Heisei Yakuhin Co. Ltd and Izutsu Kuraya Sanseido Inc. and changed its corp. name to Mediceo Corpn) 2004–12, Rep. Dir and Chair. 2012–. *Address:* Medipal Holdings Corporation, 2-7-15, Yaesu, Chuo-ku, Tokyo 104-8461, Japan (office). *Telephone:* (3) 3517-5800 (office). *Fax:* (3) 3517-5011 (office). *E-mail:* info@medipal .co.jp (office). *Website:* www.medipal.co.jp (office).

KUMALO, Dumisani Shadrack, MA; South African journalist and diplomatist; *Special Envoy to the Great Lakes Region;* b. 16 Sept. 1947; m. (divorced); one s.; ed Univ. of South Africa, Indiana Univ., USA; reporter for Golden City Post 1967–79; feature writer Drum magazine 1969–70; political reporter Sunday Times, Johannesburg 1970–76; Marketing Exec. Officer, Total Oil Co. 1976–77; in exile 1977; Int. Educ. Program Co-ordinator, Phelps Stokes Fund, New York 1978–80; Projects Dir Africa Fund and American Cttee on Africa 1980–97; Dir of US Desk, Dept of Foreign Affairs 1997–99; Perm. Rep. to UN, New York 1999–2009; Special Envoy to the Great Lakes Region 2009–. *Address:* Office of the Special Envoy to the Great Lakes Region, Ministry of International Relations and Co-operation, Union Bldgs, East Wing, 1 Government Ave, Arcadia, Pretoria 0002, South Africa (office). *Telephone:* (12) 3510002 (office). *Fax:* (12) 3231502 (office). *E-mail:* minister@ foreign.gov.za (office). *Website:* www.dfa.gov.za (office).

KUMAR, Ashwani, BA, LLB, MPhil; Indian lawyer and politician; *Governor of Nagaland;* b. 26 Oct. 1952, Delhi; s. of the late Prabodh Chandra and Adarsh Kumari; m. Madhu Kumar 1975; one s. one d.; ed St Stephen's Coll., Delhi, Univ. of Delhi, Jawaharlal Nehru Univ., New Delhi; Sec., Gurdaspur Dist Congress Cttee, Punjab 1976; Organizing Sec., Punjab Pradesh Congress Cttee 1986; Additional Solicitor-Gen. of India 1990; fmr Sr Advocate, Supreme Court of India; mem. All-India Congress Cttee 1990–2011, Spokesperson 1999–2000; mem. Rajya Sabha (upper house of Parl.) from Punjab 2002–; Union Cabinet Minister of State for Industry 2006–09, for Planning, Parl. Affairs, Science and Tech. and Earth Science 2011–12, Minister of Law and Justice 2012–13; Gov. of Nagaland 2013–, also of Manipur July–Dec. 2013; mem. Public Accounts Cttee 2009; fmr Visiting Scholar, Centre for Strategic and Int. Studies, Washington, DC; mem. numerous int. dels including to World Econ. Forum, Davos 2007 and 2012; accompanying Minister to Pres. of India on several int. state visits; Hon. LLD (Punjab Univ.) 2004. *Publications include:* Law, Ideas and Ideology in Politics: Perspectives of an Activist 2003; numerous articles in newspapers and magazines on law, econ. reforms, elections, democracy, int. affairs. *Leisure interests:* table tennis, wrestling, reading, travel, music and films. *Address:* Office of the Governor, Raj Bhavan, Kohima 797 001, India (office). *Telephone:* (370) 2242917 (office). *Fax:* (370) 2242898 (office). *E-mail:* rajbhavankohima@nic.in (office). *Website:* ashwanikumar.info/.

KUMAR, Meira, LLB, MA; Indian politician, lawyer and fmr diplomatist; *Speaker of Lok Sabha;* b. 31 March 1945, Patna, Bihar; d. of the late Shri Jagjivan Ram, fmr Deputy Prime Minister, and of Indrani Devi; m. Manjul Kumar 1968; one s. two d.; ed Indraprastha Coll., Miranda House, Delhi Univ.; joined Indian Foreign Service 1973, served at Embassy in Madrid 1976–77, Indian High Comm. in London 1977–79, Embassy in Mauritius, also served as mem. India-Mauritius Jt Comm. and at Ministry of External Affairs 1980–85; mem. eighth Lok Sabha (for Bijnor, UP) 1985–89, 11th Lok Sabha 1996–98 (mem. Jt Cttee on the Empowerment of Women and its Sub-cttee on Educ. and Health Programmes for Women 1996, Public Accounts Cttee, Cttee on Home Affairs and its Sub-cttee on Personnel Policy of Cen. Paramilitary Forces), 12th Lok Sabha (for Karol Bagh, Delhi) 1998–99 (mem. Cttee on Food and Consumer Affairs, Cttee on Environment and Forests), 14th Lok Sabha (for her father's fmr constituency of Sasaram, Bihar) 2004–09, 15th Lok Sabha 2009–, Speaker of Lok Sabha (first woman) 2009–; mem. Consultative Cttee, Ministry of External Affairs 1986–89, 1996–98; Union Minister of Social Justice and Empowerment 2004–09; briefly inducted as mem. Cabinet as Union Minister for Water Resources 2009; Gen. Sec. All India Congress Cttee 1990–92, 1996–99, mem. Congress Working Cttee 1990–2000, 2002–04; Ed. Pavan Prasad (monthly magazine) 1980–92; served as Chair. Nat. Drought Relief Cttee of Congress Party during drought of 1967, launched Family Adoption Scheme, committed to human rights and abolition of caste system; mem. Court of Jawaharlal Nehru Univ. 1996–98, Court of Univ. of Delhi 1996–98, Rajghat Samadhi Cttee 1998–99; Founder and Pres. All India Samta Movt 1990; Pres. RVAKV Soc. (Inst. of Blind Girls) 1992–98, Ravidas Smarak Soc., Varanasi 2000, Jagjivan Seva Ashram, Sasaram 2002; Chair. Meera Kala Mandir, Udaipur 2000, Jagjivan Ram Sanatorium, Dehri-on-Sone 2002; Vice-Chair. Rajendra Bhawan Trust, Delhi 1987; Man. Trustee, Jagjivan Ashram Trust, Delhi 1985–2004; mem. Senate, Bihar Univ. 1969–71, Supreme Court Bar Asscn 1980, Senate, Punjab Univ. 1987–91, Governing Body, Indian Council of Cultural Relations 1987–92, Cen. Advisory Bd of Educ. 1977–90, 2004–, Advisory Council, Delhi Devt Authority 1998–99, Nat. Comm. on Population, Nat. Integration Council; mem. India Int. Centre, New Delhi, India Habitat Centre, New Delhi, Nat. Sports Club of India, New Delhi. *Publications:* several poems. *Leisure interests:* keen sportswoman (holds medals for rifle shooting), equestrianism, painting, writing poetry, old monuments, Indian textiles and crafts, reading, Indian classical music. *Address:* Office of the Speaker, Lok Sabha Secretariat, 17 Parliament House, New Delhi 110 001 (office); D-1029, New Friends Colony, New Delhi 110 065, India (home). *Telephone:* (11) 23017795 (office); (11) 26910618 (home); (98) 10630165 (mobile). *Fax:* (11) 23792927 (office); (11) 26910618 (home). *E-mail:* speakerloksabha@ sansad.nic.in (office); lokmail@sansad.nic.in (office); meirakumar@gmail.com. *Website:* speakerloksabha.nic.in (office).

KUMAR, Narendra; Indian civil servant and government official; ed Delhi School of Econs, Shri Ram Coll. of Commerce, Univ. of Delhi; joined Admin. Service 1988, Officer on Special Duty to Chief Minister of Delhi 1999–2001; apptd Sec. and Commr Labour and Employment, Delhi 2001, 2004–05; apptd Excise Commr, Delhi 2002; Personal Sec. to Minister of State for Communication and Information Tech., Delhi 2003–04; Devt Commr and Div. Commr, Delhi 2006; Sec. and Commr Industries, Delhi 2006–08; fmr Sec., Industries and Commerce, Environment and Forests and Ex-officio Chair. Pondicherry Pollution Control Cttee; Devt Commr, Govt of Goa and Sec. to Gov. of Goa 2008–11; Admin. of Union Territories of Dadra and Nagar Haveli and of Daman and Diu 2011–12. *Address:* c/o Office of the Administration of Dadra and Nagar Haveli, Administrator's Bungalow, Moti Daman, Daman, 396 210, India. *Telephone:* (260) 2230997 (home). *E-mail:* administrator@dnh.nic.in.

KUMAR, Nikhil, MA; Indian politician and fmr police officer; b. 15 July 1941, Hajipur Dist, Vaishali; s. of Satyendra Narayan Sinha and Kishori Sinha; m. Shyama Singh; ed St Xavier's School, Patna, Allahabad Univ.; entered civil service 1963, Indian Police Service Officer assigned to fmr Union Territory of Delhi, becoming Inspector Gen., Border Security Force 1989–91, 1992–94, Commr of Police, New Delhi 1995–97, Dir-Gen. Indo-Tibetan Border Police 1997, Special Sec. in charge of Internal Security, Ministry of Home Affairs 1997–99, Dir-Gen. Nat. Security Guards 1999–2001 (retd); mem. Nat. Security Advisory Bd 2001–03; mem. Lok Sabha (parl.) for Aurangabad constituency 2004–09, mem. Cttee on External Affairs, Jt Cttee on Salaries and Allowances of MPs, Jt Cttee on Security in Parl.; Gov. of Nagaland 2009–13, of Kerala 2013–14; Pres. Anugrah Sewa Sadan, Patna; Chair. A. N. Sinha Inst. of Social Studies, Patna; Pres. Gandhi Ashram Trust, Hajipur; mem. Indian Nat. Congress party; Police Medal for Meritorious Service 1978, Pres.'s Police Medal for Distinguished Service 1985. *Address:* c/o Office of the Governor, Kerala Raj Bhavan, Thiruvananthapuram 695 099, India.

KUMAR, Nitish, BSc (Eng); Indian engineer and politician; *Chief Minister of Bihar;* b. 1 March 1951, Bakhtiarpur, Patna, Bihar; s. of the late Kaviraj Ram Lakhan Singh and Parmeshwari Devi; m. Manju Kumari Sinha 1973 (died 2007); one s.; ed Bihar Coll. of Eng, Patna; involved in JP Movt led by Jayaprakash Narayan 1974–77, detained under the Maintenance of Internal Security Act 1974, and also during Emergency 1975; mem. Bihar Legis. Ass. 1985–89, mem. Cttee on Petitions 1986–87, Cttee on Public Undertakings 1987–89; Pres. Yuva Lok Dal 1987–88; elected to Lok Sabha 1989–, mem. Janata Dal (United) party, Sec.-Gen. Janata Dal, Bihar 1989, Gen. Sec. 1991–93, Deputy Leader of Janata Dal in Parl. 1991–93, Leader 2004–, mem. House Cttee 1989–90 (resgnd), mem. Railway Convention Cttee 1991–96, Chair. Cttee on Agric. 1993–96, mem. Cttee on Estimates 1996, Gen. Purposes Cttee 1996, 2004, Jt Cttee on the Constitution 1996 (Eighty-first Amendment Bill 1996), Cttee on Defence 1998, Cttee on Coal and Steel 2004, Cttee of Privileges 2004, Union Minister of State, Agriculture and Co-operation April–Nov. 1990, Union Minister for Railways and for Surface Transport 1998–99, resgnd following railway accident at Gaisal in NE India Aug. 1999; Union Minister for Surface Transport Oct.–Nov. 1999, for Agric. Nov. 1999–March 2000; Union Minister for Agric. 2000–01, with additional charge of Railways March–July 2001, Union Minister for Railways 2001–04; led Nat. Democratic Alliance to victory in Bihar Ass. elections Nov. 2005; Chief Minister of Bihar 3 March 2000, resgnd seven days later, Chief Minister of Bihar 2005–; Founder-mem. Samata Party Movt; CNN-IBN Indian of the Year (Politics) 2008, NDTV Indian of the Year (Politics) 2009, Reformer of the Year, Economics Times 2009, Polio Eradication Championship Award, Rotary Ints 2009. *Address:* Office of the Chief Minister, Patna, (office); Vill. Hakikatpur, PO Bakhtiarpur, Distt. Patna 800 001, India (home). *Telephone:* (612) 2223886 (office); (98) 68180490 (mobile); (612) 2222079 (home). *E-mail:* cmbihar@nic.in (office). *Website:* gov.bih.nic.in (office).

KUMAR, Rajender, BTech, MA; Indian government official; b. 16 Dec. 1966; ed Indian Inst. of Tech., Kanpur, Asian Inst. of Man., Manila; joined Indian Admin. Service; fmr Dir (Educ.) Govt of Nat. Capital Territory of Delhi; Commr-cum-Sec. (Health/Finance), Union Territory of Andaman and Nicobar Islands –2006; Admin. of Lakshadweep 2006; Sec. (Information and Tech.), Delhi; Special Sec., Commonwealth Coordination and Public Grievances; Prin. Sec. (Power), Govt of Delhi 2007–11; apptd Chief Man. Dir Delhi Power Co. Ltd 2007; mem. Bd of Dirs Delhi Transco Ltd (apptd Chair. and Man. Dir 2007), Indraprastha Power Generation Co. Ltd (apptd Chair. 2007), Pragati Power Corpn Ltd (apptd Chair. 2007); fmr Chair. Lakshadweep Devt Corpn, SPORTS (Soc. for Promotion of Recreational Tourism and Sports); ex-officio Insp. Gen. of Police. *Address:* c/o Board of Directors, Delhi Transco Limited, Shakti Sadan, Kotla Marg, New Delhi 110 002, India.

KUMAR, Sanjay; American (b. Sri Lankan) fmr software industry executive; b. 1962, Colombo, Sri Lanka; emigrated from Sri Lanka to USA 1976; joined Computer Assocs Int., Inc. (CA) 1987, various sr positions in devt, strategic planning and operations, Pres. and COO 1994–2000, Pres. and CEO 2000–02, Chair. and CEO 2002–2004 (resgnd), Chief Software Architect 2004; charged with fraud related to CA accounting practices 2004, pleaded guilty to charges April 2006, sentenced to 12 years in prison Nov. 2006.

KUMARASWAMY, Haradanahalli Deve Gowda, BSc; Indian politician; b. 16 Dec. 1959, Haradanahalli, Hassan Dist, Karnataka; s. of H. D. Deve 'Mannina Maga' Gowda and Chennamma Gowda; m. Anitha Kumaraswamy 1986; one s.; ed Basavanagudi Nat. Coll., Bangalore; began career as distributor of Kannada films in Mysore, Mandya, Hassan and Coorg dists 1990–; began political career 1994, mem. Lok Sabha (Parl.) for Kanakapura (Bangalore Rural Dist) 1996–98, for Ramanagaram 2004–06, 2009–; mem. Cttee on Rural Devt 2009–; organized Daridra Narayana rally to fight for rights of the urban and rural poor 2004; Chief Minister of Karnataka 2006–07 (resgnd); Pres. Karnataka State Unit of Janata Dal (Secular) 2009–; Pres. Karnataka Cinema Theatre Owners Asscn 2002–; Founder and Pres. Film Producers Asscn 2003–. *Leisure interests:* reading, driving. *Address:* No. 281, 80 ft. Road, Padmanabhanagar, Banaskankarji, IInd stage, Bangalore 560 070 (home); No. 286, 3rd Phase, 3rd Cross, J. P. Nagar, Bangalore 560 070, India (home). *Telephone:* (80) 26582230 (home).

KUMARATUNGA, Chandrika Bandaranaike, BSc; Sri Lankan politician and fmr head of state; *Chairperson, Foundation for Democracy and Justice;* b. 29 June 1945, Colombo; d. of the late S. W. R. D. Bandaranaike and Sirimavo R. D.

Bandaranaike; m. Vijaya Kumaratunga 1978 (assassinated 1988); one s. one d.; ed St Bridget's Convent, Colombo, Institut d'Etudes Politiques de Paris (Sciences-Po), Univ. of Paris, France; mem. Exec. Cttee Women's League of SLFP 1974, Exec. Cttee and Working Cttee 1980, Cen. Cttee 1992, Deputy Leader of SLFP; Chair., Man. Dir Dinakara Sinhala (daily newspaper) 1977–85; Vice-Pres. Sri Lanka Mahajana (People's) Party (SLMP) 1984, Pres. 1988; Leader SLMP and People's Alliance; Chief Minister, Minister of Law and Order, Finance and Planning, Educ., Employment and Cultural Affairs of the Western Prov. Council 1993–94; Prime Minister Aug.–Nov. 1994, also held posts of Minister of Finance and Planning, Ethnic Affairs and Nat. Integration, of Defence, of Buddha Sasana; Exec. Pres. of Sri Lanka 1994–2005; fmrly also Minister of Defence, of Constitutional Affairs, and of Educ.; Pres. Sri Lanka Freedom Party 2000–06; Additional Prin. Dir Land Reform Comm. 1972–75; Chair. Janawasa Comm. 1975–77; Expert Consultant, FAO 1977–80; Research Fellow, Univ. of London, UK 1988–91; Guest Lecturer, Univ. of Bradford, UK 1989, Jawaharlal Nehru Univ., India 1991; Chair. Foundation for Democracy and Justice, South Asia Policy and Research Inst.; adviser on poverty alleviation to Clinton Global Initiative; Dir Club de Madrid; guest lecturer and keynote speaker at int. events and confs; ranked by Forbes magazine amongst 100 Most Powerful Women (44th) 2004, (25th) 2005, two FAO Awards. *Publications include:* several research papers on land reform, food policies, poverty alleviation, democracy and good governance, political violence and conflict management. *Leisure interests:* swimming, Kandyan (nat.) dance, music, reading, art and sculpture, drama, cinema. *Address:* Office of the Former President, #27 Independence Avenue, Colombo 10, Sri Lanka (office). *Telephone:* (11) 269-437-2 (office). *Fax:* (11) 267-415-9 (office). *E-mail:* officecbk@gmail.com (office). *Website:* www.presidentcbk.org (office); www.thesapri.org (office).

KUMARESAN, Jacob, MD, MPH, TM, DPH; Indian epidemiologist and international organization official; *Director, Centre for Health Development, World Health Organization;* ed Kilpauk Medical Coll., Univ. of Madras, Tulane Univ., New Orleans, USA; practised as surgeon in hosps around India 1978–81; Govt Medical Officer, Ministry of Health, Zimbabwe 1981, becoming Acting Provincial Medical Dir; fmr Consultant Epidemiologist, Gillis Long Hansen's Disease Center, Louisiana, USA; fmr Sr Epidemiologist, Ministry of Health, Botswana; joined WHO as Medical Officer, Global Tuberculosis Programme 1992, becoming Sr Adviser to Stop TB Initiative, Exec. Sec., Stop TB Partnership 2000, Pres. Int. Trachoma Initiative 2003–07, Co-ordinator, WHO UN Office, New York 2007, Dir, WHO Centre for Health Devt (WHO Kobe Centre-WKC) 2008–; Chair. Int. Coalition for Trachoma Control; Vice-Pres. World Lung Foundation; mem. Bd of Govs Glasses for Humanity; mem. Tech. Review Panel of Global Fund to Fight AIDS, Tuberculosis and Malaria. *Address:* Office of the Director, World Health Organization Centre for Health Development (WHO Kobe Centre-WKC), 1-5-1 Wakinohama-Kaigandori, Chuo-ku, Kobe 651-0073, Japan (office). *Telephone:* 78-230-3100 (office). *Fax:* 78-230-3178 (office). *E-mail:* wkc@wkc.who.int (office). *Website:* www.who.or.jp (office).

KUMBA, Jemma Nunu, BSc; South Sudanese politician; *Minister of Lands, Housing and Physical Planning;* m. Festo Kumba; one s. three d.; ed Univ. of Namibia; served for four years as coordinator for relief for New Sudan Council of Churches; mem. Sudan People's Liberation Movement (SPLM) 1983–, acted as SPLM peace negotiator in Machakos and Naivasha, Kenya 2002; Gender Adviser for Christian Aid, Southern Sudan Programme 2003–05; mem. Nat. Parl., Khartoum, Chair. Econ. Affairs Cttee 2005–; head of del. and mem. Pan-African Parl. 2005–, mem. Cttee for Cooperation, Int. Relations and Conflict Man. 2006–08 (Deputy Chair. 2007–08); Gov. Western Equatoria State 2009–10; Minister of Lands, Housing and Physical Planning, Govt of South Sudan 2011–; mem. Initiative for Inclusive Security. *Address:* Ministry of Lands, Housing and Physical Planning, Ministries Complex, Juba, South Sudan (office).

KUMBLE, Anil Radhakrishna; Indian fmr professional cricketer; b. 17 Oct. 1970, Bangalore, Karnataka; s. of the late K N Krishna Swamy and Saroja Krishna Swamy; m. Chethana Ramatheertha; one s. two d.; ed Nat. High School, Nat. Coll., Basavanagudi, Rashtreeya Vidyalaya Coll. of Eng; leg-break and googly bowler; right-handed lower order batsman; teams played for Karnataka 1989–2009, Northants. 1995, Leics. 2000, Surrey 2006, India 1990–2008 (Capt. 2007–08); First-class debut: 1989/90; Test debut: England v India, Manchester 9–14 Aug. 1990; One-Day Int. (ODI) debut: India v Sri Lanka, Sharjah, UAE 25 April 1990; took 619 wickets in 132 tests (average 29.65); took 337 wickets in 271 ODIs (average 30.89); took 1,136 wickets in 244 First-class matches (average 25.83); India's highest-ever wicket-taker in tests and third highest wicket-taker in tests internationally and one of only three bowlers to have taken more than 600 Test wickets; became second player, after Jim Laker of England, to capture all 10 wickets in a test innings (India v Pakistan) 7 Nov. 1999; announced retirement 2 Nov. 2008; Vice-Chair. Karnataka State Wildlife Bd 2009–; currently Capt. Royal Challengers, Bangalore; mem. Athlete Cttee World Anti-Doping Agency 2009–; Arjuna Award, Govt of India 1995, a Wisden Cricketer of the Year 1996, Padma Shri 2005; prominent intersection in M. G. Road, Bangalore named after him. *Leisure interests:* photography, wildlife. *Address:* c/o Board of Control for Cricket in India, 'Kairali', GHS Lane, Manacaud, Trivandrum 695 009,; The UB Group, Level 12–16, UB Tower, UB City 24, Vittal Mallya Road, Bangalore 560 001, India. *Telephone:* (80) 39856000. *Fax:* (80) 39856034. *E-mail:* rcbsupport@royalchallengers.com; info@wada-ama.org. *Website:* www.royalchallengers.com; www.wada-ama.org.

KÜNAST, Renate; German lawyer and politician; b. 15 Dec. 1955, Recklinghausen, North-Rhine/Westphalia; ed Düsseldorf Polytechnic, Freie Universität Berlin; social worker at youth correctional facility in Berlin-Tegel 1977–79; Co-founder and mem. West Berlin Alternative List 1979, now Bündnis 90/Die Grünen MdB (Alliance 90/Greens), Chair. 1990–93, 1998–2000 (Deputy Chair. 1995–98), Chair. Nat. Exec. Cttee 2000–01; mem. Berlin Senate 1985–87, 1989–2000; mem. Parl. 2002–, Co-Chair. Green Parl. party 2005–; Fed. Minister for Consumer Protection, Food and Agric. 2001–05; mem. Bd of Dirs Telefonseelsorge Berlin 2011–, Förderkreis politische Rhetorik und Kommunikation; mem. Advisory Bd Humanist Union, Dispute Berlin; mem. Women's Business Club, Criminal Defense Lawyers Asscn, Slow Food Berlin, Dr. Hauschka Community; Trustee, Berlin AIDS-Hilfe; Hon. mem. Raoul Wallenberg Foundation, Angelo Roncalli Cttee, Interessengemeinschaft für gesunde Lebensmittel; Rachel Carson Prize 2001,

German-British Forum Award 2001, Michael Kay Award 2005, Eurogroup Medal 2005. *Publications:* Klasse statt Masse 2002, Die Dickmacher 2004. *Address:* Bündnis 90/Die Grünen MdB, Deutscher Bundestag, Platz der Republik 1, 11011 Berlin, Germany (office). *Website:* bundestag.de/mdb/bio/K/kuenare0.html (office); www.renate-kuenast.de.

KUNCZE, Gábor, BSc, PhD; Hungarian politician; b. 4 Nov. 1950, Pápa; m.; ed Ybl Miklós Coll. of Tech., Budapest, Karl Marx Univ. of Econs, Budapest; fmr economist and engineer, various industrial man. roles –1983; dept head then div. chief, Industrial Mechanisation Co. 1983–85; Deputy Dir EPGEPTERV Co. 1985–90; mem. Parl. 1990–; joined Alliance of Free Democrats (Szabad Demokraták Szövetsége—SzDSz) 1992, mem. Nat. Council 1992, leader of Parl. group 1993–94, 1998–2000, 2002–07, mem. Nat. Governing Cttee 1994–97, Pres. SzDSz 1997–98, 2001–07; mem. Council of Elders 1993–94, 1998–2000, 2002–; apptd Minister of the Interior and Deputy Prime Minister after his party signed coalition agreement with HSP (Magyar Szocialista Párt—MSZP) 1994–98. *Address:* Hungarian National Assembly, 1357 Budapest, Kossuth tér 1–3, Hungary (office). *Telephone:* (1) 441-5000 (office); (1) 441-5820 (office). *Fax:* (1) 441-5952 (office). *Website:* www.parlament.hu (office).

KUNDERA, Milan; Czech/French novelist; b. 1 April 1929, Brno; s. of Dr Ludvik Kundera and Milada Kunderová-Janosikova; m. Věra Hrabánková 1967; ed Film Faculty, Acad. of Music and Dramatic Arts, Prague; Asst, later Asst Prof., Film Faculty, Acad. of Music and Dramatic Arts, Prague 1958–69; Prof., Univ. of Rennes 1975–80; Prof., Ecole des hautes études en sciences sociales, Paris 1980–94; mem. Union of Czechoslovak Writers 1963–69; mem. Editorial Bd Literární noviny 1963–67, 1968; Dr hc (Michigan) 1983; Commonwealth Award 1981, Prix Europa-Littérature 1982, Jerusalem Prize 1985, Prix de la critique de l'Acad. française 1987, Nelly Sachs Preis 1987, Österreichische Staatspreis für Europäische Literatur 1988, Jaroslav-Seifert Prize (Czech Repub.) 1994, Medal of Merit (Czech Repub.) 1995, J. G. Herder Prize (Austria) 2000, Grand Prize Acad. française (for novels Slowness, Identity and Ignorance) 2001, Prix mondial Cino Del Duca 2009, Prix de la Bibliothèque nationale de France 2012. *Publications:* drama: Jacques and his master, an homage to Diderot 1971–81; short stories: Laughable Loves (Czechoslovak Writers' Publishing House Prize) 1970; novels: The Joke (Union of Czechoslovak Writers' Prize 1968) 1967, Life is Elsewhere (Prix Médicis) 1973, La Valse aux adieux (The Farewell Waltz) (Premio letterario Mondello 1978) 1976, Livre du rire et de l'oubli (The Book of Laughter and Forgetting) 1979, The Unbearable Lightness of Being (Los Angeles Times Prize) 1984, Immortality (The Independent Prize, UK 1991) 1989, Slowness 1995, L'Identità (Identity) 1997, La Ignorancia (Ignorance) 2000; essays: The Art of the Novel 1987, Les Testaments trahis (Aujourd'hui Prize, France) 1993, Le Rideau (The Curtain) 2005, Une rencontre (The Encounter) 2009, Œuvre I and II 2011. *Website:* www.faber.co.uk (office).

KUNERT, Günter; German writer and painter; *President, PEN Centre of German-speaking Writers Abroad;* b. 6 March 1929, Berlin; s. of Adolf Kunert and Edith Warschauer; m. 1st Marianne Todten 1951; m. 2nd Erika Hinckel; ed Basic-School, Berlin; Visiting Assoc. Prof., Univ. of Texas at Austin, USA 1972; Writer-in-Residence, Univ. of Warwick, UK 1975; mem. Akad. der Künste (Hamburg and Mannheim), Akad. für Sprache und Dichtung, Darmstadt; Pres. PEN Centre of German-speaking Writers Abroad 2005–; Bundesverdienstkreuz (First Class), Grosses Bundesverdienstkreuz mit Stern 2012; Dr hc (Allegheny Coll., Pa) 1988, (Juniata Coll.) 2005, (Univ. of Turin) 2005, (Dickinson Coll., Pa) 2010; Heinrich Mann Prize, Akad. der Künste (East Berlin) 1962, Becher Prize for Poetry 1973, Heinrich Heine Prize (City of Düsseldorf) 1985, Hölderlin Prize 1991, E.R. Curtius Prize 1991, Hans-Sahl-Preis 1996, Georg-Trakl-Preis (Austria) 1997, EU Prix Aristeion 1999, Preis der Frankfurter Anthologie 2012, America Award. *Film:* Abschied and others. *Play:* The Time Machine (based on the novel by H. G. Wells). *TV screenplays include:* King Arthur 1990, An Obituary of the Wall 1991, Endstation: Harembar 1991 and 13 others. *Radio:* 10 radio plays. *Publications:* 60 volumes of poetry, prose, satire, essays, novels, short stories and lectures; Augenspiele (catalogue of exhibition of Kunert-Paintings in Hamburg with short prose). *Leisure interests:* travel, collecting tin toys. *Address:* Schulstrasse 7, 25560 Kaisborstel, Germany (home). *Telephone:* (4892) 1414 (home). *Fax:* (4892) 8403 (home).

KUNEVA, Meglena Shtilianova, LLM; Bulgarian lawyer and politician; *Chairwoman, Movement 'Bulgaria of the Citizens';* b. 22 June 1957, Sofia; m. Andrey Pramov; one s.; ed St Kliment Ohridski Univ. of Sofia; Ed. and presenter, Bulgarian Nat. Radio 1987–91; Asst Prof., Faculty of Law St Kliment Ohridski Univ. of Sofia 1988–89; Sr Legal Advisor Council of Ministers 1990–2001; legal consultant 1992–98; Lecturer, Free Univ. of Burgas and New Bulgarian Univ. 1992–94; legal specialist, Human Rights Inst. Turku, Finland 1993 and in Int. Relations and Environmental Law, Georgetown Univ. 1995, 1999–2000, and Environmental Law at Oxford Univ. 1996; mem. Bulgarian Del. to 4th session of UN Comm. on Sustainable Devt 1995; mem. Nat. Ass. 2001–07, Deputy Minister, Ministry of Foreign Affairs and chief negotiator with EU 2001–02, Minister of European Affairs 2002–07, Special Rep. at Convention for Future of Europe 2002; Commr for Consumer Protection, EC 2007–10; third placed presidential cand. 2011; Chair. Movement 'Bulgaria of the Citizens' 2012–; mem. Berlin Conference on European Cultural Policy; mem. Nat. Movement Simeon II, Atlantic Club, Union of Bulgarian Jurists, UN Int. Council of Environmental Law, Advisory Bd Time Eco-projects Foundation; Order for Civil Merit, Spain 2002, Légion d'honneur 2003, Order Prince Enrique, Portugal 2004, Order of the Star of Italian Solidarity 2005, Gold Distinction of the Atlantic Club, Bulgaria 2005; Face of Bulgaria Award, Politika (newspaper) 2006. *Address:* Movement 'Bulgaria of the Citizens' (Dvizhenie 'Bulgariya na grazhdanite'), Sofia 1113, Park-Hotel 'Moscow', ul. Nezabravka No. 25, et. 5, Bulgaria (office). *Telephone:* (2) 8433800 (office). *E-mail:* office@grajdani.bg (office). *Website:* grajdani.bg (office).

KUNG, Arthur Hsiang-Yun; Taiwanese business executive; *President, CPC Corporation;* fmr Vice-Pres. CPC Corpn, Chair. China American Petrochemical Co. Ltd (CAPCO) –2012, Pres. CPC Corpn 2012–. *Address:* CPC Corporation, 3 Sungren Road, Shinyi Chiu, Taipei 11010, Taiwan (office). *Telephone:* (2) 8789-8989 (office). *Fax:* (2) 8789-9000 (office). *E-mail:* ir@cpc.com.tw (office). *Website:* www.cpc.com.tw (office).

KÜNG, Hans, DTheol; Swiss theologian and academic; *President, Global Ethic Foundation;* b. 19 March 1928, Sursee, Lucerne; ed Gregorian Univ., Rome, Italy, Inst. Catholique and Univ. of the Sorbonne, Paris, France; ordained priest 1954; mem. practical ministry, Lucerne Cathedral 1957–59; Scientific Asst for Dogmatic Catholic Theology, Univ. of Münster Westfalen 1959–60; Prof. of Fundamental Theology, Univ. of Tübingen 1960–63; Prof. of Dogmatic and Ecumenical Theology and Dir, Inst. Ecumenical Research 1963–80, Prof. of Ecumenical Theology, Dir Inst. of Ecumenical Research (under direct responsibility of Pres. and Senate Univ. of Tübingen) 1980–96, Prof. Emer. 1996–; Guest Prof., Univ. of Chicago 1981, of Mich. 1983, of Toronto 1985, of Rice Univ., Houston 1987; numerous guest lectures at univs worldwide; mem. PEN; Pres. Global Ethic Foundation, Germany 1995–, Switzerland 1997–; Co-Pres. World Conf. on Religion and Peace, New York; Founding mem. Int. Review of Theology, Concilium; Hon. Citizen City of Syracuse, Italy 2002, Tübingen, Germany 2002, Mozart Hon. Chair, European Acad. of Yuste, Spain 2004; Grosses Bundesverdienstkreuz mit Stern 2003; numerous hon. doctorates, including Hon. DD (Univ. of Wales) 1998, (Florida Int. Univ.) 2002, (Ecumenical Theological Seminary, Detroit) 2003, Hon. LHD (Ramapo Coll., NY) 1999, (Hebrew Union Coll., Cincinnati) 2000, Hon. DPhil (Genoa) 2004, (Universidad Nacional de Educación a Distancia, Madrid) 2011; Ludwig-Thoma Medal 1975, Oskar Pfister Award, American Psychiatric Asscn 1986, Karl Barth Prize, Evangelische Kirche der Union, Berlin 1992, Hirt Prize, Zürich 1993, Prize for Zivilcourage Zürich 1995, Univ. of Tübingen 1996, Theodor Heuss Prize, Stuttgart 1998, Interfaith Gold Medallion of the Int. Council of Christians and Jews 1998, Martin Luther Towns Prize 1999, Ernst-Robert-Curtius Literary Award Bonn 2001, Göttingen Peace Award 2002, Juliet Hollister Award of the Temple of Understanding 2004, Niwano Peace Prize 2005, Lev Kopelev Prize 2006, Cultural Award, German Freemasons 2007, Croatian Academic Soc. Award 2007, Steiger Award 2008, Lifetime Achievement Award, Prince Alwaleed Bin Talal Center for Muslim-Christian Understanding, Georgetown Univ., Washington 2008, Award for Civil Courage, Freundeskreis Heinrich Heine 2008, Otto Hahn Peace Medal 2008, Abraham Geiger Award 2009, Nonino Prize 2012. *Publications:* The Council: Reform and Reunion 1961, That the World May Believe 1963, The Council in Action 1963, Justification: The Doctrine of Karl Barth and a Catholic Reflection 1964, (with new introductory chapter and response of Karl Barth 1981), Structures of the Church 1964, (with new preface) 1982, Freedom Today 1966, The Church 1967, Truthfulness 1968, Menschwerdung Gottes 1970, Infallible? – An Inquiry 1971, Why Priests? 1972, Fehlbar? – Eine Bilanz 1973, On being a Christian 1976, Signposts for the Future 1978, The Christian Challenge 1979, Freud and the Problem of God 1979, Does God Exist? 1980, The Church – Maintained in Truth 1980, Eternal Life? 1984, Christianity and the World Religions: Paths to Dialogue with Islam, Hinduism and Buddhism (with others) 1986, The Incarnation of God 1986, Church and Change: The Irish Experience 1986, Why I am still a Christian 1987, Theology for the Third Millennium: An Ecumenical View 1988, Christianity and Chinese Religions (with Julia Ching) 1989, Paradigm Change in Theology: A Symposium for the future 1989, Reforming the Church Today 1990, Global Responsibility: In Search of a New World Ethic 1991, Judaism 1992, Credo: The Apostles' Creed Explained for Today 1993, Great Christian Thinkers 1994, Christianity 1995, A Dignified Dying: a plea for personal responsibility (with Walter Jens) 1995, Yes to a Global Ethic (ed.) 1996, A Global Ethic for Global Politics and Economics 1997, Breaking Through (with others) 1998, The Catholic Church: A Short History 2001, Women in Christianity 2001, Tracing the Way: Spiritual Dimensions of the World Religions 2002, My Struggle for Freedom (memoirs) 2003, Islam: Past, Present and Future 2006, The Beginning of all Things: Science and Religion 2006, Disputed Truth (memoirs) 2008, How to Do Good and Avoid Evil: A Global Ethic from the Sources of Judaism (with Walter Homolka) 2009, What I Believe 2010. *Leisure interests:* water sports, classical music. *Address:* Waldhäuserstrasse 23, 72076 Tübingen, Germany (office). *Telephone:* (7071) 62646 (office). *Fax:* (7071) 610140 (office). *E-mail:* office@global -ethic.org (office). *Website:* www.global-ethic.org (office).

KUNIN, Madeleine May, MA, MS; American journalist, diplomatist, academic and fmr politician; *Chairman, Institute for Sustainable Communities;* b. 28 Sept. 1933, Zürich, Switzerland; d. of Ferdinand May and Renee Bloch; m. Arthur S. Kunin 1959 (divorced 1995); three s. one d.; ed Univ. of Massachusetts, Columbia Univ. and Univ. of Vermont; moved to USA in 1940; reporter, Burlington Free Press, Vt 1957–58; Asst Producer, WCAX-TV, Burlington 1960–61; freelance writer and instructor in English, Trinity Coll., Burlington 1969–70; mem. Vermont House of Reps 1973–78; Lt.-Gov. of Vermont 1979–82, Gov. of Vermont 1985–91; Deputy Sec., US Dept of Educ., Washington, DC 1993–96; Fellow, Inst. of Politics, Kennedy School of Govt, Harvard Univ. 1983–93; Amb. to Switzerland 1996–99; Lecturer, Middlebury Coll., also fmr Scholar-in-Residence 1999–2002; Distinguished Visiting Prof., Univ. of Vermont and St Michael's Coll. 2003–; James Marsh Scholar Prof.-at-Large, Univ. of Vermont 2007–; Founder and Chair. Inst. for Sustainable Communities 1991–; Fellow, Bunting Inst., Radcliffe Coll., Cambridge, Mass. 1991–92; Democrat; more than 15 hon. degrees. *Publications:* The Big Green Book (with M. Stout) 1976, Living a Political Life 1995, Pearls, Politics, and Power: How Women Can Win and Lead 2008, The New Feminist Agenda: Defining the Next Revolution for Women, Work and Family 2012; articles in professional journals, magazines and newspapers. *Address:* Institute for Sustainable Communities, 535 Stone Cutters Way, Montpelier, VT 05602 (office); 9 Harbor Watch Road, Burlington, VT 05401, USA (home). *Telephone:* (802) 229-2900 (office). *Fax:* (802) 229-2919 (office). *E-mail:* isc@iscvt.org (office). *Website:* www .iscvt.org (office); www.madeleinekunin.org.

KUNITZSCH, Paul Horst Robert, DPhil; German professor of Arabic Studies (retd); b. 14 July 1930, Neu-Krüssow; ed Free Univ. of West Berlin; Lecturer in Arabic, Univ. of Göttingen 1956–57; taught German, Cairo 1957–60; lecturer, Goethe Inst., FRG 1960–63; Special Adviser, Radio Deutsche Welle, Cologne 1963–68; Research Fellow, Deutsche Forschungsgemeinschaft 1969–75; Lecturer in Arabic, Univ. of Munich 1975–77; Prof. of Arabic Studies 1977–95; mem. Bavarian Acad. of Sciences, Acad. Int. d'Histoire des Sciences, Paris; Corresp. mem. Acad. of Arabic Language, Cairo; Göttingen Acad. of Sciences Prize 1974. *Publications:* Arab. Sternnamen in Europa 1959, Der Almagest 1974, The Arabs and the Stars 1989, Stars and Numbers 2004, C. Ptolemäus, Der Sternkatalog (ed.; three vols) 1986–91. *Address:* Davidstr. 17, 81927 Munich, Germany (home). *Telephone:* (89) 916280 (home).

KÜNSCH, Hans Rudolf, PhD; Swiss mathematician and academic; *Professor, Seminar für Statistik, Eidgenössische Technische Hochschule Zürich (ETH Zürich);* b. 17 Oct. 1951; ed Eidgenössische Technische Hochschule Zürich; fmr Research Student, Univ. of Tokyo, Japan; joined faculty of Eidgenössische Technische Hochschule Zürich (ETH Zürich) 1983 as Prof. of Math., Seminar für Statistik 1983–, Chair., Dept of Math. 2003–07; Co-Ed. Annals of Statistics 1998–2000; mem. Council Inst. of Math. Statistics 2003–06. *Address:* Seminar für Statistik, ETH Zürich, LEO D1, Leonhardstr. 27, 8092 Zürich, Switzerland (office). *Telephone:* 446323416 (office). *Fax:* 446321228 (office). *E-mail:* kuensch@ stat.math.ethz.ch (office). *Website:* www.ethz.ch (office); www.stat.math.ethz.ch/ ~kuensch (office).

KUNTJORO-JAKTI, Dorodjatun, PhD; Indonesian politician, diplomatist and business executive; *Chairman, PT Bank Tabungan Pensiunan Nasional (BTPN);* b. 1939, Rangkasbitung; ed Univ. of Indonesia and Univ. of Calif., Berkeley, USA; Lecturer and fmr Dean of Econs, Univ. of Indonesia; Amb. to USA 2000–01; Co-ordinating Minister for the Economy, Finance and Industry 2001–04; apptd Co-Chair. Panel 45 to formulate Indonesia's position with regard to UN reforms 2005; Chair. PT Bank Tabungan Pensiunan Nasional (BTPN); mem. Bd of Govs Nat. Resilience Inst. (LEMHANNAS); Ind. Comm. American Int. Assurance/American Int. Group, Inc. (AIA/AIG), PT Hero Supermarket; Dr hc (Univ. Tech. Malaysia). *Address:* PT Bank BTPN KC Kebayoran Baru, Jl Petogogan II, No 6-8, Blok A, Kebayoran Baru, Indonesia.

KUNZE, Reiner; German writer; b. 16 Aug. 1933, Oelsnitz/Erzgebirge; s. of Ernst Kunze and Martha Kunze (née Friedrich); m. Dr Elisabeth Mifka 1961; one s. one d.; ed Univ. of Leipzig; mem. Bavarian Acad. of Fine Arts, Acad. of Arts, West Berlin 1975–92, German Acad. for Languages and Literature, Darmstadt, Free Acad. of Arts Mannheim, Sächsische Akad. der Künste, Dresden; Hon. mem. Collegium Europaeum Jenense of Friedrich-Schiller-Universität Jena; Dr hc; numerous awards and prizes including Literary Prize of Bavarian Acad. of Fine Arts 1973, Georg Trakl Prize (Austria) 1977, Andreas Gryphius Prize 1977, Georg Büchner Prize 1977, Bavarian Film Prize 1979, Eichendorff Literature Prize 1984, Bayerischer Verdienstorden 1988, Grosses Verdienstkreuz der BRD 1993, Weilheimer Literaturpreis 1997, Europapreis für Poesie, Serbia 1998, Friedrich Hölderlin-Preis 1999, Hans Sahl Prize 2001, Bayerischer Maximiliansorden für Wissenschaft und Kunst 2001, Kunstpreis zur Deutsch-tschechischen Verständigung 2002, Ján Smrek Preis 2003, STAB Preis 2004, Übersetzer Preis 'Premia Bohemica' 2004, Thüringer Verdienstrorden 2008, Memminger Freiheitspreis 2009, Thüringer Literaturpreis 2009. *Publications:* Sensible Wege 1969, Der Löwe Leopold 1970, Zimmerlautstärke 1972, Brief mit blauem Siegel 1973, Die wunderbaren Jahre 1976, Auf eigene Hoffnung 1981, Eines jeden einziges Leben 1986, Das weisse Gedicht 1989, Deckname 'Lyrik' 1990, Wohin der Schlaf sich schlafen legt 1991, Mensch ohne Macht 1991, Am Sonnenhang 1993, Wo Freiheit ist... 1994, Steine und Lieder 1996, Der Dichter Jan Skácel 1996, Bindewort 'deutsch' 1997, Ein Tag auf dieser Erde 1998, Die Aura der Wörter 2002, Der Kuss der Koi 2002, Wo wir zu Hause das Salz haben 2003, Die Chausseen der Dichter (with Mireille Gansel) 2004, Bleibt nur die eigene Stirn 2005, Lindennacht 2007, Mensch im Wort 2008, Die Sprache, die die Sprache spricht 2009, Was macht die Biene auf dem Meer? 2011, Wenn wieder eine Wende kommt 2011. *Address:* Am Sonnenhang 19, 94130 Obernzell, Germany. *Telephone:* 8591-2989 (home). *Website:* www.reiner-kunze.com (home).

KUNZRU, Hari Mohan Nath, BA, MA; British writer and journalist; b. 1969, Woodford Green, Essex, England; s. of Krishna Mohan Nath Kunzru and Hilary Ann David; ed Wadham Coll., Oxford and Univ. of Warwick; fmr journalist, Music Ed. Wallpaper magazine, Assoc. Ed. Wired magazine, Contrib. Ed. Mute magazine; Somerset Maugham Award 2003, John Llewellyn Rhys Prize 2003, Granta Best of Young British Novelists 2003, Lire 50 Ecrivains Pour Demain 2005, British Book Award for Decibel Writer of the Year 2005. *Publications:* novels: The Impressionist (Observer Young Travel Writer of the Year 1999, Betty Trask Prize 2002) 2002, Transmission 2004, My Revolutions 2007; other: short stories, journalism; contrib. to Wired, London Review of Books, Guardian, Observer, New York Times, Daily Telegraph, BBC Midnight Review. *Leisure interest:* staring out of the window. *Address:* 435 West 23rd Street, Apt 7D, New York, NY 10011, USA. *Website:* www.harikunzru.com.

KUO, Way, BS, PhD, JP; American engineer, professor of engineering and university administrator; *President and University Distinguished Professor, City University of Hong Kong;* b. 5 Jan. 1951, Taipei, Taiwan; ed Kansas State Univ., USA, Nat. Tsing Hua Univ., Taiwan; with Bell Labs 1981–84; Wisenbaker Chair of Eng in Innovation, Texas A&M Univ. 1993–2003, also Exec. Assoc. Dean of Eng and Head of Dept of Industrial Eng 1993–2000; Univ. Distinguished Prof. and Dean of Eng, Univ. of Tennessee 2003–08; Pres. and Univ. Distinguished Prof., City Univ. of Hong Kong 2008–; Foreign mem. Chinese Acad. of Eng 2008; mem. US Nat. Acad. of Eng, Academia Sinica, Taiwan, Int. Acad. for Quality; Fellow, American Soc. for Quality, IEEE, Inst. for Operations Research and Man. Science, American Statistical Asscn, Inst. of Industrial Engineers; David F Baker Distinguished Research Award, Albert G Holzman Distinguished Educator Award, Award for Technical Innovation in Industrial Eng, Pan Wen-Yuan Foundation Award for Outstanding Research, IEEE Millennium Medal, Austin Bonis Award for Outstanding Achievement in the Advancement of Reliability Research. *Publications:* co-author of nine textbooks on reliability and education. *Address:* Office of the President, City University of Hong Kong, Level 6, Cheng Yick-chi Building, Tat Chee Avenue, Kowloon, Hong Kong Special Administrative Region, People's Republic of China (office). *Telephone:* (852) 3442-9400 (office). *Fax:* (852) 3442-0386 (office). *E-mail:* office.president@cityu.edu.hk (office). *Website:* www.cityu.edu.hk (office).

KUOK, Khoon Hong, BBA; Singaporean (b. Malaysian) business executive; *Chairman and CEO, Wilmar International Limited;* nephew of Robert Kuok; m.; four c.; ed Univ. of Singapore; joined uncle's palm oil business PPB Oil Palms, Malaysia 1973; Gen. Man. Federal Flour Mills Bhd 1986–91; Man. Dir Kuok Oils & Grains Pte Ltd 1989–91; Co-founder, Chair. and CEO Wilmar International Ltd (palm oil producer) 1991, merged with uncle's business and head of combined group 2006–. *Address:* Wilmar International Ltd, 56 Neil Road, Singapore 088830 (office). *Telephone:* 6216-0244 (office). *Fax:* 6223-6635 (office). *E-mail:* info@wilmar .com.sg (office). *Website:* www.wilmar-international.com (office).

KUOK, Robert; Malaysian business executive; b. (Kuok Hock Nien), 6 Oct. 1923, Johor Bahru, Johor; m. twice; eight c.; ed Raffles Coll., Singapore; father arrived in Malaya from Fujian, China early 20th century; worked in grains dept of Mitsubishi 1942–45; worked for father's food distribution co. (supplying produce for Japanese POWs in British Malaya) 1945–48, Co-founder (with other family mems) Kuok Brothers Co. (now Kuok Group) 1948, moved business to Singapore and began sugar trade 1953, built first sugar refinery in Singapore, also trading in sugar futures, palm oil, merged with Wilmar International and combined group now headed by nephew Kuok Khoon Hong 2007; built first of chain of Shangri-La hotels in Singapore early 1970s; acquired real estate in Malaysia, Singapore and China throughout the 1970s and 1980s; Head, Kerry Group (Hong Kong) –1993 (retd) with holdings in South-East Asia, People's Repub. of China, Australia and Canada; acquired holding in TV Broadcasts Ltd (Hong Kong) 1988, majority shareholding in Coca-Cola plant in China 1993, controlling share of South China Morning Post newspaper 1993 (Chair. South China Morning Post Publrs 1993–97); also owns significant shareholding in Citic Pacific, Chinese Govt's overseas conglomerate; currently Head, Kuok (Singapore) Ltd (investment holding co.), Transmile Group (air cargo outfit); est. several charitable foundations; majority of day-to-day businesses operations now handled by his son. *Address:* Kuok (Singapore) Ltd, No. 1 Kim Seng Promenade, #07-01 Great World City, Singapore 237994 (office). *Telephone:* 67333600 (office). *Fax:* 67389300 (home). *E-mail:* corporate@kuokgroup .com.sg (office). *Website:* www.kuokgroup.com.sg (office).

KURATA, Hiroyuki; Japanese politician; fmr Parl. Vice-Minister of Int. Trade and Industry; Minister of Home Affairs Jan.–Oct. 1996; mem. House of Councillors, Pres. 2002–04; mem. advisory panel to LDP drafting cttee for new Japanese constitution 2005 LDP. *Address:* c/o Liberal-Democratic Party—LDP (Jiyu-Minshuto), 1-11-23, Nagata-cho, Chiyoda-ku, Tokyo 100-8910, Japan.

KURBI, Abu Bakr al-; Yemeni politician; currently Minister of Foreign Affairs. *Address:* Ministry of Foreign Affairs, PO Box 1994, San'a, Yemen (office). *Telephone:* (1) 276612 (office). *Fax:* (1) 286618 (office). *E-mail:* mofa1@mofa.gov .ye (office). *Website:* www.mofa.gov.ye (office).

KURDAHI, George; Lebanese broadcaster; b. 16 Jan. 1960, Acre; s. of Gebrail Kurdahi and Lapinia Kassis; m. Ida Al Kassar; three c.; began career as journalist for Lisan ul-Hal (Lebanese daily newspaper); with Radio Monte Carlo, Paris 1979–92; Head of News, Radio Orient, Beirut 1992; fmr Gen. Man. MBC FM; currently TV presenter. *Television:* Man sa yarbah al malyoon (Who Wants to be a Millionaire?), MBC 1, Man sa yarbah 2 malyoon 2005, 2006, Eftah Albak, LBC TV, Power of 10, Al Tahaddi, MBC 1. *Address:* c/o Middle East Broadcasting Center (MBC), PO Box 76267, Dubai, United Arab Emirates (office). *Telephone:* (4) 3919999 (office). *Fax:* (4) 3919900 (office). *E-mail:* infotv@mbc.ae (office). *Website:* www.mbc.net (office).

KUREISHI, Hanif, CBE, BA; British writer and dramatist; b. 5 Dec. 1954, Bromley, England; m. Tracey Scoffield; three c.; ed King's Coll., London; worked as typist at Riverside Studios; Writer-in-Residence, Royal Court Theatre, London 1981, 1985–86; Chevalier des Arts et Lettres 2002; George Devine Award 1981, PEN/Pinter Prize 2010. *Stage plays:* Soaking the Heat 1976, The Mother Country (Thames TV Playwright Award) 1980, The King and Me 1980, Outskirts (RSC) 1981, Cinders (after the play by Janusz Glowacki) 1981, Borderline (Royal Court) 1981, Artists and Admirers (after a play by Ostrovsky, with David Leveaux) 1981, Birds of Passage (Hampstead Theatre) 1983, Mother Courage (adaptation of a play by Brecht, RSC) 1984, Sleep With Me (Nat. Theatre) 1999, When the Night Begins (Hampstead Theatre) 2004. *Screenplays:* My Beautiful Laundrette (Evening Standard Best Film Award 1986, New York Critics' Best Screenplay Award 1987) 1986, Sammy and Rosie Get Laid 1988, London Kills Me (also directed) 1991, My Son The Fanatic 1997, The Mother 2002. *Television:* The Buddha of Suburbia (BBC) 1993. *Publications:* fiction: The Buddha of Suburbia (Whitbread Award for Best First Novel) 1990, The Black Album 1995, Love in a Blue Time (short stories) 1997, Intimacy 1998, Midnight All Day (short stories) 1999, Gabriel's Gift 2000, The Body 2002, Telling Tales (contrib. to charity anthology) 2004, Something to Tell You 2008, Collected Stories 2010, The Last Word 2013; non-fiction: The Rainbow Sign (autobiog.) 1986, Eight Arms to Hold You (essay) 1991, Dreaming and Scheming: Reflections on Writing and Politics (essays) 2002, My Ear at His Heart (autobiog.) (Prix France Culture littérature étrangère, France 2005) 2004, The Word and The Bomb (essays) 2005; ed.: The Faber Book of Pop (co-ed.) 1995; stories in Granta, Harpers (USA), London Review of Books and The Atlantic; regular contrib. to New Statesman and Society. *Leisure interests:* jazz, cricket. *Address:* c/o Rogers, Coleridge & White Literary Agency, 20 Powis Mews, London, W11 1JN, England (office). *Telephone:* (20) 7221-3717 (office). *Fax:* (20) 7229-9084 (office). *E-mail:* info@rcwlitagency.co.uk (office). *Website:* www.rcwlitagency.co.uk (office).

KŪRIS, Egidijus, DJur; Lithuanian judge and professor of law; *Judge, European Court of Human Rights;* b. 26 Oct. 1961, Vilnius; s. of Pranas Kūris and Vanda Kūrienė; m. Andronė Kūrienė; two s. one d.; ed Vilnius Univ., Moscow State Univ., USSR; Lecturer and Assoc. Prof., Faculty of Law, Vilnius Univ. 1984–94, Assoc. Prof. then Prof., Dept of Political Theory, Inst. of Int. Relations and Political Science 1992–2013, Dir of Inst. 1994–99, Prof., Dept of Public Law, Faculty of Law 2008–, Head of Dept 2008–13; Justice of Constitutional Court 1999–2008, Pres. 2002–08; Judge, European Court of Human Rights 2013–; Great Cross of Royal Order of Gediminas from the Grand Duke of Lithuania 2003, Grand Croix Ordre de Leopold II (Belgium) 2006, A Magyar Köztársasági Érdemrend Középkeresztje a Csillagal (Hungary) 2006, Grosse Verdienstkreuz des Verdienstordens (Germany) 2006, Ordinus Nat. 'Servinius Credencios' in gradul de Mare Cruce (Romania) 2007, Krzyż Komandorski Orderu Zasługi Rzeczypospolitej Polskej (Poland), 2008; Medal of Ministry of Foreign Affairs 2004, Gold Medal, Yerevan Univ. (Armenia) 2005, 'Pro Merito' Medal of EC 'Democracy Through Law', Council of Europe 2007, Mykolas Romeris Award 2008, Constitution Cup 2013. *Publications include:* Self-Government, Democracy and Law, Lithuania's National Interest and Her Political System (ed.), Democracy in Lithuania: Elite and Masses (ed.), Lithuania and Her Neighbours (ed.), Lithuanian Political Parties and Party System (Vols 1–2) (ed.), Interest Groups, Power and Politics (ed.), Lithuanian Constitutional Law (co-author), Lithuanian Legal Institutions, Twenty Years of the Constitution of the Republic of Lithuania: Experience and Challenges (ed. and co-author) (all in Lithuanian), Constitutional Justice in Lithuania (co-author, in English), On

Stability of the Constitution: Sources of Constitutional Law and Ostensible Omnipotence of Constitutional Courts (in Russian); more than 80 articles in Lithuanian, English, Russian, French, Polish, Latvian and Azeri. *Address:* European Court of Human Rights, 67075 Strasbourg Cedex, France (office). *Telephone:* (3) 33-88-41-26-16 (office). *E-mail:* egidijus.kuris@echr.coe.int (office). *Website:* www.echr.coe.int (office).

KURMANOV, Zainidin Karpekovich, PhD; Kyrgyzstani politician; b. 1955, Frunze (now Bishkek); m.; two c.; ed Leningrad Univ., Marshall Centre for Security Studies, Germany; fmr Prof., Interior Ministry School of Kyrgyz Repub., Kyrgyz-Russian Slavonic Univ., Arabaev Kyrgyz State Univ. 2005–07; Deputy, Supreme Council (Zhogorku Kenesh, Parl.) 2000–05, Chair., Cttee on Constitutional Legislation, State Structure, Law and Human Rights 2007–, Chair. Supreme Council 2009–11; mem. Bright Road People's Party (Ak Jol); Honoured Educator 2002, State Adviser of II rank. *Publications:* about 230 scientific publications, including 12 books, textbooks and booklets. *Address:* Supreme Council (Zhogorku Kenesh), 720053 Bishkek, ul. Abdymomunov 207, Kyrgyzstan (office). *Telephone:* (312) 61-16-04 (office). *Fax:* (312) 62-50-12 (office). *E-mail:* zs@ kenesh.gov.kg (office). *Website:* www.kenesh.kg (office).

KURODA, Haruhiko, BA, MPhil; Japanese central banker and international banking official; *Governor, Bank of Japan;* b. 25 Oct. 1944; m. Kumiko Kuroda; two s.; ed Univ. of Tokyo, Univ. of Oxford, UK; joined Ministry of Finance 1967; secondment to IMF, Washington, DC 1975–78; Dir Int. Orgs Div., Int. Finance Bureau 1987–88; Sec. to Minister of Finance 1988–89; Dir of several divs, Tax Bureau 1989–92; Deputy Vice-Minister of Finance for Int. Affairs 1992–93; Commr Osaka Regional Taxation Bureau 1993–94; Deputy Dir-Gen., Int. Finance Bureau 1994–96, Dir-Gen. 1997–99; Pres. Inst. of Fiscal and Monetary Policy 1996–97; Vice-Minister of Finance for Int. Affairs 1999–2003; Special Adviser to Cabinet 2003–05; Chair. Bd of Dirs and Pres. Asian Devt Bank 2005–13 (resgnd); Gov. Bank of Japan 2013–; Prof., Grad. School of Econs, Hitotsubashi Univ. 2003–05; ranked by Forbes magazine amongst The World's Most Powerful People (39th) 2013. *Publications include:* several books on monetary policy, exchange rates, int. finance policy, int. taxation and int. negotiations. *Address:* Bank of Japan, 2-1-1, Motoishi-cho, Nihonbashi, Chuo-ku, Tokyo 103-0021 Metro Manila, Japan (office). *Telephone:* (3) 3279-1111 (office). *E-mail:* prdmail@boj.or.jp (office). *Website:* www .boj.or.jp (office).

KURODA, Reiko, PhD; Japanese chemist and academic; *Professor, Department of Life Sciences, Tokyo University of Science;* b. 7 Oct. 1947; ed Univ. of Tokyo; Prof., Dept of Life Sciences, Univ. of Tokyo, mem. Admin. Council, Univ. of Tokyo; Gov., Cambridge Crystallographic Data Centre 2006–; Vice-Pres. Int. Council for Science; mem. Science Council of Japan; Foreign mem. Royal Swedish Acad. of Sciences 2009; Laureate for Asia Pacific, L'Oréal-UNESCO Awards for Women in Science 2013. *Publications:* numerous papers in professional journals on the chirality of organic and inorganic compounds. *Address:* Department of Life Sciences, Graduate School of Arts and Sciences, University of Tokyo, 3-8-1 Komaba, Meguro-ku, Tokyo 153-8902, Japan (office). *Telephone:* (3) 5454-6600 (office). *Fax:* (3) 5454-6600 (office). *E-mail:* ckuroda@mail.ecc.u-tokyo.ac.jp (office). *Website:* bio.c.u-tokyo.ac.jp/labs/kuroda/englishpage.htm (office).

KUROKAWA, Hiroaki, LLB; Japanese computer and electronics industry executive; *Senior Executive Advisor, Fujitsu Limited;* ed Tokyo Univ.; joined Fujitsu 1967, various posts in Services, Software and Systems Engineering Depts, mem. Bd 1999–, Group Pres., Network Services Group, later Corp. Sr Vice-Pres. and Group Pres. of Software and Services Business Promotion Group 2002, Corp. Sr Exec. Vice-Pres. April–June 2003, Pres. and Rep. Dir June 2003–08, Sr Exec. Advisor 2008–, Pres. and Rep. Dir PT Fujitsu Indonesia. *Leisure interests:* mountaineering, trekking, soccer, nature, Japanese history. *Address:* Fujitsu Headquarters, Shiodome City Center, 1-5-2 Higashi-Shimbashi, Minato-ku, Tokyo 105-7123, Japan (office). *Telephone:* (3) 6252-2220 (office). *Fax:* (3) 6252-2783 (office). *E-mail:* info@fujitsu.com (office). *Website:* www.fujitsu.com (office).

KUROYANAGI, Nobuo; Japanese financial services industry executive; *Advisor, Honda Motor Co. Ltd;* b. 1941; joined Mitsubishi Bank Ltd 1965, Dir Bank of Tokyo-Mitsubishi Ltd (later Bank of Tokyo-Mitsubishi UFJ Ltd) 1992–96, Man.-Dir 1996–2002, Deputy Pres. 2002–04, Prin. Exec. Officer 2004–05, Pres. 2006–08, Chair. 2008–10; Dir Mitsubishi Tokyo Financial Group Inc. 2003–, Pres. and CEO 2004–05, Pres. and CEO Mitsubishi UFJ Financial Group, Inc. (after merger with UFJ Holdings) 2005–10; Outside Dir, Isetan Mitsukoshi Holdings Ltd, Isetan Co. Ltd; Dir, UnionBanCal Corpn 2008–, Honda Motor Co. Ltd 2009– (Advisor 2010–); Statutory Auditor, Mitsubishi Heavy Industries Ltd. *Address:* Honda Motor Co. Ltd, 2-1-1 Minami-Aoyama, Minato-ku, Tokyo 107-8556, Japan (office). *Telephone:* (3) 3423-1111 (office). *Fax:* (3) 5412-1515 (office). *E-mail:* info@honda.com (office). *Website:* www.honda.co.jp (office); world.honda.com (office).

KUROYEDOV, Adm. Vladimir Ivanovich; Russian naval officer; b. 5 Oct. 1944, Bamburovo, Primorsk Territory, Russia; m.; one s.; ed Pacific Higher S.O. Makarov Navy School, Navy Mil. Acad. of Gen. Staff; service in Pacific Ocean Fleet 1967–93; Head of Staff Pacific Fleet, Commdr 1996–97; First Deputy Commdr Baltic Fleet 1993–96; First Deputy Commdr Russian Navy 1997, Commdr Nov. 1997–2005; Corresp. mem. Russian Acad. of Rocket and Artillery; several decorations. *Publications:* numerous publications on mil. sciences and political problems. *Address:* c/o General Staff of Russian Navy, Bolshoi Kozlovski per. 6, 103175 Moscow, Russia (office).

KURTÁG, György; Hungarian composer; b. 19 Feb. 1926, Lugos (Lugoj, Romania); ed Franz Liszt Music Acad., Budapest and in Paris with Marianne Stein; Repetiteur, Bela Bartok Music Secondary School, Budapest 1958–63, Nat. Philharmonic 1960–68; Asst to Pal Kadosa, Franz Liszt Acad. of Music, Budapest 1967, Prof. of Chamber Music 1967–86; Composer in Residence, Wissenschaftskolleg zu Berlin 1993–95, Wiener Konzerthaus, Vienna 1995–96; mem. Bayerische Akad. der Schönen Künste, Munich 1987, Akad. der Künste, Berlin 1987; Merited Artist of Hungarian People's Repub. 1980, Outstanding Artist 1984, Officier des Arts et Lettres 1985; Erkel Prize 1954, 1956, 1969, Kossuth Prize 1973, Bartok-Pasztory Award 1984, Herder Prize, Freiherr vom Stein, Hamburg 1993, Feltrinelli Prize, Accad. dei Lincei, Italy 1993, Austrian State Award for European Composers 1994, Denis de Rougemont Prize 1994, Kossuth Prize 1996, Ernst von Siemens Music Prize, Munich 1998. *Compositions include:* Viola Concerto 1954,

String Quartet, Op. 1 1959, Wind Quintet 1959, The Sayings of Péter Bornemissza 1963–68, Hommage à Mihály András 1977, Bagatelles 1981, Scenes from a Novel 1981–82, Three Old Inscriptions 1967–86, Kafka-Fragmente 1985–87, Requiem for the Beloved 1982–87, Officium breve in memoriam Andreae Szervánszky 1988–89, Ligatura–Message to Frances-Marie 1989, Hommage à R. Sch. 1990, Transcriptions from Machaut to Bach 1974–91, Attila József Fragments 1981, Three in memoriam 1988–90, Games, two series, Beads 1994, Omaggio a Luigi Nono 1979, eight Choruses 1981–82, Songs of Despondency and Grief 1980–94, Inscriptions on a Grave in Cornwall 1994, Rückblick (Altes und Neues für vier Spieler, Hommage à Stockhausen) 1986, Three Songs to poems by János Pilinszky 1986, Mémoire de Laïka 1990, Curriculum Vitae 1992, Messages of the late Miss R. V. Troussova, Grabstein für Stephan for guitar and Instrumentengruppen, Op. 15c (Prix de Composition Musicale, Fondation Prince Pierre de Monaco 1993) 1989, …quasi una fantasia…, Double Concerto for piano, cello and 2 chamber ensembles Op. 27.2 (Prix de Composition Musicale, Fondation Prince Pierre de Monaco 1993) 1989–90, Ligature e Versetti for organ 1990, Layka- Emlèk for synthesizer and real sounds (co-composition with his son) 1990, Samuel Beckett: What is the Word for solo voice, voices and chamber ensemble Op. 30b 1991. *Address:* Lihegő v.3, 2621 Verőce; Liszt Ferenc tér 9.I.6, 1061 Budapest, Hungary. *Telephone:* (1) 2735-0177; (91) 121-3994.

KURTEŠ, Predrag; Bosnia and Herzegovina politician and fmr athlete; *Minister of Internal Affairs, Federation of Bosnia and Herzegovina;* b. 18 Aug. 1953, Sarajevo; m.; one c.; ed High School of Electrical Eng, School of Admin, Faculty for Business Studies, Fed. Bureau of Investigation (FBI) Acad., USA, Int. Law Enforcement Acad., Budapest, Hungary; professional athlete 1970–84; graduated as Admin. Lawyer and Grad. Economist, later Anti-Terrorism Specialist; with Ministry of Internal Affairs 1987–, held several positions, including police station investigator, several man. positions in Depts of the Criminal Police, Ministry of Internal Affairs of Sarajevo Canton, and Head of Sector of the Criminal Police with rank of Chief Inspector 2007–11; also held position of Asst Minister for Criminal Police and Acting Minister, Ministry of Internal Affairs of Sarajevo Canton; Minister of Internal Affairs, Fed. of Bosnia and Herzegovina 2011–; several nat. and int. awards and medals. *Address:* Ministry of Internal Affairs, 71000 Sarajevo, Mehmeda Spahe 7, Bosnia and Herzegovina (office). *Telephone:* (33) 280020 (office). *Fax:* (33) 280020 (office). *E-mail:* info@fmup.gov.ba (office). *Website:* www .fmup.gov.ba (office).

KURTI, Albin; Kosovo engineer and politician; *Chairman, Self-Determination! (Vetëvendosje!);* b. 24 March 1975, Prishtina; Vice-Pres. UPSUP, Univ. of Prishtina Student Union 1997, organizer of nonviolent demonstrations autumn 1997, spring 1998; worked in office of Adem Demaçi when latter became political rep. of Kosovo Liberation Army (KLA); arrested by Serbian forces during NATO air strikes on Yugoslavia April 1999, charged with 'jeopardizing Yugoslavia's territorial integrity and conspiring to commit an enemy activity linked to terrorism', sentenced to 15 years in prison, freed by Serbia's post-Milošević govt Dec. 2001; organized nonviolent protests in support of families of those who disappeared in the war and in favour of Kosovo self-determination; arrested following protest Feb. 2007, detained until July, then kept under house arrest, trial not concluded; mem. Ass. of Kosovo, Chair. Cttee on Foreign Affairs; Chair. Self-Determination! (Vetëvendosje!) (ethnic Albanian nationalist party) 2004–; columnist, Express, Zëri (local newspapers). *Address:* Self-Determination! (Vetëvendosje!), 10000 Prishtina, Rruga Bajram Kelmendi 10/a, Kosovo (office). *Telephone:* (44) 411172 (office). *E-mail:* info@vetevendosje.org (office). *Website:* www.vetevendosje.org (office).

KURTZER, Daniel C., BA, PhD; American diplomatist and academic; *Lecturer and S. Daniel Abraham Visiting Professor in Middle East Policy Studies, Woodrow Wilson School of Public and International Affairs, Princeton University;* m. Sheila Kurtzer; three s.; ed Yeshiva Univ., Columbia Univ.; joined Foreign Service 1976; Dean, Yeshiva Coll. 1977–79; political officer, Bureau of Int. Organizational Affairs, embassies in Cairo and Tel-Aviv; Deputy Dir Office of Egyptian Affairs 1996; on Policy Planning Staff 1987; Deputy Asst Sec. for Near Eastern Affairs 1989; Prin. Deputy Asst Sec. for Intelligence and Research 1994, then Acting Asst Sec.; Amb. to Egypt 1997–2001, to Israel 2001–05; Lecturer and S. Daniel Abraham Visiting Prof. in Middle East Policy Studies, Woodrow Wilson School of Public and Int. Affairs, Princeton Univ. 2005–; Commr Israel Baseball League; Pres.'s Distinguished Service Award, Henrietta Szold Award by Hadassah 2005, Dir-Gen. of Foreign Service Award for Reporting. *Address:* 418 Robertson Hall, Woodrow Wilson School, Princeton University, Princeton, NJ 08544-1013, USA (office). *Telephone:* (609) 258-9859 (office). *E-mail:* dkurtzer@princeton.edu (office). *Website:* www.wws.princeton.edu (office); www.israelbaseballleague.com.

KURZ, Sebastian; Austrian politician; *Federal Minister for European and International Affairs;* b. 27 Aug. 1986, Vienna; ed Univ. of Vienna; mil. service 2004–05; State Chair., Young ÖVP, Vienna 2008–11, Fed. Pres., Young ÖVP 2009; mem. Vienna State Parl. and Municipal Council 2010–11; State Sec. for Integration (part of Ministry of Internal Affairs) 2011–13; mem. Parl. (Österreichische Volkspartei) 2013–; Fed. Minister for European and Int. Affairs 2013–. *Address:* Federal Ministry of European and International Affairs, Minoritenplatz 8, 1014 Vienna, Austria (office). *Telephone:* (5) 011-50-0 (office). *Fax:* (5) 011-59-0 (office). *E-mail:* Sebastian.kurz@bmeia.gv.at (office). *Website:* www.bmeia.gv.at (office); www.sebastian-kurz.at.

KURZWEIL, Raymond (Ray) C., BS; American computer scientist and business executive; *Chairman and CEO, Kurzweil Technologies;* b. 12 Feb. 1948, Queens, NY; m. Sonya R. Kurzweil; ed Massachusetts Inst. of Tech.; aspired to become an inventor from age of five; built and programmed his own computer to compose original melodies aged 15; founder and fmr CEO Kurzweil Computer Products, Inc. 1974–80, Kurzweil Music Systems, Inc. 1982–90, Kurzweil Applied Intelligence, Inc. 1982–97, Kurzweil Educational Systems, Inc. 1996; Chair. Strategy and Tech. Cttee Bd Dirs, Wang Laboratories, Inc. 1993–98; Founder, Chair. and CEO Kurzweil Technologies, Inc. 1995–, FAT KAT, Inc. 1999–, Kurzweil Cyber Art Technologies, Inc. 2000–; Founder, Pres. and CEO Medical Learning Co., Inc. and FamilyPractice.com 1997; Founder, CEO and Ed.-in-Chief www.KurzweilAI.net 2001–; Co-Founder, Chair. and Co-CEO Ray & Terry's Longevity Products, Inc. 2003; mem. Bd Dirs Medical Manager Corpn 1997–2000, Inforte 1999–, United Therapeutics 2002–; Chair. and Founder The Kurzweil Foundation; Dir Massachusetts Computer Software Council; fmr Dir Boston Computer Soc.; mem. MIT

Corpn Visiting Cttee, MIT School of Humanities, MIT School of Music, Bd of Overseers, New England Conservatory of Music; developed first computerized Four-Way Analysis of Variance (statistical program) 1964, first computer-based Expert System for College Selection 1967, first Text-to-Speech speech synthesis 1975, first CCD Flatbed Scanner 1975, first Print-to-Speech Reading Machine for the Blind (Kurzweil Reading Machine) 1976, first Omni-Font (any-type font) Optical Character Recognition (now Xerox TextBridge) 1976, first Computer Music Keyboard capable of accurately reproducing sounds of the grand piano and other orchestral instruments (Kurzweil 250) 1984, first Knowledge Base System for Creating Medical Reports (Kurzweil VoiceMED) 1985, first commercially marketed Large Vocabulary Speech Recognition (Kurzweil Voice Report) 1987, first Speech Recognition Dictation System for Windows (Kurzweil Voice for Windows) 1994, first Continuous Speech Natural Language Command and Control Software (Kurzweil VoiceCommands) 1997, first Print-to-Speech Reading System for Persons with Reading Disabilities (Kurzweil 3000), first Virtual Performing and Recording Artist (Ramona) to perform in front of a live audience with a live band 2001, first 'host/hostess' Avatar on the Web to combine lifelike photo-realistic, moving and speaking facial image with a conversational engine 2001; Fellow, American Acad. of Arts and Sciences 2009–; Hon. Chair. for Innovation, White House Conf. on Small Business 1986; Hon. DHumLitt (Hofstra Univ.) 1982, (Misericordia Coll.) 1989, (Landmark Coll.) 2002, Worcester Polytechnic Inst. 2005; Hon. DMus (Berklee Coll. of Music) 1987; Hon. DSc (Northeastern Univ.) 1988, (Rensselaer Polytechnic Inst.) 1988, (New Jersey Inst. of Tech.) 1990, (City Univ. of New York) 1991, (Dominican Coll.) 1993; Hon. DEng (Merrimack Coll.) 1989; Dr hc in Science and Humanities (Michigan State Univ.) 2000; numerous awards including Mass's Gov.'s Award 1977, Grace Murray Hopper Award, Asscn for Computing Machinery (ACM) 1978, Nat. Award, Johns Hopkins Univ. 1981, admitted to Computer Industry Hall of Fame 1982, Pres.'s Computer Science Award 1982, The White House Award for Entrepreneurial Excellence 1986, Inventor of the Year Award, awarded by MIT, Boston Museum of Science and Boston Patent Law Asscn 1988, MIT Founders Award 1989, Engineer of the Year Award, Design News magazine 1990, Louis Braille Award, Associated Services for the Blind 1991, Massachusetts Quincentennial Award for Innovation and Discovery 1992, ACM Fellow Award 1993, Gordon Winston Award, Canadian Nat. Inst. for the Blind 1994, Dickson Prize, Carnegie Mellon Univ. 1994, Software Industry Achievement Award, Massachusetts Software Council 1996, Pres.'s Award, Asscn on Higher Educ. and Disability 1997, Stevie Wonder/SAP Vision Award for Product of the Year (for the Kurzweil 1000) 1998, Nat. Medal of Tech. 1999, Lemelson-MIT Prize 2000, inducted into Nat. Inventors' Hall of Fame, US Patent Office 2002. *Film:* The Age of Intelligent Machines (The Chris Plaque, Columbus Int. Film Festival 1987, Creative Excellence Award, US Industrial Film and Video Festival 1987, Gold Medal – Science Educ., Int. Film and TV Festival of New York 1987, CINE Golden Eagle Award 1987, Tech. Culture Award, Int. Festival of Scientific Films, Belgrade 1988, Prize of the President of the Festival, Int. Film Festival of Czechoslovakia 1988) 1987. *Publications:* The Age of Intelligent Machines (MIT Press Best Seller 1991, Silicon Valley Best Seller 1991, Most Outstanding Computer Science Book of 1990 Award, Asscn of American Publishers 1991) 1990, The 10% Solution for a Healthy Life (Regional Best Seller 1993) 1993, The Age of Spiritual Machines, When Computers Exceed Human Intelligence (Nat. and Regional Best Sellers 1999, 2000, Literary Lights Prize, Boston Public Library 1999) 1999, Are We Spiritual Machines, Ray Kurzweil versus the Critics of Strong AI 2002, Fantastic Voyage: Live Long Enough to Live Forever (co-author) 2004, The Singularity is Near, When Humans Transcend Biology 2005. *Address:* Kurzweil Technologies, Inc., PMB 193 733, Turnpike Street, North Andover, MA 01845 (office); Kurzweil Technologies, Inc., 15 Walnut Street, Wellesley Hills, MA 02481, USA (office). *Telephone:* (718) 263-0000 (office). *Fax:* (718) 263-9999 (office). *E-mail:* raymond@kurzweiltech.com (office). *Website:* www.KurzweilTech.com (office); www.KurzweilAI.net (office).

KUSAKARI, Takao, BA; Japanese transport industry executive; *Board Counsellor and Consultant, Nippon Yusen Kabushiki Kaisha (NYK Line);* b. 1940; ed Keio Univ.; joined Nippon Yusen Kabushiki Kaisha (NYK Line) 1964, Gen. Man. of Cen./S America, Africa and Specialized Cargo Div. 1990, Dir 1994–97, Man. Dir 1997–99, Sr Man. Dir 1999, Pres. 1999–2004, Chair. 2004–09, Bd Counsellor and Consultant 2009–; Corp. Auditor, Nippon Steel Corpn; fmr mem. Corp. Auditor's Bd, AOC Holdings Inc.; Pres. Japanese Shipowners' Asscn; Chair. Council for the Promotion of Regulatory Reform, Cabinet Office 2007–; Dir Nomura Securities Co. Ltd 2011–, Outside Dir, Nomura Holdings, Inc. 2011–; Dir, Japan Productivity Centre for Socio-econ. Devt; Chair. Shipping Econs Review Cttee, Asian Shipowners' Forum; mem. Int. Advisory Council, PSA Corpn; Commdr, Ordre de la Couronne (Belgium) 2010; Official Commendation by Minister of Land, Infrastructure and Transport 2004, Medal with Blue Ribbon by Japanese Govt 2005. *Address:* Nippon Yusen Kabushiki Kaisha, 3-2, Marunouchi 2-chome, Chiyoda-ku, Tokyo 100-0005, Japan (office). *Telephone:* (3) 3284-5151 (office). *Fax:* (3) 3284-6359 (office). *E-mail:* info@nyk.com (office). *Website:* www.nyk.com (office).

KUSAMA, Saburo, BEng; Japanese manufacturing executive; *CEO, Seiko Epson Corporation;* b. 12 Oct. 1939, Aichi; m. Mizue Kusama; two s.; ed Univ. of Shizuoka; began work in Crystal Devices and Circuits Div., Seiko Epson Corpn 1963, various man. positions in Clocks and Tech. Design Divs, Gen. Man. Semiconductors Div. 1986, CEO Semiconductors Div. 1990, mem. Exec. Council 1990–, CEO Display and Liquid Crystals Div. 1994, Pres. Seiko Epson Corpn 2001–2005, CEO 2005–; Medal with Blue Ribbon 2006. *Leisure interests:* golf, classical music, museums. *Address:* Seiko Epson Corporation, 3-3-5 Owa Suwa, Nagano 392-8502, Japan (office). *Telephone:* (266) 52–3131 (office). *Fax:* (266) 53–4844 (office). *Website:* www .epson.com (office).

KUSHERBAYEV, Krymbek Ye., DrPolSci; Kazakhstani diplomatist and politician; *Akim (Governor) of Kyzylorda Oblast;* b. 20 May 1955, Kazalinsk, Kyzylorda oblast; ed Kazakh Polytechnic Inst.; Asst to the Deputy Prime Minister 1991–94; headed Kalinin regional Admin of Almaty 1994–95; Deputy Head of the Office and Head of Dept of Internal Policies, Office of the Cabinet 1995; Deputy Head of the Office and Head of Dept of Territorial Devt, Office of the Govt 1995–96; Press Sec. and Head of Press Service of the Pres. 1996–97; Minister of Educ., Culture and Healthcare 1997–99, of Healthcare, Educ. and Sport following reorganization of the Ministry Jan.–Oct. 1999, of Educ. and Science Oct. 1999–2000; Akim (Gov.) of West Kazakhstan Oblast 2000–03; Amb. to Russian Fed. (also accred to Finland

and Armenia 2003–06; Akim (Gov.) of Mangystau Oblast 2006–11; adviser to the Pres. of Kazakhstan July–Oct. 2012; First Deputy Prime Minister and Minister of Regional Devt 2012–13; Akim (Gov.) of Kyzylorda Oblast 2013–; Parasat Medal 2003, Friendship Medal (Russian Fed.) 2006, Barys Medal, Second Degree 2009. *Address:* Kyzylorda Oblast Administration, Kyzylorda 120014, Y. Zhakhayev Str., 76, Kazakhstan (office). *Telephone:* (7242) 26-16-44 (office). *Fax:* (7242) 26-12-25 (office). *E-mail:* oblakimat@orda.gov.kz (office). *Website:* www.e-kyzylorda.gov.kz (office).

KUSHNER, Aleksandr Semyonovich; Russian poet; b. 14 Sept. 1936, Leningrad; s. of Semyon Semyonovich Kushner and Asya Aleksandrovna Kushner; m. Elena Vsevolodovna Nevzglyadova 1981; one s.; ed Leningrad Pedagogical Inst.; lecturer in literature 1959–69; Northern Palmira Award 1995, Russian Fed. State Award 1995, German Pushkin Award, Alfred Toepfer Foundation 1999, Russian Fed. Alexander Pushkin Award 2001, Nat. 'The Poet' Award 2005. *Publications include:* First Impression 1962, Night Watch 1966, Omens 1969, Letter 1974, Direct Speech 1975, Voice 1978, Canvas 1981, The Tavrichesky Garden 1984, Daydreams 1986, Poems 1986 (Selected Poems), The Hedgerow 1988, A Night Melody 1991, Apollo in the Snow (selected essays on Russian literature of the nineteenth and twentieth centuries and personal memoirs) 1991, Apollo in the Snow (selected poems trans. into English) 1991, On the Gloomy Star (State Prize) 1995, Selected Poetry 1997, The Fifth Element 1999, The Bush 2002, Cold Month of May 2005, Selected Poems 2005, Apollo in the Grass (essays on poetry) 2005, In the New Century 2006, The Time is Not to Be Chosen 2007, Clouds Opt for Anapest 2008, With Chalk and Coal 2010, Facing the Mysterious Line 2011, The Evening Light 2013; essays in literary journals. *Leisure interests:* reading, world painting. *Address:* Kaluzhsky pereulok No. 9, Apt 48, 193015 St Petersburg, Russia (home). *Telephone:* (812) 577-32-56 (home). *E-mail:* kushner@mail.lanck.net (home).

KUSHNER, Anthony (Tony) Robert, BA, MFA; American playwright and screenwriter; b. 16 July 1956, New York City; s. of William Kushner and Sylvia Deutscher; m. Mark Harris 2008 (civil partner since 2003); ed Columbia Univ., New York Univ. Grad. Acting Program at the Tisch School of the Arts; family moved to Lake Charles, La 1956, moved to New York 1974; spent summers directing early original works (Masque of Owls and Incidents and Occurrences During the Travels of the Tailor Max) and plays by Shakespeare (A Midsummer Night's Dream and The Tempest) for children attending the Gov.'s Program for Gifted Children, Lake Charles, La 1978–81; Playwright-in-Residence, Juilliard School, New York 1990–92; Hon. DLitt (Purchase Coll., State Univ. of NY) 2008; Dr hc (John Jay Coll. of Criminal Justice, CUNY) 2011; Cultural Achievement Award, Nat. Foundation of Jewish Culture, Lila Wallace/Reader's Digest Fellowship, Whiting Writers' Award 1990, Tony Award for Best Play 1993, 1994, Drama Desk Award for Outstanding Play 1994, Critics' Circle Award, London Evening Standard Award, Obie Award, New York Drama Critics' Circle, American Academy of Arts and Letters Award, PEN/Laura Pels International Foundation for Theater Award for a playwright in mid-career 2002, Steinberg Distinguished Playwright Award 2008, Puffin/Nation Prize for Creative Citizenship 2011, St Louis Literary Award 2012, Nat. Medal of Arts 2012. *Screenplays:* Angels in America (HBO mini-series) (Primetime Emmy Award for Outstanding Writing for a Miniseries, Movie or a Dramatic Special 2004) 2003, Munich (with Eric Roth) 2005, Lincoln (New York Film Critics Circle Award for Best Screenplay 2012) 2012. *Television includes:* American Playhouse (series) 1993, Angels in America (film) 2004. *Publications:* Yes, Yes, No, No 1985, Actors on Acting 1986, Stella 1987, A Bright Room Called Day 1987, Hydriotaphia 1987, The Illusion 1988, The Persistence of Prejudice 1989, Widows (with Ariel Dorfman) 1991, Angels in America: A Gay Fantasia on National Themes, Part One: Millennium Approaches (Pulitzer Prize for Drama 1993, Drama Desk Award for Outstanding Play 1993) 1991, Part Two: Perestroika 1992, Slavs! 1994, Holocaust and the Liberal Imagination 1994, Thinking About the Longstanding Problems of Virtue and Happiness 1995, Homebody/Kabul 2001, Caroline, or Change (Best New Musical, Olivier Awards 2007) 2006, The Intelligent Homosexual's Guide to Capitalism and Socialism with a Key to the Scriptures 2009. *Address:* c/o Steven Barclay Agency, 12 Western Avenue, Petaluma, CA 94952, USA (office). *Telephone:* (707) 773-0654 (office). *Fax:* (707) 778-1868 (office). *E-mail:* steven@barclayagency.com (office). *Website:* www.barclayagency.com (office).

KUSHNER, Eva, OC, PhD, FRSC; Canadian academic; *Mary Rowell Coyne Professor, Victoria University and Professor Emerita of French and Comparative Literature, University of Toronto;* b. 18 June 1929, Prague, Czechoslovakia; d. of late Josef Dubsky and Anna Dubsky-Cahill (née Kafka); m. 1st Donn J. Kushner 1949 (deceased); three s.; m. 2nd Rev. Canon Bruce Mutch 2005; ed McGill Univ., Montreal; Prof., Carleton Univ. 1961–76; Prof., McGill Univ. 1976–87, Chair. French Dept 1976–80; Prof., Pres. Vic. Univ. at Univ. of Toronto 1987–94, Dir Comparative Literature, Univ. of Toronto 1994–95, Mary Rowell Coyne Prof., Victoria Univ. 2001–, also Prof. Emer. of French and Comparative Literature; Pres. Int. Comparative Literature Asscn 1979–82; Vice-Pres. Int. Fed. for Modern Languages and Literatures 1987–93, Pres. 1996–99; Vice-Pres. RSC 1980–82, Conseil Int. de la Philosophie et des Sciences Humaines 2006–10; Visiting Prof., Princeton Univ. 2000, Univ. of Athens 2003; Hon. LitD (Acadia Univ.) 1988, Hon. DD (United Theological Coll., Montreal) 1992, Hon. DLitt (Univ. of St Michael's Coll.) 1993, (Univ. of Western Ont.) 1996, Dr hc (Szeged) 1997, Hon. Dr of Sacred Letters (Victoria Univ., Toronto) 2006; Lifetime Achievement Award, Canadian Soc. for Renaissance Studies 2002. *Publications:* Patrice de la Tour du Pin 1961, Le Mythe d'Orphée dans la littérature française contemporaine 1961, Chants de Bohème 1963, Rina Lasnier (two edns) 1964, 1969, Saint-Denys Garneau 1967, François Mauriac 1972, L'avènement de l'esprit nouveau 1400–80 (co-author) 1988, Théorie littéraire: problèmes et perspectives (co-author) 1989, Le problématique du sujet chez Montaigne (co-author) 1995, Histoire des poétiques (co-author) 1997, Crises et essors nouveaux 1560–1610 (co-author) 2000, Pontus de Tyard et son œuvre poétique 2001, The Living Prism: Itineraries in Comparative Literature 2001, Le Dialogue à la Renaissance: Histoire et Poétique 2004, Maturations et mutations (1520–60) 2011. *Address:* Victoria University, University of Toronto, 73 Queen's Park, Toronto, ON M5S 1K7 (office); 63 Albany Avenue, Toronto, ON M5R 3C2, Canada (home). *Telephone:* (416) 585-4592 (office); (416) 538-0173 (home). *E-mail:* eva.kushner@utoronto.ca (office). *Website:* (office).

KUSHNER, Robert Ellis, BA; American artist; b. 19 Aug. 1949, Pasadena, Calif.; s. of Joseph Kushner and Dorothy Browdy; m. Ellen Saltonstall 1978; two s. one d.; ed Univ. of Calif., San Diego; has participated in numerous group shows at Whitney Museum and Museum of Modern Art, New York etc.; Venice Biennale 1980, 1984; works represented in maj. permanent collections in USA, Tate Gallery, London etc. *Address:* c/o Shark's Ink, 550 Blue Mountain Road, Lyons, CO 80540; c/o DC Moore Gallery, 724 Fifth Avenue, New York, NY 10019, USA. *E-mail:* rzkushner@asan.com (office).

KUSSA, Mussa Muhammad, BA; Libyan government official and diplomatist; b. Benghazi; ed Michigan State Univ., East Lansing, Mich., USA; worked as a security specialist for Libyan embassies in Europe before being apptd Amb. to UK 1979–80 (expelled); Deputy Sec. for Foreign Affairs 1992–94; Head of Libyan Intelligence Agency 1994–2009; Sec. for Foreign Liaison and Int. Co-operation (Minister of Foreign Affairs) 2009–11 (fled to UK and resgnd 30 March 2011); played key role in securing the release of Pan Am Flight 103 bomber Abdelbaset al-Megrahi. *Address:* c/o Secretariat for Foreign Liaison and International Co-operation, El-Shat Street, Tripoli, Libya. *Telephone:* (21) 3400461. *Fax:* (21) 3402921. *Website:* www.foreign.gov.ly.

KUSSBACH, Erich, LLM, Dr. rer. pol, DrIur; Austrian academic and fmr diplomat; *Honorary Professor of International Humanitarian Law, Johannes Kepler University;* b. 5 May 1931; ed Eötvös Lóránd Univ., Budapest, Hungary, Univ. of Vienna, Yale Univ., USA; served in Austrian Diplomatic Service 1963–96, sr positions included Head of Dept of Legal and Consular Affairs; served as legal advisor of Austrian Del. negotiating Free-Trade-Agreements with EEC; Deputy Rep. to Council of Europe and Consul Gen. in Strasbourg 1981–85; Amb. to Hungary 1993–96, also Perm. Rep. to Int. Danube Comm.; Hon. Prof. of Int. Humanitarian Law, Faculty of Law, Johannes Kepler Univ., Linz; fmr Prof. of Public Int. Law and Int. Criminal Law, Catholic Pázmány Péter Univ., Budapest; Founding Pro-rector and fmr Prof. of Diplomacy, Faculty of Int. Relations, Andrássy Gyula German Speaking Univ., Budapest; mem. Arbitration Panel, Nat. Fund for Victims of Nat. Socialism 2001–; Dr hc (Eoetvoes Lorand Univ.). *Address:* c/o National Fund of the Republic of Austria for Victims of National Socialism, Kirchberggasse 33, 1070 Vienna, Austria.

KUSTURICA, Emir; Bosnia and Herzegovina film director and musician (guitar); b. 24 Nov. 1954, Sarajevo; ed FAMU School, Prague, Czechoslovakia; teacher, Columbia Univ., New York, USA; mem. rock and roll band, No Smoking Orchestra 1986–; Chair. of Jury, Cannes Film Festival 2005. *Films include:* Do You Remember Dolly Bell? (Golden Lion Award, Venice) 1981, When Father Was Away On Business (Palme d'Or, Cannes 1984) 1984, Time of the Gypsies (Best Dir, Cannes) 1988, Arizona Dream (Special Jury Prize, Berlin) 1993, Underground (Palme d'Or, Cannes) 1995, Black Cat White Cat 1998, La Veuve de Saint-Pierre 2000, Super Eight Stories 2001, Life is a Miracle 2004, Maradona (documentary) 2008. *Recordings include:* albums with No Smoking Orchestra: Das ist Walter 1984, Dok cekaš sabah sa šejtanom 1985, Pozdrav iz zemlje Safari (Greetings from Safari Land) 1987, Male price o velikoj ljubavi (A Little Story of a Great Love) 1989, Ja nisam odavle 1997, Black Cat White Cat 1998, Unza Unza Time 2000, La Vie est un miracle (soundtrack to film) 2004. *Address:* c/o Rasta Films, Belgrade, Serbia (office). *Telephone:* (11) 308-64-60 (office). *Fax:* (11) 308-64-61 (office). *E-mail:* marie-christine.malbert@libertysurf.fr (office). *Website:* www.kustu.com (office).

KUSUMAATMADJA, Mochtar, LLD; Indonesian politician; b. Feb. 1929, Jakarta; ed Univ. of Indonesia, Yale and Harvard Law Schools and Univ. of Chicago Law School, USA; Minister of Justice 1974–77; Acting Foreign Minister 1977–78, then Minister of Foreign Affairs 1978–88, fmr Head of UN Comm. responsible for the demarcation of the Iraq–Kuwait Border, resgnd 1992; Indonesian Rep. at Law of the Sea Conf., Geneva and at Seabed Cttee sessions, New York; involvement in numerous int. orgs. *Address:* c/o Ministry of Foreign Affairs, Jalan Taman Pejambon 6, Jakarta, Indonesia.

KUSZNIEREWICZ, Mateusz Andrzej; Polish yachtsman; b. 29 April 1975, Warsaw; s. of Zbigniew Kusznierewicz and Irena Kusznierewicz; m. Agnieszka Kusznierewicz; ed Acad. of Physical Educ., Warsaw; began sailing aged nine, competed in Club Championship, Zalew Zegrzynski 1984; won first event Puchar Spojnii, Zalew Zegrzynski 1985; Polish Youth Champion, OK-Dinghy Class 1989; European Champion, OK-Dinghy Class 1991; Olympic Champion, Finn Class, Atlanta 1996, Bronze Medal, Athens 2004; World Champion, Finn Class 1998, 2000; European Champion, Finn Class 2000; mem. Yacht Klub Polski, Warsaw; Kt's Cross of Order of Polonia Restituta 1999; Int. Sailing Fed. Sailor of the Year (Int. Sailing Fed.) 1999, Most Popular Sportsman in Poland 1999. *Leisure interests:* electromechanics, other sports (especially golf, tennis and skiing). *Address:* No Limit Kusznierewicz Events, ul. Ostrobramska 75C, 04-175 Warsaw, Poland (office). *Telephone:* (22) 6117272 (office). *Fax:* (22) 6117273 (office). *E-mail:* mkusznierewicz@akademia.org.pl (office). *Website:* www.kusznierewicz.pl (office).

KUTAFIN, Oleg Ye., Dr Jur.; Russian lawyer; *Rector, Moscow State Academy of Law;* b. 26 June 1937; m.; two c.; ed Moscow State Univ.; Asst Prof., then Prof. Moscow All-Union Extra-Mural Law Inst. 1964–71; Prof. Moscow State Univ. 1971–, Deputy Chair. Acad. of Law 1971–87, Chair. and Rector Acad. of Law 1987–; mem. Presidium Russian Acad. of Sciences 2003–, Supreme Scientific Qualification Bd, Higher Qualification Bd of Judges; Chair. Comm. on Citizenship; Co-Chair. Assn of Russian Lawyers; mem. Presidential consultative bodies; mem. editorial bds of leading Russian law journals; merited worker of science and of justice, Hon. worker of higher education and procuracy, Hon. mem. Russian Acad. of Educ., Hon. Attorney; Orders of Merit to Motherland of II, III and IV degrees, other govt awards; Presidential Prize in the field of education. *Publications include:* Municipal Law of Russia, Constitutional Law of Russia; more than 300 scientific works, including Russian Citizenship, Immunity in the Constitutional Law of the Russian Federation, Russian Autonomy, Subjects of Constitutional Law of Russian Federation as Legal and Equated to them Persons; textbooks, manuals and articles on constitutional and municipal law. *Leisure interests:* classical music, literature, history. *Address:* Moscow State Law Academy, Sadovo-Kudrinskaya str. 9, Moscow 123995, Russia (office). *Telephone:* (495) 254-99-72 (office). *E-mail:* msal@msal.ru. *Website:* www.msal.ru.

KUTARAGI, Ken, BE; Japanese computer entertainment executive (retd) and game console designer; b. 8 Aug. 1950, Tokyo; ed Denki Tsushin Univ.; joined Sony Corpn 1975, various positions in eng and digital research labs 1980s, worked on liquid crystal displays and digital camera projects; designed PlayStation game console 1989 and persuaded Sony to produce it after initiation of jt venture with Nintendo failed, headed team to create Sony PlayStation, released in 1994, began work on PlayStation 2 1996, released 2000, Playstation 3 released 2006; apptd Chair. US Div. 1997, Pres. and CEO Sony Computer Entertainment Int. 1999–Dec. 2006, Chair. and CEO Dec. 2006–June 2007 (retd); fmr mem. Bd of Dirs Sony Corpn. *Address:* c/o Sony Computer Entertainment International, 2-6-21 Minami-aoyama, Minato-ku, Tokyo 107-0062, Japan (office).

KUTCHER, (Christopher) Ashton; American actor, producer, fmr fashion model and comedian; b. 7 Feb. 1978, Cedar Rapids, Ia; s. of Larry Kutcher and Diane Kutcher; m. Demi Moore 2005 (divorced 2013); ed Clear Creek-Amana High School, Tiffin, Ia, Univ. of Iowa; discovered by local talent scout while a biochemical engineering student at Univ. of Iowa 1997; won Fresh Faces of Iowa modelling contest 1997, pursued modelling career in New York; cr., produced and hosted Punk'd; producer and co-creator of supernatural TV programme Room 401 and reality TV programme Beauty and the Geek; co-f. Demi and Ashton Foundation 2010; Co-founder Katalyst (studio for social media); joined State Dept and sr execs from eBay and Twitter on trip to Russia to help start up a Russian Silicon Valley 2010, also part of Pres. Obama's first US-Russia Innovation Del.; One of Teen People Magazine's 25 Hottest Stars Under 25 2002, named one of TIME Magazine's Top 100 Most Influential People 2010. *Film roles:* Coming Soon 1999, Down to You 2000, Deception 2000, Dude, Where's My Car? 2000, Texas Rangers 2001, Just Married 2003, My Boss's Daughter (also co-producer) 2003, Cheaper by the Dozen (uncredited) 2003, The Butterfly Effect (also exec. producer) 2004, Guess Who 2005, A Lot Like Love 2005, Bobby 2006, The Guardian 2006, Open Season (voice) 2006, Boog and Elliot's Midnight Bun Run (video short) (voice) 2006, What Happens in Vegas 2008, Spread (also producer) 2009, Personal Effects 2009, Valentine's Day 2010, Killers (also producer) 2010, No Strings Attached 2011, New Year's Eve 2011, Jobs 2013. *Television roles:* Just Shoot Me! (series) 2001, Grounded for Life (series) 2002, Robot Chicken (series) (voice) 2005, That '70s Show (series) 1998–2006, Miss Guided (series) 2008, Two and a Half Men (CBS series) (also writer) 2011–13, Men at Work (series) 2013. *Television produced:* exec. producer: Punk'd (series) (also writer) 2003–12, You've Got a Friend (series documentary) 2004, Beauty and the Geek (series) 2005–08, The Real Wedding Crashers (series) 2007, Adventures in Hollyhood (series documentary) 2007, Room 401 (series) 2007, Pop Fiction (series) 2008, Miss Guided (series) 2008, Opportunity Knocks (series) 2008–09, Choose Me (film) 2009, Game Show in My Head (series) 2009, The Beautiful Life: TBL (series) (also writer and co-producer) 2009, True Beauty (series) 2009–10, Numbnuts (series) 2010, Eric Finley: Comment Counselor (series) 2012, Rituals (series documentary) 2012–13, Forever Young (series) 2013. *Address:* c/o Adam Venit or Greg Siegel, WME Entertainment, 9601 Wilshire Boulevard, Beverley Hills, CA 90210, USA (office); c/o Stephanie Simon, Untitled Entertainment, 331 North Maple Drive, 3rd Floor, Beverley Hills, CA 90210, USA (office); Katalyst Films, 6430 Sunset Drive, Suite 1400, Los Angeles, CA 90028, USA (office). *Telephone:* (323) 785-2710 (office).

KUTELIA, Batu, PhD; Georgian politician and diplomatist; *Deputy Secretary, State Security Council;* b. 16 Jan. 1974, Tbilisi; m.; one s. one d.; ed Georgian Tech. Univ., Georgian Inst. of Public Affairs, NATO Defence Coll.; Deputy Head of Mil. Cooperation Div., Mil.-Political Dept, Ministry of Foreign Affairs 1997–98, Head of Div. 1998–2000, Deputy Dir Mil.-Political Dept 2000–03; Deputy Head of Mission, Embassy in London 2003–04; Dir Political Security Dept, Nat. Security Council May–June 2004; Head of Foreign Intelligence Dept, Ministry of State Security June–Oct. 2004, Deputy Minister of State Security Oct.–Dec. 2004; Head of Foreign Intelligence Special Service 2006; Deputy Minister of Foreign Affairs Sept.–Dec. 2006; Deputy Minister of Defence 2006–07, First Deputy Minister of Defence 2007–08; Amb. to USA 2008–10; Deputy Sec., State Security Council 2010–; Soros Foundation Scholarship 1994, 1995, 1996, 1997, GIPA Special Award for Academic Performance 1996, Pres. of Georgia Scholarship 1998, NATO Defence Coll. Scholarship 2000, Certificate of Appreciation of Pres. of Georgia 2000. *Address:* State Security Council, 0134 Tbilisi, Ingorokva 7, Georgia (office). *Telephone:* (32) 28-77-11 (office).

KUTESA, Sam; Ugandan lawyer and politician; *Minister of Foreign Affairs;* b. 1 Feb. 1949; in pvt. law practice with Kutesa and Co. Advocates 1973–2001; Attorney-Gen. 1985–86; mem. Parl. representing Mawogola Co. 1996; fmr Minister of State for Investment, Ministry of Finance, Planning and Econ. Devt 2001–05; Minister of Foreign Affairs 2005–11 (resgnd), 2012–. *Address:* Ministry of Foreign Affairs, Embassy House, POB 7048, Kampala, Uganda (office). *Telephone:* (41) 4345661 (office). *Fax:* (41) 4258722 (office). *E-mail:* info@mofa.go.ug (office). *Website:* www.mofa.go.ug (office).

KUTSYN, Lt-Gen. Mykhaylo Nikolayevich; Ukrainian army officer and fmr government official; *Chief of the General Staff and Chief of the Armed Forces;* b. 15 Aug. 1957, Svoboda, Berehove Raion, Zakarpattia Oblast; m.; two d.; ed Annunciation Higher Tank Command School, Mil. Acad. of Armoured Forces, Moscow, Operational and Strategic Nat. Defence Acad. of Ukraine; served as Tank Platoon Leader Group of Soviet Forces in Germany; commdr of a platoon and Co. Commdr of Cadets, Kharkov Higher Tank Command School 1980–87; Deputy Commdr of tank bn, then Commdr, then Deputy Chief of Staff, Tank Regt, Belarusian Mil. Dist 1990–92; enlisted in Armed Forces of Ukraine Dec. 1992; Chief of Staff and Commdr of Regt, Carpathian Mil. Dist, Army Forces of Ukraine 1992–96; Chief of Staff, Commdr of Mechanised Div., Western Operational Command 1996–99; Chief of Staff, Commdr of 13th Army Corps, Army of the Western Operational Command 2001–04; First Deputy Commdr of Western Operational Command 2004, Commdr 2004–10; Deputy Minister of Defence 2010–14; Chief of the Gen. Staff and Chief of the Armed Forces Feb. 2014–; Medal for Battle Merit (Soviet award), Medal For Mil. Service to Ukraine 1997, Order of Bohdan Khmelnytsky, Third Class 2005, Second Class 2008, Medal 'For Faultless Service', First, Second and Fhird Degree; numerous other medals and insignia of the Ministry of Defence. *Address:* Ministry of Defence, 01021 Kyiv, vul. M. Hrushevskoho 30/1, Ukraine (office). *Telephone:* (44) 253-11-56 (office). *Fax:* (44) 226-20-15 (office). *E-mail:* webmaster@mil.gov.ua (office). *Website:* www.mil.gov.ua (office).

KUTZ, Kazimierz; Polish film and theatre director and politician; b. 16 Feb. 1929, Szopienice, nr Katowice; m.; two s. two d.; ed State Higher School of Film, Television and Theatre, Łódź 1953; film and theatre dir 1959–; Dir Gen. Katowice Regional Television 1976–81; Lecturer, Dept of Radio and TV, Univ. of Silesia 1979–82; Co-Founder and Pres. Silesian Film Soc. 1981–; Chair. Solidarity Alliance of Creative Communities of the Silesian Region 1981; teacher, Directing Dept, State Higher School of Theatre, Kraków 1986–91; Man. Dir Krakow Regional Television 1990–91; mem. Soc. of Authors ZAiKS; Senator (Unia Wolnosci—Freedom Union) 1997–; Vice-Marshal of Senate 2001–; Dr hc (Univ. of Opole) 1997; Officer's Cross, Order of Polonia Restituta; State Prize (First Class) 1970, Award of the Minister of Culture and Art (1st Class) 1981, Award of the Chairman of State Radio and Television 1987, Nat. Cultural Award of Merit 1989, Solidarity – 1989 Award of the Independent Culture Cttee 1990, Teatr monthly Konrad Swinarski Award for Lifetime Achievement in Television 1993, (Asscn of Stage Artists and Composers) Hon. Distinction for Outstanding Creative Achievement 1993, Warsaw Mermaid Polish Film Critics' Award 1994, Silesian Cultural Award, Govt of Lower Saxony 1995, Korfanty Award for Lifetime Artistic Achievement 1995, Hon. Crown of Casimir the Great 1997, Grand Prix, 5th Talia Comedy Festival, Tarnow 2001, Hon. 'Jancio Wodnik', Prowincjonalia Festival, Wrzesnia 2002. *Films include:* Krzyż Walecznych (Cross of Valour) 1959, Nikt nie woła (Nobody's Calling) 1960, Ludzie pociagu (Night Train) 1961, Tarpany (Wild Horses) 1962, Mil czenie (Silence) 1963, Upal (Heat) 1964, Ktokol wiek wie... (Whoever May Know) 1966, Skok (The Leap) 1967, Sól ziemi czarnej (Salt of the Black Earth) 1970, Perła w koronie (Pearl in the Crown) 1972, Linia (The Line) 1974, Znikad donikad (From Nowhere to Nowhere) 1975, Paciorki jednego różańca (The Beads of One Rosary) (Golden Lion, Gdansk Film Festival 1981) 1980, Linie 1975, Na straży swej staé będę (I Shall Always Stand Guard) 1983, Wkrotce nadejda bracia (The Brothers Will Come Soon) 1985, Straszny sen dzidziusia Gorkiewicza (The Terrible Dream of Babyface Gorkiewicz) (TV) 1993, Zawrocony (The Convert) (TV) (Golden Lion, Gdansk 1994, Special Prize, Prix Europa Festival, Berlin 1994, Golden Grapes, Lubushan Film Summer, Zielona Gora 1994, Golden Calf for Best European Film, Int. Film Festival, Utrecht 1995, Int. Jury Diploma, Int. Film Festival, Moscow 1995) 1994, Śmierć jak kromka chleba (Death Like a Slice of Bread) 1994, Zawrócony 1994, Pułkownik Kwiatkowski (Colonel Kwiatkowski) (Silver Grapes, 26th Lubushan Film Summer, Lagow 1996, Golden Duck for the Best Polish Film of the 1996 1997) 1995, Slawa i chwala (Fame and Glory) (TV) 1997. *Screenplays:* Sól ziemi czarnej, Perła koronie, Paciorki jednego różańca. *Plays:* Do piachu (Down to Sand), Kartoteka roznucona (The Card Index Scattered), Kartoteka (The Card Index), Na czworakach (On All Fours), Spaghetti i miecz (Spaghetti and the Sword), Damy i huzary (Ladies and Hussar) 2001. *Address:* 40-079 Katowice, ul. Gliwicka 1; Senate, ul. Wiejska 6, 00-902 Warsaw (office); ul. Marconich 5 m. 6, 02-954 Warsaw, Poland. *Telephone:* (32) 2068803; (22) 8589259. *E-mail:* biuro@kazimierzkutz.pl; kutz@nw.senat.gov.pl (office). *Website:* www.senat.gov.pl (office).

KUUGONGELWA-AMADHILA, Saara, MSc; Namibian politician; *Minister of Finance;* b. 12 Oct. 1967; ed Univ. of London, UK, Univ. of Namibia; Dir-Gen. Nat. Planning Comm. 1997–2003; fmr Gov. African Devt Bank; Minister of Finance 2003–; Vice Chair., Eminent Bd mem. Pan Afrikan Centre of Namibia (Pacon); mem. Swapo Party Central Cttee. *Address:* Ministry of Finance, Fiscus Building, John Meinert Street, PMB 13295, Windhoek, Namibia (office). *Telephone:* (61) 2099111 (office). *Fax:* (61) 230179 (office). *E-mail:* skuugongelwa-amadhila@mof.gov.na (office).

KUWAIZ, Abdullah Ibrahim el-, MA, MBA, PhD; Saudi Arabian banker, politician and diplomatist; b. 21 Aug. 1939, Dawadmi; two s. two d.; ed King Saud Univ. Saudi Arabia, Pacific Lutheran Univ. and St Louis Univ., USA; accountant, Pensions Dept, Ministry of Finance and Nat. Economy 1959–67, economist, 1967–81 (adviser 1977–81); Exec. Dir Arab Monetary Fund, Abu Dhabi 1977–80; Co-Chair. Financial Co-operation Cttee, Euro-Arab Dialogue 1978–83; Asst Under-Sec. for Econ. Affairs 1981–87; Deputy Minister of Finance and Nat. Economy, Saudi Arabia 1987–2001; Dir-Gen. and Chair. of Bd Arab Monetary Fund, Abu Dhabi 1987–89; Chair. Saudi-Kuwait Cement Co., Saudi Arabia 1991–93; Asst Sec.-Gen. for Econ. Affairs, Co-operation Council for the Arab States of the Gulf 1981–95; mem. of Bd and mem. Exec. Cttee, Gulf Int. Bank, Bahrain 1977–90; mem. of Bd Gulf Co-operation Council's Org. for Measures and Standards 1984–95, Oxford Energy Inst., Oxford, UK 1985–, Int. Maritime Bureau, London 1985–88, Econ. Forum, Cairo 1994–2001, Islamic Devt Bank, Jeddah 1997–2003, Arab Fund for Econ. Devt, Kuwait 1998–2000; Gen. Man. Gulf Int. Bank, Bahrain 1997–2001; Chair. of Bd Bosna Bank Int. Sarajevo 2000; Amb. to Bahrain 2002–09; Medal of Merit for Accomplishment in Global Climate Coalition (GCC) from King Fahd Ibn Abdulaziz 1989, Lifetime Accomplishment Award Arab Bankers Association of North America (ABANA) 2003. *Publications:* numerous papers relating to banking, oil, finance and econ. devt and integration delivered at symposia in N America, Europe and the Middle East. *Leisure Interests:* hiking, swimming, reading, debating and writing. *Address:* PO Box 10866, Riyadh 11443, Saudi Arabia (home). *Telephone:* (1) 488-0882 (home). *Fax:* (1) 480-2190 (home). *E-mail:* kuwaiz@hotmail.com (home).

KUX, Barbara, MBA; Swiss business executive; *Head of Supply Chain Management and Chief Sustainability Officer, Siemens AG;* b. 1954, Zurich; d. of Prof. Dr Ernst Kux; m.; ed Institut Européen d'Admin des Affaires (INSEAD), Paris, France; Marketing Man., Nestlé SA, Germany 1979–84, Vice-Pres. Cen. and Eastern Europe Region, responsible for building up market leading business in Poland and Russia 1993–99; Man. Consultant, McKinsey & Co., Germany 1984–89; Vice-Pres. Asea Brown Boveri AG (ABB) responsible for entry into Cen. and Eastern Europe 1989–92, Pres. ABB Power Ventures 1989–92; Exec. Dir Ford Europe 1999–2003; Chief Procurement Office and mem. Group Man. Cttee, Royal Philips Electronics NV 2003–08; Head of Supply Chain Man. and Chief Sustainability Officer, Siemens AG 2008–, also mem. Man. Bd; mem. Bd of Dirs INSEAD 2003–, Total SA; MBA with Distinction (third best student), ranked by Fortune magazine amongst the 50 Most Powerful Women in Business outside the US (12th) 2003, (26th) 2004, (24th) 2005, (21st) 2006, (19th) 2007, (sixth) 2009, (fourth) 2010–12, elected Global Leader for Tomorrow, World Econ. Forum. *Leisure interests:* cultural activities, sports, spending time with friends and family. *Address:* Siemens AG, Wittelsbacherplatz 2, 80333 Munich, Germany (office).

Telephone: (89) 636-36669 (office). *Fax:* (89) 636-52000 (office). *E-mail:* constantin .birnstiel@siemens.com (office). *Website:* www.siemens.com (office).

KUZMANOVIĆ, Rajko, PhD; Bosnia and Herzegovina judge, academic and politician; *President, Academy of Sciences and Arts of Republika Srpska;* b. 1 Dec. 1931, Čelinac; s. of Nikola Kuzmanović and Vida Kuzmanović; m. Ljubica (Ladan) Kuzmanović; ed Univ. of Zagreb; fmr head of educ. service in municipality of Čelinac; fmr Speaker of Ass. in Čelinac; fmr Prin. of School of Politics, Banja Luka; fmr mem. Exec. Bd Municipality of Banja Luka; teacher, Faculty of Law, Univ. of Banja Luka 1975, External Collaborator-Asst 1975–77, Dean 1977–81, Assoc. Prof. 1981–85, Prof. of Constitutional Law 1985–, Head of Constitutional Science, Faculty of Law for 25 years, Deputy Dean 1979–81, a Dean of Faculty of Law 1983–85, 1996–2000, a Dean of Faculty of Business Economy, Deputy Rector Univ. of Banja Luka 1986–88, Rector 1988–92; fmr Deputy Rector Slavic Univ. Magen, Moscow; part-time Prof., Faculties of Law, Mostar and Prishtina, Faculty of Philosophy, Banja Luka, Coll. of Interior, Faculty of Business Economy, Banja Luka, Apeiron Pan-European Univ., Banja Luka; fmr Pres. Scientific Council Inst. for Int. Law and Int. Business Co-operation, Banja Luka, Veselin Masleša Scientific Council Centre for Political Studies and Research, Banja Luka, Council of History Inst., Asscn of Univ. Teachers and Scientific Cadre (Bosnia and Herzegovina), Community of Univs in Bosnia and Herzegovina, Community of Univs of Yugoslavia, Asscn of Lawyers in Republika Srpska; mem. Council of Educational and Pedagogy Inst. (Bosnia and Herzegovina), Council of Museums of Bosnian Krajina; mem. Parl., Ass. of Socialist Repub. of Bosnia and Herzegovina 1961–65; mem. numerous comms at Nat. Ass. of Republika Srpska 1995–2000, including Comm. for Creating and Altering the Constitution of Republika Srpska, Council of Law in the Govt of Republika Srpska; mem. League of Communists of Bosnia and Herzegovina, Cen. Cttee of League of Communists of Bosnia and Herzegovina, Republican Conf. of SSRN of Bosnia and Herzegovina; judge 1994–98, Pres. Constitutional Court of Republika Srpska 1998–2002, mem. High Prosecutor's Council; mem. Alliance of Ind. Social Democrats; Pres. of Republika Srpska 2007–10; Corresp. mem. Acad. of Sciences and Arts of Republika Srpska 1997–2004, mem. and Pres. 2004–; mem. European Acad. of Sciences and Arts, Salzburg 2009–, Russian Acad. of Natural and Social Sciences (RAEH), Moscow 2010, Spanish Royal Acad. for Economy and Finance (RACEF), Barcelona 2010, Acad. of Sciences of Higher Educ. of Ukraine, Kiev 2012; Order for Work, Order for Mil. Merits, Order for Merits for People, Pres. of Socialist Fed. of Repub. of Yugoslavia, Order of Honour Golden Rays of Republika Srpska, Peter the Great Medal of the First Order (Russian Fed.), Order of Republika Srpska 2012; Pres. of Republika Srpska Award, Medallion and Charter, Univ. of Banja Luka, Konji (Turkey), Katowice (Poland), Ostrava (Czech Repub.), Charter and Gold Coat of Arms of City of Banja Luka, Gold Medallion of Čelinac, Gold Medallion of Faculty of Law, Banja Luka, Veselin Masleša Medallion for scientific work, charters of several other cities, Higher Law Award' Femida' Int. Bar Asscn (Russia), Grand Prix' Leonardo da Vinci. *Publications:* 28 textbooks, including Constitutional Law, Science of Managing Bases, Parallel Political Systems, Constitution and Civil Rights (co-author); more than 200 articles in scientific and professional journals on constitutional law and political systems, state man. and governing, educ. and schooling, and on numerous other gen. and social subjects, New Essays on Constitutionality and Statehood, The Time of Stabilisation, Hemeroteka. *Address:* Academy of Sciences and Arts of Republic of Srpska, Bana Lazarevića 1, 78000 Banja Luka, Bosnia and Herzegovina (office). *Telephone:* (51) 333702 (office); (51) 333706 (office). *Fax:* (51) 333701 (office). *E-mail:* predsjednik@anurs.org (office); medj.saradnja@anurs.org (office); anurs@blic.net (office). *Website:* www.anurs.org (office).

KUZMIN, Alexander Viktorovich; Russian architect; b. 12 July 1951, Moscow; s. of Victor Alexandrovich Kuzmin and Antonina Alexeevna Kuzmin; m. 1996; one s. one d.; ed Moscow Inst. of Architecture; researcher, Research and Project Inst. of the Master Plan of Moscow, Dir from 1987; Deputy Head, Chief Moscow Dept of Architecture 1991, First Deputy Chair. Moscow Cttee for Architecture and Urban Devt; elected Chief Architect of Moscow 1996–2012, Chair. Architectural and City Planning Cttee, Moscow; mem. Russian Acad. of Architecture and Building Sciences 1998; oversaw works to Voentorg Hotel Moscow, building forecourt, shopping malls, Theatre 'Et Cetera', Sretenskii Gate; chief architect of reconstruction of Moscow streets, cen. region of Moscow, building of Olympic village. *Leisure interest:* collecting old medals. *Address:* c/o Moscow Committee for Architecture and Urban Development, Triumphalnaya pl. 1, 125047 Moscow, Russia. *E-mail:* asi@mka.mos.ru.

KUZ'MUK, Col-Gen. Oleksander Ivanovich; Ukrainian military officer and politician; b. 17 April 1954, Dyatilivka, Khmelnitsk Region, Ukraine; m.; two c.; ed Kharkov Guards' Higher Tank School, Moscow Mil. Acad. of Armoured Forces; commdr tank platoon, Bn; Deputy Commdr Regt, Group of Soviet Troops in Germany 1975–83; Commdg posts in Leningrad, Carpathian, Odessa Mil. commands 1983–95; Commdr Nat. Guards of Ukraine 1995–96; Minister of Defence 1996–2001, 2004–05; Deputy Prime Minister 2006–07. *Address:* c/o Ministry of Defence, Bankova str. 6, 252005 Kiev, Ukraine (office).

KUZNETSOV, Boris Avramovich; Russian barrister and writer; b. 19 March 1944, Kirov; s. of Avram Mikhailovich Kuznetsov and Nina Aleksandrovna Ukhanova; m. 2nd Nadezhda Georgiyevna Chernaya; two c.; ed Moscow Juridical Acad., Research Inst. of USSR Ministry of Internal Affairs; mem. staff, Criminal Investigation Dept, St Petersburg and Magadan Region 1962–82; mem. Magadan Regional Bd of Lawyers 1982–85, twice expelled for disagreement with party officials; Head of Lab., Inst. of Biology Problems of the North br., USSR Acad. of Sciences, Magadan 1985–89; adviser to mems Inter-regional people's deputy 1989–91; mem. St Petersburg Bd of Lawyers 1991–95, Lawyers' Interrepublic Bd 1995–2007; fmr Head, Boris Kuznetsov and Partners Lawyer's Agency; acted in numerous high-profile criminal and human rights cases, including the families of the 118 sailors killed in the Kursk nuclear submarine, relatives of murdered journalist Anna Politkovskaya, the scientist Igor Sutyagin jailed on espionage charges, NGO dir Manana Aslamazyan; left Russia 2007, granted asylum in USA 2008; CIS Lawyer of the Year Award, Golden Sign for Defence of Russian-Speaking People and Intellectuals Outside Russia, 1998, Anatoli Koni's Medal 2001, Award Hanger from the Navy of the Russian Fed. *Publications:* Ona Utonula: Pravda O Kurske Kotoruiu Skryl Genprokuror Ustinov 2005; six other

books. *Leisure interests:* pre-Revolutionary juridical literature and literature on the navy, sailing models construction.

KUZNETSOV, Nikolai Aleksandrovich; Russian cybernetician; *Counsellor, Institute of Radioengineering and Electronics, Russian Academy of Sciences;* b. 9 March 1939, Volgogradskaya Region; m.; two c.; ed Moscow Inst. of Physics and Tech.; Jr, Sr Researcher, Deputy Dir Inst. of Problems of Man. 1965–88; Dir Gen. of Research Production Union Moskva 1988–89; Dir Inst. for Information Transmission Problems (IPPI) 1990–2006; Counsellor, Inst. of Radioengineering and Electronics, Russian Acad. of Sciences 2006–; Corresp. mem. USSR (now Russian) Acad. of Sciences 1987, mem. 1994; mem. IEEE; research in theory of automatic man. and informatics; USSR State Prize. *Publications include:* Management of Observations in Automatic Systems 1961, Synthesis of Algorithms at Variable Criterion of Optimality 1966, Methods of Study of Stability of Dissynchronized Pulse Systems 1991. *Leisure interests:* skiing, singing. *Address:* Institute of Radioengineering and Electronics, Russian Academy of Sciences, Mokhovaya 11-7, 125009 Moscow, Russia (office). *Telephone:* (495) 629-30-05 (office). *Fax:* (495) 629-30-05 (office). *E-mail:* kuznetsov@cplire.ru (office).

KUZNETSOV, Nikolai Vasilyevich; Russian mathematician; b. 24 June 1939, Hachmas, Azerbaijan; s. of Vasilii Kuznetsov and Evdokia Gureutieva; m. Galina Pavlovna Kuznetsova 1975; two c.; ed Moscow Inst. of Physics and Tech.; jr researcher, Inst. of Math., USSR Acad. of Sciences 1965–69; jr, sr researcher, Moscow V. Lenin Pedagogical Inst. 1969–70; Head of Div., Head of Dept, Cen. Research Inst. of Information and Tech.-Econ. Studies 1970–71; Head of Div., Research Inst. of Systems of Man. and Econs 1972–73; Sr Researcher, Head of Lab. Khabarovsk Research Inst. of Complex Studies 1973–81; Deputy Dir Computer's Cen., Far East br. USSR Acad. of Sciences 1989–91; Deputy Dir Inst. of Applied Math. 1991–92; Corresp. mem. USSR (now Russian) Acad. of Sciences 1987; research in spectral theory, theory of modular and automorphic functions in math. physics. *Publications:* On Eigenfunctions of One Integral Equation 1970, Poincaré Series and Extended Lemer Hypothesis 1985; numerous articles in scientific journals. *Leisure interest:* chess. *Address:* Institute of Applied Mathematics, Far East Branch of Russian Academy of Sciences, 50 Svetlanskaya str., 690950 Vladivostok, Russia (office). *Telephone:* (4232) 22-86-30 (Vladivostok) (office); (4212) 33-46-76 (Khabarovsk) (office); (4212) 22-76-36 (home). *E-mail:* info@hq .febras.ru (office).

KUZNETSOV, Oleg Leonidovich, DTech; Russian geophysicist; *President, Russian Academy of Natural Sciences;* b. 29 Aug. 1938; m.; two c.; ed Moscow S. Ordzhonikidze Inst. of Geological Research, Moscow State Univ.; researcher, Inst. of Oil, USSR (now Russian) Acad. of Sciences 1962–70; Head of lab., All-Union Inst. of Nuclear Geophysics and Geochemistry, USSR Ministry of Geology (now State Scientific Centre of All-Russian Inst. of Geosystems) 1970–79, Dir 1979–; Prof., Moscow State Univ. 1986–; Vice-Pres. Russian Acad. of Nat. Sciences 1990–93, Pres. 1993–; Founder and Rector, Int. Univ. of Nature, Soc. and Man., Dubna 1994–2008, Pres. 2008–; Gen. Constructor, Global Information System GEOS 1985–91; mem. New York Acad. of Sciences 1994, Int. Acad. of Sciences on Nature and Soc. 1993, Int. Acad. of Higher Schooling 1995, Oriental Acad. of Oil and Gas 1994; Hon. mem. Hungarian Soc. of Geophysics, Euro-Asian Geophysical Soc.; Hon. Prospector of the USSR 1985; Hon. Worker of the Oil and Gas Industry of the USSR 1986; USSR State Prize 1982, Honoured Worker of Science and Tech. of Russian Fed. 1992, Prize of German Econ. Club 1996, A. Chizhevsky Prize 1997, Medal of Honour of the Russian Fed. 1998, Golden ROSING-2002, Gratitude of the Pres. of the Russian Fed. 2002, Honoured Worker of Science and Tech., Moscow region, Moscow Region Gov.'s Award (in Econs) 2007. *Publications:* more than 300 scientific works, including 14 monographs, four reference books, 67 inventions and more than 60 patents on geophysical processes, seismoacoustics, non-linear geophysics, geoinformatics and information tech. *Address:* Russian Academy of Natural Sciences, Varshavskoye shosse 8, 117105 Moscow, Russia (office). *Telephone:* (495) 954-53-50 (office). *Fax:* (495) 958-37-11 (office). *E-mail:* info@ raen.info (office). *Website:* www.raen.info (office).

KVAMME, E. Floyd, BS, MSE; American computer scientist and government official; *Co-Chairman, President's Council of Advisors on Science and Technology (PCAST);* ed Univ. of California, Berkeley and Syracuse Univ.; Founder-mem. Nat. Semiconductor 1967, Gen. Man. Semiconductor Operations, Pres. Nat. Advanced Systems (subsidiary); Exec. Vice-Pres. of Sales and Marketing, Apple Computer 1982; Pnr, Kleiner Perkins Caufield & Byers 1984, now Pnr Emer.; Chair. Electronic Commerce Advisory Council for the State of Calif. 1998; Co-Chair. President's Council of Advisors on Science Tech (PCAST), Washington, DC 2001–; Chair. Empower America; mem. Bd of Dirs Brio Tech., Gemfire, Harmonic Lightwaves, Triquint Semiconductor, Photon Dynamics, Power Integrations; mem. of Advisory Bd Markkula Center for Applied Ethics, Santa Clara Univ., Nat. Venture Capital Asscn; mem. Exec. Cttee of The Tech. Network; fmr mem. Finance Cttee, Fong for Senate Campaign, High Tech. Advisory Cttee, Nat. Finance Cttee of the Bush for President Campaign. *Address:* President's Council of Advisors on Science and Technology (PCAST), Office of Science and Technology Policy, Executive Office of the President, Washington, DC 20502, USA (office). *Website:* www.ostp.gov/PCAST/pcast.html (office).

KVAPIL, Radoslav; Czech pianist; b. 15 March 1934, Brno; s. of Karel Kvapil and Marie Kvapilová; m. Eva Mašláňová 1960 (died 1993); one s.; ed Gymnasium Dr. Kudely, Brno and Janáček Acad. of Musical Arts; first piano recital Brno 1954; 1st prize Janáček Competition 1958, Int. Competition, Czechoslovak Radio 1968; Prof. of Piano, Prague Conservatory 1963–73; concerts in countries throughout Europe, in USA and Japan 1963–; performed world premiere of Dvořák's Cypresses 1983; Dir South Bohemia Music Festival 1991–; Pres. Yehudi Menuhin Soc., Prague 1990–, Dvořák Soc., Prague 1997–, Czech Soc. for Music and Arts 1990–; Hon. Vice-Pres. Dvořák Soc., London; Chevalier des Arts et des Lettres 2002; Janáček Medal (Cultural Ministry). *Recordings include:* complete piano works of Dvořák and Martinů, complete piano and chamber music of Janáček, complete piano works of Jan Hugo Voříšek 1973–74, complete polka cycles of Smetana, Czech contemporary piano music, Piano Concerto by A. Rejcha (first ever recording), Anthology of Czech piano music (for Unicorn-Kanchana label), eight vols, works of Dvořák performed on the composer's piano 1999, Ullman's Sonatas 5–7 2002. *Leisure interest:* chess. *Address:* c/o Margaret Murphy Management, 7 Grove Park, Wanstead, London E11 2DN, England (office); Hradecká 5, 13000 Prague 3, Czech

Republic. *Telephone:* (20) 8530-1305 (office); (2) 67312430. *E-mail:* info@ margaretmurphy.com (office); r.kvapil@ecn.cz (office). *Website:* www .margaretmurphy.com (office). *Fax:* (2) 67312430 (home).

KVASHNIN, Col-Gen. Anatoly Vassilyevich; Russian politician; b. 15 Aug. 1946, Ufa, Bashkir ASSR; ed Kurgan Machine Construction Inst., Acad. of Armoured Units, Acad. of Gen. Staff; army service, Commdr of regiment, div., army 1969–; Deputy, First Deputy Head Main Operation Dept 1993–95; Commdr Allied Group of armed forces in Chechnya 1994–95; Commdr Armed Forces of N Caucasian Command 1995–97; Chief of Gen. Staff of Armed Forces of Russian Fed. 1997–2004; First Deputy Minister of Defence, Russian Fed. 1997–2004; Rep. of Russian Pres. to Siberian Fed. Okrug (Dist) 2004–10; Légion d'honneur 2004, Order of Honour 2006. *Leisure interests:* painting, sports. *Address:* c/o Office of the Presidential Representative, 630091 Novosibirsk, ul. Derzhavina 18/120, Russia.

KVIRIKASHVILI, Giorgi; Georgian politician; *First Deputy Prime Minister and Minister of the Economy and Sustainable Development;* b. 20 July 1967; m.; four c.; ed studied Medicine and Econs at Tbilisi State Medical Univ., Univ. of Illinois, USA, Georgian Tech. Univ.; Trading Operations Officer, then Deputy Dir, Credit Dept, United Georgian Bank (now VTB Bank Georgia) 1993–96; Deputy Dir Gen. TradeInvest Bank 1996–97; Dir of Business Devt and Br. Network Man., Deputy Dir Asset-Liability Man., United Georgian Bank 1998; Exec. Man. Consultant, First Commercial Bank 2004–06; Dir Gen. Cartu Bank 2006–11; expert in financial sector and pensions reform, Lenzie Fisher Hendry LLC March–Oct. 2012; mem. Georgian Dream 2012–; mem. Parl. 1999–2004; Minister of the Economy and Sustainable Devt Oct. 2012–, First Deputy Prime Minister July 2013–. *Address:* Ministry of the Economy and Sustainable Development, 0108 Tbilisi, Chanturia 12, Georgia (office). *Telephone:* (32) 299-10-11 (office). *Fax:* (32) 293-28-46 (home). *E-mail:* ministry@economy.ge (office). *Website:* www.economy.ge (office).

KVITOVÁ, Petra; Czech professional tennis player; b. 8 March 1990, Bílovec, Czechoslovakia; d. of Jiří Kvita and Pavla Kvitová; plays left-handed (two-handed backhand); trained in her hometown until age 16; turned professional 2006; played first career events on ITF (Int. Tennis Fed.) Circuit, winning two singles titles 2006; played first WTA (Women's Tennis Asscn) main draw at Stockholm 2007, won four singles titles on ITF Circuit 2007; qualified for her first WTA Tour Main Draw in Open Gaz de France 2008; winner Moorilla Hobart Int. 2009, Brisbane Int. 2011, Paris (Indoors) 2011, Mutua Madrid Open 2011, Dubai Duty Free Tennis Championships 2013; Grand Slam results: fourth round, French Open 2008, 2011, fourth round, US Open 2009, quarter-finalist, Australian Open 2011, winner, Wimbledon 2011; mem. Federation Cup Team for Czech Repub. 2007–; ranked World No. 2 31 Oct. 2011; first Grand Slam event winner born in 1990s; coached by David Kotyza; WTA Newcomer of the Year 2010, WTA Player of the Year 2011, WTA Most Improved Player 2011, Karen Krantzcke Sportsmanship Award 2011, Fan Favorite Breakthrough Player 2011, ITF World Champion 2011, Czech Athlete of the Year 2011. *Address:* c/o Women's Tennis Association, One Progress Plaza, Suite 1500, St Petersburg, FL 33701, USA. *Telephone:* (727) 895-5000. *Fax:* (727) 894-1982. *E-mail:* info@wtatennis.com. *Website:* www.wtatennis .com.

KWAJE LASUBA, Agnes; South Sudanese politician and fmr teacher; m. Joseph Oduho (deceased); mem. Southern Sudan Legislative Ass. for Cen. Equatoria, fmr Chair. Regional and Int. Cooperation Cttee; Minister of Gender, Child and Social Welfare 2009–13; mem. Sudan People's Liberation Movt. *Address:* c/o Ministry of Gender, Child and Social Welfare, Ministries Complex, Juba, South Sudan.

KWANKWASO, Rabiu; Nigerian politician; Exec. Gov. Kano state 1999–2003; Minister of Defence 2003–07; Special Presidential Envoy to Somalia and Darfur 2007; currently Leader People's Democratic Party in Kano. *Address:* c/o People's Democratic Party, Wadata Plaza, Michael Okpara Way, Zone 5, Wuse, Abuja, Nigeria (office).

KWAPONG, Alex. A., PhD; Ghanaian academic and government official; b. 8 March 1927, Akropong, Akwapim; s. of E. A. and Theophilia Kwapong; m. Evelyn Teiko Caesar 1956; six d.; ed Achimota Coll. and King's Coll., Cambridge; Visiting Prof., Princeton Univ. 1962; fmr Pro Vice-Chancellor and Head of Classics Dept, Ghana Univ., Vice-Chancellor 1966–75; Vice-Rector for Institutional Planning and Resource Devt UN Univ. 1976–88; Lester B. Pearson Chair. in Devt Studies, Dalhousie Univ. 1988–91; Dir of African Programmes, Teacher Educ., Research and Evaluation, The Commonwealth of Learning 1991–93; mem. Council of State 2000–04, Chair. 2002–04; Chair. ARB Apex Bank Ltd.; mem. Political and Educ. Cttees., Nat. Liberation Council 1966; mem. Bd Aspen Inst. Berlin 1975–, Harold Macmillan Trust 1986–, Int. Council for Educ. Devt, Int. Foundation for Educ. and Self-help 1988–; Fellow, Ghana Acad. of Arts and Sciences; Trustee Achimota Trust; Order of Volta (Ghana); Hon. DLitt (Warwick, Ife, Ghana, Univ. of Ghana); Hon. LLD (Princeton) 1974. *Publications:* Higher Education and Development in Africa Today: A Reappraisal 1979; Under-development and the Challenges of the 1980s: The Role of Knowledge 1980, The Relevance of the African Universities to the Development Needs of Africa 1980, Medical Education and National Development 1987, Culture, Development and African Unity 1988, African Scientific and Technical Institution Building and the Role of International Co-operation 1988, The Challenge of Education in Africa 1988, Some Reflections on International Education in the 90s in the Role of Service Learning in International Education 1989, Capacity Building and Human Resource Development in Africa (co-ed. with B. Lesser) 1990, Meeting the Challenge, The African Capacity Building Initiative (co-ed. with B. Lesser) 1992. *Leisure interests:* music, learning Japanese, tennis, billiards.

KWAŚNIEWSKA, Jolanta; Polish organization executive, lawyer and charity worker; b. 3 June 1955, Gdansk; d. of Julian Konty and Anna Konty; m. Aleksander Kwaśniewski (Pres. of Poland 1995–2005) 1979; one d.; ed Faculty of Law, Univ. of Gdansk; began career as lawyer 1984; est. real estate agency 1991, co-dir with husband until his assumption of Presidency of Poland 1995; est. Communication Without Barriers Foundation (org. to help disabled people and cr. medical centre for children) 1997, Let's Open the World Programme (provides funds for Polish orphans to visit European countries), Help the Talented Youth Foundation; Patron Polish UNICEF, Nat. Coalition for Breast Cancer, Adults for Children Foundation; mem. UN Comité des Sages; mem. Hon. Bd Int. Centre for Missing and Exploited Children; Order of the Smile 1998, Grand Ribbon, Order of

Leopold (Belgium) 1999, Grand Cross, Order of Isabella the Catholic (Spain) 2001, Grand Cross, Order of Merit (Germany) 2002, Grand Cross with the Ribbon of Terra Mariana (Estonia) 2002, Grand Ribbon, Order of the Precious Crown (Japan) 2002, Order of Merit and Companion of Honour (Malta) 2002, Grand Cross, Royal Norwegian Order of Merit 2003; Woman of the Year and Warsaw Lady of the Year 1998, Holy Brother Albert–Adam Chmielowski Prize for Charitable Activities 1998, Dr Henryk Jordan Medal for Assistance to Children 1999, American Centre of Polish Culture in Washington Medal 1999, Big Golden Heart Award, St Stanislaw Kostka Foundation 2000, Medal of Merit for the Mining Industry for Aid Given to Orphaned Mining Families, TV Personality of the Year 2001, For The Future of Children of Europe Award of Hungarian Asscn, Future of Europe Asscn 2002. *Leisure interests:* literature, theatre, music, fine arts, spending time with her family, travel, skiing, tennis. *Address:* al. Przyjaciół 8 lok. 1a, 00-565 Warsaw, Poland (office). *Telephone:* (22) 8499662 (office). *Fax:* (22) 8499662 (office). *E-mail:* radafundacji@fpbb.pl (office). *Website:* www.fpbb.pl (office).

KWAŚNIEWSKI, Aleksander; Polish journalist, fmr politician and fmr head of state; b. 15 Nov. 1954, Białogard, Koszalin Prov.; s. of Zdzisław Kwaśniewski and Aleksandra Kwaśniewska; m. Jolanta Konty 1979; one d.; ed Gdańsk Univ.; fmr leader of youth movt, including Chair. Univ. Council of Polish Socialist Students' Union (SZSP) at Gdańsk Univ., Head of Culture Dept of SZSP Gen. Bd 1979–80, mem. Exec. Cttee of SZSP Chief Council 1980–81; Ed.-in-Chief ltd (student weekly newspaper), Warsaw 1981–84; Ed.-in-Chief of daily Sztandar Młodych (Banner of Youth), Warsaw 1984–85; mem. Council of Ministers 1985–89; Head, Socio-Political Cttee 1988–89; Minister for Youth Affairs 1985–87; Chair. Cttee for Youth and Physical Culture 1987–90; mem. Polish United Workers' Party (PZPR) 1977–90; mem. Social Democracy of Repub. of Poland Party (SDRP) 1990–95, Chair. 1990–95; participant in Round Table plenary debates, Co-Chair. team for trade union pluralism, mem. team for political reforms and group for asscns and territorial self-govt 1989; Co-f. Democratic Left Alliance 1991; Chair. Polish Olympic Cttee 1988–91; Deputy in Sejm (Parl.) 1991–95; Chair. Constitutional Cttee 1993–95; Supreme Commdr of Armed Forces 1995–2005; Pres. of Poland 1995–2005; Kt, Order of White Eagle and numerous int. honours and awards including Grand Croix, Légion d'honneur, Kt Grand Cross, Order of Bath, Kt Grand Cross, Order of St Michael and St George (GB), Grand Cross, Order of Merit (Italy) 1996, Order of Duke Gedyminas, First Class (Lithuania), Order of Leopold (Belgium), Golden Olympic Order, Int. Olympic Cttee 1998, Golden Order of Merit, Int. Amateur Athletic Fed. 1999, Order of Merit, European Olympic Cttee 2000, Order of the Repub. (Turkey) 2000, Great Order of King Tamislav with Ribbon and Great Star (Croatia) 2001, Order of Catholic Isabella with Chain (Spain) 2001, Nat. Order of Southern Cross (Brazil) 2002, Special Grand Cross of Merit (Peru) 2002, Grand Ribbon of the Great Order of Chrysanthemum (Japan) 2002; Common Wealth 2007 Award of Distinguished Service 2007. *Leisure interests:* sport, literature, films. *Address:* Aleja Przyjaciół 8/1, 00-565 Warsaw, Poland (office). *Telephone:* (22) 8487385. *Fax:* (22) 6294816. *E-mail:* biuro@ kwasniewskialeksander.pl. *Website:* www.kwasniewskialeksander.pl.

KWEI-ARMAH, Kwame, OBE; British actor, playwright, singer and broadcaster; *Artistic Director, Centerstage, Baltimore, Md;* b. (Ian Roberts), 24 March 1967, Hillingdon, London; m.; four c.; ed Barbara Speake Stage School; Writer-in-Residence, Bristol Old Vic 1999–2001; fmrly writer on attachment as Assoc. Artist to Nat. Theatre Studio; took part in Celebrity Fame Academy (BBC TV) 2003; fmr Assoc. Artist, Centerstage, Baltimore, Md, Artistic Dir 2011–; directing debut with Naomi Wallace's Things of Dry Hours and Esa Davis's play Dave Chappelle was Right; took part in the Bush Theatre's project Sixty Six 2011; judge, BBC World Service's Int. Radio Playwriting Competition 2009; mem. Bd Royal Nat. Theatre, Tricycle Theatre; named Goodwill Amb. for Trade for Christian Aid; Chancellor Univ. of the Arts London 2011–; Dr hc (Open Univ.) 2008. *Plays as writer:* Big Nose (adaptation of Rostand's Cyrano De Bergerac, Belgrade Theatre, Coventry) 1999, Blues Brother Soul Sister (musical, Bristol Old Vic) 2000, A Bitter Herb (Peggy Ramsey Bursary, Bristol Old Vic) 2001, Hold On (Durham Theatre Royal) 2002, Elmina's Kitchen (Royal Nat. Theatre, Charles Wintour Award for Most Promising Playwright, Evening Standard Theatre Awards 2004) 2003, Fix Up (Royal Nat. Theatre) 2004, Statement of Regret (Royal Nat. Theatre) 2007, Let There Be Love (Tricycle Theatre) 2008, Seize the Day. *Plays as actor:* Mozart and Salieri (Crucible, Sheffield). *Films:* Once Upon a Time (short) (dir and producer) 1991; as actor: Cutthroat Island 1995, Il mio West 1998, The 3 Kings 2000, Fade to Black 2006. *Television:* as actor Ian Roberts: The Latchkey Children (series) 1980, Birth of a Nation (film) 1983, The Bill (series) 1989; as actor Kwame Kwei-Armah: Between The Lines (series) 1994, Casualty (series) 1994–2004, Expert Witness (series documentary) 1996, An Unsuitable Job for a Woman (series) 1998, Der Clown (series) 1999, Holby City (series) 2000–01, The Afternoon Play (series) – Sons, Daughters and Lovers 2004, Pride (film) (voice) 2004, Robin Hood (series) 2006, Cold Blood 2 (film) 2007, Lewis (series) – The Great and the Good 2008, Hotel Babylon (series) 2008, Walter's War (film) (BBC Four) (also writer) 2008, Horne & Corden (series) 2009, Skins (series) 2010; as writer: Elmina's Kitchen (film) 2005, Christianity: A History (series documentary) 2009. *Recordings:* album: Kwame 2003. *Address:* Centerstage, 700 North Calvert Street, Baltimore, MD 21202, USA (office). *Telephone:* (410) 986-4000 (office). *E-mail:* info@centerstage.org (office). *Website:* www.centerstage.org (office).

KWEK, Leng Beng; Singaporean business executive; *Executive Chairman, Hong Leong Group Singapore;* s. of the late Kwek Hong Png; m.; two c.; father left Fujian Prov., China for Singapore and subsequently founded Hong Leong Group; joined family business in 1960s; Exec. Chair. Hong Leong Group Singapore 1990–; Chair. City Developments Ltd, Millennium & Copthorne (M&C) Hotels; mem. Bd Trustees Singapore Management Univ.; Hon. DUniv (Oxford Brookes Univ.); Hotelier of the Decade, Asia Pacific Hotel Investment Conference 2000, SIAS TopGun CEO Designation Award, Brendan Wood International 2012. *Address:* Hong Leong Group Singapore, 9 Raffles Place, #36-00, Republic Plaza, Singapore 048619 (office). *Telephone:* 6438-0880 (office). *Fax:* 6534-3060 (office). *E-mail:* gerry@cdl.com.sg (office). *Website:* www.hongleong.com.sg (office).

KWIATKOWSKI, Marek; Polish professor of history of art; *Curator and Director, Royal Łazienki Palace and Park;* b. 25 April 1930, Caen, France; m.; ed Warsaw Univ.; Curator Royal Łazienki Palace and Park for over 50 years, currently Dir, has organized numerous exhbns and displays; mem. numerous asscns including Friends of Animals Asscn; Homo Varsoviensis, Commdr's Cross, Order of Polonia Restituta; Klio Award. *Publications:* 22 books on art including Szymon Bogumił Zug 1971, Stanisław August – król architekt 1983, Architektura mieszkaniowa Warszawy XVII-XIX W 1986, Historia Warszawy XVI-XX wieku. Zabytki mówią 1999. *Leisure interests:* paintings, own museum in Sucha village. *Address:* Royal Łazienki, ul. Agrykoli 1, 00-460 Warsaw, Poland (office). *Telephone:* (22) 6218212 (office). *Fax:* (22) 6296945 (office). *Website:* www.lazienki-krolewskie.pl (office).

KWIATKOWSKI, Michał; Polish business executive; *President, Management Board, EuRoPol GAZ;* b. 1947; m.; one c.; ed Silesian Tech. Univ., Gliwice; engineer, promoted to Chief Engineer KWK Sosnica coalmine 1971–90; Deputy Dir Knurów Coalmine 1990–91, Dir 1991–93; Pres. Gliwice Coal Co. 1993–98, Weglokoks Co. 1998–2001, Polish Oil and Gas Co. (PGNiG) SA 2001–03, Man. Bd EuRoPol GAZ 2003–. *Address:* EuRoPol GAZ Transit Gas Pipeline System, Al. St. Zjednoczonych 61, 04-028 Warsaw, Poland (office). *Telephone:* (22) 517-40-00 (office). *Fax:* (22) 517-40-40 (office). *E-mail:* info@europolgaz.com.pl (office). *Website:* www.europolgaz.com.pl (office).

KWOK, Raymond, MA (Cantab.), MBA, JP; Hong Kong business executive; *Vice-Chairman and Managing Director, Sun Hung Kai Properties Ltd;* b. (Kwok Ping-luen), 1952, Hong Kong; s. of Kwok Tak-seng and Kwong Siu-hing; younger brother of Walter Kwok and Thomas Kwok; ed Jesus Coll., Cambridge, UK, Harvard Univ., USA; family originated from Zhongshan, Guangdong Prov., China; with Sun Hung Kai Properties Ltd (largest property developer in Hong Kong) 1979–, currently Vice-Chair. and Man. Dir; Chair. SUNeVision Holdings Ltd, SmarTone Telecommunications Holdings Ltd; has interest in city bus operator KMB; Dir (non-exec.) Transport International Holdings Ltd, USI Holdings Ltd; Ind. Dir (non-exec.) Standard Chartered Bank (Hong Kong) Ltd; mem. Bd of Dirs Real Estate Developers Asscn of Hong Kong; mem. Gen. Cttee of Hong Kong Gen. Chamber of Commerce, Hong Kong Port Devt Council; Vice-Chair. Council of Chinese Univ. of Hong Kong; Hon. DBA (Open Univ. of Hong Kong); Hon. LLD (Chinese Univ. of Hong Kong). *Address:* Sun Hung Kai Properties Ltd, 45th Floor, Sun Hung Kai Centre, 30 Harbour Road, Wanchai, Hong Kong Special Administrative Region, People's Republic of China (office). *Telephone:* 2827-8111 (office). *Fax:* 2827-2862 (office). *E-mail:* shkp@shkp.com (office). *Website:* www.shkp.com (office).

KWOK, Thomas, BEng (Civil), MBA, JP; Hong Kong business executive; *Vice-Chairman and Managing Director, Sun Hung Kai Properties Ltd;* b. (Kwok Ping-kwong), 1951, Hong Kong; s. of Kwok Tak-seng and Kwong Siu-hing; brother of Walter Kwok and Raymond Kwok; ed London Business School and Imperial Coll., Univ. of London, UK; family originated from Zhongshan, Guangdong Prov., China; with Sun Hung Kai Properties Ltd (largest property developer in Hong Kong) 1982–, currently Vice-Chair. and Man. Dir; Chair. Route 3 (CPS) Co. Ltd; Jt Chair. IFC Development Ltd; Exec. Dir SUNeVision Holdings Ltd; Ind. Dir (non-exec.) Bank of East Asia Ltd; Exec. Vice-Pres. Real Estate Developers Asscn of Hong Kong; Govt apptd mem. Provisional Construction Industry Co-ordination Bd, Council for Sustainable Devt; fmr Chair. Property Man. Cttee Building Contractors' Asscn; fmr mem. Business Advisory Group, Land & Building Advisory Cttee, Registered Contractors' Disciplinary Bd, Gen. Chamber of Commerce Industrial Affairs Cttee, Council of Hong Kong Construction Asscn, Bd Community Chest of Hong Kong, Social Welfare Policies and Services Cttee, Council of The Open Univ. of Hong Kong; mem. Standing Cttee Ninth CPPCC Shanghai Cttee; Hon. Citizen of Guangzhou. *Address:* Sun Hung Kai Properties Ltd, 45th Floor, Sun Hung Kai Centre, 30 Harbour Road, Wanchai, Hong Kong Special Administrative Region, People's Republic of China (office). *Telephone:* 2827-8111 (office). *Fax:* 2827-2862 (office). *E-mail:* shkp@shkp.com (office). *Website:* www.shkp.com (office).

KWOK, Walter; Hong Kong business executive; *Chairman and CEO, Sun Hung Kai Properties Ltd;* b. (Kwok Ping-sheung), 1950, Hong Kong; s. of Kwok Tak-seng and Kwong Siu-hing; brother of Raymond Kwok and Thomas Kwok; m. 1st Lydia Ku 1982 (divorced 1982); m. 2nd Wendy Lee; family originated from Zhongshan, Guangdong Prov., China; Chair. and CEO Sun Hung Kai Properties Ltd (largest property developer in Hong Kong) 1990–, handed over exec. duties of SHKP to brothers while retaining title of Chair. and CEO, temporary leave of absence to visit USA and Beijing and other large cities announced 18 Feb. 2008, brought lawsuit against his brothers May 2008. *Address:* Sun Hung Kai Properties Ltd, 45th Floor, Sun Hung Kai Centre, 30 Harbour Road, Wanchai, Hong Kong Special Administrative Region, People's Republic of China (office). *Telephone:* 2827-8111 (office). *Fax:* 2827-2862 (office). *E-mail:* shkp@shkp.com (office). *Website:* www .shkp.com (office).

KWON, O-kyu, PhD; South Korean politician; b. 1952, Gangneung, Gangwon Prov.; ed Seoul Nat. Univ., Univ. of Minnesota, USA, Chung-Ang Univ., Seoul; joined Ministry of Finance 1974, held various positions at now-defunct Econ. Planning Bd and at Ministry of Finance and Economy 1975–94; researcher, World Bank 1985, 1987; Presidential Sec. 1993–98; Alt. Exec. Dir to IMF 1997–99; Dir-Gen. Econ. Policy Bureau and Deputy Minister of Finance and Economy 1999–2001; Admin. Public Procurement Service 2002; Sr Presidential Sec. for Nat. Policy 2002–04; Perm. Rep. to OECD 2004–06; Chief Econ. Policy Adviser to the Pres. 2006; Deputy Prime Minister and Minister of Finance and Economy 2006–08. *Address:* c/o Ministry of Finance and Economy, Government Complex II, 88 Gwanmoonro, Gwacheon City, Gyeonggi Province, 427-725, South Korea (office).

KWON, Oh-hyun, BS, MS, PhD; South Korean electronics industry executive; *Vice-Chairman and CEO, Samsung Electronics Company Limited;* ed Seoul Nat. Univ., Korea Advanced Inst. of Science and Tech., Stanford Univ., USA; joined Samsung Electronics' Semiconductor Business 1985, led devt of first 64MB DRAM 1992, Vice-Pres. Memory Device Tech. 1995–98, Sr Vice-Pres. and Head of System LSI Div.'s ASIC business 1998–2000, Exec. Vice-Pres. and Head of LSI Tech. 2000–04, Pres. and Gen. Man. System LSI Div. 2004–08, Pres. Semiconductor Business 2008–11, Head of Device Solutions 2011–, Vice-Chair. Samsung Electronics Co. Ltd 2011–12, Vice-Chair. and CEO 2012–. *Publications:* numerous papers at confs and symposia including ISSCC, VLSI Symposium and IEDM, has also contributed to several technical journals on semiconductor related topics. *Address:* Samsung Electronics Bldg, 1320-10 Seocho-2-dong, Seocho-gu, Seoul 137-

857, Republic of Korea (office). *Telephone:* (2) 2255-0114 (office). *Fax:* (2) 2255-0117 (office). *E-mail:* j-npr@samsung.co.kr (office). *Website:* www.samsung.com (office).

KWON, Young-soo, BBA, MEng; South Korean business executive; ed Seoul Nat. Univ., Korea Advanced Inst. of Science and Tech.; fmr Exec. Vice-Pres. LG Electronics Inc., later Pres. and Chief Financial Officer, also served as Head of Globalization Team at LG Electronics' HQ, Seoul as well as a financial officer at LG Electronics' overseas subsidiary in NJ, USA, CEO LG Display Co. Ltd (also known as LG.Philips LCD Co. Ltd) 2007–12, Rep. Dir, LG Display Co. Ltd and Royal Philips Electronics NV 2007–12. *Address:* c/o LG Display Company Ltd, 65-228 Hangang-ro 3-ga, Seoul 140-716, Republic of Korea. *E-mail:* info@lgdisplay.com.

KWONG, Most Rev. Peter K. K., MTh, DD, DSc; Hong Kong ecclesiastic; *Archbishop Emeritus of Hong Kong Sheng Kung Hui;* b. 28 Feb. 1936, Hong Kong; s. of Kwok-Kuen Kwong and Ching-lan Chan; m. Emily Ha; one s. two d.; ed Chung Chi Coll., Kenyon Coll. and Bexley Hall, Colgate Rochester; ordained priest, Anglican Church in Hong Kong 1966; Priest-in-Charge, Crown of Thorns Church, Hong Kong 1965–66; Vicar, St James's Church, Hong Kong 1967–70; Curate, St Paul's Church, Hong Kong 1971–72; mem. teaching staff, Chinese Univ. of Hong Kong 1972–79; Diocesan Gen. Sec. Anglican Diocese of Hong Kong and Macao 1979–81; Bishop of Hong Kong and Macao 1981–98, Archbishop and Primate of Hong Kong Sheng Kung Hui 1998–2006 (retd), now Archbishop Emer., Bishop of Diocese of Hong Kong Island 1998–2006, now Bishop Emer.; Sr Adviser Community Chest of Hong Kong 1999–; mem. Exec. Cttee, Consultative Cttee for Basic Law of Hong Kong 1985–90, Chair. Finance Cttee 1987–90; Adviser on Hong Kong Affairs, State Dept of People's Repub. of China 1992–97; mem. Preparatory Cttee for Special Admin. Region 1996–97, Selection Cttee 1996–97, CPPCC 1998–; Hon. Treas. Council of the Church of East Asia 1981–83, Chair. 1999–; Hon. Dir Chinese Christian Churches Union 1981–; mem. Court, Hong Kong Univ. 1981–; Vice-Pres. Church Mission Soc. 1995–; numerous appointments in health, educ., social welfare, youth orgs etc.; Gold Bauhinia Star. *Address:* Bishop's House, 1 Lower Albert Road, Hong Kong Special Administrative Region, People's Republic of China (office). *Telephone:* 25265355 (office). *Fax:* 25212199 (office). *E-mail:* office1@hkskh.org (office).

KYAMBADDE, Amelia Kulubya, BBA; Ugandan politician; *Minister of Trade, Industry and Co-operatives;* b. Guildford, UK; d. of the late Serwano Kulubya and of Mary Kafureka; m. Wilson Kyambadde 1976; six c.; ed Makerere Univ.; Sec. to Minister Yoweri Museveni 1979–81; in exile in Sweden 1983–86; Prin. Pvt. Sec. to Pres. Museveni 1986–2010; mem. Parl. (Nat. Resistance Movt) for Mawokota North 2011–; Minister of Trade, Industry and Co-operatives 2011–. *Address:* Ministry of Trade, Industry and Co-operatives, 6/8 Parliament Ave, POB 7103, Kampala, Uganda (office). *Telephone:* (41) 4314000 (office). *Fax:* (41) 4347286 (office). *E-mail:* mintrade@mtti.go.ug (office); akyambadde@parliament.go.ug (office). *Website:* www.mtti.go.ug (office).

KYDLAND, Finn K., BS, PhD; American (b. Norwegian) economist and academic; *Jeff Henley Chair in Economics, University of California, Santa Barbara;* b. 1943; m. Judy Henley; ed Norwegian School of Econs and Business Admin, Carnegie Mellon Univ., USA; Prof. of Econs, Carnegie Mellon Univ., Tepper School of Business, Pittsburgh, Pa –2004, now Richard P. Simmons Distinguished Prof. and and Univ. Prof. of Econs; Jeff Henley Chair in Econs, Univ. of Calif., Santa Barbara 2004–; Research Assoc., Fed. Reserve Banks of Cleveland and Dallas; mem. Editorial Bd Macroeconomic Dynamics 1996–; John Stauffer Nat. Fellowship, Hoover Inst. 1982–83, Fellow, Econometric Soc. 1992–; Research Assoc., Fed. Reserve Bank of Dallas, Fed. Reserve Bank of Cleveland; Alexander Henderson Award, Carnegie Mellon Univ. 1973, Nobel Prize in Econs (jtly with Edward C. Prescott) 2004. *Publications:* author or co-author of numerous articles in professional journals. *Address:* 2127 North Hall, University of California, Santa Barbara, CA 93106, USA (office). *Telephone:* (805) 893-5464 (office). *Fax:* (805) 893-8830 (office). *E-mail:* kydland@econ.ucsb.edu (office); kydland@andrew.cmu .edu (office). *Website:* www.econ.ucsb.edu (office).

KYENGE, Cécile Kashetu; Italian/Democratic Republic of the Congo politician and ophthalmologist; *Minister for International Co-operation and Integration;* b. 28 Aug. 1964, Kambove, Katanga, Democratic Repub. of the Congo; m. Domenico 1994; two d.; ed Università Cattolica del Sacro Cuore; moved to Italy 1983; became a qualified ophthalmologist in Modena, Emilia-Romagna; f. Asscn for Intercultural (DAWA) to promote mutual awareness, integration and co-operation between Italy and Africa 2002; nat. spokesperson of asscn March First, which promotes the rights of migrants in Italy 2010–; collaborates with several Italian magazines, including Combonifem and Corriere Immmigrazione; elected in dist of Modena for the Democrats of the Left 2004, later became prov. head of the Forum of Int. Co-operation and Immigration; prov. councillor in Modena for the Democratic Party (PD) 2009–13, mem. Welfare and Social Policies Cttee; also responsible for immigration policies in Emilia-Romagna for the PD; mem. Chamber of Deputies for the PD in Emilia-Romagna Feb. 2013–; Minister (without portfolio) for Int. Co-operation and Integration April 2013–. *Address:* Ministry for Integration, Segreteria Ministra Kyenge, Largo Chigi 19, 00187 Rome (office); Camera dei Deputati, Palazzo Montecitorio, Piazza Montecitorio, 00186 Rome, Italy (office). *Telephone:* (06) 67791 (Ministry) (office); (06) 67601 (Chamber) (office). *E-mail:* cecile@cecilekyenge.it (office); segreteria.ministrakyenge@governo.it (office). *Website:* www.governo.it (office); nuovo.camera.it; www.cecilekyenge.it.

KYEREMANTEN, Alan, BEcons, LLB; Ghanaian economist, politician, diplomatist and business executive; ed Univ. of Ghana; sr corp. exec. with subsidiary of Unilever Int., Ghana; Prin. Consultant to Man. Devt Productivity Inst.; est. Empretec Programme (promoting pvt. sector devt) 1990, expanding to 11 other countries in Africa; Amb. to USA 2001–03; Minister of Trade, Industry and Presidential Initiatives 2003–05, of Trade and Industry 2005–07; cand. for Pres. of Ghana (New Patriotic Party—NPP) 2007; fmr Hubert Humphrey Fellow, Univ. of Minnesota School of Man., USA; One of Top 100 Global Leaders for a New Millennium, Time magazine 1994. *Address:* c/o New Patriotic Party (NPP), C912/2 Duade Street, Kokomlemle, POB 3456, Accra-North, Ghana. *Telephone:* (21) 227951. *Fax:* (21) 224418. *E-mail:* npp@africanonline.com.gh. *Website:* www .nppghana.org.

KYL, Jon Llewellyn, BA, LLB; American lawyer and politician; b. 25 April 1942, Oakland, Neb.; s. of John Henry Kyl and Arlene Griffith; m. Caryll Collins 1964;

one s. one d.; ed Univ. of Arizona; lawyer, Jennings, Strouss & Salmon, Phoenix, Ariz. 1966–86; legal counsel, Ariz. State Republican Party 1970–75; mem. US House of Reps, Washington, DC 1987–95; Senator from Arizona 1995–2013 (retd), Chair. Republican Policy Cttee 2003–07, Republican Conf. 2007, Senate Minority Whip 2007–13, mem. Judiciary Cttee; Republican; ranked by National Journal as the fourth most conservative US Senator 2007, recognized by TIME magazine as one of the 100 most influential people in the world for his persuasive role in the Senate 2010. *Address:* c/o 730 Hart Senate Office Building, Washington, DC 20510, USA.

KYMLICKA, Will, BA, DPhil, FRSC; Canadian philosopher and academic; *Canada Research Chair in Political Philosophy, Queen's University;* ed Queen's Univ., Univ. of Oxford, UK; Lecturer, Dept of Philosophy, Queen's Univ. 1986–87, Queen's Nat. Scholar 1998–2003, Canada Research Chair in Political Philosophy 2003–; Lecturer, Dept of Philosophy, Princeton Univ., NJ 1987–88; Lecturer, Dept of Philosophy, Univ. of Toronto 1988–89, Asst Prof. 1989–90; Sr Policy Analyst, Royal Comm. on New Reproductive Technologies 1990–91; Research Dir Canadian Centre for Philosophy and Public Policy, Univ. of Ottawa 1994–98; Visiting Prof., Univ. of Ottawa 1991–93, Carleton Univ. 1994–98, Inst. for Advanced Studies, Austria 1997, Nationalism Studies Program, Cen. European Univ., Hungary 1998–, Univ. Pompeu Fabra, Spain 1998, 2003, 2012, Sciences-Po, France 2007, Wayne State Univ., USA 2009, Libera Università Internazionale degli Studi Sociali Guido Carli Univ., Italy 2010; Visiting Fellow, European Forum, European Univ. Inst., Italy 1996, Nuffield Coll., Oxford, UK 2009–11; Pres. American Soc. for Political and Legal Philosophy 2004–06; mem. several editorial and advisory bds; Corresp. Fellow, British Acad. 2011; Dr hc (Copenhagen) 2013; Guiseppe Acerbi Prize 2001, Excellence in Research Prize, Queen's Univ. 2002, Killam Prize in Social Sciences, Canada Council 2004, North American Soc. for Social Philosophy Book Prize 2008, Premier's Discovery Award in Social Sciences, Govt of Ont. 2009, Queen's Diamond Jubilee Medal 2012, Biennial Book Prize, Canadian Philosophical Asscn 2013; several fellowships. *Publications:* Liberalism, Community and Culture 1989, Contemporary Political Philosophy 1990, Justice in Political Philosophy (ed.) 1992, Multicultural Citizenship: A Liberal Theory of Minority Rights (Macpherson Prize, Canadian Political Science Asscn 1996, Bunche Award, American Political Science Asscn 1996) 1995, The Rights of Minority Cultures 1995, Ethnicity and Group Rights (co-ed.) 1997, States, Nations and Cultures: Spinoza Lectures 1997, Finding Our Way: Rethinking Ethnocultural Relations in Canada 1998, Citizenship in Diverse Societies (co-ed.) 2000, Politics in the Vernacular: Nationalism, Multiculturalism and Citizenship 2001, Alternative Conceptions of Civil Society (co-ed.) 2001, Can Liberal Pluralism be Exported? (co-ed.) 2001, Language Rights and Political Theory (co-ed.) 2003, Ethnicity and Democracy in Africa (co-ed.) 2004, Multiculturalism in Asia (co-ed.) 2005, Multiculturalism and the Welfare State (co-ed.) 2006, The Globalization of Ethics (co-ed.) 2007, Multicultural Odysseys: Navigating the New International Politics of Diversity 2007, The Politics of Reconciliation in Multicultural Societies (co-ed.) 2008, Rooted Cosmopolitanism: Canada and the World (co-ed.) 2012, Identity Politics in the Public Realm: Bringing Institutions Back In (co-ed.) 2011, Zoopolis: A Political Theory of Animal Rights (co-author) 2011; numerous book chapters and articles in professional journals. *Leisure interest:* running marathons. *Address:* Department of Philosophy, Watson Hall 313, Queen's University, Kingston, ON K7L 3N6, Canada (office). *Fax:* (613) 533-6545 (office). *E-mail:* kymlicka@queensu.ca (office). *Website:* post.queensu.ca/~kymlicka (office).

KYNASTON, Nicolas, ARCM, FRCO; British concert organist; *Organ Professor, Royal Academy of Music;* b. 10 Dec. 1941, Morebath, Devon; s. of the late Roger Tewkesbury Kynaston and of Jessie Dearn Caecilia Kynaston (née Parkes); m. 1st Judith Felicity Heron 1961 (divorced 1989); two s. two d.; m. 2nd Susan Harwood Styles 1989; ed Westminster Cathedral Choir School, Downside, Accademia Musicale Chigiana, Siena, Conservatorio Santa Cecilia, Rome, Royal Coll. of Music; Westminster Cathedral Organist 1961–71; debut recital, Royal Festival Hall 1966; recording debut 1968; concert career 1971–, travelling throughout Europe, N America, Asia and Africa; Artistic Dir J. W. Walker & Sons Ltd 1978–82, Consultant 1982–83; organist, Athens Concert Hall 1995–2010; Organ Prof., RAM 2002–; Jury mem. Grand Prix de Chartres 1971, St Albans Int. Organ Festival 1975; Pres. Inc. Asscn of Organists 1983–85; Chair. Nat. Organ Teachers Encouragement Scheme 1993–96; mem. Westminster Abbey Fabric Comm. 2000–05; consultant for various new organ projects; recordings; Hon. FRCO 1976, Hon. RAM 2010; EMI/CFP Sales Award 1974; Deutscher Schallplattenpreis 1978. *Publication:* Transcriptions for Organ 1997. *Leisure interests:* walking, church architecture. *Address:* 28 High Park Road, Kew, Richmond-upon-Thames,

Surrey, TW9 4BH, England (home). *Telephone:* (20) 8878-4455 (home). *Fax:* (20) 8392-9314 (home).

KYPRIANOU, Markos, MA; Cypriot politician; b. 22 Jan. 1960, Limassol; ed Univ. of Athens, Greece, Univ. of Cambridge, UK, Harvard Law School, USA; Assoc., Antis Triantafyllides & Sons 1985–91; Pnr, Kyprianou & Boyiadjis 1991–95, George L. Savvides & Co. (following merger) 1995–2003; Municipal Councillor, Nicosia 1986–91; mem. Parl. for Nicosia 1991–2003, fmr Deputy Chair. Cttee on Foreign and European Affairs, fmr mem. Cttee on Legal Affairs, Chair. House Cttee on Financial and Budgetary Affairs 1999–2003; mem. and Chair. House of Reps Del. to Parl. Ass. of OSCE; fmr Parl. Leader Democratic Party; Minister of Finance 2003–04; EU Commr without Portfolio 2004, for Health and Consumer Protection 2004–06, for Health 2006–08; Minister of Foreign Affairs 2008–11; Assoc. mem. ABA.

KYRIAKOU, Minos, BA; Greek shipowner and business executive; b. 1946, Athens; s. of Xenophon Kyriakou and Athina Revidies; m. (divorced); two s. one d.; ed in France and Switzerland and Columbia Univ., New York, USA; Owner Athenian Tankers Inc. 1965–; est. Bacoil Int. and Athenian Oil Trading Inc. (oil trading corpns) 1978; Founder and Pres. Aegean Foundation 1985–; f. Antenna FM (pvt. radio station) 1987; Chair. and CEO Antenna 1988–; est. Antenna TV network 1989, through Antenna Satellite Inc. Antenna began broadcasting to whole American continent, Australia and Cyprus 1992; mem. Bd Govs Singapore Port Authority 1988; Chair. of UN org. for civil, linguistic and religious rights of nat. minorities 1989; Head, Panellinios AC 1997–; mem. Council of Int. Asscn of Athletics Feds (IAAF) 2003–05; Pres. Hellenic Olympic Cttee –2006, Pres. Int. Olympic Acad. 2006–; Chair. Hellenic-Kuwait Friendship Org. in Greece 1992–, Torch Relay Comm.; Founder Mediterranean Affairs Inc. (non-profit org.) publishing Mediterranean Quarterly, Washington, DC 1990–; Hon. Consul-Gen. of Singapore in Greece 1988–, Hon. Consul of Poland in Thessaloniki 1994–; Gold Medal, Legion of Honour of Poland 1984, Golden Cross of the Order of St George 1986, Golden Medal of Honour (Cyprus) 1988, Golden Sword of Kuwait 1992; IAAF Hon. Life Pres. Prize 2005. *Publications:* The Aegean Crisis (First Prize in literary competition 1987) 1986, Siesta on a Volcano 1988. *Leisure interests:* reading (especially of history), collecting paintings and sculpture. *Address:* c/o Office of the President, International Olympic Academy, 270 65 Ancient Olympia, Athens; 10–12 Kifisias Avenue, 15125 Marousi, Greece. *E-mail:* info@ioa.gr. *Website:* www.ioa.org.gr.

KYUCHUKOV, Lyubomir Nedkov, MA; Bulgarian diplomatist, politician and business executive; b. 14 June 1955, Sofia; m.; two c.; ed English Language Secondary School, Varna, Moscow State Univ. for Int. Relations, USSR, Georgetown Univ., Washington, DC; mem. staff, Embassy in Bucharest 1981, Desk Officer, Romania and Poland, Eastern Europe Dept, Ministry of Foreign Affairs 1981–84; Political Analyst, BBSS Gallup International 1992–94; Chief Adviser, Secr. for European Integration at the Council of Ministers 1996–97; Man. consultancy co. 1997–2005; mem. Council for European and Euro-Atlantic Integration with Pres. of Bulgaria 2001–05; Deputy Minister of Foreign Affairs 2005–09, Acting Minister of Foreign Affairs May–July 2009; Amb. to UK 2009–12; participant in Nat. Round Table and Public Council on Nat. Issues 1990; Vice-Chair. Supreme Council, Bulgarian Socialist Party 1990–91, Social Democratic Political Movt 2005–07; mem. Nat. Council of Bulgarian Asscn for Support for the UN 1988–91, Exec. Council of Bulgarian Asscn for European Security and Cooperation 1989–92, Admin. Council of Devt of Civil Society Foundation 1996–97, Bd of Diplomatic Inst. 2005–09; mem. editorial staff, New Time Magazine 1992–95, Editorial Bd International Relations Magazine 2005–; Lecturer, Japanese Agency for Int. Co-operation 1997–2000; Founder-mem. Governing Council, Inst. of Econs and Int. Relations 2003–05. *Address:* Ministry of Foreign Affairs, 1040 Sofia, ul. Al. Zhendov 2, Bulgaria (office). *Telephone:* (2) 948-20-18 (office). *Fax:* (2) 297-136-20 (office). *E-mail:* vtcherneva@mfa.bg (office). *Website:* www.mfa.government.bg (office).

KYUMA, Fumio; Japanese politician; b. 4 Dec. 1940; ed Tokyo Univ.; mem. Nagasaki Prefectural Ass. 1971–80; mem. House of Reps 1980–2009, Parl. Vice-Minister of Transport 1987, Minister of State for Defence 1996–98, Dir-Gen. Defence Agency (State Minister) 1996–99; Chair. LDP Panel on Security Issues 2000, Chair. (acting) LDP Policy Research Council 2001, Acting LDP Sec.-Gen. 2002, Chair. LDP Gen. Council 2004, Minister of State for Defence 2006–07, Minister of Defence Jan.–July 2007. *Address:* c/o Liberal-Democratic Party, 1-11-23, Nagata-cho, Chiyoda-ku, Tokyo 100-8910, Japan.

KYUNG-WHA CHUNG (see Chung, Kyung-wha).

L

LA FOREST, Gerard V., BCL, MA, LLD, JSD, DCL, FRSC; Canadian lawyer; *Distinguished Legal Scholar in Residence, University of New Brunswick;* b. 1 April 1926, Grand Falls, NB; s. of J. Alfred La Forest and Philomene Lajoie; m. Marie Warner 1952; five d.; ed St Francis Xavier Univ., Univ. of New Brunswick, St John's Coll. Oxford, UK and Yale Univ., USA; called to Bar, New Brunswick 1949; QC 1968; practising lawyer, Grand Falls 1951–52; Advisory Counsel, Dept of Justice, Ottawa 1952–55; Legal Adviser, Irving Oil and assoc. cos 1955–56; Assoc. Prof. of Law, Univ. of New Brunswick 1956–63, Prof. 1963–68; Dean of Law, Univ. of Alberta 1968–70; Asst Deputy Attorney-Gen. of Canada (Research and Planning) 1970–74; Commr Law Reform Comm. of Canada 1974–79; Prof. and Dir Legis. Drafting Program, Faculty of Law (Common Law Section), Univ. of Ottawa 1979–81; Judge, Court of Appeal of New Brunswick 1981; Judge, Supreme Court of Canada 1985–97; Counsel, Stewart McKelvie Stirling Scales 1998–; Distinguished Legal Scholar in Residence, Univ. of NB 1998–; consultant to fed. and provincial govts; mem. numerous cttees, public bodies etc.; Fellow, World Acad. of Art and Science; numerous hon. degrees and other distinctions. *Publications:* Disallowance and Reservation of Provincial Legislation 1955, Extradition to and from Canada 1961, The Allocation of Taxing Power Under the Canadian Constitution 1967, Natural Resources and Public Property Under the Canadian Constitution 1969, Water Law in Canada 1973. *Address:* Stewart McKelvie Stirling Scales, Suite 600, Frederick Square, POB 730, Fredericton, NB E3B 5B4 (office); 320 University Avenue, Fredericton, NB E3B 4J1, Canada (home).

LA GRENADE, Cécile Ellen Fleurette, OBE, GCMG, BChem, PhD; Grenadian food technologist and public servant; *Governor-General;* b. 30 Dec. 1952, Laborie, British Windward Islands (now Grenada); d. of Allan A. La Grenade and Sybil Sylvester-La Grenade; ed Univ. of the West Indies, Univ. of Maryland, USA; Man. Dir De La Grenade Industries (family food-processing co) 1992–; Chair. Public Service Comm. 2007–10; Gov.-Gen. of Grenada, Carriacou and Petite Martinique 2013–. *Address:* Office of the Governor-General, Government House, Bldg 5, Financial Complex, The Carenage, St George's, Grenada (office). *Telephone:* 440-6639 (office). *Fax:* 440-6688 (office). *E-mail:* pato@spiceisle.com (office).

LA PLANTE, Lynda, CBE; British television dramatist and novelist; *Chairman, La Plante Productions Ltd;* b. 15 March 1946, Formby; m. Richard La Plante (divorced); ed Royal Coll. of Dramatic Art; fmr actress; appeared in The Gentle Touch, Out, Minder; founder and Chair. La Plante Productions 1994–. *Television includes:* Prime Suspect 1991, 1993, 1995, Civvies, Framed, Seekers, Widows (series), Comics (two-part drama) 1993, Cold Shoulder 2 1996, Cold Blood, Bella Mafia 1997, Trial and Retribution 1997–, Killer Net 1998, Mind Games 2000, The Warden 2001, Framed 2002, Widows (mini-series) 2002, The Commander 2003. *Publications include:* The Widows 1983, The Widows II 1985, The Talisman 1987, Bella Mafia 1991, Framed 1992, Civvies 1992, Prime Suspect 1992, Seekers 1993, Entwined 1993, Prime Suspect 2 1993, Lifeboat 1994, Cold Shoulder 1994, Prime Suspect 3 1994, She's Out 1995, The Governor 1996, Cold Blood 1996, Trial and Retribution 1997, Cold Heart 1998, Trial and Retribution 2 1998, Trial and Retribution 3 1999, Trial and Retribution 4 2000, Sleeping Cruelty 2000, Trial and Retribution 5 2002, Trial and Retribution 6 2002, Royal Flush 2002, Like a Charm (short stories) 2004, Above Suspicion (novel) 2004, The Red Dahlia 2006, Clean Cut 2007, Deadly Intent 2008, Silent Scream 2009, Blind Fury 2011. *Address:* La Plante Productions Ltd, Paramount House, 162–170 Wardour Street, London, W1F 8ZX, England (office). *Telephone:* (20) 7734-6767 (office). *Fax:* (20) 7734-7878 (office). *E-mail:* admin@laplanteproductions.com (office). *Website:* www.laplanteproductions.com (office); www.lyndalaplante.com.

LA RIVIÈRE, Jan Willem Maurits, PhD; Dutch environmental biologist and academic; *Professor Emeritus, UNESCO-IHE Institute for Water Education;* b. 24 Dec. 1923, Rotterdam; m. Louise A. Kleijn 1958; one s. two d.; ed Erasmus Gymnasium, Rotterdam and Delft Univ. of Tech.; Postdoctoral Rockefeller Fellowship, Stanford Univ., USA; mem. scientific staff, Microbiology Dept, Delft Univ. of Tech. 1953–63; Prof. of Environmental Microbiology and Deputy Dir, Int. Inst. for Infrastructural, Hydraulic and Environmental Eng (now UNESCO-IHE Inst. for Water Educ.), Delft 1963–88, Prof. Emer. and Hon. Fellow 1996–; Visiting Prof., Harvard Univ. 1967–68; Sec.-Gen. ICSU 1988–93; Fellow, World Acad. of Art and Science; Hon. mem. Council, Int. Cell Research Org.; Kt, Order of the Dutch Lion 1988. *Publications:* Kefiran, A Novel Polysaccharide (with P. Kooiman and K. Schmidt) 1967, Microbiology of Liquid Waste Treatment 1977, Biotechnology in Development Cooperation 1983, Water Quality: Present Status, Future Trends 1987, Threats to the World's Water 1989, Co-operation between Natural and Social Scientists in Global Change Research: Imperatives, Realities, Opportunities 1991, The Delft School of Microbiology in Historical Perspective 1996; some 80 publs in fields of microbiology, environment, water quality and int. scientific co-operation. *Leisure interests:* gardening, travel. *Address:* Laan Floris de Vijfde 93, 2631 WR Nootdorp, Netherlands. *Telephone:* (15) 2579709. *E-mail:* lark@worldonline.nl; lark@tiscali.nl.

LA RUSSA, Ignazio; Italian lawyer and politician; b. 18 July 1947, Paternò; s. of Anthony La Russa; three s.; ed St Gallen, Switzerland, Univ. of Pavia; served in Italian mil.; early career in pvt. law practice; Regional Councillor, Lombardy 1985; mem. Camera dei Deputati (Parl.) for Liguria 1992–, Deputy Speaker 1994, Chair. Cttee on Parl. Immunity 1996–2001; Minister of Defence 2008–11; mem. Italian Socialist Movt 1992–95, Alleanza Nazionale (AN) 1995–2008, Chair. AN Parl. Group in Chamber of Deputies 2001, 2004–05, AN – Popolo della Libertà (PdL) 2008–. *Address:* c/o Ministry of Defence, Palazzo Baracchini, Via XX Settembre 8, 00187 Rome, Italy (office). *E-mail:* larussa_i@camera.it (office). *Website:* www .ignaziolarussa.it (office).

LA TOURETTE, John Ernest, BA, MA, PhD; American economist and academic; *President and Professor Emeritus, Northern Illinois University;* b. 5 Nov. 1932, Perth Amboy, NJ; s. of John C. La Tourette and Charlotte R. Jones; m. Lillie (Lili) M. Drum 1957; one s. one d.; ed Rutgers Univ., NJ; served in USAF, rank of Capt. 1955–58; Instructor in Econs, Rutgers Univ. 1960–61; Asst Prof., Assoc. Prof., Prof., State Univ. of New York, Binghamton 1961–76, Chair. Dept of

Econs 1967–75, Provost for Grad. Studies 1975–76; Vice-Provost for Research and Dean, Grad. School, Bowling Green State Univ., Ohio 1976–79; Vice-Pres. and Provost, Northern Illinois Univ. 1979–86, Pres. 1986–2000, Pres. and Prof. Emer. 2000–; Ford Foundation Fellowship 1963; Brookings Inst. Research Professorship 1966–67; Univ. Research Fellowship, State Univ. of NY 1970; Sec. Yavapai Coll. Foundation Bd, Vice-Chair. West Yavapai Guidance Clinic Foundation, Prescott, Ariz. *Publications:* Pastor Pierre Peiret and Jean Latourette in America: A Comparative History of French Protestantism in America 2008; numerous articles and reviews in econs journals and to students of Bearnais Protestantism (France), articles in the Bulletin du Centre d'Etude du Protestantisme Bearnais 2005–09. *Leisure interests:* genealogy, history of Protestantism in Bearn, France, travel, distance educ. *Address:* 218 S Deerview Circle, Prescott, AZ 86303, USA (home). *Telephone:* (928) 443-1151 (home). *E-mail:* jlatour7@commspeed.net (home).

LAAFAI, Monise; Tuvaluan politician; *Minister of Communications and Transport;* Gen. Man. Tuvalu Co-operative Soc. 1998–2010; Chef de mission, Tuvaluan Del. to Pacific Games, Samoa 2007; mem. Fale i Fono (Parl.) for Nanumaga constituency 2010–; Minister of Finance, Econ. Planning and Industries Sept.–Dec. 2010, Minister of Communications and Transport 2013–; fmr Pres. Tuvalu Athletics Asscn. *Address:* Ministry of Communications and Transport, PMB, Vaiaku, Funafuti, Tuvalu (office). *Telephone:* 20052 (office). *Fax:* 20772 (office). *E-mail:* tuvmet@tuvalu.tv (office).

LAANEOTS, Lt-Gen. Ants; Estonian military officer; *Chief of Defence;* b. 16 Jan. 1948, Kilingi-Nõmme; m.; two c.; ed Higher Mil. School, Ukraine, Malinovsky Armoured and Mechanized Forces Acad., Moscow, NATO Defence Coll., Rome, Finnish Nat. Defence Coll.; Platoon Leader, then Co. Commdr, then Battalion Commdr, 300th Tank Regt for Soviet Army in Ukraine 1970–78; posted to Soviet-Chinese border in Eastern Kazakhstan 1981–87, Exec. Officer, 96th Tank Regt 1981–83, Commdr 180th Tank Regt 1983–85, Deputy Commdr Chief of Staff, 78th Armoured Div. 1985–87; deployment to Ethiopia 1987–89, mil. advisor to infantry div. Commdr 1987, mil. advisor to Army Corps Gen. 1988–89; Chief of Regional Dept of Defence, Tartu, Estonia 1989–91; Chief of Gen. Staff 1991–94, 1997–99; Insp. Gen. of Defence Forces 1997–2000; promoted to Maj. Gen. 1998; Head of Baltic Defence Research Centre 2000–01; Commdt, Estonian Nat. Defence Coll. 2001–06; Chief of Defence 2006–; promoted to Lt Gen. 2008; Order of the Cross of the Eagle. *Address:* Ministry of Defence, Sakala 1, Tallinn 15094, Estonia (office). *Telephone:* 717-0022 (office). *Fax:* 717-0001 (office). *E-mail:* info@kmin.ee (office). *Website:* www.mod.gov.ee (office).

LAAR, Mart, MA, PhD; Estonian historian and politician; b. 22 April 1960, Viljandi; s. of Tõnis Laar and Aime Laar; m. Katrin Kask 1982; one s. one d.; ed Tartu State Univ.; history teacher in Tallinn 1983–85; Head of Dept, Ministry of Culture of Estonia 1987–90; Deputy (Christian Democratic Party), Supreme Soviet of Estonia 1989–92; mem. Constitutional Ass. 1991–92; mem. Riigikogu (Estonian Parl.) 1992–; Founder and Chair. Pro Patria Union (Isamaaliit) Party 1992–95, Leader of Union of Pro Patria and Res Publica (Isamaa ja Res Publica Liit—IRL) following merger with Res Publica 2006–; Prime Minister 1992–94, 1999–2002; Minister of Defence 2011–12; apptd mem. ISTAL by EC; mem. Advisory Bd Springfellow 2003–; Founding mem. Foundation for the Investigation of Communist Crimes; fmr Pres. Council of Historians of Foundation of Estonia Inheritance, Soc. for Preservation of Estonia History, Soc. of Univ. Students of Estonia; Estonian Order of the Nat. Coat of Arms (Second Class), Cavaliere di Gran Groce dei Santi Maurizio e Lazzaro, Das Grosskreuz des Verdienstorderns des Bundesrepublic Deutschland, Nat. Order of Merit, Malta, Grand Cross, Ordre nat. du Mérite, France; Young Politician of the World (Jr Chamber Int.) 1993, European Tax Payer Asscn Year Prize 2001, European Bull, Davastoeconomic Forum, Global Link Award 2001, Adam Smith Award 2002, Milton Friedman Prize for Advancing Liberty, Cato Inst. 2006, Faith and Freedom Award, Acton Inst. 2007. *Publications:* War in the Woods 1992, The Challenge for Europe 1994, Back to the Future: Ten Years of Freedom in Central Europe 2001, Estonia: Little Country that Could 2002, Estonia: A Land of Human Dimensions 2004, Estonia in World War II 2005, The Forgotten War 2005, Estonia's Way 2006, numerous other books in Estonian, Finnish, German, Hungarian, Latvian, Polish and Esperanto; several scientific papers. *Leisure interests:* tennis, squash, history. *Address:* c/o Ministry of Defence, Sakala 1, 15094 Tallinn, Estonia. *Website:* www.martlaar.ee.

LAÂRAYEDH, Ali; Tunisian politician; b. 15 Aug. 1955, Medenine; m. Wided Lagha; two s. one d.; trained as engineer in merchant navy; Founder mem. Hizb al-Nahdah/Ennahda Movt, political activist and Spokesman 1981–90; arrested Dec. 1990, released 2004; Minister of the Interior 2011–13; Prime Minister March–Dec. 2013. *Address:* c/o Office of the Prime Minister, pl. du Gouvernement, La Kasbah, 1030 Tunis, Tunisia (office).

LABAKI, Nadine; Lebanese actress and director; b. 18 Feb. 1974, Baabdat; d. of Antoine Labaki and Antoinette Labaki; m. Khaled Mouzanar 2007; ed Saint Joseph Univ., Beirut; contestant on televised talent show Studio el in 'directing' category with music video Habeebi Ya for amateur singer called Carla early 1990s; first video, Tayr El Gharam, for Lebanese artist Pascale Machaalani; later made another two videos for Noura Rahal, followed by music video of the song Ma Fina with Katia Harb; breakthrough came with Nancy Ajram's video Akhasmak Ah 2003; further videos with Ajram followed; co-wrote, directed and starred in her first feature film Caramel 2007, premiered at Cannes Film Festival 2007, also shown at Toronto Int. Film Festival and American Film Inst.; placed on Variety's 10 Directors to Look Out for List 2007, ranked by Arabian Business amongst the Power 500: The World's Most Influential Arabs (52nd) 2012. *Music videos include:* for Pascale Machaalani: Tayr el Gharam 2001; for Noura Rahal: Salemly Albak 2001, Shoflak Hall 2002; for Katia Harb: Ma Fina 2002; for Nancy Ajram: Akhasmak Ah 2003, Ya Salam 2003, Sehr Ouyounou 2003, Ah W Noss 2004, Lawn Ouyounak 2004, Enta Eih 2005, Yatabtab 2006, Fi Hagat 2010; for Carole Samaha: Habib Albi 2003, Tala' Fiyi 2004; for Guy Manoukian: Al-Urdun 2004; for Star Academy: Jayi el Hakika 2004; for Yuri Mrakadi: Bahebak Mot 2005; for Nawal Al Zoghbi: B'einak 2005; for Nicole Saba: Ya Shaghelny Beek 2005; for Magida El Roumi: I'tazalt El Gharam 2006. *Films:* Non métrage Libanais (short) 2003,

Ramad (short) 2003, Seventh Dog (short) 2005, Bosta 2005, Caramel (also writer and dir) 2007, Stray Bullet 2010, The Father and the Foreigner 2010, The Smallest Red Carpet, But the Biggest Heart (documentary) 2011, Where Do We Go Now? (also writer, dir and producer) (People's Choice Award, Toronto Int. Film Festival) 2011. *E-mail:* nadine@nadinelabaki.com. *Website:* www.nadinelabaki.com.

LABARDAKIS, Augoustinos; Greek ecclesiastic; *Greek Orthodox Metropolitan of Germany and Exarch of Central Europe;* b. (Georges Labardakis), 7 Feb. 1938, Voukoulies-Chania, Crete; s. of Emmanouil Labardakis and Eurydike Labardakis; ed theological schools in Chalki, Turkey, Salzburg, Austria, and Münster and West Berlin, Germany; ordained as priest, Greek Orthodox Metropolitanate of Germany 1964; served as priest, West Berlin 1963–72; elected Bishop of Elaia 1972; auxiliary bishop, Greek Orthodox Metropolitanate of Germany 1972–80; elected Greek Orthodox Metropolitan of Germany and Exarch of Cen. Europe 1980–; Chair. Orthodox Bishops' Conf. in Germany 2010–; Great Fed. Cross of Merit (Germany) 1980, Order of Merit of Fed. State of North Rhine-Westphalia 1992, Grand Commdr, Order of Honour of the Hellenic Repub. 1994, Cross of Merit of Fed. State of Lower Saxony 2009; Hon. DTheol (Bonn) 2006. *Address:* Greek Orthodox Metropolitanate of Germany, Dietrich-Bonhoeffer-Strasse 2, 53227 Bonn (office); PO Box 300555, 53185 Bonn, Germany (office). *Telephone:* (228) 9737840 (office). *Fax:* (228) 97378424 (office). *E-mail:* metropolit@orthodoxie.net (office). *Website:* www.orthodoxie.net (office).

LABIS, Attilio; French ballet dancer, academic, choreographer and writer; b. 5 Sept. 1936, Vincennes; s. of Umberto Labis and Renée Labis (née Cousin); m. Christiane Vlassi 1959; two s.; ed Ecole de danse académique de l'Opéra, Paris; mem. Corps de Ballet at the Paris Opera 1952, Premier Danseur 1959, Premier Danseur Etoile Chorégraphe 1960–65, Maître de Ballet 1965–, Prof. of Danse, fmr Chief Choreographer; Prof. of Dance, Ecole de Danse; Prof. d'Adage et de Repertoire; Guest Dancer in London, Paris, Washington, Tokyo, Moscow, Kiev, Leningrad, Rome, Milan, Berlin, Munich, Stuttgart, Rio de Janeiro, Hong Kong, Singapore and Sydney; World Amb. for l'Ecole Française; devised choreography for productions including Rencontre (TV) 1961, Arcades 1964, Romeo and Juliet 1967, Spartacus 1973, Raymonda 1973; has created and interpreted numerous ballets, including Giselle, Sleeping Beauty, Swan Lake, Don Quixote, Pas de Dieux (Gene Kelly), Marines (Georges Skibine), Icare (Serge Lifar), Pas de danse (music by Gluck), Schéhérazade, Coppélia, Sarabande, Casse-Noisette, Etudes (Harold Lander), Spartacus, Arcades, Romeo et Juliette, Raymonda, Spartacus, Romeo and Juliette, Arcades (Berlioz), Sarabande (Rossini); Chevalier des Arts et des Lettres, Légion d'honneur 2002; Prix Vaslaw Nijinsky. *Films:* Le spectre de la danse (documentary short) 1961, L'adage (short) 1964, Les cahiers retrouvés de Nina Vyroubova (documentary) 1996, Serge Lifar Musagète (documentary) 2005. *Television:* Discorama (series) 1959, L'âge en fleur (series) (actor) 1975. *Address:* Opéra de Paris, 8 rue Scribe, 75009 Paris (office); 13 Avenue Rubens, 78400 Chatou, France. *Telephone:* 1-30-53-48-07 (Paris) (home); 6-63781398 (mobile). *Fax:* 1-30-53-57-80 (Paris) (home). *E-mail:* attilio.labis.choregraphe@wanadoo.fr (home). *Website:* www.operadeparis.fr (office).

LABRIE, Fernand, OC, BA, MD, PhD, FRCP, FRSC; Canadian endocrinologist, physician and academic; *Professor of Physiology and Director, Laboratory of Molecular Endocrinology, Laval University;* b. 28 June 1937, Québec; m. Nicole Cantin; two s. three d.; ed Séminaire de Québec, Laval Univ.; residency in Internal Medicine, L'Hôtel-Dieu de Québec 1962–63; Post-doctoral research, Dept of Biochemistry, Univs of Cambridge and Sussex, UK 1966–68, Lab. of Molecular Biology, Univ. of Cambridge; Dir Lab. of Molecular Endocrinology, Laval Univ. 1969–2009, Dir Medical Research Group in Molecular Endocrinology 1973–2008, Prof., Dept of Physiology 1974–, Head, Dept of Physiology and Anatomy 1990–2002; full-time physician, Dept of Medicine, Le Centre Hospitalier de l'Université Laval (CHUL) 1972–, Head, Dept of Physiology and Anatomy 1990–2002, Dir of Research, CHUL Research Centre 1982–2008; Pres. Le Fonds de la recherche en santé du Québec 1992–95, Canadian Soc. of Endocrinology and Metabolism 1978–79; mem. Medical Advisory Bd The Gairdner Foundation, Toronto 1979–1985; Consultant, Study Section, Centre for Population Research, NICHD, NIH, Bethesda, Md 1976, 1977, 1979, 1980, 1983, 1984; mem. Exec. Int. Soc. of Endocrinology 1980–88; Invited Expert, WHO Task Force on the Regulation of Male Fertility 1981; Pres. Canadian Soc. for Clinical Investigation 1981–82; mem. Science Council of Canada 1983–87; Vice-Pres. Int. Soc. of Neuroendocrinology 1992–96; Founding Bd mem. Soc. Innovatech Québec et Chaudière-Appalaches, Pres. 2008–10, High Tech. Investment Fund 1994–, Pôle Québec-Chaudière-Appalaches 2002–; mem. Life Sciences Cttee La Caisse de Dépôt du Québec 2005–; Co-Pres. Pôle Québec Chaudière-Appalaches 2005–08, Pres. 2008–; Pres. Int. Cttee Int. Congress on Hormonal Steroids and Hormones & Cancer 2008–10; Chair. Organizing Cttees of ten Congresses held in Québec City, including 7th Int. Congress of Endocrinology 1984 and mem. Scientific or Programme Cttees of 61 congresses held worldwide; Pres. 13th Int. Congress on Hormonal Steroids and Hormones & Cancer, Québec City 2008; Assoc. Ed. Journal of Molecular and Cellular Endocrinol 1973–81; Corresp. Ed. Journal of Steroid Biochemistry and Molecular Biology 1987–95; mem. Editorial Bd Journal of Cyclic Nucleotide Research 1974–80, Endocrinology 1977–81, Endocrine-Related Cancer 1994–98, Journal of Steroid Biochemistry and Molecular Biology 1995–; mem. 53 orgs, including Canadian Soc. of Endocrinology and Metabolism, Endocrine Soc. (USA), Canadian Soc. for Clinical Investigation, American Soc. of Clinical Oncology, American Assen for Cancer Research, American Urological Assen, Soc. for Endocrinology (UK), Biochemical Soc. (GB), American Soc. for Biochemistry and Molecular Biology, American Soc. of Physiology, la Soc. Française d'Endocrinologie, Canadian Fertility and Andrology Soc., World Fed. of Scientists, Soc. for Investigative Dermatology, Canadian Acad. of Health Sciences 2005; Officer, Ordre nat. du Québec 1991; Dr hc (Université de Caen, France) 1996, (Univ. of Athens) 2006; Prince of Wales Award 1957, Medal of Gov. Gen. of Canada 1957, Award of Coll. of Physicians and Surgeons of Prov. of Quebec 1959, Grant Medal 1960, Centennial Fellow, MRC of Canada 1966–69, Scholar of MRC of Canada 1969–73, Assoc. of MRC of Canada 1973–96, Assoc. of Royal Coll. of Physicians and Surgeons of Canada 1973–, Vincent Medal, Assen Canadienne-Française pour l'Avancement des Sciences 1976, Medal of City of Nice 1977, Research Award, Soc. for the Study of Reproduction 1980, Award of Fondation de recherche en hormonologie, Paris 1981, MDS Health Group Award 1981, Medal of Collège de France, Paris 1984, Canada Award for Excellence in Business 1985, Award

'Fidéides' of Chamber of Commerce of Sainte-Foy 1985, 1990, (high-tech) 1997, Certificate of Merit Celebration of Govt of Canada 1988, French Canadian Scientist of the Year 1989, Magazine 'Aujourd'hui la Science' of CBC 1989, Michel Sarrazin Award, Canadian Physiological Soc. 1990, Michel Sarrazin Award, Club de recherches cliniques du Québec 1990, Canada Award for Excellence in Business 1990, Gloire de l'Escolle, Asscn des Diplômés de l'Université Laval 1991, Grand Québécois, Chambre de commerce et d'industrie du Québec métropolitain 1991, Antoni Nalecz Award, Canadian Soc. of Endocrinology and Metabolism 1990, 1993, Recognition Prize, Séminaire de Québec 1993, Mur des Célébrités, Québec 1994, MRC Distinguished Scientist 1996, Exceptional Merit Award, Canadian Soc. of Endocrinology and Metabolism 1998, The Izaak-Walton-Killam Memorial Prize, Canada Council for the Arts 1998, Award of Int. Acad. of Human Reproduction, 10th World Congress of Human Reproduction, Bahia 1999, Golden Spatula, Quebec Alpine Ski Fed., Career involvement in devt of Alpine Skiing 1999, Grand Bâtisseur Québécois 2000, Commdr, Laval Univ., Rector's Circle 2000–, The Queen's Golden Jubilee Medal (Canadian Govs Gen.) 2002, mem. Excelcia Circle of Bioquebec, The Quebec Bio-Industries Network 2003, Personality — Special Issue of Business Plus Oct. 2003, chosen as one of the "101 Québécois au sommet de l'action" for Entreprendre magazine 2004, Mentor Scientifique Award, Club de recherches cliniques du Québec 2004, chosen among the celebrated grads of Laval Univ. 2004, chosen by public as First Entrepreneur of the Year, Chambre de Commerce des Entrepreneurs de Québec 2005, recognized as one of top five men and women of influence in Quebec City (Le Soleil) 2005, Armand-Frappier Prize (highest distinction from Govt Quebec) 2006, Reconnaissance Prize, Le Petit Séminaire de Québec 2006, Economy Leader of Quebec City area, Le Soleil and Radio-Canada 2006, King Faisal Int. Prize in Medicine, King Faisal Foundation (co-recipient) 2007, Scientific Career Award, Asscn des Médecins de Langue Française du Canada 2007, Grad. of Influence, Laval Univ. 2008, Career Award, Int. Soc. of Endocrinological Gynecology 2009. *Publications:* Proceedings of the 12th International Congress on Hormonal Steroïds and Hormones & Cancer (ed.) 2007, Endocrinology and the Prostate, Best Practice and Research, Clinical Endocrinology and Metabolism, Vol. 22, No. 2, (Guest Ed.) 2008; 1205 publs with over 40,000 citations (most-cited Canadian scientist (all disciplines) in world literature). *Address:* Laboratory of Molecular Endocrinology and Oncology, Le Centre hospitalier de l'Université Laval, 2705 boulevard Laurier, Québec, PQ G1V 4G2 (office); 2989 de la Promenade, Ste-Foy, PQ G1W 2J5, Canada (home). *Telephone:* (418) 654-2704 (office). *Fax:* (418) 654-2735 (office). *E-mail:* fernand .labrie@crchul.ulaval.ca (office). *Website:* www.crchul.ulaval.ca (office); www .fernandlabrie.com.

LABRO, Philippe; French screenwriter, director and actor; b. 27 Aug. 1936, Menthon-Saint-Bernard (Haute-Savoie); ed Washington and Lee Univ., Va, USA; travelled across all of the USA; worked as radio and newspaper reporter on his return to Europe; soldier in Algeria 1960–62; began writing for RTL, Paris Match, and for TF1 and Antenne 2 on short films; directed programmes on RTL 1985–2000, Vice-Pres. 1992; Commdr, Légion d'honneur 2010. *Films include:* as actor: Le chat et la souris 1975; as writer: Tout peut arriver (aka Don't Be Blue) 1969, Sans mobile apparent (Without Apparent Motive) (also actor, uncredited) 1971, L'héritier (The Inheritor, adaption) (also actor, uncredited) 1973, Le hasard et la violence (Chance and Violence) 1974, L'alpagueur (aka Hunter Will Get You, USA) 1976, La crime (aka Cover Up) 1983, Rive droite, rive gauche (Right Bank, Left Bank) 1984; as writer and dir: Des feux mal éteints (Poorly Extinguished Fires) 1994, Foreign Student 1994. *Television:* Les deux D: Marie Dubois, Françoise Dorléac (dir) 1966. *Publications include:* L'Étudiant étranger (Prix Interallié 1986). *Address:* c/o Editions Gallimard, 5 rue Sébastien-Bottin, 75328 Paris Cedex 07, France.

LABUS, Miroljub, MSc, PhD; Serbian economist, academic, lawyer and politician; *Professor, Department of Economics, Faculty of Law, University of Belgrade;* b. 27 Feb. 1947, Mala Krsna; s. of Zdravko Labus and Draginja Labus (née Pavlovic); m. Olivera Labus (née Grabic); two d.; ed Belgrade Univ.; attorney in Belgrade 1970–71; Lecturer in Law, Belgrade Univ. 1971, Prof. of Econs, Faculty of Law 1971–; Fulbright Lecturer, Cornell Univ., USA 1983, Visiting Asst Prof. 1984; Sr Adviser, Fed. Statistics Office 1986–94; mem. Bd Ekonomska Misl i Ekonomske Analize journals; Fellow, Econ. Inst. 1993–99; Deputy Prime Minister and Minister of Foreign Econ. Relations, Fed. Repub. of Yugoslavia 1987–91, Deputy Prime Minister, with responsibility for econ. relations with the int. community 2001–03; unsuccessful presidential cand. 2002; Deputy Prime Minister in charge of European Integration, Repub. of Serbia 2004–06 (resgnd); mem. Fed. Parl. and Cttee on Monetary Policy; Vice-Pres. Democratic Party 1994–97; mem. Standing Cttee on Econ. Affairs, UNDMP Sarajevo 1996; with UNDP 1996–97; joined IBRD 1997; Ed. The Economic Trends, Fed. Statistics Office, Belgrade, The Economic Barometer, Econ. Inst., Belgrade 2000–; Pres. Admin. Bd G17 Plus movt (later G17 Plus party) 1999–2000, Pres. G17 Plus 2003–06 (resgnd). *Publications:* Social and Collective Property Rights 1987, General Equilibrium Modelling (co-author) 1990, Contemporary Political Economy 1991, Foundations of Political Economy 1992, Foundations of Economics 1995, other books and numerous articles on econ. problems. *Leisure interests:* woodwork, skiing. *Address:* University of Belgrade, Faculty of Law, Bulevar kralja Aleksandra 67, 11000 Belgrade, Serbia (office); Gospodar Jevremova str. 13, Belgrade, Serbia (home). *Telephone:* (11) 3027700 (office). *Fax:* (11) 3221299 (office). *E-mail:* pravni@ius.bg.ac.rs (office). *Website:* www.ius.bg.ac.rs (office).

LaBUTE, Neil; American playwright, film writer and director; b. 19 March 1963, Detroit, Mich.; m.; two c.; ed Brigham Young Univ., Univ. of Kan., New York Univ. *Films include:* In the Company of Men (writer, dir) (Sundance Film Festival Filmmakers' Trophy, Soc. of Tex. Film Critics Best Original Screenplay Award, New York Film Critics' Circle Best First Film) 1997, Your Friends and Neighbors (writer, dir) 1998, Tumble (writer) 2000, Nurse Betty (dir) 2000, Possession (screenplay writer, dir) 2002, The Shape of Things (writer, dir) 2003, The Wicker Man 2006, Lakeview Terrace 2008. *Theatre productions include:* Woyzeck, Dracula, Sangguinarians & Sycophants, Ravages, Rounder, Lepers, Filthy Talk For Troubled Times, In the Company of Men (Assen for Mormon Letters Award for Drama 1993) 1992, Bash: Latterday Plays 2000, The Shape of Things 2001, The Distance From Here (Almeida, London) 2002, The Mercy Seat 2002, Merge 2003, Wrecks (Everyman Palace, Cork) 2005, This is How it Goes (New York, and Donmar Warehouse London) 2005, Some Girl(s) 2006, Land of the Dead/Helter

Skelter 2007, Reasons to be Pretty 2008. *Television includes:* Bash: Latter-Day Plays 2001. *Publications include:* In the Company of Men 1998, Your Friends and Neighbors 1999, Bash: Latterday Plays 2000, The Shape of Things 2001, The Distance from Here 2003, The Mercy Seat 2003, Seconds of Pleasure (short stories) 2004. *Address:* William Morris Agency, One William Morris Place, Beverly Hills, CA 90212, USA. *Telephone:* (310) 859-4000 (office). *Fax:* (310) 859-4462 (office). *Website:* www.wma.com (office).

LACALLE HERRERA, Luis Alberto; Uruguayan farmer, lawyer and fmr head of state; b. 13 July 1941, Montevideo; s. of Carlos Lacalle and María Hortensia de Herrera Uriarte; m. María Julia Pou Brito del Pino 1970; two s. one d.; ed Universidad de la República Oriental del Uruguay; journalist, Clarín daily newspaper 1961; currently contributor to El Debate of Montevideo; columnist, Correo de los Viernes, La Patria de Montevideo, Spanish newspaper ABC; joined Partido Nacional (Blanco) 1958; Deputy to Legis. Ass. 1971–73; elected Senator and Vice-Pres. 1984, mem. Cttee for Public Funds, for Transportation, for Public Works; cand. for Pres. for Partido Nacional (Blanco) 1989; Pres. of Uruguay 1990–95; presidential cand. 2004, 2009; Leader Nationalist sector, Herrerismo, mem. Party Directorate; Co-founder MERCOSUR 1991; mem. Club de Madrid; Gran Collar de la Orden Nacional del Mérito del Ecuador 1990, Gran Collar de la Orden al Mérito de Chile 1991, Collar de la Orden del Libertador Gral. San Martín de Argentina 1991, Gran Collar del Cóndor de los Andes de Bolivia 1991, Gran Cruz de la Orden Cruzeiro do Sul de Brasil 1991, Grand Cross of the Most Distinguished Order of St Michael and St George; Dr hc (Universidad Complutense de Madrid) 1992, (Hebrew Univ. of Jerusalem) 1992, (Autonomous Univ. of Guadalajara, Mexico) 1993, (Nat. Univ. of Paraguay) 1993; Gold Medal of the Xunta de Galicia (Spain) 1994, Jerusalem Award 1995. *Address:* Avda. de las leyes s/n Palacio Legislativo, Montevideo, Uruguay (office). *Telephone:* (2) 2000337 (office); (2) 6002757. *Fax:* (2) 9290255 (office). *E-mail:* lacalleherrera@parlamento .gub.uy (office); lacalleherrera@gmail.com. *Website:* www.parlamento.gub.uy (office).

LACEY, Richard Westgarth, MD, PhD, FRCPath; British microbiologist and academic; b. 11 Oct. 1940, London; s. of Jack Lacey and Sybil Lacey; m. Fionna Margaret Lacey 1972; two d.; ed Felsted School, Essex, Jesus Coll., Cambridge, London Hosp.; house officer, London Hosp. 1964–66, St Mary's Hosp., Eastbourne 1966; Sr House Officer, Registrar in Pathology, Bristol Royal Infirmary 1966–68; Lecturer, Reader in Clinical Microbiology, Univ. of Bristol 1968–74; Consultant in Chemical Pathology, Queen Elizabeth Hosp., King's Lynn 1975–83; Consultant in Infectious Diseases, East Anglian Regional Health Authority 1974–83, Leeds Health Authority 1983–98; Prof. of Medical Microbiology, Univ. of Leeds 1983–98, Prof. Emer. 1998–; consultant, WHO 1983–; Dick Memorial Lecture, Edin. Veterinary School 1990; Evian Health Award Winner 1989, Caroline Walker Award 1989, Campaign for Freedom of Information Award 1990. *Publications include:* Safe Shopping, Safe Cooking, Safe Eating 1989, Unfit for Human Consumption 1991, Hard to Swallow 1994, Mad Cow Disease: the History of B.S.E. in Britain 1994, Poison on a Plate 1998 and over 200 papers and articles for journals. *Leisure interests:* gardening, painting, antique restoration (intermittently). *Address:* Carlton Manor, Near Yeadon, Leeds, LS19 7BE, England (home).

LaCHAPELLE, David; American photographer; b. 1969, Fairfield, Conn.; s. of Philip LaChapelle and Helga LaChapelle; ed North Carolina School of the Arts, School of Visual Arts, New York, Art Student's League; began career by creating fine art images for Interview Magazine; photographer advertising campaigns for Keds, Estée Lauder, Prescriptives, Volvo, MasCosmetics, Diesel Jeans; widely published in fashion, music and entertainment magazines; photography prints and TV for clients including Jean Paul Gaultier, Giorgio Armani, MTV, Pepsi and Levis; fashion portraits of celebrities include Debbie Harry, Britney Spears, Madonna, David Bowie and Elton John; Best New Photographer of the Year, French Photo Magazine 1995, American Photo Magazine 1995, Photographer of the Year, VH1 Fashion Awards 1996, Best Cutting Edge Essay and Best Style Photography, Life magazine's Alfred Eisenstaedt Awards for Magazine Photography (the Eisies) 1998, Infinity Award, Int. Centre of Photography 1997, honoured in Cover of the Year category at the Eisies 1999, Best Video for Moby's Natural Blues, MTV Europe Music Awards 2000, Adult Contemporary Video of the Year for Elton John's This Train Don't Stop There Anymore, MVPA Awards 2003, Director of the Year (Best Rock Video of the Year) for No Doubt's It's My Life, MVPA Awards 2004, Special Jury Prize, Mountainfilm in Telluride 2004, Special Jury Recognition, Sundance Film Festival 2004, Best Documentary, Aspen Film Festival 2004. *Film:* Rize (dir) 2006. *Publications:* vols of photographic images: LaChapelle Land 1996, David LaChapelle Exhibition 1999, Hotel Lachapelle 1999, Portfolio 2000, David Lachapelle Photology 2001, Barbican Gallery 2002, Eros Fotografia 2003, If You Want Reality, Take The Bus! 2003, Taschen 25th Anniversary 2005, Artists and Prostitutes 2006, David LaChapelle 2006, Heaven to Hell 2006, David LaChapelle 2007, First Step 2008, Jesus is My Homeboy 2008, David LaChapelle 2008, Al Forte Belvedere 2008, Who Shot Rock and Roll 2009, Photo Wisdom 2009, Delirios de Razon 2009, The Rape of Africa 2009, Life 2010, Maybach: Going Places 2010, Atopia 2010, Divine Comedy 2010, Popular 2010, Bliss Amongst Chaos 2010, Taschen 30th Anniversary 2010, MOCA Taipei Catalogue 2010, Earth Laughs In Flowers 2011, Borders and Frontiers 2011, David LaChapelle: Lost and Found 2011, Nosotros: La humanidad al borde 2011, Thus Spoke LaChapelle 2011, LaChapelle 2012, Earth Laughs in Flowers 2012, David LaChapelle 2012, Burning Beauty 2012, Still Life 2013, Land Scape 2014. *Address:* c/o Steven Pranica, Creative Exchange Agency, 545 West 25th Street, 19th Floor, New York, NY 10001, USA. *Telephone:* (212) 414-4100; (212) 645-6100. *E-mail:* steven@cxainc.com; studio@davidlachapelle.com. *Website:* www.cxainc .com; www.davidlachapelle.com.

LACHMANN, Henri, Diplôme d'Expertise Comptable; French business executive; *Chairman of the Supervisory Board, Schneider Electric SA;* b. 13 Sept. 1938; m.; two c.; ed Ecole des Hautes Etudes Commerciales, Paris; Auditor and Dir, Arthur Andersen 1963–70; Dir, Pompey steel co. (later Strafor Facom) 1970–81, Chair. Strafor Facom 1981–98; Dir, Schneider Electric SA 1996–, Chair. and CEO 1999–2006, Chair. Supervisory Bd 2006–; Vice-Pres. Supervisory Bd Vivendi; mem. Bd of Dirs AXA Group, CARMAT, Norbert Dentressangle; mem. Man. Cttee AXA Millésimes (SAS), Comité d'Orientation et Institut de l'Entreprise; Chair. Centre Chirurgical Marie Lannelongue; Officier, Légion d'honneur, des Palmes

académiques, Commdr, Ordre nat. du Mérite; Dr hc (Ecole de Management de Grenoble). *Publication:* report: Bien-être efficacité au travail (co-author) 2010. *Leisure interests:* rugby, skiing. *Address:* Schneider Electric SA, 35 rue Joseph Monier, 92500 Rueil-Malmaison, France (office). *Telephone:* 1-41-29-70-52 (office). *Fax:* 1-41-29-71-28 (office). *Website:* www.schneider-electric.com (office).

LACHMANN, Sir Peter Julius, Kt, ScD, FRCP, FRCPath, FRS, FMedSci; British immunologist; *Sheila Joan Smith Professor Emeritus of Immunology, University of Cambridge;* b. 23 Dec. 1931, Berlin, Germany; s. of Heinz Lachmann and Thea Heller; m. Sylvia Stephenson 1962; two s. one d.; ed Trinity Coll., Univ. of Cambridge and Univ. Coll. Hosp., London; Research Student, Dept of Pathology, Univ. of Cambridge 1958–60, Research Fellow, Empire Rheumatism Council 1962–64, Asst Dir of Research, Immunology Div. 1964–71; Prof. of Immunology, Royal Postgraduate Medical School, Univ. of London 1971–75; Hon. Consultant Pathologist, Hammersmith Hosp. 1971–75; Dir MRC Research Group on serum complement 1971–75; Sheila Joan Smith Prof. of Immunology, Univ. of Cambridge 1977–99, Prof. Emer. 1999–; Hon. Dir, MRC Molecular Immunopathology Unit 1980–97; Hon. Consultant Clinical Immunologist, Cambridge Health Dist 1976–99; Pres. Royal Coll. of Pathologists 1990–93, Acad. of Medical Sciences 1998–2002; Biological Sec. and Vice-Pres. The Royal Soc. 1993–98; Visiting Investigator Rockefeller Univ., New York Univ. 1960–61, Scripps Clinic and Research Foundation, La Jolla, Calif. 1966, 1975, 1980, 1986, Basel Inst. for Immunology 1971; Meyerhof Visiting Prof., Weizmann Inst., Rehovot 1989; Visiting Prof., Collège de France 1993; Fellow, Christ's Coll. Cambridge 1962–71, 1976–, Royal Postgraduate Medical School 1995, Imperial Coll. London 2001; mem. Medical Advisory Cttee, British Council 1983–97, Scientific Advisory Bd SmithKline Beecham 1995–2000; Chair. Science Cttee Asscn Medical Research Charities 1988–92, Medical Research Cttee Muscular Dystrophy Group 1986–90, Research Cttee, CORE (Digestive Disorders Foundation) 2003–09; Pres. Fed. of European Acads of Medicine 2004–05 (Pres. Emer. 2006–07), Henry Kunkel Soc. 2003–05; Trustee, Arthritis Research Campaign 2000–06; mem. Academia Europaea 1992; Foreign mem. Norwegian Acad. of Science and Letters 1991; Foreign Fellow, Indian Nat. Acad. of Science 1997; Foundation Fellow, Univ. Coll. London Hosp. 1999; Hon. mem. Asscn of Physicians 1998; Hon. Foreign mem. Czech Acad. of Medicine 2012; Hon. Fellow, Faculty of Pathology, Royal Coll. of Physicians of Ireland 1993, Trinity Coll. Dublin 2007; Hon. DSc (Leicester) 2005; Gold Medal, European Complement Network 1997, Medicine and Europe Senior Prize, Inst. des Sciences de la Santé 2003; Foundation Lecturer, Royal Coll. of Pathologists 1983, Langdon Brown Lecturer, Royal Coll. of Physicians 1986, Heberden Orator, British Soc. of Rheumatology 1986, Charnock Bradley Memorial Lecturer 1992, Plenary Lecturer, Vienna 1993, Congress Lecturer, BSI 1993, Frank May Lecturer, Leicester 1994, Vanguard Medical Lecture, Univ. of Surrey 1998, Lloyd Roberts Lecturer, Medical Soc. of London 1999, Jean Shanks Lecturer, Acad. of Medical Sciences, London 2001. *Publications:* Jt Ed. Clinical Aspects of Immunology 1975, 1982, 1993. *Leisure interests:* keeping bees, walking in mountains. *Address:* Department of Veterinary Medicine, Madingley Road, Cambridge, CB3 0ES (office); 36 Conduit Head Road, Cambridge, CB3 0EY, England (home). *Telephone:* (1223) 766242 (office); (1223) 354433 (home). *Fax:* (1223) 766244 (office); (1223) 300169 (home). *E-mail:* pjl1000@cam.ac.uk (office). *Website:* www .christs.cam.ac.uk/college-life/people/academic-staff/display.php?id=72 (office).

LACHOUT, Karel, MusD; Czech composer, musicologist, writer, pianist and teacher; b. 30 April 1929, Prague; s. of Ing. Karel Lachout and Marie Lachoutová; m. (divorced); ed Charles Univ., Prague, Acad. of Musical Arts, Prague; teacher of music and English (approbation for grammar schools) 1952; Ed. Music Dept. Radio Prague 1953–79; freelance artist, composer and musicologist with specialization in Spanish and Latin American folk music 1979–; recognition from Queen Sofia of Spain for promotion of Spanish music 1995, from Pres. Eduardo Frei of Chile for promotion of Chilean music in Prague 1999. *Compositions include:* Such is Cuba orchestral suite 1962, Symphonietta for grand orchestra, America Latina orchestral suite (including 'Mar del Plata'), two string quartets, piano pieces. *Radio:* scripts for music programmes on Radio Prague of authentic music from Latin America, Spain and other countries, including Music From Cristóbal Colón's Land series 1974. *Publications:* The Problem of Composer's Creation (dissertation) 1953, The World Sings (Czech Music Fund Prize) 1957, Music of Chile 1976, Music of Cuba (honoured by invitation from UNEAC to Music Festival, Havana 1986) 1979, Folk Music of Latin America (edn to commemorate 500th anniversary of discovery of S America, with two LPs and booklet) 1992, Folk Music of Spain (double LP and booklet) 1993. *Leisure interests:* languages (German, English, Spanish, Latin), travelling to explore origins of authentic folk music, relaxing in Spain at Costa Brava, philosophy of deeper sense of human life and belief in higher justice; active mem., Czech Hussite Church; big collection of folk music (books, instruments, recordings etc.) from all over the world; promotes int. summer folk music festival, Prague Fair every year. *Address:* Viklefova 11, 130 00 Prague 3, Czech Republic (home). *Telephone:* (2) 71770347 (home).

LACHOWSKI, Sławomir, BEcons, PhD; Polish banking executive and business consultant; *Founder, Consulting SL;* b. 1958; ed Univ. of Planning and Statistics, Warsaw (now Warsaw School of Econs), Gutenberg Univ., Mainz, Germany, Univ. of Zurich, Switzerland, Stanford Univ., USA, INSEAD, France; fmr Researcher, Inst. of Econ. Devt; fmr Deputy Pres., PKO BP and First Deputy Pres., PBG SA; mem. Bd of Man. and Deputy Pres. in charge of retail banking, BRE Bank SA –2001, Pres., Bd of Man. 2004–08, also CEO; Founder Consulting SL 2008–. *Address:* Consulting SL, Węgrzynowice 16, 97 212 Łódź, Poland (office). *Telephone:* 447102024 (office). *Website:* www.slawomirlachowski.pl.

LACINA, Ferdinand, MA; Austrian politician; b. 31 Dec. 1942, Vienna; s. of Anna and Ferdinand Lacina; m. Monika Lacina 1966; one s. one d.; ed Hochschule für Welthandel, Vienna; various posts in Kammer für Arbeiter und Angestellte, Vienna 1964; Beirat für Wirtschafts- und Sozialfragen 1974; Dir Dept of Financial Planning, Österreichische Industrieverwaltungs AG 1978; Dir Pvt. Office of Fed. Chancellor Kreisky 1980; Sec. of State, Fed. Chancellery 1982; Fed. Minister of Transport 1984–85, of Public Economy and Transport 1985–86, of Finance 1986–95; consultant, Montana AG, Vienna 1995–, Erste Bank AG 1996–, Bank Austria Creditanstalt AG 2001–; Chair. Man. Bd GiroCredit AG 1996–; Pres. WISE Forum, Vienna; mem. Vienna Chapter, American-Austrian Foundation, Inc. *Publications:* Auslandskapital in Österreich (with O. Grünwald); articles in trade union newspapers and political and econ. journals. *Leisure interests:* literature, walking. *Address:* Erste Bank, Graben 21, 1010 Vienna, Austria (office). *Telephone:* (50) 100-10100 (office).

LACK, Andrew, BFA; American media industry executive; *CEO, Bloomberg Multimedia Group;* b. 16 May 1947, New York, NY; m. Betsy Kenny Lack; two s. one d.; ed Sorbonne, France, Boston Univ.; joined CBS News division 1976, producer 60 Minutes 1977, Exec. Producer West 57th 1985–89, Sr Exec. Producer CBS Reports 1978–85, produced various documentaries, left CBS 1993; Pres. NBC News 1993–2001, Pres. and COO NBC 2001–03; Chair. and CEO Sony Music Entertainment Inc. 2003–04, CEO Sony BMG (following merger with Bertelsmann's BMG) 2004–06, Chair. Sony BMG Music Entertainment 2006; CEO Bloomberg Multimedia Group 2008–. *Address:* Bloomberg LLP, 731 Lexington Avenue, New York, NY 10022, USA (office). *E-mail:* bloomberg@bloomberg.net (office). *Website:* www.bloomberg.com (office).

LACKIN, Winston G.; Suriname politician; *Minister of Foreign Affairs;* Minister of Foreign Affairs 2010–; Acting Finance Minister 2011–; mem. Nationale Democratische Partij, Dir of Cabinet 2010; mem. Megacombinatie political alliance. *Address:* Ministry of Foreign Affairs, Lim A. Postraat 25, POB 25, Paramaribo, Suriname (office). *Telephone:* 471209 (office). *Fax:* 410411 (office). *E-mail:* buza@sr.net (office).

LACLOTTE, Michel René; French museum director; b. 27 Oct. 1929, Saint-Malo; s. of Pierre Laclotte and Huguette de Kermabon; ed Lycée Pasteur, Neuilly, Inst. d'art et d'archéologie de l'Univ. de Paris and Ecole du Louvre; Insp. Inspectorate of Provincial Museums 1955–66; Chief Curator of Paintings, Musée du Louvre 1966–87, of collection Musée d'Orsay 1978–86, Dir Musée du Louvre 1987–92, Pres. de l'Etablissement Public (Musée du Louvre) 1992–94; Pres. Mission de préfiguration, Institut Nat. d'Histoire de l'Art 1994–98; Commdr, Légion d'honneur, Ordre nat. du Mérite, des Arts et des Lettres; Grand prix nat. des Musées 1993; Hon. CBE 1994. *Publications:* various works on history of art, catalogues and articles in reviews mainly on Italian and French painting (14th to 15th centuries) and the Louvre Museum. *Address:* 10 bis rue du Pré-aux-Clercs, 75007 Paris, France (home).

LACOSTE, Paul, OC, PhD; Canadian university administrator; b. 24 April 1923, Montréal, Québec; s. of Emile Lacoste and Juliette (née Boucher) Lacoste; m. 1st Louise Mackay (divorced), 2nd Louise Marcil 1973 (died 1995); one s. two d.; ed Univs of Montréal, Chicago and Paris; Vice-Pres., Montréal Univ. 1966–75; Prof., Dept of Philosophy, Montréal Univ. 1948–86; lawyer 1960–; Pres. Asscn des universités partiellement ou entièrement de langue française 1978–81, Fonds Int. de coopération universitaire 1978–81, Asscn of Univs and Colls of Canada 1978-79, Conf. of Rectors and Prins of Québec Univs 1977–80, mem. Bd Asscn of Commonwealth Univs 1977–80, Ecole polytechnique Montréal 1975–85, Clinical Research Inst. of Montréal 1975–, Ecole des hautes commerciales de Montréal 1982–85; Pres., Univ. of Montréal 1975–85; Chair. Comm. and Cttees of the Fed. Environmental Assessment Review to the Great-Whale Hydroelectric Project 1991–98; Chevalier, Légion d'honneur 1985; Hon. LLD (McGill Univ.) 1975, (Univ. of Toronto) 1978; Dr hc (Laval Univ.). *Publications:* Justice et paix scolaire 1962, A Place of Liberty 1964, Le Canada au seuil du siècle de l'abondance 1969, Principes de gestion universitaire 1970, Education permanente et potentiel universitaire 1977. *Leisure interests:* reading, music, travel. *Address:* Universite de Montréal, CP 6128, Cabinet du rectur, Montréal, Québec H3C 3J7, Canada (office). *Telephone:* (514) 343-6776 (office).

LACOTTE, Urs, MBA; Swiss international organization executive; *Special Adviser, International Olympic Committee;* m. France Lacotte; two c.; ed Univ. of Berne, Univ. of Bayreuth, Germany, Univ. of St Gallen; fmr tech. official for ski competitions in Switzerland; worked with Electrowatt Eng Co. in Asia and with forerunner to Swiss Sports Asscn; fmr planner, Ministry of Defence; Dir-Gen. IOC 2003–11, Special Adviser 2011–. *Address:* International Olympic Committee, Château de Vidy, 1007 Lausanne, Switzerland (office). *Telephone:* (21) 6216111 (office). *Fax:* (21) 6216216 (office). *Website:* www.olympic.org (office).

LACROIX, Christian Marie Marc; French fashion designer; b. 16 May 1951, Arles; s. of Maxime Lacroix and Jeannette Bergier; m. Françoise Roesenstiehl 1989; ed Lycée Frédéric Mistral, Arles, Univ. Paul Valéry, Montpellier, Univ. Paris-Sorbonne and Ecole du Louvre; Asst Hermès 1978–79, Guy Paulin 1980–81; Artistic Dir Jean Patou 1981–87, Christian Lacroix Feb. 1987–, Emilio Pucci 2002–; design for Carmen, Nîmes, France 1988, for L'as-tu revue? 1991, for Les Caprices de Marianne 1994, for Phèdre, Comédie Française 1995; created costumes for Joyaux, Opera Garnier 2000; decorated the TGV Méditerranée 2001; decorated Petit Moulin Hotel, Paris; Creative Dir Emilio Gucci 2002; Commdr, Ordre des Arts et Lettres 1996; Chevalier, Légion d'honneur 2002; Dés d'or 1986, 1988, Council of Fashion Designers of America 1987, Prix Balzac 1989, Goldene Spinnrad Award (Germany) 1990, Prix Molière (for costumes in Phèdre) 1996. *Dance:* Costumes for Opera Garnier (Paris), Stadt Oper (Vienna) and several ballets. *Plays:* costumes for Phèdre, Comédie Française (Paris). *Publication:* Pieces of a Pattern 1992, illustrations for albums Styles d'aujourd'hui 1995, Journal d'une collection 1996. *Address:* 73 rue du Faubourg Saint Honoré, 75008 Paris, France. *Telephone:* 1-42-68-79-00 (office); 1-42-65-79-08. *Fax:* 1-42-68-79-57 (office). *E-mail:* fquere@christian.lacroix.fr.

LACROIX, Hubert T., LLB, MBA; Canadian lawyer and broadcasting executive; *President and CEO, Canadian Broadcasting Corporation (CBC)/ Radio-Canada;* b. 13 July 1955, Montréal; ed Collège Jean-de-Brébeuf, Montréal, McGill Univ.; admitted to Quebec Bar 1977; lawyer with O'Brien, Hall, Saunders 1977–84; Pnr McCarthy Tétrault 1984–2000; Exec. Chair. Telemedia Corpn 2000–03, Sr Adviser Telemedia Ventures Inc. 2003–05; Sr Adviser Stikeman Elliott LLP 2003–07; Pres. and CEO CBC/Radio-Canada 2008–; Adjunct Prof., Faculty of Law, Univ. of Montréal; basketball commentator Télévision de Radio-Canada during Summer Olympics 1984, 1988, 1996; fmr weekly contrib. to Hebdo-sports show, Radio Canada; mem. Bd of Dirs Zarlink Semiconductor Inc. 1992–, Transcontinental Inc., ITS Investments Ltd Partnership; Chair. SFK Pulp Fund; Dir Montréal Gen. Hosp. Foundation; fmr Dir Donohue Inc., Circo Craft Co. Inc., Adventure Electronics Inc., Cambior Inc., Secor Inc., Michelin Canada Inc.; Trustee Lucie and André Chagnon Foundation, Martlet Foundation (McGill Univ.). *Address:* Canadian Broadcasting Corporation, 181 Queen Street, Ottawa, ON K1P 1K9,

Canada (office). *Telephone:* (613) 288-6000 (office). *E-mail:* liaison@cbc.ca (office). *Website:* www.cbc.ca (office).

LACSON, Panfilo Morena 'Ping', BS (Eng), BS, MA; Philippine politician; b. 1 June 1948, Imus, Cavite; adopted s. of Cebu Lacson; m. Alice Perio de Lacson; three s.; ed High School, Imus Inst., Lyceum of the Philippines, Philippine Mil. Acad., Pamantasan ng Lungsod ng Maynila; joined Philippine Constabulary 1971, with Metrocom Intelligence and Security Group 1971–86, PC-INP Anti-Carnapping Task Force 1986–88; Prov. Commdr Prov. of Isabela 1988–89; Commdr Cebu Metrodiscom 1989–92; Prov. Dir Prov. of Laguna Feb.–July 1992; Chief, Presidential Anti-Crime Comm., Task Force Habagat 1992–95; Project Officer, Special Project Alpha 1996; Chief, Presidential Anti-Organized Crime Task Force 1998–2001; Chief, Philippine Nat. Police 1999–2001; mem. Laban ng Demokratikong Pilipino (LDP) Party; senatorial cand. Feb. 2001; elected Senator May 2001–, Asst Minority Floor Leader 2001– (mem. cttees: Accountability of Public Officers and Investigations (Blue Ribbon), Cultural Communities, Environment and Natural Resources, Finance, Games, Amusement and Sports, Justice and Human Rights, Labor, Employment and Human Resources Devt, Local Govt, Nat. Defense and Security, Public Order and Illegal Drugs, Science and Tech., Social Justice, Welfare and Rural Devt, Trade and Commerce, Ways and Means); presidential cand. 2004; One of Ten Outstanding Policemen of the Philippines 1988, Philippine Mil. Acad. Alumni Achievement Award 1988, Philippine Constabulary Metrodiscom Officer of the Year 1992, two Outstanding Achievement Medals, five Bronze Cross Medals, 17 Military Merit Medals, three Medalya ng Kadakilaan, three Medalya ng Kagalingan Awards. *Address:* Room 523, 5th Floor, Senate of the Philippines, GSIS Financial Center, Pasay City, The Philippines (office). *Telephone:* (2) 552-6601 (office). *Fax:* (2) 552-6743 (office). *E-mail:* costaff@pinglacson.ph (office); senlacson@pinglacson.ph (home).

LACY, Alan J., BS, MBA; American business executive and financial analyst; ed Georgia Inst. of Tech., Emory Univ.; began career with Kraft Foods Inc., various sr financial positions at Dart and Kraft Inc., Sr Vice-Pres. Finance and Strategy Kraft General Foods; fmr Vice-Pres. Financial Services and Systems, Philip Morris Cos Inc.; fmr Pres. Philip Morris Capital Corpn; Sr Vice-Pres. Finance, Sears Roebuck and Co. 1994–95, Exec. Vice-Pres. and Chief Financial Officer 1995–97, Pres. Credit 1997–98, Pres. Credit and Chief Financial Officer 1998–99, Pres. Services 1999–2000, Chair. and CEO 2000–05, Vice-Chair. and CEO Sears Holding Corpn (formed from merger of Sears and Kmart Holding Corpn) 2005–06; mem. Bd Dirs Bristol-Myers Squibb Company, The Economic Club of Chicago, Lyric Opera of Chicago, Nat. Retail Fed.; mem. Civic Cttee Commercial Club of Chicago; Trustee, Fidelity Funds; mem. Bd Trustees, Field Museum of Natural History; Trustee and Past Chair. Nat. Parks Conservation Asscn.

ŁĄCZKOWSKI, Paweł Julian, DSoc; Polish politician and university teacher; *Head of Political Council, Alliance of Polish Christian Democrats;* b. 31 July 1942, Kielce; m. Maria Łączkowska; one s. three d.; ed Adam Mickiewicz Univ., Poznań; fmr scientific worker, Adam Mickiewicz Univ., Poznań 1966–90 1994–; contract Prof., Collegium Polonicum, Słubice; mem. Solidarity Ind. Self-governing Trade Union 1980–; Deputy to Sejm (Parl.) 1989–93, 1997–2001, Deputy Chair. Civic Parl. Club 1989–90, Chair. Sejm Circle of Christian Democrats 1990–91, Chair. Parl. Club of Christian Democrats' Party (PChD) 1991–93, Parl. Comm. for Regulations and Deputies 1997–2001, mem. Solidarity Election Action Parl. Caucus 1997–2001; Co-founder Christian Democrats' Party (PChD) 1990, Leader 1992–99, merged with two other parties to form Alliance of Polish Christian Democrats 1999, currently Head of Political Council; Deputy Prime Minister 1992–93; Deputy Chair. Presidium Nat. Bd Solidarity Election Action 1999–2001; mem. Co-ordination Team Solidarity Election Action (AWS) 1996–99; Officer's Cross, Order of Polonia Restituta 2011. *Publications:* Circumstances for Stabilizing Worker Staff in Industrialized Districts 1977; numerous articles. *Leisure interest:* gardening. *Address:* Porozumienie Polskich Chrzescijanskich Demokratów, Sejm, ul. Wiejska 4/6, 00-902 Warsaw, Poland (office). *Telephone:* (61) 8520120 (home).

LADER, Malcolm Harold, OBE, LLB, PhD, MD, DSc, FRCPsych, FMedSci; British professor of clinical psychopharmacology; *Professor Emeritus, Institute of Psychiatry, King's College London;* b. 27 Feb. 1936, Liverpool, England; s. of Abe Lader and Minnie Lader; m. Susan Packer 1961; three d.; ed Liverpool Inst. High School and Liverpool and London Univs; external mem. of scientific staff of MRC 1966–2001; Reader, King's Coll., Univ. of London 1973–78, Prof. 1978, now Prof. Emer.; Consultant Psychiatrist, Bethlem Royal and Maudsley Hosps 1970–2001; mem. various UK Govt advisory bodies; Trustee, Psychiatry Research Trust 2002–; Hon. Fellow, American Coll. of Psychiatrists 1994, British Asscn for Psychopharmacology 1994, Soc. for the Study of Addiction 1998; Heinz Karger Memorial Foundation Prize 1974, Taylor Manor Award 1989. *Publications:* Psychiatry on Trial 1977, Biological Treatments in Psychiatry 1990, Anxiety Panic and Phobias 1997; numerous articles on psychopharmacology. *Leisure interests:* antiques, paintings. *Address:* P 056, Institute of Psychiatry, Denmark Hill, London, SE5 8AF, England (office). *Telephone:* (20) 8650-0366 (office). *Fax:* (20) 7848-0818 (office). *E-mail:* malcolm.lader@kcl.ac.uk (office). *Website:* www.kcl.ac.uk/iop (office).

LADER, Philip, BA, MA, JD; American diplomatist, government official, business executive and lawyer; *Senior Adviser, Morgan Stanley International;* b. 17 March 1946, Jackson Heights, NY; m. Linda LeSourd 1980; two d.; ed Duke Univ., Univ. of Michigan, Oxford and Harvard Univs; Pres. Sea Pines Co. 1979–83, Winthrop Univ., SC 1983–85, Bond Univ., Gold Coast, Australia 1991–93, Business Execs for Nat. Security, 1991; Exec. Vice-Pres. Sir James Goldsmith's US Holdings; Deputy Dir for Man., Office of Man. and Budget, Exec. Office of the Pres. 1993; Chair. Pres.'s Council for Integrity and Efficiency 1993, Pres.'s Man. Council, Policy Cttee, Nat. Performance Review 1993; Deputy Chief of Staff and Asst to Pres., White House 1993–94; Admin., US Small Business Admin. and mem. Pres.'s Cabinet 1995–97; Amb. to UK 1997–2001; Chair. WPP 2001–; Sr Adviser and Vice-Chair., Morgan Stanley Int. 2001–; mem. Bd of Dirs AES, WPP, Marathon Oil and RAND Corpns; mem. Council of Lloyds 2003–10, Council on Foreign Relations; mem. Chief Execs Org., Prince of Wales' Trust Advisory Bd; Trustee, British Museum, 21st Century Foundation, Windsor Leadership Trust, St Paul's Cathedral Foundation; 14 hon. doctorates; RSA Benjamin Franklin Medal 2001. *Leisure interests:* reading, tennis, walking. *Address:* 20 Bank Street, Canary

Wharf, London, E14 4AD, England (office); 151 Meeting Street, Suite 600, Charleston, SC 29401, USA (home). *Telephone:* (20) 7425-6524 (office).

LADREIT DE LACHARRIÈRE, Marc; French business executive; *President, Fimalac SA;* b. 6 Nov. 1940, Nice; s. of Pierre Ladreit de Lacharrière and Hélène Mora; m. Sibylle Lucet 1967 (divorced); one s. three d.; ed Ecole Nat. d'Admin; Asst Man. Banque de Suez et de l'Union des Mines 1970, Asst Dir 1971, Deputy Dir 1973; Vice-Pres. Masson Belfond Armand Colin 1974–95; Vice-Dir Banque de l'Indochine et de Suez 1975, Corp. Affairs Dir 1976; Financial Dir L'Oréal 1976, Man. Dir Admin. and Finance 1977, Vice-Pres. Man. Cttee 1978, mem. Strategic Cttee, Dir and Exec. Vice-Pres. 1984–91, Pres. of Finances 1987–91, mem. Bd Dirs L'Oréal Finance 1984–; Pres. La Revue des deux Mondes 1990–, Financière Marc de Lacharrière (Fimalac, holding co.) 1991–, Council Banque de la Mutuelle industrielle 1988; Vice-Pres. Sofres 1992–97; fmr Vice-Pres. Centenaire Blanzy, Pres. 1994–98; Pres. Financière Sofres 1992–97, Lille Bonnières & Colombe et Alspi 1993–96, Comptoir Lyon Allemand Louyot 1995–96; Chair. Geral, USA, Fitch Ratings, Inc., Fondation Culture & Diversité 2006, Agence France-Muséums (Louvre Abu Dhabi) 2007, Supervisory Bd Webedia 2013; Man. Dir Regefi and Holdilux, Luxembourg; Vice-Chair. L'Oréal (GB), Editions Masson; Dir Collection de l'Institut de l'Entreprise, France Télécom 1995–98, Air France 1996–97, Canal+ 1998–, Flo Group 1998–, Louvre Museum 1999–, Renault 2002–, Casino, Cassina; mem. Int. Council Renault Nissan 2000–; mem. Consultative Cttee, Banque de France; mem. Bd Conseil Artistique des Musées Nationaux, Fondation Bettencourt Schueller, Soc. des Amis du Musée du Quai Branly, Fondation Nationale des Sciences Politiques, Musée du Louvre, Le Siècle, Strategic Cttee for French Econ. Attractiveness; Lecturer, Inst. d'Études Politiques, Paris 1971, then Prof.; Adviser, Foreign Trade of France; Hon. Pres. Inst. of Research and Study for Corp. Security (IERSE); mem. Académie des Beaux-Arts 2006; Grand Croix, Légion d'honneur, Officier, Ordre Nat. du Mérite, Officier des Arts et Lettres. *Publication:* Le droit de noter 2012. *Leisure interests:* tennis, skiing. *Address:* Fimalac, 97 rue de Lille, 75001 Paris, France (office). *E-mail:* contact@fimalac.com (office). *Website:* www .fimalac.com (office).

LADSOUS, Hervé; French diplomatist and UN official; *Under-Secretary-General for Peacekeeping Operations, United Nations;* b. 12 April 1950; m.; three c.; ed École nationale des langues orientales; Vice-Consul in Hong Kong 1973–75; with Econ. Affairs Div., Ministry of Foreign Affairs 1976–81; Second Counsellor, Embassy in Canberra 1981–83, Beijing 1983–86; Second Counsellor, Perm. Mission to UN, Geneva 1986–88, First Counsellor 1988–90; Asst Dir for the Americas, Ministry of Foreign Affairs 1990–92; Acting Chargé d'affaires, Embassy in Port-au-Prince 1991–92; First Counsellor, Perm. Mission to UN, New York 1992–94, Minister Counsellor 1994–97; Perm. Rep. to OSCE, Vienna 1997–2001; Amb. to Indonesia 2001–03 (also accred to E Timor 2002–03); Communications Dir Ministry of Foreign Affairs 2003–05, Dir for Asia and Oceania 2005; Amb. to People's Repub. of China 2006–10; Chief of Staff to Minister for Foreign Affairs 2010–11; Under-Sec.-Gen. for Peacekeeping Operations, UN 2011–; Chevalier, Légion d'honneur, Officier, Ordre nat. du Mérite. *Address:* Department of Peacekeeping Operations, United Nations, Room S-3727-B, New York, NY 10017, USA (office). *Telephone:* (212) 963-8077 (office). *Fax:* (212) 963-9222 (office). *Website:* www.un.org/en/peacekeeping (office).

LADUTSKA, Mikalay Alyaksandravich; Belarusian government official; *Chairman, Minsk City Executive Committee;* b. 21 March 1959, Minsk; ed Byelorussian Polytechnic Inst., Acad. of State Admin under Aegis of Pres. of Belarus; worked as a Foreman, Deputy Sec., Sec. Cttee of Leninist Young Communist League of Byelorussia, Dept 256, Minsk Production Asscn of Industrial House-Building, First Sec. Frunze Region Cttee of Leninist Young Communist League of Byelorussia, Minsk, Deputy Section Head, Cen. Cttee of Leninist Young Communist League of Byelorussia, Instructor, Frunze Region Cttee, Head of Section, Dept 256, Minsk Production Asscn of Industrial House-Building, Head of Section, Minsk Leasing Enterprise of Industrial House-Building 'Minskzhilstroy', Head of Construction Dept 101, Dir Communal Unitary Enterprise Dept of Capital Construction, Minsk City Exec. Cttee, Head of Frunze Region Admin of Minsk, Deputy Chair., First Deputy Chair., Acting Chair. Minsk City Exec. Cttee –2010, Chair. 2010–; Merited Builder of Repub. of Belarus, Medal 'For Labour Merits'; Certificate of Honour, Council of Ministers of Repub. of Belarus. *Address:* Minsk City Executive Committee, Nezavisimosti 8, 220030 Minsk, Belarus (office). *Telephone:* (17) 2180001 (office). *E-mail:* mgik@minsk.gov.by (office). *Website:* minsk.gov.by (office).

LADY GAGA; American singer and songwriter; b. (Stefani Joanne Angelina Germanotta), 28 March 1986, New York, NY; d. of Joseph Germanotta and Cynthia Germanotta (née Bissett); ed Convent of the Sacred Heart School, New York, Tisch School of the Arts, New York Univ.; learned to play piano from age of four; wrote first piano ballad, aged 13; began performing in New York clubs, aged 14; began performing in rock music scene of New York City's Lower East Side 2003; signed with Streamline Records (imprint of Interscope Records); began solo professional singing career 2006–; has written songs for Britney Spears, the Pussycat Dolls; captured attention of Akon, who recognized her vocal abilities, and signed her to his own label, Kon Live Distribution; released her first fragrance, Lady Gaga Fame, in association with Coty, Inc. 2012; launched the Born This Way Foundation 2012; ranked by Billboard the 73rd Artist of the 2000–10 decade, Billboard Rising Star Award 2009, Int. Dance Music Awards for Best Breakthrough Artist 2009, for Best Pop Dance Track (for Just Dance) 2009, MTV Europe Music Award for Best New Act 2009, MTV Video Music Award for Best New Artist 2009, Grammy Award for Best Dance Recording (for Poker Face) 2010, BRIT Awards for Best Int. Breakthrough Act 2010, for Best Int. Female Solo Artist 2010, eight MTV Video Music Awards 2010, named by TIME magazine in its annual TIME 100 list of the most influential people in the world 2010, ranked fourth by Forbes magazine on its list of the 100 Most Powerful and Influential Celebrities in the World 2010, also ranked as the second Most Powerful Musician in the World 2010, ranked by Forbes magazine amongst The World's 100 Most Powerful Women (seventh) 2010, (11th) 2011, (14th) 2012, (45th) 2013, Grammy Award for Best Female Pop Vocal Performance (for Bad Romance) 2011, MTV Europe Music Award for Best Female 2011, MTV Europe Music Award for Biggest Fans 2011. *Tours:* The Fame Ball Tour 2009, The Monster Ball Tour 2009–11, The Born This Way Ball Tour 2012–13. *Recordings:* albums: The Fame (Grammy Award for Best

Electronic/Dance Album 2010, BRIT Award for Best Int. Album 2010) 2008, The Fame Monster (Grammy Award for Best Pop Vocal Album 2011) 2009, Born This Way (two MTV Video Music Awards 2011, MTV Europe Music Award for Best Song, 2011, MTV Europe Music Award for Best Video 2011) 2011, Artpop 2013. *Address:* c/o Interscope Records, 2220 Colorado Avenue, Santa Monica, CA 90404, USA. *Website:* www.ladygaga.com.

LAERMANN, Karl-Hans, DrIng; German politician and academic; *Professor Emeritus of Statics, Bergische Universität Wuppertal;* b. 26 Dec. 1929, Kaulhausen, Kr. Heinsberg; s. of Johann Laermann and Elisabeth Laermann; m. Hilde Woestemeyer 1955; three s. one d.; ed Rhenish-Westphalian Coll. of Advanced Tech., Aachen; Lecturer in Experimental Statics, Rhenish-Westphalian Coll. of Advanced Tech. 1966–74; Prof. of Statics, Bergische Univ. G.H. Wuppertal, Head Lab. for Experimental Stress Analysis and Measurement 1974–, now Emer.; mem. FDP 1965–, mem. Fed. Exec. Cttee 1980–90, N Rhine-Westphalian Exec. Cttee 1978–94, Chair. Fed. Cttee on Research and Tech. of FDP 1981–96; mem. Bundestag (Parl.) 1974–98; Deputy Chair. working group of FDP Parl. Group on Educ. and Science, Research and Tech. 1980–94; Fed. Minister of Educ. and Science Feb.–Nov. 1994; mem. Bd Trustees Volkswagen Foundation 1984–94, Friedrich Naumann Foundation 1984–2010, Anglo-German Foundation for the Study of Industrial Society 1989–99; mem. Admin. Bd Inter Nationes 1995–99; Extraordinary mem. Goethe Inst. 1995–98; Corresp. mem. Accad. delle Scienze dell'Istituto Bologna; Hon. mem. VDI (Verein Deutscher Ingenieure, Asscn of German Engineers); Hon. CBE (UK) 1978, Commdr Order of Orange-Nassau (Netherlands) 1982, Great Cross with Star of Order of FRG 1996; Hon. DrIng (Magdeburg); Dr hc (Tech. Univ. Prague, Transilvania Univ. Braşov, Romania, Tech. Univ. Košice, Slovakia); Gold Medal of Honour, VDI 1999. *Publications:* Konstruktiver Ingenieurbau (Ed.) 1967, Experimentelle Plattenuntersuchungen-Theoretische Grundlagen 1971, Experimentelle Spannungsanalyse I, II 1972, 1977, Perspektiven – Ein Wissenschaftler in der Politik 1984, Optical Methods in Experimental Solid Mechanics (ed.) 2000, Inverse Problems in Experimental Structural Analysis 2008; about 240 publs on science and politics in int. journals. *Leisure interests:* painting, sailing. *Address:* Bergische Universität Wuppertal, FBD, Pauluskirche str. 7, 42285 Wuppertal (office); Am Tannenberg 19, 41189 Mönchengladbach, Germany (home). *Telephone:* (202) 4394249 (office); (2166) 58164 (home). *Fax:* (202) 4394078 (office); (2166) 958077 (home). *E-mail:* laermann .kh@t-online.de (home); laermann@uni-wuppertal.de (office). *Website:* www.uni -wuppertal.de (office).

LAFER, Celso, MA, PhD; Brazilian legal scholar, academic, international organization official and fmr government official; b. 7 Aug. 1941, São Paulo; ed Faculty of Law, Univ. of São Paulo, Cornell Univ., USA; Prof. of Law, Univ. of São Paulo 1988–2011, now Prof. Emer.; Minister of Foreign Affairs 1992, 2001–02; Amb. to WTO and UN and Head of WTO Gen. Council and Dispute Settlement Comm. 1995–98, Minister of Devt, Industry and Commerce 1999–; mem. Consultative Bd to Dir Gen. 2004–, mem. Brazilian Acad. of Letters 2006–; Chair. Panel of Dispute Settlement Body 2003, 2010–; Pres. FAPESP (São Paulo Foundation for Advancement of Research) 2007; numerous decorations including Grand Cross San Martin (Argentina) 1995, Grand Cross, Infante Dom Henrique (Portugal) 2001, Grand Cross Rio Branco (Brazil) 2002, Grand Officer, Légion d'honneur 2002, Grand Cross Scientific Merit (Brazil) 2002; Dr hc (Buenos Aires Univ.) 2001, (Cordoba Univ.) 2002, (Univ. Três de Febrero) 2011, (Univ. Jean Moulin Lyon 3) 2012. *Address:* University of São Paulo, School of Law, Lgo. São Francisco, 1995 Centro, 01005-010 São Paulo SP (office); Avenida Brigadeiro Faria Lima 1306, Jardim Paulistano, 01451-914 São Paulo, Brazil (office). *Telephone:* (11) 3816-0306 (office). *Fax:* (11) 3815-6014 (office). *E-mail:* c_lafer@uol.com.br (home).

LAFFAN, Brigid, PhD, MRIA; Irish political scientist and academic; *Professor of European Politics, School of Politics and International Relations, University College Dublin;* b. 6 Jan. 1955, Co. Kerry; d. of Con Burns and Aileen Burns; m. Michael Laffan 1979; one s. two d.; ed Univ. of Limerick, Coll. of Europe, Bruges, Trinity Coll. Dublin; researcher, European Cultural Foundation 1977–78; Lecturer, Coll. of Humanities, Univ. of Limerick 1979–86; Lecturer, Inst. of Public Admin 1986–89; Newman Scholar, Univ. Coll. Dublin (UCD) 1989–90, Lecturer, Dept of Politics 1990–91, Jean Monnet Prof. of European Politics 1991–, Research Dir Dublin European Inst., UCD, Prin. Coll. of Human Sciences 2005–11, Prof. of European Politics, School of Politics and Int. Relations 2011–; Visiting Prof., Coll. of Europe, Bruges 1992–2004, European Univ. Inst., Florence, Italy 2011, Harvard Univ., USA 2012; adviser on EU enlargement, Oireachtas (Parl.) Foreign Affairs Cttee; mem. Council, Inst. of European Affairs, Dublin; mem. Irish Govt Asia Strategy Group 2005–10; Chevalier, Ordre nat. du Mérite 2010; Theseus Award for Outstanding Research on European Integration 2012. *Publications:* Ireland and South Africa 1988, Integration and Co-operation in Europe 1992, Constitution Building in the European Union (ed.) 1996, The Finances of the European Union 1997, Europe's Experimental Union: Re-thinking Integration (co-author) 1999, Renovation or Revolution: New Territorial Politics in Ireland and the United Kingdom (contributing co-ed. with J. Coakley and J. Todd) 2005, Ireland in the European Union (with Jane O'Mahoney) 2008; numerous articles on Irish foreign policy, EC budgetary policy, insts, governance and political union. *Leisure interests:* theatre, reading, swimming. *Address:* School of Politics and International Relations, University College, Belfield, Dublin 4 (office); 4 Willowbank, The Slopes, Dun Laoghaire, Co. Dublin, Ireland (home). *Telephone:* (1) 7168344 (office); (1) 2862617 (home). *Fax:* (1) 7161171 (office); (1) 2845331 (home). *E-mail:* brigid.laffan@ucd.ie (office). *Website:* www.ucd.ie/humansciences (office).

LAFFITTE, Pierre Paul; French engineer and politician; b. 1 Jan. 1925, St Paul, Alpes Maritimes; s. of Jean Laffitte and Lucie Fink; m. 1st Sophie Glikman-Toumarkine (deceased); m. 2nd Anita Garcia; ed Lycée de Nice, Ecole Polytechnique, Ecole des Mines de Paris; Dir Office of Geological, Geophysical and Mining Research 1953; Asst Dir-Gen. Office of Geological and Mining Research 1959–62, Deputy Dir 1963, Dir 1973–84; Gen. Engineer Mines 1973–; Pres. Conseil de Perfectionnement, Ecole Nat. Supérieure des Mines, Paris 1984–91; Founder Pres. Sophia-Antipolis 1969; Pres. Franco-German Asscn for Science and Tech., AFAST (German-French Asscn for Science and Tech.); Senator from Alpes Maritimes 1985–2008; Pres. Rassemblement Democratique et Social Europeen 2007–; Officier, Légion d'honneur; Officier, Ordre nat. du Mérite; Commdr Order of Polar Star (Sweden); Commdr, Order of Merit (Germany); Hon. PhD (Colorado School of Mines, USA) 1984, (Open Univ., England) 1990; De Gaulle-Adenauer Prize 1994. *Publications:* works on mining and geology, science parks, the information age, local development. *Leisure interest:* gardening. *Address:* Sophia Antipolis, place Sophie Laffitte, 06560 Valbonne (office); Palais du Luxembourg, 75291 Paris Cedex 06; Ecole des Mines, 60 boulevard Saint Michel, 75006 Paris, France. *Telephone:* (4) 92-96-78-00 (office); (4) 93-32-85-90 (home). *Fax:* (4) 93-32-95-26 (home). *E-mail:* p.laffitte@senat.fr (office). *Website:* www.sophia-antipolis .com (office).

LAFFORGUE, Laurent, DèsSc; French mathematician and academic; *Permanent Professor of Mathematics, Institut des Hautes Etudes Scientifiques;* b. 6 Nov. 1966, Antony, Hauts-de-Seine; ed Ecole Normale Supérieure, Université de Paris-Sud XI; taught at Ecole Spéciale Militaire, Saint-Cyr-Coëtquidan 1991–92; Research Fellow, CNRS 1990–2000, Research Dir 2000; Perm. Prof. of Math., Institut des Hautes Etudes Scientifiques, Bures-sur-Yvette 2000–; mem. Acad. des Sciences 2003–; mem. editorial cttee for Math. Publs, Institut des Hautes Etudes Scientifiques, editorial cttee Moscow Mathematical Journal; Chevalier, Légion d'Honneur; Prix Peccot and Cours Peccot, Collège de France 1996, Invited Lecturer, Int. Congress of Mathematicians, Berlin 1998, Bronze Medal, CNRS 1998, Clay Research Award 2 2000, Jacques Herbrand Prize in Math., Acad. des sciences, Paris 2001, Fields Medal, 24th Int. Congress of Mathematicians, Beijing (jtly) 2002. *Publications:* Chtoucas de Drinfeld et conjecture de Ramanujan-Petersson Astérisque 243 1997, Une compactification des champs classifiant les chtoucas de Drinfeld JAMS 1998, Chtoucas de Drinfeld et correspondance de Langlands Inventiones 147 2002, Chirurgie des Grassmanniennes CRM Monograph Series 19 2003, La Débâcle de l'école (with Liliane Lurçat) 2007; numerous articles in math. journals on number theory and analysis. *Address:* Institut des Hautes Etudes Scientifiques, Le Bois-Marie 35, route de Chartres, 91440 Bures-sur-Yvette, France (office). *Telephone:* 1-60-92-66-00 (office). *Fax:* 1-60-92-66-09 (office). *E-mail:* laurent@ihes.fr (office). *Website:* www.ihes.fr (office).

LAFLEY, Alan G., AB, MBA; American business executive; *Chairman, President and CEO, Procter & Gamble Company;* b. 13 June 1947, Keene, NH; ed Hamilton Coll., Harvard Business School; served with USN 1970–75; brand asst, Joy, Procter & Gamble Co. 1977–78, sales training, Denver Sales Dist 1978–80, Asst Brand Man. Tide 1978–80, Brand Man. Dawn & Ivory Snow 1980–81, Ivory Snow 1981–82, Cheer 1982–83, Assoc. Advertising Man. PS & D Div. 1983–86, Advertising Man. 1986–88, Gen. Man. Laundry Products PS & D Div. 1988–91, Vice-Pres. Laundry and Cleaning Products 1991–92, Group Vice-Pres., Pres. Laundry and Cleaning Products 1992–94, Group Vice-Pres. Far East Div. 1994–95, Exec. Vice-Pres., Pres. Asia Div. 1995–98, Exec. Vice-Pres. North American Div. 1998–99, Pres. Global Beauty Care and North America 1999–2000, Pres. and CEO Procter & Gamble Co. 2000–02, Chair., Pres. and CEO 2002–07, 2013–, Chair. and CEO 2007–09, Chair. 2009–10; Sr Advisor, Clayton, Dubilier & Rice 2010–13; Chair. Cincinnati Center City Devt Corpn (3CDC); mem. Bd Dirs General Electric Co., Dell, Inc., Grocery Mfrs of America, United Negro Coll. Fund; fmr mem. Bd Dirs General Motors Corpn; mem. The Business Council, The Business Roundtable, McKinsey Advisory Council, The Lauder Inst. Bd of Govs (Wharton School of Arts and Sciences), Harvard Business School Bd of Dean's Advisors; mem. American Soc. of Corp. Execs; fmr mem. American Chamber of Commerce in Japan, G100 (fmrly The M&A Group); Trustee, Hamilton Coll., US Council for Int. Business; fmr Trustee, Cincinnati Fine Arts Fund, Cincinnati Playhouse in the Park, Cincinnati Symphony Orchestra, Medical Center Fund of Cincinnati, The Seven Hills School, Xavier Univ. *Address:* The Proctor & Gamble Co., 1 Procter & Gamble Plaza, Cincinnati, OH 43202-3315, USA (office). *Telephone:* (513) 983-1100 (office). *Fax:* (513) 983-9369 (office). *E-mail:* info@pg .com (office). *Website:* www.pg.com (office).

LAFON, Jean-Pierre; French international organization official and fmr diplomatist; *President, Bureau International des Expositions;* ed Lycée Condorcet, Institut d'Etudes Politiques, Ecole Nationale d'Administration; mil. service in Germany 1964; Lecturer, Ecole Nationale d'Administration, Côte d'Ivoire 1964–66; joined Ministry of Foreign Affairs 1968, Second then First Sec., Embassy in London 1971–74, mem. del. to Conf. on Security and Co-operation in Europe, Geneva 1973–74; with Econ. Affairs Div., Ministry of Foreign Affairs 1974–76; Adviser, Embassy in Iran 1977–79; Inspector of Foreign Affairs 1980–83, Head of Méthodes-Formation-Informatique Div. 1983–84; Consul in Arlit, Niger 1984–85; Adviser to Cabinet of Jacques Chirac 1986–88; Dir UN Div., Ministry of Foreign Affairs 1989–94; Amb. to Lebanon 1994–97; Pres. French Council for Protection of Refugees 1997–2002; Amb. to China 2002–04; Sec.-Gen. of Foreign Affairs 2004–06; Pres. Bureau international des expositions, Paris 2007–; Chevalier de la Légion d'Honneur 1991, Officier de l'Ordre National du Mérite 2003. *Address:* Bureau International des Expositions, 34, Avenue d'Iéna, Paris 75116, France (office). *Telephone:* 1-45-00-38-63 (office). *Fax:* 1-45-00-96-15 (office). *E-mail:* info@ bie-paris.org (office). *Website:* www.bie-paris.org (office).

LAFONT, Bruno; French business executive; *Chairman and CEO, Lafarge SA;* b. 1956; ed Hautes Etudes Commerciales, Paris, Ecole Nationale d'Admin, Paris; joined Lafarge SA as internal auditor in Finance Dept 1983, Chief Financial Officer Sanitaryware Div., Germany 1984, Chief Div. Finance Dept 1986–88, Int. Devt Dept 1988–89, Vice-Pres. Lafarge Cement and Aggregates and Concrete operations, Turkey 1990–94, Group Exec. Vice-Pres., Finance and mem. Exec. Cttee 1994–98, Exec. Vice-Pres. Gypsum Div. 1998–2003, COO Lafarge SA 2003–06, mem. Bd of Dirs 2005–, CEO 2006–, Chair. 2007–; mem. Bd of Dirs EDF 2008–, Arcelor Mittal 2011–; Co-Chair. World Business Council for Sustainable Devt's (WBCSD) Cement Sustainability Initiative, also Co-Chair. Energy Efficiency in Buildings initiative launched with United Technologies under aegis of WBCSD; Special Adviser to Mayor of Chongqing, China; Pres. Enterprises for the Environment Assen 2009–. *Address:* Lafarge SA, 61 rue des Belles Feuilles, BP 40, 75782 Paris Cedex 16, France (office). *Telephone:* 1-44-34-11-11 (office). *Fax:* 1-44-34-12-00 (office). *E-mail:* info@lafarge.com (office). *Website:* www.lafarge.com (office).

LAFONTAINE, Oskar; German politician; b. 16 Sept. 1943, Saarlouis; m. Doris Vartan 1984; one step-d.; ed Univs of Bonn and Saarbrücken; Mayor of Saarbrücken 1976–85; mem. Saarland Landtag (Regional Parl.), Minister-Pres. 1985–98; Chair. SPD Regional Asscn, Saar 1977–96; mem. SPD Cen. Cttee; Vice-

Chair. SPD 1987–96; Cand. for Chancellorship 1990; Leader SPD 1995–99 (resgnd); Minister of Finance 1998–99 (resgnd); Chair. Die Linke (The Left party) 2007–10. *Publications:* Angst vor den Freunden 1983, Der andere Fortschritt 1985, Die Gesellschaft der Zukunft 1988, Das Lied vom Teilen 1989, Deutsche Wahrheiten 1990, Keine Angst vor der Globalisierung (jtly) 1998, Das Herz schlägt links (autobiog.) 2000. *Address:* c/o Die Linke, Karl-Liebknecht-Haus, Kleine Alexanderstr. 28, 10178 Berlin, Germany (office).

LAGARDE, Christine Madeleine Odette, MA; French lawyer, government official and international organization official; *Madame Chairman of the Executive Board and Managing Director, International Monetary Fund;* b. 1 Jan. 1956, Paris; d. of Robert Lallouette and Nicole Lallouette; m. (divorced); two s.; partner Xavier Giocanti from 2006; ed Lycée Claude Monet, Le Havre, Holton-Arms School, Bethesda, Md, USA, Univ. Paris X, Institut d'études politiques d'Aix-en-Provence (Sciences Po Aix); worked as an intern at US Capitol, Washington, DC as William Cohen's congressional asst; started career as Lecturer at Univ. of Paris X; joined Baker & McKenzie LLP (law firm) 1981, apptd Partner 1987, Man. Partner 1991–95, elected to Global Exec. Cttee 1995, Chair. European Regional Council and Professional Devt Cttee 1995–98, Chair. Exec. Cttee 1999–2004, Chair. Global Policy Cttee 2004–05; f. European Law Centre, Brussels; Minister for Foreign Trade 2005–07, of Agric. 2007, of Economy, Finance and Industry 2007–11; Madame Chair. Exec. Bd and Man. Dir IMF 2011–; mem. Supervisory Bd ING Group April 2005–June 2005; mem. Int. Advisory Bd Escuela Superior de Administración y Dirección de Empresas (ESADE), Barcelona; mem. Int. Bd of Overseers, Illinois Inst. of Tech.; mem. Bd and Sec., Execs Club of Chicago; mem. Strategic Council on Attractivity of France; Co-Chair. US-Europe-Poland Action Comm., Center for Strategic and Int. Studies; mem. Int. Business Advisory Bd, Mayor of Beijing; Chevalier, Légion d'honneur 2000, Officier 2012; Commdr, Ordre du Mérite agricole; Dr hc (Katholieke Universiteit Leuven, Belgium); ESADE Jaume Cordelles Award 2004, ranked by Forbes magazine amongst The World's 100 Most Powerful Women (76th) 2004, (88th) 2005, (30th) 2006, (12th) 2007, (14th) 2008, (17th) 2009, (43rd) 2010, (ninth) 2011, (eighth) 2012, (seventh) 2013, chosen by TIME magazine amongst the 100 Most Influential People in the World 2009, ranked by The Financial Times the Best Minister of Finance of the Eurozone 2009, ranked by Forbes magazine amongst The World's Most Powerful People (39th) 2011, (38th) 2012, (35th) 2013, Richard Dimbleby Lecturer 2014. *Achievements include:* mem. French nat. synchronized swimming team as a teenager. *Leisure interests:* yoga, scuba diving, swimming, gardening. *Address:* International Monetary Fund, 700 19th Street NW, Washington, DC 20431, USA (office). *Telephone:* (202) 623-7000 (office). *Fax:* (202) 623-6278 (office); (202) 623-4661 (office). *E-mail:* publicaffairs@imf.org (office). *Website:* www.imf.org (office).

LAGARDE, Paul, DenD; French academic; *Professor Emeritus of Law, University of Paris I;* b. 3 March 1934, Rennes; s. of Gaston Lagarde and Charlotte Béquignon; m. Bernadette Lamberts 1962; two s. one d.; ed Univ. of Paris; Prof., Faculty of Law, Nancy 1961–69, Nanterre 1969–71; Prof. of Private Int. Law, Univ. of Paris I 1971–2001, now Prof. Emer.; Gen. Sec. Revue critique de droit international privé 1962, Ed.-in-Chief 1976, Dir 1990–2012; Pres. Comité Français de droit int. privé 1987–90; Conseiller d'Etat en service extraordinaire 1996–2001; Gen. Sec. Comm. Int. de l'Etat Civil 2000–09; Founder-mem. Groupe européen de droit int. privé (GEDIP); mem. Inst. of Int. Law; Chevalier, Légion d'honneur; Dr hc (Freiburg im Breisgau), (Athens); Prize of Foundation Alexander von Humboldt 1992, Le droit int. privé: esprit et méthodes: Mélanges en l'honneur de Paul Lagarde (publ. in his honour) 2005, Hague Prize for Int. Law 2011. *Publications:* Recherches sur l'ordre public en droit international privé 1959, La réciprocité en droit international privé 1977, Le principe de proximité dans le droit international privé contemporain 1987, Traité de droit international privé (with Henri Batiffol) 1993, La nationalité française 2011, La reconnaissance des situations en droit international privé 2013. *Address:* 65 avenue Félix Faure, 75015 Paris, France. *Telephone:* 1-45-58-30-89. *E-mail:* paul.lagarde@orange.fr.

LAGARDÈRE, Arnaud; French media executive; *General and Managing Partner, Lagardère SCA;* b. 18 March 1961, Boulogne-Billancourt; s. of Jean-Luc Lagardère; ed Lycée Janson-de-Sailly, Paris, Univ. of Paris IX-Dauphine; Chair. Grolier Inc., USA 1994–98; Chair. and CEO Lagardère Media 1999–, Chair. Lagardère Active Broadcast (Europe 1) 2001–07, Gen. and Man. Dir Partner, Lagardère SCA 2003–, Chair. Supervisory Bd, Lagardère Services, Lagardère Active, Chair. Exec. Cttee, Lagardère Unlimited, Chair. and CEO Lagardère Capital & Management; fmr Head, Dept of Emerging Activities and Electronic Media, Matra; mem. Bd of Dirs EADS NV 2003–13, Chair. (non-exec.) 2003–07, 2012–13; mem. Supervisory Bd, Daimler AG 2005–10; Dir, Hachette Livre; Chair. Jean-Luc Lagardère Foundation; Chevalier, Légion d'honneur 2008. *Address:* Lagardère SCA, 4 rue de Presbourg, 75116 Paris, France (office). *Telephone:* 1-40-69-16-00 (office). *E-mail:* secretariatal@lagardere.fr (office). *Website:* www .lagardere.com (office).

LAGAYETTE, Philippe Ernest Georges; French government official and business executive; *Vice-Chairman, JPMorgan Europe, Middle East and Africa;* b. 16 June 1943, Tulle (Corrèze); s. of Elie Lagayette and Renée Portier; m. Marie-Louise Antoni 1979; two s. two d.; ed Ecole Polytechnique and Ecole Nat. d'Admin, Paris; Eng Génie Maritime 1965; Insp. des Finances 1970; Deputy Dir Treasury Man., Ministry of Economy, Finance and Budget 1980; Dir Cabinet of Minister of Economy, Finance and Budget 1981–84; Deputy Gov. Banque de France 1984, First Deputy Gov. 1990; Insp.-Gen. des Finances 1988–; Dir-Gen. Caisse des Dépôts et Consignations 1992–97; Chair. and CEO JP Morgan et Cie SA, JPMorgan Chase NA Group 1998–2008, Vice-Chair. JPMorgan EMEA (Europe, Middle East and Africa) 2008–; Chair. Institut des Hautes Etudes Scientifiques 1995–, French American Foundation 2003–, Fondation pour la recherche sur la maladie d'Alzheimer; Bd mem. Comm. des Operations de Bourse (French Stock Market Regulator) 1989–92, Eurotunnel 1993–2004, PPR 1999–, Fimalac 2003–, Renault 2007–; Officier, Légion d'honneur, Commdr, Ordre nat. du Mérite. *Leisure interests:* hunting, tennis, skiing, cinema. *Address:* JP Morgan, 14 Place Vendôme, 75001 Paris, France (office). *Telephone:* 1-40-15-49-88 (office). *Fax:* 1-40-15-41-36 (office). *E-mail:* philippe.lagayette@jpmorgan.com (office). *Website:* www.jpmorgan .com (office).

LAGE DÁVILA, Carlos, MD; Cuban politician; *Vice-President and Executive Secretary, Council of Ministers;* b. 15 Oct. 1951, Havana; ed Univ. of Havana;

trained as pediatrician 1970s; apptd Pres. Fed. of Univ. Students 1975; worked as physician at Hosp. Pediátrico d La Habana; sent to Ethiopia in charge of medical mission; apptd First Sec., UJOTAC 1981; mem. Grupo de Coordinación y Apoyo del Comandante en Jefe (Fidel Castro's inner staff) 1986; mem. Politburo; currently Vice-Pres. and Exec. Sec., Council of Ministers. *Address:* c/o Council of Ministers, Havana, Cuba.

LAGERFELD, Karl-Otto; German fashion designer; b. 1938, Hamburg; ed privately and at art school, Hamburg; fashion apprentice with Balmain and Patou 1959; freelance designer associated with Fendi, Rome 1963–, Chloe, Paris 1964–83, Isetan, Japan; Creative Dir, Chanel, Paris 1982–, designer Karl Lagerfeld's Women's Wear, Karl Lagerfeld France Inc. 1983–; first collection under his own name 1984; Hon. Teacher, Vienna 1983; costume design for film Comédie d'Amour 1989; awarded Golden Thimble 1986. *Publications:* Lagerfeld's Sketchbook (with Anna Piaggi), Helmut Newton 1990, Karl Lagerfeld – Off the Record 1995, The Karl Lagerfeld Diet. *Address:* Karl Lagerfeld France Inc., 75008 Paris (office); Chanel, 135 avenue Charles de Gaulle, Neuilly-sur-Seine, Paris, France (office). *Website:* www.karllagerfeld.com (office); www.chanel.com (office).

LAGHDAF, Moulaye Ould Mohamed, DèsSc; Mauritanian diplomatist and politician; *Prime Minister;* b. 1957, Nema; m.; four c.; ed Univ. of Liège, Univ. of Louvain; expert on Africa, The Caribbean and The Pacific, Centre for Industrial Devt 1991–97; Co-ordinator of devt project for Hodh Chargui region 2000–06; Amb. to Belgium and EU 2006–08, Prime Minister 2008–. *Publications include:* Enrichissement des minerais d'oxyde de cuivre 1983, Utilisation des schistes bitumineux en tant que matière minérale et organique en cimenterie 1984, Combustion des gaz dans un lit fluidisé 1992, Lutte contre les émissions d'oxyde d'azote 1992. *Address:* Office of the Prime Minister, BP 237, Nouakchott, Mauritania (office). *Telephone:* 525-33-37 (office).

LAGO, Eduardo, MA, PhD; Spanish writer and academic; *Professor of Spanish and Latin American Literature, Sarah Lawrence College;* b. 1954, Madrid; ed Universidad Autónoma de Madrid, Grad. Center, City Univ. of NY; Prof. of Spanish and Latin American Literature, Sarah Lawrence Coll. 1993–; Exec. Dir Instituto Cervantes, New York 2006–; Co-founder Order of Finnegans; Bartolomé March Award for Excellence in Literary Criticism 2001. *Publications:* Cuaderno de México 2000, Cuentos Dispersos 2000, Llámame Brooklyn (Premio Nadal Prize 2006, City of Barcelona Literary Prize for Literature 2007, National Critics Award 2007, Lara Foundation Award for Best Critical Reception 2007) 2006, Ladrón de mapas 2008. *Address:* Office of the Director, Instituto Cervantes, 211 East 49th Street, New York, NY 10017, USA (office). *Telephone:* (212) 308-7720 (office). *E-mail:* dirny@cervantes.org (office). *Website:* www.nuevayork.cervantes.es (office).

LAGOS ESCOBAR, Ricardo, PhD; Chilean economist, lawyer, politician and fmr head of state; *President, Fundación Democracia y Desarrollo (Foundation for Democracy and Development);* b. 2 March 1938, Santiago; m. Luisa Durán; five c.; ed Univ. of Chile, Duke Univ., N Carolina; Prof., Univ. of Chile 1963–72, fmr Head School of Political and Admin. Sciences, fmr Dir Inst. of Econs, Gen. Sec. 1971; Visiting Prof., Univ. of N Carolina, Chapel Hill, USA 1974–75; Chair. Alianza Democrática 1983–84, Partido por la Democracia 1987–90; Minister of Educ. 1990–92, of Public Works 1994; Pres. of Chile 2000–06; Founder and Pres. Fundación Democracia y Desarrollo (Foundation for Democracy and Devt) 2006–; Pres. Club de Madrid 2006–09, mem. Bd of Dirs 2006–; UN Sec.-Gen.'s Special Envoy on Climate Change 2007–; Prof. at Large, Brown Univ., USA. *Publications:* Población, Pobreza y Mercado de Trabajo en América Latina 1997, numerous books and articles on econs and politics. *Address:* Fundación Democracia y Desarrollo, Roberto del Rio 1151, Providencia, Santiago de Chile, Chile (office). *Telephone:* (2) 333-80-98 (office); (2) 333-94-14 (office). *Fax:* (2) 334-23-61 (office). *E-mail:* cbudnik@fdd.cl (office). *Website:* www.fundaciondemocraciaydesarrollo.cl (office).

LAGRAVENESE, Richard, BFA; American screenwriter, director and producer; b. 30 Oct. 1959, Brooklyn, New York; s. of Patrick LaGravenese and Lucille LaGravenese; m. Ann Weiss LaGravenese 1986; one d.; ed Lafayette High School, Emerson Coll. and New York Univ.; Ind. Film Project Writer of the Year, Best Original Screenplay 2000. *Films include:* Rude Awakening 1989, The Fisher King (also actor) 1991, The Ref (also producer) 1994, A Little Princess 1995, The Bridges of Madison County 1995, Unstrung Heroes 1995, The Mirror Has Two Faces 1996, The Horse Whisperer 1998, Living Out Loud (also dir) 1998, Beloved 1998, The Legend of Bagger Vance 1999, Erin Brockovich (uncredited co-writer) 2000, Blow (actor) 2001, The Defective Detective 2002, A Decade Under the Influence (also producer and dir) 2003, Monster-in-Law 2005, Paris, je t'aime (dir) 2006, Freedom Writers (dir) 2007, P.S. I Love You 2007. *Leisure interests:* theatre, books, family. *Address:* c/o Kirsten Bonelli, 8383 Wilshire Boulevard, Suite 340, Beverly Hills, CA 90211, USA.

LAGU, Lt-Gen. Joseph; South Sudanese politician, army officer and diplomatist; b. 21 Nov. 1931, Moli; s. of Yakobo Yanga and Marini Kaluma; ed Rumbek Secondary School, Mil. Acad. Omdurman; served in Sudanese Army 1960–63; joined South Sudan Liberation Movt 1963, Leader SSLM 1969; signed peace agreement with Govt of Sudan March 1972; Vice-Pres. of Sudan 1978–80, 1982–85; Pres. Supreme Exec. Council for the South 1978–80; fmr Perm. Rep. to UN; moved with his family to UK; Order of the Two Niles 1972. *Publication:* The Anya-Nya – What We Fight For 1972. *Address:* c/o Ministry of Foreign Affairs, Khartoum, Sudan.

LAGUMDŽIJA, Zlatko, MSc, PhD; Bosnia and Herzegovina politician; *Minister of Foreign Affairs;* b. 26 Dec. 1955, Sarajevo; m.; two c.; ed Univ. of Sarajevo, Harvard Univ., USA; Visiting Prof., Univ. of Arizona, USA 1988–89; Prof. of Econ. and Electrical Eng, Univ. of Sarajevo 1989–, Dir Centre for Man. and Computer Tech. 1995; Vice-Chair. Council of Ministers of Bosnia and Herzegovina 1993–96, 2012–, Chair. 2001–02; mem. House of Reps of Parl. Ass. 1996–; Minister of Foreign Affairs and Treas. of the Insts of Bosnia and Herzegovina 2001–02, Minister of Foreign Affairs 2002–03, 2012–; Co-founder Social and Democratic Party of Bosnia and Herzegovina (Socijaldemokratska Partija BiH) 1990, Chair. 1997–. *Address:* Ministry of Foreign Affairs, 71000 Sarajevo, Musala 2, Bosnia and Herzegovina (office). *Telephone:* (33) 281100 (office). *Fax:* (33) 227156 (office).

E-mail: marijana.mestrovic@mvp.gov.ba (office); info_mvpbih@mvp.gov.ba (office). *Website:* www.mfa.gov.ba (office).

LAHHAM, Duraid, BSc; Syrian actor, comedian and director; b. 27 Jan. 1934, Damascus; m. 1st May al-Husayni two c.; m. 2nd Hala Bitar; one d.; ed Univ. of Damascus; Instructor, Chem. Dept, Univ. of Damascus 1955–60; stage roles 1960–; starred in mini-series Sahret Dimashq (Damascus Evening) on Syrian TV with Nihad Qali 1960, cr. duo called Duraid & Nihad, achieved dramatic success in Arab World until Qali retired from acting due to illness in 1976; joined cast of TV drama Abwab Al Rih (Gates of the Wind) to play role of Yousif Al Nahhas 2014–; Pres. Syrian Assoc. of Artists 1967; UNICEF Rep. in Syria for Children's Affairs 1990, UNICEF Amb. for Childhood in the Middle East and North Africa 1999–2004; Medal of the Syrian Repub. (Excellence Class) 1976, Medal of the Tunisian Repub. 1979, Medal of the Libyan Repub. 1991, Order of Merit of the Lebanese Repub. 2000. *Theatre includes:* Ukd al-Lulu (The Pearl Necklace) 1966, Masrah al-Shawk (The Thorn Theatre) 1968, Qadiyyah wa Haramiyya (A Cause and Thieves) 1972, Day'at Tishreen (October Village) 1974, Ghorba (Alienation) 1976, Kasak ya Watan (Cheers to the Homeland) 1978, Shaka'ik al-Nu'man (Anemones) 1987, Sani' al-Matar (The Rainmaker) 1992, Al-Asfura al-Sa'ida (The Happy Bird) 1992. *Films include:* Ghawar La'eb al-Kura (Ghawar the Football Player), Ukd al-Lulu (The Pearl Necklace) 1965, Al-Lus al-Zarif (The Nice Thief), Al-Sa'alik (The Crooks) 1968, Al-Sadikan (The Two Friends), Al-Sheridan (The Two Homeless Men), Al-Millionera (The Millionaire), Gharam fi Istanbul (Love Affair in Istanbul) 1967, Maqlab min al-Maksik (A Prank from Mexico), Lika' fi Tadmur (Rendezvous in Palmyra), Al-Rajul al-Munasib (The Right Man), Fundok al-Ahlam (The Dream Hotel) 1966, Khayyat lil Sayyidat (A Seamstress for Women) 1969, Wahid Za'ed Wahid (One plus One), Al-Nassaben al-Thalatha (The Three Crooks), Misk wa Anbar (Misk and Anbar), Al-Muzayafun (The Imposters), Al-Tha'lab (The Fox), Zawjati min al-Hippez (My Hippie Wife), Ana Antar (I am Antar), Imra'a Taskun Wahdiha (A Women Lives on Her Own), Sah al-Nawm (Good Morning), Abd al-Latiff Fathi, Ghawar James Bond, Indama Taghib al-Zawjat (When Wives are Absent), Samak bala Hasak (Fish with no Skeleton), Imbaratoriyyat Ghawar (The Empire of Ghawar), Al-Hudud (The Border), Al-Takrir (The Report), Kafroun. *Television includes:* Al-Ijaza al-Sa'ida (The Happy Holiday) 1960, Sahret Dimashq: (Damascus Evening) 1960, Maqalib Ghawar (Ghawar's Pranks) 1966, Hammam al-Hana (Pleasant Bath) 1968, Sah al-Nawm (Good Morning) 1971, Sah al-Nawm (Part 2) 1972, Melh wa Sukkar (Salt and Sugar) 1972, Wayn al-Ghalat (Where is the Error?) 1980, Wadi al-Misk (Misk Valley) 1982, Al-Doghri (The Doghri) 1991, Ahlam Abu al-Hana (The Dreams of Abu al-Hana) 1994, Awdet Ghawar (The Return of Ghawar) 1999, A'ilati wa Ana (My Family and I) 2001, Ala Mas'uliyati (On My Responsibility) 2002, Alam Doreid (Doreid's World, Doreid haza al-Mas'a (Doreid this Evening). *Publications:* author of several comedies. *Leisure interest:* accordionist. *Address:* c/o Syrian Broadcasting Corporation, Omayya Square, Damascus, Syria. *E-mail:* info@duraidlahham.com. *Website:* www.duraidlahham .com.

LAHLAIDI, Abdelhafid, PhD; Moroccan professor of medicine and cardiovascular specialist; *Chief, Department of Morphology, Université Mohammed V;* b. 20 May 1942, Essaouira; m.; three c.; ed Univ. of Paris, France, Univ. of Geneva, Switzerland; Professorial Asst, Faculty of Medicine, Univ. of Geneva, Switzerland 1973; Prof., Faculty of Medicine, Université Mohammed V 1973–, Chief, Dept of Morphology; Fellow, Islamic Acad. of Sciences 1990–; Fellow Académie Islamique des Sciences; mem. New York Acad. of Sciences; Grand Prix Scientifique, Morocco 1986, Prix Scientifique du Président de la République Tunisienne 1987, Prix Scientifique du Président de la République Algérienne 1989, Médaille d'or de l'Académie Nationale Française de Médecine 1990, Médaille de l'Académie des Sciences, Jordan 1991. *Publications:* Anatomie topographique, Applications, Anatom-Chirurgicles (five vols) 1986. *Leisure interests:* painting, writing. *Address:* Université Mohammed V, BP 6203, Rabat Institute, Rabat (office); Temara – Les Vieux Marocains, Allée 3, Maison 121, Rabat, Morocco (home). *Telephone:* (37) 77-04-21 (office); (37) 74-10-27 (home). *Fax:* (37) 77-37-01 (office); (37) 67-30-56 (home). *E-mail:* lahlaidi@online.fr (office); lahlaidi@gmail.com (home). *Website:* www.emi.ac.ma (office).

LAHNSTEIN, Manfred, MBA; German politician, civil servant and academic; b. 20 Dec. 1937, Erkrath, Rhineland; m. Sonja Lahnstein; two c.; ed Univ. of Cologne; joined SPD 1959; at European Comm., Brussels, latterly as Chef de Cabinet to Commr Wilhelm Haferkamp 1967–73; econ. adviser, Chancellery 1973; moved to Finance Ministry 1974, successively Div. Head and State Sec. in charge of Financial and Monetary Policy 1974–80; Chancellor's Chief Civil Servant 1980–82; Minister of Finance April–Oct. 1982; mem. Bd Dirs Bertelsmann AG and Pres. Electronic Media Group 1983–94, mem. Supervisory Bd 1994–98, Special Rep. of the Bd 1998–2004; Lahnstein & Partner International Consultants 1994–; mem. Supervisory or Advisory Bds Hansa Treuhand, Korn/Ferry Europe, Thalia Theater Hamburg, Berger Lahnstein Middelhoff & Partners LLP (BLM Partners), London 2009–; adviser, Olayan Group (Saudi Arabia), Rothschild investment bank; Prof. of Cultural Man., Univ. for Music and Theatre, Hamburg; Chair. Bd Govs, Univ. of Haifa, Israel 2001–07, Vice-Chair. 2007–; Chair. Bd Trustees, Ebelin and Gerd Bucerius ZEIT Foundation, Germany; Pres. German-Israel Asscn 1993–2006; mem. Trilateral Comm. 1993–2005; Fed. Cross of Merit (First Class) 2001, Grand Cross of Merit 2007; Dr hc (Haifa) 2007, (Hamburg) 2008; Moses Mendelssohn Medal 2006. *Publications:* several books and numerous articles. *Leisure interests:* music, smoking cigars. *Address:* ZEIT-Stiftung, Feldbrunnenstrasse 56, 20148 Hamburg (office). *Telephone:* (40) 413366 (office). *Fax:* (40) 41336700 (office). *E-mail:* zeit-stiftung@zeit-stiftung.de (office). *Website:* www.zeit -stiftung.de (office).

LaHOOD, Raymond (Ray) H., BS; American politician and government official; b. 6 Dec. 1945, Peoria, Ill.; m. Kathleen LaHood; two s. two d.; ed Canton Jr Coll., Bradley Univ.; began career as teacher 1971–77; Dist Admin. Asst to US Congressman Tom Railsback 1977–82; mem. Ill. State House of Reps 1982; Chief of Staff to US Congressman and House Minority Leader Bob Michels, Washington, DC 1982–94; mem. US House of Reps from 18th Ill. Dist 1995–2009; US Sec. of Transportation, Washington, DC 2009–13; Republican; Dr hc (Lincoln Coll.) 2000, (Eureka Coll.) 2002, (Tri-State Univ.) 2004, (MacMurray Coll.) 2006. *Address:* c/o Department of Transportation, 1200 New Jersey Ave, SE, Washington, DC 20590, USA (office).

LAHOUD, Gen. Emile; Lebanese politician, naval officer and fmr head of state; b. 1936, Baabdat; s. of Gen. Jamil Lahoud and Adrinée Badjakian; m. Andrée Amadouni; two s. one d.; ed Brumana High School, also attended various courses at Naval Acads in UK and USA 1958–80; joined Mil. Acad. as cadet officer 1956, promoted to Sub.-Lt 1959, Lt 1962, Lt-Commdr 1969, Commdr 1974, Cap. 1980, Rear-Adm. 1985, Vice-Adm. 1989; Commdr of Second Fleet 1966–68, of First Fleet 1968–70; Staff of Army Fourth Bureau 1970–72; Chief of Personal Staff of Gen. Commdr of Armed Forces 1973–79; Dir of Personnel, Army HQ 1980–83; Head of Mil. Office, Ministry of Defence 1983–89; Commdr-in-Chief of Armed Forces 1989; Pres. of the Repub. of the Lebanon 1998–2007; Lebanese Medal of Merit Gen. Officer 1989; War Medals 1991, 1992; Dawn of the South Medal 1993; Nat. Unity Medal 1993; Medal of Esteem 1994; Grand Cordon Order of the Cedar 1993; numerous int. decorations including Grand Cross (Argentina) 1998; Order of Merit Sr Officer Level (Italy) 1997; Order of Hussein ibn Ali (Jordan) 1999, King Abdul-Aziz Collar (Saudi Arabia) 2000, Great Collar of the Union (UAE) 2000, Great Collar of Mubarak (Kuwait) 2000, Great Collar of the Nile (Egypt) 2000, Great Collar of Independence (Qatar) 2000, Great Collar of the Khalifite Order (Bahrain) 2000, Great Cross Légion d'honneur (France) 2001, Al Muhammadi Decoration Extraordinary Grade (Morocco) 2001, Order of November 7th (Tunisia) 2001, Great Cross Order of the Redeemer (Greece) 2001, Grand Cordon Nat. Order of Oumaya (Syria) 2002, Nat. Order of Merit Al-Athir (Algeria) 2002, Order of the Repub. (Yemen) 2002, Grand Cross of the Ipiranga Order (Brazil) 2004, Grand Cross with Chain Order of Merit (Hungary) 2004, Grand Cross of Order of Merit (Poland) 2004, Knight Grand Cross of Merit with Gold Plate of the Sacred Military Constantinian Order of St George 2005. *Publication:* Method and Style, Promise and Fulfilment. *Leisure interests:* diving, swimming, reading, music. *Address:* c/o Presidential Palace, Baabda, Lebanon (office).

LAI, Jimmy; Hong Kong business executive, journalist and publisher; *Founder and Chairman, Next Media;* b. (Lai Chee-Ying), 1948; Propr Giordano (retail clothing chain) 1980–, Chair. 1980–94; Founder and Chair. Next Media, titles include Next Magazine 1990–, Apple Daily 1995–, Sharp Daily 2006–. *Address:* Next Magazine, Next Media, 8 Chun Ying Street, T. K. O. Industrial Estate West, Tseung Kwan O, Kowloon, Hong Kong, Special Administrative Region, People's Republic of China (office). *Telephone:* 27442733 (office). *Fax:* 29907210 (office). *E-mail:* adnews@appledaily.com (office). *Website:* www.nextmedia.com (office); www.next.atnext.com (office).

LAI, Shin-yuan, MA, MPhil, DPhil; Taiwanese politician; *Minister of Mainland Affairs Council;* ed London School of Econs and Univ. of Sussex, UK; Dir and Research Fellow, Div. of Int. Affairs, Taiwan Inst. of Econ. Research 1996–2000; Dir-Gen. Chinese Taipei Pacific Basin Econ. Cttee 1996–2000; Founder and Dir Chinese Taipei APEC Study Center 1997–2000; Adjunct Assoc. Prof., Grad. School for Social Transformation Studies, Shih Hsin Univ. 1997–98; Adjunct Assoc. Prof., Dept of Int. Business Man., Tamkang Univ. 1997–2008; Dir-Gen., Confed. of Asia-Pacific Chambers of Commerce and Industry 1999–2000; Sec.-Treasurer, Asian Bankers Asscn 1999–2000; Sr Adviser, Nat. Security Council 2000–04; chief negotiator for Taiwan's accession to WTO 2001; adviser to Taiwan WTO Centre, Chung-Hua Inst. for Econ. Research 2004; mem. Legis. Yuan 2005–08; Minister, Mainland Affairs Council, Exec. Yuan 2008–. *Address:* Mainland Affairs Council, 15/F, 2-2 Chi Nan Road, Sec. 1, Taipei 10054, Taiwan (office). *Telephone:* (2) 23975589 (office). *Fax:* (2) 23975300 (office). *E-mail:* macst@mac.gov.tw (office). *Website:* www.mac.gov.tw (office).

LAIDLAW, (William) Samuel (Sam) Hugh, MBA, FRSA; British solicitor and energy industry executive; *Chief Executive, Centrica plc;* b. 3 Jan. 1956, London; m.; four c.; ed Univ. of Cambridge, Institut Européen d'Admin des Affaires (INSEAD); solicitor, Macfarlanes, London 1977–79; Corp. Planner, Société Françaises Pétroles BP, Paris 1979–80; Man. of Corp. Planning Amerada Hess Corpn, New York City, USA 1981–83, Vice-Pres. Amerada Hess Ltd, London 1983–85, Man. Dir 1986–1995, Chair. 1995, Exec. Vice-Pres. Amerada Hess Corpn 1993–95, Pres. and COO, London 1995–2001; CEO Enterprise Oil 2001–03; Exec. Vice-Pres. Chevron Corpn 2003–06; Chief Exec. Centrica plc 2006–, Chair. Exec. Cttee, Disclosure Cttee; Dir (non-exec.) Hanson plc 2003–07, HSBC Holdings plc 2008–; Lead Dir (non-exec.) Dept for Transport 2010–; mem. Bd of Dirs Business Council for Int. Understanding; mem. Prime Minister's Business Advisory Group; Trustee, RAFT (medical charity); mem. UK Council of INSEAD; fmr Pres. UK Offshore Operators Asscn; fmr Chair. Petroleum Science and Tech. Inst.; fmr mem. UK Energy Advisory Panel. *Address:* Centrica plc, Millstream, Maidenhead Road, Windsor, Berks., SL4 5GD, England (office). *Telephone:* (1753) 494000 (office). *Fax:* (1753) 494001 (office). *E-mail:* info@centrica.co.uk (office). *Website:* www.centrica .co.uk (office).

LAIDLER, David Ernest William, PhD, FRSC; Canadian/British economist and academic; *Fellow-in-Residence, C. D. Howe Institute;* b. 12 Aug. 1938, Tynemouth, UK; s. of John Alphonse Laidler and Leonora Laidler (née Gosman); m. Antje Charlotte Breitwisch 1965; one d.; ed Tynemouth School, London School of Econs, Univs of Syracuse and Chicago, USA; Asst Lecturer, LSE 1961–62; Asst Prof., Univ. of Calif., Berkeley 1963–66; Lecturer, Univ. of Essex 1966–69; Prof., Univ. of Manchester 1969–75; Prof. of Econs, Univ. of Western Ont. 1975–2004, Bank of Montreal Prof. 2000–04, Prof. Emer. 2004–, Dept Chair. 1981–84; Special Adviser, Bank of Canada 1998–99; Fellow-in-Residence, CD Howe Inst., Toronto 1990–; Visiting Economist, Reserve Bank of Australia 1977; Assoc. Ed. Journal of Money, Credit and Banking 1979–; mem. Editorial Bd Pakistan Devt Review 1987–, European Journal of the History of Econ. Thought 1993–; fmr mem. editorial Bd several other journals; Co-Founder and mem. Exec. Cttee Money Study Group 1970–75; mem. Econs Cttee, CNAA, GB 1971–75, Econs Cttee, SSRC, GB 1972–75, Consortium on Macroeconomic Modelling and Forecasting, ESRC, GB 1981–88, Econ. Advisory Panel to Minister of Finance, Canada 1982–84; Co-ordinator Research Advisory Group on Econ. Ideas and Social Issues, Royal Comm. on the Econ. Union and Devt Prospects for Canada (Macdonald Comm.) 1984–85; Dir Philip Allan Publrs Ltd 1972–99; Pres. Canadian Econs Asscn 1987–88; BAAS Lister Lecturer 1972; Canadian Econs Asscn Douglas Purvis Prize 1994, Hellmuth Prize, Univ. of Western Ontario 1999. *Publications:* The Demand for Money 1969, Essays on Money and Inflation 1975, Monetarist Perspectives 1982, Taking Money Seriously 1990, The Golden Age of the Quantity Theory 1991, The Great Canadian Disinflation (with W. P. B. Robson) 1993, Money and Macroeconomics: Selected

Essays 1998, Fabricating the Keynesian Revolution 1999, Two Percent Target (with W. P. B. Robson) (Donner Prize 2004) 2004, Macroeconomics in Retrospect: Selected Essays 2004. *Leisure interests:* going to concerts, opera and theatre. *Address:* C.D. Howe Institute, 67 Yonge Street, Suite 300, Toronto, ON M5E 1J8 (office); Department of Economics, Room 4090, SSC, University of Western Ontario, London, ON, N6A 5C2 (office); 45–124 North Centre Road, London, ON, N5X 4R3, Canada (home). *Telephone:* (416) 865-1904 (C.D. Howe) (office); (519) 661-3400 (office); (519) 673-3014 (home). *Fax:* (416) 865-1866 (C.D. Howe) (office); (519) 661-3666 (office). *E-mail:* laidler@uwo.ca (office); cdhowe@cdhowe.org (office). *Website:* www.ssc.uwo.ca/economics/faculty/Laidler (office); www.cdhowe .org (office).

LAINE, Dame Clementina (Cleo) Dinah, DBE; British singer; b. 28 Oct. 1927, Southall, Middx; m. 1st George Langridge 1947 (dissolved 1957), one s.; m. 2nd John Philip William Dankworth 1958 (died 2010), one s. one d.; joined Dankworth Orchestra 1953; lead role in Seven Deadly Sins, Edinburgh Festival and Sadler's Wells 1961; acting roles in Edinburgh Festival 1966, 1967; f. Wavendon Stables Performing Arts Centre (with John Dankworth) 1970; many appearances with symphony orchestras performing Façade (Walton) and other compositions; Julie in Showboat, Adelphi Theatre 1971; title role in Colette, Comedy Theatre 1980; Desiree in A Little Night Music, Mich. Opera House, USA 1983; The Mystery of Edwin Drood, Broadway, NY 1986; Into the Woods (US Nat. Tour) 1989; frequent tours and TV appearances, Europe, Australia and USA; Freedom of Worshipful Co. of Musicians 2002; Hon. MA (Open Univ.) 1975, Hon. DMus (Berklee School of Music) 1982, (York) 1993, (Cambridge) 2004, Hon. DA (Luton) 1994; Melody Maker and New Musical Express Top Girl Singer Awards 1956; Moscow Arts Theatre Award for acting role in Flesh to a Tiger 1958; top place in Int. Critics' Poll of American Jazz magazine Downbeat 1965; Woman of the Year (9th annual Golden Feather Awards) 1973; Edison Award 1974; Variety Club of GB Show Business Personality Award (with John Dankworth) 1977; TV Times Viewers' Award for Most Exciting Female Singer on TV 1978; Grammy Award for Best Jazz Vocalist-Female 1985; Best Actress in a Musical (Edwin Drood) 1986; Theatre World Award for Edwin Drood 1986, Nat. Asscn of Recording Merchandisers (NARM) Presidential Lifetime Achievement Award 1990, Vocalist of the Year (British Jazz Awards) 1990, Lifetime Achievement Award (USA) 1991, ISPA Distinguished Artists Award 1999, Back Stage Bob Harrington Lifetime Achievement Award (with John Dankworth) 2001, BBC British Jazz Awards Lifetime Achievement Award (with John Dankworth) 2002. *Film:* Last of the Blonde Bombshells 2000. *Recordings include:* albums: Smilin' Through (with Dudley Moore) 2005, I Hear Music 2007. *Publications:* Cleo: An Autobiography 1994, You Can Sing If You Want To 1997. *Leisure interest:* painting. *Address:* The Old Rectory, Wavendon, Milton Keynes, MK17 8LT, England (home). *Fax:* (1908) 584414 (home). *Website:* www.quartermaine.com (office).

LAINE, Jermu Tapani, LLM; Finnish politician, lawyer and author; b. 1931, Turku; m. 1954; three d.; ed Univ. of Helsinki, Univ. of Pennsylvania, USA; functionary, Ministry of Trade and Industry 1955–65; Lecturer in Commercial Studies, Valkeakoski 1965–69; Rector, Commercial Inst., Mäntta 1969–; municipal positions in Valkeakoski and Mäntta 1968–; Political Sec. to Prime Minister Sorsa 1972–73; Minister for Foreign Trade 1973–75; mem. Parl. 1975–; Minister, Ministry of Finance 1982–83; Minister for Foreign Trade 1983–87; Chair. Supervisory Bd Valmet Og 1987–88; Dir-Gen. Finnish Customs Bd 1988–94; Chair. Finnish Nat. Theatres; mem. Social Democratic Party. *Plays:* Paniikki-häiriö 2001, Marie Curie. *Publications:* Autobiography 1991, Alexis de Toqueville 1999, Finland in 1906 2006, Finnish Foreign Trade towards the West 2006. *Leisure interests:* literature, theatre, cinema.

LAING, (John) Stuart, MA, MPhil; British academic and fmr diplomatist; *Master, Corpus Christi College, Cambridge;* b. 22 July 1948, Limpsfield, Surrey; s. of Denys Laing and Judy Dods; m. Sibella Dorman 1971; one s. two d.; ed Rugby School, Corpus Christi Coll., Cambridge; joined HM Diplomatic Service in 1970, served in Jeddah 1973–75, Brussels 1975–78, Cairo 1983–87, Prague 1989–92 and Riyadh 1992–95, High Commr in Brunei 1999–2002, Amb. to Oman 2002–05, to Kuwait 2005–08; Master, Corpus Christi Coll., Cambridge 2008–. *Publication:* Unshook till the End of Time – A History of Britain and Oman (with Robert Alston) 2012. *Leisure interests:* playing chamber music, hill walking, desert travel. *Address:* Corpus Christi College, Cambridge, CB2 1RH, England (office). *Telephone:* (1223) 338029 (office). *Fax:* (1223) 338020 (office). *E-mail:* master@corpus .cam.ac.uk (office). *Website:* www.corpus.cam.ac.uk (office).

LAIRD, Sir Gavin Harry, Kt, CBE; British fmr trade union official; b. 14 March 1933, Clydebank, Scotland; s. of James Laird and Frances Laird; m. Catherine Gillies Campbell 1956; one d.; shop stewards' convener, Singer, Clydebank for seven years; Regional Officer, Amalgamated Eng Union (fmrly Amalgamated Union of Eng Workers) 1972–75, Exec. Councillor for Scotland and NW England 1975–82, Gen. Sec. (AEU Section) 1982–95; Chair. Greater Manchester Buses North 1994–97; fmr Chair. Murray Johnstone Venture Capital Trust 4; mem. Murray Johnston Private Acquisition Partnership Advisory Cttee 1999–; mem. Scottish TUC Gen. Council 1973–75; mem. TUC Gen. Council 1979–82; part-time Dir Highlands and Islands Devt Bd 1974–75; mem. Industrial Devt Advisory Bd 1979–86, Arts Council 1983–86, part-time Dir BNOC 1976–86; Chair. The Foundries EDC 1982–85; Dir Bank of England 1986–94; Dir (non-exec.) Scottish TV (Media Group) PLC 1986–99, Britannia Life 1988–2000, Britannia Investment Mans Ltd, Britannia Fund Mans (now Britannic Asset Mans) Ltd 1996–2000, GEC Scotland 1991–99, Edinburgh Investment Trust Ltd; fmr Pres. Kent Active Retirement Asscn; fmr Vice-Pres. Pre-Retirement Asscn of GB and NI; fmr Trustee Anglo-German Foundation 1994–2000, John Smith Memorial Trust; fmr mem. Editorial Bd European Business Journal; mem. Advisory Bd Know-How Fund for Poland 1990–95; mem. Armed Forces Pay Review Body 1995–98, Employment Appeal Tribunal; Fellow Paisley Coll. of Tech. 1991; Hon. DLitt (Keele Univ.), (Heriot Watt Univ.) 1994. *Leisure interests:* music, hill-walking, reading. *Address:* 9 Clevedon House, Holmbury Park, Bromley, BR1 2WG, England (home). *Telephone:* (20) 8460-8998 (home). *Fax:* (20) 8460-8998 (home). *E-mail:* laird .gavin@btopenworld.com (home).

LAIRD, Melvin Robert, BA; American fmr government official; *Senior Counsellor, National and International Affairs, The Reader's Digest Association, Inc.;* b. 1 Sept. 1922, Omaha, Neb.; s. of Melvin and Helen Laird (née Connor); m.

1st Barbara Masters 1945 (died 1992); two s. one d.; m. 2nd Carole Fleischman 1993; ed Carleton Coll., Northfield, Minn.; served with Task Force 38 and 58, US Navy Pacific Fleet 1942–46; mem. Wisconsin Senate 1946–52, Chair. Wisconsin Legis. Council; mem. US House of Reps 1952–69, served on Appropriations Cttee, Chair. House of Republican Minority, mem. Republican Coordinating Council, Vice-Chair. Republican Nat. Platform Council 1960, Chair. 1964; US Sec. of Defense 1968–73; Counsellor to Pres. for Domestic Affairs 1973–74; Senior Counsellor for Nat. and Int. Affairs, Readers' Digest Asscn 1974–, now Vice-Pres.; Chair. COMSAT Corpn 1992–96; fmr mem. Bd the Kennedy Center, George Washington Univ., Airlie Foundation; mem. Bd Nat. Defense and Energy Projects of American Enterprise Inst., Thomas Jefferson Center Foundation of Univ. of Virginia, World Rehabilitation Fund; fmr Dir The Reader's Digest Asscn Inc., Metropolitan Life Insurance Co., Northwest Airlines, IDS Mutual Funds Group, Communications Satellite Corpn (Chair. 1992–96), Martin Marietta Corpn, Science Application Int. Corpn, Dir Public Oversight Bd; fmr Trustee, DeWitt and Lila Wallace-Reader's Digest Funds; Republican; over 300 awards and hon. degrees, including Albert Lasker Public Service Award, Statesman in Medicine Award (Airlie Foundation), The Harry S. Truman Award for distinguished service in defense; Presidential Medal of Freedom (USA), Order of Merit (1st Class) (Fed. Repub. of Germany), Commdr Légion d'honneur (France). *Publications include:* A House Divided: America's Strategy Gap 1962, The Conservative Papers (Ed.) 1964, Republican Papers (Ed.) 1968. *Address:* c/o The Reader's Digest Association Inc., Reader's Digest Road, Pleasantville, NY 10570-7000; 1730 Rhode Island Avenue, NW, Suite 212, Washington, DC 20036, USA (office).

LAJČÁK, Miroslav, JUDr; Slovak diplomatist and politician; *Deputy Prime Minister and Minister of Foreign and European Affairs;* b. 20 March 1963, Poprad; m. Jarmila Lajčáková Hargašová; two d.; ed Comenius Univ., Bratislava, State Inst. of Int. Relations, Moscow, Russia, George C. Marshall European Center for Security Studies, Garmisch-Partenkirchen, Germany; joined Ministry of Foreign Affairs of Czechoslovakia 1988; served in Czechoslovak Embassy in Moscow 1991–93 (Embassy of Slovakia from 1 Jan. 1993); Dir Cabinet of Minister of Foreign Affairs 1993–94, 1998–2001; Dir Cabinet of Prime Minister of Slovakia 1993–94; Amb. to Japan 1994–98, to Yugoslavia (also accred to Albania and Fmr Yugoslav Repub. of Macedonia) 2001–05; Special Asst to UN Sec.-Gen.'s Special Envoy to the Balkans 1999–2001; Dir-Gen. of Political Affairs, Ministry of Foreign Affairs 2005–07; Special Rep. of EU for Common Foreign and Security Policy, Montenegro 2006; High Rep. of Int. Community and Special Rep. of EU, Mission in Bosnia and Herzegovina 2007–09; Minister of Foreign Affairs 2009–10; Man. Dir for Russia, Eastern Neighbourhood and the Western Balkans, EU External Action Service, Brussels 2010–12; Deputy Prime Minister and Minister of Foreign and European Affairs 2012–; Person of the Year Award from two Bosnian daily newspapers: Nezavisne novine 2007 and Dnevni Avaz 2007. *Address:* Ministry of Foreign and European Affairs, Hlboká cesta 2, 833 36 Bratislava 37, Slovakia (office). *Telephone:* (2) 5978-1111 (office). *Fax:* (2) 5978-3333 (office). *E-mail:* kami@mzv.sk (office). *Website:* www.mzv.sk (office).

LAJOLO, HE Cardinal Giovanni, BCL; Italian ecclesiastic and diplomatist; *President Emeritus, Governatorate of Vatican City State;* b. 3 Jan. 1935, Novara; ordained priest of Novara 1960; entered Vatican diplomatic service 1970, served at Vatican Nunciature in Germany and in Secr. of State; Titular Archbishop of Caesariana and Sec. of Admin of Patrimony of the Apostolic See 1988–95; Apostolic Nuncio to Germany 1995–2003; Sec. for Relations with States 2003–06; Pres. Governatorate of Vatican City State 2006–11, Pres. Emer. 2011–, Pontifical Comm. for Vatican City State 2006–11 (retd); cr. Cardinal (Cardinal-Deacon of Santa Maria Liberatrice a Monte Testaccio) 2007; participated in Papal Conclave 2013. *Publications:* I Concordati moderni 1988, Libertà di religione 1971, Le Sette Parole 2010, Maria Silenzi e Parole 2011, Passione Risurrezione 2013, Lettere alle Amiche 2014. *Address:* Città del Vaticano 00120, Italy. *Website:* www.vatican.va/vatican_city_state.

LAJUNEN, Samppa; Finnish professional skier; b. 23 April 1979, Turku; entered his first cross-country race aged two; was skiing 300 miles a year by age five; added ski jumping to pursuits aged nine; won overall World Cup title in Nordic combined 1997; Silver Medals, Individual and Team events, Winter Olympics, Nagano, Japan 1998; Gold Medals, Nordic Combined, Sprint and Team events, Winter Olympics, Salt Lake City, USA 2002; First Place, Individual Discipline, World Cup, Nayoro, Japan 2004; Second Place, Sprint Discipline, World Cup, Reit im Winkl, Germany 2004; Seefeld, Austria 2004, Individual Mass Start, Sapporo, Japan 2004, Sprint, Oslo, Norway 2004, Individual Discipline, Oslo 2004; Third Place, Individual Discipline, World Cup, Kuusamo, Finland 2003; mem. Jyvaeskylaen Hiihtoseura Ski Club; now retd. *Address:* c/o Finnish Ski Association, Radiokatu 20, 00240 Helsinki, Finland. *E-mail:* samppa.lajunen@hiihtoliitto.fi. *Website:* www.hiihtoliitto.fi.

LAKATANI, Sani; Niuean politician; Prime Minister of Niue March 1999–2001; Minister for External Affairs, Finance, Customs and Revenue, Econ. and Planning Devt and Statistics, Business and Pvt. Sector Devt, Civil Aviation, Tourism, Int. Business Co. and Offshore Banking, Niue Devt Bank March 1999–2001; fmr Leader Niue People's Party (NPP); Chancellor Univ. of the South Pacific, Fiji 2000–03; Deputy Premier and Minister for Planning, Econ. Devt and Statistics, the Niue Devt Bank, Post, Telecommunications and Information Computer Tech. Devt, Philatelic Bureau and Numismatics, Shipping, Investment and Trade, Civil Aviation and Police, Immigration and Disaster Man. 2002. *Address:* c/o Office of the Prime Minister, Alofi, Niue (office).

LAKE, (William) Anthony (Kirsopp), PhD; American academic, diplomatist, UN official and fmr government official; *Executive Director, United Nations Children's Fund (UNICEF);* b. 2 April 1939, New York City; m.; three c.; ed Harvard Coll., Trinity Coll., Cambridge, UK, Woodrow Wilson School of Public and Int. Affairs, Princeton Univ.; joined Foreign Service 1962, Special Asst to Amb. Henry Cabot Lodge, Viet Nam; aide to Nat. Security Adviser Henry Kissinger 1969–70; Head of State Dept's policy planning operation 1977–81; Prof., Amherst Coll., Mass 1981–84, Mount Holyoke Coll. 1984–92; foreign policy adviser to fmr Pres. Clinton during presidential campaign 1992; Nat. Security Adviser 1993–97; served as US Pres.'s Special Envoy to Haiti as well as Ethiopia and Eritrea from 1997; worked with third Exec. Dir of UNICEF, James P. Grant, on org.'s presentation of its flagship publication, 'The State of the World's Children', at the

White House, mem. Bd of US Fund for UNICEF 1998–2007, Chair. 2004–07, Perm. Hon. mem. 2007–, Exec. Dir UNICEF 2010–; Int. Adviser to ICRC 2000–03; Distinguished Prof. in Practice of Diplomacy, Edmund A. Walsh School of Foreign Service, Georgetown Univ. –2010; fmr Chair. Marshall Legacy Inst.; has led Int. Voluntary Services; mem. Bd Save the Children 1975–77; fmr mem. Bd Overseas Devt Council; fmr mem. Bd of Trustees, Mount Holyoke Coll.; fmr mem. Advisory Council, Princeton Inst. for Int. and Regional Studies; has served on Governance Bd of Center for the Study of Democracy at St Mary's Coll. of Maryland; co-f. journal Foreign Policy; White House Samuel Nelson Drew Award 2000. *Publications include:* The 'Tar Baby' Option: American Policy Toward Southern Rhodesia 1976, Third World Radical Regimes: US Policy under Carter and Reagan 1985, Somoza Falling: A Case Study of Washington at Work 1990, Six Nightmares 2001. *Address:* UNICEF House, 3 United Nations Plaza, New York, NY 10017, USA (office). *Telephone:* (212) 326-7000 (office). *Fax:* (212) 887-7465 (office). *E-mail:* info@unicef.org (office); lakea@georgetown.edu. *Website:* www.unicef.org (office).

LAKE-TACK, Louise Agnetha; Antigua and Barbuda nurse, magistrate and government official; *Governor-General;* b. 26 July 1944, Long Lake Estate, Parish of St Phillips, Antigua; two c.; ed Antigua Girls High School, Charing Cross Hosp., UK; worked as nurse at Nat. Heart Hosp. and Harley Street Clinic, UK; magistrate Marylebone and Horseferry Magistrate Courts 1995, also sat at Pocock Street Crown Court; Gov.-Gen. of Antigua and Barbuda (first woman) 2007–; mem. Antigua and Barbuda Nat. Asscn. *Address:* Office of the Governor-General, St John's, Antigua and Barbuda (office). *Website:* www.antigua.gov.ag (office).

LAKER, John, BEcon (Hons), MSc, PhD; Australian business executive; *Chairman, Australian Prudential Regulation Authority;* ed Univ. of Sydney, Univ. of London, UK; worked in Commonwealth Treasury and IMF before joining Int. Dept of Reserve Bank of Australia (RBA) in 1982, held sr positions in econ., bank supervision and int. areas before becoming RBA's Chief Rep. in Europe, based in London 1991–93, Asst Gov. (Corp. Services) 1993–98, Asst Gov. (Financial System) 1998–2003; mem. Bd of Dirs Australian Prudential Regulation Authority (APRA) and Deputy Chair. Payments System Bd 1998–2003, Chair. APRA 2003–, APRA's rep. on Payments System Board of RBA and APRA's rep. on Council of Financial Regulators. *Address:* Australian Prudential Regulation Authority, GPO Box 9836, Sydney, NSW 2000, Australia (office). *Telephone:* (2) 9210-3000 (office). *Fax:* (2) 9210-3411 (office). *E-mail:* J.Laker@apra.gov.au (office). *Website:* www.apra.gov .au (office).

LAKERBAYA, Leonid; Georgian (Abkhazian) politician; *Prime Minister of the 'Republic of Abkhazia';* b. 1 Jan. 1947, Kutaisi, Georgian SSR, USSR; ed Moscow Automobile and Road Inst., Russian SFSR; engineer with automotive enterprise in Abkhazia 1975–85; head of pilot plant of frozen foods co. in Gagra 1985–91; mem. Parl. 1991–96, 2000–02; First Deputy Prime Minister of Abkhazia 1992–95; Minister of Foreign Affairs 1995–96; nominated by People's Party to stand in 1999 presidential election but refused registration by Cen. Election Comm.; Chair. socio-political movt Aitaira (Revival) 2001–; Vice-Premier and First Vice-Premier in govt of Pres. Bagapsh 2005–11; Prime Minister of the 'Republic of Abkhazia' 2011–. *Address:* Office of the Prime Minister of the 'Republic of Abkhazia', 6600 Abkhazia, Sukhumi, nab. Makhajirov 32, Georgia (office). *Telephone:* (8402) 22-46-22 (office). *Fax:* (8402) 22-71-17 (office). *E-mail:* sukhum-krma@yandex.ru (office). *Website:* www.abkhaziagov.org (office).

LAKHANI, Amin Mohammed, BSc, MBA; Pakistani industrialist; *Managing Director, Lakson Group of Companies;* ed Stanford Univ., Wharton School of Business, Univ. of Pennsylvania, USA; currently Man. Dir Lakson Group, conglomerate with interests in computer software, cosmetics, insurance, fast food and textiles; CEO McDonald's Pakistan; Founding mem. Pakistan Chapter, Young Presidents' Org.; Hon. Consul-Gen. of Singapore in Pakistan; Public Service Star, Govt of Singapore. *Address:* Lakson Group of Companies, Lakson Square Building, 2 Sarwar Shaheed Road, Karachi, Pakistan (office). *Telephone:* (21) 35688243 (office). *Fax:* (21) 35680093 (office). *E-mail:* amin@cyber.net.pk (office). *Website:* www.lakson.com.pk (office).

LAKHANI, Iqbal Ali; Pakistani business executive; *Chairman, Lakson Group of Companies;* one of four brothers controlling Lakson Group of Cos, with group since 1974, currently Chair.; CEO Century Paper & Board Mills Ltd, Tritex Cotton Mills Ltd, Merit Packaging, Cyber.Net (Pvt. Ltd); Hon. Consul Gen. of Mexico in Pakistan. *Address:* Lakson Square, Bldg #2, Sarwar Shaheed Road, Karachi 74200, Pakistan (office). *Telephone:* (21) 569-8000 (office). *Fax:* (21) 568-3410 (office). *E-mail:* info@lakson.com.pk (office). *Website:* www.lakson.com.pk (office).

LAKHDAR, Zohra Ben, PhD; Tunisian physicist and academic; *Professor of Physics, University of Tunis;* ed Univ. of Tunis, Univ. of Paris VI, France; fmr Head, Spectroscopy Lab., Supervisor, postgraduate students for Tunisian DEA Diploma, Co.-Chair. Molecular Spectroscopy Group for Master's Degree and PhD courses; Prof. of Physics, Univ. of Tunis 1978–; Founder mem. Tunisian Physics Soc., Tunisian Astronomy Soc.; Founding mem. and Pres. Tunisian Optical Soc.; mem. Islamic Acad. of Sciences 1994–; Sr Assoc. Abdus Salam Int. Centre for Theoretical Physics 2001–; L'Oréal-UNESCO Women in Science Award 2005. *Publications:* numerous papers in scientific journals and contribs to textbooks. *Address:* Faculté des Sciences de Tunis Département de Physique, Campus Universitaire, Tunis 1060, Tunisia (office). *Telephone:* 873-366 (office). *Fax:* 872-055 (office).

LAKHERA, Lt-Gen. Madan Mohan, MSc; Indian army officer (retd) and government administrator; b. 21 Oct. 1937, Jakhand village, UP (now in Uttaranchal); s. of the late Jaya Nand Lakhera and Kalawati Lakhera; m. Pushpa Lakhera; four d.; ed Rashtriya Indian Mil. Coll., Dehra Dun, Nat. Defence Acad., Pune, Defence Services Staff Coll., Wellington, School of Artillery, Devlali, Coll. of Defence Man., Secundrabad; commissioned in Indian Army 1958; took part in Goa operation 1961, in Indo-Pakistan war, Jammu and Kashmir 1965, 1971; instructor School of Artillery 1967–81; commanded 4th Bn Kumaon Regt, Jammu and Kashmir 1975–78; Deputy Commdr brigade in Manipur 1981–82; rank of Brig. 1982; Commdr brigade in Kanpur 1984–85; Sub-Area Commdr in Kashmir valley 1985–90; rank of Maj.-Gen. 1990; Chief of Staff Kashmir valley-based Corps HQ 1990–92; rank of Lt-Gen. of Indian Army 1993; apptd Chief of Staff, Cen. Command HQ 1992, later Chief of Staff, Northern Command HQ; Adjutant Gen. of Indian Army 1993, Chair. Prin. Personnel Staff Officers' Cttee of three services;

Col Commdt Kumaon Regt; following retirement, joined Indian Nat. Congress party, Chair. All India Congress Cttee Ex-Servicemen's Cell; Lt.-Gov. of Pondicherry 2004–06, of Andaman and Nicobar Islands Feb.–Dec. 2006; Gov. of Mizoram 2006–11; Chief of Army Staff Commendation Card (twice) 1985, Vishisht Seva Medal 1990, Ati Vashisht Seva Medal 1991, Param Vishisht Seva Medal 1995. *Leisure interests:* golf, reading. *Address:* c/o Raj Bhavan, Aizawl 796 001, India.

LAKHOVA, Yekaterina Filippovna; Russian paediatrician and politician; b. 26 May 1948; m.; one d.; ed Sverdlovsk State Medical Inst.; Deputy Head of Div., Sverdlovsk (now Yekaterinburg) City Dept of Public Health, Deputy Head of Main Dept of Public Health, Sverdlovsk Regional Exec. Cttee 1972–90; RSFSR Peoples' Deputy, mem. Council of Repub. RSFSR Supreme Soviet, Chair. Cttee on Problems of Women, Motherhood and Childhood 1990–93; State Adviser on Problems of Family, Protection of Motherhood and Childhood 1992–; adviser to Russian Pres. on Problems of Family, Protection of Motherhood and Childhood 1992–94; Chair. Cttee on Problems of Women, Family and Demography of Russian Presidency 1992–; Founder and Chair. Women of Russia (political movt) 1993; mem. State Duma 1993–, head of State Duma Cttee on Women, Families and Children's Affairs; mem. Socialist Party of Russia 1996, Otechestvo (Homeland) political movt 1998–2000, Yedinaya Rossiya 2000–. *Address:* Committee on Women, Families and Children's Affairs, State Duma, 103265 Moscow, Okhotny ryad 1, Russia. *Telephone:* (495) 292-19-00 (office). *Fax:* (495) 292-94-64 (office). *E-mail:* www@ duma.ru (office). *Website:* www.duma.ru (office).

LAKSACI, Muhammad, PhD; Algerian economist and central banker; *Governor, Banque d'Algérie;* ed Louvain Univ., Belgium; fmr univ. prof.; joined Banque d'Algérie (central bank) in early 1990s, Gov. 2001–, also Pres. Conseil de la Monnaie et du Crédit, Comm. Bancaire; Chair. Asscn of African Central Banks 2012–. *Address:* Office of the Governor, Banque d'Algérie, Immeuble Joly, 38 ave Franklin Roosevelt, 16000 Algiers, Algeria (office). *Telephone:* (21) 23-00-23 (office). *Fax:* (21) 23-03-71 (office). *E-mail:* ba@bank-of-algeria.dz (office). *Website:* www.bank-of-algeria.dz (office).

LAL, Deepak Kumar, MA, BPhil; British academic; *James S. Coleman Professor Emeritus of International Development Studies, Department of Economics, University of California, Los Angeles;* b. 3 Jan. 1940, Lahore, India; s. of the late Nand Lal and of Shanti Devi; m. Barbara Ballis 1971; one s. one d.; ed Doon School, Dehra Dun, St Stephen's Coll., India, Jesus Coll., Oxford, UK; served in Indian Foreign Service 1963–65; Lecturer, Christ Church, Oxford 1966–68; Research Fellow, Nuffield Coll., Oxford 1968–70; Lecturer, Univ. Coll. London 1970–79, Reader 1979–84, Prof. of Political Economy, Univ. of London 1984–93, Prof. Emer. 1993–; James S. Coleman Prof. of Int. Dev. Studies, UCLA 1991–2010, Prof. Emer. 2010–; Consultant, Indian Planning Comm. 1973–74; Research Admin., World Bank, Washington, DC 1983–87; Dir Trade Policy Unit, Centre for Policy Studies 1993–96, Trade and Devt Unit, Inst. of Econ. Affairs 1997–2002; Pres. Mont Pelerin Soc. 2008–10; consultancy assignments ILO, UNCTAD, OECD, IBRD Ministry of Planning, Sri Lanka, Repub. of Korea 1970–2002; Dr hc (Univ. Paul Cézanne, Aix-Marseille III) 2009; Int. Freedom Award for Econs, Società Liberia (Italy) 2007. *Publications:* Wells and Welfare 1972, Methods of Project Analysis 1974, Appraising Foreign Investment in Developing Countries 1975, Unemployment and Wage Inflation in Industrial Economies 1977, Men or Machines 1978, Prices for Planning 1980, The Poverty of "Development Economics" 1983, Labour and Poverty in Kenya (with P. Collier) 1986, Stagflation, Savings and the State (co-ed. with M. Wolf) 1986, The Hindu Equilibrium (two vols) 1988, 1989, Public Policy and Economic Development (co-ed. with M. Scott) 1990, Development Economics (four vols) (ed.) 1991, The Repressed Economy 1993, Against Dirigisme 1994, The Political Economy of Poverty, Equity and Growth (with H. Myint) 1996, Unintended Consequences 1998, Unfinished Business 1999, Trade, Development and Political Economy (co-ed. with R. Snape) 2001, In Praise of Empires 2004, The Hindu Equilibrium 2005, Reviving the Invisible Hand: The Case for Classical Liberalism in the 21st Century 2006, Poverty and Progress: Reality and Myths about Third World Poverty 2012, Lost Causes: The Retreat from Classical Liberalism 2012. *Leisure interests:* opera, theatre, tennis, bridge. *Address:* Department of Economics, 8369 Bunche Hall, UCLA, Box 951477, Los Angeles, CA 90095-1477, USA (office); A30 Nizamuddin West, New Delhi 110013, India (home); 2 Erskine Hill, London, NW11 6HB, England (home). *Telephone:* (310) 825-1011 (office); (11) 41827013 (New Delhi) (home); (20) 8458-3713 (London) (home). *Fax:* (310) 825-9528 (office). *Website:* www.econ.ucla.edu/faculty/regular/ Lal.html (office); www.econ.ucla.edu/lal (office).

LAL, Mahesh B., BS, MBA; Indian oil industry executive (retd); *Technical Member (Petroleum and Natural Gas), Appellate Tribunal for Electricity, Ministry of Power;* b. 1947; ed Indian Inst. of Tech., Kanpur, Indian Inst. of Man., Ahmedabad; trained as chemical engineer; fmr Adviser on Refineries, Ministry of Petroleum and Natural Gas; fmr Dir of Operations, Madras Refineries Ltd; Dir of Refineries, Bharat Petroleum Corpn Ltd –2002; Chair. and Man. Dir Hindustan Petroleum Corpn Ltd 2002–07; Adviser to Tech. Mission on Cotton 2003; Technical mem. (Petroleum and Natural Gas) Appellate Tribunal for Electricity 2007–; fmr mem. Bd of Dirs Cochin Refineries, IBP Co. Ltd, Numaligarh Refineries Ltd, Kochi Refineries Ltd; Chair. Scientific Advisory Cttee, Review Cttee for Auto Fuel Policy, Ministry of Petroleum and Natural Gas; mem. Bd of Govs Indian Inst. of Man., Ahmedabad, Univ. of Petroleum and Energy Studies, Dehradun.; Hon. Fellowship, Energy Inst., London; Lifetime Achievement Award, Chemtech Foundation, UK, Strategy Award, Indira Group of Insts, Pune, HR Professional Award, ITM Business School. *Address:* Appellate Tribunal for Electricity, 7th Floor, CORE-4, Scope Complex, Lodhi Road, New Delhi 110 003, India (office). *Telephone:* (11) 2436 8477 (office). *Fax:* (11) 2436 8479 (office). *E-mail:* registrar-aptel@nic.in (office). *Website:* www.aptel.gov.in (office).

LALEAU, Wilson; Haitian economist and politician; *Minister of Trade and Industry;* ed Centre de Techniques de Planification et d'Economie Appliquée, Haiti, Univ. Paris I (Sorbonne), France, Inst. Int. d'Admin Publique, Paris, Inst. of Social Studies (ISS), The Hague, Netherlands; Project Man., Commission Nationale à la Réforme Administrative (CNRA) 1997–2001; Nat. Coordinator, state modernization programme (UNDP/Govt of Haiti) 2000–01; Prof. at several insts including, Centre de Techniques de Planification et d'Economie Appliquée, Univ. of Quisqueya, Univ. d'Etat d'Haïti (UEH), also Vice-Rector for Academic Affairs, UEH 2003, 2007; fmr Econ. Adviser to Pres.; Minister of Trade and Industry 2011–, also the Economy and Finance 2013–14; fmr consultant to Govt of Haiti and to several int. insts including UNDP, IDB, World Bank, UNICEF. *Address:* Ministry of Trade and Industry, Bureau du Ministre, 23 ave l'Amartinière, BP 6114, Port-au-Prince, Haiti (office). *Telephone:* 2943-4488 (office). *Fax:* 2943-1868 (office). *E-mail:* secretariatdumiistre@mci.gouv.ht (office). *Website:* www.mci.gouv.ht (office).

LALIBERTÉ, Guy, OQ, OC; Canadian entertainment industry executive; *Founder and CEO, Cirque du Soleil Inc.;* b. 2 Sept. 1959, Quebec City; began career as musician and street performer; joined stiltwalker troupe Les Echassiers De Baie-Saint-Paul; est. summer festival La Fête Foriane, Baie-Saint-Paul 1982; created govt-sponsored event Le Grand Tour du Cirque Du Soleil 1984, show toured Canada for several years, began touring USA 1987, grew into major int. org. producing multiple shows worldwide as Cirque du Soleil, to date over 20 differently themed shows have been produced across five continents combining traditional circus skills with various other artistic and cultural elements, currently CEO; finished fourth, Season Five World Poker Tour championship 2007; Great Montrealer, Académie des Grands Montréalais 2001, named one of the 100 most influential people in the world, Time magazine 2004, Ernst & Young Entrepreneur of the Year 2006. *Address:* Cirque du Soleil, 8400 2nd Avenue, Montreal, PQ H1Z 4M6, Canada (office). *Telephone:* (514) 722-2324 (office). *Fax:* (514) 722-3692 (office). *E-mail:* mediainfo@cirquedusoleil.com (office). *Website:* www .cirquedusoleil.com (office).

LALONDE, Brice; French politician and environmental consultant; *Advisor, United Nations Global Compact;* b. 10 Feb. 1946, Neuilly-sur-Seine; s. of Alain-Gauthier Lalonde and Fiona Lalonde (née Forbes); m. Patricia Raynaud 1986; two s. (one deceased) two d.; one s. one d. from previous m.; ed Univ. of Paris (Sorbonne); Pres. Union nationale des étudiants de france 1968; Chair. Friends of the Earth 1972, French br. 1978; cand. for Green Party, French presidential election 1981; Admin. European Environment Bureau 1983; Dir Paris Office Inst. for European Environmental Policy 1987; Sec. of State for the Environment 1988–89, for the Environment and the Prevention of Tech. and Natural Disasters 1989–90, Minister Del. 1990–91, Minister of the Environment 1991–92; Pres. Génération Ecologie (political movt) 1990–2002, Hon. Pres. 2002–; Mayor of Saint-Briac-sur-Mer 1995–2008; Chair. Cttee to Free Alexandr Nikitin 1996–; mem. Conseil Régional, Brittany 1998, Comité nat. de l'eau 1998–; Chair. Round Table on Sustainable Development, OECD 2007–08; Amb. responsible for Int. Negotiations on Climate Change 2007–10; Under-Sec. Gen. UN Exec. Co-ordinator, Rio 20 2011–12, Advisor to the UN Global Compact 2014; Chevalier, Légion d'honneur. *Publications:* L'écologie en bleu; Quand vous voudrez; Sur la vague verte. *Address:* 65 boulevard Arago, 75013 Paris, France (home). *E-mail:* lalonde@un.org (office).

LALUMIÈRE, Catherine; French politician; *President, European Association of the Schools of Political Studies, Council of Europe;* b. 3 Aug. 1935, Rennes; m. Pierre Lalumière (deceased); specialist in public law; Lecturer, Univ. of Paris; mem. Steering Cttee, Parti Socialiste 1979; mem. Nat. Ass. for Gironde 1986–89; Adviser to Pres. on civil service; Sec. of State for the Civil Service and Admin. Reforms May–June 1981, Minister for Consumer Affairs 1981–83, Sec. of State 1983–84, Minister for European Affairs 1984–86; Sec.-Gen. Council of Europe 1989–94; Urban Community Councillor, Bordeaux 1989–; Municipal Councillor, Talence 1989–95; MEP 1994–2004, Vice-Pres. 2001–04; Deputy Pres. Radical France 1996 (now Radical Socialist Party); Pres. European Radical Alliance 1994–, European Asscn of the Schools of Political Studies, Council of Europe 2008–; Pres. Maison de l'Europe, Paris, French Fed. of the Maisons de l'Europe; fmr Vice-Pres. Int. European Movt; Hon. DCL (Durham) 1995. *Address:* European Association of the Schools of Political Studies, DGDAP – Council of Europe, 67075 Strasbourg, France (office). *Telephone:* 3-90-21-53-02 (office). *Website:* www .schoolsofpoliticalstudies.eu (office).

LAM, Barry, BEng, MEng; Taiwanese electronics industry executive; *Chairman, Quanta Computer Inc.;* b. Shanghai; m.; two c.; ed Nat. Taiwan Univ.; Co-founder Kimpo (handheld calculator mfr) 1973; f. Quanta Computer Inc. (computer and components mfr) 1988, currently Chair.; Chair. Quanta Culture and Educ. Foundation; mem. Bd of Dirs Cloud Gate Theatre Group; Business Week's 50 Stars of Asia 1999, 2002, Business Week's 25 Managers of the Year 2002. *Address:* Quanta Computer Inc., 211 Wen Hwa Second Road, Kui Shan Hsiang, Taoyuan, Taiwan (office). *Telephone:* (3) 327-2345 (office). *Fax:* (3) 327-1511 (office). *E-mail:* campus@quantatw.com (office); qci.ir@quantatw.com (office). *Website:* www .quantatw.com (office).

LAM, Carrie, (Carrie Lam Cheng Yuet-ngor), JP; Hong Kong civil servant and politician; *Secretary for Development;* b. 13 May 1957, Hong Kong; m. Lam Siu-por; two s.; joined Admin. Service 1980, served in various bureaux and depts, including as Dir of Social Welfare Dept 2000–03, Perm. Sec. for Housing, Planning and Lands (Planning and Lands) 2003–04, Dir-Gen. Hong Kong Econ. and Trade Office, London, UK 2004–06, rank of Admin. Officer Staff Grade A1 2006, Perm. Sec. for Home Affairs 2006–07, Sec. for Devt 2007–; Gold Bauhinia Star 2010. *Address:* Development Bureau, 8/F West Wing, Central Government Offices, 11 Ice House Street, Central, Hong Kong Special Administrative Region, People's Repub. of China (office). *Telephone:* 2848-2718 (office). *Fax:* 2845-3489 (office). *E-mail:* devbenq@devb.gov.hk (office). *Website:* www.devb.gov.hk (office).

LAMAHET, Edouard Gnakoï; Guinean politician; Minister of Foreign Affairs and Guineans Abroad 2010–12. *Address:* c/o Ministry of Foreign Affairs and Guineans Abroad, face au Port, ex-Primature, BP 2519, Conakry, Guinea.

LAMAMRA, Ramtane; Algerian diplomatist and politician; *Minister of Foreign Affairs and International Co-operation;* b. 15 June 1952, Amizour; ed École nationale d'Admin; joined Ministry of Foreign Affairs (MFA) 1976, Amb. to Ethiopia and Djibouti 1989–91, to Austria and IAEA 1992–93, Perm. Rep. to UN, New York 1993–96, Amb. to USA 1996–99, to Portugal 2004–05, African Union (AU) Special Envoy to Liberia 2003, Sec.-Gen., MFA 2005–07, AU Commr for Peace and Security 2008–13; Minister of Foreign Affairs and Int. Co-operation 2013–. *Address:* Ministry of Foreign Affairs, place Mohamed Seddik Benyahia, el-Mouradia, Algiers, Algeria (office). *Telephone:* (21) 29-12-12 (office). *Website:* www .mae.dz (office).

LAMANDA, Vincent; French judge; *First President, Court of Cassation;* b. 31 May 1946; Prosecutor, Evry-Corbeil 1972, also Versailles; Tech. Advisor to Minister of Justice 1974; Lecturer, Univ. Paris II Panthéon-Assas 1977–94; Replacement to documentation service and studies of the Court of Cassation, made available to Prime Minister as Rapporteur of Cttee for the Study of Violence 1976; Chief of Staff of the Keeper of the Seals 1977; mem. Implementation Cttee's Report on Violence 1977; Tech. Advisor to Minister of Justice 1978–80; Counsellor at Court of Cassation 1979; Sec. Supreme Council of Magistracy 1981, reinstated to Court of Cassation 1981; Vice-Pres. TGI de Paris 1986; Presiding Judge of Bordeaux 1988; First Pres. Court of Appeal of Rouen 1992, Court of Appeal of Versailles 1996–2007; mem. Supreme Council of Magistracy 2002–06; First Pres. Court of Cassation 2007–; Vice-Pres. Network of the Presidents of the Supreme Judicial Courts of the EU; Commdr, Ordre de la Légion d'honneur 2009. *Address:* Cour de Cassation, Palais de Justice, 5 quai de l'Horloge, 75001 Paris Cedex 01, France (office). *Telephone:* 1-44-32-73-70 (office). *Fax:* 1-44-32-78-28 (office). *E-mail:* pp.courdecassation@justice.fr (office). *Website:* www.courdecassation.fr (office).

LAMB, Allan Joseph; South African business executive and fmr professional cricketer; b. 20 June 1954, Langebaanweg, Cape Prov.; s. of Michael Lamb and Joan Lamb; m. Lindsay Lamb 1979; one s. one d.; ed Wynberg Boys' High School and Abbotts Coll.; middle-order right-hand batsman; teams: Western Prov. 1972–82, 1992–93, Northants. 1978–95 (Capt. 1989–95), Orange Free State 1987–88; qualified for England 1982 and played in 79 Tests 1982–92 (three as Capt.), scoring 4,656 runs (average 36.09, highest score 142) including 14 hundreds; toured Australia 1982–83, 1986–87, 1990–91; played in 122 One-Day Ints, scoring 4,010 runs (average 39.31, highest score 118) including four hundreds; scored 32,502 first-class runs (average 48.94, highest score 294) including 89 hundreds; scored 1,000 runs in a season on 15 occasions; Dir Allan Lamb Assocs Ltd (events man. co.), Grenada Sports Ltd; contrib. to Sky Sports Cricket; with Ian 'Beefy' Botham, advertised Quality Standard English lamb and beef for English Beef and Lamb Exec., using play on their names as a selling point; Wisden Cricketer of the year 1981. *Play:* Beef and Lamb in a stew (roadshow with Ian Botham) 1994–95. *Television:* contestant on a special Cricketers' Edn of the Weakest Link (voted off in second round). *Publication:* Silence of the Lamb (autobiography) 1995. *Leisure interests:* tennis, golf, cycling, rugby, horse racing, fly-fishing, shooting. *Address:* Allan Lamb Associates Ltd, First Floor, 4 St Giles Street, Northampton, NN1 1JB, England (office). *Telephone:* (1604) 231222 (office). *Fax:* (1604) 239930 (office). *E-mail:* info@lambassociates.co.uk (office). *Website:* www.lambassociates.co.uk (office).

LAMBECK, Kurt, AO, DPhil, DSc, FRS, FAA, FRSN; Australian (b. Dutch) geophysicist and academic; *Professor Emeritus, Australian National University;* b. 20 Sept. 1941, Netherlands; ed Univ. of NSW, Univ. of Oxford, UK; Geodesist, Smithsonian Astrophysical Observatory 1967–70; Dir of Research, Paris Observatory 1970–73; Prof. of Geophysics, Univ. of Paris 1973–77; Prof. of Geophysics, Research School of Earth Sciences, ANU 1977–2007, Prof. Emer. 2007–; Blaise Pascal Prof., École normale supérieure, Paris 2011–12; Foreign mem. Royal Netherlands Acad. of Arts and Sciences 1993, Norwegian Acad. of Science and Letters 1998, Acad. des sciences 2005, NAS 2009, American Acad. of Arts and Sciences 2010; Fellow, Australian Acad. of Science 1984–, Pres. 2006–10; Chevalier, Légion d'honneur; Hon. DEng (Nat. Tech. Univ. of Greece); Hon. DSc (Univ. NSW); Macelwane Award, American Geophysical Union 1976, Whitten Medal, American Geophysical Union 1993, Jaeger Medal, Australian Acad. of Science 1995, Alfred Wegener Medal, European Union of Geosciences 1996, George Lemaître Prize 2002, Balzan Prize 2012, Wollaston Medal, Geology Soc. 2013. *Publications:* The Earth's Variable Rotation 1980, Geophysical Geodesy 1988; numerous papers on geodesy and geophysics. *Address:* Research School of Earth Sciences, Australian National University, Canberra, ACT 0200, Australia (office). *Telephone:* (2) 6125-5161 (office). *E-mail:* kurt.lambeck@anu.edu.au (office). *Website:* people.rses.anu.edu.au/lambeck_k/index.php (office).

LAMBERT, Christopher; American actor; b. (Christophe Guy Dénis Lambert), 29 March 1957, Great Neck, NY; m. 1st Diane Lane 1988 (divorced 1994); one d.; m. 2nd Jaimyse Haft 1999 (divorced 2006); m. 3rd Sophie Marceau 2012; ed L'Ecole Roche, Int. School, Lycée d'Annemasse, Coll. Floriment, Geneva, Florent School, Paris and Paris Conservatoire; family left USA when only two years old, father a UN diplomat assigned to Switzerland; mil. service with Alpine Corps, Grenoble; trainee, Barclay's Bank, London 1976. *Films include:* Ciao, les mecs 1979, Le Bar du téléphone 1980, Asphalte 1981, Une sale affaire 1981, Putain d'histoire d'amour 1981, Légitime violence 1982, Greystoke: The Story of Tarzan, Lord of the Apes 1983, Paroles et Musiques 1984, Subway 1985, Highlander 1986, I Love You 1986, The Sicilian 1987, Love Dream 1988, To Kill A Priest 1988, Why Me? 1990, Highlander II: The Quickening 1991, Knight Moves 1992, Max & Jeremie 1992, Fortress 1993, Gunmen 1994, Road Killers 1994, Highlander III: The Sorcerer 1994, The Hunted 1995, Mortal Kombat 1995, Tashunga 1996, Adrenalin: Fear the Rush 1996, Hercule et Sherlock 1996, Nirvana 1997, Arlette 1997, Mean Guns 1997, Fortress 2 1999, Operation Splitsville 1999, Beowulf 1999, Resurrection 1999, Gideon 1999, Highlander: Endgame 2000, Aparté 2001, Vercingétorix 2001, The Point Men 2001, The Piano Player 2002, Absolon 2003, Qui veut la peau de Roberto Santini? (short) 2003, Janis et John 2003, A ton image 2004, Game of Swords 2006, Southland Tales 2006, Le lièvre de Vatanen 2006, Metamorphosis 2007, Trivial 2007, The Chauffeur 2008, White Material 2009, Cartagena 2009, The Gardener of God 2010, Ghost Rider: Spirit of Vengeance 2011, The Foreigner 2012, My Lucky Star 2012, Blood Shot 2013, Electric Slide 2014. *Television includes:* Douchka 1981, La Dame de coeur 1982, King of Bandit Jing (mini-series) 2002, Dalida (film) 2005, Les associés (film) 2009, The Secret of the Whales (film) 2010, Very Bad Blagues (series) 2012, L'una e l'altra (film) 2012, NCIS: Los Angeles 2012–, La source (series) 2013–.

LAMBERT, Phyllis, CC, GOQ, CAL, BA, MS (Arch), FRSC; Canadian architect and museum director; *Founding Director and Chair of the Board of Trustees, Centre Canadien d'Architecture / Canadian Centre for Architecture, Montréal;* b. 24 Jan. 1927, Montréal, Québec; d. of Samuel Bronfman and Saidye Bronfman (née Rosner); ed The Study, Montréal, Vassar Coll., New York, Illinois Inst. of Tech., Chicago; Adjunct Prof., School of Architecture, McGill Univ. 1986–; Assoc. Prof., Faculté de l'aménagement, École d'architecture, Univ. de Montréal 1989–; Bd

Chair. and Prin., Ridgway Ltd, Architects/Developers, Los Angeles 1972–84; Founding Dir and Chair. Bd of Trustees, Centre Canadien d'Architecture (CCA), Montréal 1979–, Consulting Architect and Client CCA 1984–89; cr. Fonds d'investissement de Montréal, pvt. fund for revitalization of Montréal neighbourhoods 1996; est. Int. Foundation for the Canadian Centre for Architecture Prize for Design of Cities 1999; jury mem. several cttees for architectural and urban design projects; numerous exhbns; mem. Bd of Trustees Inst. of Fine Arts, New York Univ. 1973–, Bd of Advisors Temple Hoyne Buell Center for the Study of American Architecture, Columbia Univ., New York 1984– (Founding Chair. 1984–89), Advisory Council School of Architecture, Princeton Univ. 1990–2003, 2006–, Bd Acquisitions Cttee Nat. Gallery of Canada 1991–, Provost's Advisory Bd Faculty of Architecture, Univ. of Toronto 1992–2004, Visiting Cttee Grad. School of Design, Harvard Univ. 1993–2005, and several other bodies; Founding mem. Bd Int. Confed. of Architectural Museums 1984– (Pres. 1984–87); fmr mem. Bd of Overseers, Coll. of Architecture and Planning, Ill. Inst. of Tech.; frequent guest lecturer at univs and professional orgs in N America and abroad; Academician, RCA 1977; Life mem. Council of the Ontario Asscn of Architects 2003–; Fellow, Royal Architectural Inst. of Canada (RAIC) 1983; Foreign Hon. mem. American Acad. of Arts and Sciences 1995; Hon. FRIBA 2001; Hon. FAIA 2003; Chevalier, Ordre de la Pléiade, Assemblée parlementaire de la Francophonie 1998, Grand Oficier, Ordre nat. du Québec 2005, Commdr, Ordre des Arts et des Lettres 2006; 27 hon. degrees from univs in N America and Europe; numerous awards and prizes, including Médaille de l'Acad. d'Architecture de France 1988, Gabrielle Léger Medal, Heritage Canada Foundation 1988, Prix d'excellence en architecture, Ordre des Architectes du Québec (for CCA) 1989, Médaille d'Honneur, Soc. Historique de Montréal 1990, RAIC Gold Medal 1991, AIA Inst. Honor (for CCA) 1992, Lescarbot Award, Govt of Canada 1992, Prix Gérard-Morisset, Gov. of Québec 1994, Hadrian Award, World Monuments Fund 1997, Montblanc Int. Arts Patronage Award 2001, Chrysler Design Award (as Design Champion) 2002, Prix Blanche Lemco van Ginkel, Ordre des Urbanistes du Québec 2003, Award of Excellence, Advocate for Architecture, RAIC 2005, Vincent J. Scully Prize, Nat. Building Museum 2006, Prix d'excellence de l'Opération patrimoine architectural de Montréal, Ville de Montréal et Héritage Montréal 2007, Pillar of New York Award, Preservation League of New York State 2007, Woodrow Wilson Award for Public Service, Canada Inst. of the Woodrow Wilson Int. Centre for Scholars 2007. *Projects include:* Seagram Bldg, New York (Dir of Planning) (AIA 25-Year Award 1984, New York Landmarks Conservancy Award 1989) 1954–58, Toronto-Dominion Centre, Toronto (consultant) 1962, Saidye Bronfman Centre, YM-YWHA, Montréal (architect) (RAIC Massey Medal 1970) 1963–68, Les Promenades St-Bruno Shopping Centre, St Bruno, Québec (consultant) 1974, Jane Tate House renovation, Montréal (architect) 1974–76, Biltmore Hotel renovation, Los Angeles (architect and developer) (AIA Award of Honor 1978) 1976, renovation of housing units, St-Hubert Street, Montréal (developer) 1978, 700-unit co-operative housing renovation project, Milton Park, Montréal (Pres.) 1979–85, Ben Ezra Synagogue Restoration Project, Cairo, Egypt (Dir) 1981–94. *Publications:* Court House: A Photographic Document 1978, Photography and Architecture: 1839–1939 1982, Architecture and its Image 1989, Canadian Centre for Architecture: Building and Gardens 1989, Opening the Gates of Eighteenth-Century Montréal (ed.) 1992, Fortifications and the Synagogue: The Fortress of Babylon and the Ben Ezra Synagogue, Cairo (ed.) 1994, Viewing Olmsted: Photographs by Robert Burley, Lee Friedlander and Geoffrey James (ed.) 1996, Autonomy and Ideology: Positioning an Avant-Garde in America 1997, Mies in America (ed.) 2001; numerous essays in architectural periodicals. *Address:* Centre Canadien d'Architecture, 1920 rue Baile, Montréal, PQ H3H 2S6, Canada (office). *Telephone:* (514) 939-7025 (office). *Fax:* (514) 939-7032 (office). *E-mail:* plambert@cca.qc.ca (office). *Website:* www.cca.qc.ca (office).

LAMBERT, Sir Richard Peter, Kt, BA; British journalist, organization official and university chancellor; *Chancellor, University of Warwick;* b. 23 Sept. 1944, Bucks., England; s. of Peter Lambert and Mary Lambert; m. Harriet Murray-Browne 1973; one s. one d.; ed Fettes Coll., Edinburgh, Balliol Coll. Oxford; mem. staff, Financial Times 1966–2001, Lex Column 1972, Financial Ed. 1978, New York Corresp. 1982, Deputy Ed. 1983, Ed. Financial Times 1991–2001; lecturer and contrib. to The Times 2001–; external mem. Bank of England Monetary Policy Cttee 2003–06; Dir-Gen. CBI, London 2006–11; Chancellor Univ. of Warwick 2008–; Dir (non-exec.) London Int. Financial Futures Exchange (LIFFE), AXA Investment Mans, Int. Rescue Cttee UK; Chair. Visiting Arts; Gov. Royal Shakespeare Co.; UK Chair. Franco-British Colloque; mem. UK-India Round Table; mem. Int. Advisory Bd British-American Business Inc., Bd of British Museum; Hon. DLitt (City Univ. London) 2000; Hon. LLD (Warwick) 2004; Dr hc (Brighton, Exeter), (York) 2007; Princess of Wales Amb. Award 2001, World Leadership Forum Business Journalist Decade of Excellence Award 2001. *Address:* Office of the Chancellor, University of Warwick, Coventry, CV4 7AL, England (office). *Telephone:* (24) 7652-3523 (office). *Fax:* (24) 7646-1606 (office). *Website:* www2.warwick.ac.uk/about/management/chancellor (office).

LAMBERT, Yves Maurice; French international organization official and engineer; b. 4 June 1936, Nancy, Meurthe-et-Moselle; s. of André Arthur Lambert and Paulette Franck; m. Odile Revillon 1959; three s. two d.; ed Ecole Polytechnique, Paris, Nat. Civil Aviation School, Centre de Préparation à l'Admin des Entreprises; Dir Org. de Gestion et de Sécurité de l'Algérie (OGSA), Algeria 1965–68; Tech. Adviser to Minister of Transport, France 1969–72; Rep. of France to ICAO Council 1972–76; Sec.-Gen. ICAO Aug. 1976–88, Dir of Air Navigation, Ministry of Equipment and Housing, Transport and the Sea 1989–93; Dir-Gen. Eurocontrol 1994–2001; Fellow Royal Aeronautical Soc. (UK); mem. Acad. Nat. de l'Air et de l'Espace; Officier, Légion d'honneur, Ordre nat. du Mérite; Médaille de l'Aéronautique, Glen Gilbert Award, Air Traffic Control Asscn 1997. *Address:* c/o Eurocontrol, 96 rue de la Fusée, 1130 Brussels, Belgium.

LAMBRINIDIS, Stavros, BA, JD; Greek lawyer, politician and diplomatist; b. 6 Feb. 1962, Athens; ed Amherst Coll. and Yale Univ. Law School, USA; attorney at Wilmer, Culter & Pickering, Washington, DC 1988–93; Special Advisor to the Under-Sec. of Foreign Affairs and subsequently the Minister of Educ., Giorgos Papandreou 1994–96; Head of Staff for Minister of Foreign Affairs, Theodoros Pangalos 1996; Sec.-Gen. for the Expatriate Greeks Section, Ministry of Foreign Affairs 1996–99; mem. PASOK Cttee for Expatriate Greeks 1996–99, PASOK Nat. Council; Amb. ad personam of the Hellenic Repub. 1999–2004; Dir-Gen. Int.

Olympic Truce Centre (an IOC org.) 2000–05; fmr mem. Steering Cttee on the negotiation and implementation of nine bilateral agreements with Turkey; mem. European Parl. for the Panhellenic Socialist Movt (PASOK) 2004–11, Head of Greek Socialist Del. to European Parl., Vice-Chair. Cttee on Civil Liberties, Justice and Home Affairs, Rapporteur on the Integration of Immigrants in Europe and on the Protection of Critical Infrastructures; fmr Vice-Pres. Party of European Socialists; Minister of Foreign Affairs June–Nov. 2011; represented Greece on 66th UN Gen. Ass. Sept. 2011; Ed.-in-Chief The Yale Journal of International Law 1998; Prof. Emer., Donetsk Univ. Inst. of Humanities, Ukraine 1999; Visiting Prof., Int. Olympic Acad., Greek Diplomatic Acad., Greek Police Acad. 1998–2004; Chair. DC (USA) Civil Rights Cttee 1990; Dr hc (Donetsk Nat. Univ., Ukraine); Award of Hellenic Leadership Conf. *Publications:* author of the Parl.'s reports on the 'Integration of Immigrants into the EU' and on 'Promoting Security and Fundamental Rights in the Electronic Age'. *Address:* c/o Ministry of Foreign Affairs, Odos Sofias 1, 106 71 Athens, Greece. *Website:* www.lambrinidis.gr.

LAMBRON, Marc; French journalist and writer; b. 4 Feb. 1957, Lyon; s. of Paul Lambron and Jacqueline Lambron (née Denis); m. Sophie Missoffe 1983; one s. two d.; ed Ecole normale supérieure, Institut d'études politiques, Ecole nationale d'admin; columnist, Point 1986–, Madame Figaro; mem. Conseil d'Etat 1985–; Commdr, Ordre des Arts et des Lettres, Chevalier, Légion d'honneur 2004. *Publications include:* L'Impromptu de Madrid (Prix des Deux Magots 1989) 1988, La nuit des masques (Prix Colette 1991) 1990, Carnet de bal 1992, L'oeil du silence (Prix Fémina 1993) 1993, 1941 1997, Etrangers dans la nuit 2001, Carnet de bal II 2003, Les Menteurs 2004, Une saison sur la terre 2006, Mignonne, allons voir 2006, Eh bien, dansez maintenant 2008, Théorie du chiffon 2010, Carnet de bal III 2011, Nus vénitiens 2012, Tu n'as pas tellement changé 2014. *Leisure interests:* music, cinema. *Address:* 17 rue Lagrange, 75005 Paris, France (home). *Telephone:* 1-40-51-02-12 (home). *Fax:* 1-46-33-43-18.

LAMEDA, Guaicaipuro, MA; Venezuelan business executive, engineer and army officer (retd); b. 6 Aug. 1954, Barquisimeto, Estada Lara; ed Mil. Acad. of Venezuela, Pacific Univ., USA, Inst. of Advanced Studies of Nat. Defense, Gen. Staff and Command School, USA; numerous managerial and educational posts in Venezuelan army and govt, including Chief Planning Officer, Venezuelan Co. of Mil. Industries (CAVIM) 1992, Dir of Budget Office, Ministry of Defence 1996, Dir Govt Cen. Budget Office 1998; Chair. Petróleos de Venezuela SA (PDVSA) 2000–02; Pres. of the Repub. Award, Nat. School for Advanced Defense Studies; 15 nat. and foreign distinctions; 3 mil. merit badges, 23 mil. honour awards. *Address:* c/o Edif. Petróleos de Venezuela, Torre Est, Avda Libertador, La Campina, Apdo 169, Caracas 1010-A, Venezuela.

LAMFALUSSY, Baron Alexandre, LèsSc (Econ), DPhil; Belgian banker and academic; b. 26 April 1929, Kapuvar, Hungary; m. Anne-Marie Cochard 1957; two s. two d.; ed Catholic Univ. of Louvain and Nuffield Coll., Oxford, UK; economist, then econ. adviser, Banque de Bruxelles 1955–65; Visiting Lecturer, Yale Univ., USA 1961–62; Exec. Dir and Chair. Exec. Bd Banque de Bruxelles 1965–75; Exec. Dir Banque Bruxelles Lambert 1975; Econ. Adviser, Head of Monetary and Econ. Dept, BIS 1976–81, Asst Gen. Man. 1981–85, Gen. Man. 1985–93; Pres. European Monetary Inst. 1994–97; Chair. Cttee of Wise Men on the Regulation of European Securities Markets, European Council 2000–01; currently teaching and involved in research at Institut d'études européennes, Catholic Univ. of Louvain; Chair. High Level Cttee on a New Financial Architecture 2008–. *Publications include:* Investment and Growth in Mature Economies: The Case of Belgium 1961, The UK and the Six: An Essay on Growth in Western Europe 1963, Les marchés financiers en Europe 1968, Financial Crises in Emerging Markets: An Essay on Financial Globalization and Fragility 2000. *Address:* Institut d'études européennes, Université catholique de Louvain, Ottignies-Louvain-la-Neuve, Louvain, Belgium (office); Postfach 102031, 60020 Frankfurt, Germany. *Telephone:* (69) 272270. *Fax:* (69) 27227227. *Website:* www.uclouvain.be/262380.html (office).

LAMINE LOUM, Mamadou; Senegalese politician; fmr Minister of Econ., Finance and Planning; Prime Minister of Senegal 1998–99; mem. Parti Socialiste (PS). *Address:* c/o Office of the Prime Minister, ave. Léopold Sedar Senghor, Dakar, Senegal. *Telephone:* 823-10-88. *Fax:* 822-55-78.

LAMIZANA, Mariam, MA; Burkinabè politician and organization official; *Honorary President, Inter-African Cttee (IAC) on Traditional Practices;* b. 26 July 1951, Bobo-Dioulasso; m.; four c.; ed Univ. of Paris X–Nanterre and Institut de Service Social et de Recherches Sociales, Montrouge, France; Attaché d'Etudes, Soc. of African Studies and Devt, Ouagadougou 1976; Social Asst Bureau of Social Aid 1979–90; Prof. of Sociology, Institut Nat. d'Educ. 1981–84; Prov. Dir of Family Expansion and Nat. Solidarity, Houet—Bobo-Dioulasso 1984–86; Sec.-Gen. Ministry of Family Expansion and Nat. Solidarity 1986–88; Tech. Adviser to Minister of Social Action and the Family 1988–97; Pres. Inter-African Cttee (IAC) on Traditional Practices, Nat. Cttee of the Struggle against Circumcision (CNLPE) 1988–97, Perm. Sec. 1997–2000, now Hon. Pres.; mem. House of Reps 1996–99; Regional Councillor for Francophone Africa, RAINBO (Research, Action and Information Network for Bodily Integrity of Women), New York, USA 1997–2000; Dir-Gen. of Nat. Solidarity, Ministry of Social Action and Nat. Solidarity 2001, Minister for Social Action and Nat. Solidarity 2002–05; Pres. Voice of Women Asscn, Burkina Faso 2000; mem. Ind. Nat. Election Cttee 2001; chair. numerous govt cttees; del. to int. org. including UN, UNICEF, OAU, Inter-African Cttee; Chevalier Ordre du Mérite (Burkina Faso); Nathalie Masse Int. Prize, Centre Int. de l'Enfant 1995. *Publications include:* Développement Communautaire au Burkina Faso, Mémoire de Maîtrise 1980. *Address:* Inter-African Committee on Traditional Practices, c/o ECA, PO Box 3001, Addis Ababa, Ethiopia. *E-mail:* iac -htps@uneca.org. *Website:* www.iac-ciaf.net.

LAMJAV, Banzrachiin; Mongolian fmr politician; b. 1920; ed Higher School for Party Cadres, Ulaanbaatar and Higher Party School of the CPSU Cen. Cttee; Instructor at Prov. Cttee of the Mongolian Revolutionary Youth League; served in army as private, elected as Bureau secretary of the Youth League Cttee, worked as asst and deputy chief of political dept of regt, then a brigade; Head of Section, Political Directorate, Mongolian People's Army (MPRP), then Deputy Chief of Dept; Deputy Chair. Party Cen. Cttee of MPRP Cen. Cttee 1954–56; First Sec. Party Cttee of Zavkhan Aimak (Prov.) 1956–58; Instructor at the MPRP Cen. Cttee 1958–62; Head of Personnel Dept MPRP Cen. Cttee 1962–86; concurrently First

Deputy Chair. Party Control Cttee of MPRP Cen. Cttee 1979–86; Alt. mem. Political Bureau of MPRP Cen. Cttee 1986–87, mem. 1987–90 and Chair. Party Control Cttee MPRP Cen. Cttee 1986–90 (resgnd); fmr Deputy to the Great People's Hural; mem. of Presidium of Great People's Hural 1976–86.

LAMM, Donald Stephen, BA; American publisher; *Literary Agent, Fletcher & Company;* b. 31 May 1931, New York; s. of Lawrence W. Lamm and Aleen A. Lassner; m. Jean S. Nicol 1958; two s. one d.; ed Fieldston School, Yale Univ., Univ. of Oxford, England; Counter-intelligence Corps, US Army 1953–55; joined W.W. Norton & Co. Inc. 1956, coll. rep. 1956–59, Ed. 1959–2000, Dir 1964–2000, Vice-Pres. 1968–76, Chair. 1984–2000; Pres. Yale Univ. Press 1984–2000; fmr Literary Agent, Carlisle & Co.; currently Literary Agent, Fletcher & Co.; mem. Editorial Bd The American Scholar; Regents Lecturer, Univ. of Calif., Berkeley 1997–99; mem. Advisory Council Inst. of Early American History and Culture 1979–82; mem. Council on Foreign Relations 1978; mem. Council, Woodrow Wilson Center, Int. Advisory Bd, Logos; Guest Fellow, Yale Univ. 1980, 1985; Trustee, The Roper Center 1984; Fellow, Branford Coll. Yale Univ. 1985–2000, Center for Advanced Study in Behavioral Sciences 1998–99; Guest Fellow Woodrow Wilson Center 1996; Pres. Bd of Govs Yale Univ. 1986; Ida H. Beam Distinguished Visiting Prof. Univ. of Iowa 1987–88; mem. American Acad. of Arts and Sciences (first book publisher elected in AAAS history); Vice-Pres. Phi Beta Kappa Soc. 2003; Trustee Univ. of Calif. Press. *Publications include:* Economics and the Common Reader 1989, Beyond Literacy 1990, Book Publishing in the United States Today 1997, Perception, Cognition and Language 2000. *Leisure interests:* wilderness canoeing, skiing. *Address:* Fletcher & Company, 78 Fifth Avenue, 3rd Floor, New York, NY 10011, USA (office). *Website:* www.fletcherandco.com (office).

LAMM, Richard D., LLB, JD, CPA; American lawyer, academic and politician; *University Professor, Co-Director of the Institute for Public Policy Studies and Executive Director of the Center for Public Policy and Contemporary Issues, University of Denver;* b. 8 Aug. 1935, Madison, Wis.; s. of A. E. Lamm; m. Dottie Lamm; one s. one d.; ed Univ. of Wisconsin and Univ. of California, Berkeley; Certified Public Accountant, Ernst & Ernst, Denver 1961–62; lawyer, Colo Anti-Discrimination Comm. 1962–63; lawyer, Jones, Meiklejohn, Kilroy, Kehl & Lyons 1963–65; pvt. practice 1965–74; mem. Colo House of Reps 1966–74; Assoc. Prof. of Law, Univ. of Denver 1969–74, Univ. Prof., Co-Dir Inst. for Public Policy Studies and Exec. Dir Center for Public Policy and Contemporary Issues 1987–; Gov. of Colo 1975–87 (three terms); Chair. Advisory Bd Fed. for American Immigration Reform; mem. Bd of Dirs Diversity Alliance for a Sustainable America; Founding mem. Colo Trail Foundation; mem. Bd of Advisors, Foundation for Defense of Democracies; has continued to speak publicly on environmental, immigration reduction, and health care issues; selected as one of TIME magazine's 200 Young Leaders of America 1974, winner Christian Science Monitor Peace 2020 essay 1985, selected by the Denver Post and Historic Denver, Inc. amongst the Colorado 100 1992, Humanist of the Year Award, American Humanist Asscn 1993. *Publications:* Population and the Law 1972, Some Reflections on the Balkanization of America 1978, Megatraumas: America at the Year 2000 1980, Energy Activities in the West 1980, The Angry West: A Vulnerable Land and Its Future (with Michael McCarthy) 1982, Campaign for Quality: An Education Agenda for the 80's 1983, Pioneers and Politicians: Ten Colorado Governors in Profile 1984, Copernican Politics 1984, The American West: A Poem 1985), Immigration Time Bomb: The Fragmenting of America 1985, 1988 (novel) (with Arnie Grossman) 1985, Megatraumas 1985, The Immigration Time Bomb 1985, The Lamm Administration: A Retrospective 1986, A California Conspiracy (with Arnold Grossman) 1988, Hard Choices 1989, Crisis: The Uncompetitive Society 1989, The Fall and Rise of the American Economy 1989, Indicators of Decline: An Article from The Futurist 1993, The Supply Factor in Health Care Cost Containment 1993, The Ethics of Excess: An Article from The Hastings Center Report 1994, Health Care Workforce Reform: An Article from State Legislatures 1994, The West at Risk 1994, Futurizing America's Institutions: An Article from The Futurist 1996, The Price of Modern Medicine 1997, Mountains of Colorado 1999, Government Does, Indeed, Ration Health Care: An Article from State Legislatures 1999, Redrawing the Ethics Map: An Article from The Hastings Center Report 1999, Vision for a Compassionate and Affordable Health System 2001, Brave New World of Health Care 2003, The Brave New World of Health Care 2004, The Challenge of an Aging Society: The Future of U.S. Health Care 2005, Two Wands, One Nation: An Essay on Race and Community in America 2006, Condition Critical: A New Moral Vision of Health Care 2007. *Leisure interests:* mountain climbing, reading, bicycling. *Address:* Institute for Public Policy Studies, University of Denver, Mary Reed Building 107, 2199 South University Blvd, Denver, CO 80208, USA (office). *Telephone:* (303) 871-2468 (office). *Fax:* (303) 871-3066 (office). *E-mail:* ipps@du .edu (office). *Website:* www.du.edu/ahss/ipps (office).

LAMM, Vanda Éva, PhD, DSc; Hungarian professor of international law and international legal official; *Director, Institute for Legal Studies, Hungarian Academy of Sciences;* b. 26 March 1945, Budapest; d. of Robert T. Lamm and Hedvig Lamm (née Vandel); ed Univ. of Budapest, Faculté int. pour l'enseignement du droit comparé, Strasbourg, France, Hague Acad. of Int. Law, Netherlands, Columbia Univ., USA; Research Fellow, Inst. for Legal Studies, Hungarian Acad. of Sciences, Dir 1991–; Prof. of Int. Law Univ. of Miskolc 1998, Univ. of Budapest-Győr; Head, Dept of Int. Law, Széchenyi István Univ.; mem. Perm. Court of Arbitration 1999–; Deputy mem. Court of Arbitration of OSCE; mem. UN CEDAW Cttee monitoring implementation of 1979 Convention on Elimination of Discrimination against Women; Pres. Int. Nuclear Law Asscn 2000–01, Hon. Pres. and mem. Bd of Man. 2004–05; Sec.-Gen. Hungarian Br., Int. Law Asscn; Vice-Chair. Group of Governmental Experts on Third Party Liability, OECD-NEA; Assoc. mem. Inst. of Int. Law 2001–; Ed.-in-Chief Allam-és Jogtudomány; Ed. Acta Juridica Hungarica; mem. European Acad. of Sciences and Arts. *Publications:* numerous publs on nuclear law and int. law. *Address:* Institute for Legal Studies, Hungarian Academy of Sciences, PO Box 25, I. Országház u. 30, 1250 Budapest (office); Department of International Law, Széchenyi István University, Egyetem tér 1, 9026 Győr, Hungary. *Telephone:* (1) 355-7384 (office); (96) 503-478. *Fax:* (1) 375-7858 (office); (96) 503-400/3535. *E-mail:* lamm@jog.mta.hu (office); lammv@ mail.sze.hu. *Website:* www.mta-ius.hu (office).

LAMO DE ESPINOSA Y MICHELS DE CHAMPOURCÍN, Jaime, Marqués de Mirasol and Barón de Frignani y Frignestani; Spanish agronomic engineer, academic, national organization official and fmr politician; *Chairman, Asociación Nacional de Constructores Independientes;* b. 4 April 1941, Madrid; s. of Emilio Lamo de Espinosa y Enríquez de Navarra and María Luisa Michels de Champourcín; m. Carmen Rocamora 1965; four d.; ed Colegio de Nuestra Señora del Pilar, Escuela Técnica Superior de Ingenieros Agrónomos, Univ. of Madrid; Asst Engineer, Study Group, Servicio Nacional de Concentración Parcelaria 1964–69; Tech. Dir Fondo de Ordenación y Regulación de Productos y Precios Agrarios (FORPPA) 1969–73; Sub-commissar for Devt Plan 1973; Dir of Tech. Cttee, Ministry of Agric. 1974; Dir-Gen. Food Industries 1974–76; Under-Sec. of Agric. 1976; Asst to Third Vice-Pres. of Govt 1977–78; Minister of Agric. and Fisheries 1978–81; Minister Asst to Pres. Council of Ministers 1981–82; mem. Congress of Deputies for Castellón 1979–82; mem. Unión de Centro Democrático (UCD); Chief UCD spokesman in Congress 1981–82; briefly mem. Partido Liberal 1986; Pres. 20th FAO World Conf. 1979–81; Pres. Conf. of OECD Ministers of Agric. 1980; Prof., Int. Centre for Advanced Mediterranean Agronomic Studies, Montpellier, France (OECD) 1980; fmr Prof. of Econs, School of Agricultural Eng, Univ. of Valencia; fmr Prof. of Econs and Politics, School of Agricultural Eng, Polytechnic Univ. of Madrid; EC Jean Monnet Chair 1991; apptd adviser to the Pres. of the Generalidad Valenciana 1995; Chair. Asociación Nacional de Constructores Independientes 2004–; mem. Social Council of Universidad Jaime I de Castellón; mem. Bd of Dirs of several cos; Gran Cruz del Mérito Agrícola, Gran Cruz del Mérito Civil, Encomienda del Mérito Agrícola, Cross of Merit (FRG), Croix du Mérite Civil (France), Gran Cruz de la Orden de Isabel la Católica 2002; King Jaime I Prize for Econs 1999. *Publications:* Agricultura a tiempo parcial y minifundios, Reflexiones sobre la política de precios y su armonización con la política general agraria, Los latifundios y el desarrollo agrario, Interrelación de las políticas de precio y de estructura en la agricultura, La agricultura en una sociedad democrática, El sistema de cuotas lácteas (co-author) 1996, La década perdida: 1985–1996 (La agricultura española en la UE) 1998, La nueva política agraria común 1998, Agricultura sostenible 1999, Los problemas actuales de la contratación de obras públicas (co-author) 2000. *Leisure interests:* reading, music, painting. *Address:* Asociación Nacional de Constructores Independientes, Pº de la Castellana 119, 2º dcha. Madrid 28046 (office); José Abascal 46, Madrid, Spain. *Telephone:* (91) 5550539 (office); (91) 5554005 (office); 4413415. *E-mail:* anci@ ancisa.com (office). *Website:* www.ancisa.com (office).

LAMONT, Donald Alexander, MA; British diplomatist (retd); b. 13 Jan. 1947; s. of Alexander Lamont and Alexa Lee Will; m. Lynda Margaret Campbell 1981; one s. one d.; ed Univ. of Aberdeen; with British Leyland Motor Corpn 1970; Second Sec., then First Sec. FCO 1974; First Sec., UNIDO/IAEA, Vienna 1977; First Sec. (Commercial), Embassy in Moscow 1980; First Sec., FCO 1982; Counsellor on secondment to IISS 1988; Political Adviser and Head of Chancery, British Mil. Govt, Berlin 1988–91; Amb. to Uruguay 1991–94; Head of Repub. of Ireland Dept, FCO 1994–97; Chief of Staff and Deputy High Rep., Sarajevo 1997–99; Gov. of Falkland Islands and Commr for S Georgia and S Sandwich Islands 1999–2002; Amb. to Venezuela 2003–07; CEO Wilton Park (FCO conference unit) 2007–09; mem. Bd of Dirs Sistema Scotland.

LAMONT OF LERWICK, Baron (Life Peer), cr. 1998, of Lerwick in the Shetland Islands; **Rt Hon. Norman Stewart Hughson Lamont,** PC; British politician and writer; b. 8 May 1942, Lerwick, Shetland, Scotland; s. of the late Daniel Lamont and of Helen Irene Hughson; m. Alice Rosemary White 1971 (separated 1999); one s. one d.; ed Loretto School, Fitzwilliam Coll., Cambridge; personal Asst to Rt Hon Duncan Sandys MP 1965; mem. staff Conservative Research Dept 1966–68; MP for Kingston upon Thames 1972–97; Merchant Banker with NM Rothschild & Sons 1968–79, Dir Rothschild Asset Man.; Parl. Pvt. Sec. to Norman St John Stevas (Lord St John of Fawsley) 1974; Opposition Spokesman on Prices and Consumer Affairs 1975–76, on Industry 1976–79; Parl. Under-Sec. of State, Dept of Energy 1979–81; Minister of State, Dept of Trade and Industry 1981–85, of Defence Procurement 1985–86; Financial Sec. to Treasury 1986–89, Chief Sec. 1989–90; Chancellor of the Exchequer 1990–93; Chair. Conservatives Against a Fed. Europe 1998–99; Chair. East European Food Fund 1995–; Chair. Bruges Group 2003–; mem. House of Lords Select Cttee on EU 2001–03; Dir (non-exec.) N.M. Rothschild & Sons Ltd 1993–95; Dir Balli Group, Scottish Re Group, RAB Capital; Adviser, Rotch Property Group; Chair. Cambridge Univ. Conservative Asscn 1963; Pres. Cambridge Union 1964. *Publication:* Sovereign Britain 1995, In Office 1999. *Leisure interests:* ornithology, theatre, literature. *Address:* House of Lords, Westminster, London, SW1A 0PW (office); c/o Balli Group PLC, 5 Stanhope Gate, London, W1Y 5LA, England. *Telephone:* (20) 7306-2138 (office). *E-mail:* catherinep@balli.co.uk (office).

LAMOTHE, Laurent Salvador, BSc, MBA; Haitian business executive and politician; *Prime Minister;* b. 14 Aug. 1972, Port-au-Prince; s. of Louis G. Lamothe and Ghislaine Fortuney Lamothe; m.; two d.; ed Barry Univ., Miami, St Thomas Univ.; co-f. Global Voice Group (int. telecoms co.) 1998, CEO –2011; mem. Interim Haiti Recovery Comm. 2011; involved with electoral campaign of Michel Martelly 2011, Special Adviser to Pres. Michel Martelly 2011; Minister of Foreign Affairs 2011–12, Prime Minister May 2012–, also Minister of Planning and External Co-operation Aug. 2010–; Co-Chair. (with fmr US Pres. Bill Clinton) Presidential Advisory Council for Econ. Devt and Investment in Haiti 2011; Ernst and Young Entrepreneur of the Year Award 2008. *Leisure interest:* tennis (represented Haiti in Davis Cup 1994 and 1995). *Address:* Office of the Prime Minister, Villa d'Accueil, 1 rue Prosper, Musseau, Port-au-Prince, Haiti (office). *Telephone:* 2228-6000 (office). *E-mail:* primature@primature.gouv.ht (office). *Website:* www .primature.gouv.ht (office); www.laurentlamothe.com.

LAMOUR, Jean-François; French government official and fmr fencer; b. 2 Feb. 1956; fmr sabre fencer; Silver Medal (team), Gold Medal (individual) LA Olympics 1984; Gold Medal (individual) Seoul Olympics 1988; Bronze Medal (team) Barcelona Olympics 1992; World Champion Lausanne 1987; Adviser on Youth and Sports, Office of the Mayor of Paris 1993–95, to the Presidency 1995; Minister of Youth, Sports and Social Asscns –2007. *Address:* c/o Ministry of Youth, Sports and Social Associations, 95 ave de France, 75650 Paris Cédex 13, France (office).

LAMPERT, Edward (Eddie) S., BEcons; American retail executive; *Chairman and CEO, Sears Holdings Corporation;* b. 1963, Greenwich, Conn.; m. Kinga Lampert 2001; one d.; ed Yale Univ.; sales and training internship Goldman Sachs & Co. 1984, held positions in Risk Arbitrage Dept 1985–88; Founding Chair. and

CEO ESL Investments Inc. (pvt. investment fund), Greenwich, Conn. 1988–; Chair. Kmart Holding Corpn 2003–, then Sears Holdings Corpn (after merger of Kmart Holding and Sears, Roebuck 2005), CEO 2013–; mem. Bd of Dirs AutoNation Inc., AutoZone Inc. *Address:* Sears Holdings Corpn, 3333 Beverly Road, Hoffman Estates, IL 60179 (office); ESL Investments, 200 Greenwich Avenue, Greenwich, CT 06830, USA. *Telephone:* (847) 286-2500 (office). *Fax:* (847) 286-7829 (office). *E-mail:* info@searshc.com (office). *Website:* www.searshc.com (office).

LAMRANI, Mohammed Karim (see KARIM-LAMRANI, Mohammed).

LAMY, Pascal Lucien Fernand, MBA; French civil servant and international organization official; *Honorary President, Jacques Delors Institute, Notre Europe;* b. 8 April 1947, Levallois-Perret (Seine); s. of Jacques Lamy and Denise Dujardin; m. Geneviève Luchaire 1972; three s.; ed Lycée Carnot, Paris, Ecole des Hautes Etudes Commerciales, Paris, Inst. d'Etudes Politiques, Ecole Nationale d'Admin, Paris; Lt Commdr (navy); served in Inspection Générale des Finances 1975–79; Sec.-Gen. Mayoux Cttee 1979; Deputy Sec.-Gen., then Sec.-Gen. Inter-ministerial Cttee for the Remodelling of Industrial Structures (CIASI) Treasury Dept 1979–81; Tech. Adviser, then Deputy Dir Office of the Minister for Econ. and Financial Affairs 1981–82; Deputy Dir Office of the Prime Minister (Pierre Mauroy) 1983–84; Chef de Cabinet to Pres. of Comm. of EC (Jacques Delors) 1984–94; Dir-Gen. and mem. Exec. Cttee Crédit Lyonnais 1994–99; Commr for Trade, European Comm. 1999–2004; Pres. Jacques Delors Inst., Notre Europe 2004–05, Hon. Pres. 2005–; apptd Assoc. Prof., Institut d'Etudes Politiques, Paris 2004; Dir-Gen. WTO 2005–13; Officier, Légion d'honneur 1990, Kt Commdr's Cross (Badge and Star) of the Order of Merit (Germany) 1991, Commdr Order of Merit (Luxembourg) 1995, Officer of the Order of Merit (Gabon) 2000, Order of the Aztec Eagle (Mexico) 2003, Order of Merit (Chile) 2004, Commdr, Légion d'honneur 2013; Dr hc (Louvain) 2003, (Geneva) 2009, (Montreal) 2010, (Dhaka) 2012; Global Economy Prize, Kiel Inst. 2010. *Publications include:* Report on Welfare Assistance for Children (co-author) 1979, Report on "Monde-Europe" (XI Plan of the Commissariat Général au Plan) 1993, L'Europe en première ligne 2002, L'Europe de nos volontés (co-author) 2002, La démocratie monde 2004. *Leisure interests:* Nordic skiing, jogging, marathon running. *Address:* Jacques Delors Institute, Notre Europe, 19, rue de Milan, 75009 Paris, France (office). *Telephone:* 1-44-58-97-97 (office). *Fax:* 1-44-58-97-99 (office). *Website:* www.eng.notre-europe .eu (office).

LAN, Lijun, BA, MPA; Chinese diplomatist; b. 5 Dec. 1952, Jiangsu Prov.; m. Gu Langlin; one d.; ed Beijing Foreign Languages Inst., Queen's Univ. and McGill Univ., Canada, Kennedy School of Govt, Harvard Univ., USA; Deputy Dir-Gen. Dept of N American and Oceanian Affairs, Ministry of Foreign Affairs 1996–2000, Consul Gen., with rank of Amb., Consulate Gen. in Los Angeles and Minister at Embassy in Washington, DC 2002–05, Amb. to Indonesia 2005–08, to Canada 2009–11, to Sweden 2011–13. *Address:* Ministry of Foreign Affairs, 2 Chao Yang Men Nan Dajie, Chao Yang Qu, Beijing 100701, People's Republic of China (office). *Telephone:* (10) 65961114 (office). *E-mail:* webmaster@mfa.gov.cn (office). *Website:* www.fmprc.gov.cn (office).

LANCASTER, (Christopher Ronald) Mark, BA; British/American artist and set designer; b. 14 May 1938, Holmfirth, W Yorks., England; s. of Charles Ronald Lancaster and Muriel Roebuck; m. David Bolger; ed Holme Valley Grammar School, Bootham School, York, Newcastle Univ.; asst to Andy Warhol, New York 1964; Lecturer, Newcastle Univ. 1965–66, Bath Acad. of Art 1966–68; Artist in Residence, King's Coll., Cambridge 1968–70; moved to USA permanently 1973; Pvt. Sec. to Jasper Johns, New York 1974–85; Resident Designer, Merce Cunningham Dance Co., New York 1975–80, Prin. Designer and Artistic Adviser 1980–84, designed sets, costumes and lighting for dance works including Sounddance 1975, Rebus 1975, Torse 1976, Squaregame 1976, Fractions (both video and stage versions) 1977, Tango 1978, Roadrunners 1979, Duets, 1980, Tens with Shoes 1981, Gallopade 1981, Trails 1982, Quartet 1982, Roaratorio 1983, Inlets 2 1983, Fielding Sixes 1983, Pictures 1984, Doubles 1984, also designed Duets for the American Ballet Theatre 1982, Fielding Sixes for Ballet Rambert 1983 and Ballet Royal de Wallonie 1983, returned in 1988 to design Five Stone Wind in Berlin, Avignon and New York (Bessie Award, New York Dance and Performance Awards 1989), Neighbors 1991, Touchbase for Rambert Dance Company 1992 and Cunningham Company 1992, CRWDSPCR 1993 and new versions of Sounddance and Rune 1994; US citizen 1999; New York Dance and Performance Award 1989. *Address:* c/o Robert Rogal, Rogallery.com, 47-15 36th Street, Long Island City, NY 11101, USA. *Telephone:* (718) 937-0901. *Fax:* (718) 937-1206. *E-mail:* art@rogallery.com. *Website:* www.rogallery.com/Lancaster/ Lancaster-hm.htm.

LANCE, James Waldo, AO, CBE, MD, FRCP, FRACP, FAA; Australian neurologist and academic; *Professor Emeritus of Neurology, University of New South Wales;* b. 29 Oct. 1926, Wollongong, NSW; s. of Waldo Lance and Jessie Lance (née Stewart); m. Judith L. Logan 1957; one s. four d.; ed Geelong Grammar School, The King's School, Parramatta and Univ. of Sydney; Chair. Div. of Neurology, Prince Henry and Prince of Wales Hosps, Sydney 1961–91; Prof. of Neurology, Univ. of NSW 1975–91, Prof. Emer. 1992–; Pres. Australian Asscn of Neurologists 1978–81, Int. Headache Soc. 1987–89; Vice-Pres. Australian Acad. of Sciences 1984–85, World Fed. of Neurology 1991–93; Hon. DSc 1991; Harold G. Wolff Award of American Asscn for Study of Headache 1967, 1983. *Publications include:* Headache 1975, The Golden Trout 1978, A Physiological Approach to Clinical Neurology (with J. G. McLeod 1981), Introductory Neurology (with J. G. McLeod) 1995, The Mechanism and Management of Headache with P. J. Goadsby 1998, Migraine and Other Headaches (2nd edn) 2000. *Leisure interests:* swimming, trout fishing, travel. *Address:* Medicolegal Opinions, Level 8, 179 Elizabeth Street, Sydney, NSW 2000 (office); 54 Queen Street, Woollahra, NSW 2025, Australia (home). *Telephone:* (2) 8262-9536 (office); (2) 9362-1876 (home). *Fax:* (2) 9362-9782 (home). *E-mail:* jimlance@bigpond.com (home).

LANCE, Ryan M., BS; American oil engineer and business executive; *Chairman and CEO, ConocoPhillips Company;* ed Montana Tech, Butte; joined ARCO 1984, held various man., eng and operations positions, later Vice-Pres. of Western North Slope operations in Alaska (acquired by Phillips) –2001, Gen. Man. Lower 48 and Canadian operations for Phillips 2001–02, Vice-Pres. Lower 48 (upon merger with

Conoco) 2002–03, Pres. Asia Pacific Exploration and Production 2003–05, Pres. Downstream Strategy, Integration and Specialty Functions 2005–06, Sr Vice-Pres. Tech. and Major Projects 2006–07, Sr Vice-Pres. Tech. 2007–09, Pres., Exploration and Production – Asia, Africa, Middle East and Russia/Caspian 2007–09, Sr Vice-Pres., Exploration & Production – International 2009–12, Chair. and CEO ConocoPhillips 2012–; mem. Bd of Dirs Spindletop International, Montana Tech Foundation; mem. Energy Advisory Bd, Univ. of Houston; mem. Soc. of Petroleum Engineers. *Address:* ConocoPhillips Company, Conoco Center, 600 North Dairy Ashford, Houston, TX 77079-1175, USA (office). *Telephone:* (281) 293-1000 (office). *Fax:* (281) 293-1440 (office). *E-mail:* info@conocophillips.com (office). *Website:* www .conocophillips.com (office).

LANCELOT, Alain, DèsSc et LHum; French political scientist and academic; *Professor Emeritus, Institut d'Etudes Politiques, Paris;* b. 12 Jan. 1937, Chêne-Bougeries, Geneva, Switzerland; s. of Elisée Lancelot and Suzanne Perrin-Lancelot; m. Marie Thé Merlet 1958; one s. one d.; ed Inst. d'Etudes Politiques, Paris and Univ. of Paris-Sorbonne; Asst French Political Science Asscn 1959–62, Sec.-Gen. 1970–75; naval service 1962–63; Researcher, CNRS 1963–67; Prof. Inst. d'Etudes Politiques, Paris 1967–99, Prof. Emer. 1999–; Dir Centre for Study of French Political Life 1975–86; Dir Inst. d'Etudes Politiques de Paris and Exec. Officer Fondation Nat. des Sciences Politiques 1987–96, mem. Bd 2001–; Pres. Observatoire Interrégional du Politique; mem. Conseil Constitutionnel 1996–2001, Council for Democratic Elections 2002–, Bd Fondation Robert Schuman 2003–; substitute mem. Venice Comm. for Democracy Through Law 2002–; Grand Officier, Légion d'honneur, Officier Ordre Nat. du Mérite, des Arts et des Lettres, des Palmes Académiques; decorations from Germany and Italy. *Publications:* L'abstentionnisme électoral en France 1968, La vie politique en France depuis 1940 1975, Les élections sous la cinquième république 1983. *Leisure interest:* sailing. *Address:* Fondation Nationale des Sciences Politiques, 27 rue Saint-Guillaume, 75007 Paris (office); 4 ter rue du Cherche-Midi, 75006 Paris, France (home). *Telephone:* 1-45-49-50-50 (office). *Website:* www.sciences-po.fr (office).

LANCI, Gianfranco; Italian business executive; *Consultant, Lenovo Group;* b. 1954, Turin; m.; several c.; ed Politecnico of Turin; joined Texas Instruments (TI) Italia 1981, Country Man. for Portable Computers and Printers Div. in Italy, Middle East and Africa 1991–96, Pres. Europe, Middle East, Africa (EMEA) for TI's Personal Productivity Products Div. 1996–97, Man. Dir Acer Italy (following merger of TI's portable PC business with Acer in 1997) 1997–2000, Pres. Acer Europe 2000–02, Pres. Acer EMEA 2002–03, Pres. Acer's Int. Operations Business Group 2003–04, Pres. Acer Inc. 2005–11, CEO 2008–11; consultant, Lenovo 2011–. *Leisure interests:* reading, playing tennis. *Address:* Lenovo Group, 6 Shangdi West Roade, Haidan District, Beijing 100085, People's Republic of China (office). *Telephone:* (10) 58868888 (office). *E-mail:* info@lenovo.com (office). *Website:* www .lenovo.com (office).

LAND, Michael Francis, MA, PhD, FRS; British neurobiologist and academic; *Professor of Neurobiology, University of Sussex;* b. 12 April 1942, Dartmouth, Devon, England; s. of the late Prof. F. W. Land and of Mrs N. B. Land; m. 1st Judith Drinkwater 1966 (divorced 1980), one s.; m. 2nd Rosemary Roper 1980; two d.; ed Birkenhead School, Jesus Coll. Cambridge, Univ. Coll. London and Univ. of California, Berkeley (Miller Fellowship); Asst Prof., Univ. of California, Berkeley 1969–71; Lecturer, School of Biological Sciences, Univ. of Sussex 1971–77, Reader 1977–84, Prof. of Neurobiology 1984–; Fellow, Univ. Coll. London 1998; Visiting Prof., Univ. of Ore. 1980; Sr Visiting Fellow, ANU 1982–84; Foreign mem. Royal Physiographical Soc., Sweden 1995; Frank Smart Prize in Zoology, Cambridge 1963, ALCON Prize for Vision Research 1996, Rank Prize for Opto-electronics 1998, Frink Medal, Zoological Soc. of London 1994. *Publications include:* Animal Eyes (with D. E. Nilsson) 2002 (revised edn 2012), Looking and Acting (with B. W. Tatler) 2009; 190 articles and papers on aspects of vision in animals from visual optics to behaviour. *Leisure interests:* gardening, music. *Address:* School of Life Sciences, University of Sussex, Brighton, BN1 9QG (office); White House, Cuilfail, Lewes, BN7 2BE, England (home). *Telephone:* (1273) 678505 (office); (1273) 476780 (home). *Fax:* (1273) 678433 (office). *E-mail:* m.f.land@sussex.ac.uk (office). *Website:* www.sussex.ac.uk/lifesci (office).

LANDABURU ILLARRAMENDI, Eneko; Spanish international organization official; *Head of EU Delegation in Morocco;* b. 11 March 1948, Paris; s. of Francisco Javier Nicolas Landaburu and Prudencia Francisca Constantina Illarramendi; m. Dominique Rambaud 1971; two s. one d.; ed Univ. of Paris, France; mem. staff Admin. and Financial Man. Dept, Société Labaz, Paris 1971–73, Asst to Man. Belgian subsidiary SA Labaz NV, Brussels 1973–75; Head of Study and Lecture Programmes, Centre Européen d'Etudes et d'Information sur les Sociétés Multi-nationales (CEEIM), Brussels 1975–79; PSOE Deputy, Spanish Basque Regional Parl. 1980–81; Adviser to Latin American Dept, Nestlé, Vevey, Switzerland 1981–82; Dir Institut de Recherche sur les Multinationales (IRM), Geneva, Switzerland 1983–86; Dir-Gen. for Regional Politics, European Comm., Brussels 1986–2000, for Enlargement (later External Relations) 2000–09; Head, EU Del. to Morocco 2009–; Lecturer, Institut d'Etudes Européennes, Free Univ. of Brussels 1990–94; Alt. mem. Bd of Dirs of EIB 1993–; mem. Supervisory Bd European Investment Fund FEI-EIF 1994–; mem. Bd of Dirs Fondation 'Notre Europe' 1996–. *Address:* Délégation de la Commission Européenne, RIAD Business Center Aile Sud, Boulevard Er-Riad Quartier Hay Riad, Boîte Postale 1302, Rabat, Morocco (office); Avenue Brugmann 125, 1190 Brussels, Belgium (home). *Telephone:* (0) 537-57-98-00 (office). *Fax:* (0) 537-57-98-10 (office). *E-mail:* delegation -morocco@ec.europa.eu (office). *Website:* www.delmar.ec.europa.eu (office).

LANDAU, Igor, MBA; French business executive; b. 13 July 1944, Saint-Flour, Cantal; ed Hautes Etudes Commerciales, Institut Européen d'Admin des Affaires (INSEAD); Pres. La Compagnie du Roneo (German subsidiary), Frankfurt 1968–70; consultant, McKinsey Co., Paris 1971–75; Deputy to Pres. of Health Div., Rhône-Poulenc Inc. 1975, Exec. Vice-Pres. of Div. 1977–80, Chair. Health Sector 1987, mem. Exec. Cttee 1987, Group Pres. 1992, mem. Bd of Dirs 1998; mem. Man. Bd Aventis 1999–2002, Chair. Man. Bd 2000–, Chair. Supervisory Bd Aventis Pharma AG 1999–2002, mem. Bd of Dirs Sanofi-Aventis 2004–; Pres. Supervisory Bd Centre Européen d'Educ. Perm.; mem. Institut pour le Dével-oppement Industrial; mem. Bd Dirs Essilor. *Address:* Sanofi-Aventis, 174 avenue

de France, 75013 Paris, France (office). *Telephone:* 1-53-77-44-50 (office). *Fax:* 1-53-77-46-22 (office). *Website:* www.sanofi-aventis.com (office).

LANDAU, Jean-Pierre; French economist; *Second Deputy Governor, Banque de France;* b. 7 Nov. 1946, Paris; s. of André Landau and Andrée Pestre; m. Evelyne Dova 1979; ed Inst. d'études politiques de Paris, Ecole nat. d'admin; served in Ministry of Health and Social Security 1978–79; Asst Sec. for Trade Policy, Direction des Relations Economiques Extérieures 1986–89, various other positions in Ministry of Econ. and Finance; Exec. Dir IMF 1989–93; Dir Relations Economiques Extérieures (DREE) 1993–96; Dir-Gen. French Asscn of Banks 1999–2000; Financial Counsellor, French Embassy in UK 2001–06; Dir EBRD 2001–06; Second Deputy Gov. and mem. Gen. Council Banque de France 2006–, Chair. Credit Insts and Investment Firms Cttee, Supervisory Bd Institut d'émission des départements d'Outre-Mer, mem. Supervisory Bd Caisse des dépôts et consignations; fmr Teacher of Econs, Inst. d'études politiques; fmr mem. of Bd, Renault. *Address:* Banque de France, 31 rue Croix des Petits Champs, 75001 Paris (office); 13 rue de l'Odéon, 75006 Paris, France. *Telephone:* 1-42-92-42-92 (office). *E-mail:* infos@banque-france.fr (office). *Website:* www.banque-france.fr (office).

LANDAU, Peter, DJur; German professor of law and research institute director; *President, Stephan Kuttner Institute of Medieval Canon Law;* b. 26 Feb. 1935, Berlin; m. Angelika Linnemann 1971; one s. one d.; ed Univs of Berlin, Freiburg, Bonn and Yale Univ., USA; Prof., Univ. of Regensburg 1968–87; Prof. of Law, Univ. of Munich 1987–2003, Prof. Emer. 2003–, Pres. Stephan Kuttner Inst. of Medieval Canon Law; mem. Inst. for Advanced Study, Princeton, USA 1990–91; mem. Bayerische Akad. der Wissenschaften; Corresp. mem. Medieval Acad. of America, Accad. Senese degli Intronati; Hon. DrIur (Basel) 1981; Dr hc (Munich) 1997, (Paris) 2001, (Panthéon-Assas Univ.). *Publications:* Die Entstehung des kanonischen Infamiebegriffs von Gratian bis zur Glossa ordinaria. Forschungen zur kirchlichen Rechtsgeschichte und zum Kirchenrecht Bd 5 1966, Ius Patron-atus 1975, Strafrecht, Strafprozess und Rezeption (co-ed.) 1984, Officium und Libertas christiana 1991, Heinrich Mitteis nach hundert Jahren (1889–1989) 1991, Stufen der Gerechtigkeit 1995, Proceedings of the 9th International Congress of Medieval Canon Law, Munich, July 13–18, 1992 1997, Kanones und Dekretalen 1997, Karl von Amira zum Gedächtnis 1999, Große jüdische Gelehrte an der Münchener Juristischen Fakultät 2000, Recht und Politik in Bayern zwischen Prinzregentenzeit und Nationalsozialismus (co-ed.) 2004, Magistri Honorii Summa 'De iure canonico tractaturus' I (Monumenta Iuris Canonici, Ser. A, Vol. 5) 2004, Die Lex Baiuvariorum. Entstehungszeit, Entstehungsort und Charakter von Bayerns ältester Rechts- und Geschichtsquelle 2004, Goethes verlorene juristische Dissertation und ihre Quellen. Versuch einer Rekonstruktion 2007, Die Collectio Francofurtana: Eine französische Decretalensammlung. Analyse beruhend auf Vorarbeiten von Walther Holtzmann (Monumenta Iuris Canonici, Series B, Vol. 9) (co-ed.) 2007, Summa 'Omnis qui iuste iudicat' sive lipsiensis. Tom. I (Monumenta Iuris Canonici, Series A, Vol. 7/I) 2007, Die Kölner Kanonistik des 12. Jahrhunderts; Ein Höhepunkt der europäischen Rechtswis-senschaft. In: Kölner Rechtsgeschichtliche Vorträge, Heft 1 2008, Grundlagen und Geschichte des evangelischen Kirchenrechts und des Staatskirchenrechts 2010, Magistri Honorii Summa 'De iure canonico tractaturus', Tom. II (Monumenta Iuris Canonici, Series A, Corpus Glossatorum 5/II) (co-ed.) 2010, Magistri Honorii Summa 'De iure canonico tractaturus', Tom. III (Monumenta Iuris Canonici, Series A, Corpus Glossatorum 5/III) (co-ed.) 2010, Der Archipoeta – Deutschlands erster Dichterjurist. Neues zur Identifizierung des politischen Poeten der Barbarossazeit 2011, Canon Law, Religion and Politics. Liber Amicorum Robert Sommerville (co-ed.) 2012, Summa 'Omnis qui iuste iudicat' sive Lipsiensis', Tom. 7/II (co-ed.) 2012, Europäische Rechtsgeschichte und kanonisches Recht im Mittelalter 2013; numerous essays and reviews. *Leisure interest:* art. *Address:* Stephan Kuttner Institute of Medieval Canon Law, Professor-Huber-Platz 2, 80539 Munich (office); Sperberstr. 21C, 81827 Munich, Germany (home). *Tele-phone:* (89) 21802122 (office); (89) 21801370 (office); (89) 4300121 (home). *Fax:* (89) 21802714 (office). *E-mail:* peter.landau@jura.uni-muenchen.de (office). *Website:* www.jura.uni-muenchen.de/personen/l/landau_peter/index.html (office) (office); .kuttner-institute.jura.uni-muenchen.de (office).

LANDAU, Uzi, PhD; Israeli systems analyst and politician; *Minister of Tourism;* b. 1943, Haifa; m.; three c.; ed Haifa Technion, Massachusetts Inst. of Tech., USA; served as paratrooper officer during mil. service; mem. Knesset (Likud Party) 1984–2006, (Israel Beytenu) 2008–, Chair. Foreign Affairs and Defense Cttee, State Control Cttee; Knesset Observer at the European Council; mem. Israeli Del. to Madrid Peace Conf.; Observer at the European Council; Minister of Public Security 2001–03, of Nat. Infrastructure 2008–13, of Tourism 2013–; fmr Minister in charge of overseeing the intelligence services and the US–Israel strategic dialogue in the Prime Minister's Office; Dir-Gen. Ministry of Transport; Lecturer, Israel Inst. of Tech. (Technion), Haifa; mem. Bd El-Al Airlines, Israel Port Authority, Israel Airport Authority, Soc. for the Protection of Nature, Si'ah Vasig (Israel Debating Soc.). *Publications:* articles in professional journals on transport planning, articles in the press on foreign policy, strategic and security affairs. *Address:* Ministry of Tourism, POB 1018, 5 Bank of Israel Street, Jerusalem 91009 (office); The Knesset, Jerusalem 91181, Israel. *Telephone:* 2-6664331 (office). *Fax:* 2-6514629 (office). *E-mail:* sarb@tourism.gov.il (office); klandau@knesset.gov.il (office). *Website:* www.tourism.gov.il (office).

LANDEL, Michel; French business executive; *Group CEO, Sodexo SA;* b. 1951; m.; three c.; ed European Business School, Paris; Gen. Man. Poliet Group 1980–84; Chief Operating Man. for E and N Africa, Sodexho (renamed Sodexho Alliance SA 1997, renamed Sodexo SA 2008) 1984–86, Pres. Group Remote Site Operations, Africa 1986–89, Head of N American Operations 1989–99, CEO Sodexho Inc. 1989–2000, Vice-Chair. Exec. Cttee, Sodexho Alliance SA 2000–03, COO Sodexho Alliance SA 2003–05, Group CEO 2005–, Pres. Group Exec. Cttee, Pres. Sodexo STOP Hunger Asscn; Golden Chain Award for Multi-Unit Food Service Operators 1997, Ivy Award for Restaurant & Institutions 1998, Penn State Hotel and Restaurant Soc. Hospitality Exec. of the Year 2002, Diversity Best Practice CEO Leadership Award, Asian Enterprise CEO Advocate of the Year 2004. *Leisure interests:* travel, relaxing in the kitchen preparing delicious and unique dishes for family and friends. *Address:* Sodexo SA, 255 quai de la Bataille de Stalingrad, 92130 Issy-les-Moulineaux, France (office). *Telephone:* 1-30-85-75-00 (office). *Fax:*

1-30-43-09-58 (office). *E-mail:* info@sodexho.com (office). *Website:* www.sodexho .com (office).

LANDER, Eric S., DPhil; American biologist and academic; *Director, The Broad Institute;* b. 3 Feb. 1957, Brooklyn, NY; ed Princeton Univ. and Univ. of Oxford, UK (Rhodes Scholar); taught econs to business students at Harvard Univ., Prof. of Systems Biology, Harvard Medical School; Fellow, Whitehead Inst. for Biomedical Research MIT 1985–89, f. Center for Genome Research at MIT 1990, fmr Assoc. Prof. of Biology, now Prof. of Biology and Dir Whitehead Inst. for Biomedical Research/MIT Center for Genome Research, Founding Dir The Broad Inst. 2003–; Co-Chair. Council of Advisors on Science and Technology in the Obama administration 2008–; mem. Advisory Bd USA Science and Eng Festival; serves on numerous govt advisory cttees; Founder and Dir Millennium Pharmaceuticals; fmr Chair. Jt Steering Cttee for Public Policy; Fellow, American Acad. of Arts and Sciences 1990; MacArthur Fellowship 1987, J. Allyn Taylor Int. Prize in Medicine, John P. Robarts Research Inst. (co-recipient) 2001, named to the TIME 100 2004, Harvey Prize, Technion Israel 2012, Dan David Prize 2012, Breakthrough Prize in Life Sciences 2013. *Publications:* In Wake of Genetic Revolution, Questions About Its Meaning 2000; numerous articles in scientific journals; led group of bioinformatics specialists who produced an analysis of draft human genome for publication in Nature 2001. *Address:* Office of the Provost, NE125-2246, The Broad Institute, 320 Charles Street, Cambridge, MA 02141-2023, USA (office). *Telephone:* (617) 252-1906 (office); (617) 258-5192 (Whitehead Inst.) (office). *Fax:* (617) 258-0903 (office). *E-mail:* lander@broad.mit.edu (office); lander@genome.wi.mit .edu (office). *Website:* biology.mit.edu/people/eric_lander (office); www.broad.mit .edu (office).

LANDER, Sir Stephen James, Kt, KCB, CB, MA, PhD; British public servant; *Independent Commissioner, The Law Society;* m. Felicity Lander 1972; one s. (died 2002) one d.; ed Bishop's Stortford Coll., Herts., Queens' Coll., Cambridge Univ., with Inst. of Historical Research, London Univ. 1972–75; joined Security Service 1975–, Dir 1992–96, Dir-Gen. 1996–2002; Ind. Commr (overseeing complaints against solicitors) The Law Soc. 2002–; Dir (non exec.) HM Customs and Excise 2002–, Northgate Information Solutions 2004–; Chair. Serious and Organised Crime Agency (SOCA) 2004–. *Address:* The Law Society, 113 Chancery Lane, London, WC2A 1PL, England (office). *Telephone:* (1926) 822057 (office) *Fax:* (1926) 823140 (office). *Website:* www.lawsociety.org.uk (office).

LANDGREN, Karin, BSc, LLM; Swedish UN official and academic; *Special Representative of the Secretary-General and Head, Mission in Liberia (UNMIL) United Nations;* b. 13 Oct. 1957; two c.; ed London School of Econs, UK; grew up in Japan; spent nearly 20 years with UNHCR, worked extensively with Afghan, Iranian and Vietnamese asylum seekers as Protection Officer for UNHCR in India and as Deputy Rep. in the Philippines 1980s, headed UNHCR office in Bosnia-Herzegovina during the war 1990s, as well as offices in Eritrea and Singapore, later Chief of Standards and Legal Advice, UNHCR, Head of Child Protection, UNICEF 1998–2008, UN Deputy Special Rep. of Sec.-Gen. for Nepal 2008–09, UN Rep. for Nepal and Head of UN Mission in Nepal (UNMIN) 2009–10, Special Rep. and Head, UN Office in Burundi (BNUB) 2010, Special Rep. of Sec.-Gen. and Head of UN Mission in Liberia (UNMIL) 2012–; Corresp. Ed. International Legal Materials; mem. Editorial Bd Sec.-Gen.'s Study on Violence against Children 2006; Adjunct Prof., School of Int. and Public Affairs, Columbia Univ., New York, USA. *Publications include:* has published widely on humanitarian, refugee and child protection issues. *Address:* UNMIL, PO Box 4677, Grand Central Station, New York, NY 10163-4677, USA (office); UNMIL Headquarters, Pan African Plaza, Tubman Boulevard, 1st Street, Monrovia, Liberia. *Telephone:* (212) 963-9925 (New York) (office). *Website:* unmil.unmissions.org (office).

LANDRIEU, Mary L., BA; American politician; *Senator from Louisiana;* b. 23 Nov. 1955, Arlington, Va; d. Moon Landrieu; m. E. Frank Snellings; two c.; ed Ursuline Academy, New Orleans and Louisiana State Univ., Baton Rouge; Louisiana State Rep., Dist 90 1980–88, State Treas. 1986–96; Del. Democratic Nat. Convention 1980; cand. for Democratic gubernatorial nomination 1995; Senator from Louisiana 1997–; mem. Women Execs in State Govt, Fed. of Democratic Women. *Address:* 431 Dirksen Senate Office Building, Washington, DC 20510, USA (office). *Telephone:* (202) 224-5824 (office). *Fax:* (202) 224-9735 (office). *Website:* landrieu.senate.gov (office); www.marylandrieu.com (office).

LANDRY, Donald W., BS, PhD, MD; American professor of medicine; *Samuel Bard Professor of Medicine and Chairman, Department of Medicine, Columbia University College of Physicians and Surgeons;* b. 19 May 1954, Jersey City, NJ; s. of Donald O. Landry and Gloria A. Landry; m. Maureen O'Reilly Landry; two s.; ed Lafayette Coll., Harvard Univ., Columbia Univ.; Resident in Medicine, Massachusetts Gen. Hosp., Boston, Harvard Medical School 1983–85; Dir Div. of Experimental Therapeutics, Columbia Univ. Coll. of Physicians and Surgeons 1998–, Dir of Nephrology 2003–08, Chair. Dept of Medicine 2008–, currently Samuel Bard Prof. of Medicine; Physician-in-Chief, New York Presbyterian Hosp./ Columbia; mem. Pres.'s Council on Bioethics 2008–09; mem. American Soc. for Clinical Investigation, American Asscn of Physicians; Presidential Citizen's Medal 2009. *Publications include:* more than 160 articles in learned journals. *Address:* Columbia University College of Physicians and Surgeons, Presbyterian Hospital, Room 8 East, 105 622 West 168th Street, New York, NY 10032, USA (office). *Telephone:* (212) 305-5839 (office). *E-mail:* dwl1@columbia.edu (office). *Website:* asp.cpmc.columbia.edu (office).

LANDSBERGIS, Vytautas, (Jonas Zemkalnis); Lithuanian politician, musicologist, pianist and fmr head of state; b. 18 Oct. 1932, Kaunas; s. of Vytautas Landsbergis-Zemkalnis and Ona Jablonskytė-Landsbergienė; m. Grazina Ručyte; one s. two d.; ed J. Gruodis School of Music, Kaunas, Aušra Gymnasium, Kaunas, Lithuanian Acad. of Music, Vilnius; teacher of piano and Prof. of Musicology, Vilnius Conservatoire, Vilnius Pedagogical Inst.; fmr mem. Exec. Council and Secr. Composers' Union; Pres. M.K. Čiurlionis Soc.; mem. various arts and science bodies; elected to Initiative Group, Sajūdis Reform Movt, then to Sajūdis Seimas (Ass.) and Council 1988, Pres. Sajūdis Seimas Council 1988–90, Hon. Pres. Sajūdis Dec. 1991–; f. Lithuanian Conservative Party, Chair. 1993–2003; elected Deputy to USSR Congress of People's Deputies 1989–90; elected to Supreme Council of Lithuania Feb. 1990, Pres. Supreme Council (Head of State) 1990–91; mem. Seimas (Parl.) 1992–2004, Leader of Parl. Opposition 1992–96, Pres. Seimas

1996–2000; cand. for presidential elections 1997; mem. European Parl. 2004–; Paul Harris Fellow (Rotary) 1991; Academician, Lithuanian Catholic Acad. 1997; gave concert at Moscow Conservatoire with Russian Nat. Acad. Symphonic Orchestra 1999; piano recitals in Calw, Hanover, Helsinki, Guangzhou, Moscow, New York, Paris, Tokyo, Trieste, Uznam, Vilnius, Warsaw, etc.; Hon. Fellow, Univ. of Cardiff, UK 2000; Hon. Citizen of Turin, Italy 2007; Grand Officer, European St Sebastian's Order of Kts 1995, Chevalier, Légion d'Honneur 1997, Order of Grand Duke Vytautas, First Class (Lithuania) 1998, Grand Cross, Royal Norwegian Order of Merit 1998, Grand Cross Order of the Repub. (Poland) 1999, Order of Merit (Grand Cross), Order of Malta 1999, Grand Cross, Order of Honour (Greece) 1999, Pléiade Ordre de la Francophonie (France) 2000, Three Stars Order (Second Class) (Latvia) 2001, Order of the Cross of St Mary's Land (First Class) (Estonia) 2002, Kt Grand Cross, Order of Orange-Nassau (Netherlands) 2008; Hon. LLD (Loyola Univ., Chicago) 1991; Hon. PhD (Vytautas the Great Univ., Kaunas) 1992, (Klaipėda Univ., Lithuania) 1997; Hon. HD (Weber Univ., USA) 1992; Hon. DIur (Lithuanian Acad. of Law) 2000; Dr hc (Helsinki) 2000, (Sorbonne) 2001, (Lithuanian Acad. of Art) 2003, (St Lucas Acad., Netherlands-Germany) 2004; Lithuanian State Award (for monograph on M. K. Čiurlionis) 1975; Norwegian People's Peace Prize (for role in restoration of Lithuanian independence; has used prize to establish Landsbergis Foundation to help disabled children and young musicians) 1991, Award of France Fund of Future 1991, Hermann-Ehlers Prize 1992, Catalan Ramon Llull IX Int. Prize 1994, Vibo Valentia Testimony Prize (Italy) 1998, Truman-Reagan Freedom Award (USA) 1999, Constitutional Medallion of Saxonian Parl. (Germany) 2003, Lithuanian Foundation Award 2004, Aschaffenburger Mutig-Preis, Germany 2004, Robert Schuman Medal, European Parl. 2005, Mérite Européen Medal (Luxembourg) 2006. *Recording:* Čiurlionis, Born of the Human Soul (works for solo piano) 1998. *Publications:* 24 books on musicology, art and music history (especially on artist and composer M. K. Čiurlionis) and politics, including M. K. Čiurlionis – Time and Content 1992, Lithuania Independent Again 2000; numerous edns of scores (mostly of works by M. K. Čiurlionis); M. K. Čiurlionis – Thoughts, Pictures, Music (film script) 1965; poetry collections: Intermezzo 1991, Intermezzo non finito 2004, Who Are We? (under pseudonym Jonas Zemkalnis) 2004, Glimmers of History 2006, It's Serious, Children (poems) 2006, memoirs, essays, Un peuple sort de prison 2007, Crossroad of Europe 2008. *Leisure interests:* history, poetry. *Address:* Traidenio Street 34–15, Vilnius 08116, Lithuania (office); European Parliament, Bâtiment Altiero Spinelli, 11E157, 60 rue Wiertz, 1047 Brussels, Belgium (office). *Telephone:* (52) 663676 (office); (52) 724466 (home); (2) 284-55-50 (Brussels) (home). *Fax:* (52) 663675 (office); (52) 790505 (home); (2) 284-95-50 (Brussels) (home). *E-mail:* vyland@lrs.lt (office); vytautas.landsbergis@europarl.europa.eu (office). *Website:* www .landsbergis.lt (office); www.europarl.europa.eu (office).

LANE, (Alan) Piers, AO, BMus, ARCM, LMusA, AMusA; British/Australian pianist, artistic director and broadcaster; b. 8 Jan. 1958, London, England; s. of Peter Alan Lane and Enid Muriel Hitchcock; ed Queensland Conservatorium of Music, Royal Coll. of Music, London; broadcaster for BBC Radio 3; critic CD Review; has appeared with numerous orchestras, including London Philharmonic, Philharmonia, Royal Philharmonic, all BBC orchestras, City of Birmingham Symphony, Halle, Australian Chamber Orchestra, all ABC orchestras, New Zealand Symphony Orchestra, Auckland Philharmonic, Christchurch Symphony, Southern Sinfonia, Orchestra Ensemble Kanazawa (Japan), Orchestre National de France, Orchestre Philharmonique de Montpellier, American Symphony Orchestra, Czech Philharmonic, Warsaw Philharmonic, Gothenberg Symphony; has toured extensively in Australia, Africa, Europe, India, Japan, NZ, Russia, Scandinavia, S America, USA; has appeared at festivals including Aldeburgh, Bard, BBC Promenade Concerts, Huntington, Husum Festival of Piano Rarities (Germany), Blair Atholl, Speedside, Toronto, Singapore Piano Festival, Newport Festival, Rhode Island, Duznicki Chopin Festival, Poland, Ruhr Piano Festival, Bergen Festival, Bridgewater Piano Festival, Manchester 2003, Bagatelles Chopin Festival, Paris; La Roque d'Anthéron, Storioni Festival (Netherlands), El Paso Promusica, Sitka Summer Music Festival, Alaska; Int. Adjudicator Tbilisi and Sydney Int. Piano Competitions; Prof., RAM 1989–2011; Dir Myra Hess Day Nat. Gallery 2006–, Australian Festival of Chamber Music 2007–; Dir and Trustee The Hattori Foundation; Patron, European Piano Teachers' Asscn (UK), The Old Granary Studio, Queensland Music Teachers' Asscn, Accompanists' Guild of Queensland, Youth Music Foundation of Australia, Tait Memorial Trust; Vice-Pres. Putney Music Club; Hon. ARAM 1994; Hon. DUniv (Griffith Univ.) 2007; Bartók Special Prize, Liszt Int. Competition, Budapest 1976, Best Australian Pianist, Sydney Int. Piano Competition 1977, Winner Royal Overseas League Competition 1982. *Recordings include:* Moskowski, Paderewski Concertos 1990, Complete Etudes of Scriabin 1992, Piano Quintet by Brahms (New Budapest Quartet) 1992, Violin Virtuoso (with Tasmin Little) 1992, Cello Sonatas (with Alexander Baillie) by Shostakovich, Prokofiev, Schnittke and Rachmaninoff, d'Albert Concertos 1994, Vaughan-Williams and Delius Concertos plus Finzi Eclogue 1994, Elgar Piano Quintet (with Vellinger String Quartet) 1994, Delius Violin Sonatas (with Tasmin Little) (Diapason d'Or) 1997, d'Albert Solo Piano Works 1997, Saint-Saëns Complete Etudes 1998, Kullak & Dreyschock Concertos (with Niklas Willen) 1999, Complete Scriabin Preludes 2000, Grainger Piano Transcriptions 2001, Bach Transcriptions 2002, Moscheles Etudes 2003, Henselt Etudes 2004, Stanford Quintet (with Vanburgh Quartet) 2004, Delius and Ireland Piano Concertos 2005, Alnaes and Sinding Concertos 2005, Bloch Piano Quintets (with Goldner String Quartet) 2008, Bridge Piano Quintet (with Goldner String Quartet) 2008, Dvořák Piano Quintets (with Goldner String Quartet) 2009, Bach/ d'Albert organ transcriptions 2010, Elgar Piano Quintet (with Goldner String Quartet) 2010, Virtuoso Clarinet (with Michael Collins) 2012, Harty Piano Quintet (with Goldner String Quartet) 2011, Strauss and Respighi Violin Sonatas (with Tasmin Little) 2012, Piers Lane Goes to Town 2013, Mozart Piano Concertos K482 and K491 (with Queensland Symphony) 2013, Walton and Ferguson Violin Sonatas (with Tasmin Little) 2013, Liszt/Berlioz Harold in Italy and Roger Viola Sonata (with Philip Dukes) 2013, Taneyev and Arensky Piano Quintets (with Goldner String Quartet) 2013. *Address:* c/o Hazard Chase, 25 City Road, Cambridge, CB1 1DP, England (office). *Telephone:* (1223) 312400 (office). *Fax:* (1223) 460827 (office). *E-mail:* sibylle.jackson@hazardchase.co.uk (office). *Website:* www.hazardchase.co.uk (office); www.pierslane.com.

LANE, Sir David Philip, Kt, PhD, FRS, FRSE, FRCPath, FRCSE, FMedSci; British oncologist and academic; *Professor of Molecular Oncology, University of Dundee;* b. 1 July 1952; s. of John Wallace Lane and Cecelia Frances Evelyn Wright; m. Prof. Ellen Birgitte Muldal 1975; one s. one d.; ed Univ. Coll., London; Research Fellow, Imperial Cancer Research Fund 1976–77, Staff Scientist 1985–90; Lecturer, Imperial Coll., London 1977–85; Prof. of Molecular Oncology, Univ. of Dundee 1990–, Dir Transformation Research Group, Cancer Research Campaign 1990–; Exec. Dir Agency for Science, Tech. and Research (A*STAR) Inst. of Molecular and Cell Biology, Singapore 2004–07, Chief Scientist and NUS Dept of Medicine Adjunct Prof. 2009–; first Chief Scientist, Cancer Research UK 2007–10; CEO Experimental Therapeutics Centre,Singapore 2007–09; Chair. Biomedical Research Council, Singapore 2007–09, Chugai Pharmabody Research Pte Ltd, Singapore 2012–; Visiting Fellow, Cold Spring Harbor Labs, NY, USA 1978–80; Gibb Fellow, Cancer Research UK; mem. European Molecular Biology Org. 1990; Co-founder Acad. of Medical Sciences 1998; Hon. DSc (Abertay, Dundee) 1999, (Stirling) 2000, (Aberdeen) 2002, (Birmingham) 2002, (Nottingham) 2006, (University Paul Sabatier, France) 2007, (Liverpool) 2010; Doctor of Laws honoris causa 2011 University of Dundee/ United Kingdom 2011; Charles Rodolphe Brubacher Foundation Prize 1993, Joseph Steiner Foundation Prize 1993, Yvette Mayent Prize, Inst. Curie 1994, Swedish Soc. of Oncology Medal 1994, Meyenberg Foundation Prize 1995, Silvanus Thompson Medal, British Inst. of Radiology 1996, Henry Dryerre Prize 1996, Paul Ehrlich Prize 1998, Tom Conors Prize 1998, Bruce Preller Prize 1998, Soc. of Chemical Industry Medal 2003, Buchanan Medal, Royal Soc. 2004, Biochemistry Soc. Medal 2004, Anthony Dipple Carcinogenesis Award, EACR International 2004, Sergio Lombroso Award in Cancer Research, Weizmann Inst. of Science 2005, Int. Agency for Research on Cancer Medal (France) 2005, Inserm Award (France) 2006, David Hungerford Lecture Medal, Bangalore 2007, Asscn for Int. Cancer Research Colin Thomson Memorial Medal Lecturer, Beatson Inst. for Cancer Research, UK 2007, Gregor Mendel Memorial Medal, Brno, Czech Repub. 2007, Royal Medal, Royal Soc. of Edinburgh 2008, Datta Medal, Fed. of European Biochemical Socs 2009, Extraordinary Prof. to the TEFAF Oncology Chair (Netherlands) 2011, Lifetime Achievement Award, Cancer Research UK 2012. *Address:* Cancer Research UK, College of Life Sciences, University of Dundee, Dow Street, Dundee, DD1 5EH, Scotland (office). *E-mail:* dplane@p53Lab.a-star.edu.sg (office). *Website:* www .cancerresearchuk.org/science/research/who-and-what-we-fund/browse-by-location/dundee/university-of-dundee/david-lane-8 (office); www.a-star.edu.sg/p53lab (office).

LANE, Nathan; American actor and producer; b. (Joseph Lane), 3 Feb. 1956, Jersey City, NJ; ed St Peter's Preparatory High School, Jersey City; co-hosted Tony Awards 1995, 1996. *Plays include:* Lips Together, Teeth Apart 1991, The Nance (Drama League Award for Distinguished Performance 2013, Outer Critics Circle Award for Outstanding Actor in a Play 2013) 2013. *Musicals include:* Guys and Dolls, Broadway 1992, The Producers, Broadway (Tony Award) and Theatre Royal, London 2004, A Funny Thing Happened on the Way to the Forum (Tony Award). *Films include:* Ironweed 1987, Joe Versus the Volcano 1990, The Lemon Sisters 1990, He Said, She Said 1991, Frankie and Johnny 1991, Life with Mikey (aka Give Me a Break) 1993, Addams Family Values 1993, The Lion King (voice) 1994, Stand by Me 1995, Jeffrey 1995, The Birdcage 1996, Timon and Pumbaa's Wild Adventure: Live and Learn (video, voice) 1997, Mousehunt 1997, Merry Christmas, George Bailey 1997, The Lion King II: Simba's Pride (video, voice) 1998, The Best Man 1999, At First Sight 1999, Stuart Little (voice) 1999, Isn't She Great 2000, Love's Labour's Lost 2000, Titan A.E. (voice) 2000, Trixie 2000, Stuart Little 2 (voice) 2002, Austin Powers in Goldmember 2002, Nicholas Nickleby 2002, Teacher's Pet (voice) 2004, Win a Date with Tad Hamilton! 2004, The Lion King 1½ (video, voice) 2004, Behind the Legend: Timon (video, voice) (uncredited) 2004, The Producers 2005. *Television includes:* Jacqueline Susann's Valley of the Dolls (aka Valley of the Dolls) 1981, One of the Boys (series) 1982, Alice in Wonderland 1983, The Last Mile 1992, The Wizard of Oz in Concert: Dreams Come True 1995, Timon and Pumbaa (series) 1995, The Boys Next Door 1996, Encore! Encore! (series) 1998, George and Martha (series) 1999, The Man Who Came to Dinner 2000, Teacher's Pet (series) (voice) 2000–02, One Saturday Morning (series) (voice) 2000, Laughter on the 23rd Floor 2001, Charlie Lawrence (series) (also producer) 2003. *Address:* c/o Scott Bankston, Propaganda Management, 940 N. Mansfield Avenue, Hollywood, CA 90038, USA (office); c/o Bryan Lourd, Creative Artists Agency, 9830 Wilshire Blvd, Beverly Hills, CA 90212-1825, USA. *Telephone:* (310) 288-4545. *Fax:* (310) 288-4800. *Website:* www.caa.com.

LANE, Neal Francis, BS, MS, PhD; American physicist and academic; *Malcom Gillis University Professor and Senior Fellow in Science and Technology, James A. Baker III Institute for Public Policy, Rice University;* b. 22 Aug. 1938, Oklahoma; s. of Walter Lane and Harietta Hollander; m. Joni Sue Williams 1960; one s. one d.; ed Univ. of Oklahoma; NSF Postdoctoral Fellow 1964–65; Asst Prof. of Physics, Rice Univ. Houston 1966–69, Assoc. Prof. 1969–72, Prof. 1972–84, 1986–93, Prof. of Space Physics and Astronomy 1972–84, Chair. Dept of Physics 1977–82, Provost 1986–93; Dir Div. of Physics, NSF, Washington, DC 1979–80, Dir NSF 1993–98; Chancellor, Univ. of Colorado at Colorado Springs 1984–86; Asst to Pres. for Science and Tech., Dir Office of Science and Tech. Policy, Washington 1998–2001; Univ. Prof. and Sr Fellow in Science and Tech. and Gillis Univ. Prof., James A. Baker III Inst. of Public Policy, Rice Univ. 2001–; Visiting Fellow, Jt Inst. for Lab. Astrophysics, Univ. of Colo at Boulder 1965–66, 1975–76, non-resident Fellow 1984–93; Distinguished Visiting Scientist, Ky Univ., Lexington 1980; mem. Comm. on Physics, Science, Math. and Applications, Nat. Research Council 1989–93, Bd Overseers Superconducting Super Collider (SSC), Univs Research Asscn 1985–93, Advisory Cttee, Math. and Physical Sciences, NSF 1992–93; mem. American Inst. of Physics; Fellow, American Physics Soc., American Acad. of Arts and Sciences (Co-Chair. Governing Council 2010), AAAS, Asscn for Women in Science; Hon. DHL (Univ. of Oklahoma) 1995, (Marymount Univ.) 1995, (Illinois Inst. of Tech.) 1999; Hon. DSc (Univ. of Alabama) 1994, (Michigan State Univ.) 1995, (Ohio State Univ.) 1996, (Washington Coll.) 1998, (Univ. of Colorado) 1999, (Illinois Inst. of Tech.) 1999, (Queen's Univ. Belfast) 2000, (North Carolina State Univ.) 2001, (Mt Sinai School of Medicine) 2002, (State Univ. of NY) 2002, (Univ. of Tulsa) 2006; Alfred P. Sloan Foundation Fellow 1967–71, Philip Hauge Abelson Award, AAAS 2000, William D. Carey Award, AAAS 2001, President's Award, ASME, ACS Public Service Award, Public Welfare Award, American Astronomical Soc./American Math. Soc./American Physical Soc., NASA Distinguished Service Award, Support of Science Award, Council of Science Socs Presidents, Distinguished Alumni Award, Univ. of Oklahoma, Public Welfare Medal, NAS 2009, K.T. Compton Medal for Leadership in Physics, American Inst. of Physics 2009, Gold Medal for service to Rice University, Asscn of Rice Alumni 20009, Distinguished Friend of Science Award, Southeastern Univs Research Asscn 2011, Vannevar Bush Award, Nat. Science Bd of NSF 2013. *Publications:* Quantum States of Atoms, Molecules and Solids, Understanding More Quantum Physics; several book chapters, and articles in professional journals. *Leisure interests:* tennis, squash. *Address:* Department of Physics and Astronomy, MS 108, Rice University, PO Box 1892, Houston, TX 77251-1892 (office); James A. Baker III Institute for Public Policy, MS 40, 6100 Main Street, Rice University, Baker Hall, Suite 120, Houston, TX 77005, USA (office). *Telephone:* (713) 348-2925 (office). *Fax:* (713) 348-5143 (office). *E-mail:* neal@rice.edu (office). *Website:* bakerinstitute.org/experts/neal-f-lane (office).

LANE, Raymond J., BA; American business executive; spent ten years with IBM in various product man., sales and marketing positions; Div. Vice-Pres., Electronic Data Systems Corpn (acquired by Hewlett-Packard 2008); Sr Partner, Booz-Allen & Hamilton (consulting co.), mem. Dirs and Exec. Man. Cttee; joined Oracle Corpn (software co.) as Pres. of Oracle USA 1992, Exec. Vice-Pres. and Pres. of Worldwide Operations 1993–97, mem. Bd of Dirs 1995–2000, Pres. and COO Oracle Corpn 1997–2000; Man. Partner, Kleiner Perkins Caufield & Byers (pvt. equity firm) 2000–; mem. Bd of Dirs Hewlett-Packard Co. 2010–, Chair. (non-exec.) 2010–11, Exec. Chair. 2011–13; Advisor, Meakem Becker Venture Capital, LLC; served as Interim CEO of V-Vehicle Inc.; Chair. Hara Software, Inc.; Chair. Exec. Cttee, Carnegie Mellon Univ. 2009–, mem. Bd of Trustees, co-creator of a High Dependability Computing Consortium with Carnegie Mellon and NASA; Chair. Elance Inc., SeeBeyond 2001– (mem. Bd of Dirs 1998–); mem. Bd of Dirs Quest Software Inc. 2000– (mem. Compensation Cttee, fmr mem. Audit Cttee), Kenandy, Inc., Enigma, Inc., MetaMatrix, Inc., Fisker Automotive, Inc., Visible Path Corpn, Xsigo Systems, SpikeSource, PodShow, Marimba Inc. 1997– (mem. Compensation Cttee), C-Bridge Internet Solutions Inc. 1999–, FreeMarkets Inc. 2001–; fmr mem. Bd of Dirs eXcelon Corporation, Sheer Networks, Asera, Inc.; fmr mem. Exec. Advisory Bd InSight Venture Partners; mem. Bd of Govs West Virginia Univ., mem. Acad. of Distinguished Grads of West Virginia Univ., mem. Univ.'s Foundation Bd; Vice-Chair. Special Olympics International, fmr mem. Int. Bd of Special Olympics; Hon. PhD (West Virginia Univ., Golden Gate Univ.); honoured by West Virginia Univ. with naming of Lane Dept of Computer Science and Electrical Eng 2011. *Address:* Hewlett-Packard Co., 3000 Hanover Street, MS 1050, Palo Alto, CA 94304-1185, USA (office). *Telephone:* (650) 857-1501 (office). *Fax:* (650) 857-5518 (office). *E-mail:* bod@hp.com (office). *Website:* www.hp.com (office).

LANE, Robert W., MBA; American business executive; b. 14 Nov. 1949, Washington, DC; m. Patricia Lane; three c.; ed Wheaten Coll., Ill., Univ. of Chicago Grad. School of Business; began career in corp. banking; joined Deere & Co. 1982, various positions in Worldwide Construction Equipment Div., Pres. and COO Deere Credit Inc., Sr Vice-Pres. World Agric. Equipment Div., Sr Vice-Pres. and Chief Financial Officer Deere & Co. 1996–97, Sr Vice-Pres. and Man. Dir for Operations Europe, Middle East, India and fmr USSR 1997–98, Pres. Worldwide Agric. Equipment Div. 1998–2000, Pres. and COO Jan.–Aug. 2000, Chair., Pres. and CEO Aug. 2000–09, Chair. 2009–10 (retd); mem. Bd of Dirs BMW AG, General Electric Co., Verizon Communications Inc.; Nat. Dir Lyric Opera of Chicago; mem. The Business Roundtable, Business Council, Council on Foreign Relations, New York; mem. Bd Trustees Cttee for Devt, Univ. of Chicago; Hon. Dir, Lincoln Park Zoo, Chicago. *Address:* c/o Deere & Co. World Headquarters, One John Deere Place, Moline, IL 61265, USA. *Telephone:* (309) 765-8000. *E-mail:* info@deere.com. *Website:* www.deere.com.

LANE FOX, Martha, CBE, BA; British entrepreneur; *UK Digital Champion, Cabinet Office;* b. 10 Feb. 1973; ed Oxford High School, Westminster School, Magdalen Coll., Oxford; Business Analyst, Spectrum Strategy Consultants 1994–96, Assoc. 1996–97; Business Devt Dir Carlton Communications 1997–98; Co-founder (with Brent Hoberman q.v.) and COO lastminute.com 1998–2003; co-f. Lucky Voice Private Karaoke 2005; Founder and Chair. Antigone (charity trust) 2008–; Dir (non-exec.) Channel 4 2005–, Marks and Spencer 2007–, Mydeco.com 2008–; apptd Champion for Digital Inclusion by Prime Minister Gordon Brown 2009–10; f. the Race Online 2012 Campaign 2009–; re-apptd UK Digital Champion by Prime Minister David Cameron 2010–; mem. Cabinet Office's Efficiency and Reform Bd 2010–. *Address:* Race Online 2012, 4th Floor, 6–10 Lexington Street, London, W1F 0LB, England (office). *Telephone:* 7771-332282 (mobile) (office). *Website:* www.antigone.org.uk (office); www.marthalanefox.com.

LANG, Brian Andrew, MA, PhD, FRSE; British university vice-chancellor and management consultant; *Principal Emeritus, University of St Andrews;* b. 2 Dec. 1945, Edinburgh; s. of Andrew Lang and Mary Lang; m. 1st 1975 (divorced 1982); m. 2nd 1983 (divorced 2000); two s. one d.; m. 3rd 2002; ed Royal High School, Edinburgh and Univ. of Edinburgh; social anthropological field research, Kenya 1969–70; Lecturer in Social Anthropology, Århus Univ., Denmark 1971–75; mem. scientific staff, Social Science Research Council 1976–79; Sec., Historic Building Br., Scottish Office 1979–80; Sec. Nat. Heritage Memorial Fund 1980–87, Deputy Chair. 2005–; Dir of Public Affairs, Nat. Trust 1987–91; Chief Exec. and Deputy Chair. British Library 1991–2000; Prin. and Vice-Chancellor Univ. of St Andrews 2001–08, now Prin. Emer.; Visiting Prof., Napier Univ., Edin. 1999–; Visiting Scholar, Getty Inst., Calif. 2000; Chair. European Nat. Libraries Forum 1993–2000, Heritage Lottery Fund Cttee for Scotland 2005–, Royal Scottish Nat. Orchestra 2008–; Pres. Inst. of Information Scientists 1993–94; mem. Council, Nat. Trust for Scotland 2001–04, Council, St Leonard's School, St Andrews 2001–08, Bd Scottish Enterprise, Fife 2003–08, Scottish Exec. Cultural Cttee 2004–05; Trustee, Hopeton House Preservation Trust 2001–05, Newbattle Abbey Coll. 2004–08; Hon. LLD (St Andrews), Hon. Dr (Edinburgh); Hon. Fellow, The Library Asscn 1997. *Leisure interests:* reading, music, museums, galleries, pottering. *Address:* 10 Wiltshire House, Maidstone Building Mews, Borough High Street, London, SE1 1GH, England (home); 10 Carlton Terrace, Edinburgh, EH7 5DD, Scotland (home). *Telephone:* (20) 7207-3236 (London) (home); (131) 558-8455 (Edinburgh) (home). *E-mail:* brian@lang-uk.com (home). *Website:* www.lang -uk.com (office).

LANG, David, PhD; American composer; b. 1 Aug. 1957, LA; m.; three c.; ed Stanford Univ., Univ. of Iowa, Yale School of Music; studied with Jacob Druckman, Hans Werner Henze (q.v.) and Martin Bresnick; Jr Composer-in-Residence, Horizons Summer Festival 1980s; commissioned by Boston Symphony Orchestra, Cleveland Orchestra, St Paul Chamber Orchestra, BBC Singers, American Composers Orchestra and Santa Fe Opera and Settembre Musica Festival, Turin; co-f. (with Michael Gordon and Julia Wolfe) New York annual music festival Bang on a Can 1987–; composed albums Cheating, Lying, Stealing 1996 and Brian Eno: Music for Airports 1998 for group Bang on a Can All-Stars; Rome Prize, American Acad., Rome; BMW Prize, Munich Biennale for New Music Theatre; Friedheim Award, Kennedy Center; Revson Fellowship with New York Philharmonic; grants from Guggenheim Foundation, New York Foundation of Arts and Nat. Endowment for the Arts. *Compositions include:* chamber music: Frag 1984, Dance/Drop 1987, Burn Notice 1989, Music for Gracious Living 1992, Cheating, Lying, Stealing 1993, Face so Pale 1992, Wreck/Wed 1995, Slip 1996, Follow 1996, Little Eye 1999, My Very Empty Mouth 1999, Sweet Air 1999, Short Fall 2000, Birds of Minnesota 2000; for chorus: By Fire 1984, Hecuba 1995, This Condition 2000, I Lie 2001, Again (After Ecclesiastes) 2005, Evening Morning Day 2007, The Little Match Girl Passion (Pulitzer Prize for Music 2008) 2007; opera: Judith and Holofernes 1989, Music for Gracious Living 1992, Modern Painters 1995, The Carbon Copy Building 1999, The Difficulty of Crossing a Field 2000, Lost Objects 2001; orchestral and large ensemble: Hammer Amour 1984, Eating Living Monkeys 1985, Spud 1986, Are You Experienced? 1987–89, Bonehead 1990, International Business Machine 1990, Fire and Forget 1992, My Evil Twin 1992, Slow Movement 1993, Under Orpheus 1994, Grind to a Halt 1996, The Passing Measures 1998, I Fought the Law 1998, Ariel's Version 1998, Haircut 2000, How to Pray 2002, Fur 2004, Loud Love Songs 2004, Pierced 2007, Every Ounce of Strength 2007. *Address:* Red Poppy Music, 222 East Fifth Street, No. 12, New York, NY 10003, USA (office). *Telephone:* (646) 498-8822 (office). *Fax:* (212) 388-1727 (office). *E-mail:* info@redpoppymusic.com (office). *Website:* www.redpoppymusic.com (office).

LANG, Helmut; Austrian artist and fashion designer; b. 10 March 1956, Vienna; est. own studio in Vienna 1977; made-to-measure shop opened in Vienna 1979; development of ready-to-wear collections 1984–86; presented Helmut Lang women's wear, Paris fashion week from 1986, menswear from 1987; began licence business 1988; Helmut Lang Underwear 1994; Helmut Lang Protective Eyewear 1995; Prof. of Masterclass of Fashion, Univ. of Applied Arts, Vienna 1993–97; moved to New York 1997; sold a 51% stake in co. to the Prada Group 1999, retained control of design and advertising, Prada later developed a line of Helmut Lang accessories, including shoes, belts and bags and opened Helmut Lang stores in Hong Kong and Singapore; used unconventional materials including rubber, feathers and metallic fabrics and redefined the silhouette of the 1990s and early 2000s; first designer to stream his collection online; four different scents cr. by Lang in co-operation with Procter & Gamble, all discontinued with closing of the brand 2005; retd from fashion in 2005; collaborations with artists Jenny Holzer and Louise Bourgeois; recent works explore abstract sculptural forms and physical arrangements and space beyond the limitations of the human body; lives and works in New York and on Long Island; Österreichisches Ehrenzeichen für Wissenschaft u. Kunst 2009; Best Int. Designer of the Year, Council of Fashion Designers of America (CFDA) 1996, VH-1/Vogue Award for Best Menswear Designer of the Year 1997, Fine Arts of Vienna 1997, Pitti Immagine Award for Best Designer of the Nineties 1998, New York Magazine Best Designer of the Year Award 1998, Design Distinction Award for Environments, I.D. Magazine 1998, Award for Interiors, New York City Chapter of AIA 1998, Architectural Record Award, Business Week 1999, AIA Award for Interior Architecture 1999, CFDA Menswear Designer of the Year 2000, GQ Designer of the Year 2004, 'The Imagineers of Our Time' Award, Fashion Group International 2004, LEAD Award 2005. *Publications:* has published excerpts from ongoing art projects, Long Island Diaries, and The Selective Memory Series, in several publs, including BUTT Magazine, Fannzine 137, Visionaire, The Travel Almanac. *E-mail:* helmutlangstudio@culture-edit.com. *Website:* www.helmutlangstudio.com.

LÁNG, István; Hungarian agrochemist; *Research Professor Emeritus, Hungarian Academy of Sciences*; b. 26 Dec. 1931, Mohács; s. of József Láng and Anna Világi; m. Etelka Sorosinszki; one d.; ed Agricultural Univ. of Ivanovo, USSR; Fellow, Research Inst. for Soil Sciences and Agricultural Chem., Budapest 1955–63; Exec. Sec. Section of Biological Sciences, Hungarian Acad. of Sciences 1963–70, Deputy Sec.-Gen. 1970–85, Sec.-Gen. 1985–93, Science Policy Adviser 1993–, Research Prof. 2002–11, now Emer.; Chair. Advisory Bd, Ministry of Environmental and Regional Policy 1994–96, Vice-Chair. 1998–; Chair. Hungarian Research Fund 1986–90; Chair. Local Preparatory Cttee for the World Conf. on Science 1998; mem. World Comm. on Environment and Devt (Brundtland Comm.), Advisory Cttee on Environment, Int. Council for Science; mem. Hungarian Acad. of Sciences; Hon. Chair, Nat. Cttee for Environment; Albert Einstein Medal (Silver), UNESCO 1999. *Publications include:* Agricultural Production and Global Environment Protection 2003. *Leisure interests:* philately, bird watching. *Address:* c/o Library of the Hungarian Academy of Sciences, Arany János u.1, 1051 Budapest; Szilágyi E. Fasor 51, 1026 Budapest, Hungary (home). *Telephone:* (1) 2692656 (office); (1) 2010800 (home). *Fax:* (1) 2692655 (office). *E-mail:* ilang@mtak.hu (office).

LANG, Jack Mathieu Émile, DenD; French politician and UN official; *President, Arab World Institute*; b. 2 Sept. 1939, Mirecourt (Vosges); s. of Roger Lang and Marie-Luce Bouchet; m. Monique Buczynski 1961; two d. (one deceased); ed Lycée Henri-Poincaré, Nancy, Inst. of Political Studies, Paris; Founder and Dir World Festival of Univ. Theatre, Nancy 1963–77; Dir Théâtre du palais de Chaillot 1972–74; apptd Prof. of Int. Law 1976; apptd Dir Educ. and Research Unit for econ. and legal sciences, Nancy 1977; Councillor, Paris 1977–81; Deputy Nat. Ass. for Loir-et-Cher 1986–88, March–Dec. 1993, 1997–2000, Pres. Foreign Affairs Cttee 1997–2000, Deputy for Pas-de-Calais 6th constituency 2002–12; Special Adviser to First Sec., Parti Socialiste (PS) 1978–81, PS Nat. Del. for Culture 1979–81, Nat. Sec. 2005–07; Minister of Culture and Communications 1981–83, 1984–86, May–June 1988, 1991–92, of Educ. and Culture 1992–93, also Minister for Major Public Works and Bicentenary 1988–89, apptd Govt Spokesman 1991, Minister of Educ. 2000–02; Mayor of Blois 1989–2001; mem. European Parl. 1994–97; apptd Vice-Pres. Comité sur la réforme des institutions 2007; served as Pres. Nicolas Sarkozy's Special Envoy to Cuba Feb. 2009, to the Democratic People's Repub. of Korea Nov. 2009; Special Adviser to the Sec.-Gen. on Legal Issues related to Piracy off the Coast of Somalia, UN 2010–12; Pres. Arab World Inst. 2013–; Chevalier, Légion d'honneur; Commdr des Palmes académiques; Hon. DLitt (Nottingham) 1990; Dr hc (RCA) 1993; Prix Antonio de Sancha (Spain) 1997, Prix Wartburg (Germany) 1998. *Publications include:* L'État et le théâtre 1968, Le Plateau Continental de la mer du Nord: Arrêt de la Cour Internationale de Justice 1969, Demain les femmes 1995, Lettre à Malraux 1996, François Premier 1997, Les Araignées 2000, Anna au Muséum 2002, Une Ecole Elitaire pour tous 2003, Un Nouveau Régime Politique pour la France 2004, Nelson Mandela: Leçon de vie pour l'avenir 2005, Faire la Révolution Fiscale 2006, Demain Comme Hier (with Jean-Michel Helvig) 2009, La bataille du Grand Louvre 2010, Ce que je sais de François Mitterrand 2011, François Mitterrand: fragments de vie partagée 2011, Pourquoi ce vandalisme d'État Contre l'École: Lettre au Président de la République 2011. *Address:* 17 place des Vosges, 75004 Paris, France. *Telephone:* 6-68-54-54-88 (mobile). *E-mail:* j.lang@wanadoo.fr.

LANG, Kathryn Dawn (k.d.); Canadian singer and songwriter; b. 2 Nov. 1961, Consort, Alberta; d. of Adam Lang and Audrey L. Lang; began playing guitar aged 10; formed band The Reclines in early 1980s, played N American clubs 1982–87; performed at closing ceremony, Winter Olympics, Calgary 1988; performed with Sting, Bruce Springsteen, Peter Gabriel and Tracy Chapman in Amnesty Int. tour 1988; headline US tour 1992; Canadian Country Music Asscn Awards for Best Entertainer of Year 1989, Best Album of Year 1990, Grammy Awards for Best Female Country Vocal Performance 1990, Best Pop Vocal 1993, American Music Awards, Favourite New Artist 1993, Songwriter of the Year (with Ben Mink) 1993, BRIT Award for Best Int. Female 1995. *Film appearances:* Salmonberries 1991, Teresa's Tattoo 1994, The Last Don 1997, Eye of the Beholder 1999; features on soundtrack to Dick Tracy. *Recordings include:* albums A Truly Western Experience 1984, Angel With A Lariat 1987, Shadowland 1988, Absolute Torch And Twang 1989, Ingénue (Album of the Year 1993) 1992, Even Cowgirls Get The Blues (film soundtrack) 1993, All You Can Eat 1995, Drag 1997, Australian Tour 1997, Invincible Summer 2000, Live By Request 2001, A Wonderful World (with Tony Bennett; Grammy Award for Best Traditional Pop Vocal Album 2004) 2003, Hymns of the 49th Parallel 2004, Reintarnation 2006, Watershed 2008, Recollection 2010, Sing It Loud 2011. *Address:* Direct Management Group, 947 North La Cienega Blvd, Suite G, Los Angeles, CA 90069, USA (office). *Website:* www.kdlang .com (office).

LANG, Larry H. P., BA, MA, PhD; Taiwanese economist and academic; *Chair Professor of Finance, Chinese University of Hong Kong*; ed Tunghai Univ., Nat. Taiwan Univ., Wharton School of Business, Univ. of Pennsylvania, USA; fmr Lecturer, Wharton School of Business; fmr Prof. of Finance, Grad. School of Business, Michigan State Univ., Coll. of Business, Ohio State Univ., Stern School of Business, New York Univ.; fmr Visiting Prof. of Finance, Grad. School of Business, Univ. of Chicago; currently Chair Prof. of Finance, Faculty of Business Admin, Chinese Univ. of Hong Kong; Pnr, GITIC-Lehman Infrastructure Fund, Lehman Brothers 1994–96; Consultant on Corp. Governance Projects to World Bank, Washington, DC 1998–2000, on WTO/Banking Issues to OECD 2000, on Corp. Governance to China Shenzhen Stock Exchange, Hong Kong Govt; presenter, half-hour talk show, Larry Lang Live 2004–06, show cancelled following criticism of Chinese Politburo. *Publications:* numerous articles and research papers in professional journals. *Address:* Room 225, Leung Kau Kui Building, Department of Finance, Chinese University of Hong Kong, Shatin, New Territories, Hong Kong Special Administrative Region, People's Republic of China (office). *Telephone:* 2609-7761 (office). *Fax:* 2603-6586 (office). *E-mail:* llang@baf.msmail .cuhk.edu.hk (office). *Website:* www.cuhk.edu.hk (office).

LANG, Laura, BA, MBA; American media executive; *CEO, Time Inc.*; b. Warwick, RI; ed Tufts Univ., Univ. of Pennsylvania Wharton School of Business; worked in product man. at Bristol Myers and Quaker Oats Co.; worked in strategic planning for Pfizer Pharmaceuticals; led consulting practice at Yankelovich Clancy Shulman; Pres. Marketing Corpn of America –1999; joined Digitas (digital agency) 1999, ran New York office for several years, CEO Digitas North America 2004–08, Worldwide CEO 2008–12, also headed parent co. Publicis Groupe's pure-play digital agencies, including Denuo, Big Fuel, Razorfish and Phonevalley; CEO Time Inc. 2012–; mem. Bd of Dirs VF Corpn, Benchmark Electronics, Nutrisystem; Co-Chair. The One Hundred; mem. Advisory Bd Tufts Univ. Entrepreneurial Leadership Program; named by Advertising Age as one of its Women to Watch 2007, named to BtoB Magazine's Who's Who list 2006, 2007, 2009, ranked by Forbes magazine amongst The World's 100 Most Powerful Women (44th) 2012, ranked by Fortune magazine amongst the 50 Most Powerful Women in Business in the US (46th) 2012. *Address:* Time Inc., Rockefeller Plaza, New York, NY 10019, USA (office). *Telephone:* (212) 484-8000 (office). *E-mail:* info@timeinc.com (office). *Website:* www.timeinc.com (office).

LANG, Hon. Otto, PC, OC, QC, BA, LLB, BCL, LLD; Canadian lawyer, politician, business executive and consultant; b. 14 May 1932, Handel, Sask.; s. of Otto T. Lang and Maria Theresa Wurm; m. 1st Adrian Ann Merchant 1963 (divorced 1988); three s. four d.; m. 2nd Deborah J. McCawley 1989; one step-s. one step-d.; ed Univ. of Sask. and Oxford Univ., UK; admitted to Sask. Bar 1956, to Ont., Yukon and NWT Bars 1972, Manitoba Bar 1988; Asst Prof., Univ. of Sask., Faculty of Law 1956, Assoc. Prof. 1957, Prof. 1961, Dean of Law School 1961–68; MP for Saskatoon-Humboldt 1968–79; Minister without Portfolio 1968, with responsibility for Energy and Water Resources 1969, with responsibility for Canadian Wheat Bd 1969–79; Minister of Manpower & Immigration 1970–72, of Justice 1972–75, of Transport 1975–79, of Justice and Attorney-Gen. Aug.–Nov. 1979; Pres. Asscn of Canadian Law Teachers 1962–63; Vice-Pres. Sask. Liberal Asscn 1956–63; Fed. Campaign Chair. Liberal Party 1963–64; Past Pres. Saskatoon Social Planning Council; Exec. Vice-Pres. Pioneer Grain Co. Ltd 1979–88; mem. Bd of Dirs Investor Group Trust Co. 1985–2009, Ind. Review Cttee 2009–; Company Secretary, Friends of Upper Fort Garry Gate 2007–; Chair. Transport Inst., Univ. of Manitoba 1988–93; Pres. and CEO Central Gas Manitoba Inc. 1993–99; consultant with GPC 2000–07; Vice-Chair. of Bd, Winnipeg Airports Authority 1995–2008; Campaign Chair. Winnipeg United Way 1983; Chair. Royal Winnipeg Ballet Capital Campaign 1996–2000; Rhodes Scholar 1953; QC for Ont. 1972, for Sask. 1972; Hon. Consul-Gen. of Japan 1992–97. *Publication:* Contemporary Problems of Public Law in Canada (ed.) 1968. *Leisure interests:* tennis, bridge, golf. *Address:*

135 Ash Street, Winnipeg, Man., R3N 0P4, Canada (home). *Telephone:* (204) 334-9476 (home). *E-mail:* ottolang@mts.net (home).

LANG, Rein, LLM; Estonian politician; *Minister of Justice;* b. 4 July 1957, Tartu; s. of Ants Lang and Ulve Lang; one d.; ed Tartu State Univ.; previous positions include Deputy Man. Linnahall arena, Deputy Dir Muusik club, Chair., then Head Supervisory Council, Trio media co.; apptd Deputy Mayor of Tallinn 2001; mem. Tallinn City Council 2002; founding mem. Reform Party; mem. Parl. 2003–, First Deputy Speaker –2005; Minister of Foreign Affairs 2005, of Justice 2005–, Acting Minister of the Interior 2009–; mem. Rotary Club of Tallinn; Commdr Ordre Nat. (France) 2004, Order of the White Star (2nd class) 2006; Estonian Police Award (2nd class) 2003. *Address:* Ministry of Justice, Tõnismägi 5a, Tallinn 15191, Estonia (office). *Telephone:* 620-8100 (office). *Fax:* 620-8109 (office). *E-mail:* rein.lan@just.ee (office); rein@kuku.ee (home). *Website:* www.just.ee (office); www.lang.ee (home).

LANG OF MONKTON, Baron (Life Peer), cr. 1997, of Merrick and the Rhinns of Kells in Dumfries and Galloway; **Ian (Bruce) Lang,** OStJ, BA, PC, DL; British politician and businessman; *Chairman, Marsh & McLennan Companies Inc.;* b. 27 June 1940; s. of the late James F. Lang, DSC and of Maude Stewart; m. Sandra Montgomerie 1971; two d.; ed Lathallan School, Kincardineshire, Rugby School and Sidney Sussex Coll. Cambridge; MP for Galloway 1979–83, for Galloway and Upper Nithsdale 1983–97; Asst Govt Whip 1981–83; a Lord Commr of HM Treasury 1983–86; Parl. Under-Sec. of State, Dept of Employment 1986, Scottish Office 1986–87; Minister of State, Scottish Office 1987–90; Sec. of State for Scotland and Lord Keeper of the Great Seal of Scotland 1990–95; Pres. Bd of Trade 1995–97; mem. House of Lords Select Cttee on the Constitution 2001–05, 2012–; Chair. Patrons of Nat. Galleries of Scotland 2001–08; Chair. Prime Minister's Advisory Cttee on Business Appointments 2009–; Dir Marsh & McLennan Companies Inc. 1997– (Chair. 2011–), Lithgows Ltd 1997–2009, Charlemagne Capital Ltd 2006–; Gov. Rugby School 1997–2007; mem. Queen's Bodyguard for Scotland (Royal Co. of Archers) 1974–; DL Ayrshire and Arran 1998–; mem. Conservative Party, Privy Council 1990–; Hon. Pres. St Columba's School, Renfrewshire 1999–2008. *Publication:* Blue Remembered Years 2002. *Address:* House of Lords, London, SW1A 0PW, England.

LANGAT, Nancy Jebet; Kenyan athlete; b. 22 Aug. 1981; middle-distance runner; gold medallist 800m, World Junior Championships 2000, African Championships 2004; gold medallist 1500m, Olympic Games, Beijing 2008; gold medallist 1500m World Athletics Final 2009; gold medallist 800m, 1500m, Commonwealth Games, New Delhi, African Championships, Kenya 2010. *Address:* c/o Kenya Athletics Federation, PO Box 46722, Aerodrome Road, Riadha House, 00100 Nairobi West, Kenya. *Telephone:* (2) 605021. *Fax:* (2) 605020. *E-mail:* athleticskenya@gt.co.ke.

LÅNGBACKA, Ralf Runar, MA; Finnish theatre director and professor of theatre science; b. 20 Nov. 1932, Närpes; s. of Runar Emanuel Långbacka and Hulda Emilia Långbacka (née Backlund); m. Runa Birgitta Danielsson 1961; two s. one d.; ed Abo Akademi, Munich Univ. and Freie Univ., Berlin; Ed. Finnish Radio literary programmes 1956; Asst and Dir Lilla Teatern, Helsinki 1958–60; Man. and Artistic Dir Swedish Theatre, Turku 1960–63; Dir Finnish Nat. Theatre 1963–65; Artistic Dir Swedish Theatre, Helsinki 1965–67; Dir Municipal Theatre, Gothenburg, Sweden; mem. Finnish State Comm. of Dramatic Art 1967–70; Artistic Dir Municipal Theatre, Turku 1971–77; Head Finnish Dirs Asscn 1978–82; Artistic and Man. Dir Municipal Theatre, Helsinki 1983–87, Artistic Prof. 1979–83, 1988–93; Prof. of Theatre Science, Abo Akademi, Turku 1994–97; Pres. Finnish Centre, Int. Theatre Inst. (ITI) 1983–96, mem. Bd (Excom) of ITI 1991–95; Corresp. mem. Akad. der Künste, Berlin 1979; freelance dir in Finland, Sweden, Denmark, Germany, Norway, Russia, USA, Chile, China 1960–2009; Academician, Finnish Acad. 2004–; The Critics Spurs 1963, Pro Finlandia 1973, Henrik-Steffens Award (Germany) 1994, Finland Prize, Swedish Acad., Sweden 1999, Finland Prize for Theatre 2001. *Film:* Puntila 1979. *Music:* directed operas: Wozzeck (Berg) 1967, 2001, Carmen (Bizet) 1969, Don Giovanni (Mozart) 1973, 1984, Macbeth (Verdi) 1980, 1993, Don Carlos (Verdi) 1995, Rigoletto (Verdi) 2000, 2001. *Plays:* directed over 100 performances of plays, including Shakespeare, Chekhov, Brecht and Büchner. *Television:* Premiär (four-part feature) 1992. *Publications:* Teatterikirja (The Theatre Book) (with Kalle Holmberg) 1977, Bland annat om Brecht (On Brecht and Others) 1981, Möten med Tjechov (Meetings with Chekhov) 1986, Denna långa dag, detta korta liv (This long day, This short life: poems) 1988, Krocketspelaren (The Croquet Player, play) 1990, Olga, Irina och jag (Olga, Irina and I, play) 1991, Brecht og det realistiske teater (Brecht and the Realistic Theatre) 1998, Att fånga ödets vindar (To Catch the Winds of Destiny), Memoirs 1 2009, På jakt efter en konstnärlig teater (Chasing an Artistical Theatre), Memoirs 2, 2011; numerous articles. *Leisure interests:* music, mushrooms, sailing. *Address:* Hopeasalmenranta 1B, 00570 Helsinki 57, Finland (home). *Telephone:* (9) 6849508 (home); (40) 7323323 (home). *E-mail:* ralf.langbacka@gmail.com (home).

LANGBO, Arnold G.; Canadian business executive; b. 13 April 1937, Richmond, BC; s. of Osbjourn Langbo and Laura Marie Langbo (née Hagen); m. Martha M. Miller 1959; eight c.; ed Univ. of British Columbia, Vancouver; sales rep., Kellogg Canada Inc. 1956–67, Int. Div. 1967–69, Admin. Asst to Kellogg Co., Pres. 1969–70, Exec. Vice-Pres. 1970–71, Vice-Pres. of Kellogg Canada 1971–76, Salada Foods Ltd 1971–76, Pres. and CEO Kellogg Salada Canada Ltd Inc. 1976–78, Pres. US Food Products Div. of Kellogg Co. 1978–79, Corp. Vice-Pres. 1979–81, Exec. Vice-Pres. 1981–83, Group Exec. Vice-Pres., Kellogg Co. 1983–86, Pres. Kellogg International 1986–90, Pres., COO and Dir, Kellogg Co. 1990–91, Chair. and CEO 1992–99 (retd); mem. Bd of Dirs, Johnson & Johnson 1991–2010, Whirlpool Corpn 1994–2009, Atlantic Richfield Co. from 1998, Weyerhaeuser Co. 1999–2011, Int. Youth Foundation; Ind. Dir, Hershey Co. 2007–09; fmr mem. Bd of Dirs, Grocery Mfrs of America; fmr mem. Int. Advisory Council of CGI Group Inc.; mem. Advisory Bd J.L. Kellogg Grad. School of Man., Northwestern Univ.; Trustee, W.W. Kellogg Trust, Albion Coll.; Adrian Trimpe Distinguished Service Award, Haworth Coll. of Business, Western Mich. Univ. 2000. *Address:* c/o Board of Directors, Johnson & Johnson, 1 Johnson & Johnson Plaza, New Brunswick, NJ 08933; 7614 La Corniche Circle, Boca Raton, FL 33433, USA (home).

LANGDALE, Mark, BBA, LLB; American lawyer, business executive and fmr diplomatist; *President, George W. Bush Foundation;* b. 1954; m. Patty Langdale 1982; one s. one d.; ed Univ. of Texas and Univ. of Houston School of Law; practised law in Houston, Tex. for ten years; Pres. Posadas USA, Inc. (US subsidiary of Grupo Posadas) 1989–2005, mem. Bd Dirs Grupo Posadas 1992–2004; Co-founder CapRock Communications Corpn; Chair. Texas Dept of Econ. Devt 1997–2001; Amb. to Costa Rica 2005–08; Pres. George W. Bush Foundation, Dallas 2008–; mem. Young Presidents Org. 1992–2004; YPO Legacy Award 2004. *Address:* George W. Bush Foundation, POB 600610, Dallas,, TX 75206, USA (office). *Telephone:* (214) 890-9943 (office). *E-mail:* info@georgewbushlibrary.com (office). *Website:* www.georgewbushcenter.com (office).

LANGE, Hartmut; German author and dramatist; b. 31 March 1937, Berlin; s. of Karl Lange and Johanna Lange; m. Ulrike Ritter 1971; ed Babelsberg Film School; playwright at Deutsches Theater, Berlin 1961–65; freelance writer, W Berlin 1965–; Gerhart-Hauptmann-Preis 1968, Literatur Preis der Adenauer Stiftung 1998, Ehrengabe der Schiller-Stiftung von 1859 2000, Italo Svevo Preis 2003, Preis der LiteraTour Nord 2004. *Publications:* Die Revolution als Geisterschiff 1974, Die Selbstverbrennung 1982, Deutsche Empfindungen 1983, Die Waldsteinsonate 1984, Das Konzert 1986, Die Ermüdung 1988, Vom Werden der Vernunft 1988, Gesammelte Theaterstücke (Collected Plays) 1988, Die Wattwanderung 1990, Die Reise nach Triest 1991, Die Stechpalme 1993, Schnitzlers Würgeengel 1995, Der Herr im Café 1996, Italienische Novellen 1998, Eine andere Form des Glücks 1999, Die Bildungsreise 2000, Das Streichquartett 2001, Irrtum als Erkenntnis 2002, Leptis Magna 2003, Der Wanderer 2005, Der Therapeut 2007, Der Abgrund des Endlichen 2009, Im Museum 2010, Das Haus in der Dorotheenstrasse 2012, Positiver Nihilismus 2012. *Leisure interest:* chess. *Address:* Hohenzollerndamm 197, 10717 Berlin, Germany (home); 06010 Niccone, Perugia, Italy (home).

LANGE, Hermann, DJur; German professor of law; *Professor Emeritus, University of Tübingen;* b. 24 Jan. 1922, Dresden; s. of Arno Lange and Käthe (née Braun) Lange; m. Ulrike Moser 1960; one s. one d.; ed Kreuzgymnasium, Dresden and Univs of Leipzig, Munich and Freiburg/Breisgau; Asst Inst. of Legal History, Univ. of Freiburg/Breisgau 1949–53; Privatdozent, Freiburg/Breisgau 1953–55; Extraordinary Prof. Univ. of Innsbrück 1955–57; Prof. Univ. of Kiel 1957–62, Univ. of Mainz 1962–66, Univ. of Tübingen 1966– (now Emer.); mem. Akad. der Wissenschaften und Literatur, Mainz. *Publications:* Schadensersatz und Privatstrafe in der mittelalterlichen Rechtstheorie 1955, Familienrecht (Kommentar) 1962, 1989 (12), Die Consilien des Baldus de Ubaldis 1974, Schadensersatz 1979, 2003 (3), Schadensersatzrecht 1979, 2003 (3), Wandlungen des Schadenersatzrechts 1987, 2003 (3) Die Anfänge der modernen Rechtswissenschaft 1993, Römisches Recht im Mittelalter I 1997, 100 Jahre Bürgerliches Gesetzbuch 2001, Die Universitäten des Mittelalters und das Römische Recht 2006, Römisches Recht im Mittelalter II 2007, Recht und Macht: Politische Streitigkeiten Im Sptmittelalter 2010. *Address:* Ferdinand-Christian-Baur-Strasse 3, 72076 Tübingen, Germany. *Telephone:* (7071) 61216.

LANGE, Jessica Phyllis; American actress; b. 20 April 1949, Cloquet, Minn.; d. of Albert John Lange and Dorothy Florence Lange (née Sahlman); m. Francisco (Paco) Grande 1970 (divorced 1981); one d. (with Mikhail Baryshnikov); one s. one d. (with Sam Shepard); ed Univ. of Minnesota; student of mime with Etienne DeCroux, Paris; Dancer Opéra Comique, Paris; model, Wilhelmina Agency, New York; Star Showtime TV production Cat On A Hot Tin Roof 1984; in summer stock production Angel On My Shoulder, NC 1980. *Theatre includes:* A Streetcar Named Desire, London (Theatre World Award, Golden Globe for TV performance 1996) 1992, Long Day's Journey into Night 2000, The Glass Menagerie 2005. *Films include:* King Kong 1976, All That Jazz 1979, How to Beat the High Cost of Living 1980, The Postman Always Rings Twice 1981, Frances 1982, Tootsie 1982 (Acad. Award for Best Supporting Actress 1982), Country (also producer) 1984, Sweet Dreams 1985, Crimes of the Heart 1986, Everybody's All American 1989, Far North 1988, Music Box 1989, Men Don't Leave 1989, Cape Fear 1991, Night and the City 1993, Blue Sky (Acad. Award for Best Actress 1995) 1994, Losing Isaiah 1995, Rob Roy 1995, A Thousand Acres 1997, Hush 1998, Cousin Bette 1998, Titus 1999, Prozac Nation 2001, Masked and Anonymous 2003, Great Performances 2003, Big Fish 2003, Don't Come Knockin' 2005, Broken Flowers 2005, Neverwas 2005, Bonneville 2006, The Vow 2012, The Big Valley 2012, Therese Raquin 2012. *Television includes:* The Best Little Girl in the World 1981, Notre Dame of the Cross (documentary) 1981, Cat on a Hot Tin Roof 1985, O Pioneers! 1992, A Streetcar Named Desire 1995, Off the Menu: The Last Days of Chasen's (documentary) 1997, Normal (film) 2003, XXI Century (documentary) 2003, Peace by Peace: Women on the Frontlines (narrator) 2004, The Needs of Kim Stanley (documentary) 2005, Sybil 2007, Grey Gardens (Emmy Award for Outstanding Lead Actress in a Miniseries or Movie) 2009, American Horror Story (Golden Globe Award for Best Supporting Actress in a Series, Mini-Series or Motion Picture Made for Television 2012, Emmy Award for Supporting Actress in a Miniseries or Movie 2012) 2011–. *Plays:* Long Day's Journey into Night 2000, A Glass Menagerie 2005, 2007. *Address:* c/o Toni Howard, ICM, Constellation Boulevard, Los Angeles, CA 90067, USA (office); 9401 Wilshire Blvd, Beverly Hills, CA 90212. *Telephone:* (310) 550-4000 (office). *Website:* www.icmtalent.com (office).

LANGE, Otto Ludwig, Dr rer. nat; German professor of botany (retd); *Professor Emeritus, Julius-von-Sachs-Institut für Biowissenschaften, Universität Würzburg;* b. 21 Aug. 1927, Dortmund; s. of Otto Lange and Marie Lange (née Pralle); m. Rose Wilhelm 1959; two d.; ed Univs of Göttingen and Freiburg; Asst Prof., Univ. of Göttingen 1953–61; Dozent, Technische Hochschule Darmstadt 1961–63; Prof. of Forest Botany, Univ. Göttingen 1963–67; Prof. of Botany, Univ. of Würzburg 1967–92, Prof. Emer. 1992–; Visiting Scientist, Utah State Univ. 1973, 1985, ANU, Canberra 1978–79; Dir Botanical Garden, Univ. of Würzburg 1967–92; Co-Ed. scientific journal Flora; mem. Deutsche Akad. der Naturforscher Leopoldina, Bayerische Akad. der Wissenschaften, Academia Europaea, Acad. Scientiarum et Artium Europaea; Corresp. mem. Akad. der Wissenschaften, Göttingen; Foreign Hon. mem. American Acad. of Arts and Sciences 1994; Bundesverdienstkreuz (1st Class) 1985; Dr hc (Bayreuth) 1995, (Tech. Univ., Lisbon) 1996, (Darmstadt) 2001; Antarctic Service Medal, US Govt 1974, Gottfried-Wilhem-Leibniz Prize, Deutsche Forschungsgemeinschaft 1986, Balzan Prize 1988, Adalbert Seifriz Prize 1990, Bayerische Maximiliansorden for Science and Art 1991, Acharius Medal, Int. Asscn of Lichenology 1992. *Publications:* ed. (with others) four vols of Physiological

Plant Ecology in Encyclopedia of Plant Physiology 1981–83; books on water and plant life, plant response to stress, forest decline, air pollution and biological soil crusts; book series Ecological Studies; 360 scientific papers. *Address:* Julius-von-Sachs-Institut für Biowissenschaften der Universität Würzburg, Julius-von-Sachs-Platz 3, 97082 Würzburg (office); Leitengraben 37, 97084 Würzburg, Germany (home). *Telephone:* (931) 8886205 (office); (931) 65249 (home). *Fax:* (931) 6193178 (home). *E-mail:* ollange@botanik.uni-wuerzburg.de (office). *Website:* www.botanik.uni-wuerzburg.de.

LANGELLA, Frank, BA; American actor; b. 1 Jan. 1940, Bayonne, NJ; s. of Frank A. Langella, Sr; m. Ruth Weil 1977 (divorced); ed Syracuse Univ. *Plays include:* numerous stage appearances on Broadway and elsewhere including Seascape (Tony Award for Best Featured Actor in a Play) 1975, Fortune's Fool (Tony Award for Best Featured Actor in a Play) 2002, Sherlock's Last Case 1987, Frost/Nixon (Tony Award for Best Leading Actor in a Play) 2007, A Man for All Seasons 2008. *Films include:* Diary of a Mad Housewife 1970,The Twelve Chairs 1970, The Wrath of God 1972, The Mark of Zorro 1974, Dracula 1979, And God Created Woman 1988, Body of Evidence 1993, The Beast 2001, Now You See It 2005, Good Night and Good Luck 2005, Starting Out in the Evening (Boston Soc. of Film Critics Award) 2007, Frost/Nixon 2008, The Box 2009. *Television:* Sherlock Holmes 1981. *Publications:* Dropped Names: Famous Men and Women As I Knew Them 2012. *Address:* CESD Talent Agency NY, 257 Park Avenue South, Suite 900, New York, NY 10010, USA (office). *Telephone:* (212) 477-1666 (office). *Fax:* (212) 979-2011 (office). *Website:* www.cesdtalent.com (office).

LANGER, Ivan, MD, MCL; Czech politician; b. 1 Jan. 1967, Olomouc; m. Markéta Vobořilová; one s. one d.; ed Univ. of Palacký, Charles Univ., Prague; Secr. Ministry for Justice of Czech Repub. 1993–96; mem. Council Olomouc 1994; mem. of Civic Democratic Party (ODS), Vice-Chair. 1998–2002, 2004–; mem. Parl. 1996–; Shadow Minister of the Interior 1999–2002; Vice-Chair. Chamber of Deputies (Parl.) 1998–2006; Minister of the Interior June–Oct. 2006 (resgnd), reinstated Jan. 2007–09, of Information 2007; Hon. mem. Maltese Order of Help 1994–. *Publications:* Rational Anti-drug Policy, After the Velvet Revolution. *Leisure interests:* tennis, music, theatre, film, golf. *Address:* Civic Democratic Party (Občanská demokratická strana), Jánský vršek 13, 118 00 Prague 1, Czech Republic (office). *Telephone:* 234707111 (office). *Fax:* 234707101 (home). *E-mail:* hk@ods.cz (office). *Website:* www.ods.cz (office); www.langer.cz.

LANGER, Robert Samuel, ScD, BS; American chemical engineer and academic; *David H. Koch Institute Professor, Department of Chemical Engineering, Massachusetts Institute of Technology;* b. 29 Aug. 1948, Albany, NY; m. Laura Langer; three c.; ed Cornell Univ. and Massachusetts Inst. of Tech.; Chair. Math. and Science Depts, The Group School, Cambridge, Mass 1972–73; Research Asst, MIT 1972–74, Visiting Asst Prof. of Nutritional Biochemistry, Dept of Nutrition and Food Sciences 1977–78, Asst Prof. of Nutritional Biochemistry 1978–81, Assoc. Prof. of Biochemical Eng, Dept of Nutrition and Food Sciences and the Whitaker Coll. of Health Sciences Tech. and Management, and the Harvard-MIT Div. of Health Sciences and Tech. 1981–85, Prof. of Biochemical Eng, Dept of Applied Biological Sciences etc. 1985–88, Germeshausen Prof. of Chemical and Biomedical Eng, Dept of Chemical Eng 1988–2005, Inst. Prof. 2005–09, David H. Koch Inst. Prof. 2009–; Research Assoc., Children's Hosp. Medical Center, Harvard Medical School, Boston 1974–, Sr Lecturer on Surgery, Harvard Medical School, Harvard Univ. 1999–; mem. SCIENCE Bd, US Food and Drug Admin 1995–2002, Chair. 1999–2002; mem. Bd of Dirs or Scientific Advisory Bd Wyeth, Alkermes, Mitsubishi Pharmaceuticals, Warner-Lambert, Momenta Pharmaceuticals, Pure-tech Ventures; has helped start 25 cos; mem. Inst. of Medicine (NAS) 1989, NAS, Nat. Acad. of Eng (NAE) 1992 (one of only a few people ever elected to all three US Nat. Acads and the youngest in history aged 43); Fellow, ACS 2011, American Inst. of Chemical Engineers 2012; Dr hc (ETH, Switzerland, Technion Univ., Israel, Hebrew Univ. of Jerusalem, Université Catholique de Louvain, Belgium, Univ. of Liverpool, UK, Univ. of Nottingham, UK, Albany Medical Coll., Pennsylvania State Univ., Uppsala Univ., Sweden, Yale Univ., Northwestern Univ., Yale Univ., Mount Sinai School of Medicine, Harvard Univ., Willamette Univ., Rensselaer Polytechnic Inst., Bates Coll., Ben Gurion Univ., Israel, Tel-Aviv Univ., Israel, Boston Univ.); more than 220 honours and major awards, including being named by Bio World as one of the 25 most important individuals in biotechnology in the world 1990, ACS Award for Applied Polymer Science (Phillips Award) 1992, Gairdner Foundation Int. Award 1996, AIChE William Walker Award 1996, Lemelson-MIT Prize for Invention and Innovation 1998, ACS Award in Polymer Chem. 1999, named by Forbes Magazine 1999, ACS (Delaware Section) Wallace Carothers Award 2000, named by TIME Magazine and CNN as one of the 100 most important people in America and one of the 18 top people in science or medicine in America 2001, named by Discover Magazine as one of the 20 most important people in this area 2002, selected by Forbes Magazine as one of the 15 innovators world-wide who will re-invent our future 2002, NAE Charles Stark Draper Prize 2002, Dickson Prize for Science 2002, Heinz Award for Tech., Economy and Employment 2003, Harvey Prize 2003, John Fritz Award 2003, General Motors Kettering Prize for Cancer Research 2004, selected by Parade Magazine as one of six "Heroes whose research may save your life" 2004, Dan David Prize in Materials Science 2005, Albany Medical Center Prize in Medicine and Biomedical Research 2005, Nat. Medal of Science 2006, inducted into Nat. Inventors Hall of Fame 2006, Millennium Tech. Prize 2008, Max Planck Research Award 2008, Prince of Asturias Award for Tech. and Scientific Research 2008, Nat. Medal of Tech. and Innovation 2011, Warren Alpert Foundation Prize 2011, Terumo Int. Prize 2012, ACS Priestley Medal 2012, Industrial Research Inst. Medal (co-recipient) 2013, Wolf Prize in Chem., Wolf Foundation 2013. *Publications:* more than 1,200 articles in scientific journals on drug delivery, biomaterials, tissue engineering, biotechnology, immobilized enzymes, biomedical engineering, and more than 800 issued or pending patents world-wide. *Address:* Langer Lab, Massachusetts Institute of Technology, Room 76-661, The David H. Koch Institute Building, 77 Massachusetts Avenue, Cambridge, MA 02139-4307, USA (office). *Telephone:* (617) 253-3107 (office). *Fax:* (617) 258-8827 (office). *E-mail:* rlanger@mit.edu (office); langeroffice@mit.edu (office). *Website:* web.mit.edu/langerlab (office); web.mit.edu/be/people/langer.shtml (office).

LANGHOFF, Stephanie R., BS, MBA, PhD; American chemist; *Chief Scientist, NASA Ames Research Center;* ed Colorado Coll., Univ. of Washington, Massachu-

setts Inst. of Tech.; Post-Doctoral Fellow, Battelle Memorial Inst., Columbus, OH 1973–76; Nat. Research Council Fellow, NASA Ames Research Center 1976–78, Research Scientist, Computational Chem. Br. 1978–92, Br. Chief 1992–97, Chief Scientist 1998–, Chair. NASA Ames Basic Research Council 1999–2002; Sloan Fellow, MIT 1997–98; mem. American Physical Soc.; mem. US Dept of Energy Panel on Combustion Research, Panel on Innovative Concepts in Nuclear Propulsion. *Address:* NASA Ames Research Center, MS 230–3, Moffett Field, CA 94035, USA (office). *Telephone:* (650) 604-6213 (office). *Fax:* (650) 604-0350 (office). *E-mail:* stephanie.r.langhoff@nasa.gov (office). *Website:* www.nasa.gov/centers/ames (office).

LANGLANDS, Sir (Robert) Alan, Kt, FRSE; British university administrator and health care manager; *Vice-Chancellor, University of Leeds;* b. 29 May 1952, Glasgow, Scotland; s. of James Langlands and May Langlands (née Rankin); m. Elizabeth McDonald 1977; one s. one d.; ed Allan Glen's School, Univ. of Glasgow; grad. trainee Nat. Health Service Scotland 1974–76; with Argyll and Clyde Health Bd 1976–78; with Simpson Memorial Maternity Pavilion, Elsie Inglis Hosp. 1978–81; Unit Admin. Middx and Univ. Coll. Hosps and Hosp. for Women, Soho 1981–85; Dist Gen. Man. Harrow Health Authority 1985–89; Practice Leader Health Care, Towers Perrin 1989–91; Gen. Man. NW Thames Regional Health Authority 1991–92; Deputy Chief Exec. Nat. Health Service 1993–94, Chief Exec. 1994–2000; Prin. and Vice-Chancellor Univ. of Dundee 2000–09; Chief Exec. Higher Educ. Funding Council for England 2009–13; Vice-Chancellor Univ. of Leeds 2013–; mem. Cen. Research and Devt Cttee Nat. Health Service 1991–92, Inst. of Health Services Man., Nat. Forum for Research and Devt 1994–2000, Advisory Bd Centre for Corp. Strategy and Change, Univ. of Warwick 1995–2000, Nat. Advisory Bd, Healthcare Advisory Bd Institut Européen d'Admin des Affaires (INSEAD) 1998–2000; Chair. UK Biobank 2004–12, The Health Foundation 2009–; Hon. Prof., Warwick Business School 1996, Johns Hopkins Univ. 2000–04; Hon. FFPHM 1994; Hon. FIA 1999; Hon. FCGI 2000; Hon. CCMI CIMgt 2000; Hon. Fellow, Royal Coll. of Gen. Practitioners 2001; Hon. FRCP 2001; Hon. FRCSE 2001; Hon. FRCPSGlas 2002; Hon. FMedSci 2009; Hon. DUniv Glasgow 2001; Hon. LLD (Dundee) 2010; Dr hc (Edinburgh) 2010. *Leisure interests:* walking in Yorkshire and Scotland. *Address:* Office of the Vice-Chancellor, University of Leeds, Leeds, LS2 9JT, England (office). *Telephone:* (113) 343-3000 (office). *Fax:* (113) 244-3923 (office). *E-mail:* vice-chancellor@leeds.ac.uk (office). *Website:* www.leeds.ac.uk/info/20015/senior_officers (office).

LANGLANDS, Robert Phelan, MA, PhD, FRS, FRSC; Canadian/American mathematician and academic; *Hermann Weyl Professor Emeritus, School of Mathematics, Institute for Advanced Study, Princeton;* b. 6 Oct. 1936, New Westminster, BC; s. of Robert Langlands and Kathleen J. Phelan; m. Charlotte Cheverie 1956; two s. two d.; ed Univ. of British Columbia, Yale Univ., USA; Instructor, Assoc. Prof. Princeton Univ. 1960–67; Prof. Yale Univ. 1968–72; Hermann Weyl Prof. Inst. for Advanced Study, Princeton 1972–2007, Prof. Emer. 2007–; mem. NAS, American Math. Soc.; Wolf Prize 1995/96, Grande Medaille d'Or, Paris 2000, Frederic Esser Nemmers Prize in Math. 2006, Shaw Prize 2007. *Publications:* Automorphic Forms on GL(2) (with H. Jacquet) 1970, Euler Products 1971, On the Functional Equations Satisfied by Eisenstein Series 1976, Base Change for GL (2) 1980, Les Débuts d'une Formule des Traces Stable 1983. *Leisure interests:* reading, travel. *Address:* School of Mathematics, Fuld Hall 115, Institute for Advanced Study, Einstein Drive, Princeton, NJ 08540 (office); 60 Battle Road, Princeton, NJ 08540, USA (home). *Telephone:* (609) 734-8117 (office); (609) 921-7222 (home). *E-mail:* rpl@ias.edu (office). *Website:* publications.ias.edu/rpl (office).

LANGLEY, Donna; British film industry executive and film producer; *Co-Chairman, Universal Pictures;* b. Isle of Wight, England; m.; two s.; began career as asst at New Line Cinema, later served as Sr Vice-Pres. of Production; joined Universal Pictures as Sr Vice-Pres. of Production 2001, Pres. of Production –2009, Co-Chair. Universal Pictures (first British woman to run a Hollywood studio) 2009–; Global Amb. for Vital Voices Global; mem. Advisory Bd Chrysalis (charity), Co-Chair. Chrysalis' Annual Butterfly Ball; helped start The Hollywood Reporter's Women in Film Mentorship programme; Crystal Award for excellence in film-making, Women in Film 2010, Grace Kelly Award, March of Dimes 2011. *Films include:* exec. producer: Austin Powers: The Spy Who Shagged Me 1999, Drop Dead Gorgeous 1999, The Astronaut's Wife 1999, The Bachelor 1999, The Cell 2000, Lost Souls 2000, Highway 2002; other film roles: Summer School (production sec.) 1987, Born in East L.A. (production sec.) 1987, Austin Powers: International Man of Mystery (creative exec.) 1997, Northfork (office production asst) 2003. *Television includes:* Bakugan Battle Brawlers: Gundalian Invaders (series) (production exec.) 2010; other TV film roles: The Night Train to Kathmandu (film) (production office coordinator) 1988, Ancient Mysteries (series documentary) (production coordinator) 1996–97, Biography (series documentary) (post-production manager) 1998. *Leisure interest:* organic gardening. *Address:* Universal Pictures, 100 Universal City Plaza, Universal City, CA 91608-1002, USA (office). *Telephone:* (818) 777-1000 (office). *Fax:* (818) 866-3600 (office). *Website:* www.universalpictures.com (office).

LANGSLET, Lars Roar, MA; Norwegian writer and politician; *Chairman, National Ibsen Committee;* b. 5 March 1936, Nesbyen; s. of Knut Langslet and Alma Langslet; ed Univ. of Oslo; Assoc. Prof. 1969–89; MP 1969–89; Minister of Culture and Science 1981–86; writer Aftenposten newspaper 1990–97; Ed. Ordet 1997–; State Scholarship 1997–99; Pres. of Norwegian Acad. for Language and Literature 1995–; Chair., Nat. Ibsen Cttee; Commdr Order of St Olav, Dannebrog, Order of Gregory the Great, etc. . *Publications:* Karl Marx 1963, Conservatism 1965, (biogs of) John Lyng 1989, King Olav V 1995, St Olav 1995, King Christian IV 1997, King Christian VIII 1998–99, Ludvig Holberg 2001. *Address:* Ibsen.net, c/o The National Library of Norway, PO Box 2674, Solli, 0203 Oslo, Norway (office). *Telephone:* 23-27-60-15 (office). *Fax:* 23-27-60-10 (office). *Website:* www.ibsen.net (office).

LANGUETIN, Pierre; Swiss diplomatist and fmr central banker; b. 30 April 1923, Lausanne; m. Florentina Lobo 1951; one s. one d.; ed Univ. de Lausanne and LSE, UK; diplomatic career 1949–; in Div. of Exchange, OEEC, Paris; in Div. of Commerce, Fed. Dept of Public Economy 1955–76, Head of Secr. 1957–61, Chief of Section IA 1961–63; Chief of Subdiv. 1963; has been concerned with problems of European econ. co-operation; Asst Head of Bureau of Integration, Fed. Political Dept and Dept of Public Economy 1961; Swiss Del. to Trade Cttee, OECD, Paris

1961–76, Vice-Pres. 1963–76; mem. Swiss Del. to UNCTAD, Geneva 1964, New Delhi 1968; Swiss Rep. at various int. orgs 1965–66; Del. of Fed. Council for Trade Negotiations, title of Minister Plenipotentiary 1966–68; Head of Swiss Del. to EFTA Geneva 1967–76, title of Amb. 1968–76; Deputy Head of Swiss Negotiating Team with EEC 1970–72; Head of Swiss Del. to Exec. Cttee in special session OECD 1972–76; Head of Swiss Del. for accession negotiations to Int. Energy Agency 1974, Rep. for Switzerland to Governing Bd 1974–76; mem. Governing Bd of Swiss Nat. Bank 1976–81, Vice-Chair. 1981–84, Chair. 1985–88; mem. Bd of Dirs BIS 1985–88; Chair. Inst. for Public Admin. Studies, Lausanne 1988–97, Inst. for Bank and Financial Man., Lausanne 1990–96; Vice-Chair. Sandoz SA 1988–95; Chair. Rosbank (fmrly Unexim), Switzerland 1995–2009; mem. Bd of Dirs Ludwig Inst. 1987–2007, Swiss Reinsurance Co. 1988–93, Pargesa Holding SA 1988–2002, Paribas (Suisse) 1989–96 (Vice-Chair. 1992), Renault Finance 1989–99, Fin. Cpy Tradition 1995–; mem. Advisory Bd American Int. Group 1989–97, Arthur Andersen (Switzerland) 1991–97; mem. Bd of Dirs Chase Manhattan Pvt. Bank (Switzerland) 1991–2001, Dryden Bank (formerly Prumerica Pvt. Bank) (Switzerland) 2002–05; mem. Int. Red Cross Cttee 1988–93; Dr hc (Lausanne) 1979. *Address:* 33, Chemin des Roches 1470 Estavager-le-Lac, Switzerland (home). *Telephone:* (26) 6633325 (home). *Fax:* (26) 6633325 (home).

LANKESTER, Sir Timothy Patrick, Kt, KCB, BA, MA; British fmr government official and university administrator; *Chairman, Council, London School of Hygiene and Tropical Medicine;* b. 15 April 1942, Cairo, Egypt; s. of the late Robin P. A. Lankester and of Jean D. Gilliat; m. Patricia Cockcroft 1968; three d.; ed Monkton Combe School, St John's Coll., Cambridge and Jonathan Edwards Coll., Yale; reacher with VSO, St Michael's Coll., British Honduras (now Belize) 1960–61; Faraday Fellow, St John's Coll. Oxford 1965–66; Economist, IBRD, Washington, DC 1966–69, New Delhi 1970–73; HM Treasury 1973–78, Under-Sec. 1983–85, Deputy Sec. 1988–89; Pvt. Sec. to Prime Minister Callaghan 1978–79, to Prime Minister Thatcher 1979–81; seconded to S.G. Warburg & Co. 1981–83; Econ. Minister, Washington, DC and UK Exec. Dir IMF and IBRD 1985–88; Perm. Sec., Overseas Devt Admin., FCO 1989–93, Dept for Educ. 1994–95; Dir SOAS, Univ. of London 1996–2000, Hon. Fellow 2002–; Pres. Corpus Christi Coll. Oxford 2001–10; Chair. Council of the London School of Hygiene and Tropical Medicine; mem. Jt Advisory Bd Georgetown University School of Foreign Service, Qatar; Dir European Investment Bank 1988–89, Smith and Nephew 1996–2003, London Metal Exchange 1997–2001, Mitchells and Butler plc 2003–, Actis 2004–; Gov. Asia-Europe Foundation 1997–; Deputy Chair. British Council 1998–2003; Trustee, Contemporary Dance Trust; Hon. Fellow, St John's Coll., Cambridge, Corpus Christi Coll., Oxford. *Address:* London School of Hygiene & Tropical Medicine, Keppel Street, London, WC1E 7HT, England (office). *Telephone:* (20) 7636-8636 (office). *Fax:* (20) 7436-5389 (office). *E-mail:* council@lshtm.ac.uk (office). *Website:* www.lshtm.ac.uk (office).

LANKHORST, Gertjan, AB; Dutch energy industry executive; *CEO, GasTerra BV;* b. 22 Dec. 1957, Amsterdam; ed Atheneum B, Amsterdam Free Univ.; held teaching position at Amsterdam Free Univ. 1982–86; joined Gen. Econ. Policy Dept, Ministry of Econ. Affairs 1986, becoming Dir of Oil and Gas 1996–99, Competition Dir 1999–2003, Dir-Gen. for Energy 2004–05; CEO GasTerra BV (fmrly Gasunie Trade & Supply BV) 2006–. *Address:* GasTerra BV, PO Box 477, 9700 AL Groningen; GasTerra BV, Rozenburglaan 11, 9727 DL Groningen, Netherlands (office). *Telephone:* (50) 364-86-48 (office). *Fax:* (50) 364-86-00 (office). *E-mail:* communicatie@gasterra.nl (office). *Website:* www.gasterra.com (office).

LANOTTE, Johan Vande, MA, PhD; Belgian politician; *Deputy Prime Minister and Minister of Economy, Consumers and the North Sea;* b. 6 July 1955, Poperinge; ed Sint-Stanislascollege, Univ. of Antwerpen (UIA), Rijksuniversiteit Gent (RUG); Asst Dept of Political and Social Sciences, UIA 1982–83; Asst Special Admin. Law, RUG 1983–87; Head of Office for Minister of the Interior 1988–91; Minister of the Interior and the Civil Service 1994–95; Deputy Prime Minister and Minister of the Home Dept 1995–98; Deputy Prime Minister and Minister of the Budget, Social Integration and Social Economy 1999; Deputy Prime Minister and Minister for the Budget and Public Enterprise, Deputy Prime Minister and Minister of Economy, Consumers and the North Sea 2011–; Chair. Sociaal Progressief Alternatief (Socialist Party—Flemish wing). *Publications:* Krachtlijnen van een vernieuwd gemeentebeleid 1983, Wonen in België. Mythen en werkelijkheid (co-author) 1985, Petitierecht 1987, De noodzakelijke decentralisatie 1988, De recente evolutie en de knelpunten in de ruimtelijke ordening en de stedebouw (co-author) 1988, De geschiedenis van de Provinciewet (co-author) 1990, De nieuwe gemeentelijke comptabiliteit (co-author) 1990, Inleiding tot het publiek recht 1994, Overzicht van het Belgisch Administratief Recht (co-author) 1996, Het Europees verdrag tot bescherming van de Rechten van de Mens: In Hoofdlijnen (co-author), 1997, België voor beginners: Wegwijs in het Belgisch labyrint (co-author) 1998, Handboek Europees Verdrag voor de Rechten van de Mens (co-author) 2004. *Leisure interest:* basketball. *Address:* Federal Public Service of the Economy, 50 rue de Progrès, 1210 Brussels, Belgium (office). *Telephone:* (2) 277-51-11 (office). *Fax:* (2) 277-51-07 (office). *E-mail:* info.eco@economie.fgov.be (office); info@johanvandelanotte.be (office). *Website:* www.economie.fgov.be (office).

LANOVOY, Vasilii Semenovich; Russian actor; b. 16 Jan. 1934, Moscow; s. of Semion Petrovich Lanovoy and Agafia Ivanovna Yakubenko; m. Irina Petrovna Kupchenko 1972; two s.; ed Shchukin Theatre School; actor with Vakhtangov Theatre 1957–; also works as narrator; Prof., Faculty of Artistic Speech, Shchukin's Theatre School, Moscow 1995–; mem. CPSU 1968–90; Lenin Prize 1980, People's Artist of USSR 1985. *Theatrical roles include:* Ognev in Korneichuk's Front, Prince Calaf in Gozzi's Princess Turandot, Caesar in Shaw's Antony and Cleopatra, Sagadeev in Abdullin's Thirteenth President, Don Juan in Pushkin's The Stone Guest, Trotsky in M. Shatrov's Peace of Brest, Oscar in La Bize's Murder at Lursin Street, Astrov in Uncle Vanya, J.B. Shaw in I. Kiltye's Dear Liar, King Henry in The Lion in Winter. *Films include:* War and Peace, Anna Karenina, The Strange Woman, Going in a Thunderstorm, The Picture, The Scarlet Sails, The Officers, Unknown War, The Colleges, Strategy for Victory, The Trifles of Life, Barin's Daughter. *Leisure interests:* volleyball, badminton, hunting, skiing, dogs. *Address:* 121002 Moscow, Starokonyushenny per. 39, Apt 18, Russia. *Telephone:* (495) 203-94-03.

LANSBURY SHAW, Angela Brigid, (Angela Lansbury), DBE, CBE; British actress; b. 16 Oct. 1925, London, England; d. of Edgar Lansbury and Moyna Macgill (Charlotte Lillian McIldowie); m. 1st Richard Cromwell 1945 (divorced 1946); m. 2nd Peter Shaw 1949 (died 2003); one s. one d. one step-s.; ed Webber Douglas School of Singing and Dramatic Art, Kensington, Feagin School of Drama and Radio, New York; film debut in Gaslight 1944; numerous appearances on London and New York stages and on TV; Hon. DHumLitt (Boston) 1990; Silver Mask for Lifetime Achievement BAFTA 1991, Lifetime Achievement Award, Screen Actors' Guild 1997, Stephen Sondheim Award 2009, Hon. Academy Award 2013, numerous other awards. *Stage appearances include:* Hotel Paradiso 1957, Dear World (Tony Award) 1969, The King and I 1978, A Little Family Business 1983, Deuce 2007, A Little Night Music 2009, Blithe Spirit 2014. *Films include:* Manchurian Candidate, In the Cool of the Day, Harlow, Moll Flanders, Bedknobs and Broomsticks, Death on the Nile, The Lady Vanishes 1980, The Mirror Cracked 1980, The Pirates of Penzance 1982, Company of Wolves 1983, Beauty and the Beast 1991, Anastasia (voice) 1997, Nanny McPhee 2005, Heidi 4 Paws (voice) 2009, Mr. Popper's Penguins 2011. *Television includes:* Murder She Wrote 1984–96 (with special episodes thereafter, including Murder, She Wrote: The Celtic Riddle 2003), The Shell Seekers 1989, South by Southwest 1997, A Story to Die For 2000, Touched by an Angel (series) 2002, The Blackwater Lightship (film) 2004, Law & Order: Trial by Jury (series) 2005, Law & Order: Special Victims Unit (series) 2005, At the Paley Center (series) 2010. *Publication:* Angela Lansbury's Positive Moves (with Mimi Avins) 1990. *Address:* c/o WME Entertainment, 9601 Wilshire Boulevard, Beverley Hills, CA 90210-5213, USA (office). *Telephone:* (310) 285-9000 (office). *Fax:* (310) 285-9010 (office). *Website:* www.wma.com (office).

LANSING, Sherry, BS; American film producer and business executive; *CEO, Sherry Lansing Foundation;* b. (Sherry Lee Heimann), 31 July 1944, Chicago, Ill.; d. of Norton Lansing and Margot Lansing; m. 2nd William Friedkin 1991; ed Northwestern Univ.; math. and English teacher, Public High Schools, LA, Calif. 1966–69; model, TV commercials, Max Factor Co. and Alberto-Culver 1969–70; appeared in films Loving and Rio Lobo 1970; Exec. Story Ed., Wagner Int. 1970–73; Vice-Pres. for Production, Heyday Productions 1973–75; Exec. Story Ed., then Vice-Pres. for Creative Affairs, MGM Studios 1975–77; Vice-Pres., then Sr Vice-Pres. for Production, Columbia Pictures 1977–80; Pres. 20th Century-Fox Productions 1980–83; Co-Founder Jaffe-Lansing Productions, LA 1982; Chair. Paramount Pictures 1992–2005; Founder and CEO Sherry Lansing Foundation 2005–; mem. Bd of Regents, Univ. of Calif. 1999–; mem. Bd of Dirs Encore.org, Entertainment Industry Foundation, W.M. Keck Foundation, Teach for America, American Film Inst., The Carter Center, DonorsChoose, American Asscn for Cancer Research, Friends of Cancer Research; Trustee Calif. Museum for History, Women and the Arts; Dr hc (American Film Inst.); Woodrow Wilson Award for Corporate Citizenship, Milestone Award from Producers Guild of America, Overcoming Obstacles Achievement Award for Business, YWCA Silver Achievement Award, Outstanding Woman in Business Award frome Women's Equity Action League, Distinguished Community Service Award from Brandeis Univ., Alfred P. Sloan, Jr. Memorial Award, Pioneer of the Year by Foundation of Motion Picture Pioneers 1996, first woman studio head to receive a star on Hollywood Walk of Fame 1996, named on Power 100 List in Women in Entertainment Report, The Hollywood Reporter No. 1 2002, No. 4 2003, ranked by Fortune magazine amongst 50 Most Powerful Women in Business in the US (19th) 2002, (20th) 2003, (27th) 2004, ranked 71st by Forbes magazine amongst 100 Most Powerful Women 2004, Exemplary Leadership in Management Award, UCLA Anderson School of Man. 2005, Jean Hersholt Humanitarian Award 2007, Double Helix Medal, Cold Spring Harbor Laboratory 2008, Centennial Medal for Distinguished Public Service, American Asscn for Cancer Research 2009, Stem Cell Action Leadership Award, World Stem Cell Summit 2011, Lifetime Achievement Award, Israel Film Festival, Los Angeles 2013. *Films produced include:* Racing with the Moon 1984, Firstborn 1984 (exec. producer), When the Time Comes (TV) (exec. producer), Fatal Attraction 1987, The Accused 1988, Black Rain 1989, School Ties 1992, Indecent Proposal 1993, The Untouchables: Capone Rising 2006. *Address:* Sherry Lansing Foundation, 2121 Avenue of the Stars, Suite 2020, Los Angeles, CA 90067, USA (office). *Telephone:* (310) 788-0057 (office). *E-mail:* slfasst@sherrylansingfoundation.org (office). *Website:* www.sherrylansingfoundation.org (office).

LANSLEY, Rt Hon. Andrew David, PC, CBE, BA; British politician; *Leader of the House of Commons and Lord Privy Seal;* b. 11 Dec. 1956, Hornchurch, Essex, England; s. of Thomas Lansley; m. 1st Dr Marilyn Biggs (divorced 1997); three d.; m. 2nd Sally Low; one s. one d.; ed Brentwood School, Essex, Univ. of Exeter; fmr Pres. Guild for Students, Univ. of Exeter; began career as civil servant at Dept of Trade & Industry; Prin. Pvt. Sec. to Rt Hon. Norman Tebbit MP 1984–87; Deputy Dir-Gen. British Chambers of Commerce 1987–90; Dir Conservative Research Dept 1990–95; ran Conservative Party campaign for 1992 Gen. Election; Vice-Chair. Conservative Party (with responsibility for Policy Renewal) 1998–99; MP for South Cambridgeshire 1997–2010, for South Cambridgeshire (revised boundary) 2010–; Shadow Minister for Cabinet Office and Policy Renewal 1999–2001, Shadow Chancellor of Duchy of Lancaster 1999–2001, Shadow Sec. of State for Health 2003–10; Sec. of State for Health 2010–12; Leader of the House of Commons and Lord Privy Seal 2012–; mem. Health Select Cttee 1997–98, Trade and Industry Select Cttee 2001–04, House of Commons Comm. 2012–, Speaker's Cttee for the Ind. Parl. Standards Authority 2012–, Public Accounts Comm. 2012–; Vice-Pres. Local Govt Asscn 1996–; Conservative. *Leisure interests:* spending time with family, history, cricket, theatre, films, travel. *Address:* Office of the Leader of the House of Commons, 26 Whitehall, London, SW1A 2WH (office); House of Commons, Westminster, London, SW1A 0AA (office); Constituency Office, 153 St Neots Road, Hardwick, Cambs., CB23 7QJ, England (office). *Telephone:* (20) 7276-1005 (London) (office); (1954) 212707 (Hardwick) (office). *Fax:* (20) 7276-1006 (London) (office); (1954) 211625 (Hardwick) (office). *E-mail:* Leader@CommonsLeader.x.gsi.gov.uk (office); lansleya@parliament.uk (office). *Website:* www.cabinetoffice.gov.uk/content/office-leader-house-commons-information (office); www.parliament.uk/biographies/commons/andrew-lansley/25555; www.andrewlansley.co.uk.

LANTIGUA, José Rafael, BEd; Dominican Republic writer and politician; *Secretary of State for Culture;* b. 17 Sept. 1949, Moca; ed Pedro Henríquez Ureña Nat. Univ.; Ed. Literary Section, Ultima Hora (newspaper) 1985–2000; Chair. Nat. Book Fair Standing Cttee 1996–2000; Sec. of State for Culture 2004–; mem. Dominican Acad. of Language 2008–; Nat. Essay Prize 1976, Nat. Prize for

Journalism 1988, Caonabo de Oro Prize 1999. *Publications:* poetry: Sobre un tiempo de esperanza 1982, Semblanzas del corazón 1985; essays: Domingo Moreno Jimenes: biografía de un poeta 1976, Hacia una revalorización del ideal duartiano 1985, La conjura del tiempo 1994, El oficio de la palabra 1995; anthology: del cuento cubano y dominicano 1999. *Address:* Secretariat of State for Culture, Centro de Eventos y Exposiciones, Avda George Washington, esq. Presidente Vicini Burgos, Santo Domingo, Dominican Republic (office). *Telephone:* 221-4141 (office). *Fax:* 221-3342 (office). *E-mail:* contacto@cultura.gov.do (office). *Website:* www.cultura.gov.do (office).

LANXADE, Adm. Jacques; French naval officer; *Chairman, Fondation Méditerranéenne d'Etudes stratégiques;* b. 8 Sept. 1934, Toulon; m. Loïse Rostan d'Ancezune 1959; one s. three d.; ed Ecole Navale, Institut d'Admin des Affaires (Université Dauphiné); Commdr destroyers Le Champenois 1970–72, La Galissonnière 1976–77, frigate Duguay-Trouin 1980–81; rank of Rear-Adm. 1984; Commdr Indian Ocean maritime zone 1984–86; Commdr French fleet in the Indian Ocean 1986; rank of Vice-Adm. 1987; Chef du Cabinet Militaire to Minister of Defence 1988–89; Chief of Staff, Elysée Palace 1989; Chief of Staff of French Armed Forces 1991–95; Amb. to Tunisia 1995–99; Chair. Fondation Méditerranéenne d'Etudes stratégiques; mem. Atomic Energy Cttee 1991–95, Initiative for a Renewed Transatlantic Partnership, Center for Strategic and Int. Studies 2003–, Acad. de Marine 2008–, Int. Cttee of Patronage of the French journal Politique américaine; Grand Officier Légion d'honneur, Officier, Ordre nat. du Mérite, Croix de la Valeur Militaire. *Publications:* Quand le monde a basculé 2001, Organizer la politique européenne et internationale de la France (report) 2002. *Leisure interests:* tennis, skiing. *Address:* Fondation Méditerranéenne d'Etudes stratégiques, Maison des technologies, place Georges Pompidou, 83000 Toulon, France (office); 41 rue Saint-André des Arts, 75006 Paris, France (home). *Telephone:* (4) 94-05-55-55 (office); 1-46-33-39-05 (home). *Fax:* (4) 94-05-55-59 (office). *E-mail:* info@fmes-france.org (office); jacqueslanxade@noos.fr (office). *Website:* fmes-france .org (office).

LANYON, Lance Edward, CBE, BVSc, PhD, DSc, FMedSci, MRCVS; British professor of veterinary anatomy and university administrator; b. 4 Jan. 1944; s. of the late Henry Lanyon and Heather Gordon (née Tyrrell); m. Mary Kear (divorced 1997); one s. one d.; ed Christ's Hosp., Univ. of Bristol; Lecturer, Univ. of Bristol 1967, Reader in Veterinary Anatomy 1967–79, currently Visiting Prof.; Assoc. Prof., Tufts School of Veterinary Medicine, Boston, USA 1980–83, Prof. 1983–84; Prof. of Veterinary Anatomy, Royal Veterinary Coll., Univ. of London 1984–89, personal title 1989–2004, Head of Dept of Veterinary Anatomy 1984–87, of Veterinary Basic Sciences 1987–88, Prof. Emer. 2004–, Prin. Royal Veterinary Coll. 1989–2004 (retd); Pro-Vice-Chancellor, Univ. of London 1997–99; Hon. Fellow, Royal Coll. of Veterinary Surgeons (RCVS) 2012; Hon. DSc (Bristol) 2004; RCVS Share Jones Lecturer 1989, Wooldridge Lecturer, British Veterinary Asscn 1996. *Publications include:* numerous articles in professional journals; chapters in books on osteoporosis, orthopaedics and athletic training. *Leisure interests:* building, home improvements, sailing. *Address:* Royal Veterinary College, Royal College Street, London, NW1 0UT, England. *Telephone:* (20) 7468-5000. *E-mail:* info@rvc.ac.uk. *Website:* www.rvc.ac.uk.

LANZER, Toby, BA, MIA, DPhil; British UN official; *Deputy Special Representative of the Secretary-General, Resident Coordinator and Resident Representative, United Nations Mission in the Republic of South Sudan (UNMISS);* b. 1965; m.; three c.; ed Univ. of Oxford, Columbia Univ., Univ. of New Hampshire, USA; joined UNDP 1992, Jr Professional Officer, Angola 1992–93, Field Adviser, Angola, Dept of Humanitarian Affairs (DHA) 1994–95, Head of Office, Georgia 1996–98, Head of Office for Coordination of Human Affairs (OCHA) in Russian Fed. 1999–2003, Chief of Consolidated Appeals Process (CAP), UN, Geneva 2003–05, UNDP Resident Rep. in Cen. African Repub. 2006–12, Chief of Staff, UN Integrated Mission in Timor-Leste –2012, Deputy Resident Coordinator and Humanitarian Coordinator, UN Mission in Sudan 2012–, Deputy Special Rep. of Sec.-Gen. 2012–, UN Resident Coordinator, Humanitarian Coordinator and Resident Rep., UNDP 2012–. *Address:* United Nations Mission in South Sudan Headquarters, PO Box 29, Juba, 081111, South Sudan (office); United Nations Development Programme, One United Nations Plaza, New York, NY 10017, USA (office). *Telephone:* 91206-2000 (Juba) (office); (212) 906-5000 (New York) (office). *Fax:* 91206-6200 (Juba) (office); (212) 906-5001 (New York) (office). *E-mail:* unmiss@spokesperson@un.org (office). *Website:* unmiss.unmissions.org (office); www.undp.org (office).

LANZMANN, Claude; French filmmaker and director; *Professor of Documentary Film, European Graduate School, Saas-Fee, Switzerland;* b. 27 Nov. 1925, Paris; ed Univ. of Tübingen, Germany, studied in Paris (Diplomé d'Etudes Supérieures de Philosophie); fmr journalist, France-Soir, France-Dimanche; fmr Lecturer in French Literature and Philosophy, Free Univ. of Berlin; Prof. of Documentary Film, European Grad. School, Saas-Fee, Switzerland; Ed.-in-Chief, Les Temps Modernes magazine; Hon. PhD (European Grad. School) 2004. *Films:* Elise ou la vraie vie (writer) 1970, Pourquoi Israel (Israel, Why) 1974, Shoah (Special Award, Los Angeles Film Critics' Asscn 1985, Caligari Film Award, FIPRESCI Prize, Forum of New Cinema and OCIC Award – Honorable Mention, Berlin Int. Film Festival 1986, Hon. César 1986, IDA Award, Int. Documentary Asscn 1986, Rotterdam Award for Best Documentary 1986, Rotterdam Int. Film Festical 1986, BAFTA Flaherty Documentary Award and Flaherty Documentary Award (TV) 1987) 1985, Tsahal (also writer) (1994), Un vivant qui passe (A Visitor from the Living) (also producer) 1997, Sobibór, 14 octobre 1943, 16 heures (Sobibor, Oct. 14, 1943, 4 p.m.) (also writer) (Reader Jury of the 'Standard' Award, Viennale Film Festival 2001) 2001. *Publications:* The Complete Text of the Acclaimed Holocaust Film Shoah 1997, Le Lièvre de Patagonie (The Patagonian Hare) (auto-biog.) 2009. *Address:* European Graduate School, Media & Communications Division, Ringacker, 3953 Leuk-Stadt, Switzerland (office). *Telephone:* (27) 474-9917 (office). *Fax:* (27) 474-9969 (office). *E-mail:* info@egs.edu (office). *Website:* www.egs.edu (office).

LAO, Chongpin; Chinese artist; b. 3 Nov. 1936, Xinxing City, Guangdong Prov.; s. of Lao Xianguang and Chen Ermei; m. Luo Yuzing 1956; two s. one d.; ed Fine Arts Dept, Cen. China Teachers' Coll.; has painted more than 1000 landscapes and human figures in Japan, Canada, France, Egypt, Yugoslavia, Democratic People's Repub. of Korea, Pakistan, Burma, Jordan, Hungary, USSR, Albania 1973–; Dir Poetry Inst. 1987–; mem. staff Chinese Exhbn Agency, Ministry of Culture; mem. Chinese Artists' Asscn, Advisory Cttee, Beijing Children's Fine Arts Research

Acad., Chinese Poetry Asscn, Int. Biographical Asscn; Hon. Dir Hanlin Forest of Steles, Kaifeng, China Shaolin Research Inst. of Painting and Calligraphy 1989. *Major works:* Harvest Time, Spring Ploughing, Harbour, Riverside, Arashiyama in Rain, Mosque in Lahore, Golden Pagoda of Rangoon, Pyramid and Sphinx, Autumn in Amman, Morning Glory on Seine River, Niagara Falls; group exhbns include Seven Star Cliff, Japan 1979, Scenery on Xinghu Lake, Mexico 1980, Drum Beaters, Hong Kong 1982, Panda, Wulongtang Waterfall, Belgium 1982, Scenery on Huangshan Mountain, Jordan 1983, Light Boats on the Yangtze River (Nat. Arts Museum, Romania) 1986, Scenes of Petra (Sact City Museum, Jordan) 1987, Waterfall of Lushan Mountain (Zacheta Art Museum, Poland) 1987; one-man exhbns in many Chinese cities and provs 1979–, Hong Kong 1988, Philippines 1989, Jordan 1990, Singapore 1995, India 1996; Sixth Asian Art Biennale, Bangladesh 1993. *Publication:* An Album of Sketches of Life in Foreign Countries 1986. *Leisure interests:* travel, music. *Address:* 1-301 Building No. 43, Xidahe Dongli, Chaoyang Qu, Beijing 100028, People's Republic of China. *Telephone:* (10) 64672946.

LAOKPESSI, Col Pitalouna-Ani; Togolese government official and military officer; fmr Commdr, fmr Asst Chief of Army Staff; Minister of Security 2005. *Address:* c/o Ministry of Security, rue Albert Sarraut, Lomé, Togo (office).

LAOUROU, Grégoire; Benin politician; *President, Union pour la Majorité Présidentiel Plurielle;* Pres. Council of Ministers, W African Econ. and Monetary Union (UEMOA); mem. Minister of Finance and the Economy 2003–05; mem. Assemblée nationale (Force cauris pour un Bénin émergent—FCBE) 2007–, Pres. Union pour la Majorité Présidentiel Plurielle (UMPP) 2009–. *Address:* Assemblée nationale BP 371, Porto-Novo, Benin (office). *Telephone:* 20-21-22-19 (office). *Fax:* 20-21-36-44 (office). *E-mail:* assemblee.benin@yahoo.fr (office). *Website:* www .assembleebenin.org (office).

LAPANG, D. Dethwelson, BA; Indian politician; b. 10 April 1934; s. of the late Donwa War; m. Amethyst Lynda Jomes Blah 1958; one s. one d.; ed Shillong Govt High School, St Anthony's Coll., Shillong; mem. Meghalaya Legis. Ass. 1972, Minister of State for Co-operation, Jails, Educ. and Civil Defence 1978–79, Health and Family Welfare, Labour, Information and Public Relations 1979–83, Planning, Finance, Home, Revenue, Food & Civil Supply 1983–85, Finance, Planning, Evaluation, Home and Revenue 1985–87, Planning and Programme Implementation 1987–88, Home, Revenue and Excise 1987–88; Deputy Minister of Internal Affairs 1988–90; Chief Minister of Meghalaya 1992–93, 2003–06, 2007–08 (resgnd), 2009–10 (resgnd); Deputy Chief Minister 1998–2003; Chair. State Planning Board 1993–95, Comm. on Resources Mobilization 1995–97; Pres. Meghalaya State Council of Indo-Soviet Cultural Soc. 1979, Meghalaya State Indo-GDR Friendship Asscn; Founder Pres. Bhoi Student Asscn, Meghalaya State Basketball Asscn, Meghalaya Eds and Publrs Asscn, Affiliated State Olympic Asscn. *Address:* c/o Office of the Chief Minister, Government of Meghalaya, Shillong, Meghalaya 793 001 (office); Jaiaw Main Road, Shillong, Meghalaya, India (office). *E-mail:* cmoffice@shillong.meg.nic.in (office). *Website:* www .meghalaya.nic.in (office).

LAPHAM, Lewis H., BA; American writer and editor; *Editor, Lapham's Quarterly;* b. 8 Jan. 1935, San Francisco; m.; three c.; ed Yale Univ., Univ. of Cambridge, UK; reporter San Francisco Examiner newspaper 1957–59, New York Herald Tribune 1960–62; Ed. Harper's Magazine 1976–81, 1983–2006, Ed. Emer. and columnist 2006–; syndicated newspaper columnist 1981–87; univ. lecturer; Founder and Ed., Lapham's Quarterly magazine 2008–; appearances on American and British TV, broadcasts on Nat. Public Radio; Nat. Magazine Award for Essays 1995, Thomas Paine Journalism Award 2002. *Publications include:* Fortune's Child (essays) 1980, Money and Class in America 1988, Imperial Masquerade 1990, Hotel America: Scenes in the Lobby of the Fin-de-Siècle 1995, Waiting for the Barbarians 1997, The Agony of Mammon 1999, Lapham's Rules of Influence 1999, Theater of War 2002, 30 Satires 2003, Gag Rule 2004, Pretensions to Empire: Notes on the Criminal Folly of the Bush Administration 2007; contrib. 'Notebook' monthly essay Harper's Magazine; also contrib. to Commentary, Nat. Review, Yale Literary Magazine, Elle, Fortune, Forbes, American Spectator, Vanity Fair, Parade, Channels, Maclean's, London Observer, New York Times, Wall Street Journal. *Address:* Lapham's Quarterly, 33 Irving Place, Eighth Floor, New York, NY 10003, USA (office). *E-mail:* editorial@laphamsquarterly.org (office). *Website:* laphamsquarterly.org (office).

LAPHEN, Michael W., MBA; American information technology executive; m.; ed Pennsylvania State Univ., Wharton School, Univ. of Pennsylvania; served in USAF and Pa Air Nat. Guard; joined Computer Sciences Corpn 1977, has held numerous man. positions, including Vice-Pres. Finance and Admin, Pres. Integrated Systems Div. 1992–98, Pres. Fed. Sector Civil Group 1998–2000, Pres. European Group 2000–03, Pres. and COO 2003–07, Chair., Pres. and CEO 2007–12; mem. Information Technology Asscn of America, Armed Forces Communications and Electronics Asscn, Nat. Defense Industrial Asscn. *Address:* c/o Computer Sciences Corporation, 3170 Fairview Park Drive, Falls Church, VA 22042, USA. *E-mail:* info@csc.com.

LAPID, Yair; Israeli politician, journalist, actor, author and fmr television presenter; *Minister of Finance;* b. 5 Nov. 1963, Tel-Aviv; s. of the late fmr Deputy Prime Minister Yosef 'Tommy' Lapid and Shulamit Lapid; m. Lihi Lapi; three c.; one-time amateur boxer; began career in journalism as mil. corresp. for Israeli Defense Force's weekly magazine, Ba-Mahaneh (In the Camp); also wrote for daily Maariv; apptd Ed. of Tel-Aviv local newspaper published by the Yedioth Ahronoth group 1988; began writing weekly column, Where's the Money?, in a nat. newspaper's weekend supplement, at first for Maariv and later for its competitor, Yedioth Ahronoth 1991; hosted talk show on Israel TV's Channel 1 1994, talk show on Channel 3 1994, talk show on Channel 2 1999–; host of Ulpan Shishi (Friday Studio) on Channel 2 2008; left journalism to enter politics 2012; Founder and Chair. Yesh Atid party 2012–; Minister of Finance 2013–. *Play:* The Right Age for Love, performed by the Cameri Theatre 2008. *Television includes:* Ha-Hofesh Ha'Acharon (series) (screenplay) 1989, Shevet Cohen (series) (writer) 1991, Me'ever Layam 1992, Shirat Ha'Sirena 1994, Sogrim Shavua (series) 1995, Yair Lapid Chai Be'Eser (series) (host) 1997, Yair Lapid (series) (host) 2000, Mischak Machur (series) 2005, Hadar Milhama (series) (actor and producer) 2005, Lemon Tree (played a TV presenter as himself) 2008. *Publications include:* The Double

Head 1989, Yoav's Shadow (children's book) 1992, One-Man Play 1993, Elbi – A Knight's Story (children's book) 1998, The Sixth Riddle 2001, Standing in a Row (collection of newspaper columns) 2005, The Second Woman 2006, Sunset in Moscow 2007, Memories After My Death 2010. *Address:* Ministry of Finance, POB 13195, 1 Kaplan Street, Kiryat Ben-Gurion, Jerusalem, 91030, Israel (office). *Telephone:* 2-5317111 (office). *Fax:* 2-5637891 (office). *E-mail:* webmaster@mof.gov .il (office); ylapid@knesset.gov.il (office); english@yeshatid.org.il (office). *Website:* www.mof.gov.il (office); www.yeshatid.org.il (office).

LAPIERRE, Dominique; French journalist, writer and philanthropist; b. 30 July 1931, Châtelaillon, Charente-Maritime; s. of Jean Lapierre and Luce Lapierre (née Andreotti); m. 2nd Dominique Conchon 1980; one d. (by first m.); ed Lycée Condorcet, LaFayette Univ., USA; Ed. Paris Match Magazine 1954–67; Founder and Pres. Action Aid for Lepers' Children of Calcutta; Hon. Founder and Chair City of Joy (NGO); Citizen of Honour of the City of Calcutta; Commdr, Confrérie du Tastevin 1990, Chevalier, Légion d'honneur 2000, Grand Cross of the Order of Social Solidarity (Spain) 2002, Padma Bhushan (India) 2008; Dr hc (Lafayette Univ.) 1982; Christopher Book Award 1986, 2002, Gold Medal of Calcutta, Int. Rainbow Prize, UN 2000, Vatican Prize for Peace 2000, Gold Medal of the City of Milan 2006. *Publications include:* Un dollar les mille kilomètres 1949, Honeymoon around the World 1953, En liberté sur les routes d'U.R.S.S. 1957, Russie portes ouvertes 1957, Les Caïds de New York 1958, Chessman m'a dit 1960, The City of Joy 1985, Beyond Love 1991, A Thousand Suns 1998, Five Past Midnight in Bhopal 2002, It Was Once the USSR 2006, Un Arc-en-Ciel dans la Nuit 2008, India mon amour 2010; with Larry Collins: Is Paris Burning? 1964, Or I'll Dress You In Mourning 1967, O Jerusalem 1971, Freedom at Midnight 1975, The Fifth Horseman 1980, Is New York Burning? 2004. *Leisure interests:* riding, tennis, collecting antiques, vintage cars. *Address:* 37 Rue Charles-Laffitte, 92200 Neuilly; Les Bignoles, Val de Rian, 83350 Ramatuelle, France. *Telephone:* 1-46-37-34-34 (Neuilly); (4) 94-97-17-31 (Ramatuelle). *Fax:* (4) 94-97-38-05. *E-mail:* D.Lapierre@ wanadoo.fr (home). *Website:* cityofjoyaid.org (office).

LAPIS, Károly, PhD, DSci; Hungarian pathologist, clinical oncologist, cyto-pathologist and academic; *Professor Emeritus, Semmelweis University of Budapest;* b. 14 April 1926, Túrkeve; s. of Károly Lapis and Eszter Földesi; m. Ibolya Keresztes 1955; one s. one d.; ed Lóránd Eötvös Univ. Budapest; trainee, First Inst. of Pathology and Experimental Cancer Research, Eötvös Loránd Univ., Budapest 1950–51; Asst, Inst. of Pathology Medical Univ., Debrecen 1951–54; Scientific worker Oncopathological Research Inst. 1954–63; Prof. Postgraduate Medical School, Budapest 1963–68; Prof. 1st Inst. of Pathology and Experimental Cancer Research, Semmelweis Univ. of Budapest 1968–96, Prof. Emer. 1998– (Dir 1968–93); Gordon Jacob Fellow Chester Beatty Research Inst., London 1959–60; Eleanor Roosevelt Fellow, Paris 1963–64; Visiting Prof., Duke Univ. Medical School, Durham, NC 1972; Fogarty Scholar, Nat. Cancer Inst., Bethesda 1984–85; Corresp. mem. Hungarian Acad. of Sciences 1970, mem. 1979–; Foreign mem. Medical Acad. of the USSR (now Acad. of Medical Sciences of Russia) 1987, Serbian Acad. of Sciences and Arts 1989; Pres. 14th Int. Cancer Congress of the UICC, Budapest 1986; Vice-Pres. European Assoc. for Cancer Research 1979–85; mem. Exec. Cttee European Soc. of Pathology 1989–93, French Electron Microscope Soc., German Soc. of Pathology, Int. Gastro-Surgical Club, Hungarian Cancer Soc. (Pres. 1974–84), Hungarian Soc. of Gastroenterology, Hungarian Soc. of Pathologists, Int. Acad. of Pathology (Hungarian section); Corresp. mem. American Asscn for Cancer Research; Dir Metastasis Research Soc. 1986–90; Chief Ed. Acta Morphologica Hungarica 1985–94; Hon. Citizen of Mezotur 1997; Labour Order of Merit 1978, 4th of April Order of Merit 1986; Krompecher Memorial Medal 1985, Semmelweis Memorial Medal 1987, Baló József Memorial Medal 1987, Hetényi Géza Memorial Medal 1990, 'Pro Optimo Merito in Gastroenterologia' Memorial Medal 1992, Golden seal ring of the Semmelweis University,Genersich Prize 1994, Széchényi Prize 1996, George Weber Foundation Prize 1997. *Publications include:* Lymphknotengeschwülste (co-author) 1966, The Liver 1979, Sejtosztodas Szabalyozasa es Befolyasolasa (co-author) 1981, Mediastinal Tumors and Pseudotumors (co-author) 1984, Liver Carcinogenesis (co-ed.) 1979, Ultrastructure of Tumours in Man 1981, Regulation and Control of Cell Proliferation (co-author) 1984, Tumour Progression and Markers 1982, Models, Mechanisms and Etiology of Tumour Promotion 1984, Biochemistry and Molecular Genetics of Cancer Metastasis (co-author) 1986, Abstracts of Lectures, Symposia, and Free Communications (co-author) 1986, Lectures and Symposia of the 14th International Cancer Congress (co-author) 1987, Molecular Biology and Differentiation of Cancer Cells (Oncogenes, Growth Factors, Receptors) (co-author) 1987, Carcinogenesis and Tumour Progression (co-author) 1987, Radiotherapy, Paediatric Oncology, Neurooncology (co-author) 1987, Biological Response Modifiers, Leukaemias and Lymphomas (co-author) 1987, Medical Oncology (co-author) 1987, Morphological Diagnosis of Liver Diseases (in Russian) 1989, Pathology (textbook in Hungarian) 1989, Sincerely About Cancer for Men and Women (in Hungarian) 2001. *Leisure interests:* tennis, gardening. *Address:* First Institute of Pathology and Experimental Cancer Research, Semmelweis University, Üllői út 26, 1085 Budapest (office); Lónyay u. 25, 1093 Budapest, Hungary (home). *Telephone:* (1) 459-1500 (office); (1) 217-9699 (home). *Fax:* (1) 317-1074 (office). *E-mail:* klapis@korb1.sote.hu (office); lapkar@t-online.hu (home).

LAPLI, Father Sir John Ini, Kt, DipLicTheol; Solomon Islands government official and Anglican priest; b. June 1955; s. of Christian Mekope and Ellen Lauai; m. Helen Lapli 1985; three s. one d.; ed Selwyn Coll., Guadalcanal, St John's Theological Coll., Auckland, New Zealand; tutor Theological Coll., Auckland 1982–83; teacher Catechist School, Rural Training Centre 1985; Parish Priest 1986; Bible Translator 1987–88; Premier of Temotu Prov. 1988–99; Gov.-Gen. of Solomon Is July 1999–2004; Order of St Michael and St George; Order of Propitious Clouds with Special Grand Cordon (ROC). *Leisure interest:* gardening, research and writing on oral local tradition and culture. *Address:* Luepe Village, Graciosa Bay, c/o Lata Post Office, Temotu Province, Solomon Islands (home). *Telephone:* 53111 (home).

LAPOINTE, Carman L; Canadian accountant, auditor and UN official; *Under-Secretary-General, United Nations Office of Internal Oversight Services;* b. 1951, Virden, Manitoba; three c.; ed Algonquin Coll., Colorado State Univ., USA; has held chief oversight positions in several Canadian crown corpns, including Corp. Auditor with Canada Post Corpn, Auditor of Bank of Canada, Vice-Pres. Internal

Audit and Evaluation with Export Development Canada; fmr Chair. and mem. OSCE Audit Cttee; fmr mem. UNRWA Audit Cttee; Chair. Inst. of Internal Auditors 1994–95; Auditor Gen. World Bank Group 2004–09; Dir Office of Audit and Oversight, IFAD 2009–10; Under-Sec.-Gen., Office of Internal Oversight Services, UN, New York 2010–; mem. Standards Task Force, International Federation of Accountants; mem. Criteria of Control Bd, Canadian Inst. of Chartered Accountants. *Address:* Office of Internal Oversight Services, United Nations, New York, NY 10017, USA (office). *Telephone:* (212) 963-1234 (office). *Fax:* (212) 963-4879 (office). *Website:* www.un.org/Depts/oios (office).

LAPTEV, Ivan Dmitrievich; Russian editor and journalist; b. 15 Oct. 1934, Sladkoye, Omsk Dist; m. Tatyana Kareva 1966; one d.; ed Siberian Road Transport Inst., Acad. of Social Sciences; worked for CPSU Cen. Cttee; mem. CPSU 1960–91; worked at Omsk River Port 1952–60; teacher 1960–61; instructor, Soviet Army Sports Club 1961–64, literary collaborator and special corresp. Sovietskaya Rossiya 1964–67; Consultant for Kommunist (later named Free Thought) 1967–73; work with CPSU Cen. Cttee 1973–78; Section Ed. Pravda 1978–82, Deputy Ed. 1982–84; Chief Ed. Izvestiya 1984–90; mem. USSR Supreme Soviet 1989–91; People's Deputy of the USSR 1989–91; Chair. Council of Union 1990–91; Gen. Man. Izvestiya Publrs 1991–94; Deputy Chair. Fed. Press Cttee 1994–95, Chair. 1995–99; apptd Head of Sector Professional Acad. of State Service to Russian Presidency 1995; mem. Int. Acad. of Information 1993; Pres. Asscn of Chief Eds and Publrs 1993. *Publications include:* Ecological Problems 1978, The World of People in the World of Nature 1986; over 100 scientific articles on ecological problems. *Leisure interests:* reading, automobile engineering, cycle racing.

LAPTEV, Vladimir Viktorovich, DJur; Russian jurist; *Chief Scientific Researcher, Institute of State and Law, Russian Academy of Sciences;* b. 28 April 1924, Moscow; s. of V. I. Laptev and V. A. Lapteva; m. 1950; two s.; ed Law Dept, Moscow Inst. for Foreign Trade; mem. staff, Inst. of State and Law, Russian Acad. of Sciences, Moscow 1955, Head Section, Econ. Law 1959, Head Centre of Entrepreneurial and Econ. Law 1992–97, Chief Scientific Researcher 1997–; Head, Chair of Entrepreneurial Law, Academic Law Univ., Moscow 1997–2009; Visiting Prof., Emory Univ., Atlanta, Ga, USA 1992–93; Corresp. mem. USSR (now Russian) Acad. of Science 1979–87, mem. 1987–; Honoured Scientist of Russian Fed. 1977. *Publications:* more than 360 books and articles on econ. law, including Legal Status of Enterprises in Russia 1993, Introduction to Entrepreneurial Law 1994, Entrepreneurial Law: Notion and Subjects 1997, Joint Stock Company Law 1999, Subjects of Entrepreneurial Law 2003, Entrepreneurial (Economic) Law, Selected Works 2008, Entrepreneurial (Economic) Law and Real Sector of Economy 2010. *Address:* Institute of State and Law, Znamenka Str. 10, 119991, Moscow, Russia (office). *Telephone:* (495) 691-86-03 (office). *Fax:* (495) 691-85-74 (office).

LAPTHORNE, Sir Richard Douglas, Kt, CBE, BCom; British business executive; *Chairman, Cable & Wireless Communications PLC;* b. 25 April 1943; m. Valerie Lapthorne; two s. two d.; ed Calday Grange Grammar School, West Kirby, Univ. of Liverpool; Group Financial Controller Courtaulds PLC –1986, Finance Dir 1986–92; Finance Dir British Aerospace PLC 1992–98, Vice-Chair. 1998–99; Dir (non-exec.) Amersham International PLC 1998, later Chair. Amersham PLC 1999; Chair. and Dir (non-exec.) Cable & Wireless PLC 2003–10; Chair. Cable & Wireless Communications PLC 2010–; Chair. (non-exec.) McLaren Group, Morse PLC, Avecia PLC Tunstall Holdings Ltd, TI Automotive, Oasis International Leasing Co. P.J.S.C. (Abu Dhabi); Vice-Chair. JP Morgan Investment Bank. *Address:* Cable & Wireless Communications PLC, 3rd Floor, 26 Red Lion Square, London, WC1R 4HQ, England (office). *Telephone:* (20) 7315-4000 (office). *Website:* www.cwc.com (office).

LAQUEUR, Walter; American historian, academic, editor and political commentator; *Academic Director, Center for Strategic and International Studies;* b. 26 May 1921, Breslau, Germany (now Wrocław, Poland); s. of Fritz Laqueur and Else Berliner; m. 1st Barbara Koch 1941 (deceased); m. 2nd C. S. Wichmann; two d.; Ed. Survey 1955–65; Dir Inst. of Contemporary History and Wiener Library, London 1964–91; Founding Ed. Journal of Contemporary History 1965–; Prof. of History Brandeis Univ. 1967–72; Prof. of History, Tel-Aviv Univ. 1970–87; Prof. of Govt Georgetown Univ. 1977–90; Chair. Int. Research Council, Center for Strategic and Int. Studies, Washington DC 1973–2001, currently Academic Dir; Ed. Washington Papers 1973–2001, Washington Quarterly 1978–2001; Visiting Prof. of History, Harvard Univ. 1977; Rockefeller Fellow, Guggenheim Fellow; several hon. degrees. *Publications:* Young Germany 1962, The Road to War 1967 1968, Europe Since Hitler 1970, A History of Zionism 1972, Confrontation 1974, Weimar 1974, Guerrilla 1976, Terrorism 1977, A Continent Astray: Europe 1970–78 1979, The Missing Years (novel) 1980, The Terrible Secret 1981, Farewell to Europe (novel) 1981, Germany Today 1985, A World of Secrets 1985, Breaking the Silence 1986, The Age of Terrorism 1987, The Long Road to Freedom 1989, Stalin 1990, Thursday's Child has Far to Go (autobiog.) 1993, Black Hundred 1993, The Dream That Failed 1994, Fascism 1997, Generation Exodus 2001, Yale Encyclopedia of the Holocaust (Ed.) 2001, No End to War 2003, The Changing Face of Antisemitism 2006, The Last Days of Europe 2007, Best of Times, Worst of Times 2009. *Leisure interest:* swimming. *E-mail:* walter@laqueur.net (home).

LARA, Brian Charles; Trinidad and Tobago professional cricketer; b. 2 May 1969, Santa Cruz; s. of the late Bunty Lara and Pearl Lara; one d. with Leasel Rovedas; ed San Juan Secondary, Fatima Coll., Port of Spain; started playing cricket aged six; played football for Trinidad Under-14; played cricket for West Indies Under-19; captained a West Indies Youth XI against India, scoring 186; left-hand batsman; teams: Trinidad and Tobago 1987– (Capt. 1993–), Warwicks. 1994, 1998 (Capt.), making world record first-class score of 501 not out, including most runs in a day (390) and most boundaries in an innings (72) vs Durham, Edgbaston 3–4 June 1994; played in 131 Tests for West Indies 1990–2006 (37 as Capt.), scoring 11,953 runs (average 52.88) including 34 hundreds, highest score 400 not out (world record vs England, St John's, Antigua 10–12 April 2004); played in 299 One Day Ints, scoring 10,405 runs (average 40.48, highest score 169) including 19 hundreds; scored 22,156 first-class runs (average 51.88, highest score 501 not out) including 65 hundreds; scored 2,066 runs off 2,262 balls for Warwicks. 1994, with six hundreds in first seven innings; holds Test record of scoring most number of runs in a single over in a Test match, 28 runs off an over by Robin Peterson of S

Africa 2003; only batsman to have ever scored a hundred, a double century, a triple century, a quadruple century and a quintuple century in First-class games over the course of a sr career; retd from int. cricket 19 April 2007; signed for breakaway Indian Cricket League 2007, currently Capt. Mumbai Champs; f. Pearl and Bunty Lara Foundation (charity); Amb. for Sport of Repub. of Trinidad and Tobago; Hon. AO 2009; Dr hc (Univ. of Sheffield) 2007; Wisden Leading Cricketer in the World Award 1994, 1995, Wisden Cricketer of the Year 1995, Fed. of Int. Cricketers' Asscns Int. Cricketer of the Year 1999, BBC TV Overseas Sports Personality of the Year (one of only three cricketers). *Publication:* Beating the Field (autobiography) 1995. *Leisure interests:* golf, horse racing. *Address:* c/o West Indies Cricket Board, PO Box 616 W, St John's, Antigua. *Telephone:* 481-2450. *Fax:* 481-2498. *E-mail:* wicb@windiescricket.com; *Website:* www.windiescricket.com; www .pearlandbuntylara.org.

LARA BOSCH, José Manuel; Spanish economist and media executive; *President, Grupo Planeta;* b. 8 March 1946, Barcelona; s. of the late José Manuel Lara Hernández and María Teresa Bosch Carbonell; m.; four c.; CEO Grupo Planeta (owns TV and radio stations, publishing imprints, chain of bookshops, newspapers and real estate firms) 1998–2003, Pres. 2003–; Pres. Antena 3, UTECA; Chair. Inst. of Family Businesses 2000–03, Fundación José Manuel Lara; Pres. Círculo de Economía 2005–08. *Address:* Grupo Planeta SA, Edificio Planeta, Diagonal 662–664, 08034 Barcelona, Spain (office). *Telephone:* (93) 4928999 (office). *Fax:* (93) 4928562 (office). *E-mail:* direccion@planeta.es (office).

LARA CASTRO, Jorge, MA; Paraguayan diplomatist, sociologist, academic and government official; b. 5 Aug. 1945, Asunción; s. of Mariano Lara Castro and Carmen Casco; m.; ed Catholic Univ., Asunción, Latin American Faculty of Social Sciences, Mexico City; Prof., Autonomous Nat. Univ. of Mexico 1979–81; Prof., Catholic Univ., Asunción 1974–75; Prof., Centre for Econ. Research and Teaching, Mexico City 1980–91; Prof., Faculty of Philosophy and Human Sciences, Catholic Univ. of Asunción, Paraguay 1992–98, Dir Dept of Sociology 1997–99; Pres. Inst. of San Martín, Paraguay; Amb. and Perm. Rep. to UN, New York 2000–01; Minister of Foreign Affairs 2011–12. *Publications:* numerous publs on capitalism in Brazil, the birth of campesino movt, Latin American political systems and educ. and human rights in Paraguay. *Address:* c/o Ministry of Foreign Affairs, Edif. Benigno López, Palma, esq. 14 de Mayo, Asunción, Paraguay. *E-mail:* sistemas@mre.gov .py.

LARAKI, Moulay Ahmed; Moroccan politician, physician and diplomatist; b. 15 Oct. 1931, Casablanca; ed Univ. de Paris, France; with Ministry of Foreign Affairs 1956–57; Amb. and Perm. Rep. to UN, New York 1957–59; Head of Hosp. Services, Casablanca 1956–61; Amb. to Spain 1962–65, to Switzerland 1965–66, to USA (also accred to Mexico, Canada and Venezuela) 1966–67; Minister of Foreign Affairs 1967–69; Prime Minister 1969–71; Minister of Medical Affairs 1971–74; Minister of State for Foreign Affairs 1974–77; Minister of the Environment c. 1998; Pres. Soc. marocaine des sciences médicales. *Address:* c/o Office of the Prime Minister, Palais Royal, Touarga, Rabat, Morocco. *E-mail:* courrier@pm.gov.ma.

LARCOMBE, Brian, BCom; British business executive; b. 27 Aug. 1953; s. of John George Larcombe and Joyce Lucile Larcombe; m. Catherine Bullen 1983; ed Bromley Grammar School, Univ. of Birmingham, Advanced Management Program, Harvard Business School, USA; joined 3i Group PLC 1974, Local Dir 1982–88, Regional Dir 1988–92, Finance Dir and mem. Exec. Cttee 1992–2004, CEO 1997–2004; Chair. Bramdean Asset Management LLP, Aberdeen Private Equity Fund Ltd 2007–09; mem. Bd of Dirs, Gategroup Holding AG 2008–; Dir, Gallaher Group Ltd 2006–; Dir (non-exec.), Incisive Media Ltd, NXD Smith & Nephew PLC (also mem. Remuneration Cttee), F&C Asset Management plc 2005–11; Advisor, Lighthouse Advisors India Pvt. Ltd; fmr Chair. British Venture Capital Assen. *Address:* Gategroup Holding AG, Balz-Zimmermannstrasse 7, Kloten, 8302 Zurich, Switzerland. *Telephone:* (43) 5337000. *Fax:* (44) 5337173. *E-mail:* communications@gategroup.com. *Website:* www.gategroup.com.

LARGE, Sir Andrew Mcleod Brooks, Kt, MA (Econ.), MBA; British banker and public policy adviser; *Founder-Partner, Systemic Policy Partnership;* b. 7 Aug. 1942, Goudhurst, Kent; s. of the late Maj.-Gen. Stanley Large and of Janet Brooks Large; m. Susan Melville 1967; two s. one d.; ed Winchester Coll., Univ. of Cambridge, Institut Européen d'Admin des Affaires (INSEAD), France; British Petroleum 1964–71; Orion Bank Ltd 1971–79; Swiss Bank Corpn 1980–89, Man. Dir SBCI London 1980–83, Chief Exec. and Deputy Chair. SBCI London 1983–87, Group Chief Exec. SBCI London 1987–88, mem. Bd SBC 1988–90; Chair. Large, Smith & Walter 1990–92; Chair. Securities & Investments Bd (SIB) 1992–97; Deputy Chair. Barclays Bank 1998–2002, Dir 1998–2002; Chair. Euroclear 1998–2000; mem. Bd on Banking Supervision, Bank of England 1996–97, Deputy Gov. 2002–06; Chair. Risk Cttee, Axis 2006–, Sr Advisory Bd, Oliver Wyman 2009–, Supervisory Cttee, Marshall Wace 2009–; Sr Adviser, Hedge Fund Standards Bd 2009–; Founder-Partner Systemic Policy Partnership 2012–. *Publication:* The Future of Finance, an LSE Report 2010. *Leisure interests:* skiing, walking, gardening, growing ancient apple varieties, photography, music. *Address:* Marshall Wace, 13th Floor, The Adelphi, 1–11 John Adam Street, London, WC2N 6HT, England (office). *Telephone:* (20) 7925-4826 (office). *Fax:* (20) 7316-2281 (office).

LARGE, David Clay, PhD; American historian, academic and writer; *Professor Emeritus of European History, Montana State University;* b. 13 Aug. 1945, Scott Field, Ill.; s. of H. R. Large, Jr; m. 1st Jacque Hambly 1968 (divorced 1977); one s.; m. 2nd Margaret Wheeler 1980; one d.; ed Univ. of Washington, Univ. of California, Berkeley; taught Modern European History, Smith Coll. 1973–78, Yale Univ. 1978–83, Dean, Pierson Coll. 1981–83; Prof. of European History, Mont. State Univ. 1983–2012; Contrib. Ed. Military History Quarterly 1989; Woodrow Wilson Fellowship, Morse Fellowship (Yale), Nat. Endowment for the Humanities Fellowship, German Marshall Fund Fellowship. *Publications include:* The Politics of Law and Order: A History of the Bavarian Einwohnerwehr 1980, Wagnerism in European Culture and Politics 1984, Between Two Fires: Europe's Path in the 1930s 1990, Contending with Hitler: Varieties of German Resistance in the Third Reich 1991, Germans to the Front: West German Rearmament in the Adenauer Era 1996, Where Ghosts Walked: Munich's Road to the Third Reich 1997, Berlin 2000, And the World Closed Its Doors: One Family Abandoned to the Holocaust 2003, Nazi Games: The Olympics of 1936 2007, Munich 1972: Tragedy, Terror and

Triumph at the Olympic Games 2012. *Leisure interests:* running, skiing, music, hiking. *Address:* Department of History and Philosophy, Montana State University, 2-162 Wilson Hall, Bozeman, MT 59717-2320 (office); 995 Dolores Street, San Francisco, CA 94110, USA (home). *Telephone:* (415) 515-3529 (office); (415) 643-4584 (home). *E-mail:* largedavid3@gmail.com. *Website:* www.montana.edu/ ~wwwhi (office).

LARIJANI, Ali Ardashir, BSc, MS, PhD; Iranian politician; *Speaker, Majlis-e-Shura-e Islami (Parliament);* b. 1958, Najaf, Iraq; s. of Ayatollah Mirza-Hashem Amoli; ed Sharif Univ., Tehran Univ.; began career after 1979 revolution as dir of state TV; served in sr positions at Ministry of Revolutionary Guards, including Deputy Minister; Minister of Culture and Islamic Guidance 1992–94; Head Islamic Repub. of Iran Broadcasting 1994–2004; Sec. Shura-ye Ali-ye Amniyyat-e Melli (Supreme Nat. Security Council) (one of two reps of Supreme Leader of Iran, Ayatollah Khamenei) 2005–07 (resgnd), roles included chief nuclear negotiator; Speaker Majlis-e-Shura-e Islami (Parliament) 2008–; presidential cand. 2005. *Address:* Office of the Speaker, Majlis-e-Shura-e Islami (Parliament), Tehran, Iran. *E-mail:* info@abadgaran.ir (office). *Website:* www.abadgaran.ir (office).

LARIJANI, Sadeq Ardeshir; Iranian cleric and government official; *Head of Judiciary;* b. 1960, Najaf, Iraq; s. of Ayatollah Hashem Amoli; younger brother Ali Larijani, Speaker of Iranian Parl.; taught courses on Islamic ideology, both at seminary in Qom and at various Iranian Revolutionary Guard Corps bases around Iran; apptd youngest-ever jurist to Guardian Council (oversaw Iran's disputed presidential election June 2009) 2001–09; Head of Judiciary 2009–. *Achievements include:* learned English in order to translate several philosophical works, including article by Karl Popper on philosophy of science and G. J. Warnock's Contemporary Moral Philosophy (annotated and critiqued from Islamic point of view). *Address:* Office of the Head of the Judiciary, Tehran, Iran (office). *E-mail:* info@iranjudiciary.org (office). *Website:* www.iranjudiciary.org (office).

LARKINS, Richard, AO; Australian university administrator, endocrinologist and academic; b. 17 May 1943; James Stewart Chair of Medicine, Royal Melbourne Hosp. 1984–97; Dean of Medicine, Dentistry and Health Sciences, Melbourne Univ. 1998–2003; Vice-Chancellor and Pres. Monash Univ. 2003–08 (retd); Chair. Nat. Health and Medical Research Council of Australia 1997–2000; Pres. Endocrine Soc. of Australia 1982–84, Royal Australasian Coll. of Physicians 2000–02; Chair. Accreditation Cttee, Australian Medical Council 1991–95; mem. Nat. Aboriginal and Torres Strait Islander Health Council 1997–2000; Eric Susman Prize 1982, Sir William Upjohn Medal 2002. *Address:* c/o Office of the Vice-Chancellor, Monash University, Wellington Road, Clayton, Vic. 3800, Australia (office).

LAROCCO, James A., BA, MA, PhD; American diplomatist; *Visiting Distinguished Lecturer, Near East South Asia Center for Strategic Studies, National Defense University;* b. Chicago, Ill.; m. Janet Larocco; three c.; ed Univ. of Portland, Johns Hopkins School of Advanced Int. Studies; entered Foreign Service 1973; Staff Asst Office of Congressional Relations, State Dept; Commercial Attaché, Jeddah 1975–77; Econ. Officer, Cairo 1978–81; Econ. Section Chief Kuwait 1981–83; Deputy Dir, Office of Pakistan, Afghanistan and Bangladesh Affairs, Near East Asia Bureau 1984; Minister-Counsellor for Econ. Affairs, Beijing; Kuwait Task Force Co-ordinator, State Operations Center, Operation Desert Storm 1990; Deputy Dir American Inst. in Taiwan 1991; Deputy Chief of Mission, Tel-Aviv 1993–96; Amb. to Kuwait 1997–2001; Prin. Deputy Asst Sec. Bureau of Near Eastern Affairs, Dept of State 2001–; Dir Gen. Sinai Multinational Force and Observers (ind. (non-UN) peacekeeping mission) 2004–09; Visiting Distinguished Lecturer, Near East South Asia Center for Strategic Studies, Nat. Defense Univ., Washington, DC 2009–; Congressional Fellowship 1983; US State Dept Distinguished Service Award and numerous other awards. *Address:* NESA Center for Strategic Studies, 2100 2nd Street, SW, Suite 4308, Washington, DC 20593, USA (office). *Telephone:* (202) 685-4131 (office). *Fax:* (202) 685-4999 (office). *Website:* nesa-center.org (office).

LAROCQUE, Irwin, MA; Dominican international organization official; *Secretary-General, Caribbean Community and Common Market (CARICOM);* m.; c.; ed Queen's Coll., New School for Social Research, New York Univ., USA; served in numerous civil service positions for more than 18 years in Dominica including as Perm. Sec. in Ministries of Trade, Industry, Enterprise Devt, Tourism, and Foreign Affairs, also Prin. Adviser to govt on regional integration and int. trade, Sr Policy Adviser on revision of Treaty of Chaguaramas; Asst Sec.-Gen. for Trade and Econ. Integration, Caribbean Community and Common Market (CARICOM) Secr. 2005–11, Sec.-Gen. CARICOM 2011–. *Address:* Caribbean Community and Common Market (CARICOM), POB 10827, Georgetown, Guyana (office). *Telephone:* (2) 222-0001 (office). *Fax:* (2) 222-0171 (office). *E-mail:* info@caricom.org (office). *Website:* www.caricom.org (office).

LAROQUE, Michèle; French actress; b. 15 June 1960, Nice; d. of Claude Laroque and Doïna Trandabur; m. Dominique Deschamps (divorced); one d.; ed Univ. of Nice; f. own production co. PBOF (Please Buy Our Films); Chevalier des Arts et Lettres, Chevalier de l'Ordre de mérite. *Films include:* Suivez cet avion 1989, The Hairdresser's Husband 1990, Une époque formidable 1991, Max & Jeremie 1992, La Crise 1992, Paranoïa 1993, Tango 1993, Louis, enfant roi 1993, Chacun pour toi 1994, Personne ne m'aime 1994, Aux petits bonheurs 1994, Le Fabuleux destin de Madame Petlet 1995, Nelly & Monsieur Arnaud 1995, Pédale Douce 1995, Les Aveux de l'innocent 1996, Passage à l'acte 1996, Fallait pas! 1996, Le Plus Beau Métier du Monde 1996, Ma Vie en Rose 1996, Serial Lover 1997, Doggy Bag 1999, Epouse-moi 2000, Le Placard 2001, Malabar Princess 2003, Pedale Dure 2004, L'Anniversaire 2005, Comme t'y es belle! 2006, La Maison du bonheur 2006, L'Entente cordiale 2006, Enfin veuve 2007, The Neighbor 2007. *Theatre:* Silence en coulisses, Ornifle 1991, La Face cachée d'Orion, Une Folie 1993, Ils s'aiment 1996, Ils se sont aimés 2003. *Television includes:* Vivement lundi 1988, Le Retour d'Arsène Lupin 1989, La Télé des inconnus 1990, Imogène 1990, Bébé express 1991, C'est quoi ce petit boulot? 1992, Les Cravates léopards 1992, Navarro 1993, B comme Bolo 1994, Quatre pour un loyer 1995, Une journée dans mon coeur 1995, Le Nid tombé de l'oiseau 1995, Mouton noir 1995, Elvis Aziz 1996, Week-end 1998, Le Mur 1998, Une femme neuve 2000, L'Oiseau rare 2001, La Chose publique 2003, Mon voisin du dessus 2003, Petits secrets et gros mensonges 2006, En marge des jours 2007, Faisons un rêve 2007, Dans tes bras 2008, Oscar et la dame rose 2008.

Leisure interests: tennis, skiing, riding, golf. *Address:* c/o Agent associés Guy Bonnet, 201 rue du fbg Saint-Honoré, 75008 Paris, France (office). *Telephone:* 1-42-56-04-57. *Website:* www.michelelaroque.com.

LAROVERE, Joan, BA, MD, MSc; British physician; ed St Andrews Univ., Harvard Univ. and Columbia Univ., USA; clinical training in paediatrics and paediatric intensive care, Great Ormond Street Hosp., London and Boston Children's Hosp., USA; fmr Dir Paediatric Cardiac Intensive Care Unit and Consultant Intensivist, Royal Brompton Hosp., London; Sr Lecturer, Imperial Coll. London School of Medicine and mem. Admissions Cttee; Co-founder and Vice-Pres. Virtue Foundation (non-profit org.); Dir Int. Medical Educ. Trust 2000; mem. Chief Medical Officer for England's Working Group on Revalidation and Medical Educ.; Fellow, American Acad. of Pediatrics, American Coll. of Critical Care Medicine. *Address:* Virtue Foundation, 1040 First Avenue, Suite 116, New York, NY 10022, USA (office). *Telephone:* (212) 355-2227 (office). *E-mail:* info@virtuefoundation.org (office). *Website:* www.virtuefoundation.org (office).

LARQUIÉ, André Olivier, LenD; French civil servant; *President, Palais Multisports Paris-Bercy;* b. 26 June 1938, Nay; s. of Henri Larquié and Simone Tauziède; ed Lycée Louis-le-Grand, Univ. of Paris and Ecole nat. d'Admin.; Deputy Dir Musique Art lyrique et Danse, Ministry of Culture and Communications 1978–79, Official Rep. 1981–83, 1987; Govt Commr Centre nat. d'art et de Culture Georges Pompidou 1981–84; Pres. Paris Opera 1983–87; Tech. Adviser to the Prime Minister May 1988–89; Pres. Théâtre Contemporain de la Danse, Asscn pour le Dialogue entre les Cultures 1985; Pres. Radio France Int. 1989–95; Pres. Cité de la Musique, Paris –2002, Ballet de Nancy et Lorraine, Théâtre du Chatelet, Paris; Departmental Head, Gen. Inspectorate, Ministry of Culture and Communication 2001; Pres. Communication Cttee, French Comm. for UNESCO; Pres. Palais Multisports Paris-Bercy 2004–; Commdr des Arts et Lettres 1983 Officier, Légion d'honneur 1996 Chevalier dans l'Ordre de la Pléiade 1997 Officier Ordre du Mérite agricole 1998 Commdr Ordre nat. du Mérite 2000 Commdr des Palmes académiques 2002–. *Publications:* official reports. *Leisure interests:* song and dance. *Address:* 8 blvd de Bercy, 75012 Paris (office); 26 blvd Raspail, 75007 Paris, France (home). *Telephone:* 1-40-02-60-28 (office); 1-40-02-60-29 (office); 1-45-48-48-30 (home). *E-mail:* alarquie@bercy.fr (office). *Website:* www.alarquie-chatelet-theatre.com.

LARRAIN, Juan, BA; Chilean diplomatist, UN official and academic; *Visiting Assistant Professor, Department of International Studies, University of Miami;* b. 29 Aug. 1941, Santiago; m. Mariel Cruchaga Belaunde; four c.; ed German School and Mil. Acad., Chile, Univ. of Chile, Diplomatic Acad., Ministry of Foreign Affairs; Asst Prof. School of Journalism, Catholic Univ. of Chile 1964–65; Prof. of Contemporary History Diplomatic Acad., Ministry of Foreign Affairs and Ed. Diplomacia (publ. of Acad.) 1978–79; Deputy Chief of Mission, OAS 1983–87, London 1988–90, Head of First Commercial Mission to Ireland 1991, Deputy Dir Multilateral Econ. Affairs 1991–92, Consul-Gen. New York 1992–94, Deputy Perm. Rep. to UN 1994–99, Perm. Rep. 1999–2001, also Deputy Perm. Rep. to UN Security Council 1996–97; fmr Head Monitoring Mechanism for Angola; Expert Adviser UN Security Council Counter Terrorism Cttee Exec. Directorate 2003–07; Visiting Asst Prof., Dept of Int. Studies, Univ. of Miami, USA 2007–. *Leisure interests:* history, classical music, reading, golf. *Address:* 721 Biltmore Way, # 602, Coral Gables, FL 33134, USA (office). *Telephone:* (305) 284-4796 (office); (305) 446-6280 (home). *E-mail:* j.larrain@miami.edu (office); december79@aol.com (home). *Website:* www.as.miami.edu/international-studies (office).

LARRAÍN BASCUÑÁN, Felipe, BA, MA, PhD; Chilean economist and politician; b. 14 Feb. 1958, Santiago; m. Francisca Cisternas Lira; five c.; ed Univ. Católica de Chile, Harvard Univ., USA; Prof. of Econs, Univ. Católica de Chile; fmr Visiting Prof., Robert Kennedy Chair of Latin American Studies, Harvard Univ., USA; consultant on macroeconomic issues to World Bank, UN, ECLAC, IDB; mem. Int. Advisory Bd Asian Devt Bank; Pres. Felipe Larraín & Associates (econ. consultancy); econ. adviser to several Latin American govts; Minister of Finance 2010–14; mem. Bd of Dirs Antarchile SA; several honours and awards including Premio Luis Cruz Martínez 1976, Premio Raúl Yver Oxley 1980. *Publications include:* ed. and author of 10 books including Desarrollo Económico en Democracia: Proposiciones para una Sociedad Libre y Solidaria 1987, Debt, Adjustment and Recovery: Latin America's Prospects for Growth and Development 1989, The Public Sector and the Latin American Crisis 1990, Chile Hacia el 2000 1995, Macroeconomics in the Global Economy (with Jeffrey Sachs) 2002, Chile: A developed nation 2007. *Address:* c/o Ministry of Finance, Teatinos 120, 12°, Santiago, Chile (office).

LARROULET VIGNAU, Christian, BBA, MA; Chilean academic and politician; b. 26 July 1953, Santiago; ed Univ. Católica de Chile, Univ. of Chicago, USA; Head of Planning Dept, Nat. Planning Office (Odeplan) 1980–82; Head, Antitrust Comm. 1982–84; Co-ordinator of Econ. Council, Ministry of Economy 1982–85; mem. Nat. Comm. for Privatization 1985–89; Chief of Staff to Finance Minister 1985–89; fmr Prof., Univ. Católica de Chile, Univ. de Chile; Visiting Researcher, Inst. of The Americas, Univ. of California, San Diego, USA; Dean and Prof. of Econs, Faculty of Business and Economy, Univ. del Desarrollo, Santiago; Co-founder and Exec. Dir Instituto Libertad y Desarrollo (private research and study centre) 1990–; Minister of the Presidency 2010–14; mem. The Mont Pelerin Soc. 1996, Academia Chilena de Ciencias Sociales, Políticas y Morales 2002; Premio Editorial Los Andes 1996, Premio Generación Empresarial 1997, Premio Ingeniero Comercial 2007, Premio Educación - Empresa 2007. *Publications include:* Soluciones privadas a problemas públicos (ed.) (Antony Fisher Award of the Atlas Economic Research Foundation 1995) 1993, El Gobierno de las Personas 1999, Chile 2010: el desafío del desarrollo. *Address:* c/o Office of the Minister, Secretary-General of the Presidency, Palacio de la Moneda, Santiago, Chile (office).

LARSEN, Ralph Stanley, BBA; American business executive; b. 19 Nov. 1938, Brooklyn, NY; s. of Andrew Larsen and Gurine Larsen (née Henningsen); m. Dorothy M. Zeitfuss 1961; one s. two d.; ed Hofstra Univ.; served in USN 1956–58; manufacturing trainee, then Supervisor of Production and Dir, Marketing, Johnson & Johnson, New Brunswick, NJ 1962–77, Vice-Pres. Operations and Marketing, McNeil Consumer Products Co. Div. 1977–81, Pres. Chicopee Div. 1982–83, Co. Group Chair. 1985–86, Vice-Chair. Exec. Cttee, Bd of Dirs 1986–89, Chair. and CEO 1989–2002, also Pres.; Pres. Becton Dickenson Consumer

Products, Paramus, NJ 1981–83; mem. Bd of Dirs, Xerox 1998–2000, General Electric, AT&T; fmr mem. Int. Advisory Bd, Salomon Smith Barney; Chair. The Business Council 1999–2000; Trustee, Robert Wood Johnson Foundation; Fellow, American Acad. of Arts and Sciences. *Leisure interests:* skiing, boating, art. *Address:* c/o Johnson & Johnson, 1 Johnson & Johnson Plaza, New Brunswick, NJ 08933, USA.

LARSON, Alan P., PhD; American economist; *Senior Advisor, Covington & Burling LLC;* ed Univ. of Iowa; joined State Dept 1973, serving in sr positions covering econs, trade, finance, energy, sanctions, transport, telecommunications; Amb. to OECD 1990–93; served in econ. sections of Embassies in Jamaica, Zaire, Sierra Leone; Under Sec. of State for Econ., Business and Agric. Affairs 1999–2005; Sr Advisor, Covington & Burling LLC 2005–; Distinguished Fellow, Council on Competitiveness; consultant, World Econ. Forum; Chair. Bd of Dirs Transparency Int. (US chapter); mem. Bd of Dirs Bread for the World; Univ. of Iowa Distinguished Alumnus Award 2003. *Address:* Covington & Burling LLP, 1201 Pennsylvania Avenue, NW, Washington, DC 20004-2401, USA (office). *Telephone:* (202) 662-5756 (office). *E-mail:* alarson@cov.com (office). *Website:* www.cov.com/lawyers/alarson/biography.html (office).

LARSON, Gary, BA; American cartoonist; b. 14 Aug. 1950, Tacoma, Wash.; s. of Vern Larson and Doris Larson; m. Toni Carmichael 1988; ed Washington State Univ.; performed in jazz duo 1972–75; worked in a music store; sold first cartoons to Pacific Search magazine; subsequently sold cartoons to Seattle Times, San Francisco Chronicle, Chronicle Features Syndicate; f. FarWorks Inc., creator of The Far Side, a single-panel cartoon series that was syndicated internationally to more than 1,900 newspapers for 15 years; announced retirement Oct. 1994; Nat. Cartoonists Soc. Award for best syndicated panel of 1985, Outstanding Cartoonist of the Year Award 1991, 1994, Max and Moritz Prize for Best Int. Cartoon 1993, insect named after him: Strigiphilus garylarsoni (biting louse), also butterfly Serratoterga larsoni. *Films:* Gary Larson's Tales From The Far Side 1994 (Grand Prix, Annecy Film Festival 1995), Gary Larson's Tales From The Far Side II 1997. *Publications:* 23 books, including The Far Side, Beyond The Far Side, In Search of The Far Side, Bride of The Far Side, Valley of The Far Side, It Came From The Far Side, Hound of The Far Side, The Far Side Observer, Night of the Crash-test Dummies, Wildlife Preserve, Wiener Dog Art, Unnatural Selections, Cows of Our Planet, The Chickens Are Restless, The Curse of Madame "C", Last Chapter and Worse 1996; Anthologies: The Far Side Gallery 1, 2, 3, 4 and 5, The PreHistory of The Far Side, There's A Hair in my Dirt! A Worm's Story 1998; published a 2007 calendar with all author royalties donated to Conservation International. *Leisure interests:* jazz guitar, pickup basketball. *Address:* c/o Creators Syndicate, 737 3rd Street, Hermosa Beach, CA 90254; c/o Andrews McMeel Publishing, 1130 Walnut Street, Kansas City, MO 64106-2109, USA. *E-mail:* farside@creators.com; farside@amuniversal.com. *Website:* www.thefarside.com.

LARSON-GREEN, Julie, BBA, MS; American computer software industry executive; *Executive Vice-President, Devices and Studios Engineering Group, Microsoft Corporation;* m. Gareth Green; two c.; ed Western Washington Univ., Seattle Univ.; fmr Sr Devt Engineer on Adobe PageMaker desktop publishing software for Macintosh and Windows, Seattle; joined Microsoft Corpn 1993, joined Office team 1997, Corp. Vice-Pres. Windows Experience 2007, Exec. Vice-Pres. Devices and Studios Engineering Group 2013–; mem. Bd of Dirs Western Washington Univ. Foundation. *Address:* Microsoft Corporation, 1 Microsoft Way, Redmond, WA 98052-6399, USA (office). *Telephone:* (425) 882-8080 (office). *Fax:* (425) 936-7329 (office). *Website:* www.microsoft.com (office).

LARSSON, Commr Freda; British Salvation Army officer (retd); b. (Freda Turner), 1939, Scotland; m. Gen. John Larsson 1969; two s.; officer, Upper Kingston-upon-Thames Corps, Salvation Army 1965, served as Corps Officer, Area Youth Officer, Area Sec. 1965–69, Corps Officer, Territorial Guide Organiser in Scotland, Asst Youth Dept, Nat. HQ 1969–80; S America W Territorial Home League Sec. 1980–84; Coll. Librarian, Int. Training Coll. 1984; Coordinator of Married Women Officers, Int. HQ 1988–90; UK Territorial Pres. of Women's Org. 1990; served in NZ and Fiji Territory 1993–96, Sweden and Latvia Territory 1996–99; World Sec. for Women's Ministries and World Pres. Boy Scouts, Guides and Guards, Int. HQ 1999–2003, World Pres. of Women's Ministries 2003–06 (retd). *Address:* c/o Salvation Army HQ, 101 Newington Causeway, London, SE1 6BN, England.

LARSSON, Gen. (retd) John, BD; Swedish Salvation Army officer (retd); b. 2 April 1938; s. of Sture Larsson and Flora Larsson; m. Freda Turner 1969; two s.; ed Univ. of London, UK; commissioned as Officer, Upper Norwood Corps, The Salvation Army 1957; various appointments in UK including Corps Officer, Trainer, Territorial Youth Sec. for Scotland, British Territory Nat. Youth Sec.; apptd Chief. Sec., S America W 1980–84; Prin. William Booth Memorial Training Coll., London 1984–88; Asst Admin. Planning to Chief of Staff for UK 1988–90; Territorial Commdr of UK and Repub. of Ireland Territory 1990–93, of NZ and Fiji Territory 1993–96, of Sweden and Latvia Territory 1996–99; Chief of Staff of the Salvation Army 1999–2002, 17th Gen. of the Salvation Army 2002–06 (retd). *Music includes:* co-author with Gen. John Gowans (retd) of 10 full-length musicals, Take-Over Bid 1967, Hosea 1969, Jesus Folk 1972, Spirit 1973, Glory 1975, White Rose 1977, The Blood of the Lamb 1978, Son of Man 1983, Man Mark II 1985, and The Meeting 1990. *Publications include:* Doctrine Without Tears 1974, Spiritual Breakthrough 1983, The Man Perfectly Filled with the Spirit 1986, How Your Corps Can Grow 1988, Saying Yes to Life 2006, '1929' 2009. *Leisure interests:* music, reading, walking.

LARSSON, Per; Swedish business executive; *CEO, Borse Dubai;* b. Feb. 1961, Harnosand; m.; four c.; ed Uppsala Univ.; fmr broker, Föreningssparbanken; Chief Exec. OM Group (Swedish trading tech. firm) 1985–2003 (resgnd after OM merger with HEX exchange); CEO Dubai Int. Financial Exchange (DIFX) 2006–07, CEO Borse Dubai 2007–; Global Leader for Tomorrow, World Econ. Forum 2001. *Leisure interests:* sport, spending time at second home in France, tennis. *Address:* Borse Dubai, PO Box 506690, Dubai, United Arab Emirates (office). *Telephone:* (4) 3612222 (office). *Fax:* (4) 3612130 (office). *E-mail:* info@dubaigroup.com (office). *Website:* www.borsedubai.ae (office).

LASHARI, Kamran, LLB, MSc; Pakistani civil servant and business executive; b. 7 July 1968, Sindh; ed Virginia Commonwealth Univ., USA; worked for years as

Chair. Capital Devt Authority; later served as Chief Commr of Islamabad before being posted as Environment Sec. 2009–10; belongs to Dist Man. Group and has headed various Prov. and Fed. Govt Depts and Ministries, apptd Sec. to Ministry of Petroleum and Natural Resources 2010; Chair. Oil & Gas Devt Co. Ltd–Sept. 2010; fmr Chief Sec., Govt of Sindh, currently Officer on Special Duty, Establishment Div.; Pres. Govt Coll. Univ. Lahore; mem. Bd of Dirs Org. for Human Resource Devt; mem. Advisory Bd Fatima Foundation; Visiting Faculty, Civil Services Acad.; fmr Dir.-Gen. Parks & Horticulture Authority; Pres. Pakistan Swimming Fed.; Pres. Old Ravians Unions. *Address:* c/o Board of Directors, Organization for Human Resource Development (OHRD), 293/2-W, Phase-III, Defence Housing Society, Lahore 54792, Pakistan. *Telephone:* 3005001718 (mobile). *E-mail:* lashari -27@hotmail.com.

LASICA, Milan, AM; Slovak actor, dramatist and scriptwriter; b. 3 Feb. 1940, Zvolen; s. of Vojtech Lasica and Edita Smáliková; m. Magdalena Vašáryová; two d.; ed Univ. of Musical Arts, Bratislava; dramatist Slovak TV 1964–67; actor with theatres Divadlo na Korze 1967–71, Divaldo Večerní Brno 1971–72, Nová scéna 1972–89; Founder-Dir Stúdio Lasica-Satinský (previously Stúdio S-Bratislava) 1989–; co-operation as actor, dramatist and scriptwriter with Slovak and Czech TV, radio and theatres Semafor, Divadlo bez zábradlí and Labyrint; TV Prize Monte Carlo Festival. *Films directed include:* Sladké hry minulého léta (TV) 1969, Srdečný pozdrav ze zeměkoule (also screenwriter) 1982, Tři veteráni (Three Veterans) 1983, Vážení přátelé 1989, Tajomstvo alchymistu Storitza 1991, Vystrel na Bonaparta (TV) 1992, O psíčkovi a macicke 1993, Mimozemštané, Saturnin 1994, Výchova dívek v Čechách (Bringing Up Girls in Bohemia) 1997, Pasti, pasti, pastičky (Traps) 1998, Hanele 1999, Talár a ptači zob 2003, Dámská stanica 2005, Obsluhoval jsem anglíckého krále 2006. *Television:* Hlava Medúzy 1997, Talár a ptačí zob 2003, Ulet 2003, Nadměrné maličkosti: Duch modrého pokoje 2004. *Films include:* Ulet (TV) 2002. *Plays include:* Cyrano, Don Juan, Mrtvé duše. *Publications include:* Spoza dverí 2003, Piesne a iné texty 2003, Bledomodrý svet Júliusa Satinského 2004, Bodka – Fejtóny 2003–2006 2007, Dialógy 2008, Slávne texty slávnych piesní 2008, Bodka 2 – Fejtóny 2007–2009 2009. *Leisure interest:* golf. *Address:* Stúdio Lasica-Satinský, Námestie 1. Mája 5, 811 06 Bratislava, Slovakia (office). *Website:* www.studios.sk (office).

LASKAWY, Philip A.; American business executive and management consultant; *Chairman, Fannie Mae (Federal National Mortgage Association);* b. 1941; m.; two s.; Partner, Ernst & Whinney 1978–81, Man. Partner 1981–85; Vice-Chair., Regional Man. Partner, Ernst & Young (formed from merged cos Ernst & Whinney and Arthur Young) 1985–93, Deputy Chair. 1993, Chair. and CEO 1994–2001, Chair. Ernst & Young Int. 1997–2001; Chair. Fannie Mae (Fed. Nat. Mortgage Asscn) 2008–; mem. Bd Dirs Cap Gemini, Ernst & Young, General Motors Corpn, Heidrick & Struggles Int., Inc., Henry Schein, Inc., Loews Corpn 2003–, The Progressive Corpn; Chair. of Trustees, Int. Accounting Standards Bd 2006–08; mem. Constitution Cttee, Int. Accounting Standards Cttee Foundation Trustee Cttee (Chair. 2006–07); mem. Bd Dirs General Motors Corpn, Henry Schein, Inc., Lazard Ltd, Loews Corpn; mem. Bd Dance Theater Foundation (Alvin Ailey American Dance Theater), Educational Broadcasting Corpn (Thirteen WNET/New York), The Philharmonic Symphony Soc. of New York, Inc. *Address:* Fannie Mae, 3900 Wisconsin Avenue, NW, Washington, DC 20016-2892, USA (office). *Telephone:* (202) 752-7000 (office). *E-mail:* headquarters@fanniemae.com (office). *Website:* www.fanniemae.com (office).

LASKEY, Ronald Alfred, CBE, MA, DPhil, FRS, FMedSci, FLSW; British professor of molecular biology and embryology; *Professor Emeritus of Animal Embryology, University of Cambridge;* b. 26 Jan. 1945, High Wycombe, Bucks., England; s. of Thomas Leslie Laskey and Bessie Laskey; m. Margaret Anne Page 1971; one s. one d.; ed High Wycombe Royal Grammar School, Queen's Coll., Oxford; scientific staff mem., Imperial Cancer Research Fund 1970–73, Lab. of Molecular Biology, MRC 1973–83; Co-Dir Molecular Embryology Group, Cancer Research Campaign (CRC) 1983–91; Dir CRC, Wellcome CRC Inst. 1991–; Charles Darwin Prof. of Animal Embryology, Univ. of Cambridge 1983–2012, Prof. Emer. 2012–, Fellow, Darwin Coll. Cambridge 1982–; Hon. Dir MRC Cancer Cell Unit, Hutchison/MRC Research Centre, Cambridge 2001–10; Distinguished Visitor, Agency for Science, Tech. and Research (A*STAR), Singapore 2002; mem. Scientific Advisory Cttee, European Molecular Biology Lab., Heidelberg; Assoc. Ed. Cell; Pres. British Soc. of Cell Biology 1996–99, Biochemical Soc. 2012–; Vice-Pres. Acad. of Medical Sciences 2007–12, Scientific Cttee, Louis Jeantet Foundation 2010–; Trustee, Strangeways Research Lab. 1993–2009, Inst. of Cancer Research 2007–12; mem. Academia Europaea 1989; Fellow, Learned Soc. of Wales; Colworth Medal, Biochemical Soc. 1979, CIBA Medal, Biochemical Soc. 1997, Feldberg Foundation Prize 1998, Louis Jeantet Prize for Medicine, Jeantet Foundation, Geneva 1998, Medal of Medical Faculty, Charles Univ., Prague 1999, BBC Tomorrow's World Health Innovation Award for devt of new screening test for cancer 2000, Royal Medal, Royal Soc. 2009; his research papers have been listed amongst the 100 most highly cited papers in scientific literature, and two research papers were distinguished with the Citation Classics Honour 1983. *Recordings:* albums: Songs for Cynical Scientists, More Songs for Cynical Scientists, Selected, Songs for Cynical Scientists. *Publications include:* articles on cell biology in professional journals. *Leisure interests:* music, mountains. *Address:* Department of Zoology, Downing Street, Cambridge, CB2 3EA, England (office). *Telephone:* (1223) 334106/7 (office). *E-mail:* ral19@cam.ac.uk (office). *Website:* www.zoo.cam .ac.uk/directory/professor-ron-laskey (office); www.darwin.cam.ac.uk (office).

LASORDA, Thomas (Tom) W., BA, MBA; Canadian automobile industry executive; b. 24 July 1954, Windsor, Ont.; ed Univ. of Windsor; with General Motors Corpn 1977–2000; Sr Vice-Pres. Powertrain Manufacturing, Chrysler Group, DaimlerChrysler Corpn 2000–02, Sr Vice-Pres. Production 2002–04, COO DaimlerChrysler Corpn, Auburn Hills, Mich. 2004–06, Pres. and CEO 2006–07, Pres. and CEO Chrysler LLC (after acquisition of Chrysler group by Cerberus Capital Man. LP) –Aug. 2007, Pres. and Vice-Chair. Aug. 2007–09; CEO Fisker Automotive Inc. 2011–12; Co-founder IncWell LP (venture capital firm) 2013; Deputy mem. Bd of Man. DaimlerChrysler AG 2004–05, mem. 2005–07.

LASSALLE, Jacques Louis Bernard; French theatre director, actor and writer; b. 6 July 1936, Clermont-Ferrand; s. of Antoine Lassalle and Louise Lassalle (née Courbouleix); m. Françoise Marty 1958; three s.; ed Sorbonne, Paris, Conservatoire National Supérieur d'Art Dramatique de Paris; Asst Teacher, Institut

d'Etudes Théâtrales 1969–77; f. Studio Théâtre de Vitry 1970; Teacher Conservatoire Nat. Supérieur de Paris 1981–83, 1994–2001; Dir-Gen. Théâtre Nat. de Strasbourg 1983–90; Administrateur Général, Comédie Française 1990–93; Dir Compagnie pour Mémoire; Chevalier, Ordre nat. du Mérite 1988, Officier, Légion d'honneur 1992, Commdr des Arts et des Lettres 1996; Grand prix nat. du théâtre 1998. *Film:* Après 2002, Black Billie (writer/director) 2013. *Plays:* Dir about 100 plays, particularly by Molière, Corneille, Racine, Euripides, Marivaux, Goldoni, Shakespeare, Labiche, Pirandello, Chekhov, Ibsen, Svevo, Lessing, Büchner, Hofmannsthal, Kundera, Sarraute, Brecht, Hare and Vinaver, also operas; recent productions include: La vie de Galilée 2000, Médée 2000, Le malin plaisir 2000, L'Ecole de danse 2000, Un jour d'été 2000, L'Ecole de femmes 2001, The Aspern Papers 2002, Don Juan 2002, Iphigénie en Tauride, La douleur, Platonov, Le Danse de Mort, Le Bête dans la Jungle, Le Jeu de l'Amour et du Hasard, Tartuffe 2006, La Fausse suivante 2009, Lorenzaccio 2010, La seconde surprise de l'amour, Parlez-moi d'amour 2010–11, L'école des femmes 2011, Le fils 2012, Loin de Corpus Christi 2012, Le Roi Lear 2013, Roméo et Juliette 2013. *Television:* Ferveur Jacques Lassalle, Medée (Festival d'Avignon) 2000, Don Juan 2002. *Publications:* Jonathan des années 30, Un couple pour l'hiver, Pauses 1991, Conversations sur Don Juan 1994, L'amour d'Alceste 2000, Après 2002, Nathalie Sarraute ou l'obscur commencement de la parole 2002, Conversations sur la Formation de l'Acteur, La Madone des poubelles (play) 2004, Un dimanche indécis dans la vie d'Anna 2011, Ici ou ailleurs 2011. *Leisure interests:* walking, swimming, reading, music, pre-1970 American films. *Address:* 47 boulevard Voltaire, 75011 Paris, France (home). *Telephone:* 1-47-00-32-78 (home). *Fax:* 1-47-00-32-78 (home). *E-mail:* lassalle.fra@ wanadoo.fr (home).

LASSERRE, Bruno Marie André, MPL; French public servant; *President, Autorité de la concurrence;* b. 4 Jan. 1954, Talence, Gironde; s. of Jacques Lasserre and Marie Garrigou-Lagrange de David de Lastours; m. Marie-Laure Sergent 1988; two d.; ed Bordeaux Faculty of Law, Inst. of Political Studies, Bordeaux, Ecole Nat. d'Admin, Paris; mem. Conseil d'Etat 1978–, Public Rapporteur, Litigation Chamber of Conseil d'Etat 1984–86, Deputy Pres. 2002–04; Gen. Rapporteur, Comm. on Right of Reply on Radio and TV 1980–82, Comm. on Access to Documents 1982–86; Legal Counsel, then Head of Regulatory Directorate, then Dir-Gen. of Posts and Telecommunications, Ministry of Posts and Telecommunications 1986–97; consultant on int. telecommunications to Ministers for Industry and Foreign Affairs 1997–98; Pres. Comm. of Selection of Inspectors of Finance 1998–2000; Supervisor of Privatization, Soc. française de production 2001; Pres. Press Modernization Fund 1999–2004; mem. Comm. of Selection of Banks Advising the State 1998–2004; mem., later Pres. Conseil de la concurrence (Competition Council, regulatory body) 1998–2008 (renamed Autorité de la concurrence, Competition Authority 2008), Pres. Autorité de la concurrence 2008–; mem. Comm. for the Liberation of French Econ. Growth 2007–08; Officier, Légion d'honneur, Commdr, Ordre nat. du Mérite. *Publications:* Open Government 1987, Government and Information Technologies 2000, Quality Regulation and Impact Assessment 2004. *Address:* Autorité de la concurrence, 11 rue de l'Echelle, 75001 Paris (office). *Telephone:* 1-55-04-00-00 (office). *Fax:* 1-55-04-00-22 (office). *E-mail:* bruno.lasserre@autoritedelaconcurrence.fr (office). *Website:* www .autoritedelaconcurrence.fr (office).

LASSETER, John A., BFA; American animator and film industry executive; *Chief Creative Officer, Pixar and Disney Animation Studios;* b. 12 Jan. 1957, Hollywood, Calif.; m. Nancy Lasseter; five s.; ed California Inst. of the Arts; joined The Walt Disney Company as Jungle Cruise skipper at Disneyland, Anaheim, Calif., later animator at Walt Disney Feature Animation 1979–84; worked as 'interface designer' at Lucasfilm Computer Graphics Group 1984–86, worked on project that resulted in his first computer-animated short The Adventures of André and Wally B, later made first computer-animated feature Toy Story; Founding mem. and Exec. Producer, Pixar 1986 (bought by Disney 2006), Chief Creative Officer of both Pixar and Disney Animation Studios 2006–, Prin. Creative Advisor, Walt Disney Imagineering 2006–; Fellow, American Acad. of Arts and Sciences; mem. Acad. of Motion Picture Arts and Sciences, Sec. 2009–; Contribution to Cinematic Imagery Award, Art Dirs Guild 2003, Lifetime Achievement Award, Venice Film Festival 2009, David O. Selznick Achievement Award, Producers Guild of America 2010. *Films include:* as dir: Lady and the Lamp 1979, Luxo Jr. 1986, Red's Dream 1987, Tin Toy (Academy Award for Animated Short Film) 1988, Knick Knack 1989, Toy Story (Special Achievement Academy Award) 1995, A Bug's Life 1998, Toy Story 2 1999, Who Is Bad Luckey? 2004, Cars 2006, Mater and the Ghostlight 2006; as exec. producer: Geri's Game 1997, It's Tough to Be a Bug 1998, For the Birds 2000, Monsters, Inc. 2001, Sen to Chihiro no kamikakushi (aka Spirited Away) 2001, Finding Nemo 2003, Boundin' 2003, The Incredibles 2004, Hauru no ugoku shiro (aka Howl's Moving Castle) 2004, One Man Band 2005, Mater and the Ghostlight 2006, Lifted 2006, Meet the Robinsons 2007, Ratatouille 2007, How to Hook Up Your Home Theater 2007, Presto 2008, Glago's Guest 2008, Bolt 2008, Wall-E 2008, Ponyo 2008, Bolt 2008, Up 2009. *Address:* Pixar Animation Studios, 1200 Park Avenue, Emeryville, CA 94608 (office); Walt Disney Feature Animation, 500 South Buena Vista Street, Burbank, CA 91521, USA (office). *Telephone:* (510) 922-3000 (Emeryville) (office); (818) 560-1000 (Burbank) (office). *Fax:* (510) 922-3151 (Emeryville) (office); (818) 560-1930 (Burbank) (office). *E-mail:* info@pixar.com (office). *Website:* www.pixar.com (office); www.disneyanimation.com (office); corporate.disney.go.com/careers/ who_imagineering.html (office). disney.go.com/disneypictures (office).

LASSEZ, Jean-Louis, MSc, DEA, PhD; French computer scientist and academic; *Professor and Chairman, Department of Computer Science, Coastal Carolina University;* b. 24 Dec. 1944; Lecturer, Acad. Commerciale Inte 1968–70, Dept of Mathematics, Sherbrooke Univ., Canada 1970–72; Research Fellow and Asst Prof., Dept of Computer Science, Purdue Univ., USA 1972–73; Adjunct Prof., Dept of Math., Univ. of Moncton, Canada 1974–79; Reader, Dept of Computer Science, Univ. of Melbourne, Australia 1976–85; Researcher, IBM T. J. Watson Research Center, Yorktown Heights, NY 1985–96; Prof., New York Univ. 1993–96; Prof. of Computer Science, New Mexico Inst. of Tech. 1996–2002; Prof. and Chair. Dept of Computer Science, Coastal Carolina Univ., SC 2002–. *Publications:* Logic Programming: The 4th International Conference (ed.) 1987, Computational Logic – Essays in Honor of Alan Robinson (co-ed.) 1991; numerous articles in scientific journals. *Address:* Coastal Carolina University, Coastal Science Center 111,

Conway, SC 29528-6054, USA (office). *Telephone:* (843) 349-2359 (office). *E-mail:* jlassez@coastal.edu (office). *Website:* www.coastal.edu (office).

LÁSZLÓ, Géza, BEcons, PhD; Hungarian business executive; b. 1963; m.; three c.; ed Univ. of Econ. Sciences, Budapest, Princeton Univ., USA; Man., Budapest Bank Rt. 1992–93; Sr Economist, Investel Rt. 1993–96; Strategic and Business Devt Dir, MATÁV Rt. 1996–98; Chair. Antenna Hungária 1998–2002, CEO 1999–2008; mem. Bd VRAM Rt (Vodafone Hungary) 2000–04; mem. Hungarian Acad. of Sciences 1996. *Address:* c/o Petzvál József u. 31–33, 1119 Budapest, Hungary. *E-mail:* antennah@ahrt.hu.

LATASI, Sir Kamuta, KCMG, OBE; Tuvaluan politician; b. 4 Sept. 1936, Samoa; m. Naama Latasi; ed South Devon Technical Coll., UK; Lands Officer 1965–66; Minister of Natural Resources 1967, of Works and Utilities 1968–70; First High Commr to Fiji and Papua New Guinea and Perm. Rep. to S Pacific Comm. (currently Secr. of the Pacific Community), Noumea, New Caledonia and 1978–83; Sec. British Petroleum Co., Tuvalu 1983–93; Prime Minister of Tuvalu 1993–96, Minister of Foreign Affairs and Econ. Planning 1993–97; Speaker of Parliament 2006–14. *Leisure interests:* fishing, gardening. *Address:* c/o Office of the Speaker of Parliament, Vaiaku, Funafuti, Tuvalu. *E-mail:* klatasi@yahoo.com.

LATHAM, Mark, BEc; Australian politician; b. 28 Feb. 1961, Ashcroft, NSW; s. of Donald Charles Latham and Lorraine Lillian Latham; m. Janine Lacey; two s.; ed Univ. of Sydney; Councillor, Liverpool Council 1987–94; mem. Fed. Parl. (Australian Labour Party) for Werriwa 1994–2005; Shadow Minister for Urban Devt and Housing 2001–02, for Econ. Ownership and Community Security 2002–03; Leader Australian Labor Party and Leader of the Opposition in Fed. Parl. 2003–05 (resgnd due to ill health). *Publications:* Reviving Labor's Agenda 1990, Social Capital 1998, Civilising Global Capital 1998, What Did You Learn Today? 2001, The Enabling State (co-ed.) 2001, A Conga Line of Suckholes 2006. *Address:* c/o Australian Labor Party, 5/9 Sydney Avenue, Barton, ACT 2600, Australia. *E-mail:* info@alp.org.au. *Website:* www.alp.org.au.

LATHEEF, Mohamed; Maldivian politician; one d.; fmr mem. Parl.; fmr Vice-Pres. Maldives Nat. Chamber of Commerce; Co-Founder Maldivian Democratic Party (banned opposition group), later Spokesperson; apptd Amb. for Human Rights 2008. *Address:* Maldivian Democratic Party, H. Sharasha, 2nd Floor, Sosun Magu, Malé, Maldives (office). *Telephone:* 3340044 (office). *Fax:* 3322960 (office). *E-mail:* secretariat@mdp.org.mv (office). *Website:* www.mdp.org.mv (office).

LATHEEF, Mohamed, MEd, PhD; Maldivian diplomatist, politician and civil servant; *Commissioner, Civil Service Commission;* m.; three c.; ed Univ. of Wales, UK, postgraduate studies in Cardiff Univ., Wales; Dir-Gen. Maldives Centre for Man. and Admin 1992–93; Nat. Dir Project for Public Admin. Reform 1992–93; Deputy Minister, Ministry of Atolls Admin 1993; Minister of Educ. 1993–2002; mem. and Deputy Speaker People's Special Majlis (Ass.) 1993–97; Vice-Chair. Nat. Educ. Council 1993–2002; mem. Parl. 2000–02; held posts at Ministry of Foreign Affairs and Embassy in Sri Lanka; Perm. Rep. to UN 2002–07; Amb. to USA 2003–07; Commr Civil Service Comm. 2008–. *Address:* Civil Service Commissioners' Bureau, MATI Building, Second Floor, Raadhafathi Hingun, Malé, Maldives (office). *Website:* en.csc.gov.mv/ (office).

LATORTUE, Gerald; Haitian academic, business consultant and politician; b. Gonaives; ed Inst. of Political Sciences and Inst. of Econ. and Social Devt, Paris; returned to Haiti to work as lawyer and law school Prof. 1960; fled Haiti 1963, lived in Jamaica, Washington DC, Puerto Rico working as econs teacher; joined UNO for Industrial Devt, living in Togo, Ivory Coast, and Vienna; returned to Haiti and named Minister of Foreign Affairs 1988; after coup four months later returned to UN; int. business consultant and radio show host, Fla 1994; Host of Haitian TV Network of America talk shows Revue de la semaine and L'inviter 2003; Interim Prime Minister of Haiti March 2004–06. *Address:* c/o Office of the Prime Minister, Villa d'Accueil, Delmas 60, Musseau, Port-au-Prince, Haiti (office).

LATOUR, Lamuré; Suriname lawyer and politician; *Minister of Defence;* Minister of Defence 2010–; mem. Megacombinatie political alliance. *Address:* Ministry of Defence, Kwattaweg 29, Paramaribo, Suriname (office). *Telephone:* 474244 (office). *Fax:* 420055 (office). *E-mail:* defensie@sr.net (office).

LATTRE, André Marie Joseph de; French banker; b. 26 April 1923, Paris; m. Colette Petit 1947; three s. two d.; ed Univs de Paris à la Sorbonne and Grenoble and Ecole Libre des Sciences Politiques; Insp. of Finance 1946; with Ministry of Finance 1948–; Dept of External Finance 1949–54, Deputy Dir 1955–58; Alt. Exec. Dir IMF 1954; Prof. Inst. d'Etudes Politiques, Paris 1958–83; Financial Adviser to Pres. of the Repub. 1958–60; Perm. Sec. Ministry of Finance 1960–61; Dir of External Finance 1961; Censor, Bank of France 1962, Vice-Gov. 1966–74; Mission to India for Pres. IBRD 1965; Alt. Dir BIS 1973; Pres. Crédit National 1974–82; World Bank Special Rep. to IDA 1983; Man. Dir Inst. of Int. Finance, Washington 1983–86; Chair. Banque Française Standard-Chartered 1987–89; Chair. Banque Française de Service et de Crédit 1990–97; Commdr, Légion d'honneur and foreign awards. *Publications:* Les Finances extérieures de la France 1959, Politique économique de la France depuis 1945 1967, Servir aux Finances 1999. *Leisure interests:* skiing, tennis. *Address:* 69 rue Perronet, 92200 Neuilly, France (home). *Telephone:* 1-46-24-79-00 (home).

LATULIPPE, Gérard, LLL, DSA; Canadian lawyer, politician and diplomatist; *High Commissioner to Trinidad and Tobago;* b. 5 Nov. 1944, Montréal; s. of Gérard Latulippe and Eugénie Dufort; m. Odette Dumontier; ed Université Sir George Williams (now Concordia Univ.), Univ. of Montréal, Univ. Libre de Bruxelles, Belgium; admitted to Québec Bar 1968; practised admin. and labour law with Malo, Wilhelmy and Associés 1968–76; Sr Assoc., Latulippe, L'Ecuyer et Associés 1977–81, McDougall, Lemay et Associés 1981–85; Vice-Chair., Political Cttee. Québec Liberal Party 1984–85; mem. Québec Nat. Ass. 1985–89; Solicitor-Gen. of Québec 1985–87; Gen. Del. of Québec in Mexico 1989, in Brussels (responsible for relations with EU and Benelux) 1994–97; Deputy Minister, Québec Ministry of Int. Relations 1997; Exec. Vice-Pres. Société internationale des organismes de développement économique du Canada (SIODE) 1998–2002; joined Nat. Democratic Inst., Washington, DC 2003 as Morocco Country Dir and Sr Rep. in Maghreb region, becoming Resident Dir in Haiti –2010; Pres. Int. Centre for Human Rights and Democratic Devt (Rights & Democracy), Montréal 2010–12; High Commr to Trinidad and Tobago 2012–; mem. Bd of Dirs Saint-Luc Hosp., Montréal 1978–80.

Address: Canadian High Commission, Maple House, 3–3a Sweet Briar Road, St Clair, POB 1246, Port of Spain, Trinidad and Tobago (office). *Telephone:* 622-6232 (office). *Fax:* 628-1830 (office). *E-mail:* pspan@international.gc.ca (office). *Website:* www.canadainternational.gc.ca/trinidad_and_tobago-trinite_et_tobago (office).

LAU, Andy; Hong Kong singer, actor, film producer and television presenter; b. (Liu Dehua), 27 Sept. 1961, Tai Po, Hong Kong; m. Carol Chu; ed Band One Secondary School, Ho Lap Coll., San Po Kong, Kowloon, Ho Lap Coll., TVB Acad.; has performed in more than 160 films while maintaining a successful singing career; branded by the media as one of the 'Four Heavenly Kings' of Cantopop, along with Jacky Cheung, Aaron Kwok and Leon Lai 1990s; f. own film production co. Teamwork Motion Pictures Ltd (renamed Focus Group Holdings Ltd 2002); has own production house New Melody Production (renamed NMG 2000) 1992–; apptd Summer Paralympics Goodwill Amb. and sang theme song Flying with the Dream with Han Hong during Paralympics opening ceremony, Beijing 2008; involved with charity organizations Life Education Activity Program, Hong Kong Marrow Match Foundation, Ocean Park Conservation Foundation; f. Andy Lau Charity Foundation 1994; Hon. Fellow, Hongkong Acad. of Performing Arts; Medal of Honour (Hong Kong); Dr hc (Univ. of New Brunswick, Canada) 2010; Jade Solid Gold Top 10 Award, entered into Guinness World Records for Most Awards Won By A Cantopop Male Artist, Most Popular Male Artist 1990–92, 1994, 1999, 2004, Asia Pacific Most Popular Hong Kong Male Artist 1993, 1995–96, 2000–06, named of Ten Outstanding Young Persons of the World 1999, Honorary Award, Power Acad. Awards 2000, 2006, Performance Power Award, Power Acad. Awards 2001, 2005, Asian Filmmaker of the Year, Pusan Int. Film Festival 2006, Justice of Peace Award, Govt of Hong Kong Special Admin. Region 2008, World Outstanding Chinese Award 2010. *Recordings include:* albums: I Only Know I Love You 1985, Would It Be Possible (RTHK Top 10 Gold Songs Award 1990) 1990. *Films include:* Tau ban no hoi 1982, On the Wrong Track 1983, Ga joi Heung Gong 1983, Shanghai 13 1984, Ting bu liao de ai 1984, Xia ri fu xing 1985, Fat ngoi ching 1985, Zui jia fu xing 1986, Mo fei cui 1986, Ying hung ho hon 1987, Gan dan xiang zhao 1987, Gong woo ching 1987, Zhong Guo zui hou yi ge tai jian 1988, Qun long duo bao 1988, Long zhi jia zu 1988, Lie ying ji hua 1988, Fa nei qing 1988, Jing zhuong zhui nu zi zhi er 1988, Zui jia sun you 1988, As Tears Go By 1988, In the Blood 1988, Zui jia sun you chuang qing guan 1988, Shen xing tai bao 1989, Zhi zun wu shang 1989, Sheng gang qi bing di san ji 1989, Ren hai gu hong 1989, Juen diu daai ngok 1989, Fu gui bing tuan 1989, Fa nei qing da jie ju 1989, Tong gen sheng 1989, Biao cheng 1989, Zui jie nan peng you 1989, Ao qi xiong ying 1989, Di yi jian 1989, Xiao xiao xiao jing cha 1989, China White 1989, God of Gamblers 1989, Lang zhi yi zu 1989, Stars & Roses 1989, No Risk, No Gain: Casino Raiders – The Sequel 1990, Zai zhan jiang hu 1990, Forbidden Imperial Tales (singing voice) 1990, Island of Fire 1990, A Moment of Romance 1990, Ma deng ru lai shen zhang 1990, Yi daam hung sam 1990, Yu zhong long 1990, A Home Too Far 1990, Days of Being Wild 1990, Tian zi men sheng 1991, Tricky Brains 1991, God of Gamblers II 1991, Zhong Huan ying xiong 1991, The Last Blood 1991, Casino Raiders II 1991, Wu hu jiang zhi jue lie (Jin pai wu hu jiang) 1991, Ji dao zhui zong 1991, Lee Rock 1991, Lee Rock II 1991, Saviour of the Soul 1991, Xia sheng 1992, Lee Rock III 1992, Fan dou ma liu 1992, Do sing dai hang san goh chuen kei 1992, Do sing daai hang II ji ji juen mo dik 1992, Hua! ying xiong 1992, Long teng si hai 1992, Ji Boy xiao zi zhi zhen jia wai long 1992, Chuan dao fang zi 1992, Miu kai sup yi siu 1992, Handsome Siblings 1992, Zhan shen chuan shuo 1993, Chao ji xue xiao ba wang 1993, Ji jun sam sap lok gai ji Tau tin wun yat 1993, Sat sau dik tung wah 1994, Dao jian xiao 1994, Tian chang di jiu 1994, The Legend of Drunken Master 1994, Tian yu di 1994, Yu long gong wu 1994, Jui kuen III 1994, Da mao xian jia 1995, Full Throttle 1995, A Moment of Romance III 1996, Ding Lik (as Andy T. W. Lau), San Seung Hoi tsan 1996, ½ Chi tung chong 1996, Qi yi lu cheng zhi: Zhen xin ai sheng ming 1996, Tin dei hung sam 1997, Kau luen kei 1997, Island of Greed 1997, A True Mob Story 1998, Du xia 1999 1998, Ai qing meng huan hao 1999, Hei ma wang zi 1999, Du xia da zhan Lasi Weijiasi 1999, Running Out of Time 1999, Century of the Dragon 1999, Kuet chin chi gam ji din 2000, Needing You… 2000, A Fu (also producer) 2000, Love on a Diet 2001, Fulltime Killer (also producer) 2001, Oi gwan yue mung (also producer) 2001, Kap sze moon yat goh gei kooi 2002, Fat Choi Spirit 2002, Wai See Lee ji lam huet yan 2002, Infernal Affairs 2002, Love Under the Sun (short) 2003, Lou she oi sheung mao 2003, Running on Karma 2003, Mou gaan dou III: Jung gik mou gaan 2003, Golden Chicken 2 2003, Moh waan chue fong 2004, House of Flying Daggers 2004, Gong wu (also exec. producer) 2004, McDull, Prince de la bun (voice) 2004, Yesterday Once More 2004, A World Without Thieves 2004, Wait 'Til You're Older 2005, The Shoe Fairy (voice) (also exec. producer) 2005, All About Love (also exec. producer) 2005, I'll Call You (also exec. producer) 2006, My Mother Is a Belly Dancer (also producer) 2006, Battle of Wits 2006, Protégé 2007, Brothers 2007, The Warlords (as Dehua Liu) 2007, Three Kingdoms: Resurrection of the Dragon 2008, Yau lung hei fung 2009, The Founding of a Republic 2009, Future X-Cops 2010, Detective Dee: Mystery of the Phantom Flame 2010, Shaolin 2011, What Women Want (also exec. producer) 2011, Beginning of the Great Revival 2011, A Simple Life (also exec. producer) 2011; exec. producer: Made in Hong Kong 1997, Runaway Pistol (uncredited) 2002, Invisible Waves 2006, Gallants 2010; producer: Hui nin yin fa dak bit doh 1998, Crazy Stone 2006. *Television includes:* Choi wan kuk 1982, Sou hat yi (series) 1982, Return of the Condor Heroes (series) 1983, Lao dong (series) 1983, Luk ding gei (series) 1984, The Last Performance (series) 1985, Yang ka cheung (series) 1986, Hao men ye yan (presenter) 1991, Shin chou kyou ryo: Condor Hero (series) (title theme, singing voice) 2001. *Leisure interest:* Chinese calligraphy. *Address:* Focus Films, Focus Group Holdings Ltd, 9/F, Tower A, Billion Centre, 1 Wang Kwong Road, Kowloon Bay, Kowloon, Hong Kong Special Administrative Region, People's Republic of China (office). *Telephone:* 3120-3388 (office). *Fax:* 3120-3328 (office). *E-mail:* info@andylau.com (office). *Website:* www.focusgroup.cc (office); www.andylau.com.

LAU, John C. S.; Hong Kong business executive; *President and CEO, Husky Energy Inc.;* held several sr exec. roles with Cheung Kong (Holdings) Ltd and Hutchison Whampoa Ltd group of cos, Hong Kong; currently mem. Bd of Dirs, Pres. and CEO Husky Energy Inc.; Fellow, Inst. of Chartered Accountants, Australian Soc. of Accountants, Hong Kong Soc. of Accountants, Taxation Inst. of Hong Kong, Inst. of Chartered Secs of Admins of UK. *Address:* Husky Energy Inc., 707-8th Avenue SW, Box 6525, Station 'D', Calgary, Alberta, T2P 3G7, Canada (office). *Telephone:* (403) 298-6111 (office). *Fax:* (403) 298-7464 (office). *E-mail:* info@huskyenergy.com (office). *Website:* www.huskyenergy.com (office).

LAU, Joseph, BSc; Hong Kong real estate executive; *Chairman and CEO, Chinese Estates Holdings Limited;* b. (Lau Luen-hung), Hong Kong; m. (divorced); three c.; ed Univ. of Windsor, Canada; family originated in Chaozhou, Guangdong Prov., China; has over 32 years' experience in corp. finance, manufacturing and property investment and devt; joined Chinese Estates Holdings Ltd 1989, currently Chair. and CEO; Dir (non-exec.) Lifestyle International Holdings Ltd. *Leisure interest:* collecting art. *Address:* Chinese Estates Holdings Ltd, 26/F, MassMutual Tower, 38 Gloucester Road, Wanchai, Hong Kong Special Administrative Region, People's Republic of China (office). *Telephone:* 2866-6999 (office). *Fax:* 2866-2822 (office). *E-mail:* corpcomm@chineseestates.com (office). *Website:* www.chineseestates.com (office).

LAU, Lawrence J., BS, MA, PhD, JP; Chinese economist, business executive, fmr university administrator and academic; *Chairman, CIC International (Hong Kong) Company Limited;* b. (Liu Zunyi), 12 Dec. 1944, Guizhou Prov.; s. of Liu Shait-Tat and Liu Chi-Hing Yu; m. Ayesha A. Macpherson; one s.; ed Stanford Univ. and Univ. of California, Berkeley, USA; Acting Asst Prof. of Econs, Stanford Univ., USA 1966–67, Asst Prof. of Econs 1967–73, Assoc. Prof. of Econs 1973–76, Prof. of Econs 1976–2006, Kwoh-Ting Li Prof. of Econ. Devt 1992–2006, Kwoh-Ting Li Prof. in Econ. Devt Emer. 2006–, Vice-Chair. Dept of Econs 1990–92, Co-Dir Asia/Pacific Research Center 1992–96, Dir Stanford Inst. for Econ. Policy Research 1997–99, Sr Fellow, Inst. for Int. Studies 1992–2004, Sr Fellow, Hoover Inst. on War, Revolution and Peace 1997–2004, Sr Fellow, Stanford Inst. for Econ. Policy Research 1997–2013; Visiting Asst Research Economist, Univ. of California, Berkeley 1968–69; Visiting Prof. of Econs, Harvard Univ. 1978–79; Prof. of Econs, Chinese Univ. of Hong Kong 2004–07, Ralph and Claire Landau Prof. of Econs 2007–, also Pres. (Vice-Chancellor) 2004–10; JP, Hong Kong Special Admin. Region (SAR) 2007–; Chair. CIC International (Hong Kong) Co. Ltd 2010–; Vice-Chair. CITIC Capital Holdings Ltd 2010–; mem. Bd of Dirs Far EasTone Telecommunications Co. Ltd, Taipei 2005–, CNOOC Ltd, Hong Kong 2005–, Shin Kong Life Insurance Co. Ltd, Taipei 2008–11, Semiconductor Manufacturing Int. Corpn, Shanghai 2011–; Non-official mem. Exec. Council, Govt of Hong Kong SAR 2009–12; mem. 11th Nat. Cttee, CPPCC, People's Repub. of China 2008–13, Vice-Chair. Sub-Cttee on Population, Resources and the Environment 2010–13; mem. editorial bds of several journals; Academician, Academia Sinica, Taipei 1982, Int. Eurasian Acad. of Sciences 1999; mem. American Econ. Asscn; Fellow, Econometric Soc.; Trustee, Hong Kong/Stanford Univ. Charitable Trust 1994–2004; Hon. Prof., Coll. of Man., Tsinghua Univ., Beijing 1987–, People's Univ. of China 1994–, Shantou Univ., 1994–, Inst. of Systems Science, Chinese Acad. of Sciences, Beijing 1996–, Nankai Univ., Tianjin 1998–, Nanjing Univ. 2000–, Southeast Univ., Nanjing 2000–; Hon. Research Fellow, Inst. of Quantitative and Tech. Econs, Chinese Acad. of Social Sciences, Beijing 1989–, Shanghai Acad. of Social Sciences 1998–; Hon. Mem. Chinese Acad. of Social Sciences, Beijing, 1997, Bd of Trustees, San Yuan Yu You-Ren Memorial Museum, San Yuan, Shaanxi, China 1997–; Gold Bauhinia Star; Hon. DScS (Hong Kong Univ. of Science and Tech.) 1999; Hon. LLD (Waseda Univ.) 2007; Hon. DEcon (Fudan Univ.) 2011; Hon. Dr Man. Science (Nat. Cen. Univ.) 2010; Dr hc (Soka Univ.) 2007. *Publications:* Farmer Education and Farm Efficiency (co-author) 1982, Models of Development: A Comparative Study of Economic Growth in South Korea and Taiwan (ed. and contrib.) 1986, Econometrics and the Cost of Capital: Essays in Honor of Dale W. Jorgenson (ed. and contrib.) 2000, North Korea in Transition: Prospects for Economic and Social Reform (co-ed. and contrib.) 2001, US Direct Investment in China (co-author) 2002; more than 170 articles and notes in professional journals. *Address:* 25/F, CITIC Tower, 1 Tim Mei Avenue, Central, Hong Kong Special Administrative Region, People's Republic of China (office). *Telephone:* 3550-7070 (office). *Fax:* 2104-6938 (office). *E-mail:* lawrence@lawrencejlau.hk (office). *Website:* www.igef.cuhk.edu.hk/index.php/en/professor-lawrence-j-lau (office).

LAU, Siu-Kai, JP, BSocSc, PhD; Chinese academic and political adviser; *Professor Emeritus of Sociology, Chinese University of Hong Kong;* b. 7 June 1947, Hong Kong; s. of Keng-por Lau and Wai-sin Fong; m. Sophie Lai-mui Kwok 1972; one s.; ed Univ. of Hong Kong, Univ. of Minnesota, USA; Assoc. Dir Hong Kong Inst. of Asia-Pacific Studies, Chinese Univ. of Hong Kong 1990–2002, Prof. of Sociology 1990–2007, Prof. Emer. 2007–, Chair. Dept of Sociology 1994–2002; mem., Preparatory Cttee for Hong Kong Special Admin. Region 1996–97; Head, Central Policy Unit, Hong Kong Special Admin. Region 2002–12; mem. CPPCC 2003–08; political commentator on Hong Kong issues on TV, radio and in newspapers and magazines; Gold Bauhinia Star. *Publications:* Society and Politics in Hong Kong 1982, The Ethos of the Hong Kong Chinese 1988, Governance and New Regime Building in Hong Kong after the Handover (in Chinese) 2012. *Leisure interests:* reading, walking. *Address:* Department of Sociology, Chinese University of Hong Kong, Shatin, NT, Hong Kong Special Administrative Region (office); Flat B3, 8/F Cloudview Mansion, 8 Lok Fung Path, Fotan, NT, Hong Kong Special Administrative Region, People's Republic of China (home). *Telephone:* 39436631 (office); 26036438 (home). *Fax:* 26035213 (office); 26036438 (home). *E-mail:* siukailau@cuhk.edu.hk (office). *Website:* www.cuhk.edu.hk (office).

LAUDA, Andreas-Nikolaus (Niki); Austrian fmr racing driver; *Non-Executive Chairman, Mercedes AMG Petronas Formula One Team;* b. 22 Feb. 1949, Vienna; s. of Ernst Peter Lauda and Elisabeth Lauda; m. 1st Marlene Knaus 1976 (divorced 1991); two s. one d. and one s. from another relationship; m. 2nd Birgit Lauda 2008; one s. one d. (twins); competed in hill climbs 1968, later in Formula 3, Formula 2 and sports car racing; winner John Player British Formula 2 Championship 1972; started Formula 1 racing 1971; World Champion 1975, 1977, 1984, runner-up 1976; retd 1979; returned to racing 1981, won US Formula 1 Grand Prix, British Grand Prix 1982, Dutch Grand Prix 1985 171 starts, 25 wins, 54 podiums; retd again 1985; f. LaudaAir 1979, Chair. –2000, ceased operations 2013; commentator on Grands Prix for Austrian and German TV on RTL 1996–; CEO Ford Motor Co. Premier Performance Div. 2001–02; Head of Jaguar Racing Team 2001–02; f. FlyNiki airline 2003 (acquired by Air Berlin 2011); Chair. (non-exec.) Mercedes AMG Petronas Formula One Team 2012–; winner Victoria Sporting Club's Int. Award for Valour following recovery from near-fatal crash in 1976 German Grand Prix at Nürburgring 1977, Austrian Sportsman of the Year 1977, BBC Overseas Sports Personality of the Year 1977, Autosport Int. Racing Driver Award 1984, inducted into Int. Motorsports Hall of Fame 1993, stamp honouring him issued by Austrian post office 2005, ranked 22nd by ESPN TV network on their top drivers of all-time 2008. *Grand Prix wins:* Spanish (Ferrari) 1974, Dutch (Ferrari) 1974,

Monaco (Ferrari) 1975, Belgian (Ferrari) 1975, Swedish (Ferrari) 1975, French (Ferrari) 1975, US (Ferrari) 1975, Brazilian (Ferrari) 1976, South African (Ferrari) 1976, Belgian (Ferrari) 1976, British (Ferrari) 1976, South African (Ferrari) 1977, German (Ferrari) 1977, Dutch (Ferrari) 1977, Swedish (Brabham-Alfa Romeo) 1978, Italian (Brabham-Alfa Romeo) 1978. *Film:* cameo appearance in Rush (which portrayed the 1976 F1 battle between Niki Lauda and James Hunt) 2013. *Publications:* The Art and Science of Grand Prix Driving (also titled Formula 1: The Art and Technicalities of Grand Prix Driving) 1975, My Years with Ferrari 1978, The New Formula One: A Turbo Age 1984, Meine Story (also titled To Hell and Back) 1986, Das dritte Leben 1996. *Leisure interests:* music, skiing. *Address:* Mercedes AMG Petronas Formula One Team, Operations Centre, Brackley, Northants., NN13 7BD, England. *E-mail:* enquiries@mercedes-amg-f1.com. *Website:* www.mercedesamgf1.com.

LAUDER, Leonard Alan; American business executive and philanthropist; *Chairman Emeritus, The Estée Lauder Companies Inc.;* b. 19 March 1933, New York, NY; s. of Joseph Lauder and Estée Lauder (née Mentzer); m. Evelyn Hausner 1959; two s.; ed Wharton School, Univ. of Pennsylvania, Columbia Univ. Grad. School of Business; served as Lt in USN; with Estée Lauder Inc. (cosmetics and fragrance co.) New York 1958–, Exec. Vice-Pres. 1962–72, Pres. 1972–82, Pres. and CEO 1982–99, Chair. 1995–2009, Chair. Emer. 2009–; Gov. Joseph H. Lauder Inst. of Man. and Int. Studies 1983–; Chair. Emer. Bd of Trustees, Whitney Museum of American Art; Trustee, The Aspen Inst. for Humanistic Studies 1978– (Chair. Int. Cttee); Charter Trustee, Univ. of Pennsylvania 1977–; Pres. Whitney Museum of American Art 1977–; Co-founder and Chair. Alzheimer's Drug Discovery Foundation; mem. Council on Foreign Relations, Pres.'s Council of Memorial Sloan-Kettering Hosp.; donated collection of 78 pieces of Cubist painting (Pablo Picasso, Georges Braque, Fernand Léger and Juan Gris) to Metropolitan Museum of Art, New York 2013. *Address:* The Estée Lauder Companies Inc., 767 Fifth Avenue, New York, NY 10153, USA (office). *Telephone:* (212) 572-4200 (office). *Fax:* (212) 893-7782 (office). *E-mail:* mediarequests@estee.com (office). *Website:* www.elcompanies.com (office).

LAUDER, Ronald Stephen, BS; American business executive and diplomatist; *President, World Jewish Congress;* b. 26 Feb. 1944, New York, NY; s. of the late Joseph Lauder and Estée Lauder (née Mentzer); m. Jo Carole Knopf 1967; two d.; ed Bronx High School of Science, Wharton School of the Univ. of Pennsylvania, Univ. of Paris (Sorbonne), France, Univ. of Brussels, Belgium; Estée Lauder NV Belgium 1965–67, Estée Lauder SA France 1967, Estée Lauder Sales Promotion Dir 1968–69, Vice-Pres. Sales Promotion, Clinique 1969–72, Exec. Vice-Pres., Gen. Man. Clinique, Inc. 1972–75, Exec. Vice-Pres. Estée Lauder Int. 1975–78, Exec. Vice-Pres. Estée Lauder Inc., Chair. Estée Lauder Int. 1978–83; Deputy Asst Sec. of Defense for European and NATO Policy 1983–86; Amb. to Austria 1986–87, pvt. investment man. New York 1987–, now E and Cen. Europe; Trustee, Museum of Modern Art 1975– (Chair. 1995–), Mt. Sinai Medical Center 1981–; Chair. and Pres. Lauder Investments; Chair. (non-exec.) Cen. European Devt Corpn (now Cen. European Media Enterprises Ltd); Pres. Jewish Nat. Fund 1997–; Pres. Ronald S. Lauder Foundation; Pres. World Jewish Congress 2007–; mem. New York Landmarks Conservancy's Advisory Bd, Bd of Govs Joseph H. Lauder Inst. of Man. and Int. Studies at Univ. of Pennsylvania, Visiting Cttee Wharton School, Int. Bd of Govs Tel-Aviv Museum, Chair. Bd Trustees Sakharov Archive at Brandeis Univ., US Holocaust Memorial Council, Bd Dirs Jewish Theological Seminary, Bd Dirs American Jt Jewish Distribution Cttee, Bd Trustees Anti-Defamation League Foundation, Bd Trustees Abraham Fund; Chevalier, Ordre nat. du Mérite, Great Cross of the Order of Aeronautical Merit with White Ribbon (Spain), Dept of Defense Medal for Distinguished Public Service; Dr hc (Ben-Gurion Univ. of the Negev); ranked 12 on ArtReview magazine's Power 100 list 2005. *Address:* World Jewish Congress, 501 Madison Avenue, New York, NY 10022 (office); Lauder Investments Inc., 767 Fifth Avenue, Suite 4200, New York, NY 10153, USA. *Telephone:* (212) 755-5770 (office). *Fax:* (212) 755-5883 (office). *E-mail:* info@worldjewishcongress.org (home). *Website:* www.worldjewishcongress.org (office).

LAUDER, William P.; American business executive; *Executive Chairman, The Estée Lauder Companies Inc.;* grandson of co-founder Estée Lauder; m.; several c.; ed Wharton School, Univ. of Pennsylvania and Univ. of Grenoble, France; completed Macy's exec. training program, New York, later Assoc. Merchandising Man. New York Div./Dallas 1985; Regional Marketing Dir Clinique USA, The Estée Lauder Companies 1986, Vice-Pres./Gen. Man., later Pres. of Origins Natural Resources Inc. 1990–98, Pres. Clinique Laboratories 1998–2001, Pres. Clinique Worldwide and Group Pres. The Estée Lauder Companies 2001–03, COO The Estée Lauder Companies Inc. 2003–04, Pres., CEO and mem. Bd of Dirs 2004–09, Exec. Chair. and Chair. Bd of Dirs 2009–; mem. Bd of Dirs Univ. of Pennsylvania, The Fresh Air Fund, The 92nd Street Y; mem. Bd of Trustees The Trinity School. *Leisure interests:* golf, skiing, mountain biking, hiking. *Address:* The Estée Lauder Companies Inc., 767 Fifth Avenue, New York, NY 10153-0023, USA (office). *Telephone:* (212) 572-4200 (office). *Fax:* (212) 572-6633 (office). *Website:* www.elcompanies.com (office).

LAUER, Reinhard, DPhil; German philologist and academic; *Professor Emeritus of Slavonic Philology, University of Göttingen;* b. 15 March 1935, Bad Frankenhausen; s. of Erich Lauer and Rose Fischer; m. Stanka Ibler 1962; one d.; ed Univs of Marburg, Belgrade and Frankfurt and Freie Univ. of Berlin; Reader in German Language, Univ. of Zagreb, Yugoslavia 1960–62; Research Fellow, Univ. of Frankfurt 1962–69; Prof. of Slavonic Philology and Head of Dept of Slavonic Philology, Univ. of Göttingen 1969–, now Prof. Emer.; Head of Göttingen br., Southeast Europe Asscn 1973–; mem. Göttingen Acad. of Sciences 1980, Chair. Comm. for Interdisciplinary Southeastern Europe Research 1987–; Corresp. mem. Serbian Acad. of Sciences and Arts 1987, Croatian Acad. of Sciences and Arts 1989, Austrian Acad. of Sciences 1995, Slovenian Acad. of Sciences and Arts 2003; Hon. mem. Bulgarian Philology Soc.; Valjavec Prize 1960, Yugoslav Flag with Golden Garland 1989. *Publications:* Heine in Serbien 1961, Gedichtform zwischen Schema und Verfall 1975, Europäischer Realismus (ed.) 1980, M. Krleža und der deutsche Expressionismus 1984, Sprachen und Literaturen Jugoslaviens (ed.) 1985, Poetika i ideologija 1987, Sprache, Literatur und Folklore bei Vuk St Karadžić (ed.) 1989, Kulturelle Traditionen in Bulgarien (co-ed.) 1989, Künstlerische Dialektik und Identitätssuche (ed.) 1990, Die Moderne in den Literaturen Südosteuropas (ed.)

1991, Höfische Kultur in Südosteuropa (co-ed.) 1994, Serbokroatische Autoren in deutscher Übersetzung (ed.) 1995, Slavica Gottingensia (ed.) 1995, Die Kultur Griechenlands in Mittelalter und Neuzeit (co-ed.) 1996, Die russische Seele 1997, Geschichte der russischen Literatur 2000, Deutsche und Slovakische Literatur (ed.) 2000, A. S. Puškins Werk und Wirkung (co-ed.) 2000, Philologie in Göttingen (ed.) 2001, Die literarische Avantgarde in Südosteurope und ihr politische und gesellschaftliche Bedeutung (ed.) 2001, Studije i rasprave 2002, Kleine Geschichte der russischen Literatur 2005. *Leisure interests:* music, painting, ornithology. *Address:* Seminar für Slavische Philologie, Universität Göttingen, Humboldtallee 19, 37073 Göttingen (office); Allensteiner Weg 32, 37120 Bovenden, Germany. *Telephone:* (551) 394197 (office); (551) 81375 (home). *E-mail:* rlauer@uni-goettingen.de (office). *Website:* www.uni-goettingen.de/en/51177.html (office).

LAUGHLIN, Robert Betts, BA, PhD; American theoretical physicist and academic; *Anne T. and Robert M. Bass Professor of Physics, Stanford University;* b. 1 Nov. 1950, Visalia, Calif.; m. Anita Rhona Perry 1979; two s.; ed Univ. of California, Berkeley, Massachusetts Inst. of Tech.; mil. service, US Army 1972–74; Postdoctoral Fellow, Bell Telephone Labs 1979–81; Research Scientist, Lawrence Livermore Nat. Lab. 1981–2004; Assoc. Prof. of Physics, Stanford Univ. 1985–89, Prof. of Physics 1989–, Prof. of Applied Physics (dual appointment with Physics) 1993–2007, Anne T. and Robert M. Bass Prof. of Physics and Applied Physics –2004, 2006–; Pres. Korea Advanced Inst. of Science and Tech. (KAIST), Daejon 2004–06; Pres. Asia-Pacific Centre for Theoretical Physics 2004–06; mem. Bd Science Foundation Ireland 2002–03; mem. NAS 1994; Fellow, AAAS, American Physics Soc., American Acad. of Arts and Sciences; Hon. DLitt (Univ. of Maryland) 2005; E.O. Lawrence Award for Physics 1985, Oliver E. Buckley Prize 1986, Benjamin Franklin Medal for Physics, Franklin Inst. 1998, Nobel Prize in Physics (shared with Horst L. Störmer and Daniel C. Tsui for discovery of a new form of quantum fluid with fractionally charged excitations—fractional quantum Hall effect) 1998, Golden Plate Award, Acad. of Achievement 1999, Onsager Medal 2007. *Publications:* A Different Universe: Reinventing Physics from the Bottom Down 2005, Looking for a Hero 2006, The Crime of Reason: And the Closing of the Scientific Mind 2008, Mente y materia. ¿Qué es la vida? Sobre la vigencia de Erwin Schrödinger (co-author) 2010, Powering the Future: How We Will (Eventually) Solve the Energy Crisis and Fuel the Civilization of Tomorrow 2011; numerous papers in scientific journals. *Address:* Department of Physics, Stanford University, McCullough 301, Stanford, CA 94305, USA (office). *Telephone:* (650) 723-4563 (office). *Fax:* (650) 724-3681 (office). *E-mail:* rbl@large.stanford.edu (office). *Website:* large.stanford.edu (home).

LAUGHTON, Sir Anthony Seymour, Kt, PhD, FRS; British oceanographic scientist; b. 29 April 1927; s. of Sydney T. Laughton and Dorothy (Chamberlain) Laughton; m. 1st Juliet A. Chapman 1957 (dissolved 1962), one s.; m. 2nd Barbara C. Bosanquet 1973, two d.; ed Marlborough Coll. and King's Coll. Cambridge; RNVR 1945–48; John Murray Student, Columbia Univ., New York 1954–55; Nat. Inst. of Oceanography, later Inst. of Oceanographic Sciences 1955–88, fmr Dir; mem. Jt IOC/IHO Guiding Cttee GEBCO (ocean charts) 1974–2003, Chair. 1986–2003; mem. Council, Univ. Coll. London 1983–93; mem. Co-ordinating Cttee for Marine Science and Tech. 1987–91; Pres. Challenger Soc. for Marine Science 1988–90, Soc. Underwater Tech. 1995–97, Hydrographic Soc. 1997–99; mem. Governing Body Charterhouse School 1981–2000, Chair. 1995–2000; Trustee Natural History Museum 1990–95; Royal Soc. of Arts Silver Medal 1958, Prince Albert 1er Monaco Gold Medal 1980, Founders Medal, Royal Geographical Soc. 1987, Murchison Medal, Geological Soc. 1989, Pres.'s Award, Soc. for Underwater Tech. 1998. *Publications:* papers on marine geophysics. *Leisure interests:* music, gardening, sailing, woodwork. *Address:* Okelands, Pickhurst Road, Chiddingfold, Surrey, GU8 4TS, England (home). *Telephone:* (1428) 683941 (home). *E-mail:* aslaughton@googlemail.com (home).

LAUNDER, Brian Edward, ScD, DSc (Eng), DEng, FRS, FREng, FCGI, FIMechE, FRAeS; British engineer, academic and editor; *Research Professor (part-time), University of Manchester;* b. 20 July 1939, London; s. of Harry Edward Launder and Elizabeth Ann Launder (née Ayers); m. Dagny Simonsen 1968; one s. one d.; ed Enfield Grammar School, Imperial Coll., London, Massachusetts Inst. of Tech., USA; Lecturer, then Reader, Mechanical Eng Dept, Imperial Coll. London 1964–76; Prof. of Mechanical Eng, Univ. of California, Davis 1976; Prof. of Mechanical Eng, UMIST (now Univ. of Manchester) 1980–98, Head, Mechanical Eng Dept 1983–85, 1993–95, Research Prof. 1998–; Dir Environmental Strategy Group 1998–2004; Regional Dir Tyndall Centre for Climate Change Research 2001–06; Ed.-in-Chief International Journal of Heat and Fluid Flow 1987–2013; mem. Scientific Advisory Bd CERFACS, Toulouse 1992–2013; assessor, Center for Turbulence Research, Stanford Univ., Calif. 1996–2004; Hon. Prof., Nanjing Aerospace Inst. 1993; Dr hc (Inst. Nat. Polytechnique, Toulouse) 1999, (Univ. Paul Cézanne, Aix-en-Provence) 2008; Hon. DSc (Aristotle Univ., Thessaloniki, Greece) 2005; Hon. Diploma, Russian Acad. of Sciences (Novosibirsk Br.) 2013; Busk Prize, Royal Aeronautical Soc. 1995, Computational Mechanics Award, Japan Soc. of Mechanical Engineers 1995, Daniel & Florence Guggenheim Award, Int. Council of Aeronautical Sciences 2000, Nusselt-Reynolds Prize, Council of World Confs in Fluid Mechanics, Heat Transfer and Thermodynamics 2013. *Publications include:* Mathematical Models of Turbulence 1972, Turbulent Shear Flows, Vols 1–9 (ed.), Computational Strategies for Turbulent and Transitional Flows (ed.) 2002, Geoengineering Climate Change: Environmental Necessity or Pandora's Box? 2009, Modelling Turbulence in Engineering and the Environment 2011; more than 250 papers on measurement and modelling of turbulent flow. *Leisure interests:* French culture and cuisine, walking, photography. *Address:* C31, George Begg, School of Mechanical, Aerospace and Civil Engineering, University of Manchester, Manchester, M13 9PL, England (office). *Telephone:* (161) 306-3801 (office). *Fax:* (161) 306-3723 (office). *E-mail:* brian.launder@manchester.ac.uk (office). *Website:* www.manchester.ac.uk (office).

LAURA, Ernesto Guido; Italian film director, film critic and fmr film festival director; b. 4 May 1932, Villafranca, Veronese; s. of Manuel Laura and Pia Romei Laura; m. Anna Maria Vercellotti 1958; two s.; ed Dept of Law, Catholic Univ., Milan; Co-Nat. Sec. Centri Universitari Cinematografici 1953–54; Admin. Nat. Sec. Federazione Italiana Circoli del Cinema 1954–55; Chief Ed. Bianco e Nero 1956–58, Filmlexicon 1968; Film Critic, Il Veltro from 1958; mem. Editorial Bd Rivista del Cinematografo from 1967; Pres. Immagine, Centro Studi Iconografici

from 1968, now Hon. Pres.; Dir Venice Film Festival 1969–70; Premio Charlie Chaplin (co-recipient) 2012. *Films include:* Diario di Una Dama Veneziana (documentary) 1958, Riscoperta di un Maestro (documentary) 1960, Alla Ricerca di Franz Kafka (documentary) 1964, Spielberg (documentary) 1964, Don Minzoni (documentary) (Special Award) 1967, I mari della mia fantasia (short, also writer) 1971, La caduta del fascismo (documentary, also writer) 1983, Le Stagioni Dell'Aquila (Years of the Eagle) (documentary, writer) 1997. *Publications:* Il Film Cecoslovacco 1960, La Censura Cinematografica 1961, Ladri di Biciclette 1969, Immagine del Fascismo. Volume primo: La conquista del potere (1915–1925) 1973, Comedy Italian Style 1980, Teleconfronto: IV Mostra internazionale del telefilm, 23 maggio-1 giugno 1986 1986, L'immagine bugiarda: mass-media e spettacolo nella Repubblica di Salo (1943–1945) 1986, Quando Los Angeles si chiamava Hollywood. Cinema americano tra le due guerre 1996, Le stagioni dell'aquila: Storia dell'Istituto Luce (Immagini allo specchio) 2000, Hitchcock e il surrealismo. Il filo inesplorato che lega il maestro del cinema all'arte del Novecento 2005, La gola (Piemme Shots) (co-author) 2012.

LAURANCE, Dale R., BS, MS, PhD; American chemical engineer and business executive; *Chairman, Ingram Micro Inc.;* m.; ed Oregon State Univ., Univ. of Kansas; worked at E.I. DuPont de Nemours 1967–77; with Olin Corpn 1977–83; served in various man. and exec. positions with Occidental Petroleum Corpn 1983–96, mem. Bd of Dirs 1990–2004, Pres. 1996–2004; Owner, Laurance Enterprises LLC (pvt. advisory services co.), Nightingale Properties LLC (Hawaiian real estate devt co.); mem. Bd of Dirs Ingram Micro Inc. 2001–, Chair. 2007–; Chair. Advisory Bd, Dept of Chemical Eng, Univ. of Kansas 1985–97; mem. Oregon State Univ. Coll. of Eng Acad. of Distinguished Engineers 1999–; mem. Bd of Dirs Jacobs Engineering Group 1994–, Saint John's Health Center; mem. Advisory Bd Hancock Park Assocs; mem. Bd of Trustees Polytechnic School, Children's Bureau; mem. Advisory Bd Golden West Humanitarian Foundation; mem. American Chem. Council; Hon. mem. Oregon State Univ.'s Chemical Eng Advisory Bd 1997–; mem. Hall of Fame, Dept of Chemical Eng, Univ. of Kansas. *Publications:* several US patents. *Address:* Ingram Micro Inc., 1600 East St Andrew Place, PO Box 25125, Santa Ana, CA 92799-5125, USA (office). *Telephone:* (714) 566-1000 (office). *E-mail:* info@ingrammicro.com (office). *Website:* www .ingrammicro.com (office).

LAURANCE, William (Bill) F., BSc, PhD; American biologist, environmental scientist and academic; *Distinguished Research Professor, James Cook University;* b. 12 Oct. 1957; m. Dr Susan G. Laurance; two c.; ed Boise State Univ., Univ. of California, Berkeley; Dir S.F.S. Centre for Rainforest Studies, Yungaburra, Qld, Australia 1989–91; Sr Prin. Scientist, Wet Tropics Man. Authority, Qld 1992–94; Wet Tropics Postdoctoral Fellow, CSIRO Tropical Forest Research Centre, Atherton, Qld 1994–96; Sr Scientist, Biological Dynamics of Forest Fragments Project, Smithsonian Inst. and Nat. Inst. for Amazonian Research (INPA), Manaus, Brazil 1996–2000; Sr Staff Scientist, Smithsonian Tropical Research Inst., Balboa, Panamá 2000–; Distinguished Research Prof., School of Marine and Tropical Biology, James Cook Univ., Australia 2009–; Prince Bernhard Chair in Int. Nature Conservation, WWF-Netherlands and Univ. of Utrecht, Netherlands 2010–14; Research Assoc., Arnold Arboretum, Harvard Univ. 2009–; John A. Erskine Fellow, Univ. of Canterbury, NZ 2005; Pres. Asscn for Tropical Biology and Conservation 2006; mem. Editorial Bd, Biotropica 1998–2000, Biological Conservation 1998–, Ecology Letters 2002–04, Natureza e Conservação 2002–, Trends in Ecology and Evolution 2003–, Tropical Conservation Science 2007–, Environmental Conservation 2009–, Research and Reports in Biodiversity Studies 2010–; Fellow, AAAS 2003; Hon. Fellow, World Innovation Foundation 2005; Silver and Gold Award for Outstanding Contribs, Boise State Univ. 1981, Biology Dept Scholarship, Boise State Univ. 1982, National Dean's List 1982, Outstanding Teaching Asst, Dept of Instruction in Biology, Univ. of California, Berkeley 1985, American Soc. of Mammalogists Award 1989, Award for Outstanding Scientist in the 25-year History of the Biological Dynamics of Forest Fragments Project, Manaus, Brazil 2004, John L. Boething Award for Conservation Research, Stanford Univ. 2005, BBVA Frontiers in Ecology and Conservation Biology Award 2008, Distinguished Alumni Award, Boise State Univ. 2010, Australian Laureate Award 2010–15, Distinguished Service Award, Soc. for Conservation Biology 2011, Australia's Best Science Writing Prize 2012, Winner, Faculty of 1000 Selection for Outstanding Articles 2012, Dr A.H. Heineken Prize for Environmental Sciences, Royal Netherlands Acad. of Arts and Sciences 2012. *Publications:* five books and more than 300 scientific and popular articles on the impacts of intensive land-uses, such as habitat fragmentation, logging, and wildfires, on tropical forests and species, as well as climate change and conservation policy. *Address:* Centre for Tropical Environmental & Sustainability Science (TESS), School of Marine and Tropical Biology, James Cook University, Cairns, Qld 4870, Australia (office). *Telephone:* (7) 4042-1819 (office); (7) 4038-1518 (home). *E-mail:* bill.laurance@jcu .edu.au (office). *Website:* research.jcu.edu.au/portfolio/bill.laurance (office); laurancelab.org/prof-william-laurance (office).

LAUREDO, Luis J., BA; American diplomatist, lawyer and business executive; m. Maria Regina Lauredo; two d.; ed Columbia Univ., Univ. of Madrid, Spain and Georgetown Univ.; Commr, Fla Public Service Comm. 1992–94; Chair. Int. Relations Cttee, Nat. Asscn of Regulatory Utility Commrs 1992–94; Nat. Co-ordinator Summit of the Americas 1994–95; Pres. Greenberg Taurig Consulting Inc. 1995–99; Perm. Rep. to OAS 1999–2001; consultant, Hunton & Williams law firm 2001–; mem. Presidential Advisory Cttee for Trade Promotion Negotiations 2003–; Exec. Dir FTAA Ministerial and American Business Forum 2003; Sr Vice-Pres., Export-Import Bank of the USA; Chair. Miami Int. Press Center; Dir, Rica Foods Inc. 1996–99, 2001–07, Colonial Bank of South Florida 2001–; Founding Dir, Hispanic Council on Foreign Affairs, Washington, DC; mem. Int. Advisory Bd, Baptist Health South Florida Inc. 2008–; Trustee, Pan-American Devt Foundation; represented US Pres. as Special US Amb. to the inaugurations of the Presidents of Columbia, Venezuela, Brazil and Costa Rica. *Address:* Baptist Health South Florida Inc., 6855 Red Road, Suite 600, Coral Gables, Miami, FL 33143-3632, USA (office). *Telephone:* (786) 662-6000 (office). *Fax:* (786) 662-6000 (office). *E-mail:* corporatepr@baptisthealth.net. *Website:* baptisthealth.net (office).

LAUREN, Ralph; American couturier; b. 14 Oct. 1939, Bronx, NY; s. of Frank Lifschitz and Frida Lifschitz; m. Ricky Low-Beer 1964; two s. one d.; ed DeWitt Clinton High School, the Bronx, NY and City Coll. of New York; changed name from Lifschitz to Lauren aged 16; served in US Army 1962–64; salesman, Bloomingdale's, New York, Brooks Bros New York (cr. Polo label for them); Asst Buyer, Allied Stores, New York; Rep. Rivetz Necktie Mfrs New York; neckwear designer, Polo Div., Beau Brummel, New York 1967–69; est. Polo Menswear Co., New York 1968–, Ralph Lauren's Women's Wear, New York 1971–, Polo Leathergoods 1978–, Polo Ralph Lauren Luggage 1982–, Ralph Lauren Home Collection 1983–; Chair. Polo Ralph Lauren Corpn (66 stores in USA, over 140 world-wide); cr. other brands, including Chaps, Club Monaco, Purple Label, Polo Jeans Co., Ralph Lauren Rugby 2004; recipient of many fashion awards including American Fashion Award 1975, Council of Fashion Designers of America Award 1981, CFDA Lifetime Achievement Award 1992, CFDA American Fashion Legend Award 2007. *Publication:* Ralph Lauren 2007. *Leisure interest:* collecting and showing classic automobiles. *Address:* Polo Ralph Lauren Corporation, 650 Madison Avenue, New York, NY 10022, USA (office). *Telephone:* (212) 318-7000 (office). *Fax:* (212) 888-5780 (office). *Website:* www.polo.com (office).

LAURÉN, Reidunn, BA, DIur; Swedish lawyer and politician; m.; three c.; fmr Judge Admin. Court of Appeal, Stockholm; fmr Deputy Sec. Parl. Standing Cttee on Social Affairs; Legal Adviser Ministry of Labour; Perm. Under-Sec. Ministry of Housing and Physical Planning; Justice of the Supreme Admin. Court; Chair. Labour Court; Chair. Equal Opportunities Tribunal; Minister for Constitutional and Civil Law 1991–93; Pres. Admin. Court of Appeal 1994–97; Chair. Queen Sophia's Hosp. 1995–2002; King's Medal for distinguished legal service 2000. *Publications:* Equal Opportunities at Work for Women and Men; numerous articles on legal matters. *Address:* Administrative Court of Appeal, Box 2302, 103 17 Stockholm, Sweden. *Telephone:* 700-3801.

LAURENS, André Antoine; French journalist; *Vice-President and Director-General, L'Indépendant;* b. 7 Dec. 1934, Montpellier (Hérault); s. of André Laurens and Mme Laurens (née Raymonde Balle); ed Lycée de Montpellier; journalist, L'Eclaireur Meridional (fortnightly), Montpellier 1953–54, Agence centrale de Presse, Paris 1958–62; mem. political staff, Le Monde 1963–69, Asst to head of political Dept 1969–82; Dir Le Monde 1982–84, Chief writer 1986–, Ombudsman 1994–; Vice-Pres. Soc. des Rédacteurs; Vice-Pres. and Dir-Gen. L'Indépendant 2000–. *Publications:* Les nouveaux communistes 1972, D'une France à l'autre 1974, Le Métier politique ou la conquête du pouvoir 1980. *Address:* L'Independant, Mas de la Garrigue, 2 avenue Alfred Sauvy, BP 105, 66605 Rivesaltes (office); 58 rue de la Roquette, Paris 75011 (home); 1 Espace Mediterraneé, Perpignan 66605, France (home). *Telephone:* 4-68-64-88-88 (office). *Fax:* 4-68-54-88-49 (office). *Website:* www.lindependant.com (office).

LAURENT, Jean, MSc, CE; French banking executive and administrator; *Chairman, Board of Directors, Calyon;* b. 31 July 1944, Mazamet; m.; five c.; ed École Nat. Supérieure d'Aéronautique, Wichita State Univ., USA; Dir AMACAM Co. 1994–, Indocam 1996–, Indosuez Bank of Pvt. Man. 1998–, Crédit Lyonnais Oct. 1999–; Chair. Bd Segespar May 1999– (Dir 1994–), Union of Studies and Investments June 1999–, (Dir 1996–); fmr CEO Crédit Agricole SA; Vice-Pres. Banca Intesa and Bank Espirito Santo 1999–, Bd of Trustees Crédit Agricole Indosuez 2000–; Pres. Fédération Bancaire Française, A.F.E.C.E.I. 2001–; currently Chair. Bd of Dirs Calyon; Chevalier, Légion d'honneur, Officier, Ordre du Mérite agricole. *Address:* Calyon, 9 Quai du President Paul Dourner, 9290 La Défense cedex, Paris, France (office). *Telephone:* 1-41-89-00-00 (office). *Fax:* 1-57-87-04-23 (office). *Website:* www.calyon.com (office).

LAURENT, Mélanie; French actress, director, model, singer and writer; b. 21 Feb. 1983, Paris; d. of Pierre Laurent and Annick Laurent; career began when Gérard Depardieu gave her a part in The Bridge 1999; abandoned plans to direct her first play, Mi-cuit cœur pistache at Théâtre Marigny, Paris, when she was cast as Shosanna Dreyfus in the Quentin Tarantino film Inglourious Basterds 2009; hostess of opening and closing ceremonies of 64th Cannes Film Festival 2011; a Climate Amb. for Kofi Annan's Global Humanitarian Forum 'Tck Tck Tck' Campaign; co-recipient, with Belgian actor Jérémie Renie, of the Romy Schneider and Jean Gabin Prizes for "most promising actor and actress" 2006. *Theatre includes:* Promenade de santé by Nicolas Bedos 2010. *Films include:* acted in: The Bridge 1999, Ceci est mon corps 2001, Summer Things 2002, La faucheuse (short) 2003, Snowboarder 2003, Une vie à t'attendre 2004, Rice Rhapsody 2004, The Last Day 2004, The Beat That My Heart Skipped 2005, Les visages d'Alice (short) 2005, Days of Glory 2006, Dikkenek (Étoiles d'Or for Best Female Newcomer) 2006, Don't Worry, I'm Fine (César Award for Most Promising Actress, Lumière Award for Most Promising Young Actress, NRJ Ciné Award for Best Young Talent in a Debut Film, Étoiles d'Or for Best Female Newcomer) 2006, Hidden Love 2007, Beluga 2007, Le tueur 2007, La chambre des morts 2007, Paris 2008, The Business Trip (short) 2008, Inglourious Basterds (Austin Film Critics Asscn Award for Best Actress, Broadcast Film Critics Asscn Award for Best Cast, Central Ohio Film Critics Asscn for Best Ensemble, Best Actress, Online Film Critics Soc., Screen Actors Guild Award for Outstanding Performance by a Cast in a Motion Picture) 2009, Jusqu'à toi 2009, The Concert 2009, The Round Up 2010, Beginners 2010, Requiem pour une tueuse 2011, Et soudain tout le monde me manque 2011 (writer and director: De moins en moins (short) 2008. *Television includes:* acted in; Route de nuit (film) 2000, Jean Moulin, une affaire française (film) 2003; writer and director: X Femmes (series) (A ses pieds) 2008. *Recording:* En t'Attendant (debut album) 2011.

LAUREY, Nuihau; French Polynesian politician; *Vice-President and Minister of Economy;* b. 1964, Tahiti; ed Univ. of Nice Sophia Antipolis, France; several years working in information technology and financial sectors; fmr teacher of econs and finance; consultant in field of renewable energy and natural gas; technical adviser to Minister of Energy Teva Rohfritsch 2010; Man. Dir SARL INTIA (renewable energy co.) 2011–13; Vice-Pres. and Minister of Economy 2013–; mem. Tahoera'a Huiraatira (People's Rally). *Publication:* Plaidoyer pour une véritable politique de l'énergie en Polynésie Française 2009. *Address:* Office of the Vice-President of the Government, ave Pouvana'a A Opa, BP 2551, 98713 Papeete, French Polynesia (office). *Telephone:* 472500 (office). *Website:* www.presidence.pf (office).

LAURIE, (James) Hugh Callum, OBE; British actor, writer and musician; b. 11 June 1959, Oxford, England; s. of the late (William George) Ranald (Mundell) Laurie and Patricia Laurie (née Laidlaw); m. Jo Green 1989; two s. one d.; ed Eton Coll., Windsor, Univ. of Cambridge; fmr Pres. Footlights, Univ. of Cambridge.

Films: Peter's Friends 1992, A Pin for the Butterfly 1994, Sense and Sensibility 1995, 101 Dalmatians 1996, The Snow Queen's Revenge 1996, The Borrowers 1997, Spice World 1997, The Ugly Duckling 1997, The Man in the Iron Mask 1998, Cousin Bette 1998, Stuart Little 1999, Carnivale 2000, Maybe Baby 2000, Lounge Act 2000, The Piano Tuner 2001, Chica de Río 2001, Stuart Little 2 2002, Flight of the Phoenix 2004, Valiant (voice) 2005, Street Kings 2008, Monsters vs Aliens (voice) 2009, The Oranges 2011. *Television appearances include:* Alfresco (series, also writer) 1983, The Crystal Cube (also writer) 1983, Mrs Capper's Birthday (film) 1985, Saturday Live (writer) 1986, A Bit of Fry and Laurie (series, also writer) 1986–95, The Laughing Prisoner (also writer) 1987, Blackadder the Third (series) 1987, Up Line 1987, Blackadder: The Cavalier Years 1988, Les Girls (series) 1988, Blackadder's Christmas Carol 1988, Blackadder Goes Forth (series) 1989, Hysteria 2! 1989, Jeeves and Wooster (series) 1990–92, Treasure Island (series) 1993, All or Nothing at All 1993, Look at the State We're In! (series, also dir) 1995, The Adventures of Mole 1995, The Best of Tracey Takes On… 1996, The Place of Lions 1997, Blackadder Back & Forth 1999, Santa's Last Christmas (voice) 1999, Little Grey Rabbit (series) 2000, Preston Pig (series) 2000, Life with Judy Garland: My and My Shadows 2001, Second Star to the Left 2001, Family Guy (series) 2001–09, Spooks (series) 2002, Stuart Little (series) 2003, Fortysomething (series, also dir) 2003, The Young Visiters [sic] 2003, House (Satellite Award for Outstanding Actor in a Series, Drama 2005, 2006, Television Critics Association Award for Individual Achievement in Drama 2005, 2006, Golden Globe Award for Best Performance in a Drama TV Series 2006, Golden Globe Award for Best Actor in a Drama TV Series 2007, Screen Actors' Guild Award for Outstanding Performance by a Male Actor in a Drama Series 2007, 2009, Teen Choice Award for TV Actor: Drama 2007, People's Choice Award for Favourite Male TV Star 2008, 2009, for Favourite TV Drama Actor 2010, 2011, for Favourite TV Doctor 2011) 2004–, Monsters vs Aliens: Mutant Pumpkins from Outer Space (film) 2009, The Simpsons (voice) 2010, Fry and Laurie Reunited 2010. *Recordings:* albums: Let Them Talk 2011, Didn't It Rain 2013. *Publications:* Fry and Laurie 4 (with Stephen Fry) 1994, The Gun Seller 1996, The Paper Soldier 2009. *Leisure interest:* motorcycle enthusiast. *Address:* c/o Lorraine Hodell, Hamilton Hodell Ltd, 5th Floor, 66–68 Margaret Street, London, W1W 8SR, England (office). *Telephone:* (20) 7636-1221 (office). *Fax:* (20) 7636-1226 (office). *E-mail:* info@hamiltonhodell.co.uk (office). *Website:* www.hamiltonhodell.co.uk (office); hughlaurieblues.com (office).

LAURIE, Robert Stephen, AM, BA; Australian diplomatist (retd); b. 5 Nov. 1936, Sydney, NSW; s. of William Robert Laurie; m. Diana Victoria Mary Doyne 1969; one s. one d.; ed Knox Grammar School and Univ. of Sydney; joined Dept of External Affairs (now Dept of Foreign Affairs and Trade) 1958; served in Colombo 1960, Moscow 1960–63; First Sec., Washington, DC 1965–68; Counsellor, Hong Kong 1968–69; Deputy High Commr in India 1969–71; Amb. to Burma 1975–77, to Poland 1977–80; High Commr in Canada 1985–89, in NZ 1989–92; First Asst Sec., South Pacific, Middle East and Africa Divs, Dept of Foreign Affairs and Trade 1993–97; High Commr in India 1997–2001. *Leisure interests:* tennis, cricket, golf, music. *Address:* 31 Arthur Circle, Manuka, Griffith, ACT 2603; c/o Department of Foreign Affairs and Trade, R.G. Casey Building, John McEwen Crescent, Barton ACT 0221, Australia.

LAURISTIN, Marju, PhD; Estonian politician, sociologist and academic; *Professor Emerita of Social Communication, Tartu University;* b. 7 April 1940, Tallinn; d. of Johannes Lauristin and Olga Lauristin; m. Peeter Vihalemm 1978; two d.; ed Tartu Univ.; Head of Dept of Journalism, Tartu Univ. –1989, Prof. 1993, Prof. of Social Communication 2003, now Prof. Emer.; mem. CPSU –1990; f. Popular Front of Estonia 1988–92; Chair. Estonia Social-Democratic Party 1990–94; USSR People's Deputy 1989–90; Deputy Speaker of Estonian Supreme Soviet (now Parl.) 1990–92; mem. Estonian Parl. 1992–95, 1999–2003; Minister of Social Affairs 1992–94; mem. Advisory Cttee for the Protection of Nat. Minorities, Council of Europe 2004–; mem. Bd European Sociological Asscn 2007–; mem. United Nations Univ. Council 2004–; Order of Nat. Coat of Arms, Third Class 1998, Second Class 2003, Kt, Order of the White Rose, First Class, Finland 2003; Dr hc (Univ. of Helsinki) 2006; Democracy and Civil Soc. Award, USA and EU 1998. *Publication:* Return to the Western World: Cultural and Political Perspectives on the Estonian Post-Communist Transition (ed. with P. Vihalemm), The Challenge of the Russian Minority: Emerging Multicultural Democracy in Estonia (jt ed.) 2002. *Leisure interest:* literature. *Address:* Siili 6, Apt 35, Tartu 50104 (home); Ülikooli 18, Tartu 50090, Estonia (office). *Telephone:* (7) 375-188 (office); (7) 471-532 (home). *Fax:* (7) 376-355 (office). *E-mail:* marju.lauristin@ut.ee (home). *Website:* www.jrnl.ut.ee (office).

LAUTI, Sir Toaripi, GCMG, PC; Tuvaluan politician; b. 28 Nov. 1928, Papua New Guinea; m.; three s. two d.; ed Queen Victoria School, Fiji, Wesley Coll., Paerata, NZ, St Andrew's Coll., Christchurch, Christchurch Teachers' Coll.; teacher in Tarawa, Gilbert Is (now Kiribati) 1953–62; Labour Relations and Training Officer for Nauru and Ocean Is Phosphate Comm. 1962–74; returned to Ellice Is (now Tuvalu) 1974; Chief Minister of Tuvalu 1975–78, Prime Minister 1978–81 (replaced as a result of his alleged involvement in investment scandal); Leader of the Opposition 1981–90; Gov. Gen. of Tuvalu 1990–93; also fmr Minister of Finance and Foreign Affairs. *Address:* PO Box 84, Funafuti, Tuvalu.

LAUTMANN, Rüdiger, DPhil, DJur; German sociologist and academic; *Professor, Department of Sociology, University of Bremen;* b. 22 Dec. 1935, Koblenz; s. of Kurt Lautmann and Sibylle Lautmann; partner, Heiko Hinrichs; ed Univs of Bonn, Berlin, Würzburg and Munich; Research Asst, Univ. of Bielefeld and Dortmund 1968–71; Prof. of Sociology, Law School, Univ. of Bremen 1971–82, Dept of Sociology 1982–; Ed. Journal of the German Sociological Association 1995–99; Speaker of Beirat, Kriminologisches Journal 2008–09; Pres. Inst. of Research in Security and Prevention, Hamburg 2001–10; mem. Kuratorium, Stenden Univ., Berlin 2010. *Publications:* Wert und Norm 1969, Die Funktion des Rechts in der modernen Gesellschaft (co-ed.) 1970, Die Polizei (co-ed.) 1971, Soziologie vor den Toren der Jurisprudenz 1971, Justiz–die stille Gewalt 1972, Seminar Gesellschaft und Homosexualität 1977, Rechtssoziologie–Examinatorium (co-ed.) 1980, Der Zwang zur Tugend 1984, Die Gleichheit der Geschlechter und die Wirklichkeit des Rechts 1990, Das pornographische Begehren (co-author) 1990, Männerliebe im alten Deutschland (co-ed.) 1992, Homosexualität (ed.) 1993, Vom Guten, das noch stets das Böse schafft (co-ed.) 1993, Die Lust am Kind 1994, Der Homosexuelle und sein Publikum 1997, Ausgrenzung macht krank (co-author) 2000, Soziologie der

Sexualität 2002, NS–Terror gegen Homosexuelle (co-ed.) 2002, Punitivität (co-ed.) 2004, Lexikon zur Soziologie (co-ed.) 2010, Migranten in der Zuwanderungsgesellschaft Deutschland (co-author) 2011. *Leisure interest:* theatre, e-music. *Address:* University of Bremen, Fachbereich 8, 28334 Bremen (office); Lindauer Str. 7, 10781 Berlin, Germany (home). *Telephone:* (30) 53091193 (home). *E-mail:* lautmann@uni-bremen.de (office); lautmannhh@aol.com (home). *Website:* www .lautmann.de (office).

LAUVERGEON, Anne Alice Marie; French government official and business executive; b. 2 Aug. 1959, Dijon; d. of Gérard Lauvergeon and Solange Martellière; m. Jean-Eric Molinard 1986; ed Lycées Lakanal, Sceaux, Lycée Voltaire, Orléans, Ecole Normale Supérieure and Ecole Nat. Supérieure des Mines, Paris; began her professional career in iron and steel industry, first in Canada, then with Usinor 1983–84; Eng Inst. for Protection and Nuclear Safety, Centre d'Energie Atomique and Head of Div. Direction Régionale de l'Industrie et de la Recherche, Ile-de-France 1985–88; Asst to Head of Service of Conseil-Général des Mines 1988–89; Adviser on int. econ. and foreign trade, Presidency of Repub. 1990; Deputy Sec.-Gen. Presidency of Repub. 1990–95; Partner and Man. Lazard Frères & Cie 1995–98; Deputy Dir-Gen. Alcatel Alsthom 1997, mem. Exec. Cttee Alcatel Group 1998; Pres., Dir-Gen. Compagnie générale des matières nucléaires (Cogema) 1999–2001, Chair. Exec. Bd and CEO Areva Group (formed by merger of Cogema, CEA-Industrie, Framatome) 2001–11, also Dir Arreva Enterprises Inc.; Chair. Supervisory Bd Libération (daily newspaper) 2011–; Chair. Ecole Nationale Superieure des Mines de Nancy; Vice-Pres. Bd of Dirs Société d'applications générales d'électricité et de mécanique (Sagem) 2000; mem. Strategy, Ethics and Environment Cttees, Suez Lyonnaise Group 2000; mem. Bd of Dirs Pechiney 1996–, Framatome 1998, Total Fina Elf 2000–, GDF-SUEZ, Vodafone Group Plc, EADS 2013–; Officier, Légion d'honneur; ranked by Fortune magazine amongst the 50 Most Powerful Women in Business outside the US (second) 2001, (third) 2002–03, (first) 2004–05, (second) 2006–07, (sixth) 2008, (fourth) 2009, (16th) 2010, ranked by Forbes magazine amongst The World's 100 Most Powerful Women (53rd) 2004, (11th) 2005, (eighth) 2006, (14th) 2007, (ninth) 2008–09, (24th) 2010, ranked by the Financial Times amongst Top 25 Businesswomen in Europe (second) of 2005, (second) 2006, (first) 2007. *Publication:* Sur les traces des dirigeants ou la vie du chef dans les grandes entreprises (co-author) 1988. *Address:* Libération, 11 rue Béranger, 75114 Paris Cedex 03, France. *Telephone:* 1-42-76-17-89. *Fax:* 1-42-72-94-93. *Website:* www.liberation.com.

LAVADOS MONTES, Hugo, MA; Chilean politician; b. Aug. 1949, Talca; m.; two c.; ed Univ. of Chile, Boston Univ., USA; Gen. Man. Manpower Chile 1983–90; Supervisor, Valores y Seguros 1990–94; Gen. Man. Banco BHIF 1994–98; Dir ProChile (govt agency to promote exports) 2003–06; Minister of the Economy, Econ. Promotion and Reconstruction 2008–10; mem. Anti-Trust Comm. 1990–94; Prof. of Econs, Univ. of Chile; fmr consultant to World Bank and Inter-American Devt Bank. *Address:* c/o Ministry of the Economy, Economic Promotion and Reconstruction, Teatinos 120, 10°, Santiago, Chile.

LAVAGNA, Roberto; Argentine politician and economist; b. 24 March 1942, Buenos Aires; m. Claudine Marechal; ed Univ. of Buenos Aires, Univ. of Brussels, Belgium; fmr mem. Radical Party; Sec. of Industry and Foreign Trade –1987; mem. Justicialist Party; Visiting Researcher, Center for Int. Affairs, Harvard Univ., USA 1995; fmr Prof., Univ. of Buenos Aires; Dir Ecolatina consulting firm 1995; Amb. to EU 2000–02; Minister of the Economy 2002–05; formed a front (Una Nacion Avanzada—An Advanced Nation) to run against the govt's cand., Cristina Fernández de Kirchner, in the presidential elections Oct. 2007; co-f. Unidos Para Cambiar (United for Change) 2013; Konex Award 2006. *Address:* c/o Ministry of the Economy and Public Finance, Hipólito Yrigoyen 250, C1086AAB Buenos Aires, Argentina. *E-mail:* ciudadano@mecon.gov.ar. *Website:* www.planlavagna.com.

LAVANT, Denis; French actor; b. 17 June 1961, Neuilly-sur-Seine, Hauts-de-Seine. *Films include:* Les Misérables 1982, Paris ficelle 1983, Coup de foudre 1983, L'homme blessé (The Wounded Man) 1983, Viva la vie! (Long Live Life) 1984, Boy Meets Girl 1984, Partir, revenir (Going and Coming Back) 1985, Mauvais sang (Bad Blood) 1986, L'étendu 1987, Un tour de manège (Roundabout) 1989, Mona et moi (Mona and I) 1989, C'est merveilleux 1991, Les amants du Pont-Neuf (The Lovers on the Bridge, USA) 1991, Drôle d'immeuble 1992, Fuis la nuit 1993, De force avec d'autres (Forced to Be with Others) 1993, La partie d'échecs (The Chess Game) 1994, L'ennemi 1995, Visiblement je vous aime (Obviously I Need You) 1995, Yasaeng dongmul bohoguyeog (Wild Animals) 1996, Don Juan 1998, Le monde à l'envers 1998, Cantique de la racaille (Melody for a Hustler, USA) 1998, Beau travail (Good Work) 1999, Tuvalu 1999, Promenons-nous dans les bois (Deep in the Woods) 2000, La squale (The Squale) 2000, Married/Unmarried 2001, Affaire Libinski 2001, La merveilleuse odyssée de l'idiot Toboggan (voice) 2002, Luminal 2004, Un long dimanche de fiançailles (A Very Long Engagement) 2004, Camping sauvage 2005, Mister Lonely 2006, Holy Motors 2012. *Television includes:* L'ombre sur la plage 1982, Hôtel du siècle (series) 1985, Oscar et Valentin 1986.

LAVAUDANT, Georges; French theatre director; b. 18 Feb. 1947, Grenoble (Isère); first production Lorenzaccio by Musset, Théâtre Partisan, Grenoble 1975; Co-Dir Centre Dramatique Nat. des Alpes 1976–, Maison de la Culture de Grenoble 1981, Théâtre nat. populaire de Villeurbanne (Rhône) 1986–96; Dir Odéon-Théâtre de l'Europe, Paris 1996–2007. *Productions include:* Le Régent by Jean-Christophe Bailly 1987, texts of Denis Roche (Louve basse), Pierre Bourgeade (Palazzo Mentale), Jean-Christophe Bailly (Les Céphéides and Pandora), Michel Deutsch (Féroé, la nuit. . .), Le Clézio (Pawana), Veracruz, Les Iris, Terra Incognita, Ulysse/Matériaux, interspersed with productions of works by Musset, Shakespeare, Chekhov, Brecht, Labiche, Pirandello, Genet and others; Comédie Française: Lorenzaccio, Le Balcon, Hamlet; Opéra de Paris: Roméo et Juliette by Gounod; Opéra de Lyon: L'enlèvement au sérail by Mozart, Malcolm by Gérard Maimone, Rodrigue et Chimène by Debussy; in Mexico City: Le Balcon, Pawana; in Montevideo: Isidore Ducasse/Fragments; in Bhopal: Phèdre; in Hanoi: Woyzeck; in St Petersburg: Reflets, Lumières (I) 'Près des ruines' 1995, Lumières (II) 'Sous les arbres' 1996, Théâtre Maly de St Petersburg in Russian adapation of Lumières: Reflets 1997, Prova d'orchestra by Giorgio Battistelli, Opéra du Rhin 1997; Odéon-Théâtre de l'Europe: Le Roi Lear by Shakespeare 1996, Bienvenue by Lavaudant 1996, Reflets by Jean-Christophe Bailly 1997, Ajax et Philoctète by Sophocle (Petit Odéon) 1997, Histoires de France (in collaboration with Michel

Deutsch) 1997, Un chapeau de paille d'Italie by Eugène Labiche 1997, La dernière nuit by Lavaudant (Petit Odéon) 1997, Pawana by Jean-Marie Le Clézio 1997, La noce chez les petits bourgeois et Tambours dans la nuit by Bertolt Brecht 1998, L'Orestie by Aeschylus 1999, Les Géants de la Montagne by Pirandello (in Catalan) 1999, Fanfares 2000, Un fil à la patte by Feydeau 2001, La mort de Danton by Büchner 2002, El Pelele by Jean-Christophe Bailly 2003, The Cherry Orchard by Chekhov 2004, La rose et la hache 2004, Les Cenci 2007; Ateliers Berthier, Paris: Cassandre 2006; Centre dramatique nat. de Montreuil: Troïlus et Cressida 2007; various theatres: La Mort d'Hercule, after the tragedies Les Trachiniennes by Sophocles and Héraklès furieux by Euripides 2007, 20e/ PREMIERES, Ecole nationale supérieure des arts du cirque, La Villette 2009, Allegro ricordando by Ami Flammer 2009, La Nuit de l'iguane by Tennessee Williams 2009, Roberto Zucco by Bernard-Marie Koltès 2009, La Tempête by William Shakespeare 2010, Macbeth Horror Suite by Carmelo Bene 2010, Etat civil, after António Lobo Antunes, with the junior students of École Supérieure de Théâtre de Montpellier 2010, Fado Alexandrino by António Lobo Antunes 2011, La mort de Danton by Georg Büchner 2012; abroad: Le Balcon in Mexico, Pawana in Mexico, Phèdre by Racine, with Jean-Christophe Bailly, in Hindi in Bhopal 1990, Isidore Ducasse/Fragments after Les Chants de Maldoror by Lautréamont, Montevideo 1993, Woyzeck, Hanoi, Otsviety (Reflets), Theatre Maly, St Petersburg 1997, Els gegants de la muntanya (Les géants de la montagne) by Luigi Pirandello, in Catalan, Nat. Theatre of Catalonia, Barcelona 1999, Impressions d'Afrique, Goldoni Theatre, Florence 2000, Coriolà (Coriolano) by William Shakespeare, in Catalan, Nat. Theatre of Catalonia 2002, Començaments sense fi after Franz Kafka, in Catalan, Nat. Theatre of Catalonia 2003, Play Strindberg by Friedrich Dürrenmatt, in Spanish, Madrid and Barcelona 2006, 2007, Hay que purgar a Totó (On purge bébé) after Georges Feydeau, in Spanish, Madrid 2008, El misantrop (Le misanthrope) by Molière, in Catalan, Nat. Theatre of Catalonia 2011, Cyrano de Bergerac by Edmond Rostand, premiered at Maly Theatre, Moscow 2013. *Opera productions:* Prova d'orchestra compositeur by Giorgio Battistelli after the film by Federico Fellini 1995, Impressions d'Afrique, libretto by Georges Lavaudant and Daniel Loayza, Théâtre Goldoni, Florence, Opéra national du Rhin 2000, Roméo et Juliette by Charles Gounod, Opéra de Paris, L'Enlèvement au sérail by Mozart, Opéra de Lyon, Malcolm by Gérard Maimone, Rodrigue et Chimène by Claude Debussy, Tristan et Isolde by Richard Wagner, Corum Opéra Berlioz de Montpellier 2006, Scènes de chasse after Penthésilée by Heinrich von Kleist, Opéra Berlioz 2008, Andromaque by André-Ernest-Modeste Grétry, libretto by Louis-Guillaume Pitra, Opéra national de Montpellier Languedoc-Roussillon 2010, La Cerisaie by Philippe Fénelon, libretto by Alexei Parine after Chekhov, Palais Garnier 2012, Eine florentinische Tragödie (Une tragédie florentine) by Alexander von Zemlinsky, Opéra de Lyon 2012. *Films:* Spécial police (actor) 1985, Régime sans pain (producer) 1985, The Birth of Love (actor) 1993. *Publications:* Veracruz (novel) 1989, Les Iris (novel) 1992, Terra Incognita (novel) 1992, Ulysse/ Matériaux, Théâtre et histoire contemporains III (with Jean-Christophe Bailly) 2004. *Address:* c/o Union of the Theatres of Europe, 1 boulevard Lénine, 93000 Bobigny, France. *Telephone:* 1-57-14-84-65. *E-mail:* ute.heynen@ymail.com.

LAVE, Lester B., BA, PhD; American economist and academic; *Harry B. and James H. Higgins Professor of Economics and University Professor, Tepper School of Business, Carnegie-Mellon University;* b. 5 Aug. 1939, Philadelphia, Pa; m. Judith Rice 1965; one s. one d.; ed Reed Coll., MIT and Harvard Univ.; Prof. of Econs, Carnegie-Mellon Univ. 1963–, Harry B. and James H. Higgins Prof. of Econs 1984, 1992–, also Univ. Prof., also currently Dir, Carnegie Mellon Green Design Initiative, Co-Dir, Carnegie Mellon Electricity Industry Center; Sr Fellow, Brookings Inst. 1978–82; Visiting Asst Prof., Northwestern Univ. 1965–66; consultant, Gen. Motors Research Labs, US Depts of Justice, Defense, Transportation, Health and Welfare, Environmental Protection Agency, Nuclear Regulatory Comm., NSF, Office of Tech. Assessment; Pres. Soc. for Risk Analysis 1985–86; George Leland Bach Teaching Award 1987. *Publications:* Technological Change 1966, Air Pollution and Human Health 1977, The Strategy of Social Regulation 1981, Scientific Basis of Health & Safety Regulation 1981, Clearing the Air 1981, Quantitative Risk Assessment 1982, Toxic Chemicals, Health and the Environment (with A. Upton) 1987; more than 200 scientific articles. *Leisure interests:* swimming, skiing. *Address:* Graduate School of Industrial Administration, Carnegie-Mellon University, 5000 Forbes Avenue, Pittsburgh, PA 15213, USA (office). *Telephone:* (412) 268-2000 (office). *Fax:* (412) 268-7838 (office). *E-mail:* LL01@andrew.cmu.edu (office). *Website:* public.tepper.cmu.edu (office).

LAVELLI, Jorge; French theatre and opera director; b. Buenos Aires, Argentina; ed Ecole Charles Dullin et Jacques Lecoq, Paris, Université du Théâtre des Nations; Dir Théâtre Nat. de la Colline 1987–96; fmr Pres. Centre français de l'Institut Int. du Théâtre (UNESCO); Chevalier de la Légion d'honneur; Chevalier, Ordre nat. du Mérite, Commdr, Ordre des Arts et Lettres; Cross of Commdr Order of Merit, Poland. *Plays include:* Le Mariage, Paris 1963, Berlin Festival 1964 (Grand Prix at Concours nat. des jeunes compagnies), Jeux de Massacre, Paris 1970 (Prix de la Critique), Le Roi se meurt, Paris 1976 (Prix Dominique de la mise en scène, Prix de la Critique), Doña Rosita La Soltera, Madrid, Jerusalem and Caracas Festivals and Paris 1980; at Théâtre Nat. de la Colline: Une Visite inopportune by Copi 1988 (Prix de la meilleure création française, Syndicat de la Critique), Réveille-toi Philadelphie 1988 (Prix de la meilleure création d'une pièce française, Syndicat de la Critique), La Veillée 1989, Greek 1990 (Molière Prize for best production), La Nonna 1990, Heldenplatz 1991, 1992, Le Désarroi de Monsieur Peters 2002, La Hija del aire 2004, Merlin ou la terre dévastée 2005, Himmelweg 2007. *Operas include:* The Trial (by Von Einem), Vienna State Opera 1970, Idomeneo, Angers 1975, Faust, Opéra de Paris 1975, L'Heure Espagnole and L'Enfant et les Sortilèges, La Scala Milan 1975, La Traviata, Aix-en-Provence Festival 1976, Faust, Metropolitan Opera, New York, Kennedy Center, Washington 1976, Pelléas et Mélisande, Opéra de Paris 1977, Fidelio, Toulouse 1977, Madame Butterfly, La Scala, Milan and Opéra de Paris 1978, Alcina, Aix-en-Provence Festival 1978, Carmen, Strasbourg, Brussels 1978, Oedipus Rex, Opéra de Paris 1979, Le Nozze di Figaro, Aix-en-Provence Festival, Liège 1979, Dardanus (by Rameau), Opéra de Paris 1980, Les Arts Florissants (by Charpentier), Versailles 1982, Norma, Bonn 1983, Salome, Zürich 1986, La Clemenza di Tito, Hamburg 1986, The Makropoulos Affair, Buenos Aires 1986, Die Zauberflöte, Aix-en-Provence Festival 1989, Die Entführung aus dem Serail, Aix-en-Provence Festival 1990, Cecilia 2000, Siroe 2000, Ariodante 2001, Medea 2001–02, L'Enfant et les sortilèges 2002–03, Faust 2003; several opera productions for TV. *Address:* c/o Théâtre National de la Colline, 15 rue Malte Brun, 75020 Paris, France.

LAVENIR, Frédéric; French business executive; *CEO, CNP Assurances SA;* b. 1960; ed École des Hautes Études Commerciales, École Nationale d'Admin; Finance Insp. 1986–90; joined the French Treasury, initially as Head of Banking Regulations, then as Dir of Insurance Co. Office, Sec. Gen. of Interministerial Cttee for Industrial Restructuring (CIRI) 1995–97, Deputy Dir Office of Minister of Economy and Finance 1997–2000; joined BNP Paribas 2001, COO BNP Paribas Lease Group 2001–02, Chair. and CEO 2002–07, Head of Group Human Resources, BNP Paribas and mem. Exec. Cttee 2007–12; CEO CNP Assurances SA 2012–; Vice-Pres. Assen for Right to Econ. Initiative (ADIE). *Address:* CNP Assurances SA, 4 place Raoul Dautry, 75716 Paris Cedex 15, France (office). *Telephone:* 1-42-18-88-88 (office). *Fax:* 1-42-18-93-66 (office). *E-mail:* edmond .alphandery@cnp.fr (office). *Website:* www.cnp.fr (office).

LAVENTHOL, David, BA, MA; American publisher; b. 15 July 1933, Philadelphia; s. of Jesse Laventhol and Clare Horwald; m. Esther Coons 1958; one s. one d.; ed Yale Univ., Univ. of Minnesota; reporter, later News Ed., St Petersburg Times 1957–63; City Ed. New York Herald Tribune 1963–66; Asst Man. Ed. The Washington Post 1966–69; Assoc. Ed. Newsday 1969, Exec. Ed. 1969–70, Ed. 1970–78, Publr and CEO 1978–86, Chair. 1986–87; Group Vice-Pres. Times Mirror 1981–86, Sr Vice-Pres. 1986, Pres. 1987–93; CEO and Publr Los Angeles Times 1989–93; Ed.-at-Large Times Mirror Co., Los Angeles 1994–98, Consultant Ed. 1998–99; Ed. and Publr Columbia Journalism Review 1999–2003; Chair. Pulitzer Prize Bd 1988–89; Vice-Chair. International Press Inst. 1985–92, Chair. 1992–95; Chair. Museum of Contemporary Art, Los Angeles 1993–97, Cttee to Protect Journalists 2002–05, currently mem. Bd of Dirs; apptd Dir Newspaper Advertising Bureau, American Press Inst. 1988, Los Angeles Times Washington Post/News Service, Times Mirror Foundation, United Negro Coll. Fund; mem. Bd of Dirs Assoc. Press 1993–96, Saratoga Performing Arts Center 1993–96, Columbia Journalism School 1995, Nat. Parkinson Foundation 1995; mem. American Soc. of Newspaper Eds Writing Awards Bd, American Newspaper Publr Asscn, Century Asscn, Council on Foreign Relations; Hon. LittD (Dowling Coll.) 1979, Hon. LLD (Hofstra Univ. 1986); Columbia Journalism award for Distinguished Service 1994. *Publication:* Family Business 2007. *Address:* c/o Board of Directors, Committee to Protect Journalists, 330 7th Avenue, 11th Floor, New York, NY 10001, USA.

LAVER, Rod(ney) George, MBE, OBE; Australian fmr tennis player; b. 9 Aug. 1938, Rockhampton, Queensland; s. of R. S. Laver; m. Mary Benson 1966; one s.; ed Rockhampton Grammar and High Schools; turned professional 1963; Australian Champion 1960, 1962, 1969; Wimbledon Champion 1961, 1962, 1968, 1969; French Champion 1962, 1969; only player to win two Grand Slams 1962, 1969; played Davis Cup for Australia 1958, 1959, 1960, 1961, 1962 and 1973 (first open Davis Cup); in a 23-year career won 47 professional titles; Int. Tennis Hall of Fame 1981; Melbourne Park centre court renamed Rod Laver Arena in his honour 2000. *Publications:* How to Play Winning Tennis 1964, Education of a Tennis Player 1971, A Memoir 2012. *Leisure interests:* golf, fishing, skiing. *Address:* c/o Tennis Australia, Private Bag 6060, Richmond South, Vic. 3121, Australia (office); 3009 Via Conquistador, Carlsbad, CA 92009, USA (home). *Telephone:* (760) 476-0658 (home). *E-mail:* rglaver@gmail.com (home).

LAVEROV, Nikolai Pavlovich, DGeolMineralSc; Russian geologist; *Vice-President, Russian Academy of Sciences;* b. 12 Jan. 1930, Pozharishche, Archangel Region; s. of Pavel Nikolavich Laverov and Klavdia Savvateevna Laverova; m.; two d.; ed Moscow Inst. of Nonferrous Metals; mem. CPSU 1959–91; participated in geological expeditions, Jr researcher, scientific sec. on geological stations of Inst. of Geology, Ore Deposits, Mineralogy and Chemistry 1958–66; Deputy Chief Dept of research orgs., USSR Ministry of Geology 1966–68, Chief 1968–72; Scientific Leader on research of Resources of Urals Project 1972–87; Corresp. mem. USSR (now Russian) Acad. of Sciences 1979, mem. 1987, Vice-Pres. 1988–; Prof., Prorector, Head of Chair of Ecology and rational use of natural resources, Acad. of Nat. Econs, USSR Council of Ministers 1983–87; Pres. Acad. of Sciences of Kirghiz SSR 1987–89; Vice-Chair. USSR Council of Ministers, Chair. Cttee on Science and Tech. 1989–91; mem. Cen. CPSU Cttee 1990–91; Head of Comms of Acad. of Sciences investigating consequences of earthquake in Armenia 1988–; Chair. USSR Nat. Cttee of Geologists 1990–91; Pres. Lomonosov Fund 1992–; Head Comm. on problem of safe burial of radioactive waste; Ed.-in-Chief Geology of Ore Deposits; Lomonosov Gold Medal 2006. *Publications:* works on geology of uranium deposits, continental volcanism, econs of mineral products. *Address:* Presidium of Russian Academy of Sciences, Leninsky prospekt 14, 11991 Moscow, Russia (office). *Telephone:* (495) 954-03-09 (office). *Fax:* (495) 954-33-20 (office). *E-mail:* math-net2014_03@mi.ras.ru (office). *Website:* www.ras.ru (office).

LAVIER, Bertrand; French artist; b. 14 June 1949, Châtillon-sur-Seine; s. of Jean Lavier and Geneviève Duteil; m. Gloria Friedmann 1989; ed Ecole Nat. Supérieure d'Horticulture; landscape artist and town planner, Marne Lavallée New Town 1971–72; at Centre de Recherches et d'Etudes sur le Paysage, Paris 1973–75; artist 1974–; First Prize (Sculpture), Biennale, Budapest 1984, Grand Prix Nat. de la Sculpture 1994. *Publication:* Bertrand Lavier présente la peinture des Martin de 1603 à 1984 1984. *Leisure interests:* hunting, motor-racing, tennis. *Address:* Galerie Durand-Dessert, 28 rue de Lappe, 75011 Paris (office); rue La Demoiselle, 21510 Aignay-le-Duc, France (home).

LAVILLENIE, Renaud; French pole vaulter; b. 18 Sept. 1986, Barbezieux-Saint-Hilaire; vaulted 5.81 m. in Aulnay-sous-Bois 2008; bronze medal, World Championships 2009, 2011; gold medal, European Indoor Championships 2009, 2011; silver medal, Continental Cup 2010; gold medal, European Championships 2010, 2012; gold medal, Int. Asscn of Athletics Feds. (IAAF) World Indoor Championships 2012, gold medal, Olympic Games, London 2012 (new Olympic record); mem. Clermont Athletisme Auvergne club; Best Male Athlete Award, Asscn Internationale De La Presse Sportive (AIPS) 2012. *Address:* c/o House of Sport, 1 avenue Pierre de Coubertin, 75640 Paris Cedex 13, France. *Website:* www .renaud-lavillenie.com.

LAVIN, Franklin L., BSc, MSc, MA, MBA; American business executive, fmr government official and fmr diplomatist; *CEO, Export Now;* b. Canton, Ohio; m. Ann Lavin; three c.; ed Georgetown Univ., Johns Hopkins Univ., Wharton School, Univ. of Pennsylvania; served as Deputy Exec. Sec., Nat. Security Council and Dir Office of Political Affairs during Reagan Admin; Deputy Asst Sec. of Commerce for Asia and Pacific during George H. W. Bush Admin; Sr Man. positions Citibank and Bank of America in Hong Kong and Singapore 1996–2001; Amb. to Singapore 2001–05; Under-Sec. of Commerce for Int. Trade, US Int. Trade Admin, Washington, DC 2005–07; Man. Dir and COO Cushman & Wakefield Investors Asia, Hong Kong 2007–09; Chair. Public Affairs Practice, Edelman Asia Pacific 2009–; CEO and Chair., Export Now 2010–; mem. Bd of Dirs Consistel, Globe Specialty Metals; fmr Lt Commdr in USNR; fmr mem. Council on Foreign Relations, IISS. *Publication:* Export Now 2011. *Address:* Export Now, 526 South Main Street, Akron, OH 44311, USA (office). *Telephone:* (330) 510-1069 (office). *E-mail:* www.exportnow.com (office).

LAVÍN, Joaquín José Infante; Chilean politician and economist; *Minister of Education;* b. 23 Oct. 1953, Santiago; s. of Joaquín Lavín Pradenas and Carmen Infante Vial; m. María Estela León Ruiz; seven c.; ed Pontificia Univ. Católica de Chile, Univ. of Chicago; econ. adviser, ODEPLAN (Ministry for Planning) 1975–77, Dean Faculty of Econ. and Admin. Sciences, Concepción Univ. 1979–81; Econ. Ed. El Mercurio 1986–88; fmr Sec.-Gen. UDI (Ind. Democratic Union); Dean Faculty of Econs and Business, Univ. del Desarrollo 1996–98; Mayor Las Condes 1992–96, 1996–2000; presidential cand. 1999, 2005; Mayor of Santiago 2000–04; Minister of Educ. 2010–; Founder La Vaca (NGO); mem. Opus Dei. *Publications:* Miguel Kast: Pasión de Vivir 1986, Chile Revolución Silenciosa 1987. *Address:* Ministry of Education, Alameda 1371, 7°, Santiago (office); Partido Unión Demócrata Independiente, Suecia 286, Santiago, Chile (office). *Telephone:* (2) 390-4000 (office). *E-mail:* joaquin@joaquinlavin.cl (office). *Website:* www.joaquinlavin .cl (office); www.mineduc.cl (office).

LAVIZZO-MOUREY, Risa, MBA, MD; American physician and foundation executive; *President and CEO, The Robert Wood Johnson Foundation;* b. 1954, Seattle, Wash.; m. Dr Robert Lavizzo-Mourey; two c.; ed State Univ. of NY at Stony Brook, Harvard Medical School and Wharton School, Univ. of Pennsylvania; residency in internal medicine, Brigham and Women's Hosp., Boston, Mass; fmr Robert Wood Johnson Clinical Scholar, Univ. of Pennsylvania; fmr Deputy Admin. Agency for Health Care Policy and Research (now Agency for Health Care Research and Quality), Dept of Health and Human Services; fmr Co-Chair. Working Group on Quality of Care, White House Task Force on Health Care Reform; Sylvan Eisman Prof. of Medicine and Health Care Systems and Dir Inst. on Aging, Univ. of Pennsylvania –2001; Sr Vice-Pres. and Dir Health Care Group, The Robert Wood Johnson Foundation 2001–03, Pres. and CEO (first woman and first African-American) 2003–; mem. or fmr mem. several cttees, including Nat. Cttee for Vital and Health Statistics (Chair. Sub-cttee on Minority Populations), Pres.'s Advisory Comm. on Consumer Protection and Quality in the Health Care Industry, Bd of Dirs American Bd of Internal Medicine, Bd of Regents American Coll. of Medicine; Co-Dir Inst. of Medicine study on racial disparities in health care, resulting in the publication of Unequal Treatment, Confronting Racial and Ethnic Disparities in Health Care 2004; mem. Inst. of Medicine (NAS); two hon. doctorates; numerous awards, including those from Harvard School of Public Health, Dept of Health and Human Services, NAS, American Coll. of Physicians, Nat. Library of Medicine, American Medical Women's Asscn, Nat. Medical Asscn, Univ. of Pennsylvania, ranked by Forbes magazine amongst The World's 100 Most Powerful Women (22nd) 2008, (30th) 2009, (95th) 2011, (90th) 2012, (84th) 2013, ranked by Modern Healthcare magazine amongst the 100 Most Influential People in Healthcare (51st) 2011. *Publications:* several books and numerous articles. *Address:* The Robert Wood Johnson Foundation, PO Box 2316, College Road East and Route 1, Princeton, NJ 08543, USA (office). *Telephone:* (888) 631-9989 (office). *Website:* www.rwjf.org (office).

LAVRENTYEV, Mikhail Mikhailovich; Russian mathematician; b. 21 July 1932, Krasny Liman, Ukraine; m.; three c.; ed Moscow State Univ.; jr, then sr researcher, then Head of Lab. S.L. Sobolev Inst. of Math., Siberian Br., USSR (now Russian) Acad. of Sciences 1957–64, Dir from 1986, Head of Lab., then Deputy Dir Computation Centre 1964–86; mem. Russian Acad. of Sciences 1981; Lenin Prize 1962, USSR State Prize 1987. *Address:* c/o S.L. Sobolev Institute of Mathematics, 4 Acad. Koptyug avenue, 630090 Novosibirsk, Russia. *E-mail:* im@math.nsc.ru.

LAVROV, Sergei Viktorovich; Russian diplomatist and politician; *Minister of Foreign Affairs;* b. 21 March 1950, Moscow; m. Mariya Lavrova; one d.; ed Moscow State Inst. of Int. Relations; has served in diplomatic service since 1972; attaché, USSR Embassy in Sri Lanka 1972–76, Sec., Dept of Int. Econ. Orgs, Ministry of Foreign Affairs 1976–81, Sec. and Counsellor, Perm. Mission of USSR to UN, New York 1981–88; Deputy Chair., then Chair. Dept of Int. Econ. Relations, Ministry of Foreign Affairs 1988–90; Dir Dept of Int. Orgs and Global Problems, Ministry of Foreign Affairs 1990–92, Deputy Minister of Foreign Affairs 1992–94, Perm. Rep. to UN, New York 1994–2004, Minister of Foreign Affairs 2004–; Order of Heydar Aliyev, Order of Honour 1996, Order of Service to the Nation 1997, Order of Merit for the Fatherland (Fourth Class) 1998, (Third Class) 2005, (Second Class) 2010; Honoured Worker of the Diplomatic Service of the Russian Fed. 2004, Order of the Holy Prince Daniel of Moscow (Second Class) (Russian Orthodox Church), (First Class) 2010; Hon. Medal, UN Asscn of Russia 2005, Order of Friendship (Kazakhstan) 2005, Order of Friendship of Peoples (Belarus) 2006, Grand Cross of the Order of the Sun (Peru) 2007, Order of Friendship (Viet Nam) 2009, Order of Friendship (Laos), Medal of Honour (South Ossetia) 2010, Order of St Mashtots (Armenia) 2010; Gold Medal, Yerevan State Univ., Armenia 2007. *Leisure interest:* white-water rafting, playing the guitar, writing songs and poetry. *Address:* Ministry of Foreign Affairs, 119200 Moscow, Smolenskaya-Sennaya pl. 32/34, Russia (office). *Telephone:* (499) 244-16-06 (office). *Fax:* (499) 244-34-48 (office). *E-mail:* ministry@mid.ru (office). *Website:* www.mid.ru (office).

LAVROVA, Olga V.; Kyrgyzstani economist and politician; *Minister of Finance;* b. 14 May 1956, Barnaul, Altai Region; ed Kyrgyz State Univ.; started career as economist, Pervomaisky Br., State Bank of USSR, Frunze City (now Bishkek); Economist, later Sr Economist and Lead Economist, Ministry of Finance 1978–85; Deputy Divisional Dir, later Dir, Frunze City Dept of Finance 1985–93; Inspector, Divisional Dir, Jogorku Kenesh (Supreme Council, Parl.) Control Chamber 1983–96; Auditor, Adviser to Chair. of Accounts Chamber of Kyrgyz Repub. 1996–2004; Deputy Minister of Finance 2004–05, Minister 2005–07, 2012–; Chair. Social Security Fund of the Kyrgyz Repub. 2005–07; Dir, Gazpromneft Asia Ltd 2007–12; mem. Dignity Political Party (Ar-Namys); Certificate of Merit of the

Kyrgyz Repub. *Address:* Ministry of Finance, 720040 Bishkek, bul. Erkindik 58, Kyrgyzstan (office). *Telephone:* (312) 66-12-27 (office). *Fax:* (312) 66-16-45 (office). *E-mail:* minfin@mf.gov.kg (office). *Website:* www.minfin.kg (office).

LAVROVSKY, Mikhail Leonidovich, MA; Russian ballet dancer, choreographer and academic; *Choreographer, Bolshoi State Theatre;* b. (Mikhail Ivanov-Lavrovsky), 29 Oct. 1941, Tbilisi, Georgia; s. of Leonid Lavrovsky and Elena Chikvaidze; m. Dolores García Ordonyez 1958; one s.; ed Moscow Choreographic School (now the Moscow State Choreographic Acad.), studied under O. Khodot, N. Tarassov and G. Evdokimo, studied ballet under Alexei Ermolaev, Moscow State Acad. of Theatre Art (now the Russian Univ. of Theatrical Arts—GITIS); Artistic Dir, Tbilisi State Academic Opera and Ballet Theatre Z. Paliashvili 1983–85, left the troupe 1988; Ballet Master/Repetiteur, Bolshoi Theatre 1987–; Artistic Dir, Moscow Academic Music Theatre K.S. Stanislavsky and Vl.I. Nemirovich-Danchenko ballet co. 2005–08; Artistic Dir, Moscow State Acad. of Choreography 2010–; Mikhail Lobukhin, Vladislav Lantratov and other ballet dancers rehearse under his guidance; repertoire: Slave (A. Khachaturian's Spartacus, choreography by L. Yakobson) 1962, Georgy's Son (The Pages of Life, A. Balanchivadze, L. Lavrovsky production) 1961, Philippe (Boris Asfiev's The Flames of Paris, choreography by Vasily Vainonen) 1962, Prince (Cinderella by S. Prokofiev, choreography by R. Zakharov) 1963, Vatslav (Boris Asafiev's The Fountain of Bakhchisaray, choreography by R. Zakharov) 1963, Albrecht (Giselle by A. Adam, choreography by J. Coralli, J. Perrot and M. Petipa in L. Lavrovsky version) 1963, Bluebird (The Sleeping Beauty by Tchaikovsky, choreography by M. Petipa in the version by Y. Grigorovich) 1963, Coral (Rodion Shchedrin's The Humpbacked Horse, choreography by A. Radunsky) 1963, Frondoso (Laurencia by A. Crain, choreography by V. Chabukiani) 1964, Qays (Majnun) (Layla and Majnun by S. Balasanyan, production by K. Goleyzovsky) 1965, Ferkhad (Arif Melikov's A Legend of Love, choreography by Yuri Grigorovich) 1965, The Nutcracker-Prince (Nutcracker by Tchaikovsky, choreography by Y. Grigorovich) 1966, Basil (Don Quixote by L. Minkus, choreography by A. Gorsky) 1967, Spartacus (A. Khachaturian's Spartacus, production by Yuri Grigorovich) 1968, Romeo (Romeo and Juliet by Prokofiev, choreography by L. Lavrovsky) 1969, Prince (Swan Lake by Tchaikovsky, choreography by A. Gorsky, M. Petipa. L. Ivanov in the version by Y. Grigorovich) 1970, Viktor (Angara by A. Eshpai, Y. Grigorovich production) 1976), cr. role of Ivan the Terrible (Ivan the Terrible, to music by Prokofiev, choreography by Y. Grigorovich) 1978, Paganini (Paganini to music of Rachmaninov, choreography by L. Lavrovsky) 1979, Claudio (Love for Love, music by Tikhon Khrennikov, Vera Boccadoro production, Shakespeare's Much Ado About Nothing adaptation) 1979, Artynov (Anyuta to music of V. Gavrilin, choreography by V. Vassiliev) 1986, Fantasy on the Theme of Casanova (to music by W.A. Mozart) 1993, cr. role of Capulet at the Bolshoi Theatre (Romeo and Juliet, music by Prokofiev, Declan Donnelan and Radu Poklitary production) 2003; starred in the original TV ballets: Romeo and Juliet (music by Prokofiev, choreography by N. Ryzhenko and V. Smirnov-Golovanov, dir M. Volodarsky) 1968, White Nights (after the novel by F. Dostoevsky, to music by Schoenberg, choreography and production by N. Ryzhenko and V. Smirnov-Golovanov) 1972, Fedra (music by A. Lokshin, performed part of Ippolit, choreography and production by N. Ryzhenko and V. Smirnov-Golovanov) 1972, Three Cards (after Pushkin's story The Queen of Spades, music by K. Molchanov) 1983, staged the ballets: Romeo and Juliet (after L. Lavrovsky, Tbilisi Theatre Z. Paliashvili, danced Romeo) 1983, Saratov Academic Opera and Ballet Theatre 2004, Porgy and Bess (jazz-ballet, to music by Gershwin, Tbilisi Theatre Z. Paliashvili, danced Porgy) 1983, Choreographic novellas to music by J.S. Bach, Franz Liszt and others, Arizona Ballet, Phoenix, USA 1987, Suite No. 2 for Flute by J.S. Bach, Arizona Ballet 1989, Casanova to music by W.A. Mozart, Atlanta Ballet, USA 1989, Revelations to music by V. Kikta, theatre-studio A Group of Citizens (premier took place on the stage of the Moscow Academic Musical Theatre K.S. Stanislavsky and Vl.I. Nemirovich-Danchenko) 1991, Mziri D. Toradze, Houston Ballet, USA 1992, More Powerful than Gold and Death, to music by Wagner, Russian Chamber Ballet 'Moscow' 1996, Café-Block, to music by Gershwin (premier took place on the stage of the Moscow Operetta Theatre) 1995, Nijinsky, to music by Rachmaninov (with the participation of the Bolshoi Theatre dancers, danced part of Sergei Diaghilev, premier took place on the stage of Maly Theatre) 2000, Richard III, to music by Ravel (danced the title role, premier took place on the stage of the Concert Hall P.I. Tchaikovsky) 2000, Matador, to music by de Falla (with the participation of the Bolshoi Theatre dancers, premier took place on the stage of the Bolshoi Theatre) 2001; revived Giselle in the version of his father for the troupe of the Russian Chamber Ballet 'Moscow' 1996; staged original TV ballets: Mziri (to music by D. Toradze, dir Z. Kakabadze, danced title role, Georgian TV films studio) 1977 (won Grand Prix at Int. Festival of the Dance-Video Films Asscn, New-York 1978), Prometheus (to music by Scriabin, dir Z. Kakabadze, danced title role, Georgian TV films studio) 1981, Choreographic novellas 1986, A Dreamer (video version of jazz ballet Blues, danced title role, dir V. Bunin, Mosfilm) 1989; staged dance and stage movement at drama theatres: Anna Karenina (one-person production after the novel by Tolstoy, dir A. Eshpay, Theatre Agency BOGIS) 1998, The Last Night of the Last Tsar (after the play by E. Radzinsky, dir V. Fokin, BOGIS) 1998, Evgeny Onegin... Pushkin (dir M. Krylov, BOGIS) 2000, An Excellent Cure for Melancholy (after the play by S. Zlotnikov, School of the Modern Play, dir I. Raikhelgauz) 2001, Le Petit Prince (after the story by A. de Saint-Exupéry, dir M. Krylov) 2001; actively engaged in pedagogical activities, conducts workshops; took part in seminars in Germany, USA (Houston Ballet), Japan (Tokyo Ballet), Italy (Nat. Dance Acad. of Rome), Yugoslavia (Ballet Co. of the Serbian Nat. Theatre, Novi Sad); est. Choreographic School L.M. Lavrovsky, Moscow; People's Artist of the USSR, Honour Order 2002; prizewinner, Int. Competition in Varna, Bulgaria 1965, Lenin Prize 1970, Nizhinsky Prize, Paris Acad. of Dance 1972, USSR People's Artist 1976, USSR State Prize 1977. *Films include:* choreography and lead role Ali Baba and the Forty Thieves (Dir Kakhagadze), Fantasior (Dir Bunin). *Publication:* From Myself to My Friends. *Leisure interests:* sport, fencing, reading, painting, philosophy, drama, cinema. *Address:* Bolshoi Theatre, Teatralnaya pl. 1, Moscow (office); Voznesensky per. 16/4, Apt 7, 125009 Moscow, Russia (home). *Telephone:* 916-576-24-43 (Russia, mobile); (495) 629-27-71 (office), (495) 505-95-61 (home). *E-mail:* lavrovsky@mail.ru (office). *Website:* www.lavrovsky.ru (office).

LAW, HE Cardinal Bernard F., BA; American ecclesiastic; b. 4 Nov. 1931, Torreón; s. of Bernard A. Law and Helen Stubblefield; ed Harvard Univ.; ordained 1961; Bishop of Springfield-Cape Girardeau 1973; Archbishop of Boston 1984–2002 (resgnd); cr. Cardinal by Pope John Paul II 1985 and maintained that rank despite resignation; Archpriest of St Mary Major Basilica and Pope's representative to Liberian Basilica 2004-11 (resgnd).

LAW, Jude; British actor; b. 29 Dec. 1972, London; s. of Peter Law and Maggie Law; m. Sadie Frost 1997 (divorced 2003); one step-s. two s. one d.; fmrly with Nat. Youth Music Theatre; co-f. Natural Nylon (production co.), Dir 2000–03; Chevalier, Ordre des Arts et des Lettres 2007; Hon. César Award 2007. *Stage appearances include:* Joseph and the Amazing Technicolor Dreamcoat, Les Parents Terribles 1994, Ior 1995, Tis A Pity She's A Whore 1999, Doctor Faustus 2002, Hamlet (Donmar Warehouse, London) 2009. *Film appearances include:* Shopping 1994, I Love You I Love You Not 1996, Wilde 1997, Gattaca 1997, Midnight in the Garden of Good and Evil 1997, Bent, Music From Another Room 1998, Final Cut 1998, The Wisdom of Crocodiles 1998, eXistenZ 1999, The Talented Mr Ripley (BAFTA Award for Best Supporting Actor) 1999, Enemy at the Gates 2000, Love Honour and Obey 2000, AI: Artificial Intelligence 2001, Road to Perdition 2002, Cold Mountain 2003, Sky Captain and the World of Tomorrow 2004, Alfie 2004, I Heart Huckabees 2004, The Aviator 2004, Lemony Snicket's A Series of Unfortunate Events (voice) 2004, Breaking and Entering 2006, All the King's Men 2006, The Holiday 2006, My Blueberry Nights 2007, Sleuth 2007, The Imaginarium of Doctor Parnassus 2009, Sherlock Holmes 2009, Repo Men 2010, Sherlock Holmes: A Game of Shadows 2011, Anna Karenina 2012. *Address:* c/o WME, Centre Point, 103 New Oxford Street, London, WC1A 1DD, England (office). *Telephone:* (20) 7534-6800 (office). *Fax:* (20) 7534-6900 (office). *Website:* www.wma.com (office).

LAWLER, James Ronald, MA, DUP; Australian academic; *Professor Emeritus, Department of Romance Languages and Literatures, University of Chicago;* b. 15 Aug. 1929, Melbourne; m. Christiane Labossière 1954 (died 2004); one s. one d.; ed Univs of Melbourne and Paris, France; lecturer in French, Univ. of Queensland 1955–56; Sr Lecturer, Univ. of Melbourne 1957–62; Prof. of French, Head of Dept, Univ. of Western Australia 1963–71; mem., Australian Research Grants Cttee 1969–72; Prof. of French, Chair., Univ. of Calif., Los Angeles 1971–74; McCulloch Prof. of French, Dalhousie Univ. 1974–79; Prof. of Romance Languages, Univ. of Chicago 1979, Edward Carson Waller Distinguished Service Prof. 1983–97, Prof. Emer. 1998–; Visiting Prof. Collège de France 1985; Pres. Asscn Int. des Etudes Françaises 1998–2002; Pres. Soc. des Amis de Rimbaud 2006–11; Ed. Rimbaud Vivant 2006–11; Carnegie Fellowship 1961–62; Myer Fellow, Australian Acad. of the Humanities; Commonwealth Interchange Visitor 1967; Foundation Fellow, Australian Acad. of the Humanities 1969; Guggenheim Fellowship 1974; Nat. Endowment of Humanities Fellowship 1984–85; Prix Int. des Amitiés Françaises 1986, Prix du Rayonnement de la Langue Française, Acad. Française 1999; Officier, Ordre des Palmes académiques. *Publications:* Form and Meaning in Valéry's Le Cimetière Marin 1959, An Anthology of French Poetry 1960, Lecture de Valéry: Une Etude de Charmes 1963, The Language of French Symbolism 1969, The Poet as Analyst: Essays on Paul Valéry 1974, Paul Valéry: An Anthology 1976, René Char: The Myth and the Poem 1978, Edgar Poe et les Poètes français 1989, Paul Valéry (ed.) 1991, Rimbaud's Theatre of the Self 1992, Poetry and Moral Dialectic: Baudelaire's Les Fleurs du Mal 1997, Paul Claudel: Knowing the East 2004, Edgar Allan Poe (with others) 2006; Founding Ed.: Essays in French Literature 1964, Dalhousie French Studies 1979. *Address:* c/o Department of Romance Languages and Literatures, 1050 East 59th Street, Chicago, IL 60637, USA (office); 72 bis rue Michel Ange, 75016 Paris, France (home). *Telephone:* (312) 702-8481 (office); 1-46-51-45-57 (home).

LAWRENCE, Carmen Mary, PhD; Australian politician and fmr psychologist; b. 2 March 1948, Morawa, WA; d. of Ern Lawrence and Mary Lawrence; m. 1979; one s.; ed Santa Maria Coll., Perth and Univ. of Western Australia; Sr Tutor, Dept of Psychiatry and Behavioural Science, Univ. of Western Australia 1979, Lecturer and Course Controller in Behavioural Science applied to Medicine 1980–83; Lecturer and Tutor, Curtin Univ., Univ. of Melbourne; Research Psychologist in Research and Evaluation Unit, Psychiatric Services, Health Dept of WA 1983–86; mem. (for Subiaco) Western Australia State Ass. 1986–89, Glendalough 1989, apptd Minister for Educ. 1988, fmr Minister for Educ. and Aboriginal Affairs, Premier of WA 1990–93, also Treas., Minister for the Family and for Women's Interests; Leader of the Opposition, Shadow Treas., Shadow Minister for Employment, for Fed. Affairs 1993–94; Fed. Shadow Minister of Health 1994–96, on Status of Women and on Environment and the Arts 1996–97; mem. Fed. Parl. for Fremantle 1994–2007 (retd); Minister for Human Services and Health and Minister Assisting the Prime Minister for the Status of Women 1994–97; Shadow Minister for the Environment, the Arts and Asst to the Leader of the Opposition on the Status of Women 1996–97; Shadow Minister for Industry, Innovation and Tech. 2000, for the Status of Women 2000–02, for Reconciliation, Aboriginal and Torres Strait Islander Affairs 2000–02; Professorial Fellow, Univ. of Western Australia 2008, currently mem. Faculty Advisory Bd Faculty of Arts, Humanities and Social Sciences; Benjamin Rosenstamm Prize in Econs, British Psychological Soc. Prize for Psychology, Australian Psychological Soc. Prize for Psychology, H. I. Fowler Prize for Research in Psychology, J. A. Wood Memorial Prize and other awards and prizes. *Publications:* several academic papers on psychology. *Leisure interests:* reading, theatre, classical music, cooking. *Address:* Faculty of Arts, Humanities and Social Sciences, University of Western Australia, 35 Stirling Highway, Crawley, Perth, WA 6009; Unit 7, Queensgate Mall, William Street, Fremantle, WA 6160, Australia (office).

LAWRENCE, Jennifer Shrader; American actress; b. 15 Aug. 1990, Louisville, Ky; d. of Gary Lawrence and Karen Lawrence; ed Kammerer Middle School, Louisville, Ky. *Films include:* Garden Party 2008, The Poker House 2008, The Burning Plain 2008, Winter's Bone (Detroit Film Critics Soc. Award for Best Actress, San Diego Film Critics Soc. Award for Best Actress, Stockholm Int. Film Festival Award for Best Actress, Toronto Film Critics Asscn Award for Best Actress) 2010, Like Crazy 2011, The Beaver 2011, X-Men First Class 2011, The Hunger Games 2012, Silver Linings Playbook (Golden Globe Award for Best Actress in a Motion Picture - Comedy or Musical 2013, Academy Award for Best Actress 2013) 2012, House at the End of the Street 2012, The Devil You Know 2013, The Hunger Games: Catching Fire 2013, American Hustle (Best Supporting Actress, Nat. Soc. of Film Critics 2014, Golden Globe Award for Best Supporting Actress in a Motion Picture 2014, BAFTA Award for Best Supporting Actress 2014)

2013, Serena 2014, X-Men: Days of Future Past 2014. *Television:* Company Town (film) 2006, Monk (series) 2006, Cold Case (series) 2007, Not Another High School Show (film) 2007, Medium (series) 2007–08, The Bill Engvall Show 2007–09. *Address:* c/o Creative Artists Agency, 2000 Avenue of the Stars, Los Angeles, CA 90067, USA (office). *Telephone:* (424) 288-2000 (office). *Fax:* (424) 288-2900 (office). *Website:* www.caa.com (office).

LAWRENCE, Peter Anthony, PhD, FRS; British biologist; *Scientist Emeritus, Medical Research Council Laboratory of Molecular Biology and Department of Zoology, University of Cambridge;* b. 23 June 1941, Longridge, Lancs., England; s. of Ivor D. Lawrence and Joy Liebert; m. Birgitta Haraldson 1971; ed Univ. of Cambridge; Commonwealth Fellowship, USA 1965–67; Dept of Genetics, Univ. of Cambridge 1967–69, Staff Scientist, MRC Lab. of Molecular Biology, Zoology Dept 1969–2007, Jt Head, Cell Biology Div. 1984–87, Scientist Emer. 2007–; Foreign mem. Swedish Royal Acad. of Sciences 2000; Medal of Zoological Soc. of London 1977, Darwin Medal, Royal Soc. 1994, Prize Vinci d'Excellence Moët et Chandon, Paris 1996, Waddington Medal, British Soc. of Developmental Biology 2006, Prince of Asturias Award for Scientific and Tech. Research, Oviedo (co-recipient) 2007. *Publications include:* The Making of a Fly 1992; numerous scientific papers. *Leisure interests:* garden, golf, trees, fungi, ascalaphidae, theatre. *Address:* Department of Zoology, University of Cambridge, Downing Street, Cambridge, CB2 3EJ (office); MRC Laboratory of Molecular Biology, Hills Road, Cambridge, CB2 0QH (office); 9 Temple End, Great Wilbraham, CB1 5JF, England (home). *Telephone:* (1223) 769015 (office); (1223) 880505 (home). *E-mail:* pal38@cam.ac.uk (office). *Website:* www.mrc-lmb.cam.ac.uk/PAL (office).

LAWRENCE, Robert Swan, BA; American physician and academic; *Center for a Livable Future Professor, Bloomberg School of Public Health, Johns Hopkins University;* b. 6 Feb. 1938, Philadelphia, Pa; s. of Thomas George Lawrence and Catherine Swan Lawrence; m. Cynthia Starr Cole 1960; three s. two d.; ed Harvard Coll. and Medical School; Internal Medicine Residency, Mass Gen. Hosp. 1964–66, 1969–70; Medical Epidemiologist, Center for Disease Control, US Public Health Service, Atlanta 1966–69; Asst to Assoc. Prof. of Medicine, Dir Div. of Community Medicine, NC Univ. School of Medicine 1970–74; Dir Div. of Primary Care, Asst to Assoc. Prof. of Medicine, Harvard Medical School 1974–91, Charles Davidson Assoc. Prof. of Medicine 1981–91; Assoc. Chief of Medicine, Cambridge Hosp. 1974–77, Chief of Medicine, Dir Dept of Medicine 1980–91; Dir Health Sciences, Rockefeller Foundation 1991–95; Adjunct Prof. of Medicine, New York Univ. 1991–95; Prof. of Health Policy, Assoc. Dean for Professional Educ. and Dir Center for a Livable Future, Bloomberg School of Public Health, Johns Hopkins Univ., 1995–2006, Prof. of Medicine, Johns Hopkins School of Medicine 1996–, Edyth Schoenrich Prof. of Preventive Medicine 2000–06, Prof. of Environmental Health Sciences 2006–, inaugural Center for a Livable Future Prof. 2008–; Chair. US Preventive Services Task Force, Dept of Health and Human Services, US Govt 1984–89, mem. 1990–95; Ed. American Journal of Preventive Medicine 1990–92; Pres. Physicians for Human Rights 1998–2002, Chair. Bd Trustees 2007–13; mem. Inst. of Medicine, NAS 1978; Trustee, Teachers' Coll., Columbia Univ. 1991–97; Fellow, American Coll. of Preventive Medicine; Master, American Coll. of Physicians; Maimonides Prize 1964, John Atkinson Ferrell Prize, UNC 1998, Special Recognition Award, American Coll. of Preventive Medicine 1988, Duncan Clark Lecturer, Asscn of Teachers of Preventive Medicine 1993, Leadership Award, Soc. for Gen. Internal Medicine 1996, Albert Schweitzer Humanitarian Award 2002, Sedgwick Memorial Medal, American Public Health Asscn 2009. *Publications:* Co-Ed. Preventing Disease: Beyond the Rhetoric 1990, Health Promotion and Disease Prevention in Clinical Practice 1996, International Perspectives on Environment, Development and Health 1997; 90 articles in scientific journals. *Address:* Johns Hopkins Bloomberg School of Public Health, 615 N Wolfe Street, Room W7010, Baltimore, MD 21205 (office); Highfield House 1112, 4000 N Charles Street, Baltimore, MD 21218-1737, USA (home). *Telephone:* (410) 614-4590 (office), (410) 235-5474 (home). *Fax:* (410) 502-7579 (office). *E-mail:* rlawrenc@jhsph.edu (office). *Website:* www.jhsph.edu/clf (office).

LAWRENCE, Walter Nicholas Murray, MA; British underwriting agent; b. 8 Feb. 1935, London, England; s. of Henry Walter Neville Lawrence and Sarah Schuyler Lawrence (née Butler); m. Sally Louise O'Dwyer 1961; two d.; ed Winchester Coll., Trinity Coll., Oxford; with C.T. Bowring & Co. Ltd 1957–62, 1976–84, Treaty Dept 1957–62, Dir 1976–84; with Harvey Bowring and Others 1962–84, Asst Underwriter 1962–70, Underwriter 1970–84; Dir C.T. Bowring (Underwriting Agencies) Ltd 1973–84; Chair. Fairway Underwriting Agencies Ltd 1979–85; mem. Lloyd's Underwriter's Non-Marine Asscn, Deputy Chair. 1977, Chair. 1978; served Cttee of Lloyd's 1979–82, 1991, Deputy Chair. 1982, mem. Council of Lloyd's 1984–91, Deputy Chair. 1984–87, Chair. 1988–90; Dir, Chair. Murray Lawrence Holdings Ltd 1988–94, Murray Lawrence Members Agency Ltd 1988–92, Murray Lawrence & Partners Ltd (now Amlin Underwriting Ltd) 1989–93; Dir, Cbs Services No 1 Ltd 1991–95, Amlin Underwriting Ltd 1991–96, Amlin Corporate Services Ltd 1992–97, Amlin Dedicated Ltd 1994–96, Amlin Corporate Member Ltd 1994–96, Asta Management Services Ltd 1993–96, Benenden School (Kent) Ltd 1992–98, The Benenden School Trust 1998–2008. *Leisure interests:* golf, opera, travel. *Address:* c/o Amlin Underwriting Ltd, St Helen's, 1 Undershaft, London, EC3A 8ND, England.

LAWRENSON, Peter John, DSc, FIEEE, FREng, FRS; British fmr electrical engineer and fmr business executive; b. 12 March 1933, Prescot; s. of John Lawrenson and Emily Houghton; m. Shirley H. Foster 1958; one s. three d.; ed Prescot Grammar School and Manchester Univ.; research Eng General Electric Co., Ltd 1956–61; Lecturer, Univ. of Leeds 1961–65, Reader 1965–66, Prof. of Electrical Eng 1966–91, Head, Dept of Electrical and Electronic Eng 1974–84, Chair. Faculty of Science and Applied Science 1978–80; Dir of major, fully int. product exhbns, coordinated with conf. in UK (Nat. Exhbn Centre Birmingham), Dusseldorf, Paris, Hong Kong 1980–90; Chair. Switched Reluctance Drives Ltd 1981–97, Dir 1997–2002; Consultant Rolls-Royce 2000–02; Pres. IEE 1992–93; James Alfred Ewing Medal 1983, Royal Soc. Esso Medal 1985, Faraday Medal (IEE) 1990, RAE Sir Frank Whittle Medal 2005, IEEE (NY) Thomas Edison Medal 2005, and other awards. *Publications:* The Analytical and Numerical Solution of Electromagnetic Field Problems 1992, other books and over 160 articles and patents in the field of electrical eng, particularly electromagnetics and electro-mechanics. *Leisure interests:* lawn tennis, bridge, chess, jewellery making, large

garden. *Address:* Hard Gap, Linton, Wetherby, Yorks., LS22 4HT; Switched Reluctance Drives Ltd, East Park House, Otley Road, Harrogate, HG3 1PR, England (office). *Telephone:* (1423) 845200 (office); (1937) 588883 (home). *Fax:* (1937) 588801 (home). *E-mail:* peterlawrenson100@btinternet.com (home).

LAWS, Richard Maitland, CBE, ScD, FRS, FIBiol; British scientist; b. 23 April 1926, Whitley Bay; s. of Percy Malcolm Laws and Florence May Heslop; m. Maureen Isobel Holmes 1954; three s.; ed Dame Allan's School, Newcastle and St Catharine's Coll., Cambridge; Biologist and Base Leader, Falkland Islands Dependencies Survey 1947–53; Whaling Insp., F/F Balaena 1953–54; Prin. Scientific Officer, Nat. Inst. of Oceanography, Godalming 1954–61; Dir, Nuffield Unit of Tropical Animal Ecology, Uganda 1961–67; Dir, Tsavo Research Project, Kenya 1967–68; Head, Life Sciences Div., British Antarctic Survey 1969–73; Dir, British Antarctic Survey, Cambridge 1973–87; Dir Sea Mammal Research Unit, Cambridge 1977–87; Master, St Edmund's Coll. Cambridge 1985–96; Sec. Zoological Soc. of London 1984–88; mem. Council of the Senate, Univ. of Cambridge 1989–92, Financial Bd 1988–91; Pres. Scientific Cttee for Antarctic Research 1990–94, Hon. mem. 1996; Foreign mem. Norwegian Acad. of Science and Letters 1998; 36th Annual Lecture, Ciba Foundation 1984, 2nd Cranbrook Memorial Lecture, Mammal Soc. 1987, 4th Annual Dice Lecture, Univ. of Kent 1997; Hon. mem. Soc. for Marine Mammalogy 1994; Hon. Warden, Uganda Nat. Parks 1996; Hon. Fellow St Catharine's Coll. 1982, St Edmund's Coll. 1996; Hon. DSc (Bath) 1991; Bruce Medal 1954, Scientific Medal, Zoological Soc., London 1965, Polar Medal 1976 and Second Clasp 2001. *Publications:* The Elephant Seal: Growth and Age 1953, The Elephant Seal: General Social and Reproductive Behaviour 1956, The Elephant Seal: The Physiology of Reproduction 1956, Reproduction, Growth and Age of Southern Fin Whales 1961, Elephants and Their Habitats (co-author) 1975, Scientific Research in Antarctica (ed.) 1977, Antarctic Ecology (ed.) 1984, Antarctic Nutrient Cycles and Food Webs (co-ed.) 1985, Antarctica: The Last Frontier 1989, Life at Low Temperatures (co-ed.) 1990, Antarctica and Environmental Change (co-ed.) 1992, Antarctic Seals: Research Methods and Techniques (ed.) 1993, Elephant Seals: Population Ecology, Behaviour and Physiology (co-ed.) 1994. *Address:* 3 The Footpath, Coton, Cambs., CB23 7PX, England (home). *Telephone:* (1954) 210567 (home).

LAWSON, Dominic Ralph Campden, BA, FRSA; British journalist and editor; b. 17 Dec. 1956, London; s. of Nigel Lawson, now Lord Lawson of Blaby (q.v.) and the late Lady (Vanessa) Ayer; m. 1st Jane Fiona Wastell Whytehead 1982 (divorced 1991); m. 2nd Rosamond Monckton 1991; two d.; ed Westminster School, Christ Church, Oxford; mem. staff, World Tonight and The Financial World Tonight, BBC 1979–81; mem. staff, Financial Times (Energy Corresp. and Lex column) 1981–87; Deputy Ed. The Spectator 1987–90, Ed. 1990–95; Ed. The Sunday Telegraph 1995–2005; columnist, Sunday Corresp. 1990, The Financial Times 1991–94, Daily Telegraph 1994–95, The Independent 2006–, The Sunday Times 2008–; Harold Wincott Prize for Financial Journalism, Ed. of the Year, Soc. of Magazine Eds 1990. *Publications include:* Korchnoi, Kasparov 1983, Britain in the Eighties (jtly) 1989; ed. The Spectator Annual 1992, 1993, 1994, The Inner Game 1993. *Leisure interests:* chess, cricket. *Address:* The Sunday Times, 1 Pennington Street, London, E98 1ST, England (home). *Telephone:* (20) 7782-5000 (office). *Fax:* (20) 7782-5658 (office). *Website:* www.sunday-times.co.uk (home).

LAWSON, Lesley (Twiggy); British model, singer and actress; b. 19 Sept. 1949, London; d. of William Hornby and Helen Hornby (née Reeman); m. 1st Michael Whitney Armstrong 1977 (died 1983); one d.; m. 2nd Leigh Lawson 1988; ed Brondesbury and Kilburn Grammar School; model 1966–70; Man. and Dir Twiggy Enterprises Ltd 1966–; f. Twiggy & Co. 1998–; launched Twiggy skin care range 2001; own British TV series; has made several LP records; two Golden Globe Awards 1970. *Films include:* The Boy Friend 1971, W, There Goes the Bride 1979, Blues Brothers 1981, The Doctor and the Devils 1986, Club Paradise 1986, Harem Hotel, Istanbul 1988, Young Charlie Chaplin (TV) 1989, Madame Sousatzka 1989, Woundings 1998, The Taming of the Shrew-Shakespeare Re-Told 2005. *Plays:* Cinderella 1976, Captain Beaky 1982, My One and Only 1983–84, Blithe Spirit, Chichester 1997, Noel and Gertie, USA 1998, If Love Were All, New York 1999, Blithe Spirit, New York 2002, Play What I Wrote 2002, Mrs Warren's Profession 2003. *Television:* own musical series 1975–76; has appeared in numerous TV dramas in UK and USA; chat shows: Twiggy's People 1998, Take Time with Twiggy 2001, This Morning 2001. *Publications include:* Twiggy: An Autobiography 1975, An Open Look 1985, Twiggy in Black and White 1997. *Leisure interests:* music, design. *Address:* Caroline Michel, Peter, Fraser and Dunlop Group Ltd., Drury House, 34-43 Russell Street, London, WC2B 5HA, England (office). *Telephone:* (20) 7344-1000 (office). *Fax:* (20) 7836-9539 (office). *E-mail:* info@twiggylawson.co.uk. *Website:* www.twiggylawson.co.uk.

LAWSON, Sonia, MA, RA, RWS; British artist; b. 2 June 1934, Darlington, Co. Durham; d. of the late Frederick Lawson and Muriel Metcalfe; m. Charles William Congo 1969; one d.; ed Royal Coll. of Art, London; travelling scholarship to France 1956–60; one of four young artists for John Schlesinger's BBC TV documentary 1960; Visiting Lecturer, Royal Acad. Schools 1985–; Lorne Scholarship, Univ. of London 1986–87; works in collections including Arts Council, Great Britain, Belfast Art Gallery, Bolton Art Gallery, Carlisle Art Gallery, Cartwright Hall, Bradford, Chatsworth Collection, Graves Art Gallery, Sheffield, Harrogate Art Gallery, Huddersfield Art Gallery, Imperial War Museum, Leeds Univ., Middlesbrough Art Gallery, Nuffield Collection, Rochdale Art Gallery, RCA Collection, Royal Acad. of Arts Collection, Univ. of Birmingham, The Vatican, Rome, Wakefield Art Gallery; works commissioned by Imperial War Museum, BAOR 1984, Lambeth Palace for the Pope 1989, drawings for Look at it This Way! (collection of poems) by James Kirkup 1993, two related works for Univ. Centre, Birmingham 1994, New Year's Eve (short story) by Fay Weldon 1995, Barclays Capital Paris 1998; Rowney Drawing Prize 1984, Eastern Arts Drawing Prize 1984, 1989, Lorne Award 1987, Eastern Art Drawing Prize 1990. *Address:* c/o Royal Academy of Arts, Burlington House, Piccadilly, London, W1V 0DS, England. *Telephone:* (20) 7300-5680 (Academicians' Affairs Office). *Fax:* (20) 7300-5812. *E-mail:* art@sonialawson.co.uk (home). *Website:* www.sonialawson.co.uk.

LAWSON OF BLABY, Baron (Life Peer), cr. 1992, of Newnham in the County of Northamptonshire; **Nigel Lawson,** BA (Hons PPE), MA, PC; British politician and business executive; *Chairman, Central Europe Trust Co. Ltd;* b. 11 March 1932, London; s. of Ralph Lawson and Joan Elisabeth Lawson (née Davis); m. 1st

Vanessa Salmon 1955 (divorced 1980); m. 2nd Thérèse Mary Maclear 1980; two s. four d. (one deceased); ed Westminster School and Christ Church, Oxford (Scholar); Sub-Lt, RNVR 1954–56, CO HM MTB Gay Charger; mem. editorial staff, Financial Times 1956–60; City Ed. Sunday Telegraph 1961–63; Special Asst to Prime Minister Sir Alec Douglas-Home 1963–64; Financial Times columnist and BBC broadcaster 1965; Ed. The Spectator 1966–70; regular contributor to Sunday Times and Evening Standard 1970–71, The Times 1971–72; Fellow, Nuffield Coll. Oxford 1972–73; Special Political Adviser, Conservative Party HQ 1973–74; MP for Blaby, Leics. 1974–92; Opposition Whip 1976–77; Opposition spokesman on Treasury and Econ. Affairs 1977–79; Financial Sec. to the Treasury 1979–81; Sec. of State for Energy 1981–83, Chancellor of the Exchequer 1983–89; mem. (Conservative) House of Lords 1992–, House of Lords Econ. Affairs Cttee 1992–; Dir (non-exec.) Barclays Bank 1990–98; Chair. Central Europe Trust Co. Ltd 1990–; Chair. Oxford Investment Partners (OXIP) 2006–; Founding Chair. Global Warming Policy Foundation 2009–; Pres. British Inst. of Energy Econs 1995–2003; Dir Inst. for Int. Econs, Wash. 1991–2001; mem. Governing Body, Westminster School 1999–2005, Fellow 2005–; Hon. Student, Christ Church, Oxford 1996; Hon. DSc (Buckingham) 2011; Finance Minister of the Year, Euromoney Magazine 1988, IEA Nat. Free Enterprise Award 2008 Mousquetaire d'Armagnac 2010. Publications: The Power Game (with Jock Bruce-Gardyne) 1976, The View from No. 11 1992 (revised edn as Memoirs of a Tory Radical 2010), The Nigel Lawson Diet Book (with Thérèse Lawson) 1996, An Appeal to Reason: A Cool Look at Global Warming 2008; various pamphlets. Address: House of Lords, Westminster, London, SW1A 0PW, England (office). Telephone: (20) 7219-3000 (office). E-mail: rathbonea@parliament.uk (office). Website: www.parliament.uk/biographies/lords/nigel-lawson/27077 (office).

LAWTON, Sir John Hartley, Kt, CBE, BSc, PhD, FRS; British ecologist and academic; b. 24 Sept. 1943, Preston, Lancs.; s. of Frank Hartley and Mary Lawton; m. Dot (Lady Dorothy) Lawton; one s. one d.; ed Univ. of Durham; Lecturer in Zoology, St Anne's and Lincoln Coll., Univ. of Oxford 1968–71; Lecturer, Sr Lecturer, Reader then Prof. of Biology, York Univ. 1972–89; Founding Dir Centre for Population Biology, Natural Environment Research Council (NERC), Imperial Coll. London, Silwood Park 1989–99, Chief Exec. Natural Environment Research Council 1999–2005; Adviser to Royal Comm. on Environmental Pollution 1986–89, mem. 1990–96, Chair. 2005–11; Chair. Royal Soc. for the Protection of Birds 1993–98, currently Vice-Pres.; Pres. Council of British Ecological Soc. 2005–07; Vice-Pres. British Trust for Ornithology 2002–08; Trustee, WWF-UK 2002–08, currently Fellow; Chair. Yorkshire Wildlife Trust 2009–; Scientific Adviser and Presenter, The 300 Million Years War, BBC 1985 and The State of the Planet 2000; Foreign mem. American Acad. of Arts and Sciences, Nat. Acad. of Sciences; Patron, Inst. of Ecology and Environmental Man. 2011; Hon. Fellow, Royal Entomological Soc. 2001, Zoological Soc. of London 2007, British Ecological Soc. 2009, Inst. of Environmental Sciences 2011, Soc. for the Environment 2013; Hon. DSc (Lancaster), (Birmingham), (East Anglia), (York), (Aberdeen), (Imperial Coll.); Pres.'s Gold Medal, British Ecological Soc. 1987, Frink Medal, Zoological Soc. of London 1998, La Roe Award, Soc. for Conservation Biology 2002, Japan Prize for Science and Tech. for Conservation of Biodiversity 2004, Ramon Margalef Prize in Ecology and Environmental Science 2006, RSPB Medal 2011. Publications: author or ed. of five books and more than 320 papers, articles and book chapters. Leisure interests: bird watching, gardening, natural history, walking, cooking, playing with his grandchildren.

LAWZI, Ahmed Abdel Kareem al-; Jordanian politician; b. 1925, Jubeiha, nr Amman; m.; ed Teachers' Training Coll., Baghdad, Iraq; teacher 1950–53; Asst to Chief of Royal Protocol 1953–56; Head of Ceremonies, Ministry of Foreign Affairs 1957; mem. Parl. 1961–62, 1962–63; Asst to Chief of Royal Court 1963–64; Minister of State, Prime Minister's Office 1964–65; mem. Senate 1965, 1967; Minister of the Interior for Municipal and Rural Affairs April–Oct. 1967; Minister of Finance 1970–71; Prime Minister 1971–73; Pres. Nat. Consultative Council 1978–79; various Jordanian and foreign decorations. Address: c/o Ministry of Foreign Affairs, PO Box 35217, Amman 11180, Jordan.

LAX, Peter D., AB, PhD; American mathematician and academic; Professor Emeritus of Mathematics, Courant Institute of Mathematics, New York University; b. 1 May 1926, Budapest, Hungary; s. of Henry Lax and Klara Kornfeld; m. Anneli Cahn 1948 (died 1999); two s.; ed New York Univ.; with Los Alamos Scientific Lab., Manhattan Project 1945–46; Asst Prof., New York Univ. 1951, Prof. 1957–99, Prof. Emer. 1999–, Dir AEC Computing and Applied Math. Center 1964–72, Courant Inst. of Math. Sciences 1972–80, Courant Math. and Computing Lab. 1980–; Fulbright Lecturer in Germany 1958; Visiting Lecturer, Univ. of Oxford 1969; Vice-Pres. American Math. Soc. 1969–71, Pres. 1978–80; mem. Nat. Science Bd 1980–86; mem. American Acad. of Arts and Sciences 1982, NAS 1982, American Philosophical Soc. 1996, Moscow Math. Soc. 1995, Norwegian Acad. of Science and Letters; Foreign Assoc. French Acad. of Sciences 1982, Academia Sinica 1993, Hungarian Acad. of Sciences 1993; Foreign mem. Soviet (now Russian) Acad. of Sciences 1989; Fellow, American Math. Soc.; Hon. Life mem. New York Acad. of Sciences 1982; Dr hc (Kent State) 1975, (Paris) 1979, (Tech. Univ. of Aachen) 1988, (Heriot Watt) 1990, (Tel-Aviv) 1992, (Univ. of Maryland, Baltimore) 1993, (Brown) 1993, (Beijing) 1993, (Texas A&M) 2000; Lester R. Ford Award 1966, 1973, Von Neumann Lecturer, S.I.A.M. 1969, Hermann Weyl Lecturer 1972, Hedrick Lecturer 1973, Chauvenet Prize, Math. Asscn of America 1974, Norbert Wiener Prize, American Math. Soc. and Soc. of Industrial and Applied Math. 1975, NAS Award in Applied Math. and Numerical Sciences 1983, Nat. Medal of Science 1986, Wolf Prize 1987, Steele Prize, American Math. Soc. (co-winner) 1992, Distinguished Teaching Award, New York Univ. 1995, Abel Prize, Norwegian Acad. of Arts and Letters 2005, Gibbs Lecturer, American Math. Soc. 2007, Lomonosov Gold Medal 2013. Publications: Recent Advances in Partial Differential Equations, Mathematical Aspects of Production and Distribution of Energy, Nonlinear Partial Differential Equations in Applied Science, Decay of Solutions of Systems of Nonlinear Hyperbolic Conservation Laws (co-author) 1970, Calculus with Applications and Computing (co-author) 1979, Hyperbolic Systems of Conservation Laws and the Mathematical Theory of Shock Waves 1987, Scattering Theory (co-author) 1989, Recent Mathematical Methods in Nonlinear Wave Propagation (co-author) 1996, Scattering Theory for Automorphic Functions (co-author) 2001, Functional Analysis 2002, Selected Papers. Vol. I 2005, Vol. II 2005, Hyperbolic Partial Differential Equations 2006, Linear Algebra and Its Applications (second

edn) 2007; numerous papers in learned journals. Address: Courant Institute of Mathematics, New York University, Warren Weaver Hall, Room 912, 251 Mercer Street, New York, New York, NY 10012, USA (office). Telephone: (212) 998-3232 (office). Fax: (212) 995-4121 (office). E-mail: lax@cims.nyu.edu (office). Website: www.math.nyu.edu (office).

LAXMAN, Rasipuram Krishnaswamy, BA; Indian cartoonist and illustrator; b. 23 Oct. 1924, Mysore; m. Kamala Laxman; ed Univ. of Mysore; cartoonist, Swarajya, Blitz, Swatantra, Koravanji; Political Cartoonist, Free Press Journal; joined Times of India, illustrations for Illustrated Weekly, comic strips for Junior (children's magazine); best known for his creation The Common Man; Hon. DLit (Univ. of Marathawada); Ramon Magsaysay Award 1984, B.D. Goenka Award, Indian Express, Durga Ratan Gold Medal, Hindustan Times, Padma Bhushan, Padma Vibhushan, Lifetime Achievement Award, CNN IBN TV18 2008, Art and Music Foundation Pune Pandit Award (Scholar of Pune Award) for Excellence in Creative Communication 2012. Publications include: Sorry, No Room 1969, Doodles 1975, The Emerald Route 1977, Madhya Pradesh 1985, Hotel Riviera 1989, Calcutta Images 1990, Grandmother's Tale 1992, The Messenger 1993, The Tunnel of Time (autobiography) 1998, Faces 2000, Distorted Mirror 2004, Brushing Up the Years: a Cartoonist's History of India 1947–2004 2005. Address: c/o Times of India, 7 Bahadur Shah Zafar Marg, Darya Ganj, Bahadur Shah Zafar Marg, New Delhi 110 002, India.

LAXMAN, V(angipurappu) V(enkata) S(ai); Indian professional cricketer; b. 1 Nov. 1974, Hyderabad, AP; s. of Dr Shantaram Laxman and Dr Satyabhama Laxman; m. G. R. Sailaja 2004; one s. one d.; ed Little Flower High School, St John's School, studied medicine at univ.; right-handed batsman; occasional right-arm off-break bowler; plays for Hyderabad 1992–, India 1996–2012, Lancs. 2007, 2009, Deccan Chargers 2008–10 (Capt. 2008), Kochi Tuskers Kerala 2011; First-class debut: 1992/93; Test debut: India v S Africa, Ahmedabad 20–23 Nov. 1996; One-Day Int. (ODI) debut: India v Zimbabwe, Cuttack 9 April 1998; has played in 134 Tests, scored 8,781 runs (17 centuries, 56 half-centuries), highest score 281, average 45.97, best bowling 1/2; ODIs: 86 matches, 2,338 runs, highest score 131, average 30.76; First-class: 267 matches, 19,730 runs, highest score 353, average 52.64, took 22 wickets, best bowling 3/11; announced retirement from int. cricket 18 Aug. 2012; Arjuna Award, Govt of India 2001, Wisden Cricketer of the Year 2002, Padma Shri 2011, Northern Stand at Rajiv Gandhi Int. Cricket Stadium named after him 2012. Address: c/o Honorary Secretary, Hyderabad Cricket Association, Gymkhana Grounds, Secunderabad, Hyderabad Urban 500 039; Hyderabad Cricket Association, Rajiv Gandhi International Cricket Stadium, Uppal, Hyderabad 500 039, India.

LAYARD, Baron (Life Peer), cr. 2000, of Highgate in the London Borough of Haringey; **Peter Richard Grenville Layard,** BA, MSc, FBA; British economist and academic; Director, Wellbeing Programme, Centre for Economic Performance, London School of Economics; b. 15 March 1934, Welwyn Garden City, Herts.; s. of John Willoughby Layard and Doris Layard; m. Molly Meacher 1991; ed Univ. of Cambridge, London School of Econs; school teacher, London Co. Council 1959–61; Sr Research Officer, Robbins Cttee on Higher Educ. 1961–64; Deputy Dir Higher Educ. Research Unit, LSE 1964–74, Lecturer, LSE 1968–75, Reader 1975–80, Prof. of Econs 1980–99, Prof. Emer. 1999–, Hon. Fellow 2000–, Head, Centre for Labour Econs 1974–90, Co-Dir Centre for Econ. Performance 1990–2003, currently Dir Wellbeing Programme; Consultant, Centre for European Policy Studies, Brussels 1982–86; mem. Univ. Grants Cttee 1985–89; Chair. Employment Inst. 1987–92; Co-Chair., World Economy Group of the World Inst. for Devt Econs Research 1989–93; Econ. Adviser to Russian Govt 1991–97; Fellow, Econometric Soc. 1986, European Econ. Asscn 2004; mem. (Labour) House of Lords 2000–; W.W. Leontief Medal, Russian Acad. of Natural Sciences for "achievements in economics" 2005, IZA Prize in Labor Econs (co-recipient with S. Nickell), Inst. for the Study of Labor 2008. Publications: Cost Benefit Analysis 1973, Causes of Poverty (with D. Piachaud and M. Stewart) 1978, Microeconomic Theory (with A. A. Walters) 1978, More Jobs, Less Inflation 1982, The Causes of Unemployment (co-ed.) 1984, The Rise in Unemployment (co-ed.) 1986, How to Beat Unemployment 1986, Handbook of Labor Economics (co-ed.) 1987, The Performance of the British Economy (co-author) 1988, Unemployment: Macroeconomic Performance and the Labour Market (co-author) 1991 (second edn 2005), East-West Migration: the alternatives (co-author) 1992, Post-Communist Reform: Pain and Progress 1993 (co-author), Macroeconomics: A Text for Russia 1994, The Coming Russian Boom 1996 (co-author), What Labour Can Do 1997, Tackling Unemployment 1999, Tackling Inequality 1999, What the Future Holds (co-ed.), Happiness: Lessons from a New Science 2005 (second edn 2011), A Good Childhood (with J. Dunn) 2009. Leisure interests: walking, tennis. Address: Centre for Economic Performance, London School of Economics, Houghton Street, London, WC2A 2AE (office); 45 Cholmeley Park, London, N6 5EL, England (home). Telephone: (20) 7955-7281 (office). Fax: (20) 7955-7595 (office). E-mail: r.layard@lse.ac.uk (office). Website: cep.lse.ac.uk/layard (office); www.parliament.uk/biographies/lords/peter-layard/26890.

LAYDEN, Anthony Michael, CMG, LLB (Hons); British diplomatist (retd); b. 27 July 1946; m. Josephine Layden; three s. one d.; ed Holy Cross Acad., Edinburgh, Univ. of Edinburgh; Lt 15th (Scottish Volunteer) Battalion, Parachute Regiment 1966–69; joined British Diplomatic Service 1968, Desk Officer, Atomic Energy and Disarmament Dept, FCO 1968–69; at Middle East Centre for Arab Studies 1969–71; Second Sec., Jedda 1971–73, First Sec. and Head of Chancery, Rome 1973–77, Desk Officer, Middle East Dept 1977–79, Rhodesia Dept 1979–80, Personnel Operations Dept 1980–82, Head of Chancery, Jedda 1982–85, Deputy Head of Hong Kong Dept, FCO 1985–87, Deputy Head of Mission, Muscat 1987–91, Counsellor, later Deputy Head of Mission, Copenhagen 1991–95, Head of W European Dept, FCO 1995–98, Amb. to Morocco 1999–2002, to Libya 2002–06; Foreign Sec.'s Special Rep. for Relations with Assurances 2006; Chair. The British Moroccan Soc. 2007; Pres. Soc. for Libyan Studies 2009; Chair. Travellers Club 2010. Leisure interests: sailing, hill walking, bridge. Address: Foreign and Commonwealth Office, Room K 143, King Charles Street, London, SW1A 2AH, England (office). Telephone: (20) 7008-2076 (office). Website: www.gov.uk/government/organisations/foreign-commonwealth-office (office); www.britishmoroccansociety.org (office).

LAYNE, Kingsley, BA; Saint Vincent and the Grenadines civil servant and diplomatist; b. 1949; ed Univ. of the West Indies, Univ. of British Columbia, Inst.

for Applied Behavioural Sciences; economist, Ministry of Trade, Agric. and Tourism 1973–74; Sr Official, Econ. Affairs Secr., Org. of Eastern Caribbean States, St John's, Antigua 1982–86; Perm. Sec., Ministry of Trade, Agric. and Industry 1986–87, Tourism, Aviation and Culture 1987–89, Trade and Tourism 1989–90; Perm. Rep. of Saint Vincent and the Grenadines to UN, New York 1990–94; Amb. to USA 1991–2000; Perm. Rep. to OAS, Vice-Chair. –1999; mem. New Democratic Party. *Publications:* several publs on staff devt and man. training. *Address:* c/o New Democratic Party (NDP), Murray Road, POB 1300, Kingstown, Saint Vincent and the Grenadines. *Telephone:* 457-2647.

LAYTON, Donald H., BS, MS, MBA; American business executive; *CEO, Freddie Mac (Federal Home Loan Mortgage Corporation);* ed Massachusetts Inst. of Tech., Harvard Business School; joined predecessor of JPMorgan Chase as a trainee 1980s, responsible for Treasury & Securities (operating services unit of the co.) 1999–2004, responsible for Chase's worldwide capital markets and trading activities prior to merger of Chase Manhattan and J.P. Morgan 2000, Co-CEO J.P. Morgan (investment bank of the co.) 2000–02, responsible for Chase Financial Services 2002–04, Vice-Chair. and mem. of three-person Office of the Chair., retd 2004; Chair. and then CEO E*TRADE Financial 2007–09; mem. bds of several financial services firms; Sr Advisor, Securities Industry and Financial Markets Asscn 2006–08; CEO Freddie Mac (Fed. Home Loan Mortgage Corpn) 2012–; Chair. Partnership for the Homeless, New York City. *Address:* Freddie Mac, 8200 Jones Branch Drive, McLean, VA 22102-3110, USA (office). *Telephone:* (703) 903-2000 (office). *E-mail:* info@freddiemac.com (office). *Website:* www.freddiemac.com (office).

LAZAR, Philippe; French scientist and administrator (retd); b. 21 April 1936, Paris; s. of Maximilien Lazar and Françoise Lazar; m. Monique Lazar 1960; one s. one d.; ed Ecole Polytechnique, Paris; researcher, Nat. Inst. of Hygiene 1960, Dir of Research Institut Nat. de la Santé et de la Recherche Médicale (INSERM) 1964, Dir Environmental Health Research Unit 1977, Chair. Scientific Council 1981, Dir-Gen. INSERM 1982–96; Chair. European Medical Research Councils (EMRC) 1994–96; Chair. Bd Research Inst. for Devt (IRD) 1997–2001; with Cour des Comptes 2001–05; Visiting Prof. Harvard School of Public Health 1975; Officier, Légion d'honneur 1994, Chevalier, Ordre des Arts et des Lettres 1994, Commdr, Ordre nat. du Mérite 1999. *Publications:* Eléments de probabilités et statistiques 1967, Méthodes statistiques en expérimentation biologique 1974, Les explorateurs de la santé 1989, L'éthique biomédicale en question 1995, La République a-t-elle besoin de savants? 1998, Autrement dit laïque 2003, Court traité de l'âme 2008. *Leisure interests:* arts, literature. *Address:* 9 rue Friant, 75014 Paris, France. *Telephone:* (6) 81-11-80-67. *E-mail:* philippe.lazar@orange.fr.

LAZĂR, Valeriu, BEng; Moldovan politician; *Deputy Prime Minister and Minister of the Economy;* b. 20 May 1968, Mingir, Hîncești Dist; m.; two c.; ed Agrarian State Univ. of Moldova, Inst. Int. d'Admin Publique, Paris, France, European Inst. of Public Admin, Bruges, Belgium; joined Ministry of Devt 1994, Special Co-ordinator, Nat. Agency for Promoting Foreign Investment 1994, Dir Foreign Econ. Relations Dept 1994–96, Adviser to Minister of Economy 1996–98, Adviser to Deputy Prime Minister 1998–99, Deputy Prime Minister 1999, Deputy Minister of Economy 2004–05, Deputy Prime Minister and Minister of the Economy 2009–; Rep. for Moldova to EBRD and Multilateral Investment Guarantee Agency 2005–06; Exec. Dir Business Intelligent Services SRL 2000–04, 2006–09; Exec. Dir BIS-Capital Investment House Ltd 2007–09; mem. Parl. 2009–; mem. Democratic Party of Moldova (Partidului Democrat din Moldova), currently Sec.-Gen. *Address:* Ministry of the Economy, 2033 Chișinău, Piața Marii Adunări Naționale 1 (office); Democratic Party of Moldova (PDM— Partidul Democrat din Moldova) 2001 Chișinău, str. Tighina 32, Moldova. *Telephone:* (22) 23-74-48 (office); (22) 27-82-29. *Fax:* (22) 23-40-64 (office); (22) 27-82-30. *E-mail:* mineconcom@mec.gov.md (office); pdm@mtc.md. *Website:* www .mec.gov.md (office); www.pdm.md.

LAZARAN, Frank, BSc; American retail executive; *Founder, Galazarano Investments & Consulting;* b. 1957; ed California State Univ.-Long Beach, Univ. of Southern Calif.; joined Ralphs Grocery Co., Compton, Calif. 1974, various positions including Group Vice-Pres. of Sales, Advertising and Merchandising –1997; Sr Vice-Pres. of Sales, Merchandising and Logistics, Randalls Food Markets, Inc., Houston, Tex. 1997–99, Pres. 1999–2002; Exec. Vice-Pres. and COO Winn-Dixie Stores Inc., Jacksonville, Fla 2002–03, Pres., CEO and Dir 2003–04; Chair. City Markets 2003–04; Chair., Pres. and CEO Marsh Supermarkets, Inc. 2006–11; Founder Galazarano Investments & Consulting 2012–; mem. Gov.'s Advisory Bd, State of Tex. 1999–2002, Greater Houston Partnership 1999–2002; mem. Gator Bowl Cttee Asscn 2003–04, 2004 Super Bowl Host Cttee 2004; mem. Bd Jacksonville Zoo and Gardens 2003–04; mem. Advisory Bd NGB Markets 2012–, Magical Brands 2013–. *Address:* NGB Markets, 555 Bryant Street, #237, Palo Alto, CA 94301, USA. *Telephone:* (650) 646-4931. *E-mail:* info@ ngbmarkets.com. *Website:* www.ngbmarkets.com.

LAZAREV, Alexander Nikolayevich; Russian conductor; *Principal Conductor, Japan Philharmonic Orchestra;* b. 5 July 1945; m. Tamara Lazarev; one d.; ed Leningrad and Moscow Conservatoires; conducting debut at Bolshoi Theatre 1973, conducted numerous ballets and operas of the Bolshoi Theatre's European and Russian repertoires, founder and conductor Ensemble of Soloists of the Bolshoi Theatre 1978–89, Chief Conductor, Artistic Dir, Bolshoi Theatre 1987–95; Chief Conductor Duisburg Symphony Orchestra 1988–93; has conducted numerous orchestras including Berlin Philharmonic, Munich Philharmonic, Orchestra Sinfonica del Teatro alla Scala di Milano, Orchestre Nat. de France and others; UK debut with Royal Liverpool Philharmonic Orchestra 1987; subsequently performed with the City of Birmingham Symphony Orchestra, the Royal Scottish Nat. Orchestra, etc.; Prin. Guest Conductor BBC Symphony Orchestra, 1992–95, Royal Scottish Nat. Orchestra 1994–97, Prin. Conductor 1997–2005, Conductor Emer. 2005–; Prin. Conductor, Japan Philharmonic Orchestra 2007–; Hon. Prof., Univ. of Glasgow 2005 First Prize USSR Nat. Competition 1971, First Prize and Gold Medal Karajan Competition (Berlin) 1972. *Address:* c/o Tennant Artists, Unit 2, 39 Tadema Road, London, SW10 0PZ, England (office). *Telephone:* (20) 7376-3758 (office). *Fax:* (20) 7351-0679 (office). *E-mail:* info@tennantartists.com (office). *Website:* www.tennantartists.com (office).

LAZARIDIS, Mike, OC, FRSC; Canadian engineer, inventor and business executive; b. Istanbul, Turkey; s. of Nick Lazaridis and Dorothy Lazaridis; m. Celia Lazaridis; one s. one d.; ed Univ. of Waterloo; emigrated to Canada with family aged five 1966; awarded industrial automation contract by General Motors 1984; Founder, Co-Chair., Pres. and Co-CEO Research in Motion Ltd (name changed to BlackBerry 2013) (designer and manufacturer of wireless electronic products) 1984–2012 (resgnd), mem. Bd of Dirs 1984–; est. Perimeter Inst. for Theoretical Physics, Univ. of Waterloo 2000; Chancellor Univ. of Waterloo 2003–; inventor of BlackBerry wireless e-mail pager device 1991; Order of Ont.; Hon. DEng (Waterloo); Dr hc (McMaster, Windsor, Laval); numerous industry and community awards for innovations for wireless radio tech. and software, including Academy Award for Tech. Achievement for invention of digital barcode reader for film editing 1999; named by readers of newspaper The Globe and Mail as Canada's Nation Builder of the Year 2002, Ernest C. Manning Principal Award, listed on the TIME 100 List of Most Influential People. *Publications:* more than 30 patents. *Leisure interests:* cinema, cars. *Address:* Board of Directors, BlackBerry, 295 Phillip Street, Waterloo, ON N2L 3W87, Canada (office). *Telephone:* (519) 888-7465 (office). *Fax:* (519) 888-7884 (office). *E-mail:* info@blackberry.com (office). *Website:* www.blackberry.com (office).

LAZARUS, Rochelle (Shelly), BA, MBA; American advertising executive; *Chairman Emeritus, Ogilvy & Mather Worldwide;* b. 1 Sept. 1947, New York; m. George Lazarus; three c.; ed Smith Coll., Columbia Univ. Business School; with Clairol 1970; with Ogilvy & Mather 1971–74, 1976–, Pres. Ogilvy & Mather Direct US 1989–91, Pres. Ogilvy & Mather Advertising, New York 1991–94, Pres. Ogilvy N America 1994–95, Pres. and COO Ogilvy & Mather Worldwide 1995–96, CEO 1996–2009, Chair. 1997–2012, Chair. Emer. 2012–; mem. Bd of Dirs General Electric, New York Presbyterian Hosp., World Wildlife Fund, Merck & Co. 2004–, The Blackstone Group, FINRA; mem. Bd of Dirs Partnership for New York City, Lincoln Center for Performing Arts; mem. Bd Overseers Columbia Business School, Cttee to Encourage Corp. Philanthropy; mem. Council on Foreign Relations, Business Council, Advertising Women of New York, Cttee of 200, Women's Forum, American Asscn of Advertising Agencies' Advisory Council, Yale Pres.'s Council on Int. Activities, Advisory Bd Judge Inst. of Man. Studies, Cambridge Univ. (UK); fmr Chair. American Asscn of Advertising Agencies, Bd Trustees Smith Coll.; ranked by Fortune magazine amongst 50 Most Powerful Women in Business in the US 1998–2001, (14th) 2002, (16th) 2003, (26th) 2004, (26th) 2005, (30th) 2006, (34th) 2007, ranked by Forbes magazine amongst 100 Most Powerful Women (93rd) 2004, (78th) 2005, (87th) 2006, (96th) 2007, Distinguished Leadership Award in Business, Columbia Business School (first woman recipient), Lifetime Achievement Award, Advertising Educational Foundation, inducted into Direct Marketing Asscn Hall of Fame, American Advertising Fed. Hall of Fame 2013, numerous advertising, communications, and business leadership awards. *Address:* Ogilvy & Mather Worldwide, 636 11th Avenue, New York, NY 10036, USA (office). *Telephone:* (212) 237-4000 (office). *Fax:* (917) 475-3628 (office). *Website:* www.ogilvy.com (office).

LAZENBY, Alec, AO, ScD, FTSE, FIBiol, FAIAST; Australian/British agronomist and university administrator (retd); b. 4 March 1927, UK; s. of G. Lazenby and E. Lazenby; m. Ann J. Hayward 1957; one s. two d.; ed Univ. Coll. of Wales and Univ. of Cambridge, UK; Scientific Officer, Welsh Plant Breeding Station 1949–53; Demonstrator, Agricultural Botany, Univ. of Cambridge 1953–58, Lecturer in Agricultural Botany 1958–65, Fellow and Asst Tutor, Fitzwilliam Coll. 1962–65; Foundation Prof. of Agronomy, Univ. of New England, NSW 1965–70, Vice-Chancellor 1970–77; Dir Grassland Research Inst. 1977–82; Visiting Prof. Reading Univ. 1978–82; Hon. Professorial Fellow, Univ. of Wales 1979–82; Vice-Chancellor, Univ. of Tasmania 1982–91; consultant in higher educ. and agricultural research and man. 1991–2012; Fellow, Australian Acad. of Technological Sciences, Australian Inst. of Agricultural Science and Tech.; Hon. Prof., Victoria Univ. of Tech. 1992; Hon. DRurSci (New England) 1981; Hon. LLD (Tasmania) 1992; Centenary Medal for Contrib. to Rural Science and Tech. 2003. *Publications:* Intensive Pasture Production (co-ed.) 1972, Australian Field Crops (co-ed.), Vol. I 1975, Vol. II 1979, Australia's Plant Breeding Needs 1986, The Grass Crop (co-ed.) 1988, The Story of IDP 1999, Competition and Succession in Pastures (co-ed.) 2001; papers on pasture plant breeding, agronomy and weed ecology in various scientific journals. *Leisure interests:* golf, gardening, current affairs. *Address:* 16/99 Groom Street, Hughes, ACT 2605, Australia. *Telephone:* (2) 6281-2898. *Fax:* (2) 6281-0451. *E-mail:* alazenby@netspeed.com.au.

LAZIO, Enrico (Rick) Anthony, AB, JD; American lawyer, business executive and politician; *Executive Vice-President of Global Government Affairs and Public Policy, JPMorgan Chase & Company;* b. 13 March 1958, Amityville, Suffolk Co., NY; s. of Anthony Lazio and Olive E. Lazio (née Christensen); m. Patricia Moriarty; two d.; ed Vassar Coll., American Univ. Washington Coll. of Law; called to New York Bar 1984; Asst Dist Attorney, Suffolk Co. Rackets Bureau, Hauppage, NY 1983–88, Exec. Asst Dist Attorney, Suffolk Co. 1987–88, Village Attorney, Village of Lindenhurst, NY 1988–93; Man. Partner, Glass, Lazio & Glass, Babylon, NY 1989–93; mem. Suffolk Co. Legis. from 11th Dist, NY 1989–93, mem. House of Reps, Deputy Majority Whip, then Asst Majority Leader 1993–2000; cand. for Senate, New York State 2000; Pres. and CEO Financial Services Forum 2001–05; Exec. Vice-Pres. Global Govt Affairs and Public Policy, JPMorgan Chase & Co., also mem. Exec. Cttee; mem. Bd of Dirs, Polaroid Corpn, TB Woods Corpn, World Rehabilitation Fund, Audubon New York; mem. Advisory Cttee The Ad Council; mem. Suffolk Co. Bar Asscn; unsuccessfully cand. for New York Republican gubernatorial nomination 2010. *Leisure interests:* numismatics, guitar. *Address:* JPMorgan Chase & Co., 270 Park Avenue, New York, NY 10017 (office); PO Box 5063, Bay Shore, NY 11706, USA. *Telephone:* (212) 270-6000 (office); (631) 981-7533. *Fax:* (212) 270-1648 (office). *E-mail:* ricklazio@optonline.net. *Website:* www .jpmorganchase.com (office); lazio.com.

LAZOVIĆ, Vujica, PhD; Montenegrin economist, academic and politician; *Deputy Prime Minister, responsible for Economic Policy and the Financial System, and Minister of the Information Society and Telecommunications;* b. 10 March 1963, Plav; m.; one d.; ed Univ. of Podgorica; fmr mem. Faculty of Econs, Univ. of Montenegro, Vice-Dean 1998–2000, Dean 2001–06; currently Prof. of Econs and Dean of Faculty of Econs, Univ. of Podgorica; Deputy Prime Minister, responsible for Econ. Policy 2006–09, Deputy Prime Minister, responsible for Econ. Policy and the Financial System and Minister of the Information Society and Telecommunications 2009–; several awards, including Award Liberation Podgorica '19 December', Veljko Vlahović Univ. Award for the best success in final year of study. *Publications include:* numerous books and articles on economics; conducted several studies in UK and USA. *Address:* Ministry of the Information Society and Telecommunications, 81000 Podgorica, Montenegro (office). *Telephone:* (20) 241412 (office). *Fax:* (20) 241790 (office). *E-mail:* kabinet@mid.gov.me (office). *Website:* www.mid.gov.me (office).

LAZRAQ, Alami; Moroccan business executive; *President and Director-General, Groupe Alliances;* m.; three c.; ed Ecole Speciale d'Architecture, France; started career as Head of Studies and Realization Dept, Ministry of Habous (Islamic land legislation) 1976; Man. Dir Etablissement Regional d'Amenagement et de Construction du Tensift 1978; joined Groupe Omnium Nord Africain 1989; f. Groupe Alliances 1994, currently Pres. and Dir-Gen.; Chair. Al Maaden Golf Resort. *Address:* Groupe Alliances, 16, rue Ali Abderazak, Casablanca, Morocco (office). *Telephone:* (522) 993480 (office). *Fax:* (522) 993481 (office). *Website:* www.alliances.co.ma (office).

LAZUTKIN, Valentin Valentinovich, CandPhil; Russian politician and journalist; b. 10 Jan. 1945, Kraskovo, Moscow Region; m.; one s. one d.; ed Moscow State Univ., Acad. of Social Sciences Cen. Cttee CPSU; Head Div. of Press and Information Cttee of Youth Orgs 1967–73; Deputy Head, Head Dept of Int. Relations, mem. Exec. Bd, Deputy Chair. USSR State Cttee on Radio and TV 1974–91; First Deputy Chair. 1991, Deputy Chair., Dir-Gen. of Int. Relations, Russian State TV-Radio Broadcasting Co. Ostankino 1991–93; First Deputy Chair. Feb.–Dec. 1993, First Deputy Head Russian Fed. Service on TV and Radio Broadcasting, concurrently Dir-Gen. Russian State TV-Radio Broadcasting Co. Ostankino 1993–95; Head Russian Fed. Service on TV and Radio Broadcasting 1995–98; Rector Humanitarian Inst. of Television and Radio Broadcasting 1998–; Chair. Interstate TV Service, Union of Russia and Belarus 1998–; Coordinating Bd Soyuz (Union) Media Group 2001–, Moscow TV Center Channel –2005; Deputy Head Exec. Cttee Union of Russia and Belarus 2000–; Dir Nat. TV Broadcasters Asscn, Russian CATV Asscn; mem. Bd Dirs Moscow CableCom 2004–; mem. Russian TV Acad., Int. TV Acad., Russia Acad. of Natural Sciences; Officier des Arts et Lettres, Peter the Great Prize and other decorations. *Leisure interests:* history, military heraldry. *Address:* c/o M. Sufott, Porzio, Bromberg & Newman, 156 West 56th Street, New York, NY 10019, USA; Humanitarian Institute of Television and Radio Broadcasting, Brodnikov per. 3, 109186 Moscow, Russia (office). *Telephone:* (495) 238-19-75 (office).

LE, Duc Thuy, PhD; Vietnamese fmr central banker; b. 1948, Ha Tinh Prov.; ed Nat. Econs Univ., Hanoi, postgraduate studies in USSR; mem. Party Cen. Cttee; Asst in Econs to Prime Minister and to Gen. Sec. of CP early 1990s; joined State Bank of Viet Nam 1996, Deputy Gov. –1999, Gov. 1999–2007, Gov. for Viet Nam, IMF, Washington, DC; Vice-Chair. Nat. Financial, Monetary Policy Advisory Council 2007–11; Visiting Scholar, Harvard Inst. for Int. Devt, USA 1991–92. *Address:* c/o National Financial, Monetary Policy Advisory Council, Ministry of Finance, 28 Tran Hung Dao, Hoan Kiem District, Hanoi, Viet Nam (office).

LE, Jingyi; Chinese fmr swimmer; b. 19 March 1975, Shanghai; entered Chinese Women's Swimming Team 1991; fmr world record-holder at 50m and 100m freestyle; broke Olympic record for women's 100m freestyle; affected by illness in the build-up to 27th Olympics, Sydney 2000; gold medallist 50m freestyle, World Championships, Palma 1993, Summer Universiade, Buffalo 1993, World Championships, Rome 1994, World Championships, Rio 1995, Pan Pacific Championships, Fukuoka 1997; gold medallist 100m freestyle, World Championships, Palma 1993, World Championships, Rio 1995, Atlanta Olympics 1996; gold medallist 4x100 m freestyle relay, World Championships, Palma 1993, World Championships, Rome 1994, World Championships, Rio 1995, Gothenburg 1997; silver medal 100m freestyle, 200m freestyle, Pan Pacific Championships, Fukuoka 1997; bronze medal 50m freestyle, World Championships, Gothenburg 1997, 100m freestyle, World Championships, Gothenburg 1997; United Press Int. Athlete of the Year 1994, World Pacific Rim Swimmer of the Year 1996, State Physical Culture and Sports Comm. Nat. Sports Medal of Honour and First Prize 1996. *Address:* c/o State General Bureau for Physical Culture and Sports, 9 Tiyuguan Road, Chongwen District, Beijing, People's Republic of China.

LE, Gen. Kha Phieu; Vietnamese army officer and politician; b. 27 Dec. 1931, Dong Khe Commune, Dong Son Dist, Thanh Hoa Prov.; ed Viet Nam Mil. Coll.; joined CP 1949, served in several positions 1964–93 including Regt's Political Commissar and Commdr of the Regiment, Deputy Chief Army Political Dept of Second Army Corps, Deputy Political Commissar and Chief Political Dept of Ninth Mil. Zone, Maj.-Gen., Chief of Political Dept and Deputy Political Commdr of 719 Front, Lt-Gen., Deputy Chief and then Sr Lt-Gen. and Chief Gen. Political Dept Vietnamese People's Army; Gen. Sec. CP of Viet Nam 1997–2001, mem. Politburo, Politburo Standing Bd. *Address:* c/o Communist Party of Viet Nam, 1 Hoang Van Thu, Hanoi, Viet Nam.

LE BESCO, Maïwenn; French actress and film director; b. 17 April 1976, Les Lilas, Seine-Saint-Denis, Île-de-France; d. of Catherine Belkhodja; one d. with Luc Besson; m. Jean-Yves Le Fur; one s.; performed as stand-up comedian in one-woman shows Le Pois Chiche and I'm an Actress. *Theatre writing:* Café de la Gare 2003. *Films include:* L'Année prochaine… si tout va bien 1981, L'été meurtrier 1983, L'état de grâce 1986, L'autre nuit 1988, Lacenaire 1990, La Gamine 1992, Leon 1994, The Professional 1994, The Fifth Element (dir Luc Besson) 1997, Coquillettes (short) 1998, Keskidi? (short) 1998, Le marquis (short) 2000, The Mechanics of Women 2000, 8 rue Charlot 2001, Haute Tension 2003, Osmose 2003, Switchblade Romance 2003, Les Parisiens 2004, Le genre humain – 1ère partie: Les Parisiens 2004, Le courage d'aimer 2005, Star Stuff (short) 2005, Pardonnez-moi (also screenwriter, dir and producer) 2006, Le bal des actrices (also screenwriter and dir) 2009, Polisse (also screenwriter and dir) (Jury Prize, Cannes Film Festival 2011) 2011; dir: I am an actrice (short) 2004. *Music video:* played The Scarecrow in The Cranberries: The Best Videos 1992–2002 2002. *Television includes:* Cinéma 16 (series) 1983, Les enquêtes du commissaire Maigret (series) 1983, Double face (film) 1987, La famille Ramdam (series) 1990, L'oiseau rare (film) 2001, Nestor Burma (series) 2002, Caméra café (series) 2002.

LE BLANC, Bart, PhD; Dutch banker and academic; *Senior Partner, Andreas Capital Group SA (Luxembourg);* b. 4 Nov. 1946, Bois-le-Duc; s. of Christian Le Blanc and Johanna Bogaerts; m. Gérardine van Lanschot; one s. two d.; ed Leiden and Tilburg Univs; Special Adviser, Prime Minister's Office, Deputy Sec. to Cabinet 1973–79; Deputy Dir-Gen. for Civil Service at Home Office 1979–80; Dir-Gen. for Budget at Treasury 1980–83; Deputy Chair. Man. Bd F. van Lanschot Bankiers NV, 's-Hertogenbosch 1983–91; Sec.-Gen. EBRD, London 1991–94, Vice-Pres. of Finance 1994–98; Dir Int. Finance, Caisse des Dépôts et Consignations, Paris 1998; Chief Financial Officer, Urenco Ltd 2004–11; Chair. ETC, UK 2006–13, Andreas Capital Group SA (Luxembourg) 2010–; Kt, Order of Netherlands Lion 1986. *Publications:* books and contribs on econ. and fiscal policy to nat. and int. journals. *Leisure interest:* farming in France. *Address:* Andreas Capital Group SA, 10–12 Rue de Medernach, Larochette, 7601 Luxembourg, Luxembourg (office). *Telephone:* 8782971 (office). *E-mail:* blb@andreas-capital.com (office). *Website:* www.andreas-capital.com (office).

LE BRIS, Raymond-François; French professor of law and university administrator; b. 18 Sept. 1935, Gouesnou; s. of François Le Bris and Bernadette Le Bris (née Lunven); m. Jacqueline Pareau 1964; one s. two d.; ed Coll. Notre-Dame-de-Bon-Secours, Brest, Univ. of Rennes; Asst Lecturer, Law Faculty, Univ. of Rennes 1958–63, Lecturer 1963–65; Prof., Univ. of Bordeaux 1965–68; Asst Dir Institut Henry-Vizioz des Antilles-Guyanne 1966; Prof., Univ. of Bretagne Occidentale 1969, 1976–77, Pres. 1971; Dir Institut de droit et des sciences économiques, Brest 1969; Deputy Dir for higher educ. and research, Ministry of Nat. Educ. 1972, Dir-Gen. 1972–74; Dir de Cabinet of Sec. of State for Univs 1974–76; Préfet, L'Ariège 1977–79, L'Ain 1979–81, Seine-Saint-Denis 1986–90; Prof. Univ. of Paris IX – Dauphiné 1981–86; Sec.-Gen. Conseil pour l'avenir de la France 1982–86; Dir-Gen. Chambre de commerce et d'industrie de Paris 1990–95; Dir Ecole Nat. d'Admin 1995–2000; expert consultant to Tekelec Airtronic, Sociovision CoFremca, NN France, Tilder Associates; mem. Bd MIT France, Bd of Trustees, Int. Council for Educational Devt; Prefet Honoraire; Officier, Légion d'Honneur; Commdr, Ordre Nat. du Mérite; Commdr des Palmes Académiques; Grand Officier, Ordre de Castello Branco (Brazil). *Publications:* La relation de travail entre epoux 1965, Les universités à la loupe 1986, L'Etat quand même 2005, Réflexion et propositions sur l'organisation et le fonctionnement des services de l'Etat à l'étranger 2005. *Leisure interest:* cross-country and marathon running. *Address:* Tekelec Airtronic, 5 rue Carle Vernet, Sèvres 92 (office); CoFremca, 16 rue d'Athènes, 75009, Paris (office); 34 rue des Vignes, 75007 Paris, France (home); Tilder Associates, 57 boulevard de Montmorency, 75026, Paris. *Telephone:* 1-46-90-23-50 (office); 1-59-70-60-00 (office); 1-45-25-14-32 (home). *Fax:* 1-46-90-23-92 (office). *E-mail:* raymond-francois.lebris@temex.fr (office).

LE BRUN, Christopher Mark, MA, DFA, RA; British artist; *President, Royal Academy of Arts;* b. 20 Dec. 1951, Portsmouth; s. of John Le Brun, BEM and Eileen B. Le Brun (née Miles); m. Charlotte Verity 1979; two s. one d.; ed Portsmouth Southern Grammar School, Slade School of Fine Art and Chelsea School of Art; Visiting Lecturer, Brighton Polytechnic 1975–82, Slade School of Fine Art 1978–83, Wimbledon School of Art 1981–83; Prof. of Drawing RA 2000–02; mem. Advisory Cttee, Prince of Wales's Drawing Studio 2000–; Chair. Educ. Cttee RA 2000–, Pres. Royal Acad. of Art 2011–; work in numerous public collections including Tate Gallery, London and Museum of Modern Art, New York; Trustee Tate Gallery 1990–95, Nat. Gallery 1996–2003, Dulwich Picture Gallery 2000–; major comms include Liverpool Anglican Cathedral 1996; Chair. Academic Advisory Bd, Prince of Wales Drawing School 2004–; Trustee, Princes' Drawing School 2004–; Honorary Fellow, Univ. of the Arts London 2010; Gulbenkian Printmakers Award 1983, DAAD Award, W Berlin 1987–88 and other prizes. *Publication:* Christopher Le Brun 2001, Booth-Clibborn Edns. *Address:* The Royal Academy of Arts, Burlington House, Piccadilly, London W1V 0DS, England (office). *Telephone:* (20) 7300-8000 (office). *E-mail:* press.office@royalacademy.org.uk (office). *Website:* www.royalacademy.org.uk (office).

Le CARRÉ, John (see Cornwell, David John Moore).

LE CLÉZIO, Jean Marie Gustave; British/French writer; b. 13 April 1940, Nice; s. of Raoul Le Clézio and Simone Le Clézio; m. 1st Rosalie Piquemal 1961; one d.; m. 2nd Jemia Jean 1975; ed Bristol Univ., Univ. de Provence, Univ. de Perpignan; lived in Nigeria as a child 1948–50; has taught at univs in Bangkok, Mexico City, Boston, Austin, Albuquerque; Chevalier des Arts et Lettres, Légion d'honneur; Prix Larbaud 1972, Grand Prix Paul Morand (Acad. française) 1980, Grand Prix Jean Giono 1997, Prix Prince de Monaco 1998, Stig Dagermanpriset 2008, Nobel Prize for Literature 2008. *Publications include:* Le procès-verbal (The Interrogation) (Prix Renaudot) 1963, Le jour où Beaumont fit connaissance avec sa douleur 1964, La fièvre (Fever) 1965, Le procès 1965, Le déluge 1966, L'extase matérielle 1967, Terra amata 1967, Le livre des fuites 1969, La guerre 1970, Haï 1971, Conversations 1971, Les géants 1973, Mydriase 1973, Voyages de l'autre côté 1975, Mondo et autres histoires 1978, L'inconnu sur la terre 1978, Vers les Icebergs 1978, Voyages au pays des arbres 1978, Désert 1980, Trois villes saintes 1980, Lullaby 1980, Celui qui n'avait vu la mer suivi de la Montagne du dieu vivant 1982, La ronde et autres faits divers 1982, Journal du chercheur d'or 1985, Balaabilou 1985, Villa Aurore 1985, Voyage à Rodrigues 1986, Le rêve mexicain ou la pensée interrompue 1988, Printemps et autres saisons 1989, La Grande Vie 1990, Sirandanes, Suivi de Petit lexique de la langue créole et des oiseaux (jtly) 1990, Onitsha 1991, Étoile errante 1992, Pawana 1992, Diego et Frida 1993, La Quarantaine 1995, Le Poisson d'or 1997, La Fête chantée 1997, Hasard et Angoli Mala 1999, Coeur brûlé et autres romances 2000, Révolutions 2003, L'Africain 2004, Ourania 2005, Raga: approche du continent invisible 2006, Ballaciner 2007, Ritornelle de la faim 2008. *Address:* c/o Editions Gallimard, 5 rue Gaston-Gallimard, 75328 Paris, France. *Telephone:* 1-49-54-42-00. *Fax:* 1-45-44-94-03. *Website:* www.gallimard.fr.

LE COZ, Martine; French novelist; b. 13 Sept. 1955, Prix Renaudot 2001. *Publications include:* Gilles de Raiz ou La confession imaginaire 1989, Le pharaon qui n'avait pas d'ombre 1992, Hypnose et graphologie 1993, La palette du jeune Turner 1993, Le journal de l'autre 1995, Gilles de Rais ignoble et chrétien 1995, Les confins du jour 1996, Léo la nuit 1997, Le Briquet 1997, Le chagrin du zèbre 1998, Le nègre et la Méduse 1999, Catherine d'Alexandrie ou La philosophie défaite par la foi 1999, La beauté 2000, Le rire de l'arbre au milieu du jardin 2000, Céleste (Prix Renaudot) 2001, Hosana! 2003, Nos lointains et nos proches 2004, La reine écarlate 2007, Le Jardin d'Orient 2008, L'Homme Électrique 2009, Signe de ferveur noir 2010. *Address:* c/o Les Éditions Michalon, 34 rue de Lancry, 75010 Paris, France. *Website:* www.michalon.fr.

LE DRIAN, Jean-Yves; French politician; *Minister of Defence;* b. 30 June 1947, Lorient (Morbihan); s. of Jean Le Drian and Louisette Le Drian; m. 2nd Maria Vadillo; ed Univ. of Rennes 2 Haute Bretagne; mem. Socialist Party (Parti socialiste—PS); Deputy to Nat. Ass. for Fifth Dist of Morbihan 1978–86, 1988–91, 1997–2007; Deputy Mayor of Lorient 1977–81, Mayor of Lorient 1981–98, mem. City Council 1998–2004; Sec. of State for Maritime Affairs under Edith Cresson 1991–92; mem. Regional Council of Brittany 1998–2004, Pres. 2004–12; Pres. Conf. of Peripheral Maritime Regions 2010–; Minister of Defence 2012–. *Address:* Ministry of Defence and Veterans, 14 rue Saint Dominique, 75007 Paris, France (office). *Telephone:* 1-42-19-30-11 (office). *Fax:* 1-47-05-40-91 (office). *E-mail:* courrier-ministre@sdbc.defense.gouv.fr (office). *Website:* www.defense.gouv.fr (office); www.bretagne.fr.

LE FLOCH-PRIGENT, Loïk; French business executive; b. 21 Sept. 1943, Brest; s. of Gérard Le Floch and Gabrielle Julienne; m.; one s. two d.; ed Institut Nat. Polytechnique, Grenoble and Univ. of Missouri, USA; scientific and tech. research, DGRST 1969–81; Dir of Cabinet of Industry Minister, Pierre Dreyfus 1981–82; Chair. and CEO Rhône-Poulenc 1982–86, Elf Aquitaine 1989–93, SNCF 1995–96; Chair. Gaz de France 1993–95, Asscn Europe et Entreprises 1994–, Club des présidents d'université et entreprise, Ecole Nat. Supérieure de Création Industrielle 1992–95; Dir Crédit Nat. 1985–97, Compagnie Gén. des Eaux 1990–96, Banco Cen. Hispano Americano 1990–94, Pallas 1991–, Pinault Printemps Redoute 1991–, Entrepose-Montalev 1994–; imprisoned for involvement in Elf Affair (financial scandal) May 2001, sentenced to five years in prison Nov. 2003, released in April 2004 for health reasons, ordered to return to prison June 2007 to serve remainder of his sentence; Officier, Légion d'honneur, Ordre nat. du Mérite.

LE FOLL, Stéphane, DEA (Econ); French politician; *Minister of Agriculture and Food;* b. 9 Feb. 1960, Le Mans; ed Nat. Conservatory for Industrial Arts and Crafts; econs teacher 1987–91; Head of the Office of First Sec. of the Socialist Party (Parti socialiste—PS) 1997–2004; Vice-Chair. Le Mans Urban Community Council and mem. Le Mans Municipal Council 2002–04; mem. (PS) European Parl. for the West of France (Group of the Progressive Alliance of Socialists and Democrats in the European Parl.) 2004–, mem. Cttee on Agric. and Rural Devt, Del. for relations with the Palestinian Legis. Council; Minister of Agric. and Food 2012–, also Govt Spokesman 2014–; Chevalier du Mérite agricole. *Address:* Ministry of Agriculture and Food, Hôtel de Villeroy, 78 rue de Varenne, 75349 Paris Cedex 07, France (office). *Telephone:* 1-49-55-49-55 (office). *Fax:* 1-49-55-40-39 (office). *E-mail:* infodoc@agriculture.gouv.fr (office). *Website:* www.agriculture.gouv.fr (office).

LE FUR, Gérard; French physician and pharmaceuticals industry executive; b. 1950; trained as doctor of pharmacy and science with specialisation in area of cen. nervous system disorders; Head of Lab., Dept of Pharmacological Biochemistry, Pharmuca 1973–82; Dir of Biology Dept, Rhône-Poulenc 1982–86; Assoc. Dir of Research and Devt, Sanofi 1986–95, Dir of Research and Devt 1995–98, Man.-Dir in charge of Scientific Depts 1998, Dir of Research, Sanofi-Synthélabo (following merger of Sanofi and Synthélabo 1998) 1999–2002, Group Man.-Dir 2002–04; Chair. Man. Bd Aventis 2004–06, CEO Sanofi-Aventis SA (following merger of Sanofi-Synthélabo and Aventis) 2006–08, consultant 2008–; mem. Acad. des Sciences 1999–2003, Corresp. mem. 2003–04; Galien Prize 1983, 2000. *Publications:* more than 300 scientific papers in int. publs. *Address:* Sanofi-Aventis SA, 174 Avenue de France, 75013 Paris, France (office). *Telephone:* 1-53-77-42-23 (office). *Fax:* 1-53-77-42-65 (office). *E-mail:* info@sanofi-aventis.com (office). *Website:* www.sanofi-aventis.com (office).

LE GENDRE, Bertrand, BA, LLB; French journalist; b. 25 Feb. 1948, Neuilly-sur-Seine; s. of Bernard Le Gendre and Catherine Chassaing de Borredon; m. 1st Jacqueline de Linares 1987 (divorced 1995); one s.; m. 2nd Nadia du Luc-Baccouche 1995; one s.; ed Collège Sainte-Croix-de-Neuilly, Univ. of Paris X, Institut d'études politiques, Paris, Institut des hautes études de défense nationale; joined Le Monde as journalist 1974, in charge of judicial desk 1983, Reporter 1987, Ed.-in-Chief 1993–2000; Visiting Assoc. Prof., Univ. de Paris II 2000–11; Sub-Ed. Gallimard 1986–89; Prix de la Fondation Mumm pour la presse écrite 1986. *Publications include:* Confessions du n° 2 de l'OAS. Entretiens avec Jean-Jacques Susini 2012, 1962, L'année prodigieuse 2012. *Address:* 16 rue de la Glacière, 75013 Paris, France (home).

LE GREW, Daryl John, MArch; Australian university administrator and professor of architecture; *Vice-Chancellor Professorial Fellow, Monash University;* b. 17 Sept. 1945, Melbourne, Vic.; s. of A. J. Le Grew; m. Josephine Le Grew 1971; one s. two d.; ed Trinity Grammar School, Kew and Univ. of Melbourne; Lecturer, Dept of Town and Regional Planning, Univ. of Melbourne 1969–73, Lecturer and Sr Lecturer, Dept of Architecture and Building 1973–85; Prof. of Architecture, Deakin Univ. 1986–98, Dean Faculty of Design and Tech. 1992–93, Chair. Academic Bd 1992–98, Pro-Vice-Chancellor (Academic) 1993–94, Deputy Vice-Chancellor and Vice-Pres. (Academic) 1994–98; Vice-Chancellor Univ. of Canterbury, New Zealand 1998–2002; Vice-Chancellor and Pres. Univ. of Tasmania 2003–11; Vice-Chancellor Professorial Fellow, Univ. of Melbourne 2010–; Monash Univ. 2010–; Senate Pres., Australian Acad. of Design 2010–; Dir LeGrew Design Pty Ltd 2010–; Sr Consultant Gehl Architects, Copenhagen 2010–; Consultant, UK Science Research Council Training Programme; Architectural Consultant and Adviser to Dir and Trustees of Nat. Gallery of Victoria, Melbourne for redevelopment of gallery site, to Dir and Council Museum of Victoria, Melbourne for its redevelopment, mem. Council; several sr appointments in business and higher educ.; Life Fellow, Museum of Vic. 1997; Visiting Fellow, Bartlett School of Architecture and Planning, Univ. Coll. London; Fellow, Australian Inst. of Man.; Hon. Fellow, Certified Practising Accountant of Australia; Hon. DLitt (Univ. of Tasmania). *Leisure interests:* swimming, music, poetry, philosophy. *Address:* Office of the Vice-Chancellor, Monash University, Clayton, Vic., Australia (office); PO Box 118, Aireys Inlet, Vic. 3231, Australia. *Telephone:* (3) 9903-2709 (office); (3) 6289-6354. *E-mail:* daryl.legrew@monash.edu (office); daryllegrew@gmail.com (office). *Website:* www.monash.edu (office); www.legrew.com.

LE MAIRE, Bruno; French politician; b. 15 April 1969, Neuilly-sur-Seine (Hauts-de-Seine); s. of Maurice Le Maire and Viviane Fradin de Belabre; ed École nationale d'admin, Paris; Adviser to Dominique de Villepin, Ministry of Foreign Affairs 2002–04, Adviser, Ministry of the Interior 2004–05, Political Adviser to Prime Minister (Dominique de Villepin) 2005–06, Head of PM's Cabinet 2006–07; mem. Assemblée nationale (Parl.) for Eure 2007–12; mem. Municipal Council, Évreux (Eure) 2008–; Regional Councillor, Haute-Normandie 2010–; Sec. of State in charge of European Affairs 2008–09; Minister of Food, Agric. and Fisheries 2009, of Agric., Food, Fisheries, Rural Affairs and Town and Country Planning (Regional Devt) 2009–12; mem. Union pour un Mouvement Populaire (UMP), Political Adviser 2008–09, Regional Sec. for Eure 2008–; Prix du Livre Politique 2013. *Publications:* Le Ministre 2004, Des hommes d'État (Prix Edgar Faure 2008) 2007, Sans mémoire, le présent se vide 2010, Musique absolue. Une répétition avec Carlos Kleiber 2012, Jours de Pouvoir 2013. *Address:* Assemblée nationale, 126 rue de l'Université, 75007 Paris, France (office). *Telephone:* 1-40-63-54-96 (office). *Fax:* 1-40-63-56-91 (office). *E-mail:* blemaire@assemblee-nationale.fr (office). *Website:* www.brunolemaire.fr.

LE PEN, Jean-Marie, LenD; French politician; b. 20 June 1928, La Trinité-sur-Mer, Morbihan; s. of Jean Le Pen and Anne-Marie Hervé; m. 1st Pierrette Lalanne, 1960 (divorced); three d.; m. 2nd Jeanne-Marie Paschos 1991; ed Coll. des Jésuites Saint-François-Xavier, Vannes, Lycée de Lorient, Univ. de Paris; Pres. Corpn des étudiants en droit de Paris 1949–51; Sub-Lt 1st foreign Bn of paratroopers, Indochina 1954–55; Political Ed. Caravelle 1955, Nat. Del. for Union de défense de la jeunesse française, then Deputy 1st Sector, La Seine; mem. Groupe d'union et de fraternité at Nat. Ass., independent Deputy for la Seine 1958–62; Gen. Sec. Front Nat. Combattant 1956, of Tixier Vignancour Cttee 1964–65; Dir Soc. d'études et de relations publiques 1963–; Pres. Front Nat. 1972–2011, Front Nat. Provence-Alpes-Côte d'Azur 1992–2000; mem. Nat. Ass. 1986–88; mem. European Parl. 1984–2000, Pres. groupe des droites européennes 1984–2000; presidential cand. 1988, 2002, 2007; guilty of physical assault and banned from holding or seeking public office for two years, given three-month suspended prison sentence April 1998; sentence on appeal: immunity removed by European Parl. Oct. 1998; Croix de la Valeur militaire. *Publications:* Les Français d'abord 1984, La France est de retour 1985, L'Espoir 1986, J'ai vu juste 1998. *Address:* Serp, 6 rue de Beaune, 75007 Paris (office); 8 parc de Montretout, 92210 St-Cloud, France (home).

LE PENSEC, Louis; French politician; b. 8 Jan. 1937, Mellac; s. of Jean Le Pensec and Marie-Anne Hervé; m. Colette Le Guilcher 1963; one s.; Personnel Officer, Soc. nationale d'étude et de construction de moteurs d'aviation 1963–66, Soc. anonyme de véhicules industriels et d'équipements mécaniques 1966–69; Teacher of Personnel Man., Legal Sciences Teaching and Research Unit, Univ. of Rennes 1970–73; Mayor of Mellac 1971–97; Deputy (Finistère) to Nat. Ass. 1973–81, 1983–88, 1993; Councillor for Finistère 1976–, Senator 1998–; mem. Steering Cttee, Parti Socialiste 1977, Exec. Bureau 1979; Minister for the Sea 1981–83, 1988, of Overseas Depts and Territories 1988–93; Govt Spokesperson 1989–91; Vice-Pres. for Europe, Council of European Communities 1983–; Minister of Agric. and Fisheries 1997–98; Vice-Pres. County Council (Finistère) 1998–2008; Head ASEAN Mission for External Trade; mem. Senate Del. for EU 1999–; Vice-Pres. Council of European Municipalities and Regions 2007–; Commdr du Mérite maritime, du Mérite agricole, Order du Mérite (Côte d'Ivoire), Grand-croix du Royaume (Thailand). *Publication:* Ministre à Babord 1997. *Leisure interest:* golf. *Address:* Kerviguennou, 29300 Mellac (home); Hôtel du département, 32 quai Dupleix, 29196 Quimper Cedex, France. *Telephone:* (2) 98-76-20-24 (office); (2) 98-35-08-00 (home). *Fax:* (2) 98-76-21-96 (office); (2) 98-35-08-09 (home). *E-mail:* louis.le-pensec@wanadoo.fr (office).

LE PICHON, Xavier, PhD; French geologist and academic; *Honorary Professor and Chair of Geodynamics, Collège de France;* b. 18 June 1937, Quinhon, Viet Nam; s. of Jean-Louis Le Pichon and Hélène Tyl; m. Brigitte Barthélemy 1962; five c.; ed Sciences Physiques, Strasbourg; Research Asst Columbia Univ., New York 1963; Scientific Adviser, Centre Nat. pour l'Exploitation des Océans 1968, 1973; Head, Dept of Oceanography, Centre Océanologique de Bretagne, Brest 1969; Prof. Univ. P. & M. Curie, Paris 1978; Dir Dept of Geology, Ecole Normale Supérieure, Paris 1984–91, Dir Lab. of Geology 1984–2000; Hon. Prof. and Chair. of Geodynamics, Collège de France 1986–; Pres. Ifremer Scientific Council 1991–2000, Sr Jury Inst. Universitaire de France 1997; Visiting Prof. Oxford Univ. 1994, Univ. of Tokyo 1995, Rice Univ. Houston 2002; mem. Acad. des Sciences; Founder mem. Acad. Europaea 1988, NAS, USA 1995; Officier, Légion d'Honneur, Commdr Ordre Nat. du Mérite; Dr hc (Dalhousie Univ.) 1989, (ETH, Zürich) 1992; Maurice Ewing Medal, American Geophysical Union 1984, Huntsman Award (Canada) 1987, Japan Prize 1990, Wollaston Medal (Geological Soc. of London) 1991, Balzan Prize 2002, Wagener Medal 2003. *Publications:* Plate Tectonics (with others) 1973, Expédition Famous, à 3000m sous l'Atlantique (with C. Riffaud) 1976, Kaiko, voyage aux extrémités de la mer 1986, Aux racines de l'homme, De la Mort à l'Amour 1997, La Mort, Desclée de Brouwer 1999. *Address:* Chaire de Géodynamique, Collège de France, BP 80, 13545, Aix-en-Provence, Cedex 04, France (office). *Telephone:* 4-42-50-74-02 (office). *Fax:* 4-42-50-74-01 (office). *E-mail:* lepichon@cdf.u-3mrs.fr. *Website:* www.cdf.u-3mrs.fr (office).

LE PORS, Anicet; French politician, economist and jurist; *Section President, National Court of Asylum;* b. 28 April 1931, Paris; s. of François Le Pors and Gabrielle Croguennec; m. Claudine Carteret 1959; one s. two d.; ed Collège Arago, Paris, Ecole de la Météorologie, Univ. of Paris, Centre d'étude des programmes économiques; Meteorological Eng, Marrakesh, Morocco 1953, Paris 1957–65; trade union official (CGT) 1955–77; Consultant, World Meteorological Org., Léopoldville, Congo (now Kinshasa, Democratic Repub. of Congo) 1960; Sec. Communist section of Metropolitan Office 1962; Head of Dept, Ministry of Economy and Finance 1965; Sec. Cttee of Cen. Admin., Parti Communiste Français (PCF) 1976–77, Head of Nationalizations, Industrial Policy and Insts Dept, then of Int. Dept, PCF 1978, mem. Cen. Cttee 1979; Head of Interministerial Comm., Univ. of Paris XIII 1976–77 and Ecole supérieure des Sciences Economiques et Commerciales 1978; Senator (Hauts-de-Seine) 1977–81; Minister-Del. for the Civil Service and Admin. Reforms, attached to Prime Minister 1981–83; Sec. of State in charge of Public and Admin. Reform 1983–84; Sr mem. Council of State 1985–; mem. Higher Council for Integration; Councillor-Gen. from Hauts-de-Seine 1985–98; Vice-Pres. Nat. Council of Tourism 2000–; Chair. Youth Employment Programme, Cttee de pilotage pour l'égal accès des femmes et des hommes (cttee for equal rights for men and women); Section Pres. Comm. de recours des réfugiés (now Cour nationale du droit d'asile, Nat. Court of Asylum) 2000–; Officier, Légion d'honneur; Officier, Ordre nat. du mérite. *Publications:* Les transferts Etats-industries en France et dans les pays occidentaux 1976, Les béquilles du capital 1977, Marianne à l'encan 1980, Contradictions 1984, L'état efficace 1985, Pendant la mue, le serpent est aveugle 1993, Le Nouvel Age de la citoyenneté 1997, La Citoyenneté 1999, Eloge de l'échec 2001, Le droit d'asile 2005. *Leisure interests:* swimming, sailing. *Address:* Conseil d'Etat, place du Palais-Royal, 75001 Paris (office); 189 boulevard de la République, 92210 St-Cloud, France (home). *Telephone:* (6) 80-20-81-67 (office). *E-mail:* anicetlp@club-internet.fr (office).

LE ROY, Alain; French diplomatist and UN official; *Ambassador to Italy;* b. 5 Feb. 1953; m.; one s.; ed Ecole nationale supérieure des Mines, Paris, Paris 1 (Sorbonne) Univ.; early career as petroleum engineer for Total; with Sous-préfet d'Avallon 1991–92; Cabinet Chief, Ministry of Agric. 1992–93; Counsellor, Cour des comptes 1993–95, 1995–99; Deputy to UN Special Co-ordinator for Sarajevo and Dir of Operations for restoration of essential public services March–Sept. 1995; UN Regional Admin. in Kosovo (Western Region) 1999–2000; Nat. Co-ordinator for Stability Pact for SE Europe, Ministry of Foreign Affairs 2000; fmr EU Special Rep. in Fmr Yugoslav Repub. of Macedonia; fmr Asst Sec. for Econ. and Financial Affairs, Ministry of Foreign Affairs; Amb. to Madagascar 2006–07; Conseiller Maître, Cour des comptes and Amb. in charge of Union for Mediterranean Initiative 2007–08; UN Under-Sec.-Gen. for Peacekeeping Operations 2008–11; Amb. to Italy 2011–; Commandeur, Ordre nat. de Madagascar. *Address:* Embassy of France, Piazza Farnese 67, 00186 Rome, Italy (office). *Telephone:* (06) 686011 (office). *Fax:* (06) 68601418 (office). *Website:* www.ambafrance-it.org (office).

LE ROY LADURIE, Emmanuel, DèsSc; French historian and academic; *Professor Emeritus of History of Modern Civilization, Collège de France;* b. 19 July 1929, Les Moutiers en Cinglais (Calvados); s. of Jacques Le Roy Ladurie and Léontine Dauger; m. Madeleine Pupponi 1956; one s. one d.; ed École Normale Supérieure; taught at Lycée de Montpellier 1955–57; research attaché, CNRS 1957–60; Asst Faculté des Letters, Montpellier 1960–63; Asst Lecturer and Dir of Studies, École des Hautes Études 1963; Lecturer, Univ. of the Sorbonne 1970–71, Univ. of Paris VII 1971–73; Prof. of History of Modern Civilization, Collège de France 1973–99, Prof. Emer. 1999–; Gen. Admin. Bibliothèque Nat. 1987–94, Pres. Scientific Council 1994–; mem. Conseil scientifique de l'École Normale Supérieure 1998–; mem. Acad. des Sciences morales et politiques; writes for Le Nouvel Observateur, L'Express, Le Monde newspapers; appears on French TV; Foreign Hon. mem. Acad. des Sciences américaines 1984; Commdr, Légion d'honneur, Ordre des Arts et des Lettres; 15 hon. degrees; Medal of Center for French Civilization and Culture, New York Univ. 1985. *Publications include:* Les paysans de Languedoc 1966, Histoire du climat depuis l'an mil 1967, Le territoire de l'historien Vol. I 1973, Vol. II 1978, Montaillou, village occitan de 1294 à 1324 1975, Le carnaval de Romans 1579–80 1980, L'argent, l'amour et la mort en pays d'oc 1980, Histoire de la France urbaine, Vol. III 1981, Paris-Montpellier PC-PSU 1945-1963 1982, La Sorcière de Jasmin 1983, Parmi les historiens 1983, The French Peasantry 1450–1680, Pierre Prion, scribe 1987, Monarchies 1987, L'Histoire de France de: L'Etat Royal 1460–1610 (co-author) 1987, L'Ancien Régime 1610–1770 (co-author) 1991, The Royal French State 1460–1610 1994, Le Siècle des Plaeter (1499–1628) 1995, The Ancien Régime: A History of France 1610–1774 1996, Mémoires 1902–1945 1997, L'Historien, le chiffre et le texte 1997, Saint-Simon, le système de la Cour 1997, Le Voyage de Thomas Plaeter 2000, Histoire de France des Régions 2001, Histoire des paysans français de la Peste Noire à la Revolution 2002, Histoire humaine et comparée du climat 2004, Abrégé d'Histoire du climat 2007. *Leisure interests:* cycling, swimming. *Address:* Collège de France, 11 place Marcelin-Berthelot, 75005 Paris (office); 88 rue d'Alleray, 75015 Paris, France (home). *Telephone:* 1-44-27-10-38 (office); 1-48-42-01-27 (home). *Fax:* 1-44-27-12-40 (office). *E-mail:* e.m.ladurie@wanadoo.fr (home).

LEA, Ruth Jane, BA, MSc, FRSA; British economist; *Economic Adviser and non-Executive Director, Arbuthnot Banking Group;* b. 22 Sept. 1947, Cheshire, England; d. of Thomas Lea and of the late Jane Lea (née Brown); ed Lymm Grammar School, Univs of York and Bristol; asst statistician, Sr Econ. Asst, HM Treasury 1970–73, statistician 1977–78; Lecturer in Econs, Thames Polytechnic 1973–74; statistician, Civil Service Coll. 1974–77, Cen. Statistics Office 1978–84; briefing and policy posts, Dept of Trade and Industry 1984–88; with Mitsubishi Bank 1988–93, Chief Economist 1990–93; Chief UK Economist, Lehman Brothers 1993–94; Econs Ed. Ind. TV News 1994–95; Head of Policy Unit, Inst. of Dirs 1995–2003; Dir Centre for Policy Studies 2004–07; mem. Bd Dirs Arbuthnot Banking Group 2005–, Econ. Adviser 2007–; Dir Global Vision 2007–10; mem. Retail Prices Advisory Cttee 1992–94, Nat. Consumer Council 1993–96, Rowntree Foundation Income and Wealth Inquiry Group 1993–94, Nurses' Pay Review Body 1994–98, Research Centres Bd ESRC 1996, Research Priorities Bd 1996–97, Statistics Advisory Cttee Office of Nat. Statistics 1996–97; Trustee, New Europe Research Trust 1999–2005; Council mem. Univ. of London 2001–06; Gov. LSE 2003–08; Hon. DBA (Greenwich) 1997, (BPP Univ. Coll.) 2010. *Publications:* numerous publs on business and econ. topics and the EU. *Leisure interests:* music, philately, natural history and countryside, heritage. *Address:* Arbuthnot Banking Group, Arbuthnot House, 20 Ropemaker Street, London, EC2Y 9AR (office); 25 Redbourne Avenue, Finchley, London, N3 2BP, England (home). *Telephone:* 7800-608674 (mobile); (20) 8346-3482 (home). *E-mail:* ruth.lea@btinternet.com (home); ruthlea@arbuthnot.co.uk (home). *Website:* www.arbuthnotgroup.com (office).

LEACH, James Albert Smith (Jim); American government official and fmr politician; *Chairman, National Endowment for the Humanities;* b. 15 Oct. 1942, Davenport, Ia; m. Elisabeth 'Deba' Leach; one s. one d.; ed Princeton Univ., Johns Hopkins Univ., London School of Econs, UK; staffer for then US Rep. Donald Rumsfeld 1970s; entered US Foreign Service, del. to Geneva Disarmament Conf. and UN Gen. Ass., New York –1973 (resgnd); returned to Iowa to head family business 1973–76; mem. US House of Reps from Iowa's 2nd Congressional Dist (numbered as 1st Dist 1977–2003) 1977–2007, Chair. House Cttee on Banking and Financial Services 1995–2001, Sr mem. House Cttee on Int. Relations (Chair. Sub-cttee on Asian and Pacific Affairs 2001–06), Founder and Co-Chair. Congressional Humanities Caucus; John L. Weinberg Visiting Prof. of Public and Int. Affairs,

Woodrow Wilson School, Princeton Univ. –2007; Dir Inst. of Politics, John F. Kennedy School of Govt, Harvard Univ. 2007–08; Chair. Nat. Endowment for the Humanities 2009–; Vice-Chair. Century Foundation; mem. Council on Foreign Relations; fmr Chair. Ripon Soc., Republican Mainstream Cttee; fmr Pres. Parliamentarians for Global Action; fmr mem. Bd Social Science Research Council, Carnegie Endowment for Int. Peace, Kettering Foundation; fmr Trustee, Princeton Univ.; Republican; decorations from two foreign govts; eight hon. degrees; Wayne Morse Integrity in Politics Award, Woodrow Wilson Award, Johns Hopkins, Univ., Adlai Stevenson Award, UNA, Edger Wayburn Award, Sierra Club, elected to Wrestling Hall of Fame, Stillwater, Okla, Int. Wrestling Hall of Fame, Waterloo, Ia. *Achievements include:* won state wrestling championship at 138-pound weight class for Davenport High School 1960. *Address:* Office of the Chairman, Room 503, National Endowment for the Humanities, 1100 Pennsylvania Avenue, NW, Washington, DC 20506, USA (office). *Telephone:* (202) 606-8310 (office). *E-mail:* jleach@neh.gov (office). *Website:* www.neh.gov (office).

LEAHY, Sir John H. G., KCMG, MA; British diplomatist (retd); b. 7 Feb. 1928, Worthing, Sussex, England; s. of the late William H. G. Leahy and Ethel Leahy; m. Elizabeth Anne Pitchford 1954; two s. two d.; ed Tonbridge School, Clare Coll. Cambridge, Yale Univ., USA; joined diplomatic service 1951, Third Sec., Singapore 1955–57; Second Sec., then First Sec., Paris 1958–62; First Sec., Tehran 1965–68; Counsellor, Paris 1973–75; attached to Northern Ireland Office, Belfast 1975–76; Amb. to South Africa 1977–82; Deputy Under-Sec. (Africa and the Middle East), FCO 1982–84; High Commr to Australia 1984–88; Dir Observer newspaper 1989–92; Dir (non-exec.) Lonrho PLC 1993–98, Chair. 1994–97; Master, Skinners' Co. 1993–94; Chair. Britain-Australia Soc. 1994–97; mem. Franco-British Council (Chair. 1989–93); Chair. Govs' Cttee Tonbridge School 1994–99; Pro-Chancellor City Univ. 1991–97; Officier, Légion d'honneur; Hon. DCL (City Univ.) 1997. *Publication:* A Life of Spice 2006. *Address:* 16 Ripley Chase, The Goffs, Eastbourne, East Sussex, BN21 1HB, England. *Telephone:* (1323) 725368. *E-mail:* johnleahy@dsl.pipex.com.

LEAHY, Patrick Joseph, JD; American politician and lawyer; *Senator from Vermont;* b. 31 March 1940, Montpelier, Vt; s. of Howard Leahy and Alba Leahy (née Zambon); m. Marcelle Pomerleau 1962; two s. one d.; ed St Michael's Coll., Colchester, Vt and Georgetown Univ. Law Center, Washington, DC; admitted to practise law, State of Vermont 1964, US Supreme Court, Second Circuit Court of Appeals, New York, US Fed. Dist Court of Vt; Senator from Vermont 1975–, Vice-Chair. Intelligence Cttee 1985–86, Chair. Judiciary Cttee 2001, 2007–, sr mem. Agric. Cttee and Appropriations Cttee, Co-Chair. Senate Nat. Guard Caucus; mem. Vt Bar Asscn 1964–; Vice-Pres. Nat. Dist Attorneys' Asscn 1971–74; Democrat; Distinguished Service Award of Nat. Dist Attorneys' Asscn 1974, Harry S. Truman Award, Nat. Guard Asscn 2003. *Leisure interests:* photography, reading, hiking, cross-country skiing. *Address:* 437 Russell Senate Office Building, Washington, DC 20510, USA (office). *Telephone:* (202) 224-4242 (office). *Website:* leahy.senate.gov (office).

LEAHY, Sir Terence Patrick, Kt, BSc; British business executive; b. 28 Feb. 1956, Belle Vale, Liverpool, England; m. Alison Leahy; two s. one d.; ed St Edward's Coll., Liverpool, Univ. of Manchester Inst. of Science and Tech.; mem. of staff Co-op supermarket group 1977–79; joined Tesco plc 1979, Marketing Dir 1992–95, Deputy Man. Dir 1995–97, Chief Exec. 1997–2011; Chancellor UMIST 2002–04, Co-Chancellor Univ. of Manchester 2004–; Special Adviser, Everton Football Club 2004–; Freeman of the City of Liverpool 2002; Hon. DSc (Cranfield Univ.) 2007; Business Leader of the Year 2003, Fortune European Businessman of the Year 2004, selected as Britain's most admired business leader by Management Today 2005, "most influential non-elected person in Britain" Guardian Unlimited Politics panel 2007. *Leisure interests:* sport, reading, theatre, architecture. *Address:* c/o Tesco plc, Tesco House, PO Box 18, Delamare Road, Cheshunt, Herts., EN8 9SL, England. *Telephone:* (1992) 632222. *Website:* www.tesco.com.

LEAKEY, Louise Nicol, BS, PhD; Kenyan palaeontologist and academic; *Director, Turkana Basin Institute;* b. 21 March 1972, Kenya; d. of Richard Leakey and Meave Leakey (née Epps); grand-d. of the late Louis Leakey; m. Emmanuel de Merode; two d.; ed Univs of Bristol and London, UK; worked with parents from early age in Turkana Basin, Kenya; currently Dir Turkana Basin Inst.; Research Asst Prof., Dept of Anthropology, Univ. of Stony Brook, NY; named (with mother) Nat. Geographic Soc. Explorer-in-Residence 2002; Chair. Nat. Museums of Kenya 2014. *Achievements include:* discovery of *Kenyanthropus platyops*, a new human species that extended diversity in hominid family record back to 3.5 million years. *Address:* Turkana Basin Institute, PO Box 24926, Nairobi 00502, Kenya (office); Department of Anthropology, University of Stony Brook, N507 Social and Behavioural Sciences, Stony Brook, NY 11794-4364, USA (office). *Telephone:* (631) 632-5800 (Stony Brook) (office). *Fax:* (631) 632-5810 (Stony Brook) (office). *E-mail:* louise.leakey@stonybrook.edu (office). *Website:* www.turkanabasin.org (office); www.stonybrook.edu/anthro/staff.shtml (office); www.leakey.com; www .africanfossils.org.

LEAKEY, Richard Erskine Frere, FRAI; Kenyan politician, palaeontologist and conservationist; b. 19 Dec. 1944, Nairobi; s. of the late Louis Leakey and Mary Leakey; m. 1st Margaret Cropper 1965; m. 2nd Meave Gillian Epps 1970; three d.; ed Duke of York School (later known as Lenana School), Nairobi; trapper of primates for research 1961–65; co-leader of research expeditions to Lake Natron 1963–64, Omo River 1967; Dir Root & Leakey Safaris (tour co.) 1965–68; archaeological excavation, Lake Baringo 1966; Admin. Dir Nat. Museums of Kenya 1968–74, Dir and Chief Exec. 1974–89; research in Nakali/Suguta Valley 1978; leader of research projects, Koobi Fora 1979–81, W Turkana 1981–82, 1984–89, Buluk 1983; Dir Wildlife Conservation and Man. Dept 1989–90; Dir Kenya Wildlife Service 1990–94, 1998–99; Man. Dir Richard Leakey & Assocs Ltd 1994–98; Co-Founder and Gen.-Sec. Safina Party 1995–98; nominated MP Nat. Ass. –1999; Perm. Sec., Sec. to the Cabinet, Head of the Public Service, Office of the Pres., Rep. of Kenya 1999–2001; interim Chair. Transparency International (Kenya br.) 2007; numerous hon. positions including Chair. Wildlife Clubs of Kenya 1969–80 (Trustee 1980–); Foundation for Research into the Origins of Man (USA) 1971–85, Kenya Nat. Cttee of the United World Colls 1982–, E African Wildlife Soc. 1984–89, SAIDIA 1989–; Chair. Bd of Trustees, Nat. Museums of Kenya 1989–94; Co-founder and mem. Bd Dirs Wildlife Direct 2004–; Life Trustee, L.S.B. Leakey Foundation; Trustee, Nat. Fund for Disabled in Kenya 1980–95,

Agricultural Research Foundation, Kenya 1986–; has given more than 750 public and scholarly Lectures; Foreign Hon. mem. American Acad. of Arts and Sciences 1998; Order of the Burning Spear, Kenya 1993; nine hon. degrees; numerous awards and honours, including James Smithsonian Medal, USA 1990, Gold Medal, Royal Geographical Soc., UK 1990, World Ecology Medal, Int. Centre for Tropical Ecology, USA 1997. *TV documentaries:* Bones of Contention, Survival Anglia 1975, The Making of Mankind, BBC 1981, Earth Journal (presenter), NBC 1992. *Publications:* numerous articles on finds in the field of palaeontology in scientific journals, including Nature, Journal of World History, Science, American Journal of Physical Anthropology, etc.; contrib. to General History of Africa (Vol. I), Perspective on Human Evolution and Fossil Vertebrates of Africa; Origins (book, with R. Lewin) 1977, People of the Lake: Man, His Origins, Nature and Future (book, with R. Lewin) 1978, The Making of Mankind 1981, Human Origins 1982, One Life 1983, Origins Reconsidered (with R. Lewin) 1992, Origins of Humankind (with R. Lewin) 1995, The Sixth Extinction (with R. Lewin) 1995, Wildlife Wars: My Fight to Save Africa's Natural Treasures (with V. Morrell) 2001, Wildlife Wars: My Battle to Save Kenya's Elephants 2011. *Leisure interests:* sailing and cooking. *Address:* Africa Conservation Fund, PO Box 24926, Karen 00502, Nairobi, Kenya (office). *Telephone:* (3) 865120 (office). *E-mail:* info@wildlifedirect.org (office); leakey@wananchi.com (home). *Website:* www.leakey.com; www.leakeyfoundation .org; richardleakey.wildlifedirect.org.

LEAL, Guilherme Peirão; Brazilian business executive; *Chairman, Natura Cosméticos SA;* b. 1950; five c.; ed Univ. of São Paulo, Harvard Business School, USA; joined Natura Cosméticos SA 1979, mem. Bd of Dirs 1998–, Co-Chair. 2001–; f. Instituto Ethos 1998, currently Pres. and mem. Admin. Council; mem. Superior Council on Social Responsibility, (FIESP), Nat. Council on Food Security; mem. Bd of Dirs Brazilian Fund for Biodiversity; mem. Admin. Council, Grupo 'O Estado de São Paulo', WWF Brasil; Citizen of the State of Rio de Janeiro 2004. *Address:* Natura Cosméticos SA, Rodavia Régis Bittencourt, s/n°, km 293, Potuverá, 06882-700 Itapecerica da Serra, São Paulo, Brazil (office). *Telephone:* (11) 3074-1504 (office). *E-mail:* guilhermeleal@natura.net (office). *Website:* www.natura.net (office).

LEANCĂ, Iurie, MA; Moldovan diplomatist and politician; *Prime Minister;* b. 20 Oct. 1963, Oraşul, Cimişlia Dist; m. Aida Leancă; two c.; ed Moscow State Inst. of Int. Relations; joined Ministry of Foreign Affairs 1986, served in several positions including Minister-Counselor, Embassy in Washington, DC 1993–97, Amb.-at-Large for European Integration 1998, Deputy Minister of Foreign Affairs 1998–99, First Deputy Minister of Foreign Affairs 1999–2001; Deputy CEO Ascom Group (oil co.) 2001–05, 2007–09; Sr Adviser to OSCE High Commr on Nat. Minorities 2005–07; Vice-Pres. Foreign Policy Asscn of Moldova 2005–09; mem. Parl. 2009–; Deputy Prime Minister 2009–13, Minister of Foreign Affairs and European Integration 2009–13, Acting Prime Minister April–May 2013, Prime Minister May 2013–; mem. Liberal Democratic Party of Moldova (Partidul Liberal Democrat din Moldova). *Address:* Office of the Council of Ministers, Piaţa Marii Adunări Naţionale 1, Moldova (office). *Telephone:* (22) 25-01-01 (office). *Fax:* (22) 23-38-72 (office). *E-mail:* petitii@gov.md (office). *Website:* www.gov.md (office).

LEAPE, James P.; American lawyer and international organization official; *Director-General, WWF International;* b. 1956; ed Harvard Coll. and Harvard Law School; has worked in nature conservation for more than 30 years; began his career as an environmental lawyer, working on environmental protection cases in USA, advising UNEP, Nairobi, Kenya and co-authoring a text on environmental law; joined WWF-US 1989, Exec. Vice-Pres. of its worldwide conservation programmes 1991–2001, Dir-Gen. WWF International 2005–; Dir conservation and science initiatives, David and Lucile Packard Foundation 2001–05. *Address:* WWF International, avenue du Mont-Blanc 27, 1196 Gland, Switzerland (office). *Telephone:* (22) 364-91-11 (office). *Fax:* (22) 364-88-36 (office). *E-mail:* cdoole@ wwfint.org (office). *Website:* www.wwfint.org (office); www.panda.org (office).

LÉAUD, Jean-Pierre; French actor; b. 28 May 1944, Paris; s. of Pierre Léaud and Jacqueline Pierreux; debut as Antoine Doinel in Truffaut's The 400 Blows 1959, first of a series of Doinel films directed by Truffaut over 20 years. *Films include:* Les quatre cents coups (The Four Hundred Blows) 1959, La Tour, prends garde! (aka Killer Spy) 1960, Boulevard 1960, Le testament d'Orphée, ou ne me demandez pas pourquoi! (The Testament of Orpheus) (uncredited) 1962, L'amour à vingt ans (Love at Twenty) 1962, Les mauvaises fréquentations (Bad Company) 1963, La peau douce (The Soft Skin) (asst dir; uncredited) 1964, L' amour à la mer (Love at Sea) 1963, Une femme mariée: Suite de fragments d'un film tourné en 1964 (asst dir) 1964, Mata-Hari (also asst dir; uncredited) 1964, Alphaville, une étrange aventure de Lemmy Caution (Alphaville, a Strange Case of Lemmy Caution) (also asst dir; uncredited) 1965, Pierrot le fou (also asst dir; uncredited) 1965, Le Père Noël a les yeux bleus (Santa Claus Has Blue Eyes) 1966, Masculin, féminin: 15 faits précis 1966, Made in U.S.A. (also asst dir) 1966, Le plus vieux métier du monde (The Oldest Profession in the World) (uncredited) 1967, Le départ 1967, La chinoise 1967, Week End 1967, Dialóg 20-40-60 1968, La Concentration 1968, Baisers volés (Stolen Kisses) 1968, Paul 1969, Der Leone have sept cabeças (The Lion Has Seven Heads) 1969, Le gai savoir (Joy of Learning) 1969, Porcile (Pigsty) 1969, Domicile conjugal (Bed & Board) 1970, Os herdeiros (The Heirs) 1970, Une aventure de Billy le Kid (aka A Girl Is a Gun, USA) 1971, Out 1, noli me tangere 1971, Les deux anglaises et le continent (Two English Girls and the Continent) 1971, Out 1: Spectre 1972, Last Tango in Paris 1972, La nuit américaine (aka Day for Night) 1973, La maman et la putain (The Mother and the Whore) 1973, De quoi s'agit-il? (dir) 1974, Umarmungen und andere Sachen 1975, Les lolos de Lola 1976, L'amour en fuite (Love on the Run) 1979, Parano 1980, La cassure 1981, Aiutami a sognare (Help Me Dream) 1981, Rebelote 1983, Paris vu par... vingt ans après (Paris Seen By... 20 Years After) 1984, Treasure Island 1985, Csak egy mozi 1985, Détective 1985, Boran – Zeit zum Zielen 1986, Corps et biens (Lost with All Hands) 1986, Osseqq oder Die Wahrheit über Hänsel und Gretel 1987, Jane B. par Agnès V. 1987, Les keufs (Lady Cops) 1987, 36 fillette (Junior Size 36) 1988, La couleur du vent (The Colour of the Wind) 1988, Bunker Palace Hôtel 1989, I Hired a Contract Killer 1990, Paris s'éveille (Paris Awakens) 1991, C'est la vie 1991, La vie de bohème (Bohemian Life) 1992, La naissance de l'amour (The Birth of Love) 1993, Personne ne m'aime (Nobody Loves Me) 1994, Les cent et une nuits de Simon Cinéma (A Hundred and One Nights of Simon Cinema) 1995, Mon homme (My Man) 1996, Le journal du séducteur (Diary of a Seducer) 1996, Irma Vep 1996,

Pour rire! 1996, Elizabeth (uncredited) 1998, Innocent 1999, Une affaire de goût (A Question of Taste) 2000, L'affaire Marcorelle (The Marcorelle Affair) 2000, Ni neibian jidian (What Time Is It There?) 2001, Le Pornographe (The Pornographer) 2001, La guerre à Paris (The War in Paris) 2002, Folle embellie 2004, Léaud de Hurle-dents (writer) 2004, J'ai vu tuer Ben Barka 2005, Visage 2009. *Television includes:* L'éducation sentimentale (mini-series) 1973, Le petit pommier 1981, Mersonne ne m'aime 1982, Le tueur assis 1985, L'herbe rouge 1985, Néo Polar (series; episode Des choses qui arrivent) 1985, Grandeur et décadence 1986, Sei delitti per padre Brown (mini-series) 1988, Femme de papier (Front Woman) 1989, L'homme aux cercles bleus 2009.

LEAVER, Sir Christopher, Kt, GBE, KStJ, JP; British business executive; b. 3 Nov. 1937, London, England; s. of Dr Robert Leaver and Audrey Kerpen; m. Helen Mireille Molyneux Benton 1975; one s. two d.; ed Eastbourne Coll.; commissioned, Royal Army Ordnance Corps 1956–58; mem. Retail Food Trades Wages Council 1963–64; JP, Inner London 1970–83, City 1974–93; mem. Council, Royal Borough of Kensington and Chelsea 1971–74; Alderman, Court of Common Council (Ward of Dowgate), City of London 1974–2002, Sheriff, City of London 1979–80, Lord Mayor of London 1981–82; Chair. London Tourist Bd Ltd 1983–89; Deputy Chair. Thames Water PLC 1989–93, Chair. 1993–94, Vice-Chair. 1994–2000; mem. Bd of Brixton Prison 1975–78, Comm. of Lt for City of London 1982–2002, Finance Cttee of London Diocesan Fund 1983–86, Council of Mission to Seamen 1983–93; Adviser to Sec. of State on Royal Parks 1993–96; Gov. Christ's Hosp. School 1975–2002, City of London Girls' School 1975–78, City Univ. 1978–2002 (Chancellor City Univ. 1981–82), City of London Freemen's School 1980–81, Music Therapy Trust 1981–89; Chair. Young Musicians' Symphony Orchestra Trust 1979–81, London Tourist Bd 1983–89, Eastbourne Coll. 1988–2006; Pres. City of London Bowling Club 1981; Vice-Pres. Nat. Playing Fields Asscn 1983–99, Bridewell Royal Hosp. 1983–89; Chair. Pathfinder Properties PLC 1997; Dir (non-exec.) Bath & Portland Group PLC 1983–85, Thermal Scientific PLC 1985–88, Unionamerica Holdings 1994–97, Pathfinder Minerals PLC 1997–2002, Pathfinder Repossessions II Ltd 1998–2002, The Turkish Earthquake Disaster Relief Fund 1999; Trustee, Chichester Festival Theatre 1982–97, London Symphony Orchestra 1983–90; Church Warden, St Olave's Hart Street 1975–89, Church Commr 1982–93, 1996–99; Hon. mem. Guildhall School of Music 1982; Hon. Col 151 Regt RCT(V) 1983–89; Hon. Col Commdt RCT 1988–91; Hon. Liveryman, Worshipful Co. of Farmers 1980, Worshipful Co. of Environmental Cleaners; Freeman, Worshipful Co. of Watermen and Lightermen, Liveryman Co. of Water Conservators; Master Worshipful Co. of Carmen 1987–88; KStJ 1982; Order of Oman; Hon. DMus (City Univ.) 1982. *Leisure interests:* gardening, music, travel.

LEAVER, Christopher John, CBE, BSc, MA, PhD, DIC, ARCS, FRS, FRSE; British scientist and academic; *Emeritus Professor of Plant Sciences, University of Oxford;* b. 31 May 1942, Bristol; s. of Douglas P. Leaver and Elizabeth C. Leaver; m. Anne Huggins 1971; one s. one d.; ed Imperial Coll. of Science, London, Univ. of Oxford; Fulbright Scholar, Purdue Univ., Ind., USA 1966–68; Scientific Officer, ARC Unit of Plant Physiology, Imperial Coll. London 1968–69; Lecturer, Univ. of Edinburgh 1969–80, Reader 1980–86, Science and Eng Research Council Sr Research Fellow, 1985–89, Prof. of Plant Molecular Biology 1986–89; Sibthorpian Prof. of Plant Sciences, Univ. of Oxford 1990–2007, now Prof. Emer., Head of Dept of Plant Sciences 1991–2007; Nuffield Commonwealth Bursary, Sr Visiting Fellowship (SERC), CSIRO Div. of Plant Industry, Canberra 1975; European Molecular Biology Org. Long-term Fellowship, Biozentrum, Basle 1980; Trustee and mem. Governing Council, John Innes Centre, Norwich 1984–; Trustee, Nat. History Museum, London 1997–2006; mem. Council, Agric. and Food Research Council 1990–93; mem. Ministry of Agric., Fisheries and Food Priorities Bd 1990–93; mem. Royal Soc. Council 1992–94; mem. European Molecular Biology Org. (Council mem. 1992–97, Chair. 1996–97), Advisory Council on Science and Tech. 1992–93, Council Biochemical Soc. (Chair. NA & MB Group) (Vice-Chair. Exec. Cttee 2002–04, Chair. 2005–07); Dir Isis Innovation Ltd, Univ. of Oxford 1996–2002; Visiting Prof. Univ. of Western Australia 2002–; Del. Oxford Univ. Press 2002–07; mem. Individual Merit Promotion Panel, Biotechnology and Biological Sciences Research Council (BBSRC) 1996–2005 (mem. BBSRC Council 2000–03); Chair. External Scientific Advisory Bd, Inst. of Molecular and Cell Biology, Univ. of Oporto; mem. Scientific Advisory Bd, Inst. of Molecular and Cellular Biology, Singapore, Int. Advisory Panel, A*Star Graduate Acad., Singapore, ITQB Advisory Cttee, Univ. of Lisbon; mem. Academia Europaea; corresponding mem., American Soc. of Plant Biologists 2003; Emer. Fellow, St John's Coll. Oxford; Huxley Gold Medal, Imperial Coll. 1970; Tate & Lyle Award, Phytochemical Soc. of Europe 1984, Humboldt Prize 1997. *Publications:* ed. several books; numerous papers in int. scientific journals. *Leisure interests:* walking and talking in Upper Coquetdale. *E-mail:* chris.leaver@plants.ox.ac.uk (office).

LEAVER, Peter Lawrence Oppenheim, QC; British lawyer; b. 28 Nov. 1944; s. of Marcus Isaac Leaver and Lena Leaver (née Oppenheim); m. Jane Rachel Pearl 1969; three s. one d.; ed Aldenham School, Elstree, Trinity Coll., Dublin; called to Bar, Lincoln's Inn 1967, QC 1987, Recorder 1994–, Bencher 1995; Chief Exec. Football Asscn Premier League 1997–99; Chair. Bar Cttee 1989, Int. Practice Cttee 1990; mem. Cttee on Future of the Legal Profession 1986–88, Council of Legal Ed. 1986–91, Gen. Council of the Bar 1987–90; Dir Investment Man. Regulatory Org. 1994–2000; Deputy High Court Judge; Deputy Chair. Financial Services Authority Regulatory Decisions Cttee; mem. Chartered Inst. of Arbitrators, Soc. of Legal Scholars; mem. Dispute Resolution Panel for Winter Olympics, Salt Lake City 2002; recent work includes acting in large-scale arbitration in Dubai (validity of termination of man. contract governed by Middle Eastern law), acting in Grupo Torras litigation (Court of Appeal), appearing for firm of stockbrokers in MGNPT Ltd vs Invesco, acting in Girozentrale and Bank der Österreichischen Sparkassen AG vs TOSG Fund Ltd litigation, appearing for 47 banks in Walker vs Standard Chartered Bank and Jasaro SA vs Standard Chartered Bank litigation, acting in Dimskal Shipping Co. SA vs ITWF The Evia Luck case (House of Lords), appearing in Agip (Africa) Ltd vs Jackson litigation (Court of Appeal), acting in MacLaine Watson vs Dept of Trade and Industry and Int. Tin Council case. *Publication:* Pre-Trial and Pre-Hearing Procedures Worldwide (contrib.) 1990. *Leisure interests:* sport, theatre, wine, opera. *Address:* The Chambers of Lord Grabiner QC, 1 Essex Court, Temple, London, EC4Y 9AR (office); 5 Hamilton Terrace, London, NW8 9RE, England (home). *Telephone:* (20) 7583-2000 (office); (20) 7286-0208 (home).

Fax: (20) 7520-4837 (office). *E-mail:* pleaver@oeclaw.co.uk (office). *Website:* www .oeclaw.co.uk (office).

LEAVEY, Thomas Edward, MA, PhD; American international postal official (retd); b. 10 Nov. 1934, Kansas City, Mo.; m. Anne Roland 1968; ed Josephinum Coll., Columbus, Ohio, Inst. Catholique, Paris and Princeton Univ.; Prof. Farleigh Dickinson Univ. Teaneck, NJ and George Washington Univ., Washington, DC 1968–70; various man. and exec. positions in US Postal Services, Los Angeles, Chicago and Washington DC 1970–87; Asst Postmaster-Gen. Int. Postal Affairs, USPS HQ 1987–94; Chair. Exec. Council, Universal Postal Union (UPU) 1989–94, Dir-Gen. Int. Bureau of UPU 1995–2004; John Wanamaker Award 1991, Heinrich von Stephan Medal. *Leisure interests:* golf, tennis.

LEAVITT, Michael Okerlund; American politician, insurance industry executive and fmr government official; b. 11 Feb. 1951, Cedar City, Utah; s. of Dixie Leavitt and Anne Okerlund; m. Jacalyn Smith; four s. one d.; ed S Utah Univ.; Sales Rep. Leavitt Group, Cedar City 1972–74, Account Exec. 1974–76; Man. Underwriting, Salt Lake City 1976–82, COO 1982–84, Pres. and CEO 1984–92; mem. Bd of Dirs Pacificorp, Portland, Ore., Utah Power and Light Co., Salt Lake City, Great Western Thrift & Loan, Salt Lake City; mem. staff, Reagan–Bush '84; Gov. of Utah 1993–2003; Admin. US Environmental Protection Agency, Washington, DC 2003–05; US Sec. of Health and Human Services 2005–09. *Leisure interest:* golf. *Address:* c/o Department of Health and Human Services, 200 Independence Avenue, SW, Washington, DC 20201, USA.

LEBED, Aleksey Ivanovich; Russian politician; b. 14 April 1955, Novocherkassk, Rostov Region; m.; one s. one d.; ed Ryazan Higher School of Airborne Troops, Frunze Mil. Acad., St Petersburg State Univ.; mil. service in Afghanistan 1982; participated in mil. operations in different parts of USSR 1980–92; Regt Commdr, 14th Army in Chişinău 1992, resgnd 1995; mem. State Duma 1995–96; Head of Govt Repub. of Khakassia 1996–2009; mem. Council of Fed. 1996–2001; mem. Congress of Russian Communities; Order of the Red Star; Dr hc (Khakassia Katanov State Univ.); Hon. Diploma (Supreme Council, Repub. of Khakassia); Medal for Courage, Peter the Great Prize 2001. *Publication:* article on regional econ. devt. *Leisure interests:* football, table tennis, billiards, downhill skiing. *Address:* c/o House of Government, prosp. Lenina 67, 655019 Abakan, Republic of Khakassia, Russia.

LEBEDEV, Aleksander Yevgenyevich; Russian banker; *President, National Reserve Bank;* b. 16 Dec. 1960; m.; one s.; ed Moscow Inst. of Int. Relations; staff mem. Inst. mem. of Econs of World Socialist System, USSR Acad. of Sciences 1982–83; joined Ministry of Foreign Affairs 1983, First, then Second Sec. Embassy to UK 1987–92; Rep. Swiss Bank in Russia 1992–93; Founder and Chair. of Bd Russian Investment Finance Co. 1993–; Pres. Nat. Reserve Bank 1995–; Chair. Nat. Investment Bd 1999–. *Address:* National Reserve Bank, N. Barmannaya str. 37A, 107066 Moscow, Russia (office). *Telephone:* (495) 956-32-30 (office). *Fax:* (495) 596-32-30 (office).

LEBEDEV, Pavlo Valentynovych; Ukrainian economist, business executive and politician; b. 12 July 1962, Novomikhailovskii, Krasnodar Krai, Russia; m.; five d.; ed Yaroslavl Higher Mil. Financial School; began career as locksmith, Orlyatko 1979–80; performed mil. service in Chernivtsi garrison, becoming Head, Bn Financial Service, later Deputy Head of Div. Financial Service and Inspector-Auditor 1984–92; Chair. Prestige-Inter (leather goods co.) 1992–99; Councillor, Chernivtsi Municipal Council 1994–2000, also Chair. of Budget Comm. and Chair. of Privatization Comm.; Financial Dir Tytan PJSC (chemical plant), Armyansk 1999–2002; Chair. Supervisory Bd Kremenchuk Steel Plant, Kremenchuk and Dnipropetrovsk Co., Dnipropetrovsk 2002–05; Pres. Inter Car Group (investment group) 2005–06, Hon. Pres. 2006–; Pres. Sevastopol Econ. Devt Fund 2006–12; mem. Verkhovna Rada (Supreme Council, Parl.) 2006–13 (parl. mandate annulled by Parl.); Minister of Defence 2012–14 (dismissed); Medal of Distinction in Mil. Service, 1st Class, Crimean Autonomous Repub. State Prize in Industry, Merited Economist of Ukraine 2011. *Address:* c/o Ministry of Defence, 01021 Kyiv, vul. M. Hrushevskoho 30/1, Ukraine. *E-mail:* webmaster@mil.gov.ua.

LEBEDEV, Col-Gen. Sergei Nikolayevich; Russian international organization official and fmr intelligence officer; *Executive Secretary, Commonwealth of Independent States;* b. 9 April 1948, Jizzax, Uzbek SSR; m. Vera Mikhailovna; two s.; ed Kyiv Polytechnic Inst., Ukrainian SSR, Diplomatic Acad. of USSR; staff mem., Chernihiv br., Kyiv Polytechnic Inst. 1970; army service 1971–72; with state security bodies 1973–75, Foreign Intelligence Service 1975–78; Rep. of Foreign Intelligence Service to USA 1998–2000; Dir Fed. Foreign Intelligence Service (SVR) 2000–07; Exec. Sec. Commonwealth of Independent States (CIS) 2007–; numerous state awards. *Leisure interests:* travelling, Greco-Roman wrestling, shooting. *Address:* Office of the Executive Secretary, Commonwealth of Independent States, 220000 Minsk, vul. Kirova 17, Belarus (office). *Telephone:* (17) 222-35-17 (office). *Fax:* (17) 227-23-39 (office). *E-mail:* anna@cis.minsk.by (office). *Website:* www.cis.minsk.by (office).

LEBEDEVA, Tatyana Romanovna; Russian athlete; b. 21 July 1976, Sterlitamak, Volgograd; m.; one d.; specialises in triple jump and long jump; set two world records at 2004 World Indoor Championships in Budapest, finished with leap of 15.36m; produced best-ever series of triple jumps prior to 2000 Olympic Games, of 15.14m, 15.32m, 15.15m, 15.16m, 14.86m; personal best of 7.33m in long jump, Tula 2004; winner Gold Medal for triple jump, European Cup, Gateshead 2000, Bremen 2001, European Indoor Championships, Ghent 2000, Goodwill Games, Brisbane 2001, World Championships, Edmonton 2001, World Championships, Paris 2003, Russian Indoor Championships 2003, World Indoor Championships, Budapest 2004, European Championships, Gothenburg 2006; winner Gold Medal for long jump, World Indoor Championships, Budapest 2004, Olympic Games, Athens 2004, World Championships, Osaka 2007, Olympic Games, Beijing 2008; winner Silver Medal for triple jump, Int. Asscn of Athletics Feds (IAAF) World Cup, Johannesburg 1998, Goodwill Games, NY 1998, Olympic Games, Sydney 2000, World Indoor Championships, Lisbon 2001, World Championships, Osaka 2007, Olympic Games, Beijing 2008; winner Silver Medal for long jump, Olympic Games, Beijing 2008, World Championships, Berlin 2009; winner Bronze Medal for triple jump, World Jr Championships 1994, Olympic Games, Athens 2004; only athlete to record six wins in six Golden Leagues, winning Golden League jackpot 2005; mem. Volgograd Army Club, RUS. *Address:* c/o All-Russia

Athletic Federation, 8, Luzhnetskaya nab., Moscow 119992, Russia. Website: www .lebedeva.ru.

LEBEGUE, Daniel Simon Georges, BL; French independent financial director; *Chairman, Institut Français des Administrateurs;* b. 4 May 1943, Lyon; s. of Robert Lebègue and Denise Lebègue (née Flachet); m. Chantal Biron 1970; one s. one d.; ed Univ. of Lyons, Inst. for Political Sciences and Nat. School for Admin., Paris; civil servant, Ministry of Economy and Finance 1969–73; Financial Adviser, Embassy in Japan 1974–76; Head of Balance of Payments Section, Treasury 1976–79, Head of Monetary Funds Section 1979–80; Deputy Dir of Savings and Financial Market 1980–81; Counsellor in charge of Economy and Finance, Prime Minister's Office 1981–83; Head of Dept of Financial and Monetary Affairs at Treasury 1983–84, Head of Treasury 1984–87; Pres. and COO Banque Nat. de Paris 1987–96, Vice-Chair. 1996–97; Pres. and CEO Caisse des dépôts et consignations (CDC) 1997–2002, Chair. CDC Ixis (formed after merger of CDC and CNCE) 2001–02; Dir SCOR SE 2003–; Chair. Institut Français des Administrateurs 2003–, Observatoire sur la Responsibilité Sociétale des Enterprises 2008–; currently Chair. Transparency International (France); Chevalier, Légion d'honneur, Ordre nat. du Mérite. *Publications:* Le Trésor et la politique financière 1988, La fiscalité de l'épargne dans le marché unique européen 1988. *Leisure interests:* opera, cinema, hiking. *Address:* Institut Français des Administrateurs, 27 avenue de Friedland, 75382 Paris Cedex 08, France (office). *Telephone:* 1-55-65-81-40 (office). *Fax:* 1-55-65-75-99 (office). *E-mail:* president@ifa-asso.com (office). *Website:* www.ifa-asso.com (office).

LEBEL, The Hon. Denis, PC, BA; Canadian politician; *Minister of Infrastructure, Communities and Intergovernmental Affairs;* b. 26 May 1954, Roberval, Quebec; m. Danielle Girard; two c.; Mayor of Roberval 2000–07; MP for Roberval-Lac-Saint-Jean 2007–; Minister of State for the Econ. Devt Agency of Canada for the Regions of Quebec 2008–, Minister of Transport, Infrastructure and Communities 2011–13, Minister of Infrastructure, Communities and Intergovernmental Affairs 2013–; mem. Bd of Dirs Union des municipalités du Québec; fmr Chair. Caucus des municipalités voisines des Premières Nations; fmr Dir Infrastructure Québec; fmr Vice-Pres. Société d'aide au développement des collectivités Lac-Saint-Jean Ouest, Agence régionale de santé du Saguenay–Lac-Saint-Jean; mem. Conservative Party of Canada. *Address:* Department of Infrastructure, 180 Kent Street, Suite 1100, Ottawa, ON K1P 0B6, Canada (office). *Telephone:* (613) 948-1148 (office). *Fax:* (613) 948-9393 (office). *E-mail:* info@infc.gc.ca (office). *Website:* www.infrastructure.gc.ca (office).

LEBEL, Jean-Jacques; French artist and art critic; b. 1936, Neuilly-sur-Seine; ed Accad. delle Belle Arti, Florence, Italy; first one-man show Galleria Numero, Florence 1955; has exhibited in many galleries and museums in Europe, USA and Japan; ran Front Unique (poetry, art and politics magazine); worked with American Happening artists, Claes Oldenburg 1962 and Allan Kaprow 1963; involved in NO!art and took part in Involvement Show and Doom Show 1960–61, March Gallery, New York; has produced more than 80 Happenings (Direct Poetry actions or performances worldwide); set up Festival de la Libre Expression, American Center in Paris (an int. exchange of experimental arts); directed Picasso's Desire Caught by the Tail 1967; has participated in most major int. poetry festivals and art shows since 1960s; co-ed. series of re-edns of historical anarchist texts for Belfond publishing house, Paris; has curated 20 int. art shows, including shows by Erro, Paysages (Musee d'Art Moderne de la Ville de Paris 1985), Victor Hugo, peintre (Galleria d'Arte Moderna, Ca' Pesaro, Venice 1993), Disegno del nostro secolo (Fondazione Antonio Mazzotta, Milano 1994), Picabia, Maquinas y Espanolas (IVAM, Valencia, Fuindacio Tapies, Barcelona 1995), Picabia, 1922 (Musee National d'Art Moderne, Centre Georges Pompidou, Paris 1996), Juegos Surrealistas (Museo Thyssen-Bornemisza, Madrid 1996), Victor Hugo, du Chaos dans le pinceau (Museo Thyssen-Bornemisza, Madrid and Maison de Victor Hugo, Paris 2000), Picasso erotique (Musee des Beaux Arts, Montreal 2001). *Works include:* 8m high Monument to Felix Guattari (open-ended motorized multi-media desiring machine, including live performances and videos by poets, philosophers, musicians, anti-psychiatrists and artists close to Guattari and Lebel), Off Limits Exhbn, Centre Georges Pompidou, Paris 1994, large installation entitled Reliquaire pour un Culte de Venus. *Publications:* Happening (The Burial of Tinguely's Chose) 1960; has published 10 books of essays on culture and politics, including Poesie Directe, Happenings and Interventions, Paris 1994; trans of Ginsberg, Corso, Burroughs, Ferlinghetti were the first to appear in French. *Address:* c/o Berliner Kunstprojekt, Gneisenaustr. 33, Berlin -Kreuzberg, Germany (office).

LeBLANC, Matthew Steven (Matt); American actor; b. 25 July 1967, Newton, Mass; son of Paul LeBlanc and Patricia LeBlanc; m. Melissa McKnight 2003 (divorced 2006); one d.; ed Newton North High School; trained as a carpenter; appeared in TV commercials for a variety of products, New York 1987; began formal acting training 1988; f. Fort Hill Productions (production co.). *Films include:* Anything to Survive 1990, Grey Knight (int. title The Killing Box) 1993, Red Shoe Diaries 3: Another Woman's Lipstick 1993, Lookin' Italian 1993, Ed 1996, Red Shoe Diaries 7: Burning Up 1997, Lost in Space 1998, Charlie's Angels 2000, All the Queen's Men 2001, Charlie's Angels: Full Throttle 2003. *Television includes:* series: TV 101 (as Chuck Bender) 1988, Top of the Heap 1991, Vinnie & Bobby 1992, Red Shoe Diaries, Rebel Highway, Friends (as Joey Tribbiani) (Screen Actors Guild Award for Outstanding Performance by an Ensemble in a Comedy Series 1995, TV Choice Actor, Teen Choice Awards 2002, Favorite Male Television Star, People's Choice Awards 2005) 1994–2004, Joey 2004–06, Episodes (Golden Globe Award for Best Performance by an Actor in a Television Series – Comedy or Musical 2012) 2011; films: Anything to Survive 1990, Reform School Girl 1994, The Prince (dir) 2006, Jonah Hex (exec. producer) 2010. *Leisure interest:* landscape photography. *Address:* c/o United Talent Agency, 9560 Wilshire Boulevard, Suite 500, Beverly Hills, CA 90212-2401, USA. *Telephone:* (310) 273-6700. *Fax:* (310) 247-1111. *Website:* www.unitedtalent.com.

LEBOUDER, Jean-Pierre; Central African Republic politician; b. 1944; ed Ecole nationale supérieure agronomique, Toulouse, France; Dir Research Centre, Union cotonnière centrafricaine 1971–72, Dir-Gen. 1974–76; Minister of Rural Devt 1976, of Planning, Statistics and Int. Co-operation 1978–80; Prime Minister 1980–81; Minister of State, responsible for Planning, the Economy, Finance, the Budget and Int. Co-operation 2003–05.

LEBOWITZ, Joel L., MS, PhD; American mathematician and academic; *Professor, Department of Mathematics, Rutgers University;* b. 10 May 1930, Taceva, Czechoslovakia; m. 1st Estelle Mandelbaum 1953 (died 1996); 2nd Ann K. Beneduce 1999; ed Brooklyn Coll. and Syracuse Univ.; Nat. Science Foundation Postdoctoral Fellow, Yale Univ. 1956–57; Asst Prof. Stevens Inst. of Tech. 1957–59; Asst Prof. Belfer Grad. School of Science, Yeshiva Univ. 1959–60, Assoc. Prof. 1960–65, Prof. of Physics 1965–77, Chair. Dept of Physics 1968–76; Dir Center for Mathematical Sciences Research and Prof. of Math. and Physics, Rutgers Univ. 1977–; mem. NAS, AAAS, New York Acad. of Sciences, American Physical Soc.; Dr hc (Ecole Polytechnique Fédérale, Lausanne, Clark Univ.) 1999; Henri Poincaré Prize, IAMP 2000, Boltzmann Medal 1992, Max Planck Research Award 1993, Delmar S. Fahrney Medal, Franklin Inst. 1994, AAAS Scientific Freedom and Responsibility Award 1999 and other distinctions. *Publications:* more than 450 scientific papers. *Address:* Room 612, Hill Center, Building For The Mathematical Sciences, Busch Campus, Rutgers University, New Brunswick, NJ 08903, USA (office). *Telephone:* (732) 445-2390 (ext. 6025) (office). *Fax:* (732) 445-4936 (office). *E-mail:* lebowitz@math.rutgers.edu (office). *Website:* www.math .rutgers.edu/~lebowitz (office).

LEBRANCHU, Marylise; French politician and academic; *Minister of Reform of the State, Decentralization and Public Service;* b. 25 April 1947, Loudéac (Côtes-d'Armor); d. of Adolphe Perrault Lebranchu and Marie Epert; m. Jean Lebranchu 1970; three c.; ed Rennes Univ.; began career as researcher, semi-public co., Nord-Finistère 1973–78; joined Parti Socialiste Unifié (PSU) 1972, Parti Socialiste (PS) 1977; Parl. Asst to MP Marie Jacq 1978–93; Municipal Councillor, Morlaix (Finistère) 1983, Mayor 1995–97; Regional Councillor, Brittany 1986–; mem. Assemblée nationale (Parl.) for Finistère 1997, 2002–12; Minister of State attached to Minister for the Economy, Finance and Industry, with responsibility for small and medium-sized enterprises, trade and artisan activities 1997–2000, Minister of Justice and Keeper of the Seals 2000–02, Minister of Reform of the State, Decentralization and Public Service 2012–; Jr Lecturer in Econs, Univ. of Brest 1990–; Trombinoscope Politician of the Year Award 2000. *Publications:* Etre Juste, Justement, Brèves de campagne. *Leisure interest:* music. *Address:* Ministry of Reform of the State, Decentralization and Public Service, 80 rue de Lille, 75007 Paris Cedex 07, France (office). *Telephone:* 1-43-19-23-50 (office). *Fax:* 1-43-19-23-97 (office). *E-mail:* sec-mredfp-sp@action-publique.gouv.fr. *Website:* www.fonction -publique.gouv.fr (office).

LeBRETON, Marjory; Canadian politician; *Leader of the Government in the Senate and Secretary of State for Seniors;* b. 1940, Nepean, Ont.; m. Douglas LeBreton; one s. (one d. deceased); ed Ottawa Business Coll.; worked for Progressive Conservative Party of Canada (PC) nat. campaign group 1962, 1963 general elections; worked in office of John G. Diefenbaker 1963–67, in office of Robert L. Stanfield 1967–75, office of Joe Clark 1976–79; mem. Senate 1993–; fmr Chief Opposition Whip, fmr mem. several Standing Cttees including Social Affairs, Human Rights, Forestry and Agric., Internal Economy, Banking, currently Co-Chair Senate Standing Cttee on Health, Leader of the Govt in the Senate 2006–, Sec. of State for Seniors 2007–; Chair. Mothers Against Drunk Drivers, Canada. *Address:* Senate of Canada, Ottawa, ON K1A 0A4, Canada (office). *Telephone:* (613) 943-0756 (office). *E-mail:* lebrem@sen.parl.gc.ca (office). *Website:* www.parl .gc.ca (office).

LECHLEITER, John C., BSc, MSc, PhD; American pharmaceutical industry executive; *Chairman, President and CEO, Eli Lilly & Company;* m. Sarah Lechleiter; two s. one d.; ed Xavier Univ., Cincinnati, OH, Harvard Univ., Mass (NSF Fellow); joined Eli Lilly as sr organic chemist in process research and devt 1979, Pharmaceutical Product Devt Dir, Lilly Research Centre, Windlesham, UK 1983–86, Man. European Research and Devt, USA 1986–88, Dir Devt Projects Man. 1988–91, Exec. Dir Pharmaceutical Product Devt 1991–93, Vice-Pres. 1993, Vice-Pres. Regulatory Affairs 1994–96, Vice-Pres. Lilly Research Labs 1996–98, Sr Vice-Pres. Pharmaceutical Products 1998–2001, Exec. Vice-Pres. Pharmaceutical Products and Corporate Devt 2001–04, Exec. Vice-Pres. Pharmaceutical Operations 2004–05, mem. Bd Dirs, Pres. and COO 2005–08, Pres. and CEO April 2008–, Chair. Dec. 2008–; mem. Bd of Dirs United Way of Cen. Indiana, Fairbanks Inst. (also mem. Exec. Cttee), Cincinnati, Indianapolis Downtown, Inc., Pharmaceutical Research and Mfrs of America (PhRMA), Nike, Inc.; mem. Business Roundtable, Business Council; mem. Visiting Cttee, Harvard Business School 2004–, Health Policy and Man. Council, Harvard School of Public Health 2004–, Dean's Advisory Bd, Indiana Univ. School of Medicine; Distinguished Advisor, The Children's Museum of Indianapolis, Bd United Way Worldwide, Bd Life Sciences Foundation, Bd Central Indiana Corp. Partnership, 2012 Indianapolis Super Bowl Host Cttee; mem. Bd of Trustees Xavier Univ.; mem. ACS; Hon. DBA (Marian Coll., Indianapolis). *Address:* Eli Lilly & Co., Lilly Corporate Center, Indianapolis, IN 46285, USA (office). *Telephone:* (317) 276-2000 (office). *Fax:* (317) 277-6579 (office). *E-mail:* info@lilly.com (office). *Website:* www.lilly.com (office).

LECLERCQ, Patrick; French diplomatist; b. 2 Aug. 1938, Lille; m. 2nd Marie-Alice Berard; two s.; one s. from previous m.; ed Institut d'Etudes Politiques, Paris, Ecole Nat. d'Admin; joined Diplomatic Service 1966; Consul-Gen. Montréal, Canada 1982–85; Amb. to Jordan 1985–89, to Egypt 1991–96, to Spain 1996–99; Minister of State and Dir of External Relations for Monaco 2000–05; Officier, Légion d'honneur, Commdr, Ordre nat. du Mérite, several foreign decorations, including Orden del Merito and Isabel la Católica, Spain, Ordre de Saint-Charles, Monaco. *Address:* 3 rue Francisque Sarcey, 75116 Paris, France. *Telephone:* 1-40-72-65-28. *E-mail:* leclercq_patrick@hotmail.fr.

LECONTE, Patrice; French film director; b. 12 Nov. 1947, Tours; ed Institut des Hautes Etudes Cinématographiques. *Films include:* L'Espace vital 1969, Le Laboratoire de l'angoisse 1971, La Famille heureuse (Famille Gazul) 1973, Les Vécés étaient fermés de l'interieur 1976, Les Bronzés 1978, Les Bronzés font du ski 1979, Viens chez moi, j'habite chez une copine 1981, Ma femme s'appelle reviens 1982, Circulez y'a rien à voir 1983, Les Spécialistes 1985, Tandem 1987), Monsieur Hire 1989, Le Mari de la coiffeuse 1990, Contre l'oubli 1991, Le Batteur du boléro 1992, Tango 1993, Le Parfum d'Yvonne 1994, Lumière et compagnie 1996, Les Grands ducs 1996, Ridicule 1996, Une chance sur deux 1998, La Fille sur le pont 1999, La Veuve de Saint-Pierre 2000, Félix et Lola 2001, Rue des plaisirs 2002, L'Homme du train 2002, Confidences trop intimes 2004, Dogora-Ouvrons les yeux

2004, Les Bronzés 3: amis pour la vie 2006, Mon meilleur ami 2006, La Guerre des miss 2008.

LEDER, Philip, MD, FAAS; American geneticist and academic; *John Emory Andrus Professor Emeritus of Genetics and Head, Department of Genetics, Harvard Medical School;* b. 19 Nov. 1934, Washington, DC; ed Harvard Coll. and Harvard Medical School; Intern and Resident in Medicine, Univ. of Minnesota Hosps 1960–62; Research Assoc., Biochemical Genetics, NIH Nat. Heart Inst., Bethesda, Md 1962, joined lab. of Marshall Nirenberg 1963, Research Medical Officer, Biosynthesis, Lab. of Biochemistry, Nat. Cancer Inst. 1966–69; Chair. Dept of Biochemistry, Grad. Program of Foundation for Advanced Educ. in the Sciences 1968–73, mem. Bd of Dirs 1968–74 (Vice-Pres. Foundation 1970–71, Pres. 1973); Head, Section on Molecular Genetics, Lab. of Molecular Genetics, Nat. Inst. of Child Health and Human Devt 1969–71, Dir Lab. for Molecular Genetics 1972–80; John Emory Andrus Prof. of Genetics and Head Dept of Genetics, Harvard Medical School 1980–2008, Prof. Emer. 2008–, Dir Harvard Inst. of Human Genetics 1995–2008; Sr Investigator, Howard Hughes Medical Inst. 1986–2004; Visiting Scientist, Weizmann Inst., Rehovot, Israel 1965–66; Dir Pharmacia (fmrly Monsanto Co.) 1990, Genome Therapeutics, Inc. 1994, Schering-Plough Corpn 2003; mem. NAS 1979, American Acad. of Arts and Sciences 1981, Inst. of Medicine 1982; Trustee and Chair. Bd Charles A. Revson Foundation; Trustee Foundation for Advanced Educ. in the Sciences, Hadassah Medical Org. 1996–; Hon. Trustee, Massachusetts Gen. Hosp.; Hon. DSc (Yale Univ.) 1984, (Mount Sinai Medical Center) 1985, (Univ. of Guelph) 1986, (Hebrew Univ. of Jerusalem) 1996; Detur Award for Academic Excellence 1954, NIH Director's Award 1976, Drew Award in Biomedical Research, CIBA-Geigy Ltd 1978, Award in Biological and Medical Sciences, New York Acad. of Sciences 1978, Warren Triennial Prize, Massachusetts Gen. Hosp. 1980, Dickson Prize, Univ. of Pittsburgh School of Medicine 1980, NAS Richard Lounsbery Award 1981, Harvey Prize in Human Health, Technion-Israel Inst. of Tech. 1983, Award for Distinguished Research in the Biomedical Sciences, American Asscn of Medical Colls 1983, Steven C. Beering Award for Advancement of Biomedical Science, Indiana Univ. School of Medicine 1984, Bristol-Meyers Award for Distinguished Achievement in Cancer Research (co-recipient) 1985, Giovanni Lorenzini Foundation Prize for Basic Biomedical Research 1987, Albert Lasker Basic Medical Research Award 1987, Cancer Research Award in Basic Sciences Milken Family Medical Foundation 1988, V.D. Mattia Award, Roche Inst. of Molecular Biology 1988, Nat. Medal of Science 1989, Dr H.P. Heinekin Prize for Biochemistry, Royal Netherlands Acad. of Arts and Sciences 1990, Lee Kuan Yew Distinguished Visitorship, Repub. of Singapore 1990, Ernst W. Bertner Award, Univ. of Texas M.D. Anderson Cancer Center 1991, City of Medicine Award, City of Durham, NC 1991, American Coll. of Physicians Award 1991, Distinguished Alumnus Award, NIH Nat. Inst. of Child Health and Human Devt 1994, William Allan Award for Exceptional Contributions in the Field of Human Genetics, American Soc. of Human Genetics 1997, Albert Einstein Lecturer, Israel Acad. of Sciences and Humanities 2000. *Publications:* more than 240 articles in scientific journals. *Address:* Department of Genetics, Harvard Medical School, New Research Building, Room 358d, 77 Avenue Louis Pasteur, Boston, MA 02115, USA (office). *Telephone:* (617) 432-7667 (office). *Fax:* (617) 432-7944 (office). *E-mail:* leder@ receptor.med.harvard.edu (office). *Website:* genetics.med.harvard.edu/faculty/ leder (office).

LEDERMAN, Leon M., PhD; American physicist and academic; *Director Emeritus, Fermilab;* b. 15 July 1922, New York City; s. of the late Morris Lederman; m. 1st Florence Gordon; two d. one s.; m. 2nd Ellen Lederman; ed City Coll. of New York, Columbia Univ., New York; entered US Army 1943, rank of 2nd Lt Signal Corps 1946; grad. research involved building a Wilson Cloud Chamber for Cyclotron Project, Columbia Univ. 1948–51, Asst Prof. of Physics 1951–58, Prof. of Physics 1958–79; organised g-2 experiment, CERN 1958; Dir Nevis Labs 1961–78; Dir Fermi Nat. Accelerator Laboratory (now Fermilab) 1979–89, Dir Emer. 1989–; Prof. of Physics, Univ. of Chicago 1989–; fmr Pritzker Prof. of Science, Illinois Inst. of Tech.; apptd Science Adviser to Gov. of Illinois 1989; apptd Pres. American Asscn for the Advancement of Science 1991; Resident Scholar IMSA Great Minds Program 1998–2012; Founding mem. High Energy Physics Advisory Panel, Int. Cttee on Future Accelerators; Co-founder and mem. Bd of Trustees, Illinois Math. and Science Acad.; mem. American, Finnish and Argentine Nat. Acads of Science; serves on 13 bds of dirs of museums, schools, science orgs and govt agencies; recipient of fellowships from Ford, Guggenheim, Ernest Kepton Adams and Nat. Science Foundations; Hon. Prof., Beijing Normal Univ. Beijing, China 2000; Hon. DSc (City Coll. of New York, Univ. of Chicago, Illinois Inst. of Tech., Northern Illinois Univ., Lake Forest Coll., Carnegie Mellon Univ., Univ. of Pisa, Univ. of Guanajuarto), numerous others; Nat. Medal of Science 1965, Elliot Cresson Medal, Franklin Inst. 1976, Wolf Prize for Physics 1982, Nobel Prize for Physics 1988, Enrico Fermi Prize 1992, Benton Medal, Univ. of Chicago 2008, Vannevar Bush Prize 2012. *Achievements include:* discovery of Neutral K-Meson 1956, discovery of Parity Violation in Pion and Muon Decay 1957, discovery of Antideuteron 1965, discovery of Drell-Yan Process. *Publications include:* Nuclear and Particle Physics (with J. Weneser) 1969, From Quarks to the Cosmos: Tools of Discovery (with David N. Schramm) 1989, Portraits of Great American Scientists 2001, Symmetry and the Beautiful Universe (with Christopher T. Hill) 2004, Quantum Physics for Poets (co-author) 2010; numerous scientific articles. *Leisure interest:* horse-riding. *Address:* Fermilab, PO Box 500, Batavia, IL 60510-0511, USA (office). *Telephone:* (630) 840-3000 (office). *Fax:* (630) 840-4343 (office). *E-mail:* lederman@fnal.gov (office). *Website:* www.fnal.gov (office).

LEDINGHAM, John Gerard Garvin, MA, DM, FRCP; British medical scientist and academic; *Professor Emeritus of Clinical Medicine, University of Oxford;* b. 19 Oct. 1929, London, England; s. of John Ledingham and Una C. Garvin; grandson of J. L. Garvin; m. Dr Elaine Maliphant 1962; four d.; ed Rugby School, New Coll. Oxford and Middlesex Hosp. London; Registrar, Middlesex Hosp. 1960–62; Sr Registrar in Medicine, Westminster Hosp. 1962–64; Visiting Fellow, Columbia Univ., New York 1965–66; Consultant Physician, United Oxford Hosps 1966–74; May Reader in Medicine, Univ. of Oxford 1974–95, Prof. of Clinical Medicine 1989–95, Prof. Emer. 1995–, Dir of Clinical Studies 1977–81, 1990–95; Fellow, New Coll. Oxford 1974–95, Emer. Fellow 1995–, Hon. Fellow 2001–, Sub-Warden 1994–95; Hon. Clinical Dir Biochemical and Clinical NMR Unit, Medical Research

Council 1988–95; mem. Nuffield Council on Bioethics 2001–03; Trustee, Nuffield Trust 1978–2002, Beit Trust 1988–2008; Hon. Fellow, New Coll. Oxford, Distinguished Friend of Oxford 2011; Osler Memorial Medal 2000. *Publications:* Oxford Textbook of Medicine (co-ed.) 1983, Concise Oxford Textbook of Medicine 2000, We Hope to Get Word Tomorrow – The Garvin Family Letters 1914–1916 (co-ed.) 2009; contribs to medical journals. *Leisure interests:* music, reading, golf. *Address:* 124 Oxford Road, Cumnor, Oxford, OX2 9PQ, England. *Telephone:* (1865) 865806. *Fax:* (1865) 865806. *E-mail:* jeled@btopenworld.com.

LEE, Allen Peng-Fei, CBE, OBE, BS, JP; Chinese business executive; b. 24 April 1940, Chefoo; m. Maria Choi Yuen Ha; two s. one d.; ed Univ. of Michigan, USA; joined Lockheed Aircraft Ltd 1966, Test Eng Supervisor 1966–67, Test Eng Man. 1968–70; Eng Operations Man. Fabri-Teck Ltd 1967; Test Man., Ampex Ferrotec Ltd 1970–72, Man. Dir 1974–79; Gen. Man. Dataproducts Hong Kong Ltd 1972–74; Man. Dir Ampex World Operations SA 1979–83, Ampex Far East Operations 1983–; Dir, consultant Elec & Eltek Co. Ltd 1984; Chair. Hong Kong Productivity Council 1982; Chair. Hong Kong Liberal Party 1994–98; Deputy NPC 1997–2004; Chair. Pacific Dimensions Consultants Ltd; Dir Sam Woo Holdings Ltd 2003–; mem. Industry Devt Bd 1983, Hong Kong Gen. Chamber of Commerce (Cttee and Council mem.), Fed. of Hong Kong Industries, Broadcasting Review Bd 1984, Political Section of Preparatory Cttee for Hong Kong Special Admin. Region; Outstanding Young Persons of Hong Kong Award 1977. *Leisure interests:* fishing, swimming, tennis. *Address:* c/o Liberal Party, Shun Ho Tower, 2/F, 24–30 Ice House Street, Central Energy Plaza, Tsimshatsui East, Kowloon, Hong Kong Special Administrative Region, People's Republic of China (office).

LEE, Ang, BA, MFA; American (b. Taiwanese) film director; b. 23 Oct. 1954, Chaochou, Pingtung, Taiwan; m. Jane Lin 1983; two s.; ed Nat. Taiwan Coll. of Arts, Univ. of Illinois, Urbana-Champaign, Tisch School of the Arts, New York Univ.; moved to USA 1978; classmate of Spike Lee at NYU; finished a 16mm short film, Shades of the Lake that won Best Drama Award in Short Film in Taiwan 1982; winner of nat. script-writing contest (Taiwanese Govt) 1990. *Films:* Pushing Hands 1992, The Wedding Banquet (Asia-Pacific Film Festival Best Film) 1993, Eat Drink Man Woman (Asia-Pacific Film Festival Best Film) 1995, Sense and Sensibility 1996, The Ice Storm 1998, Ride with the Devil 1998, Crouching Tiger, Hidden Dragon (Acad. Award for Best Foreign Film, David Lean Award for Best Dir, BAFTA Award 2001, Golden Globe for Best Dir 2001) 1999, Chosen 2001, Hulk 2003, Brokeback Mountain (Venice Film Festival Golden Lion, Critics' Choice Award for Best Film and Best Dir, Golden Globe for Best Dir and Best Drama, Dirs Guild of America Best Dir 2006, BAFTA David Lean Award for Achievement in Direction 2006, Acad. Award for Best Dir 2006) 2005, Sè, Jiè (Lust, Caution) (Golden Lion, Venice Film Festival 2007) 2007, Taking Woodstock 2009, Life of Pi (Academy Award for Best Dir 2013) 2012. *Address:* c/o Creative Artists Agency, 2000 Avenue of the Stars, Los Angeles, CA 90067, USA (office). *Telephone:* (424) 288-2000 (office). *Fax:* (424) 288-2900 (office). *Website:* www.caa.com (office).

LEE, Brett; Australian professional cricketer and television commentator; b. 8 Nov. 1976, Wollongong, NSW; s. of Bob Lee and Helen Lee (née Buxton); m. Elizabeth Kemp 2006 (divorced 2009); one s.; ed Balarang Public School, Oak Flats High School; bowler; lower order right-handed batsman; right-arm fast bowler; plays for NSW 1995–, Australia 1999–2012, Kings XI Punjab 2008–10, Kolkata Knight Riders 2011–, Wellington 2011, Sydney Sixers 2011–; First-class debut: 1994/95; Test debut: Australia v India, Melbourne 26–30 Dec. 1999; One-Day Int. (ODI) debut: Australia v Pakistan, Brisbane 9 Jan. 2000; T20I debut: NZ v Australia, Auckland 17 Feb. 2005; played in 76 Tests, took 310 wickets and scored 1,451 runs, highest score 64, average 20.15, best bowling (innings) 5/30, (match) 9/171; ODIs: 221 matches, scored 1,176 runs, highest score 57, average 17.81, took 380 wickets, average 23.36, best bowling 5/22; First-class: 116 matches, 2,120 runs, highest score 97, average 18.59, took 487 wickets, average 28.22, best bowling 7/114; retd from Test cricket Feb. 2010, from int. cricket July 2012; ranked with Pakistani bowler Shoaib Akhtar as the fastest bowler in contemporary cricket during most of decade 2000–09; first player in Twenty20 Int. cricket to take a hat-trick; launched own fashion label 'BL' 2001; cricket commentator for Channel Nine; mem. (with brother Shane and fmr NSW cricketers Brad McNamara, Gavin Robertson and Richard Chee Quee) rock band Six & Out; inaugural Donald Bradman Young Player of the Year Award 2000, Wisden Young Cricketer of the Year 1999–2000, VB Series Player of the Series 2002–03, VB Series Player of the Series 2004–05, chosen in Australia's Greatest ODI XI (selected by fmr and current Australian ODI reps), chosen in ODI Team of the Year at ICC (Int. Cricket Council) Awards 2005, chosen in Test Team of the Year at ICC Awards 2006, chosen in ODI Team of the Year at ICC Awards 2006, Wisden Cricketer of the Year 2006, DLF Cup Player of the Tournament 2006, Warne-Muralitharan Trophy Player of the Series 2007, Border-Gavaskar Trophy Player of the Series 2007–08, McGilvray Medallist for ABC's Australian Test Player of the year 2007, Australian Test Player of the Year 2008, Allan Border Medallist 2008, chosen in ODI Team of the Year at ICC Awards 2008, chosen in Test Team of the Year at ICC Awards 2008, Champions League Twenty20 Player of the Series 2009. *Television:* fmr Host, Personal Best. *Music:* recording: You're the One For Me (duet with Asha Bhosle). *Publication:* My Life (with James Knight) (autobiog.) 2011. *Address:* c/o Cricket NSW, PO Box 333, Paddington, NSW 2021; c/o Cricket NSW, Driver Avenue, Moore Park, NSW 2021, Australia. *Telephone:* (2) 8302-6000. *Fax:* (2) 8302-6080. *E-mail:* info@cricketnsw.com. *Website:* www.cricketnsw.com.

LEE, C. Y., MArch; Taiwanese (b. Chinese) architect; *Principal, C. Y. Lee & Partners Architects/Planners;* b. 30 Dec. 1938, Guangdong, China; ed Nat. Cheng Kung Univ., Princeton Univ., USA; Prin. C. Y. Lee & Partners Architects/Planners, Taiwan 1978–; Prof., Dept of Architecture, Waseda Univ., Japan 2003–06; architect of Taipei 101, world's tallest building 2004–10; first China Outstanding Architect Award 1995, winner, Architecture Category, Nat. Awards for Arts 2008. *Major works include:* in Taiwan: Hung Kuo Building, Taipei 1989, Grand 50 Tower, Kaohsiung (Taiwan's tallest building 1992–93), Far Eastern Plaza I & II, Taipei 1994, Tuntex Sky Tower, Kaohsiung (Taiwan's tallest building 1997–2004), Grand Formosa, Taichung 1997, Taiwan Taoyuan Int. Airport-Terminal 2, Taoyuan (Buddhist temple, tallest Buddhist Building in the world 2001–06), New Chien-Cheng Circle, Taipei 2003, Taipei 101, Taipei (Taiwan's tallest building 2004–, world's tallest skyscraper 2004–10), W Taipei; in China: Post & Telecommunications Centre, Tianjin 1998, Yuda International Trade Centre, Zhengzhou 1999, Fangyuan Mansion, Shenyang 2001, Jinsha Plaza, Shenyang 2001, Pangu 7 Star Hotel, Beijing 2008. *Address:* C.Y. Lee & Partners Architects/Planners, 13th Floor, No. 178, Sec. 3, Ming-Quan East Road, Taipei, 10542, Taiwan (office). *Telephone:* (2) 2719-8288 (office). *Fax:* (2) 2719-8808 (office). *E-mail:* info@cyleearchitect.com (office). *Website:* www.cyleearchitect.com (office).

LEE, Datuk Chong Wei; Malaysian badminton player; b. 21 Oct. 1982, Georgetown, Penang; began playing badminton at age 11; winner Asian Badminton Championships 2006, Silver Medal, Olympic Games, Beijing 2008, Gold Medal, Commonwealth Games, Delhi 2010, Silver Medal, Asian Games 2010, Winner All-England Open Men's Singles 2010, 2011, Malaysia Open Grand Prix Gold 2011, India Open 2011, Indonesian Open 2011; ranked world No 1 June–July 2006, Aug.–Sept. 2006, Aug. 2008; several awards including Penang Sportsman 2005, 2007, 2008, 2009, Malaysia's Male Olympian 2008. *Address:* c/o Badminton Association of Malaysia, Stadium Juara Bukit Kiara Sports Complex Jalan 1 / 70 D, Bukit Kiara, 60000 Kuala Lumpur, Malaysia. *Website:* www.leechongwei.com.

LEE, Sir Christopher Frank Carandini, Lord of Sarzano; Kt, CBE, CStJ; British actor, author and singer; b. 27 May 1922, London; s. of the late Lt-Col Geoffrey Trollope Lee and of Contessa Estelle Marie Carandini; m. Birgit Kroencke 1961; one d.; ed Summer Fields Preparatory School, Wellington Coll.; served in RAF and Special Forces 1941–46; mentioned in despatches 1944; film industry 1947–; appeared in over 250 motion pictures and TV films; Officier des Arts, Sciences et des Lettres 1973; Officier des Arts et Lettres 2002; Life Achievement Award, Evening Standard Film Awards 2002, Life Achievement Award, Empire Magazine, World Award for Lifetime Achievement, Vienna 2002, German Video Award for Lifetime Achievement 2002, Metal Hammer Golden Gods, BAFTA Fellowship 2011. *Films include:* Corridor of Mirrors 1948, One Night with You 1948, Hamlet (uncredited) 1948, A Song for Tomorrow 1948, Penny and the Pownall Case 1948, My Brother's Keeper 1948, Saraband for Dead Lovers (uncredited) 1948, Scott of the Antarctic 1948, Trottie True 1949, They Were Not Divided 1950, Prelude to Fame 1950, Captain Horatio Hornblower R.N. 1951, Valley of Eagles 1951, The Crimson Pirate 1952, Paul Temple Returns 1952, Babes in Bagdad 1952, Destination Milan 1954, The Dark Avenger 1955, The Cockleshell Heroes 1955, Alias John Preston 1955, Storm Over the Nile 1955, Private's Progress (uncredited) 1956, Port Afrique 1956, Beyond Mombasa 1956, The Battle of the River Plate 1956, Ill Met by Moonlight 1957, Fortune Is a Woman 1957, The Traitor 1957, The Curse of Frankenstein 1957, Bitter Victory 1957, The Truth About Women 1957, A Tale of Two Cities 1958, Dracula 1958, Battle of the V-1 1958, Corridors of Blood 1958, The Hound of the Baskervilles 1959, The Man Who Could Cheat Death 1959, Hot Money Girl 1959, The Mummy 1959, Too Hot to Handle 1960, The City of the Dead 1960, The Two Faces of Dr. Jekyll 1960, The Hands of Orlac 1960, Taste of Fear 1961, The Devil's Daffodil 1961, Hercules in the Center of the Earth 1961, Stranglehold 1962, Das Rätsel der roten Orchidee 1962, The Pirates of Blood River 1962, The Devil's Agent 1962, Sherlock Holmes in, Valley of Fear 1962, The Castle of Terror 1963, The Whip and the Flesh 1963, La cripta e l'incubo 1964, The Devil-Ship Pirates 1964, Terror in the Crypt 1964, The Gorgon 1964, Dr. Terror's House of Horrors (segment 4 'Disembodied Hand') 1965, She 1965, The Skull 1965, Ten Little Indians (voice) (uncredited) 1965, The Face of Fu Manchu 1965, Dracula: Prince of Darkness 1966, Rasputin: The Mad Monk 1966, Circus of Fear 1966, The Brides of Fu Manchu 1966, The Vengeance of Fu Manchu 1967, Theatre of Death 1967, Five Golden Dragons 1967, Die Schlangengrube und das Pendel 1967, The Devil Rides Out 1968, The Blood of Fu Manchu 1968, Dracula Has Risen from the Grave 1968, Curse of the Crimson Altar 1968, Sax Rohmer's The Castle of Fu Manchu 1969, The Magic Christian 1969, Scream and Scream Again 1970, Il trono di fuoco 1970, Marquis de Sade's 'Philosophy in the Boudoir' 1970, Count Dracula 1970, Taste the Blood of Dracula 1970, The Private Life of Sherlock Holmes 1970, Scars of Dracula 1970, The House That Dripped Blood 1971, I, Monster 1971, Dracula A.D. 1972 1972, Horror Express 1972, Nothing But the Night 1973, Dark Places 1973, The Creeping Flesh 1973, The Satanic Rites of Dracula 1973, The Three Musketeers 1973, The Wicker Man 1973, The Four Musketeers 1974, The Man with the Golden Gun 1974, Diagnosis: Murder 1975, The Keeper 1976, The Diamond Mercenaries 1976, To the Devil a Daughter 1976, Dracula père et fils 1976, Airport '77 1977, End of the World 1977, Starship Invasions 1977, The Passage 1979, Arabian Adventure 1979, Nutcracker Fantasy 1979, Bear Island 1979, 1941 1979, Serial 1980, The Salamander 1981, An Eye for an Eye 1981, Safari 3000 1982, The Last Unicorn (voice) 1982, New Magic (short) 1983, The Return of Captain Invincible 1983, House of the Long Shadows 1983, The Rosebud Beach Hotel 1984, Mask of Murder 1985, Howling II: Stirba – Werewolf Bitch 1985, Roadstrip 1985, Jocks 1986, Shaka Zulu 1987, Mio in the Land of Faraway 1987, The Girl 1987, Columbian Connection 1988, Fall of the Eagles 1989, The Return of the Musketeers 1989, La révolution française 1989, Murder Story 1989, Casanova, Murder Story 1989, Honeymoon Academy 1990, L'avaro 1990, Shogun Warrior 1991, Curse III: Blood Sacrifice 1991, Beauty and the Beast (video) 1992, Jackpot 1992, Funny Man 1994, Police Academy: Mission to Moscow 1994, A Feast at Midnight 1995, The Stupids 1995, The Stupids 1996, Tale of the Mummy 1998, Jinnah 1998, Sleepy Hollow 1999, Conquest: Frontier Wars (video game) 2001, The Lord of the Rings: The Fellowship of the Ring 2001, Star Wars: Episode II – Attack of the Clones 2002, The Lord of the Rings: The Two Towers 2002, The Lord of the Rings: The Return of the King 2003, Crimson Rivers 2: Angels of the Apocalypse 2004, Greyfriars Bobby 2005, Star Wars: Episode III – The Revenge of the Sith 2005, Charlie and the Chocolate Factory 2005, The Corpse Bride (voice) 2005, The Golden Compass 2007, The Heavy 2007, The Stone of Destiny 2007, Star Wars: The Clone Wars 2008, Boogie Woogie 2009, Triage 2009, Glorious 39 2009, The Heavy 2009, Alice in Wonderland (voice) 2010, Burke and Hare 2010, The Resident 2011, Season of the Witch 2011, Monstermania! (voice) 2011, The Wicker Tree 2011, Back2Hell 2011, Hugo Cabret 2011, Dark Shadows 2012, The Hobbit: An Unexpected Journey 2012. *Music:* The King of Elfland's Daughter, Peter and the Wolf, The Soldier's Tale, The King and I, Wandering Star, It's Now or Never, Christopher Lee Sings Rogues, Devils, and Other Villains—From Broadway to Bayreuth, The Dark Secret by Rhapsody featuring Christopher Lee 2005, 'Revelation' 2007. *Television includes:* Douglas Fairbanks, Jr., Presents (series) 1953–56, Moby Dick Rehearsed (film) 1955, The Vise (series) 1955, Tales of Hans Andersen (series) 1955, Chevron Hall of Stars (series) 1956, The Scarlet Pimpernel (series) 1956, Colonel March of Scotland Yard (series) 1956, The Adventures of Aggie (series) 1956, Sailor of Fortune (series) 1956, The Errol Flynn Theatre (series) 1956–57, The Gay Cavalier (series) 1957, O.S.S. (series) 1958, Ivanhoe (series) 1958, White Hunter (series) 1958, William Tell (series) 1959, Tales of the Vikings (series) 1960, The Alfred Hitchcock Hour (series) 1964, The Avengers (series) 1967–69, Poor Devil (film) 1973, Great Mysteries (series) 1973, Space: 1999 (series) 1976, How the West Was Won (mini-series) 1978, Once Upon a Spy (film) 1980, Charlie's Angels (series) 1980, Evil Stalks This House (film) 1981, Goliath Awaits (film) 1981, Massarati and the Brain (film) 1982, Charles & Diana: A Royal Love Story (film) 1982, The Far Pavilions (mini-series) 1984, Faerie Tale Theatre (series) 1984, Shaka Zulu (mini-series) 1986, Un métier du seigneur (film) 1986, Around the World in 80 Days (mini-series) 1989, Treasure Island (film) 1990, Wahre Wunder (Germany) 1990, Young Indy 1991, Sherlock Holmes and the Leading Lady (film) 1991, Sherlock Holmes in Incident at Victoria Falls (film) 1992, The Young Indiana Jones Chronicles (series) 1992, Death Train (film) 1993, Street Gear (series) 1994–95, Tales of Mystery and Imagination (series) 1995, The Tomorrow People (series) 1995, Moses (film) 1995, Princess Alisea (film) 1996, Ivanhoe (mini-series) 1997, Soul Music (series) 1997, Wyrd Sisters (mini-series) 1997, The Odyssey (film) 1997, The New Adventures of Robin Hood (series) 1997–98, Gormenghast (mini-series) 2000, In the Beginning (film) 2000, Ghost Stories for Christmas (mini-series) 2000, Les redoutables (series) 2001, Pope John Paul II (film) 2005, The Colour of Magic (voice) 2008. *Publications:* Christopher Lee's Treasury of Terror, Christopher Lee's Archives of Evil 1975, Christopher Lee's The Great Villains 1977, Tall, Dark and Gruesome (autobiog.) 1977, (updated) 1997, (updated) 2003 as Lord of Misrule. *Leisure interests:* music, travel, golf. *Address:* Independent Talent Group Ltd, Oxford House, 76 Oxford Street, London, W1D 1BS, England (office). *Telephone:* (20) 7636-6565 (office). *Fax:* (20) 7323-0101 (office). *Website:* www.independenttalent .com (office). *E-mail:* webmaster@christopherleeweb.com (office).

LEE, David Morris, PhD; American physicist and academic; *Professor of Low Temperature Physics, Cornell University;* b. 20 Jan. 1931, Rye, NY; s. of Marvin Lee and Annette Lee (née Franks); m. Dana Thorangkul 1960; two s.; ed Harvard Univ., Univ. of Connecticut, Yale Univ.; served in US Army 1952–54; Instructor in Physics, Cornell Univ., Ithaca, NY 1959–60, Asst Prof. 1960–63, Assoc. Prof. 1963–68, Prof. 1968–97; James Gilbert White Distinguished Prof. of Physical Sciences 1997–; Visiting Scientist Brookhaven Nat. Lab., Upton, NY 1966–67; Visiting Prof., Univ. of Fla, Gainesville 1974–75, 1994, Univ. of Calif., San Diego, La Jolla 1988; Visiting Lecturer, Peking Univ., Beijing, China 1981; Chair. Joseph Fourier Univ., Grenoble, France 1994; co-discoverer superfluid 3He, tricritical point of 3He-4He mixtures; co-observation of spin waves in spin polarized hydrogen gas; Fellow AAAS; mem. American Acad. of Arts and Sciences, NAS; John Simon Guggenheim Fellow 1966–67, 1974–75; Japan Soc. for Promotion of Sciences Fellow 1977; Sir Francis Simon Memorial Prize, British Inst. of Physics 1976, Oliver Buckley Prize, American Physical Soc. 1981, shared Nobel Prize for Physics 1996, Wilber Cross Medal, Yale Univ. 1998. *Address:* 610 Clark Hall, Laboratory of Atomic and Solid Physics, Cornell University, Ithaca, NY 14853-2501, USA (office). *Telephone:* (607) 255-5286 (office). *Fax:* (607) 255-6428 (office). *E-mail:* dml20@cornell.edu (office). *Website:* www.lassp.cornell.edu/lassp_data/ dmlee (office).

LEE, David Tawei, PhD; Taiwanese editor, academic, government official and diplomatist; *Chairman, Coordination Council for North American Affairs;* b. 15 Oct. 1949, Taipei; m.; one s. one d.; ed Nat. Taiwan Univ., Univ. of Virginia, USA; Man. Ed. Asia and the World Forum 1976–77; staff consultant, Co-ordination Council for N American Affairs, Washington, DC 1982–88; Prin. Asst to Minister of Foreign Affairs 1988–89; Adjunct Assoc. Prof. of Int. Politics, Grad. School of Social Science, Nat. Taiwan Normal Univ. 1988–93; Deputy Dir Dept of Int. Information Services, Govt Information Office 1989–90; Deputy Dir Dept of N American Affairs, Ministry of Foreign Affairs 1990–93, Dir 1996, Deputy Minister 1998–2001; Assoc. in Research, Fairbank Center for E Asian Research, Harvard Univ. 1993–96; Dir-Gen. Taipei Econ. and Cultural Office, Boston 1993–96; Deputy Dir-Gen. Govt Information Office, Exec. Yuan 1996–97; Dir-Gen. Govt Information Office, Exec. Yuan and Govt Spokesman 1997–2000; Rep. to Belgium, Luxembourg and EU, Brussels 2001–04, to USA 2004–07, to Canada 2007–12; Chair. Coordination Council for N American Affairs, Taipei 2012–. *Address:* Coordination Council for North American Affairs, 133 Bo Ai Road, Taipei 10048, Taiwan (office). *Telephone:* (2) 23119212 (office). *Fax:* (2) 23148412 (office).

LEE, Gang-yon, BA (Econ), MBA; South Korean business executive; *Senior Advisor, Lee International IP & Law Group;* m.; one s. one d.; ed Yonsei Univ., New York Univ. Grad. School of Business Admin, Manufacturers Hanover Trust Co.'s Exec. Training Program, IMF's Balance of Payments Methodology Course, US Dept of State's AID Int. Capital Markets Program; began career in public admin at Ministry of Finance serving as Deputy Dir Foreign Exchange Control Div., Int. Finance Div. and Treasury Div. 1969–75, Foreign Investment Promotion Officer, then Dir of Insurance Div., Securities Div. and Foreign Fund Div. 1976–80, Dir Gen. augmented to US Customs Service and Customs Counsellor of Korean Embassy in Washington, DC 1984–90, additionally, Dir Gen. Korea Customs Service's Int. Co-operation and Valuation Bureau 1991–95, Investigation Bureau 1995–97, Korea Customs Service's Deputy Commr 1997–99, Chair. Ministry of Finance's Advisory Cttees of the Task Force for the Establishment of the Korean Financial Intelligence Unit 2000–01, Ministry of Finance & Economy's Prevention of Money Laundering Cttee 2002–05; Adjunct Prof., Grad. School of Industry and Business, Dankook Univ. 2001–07; Sr Advisor, Lee International IP & Law Group 2000–05, 2013–; Sr Advisor, Samjong KPMG 2005–12; Chair. Korea Gas Corpn (KOGAS) 2006–09; Chair. Sejong Trade & Customs Advisory Services, Inc. 2008–12, Asia Pacific Trade & Customs Advisory Services 2012–; Corp. Advisor, Fila Korea Ltd 2012–; Outside Dir (and mem. Audit Cttee) Hyundai Heavy Industries Co. Ltd 2003–06, Shin Dong-Ah Fire & Marine Insurance Co. 2002–07, CJ Freshway 2012–; Research Advisor, Korea Inst. for Int. Econ. Policy 1999–2007; mem. Asia Pacific Advisory Bd of Deutsche Bank 2008–13; Vice-Chair. Korean-American Asscn 2013–; Order of Service Merit Red Stripe 1992. *Publication:* Money Laundering (third edn). *Leisure interests:* playing golf, hiking. *Address:* Lee International IP & Law Group, 14F Poongsan Building, 23 Chungjeongro, Seodaemun-Gu, Seoul, 120-837, Republic of Korea (office). *Tele- phone:* (2) 2279-3631 (office). *Fax:* (2) 2273-4605 (office). *E-mail:* gylee@ leeinternational.com (office). *Website:* www.leeinternational.com (office).

LEE, Hae-chan; South Korean politician; fmr Vice Mayor of Seoul; fmr chief policy-maker for Millennium Democratic Party; Minister for Educ. 1998–99; Prime Minister 2004–06 (resgnd). *Address:* c/o Office of the Prime Minister, 77 Sejong-no, Jongno-gu, Seoul, Republic of Korea (office).

LEE, Han-dong, BA; South Korean politician; b. 5 Dec. 1934, Gyeonggi-do; m. Nam Sook Cho; one s. two d.; ed Kyungbok High School, Seoul Nat. Univ.; Mil. Prosecutor, Rep. of Korea Army 1959, Staff Judge Advocate with 5th Corps 1961; Judge, Seoul Dist Court 1963, Prosecutor 1969, Prosecutor, Seoul High Prosecutor's Office and Deputy Dir of Legal Affairs Training, Ministry of Justice 1974; Sr Prosecutor, Daejeon Dist Prosecutor's Office 1975, Pusan Dist Prosecutor's Office 1977, Seoul Dist Prosecutor's Office 1980; mem. Nat. Ass. 1981–, Vice-Speaker 1995; Deputy Floor Leader for Democratic Justice Party (DJP) 1981, Chief Sec. to Party Pres. 1982, DJP Sec. Gen. 1984, Floor Leader 1986, mem. Cen. Exec. Council 1990; Minister of Home Affairs 1988; Floor Leader for Democratic Liberal Party (DLP) 1993, Sr Adviser to Party Pres. 1996; Chief Exec., Chair. New Korea Party 1997, Grand Nat. Party 1997, Vice-Pres. 1998, Acting Pres. 1998; Acting Pres. United Liberal Democrats 2000, Pres. 2000–; Prime Minister of Repub. of Korea 2000–02; presidential cand. 2002; Service Merit Medal 1976. *Address:* c/o Office of the Prime Minister, 77, Sejong-no, Jongno-gu, Seoul, Republic of Korea (office).

LEE, (Nelle) Harper; American writer; b. 28 April 1926, Monroeville, Ala; d. of Amasa Coleman Lee and Frances Finch Cunningham Lee; ed Huntingdon Coll., Univ. of Ala and Univ. of Oxford, UK; worked as airline reservation clerk for Eastern Airlines and BOAC (NY) 1950s; accompanied the late Truman Capote to Holcombe, Kan., as research asst for his novel In Cold Blood; mem. Nat. Council of Arts 1966–71; Hon. DHumLitt (Spring Coll., Ala) 1997, (Notre Dame) 2006; Alabama Library Asscn Award 1961, Nat. Conf. of Christians and Jews Brother- hood Award 1961, Los Angeles Public Library Literary Award 2005, Presidential Medal of Freedom 2007, National Medal of Arts 2011. *Publications include:* fiction: To Kill A Mockingbird (Pulitzer Prize for Fiction 1961, Best Sellers' Paperback of the Year Award 1962) 1960; essays: Love: In Other Words (essay in Vogue) 1961, Christmas to Me (essay in McCalls) 1961, When Children Discover America (essay in McCalls) 1965, High Romance and Adventure (essay, part of Ala History and Heritage Festival) 1983; contribs to numerous magazines. *Leisure interest:* golf. *Address:* PO Box 278, Monroeville, AL 36461, USA.

LEE, Dame Hermione, DBE, CBE, MA, FBA, FRSL; British writer, broadcaster and academic; *President, Wolfson College, Oxford;* b. 29 Feb. 1948, Winchester, Hants., England; d. of Dr Benjamin Lee and Josephine Lee; m. John Barnard 1991; ed Univ. of Oxford; Instructor, Coll. of William and Mary, Williamsburg, Va, USA 1970–71; Lecturer, Dept of English, Univ. of Liverpool 1971–77; Lecturer, Dept of English, Univ. of York 1977–87, Sr Lecturer 1987–90, Reader 1990–93, Prof. 1993–98; Goldsmiths' Chair of English Literature and Fellow of New Coll., Oxford 1998–2008, Pres. Wolfson Coll., Oxford 2008–; presenter of Book Four on Channel Four TV (UK) 1982–86; Chair. of Judges, Man Booker Prize for Fiction 2006; Mel and Lois Tukman Fellow, Dorothy and Lewis B. Cullman Center for Scholars and Writers, New York Public Library 2004–05; Foreign Hon. mem. American Acad. of Arts and Sciences; Hon. Fellow, St Hilda's Coll. Oxford 1998, St Cross Coll. Oxford 1998; Hon. DLitt (Liverpool) 2002, (York) 2007. *Publications include:* The Novels of Virginia Woolf 1977, Elizabeth Bowen 1981 (2nd ed. 1999), Philip Roth 1982, The Secret Self I 1985 and II 1987, The Mulberry Tree: Writings of Elizabeth Bowen 1986, Willa Cather: A Life Saved Up 1989, Virginia Woolf 1996, Virginia Woolf: Moments of Being (ed.) 2002, Body Parts: Essays on Life-Writing 2005, Virginia Woolf's Nose 2005, Edith Wharton (biog.) 2007, Biography: A Very Short Introduction 2009, Penelope Fitzgerald: A Life (biog.) 2013; Co-Ed. (with David Constantine and Bernard O'Donoghue): Oxford Poets 2000: An Anthology, Oxford Poets 2001: An Anthology, Oxford Poets 2002: An Anthology; Consultant Ed., The Good Fiction Guide 2001, 2002; Assoc. Ed., The Oxford Companion to English Literature (seventh edn); *Leisure interests:* reading, music, countryside. *Address:* c/o United Agents, 12–26 Lexington Street, London, W1F 0LE, England (office); Wolfson College, Linton Road, Oxford, OX2 6UD, England (office). *Telephone:* (20) 3214-0800 (office), (18) 6527-4100 (office). *Fax:* (20) 3214-0801 (office), (18) 6527-4125 (office). *E-mail:* info@unitedagents.co.uk (office); hermione.lee@wolfson.ox.ac .uk (office). *Website:* unitedagents.co.uk (office); www.wolfson.ox.ac.uk (office); www.hermionelee.com.

LEE, Hoi-chang, BA; South Korean politician; *Leader, Liberty Forward Party;* b. 2 June 1935, Sohung, Hwanghae Prov.; m.; two s. one d.; ed Kyonggi High School, Seoul Nat. Univ., Harvard Univ., USA; service in AF, attained rank of Capt.; Judge, Incheon and Seoul Dist Court 1960–65; apptd Judge, Seoul High Court 1965, Sr Judge 1977; Prof., Judicial Research and Training Inst. 1971; Dir Planning and Co-ordination Office, Ministry of Court Admin 1980; Justice, Supreme Court 1981–86, 1988–93; practised law 1986–88, 1994–; Head of Nat. Election Comm. 1988–93; Head of Bd of Audit and Inspection 1993; Prime Minister of Repub. of Korea 1993; cand. of ruling New Korea Party in presidential elections 1997; Pres. Grand Nat. Party (GNP) 2000–02; cand. of GNP in presidential elections 2002, incl. cand. 2007; Founder and Leader, Liberty Forward Party 2007–. *Leisure interest:* listening to classical music. *Address:* Liberty Forward Party, Yeongsan Bldg, 3rd Floor, 14-14, Yeouido-dong, Yeoungdeungpo-gu, Seoul (office); 10-1401 Asia Seonsuchon Apt, Jamsil-7-dong, Songpa-gu, Seoul, Republic of Korea (home). *Telephone:* (2) 780-3988 (office); (2) 3432-2030 (home). *Fax:* (2) 780-3983 (office). *E-mail:* webmaster@jayou.or.kr (office). *Website:* www.jayou.or .kr (office).

LEE, Hong-koo, PhD; South Korean politician and political scientist; b. 9 May 1934, Seoul; m.; one s. two d.; ed Seoul Nat. Univ., Emory and Yale Univs, USA; Asst Prof., Emory Univ. 1963–64, Case Western Reserve Univ. 1964–67; Asst Prof., Assoc. Prof., Prof. of Political Science, Seoul Nat. Univ. 1968–88, Dir Inst. of Social Sciences 1979–82; Fellow Woodrow Wilson Int. Center for Scholars, Smithsonian Inst. 1973–74, Harvard Law School 1974–75; Minister of Nat. Unification 1988–90; Special Asst to Pres. 1990–91; Amb. to UN 1991–93; Sr Vice-Chair. Advisory Council for Unification; Chair. Seoul 21st Century Cttee, The World Cup 2002 Bidding Cttee 1993–94; Deputy Prime Minister and Minister of Nat. Unification April–Dec. 1994, Prime Minister 1994–95; mem. Comm. on Global Governance 1991–95; Chair. New Korea Party May 1996; Amb. to USA 1998–2001; fmr Pres. Seoul Forum for Int. Affairs; Sheth Distinguished Int. Alumni Award from Emory

Univ. 2002. *Publications:* An Introduction to Political Science, One Hundred Years of Marxism, Modernization. *Address:* c/o Ministry of Foreign Affairs and Trade, 77 1-ga, Sejong-no, Jongno-gu, Seoul, Republic of Korea (office).

LEE, Brig.-Gen. Hsien Loong, (BG Lee); Singaporean politician and fmr military officer; *Prime Minister;* b. 10 Feb. 1952; s. of Lee Kuan Yew (q.v.) and Kwa Geok Choo; m. 1st (deceased 1982), one s. one d.; m. 2nd Ho Ching 1985; two s.; ed Catholic High School, Nat. Jr Coll., Cambridge Univ., UK, Kennedy School of Govt Harvard Univ., USA; nat. service 1971; Sr Army course at Fort Leavenworth, USA; Asst Chief of Gen. Staff (Operations) 1981–82, Chief of Staff (Gen. Staff) Singapore Army 1982–84; resgnd as Brig.-Gen. Aug. 1984, Nat. Reserves –2002; Political Sec. to Minister of Defence; MP for Teck Ghee 1984–; Chair. Comm. for Restructuring of the Economy 1985; Minister of State for Defence and for Trade and Industry 1985–86, for Trade and Industry 1986–93; Deputy Prime Minister 1990–2004, also Minister of Finance, Minister of Defence 1993–95, Second Minister of Finance (Services), Head Monetary Authority of Singapore; Prime Minister of Singapore and Minister of Finance 2004–07; Prime Minister 2007–; Second Asst Sec.-Gen. People's Action Party 1989–. *Leisure interests:* swimming, reading, jogging, computers. *Address:* Office of the Prime Minister, Orchard Road, Istana Annexe, Istana, Singapore 238823 (office). *Telephone:* 2358577 (office). *Fax:* 7324627 (office). *Website:* www.pmo.gov.sg (office).

LEE, Hun-jai, MA; South Korean government official and financial analyst; b. 17 April 1944, Shanghai, China; ed Seoul Nat. Univ., IMF Inst., Boston Univ. and Harvard Business School, Mass, USA; Dir Financial Policy Div., Ministry of Finance 1974–78, Deputy Dir-Gen. Office of Public Finance and Monetary Policy 1978–79; Exec. Man. Dir and CEO Daewoo Semiconductor Co. Ltd 1984–85; Pres. and CEO Korea Investors Service Co., Ltd 1985–1991; Head of Secr. to Jt Presidential Cttee for Econ. Policy 1997–98; Chair. Financial Supervisory Comm. 1998–2000; Minister of Finance and Economy 2000, Acting Prime Minister May 19–22 2000; Chair. Korean Inst. of Dirs 2002–04; Deputy Prime Minister and Minister of Finance and the Economy 2004–05 (resgnd), Acting Prime Minister 25 May–30 June 2004; Chair. Bd of Govs Asian Devt Bank; mem. Advisory Bd, Cen. Cttee of Agric. Cooperative Union 1993–97; mem. Citizens Advisory Cttee, City of Seoul 1995–97. *Publications:* Development of the Credit Rating System in Korea 1988. *Address:* c/o Ministry of Finance and the Economy, 1 Jungang-dong, Gwacheon City, Gyeonggi Province, Republic of Korea (office).

LEE, Hyoung-keun (Hank), BEng; South Korean automotive company executive; *Vice-Chairman, President and CEO, Kia Motors Corporation;* ed Seoul Nat. Univ.; joined Hyundai Motor Group 1977, has held numerous positions including Sr Exec. Vice-Pres. and COO Int. Business Div. –2009, Pres. Kia Motors Europe and Pres. and CEO Dongfeng Yueda Kia (joint venture in China), served as a Co-Pres. Kia Motors Corpn in charge of overseas business operations 2009–10, Vice-Chair., Pres. and CEO Kia Motors Corpn 2010–. *Address:* Kia Motors Corporation, 231 Yangjae-Dong, Seocho- Gu, Seoul 137-938, Republic of Korea (office). *Telephone:* (2) 3464-1114 (office). *E-mail:* info@kiamotors.com (office). *Website:* www.kiamotors.com (office).

LEE, Hyung-koo; South Korean banker; b. 30 Aug. 1940; m. 1969; ed Seoul Nat. Univ.; Deputy Dir Planning and Man. Office, Budget Bureau, Econ. Planning Bd (EPB) 1964; Sec. for Econ. Affairs, Presidential Secr. 1969–70; Dir and Dir-Gen. EPB 1971–81; Parvin Fellow, Woodrow Wilson School of Public Admin., Princeton Univ. 1978–79; Asst Minister, Ministry of Finance 1982; Vice-Minister, Ministry of Construction 1986, Ministry of Finance 1988, EPB 1988; Gov. Korea Devt Bank 1990–96. *Publications:* Economic Development in Korea, The Korean Economy, The Korean Economy Looks to the 21st Century. *Leisure interests:* golf, tennis. *Address:* 10-2, Gwancheol-dong, Jongno-gu, CPO Box 28, Seoul, 110-111, Republic of Korea. *Telephone:* (2) 398-6114.

LEE, In-ho, BA; South Korean banking executive; *Corporate Adviser, Shinhan Bank;* b. 2 Nov. 1943; ed Yonsei Univ.; joined Shinhan Bank as incorporator 1982, later Pres. and CEO Shinhan Bank, Dir (non-exec.) Shinhan Financial Group Co. Ltd, Pres. and CEO 2005–09, currently Corporate Adviser, Shinhan Bank; Dir Samsung Electronics Co. Ltd 2010–. *Address:* Shinhan Financial Group Co. Ltd, 120 Taepyung-ro 2-ga, Jung-gu, Seoul 100-102, Republic of Korea (office). *Telephone:* (822) 6360-3072 (office). *E-mail:* info@shinhangroup.com (office). *Website:* www.shinhangroup.com (office).

LEE, Jae-joung; South Korean academic and politician; b. 1944, Jincheon, N Chungcheong prov.; m.; one d.; ed Korea Univ. and Univ. of Manitoba and Trinity Coll., Canada; ordained Anglican priest 1972; teacher then Pres. Sung Kong Hoe Univ., Seoul 1994–2000; mem. Nat. Ass. 2000–04; Chief Campaign Man. for Pres. Roh during 2002 presidential campaign; co-f. Uri Party, now Adviser; worked at House of Shalom (shelter for migrant workers) 2004; Sr Vice Chair. Nat. Unification Advisory Council and presidential advisor on N Korea policy 2004–06; Minister of Unification 2006–08; arrested for accepting illegal political funds during the 2002 presidential campaign 2004, sentenced to a fine, received presidential pardon 2006. *Address:* c/o Ministry of Unification, 77-6, Sejong-no, Jongno-gu, Seoul 110-760, Republic of Korea (office).

LEE, Jai-seong; South Korean business executive; *President and Co-CEO, Hyundai Heavy Industries;* fmr Chief Financial Officer Hyundai Heavy Industries Co. Ltd, later Chief of Admin and Assistance HQ, Sr Exec. Vice-Pres. –2010, mem. Bd of Dirs, Pres. and Co-CEO 2010–. *Address:* Hyundai Heavy Industries Co. Ltd, 1, Jeonha-dong, Dong-gu, Gyeonsang nam-do, Ulsan 682-792, Republic of Korea (office). *Telephone:* (52) 202-2114 (office). *Fax:* (52) 202-3470 (office). *E-mail:* ir@hhi .co.kr (office); webzine@hhi.co.kr (office). *Website:* www.hhi.co.kr (office).

LEE, Jang-moo, BSc, PhD; South Korean engineer, university administrator and academic; *President Emeritus, Seoul National University;* b. 14 May 1945, Seoul; ed Seoul Nat. Univ., Iowa State Univ., USA, Babes-bolyai Univ., Romania, Hokkaido Univ., Japan; Prof., Coll. of Eng, Seoul Nat. Univ. 1976–, Dean Coll. of Eng 1997–2002, Pres. Seoul Nat. Univ. 2006–10, Pres. Emer. 2010–; Visiting Scholar, MIT, USA 1982–83; Chair. Univ. Educ. Section Cttee, Educational Policy Council, Korean Ministry of Educ. 1998–2000, Industrial Tech. Evaluation Inst., Korean Ministry of Industry and Resources 1999–2005, Founding Cttee for the Nat. Science Museum 2001–06, Climate Change Center of Korea 2010–13; Pres. Korean Soc. for Precision Eng 1996–99, Nat. Asscn of Deans of Eng Colls

1998–2000, Korean Soc. of Mechanical Engineers 2000, Korean Soc. for New and Renewable Energy 2004–06; Vice-Pres. Asscn of Korean Socs of Science and Tech. 2005–; mem. Nat. Presidential Advisory Cttee on Science and Tech. 1998–99, Nat. Cttee for Innovation of Science and Tech. 2004–06; Fellow, American Soc. of Mechanical Engineers, Int. Acad. of Production Research, Korean Acad. of Science and Tech.; mem. Korean Acad. of Eng; Order of Service Merit (Blue Stripe); Dr hc (several); Korean Acad. of Science Award. *Address:* Office of the 24th President Emeritus, Seoul National University, San 56-1, Sillim-dong Gwanak-gu, Seoul 151-742, Republic of Korea (office). *Telephone:* (2) 880-7137 (office). *Fax:* (2) 889-7515 (office). *E-mail:* leejm@snu.ac.kr (office). *Website:* www.snu.ac.kr (office).

LEE, John Joseph, MA, MRIA; Irish historian and academic; *Glucksman Professor of Irish Studies and Director, Glucksman Ireland House, New York University;* b. 9 July 1942, Tralee, Co. Kerry; s. of Thomas P. Lee and Catherine Burke; m. Anne Marie Mitchell 1969; one s. two d.; ed Franciscan Coll. Gormanston, Univ. Coll. Dublin, Inst. for European History, Mainz, Germany, Peterhouse, Cambridge, UK; Admin. Officer, Dept of Finance, Dublin 1963; Asst in History, Univ. Coll. Dublin 1963–65; Research Fellow, Peterhouse, Univ. of Cambridge 1968–70, Official Fellow, Lecturer, Tutor 1970–74; Prof. of Modern History, Univ. Coll. Cork (UCC) 1974–93, Prof. of History 1993–2007, Dean Faculty of Arts 1976–79, Vice-Pres. UCC 1982–85; Visiting Mellon Prof., Univ. of Pittsburgh, USA 1979; Visiting Prof., European Univ. Inst., Florence, Italy 1981; Guest Fellow, Austrian Acad. 1989; Eisenhower Fellow, USA 1989, Distinguished Slick Visiting Prof. of World Peace, L.B.J. School, Univ. of Texas, Austin 1989–90; Visiting Prof. of Govt, Colby Coll. 1991; Visiting Sr Parnell Fellow, Magdalene Coll., Cambridge 1992–93, Visiting Arbuthnot Fellow, Univ. of Edinburgh 1996; Visiting Prof. of Irish Studies, New York Univ. 1999–2000, Glucksman Prof. of Irish Studies, Prof. of History and Dir Glucksman Ireland House 2002–; Distinguished Visiting Fellow, Queen Mary, Univ. of London 2007; Visiting Research Fellow, Trinity Coll. Dublin 2009, mem. External Advisory Bd, Long Room Hub 2007–; columnist, Sunday Tribune 1996–2002; Chair. Irish Scholarship Exchange Bd 1980–92, Irish Fulbright Comm. 1992–96; mem. Irish Senate 1993–97; mem. British-Irish Parl. Body 1993–97; Hon. DLitt (Nat. Univ. of Ireland) 2006; Irish Life/Sunday Independent Arts Award 1991, Aer Lingus/Irish Times Prize for Literature 1992, Donnelly Prize for History and Social Sciences, American Conf. for Irish Studies 1992. *Publications:* The Modernization of Irish Society 1848–1918 1973 (revised edn 2008), Labour in German Industrialisation, in Cambridge Economic History of Europe, VII 1978, Ireland 1912–1985: Politics and Society 1989, Europe and America in the 1990s (co-ed.) 1991, The Shifting Balance of Power, Exploring the 20th Century 2000, Making the Irish American (co-ed.) 2006. *Leisure interests:* sport, reading. *Address:* Glucksman Ireland House, One Washington Mews, New York, NY 10003, USA (office). *Telephone:* (212) 998-3950 (office). *Fax:* (212) 995-4373 (office). *E-mail:* jl91@nyu.edu (office). *Website:* irelandhouse.fas.nyu.edu (office).

LEE, Jye; Taiwanese naval officer; b. 6 June 1940, Tianjin City; m.; three d.; ed ROC Naval Acad., Navy Command and Staff Coll., Naval War Coll., USA; served as Submarine Commdg Officer, Submarine Squadron Commdr, Antisubmarine Warfare Commdr, Taiwan Navy 1992–94, Chief of Staff Navy Gen. HQ 1994–95, Commdg Gen. of Fleet Command 1995–96, Deputy Commdr-in-Chief Navy Gen. HQ 1996–97, Commdr-in-Chief Navy Gen. HQ 1999–2002; Vice Chief of Gen. Staff, Ministry of Nat. Defence Taiwan 1997–99, Chief of Gen. Staff 2002–04, Minister of Nat. Defence 2004–05, 2006–07 (retd); mem. Kuomintang (KMT, Nationalist Party of China) –2007. *Address:* c/o Ministry of National Defence, 2/F, 164 Po Ai Road, Taipei, Taiwan (office).

LEE, Kai-Fu, BS, PhD, FIEEE; Chinese (b. Taiwanese) computer software executive and entrepreneur; *Chairman and CEO, Innovation Works;* b. 3 Dec. 1961, Taipei, Taiwan; ed high school, Oak Ridge, Tenn., Columbia Univ., New York, Carnegie Mellon Univ., Pittsburg, Pa, USA; emigrated to USA 1973; Asst Prof., Carnegie Mellon Univ. 1988–90, developed Bill (Bayesian learning-based system for playing board game Othello that won US nat. tournament of computer players 1989); joined Apple Computer as research and devt exec. 1990, Vice-Pres. Interactive Media Group 1990–96, mem. of team that developed PlainTalk, the Apple Newton and several versions of QuickTime and QuickTime VR; Vice-Pres. and Gen. Man., Silicon Graphics Inc. (SGI) 1996–98, also Pres. Cosmo Software; joined Microsoft Corpn and moved to China to found and head up Microsoft Research Asia, Beijing 1998–2000, returned to USA 2000, Corp. Vice-Pres. Natural Interactive Services Div. 2000–05; Vice-Pres. Google and Founding Pres. Google Greater China 2005–09, responsible for launching Google.cn regional website; Founder, Chair. and CEO Innovation Works (business creation platform for creating new Chinese high-tech cos and for mentoring next generation of Chinese entrepreneurs) 2009–; Vice-Chair. Committee of 100; Sphinx (first large-vocabulary, speaker-independent, continuous speech-recognition system) selected by Business Week as the "Most Important Innovation of 1988". *Publications:* Automatic Speech Recognition: The Development of the Sphinx Recognition System, Readings in Speech Recognition (co-ed.) 1990, Making a World of Difference (autobiog.) 2011; four best-selling books in China; more than 60 papers in computer science. *Address:* Innovation Works, Tower C F16, Tsinghua Science Park, Haidian District, Beijing 100084, People's Republic of China (office). *E-mail:* contact@innovation-works.com (office). *Website:* www.innovation-works.com (office); en.chuangxin.com (office); www.kaifulee.com.

LEE, Ku-taek, BE; South Korean business executive; b. 1946; ed Kyunggi High School, Seoul, Seoul Nat. Univ.; joined POSCO (Pohang Iron and Steel Co.) 1969, various positions including steel specialist Pohang Works, Gen. Man. Export Dept, Gen. Man. Corp. Strategic Planning Dept, Sr Exec. Vice-Pres. 1996–98, Pres. 1998–2003, Chair. and CEO POSCO 2003–09 (resgnd); fmr Pres. Korea Iron and Steel Asscn; mem. Exec. Cttee, Int. Iron and Steel Inst. (renamed World Steel Asscn 2008) 2004–, Vice-Pres.; sr positions, Korea-US Econ. Council (KUSEC), Korea Inst. of Tech. (KITECH); Hon. AC (Australia) 2006. *Address:* c/o POSCO, POSCO Centre, 892 Daechi-4-dong, Kangnam-ku, Seoul, Republic of Korea (office).

LEE, Kuan Yew, MA; Singaporean politician and barrister; b. 16 Sept. 1923, Singapore; s. of the late Lee Chin Koon and Chua Jim Neo; m. Kwa Geok Choo 1950 (died 2010); two s. one d.; ed Raffles Coll., Singapore, Fitzwilliam Coll. Cambridge, UK; called to Bar, Middle Temple, London 1950, Hon. Bencher 1969;

Advocate and Solicitor, Singapore 1951; a founder of People's Action Party 1954, Sec.-Gen. 1954–92; mem. Legis. Ass. 1955–; first Prime Minister Repub. of Singapore 1959, re-elected 1963, 1968, 1972, 1976, 1980, 1984, 1988; resgnd as Prime Minister Nov. 1990; Sr Minister in the Prime Minister's Office 1990–2004; Minister Mentor 2004–11; mem. Singapore Internal Security Council 1959–; MP Fed. Parl. of Malaysia 1963–65; Chair. Singapore Investment Corpn 1981–; Fellow, Inst. of Politics, Harvard Univ. 1968; Hoyt Fellow, Berkeley Coll., Yale Univ. 1970; Hon. Fellow, Fitzwilliam Coll. Cambridge 1969, Royal Australasian Coll. of Surgeons 1973, RACP 1974; Hon. LLD (Royal Univ. of Cambodia) 1965, (Hong Kong) 1970, (Liverpool) 1971, (Sheffield) 1971; Hon. CH 1970; Hon. GCMG 1972; Bintang Republik Indonesia Adi Pradana 1973, Order of Sikatuna (Philippines) 1974, Most Hon. Order of Crown of Johore (First Class), 1984, Hon. Freeman, City of London 1982, numerous other distinctions. *Publications:* The Singapore Story – Memoirs of Lee Kuan Yew (Vol. 1), From Third World to First: The Singapore Story 1965–2000 (Vol. 2),. *Leisure interests:* jogging, swimming, golf. *Website:* www.lee-kuan-yew.com.

LEE, Kun-hee, BCom, MBA; South Korean business executive; *Chairman, Samsung Electronics;* b. 9 Jan. 1942, Uiryung, Kyongnam Prov.; s. of Lee Byung-chull and Park Doo-eul; m. Hong Ra-hee 1967; one s. two d.; ed Waseda Univ., Tokyo, Grad. School of Business, George Washington Univ., USA; Exec. Dir Joong-Ang Daily 1968–78, Tong-Yang Broadcasting Corpn 1968–78; Vice-Chair. Samsung Group 1979–87, Chair. 1987–98, Chair. and CEO Samsung Electronics Co. Ltd 1998–2008, Chair. 2010–; Vice-Chair. Korea-Japan Econ. Comm. 1981–, Fed. of Korean Industries 1987–; Pres. Korean Amateur Wrestling Fed. 1982–97, now Hon. Pres.; Vice-Pres. Korean Olympic Cttee 1993–96, now Hon. Pres.; mem. IOC 1996–; Order of Sport Merit, Maengho Medal 1984, Order of Sport Merit, Cheongryong Medal 1986, IOC Olympic Order 1991, Chevalier, Légion d'honneur 2004; Hon. DBA (Seoul Nat. Univ.) 2000, Hon. PhD (Korea Univ.) 2005, Hon. LLD (Waseda Univ.) 2010; Margaret Mead Award 1997, James A. Van Fleet Award 2006; ranked by Forbes magazine amongst The World's Most Powerful People (41st) 2013. *Publications include:* Read the World, With Your Own Thinking 1997. *Leisure interests:* horse riding, golf. *Address:* Samsung Electronics Bldg, 1320-10 Seocho-2-dong, Seocho-gu, Seoul 137-857, Republic of Korea (office). *Telephone:* (2) 2255-0114 (office). *Fax:* (2) 2255-2133 (office). *Website:* www.samsung.com (office).

LEE, Kyung-shik; South Korean politician and banker; ed Korea Univ.; joined Bank of Korea; Econ. Planning Bd 1961–72; served in Office of Pres. 1972–74; later Vice-Minister of Communications and mem. Monetary Bd of Korea; Pres. Daewoo Motor Co. 1988–93, Korea Gas Corpn until 1993; Deputy Prime Minister and Minister of Econ. Planning 1993; Gov. Bank of Korea 1995–98. *Address:* c/o Bank of Korea, 110, 3-ga, Namdaemun-no, Jung-gu, Seoul 100-794, Republic of Korea.

LEE, Martin Chu Ming, QC, JP, BA; Chinese barrister; b. 8 June 1938, Hong Kong; m. Amelia Lee 1969; one s.; ed Univ. of Hong Kong; Chair. Hong Kong Bar Asscn 1980–83; mem. Hong Kong Legis. Council 1985–2008, Hong Kong Law Reform Comm. 1985–91, Basic Law Drafting Cttee 1985–90 (expelled for criticism of People's Repub. of China); Chair. Hong Kong Consumer Council 1988–91; formed United Democrats of Hong Kong, party opposed to Chinese mil. suppression of Tiananmen Square demonstrators in 1989, Leader 1990–94 (merged with Meeting Point party to become Democratic Party of Hong Kong), Chair. 1994–2002; Goodman Fellow, Univ. of Toronto 2000; Bencher, Hon. Soc. of Lincoln's Inn 2000; Hon. LLD (Holy Cross Coll.) 1997, (Amherst Coll., USA) 1997, (Warwick Univ.) 2006; Prize for Freedom, Liberal Int. 1996, Int. Human Rights Award (American Bar Asscn) 1995, Democracy Award, Nat. Endowment for Democracy, USA 1997, Statesmanship Award, Claremont Inst., USA 1998, Schuman Medal, European Parl. 2000, Rutgers Coll. Brennan Human Rights Award 2004. *Publication:* The Basic Law: some basic flaws (with Szeto Wah) 1988. *Address:* Admiralty Centre, Room 704A, Tower I, 18 Harcourt Road, Hong Kong Special Administrative Region, People's Republic of China (office). *Telephone:* 25290864 (office). *Fax:* 28612829 (office). *E-mail:* oml@martinlee.org.hk (office). *Website:* www.martinlee.org.hk (office).

LEE, Michael Shumway (Mike), BA, JD; American lawyer and politician; *Senator from Utah;* b. 4 June 1971, Mesa, Ariz.; s. of Rex E. Lee and Janet Lee (née Griffin); m. Sharon Burr 1993; three c.; ed Timpview High School, Provo, UT, Brigham Young Univ. J. Reuben Clark Law School; served mission for Church of Jesus Christ of Latter-day Saints in Tex. Rio Grande Valley 1990–92; Pres. Student Body, Brigham Young Univ. 1993–94; admitted to Bar: Utah 1998, DC 1999; law clerk to Judge Dee V. Benson of US Dist Court for Dist of Utah 1997–98, to Judge Samuel A. Alito, Jr of US Court of Appeals for the Third Circuit Court, Newark, NJ 1998–99; joined office of Sidley & Austin LLP, Washington, DC 2000–02, specialized in appellate and Supreme Court litigation; Asst US Attorney, Salt Lake City, UT 2002–05; Gen. Counsel to Gov. of Utah, Jon M. Huntsman, Jr 2005–06; clerk at US Supreme Court with Justice Alito, Washington, DC 2006–07; Partner, Howrey LLP (law firm), Salt Lake City 2007–10; Senator from Utah 2011– (youngest senator of 112th Congress), mem. Judiciary Cttee, Energy and Natural Resources Cttee; mem. J. Reuben Clark Law Soc., Federalist Soc. for Law and Public Policy Studies; fmr mem. Alumni Bd Brigham Young Univ., Alumni Bd Brigham Young Univ. Law School; Republican; named by TIME magazine as one of The Politics 40 Under 40 2010. *Address:* 316 Hart Senate Office Building, Washington, DC 20510, USA (office). *Telephone:* (202) 224-5444 (office). *Fax:* (202) 228-1168 (office). *Website:* lee.senate.gov (office).

LEE, Myles, BE, FCA; Irish civil engineer, accountant and business executive; *Group Chief Executive, CRH plc;* worked in professional accountancy practice and in oil industry –1982; joined CRH plc 1982, Gen. Man. Finance 1988–2003, Finance Dir and mem. Bd of Dirs CRH plc 2003–09, Group Chief Exec. 2009–. *Address:* CRH plc, Belgard Castle, Clondalkin, Dublin 22, Ireland (office). *Telephone:* (1) 4041000 (office). *Fax:* (1) 4041007 (office). *E-mail:* mail@crh.com (office). *Website:* www.crh.com (office).

LEE, Myung-bak, BA; South Korean business executive, politician and fmr head of state; b. 19 Dec. 1941, then-Korean residential dist of Nakakawachi-gun, Osaka Pref., Japan (now Hirano-ku, Osaka City); s. of Lee Cheung-u and Chae Taewon; m. Kim Yun-ok; one s. three d.; ed Korea Univ., Seoul Nat. Univ., Yonsei Univ.; worked for Hyundai Group 1977–92, fmnr Pres. Hyundai Construction; Assembly-man, 16th Nat. Ass. 1996–2001; Mayor of Seoul City 2002–06; Founder and Exec.

Chair. Anguk Forum 2006; Pres. of S Korea 2008–13; Chair., Korea Atomic Industry Forum Inc. 1980; Chair. Int. Contractors Asscn of Korea 1980; Pres. Korea Amateur Swimming Fed. 1981–92; Exec. mem. Korean Olympic Cttee 1982–92; Chief, Construction Div., Econ. Cooperation Cttee in SE Asian Countries 1982; Deputy Chair. Korea Chamber of Commerce 1982; Vice Pres., Korea Man. Asscn 1983; Bureau mem. FINA 1984; Deputy Chair., Korea-USSR Econ. Asscn 1989; Exec. Dir, Korea Electric Asscn 1990; mem. NE Asia Econ. Cttee 1991; Vice-Chair., World Fed. of Korean Asscn of Commerce 1993; Founder East Asia Foundation, Chair. 1994–2002; Pres. Asian Pacific Foundation, Korea 2000–02; Commr. Sub-cttee on Future Competitiveness, Nat. Cttee, Grand Nat. Party 2001–02; Adviser, Overseas Korean Traders Asscn 2001–07; Econ. Adviser to Hun Sen, Prime Minister of Kingdom of Cambodia 2000–07; Hon. Consul Gen. of Kingdom of Bhutan to Korea 1986–99; Hon. Amb. of Arkansas State 1992–2007; Hon. Instructor, Undergraduate School of Business Admin, Korea Univ. 1993–; Hon. Instructor, Grad. School of Political Science, Kookmin Univ. 1995–, Hon. Instructor, Grad. School of Business Admin, Korea Univ. 1997–; Order of Civil Merit 1984, Order of Industrial Service Merit, Gold Tower 1985; Hon. DSc (Korea Nat. Univ. of Physical Educ.) 1998; Hon. DBA (Sogang Univ.) 2004; Hon. DEcon (Nat. Univ. of Mongolia) 2005, (Mokpo Nat. Univ.) 2005; Dr hc (Eurasia Univ., Astana, Kazakhstan) 2004; Excellent Enterprise Award by Pres. 1979, Excellent Enterprise Award, Business Admin Center, Korea Univ. 1983, selected as one of top 50 business leaders contributing to Nat. Devt, Daily Chosun 1998, selected as one of the top 30 business leaders in Korea in 20th century, Daily Maekyung and Fed. of Korean Industries 1999, Personality of the year 2005 awarded by fDi Magazine, affiliate magazine of the Financial Times 2005, Time magazine Hero of the Environment 2007, Zayed Int. Prize for the Environment (Category 1) 2011. *Publications include:* History of June 3rd Student Movement 1994, There Is No Such Thing as a Myth 1995, See Hope When Everyone Else Talks of Despair 2002, Cheonggyecheon Flows to the Future 2005, Unwavering Promise 2007, My Mother 2007. *Leisure interests:* tennis, swimming. *Address:* Saenuri Party, 14-31, Yeouido-dong, Yeongdeungpo-gu, Seoul 156-768, Republic of Korea (office). *Telephone:* (2) 3786-3000 (office). *Fax:* (2) 3786-3610 (office). *Website:* www.saenuriparty.kr (office).

LEE, Pal-seung, BL, MBA; South Korean business executive; *Chairman and CEO, Woori Finance Holdings Co. Ltd;* ed Jinkyo High School, Korea Univ., Advanced Information Man. Program, Korea Advanced Inst. of Science and Tech.; fmr Dir of Work Integration Div., Hanmi Bank, fmr Head of Busan and Gyeongnam HQ of Hanmi Bank; fmr Man. Dir Hanvit Bank; fmr Pres. and CEO Woori Securities, Hanvit Securities, CEO Woori Investment & Securities and Exec. Man. Dir Hanil Bank –2008, Chair. and CEO Woori Finance Holdings Co. Ltd 2008–, Chair. Woori Bank; Chair. KOFICE, Woori Multicultural Scholarship Foundation; CEO Seoul Philharmonic Orchestra; Hon. PhD (Chungnam Nat. Univ.). *Address:* Woori Finance Holdings Co. Ltd, 20F 203 Hoehyon-dong 1-ga, Chung-gu, Seoul 100-792, Republic of Korea (office). *Telephone:* (2) 2125-2000 (office). *Fax:* (2) 2125-2191 (office). *E-mail:* woorifg@woorifg.com (office). *Website:* www.woorifg.com (office).

LEE, Patrick A., PhD; American physicist and academic; *William and Emma Rogers Professor of Physics, Massachusetts Institute of Technology;* b. 8 Sept. 1946, British Hong Kong; ed Massachusetts Inst. of Tech.; Gibbs Instructor, Yale Univ. 1970–72; mem. tech. staff, Theoretical Physics Dept, Bell Labs 1972–73, 1974–81, Head, Theoretical Physics Dept 1981–82; Asst Prof., Univ. of Washington 1973–74; Prof. of Physics, MIT 1982–; William and Emma Rogers Prof. of Physics 1990–, fmr Div. Head, Atomic, Biological, Condensed Matter and Plasma Physics, affiliated with Quantum-Effects Devices Group of Research Lab. of Electronics; Co-Chair. Gordon Research Conf. 1984; Guest Ed. Special Issue on Disordered Solids, Physics Today 1988; mem. Editorial Bd, Chinese Physics 1980–85; mem. Proposal Review Bd, Stanford Synchrotron Radiation Lab. 1977–80, Bd of Trustees, Aspen Center for Physics 1981–87, Advisory Bd, Inst. for Theoretical Physics 1992–95; mem. NAS, American Acad. of Arts and Sciences, Academia Sinica (Taiwan); Fellow, American Physical Soc.; Oliver Buckley Prize, American Physical Soc. 1990, Dirac Medal, Int. Centre for Theoretical Physics 2005. *Publications:* numerous articles in scientific journals. *Address:* Department of Physics, Building 6C-347, Massachusetts Institute of Technology, 77 Massachusetts Avenue, Cambridge, MA 02139-4307, USA (office). *Telephone:* (617) 253-8325 (office). *Fax:* (617) 253-2562 (office). *E-mail:* palee@mit.edu (office). *Website:* web.mit.edu/physics/people/faculty/lee_patrick.html (office).

LEE, Sang-dae; South Korean business executive; *President and CEO, Housing Group, Samsung C&T Corporation;* ed Korea Univ.; has held numerous sr man. positions with Samsung Corpn including Exec. Vice-Pres. Samsung Training Inst., Exec. Vice-Pres. Planning and Man. Office, Pres. and CEO Housing Devt Div., Pres. and CEO Construction and Devt Div., Vice-Chair. and CEO Samsung C&T Corpn –2011, currently Pres. and CEO Construction Group, Housing Group, Exec. Vice-Pres. Office of Strategic Planning, Exec. Dir and Vice-Pres. Samsung Human Resources Devt Centre, Man. Dir HQ for Planning and Man., Samsung E&C Ltd. *Address:* Samsung C&T Corpn, 310 Taepyeong-Ro 1 Ga, Jung-Gu, Seoul, Republic of Korea (office). *Telephone:* (2) 2145-2114 (office). *Fax:* (2) 2145-3114 (office). *E-mail:* info@samsungcorp.com (office). *Website:* www.samsungcorp.com (office).

LEE, Gen. Sang-hee; South Korean army officer (retd) and politician; b. 12 Aug. 1945, Wonju, Gangwon Prov.; m. Kim Sun Young; one s. one d.; ed Kyung-Gi High School, Seoul, Repub. of Korea (ROK) Mil. Acad., Coll. of Liberal Arts and Science, Seoul Nat. Univ., Center for Int. Security Studies, Univ. of Maryland, USA; Commdr 29th Regt, 9th Infantry Div. 1989–91, Chief of Mil. Strategy, J-5 Directorate, Jt Chiefs of Staff 1991–92, Advisor to the Pres. for Nat. Defense Policy, Office of the Presidential Secr. 1992–94, Chief of Force Planning, G-5 Directorate, ROK Army HQ 1995–96, Commanding Gen., 30th Infantry Div. (Mechanized) 1996–98, Dir Policy Planning Bureau, Ministry of Nat. Defense 1998–99, Commanding Gen. 5th Corps 1999–2001, Chief Dir, Strategy and Plans (J5), Jt Chiefs of Staff 2001–02, Chief Dir, Operations (J3), Jt Chiefs of Staff 2002–03, promoted to four-star Gen. and Commanding Gen., Third ROK Army 2003, 32nd Chair. Jt Chiefs of Staff 2005–06 (retd); Minister of Nat. Defense 2008–09; Visiting Fellow, Brookings Inst., Washington, DC 2007; Presidential Citation, Order of Nat. Security 'Samil' Medal, Order of Nat. Security 'Chonsu' Medal, Order of Nat. Security 'Gukson' Medal, Armed Forces Merit Award

(Turkey), Legion of Merit, Commdr and Officer Grade (USA). *Address:* c/o Ministry of National Defense, 1, 3-ga, Yeongsan-dong, Yeongsan-gu, Seoul 140-701, Republic of Korea (office).

LEE, Seng Wee, MBA; Singaporean business executive; b. 1930; m.; ed Univs of Toronto and Western Ontario, Canada; mem. Bd of Dirs Oversea-Chinese Banking Corpn (Singapore's third-largest bank) 1966–, Chair. 1995–2003, mem. Bd Exec. Cttee, Bd Nominating Exec. 2003–; mem. Bd of Dirs Great Eastern Holdings Ltd, GIC Real Estate Pte Ltd, Lee Rubber Group of Cos, Lee Foundation; Chair. Temasek Trust. *Address:* Oversea-Chinese Banking Corporation, 65 Chulia Street, #29-02, OCBC Centre, Singapore 049513 (office). *Telephone:* 6318-7222 (office). *Fax:* 6533-7955 (office). *E-mail:* info@ocbc.com (office). *Website:* www.ocbc.com (office).

LEE, Seong-tae, BA, MA; South Korean fmr central banker; ed Seoul Nat. Univ., Univ. of Illinois, USA; joined Bank of Korea 1968, Chief of Monetary Policy Dept 1981–83, Chief of Research Dept 1983–86, Deputy Dir Research Dept 1986–89, Deputy Gen. Man. Pusan Br. 1989–91, Deputy Dir Monetary Policy Dept 1991–94, Gen. Man. Changwon Br. 1994–95, Dir Public Information Dept 1995–96, Dir Support Services and Properties Dept 1996–97, Dir Budget and Man. Dept 1997–98, Dir Research Dept 1998–2000, Deputy Gov. 2000–03, Sr Deputy Gov. 2003–04, Sr Deputy Gov. and mem. Monetary Policy Cttee 2004–06, Gov. Bank of Korea 2006–10. *Address:* c/o Bank of Korea, 110, 3-ga, Namdaemun-no, Jung-gu, Seoul 100-794, Republic of Korea (office).

LEE, Shau Kee; Hong Kong real estate executive; *Chairman and Managing Director, Henderson Land Development Company Limited;* b. Guangdong; m. (divorced); five c.; Founder Henderson Land Development Co. Ltd, Chair. and Man. Dir 1976–; Founder, Chair. and Man. Dir Henderson Investment Ltd; Chair. Henderson Cyber Ltd; Exec. Dir Henderson China Holdings Ltd; Chair. Hong Kong and China Gas Co. Ltd; Vice-Chair. Sun Hung Kai Properties Ltd; Dir Hong Kong Ferry (Holdings) Co. Ltd, The Bank of East Asia Ltd, Miramar Hotel and Investment Co. Ltd, Rimmer (Cayman) Ltd, Riddick (Cayman) Ltd, Hopkins (Cayman) Ltd, Henderson Development Ltd, Believegood Ltd, Cameron Enterprise Inc.; nicknamed "Asia's Warren Buffett"; Grand Bauhinia Medal 2007; Hon. DBA, Hon. DSSc, Hon. LLD. *Address:* Henderson Land Development Co. Ltd, 6th Floor, World-Wide House, 19 Des Voeux Road, Central, Hong Kong (office). *Telephone:* 29088888 (office). *Fax:* 29088838 (office). *E-mail:* corpcomm@hld.com (office). *Website:* www.hld.com (office).

LEE, Tan Sri Dato' Shin Cheng; Malaysian business executive and real estate executive; *Executive Chairman and CEO, IOI Group;* m.; two s. four d.; became field supervisor at palm oil co. aged 22; controlled small co. by 1981, bought Industrial Oxygen Inc. 1981, changed name to IOI 1995, currently Exec. Chair. and CEO IOI Group (operator of palm oil plantations, refineries and related mfg activities); mem. Council Malaysian Palm Oil Asscn, Malaysia-China Business Council; Adviser to KL & Selangor Chinese Chamber of Commerce and Industry; mem. Bd Universiti Putra Malaysia; Hon. Pres. Asscn of Eng Choon Socs of Malaysia, Fed. of Hokkien Asscn of Malaysia; Hon. Doctorate in Agric. (Universiti Putra Malaysia) 2002; FIABCI Malaysia Property Man of the Year Award 2001. *Address:* IOI Corporation Berhad, 2 IOI Square, IOI Resort, 62502 Putrajaya, Malaysia (office). *Telephone:* (3) 8947-8888 (office). *Fax:* (3) 8943-2266 (office). *E-mail:* corp@ioigroup.com (office). *Website:* www.ioigroup.com (office).

LEE, Si-chen, BS, MS, PhD; Taiwanese engineer, academic and fmr university administrator; *Distinguished Professor, Department of Electrical Engineering, National Taiwan University;* b. 13 Aug. 1952, Gon-Shan; ed Nat. Taiwan Univ., Stanford Univ., USA; Researcher, Energy Conversion Devices, Inc., Troy, Mich., USA 1980–82; Visiting Assoc. Prof., Dept of Electrical Eng, Nat. Taiwan Univ. 1982–85, Prof. of Electrical Eng, Coll. of Electrical Eng and Computer Science 1985–, now Distinguished Prof., Chair. Dept of Electrical Eng 1988–92, Dean of Academic Affairs 1996–2002, Pres. Nat. Taiwan Univ. 2005–13; Asst to Minister of Nat. Defence 1993–94; Chair. University Mobility in Asia and the Pacific 2005–; Pres. Asscn of Nat. Univs of Taiwan 2006–; Leader Bioenergy Field Group, Biology Dept, Nat. Science Council 1992–98, Microelectronics Group, Eng Dept 1988–93; mem. Directorate, Asscn of Chinese Electrical Engineers 1992–94; consultant, Electronics Research and Service Org., Industrial Tech. Research Inst. 1986–89, 1991–92; mem. Directorate, Chinese Asscn of Electromagnetism in Life Science 1999–2004; Assoc. Ed. Materials Chemistry and Physics 1992–2004, Journal of Chinese Engineers 1996–2000; Fellow, IEEE 2002 (mem. Vice-Directorate, IEEE Taipei section 2001–02); mem. Chinese Inst. of Electrical Eng, Asia-Pacific Acad. of Materials 1997; Dr hc (Kansai Univ.) 2005; five consecutive Outstanding Research Awards from Nat. Science Council 1986–96, Sun Yat-San Academic Award (Eng) 1987, Young Distinguished Engineer, Chinese Engineer Asscn 1987, Special Contracted Researcher, Nat. Science Council 1996–2002, IEEE Third Millennium Medal 2000, Annual Medal, Chinese Asscn of Electrical Engineers 2002, 47th Academic Award, Ministry of Educ. 2003. *Publications:* numerous scientific papers in professional journals. *Address:* Department of Electrical Engineering, EE Building 2 R440, National Taiwan University, Taipei 106, Taiwan (office). *Telephone:* (2) 33663640 (office). *Fax:* (2) 23675509 (office). *E-mail:* sclee@cc.ee.ntu.edu.tw (office). *Website:* www.ee.ntu.edu.tw/e_profile?id=6 (office).

LEE, Soo-chang; South Korean insurance executive; b. 1949, Yecheon, Gyeongsangbuk-do; m. three c.; ed Daechang High School, Coll. of Veterinary Medicine, Seoul Nat. Univ.; joined Samsung Life Insurance Co. Ltd 1973, Dir Cheil Jedang (subsidiary co.) 1990, Dir Shipbuilding Dept, Samsung Heavy Industries 1990–92, Dir Heavy Machinery Dept, Samsung Heavy Industries Jan.–Dec. 1993, Man. Dir Samsung Life Insurance Co. 1993–95, Man. Dir Samsung Fire 1995–95, Sr Man. Dir 1996–98, Vice-Pres. 1998–99, Vice-Pres. and CEO 1999–2001, Pres. and CEO 2001–06, Pres. and CEO Samsung Life Insurance Co. Ltd 2006–10; Iron Tower Order of Industrial Service 2000; 1st Nat. Country Love-Leader Award 2006, Forbes Korea Excellence in Leadership Award 2007. *Leisure interests:* reading, go, golf. *Address:* c/o Samsung Life Insurance Co. Ltd, 150 Taepyung-ro 2-ga, Jung-gu, Seoul 100-716, Republic of Korea.

LEE, Soo-ho, BA; South Korean business executive; b. 8 Feb. 1944, Jinju, Kyungnam Prov.; m. Young-Sook Park; one s. one d.; ed Jinju High School, Yonsei Univ.; began career with trading co. 1968–78; joined Bando International (renamed LG International) 1978, Sr Man. Gen. Merchandise Dept 1980–81,

with Br. Office, Jakarta, Indonesia 1981–84, Overseas Man. Div./Resources 1985–88, Br. Offices, Singapore and Hong Kong 1988–92, Man. Dir Sales Group/Support 1992–95, Sr Man. Dir Support 1995–96, Vice-Pres. Business Operations 1996–97, CEO LG International Corpn 1997–2003; Pres. Korea Gas Corpn (KOGAS) 2005–08; Order of Merit for Industrial Service 1997. *Address:* c/o Korea Gas Corpn, 215 Jeongja-dong, Bundang-gu, Seongnam, Gyeonggi-do, 463-754, Republic of Korea.

LEE, Soo-sung; South Korean politician and academic; fmr Pres. Seoul Nat. Univ.; Prime Minister of Repub. of Korea 1995–97; fmr Pres. Nat. Council of Saemaul-Undong Movement; Head, Screening Cttee, Asscn for Enhancing and Practising the Spirit of Manhae. *Address:* c/o National Council of Saemaul-Undong Movement, 1008-4 Daichi-dong Kangnam-Ku, Seoul, Republic of Korea (office).

LEE, Spike; American filmmaker and actor; b. (Shelton Jackson Lee), 20 March 1957, Atlanta; s. of Bill Lee and Jacquelyn Shelton; m. Tonya Lewis 1993; one d.; ed Morehouse Coll., Atlanta and New York Univ. Inst. of Film and Television; wrote scripts for Black Coll.: The Talented Tenth, Last Hustle in Brooklyn; produced, wrote, Dir Joe's Bed-Stuy Barbershop: We Cut Heads; has directed music videos, TV commercials and other short projects; f. Forty Acres and a Mule Filmworks; Commdr des Arts et des Lettres 2003; Dr hc (New York Univ.) 1998; Cannes Film Festival Best New Dir 1986, LA Film Critics' Asscn Awards 1986, 1989, Chicago Film Festival Critics' Awards 1990, 1992, Golden Satellite Best Documentary 1997; inducted into Nat. Asscn for the Advancement of Colored People (NAACP) Hall of Fame 2003. *Films include:* She's Gotta Have It 1985 (Cannes Film Festival Prize for Best New Film), School Daze 1988, Do the Right Thing 1989, Love Supreme 1990, Mo' Better Blues 1990, Jungle Fever 1991, Malcolm X 1992, Crooklyn, Girl 6, Clockers 1995, Get on the Bus, He Got Game 1998, Summer of Sam 1999, Tales from the Hood 1995 (exec. producer), Bamboozled 2000, The Original Kings of Comedy 2000, Lisa Picard is Famous 2001, A Huey P. Newton Story 2001, The 25th Hour 2003, CSA: Confederate States of America (exec. producer) 2004, She Hate Me 2004, Inside Man 2006, Miracle at St. Anna 2008, Red Hook Summer 2012. *Television:* Sucker Free City 2004. *Documentaries:* Four Little Girls 1997, When the Levees Broke 2006. *Publications:* Spike Lee's Gotta Have It: Inside Guerrilla Filmmaking 1987, Uplift the Race 1988, The Trials and Tribulations of the Making of Malcolm X 1992, Girl 6 1996, Get on the Bus 1996. *Leisure interest:* basketball. *Address:* Forty Acres and a Mule Filmworks, 124 De Kalb Avenue, Suite 2, Brooklyn, New York, NY 11217, USA. *Telephone:* (718) 624-3703. *Fax:* (718) 624-2008.

LEE, Stan; American comic book writer and film producer; *Chairman Emeritus, Marvel Comics;* b. (Stanley Martin Lieber), 28 Dec. 1922, New York, NY; s. of Jack Lieber and Celia Lieber; m. Joan Lee 1947; two c.; ed De Witt Clinton High School; fmr Asst Ed., Ed. Timely Comics Group (later known as Marvel Comics), first comic book script appeared in Captain America 1941, fmr positions at Marvel Comics include Head Writer, Art Dir, Publisher, Ed.-in-Chief, Pres. and Chair., currently Chair. Emer.; comic book creations (together with illustrators) include Fantastic Four, Hulk, Spider-Man, X-Men, The Avengers, Iron Man, Daredevil, Silver Surfer; f. Pow! Entertainment Inc. 2005; Nat. Medal of Arts 2008. *Films include:* Exec. Producer: Captain America 1991, Generation X 1996, Nick Fury: Agent of Shield 1998, Blade 1998, X-Men 2000, Blade II 2002, Spider-Man 2002, Daredevil 2003, X2 2003, Hulk 2003, The Punisher 2004, Spider-Man II 2004, Blade: Trinity 2004, Elektra 2005, Man-Thing 2005, Fantastic Four 2005. *Publication:* Excelsior! The Amazing Life of Stan Lee (autobiography) 2002. *Address:* c/o Marvel Entertainment Inc., 417 Fifth Avenue, New York, NY 10016, USA (office). *Telephone:* (212) 576-4000 (office). *Fax:* (212) 576-8517 (office). *Website:* www.marvel.com (office); www.powentertainment.com (office); www.stanleeweb.com

LEE, Sun-jin; South Korean diplomatist; m.; one s. one d.; ed Seoul Nat. Univ.; joined Ministry of Foreign Affairs 1975, overseas postings include Second Sec., Embassy in Beirut 1980, First Sec., Embassy in Washington, DC 1985, Counsellor, Embassy in Beijing 1992, Minister-Counsellor, Embassy in Tokyo; fmr Vice-Consul in Seattle, Wash., USA; Deputy Dir-Gen., Int. Trade Bureau, Ministry of Foreign Affairs and Trade 1996, Dir-Gen. for Policy Planning, Office of Policy Planning and Int. Orgs 2001, Deputy Minister for Policy Planning and Int. Orgs 2003; Amb. to Indonesia 2005–08. *Address:* Ministry of Foreign Affairs and Trade, 37, Sejong-no, Seoul 110-787, Republic of Korea (office). *Telephone:* (2) 2100-2114 (office). *Fax:* (2) 2100-7999 (office). *E-mail:* web@mofat.go.kr (office). *Website:* www.mofat.go.kr (office).

LEE, Tsung-Dao, PhD; American (b. Chinese) physicist; *University Professor Emeritus, Columbia University;* b. 25 Nov. 1926, Shanghai; s. of Tsing-Kong Lee and Ming-Chang Chang; m. Jeanette H. C. Chin 1950 (died 1995); two s.; ed Nat. Chekiang Univ., Nat. Southwest Univ., China and Univ. of Chicago, USA; Research Assoc. in Astronomy, Univ. of Chicago 1950; Research Assoc. and Lecturer in Physics, Univ. of California 1950–51; mem. Inst. for Advanced Study, Princeton, NJ 1951–53; Asst Prof. of Physics, Columbia Univ., New York 1953–55, Assoc. Prof. 1955–56, Prof. 1956–60, 1963, Enrico Fermi Prof. of Physics 1964–, Univ. Prof. 1984–2012, Univ. Prof. Emer. 2012–; Prof. Princeton Inst. for Advanced Study 1960–63; mem. NAS; naturalized as American citizen 1962; Order of the Rising Sun, Gold and Silver Star (Japan) 2007; shared Nobel Prize in Physics 1957 with Prof. Yang Chen-ning for work on elementary particles; Albert Einstein Award in Science 1957; numerous other awards including New York Acad. of Science Award 2000. *Publications:* articles in physical journals. *Address:* Department of Physics, Columbia University, Building 538, Morningside Heights, W 120th Street, New York, NY 10027 (office); 25 Claremont Avenue, New York, NY 10027, USA (home). *Telephone:* (212) 854-1759 (office). *Fax:* (212) 932-0418 (office). *E-mail:* tdl@phys.columbia.edu (office). *Website:* www.columbia.edu (office).

LEE, Teng-Hui, PhD; Taiwanese politician; b. 15 Jan. 1923, Taiwan; m. Tseng Wen-fui; two d.; ed Kyoto Imperial Univ., Japan, Nat. Taiwan Univ., Iowa State and Cornell Univs, USA; Asst Prof., Nat. Taiwan Univ. 1949–55, Assoc. Prof. 1956–58; Research Fellow, Taiwan Co-operative Bank 1953; Specialist and Econ. Analyst, Dept of Agric. and Forestry, Taiwan Prov. Govt 1954–57; Specialist, Joint Comm. on Rural Reconstruction (JCRR) 1957–61; Sr Specialist and Consultant 1961–70, Chief, Rural Economy Div. 1970–72; Prof. Nat. Chengchi Univ. 1958–78; Minister without Portfolio 1972–78; Mayor of Taipei City 1978–81; Gov. Taiwan Province 1981–84; Vice-Pres. of Repub. of China (Taiwan) 1984–88, Pres.

1988–2000; co-f. Taiwan Solidarity Union 2001; expelled from KMT (Kuomingtang) Party 2001; Hon. LLD (Southern Methodist Univ., USA) 1994; Int. Distinguished Achievement Citation, Iowa State Univ., USA and other awards. *Publications:* several works on agricultural development in Taiwan. *Leisure interests:* art, music and sport.

LEE, Gen. Tien-yu; Taiwanese military official; b. 1946, Nanjing; served in Tactical Fighter Wing, Armed Forces of Taiwan 1990–92, Commdr Combat Air Command 1998–2001, Commdr of Air Force 2002–04, Chief of Gen. Staff 2004–2007; Strategic Adviser to Pres. Chen Shui-bian Feb.–May 2007; Minister of Nat. Defense 2007–08 (resgnd); Order of Blue Sky and White Sun with Grand Cordon 2007. *Address:* c/o Ministry of National Defense, 2/F, 164 Po Ai Road, Taipei, 10048, Taiwan (office).

LEE, Ufan; South Korean painter; b. 1936, Gyeonsang Nam-do; ed Seoul Nat. Univ. and Nihon Univ., Tokyo, Japan; Leader Mono-Ha group (Japanese avantgarde art movt) 1969; Prof., Tama Art Univ., Tokyo 1973–2007; Invited Prof., Ecole Nat. Supérieure des Beaux-Arts, Paris 1997; Artists Summit, Kyoto 2005; Cultural Decoration 1990, Chevalier des Arts et des Lettres 1991, Order of the Rising Sun, Gold Rays with Rosette 2009; prize for critical writing for From Object to Being 1969, UNESCO Prize, Shanghai Biennale, Paris-Shanghai 2000, Praemium Imperiale Award (Painting), Japan Art Asscn 2001, Ho-Am Prize in the Arts 2001. *E-mail:* info@studioleeufan.org. *Website:* www.studioleeufan.org.

LEE, Won-gul; South Korean business executive; fmr Dir Aerospace Industry Div., Basic Industry Bureau, Ministry of Trade; Vice-Minister of Commerce, Industry and Energy –2006; Pres. and CEO Korea Electric Power Corpn (KEPCO) 2006–08. *Address:* c/o Korea Electric Power Corpn, 411 Yeongdong-daero, Gangnam-gu, Seoul 135-791, Republic of Korea. *E-mail:* info@kepco.co.kr.

LEE, Yeh Kwong Charles, OBE, JP, LLM, ACIS; Chinese lawyer; b. 16 July 1936, Shanghai; m. Nancy Lee 1960; one s. one d.; ed London School of Econs, UK; audit asst, Li Kwan Hung 1954–57, Peat Marwick Mitchell & Co., Hong Kong 1957–60; Asst Registrar, Registrar-Gen.'s Dept 1960–65; articled clerk, Nigel, Wallis & Apfel, Solicitors, UK 1965–68; solicitor, Registrar-Gen.'s Dept 1968–70, Johnson Stokes & Master 1970–72, Partner 1972–73; Partner Charles Lee & Stephen Lo 1973, Woo Kwan Lee & Lo 1973–; non-official mem., Exec. Council of Hong Kong 2005–12; mem. Council, Stock Exchange of Hong Kong Ltd 1988–, Chair. 1991; Dir several listed cos including Hutchison Whampoa 2013–, Cheung Kong (Holdings) Ltd 2013–; Fellow Chartered Asscn of Certified Accountants; Hon. DBA (Hong Kong Polytechnic Univ.) 2001; Gold Bauhinia Star 2000, Grand Bauhinia Medal 2006. *Leisure interests:* boating, scuba diving. *Address:* Woo Kwan Lee & Lo, 26/Fl. Jardine House, 1 Connaught Place, Hong Kong Special Administrative Region, People's Republic of China (office). *Telephone:* 8477823 (office). *Fax:* 8450239 (office).

LEE, Yock Suan, BSc; Singaporean politician; b. 30 Sept. 1946, Singapore; m. Adeline Oh Choon Neo; one s. one d.; ed Queenstown Secondary Technical School, Raffles Institution, Imperial Coll., Univ. of London, UK, Univ. of Singapore; Div. Dir (Projects), Econ. Devt Bd 1969–80; MP 1980–2006; Deputy Man. Dir Petrochemical Corpn of Singapore (Pte.) Ltd Jan.–Sept. 1981; Minister of State (Nat. Devt) 1981–83, (Finance) 1983–84, Sr Minister of State and Acting Minister for Labour 1985–86, Minister for Labour 1987–91, Second Minister of Educ. 1991–92, Minister of Educ. 1992–97, of Trade and Industry 1998–99, for Information and the Arts 1999–2001, of Environment 1999–2000, Minister in Prime Minister's Office and Second Minister of Foreign Affairs 2001–04; Deputy Chair. People's Asscn 1984–91. *Leisure interest:* badminton. *Address:* 9 Bishopsgate, 249988, Singapore. *Telephone:* 62381600. *E-mail:* leeyocksuan2004@yahoo.com.sg. *Website:* www.parliament.gov.sg.

LEE, Yong-kyung, BS, MS, PhD; South Korean telecommunications executive; b. 11 June 1943, Anyang; m.; two c.; ed Seoul Nat. Univ., Univ. of Oklahoma, Univ. of California, Berkeley, USA; Asst Prof. of Information Eng, Univ. of Illinois, Chicago 1975–77; sr researcher, Exxon Enterprises 1977–79; sr researcher, AT&T Bell Labs 1979–91; Vice-Pres. Outside Plant T Lab., Korea Telecom 1991–94, Vice-Pres. Telecommunication Systems Lab. and Software Lab. 1994–95, Vice-Pres. Wireless Tech. Lab. 1995–96, Exec. Vice-Pres. Research and Devt Group 1996–2000; CEO KT Freetel Co. 2000–02, Pres. and CEO KT Corpn (telecommunications service provider) 2002–05 (retd); participant on the future of communications panel, World Econ. Forum, Davos 2004; Exec. Leader in Residence, Kellogg School of Man., USA 2007; Adjunct Prof., KAIST Grad. School of Information and Media Man.; Visiting Scholar, Institut Européen d'Admin des Affaires (INSEAD) 2014; mem. Korea Nat. Ass. 2008–12, mem. Standing Cttee on Culture, Sports, Tourism, Broadcasting, and Telecommunications; Distinguished Eng Alumnus, Univ. of California, Berkeley 2003, Forbes magazine's Man. Leadership Award 2004, Industrial Gold Medal Korean Govt 2005. *Address:* c/o KT Corporation, 206 Jungja-dong, Bundang-gu, Sungnam, Kyonggi 463-711, Republic of Korea (office); c/o INSEAD, boulevard de Constance 77305 Fontainebleau, France. *Telephone:* 1-60-72-48-41 (Fontainebleau). *E-mail:* yongkyun.lee@insead.edu.

LEE, Yoon-woo, BSEE; South Korean business executive; b. 26 April 1946; ed Seoul Nat. Univ.; joined Display Device Business, Samsung Electronics 1968, Products Man., Semiconductor Business 1976–87, Man. Dir, Giheung Plant, Semiconductor Business 1987–92, mem. Bd of Dirs Samsung Electronics 1988–, Exec. Vice-Pres., Semiconductor Business 1992–96, Exec. Vice-Pres. and CEO 1993–96, Pres. and CEO 1996–2004, Vice-Chair., Global Collaboration, Samsung Electronics and CEO Samsung Advanced Inst. of Tech. 2004–05, Vice-Chair., Corp. Chief Tech. Officer and Global Collaboration, Samsung Electronics and Vice-Chair., Samsung Advanced Inst. of Tech. 2005–08, Vice-Chair. and CEO Samsung Electronics 2008–09, Vice-Chair., CEO and DS Business Pres. 2009–10, Vice-Chair. and Chair. Bd of Dirs 2010, Vice-Chair. 2010–12; Chair. Korea Semiconductor Industry Asscn 2000, Korea AV Equipment Research Asscn 2001–, Korea Engineers' Club 2004–, Joong Dong Foundation 2004–, Korea Inst. of Patent Information 2005–; Vice-Chair. Korea Industrial Tech. Asscn 2003–, Seoul Chamber of Commerce and Industry, Korea Fed. of Science and Tech. Socs 2005–; Dir, Korea Int. Trade Asscn 2003–; Technology and Science Award, Invention of 256K DRAM 1985, Order of Industrial Service Merit Award, Silver Tower 1993, Grand Prize of Korean Productivity Award 1995, Grand Prize of Korean Environment Man. Award 1998, Best TPM CEO Award, TPM World Conf.

1998, Order of Industrial Service Merit Award, Gold Tower 1999, Proud Korean Award, Journalist Fed. of Korea 2003, 34th CEO of the Year Award, Korea Man. Asscn 2005. *Address:* c/o Samsung Electronics Bldg, 1320-10 Seocho-2-dong, Seocho-gu, Seoul 137-857, Republic of Korea. *E-mail:* j-npr@samsung.co.kr.

LEE, Young-sun; South Korean business executive; *Chairman, Pohang Iron and Steel Company (POSCO);* fmr Pres. Hallym Univ.; fmr Prof. of Econs and Head of Inst. of State Governance Studies, Yonsei Univ.; Ind. Dir (non-exec.), POSCO (Pohang Iron and Steel Co.), Chair. POSCO 2012–, Chair. of Dir Cand. Recommendation Cttee, mem. Audit Cttee, Related Party Transactions Cttee, Evaluation and Compensation Cttee. *Address:* POSCO Head Office, 1 Goedong-dong, Nam-gu, Pohang, Kyongsangbuk-do, 790-600 (office); POSCO, POSCO Centre, 892 Daechi-4-dong, Kangnam-ku, Seoul 135-777, South Korea (office). *Telephone:* (54) 220-0114 (Head Office) (office); (2) 3457-0114 (POSCO Centre) (office). *Fax:* (54) 220-6000 (Head Office) (office); (2) 3457-6000 (POSCO Centre) (office). *E-mail:* info@posco.com (office). *Website:* www.posco.com (office).

LEE, Yuan-Tseh, PhD; Taiwanese scientist and academic; b. 19 Nov. 1936, Hsinchu; s. of Tse Fan Lee and Pei Tasi; m. Bernice Wu 1963; two s. one d.; ed Nat. Taiwan Univ., Univ. of California, Berkeley, USA; Asst Prof., James Franck Inst. and Dept of Chem., Univ. of Chicago 1968–71, Assoc. Prof. 1971–72, Prof. of Chem. 1973–74; Prof. of Chem., Univ. of California, Berkeley 1974–94, Prof. Emer. 1994–, also Prin. Investigator, Lawrence Berkeley Lab. 1974–97; Distinguished Research Fellow, Inst. of Atomic and Molecular Sciences, Academia Sinica, Taiwan 1994–, Pres. 1994–2006; Sloan Fellow 1969; Guggenheim Fellow 1976; Miller Professorship 1981–82; mem. Int. Council for Science 1993–, mem. Standing Cttee on Freedom in the Conduct of Science 1996–2005, elected Pres. 2008 to take up office 2010; mem. American Acad. of Arts and Sciences, NAS, American Physical Soc. and numerous other scholarly socs; Hon. Prof., Inst. of Chem., Chinese Acad. of Sciences, Beijing 1980–, Hon. Foreign Mem. Indian Nat. Science Acad. 1997, Hon. Mem. Chemical Soc. of Japan 2002–; E. O. Lawrence Award (US Dept of Energy) 1981, Harrison Howe Award, Rochester Section, ACS, 1983, Nobel Prize for Chem. (jtly) 1986, Nat. Medal of Science 1986, Peter Debye Award of Physical Chem., ACS 1986, Faraday Medal, Royal Soc. of Chem., UK 1992, Clark Kerr Award, Univ. of California, Berkeley 1999, Jawaharlal Nehru Centenary Medal, Indian Nat. Science Acad. 2004, and many other awards and prizes. *Publications:* articles in professional journals. *Address:* c/o Academia Sinica, 128 Academia Road, Section 2, Nanking, Taipei 11529, Taiwan (office). *Telephone:* (2) 27899400 (office). *Fax:* (2) 27853852 (office). *E-mail:* ytlee@gate.sinica.edu.tw (office). *Website:* www.sinica.edu.tw (office).

LEE, Yung-San, MA, PhD; Taiwanese economist, banking executive, company director and fmr politician; b. 7 Dec. 1938; m.; three d.; ed Nat. Taiwan Univ., Univ. of Wisconsin, Madison, USA; joined as Asst, Inst. of Econs, Academia Sinica, served successively as Asst Research Fellow, Assoc. Research Fellow, Research Fellow 1962–70, Deputy Dir 1985–87, Dir 1988–90; Prof. of Econs, Nat. Taiwan Univ. 1973–94; Visiting Scholar, Harvard Univ., USA 1976–77; Dir Econ. Research Dept, Cen. Bank of China 1977–85; Pres. Chiao Tung Bank 1990–94; Chair. Farmers Bank of China 1994–98, Int. Commercial Bank of China 1998–2002, Bankers Asscn of Taiwan 2000–02, Asian Bankers Asscn 2000–02; Minister of Finance 2002; fmr Man. Dir Chang Hwa Commercial Bank Ltd, Chair. 2007; Ind. Dir, Nan Ya Plastics Corpn; fmr Dir, International Bills Financial Corpn, Micron Memory Taiwan Co. Ltd, Rexchip Electronics Corpn. *Address:* Nan Ya Plastics Corpn, No. 35-1, Zhongshan 3rd Road, Kaohsiung City, Taiwan. *Telephone:* (2) 2712-2211. *Fax:* (2) 2717-8533. *E-mail:* nanya@npc.com.tw. *Website:* www.npc.com.tw.

LEE-CHIN, Michael; Canadian/Jamaican investment industry executive; *Chairman, AIC Limited;* b. 1951, Port Antonio, Jamaica; m. Adrian Chin 1974 (separated 1997); three c.; pnr Sonya Hamilton; two c.; ed McMaster Univ.; began career in financial services in 1977, positions included Financial Advisor, Investors Group and Regional Br Man., Regal Capital Planning; est. Berkshire Group (financial services co.) 1985; purchased Advantage Investment Council 1987 (renamed AIC) and developedit into an investment co. with funds over C$12 billion, CEO –2006, currently Chair., AIC acquired 75 per cent of Nat. Commercial Bank of Jamaica 2002, established AIC Caribbean Fund 2004; Dr hc (McMaster Univ.) 2003; Hon. LLD, Univ. of Toronto 2007; Harry Jerome Award for Business Leader of the Decade 2002, one of Time magazine's 'Canada's Heroes' 2004. *Address:* AIC Limited, 1375 Kerns Road, Burlington, ON L7R 4X8, Canada (office). *Telephone:* (905) 331-4242 (office). *E-mail:* info@aic.com (office). *Website:* www.aic.com (office).

LEE HANG, Niko; Samoan accountant and politician; *Minister of Finance;* fmr Public Trustee; elected to one of the two parl. seats reserved for Individual Voters March 2006; nominated to cabinet post by the Prime Minister; Minister of Finance 2007–. *Address:* Ministry of Finance, Private Bag, 2–4th Floors, Central Bank Building, Matafele, Apia, Samoa (office). *Telephone:* 34333 (office). *Fax:* 21312 (office). *E-mail:* treasury@samoa.ws (office); information@mof.gov.ws (office). *Website:* www.mof.gov.ws (office).

LEEBRON, David W., JD; American lawyer and university administrator; *President, Rice University;* b. 1956, Philadelphia; s. of Norman D. Leebron; m. Y. Ping Sun; one s. one d.; ed Harvard Coll., Harvard Law School; began career as clerk, US Ninth Circuit Court of Appeals; Assoc., Cleary, Gottlieb, Steen & Hamilton (law firm), New York 1981–83; Prof. of Law, New York Univ. (NYU) 1983, also Dir NYU Int. Legal Studies Program 1983–89; joined faculty, Columbia Univ. Law School 1989, Dean of Law School 1996; Pres. Rice Univ. 2004–; mem. NY State Bar; mem. American Law Inst., Council on Foreign Relations, American Soc. of Int. Law; mem. Bd of Dirs IMAX Corpn; mem. Editorial Bd Foundation Press; Commandeur de l'Ordre Nat. du Mérite 2006. *Address:* Office of the President, Rice University, PO Box 1892, Houston, TX 77251-1892, USA (office). *E-mail:* info@rice.edu (office). *Website:* www.professor.rice.edu/professor/Office_of_the_President.asp (office).

LEENHARDT, Jacques, PhD; French sociologist and academic; *Director of Studies, École des Hautes Études en Sciences Sociales;* b. 17 April 1942, Geneva, Switzerland; s. of Franz J. Leenhardt and Antoinette Chenevière; m. 1st Françoise Warnod 1964 (divorced 1970); one s.; m. 2nd Sabine Wespieser 2006; contrib. to Le Journal de Genève 1963–98, to Le Temps 1998–; Fellow, Inst. for Advanced Study,

Princeton, NJ 1979–80; Visiting Prof. to Univs in Brazil, Chile, Germany, Mexico, Portugal, Puerto Rico, USA 1974–; now Dir of Studies, School of Advanced Studies in Social Sciences, Paris; Pres. French Art Critics Asscn 1981–90, Crestet Centre d'Art 1987–2002, Int. Art Critics Asscn 1990–96, Art in Nature 1991–; mem. European Acad. of Arts and Sciences 1992–; curator of various exhbns; Chevalier des Arts et des Lettres 1983, Ordre nat. du Mérite 1987; Oficial Ordem Nacional do Cruzeiro do Sul (Brazil) 1998; Edra-Place Award 2000. *Publications include:* Lecture politique du roman 1973, Lire la lecture 1982, La force des mots 1982, Au Jardin des Malentendus 1990, Les Amériques latines en France 1992, Dans les jardins de Roberto Burle Marx 1994, Villette-Amazone 1996, Bienal do Mercosur 1998, Michel Corajoud, Paysagiste 2000, Erico Veríssimo. O romance da História 2001, Conscience du paysage: Le passant de Montreuil 2002, Reinventar o Brasil: Gilberto Freyre entre historia e ficçao 2006. *Address:* École des Hautes Études en Sciences Sociales, 13 rue de l'Abbé Grégoire, 75006 Paris, France (office). *Telephone:* (9) 66-95-66-49 (office). *Fax:* (9) 66-95-66-49 (office). *E-mail:* jacques .leenhardt@ehess.fr (office). *Website:* cral.ehess.fr (office).

LEES, Sir David (Bryan), Kt, CBIM, FCA, FRSA; British chartered accountant and business executive; *Chairman, Court of the Bank of England;* b. 23 Nov. 1936, Aberdeen, Scotland; s. of the late Rear-Adm. D. M. Lees, CB, DSO, and of C. D. M. Lees; m. Edith M. Bernard 1961; two s. one d.; ed Charterhouse, Godalming, Surrey; 2nd Lt, Royal Artillery 1955–57; articled clerk, Binder Hamlyn & Co. (Chartered Accountants) 1957–62, Sr Audit Clerk 1962–63; Chief Accountant, Handley Page Ltd 1964–68; Financial Dir Handley Page Aircraft Ltd 1969; Chief Accountant, GKN Sankey Ltd 1970–72, Deputy Controller 1972–73, Dir, Sec., Controller 1973–76; Group Finance Exec. GKN Ltd 1976–77, Gen. Man. Finance 1977–82; Finance Dir GKN PLC 1982–87, Group Man. Dir 1987–88, CEO 1988–96, Chair. 1988–2004; Chair. Courtaulds 1996–98 (Dir (non-exec.) 1991–98); Deputy Chair. Brambles Industries Ltd and Brambles Industries PLC 2001–; Chair. Tate & Lyle PLC 1998–2009; Dir (non-exec.), Bank of England 1991–99 (Chair. of the Court 2009–14), Royal Opera House 1998–2008, QinetiQ Group plc 2005– (Deputy Chair. 2005–12); Pres. Eng Employers' Fed. (EEF) 1990–92, Soc. of Business Economists 1994–99; mem. CBI Council 1988–, Chair. CBI Econ. Affairs Cttee 1988–94, mem. CBI Pres.'s Cttee 1988–96; Commr, Audit Comm. 1983–90; mem. Listed Cos Advisory Cttee 1990–97, Nat. Defence Industries Council 1995–2004, European Round Table 1995–2002, Panel on Takeovers and Mergers 2001– and other bodies; Gov. Shrewsbury School from 1986 (Chair. Governing Body 2004–07), Sutton's Hosp. in Charterhouse 1995–; DL, Shropshire 2007; Hon. Patron Shrewsbury Town Football Club 2010–; Officer's Cross, Order of Merit (FRG) 1996; ICAEW Award for Outstanding Achievement 1999. *Leisure interests:* walking, golf, opera, music. *Address:* Bank of England, Threadneedle Street, London, EC2R 8AH, England. *Telephone:* (20) 7601-4444. *Fax:* (20) 7601-4771. *E-mail:* enquiries@bankofengland.co.uk. *Website:* www.bankofengland.co.uk.

LEES, Martin, BMechEng; British engineer, international official and university administrator; *Rector Emeritus, United Nations University for Peace;* b. 1941; m.; four c.; ed Fettes Coll., Edinburgh, Univ. of Cambridge, Coll. of Europe, Belgium; joined OECD 1971; Special Adviser to Bradford Morse, Admin. UNDP 1978, Exec. Dir UN Financing System for Science and Tech. for Devt 1979–84, Asst Sec.-Gen. UN 1984; Exec. Dir InterAction Council of Former Heads of State and Govt 1983; Dir Gen. Int. Cttee for Econ. Reform and Cooperation, Bonn 1991–96; Founder mem. Toyota Int. Advisory Bd, Moderator 1995–2008; Rector and CEO UN Univ. for Peace, Costa Rica 2001–05, Rector Emer. 2005–; Sr Adviser to Chinese Govt on climate change and sustainable devt 2005–09; Sec. Gen. Club of Rome, Winterthur, Switzerland 2008–10. *Address:* c/o Club of Rome International Secretariat, Lagerhausstrasse 9, 8400 Winterthur, (Canton Zurich), Switzerland.

LEEVES, Jane; British actress; b. 18 April 1963, Ilford, Essex; d. of Colin Leeves and Ruth Leeves; m. Marshall Cohen 1996; one d.; co-f. (with Frasier co-star Peri Gilpin) Bristol Cities Production Co. 1998. *Films:* Monty Python's The Meaning of Life 1983, The Hunger 1983, To Live and Die in LA 1985, Mr Write 1994, Miracle on 34th Street 1994, James and the Giant Peach (voice) 1996, Hercules (voice) 1998, Don't Go Breaking My Heart 1998, Music of the Heart 1999, The Adventures of Tom Thumb and Thumbelina (voice) 2000, The Event 2003, Garfield: A Tail of Two Kitties (voice) 2006, Endless Bummer 2008. *Television:* The Benny Hill Show 1983–85, Double Trouble 1984, Throb 1986, Murphy Brown 1988, Seinfeld 1992, Red Dwarf 1992, Just Deserts 1992, 1999, Frasier 1993–2004, Pandora's Clock 1996, The Great War and the Shaping of the 20th Century (voice) 1996. *Theatre:* Cabaret, Broadway 2002. *Leisure interests:* reading, cooking, sports, dance classes. *Address:* Bristol Cities Productions, c/o Paramount Productions, 5555 Melrose Avenue, Los Angeles, CA 90038, USA (office). *Telephone:* (323) 956-3513 (office). *E-mail:* BrstlCty@aol.com (office).

LEFEBVRE, Georges; French postal service executive; *CEO and Director of Human Resources and Employee Relations, La Poste Group;* ed Ecole Nationale Supérieure des PTT; joined La Poste 1970, becoming Man. Human Resources and Employee Relations 1990–, CEO La Poste Group 2002–, also mem. council various subsidiary cos including Sofipost, Geopost, Banque postale, Poste Immo. *Address:* La Poste Group, 44 boulevard de Vaugirard, 75757 Paris Cedex 15, France (office). *Telephone:* 1-55-44-00-00 (office). *Fax:* 1-55-44-33-00 (office). *E-mail:* info@laposte .fr (office). *Website:* www.laposte.com (office).

LEFÈVRE, Brigitte; French ballet dancer and ballet director; *Director of Dance, Paris Opera;* entered Paris Opera Ballet School aged eight and corps de ballet aged 16, studied with Yvette Chauviré, Gérard Mulys, Serge Peretti, Yves Brieux, Rita Thalia, Janine Schwarz, Serge Perrault and Raymond Franchetti, dancing in ballets by George Balanchine, Roland Petit, Maurice Béjart, Michel Descombey and Gene Kelly, as well as in the major classical works; studied jazz with Gene Robinson and participated in numerous courses given by Alwin Nikolaïs, Merce Cunningham and Paul Taylor; choreographed first work, Mikrocosmos (to music by Bartók), for Jacques Garnier, Michaël Denard and herself 1970, presented at Avignon Festival in the Cour d'honneur; has also worked for the theatre and for musical comedy, in productions by Jean-Michel Ribes, Jean Mercure and Serge Peyrat at the Théâtre de la Ville; cr. choreography for La Révolution Française at the Palais des Sports, Paris; debut as actress in the role of Lisa, in Dostoïevsky's The Possessed, at Théâtre de la Ville, Paris; left the Paris Opera 1972; co-f., with Jacques Garnier, Théâtre du Silence, La Rochelle 1974–85, toured 21 countries world-wide, gave both classical and contemporary classes within the company and

acted as sole dir from 1980; Prin. Insp. of Dance, Ministry of Culture 1985–87, Gen. Insp. and Chief Dance Delegate 1987–92; Gen. Admin. Paris Opéra-Garnier 1992–94, Assoc. Dir and Head of Dance 1994–95, Dir of Dance, Paris Opera 1995–; Vice-Pres. Conservatoire nat. supérieur de musique et de danse de Paris; Admin. Centre Nat. de la Danse 1998–, La Soc. Radio France 2004–; Officier, Ordre nat. du Mérite, Légion d'honneur; Commdr des Arts et des Lettres. *Address:* Opéra National de Paris, Palais Garnier, 8 rue Scribe, 75009 Paris, France (office). *Telephone:* 1-71-25-24-23 (office). *E-mail:* info@operadeparis.fr (office). *Website:* www.operadeparis.fr (office).

LEFKOWITZ, Robert J., BA, MD; American biologist/biochemist and academic; *James B. Duke Professor of Medicine and Professor of Biochemistry, Duke University Medical Center;* b. 15 April 1943, New York; ed Columbia Univ.; Intern, Dept of Medicine, Columbia-Presbyterian Medical Center 1966–67, Asst Resident 1967–68; Clinical and Research Assoc., US Public Health Service, NIH, Bethesda, Md 1968–70; Sr Resident, Dept of Medicine, Mass Gen. Hosp., Boston 1970–71, Clinical and Research Fellow, Dept of Cardiology 1971–73; Teaching Fellow, Harvard Medical School, Dept of Medicine, Boston 1971–73; Assoc. Prof. of Medicine, Duke Univ. Medical Center Durham, NC 1973–77, Asst Prof. of Biochemistry 1973–85, Prof. of Medicine 1977–82, James B. Duke Prof. of Medicine 1982–, Prof. of Biochemistry 1985–, Investigator, Howard Hughes Medical Inst. 1976–; George Thorn Visiting Prof., Brigham and Women's Hosp. 1984; Sterling Drug Visiting Prof. of Pharmacology, Univ. of Mich. Medical School 1986; Sterling Drug-Maurice L. Tainter Professorship, Stanford Univ. School of Medicine 1988; Bulfinch Visiting Prof., Mass Gen. Hosp. 1999; Sec./Treasurer American Fed. for Clinical Research 1980–83; Pres. American Soc. for Clinical Investigation 1987–88; Treasurer Asscn of American Physicians 1989–94, Vice-Pres. 1999–2000, Pres. 2000–01; mem. Bd of Dirs Lexicon Pharmaceuticals 2001–; mem. American Fed. for Clinical Research, American Soc. of Biological Chemists, American Soc. for Clinical Investigation, American Heart Asscn Councils on Basic Science, Clinical Cardiology and Hypertension, American Soc. for Pharmacology and Experimental Therapeutics, Endocrine Soc., Asscn of American Physicians, American Physiological Soc.; mem. Editorial Bd Journal of Clinical Investigation 1990–, Proceedings of the Asscn of American Physicians 1995–, Molecular Biology of the Cell 1996–, Physiological Genomics 1999–, Molecular Interventions 2000–, Circulation 2000–, Fellowship, Int. Acad. of Cardiovascular Sciences 2002; Hon. mem. Japanese Biochemical Soc. 1990; Hon. DSc (Medical Univ. of South Carolina) 2004, (Mount Sinai School of Medicine, New York Univ.) 2004; numerous awards including Roche Prize for Excellence in Medical Studies 1962, Janeway Prize 1966, John J. Abel Award in Pharmacology, American Soc. for Pharmacology and Experimental Therapeutics 1978, George W. Thorn Award for Scientific Excellence, Howard Hughes Medical Inst. 1979, Gordon Wilson Lecture and Award, American Clinical and Climatological Asscn 1982, Ernst Oppenheimer Memorial Award, Endocrine Soc. 1982, Award for Outstanding Research, Int. Soc. for Heart Research 1985, Steven C. Beering Award for Outstanding Achievement in Biomedical Science, Indiana Univ. School of Medicine 1986, H.B. van Dyke Award for Excellence in Medical Research, Columbia Univ. Coll. of Physicians and Surgeons 1986, Goodman and Gilman Award, American Soc. for Pharmacology and Experimental Therapeutics 1986, Gairdner Foundation Int. Award 1988, American Heart Asscn Basic Research Prize (co-recipient) 1990, Asscn of American Medical Colls Biomedical Research Award 1990, Giovanni Lorenzini Prize for Basic Biomedical Research 1992, Bristol-Myers Squibb Award for Distinguished Achievement in Cardiovascular Research 1992, Columbia Univ. Coll. of Physicians and Surgeons Alumnus Award for Distinguished Achievements in Medicine 1992, Joseph Mather Smith Prize, Columbia Univ. Coll. of Physicians and Surgeons 1993, Glorney-Raisbeck Award in Cardiology, The New York Acad. of Medicine 1997, F.E. Shideman-Sterling Award 2000, Novartis/Drew Award in Biomedical Research 2000, Francis Gilman Blake Award, Asscn of American Physicians 2001, Peter Harris Distinguished Scientist Award, Int. Soc. for Heart Research 2001, NAS Jessie Stevenson Kovalenko Medal 2001, Louis and Artur Lucian Award for Research in Circulatory Disease 2001, Pasarow Cardiovascular Research Award 2002, Medal of Merit, Int. Acad. of Cardiovascular Sciences 2003, IPSEN Endrocrinology Prize, France 2003, Grand Prix for Science, Fondation Lefloulon-Delalande, Institut de France 2003, Founding Distinguished Scientist Award, American Heart Asscn, Distinguished Faculty Award, Duke Univ. Medical Center 2004, Albany Medical Center Prize in Medicine and Biomedical Research 2007, The Shaw Prize in Life Science and Medicine 2007, Nat. Medal of Science 2007, Research Achievement Award, American Heart Asscn 2009, BBVA Frontiers of Knowledge Award (Biomedicine Category) 2009, Nobel Prize in Chem. (jtly with Brian K. Kobilka) 2012. *Publications:* more than 800 articles in scientific and medical journals. *Address:* Department of Medicine, Howard Hughes Medical Institute, Duke University Medical Center, PO Box 3821, Durham, NC 27710, USA (office). *Telephone:* (919) 684-2974 (office). *Fax:* (919) 684-8875 (office). *E-mail:* lefko001@receptor-biol.duke.edu (office). *Website:* www.lefkolab.org (office).

LEFRANÇOIS, Jacques Roger; Belgian accountant; *Secretary-General, Conseil mondial de crise;* b. 1 March 1929, Eu, Seine Maritime, France; s. of Roger Lefrançois and Simone Boussy; m. Rosa Van Laer Londerzeel 1952; one s. one d.; ed Coll. d'Eu, Inst. Nat. de Comptabilité; second accountant (Sogeco mar) 1948–52; publicity agent (Publi-Buro) 1952–68; Spokesman, Union pour le contrôle de la democratie 1960; mem. Congress of European People (EFB-MFE) 1961–65; confidential employee 1966–78; World Citizen for Peace through Human Rights 1965; proposed UN Day for World Peace and the Environment 1970; mem. Professional Union of Int. School of Detective Experts 1950–75, Belgium Comm. World Political Union, The Hague 1978–; First Sec. Universal Charter for Survival (UFOS) 1978; Pres. Group 'L'Homme Planétaire' 1970–2012; Founder and Sec.-Gen. Conseil mondial de crise 1989–; mem. Flemish Asscn of Journalists of Periodical Press 1970–94; Ed. L'Indépandant Schaerbeek 1964–, Het Watervlietje 1975–2001; Sec. Flemish Regions, Parti Progressiste Belge 1989–93, Pres. 1985–89; Belgian Ombudsman/Médiateur Belge 1986–88; Pres. Flemish Progressive Party, European Flemish Programme 1989–92; Vice-Pres. European Progressive Party 1990–94; Hon. Pres. and Public Relations Ombudsman Parti Mondial du Coeur 1993–97; mem. Assemblée consultative du congrès des peuples 2007–; Citoyen d'honneur de la ville mondialisée de Dison 2004; Prize for Action to Promote European Federalism 1967, Diploma for services to Brussels tradition and folklore, Ordre des Amis de Manneken-Pis 1986, Action for Handicap International 1998, Action for Alzheimer 2006. *Address:* 9 Rue Leo Baekelandstraat, 2030 Antwerp, Belgium. *Telephone:* (3) 542-04-58.

LEGGESE, Addiso; Ethiopian politician; Pres. Amhara Nat. Regional State 1992–2000; mem. Parl. for Belessa 2005–; Deputy Prime Minister of Ethiopia 2005–, Minister of Agric. and Rural Devt 2005–08; Chair. Population Census Comm. 2006–. *Address:* c/o Office of the Prime Minister, POB 1013, Addis Ababa, Ethiopia (office). *Telephone:* (1) 552044 (office).

LEGGETT, Anthony J., PhD, FRS; British/American physicist and academic; *John D. and Catherine T. MacArthur Professor of Physics and Professor, Center for Advanced Study, University of Illinois at Urbana-Champaign;* ed Balliol, Merton and Magdalen Colls, Oxford; Postdoctoral Research Assoc., Univ. of Illinois, USA 1964–65, Visiting Research Assoc. 1967; Lecturer in Physics, Univ. of Sussex 1967–71, Reader 1971–78, Prof. 1978–83; Fellow, Magdalene Coll. Oxford 1965–67; John D. and Catherine T. MacArthur Prof. of Physics and Prof., Center for Advanced Study, Univ. of Illinois at Urbana-Champaign 1983–; mem. American Philosophical Soc. 1991–, American Acad. of Arts and Sciences 1996–; Foreign Assoc. NAS 1997–; Foreign mem. Russian Acad. of Sciences 1999–; Fellow, American Physical Soc., American Inst. of Physics; Hon. FInstP 1999–; Prize Fellowship, Magdalene Coll., Oxford 1963–64; Inst. of Physics (UK) Maxwell Medal and Prize 1975, Inst. of Physics Simon Memorial Prize 1981, Fritz London Memorial Award 1981, Inst. of Physics Paul Dirac Medal and Prize 1992, John Bardeen Prize (jt recipient) 1994, Wolf Prize (jt recipient) 2003, Nobel Prize in Physics (shared with Alexei Abrikosov and Vitaly Ginzburg) 2003. *Publications:* The Problems of Physics 1986; numerous articles on superconductivity, super-fluidity and theoretical condensed matter physics in scientific journals. *Address:* Department of Physics, University of Illinois at Urbana-Champaign, 1110 West Green Street, Urbana, IL 61801-3080, USA (office). *Telephone:* (217) 333-2077 (office). *Fax:* (217) 333-9819 (office). *E-mail:* aleggett@uiuc.edu (office). *Website:* www.physics.uiuc.edu/People/Faculty/profiles/Leggett (office).

LEGQOG; Chinese politician; b. Oct. 1944, Gyangze Co., Tibet; ed CCP Cen. Driver Cen. Party School; teacher, Gyangze Co., Tibet Autonomous Region 1964–71; Political Cadre, Gyangze Co., Tibet Autonomous Region 1971–73; joined CCP 1972; Sec. Gyangze Co. Autonomous Co. Cttee, CCP Communist Youth League 1973–75; mem. Standing Cttee CCP Communist Youth League Autonomous Prefectural Cttee, Xigaze Prefecture, Tibet Autonomous Region 1973–75; Sec. Org. Dept (Supervisory and Org. Divs) CCP Tibet Autonomous Regional Cttee 1975–80, Deputy Head Org. Dept and Deputy Chief Org. Div. 1980–86, Exec. Deputy Head Org. Dept 1986–91, mem. Standing Cttee CCP Tibet Autonomous Regional Cttee 1991–, Deputy Sec. CCP Tibet Autonomous Regional Cttee 1994–; Sec. CCP Lhasa City Cttee 1991–94; Vice-Chair. Tibet Autonomous Region People's Govt 1995–98, Chair. 1998–2004; Chair. Standing Cttee Tibet Autonomous Regional People's Congress 2003–10; Alt. mem. CCP 15th Cen. Cttee 1997–2002, mem. CCP 16th Cen. Cttee 2002–07, mem. CCP 17th Cen. Cttee 2007–12. *Address:* c/o People's Government of Tibetan Autonomous Region, Lhasa, Tibet, People's Republic of China.

LEGRAS, Guy; French diplomatist and international organization official; b. 19 July 1938, Angers; s. of René Legras and Pauline Legras; m. Borka Oreb 1971; one s. one d.; ed Faculté de Droit, Paris, Inst. d'Etudes Politiques, Paris and Ecole Nat. d'Admin; joined Ministry of Foreign Affairs 1967; Cabinet of Sec. of State for Foreign Affairs 1968–71; Sec.-Gen. of Interministerial Cttee (SGCI) for European Affairs (Prime Minister) 1971–74; Cabinet of Sec.-Gen. of OECD 1974–77; Counsellor, Perm. Rep. of France at European Communities, Brussels 1977–80; Asst Sec.-Gen. SGCI 1980-82; Head, Dept of Econ. Affairs, Ministry of Foreign Affairs 1982–85; Dir-Gen. for Agricultural Comm. of European Communities (now EC), Brussels 1985–99, for External Affairs 1999–2003 (retd); Adviser to Croatia for EU accession talks from 2004; Minister Plenipotentiary 1988; Officier, Ordre nat. du Mérite; Chevalier, Légion d'honneur; Order of Duke Branimir with Necklace (Croatia) 2012. *Leisure interest:* tennis. *Address:* c/o Ministry of Foreign Affairs, 37 quai d'Orsay, 75351 Paris Cedex 07, France.

LEGRIS, Manuel Christophe; French ballet dancer and ballet company director; *Director, Wiener Staatsballett;* b. 19 Oct. 1964, Paris; s. of Michel Legris and Raymonde Gazave; ed Paris Opera School of Dancing; mem. corps de ballet, Opéra de Paris 1980, 'Danseur Etoile' 1986–2009, repertoire included lead roles in works by Frederick Ashton, George Balanchine, Patrice Bart, Maurice Béjart, Trisha Brown, August Bournonville, Vladimir Burmeister, John Cranko, Nacho Duato, Mats Ek, Mikhail Fokin, William Forsythe, Jiří Kylián, Pierre Lacotte, Harald Lander, Serge Lifar, Kenneth MacMillan, John Neumeier, Rudolf Nureyev, Roland Petit, Angelin Preljocaj, Jerome Robbins, Twyla Tharp, Antony Tudor and Rudi van Dantzig; major roles at Paris Opéra include Arepo (Béjart) 1986, In the Middle Somewhat Elevated (Forsythe) 1987, Magnificat (Neumeier) 1987, Rules of the Game (Twyla Tharp) 1989, The Sleeping Beauty (Nureyev) 1989, Manon (MacMillan) 1990, Dances at the Gathering (Robbins) 1993, Variations sur Carmen (Roland Petit) 2003, Phrases de Quatuor (Maurice Béjart) 2003; in Hamburg created Cinderella Story and Spring and Fall (Neumeier); has also appeared at Bolshoi Ballet, Moscow, La Scala, Milan, Royal Ballet, London, New York City Ballet, Tokyo Ballet, Stuttgart Ballet and others; danced at Burgtheater as part of ImPulsTanz 2005, performed in ImPulsTanz ballet gala 2008, presented the gala Manuel Legris & Guests 2012; also appeared with his own ensemble, Manuel Legris et ses Étoiles; danced a solo at Vienna Philharmonic's New Year's Concert 2001; guest performances both at Paris Opéra and at other theatres in Europe, Asia and N America 2009–; Dir Wiener Staatsballett and Artistic Dir Ballet School of the Vienna State Opera 2010–, presented Rudolf Nureyev's version of Don Quixote, staged Pierre Lacotte's La Sylphide, season 2012–13 produced Rudolf Nureyev's The Nutcracker, a total amount of 30 different productions presented 2010–13, as dancer, appeared at the Wiener Staatsoper at opening ceremony of the Vienna Opera Ball 2011, at the Nureyev Galas 2011, 2012, 2013, toured with Wiener Staatsballett to Japan 2012, cr. title-role in Patrick de Bana's Ludwig II – The Swan King and also danced in Roland Petit's The Bat; Chevalier des Arts et des Lettres 1993, Officier 1998, Commdr 2009; Chevalier, Ordre nat. du Mérite 2002, Légion d'honneur 2006; Gold Medal, Osaka Competition 1984, Prix du Cercle Carpeaux 1986, Nijinsky Prize 1988, Prix Benois de la danse 1998, Nijinsky Award (Best Dancer in the World) 2000, Prix Positano 2001,

Prix Léonide Massine 2001, Prix Danza & Danza 2002. *Film appearances include:* Romeo and Juliet, Le Spectre de la Rose, Notre Dame de Paris, L'Arlésienne, The Sleeping Beauty, Don Quixote. *Address:* Wiener Staatsoper GmbH, Opernring 2, 1010 Vienna, Austria (office). *Telephone:* (1) 51444 (office). *E-mail:* information@wiener-staatsoper.at (office). *Website:* www.wiener-staatsoper.at (office).

LEGWAILA, Legwaila Joseph, MA; Botswana diplomatist; b. 2 Feb. 1937, Mathathane; s. of Madume Legwaila and Morongwa Legwaila; m. Pholile Matsebula 1975; three d.; ed Bobonong School, Brussels School, SA, Serowe Teacher Training Coll., Univs of Calgary and Alberta, Canada; early career as primary school teacher; Asst Prin. External Affairs, Govt of Botswana 1973–74, Sr Pvt. Sec. to Pres. of Botswana 1974–80; apptd Perm. Rep. to UN 1980; High Commr to Guyana 1981–2001, concurrently High Commr to Jamaica 1982–2001, Amb. to Cuba 1983–2001; Deputy Special Rep. of the UN Sec.-Gen. for Namibia 1989–90, Head of UN Mission in Ethiopia and Eritrea (UNMEE) 2000–06, Sec.-Gen.'s Special Adviser on Africa 2006–08. *Publication:* Safari to Serowe (co-author) 1970. *Leisure interests:* music, cycling. *Address:* c/o Office of the Secretary General, United Nations, New York, NY 10017, USA.

LEHMAN, Ronald (Ron) Frank, II, PhD; American security expert and government official; *Director, Center for Global Security Research, Lawrence Livermore National Laboratory;* b. 25 March 1946, Napa, Calif.; s. of Ronald Lehman and Esther Suhr; m. Susan Young 1979; ed Claremont Men's Coll. and Claremont Grad. School; served in US Army in Viet Nam 1969–71; Legis. Asst US Senate 1976–78; mem. professional staff, US Senate Armed Services Cttee 1978–82; Deputy Asst Sec. of Defense, Office of Int. Security Policy 1982–83; Sr Dir Defense Programs and Arms Control, Nat. Security Council 1983–86; Deputy US Negotiator for Strategic Nuclear Arms, Dept of State, Washington, DC 1985–86, Chief US Negotiator Geneva 1986–88; Deputy Asst to Pres. for Nat. Security Affairs 1986; Asst Sec. Dept of Defense 1988–89; Dir Arms Control and Disarmament Agency, Washington, DC 1989–93; Asst to Dir Lawrence Livermore Nat. Lab. 1993–, Dir Center for Global Security Research 1996–; mem. Presidential Advisory Bd on Arms Proliferation Policy 1995–96; Adjunct Prof. Georgetown Univ. 1982–89; mem. Bd Dirs US Inst. of Peace 1988–93, Keck Center for Int. and Strategic Studies (now Chair.), Claremont McKenna Coll.; mem. Int. Advisory Bd Inst. of Global Conflict and Cooperation, Univ. of Calif. San Diego 1994–; mem. IISS, Council on Foreign Relations, Atlantic Council. *Address:* Center for Global Security Research, Lawrence Livermore National Laboratory, PO Box 808, L-1, Livermore, CA 94551 (office); 693 Encina Grande Drive, Palo Alto, CA 94306, USA (home). *Telephone:* (925) 422-6141 (office). *Fax:* (925) 422-5252 (office). *E-mail:* lehman3@llnl.gov (office). *Website:* cgsr.llnl.gov (office).

LEHMANN, HE Cardinal Karl, DPhil, DTheol; German ecclesiastic; *Bishop of Mainz;* b. 16 May 1936, Sigmaringen; ed in Freiburg, Rome, Munich, Münster; ordained priest of Freiburg im Breisgau 1963; asst to Karl Rahner, Munich and Münster 1964–67; Prof. of Theology, Univ. of Mainz 1968–71, Univ. of Freiburg 1971–83; Bishop of Mainz 1983–; Chair. German Bishops' Conf. 1987–2008; cr. Cardinal (Cardinal-Priest of San Leone I) 2001; participated in Papal Conclave 2005, 2013; Hon. Citizen of Mainz 2001; Bundesverdienstkreuz 2000; Dr hc (Innsbruck, Washington, Maynooth, Warsaw, Graz, Opole (Poland)); FrieKarl Barth Prize, Evangelical Union of Churches 1994, 'Golden Flower from Rheydt' of the town Mönchengladbach 1995. *Publications:* ed. of numerous religious journals. *Address:* Bischofsplatz 2A, 55116 Mainz, Germany (office). *Telephone:* (6131) 253101 (office). *Fax:* (6131) 229337 (office). *E-mail:* bischof.lehmann@bistum-mainz.de (office). *Website:* www.bistum-mainz.de.

LEHMANN, Klaus-Dieter; German librarian; *President, The Goethe Institute;* b. 29 Feb. 1940, Breslau (today Wrocław, Poland); ed Max-Planck-Institut für Chemie, Mainz; trained as a librarian, graduated in Library Science 1970; worked at Municipal Library and Univ. Library, Frankfurt am Main 1973–88, Man. Dir 1978–88; Dir-Gen. Univ. Library, Frankfurt 1988–98; following re-unification, led two Nat. Libraries in Frankfurt and Leipzig (Die Deutsche Bibliothek—German Nat. Library); Pres. Prussian Cultural Heritage Foundation, Berlin 1998–2008; Vice-Pres. Goethe Inst. 2002–08, Pres. and mem. Bd of Trustees 2008–; mem. Bd of Trustees, Bertelsmann Foundation, Acad. of Sciences and Literature, Mainz, Peace Prize of German Publrs and Booksellers; Hon. Prof., Univ. of Frankfurt am Main, Humboldt Univ., Berlin; Ordre des Palmes académiques, Bundesverdienstkreuz (First Class), Order of Merit of the Land Berlin 2006, Austrian Honorary Cross for Science and Art (First Class) 2007, Culture of the German Cultural Council groschen 2008; Dr hc (Ludwig-Maximilians Univ., Munich). *Publications:* Treasures of the World Cultures in the Collections of the Stiftung Preussischer Kulturbesitz 2004, Digital Resources from Cultural Institutions for Use in Teaching and Learning 2004, Science and Culture in Libraries, Museums and Archives 2005, Phoenix Bird 2007, Picture Book and Archetypes 2008. *Address:* Goethe-Institut, Head Office, Dachauer Strasse 122, 80637 Munich, Germany (office). *Telephone:* (89) 15921-0 (office). *Fax:* (89) 15921-450 (office). *E-mail:* praesident@goethe.de (office). *Website:* www.goethe.de (office).

LEHMBERG, Stanford Eugene, PhD, LittD, FRHistS, FSA; American historian and academic; *Professor Emeritus of History, University of Minnesota;* b. 23 Sept. 1931, McPherson, Kan.; s. of W. E. Lehmberg and Helen Lehmberg; m. Phyllis Barton 1962; one s.; ed Univ. of Kansas, Univ. of Cambridge, UK; mem. History Faculty, Univ. of Tex. at Austin 1956–69; Prof. of History, Univ. of Minn. 1967–98, now Prof. Emer.; Organist and Choirmaster, St Clement's Episcopal Church, St Paul, Minn. 1970–98; Fulbright Scholarship 1954–56, Guggenheim Fellow 1955–56, 1985–86. *Publications:* Sir Thomas Elyot, Tudor Humanist 1960, Sir Walter Mildmay and Tudor Government 1966, The Reformation Parliament, 1529–1536 1970, The Later Parliaments of Henry VIII 1977, The Reformation of Cathedrals 1988, The Peoples of the British Isles from Prehistoric Times to 1688 1991, Cathedrals Under Siege 1996, The University of Minnesota 1945–2001 2001, Holy Faith of Santa Fe 2004, English Cathedrals: a History 2005, Churches for the Southwest 2005; Ed. Sir Thomas Elyot, The Book Named the Governor 1962; articles, reviews. *Leisure interests:* music, the arts. *Address:* 1005 Calle Largo, Santa Fe, NM 87501, USA. *Telephone:* (505) 986-5074. *Fax:* (505) 986-1724. *E-mail:* lehmberg@earthlink.net.

LEHN, Jacques André, LèsL; French business executive; b. 15 July 1944, Lausanne, Switzerland; s. of François-Xavier Lehn and Geneviève Jaeger; ed lycées in Rabat, Morocco and Sceaux, Sorbonne, Paris, Inst. d'Etudes Politiques, Paris and Ecole des Hautes Etudes Commerciales; Man. Consultant, Arthur Andersen 1969–76; Finance Dir Warner Lambert France 1976–79; Dir-Gen. Adams' France 1979–80; Dir Matra, Médias Br. 1980–81; Dir Hachette Group 1981–84, Deputy Dir-Gen. 1984–90, Dir-Gen. 1990; Dir-Gen. Matra-Hachette 1993–; Vice-Pres. Europe I Communication 1986–94, Deputy Pres. 1994–99; Pres., Dir-Gen. Europe développement int. 1996–; Pres. Supervisory Bd Europa Plus, France 1996–, Chair. and CEO Go Mass Media, Go Outdoor Holdings Systems 1999–; Chair. Supervisory Bd Giraudy 1999–; Founding mem. ORMA (Ocean Racing Multihull Asscn) 1993–, Pres. 1993–2004; Vice-Chair. Oceanic Subcttee, Int. Sailing Fed. (ISAF) 2005–09, Chair. Offshore and Oceanic Cttee 2009–, mem. ISAF Council 2012–; numerous other business affiliations; Chevalier, Ordre nat. du Mérite, Chevalier, Légion d'honneur. *Leisure interest:* yachting. *Address:* ORMA, 9 rue Royale, 75008 Paris (office); ISAF UK (Ltd), Ariadne House, Town Quay, Southampton, Hants., SO14 2AQ, England; 47 blvd Lannes, 75116 Paris, France (home). *Telephone:* 1-53-30-86-07 (office); (23) 8063-5111. *Fax:* (23) 8063-5789; 1-47-42-32-14 (office). *E-mail:* secretariat@isaf.co.uk (office); jacques.lehn@libertysurf.fr (office). *Website:* www.sailing.org (office).

LEHN, Jean-Marie Pierre, DèsSc, PhD; French chemist and academic; *Director, Institut de Science et d'Ingénierie Supramoléculaires, Université Louis Pasteur;* b. 30 Sept. 1939, Rosheim, Bas-Rhin; s. of Pierre and Marie (née Salomon) Lehn; m. Sylvie Lederer 1965; two s.; ed Univ. of Strasbourg; various posts, CNRS 1960–66; post-doctoral Research Assoc. with Prof. R. B. Woodward, Harvard Univ., USA 1963–64; Asst Prof., Univ. of Strasbourg 1966–70, Assoc. Prof. 1970, Prof. 1970–79; currently Dir Institut de Science et d'Ingénierie Supramoléculaires, Université Louis Pasteur; Visiting Prof. of Chem., Harvard Univ. 1972, 1974, ETH, Zurich 1977, Univ. of Cambridge 1984, Barcelona Univ. 1985; Prof., Collège de France, Paris 1979–; Pres. Scientific Council of Rhône-Poulenc 1992–, of Ministry of Nat. Educ., Youth and Sport 1989–93; mem. Research Strategy Cttee 1995, Inst. de France, Deutsche Akad. der Naturforscher Leopoldina, Accad. Nazionale dei Lincei; Foreign assoc. NAS; Foreign mem. Royal Netherlands Acad. of Arts and Sciences, Royal Soc. and many others; Foreign Hon. mem. American Acad. of Arts and Sciences; Commdr, Légion d'honneur, Officier, Ordre nat. du Mérite, mem. Order 'Pour le Mérite' 1990, Ostereizschihes Ehrenkreuz für Wissenschaft und Kunst, Erste Klasse 2001; shared Nobel Prize in Chem. 1987, Gold, Silver and Bronze Medals of CNRS, Gold Medal, Pontifical Acad. of Sciences 1981, Paracelsus Prize, Swiss Chemical Soc. 1982, von Humboldt Prize 1983, Karl Ziegler Prize (German Chemical Soc.) 1989, Davy Medal (Royal Soc.) 1997, Lavoisier Medal 1997, A.R. Day Award 1998, numerous others. *Publications:* about 900 scientific publs. *Leisure interest:* music. *Address:* Chemistry laboratory Chimie Supramoléculaire, ISIS, Allée Gaspard Monge 8, 67000 Strasbourg Cedex (office); 6 rue des Pontonniers, 67000 Strasbourg, France (home). *Telephone:* (3) 68-85-51-45 (office); (88) 37-06-42 (home). *Fax:* (3) 68-85-51-40 (office). *E-mail:* lehn@unistra.fr (office). *Website:* www-isis.u-strasbg.fr/supra/ (office).

LEHNER, Ulrich; German business executive; *Chairman of the Supervisory Board, Deutsche Telekom AG;* b. 1 May 1946, Düsseldorf; m. Johanna Ewers 1970; two s. one d.; mem. Bd of Man., Henkel KGaA 1995–2000, Chair. Exec. Bd, Pres. and CEO 2000–08, mem. Stockholder Cttee 2008–; Chair. Supervisory Bd Dial Corpn, Deutsche Telekom AG, ThyssenKrupp AG 2013– (mem. 2008–); mem. Supervisory Bd E.ON AG, Porsche Automobil Holding SE; mem. Advisory Bd Novartis AG (Switzerland), Dr August Oetker KG; Pres. Verbandes der Chemischen Industrie 2007–10; Hon. Prof., Univ. of Münster. *Address:* Deutsche Telekom AG, Friedrich-Ebert-Allee 140, 53113 Bonn, Germany (office). *Telephone:* (228) 1814949 (office). *Fax:* (228) 18194004 (office). *E-mail:* info@deutschetelekom.com (office). *Website:* www.deutschetelekom.com (office); www.telekom.com (office).

LEHOHLA, Archibald Lesao, BSc, BA, MA; Lesotho politician; *Deputy Prime Minister and Minister of Home Affairs, Public Safety and of Parliamentary Affairs;* b. 28 July 1946, Mafeteng; m.; two s. one d.; ed Mafeteng Secondary School, Basutoland High School, Univ. of Botswana, Lesotho and Swaziland, Roma, Univ. of Oxford, UK; Teaching Asst in Math., Univ. of Botswana, Lesotho and Swaziland 1971–72; Asst Teacher, Bereng High School 1975–76, Headmaster 1977–93; mem. Parl. for Mafeteng 1993–; Minister of Home Affairs (Local Govt, Rural and Urban Devt) 1993–95, of Transport, Posts and Telecommunications 1995–96, of Educ. and Manpower Devt 1996–2004, of Home Affairs and Public Safety 2004–, and of Parl. Affairs 2007–; Deputy Prime Minister 2003–; Chair. Scott Hosp. Comm. of Inquiry 1990; fmr Chair. Mafeteng Tractor Owners' Cooperative; Church Elder and mem. Mafeteng LEC consistory; fmr mem. Lesotho Headmasters' and Headmistresses' Asscn, Lesotho Evangelical Church Law Review Comm., LEC Educational Sec.'s Advisory Cttee on Educ.; rep. Lesotho at Commonwealth Seminar on Educational Admin and Supervision, Univ. of Nairobi, Kenya 1977; UNESCO Fellowship to Univ. of Oxford 1975. *Leisure interests:* gardening, singing, crop farming. *Address:* Ministry of Home Affairs and Public Safety, POB 174 Maseru 100, Lesotho (office). *Telephone:* 22320017 (office). *E-mail:* mohonoel@homeaffairs.gov.ls (office).

LEHR, Ursula M., DrPhil (Habil.); German government official, psychologist and academic; *Founding Director and Senior Researcher, Deutsches Zentrum für Alternsforschung;* b. (Ursula M. Leipold), 5 June 1930, Frankfurt am Main; d. of Georg-Josef Leipold and Gertrud Jendorff; m. 1st Helmut Lehr 1950 (died 1994); two s.; m. 2nd Hans Thomas 1998 (died 2001); Research Asst, Univ. of Bonn 1955–60, Research and Teaching Asst, Inst. of Psychology 1960–68, mem. perm. staff 1968–69, Additional Prof. and Head Dept of Developmental Psychology 1969–72, Chair. Dept of Psychology and Dir Inst. of Psychology 1976–86, Hon. Prof. 1987–; Chair. of Pedagogics and Pedagogical Psychology, Albertus Magnus Univ., Cologne 1972; Dir Inst. of Gerontology, Ruprecht Karls Univ., Heidelberg 1986–88, 1991–96; Founding Dir and Sr Consultant Deutsches Zentrum für Alternsforschung (DZFA—German Centre for Research on Aging), Heidelberg 1996–; Fed. Minister of Youth, Families, Women and Health 1988–91; mem. Families Advisory Bd, Fed. Ministry of Youth, Families and Health 1972–80, WHO Expert Advisory Panel on Health of Elderly Persons 1983–87; mem. Parl. 1990–94; Pres. Asscn of Fmr Mems of the German and European Parl. 2002–; German Nat. Asscn of Senior Citizens Orgs (BAGSO) 2009–; Vice-Pres. German Gerontological Soc. 1973–78, 1980–84, Pres. 1997–99; Founder mem. Acad. of Sciences, Berlin 1987–91; Corresp. mem. Acad. of Sciences, Austria 1994–, Sächsische Akad. der

Wissenschaften 1998–; mem. European Acad. of Yuste, Spain 2000–; Hon. mem. Socs of Gerontology of Switzerland, Spain, Mexico, Hon. Pres. BAGSO (German Nat. Asscn of Senior Citizens' Orgs) 2009–; Grosses Bundesverdienstkreuz 1996; Hon. PhD (Fribourg, Switzerland, Univ. of Vechta); Landesverdienstmedaille Baden-Württemberg 1999, Lifetime award Bund Deutscher Psychologen 2003. *Publications:* more than 900 scientific texts. *Leisure interests:* art (paintings of the Middle Ages), history of art. *Address:* Am Büchel 53B, 53173 Bonn, Germany. *Telephone:* (228) 352849. *Fax:* (228) 352741. *E-mail:* ursula.lehr@t-online.de.

LEHRER, James (Jim) Charles, AA, BJ; American broadcast journalist and writer; *Executive Editor and Anchor, The News Hour with Jim Lehrer;* b. 19 May 1934, Wichita, Kan.; m. Kate Lehrer (née Staples); three d.; ed Victoria Coll., Tex., Univ. of Missouri; served as infantry officer US Marine Corps 1956-58; reporter, Dallas Morning News (daily newspaper) 1959–61; reporter and columnist Dallas Times-Herald 1961–70; Exec. Dir of Public Affairs, on-air host, and Ed., nightly news program KERA–TV, Dallas 1970–72; Public Affairs Coordinator, Public Broadcasting Service (PBS), Washington, DC 1972–73, also mem. Journalism Advisory Bd and Fellow, Corpn for Public Broadcasting; correspondent Nat. Public Affairs Center for TV (NPACT) 1973–, co-hosted coverage of US Senate Watergate hearings and US House Judiciary Cttee Nixon impeachment inquiry, Washington correspondent, Robert MacNeil Report 1975, co-anchor MacNeil/Lehrer Report 1975–83, co-anchor MacNeil/Lehrer NewsHour 1983–96, Exec. Ed. and Anchor, The News Hour with Jim Lehrer 1996–; Fellow, American Acad. of Arts and Sciences; numerous awards for journalism including two Emmys, Fred Friendly First Amendment Award, George Foster Peabody Broadcast Award, William Allen White Foundation Award for Journalistic Merit, Medal of Honor, Univ. of Missouri School of Journalism; Nat. Humanities Medal 1999; inducted (with Robert MacNeil) TV Hall of Fame, Silver Circle of Washington, DC Chapter of Nat. Acad. of TV Arts and Sciences. *Plays:* Chili Queen 1987, Church Key Charlie Blue 1988, The Will and Bart Show 1992. *Publications include:* We Were Dreamers 1975, Kick the Can 1988, Crown Oklahoma 1989, The Sooner Spy 1990, Lost and Found 1991, Short List 1992, A Bus of My Own 1992, Blue Hearts 1993, Fine Lines 1994, The Last Debate 1995, White Widow 1997, Purple Dots 1998, The Special Prisoner 2000, No Certain Rest 2002, Flying Crows 2004, The Franklin Affair 2005, The Phony Marine 2006, Super 2010. *Address:* The NewsHour with Jim Lehrer, 3620 S 27th Street, Arlington, VA 22206, USA (office). *Telephone:* (703) 998-2813 (office). *E-mail:* newshour@pbs.org (office). *Website:* www.pbs.org/newshour/aboutus/bio_lehrer.html (office).

LEHTOMÄKI, Paula Ilona, MSc; Finnish politician; b. 29 Nov. 1972, Kuhmo; m.; one c.; acting sr teacher 1995; research asst 1998; mem. Kuhmo Town Council 1997; mem. Parl. (Centre Party) 1999–; mem. Finnish Del. to Nordic Council 1999–2003, to Council of Europe 2003; Minister for Foreign Trade and Devt and Minister at the Prime Minister's Office 2003–07, of the Environment 2007–11; mem. Supervisory Bd VR-Group Ltd 2000–03, Bd Audiator Oy 2000–03, Exec. Cttee Lasten Keskus Publishing House 2000–01, Cttee Finnish 4H Fed. 2001–03, Bd Finland-Russia Soc. 2000–03. *Leisure interest:* fitness training. *Address:* c/o Ministry of the Environment, Kasarmikatu 25, PO Box 35, 00023 Helsinki, Finland.

LEI, Lt-Gen. Mingqiu; Chinese army officer; *Political Commissar, Nanjing Military Region, People's Liberation Army;* b. March 1942, Jiangjiaqiao, Qidong Co., Hengyang City, Hunan Prov.; ed Zhuzhou Aeronautical Acad. Hunan and PLA Political Acad.; joined PLA 1962, CCP 1964; platoon leader and Deputy Political Instructor, Mortar Bn 1965–69; Deputy Section Chief of Org., Div. Political Dept 1969–71, Dir Div. Political Dept 1982–83; clerk and Deputy Chief (later Chief) of Youth Affairs Section, Political Dept, Guangzhou City, PLA Guangzhou Mil. Region 1971–80; Deputy Political Commissar, 42nd Army, Army (or Ground Force), PLA Services and Arms 1983–85, Political Commissar 1985–92; Dir Political Dept, Guangzhou Mil. Region 1992–94; Deputy Political Commissar, Nanjing Mil. Region 1994–2000 (Sec. Comm. for Discipline Inspection, CCP Party Cttee 1994–99), Political Commissar 2000–; mem. 13th CCP Cen. Cttee 1987–92, 14th CCP Cen. Cttee 1992–97, 15th CCP Cen. Cttee 1997–2002, 16th CCP Cen. Cttee 2002–07. *Address:* Office of the Political Commissar, Nanjing Military Region, People's Republic of China.

LEIBINGER, Berthold, Dr-Ing; German business executive; *Chairman of the Supervisory Board, TRUMPF GmbH & Company KG;* joined TRUMPF as engineer 1950, Pres. and Chair. Man. Bd –2005, Chair. Supervisory Bd 2005–. *Address:* TRUMPF GmbH + Co. KG, Johann-Maus-Strasse 2, 71254 Ditzingen, Germany (office). *Telephone:* (7156) 303-30231 (office). *E-mail:* berthold.leibinger@de.trumpf.com (office). *Website:* www.trumpf.com (office).

LEIBINGER-KAMMÜLLER, Nicola, DrPhil; German business executive; *President and Chairwoman of the Management Board, Trumpf Group;* b. 15 Dec. 1959, Wilmington, Ohio, USA; ed studied German, English and Japanese language and literature in Freiburg, Germany, Middlebury, VT, USA and Zurich, Switzerland; worked in Press and Public Relations Office, Trumpf Group 1984–88, for Trumpf Corpn, Japan 1988–90, Man. Dir Berthold Leibinger Foundation, GmbH 1992–2003, Exec. Vice-Pres. Trumpf GmbH & Co. KG (man. holding co. of Trumpf Group) 2003–05, Pres. 2005–, Pres. and Chair. Man. Bd Trumpf Group 2008–, responsible for strategic devt, corp. communication and real estate and facilities; mem. Supervisory Bd CLAAS KGaA mbH 2006–, Siemens AG 2008–, Voith AG, Axel-Springer-Verlag; mem. Advisory Bd Landesbank Baden-Wuerttemberg; previously served with Claas Kommanditgesellschaft auf Aktien mgh and Deutsche Lufthansa AG from 2008; ranked 38th by Fortune magazine amongst the 50 Most Powerful Women in Business outside the US (38th) 2008, (36th) 2009, (49th) 2010, (47th) 2011. *Address:* Trumpf Group, Trumpf GmbH & Co. KG, Johann-Maus-Str. 2, 71254 Ditzingen, Germany (office). *Telephone:* (7156) 303-0 (office). *Fax:* (7156) 303-30309 (office). *E-mail:* info@trumpf.com (office). *Website:* www.trumpf.com (office).

LEIBLER, Kenneth (Ken) Robert, BA; American business executive; b. 21 Feb. 1949, New York, NY; s. of Max Leibler and Martha Leibler (née Dales); m. Marcia Kate Reiss 1973; one s. one d.; ed Syracuse Univ. and Univ. of Pennsylvania; Options Man. Lehman Bros 1972–75; Vice-Pres. Options, American Stock Exchange, New York 1975–79, Sr Vice-Pres. Admin. and Finance 1979–81, Exec. Vice-Pres. Admin. and Finance 1981–85, Sr Exec. Vice-Pres. 1985–86, Pres.

1986–90; Pres. and COO Liberty Financial Cos 1990–95, Pres. and CEO 1995–2000; Chair. and CEO Boston Stock Exchange 2001–05; Chair. and CEO NASDAQ OMX BX, Inc. 2001–05; Founder Partner and Chair. Boston Options Exchange Group, LLC 2004–07; Vice-Chair. Beth Israel Medical Center 2009–12; Instructor, New York Inst. of Finance; Dir, Securities Industry Automation Corpn, Beth Israel Deaconess Care Org.; Lead Dir and Dir, The Ruder Finn Group 2005–10; mem. Finance Execs Inst. of Securities Industry Asscn, American Stock Exchange Clearing Corpn; Trustee, Northeast Utilities 2006–, Putnam Investment Management, LLC 2006–, Beth Israel Deaconess Hosp., Boston 2006–; Dir/Trustee, Optimum Funds in Fund Complex 2003–06; Ind. Trustee of various funds in the fund complex of Putnam Funds (except Putnam Investment Management) 2006–, Chair. Audit and Compliance Cttee 2012–. *Publication:* Handbook of Financial Markets: Securities, Options, Futures (contrib.) 1981. *Address:* Northeast Utilities, Prudential Building, Boston, MA 02199, USA (office). *Telephone:* (860) 665-3249 (office). *E-mail:* info@nu.com (office). *Website:* www.nu.com (office).

LEIBOVITZ, Annie; American photographer; b. 2 Oct. 1949, Westport, Conn.; ed San Francisco Art Inst. and studies with photographer Ralph Gibson; lived on a kibbutz in Israel and participated in archaeological dig at site of King Solomon's temple 1969; photographed rock 'n' roll stars and other celebrities for Rolling Stone magazine 1970–83; served as concert-tour photographer for The Rolling Stones band 1975; Chief Photographer, Vanity Fair 1983–; Propr Annie Leibovitz Studio, New York; official photographer Olympic Games, Atlanta 1996; advertising campaigns for American Express 2005, Disney 2007; celebrity portraits include John Lennon, Mick Jagger, Bette Midler, Louis Armstrong, Ella Fitzgerald, Jessye Norman, Mikhail Baryshnikov, Arnold Schwarzenegger, Tom Wolfe 1991, HM Queen Elizabeth II 2007; Photographer of the Year Award, American Soc. of Magazine Photographers 1984, Innovation in Photography Award, American Soc. of Magazine Photographers 1987, Clio Award 1987, Campaign of the Decade Award, Advertising Age magazine 1987, Infinity Award for applied photography, Int. Center for Photography 1990, Lifetime Achievement Award, Int. Center of Photography 2008, Award to Distinguished Women in the Arts, Museum of Contemporary Art, Los Angeles 2012. *Film:* Annie Leibovitz Life through a Lens 2006. *Publications:* Photographs 1970–90 1992, Women (with Susan Sontag) 2000, A Photographer's Life 1990–2005 2006, Annie Leibovitz at Work 2008. *Address:* Annie Leibovitz Studio, 443 West 18th Street, Suite 4, New York, NY 10011-3817 (office); c/o Jim Moffat, Art and Commerce, 755 Washington Street, New York, NY 10014, USA. *Telephone:* (212) 594-3817 (office). *E-mail:* als@leibovitzstudio.com (office). *Website:* www.leibovitzstudio.com (office).

LEIFERKUS, Sergey Petrovich; Russian singer (baritone); b. 4 April 1946, Leningrad; ed Leningrad Conservatory with Barsov and Shaposhnikov; stage debut in Leningrad Theatre of Musical Comedy 1972; soloist Maly Theatre of Opera and Ballet 1972–78, sang in Eugene Onegin, Iolanta, Il Barbiere di Siviglia and Don Giovanni; Kirov (now Mariinsky) Theatre of Opera and Ballet 1977–85, sang Prince Andrei in War and Peace by Prokofiev; Wexford Festival 1982–86, in Grisélidis and Le Jongleur de Notre Dame by Massenet, Hans Heiling by Marschner and Königskinder by Humperdinck; Scottish Opera from 1985, as Don Giovanni, Germont and Eugene Onegin 1988; Covent Garden 1987, as Eugene Onegin and Tomsky in The Queen of Spades, with the Kirov Company; ENO 1987, as Zurga in Les Pêcheurs de Perles; US debut 1987, in Symphony No. 13 by Shostakovich, with the Boston Symphony; Wigmore Hall debut recital, sang Luna in a new production of Il Trovatore at Covent Garden and appeared in a concert performance of Giovanna d'Arco at the Festival Hall 1989; concert performance of Mlada by Rimsky-Korsakov, Barbican Hall; US opera debut at San Francisco, as Telramund in Lohengrin, and the title role in Prince Igor at Covent Garden 1989–90; sang Rangoni in Boris Godunov at the Kirov Theatre, St Petersburg 1990; Luna at the Teatro Colón, Buenos Aires, Mazeppa at the Bregenz Festival and Netherlands Opera, Amsterdam, Ruprecht in Prokofiev's Fiery Angel at the BBC Promenade Concerts, London; Tomsky in The Queen of Spades in Boston and New York with the Boston Symphony; Onegin in Montreal, Ruprecht in St Petersburg, Tomsky at Glyndebourne and Vienna State Opera, Rangoni at San Francisco; Iago at Covent Garden and at the Metropolitan 1992; sang Carlo in La Forza del Destino for VARA Radio at the Amsterdam Concertgebouw, Shostakovich 13th Symphony with the New York Philharmonic, Scarpia, Amonasro, Escamillo and Luna 1993; debut at La Scala in The Fiery Angel, further performances as Iago at the Metropolitan, New York, Scarpia at Opéra Bastille, Paris, sang Mephistopheles in La Damnation de Faust with Ozawa and the Berlin Philharmonic in Berlin, the title role in Nabucco at the Bregenz Festival, sang Ruprecht in San Francisco and gave recitals across America, Escamillo at the Teatro Colón, Buenos Aires and Prokofiev's Ivan the Terrible at La Scala 1994; sang Iago at Covent Garden, Mazeppa at Netherlands Opera, Amsterdam, Shostakovich 13th Symphony in Leipzig with the Gewandhaus Orchestra, Gryaznoy in The Tsar's Bride for Opera Orchestra of New York in Carnegie Hall, Escamillo in a gala performance of Carmen in Stuttgart, Iago at the Vienna State Opera, recitals at Cologne and Graz, Amonasro at the Berlin State Opera under Mehta, Scarpia at the Ravinia Festival 1995; Boccanegra in the original version of Verdi's opera and Telramund in Lohengrin at Covent Garden 1997; Klingsor in Parsifal with the Royal Opera, RFH 1998; Klingsor at the Royal Albert Hall (concert), Simon Boccanegra at Melbourne and Prince Igor in Houston 2000–01; season 2001–02 in Pique Dame in Los Angeles and Washington, DC, Simon Boccanegra in Dallas, Aida in Berlin, Lohengrin in Munich, Tosca in London and Munich, solo recitals in Paris and London; season 2002–03 in Otello in Japan (tour), London and San Francisco, Pique Dame in Munich, Fidelio in Dallas, Tosca in Munich, Shostakovich Symphony No. 13 in Prague and Lohengrin in London. *Recordings include:* Songs of Borodin and Dargomizhsky 1996, Mahler's Symphony No. 8 1997, Mahler's Das klagende Lied 1997, Verdi, Tenor Arias 2001, Mussorgsky's Chansons 2003, Shostakovich's Songs and Waltzes 2006. *Address:* c/o Deutsche Grammophon, Baumwall 3, 20459 Hamburg, Germany (office). *E-mail:* deutschegrammophon@umusic.com (office). *Website:* www.deutschegrammophon.com (office).

LEIGH, Irene May, CBE, OBE, BSc, MB BS, MD, DSc (Med), FRCP, FRSE, FMedSci; British dermatologist, cell biologist and academic; *Professor Cellular and Molecular Medicine, University of Dundee;* b. 25 April 1947, Liverpool, England; d. of A. Allen and M. L. Allen; m. 1st Nigel Leigh 1969 (divorced 1999); one s. three d.; m. 2nd J. E. Kernthaler 2000; two step-s. one step-d.; ed Merchant

Taylors' Girls' School, London Hosp. Medical Coll.; Dir Cancer Research UK Skin Tumour Lab. 1989–(2016); Prof. of Dermatology, Barts and London School of Medicine and Dentistry (BLSMD) 1992–98, Research Dean 1996–2001, Prof. of Cellular and Molecular Medicine 1998–2006; Vice-Prin. and Head of the Coll. of Medicine, Dentistry and Nursing, Univ. of Dundee 2006–11, Vice-Pres. Research, Univ. of Dundee 2009–11, Prof. of Cellular and Molecular Medicine 2006–(16); Research Dir UK, I-PRI, Lyon 2011–13; Archibald Gray Medal 2012. *Publications:* more than 300 peer-reviewed publns in biomedical literature. *Leisure interests:* baroque music, opera, theatre, cinema, children, grandchildren. *Address:* College of Medicine, Dentistry and Nursing, University of Dundee, Dundee, DD1 4HN, Scotland (office); 14 Oakeshott Avenue, London, N6 6NS, England (home). *Telephone:* 7989-344212 (mobile) (office); (20) 8340-4761 (home). *E-mail:* i.m .leigh@dundee.ac.uk (office).

LEIGH, Jennifer Jason; American actress; b. 5 Feb. 1962, Los Angeles, Calif.; d. of the late Vic Morrow and of Barbara Turner; m. Noah Baumbach (divorced); one s.; ed Palisades High School; appeared in Walt Disney TV movie The Young Runaways aged 15; other TV films include The Killing of Randy Webster 1981, The Best Little Girl in the World 1981. *Films include:* Eyes of a Stranger 1981, Fast Times at Ridgemont High 1982, Grandview, USA 1984, Flesh and Blood 1985, The Hitcher 1986, The Men's Club 1986, Heart of Midnight 1989, The Big Picture 1989, Miami Blues 1990, Last Exit to Brooklyn 1990, Crooked Hearts 1991, Backdraft 1991, Rush 1992, Single White Female 1992, Short Cuts 1993, The Hudsucker Proxy 1994, Mrs Parker and the Vicious Circle 1994, Georgia 1995, Kansas City 1996, Washington Square 1997, eXistenZ 1999, The King is Alive 2000, The Anniversary Party 2001, Crossed Over 2002, Road to Perdition 2002, In the Cut 2003, The Machinist 2004, Childstar 2004, The Jacket 2005, Palindromes 2005, Rag Tale 2005, Margot at the Wedding 2007, Synecdoche, New York 2008, Greenberg 2010, Kill Your Darlings 2013, The Spectacular Now 2013, The Moment 2013. *Television includes:* Weeds (series) 2009–12, Revenge (series) 2012. *Stage appearances include:* Sunshine, Off-Broadway 1989. *Address:* c/o CAA, 2000 Avenue of the Stars, Los Angeles, CA 90067, USA (office).

LEIGH, Julia; Australian novelist, film director and screenwriter; b. 1970, Sydney, NSW; ed Univ. of Sydney; initially studied law but changed to writing; worked at Australian Soc. of Authors; mentors have included Frank Moorhouse, Toni Morrison and Jane Campion; directorial debut with screenplay for Sleeping Beauty 2011; film selected for main competition at Cannes Film Festival 2011; chosen by the Observer newspaper as one of 21 writers to watch in the millennium. *Film screenplays include:* Sleeping Beauty 2011, The Hunter 2011. *Television:* appeared as herself in episode of Cinema 3 (series) May 2011. *Publications:* novels: The Hunter (Betty Trask Award, Prix de l'Astrolabe 2001, New York Times Notable Book of the Year) (adapted into feature film 2011) 2001, Disquiet 2009. *Address:* c/o Faber and Faber Ltd (Editorial Dept), Bloomsbury House, 74–77 Great Russell Street, London, WC1B 3DA, England. *Telephone:* (20) 7927-3800. *Fax:* (20) 7927-3801. *Website:* www.faber.co.uk.

LEIGH, Sir Michael, Kt, KCMG, PhD; British fmr European Union official and international consultant; *Senior Advisor, The German Marshall Fund of the United States;* ed Univ. of Oxford, Massachusetts Inst. of Tech., USA; Lecturer in Int. Relations, Univ. of Sussex 1974–76; Asst Prof. of Int. Relations, John Hopkins Univ., USA 1976–77; with Directorate-Gen. for External Relations, Secr.-Gen., Council of the European Communities 1977–80, Int. Fisheries Negotiations, bilateral and multilateral, Directorate-Gen. for Fisheries, EC, Brussels 1980–82, Desk Officer for UK Ireland and Denmark, Press and Information, Directorate-Gen. for Information 1982–85, Directorate-Gen. for External Relations, Horizontal unit North–South Relations 1985–88, mem. Cabinet of Vice-Pres. Lord Cockfield 1988–89, mem. Cabinet of Vice-Pres. Frans Andriessen 1989–92, 1993–98, mem. Cabinet of Commr Hans van den Broek 1999, Negotiator for Czech Repub., Task Force for the Accession Negotiations 1998–2000, Dir, Directorate-Gen., Enlargement, Turkey, Cyprus, Bulgaria, Malta, Romania 2000–03, Deputy Dir-Gen., Directorate-Gen., External Relations, responsible for European Neighbourhood Policy, relations with Eastern Europe, Southern Caucasus and Cen. Asia, Middle East and S Mediterranean 2003–05, Dir-Gen. for Enlargement 2006–11; consultant and Sr Advisor to The German Marshall Fund of the US, Brussels 2012–. *Address:* The German Marshall Fund of the United States, Résidence Palace, Rue de la Loi 155 Wetstraat, 1040 Brussels, Belgium (office). *Telephone:* (2) 238-52-70 (office). *Fax:* (2) 238-52-99 (office). *E-mail:* mleigh@gmfus.org (office). *Website:* www.gmfus.org (office).

LEIGH, Mike, OBE; British dramatist and film and theatre director; b. 20 Feb. 1943, Salford, Lancs., England; s. of the late A. A. Leigh and the late P. P. Leigh (née Cousin); m. Alison Steadman (q.v.) 1973 (divorced 2001); two s.; ed Royal Acad. of Dramatic Art, Camberwell School of Arts and Crafts, Cen. School of Art and Design, London Film School; Chair. Govs London Film School 2001–; Officier des Arts et des Lettres; Hon. MA (Salford) 1991, (Northampton) 2000; Hon. DLitt (Staffs.) 2000, (Essex) 2002. *Plays:* The Box Play 1965, My Parents Have Gone to Carlisle, The Last Crusade of the Five Little Nuns 1966, Nenaa 1967, Individual Fruit Pies, Down Here and Up There, Big Basil 1968, Epilogue, Glum Victoria and the Lad with Specs 1969, Bleak Moments 1970, A Rancid Pong 1971, Wholesome Glory, The Jaws of Death, Dick Whittington and His Cat 1973, Babies Grow Old, The Silent Majority 1974, Abigail's Party 1977 (also TV play), Ecstasy 1979, Goose-Pimples (London Evening Standard and London Drama Critics' Choice Best Comedy Awards 1981) 1981, Smelling A Rat 1988, Greek Tragedy 1989 (in Australia), 1990 (in UK), It's a Great Big Shame! 1993, Two Thousand Years (Cottlesloe Theatre, Comedis, Grief 2011. *Feature films:* Bleak Moments (Golden Leopard, Locarno Film Festival, Golden Hugo, Chicago Film Festival 1972) 1971, High Hopes (Int. Critics' Prize, Venice Film Festival 1989, London Evening Standard Peter Sellers Best Comedy Film Award 1990) 1989, Life is Sweet 1991, Naked (Best Dir Cannes Film Festival 1993) 1993, Secrets and Lies (winner Palme d'Or) 1996, (Alexander Korda Award, BAFTA 1997; Career Girls 1997, Topsy-Turvy 1999 (London Evening Standard Best Film 1999, Los Angeles Film Critics' Circle Best Film 1999, New York Film Critics' Circle Best Film 1999), All or Nothing 2002, Vera Drake (Best British Ind. Film, Best Dir, British Ind. Film Awards, Best Film, Evening Standard British Film Awards 2005, David Lean Award for Achievement in Direction, BAFTA Awards 2005) 2004, Happy-Go-Lucky 2008, Another Year 2010, A Running Jump (short) 2012, Mr. Turner 2014.

Radio play: Too Much of a Good Thing 1979. *Television films:* A Mug's Game 1972, Hard Labour 1973, The Permissive Society, The Birth of the 2001 F.A. Cup Final Goalie, Old Chums, Probation, A Light Snack, Afternoon 1975, Nuts in May 1976, Knock for Knock 1976, The Kiss of Death 1977, Abigail's Party 1977, Who's Who 1978, Grown-Ups 1980, Home Sweet Home 1981, Meantime 1984, Four Days in July 1984, The Short and Curlies 1987, A Sense of History 1992. *Publications:* Abigail's Party and Goose-Pimples 1982, Ecstasy and Smelling a Rat 1989, Naked and other Screenplays 1995, Secrets and Lies 1997, Career Girls 1997, Topsy-Turvy 1999, All or Nothing 2002, Two Thousand Years 2006, Vera Drake 2008, Mike Leigh on Mike Leigh 2008. *Address:* c/o United Agents, 12–26 Lexington Street, London W1F 0LE, England (office). *Telephone:* (20) 3214-0800 (office). *Fax:* (20) 3214-0801 (office). *E-mail:* info@unitedagents.co.uk (office). *Website:* unitedagents.co.uk (office).

LEIGHTON, Allan Leslie; British business executive; *Chairman, Royal Mail Holdings PLC;* b. 12 April 1953; m.; two s. one d.; ed Magdalen Coll. School, North Oxon. Polytechnic, A.M.P. Harvard; with Mars Confectionery 1974–91, rising to Business Sector Man. UK Grocery Div.; Sales Dir Pedigree Petfoods 1991–92; joined ASDA Stores Ltd as Group Marketing Dir 1992, then successively Retail Dir, Deputy Chief Exec.; Chief Exec. 1996; Pres. and CEO Wal-Mart Europe 1999–2000; Dir (non-exec.) Wilson Connolly Holdings PLC 1995 (Deputy Chair. 2000, interim CEO 2001–02); Dir (non-exec.) BSkyB PLC 1999–, Dyson Ltd –2004, Cannons –2004, Scottish Power PLC 2001, George Weston Ltd 2001 (currently Deputy Chair.), Consignia PLC 2001; Chair. (non-exec.) lastminute.com 2000–04, Cannons Group Ltd 2001; Dir (non-exec.) Royal Mail Holdings PLC 2001–, Chair. 2002–; Chair. Race for Opportunity 2000, BHS Ltd 2000–; Deputy Chair. (non-exec.) Leeds Sporting PLC 1998, Loblaw Companies Ltd, Selfridges & Co. *Publication:* On Leadership 2007. *Address:* Royal Mail Holdings PLC, 148 Old Street, London, EC1V 9HQ, England (office). *Telephone:* (20) 7250-2888 (office). *Fax:* (20) 7659-4948 (office). *E-mail:* info@royalmailgroup.com (office). *Website:* www.royalmailgroup.com (office).

LEIGHTON, Sir John, Kt; British art historian and museum director; *Director-General, National Galleries of Scotland;* b. 1959, Belfast, Northern Ireland; ed Univ. of Edinburgh, Edinburgh Coll. of Art, Courtauld Inst. of Art; trained as art historian and taught art history at Univ. of Edinburgh; Curator of 19th Century Paintings, Nat. Gallery, London 1987–97; Dir Van Gogh Museum, Amsterdam 1997–2005, organized exhbn 'Van Gogh and Gauguin' in conjunction with Chicago Art Inst. 1997–2002; Dir-Gen. Nat. Galleries of Scotland 2006–. *Publications:* has contributed to catalogues for the above exhbns; has published and lectured on various aspects of 19th and 20th century art. *Address:* The Dean Gallery, 73 Belford Road, Edinburgh, EH4 3DS, Scotland (office). *Telephone:* (131) 624-6200 (office). *E-mail:* enquiries@nationalgalleries.org (office). *Website:* www.nationalgalleries.org (office).

LEIJONHUFVUD, Baron Axel Stig Bengt, PhD; Swedish economist and academic; *Professor Emeritus, University of Trento;* b. 9 June 1933, Stockholm; s. of Erik G. Leijonhufvud and Helene A. Neovius; m. 1st Marta E. Ising 1955 (divorced 1977), 2nd Earlene J. Craver 1977; one s. two d.; ed Univ. of Lund, Univ. of Pittsburgh and Northwestern Univ., USA; Acting Asst Prof. of Econs, UCLA 1964–67, Assoc. Prof. 1967–71, Prof. of Econs 1971–94, now Prof. Emer., Chair. Dept of Econs 1980–83, 1990–92, Dir Center for Computable Econs 1991–97; Prof. of Monetary Econs, Univ. of Trento 1995–2008, Prof. Emer. 2008–; Visiting Prof., Stockholm School of Econ. and Commerce 1979–80, 1986, 1987, 1996, Inst. for Advanced Studies, Vienna 1976, 1987, Inst. for Advanced Studies, Jerusalem 1987, Nihon Univ. Tokyo 1980, European Univ. Inst., Florence 1982, 1986–87, 1989, Istituto Torcuato di Tella, Buenos Aires 1989, 1995; Ständiger Gastprofessor Univ. of Konstanz 1982–85; mem. Econ. Export Cttee of Pres. of Kazakhstan 1991; other professional appointments, Cttee memberships etc.; Brookings Inst. Fellow 1963–64; Marshall Lecturer, Univ. of Cambridge 1974; Overseas Fellow, Churchill Coll. Cambridge 1974; Inst. for Advanced Study Fellow 1983–84; Dr hc (Lund) 1983, (Nice, Sophia Antipolis) 1995; Macroeconomics in the Small and the Large: Essays on Microfoundations, Macroeconomic Applications and Economic History in Honour of Axel Leijonhufvud (ed. by Roger E. A. Farmer) 2008, Inflation, Institutions and Information: Essays in Honour of Axel Leijonhufvud (co-ed. by Daniel Vaz and Kumaraswamy Velupillai) 2010. *Publications:* On Keynesian Economics and the Economics of Keynes: A Study in Monetary Theory 1968, Keynes and the Classics: Two Lectures 1969, Information and Coordination: Essays in Macroeconomic Theory 1981, High Inflation (co-author) 1995, Macro-economic Instability and Coordination 2000, Monetary Theory as a Basis for Monetary Policy (ed.) 2001, Monetary Theory and Policy Experience (ed.) 2001, Informazione, coordinamento e instabilità macroeconomica (a cura di Elisabetta De Antoni) 2004, Organización e inestabilidad económica: Ensayos elegidos 2006; contribs to professional journals. *Telephone:* (805) 474-1540 (office). *Fax:* (805) 474-9896 (office). *E-mail:* stigaxel33@gmail.com (office); axel@ucla.edu (office); axel@economia.unitn.it (office). *Website:* www-ceel.economia.unitn.it/staff/leijonhufvud (office).

LEIMAN, Ricardo, BComm, MBA; Brazilian business executive; *CEO, Noble Group Ltd;* ed Univ. of São Paulo, Univ. of Rochester, NY, USA, Univ. of Nyenrode, The Netherlands; began career with Credit Lyonnais Bank in Brazil followed by man. positions with Louis Dreyfus in Brazil, Eximcoop in The Netherlands and Trader Classified Media in London and Paris; rejoined Louis Dreyfus as COO, North America, EMEA (Europe, Middle East, Africa and Asia) 2002, later COO, Soft Commodities; joined Noble Resources Ltd 2006, COO Noble Group Ltd 2006–09, mem. Bd of Dirs 2009–, CEO 2010–; mem. Bd of Dirs Gloucester Coal Ltd 2009–; Dir (non-exec.) Windimurra Vanadium Ltd (alternatively, Precious Metals Australia Ltd) 2006–09. *Address:* Noble Group Ltd, 18th Floor, MassMutual Tower, 38 Gloucester Road, Hong Kong Special Administrative Region, People's Republic of China (office). *Telephone:* 2861-3511 (office). *Fax:* 2527-0282 (office). *E-mail:* richard@thisisnoble.com (office). *Website:* www.thisisnoble.com (office).

LEINEN, Margaret, BS, MS, PhD; American oceanographer, academic and research institute director; *Director, Scripps Institution of Oceanography, Vice-Chancellor for Marine Sciences and Dean, School of Marine Sciences, University of California, San Diego;* ed Univ. of Illinois, Oregon State Univ., Univ. of Rhode Island; fmr Chief Science Officer, Climos, Inc.; Founder and Pres. Climate Response Fund; Asst Dir for Geosciences and Co-ordinator of Environmental Research and Educ., NSF for seven years; Vice-Provost for Marine and Environmental Initiatives and Exec. Dir Harbor Br. Oceanographic Inst., Florida Atlantic Univ. –2013; Prof., Geosciences Research Div., Univ. of California, San Diego and Dir Scripps Inst. of Oceanography 2013–, also Vice-Chancellor for Marine Sciences and Dean, School of Marine Sciences; fmr Vice-Provost for Marine and Environmental Programs and Dean of Grad. School of Oceanography, Univ. of Rhode Island; Pres.-elect, American Geophysical Union; Vice-Chair. Research Bd, Gulf of Mexico Research Initiative; fmr Vice-Chair. Int. Geosphere-Biosphere Programme; fmr Pres. The Oceanography Soc.; fmr Chair. Atmospheric and Hydrospheric Science Section of AAAS; mem. Bd Nat. Council for Science and the Environment; fmr mem. Bd on Global Change of Nat. Research Council/NAS; fmr mem. Nat. Ecological Observatory Network; Fellow, AAAS, Geological Soc. of America; Distinguished Alumni Awards, Univ. of Illinois, Oregon State Univ. and Univ. of Rhode Island. *Publications:* numerous papers in professional journals on ocean sediments and their relationship to global biogeochemical cycles and the history of Earth's ocean and climate. *Address:* Scripps Institution of Oceanography, University of California, San Diego, 9500 Gilman Drive, #0210, La Jolla, CA 92093-0210, USA (office). *Telephone:* (858) 534-2827 (office). *Fax:* (858) 534-0167 (office). *E-mail:* mleinen@ucsd.edu (office). *Website:* scripps.ucsd.edu/about/leadership/director (office). scrippsscholars.ucsd.edu/mleinen/biocv (office).

LEINONEN, Tatu Einari, MSc, DTech; Finnish engineer and academic; *Professor of Machine Design, University of Oulu;* b. 21 Sept. 1938, Kajaani; s. of Aate Leinonen and Aili Leinonen (née Nieminen); m. Tuula Tuovinen 1968; one s. two d.; Lecturer, Tech. Inst. of Helsinki 1963; Researcher, Tech. Research Centre of Finland 1965; Design Engineer, State Railway Co. 1966; Prof. of Machine Design, Univ. of Oulu 1968–; Visiting Prof., Univ. of Vt, USA 1976, Mich. Tech. Univ., USA 1977, 1981–82, 1991, Univ. of Fla, USA 1991, Lakehead Univ., Canada 1991, 2000, Toin Univ. of Yokohama, Japan 1994, Yanshan Univ., China 2000; fmr Sec.-Gen IFToMM. *Publications:* more than 300 papers and books 1966–. *Leisure interests:* cross-country skiing, golf. *Address:* Department of Mechanical Engineering, PO Box 4900, University of Oulu, 90014 Oulu (office); Tuulastie BA6, 90550 Oulu, Finland (home). *Telephone:* (8) 5532050. *Fax:* (8) 5532026. *E-mail:* tatu.leinonen@oulu.fi (office). *Website:* www.oulu.fi (office).

LEIPER, Quentin John, CBE, MSc, PhD, CEng, CEnv, FICE; British civil engineer, academic and business executive; *Director for Engineering and the Environment, Carillion plc;* m. Dorothy Leiper; three c.; ed Univ. of Glasgow; spent 16 years working for specialist sub-contractors in foundations, ground treatment and geotechnical eng; joined Carillion plc 1991, currently Dir for Eng and the Environment, major projects include Canary Wharf and Canada Water stations, Tees Barrage and Copenhagen Metro; led formation of and fmrly served as Chair. British Geotechnical Asscn; Pres. ICE 2006–07; fmr Dir and Council mem. Construction Industry Research and Information Asscn; fmr mem. two British Standards cttees, two working groups set up by Sustainable Procurement Task Force and UK Construction Industry Sustainability Forum, Eng and Physical Sciences Research Council's Built Environment Coll. and several research steering groups; Founding Ed. ICE's Proceedings journal, Engineering Sustainability, fmr mem. ICE Proceedings journal, Geotechnical Engineering editorial panel; Visiting Prof., School of Civil and Environmental Eng, Univ. of Edinburgh 1998–, Chair. School Advisory Bd; fmr mem. Civil Eng Advisory Bds, Univs of Nottingham, Southampton, City Univ.; Judge, Science, Eng and Tech. Student of the Year Award 1997–. *Publications:* about 50 papers and articles on a range of subjects, including sustainability, environmental and supply chain management, the training and development of engineers, earthworks, construction, foundations, piling, reinforced soil and ground radar. *Leisure interests:* hockey, flying kites, playing tenor sax and clarinet. *Address:* Carillion Head Office, 24 Birch Street, Wolverhampton, WV1 4HY, West Midlands, England (office). *Telephone:* (1902) 422431 (office). *Fax:* (1902) 316165 (office). *E-mail:* info@carillionplc.com (office). *Website:* www.carillionplc.com (office).

LEIPOLD, Gerd, PhD; German environmentalist; *Executive Director, Greenpeace International;* b. 1 Jan. 1951, Rot an der Rot; two c.; ed Max Planck Inst. for Meteorology, Hamburg; trained as scientist; joined Greenpeace Germany as volunteer 1980, joined full-time 1983, later mem. Exec. Cttee and Trustee, Int. Co-ordinator Nuclear Free Seas Campaign 1987, fmr Chair. Bd Green Peace Nordic, mem. Bd Greenpeace USSR, Dir Greenpeace Nuclear Disarmament Campaign, London, Acting Int. Exec. Dir Greenpeace International Feb.–June 2001, Int. Exec. Dir June 2001–; set up own consultancy, GEM Partners Ltd, London to advise NGOs on strategy and communications 1993, Dir 1993–2001. *Leisure interests:* playing piano, literature, soccer, history. *Address:* Greenpeace International, Ottho Heldringstraat 5, Amsterdam 1066 AZ, Netherlands (office); Im Hebsack 4, 88430 Rot, Germany (home). *Telephone:* (20) 718-2081 (office). *Fax:* (20) 718-2578 (office). *E-mail:* gerd.leipold@int.greenpeace.org (office). *Website:* www.greenpeace.org (office).

LEIRNER, Sheila Anne; Brazilian journalist, art critic, curator and writer; b. (Sheila Anne Klinger), 25 Sept. 1948, São Paulo; d. of Abraham L. Klinger and Giselda Leirner Klinger; m. 1st Décio Tozzi 1970 (divorced 1972); one s.; m. 2nd Gustavo Halbreich 1974 (divorced 1988); one s.; m. 3rd Jean-Louis Andral 1991 (divorced 2000); m. 4th Patrick Corneau 2007; ed Univ. of Vincennes, Ecole Pratique des Hautes Etudes, Sorbonne, Paris; art critic, O Estado de São Paulo 1975–90; Gen. Curator, 18th and 19th São Paulo Biennial 1985, 1987; curator of various exhbns in Brazil and abroad; now ind. curator and art critic; apptd to Ile-de-France regional comm. to examine projects of the "1% artistic", French Ministries of the Interior and Educ.; mem. French and Brazilian sections, Int. Asscn of Art Critics; mem. juries and invited lecturer in Latin America, Africa, USA, Asia and Europe; corresp. for nat. and foreign publs; lives and works in Paris; Chevalier, Ordre des Arts et des Lettres; Critic of the Year Award, Brazilian Asscn of Art Critics and Sec. of Culture of the State of São Paulo, Artistic Personality of the Year in Latin America, Argentine Asscn of Art Critics. *Publications:* selected works of art criticism, anthologies and monographies, including Leopoldo Nóvoa, Art as Measure 1982, Art and Its Time 1991, Ars in Natura 1996, Lateinamerikanische Kunst 1993, Sky Above – A Tombeau for Haroldo de Campos 2005, The Surrealism (with J. Guinsburg) 2009. *Leisure interests:* literature, music, collecting miniatures and dolls houses. *Address:* c/o Editora Perspectiva, Avenida

Brigadeiro Luis Antônio 3025–3035, 01401-000 São Paulo, Brazil. *E-mail:* sheila .leirner@gmail.com (home). *Website:* sheila.leirner.pagesperso-orange.fr.

LEISINGER, Klaus Michael, Dr rer. pol; German sociologist, academic, foundation executive and UN official; *President and CEO, Novartis Foundation for Sustainable Development;* b. 6 July 1947, Lörrach; ed Univ. of Basel, Switzerland; Prof. of Devt Sociology, Univ. of Basel; fmr Man. of Ciba Pharmaceuticals, East Africa, headed co.'s Dept for Developing-country Relations, Basel; Exec. Dir and Del. of Novartis Foundation's Bd of Trustees –2002, Pres. and CEO Novartis Foundation for Sustainable Devt 2002–; Special Advisor on the Global Compact, UN, New York 2005–06; adviser to various nat. and int. orgs dealing with sustainable devt, including UNDP, World Bank (CGIAR), Asian Devt Bank, and ECLA; mem. Exec. Cttee German Soc. for UN; mem. Advisory Council of Mary Robinson's Ethical Globalization Initiative; mem. European Acad. of Science and Arts 1994; mem. Bd of Trustees German Network Business Ethics; Hon. D'Theol (Univ. of Fribourg, Switzerland) 2004. *Publications:* Unternehmensethik. Globale Verantwortung und modernes Manageme 1997, Die sechste Milliarde. Weltbevölkerungswachstum und nachhaltige Entwicklung 1999; several articles. *Address:* Novartis Foundation for Sustainable Development, Schwarzwaldallee 215, 4058 Basel, Switzerland (office). *E-mail:* info@novartisfoundation.org (office). *Website:* www.novartisfoundation.org (office).

LEITE, Arcangelo; Timor-Leste politician; *Minister of Internal Administration;* has held several govt posts including Dir Nat. Directorate for State Admin, Acting Dir (Territories), Ministry of State Admin; Minister of Internal Admin 2007–. *Address:* Ministry of Internal Administration, Dili, Timor-Leste (office).

LEITER, Michael E., BA, JD; American naval officer, lawyer and government official; ed Columbia Univ., Harvard Law School; Naval Flight Officer, USN 1991–97, served on US, NATO and UN missions in fmr Yugoslavia and Iraq; fmr Harvard Law School Human Rights Fellow, Int. Criminal Tribunal for the Fmr Yugoslavia, The Hague; fmr law clerk to Assoc. Justice Stephen G. Breyer of US Supreme Court and to Chief Judge Michael Boudin of US Court of Appeals for the First Circuit; Asst US Attorney, Eastern Dist of Va, US Dept of Justice 2002–05; Deputy Gen. Counsel and Asst Dir, Pres.'s Comm. on Intelligence Capabilities of US Regarding Weapons of Mass Destruction (Robb-Silberman Comm.) 2005; Deputy Chief of Staff, Office of Dir of Nat. Intelligence 2005–07; Prin. Deputy Dir Nat. Counterterrorism Center Feb.–Nov. 2007, Acting Dir 2007–08, Dir 2008–11. *Address:* c/o United States National Counterterrorism Center, c/o Director of National Intelligence, Washington, DC 20511, USA (office).

LEITH, Prudence Margaret (Prue), CBE, DL, FRSA; British caterer and author; b. 18 Feb. 1940, Cape Town, South Africa; d. of the late Stewart Leith and of Margaret Inglis; m. Rayne Kruger (died 2002); one s. one d.; ed Haywards Heath, Sussex, St Mary's, Johannesburg, Cape Town Univ., Sorbonne, Paris and Cordon Bleu School, London; started Leith's Good Food (commercial catering co.) 1965, Leith's restaurant 1969; cookery corresp. Daily Mail 1969–73; Man. Dir Prudence Leith Ltd 1972–94, Chair. Leith's Ltd 1994–96; opened Leith's School of Food and Wine 1975; added Leith's Farm 1976; Cookery Corresp., Daily Express 1976–80; Cookery Ed., The Guardian 1980–85, columnist 1986–90; subject of TV documentaries by BBC and Channel 4; presented series Tricks of the Trade, BBC 1; judge, Great British Menu, BBC 2 2006–; Vice-Pres. Restaurateurs' Assocn of GB; Gov. Nat. Inst. of Econ. and Social Research; Vice-Patron Women in Finance and Banking; Chair. UK Cttee New Era Schools' Trust 1994–2000, Royal Soc. of Arts 1995–97 (Deputy Chair. 1997–2000), The British Food Heritage Trust 1997–2006; Dir (non-exec.) Halifax PLC 1992–99, Whitbread PLC 1995–2005, Argyll Group 1989–96, Woolworths 2001–06, Orient Express Hotels 2006–; Hon. Fellow, Univ. Salford 1992; Visiting Prof., Univ. of North London 1993–; Chair. School Food Trust 2006–10; mem. Nat. Council for Vocational Qualifications and UK Skills, Stamp Cttee 1997–2003; Gov. Kingsmead City Tech. Coll., Ashridge Man. Coll.; Reader for Queen's Anniversary Prizes; Patron Prue Leith Coll. of Food and Wine, Johannesburg 1997–, Prue Leith Group; Chair. 3Es Enterprises 1998–2006, King's Coll. 1998–2007; Trustee, Forum for the Future 1998–2003; Training for Life 1999–2006, Places for People 1999–2003; DL Greater London 1998; Freeman, City of London 1994; Dr hc (Open Univ.) 1997; Hon. DUniv (Oxford Brookes) 2000; Business Woman of the Year 1990. *Publications include:* Leith's All-Party Cook Book 1969, Parkinson's Pie 1972, Cooking for Friends 1978, The Best of Prue Leith 1979, Leith's Cookery Course (with J. B. Reynaud) 1979–80, The Cook's Handbook 1981, Prue Leith's Pocket Book of Dinner Parties 1983, Dinner Parties 1984, Leith's Cook Book 1985, Leith's Cookery School (with Caroline Waldegrave) 1985, Entertaining with Style (with P. Tyrer) 1986, Confident Cooking (part-work) 1989–90, Leith's Cookery Bible (with Caroline Waldegrave) 1991, Leith's Complete Christmas 1992, Sunday Times Slim Plan: The 21-Day Diet for Slimming Safely 1992, Leith's Baking (with Caroline Waldegrave) 1993, Leith's Vegetarian Cookery 1993, Leith's Step by Step Cookery 1993, Salads 1993, Chicken Dishes 1993, Starters 1993, Fruit 1993, Quick and Easy 1993, Leith's Contemporary Cooking (with Caroline Yates and Alison Cavaliero) 1994, Leith's Guide to Wine (with Richard Harvey) 1995, Leaving Patrick (novel) 1999, Sisters (novel) 2001, A Lovesome Thing (novel) 2004, Choral Society (novel) 2009, A Serving of Scandal (novel) 2010, Relish: My Life on a Plate (memoir) 2012. *Leisure interests:* travelling, walking, fishing, gardening, old cookbooks, kitchen antiques, Trollope. *Address:* c/o Hilary Knight Management, Grange Farm, Church Lane, Old, Northampton, Northants., NN6 9QZ, England (office); The Office, Chastleton Glebe, Chastleton, nr Moreton-in-Marsh, Glos., GL56 0SZ, England (home). *E-mail:* hilary@hkmanagement.co.uk (office); pmleith@prue-leith.com (office). *Website:* www.hkmanagement.co.uk (office); www.prue-leith.com. *Telephone:* (1608) 674908 (office). *Fax:* (1608) 674083 (office).

LEKHANYA, Maj.-Gen. Justin Metsing; Lesotho politician and army officer; *Leader, Basotho National Party;* b. 7 April 1938, Thaba-Tseka; Commdr of Lesotho Army; overthrew Prime Minister Leabua Jonathan in a mil. coup 1986; Head Mil. Council and Council of Ministers 1986–91, Minister of Defence and Internal Security 1986–91, also Minister of Public Service, Youth and Women's Affairs, Food Man. Units and Cabinet Office; deposed King of Lesotho in mil. coup 1990, later restored; Lekhanya ousted in coup 1991; now Leader Basotho Nat. Party. *Address:* Basotho National Party, PO Box 124, Maseru 100, Lesotho.

LEKISHVILI, Niko Mikhailovich; Georgian politician; b. 20 April 1947, Tbilisi; m.; two d.; ed Tbilisi Polytech. Inst., Moscow Acad. of Nat. Econ.; Sr Lab. Asst Georgian Polytech. Inst. 1971–72; Komsomol functionary 1972–77; Second Sec., Chair. Dist Exec. Cttee, First Sec. Pervomay Dist CP Cttee, Tbilisi 1977–89; Second Sec., First Sec. Tbilisi City CP Cttee 1989–90; Chair. Tbilisi City Soviet 1990; Deputy Supreme Soviet Georgian SSR 1990–91; Chief State Counsellor Georgian Cabinet of Ministers Jan.–Nov. 1992; mem. Parl. Repub. of Georgia 1992–95, 1999–; Deputy Prime Minister Sept.–Oct. 1993; Mayor of Tbilisi 1993–95; State Minister of Georgia 1995–98; Chair. Union of Tax-Payers. *Leisure interests:* music, football, travel. *Address:* Kargareteli Str. 3a, 380064 Tbilisi, Georgia (home); Ingorokva str. 7, 380034, Tbilisi, Georgia.

LEKO, Josip; Croatian lawyer and politician; *Speaker of the Sabor (Parliament);* b. 19 Sept. 1948, Plavna, Bač, Serbia; m.; two c.; ed Faculty of Law, Univ. of Zagreb; legal admin. in 'Slavonija DI', Slavonski Brod 1975–76; volunteer at Municipality Court, Zagreb 1976, 1977; legal adviser, Novi Zagreb Municipality 1976–82; Sec. Exec. Bd, Novi Zagreb Municipality 1982–86; State Ombudsmen for Self-Man. 1986–89; Dir Working Community and Vice-Gen. Dir 'Zagrepčanka' co. for trade, production and catering 1989–91; mem. Social Democratic Party of Croatia (SDP), Business Dir SDP 1991–2000, Pres. Standing Cttee of SDP 2008–; mem. (SDP) Parl. 2000–, Chair. Legislation Cttee 2000–03, mem. Cttee on the Constitution, Standing Orders and Political System 2000–03, Judiciary Cttee 2000–03, Pres. Supervisory Bd Croatian Radiotelevision 2000–03, Pres. Comm. for Conflict of Interest of the Repub. of Croatia 2003–07, Chair. then Deputy Chair. Legislation Cttee 2003–07, mem. Judiciary Cttee 2003–07, Deputy Chair. Cttee on the Constitution, Standing Orders and Political System 2007–11, mem. Legislation Cttee and Judiciary Cttee 2007–11, mem. State Judiciary Council, Nat. Water Council and Comm. for Conflict of Interest 2007–11, Chair. Cttee on the Constitution, Standing Orders and Political System 2011–12, Deputy Speaker of the Sabor (Parl.) 2011–12, Interim Speaker 1–10 Oct. 2012, Speaker 10 Oct. 2012–. *Address:* Office of the Speaker of the Sabor, 10000 Zagreb, trg sv. Marka 6–7, Croatia (office). *Telephone:* (1) 4569444 (office); (1) 6303544 (office). *Fax:* (1) 1 6303010 (office). *E-mail:* predsjednik@sabor.hr (office). *Website:* www.sabor.hr (office).

LEKOTA, Mosiuoa Patrick (Terror); South African politician; *President, Congress of the People (COPE);* b. 13 Aug. 1948, Senekal, Orange Free State; s. of the late Mapiloko Lekota and Mamosiuoa Lekota; m. Cynthia Lekota 1975; two s. two d. (deceased); ed Univ. of the North (Turfloop); perm. organizer, South African Students' Org. (SASO) 1972–74; charged under Terrorism Act 1974; tried and imprisoned on Robben Island 1976–82; Nat. Publicity Sec. United Democratic Front (UDF) 1983–91; fmrly with African Nat. Congress (ANC) in Natal; organizer for ANC in Northern Free States 1990; mem. ANC Working Cttee 1991–, Nat. Chair. ANC Nat. Exec. Cttee 1991–, Chair. Southern OFS of Nat. Exec. Comm. 1991, Sec. Elections Comm. 1992–94; Nat. Chair. ANC 1997–2007, detained 1983, 1984, 1985; on trial with 21 others charged with treason and murder in Delmas case 1986, convicted 1988, sentenced to 12 years imprisonment after being held in custody for four years; conviction overturned by Appeal Court 1989; in exile, returned to S Africa 1990; Premier Free State Prov. Legislature 1994; Chair. Nat. Council of Provinces 1997–99; Minister of Defence 1999–2008 (resgnd); Co-founder and Pres. Congress of the People party 2008–. *Leisure interests:* cycling, reading, soccer, rugby and studying wildlife. *Website:* www.congressofthepeople.org.za.

LELEU, Romain; French trumpeter; ed Paris Conservatoire, Karlsruhe Hochschule fur Musik, Germany; numerous performances at music festivals and in concert halls, including Festival de la Roque d'Anthéron, Festival Radio France, Montpellier, Folle Journée de Nantes, Folle Journée, Tokyo, Flâneries Musicales, Reims, Festival de Saint-Denis, Festival d'Auvers-sur-Oise, Festival de Prades, Festival Estival d'Annecy, Salle Cortot, Salle Gaveau; soloist with Orchestre Nat. de Lorraine, Ensemble Orchestral de Paris, Orchestre de Bretagne, Orchestre Régional de Cannes PACA, Orchestre Philharmonique de l'Opéra de Marseille, Orchestre d'Auvergne, Orchestre des Concerts Colonne, Württembergisches Kammerorchester Heilbronn, Baltic Chamber Orchestra, Slovak Sinfonietta in France and abroad in Switzerland, Belgium, Spain, Portugal, Athenaeum Concert Hall, Romania, in Turkey, Algeria, Israel, Cuba, Egypt, Japan; has collaborated with Karol Beffa (premiere of Subway and Nuit Etoilée), Philippe Hersant (premiere of Folk Tunes), Martin Matalon and others; f. Feeling Brass Quintet 2000; Yamaha Performing Artist 2002–; Laureate of the Fondation Meyer 2002–; regularly invited to perform on radio and TV, including France 2, France 3, Direct 8 TV, France Musique, France Inter, Radio Suisse Romande, Radio Romania Muzical; season 2011–12 performed in Korea for Seoul Spring Festival, in Sweden, Belgium, and in France with Orchestre d'Auvergne in Vichy Opera for Martin Matalon piece, Orchestre Lyrique de Nancy, Orchestre Nat. de Lille for Arutunian concerto and in Grenoble Auditorium Museum, Festival de l'Epau; gives numerous master classes in France, Korea, Japan and elsewhere; winner Festival Musical d'Automne de Jeunes Interprètes, Special Interpretation Prize, Finnish Int. Competition, Lieksa Brass Week 1999, Adami's Classical Revelation, First Prize for Trumpet, Paris Conservatoire 2003, First Prize for Chamber Music 2003, Third Prize, Int. Competition of Chamber Music, Lyon 2005, Victoires de la Musique (category Revelation) 2009, Prix Del Duca, Acad. des Beaux Arts 2011. *Recordings include:* Famous Trumpet Sonatas 2008, Outrageously French – Wind Music from France 2008, L'école française des vents 2009, Classical Concertos with Baltic Chamber Orchestra (St Petersburg Philharmonic) 2011. *Address:* c/o M. Jérémie Barret, Musicaglotz, 29 rue Violet, 75015 Paris, France (office). *Telephone:* 1-42-34-53-44 (office). *E-mail:* jeremie.barret@musicaglotz.com (office); contact@romainleleu.com. *Website:* www.musicaglotz.com (office); www.romainleleu.com.

LELONG, Pierre Alexandre; French administrative official; b. 22 May 1931, Paris; s. of Prof. Marcel Lelong; m. Catherine Demargne 1958; four s. one d.; ed Coll. Stanislas, Paris, Univ. of Paris and Ecole Nat. d'Admin.; Ministry of Finance and Econ. Affairs 1958–62; Econ. Adviser to Prime Minister Pompidou 1962–67; Gen. Man. Fonds d'Orientation et de Régularisation des Marchés Agricoles (FORMA) 1967–68; MP for Finistère 1968–74; Sec. of State for Posts and Telecommunications 1974–75; Judge, Court of Accounts 1975–77; mem. European Court of Auditors 1977–84, Pres. 1981–84; Pres. of Section (Defence) at Court of Accounts 1990–94, Pres. of Chamber (European Affairs) 1994–97; Pres. Interministerial Cttee for Mil., Aeronautic and Mechanical State Procurements

1997–2004; Pres. Consultative Cttee on Secret Defence Affairs 1999–2005; Pres. Commission des Marchés Publics de l'Etat 2005–08; Commdr, Légion d'honneur, Officier, Ordre nat. du Mérite, Grand Cross, Ordre de la Couronne de Chêne (Luxembourg). *Address:* 130 rue de Rennes, 75006 Paris, France (home). *Telephone:* 1-45-44-12-49 (home). *Fax:* 1-45-44-12-49 (home). *E-mail:* lelongdemargne@noos.fr (home).

LELOUCH, Claude; French film director, producer and writer; b. 30 Oct. 1937, Paris; s. of Simon Lelouch and Charlotte Abeilard; m. Christine Cochet 1968 (divorced); m. 2nd Marie-Sophie Pochat; four c., three c. from previous relationships; m. 3rd Alessandra Martines 1995; Pres. and Dir-Gen. Société Les Films 13, 1966–; Chevalier, Ordre nat. du Mérite, Officier des Arts et des Lettres, Grand Prix Nationaux 1993; Dr hc (UMIST) 1996; Palme d'or, Cannes 1966, Acad. Award 1966. *Films include:* L'amour des si... (In the Affirmative) 1962, La femme-spectacle (Night Women) 1964, Une fille et des fusils 1964, Les grands moments 1965, ...pour un maillot jaune (For a Yellow Jersey) 1965, Jean-Paul Belmondo 1965, Un homme et une femme (A Man and a Women) (uncredited) 1966, Loin du Vietnam (Far from Vietnam) 1967, Vivre pour vivre (Live for Life) 1967, 13 jours en France (aka Challenge in the Snow) 1968, Un homme qui me plaît (A Man I Like) 1969, La vie, l'amour, la mort (Life Love Death) 1969, Le voyou (The Crook) 1970, Smic Smac Smoc 1971, L'Aventure c'est l'aventure (aka Money Money Money) 1972, La bonne année (Happy New Year) 1973, Visions of Eight (also co-dir) 1973, Toute une vie (also producer, dir, author) 1974, Mariage 1974, Le chat et la souris (Cat and Mouse) 1975, C'était un rendez-vous 1976, Le bon et les méchants (The Good Guys and the Bad Guys) 1976, Si c'était a refaire (If I Had to Do It All Over Again) 1976, Un autre homme, une autre chance (Another Man, Another Chance) 1977, Robert et Robert 1978, A nous deux (Us Two) 1979, Les uns et les autres (aka Within Memory) 1981, Edith et Marcel 1983, Viva la vie! 1984, Partir, revenir (Going and Coming Back) 1985, Un homme et une femme, 20 ans déjàs (A Man and a Woman: 20 Years Later) 1986, Attention bandits 1986, Itinéraire d'un enfant gâté 1988, Il y a des jours... et de lunes 1990, La belle histoire (The Beautiful Story) 1992, Tout ça... pour ça! (All That... for This?!) 1993, Les Misérables (Golden Globe 1996, Ephèbe d'or 1996) 1995, Lumière et compagnie 1996, Hommes, Femmes, mode d'emploi (Men, Women: A User's Manual) 1996, Hasards ou coïncidences 1998, Une pour toutes (One 4 All) 1999, And Now... Ladies and Gentlemen... 2002, 11'09"01 – September 11 2002, Le genre humain – 1ère partie: Les parisiens 2004, Le courage d'aimer 2005, Chachun son cinéma 2007, Roman de Gare 2007. *Television includes:* Les uns et les autres (mini-series) 1983. *Publication:* Itinéraire d'un enfant très gâté (autobiog.) 2000. *Address:* 15 avenue Hoche, 75008 Paris, France. *Telephone:* 42-25-00-89.

LELYVELD, Joseph Salem; American journalist; b. 5 April 1937, Cincinnati; s. of Arthur Joseph Lelyveld and Toby Bookholz; m. Carolyn Fox 1958; two d.; ed Columbia Univ., New York; reporter, Ed. New York Times 1963–2001, Foreign Corresp. Johannesburg, New Delhi, Hong Kong, London 1965–86, columnist, staff writer 1977, 1984–85, Foreign Ed. 1987–89, Deputy Man. Ed. 1989–90, Man. Ed. 1990–94, Exec. Ed. 1994–2001 (retd), Interim Exec. Ed. 2003; Trustee, Thomson Reuters 2004–; Hon. DHumLitt (CUNY Graduate Center) 2007; George Polk Memorial Award 1972, 1984. *Publications include:* Move Your Shadow (Pulitzer Prize) 1985, Omaha Blues: A Memory Loop 2005, Great Soul: Mahatma Gandhi and His Struggle With India 2011. *Address:* c/o Thomson Reuters, 3 Times Square, New York, NY 10036, USA.

LEMANN, Jorge Paulo; Swiss/Brazilian business executive; *Principal, 3G Capital;* b. 26 Aug. 1939, Rio de Janeiro; m. Susanna Lemann; five c.; ed Harvard Univ., USA; trainee at Credit Suisse 1961–62; co-f. Banco de Investimentos Garantia 1971, Sr Pnr 1971–98, bought control of a Brazilian brewery that eventually became AmBev; CEO Brahma 1990–99, mem. Bd of Dirs, Companhia de Bebidas das Américas/Ambev (formed after merger of Brahma and Antarctica) 1999–2004, mem. Admin. Council, InBev NV/SA (after merger of Interbrew and Ambev) 2004–08 (following acquisition of Anheuser-Busch); Co-founder and Prin., 3G Capital, New York 2004–, bought Burger King 2010, acquired H.J. Heinz Co. and Warren Buffet's Berkshire Hathaway 2013; mem. Admin. Council, Gillette Corpn 1998–2005, Lojas Americanas SA; mem. Advisory Cttee, New York Stock Exchange 1998–2005, Chair. Latin American Advisory Cttee; mem. Int. Advisory Bd, Credit Suisse, DaimlerChrysler AG; Founder and mem. Advisory Council, Fundação Estudar; mem. Bd of Deans Advisors, Harvard Business School; est. Lemann Scholarships 2005; has lived in Switzerland since 1999 following an attempted kidnapping of his children. *Sporting achievements:* Swiss nat. tennis champion 1963, played at Wimbledon. *Leisure interest:* tennis. *Address:* 3G Capital, 600 Third Avenue, 37th Floor, New York, NY 10016, USA (office). *Telephone:* (212) 893-6727 (office). *E-mail:* ir@3g-capital.com (office). *Website:* www .3g-capital.com (office).

LEMANN, Nicholas Berthelot, BA; American journalist and academic; *Dean and Henry R. Luce Professor, Graduate School of Journalism, Columbia University;* b. 11 Aug. 1954, New Orleans, La; m. 1st Dominique Alice Browning 1983; two s.; m. 2nd Judith Anne Shulevitz 1999; one s. one d.; ed Harvard Coll.; Assoc. Ed. and Man. Ed., Washington Monthly magazine 1976–78; Assoc. Ed. and Exec. Ed. Texas Monthly magazine 1978–79, Exec. Ed. 1981–83; Nat. Staff Reporter, Washington Post 1979–81; Nat. Corresp. The Atlantic Monthly magazine 1983–99; staff writer, The New Yorker magazine 1999–, Washington Corresp. 2000–03, currently Contrib.; Henry R. Luce Prof., Grad. School of Journalism, Columbia Univ. 2003–, Dean Grad. School of Journalism 2003–; fmr contrib. to numerous publs including New York Times, New York Review of Books, New Republic, Slate, American Heritage; mem. Bd of Dirs Authors Guild, Center for Humanities, CUNY Grad. Center, Soc. of American Historians; mem. New York Inst. for Humanities. *Television:* documentary projects for Blackside Inc., Frontline, Discovery Channel, BBC. *Publications:* The Fast Track: Texans and Other Survivors 1981, Out of the Forties 1983, The Promised Land: The Great Black Migration and How It Changed America 1991, The Big Test: The Secret History of the American Meritocracy 1999 (Washington Monthly Political Book Award), Redemption: The Last Battle of the Civil War 2006. *Address:* Columbia University Graduate School of Journalism, 2950 Broadway, New York, NY 10027, USA (office). *Telephone:* (212) 854-6056 (office). *E-mail:* lemann@columbia.edu (office). *Website:* www.journalism.columbia.edu (office).

LEMBERGS, Aivars; Latvian politician and business executive; *Mayor of Ventspils;* b. 26 Sept. 1953, Jēkabpils; ed Latvian State Univ. (now Univ. of Latvia); worked in various positions in CP of Latvia; Mayor of Ventspils 1988–; Founder and Leader of local political party, Latvijai un Venstpilij (For Latvia and Ventspils) 1994–, formed alliance with Union of Greens and Farmers; fmr business partner of Ainars Gulbis; unsuccessful cand. for post of Prime Minister; detained on charges of money laundering, abuse of public office, and bribery charges March 2007, spent several months in Matisa Prison, later placed under house arrest 2008, subject of court proceedings Feb. 2009; Order of Three Stars (Third Class) 2008. *Address:* Office of the Mayor, Ventspils City Council, Jūras iela 36, 3601 Ventspils, Latvia (office). *Telephone:* 6360-1113 (office). *Fax:* 6360-1118 (office). *E-mail:* atbalsts@ventspils.gov.lv (office). *Website:* www.ventspils.lv (office); www .aivarslembergs.lv.

LEMERCIER GEORGES, André; Haitian lawyer and politician; *Minister of the Economy and Finance;* served in pvt. legal practice; fmr consultant, Domus Conseil; Minister of the Economy and Finance 2011–. *Address:* Ministry of the Economy and Finance, Palais des Ministères, rue Mgr Guilloux, Port-au-Prince, Haiti (office). *Telephone:* 2223-7113 (office). *Fax:* 2223-1247 (office). *E-mail:* mef@ mefhaiti.gouv.ht (office). *Website:* www.mefhaiti.gouv.ht (office).

LEMIERRE, Jean; French international civil servant and international business consultant; *Senior Advisor to the Chairman, BNP Paribas;* b. 6 June 1950, Sainte Adresse; m.; three c.; ed Institut d'Etudes Politiques de Paris, Ecole Nationale d'Admin; Inspection Générale des Finances 1976; various positions, Tax Policy Admin 1980–87, Head 1987–89; Directeur Général des Impôts 1989–95; Directeur de Cabinet, French Pvt. Office, Minister of Economy and Finance, Paris 1995; Head of Treasury 1995–2000; mem. European Monetary Cttee 1995–98; Chair. European Econ. and Finance Cttee 1999–2000, Paris Club 1999–2000; Pres. EBRD 2000–08; Sr Advisor to the Chair., BNP Paribas Group 2008–. *Address:* BNP Paribas, 16 boulevard des Italiens, 75009 Paris, France (office). *Telephone:* 1-40-14-45-46 (office). *Fax:* 1-40-14-69-73 (office). *Website:* www.bnpparibas.com (office).

LEMIEUX, Joseph Henry, BS; American business executive; b. 2 March 1931, Providence, RI; s. of Joseph C. Lemieux and Mildred L. Lemieux; m. Frances J. Schmidt 1956; three s. two d.; ed Stonehill Coll., Univ. of Rhode Island, Bryant Coll., Providence; joined Glass Container Div., Owens-Illinois as trainee 1957, numerous posts include Plant Comptroller 1961, Admin. Man. 1964, Plant Man. 1965–72, Vice-Pres. 1972–78, Group Vice-Pres. 1979–84, Exec. Vice-Pres. and Pres. Packaging Operations 1984–86, Pres. and COO 1986–90, CEO 1990–2003, Chair. 1991–2004; Chair. Health Care and Retirement Corpn of America 1986, ACI America Holdings, Inc.; mem. Bd of Dirs Manor Care, Inc. 1991–2005; Hon. DBA (Bryant Coll.) 1994; Outstanding Young Man of America, US Jr Chamber of Commerce 1965, Ellis Island Medal of Honor 2001. *Leisure interests:* golf, tennis. *Address:* c/o Owens-Illinois Inc., One Sea Gate, Toledo, OH 43666, USA.

LEMIEUX, Mario, OC, CQ; Canadian ice hockey executive and fmr ice hockey player; *Co-Owner and Chairman, Pittsburgh Penguins;* b. 5 Oct. 1965, Montreal; m. Nathalie Asselin; four c.; picked first overall in 1984 Nat. Hockey League (NHL) Entry Draft by Pittsburgh Penguins; winner of Stanley Cup 1991, 1992, 2009 (as owner); retd 1997; led group that acquired Penguins 1999, returned as player 2000, retd 2006, currently Co-Owner and Chair.; played for Canadian nat. team in Canadian Cup 1988, gold medal, Olympic Games, Salt Lake City 2002; est. Mario Lemieux Foundation 1993; regular competitor at the American Century Championship, Edgewood Tahoe Golf Course, Lake Tahoe, NV, won tournament 1998; Chevalier, Ordre nat. du Québec; CHL Player of the Year 1984, Calder Memorial Trophy 1985, NHL All-Rookie Team 1985, Chrysler-Dodge/NHL Performer of the Year 1985, 1986, 1987, NHL All-Star Game MVP 1985, 1988, 1990, Dapper Dan Athlete of The Year 1986, 1989, Lester B. Pearson Award 1986, 1988, 1993, 1996, NHL Second All-Star Team 1986, 1987, 1992, 2001, Art Ross Trophy 1988, 1989, 1992, 1993, 1996, 1997, NHL First All-Star Team 1988, 1989, 1993, 1996, 1997, Hart Memorial Trophy 1988, 1993, 1996, Conn Smythe Trophy 1991, 1992, Bill Masterton Memorial Trophy 1993, Lou Marsh Trophy 1993, NHL Plus/Minus Award 1993, ESPY Award NHL Player of the Year 1993, 1994, 1998, inducted into Hockey Hall of Fame 1997, ranked No. 4 on The Hockey News' list of the 100 Greatest Hockey Players (highest-ranking French-Canadian player) 1998, Lester Patrick Trophy 2000, ESPN Hockey Player of the Decade 2000, featured as the cover athlete on EA Sports' 2002 edn of its popular NHL series for multiple platforms, inducted into Canada's Walk of Fame 2004. *Leisure interest:* golf. *Address:* Pittsburgh Penguins, CONSOL Energy Center, 1001 Fifth Avenue, Pittsburgh, PA 15219, USA (office). *Telephone:* (412) 642-1300 (office). *Fax:* (412) 255-1980 (office). *E-mail:* info@penguins.nhl.com (office). *Website:* penguins.nhl .com (office).

LEMINE, Mohamed Mahmoud Ould Mohamed, DEcon; Mauritanian politician; *Chairman, Union for the Republic;* b. 1952, Hodh El Gharbi; m.; ed studied in Cairo, Egypt; fmr Prof. of Econs, Univ. of Nouakchott –1996; Dir-Gen. Ecole Nationale de l'Administration (ENA), Nouakchott 1996–2007; Minister of Nat. Defence 2007–08; Chair. Union for the Repub. 2009–. *Address:* Union for the Republic, Nouakchott, Mauritania (office).

LeMOND, Gregory James (Greg); American motor racing driver, fmr professional road racing cyclist and entrepreneur; b. 26 June 1961, Lakewood, Calif.; m. Kathy Morris 1981; two s. one d.; began professional competitive cycling career 1980; won Coors Classic stage race 1981, 1985; World Road Race Champion 1983, 1989; won Tour de France 1986, 1989, 1990; retd from cycling due to injury 1994; currently designer of bicycles; also leads cycling tours; now engaged in auto racing, professional series debut 1997 (with US F2000); Sports Illustrated Sportsman of the Year 1989, ABC Wide World of Sports Athlete of the Year 1989, 1990, World's Most Outstanding Athlete, Jesse Owens Int. Trophy Awards 1991, twice winner of the Pernod Trophy (for best cyclist in the world), inducted into Cycling Hall of Fame. *Leisure interests:* outdoor enthusiast, fly fishing. *Address:* c/o Trek Travel, 801 West Madison, Waterloo, WI 53594, USA. *E-mail:* info@greglemond.com. *Website:* www.lemondbikes.com; greglemond.com.

LEMOS, Nikolas Spyridon; Greek business executive; b. 8 Sept. 1933, Oinoussai, Chios; s. of Spyros A. Lemos and Irene N. Pateras; m. Irini Doxiadis 1976; three s. three d.; ed Univ. School of Navigation, Southampton, Edinburgh Univ.; officer, Capt. on various types of merchant ships; port capt. several shipyards in numerous countries; Man. Dir Lemos & Pateras 1966–83; Founder and Chair. NS Lemos & Co. Ltd (Shipbrokers) 1983–99; Pres. Maritime Museum Oinoussai; mem. Council Det Norske Veritas; Trustee, Thyateira and St Nicholas Trust; Actuarius of Ecumenical Patriarche Constantinopoleos; Lifetime Achievement Award, Annual Lloyds List Greek Shipping Awards 2008. *Leisure interests:* fishing, sailing, scuba diving, skiing, swimming. *Address:* 23A Vas Sofias Avenue, 10674 Athens, Greece (office). *Telephone:* (1) 07260500 (office). *Fax:* (1) 07260552 (office).

LEMOS SIMMONDS, Carlos, DrIur; Colombian politician; b. Popayán, Cauca; m. Martha Blanco Guake; four c.; ed Lycée of Cauca Univ. and Cauca Univ.; Prof. of Colombian Political History, Universidad Javeriana; Prof. of Colombian Econ. History, Free Univ. of Colombia; Dir of Consigna magazine 1982–87; mem. of Bogotá Council 1972–74, 1986–88; mem. House of Reps 1974–78; Gov. of Cauca Prov. 1976–77; Sec.-Gen. of the Presidency 1978–79; Senator 1978–81; Minister of Foreign Affairs 1981–82; Amb. to the OAS 1987–89; Minister of Communications Feb.–Oct. 1989; Minister of Government (Interior) 1989–90; Del. to Nat. Constitutional Ass. 1990–91; Chair of Bogotá Council 1992; cand. for Pres. of Colombia 1992; Amb. to Austria 1995, to UK 1995; Vice-Pres. of Colombia 1996–98; Orders of Boyacá, San Carlos, Civil Merit (Spain), Independence (Equatorial Guinea), Merit (Italy, Chile and Ecuador), Sol (Peru) and Balboa (Panama), Commdr Order of Isabel la Católica. *Publications include:* Francisco de Paula Santander, An Iconography, The Pre-Columbian Economy. *Address:* Palacio de Nariño, Carrera 8A, 7–26, Bogotá, DC, Colombia.

LEMPER, Ute; German singer, dancer and actress; b. 4 July 1963, Münster; pnr Todd Turkisher; two s. one d.; ed Dance Acad., Cologne, Max Reinhardt Seminary for Dramatic Art, Vienna; leading role in Viennese production of Cats 1983; appeared in Peter Pan, Berlin, Cabaret, Düsseldorf and Paris (recipient of Molière Award 1987), Chicago (Laurence Olivier Award) 1997–99 an in London and New York, Life's a Swindle tour 1999, Punishing Kiss tour 2000, The Last Tango in Berlin tour 2009; Die sieben Todsünden (Weill) at Covent Garden Festival, London 2000; collaborations with Michael Nyman; French Culture Prize 1993. *Recordings include:* Life is a Cabaret 1987, Ute Lemper Sings Kurt Weill 1988, (Vol. 2) 1993, The Threepenny Opera 1988, Mahagonny Songspiel 1989, Crimes of the Heart 1989, The Seven Deadly Sins 1990, Songbook (with Michael Nyman) 1992, Illusions 1992, Espace Indécent 1993, Portrait of Ute Lemper 1995, City of Strangers 1995, Berlin Cabaret Songs 1996, Nuits Étranges 1997, All that Jazz/ The Best of Ute Lemper 1998, Punishing Kiss 2000, But One Day 2002, Blood and Feathers 2006, Between Yesterday and Tomorrow 2008. *Television appearances include:* L'Affaire Dreyfus (Arte), Tales from the Crypt (HBO), Illusions (Granada) and The Look of Love (Gillian Lynne). *Film appearances include:* L'Autrichienne 1989, Moscou Parade 1992, Coupable d'Innocence 1993, Prêt à Porter 1995, Bogus 1996, Combat de Fauves, A River Made to Drown In, Appetite 1997. *Address:* Les Visiteurs du Soir, 40 rue de la Folie Régnault, 75011 Paris, France (office). *Telephone:* 1-44-93-02-02 (office). *Fax:* 1-44-93-04-40 (office). *E-mail:* ogluzman@visiteursdusoir.com (office). *Website:* www.visiteursdusoir.com (office); www.utelemper.com.

LENAERTS, Baron; Koen, Lic.iuris, LLM, MPA, PhD; Belgian judge; *Vice-President, Court of Justice of the European Union;* b. (Koenraad Lenaerts), 20 Dec. 1954, Mortsel; m. Kris Grimonprez; six d.; ed Univs of Namur and Leuven, Belgium and Harvard Univ., USA; Asst Prof., Leuven Univ. 1979–82, Assoc. Prof. 1982–83, Prof. of EC Law 1983–; Prof. of European Insts, Coll. of Europe, Bruges 1984–89; law clerk to Judge R. Joliet, Court of Justice of the European Communities 1984–85; mem. Brussels Bar 1986–89; Judge, Court of First Instance of the European Communities, Luxembourg 1989–2003, Court of Justice of the European Union 2003– (currently Vice-Pres.); Visiting Prof. of Law, Univ. of Burundi 1983, 1986, Univ. of Strasbourg 1986–89, Harvard Univ. 1988–89; numerous academic distinctions, fellowships and prizes. *Publications:* 'The Negative Implications' of the Commerce Clause and 'Preemption' Doctrines as Federalism Related Limitations on State Power: a Historical Review 1978, Constitutie en rechter 1983, International privaatrecht (with G. Van Hecke) 1986, Le juge et la constitution aux Etats-Unis d'Amérique et dans l'ordre juridique européen 1988, Two Hundred Years of U.S. Constitution and Thirty Years of EEC Treaty: Outlook for a Comparison 1988, Constitutional Law of the European Union (with P. Van Nuffel) 1999 (second edn 2005), Procedural Law of the European Union (with D. Arts and I. Maselis) 1999 (second edn 2006), European Union Law (third edn) 2011, articles and contribs to reviews etc. *Address:* Court of Justice of the European Union, blvd Konrad Adenauer, 2925 Luxembourg (office). *Telephone:* 4303-3553 (office). *Fax:* 4303-3541 (office). *E-mail:* koen.lenaerts@curia.europa.eu (office). *Website:* www.curia.europa.eu (office).

LENDL, Ivan; American (b. Czech) fmr professional tennis player; b. 7 March 1960, Ostrava, Czechoslovakia; s. of Jiri Lendl and Olga Lendlova; m. Samantha Frankel 1989; five d.; Davis Cup player 1978–85, winner 1980; winner, Italian Jr Singles 1978, French Jr Singles 1978, Wimbledon Jr Singles 1978, Spanish Open Singles 1980, 1981, S. American Open Singles 1981, Canadian Open Singles 1980, 1981, WCT Tournament of Champion Singles 1982, WCT Masters Singles 1982, WCT Finals Singles 1982, Masters Champion 1985, 1986, French Open Champion 1984, 1986, 1987, US Open Champion 1985, 1986, 1987, US Clay Court Champion 1985, Italian Open Champion 1986, Australian Open Champion 1989, 1990; finalist Wimbledon 1986; held World No. 1 ranking for a record 270 weeks 1985–87, 1989; won 94 singles titles and six doubles; named World Champion (Int. Tennis Fed.) 1985, 1986, 1990; competed in 19 Grand Slam singles finals, a record surpassed by Roger Federer 2009; remains the only male tennis player with at least 90% match wins in five different years (1982 the first, 1989 the last); retd Dec. 1994; returned to play his first tournament since retirement in the Caesars Tennis Classic exhibition match in Atlantic City, NJ against Mats Wilander, losing the one-set match 3–6 April 2010; played exhibition match with John McEnroe at Madison Square Garden Feb. 2011; played in Prague for the first time since the 1970s as part of Sparta Prague Open tournament, beating Jiří Novák May 2012; apptd coach to Andy Murray Dec. 2011, credited with guiding Murray to his first two Grand Slam victories in US Open 2012 and Wimbledon Championships 2013; mem. Laureus World Sports Acad.; granted US citizenship 1992; ATP Most Improved Player 1981, ITF World Champion: 1985, 1986,1987, 1990, ATP Player of the Year 1985, 1986, 1987, inducted into Int. Tennis Hall of Fame 2001.

Publication: Ivan Lendl's Power Tennis. *Leisure interests:* golf, collecting art. *Address:* c/o Laureus World Sports Academy, 460 Fulham Road, London, SW6 1BZ, England.

LENDLEIN, Andreas, DrScNat; German scientist and academic; *Vice-Director and Co-ordinator of Research Field 'Bio-Engineering', Berlin-Brandenburg School for Regenerative Therapies;* ed Univ. of Technology (RWTH), Aachen; Postdoctoral Fellow, Dept for Material Science, ETH, Zurich, Switzerland 1996–97; Visiting Scientist, Dept of Chemical Eng, MIT, USA 1997–98; Head of Dept, Devt and Eng of Biocompatible Polymer Systems, German Wool Research Inst., Univ. of Tech. (RWTH), Aachen 1997–2002; Man. Dir Nemoscience GmbH, Aachen 1998–2003; Prof., Materials in Life Sciences, Faculty of Math. and Natural Sciences, Univ. of Potsdam 2002–; Dir Inst. of Polymer Research, Helmholtz-Zentrum Geesthacht Research Centre, Teltow 2002–13; Dir Inst. for Tech. and Devt, Medical Devices (ITEMP), RWTH 2004–06; Prof., Medical Faculty, RWTH 2004–06; Vice-Dir and Co-ordinator of Research Field 'Bio-Engineering', Berlin-Brandenburg School for Regenerative Therapies, Virchow Charité, Berlin 2006–, mem. Medical Faculty Bd; Speaker, Research Programme 'Regenerative Medicine', Helmholtz Asscn of German Research Centres 2002–07; Guest Prof., Tianjin Univ., People's Repub. of China 2006; Authorised Officer for Health Sciences, Health Capital Network, Berlin-Brandenburg 2006; Scientific Amb. of Brandenburg 2008; Hon. Prof. of Chem., Free Univ., Berlin 2008–; World Tech. Award in Health and Medicine, The World Tech. Network 2005. *Publications:* numerous scientific papers in professional journals on biomaterials for clinical applications in regenerative medicine. *Address:* Berlin-Brandenburg School for Regenerative Therapies Charité Campus Virchow Klinikum, Augustenburger Platz 1, 13353 Berlin, Germany (office). *Telephone:* 30 450539417 (office). *Fax:* 30 450539918 (office). *E-mail:* info@bsrt.de (office). *Website:* www.bsrt.de (office).

LENG, James (Jim) W.; British steel industry executive and mining industry executive; b. 1945; CEO Low & Bonar PLC –1995; CEO Laporte PLC 1995–2001; apptd Dir (non-exec.) Corus Group PLC (fmrly British Steel) 2001, Deputy Chair. and Sr Ind. Dir 2002–03; Chair. 2003–09; European Chair. and Chair. European Advisory Bd, AEA Investors Ltd; mem. Bd of Dirs Alston 2003–, Pilkington PLC –2006, IMI PLC –2005, JP Morgan Fleming Mid Cap Investment Trust PLC –2004, Hanson PLC 2004–07, TNK–BP, Doncasters –2010; Gov. Nat. Inst. of Econ. and Social Research. *Address:* AEA Investors Ltd, 78 Brook Street, London, W1K 5EF, England (office). *Telephone:* (20) 7659-7800 (office). *Fax:* (20) 7491-2155 (office). *Website:* www.aeainvestors.com (office).

LENG, Rongquan, MSc; Chinese telecommunications executive; b. 1949, Liaoning Prov.; ed Beijing Inst. of Posts and Telecommunications; Chief Engineer, Beijing Long Distance Telephone Bureau 1989–94, Deputy Chief Engineer, Telecommunications Bureau, Ministry of Posts and Telecommunications 1994–99, Deputy Dir Gen. 1999–2000, Exec. Dir 2004–11, China Telecommunications Corpn 2004–, Pres. and COO 2004–08, Vice-Pres. 2008–11, also Deputy Gen. Man., China Network Communications Group Corpn –2004, Vice-Chair. China Netcom Group Corpn (HK) Ltd –2004; Dir Alcatel-Lucent Shanghai Bell Co. Ltd; Ind. Dir, China Finance Online Co. Ltd 2012–; Chair. China Inst. of Communications. *Address:* China Finance Online Co. Ltd, 9th Floor, Tower C, Corporate Square, 35 Financial Street, Xicheng District, Beijing 100033, People's Republic of China (office). *Telephone:* (10) 58325388 (office). *Fax:* (10) 58325300 (office). *E-mail:* info@chinafinanceonline.com (office). *Website:* www.chinafinanceonline.com (office).

LENK, Hans Albert Paul, PhD; German fmr rower and academic; *Professor Emeritus of Philosophy, Karlsruhe Institute of Technology;* b. 23 March 1935, Berlin; s. of Albert Lenk and Annemarie Lenk; m. Ulrike Reincke; two s. one d.; ed Lauenburgische Gelehrtenschule, Ratzeburg, Freiburg and Kiel Univs, Tech. Univ. of Berlin; early career as rower (competed for Unified Team of Germany in 1960 Summer Olympics); Asst Prof., Tech. Univ. of Berlin 1962, Assoc. Prof. 1966, Prof. 1969; Chair. and Prof. of Philosophy, Karlsruhe Univ. (now Karlruhe Inst. of Tech.) 1969, now Prof. Emer., Dean, Coll. of Humanities and Social Sciences 1973–75; Dean and Prof. Philosophy of Social Sciences and Theory of Planning, European Faculty of Land Use and Devt, Strasbourg 1983–2006; Visiting Prof. numerous foreign univs; Hon. Prof. Tech. Univ., Budapest 1992; Green Honors Prof., Tex. Christian Univ., Fort Worth 1987; Pres. Int. Philosophic Soc. for Study of Sport 1980–81, Int. Olympic Union 1980–90, European Forum, Baden 1980–; Vice-Pres. European Acad. of Sciences and Philosophy of Law 1986–; Pres. Gen. Soc. for Philosophy in Germany 1991–93; Pres. Argentine-German Soc. of Philosophy 1992–, German-Hungarian Soc. of Philosophy 1993–2005, Chilean-German Soc. of Philosophy 1995–, German-Romanian Soc. of Philosophy 2000–, German-Russian Soc. for the Philosophy of Science and Technology 2002–, Int. Inst. of Philosophy (World Acad.) 2005–08; Vice-Pres. Féd. Int. des Sociétés de Philosophie 1998–2003; mem. American Acad. of Kinesiology and Physical Educ., Russian Acad. of Science 2003, Nat. Olympic Cttee for Germany –1992, German UNESCO Comm. –1992, Inst. Int. de Philosophie 1994 (mem. Bd 1996–2000, Pres. 2005–08), Int. Acad. of Philosophy of Science 1995–; Hon. mem. Int. Olympic Acad., Romanian Acad. of Science, Dept of Philosophy 2001; Dr hc (Deutsche Sporthochschule, Cologne) 1986, (Córdoba/Argentina) twice 1992, (Tech. Univ. Budapest) 1993, (Univ. Pécs) 1994, Moscow (Univ. of Humanistic Studies) 1995, (Int. Ind. Univ. for Ecology and Politology) 2001, Rostov 2002; four German, two European and one Olympic title for rowing, Silver Leaf of Fed. Pres. 1959, 1960, Scientific Diem Plaque 1962, Sievert Award (Olympian Int.) 1973, Noel Baker Prize (UNESCO) 1978, Fed. Pres. of Germany's Great Merit Cross 2005, Ethics Prize (German Olympic Sports Confed.) 2010, Hall of Fame of German Sports 2012. *Achievements include:* Olympic Champion, Eight Oar Crew 1960, two European championships in rowing, Amateur Coach World Champion Eight Oar Crew 1966. *Publications:* more than 140 books, including Kritik der logischen Konstanten 1968, Team Dynamics 1977, Pragmatische Vernunft 1979, Social Philosophy of Athletics 1979, Zur Sozialphilosophie der Technik 1982, Eigenleistung 1983, Zwischen Wissenschaftstheorie und Sozialwissenschaft 1985, Zwischen Sozialpsychologie und Sozialphilosophie 1987, Kritik der kleinen Vernunft 1987, Das Prinzip Fairness 1989, Tagebuch einer Rückreise 1991, Prometheisches Philosophieren zwischen Praxis und Paradox 1991, Zwischen Wissenschaft und Ethik 1992, Philosophie und Interpretation 1993, Interpretationskonstrukte 1993, Macht und Machtbarkeit der Technik 1994, Schemaspiele 1995, Interpretation und Realität 1995, Einführung in die angewandte Ethik 1997, Einführung in die Erkenntnistheorie 1998, Konkrete Humanität 1998, Praxisnahes Philosophieren 1999, Erfassung der Wirklichkeit 2000, Kreative Aufstiege 2000, Albert Schweitzer – Ethik als Konkrate Humanität 2000, Advances and Problems in the Philosophy of Technology (ed.) 2001, Das Denken und sein Gehalt 2001, Kleine Philosophie des Gehirns 2001, Denken und Handlungsbindung 2001, Erfolg oder Fairness? 2002, Natur-Umwelt-Ethik 2003, Grasping Reality 2003, Bewurstein als Schema interpretation 2004, Wittgenstein y el giro pragmático en la Filosofía (co-author) 2005, Veranwortung und Gewissen des Forschers 2006, Das Gefass 2006, Ethics Facing Globalization (co-ed.) 2006, Kant Today (chief ed.) 2006, Bewusstsein Kreativität und Leistung 2007, Global Technoscience and Responsibility 2007, Filosofia pragmática y humanidad concreta 2007, Humanitätsforschung als interdisziplinäre Anthropologie 2008, Von der Arbeitsz- zur Selbstbildungs- und Eigenleistungsgesellschaft 2008, Conciencia: Conciencia, acción y humanidad como interpretación 2008, Saeron Hyunsil – Tschulhak-ui Dochun 2008, Wittgenstein und die schema-pragmatische Wende (co-author) 2009, Land Development Strategies: Patterns, Risks and Responsibilities (co-ed.) 2009, Umweltverträglichkeit und Menschenzuträglichkeit 2009, Aesthetics in Contemporary Philosophy (co-ed.) 2009, Comparative and Intercultural Philosophy (ed.) 2009, Acción, Responsabilidad, Tolerancia y Humanidad 2010, Das flexible Vielfachwesen 2010, Gold-Achter 2010, Sport von Kopf bis Fuss(ball) 2010, Responsabilidad, Ciencia, Tecnología y Bioética 2012, S.O.S. – Save Olympic Spirit: Toward a Social Philosophy of the Olympics (co-ed.) 2012, Mala Filosofija Mozga 2012, LiLun, Lunlixue He Tiyu Jian de Jutirenxin 2013, Kreative Pluralität 2013; more than 2,000 articles. *Address:* Karlsruhe Institute of Technology (Universität Karlsruhe Institut für Philosophie), Kollegium am Schloss, Bau 2, 76128 Karlsruhe (office); Neubrunnenschlag 15, 76337 Waldbronn, Germany (home). *Telephone:* (721) 60842149 (office); (7243) 67971 (home). *Fax:* (721) 60843084 (office). *E-mail:* sekretariat@philosophie.kit.edu (office); hans.lenk@kit.edu (home). *Website:* www.philosophie.kit.edu (office).

LENK, Thomas; German sculptor and graphic artist; b. 15 June 1933, Berlin; s. of Franz Lenk and Anneliese Lenk (née Hoernecke); m. Maria Bendig 1959; two d.; Guest Prof., Heluwan Univ., Cairo 1978; mem. Humboldt-Gesellschaft 1992; Hon. Life mem. Art Gallery of Ont., Toronto 1988; Carnegie Int. Purchase Award 1967, Third Prize, Socha Piestanskych Parkov, Bratislava 1969, Prize of Second Norwegian Graphics Biennale 1974, Verleihung des Professorentitels 1989. *Address:* Hübscher Weg 20/17, 74523 Schwäbisch Hall, Germany. *Telephone:* (791) 49390042. *E-mail:* miralenk@yahoo.com.

LENNOX, Annie, OBE, ARAM; British rock singer and lyricist; b. 25 Dec. 1954, Aberdeen, Scotland; d. of the late Thomas A. Lennox and of Dorothy Lennox (née Ferguson); m. 1st Rahda Raman 1984 (divorced); m. 2nd Uri Fruchtmann; one s. two d.; m. 3rd Mitch Besser 2012; ed Aberdeen High School for Girls, Royal Acad. of Music; Founder-mem. (with Dave Stewart q.v.) The Catch 1977, renamed The Tourists 1979–80, Eurythmics 1980–89, 1999–; numerous Eurythmics tours world-wide; solo artist 1988–; Dr hc (Royal Scottish Acad. of Music and Drama, Glasgow) 2006, (Berklee Coll. of Music) 2013; American Soc. of Composers Award, BPI Award for Best Female Vocalist 1982/83, 1987/88, 1989/90, 1992/93, Grammy Award for Best Female Performance (for Sweet Dreams) 1983, Ivor Novello Award for Best Pop Song (for Sweet Dreams, with Dave Stewart) 1983, MTV Music Award for Best New Artist Video (for Sweet Dreams (Are Made of This)) 1984, Ivor Novello Award for Best Song (for It's Alright (Baby's Coming Back), with Dave Stewart) 1987, Ivor Novello Award for Best Song (for Why) 1992, BRIT Award for Best Female Solo Artist 1996, Grammy Award for Best Female Pop Vocals (for No More I Love Yous) 1996, BRIT Award for Outstanding Contrib. to Music 1999, Tartan Cleff Award 2001, Acad. Award for Best Song (for Into the West and Use Well the Days, from the film Lord of the Rings: The Two Towers) 2004, ASCAP Founders Award 2006, Woman of Peace Award, World Summit of Nobel Peace Prize Laureates 2009, Music Industry Trust Award 2013. *Film:* Revolution 1985. *Recordings include:* albums: with The Tourists: The Tourists 1979, Reality Affect 1980, Luminous Basement 1980; with Eurythmics: In The Garden 1981, Sweet Dreams (Are Made of This) (Grammy Award for Best Video Album) 1982, Touch 1983, 1984 (For The Love of Big Brother) 1984, Be Yourself Tonight 1985, Revenge 1986, Savage 1987, We Too Are One 1989, Peace 1999, The Ultimate Collection 2005; solo: Diva (BPI Award for Best Album) 1992, Medusa 1995, Train In Vain 1995, Bare 2003, Songs of Mass Destruction 2007, A Christmas Cornucopia 2010. *Address:* c/o 19 Management, 33 Ransomes Dock, 35–37 Parkgate Road, London, SW11 4NP, England (office). *Telephone:* (20) 7801-1919 (office). *Fax:* (20) 7801-1920 (office). *Website:* www.annielennox.co.uk; www.eurythmics.com.

LENNOX-BOYD, Simon Ronald Rupert (see BOYD OF MERTON, 2nd Viscount).

LENO, Jay, BA; American comedian and TV presenter; b. (James Douglas Muir Leno), 28 April 1950, New Rochelle, NY; m. Mavis Nicholson; ed Emerson Coll.; started career as stand-up comedian and comedy writer in 1970s; named one of several guest hosts Tonight Show (NBC) 1986, exclusive guest host 1987–92, Host 1992–2009 2010–14; host, The Jay Leno Show (NBC) 2009–10; Emmy Award 1995. *Films include:* American Hot Wax 1978, Silver Bears 1978, Americathon 1979, What's Up, Hideous Sun Demon (voice) 1983, Collision Course 1989, We're Back! A Dinosaur's Story (voice) 1993, The Flintstones 1994, Robots (voice) 2005, Ice Age: The Meltdown (voice) 2006, Cars (voice) 2006, Ice Age 2: The Meltdown (voice) 2006, Christmas is Here Again (voice) 2007, Unstable Fables: Tortoise vs. Hare (voice) 2008, Igor (voice) 2008, Scooby-Doo and the Goblin King (voice) 2008. *Leisure interests:* classic cars and motorcycles. *Address:* ICM, 10250 Constellation Boulevard, Los Angeles, CA 90067, USA (office). *Telephone:* (310) 550-4000 (office). *Website:* www.icmtalent.com (office).

LENZ, Carl Otto, DJur; German lawyer; b. 5 June 1930, Berlin; s. of the late Dr Otto Lenz and of Marieliese Pohl; m. Ursula Heinrich 1960; two s. three d.; ed schools in Germany and Switzerland, Univs of Bonn, Freiburg and Munich, Germany, Univ. of Fribourg, Switzerland, and Harvard and Cornell Univs, USA; Sec.-Gen. Christian Democratic Group, European Parl. 1956–66; mem. Bundestag 1965–84; Advocate-Gen. European Court of Justice 1984–97; Hon. Prof. of European Law, Saarland Univ. 1990–; Grosses Bundesverdienstkreuz 1976, Grosseskreuz des Verdienstordens (Grand Duchy of Luxembourg) 1998 and numerous other honours. *Publications:* Die Notverstandsverfassung des GG 1971,

EG Handbuch Recht im Binnenmarkt 1994, EG-Vortrag Kommentar 1994. *Address:* Baker & McKenzie LLP, Bethmannstrasse 50-54, 60311 Frankfurt am Main (office); Rodensteinstrasse 22, 64625 Bensheim, Germany. *Telephone:* (69) 29908-189 (office). *Fax:* (69) 29908-108 (office). *E-mail:* otto.c.lenz@bakernet.com (office). *Website:* www.bakernet.com.

LENZ, Guy; Luxembourg army officer; b. 28 Jan. 1946, Pétange; s. of Louis Lenz and Hélène Ludovicy; m. Liliane Wetz; two d.; ed Belgian Infantry School, Armed Forces Staff Coll., Norfolk, Va, USA; rank of Lt 1973, Capt. 1976, Maj. 1982, Lt-Col 1986, Col 1998; Chief of Staff of the Luxembourg Army 1998–2002; served as Head of Operations and Training, Deputy Commdr of the Mil. Training Centre; Head of GIVO at HQ, Mil. Councillor at NATO; Mil. Rep. at SHAPE; Perm. Rep. to NATO Mil. Cttee; Mil. Del. WEU Perm. Council; Commdr, Ordre de Mérite, Cross for 25 years service; Kt, Order of Civilian and Mil. 'Mérite de Adolphe de Nassau', Meritorious Service Medal (USA), Commdr, Ordre de la Couronne de Chêne (Belgium); Kt, Order of Orange Nassau (Netherlands). *Address:* Headquarters of the Armed Forces, BP 1873, 1018 Luxembourg (office); 50 rue um Böchel, 9017 Ettelbruck, Luxembourg (home). *Telephone:* (26) 848-1 (office); 819680 (home). *Fax:* (26) 845601 (office); 819680 (home). *E-mail:* info@armee.lu (office). *Website:* www.armee.lu (office).

LENZ, Siegfried; German writer; b. 17 March 1926, Lyck, East Prussia; m. Liselotte Lenz; ed High School, Samter and Univ. of Hamburg; Cultural Ed. Die Welt 1949–51; freelance writer 1952–; Hon. Citizen of Hamburg 2001–; Gerhart Hauptmann Prize 1961, Bremer Literaturpreis 1962, German Freemasons' Literary Prize 1970, Kulturpreis, Goslar 1978, Bayern Literary Prize 1995, Goethe Prize 1999, Lev Kopelev Prize for Peace and Human Rights 2009. *Publications include:* Es waren Habichte in der Luft 1951, Duell mit dem Schatten 1953, So zärtlich was Suleyken 1955, Das schönste Fest der Welt 1956, Das Kabinett der Konterbande 1956, Der Mann im Strom 1957, 1958, Jäger des Spotts 1958, Lukas, sanftmütiger Knecht 1958, Brot und Spiele 1959, Das Feuerschiff 1960, Zait der Schuldlosen 1961, Stimmungen der See 1962, Stadtgespräche 1963, Das Gesicht 1964, Lehmanns Erzählungen 1964, Der Spielverderber 1965, Haussuchung 1967, Deutschstunde 1968, Leute von Hamburg 1968, Die Augenbinde 1970, Das Vorbild 1973, Wie bei Gogol 1973, Einstein überquert die Elbe bei Hamburg 1975, Heimatmuseum 1978, Drei Stücke 1980, Der Verlust 1981, Ein Kriegsende 1984, Das serbische Mädchen 1987, Die Auflehnung 1994, Ludmilla 1996, Arnes Nachlass 1999, Fundbüro 2003, Zaungast 2004, Die Erzählungen 2006, Ein Freund der Gesamtausgabe 2006, Schweigeminute 2008, Kummer mit jütländischen Kaffeetafeln 2008, Der Anfang von etwas 2009; stories: So zärtlich war Suleyken 1955, Jäger des Spotts 1958, Das Feuerschiff 1960, Der Spielverderber 1965, Einstein überquert die Elbe bei Hamburg 1975; plays: Zeit der Schuldlosen 1961, Das Gesicht 1963, Haussuchung (radio plays) 1967. *Address:* c/o Hoffman und Campe Verlag, Harvestehuder Weg 42, 20149 Hamburg, Germany (office). *E-mail:* email@hoca.de (office). *Website:* www.hoca.de (office).

LEO, Melissa; American actress; b. 14 Sept. 1960, New York, NY; d. of Arnold Leo and Peggy Leo; one s. with John Heard; ed Mountview Theatre School, London, UK. *Films include:* Always 1985, A Time of Destiny 1988, The Ballad of Little Jo 1993, 21 Grams 2003, Hide and Seek 2005, American Gun 2006, The Cake Eaters 2007, One Night 2007, Frozen River (several awards including Central Ohio Film Critics Asscn Award for Best Actress, Central Ohio Film Critics Asscn Award for Best Breakthrough Film Artist, Florida Film Critics Circle Award for Best Actress, Gotham Independent Film Award for Breakthrough Actor, Independent Spirit Award for Best Female Lead, San Sebastián Int. Film Festival Award for Best Actress) 2008, Lullaby 2008, Righteous Kill 2008, Welcome to the Rileys 2010, The Dry Land 2010, Conviction 2010, The Fighter (several awards including Broadcast Film Critics Asscn Award for Best Supporting Actress, Dallas-Fort Worth Film Critics Asscn Award for Best Supporting Actress, Denver Film Critics Soc. Award for Best Supporting Actress, Florida Film Critics Circle Award for Best Supporting Actress, New York Film Critics Circle Award for Best Supporting Actress, Academy Award for Actress in a Supporting Role 2011) 2010, Red State 2011, Lost Revolution 2011, Francine 2011, The Sea Is All I Know (short) 2011, Seven Days in Utopia 2011. *Television includes:* Silent Witness 1985, Nasty Boys 1989, The Bride in Black 1990, Carolina Skeletons 1991, Homicide: Life on the Street 1993–99, In the Line of Duty: Hunt for Justice 1995, Legacy 1998, Homicide: The Movie 2000, Cold Case 2007, Treme (series) 2010. *Address:* c/o Untitled Entertainment, 1801 Century Park East, Suite 700, Los Angeles, CA 90067, USA (office). *Telephone:* (310) 601-2100 (office). *Fax:* (310) 601-2344 (office).

LEÓN PORTILLA, Miguel, PhD; Mexican anthropologist and historian; b. 22 Feb. 1926, Mexico City; s. of Miguel León Ortiz and Luisa Portilla Nájera; m. Ascensión Hernández Triviño 1965; one d.; ed Loyola Univ. of Los Angeles and Nat. Univ. of Mexico; Sec.-Gen. Inter-American Indian Inst. 1955–59, Asst Dir 1959–60, Dir 1960–66; Asst Dir Seminar for Náhuatl Culture, Nat. Univ. of Mexico 1956, Dir Inst. of Historical Research 1963–78, Prof. Emer. 1988–; Dir América Indígena 1960; Adviser, Int. Inst. of Different Civilisations 1960; Perm. Rep. of Mexico to UNESCO, Paris 1987; mem. Bd Govs Nat. Univ. Mexico 1976; mem. American Anthropological Asscn 1960–, Mexican Acad. of Language 1962–, Société des Américanistes de Paris 1966–, Mexican Acad. of History 1969–, Nat. Coll. of Mexico 1971–; Corresp. mem. Royal Spanish Acad. of History 1969–; Guggenheim Fellow 1969; Fellow, Portuguese Acad. of History, Lisbon 1995; Hon. mem. American Historical Asscn 1991, NAS 1995; Commendatore Repub. Italiana 1977, Great Cross of Alfonso X el sabio (Spain) 1998, Ordre des Palmes académiques 2000, Orden del Mérito Civico (en grado de Gran Cruz) (Spain) 2003; Hon. PhD (Southern Methodist Univ., Dallas, Tex.) 1980, (California) 1986, (Tel-Aviv) 1987, (Toulouse) 1990, (Colima) 1993, (San Andrés, Bolivia) 1994, (Brown Univ.) 1996, (Carolina Univ., Prague) 2000; Fifth Distinguished Lecturer, American Anthropological Asscn 1974, Serra Award 1978, Nat. Prize in the Social Sciences (Mexico) 1981, Manuel Gamio Anthropological Award 1983, Nat. Univ. of Mexico Prize 1994, Belisario Domínguez Medal (Mexico) 1997, Bartolomé de las Casas Prize (Spain) 2001, Investigador Nacional de Excelencia (Mexico) 2002, Presea 'Estado de Mexico 2001' 2002, Universidad Latinoamericana Prize, 2003, Veracruz Prize 2003, Medalla Ignacio de la Llave 2003, recognized for his historical investigations over 46 years by UNAM 2003, Toltecáyod Prize, Universidad de Tula Hidalgo 2005, Tlamatili Prize, Universidad Iberoamericana, Mexico 2005, Fundación

México Unido Prize 2005, Chiapas Prize 2006, US Library of Congress Living Legend Award 2013. *Publications include:* La Filosofía Náhuatl 1956, Visión des los Vencidos 1959, Los Antiguos Mexicanos 1961, The Broken Spears, Aztec Account of the Conquest of Mexico 1962, Aztec Thought and Culture 1963, Literaturas Precolombinas de México 1964, Imagen del México Antiguo 1964, Le Crépuscule des Aztèques 1965, Trece Poetas del Mundo Azteca 1967, Pre-Columbian Literatures of Mexico 1968, Tiempo y Realidad en el Pensamiento Maya 1968, Testimonios Sudcalifornianos 1970, De Teotihuacan a los Aztecas 1971, The Norteño Variety of Mexican Culture 1972, The Voyages of Francisco de Ortega to California 1632–1636 1972, Time and Reality in the Thought of the Maya 1973, Historia Natural y Crónica de la Antigua California 1973, Il Rovescio della Conquista, Testimonianze Asteche, Maya e Inca 1974, Aztecs and Navajos 1975, Endangered Cultures: The Indian in Latin America 1975, L'Envers de la conquête 1977, Los Manifestos en Náhuatl de Emiliano Zapata 1978, Toltecayotl, Aspectos de la Cultura Náhuatl 1980, Mesoamerican Spirituality 1980, Literaturas de Anahuac y del Imcario 1982, Mesoamerica before 1519 1984, Codex Fejérváry-Mayer, a Book of the Merchants, 1985, La Pensée Aztèque 1985, Libro de los Coloquios 1986, Das Alte Mexiko: Religion 1986, Huehuehtlahtolli, Testimonies of the Ancient Word 1988, Mesoamerica in 1492 and on the eve of 1992, 1988, Poésie Náhuatl d'amour et d'amitié 1991, Fifteen Poets of the Aztec World 1992, The Aztec Image of Self and Society 1992, Raíces indígenas, presencia hispánica 1993, La flecha en el blanco 1995, Bernardino de Sahagún: Pionero de la antropología 1999, Tonantzin Guadalupe 2000, La Visión de los Vencidos (published in English as The Broken Spear), La Filosofía Náhuatl (published as Aztec Thought and Culture), Motivos de la Antropología Americanista, Indagación en la Diferencia 2001, In the Language of Kings – An Anthology of Mesoamerican Literature Pre-Columbian to the Present 2001, México an 1554, Ordenanzas de Tema Indígena en Castella y náhuatl – Expedidas par Maximiliano de Habsburgo 2003, Codices – Los antiguos libros del Nuevo Mundo 2003, Obras de Miguel León-Portillo, Pueblos Indígenas de México – Autonomía y Diferencia Cultural 2003, Obras de Miguel León-Portillo – En torno a la Historia de Mesoamérica 2004, Aztecas-Mexicas – Desarrollo de una civilización originaria 2005. *Leisure interests:* scouting and gardening. *Address:* Instituto de Investigaciones Históricas, Circuitro Mtro. Mario de la Cueva, Zona Cultural, Ciudad Universitaria, UNAM, 04510 México, DF (office); Alberto Zamora 131 antes 103, Col. Coyoacán, 04520 Delegación, México, DF, Mexico (home). *Telephone:* (5) 665-44-17 (office); (55) 54-08-02 (home). *Fax:* (5) 665-0070 (office). *E-mail:* portilla@servidor.unam.mx (office).

LEONARD, Brian Edmund, PhD, DSc, MRIA; Irish pharmacologist and academic; *Professor Emeritus of Pharmacology, National University of Ireland, Galway;* b. 30 May 1936, Winchester, Hants., England; s. of Harold E. Leonard and Dorothy Coley; m. Helga F. Mühlpfordt 1959; two d.; ed Univ. of Birmingham; Dept of Medical Biochemistry, Univ. of Birmingham 1956–62; Lecturer in Pharmacology, Univ. of Nottingham 1962–68; Tech. Officer, CNS Research, ICI Pharmaceuticals Div. Alderley Park, Cheshire 1968–71; Group Leader, CNS Pharmacology, Organon International BV, Oss, Netherlands 1971–74; Prof. of Pharmacology, Univ. Coll. (now Nat. Univ. of Ireland) Galway 1974–, Prof. Emer. 1999–; Councillor, CINP 1996–2000, Treas. 1992–96, Pres. Elect 2002–04, Pres. 2004–06; Visiting Prof., Brain and Behaviour Research Inst., Maastricht Univ.; Pres. British Asscn Psychopharmacology 1988–90; Past Pres. Int. Soc. for the Investigation of Stress; Assoc. mem. Royal Coll. of Psychiatrists; Foreign Corresp. mem. American Coll. Neuropsychopharmacology; Visiting Fellow, Magdalen Coll. Oxford 1990–91; Hon. Prof., Faculty of Medicine, Queen's Univ. Belfast, NI, Dept of Psychiatry, Univ. of Hong Kong 2004–06, Hon. mem. S African Asscn of Psychiatrists; Silver Medal, Royal Irish Acad. 1996. *Publications:* Fundamentals of Psychopharmacology 1992, Fundamentals of Psychoimmunology 2000; over 400 articles in int. scientific journals. *Leisure interests:* entomology, classical music, political science. *Address:* Pharmacology Department, National University of Ireland, University Road, Galway (office); Currabhaitia, Tullykyne, Moycullen, Co. Galway, Ireland (home). *Telephone:* (91) 524411 (ext. 3837) (office); (91) 555292 (home). *Fax:* (91) 525700 (office). *E-mail:* belucg@iol.ie. *Website:* www.nuigalway .ie/pharmacology (office).

LEONARD, Hugh Terence; New Zealand broadcasting executive; b. 20 July 1938, Greymouth; s. of Michael James Leonard and Elizabeth Leonard (née Storey); m. Pauline Lobendahn 1965; one s. two d.; joined NZ Broadcasting Service 1956, Fiji Broadcasting Comm. 1960, Gen. Man. 1973–85; Sec.-Gen. Asia-Pacific Broadcasting Union 1985–2002, Special Adviser to the Pres. 2002–03 (retd); Fiji Independence Medal 1970. *Leisure interests:* classic motorcycles, remote-controlled model aircraft, computers. *Address:* c/o Asia-Pacific Broadcasting Union, PO Box 1164, 59700 Kuala Lumpur, Malaysia. *Telephone:* (3) 22823592.

LEONARD, Jason, OBE; British professional rugby football player (rugby union); b. 14 Aug. 1968, Barking, Essex; s. of Frank Leonard and Maria Leonard; two s. one d.; ed Warren Comprehensive, Chadwell Heath, Essex; prop forward (usually loose-head); teams: Barking, Saracens, Harlequins 1990– (264 appearances, five tries), England Under-21, England A (2 caps), England 1990– (debut versus Argentina); 114 Tests (world record) for England (as 2 as Capt.), one try, to 31 March 2004; mem. Grand Slam winning squads 1991, 1992, 1995, 2003, Five Nations Championship winners 1999, Six Nations Championship winners 2000, 2001, World Cup winning squad 2003, runners-up 1991, 4th place 1995; mem. British Lions' team, New Zealand (2 Tests) 1993, South Africa (1 Test), 1997 Australia (2 Tests) 2001; Freeman, City of Greater London.

LEONARD, Ray Charles ("Sugar Ray"); American fmr professional boxer; b. 17 May 1956, Wilmington, NC; s. of Cicero Leonard and Getha Leonard; m. 1st Juanita Wilkinson 1980 (divorced 1990); two s.; m. 2nd Bernadette Robi 1993; one s. one d.; ed Palmer Park High School, Md; amateur boxer 1970–77; won 140 of 145 amateur fights; world amateur champion 1974, US Amateur Athletic Union champion 1974, Pan-American Games gold medallist 1975, Olympic gold medallist 1976; guaranteed record purse of US $25,000 for first professional fight Feb. 1977; won North American welterweight title from Pete Ranzany August 1979; won World Boxing Council version of world welterweight title from Wilfred Benitez Nov. 1979; retained title against Dave Green March 1980, lost it to Roberto Durán (q.v.), Montréal, June 1980, regained it from Durán, New Orleans, Nov. 1980; world jr middleweight title, World Boxing Asscn (WBA) June 1981; won WBA world welterweight title from Tommy Hearns to become undisputed world

champion Sept. 1981, drew rematch June 1989; 36 professional fights, 33 wins, lost two, drawn one; retd from boxing Nov. 1982; returned to the ring April 1987; won World middleweight title, lost to Terry Norris 1991, retd from boxing 1991; returned to ring March 1997; lost Int. Boxing Council middleweight title fight to Hector Camacho 1997; boxing promoter (Sugar Ray Leonard Boxing); commentator for Home Box Office TV Co.; motivational speaker; Ring magazine's Fighter of the Decade for the 1980s. *Television:* The Contender 2005. *Publication:* The Big Fight 2011. *Address:* Suite 206-B, 4401 East West Highway, Bethesda, MD 20814, USA. *Telephone:* (310) 471-3100 (office). *Website:* www.srlboxing.com (office).

LEONARDO, Anne Itto; South Sudanese politician; d. of the late Leonardo Tongun Itto; Deputy Sec. Gen., Sudan People's Liberation Movt (southern sector); Chair. Political Cttee, Jt Nat. Transitional Team 2005–; Minister of State for Agric. and Forestry, Govt of Nat. Unity, Sudan 2005–2010; mem. Nat. Ass. 2005–; Minister of Agric. and Forestry, Govt of South Sudan 2011. *Address:* c/o Ministry of Agriculture and Forestry, Juba, South Sudan (office).

LEONG, Alan, LLB, LLM; Chinese barrister and politician; b. 22 Feb. 1958, Hong Kong; m.; three c.; ed Wah Yan Coll., Kowloon, Univ. of Hong Kong, Univ. of Cambridge, UK; called to Hong Kong Bar 1983, to Inner Bar 1998 (first to be apptd after establishment of Hong Kong Special Admin. Region; mem. Legis. Council (Civic Party) representing Kowloon East 2004–10 (resgnd) (nominated as Civic Party cand. for 2007 election for Chief Exec.); Chair. Special Cttee on Mainland Practice and Relations; Chair. Asscn of Heads of Secondary Schools of Tsuen Wan, Kwai Chung and Tsing Yi Dist 1998–; Chair. Water Pollution Control Appeal Bd 2001–; Dir Applied Research Council 2000–; mem. Criminal and Law Enforcement Injuries Compensation Bd 2000–, Ind. Police Complaints Council 2000–, Hong Kong Bar Asscn 2000– (Chair. 2001–03); Professional Services Advisory Cttee Hong Kong Trade Devt Council 2002–, Chief Justice's Steering Cttee on Implementation of Use of Chinese in the Courts 1996–2003, Task Group on Promotion of English Standards in the Workplace, Standing Cttee on Language Educ. and Research 1999–2000, Cen. Policy Unit Panel on Social Cohesion 2002–03, Cttee of Bilingual Legal System in Hong Kong 1998–2004; Pres. Kwai Tsing Lions Club 1998–99; Chair. Task Force on Accreditation re Internship, Advisory Cttee on Teacher Educ. and Qualification 2003; Bar's Rep. on the Working Group on Review of Legal Educ. and Training 1999–2002; Hon. Lecturer, Dept of Professional Legal Educ., Univ. of Hong Kong 2002–. *Address:* Room 601D, Citibank Tower, 3 Garden Road, Central, Hong Kong Special Administrative Region, People's Republic of China (office). *Telephone:* 25093116 (office). *Fax:* 25093101 (office). *E-mail:* al@alanleong.net (office); contact@alanleong.net (office). *Website:* www.alanleong.net (office).

LEONG, Lampo, BFA, MFA, PhD; American (b. Chinese) artist and academic; *Professor of Art, University of Missouri-Columbia;* b. (Liang Lanbo), 3 July 1961, Guangzhou, Guangdong Prov., People's Repub. of China; ed Guangzhou Acad. of Fine Arts, California Coll. of the Arts, San Francisco and Univ. of California, Berkeley, USA, Cen. Acad. of Fine Arts, Beijing; Instructor, California Coll. of Arts and Crafts 1986–87, Chabot Coll., Hayward, Calif. 1989–94, Univ. of California, Berkeley 1989–99, Diablo Valley Coll., Pleasant Hill, Calif. 1998–99; Visiting Asst Prof., San Francisco State Univ. 1996–2001; Prof. of Art, Univ. of Missouri-Columbia 2001–, Chair. Art Dept 2007–09; Weiner Distinguished Prof., Missouri Univ. of Science and Tech. 2012; Guest Speaker Asian Art Museum of San Francisco 1985, 1990, 1992, 1994, 1996–2001, Univ. of California, Berkeley, Dept of Art History 1997, 1998, 2001, 2006, Stanford Univ. Inst. for Int. Studies 1999, 2000, Univ. of Minnesota 2005, 2006, Univ. of California, Davis 2010, Luxun Acad. of Fine Arts, People's Repub. of China 2010, Guangzhou Acad. of Fine Arts 2008, 2009, 2011, 2012, Harbin Inst. of Tech. 2012, Guangxi Acad. of Arts 2012; works in 15 museums and more than 70 public collections world-wide, including Japan, China, Hong Kong, Macao, Taiwan, Indonesia, Canada, France, Germany; Hon. Visiting Prof., Guangzhou Acad. of Fine Arts 2009–, South China Normal Univ. 2011–, Huazhong Normal Univ., Wuhan 2012–; numerous awards, including Gold Medal Award, XV Exposição Colectiva dos Artistas de Macau 1998, Mayoral Proclamation: Lampo Leong Day (Nov. 19th), City of San Francisco 1999, Best of Show, 42nd Annual Int. Exhbn, Sumi-e Soc. of America 2005, Diploma of Excellence, Medial 1.Art Biennial, Medial Museum, London 2005, Top Ten Award, Exposição Annual de Artes Visuais, Instituto Cultural do Governo da Macao 2007, 2009, 2011, 2012, Faculty-Alumni Awards, Univ. of Missouri-Columbia 2007, Cover Award, New Art International, New York 2009, Gold Medal Award, Creative Quarterly (No. 18), New York 2010, Best of Show, 48th Annual Int. Exhbn, Sumi-e Soc. of America 2011. *Publications:* contrib. to numerous art books and journals, including 50 essays and more than 900 reviews and publs internationally. *Leisure interests:* photography, film, travel, ballroom dancing. *Address:* Department of Art, A129 Fine Arts, University of Missouri-Columbia, Columbia, MO 65211, USA (office). *Telephone:* (573) 882-9446 (office). *Fax:* (573) 884-6807 (office). *E-mail:* leongl@missouri.edu (office). *Website:* web.missouri.edu/ ~leongl (office).

LEONI, Téa; American actress; b. 25 Feb. 1966; m. 1st Neil Tardio; m. 2nd David Duchovny (q.v.) 1997; two c. *Films include:* Switch 1991, A League of Their Own 1992, Wyatt Earp 1994, Bad Boys 1995, Flirting with Disaster 1996, Deep Impact 1998, There's No Fish Food in Heaven 1999, Life in the Fast Lane 1999, The Family Man 2000, Jurassic Park III 2001, Hollywood Ending 2002, People I Know 2003, House of D 2004, Spanglish 2004, Fun with Dick and Jane 2005, You Kill Me 2007, Ghost Town 2008, The Smell of Success 2009, Tower Heist 2011. *Television:* (sitcoms) Naked Truth, Flying Blind 1995. *Address:* ICM, 8942 Wilshire Boulevard, Beverly Hills, CA 90211, USA (office).

LEONI-SCETI, Elio; Italian business executive; *CEO, Iglo Foods Group Ltd;* b. Rome; m.; four c.; began career in brand man., Proctor and Gamble 1988–92; Marketing Man., Reckitt Benckiser 1992–93, Marketing Dir, Benckiser USA 1993–95, Gen. Man., Benckiser Germany 1995–97, Gen. Man., Benckiser Italy 1997–99, Sr Vice-Pres. and Regional Dir, North America 1999–2001, Exec. Vice-Pres., Category Devt 2001–06, Exec. Vice-Pres., Europe 2001–08; CEO, EMI Music 2008–10, also Pres., New Music Div.; CEO Iglo Foods Group Ltd 2013–; Co-Founder and Chair. LSG Holdings. *Address:* Iglo Foods Group Ltd, 5 New Square, Feltham, Middlesex, TW14 8HA, England (office). *Telephone:* (20) 8918-3200. *E-mail:* igloenquiry@iglo.com. *Website:* www.iglo.com.

LEONOV, Maj.-Gen. Aleksey Arkhipovich; Russian fmr cosmonaut and banking executive; *Advisor to the First Deputy Chairman, Alfa Bank;* b. 30 May 1934, Listvianka, Kamerovo Region; s. of Arkhip Leonov and Yevdokia Leonova; m. Svetlana Leonova; two d.; ed Kremenchug Air Force School for Pilots, Chuguev Air Force School for Pilots and Zhukovsky Air Force Eng Acad.; pilot 1956–59; mem. CPSU 1957–91; cosmonaut training 1960; first man to walk in space 18 March 1965: took part in flight of space-ship Voskhod 2 and spent 12 minutes and 9 seconds outside the spaceship, connected by a 5.35-m tether; Deputy Commdr Gagarin Cosmonauts Training Centre 1971; took part in joint flight Soyuz 19–Apollo 1975; rank of Maj.-Gen. 1975; Chair. Council of Founders of Novosti Press Agency 1969–90; Deputy Head, Centre of Cosmonaut Training 1975–92, Commdr of Cosmonauts 1976–92; Dir Checteck-Cosmos Co. 1981–92, Pres. Investment Fund Alfa-Capital 1993–; Vice-Pres. Alfa Bank from 1998, currently Advisor to the First Deputy Chair.; Co-Chair. Int. Asscn of Cosmonauts; mem. Int. Acad. of Astronautics, Soviet Artists Union; Acting mem. and Academician, Russian Acad. of Arts; Acting mem. New York Acad. of Arts; Hon. Citizen of Belgorod, Vologda, Kaliningrad, Kaluga, Kemerovo, Nalchik, Perm, Arkalyk (Kazakhstan), Kremenchug (Ukraine), Veliko Tarnovo, Vidin, Svishtov (Bulgaria), Usti nad Labem (Czech Repub.), San Antonio (Chile); Hon. mem. Russian Acad. of Fine Arts; Order for Service to the Homeland in the Armed Forces of the USSR, 3rd Class, five Jubilee Medals, Order of the Red Star 1961, Hero of the Soviet Union 1965, 1975, Hero of Socialist Labour (Bulgaria) 1965, Hero of Viet Nam, Hero of Labour (Viet Nam) 1966, Order of Karl Marx (DDR) 1966, Order 'For Merit', 1st Class (Syria) 1966, Order of Georgi Dimitrov (Bulgaria), Order of the Banner of the Hungarian People's Repub., Pilot-Cosmonaut of USSR 1966, Yuri Gagarin Gold Medal 1965, Hero of Bulgaria 1965, Hero of Vietnam 1965, Master of Sports 1965, Order of Lenin 1965, 1975, USSR State Prize 1981, Order for Merit to the Fatherland, 4th Class 2000, Order the 'Pride of Russia', Foundation for the 'Pride of the Fatherland' 2007, Order 'The Glory of the Fatherland', 2nd Class 2008, Order of Friendship 2011, Order of Merit, 3rd Class (Ukraine) 2011, Commdr, Order of St Anne, II Degree, Head of the Russian Imperial House Maria Vladimirovna Romanova 2011; Hon. DrScEng 1981; Honoured Master of Sport of the USSR 1965, Lenin Komsomol State Prize 1979, USSR State Prize 1981, Ludwig Nobel Prize 2007, Nat. Award 'To the Glory of the Fatherland' in the 'Glory to Russia', Int. Acad. of Social Sciences and Int. Acad. of Patronage 2008. *Publications:* Two Sides of the Moon: Our Story of the Cold War Space Race (with David Scott) 2006, Into That Silent Sea (contrib.) 2007; numerous books, papers and articles, notably on the psychological activity of cosmonauts. *Leisure interests:* painting, shooting movies. *Address:* Alfa Bank, 27 Kalanchevskaya Street, 107078 Moscow, Russia (office). *Telephone:* (495) 620-91-91 (office). *E-mail:* mail@alfabank.ru (office). *Website:* alfabank.com (office).

LEONTYEV, Leopold Igorevich, DrTechSci; Russian metallurgist; b. 1 Dec. 1934, Sverdlovsk (now Yekaterinburg); m.; two s.; ed Urals Polytechnic Inst.; researcher, Head of Lab., then Deputy Dir Inst. of Metallurgy, Ural br. of USSR (now Russian) Acad. of Sciences 1957–93, Deputy Chair. 1993, currently mem. Presidium, also mem. Russian Acad. of Sciences 1997, mem. Presidium 2000; First Deputy Minister of Science and Tech. 1993–96, 1997–2000; First Deputy Chair. State Cttee on Science and Tech. 1996–97; mem. editorial bds of seven journals; Russian Federation Government Award, Labor Red Star Medal 1987, Medal of Honour 1999, Balkin IP Award, Russian Acad. of Sciences 2005. *Publications:* more than 400 scientific publs on the devt of physical and chemical fundamentals and processes of complex use of metallurgic raw materials; more than 80 patents. *Address:* Presidium of Ural Branch of Russian Academy of Sciences, Yekaterinburg, Pervomayskaya str. 91, 620219 Yekaterinburg, Russia Federation (office). *Telephone:* (495) 237-39-31 (Moscow) (office); (3432) 74-53-85 (Yekaterinburg) (office).

LEONTYEV, Mikhail Vladimirovich; Russian journalist; b. 12 Oct. 1958, Moscow; m.; two c.; ed Moscow Plekhanov Inst. of Nat. Econs; political reviewer Kommersant (newspaper) 1987–90; on staff newspaper Atmoda (Riga) and Experimental Creative Cen. in Moscow 1989–91; Ed. Div. of Politics Nezavisimaya Gazeta (newspaper) 1990–92; First Deputy Ed.-in-Chief Business MN (daily) 1992–93; First Deputy Ed.-in-Chief Segodnya (newspaper) 1993–97; political reviewer TV-Cen. Channel 1997–98, ORT Channel 1999–; Ed.-in-Chief journal Fas 2000–. *Address:* Obshchestvennoye Rossiyskoe Televideniye (ORT), Akademika Koroleva str. 12, 127000 Moscow, Russia (office). *Telephone:* (495) 217-94-72 (office); (495) 217-94-73 (office).

LEOPHAIRATANA, Prachai, BE, MSEE; Thai business executive; *CEO, TPI Polene Public Co. Ltd;* b. 28 Aug. 1944; s. of Phorn Leophairatana and Boonsri Leophairatana; m. Orapin Leophairatana 1974; ed Canterbury Univ., New Zealand, Univ. of California, Berkeley, USA, Directors Accreditation Program, Thai Inst. of Dirs; CEO International Plastic Trading Co. Ltd 1981–2006; CEO Thai Petrochemical Industry Public Co. Ltd (PCL) (now IRPC PCL) 1988–2006, TPI Group of Cos 1988–2006, TPI Polene PCL 2001–; Man. Dir Hong Yiah Seng Co. Ltd 1986–; mem. Senate; Chair. United Grain Industry Co. Ltd from 1986, Bangkok Union Insurance PCL from 1986, Thai Industrial Estate Corp. Ltd from 1988, Exec. Bd Thai Caprolactam PCL from 1989, Uhde (Thailand) Co. Ltd from 1990, Thai Int. Tankers Co. Ltd from 1994; Vice-Chair. Thai Alliance Textile Co. Ltd from 1986; Dir, Bangkok Union Insurance Public Co. Ltd 2012–; Dir Rice Export Asscns, Thai–Chinese Friendship Asscn, Thai–Chinese Promotion of Investment and Trade Asscn, Bd of Trade of Thailand; Sec.-Gen. Environment for Better Life Foundation; Kt Grand Cross, Most Noble Order of the Crown of Thailand, Kt Grand Cross (1st Class), Exalted Order of the White Elephant, Kt Grand Cordon (Special Class), Most Noble Order of the Crown of Thailand, Companion (4th Class), Most Admirable Order of the Direkgunabhom. *Address:* TPI Polene Public Co. Ltd, TPI Tower, 26/56 Chan Tat Mai Road, Tungmahamek, Sathorn, Bangkok 10120, Thailand (office). *Telephone:* (2) 2855090 (office). *Fax:* (2) 2131035 (office). *E-mail:* info@tpipolene.co.th (office). *Website:* www.tpipolene.co.th (office).

LÉOTARD, François Gérard Marie; French politician, diplomatist and civil servant; b. 26 March 1942, Cannes; s. of André Léotard and Antoinette Tomasi; m. 1st France Reynier 1976; m. 2nd Ysabel Duret 1992; one s. one d.; ed Lycées Charlemagne and Henri IV, Paris, Faculté de Droit and Inst. d'Etudes Politiques, Paris and Ecole Nat. d'Admin; Sec. of Chancellery, Ministry of Foreign Affairs

1968–71; Admin. Town Planning 1973–75; Sous-préfet 1974–77; Mayor of Fréjus 1977–92, 1993–97, Municipal Councillor 1992; Deputy to Nat. Ass. (UDF-PR) 1978–86, 1988–92; Conseiller-Gen., Var 1980–88; Sec.-Gen. Parti Républicain 1982–88, Pres. 1988–90, 1995–97, Hon. Pres. 1990–95; Vice-Pres. Union pour la Démocratie Française (UDF) 1983–84, Pres. 1996–98; Minister of Culture and Communications 1986–88, of Nat. Defence (oversaw peace-keeping operations in Bosnia) 1993–95; Deputy for Var 1988–92, 1995–97, 1997–2002; apptd EU Special Envoy to Macedonia 2001; Insp. Gen. des Finances pour l'extérieur 2001; convicted of money-laundering and illegal party funding, received ten month suspended sentence Feb. 2004; Chevalier, Ordre nat. du Mérite. *Publications:* A Mots Decouverts 1987, Culture: Les Chemins de Printemps 1988, La Ville aimée: mes chemins de Fréjus 1989, Pendant la Crise, le spectacle continue 1989, Adresse au Président des Républiques françaises 1991, Place de la République 1992, Ma Liberté 1995, Pour l'honneur 1997, Je vous hais tous avec douceur 2000, Paroles d'immortels 2001, La Couleur des Femmes 2002, A mon frère qui n'est pas mort 2003, Ça va mal finir 2008. *Leisure interests:* running, tennis, parachuting. *Address:* c/o Assemblée Nationale, 75355 Paris, France.

LEPAGE, Corinne Dominique Marguerite; French lawyer and politician; *Leader, CAP 21-Citoyenneté Action Participation pour le 21è siècle;* b. 11 May 1951, Boulogne-Billancourt; d. of Philippe Lepage and Jacqueline Schulmann; m. 1st Christian Jessua, one d.; m. 2nd Christian Huglo, one s.; ed Lycée Molière, Univ. of Paris II and Inst. d'Etudes Politiques, Paris; in legal partnership 1971–76; barrister, Paris 1978–; Dir of Studies, Univ. of Paris II 1974–77; Dir of Educ. Univ. of Metz 1978–80; Deputy Mayor of Cabourg 1989–2001; Lecturer, Inst. d'Etudes Politiques, Paris 1979–87, 1989–94; Course Dir Univ. of Paris II 1982–86, Univ. of Paris XII 1987–92; mem. Bar Council 1987–89; Vice-Pres. then Pres. Asscn of Admin. Law Advocates 1989–95; Minister of the Environment 1995–97; Pres. Asscn nationale des docteurs en droit 1998–2003; Vice-Pres. Environnement sans frontières 1998–, Modem; Pres. Comité de Recherche Indépendante et d'Information sur le Génie Génétique (CRII-GEN); Leader CAP 21-Citoyenneté Action Participation pour le 21è siècle; Prof., Inst. d'Etudes Politiques de Paris 1994–; Pres. Observatoire de vigilance et d'alerte écologique; Chevalier, Légion d'honneur. *Publications:* Code annoté des procédures administratives contentieuses 1990, Les audits de l'environnement 1992, On ne peut rien faire, Madame le ministre 1998, Bien gérer l'environnement, une chance pour l'entreprise 1999, La Politique de Précaution 2001, Oser l'Espérance, Robert Jauze 2002, De l'Écologie, Hors de l'Imposture et l'Opportunisme 2003, Santé et Environnement, l'Abécédaire 2005, Ecoresp I et II, Et si c'était elle? 2006; numerous articles in La Gazette du Palais. *Leisure interests:* cinema, reading, tennis, skiing, swimming. *Address:* CAP 21, 40 rue de Monceau, 75008 Paris, France (office). *Telephone:* 1-56-59-29-59 (office). *Fax:* 1-56-59-29-39 (office). *E-mail:* corinne.lepage@huglo-lepage .com (home). *Website:* www.cap21.net (office); www.huglo-lepage.com (home).

LePAGE, Paul Richard, BS, MBA; American business executive, politician and state governor; *Governor of Maine;* b. 9 Oct. 1948, Lewiston, Me; s. of Gerard A. LePage and Theresa B. LePage (née Gagnon); eldest s. of 18 c.; m. 1st Ann S. Crabbe 1971 (divorced 1980); two d.; m. 2nd Ann M. Derosby 1984; two c. one adopted s.; ed Husson Coll. (now Husson Univ.), Bangor, Me, Univ. of Maine; left home aged 11 and lived on streets of Lewiston for two years, various jobs including shining shoes, washing dishes and loading boxes aged 13, later worked at a rubber co., a meat packing plant, and was a short order cook and bartender; ed. of coll. newspaper as a student; Treas. and Gen. Man. Arthurette Lumber Co., Canada 1971–77; Task Force Leader, Town of Perth-Andover, Canada 1976–77; Vice-Pres. Mid-Maine United Way Program, Waterville 1985–86; Dir of Finance, Maine State Housing Authority, Augusta 1977–79; Controller, Scott Paper Co., Winslow 1979–83; Dir of Finance and Admin, Interstate Food Processing Corpn, Fort Fairfield 1983–84; Chief Financial Officer, Forster Manufacturing Co., Inc., Wilton 1984–85; Pres. Paul LePage Assocs., Inc., Waterville 1985–; teacher, Kennebec Vallery Vocational Inst., Waterville 1986–; Gen. Man. Marden's Surplus and Salvage 1996–; Head of LePage & Kasevich (pvt. consultancy); served two terms as City Councillor, Waterville –2003, Mayor of Waterville 2003–10; Gov. of Maine 2011–; mem. Maine Forest Products Council, American Asscn Council, Nat. Asscn of Accountants, Mid-Maine Chamber of Commerce, Maine Chamber of Commerce and Industry, Toastmasters, Rotary, Elks; Republican; Dr hc (Thomas Coll., Waterville) 2012; voted Mid-Maine Chamber of Commerce's Businessman of the Year 2006, named by Nat. Fed. of Ind. Business as Maine Business Champion 2007. *Leisure interests:* furniture making, softball, racquetball, ice hockey. *Address:* Office of the Governor, 1 State House Station, Augusta, ME 04333, USA (office). *Telephone:* (207) 287-3531 (office). *Fax:* (207) 287-1034 (office). *Website:* www.maine.gov/governor (office).

LEPAGE, Robert, CC; French-Canadian actor and theatre and opera director; *Artistic Director, Ex Machina;* b. 1957, Québec City; ed Conservatoire d'Art Dramatique Québec, Canada; Artistic Co-Dir Théatre Repère 1986–89; Founder and Pres. Robert Lepage Inc. 1988–; Artistic Dir Nat. Arts Centre Ottawa, Canada 1989–93; Artistic Dir Ex Machina 1994–; Founder, Pres. and Artistic Dir In Extremis Inc. 1995–2004; Founder La Caserne Dalhousie 1997–; Officier, Order nat. du Quebec 1999, Légion d'honneur 2002; Hon. PhD (Laval) 1994, Hon. DLitt (Toronto, McGill) 1997, Hon. LLD (Concordia) 1999; Evening Standard Award for Best Play 2001, Herbert Whittaker Drama Bench Award 2002, Denise Pelletier Prize 2003, Hans Christian Andersen Prize 2004, Samuel de Champlain Prize 2005, Stanislavski Award 2005, Europe Theatre Prize 2007, Gov.-Gen's Performing Arts Award 2009, Eugene McDermott Award, MIT 2012. *Films:* (scriptwriter, dir): The Confessional 1995, The Polygraph 1996, Nô 1998, Possible Worlds 2000, The Far Side of the Moon 2003. *Operas:* (dir): Bluebeard's Castle 1993, Erwartung 1993, The Damnation of Faust 1999, The Busker's Opera 2004, 1984 2005, The Rake's Progress 2007, The Nightingale an Other Short Fables 2008, Der Ring des Nibelungen (Das Rheingold) 2010, (Die Walküre and Siegfried) 2011, (Götterdämmerung) 2012. *Productions include:* Circulations 1984, Dragon's Trilogy (co-writer, dir and actor) 1985, Vinci (writer, dir and actor) 1986, Polygraph (writer, dir and actor) 1987, Tectonic Plates (co-writer, dir and actor) 1988, Needles and Opium (dir) 1991, A Midsummer Night's Dream (dir) 1992, Coriolanus (dir) 1992, Macbeth (dir) 1992, The Tempest (dir) 1992, The Seven Streams of the River Ota (writer and dir) 1994, Elsinore (writer and dir) 1995, The Geometry of Miracles (co-writer, dir) 1998, Zulu Time (writer and dir) 1999, The Far Side of the Moon (writer, dir and actor) 2000, La Casa Azul (writer and dir) 2001, The Andersen

Project (writer and dir) 2005, Lipsynch (writer and dir) 2007, The Blue Dragon (writer and dir) 2008, Eonnagata 2009, La Tempête 2011. *Publications:* Connecting Flights 1995; (in French): La Trilogie des Dragons 2005, Le Projet Andersen 2007, La Face cachée de la Lune 2007, Chantiers d'écriture scénique 2007, The Image Mill 2008, The Blue Dragon 2011, Le Rossignol, Renard et autres fables 2011. *Address:* 103 Dalhousie, Québec City, PQ G1K 4B9, Canada (office). *Telephone:* (418) 692-0055 (home). *Fax:* (418) 692-2390 (office). *E-mail:* rli@exmachina.qc.ca (office). *Website:* www.lacaserne.net (office).

LEPAON, Thierry; French trade union official; *Secretary-General, Confédération Générale du Travail;* b. 31 Jan. 1960, Caen (Calvados); entered work force aged 17; worked as welder at Caterpillar factory near Caen; employed in large metallurgical co. in Caen region, Spie Batignolles –1983; worked for Moulinex in Cormelles-le-Royal from 1983; joined Confédération Générale du Travail (CGT), elected to Exec. Cttee of Fed. of CGT Metalworkers 1986–90, Sec. of CGT union in Caen 1990–2001, Gen. Sec. Departmental Union of Calvados 2001–06, elected to Exec. Cttee of Cen. Trade Union Part of CGT Fed. of Metallurgy 2006–08, apptd by CGT to Conseil d'orientation pour l'emploi est. under Prime Minister 2006–11, Regional Head of CGT for Basse-Normandie 2008–12, also led del. of CGT in negotiations for the reform of vocational training 2008, Sec.-Gen. CGT 2013–. *Address:* Confédération Générale du Travail, 263 rue de Paris, 93516 Montreuil Cedex, France (office). *Telephone:* 1-55-82-80-00 (office). *Fax:* 1-49-18-18-57 (office). *E-mail:* info@cgt.fr (office). *Website:* www.cgt.fr (office).

LEPPING, Sir George, GCMG, MBE; Solomon Islands politician and government official; b. 22 Nov. 1947; s. of Chief Dionisio Tanutanu and Regina Suluki; m. Margaret Kwalea Teioli 1972; two s. five d.; ed King George VI Secondary School, Agric. Coll., Vudal, Univ. of Reading, UK; field officer, Dept of Agric. and Rural Econ. 1968, Pres. Solomon Is. Amateur Athletics Union 1970–73, 1981–82; Sr Field Officer then Under-Sec. (Agric.), Ministry of Agric. 1979–80; Perm. Sec. Ministry of Home Affairs and Nat. Devt 1981–84; Project Dir Rural Services Project 1984–87; Minister of Finance 1988; Gov.-Gen. 1988–94; Leader, then Pres. People's Alliance Party 1996–; Perm. Sec., Policy Evaluation Unit 2002; Chair. 2012 Festival Pacific Arts Organising Cttee 2010–. *Leisure interests:* reading, swimming, lawn tennis, snooker, snorkelling, high-speed boat driving, fishing; first Solomon Islands athlete to win int. sports medals; KStJ 1991. *Address:* PO Box 1431, Honiara; People's Alliance Party, PO Box 722, Honiara, Solomon Islands.

LERCHE, Peter Fritz Franz, DJur; German legal scholar and academic; *Professor of Public Law, University of Munich;* b. 12 Jan. 1928, Leitmeritz; s. of Dr Fritz Lerche and Karoline Lerche (née Artmann); m. Dr Ilse Lerche (née Peschek) 1955; two s.; ed Univ. of Munich; Prof. Freie Universität Berlin 1960; Prof. of Public Law, Univ. of Munich 1965–; mem. Bavarian Acad. of Sciences; fmr mem. Council of Science; First Pres. Union of German Lecturers in Public Law 1982; fmr mem. numerous govt comms and attorney in governmental lawsuits, etc.; Bavarian Order of Merit, Maximiliansorden, Bavarian Constitution Gold Medal; Hon. DJur; numerous other awards. *Publications:* Ordentlicher Rechtsweg und Verwaltungsrechtsweg 1953, Übermass und Verfassungsrecht 1961, 1999, Werbung und Verfassung 1967, Rundfunkmonopol 1970, Verfassungsrechtliche Fragen zur Pressekonzentration 1971, Verfassungsrechtliche Aspekte der 'inneren Pressefreiheit' 1974, Kernkraft und rechtlicher Wandel 1981, Städte und Kabelkommunikation 1982, Mitarbeit an Maunz/Dürig, Kommentar zum Grundgesetz, Verfassungsgerichtsbarkeit in besonderen Situationen 2001. *Leisure interest:* study of the hippopotamus. *Address:* Junkersstrasse 13, 82131 Gauting, Germany (home). *Telephone:* (89) 8502088 (home).

LERNER, Randolph Dale, LLB; American lawyer and business executive; *Chairman, Aston Villa Football Club;* b. 21 Feb. 1962, Brooklyn, NY; s. of Alfred Lerner and Nancy Wolkoff; ed Columbia Coll., Clare Coll., Cambridge, UK, Columbia Univ. Law School; mem. NY and DC Bar Asscns; began career as Investment Analyst, Progressive Corpn; Founder and Man.-Dir Securities Advisors Inc. 1991–2001; apptd Dir MBNA Corpn 1993, Chair. 2002–06, involved in its sale to Bank of America 2006, also Dir MBNA America Bank 1993–2006; Chair. New York Acad. of Arts 1998–2003; Owner Cleveland Browns Football Club, Nat. Football League (NFL) 2002–12, mem. NFL Business Ventures Cttee; Owner/Chair. Aston Villa Football Club, Premier League, UK 2006–; Trustee, Hosp. for Special Surgery, New York City 1996–; fmr Trustee, Corcoran Museum, Washington DC. *Address:* Aston Villa Football Club, Villa Park, Birmingham, B6 6HE, England (office). *Telephone:* (121) 327-2299 (office). *Fax:* (121) 322-2107 (office). *E-mail:* info@avfc.co.uk (office). *Website:* www.avfc.co.uk (office).

LERNER, Richard A., BS, MD, PhD; American chemist and academic; *Lita Annenberg Hazen Professor of Immunochemistry, Institute Professor and Professor, Department of Cell and Molecular Biology, Scripps Research Institute;* b. 28 Aug. 1938, Chicago, Ill.; m. 1st Diana Pickett; two s. one d.; m. 2nd Nicola Greed 1981; ed Northwestern Univ., Stanford Medical School; fmr intern, Palo Alto Stanford Hosp.; Postdoctoral Research Fellow, Scripps Clinic and Research Foundation, later Chair., Dept of Molecular Biology, Scripps Research Inst. 1982–86, Pres. Scripps Research Inst. 1986–2012, also Lita Annenberg Hazen Prof. of Immunochemistry, Inst. Prof. and fmr Cecil H. and Ida M. Green Chair. in Chem., mem. Skaggs Inst. for Chemical Biology 1996–; Staff mem., Wistar Inst., Phila 1970–; mem. Scientific Advisory Bd, Dyadic Group 2004–, Senomyx; mem. Scientific Policy Advisory Cttee, Uppsala Univ., Sweden 1991; mem. Scientific Advisory Bd, Econ. Devt Bd, Singapore 1991; mem. ETH Inst. of Biotechnology Advisory Bd, Zurich, Switzerland 1994; mem. Stanford Linear Accelerator Center Scientific Policy Cttee, Stanford, Calif. 1995–98; mem. Center for Nanoscale Science and Tech. Scientific Advisory Bd 1996; mem. Bd of Dirs, Calif. Council on Science and Tech. 1996–97; mem. Advisory Steering Group for Chem., Calif. State Univ. 1996; mem. Academic Cttee, Bd of Govs, Technion Israel Inst. of Tech., Haifa, Israel 1998; Sr Contributing Ed. PNAS, Chem. and Biology, Bioorganic and Medicinal Chem., Molecular Medicine, Catalysis Technology, Angewandte Chemie; mem. Editorial Bd Journal of Virology, Molecular Biology and Medicine, Vaccine, Bioorganic and Medicinal Chemistry Letters, Drug Targeting and Delivery, Bioorganic and Medicinal Chemistry, Molecular Medicine, Catalysis Technology, Angewandte Chemie; mem. Advisory Bd Chemical and Engineering News 1994–96; mem. NAS 1991, American Acad. of Arts and Sciences 2000, American Soc. for Experimental Pathology, American Soc. of Microbiology, New York Acad. of Sciences, Biophysical Soc., Pluto Soc.; Foreign mem. Royal Swedish

Acad. of Sciences 1985; AAAS Fellow 2005; Trustee, Neurosciences Research Foundation, Inc. 1992–; Distinguished Visiting Scientist, IBM T.J. Watson Research Center, NY 2006; Hon. DSc (Technion Israel Inst. of Tech.) 2001, (Northwestern Univ.) 2002, (Oxford) 2006; Hon. DHumLitt (Florida Atlantic Univ.) 2004; Dr hc (Ben-Gurion Univ. of the Negev, Israel) 2004; Parke Davis Award 1978, John A. Muntz Memorial Prize 1990, San Marino Prize 1990, Arthur C. Cope Scholar Award 1991, Jeanette Piperno Memorial Award 1991, CIBA-GEIGY Drew Award in Biomedical Research 1992, Humboldt Research Award 1994, Wolf Prize in Chem. 1994, Calif. Scientist of the Year Award 1996, Coley Award for Distinguished Research in Basic and Tumor Immunology 1999, Univ. of Calif. Presidential Medal 2002, Scientist of the Year Award, ARCS Foundation, Inc. 2002, Paul Ehrlich and Ludwig Darmstaedter Prize, Frankfurt, Germany 2003, Pres.'s Medal, Univ. of California 2003, DART/NYU Biotechnology Achievement Award in Basic Biotechnology, New York 2005. *Address:* Scripps Research Institute, 10550 North Torrey Pines Road, La Jolla CA 92037, USA (office). *Telephone:* (858) 784-8265 (office). *Fax:* (858) 784-9899 (office). *E-mail:* rlerner@scripps.edu (office). *Website:* www.scripps.edu/research/faculty/lerner (office); www.scripps.edu/lerner (office).

LERNMARK, Åke, PhD; Swedish/American medical scientist, biologist and academic; *Professor of Experimental Diabetes, Lund University;* b. 11 Aug. 1945, Stockholm; ed Univ. of Umeå; Instructor, Dept of Histology, Univ. of Umeå 1968–70, Research Assoc. 1970–73, Asst Prof. (Docent) of Histology 1973–79; Visiting Scientist, Dept of Biochemistry, Univ. of Chicago 1974–75, Visiting Asst Prof., Dept of Biochemistry and Univ. of Chicago Diabetes Research and Training Center 1977–78; Dir of Research, Hagedorn Research Lab., Gentofte, Denmark 1979–87; Robert H. Williams Prof. in Medicine, Dept of Medicine, Univ. of Washington, Seattle, Wash. 1988–92, 1995–2008, Adjunct Prof., Dept of Pathology 1991–93, Affiliate Prof., Dept of Medicine 1993–94, Adjunct Prof., Dept of Immunology 1995–2007, mem. Grad. Faculty 1997–; Prof. of Experimental Endocrinology, Dept of Molecular Medicine (Chair.), Karolinska Inst., Stockholm 1993–94, Adjunct Prof., Experimental Endocrinology, Dept of Molecular Medicine 1995–2001; Adjunct Prof. of Medical Cell Biology, Lund Univ., Malmö, Sweden 1984–89, Prof. in Diabetes Research, Malmö Gen. Hosp. (leave of absence) 1989–91, Adjunct Prof., Dept of Endocrinology 1998–2005, Adjunct Prof., Dept of Clinical Sciences 2006–08, Prof. of Experimental Diabetes, Dept of Clinical Sciences 2009–; C.C. Sturgis Visiting Prof., Univ. of Michigan Medical School 1985; Visiting Prof., Vrije Universiteit Brussel, Belgium 1990–2000; David Pyke Prof., King's Coll., London, UK 1994; Hillblom Visiting Prof., UCLA 2007; Enz Visiting Prof., Univ. of Kansas, Lawrence 2007; Assoc. Ed. Diabetologia 1989–94; Co-Ed.-in-Chief Hormone and Metabolic Research 1996–2003; mem. Editorial Bd Diabetes 1982–89, Diabetes Research 1984–89, Regional Immunology 1990–99, Diabetes Research and Clinical Practice 1989–2006, Diabetes Technology & Therapeutics 2000–06, Endocrine Reviews 2006–; mem. Editorial Advisory Bd Journal of Clinical Investigation 1998–2002; mem. Advisory Bd Autoimmunity 2002–; mem. Scandinavian Soc. for the Study of Diabetes 1969, European Asscn for the Study of Diabetes 1970 (Hon. Sec. 1986–88), American Diabetes Asscn 1979, AAAS 1980, Danish Acad. of Natural Sciences 1981, Bd Swedish Endocrine Soc. 1986–89, Immunology and Diabetes Workshops 1988–91 (Chair. 1989–91), Juvenile Diabetes Foundation International 1992, Immunology of Diabetes Soc. 1996 (Pres. 1996–98), Asscn of American Immunologists 2001, Royal Physiographic Soc. in Lund 2002; Fellow, American Coll. of Physicians 2008; CIBA Fellow, Swedish Soc. of Endocrinology 1974, C.G. Bergstrand Lecturer, Swedish Pediatric Soc. 1982, Minkowski Award, European Asscn for the Study of Diabetes 1984, David Rumbough Award, Juvenile Diabetes Foundation International 1985, Kellion Medal, Australian Diabetes Foundation 1985, Paul E. Lacy Award, Nat. Diabetes Research Interchange 1985, E.F.F. Copp Lecturer, California Metabolic Research Foundation and Los Angeles Co. Medical Asscn 1986, Nordisk Lecturer, McGill Univ. 1986, Pehr Dubb Lecturer, Göteborgs Läkaresällskap 1986, Jacob E. Poulsen Grant, Scandinavian Soc. for the Study of Diabetes 1991, Arnold Lazarow Memorial Lecturer, Univ. of Minnesota 1993, API-Novo Nordisk Lecturer, Madras, India 1995, Kroc Lecturer, Baylor Coll., Houston, Tex. 1996, Dorothy Hodgkin Lecturer, British Diabetes Asscn 1998, John K. Davidson Diabetes Lectureship, Emory Univ., Atlanta, Ga 1999, Hamdan Award for Medical Science Excellence, Dubai, UAE 2002, J. Allyn Taylor Int. Prize in Medicine 2002, Langerhans-Virchow Lecturer, Pacific Northwest Research Inst., Seattle, Wash. 2006. *Publications:* 50 book chapters and more than 400 articles in peer-reviewed journals on genetic causes of diabetes. *Address:* Department of Clinical Sciences, Lund University, CRC, Entrance 72, 20502 Malmö, Sweden (office). *Telephone:* (40) 391901 (office); 70-6164779 (mobile). *Fax:* (40) 337042 (office). *E-mail:* ake.lernmark@med.lu.se (office). *Website:* www.lu.se/lucat/user/endo-ale (office).

LEROI, Armand Marie, BSc, PhD; Dutch evolutionary biologist; *Professor of Evolutionary Developmental Biology, Division of Ecology and Evolution, Imperial College London;* b. 16 July 1964, Wellington, New Zealand; ed Dalhousie Univ., Canada, Univ. of California at Irvine, USA; postdoctoral work at Albert Einstein Coll. of Medicine, New York; Lecturer, Imperial Coll. London 1996–2001, apptd Reader in Evolutionary Developmental Biology 2001, currently Prof. of Evolutionary Developmental Biology. *Television:* Mutants (three-part series, Channel 4) 2004, Alien Worlds (Channel 4) 2005, What Makes Us Human (Channel 4) 2006, What Darwin Didn't Know (documentary) (BBC 4) 2009, Aristotle's Lagoon (documentary) (BBC 4) 2010. *Publication:* Mutants: On the Form, Varieties and Errors of the Human Body (Guardian First Book Award 2004) 2003; contrib. to London Review of Books; numerous research papers. *Address:* Division of Ecology and Evolution, Imperial College London, Silwood Park Campus, Buckhurst Road, Ascot, SL5 7PY, England (office). *Telephone:* (20) 7594-2396 (office). *E-mail:* a.leroi@imperial.ac.uk (office). *Website:* www3.imperial.ac.uk/people/a.leroi (office).

LEROY, Maurice; French economist and politician; *President, General Council of Loir-et-Cher;* b. 2 Feb. 1959, Paris; m.; three c.; Head of Cabinet for Mayor of Orly 1982–84; Sec. Gen., Communist Group in Senate 1984–90; Mayor of Poislay 1989–2001; Head of Cabinet of Pres., Val-de-Marne Gen. Council 1990–91; Head of Cabinet of Mayor of Nanterre, then of Mayor of Colombes 1991–93; Chargé de Mission for Charles Pasqua (Minister of State) 1993–97; Gen. Councillor, canton of Droué 1994–; Chargé de Mission of Éric Raoult, responsible for Urban Affairs 1995–97; mem. Assemblée nationale (Parl.) for Vendôme 1997–2010, Vice Pres.

Assemblée nationale 2009–10; Pres. Loir-et-Cher Gen. Council 2004–; Vice-Pres. Union des conseillers généraux de France 1998–2001, Pres. 2001–08; mem. Nouveau Centre (Nouveau Centre), also Spokesman; Minister of Urban Affairs 2010–12. *Address:* Conseil général de Loir-et-Cher, Place de la République, 41020 Blois Cedex, France (office). *Telephone:* (2) 54-58-41-41 (office). *Fax:* (2) 54-58-42-13 (office). *E-mail:* info@le-loir-et-cher.fr (office); mleroy.depute@wanadoo.fr (office). *Website:* www.le-loir-et-cher.fr (office).

LESAR, David J., BS, MBA; American business executive; *Chairman, President and CEO, Halliburton Company;* b. 1954, Madison, Wis.; ed Univ. of Wisconsin-Madison; Partner and Commercial Group Dir, Arthur Anderson Co., Dallas, Tex. –1993; Exec. Vice-Pres. Finance and Admin, Halliburton Energy Services 1993–95, Exec. Vice-Pres. and Chief Financial Officer Halliburton 1995–96, Pres. and CEO 1997–2000, Chair., Pres. and CEO 2000–; Pres. and CEO Brown & Root Inc. 1996–97; mem. Bd of Dirs Lyondell Chemical Co., Mirant Corpn; mem. Upstream Cttee, American Petroleum Inst., Bd of Dirs American Iranian Council. *Address:* Halliburton Company, 3000 North Sam Houston Parkway East, Houston, TX 77032, USA (office). *Telephone:* (281) 871-4000 (office). *E-mail:* info@halliburton.com (office). *Website:* www.halliburton.com (office).

LESCHLY, Jan, BSc, MSc; Danish business executive and fmr professional tennis player; *Partner and Chairman, Care Capital, LLC;* b. 11 Sept. 1940; m. Lotte Enngelbred 1963; four s.; ed Copenhagen Coll. of Pharmacy, Copenhagen School of Econ. and Business Admin, Princeton Univ., USA; tour tennis professional 1960s and early 1970s, participated in nine Wimbledon Championships 1959–71, best result reaching fourth round of singles event and quarterfinals of doubles with Jorgen Ulrich 1966, reached semifinals of US Open 1967; ranked World No. 10 for 1967 by Lance Tingay of The Daily Telegraph; Novo Industries A/S 1972–1979; Vice-Pres. Commercial Devt, Squibb Corpn 1979, US Pres. 1981, Group Vice-Pres. and Dir 1984, Exec. Vice-Pres. 1986, Pres. and COO 1988–90; Chair. SmithKline Beecham Pharmaceuticals 1990, CEO 1994–2000; Founding Partner and Chair. Care Capital LLC 2000–; Chair. Epigenesis Pharmaceuticals, LLC; Dir, Dampskibsselskabet AF 1912 AS, Inotek Pharmaceuticals Corpn, LifeTecNet, Vaxart, Squibb Corpn 1984–90, SmithKline Beecham Ltd 1990, Inc., American Express Co. 1997–2013, CBS Corpn 1998, A.P. Møller – Mærsk A/S (fmrly Dampskibsselskabet Svendborg A/S) 2000–, APM-Maersk Group, Viacom 2000–, D-pharm Ltd 2001–, Dynavax Technologies Corpn 2004–06; mem. Int. Advisory Bd DaimlerChrysler AG, Emory Univ. Goizueta Business School Dean's Advisory Council; mem. pharmaceutical asscns and educational bodies; Chair. Int. Tennis Hall of Fame. *Address:* Care Capital LLC, 47 Hulfish Street, Suite 310, Princeton, NJ 08542, USA. *Telephone:* (609) 683-8300. *Fax:* (609) 683-5787. *E-mail:* info@carecapital.com. *Website:* www.carecapital.com.

LESCURE, Pierre François Amar; French business executive and actor; *President, Cannes Film Festival;* b. 2 July 1945, Paris; s. of François Lescure and Paulette Baudoin; m. Frédérique Fayles-Bernstein 1996; ed Lycée Turgot, Paris, Centre de formation des journalistes; reporter and newsreader, Radio Télé Luxembourg 1965–68; with Radio Caroline and Radio Monte Carlo 1968–72; newsreader and presenter, Office de radiodiffusion télévision française (ORTF) 1973–77, Deputy Ed., weekend programmes 1977–80, Dir Programmes Europe 1 1980–81; Ed.-in-Chief Antenne 2 1982–84, Head of Programmes 1984–86; Dir-Gen. Canal+ 1986–94, Chair. and Man. Dir 1994–2000, Chair. 2000–02; Chair. Canal Jimmy 1991–2002; Chair. and Man. Dir Paris Saint-Germain Football SA 1994–, Le Studio Canal+ 1991–2002, Le Monde Presse 1994–; Chair. UGCDA (audiovisual rights co.) 1997–, CanalPro 1997–2002, Multithématiques 2001–; Deputy Chair. Exec. Cttee Havas 1997–; Co-CEO Vivendi Universal 2000–02; Dir and mem. Strategic Cttee, Havas Group 1993–; mem. Advisory Bd, Lagardère Group 2000–; mem. Bd Dirs, Kudelski Group 2004–; Pres. of the Jury, American Film Festival, Deauville 2002, mem. Bd 2013–; Producer and Dir of Operations, Marigny Theatre 2008–; Perm. mem. of the jury, Prix des prix littéraires 2011–; Pres. Cannes Film Festival 2014–; Chevalier, Ordre nat. du Mérite, Officier des Arts et Lettres; Homme de la décennie de la télévision, CB News 1996, Manager of the Year, le Nouvel économiste 1996, Le Laurier d'Or d'honneur de la télévision 2014 and other awards. *Films include:* 5% de risques (voice) 1980, Le quart d'heure américain 1982, La Cité de la peur 1994, Mon petit doigt m'a dit... 2005, Le Grand appartement 2006, Musée haut, musée bas 2008. *Television includes:* 24½ (presenter) 2003, Graffiti 60 (mini-series) (presenter and screenplay) 2004, Graffiti 70 2005, Ça balance in Paris (Paris Première) 2006–10, Master classe (France 4) 2012. *Publications:* A nous la radio, In the baba (memoir) 2012. *Address:* Association française du festival international du film, 3 rue Amélie, 75007 Paris, France (office). *Telephone:* 1-53-59-61-00 (office). *Fax:* 1-53-59-61-10 (office). *E-mail:* info@festival-cannes.fr (office). *Website:* www.festival-cannes.fr (office). www.festival-cannes.org (office).

LESIN, Mikhail Yuryevich; Russian politician and journalist; b. 11 July 1958; m.; one s.; ed Moscow Inst. of Eng and Construction; fmr eng constructor; f. Igrotechnika (later Intelleks) Co-operative 1989–91; Founder and Chair. Bd of Dirs Videoint. (advertising co.) 1991–94; mem. of staff RIA Novosti, Dir-Gen. Novosti-TV Co. 1993–96; Head of Dept of Public Relations, Russian Presidency 1996–97 (resgnd); First Deputy Chair. All-Russian State TV Co. 1997–99; Minister of Press, TV, Broadcasting and Telecommunications (subsequently the Press, Broadcasting and Mass Media) 1999–2004; Adviser to the Pres. 2004–08; mem. Bd of Dirs Pervyi Kanal 2004–. *Address:* c/o Office of the President, Kremlin, 103073 Moscow, Russia (office).

LESJAK, Catherine A. (Cathie), BS, MBA; American business executive; *Executive Vice-President and Chief Financial Officer, Hewlett Packard Company;* b. 1959; m.; ed Stanford Univ., Univ. of California, Berkeley; joined Hewlett Packard Co. 1986, Controller and Credit Man., Commercial Customer Org. 2000–02, Vice-Pres. of Finance for Enterprise Marketing and Solutions and Vice-Pres. of Finance for Software Global Business Unit 2002–03, Group Controller, Software Solutions Org. and Sr Vice-Pres. 2003–06, Treas. 2003–07, Exec. Vice-Pres. and Chief Financial Officer (CFO) 2007–Aug. 2010, Oct. 2010–, Interim CEO and CFO Aug.–Oct. 2010; ranked by Forbes magazine amongst The World's 100 Most Powerful Women (50th) 2007, (32nd) 2009, ranked by Fortune magazine amongst the 50 Most Powerful Women in Business in the US (42nd) 2009, (28th) 2010. *Address:* Hewlett Packard Company, 3000 Hanover Street, Palo Alto, CA

94304-1185, USA (office). *Telephone:* (650) 857-1501 (office). *Fax:* (650) 857-5518 (office). *Website:* www.hp.com (office).

LESOURNE, Jacques François; French newspaper editor, economist and academic; *President, Futuribles International;* b. 26 Dec. 1928, La Rochelle; s. of André Lesourne and Simonne Lesourne (née Guille); m. Odile Melin, 1961; one s. two d.; ed Lycée Montaigne, Bordeaux, École Polytechnique, École Nationale Supérieure des Mines de Paris; Head Econ. Service of French Collieries 1954–57; Dir Gen., later Pres. METRA Int. and SEMA 1958–75; Prof. of Econs École des Mines de Saint-Étienne 1958–61; Prof. of Industrial Econs École Nationale Supérieure de la Statistique 1960–63; Pres. Asscn Française d'Informatique et de Recherche Operationnelle 1966–67; mem. Council Int. Inst. of Applied Systems Analysis, Vienna 1973–79, Inst. of Man. Science 1976–79; Prof. Conservatoire Nat. des Arts et Métiers 1974–; Dir Projet Interfuturs OECD 1976–79; Dir of Studies, Inst. Auguste Comte 1979–81; Pres. Comm. on Employment and Social Relations of 8th Plan 1979–81; mem. Comm. du Bilan 1981, Council European Econ. Asscn 1984–89; Pres. Asscn Française de Science Économique 1981–83, Int. Federation of Operational Research Socs 1986–89; Dir and Man. Ed. Le Monde 1991–94; Pres. Futuribles Int. 1993–, Centre for Study and Research on Qualifications 1996–; Bd mem. Acad. des Technologies; Officier, Légion d'honneur 1993, Commdr 2009, Commdr, Ordre nat. du Mérite, Officier des Palmes académiques. *Publications:* Economic Technique and Industrial Management 1958, Du bon usage de l'étude économique dans l'entreprise 1966, Les systèmes du destin 1976, L'entreprise et ses futurs 1985, Éducation et société, L'après-Communisme, de l'Atlantique à l'Oural 1990, The Economics of Order and Disorder 1991, Vérités et mensonges sur le chômage 1995, Le Modèle français: Grandeur et Décadence 1998, Un Homme de notre Siècle 2000, Ces Avenirs qui n'ont pas eu lieu 2001, Leçons de Microéconomie évolutionniste (with André Orléan and Bernard Walliser) 2002, Democratie: Marché et Gouvernance, Quels Avenirs? 2004, Evolutionary Microeconomics (with André Orléan and Bernard Walliser) 2006, La recherche et l'innovation en France (with Denis Radet) 2007, 2008, 2009, Les crises et le XXIème siècle 2009, L'humanité face au changement climatique (with R. Dautray) 2009. *Leisure interest:* piano. *Address:* 52 rue de Vaugirard, 75006 Paris, France. *Telephone:* 1-43-25-66-05. *Fax:* 1-56-24-47-98. *E-mail:* jolesourne@wanadoo.fr. *Website:* www.futuribles.com.

LESSARD, Claude; Canadian business executive; *Chairman and CEO, Vision7 International;* b. 29 July 1949, Notre Dame du Portage; s. of Jean-Luc Lessard and Carmen Cerat; m. Marie Lortie 1971; three s.; ed Univ. Laval, Québec; joined Groupe Cossette Communication 1972, Chair. and CEO 1980– and of Vision7 International (holding co.) 2010–; Dir Canam-Manac, Inst. de cardiologie de Québec, Opéra de Québec, Faculté des Sciences de l'Admin, Univ. Laval, Fondation Communautaire du Grand Québec, DiagnoCure Inc., Ronald McDonald Children's Charities of Canada, Faculté des sciences de l'admin at l'Université Laval; Co.-Chair. Canadian Congress of Advertising 1995; Hermes Prize (Univ. of Laval) 1984, Dimensions Prize 1987, 'Spiess' Bessies Award 1993, ACA Gold Medal 1994. *Leisure interests:* golf, skiing, riding. *Address:* Vision7 International, 300 St Paul Street, Suite 300, Québec, PQ, G1K 7R1, Canada (office). *Telephone:* (418) 647-2727 (office). *Fax:* (418) 647-2564 (office). *E-mail:* information@v7international.com (office). *Website:* vision7international.com (office).

LESSELS, Norman, CBE, CA; British chartered accountant; b. 2 Sept. 1938, Edinburgh, Scotland; s. of John Clark Lessels and Gertrude Margaret Ellen Lessels (née Jack); m. 1st Gillian Durward Clark 1960 (died 1979); one s. (and one s. one d. deceased); m. 2nd Christine Stevenson Hitchman 1981; ed Melville Coll., Edin., Edin. Acad.; apprentice with Graham Smart & Annan, Edin. 1955–60, with Thomson McLintock & Co., London 1960–61; Pnr, Wallace & Somerville, Edin., subsequently merged with Whinney Murray & Co., latterly Ernst & Whinney 1962–80; Pnr, Chiene & Tait, CA 1980–93, Sr Pnr 1993–98; Dir (non-exec.) The Standard Life Assurance Co. 1978–2002 (Chair. 1988–98), Cairn Energy PLC 1988–2002 (Chair. 1995–2002), Bank of Scotland 1988–97, General Surety & Guarantee Co. Ltd 1988–97, Havelock Europa PLC –1998 (Chair. 1993–98), NWS Bank PLC 1989–97, Robert Wiseman Dairies PLC 1994–2003, Martin Currie Portfolio Investment Trust PLC 1999–2001; Pres. Inst. of Chartered Accountants of Scotland 1987–88; Chair. Tilney & Co. 1993–98. *Leisure interests:* golf, bridge, music. *Address:* 17 India Street, Edinburgh, EH3 6HE, Scotland (home).

LESSIG, Lawrence (Larry), BA, BS, MA, JD; American professor of law and institute director; *Professor of Law, Harvard Law School and Director, Edmond J. Safra Foundation Center for Ethics, Harvard University;* b. 3 June 1961, Rapid City, SDak; m. Bettina Neuefeind; two s. one d.; ed Univ. of Pennsylvania, Trinity Coll., Cambridge, UK, Yale Univ. Law School; grew up in Williamsport, Pa; active Teenage Republican, serving as Youth Gov. for Pennsylvania through YMCA Youth & Govt Program 1978; law clerk for Judge Richard Posner, 7th Circuit Court of Appeals, Chicago, Ill. 1989–90, for Justice Antonin Scalia, US Supreme Court, Washington, DC 1990–91; Asst Prof. of Law, Univ. of Chicago Law School 1991–95, Prof. of Law 1995–97; Visiting Prof. of Law, Yale Law School 1995; Fellow, Program on Ethics and the Professions, Harvard Univ. 1996–97, Visiting Prof. of Law, Harvard Law School 1997, Prof. of Law 1997–2000, Jack N. and Lillian R. Berkman Prof. for Entrepreneurial Legal Studies 1998, Prof. of Law and Dir Edmond J. Safra Foundation Center for Ethics, Harvard Univ. 2009–; joined Stanford Law School 2000, Co-Dir Center for Internet and Society 2000–, Wilson Faculty Scholar 2002, Prof. of Law 2000–02, John A. Wilson Distinguished Faculty Scholar 2003–05, C. Wendell and Edith M. Carlsmith Prof. of Law 2005–09; Lecturer in LLM programme for Eastern and Cen. European lawyers, Legal Studies Programme, CEU Budapest Coll., Budapest, Hungary 1992, 1993, 1995, Moscow 1994; Moderator, Constitutional Law Discussion Group, Lexis Counsel Connect, Miamisburg, Ohio 1994–95; Chair. Creative Commons, San Francisco 2001–07, mem. Bd 2007–; mem. Bd of Dirs Public Library of Science, San Francisco 2003–07; mem. Bd Red Hat Center for the Public Domain, Durham, NC 2000–01, Electronic Frontier Foundation, San Francisco 2002–07, Public Knowledge, Washington, DC 2002–07, Free Software Foundation, Cambridge, Mass 2004–07, Software Freedom Law Center, New York 2005–08, iCommons, London, UK 2005–, Brave New Films Foundation, Los Angeles 2007–08 (Chair. 2008–), Free Press, Washington, DC 2007–09, Change Congress, San Francisco 2008–, American Acad. in Berlin, Germany 2008–, MAPLight.org, Berkeley, Calif. 2008–, Freedom House, Washington, DC 2008–; mem. Editorial Advisory Bd Lexis-Nexis

Electronic Authors Press 1995–97; mem. Advisory Bd LifeJournal, San Francisco 2008–09, Sunlight Foundation, Washington, DC 2008–, Journal of Academic Legal Studies 2008–; Comm. mem. Pennsylvania Nat. Comm. on Soc., Culture and Community, Philadelphia 1997–98; columnist, The Industry Standard, San Francisco 1998–2001, Red Herring 2002–03, CIO Insight, New York 2002–03, Wired Magazine 2003–07; Fellow, Wissenschaftskolleg zu Berlin 1999–2000, Business Law Center, Tokyo Univ., Japan 2002, American Acad. in Berlin 2007–08, American Acad. of Arts and Sciences 2006, American Philosophical Soc. 2007; Dr hc (Amsterdam) 2010; hon. degrees from Athabasca Univ., Georgian-American Univ.; Award for the Advancement of Free Software, Free Software Foundation 2003, National Law Journal 100 Most Influential Lawyers in America 2000, 2006, BusinessWeek 25 Top eBiz Leaders 2000, 2001, World Technology Award for Law 2001, 2009, named as one of Scientific American's Top 50 Visionaries 2002, Editors' Choice, Best Non-Technical Book, Linux Journal 2002, Monaco Media Prize 2008. *Achievements include:* best known as a proponent of reduced legal restrictions on copyright, trademark and radio frequency spectrum, particularly in technology applications; has served as lead counsel in several key cases marking boundaries of copyright law in digital age, including Eldred v. Ashcroft, a challenge to the 1998 Sonny Bono Copyright Term Extension Act, and Golan v. Holder. *Publications:* Code and Other Laws of Cyberspace 2000, The Future of Ideas: The Fate of the Commons in a Connected World 2001, Free Culture: The Nature and Future of Creativity 2004, Code: Version 2.0 2006, Remix: Making Art and Commerce Thrive in the Hybrid Economy 2008; numerous articles in professional journals. *Address:* Edmond J. Safra Center for Ethics, Harvard University, Areeda 235, 124 Mount Auburn Street, Suite 520N, Cambridge, MA 02138 (office); 20 Amory Street, Brookline, MA 02446, USA. *Telephone:* (617) 496-8853 (office); (617) 487-5307. *Fax:* (617) 496-6104 (office). *E-mail:* sgray@law.harvard.edu (office); ethics@harvard.edu (office). *Website:* www .ethics.harvard.edu (office); www.lessig.org.

LESTER, Adrian Anthony, OBE; British actor; b. 14 Aug. 1968, Birmingham, England; m. Lolita Chakrabarti; two d.; ed Royal Acad. of Dramatic Art; mem. Council, Royal Acad. of Dramatic Art, Artistic Bd Royal Nat. Theatre; Amb., The Prince's Foundation for Children and the Arts; Time Out Award 1992, Olivier Award 1996, Carlton Theatre Award 2001. *Theatre appearances include:* Cory in Fences, Garrick 1990, Paul Poitier in Six Degrees of Separation (Time Out Award), Royal Court and Comedy Theatre 1992, Anthony Hope in Sweeney Todd, Royal Nat. Theatre 1994, Rosalind in As You Like It (Time Out Award), Albery and Bouffes du Nord 1995, Company (Olivier Award), Albery and Donmar 1996, Hamlet, Bouffes du Nord and Young Vic 2001, Henry V, Royal Nat. Theatre 2003, Brick, Cat on a Hot Tin Roof, Novello, Red Velvet, Tricycle Theatre, Othello, Royal Nat. Theatre. *Films include:* Les Soeurs Soleil 1997, Primary Colors 1997, Storm Damage, Love's Labour's Lost 2000, Best 2000, Maybe Baby 2000, Born Romantic 2000, Dust 2001, The Final Curtain 2002, The Day After Tomorrow 2004, As You Like It 2006, Scenes of a Sexual Nature 2006, Starting Out in the Evening 2007, The Key (video) 2007, Doomsday 2008, Case 39 2009, All is by My Side 2013. *Radio:* The Making of Slavery (BBC Radio 4) 2007. *Television includes:* The Affair 1995, Company 1996, Storm Damage 1998, Jason and the Argonauts 2000, The Tragedy of Hamlet 2002, Girlfriends (episodes) 2002–03, Hustle (as Mickey Stone) 2004–12, Afterlife (episode) 2005, The Ghost Squad (episode) 2005, Beyond (film) 2006, Empire's Children (film) 2007, Ballet Shoes (film) 2007 Being Human (series) 2008, Bonekickers (series) 2008, Merlin (series) 2009, Sleep with Me (film) 2009, Robot Chicken (series) 2013. *Leisure interests:* Tae Kwon Do (Black Belt 2nd Dan), music. *Address:* c/o Tina Price Consultants, Bay Tree House, Haywards Lane, Child Okeford, Dorset, DT11 8DX (office); c/o Artists Rights Group (ARG), 4 Great Portland Street, London, W1W 8PA, England (office). *Telephone:* (1258) 861221 (Tina Price) (office); (20) 7436-6400 (ARG) (office). *Fax:* (20) 7436-6700 (ARG) (office). *E-mail:* tina@tinapriceconsultants.com (office); latimer@argtalent.com (office). *Website:* www.argtalent.com (office).

LESTER, Richard; American film director; b. 19 Jan. 1932, Philadelphia; s. of Elliott Lester and Ella Young; m. Deirdre V. Smith 1956; one s. one d.; ed William Penn Charter School, Univ. of Pennsylvania; TV Dir, CBS 1952–54, ITV 1955–59; composer 1954–57; film director 1959– (noted for work with The Beatles); Grand Prix, Cannes Festival 1965; Best Dir, Rio de Janeiro Festival 1966; Gandhi Peace Prize, Berlin Festival 1969; Best Dir, Tehran Festival 1974. *Films directed:* The Running, Jumping and Standing Still Film 1959, It's Trad, Dad 1962, The Mouse on the Moon 1963, A Hard Day's Night 1963 (re-release 2000), The Knack 1965, Help! 1965, A Funny Thing Happened on the Way to the Forum 1966, How I Won the War 1967, Petulia 1969, The Bed Sitting Room 1969, The Three Musketeers 1973, Juggernaut 1974, The Four Musketeers 1974, Royal Flash 1975, Robin and Marian 1976, The Ritz 1976, Butch and Sundance: The Early Days 1979, Cuba 1979, Superman II 1980, Superman III 1983, Finders Keepers 1984, The Return of the Musketeers 1989, Get Back 1991. *Leisure interests:* tennis, music. *Address:* c/o Creative Artists Agency, 9830 Wilshire Boulevard, Beverly Hills, CA 90212, USA.

LESTER OF HERNE HILL, Baron (Life Peer), cr. 1993, of Herne Hill in the London Borough of Southwark; **Anthony Paul Lester,** QC, BA, LLM; British barrister; b. 3 July 1936, London, England; s. of Harry Lester and Kate Lester; m. Catherine Elizabeth Debora Wassey 1971; one s. one d.; ed City of London School, Trinity Coll. Cambridge, Harvard Law School; called to the Bar, Lincoln's Inn 1963, Bencher 1985; Special Adviser to Home Sec. 1974–76; QC 1975; Special Adviser to Northern Ireland Standing Advisory Comm. on Human Rights 1975–77; Recorder, South-Eastern Circuit 1987–93; Hon. Visiting Prof., Univ. Coll. London 1983–; mem. Bd of Dirs Salzburg Seminar 1996–2000; mem. Bd of Overseers, Univ. of Pa Law School 1977–90, Council of Justice; mem. Court of Govs, LSE 1980–94; Pres. Interights 1983–; UK legal expert EEC Comm. Network Cttee on Equal Pay and Sex Discrimination 1983–93; mem. House of Lords Select Cttee on European Communities Sub-cttee E (Law and Insts) 2000–Jan. 2004, rejoined Dec. 2004, Sub cttee on 1996 Inter-Governmental Conf., Sub-cttee F (Social Affairs, Educ. and Home Affairs) 1996–2000; Co-Chair. of Bd European Roma Rights Centre, Budapest 1999–2001; Gov. British Inst. of Human Rights; Chair. Bd of Govs, James Allen's Girls' School 1987–93; Chair. Runnymede Trust 1990–93; mem. Advisory Cttee Centre for Public Law, Univ. of Cambridge 1999–, Int. Advisory Bd, Open Soc. Inst. Justice Initiative 2000–, Parl. Jt Human Rights Comm. 2001–04, 2005–; Ind. Adviser to Justice Sec. on Constitutional Reform 2007–08; Foreign Hon. mem. American Acad. of Arts and Sciences 2002, Foreign

mem. American Philosophical Soc. 2003; Hon. Adjunct Prof. of Law, Univ. Coll. London 2007; hon. degrees/fellowships from Open Univ., Univ. Coll., London Univ., Ulster Univ., South Bank Univ., Stirling Univ.; Liberty Human Rights Lawyer of the Year 1997, Liberty and Justice Judges Award for Lifetime Achievement 2007. *Publications:* Justice in the American South (Amnesty International) 1964, Race and Law (co-author) 1972; Ed.-in-Chief Butterworths Human Rights Cases; Consultant Ed. and Contrib. Halsbury's Laws of England Title Constitutional Law and Human Rights (4th edn 1996), Human Rights Law and Practice (co-ed.) 1999 (3rd edn 2009), and articles on race relations, public affairs and int. law. *Leisure interests:* painting, walking. *Address:* Blackstone Chambers, Blackstone House, Temple, London, EC4Y 9BW, England (office). *Telephone:* (20) 7583-1770 (office). *E-mail:* anthonylester@blackstonechambers .com (office). *Website:* www.blackstonechambers.com (office).

LETERME, Yves Camille Désiré, LLB, BSc, LLM, MPA; Belgian politician and international organization official; *Deputy Secretary General, Organisation for Economic Co-operation and Development;* b. 6 Oct. 1960, Wervik, West Flanders; ed Catholic Univ. of Leuven, Ghent Univ.; served as auditor at Court of Audit (Rekenhof/Cour des Comptes); Adjunct, then Nat. Sec. CVP, resigned to become civil servant with EU, indefinite leave 1997, apptd mem. Belgian Parl. (House of Reps) 1997–, elected 1999, 2003; mem. City Council of Ypres 1995–2001, Alderman of Ypres 1995–2001; Chair. Christen-Democratisch en Vlaams (Christian Demo-cratic and Flemish party—CD&V) 2003–04; Minister-Pres. of Flanders 2004–07; fmr Flemish Minister of Agric. and Fisheries; fmr Deputy Prime Minister and Minister of Budget, Institutional Reforms, Transport and the North Sea in Belgian Fed. Govt; Prime Minister of Belgium March–Dec. 2008, 2009–11; Minister of Foreign Affairs July–Nov. 2009; Deputy Sec. Gen., OECD 2011–. *Address:* Diksmuidsestraat 58, 8900 Ypres, Belgium (home). *Telephone:* (57) 20-63-61 (office). *Fax:* (57) 20-08-14 (office). *E-mail:* secr.leterme@skynet.be (office). *Website:* www.yvesleterme.be.

LETH, Jørgen; Danish filmmaker; b. 14 June 1937, Århus; has also written, produced, edited, filmed, designed production for and acted in many of his own films; cycling commentator, Tour de France on Danish TV2. *Films include:* as Dir (English titles): Stop for Bud 1963, Look Forward to a Time of Security 1964, The Perfect Human 1967, Ophelia's Flowers 1968, Near Heaven, Near Earth, 1968, Jens Otto Krag 1969, The Deer Garden 1969, Without Kin 1970, Teatret i de grønne bjerge 1970, Motional Picture 1970, The Search 1970, Life in Denmark 1971, Chinese Ping-Pong 1972, Eddy Merckx in the Vicinity of a Cup of Coffee (TV) 1973, The Impossible Hour 1974, Stars and the Water Carriers 1974, Klaus Rifbjerg 1974, The Good and the Bad 1975, Sunday in Hell 1976, Peter Martins: A Dancer 1978, A Midsummer's Play (TV) 1979, Kalule 1979, At danse Bournonville 1979, Step on Silence 1982, 66 Scenes from America 1982, Haiti Express 1983, Pelota 1984, Notebook from China 1986, Moments of Play 1986, Composer Meets Quarter 1987, Notes on Love 1989, Dansk litteratur 1989, Traberg 1992, Michael Laudrup: A Football Player 1993, Haiti, Untitled 1996, I Am Alive 1999, Dreamers 2002, New Scenes from America 2003, The Five Obstructions 2003. *Address:* c/o Zentropa Production, Filmbyen 22, 2650 Hvidovre (home); c/o Danish Film Institute, Gothersgade 55, 1123 Copenhagen K, Denmark (office).

LETO, Jared Joseph; American singer, songwriter, musician (guitar) and actor; b. 26 Dec. 1971, Bossier City, La; s. of Constance Leto; ed Emerson Preparatory School, Washington, DC, Univ. of the Arts, Philadelphia, New York City School of Visual Arts; TV and film actor 1992–; Founder-mem. 30 Seconds to Mars 1998–; MTV2 Award at MTV Video Music Awards 2006, MTV Australia Video Music Awards for Best Rock Video and Video of the Year 2007, Kerrang! Awards for Best Int. Newcomer 2007, for Best Single 2007, 2008, 2011, for Best Int. Band 2010, 2011, TRL Award for Best New Artist 2007, Bandit Rock Award for Best Int. Breakthrough 2008, Los Premios MTV Award for Best Int. Rock Artist 2008, MTV Europe Music Rock Out Award 2008, MTV Europe Music Video Star Award 2008, MTV Video Music Award for Best Rock Video 2010, 2013, MTV Europe Music Award for Best Rock Act 2010, for Best Alternative Act 2013. *Recordings include:* with 30 Seconds to Mars: 30 Seconds to Mars 2002, A Beautiful Lie (MTV Asia Video Star Award 2008) 2005, This is War 2009, Love, Lust, Faith and Dreams 2013. *Films include:* How to Make an American Quilt 1995, The Last of the High Kings 1996, Switchback 1997, Prefontaine 1997, Basil 1998, Urban Legend 1998, The Thin Red Line 1998, Black and White 1999, Girl, Interrupted 1999, Fight Club 1999, American Psycho 2000, Sunset Strip 2000, Requiem for a Dream (Boston Society of Film Critics Award for Best Actor 2000, Stockholm Film Festival Award for Best Actor 2000) 2000, Highway 20902, Panic Room 2002, Phone Booth 2002, Alexander 2004, Lord of War 2005, Hubert Selby Jr.: It'll Be Better Tomorrow (documentary) 2005, Lonely Hearts 2006, Chapter 27 2007, Mr. Nobody (Sitges International Fantastic Film Festival Award for Best Performance 2009, Sitges Film Festival Award for Best Actor 2009) 2009, TT3D: Closer to the Edge (narrator for documentary) 2011, Dallas Buyers Club (Golden Globe Award for Best Supporting Actor in a Motion Picture, Screen Actors Guild Award for Outstanding Performance by a Male Actor in a Supporting Role, Academy Award for Best Supporting Actor 2014) 2013. *Television includes:* Camp Wilder (series) 1992, Almost Home (series) 1993, Rebel Highway (series) 1994, Cool and the Crazy (film) 1994, My So-Called Life (series) 1994. *Website:* jaredleto.com/thisiswhoireallyam.

LETO, Shannon Christopher; American musician (drums); b. 9 March 1970, Bossier City, La; occasional actor in TV and film during 1990s; Founder-mem. 30 Seconds to Mars 1998–; mem. supergroup The Wondergirls 1999; Awards: MTV2 Award at MTV Video Music Awards 2006, MTV Australia Video Music Awards for Best Rock Video and Video of the Year 2007, Kerrang! Awards for Best International Newcomer 2007, for Best Single 2007, 2008, 2011, for Best International Band 2008, 2010, 2011, TRL Award for Best New Artist 2007, Bandit Rock Award for Best International Breakthrough 2008, Los Premios MTV Award for Best International Rock Artist 2008, MTV Asia Video Star Award 2008, MTV Europe Music Rock Out Award 2008, MTV Europe Music Video Star Award 2008, MTV Video Music Award for Best Rock Video 2010, 2013, MTV Europe Music Award for Best Rock Act 2010, for Best Alternative Act 2013. *Recordings:* with 30 Seconds to Mars: 30 Seconds to Mars 2002, A Beautiful Lie (MTV Asia Video Star Award 2008) 2005, This is War 2009, Love, Lust, Faith and Dreams 2013. *Television:* as actor: My So-Called Life 1994. *Films:* as actor: Prefontaine 1997, Highway 2002. *Address:* c/o Virgin Records America Inc., 304 Park Avenue South,

5th Floor, New York, NY 10010-4316, USA (office). *Website:* thirtysecondstomars .thisisthehive.net/EMAs.

LETOKHOV, Vladilen Stepanovich, PhD, DSc; *Russian physicist; Head, Laser Spectroscopy Department, Institute of Spectroscopy, Russian Academy of Sciences;* b. 10 Nov. 1939, Irkutsk; s. of Stepan G. Letokhov and Anna V. Letokhova (née Sevastianova); m. 2nd Tina Karu 1979; one d.; ed Moscow Physical Tech. Inst., P.N. Lebedev Physical Inst.; researcher, P.N. Lebedev Physical Inst. 1966–70; Head Laser Spectroscopy Dept, Inst. of Spectroscopy, USSR (now Russian) Acad. of Sciences 1970–, Vice-Dir for Research 1970–89; Prof., Moscow Physical-Tech. Inst. 1973–; Dir Laser Lab., Soviet (now Russian) Branch of World Lab. 1990–; Fellow American Optical Soc.; mem. New York Acad. of Sciences, Max Planck Soc., Germany, European Acad. of Arts and Science, Academia Europaea; Lenin Prize for Science and Tech. 1978, Jubilee Medal of 600th Anniversary of Heidelberg Union 1985, European Physics Soc. Prize for Quantum Electronics 1998, State Prize for Science and Tech. 2002. *Publications:* Nonlinear Laser Spectroscopy 1977, Nonlinear Laser Chemistry 1987, Photoionization Laser Spectroscopy 1987, Laser Control of Atoms and Molecules 2007, Dalla Siberia alla Scienza del Laser 2008, Astrophysical Lasers 2009, 10 other scientific books and more than 900 publs in scientific journals. *Leisure interests:* music, swimming, house design. *Address:* Institute of Spectroscopy of the Russian Academy of Sciences, Troitsk, 142190 Moscow Region (office); Puchkovo-66, Troitsk, Moscow Region, Russia (home). *Telephone:* (496) 751-05-78 (office). *Fax:* (496) 751-08-86 (office). *E-mail:* letokhov@ isan.troitsk.ru (office). *Website:* www.isan.troitsk.ru (office).

ŁĘTOWSKA, Ewa Anna, MA, LLD; *Polish lawyer and judge;* b. 22 March 1940, Warsaw; m. Janusz Łętowski (deceased); ed Faculty of Law, Warsaw Univ.; scientific worker, Inst. of Legal Sciences, Polish Acad. of Sciences, Warsaw 1962–; Lecturer, Dept of Law, Warsaw Univ. 1963–83; first Commr for Civil Rights Protection 1987–92; lecturer and author of educational material, Helsinki Foundation for Human Rights, Warsaw 1992–99; mem. Expert Cttee, ILO 1993–2002; Judge, Supreme Administrative Court 1999–2002; Judge, Polish Constitutional Tribunal 2002–11; mem. Int. Comm. of Jurists 1995–, mem. Exec. Cttee 1995–98, Vice-Pres. 1998–2001; fmr mem. Bd of Stichting European Human Rights Foundation, Legis. Council at Chair. of Council of Ministers, Codifying Comm. for the Reform of Civil Law; Corresp. mem. Polish Acad. of Arts and Sciences, Kraków and Acad. of Comparative Law, Paris; mem. Polish Helsinki Cttee 1991–; Kt's Cross, Order of Polonia Restituta; Friedrich Ebert Stiftung Award; recipient of many scientific awards. *Publications:* 19 books on civil law, consumer protection and constitutional law; co-author of three books about music; introductions to theatre programmes, concerts and opera reviews; over 30 articles. *Leisure interests:* classical music, vocalism. *Address:* Instytut Nauk Prawnych PAN, ul. Nowy Świat 72, 00-330 Warsaw, Poland (office). *Telephone:* (22) 8267853 (office).

LETSIE III, King of Lesotho, BLL; b. (David Mohato Bereng Seeiso), 17 July 1963, Morija; s. of the late King Moshoeshoe II and Queen Mamohato Berenc Seeiso; m. Anna Karabo Motšoeneng (now Queen 'Masenate Mohato Seeiso) 2000; children: Princess Mary Senate Mohato Seeiso, b. 7 Oct. 2001, Princess 'M'aSeeiso, b. 20 Nov. 2004, Prince Lerotholi David Mohato Bereng Seeiso, b. 18 April 2007; ed Ampleforth Coll., UK, Nat. Univ. of Lesotho, Univs of Bristol, Cambridge and London; Prin. Chief of Matsieng 1989; installed as King Nov. 1990, abdicated Jan. 1995, reinstated following his father's death Feb. 1996–; Patron of Prince Mohato Award (Khau Ea Khosana Mohato). *Leisure interests:* classical and traditional music, horse riding, rugby, squash, tennis. *Address:* Royal Palace, Maseru, Lesotho.

LETTA, Enrico, PhD; *Italian politician;* b. 20 Aug. 1966, Pisa; m. Gianna Letta; three s.; ed Univ. of Pisa, Sant'Anna School of Advanced Studies; researcher, Agency for Research and Legislation, Rome 1991–94, Sec.-Gen. 1994–; Chair. European Young Christian Democrats 1991–95; Head of Secr. of Foreign Minister Beniamino Andreatta 1993–94; Sec.-Gen. Cttee for the Euro, Ministry of the Treasury, the Budget and Econ. Planning 1996–97; Deputy Sec. Italian People's Party 1997–98; Minister for Community Policies 1998–99, for Industry, Trade and Crafts Jan.–April 2000, for Industry and Foreign Trade 2000–01; nat. official of Margherita party responsible for the economy 2001–07; mem. Chamber of Deputies 2001–04, 2006– (Olive Tree coalition); mem. Partito Democratico 2007–; mem. European Parl. for NE Italy 2004–06, part of Alliance of Liberals and Democrats for Europe, mem. Cttee on Econ. and Monetary Affairs, mem. Del. for relations with the Maghreb countries and the Arab Maghreb Union (including Libya); Under-Sec. of State to the Presidency of the Council of Ministers 2006–08; Shadow Minister for Welfare 2008–13; Prime Minister 2013–14 (resgnd), Minister of Agric. Jan.–Feb. 2014; Vice-Pres. Aspen Inst. Italy 2004–; Prof. under contract, Libera Università Cattaneo 2001–03, la Scuola superiore S. Anna di Pisa 2003, Haute école de commerce, Paris 2004, 2005; mem. Trilateral Comm. *Publications include:* Passaggio a Nord-Est 1994, Euro sì – Morire per Maastricht 1997, La Comunità competitiva 2001, Dialogo intorno all'Europa (with L. Caracciolo) 2002, L'allargamento dell'Unione europea 2003, Viaggio nell'economia italiana (with P. Bersani) 2004), L'Europa a Venticinque 2005. *Address:* Partito Democratico, Piazza Saint'Anastasia 7, 00186 Rome, Italy (office). *Telephone:* (06) 675471 (office). *Fax:* (06) 67547319 (office). *E-mail:* info@partitodemocratico.it (office). *Website:* www.partitodemocratico.it (office).

LETTE, Kathy; *Australian author and playwright;* b. 11 Nov. 1958, Sydney; d. of Mervyn Lette and Val Lette; m. Geoffrey Robertson (q.v.) 1990; one s. one d.; fmr columnist, Sydney and NY; fmr satirical news writer and presenter Willasee Show, Channel 9; fmr TV sitcom writer Columbia Pictures, LA; fmr guest presenter This Morning with Richard and Judy, ITV; writer-in-residence, The Savoy, London 2003; Australian Literature Board Grant 1982. *Plays include:* Wet Dreams 1985, Perfect Mismatch 1985, Grommits 1986, I'm So Happy For You, I Really Am 1991. *Films:* Puberty Blues 1982, Mad Cows 2001. *Publications:* Puberty Blues (with G. Carey) 1979, Hit and Ms 1984, Girls' Night Out 1987, The Llama Parlour 1991, Foetal Attraction 1993, Mad Cows 1996, She Done Him Wrong (essays), The Constant Sinner by Mae West (introduction) 1995, Altar Ego 1998, Nip 'n Tuck 2001, Dead Sexy 2003, How to Kill Your Husband 2005, A Stitch in Time 2005, To Love, Honour, and Betray 2009; contribs to Sydney Morning Herald, The Bulletin, Cleo Magazine. *Leisure interests:* scuba diving, opera, feminism. *Address:* c/o Ed Victor, 6 Bayley Street, London, WC1B 3HB, England. *Telephone:* (20) 7304-4100

(office). *Fax:* (20) 7304-4111 (office). *E-mail:* kathy.lette@virgin.net (office). *Website:* www.kathylette.com.

LETTERMAN, David Michael; *American comedian, talk show host and producer; Host, Late Show with David Letterman;* b. 12 April 1947, Indianapolis, Ind.; s. of Joseph Letterman and Dorothy Letterman; m. 1st Michelle Cook 1969 (divorced 1977); m. 2nd Regina Lasko 2009; one s.; ed Ball State Univ.; began career as a radio talk show host on WNTS (AM) and on Indianapolis TV station WLWI (now WTHR) as an anchor and weatherman; radio and TV announcer in Indianapolis 1970–75; performer, The Comedy Store, LA 1975; frequent guest host on The Tonight Show; host, David Letterman Show 1980, Late Night with David Letterman (NBC) 1982–93; Late Show with David Letterman (CBS, also writer and producer) 1993–; Host of the Academy Awards 1995; Founder and Chair. Worldwide Pants Inc. (production co.) 1993–; TV scriptwriter including Bob Hope Special, Good Times, Paul Lynde Comedy Hour, John Denver Special; Co-owner Rahal Letterman Racing 1996–; Emmy Awards for Outstanding Host or Hostess in a Variety Series 1981, Outstanding Individual Achievement – Writers 1981, Outstanding Writing in a Variety or Music Program 1984, 1985, 1986, 1987, Outstanding Variety, Music or Comedy Series 1994; American Comedy Awards for Funniest Male Performer in a TV Special (Leading or Supporting) Network, Cable or Syndication 1989, 1995, Funniest Male Performer in a TV Series (Leading Role) Network, Cable or Syndication 1994, 2001, Kennedy Center Honor 2012. *Publications include:* The Late Night with David Letterman Book of Top Ten Lists 1990, An Altogether New Book of Top Ten Lists, 1991, David Letterman's Book of Top Ten Lists 1996. *Leisure interests:* baseball, basketball, running, auto racing. *Address:* Late Show with David Letterman, Ed Sullivan Theater, 1697 Broadway, New York, NY 10019 (office); Worldwide Pants Inc., 1697 Broadway, Suite 805, New York, NY 10019, USA. *Telephone:* (212) 975-5300 (Worldwide Pants). *Fax:* (212) 975-4780 (Worldwide Pants). *Website:* www.cbs.com/shows/ late_show (office); www.rahal.com.

LETTINGA, Gatze, DrIr; *Dutch chemical engineer and academic; Adviser to the Board, Lettinga Associates Foundation;* b. 4 Jan. 1936, Dongjum, Friesland; ed RHBS High School, Harlingen, Tech. Univ., Delft, Inter Univ. Reactor Inst., Delft; began his work on devt and implementation of anaerobic treatment systems in 1971, developed Upflow Anaerobic Sludge Bed Reactor system 1972, succeeded in implementing it in sugar beet industry for treatment of wastewater; joined Dept of Environmental Tech., Wageningen Agricultural Univ. 1970, Prof. in Environmental Tech. 1988–2001 (retd); currently Consultant and mem. Bd of Dirs Lettinga Associates Foundation (LeAF—fmrly Environmental Protection and Resources Conservations Foundation, Chair. 1997–2002); has served on organizing or scientific cttees of several nat. and int. confs, including Second Int. AD-Symposium 1981, Third Int. AD-Symposium, Boston 1983; organized yearly int. courses on Anaerobic Digestion for developing countries; fmr mem. Editorial Bd Agricultural Wastes (now Bioresources Technology), Re/Views in Environmental Science and Bio/Technology, Journal of Environmental Science and Health; mem. Dutch Asscn of Water Pollution Control (NVA), Dutch Asscn of Biotechnology (NBV), Int. Water Asscn; Dr hc (Univ. of Valladolid, Spain) 2001; NVA Prize, Dutch Asscn on Wastewater Treatment 1979, Medaille d'argent de la Ville de Paris 1981, Karl Imhoff Award, Int. Asscn of Water Pollution Research Control 1992, Royal Shell Prize for Sustainable Devt and Energy 2001, Tyler Prize for Environmental Achievement 2007. *Achievements include:* was involved in more than 15 env projects on anaerobic wastewater treatment plants in developing countries, including Cuba, Brazil, Indonesia, India and Viet Nam 1980s, Morocco present day. *Publications:* more than 500 scientific papers in professional journals on anaerobic digestion and treatment of solid and liquid wastewater in modern high-rate treatment systems under psychrophilic, mesophilic and thermophilic conditions for remediation and energy production. *Address:* Lettinga Associates Foundation, PO Box 500, 6700 AM Wageningen, Netherlands (office). *Telephone:* (317) 482023 (office). *Fax:* (317) 482108 (office). *E-mail:* gatze.lettinga@wur.nl (office). *Website:* www.lettinga-associates.wur.nl (office).

LETWIN, Rt Hon. Oliver, PC, MA, PhD, FRSA; *British politician; Minister of State for Policy, Cabinet Office;* b. 19 May 1956, Hampstead, London; s. of the late Prof. William Letwin and Shirley R. Letwin; m. Isabel Grace Davidson 1984; one s. one d. (twins); ed Eton Coll., Trinity Coll., Cambridge, London Business School; visiting research fellow Princeton Univ. 1980–81; research fellow Darwin Coll. Cambridge 1981–82; special adviser Dept of Educ. and Science 1982–83; mem. Prime Minister's Policy Unit 1983–86; Dir N.M. Rothschild and Sons Ltd 1991–; MP (Conservative) Dorset W 1997–; Opposition Front Bench Spokesperson on Constitutional Affairs 1998–99; Shadow Financial Sec. to Treasury 2000–01; Shadow Chief Sec. to Treasury 2000–01; Shadow Sec. of State for Home Affairs 2001–02; Privy Councillor 2002; Shadow Sec. of State for Econ. Affairs and Shadow Chancellor of the Exchequer 2003–May 2005; Shadow Sec. of State for Environment, Food and Rural Affairs May–Dec. 2005; Chair. of Policy Review and Chair. of Conservative Research Dept 2005–; Minister of State for Policy (Cabinet Office) 2010–; fmr Visiting Fellow (Procter Fellow), Princeton Univ., USA; Research Fellow, Darwin Coll., Cambridge 1981–83. *Publications include:* Ethics, Emotion and the Unity of Self 1984, Privatising the World 1987, Aims of Schooling 1988, Drift to Union 1990, The Purpose of Politics 1999; numerous articles in professional and popular journals. *Leisure interests:* philosophy, walking, skiing, tennis. *Address:* House of Commons, Westminster, London, SW1A 0AA (office); Constituency Office, Chapel House, Dorchester Road, Maiden Newton, DT2 0BG, England. *Telephone:* (20) 7219-0826 (Westminster) (office); (20) 7219-0292 (Westminster) (office); (1308) 321188 (Maiden Newton); (1308) 456891 (Maiden Newton). *Fax:* (1308) 321233 (Maiden Newton). *E-mail:* letwino@parliament.uk (office); publiccorrespondence@cabinet-office.gsi.gov.uk (office); anthonystanley@ westdorsetconservatives.com. *Website:* www.gov.uk/government/organisations/ cabinet-office (office); www.parliament.uk/biographies/commons/mr-oliver-letwin/ 247 (office); www.oliverletwinmp.com; www.westdorsetconservatives.com.

LEUENBERGER, Moritz; *Swiss politician and lawyer;* b. 21 Sept. 1946, Biel/ Bienne; s. of Robert Leuenberger and Ruth Leuenberger; m. Gret Loewensberg 2003; two s.; ed Univ. of Zürich; pvt. practice as lawyer 1972–91; joined Social Democratic Party (SP) 1969, Leader Zürich SP 1972–80; mem. Zürich City Council 1974–83; Pres. Swiss Tenants' Asscn 1986–91; elected to Nat. Council 1979; elected to Zürich Cantonal Council 1991, Dir of Justice and Internal Affairs 1991–95; Fed.

Councillor 1995–2010; Minister, Fed. Dept of Transport, Communications and Energy 1995–2010, Head of Fed. Dept of Environment, Transport, Energy and Communications (subsequently Transport, Energy and Communications) 2001–2010; Vice-Pres. Swiss Federal Council 2000, 2005, 2010, Pres. 2001, 2006. *Address:* c/o Federal Department of Transport, Energy and Communications, Bundeshaus-Nord, 3003 Berne, Switzerland (office).

LEUNG, C. C., BSc; Taiwanese business executive; *Vice-Chairman and President, Quanta Computer Inc.;* ed Nat. Taiwan Univ.; co-f. Quanta Computer Inc. 1988, Pres. 1993–2006, 2007–, also Vice-Chair. and Chief Research and Devt Officer; Pres. Quanta Research Inst. *Address:* Quanta Computer Inc., 211 Wen Hwa Second Road, Kui Shan Hsiang, Taoyuan, Taiwan (office). *Telephone:* (3) 327-2345 (office). *Fax:* (3) 327-1511 (office). *E-mail:* campus@quantatw.com (office); qci.ir@quantatw.com (office). *Website:* www.quantatw.com (office).

LEUNG, Hon. Chun-ying, JP; Chinese civil servant; *Chief Executive, Executive Council of Hong Kong;* b. 1954, Hong Kong; m. Regina Tong Ching Yee; three c.; ed Hong Kong Univ. of Science and Tech., Bristol Polytechnic and King's Coll. London, UK; fmr Sec. Gen. Basic Law Consultative Cttee; Vice-Chair. Preparatory Cttee, Hong Kong Special Admin. Region 1995–96; Convenor Exec. Council, Non-Official Mem. 1997–2012; Chief Exec., Exec. Council of Hong Kong 2012–; Chair. DTZ Debenham Tie Leung Ltd, One Country Two Systems Research Inst. Ltd; mem. Nat. Cttee and Standing Cttee, 10th CPPCC 2008–08, 11th CPPCC 2008–13; Chancellor The Chinese Univ. of Hong Kong; Fellow, Hong Kong Inst. of Surveyors; Gold Bauhinia Star; Hon. DBA. *Leisure interests:* gardening, sports. *Address:* Office of the Chief Executive, 5/F, Main Wing, Central Government Offices, Lower Albert Rd, Central, Hong Kong Special Administrative Region, People's Republic of China (office). *Telephone:* 28783300 (office). *Fax:* 25090577 (office). *E-mail:* ceo@ceo.gov.hk (office). *Website:* www.ceo.gov.hk (office).

LEUNG, Oi Sie (Elsie), GMB, LLM, JP; Chinese politician, solicitor and legal official; *Vice-Director, Hong Kong Basic Law Committee, National People's Congress Standing Committee;* b. 24 April 1939, Hong Kong; ed Univ. of Hong Kong, Coll. of Law, England; admitted as solicitor of Hong Kong 1968, registered as overseas solicitor, UK Supreme Court 1976; Notary Public 1978; admitted as solicitor and barrister of Vic., Australia 1982; Founding mem. Hong Kong Fed. of Women Lawyers 1975, Hong Kong Fed. of Women 1993; Pres. Int. Fed. of Women Lawyers 1994; del. 7th People's Congress of Guangdong Prov. 1989–93, 8th Nat. People's Congress, People's Repub. of China 1993–97; Sec. for Justice of Hong Kong Special Admin. Region 1997–2005, also Chief Legal Adviser and Ex-Officio mem. Exec. Council of Hong Kong 1997–2005; resumed practice as solicitor 2006–; Vice-Dir Hong Kong Basic Law Cttee, Nat. People's Congress Standing Cttee, People's Repub. of China 2006–; Fellow, Int. Acad. of Matrimonial Lawyers 1994; Hon. LLD (China Univ. of Political Science and Law) 2004, (Warwick) 2005, (Hong Kong Shue Yan Univ.) 2010, (Univ. of Science and Tech., Hong Kong) 2011; Grand Bauhinia Medal (Hong Kong) 2002. *Address:* 2201–2202 Admiralty Centre, Tower 1, 18 Harcourt Road, Hong Kong Special Administrative Region, People's Republic of China (office). *Telephone:* 25249995 (office). *Fax:* 25372609 (office). *E-mail:* elsie.leung@iulaili.com (office).

LEUNG, Tony Chiu Wai; Hong Kong actor; b. 27 June 1962, Hong Kong. *Films:* Feng kuang ba san (Mad Mad 83) 1983, Qing chun chai guan (Young Cops) 1985, Din lo jing juen (The Lunatics) 1986, Deiha tsing (Love Unto Waste) 1986, Yan man ying hung (The People's Hero) 1987, Sha shou hu die meng (My Heart is that Eternal Rose) 1987, Kai xin kuai huo ren (Happy Go Lucky) 1987, Tie jia wu di Ma Li A (I Love Maria) 1988, Beiqing chengshi (City of Sadness) 1989, Zhong yi qun ying (Seven Warriors) 1989, Liang ge you qi jiang (Two Painters) 1989, Die xue jie tou (Bullet in the Head) 1990, A Fei jing juen (Days of Being Wild) 1991, Hoyat gwan tsoi loi (Au revoir mon amour) 1991, Sinnui yauman III (Chinese Ghost Story 3) 1991, Zhong huan ying xiong (Don't Fool Me) 1991, Wu hu jiang zhi jue lie (The Tigers) 1991, Sha Tan-Zi yu Zhou Shih-Nai (Royal Scoundrel) 1991, Qian Wang (The Great Pretenders) 1991, Haomen yeyan (The Banquet) 1991, Lashou shentan (Hard Boiled) 1992, Ge ge de qing ren (Three Summers) 1993, Ya Fei yu Ya Ji (The Days of Being Dumb) 1992, Ti dao bao (Lucky Encounter) 1992, Fan dou ma liu (Come Fly the Dragon) 1992, Yi yu zhi mo lu ying xiong (End Of The Road) 1993, Xin xian hao shen zhen (The Magic Crane) 1993, Xin nan xiong nan di (He Ain't Heavy, He's My Father) 1993, Xin liu xing hu die jian (Butterfly and Sword) 1993, Wei Xiao Bao zhi feng zhi gou nu (Hero Beyond The Boundary Of Time) 1993, Seidu yinghung tsun tsi dung sing sai tsau (The Eagle Shooting Heroes) 1993, Mo hua qing (Fantasy Romance) 1993, Feng chen san xia (Tom, Dick, and Hairy) 1993, Chong qing sen lin (Chungking Express) 1994, Dung che sai duk (Ashes of Time) 1994, Shen long du sheng zhi qi kai de sheng (Always Be the Winners) 1994, Dun jeuk nai guay loy (The Returning) 1994, Xich lo (Cyclo) 1995, Ming yat tin aai (Tomorrow) 1995, Liu mang yi sheng (Dr Mack) 1995, Jushi shengun (Heaven Can't Wait) 1995, Tou tou ai ni (Blind Romance) 1996, Hong xing zi zhi jiang hu da feng bao (War of the Underworld) 1996, Cheun gwong tsa sit (Happy Together) 1997, Zui jia pai dang zhi zui jie pai dang (97 Aces Go Places) 1997, Aau dut (The Longest Nite) 1998, Hai shang hua (Flowers of Shanghai) 1998, Mooi tin oi lei siu shut (Your Place or Mine) 1998, Hei yu duan chang ge zhi qi sheng zhu rou (Chinese Midnight Express) 1998, Chiu si hung yiu oi (Timeless Romance) 1998, Bor lei jun (Gorgeous) 1999, Dong jing gong lue (Tokyo Raiders) 2000, Fa yeung nin wa (In the Mood for Love) (Best Actor Cannes Film Festival) 2000, Tung gui mat yau (Fighting for Love) 2001, Hap gwat yan sam (Healing Hearts) 2001, Yau ching yam shui baau (Love Me, Love My Money) 2001, Tian xia wu shuang (Chinese Odyssey 2002) 2002, Ying xiong (Hero) 2002, Wu jian dao (Infernal Affairs) 2002, Xing yun chao ren (My Lucky Star) 2003, Wu jian Dao 3 (Infernal Affairs III) 2003, Dei gwong tit 2003, Di xia tie 2003, 2046 (Best Actor Hong Kong Film Critics' Society 2005) 2004, Han chang gong lue 2005, Seung sing (Confession of Pain) 2006, Se, jie (Lust, Caution) 2007, Chi bi (Red Cliff) 2008. *Address:* c/o Jet Tone Productions Limited, Flat E, 3/F, Kalam Court 9, Grampion Road, Kowloon, Hong Kong Special Administrative Region, People's Republic of China (office).

LEUNG KAM CHUNG, Antony, BSc; Hong Kong government official and financial services industry executive; *Senior Managing Director and the Chairman of Blackstone Greater China, The Blackstone Group (HK) Ltd;* b. 29 Jan. 1952, Hong Kong; m. 1st Sophie Leung; m. 2nd Fu Mingxia 2002; one d.; ed Univ. of Hong Kong, Harvard Business School, USA; Man. Dir and Regional Man. for Greater China and the Philippines, Chase Manhattan Bank; Chair. Univ. Grants Cttee

1993–98; Dir Hong Kong Futures Exchange 1987–90, Hong Kong Policy Research Inst. 1996–; Arbitrator, China Int. Econ. and Trade Arbitration Comm. 1994–; mem. Exec. Council Hong Kong Special Admin. Region 1997–2001; Financial Sec. of Hong Kong 2001–03 (resgnd); Sr Man. Dir and Chair. Blackstone Greater China, Blackstone Group HK Ltd, Hong Kong 2007–; mem. Industrial Devt Bd 1985, Univ. and Polytechnic Grants Cttee 1990–93, Bd Provisional Airport Authority 1990–95, Bd Airport Authority 1995–99, Cen. Policy Unit 1992–93, Bd Hong Kong Community Chest 1992–94, Educ. Comm. 1993–98 (Chair. 1998), Standing Council Chinese Soc. of Macroeconomics, State Planning Comm. 1994, Exchange Fund Advisory Cttee 1993, Prep. Cttee of Hong Kong Special Admin. Region 1996–97; Trustee, Queen Mary Hosp. Charitable Trust 1993–, Hong Kong Centre for Econ. Research 1995–98; Hong Kong Affairs Adviser 1994–97. *Leisure interest:* golf. *Address:* The Blackstone Group (HK) Ltd, Suite 9021, 9th Floor, Two International Finance Centre, 8 Finance Street Central, Hong Kong Special Administrative Region, People's Republic of China (office). *Telephone:* 36568600 (office). *Fax:* 36568601 (office). *Website:* www.blackstone.com (office).

LEUTHARD, Doris; Swiss politician; *Head of the Federal Department of the Environment, Transports, Energy and Communications;* b. 10 April 1963; m. Roland Hausin; ed Zürich Univ.; mem. Swiss Nat. Council 1999–2006; Grossrätin, Aragau Canton 1997–2000; Vice-Pres. Christian Democratic Party 2001–04, Pres. 2004–06; mem. Fed. Council and Head of Fed. Dept of Econ. Affairs 2006–10, also responsible for Agric., Veterinary Affairs, Consumer Affairs, Housing, Vocational Training, European Integration, Vice-Pres. Fed. Council 2009, Pres. 2010, Head of Fed. Dept of the Environment, Transports, Energy and Communications 2010–. *Address:* Federal Department of the Environment, Transport, Energy and Communications, Bundeshaus Nord, 3003 Bern, Switzerland (office). *Telephone:* (31) 3225502 (office). *Fax:* (31) 3225934 (office). *E-mail:* info@gs-uvek.admin.ch (office). *Website:* www.uvek.admin.ch (office).

LEVADA, HE Cardinal William Joseph, STD; American ecclesiastic; *Prefect Emeritus, Congregation for the Doctrine of the Faith;* b. 15 June 1936, Long Beach, Calif.; s. of Joseph Levada, Jr and Lorraine Nunez Levada; ed St Anthony's High School, Long Beach, Our Lady Queen of Angels Seminary, San Fernando, St John's Seminary, Camarillo, North American Coll. and Pontifical Gregorian Univ., Rome, Italy; ordained priest 1961; Assoc. Pastor, St Louis of France Parish, San Gabriel Valley community of La Puente 1962; Assoc. Pastor, St Monica's Church, Santa Monica 1963–67, where he served as high school religion teacher and chaplain of local Community Coll. Newman Center; taught theology at St John's Seminary School of Theology, Los Angeles 1970–76; served as first Dir Continuing Educ. for the Clergy, Archdiocese of Los Angeles 1973; Pres. Senate of Priests 1975–76; official of Congregation for the Doctrine of the Faith, Vatican City 1976–82; part-time Instructor, Pontifical Gregorian Univ. 1976–82; Exec. Dir California Catholic Conf. of Bishops, Sacramento 1982–84; Auxiliary Bishop of Los Angeles (Titular Bishop of Capri) 1983–86; Episcopal Vicar for Santa Barbara Co. 1984–86; Chancellor and Moderator of the Curia 1986; Archbishop of Portland, Ore. 1986–95; Coadjutor Archbishop of San Francisco Aug.–Dec. 1995, Archbishop of San Francisco 1995–2005; Apostolic Admin. Diocese of Santa Rosa 1999–2000; Bishop Co-Chair. Anglican–Roman Catholic Dialogue in the US 2000–05; mem. Congregation for the Doctrine of the Faith 2000–05, Prefect 2005–12, Prefect Emer. 2012–; cr. Cardinal (Cardinal-Deacon of Santa Maria in Domnica) 2006; participated in Papal Conclave 2013; Chair. US Conf. of Catholic Bishops' Cttee on Doctrine 2003–05; Pres. Int. Theological Comm. 2005–12, Pontifical Biblical Comm. 2005–12, Pontifical Comm. 'Ecclesia Dei' 2009–12. *Address:* Congregation for the Doctrine of the Faith, Palazzo del Sant'Uffizio, Piazza del S. Uffizio 11, 00193 Rome, Italy (office). *Website:* www.vatican.va/roman_curia/congregations/cfaith (office).

LEVEAUX, David; British theatre director; b. 13 Dec. 1957, Leicester, England; s. of Michael Leveaux and Eve Powell; ed Univ. of Manchester; Assoc. Dir Riverside Studios 1981–85; Artistic Dir Theatre Project Tokyo from 1993; has directed productions for Nat. Theatre, RSC, ENO, Almeida Theatre, Donmar Warehouse (Assoc. Dir) and on Broadway. *Productions include:* Broadway: A Moon for the Misbegotten 1984, Anna Christie 1993, Electra (Sophocles) 1998, The Real Thing 2000, Betrayal 2000, Nine 2003, Fiddler on the Roof 2004, Jumpers 2004, The Glass Menagerie 2005, Cyrano de Bergerac 2007, Arcadia 2011, Romeo and Juliet 2013; Almeida Theatre: Betrayal 1991, Moonlight 1993, No Man's Land 1992 (transferred to Comedy Theatre 1993), The Distance From Here 2002; Theatre Project Tokyo: Electra 1995, Lulu 1999, Modern Noh Plays, The Changeling, Hedda Gabler, Two Headed Eagle; Donmar Warehouse: Nine 1996, Electra 1997, The Real Thing 1999 (transferred to the Albery Theatre 2000); Duke of York's Theatre: Backbeat 2011. *Address:* c/o Simpson Fox Associates, 6 Beauchamp Place, London, SW3 1NG, England (office). *Telephone:* (20) 7434-9167 (office). *E-mail:* david.watson@simpson-fox.com (office). *Website:* www.simpson-fox.com (office).

LEVELT, Willem J. M. (Pim), PhD; Dutch psychologist, psycholinguist and academic; *Director Emeritus, Max-Planck-Institute for Psycholinguistics;* b. 17 May 1938, Amsterdam; s. of Dr W. H. Levelt and J. Levelt-Berger; m. Elisabeth C. M. Jacobs 1963; two s. one d.; ed Leiden Univ.; staff. mem. Inst. for Perception, Soesterberg 1962–65; Research Fellow Center for Cognitive Studies, Harvard Univ. 1965–66; Visiting Asst Prof. Univ. of Illinois 1966–67; Prof. of Experimental Psychology, Groningen Univ. 1967–70, Nijmegen Univ. 1971–79, Hon. Prof. of Psycholinguistics 1980–; Leader Max-Planck Project Group for Psycholinguistics, Nijmegen 1976–79; Dir Max-Planck-Inst. for Psycholinguistics, Nijmegen 1980–2005, now Dir Emer. 2005–; Visiting Prof. Louvain Univ. 1967–70; mem. Inst. for Advanced Study, Princeton 1971–72; mem. Royal Netherlands Acad. of Sciences, Pres. 2002–05; mem. Academia Europaea, American Philosophical Soc., NAS, Leopoldina and other acads; Hon. dgress from Univs of Maastricht, Antwerp, Louvain, Padua. *Publications:* On binocular rivalry 1968, Formal grammars in linguistics and psycholinguistics, 3 Vols 1974, Speaking: From intention to articulation 1989. *Leisure interest:* playing the traverso. *Address:* Max-Planck-Institute for Psycholinguistics, Wundtlaan 1, 6525 XD Nijmegen, Netherlands (office). *Telephone:* (24) 352-1317 (office). *Fax:* (24) 352-1213 (office). *E-mail:* PIM@mpi.nl (office). *Website:* www.mpi.nl/world/persons/profession/pim.html (office).

LEVELT SENGERS, Johanna Maria Henrica, (Anneke); American (b. Dutch) physicist; *Scientist Emerita, National Institute of Standards and Technology;* b. 4

March 1929, Amsterdam, The Netherlands; d. of Wilhelmus Levelt and Josephine Berger; m. Jan V. Sengers 1963; two s. two d.; ed Univ. of Amsterdam, Univ. of Wisconsin, Madison; joined Nat. Bureau of Standards (now Nat. Inst. of Standards and Tech.) 1963, Group Leader Chemical Science and Tech. Lab. (Physical and Chemical Properties Div.) 1978–87, Sr Fellow 1984, Scientist Emer. 1995–; Lecturer, Catholic Univ. Louvain, Belgium 1971; Research Assoc., Inst. of Theoretical Physics, Univ. of Amsterdam 1974–75; Regents Prof., Dept of Chemistry, Univ. of California, Los Angeles 1982; Fellow American Physical Soc., AAAS, Int. Asscn for the Properties of Water and Steam (IAPWS); mem. NAS, Nat. Acad. of Eng; Corresp. mem. Royal Netherlands Acad. of Arts and Sciences, Koninklijke Holland Maatschappij der Wetenschappen; fmr Pres. IAPWS and US nat. rep. to IAPWS on behalf of ASME; Jt Organizer first NATO Summer School on Supercritical Fluids 1994; co-Chair., Women for Science Working Group, InterAmerican Network of Acads of Sciences (IANAS) 2010–; Dr hc (Tech. Univ. of Delft, Netherlands); Dept of Commerce Silver Medal 1972, Gold Medal 1978, Alexander Von Humboldt Research Award, Germany 1991, N American recipient of L'Oréal-UNESCO Women in Science Award 2003, ASME Yeram S. Touloukian Award 2006. *Publications include:* How Fluids Unmix 2002; numerous papers and reviews on thermodynamics and properties of fluids and fluid mixtures near their critical points, 14 book chapters. *Leisure interests:* swimming, hiking, travelling, reading. *Address:* Physical and Chemical Properties Division, Chemical Science and Technology Laboratory, National Institute of Standards and Technology, Gaithersburg, MD 20899-8380 (office); 110 N. Van Buren Street, Rockville, MD 20850, USA (home). *Telephone:* (301) 975-2463 (office). *Fax:* (301) 869-4020 (office). *E-mail:* johanna.sengers@nist.gov (office). *Website:* www.nist.gov/mml/properties/Levelt-Sengers.cfm (office).

LEVENE OF PORTSOKEN, Baron (Life Peer), cr. 1997, of Portsoken in the City of London; **Peter Keith Levene,** KBE, BA, JP, FCIT, CIMgt; British business executive; *Chairman, NBNK Investments plc;* b. 8 Dec. 1941, Pinner, Middx, England; s. of the late Maurice Levene and Rose Levene; m. Wendy Ann Levene 1966; two s. one d.; ed City of London School and Univ. of Manchester; joined United Scientific Holdings 1963, Man. Dir 1968, Chair. 1982; Personal Adviser to Sec. of State for Defence 1984; Chief of Defence Procurement, Ministry of Defence 1985–91; mem. SE Asia Trade Advisory Group 1979–83, Council, Defence Mfrs Asscn 1982–85, Vice-Chair. 1983–84, Chair. 1984–85; Chair. European NATO Nat. Armaments Dirs 1990–91, Docklands Light Railway Ltd 1991–94; Special Adviser to Sec. of State for the Environment 1991–92; Adviser to Prime Minister on Efficiency 1992–97; Special Adviser to Pres. of the Bd of Trade 1992–95; Chair. Public Competition and Purchasing Unit, HM Treasury 1991–92; Deputy Chair. Wasserstein Perella & Co. Ltd 1991–94; Chair. and CEO Canary Wharf Ltd 1993–96; Sr Adviser Morgan Stanley & Co. Ltd 1996–98; Chair. Bankers Trust Int. 1998–99, Investment Banking Europe, Deutsche Bank AG 1999–2001 (Vice-Chair. Deutsche Bank UK 2001–02), General Dynamics UK Ltd 2001–, Lloyd's 2002–11, NBNK Investments plc 2011–; mem. Bd of Dirs Haymarket Group Ltd 1997–, J. Sainsbury PLC 2001–04, China Construction Bank 2006–11; mem. Supervisory Bd Deutsche Boerse AG 2004–05; Alderman, City of London 1984–, Sheriff 1995–96, Lord Mayor of London 1998–99; Fellow, Queen Mary and Westfield Coll., Univ. of London 1995; Hon. Col Commdt, Royal Corps of Transport 1991–93, Royal Logistics Corps 1993–; Master, Worshipful Co. of Carmen 1992–93; KStJ 1989; Commdr, Order nat. du Mérite 1996; Kt Commdr, Order of Merit (Germany) 1998, Middle Cross Order of Merit (Hungary) 1999; Hon. DSc (City Univ.) 1998, (Univ. of London) 2005. *Leisure interests:* skiing, travel, watching Association football. *Address:* One Angel Court, London, EC2R 7HJ, England (office). *Telephone:* (20) 7710-7432 (office). *Fax:* (20) 7710-7418 (office). *E-mail:* peter.levene@nbnki.com (office). *Website:* www.nbnki.com (office).

LEVENS, Marie E.; Suriname politician and international organization official; *Director, Department of Human Development and Employment, Organization of American States;* b. 1950; fmr Sr Policy Adviser, Higher Educ. Devt Scholarship and Exchange Programs, Ministry of Educ. and Community Devt; Consultant, Inter-American Devt Bank 1998; Minister of Foreign Affairs 2000–05; mem. Suriname Nat. Party (NPS-Nationale Partij Suriname); currently Dir Dept of Human Devt and Employment, OAS, Washington, DC. *Address:* Organization of American States, General Secretariat Building (GSB), Office 760, 1889 F Street NW, Washington, DC 20006, USA (office). *Telephone:* (202) 370-9771 (office). *Website:* www.oas.org (office).

LEVENTAL, Valery Yakovlevich; Russian artist and stage designer; b. 17 Aug. 1942, Moscow; ed All-Union State Cinematography Inst.; with Bolshoi Theatre 1965–95, Chief Designer 1988–95; Chief Designer, Moscow A.P. Chekhov Art Theatre from 2001; designs and sets for Cinderella, Romeo and Juliet, Anna Karenina, Khovanshchina, Prince Igor (Vilnius and Sofia), Tosca, Così fan tutte, Madame Butterfly, Otello, Till Eulenspiegel, Icarus, décor for experimental ballets of Maiya Plisetskaya (q.v.) and Vladimir V. Vasiliyev; also for Love for Three Oranges (Berlin), War and Peace, Dead Souls (Bolshoi); Corresp. mem. USSR (now Russian) Acad. of Arts 1988; People's Artist of the USSR 1989; State Prize of the Russian Fed. 1994. *Theatrical designs:* Woe from Wit, The Bedbug, The Wedding (Gogol), The Marriage of Figaro, The Duenna, Macbeth 1979, The Seagull 1979, Boris Godunov. *Film designs:* Romeo and Juliet, Phèdre. *Address:* Sadovaya-Spasskaya Street 19, Apt 88, 107078 Moscow, Russia. *Telephone:* (495) 975-14-94.

LEVER, Sir Jeremy Frederick, Kt, KCMG, MA, QC, FRSA; British lawyer; b. 23 June 1933, London; s. of the late Arnold Lever and of Elizabeth Cramer (née Nathan); ed Bradfield Coll., Berks., University Coll. Oxford, Nuffield Coll., Oxford; Fellow, All Souls Coll. Oxford 1957–, Sub-Warden 1982–84, Sr Dean 1988–; QC (England and Wales) 1972, (Northern Ireland) 1988; Bencher, Gray's Inn 1986–; Dir (non-exec.) Dunlop Holdings Ltd 1973–80, The Wellcome Foundation 1983–94; mem. arbitral tribunal, US/UK Arbitration concerning Heathrow Airport user charges 1989–94, Univ. of Portsmouth Ind. Inquiry 1995; Chair. Oftel Advisory Body on Fair Trading in Telecommunications 1996–2000, Performing Rights Soc. Appeals Panel 1997–2001; Visiting Prof. Wissenschaftszentrum Berlin für Sozialforschung Jan.–March 1999; Pres. Oxford Union Soc. 1957; mem. Council British Inst. of Int. and Comparative Law 1987–2005; Africa Gen. Service Medal 1953. *Publications:* The Law of Restrictive Trading Agreements 1964, Comparative Law Casebook, Torts (with W. van Gerven) and other legal works. *Leisure interests:* porcelain, music. *Address:* All Souls College, Oxford, OX1 4AL;

Monckton Chambers, 1–2 Raymond Buildings, Gray's Inn, London, WC1R 5NR, England (office). *Telephone:* (1865) 279379 (Oxford); (20) 7405-7211 (office). *Fax:* (1865) 279299 (Oxford); (20) 7405-2084 (office). *E-mail:* chambers@monckton.co.uk (office). *Website:* www.monckton.co.uk (office).

LEVER, Sir Paul, KCMG, CMG, MA; British diplomatist (retd) and business executive; *Vice-President of the Council, Royal United Services Institute;* b. 31 March 1944; s. of John Morrison Lever and Doris Grace Lever (née Battey); m. Patricia Anne Ramsey 1990; ed St Paul's School, Queen's Coll., Oxford; Third Sec. FCO 1966–67; Third, then Second Sec., Embassy in Helsinki 1967–71; Second, then First Sec., UK Del. to NATO 1971–73; with FCO, London 1973–81; Asst Pvt. Sec. to Sec. of State for Foreign and Commonwealth Affairs 1978–81; Chef de Cabinet to Vice-Pres. of EEC 1981–85; Head of UN Dept, FCO 1985–86, Head of Defence Dept 1986–87, Security Policy Dept 1987–90; Amb. and Head of UK Del. to Conventional Arms Control Negotiations, Vienna 1990–92; Asst Under-Sec. of State, FCO 1992–94, Deputy Sec. Cabinet Office and Chair. Jt Intelligence Cttee 1994–96; Deputy Under-Sec. of State (Dir for EU and Econ. Affairs), FCO 1996–97; Amb. to Germany 1998–2003; Global Devt Dir RWE Thames Water PLC 2003–06 (co. sold to Kemble Water Ltd); mem. Bd of Dirs Königswinter 2003–; Chair. Royal United Services Inst. for Defence and Security Studies 2004–09, now Vice-Pres. of the Council; Hon. LLD (Birmingham) 2001. *Leisure interests:* walking, art deco pottery, the music of Sandy Denny. *Address:* Royal United Services Institute, 61 Whitehall, London, SW1A 2ET, England (office). *Telephone:* (20) 7747-2600 (office). *E-mail:* info@rusi.org (office). *Website:* www.rusi.org (office).

LEVETT, Michael John (Mike), BComm, FIA, FFA, FASSA; South African insurance executive; b. 6 June 1939, Cape Town; m. Mary Gillian Aston 1966; two s. one d.; ed Christian Brothers Coll., Cape Town, Univ. of Cape Town; joined Old Mutual Life Assurance Soc. 1959, Gen. Man. 1981–85, Man. Dir 1985–2001, Exec. Chair. 1990–2001, Chair. (non-exec.) 2001–05; Chair. South African Mutual Life Assurance Soc. 1990–99, Mutual & Federal Insurance Co. Ltd 1993–99, South Africa Growth Equities 1995–; Deputy Chair. Mutual & Federal Insurance Co. Ltd –2005; Dir, Central Africa Building Soc. 1985–2005, South African Breweries (now SABMiller) 1999–2004; Dir (non-exec.), Barloworld Ltd 1985–2009, Mutual & Federal Insurance Co. Ltd –2005, Nedbank Group Ltd (fmrly Nedcor Ltd) 1987–2004, Sasol 1991–2000, Old Mutual South Africa Trust plc 1994–; Trustee, World Wide Fund for Nature (South Africa) 1990–, Nelson Mandela Children's Fund 1994–, The Coll. of Medicine Foundation 1995–; Patron Free Market Foundation 1990–; Founding Patron The Children's Hospital Trust 1996–; Hon. DEconSc (Cape Town) 1997; Businessman of the Year, Sunday Times Business Times Top 100 Companies 1999. *Leisure interests:* skiing, tennis. *Address:* c/o Old Mutual PLC, 5th Floor, Millennium Bridge House, 2 Lambeth Hill, London, EC4V 4GG, England. *E-mail:* michael.levett@omg.co.uk.

LEVEY, Gerald Saul, AB, MD; American physician and academic; *Dean, David Geffen School of Medicine, University of California, Los Angeles;* b. 9 Jan. 1937, Jersey City, NJ; m. Barbara Ann Levey (née Cohen) 1961; two c.; ed Univ. of Medicine and Dentistry of New Jersey; intern, Jersey City Medical Center 1961–62, resident 1962–63; Postdoctoral Fellow, Dept of Biological Chem., Harvard Univ. Medical School 1963–65; Medical Resident, Mass Gen. Hosp., Boston 1965–66; Clinical Assoc., Clinical Endocrinology Br., Nat. Inst. of Arthritis and Metabolic Diseases, NIH, Bethesda, Md 1966–68; Clinical Assoc., Nat. Heart and Lung Inst. 1968–69, Sr Investigator 1969–70; Assoc. Prof. of Medicine, Univ. of Miami School of Medicine 1970–73, Prof. of Medicine 1973–79, also Howard Hughes Medical Inst. Investigator; Prof. and Chair. Dept of Medicine, Univ. of Pittsburgh School of Medicine 1979–91, also Physician-in-Chief, Presbyterian Univ. Hosp.; Sr Vice-Pres. for Medical and Scientific Affairs, Merck and Co. 1991–94; Prof. and Vice Chancellor, Medical Sciences, David Geffen School of Medicine, UCLA 1994–, also Provost of Medical Sciences and Dean; Co-Chair. Nat. Study of Internal Medicine Manpower; Fellow, ACP; fmr Pres. Asscn of Profs of Medicine; mem. Bd of Govs American Bd of Internal Medicine; mem. American Medical Asscn, Asscn of American Physicians, Soc. of Gen. and Internal Medicine, Southern Soc. for Clinical Investigation, Endocrine Soc., American Soc. for Clinical Investigation, American Fed. for Clinical Research, American Thyroid Asscn. *Address:* Office of the Dean, David Geffen School of Medicine, 12-138 CHS, Los Angeles, CA 90095-1722, USA. *Telephone:* (310) 825-5687 (office). *Fax:* (310) 206-2142 (office). *E-mail:* glevey@mednet.ucla.edu (office). *Website:* dgsom.healthsciences.ucla.edu/deans-site/levey (office).

LEVI, Arrigo, PhD; Italian journalist and political writer; b. 17 July 1926, Modena; s. of Enzo Levi and Ida Levi (née Donati); m. Carmela Lenci 1952; one d.; ed Univs of Buenos Aires and Bologna; refugee in Argentina 1942–46; Negev Brigade, Israeli Army 1948–49; BBC European Services 1951–53; London Corresp. Gazzetta del Popolo and Corriere d'Informazione 1952–59; Moscow Corresp. Corriere della Sera 1960–62; news anchorman on Italian State Television 1966–68; special corresp. La Stampa 1969–73, Ed. in Chief 1973–78, Special Corresp. 1978; columnist on int. affairs, The Times 1979–83; Leader Writer, Corriere della Sera 1988–; Adviser for External Relations to two Italian Pres. Carlo Azeglio Ciampi and Giorgio Napolitano 1998–2007; Premio Trento 1987, Premio Luigi Barzini 1995, Premio Ischia Internazionale di Giornalismo 2001, Guidarello Prize 2006. *Publications include:* L'economia degli Stati Uniti oggi 1966, Il potere in Russia 1965, La televisione all'italiana 1969, Viaggio fra gli economisti 1970, PCI, la lunga marcia verso il potere 1971, Un'idea dell'Italia 1983, La Democrazia nell'Italia che cambia 1984, Intervista sulla Dc 1986, Noi: gli italiani 1988, Tra Est e Ovest 1990, Yitzhak Rabin 1996, Le due fedi 1996, La vecchiaia può attendere 1997, Rapporto sul Medio Oriente 1998, Russia del '900 1999, Dialoghi di fine Millennio 1999, Dialoghi sulla fede 2000, America Latina: Memorie e ritorni 2004, Cinque discorsi tra due secoli 2004. *Address:* c/o Palazzo Del Quirinale, 00186 Rome, Italy.

LEVI, Isaac, PhD; American philosopher and academic; *John Dewey Professor Emeritus of Philosophy, Columbia University;* b. 30 June 1930, New York, NY; s. of Eliezer Asher Levi and Eva Lunenfeld; m. Judith R. Levi 1951; two c.; ed New York and Columbia Univs; Asst Prof. of Philosophy, Case Western Reserve Univ. 1957–62, The City Coll. of New York 1962–64; Assoc. Prof. then Full Prof. of Philosophy, Case Western Reserve Univ. 1964–67, Chair. Dept 1968–70; Prof. of Philosophy, Columbia Univ. 1970–, Chair. Dept 1973–76, 1989–91, apptd John Dewey Prof. of Philosophy 1992, now Emer.; Visiting Fellow, Corpus Christi Coll. Cambridge, UK 1973, Darwin Coll. 1989, All Souls Coll. Oxford, UK 1988, Inst. of

Advanced Study, Princeton, Hebrew Univ. of Jerusalem 1994, Wolfson Coll. Cambridge, UK 1997; mem. American Acad. of Arts and Sciences; Dr hc (Lund) 1988; Guggenheim Fellow, Fulbright Scholar; Univ. of Helsinki Medal and other awards. *Publications:* For the Sake of the Argument 1966, 1996, Gambling with Truth 1967, Enterprise of Knowledge 1980, Decisions and Revisions 1984, Hard Choices 1986, The Fixation of Belief and its Undoing 1991, For the Sake of the Argument 1996, The Covenant of Reason 1997, Mild Contradiction 2004. *Address:* 25 Claremont Avenue, New York, NY 10027, USA (home). *Telephone:* (212) 864-3615 (home). *E-mail:* levi@columbia.edu (office). *Website:* philosophy.columbia .edu/directories/faculty/isaac-levi (office); (office).

LEVI, Noel, CBE, BA; Papua New Guinea politician and diplomatist; b. (Wasangula Noel Levi), 6 Feb. 1942, Nonopai, Kavieng; m. Josepha Muna Levi; two s. two d.; ed Scots Coll., Queensland, Papua New Guinea Admin. Coll., Cromwell Coll. Univ. of Queensland and Univ. of Papua New Guinea; patrol officer Dept of Dist Admin., Papua New Guinea 1967, later Asst Dist Commr; Asst Sec. Dept of Chief Minister 1973; Sec. Dept of Defence 1974; Minister of Foreign Affairs 1980; Amb. to People's Repub. of China 1987; High Commr to UK (also accred to Israel, Zimbabwe and Egypt) 1991; Sec., Dept of the Prime Minister and Nat. Exec. Council 1995; Sec.-Gen. Pacific Islands Forum Secr. 1998–2003; currently Chair. New Ireland Tourism Bureau. *Leisure interests:* reading, walking, watching rugby. *Address:* New Ireland Tourism Bureau, Cnr Coronation Drive and Tanga Street, PO Box 419, Kavieng, New Ireland Province, Papua New Guinea (office); House No. 4, Forum Secretariat Compound, Ratu Sukuna Road, Suva, Fiji (home). *Telephone:* (675) 9842441 (office); (679) 3306535 (home). *Fax:* (675) 9842254 (office). *E-mail:* nitb@global.net.pg (office). *Website:* www.newirelandtourism.org .pg (office).

LEVI, Yoel, MA; Romanian/American conductor; *Principal Conductor, Orchestre national d'Ile de France;* b. 16 Aug. 1950, Romania; m.; ed Tel-Aviv and Jerusalem Acads of Music, Guildhall School of Music, London; grew up in Israel; studied under Mendi Rodan, Franco Ferrara, Kiril Kondrashin; won First Prize Conductors' Int. Competition Besançon, France 1978; Asst to Lorin Maazel Cleveland Orchestra for six years, Resident Conductor 1980–84; Music Dir Atlanta Symphony Orchestra (ASO) 1988–2000, extensive European tour 1991, Music Dir Emer. 2000–; Principal Guest Conductor Israel Philharmonic Orchestra, US tour 2004; Music Adviser to Flemish Radio Orchestra; Principal Conductor Orchestre Nat. d'Ile de France 2005–; frequent guest conductor of orchestras throughout N America, Europe and the Far East; conducted Stockholm Philharmonic at Nobel Prize Ceremony 1991; performed at Opening Ceremonies of Centennial Olympic Games 1996; apptd first Music Adviser to Israel Festival for 1997/98 seasons; opera conducting debut La Fanciulla del West at Teatro Comunale, Florence 1997; has also conducted Carmen at Lyric Opera of Chicago, Makropoulus Case by Janacek in Prague, Puccini's Edgar with Orchestra Nat. de France (released as live performance on CD by Radio France), with ASO: Mozart's Magic Flute, The Abduction from the Seraglio, Bartok's Bluebeard's Castle; Distinguished Visiting Prof., Univ. of Georgia School of Music; Chevalier des Arts et des Lettres 2001; Hon. DFA (Oglethorpe Univ., Atlanta) 1997; Best Orchestra of the Year (awarded to ASO), Int. Classical Music Awards 1991–92. *Recordings:* more than 40 recordings on different labels with various orchestras, including Cleveland Orchestra, London Philharmonic, Philharmonia Orchestra, Atlanta Symphony Orchestra, of music by Barber, Beethoven, Brahms, Copland, Dohnanyi, Dvorak, Hindemith, Kodaly, Mahler, Mendelssohn, Mussorgsky, Nielsen, Prokofiev, Puccini, Ravel, Rossini, Saint-Saens, Schoenberg, Shostakovich, Sibelius, Stravinsky and Tchaikovsky. *Address:* La maison de l'Orchestre national d'Ile de France, 19 rue des Ecoles, 94140 Alfortville, France (office). *Telephone:* 1-43-68-76-00 (office). *Fax:* 1-41-79-03-50 (office). *E-mail:* courrier@ orchestre-ile.com (office). *Website:* www.orchestre-ile.com (office).

LEVIE, Simon Hijman; Dutch art historian (retd); b. 17 Jan. 1925, Rheden; m. Mary Levie-Lion 1955; one s. two d.; ed Univ. of Basel, Switzerland; Keeper, Central Museum, Utrecht; Dir, Historical Museum, Amsterdam; Dir Rijksmuseum Amsterdam 1975–89; Dir Simart Art Consultancy, Amsterdam 1990–2010. *Address:* Minervalaan 70 II, 1077 PG Amsterdam, The Netherlands. *Telephone:* (20) 6718895. *E-mail:* simart@hetnet.nl.

LEVIN, Carl, JD; American politician; *Senator from Michigan;* b. 28 June 1934, Detroit, Mich.; s. of Saul R. Levin and Bess Levin (née Levinson); m. Barbara Halpern 1961; three d.; ed Detroit Central High School, Swarthmore Coll., Pa and Harvard Law School; Mich. Asst Attorney Gen. and Gen. Counsel for Mich. Civil Rights Comm. 1964–67; Special Asst Attorney Gen. and Chief Appellate Attorney for Defender's Office of Legal Aid and Defender Assoc. of Detroit 1968–69; elected to Detroit City Council 1969, re-elected as City Council Pres. 1973; Senator from Michigan 1979–, Chair. Armed Services Cttee 2001–03, 2007–, mem. Governmental Affairs Cttee; Democrat; Christian A. Herter Award, WorldBoston 2002, Distinguished Public Service Award, Sec. of the Navy 2003, Harry S. Truman Award, Nat. Guard Asscn 2004, Stewardship Award, Nat. Marine Sanctuary 2005, one of TIME's 10 Best Senators 2006, Four Freedoms Medal, Franklin and Eleanor Roosevelt Foundation 2007, Global Service Award, World Affairs Council 2007. *Address:* 269 Russell Senate Office Building, Washington, DC 20510-2202, USA (office). *Telephone:* (202) 224-6221 (office). *Fax:* (202) 224-1388 (office). *Website:* levin.senate.gov (office).

LEVIN, Gerald Manuel, BA, LLB; American fmr media executive; *Presiding Director, Moonview Sanctuary;* b. 6 May 1939, Philadelphia, Pa; s. of David Levin and Pauline Schantzer; m. 1st Carol S. Needleman 1959 (divorced 1970), two s. (one deceased), one d.; m. 2nd Barbara Riley 1970, one s. one d.; m. 3rd Laurie Perlman 2005; ed Haverford Coll. and Univ. of Pennsylvania; Assoc., Simpson, Thatcher & Bartlett, New York 1963–67; Gen. Man. and COO, Devt and Resources Corpn, New York 1967–71; Rep., Int. Basic Economy Corpn, Tehran 1971–72; Vice-Pres. Programming, Home Box Office, New York 1972–73, Pres. and CEO 1973–76, Chair. and CEO 1976–79; Group Vice-Pres. (Video), Time Inc. New York 1979–84, Exec. Vice-Pres. 1984–88, Vice-Chair. 1988–90, Vice-Chair. Time-Warner Inc. 1990–92, Jt CEO 1992–93, CEO and Chair. 1992–2001, CEO AOL Time Warner (created after merger of Time Warner and American Online 2000) 2001–02 (retd); Presiding Dir Moonview Sanctuary (spiritual healing firm) 2004–; Chair. StartUp Health 2011–; mem. Bd of Dirs Organized Wisdom; Hon. LLD (Texas Coll.) 1985, (Middlebury Coll.) 1994, Hon. LHD (Univ. of Denver) 1995;

Media Person of the Year Award, Cannes Lions Int. Advertising Festival 2001. *Leisure interests:* reading, jogging. *Address:* Moonview Sanctuary, PO Box 1518, Santa Monica, CA 90406, USA (office). *Telephone:* (866) 601-0601 (office). *E-mail:* glevin@moonviewsanctuary.com (office). *Website:* www.moonviewsanctuary.com (office).

LEVIN, Richard Charles, BA, BLitt, PhD; American economist, academic and fmr university administrator; *CEO, Coursera Inc.;* b. 7 April 1947, San Francisco, Calif.; s. of Derek Levin and Phylys Goldstein; m. Jane Aries 1968; two s. two d.; ed Lowell High School, San Francisco, Stanford and Yale Univs and Merton Coll., Oxford, UK; Asst Prof. of Econs, Yale Univ. 1974–79, Assoc. Prof. 1979–82, Prof. of Econs and Man. 1982–92, Dir Grad. Studies in Econs 1984–86, Chair. Dept of Econs 1987–92, Frederick William Beinecke Prof. of Econs 1992–, Dean, Grad. School 1992–93, Pres. Yale Univ. 1993–2013; CEO Coursear Inc. (online learning co.) 2014–; Fellow, Merton Coll. Oxford 1996; mem. Yale-New Haven Hosp. Bd of Trustees 1993, Yale-New Haven Health Services Corpn Inc. 1993; mem. Bd of Dirs Hewlett Foundation, Lucent Technologies, Satmetrix; Trustee, Hewlett Foundation, Univs Research Asscn 1994–99; mem. American Econ. Asscn, Econometric Soc.; Fellow, American Acad. of Arts and Sciences; Hon. LLD (Princeton) 1993, (Harvard) 1994; Hon. DCL (Oxford) 1998. *Publication:* The Work of the University 2003. *Address:* Coursera Inc., 1975 El Camino Real West, Mountain View, CA 94040, USA (office). *Website:* www.coursera.org (office).

LEVIN, Richard I., BS, MD; American physician, academic, university administrator and foundation president; *President and CEO, Arnold P. Gold Foundation;* b. 28 July 1948, Long Branch, NJ; s. of Jack Levin and Sally Stark; m. Jane Bressman 1970; two c.; ed Peddie School, Yale Univ., New York Univ. (NYU) School of Medicine, Cornell Univ. Medical Coll.; Postdoctoral Fellowship, Cornell Univ. Medical Coll. 1979–83; Founder, Vice-Pres. and Medical Dir Q-Med, Inc. 1983–2008; practised and taught medicine for 35 years at NYU and Bellevue Hosp. Center, New York City; Prof. of Medicine, NYU 1996–2006, Prof. Emer. 2006–, also Vice-Dean for Educ., Faculty and Academic Affairs, NYU School of Medicine; Vice-Prin. (Health Affairs), McGill Univ., Montreal, also Dean, Faculty of Medicine 2006–11, Prof. Emer. 2013–; Pres. and CEO Arnold P. Gold Foundation 2012–; Clinical Investigator, Nat. Heart, Lung, and Blood Inst.; consultant to Liposome Co., Princeton 1988–; mem. American Fed. for Medical Research (Councillor 1986–88), Harvey Soc., New York Heart Asscn, Fed. of American Socs for Experimental Biology, American Osteopathic Asscn; Fellow, American Coll. of Physicians, American Coll. of Cardiology, American Heart Asscn (AHA, Clinician Scientist), Canadian Acad. of Health Science 2011; AHA Beller Research Award, AHA Mission Achievement Award, David L. Johnston Award, McGill Univ., Aaron Diamond Res Award, Dana Award. *Publications:* more than 75 publs in int. journals. *Address:* APGF, 619 Palisade Avenue, Englewood Cliff, NJ 07632, USA (office). *Telephone:* (201) 567-7999 (office). *Fax:* (201) 567-7880 (office). *E-mail:* rlevin@gold-foundation.org (office). *Website:* www.humanism-in-medicine.org (office).

LEVIN, Simon Asher, PhD; American mathematician, ecologist and academic; *George M. Moffett Professor of Biology, Department of Ecology and Evolutionary Biology and Director, The Center for BioComplexity, Princeton University;* b. 22 April 1941, Baltimore, Md; s. of Theodore S. Levin and Clara G. Levin; m. Carole Lotte Leiffer; one s. one d.; ed Johns Hopkins Univ., Baltimore, Univ. of Maryland, College Park; Asst Prof., Cornell Univ. 1965–70, Assoc. Prof. 1971–77, Chair. Section of Ecology and Systematics, Div. of Biological Sciences 1974–79, Prof. of Applied Math. and Ecology 1977–92, Charles A. Alexander Prof. of Biological Sciences 1985–92, Adjunct Prof. 1992–, Dir Ecosystems Research Center 1980–87, Dir Center for Environmental Research 1987–90; Affiliated Faculty, Program in Applied and Computational Math., Princeton Univ. 1992–, George M. Moffett Prof. of Biology 1992–, Affiliated Faculty, Princeton Environmental Inst. 1993–, Dir Princeton Environmental Inst. 1992–98, Dir The Center for BioComplexity 2001–, Participating Faculty, Biophysics Program 2009–; numerous visiting positions including Univ. of Maryland, College Park 1968, Univ. of British Columbia, Vancouver 1979–80, Weizmann Inst., Rehovot, Israel 1977, 1980, Univ. of Kyoto, Japan 1983–84, Colorado State Univ. (Visiting Distinguished Ecologist) 1987, Stanford Univ., Calif. 1988, All Souls Coll., Oxford, UK (Visiting Fellow) 1988, Inst. for Advanced Study, Princeton 1999, 2008–09, Univ. of Miami 2004–05, Univ. of California, Irvine 2007, 2009; Visiting Miller Research Prof., Univ. of California, Berkeley 2003, Univ. of Miami 2004–05; Chair. Council Int. Inst. for Applied Systems Analysis (IIASA), Laxenburg, Austria 2003–08, (Vice-Chair. 2009–12), US Nat. Cttee for IIASA, The Nat. Academies 2003–; mem. numerous advisory bds including Biodiversity Science and Educ. Initiative (BSEI), Smithsonian Inst. 2005–, DIMACS, Rutgers Univ. 2008–11, Center for Social and Econ. Dynamics, Brookings Inst. 2008–, Miller Inst. for Basic Research in Science, Univ. of California, Berkeley 2009–12; mem. Science Bd Inst. for Medical BioMathematics, Bene Ataroth, Israel 1999–, Santa Fe Inst., NM 1991–99, 2001–; Ed.-in-Chief Encyclopedia of Biodiversity, Online Edn 2005–; Co-Man. Ed. Monographs in Population Biology 1992–, Complexity Series 1992–; mem. Editorial Bd numerous journals including Evolutionary Theory 1976–, Mathematical and Computer Modelling 1979–, Applied Mathematics Letters 1987–, Mathematical Biosciences 1987–, Conservation Ecology 1995–, Issues in Ecology 1995–, Journal of Biomathematics (China) 1999–, Journal of Mathematical Biology 1995–; mem. Advisory Bd severala journals including Journal of Environmental and Ecological Statistics 1992–, Ecological Research 1996–, Ecological Complexity 2004–, Mathematical Biosciences and Engineering 2004–; Fellow, American Acad. of Arts and Sciences 1992, AAAS 1992, Ecological Soc. of America 2012; mem. American Inst. of Biological Sciences, American Soc. of Naturalists, British Ecological Soc., Ecological Soc. of America (Pres. 1990–91), Soc. for Industrial and Applied Math., Soc. for Math. Biology (Pres. 1987–89, Past Pres. and Vice-Pres. 1989–91), Soc. for the Study of Evolution, NAS 2000, American Philosophical Soc. 2003; Foreign mem. Istituto Veneto di Scienze, Lettere ed Arti, Venice 2008; Beijer Fellow 2007; Fellow, Soc. for Industrial and Applied Math. 2009; Hon. Ed. several journals; Hon. mem. Lund (Sweden) Ecological Soc. 1999, Eastern Europe Soc. of Math. Ecology 1995, Asian Math. Ecology Soc. 1995, World Innovation Foundation 2003; Hon. DSc (Eastern Michigan Univ.) 1990, (Michigan State Univ.) 2009; Hon. DHumLitt (Whittier Coll.) 2004; numerous awards including MacArthur Award, Ecological Soc. of America 1988, Distinguished Statistical Ecologist Award, Int. Asscn for Ecology 1994, Distinguished Service Citation, Ecological Soc. of America 1998,

First Okubo Lifetime Achievement Award, Soc. for Math. Biology and Japanese Soc. for Theoretical Biology 2001, Medallion of Université de Montpellier 2004, A. H. Heineken Prize for Environmental Sciences, Royal Netherlands Acad. of Arts and Sciences 2004, Kyoto Prize in Basic Sciences, Inamori Foundation, Japan 2005, SIAM I.E. Block Community Lecture Award 2006, Distinguished Scientist Award, American Inst. of Biological Sciences 2007, Margalef Prize for Ecology 2010, Eminent Ecologist Award, Ecological Soc. of America 2010. *Publications:* numerous publs on modelling of ecological systems, dynamics of populations and communities, spatial heterogeneity and problem of scale, evolutionary, math. and theoretical ecology. *Address:* Department of Ecology and Evolutionary Biology, 203 Eno Hall, Princeton University, Princeton, NJ 08544-1003, USA (office). *Telephone:* (609) 258-6880 (office). *Fax:* (609) 258-6819 (office). *E-mail:* slevin@princeton.edu (office). *Website:* www.eeb.princeton.edu/~slevin (office).

LEVINE, Alan J., BS, JD; American lawyer, entertainment industry executive and lecturer; *Managing Partner, Canon Media Partners, LLC;* b. 8 March 1947, Los Angeles, Calif.; s. of Phil Levine and Shirley Lauber; m. Judy Birnbaum 1973; two c.; ed Univ. of Southern California (USC); called to the California Bar 1972, US Dist Court (South Dist) Calif. 1972; Partner, Pacht, Ross, Warne, Bernhard & Sears, LA 1971–78, Schiff, Hirsch & Schreiber, Beverly Hills, Calif. 1978–80, Armstrong, Hirsch & Levine, LA 1980–89; Pres. and COO SONY Pictures Entertainment Inc., Culver City, Calif. 1989–96, Chair. 1994–96, entertainment and media consultant 1996–99; Of Counsel, Ziffren, Brittenham, Branca & Fischer (now Ziffren, Brittenham, Branca, Fischer, Gilbert-Lurie, Stiffleman & Cook LLP), LA from 1999; Founder J.P. Morgan Entertainment Advisors 2007 (became Canon Media Partners, LLC), Man. Partner 2010–; mem. Bd of Councilors, School of Cinema-TV; fmr mem. Bd of Dirs, DreamWorks Studios, Castle Rock Entertainment, and several other civic, charitable and education bds and cttees, including Frank Sinatra Foundation, Bd Govs, Cedars-Sinai Medical Center, Los Angeles, Bd of Councilors, USC School of Cinematic Arts and USC Law School, Roundtable of the Museum of Radio & Television; has lectured at numerous entertainment and media confs at Harvard Business School, Howard Univ., UCLA and USC; mem. Acad. of Motion Picture Arts & Sciences, Acad. of Television Arts & Sciences. *Address:* Gould School of Law, University of Southern California, 699 Exposition Boulevard, Los Angeles, CA 90089 (office). Canon Media Partners, LLC, 100 North Crescent Drive, Suite 300, Beverly Hills, CA 90210, USA. *Telephone:* (213) 740-7331 (Los Angeles) (office); (310) 385-3676 (Beverly Hills). *Fax:* (310) 432-5000 (Beverly Hills). *E-mail:* alevine@law.usc.edu (office). *Website:* weblaw.usc.edu/contact/contactInfo.cfm?detailID=71043 (office); www.canonmp.com.

LEVINE, James; American musician, conductor and pianist; *Music Director, Metropolitan Opera;* b. 23 June 1943, Cincinnati, Ohio; s. of Lawrence M. Levine and Helen Levine (née Goldstein); ed Walnut Hills High School, Cincinnati, The Juilliard School, New York; Asst Conductor, Cleveland Orchestra 1964–70; Prin. Conductor, Metropolitan Opera, New York 1973–, Music Dir 1976–, Artistic Dir 1986–2004; Music Dir Ravinia Festival 1973–93, Cincinnati May Festival 1974–78; Chief Conductor, Munich Philharmonic 1999–2004; Music Dir UBS Verbier Festival Youth Orchestra 2000–04; Music Dir Boston Symphony Orchestra 2004–11; regular appearances as conductor and pianist in Europe and the USA with orchestras including Vienna Philharmonic, Berlin Philharmonic, Chicago Symphony, Philadelphia Orchestra, Philharmonia, Dresden Staatskapelle, Boston Symphony, New York Philharmonic, Israel Philharmonic, Salzburg and Bayreuth Festivals; conducted Metropolitan Opera premieres of I Vespri Siciliani, Stiffelio, I Lombardi (Verdi), The Rise and Fall of the City of Mahagonny (Weill), Lulu (Berg), Porgy and Bess (Gershwin), Oedipus Rex (Stravinsky), Idomeneo, La Clemenza di Tito (Mozart), Erwartung, Moses und Aron (Schönberg), La Cenerentola (Rossini), Benvenuto Cellini (Berlioz), The Ghosts of Versailles (Corigliano) (world premiere), The Great Gatsby (Harbison) (world premiere); Conductor of Salzburg Festival premieres of Offenbach's Les contes d'Hoffmann 1980 and Schönberg's Moses und Aron 1987; conducted Munich Philharmonic Orchestra at the BBC Proms 2002, Boston Symphony 2007; Dr hc (Univ. of Cincinnati, New England Conservatory, Northwestern Univ., State Univ. of New York, The Juilliard School); Grammy Awards for audio recordings of Orff's Carmina Burana, Mahler's Symphony No. 7, Brahms' A German Requiem, Verdi's La Traviata (film soundtrack), Wagner's Das Rheingold, Die Walküre, Götterdämmerung, Strauss' Ariadne auf Naxos, Ravel's Daphnis et Chloé; Cultural Award of New York City 1980, Smetana Medal 1987, Musical America's Musician of the Year Award, Gold Medal, Nat. Inst. of Social Sciences 1996, Nat. Medal of Arts 1997, Anton Seidl Award 1997, Lotus Award 1997, Kennedy Center Honors 2002, World Econ. Forum Crystal Award 2003, Metropolitan Opera Guild Opera News Award 2006, Nat. Endowment for the Arts Opera Award 2008. *Recordings:* over 100 albums of symphonic works, chamber music, lieder and song recitals, solo piano music and 36 complete operas, including Wagner: Der Ring Des Nibelungen (Grammy Award for Best Opera Recording 2013). *Address:* Metropolitan Opera, Lincoln Center, New York, NY 10023, USA (office). *Telephone:* (212) 799-3100 (office). *Website:* www.metopera.org (office).

LEVINE, Philip, BA, AM, MFA; American poet, writer and academic (retd); b. 10 Jan. 1928, Detroit, Mich.; m. Frances Artley 1954; three s.; ed Wayne State Univ., Detroit, Univ. of Iowa, studied with John Berryman; worked in several automobile mfg plants, Detroit; Instructor, California State Univ. at Fresno 1958–69, Prof. of English 1969–92; Elliston Prof. of Poetry, Univ. of Cincinnati 1976; Poet-in-Residence, ANU, Canberra 1978; Visiting Prof. of Poetry, Columbia Univ. 1978, 1981, 1984, New York Univ. 1984, 1991, Brown Univ. 1985; Poet Laureate of the US 2011–12; Chair. Literature Panel, Nat. Endowment for the Arts 1985; NEA grants 1969, 1976, 1981, 1987; Guggenheim Fellowships 1974, 1981; mem. American Acad. of Arts and Letters, Acad. of American Poets (Chancellor 2000–); San Francisco Foundation Joseph Henry Jackson Award 1961, Frank O'Hara Prizes 1973, 1974, American Acad. of Arts and Letters Award of Merit 1974, Levinson Prize 1974, Univ. of Chicago Harriet Monroe Memorial Prize for Poetry 1976, Leonore Marshall Award for Best American Book of Poems 1976, American Book Award for Poetry 1979, Nat. Book Critics Circle Prize 1979, American Library Asscn Notable Book Award 1979, New England Poetry Soc. Golden Rose Award 1985, Ruth Lilly Award 1987, New York Univ. Elmer Holmes Bobst Award 1990, Commonwealth Club of California Silver Medal in Poetry 1992, 2000. *Publications:* poetry: On the Edge 1961, Silent in America: Vivas for Those Who Failed 1965, Not This Pig 1968, 5 Detroits 1970, Thistles: A Poem of Sequence

1970, Pili's Wall 1971, Red Dust 1971, They Feed, They Lion 1972, 1933 1974, New Season 1975, On the Edge and Over: Poems Old, Lost, and New 1976, The Names of the Lost 1976, 7 Years from Somewhere 1979, Ashes: Poems New and Old 1979, One for the Rose 1981, Selected Poems 1984, Sweet Will 1985, A Walk with Tom Jefferson 1988, New Selected Poems 1991, What Work Is (Nat. Book Award for Poetry) 1991, The Simple Truth: Poems (Pulitzer Prize in Poetry 1995) 1994, The Mercy 1995, Breath 2004, News of the World 2009; non-fiction: Don't Ask (interviews) 1979, Earth, Stars, and Writers (with others, lectures) 1992, The Bread of Time: Toward an Autobiography 1994; contrib. to many anthologies and reviews. *Address:* 4549 North Van Ness Blvd, Fresno, CA 93704, USA (home). *Telephone:* (209) 226-3361 (home). *E-mail:* pl24@nyu.edu (home). *Website:* www.loc.gov.poetry.

LEVINGSTON, Gen. Roberto Marcelo; Argentine politician and army officer; b. 10 Jan. 1920, San Luis; s. of Guillermo Levingston and Carmen Laborda; m. Betty Nelly Andrés 1943; two s. (one deceased) one d.; ed Pius IX Coll., Nat. Mil. Coll., Army Intelligence School, Escuela Superior de Guerra and Center for High Mil. Studies; entered army as cadet, Nat. Mil. Coll. 1938, Sub-Lt 1941, Brig.-Gen. 1966; Army Information Officer 1947–50; mem. Gen. Staff 1951–57; Prof., Escuela Superior de Guerra 1958–62; Head of Army Information Services 1963–64; Dir-Gen. Lemos School of Logistics 1965–66; Head of Intelligence of Jt Chiefs of Staff 1967–68; Mil. Attaché Army Del. to Interamerican Defense Bd and Pres. Special Comm. on Acquisitions in USA 1969–70; Pres. and Prime Minister of Argentina 1970–71; Pres. Circle of Studies of Nat. Argentine Movt. *Publications:* political and military works. *Leisure interests:* reading of all kinds, particularly on politics, economics and military subjects, music and sport. *Address:* 11 de Septiembre 1735-17 A, Buenos Aires, Argentina. *Telephone:* 782-4433 (home).

LEVINSOHN, James, BA, MPA, PhD; American economist and academic; *Director, Jackson Institute of Global Affairs, Yale University;* ed Williams Coll., Woodrow Wilson School, Princeton Univ.; joined faculty of Univ. of Michigan 1987, becoming Assoc. Dean, Gerald R. Ford School of Public Policy 2003–07, also J. Ira and Nicki Harris Family Prof. of Public Policy and Prof. of Econs; Visiting Prof., Cowles Foundation, Yale Univ. 2008; Charles W. Goodyear Prof. in Global Affairs, Prof. of Econs and Man. and Dir, Jackson Inst. of Global Affairs, Yale Univ. 2010–; fmr Visiting Prof., Univ. of Cape Town, Tel-Aviv Univ.; fmr Visiting Fellow, Inst. for Int. Econ. Studies, Stockholm; Nat. Fellow, Hoover Inst., Stanford Univ.; served on editorial bds of numerous econs publs, including American Economic Review, Review of Economics and Statistics. *Address:* Office of the Director, Jackson Institute of Global Affairs, Yale University, Rosenkranz Hall, 115 Prospect Street, PO Box 208206, New Haven, CT 06520, USA (office). *Telephone:* (203) 432-6253 (office). *E-mail:* jackson.institute@yale.edu (office). *Website:* jackson.yale.edu (office).

LEVINSON, Arthur D., BS, PhD; American biochemist and business executive; *Chairman, Apple Inc.;* b. 31 March 1950, Seattle, Wash.; s. of Sol Levinson and Malvina Levinson (née Lindsay); m. Rita May Liff 1978; two c.; ed Univ. of Washington, Princeton Univ.; Postdoctoral Fellow, NIH 1972–77, Univ. of California, San Francisco 1977, American Cancer Soc. 1978–80; Sr Scientist, Genentech Inc. 1980–83, Staff Scientist 1983–87, Dir Cell Genetics Dept 1987–89, Vice-Pres. Research Tech. 1989–90, Vice-Pres. Research 1990–92, Sr Vice-Pres. Research 1992–93, Sr Vice-Pres. Research & Devt 1993–95, Pres. and CEO Genentech Inc. 1995–99, Chair. and CEO 1999–2009, Chair. 2009–; Chair. Apple Inc. 2011–; mem. Editorial Bd Virology 1984–87, Molecular Biology and Medicine 1986–89, Molecular and Cellular Biology 1987–96, Journal of Virology 1988–91; mem. AAAS, New York Acad. of Sciences, Pharmaceutical Research & Mfrs of America (Dir 1997–2001), Biotechnology Industry Org. 1995–2000, American Soc. of Biochemistry & Molecular Biology, American Soc. of Microbiology; Fellow, American Acad. of Arts and Sciences; numerous awards, including Salk Translational Medicine Award, Univ. of California, San Diego 1999, James Madison Medal, Princeton Univ. 2006, Biotechnology Heritage Award, Chemical Heritage Foundation/Biotechnology Industry Org. 2010, Margaret Foti Award, American Asscn for Cancer Research 2011, Cold Spring Harbor Laboratory Double Helix Medal Honoree 2012. *Publications include:* author or co-author of more than 80 scientific articles; named inventor on 11 US patents. *Address:* Apple Inc., 1 Infinite Loop, Cupertino, CA 95014, USA (office). *Telephone:* (408) 996-1010 (office). *Fax:* (408) 974-2113 (office). *E-mail:* media.help@apple.com (office). *Website:* www.apple.com (office).

LEVINSON, Barry; American screenwriter, film director and producer; b. 6 April 1942, Baltimore, Md; m. 1st Valerie Curtin 1975 (divorced); m. 2nd Diana Rhodes; ed American Univ.; fmrly wrote and acted on TV comedy show in LA; later worked on network TV; wrote and appeared, The Carol Burnett Show; worked on film scripts for Silent Movie and High Anxiety (with Mel Brooks q.v.); f. Baltimore Pictures, Inc. and The Levinson/Fontana Co. (Exec. Producer); Hon. DFA (American Univ.) 1999; ShoWest Director of the Year Award 1998, named one of Variety Winners 'Billion Dollar Directors' 1998, Creative Achievement Award, 13th Annual American Comedy Awards 1999, ACE Golden Eddie Filmmaker of the Year Award 2002. *Actor:* High Anxiety 1977, Rain Man 1988, Quiz Show 1994, Bee Movie (voice) 2007. *Writer:* Diner, Tin Men, Avalon; co-wrote screenplays (with Valerie Curtin) for And Justice for All, Inside Moves, Best Friends, Unfaithfully Yours, Toys, Liberty Heights. *Films directed:* Diner 1982, The Natural 1984, Young Sherlock Holmes 1985, Tin Men 1987, Good Morning Vietnam 1987, Rain Man (Academy Award for Best Picture 1988, Academy Award for Best Dir 1988, Directors Guild Award for Best Dir 1988) 1988, Disclosure 1994; directed and produced Avalon (Writers Guild Award for Best Screenplay 1989) 1990, Bugsy (Golden Globe Award for Best Picture 1991) 1991, Toys 1992, Jimmy Hollywood (dir, writer) 1994, Sleepers 1996, Wag the Dog 1997, Sphere 1998, Liberty Heights 2000, An Everlasting Piece 2001, Bandits 2001, Envy 2004, Man of the Year 2006, What Just Happened? 2008. *Television includes:* writer for Tim Conway Comedy Hour, The Marty Feldman Comedy Machine, The Carol Burnett Show (Emmy Awards for TV Comedy Writing 1974, 1975); exec. producer: Harry, 30 Minutes of Investigative Ticking, Diner, Homicide: Life on the Street (series) (Emmy Award for Best Dir 1993, Peabody Award 1993, 1995, 1997, Writers Guild Award 1994, 1995, The Nancy Susan Reynolds Award for Outstanding Portrayal of Sexual Responsibility in a Dramatic Series 1996, The Prism Commendation from the Nat. Inst. Inst. on Drug Use and The Entertainment Industries Council 1997, DGA

Award for Outstanding Directorial Achievement for Dramatic Series 1998, TCA Award for Program of the Year and Drama of the Year 1998, Emmy Award for Best Male Actor in a Drama Series 1998, Emmy Award for Best Casting in a Drama Series 1998, Humanitas Award 1999), Oz, The Beat 2000, Shot in the Heart 2001, Baseball Wives 2002, Possession 2002, Analyze That 2002, Deliver Us from Eva 2003, Strip Search 2004, Envy 2004, The Jury (series) 2004, The Bedford Diaries (series) 2006. *Publications:* Levinson on Levinson 1992, Sixty-Six (novel) 2003. *Address:* Baltimore Pictures, Inc., 8306 Wilshire Boulevard, PMB 1012, Beverly Hills, CA 90211, USA (office). *Website:* www.levinson.com (office).

LEVITIN, Igor Yevgenyevich; Russian politician and government official; *Presidential Aide;* b. 21 Feb. 1952; m.; one d.; ed Mil. Acad. of Rear Services and Transportation; served in Soviet armed forces in Odessa 1970–80, with Armies Southern Div. 1980–83, Mil. Commdt of Urgal station and Baikal 1983–85, Mil. Commdt and Deputy Head of Moscow Mil. Railway Communications Service 1985–94; Head of Transport Dept, Phoenix-Trans Co. 1995–98; Head of Railway Dept, worked for Severstaltrans 1996–2004, Deputy Dir 1998–2004; Minister of Transport 2004–12; Presidential Aide 2012–; Order 'For Merit to the Fatherland', 4th Class, then 3rd Class, Medal 'For the Development of Railways'. *Address:* c/o Presidential Executive Office, 103132 Moscow, Staraya Square 4 (office). *Telephone:* (495) 925-35-81 (office). *Fax:* (495) 206-07-66 (office). *E-mail:* president@gov .ru (office). *Website:* www.kremlin.ru (office); www.state.kremlin.ru (office).

LEVITIN, Mikhail Zakharovich; Russian stage director and writer; *Artistic Director, Hermitage Theatre;* b. 27 Dec. 1945, Odessa, Ukraine; m.; one d. one s.; ed Moscow Inst. of Theatre Arts; Founder and Artistic Dir Moscow Hermitage Theatre 1981–; People's Artist of Russia, Order of Honour 2006; Moscow State Prize Laureate 2010. *Stage productions include:* Wanderings of Pilgrim Billy, Faryatyev's Fantasies in Moscow Theatre of Soviet Army, Alice Behind the Mirror, Moscow Theatre of Young Spectators, Harm! Harms! Shardam! or Clowns' School 1981, Pauper or Zanda's Death 1986, Evening in a Lunatic Asylum 1991, Maria, Hermitage Theatre 1996, New Year Tree at Ivanovs', Omsk Drama Theatre 1996; Hermitage Theatre: Fiend 2003, Suyer-Viyer 2005, Rescue Cantata 2005, Dissecting Room of Engineer Evno Azef 2005, A Feast in the Time of Plague 2005–06, Erendira and Her Grandmother 2006, Under the Bed 2006, Golden Calf or Back to Odessa 2007, The Secret Notes of a Secret Counselor 2009, Kapnist Round Trip 2009, These Bitches Wanted to Kill Me 2011. *Television:* series of broadcasts '…and others' 2011–. *Publications:* Other Man's Spectacle, My Friend Believes, Bolero, Sheer Indecency, Plutodrama, Dog's Shit, Dissecting Room of Engineer Evno Azef, Clowns' School, Tairov. *Address:* Moscow Hermitage Theatre, Karentny Ryad 3, 103006 Moscow, Russia (office). *Telephone:* (495) 209-20-76 (office). *E-mail:* ermitazh@theatre.ru (office). *Website:* ermitazh.theatre.ru/people/ levitin (office).

LEVITIS, Yefim Zavelyevich; Russian religious leader; b. 29 Nov. 1930; m.; one s.; ed Moscow Inst. of Aviation, Jewish seminary at Moscow Choral Synagogue, Higher Rabbis' School, Budapest; Scientific Sec. Moscow Jewish community 1975–80; Rabbi, St Petersburg 1980–91, Chief Rabbi, Grand Choral Synagogue 1991–97; Deputy Chief Rabbi of Russia responsible for co-operation with non-Jewish orgs; mem. Jewish Conf. of Rabbis; mem. Working Group, Consultative Council of Confession Heads, St Petersburg. *Address:* c/o Grand Choral Synagogue, 2 Lermontovsky pr., St Petersburg, Russia.

LEVITT, Arthur, Jr; American business executive and fmr government official; *Senior Advisor, The Carlyle Group;* b. 3 Feb. 1931, Brooklyn; s. of Arthur Levitt and Dorothy Wolff; m. Marylin Blauner 1955; one s. one d.; ed Williams Coll.; Asst Promotion Dir Time Inc. New York 1954–59; Exec. Vice-Pres., Dir Oppenheimer Industries Inc. Kansas City 1959–62; with Shearson Hayden Stone Inc. (now Shearson Lehman Bros Inc.), New York 1962–78, Pres. 1969–78; Chair., CEO, Dir American Stock Exchange, New York 1978–89; Chair. Levitt Media Co. New York 1989–93, New York City Econ. Devt Corpn 1990–93; Chair. SEC 1993–2001; Sr Advisor, The Carlyle Group 2001–; Hon. LLD (Williams Coll.) 1980, (Pace) 1980, (Hamilton Coll.) 1981, (Long Island) 1984, (Hofstra) 1985. *Address:* The Carlyle Group, 520 Madison Avenue, New York, NY 10022, USA (office). *Telephone:* (212) 381-4900 (office). *Fax:* (212) 381-4901 (office). *Website:* www.thecarlylegroup.com (office).

LEVITT, Brian Michael, BASc, LLB; Canadian business executive; *Chairman, TD Bank Financial Group;* b. 26 July 1947, Montreal; s. of Eric Levitt and Rya Levitt; m. Claire Gohier 1992; two d.; ed Univ. of Toronto; Special Asst to Provost, Univ. of Toronto 1969–73; called to Bar, Ont. 1974; Dir Interpretation, Prices and Profits Branch, Anti-Inflation Bd, Govt of Canada 1975–76; Assoc., Osler, Hoskin & Harcourt LLP, Toronto 1976–79, Partner 1979–91, Counsel, Montreal office 2001–; Pres. IMASCO Ltd, Montreal 1991–2000, also COO, CEO 1995–2000; mem. Bd of Dirs TD Bank Financial Group 2008–, Chair. 2011–; mem. Bd of Dirs Domtar Corpn (Chair. until merger with Weyerhauser's –2007), Bell Canada, BCE Inc.; Chair. Bd of Trustees, Montreal Museum of Fine Arts; Vice-Chair. C.D. Howe Inst.; apptd to five-person Competition Policy Review Panel cr. by Govt of Canada 2007; Chair. Judicial Compensation and Benefits Comm. of Canada. *Publications:* various articles on business law. *Leisure interests:* skiing, riding, sailing. *Address:* TD Bank Financial Group, Toronto-Dominion Centre, King Street West and Bay Street, Toronto, ON M5K 1A2, Canada (office). *Telephone:* (416) 982-8222 (office). *Fax:* (416) 982-5671 (office). *E-mail:* td.capa@td.com (office). *Website:* www.td.com (office).

LEVITT, Michael, PhD, FRS; American/British/Israeli biologist and academic; *Robert W. and Vivian K. Cahill Professor in Cancer Research in the School of Medicine and Professor, by courtesy, of Computer Science, Stanford University;* b. 1947, Pretoria, South Africa; s. of Gertrude Levitt; m. Rina Levitt; three s.; ed King's Coll. London, Peterhouse, Cambridge, UK; Postdoctoral Fellow, Weizmann Inst. of Science, Israel 1972–74, Assoc. Prof. of Chemical Physics 1979–84, Full Prof. 1984–87, Chair. of Dept 1980–83; Staff Scientist, MRC Lab. of Molecular Biology, Cambridge 1974–79; Visiting Scientist, Salk Inst., Calif. 1977–79; Prof. of Structural Biology, Stanford Univ. School of Medicine 1987–, Chair., Dept of Structural Biology 1993–2004, currently Robert W. and Vivian K. Cahill Prof. in Cancer Research and Prof., by courtesy, of Computer Science; Blaise Pascal Prof. of Research, Fondation de l'Ecole Normale Superieure, Paris 2003–04; mem. NAS 2002; Nobel Prize in Chemistry (jtly with Martin Karplus and Arieh Warshel)

2013. *Address:* Stanford University, Department of Structural Biology, 450 Serra Mall, Room D-109, Stanford, CA 94305-5345, USA (office). *E-mail:* michael.levitt@ stanford.edu (office). *Website:* csb.stanford.edu/levitt (office).

LEVITZKI, Alexander, PhD; Israeli biochemist and academic; *Wolfson Family Professor of Biochemistry and Director, Institute for Advanced Studies, Hebrew University of Jerusalem;* ed Hebrew Univ. of Jerusalem, Weizmann Inst. of Science, Rehovot and Univ. of California, Berkeley, USA; Fulbright-Hayes Fellow 1968–71; Sr Scientist, Dept of Biophysics, Weizmann Inst. of Science 1970, Assoc. Prof. 1974–76; Assoc. Prof., Hebrew Univ. of Jerusalem 1974, Prof. 1976–, Wolfson Family Prof. of Biochemistry 1985–, Dir Inst. for Advanced Studies 1998–2001, currently with Dept of Biological Chem., Alexander Silberman Inst. of Life Sciences; Visiting Prof. of Chem. and Research Assoc., Inst. of Molecular Biology, Univ. of Ore. Eugene 1974; Visiting Prof. of Biochemistry, Univ. of California, Berkeley 1974, Visiting Miller Research Professor, Miller Inst. for Basic Research in Science 2008; Visiting Scientist, Nat. Cancer Inst., NIH, Bethesda, Md 1979–80; Fogarty Scholar-in-Residence, NIH, Bethesda, Md 1984–85; Visiting Scholar, Stanford Univ., Calif. 1993–94; Visiting Prof., Comprehensive Cancer Center, Univ. of California, San Francisco 2001–03; Edward Rotan Visiting Prof., The M.D. Anderson Cancer Center, Houston, Tex. 2002–, John H. Blaffer Endowed Professorship 2005; Sr Consultant, Biotechnology Research Consultants, Tel-Aviv 1982–86, Rorer Biotechnology, King of Prussia, Pa, USA 1987–92; consultant and mem. Bd of Dirs Int. Diagnostic Labs, Jerusalem 1984–88; consultant, Eldan-Tech 1987–91; mem. Scientific Advisory Bd SUGEN, Inc., Redwood City, Calif. 1993–97, Vice-Pres. Research 1993–94; Chief Scientific Advisor and mem. Scientific Advisory Bd Peptor Ltd 1997–2003; Co-founder TK Signal, Israel 2000, UnResto 2001; Founder Algen Biopharmaceuticals, Israel and USA 2001; mem. Scientific Advisory Bd, ProteoLogics, Rehovot 2002–05; Teva Pharmaceutical Industries Ltd 2008; Founder NovoTyr Pharmaceuticals 2005; Vice-Pres. Fed. of Israeli Socs of Experimental Biology 1999, Pres. 2002–05; mem. Bd Govs, Israel Cancer Asscn 2007–; Ed. Current Topics in Cellular Regulation 1987–91; Assoc. Ed. Cellular Signalling 1987–; mem. Editorial Bd European Journal of Biochemistry 1975–81, Molecular Physiology 1982–85, Journal of Cyclic Nucleotide Research 1982–94, Pharmacology 1991–, Science 1993–96, Anti-cancer Drug Design 1995–2002, Molecular Biology Research Communications 1998–2001, European Journal of Chemical Biology (ChemBiochem) 2000, Oncology Research 2002, Journal of Biological Chemistry 2003, Current Signal Transduction Therapy 2006; mem. European Molecular Biology Org. 1978, Israel Acad. of Sciences 1999 (Chair. Div. of Natural Sciences 2004), Academia Europaea 2010; Hon. mem. American Soc. of Biological Chemists 1985; Hon. Scholar, Tel-Hai Academic Coll., Tel Hai, Israel 2006; Dr hc (Ben-Gurion Univ.) 2006; Bi-Annual Shlomo Hestrin Prize, Israel Biochemical Soc. 1975, Bronze Medal for Biochemistry, Free Univ. of Brussels 1983, Israel Prize in Biochemistry 1990, Rothschild Prize in Biology 1990, Lectureship Award, Fed. of European Biochemical Socs 1991, Schender Prize for Pharmacology and Drug Research 1998, Lichtenstein Memorial Lecturer 1998, Hamilton-Fairley Award, European Soc. of Medical Oncology 2002, Medal of the Univ., Univ. of Helsinki 2003, Al Wolf Lectureship (IRSC), Australia 2003, Wolf Prize for Medicine 2005 (jt winner), Research Award, The Jacqueline Seroussi Memorial Foundation for Cancer, Tel-Aviv 2006, Research Award, Prostate Cancer Foundation 2006, 2007, Paul Ehrlich Magic Bullet Lifetime Achievement Award in Oncology, 100th Anniversary Paul Ehrlich meeting, Nuremberg, Germany 2008, Karl Friedrich Bonhöffer Lecturer, Max Plank Inst. for Biophysical Chemistry, Göttingen 2011, The Nauta Award in Pharmacochemistry, European Fed. of Medicinal Chem. 2012, Award for Outstanding Achievement in Chem. in Cancer Research, American Asscn for Cancer Research 2013. *Publications:* numerous articles in scientific journals on developing techniques for targeted destruction of cancer cells through biochemical means. *Address:* The Levitzki Lab, Unit of Cellular Signalling, Department of Biological Chemistry, The Alexander Silberman Institute of Life Sciences, The Hebrew University of Jerusalem, 91904 Jerusalem, Israel (office). *Telephone:* (2) 6585404 (office). *Fax:* (2) 6512958 (office). *E-mail:* alex.levitzki@mail.huji.ac.il (office). *Website:* biolchem .huji.ac.il/levitzki/levitzki.html (office).

LEVY, Alain M., MBA; French record company executive; b. 19 Dec. 1946; ed Ecole des Mines, Univ. of Pennsylvania, USA; Asst to the Pres. CBS Int., New York 1972–73, Vice-Pres. Marketing for Europe, Paris 1973, Vice-Pres. of Creative Operations for Europe, also Man. CBS Italy 1978; Man. Dir CBS Disques, France 1979, CEO PolyGram France 1984, Exec. Vice-Pres. PolyGram Group, France and FRG 1988, Man. US Operations PolyGram Group 1990–98, Pres., CEO, mem. Bd Man. PolyGram USA 1991–98; mem. Group Man. Cttee Philips Electronics, majority shareholder PolyGram USA 1991–98; Chair. Bd EMI Group PLC 2001–07, Chair. and CEO EMI Recorded Music 2001–07; mem. advisory bd Film Business Academy 2006–. *Address:* c/o Film Business Academy, Cass Business School, 106 Bunhill Row, London, EC1Y 8TZ, England.

LEVY, Andrea, BA (Hons); British writer; b. 7 March 1956, London; d. of Winston Levy and Amy Levy; m. Bill Mayblin; two step-d.; ed Highbury Hill High School, London and Middlesex Polytechnic; fmr graphic designer; Dr hc (Middlesex); Arts Council Award 1998. *Publications:* Every Light in the House Burnin' 1994, Never Far from Nowhere 1996, Fruit of the Lemon 1999, Small Island (Orange Prize 2004, Whitbread Novel of the Year and Whitbread Prize 2005, Commonwealth Writers Prize 2005, Orange Prize for Fiction tenth anniversary award 2005) 2004, The Long Song 2010. *Leisure interests:* reading, films, TV and swimming. *Address:* David Grossman Literary Agency, 118B Holland Park Avenue, London, W11 4VA, England (office); c/o Review Press, Hodder Headline, 338 Euston Road, London, NW1 3BH, England. *Telephone:* (20) 7221-2770 (office). *Fax:* (20) 7221-1445 (office).

LÉVY, Bernard-Henri; French writer and philosopher; *Director, La Règle du jeu;* b. 5 Nov. 1948, Beni-Saf, Algeria; s. of André Lévy and Ginette Lévy; m. 1st Isabelle Doutreluigne; one d.; m. 2nd Sylvie Bouscasse 1980; one s. one d.; m. 2nd Arielle Sonnery 1993; ed Ecole Normale Supérieure (rue d'Ulm), Paris; War Corresp. for Combat 1971–72; Lecturer in Epistemology, Univ. of Strasbourg, in Philosophy, Ecole Normale Supérieure 1973; mem. François Mitterrand's Group of Experts 1973–76; joined Editions Grasset as Ed. 'nouvelle philosophie' series 1973; Ed. Idées section, Quotidien de Paris; Contrib. to Nouvel Observateur and Temps Modernes 1974; Co-founder Action International contre la Faim 1980, Radio Free

Kabul 1981, SOS Racisme; Founder-Dir La Règle du jeu 1990–; apptd Pres. Supervisory Council Sept-Arte 1993; appointed by French Govt to head fact-finding mission to Kabul, Afghanistan 2002. *Film:* directed: Le Jour la Nuit 1997. *Publications include:* Bangladesh: Nationalisme dans la révolution 1973, Les Indes rouges 1973, La barbarie à visage humain (Prix d'honneur) 1977, Le testament de Dieu 1979, L'idéologie française 1981, Questions de principe 1983, Le diable en tête (Prix Médicis) 1984, Impressions d'Asie 1985, Questions de principe II 1986, Eloge des intellectuels 1987, Les derniers jours de Charles Baudelaire (Prix Interallié) 1988, Questions de principe III 1990, Frank Stella: Les années 80 1990, Les bronzes de César 1991, Les aventures de la liberté 1991, Piet Mondrian 1992, Piero Della Francesca 1992, Le jugement dernier (play) 1992, Questions de principe IV 1992, Les hommes et les femmes (jtly) 1993, Un jour dans la mort de Sarajevo (screenplay, jtly) 1993, Bosna! (screenplay, jtly) 1994, La pureté dangereuse 1995, Questions de principe V 1995, Le lys et la cendre 1996, Comédie 1997, The Rules of the Game 1998 (revised edn What Good Are Intellectuals?: 44 Writers Share Their Thoughts 2000), Le siècle de Sartre 2000, Réflexion sur la guerre, Le mal et la fin de l'histoire 2001, Mémoire vive 2001, Qui a tué Daniel Pearl? 2003, American Vertigo 2006, Ce grand cadavre à la renverse 2007, Ennemis publics (with Michel Houellebecq) 2008, Left in Dark Times: A Stand Against the New Barbarism 2009, Pièces d'identité 2010, La Guerre sans l'aimer 2011. *Leisure interests:* skiing, judo, water-skiing. *Address:* La Règle du jeu, 61, rue des Saints-Peres, 75006 Paris, France (office). *Telephone:* 1-45-44-98-74 (office). *E-mail:* redaction@laregledujeu.org (office). *Website:* www.laregledujeu.org (office).

LEVY, David; Israeli politician; b. 1938, Morocco; emigrated to Israel 1957; construction worker; joined Histadrut (trade union); elected to Knesset (Parl.), representing Herut (Freedom) group of Gahal 1969–2006 (subsequently of Likud Bloc); Likud cand. for Sec.-Gen. of Histadrut 1977, 1981; Minister of Immigrant Absorption 1977–78, of Construction and Housing 1978–90, of Foreign Affairs 1990–92, 1996–97, 1999–2000, Deputy Prime Minister 1981–84, 1988–92, Minister without portfolio –2002; f. Gesher Party 1996 (merged with Likud 2003). *Address:* c/o Likud, 38 Rehov King George, Tel-Aviv 61231, Israel.

LEVY, Itzhak; Israeli rabbi and politician; b. 1947, Morocco; m.; five c.; ed Kerem B'Yavne and Yeshivat Hakotel; emigrated to Israel in 1957; ordained rabbi; served in Israeli Defence Forces, to rank of Maj.; mem. Knesset (Parl.) (Nat. Religious Party, now Jewish Home—HaBayit HaYehudi) 1988–2009 (retd), mem. Knesset House Cttee, Cttees on Finance, on Constitution, Law and Justice, on Labour and Social Welfare 1988–92, on Knesset House Cttee and Cttee on Constitution, Law and Justice 1992–96; Minister of Transport 1996–98, of Educ. 1998–99 (also Minister of Religious Affairs), of Housing and Construction 1999–2000, without Portfolio 2002, of Tourism 2002–03; Deputy Prime Minister 2003–04; mem. Bnei Akiva Exec. and World Secr.; Leader Nat. Religious Party 1998–2002; Chair. Israel–Argentina Parl. Friendship League. *Address:* c/o Jewish Home (HaBayit HaYehudi), Jerusalem, Israel.

LÉVY, Jacques Bernard, DèsSc; French metallurgist; *President, Fondation Industries Minerales, Minières et Metallurgiques;* b. Jan. 1937, Constantine, Algeria; s. of Gilbert Lévy and Renée Cassin; m. Marianne Neuburger 1964; two s. one d.; ed Ecole Polytechnique, Ecole des Mines de Paris, Univ. de Paris VI; Prof. of Metallurgy, Ecole des Mines de St-Étienne 1962, Dir Dept of Metallurgy 1974; Post-doctoral Fellow, Univ. of Waterloo, Ont., Canada 1968; Scientific Dir Ecole des Mines de Paris 1976, Dir 1984–2001; Ingénieur général du corps des mines 1983; Chair. (Research Comm.) Conf. des Grandes Ecoles 1984; mem. Royal Swedish Acad. of Eng Sciences 1989; Pres. Conf. of European Schools for Advanced Eng Educ. and Research 1990; Pres. Conf. des Grandes Ecoles 1993, Fondation Industries Minerales, Minières et Metallurgiques 2001–; mem. Conseil pour les Applications de l'Académie des Sciences 1999, Acad. des Technologies 2000–; Officier, Légion d'honneur, Commdr, Ordre nat. du mérite, Commdr, Ordre des Palmes académiques; Dr hc (Catholic Univ. of Louvain) 1996; Prix Jean Rist (Soc. Française de Métallurgie) 1972. *Publications:* about 30 publs on physical metallurgy (grain boundaries and interfaces, structure and properties of metals and alloys), official reports on materials science and eng higher educ. *Leisure interests:* skiing, tennis. *Address:* Ecole Nationale Supérieure des Mines, 60 boulevard Saint-Michel, 75272 Paris Cedex 06; 34 rue Dareau, 75014 Paris, France. *Telephone:* 1-40-51-90-18 (office); 1-53-62-05-13 (home). *Fax:* 1-40-51-90-25 (office). *E-mail:* jacques.levy@ensmp.fr (office). *Website:* www.ensmp.fr (office).

LÉVY, Jean-Bernard; French media and telecommunications executive; b. 18 March 1955; ed École Polytechnique, École Nationale Supérieure des Télécommunications; engineer with France Telecom 1978–86; Tech. Adviser to Minister for Postal Services and Telecommunications 1986–88; Gen. Man. Communication Satellites, Matra Marconi Space 1988–93; Chief of Staff to Minister for Industry, Postal Services, Telecommunications and Foreign Trade 1993–94; Chair. and CEO Matra Communication (Lagardère Group) 1995–98; Man. Partner, Corp. Finance, Oddo Pinatton (equities broker) 1998–2002; COO Vivendi Universal (now Vivendi) 2002–05, Chair. Man. Bd and CEO 2005–12 (resgnd), mem. Bd of Dirs Vivendi Games, Inc. (USA) –2009; Chair. Activision Blizzard, Inc. (USA) 2011–12, GVT Holdings SA (Brazil), Institut Télécom; Chair. Supervisory Bd Canal+ France, Viroxis; Vice-Chair. Supervisory Bd Groupe Canal+, Maroc Telecom; mem. Supervisory Bd Canal+ Group; mem. Bd of Dirs NBC Universal Inc., SFR, Société Générale, Vinci, Institut Pasteur; fmr mem. Bd of Dirs UGC; mem. Orientation Cttee, Paris Europlace; Chevalier, Légion d'honneur; Officier, Ordre nat. du Mérite. *Address:* c/o Vivendi, 42 avenue de Friedland, 75380 Paris Cedex 08, France. *E-mail:* info@vivendi.com.

LÉVY, Maurice; French advertising executive; *Co-CEO, Publicis Omnicom Group;* b. 18 Feb. 1942, Oudja, Morocco; m.; three s.; joined Publicis Groupe SA and given responsibility for data processing and information tech. systems 1971, apptd Corp. Sec. 1973, Man. Dir 1976, Chair. and CEO Publicis Conseil 1981, Vice-Chair. Publicis Groupe SA 1986, Vice-Chair. Man. Bd 1988, Chair. Man. Bd and CEO 1987, Chair. and CEO Publicis Group 1988–2013, Co-CEO Publicis Omnicom Group (following merger with Omnicon) 2013–; mem. Foundation Bd World Econ. Forum, Supervisory Bd Deutsche Bank; French Pres. French-American Business Council; Dir Musée des Arts Décoratifs, Paris, Council on Foreign Relations, New York; Commdr, Légion d'honneur, Grand Officier, Ordre nat. du Mérite. *Address:* Publicis Groupe SA, 133 avenue des Champs Elysées, 75008 Paris, France (office).

Telephone: 1-44-43-70-00 (office). *Fax:* 1-44-43-75-25 (office). *E-mail:* contact@publicisgroupe.com (office). *Website:* www.publicisgroupe.com (office).

LEVY, Baron (Life Peer), cr. 1997, of Mill Hill in the London Borough of Barnet; **Michael Abraham Levy,** FCA, CA; British consultant; b. 11 July 1944, London, England; s. of Samuel Levy and Annie Levy; m. Gilda Altbach 1967; one s. one d.; ed Hackney Downs Grammar School; chartered accountant, Lubbock Fine 1961–66; Prin. M. Levy & Co. 1966–69; Partner, Wagner, Prager, Levy & Partners 1969–73; Chair. Magnet Group of Cos 1973–88, D & J Securities Ltd 1988–92, M & G Records 1992–97; Vice-Chair. Phonographic Performance Ltd 1979–84, British Phonographic Industry Ltd 1984–87; Chair. British Music Industry Awards Cttee 1992–95, Patron 1995–; Nat. Campaign Chair. United Jt Israel Appeal 1982–85, Hon. Vice-Pres. 1994–2000, Hon. Pres. 2000–; Special Envoy of Prime Minister and Adviser on Middle East, South America and Kazakhstan 1997–2007; mem. (Labour), House of Lords 1997–; Chair. Jewish Care 1992–97, Pres. 1998–; fmr Chair. Jewish Care Community Foundation, Foundation for Educ.; Vice-Chair. Cen. Council for Jewish Community Services 1994–, Chair. Chief Rabbinate Awards for Excellence 1992–2007; mem. Jewish Agency World Bd of Govs 1990–95, World Chair. Youth Aliyah Cttee 1991–95; mem. Keren Hayesod World Bd of Govs 1991–95, World Comm. on Israel–Diaspora Relations 1995–, Int. Bd Govs Peres Centre for Peace 1997–, Advisory Council Foreign Policy Centre 1997–, Nat. Council Voluntary Orgs Advisory Cttee 1998–, Community Legal Service Champions Panel 1999–, Hon. Cttee Israel, Britain and the Commonwealth Asscn 2000–; Pres. CSV (Community Service Volunteers) 1998–, Jewish Lads & Girls Brigade 2006–; Chair. Wireart Ltd and Chase Music Ltd (fmrly M & G Music Ltd) 1992–2008, International Standard Asset Management 2008–11; Chair. Bd of Trustees, New Policy Network Foundation 2000–07; Vice-Pres. JLC 2010–11; mem. Devt Bd British Library 2008–; mem. Exec. Cttee Chai-Lifeline 2001–02; Gov. Jewish Free School 1990–95, Hon. Pres. 2001–; Trustee, Holocaust Educ. Trust 1998–2007; Patron Prostate Cancer Charitable Trust 1997–, Friends of Israel Educ. Trust 1998–, Save a Child's Heart Foundation 2000–, Simon Mark's Jewish Primary School Trust 2002–, Mathilda Marks-Kennedy Jewish Primary School 2011–; Hon. Patron, Cambridge Univ. Jewish Soc. 2002–; Hon. PhD (Middlesex Univ.) 1999; B'nai B'rith First Lodge Award 1994, Scopus Award Hebrew Univ. of Jerusalem 1998, Israel Policy Forum Special Recognition Award (USA) 2003. *Publication:* A Question of Honour (memoir) 2008. *Leisure interests:* tennis, swimming. *Address:* House of Lords, Westminster, London, SW1A 0PW, England (office). *Telephone:* (20) 7487-5174 (office). *Fax:* (20) 7486-7919 (office). *E-mail:* ml@lordlevy.com (office). *Website:* www.parliament.uk/biographies/lords/lord-levy/2033 (office).

LÉVY, Thierry; French lawyer and writer; b. 13 Jan. 1945, Nice (Alpes-Maritimes); s. of Paul Lévy; admitted to the Bar, Paris 1969, assigned to defend Claude Buffet who was later executed by guillotine 1972, won acquittal of Roger Knobelspiess 1986; Chair. Int. Observatory of Prisons 2000–04. *Publications:* Convaincre, Dialogue sur l'éloquence (with Jean-Denis Bredin) 1997, Eloge de la barbarie judiciaire 2004, Nos têtes sont plus dures que les murs des prisons 2006, Lévy oblige 2008; numerous legal articles. *Address:* c/o Éditions Grasset & Fasquelle, 61 rue des Saints-Pères, 75006 Paris, France. *Telephone:* 1-44-39-22-00. *Fax:* 1-42-22-64-18. *E-mail:* info@grasset.fr. *Website:* www.grasset.fr.

LEW, Jacob (Jack), AB, JD; American government official; *Secretary of the Treasury;* b. 29 Aug. 1955, New York; ed Harvard Coll., Georgetown Univ.; began career as legislative aide to US Rep. Joe Moakley, Washington, DC 1973–75; Prin. Domestic Policy Advisor to US House Speaker Tip O'Neill 1979–87, Asst Dir US House Democratic Steering and Policy Cttee, later Exec. Dir; Partner, Van Ness, Feldman and Curtis (law firm), Washington, DC 1988–93; Special Asst to Pres. Clinton 1993–94, Deputy Dir Office of Program Analysis, Office of Man. and Budget (OMB) 1995–98, Dir of OMB 1998–2001, 2010–12, mem. Nat. Security Council 1998–2001; Exec. Vice-Pres. and Prof. of Public Admin, Wagner School of Public Service, New York Univ. 2001–06; Man. Dir and COO Citi Global Wealth Man., Citigroup 2006–08, Citi Alternative Investments 2008–09; Deputy Sec. of State for Man. and Resources, Dept of State 2009–10; Chief of Staff to Pres. 2012–13; Sec. of the Treasury 2013–; Exec. Dir Center for Middle East Research; Issues Dir Democratic Nat. Cttee's Campaign 88; Chair. Corpn for Nat. and Community Service Bd, Man., Admin and Govt Cttee 2004–08; Co-Chair. Advisory Bd for City Year New York; Co-leader Quadrennial Diplomacy and Devt Review; mem. Council on Foreign Relations, Brookings Inst. Hamilton Project Advisory Bd, Nat. Acad. of Social Insurance; mem. Massachusetts and District of Columbia Bar. *Address:* Office of the Secretary, Department of the Treasury, 1500 Pennsylvania Avenue, NW, Washington, DC 20220, USA (office). *Telephone:* (202) 622-2000 (office). *Fax:* (202) 622-6415 (office). *E-mail:* dcfo@do.treas.gov (office). *Website:* www.ustreas.gov (office).

LEWIN, Ben; Australian/American film director and screenwriter; b. 6 Aug. 1946, Poland; ed Univ. of Melbourne, Nat. Film and Television School, UK. *Films include:* Welcome to Britain (documentary) 1975, Georgia 1988, The Favour, the Watch and the Very Big Fish 1991, Lucky Break 1994, Hollywood Gold (documentary) 2003, The Sessions (also writer and producer) 2012. *Television includes:* ITV Playhouse (series) – The Case of Cruelty to Prawns 1979, Destination Australia: The Migrant Experience Since 1788 (series documentary) 1984, The Dunera Boys (film) 1985, Rafferty's Rules (series) 1987, A Matter of Convenience (film) 1987, Ally McBeal (series) – Let's Dance 1999, SeaChange (series) 2000, Touched by an Angel (series) – The Good Earth 2003.

LEWIN, Harris A., BS, MS, PhD; American geneticist, immunologist, academic and university administrator; *Vice-Chancellor of Research and Professor of Evolution and Ecology, University of California, Davis;* ed Cornell Univ., Univ. of California, Davis; Asst Prof. of Immunogenetics, Dept of Animal Sciences, Univ. of Illinois, Urbana, Ill. 1984–89, Assoc. Prof. of Immunogenetics 1989–94, Prof. of Immunogenetics 1994–2011, Dir Univ. of Illinois Biotechnology Center 1996–98, Founding Dir W. M. Keck Center for Comparative and Functional Genomics 1998–2003, Sr Scientist, Nat. Center for Supercomputing Applications 1998–2003, E.W. and J.M. Gutgsell Endowed Chair 1999–2011, Resident Assoc., Center for Advanced Study 2001–02, Research Prof., Microelectronics Lab. 2002–11, Founding Dir Inst. for Genomic Biology 2003–11, Affiliate, Micro and Nanotechnology Lab. 2008–11, Prof., Center for Advanced Study 2009–11; Vice-Chancellor of Research and Prof. of Evolution and Ecology, Univ. of California, Davis 2011–;

Visiting Scientist, Dept of Animal Genetics, Nat. Veterinary Inst., Oslo, Norway Aug. 1989; Visiting Assoc. Prof., Section of Molecular Biology, Univ. of Southern California, Los Angeles 1991; mem. Bd of Dirs Stormont Laboratories, Woodland, Calif. 1984–2006; Founder and Scientific Dir Midwest Molecular Diagnostics, Champaign 1987–89; consultant, American Cyanamid Co., Princeton, NJ 1990–94, Applied Biosystems, Inc., Foster City, Calif. 1993–98, Protiva/Monsanto Chesterfield, Mo. 1997–99, ELANCO, Greenfield, Ia 2000–02, Pfizer Inc., New York, NY 2007, Hebrew Univ. of Jerusalem, Israel 2009, Washington Advisory Group, Washington, DC 2010; mem. External Advisory Cttee, Food Animal Biotechnology Center, Univ. of Minnesota 1994–2001; Chair. Scientific Advisory Bd, GenoMar AS, Norway 1997–2003; mem. Scientific Advisory Bd, Burrill & Co., Animal Health Venture Fund, San Francisco 1999–2003; Founder-mem. Scientific Advisory Bd, Pyxis Genomics, Inc., Chicago 2000–07; Assoc. Ed. Animal Biotechnology 1990–; Man. Ed. National Animal Genome Research Program (NAGRP) Newsletter 1993–96; Founding Ed. Annual Reviews of Animal and Veterinary Biosciences; Section Ed. Encyclopedia of Genetics, Genomics, Proteomics and Bioinformatics 2002–; mem. Editorial Bd Physiological Genomics 1999–, Faculty of 1000, Genomics Section, Genetics and Genomics Faculty, BioMed Central 2002–03; mem. Editorial Cttee, Annual Reviews of Genomics and Human Genetics 2009–; mem. American Asscn of Immunologists, American Asscn of Veterinary Immunologists, Int. Soc. for Animal Genetics, American Asscn of Animal Science; Foreign mem. Royal Swedish Acad. of Agric. and Forestry 2007; Fellow, AAAS 2004; American Asscn of Veterinary Immunologists Travel Award, William and Flora Hewlett Foundation Int. Travel Award 1989, Young Faculty Award for Excellence in Research, Coll. of Agric., Univ. of Illinois 1992, Univ. Scholar, Univ. of Illinois 1993–96, H.H. Mitchell Award for Grad. Teaching and Research 1995, Paul A. Funk Recognition Award, Coll. of Agricultural, Consumer and Environmental Sciences, Univ. of Illinois 1996, Arnold O. Beckman Research Award, Univ. of Illinois 1997, Wellcome Visiting Professorship in Basic Biomedical Sciences, Washington State Univ. 1999–2000, C.R. Henderson Lecturer in Animal Breeding and Genetics, Cornell Univ. 2000, Pres.'s Distinguished Speakers, Univ. of Illinois 2000-01, Sir Frederick McMaster Fellowship (declined after award) 2001, ACES Team Award for Excellence in Research 2003, Alltech Distinguished Lecturer in Nutrigenomics, Univ. of Kentucky, Lexington 2009, Wolf Prize in Animal Sci. (with R. James Cook) 2011. *Publications:* Gene Mapping: Techniques and Applications (co-ed.) 1991, Comparative Analysis and Phylogeny (Section Ed.). In, S. Subramaniam (ed.) Encyclopedia of Genetics, Genomics, Proteomics and Bioinformatics 2005; 21 book chapters and more than 160 papers in professional journals on mammalian comparative and functional genomics. *Address:* Office of the Vice-Chancellor of Research, 1850 Research Park Drive, Suite 300, Davis, CA 95618-6153, USA (office). *Telephone:* (530) 754-7764 (office). *Fax:* (530) 754-7894 (office). *E-mail:* lewin@ucdavis.edu (office); ORExecutiveMgtAsst@ad3.ucdavis.edu (office). *Website:* www.research.ucdavis.edu

LEWINTON, Sir Christopher, Kt, CEng, FEng, FIMechE.; British/American engineer and industrialist; *Chairman, Camper & Nicholsons Marina Investments Limited;* b. 6 Jan. 1932, London; s. of Joseph Lewinton and Elizabeth Lewinton; m. 1st Jennifer Alcock (divorced); two s.; m. 2nd Louise Head 1979; two step-s.; ed Acton Tech. Coll.; commissioned army service in REME; Pres. Wilkinson Sword, N America 1959–71, CEO Wilkinson Sword Group 1970–85; Pres. Int. Group, Allegheny Int. 1978–85; Chief Exec. TI Group 1986–99, Chair. and CEO 1989–2000; Dir Reed Elsevier 1993–99, Messier-Dowty 1994–1998, Y&R/WPP 1996–2003; mem. Supervisory Bd Mannesmann AG 1995–99, J. F. Lehman Exec. Bd 2000–03; Adviser to Booz Allen Hamilton Inc. 2000–03, to Morgan Stanley Capital Pnrs (now Metalmark Capital) 2000–, Compass Advisers 2004–10; Chair. Camper & Nicholsons Marina Investments Ltd 2008–; Hon. FRAeS 1993; Hon. DTech (Brunel) 1997. *Leisure interests:* golf, tennis, travel, reading. *Address:* Camper & Nicholsons Marina Investments Limited, Richmond Place, 15 Petersham Road, Richmond, TW9 6TP, England (office). *Telephone:* (20) 7201-5490 (office). *Fax:* (20) 7201-5499 (office). *Website:* www.cnmarinas.com (office).

LEWIS, Anthony Robert (Tony), CBE, DL, MA; British sports commentator, writer, fmr cricketer and opera administrator; *Director, Welsh National Opera;* b. 6 July 1938, Swansea, Wales; s. of Wilfrid Lewis and Florence Lewis (née Flower); m. Joan Pritchard 1962; two d.; ed Neath Grammar School, Christ's Coll. Cambridge; right-hand batsman; teams: Glamorgan, Cambridge Univ.; double blue and debut at int. level; led Glamorgan to their second Co. Championship title 1969; played in nine Tests (eight as Capt. 1972–73) scoring 457 runs (average 32.64, highest score 125) including one hundred; scored 20,495 First-class runs (average 32.42, highest score 223) including 30 hundreds; retd 1974; became cricket commentator and journalist; Pres. Marylebone Cricket Club (MCC) 1998–2000, secured admission of women into MCC Club, Trustee 2002–; fmr Chair. Glamorgan Co. Cricket Club, Pres. 1987–93, 2003–; Chair. Welsh Tourist Bd 1992–2000; led successful Welsh campaign to host 2010 Ryder Cup; Chair. (non-exec.) World Snooker Ltd 2003–; Dir Welsh Nat. Opera 2003–; Hon. Fellow, St David's Univ. Coll., Lampeter 1993, Univ. of Glamorgan 1995, Univ. of Wales, Swansea 1996, Univ. of Cardiff 1999. *Publications:* A Summer of Cricket 1976, Playing Days 1985, Double Century 1987, Cricket in Many Lands 1991, MCC Masterclass 1994, Taking Fresh Guard 2003. *Leisure interests:* classical music, golf. *Address:* Castellau, Near Llantrisant, Mid Glamorgan, CF72 8LP, Wales (home); c/o Angie Bainbridge Management, 3 New Cottages, The Holt, Washington, West Sussex, RH20 4AW, England (office). *Telephone:* (1903) 8933748 (office). *Fax:* (1903) 891320 (office). *E-mail:* angie .bainbridge@btopenworld.com (office).

LEWIS, Aylwin B., BA, MBA; American retail executive; ed Univ. of Houston; started career as Dist Man. of Operations Jack in the Box restaurants in Tex.; held various exec. positions at food retailers including KFC Corpn, COO Pizza Hut 1996–2000, Exec. Vice Pres. of Operations and New Business Devt Tricon Global Restaurants Inc. then Pres., Chief Multibranding and Operating Officer YUM! Brands Inc. (fmrly Tricon) 2000–03; Pres. and CEO Kmart Holdings Corpn 2004, Pres. and CEO Sears Holding Corpn (after merger of Kmart and Sears, Roebuck) 2005–08, also mem. Bd of Dirs; mem. Bd of Dirs Halliburton Co., Walt Disney Co. *Address:* c/o Sears Holding Corporation, 3333 Beverly Road, Hoffman Estates, IL 60179, USA (office).

LEWIS, Bernard, PhD, FBA, FRHistS; American writer and academic; b. 31 May 1916, London, England; m. Ruth Hélène Oppenhejm 1947 (divorced 1974); one s.

one d.; ed Univs of London and Paris; Lecturer in Islamic History, School of Oriental Studies, Univ. of London 1938; served in RAC and Intelligence Corps 1940–41; attached to Foreign Office 1941–45; Prof. of History of the Near and Middle East, Univ. of London 1949–74; Cleveland E. Dodge Prof. of Near Eastern Studies, Princeton Univ. 1974–86, later Prof. Emer.; Dir Annenberg Research Inst., Philadelphia 1986–90; Visiting Prof. of History, UCLA 1955–56, Columbia Univ. 1960, Ind. Univ. 1963, Princeton Univ. 1964, Univ. of Calif. at Berkeley 1965, Coll. de France 1980, École des Hautes Études en Sciences Sociales, Paris 1983, 1988, Univ. of Chicago 1985; Visiting mem. Inst. for Advanced Study, Princeton Univ. 1969, mem. 1974–86; A.D. White Prof.-at-Large, Cornell Univ. 1984–90; mem. Bd of Dirs, Institut für die Wissenschaften von Menschen, Vienna 1988; Jefferson Lecturer in the Humanities, US Nat. Endowment for the Humanities 1990; Tanner Lecturer, Brasenose Coll., Oxford 1990; Henry M. Jackson Memorial Lecturer (Seattle) 1992; mem. British Acad., American Philosophical Soc. 1973, American Acad. of Arts and Sciences 1983; American Oriental Soc., Corresp. mem. Inst. d'Egypte, Cairo 1969, Inst. de France 1994; Fellow, Univ. Coll., London 1976; Hon. mem. Turkish Historical Soc., Société Asiatique, Paris, Atatürk Acad. of History, Language and Culture, Ankara, Turkish Acad. of Sciences, Hon. Fellow, SOAS, London 1986; 15 hon. doctorates including (Hebrew Univ., Jerusalem) 1974, (Tel-Aviv) 1979, (State Univ. of New York, Binghamton, Univ. of Penn., Hebrew Union Coll., Cincinnati) 1987, (Univ. of Haifa, Yeshiva Univ., New York) 1991, (Bar-Ilan Univ.) 1992, (Brandeis) 1993, (Ben-Gurion, Ankara) 1996, (Princeton Univ.) 2002; Citation of Honour, Turkish Ministry of Culture 1973, Harvey Prize, Technion-Israel Inst. of Tech. 1978, Educ. Award for Outstanding Achievement in Promotion of American-Turkish Studies 1985, Atatürk Peace Prize 1998, Golden Plate Award, Acad. of Achievement, Washington, DC 2004, Nat. Endowment for the Humanities 2007, Irving Kristol Award 2007. *Publications:* The Origins of Ismā'ilism: A Study of the Historical Background of the Fatimid Caliphate 1940, Turkey Today 1940, British Contributions to Arabic Studies 1941, Handbook of Diplomatic and Political Arabic 1947, Land of Enchanters (ed.) 1948, The Arabs in History 1950, Notes and Documents from the Turkish Archives: A Contribution to the History of the Jews in the Ottoman Empire 1952, Encyclopedia of Islam (co-ed.) 1956–86, The Emergence of Modern Turkey 1961, The Kingly Crown 1961, Historians of the Middle East (co-ed. with P.M. Holt) 1962, Istanbul and the Civilization of the Ottoman Empire 1963, The Middle East and the West 1964, The Assassins: A Radical Sect in Islam 1967, The Cambridge History of Islam (ed. with P. M. Holt and Ann K. S. Lambton, two vols) 1970, Race and Colour in Islam 1971, Islam in History: Ideas, Men and Events in the Middle East 1973, Islamic Civilization (ed.) 1974, Islam from the Prophet Muhammad to the Capture of Constantinople (ed. and trans., two vols) 1974, History: Remembered, Recovered, Invented 1975, Studies in Classical and Ottoman Islam: Seventh to Sixteenth Centuries 1976, The World of Islam: Faith, People, Culture (ed.) 1976, Population and Revenue in the Towns of Palestine in the Sixteenth Century (with Amnon Cohen) 1978, The Muslim Discovery of Europe 1982, Christians and Jews in the Ottoman Empire (two vols) 1982, The Jews of Islam 1984, Semites and Anti-Semites: An Inquiry into Conflict and Prejudice 1986, As Others See Us (co-ed.) 1986, The Political Language of Islam 1988, Race and Slavery in the Middle East: A Historical Enquiry 1990, Islam and the West 1993, The Shaping of the Modern Middle East 1994, Cultures in Conflict: Christians, Muslims and Jews in the Age of Discovery 1995, The Middle East: Two Thousand Years of History from the Rise of Christianity to the Present Day 1995, The Future of the Middle East 1997, The Multiple Identities of the Middle East 1998, A Middle East Mosaic: Fragments of Life, Letters and History 2000, Music of a Distant Drum, Classical Arabic, Persian, Turkish and Hebrew Poems 2001, What Went Wrong? Western Impact and Middle Eastern Response 2002, The Crisis of Islam: Holy War and Unholy Terror 2003, From Babel to Dragomans: Interpreting the Middle East 2004, Political Words and Ideas in Islam 2008, Islam: The Religion and The People (co-author) 2008, Faith and Power: Religion and Politics in the Middle East 2010, The End of Modern History in the Middle East 2011, Notes on a Century: Recollections of a Middle East Historian (co-author) 2012; numerous contribs to professional journals. *Telephone:* (609) 258-4280.

LEWIS, Charles Edwin; American professor of medicine; *Professor of Health Services, Medicine, and Nursing, School of Public Health and Director, Center for Health Promotion and Disease Prevention, University of California, Los Angeles;* b. 28 Dec. 1928, Kansas City, Mo.; s. of Claude Herbert Lewis and Maudie Friels (née Holaday); m. Mary Ann Gurera 1963; three s. one d.; ed Univs of Kansas and Cincinatti and Harvard Medical School; USAF 1955–56; Fellow, The Kettering Lab. 1956–59; Asst Prof. Epidemiology, Baylor Univ. 1959–61; Assoc. Prof. of Medicine, Univ. of Kansas 1962–64, Prof. and Chair. Dept of Community Medicine 1964–69; Prof. and Head of Div. of Health Services and Prof. of Medicine, UCLA 1970–72, Chief, Div. of Gen. Internal Medicine 1972–90, Prof. of Nursing, School of Nursing 1973–, Dir UCLA Center for Health Promotion and Disease Prevention 1991–, Head Div. of Preventive and Occupational Medicine 1991–93, Dir Health Services Research Center 1991–93, Chair. Academic Senate 1995–96; Regent, ACP 1989; Master American Coll. of Physicians; mem. Inst. of Medicine (NAS); Ginsberg Prize, Univ. of Kan., Rosenthal Award (ACP) 1980. *Publications:* more than 120 research publns in journals and 15 chapters in books. *Leisure interests:* music, travel. *Address:* UCLA School of Public Health, Box 951772, Los Angeles, CA 90095-1772 (office); 221 Burlingame Avenue, Los Angeles, CA 90049, USA (home). *Telephone:* (310) 825-6709 (office); (310) 206-6322 (office). *Fax:* (310) 206-5717 (office); (310) 394-8929 (home). *E-mail:* lewis@admin.ph.ucla.edu (office). *Website:* www.ph.ucla.edu (office).

LEWIS, Hon. Douglas (Doug) Grinslade, PC, LLB, FCA, QC; Canadian lawyer, chartered accountant and fmr politician; b. 17 April 1938, Toronto, Ont.; s. of Horace Grinslade and Brenda Hazeldine Lewis (née Reynolds); m. Linda Diane Haggans 1962; two s. three d.; ed Univ. of Toronto, Osgoode Hall Law School; Progressive Conservative MP for Simcoe N 1979–93; Parl. Sec. to Minister of Supply and Services 1979; Deputy Opposition House Leader 1981, Opposition House Leader 1983; Parl. Sec. to Pres. of Treasury Bd 1984, to Pres. of Privy Council 1985, to Deputy Prime Minister and Pres. of Queen's Privy Council for Canada 1986–87; Minister of State (Deputy House Leader) and Minister of State (Treasury Bd) 1987–88; Acting Pres. Treasury Bd 1988; Minister of Justice, Attorney-Gen. and Govt House Leader 1989–90; Minister of Transport 1990–91; Solicitor-Gen. 1991–93; currently practising law with Lewis Downey Tornosky

Lassaline & Timpano Professional Corpn; Chair. Fed. Govt Panel on Railway Safety in Canada 2007; currently Chair. Audit Cttee, Ministry of the Attorney Gen.; Bencher, Law Soc. of Upper Canada 2007–11; mem. Orillia Soldiers' Memorial Hosp. Foundation Bd 2001–06; Orillia Citizen of the Year 1972, 2002. *Address:* Lewis Downey Tornosky Lassaline & Timpano Professional Corpn, 77 Coldwater Street East, Orillia, ON L3V 1W6, Canada. *Telephone:* (705) 327-2600. *Fax:* (705) 327-7532. *E-mail:* dlewis@greatlaw.ca. *Website:* www.greatlaw.ca.

LEWIS, Frederick Carlton (Carl); American fmr professional athlete; b. 1 July 1961, Birmingham, Ala; s. of the late William Lewis and of Evelyn Lawler Lewis; ed Univ. of Houston; bronze medal for long jump, Pan-American Games 1979; won World Cup competition 1981, first World Championships (with 8.55m); achieved world record 8.79m jump 1983; gold medals at Olympic Games 1984 for 100m, 200m., long jump and 4×100m; athlete in fields of sprints and long jump; silver medal for 200m, gold medal for 100m, Olympic Games 1988; jumped 8.64m New York 1991; world record for 100m 9.86 seconds Aug. 1991 (surpassed 1994); gold medal, long jump Olympic Games 1992; gold medal for long jump (8.50m), Olympic Games 1996; only man to defend an Olympic long jump title successfully; retd 1997; has won a total of nine Olympic gold medals; revealed in 2003 to have failed a drugs test at Seoul Olympics 1988, disqualified at the time, but case dismissed after an appeal; f. Carl Lewis Fund to help disadvantaged youths; official supporter of Ronald McDonald House Charities, mem. Friends of RMHC celebrity bd; appeared in several TV and film projects produced by the Carl Lewis Entertainment Group; nominated a Goodwill Amb. for the UN FAO 2009; filed petitions to run as a Democrat for NJ Senate 2011, disqualified by Lt Gov. for failing to meet state's residency requirements, appeal to Third Circuit Court of Appeals eventually rejected; Hon. Chair. Negro Coll. Fund; Track and Field News Athlete of the Decade 1980–89, World Athlete of the Year 1982, 1983, 1984, Athlete of the Century, Int. Asscn of Athletics Feds 1999, voted Sportsman of the Century by IOC 1999, named Olympian of the Century by Sports Illustrated 1999, Univ. of Houston named the Carl Lewis Int. Complex in his honour 2000. *Films:* has appeared in numerous films, including playing himself in cameos in Perfect Strangers, Speed Zone!, Alien Hunter and Material Girls. *Television:* appeared on The Weakest Link; played Stu in TV film Atomic Twister and appeared in short documentary Challenging Impossibility 2011; guest on ESPN TV show College GameDay 2011. *Address:* c/o Cleve Lewis Management, 5170 Pinyon Jay Road, Parker, CO 80134 (office); c/o Carl Lewis Foundation, 3350 Wilshire Blvd, Suite 675, Los Angeles, CA 90010, USA. *Telephone:* (303) 531-4469 (office); (310) 578-1885. *Fax:* (303) 531-5340 (office). *E-mail:* carl@clevelewis.com. *Website:* www.iaaf .org/athletes/united-states/carl-lewis-1622; www.carllewis.com.

LEWIS, Geoffrey David, MA, FSA, FMA; British museum director, museum consultant and university teacher; b. 13 April 1933, Brighton, Sussex, England; s. of David Lewis and Esther Lewis; m. Frances May Wilderspin 1956; three d.; ed Varndean Grammar School, Brighton, Univ. of Liverpool; Asst Curator, Worthing Museum and Art Gallery 1950–60; Deputy Dir (and Keeper of Antiquities) Sheffield City Museum 1960–65; Dir Sheffield City Museums 1966–72, Liverpool City Museums 1972–74, Merseyside Co. Museums 1974–77; Dir of Museum Studies, Univ. of Leicester 1977–89, Assoc. Teacher 1989–92; Fellow, Museums Asscn London 1966, Pres. 1980–81, Pres. Int. Council of Museums 1983–89, Chair. Advisory Cttee 1974–80, Chair. Ethics Cttee 1996–2004; currently a museum consultant; mem. Bd of Trustees, Royal Armouries 1990–99, Chair. Design Cttee 1995–99; Chair. Printing Matters (Bude) Ltd 1991–96; Deputy Chair. The Genesis Agendum 1996–2008; Gov. Wolvey School 1993–2003, Chair. of Govs 1998–2003; Hon. Lecturer in British Prehistory, Univ. of Sheffield 1965–72, Hon. Fellow, Museums Asscn 1989, Hon. mem. Int. Council of Museums 2004. *Publications include:* The South Yorkshire Glass Industry 1964, Prehistoric and Roman Times in the Sheffield Area (co-author) 1968, For Instruction and Recreation: A Centenary History of the Museums Association 1989, Manual of Curatorship (co-ed.) 1984, 1992; contrib. to Encyclopaedia Britannica 2012 and Britannica Online 2013; many articles relating to archaeology, museums and professional ethics. *Leisure interests:* reading, computing. *Address:* 4 Orchard Close, Wolvey, Hinckley, Warwicks., LE10 3LR, England. *Telephone:* (1455) 220708. *E-mail:* mail@geoffreylewis.co.uk. *Website:* www.geoffreylewis.co.uk.

LEWIS, Gwyneth, MA, DPhil, FRSL; British poet and writer; b. 1959, Cardiff, Wales; d. of Gwilym Lewis and Ann Eryl James; m. Leighton Denver Davies; ed Girton Coll., Cambridge, Harvard and Columbia Univs, USA, Balliol Coll., Oxford; fmr freelance journalist in New York, USA and documentary prod. and dir, BBC Wales; composed the bilingual inscription on the front of Cardiff's Wales Millennium Centre, opened in 2004; Nat. Poet of Wales 2005–06; Fellow, Radcliffe Inst. for Advanced Studies, Harvard Univ. 2008–09, Stanford Humanities Center 2009–10; Mary Amelia Cummins Harvey Visiting Fellow Commonership, Girton Coll. Cambridge 2011; Royal Literary Fund Fellow, Swansea Univ. 2011–12; Writing Fellow, Centre for New Writing, Univ. of Manchester 2012; Hon. Fellow, Univ. of Cardiff 2005, Univ. of Liverpool 2011, Bangor Univ. 2012; Dr hc (Glamorgan) 2012; Harkness Fellow 1982–84, Eric Gregory Award 1987, Aldeburgh Festival Prize 1996, Nat. Endowment for Science, Tech. and the Arts Fellowship 2002–07, Wellcome Trust Sciart Award, Creative Wales Award, Cholmondeley Award 2010, Roland Mathias Poetry Award 2012. *Play:* Clytemnestra (Sherman Cymru). *Radio:* Sunbathing in the Rain (BBC Radio 4), Stardust: A Love Story (BBC Radio 4). *Television:* Zero Gravity (BBC 2). *Publications:* Llwybrau bywyd (poetry) 1977, Ar y groesffordd (poetry) 1978, Sonedau Redsa a Cherddi Eraill 1990, Parables and Faxes (poetry) (Aldeburgh Poetry Festival Prize) 1995, Cyfrif Un ac Un yn Dri (poetry) 1996, Zero Gravity (poetry) 1998, Y Llofrudd Iaith (poetry) (Welsh Arts Council Book of the Year) 2000, Sunbathing in the Rain: A Cheerful Book About Depression (non-fiction) 2002, Keeping Mum (poetry) 2003, Redflight/Barcud (libretto) 2005, The Most Beautiful Man from the Sea (oratorio) 2005, Two in a Boat: A Marital Voyage 2005, Tair mewn Un (poetry) 2005, Chaotic Angels (poetry) 2005, Dolffin (libretto) 2006, The Hospital Odyssey (poetry) 2010, The Meat Tree (stories) 2010, Sparrow Tree 2011, Clytemnestra (play) 2012, Y Storm (trans. of The Tempest) 2012. *Address:* c/o David Miller, Rogers, Coleridge & White Literary Agency, 20 Powis Mews, London, W11 1JN, England (office). *Telephone:* (20) 7243-9504 (office). *E-mail:* davidmiller@ rcwlitagency.com (office); gl@gwynethlewis.com. *Website:* www.rcwlitagency.com (office); www.gwynethlewis.com.

LEWIS, Baron (Life Peer), cr. 1989, of Newnham; **Jack Lewis,** PhD, FRSC, FRS; British chemist and academic; *Professor Emeritus of Chemistry, University of Cambridge;* b. 13 Feb. 1928, Barrow; m. Elfreida M. Lamb 1951; one s. one d.; ed Barrow Grammar School and Univs of London and Nottingham; Lecturer, Univ. of Sheffield 1954–56, Imperial Coll. London 1956–57; Lecturer-Reader, Univ. Coll. London 1957–61; Prof. of Chem., Univ. of Manchester 1961–67, Univ. Coll. London 1967–70, Univ. of Cambridge 1970–95, now Prof. Emer.; Warden, Robinson Coll. Cambridge 1975–2001; mem. numerous cttees etc.; Foreign Assoc. NAS; Foreign mem. American Philosophical Soc. 1994, Accad. Naz. dei Lincei 1995; Hon. FRSC; Hon. Fellow, Sidney Sussex Coll. Cambridge (Fellow 1970–77); Chevalier, Ordre des Palmes Académiques, Commdr Cross of the Order of Merit (Poland) and other distinctions; 22 hon. degrees; Davy Medal, Royal Soc. 1985, Royal Medal 2004, and other awards. *Publications:* papers in scientific journals. *Address:* Robinson College, Grange Road, Cambridge, CB3 9AN, England (office). *Telephone:* (1223) 339198 (office); (1223) 360222 (home).

LEWIS, Jerry; American comedian, writer, director, producer and actor; b. (Joseph Levitch), 16 March 1926, Newark, NJ; s. of Danny Lewis and Rachael Lewis; m. 1st Patti Palmer 1944 (divorced); five s.; m. 2nd SanDee Pitluck 1983; one d.; performed in nightclubs as a comedian before teaming with Dean Martin in 1946 at the 500 Club, Atlantic City, NJ; Nat. Chair. Muscular Dystrophy Asscn of America 1951–; Prof. of Cinema at Univ. of Southern Calif.; mem. Screen Directors Guild; Chevalier, Légion d'honneur 1984; Commdr des Arts et Lettres 1984; Hon. DHumLitt (Mercy Coll., Westchester, NY) 1987, (Emerson Coll., Boston, Mass) 1993; N. Neal Pike Prize for Service to the Handicapped, Boston Univ. School of Law 1984; numerous awards and honours including Best Dir of the Year Award (8 times), Lifetime Achievement Award, American Medical Asscn 1996, Golden Lion Award, Venice Int. Film 1999. *Films:* made film début with Dean Martin in My Friend Irma 1949; other films (many also as producer and/or Dir) include: My Friend Irma Goes West 1950, That's My Boy 1951, The Caddy 1952, Sailor Beware 1952, Jumping Jacks 1953, The Stooge 1953, Scared Stiff 1953, Living it Up 1954, Three Ring Circus 1954, You're Never Too Young 1955, Partners 1956, Hollywood or Bust 1956, The Delicate Delinquent 1957, The Sad Sack 1958, Rock a Bye Baby 1958, The Geisha Boy 1958, Visit to a Small Planet 1959, The Bellboy 1960, Cinderfella 1960, It's Only Money 1961, The Errand Boy 1962, The Patsy 1964, The Disorderly Orderly 1964, The Family Jewels 1965, Boeing-Boeing 1965, Three On a Couch 1965, Way Way Out 1966, The Big Mouth 1967, Don't Raise the Bridge, Lower the River 1968, One More Time 1969, Hook, Line and Sinker 1969, Which Way to the Front? 1970, The Day the Clown Cried 1972, Hardly Working 1979, King of Comedy 1981, Slapstick of Another Kind 1982, Smorgasbord 1983, How Did You Get In? 1985, Mr Saturday Night 1992, Funny Bones 1995. *Play:* Damn Yankees 1995, on tour 1995–97. *Television appearances include:* Startime, The Ed Sullivan Show and the Jazz Singer, Martin & Lewis – Colgate Comedy Hour. *Publications:* The Total Film-Maker 1971, Jerry Lewis in Person 1982, Dean and Me (memoir, with James Kaplan) 2006. *Leisure interests:* golf, sailing. *Website:* www.jerrylewiscomedy.com (office).

LEWIS, Jerry Lee; American rock singer and musician (piano); b. 29 Sept. 1935, Ferriday, La; m. 6th Kerrie Lynn McCarver Lewis 1984 (divorced 2005); two s. (one deceased); one d.; ed Waxahachie Bible Inst., Texas; numerous concert tours, festival appearances. *Films include:* Jamboree 1957, High School Confidential 1958, Be My Guest 1965. *Theatre includes:* Iago in Catch My Soul. *Recordings include:* albums: Jerry Lee Lewis 1957, Jerry Lee's Greatest 1961, Live At The Star Club 1965, The Greatest Live Show On Earth 1965, The Return Of Rock 1965, Whole Lotta Shakin' Goin' On 1965, Country Songs For City Folks 1965, By Request – More Greatest Live Show On Earth 1967, Breathless 1967, Together (with Linda Gail Lewis) 1970, Rockin' Rhythm And Blues 1971, Sunday Down South (with Johnny Cash) 1972, The Session (with Peter Frampton and Rory Gallagher) 1973, Jerry Lee Lewis 1979, When Two Worlds Collide 1980, My Fingers Do The Talking 1983, I Am What I Am 1984, Keep Your Hands Off It 1987, Don't Drop It 1988, Great Balls of Fire! 1989, Rocket 1990, Young Blood 1995, Keep Your Eyes Off Of It 2000, By Invitation Only 2000, Last Man Standing 2006, Mean Old Man 2010. *Address:* Al Embry International, PO Box 23162, Nashville, TN 37202, USA (office); The Lewis Ranch, Box 384, Nesbit, MS 38651, USA (office). *E-mail:* phoebemedia@aol.com (office). *Website:* www .jerryleelewis.com.

LEWIS, Joseph C. (Joe); British business executive; b. 5 Feb. 1937, Bow, London, England; s. of the late Charles Lewis; m. 1st Esther Browne (divorced); one s. one d.; m. 2nd Jane Lewis; joined father's small catering business 1958; with father ran Hanover Grand chain of banqueting suites, London 1970s; moved to New Providence, Bahamas 1979 (tax exile); moved into currency trading 1980s and 1990s; teamed up with George Soros to bet on pound crashing out of European Exchange Rate Mechanism (Black Wednesday) Sept. 1992; Founder and Owner Tavistock Group of financial services, property and retail businesses (more than 200 cos in 15 countries); shareholder Rapallo Ltd, London, English Nat. Investment Corpn, Tamarind Int., Hong Kong, auction house Christie's, London. *Leisure interest:* art collection includes works by Picasso, Matisse, Lucian Freud and Francis Bacon and sculptor Henry Moore. *Address:* PO Box N7776, Lyford Cay, New Providence, Bahamas. *E-mail:* info@tavistock.com. *Website:* www .tavistock.com.

LEWIS, Juliette; American film actress and musician; b. 21 June 1973, Los Angeles, Calif.; d. of Geoffrey Lewis and Glenis Batley Lewis; m. Steve Berra 1999; f. band Juliette & The Licks 2003; Chicago Film Critics' Asscn Most Promising Actress 1991, NATO/ShoNest Female Star of Tomorrow 1993, Venice Film Festival Pasinetti Prize 1994. *Films include:* My Stepmother is an Alien 1988, Meet the Hollowheads 1989, National Lampoon's Christmas Vacation 1989, Cape Fear 1991, Crooked Hearts 1991, Husbands and Wives 1992, Kalifornia 1993, One Hot Summer, That Night 1993, What's Eating Gilbert Grape 1993, Romeo is Bleeding 1994, Natural Born Killers 1994, Mixed Nuts 1994, The Basketball Diaries 1995, Strange Days 1995, From Dusk Till Dawn 1996, The Evening Star 1996, The Audition, Full Tilt Boogie 1997, The Other Sister 1999, The 4th Floor 1999, Way of the Gun 2000, My Louisiana Sky 2002, Hysterical Blindness 2002, Enough 2002, Gaudi Afternoon 2003, Old School 2003, Cold Creek Manor 2003, Blueberry 2004, Starsky and Hutch 2004, Aurora Borealis 2005, Daltry Calhoun 2005, Lightfield's Home Videos 2006, The Darwin Awards 2006, Grilled 2006, Catch and Release

2006. *Television appearances include:* Homefires (mini-series), I Married Dora 1988, Too Young To Die (movie) 1989, A Family For Joe 1990. *Theatre:* Fool for Love (Apollo Theatre, London) 2006. *Recordings include:* albums: You're Speaking My Language 2005, Four on the Floor 2006. *Address:* c/o Norman Brokaw, William Morris Agency, 1 William Morris Place, Beverly Hills, CA 90212, USA (office). *Website:* www.julietteandthelicks.com (office).

LEWIS, Kenneth D., BA; American banking executive; b. 9 April 1947, Meridian, Miss.; ed Georgia State Univ., Stanford Univ.; credit analyst, North Carolina Nat. Bank (NCNB, predecessor to NationsBank and Bank of America), Charlotte, NC 1969–77, Man. NCNB Int. Banking Corpn, NY 1977–79, Sr Vice-Pres. and Man. US Dept 1979–83, Middle Market Group Exec. (following creation of Bank of America group) 1983–86, Pres. Fla Div. 1986–88, Pres. Tex. Div. 1988–90, Pres. Consumer and Commercial Banking 1990–99, Pres. and COO Bank of America Corpn 1999–2001, Pres. and CEO 2001–09, Chair. 2001–09; mem. Bd of Dirs Health Man. Assocs Inc., Homeownership Educ. and Counseling Inst., Lowe's Cos Inc., Presbyterian Hosp. Foundation (fmr Chair.); fmr Chair. Nat. Urban League; Vice-Chair. Corp. Fund Bd of The John F. Kennedy Center for the Performing Arts; mem. Financial Services Roundtable, Financial Services Forum, Cttee to Encourage Corporate Philanthropy; Fifth Dist's Rep. on Fed. Advisory Cttee; mem. Bd, Exec. Cttee and past Chair. United Way of Central Carolinas, Inc.; mem. Bd Dirs Homeownership Educ. and Counseling Inst.; Banker of the Year, American Banker 2002, Top CEO, US Banker 2002, named by Time Magazine to The Time 100 List 2007. *Address:* c/o Bank of America Corporate Center, 100 North Tryon Street, Charlotte, NC 28255, USA (office). *E-mail:* info@bankofamerica.com (office). *Website:* www.bankofamerica.com (office).

LEWIS, Lennox, CBE; British professional boxer; b. 2 Sept. 1965, London; s. of Violet Blake; defeated Jean Chanet to win European heavyweight title, Crystal Palace 1990; defeated Gary Mason to win British heavyweight title, Wembley 1991; Commonwealth heavyweight; WBC heavyweight 1992; defeated Frank Bruno (q.v.) 1993; WBC world champion 1993–94, 1997–; defended WBC title and challenged for World Boxing Asscn (WBA) and Int. Boxing Fed. (IBF) titles against Evander Holyfield (q.v.) March 1999, bout declared a draw; undisputed world heavyweight champion 1999–2001 (lost WBC and IBF titles when defeated by Hasim Rahman April 2001); regained title of world heavyweight champion from Hasim Rahman Nov. 2001; retained title of undisputed world heavyweight champion June 2002 (after beating Mike Tyson q.v.) and June 2003 (after beating Vitali Klitschko); 41 professional wins (two draws, one draw, 31 knock-outs); announced retirement Feb. 2004; f. Lennox Lewis Coll., Hackney 1994; Dr hc (Univ. of London) 1999. *Film:* Ocean's Eleven 2002. *Publications include:* Lennox Lewis (autobiog.) 1993, Lennox 2002. *Leisure interests:* action movie watching, urban music, cross training, golf, chess. *Website:* www.lennoxlewis.com.

LEWIS, Patrick Albert, PhD; Antigua and Barbuda diplomatist and historian; b. 27 Nov. 1938, St John's; m.; two c.; ed Hampton Inst. and Univ. of Cincinnati; Asst Prof. Univ. of Cincinnati 1971–73, Asst Prof., Assoc. Prof., Prof. of History, Hampton Univ. 1973–84; Adviser to Deputy Prime Minister of Antigua and Barbuda 1984–87, Minister-Counsellor, Perm. Mission to the UN 1987–91, apptd Amb. to UN 1995, to Brazil 1999. *Leisure interests:* cricket, movies, theatre, music. *Address:* c/o Ministry of Foreign Affairs, Queen Elizabeth Highway, St John's, Antigua and Barbuda (office).

LEWIS, Roger Charles, BMus, FRWCMD; British sports executive and fmr broadcasting executive; *Group Chief Executive, Welsh Rugby Union;* b. 24 Aug. 1954, Bridgend, Glamorgan, Wales; s. of the late Griffith Charles Job Lewis and Dorothy Lewis (née Russ); m. Christine Trollope 1980; two s.; ed Cynffig Comprehensive School, Bridgend, Univ. of Nottingham; freelance musician 1976–80; Music Officer Darlington Arts Centre 1980–82; presenter Radio Tees 1981–84; producer Capital Radio 1984–85; BBC Radio 1 1985–87, Head of Music Radio 1 1987–90; Dir Classical Div. EMI Records 1990–95, Man. Dir 1995, Man. Dir EMI Premier 1995–97; Pres. Decca Record Co. 1997–98; Man. Dir and Programme Controller Classic FM 1998–2004; Man. Dir ITV Wales 2004–06; Group CEO Welsh Rugby Union (WRU) 2006–; Deputy Chair. Boosey & Hawkes 2004–; Chair. Classic FM Charitable Trust 1998–2004, Music and Dance Scheme Advisory Group, Dept for Educ. and Skills 2000–04, Barchester Group 2001–06; Dir, GWR PLC 1998–2004, The Radio Corpn Ltd 1999–2004, Digital One 2003–04, Liverpool Capital of Culture 2003–06 (mem. Bd Liverpool Culture Co.), Wales Millennium Centre 2004–06, ERC Ltd 2006–, Celtic Rugby Ltd 2006–; Dir (non-exec.), RMG Ltd 2012–; Pres. Bromley Youth Music Trust 2000–05; Chair. Royal Liverpool Philharmonic 2003–06, Int. Advisory Bd Cardiff Univ. Business School 2008–, Yes for Wales Referendum Campaign 2010–11, South East Wales City Region Bd 2013–; Vice-Pres. London Welsh Male Voice Choir 2004–; mem. British Phonographic Inst. (Classical Cttee 1990–98, Chair. 1996–98), Six Nations Council 2012–; Chair. of Trustees, Ogmore Centre 1996–2008; Trustee, Masterprize (Int. Composers' Competition) 1995–2010, Masterclass Charitable Trust 2000–04; Fellow, Cardiff Univ.; Hon. Fellow, Royal Welsh Coll. of Music and Drama; Hon. mem. Royal Coll. of Music; Dr hc (Nottingham), (Glamorgan); Sony Radio Award 1987, 1988, 1989; Grand Award Winner and Gold Medal, New York Radio Festival 1987, One World Broadcasting Trust Award 1989, NTL Commercial Radio Programmer of the Year 2002. *Leisure interests:* rugby, walking, skiing. *Address:* Welsh Rugby Union Ltd, Millennium Stadium, Westgate Street, Cardiff, CF10 1NS, Wales (office). *Telephone:* (844) 249-1999 (office). *E-mail:* info@wru.co.uk (office). *Website:* www.wru.co.uk (office).

LEWIS, Russell T., BA, JD; American newspaper executive; b. 1948; ed State Univ. of New York at Stony Brook, Brooklyn Law School; joined New York Times as a copy boy, while attending coll. 1966; litigation assoc., Cahill, Gordon and Reindel 1973; staff attorney, New York Times legal dept 1977; Pres., Gen. Man. The New York Times, New York 1993–97, Pres., CEO 1997–2004 (retd); Acad. of Man. Distinguished Exec. of the Year 2002, American Lung Asscn of NY Life & Breath Award 2002, Nat. Human Relations Award, American Jewish Cttee 2003. *Leisure interests:* fitness, running, golf.

LEWIS, Stephen, CC; Canadian international advocate and academic; *Co-Director, AIDS-Free World;* b. 11 Nov. 1937, Ottawa, Ont.; s. of David Lewis and Sophie Lewis; m. Michele Landsberg 1963; three c.; ed Univs of Toronto and British Columbia; spent one year teaching and travelling in Africa; Prov. Leader,

New Democratic Party (NDP) 1970–77; MP for Scarborough W, Ont. Legis. 1963–78; Canadian Amb. to UN 1984–88; Special Adviser to UN Sec.-Gen. on Africa 1986–91; Special Rep. to UNICEF 1990, Deputy Exec. Dir 1995–99; mem. Int. Panel of Eminent Personalities to investigate genocide in Rwanda 1998; UN Special Envoy for HIV/AIDS in Africa 2001–06; Co-Dir AIDS-Free World 2007–; Prof., McMaster Univ. 2007–; Founder and Chair. Stephen Lewis Foundation 2003–; Hon. LLD from 30 univs; Gordon Sinclair ACTRA Award 1982, Maclean's Magazine Canadian of the Year 2003, listed by TIME magazine as one of 100 most influential people in the world 2005. *Publications:* Art Out of Agony 1983, Race Against Time 2005. *Address:* Stephen Lewis Foundation, 260 Spadina Avenue, Suite 501, Toronto, ON M5T 2E4, Canada (office). *Telephone:* (416) 533-9292 (office). *Fax:* (416) 850-4910 (office). *E-mail:* info@stephenlewisfoundation.org (office); info@aids-freeworld.org (office). *Website:* www.stephenlewisfoundation .org (office); www.aids-freeworld.org (office).

LEWIS, Vaughan Allen, PhD, CBE; Saint Lucia politician and academic; *Professor Emeritus of International Relations, University of the West Indies;* b. 17 May 1940; m. Shirley May Lewis; two d.; ed Univ. of Manchester, UK; temporary Asst Lecturer, Dept of Political Theory, Univ. Coll. Swansea, Wales 1963–64; Asst Lecturer, Dept of Politics, Univ. of Liverpool 1964–66; Research Fellow Dept of Govt, Univ. of Manchester 1966–68; Lecturer, Dept of Govt, Univ. of the West Indies, Mona, Jamaica 1968–72, Part-time Lecturer, Inst. of Int. Relations, Univ. of the West Indies, St Augustine, Trinidad 1974–80, Acting Dir Inst. of Social and Econ. Research, Univ. of the West Indies 1974, Dir (rank of Full Prof.) 1977–82; Dir-Gen. Org. of Eastern Caribbean States, Castries, St Lucia 1982–95; Prime Minister of Saint Lucia 1996–97; Prof. of Int. Relations, Inst. of Int. Relations, Univ. of the West Indies 1999, now Prof. Emer.; Visiting Prof., Fla Int. Univ. 1980, Ford Foundation Visiting Fellow, Yale Univ. 1981. *Publications:* numerous books, papers and articles on int. relations, particularly concerning the Caribbean. *Address:* Institute of International Relations, University of the West Indies, St Augustine Campus, St Augustine, Trinidad and Tobago. *E-mail:* iirt@sta.uwi.edu (office). *Website:* sta.uwi.edu/iir (home).

LEWIS, W. Joe, BS, MS, PhD; American entomologist and government scientist; *Research Entomologist, Crop Protection and Management Research Unit, Agricultural Research Service, US Department of Agriculture;* b. Miss.; ed Mississippi State Univ.; currently Research Entomologist, Crop Protection and Man. Research Unit, Agricultural Research Service (ARS), US Dept of Agric. (USDA), Tifton, Ga; Charter Ed. Biological Control: Theory and Applications in Pest Management 1991; Founders' Memorial Lecturer Award, Entomological Soc. of America 1990, USDA-ARS Outstanding Scientist of the Year Award 1999, Special Congressional Recognition for Outstanding Achievement, Service and Public Distinction 2000, Jean-Marie Delwart Prize for Science of Chemical Communications (co-recipient) 2003, Invitational Fellowship for Research, Japan Soc. for Promotion of Science 2003, Wolf Prize in Agric. (Israel) (co-recipient) 2008. *Publications:* several book chapters and more than 200 peer-reviewed papers in professional journals. *Address:* Crop Protection and Management Research Unit, USDA-ARS, PO Box 748, Tifton, GA 31793-0748, USA (office). *Telephone:* (229) 387-2369 (office). *Fax:* (229) 387-2321 (office). *E-mail:* wjl@tifton.usda.gov (office). *Website:* www.ars.usda .gov (office).

LEWIS, William; British journalist and newspaper editor; *Group General Manager, News International;* b. 2 April 1969; m. Rebecca Lewis; three c.; worked on financial section of Mail on Sunday (UK) 1991–94; Global News Ed., later Mergers and Acquisitions Ed. (based in New York), later Investment Corresp., Financial Times 1994–2002; Business Ed. Sunday Times 2002–05; Jt Deputy Ed. Daily Telegraph 2005–06, Man. Dir (Editorial) 2006, Ed. 2006–09, Ed.-in-Chief 2007–09, also of Sunday Telegraph 2007–09, Digital Man. Dir 2009–10; Group Gen. Man., News International 2010–; several awards, including Wincott Young Financial Journalist of the Year, Journalist of the Year, British Press Awards 2010. *Address:* News International PLC, 1 Virginia Street, London, E98 1XY, England (office). *Telephone:* (20) 7782-6000 (office). *Fax:* (20) 7782-6097 (office). *Website:* www.newsint.co.uk (office).

LEXDEN, Baron (Life Peer), cr. 2010, of Lexden in the County of Essex and of Strangford in the County of Down; **Alistair Cooke,** OBE; British political historian; b. 20 April 1945, Colchester, Essex; s. of Dr Basil Cooke and Nancy Cooke (née Neal); ed Peterhouse, Cambridge; spent majority of career in cen. org. of Conservative Party; taught and researched modern British and Irish history at Queen's Univ., Belfast 1971–77; political adviser to Airey Neave, Conservative Spokesman on NI 1977–79; Asst Dir, then Deputy Dir Conservative Research Dept 1983–97, consultant 2004–, Dir Conservative Political Centre 1988–97; Gen. Sec. Independent Schools Council 1997–2004; Official Historian and Archivist, Carlton Club 2007–, Conservative Party 2009–; mem. (Conservative) House of Lords 2010–; historical consultant to Conservative Party Archive; Pres. NI Schools Debating Competition; has reviewed history books for The Daily Telegraph, Northern Ireland magazine Fortnight and for national journals; obituarist for several nat. newspapers. *Publications include:* as author: Ulster: The Unionist Options, Ulster: The Origins of the Problem, Making Unionism Positive A Party of Change: A Brief History of the Conservatives (co-author), Government and Party Politics in Britain 1885–86, The Governing Passion: Cabinet (with John Vincent), The Carlton Club 1832–2007 (with Sir Charles Petrie) 2007, A Party of Change: A Brief History of the Conservatives 2008, Tory Heroine: Dorothy Brant and the Rise of Conservative Women 2008, Tory Policy-Making: The Conservative Research Department 1929–2009 2009, A Gift from the Churchills: The Primrose League 1883–2004 2010; as editor of historical series: The Conservative Party: Seven Historical Studies 1680 to the 1990s, A Conservative Party Leader in Ulster: Sir Stafford Northcote's Diary of a Visit to the Province, October 1883, The Conservative Research Department 1929–2004, Ireland and Party Politics, 1885–87: An Unpublished Conservative Memoir, The Ashbourne Papers 1869–1913 (co-ed.); as editor of party publs: The Campaign Guide, Seven Volumes, 1987–2005, Collected Speeches: Margaret Thatcher, John Major and David Cameron, Conservative Political Centre: 120 pamphlets, 1988–97, Politics Today, published 12 times a year by the Research Dept 1986–97; frequent letters on historical subjects in nat. press. *Address:* Conservative Party, 30 Millbank, London, SW1P 4DP (office); House of Lords, Westminster, London, SW1A 0PW, England (office). *Telephone:* (20) 7222-9000 (Millbank) (office); (20) 7219-8216

(House of Lords) (office). *Fax:* (20) 7219-5979 (House of Lords) (office). *E-mail:* lexdena@parliament.uk (office). *Website:* www.alistairlexden.org.uk.

LEY, Steven Victor, CBE, BSc, PhD, FRS, FRSC, FMedSci; British chemist and academic; *BP (1702) Professor of Organic Chemistry, University of Cambridge;* b. 10 Dec. 1945, Stamford, Lincs., England; ed Loughborough Univ.; Postdoctoral Fellow, Ohio State Univ., USA 1972–74; Postdoctoral Fellow, Imperial Coll., London 1974–75, Probationary Lecturer 1975–76, Lecturer 1976–83, Prof. of Organic Chem. 1983–92, Head of Dept 1989–92, Fellow 2001–; BP (1702) Prof. of Organic Chem., Univ. of Cambridge 1992–2014, Head of Organic Chem. 1992–, Fellow, Trinity Coll. 1993–; numerous hon. lectureships including at univs in USA, Canada, Japan, Australia; Pres. RSC 2002–03; Hon. Fellow, Chemical Research Soc. of India 2001; Hon. DSc (Loughborough) 1994, (Salamanca, Spain) 2000, (Huddersfield) 2003; 29 major prizes and awards, including Corday-Morgan Medal and Prize, Royal Inst. of Chem. 1980, Davy Medal, Royal Soc. 2000, Gesellschaft Deutscher Chemiker August-Wilhelm-von Hofmann Medal 2001, Wolfson Merit Award 2003, ACS Ernest Guenther Award in the Chem. of Natural Products 2003, RSC Teamwork in Innovation Award 2004, iChemE Award for Innovation in Applied Catalysis 2004, Alexander-von-Humboldt Award 2004, Innovation of the Year Award (jtly with AstraZeneca, Avecia and Syngenta), Chemical Industries Asscn 2004, Messel Medal Lecture, Soc. of Chemical Industry 2004, Yamada-Koga Prize 2005, RSC Robert Robinson Award and Medal 2006, Nagoya Gold Medal, Banyu Life Science Foundation International, Japan 2006, ACS Award for Creative Work in Synthetic Organic Chem. 2007, SCI Innovation Award 2007, Hans Herloff Inhoffen Medal, Helmholtz Zentrum für Infektionsforschung, Germany 2008, Prous Inst.-Overton and Meyer Award for New Technologies in Drug Discovery, European Fed. of Medicinal Chem. 2008, RSC High Throughput Drug Discovery Methodologies Award 2008, U.R. Ghatak Endowment Lecture and Gold Medal, Indian Asscn for the Cultivation of Science 2009, first recipient of the RSC Perkin Prize for Organic Chem. 2009, Heinrich Wieland Prize, Boehringer Ingelheim 2009, Tetrahedron Prize for Creativity in Organic Chem. 2009, Paracelsus Prize, Swiss Chemical Soc. 2010, Royal Medal, Royal Soc. 2011, included by The Times in its list of the "100 most important people in British science" 2011, Franco Brittanique Prize, Soc. Chimie de France 2013, RSC Longstaff Prize 2013. *Publications:* more than 770 papers in scientific journals. *Address:* Department of Chemistry, University of Cambridge, Lensfield Road, Cambridge, CB2 1EW, England (office). *Telephone:* (1223) 336398 (office). *E-mail:* svl1000@cam.ac.uk (office). *Website:* www.leygroup.ch.cam.ac.uk (office).

LEYE, Jean-Marie; Ni-Vanuatu fmr head of state; *Pres. of Vanuatu 1994–99.* *Address:* c/o Office of the President, Port Vila, Vanuatu.

LEYSEN, Thomas; Belgian business executive; *Chairman, KBC Group NV;* b. 1960; ed Univ. of Leuven; began career in maritime business in Hamburg, London and Tokyo; managed Transcor group 1983–88; managed restructuring of General Trading Cy (subsidiary of Société Générale de Belgique) 1989; joined Umicore as mem. Exec. Cttee 1993, successively managed several industrial divisions, Exec. Vice-Pres. 1998–2000, CEO 2000–08, Chair. 2008–; Chair. Fed. of Belgian Enterprises 2008–11; Chair. KBC Group NV 2011–; Chair. Corelio (newspaper publishing group); mem. Supervisory Bd Bank Metzler, Frankfurt, Global Advisory Council of Toyota Motor Corpn (Japan); mem. Trilateral Comm., European Round Table of Industrialists; Chair. Belgium-Japan Asscn, Rubenianum Fund, Heritage Fund of the Fondation Roi Baudouin, European Friends of Versailles; Vice-Pres. Vrienden van het Rubenshuis. *Address:* KBC Group NV, Havenlaan 2, Brussels 1080, Belgium (office). *Telephone:* (2) 429-50-45 (office). *Fax:* (2) 429-63-40 (office). *E-mail:* thomas.leysen@kbc.be (office). *Website:* www .kbc.be (office).

LHENDUP, Kesang; Bhutanese politician; *President, Druk National Congress;* joined Druk Nat. Congress 1994, served as Gen. Sec. and Vice-Pres., Pres. 2011–; also worked in Dept of Revenue and Custom. *Address:* Druk National Congress, Boudha 6, POB 5754, Kathmandu, Nepal (office). *Telephone:* (1) 2298060 (office). *E-mail:* dnc@bhutandnc.com (office); dnc2006@gmail.com (office). *Website:* www .bhutandnc.com (office).

LHO, Shin-yong; South Korean politician and diplomatist; b. 28 Feb. 1930, S Pyongyang Prov.; ed Law Coll. of Seoul Nat. Univ., Kentucky State Univ., USA; joined diplomatic service 1956, Dir Planning and Man. Office, Ministry of Foreign Affairs 1967; Consul-Gen., Los Angeles, USA 1969–72; Amb. to India 1973, to Geneva 1976; Vice-Foreign Minister 1974, Foreign Minister 1980–82; Acting Prime Minister Feb.–May 1985, Prime Minister May 1985–87; Head, Agency of Nat. Security Planning 1982–85; mem. Democratic Justice Party (later New Korea Party to be merged with Democratic Party to form Grand Nat. Party); elected Chair. Lotte Foundation 1995. *Publications:* The U.S.–Korea Success Story (The Heritage Lectures) 1969, Forging an Asia Pacific Community: The East-West Center's Role in the 21st Century 1969, No Sin-yong hoegorok 2000. *Address:* Lotte Foundation, 24th Floor, Lotte Building, 81 Namdaemun-ro, Jung-Gu, Seoul 100-721 South Korea. *Telephone:* (2) 776-6723. *Fax:* (2) 318-4823. *E-mail:* scholarship@ lotte.net; welfare@lotte.net. *Website:* www.lottefoundation.or.kr.

LI, Arthur K. C., GBS, BChir, MA, MD, JP; British surgeon and academic; *Secretary for Education and Manpower, Hong Kong Special Administrative Region;* b. 23 June 1945, Hong Kong; ed St Paul's Co-educational Coll., King's Coll., Cambridge, Middlesex Hosp. Medical School, Harvard Medical School, USA; house physician, Addenbrooke's Hosp., Cambridge 1969–70, Rotational Sr House Officer 1970–71; house surgeon, Middx Hosp., London 1970; Rotational Surgical Registrar, Queen Elisabeth II Hosp. 1971-71, Hillingdon Hosp., Uxbridge 1972–73; Surgical Registrar, St Mary's Hosp., London 1973–75; Lecturer in Surgery and Sr Surgical Registrar, Royal Free Hosp., London 1975–77, Chair. Div. of Jr Hosp. Doctors 1975–77, Consultant Surgeon and Sr Lecturer in Surgery 1980–82; Stanley Thomas Johnson Foundation Research Fellow, Harvard Medical School, Massachusetts Gen. Hosp. and Shriners Burns Inst., Boston 1977–78, Clinical and Research Fellow 1978–79, Surgical Staff and Instructor in Surgery 1979–80; Foundation Prof. of Surgery and Chair. of Surgical Services, Chinese Univ. of Hong Kong and the Prince of Wales Hosp. 1982–95, Assoc. Dean, Faculty of Medicine 1986–92, Dean 1992–96, Prof. of Surgery 1995, Vice-Chancellor (Pres.) and mem. Univ. Council 1996–2002; Chair. Hosp. Gov. Cttee, United Christian Hosp. 1987–97; mem. Exec. Council and Sec. for Educ. and Manpower, Hong Kong Special Admin. Region 2002–; Visiting Prof., Royal Australian Coll. of Surgeons 1984, 1986, Nat. Univ. of Singapore 1986, Yale Univ. 1989; Pearce Gould Visiting Prof. in Surgery, Univ. Coll. London and Middlesex School of Medicine 1993; Edward Tooth Prof., Royal Brisbane Hosp. 1995; mem. Bd United Christian Medical Services 1987–; fmr mem. Bd Dirs Hong Kong Science and Tech. Parks Corpn, Hong Kong Applied Science and Tech. Research Inst.; mem. Int. Advisory Panel Ministry of Health, UAE 1993–; fmr Vice-Pres. Asscn of Univ. Pres of China; Hon. Prof. of Surgery, Sun Yat-sen Univ. of Medical Sciences, Guangzhou 1986, People's Hosp., Beijing Medical Univ. 1987, Mil. Postgraduate Medical School and Chinese PLA Gen. Hosp., Beijing 1994; Hon. Prof., Peking Union Medical Coll. 1996, Shanghai Medical Univ.; Hon. Fellow, Sidney Sussex Coll. Cambridge, Philippines Coll. of Surgeons 1994, Asscn of Surgeons of GB and Ireland 1998; Hon. FRCS (Glasgow) 1995; Hon. FRCS (Ireland); Hon. FRSM 1997; Hon. FACS 2000; Hon. FRCP; Hon. DSc (Hull) 1999; Hon. DLitt (Hong Kong Univ. of Science and Tech.) 1999; Dr hc (Soka Univ., Tokyo) 1999; European Soc. for Surgical Research Prize 1980, Moynihan Medal 1982, Royal Coll. of Surgeons Gordon Watson Medal 1987, Stanford Cade Memorial Medal 1988, Royal Marsden Surgical Soc. Ernest Miles Memorial Medal 1990, Edward Hallaran Bennett Lecturer, Trinity Coll. Dublin 1995, Pres.'s Gold Medal Royal Coll. of Surgeons of Edin. 1996, Sir Edward Dunlop Memorial Lecturer, Royal Australian Coll. of Surgeons 2000, Gold Bauhinia Star, Govt of Hong Kong Special Admin. Region 2000, Shaw Prize 2004. *Publications:* numerous research papers in learned journals. *Leisure interests:* reading, skiing, scuba diving. *Address:* Education and Manpower Bureau, 15/F, Wu Chung House, 213 Queen's Road East, Wan Chai, Hong Kong Special Administrative Region, People's Republic of China (office). *Telephone:* (852) 28910088 (office). *Fax:* (852) 28930858 (office). *E-mail:* embinfo@ emb.gov.hk (office). *Website:* www.emb.gov.hk (office).

LI, Baomin; Chinese economist and business executive; *Chairman, Jiangxi Copper Company Limited;* ed Faculty of History, Jiangxi Teachers' Univ., Corp. Man. Coll. of Fudan Univ., Postgraduate Programme of Econs of Jiangxi Prov. Party Cttee Coll.; fmr Deputy Sec. of Party Cttee, Jiangxi Copper Co. Ltd, now Sec., Supervisor, Jiangxi Copper Co. Ltd 2003–, has held several man. positions, Exec. Dir and Vice-Chair. 2007–13, Chair. 2013–. *Address:* Jiangxi Copper Co. Ltd, 15 Yejin Avenue, Guixi 335424, People's Republic of China (office). *Telephone:* (701) 3777070 (office). *E-mail:* webmaster@jxcc.com (office). *Website:* www.jxcc .com (office).

LI, Baotian; Chinese actor; b. Dec. 1946, Xuzhou, Jiangsu Prov.; ed Cen. Acad. of Drama; teacher, Cen. Acad. of Drama 1981–; acted in Judou, Shanghai Triad, Prime Minister Hunchback Liu (TV series); Best Supporting Actor, 8th Golden Rooster Awards. *Films include:* Ju Dou 1990, Shanghai Triad 1995, Keep Cool 1997, Courthouse on Horseback 2006, The Nightingale 2013. *Address:* Central Academy of Drama, Beijing, People's Republic of China.

LI, Bin, BA, DEcon; Chinese government official; *Minister, National Health and Family Planning Commission;* b. 1954, Fushun City, Liaoning Prov.; ed Jilin Univ.; joined CCP 1981; Asst to Gov., Jilin Prov. 2000–01, mem. People's Govt 2001–07, Vice-Gov. 2001–07; Deputy Dir, Nat. Population and Family Planning Comm. 2007–08, Dir 2008–11, also Sec., CCP Leading Party Group 2007–11; Vice-Gov., Anhui Prov. 2011–12, Gov. 2012–13, also mem. and Deputy Sec., CCP Prov. Standing Cttee 2011–13; Minister, Nat. Health and Family Planning Comm. 2013–; mem. 17th CCP Cen. Cttee 2007–12, 18th CCP Cen. Cttee 2012–, also mem. CCP Cen. Cttee Central Guidance Cttee on Ethical and Cultural Construction 2008–11. *Address:* National Population and Family Planning Commission, 1 Xizhinenwai Nan Lu, Xicheng Qu, Beijing 100044, People's Republic of China (office). *Telephone:* (10) 68792114 (office). *Fax:* (10) 64012369 (office).

LI, Boyong; Chinese state official and engineer; b. 1932, Tianjin City; ed Air Force Inst. of Mil. Eng, fmr USSR; Vice-Minister, Labour and Personnel 1986–93; mem. 14th CCP Cen. Cttee 1992–97; Minister of Labour 1993–98; Vice-Chair. Legal Affairs Cttee of 9th NPC 1998–2003. *Address:* c/o Standing Committee of National People's Congress, Beijing 100716, People's Republic of China.

LI, Chang'an; Chinese party and state official; b. 1935, Tai'an Co., Liaoning Prov.; ed Shandong Tech. Coll.; joined CCP 1961; Alt. mem. 12th CCP Cen. Cttee 1982, mem. 1985; Deputy Sec. CCP Cttee, Shandong Prov. 1983–88; Gov. of Shandong 1985–88; Deputy Sec.-Gen. CCP State Council 1987; Deputy Head State Flood Control HQ 1988, Cen. Forest Fire Prevention 1987; Deputy Head Leading Group for Comprehensive Agricultural Devt 1990–; Vice-Chair. State Tourism Cttee 1988; Exec. Vice Chair. China Poly Group Corpn 1993–2001; Chair. China Orient Telecomm Satellite Co. Ltd 1995–2003; Dir (non-exec.) PYI Corpn 2007. *Address:* c/o PYI (Shanghai) Enterprise Management Co., Ltd 38/F, Building B, No. 391 Guiping Road, Xuhui District, Shanghai, People's Republic of China.

LI, Changchun; Chinese party and government official; b. Feb. 1944, Dalian City, Liaoning Prov.; m. Zhang Shurong; ed Harbin Inst. of Tech.; joined CCP 1965; at Harbin Inst. of Tech. 1966–68; technician, Shenyang Switchgear Plant, Liaoning Prov. 1968–75; Deputy Man. later Man. Shenyang Electrical Equipment Co. 1975–80 (Vice-Chair. CCP Revolutionary Cttee, mem. Standing Cttee and Deputy Sec. CCP Party Cttee 1975–80); Deputy Dir Bureau of Mechanical and Electrical Industry, Shenyang City 1980–81 (Deputy Sec. CCP Party Cttee 1980–81); Deputy Sec.-Gen. CCP Municipal Cttee, Shenyang City 1981–82; Vice-Mayor Shenyang City 1982–83, Mayor 1983–85; Sec. Shenyang Municipal CCP Cttee 1983–86 (Chair. Econ. Cttee 1982–83); Deputy Sec. Liaoning Prov. CCP Cttee 1985–90; Vice-Gov. (also Acting Gov.) of Liaoning Prov. 1986–87, Gov. 1987–90; Vice-Gov. (also Acting Gov.) of Henan Prov. 1990–91, Gov. 1991–92; Sec. CCP 5th Henan Prov. Cttee 1992–98; Chair. Standing Cttee Henan Prov. People's Congress 1993–98; Alt. mem. 12th CCP Cen. Cttee 1981–82, mem. 13th CCP Cen. Cttee 1987–92, 14th CCP Cen. Cttee 1992–97, 15th CCP Cen. Cttee 1997–2002, Politburo 15th CCP Cen. Cttee 1997–2002, 16th CCP Cen. Cttee 2002–07, Politburo 16th CCP Cen. Cttee 2002–07, Standing Cttee Politburo 16th CCP Cen. Cttee 2002–07, 17th CCP Cen. Cttee 2007–12, Standing Cttee Politburo 17th CCP Cen. Cttee 2007–12; Sec. CCP Guangdong Prov. Cttee 1998–2002; Chair. CCP Central Guidance Comm. for Building Spiritual Civilization 2002–12; ranked by Forbes magazine amongst The World's Most Powerful People (19th) 2009, (32nd) 2010. *Address:* Standing Committee of the Politburo, Chinese Communist Party Central Committee, Beijing, People's Republic of China (office).

LI, Changjin, MEng; Chinese railway industry executive; *Chairman, President and Executive Director, China Railway Group;* ed Changsha Railway Inst., Southwest Jiaotong Univ.; Vice-Pres. The Fourth Survey and Design Inst., MOR Jan.–Dec. 1995, Deputy Dir and Sr Engineer, The Second Eng Bureau of MOR (predecessor of China Railway No. 2 Eng Group Co. Ltd) 1996–98, Vice-Chair. and Gen. Man. China Railway No. 2 Eng Group Co. Ltd 1998–2002, also Chair. and Sec. to CCP Cttee, Deputy Gen. Man. China Railway Eng Corpn (CRECG) 2002–06, mem. Bd of Dirs 2006–, Pres. and Exec. Dir China Railway Group Ltd –2010, Chair. and Exec. Dir 2010–13, Chair., Pres. and Exec. Dir 2013–; recognized as prof.-level sr engineer by Ministry of Personnel 2003. *Address:* China Railway Group Ltd, 26 Lianhuachi Nanli, Beijing 100055, People's Republic of China (office). *E-mail:* info@crecg.com (office). *Website:* www.crecg.com (office); www.crec.cn/en (office).

LI, Changyin; Chinese engineer and business executive; *General Manager and President, China Shipbuilding Industry Corporation;* Chair. China Shipbuilding Industry Co. Ltd 2008–, fmr Deputy Gen. Man. China Shipbuilding Industry Corpn, currently Gen. Man. and Pres. *Address:* China Shipbuilding Industry Corporation, 72 Kunminghu Nan Lu, Haidian District, Beijing 100097, People's Republic of China (office). *Telephone:* (10) 88598000 (office). *Fax:* (10) 88599000 (office). *E-mail:* csic@csic.com.cn (office). *Website:* www.csic.com.cn (office).

LI, Chunting; Chinese provincial governor; b. Oct. 1936, Luotang village, Zhaili, Qixia Co., Shandong Prov.; joined CCP 1958; worked as farmer; assumed leading posts at village, township, co., prefectural and city level; fmr Deputy Sec. CCP Qixia Co. Cttee, Deputy Sec. CCP Yantai Prefectural Cttee, Head Prov. Metallurgical Dept; Vice-Gov. Shandong Prov. 1988–95, Gov. 1995–97; Deputy Sec. CCP Shandong Prov. Cttee 1992–2001; mem. 15th CCP Cen. Cttee 1997–2002; Vice-Chair. NPC Agric. and Rural Affairs Cttee 2001–. *Address:* National People's Congress, Tiananmen, Beijing, People's Republic of China.

LI, Dadong; Chinese engineer; b. 24 Feb. 1938, Beijing; ed Peking Univ.; joined Research Inst. of Petroleum Processing (RIPP) 1962, becoming Group Leader, Dir, Research Dept, Deputy Chief Engineer 1987–88, Vice-Pres. 1988–91, Pres. 1991–2003, Dir Science Cttee 2004–; Fellow Chinese Acad. of Eng 1994–, Chair. Standing Cttee of Chemical Eng, Metallurgy and Material Eng Dept; many nat., prov. and ministerial prizes. *Publications:* published 70 research papers. *Address:* Petrochemical Science Research Institute, 18 Xueyuan Road, Beijing 100083, People's Republic of China (office). *Telephone:* (10) 62310757 (office). *Fax:* (10) 62311290 (office). *E-mail:* ripp@mimi.cnc.ac.cn (office).

LI, Daoyu; Chinese diplomatist; *President, Chinese International Public Relations Association;* b. 7 Aug. 1932, Shanghai; m. Ye Zhao Lie 1956; two s.; ed Univ. of Shanghai; joined Foreign Service 1952; held various posts Dept of Int. Orgs and Confs; Deputy Perm. Rep. to UN at Geneva 1983–84; Dir Dept of Int. Orgs, Foreign Ministry 1984–88; Asst Foreign Minister 1988–90; Perm. Rep. to UN, New York 1990–93, Amb. to USA 1993–98; led Chinese Del. to ESCAP session 1989; fmr Vice-Chair. Chinese Nat. Comm., UNESCO, Nat. Cttee for Pacific Econ. Co-operation, Preparatory Cttee of China for Int. Space Year 1992, Nat. Cttee for Int. Decade for Natural Disaster Reduction; fmr rep. of China on Comm. on Human Rights, ECOSOC and UNCTAD; Vice-Chair. Overseas Chinese Affairs Cttee of 9th NPC 1998; mem. Standing Cttee NPC 1998–2003; Prof. School of Int. Studies, Beijing Univ., Inst. of Int. Studies, Tsinghua Univ., Foreign Affairs Coll., Center for American Studies, Fudan Univ., Pacific Inst., Tongji Univ.; Pres. China Int. Public Relations Asscn 1999–, Chinese Asscn of Arms Control and Disarmament 2001–; Vice-Pres. China Int. Friendship Exchange Asscn, China Women Devt Fund; mem. Council Chinese People's Inst. of Foreign Affairs; Sr Adviser China Inst. of Int. Strategic Studies; Adviser China Int. Law Soc., Centre for Across-the-Straits Relationship Studies, Shanghai WTO Affairs Consulting Centre. *Address:* China International Public Relations Association, Room 918, 7 Fuchengmenwai Street, Beijing, 100037, People's Republic of China (office). *Telephone:* (10) 68095777 (office). *Fax:* (10) 68095775 (office). *E-mail:* info@cipra.org.cn (office). *Website:* www.cipra.org.cn (office).

LI, Dezhu, (Li Dek Su); Chinese party and government official; b. 1943, Wangqing Co., Jilin Prov.; ed Yanbian Univ.; joined CCP 1965; Vice-Gov. of Jilin Prov. 1988–93; Deputy Head United Front Work Dept 1992; Pres. Chinese Asscn of Ethnic Minorities for External Exchanges 1992–98; Minister State Comm. of Ethnic Affairs 1998–2008; mem. 14th CCP Cen. Cttee 1992–97, 15th CCP Cen. Cttee 1997–2002, 16th CCP Cen. Cttee 2002–07. *Address:* c/o State Ethnic Affairs Commission, 252 Teipingqiao Street, Beijing 100800, People's Republic of China.

LI, Dongsheng; Chinese electronics industry executive; *Chairman, TCL–Thomson Electronics Company Limited (TTE);* b. July 1957; ed Huanan Tech. Inst.; started career as technician with TTK Home Appliances Co. Ltd 1982, later Deputy Workshop Dir, Business Man.; Gen. Man. TCL Communication Equipment Co. 1985–93, Gen. Man. TCL Corpn 1993–96, Chair. and Pres. 1996–2004, Chair. TCL–Thomson Electronics Co. Ltd (TTE) 2004–; mem. 16th CCP Cen. Cttee 2002–07; Special Contributor to China Household Appliance Industry 1994, Nat. Excellent Young Entrepreneur 1995, Nat. Model Worker 2000, Meritorious Figure of Chinese Brands 2009. *Address:* TCL Corporation, East Yunshan Road, Jiangbei Huizhou, Guangdong 516003, China (office). *Telephone:* (752) 2803898 (office). *Fax:* (752) 2803188 (office). *Website:* (office).

LI, Fanghua, BS; Chinese physicist; *Professor, Institute of Physics, Chinese Academy of Sciences;* b. 6 Jan. 1932, Hong Kong; d. of Jiong Li and Jiqing Liu; m. Haifu Fan 1960; one s. one d.; ed Beijing Furen and Peidao High Schools, Lingnan and Zhongshan Univs, Guangzhou, Wuhan Univ., Hubei Prov., Leningrad (now St Petersburg) Univ., USSR; Research Asst, Inst. of Physics, Chinese Acad. of Sciences 1956–61, Research Assoc. 1962–78, Assoc. Prof. 1979–86, Prof. 1986–; Visiting Scientist, Osaka Univ. 1982–83; Visiting Prof., City Univ. of Hong Kong 1998–99; Pres. Chinese Electron Microscopy Soc. 1996–2000; mem. Chinese Acad. of Sciences 1993, Third World Acad. of Science (now named TWAS, the academy of sciences for the developing world) 1998; Asia-Pacific recipient, L'Oréal-UNESCO For Women in Science Award (first Chinese woman) 2003, State Natural Science Awards (Second Class) 2005, Ho Leung Ho Lee Prize for Scientific and Technological Progress 2009. *Publications include:* Electron Crystallography and Image Processing (in Chinese) 2009; numerous articles in scientific journals. *Leisure interest:* singing. *Address:* Institute of Physics, Chinese Academy of Sciences, PO Box 603, Beijing, 100190, People's Republic of China (office). *Telephone:* (10) 82649170 (office). *Fax:* (10) 82649531 (office). *E-mail:* lifh@aphy.iphy.ac.cn (office). *Website:* www.iphy.ac.cn (office).

LI, Fanrong, BSc, MBA; Chinese engineer and oil industry executive; *CEO and President, China National Offshore Oil Corporation;* b. Oct. 1963; ed Jianghan Petroleum Univ., Cardiff Business School, UK; joined China National Offshore Oil Corpn (CNOOC) 1984, engaged in well testing, CNOOC Nanhai East Corpn 1984–89, Production Supervisor and Platform Man., ACT (Agip-Chevron-Texaco) Operators Group 1990–95, becoming Production Dept Man., Liuhua Oilfield Jt Operation Org., Gen. Man., Lufeng 22-1 Oilfield Jt Operation Org., Deputy Gen. Man., CNOOC (China) Ltd-Shenzhen Br. and concurrently Chinese Chief Rep. at CACT (CNOOC-Agip-Chevron-Texaco) Operators Group 1995–2005, Gen. Man., Devt and Production Dept, CNOOC Ltd 2005–07, Gen. Man., CNOOC (China) Ltd-Shenzhen Br. 2007, Asst Pres., CNOOC 2009, also Gen. Man. CNOOC Energy Technology & Services Ltd 2009, Vice-Pres. and Party Leadership Group mem., CNOOC May–Sept. 2010, Pres. CNOOC Sept. 2010–, CEO 2011–. *Address:* China National Offshore Oil Corpn (CNOOC), 25 Chaoyangmen Bei Dajie, Dongcheng Qu, Beijing 100010, People's Republic of China (office). *Telephone:* (10) 84521010 (office). *Fax:* (10) 64602600 (office). *E-mail:* cnooc@cnooc.com.cn (office). *Website:* www.cnooc.com.cn (office).

LI, Furong; Chinese sports administrator; b. 1942, Shanghai City; Deputy, 5th NPC 1978–83; Deputy Dir Training Bureau under the Comm. for Physical Culture and Sports 1983, Dir 1986–; Vice-Chair. Youth Fed. 1983; Vice-Minister of the Physical Culture and Sports Comm. 1987; Sec.-Gen. Chinese Olympic Team, Seoul 1988; Vice-Pres. Chinese Olympic Cttee 1989–; apptd Vice-Minister in charge of State Gen. Admin for Sports 1999; Pres. Asian Table Tennis Union 2001–09, Hon. Life Pres. 2010–; Head of Chinese Delegation, World Univ. Games 2008. *Address:* 9 Tiyuguan Road, Beijing 100763, People's Republic of China.

LI, Fushan; Chinese artist and engraver; b. June 1940, Quinhuangdao, Hebei; s. of Li Yinchang and Wang Lihui; m. Lei Suoxia 1961; one s. two d.; worked at Quinhuangdao Cultural Centre 1959–62, at Shanhaiguan Cultural Centre 1962–, deputy researcher 1994–; his works are in pvt. collections in Canada, USA, Italy, NZ and countries in SE Asia; Dir Quinhuangdao Arts Asscn; mem. Hebei Br. China Arts Asscn, Hebei Prov. Research Asscn of Etched Plates. *Leisure interests:* classical literature, photography. *Address:* Shanhaiguan Cultural Centre, Quinhuangdao, Hebei Province, People's Republic of China. *Telephone:* 5051418; 3069987.

LI, Genshen, DSc; Chinese party official and engineer; b. 1 July 1930, Huzhou City, Zhejiang Prov.; s. of Li Xin-pei and Zhang Zhu-bao; m. Xu Ying; one s. two d.; ed Jiaotong Univ., Shanghai and in USSR; Dir and Chief Engineer, No. 3 Research Inst., No. 7 Research Acad., China Shipbuilding Industrial Corpn; Chair. Bd Harbin Power Equipment Co. 1993–97, Dir (non-exec.) 1997–; mem. Standing Cttee Heilongjiang Prov. CCP Cttee 1983–92, Sec.-Gen. 1984, Deputy Sec. 1985–86; Vice-Chair. Heilongjiang Prov. 8th People's Congress 1993–96; Sec. Harbin Mun. CCP Cttee 1985, Chair. 1983–; Standing Cttee CCP Heilongjiang Prov. Cttee 1988; mem. 13th CCP Cen. Cttee 1987–92; mem. Standing Cttee 1988. *Publication:* Principles, Design and Testing of Marine Steam and Gas Turbines. *Leisure interest:* reading. *Address:* 1 Guomin Street, Nangang District, Harbin 150001, Heilongjiang Province, People's Republic of China (office). *Telephone:* (451) 84616291 (office); (451) 53624054 (home).

LI, Gong; Chinese actress; b. 31 Dec. 1965, Shenyang, Liaoning; m. Ooi Hoe-Seong 1996. *Films include:* Red Sorghum 1987, Evil Empress 1988, Operation Cougar 1988 (Hundred Flowers Award for Best Supporting Actress 1989), The Terracotta Warrior 1989, Ju Dou 1990, The Banquet 1991, God of Gamblers II: Back to Shanghai 1991, Raise the Red Lantern 1991 (Hundred Flowers Award for Best Actress 1993), The Story of Qiu Ju 1991 (Golden Rooster Awards for Best Actress, 1993, Venice Film Festival Volpi Cup for Best Actress), Mary from Beijing 1992, Farewell, My Concubine 1993 (New York Film Critics Circle Award 1993), Flirting Scholar 1993, To Live 1994, La Peintre 1994, The Great Conqueror's Concubine 1994, Semi-Gods and Semi-Devils 1994, Shanghai Triad 1995, Temptress Moon 1996, The Empress and the Assassin 1997, Chinese Box 1998, Breaking the Silence 1999 (Golden Rooster Awards for Best Actress 2000, Montreal World Film Festival for Best Actress 2000), Zhou Yu's Train 2002, Eros 2004, 2046 2004, Miami Vice 2006, Man cheng jin dai huang jin jia (Curse of the Golden Flower) 2006 (Hong Kong Film Awards for Best Actress, 2007), Hannibal Rising 2007, Shanghai 2010, What Women Want 2011.

LI, Guixian; Chinese party official; *Vice-Chairman, 10th National Committee, Chinese People's Political Consultative Conference;* b. 1938, Gaixian Co., Liaoning Prov.; ed Chinese Univ. of Science and Tech., Mendeleyev Chemical Tech. Inst., Moscow, USSR; joined CCP 1962; worker, Research Inst., Ministry of Public Security 1966–67; technician, later Workshop Dir, later Deputy Dir, later Chief Engineer, No. 777 Factory 1967–77 (Deputy Sec. CCP Party Cttee 1967–77); Deputy Dir, Chief Engineer Jinzhou City Bureau of Electronics Industry 1977–79; Deputy Dir Liaoning Provincial Bureau of Electronics Industry 1979–82 (Deputy Sec. CCP Leading Party Group 1979–82); Vice-Gov. Liaoning Prov. 1982–85; Chair. Science and Tech. Comm. CCP Liaoning Prov. Cttee, CCP Leading Party Group 1982–83; Sec. CCP Cttee, Liaoning Prov. 1985–86, Anhui Prov. 1986–87; Gov. People's Bank of China 1988–93 (resgnd); State Councillor 1988–98; mem. 12th CCP Cen. Cttee 1982–87, 13th CCP Cen. Cttee 1987–92, 14th CCP Cen. Cttee 1992–97, 15th CCP Cen. Cttee 1997–2002, 16th CCP Cen. Cttee 2002–07; Vice-Chair. Nat. Cttee of 9th CPPCC 1998–2003, Nat. Cttee of 10th CPPCC 2003–08; Pres. Chinese Asscn for Int. Understanding 1999–; fmr Dir China Cttee of Int. Decade for Natural Disaster Reduction. *Address:* National Committee of Chinese People's Political Consultative Conference, 23 Taipingqiao Street, Beijing, People's Republic of China. *Website:* www.cafiu.org.cn.

LI, Guohua; Chinese business executive; *President, China Post Group;* Vice-Pres. China Post Group –2012, Pres. and Deputy Sec. CCP Cttee of China Post Group 2012–. *Address:* China Post Group, 3 Financial Street, Beijing, 100080, People's Republic of China (office). *E-mail:* info@chinapost.com.cn (office). *Website:* www .chinapost.com.cn (office).

LI, Guorui; Chinese engineer and business executive; *Chairman and General Manager, China Railway Construction Corporation Ltd;* b. 1950; ed Southwest Jiaotong Univ.; Sec. to CCP Cttee, China Railway Engineering Corpn 1996–97; joined China Railway Construction Corpn (CRCC) Ltd 1997, Sec. to CRCC CCP Cttee 1997–2007, Deputy Gen. Man. CRCC 2002–05, Chair. 2005–, also Gen. Man. 2007–; Chair. Nanjing Changjiang Tunnel Co. Ltd; mem. 17th CCP Congress. *Address:* China Railway Construction Corpn Ltd, 40 Fuxing Road, Haidian District, Beijing 100855, People's Republic of China (office). *Telephone:* (10) 51886971 (Directorate) (office); (10) 51889515 (Supervisory Bd) (office); (10) 52688600 (office); (10) 51888114 (office). *Fax:* (10) 68217382 (office); (10) 52688302 (office). *E-mail:* ir@crcc.cn (office). *Website:* www.crccg.com (office); www.crcc.cn (office).

LI, Hao; Chinese politician; b. Dec. 1926, Dianbai Co., Guangdong Prov.; s. of Li Hansan and Cheng Li; m. Cheng Huizheng 1943; one s. two d.; ed Zhongshan Univ., Guangzhou; joined CCP 1949; Deputy Sec.-Gen. of State Council, Beijing 1983–85; Vice-Gov. Guangdong Prov. 1985–88; Mayor, Shenzhen City, Sec. of CCP Shenzhen Cttee 1985–93; mem. and Vice-Chair. Financial and Econ. Cttee 8th NPC 1993–98; part-time Prof., Beijing Univ. and People's Univ. of China. *Address:* Shenzhen People's Government, Guangdong, People's Republic of China. *Telephone:* (755) 2239440.

LI, Hongzhi; Chinese spiritual leader; b. 13 May 1951, Jilin Prov.; m.; one d.; fmr stud farm worker, trumpeter in police band and grain clerk; Leader, Falun Gong spiritual movt 1992–; lives in exile in New York, USA. *Publication:* Zhuan Falun (Law of the Wheel) 1996. *Address:* c/o The Universe Publishing, PO Box 193, Gillette, NJ 07933, USA (office). *Telephone:* (888) 353-2288 (office). *Fax:* (888) 214-2172 (office).

LI, Huaji; Chinese artist; b. 16 Feb. 1931, Beijing; s. of Li Jue-Tian and Zhang Yun-Zheng; m. Quan Zhenghuan 1959; two d.; mem. Acad. Cttee and Dir Mural Painting Dept, Cen. Acad. of Fine Arts; Vice-Dir Mural Painting Cttee, Artists' Asscn of China; mem. Oil Painting Research Asscn 1988–; important murals include Hunting (Harbin Swan Hotel), 5,000 Years of Culture (Beijing Nat. Library). *Leisure interests:* classical music, Beijing opera. *Address:* 6/F Hongmiao Beili, 100025 Beijing 3-601, People's Republic of China. *Telephone:* (1) 552213.

LI, Jennifer, BA, MBA; Chinese business executive; *Chief Financial Officer, Baidu, Inc.;* m.; two c.; ed Tsinghua Univ., Univ. of British Columbia, Canada; held several finance positions at General Motors in Canada, USA and Singapore 1994–2001, worked at General Motors China, responsible for overseeing finance functions of General Motors' wholly owned and joint venture businesses in China 2001–04, later Chief Financial Officer; Controller, General Motors Acceptance Corpn North American Operations 2005–08; Chief Financial Officer, Baidu, Inc. 2008–; mem. Bd of Dirs Philip Morris International, Inc. 2010–; ranked by Forbes magazine amongst The World's 100 Most Powerful Women (98th) 2013. *Address:* Baidu, Inc., Baidu Campus, No. 10, Shangdi 10th Street, Haidian District, Beijing 100085, People's Repub. of China (office). *Telephone:* (10) 59928888 (office). *Fax:* (10) 59920000 (office). *E-mail:* info@baidu.com (office). *Website:* www.baidu.com (office).

LI, Jet; Chinese actor, producer and martial artist; b. 26 April 1963, Beijing; m. 1st Qiuyan Huang 1987 (divorced 1990); two d.; m. 2nd Nina Li Chi 1999; two d.; began training at Wu Shu (martial arts) Acad., Beijing aged nine; winner of five gold medals in Chinese Wu Shu Championships aged 11; world Wu Shu champion on several occasions; became Wu Shu nat. coach age 20; film debut in Shao Lin tzu (The Shaolin Temple) 1979. *Films include:* Shao Lin tzu 1979, Shao Lin xiao zi 1983, Zhong hua ying xiong 1986, Nan bei Shao Lin 1986, Long zai tian ya 1988, Once upon a Time in China 1991, The Legend (also producer) 1993, Lord of the Wu Tang (also producer) 1993, Claws of Steel (also producer) 1993, Tai-Chi (also producer) 1993, The Legend 2 (also producer) 1993, The Defender (also producer) 1994, High Risk 1995, The Enforcer 1995, Adventure King 1996, Lethal Weapon 4 1998, Romeo Must Die 2000, Kiss of the Dragon (also producer) 2001, The One 2001, Ying xiong 2002, The Contract Killer 2002, Legend of the Red Dragon (also producer) 2002, Legend of the Swordsman 2002, Rise to Honor 2003, Danny the Dog 2005, Huo Yuan Jia 2006, War 2007, The Warlords 2007, The Forbidden Kingdom 2008, The Mummy: Tomb of the Dragon Emperor 2008, The Founding of a Republic 2009, Ocean Heaven 2010, The Expendables 2010, The Expendables 2 2012. *Website:* www.jetli.com.

LI, Jianguo; Chinese politician; b. April 1946, Juanchen Co., Shandong Prov.; ed Shandong Univ., joined CCP 1971; joined CCP 1971; worker, Culture and Educ. Bureau, Ninghe Co., Shandong Prov., Publicity Dept, CCP Co. Cttee, Ninghe Co., Publicity Div., Agricultural Cttee, Tianjin Municipality, Gen. Office CCP Tianjin Municipal Cttee (Deputy Office Dir 1981, Dir 1983, Deputy Sec.-Gen. CCP Tianjin Municipal Cttee 1988, Sec.-Gen. 1989, Deputy Sec. 1992–97); Sec. CCP Heping Dist Cttee, Tianjin 1991–92; Vice-Sec. CCP Tianjin Mun. Cttee 1992; apptd Sec. CCP Shaanxi Prov. Cttee 1997–98, elected Sec. 1998–2002, Chair. Standing Cttee of Shaanxi Prov. People's Congress 1998–; Alt. mem. 14th CCP Cen. Cttee 1992–97, mem. 15th CCP Cen. Cttee 1997–2002, 16th CCP Cen. Cttee 2002–07, 17th CCP Cen. Cttee 2007–12, 18th CCP Cen. Cttee 2012–, 18th CCP Cen. Cttee Politburo 2012–; Sec.-Gen. and Vice-Chair. 11th NPC Standing Cttee 2008–13; Vice-Chair. 12th NPC Standing Cttee 2013–. *Address:* Chinese Communist Party, Zhongnanhai, Beijing, People's Republic of China (office). *Website:* cpc.people.com .cn (office).

LI, Jiating; Chinese politician; b. April 1944, Shiping, Yunnan Prov.; ed Tsinghua Univ.; joined CCP 1964; cadre CCP Heilongjiang Prov. Cttee; Vice-Dir Office of Heilongjiang Prov. Econ. Comm. then Vice-Dir of Comm.; Vice-Mayor then Mayor of Harbin; Asst Sec. of Heilongjiang Prov. 1968–93; Vice-Gov. Yunnan Prov. 1993–98, Gov. 1998–2001; Alt. mem. CCP 14th and 15th Cen. Cttees 1992–2002; arrested and detained pending trial on corruption charges 2002, convicted of corruption, received suspended death sentence 2003.

LI, Ji'nai; Chinese army officer; b. July 1942, Tengzhou City, Shandong Prov.; ed Harbin Acad. of Mil. Eng; joined CCP 1965; joined PLA 1967; various posts, PLA 2nd Artillery; Dir Cadre Dept PLA Gen. Political Dept 1987–90, Deputy Dir 1990–92; Deputy Political Commissar, State Comm. of Science, Tech. and Industry for Nat. Defence 1992–95, Political Commissar 1995, PLA Gen. Equipment Dept

1998–2002; rank of Maj.-Gen. 1988, Lt-Gen. 1993, Gen. 2000; Alt. mem. 14th CCP Cen. Cttee 1992–97, mem. 15th CCP Cen. Cttee 1997–2002, 16th CCP Cen. Cttee 2002–07; mem. 16th CCP Cen. Cttee Cen. Military Comm. 2002–07, 17th CCP Cen. Cttee Cen. Military Comm. 2007–12. *Address:* State Commission of Science, Technology and Industry for National Defence, Jingshanqian Jie, Beijing, People's Republic of China. *Telephone:* (1) 6370000.

LI, Adm. Jing; Chinese naval officer and party official; b. 1930; ed Air Force Aviation Acad. of China; joined PLA 1946, CCP 1949; Deputy Chief PLA Navy Staff 1973–80; Deputy Commdr Naval Air Force 1980–82; Deputy Commdr PLA Navy 1982–92 and concurrently Commdr Naval Air Force 1985–90; Deputy Chief of PLA Gen. Staff HQ 1992–95; rank of Vice-Adm. 1988, Adm. 1994; mem. 7th NPC 1987–92; mem. 14th CCP Cen. Cttee 1992–97; mem. Standing Cttee, Vice-Chair. Foreign Affairs Cttee, 9th Nat. Cttee of CPPCC 1998–2003; mem. Standing Cttee 9th NPC 1998–2008; Sr Adviser Int. Strategy Soc. 1998–. *Address:* c/o National Committee of Chinese People's Political Consultative Conference, 23 Taipingqiao Street, Beijing, People's Republic of China (office).

LI, Jinhua; Chinese politician; b. 1943, Rudong Co., Jiangsu Prov.; ed Cen. Inst. of Finance and Banking, CCP Cen. Cttee Cen. Party School; joined CCP 1965; fmr teacher, Northwest China Inst. of Finance and Banking, Shaanxi Prov.; fmr Deputy Dir later Dir Factory, Ministry of Aeronautics Industry (Deputy Sec. CCP Party Cttee); Dir Econ. and Trade Dept of Shaanxi Prov. 1985; Deputy Auditor Gen. Nat. Audit Office 1985–98, Auditor-Gen. 1998–2008; mem. 14th CCP Cen. Cttee for Discipline Inspection 1992–97, 15th CCP Cen. Cttee 1997–2002, 16th CCP Cen. Cttee 2002–07; Vice-Chair. 11th CPPCC Nat. Cttee 2008–13; Chair. Environmental Auditing Cttee (and mem. Governing Bd), Asian Org. of Supreme Audit Insts; Hon. Prof. Peking Univ., Nankai Univ., Cen. Univ. of Finance and Banking, Nanjing Audit Inst. *Leisure interests:* calligraphy, bridge, swimming, climbing. *Address:* c/o Chinese People's Political Consultative Conference, No. 23, Taipingqiao Street, Beijing 100811, People's Republic of China (office).

LI, Jinping; Chinese business executive; *Chairman and President, Shanxi Lu'An Mining Industry (Group) Company Limited;* Chair. Shanxi Lu'an Environmental Energy Development Co. Ltd 2011–; fmr Gen. Man. and Dir, Shanxi Lu'an Mining Industry (Group) Co. Ltd, currently Chair. and Pres. *Address:* Shanxi Lu'An Mining Group, Houbu Town, Changzhi 046204, People's Republic of China (office). *Telephone:* (355) 5922-141 (office). *Fax:* (355) 5921-972 (office). *E-mail:* webmaster@cnluan.com (office). *Website:* www.cnluan.com (office).

LI, Jinyuan, MBA; Chinese business executive; *Chairman and President, Tiens Group;* b. June 1958, Changzhou, Hebei Prov.; ed Nankai Univ.; left school at 14 and worked in oil field and plastics factory for seven years before starting own business in 1985, set up printing co., flour mill and fodder factory; Chair. and Pres. Tiens Group 1995–, also Chair. and CEO Tiens Bio-Tech Group (USA) Inc.; numerous awards for philanthropy including title of Patriotic Entrepreneur by Patriotic Chinese Businessmen New Year Gathering and Forum of Econ. and Business Cooperation 2005, named as one of Top 10 Philanthropists in Mainland China 2005, honoured with title of State Advanced Individual in Nat. Unity 2005, named as one Top 10 Econ. Talents in China 2005, named China's Top Business Education Leader 2008, China Most Philanthropic Entrepreneur 2010. *Address:* Tiens Group, F20 No. 1 Building, Henderson Center, No. 18, JianGuoMen Nei Street, Beijing 100005, People's Republic of China (office). *Telephone:* (10) 65186239 (office). *E-mail:* support.china@tiens.com.cn (office). *Website:* www .tiens.com/tiens/group/en (office).

LI, Jun, MA; Chinese economist and banking executive; *Chairman of the Board of Supervisors, Bank of China Ltd;* ed Huazhong Univ. of Science and Tech.; joined Bank of Communications 1990, Deputy Gen. Man. and Gen. Man. Wuhan Branch 1990–98, Controller Gen. 1998–2001, Exec. Dir 2000–09, Exec. Vice-Pres. 2000–06, Vice-Chair. and Pres. 2006–09; Chair. Bd of Supervisors, Bank of China Ltd 2010–, Vice-Party Sec. 2009–. *Address:* Bank of China Ltd, 1 Fuxingmen Nei Dajie, Beijing 100818, People's Republic of China (office). *Telephone:* (10) 6659-6688 (office). *Fax:* (10) 6659-3777 (office). *E-mail:* info@boc.cn (office). *Website:* www.boc.cn (office).

LI, Ka-shing, KBE, JP; Chinese entrepreneur and business executive; *Chairman, Cheung Kong (Holdings) Ltd;* b. 1928, Chaozhou, Guangdong Prov.; m. Chong Yuet-ming (deceased); two s.; moved with family from mainland to Hong Kong 1940; worked in watch-strap co. 1942; salesman, later Man. then Gen. Man., for watch strap co. 1945–47; est. Cheung Kong Plastics Co. 1950; est. Cheung Kong Real Estate Co. Ltd 1971; listed Cheung Kong (Holdings) Ltd in Hong Kong 1972, Chair. 1971–; acquired Hutchison Whampoa Ltd 1979, Chair. 1981–; est. Li Ka Shing Foundation 1980; f. Shantou Univ. 1981; acquired Hongkong Electric Holdings Ltd (later renamed Power Assets Holdings Ltd) 1985, Cheung Kong Infrastructure Holdings Ltd spun off in listing 1996, Tom.com (later renamed TOM Group) listed on GEM Stock Exchange 2000, CK Life Sciences International (Holdings) Inc. listed on GEM Stock Exchange 2002, TOM Group advanced to Main Bd of Hong Kong Stock Exchange (HKSE) 2004, CK Life Sciences International (Holdings) Inc. advanced to Main Bd of HKSE 2008; has investments in 52 countries; mem. Drafting Cttee for Basic Law of Hong Kong Special Admin. Region (HKSAR) 1985–90; Hong Kong Affairs Adviser 1992–97; mem. Preparatory Cttee for the HKSAR 1995–97, mem. Selection Cttee of Govt of HKSAR 1996–; mem. Int. Business Advisory Council of the UK 2006; Hon. Citizen of a number of cities in People's Repub. of China (PRC) and overseas; Grand Officer, Order Vasco Nuñez de Balboa (Panama) 1982, Commdr, Order of the Crown (Belgium) 1986, Hon. KBE 2000, Commdr, Order of Leopold (Belgium) 2000, Grand Bauhinia Medal (HKSAR) 2001, Commdr, Légion d'honneur 2005; Hon. LLD (Univ. of Hong Kong) 1986, (Univ. of Calgary, Canada) 1989, (Chinese Univ. of Hong Kong) 1997, (Univ. of Cambridge, UK) 1999; Hon. DScS (Hong Kong Univ. of Science and Tech.) 1995, (City Univ. of Hong Kong) 1998, (Open Univ. of Hong Kong) 1999; Dr hc (Peking Univ.) 1992; Entrepreneur of the Millennium Award, The Times newspaper and Ernst & Young, UK 1999, Int. Distinguished Entrepreneur Award (Univ. of Manitoba, Canada) 2000, Malcolm S. Forbes Lifetime Achievement Award 2006, Special Hon. Award for Econ. Contrib., China Central Television 2007, Lifetime Achievement Award for Philanthropy, PRC Ministry of Civil Affairs 2007, Presidential Award, Teachers of English to Speakers of Other Languages, Inc. 2007, The Robert H. Alway Lifetime Achievement Award, Stanford Univ.,

USA 2010, Lifetime Achievement Award, DHL/SCMP Hong Kong Business Awards 2010, Carnegie Medal of Philanthropy, Carnegie Corpn 2011, Berkeley Medal, Univ. of California, Berkeley 2011, ranked by Forbes magazine amongst The World's Most Powerful People (44th) 2011, (31st) 2012, (30th) 2013. *Address:* 70/F, Cheung Kong Center, 2 Queen's Road, Central, Hong Kong Special Administrative Region, People's Republic of China (office). *Telephone:* (852) 21288888 (office). *Fax:* (852) 21288348 (office). *E-mail:* contactckh@ckh.com.hk (office). *Website:* www.ckh.com.hk (office).

LI, Keqiang, MA, PhD; Chinese economist and politician; *Premier;* b. July 1955, Dingyuan Co., Anhui Prov.; m. Cheng Hong; ed Beijing Univ.; sent to do manual labour, Dongling Production Brigade, Damiao Commune early 1970s (Sec. CCP Party Br. 1976–78); joined CCP 1976; Head, Beijing Univ. Students' Fed. 1978–82; Sec. Communist Youth League, Beijing Univ. 1978–82; fmr Deputy Dir Dept of Schools and Colls of Communist Youth League Cen. Cttee; Sec.-Gen. All-China Students' Fed. 1982, Vice-Chair. 1990; Sec. Secr. of Communist Youth League Cen. Cttee 1982–93, First Sec. 1993–98; Pres. China Youth Political Coll. 1993; Deputy Sec. CCP Henan Prov. Cttee 1998–2002 (mem. Standing Cttee 2001–04), Sec. 2002–04; Deputy Gov. Henan Prov. 1998, Acting Gov. 1998–99, Gov. 1999–2003; Chair. Standing Cttee Henan Prov. People's Congress 2003–04, Standing Cttee Liaoning Prov. People's Congress 2004–07; Sec. CCP Liaoning Prov. Cttee 2004–07; mem. Standing Cttee of NPC 1993–98; mem. 15th CCP Cen. Cttee 1997–2002, 16th CCP Cen. Cttee 2002–07, 17th CCP Cen. Cttee 2007–12, 17th CCP Politburo 2007–12 and Politburo Standing Cttee 2007–12; mem. 18th CCP Cen. Cttee 2012–, also mem. 18th CCP Cen. Cttee Politburo 2012– and Politburo Standing Cttee 2012–; First Vice-Premier 2008–13, Premier 2013–; Deputy Sec. State Council Leading Party mems group 2008–13; Party Sec., State Council; Dir State Council Leading Group for Western Region Devt 2013–; Deputy Dir State Energy Cttee. 2008–13, Dir 2013–; ranked by Forbes magazine amongst The World's Most Powerful People (13th) 2012, (14th) 2013. *Address:* Office of the Premier, Great Hall of the People, West Edge, Tiananmen Square, Beijing, People's Republic of China (office). *Telephone:* (10) 88050813 (office). *Fax:* (10) 63070900 (office). *Website:* english.gov.cn/2008-03/16/content_921792.htm (office).

LI, Keyu; Chinese fashion and costume designer; b. 15 May 1929, Shanghai; m. Yuan Mao 1955; ed Cen. Acad. of Fine Arts; Chief Costume Designer of Cen. Ballet; Deputy Dir Chinese Soc. of Stage Design; mem. Bd All-China Artists' Asscn, Chinese Dancers' Asscn; Deputy Dir China Export Garments Research Centre; Prof. and Sr consultant, Beijing Inst. of Fashion Tech. and Head Apparel Research Inst.; has designed costumes for many works, including Swan Lake, Le Corsaire, The Maid of the Sea, The Fountain of Bakhchisarai, La Esmeralda, The Red Detachment of Women, The East is Red, The New Year Sacrifice (Ministry of Culture costume design prize), Zigeunerweisen (Ministry of Culture costume design prize), Othello (for Peking Opera, Beijing's costume design prize), Tang Music and Dance, Zheng Ban Qiao (Houston Ballet), Fu (Hongkong Ballet), La Péri (Houston Ballet); winner sole costume design prize, 4th Japan World Ballet Competition, Osaka 1984. *Publications:* two vols of sketches. *Address:* 21 Gongjian Hutong, Di An-Men, Beijing 100009, People's Republic of China. *Telephone:* 4035474.

LI, Hon. Kwok Nang Andrew, CBE, MA, LLM, QC, JP; Chinese fmr judge; b. 12 Dec. 1948, Hong Kong; s. of Li Fook Kow and of the late Edith Kwong Li; m. Judy Mo Ying Li; two d.; ed St Paul's Co-Educational Coll., Hong Kong, Repton School, Univ. of Cambridge, UK; called to the Bar, Middle Temple 1970, Hong Kong 1973; practised at Hong Kong Bar 1973–97; QC 1988, Chief Justice, Court of Final Appeal Hong Kong 1997–2010; Hon. Bencher Middle Temple 1997; Hon. Fellow, Fitzwilliam Coll. Cambridge 1999; Grand Bauhinia Medal 2008; hon. degrees (Hong Kong Univ. of Science and Tech.) 1993, (Baptist Univ.) 1994, (Open Univ. of Hong Kong) 1997, (Univ. of Hong Kong), (The Griffith Univ.) 2001, (Univ. of NSW) 2002, (Univ. of Tech., Sydney) 2005, (Chinese Univ. of Hong Kong) 2006, (Hong Kong Shue Yan Univ.) 2009, (Lingnan Univ. Hong Kong) 2010, (City Univ. of Hong Kong) 2010. *Leisure interests:* reading, tennis, hiking.

LI, Gen. Laizhu; Chinese army officer and party official; b. 1932, Shen Co., Shandong Prov.; ed PLA Mil. and Political Acad.; joined PLA 1947, CCP 1948; Deputy Commdr of Beijing Mil. Area Command 1985; rank of Lt-Gen., PLA 1988; Commdr Beijing Mil. Region 1994–97; Gen. mem. 14th CCP Cen. Cttee 1992–97; rank of Gen. 1994–. *Address:* Beijing Military Area Command, People's Liberation Army, Beijing, People's Republic of China.

LI, Lanqing; Chinese government and party official; b. May 1932, Zhengjiang Co., Jiangsu Prov.; ed Fudan Univ., Shanghai; joined CCP 1952; worker, No. 1 Automobile Works, Changchun City Jilin Prov. 1952, Chief of Planning Section 1957–59; trainee, Liharchev and Gorky Automobile Factories, USSR 1956–57; worker, First Ministry of Machine-Building Industry 1959–81, State Econ. Comm. 1959–81, No. 2 Automobile Works 1959–81, No. 3 Automobile Factory 1959–81; Chief, Govt Loan Office, State Admin Comm. on Import and Export Affairs 1981–82; Dir Foreign Investment Admin. Bureau, Ministry of Foreign Econ. Relations and Trade 1982; Vice-Mayor Tianjin 1983–85; Vice-Minister of Foreign Econ. Relations and Trade 1986–90, Minister 1990–92; Vice-Premier, State Council 1993–2003; Head Nat. Leading Group for Foreign Investments (State Council) 1994–; Deputy Head Cen. Leading Group for Party Bldg Work 1994–; Chair. Academic Degrees Cttee 1995–; Dir Nat. Cttee for the Patriotic Public Health Campaign 1998–; Deputy Head, State Steering Group of Science, Tech. and Educ. 1998–; mem. 8th NPC 1993–98; Alt. mem. 13th CCP Cen. Cttee 1987–92, mem. 14th CCP Cen. Cttee 1992–97 (mem. Politburo 1992–97), 15th CCP Cen. Cttee 1997–2002 (mem. Standing Cttee of Politburo 1997–2002). *Address:* c/o Zhongguo Gongchan Dang (Chinese Communist Party), Zhongnanhai, Beijing, People's Republic of China (office).

LI, Ligong; Chinese party official; b. 20 Feb. 1925, Jiaocheng, Shanxi; s. of Li Zhengliang and Li Shi; m. Xie Bin; two s. three d.; Sec. CCP County Cttee, Sec. CCP Pref. Cttee, Sec. Communist Youth League of Shanxi Prov., mem. Cen. Cttee Communist Youth League 1953–65; Sec. Communist Youth League, Beijing Municipal Cttee 1966; Vice-Dir Beijing Municipal Revolutionary Cttee 1977; Sec. CCP Beijing Municipal Cttee 1978–81; Exec. Sec. CCP Shanxi Prov. Cttee 1981–83, Sec. 1983–91; Dir CCP Shanxi Advisory Cttee 1991–92; mem. CCP Cen. Comm. for Inspecting Discipline 1979–82; mem. 12th Cen. Cttee CCP 1982–87,

13th Cen. Cttee 1987–92; mem. Standing Cttee 8th NPC 1992–98, mem. 9th NPC 1998–2003. *Publication:* Shanxi in Contemporary China (Chief Ed.). *Leisure interests:* swimming, fencing, tennis, hiking. *Address:* General Office of the Chinese Communist Party Shanxi Provincial Committee, 369 Yingze Street, Taiyuan, Shanxi, People's Republic of China (office). *Telephone:* 4045093 (office).

LI, Liguo; Chinese government official; *Minister of Civil Affairs;* b. Nov. 1953, Yutian County, Tangshan, Hebei Prov.; ed Northeastern Univ.; joined CCP 1974; Chinese Communist Youth League Prov. Deputy Sec., Liaoning Prov. 1985–90; Vice-Mayor of Panjin, Liaoning Prov. 1990–93; Sec.-Gen., CCP Autonomous Regional Cttee, Tibet Autonomous Region 1993–2001, Deputy Sec. 1999–2003; Vice-Chair., CPPCC Autonomous Regional Cttee, Tibet Autonomous Region 2003; Vice-Minister of Civil Affairs 2003–05, Exec. Vice-Minister of Civil Affairs 2005–10, Minister of Civil Affairs 2010–; Deputy Dir, Nat. Cttee for Disaster Reduction 2013–; mem. 18th CCP Cen. Cttee 2012–. *Address:* Ministry of Civil Affairs, 147 Beiheyan Dajie, Dongcheng Qu, Beijing 100721, People's Republic of China (office). *Telephone:* (10) 58123114 (office). *Website:* www.mca.gov.cn (office).

LI, Lihui, DEcon; Chinese banker; *Vice-Chairman and President, Bank of China Ltd;* b. 1952, Fujian Prov.; ed Xiamen Univ., Guanghua School of Man. at Peking Univ.; with People's Bank of China, Fujian Br. 1977–84; joined Industrial and Commercial Bank, Fujian Br. 1984, served in several positions 1989–94, including Deputy Gen. Man. Fujian Br., Chief Rep. of Singapore Rep. Office and Gen. Man. Int. Business Dept, Exec. Vice-Pres. Industrial and Commercial Bank 1994–2002; Deputy Gov. Hainan Prov. 2002–04; Vice-Chair. and Pres. Bank of China Ltd 2004–; Chair. BOCI 2005–; Chair. Bohai Industry Investment Management Ltd 2006–. *Address:* Bank of China Ltd, 1 Fuxingmen Nei Dajie, Beijing 100818, People's Republic of China (office). *Telephone:* (10) 6659-6688 (office). *Fax:* (10) 6659-3777 (office). *E-mail:* info@boc.cn (office). *Website:* www.boc.cn (office).

LI, Lingwei; Chinese fmr badminton player; b. 4 Jan. 1964; won women's singles title at 3rd World Badminton Championships, Copenhagen 1982; elected 7th in list of 10 best Chinese athletes 1984; won women's singles and women's doubles (co-player Wu Dixi) at 5th ALBA World Cup, Jakarta 1985; won women's singles, at World Badminton Grand Prix finals, Tokyo 1985, at Dunhill China Open Badminton Championships, Nanjing 1987, at Malaysian Badminton Open, Kuala Lumpur 1987, at World Grand Prix, Hong Kong 1988, at China Badminton Open 1988, at Danish Badminton Open, Odense 1988, at All-England Badminton Championships 1989, at 6th World Badminton Championships, Jakarta; coached Chinese women's singles players; took part in Olympic Torch Relay as flame bearer, Hangzhou 2008; mem. Int. Badminton Fed. (IBF) Events and Devt Cttee; IBF Hall of Fame 1998, Int. Olympic Cttee Women and Sport Trophy for Asia 2008. *Address:* China Sports Federation, Beijing, People's Republic of China.

LI, Luye; Chinese diplomatist (retd); b. 1925, Beijing; Dir Dept of Int. Orgs of Foreign Ministry 1980; Perm. Rep. to UN, New York –1990; Pres. of Chinese People's Asscn for Friendship with Foreign Countries 1990–, Dir Chinese Int. Studies Centre 1990–, Vice-Chair. Foreign Affairs Cttee; Pres. China Nat. Cttee for Pacific Econ. Co-operation 1991; mem. Standing Cttee of 8th NPC 1993–98. *Address:* c/o Chinese People's Association for Friendship with Foreign Countries, Taijichang, Beijing 100002, People's Republic of China.

LI, Ming, MS, MS, PhD, FRSC; Canadian/Chinese computer scientist and academic; *University Professor and Canada Research Chair in Bioinformatics, University of Waterloo;* ed Inst. of Computing Tech., Chinese Acad. of Sciences, Wayne State Univ., Cornell Univ.; farmer, Su Jia Tuo Village, Beijing, People's Repub. of China 1974–76; Computer Programmer, Cen. Weather Bureau of China 1976–78; Asst Prof., Dept of Computer Science and Information, Ohio State Univ., USA 1985–86; Postdoctoral Fellow, Harvard Univ. 1986–87, Visiting Asst Prof., Aiken Computational Lab. 1987–88; Asst Prof., Computer Science Dept, York Univ. 1988–89; Assoc. Prof., Computer Science Dept, Univ. of Waterloo 1989–94, Prof., School of Computer Science 1994– (on leave 2000–02), Canada Research Chair in Bioinformatics, Tier I 2002–, Univ. Prof. 2009–; Prof., Computer Science Dept, Univ. of California, Santa Barbara 2000–02; Guest Prof., Academia Sinica 1995–, Univ. of Science and Tech. of China 1995–, Peking Univ. 1995–; Visiting Prof., City Univ. of Hong Kong 1996–97, 2004–05; Chang Jiang Prof., Tsinghua Univ., China 2003–; Co-Ed.-in-Chief Journal of Bioinformatics and Computational Biology 2002–; Assoc. Ed.-in-Chief Journal of Computer Science and Technology 2003–, Journal of Computer and System Sciences 1992–, SIAM Journal on Computing 2002–08, Information and Computation 1997–2006, Journal of Combinatorial Optimization 1995–, International Journal of Foundation of Computer Science 1999–2003, Journal of Software 2001–; Fellow, IEEE 2006, Asscn for Computing Machinery 2006; First-class Prize, China's Nat. Excellent Science and Tech. Book Prize 1999, Best Paper Awards: Genome Informatics Workshop, Tokyo, Japan 1999, Genome Informatics Workshop, Singapore 2007, CSB 2007, San Diego 2007, COLING 2010, Beijing 2010; E.W.R. Steacie Memorial Fellowship, NSERC 1996, Award of Merit, Fed. of Chinese Canadian Professionals 1997, Killam Research Fellowship, Canada Council for the Arts 2001, Pioneer Award, IEEE GrC Conf. 2006, Premier's Discovery Award (Innovation Leadership) 2009, Outstanding Contrib. Award, IEEE Granular Computing, San Jose 2010, Killam Prize in Engineering, Canada Council for the Arts 2010. *Publications:* An Introduction to Kolmogorov Complexity and Its Applications (with P. Vitányi) 1993 (third edn 2008), A Course on Java Programming (with H. A. Li) (in Chinese) 1997, Descriptional Complexity (with P. Vitányi) (in Chinese) 1999; numerous papers in professional journals on bioinformatics algorithms and software, Kolmogorov complexity and its applications, analysis of algorithms, computational complexity, and computational learning theory; two US patents. *Address:* Davis Center 3355, David R. Cheriton School of Computer Science, University of Waterloo, Waterloo, ON N2L 3G1, Canada (office). *Telephone:* (519) 888-4659 (office), (519) 591-3578 (mobile). *Fax:* (519) 885-1208 (office). *E-mail:* mli@ uwaterloo.ca (office). *Website:* www.cs.uwaterloo.ca/~mli (office).

LI, Na, BA; Chinese professional tennis player; b. 26 Feb. 1982, Wuhan, Hubei; d. of the late Li Shengpeng; m. Jiang Shan 2006; ed Huazhong Univ. of Science and Tech.; mem. China's Nat. Tennis Team 1997–2002; turned professional 1999; winner, Tashkent Open doubles title, Uzbekistan 2000, Guangzhou Int. Women's Open singles title 2004, AEGON Classic doubles title, Birmingham, UK 2006, Gold Coast Tournament singles title 2008, AEGON Classic singles title, Birmingham,

UK 2010, Medibank Int. Sydney tournament singles title, Australia 2011, Shenzhen Gemdale Open, Shenzhen, China 2013; Grand Slam results: quarter-finalist, Wimbledon 2006, 2010, 2013, quarter-finalist, US Open 2009, finalist, Australian Open 2011 (first Asian player to appear in a Grand Slam singles final), 2013, winner, French Open 2011 (first Asian player to win a Grand Slam singles title), Australian Open 2014, semi-finalist, US Open 2013; Laureus World Sportswoman of the Year 2011. *Address:* c/o Max Eisenbud, IMG, 1360 East 9th Street, Suite 100, Cleveland, OH 44114, USA.

LI, Peigen, BSc, MSc, PhD; Chinese engineer, academic and university administrator; *President, Huazhong University of Science and Technology;* ed Shanghai Textile Inst. of Tech., Huazhong Univ. of Science and Tech., Univ. of Wisconsin, USA; Dean, School of Mechanical Science and Eng, Huazhong Univ. of Science and Tech. (HUST) 1995–2002, Vice Pres. HUST 2002–05, Pres. 2005–; mem. Chinese Acad. of Eng 2003–; Govt of Hubei Prov. Outstanding Professionals Award 2001. *Publications:* three books and over 100 papers. *Address:* Office of the President, Huazhong University of Science and Technology, 1037 Luoyu Road, Wuchang, Wuhan, People's Republic of China (office). *Telephone:* (27) 87544088 (office). *Website:* www.hust.edu.cn/english (office).

LI, Peng; Chinese politician; b. Oct. 1928, Chengdu City, Sichuan Prov.; s. of the late Li Shuoxun and of Zhao Juntao; m. Zhu Lin 1958; two s. one d.; ed Yan'an Inst. of Natural Sciences, Zhangjiakou Vocational School of Industry, Moscow Power Inst., USSR; joined CCP 1945; technician, Shanxi-Chahar-Hebei Power Co. 1946–48; Asst Man. Harbin Grease Co. 1946–48 (Sec. CCP Party Cttee 1946–48); Chief Engineer and Deputy Dir Fengman Hydroelectric Power Plant, Jilin Prov. 1955; fmr Deputy Chief Engineer, Northeast China Power Admin, later Dir Electricity Dispatch Dept; fmr Dir Fuxin Power Plant, Liaoning Prov. (Deputy Sec. CCP Party Cttee); Acting Sec. Beijing Power Supply Bureau, CCP Party Cttee 1966–76 (Chair. CCP Revolutionary Cttee 1966–76); Deputy Sec. Power Admin, CCP Party Cttee, Beijing 1966–76; Chair. Power Admin, CCP Revolutionary Cttee, Beijing 1966–76; Dir Power Admin, Beijing 1966–76 (Sec. CCP Leading Party Group 1966–76); Vice-Minister of Electric Power Industry 1979–81, Minister 1981–82; Vice-Minister of Water Conservancy and Electric Power 1982–83 (Deputy Sec. CCP Leading Party Group); Vice-Premier of State Council 1983–87; Minister in Charge of State Educ. Comm. 1985–88; Acting Premier, State Council 1987–88, Premier 1988–98; Minister, State Comm. for Restructuring the Economy 1988–90; Chair. Standing Cttee 9th NPC 1998–2003; mem. 12th Cen. Cttee of CCP 1982–87, 13th CCP Cen. Cttee 1987–92, 14th CCP Cen. Cttee 1992–97, 15th CCP Cen. Cttee 1997–2002; mem. Political Bureau 1985–2002, Standing Cttee 1987–2002; mem. Secr. CCP Cen. Cttee 1985–87; announced retirement 2003. *Publication:* The Critical Moment – Li Peng Diaries 2010. *Address:* c/o Zhongguo Gongchan Dang (Chinese Communist Party), Zhongnanhai, Beijing, People's Republic of China (office).

LI, Qi; Chinese artist; b. Sept. 1928, Pingyao, Shanxi Prov.; ed North China United Univ.; Lecturer then Prof. of Chinese Painting, Cen. Acad. of Fine Art 1950–. *Works include:* several portraits of Chinese leaders including Portrait of Mao Zedong 1960. *Publication:* Portraits by Li Qui. *Address:* Central Academy of Fine Art, 5 Xiaowei Hutong, East District, Beijing 100730, People's Republic of China.

LI, Lt-Gen. Qianyuan; Chinese army officer (retd); b. March 1942, Linzhou, Henan Prov.; ed Zhengzhou Textile Machinery Inst., Mil. Acad. of the Chinese PLA; joined PLA 1961; joined CCP 1963; Regimental Commdr, PLA 1976; Div. Chief of Staff, PLA 1982–83, Deputy Chief of Staff 1st Army, Army (or Ground Force), PLA Services and Arms 1983–85, Army Commdr Group Army, PLA Services and Arms 1985–90 (Deputy Sec. CCP Party Cttee 1985–90); Deputy Chief of Staff, Guangzhou Mil. Command 1990–94; rank of Maj.-Gen. 1997, Lt-Gen. 1996; Chief of Staff, Lanzhou Mil. Region 1994–99, Commdr 1999–2007; Alt. mem. 14th CCP Cen. Cttee 1992–97, 15th CCP Cen. Cttee 1997–2002, mem. 16th CCP Cen. Cttee 2002–07. *Address:* c/o Headquarters, Lanzhou Military Region, Lanzhou, Gansu Province, People's Republic of China (office).

LI, Renchen, (Chen Ping); Chinese journalist; b. Oct. 1941, Changyi County, Shandong Prov.; ed Fudan Univ.; Ed. CCP 1975–; Features and Photos Service, Comm. for Cultural Relations with Foreign Countries 1964–66; Ed. Huizhou Bao, Anhui Prov., Ed. People's Daily and Deputy Dir Commentary Dept People's Daily 1983–86; Deputy Ed.-in-Chief, then Ed.-in-Chief, Renmin Ribao (People's Daily) 1986; currently Sr Visiting Prof., School of Journalism and Communication, Tsinghua Univ.; Standing mem. CPPCC Nat. Cttee; Vice-Chair. CPPCC Learning and Historical and Cultural Data Cttee. *Address:* c/o School of Journalism and Communication, Tsinghua University, Omnicom Building, Beijing 100084, People's Republic of China.

LI, Renjie, BA; Chinese economist and business executive; *President, Industrial Bank Company Limited;* fmr Dir of Planning Div., Fujian Br. of People's Bank of China; fmr Exec. Dir Hong Kong Jiang Nan Finance Ltd; fmr Chair. Great Wall Securities Co. Ltd; worked as Head of Preparatory Team, Pres. of Shenzhen Br. of Industrial Bank, later Vice-Pres. of Industrial Bank Co. Ltd, mem. Bd of Dirs 2007–, Pres. 2012–. *Address:* Industrial Bank Co. Ltd, 154 Hudong Road, Fuzhou 350003, People's Republic of China (office). *Telephone:* (591) 87839338 (office). *Fax:* (591) 87841932 (office). *E-mail:* webmaster@cib.com.cn (office). *Website:* www.cib.com.cn (office).

LI, Richard; Hong Kong computer engineer and business executive; *Chairman and CEO, Pacific Century CyberWorks Ltd;* b. (Li Tzar Kai), 1966; s. of Li Ka-shing; ed Stanford Univ., USA; cr. Star TV (first satellite cable TV network in Asia) 1992; Founder, Chair. and CEO Pacific Century Group (PCG—internet co.) 1993–, Pacific Century CyberWorks (PCCW) Ltd 1999– (PCCW merged with Cable & Wireless HKT 2000), PCCW Japan 2000–; Chair. Pacific Century Regional Devts Ltd, Singapore, Pacific Century Premium Devts Ltd; cr. Network of the World (NOW—internet and digital TV content service) 2000, NOW Japan 2001; Gov. World Econ. Forum for Information Technologies and Telecommunications; mem. Int. Councillors' Group, Center for Strategic and Int. Studies, Washington, DC, Global Information Infrastructure Comm., Panel of Advisors to UN Information and Communication Technologies Task Force. *Address:* Pacific Century Cyber-Works Ltd, Floor 39, PCCW Tower, Taikoo Place, 979 Kings Road, Quarry Bay 070, Hong Kong Special Administrative Region, People's Republic of China (office).

Telephone: 28882888 (office). *Fax:* 28778877 (office). *Website:* www.pccw.com (office).

LI, Robin, BS, MS; Chinese business executive and entrepreneur; *Co-founder, Chairman and CEO, Baidu, Inc.;* b. (Li Yanhong), 17 Nov. 1968, Yangquan, Shanxi Prov.; m. Ma Dongmin 1995; one d.; ed Yangquan First High School, Peking Univ., State Univ. of New York, Buffalo, NY, USA; joined Dow Jones & Co., NJ, USA 1994, served as sr consultant for IDD Information Services, USA (a NJ div. of Dow Jones & Co.) 1994–97; staff engineer, Infoseek 1997–99; Co-founder Baidu, Inc. (internet search engine) 2000, Chair. 2000–, CEO 2004–; named amongst "the Chinese Top Ten Innovative Pioneers" 2001, named amongst IT Ten Famous Persons 2002, 2003, elected to Chinese Software Ten Outstanding Young Persons 2004, ASEAN Youth Award 2005, named amongst CCTV Chinese Economic Figures of The Year 2005, named by American Business Weekly as World's Best Business Leader 2006, listed in CNN Money annual "50 people who matter now" 2007, ranked by Forbes magazine amongst The World's Most Powerful People (46th) 2010, (42nd) 2011, (64th) 2012, (61st) 2013. *Publications:* Business War in Silicon Valley 1998; received a US Patent for the RankDex site-scoring algorithm used for search engine results page ranking 1999. *Address:* Baidu, Inc., Baidu Campus, 10 Shangdi 10th Street, Haidian District, Beijing 100085, People's Republic of China (office). *Telephone:* (10) 59928888 (office). *Fax:* (10) 59920000 (office). *E-mail:* ir@baidu.com (office). *Website:* www.baidu.com (office); ir.baidu .com (office).

LI, Rongrong; Chinese economist and state official; b. Dec. 1944, Suzhou, Jiangsu Prov.; ed Tianjin Univ.; workshop chief, Wuxi Oil Pump and Oil Throttle Factory, Deputy Dir, then Dir 1984–86; Vice-Chair. Wuxi Municipal Econ. Comm. 1986, later Dir Wuxi Municipal Light Industry Bureau and Chair. Wuxi Municipal Planning Comm.; Vice-Chair. Jiangsu Prov. Planning and Econ. Comm. 1986–91; Production Planning Bureau, State Council Production Office 1992; Dir Foreign Econ. Cooperation Dept, State Council 1994–95; Deputy Dir, State Econ. and Trade Comm. (SETC) 1999–2001, Dir 2001–03; Dir State-Owned Assets Supervision and Admin Comm. (SASAC) 2003–10; joined CCP 1983, mem. 16th CCP Cen. Cttee 2002–07, 17th CCP Cen. Cttee 2007–12; Vice-Chair. 11th CPPCC, Nat. Cttee, Econs Cttee 2010–13; ranked 61st by Forbes magazine amongst The World's Most Powerful People 2009. *Address:* Office of the Chairman, State-Owned Assets Supervision and Administration Commission (SASAC), 26 Xuanxuan Xidajie, Beijing 100053, People's Republic of China (office). *Telephone:* (10) 63193615 (office). *Fax:* (10) 63193571 (office). *E-mail:* iecc@sasac.gov.cn (office). *Website:* www.sasac.gov.cn (office).

LI, Rui; Chinese party official; b. 1917, Pingjiang Co., Hunan Prov.; ed Wuhan Univ.; joined CCP 1937; cadre in Hunan 1950; Asst Minister of Water Conservancy and Electrical Power 1955–58; in political disgrace 1967–79; fmr Sec. to Mao Zedong; Vice-Minister, 4th Ministry of Machine Building 1979–82; Vice-Minister, Power Industry 1979–82; Dir State Bureau of Computers 1980; mem. 12th Cen. Cttee CCP 1982–87; mem. Cen. Advisory Comm. 1987; Deputy Dir State Bureau of Tech. Supervision 1991; Deputy Head Org. Dept CCP 1983. *Publications:* The Early Revolutionary Activities of Comrade Mao Zedong, Some Fundamental Problems Concerning the Total Utilization Plan for the Yellow River. *Address:* Central Committee of the Chinese Communist Party, Beijing, People's Republic of China (office).

LI, Ruihuan; Chinese party and government official; b. Sept. 1934, Baodi Co., Tianjing; ed part-time studies at an architecture eng inst.; construction worker, Beijing No. 3 Construction Co. 1951–65; Joined CCP 1959; Deputy Sec. Beijing Building Materials Co. CCP Party Cen. 1965–66; Vice-Chair. Beijing Municipal Trade Union Fed. 1971; Vice-Chair. All-China Youth Fed. 1971–80; Dir-Gen. Work Site for Mao Zedong Memorial Hall, Beijing 1977; Deputy for Beijing, 5th NPC 1978; Sec. Communist Youth League 1979–81; mem. Standing Cttee, 5th NPC 1978–83; Deputy Mayor Tianjin 1981, Acting Mayor 1982, Mayor Tianjin 1982–89; Sec. CCP Municpal Cttee, Tianjin 1982–84; mem. 12th CCP Cen. Cttee 1982–87, 13th CCP Cen. Cttee 1987–92, 14th CCP Cen. Cttee 1992–97, 15th CCP Cen. Cttee 1997–2002; mem. Politburo 1987–2002, Standing Cttee Politburo 1989, Perm. mem. Politburo 1992–2002; Chair. 8th Nat. Cttee CPPCC 1993–98, 9th Nat. Cttee CPPCC 1998–2003; Hon. Pres. Chinese Fed. for the Disabled 1993–; Hon Pres. Chinese Table Tennis Asscn 1990–; named Nat. Model Worker 1979. *Address:* c/o National Committee of the Chinese People's Political Consultative Conference, No.23, Taipingqiao Street, Beijing 100811; Zhongguo Gongchan Dang (Chinese Communist Party), Zhongnanhai, Beijing, People's Republic of China (office).

LI, Sanli, DSc; Chinese computer scientist; b. 1935, Shanghai; ed Tsinghua Univ., Acad. of Sciences, USSR; Co-Chair. Accreditation Cttee Computer Discipline of State Academic Comm. of the State Council; Deputy Chief Ed. China Computer Encyclopaedia; Exec. Dir of China Computer Fed.; Pres. IEEE in China; Dir EUROMICRO Europe 1984–97; Dir Research Inst. of Computer Sciences and Eng, Tsinghua Univ.; Jt Dean Coll. of Computer Eng and Science, Shanghai Univ.; mem. Chinese Acad. of Engineering; many awards including First Grade Award (govt of Shanghai) 2001. *Publications:* 11 books including RISC – Single and Multiple Issue Architecture and more than 100 research papers. *Address:* Research Institute of Computer Sciences and Engineering, Tsinghua University, 1 Qinghuayuan, Beijing 100084, People's Republic of China (office). *Telephone:* 62561144 (office). *Fax:* 62562768 (office). *Website:* www.tsinghua.edu.cn (office).

LI, Shenglin; Chinese politician; b. Nov. 1946, Nantong Co., Jiangsu Prov.; ed Zhejiang Coll. of Agricultural Machinery 1970; joined CCP 1973; fmr Planner, Tools Workshop, Tianjin Tractor Plant (Clerical Sec., later Deputy Sec., later Sec. CCP Communist League, later Sec. CCP Party Br.); fmr Deputy Man. Chemical Industry Machinery Co., Tianjin, later Deputy Office Dir; fmr Deputy Section Chief, Tractor Industry Co., Tianjin; fmr Cadre, Planning Div., People's Govt, Tianjin Municipality, later Deputy Sec.-Gen. People's Govt; fmr Dir CCP Party Cttee, Tianjin Municipality; fmr Dir Textile Industry Bureau, Tianjin Municipality (Deputy Sec. CCP Party Cttee); Dir Planning Cttee, Tianjin Municipality 1983; Deputy Sec. Work Cttee, CCP Tianjin Municipal Cttee 1983, Deputy Sec. Municipal Cttee 1993–98, mem. Standing Cttee of Municipal Cttee 2002–05; Vice-Mayor of Tianjin 1991–93, Mayor 1993–98; Vice-Sec. CCP Tianjin Mun. Cttee 1993; mem. 15th CCP Cen. Cttee 1997–2002, 16th CCP Cen. Cttee 2002–07, 17th CCP Cen. Cttee 2007–12; Minister of Transport 2005–13; Deputy, 9th NPC

1998–2003. *Address:* c/o Ministry of Transport, Beijing, People's Republic of China (office).

LI, Shiji; Chinese opera singer; b. May 1933, Suzhou Co., Jiangsu Prov.; Head First Troupe, Beijing Opera Theatre 1989–; mem. 7th CPPCC 1988–93, 8th 1993–98; Vice-Chair. China Fed. of Literary and Art Circles 2001. *Repertoire includes:* Tears in the Wild Mountain, The Unicorn Purse, Snow in Midsummer, The Story of Su San, Chen Sanliang Appeals at Court. *Beijing operas include:* Wenji's Return to the Hans, Concubine Mei, A Green Jade Hairpin, Wedding on the Execution Ground. *Address:* Beijing Opera Theatre, 11 Hufang Road, Xuanwu District, Beijing 100052, People's Republic of China (office).

LI, Shufu, MEng; Chinese motor company executive; *Chairman, Zhejiang Geely Holding Group Company Ltd;* b. 1963, Taizhou, Zhejiang Prov.; ed Harbin Polytechnic Univ., Yan Shan Univ.; Pres. Geely Guorun and Maple Guorun (jt ventures of Geely Automobile Holdings Ltd); Owner of Zhejiang Geely Merrie Automobile Co. Ltd; Founder and Chair. Zhejiang Geely Holding Group Co. Ltd (also known as Geely Group Co. Ltd) 1986–; Chair. Shanghai Maple Guorun Automobile Co. Ltd, Zhejiang Geely Automobile Co. Ltd, Geely Automobile Holdings Ltd 2005–; purchased Volvo Cars from Ford Motor Co. 2010, Chair. Volvo Car Corpn 2010–; mem. 9th and 10th CPPCC; honours include Operation and Management Master, one of Top 10 Private Entrepreneurs, Man of the Automobile Industry in China, Heroes of China's Automobile Industry (for 50 Years), Man of the Year of Zhejiang Merchants, Top 25 People Contributing to Chinese Brands, Top 10 Philanthropists in China, Top 10 Figures of Chinese Automobiles in 2006, Heroes Contributing to Independent Innovation of Chinese Automobile Brands, Innovation Grand Prize of Zhejiang Merchants 2007, accredited as one of 50 of 50 (Fifty Influential Persons for the Fiftieth Anniversary of the China Automobile Industry) from pertinent insts in China. *Address:* Zhejiang Geely Holding Group, 1760 Jiangling Road, Hangzhou 310051 (office); Geely International Corporation, 87 Qianyang Road, Shanghai 200333, People's Republic of China (office). *Telephone:* (571) 28001111 (Hangzhou) (office); (21) 52695666 (Shanghai) (office). *Fax:* (21) 52695771 (Shanghai) (office). *E-mail:* info@geely.com (office). *Website:* www.geely.com (office); www.geely.com/brands/international (home).

LI, Sush-der, BBA, MBA; Taiwanese government official; b. 29 Nov. 1951, Taipei; ed Tamkang Univ., Mankato State Univ., USA; Section Chief and Sr Specialist, Nat. Treasury Agency, Ministry of Finance 1980–88, Chief Sec., Nat. Treasury Agency 1988–91, Chief Sec., Taipei Nat. Tax Admin 1991–93, Deputy Dir Nat. Tax Admin of N Taiwan Prov. 1993–94, Deputy Dir-Gen. Nat. Treasury Agency 1994–96, Dir-Gen. Kaohsiung Nat. Tax Admin 1996–98; Commr, Dept of Finance, Taipei City Govt 1998–2006; Sec.-Gen. Taipei City Govt 2006–08; Minister of Finance 2008–12. *Address:* c/o Ministry of Finance, 2 Ai Kuo West Road, Taipei 10066, Taiwan (office).

LI, Tieying; Chinese state official; *Vice-Chairman, 10th Standing Committee, National People's Congress;* b. Sept. 1936, Changsha City, Hunan Prov.; s. of the late Li Weihan; m. Qin Xinhua; ed Charles Univ., Czechoslovakia; joined CCP 1955; worker, Research Inst., Ministry of Electronics Industry 1961, Chief Engineer and Dir 1976; Deputy Dir Science and Tech. Cttee, Shenyang City, Liaoning Prov. 1976; Sec. CCP Shenyang City Cttee 1981–83, CCP Liaoning Prov. Cttee 1983–86; Minister of Electronics Industry 1985–88; Minister in charge of State Comm. for Econ. Restructuring 1987–88, 1993–98, of State Educ. Comm. 1988–93; Chair. Cen. Patriotic Public Health Campaign Cttee; State Councillor 1988–98; Head Leading Group for the Reform of the Housing System 1991–; Deputy Head Nat. Leading Group for Anti-Disaster and Relief Work 1991–; Dir Nat. Cttee for the Patriotic Public Health Campaign; Vice-Chair. NPC 10th Standing Cttee 2003–; Pres. Chinese Acad. of Social Sciences 1998–2003; Del., World Conf. on Educ., Bangkok 1990, visited India, Laos 1992; Alt. mem. 12th CCP Cen. Cttee 1982, mem. 1985, mem. 13th CCP Cen. Cttee 1987–92, 14th CCP Cen. Cttee 1992–97, 15th CCP Cen. Cttee 1997–2002, mem. Politburo of CCP 1992–2002; Hon. Pres. Mao Zedong Acad. of the Arts 1997–, Athletics Asscn, Soc. of Nat. Conditions; Nat. Science Conf. Prize 1978. *Address:* Chinese Academy of Social Sciences, 5 Jianguomen Nei Da Jie, Beijing 100732, People's Republic of China (office). *Telephone:* (10) 65137744 (office).

LI, Tingye, PhD; American (b. Chinese) communications engineer (retd); b. 7 July 1931, Nanjing, China; m. Edith Hsiu-hwei Wu; two d.; ed Univ. of Witwatersrand, SA, Northwestern Univ., Evanston, Ill., USA; joined Bell Telephone Laboratories (later AT&T Bell Laboratories), Red Bank, NJ 1957, mem. Tech. Staff 1957–67, Head, Lightwave Systems Research Dept 1967–96, Div. Man., Communications Infrastructure Research Lab. 1996–98; Co-founder Zolo Technologies Inc. 1999; Fellow, Optical Soc. of America (Vice-Pres. 1993, Pres. 1995), IEEE, AAAS, Photonic Soc. of Chinese-Americans, Int. Eng Consortium; mem. Nat. Acad. of Eng 1980–, Academia Sinica (Taiwan); Foreign mem. Chinese Acad. of Eng 1996–; Hon. Prof. at several univs in People's Repub. of China including Tsinghua Univ., Shanghai Jiaotong Univ., Beijing Univ. of Posts and Telecommunications, Northern Jiaotong Univ., Fudan Univ., Nankai Univ., Tianjin Univ., Univ. of Electronic Science and Tech. of China, Qufu Normal Univ.; Hon. DEng (Nat. Chiao Tung Univ., Taiwan); numerous awards including IEEE W. R. G. Baker Prize 1975, IEEE David Sarnoff Award 1979, Optical Soc. of America/IEEE John Tyndall Award 1995, Optical Soc. of America Frederic Ives Medal/Jarus Quinn Endowment 1997, AT&T Science and Tech. Medal 1997, Northwestern Univ. Alumni Merit Award 1981, IEEE Photonics Award 2004. *Achievements include:* holder of 15 patents. *Publications include:* more than 100 journal papers, patents, books and book chapters. *Address:* c/o International Engineering Consortium, 233 South Wacker Drive, Suite 8400, Chicago, IL 60606-6338, USA.

LI, Victor Tzar Kuoi, BSc, MSc; Hong Kong business executive; *Co-Chairman, Husky Energy Inc.;* s. of Li Ka-Shing; Man. Dir and Deputy Chair. Cheung Kong (Holdings) Ltd; Exec. Dir Hutchison Whampoa Ltd 1995–, Deputy Chair. 1999–; mem. Bd of Dirs Husky Energy Inc. 2000–, currently Co-Chair.; Chair. Cheung Kong Infrastructure Holdings Ltd, CK Life Sciences International (Holdings) Inc.; Exec. Dir Hongkong Electric Holdings Ltd; Dir Hongkong and Shanghai Banking Corpn Ltd, Continental Realty Ltd, Honourable Holdings Ltd, Winbo Power Ltd, Polycourt Ltd, Well Karin Ltd; Vice-Chair. Hong Kong Gen. Chamber of Commerce; mem. Comm. on Strategic Devt, Council for Sustainable Devt of the Hong Kong Special Admin. Region; mem. Standing Cttee 11th Nat. Cttee CPPCC;

Hon. Consul of Barbados in Hong Kong; Hon. LLD. *Address:* Husky Energy Inc., 707-8th Avenue SW, Box 6525, Station 'D', Calgary, Alberta, T2P 3G7, Canada (office); Hutchison Whampoa Ltd, 22nd Floor, Hutchison House, 10 Harcourt Road, Hong Kong Special Administrative Region, People's Republic of China (office). *Telephone:* (403) 298-6111 (Calgary) (office); 2128-1188 (Hong Kong) (office). *Fax:* (403) 298-7464 (Calgary) (office); 2128-1705 (Hong Kong) (office). *E-mail:* info@huskyenergy.com (office); info@hutchison-whampoa.com (office). *Website:* www.huskyenergy.com (office); www.hutchison-whampoa.com (office).

LI, Weikang; Chinese opera singer; b. Feb. 1947, Beijing; ed China Acad. of Traditional Operas; Dir Troupe No 2, China Peking Opera Co., performer Beijing Peking Opera Co. 1987–; Prof. Nat. Acad. of Chinese Theatre Arts; Plum Blossom Award 1984, Gold Album Award for Lead Role at Nat. Theatrical Performance Ass., Gold Prize at Nat. Mei Lanfang Grand Competition, Gold Eagle Award for Best Actress. *Recordings include:* Selected Arias of Li Weikang 1995, Battle on the Plain, Unicorn Trapping Purse. *Address:* c/o Beijing Opera Company, Beijing, People's Republic of China.

LI, Wenke; Chinese business executive; *President and CEO, China Railway Materials Company Ltd;* Deputy Gen. Man. China Railway Materials Commercial Corpn (now China Railway Materials Co. Ltd) 2007–11, Pres. and CEO 2011–. *Address:* China Railway Materials Co. Ltd, 11 Huayuan Street, Xicheng District, Beijing 100032, People's Republic of China (office). *Telephone:* (10) 51895188 (office). *Fax:* (10) 51895028 (office). *E-mail:* crm@crmsc.com.cn (office). *Website:* www.crmsc.com.cn (office).

LI, Xiaolin, ME; Chinese business executive; *Chairman and CEO China Power International Development Ltd;* b. 1961; d. of Li Peng, fmr Premier, People's Repub. of China, and Zhu Lin; ed Tsinghua Univ.; worked as engineer at Equipment Introduction Office, Beijing Power Supply Bureau; fmr Assoc. Dir Int. Econ. and Trade Dept, Ministry of Energy; fmr Dir Int. Econ. and Trade Dept, Ministry of Electric Power; joined China Power Int. Devt Ltd (CPI) as Gen. Man. 1996, CEO, Vice-Chair. and mem. Exec. Bd 2004, currently CEO and Chair., also serves as Vice-Pres. CPI Group and mem. Exec. Bd CPI Holding; mem. Bd of Dirs Companhia de Electricidade de Macao; mem. Copenhagen Climate Council; fmr Visiting Scholar, Sloan School of Man., MIT; ranked by Fortune magazine amongst the 50 Most Powerful Women in Business outside the US (49th) 2007–08, (45th) 2010, (43rd) 2011. *Address:* China Power International Development Ltd, Suite 6301, 63rd Floor, Central Plaza, Wanchai, Kowloon, Hong Kong Special Administrative Region, People's Republic of China (office). *Telephone:* 28023861 (office). *Fax:* 28023922 (office). *Website:* www.chinapower.hk (office).

LI, Gen. Xinliang; Chinese army officer and party official; b. 1936, Laiyang Co., Shandong Prov.; joined PLA 1953, CCP 1956; Commdr Autonomous Region Mil. Dist, Guangxi Prov. 1983–88; Party Cttee Sec. PLA Guangxi Mil. Area Command 1986–89; mem. 13th CCP Cen. Cttee 1987–92; Deputy Commdr Guangzhou Mil. Region 1989–94; Political Commissar Shenyang Mil. Region 1994–95, Commdr Shenyang Mil. Area Command 1995–97; Commdr Beijing Mil. Area Command 1997–2002; mem. 15th CCP Cen. Cttee 1997–2002; rank of Lt-Gen. 1993, Gen. 1998. *Address:* c/o Commander's Office, Beijing Military Area Command, Beijing, People's Republic of China.

LI, Xu'e; Chinese politician and aerospace industry executive; b. 1928, Hanyang, Hubei Prov.; ed Tsinghua Univ.; joined CCP 1955; Vice-Minister of Space Industry 1982–85; Minister of Astronautics (Space) Industry 1985–88; Vice-Minister State Science and Tech. Comm. 1988–93; Chair. Bd of Dirs China Science and Tech. Consultant Corpn 1983–; Vice-Chair. Environmental Protection Cttee 1988–; a Deputy Head Co-ordination Group for Weather Change 1990–; a Vice-Chair. China Cttee of Int. Decade for Nat. Disaster Reduction 1991–; Pres. Soc. of Social Devt Science 1992–, of China Soc. of Geographic Information System 1994; mem. 12th CCP Cen. Cttee 1982–87, 8th NPC 1993–98, 9th NPC 1998–2003; Vice-Chair. Educ., Science, Culture and Public Health Cttee; Head Dels to Poland, Finland, India. *Address:* Standing Committee of National People's Congress, Beijing, People's Republic of China.

LI, Yining; Chinese economist; *Dean, Guanghua School of Management, Peking University;* b. Nov. 1930, Yizheng City, Jiangsu Prov.; ed Beijing Univ.; Prof., Dean Economy Admin. Dept, Beijing Univ. 1955–; joined CCP 1984; Vice-Chair. 8th Chinese Democratic League Cen. Cttee 1997; mem. Standing Cttee 7th NPC, 8th NPC; Vice-Chair. Finance and Econ. Cttee of 9th NPC 1998; Dean Guanghua School of Man. 1993–. *Address:* Guanghua School of Management, Peking University, 5 Yiheyuan Road, Hai Diau, Beijing 100871, People's Republic of China (office). *Telephone:* 62752114 (office). *Fax:* 627517207 (office). *Website:* www.pku.edu.cn (office).

LI, Yiyi; Chinese metallurgist; b. 20 Oct. 1933, Beijing; m. Ke Wei; one s. one d.; ed Beijing Univ. of Iron and Steel Tech.; China's first female workshop chief in charge of a blast furnace late 1950s; researcher, Metal Research Inst., Chinese Acad. of Sciences 1962–, Vice-Dir 1986, Dir 1990–98; mem. Chinese Acad. of Sciences 1993–, mem. Fourth Presidium 2000–; Vice-Pres. Chinese Soc. for Metals, Chinese Materials Research Soc.; mem. Third World Acad. of Sciences 1999–; mem. Bd Int. Cryogenic Materials Conf. 1985–; mem. Editorial Bd, Modelling of Simulation in Materials Science and Eng 2002–; developed five series of hydrogen-resistant steels and alloys; Nat. Science and Tech. Advancement Award (five times), Chinese Acad. of Sciences Award for Advancement in Science and Tech. (seven times). *Publications:* more than 200 research papers. *Address:* Metal Research Institute, Chinese Academy of Sciences, 72 Wenhua Road, Shenyang 110016, People's Republic of China (office). *Telephone:* (24) 23881881 (office). *Fax:* (24) 23891320 (office). *E-mail:* yyli@imr.ac.cn (office). *Website:* english.imr.cas.cn (office).

LI, Yuanchao, MS, PhD; Chinese politician; *Vice-President;* b. 1950, Lianshui Co., Jiangsu Prov.; ed Shanghai Fudan Univ., Beijing Univ., Cen. Party School; joined CCP 1978; Sec. Shanghai Municipal Cttee Communist Youth League (CCYL) 1983; mem. Sec. Youth League Cen. Cttee 1983–90; Dir Nat. Cttee for Young Pioneers' work 1984; Vice-Chair. Nat. Youth Fed. 1986–96; Dir First Bureau, Int. Publicity Leading Group 1990–93, Vice-Minister Int. Publicity Office under CCP Cen. Cttee 1993–96, Vice-Minister of Culture 1996–2000; Deputy Sec. CCP Jiangsu Prov. Party Cttee 2000–02, Sec. 2002–07, Chair. Standing Cttee 2003–07; Sec. CCP Party Cttee Nanjing City 2001–03; Head, CCP Central Org.

Dept 2007–12; Vice-Pres. People's Republic of China 2013–; mem. CPPCC 7th Nat. Cttee 1988–93, 8th Nat. Cttee 1993–98, 9th Nat. Cttee 1998–2003; Alt. mem. 16th CCP Cen. Cttee 2002–07; mem. 17th CCP Cen. Cttee 2007–12, 18th CCP Cen. Cttee 2012–, mem. 18th CCP Politburo 2012–. *Address:* Office of the Vice-President, Great Hall of the People, West Edge, Tiananmen Square, Beijing, People's Republic of China (office). *Website:* www.gov.cn (office).

LI, Yue, BEng, MBA, DBA; Chinese telecommunications industry executive; *Executive Director, President and CEO, China Mobile Communications Corporation;* ed Correspondence Coll. of Beijing Univ. of Posts and Telecommunications, Tianjin Univ., Hong Kong Polytechnic Univ.; began career with China Mobile Communications Corpn 1976, later Deputy Dir Gen. and Chief Engineer of Tianjin Long-Distance Telecommunications Bureau, Deputy Dir Gen. of Tianjin Posts and Telecommunications Admin, Pres. Tianjin Mobile Communications Co., Deputy Head of Preparatory Team and Vice-Pres. China Mobile Communications Corpn, Exec. Dir, Pres. and CEO 2003–; Chair. Aspire Holdings Ltd, Union Mobile Pay Ltd; Dir (non-exec.) Phoenix Satellite Television Holdings Ltd; numerous nat., prov. and ministerial-level scientific and technological progress awards. *Address:* China Mobile Communications Corpn, 29 Financial Street, Xicheng District, Beijing 100032, People's Republic of China (office). *Telephone:* (10) 3121-8888 (office). *Fax:* (10) 2511-9092 (office). *E-mail:* info@chinamobile.com (office). *Website:* www.chinamobile.com (office).

LI, Yunpeng, MA; Chinese engineer and business executive; *President, China Ocean Shipping (Group) Company (COSCO);* ed Tianjin Univ.; served as fourth engineer, then third engineer, then second engineer on China Ocean Shipping (Group) Company (COSCO)'s vessels, also served in COSCO Tianjin as Deputy Man. and Gen. Man. Human Resources Dept, Gen. Man. Admin Dept and Party Sec. Office, various posts including Deputy Gen. Man. Exec. Div., Deputy Sec. of Party Disciplinary Inspection Office, Gen. Man. Supervisory Div., Dir of Org. Div., Gen. Man. Human Resources Div., Asst to Pres., Party Cttee mem., Dir of Party Disciplinary Inspection Office and Exec. Vice-Pres. COSCO Group, mem. Bd of Dirs and Pres. COSCO 2013–. *Address:* China Ocean Shipping (Group) Company (COSCO), Ocean Plaza, 158 Fuxingmennei Street, Beiing 100031, People's Republic of China (office). *Telephone:* (10) 66493388 (office). *Fax:* (10) 66492266 (office). *E-mail:* info@cosco.com (office). *Website:* www.cosco.com (office).

LI, Zehou; Chinese philosopher; b. 1930, Changsha, Hunan Prov.; ed Hu'an No. 1 Prov. Normal School, Peking Univ.; Asst Research Fellow, Assoc. Research Fellow then Research Fellow Philosophy Inst., Chinese Acad. of Sciences 1955–; Vice-Chair. Aesthetics Soc. of China; mem. Exec. Council Chinese Writers Asscn and Soc. of Sun Yat-sen Studies. *Publications:* Critique of Critical Philosophy, The Course of Beauty, History of Chinese Aesthetics, Essays on China's Ancient Intellectual History. *Address:* Institute of Philosophy, Chinese Academy of Social Sciences, Beijing, People's Republic of China (office).

LI, Zemin; Chinese party official; *Chairman, Standing Committee, Zhejiang Provincial People's Congress;* b. 1934, Cangxi Co., Sichuan Prov.; ed People's Univ. of China; joined PLA 1950, soldier in Korean War 1952; joined CCP 1954; Deputy Dir Marxism-Leninism Teaching and Research Centre, Shenyang Agricultural Coll., Liaoning Prov. 1973–78 (Sec. CCP Party Br. 1973–78); Deputy Sec. Shenyang Mun. CCP Cttee, Liaoning Prov. 1983–85, Sec. 1986–88; Deputy Sec. Liaoning Prov. CCP Cttee 1985–86; First Sec. CCP Party Cttee, Zhejiang Mil. Dist, PLA Nanjing Mil. Region 1988; Sec. CCP Zhejiang Prov. Cttee 1988–98; Chair. Standing Cttee of Zhejiang Prov. People's Congress 1993–; mem. 13th CCP Cen. Cttee 1987–92, 15th CCP Cen. Cttee 1997–2002; Deputy, 8th NPC 1993–98. *Address:* Standing Committee of Zhejiang Provincial People's Congress, Hangzhou, Zhejiang Province, People's Republic of China (office).

LI, Zhanshu; Chinese politician; *Director, CCP Central Committee General Office;* b. 1950, Pingshan County, Hebei Prov.; ed Harbin Inst. of Tech.; joined CCP 1975; Staff mem., Document Dept, Gen. Office, CCP Prefectural Cttee, Shijiazhuang Prefecture, Hebei Prov. 1976–83; Sec., Wuji County CCP Cttee, Hebei Prov. 1983–85, Deputy Sec., Shijiazhuang City CCP Cttee 1985–86, also Commr, Shijiazhuang Prefectural Admin. Office 1985–86; Sec., Communist Youth League of China, Hebei Prov. 1986–90; Deputy Sec., CCP Dist Cttee, Chengde Prefecture 1990–93; Sec.-Gen., CCP Prov. Cttee, Hebei Prov. 1993–97; Deputy, 8th NPC 1993–98; Commr, Prov. Admin. Office, Hebei Prov. 1998–2002; Sec., Xi'an City CCP City Cttee 2002–04; Chair., Standing Cttee, Xi'an City People's Congress 2002–04; Deputy Sec., Heilongjiang Prov. CCP Prov. Cttee 2003–10; Vice-Gov., Heilongjiang Prov. 2004–07, Acting Gov. 2007–08, Gov. 2008–10; Sec., CCP Prov. Cttee, Guizhou Prov. 2010–12; Dir, CCP Cen. Cttee Gen. Office 2012–; alt. mem. 16th CCP Cen. Cttee 2002–07, mem. 17th CCP Cen. Cttee 2007–12, 18th CCP Cen. Cttee 2012–, also mem. Politburo and Secr. 2012–. *Address:* Zhongguo Gongchan Dang (Chinese Communist Party), Zhongnanhai, Beijing, People's Republic of China (office). *Website:* cpc.people.com.cn (office).

LI, Zhaoxing, MA; Chinese politician and diplomatist; b. Oct. 1940, Jiaonan, Shandong Prov.; m. Qin Xiaomei; one s.; ed Beijing Univ., Beijing Foreign Languages Inst.; joined CCP 1965; on staff, Chinese People's Inst. of Foreign Affairs 1967–70; attaché, Embassy, Nairobi, Kenya 1970–77; Third Sec., later Second Sec., later Deputy Div. Chief, Information Dept, Ministry of Foreign Affairs 1977–83; Deputy Dir-Gen., later Dir-Gen. 1985–90 (also Spokesman, Ministry of Foreign Affairs 1985–90), Asst to Vice-Minister of Foreign Affairs 1990–93; First Sec. Embassy, Maseru, Lesotho 1983–85; Chinese Rep. and Amb. to UN 1993–95; Vice-Minister of Foreign Affairs 1995–98; Amb. to USA 1998–2001; Vice-Minister of Foreign Affairs in charge of American and Latin American Affairs 2001–03; Minister of Foreign Affairs 2003–07; Alt. mem. 15th CCP Cen. Cttee 1997–2002, mem. 16th CCP Cen. Cttee 2002–07; Chair. 11th NPC Foreign Affairs Cttee 2008–13. *Address:* c/o Ministry of Foreign Affairs, 225 Chaoyangmen Nan Dajie, Chaoyang Qu, Beijing 100701, People's Republic of China (office).

LI, Zhaozhuo; Chinese politician; b. Sept. 1944, Pingguo, Guangxi Zhuang Autonomous Region; ed Guangxi Univ., Nanning, CCP Guangxi Zhuang Autonomous Regional Cttee Party School, CCP Cen. Cttee Cen. Party School; sent to do manual labour, Army Farms, Guangxi Zhuang Autonomous Region and Hunan Prov. 1968–70; technician, Du'an Commune, Debao Co., Guangxi Zhuang Autonomous Region 1970–74; joined CCP 1974; technician, Sec., later Deputy Dir Debao Co. Hydroelectric Power Bureau, Guangxi 1975–80; Deputy Dir Capital

Construction Bureau, Debao Co., Guangxi Zhuang Autonomous Region 1980–83, Deputy Dir Planning Cttee 1980–83; Dir Econ. Cttee, CCP Autonomous Co. Cttee, Debao Co., Guangxi Zhuang Autonomous Region 1983–84 (also mem. Standing Cttee), Sec. CCP Autonomous Co. Cttee 1984–85; Deputy Sec. CCP Autonomous Prefectural Cttee, Bose Prefecture, Guangxi Zhuang Autonomous Region 1985–92 (Sec. 1992–93), Commr, Prefectural Admin. Office 1985–93; Sec. CCP Fangchenggang Autonomous City Cttee, Guangxi Zhuang Autonomous Region 1993–95, Chair. Autonomous Regional People's Congress 1993–95; Sec. Nanning Autonomous City Cttee, Guangxi Zhuang Autonomous Region 1994–96; Deputy Sec. Guangxi Zhuang Autonomous Regional Cttee 1996–2002 (mem. Standing Cttee 1996–2002); Chair. People's Govt of Guangxi Zhuang Autonomous Region 1997–2003; mem. 15th CCP Cen. Cttee 1997–2002, 16th CCP Cen. Cttee 2002–07, 17th CCP Cen. Cttee 2007–12; Vice-Chair. 10th CPPCC Nat. Cttee 2003–08, 11th CPPCC Nat. Cttee 2008–13. *Address:* c/o People's Government of Guangxi Zhuang Autonomous Region, 1 Minle Road, Nanning 530012, Guangxi, People's Republic of China (office).

LI, Zhengwu; Chinese physicist; *Honorary Director, Southwestern Institute of Physics;* b. Nov. 1916; Pres. Soc. of Nuclear Fusion and Plasma 1980–; mem. Chinese Acad. of Sciences 1980–; mem. Nat. Cttee 7th CPPCC 1988–93; Hon. Dir Southwestern Inst. of Physics; mem. Ed. Bd Plasma Science and Technology (journal). *Address:* Southwestern Institute of Physics, Chengdu 610041, People's Republic of China (office). *Website:* www.swip.ac.cn (office).

LI, Zhensheng; Chinese geneticist; *Senior Research Fellow, Institute of Genetics and Developmental Biology;* b. 1931, Zibo, Shandong Prov.; ed Shandong Agricultural Coll.; Dir Northwest Botanical Research Inst.; Vice-Chair. China Science and Tech. Asscn; currently Sr Research Fellow Inst. of Genetics and Developmental Biology, Chinese Acad. of Sciences; mem. 4th Presidium, Chinese Acad. of Sciences 2000–; Fellow, Chinese Acad. of Sciences, fmr Vice-Pres.; mem. Third World Acad. of Sciences 1990–; bred super wheat varieties Xiaoyan Nos. 4, 5 and 6; created the blue-grained wheat monosomic system (BGM); pioneered 'the nullisomic back-crossing method' for fast breeding alien substitution lines of wheat and laid a foundation for wheat chromosome eng breeding; awarded title of Nat. Model Worker 1980, Nat. Supreme Scientific and Technological Award 2006. *Publications:* Outline of Distant Hybridisation of Plants, Distant Hybridisation of Wheat. *Address:* Institute of Genetics and Developmental Biology, Datun Road, Andingmenwai, Beijing 100101, People's Republic of China (office). *Telephone:* (10) 64889331 (office). *Fax:* (10) 64856610 (office). *E-mail:* zsli@genetics.ac.cn (office). *Website:* www.genetics.ac.cn (office).

LI SHAN, Rev. Joseph; Chinese ecclesiastic; *Bishop of Beijing;* b. 1965; ed Chinese Catholic Acad. of Theology and Philosophy, Beijing Theological Seminary; among first priests ordained after Cultural Revolution 1989; taught the Bible at Beijing Theological Seminary; Vice-Chair. Beijing Church Affairs Cttee; Deputy to Beijing Municipal People's Congress (local parl.); selected for appointment as bishop by mems of Patriotic Catholic Asscn, consecrated Bishop of Beijing in pvt. ceremony 2007. *Address:* Catholic Diocese of Beijing, Si-She-Ku, Beijing, People's Republic of China (office).

LI YAN, (Zhuang Bei); Chinese painter; *Professor, Academy of Arts, Tsinghua University;* b. Nov. 1943, Beijing; s. of Li Ku Chan and Li Hui Wen; m. Sun Yan Hua 1972; one d.; Prof., Cen. Inst. of Arts and Crafts and of Shandong; fmr Vice-Pres. Li Ku Chan Museum; mem. Chinese Artists' Asscn; currently Prof., Acad. of Arts, Tsinghua Univ.; Deputy Dir of Li Kuchan Memorial; Vice-Pres. Int. Soc. Yi Jing, Research Fellow Research Soc. Yi Jing; Specialist, Appraising Cttee of Chinese Arts of Calligraphy and Painting; specializes in painting figures, animals and mountains and water scenes and in calligraphy; over 10,000 sketches and paintings from life, 3,000 exercises in Chinese painting 1956–; mem. 9th CPPCC 1998–2003, 10th CPPCC 2003–08; mem. Beijing PCCC; works have been exhibited in Sweden, USA, Canada, Japan, Singapore, Philippines, Hong Kong, Tanzania; gave lectures at Hong Kong Univ. 1980; held lectures and exhbn in India 1989, in Malaysia 1991, in Indonesia 1993; subject of TV films by Shen Zhen TV 1986 and Swedish TV 1986, presenter of CCTV's The Wind of China 1995; important works include Chinese Emperor, Zhou Wen Emperor, Lao Zi, Confucian Worry about Taoism, Lao Zi and Einstein, Five-Colour Earth, Start Sailing, A Swarm of Monkeys, Cat and Chrysanthemum, Tiger Cub. *Publications:* Yi Jing Album 1993; several magazine articles on art. *Leisure interests:* writing poetry, Qigong, The Book of Changes. *Address:* No. 2-1, Building 15, Nan sha Go, San Li He, Xi Cheng District, Beijing, People's Republic of China. *Telephone:* (10) 68534056 (office). *Fax:* (10) 68512920 (office). *E-mail:* sumantar@hotmail.com (office).

LIANG, Dongcai, PhD; Chinese molecular biophysicist and protein crystallographer; b. 29 May 1932, Guangzhou, Guangdong Prov.; ed Zhongshan Univ., Inst. of Organo-Element Compounds, USSR Acad. of Sciences, Royal Inst., UK, Univ. of Oxford, UK; Prof., Inst. of Biophysics, Chinese Acad. of Sciences (Dir 1983–86); mem. Chinese Acad. of Sciences 1980–, Dir Biology Div.; Vice-Chair. Nat. Natural Science Foundation of China 1986–95, adviser 1995–98, Chair. Inspection Cttee 1998–2001; mem. Cttee on Biomacromolecule Crystallography of Int. Soc. of Crystallography 1981–84; mem. Council of Int. Soc. of Biophysics 1993–99, 4th Presidium of Depts, Chinese Acad. of Sciences 2000–; Pres. Chinese Biophysics Soc. 1983–86, 1990–98; Vice-Pres. Chinese Biochemistry Soc. 1987–90; Fellow, Third World Acad. of Sciences 1985–; Alt. mem. 12th CCP Cen. Cttee 1982–87; mem. 13th CCP Cen. Cttee 1987–92; Chinese Nat. Scientific Prize (2nd Rank) 1982, 1989, Scientific Prize (2nd Rank), Chinese Acad. of Sciences 1986, 1992, Scientific Prize (1st Rank), Chinese Acad. of Sciences 1987. *Publications:* more than 140 papers in scientific journals. *Address:* Institute of Biophysics, Chinese Academy of Sciences, Beijing 100101, People's Republic of China (office). *Telephone:* (10) 64888506 (office). *Fax:* (10) 64889867 (office).

LIANG, Gen. Guanglie; Chinese army officer and government official; b. Dec. 1940, Santai Co., Sichuan Prov.; ed Xinyang Infantry Acad. 1963, PLA Mil. Acad., Nat. Defence Univ., Henan Univ.; joined CCP 1958, PLA 1959; Vice-Div. Commdr and then Div. Commdr 1979–82; Vice-Army Commdr then Army Commdr, Vice-Commdr PLA Beijing Mil. Area Command 1983–97; rank of Lt-Gen. 1995, Gen. 2002; Commdr PLA Shenyang Mil. Area Command 1997–2000; Commdr PLA Nanjing Mil. Area Command 2000–03; Alt. mem. 13th CCP Cen. Cttee 1982–87, 14th CCP Cen. Cttee 1987–92, mem. 15th CCP Cen. Cttee 1997–2002, 16th CCP

Cen. Cttee 2002–07, 17th CCP Cen. Cttee 2007–12 (mem. Cen. Mil. Comm. 2002–); Chief, HQ of Gen. Staff, PLA 2002–07; Minister of Nat. Defence 2008–13; State Councillor 2008–. *Address:* c/o Ministry of National Defence, 20 Jingshanqian Jie, Beijing 100009, People's Republic of China (office).

LIANG, Xiaosheng; Chinese writer; b. Sept. 1949, Harbin; worker on land reclamation project; local newspaper reporter; Chinese language student, Fudan Univ. 1975; mem. Chinese Writers' Asscn, Chinese Filmmakers' Asscn; mem. and official of Chinese Film Scriptwriters' Asscn; Film Script Ed., Beijing Film Studio. *Publications:* four anthologies of short stories, an anthology of medium-length novels and two novels, most of which have been adapted as films or TV plays; works include: This is a Strange Land, Father, Literary Accomplishments, Blizzard at Midnight (all of which have won All-China Short Novel Prizes), For the Harvest, TV play based on Blizzard at Midnight (awarded All-China TV Playscript Grand Prize), Floating City 1992, Panic 2002, Deaf 2002, Growth Rings (TV series), Snow City, Bitter Love, Broken Heart Bar. *Address:* Editorial Department, 'Creative Cinema', 19 Bei-huan Xilu Street, Beijing, People's Republic of China.

LIAO, Hui; Chinese government official; b. 1942, Huiyang Dist, Guangdong Prov.; s. of the late Liao Chengzhi and Jing Puchum; ed Mil. Eng Inst. of Chinese PLA; joined CCP 1965; fmr technician, Air Force, PLA Services and Arms (Rep. in charge of Mil. Inspection); fmr Staff Officer, HQ of the Gen. Staff, PLA Beijing Mil. Region; Dir Overseas Chinese Affairs Office, State Council 1984–, Dir Leading Party Group 1984–87, Sec. Leading Party Group 1984–97; Dir Hong Kong and Macao Affairs Office of the State Council 1997–; Vice-Chair. Macao Special Admin. Region Preparatory Cttee 1998–99; Vice-Chair. 10th CPPCC Nat. Cttee 2003–08, 11th CPPCC Nat. Cttee 2008–13; mem. 12th CCP Cen. Cttee 1982–87, 13th CCP Cen. Cttee 1987–92, 14th CCP Cen. Cttee 1992–97, 15th CCP Cen. Cttee 1997–2002, 16th CCP Cen. Cttee 2002–07, 17th CCP Cen. Cttee 2007–12; Vice-Pres. China Overseas Exchanges Asscn 1991–97; mem. 21st Century Comm. for Sino-Japanese Friendship 1985–; Hon. Vice-Chair. Zhonghai Inst. of Agricultural Tech. 1987–. *Address:* c/o State Council, Zhong Nan Hai, Beijing, People's Republic of China.

LIAO, Gen. Xilong; Chinese army officer; *Director, Logistics Department, People's Liberation Army;* b. June 1940, Sinan Co., Guizhou Prov.; ed Mil. Acad. of Chinese PLA; joined PLA 1959, CCP 1963; served as Platoon Commdr 1966–67, Co. Commdr 1969–71, Deputy Chief of a regimental combat training section 1971–73, Deputy Chief of a div. mil. affairs section 1973–78, Deputy Regt Commdr 1978–79, Regt Commdr 1979–80, Deputy Div. Commdr 1981–83, Div. Commdr 1983, Army Commdr 1984–85, Deputy Commdr Chengdu Mil. Region 1985–95, Commdr 1995–2003; rank of Maj.-Gen. 1988–93, Lt-Gen. 1993–2000, Gen. 2000–; Dir Logistics Dept, PLA 2002–; mem. 15th CCP Cen. Cttee 1997–2002, 16th CCP Cen. Cttee 2002–07, 17th CCP Cen. Cttee 2007–12 (mem. Cen. Mil. Comm. 2002–). *Address:* People's Liberation Army, c/o Ministry of National Defence, 20 Jingshanqian Jie, Beijing 100009, People's Republic of China.

LIAO, Yongyuan, MA; Chinese oil industry executive; *General Manager and President, China National Petroleum Corporation (CNPC);* professor-level sr engineer; has worked in oil and gas industry since 1980s; Deputy Dir New Zone Exploration and Devt Dept, China Nat. Petroleum Corpn (CNPC) 1996–99, Standing Deputy Commdr, then Commdr Tarim Petroleum Exploration and Devt HQ 1996–99, Gen. Man. PetroChina Tarim Oilfield Co. 1999–2001, Deputy Dir Gansu Prov. Econ. and Trade Cttee 2001–04, Asst to Gen. Man. of CNPC 2004–05, concurrently Head of Co-ordination Team for Oil Enterprises in Sichuan and Chongqing and Dir Sichuan Petroleum Admin 2004–05, Vice-Pres. CNPC 2005–07, Deputy Gen. Man. Feb. 2007–13, Safety Dir July 2007–08, Dir 2008–, Gen. Man. and Pres. 2013–. *Address:* China National Petroleum Corporation, 9 Dongzhimen North Street, Dongcheng District, Beijing 100007, People's Republic of China (office). *Telephone:* (10) 62094114 (office). *Fax:* (10) 62094205 (office). *E-mail:* admin_eng@cnpc.com.cn (office). *Website:* www.cnpc.com.cn (office).

LIBAI, David, LLD; Israeli lawyer and politician; b. 22 Oct. 1934, Tel-Aviv; m.; one s. one d.; ed Ironi Alef High School, Hebrew Univ. of Jerusalem, Tel-Aviv Univ., Univ. of Chicago, USA; served as Deputy Chief Mil. Prosecutor, discharged with rank of Maj.; certified as a lawyer 1960; apptd Chief Asst to Attorney Gen. Colin Gillon and Chief Prosecutor of the State Workers' Disciplinary Court; opened a private law office 1964; Deputy Attorney-Gen.; Assoc. Prof. and Dir Inst. of Criminology and Criminal Law, Tel-Aviv Univ., fmr Dean of Students; Chair. Labour Party Constitution Cttee 1977, Israel-Britain Parl. Friendship Asscn, Public Audit (Control) Cttee 1984–92; mem. Knesset (Alignment) 1984–91, (Labour Party) 1991–99, served on various cttees; Spokesman, Ministry of Justice, then Minister of Justice 1992–96; Minister of the Interior 1995; Assoc. Prof., Herzliya Interdisciplinary Center; fmr mem. Nat. Comm. of Inquiry on Prison Conditions, Press Council; mem. Israel Labour Party; Head of Israel Bar Asscn 1983–85; Pinchas Rosen Award, Ethics Award from Minister of Justice 2005. *Publications:* Imprisonment Law 1978; numerous articles on legal issues. *Address:* c/o Israel Labour Party, PO Box 62033, Tel-Aviv, 61620, Israel. *Telephone:* 3-6899444. *Fax:* 3-6899420. *E-mail:* inter@havoda.org.il. *Website:* www.havoda.org.il.

LIBANIO CHRISTO, Carlos Alberto (Frei Betto); Brazilian Dominican friar and writer; b. 25 Aug. 1944, Belo Horizonte, Minas Gerais; s. of Antônio Carlos Vieira Christo and Maria Stella Libanio Christo; ed Univ. of Brazil, Escola Dominicana de Teologia and Seminário São Leopoldo; Vice-Pres. High School Municipal Union of Belo Horizonte 1961; Nat. Leader Catholic Young Students 1961–64; political prisoner 1964; newspaper and magazine ed. 1966–69; political prisoner held in São Paulo, accused of carrying out subversive activities 1969–73; organizer of basic Church communities 1973–79; teacher, popular educ. 1977–; writer and teacher with Workers' Pastoral 1979–; was sued, under the Media Law, by São Paulo Mil. Police for denouncing the violent acts of some its mems 1992, absolved by court 1993; Dir América Libre (magazine) 1993–2003; mem. Council Swedish Foundation for Human Rights 1991–96, Inst. for Critical Research, Amsterdam, Cajamar Inst., São Paulo, 'Sedes Sapientiae' Centre for Popular Educ., São Paulo; Consultant, Movimento dos Trabalhadores Rurais Sem Terra (MST); mem. and consultant Inst. Cidadania –2003; consultant to Itau Cultural Inst.; Special Assessor of the Presidency of the Repub., acting as Co-ordinator of

Social Mobilization for the Zero Hunger Programme 2003–04; mem. Strategic Bd Faca Parte (Join In); assisted the Popular Movts Cen. Bd Workers Pastoral in the ABC area, São Paulo, Centre of Popular Movts, Ecclesiastical Base Communities; Co-ordinator ANAMPOS (Nat. Articulation for Popular and Union Movts Sindicais); consultant to Rural Landless Workers Movt; fmr Dir America Libre magazine; has lectured and given pastoral courses in Brazil and overseas; Intellectual of the Year Prize, Brazilian Writers' Union 1985, Human Rights Prize, Bruno Kreisky Foundation, Vienna 1987, Human Rights Prize, Bruno Kreisky Foundation 1988, Crea de Meio Ambiente Prize, Conselho Regional de Engenharia e Arquitetura, Rio de Janeiro, Paolo E. Borsellino Award (Italy) for work in human rights 1998, Award of Rio de Janeiro Regional Council for Architecture and Eng 1998, Chico Mendes de Resistência Medal, Grupo Tortura Nunca Mais, Rio de Janeiro 1998, Solidarity Medal (Cuba) 2000, Prêmio Abogados de Atocha (Spain), Paulo Freire Trophy for Social Commitment, Brazilian Psychology Council 2000. *Publications:* Cartas da Prisão (Letters from the Prison) 1974, Das Catacumbas 1976, Oração na Ação (Prayers in the Action) 1977, Natal, a ameaça de um menino pobre (Christmas, a Threat of a Poor Boy) 1978, A Semente e o Fruto, Igreja e Comunidade (The Seed, the Fruit, Church and the Community) 1981, Diário de Puebla (Diary of Puebla) 1979, A Vida Suspeita do Subversivo Paul Parelo (The Suspect Life of Paul Parelo – short stories) 1979 (re-published with the title O Aquária Negro – The Black Fishbowl) 1986), Puebla para o Povo (Puebla for the People) 1979, Nicarágua Livre, o Primeiro Passo (Nicaragua Free, First Step) 1980, O que é Comunidade Eclesial de Base (What is an Ecclesiastical Base Community) 1981, O Fermento na Massa (The Baking Powder in the Dough) 1981, CEBs, Rumo à Nova Sociedade (EBC – A Step to a New Society) 1981, Batismo de Sangue, Os dominicanos e a morte de Carlos Marighella (Blood Baptism, The Dominican Friars and the Death of Carlos Marighella) (Jabuti Prize, Brazilian Book Asscn 1983) 1982, Fogãozinho, culinária em histórias infantis (Cooking in Children's Stories) (with Maria Stella Libanio Christo) 1984, Fidel e a Religião, Conversas com Frei Betto (Fidel and Religion – Talks with Frei Betto) 1985, OSPB, Introdução à Política Brasileira (Social and Political Organization of Brazil - Introduction to Brazilian Politics) 1985, O Dia de Angelo (Angelo's Day) (romance) 1987, Cristianismo & Marxismo (Christianity and Marxism) 1988, Sinal de contradição (Sign of Contradiction) (with Afonso Borges Filho) 1988, Essa escola chamada vida (A School Called Life) (with Paulo Freire and Ricardo Kotscho) 1988, Lula – Biografia Política de um Operário (Lula - Political Biography of a Worker) 1989, A Proposta de Jesus (Jesus' Proposal) (Popular Catechism, Vol. I) 1989, A Comunidade de Fé (The Faith Community) (Popular Cathecism, Vol. II) 1989, Militantes do Reino (Militants of the Kingdom) (Popular Catechism, Vol. III) 1990, Viver em Comunhão de Amor (Living in a Communion of Love) (Popular Catechism, Vol. IV) 1990, A Menina e o Elefante (The Girl and the Elephant) (teenage book) 1990, Fome de Pão e de Beleza (Hunger of Bread and Beauty) 1990, Uala, o Amor (Uala and Love) (teenage literature) 1991, Popular Catechism (condensed version) 1992, Alucinado Som de Tuba (Allucinated Sound of Tuba) (romance) 1993, O Paraiso Perdido – nos bastidores do socialismo (The Lost Paradise – In the Backstage of Socialism) 1993, Por que Eleger Lula Presidente da República (Why Elect Lula President of the Republic?) 1994, Mística e espiritualidade (Mystic and Spirituality) (with Leonardo Boff) 1994, O Desafio Ético (The Ethical Challenge) (with Eugenio Barba and Jurandir Freire Costa) 1995, A Obra do Artista – uma visão holística do Universo (The Artist's Work – A Holistic Vision of the Universe) 1995, Comer como um frade – divinas receitas para quem sabe por que temos um céu na boca (Eating like a Fries – Divine Recipes) 1996, Cotidiano & Mistério (Everyday Stories and Mystery) 1996, O Vencedor (The Winner) (romance) 1996, Sinfonia Universal, a cosmovisão de Teilhard de Chardin (Universal Symphony – The Cosmovision of Teilhard de Chardin) 1997, Entre todos os homens (Amongst All Men) (novel) 1997, Talita abre a porta dos evangelhos (Talita Opens the Doors of the Gospels) 1998, A noite em que Jesus nasceu (The Night when Jesus was Born) (Best Young Readers' Book, Art Critics Asscn of São Paulo 1998) 1998, Hotel Brasil (detective story) 1999, Mysterium Creationes – Um olhar interdisciplinar sobre o Universo (Jabuti Prize 2000) 2000, Brasil 500 Anos: trajetórias, identidades e destinos (Brazil 500 Years: Routes, Identities and Destinies) 2000, O Decálogo (The Commandments) (short stories in partnership with Moacyr Scliar, Luiz Vilela, Ivan Angelo, José Roberto Torero and others) 2000, A mula de Balaão (Balaao's Mule) 2001, Os dois irmãos (The Two Brothers) 2001, A mulher Samaritana (The Samaritan) 2001, Alfabeto – Autobiografia Escolar (Alfabetto – An Educational Self-Biography) 2002, Gosto de Uva – Textos selecionados (Taste of Grapes – Selected Articles) 2003, Típicos Tipos – Coletânea de Perfis Literários (Typical Types – Collective of Literary Profiles) 2004, Uma saborosa viagem pelo Brasil – Limonada e sua turma em histórias e receitas a bordo do Fogãozinho (A Tasteful Journey in Brazil – Lemonade and his Gang with Their Stories and Recipes on Board a Cooker) 2004, Treze contos diabólicos e um angélico 2005, A Mosca Azul 2006; numerous articles in Brazilian newspapers and magazines, including Diário Popular, O Globo, Folha de S. Paulo, O Estado de Minas, Correio Braziliense, O Dia, Caros Amigos, Brasileira, Chronica Brasil. *Leisure interests:* cooking, swimming. *Address:* Rua Atibaia 420, 01235-010 São Paulo, SP, Brazil. *Telephone:* (11) 38640844 (R. 224); (11) 38651473. *Fax:* (11) 38656941. *E-mail:* fbetto@uol.com.br.

LIBBRECHT, Kenneth G., BS, PhD; American physicist and academic; *Professor of Physics, California Institute of Technology;* b. 9 June 1958, Fargo, ND; m. Rachel Wing; two c.; ed California Inst. of Tech., Princeton Univ.; Asst Prof. of Astrophysics, California Inst. of Tech. 1984–89, Assoc. Prof. 1989–95, Prof. of Physics 1995–, Exec. Officer for Physics Dept 1997–; Fellow, AAAS 1996; Fisher Prize for Physics, California Inst. of Tech. 1979, NSF Presidential Young Investigator Award 1987, Newton Lacy Pierce Prize in Astrophysics, American Astronomical Soc. 1991, US Postal Service Stamp Set (using KGL photographs) 2006, Emile Chamot Award, State Microscopical Soc. of Ill. 2009, Swedish Postal Service Stamp Set (using KGL photographs) 2010, Lennart Nilsson Award 2010, several website awards. *Publications:* The Snowflake: Winter's Secret Beauty (with Patricia Rasmussen photography) 2003 (Benjamin Franklin Book Award 2004, Nat. Outdoor Book Award 2004), The Little Book of Snowflakes (Runner-up, Benjamin Franklin Book Award 2005) 2004, The Magic of Snowflakes 2005, Ken Libbrecht's Field Guide to Snowflakes 2006, The Art of the Snowflake: A Photographic Album 2007, Snowflakes 2008, The Secret Life of a Snowflake 2010; numerous research papers and articles in learned journals. *Address:* Physics Department, California Institute of Technology, Caltech 264–33, Pasadena, CA

91125, USA (office). *Telephone:* (626) 395-3722 (office). *Fax:* (626) 395-3814 (office). *E-mail:* kgl@caltech.edu (office). *Website:* www.its.caltech.edu/~atomic (office).

LIBERADZKI, Bogusław Marian, DEcon; Polish politician and economist; b. 12 Sept. 1948, Sochaczew; m.; two s.; ed Main School of Planning and Statistics, Warsaw and Univ. of Illinois, USA; Scientist, Main School of Planning and Statistics (now Warsaw School of Econs) Warsaw 1971–75, Asst 1971–75, Tutor 1975–82, Asst Prof. 1982–99, Prof. of Econs 1999–, Head, Dept of Transport; Dir Transport Econs Research Centre, Warsaw 1986–89; Prof., Maritime Univ., Szcecin 1998–; Deputy Minister of Transport 1989–93; mem. Transport Comm., Polish Acad. of Sciences 1988–96, European Rail Congress Council, Brussels; Chair. Supervisory Bd Polish LOT Airways –1993; Minister of Transport and Maritime Economy 1993–97; mem. Democratic Left Alliance (Sojusz Lewicy Demokratycznej-Unia Pracy—SLD-UP) Parl. Club; Deputy to Sejm (Parl.) 1997–2004, Vice-Chair. Infrastructure Cttee 2001–04, European Cttee 2003–04, Polish-Nordic Group 2001–04, Chair. Perm. Sub-cttee on Transport 2001–04, Perm. Sub-cttee for Monitoring the Utilization of EU Funds 2001–04; Observer to European Parl. 2003–04; mem. European Parl. (Socialist Group) 2004–, Cttee on Transport and Tourism 2004–, Substitute mem. Cttee on the Internal Market and Consumer Protection 2004–, mem. Del. to the EU-Russia Parl. Cooperation Cttee 2004–, Substitute mem. Del. for Relations with the United States 2004–; Golden Medal of Merit 1978; Medal of the National Education Committee, Fulbright Scholarship 1986. *Publications:* Economics of Railways 1980, Supply of Railroad Services 1981, Transport: Demand, Supply, Equilibrium 1999. *Leisure interests* biographies, gardening. *Address:* European Parliament, 07H141, 60 rue Wiertz, 1047 Brussels, Belgium (office); Biuro Poselskie, ul. Garncarska 5, 70-402 Szczecin, Poland. *Telephone:* (91) 4341918. *Fax:* (2) 284-9423 (office). *Website:* www.europarl.eu.int (office).

LIBERIA-PETERS, Maria; Curaçao politician; b. 20 May 1941, Willemstad; m. Neils Liberia; two adopted c.; fmr kindergarten teacher; mem. Curaçao Island Council 1975–82; elected mem. Staten (legislature of Netherlands Antilles) 1982–2010; Minister of Economic Affairs, Netherlands Antilles 1982–84; mem. Nat. Volkspartij (Nat. People's Party), fmr Pres.; Prime Minister of Netherlands Antilles 1984–86, 1988–94; Leader of the Opposition 1986–88, 1994–; mem. Council of Women World Leaders. *Address:* Partido Nashonal di Pueblo, Winston Churchillweg 133, Willemstad, Curaçao (office). *Telephone:* (9) 869-6777 (office). *Fax:* (9) 869-6688 (office).

LIBESKIND, Daniel, BArch, MA; American architect; *Owner and Architect, Studio Daniel Libeskind;* b. 1946, Łódź, Poland; s. of Nachman Libeskind and Dora Blaustein; m. Nina Lewis 1969; two s. one d.; ed Cooper Union School of Architecture, New York, Univ. of Essex, UK; fmr Head, Dept of Architecture, Cranbrook Acad. of Art, Bloomfield Hills, Mich. fmr Sr Scholar, John Paul Getty Centre; fmr Visiting Prof., Harvard Univ.; fmr Bannister Fletcher Prof., Univ. of London, UK; fmr holder Davenport Chair, Yale Univ.; Owner, Studio Daniel Libeskind (architectural practice), Berlin 1989–; apptd lead architect for rebuilding of World Trade Center site 2003; Prof., Hochschule für Gestaltung, Karlsruhe; holder of Creative Chair, Univ. of Pennsylvania, USA; mem. Akad. der Kunst 1990–, European Acad. of Arts and Letters, American Acad. of Arts and Letters; Hon. RA 2002; Dr hc (Humboldt Univ.) 1997, (Univ. of Essex) 1999, (Technion, Israel); Hon. DHumLitt (De Paul Univ.) 2002, (Brandeis) 2007; Hon. DScS (Edinburgh) 2002; Hon. LLD (Toronto) 2004; Commander's Cross, Order of Merit (Germany); numerous awards including Lion d'Or, Venice Biennale 1985, Berlin Cultural Prize 1996, Award for Architecture, American Acad. of Arts and Letters 1996, Goethe Medallion 2000, Hiroshima Art Prize 2001, Holocaust Educational Trust Award, Leo Baeck Inst. Award, Trebbia European Award, Prague 2006, Gold Medal Award for Architecture, Genoa, Italy, Nat. Arts Club Gold Medal for Architecture 2007, Penn State IAH Medal for Distinguished Contribution to Public Advancement of Arts and Humanities, Yivo Inst. for Jewish Research 'Lifetime Achievement' Award, New York City. *Opera:* stage sets: Tristan und Isolde (also costume design), Saarbrücken, Germany 2001, Saint Francis of Assisi, Berlin, Germany 2002. *Projects include:* (architectural) Felix-Nussbaum-Haus, Osnabrück, Germany 1998, Jewish Museum, Berlin 1999 (German Architecture Prize 1999, Art Forum Int. Best of 1998), Imperial War Museum North, Manchester 2001 (RIBA Award 2004, British Construction Industry Building of the Year), Eighteen Turns (summer pavilion) Serpentine Gallery, London 2001, Weil Gallery, Majorca 2001, Jewish Museum, Copenhagen 2002, CUBE Bar and Restaurant, Manchester 2002, London Metropolitan Univ. Graduate Centre 2004 (RIBA Award), Wohl Centre, Bar-Ilan Univ., Israel 2005 (RIBA Int. Award), Denver Art Museum Residences 2006 (American Inst. of Architects Award of Honor 2008, CNBC Americas Property Awards 2008), Royal Ontario Museum, Canada 2007 (Award of Merit for innovative steel design), Ascent at Roebling's Bridge, Ky 2008 (CNBC Americas Property Awards 2008), Jewish Museum, San Francisco 2008; Univ. Guadalajara, Mexico, Creative Media Centre, Hong Kong, Złota 44 (apartment tower), Warsaw, Poland, Reflections at Keppel Bay, Singapore. *Publications:* Radix—Matrix: Architecture and Writings 1997, The Space of Encounter 2001, Breaking Ground (with Sarah Crichton) 2004, Counterpoint: Daniel Libeskind in Conversation with Paul Goldberger 2008. *Address:* Studio Daniel Libeskind, 2 Rector Street, 19th Floor New York, NY 10006, USA (office); Architect Daniel Libeskind AG, Walchestrasse 9, 8006 Zürich, Switzerland (office). *Telephone:* (212) 497-9100 (New York); (44) 540-4700 (office). *Fax:* (212) 285-2130 (New York); (44) 540-4760 (office). *E-mail:* info@daniel-libeskind.com (office). *Website:* www.daniel-libeskind.com (office).

LICITRA, Karen, BS; American business executive; *Worldwide Chairman, Global Medical Solutions, Johnson & Johnson;* b. Bridgewater, NJ; ed Rider Coll.; joined Johnson & Johnson as sales rep. with Ethicon, Inc. 1984, advanced through positions in sales and marketing, Dir of Marketing, Ethicon Endo-Surgery, Inc. 1991–96, Vice-Pres., Product Man. 1996–97, Vice-Pres., Breast Care Man. (following acquisition of Biopsys Medical business 1997) 1997–2000, Vice-Pres. and Gen. Man. Ethicon Endo-Surgery, Inc. 2000, Pres. Dec. 2000–02, Co. Group Chair. for Johnson & Johnson and Worldwide Franchise Chair. for Ethicon Endo-Surgery, Inc., including Advanced Sterilization Products business and Johnson & Johnson Medical, Canada 2002–12, Worldwide Chair., Global Medical Solutions, Johnson & Johnson 2012–; mem. Bd of Trustees, Rider Univ., St Peter's Healthcare System Inc.; mem. Bd Campaign to End Obesity; ranked by Fortune

magazine amongst the 50 Most Powerful Women in Business in the US (40th) 2012. *Address:* Johnson & Johnson, 1 Johnson & Johnson Plaza, New Brunswick, NJ 08933, USA (office). *Telephone:* (732) 524-0400 (office). *Fax:* (732) 214-0332 (office). *E-mail:* info@jnj.com (office). *Website:* www.jnj.com (office).

LICK, Dale Wesley, BS, MS, PhD; American mathematician, academic, university administrator and business executive; *President Emeritus and Professor Emeritus, Florida State University;* b. 7 Jan. 1938, Marlette, Mich.; s. of John R. Lick and Florence May Lick (née Baxter); m. Marilyn Kay Foster 1956; one s. three d.; ed Michigan State Univ., Univ. of California, Riverside; Instructor and Chair. Dept of Math., Port Huron Jr Coll. (later St Clair Co. Community Coll.), Port Huron, Mich. 1959–60; Asst to Comptroller, Line and Staff Man., Michigan Bell Telephone Co., Detroit, Mich. 1961; Instructor of Math., Univ. of Redlands, Calif. 1961–63; Teaching Asst in Math., Univ. of Calif., Riverside, Calif., 1964–65; Asst Prof. of Math., Univ. of Tenn. 1965–67, Assoc. Prof. 1968–69; textbook and manuscript reviewer for several publrs 1966–; Visiting Research Mathematician, Applied Math. Dept, Brookhaven Nat. Lab., Upton, New York 1967–68; Consultant, Computing Tech. Center, Union Carbide Corpn, Oak Ridge, Tenn., under auspices of US Atomic Energy Comm. 1966–71; Adjunct Assoc. Prof., Dept of Pharmacology (Biomathematics), Temple Medical School, Temple Univ. 1969–72; Head and Assoc. Prof., Dept of Math., Drexel Univ., Philadelphia, Pa 1969–72; Vice-Pres. for Academic Affairs, Russell Sage Coll., Troy, New York 1972–74; Dean, School of Sciences and Health Professions and Prof. of Math. and Computing Sciences, Old Dominion Univ., Norfolk, Va 1974–78; Pres. and Prof. of Math. and Computer Sciences, Georgia Southern Coll., Statesboro, Ga 1978–86; Pres. and Prof. of Math., Univ. of Maine 1986–91; Co-founding Leader, American Univ. in Bulgaria 1991; Pres. and Prof. of Math., Florida State Univ., Tallahassee 1991–94, Univ. Prof., Learning Systems Inst. and Dept of Educ. Leadership 1993–2008, Pres. and Prof. Emer. 2008–; Co-Developer and Chair. HyLighter, LLC 2000–; mem. Editorial Bd Innovate (journal), International Journal for the Scholarship of Teaching and Learning; mem. American Asscn of Univ. Admins, American Asscn of Univ. Profs, American Math. Soc., Math. Asscn of America, Asscn Study of Higher Educ., Nat. Staff Devt Council, American Educ. Research Asscn; Pres.'s Award, US Baseball Fed. 1985, Man of the Year Award, Rotary Club of Statesboro 1985, Certificate of Appreciation, US Dept of Educ. 1985, Silver Beaver Award, Coastal Empire Council of Boy Scouts of America 1986, Medallion of Merit, US Govt Printing Office 1988, Athletic Hall of Fame, Georgia Southern Univ. 1990, Renaissance Award for Leadership and Enlightenment, Southeast Georgia, Black Image Steering Cttee 1993, honoured as one of Forty Alumni Who Make a Difference, Univ. of California, Riverside 1994, Circle of Gold, Florida State Univ. Alumni Asscn, Rosa Parks Servant Leader Award, Florida State Univ. 1996, Distinguished Alumni Award, Michigan State Univ. 2006, named by Univ. of California, Riverside "One of 40 Alumni Who Make a Difference" 2006, Int. Peace Prize, United Cultural Convention 2010. *Publications:* Fundamentals of Algebra 1970, Whole-Faculty Study Groups: A Powerful Way to Change School and Enhance Learning (co-author) 1998, New Directions in Mentoring: Creating a Culture of Synergy (co-author) 1999, Whole-Faculty Study Groups: Creating Student-Based Professional Development (co-author) 2001, Whole-Faculty Study Groups: Creating Professional Learning Communities That Target Student Learning (co-author) 2005, The Whole-Faculty Study Group Fieldbook: Improving Schools and Enhancing Student Learning (co-author) 2005, The Whole-Faculty Study Groups Fieldbook: Lessons Learned and Best Practices from Classrooms, Districts, and Schools (with Murphy) 2007, Schoolwide Action Research for Professional Learning Communities: Improving Student Learning Through the Whole-Faculty Study Groups Approach (co-author) 2008, Schools Can Change: A Step-by-Step Change Creation System for Building Innovative Schools and Increasing Student Learning (co-author) 2013; more than 100 book chapters, papers and articles in learned journals and 300 newspaper columns. *Leisure interests:* sports, reading, writing, the arts, church work. *Address:* 348 Remington Run Loop, Tallahassee, FL 32312-1402, USA (home). *Telephone:* (850) 284-3219 (office); (850) 553-4080 (home). *Fax:* (850) 553-4081 (office). *E-mail:* dwlick@comcast.net (home); dlick@lsi.fsu.edu (office).

LIDDELL OF COATDYKE, Baroness (Life Peer), cr. 2010, of Airdrie in Lanarkshire; **Helen Lawrie Liddell,** PC; British economist, politician and diplomatist; b. (Helen Reilly), 6 Dec. 1950, Coatbridge, Lanarkshire, Scotland; d. of Hugh Reilly and the late Bridget Lawrie Reilly; m. Alistair Henderson Liddell 1972; one s. one d.; ed St Patrick's High School, Coatbridge, Univ. of Strathclyde; Head, Econ. Dept Scottish TUC 1971–75, Asst Sec. 1975–76; Econ. Corresp. BBC Scotland 1976–77; Scottish Sec. Labour Party 1977–88; Dir Personnel and Public Affairs, Scottish Daily Record and Sunday Mail Ltd 1988–92; Chief Exec. Business Venture Programme 1993–94; MP for Monklands E 1994–97, for Airdrie and Shotts 1997–2005, Opposition Spokeswoman on Scotland 1995–97; Econ. Sec. HM Treasury 1997–98, Minister of State Scottish Office 1998–99; Minister of Transport 1999, Minister for Energy and Competitiveness in Europe 1999–2001; Sec. of State for Scotland 2001–03; High Commr to Australia 2005–09; Commr, BBC Privacy Comm. 2011; mem. Inquiry into the Mull of Kintyre Helicopter Accident 2010–11; currently mem. Bd of Dirs VisitBritain; Trustee, Northcote Trust; Hon. LLD (Strathclyde). *Publication:* Elite (novel) 1990. *Leisure interests:* cooking, hill-walking, music, writing. *Address:* House of Lords, Westminster, London, SW1A 0PW, England (office). *Telephone:* (20) 7219-5353 (office). *E-mail:* liddellh@parliament.uk (office). *Website:* www.parliament.uk/biographies/lords/helen-liddell/25562 (office).

LIDDY, Edward Michael, BA, MBA; American business executive; b. 28 Jan. 1946, New Brunswick, NJ; m. Marcia Liddy; three c.; ed Catholic Univ. of America, George Washington Univ.; joined G.D. Searle & Co. 1979, Sr Vice-Pres. and COO –1986; Exec. Vice-Pres. ADT 1986–88; sr financial and operation positions Sears, Roebuck & Co. 1988–91, Chief Financial Officer 1991–94; Pres. and COO The Allstate Corpn 1994–99, Chair. 1999–2008, also Pres. and CEO 1999–2005, CEO 1999–2006; Chair. and CEO American International Group (AIG), Inc. 2008–09; mem. Bd of Dirs Goldman Sachs 2003–08, The Kroger Co., 3M, Insurance Information Inst., Insurance Inst. for Highway Safety, Northwestern Memorial Hosp., United Way/Crusade of Mercy, The Boeing Co. 2007–; Chair. and Nat. Gov. Boys & Girls Clubs of America (BGCA); mem. Civic Cttee Commercial Club, Financial Services Forum, Business Roundtable, Catalyst; Trustee, Northwestern

Univ. *Address:* c/o AIG, Inc., 70 Pine Street, New York, NY 10270, USA. *Telephone:* (212) 770-7000. *Website:* www.aigcorporate.com.

LIDEGAARD, Martin; Danish politician; *Minister of Foreign Affairs;* b. 12 Dec. 1966; s. of Mads Lidegaard and Else Lidegaard; m. Sniff Andersen Nexø; one d.; ed Roskilde Univ.; Bank Asst, Bikuben 1985; worked at Danish Red Cross Asylum Centre 1986–87; Ed. 'RUCNyt' (Roskilde Univ. News) 1988–92; freelance consultant, Int. Forum of the Labour Movt 1992–93; Information Officer and Man., Municipalities Mutual Insurance Co. 1993–96; Information Officer and Deputy Sec.-Gen., Danish Asscn for Int. Cooperation 1996–2001; mem. Folketing (Parl.) for W Copenhagen constituency 2001–05, for Roskilde Co. constituency 2005–07; Co-founder and Chair. CONCITO (think-tank) 2008–11; Communications Consultant, RelationPeople 2008–11; Minister for Climate, Energy and Buildings 2011–14, for Foreign Affairs 2014–; mem. Det Radikale Venstre (Social Liberals). *Address:* Ministry of Foreign Affairs, Asiatisk Pl. 2, 1448 Copenhagen K, Denmark (office). *Telephone:* 33-92-00-00 (office). *Fax:* 32-54-05-33 (office). *E-mail:* um@um.dk (office). *Website:* www.um.dk (office).

LIDSTRÖM, Nicklas Erik; Swedish fmr professional ice hockey player; b. 28 April 1970, Västerås, Västmanland; s. of Jan-Eric Lidström; m. Annika Lidström; four s.; defenseman; played for Skogsbo SK youth team, Västerås IK sr team 1988–91; played entire Nat. Hockey League (NHL) career with the Detroit Red Wings (picked 53rd overall in NHL draft in 1989) Capt. 2006–12 (retd); won Stanley Cup 1997, 1998, 2002, 2008, played for Swedish nat. team 1990–2010: gold medal, World Championships 1991, Winter Olympics, Turin 2006, silver medal, World Championships 2004, bronze medal, World Championships 1994; winner, Norris Trophy (best defensive player) 2001, 2002, 2003, 2006, 2007, 2008, 2011, Conn Smythe Trophy (most valuable player during playoffs) 2002; NHL All-Rookie Team 1992, NHL All-Star Team 1996, 1998, 1999, 2000, 2001, 2002, 2003, 2004, 2007, 2008, 2009, 2011, 17th, mem. Olympic All-Star Team 2006, Viking Award (best Swedish ice hockey player in North America) 2000, 2006, selected by The Hockey News as the Best European-trained player ever in the NHL, selected by The Sporting News and Sports Illustrated as the NHL Player of the Decade. *Leisure interests:* tennis, golf, boating. *Address:* c/o Detroit Red Wings, Joe Louis Arena, 600 Civic Center Drive, Detroit, MI 48226, USA (office).

LIEBENBERG, Christo Ferro, MPA.; South African politician and banker (retd); b. 2 Oct. 1934, Touwsriver; s. of Christiaan Liebenberg and Helene Griessel; m. Elly Liebenberg 1959; two s.; ed Worcester Boys' High School, Harvard Univ., USA, Institut Européen d'Admin des Affaires, Paris and Cranfield Polytechnic, UK; joined Nedbank, Cape Town 1952, Man. Dir Nedbank Group Ltd, Johannesburg 1988–90, CEO Nedcor 1990–94, Chair. 1997–2004; fmr Chair. Credit Guarantee Insurance Corpn of Africa Ltd, Syfrets Ltd, Cape Town; fmr Deputy Chair. NedPerm Bank; Pres. Inst. of Bankers in S Africa 1991; Minister of Finance 1994–96; fmr Dir, Mutual and Federal Insurance Co., Oceana Fishing Group; fmr mem. Policy Bd for Financial Services and Regulation, Council of Univ. of Stellenbosch School of Business; fmr Chair. Salvation Army Nat. Advisory Bd. *Leisure interests:* music, photography, theatre, ballet, reading, golf. *Address:* c/o National Treasury, 40 Church Square, Pretoria 0002, South Africa.

LIEBER, Charles Michael, BA, PhD; American chemist and academic; *Mark Hyman, Jr Professor of Chemistry, Harvard University;* b. 9 April 1959, Philadelphia, Pa; s. of Robert and Marlene Lieber; m. Jennifer Karas Lieber; one s. one d.; ed Franklin and Marshall Coll., Stanford Univ., California California Inst. of Tech.; Asst Prof. of Chem., Columbia Univ., New York 1987–90, Assoc. Prof. 1990–91; Prof. of Chem., Harvard Univ. 1991–99, holds jt appointment in Dept of Chem. and Chemical Biology, as Mark Hyman, Jr Prof. of Chem., and School of Eng and Applied Sciences 1999–; Co-Ed. Nano Letters; Consulting Ed. International Journal of Biomedical Nanoscience and Nanotechnology; mem. Editorial Bd numerous journals including Advances in Nanoscale Materials and Nanotechnology, Applied Physics Letters, Chemical and Engineering News, Current Nanoscience, Frontiers of Physics, Fullerenes, Journal of Applied Physics, Journal of Nanoscience and Nanotechnology, Journal of Physical Chemistry, Nano Research, Nano Today, Nanomedicine, Research Letters in Nanotechnology; Virtual Journal of Nanoscale Science and Technology; mem. Tech. Advisory Cttee, Samsung Electronics; has been active in commercializing nanotechnology; f. Nanosys, Inc. 2001, Vista Therapeutics 2007; mem. NAS 2004–, Optical Soc. of America, SPIE, ACS, IEEE, Int. Soc. for Optical Eng, Materials Research Soc.; Fellow, American Physical Soc. 1996–, AAAS 1996–, IUPAC 2001–, World Tech. Network 2002–, American Acad. of Arts and Sciences 2002–, Inst. of Physics 2007–, Materials Research Soc. 2008–; Hon. Prof., Zhejiang Univ. 2002, Fudan Univ. 2002, Univ. of Science and Tech. of China 2002, Peking Univ. 2008, Univ. of Science and Tech., Beijing 2011; Wilson Prize 1990, ACS Award in Pure Chem. 1992, MRS Outstanding Young Investigator Award 1993, George Ledlie Prize, Harvard Univ. 1994–95, ACS Leo Hendrik Baekeland Award 1995, NSF Creativity Award 1996, Breakthrough of the Year, Science Magazine 2002, Feynman Prize in Nanotechnology 2001, MRS Medal 2002, Harrison Howe Award, Univ. of Rochester 2002, American Physical Soc. McGroddy Prize for New Materials 2003, New York Intellectual Property Law Asscn Inventor of the Year 2003, Scientific American 50 Award in Nanotechnology and Molecular Electronics 2003, World Tech. Award in Materials, The World Tech. Network 2003, 2004, ACS Award in the Chem. of Materials 2004, Nanotech Briefs Nano 50 Award 2005, NBIC Research Excellence Award, Univ. of Pennsylvania 2007, Einstein Award, Chinese Acad. of Sciences 2008, recognised as the leading chemist in the world by Thomson Reuters for the decade 2000–10 for the impact of his scientific publs 2011, NIH Pioneer Award 2008, Wolf Foundation Prize in Chem. (shared with Paul Alivisatos) for his contribs to nanochemistry 2012, Willard Gibbs Award, ACS Chicago Section 2013. *Publications:* more than 350 papers in peer-reviewed journals on the synthesis of a broad range of nanoscale materials, and the demonstration of applications of these materials in nanoelectronics, nanocomputing, biological and chemical sensing, neurobiology and nanophotonics; prin. inventor on more than 35 patents. *Address:* Department of Chemistry and Chemical Biology, Harvard University, 12 Oxford Street, Cambridge, MA 02138, USA (office). *Telephone:* (617) 496-3169 (office). *Fax:* (617) 496-5442 (office). *E-mail:* cml@cmliris.harvard.edu (office). *Website:* cmliris.harvard.edu (office).

LIEBERMAN, Avigdor, BA; Israeli politician; *Minister of Foreign Affairs;* b. 5 June 1958, Kishinev, USSR (now Chisinau, Moldova); m. Ella Tzipkin; three c.; ed Hebrew Univ. of Jerusalem; emigrated to Israel aged 20; attained rank of corporal during mil. service; worked for Likud party as party Dir Gen. 1993–96; head of Prime Minister Benjamin Netanyahu's office 1997; Founder and Chair. Israel Beytenu Party 1999–, mem. Knesset (Israel Beytenu Party, Ihud Leumi-Israel Beytenu Party) 1999–2012, 2013–, mem. Foreign Affairs and Defence Cttee; Minister of Nat. Infrastructure 2001–02, of Transport 2003–04, Deputy Prime Minister and Minister of Strategic Affairs 2006–08, Deputy Prime Minister and Minister of Foreign Affairs 2009–12, 2013–; Sec. Nat. Workers' Union; Chair. Bd of Dirs of Information Industries; Dir, Econ. Corpn of Jerusalem 1983–88; Dir Likud Movt 1993–96; Dir Prime Minister's Office 1996–97; f. Zionist Forum. *Leisure interests:* football, tennis. *Address:* Ministry of Foreign Affairs, 9 Yitzhak Rabin Blvd, Kiryat Ben-Gurion, Jerusalem 91950, Israel (office). *Telephone:* 2-5303111 (office). *Fax:* 2-5303367 (office). *E-mail:* pniot@mfa.gov.il (office). *Website:* www.mfa.gov.il (office).

LIEBERMAN, Joseph (Joe) I., BA, JD; American politician; b. 24 Feb. 1942, Stamford, Conn.; s. of Henry Lieberman and Marcia Lieberman (née Manger); m. Hadassah Freilich 1983; two s. two d.; ed Yale Univ.; called to the Bar, Conn. 1967; mem. Conn. Senate 1971–81, Senate Majority Leader 1975–81; Pnr, Lieberman, Segaloff & Wolfson, New Haven, Conn. 1972–83; Attorney Gen., State of Conn., Hartford 1983–88, Senator for Connecticut 1989–2013 (retd), Chair. Governmental Affairs Cttee 2001–03, Homeland Security Cttee 2007–13; Chair. Democratic Leadership Council 1995–2001; cand. for Vice-Pres. of Democratic Party 2000; sought Democratic Party presidential candidacy 2004; mem. Governmental Affairs Cttee, Small Business Cttee, Trustee Wadsworth Atheneum, Univ. of Bridgeport; Democrat –2006, Ind. Democrat 2007–. *Publications:* The Power Broker 1966, The Scorpion and the Tarantula 1970, The Legacy 1981, Child Support in America 1986. *Address:* c/o 706 Hart Senate Office Building, Washington, DC 20510, USA.

LIEBLEIN, Grace D., BEng, MA; Brazilian automotive industry executive; *Vice President of Global Purchasing and Supply Chain, General Motors Company;* ed Kettering Univ., Michigan State Univ.; joined General Motors Co. (GM) 1978 as cooperative eng student at Gen. Ass. Div., Los Angeles, Calif., later Vehicle Chief Engineer, Front Wheel Drive Trucks for Product Devt, Detroit, Pres. and Man. Dir GM de Mexico 2008–11, Pres. and Man. Dir GM do Brasil 2011–12, Vice Pres. of Global Purchasing and Supply Chain, GM 2012–; mem. Bd GM Hispanic Initiative Team; mem. Bd Honeywell International, Inc.; Hispanic Business Magazine Top 50 Businesswomen, named by Hispanic Engineer & Informational Technology Magazine as one of the most powerful Hispanics in business and technology, Professional Achievement Award, Hispanic Eng Nat. Achievement Awards Conf., Automotive News Top 100 Women in the Auto Industry, Latino Executive of the Year, Urban Wheels Awards 2006, ranked by Fortune magazine amongst the 50 Most Powerful Women in Business outside the US (22nd) 2011, (34th) 2012. *Address:* General Motors Co., Renaissance Center, Detroit MI 48265, USA (office). *Telephone:* (313) 556-5000 (office). *Website:* www.gm.com (office); www.chevrolet.com (office).

LIEDTKE, Kurt W., Dr jur.; German lawyer and business executive; *Chairman, Board of Trustees, Robert Bosch Stiftung GmbH;* b. 23 March 1943, Darmstadt; m. 1966; three c.; ed Goethe School, Dieburg, Univ. of Frankfurt am Main, Univ. of Lausanne, Switzerland; began career as lawyer specializing in tax law, Frankfurt 1972–74; Gen. Counsel, Laufenberg Power Station, Switzerland 1974–77; Sr Consultant, Corp. Law and Contracts Dept, Robert Bosch GmbH, Stuttgart 1977–81, various positions, Marketing Dept, Fàbrica Española Magnetos SA, Spain 1981–82, Man.-Dir Robert Bosch Comercial Española Magnetos SA, Spain 1982–89, Man.-Dir Robert Bosch Ltd, London, UK 1989–96, Pres. Robert Bosch Australia Pty Ltd, Melbourne 1996–2001, Assoc. mem. Bd of Man. Robert Bosch GmbH 2001–02, mem. 2002–, Pres., Chair. and CEO Robert Bosch Corpn, USA 2001–05, Partner and mem. Bd of Trustees Robert Bosch Stiftung GmbH 2006–, Chair. 2007–; Deputy Chair. Royal Winter Foundation; mem. Advisory Bd Baden-Württemberg Film Acad., Bd Tanja Liedtke Foundation, German Sponsors of the Univ. of Haifa eV, Friends of the Museum Asscn eV; Trustee, Foundation of the Int. Charlemagne Prize of Aachen; Patron Asscn for the Municipal Theatre; Officier, Légion d'honneur 2012. *Leisure interests:* sports, opera, classical music. *Address:* Robert Bosch Stiftung GmbH, Postfach 10 06 28, 70005 Stuttgart, Germany (office). *Telephone:* (711) 46084-0 (office). *Fax:* (711) 46084-94 (office). *Website:* www.bosch-stiftung.de (office).

LIEN, Chan, MSc, PhD; Taiwanese politician; b. 27 Aug. 1936, Sian, Shansi; s. of Chen Tung Lien and Chao Lan-Kun Lien; m. Yui Fang; two s. two d.; ed Nat. Taiwan Univ. and Univ. of Chicago, USA; Assoc. Prof. Nat. Taiwan Univ. 1968–69, Prof. and Chair. Dept of Political Science and Dir Graduate Inst. of Political Science 1969–75; Amb. to El Salvador 1975–76; Dir Dept of Youth Affairs, Cen. Cttee Kuomintang 1976–78; Deputy Sec.-Gen. Cen. Cttee Kuomintang 1978, mem. Cen. Standing Cttee 1983, Chair. 2000–05, Chair. Emer. 2005–; Chair. Nat. Youth Comm., Exec. Yuan 1978–81; Minister of Communications 1981–87; Vice-Premier 1987–88; Minister of Foreign Affairs 1989–90; Gov. Taiwan Provincial Govt 1990–93; Premier of Taiwan 1993–97; Vice-Pres. of Taiwan 1997–2000; unsuccessful presidential cand. 2000; Pres. Chinese Asscn of Political Science 1979–82. *Publications:* The Foundation of Democracy, Taiwan in China's External Relations, Western Political Thought. *Leisure interests:* golf, swimming, music. *Address:* Kuomintang, 11 Chung Shan South Road, Taipei 100, Taiwan (office). *Telephone:* (2) 23121472 (office). *Fax:* (2) 2343524 (office). *Website:* www.kmt.org.tw (office).

LIEN, Siaou-Sze, MSc; Singaporean business executive; *Senior Executive Coach, Mobley Group Pacific Ltd;* b. Singapore; one d.; ed Nanyang Univ., Imperial Coll. of Science and Tech., Univ. of London, UK; joined Hewlett-Packard (HP) as systems engineer 1978, later Vice-Pres. and Man. Dir HP Asia Pacific, Sr Vice-Pres. HP Services Asia Pacific (following merger with Compaq; first woman vice-pres. in region) 2002–06 (retd); Sr Exec. Coach, Mobley Group Pacific Ltd 2006–; mem. Bd of Dirs Luvata Ltd, Huhtamäki Oyj 2009–; Deputy Chair. Bd Govs Republic Polytechnic (Chair. Admin. Cttee); fmr Dir PSA (Port of Singapore Authority) Int.; fmr adviser, Gov. of Guangdong Prov., People's Repub. of China; Trustee Nanyang Technological Univ.; ranked by Fortune magazine amongst 50 Most Powerful Women in Business outside the US (fifth) 2001, (eighth) 2002, (eighth) 2003, (19th) 2004, (22nd) 2005, (31st) 2006. *Leisure interests:* sports, jogging, dancing, hot-air ballooning. *Address:* Mobley Group Pacific Ltd, Room 2006-2008, 20/F, One

Corporate Avenue, 222 Hu Bin Road, Shanghai 200021, People's Republic of China (office). *Telephone:* (21) 63406222 (office). *Fax:* (21) 63406226 (office). *Website:* www .mobleygrouppacific.com (office).

LIEPA, Andris; Russian/Latvian ballet dancer and choreographer; b. 6 Jan. 1962, Moscow; s. of the late Marius Liepa and of Margarita Zhigunova; brother of Ilze Liepa (q.v.); m. Yekaterina Liepa; one d.; ed Moscow Choreographic School of Bolshoi Theatre; with Bolshoi Ballet 1980–87; Golden Medal, Moscow int. competition 1981, Silver Medal 1985, Jackson, USA (Grand Prix) 1986; has lived in the West 1987–; appeared with New York City Ballet, subsequently with American Ballet Theater; danced in Raymonda Variations, Swan Lake (Baryshnikov), Romeo and Juliet (Macmillan), Violin Concerto (Balanchine); worked with Nina Ananiashvili, Carla Fracci and other partners; choreographer 1993–, restored Fokin's masterpieces Petrushka, Scheherazade and The Firebird; has adapted Fokine ballets for film, including Return to the Firebird; guest artist with Kirov (now Mariinsky) Ballet, London tour 1990; staged The Legend of the Invisible City of Kitezh by Rimsky-Korsakov at the Mariinsky Theatre 1994, Edinburgh Festival 1995; est. Liepa Charity Foundation 1997; premiered production of Scheherazade at Latvian Nat. Opera 1998; performed with Katya Liepa the leading parts in The Firebird with the Mariinsky Theatre in Munich 1999; organized Ballet Evenings in commemoration of Maris Liepa at Moscow Operetta Theatre 2000; gala-concert for participants of Int. Conf. 'Teenagers and Youth in Changing Society' 2001; organized performance of The Firebird and Scheherazade ballets by Mariinski Co. at State Kremlin Theatre, Moscow 2002; stage director of concert to mark 300th anniversary of St Petersburg 2003; stage director for world premiere of ballet Sapphires 2004; mem. Jury, Golden Mask Contest 2004; staged The Firebird and Petrushka ballets for Dresden Opera and Ballet Theatre 2005; stage director for ballets Petrushka and The Firebird performed by Rome Opera at music festival in Aspendos, Turkey 2005; produced opening nights of ballets Petrushka and The Firebird for Opera and Ballet Theatre of Marseille, France 2006; mem. Bd of Trustees, Church of the Great Martyr Catherine, Cherry-Tree Forest Festival; works in USA, Russia and Latvia; People's Artist of Russia 2009. *Address:* Maris Liepa Charity Foundation, ul. Ilyinka 4, 103132 Moscow, Russia. *Telephone:* (495) 956-76-76; (495) 698-12-43. *E-mail:* andris@liepa.ru. *Website:* www.liepa.ru.

LIEPA, Ilze; Russian/Latvian ballerina; b. 22 Nov. 1963; d. of the late Maris Liepa and of Margarita Zhigunova; sister of Andris Liepa (q.v.); m. 1st Sergey Stadler (divorced); m. 2nd Vladislovas A. Paulius; ed Russa Academic Choreography Coll. (studied with N. V. Zolotariova), Pedagogic Faculty of Moscow Theatre Art Acad.; joined Bolshoi ballet 1982, then First Soloist; danced on various stages of Europe and America performing parts of classic repertoire, including Legend about Love, Romeo and Juliet, Firebird, Don Quixote, Corsair, Raimonda, Prince Igor; début in England concert Stars of World Ballet, Covent Garden (Firebird), tours with Bolshoi Theatre in most countries of Europe and America, independently toured in Argentina, Greece, Taiwan, Japan; Artistic Dir Golden Age Asscn 1994–98; f. Maris Liepa Foundation; Prize of Russian Trade Unions, Hon. Artist of Russian Fed. 1996, People's Artist of Russia 2002, Gold Mask (Best Female Ballet Role) 2003. *Films include:* The Shining World 1983, Bambi's Childhood 1984, Lermontov 1985, Lomononov 1987, Return of the Firebird 1994. *Plays include:* Your Sister and Captive 1999, The Empress's Dream 2000. *Publication:* Circle of the Sun (play) 2000. *Address:* Ilynka st. 4, Moscow, Russia. *Telephone:* (495) 956-76-76. *Website:* www.ilze-liepa.ru; www.liepa.ru.

LIÈS, Michel M.; Luxembourg business executive; *Group CEO, Suisse Reinsurance (Swiss Re);* b. 1954; ed Fed. Inst. of Tech. (ETH), Zurich; joined Swiss Re 1978, Head of Latin America Div. 1998–2000, Head of Europe Div. 2000–05, Head of Client Markets in charge of all client relationships world-wide, and mem. Group Exec. Cttee 2005–11, Chair. Global Partnerships 2011–12, Group CEO Suisse Reinsurance (Swiss Re) 2012–, mem. Swiss Re Advisory Panel. *Address:* Swiss Reinsurance Co., Mythenquai 50/60, 8022 Zurich, Switzerland (office). *Telephone:* (43) 285-21-21 (office). *Fax:* (43) 285-29-99 (office). *E-mail:* info@swissre.com (office). *Website:* www.swissre.com (office).

LIESEN, Klaus, DJur; German lawyer and business executive; *Honorary Chairman of the Supervisory Board, E.ON Ruhrgas AG;* b. 15 April 1931; fmr Chair. Exec. Bd E.ON Ruhrgas AG, Chair. Supervisory Bd 1996–2003, Hon. Chair. 2003–; Chair. Supervisory Bd Volkswagen AG, Allianz AG 1996–2003; mem. Supervisory Bd TUI AG 2005–11 (also mem. Presiding Cttee), Otto Wolff Industrieberatung und Beteiligungen GmbH; other directorships in steel, energy, banking and insurance cos; Great Cross of Merit of FRG with Star, Bavarian Order of Merit, Lower Saxony Medal 1992, Order of Merit of North Rhine-Westphalia 2001, Commdr, Royal Norwegian Order of Merit, Commdr, Dutch Order of Orange-Nassau, Norwegian-German Willy Brandt Prize 2001; Hon. Dr rer. pol. *Address:* E.ON Ruhrgas AG, Huttropstrasse 60, 45117 Essen, Germany (office). *Telephone:* 20118400 (office). *Website:* www.eon-ruhrgas.com (office).

LIEVONEN, Matti, BSc (Eng); Finnish business executive; *President and CEO, Neste Oil;* b. 1958; with ABB –1986; held several senior positions at UPM-Kymmene Corpn 1986–2008, including Pres. Fine and Speciality Papers Div., mem. Exec. Bd 2002–08; Pres. and CEO Neste Oil 2008–; Vice-Chair. CEPIFINE; mem. Supervisory Bd of Mutual Pension Insurance Co.; Chair. Advisory Bd Excellence Finland. *Address:* Neste Oil Oyj, Keilaranta, PO Box 95, 00095 Espoo (office); Neste Oil Oyj, Keilaranta 21, Espoo, Finland (office). *Telephone:* (10) 45811 (office). *Fax:* (10) 458-4442 (office). *E-mail:* info@nesteoil.com (office). *Website:* www.nesteoil.com (office).

LIÈVREMONT, Marc; French rugby union coach and fmr professional rugby union player; *Head Coach, French National Rugby Union Team;* b. 28 Oct. 1968, Dakar, Senegal; raised in Argelès-sur-Mer; began rugby career with amateur club Étoile sportive catalane 1974–88; played for Perpignan 1988–97, Stade Français 1997–2000 (Top 14 1998, 2000), Biarritz Olympique 2000–02; played as a back-row forward for France, gaining 25 caps 1995–99; selected in France's Rugby World Cup squad 1999; also played with French Rugby Sevens team and with French Barbarians; coach of France Under 21 team 2003–; following retirement from playing rugby, turned to coaching at US Dax 2005–07, guided team to promotion to the Top 14 2007; apptd Head Coach of French Nat. Rugby Union Team following Rugby World Cup 2007–; coached France to win Six Nations Championship and

Grand Slam beating England 12–10 2010; guided France to Rugby World Cup final where they played New Zealand, losing 7–8 at Eden Park, Auckland 2011. *Address:* Fédération Française de Rugby, 3–5 rue Jean de Montaigu, 91463 Marcoussis Cedex, France (office). *Telephone:* 1-69-63-64-65 (office). *E-mail:* info@ffr.fr (office). *Website:* www.ffr.fr (office).

LIEW, Datuk Vui Keong, LLB, JP; Malaysian lawyer and politician; *President, Liberal Democratic Party;* b. 18 Jan. 1960, Kota Belud, Sabah; s. of the late Ping-Hon Liew and Yet Liew Wong; m. Dr Lindai Lee; four c.; ed Diploma in Business and Finance, Univ. of North London, Lincoln's Inn, London, UK; active legal practitioner in criminal law and jurisdiction in Malaysia; called to Malayan Bar 1990, Borneo Bar 1992; est. own legal practice 1997; legal adviser to the Sabah United Chinese Chamber of Commerce, United Sabah Sze Yip Asscn, Sabah Motion Picture & Entertainment Asscn, Sabah Sze Yip Asscn (West Coast), Sabah Women Asscn, Kota Belud Chinese Chamber of Commerce, Kota Kinabalu Journalists Asscn, Sabah Law Asscn; joined Liberal Democratic Party (LDP) 1994, Head, Usukan Div., Kota Belud 1994–2004, Kapayan Div. 2004–, Asst Sec.-Gen. LDP 1999–2004, Sec.-Gen. 2005–06, Pres. 2006–; Vice-Pres. Barisan Nasional, Malaysia. *Leisure interests:* swimming, reading. *Address:* Messrs V. K. Liew & Partners, Lots 905-911B, 9th Floor, Wisma Merdeka Phase 2, Jalan Tun Abdul Razak, 88000 Kota Kinabalu, Sabah (office); Liberal Democratic Party, Tingkat 1, No. 33, Karamunsing Warehouse, PO Box 16033, 88868 Kota Kinabalu, Sabah, Malaysia. *Telephone:* (88) 248986 (office); (88) 246896 (office); (88) 218985; (88) 256352 (office). *Fax:* (88) 240698 (office); (88) 240598. *E-mail:* vkliew26@gmail.com (office); ldpkk@tm.net.my (office). *Website:* www.ldpsabah.com (office).

LIGACHEV, Yegor Kuzmich; Russian politician; b. 29 Sept. 1920; m.; one s.; ed Moscow Inst. of Aviation and CPSU Higher Party School; engineer 1943–49; joined CPSU 1944; Party and Local Govt Official Novosibirsk 1949–55; Vice-Chair. Novosibirsk Regional Soviet of Working People's Deputies 1955–58; Sec. Novosibirsk Regional Cttee CPSU 1959–61, mem. Cen. Cttee CPSU 1961–65; First Sec. Tomsk Regional Cttee CPSU 1965–83; Cand. mem. Cen. Cttee CPSU 1966–76, mem. 1976–90, mem. Politburo 1985–90; Deputy to Supreme Soviet 1966–89; Sec. Cen. Cttee in Charge of Personnel and Ideology 1983–88; in Charge of Agric. 1988–90; People's Deputy of the USSR 1989–91; active in Russian nat. and communist movt; Vice-Chair. Union of Communist Parties of fmr USSR 1995–; mem. State Duma (Parl.) 1999–2003. *Publication:* Inside Gorbachev's Kremlin 1993. *Address:* c/o Communist Party of Russian Federation, per. Maly Sukharevskii 3/1, 127051 Moscow, Russia. *E-mail:* inter@kprf.ru.

LIGHT, Jay, BA, PhD; American academic and university administrator; b. Ohio; m. Judy Light; two c.; ed Cornell Univ., Harvard Univ.; early career in data communications and satellite guidance at Jet Propulsion Lab. –1970; mem. of Faculty, Harvard Business School 1970–, Dwight P. Robinson, Jr. Prof. of Business Admin 1979–, held various sr positions including Chair. Finance Area 1985–88, Sr Assoc. Dean and Dir of Faculty Planning 1988–92, Sr Assoc. Dean and Dir of Planning and Devt 1998–2005, Interim Dean, Harvard Business School 2005–06, Dean 2006–10 (retd), took leave of absence from Harvard to serve as Dir of Investment and Financial Policies, Ford Foundation 1977–79; mem. Bd of Dirs Harvard Man. Co., Pnrs HealthCare, also Chair. Investment Cttee; Trustee, Groton School. *Publications:* The Financial System (with W.L. White) 1979; numerous articles in professional journals and more than 50 cases and notes. *Address:* c/o Office of the Dean, Harvard Business School, Soldiers Field, Boston, MA 02163, USA.

LIGHTFOOT, Edwin N., BS, PhD; American scientist and academic; *Hilldale Professor Emeritus of Chemical and Biological Engineering, University of Wisconsin;* m.; five c.; ed Cornell Univ., New York; joined Faculty of Univ. of Wisconsin-Madison 1953, became one of the country's first profs in biochemical eng, now Hilldale Prof. Emer. of Chemical and Biological Eng; mem. Nat. Acad. of Eng 1979, Royal Norwegian Soc. of Sciences and Letters 1985, NAS 1995; Hon. DrTech (Tech. Univ. of Norway) 1985; Fulbright Research Scholar, Tech. Univ. of Norway 1962, AIChE William H. Walker Award 1975, AIChE Warren K. Lewis Award 1991, Nat. Medal of Science (jt recipient) 2004. *Publications:* Transport Phenomena 1960 (second edn 2002), Transport Phenomena and Living Systems: Biomedical Aspects of Momentum and Mass Transport 1974; numerous scientific papers in professional journals. *Address:* Department of Chemical and Biological Engineering, 3639 Engineering Hall, 1415 Engineering Drive, Madison, WI 53706, USA (office). *Telephone:* (608) 262-6934 (office). *Fax:* (608) 262-5434 (office). *E-mail:* lightfoot@engr.wisc.edu (office). *Website:* directory.engr.wisc.edu/che/Faculty/Lightfoot_Edwin (office).

LIGHTING, Jane, FRSA; British television executive; two c.; began career with Crown Cassette Communications 1976; fmr marketing exec. for Video Arts (training film co.), then with its sister co., later worked in int. sales and distribution; Founder and Man. Dir, Minotaur International (distribution co.) 1995, acquired by Flextech (part of UK cable group Telewest) 1999; Man. Dir of Broadcast and TV, Flextech, oversaw five TV channels: Bravo, Living, Trouble, Challenge and Freeview entertainment channel FTN as well as 10-channel jt venture with BBC, including UK Gold and UK History 1999–2002, CEO Flextech 2002–03; CEO Channel 5 2003–08; Fellow, Royal TV Soc. 2006–, Chair. 2006–; Dir (non-exec.) Trinity Mirror PLC 2008–, Paddy Power 2009–; apptd Chair. Remuneration Cttee 2009; fmr Gov. Nat. Film and Television School; mem. British Screen Advisory Council; Olswang Business Award, Carlton Women in Film and TV Awards 2001. *Address:* Trinity Mirror plc, One Canada Square, Canary Wharf, London, E14 5AP, England (office). *Telephone:* (20) 7293-3000 (office); (20) 7510-3000. *Website:* www.trinitymirror.com (office).

LIGHTMAN, Alan Paige, AB, PhD; American physicist, writer and academic; *Professor of the Practice of the Humanities, Massachusetts Institute of Technology;* b. 28 Nov. 1948, Memphis, Tenn.; s. of Richard Lightman and Jeanne Lightman (née Garretson); m. Jean Greenblatt 1976; two d.; ed Princeton Univ., California Inst. of Technology; Postdoctoral Fellow, Cornell Univ. 1974–76; Asst Prof., Harvard Univ. 1976–79; staff scientist Smithsonian Astrophysical Observatory, Cambridge 1979–88; Prof. of Science and Writing, MIT 1988–2002, John E. Burchard Chair 1995–2001, f. Grad. Program in Science Writing 2001, Adjunct Prof. of Humanities, Creative Writing, Physics 2002–12, Prof. of the Practice of the Humanities 2012–; Founding Dir Harpswell Foundation to empower women leaders in Cambodia 2003; Fellow, American Acad. of Arts and Sciences, American Physical Soc.; mem. American Astronomical Soc.; Hon. DLitt (Bowdoin Coll.) 2005, Hon. DFA (Memphis Coll. of Arts) 2006; Hon. Dr of Humanities (Univ. of Maryland) 2006, Hon. DHumLitt (Univ. of Massachusetts) 2010; Asscn of American Publishers Most Outstanding Science Book in the Physical Sciences Award 1990, Boston Globe Winship Book Prize 1993, American Inst. of Physics Andrew Gemant Award 1996, Nat. Public Radio Book of the Month 1998, Distinguished Alumnus Award, California Inst. of Tech. 2003, Sigma Xi John P. McGovern Award, 2006, Gold Medal for Humanitarian Service, Govt of Cambodia 2008, Sydney Award for Best Essays 2011. *Publications:* fiction: Einstein's Dreams 1993, Good Benito 1994, The Diagnosis 2000, Reunion 2003, Ghost 2007, Song of Two Worlds 2009, Mr g 2012; non-fiction: Problem Book in Relativity and Gravitation 1974, Radiative Process in Astrophysics (with George B. Rybicki) 1976, Time Travel and Papa Joe's Pipe 1984, A Modern Day Yankee in a Connecticut Court and Other Essays on Science 1986, Origins: The Lives and Worlds of Modern Cosmologists (with Roberta Brawer) 1990, Ancient Light: Our Changing View of the Universe (adapted from Origins) 1991, Great Ideas in Physics 1992, Time for the Stars: Astronomy in the 1990s 1992, The World is Too Much with Me: Finding Private Space in the Wired World 1992, Dance for Two: Selected Essays 1996, A Sense of the Mysterious: Science and the Human Spirit 2005, The Discoveries 2005; editor: Revealing the Universe: Prediction and Proof in Astronomy (with James Cornell) 1982, The Best American Essays 2000; contrib. to professional journals and literary magazines. *Address:* Massachusetts Institute of Technology, Room 14E-303, 77 Massachusetts Avenue, Cambridge, MA 02139, USA (office). *Telephone:* (617) 253-2308 (office). *Website:* www .harpswellfoundation.org (office); www.alanlightman.com.

LIGI, Jürgen, BA, MBA; Estonian economist and politician; *Minister of Finance;* b. 16 July 1959, Tartu; m.; two s.; ed Tartu Second High School, Tartu State Univ., Estonian Business School; Economist, Estonian SSR Planning Inst. 1982–89; Chief Specialist, Saaremaa Agro-Industrial Asscn 1989–90; Head, Saaremaa Dept, Chamber of Commerce and Industry 1990–91; consultant on entrepreneurial activities 1991–92; Econ. Adviser, Kaarma Rural Municipal Govt 1992–93; Head of Br. Office, EVEA Bank, Kuressaare 1993–95; joined Reform Party 1994; mem. Riigikogu (Parl.) for Harju and Rapla Dist 1995–2005, 2007–09, Chair. Parl. Cttee for Budget Control 2007–09; Minister of Defence 2005–07, of Finance 2009–; Chair. Compensation Fund Supervisory Bd; mem. Estonian Athletic Asscn; Trustee, Tallinn Tech. Univ. *Publications:* articles in newspapers. *Address:* Ministry of Finance, Suur-Ameerika 1, Tallinn 15006, Estonia (office). *Telephone:* 611-3558 (office). *Fax:* 696-6810 (office). *E-mail:* info@fin.ee (office). *Website:* www .fin.ee; www.reform.ee

LIGRESTI, Giulia Maria; Italian business executive; *President and CEO, Premafin Finanziaria SpA;* ed Università Commericale Luigi Bocconi, Milan, Queen Mary Coll., London, UK; Pres. and CEO Premafin Finanziaria SpA 2002–, Chair. and Man. Dir Premafin Finanziaria Holding di Partecipazioni SpA; Deputy Chair. Fondiaria SAI SpA, mem. Bd of Dirs several subidiary cos; Chair. Gilli Srl, Fondazione FON-SAI; Man. Dir SAI Holding Italia SpA; mem. Bd of Dirs Finadin SpA, Milano Assicurazioni SpA, Sailux SA, Sainternational SA, Saifin SpA, Filarmonica della Scala di Milano, Helm Finance SGR SpA, ATA Hotels SpA, Istituto Europeo di Oncologia Srl. *Address:* SpA, Via Daniele Manin 37, Milan 20121, Italy (office). *Telephone:* (02) 667041 (office). *E-mail:* info@primafin.it (office). *Website:* www.premafin.it (office).

LIIKANEN, Erkki Antero, MPolSc (Econ); Finnish politician and central banker; *Governor, Bank of Finland;* b. 19 Sept. 1950, Mikkeli; m. Hanna-Liisa Issakainen 1971; ed Univ. of Helsinki; mem. Parl. 1972–90; Minister of Finance 1987–90; mem. Social Democratic Party (SDP) Cttee 1978–, Gen. Sec. 1981–87; Amb. to EU 1990–95; EC Commr for Budget, Personnel and Admin 1995–99, for Industry and Information (subsequently Enterprise, Competitiveness, Innovation and the Information Society) 1999–2004; Gov. Bank of Finland (central bank) 2004–, also mem. Governing Council, European Cen. Bank 2004–, IMF Gov. for Finland 2004–; Hon. DSc (Tech.) (Univ. of Tech.), Hon. DSc (Econ) (Aalto/Helsinki School of Econs and Business Admin). *Address:* Bank of Finland, Snellmaninaukio, PO Box 160, 00101 Helsinki, Finland (office). *Telephone:* (10) 8312001 (office). *Fax:* (10) 8312022 (office). *E-mail:* erkki.liikanen@bof.fi (office). *Website:* www.bof .fi (office).

LIKENS, Gene Elden, PhD; American ecologist, academic and research institute director; *Distinguished Senior Scientist, Ecologist, Founding Director and President Emeritus, Institute of Ecosystem Studies;* b. 6 Jan. 1935, Pierceton, Indiana; s. of Colonel and Josephine Likens; m. Phyllis C. Likens; three c.; ed Univ. of Wisconsin, Madison; joined faculty of Dartmouth Coll. 1961; Co-founder Hubbard Brook Ecosystem Study at Hubbard Brook Experimental Forest, White Mountains of NH; Founder Inst. of Ecosystem Studies, Millbrook, NY (part of New York Botanical Garden) 1983, inst. became ind. 1993, Dir and Pres. 1993–2007, Distinguished Sr Scientist, Ecologist, Founding Dir and Pres. Emer. 2007–; holds faculty positions at Yale, Cornell, Rutgers Univs, State Univ. of NY, Albany and Univ. of Connecticut; fmr Pres. Int. Soc. of Theoretical and Applied Limnology, American Inst. of Biological Sciences, Ecological Soc. of America, American Soc. of Limnology and Oceanography; mem. American Acad. of Arts and Sciences 1979, NAS 1981, American Philosophical Soc. 2006; Foreign mem. Royal Swedish Acad. of Sciences 1988, Royal Danish Acad. of Sciences and Letters 1994, Austrian Acad. of Sciences 2000; Flagship Fellowship in Water for a Healthy Country Flagship, CSIRO, Australia 2007–08; Einstein Prof., Chinese Acad. of Science 2010; Hon. Prof., Jinan Univ., China; Hon. mem. British Ecological Soc.; nine hon. doctorate degrees; Guggenheim Fellowship 1972, Tyler Prize, The World Prize for Environmental Achievement (with F. H. Bormann) 1993, Australia Prize for Science and Tech. 1994, Naumann-Thienemann Medal, Societas Internationalis Limnologiae 1995, Eminent Ecologist Award, Ecological Soc. of America 1995, Nat. Medal of Science 2001, Blue Planet Prize (with F. H. Bormann), Asahi Glass Foundation 2003, Miegunyah Fellowship, Melbourne, Australia 2004. *Achievements include:* best known for his discovery of acid rain in N America. *Publications:* author, co-author or ed. 24 books, including Pattern and Process in a Forested Ecosystem (co-author) 1979, Limnological Analyses (co-author) 1979, Biogeochemistry of a Forested Ecosystem (co-author) 1995, The Ecosystem Approach: Its Use and Abuse. Excellence in Ecology, Vol. 3 1992, Mirror Lake: Interactions among Air,

Land and Water (co-author) 2009, Effective Ecological Monitoring (co-author) 2010; more than 550 scientific papers in professional journals. *Leisure interests:* basketball, fishing. *Address:* Cary Institute of Ecosystem Studies, PO Box AB, Millbrook, NY 12545-0129, USA (office). *Telephone:* (845) 677-5343 (office). *Fax:* (845) 677-5976 (office). *E-mail:* likensg@ecostudies.org (office). *Website:* www .ecostudies.org/people_sci_likens.html (office).

LIKHACHEV, Vasily Nikolayevich, DJur; Russian politician and diplomatist; *Representative of the Legislature of the Republic of Ingushetiya in the Federation Council;* b. 5 Jan. 1952, Gorky; s. of Nina F. Likhacheva; m. Nailya Imatovna Taktasheva; two d.; ed Kazan State Univ.; Asst, then Docent Chair of State Law, Kazan State Univ. 1978–82, 1983–87; teacher, Nat. School of Law Guinea-Bissau 1982–83; Prof., Univ. of Madagascar 1987–88; Head, Div. of State Law Tatar Regional CPSU Cttee 1988–90; Chair. Cttee of Constitutional Control Tatar SSR 1990–91; elected Vice-Pres. Repub. of Tatarstan 1991–95, Chair. State Council of Tatarstan 1995–; Deputy Chair. Council of Fed. of Russian Parl. 1996–98; Amb. and Perm. Rep. of Russian Fed. to EU 1998–2003; Rep. of Legislature of Repub. of Ingushetiya in the Fed. Council 2004–; Deputy Chair. Int. Affairs Cttee, Fed. Council. *Publications:* nine books; more than 400 articles on questions of int. and state law. *Leisure interests:* music, art, sailing. *Address:* Federation Council, ul. B.Dmitrovka 26, 103426 Moscow (office); ul. Akademika Zelinskogo 6–10, 119334 Moscow, Russia (home). *Telephone:* (495) 986-60-36 (office); (495) 692-13-42 (office); (495) 135-74-93 (home). *E-mail:* VNLikhachev@council.gov.ru (office). *Website:* www.council.gov.ru (office).

LILIĆ, Zoran; Serbian politician and government official; *Chairman, Upravnog odbora JP Putevi Srbije;* b. 27 Aug. 1953, Brza Palanka, Serbia; s. of Sokol Lilić and Dobrila Lilić; m. Ljubica Brković-Lilić 1980; one s.; ed Belgrade Univ.; several posts as grad. engineer, then man., with state-owned Rekord enterprise, Belgrade; fmr Pres. Exec. Bd Yugoslav Tyre Makers Business Asscn, mem. Presidency of Belgrade Chamber of Economy, Pres. Man. Bd of Belgrade Airport, mem. Council of Faculty of Tech.; mem. Serbian League of Communists, subsequently Socialist Party of Serbia (SPS); Deputy to Nat. Ass. of Repub. of Serbia 1990, Chair. Cttee on Industry, Energy, Mining and Construction, Chief of Group of SPS Deputies; re-elected Deputy and also Pres. of Nat. Ass. 1992; Pres. of Fed. Repub. of Yugoslavia 1993–97; Vice-Prime Minister of Yugoslavia 1997–2000; Vice-Pres. Socialist Party of Serbia (SPS) 1995–2000; Chair. Upravnog odbora JP Putevi Srbije (Bd of Public Roads of Serbia) 2008–; testified against successor Slobodan Milosevic at Int. Criminal Tribunal for Fmr Yugoslavia, The Hague, Netherlands 2002. *Leisure interests:* fishing, football, chess. *Address:* Upravnog odbora JP Putevi Srbije, Bulevar kralja Aleksandra 282, Poštanski fah, Belgrade, Serbia (office). *Telephone:* (11) 3040700 (office). *Fax:* (11) 2412540 (office). *E-mail:* office@putevi-srbije.rs (home). *Website:* www.putevi-srbije.rs (office).

LILIUS, (Percy Henrik) Mikael, BSc, MSc, BBA; Finnish business executive; *Chairman, Ambea AB;* b. 1949, Helsinki; m.; three c.; ed Helsinki School of Econs; Marketing Dir Huhtamäki Oy Polarpak, Helsinki 1981–84, Pres. 1984–85, Pres. Packing Div. 1985–89, Chair. 2005–13; Pres. and CEO KF Industri AB (Nordico), Stockholm 1989–90; Pres. and CEO Incentive AB, Stockholm 1990–98; Pres. and CEO Gambro AB (medical supply co.), Stockholm 1998–2000; Pres. and CEO Fortum (Finnish state-owned energy co.), Espoo 2000–09; Chair. Ambea AB 2011–, Wärtsilä Oyj Abp 2011–, Sanitec Oy, Mehiläinen Oy; Chair. Supervisory Bd Teollisuuden Voima Oy; Vice-Chair. Ahlstrom Oyj 2001–05, OAO Lenenergo, Lite-On Mobile Oyj (fmrly Perlos Oyj); Deputy Chair. Aker Solutions ASA; Dir Gambro AB, Sweden-Japan Foundation, Huhtamäki Van Leer Oyj, Instrumentarium Oy, Perlos Oy, A. Ahlstrom Corpn, Wärtsilä Oyj Abp 2010–, Aker Solutions ASA 2011–, Metso Corpn 2013–, Aker Kvaerner Subsea AS; mem. Advisory Bd EQT; mem. Supervisory Bd Finnish Fair Corpn, Kemijoki Oy; Chair. Asscn of Finnish Energy Industries. *Address:* Ambea AB, Holländargatan 21A 4 Floor, 111 60 Stockholm, Sweden (office). *Telephone:* (8) 617-39-00 (office). *Fax:* (8) 617-39-80 (office). *E-mail:* info@ambea.com (office). *Website:* www.ambea.com (office).

LILL, John Richard, CBE, FRCM, FLCM, FTCM; British pianist; b. 17 March 1944, London; s. of George Lill and the late Margery (née Young) Lill; m. Jacqueline Clifton Smith; ed Leyton County High School and Royal Coll. of Music; London debut at Royal Festival Hall 1963; plays regularly in European capitals, the USA and the Far East, as recitalist and as soloist with most prin. orchestras; recognized as leading interpreter of Beethoven; Prof., Royal Coll. of Music; Hon. DSc (Univ. of Aston), Hon. DMus (Exeter Univ.); Hon. FTCL, FLCM; first prize Royal Overseas League Competition 1963, first prize Int. Tchaikovsky Competition, Moscow 1970, Dinu Lipatti Medal, Chappell Gold Medal. *Recordings include:* complete Beethoven piano sonatas, concertos and bagatelles, complete piano works of Rachmaninov (with BBC Nat. Orchestra of Wales/Otaka), Brahms piano concertos, Tchaikovsky Piano Concerto No. 1 (with London Symphony Orchestra), complete Prokofiev sonatas 1991. *Leisure interests:* chess, amateur radio, walking. *Address:* c/o Royal College of Music, Prince Consort Road, London, SW7 2BS, England (office). *Telephone:* (20) 7591-4300 (office). *Fax:* (20) 7591-4737 (office). *E-mail:* info@rcm.ac.uk (office). *Website:* www.rcm.ac.uk (office).

LILLEE, Dennis Keith, MBE; Australian fmr professional cricketer; *President, Western Australian Cricket Association;* b. 18 July 1949, Perth, WA; s. of K. Lillee; m. Helen Lillee 1970; two s.; ed Belmay State School, Belmont High School; right-arm fast bowler, lower-order right-hand batsman; played for WA 1969–84, Tasmania 1987–88, Northants. 1988; Test debut: Australia v England, Adelaide 29 Jan.–3 Feb. 1971; One-Day Int. debut: England v Australia, Manchester 24 Aug. 1972; played in 70 Tests for Australia 1970–84, taking then world record 355 wickets (average 23.92), including record 167 wickets in 29 Tests against England, and scoring 905 runs (average 13.71, highest score 73 not out), best bowling (innings) 7/83, (match) 11/123; toured England 1972, 1975, 1980, 1981, 1983 (World Cup), took 882 First-class wickets (average 23.46), best bowling (innings) 8/29; Coach Western Australian Cricket Asscn 2000; coaching fast bowlers, MRF Pace Foundation, Chennai, India 2001, Dennis Lillee Fast Bowling Acad. (est. June 2002) 2002–; continued playing cricket, bowling for the Australian Cricket Bd Chair.'s XI –2000; Pres. Western Australian Cricket Asscn 2004–; appeared in numerous TV commercials for carpets, work boots, glucosamine tablets to relieve osteoarthritis symptoms and solar power cos; Wisden Cricketer of the Year 1973, inducted into Australian Cricket Hall of Fame 1996, named mem. of Australia's Test Team of the Century. *Publications:* Back to the Mark 1974, The Art of Fast

Bowling 1977, Dennis Lillee's Book of Family Fitness 1980, My Life in Cricket 1982, Over and Out 1984. *Leisure Interests:* music, philately. *Address:* Western Australian Cricket Association, WACA Ground, PO Box 6045, Nelson Crescent, East Perth, WA 6892 (office); c/o Swan Sport, PO Box 158, Byron Bay, NSW 2481, Australia. *Telephone:* (8) 9265-7222 (office). *Fax:* (8) 9265-7275 (office). *E-mail:* info@waca.com.au (office). *Website:* www.waca.com.au (office).

LILLELUND BECH, Gitte, BSc, MSc; Danish politician; b. 21 Jan. 1969, Århus; d. of Jørgen Bech and Helle Lillelund Bech; m. Thomas Egebo; ed Copenhagen Business School; Financial Analyst, Den Danske Bank 1991–94; Consultant, Financial Specialist, COWI Rådgivende Ingeniører A/S 1994–98; Economist, Nykredit 1998–99; mem. Folketing (Parl.) for Venstre (Liberal Party), mem. Foreign Affairs Cttee (Chair. 2006), Defence Cttee, Naturalization Cttee; Minister of Defence 2010–11; Kt, Order of Dannebrog 2010. *Address:* c/o Ministry of Defence, Holmens Kanal 4, 10602 Copenhagen K, Denmark. *Website:* gittelillelundbech.venstre.dk (office); gittelillelundbech.dk.

LILLEY, Rt Hon. Peter Bruce, PC, MA; British politician; b. 23 Aug. 1943, Kent; s. of S. Arnold Lilley and Lilian Lilley (née Elliott); m. Gail Ansell 1979; ed Dulwich Coll., Clare Coll., Cambridge; Chair. Bow Group 1973; MP for St Albans 1983–97, for Hitchin and Harpenden 1997–; Econ. Sec. to Treasury 1987–89, Financial Sec. 1989–90; Sec. of State for Trade and Industry 1990–92, for Social Security 1992–97; Opposition Front Bench Spokesman for Treasury 1997–98; Deputy Leader of the Opposition 1998–99; fmr Dir Greenwell Montagu (Oil Analyst); Dir (non-exec.) JP Morgan Fleming Claverhouse Investment 1997–2008, IDOX PLC 2002–, Melchior Japan Investment Trust 2006–10, Tethys Petroleum Ltd 2006–; mem. Advisory Bd Yihei Capital 2013–. *Publications:* The Delusion of Incomes Policy (with Samuel Brittan) 1977, The End of the Keynesian Era 1980, Thatcherism: The Next Generation 1990, Winning the Welfare Debate 1996, Patient Power 2000, Common Sense on Cannabis 2001, Taking Liberties 2002, Save Our Pensions 2003, The Case Against ID Cards 2004, Too Much of a Good Thing? 2005, In it Together (Report of Global Poverty Group) 2007, Paying for Success (Policy Exchange) 2008, What is Wrong with Stern: the Failings of the Stern Review of the Economics of Climate Change 2012. *Leisure interest:* France (and most things French). *Address:* House of Commons, Westminster, London, SW1A 0AA, England (office). *Website:* www.peterlilley.co.uk (office).

LILLIKAS, Yiorgos, MA; Cypriot politician and consultant; b. 1 June 1960, Pafos; m. Barbara Petropoulou; one s.; ed Inst. of Political Science, Lyon, France, Inst. of Political Science, Grenoble; mem. Historic Politology Research Team, Nat. Scientific Research Centre of France 1985–87; Special Adviser to Pres. of Repub. of Cyprus 1988–90; Gen.-Sec. Secr. for New Generation 1990–93; consultant in public relations, strategic marketing and advertising 1993–2001; mem. House of Reps from Nicosia 1996–2006, fmr mem. Parl. Cttees on Finance, Foreign and European Affairs, Educ., Trade, fmr Chair. Environment Cttee; Minister of Commerce, Industry and Tourism 2003–06, of Foreign Affairs 2006–07; fmr Head of Del. to Parl. Ass. of OSCE; Vice-Pres. OSCE Political Affairs and Security Cttee Jan.–June 2006; cand. in presidential election Feb. 2013; mem. Anorthotiko Komma Ergazomenou Laou (Progressive Party of the Working People); f. BlueTree Consultants (advises in international investment) 2008. *Address:* c/o Anorthotiko Komma Ergazomenou Laou (Progressive Party of the Working People), POB 21827, 4 E. Papaioannou Street, 1075 Nicosia, Cyprus. *Website:* www.yiorgoslillikas.com.

LIM, C(hwen) J(eng), AA Dip; British architect, urban designer and academic; *Director, Studio 8 Architects;* b. 1964, Ipoh, Malaysia; s. of Kar Sun Lim and Yoke Kheng Leong; ed St Michael's Inst., Ipoh, Malaysia, Ashville Coll., Harrogate, Architectural Assccn School of Architecture, London; Prof. of Architecture and Urbanism, Bartlett School of Architecture, Univ. Coll. London (UCL) 1993–, Dir Bartlett Architecture Research Lab. 1999–2007, UCL Pro-Provost of N America 2008–11, Bartlett Vice-Dean 2011–13; Sr Lecturer Univ. of E London 1990–93, Univ. of N London 1991–99; Dir Studio 8 Architects, London 1994–; Visiting Prof., Curtin Univ., Perth, Australia 1996, Stadelschule, Frankfurt 1997–98, 2000–01, Technological Univ., Lund, Sweden 2001–, MacKintosh School of Architecture, Glasgow 2001–11, School of Architecture, Arhus, Denmark 2002, Chiba Inst. of Tech., Japan 2004, Royal Danish Acad. of Fine Arts, Denmark 2006, The Univ. of Girona, Spain 2008, Seoul Nat. Univ., South Korea 2012, RMIT Australia 2012; RIBA External Examiner 2000–; numerous exhbns Europe, Japan, Canada, USA, Australia; RIBA Pres.'s Medals for Academic Contrib. in Architecture 1997, 1998, 1999; several prizes for architectural research projects including First Prize Bldg Centre Trust Competition 'Housing: a demonstration project' 1987, UCL Cultural Centre Int. Competition 1996, Cen. Glass Int. Competition Japan: Glasshouse 2001, 2nd Prize Japanese/NCE Competition: an image of the bridge of the future 1987, Concept House 2000 (Int.) Ideal Home Exhbn 1999, Tangshan Earthquake Memorial Landscape China 2007, NanYu Shopping Park China 2008, Great Places: Environmental Design Research Asscn Int. Competition, USA 2009. *Achievements:* represented UK at the Venice Biennale 2004. *Publications:* 441/10… We'll Reconfigure the Space When You're Ready 1996, Sins + Other Spatial Relatives 2000, Realms of Impossibility: Water 2002, Realms of Impossibility: Ground 2002, Realms of Impossibility: Air 2002, How Green is Your Garden? 2003, Museums (Work in Process) 2004, Devices 2005, Neoarchitecture 2005, Virtually Venice 2006, Smartcities and Eco-warriors 2010, Short Stories: London in Two-and-a-half Dimensions 2011. *Address:* Studio 8 Architects, 95 Greencroft Gardens, London, NW6 3PG, England (office). *Telephone:* (20) 7679-4842 (office). *E-mail:* mail@cjlim-studio8.com (office). *Website:* www.cjlim-studio8.com (office).

LIM, Dong-won; South Korean politician and diplomatist; b. 25 July 1934; ed Korea Mil. Acad., Seoul Nat. Univ.; Asst Prof., Korean Mil. Acad. 1964–69; with Armed Forces, attained rank of Maj.-Gen. 1980, now retd; apptd Amb. to Nigeria 1981, to Australia 1984; Chancellor Inst. of Foreign Affairs and Nat. Security, Ministry of Foreign Affairs 1988–92; Chair. Presidential Comm. on Arms Control 1990; Del. South–North High-Level Talks 1990–92; apptd Chair. Asscn for Nat. Unification of Korea 1993; mem. Unification Policy Evaluation Cttee 1993; Sec.-Gen. Kim Dae Jung Peace Foundation for the Asia-Pacific 1995; Sr Sec. for Nat. Security and Foreign Affairs, Pres. Sec. 1998; Minister for Unification (involved in reconciliatory Sunshine Policy towards North Korea) 1999–2001; Dir-Gen. Nat. Intelligence Service 1999–2001; Special Envoy to North Korea April 2002; fmr staff mem. Sejong Inst., Chair. Sejong Foundation 2004–08. *Address:* c/o Sejong

Institute, Shihung-dong 230, Sujeong-gu, Seongnam-shi, Kyonggi-do, Seoul 461-370, Republic of Korea (office). *E-mail:* public@sejong.org (office). *Website:* www.sejong.org/foundation/eng/main01.htm (office).

LIM, Hng Kiang, BSc, MPA; Singaporean government official; *Minister of Trade and Industry;* b. 9 April 1954; m. Lee Ai Boon; two s.; ed Raffles Inst., Univ. of Cambridge, UK, Kennedy School, Harvard Univ., USA; with Singapore Armed Forces 1976–85, Ministry of Defence 1986; Deputy Sec. Ministry of Nat. Devt 1987; CEO Housing and Devt Bd 1991; mem. Parl. 1991–; Minister of State for Nat. Devt 1991–94, Acting Minister for Nat. Devt and Sr Minister of State for Foreign Affairs 1994–95, Minister for Nat. Devt 1995–99, Second Minister for Foreign Affairs 1995–98, Second Minister for Finance 1998–2004, Minister of Health 1999–2003, Minister, Prime Minister's Office 2003–04, Minister of Trade and Industry 2004–, also Deputy Chair. Monetary Authority of Singapore; mem. Bd of Dirs Govt of Singapore Investment Corpn. *Leisure interests:* swimming, golf. *Address:* Ministry of Trade and Industry, 100 High Street, 09-01 The Treasury, 179434 Singapore (office). *Telephone:* 62259911 (office). *Fax:* 63327260 (office). *E-mail:* mti_email@mti.gov.sg (office). *Website:* www.mti.gov.sg (office).

LIM, Datuk Seri Keng Yaik, MB, BCh; Malaysian politician; *Party Adviser, Parti Gerakan Rakyat Malaysia Barisan Nasional;* b. 8 April 1939, Tapah, Perak; m. Wong Yoon Chuan; three c.; ed Queen's Univ., Belfast; Senator 1972–78; Minister with Special Functions 1972–73, of Primary Industries 1986–2004, of Energy, Water and Communications 2004–07; mem. State Exec. Council, Perak 1978–86; mem. Parl. 1986–; Co-founder and Pres. Gerakan 1980–2007, Party Adviser 2007–. *Address:* Parti Gerakan Rakyat MalaysiaBarisan Nasional, Tingkat 5, Menara PGRM, 8 Jalan Pudu Ulu, Cheras, 56100 Kuala Lumpur, Malaysia. *Telephone:* (3) 22747511 (office). *Fax:* (3) 22745014 (office). *E-mail:* gerakan@gerakan.org.my (office). *Website:* www.gerakan.org.my (office).

LIM, Pin, MA, MD, FRCP, FRCPE, FRACP, FACP; Singaporean medical scientist, endocrinologist and academic; *Professor of Medicine and Senior Consultant Endocrinologist, National University Hospital, Singapore;* b. 12 Jan. 1936, Penang, Malaysia; m. Shirley Loo Ngai Seong 1964; two s. one d.; ed Raffles Inst., Singapore and Cambridge Univ.; Registrar, King's Coll. Hosp., London 1965; Medical Officer, Ministry of Health, Singapore 1965–66; Lecturer in Medicine, Nat. Univ. of Singapore 1966–70, Sr Lecturer 1971–73, Assoc. Prof. of Medicine 1974–77, Prof. and Head of Dept 1978–81, Deputy Vice-Chancellor 1979–81, Vice-Chancellor 1981–2000; Prof. of Medicine Nat. Univ. of Singapore 2000–, Prof. of Medicine and Sr Consultant Endocrinologist, Nat. Univ. Hosp. 2000–; Common-wealth Medical Fellow, The Royal Infirmary, Edin. 1970; Chair. Nat. Wages Council, Bio-ethics Advisory Cttee, Tropical Marine Science Inst., Nat. Longevity Insurance Cttee 2007–, Singapore-MIT Alliance for Research & Tech. 2007–, Special Needs Trust Co. 2008–, Singapore Millennium Foundation Ltd 2008–; Deputy Chair., Lee Kuan Yew Water Prize Council 2009–; Dir United Overseas Bank; mem. Chinese Heritage Council 1995–; Patron Mensa Singapore, Eisen-hower Fellow 1982, Dir Raffles Medical Group;; Hon. Fellow, Coll. of General Practitioners, Singapore 1982, Royal Australian Coll. of Obstetricians and Gynaecologists 1992, Royal Coll. of Physicians and Surgeons of Glasgow 1997, Royal Coll. of Surgeons of Edin. 1997, Int. Coll. of Dentists, USA 1999 (Dental Surgery), Royal Coll. of Surgeons of Edin. 1999; Officier, Ordre des Palmes académiques 1988, Singapore Distinguished Service Order 2000; Hon. DSc (Univ. of Hull) 1999; Rep. of Singapore Public Admin. Medal (Gold) 1984, Meritorious Service Medal 1990, Friend of Labour Award, NTUC 1995, Gordon Arthur Ransome Orator 2000, Lee Foundation–NHG Lifetime Achievement Award 2002, Nat. Univ. of Singapore Outstanding Service Award 2003. *Publications:* numerous articles in medical journals. *Leisure Interest:* swimming. *Address:* Department of Medicine, National University of Singapore/National University Hospital, 5 Lower Kent Ridge Road, 119074 Singapore (office). *Telephone:* 67724976 (office). *Fax:* 67735627 (office). *Website:* www.nus.edu.sg (office).

LIMA, Adriana Francesca; Brazilian fashion model and actress; b. 12 June 1981, Salvador, Bahia; m. Marko Jarić 2009; two d.; finished first in Ford's Supermodel of Brazil model search 1995, finished second in Ford's Supermodel of the World contest 1996; moved to New York City and signed with Elite Model Management 1999; best known for work with Victoria's Secret; was the face of Telecom Italia Mobile (mobile phone carrier) 2005; appeared at Givenchy fashion show 2009; carries out charitable work with orphanage, Caminhos da Luz (Ways of Light), Salvador, Bahia. *Film:* first acting role in The Follow (short film in BMW's series The Hire) 2001. *Television includes:* Pista Dupla (series) 1996, hosted What Is Sexy? programme for E! Entertainment Network 2008, appeared as guest playing herself in series How I Met Your Mother 2007, appeared on US TV series Ugly Betty playing herself 2008, appeared on Var mısın? Yok musun? (Turkish version of Deal or No Deal) 2009, Access Hollywood (series) 2009, Today (series) 2009–12, The Victoria's Secret Fashion Show (film) 2010, 2011, Super Bowl's Greatest Commercials 2012 (film) 2012, Late Night with Jimmy Fallon (series) 2012. *Address:* c/o The Society Model Management Inc., 156 5th Avenue, Suite #800, New York, NY 10010, USA (office). *Telephone:* (212) 377-5025 (office). *Fax:* (212) 377-5024 (office). *E-mail:* info@thesocietymanagement.com (office). *Website:* www.thesocietymanagement.com (office). adrianalima.com.

LIMA, Cássio Casseb, BE; Brazilian banking executive; b. 8 Aug. 1955; m.; two c.; of São Paulo; began career with Leading and Credit Dept, Bank of Boston 1976–79; Account Officer, Chief Financial Officer then Commercial Officer NW Region, Banco Francês & Brasileiro (Credit Lyonnaise) 1979–88; Chief Financial Officer then Exec. Vice-Pres. Banco Mantrust SRL 1988–92; Coordinator Industrial Restructuring Vila Romana Group 1992–93; Vice-Pres. Finance (Treas.) Citibank 1993–97; Pres. Credicard SA 1997–99; apptd Head Industrial Strategy Vichuna Textil, Fibra Dupont, Fibrasil, Companhia Siderúrgica Nacional, Vale do Rio Doce, Maxitel, Banco Fibra 1999; Pres. Banco do Brasil 2003–05; CEO Cia. Brasileira de Distribuição (Grupo Pão de Açúcar) 2006–07; mem. Bd Nat. Asscn Open Market Insts. (ANDIMA), Brazilian Banking Service Inst. (IBCB) 1993–97; mem. Bd of Dirs Vicunha, Banco Fibra, Solpart 1999, Brasilprev –2005, Aliança do Brasil –2005, Localiza SA –2006, Localiza Rent SA –2006, Sandia SA 2008–; Ind. Dir, Marisa Lojas SA 2008–, mem. Fiscal Council; Man. Inst. Reciclar; mem. Superior Econ. Council, Fed. of Industry for São Paulo (FIESP) 2006–. *Address:* Marisa Lojas SA, Rua James Holland, nº 422, 01138-909 São Paulo, Brazil.

Telephone: (11) 2109-3121. *Fax:* (11) 3392-4276. *E-mail:* info@marisa.com.br. *Website:* www.marisa.com.br.

LIMA DA VEIGA, Maria de Fátima; Cape Verde diplomatist; *Ambassador to USA;* b. 22 June 1957, São Vicente; m.; two c.; ed Univ. of Aix-ex-Provence, France, post-univ. training in devt and diplomacy at German Foundation in Berlin, training in Praia by Foreign Affairs Ministry in cooperation with the UN Inst. for Training and Research and Rio Branco Inst. of Brazil; joined Ministry of Foreign Affairs 1980, subsequently adviser, Chief of Staff, Office of the Minister for Foreign Affairs 1995–99; Amb. to Cuba 1999–2001; Sec. of State for Foreign Affairs 2001–02, Minister of Foreign Affairs, Co-operation and Communities 2002–04, Perm. Rep. to UN, New York 2004–07, Amb. to USA (also accred to Canada and Mexico) 2007–; fmr Vice-Chair. and Acting Chair. Alliance of Small Island Developing States (OASIS), New York; fmr mem. Nat. Comm. Interstate Cttee for Drought Control in the Sahel, Nat. Comm. of La Francophonie, Network of Women Ministers and Parliamentarians; Medalla de la Amistad (Cuba); Gran Cruz de la Orden del Mérito Civil (Spain). *Address:* Embassy of Cape Verde, 3415 Massachusetts Avenue NW, Washington, DC, 20007, USA (office). *Telephone:* (202) 965-6820 (office). *Fax:* (202) 965-1207 (office). *E-mail:* fatimav@caboverdeus .net (office). *Website:* www.embcv-usa.gov.cv (office).

LIMONOV, Eduard; Russian/French writer, poet and politician; *Chairman, National Bolshevik Party;* b. (Eduard Venyaminovich Savenko), 22 Feb. 1943, Dzerzhinsk, Gorkii (now Nizhnii Novgorod) Oblast; m. 1st Yelena Limonova Shchapova 1971 (divorced); m. 2nd Natalya Medvedeva (divorced); m. 6th Yekaterina Volkova 2006; one s. one d.; first wrote poetry at age of 15; in Kharkov 1965–67, moved to Moscow in 1967, worked as a tailor; left USSR 1974; settled in New York, USA 1975; moved to Paris, France 1982; participant in Russian nationalist movt 1990–; returned to Russia 1991; Chair. Nat. Radical Party 1992–93; Chair. Nat. Bolshevik Party (banned political party) 1994–; arrested on terrorism and conspiracy charges 2001, sentenced by Saratov Oblast Court to four years' imprisonment for illegal acquisition and possession of arms April 2003, released June 2003; f. Russia without Putin movt Jan. 2004. *Publications* include: verse and prose in Kontinent, Ekho, Kovcheg, Apollon –1977 (in trans. in England, USA, Austria and Switzerland); over 40 books including It's Me – Eddie (novel) 1979, Russian (Russkoye) (verse) 1979, Diary of a Failure 1982, Teenager Savenko: Memoir of a Russian Punk 1983, The Young Scoundrel (memoir) 1986, The Death of Contemporary Heroes 1993, The Murder of the Sentry 1993, Selected Works (three vols) 1999, The eXile: Sex, Drugs and Libel in the New Russia (with Mark Ames and Matt Taibbi) 2000, My Political Biography; articles in Russian Communist and nationalist newspapers 1989–. *E-mail:* nbpinfo@gmail.com (office). *Website:* www.nazbol.ru (office); limonov2012.ru.

LIN, Cho-Liang, BMus; American violinist; b. 29 Jan. 1960, Taiwan; s. of Kuo-Jing Lin and Kuo-Ling Yu; m. Deborah Lin; ed Juilliard School, New York, Sydney Conservatoire; concert tours worldwide; over 100 performances a year; soloist with leading orchestras including London Symphony Orchestra, Philharmonia, Concertgebouw, Orchestre de Paris, Chicago Symphony Orchestra, Philadelphia Orchestra and Boston Symphony Orchestra; played Tchaikovsky's Concerto at London Proms 1999; 20 solo albums; Founder, Dir Taipei Int. Music Festival; mem. Faculty Juilliard School 1991–; Gramophone Record Award 1989, Musical American's Instrumentalist of the Year 2000. *Leisure interests:* tennis, wine. *Address:* Opus 3 Artists, 470 Park Avenue South, 9th Floor North, New York, NY 10016, USA (office). *Telephone:* (212) 584-7500 (office). *Fax:* (646) 300-8200 (office). *E-mail:* info@opus3artists.com (office). *Website:* www.opus3artists.com (office).

LIN, Chuan, PhD; Taiwanese politician; b. 13 Dec. 1951; m.; two d.; ed Fu Jen Catholic Univ., Nat. Chengchi Univ., Univ. of Illinois, USA; Assoc. Research Fellow, Chung Hua Inst. for Econ. Research 1994–89; Assoc. Prof., Dept of Public Finance, Nat. Chengchi Univ. 1989–90, Prof. 1990–95, 1998–2000; Dir Bureau of Finance, Taipei City Govt 1995–98; Dir-Gen. Directorate-Gen. of Budget, Accounting and Statistics 2000–02; Minister of Finance 2002–06. *Address:* c/o Ministry of Finance, 2 Ai Kuo West Road, Taipei, Taiwan. *E-mail:* mof@mail.mof .gov.tu.

LIN, Dan; Chinese badminton player; b. 14 Oct. 1983, Longyan, Fujian; m. Xie Xingfang 2010; began playing badminton at age five; took part in winning Chinese nat. team, Asian Junior Championships 2000; began professional career 2001; mem. Chinese nat. badminton team 2001–; has won all major titles in world badminton (Olympic Games, World Championships, World Cup, Thomas Cup, Sudirman Cup, All England Open, Asian Games, Asia Championships); highest world ranking number 1 (Feb. 2004); Gold Medals (men's singles): Olympic Games, Beijing 2008, London 2012, World Championships, Madrid 2006, Kuala Lumpur 2007, Hyderabad 2009, World Cup, Yiyang 2005, 2006, Asian Games, Doha 2006, Guangzhou 2010, Asian Championships New Delhi 2010, Chengdu 2011; Laureus China Sportsman of the Year 2011. *Website:* www.cba.org.cn.

LIN, David Y. L., BCom, MSFS; Taiwanese diplomatist and government official; *Minister of Foreign Affairs;* b. March 1950; ed National Chengchi Univ., Taipei, Georgetown Univ., Washington, DC, USA; Sec., Embassy in South Africa 1980–87, Chief of Section, Dept of African Affairs and Personnel Dept, Ministry of Foreign Affairs (MFA) 1987–92, Deputy Dir-Gen., Dept of European Affairs 1992–95, Dir-Gen., Taipei Econ. and Cultural Office (TECO), Houston, Tex. 1995–97, Amb. to Grenada and St Vincent 1997–2001, Dir-Gen., Dept of European Affairs, MFA 2001–03, Rep., Taipei Econ. and Trade Office, Indonesia 2003–07, Dir-Gen., Dept of Int. Orgs, MFA 2007–08, Vice Minister of Foreign Affairs 2008–10, Rep., Taipei Representative Office in EU and Belgium 2010–12, Minister of Foreign Affairs 2012–. *Address:* Ministry of Foreign Affairs, 2 Kaitakeland Blvd, Taipei 10048, Taiwan (office). *Telephone:* (2) 23482999 (office). *Fax:* (2) 23805678 (office). *E-mail:* eyes@mofa.gov.tw (office). *Website:* www.mofa.gov.tw (office).

LIN, Hsin-i, BSc; Taiwanese politician and business executive; b. 2 Dec. 1946; m.; three c.; ed Nat. Cheng Kung Univ.; engineer, China Motor Corpn, later Deputy Man. Eng Div. 1972–76, Deputy Man. Marketing Div. 1976–79, Man. Yangmei Plant 1980–82, Vice-Pres. 1982–87, Exec. Vice-Pres. 1987–90, Pres. 1991–96, Vice-Chair. 1997–2000; Chair. Sino Diamond Motors Ltd 1993–2000, Automotive Research and Testing Centre 1996–2000, Newa Insurance Co. Ltd 1999–2000; Minister of Econ. Affairs 2000–02; Vice-Premier and Chair. Council of Econ. Planning and Devt 2002–04 (resgnd). *Address:* c/o Council for Economic Planning

and Development, 9th Floor, 87 Nanking East Road, Section 2, Taipei, Taiwan (office).

LIN, Join-sane, LLD; Taiwanese politician; *Secretary General, Kuomintang (KMT);* b. 17 Dec. 1944; ed Nat. Chengchi Univ.; Assoc. Specialist, later Specialist, Ministry of the Interior 1970–77; Section Chief, later Sr Specialist and Sr Exec. Officer, Dept of Land, Taipei City Govt 1977–83; Deputy Dir, later Dir, Dept of Land, Kaohsiung City Govt 1983–90, Sec.-Gen., Kaohsiung City Govt 1990–94, Deputy Mayor, Kaohsiung City 1995–98; Admin. Deputy Minister, later Political Deputy Minister, Ministry of the Interior 1998–2009; Sec.-Gen., Exec. Yuan (Cabinet) 2009–12; Sec.-Gen. Kuomintang (KMT) (Nationalist Party of China) 2012–. *Address:* Kuomintang, 232–234 Bade Rd, Sec. 2, Taipei 10492, Taiwan (office). *Telephone:* (2) 87711234 (office). *Fax:* (2) 23434561 (office). *Website:* www .kmt.org.tw (office).

LIN, Justin Yifu, MBA, MA, PhD; Chinese (b. Taiwanese) economist and international organization official; b. (Lin Zhengyi), 15 Oct. 1952, Yilan, Taiwan; m.; several c.; ed Nat. Chengchi Univ., Taipei (defence scholarship), Peking Univ., People's Repub. of China, University of Chicago, USA; returned to Army of Repub. of China (ROC) following his MBA 1978, achieved rank of Capt., defected to mainland China 17 May 1979; Research Asst, Dept of Econs, Univ. of Chicago 1984–86; Postdoctoral Fellow, Econ. Growth Center, Yale Univ. 1986–87; Assoc. Prof. of Econs, Peking Univ., Beijing 1987–93, Prof. of Econs 1993–, Founding Dir China Centre for Econ. Research 2005–; Deputy Dir Inst. of Rural Devt Research, Chinese Acad. of Social Sciences 1987–89; fmr Prof. of Econs, Hong Kong Univ. of Science and Tech.; Chief Economist and Sr Vice-Pres., Devt Econs, World Bank Group, Washington, DC (first Chinese citizen to hold post) 2008–12; served as a Deputy of China's People's Congress and Vice-Chair. All-China Fed. of Industry and Commerce; has served on several nat. and int. cttees, leading groups and councils on devt policy, tech. and environment, including UN Millennium Task Force on Hunger, Eminent Persons Group of Asian Devt Bank, Nat. Cttee on US-China Relations, Hong Kong-US Business Council, Working Group on the Future of the OECD, Reinventing Bretton Woods Cttee; mem. editorial bds of several int. academic econs journals; Fellow, Acad. of Sciences for the Developing World 2005; Corresp. Fellow, British Acad. 2010; Dr hc (Université D'Auvergne, Univ. of Nottingham, City Univ. of Hong Kong), (Fordham Univ.) 2009; Sun Yefang Prize (highest honour for economists in China) 1993, 2001, Policy Article Prize, Centre for Int. Food and Agricultural Policy, Univ. of Minnesota 1993, Sir John Crawford Award, Australian Agricultural and Resource Econs Soc. 1997, Best Article Prize, Australian Journal of Agricultural and Resource Economics 1999, Citation Classic Award, publisher of Social Science Citation Index 2000, Marshall Lecturer, Univ. of Cambridge, UK 2007. *Publications:* 18 books, including The China Miracle: Development Strategy and Economic Reform, Economic Development and Transition: Thought, Strategy, and Viability; more than 100 articles in refereed int. journals and collected vols on history, devt and transition. *Address:* c/o The World Bank, 1818 H Street, NW, Washington, DC 20433, USA (office). *Telephone:* (202) 473-1000 (office). *Fax:* (202) 477-6391 (office). *Website:* web.worldbank.org (office).

LIN, Liyun; Chinese state official; b. 1933, Taizhong, Taiwan; ed Minatogawa High School, Kyoga Prefecture, Japan, Beijing Univ.; teacher, Chinese School, Kobe, Japan 1952; Bureau Chief, CCP Cen. Cttee Int. Dept 1953–78; joined CCP 1963; council mem. Sino-Japanese Friendship Asscn 1973–; mem. Standing Cttee 4th NPC 1975–78, Standing Cttee 5th NPC 1978–83, Standing Cttee 6th NPC 1983–88 (mem. Presidium 6th NPC 1986–88, mem. Credentials Cttee NPC 1984–88), Standing Cttee 7th NPC 1988–93, Standing Cttee 8th NPC 1993–98; Deputy for Taiwan to 5th NPC 1978, 6th NPC 1983; Deputy Sec. CCP Langfang Prefectural Cttee, Hebei Prov. 1981; Vice-Chair. Exec. Cttee All-China Women's Fed. 1978 (mem. Secr. and Leading Party Group 1978); Vice-Chair. All-China Sports Asscn 1979; Pres. All-China Fed. of Taiwan Compatriots 1981–; mem. Overseas Chinese Affairs Cttee NPC 1988–98 (now Vice-Chair.); mem. Working Group for Unification of the Motherland 1984–; Vice-Pres. China Int. Cultural Exchange Centre 1984–; adviser Asscn for the Promotion of the Peaceful Reunification of China 1988–; Vice-Pres. All China Fed. of Returned Overseas Chinese 1994–; adviser, Asscn for Relations Across the Taiwan Straits; mem. 10th CCP Cen. Cttee 1972–77, 11th CCP Cen. Cttee 1977–82, 12th CCP Cen. Cttee 1982–87, 13th CCP Cen. Cttee 1987–92, 14th CCP Cen. Cttee 1992–97, 15th CCP Cen. Cttee 1997–2002. *Address:* Chinese Communist Party Central Committee, Beijing, People's Republic of China.

LIN, Maw-Wen; Taiwanese business executive; Vice-Pres. CPC Corpn –2010, Pres. 2010–12; Dir Taiwan Stock Exchange Corpn. *Address:* c/o CPC Corporation, 3 Sungren Road, Shinyi Chiu, Taipei 11010, Taiwan. *E-mail:* ir@cpc.com.tw.

LIN, Maya, MArch, PhD; American artist and architect; b. 5 Oct. 1959, Athens, OH; d. of Prof. Henry H. Lin and Prof. Julia Lin (née Chang); m. Daniel Wolf; two c.; ed Yale Univ.; architectural designer, Pers Forbes & Assocs, New York 1986–87; pvt. practice, New York 1987–; mem. Batey & Mack, San Francisco 1983, Fumihiko Maki Assoc., Tokyo 1985; f. Maya Lin Studio, New York 1986; William A. Bernoudy Resident in Architecture, American Acad., Rome, Italy 1998–99; artwork rep. by Pace Wildenstein; mem. Bd Nat. Resources Defense Council; subject of Acad. Award-winning documentary Maya Lin: A Strong Clear Vision 1995; mem. Bd of Trustees, Natural Resources Defense Council; mem. American Acad. of Arts and Letters, American Acad. of Arts and Sciences; fmr mem. Yale Corpn, Energy Foundation; William A. Bernoudy Resident in Architecture Fellowship, American Acad., Rome; inducted into National Women's Hall of Fame 2005; Dr hc (Yale), (Harvard), (Williams), (Smith College); American Acad. of Arts and Letters Award in Architecture, Finn Juhl Architecture Award 2003; Presidential Design Award, Artist Award from National Endowment for the Arts; AIA Honor Award, Finn Juhl Prize, Nat. Medal of Arts 2009. *Major projects include:* Vietnam Veterans' Memorial, Washington, DC 1982; Peace Chapel, Juniata Coll., Pennsylvania; Langston Hughes Library, Clinton, Tennessee; Civil Rights Memorial, Montgomery, AL 1989; The Women's Table, Yale Univ., CT 1993; Groundswell, Wexner Center for the Arts, Columbus, OH 1993, Museum for African Art, New York 1993, Eclipsed Time, Pennsylvania Station, New York 1994, The Wave Field, Univ. of Michigan Coll. of Eng, Ann Arbor 1995, Langston Hughes Library, Clinton, Tenn. 1999, Federal Courthouse, Manhattan, New York, Ecliptic, Grand Rapids, Mich. 2000, the character of a hill, under glass, American Express Financial Advisors, Minneapolis, Minn., Aveda HQ, Manhattan 2002,

Where the Land Meets the Sea 2005, Confluence Project 2006–, Maya Lin: Systematic Landscapes 2006–, Storm King Wavefield 2008, What is Missing? 2009. *Publications:* Maya Lin: Public/Private 1994, Boundaries 2000, Maya Lin: Systematic Landscape Catalogue 2006. *Address:* 52 East 78th Street, New York, NY 10075-1810, USA (office). *Website:* www.mayalin.com.

LIN, Rong-San; Taiwanese publisher and business executive; *Owner, Liberty Times;* b. 27 May 1939, Lujhou, Taipei; brother of Lin Yu-Lin; m.; four c.; began in business growing vegetables and selling rice, began developing property late 1960s; fmr Publr of Liberty Times (daily newspaper), Taipei Times (daily newspaper) 1999–; Founder Union Bank of Taiwan (still retains holding); fmr Taiwan legislator and nat. policy adviser to two past presidents; Founder and Chair. Lin Rong San Foundation of Culture and Social Welfare. *Address:* Liberty Times, 399 Rueiguang Road, Nei-Hu District, Taipei 11492, Taiwan (office). *Telephone:* (2) 26562828 (office). *Fax:* (2) 26561034 (office). *E-mail:* newstips@ libertytimes.com.tw (office). *Website:* www.libertytimes.com.tw (office); www .taipeitimes.com.

LIN, See-Yan, MA, MPA, PhD, CStat, FIB, FRSS, FIBM; Malaysian banker and financial consultant; *Chairman and CEO, Lin & Associates;* b. 3 Nov. 1939, Ipoh; ed Univ. of Malaya in Singapore, Harvard Univ., USA; Tutor in Econs, Univ. of Malaya 1961–63, Harvard Univ. 1970–72, 1976–77; Statistician, Dept of Statistics 1961–63; Econ. Adviser, Minister of Finance 1966–69; Dir Malaysian Rubber Exchange and Licensing Bd 1974–85; mem. Council on Malaysian Invisible Trade 1981–85, Econ. Panel of the Prime Minister 1982–87, Capital Issues Cttee 1985–86; Chief Economist, Bank Negara Malaysia (Cen. Bank of Malaysia) 1973–77, Econ. Adviser 1977–80, Deputy Gov. 1980–94; Chair., Pres. and CEO Pacific Bank Group 1994–98; Chair. Credit Guarantee Corpn Malaysia Berhad, Malaysian Insurance Inst.; Deputy Chair. Industrial Bank of Malaysia Berhad (Bank Industri); Dir Malaysia Export Credit Insurance Berhad, Govt Officers Housing Corpn, Seacen Research and Training Centre, Malaysian Wildlife Conservation Foundation; mem. Malaysia Program Advisory Council, US-ASIAN Centre for Tech. Exchange, Commonwealth Group of Experts on the Debt Crisis 1984, IMF Working Party on Statistical Discrepancy in World Currency Imbalances 1985–87, IMF Cttee of Balance of Payments Compilers 1987; Chair. and CEO Lin & Associates; Pres. Malaysian Econ. Asscn; mem. Nat. Econ. Action Council Working Group, Asian Financial Regulatory Shadow Committee, USA; Econ. Adviser, Associated Chinese Chambers of Commerce and Industry of Malaysia; Trustee Malaysia Univ. for Science and Tech.; mem. Bd Dirs Monash Univ. (Sunway Campus) Malaysia; Gov. Asian Inst. of Man., Manila; mem. bds several publicly listed and pvt. cos in Malaysia, Singapore and Indonesia; Chair. Harvard Grad. School Alumni Asscn Council, Harvard Univ., Regional Dir for Asia, Harvard Alumni Asscn, mem. Visiting Cttee for Asian Studies; Pres. Harvard Club of Malaysia; Pro-Chancellor Universiti Sains Malaysia –2011; Adjunct Prof. of Econs, Universiti Utara Malaysia; Trustee Tun Ismail Ali Foundation (PNB), Harvard Club of Malaysia Foundation, Malaysian Econ. Asscn Foundation, MAKNA (Nat. Cancer Council); Eisenhower Fellow 1986, mem. Eisenhower Fellowships' International Advisory Council, Phila, USA; Distinguished Fellow, Inst. of Strategic and Int. Studies; Fellow, Inst. of Statisticians, Malaysian Inst. of Man., Malaysian Econ. Asscn; Hon. PhD (Universiti Utara Malaysia); Hon. Fellow, Malaysian Insurance Inst. *Publications:* numerous articles in academic, banking and business journals. *Address:* Lin and Associates, B-610, First Floor, Jalan Air Putih, Pusat Komersial Air Putih, 25300 Kuantan, Pahang, Malaysia (office).

LIN, Sheng-chung; Taiwanese politician and business executive; *Chairman, CPC Corporation;* fmr Taiwan Rep. at WTO, Zurich, Switzerland; also worked at Taiwanese office in Boston and at Taipei City Govt; fmr Vice-Minister of Econs; Chair. CPC Corpn, Taiwan (state-run oil co.) 2012–. *Address:* CPC Corporation, 3 Songren Road, Sinyi Chiu, Taipei 11010, Taiwan (office). *Telephone:* (2) 8789-8989 (office). *Fax:* (2) 8789-9000 (office). *E-mail:* ir@cpc.com.tw (office). *Website:* www .cpc.com.tw (office).

LIN, Simon; Taiwanese computer industry executive; *Chairman and CEO, Wistron Corporation;* ed Nat. Chiao Tung Univ.; fmr Pres. Acer Inc.; currently Chair. and CEO Wistron Corpn; Chair. AOpen Inc., Wistron NeWeb, Wistron Information and Technology Services Corpn; Outstanding Man. of the Repub. of China Award, Govt of Taiwan 1989, named Outstanding Alumnus, Nat. Chiao Tung Univ. 1996. *Address:* Wistron Corporation, 158 Singshan Road, Neihu, Taipei 11469, Taiwan (office). *Telephone:* (2) 66169999 (office). *Fax:* (2) 66125188 (office). *E-mail:* info@wistron.com (office). *Website:* www.wistron.com (office).

LIN, Yi-shih, BS; Taiwanese politician; *Secretary-General, Executive Yuan;* b. 19 Aug. 1968; ed Dept of Dentistry, Taipei Medical Coll., Nat. Sun Yat-sen Univ.; mem., Legis. Yuan (Parl.) for 2nd electoral Dist, Kaohsiung City 1999–2012; mem. Kuomingtang (KMT), Sec.-Gen., KMT caucus 2002–, Dir, KMT Youth League 2006–07, Vice-Chair. KMT 2006–08, Exec. Dir, KMT Central Policy Cttee 2008–12, Sec.-Gen., Exec. Yuan (cabinet) 2012–. *Address:* Executive Yuan, No.1, Sec. 1, Zhongxiao E. Rd., Zhongzheng Dist., Taipei 10058, Taiwan (office). *Telephone:* (2) 33566500 (office). *E-mail:* eyemail@eyemail.gio.gov.tw. (office). *Website:* www.ey.gov.tw (office).

LIN, Yu-Lin; Taiwanese real estate executive; *Chairman, Hung Tai Group;* brother of Lin Rong-San; m.; seven c.; Chair. Hung Tai Group (property devt co.), Owner Hung Tai Center and Exchange Square (office bldgs); owns stakes in Hung Sheng Construction and Capital Securities. *Address:* Hung Tai Center, 168 Tun Hwa North Road, Taipei 105, Taiwan (office).

LIN, Zhaohua, BA; Chinese theatre director; *Senior Director, Beijing People's Art Theatre;* b. 1 July 1936, Tianjin; s. of Lin Baogui and Zhang Shuzhen; m. He Binzhu 1964; one s. one d.; ed Cen. Acad. of Drama, Beijing; Vice-Pres. and Dir Beijing People's Art Theatre 1984–, Chair. Art Cttee 1984–; Artistic Dir Lin Zhaohua Drama Studio 1990–; mem. Standing Cttee, China Theatre Asscn 1984–; Chair. Peking Univ. Theatre Research Inst. 2005–; Lin Zhaohua Theatre Arts Festival 2010–. *Theatre productions include:* The Red Heart 1978, Just Opinion 1980, Absolute Signal 1982, Bus Stop 1983, Festivities of Marriage and Funeral 1984, Wildman 1985, Schweyk in the Second World War 1986, Uncle Doggie's Nirvana 1986, Peace Lake 1988, Filed…Filed 1989, Peking Man 1989, Chinese Orphan 1990, Hamlet 1990, Countryside Anecdote 1990, A Report from Hu-Tuo

River 1991, Birdman, Romulus the Great 1992, Ruan Lingyu 1994, Faust 1994, Chessman 1995, Fisherman 1997, The Three Sisters Waiting For Godot (adapted from Chekhov's Three Sisters and Beckett's Waiting for Godot) 1998, The Teahouse 1999, Boundless Love 2000, A Parody 2000, Richard III 2001, Cai Wen Ji (Anhui Opera) 2002, Zhao's Orphan 2003, Toilet 2004, The Cherry Orchard 2004, The Dream Play 2005, Bird People, Antiques, Tea House, Frameless Wind and Moon, Beijingers, The Master Builder 2006, Coriolanus 2007, The Assassin 2008, The Lobbyist 2010, Ivanov 2011, The Book of Mountains and Sea 2012. *Beijing Opera productions include:* Mountain Flower 1991, Turandot, The Humpbacked Prime Minister Liu 2000, The Minister Liu Luoguo I 2000, The Minister Liu Luoguo II 2001, The Minister Liu Luoguo III 2002, The Bravest and Cleverest Soldier Sun Wu 2002, Farewell My Concubine 2003, The Very Best Zhangxie 2003. *Videos:* The Ape and His Six Roars – An Anthology of Lin Zhaohua Drama 2003, The Anthology of Lin Zhaohua Drama Studio (eight dramas and interview with Lin Zhaohua) 2004. *Publications:* Stage Art of Absolute Signal (ed.) 1985, Stage Art of Marriage and Funeral 1997, Lin Zhaohua on Theatrical Directing 1992. *Leisure interests:* Chinese yoga, swimming, music, playing the erhu. *Address:* Beijing People's Art Theatre, 22 Wangfujing Street, Beijing (office); 3-7-503, East Block, Ditan Beili, Heping li, Beijing, People's Republic of China (home). *Telephone:* (10) 65254346 (office); (10) 84043339 (home). *Fax:* (10) 62753253 (office). *E-mail:* linzhaohua1936@hotmail.com (home); lzh@linzhaohua .org (office). *Website:* www.linzhaohua.org (home).

LIN, Zuoming, PhD; Chinese aviation industry executive; *President, Aviation Industry Corporation of China (AVIC);* b. 1957, Zhangzhou City, Fujian Prov.; ed Nanjing Aeronautical Inst., Beijing Univ. of Aeronautics and Astronautics; began career 1976, successively, mem. staff and Deputy Dir Human Resource Div., Deputy Dir of Eng and Tech. Div., Deputy Dir Gen. Tech. Research Inst., Deputy Chief Engineer, Deputy Gen. Man., Gen. Man. and Chair. Chengdu Engine Co. Ltd; Gen. Man. Shenyang Liming Aero-Engine (Group) Corpn Ltd 1998–2001; Vice-Pres. and mem. Leading Party Group of CCP, Aviation Industry Corpn of China (AVIC) 2001–06, Sec. 2006–, Pres. Aviation Industry Corpn of China 2006–; Chair. AVIC I Commercial Aircraft Co. Ltd, AVIC I Investment Co. Ltd, AVIC I Consultant Co. Ltd, AviChina 2008–; Vice-Chair. Commercial Aircraft Corpn of China Ltd; Alt. mem. 16th CCP Cen. Cttee 2002–07, 17th CCP Cen. Cttee 2007–12, mem. 18th CCP Cen. Cttee 2012–. *Address:* Aviation Industry Corpn of China, PO Box 2399, AVIC Plaza, 128 Jianguo Road, Chaoyang District, Beijing 100022, People's Republic of China (office). *Telephone:* (10) 65665922 (office). *Fax:* (10) 65666518 (office). *E-mail:* info@avic.com.cn (office). *Website:* www.avic.com.cn (office).

LINACRE, Sir (John) Gordon Seymour, Kt, CBE, AFC, DFM, CCMI; British newspaper executive; b. 23 Sept. 1920, Sheffield; s. of John J. Linacre and Beatrice B. Linacre; m. Irene A. Gordon 1943; two d.; ed Firth Park Grammar School, Sheffield; served RAF, rank of Squadron Leader 1939–46; journalistic appointments Sheffield Telegraph/Star 1937–47; Kemsley News Service 1947–50; Deputy Ed. Newcastle Journal 1950–56, Newcastle Evening Chronicle 1956–57; Ed. Sheffield Star 1958–61; Asst Gen. Man. Sheffield Newspapers Ltd 1961–63; Exec. Dir Thomson Regional Newspapers Ltd, London 1963–65; Man. Dir Yorkshire Post Newspapers Ltd 1965–83, Deputy Chair. 1981–83, Chair. 1983–90, Pres. 1990–2009; Dir United Newspapers PLC 1969–91, Deputy Chair. 1981–91, Chief Exec. 1983–88; Deputy Chair. Express Newspapers PLC 1985–88; also fmr Chair. United Provincial Newspapers Ltd, Sheffield Newspapers Ltd, Lancashire Evening Post Ltd, Northampton Mercury Co. Ltd, East Yorkshire Printers Ltd etc.; Dir Yorkshire TV 1969–90; Chair. Leeds Univ. Foundation 1989–2000; Chair. Chameleon TV Ltd 1994–2008; Chair. Opera North Ltd 1978–98, Pres. 1998–; many other professional and public appointments; Commendatore, Ordine al Merito della Repubblica Italiana 1973, Grand Ufficiale 1987; Kt Order of the White Rose, Finland 1987; Hon. LLD (Leeds) 1991. *Leisure interests:* fly-fishing, hill-walking, golf, music, theatre.

LINCOLN, Blanche Meyers Lambert, BA; American politician and business executive; *Director, Entergy Corporation;* b. 30 Sept. 1960, Helena, Phillips Co., Ark.; d. of Jordan Bennett Lambert and Martha Lambert (née Kelly); m. Dr Steve Lincoln; two s. (twins); ed Central High School, Helena, Randolph-Macon Woman's Coll., Lynchburg, Va, Univ. of Arkansas, Fayetteville; served as staff asst to US Rep. Bill Alexander (Democrat from Ark.'s 1st Congressional Dist) 1982–84; mem. US House of Reps 1993–97; Senator from Ark. 1999–2011 (youngest ever female senator), mem. Senate Finance Cttee 2001–11, also mem. Agric., Nutrition and Forestry Cttee (Chair. 2009–11), Special Cttee on Aging, Select Cttee on Ethics, Social Security Task Force, Rural Health Caucus, Chair. of Rural Outreach for Senate Democratic Caucus; mem. Bd of Dirs Entergy Corpn 2011–; Democrat. *Address:* Entergy Corporation, 639 Loyola Avenue, New Orleans, LA 70113 (office); Entergy Corporation, PO Box 61000, New Orleans, LA 70161, USA (office). *Telephone:* (504) 576-4000 (office). *Fax:* (504) 576-4428 (office). *E-mail:* info@ entergy.com (office). *Website:* www.entergy.com (office).

LINDAHL, George, III, BS; American petroleum industry executive; ed Univ. of Alabama, Tulane Univ., Advanced Man. Program at Harvard Business School; began career as geologist and Man. Amoco Production Co.; Exec. Vice-Pres., Dir and Partner Walker Energy Partners of Houston –1987; joined Union Pacific Resources (UPR) Group, Inc. 1987, Pres. and COO 1996–99, Chair., Pres. and CEO 1999–2000; Dir Anadarko Petroleum Corpn, Vice-Chair. 2000–01; Man. Partner, Sandefer Capital Partners 2001–07; Dir, EV Energy Partners LP 2006–; mem. or fmr mem. Advisory Bd NAPE (fmrly North American Prospect Expo), True North Energy Corpn; mem. Pres.'s Council, Univ. of Ala; mem. Visiting Cttee, Petroleum and Geosystems Engineering Dept, Univ. of Texas at Austin; mem. Texas Hall of Fame Foundation; fmr Pres. Fort Worth Petroleum Club; mem. All-American Wildcatters 1999. *Address:* EV Energy Partners LP, 1001 Fannin Street, Houston, TX 77002 (office); c/o Sandefer Capital Partners, 515 Congress Avenue, Suite 1875, Austin, TX 78701-3518, USA. *Telephone:* (713) 651-1144 (office); (512) 495-9925. *Fax:* (713) 651-1260 (office). *E-mail:* info@evenergypartners.com (office). *Website:* www.evenergypartners.com (office).

LINDAHL, Tomas, MD, FRS; Swedish scientist; *Director Emeritus, London Research Institute, Cancer Research UK;* b. 28 Jan. 1938, Stockholm; ed Karolinska Inst., Stockholm; joined Cancer Research 1981, Deputy Dir of Research, Cancer Research UK, London Research Inst., later Researcher,

Mutagenesis Lab., now Dir Emer. London Research Inst.; INSERM (French Nat. Inst. for Health and Medical Research) Prix Etranger 2007, Royal Medal, Royal Soc. 2007, Copley Medal, Royal Soc. 2010. *Address:* London Research Institute, Clare Hall Laboratories, Blanche Lane, South Mimms, Herts., EN6 3LD, England (office). *Telephone:* (1707) 625993 (office). *Fax:* (1707) 625801 (office). *E-mail:* tomas.lindahl@cancer.org.uk (office). *Website:* www.cancerresearchuk.org/science (office).

LINDBÆK, Jannik; Norwegian petroleum industry executive; b. 1939; ed Norwegian School of Econs and Business Admin, Bergen; Pres. and CEO Storebrand Group 1976–85; Pres. and CEO Nordiska Investeringsbanken (Nordic Investment Bank), Helsinki 1986–94; Exec. Vice-Pres. Int. Finance Corpn (World Bank Group), Washington, DC, USA 1994–99; Chair. Statoil ASA 2003–07 (until merger with Norsk Hydro to form StatoilHydro); Chair. Bergen Int. Festival, Transparency Int. Norge, Plan Int. Norge, Gearbulk; fmr Chair. Gaz de France Norge, Saga Petroleum, Den Norske Bank; mem. Bd of Dirs Kristian Gerhard Jebsen Skipsrederi (shipping co.); Fulbright Scholar, Univ. of Kansas, USA 1961–62. *Address:* c/o StatoilHydro, Forusbeen 50, 4035 Stavenger 4035, Norway. *Telephone:* 51-99-00-00. *Fax:* 51-99-00-50. *E-mail:* statoil@statoilhydro.com. *Website:* www.statoilhydro.com.

LINDBECK, Assar, PhD; Swedish economist and academic; *Professor of International Economics, Institute for International Economic Studies, University of Stockholm;* b. 26 Jan. 1930, Umeå; s. of Carl Lindbeck and Eugenia Lindbeck (née Sundelin); m. Dorothy Nordlund 1953; one s. one d.; ed Univs of Uppsala and Stockholm; Asst Prof., Univ. of Michigan, USA 1958; with Swedish Treasury 1953–56; Asst Prof. of Econs, Univ. of Stockholm 1962–63, Prof., Stockholm School of Econs 1964–71, Prof. of Int. Econs 1971–, Dir Inst. of Int. Econs 1971–94; Visiting Prof., Columbia Univ., USA 1968–69, Univ. of California, Berkeley 1969, ANU 1970, Yale Univ. 1976, Stanford Univ. 1977; Research Fellow, Research Inst. of Industrial Econs, Stockholm, CESifo, Munich, Kiel Inst. of World Econs, Kiel; Consultant, World Bank 1986–87; mem. Nobel Prize Cttee on Econs 1969–94 (Chair. 1980–94). *Music:* Sonata for Clarinet and piano: Fantasi i folkton 1948, performed in City Hall, Luleå 1948. *Publications:* A Study in Monetary Analysis 1963, The Political Economy of the New Left 1971, Economics of the Agricultural Sector 1973, Swedish Economic Policy 1975, The Insider-Outsider Theory (with Dennis Snower) 1988, Unemployment and Macroeconomics 1993, The Swedish Experiment 1997. *Leisure interest:* painting. *Address:* Institute for International Economic Studies, Stockholm University, 106 91 Stockholm (office); Karlavägen 78, 114 59 Stockholm, Sweden (home). *Telephone:* (8) 16-30-78 (office); (8) 21-23-37 (home). *Fax:* (8) 16-29-46 (office); (8) 21-23-37 (home). *E-mail:* assar@iies.su.se (office). *Website:* people.su.se/~alind.

LINDBLOM, Seppo Olavi, LicPolSc; Finnish bank executive and politician; b. 9 Aug. 1935, Helsinki; s. of Olavi Lindblom and Aura Lindblom (née Sammal); m. Anneli Johanson 1958; four d.; ed Univ. of Helsinki; Man. br. office, Finnish Workers' Savings Bank 1958–60; Economist, Bank of Finland 1960–68; Sec. to Prime Minister 1968–70; Head, Labour Inst. for Econ. Research 1970–72; Minister in Ministry of Trade and Industry 1972; Head, Dept of Nat. Econ. Research 1973–74; Nat. Conciliator for Incomes Policy 1973–74; Dir Bank of Finland 1974–82, mem. Bd of Man. 1982–87; Minister of Trade and Industry 1983–87; Chair. and Chief Exec. Postipankki Ltd 1988–96. *Publications:* (in Finnish): SAK's Remuneration Policy is the Main Principle of the Second World War 1959, Investment Theory of Investment Surveys Theoretical Basis 1966, Political Negotiation Process Problems in the Industrialized Market Economy Countries 1967, Left Qualm 1970, Finland and the European Economy 1992, People's Home Report – The Welfare State Accountability Review 2002, Policy on the Run 2007, Manu in the Ointment 2009, Wobbly Republic 2013. *Leisure interests:* music, chess.

LINDE DE CASTRO, Luis María, BEcons; Spanish economist and central banker; *Governor, Banco de España;* b. 1945, Madrid; ed Univ. Complutense de Madrid; Head, Directorate-Gen. for Foreign Trade, Ministry of Trade 1969–71, Head, Balance of Payments Office 1971–73; Head, Spanish Trade Office, Moscow 1974–78; Technical Sec.-Gen., Ministry of Economy and Trade 1978–82; Deputy Dir-Gen., Foreign Dept, Banco de España (central bank) 1983–87, Dir-Gen. of Int. Affairs 1987–2000, Dir, Country Risk Dept 2001–04, Adviser to Assoc. Directorate-Gen. of Int. Affairs 2009–11, mem. Council 2012–, Gov. Banco de España 2012–; Dir Official Credit Inst. 1989–92; Exec. Dir for Spain, IDB 2005–08; Econs Coordinator, Revista de Libros (magazine) of Fundación Caja Madrid 1998–2012; Founding mem. and sponsor, Fundación Transición Española (Spanish Transition Foundation) 2007–. *Address:* Office of the Governor, Banco de España, Alcalá 48, 28014 Madrid, Spain (office). *Telephone:* (91) 3386063 (office). *Fax:* (91) 3385884 (office). *E-mail:* bde@bde.es (office). *Website:* www.bde.es (office).

LINDEGAARD, Jørgen, MEng; Danish business executive; *Vice-Chairman, Zealand Pharma A/S;* b. 7 Oct. 1948; ed Tech. Univ. of Denmark; worked as exec. in telecommunications eng with Philips Telekommunikation (subsidiary of the Dutch Philips conglomerate) –1977; Pres. Fyns Telefon A/S 1977–91, Københavns Telefon A/S 1991–95; fmr mem. Exec. Bd Tele Danmark; Chair. Sonofon Holding A/S 1996–2004; Pres. and CEO GN Store Nord 1997–2001; Pres. and CEO SAS Group 2001–06; CEO ISS A/S (world's largest facilities man. co.) 2006–10, Dir 2010–11; Vice-Chair. and mem. Remuneration and Nomination Cttee, Zealand Pharma A/S 2011–; mem. Bd of Dirs Cimber Sterling Group A/S 2011–; Fellow, Norwegian Acad. of Technological Sciences. *Address:* Zealand Pharma A/S, Smedeland 36, 2600 Glostrup (Copenhagen), Denmark (office). *Telephone:* 88-77-36-00 (office). *Fax:* 88-77-38-98 (office). *E-mail:* info@zealandpharma.com (office). *Website:* www.zealandpharma.com (office).

LINDEMAN, Fredrik Otto, DPhil; Norwegian academic; *Professor Emeritus of Indo-European Linguistics, University of Oslo;* b. 3 March 1936, Oslo; s. of Carl Fredrik Lindeman and Agnes Augusta Lindeman; m. Beate Konow Taranger 1960; one s. one d.; ed Univ. of Oslo, Sorbonne, Paris; Prof. of Indo-European Linguistics, Univ. of Copenhagen 1970–76; Prof. of Indo-European Linguistics, Univ. of Oslo 1976–2005, now Emer.; Visiting Prof., Dublin Inst. for Advanced Studies, School of Celtic Studies 1982–83; Dals Prize for Outstanding Achievement, Univ. of Oslo 1997. *Publications:* Les Origines Indo-Européennes de la 'Verschärfung' Germanique 1964, Einführung in die Laryngaltheorie 1970, The

Triple Representation of Schwa in Greek and some related problems of Indo-European Phonology 1982, Studies in Comparative Indo-European Linguistics 1996, Introduction to the 'Laryngeal Theory' 1997, Våre Arveord Etymologisk Ordbok (with Harald Bjorvand) 2000 (enlarged and revised edn) 2007. *Leisure interest:* music. *Address:* Abbedikollen 13, 0280 Oslo 2 (home); Institutt for lingvistiske og nordiske studier, Universitetet i Oslo, PB 1102 Blindern, 0317 Oslo, Norway (office). *Telephone:* 22-50-92-78 (home). *E-mail:* bente.lindeman@c2i.net (home).

LINDENSTRAUSS, Elon, BSc, MSc, PhD; Israeli mathematician and academic; *Professor, Einstein Institute of Mathematics, Hebrew University of Jerusalem;* b. 1 Aug. 1970, Jerusalem; s. of Joram Lindenstrauss and Naomi Lindenstrauss; ed Hebrew Univ. Secondary School, Hebrew Univ. of Jerusalem; fmr mem. Inst. for Advanced Study, Princeton, NJ, USA; fmr Szego Asst Prof., Stanford Univ., USA; Long Term Prize Fellow, Clay Math. Inst. 2003–05; Prof., Princeton Univ., USA 2004–; Prof., Einstein Inst. of Math., Hebrew Univ. of Jerusalem 2009–; represented Israel at Int. Math. Olympiad and won a bronze medal 1988, Israel Defense Prize, Israel Defense Forces, Salem Prize (co-recipient) 2003, European Math. Soc. Prize 2004, Michael Bruno Memorial Award 2008, Erdős Prize 2009, Fermat Prize 2009, Fields Medal (co-recipient) 2010. *Publications:* more than 40 papers in professional journals on ergodic theory and its applications to number theory. *Address:* Einstein Institute of Mathematics, Edmond J. Safra Campus, Givat Ram, Manchester House 103, Hebrew University of Jerusalem, Jerusalem 91904, Israel (office). *Telephone:* 2-6586834 (office). *Fax:* 2-6537266 (office). *E-mail:* elon@math.huji.ac.il (office). *Website:* www.math.huji.ac.il/~elon (office); www .math.princeton.edu/~elonl.

LINDENSTRAUSS, Joram, PhD; Israeli mathematician and academic; *Professor Emeritus, Einstein Institute of Mathematics, Hebrew University of Jerusalem;* b. 28 Oct. 1936, Tel-Aviv; m. Naomi Salinger 1962; one s. three d.; ed Hebrew Univ., Jerusalem; Sr Lecturer in Math., Hebrew Univ. 1965, Assoc. Prof. 1967, Prof. 1970–2007, Prof. Emer. 2007–; Visiting Prof., Yale Univ., Univs of Washington, California and Texas, Texas A&M Univ., Inst. Mittag Leffler, Inst. for Advanced Study, Princeton; mem. Israel Acad. of Science and Humanities; Foreign mem. Austrian Acad. of Sciences; Dr hc (Kent State Univ., Ohio); Israel Prize in Math. 1981, Banach Medal, Polish Acad. of Sciences. *Publications:* Classical Banach Spaces, Vols I–II, 1977, 1979, Geometric Non Linear Functional Analysis, Vol. I (co-author) 2000, Handbook of the Geometry of Banach Spaces, Vol. I (co-ed.) 2001. *Address:* Einstein Institute of Mathematics, Edmond J. Safra Campus, Givat Ram, Manchester House 101, Hebrew University of Jerusalem, Jerusalem 91904, Israel (office); 36 Habanai Street, Jerusalem, Israel. *Telephone:* (2) 6522762 (home). *Fax:* (2) 6537266 (office). *E-mail:* joram@math.huji.ac.il (office). *Website:* www.math.huji.ac.il (office).

LINDERBERG, Jan Erik, FD; Danish chemist and academic; *Professor Emeritus of Theoretical Chemistry, Aarhus University;* b. 27 Oct. 1934, Karlskoga, Sweden; s. of David Linderberg and Sara Bäckström; m. Gunnel Björstam 1957; two s.; ed Uppsala Univ.; Docent, Uppsala Univ. 1964–68; Prof. of Theoretical Chem., Aarhus Univ., Denmark 1968–, now Prof. Emer.; Adjunct Prof. of Chem., Univ. Florida, Gainesville and Univ. of Utah, USA; mem. Royal Danish Soc. of Sciences and Letters, Int. Acad. of Quantum Molecular Science, Royal Soc. of Science (Uppsala). *Publications:* Role of Correlation in Electronic Systems 1964, Propagators in Quantum Chemistry (co-author), Quantum Science (with others) 1976; more than 100 papers in refereed journals. *Leisure interest:* orienteering. *Address:* Aarhus University, Department of Chemistry, Langelandsgade 140, 8000 Aarhus C (office); Janus la Cours gade 20, 8000 Aarhus C, Denmark (home). *Telephone:* 87-15-53-45 (office); 86-12-02-41 (home). *Fax:* 86-19-61-99 (office). *E-mail:* jan@chem.au.dk (office). *Website:* pure.au.dk/portal/da/persons/id(aff9b4bb-2f80-47d3-a4a5-59efc1370df0).html (office).

LINDNER, Christian; German business executive and politician; *Chairman, Free Democratic Party;* b. 7 Jan. 1979, Wuppertal; s. of Wolfgang Lindner; m. Dagmar Rosenfeld-Lindner; ed Rheinischen Friedrich-Wilhelms-Univ.; freelance business consultant 1997–99, 2002–04; Partner, Knüppel Lindner Communications GmbH 1999–2002; co-f. Moomax GmbH (internet co.) 2000; mem. North Rhine-Westphalia Landtag (State Parl.) 2000–09, 2012–; mem. Bundestag (Parl.) 2009–12; mem. Freie Demokratische Partei (FDP, Free Democratic Party) 1995–, mem. Exec. Bd, FDP North Rhine-Westphalia 1998–, Sec.-Gen. 2004–10, mem. Exec. Bd, FDP (Fed. level) 2007–, Sec.-Gen. 2009–11, Chair. 2013–. *Address:* Freie Demokratische Partei, Reinhardtstr. 14, 10117 Berlin, Germany (office). *Telephone:* (30) 28495820 (office). *Fax:* (30) 28495822 (office). *E-mail:* fdp-point@fdp.de (office). *Website:* www.fdp-bundespartei.de (office); www.christian-lindner.de.

LINDSAY, Most Rev. and Hon. Orland Ugham, OD, OJ, BD, DD; Jamaican/Antiguan ecclesiastic (retd); b. 24 March 1928, Jamaica; s. of Hubert Lindsay and Ida Lindsay; m. Olga Daphne Wright 1959; three s.; ed Mayfield Govt School, Southfield, Jamaica, Culham Coll. Oxford, England, St Peter's Theological Coll., Jamaica, Montréal Diocesan Theological Coll. at McGill Univ., Canada; served in RAF 1944–49; teacher Franklin Town Govt School 1949–52; Asst Master Kingston Coll. 1952–53, 1958–63; ordained Deacon, Jamaica 1956; Asst Curate St Peter's Vere Cure 1956–57; ordained Priest 1957; Chaplain Kingston Coll. 1958–63; Asst Curate in charge of Manchioneal Cure 1960–63; Sec. Jamaica Diocesan Synod 1962–70; Chaplain Jamaica Defence Force 1963–67; Prin. Church Teachers' Coll., Mandeville, Jamaica 1967–70; Bishop of Antigua, latterly of NE Caribbean and Aruba 1970–98; Archbishop of the West Indies 1986–98; Order of Distinction (Antigua) 1996, Order of Jamaica 1997; Hon. DD (Berkeley Divinity School, Yale Univ.) 1978, (St Paul's Coll., S Va) 1998; Hon. STD (Diocesan Theological Coll., Montreal) 1997. *Leisure interests:* swimming, listening to music, reading, photography. *Address:* Crosbies, PO Box 3456, Antigua, West Indies (home). *Telephone:* 560-1724 (home). *Fax:* 462-2090 (home). *E-mail:* orland@candw.ag (home).

LINDSAY, Robert; British actor; b. (Robert Lindsay Stevenson), 13 Dec. 1949, Ilkeston, Derbyshire; s. of Norman Stevenson and the late Joyce Stevenson; m. 1st Cheryl Hall (divorced); m. 2nd Rosemarie Ford; two s.; one d. by actress Diana Weston; ed Royal Acad. of Dramatic Art; began career as dialect coach with repertory company in Exeter, later joined regional theatre group, then moved on to West End and to television roles; first became household name in UK as Wolfie in sitcom Citizen Smith 1977; stage career commenced at Manchester Royal

Exchange; Patron of New Arts Course, NCN (fmrly Clarendon Coll.) – Robert Lindsay Theatre; Hon. Fellow, Univ. of Manchester; Dr hc (Nottingham, Derby). *Theatre includes*: Hamlet, Royal Exchange, Manchester (then tour of UK) 1983, Bill Snibson in Me and My Girl, Adelphi Theatre, London, Broadway and LA (Laurence Olivier Award for Outstanding Performance by an Actor in a Musical, Tony Award for Best Actor in a Musical, Drama Desk Best Actor Award, Outer Critics' Best Actor Award, Fred Astaire Award for Best Dancer on Broadway) 1985–87, Henry II in Anouilh's Beckett, West End, London (Variety Club Best Theatre Actor) 1991, Cyrano de Bergerac, Theatre Royal, London 1992, Oliver! (Laurence Olivier Award for Best Actor), Beaux Stratagem/Philoctetes, Royal Exchange, Manchester (Manchester Evening News Award), Richard III, tour by RSC then at Stratford-upon-Avon then at Savoy Theatre, London 1998, The Changeling, Riverside Studios, London, The Cherry Orchard, The Roundhouse, London, Godspell, Wyndhams Theatre, How I Got That Story, Hampstead Theatre, Octavius in Julius Caesar, Royal Exchange, Manchester, Leaping Ginger, Royal Exchange, Manchester, Lower Depths, The Roundhouse, London, Power, Royal Nat. Theatre, London, D'Artagnan in Three Musketeers, Royal Exchange, Manchester, Trelawny of The Wells, Old Vic, London, The Entertainer, Old Vic, London. *Films include*: That'll Be the Day 1973, Three for All 1974, Adventures of a Taxi Driver 1976, Bert Rigby, You're a Fool 1989, Strike It Rich (aka Loser Takes All; Money Talks) 1990, Goodbye My Love 1996, Fierce Creatures 1997, Remember Me? 1997, The Canterbury Tales (voice) 1998, Divorcing Jack 1998, Wimbledon 2004; training videos: The Dreaded Appraisal, The Helping Hand, I Wasn't Prepared For That, Meeting Breaks – Bosses From Hell, From 'No' To 'Yes', Sell It To Me!. *Radio includes*: Puttin' On The Style (BBC Radio 2), Peer Gynt (BBC Radio 4) (Sony Award), Oedipus (Radio 4), Frankenstein (BBC World Service), Nineteen Ninety Four, (Radio 4) Nobody Will Laugh (Milan R3), as Iago with Robert Stephens as Othello (Prince's Trust CD); audiobooks: Pinocchio, Fortysomething, Falling, Tom Jones, Virgin And The Gypsy, Sherlock Holmes, Mary Shelley's 'Frankenstein', Can't You Sleep Little Bear?. *Television includes*: Get Some In! (series) 1975–77, Wolfie in Citizen Smith (series) 1977, Twelfth Night 1980, Seconds Out (series) 1981, All's Well That Ends Well 1981, A Midsummer Night's Dream 1981, Cymbeline 1982, Give us a Break (series) 1983, Edmund in King Lear (Granada) 1984, Much Ado About Nothing 1984, Confessional 1989, Nightingales (series) 1990, Michael in GBH (mini-series; Channel 4) (BAFTA Award for Best Actor, Royal Television Soc. Award for Best Actor) 1991, Genghis Cohn 1993, The Wimbledon Poisoner (mini-series) 1994, Jake's Progress (mini-series) 1995, The Office 1996, Brazen Hussies 1996, In Your Dreams (series; voice) 1998, Capt. Pellew in Hornblower: The Even Chance (aka Horatio Hornblower: The Duel, USA) 1998, Hornblower: The Examination for Lieutenant (Horatio Hornblower: The Fire Ship, USA) 1998, Hornblower: The Duchess and the Devil (Horatio Hornblower: The Duchess and the Devil, USA) 1999, Hornblower: The Frogs and the Lobsters (Horatio Hornblower: The Wrong War, USA) 1999, Oliver Twist (mini-series) 1999, My Family (series) 2000–10, Hawk (aka Hawkins, UK) (mini-series) 2001, The Heat Is On (series) 2001, Hornblower: Mutiny 2001, Hornblower: Retribution (aka Horatio Hornblower: Retribution, USA) 2001, Don't Eat the Neighbours (series) 2001, Out of Eden (voice) 2002, Hornblower: Duty 2003, Hornblower: Loyalty (aka Horatio Hornblower 3, USA) 2003, Friends and Crocodiles 2005, A Very Social Secretary 2005, Jericho (series) 2005, Space Race (BBC series) (narrator) 2005, Friends and Crocodiles 2006, Gideon's Daughter 2006, The Trial of Tony Blair 2007, Extras (Series 2; as himself) 2007; guest appearances in Absolutely Fabulous (BBC), Whodunnit! (episode 'Pop Goes The Weasels'), The Good Life (episode 'Our Speaker Today') (BBC), Tales From The Crypt (episode 'Ear Today... Gone Tomorrow'), Victoria Wood With All The Trimmings (BBC), The Parkinson Show (ITV) 2005. *Address*: c/o Lorraine Hamilton, Hamilton Hodell Ltd, 5th Floor, 66–68 Margaret Street, London, W1W 8SR, England (office). *Telephone*: (20) 7636-1221 (office). *Fax*: (20) 7636-1226 (office). *E-mail*: lorraine@hamiltonhodell.co.uk (office). *Website*: www .hamiltonhodell.co.uk (office); www.robertlindsay.net.

LINDSEY, Lawrence B., AB, MA, PhD; American economist and fmr government official; *President and CEO, Lindsey Group*; b. 18 July 1954, Peekskill, NY; s. of Merritt Lindsey and Helen Hissam; m. Susan Lindsey 1982; three c.; ed Bowdoin Coll., Harvard Univ.; on staff of Pres. Reagan's Council of Econ. Advisers; Special Asst for Policy Devt to Pres. George H.W. Bush; fmr Prof. of Econs, Harvard Univ.; mem. Bd of Govs Fed. Reserve System 1991–97; Man. Dir Econ. Strategies Inc. 1997–2001; Econ. Adviser to Pres. 2001–02; Dir Nat. Econ. Council 2001–02; Pres. and CEO Lindsey Group 2003–; Chair. Bd Neighborhood Reinvestment Corpn 1993–97; Resident Scholar and holder Arthur C. Burns Chair., American Enterprise Inst. 1997–2001, now Visiting Scholar; Hon. JuD (Bowdoin Coll.) 1993; Distinguished Public Service Award, Boston Bar Asscn 1994. *Publications*: The Growth Experiment: How the New Tax Policy is Transforming the US Economy 1990, Econ. Puppermasters: Lessons From the Halls of Power 1999; numerous articles in professional publs. *Address*: The Lindsey Group, 11320 Random Hills Road, Suite 310, Fairfax, VA 22030; American Enterprise Institute, 1150 17th Street, NW, Washington, DC 20036, USA (office). *Telephone*: (703) 621-1170 (office). *Fax*: (703) 218-3956 (office). *E-mail*: info@thelindseygroup.com (office); LLindsey@aei.org (office). *Website*: www.thelindseygroup.com (office).

LINDSTEN, Jan Eric, PhD, MD; Swedish geneticist and academic; *Professor Emeritus of Medical Genetics, Karolinska Institute*; b. 23 Jan. 1935, Stockholm; s. of Carl-Eric Lindsten and Lisa M. Hallberg; m. Marianne E. Östling 1960; two s. one d.; ed Uppsala Univ., Karolinska Inst., Stockholm; Prof. of Human Genetics, Århus 1968–70; Prof. of Medical Genetics, Karolinska Inst. 1969–2000, Prof. Emer. 2000–, Head, Dept of Clinical Genetics 1970–90; Chief Medical Officer, Karolinska Hosp. 1987–90, Man. Dir 1990–94; Man. Dir Nat. Univ. Hosp. Copenhagen 1994–96; Dean Medical Faculty, Karolinska Inst. 1996–98; Sec. Nobel Ass. and Medical Nobel Cttee Karolinska Inst. 1979–90; Pres. Royal Swedish Acad. of Sciences 2003–06. *Publications*: more than 300 publs in the field of medical genetics, especially clinical genetics. *Address*: Council of Cultural Affairs, Karolinska Institutet, 17177 Stockholm, Sweden (office). *Telephone*: (8) 52-48-39-29 (office). *Fax*: (8) 31-67-74 (office). *E-mail*: jan.lindsten@ki.se (office).

LINEHAN, Fergus; Irish theatre director; *Director and Chief Executive, Edinburgh International Festival*; began career in Dublin, producing numerous shows and then directing Dublin Theatre Festival; Chief Exec. and Artistic Dir Sydney Festival 2004–09; Head of Music, Sydney Opera House 2010–12; Dir (part-time), Edinburgh Int. Festival 2013–14, Dir and Chief Exec. 2014–; Festival Dir Vivid LIVE. *Address*: Edinburgh International Festival, The Hub, Castlehill, Edinburgh, EH1 2NE, Scotland (office). *Telephone*: (131) 473-2099 (office). *E-mail*: marketing@eif.co.uk (office). *Website*: www.eif.co.uk (office).

LINEKER, Gary Winston, OBE; British television presenter, journalist and fmr professional footballer; *Presenter, Match of the Day, British Broadcasting Corporation*; b. 30 Nov. 1960, Leicester, Leics., England; s. of Barry Lineker and Margaret Patricia Morris Lineker (née Abbs); m. 1st Michelle Denise Cockayne 1986 (divorced 2006); four s.; m. 2nd Danielle Bux 2009; ed City of Leicester Boys' Grammar School; striker; youth player, Leicester City 1976–78, sr team 1978–85 (won Football League Second Div. 1979/80); played for Everton 1985–86 (won FA Charity Shield 1985), Barcelona 1986–89 (won Copa del Rey 1988, European Cup Winners' Cup 1989), Tottenham Hotspur 1989–92 (won FA Cup 1991, shared FA Charity Shield 1991), Nagoya Grampus Eight, Japan 1992–94 (retd); mem. England team 1984–92, scoring 48 goals in 80 appearances (won Rous Cup 1986, 1988, 1989, 1991, England Challenge Cup 1991), rep. England World Cup, Mexico 1986, World Cup, Italy 1990, Capt. of England 1990–92; never booked in 16-year career; began working as football pundit on BBC Radio 5 Live and on BBC TV's Match of the Day, went on to present show, has also worked on other programmes; led consortium that invested in Leicester City FC, saving it from bankruptcy 2002, now Hon. Vice-Pres.; has featured in several TV commercials for Walkers Crisps 1994–; Freeman of City of Leicester 1995; Hon. MA (Leicester) 1992, (Loughborough) 1992; English league top scorer 1985, 1986, 1990, only English player to win Golden Boot Award (for scoring most goals in a World Cup) 1986, Football Writers' Asscn Player of the Year 1986, 1992, Professional Footballers' Asscn Players' Player of the Year 1986, Runner-up, European Footballer of the Year 1986, FIFA Fair Play Award 1990, Third Place, FIFA World Player of the Year 1991, inducted into English Football Hall of Fame 2003, TRIC Awards Sports Presenter/Reporter of the Year 2003, 2006, 2007, 2009, 2010, 2011, north stand of Leicester City Football Club's Walkers Stadium named in his honour, voted by Leicester City fans as club's greatest ever player in poll by Sky Sports 2009. *Television includes*: presenter, Match of the Day, BBC TV 1995–, team capt. They Think It's All Over (quiz show) 1995–2003, presenter for BBC's golf coverage, co-presenter BBC Sports Personality of the Year, presented six-part BBC series called Golden Boots 1998, co-hosted, with wife Danielle, series of BBC's Northern Exposure 2009, main presenter of London Olympics for the BBC 2012. *Leisure interests*: cricket, golf, snooker. *Address*: c/o Diana van Bunnens, Jon Holmes Media Ltd, 3 Wine Office Court, London, EC4A 3BY, England (office). *Telephone*: (1582) 469233 (office). *E-mail*: diana@jonholmesmedia.com (office). *Website*: www.jonholmesmedia.com (office).

LING, Jiefang, (Er Yuehe); Chinese writer; b. Oct. 1945, Xiyang, Shanxi Prov.; Chair. Nanyang Literary and Art Circles 1985–; Vice-Chair. He'nan Prov. Asscn of Writers 1996–; Dean Zhengzhu Univ.; Deputy, 11th NPC 2008–13; Nat. Achievement by Self-Study Medal 1996, Nat. Wuyi Labour Medal 1998. *Publications*: The Great Emperor Kangwi (four vols), Emperor Yongzheng (three vols, Nat. Excellent Novel 1997), Emperor Qianlong (six vols). *Leisure interests*: chess, card games. *Address*: 13 South Square Street, Nanyang 473000, He'nan Province (office); Literary and Art Circles of Wolong District, Nanyang 473000, He'nan Province, People's Republic of China (home). *Telephone*: (377) 3161798 (office); (377) 3219098 (home). *Fax*: (377) 3219098 (home).

LING, Jihua, MBA; Chinese party official; *Head, CCP Central Committee United Front Work Department*; b. 1956, Shanxi Prov.; m. Gu Liping; ed China Youth Univ. for Political Sciences, Beijing, Hunan Univ.; joined CCP 1976; Cadre, Propaganda Dept, Communist Youth League of China (CYLC) Cen. Cttee 1979–83, Deputy Dir 1985–88, Dir 1994–95; Dir Gen. Office, CYLC Cen. Cttee Secr. 1988–90, Deputy Dir-Gen. 1990–94; Ed.-in-Chief, Youth League Journal 1990–94; Deputy Dir CCP Cen. Cttee Investigation and Research Office 1997–99, Dir 1999–2003, Dir, CCP Cen. Cttee Research Office 1998–2007, Deputy Dir, CCP Cen. Cttee Org. Dept 2000–12, Dir CCP Cen. Cttee Gen. Office 2007–12; Alt. mem. 16th CCP Cen. Cttee 2002–07, mem. 17th CCP Cen. Cttee 2007–12, also mem. 17th CCP Cen. Cttee Politburo Secr. 2007–12, mem. 18th CCP Cen. Cttee 2012–, also Head, CCP Cen. Cttee United Front Work Dept 2012–; Vice-Chair. 12th CPPCC Nat. Cttee 2013–. *Address*: United Front Work Department, Chinese Communist Party, Quanguo Renmin Diabiao Dahui, Zhongguo Gongchan Dang, 1 Zhongnanhai, Beijing, People's Republic of China (office). *Website*: www.cppcc.gov.cn (office).

LING, Tun Liong Sik, MB, BS; Malaysian university administrator and fmr politician; b. 18 Sept. 1943, Kuala Kangsar, Perak; m. Datin Ee Nah Ong 1968; two c.; ed King Edward VII School, Royal Mil. Coll. and Univ. of Singapore; Parl. Sec. Ministry of Local Govt and Fed. Territory 1976–77; Deputy Minister of Information 1978–82, of Finance 1982–84, of Educ. 1985–86; fmr Minister of Transport; Deputy Pres. Malaysian Chinese Asscn 1985–87, Pres. 1987–2003; currently Chair. Univ. Council, Tunku Abdul Rahman Univ. *Leisure interests*: reading, golf. *Address*: Office of the Chairman, Tunku Abdul Rahman University, 13, Jalan 13/6, 46200, Petaling Jaya, Selangor, Malaysia (office). *Telephone*: (3) 79582628 (office). *Fax*: (3) 79561923 (office). *E-mail*: info@utar.edu.my (office). *Website*: www.utar .edu.my (office).

LING, Sergei Stepanovich; Belarusian politician, diplomatist and agronomist; *Chairman, State Committee on Economics and Planning*; b. 7 May 1937; m.; three c.; ed Belarus Agricultural Acad., Higher CPSU School, CPSU Cen. Cttee; agronomist sovkhoz, Lesnoye Kopylsk Dist, Chief Agronomist Sovkhoz, Krynitsa Kopylsk Dist, Chief Agronomist, Deputy Dir Lyuban Production Co., Chief Soligorsk Production Agric. Admin; Deputy Chair. then Chair. Slutsk Dist Exec. Cttee, Sec. Smolevichi Dist CPSU Cttee 1960–72; Chief Agric. Div., Sec. Minsk Regional Belarus CP Cttee 1972–82; First Deputy Chair. then Chair. Exec. Cttee Minsk Regional Soviet 1982–86; Chair. Belarus State Cttee on Prices, Deputy Chair. State Planning Cttee 1986–90; Head Agric. Div., Sec. Cen. Cttee Belarus CP 1990–91; Deputy Chair. Belarus Council of Ministers; Chair. State Cttee on Econs and Planning 1991–; Deputy Prime Minister of Belarus 1994–96, Acting Prime Minister 1996–97, Prime Minister 1997–2000; Amb. and Perm. Rep. to UN 2000–02. *Address*: Ministry of Economy, 220050 Minsk, vul. Bersona 14, Belarus. *Telephone*: (17) 200-53-16. *Fax*: (17) 200-37-77. *E-mail*: minec@economy.gov.by. *Website*: www.economy.gov.by.

LINGFIELD, Baron (Life Peer), cr. 2010, of Lingfield in the County of Surrey; **Robert George Alexander Balchin**, Kt; English educationalist; *Chairman, The Chartered Institution for Further Education;* b. 31 July 1942, Dulverton, Somerset; m. Jennifer Kinlay; two s. (one deceased); ed Bec School, Univ. of London, Univ. of Hull; teacher 1964–69; researcher, Inst. of Educ., Univ. of Hull 1969–71; Chair. Grant-Maintained Schools Centre (fmrly Foundation) 1989–99, Centre for Educ. Man. (now Centre for Educ. and Finance Man.) 1995–; Asst Dir-Gen. St John Ambulance 1982–84, Dir-Gen. 1984–90; Founding Chair. Balchin Family Soc. 1993–; Chair. St John Nat. Schools Project 1990–95, ARNI Inst. 2000–, Educ. Comm. 2003–10, Maritime Heritage Foundation 2012–; Pres. English Schools Orchestra 1991–, League of Mercy 1999–; mem. Court of Univ. of Leeds 1995–2001, Council of Goldsmiths Coll., London 1997–2005 (Deputy Chair. 1999–2005); Pro-Chancellor Brunel Univ. 2006–12; mem. Council Imperial Soc. of Kts Bachelor 1995–, Kt Registrar 1998–2006, Kt Prin. 2006–12, Kt Pres. 2012–; mem. Funding Agency for Schools 1994–97; Deputy Patron Nat. Asscn for Gifted Children 1998–; DL of Greater London 2001–; Liveryman, Worshipful Co. of Goldsmiths 1987 (Freeman 1981); Hon. Fellow, Coll. of Preceptors 1987 (Fellow 1971), Hon. Fellow, Heraldry Soc. 1987, Hon. FCGI 1997; Hon. Col, Humberside and S Yorks. Army Cadet Force 2004–12; KStJ 1984, Commdr's Cross (Pro Merito Melitensi SMOM) 1987; Hon. DLitt (Hull) 2006, Hon. EdD (Brunel) 2013. *Publications:* Emergency Aid in Schools 1984, Choosing a State School (co-author) 1989), Emergency Aid at Work (co-author) 1990, Lingfield Report on Professionalism in Further Education (Dept of Business, Innovation and Skills) 2012; numerous articles on education and politics. *Leisure interest:* restoring an ancient house. *Address:* House of Lords, Westminster, London, SW1A 0PW, England (office). *Telephone:* (20) 7219-5353 (office). *Fax:* (20) 7219-5979 (office).

LINGHU, An; Chinese politician; *Deputy Auditor-General, National Audit Office;* b. Oct. 1946, Pinglu Co., Shanxi Prov.; ed Beijing Eng Inst.; joined CCP 1965; fmr Deputy Dir City Machin-Building Industry Bureau, Dalian City, Liaoning Prov., City Instrument, Meter and Electronics Bureau, Dalian City (later Deputy Gen. Man.); fmr Deputy Sec. CCP Dalian City Cttee; fmr Chair. Dalian Fed. of Trade Unions; fmr Vice-Chair. Comm. for Restructuring the Economy, Dalian City; Exec. Vice-Mayor Dalian City 1988; fmr mem. CCP Standing Cttee, Dalian City Cttee; fmr Dir Gen. Office, People's Govt, Dalian City; fmr Dir Retired Cadres Bureau, Ministry of Labour; Vice-Minister of Labour 1989–93; Deputy Sec. CCP Yunnan Prov. Cttee 1993–97, Sec. 1997–2001; Chair. Yunnan Prov. People's Political Consultative Conf. 1998–2001; Deputy Auditor-Gen. Nat. Audit Office 2001–; mem. 15th CCP Cen. Cttee 1997–2002; Del., 14th CCP Nat. Congress 1992–97. *Address:* National Audit Office of China, 1 Beiluyuan, Zhanlan Road, Beijing, 100830 People's Republic of China. *Telephone:* (10) 68301520 (office). *E-mail:* cnao@audit.gov.cn (office).

LINGWOOD, James Peter Boyce, MBE; British gallery curator; *Co-Director, Artangel;* b. 28 May 1959; Exhbns Curator, Inst. of Contemporary Arts, London 1986–90; ind. curator 1991–; Co-Dir, with Michael Morris, Artangel 1991–, Artangel Media Ltd 2000–; has curated exhbns for nat. and int. arts insts, including Juan Muñoz's Double Bind in Tate Modern's Turbine Hall 2001, Field Trips – Robert Smithson and Bernd and Hilla Becher at Museu Serralves, Porto and Douglas Gordon's exhbn What Have I Done at Hayward Gallery, London 2002, Susan Hiller's exhbn at Baltic, Gateshead 2004; has organized major survey exhbns with Vija Celmins, Juliao Sarmento, Thomas Struth and Thomas Schütte; Trustee, Paul Hamlyn Foundation 2003–, Art Fund 2008–, Cubitt Studios, London; mem. Int. Advisory Bd Museu Serralves, Porto, Atelier Calder, Saché, France, Capc, Bordeaux. *Publications include:* Juan Muñoz: Double Bind at Tate Modern 2001, Robert Smithson, Bernd and Hilla Becher: Field Trips 2001, Off Limits – 40 Artangel Projects 2002, Susan Hiller: Recall 2004. *Address:* Artangel, 31 Eyre Street Hill, London, EC1R 5EW, England (office). *Telephone:* (20) 7713-1400 (office). *Fax:* (20) 7713-1401 (office). *E-mail:* info@artangel.org.uk (office). *Website:* www.artangel.org.uk (office).

LINI VANUAROROA, Ham; Ni-Vanuatu politician; b. 8 Dec. 1951; m. Ruth Lini; mem. Nat. United Party (NUP), Pres. 1999–; Deputy Prime Minister 2003–04, also Minister of Home Affairs, of Infrastructure and Public Utilities and of Civil Aviation; Prime Minister of Vanuatu 2004–08; Minister of Public Works and Utilities 2008, Deputy Prime Minister and Minister of Justice and Social Welfare 2008–09, Deputy Prime Minister and Minister of Trade, Industry and Tourism 2010–11, 2011–13. *Address:* c/o Ministry of Trade, Industry and Tourism, POB 9056, Port Vila, Vanuatu.

LINIĆ, Slavko; Croatian economist and politician; b. 19 Sept. 1949, Grobnik (Čavle); ed Univ. of Rijeka; began career with Avtotehna, Ljubljana 1972; worked in Viktor Lenac naval shipyard, Rijeka 1974–76; Chief Financial Officer, Gradšped 1976–78; Chief Financial Officer, Kvarnertrans 1979; Dir of Financial Accounting Services, Rijeka Oil Refinery 1979–90; Mayor, City of Rijeka 1990–2000; mem. Sabor (Parl.) 1997–2000, 2004–, mem. Tourism Cttee, Maritime Affairs Cttee, Transportation and Communications Cttee, Planning and Building Cttee; Deputy Prime Minister 2000–03, Minister of Finance 2011–14; mem. Social Democratic Party of Croatia (Socijaldemokratska partija Hrvatske) 1990–. *Leisure interest:* skiing. *Address:* c/o Ministry of Finance, 10000 Zagreb, ul. Katančićeva 5, Croatia (office).

LINK, Christoph, DJur; German/Austrian legal scholar and academic; *Professor Emeritus of State, Administration and Church Law, University of Erlangen;* b. 13 June 1933, Dresden; s. of late Hellmuth Link and of Gerda Link; m. 1st Eva Link 1957; m. 2nd Sibylle Obermayer 1991; two s. one d.; ed Kreuzschule, Dresden and Univs of Marburg, Cologne and Munich; Prof. Vienna 1971–77, Salzburg 1977–79, Hon. Prof. 1979–, Göttingen 1979–86; Prof. of State Admin and Church Law, Univ. of Erlangen 1986, now Prof. Emer.; Dir Hans-Liermann-Inst. für Kirchenrecht 1986–2001; mem. Akad. der Wissenschaften, Göttingen; DTheol hc (Vienna), (Tübingen); Österreichisches Ehrenkreuz für Wissenschaft und Kunst, 1st Klasse 2004. *Publications:* Die Grundlagen der Kirchenverfassung im lutherischen Konfessionalismus des 19ten Jahrhunderts 1966, Herrschaftsordnung und bürgerliche Freiheit 1979, Hugo Grotius als Staatsdenker 1983, Kirchen und privater Rundfunk (with A. Pahlke) 1985, Staat und Kirche in der neueren deutschen Geschichte 2000, Kirchliche Rechtsgeschichte 2009. *Address:* Hans-Liermann-Institut für Kirchenrecht, 91054 Erlangen, Hindenburgstrasse 34 (office); Ruehlstrasse 35, 91054 Erlangen, Germany (home). *Telephone:* (9131)

8522242 (office); (9131) 209335 (home). *Fax:* (9131) 8524064 (office); (9131) 534566 (home). *E-mail:* hli@jura.uni-erlangen.de (office); linkerta@t-online.de (home). *Website:* www.jura.uni-erlangen.de (office).

LINKEVIČIUS, Linas Antanas; Lithuanian politician and diplomatist; *Minister of Foreign Affairs;* b. 6 Jan. 1961, Vilnius; m. Danguolė Linkevičienė 1982; two d.; ed Kaunas Polytechnical Inst.; worked in technical insts 1983–92; reviewer, newspaper Tiesa 1992–93; mem. Council of Democratic Labour Party 1991–96; mem. Seimas (Parl.) 1992–96; Chair. Parl. Del. to N Atlantic Ass. 1992–93; Deputy Chair. Parl. Comm. on Foreign Affairs 1992–93; Chair. Labour Youth Union 1992–93; Observer, Lithuanian daily 'Tiesa'; Minister of Nat. Defence 1993–96, 2000–04; Amb. and Head of Lithuanian Mission to NATO and WEU 1997–99; Amb. for Special Missions, Ministry of Foreign Affairs 2004–05; Amb. and Perm. Rep. to NATO, Brussels 2005–11; Minister of Foreign Affairs Dec. 2012–; mem. Exec. Bd European Leadership Network for Multilateral Nuclear Disarmament and Non-proliferation. *Address:* Ministry of Foreign Affairs, J. Tumo-Vaižganto g. 2, Vilnius 01511, Lithuania (office). *Telephone:* (5) 236-2444 (office). *Fax:* (5) 231-3090 (office). *E-mail:* urm@urm.lt (office). *Website:* www.urm.lt (office).

LINKLATER, Richard; American film director; b. 1967; f. Detour Films, Austin, Tex.; founder and Artistic Dir Austin Film Soc. *Films:* Slacker 1991, Dazed and Confused 1993, Before Sunrise (Berlin Film Festival Silver Bear) 1995, Suburbia 1997, The Newton Boys 1998, Waking Life 2001, Tape 2001, Live from Shiva's Dance Floor 2003, School of Rock 2003, Before Sunset 2004, Bad News Bears 2005, A Scanner Darkly 2006, Fast Food Nation 2006, Me and Orson Welles 2009, Bernie 2011. *Address:* c/o Creative Artists Agency, Inc., 9830 Wilshire Blvd., Beverly Hills, CA 90212-1825, USA.

LINNANE, Anthony William, AM, PhD, DSc, FRS, FAA, FTSE; Australian biochemist and academic; *Managing Director, Centre for Molecular Biology and Medicine;* b. 17 July 1930, Sydney, NSW; s. of W. P. Linnane; m. 1st Judith Neil 1956 (divorced 1979); one s. one d.; m. 2nd Daryl Woods 1980; one s. one d.; ed Univ. of Sydney, Univ. of Wisconsin, USA; Postdoctoral Fellow, Univ. of Wisconsin 1956–58; Lecturer, then Sr Lecturer, Univ. of Sydney 1958–62; Reader, Monash Univ. 1962–65, Prof. of Biochemistry 1965–95, Prof. Emer. 1996–; Dir Centre for Molecular Biology and Medicine, Epworth Medical Centre 1984–, Man. Dir 1996–; Man. Dir Magral Ltd 2002–; Ed.-in-Chief Biochemistry and Molecular Biology International 1980–98; Visiting Prof., Univ. of Wisconsin 1967–68; Pres. Australian Biochemical Soc. 1974–76, Fed. of Asian and Oceanic Biochemical Socs 1975–77, 12th Int. Congress of Biochemistry, Perth 1982; Foundation Pres. Australian Soc. for Cellular and Molecular Gerontology 2000; Treas., Int. Union of Biochemistry and Molecular Biology 1988–97; Hon. Prof., Univ. of Melbourne 1996–; Centenary Medal of Australia 2003; Distinguished Service Award, Int. Union of Biochemistry and Molecular Biology 2000. *Publications:* over 300 scientific publs. *Leisure interests:* golf, reading, horseracing. *Address:* 24 Myrtle Road, Canterbury, Vic. 3126 (home); Centre for Molecular Biology and Medicine, Epworth Medical Centre, 185–187 Hoddle Street, Richmond, Vic. 3121, Australia (office). *Telephone:* (3) 9888-6526 (home); (3) 9426-4200 (office). *Fax:* (3) 9830-5415 (home); (3) 9426-4201 (office). *E-mail:* tlinnane@cmbm.com.au (office). *Website:* www.cmbm.com.au (office).

LINNEY, Laura, BFA; American actress; b. 5 Feb. 1964, New York, NY; m. David Adkins 1995 (divorced 2000); ed Northfield Mount Hermon School, Northwestern Univ., Brown Univ., Juilliard School; Theatre World Award 1992, Calloway Award 1994, Best Actress, Toronto Film Critics Asscn 2000, Best Actress, Nat. Soc. Film Critics 2000, Best Actress, NY Film Critics Circle 2000, Best Actress, Boston Soc. Film Critics 2000, Emmy Award, Outstanding Lead Actress 2002, Best Supporting Actress, Nat. Bd of Review 2004, Desert Palm Award for Best Actress, Palm Springs Int. Film Festival 2004, Emmy Award, Best Guest Actress in a Comedy Series 2004, Special Civil Rights Award, Pride Awards 2004, Best Supporting Actress, Broadcast Film Critics Asscn 2004. *Plays include:* The Seagull, Six Degrees of Separation, Sight Unseen, Hedda Gabler, Holiday 1995, Honour 1998. *Films include:* Lorenzo's Oil 1992, Dave 1993, Blind Spot 1993, Searching for Bobby Fischer 1993, A Simple Twist of Fate 1994, Congo 1995, Primal Fear 1996, Absolute Power 1997, The Truman Show 1998, You Can Count on Me 2000, The House of Mirth 2000, Lush 2000, Maze 2000, Running Mates 2000, The Laramie Project 2001, The Mothman Prophecies 2002, The Life of David Gale 2003, Mystic River 2003, Love, Actually 2003, P.S. 2004, Kinsey 2004, The Squid and the Whale 2005, The Exorcism of Emily Rose 2005, Driving Lessons 2006, Jindabyne 2006, The Hottest State 2006, Man of the Year 2006, The Savages 2007, Breach 2007, The Nanny Diaries 2007, The Other Man 2008, The City of Your Final Destination 2009, Sympathy for Delicious 2010, Morning 2010, The Details 2011, Hyde Park on Hudson 2012, The Fifth Estate 2013. *Television includes:* Armistead Maupin's Tales of the City 1993, Class of '61 1993, More Tales of the City 1998, Love Letters 1999, Wild Iris 2001, Further Tales of the City 2002, Frasier (series) 2003–04, John Adams (mini-series, HBO) (Golden Globe Award for Best Performance by an Actress in a Mini-Series 2009) 2008–, The Big C (series) (Golden Globe Award for Best Performance by an Actress in a TV Series – Comedy or Musical 2011, Emmy Award for Best Actress in a mini-series 2013) 2010–13. *Address:* c/o Toni Howard, ICM, Constellation Boulevard, Los Angeles, CA 90067, USA (office). *Telephone:* (310) 550-4000 (office). *Website:* www.icmtalent.com (office).

LINTOTAWELA, Vivien; Sri Lankan business executive; Dir John Keells Holdings Ltd 1986–, Deputy Chair. 1997–2000, Chair. 2000–05; Chair. Ceylon Cold Stores (subsidiary of John Keells Holdings Ltd); Vice-Chair. Employers' Fed. of Sri Lanka. *Address:* c/o John Keells Holdings Ltd, 130 Glennie Street, PO Box 76, Colombo 2, Sri Lanka.

LIONS, Pierre-Louis, DèsSc; French mathematician and academic; *Professor of Mathematics, Collège de France;* b. 11 Aug. 1956, Grasse, Alpes-Maritime; s. of Jacques-Louis Lions and Andrée Olivier; m. Lila Laurenti 1979; one s.; ed Lycée Pasteur and Lycée Louis-le-Grand, Paris, Ecole Normale Supérieure, Paris, Univ. of Paris VI; Researcher, CNRS 1979–81, Dir of Research 1995–; Prof. of Math., Univ. of Paris-Dauphine 1981–2002; Prof. of Applied Math., Ecole Polytechnique, Palaiseau 1992–; Prof., Collège de France 2002–; mem Acad. des sciences, Paris, Naples Acad., Academia Europaea; mem. Editorial Bd 25 int. journals; Chevalier, Légion d'honneur; Dr hc (Heriot-Watt Univ., Edinburgh, UK, Univ. of Hong Kong); Doistau-Blutet Foundation Prize, Acad. des sciences 1986, IBM Prize 1987, Philip

Morris Prize 1991, Ampère Prize, Acad. des sciences 1992, Fields Medal, Int. Congress of Mathematicians, Zürich 1994, Prix d'équipe Institut de Finance Europlace 2003, Thomson Prize 2004. *Publications:* numerous articles in math. journals on theory of nonlinear partial differential equations. *Leisure interests:* cinema, reading, rugby, swimming. *Address:* (office); Collège de France, 11 place Marcelin Berthelot, 75005 Paris, France (office). *Telephone:* 1-44-27-12-11 (office). *Fax:* 1-44-05-49-08 (office). *E-mail:* lions@dmi.ens.fr (office). *Website:* www.college-de-france.fr (office).

LIOTTA, Ray, BFA; American actor; b. 18 Dec. 1955, Newark, NJ; s. of Alfred Liotta and Mary Liotta; m. Michelle Grace 1997; one d.; ed Univ. of Miami. *Films:* The Lonely Lady 1983, Something Wild 1986, Arena Brains 1987, Dominick and Eugene 1988, Field of Dreams 1989, Goodfellas 1990, Article 99 1992, Unlawful Entry 1992, No Escape 1994, Corrina, Corrina 1994, Operation Dumbo Drop 1995, Unforgettable 1996, Turbulence 1997, Phoenix 1997, Copland 1997, The Rat Pack 1998, Forever Mine 1999, Muppets From Space 1999, Blow 2001, Heartbreakers 2001, Hannibal 2001, John Q. 2002, A Rumor of Angels 2002, Narc 2002, Identity 2003, Last Shot 2004, Control 2004, Happy Endings 2005, Slow Burn 2005, Revolver 2005, Take the Lead 2006, Even Money 2006, Local Color 2006, Comeback Season 2006, Smokin' Aces 2006, Wild Hogs 2007, Battle in Seattle 2007, Bee Movie (voice) 2007, Hero Wanted 2008, Chasing 3000 2008, La Linea 2008, Powder Blue 2009, Crossing Over 2009, Observe and Report 2009, Youth in Revolt 2010, Date Night 2010, The River Sorrow 2010, Killing Them Softly 2012. *Television appearances include:* Another World, NBC 1978–80, Hardhat & Legs (CBS movie) 1980, Crazy Times (ABC pilot) 1981, Casablanca, NBC 1983, Our Family Honor, NBC 1985–86, Women & Men 2–In Love There Are No Rules 1991, The Rat Pack 1998, Point of Origin 2002, Smith (series) 2006. *Address:* c/o Endeavor Talent Agency, 9701 Wilshire Boulevard, 10th Floor, Beverly Hills, CA 90212, USA.

LIPENGA, Ken, BEd, PhB; Malawi journalist, editor and politician; b. 14 Feb. 1952; ed Univ. of Malawi, Univ. of New Brunswick; Ed.-in-Chief Blantyre Newspapers Ltd and Gen. Man. Blantyre Printing and Publishing Co. 1986–92; Founding Ed.-in-Chief The Malawi Nation 1993–95; Minister of Educ., Sports and Culture 1999–2004, of Labour and Vocational Training 2005–06, Deputy Minister of Finance 2006–08, Minister of Econ. Planning and Devt 2008–11, of Finance and Devt Planning 2011–13; mem. Parl. for Phalombe East 2004–; mem. Democratic Progressive Party. *Address:* c/o Ministry of Finance and Development Planning, Capital Hill, POB 30049, Lilongwe 3, Malawi (office).

LIPIČ, Maj.-Gen. Ladislav, BSc; Slovenian army officer; b. 30 Nov. 1951, Murska Sobota; ed Univ. of Ljubljana; Asst for Organizational and Mobilization Affairs, Murska Sobota Municipal Territorial Defence HQ 1987–90; Chief of Logistics, Territorial Defence Regional Command (Vzhodna Stajerska Region) 1990–94, Commdr 1994–97; Chief of Logistics, Slovenian Armed Forces Gen. Staff 1997–2000, Deputy Chief of Gen. Staff 2000–01, Chief of Gen. Staff 2001–06; Co-Dir CAE 98 Exercise (jt NATO and PfP member countries exercise), Slovenia 1998; apptd Brig. 1998, Maj.-Gen. 2003; guest lecturer, Faculty of Social Sciences, Univ. of Ljubljana. *Address:* c/o Ministry of Defence, General Staff, Kardeljeva ploščad 25, 1000 Ljubljana, Slovenia (office).

LIPMAN, David J., BA, MD; American biologist, biochemist and academic; *Director, National Center for Biotechnology Information, National Institutes of Health;* ed Brown Univ., Univ. at Buffalo, State Univ. of NY; Founding Dir Nat. Center for Biotechnology Information, Nat. Library of Medicine, NIH, Bethesda, Md 1989–; cr. GenBank (world's largest public database of DNA data), introduced PubMed Central to provide free, permanent electronic access to articles from participating journals 2000; one of the originators of the Influenza Genome Sequencing Project; Ed.-in-Chief Biology Direct online journal; mem. NAS 2005; Fellow, American Coll. of Medical Informatics 2001; Asscn of Biomolecular Resource Facilities Award 1996, Accomplishment by a Sr Scientist Award, Int. Soc. for Computational Biology 2004. *Publications:* numerous articles in scientific journals on sequence comparison methods, comparative genomics and molecular evolution. *Address:* National Center for Biotechnology Information, Building 38A, Room N807, 8600 Rockville Pike MSC 6075, Bethesda, MD 20894-6075, USA (office). *Telephone:* (301) 496-2475 (office). *Fax:* (301) 480-2288 (office). *E-mail:* lipman@ncbi.nlm.nih.gov (office). *Website:* www.ncbi.nlm.nih.gov/research/staff/lipman (office).

LIPP, Robert I., BA, MBA, JD; American insurance industry executive; *Senior Advisor, Stone Point Capital LLC;* m. 1st Bari Lipp (deceased); m. 2nd Martha Berman; five c.; ed Williams Coll., Harvard Univ., New York Univ.; various positions with Chemical NY Corpn (now JPMorgan Chase & Co.) 1963–86; joined Citigroup 1986, Chair. and CEO CitiFinancial Credit Co. 1991–93, Co-Chair. Citigroup Inc. 1998–99, Vice-Chair. and mem. Office of Chair. 2000, Chair. and CEO Global Consumer Business 1999–2000; Vice-Chair. and Dir Travelers Group Inc. 1991–98; Chair. and CEO Travelers Insurance Group Inc. 1993–2000; CEO and Pres. Travelers Insurance Group Holdings Inc. 1996–98, Chair. 1996–2000, 2001, Chair. and CEO Travelers Property Casualty Corpn 2001–04, Chair. The St Paul Travelers Cos Inc. (following merger of The St Paul Co. and Travelers Insurance Group 2004) 2004–05; Sr Advisor, Brysam Global Partners, LLC 2008–09; Sr Advisor, Stone Point Capital LLC and Exec. Chair. StoneRiver Group, LP 2009–; mem. Bd of Dirs The Travelers Cos, Inc. 2001–10, Accenture Ltd 2001–, Bank One Corpn 2003–, JPMorgan Chase & Co. 2005–08, GENEX Services, Inc.; Pres. New York City Ballet; Chair. Bd Trustees, Williams Coll.; Founder Bari Lipp Foundation; Treas. Massachusetts Museum of Contemporary Art; Trustee Carnegie Hall. *Address:* Stone Point Capital LLC, 20 Horseneck Lane, Greenwich, CT 06830-6327, USA (office). *Telephone:* (203) 862-2900 (office). *Fax:* (203) 625-8357 (office). *E-mail:* info@stonepoint.com (office). *Website:* www.stonepoint.com (office); www.stoneriver.com (office).

LIPPARD, Stephen J., BA, PhD, MRIA; American chemist and academic; *Arthur Amos Noyes Professor of Chemistry, Massachusetts Institute of Technology;* b. 12 Oct. 1940, Pittsburgh, Pa; m. Judith Ann Lippard 1964 (died 2013); two s.; ed Haverford Coll., Haverford, Pa, Massachusetts Inst. of Tech.; Asst Prof. of Chem., Columbia Univ. 1966–69, Assoc. Prof. 1969–72, Prof. 1972–82; Prof. of Chem., MIT 1983–89, Arthur Amos Noyes Prof. of Chem. 1989–, Head, Dept of Chem. 1995–; mem. NAS 1989, Nat. Inst. of Medicine 1993, Italian Chemical Soc. 1996, Deutsche

Akad. der Naturforscher Leopoldina 2004; Scientific mem. Max-Planck-Gesellschaft 1996–; Fellow, Alfred P. Sloan Foundation 1968–70, John Simon Guggenheim Foundation 1972–, John E. Fogarty Int. Center 1979–, AAAS 1980–, American Acad. of Arts and Sciences 1986–; Hon. Fellow, Woodrow Wilson Foundation 1962, Hon. mem. Italian Chemical Soc. 1996; Hon. DSc (Texas A&M Univ.) 1995, (Haverford Coll.) 2000; Int. Precious Metals Inst. Henry J. Albert Award 1985, ACS Award in Inorganic Chem. 1987, Remsen Award 1987, Alexander von Humboldt Sr US Scientist Award 1988, John C. Bailar, Jr Award, Univ. of Illinois 1993, ACS Award for Distinguished Service in Inorganic Chem. 1994, William H. Nichols Medal 1995, Frontiers in Biological Chem. Award, Max-Planck-Institut für Strahlenchemie 1995, Basolo Medal 2002, Richards Medal 2002, ACS Alfred Bader Award in Bio-organic or Bio-inorganic Chem. 2004, Nat. Medal of Science 2004, Linus Pauling Medal 2009, Breslow Award for Achievement in Biomimetic Chem. 2010, RSC Centenary Medal 2010, Sacconi Medal, Italian Chemical Soc. 2012, James R. Killian Jr Faculty Achievement Award, MIT 2013, ACS Priestley Medal 2014. *Leisure interests:* playing the harpsichord, supporting Boston Red Sox baseball team. *Address:* Department of Chemistry, Massachusetts Institute of Technology, Room 18-498, Cambridge, MA 02139, USA (office). *Telephone:* (617) 253-1892 (office). *Fax:* (617) 258-8150 (office). *E-mail:* lippard@mit.edu (office). *Website:* web.mit.edu/lippardlab (office); chemistry.mit.edu/people/lippard-stephen (office).

LIPPE, Stefan, PhD; German insurance industry executive; *CEO, Swiss Reinsurance Company (Swiss Re);* b. 1955; ed Univ. of Mannheim; joined Bavarian Re 1983, Head of Non-proportional Underwriting Dept 1986, Deputy Mem. Bd of Dirs 1988–91, Full Mem. Bd of Dirs 1991–93, Chair. Bd of Man. 1993, mem. Exec. Cttee Swiss Reinsurance Co. (Swiss Re; as Head of Bavarian Re Group) 1995–, Head of Property and Casualty Business Group, Swiss Re Co. 2001–05, Head of Reinsurance Products 2005–08, COO and Deputy CEO 2008–09, CEO 2009–; Kurt Hamann Foundation Prize. *Address:* Swiss Reinsurance Co., Mythenquai 50/60, 8022 Zürich, Switzerland (office). *Telephone:* (43) 285-21-21 (office). *Fax:* (43) 285-29-99 (office). *E-mail:* stefan_lippe@swissre.com (office). *Website:* www.swissre.com (office).

LIPPONEN, Paavo Tapio, MA; Finnish writer, international affairs scholar, business consultant and fmr politician; b. 23 April 1941, Turtola (now Pello); s. of Orvo Lipponen and Hilkka Lipponen; m. Päivi Lipponen 1998; three d.; ed Univ. of Helsinki, Dartmouth Coll., USA; journalist 1963–67; Research and Int. Affairs Sec. and Head Political Section Finnish Social Democratic Party (SDP) 1967–79; Pvt. Sec. (Special Political Adviser) to Prime Minister 1979–82; Political Sec. to Minister of Labour 1983; Man. Dir Viestintä Teema Oy 1988–93; Head Finnish Inst. of Int. Affairs 1989–91; Chair. Supervisory Bd Outokumpu Oy 1989–90; mem. Helsinki City Council 1985–95; MP 1983–87, 1991–2007 (retd); mem. SDP Party Cttee 1987–90, Chair. SDP Helsinki Dist 1985–92, Chair. of SDP 1993–2005; Speaker of Parl. March–April 1995, 2003–07; Prime Minister of Finland 1995–2003; SDP cand. (unsuccessful) in presidential election 2012; writer-columnist; consultant to Pohjolan Voima Oy (Finland) on nuclear energy 2007–, to Nord Stream 2008–; Dr hc (Dartmouth Coll., USA) 1997, (Finlandia Univ.) 2000, (Acad. of Arts and Design, Helsinki) 2008, (Abo Akademi, Turku) 2007, (Univ. of Joensuu) 2007; Theodor Aue Prize 2007, Konstsamfundet 2008. *Publications:* Muutoksen suunta 1986, Kohti Eurooppaa 2001, Järki voittaa 2008, Muistelmat I 2009. *Leisure interests:* architecture, swimming. *E-mail:* paavo.t.lipponen@gmail.com.

LIPŠIC, Daniel, LLM, JUDr; Slovak politician and lawyer; b. 8 July 1973, Bratislava; m. Beáta Oravcová; ed Comenius Univ., Bratislava, Harvard Law School, USA; Chair. Civil Democratic Youth 1991–95; Project Leader Advisory Centre for Slovak Businesses and Banks 1996–97; with Dist Mil. Prosecutor, Prešov 1997–98; Ernest Valko legal firm 1998; Head, Office of Ministry of Justice 1998–2002; Deputy Prime Minister and Minister of Justice 2002–06; mem. Nat. Council of the Slovak Repub. 2006–10; Minister of the Interior 2010–12; Deputy Chair. for Internal Policy, Christian Democratic Movt; mem. Council of Experts, Inst. of Bankruptcy Law 1997–. *Address:* c/o Ministry of the Interior, Pribinova 2, 812 72 Bratislava, Slovakia.

LIPSKA, Ewa; Polish poet; b. 8 Oct. 1945, Kraków; ed Acad. of Fine Arts, Kraków; Co-Ed. Pismo 1981–83; mem. editorial Bd Dekada Literacka 1990–92; First Sec., Polish Embassy, Vienna 1991–95, Adviser 1995–97; Deputy Dir Polish Inst., Vienna 1991–95, Dir 1995–97; mem. Asscn of Polish Writers, Polish and Austrian PEN Club; Koscielscy Foundation Award (Switzerland) 1973, Robert Graves PEN Club Award 1979, Ind. Foundation for Polish Culture, Polcul Foundation Award 1990, PEN Club Award 1992, Alfred Jurzykowski Foundation Award (USA) 1993, City of Kraków Award 1995, Andrzej Bursa Award 1997, Literary Laurel 2002, Samuel Bogumil Linde Twin Cities Göttingen-Toruń 2007, Zlatni Kljuc Smedereva 2009, Naim Frasheri Prize 2010, Cape of Good Hope Award, Ministry of Culture, Repub. of Kosovo 2010, Gdynia Literary Award 2011. *Publications include:* Wiersze (Poems) 1967, Drugi zbiór wierszy (Second Vol. of Poems) 1970, Trzeci zbiór wierszy (Third Vol. of Poems) 1972, Czwarty zbiór wierszy (Fourth Vol. of Poems) 1974, Piaty zbiór wierszy (Fifth Vol. of Poems) 1978, Zywa smierc (Living Death) 1979, Dom Spokojnej Mlodosci (House of the Quiet Youth) 1979, Nie o smierc tutaj chodzi, lecz o bialy kordonek 1982, Utwory wybrane (Selected Poems) 1986, Przechowalnia ciemnosci 1985, Strefa ograniczonego postoju 1990, Wakacje Mizantropa (Misanthrope's Holidays) 1993, Stypendysci czasu 1994, Wspólnicy zielonego wiataczka 1996, Ludzie dla poczatkujacych (People for Beginners) 1997, Zycie zastepcze (Substitute Life) (Polish-German edition 1998), Godziny poza godzinami (After-hours Hours) 1999, Biale truskawki (White Strawberries) 2000, Sklepy zoologiczne (Pet Shops) 2001, Uwaga stopien 2002, Ja 2003, Gdzie indziej 2005, Drzazga 2006, Pomarańcza Newtona 2007, Sefer (prose) 2009; selections of poems translated include Versei (Hungary) 1979, Vernisaz (Czechoslovakia) 1979, Such Times (Canada) 1981, Huis voor een vredige jeugd 1982, Auf den Dächern der Mausoleen (Germany) 1983, En misantrops ferie (Denmark) 1990, Meine Zeit. Mein Leib. Mein Leben (Austria) 1990, Poet? Criminal? Madman? (UK) 1991, Wakancitie na mizantropa (Bulgaria) 1994, Zon (Sweden) 1997, Stipendisti Wremiena (Yugoslavia) 1998, Mennesker for Begyndere (Denmark) 1999, Mesohu me vdekjen (Albania) 2000, Menseen voor beginners (Netherlands) 2000, Sedemnast cervenych vevericiek (Slovakia) 2001,

Selection of Poems (Israel) 2001, Fresas Blancas (Spain) 2001, Pet Shops (UK) 2002.

LIPSKY, John, BA, MA, PhD; American academic, business executive and fmr international organization official; *Distinguished Visiting Scholar, Paul H. Nitze School of Advanced International Studies, Johns Hopkins University;* b. 1947; s. of Abbott Lipsky and Joan Lipsky; m.; one s. two d.; ed Wesleyan and Stanford Univs; spent a decade at IMF, where he helped manage exchange rate surveillance procedure and analysed devts in int. capital market, also participated in negotiations with several mem. countries and served as IMF Resident Rep. in Chile 1978–80; joined Salomon Brothers Inc. 1984, directed European Econ. and Market Analysis Group, London, UK 1989–92, Chief Economist 1992–97; Chief Economist and Dir of Research, Chase Manhattan Bank 1997; fmr Chief Economist, JPMorgan, later Vice-Chair. JPMorgan Investment Bank; Chair. Financial Sector Review Group, IMF 2000, First Deputy Man. Dir IMF 2006–11, Acting Man. Dir (following resignation of Dominique Strauss-Kahn) May–July 2011, Special Advisor to Man. Dir Sept.–Nov. 2011; Distinguished Visiting Scholar, Paul H. Nitze School Advanced International Studies, Johns Hopkins Univ. 2012–; Co-Dir Program on Global Economy, Aspen Inst.; mem. Bd of Dirs HSBC Holdings PLC 2012–, Nat. Bureau of Econ. Research; Trustee, Stanford Inst. for Econ. Policy Research. *Address:* Paul H. Nitze School of Advanced International Studies, Johns Hopkins University, 1740 Massachusetts Aveue, NW, Washington, DC 20036, USA (office). *Telephone:* (202) 663-5600 (office). *Fax:* (202) 663-5656 (office). *Website:* www.sais-jhu.edu (office).

LIPSTOK, Andres; Estonian fmr central banker; b. 6 Feb. 1957, Haapsalu; m.; one s. one d.; ed Haapsalu Secondary School No. 1, Univ. of Tartu; Deputy Head 1980–83, Head 1983–86, Finance Dept of the Exec. Cttee of Haapsalu District; Chair. Planning Comm. 1986–89; Deputy Minister of Finance of Estonian SSR 1989; mem. Council of Lääne Co. 1989–93, Gov. Lääne Co. 1989–94; Minister of Finance 1994–95, of Econ. Affairs 1995–96; mem. Riigikogu (Parl.) 1995–2005; Gov. Bank of Estonia 2005–12; mem. Estonian Liberal Democratic Party 1993–94, Estonian Reform Party 1994–2005, Congress of Estonia, Lions Club 1992; Vice-Pres. Estonian Olympic Cttee 2004–08; IV Class Order of the Nat. Coat of Arms. *Address:* c/o Bank of Estonia (Eesti Pank), Estonia pst. 13, Tallinn 15095, Estonia. *E-mail:* info@eestipank.ee.

LIPTON, David, BA, MA, PhD; American economist, government official and international organization official; *First Deputy Managing Director, International Monetary Fund;* ed Wesleyan Univ., Harvard Univ.; economist, IMF, Washington, DC 1981–89; econ. advisor (with Harvard Univ. Prof. Jeffrey Sachs) to govts of Russia, Poland, Slovenia 1989–92; Fellow, Woodrow Wilson Center of Scholars 1992–93; Under-Sec. for Int. Affairs, US Treasury Dept, Washington, DC 1993–98; Man. Dir Moore Capital Strategy Group, Moore Capital Management 2000–05; Man. Dir and Head of Global Country Risk Man. Citigroup 2005–08; Special Asst to US President Obama, Sr Dir for Int. Econ. Affairs, Nat. Econ. Council and Nat. Security Council, The White House 2008–11; Special Advisor to Man. Dir, IMF July–Nov. 2011, First Deputy Man. Dir 2011–; mem. Nat. Advisory Bd, Merage Foundation for the American Dream. *Address:* International Monetary Fund, 700 19th Street, NW, Washington, DC 20431, USA (office). *Telephone:* (202) 623-7000 (office). *Fax:* (202) 623-4661 (office). *Website:* www.imf.org (office).

LIPTON, Stuart A., MD, PhD; American neuroscientist and academic; *Professor and Scientific Director, Del E. Webb Center for Neuroscience and Aging, The Burnham Institute;* b. 11 Jan. 1950, Danbury, Conn.; ed Cornell and Harvard Univs, Univ. of Pennsylvania; Intern in Medicine, Beth Israel Hosp., Boston, Mass 1977–78, Chief Resident in Neurology 1980, Asst in Neurology 1981–86, Assoc. in Neurology 1986–93, Sr Assoc. in Neurology, Beth Israel Deaconess Medical Center 1993–99; Jr and Sr Asst Resident, Longwood Area Neurology Program, Harvard Medical School, Boston 1978–80, Instructor in Neurology 1981–83, Asst Prof. of Neurology (Neuroscience) 1983–87, Assoc. Prof. of Neurology (Neuroscience) 1987–97, Assoc. Prof. of Neuroscience (Neurosurgery) 1997–2001; Chief Resident in Neurology, Children's Hosp. 1980, Asst in Neurology 1981–88, Dir Lab. of Cellular and Molecular Neuroscience 1987–97, Assoc. in Neurology 1988–97; Chief Resident in Neurology, Brigham and Women's Hosp. 1980, Assoc. in Neurology 1988–97, Chief, CNS Research Inst. 1997–99; Clinical Asst in Neurology, Massachusetts Gen. Hosp. Boston 1991–92, Clinical Assoc. in Neurology 1992–97; Prof. and Scientific Dir, Center for Neuroscience and Aging, The Burnham Inst., La Jolla, Calif. 1999–; Attending Neurologist, Medical Center, Univ. of California, San Diego, La Jolla 1999–; Adjunct Prof., Depts of Neurosciences and Psychiatry 1999–; Adjunct Prof., Dept of Neuropharmacology and Molecular and Experimental Medicine, Scripps Research Inst., La Jolla 1999–; Adjunct Prof. of Neuroscience, Salk Inst., La Jolla 2002–; Established Investigator, American Heart Asscn 1988–93; mem. Asscn for Research in Vision and Ophthalmology 1974–, American Acad. of Neurology 1979–98 (Fellow 1998–), AAAS 1980–, Soc. for Neuroscience 1982–, Biophysical Soc. 1986–; mem. Scientific Advisory Bd, HIV Neurobehavioral Research Center, School of Medicine, Univ. of California, San Diego 1995–99, Center for Neurovirology and Neurodegenerative Disorders, Univ. of Nebraska and Creighton Univ. 1997–, AIDS Research Center, Scripps Research Inst. 1997–; Assoc. Ed. Neuron 1995–; Reviewing Ed. Cell Death and Differentiation 2000–; mem. Editorial Bd several journals on neuroscience; Hon. mem. British Brain Research Association 1982–, European Brain and Behaviour Soc. 1982–; Ford Foundation Scholarship 1968–72, NIH MD-PhD Fellowship 1972–77, Mary Ellis Bell Prize for Research, Univ. of Pennsylvania School of Medicine 1973, Baluin-Lucke Memorial Prize for Research 1976, Von L. Meyer Research Award, Children's Hosp., Boston 1979, Hartford Foundation Fellowship 1981–84, NIH Teacher-Investigator Development Award 1984–89, Pattison Award in Neuroscience, Research Inst. for Child Devt Research, Inc. 1989, Nobel Foundation Lectureship, Karolinska Institutet, Stockholm 1994, Grass Foundation Lectureship 1995, San Diego Health Hero Award, American Parkinson's Disease Asscn 2002, Ernst Jung Prize for Medicine 2004. *Publications:* more than 520 articles in scientific and medical journals. *Address:* Center for Neuroscience and Aging, The Burnham Institute, 10901 Torrey Pines Road, La Jolla, CA 92037, USA (office). *Telephone:* (858) 713-6261 (office). *Fax:* (858) 713-6262 (office). *E-mail:* slipton@burnham.org (office). *Website:* www.burnham.org (office).

LIPTON, Sir Stuart Anthony, Kt; British property developer; *Deputy Chairman, Chelsfield Partners LLP;* b. 9 Nov. 1942; s. of Bertram Green and Jeanette Lipton; m. Ruth Marks 1966; two s. one d.; ed Berkhamsted School; Dir Sterling Land Co. 1971–73, First Palace Securities Ltd 1973–76; Man. Dir Greycoat PLC 1976–83; Founder and Chair. Stanhope Properties PLC 1983–95, Stanhope PLC 1995–2006; Deputy Chair. Chelsfield Partners LLP 2006–; Chair. Comm. for Architecture and the Built Environment 1999–2005; adviser, new Glyndebourne Opera House 1988–94; Dir Nat. Gallery Trust Foundation 1998–; mem. Bd Royal Nat. Theatre 1988–98, Royal Opera House 1998–2006; mem. Governing Body Imperial Coll. 1987–2000, Royal Fine Art Comm. 1988–99, LSE 2000–06; Trustee, Whitechapel Art Gallery 1987–94, Architecture Foundation 1991–, Urban Land Inst.; Hon. FRIBA; Hon. Fellow, Imperial Coll.; Hon. LLD (Bath) 2005. *Address:* Chelsfield Partners LLP, 53 Grosvenor Street, London, W1K 3HU, England (office). *Telephone:* (20) 7290-2388 (office). *Fax:* (20) 7493-7667 (office). *E-mail:* slipton@chelsfield.com (office).

LIPWORTH, Sir (Maurice) Sydney, Kt, BCom, LLB; British barrister and business executive; b. 13 May 1931, Johannesburg, South Africa; s. of Isidore Lipworth and Rae Lipworth; m. Rosa Liwarek 1957; two s.; ed King Edward VII School, Johannesburg, Univ. of the Witwatersrand; practising barrister, Johannesburg 1956–64; Dir (non-exec.) Liberty Life Asscn of Africa Ltd 1956–64; Exec. Pvt. Trading Cos. 1964–67; Exec. Dir Abbey Life Assurance PLC 1968–70; Vice-Pres. and Dir Abbey Int. Corpn Inc. 1968–70; one of co-founders and Dir Allied Dunbar Assurance PLC 1970–88, Deputy Man. Dir 1977–79, Jt Man. Dir 1979–84, Deputy Chair. 1984–88; Dir J. Rothschild Holdings PLC 1984–87, BAT Industries PLC 1985–88; Deputy Chair., Dir (non-exec.) Nat. Westminster Bank 1993–2000; Chair., Dir (non-exec.) Zeneca Group PLC 1995–99 (Dir 1994–99); Dir (non-exec.), Carlton Communications PLC 1993–, Centrica PLC 1999–2002; Chair. Monopolies and Mergers Comm. 1988–92, Bar Asscn for Commerce, Finance and Industry 1991–92 (Vice-Pres. c. 2012), Financial Reporting Council 1993–2001; Arbitrator/Mediator, One Essex Court (The Chambers of Lord Grabiner QC) 2004–; mem. Sr Salaries Review Body 1994–, Panel of Conciliators and of Arbitrators, Int. Centre for Settlement of Investment Disputes, Int. Advisory Bd, SOAS 2004–, Constitution Committee, Int. Accounting Standards Cttee Foundation Trust 2000–, European Policy Forum; Vice-Chair. of Trustees, Philharmonia Orchestra 1986–93, Chair. 1993–; Trustee, South Bank Ltd 1996–; Hon. QC 1993; Hon. LLD (Univ. of the Witwatersrand) 2003. *Publications:* The Monopolies and Mergers Yearbook: March 1989–December 1990 Vol. 1 1991, Major Issues in Regulation: Regulation Lectures (co-author) 1992. *Leisure interests:* music, theatre, tennis. *Address:* One Essex Court, Temple, London, EC4Y 9AR (office); International Accounting Standards Board, 30 Cannon Street, London, EC4M 6XH, England. *Telephone:* (20) 7583-2000 (office); (20) 7726-1000. *Fax:* (20) 7583-0118 (office); (20) 7726-1038. *E-mail:* clerks@oeclaw.co.uk (office). *Website:* www.oeclaw.co.uk (office); www.ifrs.org.

LISITSYN, Aleksander Petrovich; Russian marine geologist, geophysicist and geochemist; *Head of Department, P.P. Shirshov Institute of Oceanology, Russian Academy of Sciences;* b. 3 July 1923; m.; two c.; ed Moscow Geological Prospecting Inst.; Jr, Sr Researcher, Head of Lab., Head of Div., P.P. Shirshov Inst. of Oceanology, USSR (now Russian) Acad. of Sciences 1953–81, Head of Dept 1981–; Corresp. mem. USSR (now Russian) Acad. of Sciences 1974, mem. 1994–; research in marine geology, geophysics and geochemistry of seas and oceans; USSR State Prize, F. Shepard Award. *Publications include:* Sedimentation in the World Ocean 1972, Processes of Oceanic Sedimentation 1978, Geological History of Oceans 1980, Biogeochemistry of Oceans 1983, Avalanche Sedimentation and Gapes in Sedimentation in Seas and Oceans 1988, Marine Glacial and Marine Ice Sedimentation 1994, Oceanic Sedimentation, Lithography and Geochemistry 1996, Litology of Lithospheric Plates 2001, Sea-Ice and Iceberg Sedimentation in the Ocean 2002; numerous journal contribs. *Address:* P.P. Shirshov Institute of Oceanology, Russian Academy of Sciences, Nachimovsky Prospect 36, 117851 Moscow (office); Ivanovskaya 8A, 1 127434 Moscow, Russia (home). *Telephone:* (495) 124-85-28 (office); (495) 977-97-02 (home). *Fax:* (495) 124-85-28 (office). *Website:* www.ocean.ru (office).

LISITSYN, Anatoly Ivanovich; Russian politician; *Governor of Yaroslavl Region;* b. 26 June 1947, Bolshiye Smenki, Kalinin Region; m.; one c.; ed Leningrad Acad. of Forest Tech.; Rybinsk furniture factory 1987, also Chair., Rybinsk City Dist Exec. Cttee 1987–90; Chair. Rybinsk City Exec. Cttee 1990–91; Deputy Head, Head, Yaroslavl Regional Admin 1991–92; mem. Council of Fed. 1993–; mem. Movt Our Home is Russia (resgnd); mem. People's Democratic Party 1995; Gov. Yaroslavl Region 1995–; Chair. Interregional Asscn Cen. Russia; mem. Council of Russian Fed. 1996–2000; mem. Bd Union of Russian Govs. *Address:* Office of the Governor, Sovetskaya pl. 3, 150000 Yaroslavl, Russia (office). *Telephone:* (852) 72-81-28 (office). *Fax:* (852) 32-84-14 (office). *E-mail:* gubern@adm.yar.ru (office). *Website:* www.adm.yar.ru (office).

LIŠKA, Juraj; Slovak politician; b. 29 Nov. 1964, Trenčín; m.; two c.; ed Slovak Tech. Univ., Univ. of Transport, Zilina; employed in State Forest 1982–84; TOS Trenčín 1989–91; entrepreneur in wood production, Finnish saunas 1991–; Chair. Regional Asscn, Slovak Democratic Christian Union 2000; elected mem. Národná rada Slovenskej republiky (Parl.) 2002–, mem. Finances, Budget and Currency Cttee, Standing Del. to Parl. EU Cttee; apptd Mayor of Trenčín 2002; Minister of Defence 2003–06 (resgnd); resgnd as Deputy Chair. Slovak Democratic and Christian Uniion (SDKU) 2008. *Address:* Národná rada Slovenskej republiky (National Council of the Slovak Republic), nám. Alexandra Dubčeka 1 1, 812 80 Bratislava, Slovakia (office). *Telephone:* (2) 5972-1111 (office). *Fax:* (2) 5441-9529 (office). *E-mail:* info@nrsk.sk (office). *Website:* www.nrsk.sk (office).

LISKOV, Barbara, BA, MS, PhD; American computer scientist and academic; *Institute Professor, Department of Electrical Engineering and Computer Science, Massachusetts Institute of Technology;* b. 7 Nov. 1939, Calif.; m. Nathan Liskov; one s.; ed Univ. of California, Berkeley, Stanford Univ.; Applications Programmer, The Mitre Corpn, Bedford, Mass 1961–62, mem. of Tech. Staff, Computer Science Research and Devt 1968–72; Programmer, Language Trans. Project, Harvard Univ. 1962–63; Grad. Research Asst in Artificial Intelligence, Stanford Univ. 1963–68; Asst Prof., Dept of Electrical Eng and Computer Science, MIT 1972–76, Assoc. Prof., 1976–80, Prof. 1980–, NEC Prof. of Software Science and Eng 1986–97, Ford Prof. of Eng 1997–2008, Inst. Prof. 2008–, Assoc. Head for

Computer Science 2001–04, Assoc. Provost for Faculty Equity 2007–; fmr Assoc. Ed. ACM, Transactions on Programming Languages and Systems; consultant, Bolt, Beranek, and Newman, Cadence, Digital Equipment Corpn, Hewlett-Packard, Intermetrics, NCR, Prime Computer; mem. American Acad. of Arts and Sciences, Nat. Acad. of Eng, IEEE; Fellow, Asscn for Computing Machinery (ACM); Dr hc (ETH Zurich) 2005; Achievement Award, Soc. of Women Engineers 1996, named by Open Computing magazine amongst the top 100 women in computing 1996, named by Discover magazine amongst the 50 most important women in science 2003, ACM SIGPLAN Programming Languages Lifetime Achievement Award 2007, ACM SIGSOFT Impact Paper Award 2007, IEEE John von Neumann Medal 2004, ACM A.M. Turing Award 2008. *Publications:* CLU Reference Manual (co-author) 1984, Abstraction and Specification in Program Development (co-author) 1986, Program Development in Java: Abstraction, Specification, and Object-Oriented Design 2001; 137 papers in professional journals and 102 reports. *Address:* Computer Science and Artificial Intelligence Laboratory, Massachusetts Institute of Technology, Room 32-G942, 32 Vassar Street, Cambridge, MA 02139, USA (office). *Telephone:* (617) 253-5886 (office). *Fax:* (617) 253-8460 (office). *E-mail:* liskov@csail.mit.edu (office). *Website:* www.pmg .csail.mit.edu/~liskov (office).

LISNYANSKAYA, Inna Lvovna; Russian writer and poet; b. 24 June 1928, Baku, Azerbaijan SSR, USSR; d. of Lev Lisnyansky, Raisa Adamova; m. Semen I. Lipkin (died 2003); one d.; ed Baku Univ., literary courses, Moscow; began writing poetry aged 10; first works published 1948; poems published in Moscow literary journal Novyi mir (New World) and Yunost (Youth) 1957–; in internal exile 1979–89, following contribs to literary almanac Metropole; resgnd from Union of Writers 1980 (membership restored 1989); Chair. Bd, 'Poet' Award of Russia 2010; mem. Russian PEN Centre; Arion Prize 1994, Streletz Prize 1995, Druzhba Narodov magazine Prize 1996, State Literary Prize of Russia 1998, Alexander Solzhenitsyn Prize 1999, Znamya magazine Prize 2000, 'Poet' Award of Russia 2009. *Publications include:* This Happened to Me 1957, Faithfulness 1958, Not Simply Love 1963, At First Hand 1966, Grape Light 1978, Rains and Mirrors 1983, Verse 1970–83, 1984, On the Edge of Sleep 1984, The Circle 1985, Airy Layer 1990, Poetry 1991, The Music of Akhmatova's 'Poem without a Hero' 1991, After Everything 1994, The Lonely Gift 1995, 2003, The Box with a Triple Bottom (Study on Akhmatova's Poem without the Hero) 1995, The First-hand World 1996, Wind of Calmness 1998, Selected Poetry 2000, Far from Sodom 2002 (English trans. 2005), Without You 2003, The Echo 2005 (Bulgarian trans. 2010), Dreams of Old Eve 2005, She-Boaster 2006, Inna Lisnyanskaya 2009, Replaced Windows 2011, Verses (Chinese) 2010, Color Visions 2011; contribs to literary journals including Novyi mir, Oktiabr, Znamia, etc. *Address:* c/o Russian PEN Centre, 107031 Moscow, Neglinnaya str. 18/1, p. 2, Russia; Hess Street 33, Apt 5, 33397 Haifa, Israel (home). *Telephone:* 77-5633023 (Voip, Internet phone) (home); 547-994732 (Israel, mobile) (office). *Fax:* (495) 625-35-73 (office). *E-mail:* penrussian@mail.ru; inlist@ rambler.ru.

LISOV, Yevgeny Kuzmich; Russian politician and lawyer; b. 1940, Ivanovo Region; ed Saratov State Univ.; investigator, Dist Prosecutor's Office, Kursk Region, Sr Investigator, Head of Div., Deputy Head, Investigation Dept, RSFSR Prosecutor's Office; Deputy Gen. Prosecutor of Russian Fed. 1991–93; investigated coup d'état 1991; Deputy Prosecutor of Moscow 1993–95; attorney, Moscow Regional Coll. of Barristers; expert, magazine Ogonyok 1995–98; Deputy Head, Admin of Russian Presidency, Head, Main Control Dept, Admin of Russian Presidency 1998–2004. *Publications:* Kremlin Conspiracy (with V. G. Stepankov q.v.); articles in magazines and newspapers. *Address:* c/o Administration of the President, Staraya pl. 4, 103132 Moscow, Russia. *Telephone:* (495) 206-48-51.

LISSAKERS, Karin Margareta, MA; American economist and fmr government official; *Director, Revenue Watch Institute;* b. 16 Aug. 1944; m.; two c.; ed Ohio State Univ. and Johns Hopkins Univ.; mem. staff, Cttee on Foreign Relations, US Senate, Washington, DC 1972–78; Deputy Dir Econ. Policy Planning Staff, US Dept of State 1978–80; Sr Assoc. Carnegie Endowment for Int. Peace, New York 1981–83; Lecturer in int. banking, Dir int. business and banking programme, School of Int. Public Affairs, Columbia Univ. 1985–93; US Exec. Dir IMF 1993–2001; mem. Council on Foreign Relations; Chief Adviser to George Soros on globalization issues, Soros Fund Management LLC 2001–06; Dir Revenue Watch Inst. 2006–. *Publications:* Banks, Borrowers and the Establishment 1991; articles in professional journals. *Address:* Revenue Watch Institute, 400 West 59th Street, New York, NY 10019, USA (office). *Telephone:* (212) 548-0696 (office). *E-mail:* klissakers@revenuewatch.org (office). *Website:* www.revenuewatch.org (office).

LISSNER, Stéphane Michel; French theatre director; *Director General, Opéra National de Paris;* b. 23 Jan. 1953, Paris; s. of Georges Lissner and Elisabeth Landenbaum; two s. one d.; ed Coll. Stanislas and Lycée Henri IV, Paris; f. his first theatre, Théâtre Mécanique 1971; Sec.-Gen. Centre dramatique, Aubervilliers 1977–78; Co-Dir Centre dramatique, Nice 1978–83; Admin., Théâtre du Châtelet, Paris 1983–88, Gen. Man. 1988–98; Dir-Gen. Orchestre de Paris 1993–95; Artistic Dir Teatro Real de Paris 1996–97; Dir Aix-en-Provence Int. Festival 1998–2006; Co-Dir, with Peter Brook (q.v.), Théâtre des Bouffes du Nord, Paris 1998–; currently Dir Théâtre de la Madeleine, Paris, and Music Dir Vienna Festival; Supt and Artistic Dir Teatro alla Scala, Milan 2005–14; Musical Dir Wiener Festwochen 2005–; Dir-Gen.-designate Opéra Nat. de Paris 2012–14, Dir-Gen. 2014–; Chevalier, Légion d'honneur, Officier, Ordre nat. du Mérite, Ufficiale Ordine al Merito della Repubblica Italiana. *Publication:* Métro Chapelle 2000. *Address:* c/o Théâtre de la Madeleine, 19 rue de Surène, 75008 Paris; Opéra Natonal de Paris, Palais Garnier, 8 rue Scribe, 75009 Paris, France. *Website:* www.theatremadeleine .com; www.festwochen.at; www.operaparis.fr; www.bouffesdunord.com

LISSOUBA, Pascal, DèsSc; Republic of the Congo fmr head of state; b. 15 Nov. 1931, Tsinguidi, Congo (Brazzaville); s. of Albert Lissouba and Marie Bouanga; m. 2nd Jocelyne Pierrot 1967; one s. six d.; ed secondary education in Nice, France and Ecole Supérieure d'Agric., Tunis, Tunisia; fmr agricultural specialist; Prime Minister of Congo (Brazzaville) 1963–66, concurrently Minister of Trade and Industry and Agric.; Prof. of Genetics, Brazzaville 1966–71, concurrently Minister of Planning 1968, Minister of Agric., Waterways and Forests 1969; Dir Ecole Supérieure des Sciences, Brazzaville 1970; sentenced to life imprisonment for complicity in assassination of Pres. Ngouabi 1977, subsequently released and

exiled; Dir African Bureau for Science and Tech., Nairobi from 1981; Leader Union panafricaine pour la Démocratie sociale (UPADS); Pres. Repub. of the Congo 1992–97; living in exile in London, UK; convicted *in absentia* on charges of treason and corruption, related to a $150m oil deal with the American co. Occidental Petroleum, and sentenced to 30 years' by the high court in Brazzaville 2001. *Leisure interests:* geology, music.

LISSOWSKI, Antoine; French business executive; *Deputy CEO, CNP Assurances;* ed Institut d'Études Politiques de Paris, École Nationale d'Admin; began career at Caisse des Dépôts et Consignations as Head of the Treasury and currency eurocredits; Special Adviser to Securities and Exchange Comm. 1985–88; returned to Caisse des Dépôts 1988 as Head of Business Devt activities on money and bond markets 1988–90, Man. Dir Fund Autonomous Refinancing (CAR – Groupe Caisse des Dépôts), Chief Financial Officer (CFO) Banking and Financial Deposit 1990–2000; CFO CDC IXIS 2000–03, mem. Exec. Bd 2002–03; mem. Bd of Dirs CNP Assurances 2003–07, Deputy Dir Gen. and CFO CNP Assurances 2007–12, Acting CEO and CFO June–Sept. 2012, Deputy CEO 2012–; Chair. Econ. and Financial Plenary Cttee, FSSA 2003–, Pres. (Solvency), Centre Européen des Assurances 2003–. *Address:* CNP Assurances, 4 place Raoul Dautry, 75716 Paris, France (office). *Telephone:* 1-42-18-88-88 (office). *Fax:* 1-42-18-86-55 (office). *E-mail:* info@cnp.fr (office). *Website:* www.cnp.fr (office).

LIST, Benjamin, PhD; German chemist and academic; *Director, Max Planck Institute for Coal Research;* b. 1968, Frankfurt; ed Free Univ., Berlin, Univ. of Frankfurt; postdoctoral researcher, Scripps Research Inst., La Jolla, Calif., USA 1997–98, Asst Prof. (Tenure Track) 1999–2003; Group Leader, Max-Planck-Institut für Kohlenforschung, Mülheim 2003–05, Dir 2005–, Acting Dir 2012–; Visiting Prof., Gakushuin Univ., Tokyo, Japan 2005, Sungkyunkwan Univ., Korea 2008; Hon. Prof., Univ. of Cologne 2004–; NaFöG-Award from City of Berlin 1994, Feodor-Lynen Fellowship, Alexander von Humboldt Foundation 1997, Synthesis-Synlett Journal Award 2000, Carl-Duisberg-Memorial Award, German Chemical Soc. 2003, Degussa Prize for Chiral Chem. 2004, Lecturer's Award, Fonds der Chemischen Industrie 2004, Lieseberg Prize, Univ. of Heidelberg 2004, Lectureship Award, Soc. of Synthetic Chem., Japan 2005, AstraZeneca European Lecturer 2005, Novartis Young Investigator Award 2005, JSPS Fellowship Award (Japan) 2006, 100 Masterminds of Tomorrow (Germany) 2006, Award of the Fonds der Chemischen Industrie (Silver) 2007, OBC-Lecture Award 2007, AstraZeneca Award in Organic Chem. 2007, Boehringer-Ingelheim Lectureship (Canada) 2009, Organic Reactions Lectureship (USA) 2009, ERC Advanced Grant 2011, Boehringer-Ingelheim Lectureship, Harvard Univ., USA 2011. *Publications:* more than 120 papers in professional journals on new synthetic methodologies, asymmetric catalysis, organocatalysis, bio-organic chemistry and natural product synthesis. *Address:* Max-Planck-Institut für Kohlenforschung, Kaiser-Wilhelm-Platz 1, 45470 Mülheim an der Ruhr, Germany (office). *Telephone:* (208) 306-2410 (office). *Fax:* (208) 306-2999 (office). *E-mail:* list@mpi-muelheim.mpg.de (office); list@kofo.mpg.de (office). *Website:* www.kofo.mpg.de/de/forschung/homogene -katalyse (office).

LIST, Roland, DrScNat, CCM, FRSC; Canadian/Swiss physicist and international official; *Professor Emeritus of Physics, University of Toronto;* b. 21 Feb. 1929, Frauenfeld, Thurgau, Switzerland; s. of August Joseph List and Anna Kaufmann; m. Gertrud K. Egli 1956 (died 1996); two c.; ed Swiss Fed. Inst. of Tech., Zurich; Head, Hail Section, Swiss Fed. Inst. for Snow and Avalanche Research, Davos 1952–63; Prof. of Physics (Meteorology), Dept of Physics, Univ. of Toronto 1963–82, 1984–94, Prof. Emer. 1994–, Assoc. Chair. Dept of Physics 1969–73; Deputy Sec.-Gen. WMO 1982–84; Chair. Exec. Cttee Panel of Experts on Weather Modification, WMO, Geneva 1969–82; Dir Univ. Corpn for Atmospheric Research, Boulder, Colo 1974–77; mem. Science Council, Space Shuttle Program (NASA) 1978–80; Chair. Italian Scientific Cttee for Rain Enhancement 1990–98; Sec.-Gen. Int. Asscn of Meteorology and Atmospheric Sciences 1995–2007; Rep. of Int. Union for Geodesy and Geophysics with WMO and World Climate Research Program 1995–2007; mem. and Chair. Planned and Inadvertent Weather Modification Cttee, American Meteorological Soc. 1996–2003; mem. or chair. many int., Canadian, US and Swiss cttees; consultant to UN, UNEP, World Bank, Inco and many other orgs; Visiting Prof., Swiss Fed. Inst. of Tech., Zürich 1974, 1998; Pres. Rotary Club of Toronto–Don Mills 1995–96; mem. Canadian and Swiss Acads of Sciences, Canadian Meteorological and Oceanic Soc., American Geophysical Union, American and Swiss Physical Socs, etc.; Fellow, Royal Meteorological Society (UK) 1963, American Meteorological Soc. 1973; Hon. Prof., Chinese Acad. of Meteorological Sciences 2005; Hon. Life Mem. Int. Comm. on Cloud Physics 2008; Sesquicentennial Medal, Univ. of Leningrad 1970, Patterson Medal, Canadian Meteorological Service 1979, Plaque of Recognition (Thailand) 1986, Paul Harris Medal, Rotary International 2004, Golden Cumulonimbus Award, Spanish Inst. of Meteorology 2005, Weather Modification Trophy (UAE) 2005, Thunderbird Award, American Weather Modification Asscn, Special Award and Trophy, Int. Asscn for Meteorology and Atmospheric Sciences 2007. *Publications:* more than 260 papers and many reports in the field of cloud physics, cloud dynamics, weather modification, classical physics, heat and mass transfer and aerodynamics. *Address:* Department of Physics, University of Toronto, Toronto, ON M5S 1A7 (office); Ph-8, 1555 Finch Avenue E, North York, ON M2J 4X9, Canada (home). *Telephone:* (416) 978-2982 (office); (416) 494-3621 (home). *Fax:* (416) 978-8905 (office). *E-mail:* list@atmosp.physics.utoronto.ca (office); roland .list@rogers.com (home).

LISTER, Gwen, BA; Namibian journalist; *Chairperson, Namibia Media Trust;* b. 5 Dec. 1953, East London, S Africa; one s. one d.; ed Univ. of Cape Town; began career as journalist with Windhoek Advertiser 1975; Co-founder (with Hannes Smith) Windhoek Observer 1978, Political Ed. 1978–84 (S African authorities banned newspaper during coverage of independence talks 1984, ban defeated, resgnd because of accusations by newspaper sr staff 1984); Founder The Namibian newspaper 1985, Ed. 1985–2011 (copies confiscated by authorities, advertising boycott by business community, office bldg burned down 1988, prohibition of govt advertising in newspaper 2001); currently Chair. Namibia Media Trust; Exec. Dir Free Press of Namibia (Pty) Ltd (publishes The Namibian); Co-founder Media Inst. of Southern Africa, fmr Chair. Governing Council and mem. Trust Funds Bd; mem. UNESCO Press Freedom Council, African Advisory Bd Int. Women's Media Foundation, Advisory Bd Int. Consortium of Investigative Journalists; various speeches on media freedom/democracy and ethics worldwide, including at several UNESCO confs; Namibian nat. colours for squash, Inter Press Service Int. Journalism Award 1988, S African Soc. of Journalists Pringle Prize for Journalism 1988, Cttee to Protect Journalists Int. Journalism Award 1991, Nieman Fellowship, Harvard Univ. 1995–96, Media Inst. of S Africa Press Freedom Award 1997, named Int. Press Inst. Press Freedom Hero 2000, Int. Women's Media Foundation Courage in Journalism Award 2004. *Publications:* several book chapters. *Address:* The Namibian, PO Box 20783, 42 John Meinert Street, Windhoek, Namibia (office). *Telephone:* (61) 279600 (office). *Fax:* (61) 279602 (office). *E-mail:* gwen@namibian.com.na (office). *Website:* www.namibian.com.na (office).

LISTER OF BURTERSETT, Baroness (Life Peer), cr. 2011, of Nottingham in the County of Nottinghamshire; **Ruth Lister,** CBE, BA (Hons), MA, FBA, AcSS; British sociologist and academic; *Professor Emerita of Social Policy, Loughborough University;* b. (Margot Ruth Aline Lister), 3 May 1949, Huddersfield, West Yorks.; d. of Werner Bernard Lister and Daphne Lister; ed Univs of Essex and Sussex; worked for Child Poverty Action Group 1971–87, Dir 1979–87; Prof. and Head of Dept of Applied Social Studies, Univ. of Bradford 1988–94; Prof. of Social Policy, Dept of Sociology, Loughborough Univ. 1994–2010, Prof. Emer. of Social Policy 2010–; consultant on a Joseph Rowntree Foundation funded project, Living through Change in Challenging Neighbourhoods, Sheffield Hallam Univ.; mem. Social Policy Asscn; Chair. Jt Univ. Council Social Policy Cttee 1994–96; Founding Academicians, Acad. of Social Sciences; first Donald Dewar Visiting Prof. of Social Justice, Univ. of Glasgow 2005–07; Chair. Editorial Bd Social Policy & Administration 2003–09; mem. several journal editorial bds; mem. Bd, Smith Inst.; fmr mem. Comm. on Social Justice, Opsahl Comm. on the future of Northern Ireland, Comm. on Poverty, Participation and Power (est. by UK Coalition against Poverty as part of their Voices for Change consultation project), Fabian Comm. on Life Chances and Child Poverty, Nat. Equality Panel, task group on social protection as part of Sir Michael Marmot's Strategic Review of Health Inequalities in England, Post 2010; Trustee, Community Devt Foundation 2000–10; sits on various other voluntary sector and research advisory cttees; mem. House of Lords (Labour) 2011–; Hon. Pres. Child Poverty Action Group 2010–; Hon. LLD (Manchester), (Brighton) 2012; Hon. DLitt (Glasgow Caledonian), (Essex) 2012; Eleanor Rathbone Memorial Lecturer 1989, Queen's Anniversary Prize for Higher and Further Educ. (co-recipient) 2005, 2006 Jill Vickers Prize, Canadian Political Science Asscn (co-recipient) 2006, Lifetime Achievement Award, Social Policy Asscn 2010. *Publications:* Social Justice. Strategies for National Renewal (report co-author) 1994, Citizenship: Feminist Perspectives 1998 (second edn 2003, translated into Chinese), Listen Hear: The Right to be Heard (report co-author) 2000, Young Peoples Voices. Citizenship Education (with S. Middleton and N. Smith) 2002, Poverty 2004 (translated into Polish, Macedonian and Japanese), Narrowing the Gap (report co-author) 2006, Why Money Matters (co-ed.) 2008, Understanding Theories and Concepts in Social Policy (Understanding Welfare series) 2010, An Anatomy of Economic Inequality in the UK (report co-author) 2010; numerous book chapters and articles in academic journals. *Leisure interests:* walking, watching tennis, music, films and theatre, meditation, Tai Chi. *Address:* House of Lords, Westminster, London, SW1A 0PW, England (office). *Telephone:* (20) 7219-5353 (office); (20) 7219-8984 (office). *Fax:* (20) 7219-5979 (office); (1509) 223944 (office). *E-mail:* m.r.lister@lboro.ac.uk (office); listerr@parliament.uk (office). *Website:* www.lboro.ac.uk/departments/socialsciences/staff/ruth-lister.html (office); www.parliament.uk/biographies/lords/margot-aline/90403 (office).

LITHERLAND, Albert Edward, PhD, DSc, FRS, FRSC; Canadian physicist and academic; *University Professor Emeritus, University of Toronto;* b. 12 March 1928, Wallasey, Merseyside, England, UK; s. of Albert Litherland and Ethel Clement; m. Anne Allen 1956; two d.; ed Wallasey Grammar School and Univ. of Liverpool; Scientific Officer, Atomic Energy of Canada 1955–66; Prof. of Physics, Univ. of Toronto 1966–79, Univ. Prof. 1979–93, Univ. Prof. Emer. 1993–, Dir Isotrace Lab. 1982–2008; Guggenheim Fellow 1986; Hon. DSc (Toronto) 1998; Gold Medal, Canadian Asscn of Physicists 1971, Rutherford Medal and Prize, Inst. of Physics 1974, Silver Medal, Journal of Applied Radiation and Isotopes 1981, Henry Marshall Tory Gold Medal, Royal Soc. of Canada 1993. *Publications:* numerous scientific papers. *Leisure interests:* reading, travel. *Address:* Apartment 801, 120 Rosedale Valley Road, Toronto, ON M4W 1P8, Canada (home). *Telephone:* (416) 978-3785 (office); (416) 978-5685 (office); (416) 923-5616 (home). *E-mail:* ted.litherland@utoronto.ca (office).

LITHGOW, John Arthur; American actor; b. 19 Oct. 1945, Rochester, New York; s. of Arthur Lithgow and Sarah Jane (née Price); m. 1st Phoebe Jean Taynton 1966; m. 2nd Mary Yeager 1981; ed Harvard Univ., London Acad. of Music and Dramatic Art, UK; Broadway debut in The Changing Room 1973; also writes children's literature. *Films include:* Obsession 1976, All That Jazz 1979, The World According to Garp 1982, Terms of Endearment 1983, The Day After 1983, Footloose 1984, Harry and the Hendersons 1987, Raising Cain 1992, The Pelican Brief 1993, Don Quixote 2000, Shrek (voice) 2001, Orange County 2002, The Life and Death of Peter Sellers 2004, Kinsey 2004, Dreamgirls 2006, Leap Year 2010, Shrek Forever After 2010, The Campaign 2012. *Theatre includes:* The Changing Room (Tony Award for Best Featured Actor in a Play) 1973, Boy Meets Girl 1976, Comedians 1976, Division Street 1980, Requiem for a Heavyweight 1985, M. Butterfly 1988, Sweet Smell of Success (Tony Award for Best Actor in a Musical) 2002, Dirty Rotten Scoundrels 2005, All My Sons 2008, Mr & Mrs Fitch 2010. *Television includes:* 3rd Rock from the Sun (Primetime Emmy Award for Outstanding Lead Actor in a Comedy Series 1996, 1997, 1999) 1996–2001, Twenty Good Years 2006, Dexter (Golden Globe Award) 2009. *Publications include:* children's stories: Remarkable Farkle Mcbride 2000, Marsupial Sue 2001, Micawber 2002, I'm a Manatee 2003, A Lithgow Palooza 2004, Carnival of the Animals 2004, Mahalia Mouse Goes to College 2007, I Got Two Dogs 2008; Drama: An Actor's Education 2011. *Address:* Brady, Brannon & Rich, 5670 Wilshire Blvd, Suite 820, Los Angeles, CA 90036, USA (office). *Telephone:* (323) 852-9559 (office). *Fax:* (323) 852-9579 (office). *Website:* www.bbrtalentagency.com (office).

LITTELL, Robert; American writer; b. 8 Jan. 1935, New York, NY; journalist, Newsweek 1964; writer of Cold War espionage fiction. *Publications include:* Read America First 1968, If Israel Lost the War (with Richard Z. Cheznoff and Edward Klein) 1969, The Czech Black Book 1969, The Defection of A. J. Lewinter (Gold Dagger Award for Fiction) 1973, Sweet Reason 1974, The October Circle 1976,

Mother Russia 1978, The Debriefing 1979, The Amateur 1981, The Sisters 1985, The Revolutionist 1988, The Once and Future Spy 1990, An Agent in Place 1991, The Visiting Professor 1994, Walking Back the Cat 1996, For the Future of Israel (with Shimon Peres) 1998, The Company 2002, Legends: A Novel of Dissimulation (Los Angeles Times Book Prize) 2005, Vicious Circles 2007, The Stalin Epigram 2009, Young Philby 2011. *Address:* c/o Author Mail, Simon and Schuster, 1230 Avenue of the Americas, 11th Floor, New York, NY 10020, USA. *Website:* www.simonandschuster.com.

LITTLE, (Robert) Alastair, MA; British restaurateur and chef; b. 25 June 1950, Colne, Lancs., England; s. of R. G. Little and M. I. Little; m. 1st Kirsten Pedersen 1981; one s. one d.; m. 2nd Sharon Jacob 2000; ed Kirkham Grammar School, Downing Coll., Cambridge; self-taught chef; Head Chef, Old Compton Wine Bar 1974–76; Chef/Propr, Le Routier Wrentham Suffolk 1976–79, Simpsons, Putney, London 1979–81; Chef, L'Escargot, London 1981–82, 192 Kensington Park Road 1982–85; Chef/Propr, Alastair Little, Frith Street 1985–2002, Lancaster Road 1996–2002; Propr Tavola (delicatessen), Westbourne Grove, London 2003–; food columnist, Daily Mail 1993–; mem. Acad. Culinaire; Times Restaurant of Year 1993. *Publications:* Keep it Simple 1993, Mediterranean Redefined (with Richard Whittington) 1995, Alastair Little's Italian Kitchen 1996, Soho Cooking 2000. *Leisure interests:* jigsaws, trashy novels, travel, wine, reading, mycology, watching sport. *Address:* Tavola, 155 Westbourne Grove, Notting Hill, London, W11 2RS, England. *Telephone:* (20) 7229-0571.

LITTLE, Tasmin E., OBE, ARCM, FGSM; British violinist; b. 13 May 1965, London, England; d. of George Little and Gillian Little; one s. one d.; ed Yehudi Menuhin School, Guildhall School of Music; studied privately with Lorand Fenyves in Canada; performed with New York Philharmonic, Berlin Philharmonic, Leipzig Gewandhaus, Cleveland Orchestra, Berlin Symphony, London Symphony, London Philharmonic, Philharmonia, Royal Philharmonic, New Japan Philharmonic, Royal Stockholm Philharmonic, Hong Kong Philharmonic, BBC Symphony, Royal Liverpool Philharmonic, European Community Chamber, Royal Danish and Stavanger Symphony Orchestras; has played with orchestras conducted by Gustavo Dudamel, Kurt Masur, Vladimir Ashkenazy, Leonard Slatkin, Tadaaki Otaka, Sir Charles Groves, Sir Andrew Davis, Vernon Handley, Yan Pascal Tortelier, Sir Edward Downes, Yehudi Menuhin and Sir Simon Rattle; played at the Proms since 1990; concerto and recital performances in UK, Europe, Scandinavia, S America, Hong Kong, Oman, Zimbabwe, Australia, NZ, USA and Japan; numerous TV appearances, including BBC Last Night of the Proms 1995, 1998, Wallace and Gromit Prom 2012; Hon. DLitt (Bradford) 1996; Hon. DMus (Leicester) 2002; Hon. DArts (Hertfordshire) 2007, (City) 2008. *Recordings include:* works by Bruch, Dvořák, Brahms, Sibelius, Delius, Rubbra, Saxton, George Lloyd, Ravel, Debussy, Poulenc, Delius, Elgar, Bax, Finzi; Dohnányi violin sonatas, Bruch Scottish Fantasy, Lalo Symphonie Espagnole, Pärt Spiegel im Spiegel and Fratres, The Naked Violin (Gramophone/Classic FM Award for Innovation 2008) 2007, Elgar Violin Concerto (Classic BRIT Award, Critic's Choice 2011) 2010, Strauss and Respighi sonatas, British Violin Sonatas 2013, Moeran Concerto, Lark Ascending 2013. *Publication:* paper on Delius' violin concerto. *Leisure interests:* theatre, cinema, swimming, languages. *Address:* 67 Teignmouth Road, London, NW2 4EA, England (office). *Telephone:* (20) 8208-2480 (office). *Fax:* (20) 8208-2490 (office). *E-mail:* d.kantor.kcm@btinternet.com (office). *Website:* www.tasminlittle.net.

LITTLE RICHARD, American rock singer and songwriter; b. (Richard Wayne Penniman), 5 Dec. 1932, Macon, Ga; adopted s. of Enotris Johnson and Ann Johnson; R&B singer in various bands, including own band The Upsetters; gospel singer 1960–62; worldwide tours and concerts; announced retirement 2002; Grammy Lifetime Achievement Award 1993. *Recordings include:* albums: Cast A Long Shadow 1956, Little Richard Vol. 1 1957, Little Richard Vol. 2 1957, Little Richard Vol. 3 1957, Here's Little Richard 1957, The Fabulous Little Richard 1959, Clap Your Hands 1960, Pray Along With Little Richard Vol. 1 1960, Pray Along With Little Richard Vol. 2 1960, King Of The Gospel Singers 1962, Sings Spirituals 1963, Sings the Gospel 1964, Little Richard Is Back 1965, The Wild and Frantic Little Richard 1965, The Explosive Little Richard 1967, Rock 'n' Roll Forever 1967, Good Golly Miss Molly 1969, Little Richard 1969, Right Now 1970, Rock Hard Rock Heavy 1970, Little Richard 1970, Well Alright! 1970, Mr Big 1971, The Rill Thing 1971, The Second Coming 1971, Dollars 1972, The Original 1972, You Can't Keep A Good Man Down 1972, Rip It Up 1973, Talkin' 'Bout Soul 1974, Recorded Live 1974, Keep A Knockin' 1975, Sings 1976, Little Richard Live 1976, Now 1977, Lucille 1988, Shake It All About 1992, Shag On Down By The Union Hall 1996. *Films include:* Don't Knock the Rock 1956, Mr Rock 'n' Roll 1957, The Girl Can't Help It 1957, Keep On Rockin' 1970, Down and Out in Beverly Hills 1986, Mother Goose Rock 'n' Rhyme (Disney Channel) 1989. *Address:* Richard de la Font Agency Inc., 4845 South Sheridan Road, Suite 505, Tulsa, OK 74145-5719, USA (office). *Website:* www.delafont.com (office).

LITTLECHILD, Stephen Charles, PhD; British economist and public servant; b. 27 Aug. 1943, Wisbech; s. of Sidney F. Littlechild and Joyce M. Littlechild; m. Kate Crombie 1974 (died 1982); two s. one d.; ed Wisbech Grammar School, Univ. of Birmingham, Univ. of Texas, USA; Harkness Fellow 1965–67; Sr Research Lecturer in Econs, Graduate Centre for Man. Studies, Birmingham 1970–72; Prof. of Applied Econs and Head of Econs, Econometrics, Statistics and Marketing Subject Group, Aston Man. Centre, Birmingham 1972–75; Prof. of Commerce, Univ. of Birmingham 1975–94, Head, Dept of Industrial Econs and Business Studies 1975–89, Hon. Prof. 1994–2004, Prof. Emer. 2004–; Visiting Scholar, Dept of Econs, UCLA, USA 1975; Visiting Prof., New York, Stanford and Chicago Univs and Virginia Polytechnic 1979–80; mem. Monopolies and Mergers Comm. 1983–89, Sec. of State for Energy's Advisory Council on Research and Devt 1987–89; Dir-Gen. of Electricity Supply 1989–98; Prin. Research Fellow, Judge Business School, Univ. of Cambridge 2000–04, Sr Research Assoc. 2004–; mem. Postcomm 2006–; Hon. DSc (Birmingham) 2001; Hon. DCL (East Anglia) 2004. *Publications:* Operational Research for Managers 1977, (with M. F. Shutler) 1991, The Fallacy of the Mixed Economy 1978, 1986, Elements of Telecommunications Economics 1979, Energy Strategies for the UK (with K. G. Vaidya) 1982, Regulation of British Telecommunications' Profitability 1983, Economic Regulation of Privatised Water Authorities 1986. *Leisure interest:* family history.

Address: White House, The Green, Tanworth-in-Arden, Solihull, West Midlands, B94 5AL, England (home). *E-mail:* sclittlechild@tanworth.mercianet.co.uk (office).

LITTLEWOOD, Peter Brent, BA, PhD, FInstP; British physicist and academic; *Associate Laboratory Director, Argonne National Laboratory;* b. 18 May 1955, Pembury, Kent, England; m. Elizabeth Littlewood 1978; one s. one d.; ed Cavendish Lab., Univ. of Cambridge; worked at Bell Labs, Murray Hill, NJ, USA 1980–97, Head of Theoretical Physics Research Dept 1992–97; Prof. of Physics, Cavendish Lab., Univ. of Cambridge 1997–2005, Head of Theory of Condensed Matter Group, Cavendish Lab. 1997–2005, Head of Dept of Physics, Cavendish Lab. 2005–11, Head of Cavendish Lab. 2005–11, Fellow, Trinity Coll.; Assoc. Lab. Dir, Argonne Nat. Lab., Ill., USA 2011–; Prof. of Physics, Univ. of Chicago, USA 2011–; mem. Royal Soc. 2008–; Fellow, American Physical Soc. *Address:* Argonne National Laboratory, 9700 South Cass Avenue, Argonne, IL 60439, USA (office). *Telephone:* (630) 252-5858 (office). *E-mail:* pblittlewood@anl .gov (office). *Website:* www.anl.gov/Administration/Bios/littlewood.html (office).

LITTMAN, Mark, QC; British barrister-at-law and business executive; b. 4 Sept. 1920, London; s. of Jack Littman and Lilian Littman; m. Marguerite Lamkin 1965; ed Owen's School, London School of Economics, Queens Coll. Oxford; Lt, RNVR 1941–46; called to Bar, Middle Temple 1947; Dir Rio Tinto-Zinc Corpn 1968–91; Pres. Bar Asscn for Commerce, Finance and Industry 1974–80; mem. Bar Council 1973–75, mem. of Senate of the Inns of Court and the Bar 1974–75; Deputy Chair. British Steel Corpn 1970–79; Dir Commercial Union Assurance Co. Ltd 1970–81, Granada Group Ltd 1977–93, British Enkalon Ltd 1972–80; Amerada Hess Corpn 1973–86, Envirotech Corpn 1974–78, Burton Group PLC 1983–93; Treas. Middle Temple 1988; Bencher of the Middle Temple 1970; mem. Royal Comm. on Legal Services 1976; mem. Int. Council for Commercial Arbitration 1978–; mem. Court of Govs, LSE 1980–; Vice-Chair. London Int. Arbitration Trust 1980–. *Address:* 12 Gray's Inn Square, London, WC1R 5JP, England (office). *Telephone:* (20) 7404-3072 (office). *E-mail:* 101712.2534@compuserve.com (office). *Website:* www .littmanchambers.com (office).

LITTON, Andrew, MM; American conductor and pianist; *Music Director, Bergen Philharmonic Orchestra;* b. 16 May 1959, New York; ed Fieldston High School, New York, Mozarteum, Juilliard School; Asst Conductor La Scala, Milan 1980–81; Exxon/Arts Endowment Asst Conductor, then Assoc. Conductor, Nat. Symphony Orchestra, Washington, DC 1982–86; Prin. Guest Conductor Bournemouth Symphony Orchestra 1986–88, Prin. Conductor and Artistic Adviser 1988–94, Conductor Laureate 1994–; Prin. Conductor and Music Dir Dallas Symphony Orchestra 1994–2006, Music Dir Emeritus 2006–; guest conductor many leading orchestras worldwide, including Chicago Symphony, Philadelphia, Los Angeles Philharmonic, Pittsburgh Symphony, Toronto Symphony, Montréal Symphony, Vancouver Symphony, London Philharmonic, Royal Philharmonic, London Symphony, English Chamber Orchestra, Leipzig Gewandhaus, Moscow State Symphony, Stockholm Philharmonic, RSO Berlin, RAI Milan, Orchestre Nat. de France, Suisse Romande, Tokyo Philharmonic, Melbourne Symphony and Sydney Symphony orchestras; debut at Metropolitan Opera, New York with Eugene Onegin 1989; also conducted at St Louis Opera, LA Opera, Royal Opera House, Covent Garden and ENO; music consultant to film The Chosen; Prin. Conductor Bergen Philharmonic Orchestra 2002–15; Music Dir 2005–(15); Artistic Dir Minnesota Orchestra's Sommerfest 2003–; winner Bruno Walter Conducting Fellowship 1981, Hon. DMus (Bournemouth) 1992; winner William Kapell Memorial US Nat. Piano Competition 1978, BBC/Rupert Foundation Int. Conductors Competition 1982, Yale Univ. Sanford Medal. *Recordings include:* Mahler Symphony No. 1 and Songs of a Wayfarer, Elgar Enigma Variations, complete Tchaikovsky symphony cycle, complete Rachmaninov symphony cycle, Shostakovich Symphony No. 10, Gershwin Rhapsody in Blue, Concerto in F and Ravel Concerto in G (as piano soloist and conductor), Bernstein Symphony No. 2, Brahms Symphony No. 1, Walton's Belshazzar's Feast (with Bryn Terfel and Bournemouth Symphony) (Grammy Award), Rachmaninov Piano Concertos (with Stephen Hough and Dallas Symphony Orchestra) (Classical BRIT Critics' Award 2005) 2004. *Address:* c/o Columbia Artists Management, 1790 Broadway, New York, NY 10019-1412, USA (office). *Telephone:* (212) 841-9500 (office). *Fax:* (212) 841-9744 (office). *E-mail:* info@cami.com (office). *Website:* www.cami.com (office); www.filharmonien.no; www.andrewlitton.com.

LITVINOV, Boris Vasilyevich; Russian physicist and engineer; b. 12 Nov. 1929; m.; three c.; ed Moscow Inst. of Mechanics; lab. engineer, Sr Engineer, Sr Researcher, Deputy Head of Div., Research Inst. of Experimental Physics 1952–61; Chief Constructor, All-Union Inst. of Tech. Physics, USSR (now Russian) Ministry of Medium Machine Bldg (now Ministry of Atomic Energy) 1961–77; First Deputy Scientific Dir 1978–97, Deputy Scientific Dir from 1997; Corresp. mem. USSR (now Russian) Acad. of Sciences 1991, mem. 1997; main research in applied physics, devt of new constructions of exploding devices; Labour Banner 1956, Order of Lenin 1962, 1977, 1981, Order of October Revolution 1971; Lenin Prize 1966, Hero of Socialist Labour 1981, Merit to Motherland (Third Class) 1995. *Publications:* Metals and Minerals Research in Spherical Shockwaves, Power Engineering of Deuterium Explosion, Basic Engineering Activity. *Leisure interest:* carving. *Address:* Institute of Technical Physics, PO Box 245, 456770 Chelyabinsk, Russia (office). *E-mail:* litvinov@snezhinsk.ru (home); lit@kbone.ch70.chel.ru (office).

LITVINOVA, Renata Muratovna; Russian actress and scriptwriter; b. 11 Jan. 1968, Moscow; d. of Murat Vergazov and Alissa Litvinova; m. Mikhail Dobrovsky; ed All-Union State Inst. of Cinematography; mem. Union of Theatre Workers; mem. jury, Moscow International Film Festival 2007; Honoured Artist of the Russian Fed. 2003, Pushkin Medal 2012. *Films include:* The Border–Taiga Romance, Dve strely. Detektiv kamennogo veka (Two Arrows: The Crime Story from the Stone Age) 1989, Uvlecheniya (Passions) 1994, Tri istorii (Three Stories) 1997, 8½ $ (voice) 1999, Aprel (April) 1992, Nebo. Samolyot. Devushka. (Sky. Plane. Girl.) (also writer and producer) 2002, Net smerti dlya menya (There is No Death for Me) (dir) 2002, The Tulse Luper Suitcases, Part 3: From Sark to the Finish 2003, Nastroyshchik (The Tuner) 2004, Boginya: kak ya polyubila (Goddess: How I Felt in Love) (also writer and dir and producer) 2004, Zhmurki 2005, Vokaldy paraleldei 2005, Zhest 2006, Mne ne bolno 2006, Dva v odnom 2007, Zhestokost 2007, Wow! (Generation P) 2011, Heart's Boomerang 2011, Poslednyaya skazka Rity 2012, The Girl and Death 2012, Vechnoye vozvrashcheniye 2012. *Scriptwriter for films:* Leningrad, November, Nelyubov (No Love) 1991,

Traktoristy (Tractor Drivers) 1992, Muzhskiye otkroveniya (Revelations of Men) 1995, Principal and Compassionate Eye, Tri istorii (Three Stories) 1997, Strana glukhikh (The Country of Deaf People) 1998. *Television includes:* Granitsa. Tayozhnyy roman (mini-series) 2001, Diversant (mini-series) 2004. *Publications:* Prize of Film Festival Centaurs for Passions. *Leisure interests:* antiques, cats. *E-mail:* info@renatalitvinova.ru. *Website:* renatalitvinova.ru.

LIU, Andong; Chinese business executive; b. 1946, Fengcheng Co., Liaoning Prov.; ed Beijing Inst. of Posts and Telecommunications; joined CCP 1966; technician, Petrochemical Research Inst., Ministry of Petroleum Industry 1970–85, Assoc. Engineer 1970–85; technician, Computer Bureau, Ministry of Foreign Trade and Econ. Cooperation 1970–85; Office Sec., Work Group for Special Econ. Zones, Gen. Office of the State Council 1970–85, Deputy Div. Head, Open City Group 1985–88, Deputy Div. Head, Foreign Investment Dept 1985–88, Deputy Dir Foreign Investment Dept 1988–98, Deputy Dir Open Zones Dept 1988–98, Deputy Dir Open Coastal Regions Dept 1988–98, Dir Foreign Investment Dept 1988–98, Dir Open Zones Dept 1988–98, Dir Coastal Regions Dept 1988–98; Vice-Pres. China Post Group 1998–2003, Pres. 2003–12. *Address:* c/o China Post Group, 3 Financial Street, Beijing, 100080, People's Republic of China. *E-mail:* info@chinapost.com.cn.

LIU, Benren; Chinese engineer and business executive; b. 1942; ed Wuhan Iron and Steel Univ., Training Dept of Party School of CCP; fmr Man. Wuhan Hot Rolling Plant, later Vice-Chief Engineer, later Vice-Gen. Man. and Party Cttee mem. Wuhan Iron and Steel Plant Gen. Man., also Party Cttee mem. and Vice-Sec. Party Cttee Wuhan Iron and Steel Group Corpn (WISCO) 1993–2004; Chair. and External Dir China Metallurgical Group Corpn 2004–10; mem. Nat. Cttee CPPCC. *Address:* c/o China Metallurgical Group Corpn, 11 Gaoliangqiao Xiejie, Haidian, Beijing 100081, People's Republic of China (office).

LIU, Bingsen; Chinese calligrapher; b. Aug. 1937, Shanghai; ed Beijing Acad. of Arts; asst technician, Asst Research Fellow, Assoc. Research Fellow, Research Fellow, Nat. Palace Museum, Taipei, Taiwan 1962–86; mem. Nat. Cttee 7th, 8th and 9th CPPCC 1988–2003; Vice-Chair. and mem. Exec. Council Chinese Calligraphers' Asscn; Vice-Chair. China Fed. of Literary and Art Circles 2001; Exec. mem. All-China Youth Fed.; Fushi Fine Arts Award (Japan) 1990. *Publications:* Travel Notes of Past Dynasties; Purple Wall and Autumn Grass. *Address:* Chinese Calligraphers Association, No.10, Nanli, Nong Zhanguan (Agricultural Exhibition Hall), Beijing 100026, People's Republic of China (office).

LIU, Bosu; Chinese professor of fine art; b. Nov. 1935, Nanchang City, Jiangxi Prov.; ed Cen. Inst. of Fine Arts 1955; Assoc. Prof. Cen. Inst. of Fine Arts 1981–83, Prof. 1983–, Vice Dir 1986–; Dir Chinese Painting Acad. 1993–; mem. 7th CPPCC 1988–93, 8th CPPCC 1993–98. *Address:* c/o Central Academy of Fine Arts, No.2 West Wanhong Street, Jiuxianqiao, Beijing 100015, People's Republic of China.

LIU, Chao-shiuan, BS, MS, PhD; Taiwanese politician; b. 10 May 1943; ed Nat. Taiwan Univ., Univ. de Sherbrooke and Univ. of Toronto, Canada; Assoc. Prof., Nat. Tsing Hua Univ. 1971–75, Prof. 1975–79, Dean, Coll. of Science 1982–84, Pres., Nat. Tsing Hua Univ. 1987–93, Chair Prof. 2000; Dir-Gen. Dept of Planning and Evaluation, Nat. Science Council, Exec. Yuan 1979–82, Deputy Minister 1984–87, Minister 1996–97; Minister of Transportation and Communications 1993–96; Vice Premier 1997–2000, Premier 2008–09 (resgnd); Pres. Soochow Univ. 2004–08; Pres. Asscn of Pvt. Univs and Colls 2006–08; Vice-Chair. Nat. Policy Foundation 2000–04; Chair. Monte Jade Science and Tech. Asscn of Taiwan 2001–05, K.T. Li Foundation for Devt of Science and Tech. 2000–08; Pres. Chemical Soc. 1986–87.

LIU, Chiu-Te; Taiwanese insurance industry executive; Pres. Cathay Life Insurance Co. Ltd 1998–2008; Dir The Life Assurance Asscn of the Repub. of China, Cathay Financial Holding Co. *Address:* c/o Cathay Life Insurance Co. Ltd, 296 Jen Ai Road, Section 4, Taipei 10639, Taiwan. *Telephone:* (2) 2755-1399.

LIU, Christina Y., BA, MBA, PhD; Taiwanese economist, academic and politician; *Minister of Finance;* b. 7 April 1955, Taipei; m. Johnsee Lee (divorced 1995); ed Nat. Taiwan Univ., Univ. of Chicago, USA; Lecturer, Dept of Econs, Univ. of Chicago 1983–86; Asst Prof. of Econs and Finance, CUNY 1987–92, Assoc. Prof. 1992–93; Visiting Prof., Coll. of Business and Econs, ANU 1992–98; Prof., Dept of Finance, Nat. Taiwan Univ. 1993–97, Adjunct Prof. 1997–, Chair., Dept and Graduate Inst. of Finance 1994–96; mem. Securities Listing Review Cttee, Taiwan Stock Exchange Corpn 1994–2001, mem. Public Interest Bd 1995–2001; mem. Ministry of Finance Financial Reform Comm. 2001–03; Adjunct Prof. of Business Admin, Tsinghua Univ., Beijing, Chinese Univ. of Hong Kong 2001–09; mem. and Convenor, Legis. Yuan Finance Cttee 2002–07, Commr, Exec. Yuan Tax Reform Comm. 2008–09, Chief Economist, Exec. Yuan 2009–10; Chief Econ. Adviser, Daiwa Inst. of Research 2008–09; Adviser, Chinese Nat. Fed. of Industries 2009–10; Chief Econ. Adviser, Chinatrust Financial Holding Co. Ltd 2009–10; Minister for Council for Econ. Planning and Devt 2010–12, Minister of Finance 2012–. *Address:* Ministry of Finance, 2 Ai Kuo West Rd, Taipei 10066, Taiwan (office). *Telephone:* (2) 23228000 (office). *Fax:* (2) 23568774 (office). *E-mail:* mof@mail.mof.gov.tu (office). *Website:* www.mof.gov.tw (office).

LIU, Chuanzhi; Chinese computer scientist and business executive; *Chairman, Legend Holdings Ltd;* b. 29 April 1944, Zhenjiang, Jiangsu Prov.; m.; three c.; ed Xi'an Mil. Telecommunications Inst.; researcher, Research Inst. No. 10 of State Science and Tech. Comm., Chengdu 1967–70; researcher, Computational Science Research Inst. of Chinese Acad. of Sciences 1970–83, later Dir; Cadre, Cadre Bureau, Chinese Acad. of Sciences 1983; Founder and Pres. Computational Science Research Inst. Inc. 1984; Founder, Chair. and Pres. Legend Holdings Group Inc., Hong Kong Special Admin. Region 1984–2012 (largest computer co. in China and parent co. of Lenovo), Chair. 2012–, Chair. and Pres. Lenovo Group Ltd 1994–2005, Chair. 2009–11, Hon. Chair. 2011–; Deputy, 10th NPC 2003–08; Vice-Chair. Exec. Cttee All-China Fed. of Industry and Commerce 2002; Dir, Computer Tech. Research Inst. of Chinese Acad. of Sciences 2004–; elected one of China's Top Ten Econ. Figures 2000, named by TIME magazine as one of the 25 Most Influential Worldwide Business Leaders, named by Forbes magazine as one of the Best Asian Business Leaders, named by BusinessWeek as one of the Stars of Asia. *Address:* Lenovo Group Ltd, 23rd Floor, Lincoln House, Taikoo Place, 979 King's Road, Quarry Bay, Hong Kong Special Administrative Region (office); Legend

Holdings Ltd, 10/F, Tower A, Raycom Info Tech Park, No. 2 Ke Xue Yuan Nanlu, Zhongguancun, Haidian District, Beijing 100190, People's Republic of China (office). *Telephone:* 25900228 (Hong Kong) (office); (10) 62572078 (Beijing) (office). *Fax:* 25165384 (Hong Kong) (office); (10) 62561056 (Beijing) (office). *E-mail:* info@lenovo.com (office). *Website:* www.lenovo.com (office); www.legendholdings.com.cn (office).

LIU, Chunhong; Chinese weightlifter; b. 29 Jan. 1985, Yantai, Shandong Prov.; ed Yantai Sports School; switched from judo to weightlifting at Sports School 1996; mem. Shandong Prov. Weightlifting Team 1998–; mem. nat. team 2002–; competes in 63–69kg weight div.; silver medal at clean and jerk World Championships, Warsaw 2002; gold medals at snatch (with world record weight of 120kg), clean and jerk (world record 150kg) and combined (world record 270kg) World Championships, Vancouver 2003; gold medal, Olympic Games, Athens 2004, broke world records at snatch (122.5kg), clean and jerk (152.5kg), combined (275kg); gold medal, Olympic Games, Beijing 2008; gold medal (69kg weight div.) Nat. Games 2009; gold medal (69kg weight div.) Asian Games 2010; broke world records at snatch (128kg), clean and jerk (158kg), combined (286kg); has set 27 world records (12 jr, 15 sr) throughout career. *Leisure interests:* music, reading, painting. *Address:* 9 Tiyuguan Road, Beijing, 100763, People's Republic of China (office). *Telephone:* (10) 67116669 (office). *Fax:* (10) 67115858 (office). *E-mail:* coc@olympic.cn (office). *Website:* www.olympic.cn (office).

LIU, Dehai; Chinese musician and university professor; b. May 1937, Cangxian Co., Hebei Prov.; ed Centre Music Inst.; began learning Pipa and other traditional Chinese instruments (including Erhu and Sanxian) at age 13; toured extensively abroad and performed with many famous orchestras including Boston Symphony Orchestra, Berlin Symphony Orchestra; Prof., Centre Music Inst. 1984–; mem. 7th CPPCC Nat. Cttee 1988–93, 8th 1993–98. *Address:* c/o CRC Jianian, Inc., No. 18, Jianguo Mennei Street, Rm 1706-1708, Henderson Center, Dongcheng District, Beijing 100005, People's Republic of China.

LIU, Deshu, BEng, EMBA; Chinese petrochemical industry executive; *President and CEO, Sinochem Corporation;* b. Nov. 1952; ed Tsinghua Univ., China-Europe Int. Business School; active in foreign trade for more than 20 years; Vice-Gen. Man., later Gen. Man. China Nat. Machinery Import and Export Corpn –1998; Pres. and CEO Sinochem Corpn 1998–; Sinofert Holdings Ltd, Sinochem Quanzhou Petrochemical Co. Ltd, Far East Horizon Ltd; mem. 10th CPPCC, 11th CPPCC; del., 16th CCP Nat. Cttee 2002–07, 17th CCP Nat. Cttee 2007–12; Dir, Int. Acad. of Man. 2003–. *Address:* Sinochem Corpn, Sinochem Tower A2, 28 Fuxingmenwai Dajie, 100031 Beijing, People's Republic of China (office). *Telephone:* (10) 8807-8898 (office). *Fax:* (10) 8807-8890 (office). *E-mail:* webmaster@sinochem.com (office). *Website:* www.sinochem.com (office).

LIU, Lt-Gen. Dongdong; Chinese army officer; *Political Commissar, Jinan Military Region, People's Liberation Army;* b. Oct. 1945, Wuhan, Hubei Prov.; ed PLA Political Acad., Military Acad.; joined PLA 1961, CCP 1963; soldier, later staff mem., later Head of Propaganda Dept, later Deputy Political Commissar Artillery Regt, later Dir Artillery Regt (Political Section), later Section Head Org. Section (Army Political Dept), later Dir Political Dept, later Deputy Political Commissar, later Political Commissar, 139th Div., 47th Group Army, PLA Services and Arms, later Dir Political Dept, 47th Group Army, later Deputy Political Commissar 47th Group Army; Dir Political Dept, PLA Lanzhou Mil. Region, Gansu Prov. –2000, Political Commissar 2000–03; Political Commissar PLA Jinan Mil. Region, Shandong Prov. 2003–; rank of Maj.-Gen. 1992, Lt-Gen. 1999; Deputy, 11th NPC 2008–13; mem. 16th CCP Cen. Cttee 2002–07, 17th CCP Cen. Cttee 2007–12. *Address:* People's Liberation Army Lanzhou Military Area Command, Lanzhou, Gansu Province, People's Republic of China (office).

LIU, Fangren; Chinese party official; b. 1936, Wugong, Shaanxi Prov.; ed Shenyang Building Materials Eng Coll.; joined CCP 1954; worker, later technician, later Deputy Workshop Head, later Deputy Chief Engineer, later Deputy Factory Dir, Ministry of Ordnance Industry; fmr Deputy Sec., later Sec. CCP Jiujiang City Cttee, Jiangxi Prov.; Deputy Sec. Jiangxi Prov. CCP Cttee 1985–93; First Sec. CCP Party Cttee Guizhou Mil. Dist, PLA Chengdu Mil. Region 1993; Sec. CCP 7th Guizhou Prov. Cttee 1993–2001; Chair. Standing Cttee Guizhou Prov. People's Congress 1998; Alt. mem. 13th CCP Cen. Cttee 1987–92, 14th CCP Cen. Cttee 1992–97, mem. 15th CCP Cen. Cttee 1997–2002; Deputy, 8th NPC 1993–98, 9th NPC 1998–2003 (Vice-Chair. Agriculture and Rural Affairs Cttee 1998–2003); expelled from CCP following accusations of corruption 2003; sentenced to life imprisonment for taking bribes 2004.

LIU, Fuchun; Chinese business executive; b. 1949; ed Beijing Foreign Trade Junior Coll., Beijing Foreign Trade Inst.; several years' work experience in N America and Europe, including as Deputy Consul, Chinese Consular Section, Vancouver 1981–85; Deputy Division Dir, Division Dir, Oils and Fats Division, Cereals, Oils & Foodstuffs Import and Export Corpn (COFCO) 1985–91, Exec. Dir and Man. Dir COFCO 2000–07, also Pres. and Vice-Chair. 2000; Man. Dir COFCO HK; Gen. Man. Top Glory (London) Ltd 1991–2000; Dir China Aviation Oil (Singapore) Corpn Ltd 2006–, DaChan Food (Asia) Ltd 2007–. *Address:* c/o China National Cereals, Oils & Foodstuffs Import and Export Corporation (COFCO), 11th Floor, COFCO Plaza, 8 Jian Gou Men Nei Avenue, Beijing 100005, China (office).

LIU, Gang, MS; Chinese dissident; b. Liaoyuan city, Jilin; m. Yinghua Guo; one d.; ed Peking Univ., Columbia Univ., USA; leader of Tiananmen Square pro-democracy demonstrations 1989; imprisoned 1989–95; fled China; granted temporary asylum in USA 1996; trader with Morgan Stanley, New York 2009–11.

LIU, Guchang; Chinese diplomatist; b. 1946, Jiangsu Prov.; entered Foreign Ministry 1973; assigned to Embassy in Bucharest, Romania 1973–80, Third Sec. 1986–90, First Sec. 1990–92; Deputy Chief, Soviet Union and E European Affairs Dept 1980–86, Chief 1990–92; Chief, Europe-Asia Dept, Ministry of Foreign Affairs 1992–95; Amb. to Romania 1996–99; Asst to Minister of Foreign Affairs 1999–2002, Vice-Minister of Foreign Affairs 2002–03; Amb. to Russia 2003–09. *Address:* c/o Embassy of the People's Republic of China, 117330 Moscow, ul. Druzhby 6, Russian Federation (office).

LIU, Guoguang; Chinese economist; *Special Invited Consultant, Chinese Academy of Social Sciences;* b. 23 Nov. 1923, Nanjing; s. of Liu Zhihe and Zhiang

Shulang; m. Liu Guoshiang 1948; two s. one d.; ed Southwest China United Univ., Kunming and Moscow State Inst. of Econs, USSR; joined CCP 1961; Deputy Dir-Gen. Nat. Bureau of Statistics 1980–82; Dir Inst. of Econs, Chinese Acad. of Social Sciences 1982–85, Vice-Pres. Chinese Acad. of Social Sciences 1982–93, Special Invited Consultant 1993–; Prof., Beijing Univ.; Alt. mem. 12th Cen. Cttee, CCP 1982–87, 13th Cen. Cttee 1987–92; mem. 8th NPC Standing Cttee 1993–98, mem. Financial and Econ. Cttee; mem. State Academic Degree Comm. 1988–95; mem. State Council Project Review Cttee for Three Gorges Project 1990–93; China Econs Award 2005. *Publications include:* The Problem Concerning the Reform of the Management System of the National Economy, Problems Concerning China's Strategy of Economic Readjustment, Economic Reform and Economic Readjustment, Developing Marxist Theory in the Practice of Reform, Reform, Stability and Development: Macroeconomic Management under the Dual-Track System, New Stage of China's Economic Reform and Development, Two Fundamental Transformations in China's Economy. *Leisure interest:* music. *Address:* Chinese Academy of Social Sciences, Beijing, People's Republic of China (office). *Telephone:* (10) 85195012 (office); (10) 87752681 (home). *Fax:* (10) 65137435 (office); (10) 87752680 (home). *E-mail:* liugg2005@yahoo.com.cn (home).

LIU, Haibin, BA; Chinese editor and business executive; *Chairman of Supervisory Board, Shanghai Pudong Development Bank Company Limited;* b. 1952; fmr Deputy Ed.-in-Chief; fmrly worked as Special Commr of State Audit Bureau to Nanjing, Special Commr to Shanghai from State Audit Bureau; currently Chair. Supervisory Bd, Shanghai Pudong Development Bank Co. Ltd; mem. Bd of Dirs, Shanghai International Group Co. Ltd. *Address:* Shanghai Pudong Development Bank Co. Ltd, 12 Zhongshan Dong Yi Road, Shanghai 200002, People's Republic of China (office). *Telephone:* (21) 6161-8888 (office). *E-mail:* webmaster@spdb.com.cn (office). *Website:* www.spdb.com.cn (office).

LIU, Hongliang; Chinese scientist; b. 20 June 1932, Dalian, Liaoning Prov.; s. of Liu Changchun (China's first Olympic athlete); ed Tsinghua Univ., Beijing; Fellow, Chinese Acad. of Eng 1994–; Pres. and Prof., Chinese Research Acad. of Environmental Sciences (CRAES) 1982, now Research Fellow; Chair. Agric., Textile and Environment Eng Div., Chinese Acad. of Eng; Deputy Dir, Consultant Cttee on Science and Tech., Ministry of Environmental Protection; Chief Ed. Environmental Science Research journal (Huanjing Kexue Yanjiu); travelled to Greece to take part in Olympic torch handover procession 2008; environmental consultant to Beijing Organizing Cttee for Olympic Games; pioneer in research on water environment. *Publications:* over 20 research papers and a number of monographs. *Address:* Chinese Research Academy of Environmental Sciences (CRAES), Dayangfang, Beiyuan, Andingmen Wai, Beijing 100012, People's Republic of China (office). *Telephone:* (10) 64232542 (office). *Fax:* (10) 64232542 (office). *E-mail:* engach@mail.cae.ac.cn (office).

LIU, Hongru; Chinese business executive; b. 1930, Yushu, Jilin; ed Northeast Mil. Coll., Chinese People's Univ., Moscow Univ., Moscow Financial Coll., USSR; joined CCP 1948; Vice-Gov. Agricultural Bank of China 1979–80; Vice-Gov. People's Bank of China 1981–89, Vice-Pres. Council People's Bank of China 1980; Vice-Minister State Economic Restructuring Comm. 1988–93; Vice-Gov. People's Bank of China 1981–89; Vice-Chair. Securities Comm. of the State Council 1992–95; Part-time Prof., Beijing, Qinghua and Nankai Univs; Pres. Financial and Banking Inst. of China, China Monetary Coll. 1989–, China Finance and Economics Univ.; Deputy Head Leading Group for the Reform of the Housing System 1991–; Chair. China Securities Regulatory Comm. 1992–95; Alt. mem. 13th CCP Cen. Cttee 1987–92; Vice-Chair. Econ. Sub-cttee 8th and 9th Nat. Cttees. of CPPCC 1993–2003; Ind. Supervisor PetroChina 1999–2002, Ind. Dir (non-exec.) 2002–; Chair. Chinese Financial Educ. Devt Foundation, Capital Market Research Inst.; Vice-Pres. China Finance and Banking Soc., China Nat. Debt Asscn; Hon. Pres. Securities and Futures Coll., Univ. of Hanzhou 1995–; Hon. Chair. Oriental Patron (ind. financial services group). *Publications include:* Questions on Socialist China's Currency and Banking, Questions on Socialist Credit. *Address:* National Committee of Chinese People's Political Consultative Conference, 23 Taipingqiao Street, Beijing, People's Republic of China.

LIU, Huan; Chinese singer; b. Aug. 1963, Tianjin; ed Beijing Int. Relations Inst.; solo artist; univ. teacher; performed official theme song "You and Me" at Summer Olympic Games Opening Ceremony, Beijing, August 2008. *Stage production:* Sister Liu (opera) 2003. *Compositions include:* themes to TV dramas: Plainclothes Cop 1986, The Water Margin, A Native of Beijing in New York, Snow City, Sun Rises in the East and Rain Drops in the West; songs: Asking Myself a Thousand Times for That, Helpless Love. *Address:* c/o Beijing International Relations Institute, Beijing, People's Republic of China (office).

LIU, Huanzhang; Chinese sculptor; b. 30 Dec. 1930, Balihan, Inner Mongolia; m. Shen Chaohui 1968; one d.; ed Beijing Yuying Pvt. School, Beijing Cen. Acad. of Fine Arts; Assoc. Prof., Sculpture Studio, Beijing Cen. Acad. of Fine Arts 1956–; works at Tangshan No. 1 Middle School, Chen Jinlun Middle School, Beijing, Meixian, Guangdong Prov., Lanzhou Inst., Gansu Prov. *Publications:* Liu Huanzhang Carre Works Selection 1984, Sculpture Works Selection 1985, Seals Selection 1988. *Leisure interests:* sports, growing flowers. *Address:* Building No. 3, 1-102, Hong Miao Beili Chao Yang, Beijing, People's Republic of China.

LIU, Huaqiu; Chinese diplomatist; *Director of Foreign Affairs Office, State Council;* b. Nov. 1939, Wuchuan Co., Guangdong Prov.; ed Foreign Affairs Inst., Beijing; joined CCP 1965; Second Sec., Embassy, Accra, Ghana 1973–81; Clerk, Gen. Office of State Council 1981; Counsellor then Minister, Embassy, Sydney, Australia 1984–86; Dir Dept of Affairs of the Americas and Oceania, Ministry of Foreign Affairs 1986–87; Asst Minister of Foreign Affairs 1987–89; Vice-Minister of Foreign Affairs 1989–98; Dir Foreign Affairs Office, State Council 1994–; Alt. mem. 14th CCP Cen. Cttee 1992–97, mem. 15th CCP Cen. Cttee 1997–2002, 16th CCP Cen. Cttee 2002–07; Dir Cen. Foreign Affairs Office, CCP Cen. Cttee 1998–; fmr Deputy Dir China Cttee of the Int. Decade for Natural Disaster Reduction; fmr Vice-Chair. Chinese Preparatory Committee, UN World Summit on Social Devt. *Address:* c/o Ministry of Foreign Affairs, 225 Chaoyangmen Nan Dajie, Chaoyang Qu, Beijing 100701, People's Republic of China. *Telephone:* (10) 65961114. *Fax:* (10) 65962146. *E-mail:* webmaster@mfa.gov.cn. *Website:* www.fmprc.gov.cn/eng/default.htm.

LIU, Jianfeng; Chinese politician and government official; b. 1936, Ninghe Co., Hebei Prov.; ed Kiev Eng Coll., USSR; joined CCP 1956; Deputy Dir, later Dir No. 1425 Research Inst., 4th Ministry of Machine-Building Industry 1968–84 (Acting Sec. CCP Party Cttee 1968–84); Vice-Minister of Electronics Industry 1984–88; Sec. Work Cttee, CCP Hainan Prov. Cttee 1988; Deputy Sec. CCP Hainan Prov. Cttee 1988–93; Gov. Hainan Prov. 1989–93; Vice-Minister of Electronics Industry 1993–98; Vice-Minister of Information Industry 1998–2003; Dir, Gen. Admin, Civil Aviation Admin of China 1998–2008; mem. 14th CCP Cen. Cttee 1992–97, 15th CCP Cen. Cttee 1997–2002, 16th CCP Cen. Cttee 2002–07; Del., 13th CCP Nat. Congress 1987–92; Pres. Electronics Br., China Council for the Promotion of Int. Trade. *Address:* c/o Civil Aviation Administration of China, 155 Four East West Main Streets, Dongcheng District, Beijing, People's Republic of China (office).

LIU, Jiang; Chinese government official; *Vice-Chairman, National Development and Reform Commission;* b. 1940, Beijing; m.; two d.; ed Shihezi Agricultural Coll., Xinjiang Uygur Autonomous Region, CCP Cen. Cttee Cen. Party School; technician, later Chief, Mil. Farm, Tibet Autonomous Region; Farm Head, later Dir Animal Husbandry Bureau, Beijing 1972–84 (Sec. CCP Party Cttee 1972–84); joined CCP 1978; Vice-Minister of Agric., Animal Husbandry and Fishery 1986–90; Vice-Chair. State Planning Comm. 1990–93; Minister of Agric. 1993–98; Chair. Beijing Greening Cttee 1997; Vice-Chair. Nat. Devt and Reform Comm. 1998–; Deputy Head State Working Group for Comprehensive Agricultural Devt, Leading Group, Aid-the-Poor Projects 1998–; mem. 15th CCP Cen. Cttee 1997–2002; Vice-Chair. China Council for Int. Cooperation on Environment and Devt. *Address:* National Development and Reform Commission, 38 Yuetan Nan Jie, Xicheng Qu, Beijing, People's Republic of China.

LIU, Jianzhong; Chinese business executive; *President, Shanxi Coal Transportation and Sales Group Company Ltd;* Sec., Party Cttee, Shanxi International Electricity Group Co. Ltd, currently Pres. Shanxi Coal Transportation and Sales Group Co. Ltd. *Address:* Shanxi Coal Transportation and Sales Group Co. Ltd, 82 Kaihuasi Street, Taiyuan 030002, Shanxi Province, People's Republic of China (office). *Telephone:* (351) 4924076 (office). *Fax:* (351) 4924061 (office). *E-mail:* sxct@jmxs.com (office). *Website:* www.sxmx.com.cn (office).

LIU, Jiayi; Chinese government official; *Auditor-General;* b. 1956, Chongqing Municipality, Kaixian County; ed CCP Cen. Cttee Cen. Party School; joined CCP 1976; Staff mem., Finance Dept, Supervision Div., Sichuan Prov. 1984–88; Cadre, Nat. Audit Office, Special Correspondent Office, Chengdu 1988–89, Deputy Special Commr 1989–92; Deputy Dir-Gen., Trade Audit Dept, Nat. Audit Office 1992–93, Dir-Gen. 1993–96, Deputy Auditor-Gen. 1996–2008, Auditor-Gen. 2008–; Chair., UN Bd of Auditors 2011–; mem. 16th CCP Cen. Cttee 2002–07, 17th CCP Cen. Cttee 2007–12, 18th CCP Cen. Cttee 2012–. *Address:* National Audit Office of China, No.1 Beiluyuan, Zhanlan Road, Beijing 100830, People's Republic of China (office). *Fax:* (10) 6833-0958 (office). *E-mail:* CNAO@audit.gov.cn (office). *Website:* www.cnao.gov.cn (office).

LIU, Jibin; Chinese politician; b. Dec. 1938, Longkou, Shandong Prov.; ed Beijing Aeronautics Inst.; joined CCP 1966; engineer, Section Dir then Vice-Man. Shenyang Songling Machinery Factory 1981–85; Deputy Chief Engineer, Ministry of Aeronautics Industry 1985; Minister of Aeronautics Industry 1985–88; Dir State Admin of State Property 1985–88; Vice-Minister of Finance 1988–98; Minister in Charge of Comm. of Science, Tech. and Industry for Nat. Defence 1998–2003; Del., 14th CCP Nat. Congress 1992–97; mem. Cen. Comm. for Discipline Inspection, CCP Cen. Cttee 1992–2002, Nat. Narcotics Control Comm. 1993, State Academic Degrees Cttee 1995–97, Hong Kong Special Admin. Region Preparatory Cttee 1995–97 (mem. Govt Del., Hong Kong Hand-Over Ceremony 1997), State Steering Group of Science, Tech. and Educ. 1998–; Vice Chair., Sr Advisory Cttee, Great Wall Securities Co. Ltd. *Address:* Great Wall Securities Co., Ltd., 6008 Shennan Road, Shenzhen 518034, Guangdong Province, People's Republic of China (office).

LIU, Jie; Chinese business executive; *President of the Board of Supervisors, China State Construction Engineering Corporation;* b. 22 Nov. 1943, Shucheng, Anhui Prov.; ed Wuhan Iron and Steel Inst., E.M. Beijing Iron and Steel Inst.; technician, Wuhan Iron and Steel Co. 1968; Chair. and Gen. Man., Anshan Iron and Steel Group Inc. 1994–2007 (retd); Pres. Bd of Supervisors China State Construction Eng Corpn 2008–; Alt. mem. 15th CCP Cen. Cttee 1997–02, 16th CCP Cen. Cttee 2002–07; Fellow, Chinese Acad. of Eng 1996–; State Science and Tech. Progress, Ministry of Metallurgical Industry of China: First Prize, Third Prize and Special Class Prize 1985, Third Prize 1987, Special Class Prize 1990, Second Prize 1997. *Publications:* more than 10 specialized articles, treatises and tech. reports. *Address:* China State Construction Eng Corpn, CSCEC Mansion, 15 Sanlihe Road, Haidian District, Beijing 100037, People's Republic of China (office). *Telephone:* (10) 8808-2888 (office). *E-mail:* info@cscec.com (office). *Website:* www.cscec.com (office).

LIU, Jingsheng; Chinese writer and dissident; b. 1954, Beijing; m. Jin Yanming; one c.; ed Middle School; factory worker; pro-democracy campaigner; Co-founder and fmr Co-ed. Tansuo (Explorations) journal late 1970s; joined Democracy Wall movt 1978, this involvement leading to theft charge and arrest for producing and distributing the journal; released from prison and resumed job as bus driver; helped establish China Freedom and Democracy Party after Tiananmen Square incident 1989; detained incommunicado for two years in 1992, trial July 1994, found guilty of membership in counter-revolutionary orgs, most notably Chinese Progressive Alliance, Liberal Democratic Party of China, and Free Labour Union of China; sentenced to eight years' imprisonment in Beijing Prison No. 2 for "organising and leading a counter-revolutionary organisation" and a further eight years for "inciting counter-revolutionary subversion" 1994; these were combined into 15-year prison sentence and four years' deprivation of political rights, sentence reduced by one year and three months in 2000 and 2001 for "good behaviour"; released early from prison 27 Nov. 2004; est. Beijing Huaxia Gongwei Consultation Center April 2005, forcefully locked out by govt; est. Jingsheng Work House Sept. 2005; Hon. mem. UK, German, NZ, Netherlands and Swedish PEN Centres; PEN/Barbara Goldsmith Freedom to Write Award 1998. *Address:* Zhongguan Village A21-203, Haidan District, Beijing 100080, People's Republic of China (home). *Telephone:* (10) 82591379 (home); 13718766884 (mobile). *E-mail:* ljs6454@hotmail.com (home). *Website:* www.chinesepen.org.

LIU, Gen. Jingsong; Chinese army officer; b. 1933, Shishou, Hubei Prov.; ed PLA 7th Infantry Acad.; joined CCP 1954; platoon leader, Training Bn, First Mechanized Div., PLA Services and Arms, later Commdr Artillery Gun Co., Tank Regt; Regimental Staff Officer, Operations and Training Dept, PLA Regimental Office, later Div. Staff Officer; Deputy Commdr, later Chief of Staff, Artillery Gun Regt, PLA Services and Arms; Div. Commdr, later Div. Chief of Staff, later Army Commdr, PLA; Commdr, Shenyang Mil. Region, PLA 1985–; rank of Lt-Gen., PLA 1988, Gen. 1994; Commdr Lanzhou Mil. Region 1992–97; Pres. PLA Acad. of Mil. Sciences 1997–99; mem. 12th CCP Cen. Cttee 1985–87, 13th CCP Cen. Cttee 1987–92, 14th CCP Cen. Cttee 1992–97, 15th CCP Cen. Cttee 1997–2002. *Address:* c/o PLA Academy of Military Sciences, Beijing, People's Republic of China (office).

LIU, Jiyuan; Chinese aeronautical engineer; *General Manager, China Aerospace Science and Technology Corporation;* b. 1933, Xing Co., Shanxi Prov.; ed higher industrial inst. Moscow, USSR; joined CCP 1952; technician, No. 5 Research Acad. Ministry of Nat. Defence 1960–64; Dir and Sr Engineer No. 12 Research Inst. of No. 1 Research Acad. under 7th Ministry of Machine-Bldg Industry 1980–83; Deputy Dir No. 1 Research Acad. under Ministry of Astronautics Industry 1983–84; Vice-Minister of Astronautics Industry 1984–88; Vice-Minister of Aeronautics and Astronautics Industry 1988–93; Dir China Nat. Aerospace Admin 1993–98; Gen. Man. China Aerospace Science and Tech. Corpn 1993–; mem. 14th CCP Cen. Cttee 1992–97, 15th CCP Cen. Cttee 1997–2002; mem. 9th Standing Cttee of NPC 1998–2003; Pres. China Astronautics Soc.; mem. Russian Acad. of Navigation 1997; Von Karman Award, Int. Acad. of Astronautics 2011. *Address:* China Aerospace Science and Technology Corporation, No 9 Fuchenglu, Haidian District, Beijing 100830, People's Republic of China (office).

LIU, Liehong, MBA; Chinese business executive; *President, China Electronics Corporation;* b. Oct. 1968; ed Automation Control Dept, East China Univ. of Science and Tech., School of Man., Xi'an Jiaotong Univ.; Research Fellow-level Sr Engineer; positions held include Deputy Dir No. 29 Research Inst., Dir and Party Sec. No. 2 Research Inst., Vice-Pres. and mem. Party Leadership Group, China Electronics Technology Group Corpn, Pres. China Center for Information Industry Group and Beijing CCID Info Tech Co. Ltd 2006–; Dir, Pres. and mem. Party Leadership Group, China Electronics Corpn 2008–; winner Special Govt Allowance from the State Council. *Address:* China Electronics Corporation, 27 Wanshou Road, Haidian District, Beijing 100846, People's Republic of China (office). *Telephone:* (10) 68218529 (office). *Fax:* (10) 68213745 (office). *E-mail:* webmaster@cec.com.cn (office). *Website:* www.cec.com.cn (office).

LIU, Lucy; American actress and artist; b. 2 Dec. 1968, Jackson Heights, Queens, NY; ed Brooklyn Technical High School, Stuyvesant High School, New York Univ., Univ. of Mich.; UNICEF Amb. 2005–; Asian Excellence Award. *Films include:* Bang 1995, Jerry Maguire 1996, Payback 1999, Play it to the Bone 1999, Shanghai Noon 2000, Charlie's Angels 2000, Cypher 2002, Chicago 2002, Charlie's Angels: Full Throttle 2003, Kill Bill Vol. 1 2003, Domino 2005, Lucky Number Slevin 2005, 3 Needles 2005, Rise 2005, The Year of Getting to Know Us 2007, Code Name: The Cleaner 2007, Rise: Blood Hunter 2007, Watching the Detectives 2007, Kung Fu Panda (voice) 2008, The Year of Getting to Know Us 2008, Tinker Bell 2008, Tinker Bell and the Lost Treasure 2009, Tinker Bell and the Great Fairy Rescue 2010, Nomads 2011, East Fifth Bliss 2011, Detachment 2011, Tinker Bell and the Mysterious Winter Woods 2011, Kung Fu Panda 2 2011, Someday This Pain Will Be Useful to You 2011, The Man with the Iron Fist 2011, Detachment 2011, Secret of the Wings 2012; as producer: Freedom's Fury 2006, Code Name: The Cleaner 2007. *Television:* Beverly Hills 90210 1991, L.A. Law 1993, Coach 1994, Home Improvement 1995, ER 1995, Pearl 1996, The X-Files 1996, Nash Bridges 1996, NYPD Blue 1997, Ally McBeal (series) 1998–2002, Futurama (voice) 2001–02, Joey 2004–05, Game Over 2004, Ugly Betty 2007, Cashmere Mafia 2008, Dirty Sexy Money 2008–09, Afro Samurai Resurrection 2009, Marry Me (mini-series) 2010, Ni Hao, Kai-Lan 2010, Pixie Hollow Games (film) 2011, Southland (series) 2012, Kung Fu Panda: Legends of Awesomeness 2011–12, Elementary (series) 2012. *Address:* Creative Artists Agency, 2000 Avenue of the Stars, Los Angeles, CA 90067, USA. *Telephone:* (424) 288-2000. *Fax:* (424) 288-2900. *Website:* www.caa.com.

LIU, Mingkang, MBA; Chinese banker and public servant; b. 1946, Fuzhou, Fujian Prov.; m.; two s.; ed City Univ., London, UK, Cass Business School; Vice-Pres. Bank of China Fujian Branch 1988–92, Pres. 1992–93, Chair. and Pres. Bank of China 2000–03; Deputy Gov. Fujian Prov. 1993–94; Deputy Gov. State Devt Bank of China 1994–98; First Deputy Gov. People's Bank of China and Vice-Chair. Monetary Policy Cttee 1998–99; Chair. China Everbright Group, Hong Kong 1999–2000; Chair. China Banking Regulatory Comm. 2003–11; Alt. mem. 16th CCP Cen. Cttee 2002–07, mem. 17th CCP Cen. Cttee 2007–12; Distinguished Fellow, Fung Global Inst.; mem. Bd of Dirs Int. Centre for Leadership in Finance, Bank Negara Malaysia; mem. Consultant Cttee for Chair. of Financial Stability Forum, BIS; mem. Int. Advisory Council, Faculty of Business Admin, Chinese Univ. of Hong Kong; Hon. Dir Fudan Univ. Int. Financial Centre, Hon. Prof. Chinese Univ. of Hong Kong. *Leisure interests:* jogging, swimming. *Address:* c/o China Banking Regulatory Commission, Jia No. 15, Financial Street, Xiacheng District, Beijing 100800, People's Republic of China.

LIU, Mingzhong, DEng; Chinese engineer and business executive; *Chairman, Xinxing Cathay International Group Company Ltd;* Vice-Chair. Xinxing Ductile Iron Pipes Co. Ltd 1997–2000, Chair. and Gen. Man. 2000–05, Chair. 2005–, Chair. Wuhu Xinxing Ductile Iron Pipes Co. Ltd 2003–05, currently Chair. Xinxing Cathay International Group Co. Ltd (fmrly Xinxing Ductile Iron Pipes Co. Ltd), Sec. of the Party Cttee. *Address:* Xinxing Cathay International Group, 27F Office Tower, Beijing Fortune Plaza, 7 Dongsanhuan Zhong Road, Beijing 100020, People's Republic of China (office). *Telephone:* (10) 59290000 (office). *Fax:* (10) 59290029 (office). *E-mail:* service@xxpgroup.com (office). *Website:* english.xxcig.com (office).

LIU, Mingzu; Chinese party official; *Chairman, Agriculture and Rural Affairs Committee, National People's Congress;* b. 1936, Weihai City, Shandong Prov.; joined CCP 1959; fmr Deputy Dir Office of CCP Weihai City Cttee, later Deputy Sec. then Sec. Weihai City Cttee; fmr Sec. CCP Rushan Co. Cttee, Shandong Prov.; fmr Deputy Sec. CCP Yantai Prefectural Cttee, Shandong Prov.; fmr Sec. CCP Linyi Prefectural Cttee, Shandong Prov.; Chair. Guangxi Regional People's

Congress 1993–94; Deputy Sec., Standing Cttee and mem. CCP Guangxi Regional Cttee 1988–94; mem., Standing Cttee, mem. and Sec. CCP Inner Mongolia Autonomous Region Cttee 1994–2000; Chair. Inner Mongolia Regional People's Congress 1997–99; Alt. mem. 14th CCP Cen. Cttee 1992–97, mem. 15th CCP Cen. Cttee 1997–2002; Deputy, 8th NPC 1993–98, 9th NPC 1998–2003, Vice-Chair. Ethnic Affairs Cttee 2002, Chair. Agric. and Rural Affairs Cttee 2003–; Del., 12th CCP Nat. Congress 1982–87, 13th CCP Nat. Congress 1987–92. *Address:* Agriculture and Rural Affairs Committee, National People's Congress, Beijing, People's Republic of China (office).

LIU, Nianqu; Chinese composer; b. 24 Nov. 1945, Shanghai; s. of Liu Jin Chuang and Wang Yun Cong; m. Cai Lu 1973; one d.; ed Shanghai Conservatory of Music; Art Inspector Gen. Shanghai Int. Arts Festival 1987; Art Dir Shanghai Creation Centre; Vice Sec.-Gen. Org. Cttee 1990, Shanghai Art Festival; Vice-Chair. Exec. Cttee 1991, Shanghai Spring Arts Festival; Vice-Chair. Shanghai Musicians' Asscn; Councillor China Musicians' Asscn. *Compositions include:* Phoenix Singing at Qi San Mountain (dance drama) 1983, 1989, Spring of Life and Universe (oratorio) 1989 (1st Prize Shanghai Art Festival). *Leisure interests:* table tennis, football. *Address:* Shanghai Municipal Bureau of Culture, 709 Ju Lu Road, Shanghai, People's Republic of China (office).

LIU, Qi; Chinese government official; b. 1942, Wujin Co., Jiangsu Prov.; ed Beijing Inst. of Iron and Steel Eng; joined CCP 1975; gas controller, furnaceman and founder, No. 2 Blast Furnace, Steel Works, Wuhan Iron and Steel Co. 1968–78, technician and Deputy Head, No. 3 Blast Furnace 1978–83, Deputy Dir Steel Works and Head Production Dept 1983–85, First Deputy Man. Wuhan Iron and Steel Co. 1985–90 (mem. Standing Cttee CCP Party Cttee 1985–93), Man. 1990–93; Minister of Metallurgical Industry 1993–98 (Sec. CCP Leading Party Group at Ministry 1993–98); Deputy Sec. CCP Beijing Municipal Cttee 1998–2002, Sec. 2002–12; Vice-Mayor of Beijing 1998–99, Mayor of Beijing 1999–2002; Alt. mem. 14th CCP Cen. Cttee 1992–97, mem. 15th CCP Cen. Cttee 1997–2002, 16th CCP Cen. Cttee 2002–07 (mem. Politburo 2002–07), 17th CCP Cen. Cttee 2007–12 (mem. Politburo 2007–12); Chair. Chinese Olympic Cttee, Beijing Municipality 2007–; Deputy Dir, CCP Cen. Cttee Central Guidance Cttee on Ethical and Cultural Construction 2012–. *Address:* c/o CCP Central Guidance Committee Ethical and Cultural Construction, Beijing, People's Republic of China (office).

LIU, Qibao; Chinese government official; *Director, CCP Central Committee Propaganda Department;* b. 1953, Susong, Anhui Prov.; ed Anhui Normal Univ., Jilin Univ.; sent to countryside during Cultural Revolution 1968–72; joined CCP 1971, Worker, Publicity Dept, CCP Prov. Cttee, Anhui Prov. 1974–77; Deputy Dir, Publicity Dept, Communist Youth League of China (CYLC), Anhui Prov. 1980–82, Dir 1982–83; Deputy Sec., CYLC, Anhui Prov. 1982–83; Deputy Sec., CCP City Cttee, Suzhou City 1984–85; Mayor of Suzhou City 1984; Sec., CYLC Cen. Cttee 1985–93; Deputy Ed.-in-Chief, People's Daily 1993–94; Deputy Sec.-Gen., State Council 1994–2000; Deputy, 10th NPC 2003–08; Sec., CCP Autonomous Regional Cttee, Guangxi Zhuang Autonomous Region 2006–07; Sec., CCP Prov. Cttee, Sichuan Prov. 2007–12, Chair. Standing Cttee, Sichuan Prov. People's Congress 2008–12; Dir CCP Cen. Cttee Propaganda Dept 2012–; alt. mem. 16th CCP Cen. Cttee 2002–07, 17th CCP Cen. Cttee 2007–12, 18th CCP Cen. Cttee 2012–, also mem. Politburo 2012–, Secr. 2012–. *Address:* CCP Central Committee Propaganda Department, Zhongnanhai, Beijing, People's Republic of China (office). *Website:* cpc.people.com.cn (office).

LIU, Qitao; Chinese business executive; *Executive Director, Chairman and President, China Communications Construction Company Ltd;* ed Dalian Inst. of Tech. (now known as Dalian Univ. of Tech.); worked at Sinohydro Bureau 13 1982–98, Deputy Head of Bureau 1995–98; held positions as Asst to Gen. Man. and Deputy Gen. Man. with China Nat. Water Resources and Hydropower Engineering Corpn, Gen. Man. Dept of Overseas Operations 1997–2003; Deputy Gen. Man. Sinohydro Corpn 2003–09, Gen. Man. Sinohydro International Engineering Co. Ltd 2004–06, Dir and Gen. Man. Sinohydro Group Ltd 2009–10; Pres. China Communications Construction Co. Ltd 2010–, Exec. Dir 2011–, Chair. 2013–; Top Ten Young and Middle-Aged Leaders of Technical Expertise, China Nat. Water Resources and Hydropower Engineering Corpn 1995. *Address:* China Communications Construction Co. Ltd, B88 Andingmenwai Dajie, Beijing 100011 (office); China Communications Construction Co. Ltd, 85 Deshengmenwai Street, Xicheng District, Beijing 100088, People's Republic of China (office). *Telephone:* (10) 82016655 (office). *Fax:* (10) 82016500 (office). *E-mail:* info@ccgrp.com.cn (office). *Website:* www.ccgrp.com.cn (office).

LIU, Shahe; Chinese poet; b. (Wu Xuntan), 11 Nov. 1931, Chengdu, Sichuan Prov.; m. 1st 1966; one s. one d.; m. 2nd 1992; ed Sichuan Univ.; mem. editorial staff The Stars (poetry magazine) –1957, 1979–; satirical poem Verses of Plants (1957) led to condemnation as 'bourgeois rightist'; in labour camp during Cultural Revolution 1966–77, rehabilitated 1979. *Publications include:* Night on the Farm 1956, Farewell to Mars 1957, Liu Shahe Poetic Works (Nat. Prize) 1982, Travelling Trace 1983, Farewell to my Home 1983, Sing Alone 1989, Selected Poems of Seven Chinese Poets 1993, Random Notes by Liu Shahe 1995, River of Quicksand (poetry) 1995, River of Quicksand (short texts) 2001. *Address:* 30 Dacisi Road, Chengdu, Sichuan Province, People's Republic of China (home). *Telephone:* (28) 6781738 (home).

LIU, Shao Yong; Chinese airline executive; *President, China Southern Air Holding Company;* b. Nov. 1958; ed Civil Aviation Flight Univ. of China, Tianjin Univ. of Finance and Econs; Pres. China Eastern Airlines Co. Ltd (state-owned airline) 2000–02; Vice-Minister Civil Aviation Admin of China 2002–04; Pres. China Southern Air Holding Co. 2004–, Chair. China Southern Airlines Co. Ltd 2004–. *Address:* China Southern Air Holding Co., 278 Airport Road, Guangzhou 510405, Guangdong, People's Republic of China (office). *Telephone:* (20) 86130870 (office), (20) 86130873 (office). *E-mail:* webmaster@cs-air.com (office). *Website:* www.csair.com/en/index.shtml (office).

LIU, Shaohui; Chinese artist; b. 27 Aug. 1940, Szechuan; s. of Liu Veizheng and Xiong Wenying; m. Yang Yijing 1968; one s. one d.; ed Cen. Inst. of Applied Arts, Beijing; fmr Dir Art Layout Office, Yunnan People's Publishing House; Assoc. Prof., Pedagogical Inst., Guilin Pref.; mem. Chinese Artists Asscn; Assoc. Pres. Guilin Chinese Painting Acad. 1995–; engaged in design and research; exhbns in USA, Japan, Bulgaria, Hong Kong, Italy, Taiwan; works at Guilin Arts Garden;

main designer for film Fire Boy (1st Prize, Int. Animated Film Festival, Japan 1984); Prize of Nat. Art Works of Excellence 1981, 1983, Japanese Int. Fine Arts Exhbn Prize of the Highest Honour. *Works include:* Zhaoshutun – Legend of a Dai Prince, An Elementary Theory on Binding and Layout of Books, The Candlewick Fairy 1985, Cowrie and a Little Girl 1986, Fine Arts Collection 1989. *Publications:* Yunnan School – A Renaissance in Chinese Painting 1988, Selected Paintings by Liu Shaohui 1989, The Third Sister Liu 1993, Selected Paintings of Guilin Chinese Painting Academy 1995. *Leisure interests:* music, travel, table-tennis. *Address:* Pedagogical Institute, Guilin Prefecture, 45 Xing Yi Road, Guilin, People's Republic of China (office).

LIU, Shunda; Chinese engineer and business executive; mem. CCP; fmr Deputy Head of Gen. Services Dept, Electric Power Div., Ministry of Energy; fmr Deputy Dir Office of the Minister of Electricity; fmr Party Cttee mem. and Asst to the Chief and Deputy Chief (Deputy Gen. Man.) Electric Power Bureau (Power Co.), Hunan Prov.; fmr Party Cttee mem. and Deputy Chief (Deputy Gen. Man.) East China Power Adm. Bureau (Power Corpn); fmr Party Sec. and Chief (Chair./Gen. Man.) Electric Power Bureau (Power Co. Ltd), Fujian Prov.; fmr Party Cttee mem. and Deputy Gen. Man. China Datang Corpn, Chair. Datang Huayin Electric Power Co. Ltd 2006–10, Chair. and Party Sec. China Datang Corpn 2010–13, Chair. Datang International Power Generation Co. Ltd 2010–13. *Address:* c/o China Datang Corporation, 1 Guangningbo Street, Xicheng District, Beijing 100032, People's Republic of China. *E-mail:* webmaster@china-cdt.com.

LIU, Lt-Gen. Shutian; Chinese army officer; b. 1940, Tengzhou Co., Shandong Prov.; ed Nanjing Political Coll. of the Chinese PLA; joined PLA 1958, CCP 1960; platoon leader, later staff mem., later Deputy Section Head, later Section Head, Cadre Section, Div. Political Dept; Political Commissar, Regt 1983; Political Commissar, 8th Div., Artillery Force, PLA Services and Arms 1983–86; Dir 26th Army (Political Dept), Army (or Ground Force), PLA Services and Arms 1986–88, Political Commissar 26th Army 1988–92; Deputy Political Commissar, Guangzhou Mil. Area Region 1994–98, Political Commissar 1998, Political Commissar, Chengdu Military Command –2012; mem. 15th CCP Cen. Cttee 1997–2002, 16th CCP Cen. Cttee 2002–07. *Address:* c/o Chengdu Military Area Command Headquarters, Chengdu, People's Republic of China (office).

LIU, Xiang; Chinese athlete; b. 13 July 1983, Shanghai; ed Jr Sports School, Putuo District, Shanghai, East China Normal Univ., Shanghai; began competitive athletics career as a high jumper, switched to 110m. hurdles in 1998; set world jr and Asian records for 110m. hurdles Lausanne, 2001; won titles at World Univ. Games, Asian Games and Asian Championships in 2001–02; bronze medal 110m. World Indoor Championships, Birmingham, UK 2003; silver medal 110m. World Indoor Championships, Budapest 2004; bronze medal 110m. hurdles World Championships, Paris 2003; three Grand Prix victories in 2004; gold medal 110 m. hurdles Olympic Games, Athens 2004 in world-record equalling time of 12.91 seconds; set world-record time of 12.88 seconds, Lausanne 2006; first Chinese man to win Olympic track and field gold medal; 1st place, 60m. hurdles, IAAF World Indoor Championships, Valencia 2008; forced to withdraw from Beijing Olympics due to injury 2008; elected as a Deputy Sec. China Communist Youth League Shanghai Sports Bureau Cttee 2011; Male Athlete of the Year 2003 by Chinese Sports Journalists, Laureus China Most Popular Sportsman of the Year 2011. *Leisure interests:* music, video games, karaoke. *Website:* liuxiang.sports.cn.

LIU, Xiaobo, BA, MA, PhD; Chinese writer and literary critic; b. 28 Dec. 1955, Changchun, Jilin Prov.; m. Liu Xia 1996; ed Jilin Univ., Beijing Normal Univ.; taken by his father to Horqin Right Front Banner of Inner Mongolia during the Down to the Countryside Movt 1969–73; worked in village in Jilin Prov. aged 19 and later at a construction co.; following graduation, joined faculty at Beijing Normal Univ. 1984; visiting scholar at several univs outside of China, including Univ. of Oslo, Norway and Columbia Univ. and Univ. of Hawaii, USA 1988–89; decided to return to China during Tiananmen Square protests to join the movement 1989, later named as one of the "Four gentlemen of Tiananmen Square" (Junzi) for persuading students to leave the square; charged counter-revolutionary behaviour and imprisoned in Qincheng Prison June 1989, discharged after signing "letter of repentance" Jan. 1991; charged with being involved in democracy and human rights movement May 1995, released after six months Jan. 1996; charged with disturbing the social order Oct. 1996, jailed in a labour education camp for three years 1996–99; Pres. Ind. Chinese PEN Centre (ICPC) 2003–09; detained in response to his participation with Charter 08 Dec. 2008, formally arrested on suspicion of inciting subversion of state power June 2009, tried and sentenced to 11 years' imprisonment and two years' deprivation of political rights, Jinzhou Prison, Liaoning Prov. 25 Dec. 2009; Hellman-Hammett Grant 1990, 1996, Fondation de France Prize 2004, Hong Kong Human Rights Press Awards 2004, 2005, 2006, Homo Homini Award, One World Film Festival 2009, PEN/Barbara Goldsmith Freedom to Write Award 2009, Hermann Kesten Award 2010, Nobel Peace Prize in recognition of "his long and non-violent struggle for fundamental human rights in China" 2010, PEN Canada One Humanity Award 2012. *E-mail:* penchinese@gmail.com (office). *Website:* www.chinesepen .org/english (office).

LIU, Xiaoming; Chinese diplomatist and government official; *Ambassador to UK;* m. Hu Pinghua; one s.; ed Dalian Univ. of Foreign Languages, Fletcher School of Law and Diplomacy, Tufts Univ., USA; Desk Officer, Ministry of Foreign Affairs 1974–75; Political Officer, Embassy in Lusaka, Zambia 1975–78; Desk Officer, Div. of US Affairs, Dept of American and Oceanian Affairs, Ministry of Foreign Affairs 1978–82, Deputy Dir, Div. of US Affairs 1983–89; Second Sec., Embassy in Washington, DC 1989–90, First Sec. 1990–93; Dir, Div. of US Affairs, Dept of N American and Oceanian Affairs, Ministry of Foreign Affairs 1993–94, Counsellor 1994–95, Deputy Dir-Gen. 1995–98; Minister (Deputy Chief of Mission), Embassy in Washington, DC 1998–2001; Amb. to Egypt 2001–03; Amb., Ministry of Foreign Affairs 2003–04; Deputy Sec.-Gen., Govt of Gansu Prov. 2004, Asst Gov. 2004–05; Vice-Minister, Cen. Foreign Affairs Office of China 2005–06; Amb. to N Korea 2006–09, to UK 2009–; mem. Eighth Nat. Cttee of the All-China Youth Fed., First and Second Cttee of the Youth Fed. of the Cen. Govt of China; The Fletcher Dean's Medal, Fletcher School of Law and Diplomacy, Tufts Univ. 2007, First Class Friendship Medal (N Korea) 2010. *Address:* Embassy of the People's Republic of China, 49–51 Portland Place, London, W1B 4JL, England (office). *Telephone:* (20)

7299-4049 (office). *Fax:* (20) 7636-5578 (office). *E-mail:* secretary_uk@mfa.gov.cn (office). *Website:* www.chinese-embassy.org.uk (office).

LIU, Xiaoqing; Chinese actress and business executive; b. 30 Oct. 1955, Chengdu City, Sichuan Prov.; d. of Ran Changru and Liu Huihua; m. Chen Guojun (divorced 1991); ed Sichuan Music Coll. Affiliated High; joined Chengdu's Army Performing Group 1973; head of business empire ranging from film production to real estate (45th richest person in China), including Xiaoqing Cultural Arts Ltd, Beijing; detained, convicted of tax-dodging and imprisoned 2002; also sued for defamation, Nanjing 2002. *Films include:* Great Wall of South China Sea 1976, Spring Song 1978, Wedding 1978, Little Flower 1979, Look at this Family (3rd Hundred Flowers (Baihua) Best Actress Award) 1980, Burning Down Yuan Ming Yuan 1983, Furong Zhen (Lotus Town) (10th Hundred Flowers Best Actress Award, 7th Golden Cock Best Actress Award 1986) 1986, Loveless Lover 1986, Hibiscus Town 1986, Yuanye (11th Hundred Flowers Best Actress Award) 1988, A Woman For Two 1988, Evil Empress 1988, Dream of Red Mansion 1, 1988, 2 1988, 3, 1989, 4 1989, 5 1989, 6 1989, Chuntao (12th Hundred Flowers Best Actress Award) 1989, Li Lianying, the Imperial Eunuch 1991, Town of Furong (Baihua Best Actress Award), Plastic Flowers 2004. *Television includes:* Wu Ze Tian 1995, Huo Shao E Pang Gong 1998, Tian Gui Hua 2000, Huo Feng Huang 2001, Lotus Lantern 2005. *Plays:* The Last Night of Taipan Chin, Taipei 2008. *Publication:* My Way, My Eight Years, From a Movie Star to Billionaire. *Address:* PO Box 38, Asia Sport Village, Beijing, People's Republic of China. *Telephone:* (10) 4915988. *Fax:* (10) 4915899.

LIU, Xinwu; Chinese writer; b. 4 June 1942, Chengdu, Sichuan Prov.; s. of Liu Tianyan and Wang Yuntao; m. Lu Xiaoge 1970; one s.; ed Beijing Teachers' Coll.; school teacher 1961–76; with Beijing Publishing House 1976–80; lived in Beijing 1950–; Ed.-in-Chief, People's Literature 1987–89; professional writer 1980–; mem. Standing Cttee, China All Nation Youth Fed. –1992; mem. Council, Chinese Writers' Asscn. *Publications include:* Class Counsellor (Nationwide Short Story Prize) 1977, The Position of Love 1978, I Love Every Piece of Green Leaves (Nationwide Short Story Prize) 1979, Ruyi (As You Wish) 1980, Overpass 1981, Black Walls 1982, Drum Tower (Mao Dun Literature Prize) 1984, A Scanning over the May 19th Accident 1985, Liu Xinwu Collected Works (eight vols) 1993, A Small Block of Wood, Four Decorated Archways, Wind Passing through the Ear; non-fiction: Construction and Environment in My Eyes 1998, The Beauty of Material 2004. *Leisure interests:* reading, travelling, painting, stamp collecting, music, gardening, football. *Address:* 8 Building No. 1404, Anding Menwai Dongheyan, Beijing 100011, People's Republic of China. *Telephone:* 4213965 (home).

LIU, Yandong; Chinese politician; *Vice-Premier;* b. 1945, Nantong City, Jiangsu Prov.; d. of Liu Ruiling; ed Jilin Univ.; joined CCP 1964; Sec. Org. Dept, CCP Beijing Municipal Cttee 1980–81; Deputy Sec. CCP Chaoyang Dist Cttee, Beijing 1980–81; mem. Secr. CCP Communist Youth League of China 1982–87; Vice-Pres. All-China Youth Fed. 1982, later Pres.; mem. Standing Cttee, CPPCC Nat Cttee 1983–2003; Deputy Dir Youth Ideological Educ. Research Centre 1988–93; Deputy Head United Front Work Dept 1991–2002; Alt. mem. 15th CCP Cen. Cttee 1997–2002, mem. 16th CCP Cen. Cttee 2002–07, 17th CCP Cen. Cttee 2007–12 (mem. Politburo 2007–12), 18th CCP Cen. Cttee 2012– (mem. Politburo 2012–); Vice-Chair. 10th CPPCC Nat. Cttee 2003–08; State Councillor 2008–; Vice-Premier 2013–; fmr Pres., later Sec.-Gen. China Youth Devt Foundation; Vice-Pres. China Inventors' Asscn 1988–93; mem. Sino-Japanese Friendship Asscn. *Address:* State Council, 22 Xi'anmen Avenue, Beijing, People's Republic of China (office). *Telephone:* (10) 66036884 (office).

LIU, Yang, BEcons; Chinese business executive; *Chairman and Chief Investment Officer, Atlantis Investment Management Group;* ed Central Univ. of Finance and Investment, Beijing, Grad. Diploma in Applied Finance and Investment, Securities Inst. of Australia; joined CITIC Group, Beijing 1988; joined CMG CH China Investment Ltd 1993, later Chief Investment Officer CMG CH China Fund (later renamed New Era PRC Fund); Head of China equities at First State Investment Management (HK) 2001–02; joined Atlantis 2002, later Fund Man. of Atlantis China Fund, Atlantis New China Fortune Fund and Atlantis China Healthcare Fund, currently Chair. and Chief Investment Officer Atlantis Investment Management Ltd and Atlantis Investment Management (HK) Ltd; Co-founder China Times Investments; Man. Dir Riverwood Asset Management (Cayman) Ltd; ranked by Fortune magazine amongst the 50 Most Powerful Women in Business outside the US (48th) 2012. *Address:* Atlantis Investment Management (Hong Kong) Ltd, Room 3501, The Centrium, 60 Wyndham Street, Central, Hong Kong Special Administrative Region, People's Republic of China (office). *Telephone:* 2110-6320 (office). *Fax:* 2110-9378 (office). *E-mail:* annie@atlantis-hk.com (office). *Website:* www.atlantis-investment.com (office).

LIU, Yonghao; Chinese business executive; b. 1951, Xinjin, Sichuan Prov; brother of Liu Yongxing; fmr Lecturer, Cadres' Inst., Sichuan Machinery Ministry; co-f. New Hope Group 1982, co. restructured in 1995, Pres. New Hope Group –2013, Dir New Hope Liuhe Co. Ltd 2003–; Vice-Chair. Chinese Minsheng Bank Co. Ltd 1996–2003; Deputy Pres. Chinese Feed Industry Asscn, Chinese Dairy Industry Asscn, Chinese Glory Undertaking Enhance Asscn; mem. 9th CPPCC Standing Cttee 1998–2003, Deputy Dir Econ. Cttee 2003–; named as one of Top Ten Private Entrepreneurs of China, Man of China's Reform, Top Ten Poverty-fighters, The Most Outstanding Enterprise Admin Talent, Man of China Real Estate and Star of Asia (Business Weekly) 2000, Ernst & Young Entrepreneur of the Year 2007. *Address:* New Hope Group, 4th Floor, Block B, Waltz Plaza #7, Hangkong Road, Chengdu 610041, Sichuan, People's Republic of China (office). *Website:* www.newhopegroup.com (office).

LIU, Yongxing, BS; Chinese business executive; *Chairman, East Hope Group;* b. June 1948, Xinjin, Sichuan Prov.; brother of Liu Yonghao; one s.; started family business, Hope Group, raising quail and chickens in Sichuan with his three brothers 1982, grew into second largest animal feed producer in China, co. later restructured into four entities each owned by one of the brothers; East Hope Group relocated from Sichuan to Shanghai 1999; Chair. East Hope Group 1995–; maintains portfolio interests in MinSheng Bank, MinSheng Insurance, Bright Dairy; mem. Shanghai Pudong New Area CPPCC Standing Cttee; recognized by Forbes magazine as one of most successful entrepreneurs in mainland China 2001, 2002, honoured by CCTV as one of Top 10 Economic People of 2001, by Sohu.com as one of Top 10 Financial People of 2001, recognized by Asia Week magazine as one of the Most Influential Entrepreneurs in China in the 21st Century, awarded hon. title of "30 Rural People in 30-Year China's Reform and Opening-up" 2008. *Address:* East Hope Group, 57 Songlin Road, Pudong, Shanghai 200120, People's Republic of China (office). *Telephone:* (21) 5831-2099 (office). *Fax:* (21) 6876-8702 (office). *Website:* www.easthope.com.cn (office).

LIU, Gen. Yuan; Chinese army officer and government official; *Political Commissar, PLA General Logistics Department;* b. 1951, Beijing; s. of the late Liu Shaoqi and Wang Guangmei; joined CCP 1982; Vice-Mayor Zhengzhou City, Henan Prov. 1985–88, Vice-Gov. Henan 1988–92; Second Political Commissar, PRC Police Force 1992–98; rank of Maj.-Gen. 1992, Lt-Gen. 2003, Gen. 2009; Deputy Political Commissar, PLA Gen. Logistics Dept 2003–05, Political Commissar 2011–; Political Commissar, Acad. of Military Sciences 2005–11; mem. 17th CCP Cen. Cttee 2007–12, 18th CCP Cen. Cttee 2012–. *Address:* People's Liberation Army Academy of Military Sciences, Beijing, People's Republic of China.

LIU, Yunshan; Chinese politician; *President, CCP Central Party School;* b. July 1947, Xinzhou, Shanxi Prov.; ed Jining Normal School, Inner Mongolia, CCP Cen. Cttee Cen. Party School; teacher, Baishi School, Inner Mongolia 1968; sent to do manual labour, Sobugai People's Commune, Inner Mongolia 1968–69; clerk, Publicity Dept, CCP Inner Mongolia Autonomous Prefectural Cttee 1969–75; joined CCP 1971; reporter, Div. Head, Xinhua News Agency, Inner Mongolia Autonomous Region 1975–82; Deputy Sec. Communist Youth League Inner Mongolia Autonomous Regional Cttee 1982–84; Deputy Head Publicity Dept CCP Inner Mongolia Autonomous Regional Cttee 1984–86, Head 1986–87 (mem. Standing Cttee 1986–92), Sec.-Gen. CCP Inner Mongolia Autonomous Regional Cttee 1987–91 (Sec. Insts of Higher Learning Work Cttee 1987–91), Deputy Sec. 1992–93; Sec. CCP Chifeng Municipal Cttee, Inner Mongolia Autonomous Region 1991–93; Sec. CCP Inner Mongolia Autonomous Regional Cttee; Vice-Dir Propaganda Dept of CCP Cen. Cttee 1993; Pres. CCP Central Party School 2013–; alt. mem. 12th CCP Cen. Cttee 1987–92, 14th CCP Cen. Cttee 1992–97, mem. 15th CCP Cen. Cttee 1997–2002, 16th CCP Cen. Cttee 2002–07 (mem. Politburo 2002–07, Secr. of Politburo 2002–07), 17th CCP Cen. Cttee 2007–12 (mem. Politburo 2007–12); Deputy Head, Publicity Dept CCP Cen. Cttee 1993–97, Head 1997–2002; Head, Office of Spiritual Civilization Steering Cttee, Offices Under Cen. Cttee CCP Cen. Cttee 2002–07; mem. 18th CCP Cen. Cttee 2012–, Politburo 2012–, Politburo Standing Cttee 2012–; First Sec., CCP Cen. Secr. 2012–. *Address:* CCP Central Party School, Beijing, People's Republic of China (office). *E-mail:* tgwww@ccps.gov.cn (office). *Website:* www.ccps.gov.cn (office).

LIU, Gen. Zhenwu; Chinese army officer; b. 1944, Nanxian Co., Hunan Prov.; joined PLA 1961; squad leader, later platoon leader, 42nd Army (124 Div., 370 Regt, 4th Co.), Army (or Ground Force), PLA Services and Arms, Deputy Army Commdr and Chief of Staff 42nd Army 1983–92, Army Commdr 1992–94; Commdr PLA Hong Kong Garrison 1994–99; fmr staff mem., later Head, Regimental Combat Training Br., PLA Guangzhou Mil. Region, Guangdong Prov., later Section Head, Combat Training Dept, later Deputy Dir Mil. Training Dept, Deputy Commdr PLA Guangzhou Mil. Region 1999–2002, Commdr 2002–07; Alt. mem. 15th CCP Cen. Cttee 1997–2002, 16th CCP Cen. Cttee 2002–07; Deputy Chief of Gen. Staff, PLA 2007–09; Deputy Dir, 11th NPC Foreign Affairs Cttee 2010–13; rank of Maj.-Gen. 1990, Lt-Gen. 1997, Gen. 2004. *Address:* Ministry of National Defence, Jingshanqian Jie, Beijing, People's Republic of China (office).

LIU, Zhenya; Chinese energy industry executive; *President and CEO, State Grid Corporation of China;* b. 1952, Shandong Prov.; ed Electric Power Dept, Shandong Eng and Tech. Inst.; several positions at Shandong Linyi Power Supply Utility 1984–91 including Section Chief, then Vice-Dir, then Dir; Vice-Pres. then Pres. Shandong Electric Power Bureau 1997–2004, renamed State Grid Corpn of China, Man. State Grid Corpn of China 1997–2004, Pres. and CEO 2004–; joined CCP 1984; Alt. mem. 17th CCP Cen. Cttee 2007–12. *Address:* State Grid Corporation of China, 86 West Chang'an Street, Xicheng District, Beijing 100031, People's Republic of China (office). *Telephone:* (10) 66598583 (office). *Fax:* (10) 66598794 (office). *E-mail:* sgcc-info@sgcc.com.cn (office). *Website:* www.sgcc.com.cn (office).

LIU, Zhongde; Chinese administrator; *Chairman, Sub-committee for Education, Science, Culture, Health and Sports, Chinese People's Political Consultative Conference;* b. 1933, Ji'an Co., Jilin Prov.; ed Northeast PLA Flying School, Mudanjiang City, Heilongjiang Prov., Harbin Technological Univ., Heilongjiang Prov.; joined Northeast Democratic Youth League 1948; fmr Deputy Sec. Gen. Br., CCP Communist Youth League, Harbin Technological Univ.; joined CCP 1958; worked in Harbin Civil Eng Inst.; Lecturer, later Assoc. Prof., Nanjing Eng Inst. 1962 (also Chief, Teaching and Research Office and Sec. CCP Party Cttee); fmr mem. CCP Jiangsu Prov. Cttee; Vice-Minister, State Educ. Comm. 1985; Deputy Sec.-Gen. of State Council 1988–92; Deputy Head, Propaganda Dept CCP Cen. Cttee 1990–98; mem. Cen. Group for Propaganda and Thought; Vice-Minister of Culture 1992–93 (also Acting Minister), Minister 1993–98; mem. Nat. Cttee of 7th CPPCC 1988–93, Standing Cttee of Nat. Cttee of 9th CPPCC 1998–2003, Chair. Sub-cttee for Educ., Science, Culture, Health and Sports 1998–; Pres. Asscn for Artists of Ministry of Culture 1993–; Vice-Pres. Party Bldg Research Soc.; Del., 13th CCP Nat. Congress 1987–92; mem. 14th CCP Cen. Cttee 1992–97, 15th CCP Cen. Cttee 1997–2002; mem. Govt Del., Hong Kong Hand-Over Ceremony, Hong Kong Special Admin. Region Preparatory Cttee 1997. *Address:* A 83 Beiheyan Street, Beijing 100722, People's Republic of China.

LIU, Zhongli; Chinese state official (retd); b. 1934, Ningbo City, Zhejiang Prov.; joined CCP 1954; Deputy Div. Chief, Vice-Chair., Chair. Heilongjiang Prov. Planning Comm. 1973–84, Chair. Planning and Econ. Comm. 1984–95; Vice-Gov. Heilongjiang Prov. 1985–88; Vice-Chair. State Cttee for Enterprise Man. 1988; Vice-Minister of Finance 1988–92, Minister 1992–98; Deputy Sec.-Gen. State Council 1990, Dir Econ. System Reform Office of State Council 1998–2000; Dir State Gen. Admin. of Taxation 1994–98; Deputy Head Cen. Financial and Econ. Leading Group; mem. 14th CCP Cen. Cttee 1992–97, 15th CCP Cen. Cttee 1997–2002; Pres. Nat. Social Security Fund Council 2000–04; Chair. CPPCC Sub-Cttee of Economy 2003–; Pres. Chinese Inst. of Certified Public Accountants. *Address:* c/o Chinese Institute of Certified Public Accountants, Building B, No. 16 Xisihuanzhonglu, Haidian District, Beijing 100039, People's Republic of China (office).

LIU, Zhongyi; Chinese administrator; b. 1930, Wuchang City, Hubei Prov.; ed Zhongyuan Univ., Hainan Prov.; squad leader, Sub-Regional Training Unit, PLA Cen. China Mil. Command 1949; joined CCP 1954; fmr Dir Agriculture, Forestry and Water Conservancy Planning Bureau, State Devt and Reform Comm.; Vice-Minister, State Planning and Reform Comm. 1985–90; Minister of Agric. 1990–93; Research Fellow and Deputy Dir Environmental Protection Cttee of the State Council 1992; Deputy Dir-Gen. Devt Research Centre of the State Council 1993–98; State Leading Group for Comprehensive Agricultural Devt 1990; mem. 14th CCP Cen. Cttee 1992–97; Del., 15th CCP Nat. Congress 1997–2002; mem. Standing Cttee 9th NPC 1998–2003, Vice-Chair. Agric. and Rural Affairs Cttee 1998–2003; Chair. Sino-Finnish Friendship Asscn. *Address:* c/o Standing Committee of National People's Congress, Beijing, People's Republic of China.

LIVADIOTTI, Massimo; Italian painter and sculptor; b. 20 Nov. 1959, Zavia, Libya; s. of Mario Livadiotti and Giovanna Mattera; ed Accad. di Belle Arti, Rome; major shows Rome 1987, 1989, 1994, 2000, Milan 1990, 1992, Bologna 1994; retrospectives, Petöfi Museum, Budapest 1997, Sociedade Nacional de Belas Artes, Lisbon 2000; numerous group exhbns; work inspired by San Filippo Neri acquired by the Vatican 1995. *Publications:* Monograph 1987, Anthology Monographs to accompany exhbns at Centro Ausoni, Rome, Petöfi Museum, Budapest, Sociedade Nacional de Belas Artes, Lisbon 2001, Kalós Arte Contemporanea 2001, Le anime del bosco 2009. *Leisure interests:* gardening and light exercise. *Address:* Piazza Vittorio Emanuele II, N 31, 00185 Rome, Italy. *Telephone:* (06) 4468302; (06) 77590553. *Fax:* (06) 77261541. *E-mail:* maxlivadia@gmail.com (office).

LIVELY, Dame Penelope Margaret, DBE, CBE, OBE, FRSL; British writer; b. (Penelope Margaret Low), 17 March 1933, Cairo, Egypt; d. of Roger Low and Vera Greer; m. Jack Lively 1957; one s. one d.; ed St Anne's Coll. Oxford; mem. Bd British Library 1993–99, Bd British Council 1998–; Vice-Pres. Friends of the British Library; mem. Soc. of Authors, PEN; Hon. Fellow, Swansea Univ. 2002, St Anne's Coll., Oxford 2007; Hon. DLitt (Tufts Univ.) 1993, (Warwick) 1998. *Publications:* juvenile fiction: Astercote 1970, The Whispering Knights 1971, The Wild Hunt of Hagworthy 1971, The Driftway 1972, Going Back 1973, The Ghost of Thomas Kempe (Carnegie Medal) 1973, The House in Norham Gardens 1974, Boy Without a Name 1975, Fanny's Sister 1976, The Stained Glass Window 1976, A Stitch in Time (Whitbread Award) 1976, Fanny and the Monsters 1978, The Voyage of QV66 1978, Fanny and the Battle of Potter's Piece 1980, The Revenge of Samuel Stokes 1981, Uninvited Ghosts and Other Stories 1984, Dragon Trouble, Debbie and the Little Devil 1984, A House Inside Out 1987, The Cat, the Crow and the Banyan Tree 1994, Good Night, Sleep Tight 1995, Two Bears and Joe 1995, Staying with Grandpa 1995, A Martian Comes to Stay 1995, Heatwave 1996, Lost Dog 1996, One, Two, Three. . . Jump! 1998, Beyond the Blue Mountains: Stories 1997, Spiderweb 1998, In Search of a Homeland: The Story of the Aeneid 2001; adult fiction: The Road to Lichfield 1977, Nothing Missing but the Samovar and Other Stories (Southern Arts Literature Prize) 1978, Treasures of Time (Nat. Book Award) 1979, Judgement Day 1980, Next to Nature, Art 1982, Perfect Happiness 1983, Corruption and Other Stories 1984, According to Mark 1984, Moon Tiger (Booker-McConnell Prize 1987) 1986, Pack of Cards: Stories 1978–86 1986, Passing On 1989, City of the Mind 1991, Cleopatra's Sister 1993, The Photograph 2003, Making It Up 2005, Family Album 2009, How It All Began 2011; non-fiction: The Presence of the Past: An Introduction to Landscape History 1976, Oleander, Jacaranda: A Childhood Perceived (autobiog.) 1994, A House Unlocked (memoir) 2001, Consequences 2007; TV and radio scripts; contrib. to numerous journals and magazines. *Leisure interests:* gardening, landscape history, talking, listening. *Address:* c/o David Higham Associates, 5–8 Lower John Street, Golden Square, London, W1F 9HA, England (office). *Telephone:* (20) 7434-5900 (office). *Fax:* (20) 7437-1072 (office). *E-mail:* dha@davidhigham.co.uk (office). *Website:* www .davidhigham.co.uk (office); www.penelopelively.net.

LIVERIS, Andrew N., BSc, FIChemE, FAATS; Australian chemical industry executive; *Chairman, President and CEO, Dow Chemical Company;* b. Darwin, Northern Territory; m. Paula Liveris; three c.; ed Univ. of Queensland, Brisbane; chartered engineer; joined Dow Chemical Co. 1976, Gen. Man. Thailand 1989–92, Group Business Dir Midland, Mich. 1992–93, Gen. Man. 1993–94, Vice-Pres. 1994–95, Pres. Dow Chemical Pacific Hong Kong 1995–98, Vice-Pres. Specialty Chemicals, Midland 1998–2000, Business Group Pres. 2000–04, Pres. Dow Chemical 2003–, COO 2004–04, mem. Bd of Dirs and CEO 2004–, Chair. 2006–, mem. Bd of Dirs Dow Corning Corpn; mem. Bd of Dirs Citigroup, IBM; Vice-Chair. US Business Council, Business Roundtable; Pres. Int. Council of Chemical Asscn; Co-Chair. Pres. Obama's Advanced Manufacturing Partnership 2011–; fmr Chair. US-China Business Council, American Chem. Council, Soc. of Chemical Industry America Int. Group; mem. Pres.'s Export Council, US-India CEO, Peterson Inst. for Int. Econs, Int. Council of Chemical Asscns, United States Climate Action Partnership, American Australian Asscn, Detroit Econ. Club, Nat. Petroleum Council, Soc. de Chimie Industrielle; Trustee, Tufts Univ., The Herbert H. and Grace A. Dow Foundation, US Council for Int. Business; Inaugural Chair. The Univ. of Queensland in America Foundation 2011–; Co-founder and Chair. The Hellenic Initiative (to support economic renewal in Greece) 2012–; Hon. DSc (Univ. of Queensland) 2005; University Medal for year of graduation, Alumnus of the Year 2005, named by ICIS Chemical Business magazine as the greatest influential person in the global chemical markets 2010, Distinguished Performance Award for Excellence in Public Policy, Cttee for Econ. Devt 2011, Int. Leadership Award, Council for Int. Business 2011, Legend in Leadership, Yale Chief Exec. Leadership Inst. 2011, named Platts Global Energy Awards CEO of the Year 2011, named as one of the most influential people in the global chemical markets, ICIS Chemical Business magazine 2010–12, George E. Davis Medal, Inst. of Chemical Engineers 2011, Int. Palladium Medal, Soc. de Chimie Industrielle 2012, Vanguard Award, Chemical Educ. Foundation, Inspired Leadership Award, The Performance Theater 2012, Aristeio Award in Business, American Hellenic Council 2012, Archbishop Iakovos Leadership 100 Award for Excellence 2012, named a BOSS True Leader by the Australian Financial Review 2012, BENS Eisenhower Award, Business Execs for Nat. Security 2013, Chemical Industry Medal, Soc. of Chemical Industry 2013. *Publication:* Make It in America 2011. *Leisure interests:* science, maths, astronomy, sports. *Address:* Dow Chemical Co., 2030 Dow Center, Midland, MI 48674, USA (office). *Telephone:* (989) 636-1000 (office). *Fax:* (989) 636-3518 (office). *E-mail:* info@dow.com (office). *Website:* www.dow.com (office).

LIVERMORE, Ann Martinelli, BA, MBA; American computer company executive; b. 23 Aug. 1958, Greensboro, N Carolina; ed Univ. of N Carolina at Chapel Hill and Stanford Univ., Calif.; joined Hewlett-Packard in 1982, held several man. positions in Marketing, Sales, Research and Devt, Business Man. before being elected a Corp. Vice-Pres. in 1995, CEO Enterprise Computing Solutions Org. 1996, Exec. Vice-Pres. HP Services 2001–04, Exec. Vice-Pres. HP Enterprise Business 2004–11, mem. Bd Dirs 2011–; mem. Bd Dirs United Parcel Service Inc. 1997–; mem. Bd of Visitors Kenan-Flagler Business School at Univ. of N Carolina at Chapel Hill, Bd of Advisors at Stanford Business School; ranked by Fortune magazine amongst 50 Most Powerful Women in Business in the US (23rd) 2002, (24th) 2003, (22nd) 2004, (18th) 2005, (14th) 2006, (13th) 2007, (11th) 2008, (13th) 2009, (14th) 2010, ranked by Forbes magazine amongst The World's 100 Most Powerful Women (20th) 2005, (19th) 2006, (36th) 2007, (33rd) 2008, (31st) 2009. *Address:* HP, 3000 Hanover Street, Palo Alto, CA 94304-1185, USA (office).

LIVERPOOL, Nicholas Joseph Orville, LLD; Dominican fmr head of state; b. 9 Sept. 1934; ed Sheffield Univ. (UK); called to the Bar, Inner Temple, London 1961; lawyer and legal consultant 1970s; prepared new criminal code for Belize 1980; Justice of Appeal for Belize 1990–92; Law Review Commr 1992; Judge, Eastern Caribbean Court of Appeal 1993–95; fmr Judge Court of Appeal, Grenada, Bahamas and High Court of Antigua and Montserrat; Chair. Constitution Review Comm. for Grenada 2002; Pres. of Dominica 2003–12; fmr Prof. of Law, Univ. of the West Indies, Barbados; fmr Amb. of Dominica to the UN; fmr Project Dir Caribbean Justice Improvement Project; Dominica Award of Honour (DAH) 2003. *Address:* 37 Margaret's Gap, Goodwill, Roseau (home); POB 233, Roseau, Dominica. *Telephone:* 4488968 (home).

LIVINGSTONE OF PARKHEAD, Baron (Life Peer), cr. 2013; **Ian Paul Livingston,** BA; British chartered accountant, business executive and government official; *Minister of State for Trade and Investment;* b. 28 July 1964; ed Kelvinside Acad., Univ. of Manchester; held sr man. positions at 3i Group and Bank of America International; joined Dixons in 1991, held several operational and financial roles, both in UK and abroad, Group Finance Dir Dixons Group 1997–2002; Group Finance Dir BT Group plc 2002–05, Chief Exec. BT Retail 2005–08, Chief Exec. BT Group plc 2008–13; mem. (Conservative), House of Lords 2013–; Minister of State for Trade and Investment 2013–; Dir (non-exec.) Ladbrokes plc 2003–07, Celtic plc 2007–. *Address:* Department for Business, Innovation and Skills, 1 Victoria Street, London, SW1H 0ET, England (office). *Telephone:* (20) 7215-5000 (office). *Website:* www.gov.uk/government/ organisations/department-for-business-innovation-skills (office); www.parliament .uk/biographies/lords/lord-livingston-of-parkhead/4278.

LIVINGSTONE, Catherine B., AO, BA (Hons), FCA, FTSE, FAICD; Australian business executive; *Chairman, Telstra Corporation Ltd;* has held several finance and Gen. Man. roles, predominantly in medical devices sector; Chief Exec. Cochlear Ltd 1994–2000; joined Telstra Corpn Ltd as (non-exec.) Dir 2000, Chair. 2009–, Chair. Nomination and NBN Cttees, mem. Remuneration, Audit and Tech. Cttees; mem. Bd of Dirs Sydney Inst. 1998–2005, Goodman Fielder Ltd 2000–03, Rural Press Ltd 2000–03, Macquarie Bank Ltd 2003–13, Macquarie Grad. School of Man. Pty Ltd 2007–08, Macquarie Group Ltd 2007–13, WorleyParsons Ltd 2007–, Future Directions International Pty Ltd 2007–, Saluda Medical Pty Ltd 2013–; Chair. CSIRO 2001–06, Australian Business Foundation 2000–05; mem. Dept of Accounting and Finance Advisory Bd, Macquarie Univ., Business/ Industry/Higher Educ. Collaboration Cttee (BIHECC), New South Wales Innovation and Productivity Council 2007–, Fed. Govt's Nat. Innovation System Review Panel 2008, Advisory Bd for the John Grill Centre for Project Leadership at Univ. of Sydney 2013–; Pres. Australian Museum Trust 2012–; Dir, The George Inst. 2012–; mem. Royal Inst. of Australia 2009–; Fellow, Australian Acad. of Technological Sciences, Australian Inst. of Co. Dirs; Hon. DSc (Murdoch Univ.); Hon. DBus (Macquarie Univ.). *Address:* Telstra Corporation Ltd, 242 Exhibition Street, Melbourne, Vic. 3000, Australia (office). *Telephone:* (3) 9634-6400 (office). *Fax:* (3) 9632-3215 (office). *E-mail:* info@telstra.com.au (office). *Website:* www .telstra.com.au (office).

LIVINGSTONE, Kenneth (Ken) Robert; British politician; b. 17 June 1945, London; s. of Robert Moffat Livingstone and Ethel Ada Kennard; m. Christine Pamela Chapman 1973 (divorced 1982); ed Tulse Hill Comprehensive School, Phillipa Fawcett Coll. of Educ.; technician, Cancer Research Unit, Royal Marsden Hosp. 1962–70; Councillor, Borough of Lambeth 1971–78, of Camden 1978–82, of Greater London Council 1973–86 (Leader 1981–86); MP for Brent East 1987–2001; Mayor of London 2000–08; joined Labour Party 1969, mem. Regional Exec. 1974–86, Nat. Exec. Cttee 1987–89, 1997–98, NI Select Cttee 1997–99; consultant to Venezuelan Pres., Hugo Chavez 2008; mem. Council, Zoological Soc. of London 1994–2000 (Vice-Pres. 1996–98). *Publications:* If Voting Changed Anything They'd Abolish It 1987, Livingstone's Labour 1989, You Can't Say That (memoirs) 2011. *Leisure interests:* science fiction, cinema, natural history, thinking while gardening. *Address:* c/o Labour Party, 39 Victoria Street, London, SW1H 0HA, England (office).

LIVINGSTONE, Marco Eduardo, MA; American/British art historian, writer and curator; b. 17 March 1952, Detroit, Mich., USA; s. of Leon Livingstone and Alicia Arce Fernández; partner, Stephen Stuart-Smith; ed Univ. of Toronto, Courtauld Inst. of Fine Art, Univ. of London; Asst Keeper of British Art, Walker Art Gallery, Liverpool 1976–82; Deputy Dir Museum of Modern Art, Oxford 1982–86; Area Ed. for 20th Century The Dictionary of Art 1986–91, Deputy Ed. for 19th and 20th Centuries 1987–91; UK adviser to Art Life, Tokyo 1989–98; freelance writer and ind. curator 1991–. *Publications include:* Sheer Magic by Allen Jones 1979, Allen Jones Retrospective 1979, David Hockney 1981, Patrick Caulfield 1981, Peter Phillips Retrovision 1982, Duane Michals 1984, Stephen Buckley: Many Angles 1985, R. B. Kitaj 1985 (revised edn 2010), Arthur Tress: Talisman 1986, Stephen Farthing: Mute Accomplices 1987, David Hockney: Faces 1987, Michael Sandle 1988, Pop Art: A Continuing History 1990, Tim Head 1992, Tom Wesselmann 1993, Duane Hanson 1994, David Hockney in California 1994, Jim Dine: Flowers and Plants 1994, Allen Jones Prints 1995, Jim Dine: The Body and its Metaphors 1996, George Segal 1997, The Pop '60s: Transatlantic Crossing 1997, The Essential Duane Michals 1997, R. B. Kitaj: An American in Europe 1998, Jim Dine: The Alchemy of Images 1998, David Hockney: Space and Line 1999, Signature Pieces: Contemporary British Prints and Multiples 1999, Patrick

Caulfield 1999, Photographies 2000, Jim Dine: Subjects 2000, Encounters: New Art from Old (contrib.) 2000, Kienholz Tableau Drawings 2001, Callum Innes: Exposed Paintings 2001, Langlands & Bell: The Language of Places 2002, David Hockney: Egyptian Journeys 2002, Clive Barker Sculpture (with Ann Fermon) 2002, Maurice Cockrill (with Nicholas Alfrey) 2002, Blast to Freeze (contrib.) 2002, Tony Bevan: Paintings 2000–2003 2003, David Hockney's Portraits and People (with Kay Heymer) (Sir Bannister Fletcher Award for Best Book on the Arts 2004) 2003, Pop Art UK: British Pop Art 1956–1972 2004, R. B. Kitaj: Portrait of a Hispanist 2004, Patrick Caulfield: Paintings 2005, British Pop 2005, Tom Wesselmann (contrib.) 2005, British Pop 2005, Richard Woods 2006, Tilson 2007, Tony Bevan Monotypes 2007, Gary Hume: Prints 2007, Tony Bevan (contrib.) 2007, Seeing Double: The Poetic Focus of Claes Oldenburg and Coosje van Bruggen 2007. Gilbert & George: Major Exhibition (contrib.) 2007, Peter Blake: A Retrospective (contrib.) 2007, Paula Rego 2007, Antony Donaldson: French Paintings 2008, John Wesley: Works on Paper & Paintings 2008, Paula Rego: Human Cargo 2008, Colin Self: Art in the Nuclear Age (contrib.) 2008, Jim Dine: Talking about Aldo 2008, Peter Blake: One Man Show 2009, Peter Blake: Venice Fantasies (with Peter Blake) 2009, David Hockney: Just Nature (contrib.) 2009, Peter Kinley (with Catherine Kinley) 2010, Paula Rego 2010, Peter Blake: Paris Escapades 2011, David Hockney: My Yorkshire 2011, David Hockney: A Bigger Picture (contrib.) 2012, Paula Rego (contrib.) 2012, Tom Wesselmann: Beyond Pop (contrib.) 2012, Allen Jones: Off the Wall (contrib.) 2012, Pop Art Design (contrib.) 2012, Peter Blake: Rock, Paper, Scissors 2012, David Mach 2012, Joe Tilson: A Survey 2013, Patrick Caulfield 2013, Pop Imagery 2013, Clive Barker: Objects for Contemplation 2013, When Britain Went Pop (contrib.) 2013, Caroline Walker: In Every Dream Home (contrib.) 2013, Tom Wesselmann. Still Life, Nude, Landscape: The Late Prints 2013. *Leisure interests:* music, languages, travel, collecting art, drawing and painting. *Address:* 1 Empire Square, London, N7 6JN, England (office). *Telephone:* (20) 7272-8727 (office). *E-mail:* marcolivingstone@aol.com (office).

LIVNAT, Limor; Israeli politician; *Minister of Culture and Sport;* b. 22 Sept. 1950, Haifa; m.; two c.; ed Tel-Aviv Univ.; in Israel Defense Forces, served in Educ. and Social Welfare Unit; worked in advertising and public relations; mem. Knesset (Parl.) 1992–, mem. Knesset Educ. and Culture Cttee, Labour and Social Affairs Cttee 1991–96, Chair. Knesset Cttee for Advancement of Status of Women 1993–94, Sub-Cttee on Women's Representation, Parl. Comm. of Inquiry into domestic violence 1995; Chair. of Likud and of Benjamin Netanyahu's election campaign 1996; Minister of Communications 1996–99, of Educ. 2001–06 (resgnd), Minister of Culture and Sport 2002–06 (resgnd), 2009–; fmr Vice-Chair. World Likud Movt, fmr mem. Educ. and Cultural Cttee, Labour and Social Affairs Cttee, Comm. for Commercial TV. *Address:* Ministry of Culture and Sport, PO Box 57577, Tel-Aviv 61575 (office); Knesset, Kiryat Ben-Gurion, Jerusalem 91950, Israel (office). *Telephone:* 3-6367222 (office). *Fax:* 3-6873361 (office). *E-mail:* livnat@knesset.gov.il (office); ministerts@most.gov.il (office). *Website:* www.mcs.gov.il (office); www.knesset.gov.il (office).

LIVNI, Tzipi, LLB; Israeli politician and lawyer; b. 5 July 1958; d. of Eitan Livni; m.; two c.; ed Bar-Ilan Univ.; with Mossad 1980–84; practised law in pvt. firm for ten years before entering public life; Gen. Man. Govt Cos Authority 1996–99; mem. Likud Party –2005, Co-founder and mem. Kadima Party 2005–, Leader 2008–12; mem. Knesset 1999–, served as mem. Constitution, Law and Justice Cttee, Cttee on the Status of Women, Chair. Sub-cttee responsible for legislation of the Prevention of Money Laundering Law; Minister of Regional Co-operation –2001, without Portfolio 2001–02, of Agric. and Rural Devt 2002, of Immigrant Absorption; Acting Minister of Housing and Construction 2004, Minister of Housing and Construction 2004–05; Acting Minister of Justice 2004–05, 2006–07, Minister of Justice 2005–06; Minister of Foreign Affairs 2006–09, Vice-Premier May 2006–09; Champion of Good Govt Award 2004, ranked by Forbes magazine amongst 100 Most Powerful Women (40th) 2006, (39th) 2007, (52nd) 2008. *Address:* Kadima Party, Petach Tikva, Tel-Aviv, Israel (office). *Telephone:* 3-9788000 (office). *Fax:* 3-9788020 (office). *Website:* www.kadima.org.il (office).

LIVSHITZ, Aleksander Yakovlevich, DEcon; Russian economist, banker and mining industry executive; *Director for International and Special Projects, UC RUSAL;* b. 6 Sept. 1946, Berlin, Germany; s. of Yakov Livshitz and Liya Livshitz; m. Galina Markina 1966; two d.; ed G. Plekhanov Inst. of Nat. Econ.; Chair. and Prof., Moscow Machine Tool Instrumentation Inst. 1974–; Deputy Chief Analytical Centre, Admin. of Pres. 1992–94; Head of Pres.'s Advisers 1994; Asst to Pres. on problems of economy 1994–96; Deputy Prime Minister and Minister of Finance 1996–97; Deputy Head of Pres. Admin. 1997–98; Head Econ. Policy Fund 1998; Pres. Rep. for relations with G8 countries 1999–2000; Adviser to Prime Minister 2000–; Chair. Russian Credit Bank 2000–01, also Pres. Brussels Int. Banking Club; Deputy Dir-Gen. Russian Aluminium Co. (now UC RUSAL) 2001–07, Dir for Int. and Special Projects 2007–; Chair. Supervisory Bd Soyuz Bank; mem. UN Comm. on Financing of Devt 2001. *Publications:* Introduction to Market Economy 1991, Economic Reform in Russia and its Price 1994, more than 150 works on econ. problems of Russia, econ. situation in USA in 1980s. *Address:* UC RUSAL, 109240 Moscow, Nikoloyamskaya str. 13, Bldg 1, Russia (office). *Telephone:* (495) 720-51-70 (office). *Website:* rusal.ru/en (office).

LJAJIĆ, Rasim; Serbian physician and politician; *Deputy Prime Minister and Minister of Foreign and Domestic Trade and Telecommunications;* b. 28 Jan. 1964, Novi Pazar; m.; two c.; ed Medical Faculty, Sarajevo Univ.; journalist for various newspapers and periodicals across fmr 1989–2000; Founder and Pres. Coalition of Sandzak 1994–2007 (now Sandzak Democratic Party); Pres. Social Democratic Party of Serbia 2007–; Minister of Nat. and Ethnic Communities 2000–06; also Pres. Co-ordinating Body for Municipalities of Presevo, Bujanovac and Medvedja 2000–03, 2005–07; Vice-Pres. Co-ordination Centre for Kosovo and Metohija 2001–03; Minister of Human and Minority Rights of Serbia-Montenegro 2003–06; Minister of Labour and Social Policy 2007–12; Deputy Prime Minister and Minister of Foreign and Domestic Trade and Telecommunications 2012–; Co-Pres. Jt Cttee for co-operation with Arab countries 2003–06; Pres. Nat. Council for Co-operation with the Int. Criminal Tribunal for the fmr Yugoslavia (ICTY) 2004–07; mem. Forum for Int. Relations, Belgrade, East-West Inst., Prague. *Address:* Ministry of Foreign and Domestic Trade and Telecommunications, 11070 Belgrade, bul. Mihaila Pupina 2 (office); Social Democratic Party of Serbia

(Socijaldemokratska Partija Srbije), 11000 Belgrade, Terazije 16, Serbia. *Telephone:* (11) 3113432 (office); (11) 2656442. *Fax:* (11) 3114650 (office); (11) 2656333. *E-mail:* kabinet@mtt.gov.rs (office); info@sdpsrbije.org.rs. *Website:* www.mtt.gov.rs (office); www.sdpsrbije.org.rs.

LJUNGGREN, Olof, LLB; Swedish publisher and business executive; b. 5 Jan. 1933, Eskilstuna; s. of Lars Ljunggren and Elisabeth Ljunggren; m. 1st Lena Carlsöö; m. 2nd Margreth Bäcklund; three s.; ed Univ. of Stockholm; Sec. Tidningarnas Arbetsgivareförening (Swedish Newspaper Employers' Asscn) 1959–62, Pres. and CEO 1962–66; Deputy Pres. and CEO Allers Förlag AB 1967–72, Pres. and CEO 1972–74; Pres. and CEO Svenska Dagbladet 1974–78; Pres. and CEO Svenska Arbetsgivareföreningen (Swedish Employers' Confed.) 1978–89; Chair. of Bd Askild & Kärnekull Förlag AB 1971–74, Nord Artel AB 1971–78, Centralförbundet Folk och Försvar (Vice-Chair. 1978–83) 1983–86, Richard Hägglöf Fondkommission AB 1984–87, Svenska Dagbladet 1989–91, Liber AB 1990–98 (Vice-Chair. 1998–), Intentia AB 1994–, AMF 1995–, AFA 1995–2001, Addum AB 1996–99, Consolis AB Oy 1997–; Bd mem. SPP 1978–93, Investor 1989–92, Providentia 1989–92, Alfa Laval 1989–92, Trygg Hansa 1990–95, and numerous other bds; Kt Commdr Order of the White Rose of Finland 1982, The King's Medal of the 12th Dimension with the Ribbon of the Order of the Seraphim 1987, Kommendörskorset av Den Kgl. Norske Fortjenstorden; Hon. MD. *Leisure interests:* shooting, golf, classical music, playing the piano. *Address:* Skeppargatan 7, 114 52 Stockholm, Sweden. *Telephone:* (707) 472346 (office); (8) 6678785 (home). *Fax:* (8) 6678785 (home). *E-mail:* olof.ljunggren@gmail.com.

LJUNGQVIST, Bengt, BA; Swedish business executive and lawyer; b. 13 Aug. 1937, Stockholm; s. of Gunnar Ljungqvist and Solveig Ljungqvist; m. 1st Sylvia Elmstedt 1961 (divorced 1977); m. 2nd Christina (née Hedén) Ljungqvist 1978; two s. two d.; ed Stockholm Univ.; joined Malmström and Malmenfelt Advokatbyrå, Stockholm 1967, Partner 1971–; Solicitor-Royal 1995–; Pres. Bd of City Planning, Danderyd 1976–85, Chair. City Council, Danderyd 1986–; mem. Council, Swedish Bar Asscn 1983–, Vice-Pres. 1985–; Pres. Swedish Bar Asscn 1989–92; mem. Council Int. Bar Asscn 1984–90; Pres. JP-Bank Stockholm, Swedish Real Property Owners Asscn 1991–96; Vice-Pres. Union Int. de la Propriété Immobilière 1993–96; mem. Bd, Länsförsäkringar-Stockholm 1993–, Pres. 1995–.

LLEWELLYN-SMITH, Sir Chris(topher) Hubert, Kt, DPhil, FRS; British theoretical physicist and academic; *Director of Energy Research, University of Oxford;* b. 19 Nov. 1942, Gigglewsick, W.Yorks., England; s. of the late John Clare Llewellyn Smith and Margaret Emily Frances Crawford; m. Virginia Grey 1966; one s. one d.; ed Wellington Coll. and New Coll. Oxford; Royal Soc. Exchange Fellow, Lebedev Inst., Moscow 1967–68; Fellow, CERN, Geneva 1968–70, Staff mem. 1972–74, Chair. Scientific Policy Cttee 1990–92, Dir-Gen. CERN European Lab. for Particle Physics 1994–98; Research Assoc., Stanford Linear Accelerator Center (SLAC), Calif., USA 1970–72; Univ. Lecturer in Theoretical Physics, Univ. of Oxford and Fellow, St John's Coll. 1974–98, Reader in Theoretical Physics 1980–87, Prof. 1987–98 (on leave of absence 1994–98), Chair. of Physics 1987–92, Sr Research Fellow in Theoretical Physics 2002–03, Visiting Prof. 2004–, Dir of Energy Research 2011–; Pres. and Provost Univ. Coll., London 1999–2002; mem. various advisory bodies for SLAC, CERN, DESY (Deutsches Elektronen-Synchrotron, Hamburg), Science and Eng Research Council, CCLRC, Princeton Plasma Physics Lab., Max Planck Inst. for Plasma Physics, Forschung Zentrum Karlsruhe, Saclay; mem. Advisory Council on Science and Tech. 1989–92; Dir United Kingdom Atomic Energy Authority (UKAEA) Culham Division 2003–08; Chair. Consultative Cttee for Euratom on Fusion 2004–09, Council of Int. Tokamak Experimental Reactor (ITER) 2007–09; Pres. Council of Synchrotronlight for Experimental Science and its Applications in the Middle East (SESAME) 2008–; mem. Academia Europaea 1989; Fellow, American Physical Soc. 1994; Foreign Fellow, Indian Nat. Science Acad. 1998; Hon. Fellow, Univ. of Wales 1998, St John's Coll. Oxford 2000, New Coll. Oxford 2002; Hon. FInstP 2008; Hon. DSc (Bristol), (Shandong), (Granada), (York); Maxwell Medal 1979, US Dept of Energy Distinguished Assoc. Award 1984, US NSF Distinguished Service Award 1998, Medal of Japanese Assoc. of Medical Sciences 1997, Gold Medal, Slovak Acad. of Science 1998, Glazebrook Medal, Inst. of Physics 1999. *Publications:* numerous articles in scientific journals including Nuclear Physics, Physics Letters, Physical Review. *Leisure interests:* books, travel, opera. *Address:* Theoretical Physics, 1 Keble Road, Oxford, OX1 3NP, England (office). *E-mail:* c.llewellyn-smith@physics.ox.ac.uk (office). *Website:* www.physics.ox.ac.uk (office); www.energy.ox..ac.uk (office).

LLEWELLYN-SMITH, Elizabeth, CB, BA, MA; British public servant and college principal (retd); b. 17 Aug. 1934, Upshire, Essex, England; d. of the late John Clare Llewellyn-Smith and Margaret Emily Frances Crawford; sister of Sir Michael John Llewellyn-Smith (q.v.) and Sir Chris Llewellyn-Smith; ed Christ's Hosp., Univ. of Cambridge and Royal Coll. of Defence Studies; fmr civil servant; Deputy Dir-Gen. of Fair Trading 1982–87; Deputy Sec. Dept of Trade and Industry 1987–90; Dir European Investment Bank 1987–90; Prin. St Hilda's Coll., Oxford 1990–2001; mem. Council Consumers' Asscn 2002–08, Accountancy Investigation and Disciplinary Bd 2003–09; Hon. Fellow, Girton Coll., Cambridge 1994, St Mary's Coll., Durham Univ. 1999, St Hilda's Coll., Oxford 2001. *Publications:* articles in Dictionary of National Biography. *Leisure interests:* travel, books, entertaining. *Address:* Brook Cottage, Taston, nr Charlbury, Oxon., OX7 3JL, England. *Telephone:* (1608) 811874. *E-mail:* e.llewellynsmith@btopenworld.com.

LLEWELLYN-SMITH, Sir Michael John, Kt, KCVO, CMG, MA, DPhil; British diplomatist (retd) and writer; *Senior Independent Director, Coca-Cola Hellenic AG;* b. 25 April 1939, Tunbridge Wells, Kent, England; s. of John Clare Llewellyn-Smith and Margaret Emily Frances Crawford; brother of Elizabeth Llewellyn-Smith (q.v.) and Sir Chris Llewellyn-Smith; m. Colette Gaulier 1967; one s. one d.; ed Wellington Coll., Berks., New Coll. and St Antony's Coll., Oxford; at Embassy, Moscow 1973–75, at Embassy, Paris 1976–78; at Royal Coll. of Defence Studies 1979; at Embassy, Athens 1980–83; Head, Western European Dept, FCO 1984–85, Head of Soviet Dept 1985–88; Minister, Embassy, Paris 1988–91; Amb. to Poland 1991–96, to Greece 1996–99; Vice-Chair. Cathedrals Fabric Comm. for England 1999–2006; Dir (non-exec.) Coca-Cola HBC SA 2000–; Vice-Pres. British School at Athens 2009–; Council mem. Anglo-Hellenic League 1999–; Hon. Fellow, St Antony's Coll., Oxford 2007; John D. Criticos Prize 1999. *Publications:* The Great

Island: A Study of Crete 1965, Ionian Vision: Greece in Asia Minor 1919–22 1973, The British Embassy Athens 1998, Olympics in Athens 1896: The Invention of the Modern Olympic Games 2004, Athens: A Cultural and Literary History 2004, Scholars, Travels, Archives: Greek History and Culture through the British School at Athens (ed.) 2009. *Leisure interests:* music, Greek mountains. *Address:* c/o Oxford and Cambridge Club, 71 Pall Mall, London, SW1Y 5HD, England. *Website:* www.michaellllewellynsmith.co.uk.

LLORENTI SOLIS, Sacha Sergio; Bolivian lawyer and diplomatist; *Minister of the Interior;* b. 31 March 1972, Cochabamba; Lecturer, Universidad de Aquino Bolivia, Universidad Andina Simón Bolívar and Bolivia's judicial institute (Instituto de la Judicatura) 2002–05; Pres. Asamblea Permanente de Derechos Humanos de Bolivia (Human Rights Permanent Nat. Ass. of Bolivia) 2005–07; mem. Nat. Council for the Constituent's Ass.; Deputy Minister for Coordination of Social Movts and Civil Soc., Ministry of the Presidency 2007–10, Minister of the Interior 2010–. *Publications:* numerous articles and books on the defence of human rights in Bolivia. *Address:* Ministry of the Interior Avda Arce 2409, esq. Belisario Salinas, La Paz, Bolivia (office). *Telephone:* (2) 237-0460 (office). *Fax:* (2) 237-1334 (office). *E-mail:* mail@mingobierno.gov.bo (office). *Website:* www.mingobierno.gov .bo (office).

LLOWARCH, Martin Edge, CBIM, FCA, FICA; British business executive; b. 28 Dec. 1935; s. of Wilfred Llowarch and Olga Llowarch; m. Ann Marion Buchanan 1965; one s. two d.; ed Stowe School; with Buckingham, Coopers & Lybrand 1962–68; with British Steel PLC (fmrly British Steel Corpn) 1968–, Head of Special Projects 1968, Man. Dir (SA) 1971, Dir Finance and Admin. (Int.) 1973, Finance Dir Tubes Div. 1975, Financial Controller Strip Products Group 1980, Man. Dir for Finance 1983, Dir 1984–91, Deputy CEO 1986, CEO 1986–91; Chair. (part-time) Transport Devt Group PLC 1992–2000; Deputy Chair. (non-exec.) Firth Rixson (fmrly Johnson and Firth Brown PLC) 1992–93, Chair. 1993–2001; Dir (non-exec.) Abbey Nat. PLC 1989–99 (Deputy Chair. 1994–99), Hickson Int. PLC 1992–99; mem. Accounting Standards Cttee 1985–87. *Leisure interests:* sport, music, gardening, reading.

LLOYD, Chris(tine) Marie Evert (see EVERT, Chris(tine) Marie).

LLOYD, Christopher; American actor; b. 22 Oct. 1938, Stamford, Conn.; ed Neighborhood Playhouse, New York. *Plays:* Red White & Madox, Possessed, Midsummer Night's Dream, Kaspar (Drama Desk and Obie Awards 1973), Unexpected Man 2002, Mornings at 7 (Broadway) 2002, Twelfth Night (Shakespeare in the Park) 2002. *Films include:* One Flew Over the Cuckoo's Nest 1975, Three Warriors 1978, Goin' South 1978, Butch and Sundance: The Early Days 1979, The Onion Field 1979, The Black Marble 1980, The Legend of the Lone Ranger 1981, Mr Mom 1983, To Be or Not To Be 1983, Star Trek III: The Search for Spock 1984, The Adventures of Buckaroo Banzai Across the 8th Dimension 1984, Back to the Future 1985, Clue 1985, Walk Like a Man 1987, Who Framed Roger Rabbit? 1988, Track 29 1988, Eight Men Out 1988, The Dream Team 1989, The Real Blonde, Back to the Future Part II 1989, Why Me? 1990, Back to the Future Part III 1990, The Addams Family 1991, Twenty Bucks (Independent Spirit Award for Best Dramatic Actor) 1993, Dennis the Menace 1993, Addams Family Values 1993, Angels in the Outfield 1994, The Pagemaster 1994, Camp Nowhere 1994, Radioland Murders 1994, Things To Do in Denver When You're Dead 1995, Cadillac Ranch 1996, Changing Habits 1997, Anastasia 1997, Dinner at Fred's 1999, Baby Geniuses 1999, My Favorite Martian 1999, Man on the Moon 1999, Wish You Were Dead 2002, Interstate 60 2002, Hey Arnold! The Movie (voice) 2002, Haunted Lighthouse 2003, Merry Christmas Space Case (voice) 2003, Admissions 2004, A Fate Totally Worse Than Death 2005, Enfants terribles 2005, Flakes 2007, Fly Me to the Moon (voice) 2007. *Television includes:* Lacy and the Mississippi Queen 1978, The Word (mini-series) 1978, The Fantastic Seven 1979, Barney Miller 1978, 1979, Taxi (series) (two Emmy Awards including Best Supporting Actor) 1978–83, Visions 1980, Best of the West (series) 1981, Pilgrim, Farewell 1982, Money on the Side 1982, September Gun 1983, Cheers 1984, Old Friends 1984, The Cowboy and the Ballerina 1984, Street Hawk 1985, Amazing Stories 1986, Tales from the Hollywood Hills: Pat Hobby Teamed with Genius 1987, Back to the Future (series) 1991, Road to Avonlea (Emmy Award for Best Supporting Actor) 1992, T Bone N Weasel 1992, Dead Ahead: The Exxon Valdez Disaster 1992, Fallen Angels 1993, Mrs. Piggle-Wiggle (series) 1994, In Search of Dr. Seuss 1994, Deadly Games (series) 1995, Rent-a-Kid 1995, The Right to Remain Silent 1996, Quicksilver Highway 1997, Angels in the Endzone 1997, The Ransom of Red Chief 1998, Spin City - Back to the Future IV - Judgment Day 1999, Alice in Wonderland 1999, It Came from the Sky 1999, On the Edge 2001, The Tick 2001, Chasing Destiny 2001, The Big Time 2001, When Good Ghouls Go Bad 2001, Cyberchase (series; voice) 2002, Malcolm in the Middle 2002, Ed 2003, Tremors (episodes) 2003, Grim & Evil (voice) 2004, I Dream (series) 2004, Clubhouse (series) 2004, King of the Hill (voice) 2005, The West Wing (episode The Wake Up Call) 2005, Stacked (series) 2005, Detective 2005, Here Comes Peter Cottontail: The Movie (voice) 2005, Stacked (series) 2005–06, A Perfect Day 2006. *Address:* c/o The Gersh Agency, 9465 Wilshire Blvd, 6th Floor, Beverly Hills, CA 90212, USA (office).

LLOYD, Clive Hubert, AO, CBE; Guyanese sports administrator and fmr professional cricketer; *Chairman, Cricket Committee, International Cricket Council;* b. 31 Aug. 1944, Georgetown, British Guiana (now Guyana); s. of the late Arthur Christopher Lloyd and Sylvia Thelma Lloyd; cousin of Lance Gibbs; m. Waveney Benjamin 1971; one s. two d.; ed Chatham High School, Georgetown; left-hand batsman; right-arm medium-paced bowler; played for British Guiana/ Guyana 1963–83, Lancashire 1968–86 (Capt. 1981–83, 1986); played in 110 Tests for W Indies 1966–85, record 74 as Capt., scoring 7,515 runs (average 46.67, highest score 242 not out) including 19 hundreds; scored 31,232 First-class runs (average 49.26) including 79 hundreds; W Indies Team Man. 1988–89, 1996–99; Int. Cricket Council (ICC) Referee 1992–95, Match Referee 2001–06, Chair. ICC Cricket Cttee and Ex-Officio mem. ICC Chief Execs' Cttee 2008–; Exec. Promotions Officer, Project Fullemploy 1987–; Dir Red Rose Radio PLC 1981; Patron Nat. Lottery Charities Bd, Major League Cricket for inaugural Interstate Cricket Cup (named the Sir Clive Lloyd Cup), USA 2005; Hon. Fellow, Manchester Polytechnic, Lancs. Polytechnic 1986; Hon. MA (Manchester, Hull); Hon. DLitt (Univ. of W Indies, Jamaica); Golden Arrow of Achievement (Guyana) 1975, Wisden Cricketer of the Year 1971. *Publications:* Living for Cricket (with Tony Cozier) 1980,

Winning Captaincy (with Mihir Bose) 1995. *Address:* International Cricket Council, PO Box 500 070, Street 69, Dubai Sports City, Emirates Road, Dubai, UAE (office); c/o Harefield, Harefield Drive, Wilmslow, Cheshire, SK9 1NJ, England. *Telephone:* (4) 382-8800 (office). *Fax:* (4) 382-8600 (office). *E-mail:* enquiry@icc-cricket.com (office). *Website:* icc-cricket.yahoo.net (office).

LLOYD, David Robert, MA, PhD, ScD, MRIA, FInstP; British chemist and academic; *Fellow Emeritus, Department of Chemistry, Trinity College Dublin;* b. 19 May 1937, Derby, England; s. of George Lloyd and Effie Lloyd; m. Heidi Hoffman 1964; one s. one d.; ed Halesowen Grammar School, Worcs. and Selwyn Coll., Cambridge; temporary Lecturer, Chem. Dept, Northwestern Univ., Evanston, USA 1963–65; Lecturer in Chem., Univ. of Birmingham 1965–78; Prof. of Chem., Trinity Coll. Dublin, Ireland 1978–2000, now Fellow Emer., Head of Chem. Dept 1978–85, 1992–94; A. von Humboldt Fellowship 1962–63; Fellow, Trinity Coll. Dublin. *Publications:* approx. 118 papers on aspects of chemistry and physics, three on Plato's view of the elements. *Leisure interests:* music, hill walking, domestic chores, theology, classical Greek. *Address:* Department of Chemistry, University of Dublin, Trinity College, Dublin 2, Ireland (office). *Telephone:* (1) 6081726 (office). *E-mail:* chemdept@tcd.ie (office). *Website:* www.tcd.ie/Chemistry (office).

LLOYD, Sir Geoffrey Ernest Richard, Kt, PhD, FBA; British academic; *Professor Emeritus of Ancient Philosophy and Science, University of Cambridge;* b. 25 Jan. 1933, London, England; s. of William Ernest Lloyd and Olive Irene Neville Lloyd; m. Janet Elizabeth Lloyd 1956; three s.; ed Charterhouse and King's Coll. Cambridge; Asst Lecturer in Classics, Univ. of Cambridge 1965–67, Lecturer 1967–74, Reader in Ancient Philosophy and Science 1974–83, Prof. 1983–2000, Prof. Emer. 2000–; Master, Darwin Coll., Cambridge 1989–2000, Hon. Fellow 2000–; Fellow, King's Coll. 1957–89, Hon. Fellow 1990–; A. D. White Prof.-at-Large, Cornell Univ., Ithaca, NY, USA 1990–96; Chair. East Asian History of Science Trust 1992–2002; mem. Japan Soc. for the Promotion of Science, Int. Acad. of the History of Science; Zhu Kezhen Visiting Prof., Inst. for the History of Natural Science, Beijing 2002; Foreign Hon. mem. American Acad. of Arts and Sciences 1995; Hon. LittD (Athens) 2003; Sarton Medal 1987, Kenyon Medal 2007. *Publications:* Polarity and Analogy 1966, Aristotle, the Growth and Structure of his Thought 1968, Early Greek Science: Thales to Aristotle 1970, Greek Science after Aristotle 1973, Hippocratic Writings (ed.) 1978, Aristotle on Mind and the Senses (co-ed. with G. E. L. Owen) 1978, Magic, Reason and Experience 1979, Science, Folklore and Ideology 1983, Science and Morality in Greco-Roman Antiquity 1985, The Revolutions of Wisdom 1987, Demystifying Mentalities 1990, Methods and Problems in Greek Science 1991, Adversaries and Authorities 1996, Aristotelian Explorations 1996, Greek Thought (ed.) 2000, The Ambitions of Curiosity 2002, The Way and the Word (with N. Sivin) 2002, In the Grip of Disease, Studies in the Greek Imagination 2003, Ancient Worlds, Modern Reflections 2004, The Delusions of Invulnerability 2005, Principles and Practices in Ancient Greek and Chinese Science 2006, Cognitive Variations, Reflections on the Unity and Diversity of the Human Mind 2007, Disciplines in the Making, Cross-Cultural Perspectives on Elites, Learning and Innovation 2009. *Leisure interest:* travel. *Address:* Needham Research Institute, 8 Sylvester Road, Cambridge, CB3 9AF (office); 2 Prospect Row, Cambridge, CB1 1DU, England (home). *Telephone:* (1223) 311545 (office); (1223) 355970 (home). *E-mail:* eahost1@hotmail.com (office); gel20@cam.ac.uk (office).

LLOYD, John Nicol Fortune, MA; British journalist; *Contributing Editor, Financial Times;* b. 15 April 1946; s. of Christopher Lloyd and Joan A. Fortune; m. 1st Judith Ferguson 1974 (divorced 1979); one s.; ed Waid Comprehensive School and Univ. of Edinburgh; Ed. Time Out 1972–73; reporter, London Programme 1974–76; Producer, Weekend World 1976–77; industrial reporter, labour corresp., industrial and labour ed., Financial Times 1977–86; Ed. New Statesman 1986–87, Assoc. Ed. 1996–2003; with Financial Times 1987–, posts include East Europe Ed., Financial Times Magazine Ed., Moscow Corresp. 1991–95, currently Contributing Ed.; columnist, Reuters.-com, La Repubblica, Rome; Dir of Journalism, Reuters Inst., Univ. of Oxford; Chair. Advisory Council, Moscow School of Political Studies; Journalist of the Year, Granada Awards 1984, Specialist Writer of the Year, IPC Awards 1985, Rio Tinto David Watt Memorial Prize 1997. *Publications include:* The Politics of Industrial Change (with Ian Benson) 1982, The Miners' Strike: Loss Without Limit (with Martin Adeney) 1986, In Search of Work (with Charles Leadbeater) 1987, Counterblasts (contrib.) 1989, Rebirth of a Nation: An Anatomy of Russia 1998, Re-engaging Russia 2000, The Protest Ethic 2001, What the Media are Doing to Our Politics 2004, Scandal! 2011. *Leisure interests:* opera, Italy. *Address:* c/o CA Holdings, Branch Hill Mews, Branch Hill, London, NW3 7LT, England (office). *Telephone:* (20) 7472-6500 (office). *E-mail:* john.lloyd@ft.com (office). *Website:* www .reutersinstitute.politics.ox.ac.uk (office).

LLOYD, Robert Andrew, CBE, MA; British singer (bass); b. 2 March 1940, Southend; s. of William Edward Lloyd and May Lloyd (née Waples); m. 1st Sandra D. Watkins 1964 (divorced 1990); one s. three d.; m. 2nd Lynda A. Hazell (née Powell) 1992; ed Southend High School for Boys, Keble Coll. Oxford, London Opera Centre; served as Lt in Royal Navy 1963–66; Lecturer, Bramshill Police Coll. 1966–68; Prin. Bass, Sadler's Wells Opera 1969–72, Royal Opera House 1972–83, Sr Artist, Royal Opera House 2005–10; freelance singer with all maj. opera houses and orchestras world-wide, frequent broadcasts as presenter, BBC radio and TV 1983–; film appearances: Parsifal, Bluebeard's Castle; performed title role in Tarkovsky production of Boris Godunov at Kirov Opera, Leningrad 1990; created role of Tyrone in Tower by Alun Hoddinott; Visiting Prof. Royal Coll. of Music, London 1996–; Pres. British Youth Opera 1988–94, Southend Choral Soc. 1996–; mem. Exec. Cttee Musicians' Benevolent Fund 1989–92; mem. Conservatoires Advisory Group 1993–99; Pres. Inc. Soc. of Musicians 2006; Fellow, Royal Welsh Coll. of Music and Drama; Hon. Fellow Keble Coll. 1990; Patron Carl Rosa Trust 1994–; Hon. mem. Royal Acad. of Music; Artist of the Year, Teatro Colón, Buenos Aires 1996, Charles Santley Award 1997, Chaliapin Commemoration Medal (St Petersburg) 1998. *Radio:* regular presenter for BBC Radio 3. *Television:* wrote and presented documentary Six Foot Cinderella 1990, subject of BBC documentary Bob the Bass. *Publications:* numerous contribs to magazines. *Leisure interests:* sailing, hill walking, history.

LLOYD-JONES, David Mathias, BA; British musician and conductor; b. 19 Nov. 1934, London; s. of the late Sir Vincent Lloyd-Jones and Margaret Alwena Mathias; m. Anne Carolyn Whitehead 1964; two s. one d.; ed Westminster School, Magdalen Coll. Oxford; Repetiteur, Royal Opera 1959–61; Chorus Master, New Opera Co. 1961–64; conducted at Bath Festival 1966, City of London Festival 1966, Wexford Festival 1967–70, Scottish Opera 1968, Welsh Nat. Opera 1968, Royal Opera, Covent Garden 1971, Sadler's Wells Opera Co. (now ENO) 1969; Asst Music Dir ENO 1972–78; Artistic Dir Opera North 1978–90; also conductor for TV operas (Eugene Onegin, The Flying Dutchman, Hansel and Gretel) and has appeared with most British symphony orchestras and conducted worldwide; Chair. Delius Trust 1997–, Gen. Ed. William Walton Edn 1996–; Hon. mem. Royal Philharmonic Soc. 2007; Hon. DMus (Leeds) 1986. *Music:* many acclaimed recordings of British and Russian music; has edited works by composers, including Mussorgsky, Bizet, Walton, Berlioz, Elgar and Sullivan. *Publications:* Boris Godunov–Translation, Vocal Score, Eugene Onegin–Translation, Vocal Score, Boris Godunov–Critical Edition of Original Full Score, numerous contribs to publs including Grove's Dictionary of Music and Musicians, Musik in Geschichte und Gegenwart, Music and Letters, The Listener. *Leisure interests:* theatre, French cuisine, rose growing. *Address:* c/o Allied Artists, 42 Montpelier Square, London SW7 1JZ, England (office); 94 Whitelands House, Cheltenham Terrace, London, SW3 4RA, England (home). *Telephone:* (20) 7589-6243 (office); (20) 7730-8695. *E-mail:* info@alliedartists.co.uk (office). *Website:* www.alliedartists.co.uk (office).

LLOYD WEBBER, Baron (Life Peer), cr. 1997, of Sydmonton in the County of Hampshire; **Andrew Lloyd Webber,** FRCM; British composer; *Chairman, The Really Useful Group Ltd;* b. 22 March 1948, Kensington, London; s. of the late William Southcombe Lloyd Webber and Jean Hermione Johnstone; brother of Julian Lloyd Webber (q.v.); m. 1st Sarah Jane Tudor (née Hugill) 1971 (divorced 1983); one s. one d.; m. 2nd Sarah Brightman 1984 (divorced 1990); m. 3rd Madeleine Astrid Gurdon 1991; two s. one d.; ed Westminster School, Magdalen Coll. Oxford, Royal Coll. of Music; Chair. The Really Useful Group Ltd; owner of seven London theatres including the Palace Theatre, Theatre Royal Drury Lane, The London Palladium; seven Tony Awards, four Drama Desk Awards, seven Laurence Olivier Awards, 14 Ivor Novello Awards from British Acad. of Songwriters, Composers and Authors, Triple Play Awards 1996, ASCAP 1988, Star on the Hollywood Walk of Fame for live theatre 1993, Praemium Imperiale Award 1995, four Grammy Awards, Golden Globe Award, Academy Award 1996, Richard Rodgers Award for Excellence in Musical Theatre 1996, Kennedy Center Honor 2006, Woodrow Wilson Award for Public Service 2008, American Songwriter's Hall of Fame; Commdr's Cross of the Order of Merit (Hungary) 2005. *Works:* musicals: Joseph and the Amazing Technicolor Dreamcoat (lyrics by Tim Rice) 1968 (revised 1973, 1991), Jesus Christ Superstar (lyrics by Tim Rice) 1970 (revised 1996), Jeeves (lyrics by Alan Ayckbourn) 1975 (revised as By Jeeves 1996), Evita (lyrics by Tim Rice) 1976 (stage version 1978), Tell Me on a Sunday (lyrics by Don Black) 1980, revised 2003, Cats (based on T. S. Eliot's Old Possum's Book of Practical Cats) (Tony Awards for Best Score and Best Musical 1983) 1981, Song and Dance (lyrics by Don Black) 1982, Starlight Express (lyrics by Richard Stilgoe) 1984, The Phantom of the Opera (Tony Award for Best Musical 1988) (lyrics by Richard Stilgoe and Charles Hart) 1986, Aspects of Love (lyrics by Don Black and Charles Hart) 1989, Sunset Boulevard (Tony Awards for Best Score and Best Musical 1995) (lyrics by Christopher Hampton and Don Black) 1993, Whistle Down the Wind (lyrics by Jim Steinman) 1996, The Beautiful Game (with lyrics by Ben Elton) (London Critics' Circle Best Musical 2000) 2000, The Woman in White (lyrics by David Zippel) 2004, Love Never Dies (lyrics by Glenn Slater) 2010; other compositions: Variations (based on A minor Caprice No. 24 by Paganini) 1977 (symphonic version 1986), Requiem Mass 1985, Amigos Para Siempre (official theme for 1992 Olympic Games, UK Eurovision entry, It's My Time (co-written with Diane Warren), Moscow 2009; film scores: Gumshoe 1971, The Odessa File 1974. *Producer:* Joseph and the Amazing Technicolor Dreamcoat 1973, 1974, 1978, 1980, 1991, Jeeves Takes Charge 1975, Cats 1981, Song & Dance 1982, Daisy Pulls it Off 1983, The Hired Man 1984, Starlight Express 1984, On Your Toes 1984, The Phantom of the Opera 1986, Café Puccini 1986, The Resistible Rise of Arturo Ui 1987, Lend Me a Tenor 1988, Aspects of Love 1989, Shirley Valentine (Broadway) 1989, La Bête 1992, Sunset Boulevard 1993, By Jeeves 1996, Whistle Down the Wind 1996, 1998, Jesus Christ Superstar 1996, 1998, The Beautiful Game 2000, Bombay Dreams 2002, Tell Me On A Sunday 2003, The Woman in White 2004, The Sound of Music 2006 and others. *Film:* The Phantom of the Opera (directed by Joel Schumacher) 2004. *Publications:* Evita (with Tim Rice) 1978, Cats: the book of the musical 1981, Joseph and the Amazing Technicolor Dreamcoat (with Tim Rice) 1982, The Complete Phantom of the Opera 1987, The Complete Aspects of Love 1989, Sunset Boulevard: from movie to musical 1993. *Leisure interests:* architecture, art. *Address:* The Really Useful Group Ltd, 22 Tower Street, London, WC2H 9TW, England (office). *Telephone:* (20) 7240-0880 (office). *Fax:* (20) 7240-1204 (office). *Website:* www.reallyuseful.com (office).

LLOYD WEBBER, Julian, FRCM; British cellist and writer; *Chairman, In Harmony Sistema England;* b. 14 April 1951, London; s. of the late William Southcombe Lloyd Webber and of Jean Hermione Johnstone; brother of Andrew Lloyd Webber (q.v.); m. 1st Celia M. Ballantyne 1974 (divorced 1989); m. 2nd Zohra Mahmoud Ghazi 1989 (divorced 1999); one s.; m. 3rd Kheira Bourahla 2001 (divorced 2007); m. 4th Jiaxin Cheng 2009; one d.; ed Univ. Coll. School, Royal Coll. of Music (scholar), studied with Pierre Fournier in Geneva; debut with first London performance of Bliss Cello Concerto at Queen Elizabeth Hall 1972; debut, Lincoln Center, New York 1980; debut with Berlin Philharmonic Orchestra 1984; appears at major int. concert halls and on concert tours throughout Europe, N and S America, S Africa, Australasia, Singapore, Japan, China, Hong Kong and S Korea; numerous radio and TV appearances and broadcasts in UK, Netherlands, Africa, Germany, Scandinavia, France, Belgium, Spain, Australasia and USA; Patron Jacqueline du Pré Charity Concerts 2006–, BSO (Bournemouth Symphony Orchestra) Vibes 2012–; Chair. In Harmony Sistema England charity 2008–; Pres. Elgar Soc. 2009; Dr hc (Hull) 2003, (Thames Valley) 2004; Suggia Gift 1968, Brit Award for Elgar Cello Concerto recording 1987, Crystal Award, World Economic Forum (Switzerland) 1998, Classic FM Red Award for outstanding services to music 2005. *Recordings:* world premiere recordings of Britten's 3rd Suite for Solo Cello, Bridge's Oration, Rodrigo's Cello Concerto (Spanish Ministry of Culture Award for world premiere recording 1982), Holst's Invocation, Gavin Bryars' Cello

Concerto, Michael Nyman's Cello and Saxophone Concerto, Sullivan's Cello Concerto, Vaughan Williams' Fantasia on Sussex Folk Tunes, Andrew Lloyd Webber's Variations (Gold disc 1978), Elgar's Cello Concerto (British Phonographic Industry Award for Best Classical Recording 1986), Dvořák Concerto, Saint-Saëns Concerto, Lalo Concerto, Walton Concerto, Britten Cello Symphony; Philip Glass Cello Concerto. *Publications:* Classical Cello 1980, Romantic Cello 1981, French Cello 1981, Frank Bridge, Six Pieces 1982, Young Cellist's Repertoire (three vols) 1984, Holst's Invocation 1984, Travels with my Cello 1984, Song of the Birds 1985, Recital Repertoire for Cellists (four vols) 1986, Short Sharp Shocks 1990, The Great Cello Solos 1992, The Essential Cello 1997, Cello Moods 1999, String Quartets, 2003; Made in England 2003; columnist, Daily Telegraph 2003–; contrib. to: The Times, The Sunday Times, USA Today. *Leisure interests:* topography (especially British), football (Leyton Orient), turtles. *Address:* c/o IMG Artists Europe, The Light Box, 111 Power Road, London, W4 5PY, England (office). *Telephone:* (20) 7957-5800 (office). *Fax:* (20) 7957-5801 (office). *E-mail:* labrahams@imgartists.com (office). *Website:* www.imgartists.com (office); www.julianlloydwebber.com (office).

LO, Vincent Hong Sui; Chinese business executive; *Chairman and Chief Executive, Shui On Group;* b. 18 April 1948, Hong Kong; m. Jean Lo 1981; one s. one d.; ed Univ. of New South Wales, Australia; f. Shui On Group 1971, now Chair. and Chief Exec.; Chair. Hong Kong Gen. Chamber of Commerce 1991–92; mem. Exec. Cttee Basic Law Consultative Cttee 1985–90; mem. Bd Land Devt Corpn 1988–90; mem. Hong Kong Trade Devt Council 1991–92, Hong Kong Baptist Coll. 1987–89; mem. Council, Exec. Cttee Hong Kong Man. Asscn 1984–94; Pres. Business and Professionals Fed. of Hong Kong; mem. Preparatory Cttee for the Hong Kong Special Admin. Region 1996–97; Hong Kong Affairs Adviser, People's Repub. of China State Council's Office of Hong Kong and Macao Affairs/Xinhua News Agency, Hong Kong Br. 1994–97; Adviser China Soc. of Macroeconomics, Peking Univ. China Centre for Econ. Research; mem. Gov.'s Business Council 1992–97, Airport Authority 1990–99, Hong Kong/United States Econ. Co-operation Cttee; mem. Nat. Cttee, 12th CPPCC 2013–; Dir The Real Estate Developers Asscn of Hong Kong, The Community Chest of Hong Kong 1990–95, Great Eagle Holdings Ltd; Dir (non-exec.) Hang Seng Bank Ltd, New World China Land Ltd; Chair. Council Hong Kong Univ. of Science and Tech.; JP 1999; Advisory Professorship (Shanghai Tongji Univ.) 1996, (Shanghai Univ.) 1998; Hon. Citizen of Shanghai 1998; Gold Bauhinia Star 1998, Chevalier des arts et des lettres (France) 2005; Hon. DBA (Hong Kong Univ. of Science and Tech.) 1996; World Chinese Economic Forum Lifetime Achievement Award for Leadership in Property Sector 2012. *Address:* 34/F Shui On Centre, 6–8 Harbour Road, Hong Kong Special Administrative Region, People's Republic of China. *Website:* www.shuion.com (office).

LOACH, Kenneth, BA; British film director; b. 17 June 1936, Nuneaton; s. of the late John Loach and of Vivien Loach (née Hamlin); m. Lesley Ashton 1962; three s. (one deceased) two d.; ed King Edward VI School, Nuneaton, St Peter's Hall (now Coll.), Oxford; BBC trainee, Drama Dept 1963; freelance film dir 1963–; Hon. DLitt (St Andrews), (Staffs. Univ., Bristol); Dr hc (Royal Coll. of Art) 1998; Hon. Fellow, St Peter's Coll. Oxford; Praemium Imperiale 2003, Léopard d'honneur for Lifetime Achievement, Locarno Film Festival 2003, London Film Critics' Circle Award for Outstanding Contrib. to Cinema 2005, Hon. Golden Bear, Berlin Film Festival 2014. *Films:* Poor Cow 1967, Kes 1969, In Black and White 1970, Family Life 1971, Black Jack 1979, Looks and Smiles 1981, Fatherland 1986, Hidden Agenda 1990, Riff-Raff 1991, Raining Stones 1993, Ladybird, Ladybird 1994, Land and Freedom 1995, Carla's Song 1996, My Name is Joe 1998, Bread and Roses 2000, 11.09.01 UK Segment 2002, Sweet Sixteen 2003, A Fond Kiss 2004, Tickets (with others) 2005, The Wind That Shakes the Barley (Palme d'Or, Cannes Film Festival 2006, Best Film, Irish Film and TV Awards 2007) 2006, It's a Free World 2007, Looking for Eric 2009, Route Irish 2010, The Angels' Share (Jury Prize, Cannes Film Festival 2012) 2012, The Spirit of '45 (documentary) 2013. *Television:* Diary of a Young Man 1964, Three Clear Sundays 1965, The End of Arthur's Marriage 1965, Up the Junction 1965, Coming Out Party 1965, Cathy Come Home 1966, In Two Minds 1966, The Golden Vision 1969, The Big Flame 1970, After a Lifetime 1971, The Rank and File 1972, Days of Hope (four films) 1975, The Price of Coal 1977, The Gamekeeper 1979, Auditions 1980, A Question of Leadership 1980, The Red and the Blue 1983, Questions of Leadership 1983, Which Side are You on? 1984, The View from the Woodpile 1988, Time to Go 1989, Dispatches: Arthur Scargill 1991, The Flickering Flame 1996, Another City 1998, The Navigators 2001. *Address:* c/o Sixteen Films, 2nd Floor, 187 Wardour Street, London, W1F 8ZB, England.

LOADER, Danyon Joseph, ONZ; New Zealand fmr swimmer; b. 21 April 1975, Timaru; s. of Peter Loader and Daphne Loader; ed Berkeley Univ., San Francisco, USA; world short-course record in 200m butterfly 1991; silver medallist, Olympic Games, Barcelona 1992; gold, silver (three times) and bronze medallist, Commonwealth Games, Victoria, BC 1994; gold medallist, 200m and 400m freestyle, Olympic Games Atlanta 1996; est. over 40 NZ records; retd 2000; motivational speaker with Speakers New Zealand; NZ Sportsman of the Decade (1990s), Lonsdale Cup, NZ Olympic Cttee. *Leisure interests:* reading, films, surfing, scuba diving, socializing. *Address:* 9 Prince Albert Road, St Kilda, Dunedin, New Zealand. *Telephone:* (3) 455-2486.

LOAYZA MARIACA, Armando; Bolivian government official; b. 8 Dec. 1943, La Paz; m. Teresita Keel de Loaiza; one s.; ed Univ. of Montevideo, Uruguay; Under-Sec. of Econ. Integration 1980; Gen. Adviser of the Chancellery 1991; Under-Sec. of Bilateral Policy 1993; diplomatic postings in Montevideo, Caracas, Geneva, Brussels; Dir Academia Diplomática Boliviana Rafael Bustillo 1993, 1998–2003; Consul-Gen. in Santiago 1993; Amb. to Santa Sede (Vatican) 1994–98; Amb. to Uruguay and Perm. Rep. to ALADI 2003; Minister of Foreign Affairs and Worship –2006. *Address:* c/o Ministry of Foreign Affairs and Worship, Calle Ingavi, esq. Junín, La Paz, Bolivia (office).

LOBASHEV, Vladimir Mikhailovich; Russian nuclear physicist; b. 29 July 1934, Leningrad (now St Petersburg); s. of Mikhail Yefimovich Lobashev and Nina Vladimirovna Yevropeitseva; m. Muza Romanovna Lobasheva; two s. one d.; ed Leningrad Univ.; mem. CPSU 1970–91; mem. of staff of Physical-Tech. Inst. 1957–72; Scientific Leader, Moscow Meson Factory Programme; Head, Experimental Physics Div. of Inst. for Nuclear Research at USSR (now Russian) Acad. of Sciences 1972–; Leader, Lab. for Weak Interaction Study, Leningrad (now St

Petersburg) Inst. for Nuclear Physics 1972–; Corresp. mem. USSR (now Russian) Acad. of Sciences 1970–2003, Academician, Russian Acad. of Sciences 2003–; Bruno Pontecorvo Prize, Jt Inst. for Nuclear Research, Dubna 1998, Markov Prize 2004. *Leisure interest:* tennis. *Address:* Institute for Nuclear Research, Academy of Sciences, 142190 Troitsk, Moscow Region (office); Institute for Nuclear Research, Academy of Sciences, Prospect 60 Let Oktyabrya 7A, 117312 Troitsk, Moscow Region, Russia (office). *Telephone:* (495) 334-01-90 (office); (495) 334-03-18 (home). *E-mail:* lobashev@al20.inr.troitsk.ru (office). *Website:* www.inr.troitsk.ru (office).

LOBATO, Edson, MS; Brazilian agronomist and administrator; b. 1940; ed Nat. School of Agronomy (now Coll. of Agricultural Sciences), Southern Illinois Univ., USA; began career in soil fertility research through programme sponsored by IRI Research Inst., USAID and Brazilian Ministry of Agric. 1964; received USAID fellowship to study soil fertility in USA 1972–73; hired as researcher, Brazilian Corpn of Agricultural Research (EMBRAPA) 1973, responsible for coordinating several programmes, including outlining plan for Cerrado Agricultural Research Centre, served in variety of positions at EMBRAPA Cerrado Centre, including Tech. Dir 1975–2004; World Food Prize (co-recipient) 2006. *Publications:* Cerrado: Soil Correction and Fertilization; more than 80 publs in professional journals. *Address:* c/o Embrapa, Parque Estação Biológica - PqEB s/n°, Brasília, DF 70770-901, Brazil. *Telephone:* (61) 3448-4433. *Fax:* (61) 3347-1041. *E-mail:* sac@embrapa .br. *Website:* www.embrapa.br.

LOBKOWICZ, Michal; Czech business executive and fmr politician; *Partner, Corsum Group;* b. 20 July 1964, Prague; m.; one s.; ed Charles Univ., Prague; mem. Parl. for Civic Democratic Party (ODS) 1992–98, for Freedom Union (FU) 1998–2002; Chef de Cabinet for Minister of Foreign Affairs 1993–96; Minister of Defence Jan.–July 1998; mem. Cttee for European Integration 1998–2002, Cttee for Defence and Security 1998–2002; left parl. functions following elections in 2002; Partner, Corsum Group 2002–; mem. Supervisory Bd Massag Bílovec, SK Slavia Prague soccer club. *Address:* Corsum Group s.r.o. Opatovická 4, 110 00 Prague 1, Czech Republic (office). *Telephone:* (2) 24934707 (office). *Fax:* (2) 24934701 (office). *E-mail:* corsum@corsum.cz (office). *Website:* www.co (office).

LOBKOWICZ, Prince; Nicholas, DPhil; American philosopher, political scientist and academic; *Director, Institute of Central and Eastern European Studies, Catholic University of Eichstätt-Ingolstadt;* b. 9 July 1931, Prague, Czechoslovakia (now Czech Repub.); s. of Prince Jan Lobkowicz and Countess Marie Czernin; m. 1st Countess Josephine Waldburg-Zeil 1953; three s. two d.; m. 2nd Aleksandra N. Cieślińska 1999; ed Collegium Maria Hilf, Switzerland, Univs of Erlangen and Fribourg; Assoc. Prof. of Philosophy, Univ. of Notre Dame, Ind. 1960–67; Prof. of Political Theory and Philosophy, Univ. of Munich 1967–90, Dean School of Arts and Letters 1970–71, Rector Magnificus 1971–76, Pres. Univ. of Munich 1976–82; Pres. Catholic Univ. of Eichstätt 1984–96, Founder and Dir Inst. of Cen. and Eastern European Studies 1994–; mem. Bd of Dirs Fed. Inst. of Int. and E European Studies, Cologne 1972–75, Senate, West German Rectors' Conf. 1976–82, Perm. Cttee European Rectors' Conf. 1979–84, Council Int. Fed. of Catholic Univs 1984–91; Founding mem. Int. Metaphysical Asscn; mem. Cen. Cttee of German Catholics 1980–84; mem. Ukrainian Acad. of Arts and Science (USA) 1979–; mem. W Europe Advisory Cttee to Radio Free Europe/Radio Liberty 1980–2002, Chair. 1994–2002; Founder-mem., Vice-Pres. European Acad. of Sciences and Arts 1990–; Pres. Freier Deutscher Autorenverband 1985–91; mem. Pontifical Council for Culture 1982–93; Pres. Czechoslovak Christian Acad. in Rome 1983–90; Administrator of Faculty of Catholic Theology, Charles Univ. Prague 2002–03; Hon. Citizen of Dallas, Tex.; Hon. DHL (Wayne State Univ.); Hon. DLL (Univ. of Notre Dame); Hon. DrPhil (Seoul and Ukrainian Univ., Munich, Catholic Univ. of America); Hon. DTheol (Charles Univ., Prague). *Publications:* Theory and Practice 1967, Ende aller Religion? 1976, Marxismus und Machtergreifung 1978, Wortmeldung zu Staat, Kirche, Universität 1981, Irrwege der Angst 1983, Das europäische Erbe 1984, Das Konzil 1986, Zeitwende 1993, Czas przelomu 1996, Rationalität und Innerlichkeit 1997, Duše Evropy 2001, Večnaja filosofia 2007. *Address:* Oskar-von-Miller-Strasse 20, 82319 Starnberg (home); Katholische Universität, 85071 Eichstätt, Germany. *Telephone:* (8421) 931717 (office). *Fax:* (8421) 931780 (office). *E-mail:* zimos@ku-eichstaett.de (office); nikolaus.lobkowicz@t-online.de (home). *Website:* www.ku.de/forschung/ forschungseinr/zimos/mitarbeiter/nikolaus-lobkowicz (office).

LOBO ANTUNES, António, MD; Portuguese novelist; b. 1 Sept. 1942, Lisbon; s. of João Alfredo Lobo Antunes and Maria Margarida Almeida Lima; m. 1st Maria José Xavier da Fonseca e Costa (divorced); m. 2nd Maria João Espírito Santo Bustorff Silva (divorced); m. 3rd Cristina Ferreira de Almeida; three d.; ed higher educ. in Portugal; fmr doctor and psychiatrist, now full-time writer (his experience of the Portuguese colonial war in Angola being a major influence); Commdr, Ordre des Arts et des Lettres 2008; French Culture Prize 1996, 1997, Prix du Meilleur Livre Etranger, Rosália de Castro Prize 1999, European Literature Prize of Austria 2000, Latin Union Int. Prize 2003, Jerusalem Prize 2005, Premio Camões 2007. *Publications include:* novels: Memória de Elefante 1979, Os Cus de Judas 1979, Conhecimento do Inferno 1980, Explicação dos Pássaros 1981, Fado Alexandrino 1983, Auto dos Danados 1985, As Naus 1988, Tratado das Paixões da Alma 1990, A Ordem Natural das Coisas 1992, A Morta de Carlos Gardek 1994, O Manual dos Inquisidores 1996, O Esplendor de Portugal 1997, Livro de Crónicas 1998, Exortação aos Crocodilos 1999, Não Entres Tão Depressa Ness Noite Excura 2000, Que Farei Quando Tudo Arde? 2001, Segundo Livro de Crónicas 2002, Boa Tarde ás Coisas Aqui em Baixo 2003, Eu Hei-de Amar Uma Pedra 2004, Terceiro Livro de Crónicas 2006, Ontem Não Te Vi em Babilónia 2006, O Meu Nome é Legião 2007, O Arquipélago da Insónia 2008, Que Cavalos São Aqueles Que Fazem Sombra no Mar? 2009, Sôbolos Rios Que Vão 2010, Comissão das Lágrimas 2011; short stories: A História do Hidroavião 1994–2005 2005, The Fat Man and Infinity and Other Writings (in trans.) 2009; other: Letrinhas de Cantigas 2002, Apontar com o dedo o centro da terra 2002, D'este Viver Aqui Neste Papel Descripto 2005, Quem me assassinou para que eu seja tão doce? 2008. *Address:* c/o Publicações Dom Quixote, Rua Cidade de Códova 2, 2610-038 Alfragide, Portugal. *Website:* www.dquixote.pt.

LOBO SOSA, Porfirio (Pepe); Honduran politician, lawyer and fmr head of state; b. 22 Dec. 1947, Trujillo; ed Univ. of Miami, USA; Deputy, Nat. Congress 1990; Head, Honduran Corpn for Forestry Devt 1990–94; presidential cand. 2005; Pres. Partido Nacional; Pres., Repub. of Honduras 2010–14. *Address:* c/o Office of

the President, Palacio José Cecilio del Valle, Blvd Juan Pablo II, Tegucigalpa, Honduras (office).

LOCHHEAD, Liz; British poet, playwright, screenwriter and teacher; *Scots Makar;* b. 26 Dec. 1947, Motherwell; fmr art school teacher, Glasgow and Bristol; Lecturer, Univ. of Glasgow; Scots Makar (Nat. Poet of Scotland) 2011–; Dr hc (Edinburgh) 2000; BBC Scotland Prize 1971, Scottish Arts Council Award 1972. *Television includes:* Damages (BBC). *Publications include:* poetry: Memo for Spring 1972, The Grimm Sisters 1981, Dreaming of Frankenstein and Collected Poems 1984, True Confessions and True Clichés 1985, Bagpipe Muzak 1991, Cuba/ Dog House (with Gina Moxley) 2000, The Colour of Black and White: Poems 1984–2003 2003; plays: Blood and Ice 1982, Silver Service 1984, Dracula (adaptation) 1989, Mary Queen of Scots Got Her Head Chopped Off 1989, Molière's Tartuffe (Scots trans. in rhyming couplets), Perfect Days 1998, Medea (adaptation) 2000, Misery Guts (adaptation) 2002, Thebans 2003, Good Things 2006; screenplay: Now and Then 1972; anthology contribs: Penguin Modern Poets Vols 3 and 4, Shouting It Out 1995. *Address:* 57 Productions, 57 Effingham Green, Lee Green, London, SE12 8NT, England (office). *Telephone:* (20) 8463-0866 (office). *E-mail:* paul@57productions.com (office). *Website:* www.57productions.com (office).

LOCHTE, Karin, MSc, PhD (Habil.); German oceanographer, environmental scientist, academic and research institute director; *Director, Alfred Wegener Institute for Polar and Marine Research;* b. 20 Sept. 1952, Hanover; ed Tech. Univ., Hanover, Marine Science Labs, Menai Bridge, Univ. Coll. of N Wales, Bangor, UK, Univ. of Bremen; Post-doctoral researcher, Inst. of Oceanography, Kiel 1985–90; mem. Scientific Staff, Alfred Wegener Inst. for Polar and Marine Research, Bremerhaven, Germany 1990–94, Scientific Advisor 1999–2003, Dir 2007–; Head of Section, Biological Oceanography and Prof. of Biological Oceanography, Inst. for Baltic Sea Research, Univ. of Rostock 1995–2000; Prof. of Biological Oceanography, Leibniz Inst. for Marine Sciences, Christian-Albrechts Univ., Kiel 2000–07; Project Co-ordinator for ADEPD (Atlantic Data Base for Exchange Processes at the Deep Sea Floor —EU-funded marine research project) 1998–2000; Chair. Governing Bd Jacobs Univ., Bremen 2007–; mem. ECOPS Working Group 'Deep Sea Floor Instrumentation Development' 1991–92, Scientific Steering Cttee Jt Global Ocean Flux Studies 1995–2001, Bd of Trustees Terramare Research Centre, Wilhelmshaven 1996–98, Nat. Cttee for Global Change Research (Co-Chair. 2000–05), Scientific Cttee Int. Geosphere-Biosphere Programme (Vice-Chair. 2001-06), DFG Fachkollegiums 313 'Atmosphären- und Meeresforschung' 2004–05, Senate Cttee Deutsche Forschungsgemeinschaft for Oceanography 1995– (Chair. 2004–), Jury for Science Prize of WGL 'Society Needs Science' 2002–, Science Council 2004 (Chair. Scientific Comm. 2006–), Grant Cttee of Excellence Initiative 2005–, Exec. Cttee Acad. of Sciences, Hamburg 2005–; Scientific Advisor, Royal Netherlands Inst. for Sea Research (NIOZ), Texel 1998–2004, Instituts Chemie und Biologie des Meeres, Universität Oldenburg 1998–2006 (Chair. 2003–), Potsdam Instituts für Klimafolgenforschung 2002–05, Max Plank Inst. for Marine Microbiology, Bremen 2006–; Consultant, Third World Aid Programme to S America, Deutscher Akademischer Austausch Dienst 2003–; Mentor, Advancement Programme for Young Scientists, Univ. of Bremen 2005–07. *Publications:* numerous scientific papers in professional journals. *Address:* Alfred Wegener Institute, Building E-3226, Am Handelshafen 12, 27570 Bremerhaven, Germany (office). *Telephone:* (471) 4831-1101 (office). *E-mail:* karin.lochte@awi.de (office). *Website:* www.awi.de (office).

LOCHTE, Ryan Steven; American swimmer; b. 3 Aug. 1984, Rochester, New York; s. of Steven R. Lochte and Ileana M. Lochte; ed Spruce Creek High School, Port Orange, Univ. of Florida; raised in Daytona Beach, Fla where his parents were swimmers who coached him up until coll.; mem. Florida Gators swimming and diving team; NCAA Swimmer of the Year twice, seven-time NCAA champion, seven-time SEC champion, 24-time All-American; won individual titles in three individual events at NCAA Men's Swimming and Diving Championships 2006, set US Open and American records in 200-yard individual medley and 200-yard backstroke; also broke NCAA record in 400-yard individual medley; currently trains under Coach Gregg Troy at Univ. of Florida; Pan American Games, Santo Domingo 2003: gold medal, 4×200m freestyle; Olympic Games, Athens 2004: gold medal, 4×200m freestyle, silver medal, 200m medley; Beijing 2008: gold medal, 200m backstroke, 4×200m freestyle, bronze medal, 200m medley, 400m medley, London 2012: gold medal, 400m individual medley, 4×200m. freestyle relay, silver medal, 4×100m. freestyle relay, 200m individual medley, bronze medal, 200m. backstroke; World Championships (short course), Indianapolis 2004: gold medal, 4×200m freestyle, silver medal, 200m medley, bronze medal, 200m freestyle, Shanghai 2006: gold medal, 200m backstroke, 200m medley, 400m medley, silver medal, 4×100m medley, bronze medal, 4×100m freestyle, 4×200m freestyle, Manchester 2008: gold medal, 100m medley, 200m medley, 400m medley, 4×100m freestyle, silver medal, 200m backstroke, 4×100m medley, Dubai 2010: gold medal, 200m backstroke, 200m freestyle, 100m medley, 200m medley, 400m medley, 4×100m medley, silver medal, 4×200m freestyle; World Championships (long course), Montreal 2005: gold medal, 4×200m freestyle, bronze medal, 200m backstroke, 200m medley, Melbourne 2007: gold medal, 200m backstroke, 4×200m freestyle, silver medal, 100m backstroke, 200m medley, 400m medley, Rome 2009: gold medal, 200m medley, 400m medley, 4×100m freestyle, 4×200m freestyle, bronze medal, 200m backstroke, Shanghai 2011: gold medal, 200m backstroke, 200m freestyle, 200m medley, 400m medley, 4×200m freestyle, bronze medal, 4×100m freestyle, Barcelona 2013: gold medal, 200m backstroke, 200m medley, 4×200m freestyle, silver medal, 4×100m freestyle; Pan Pacific Championships, Victoria 2006: gold medal, 4×200m freestyle, silver medal, 100m backstroke, 200m medley, Irvine 2010: gold medal, 200m backstroke, 200m freestyle, 200m medley, 400m medley, 4×100m freestyle, 4×200m freestyle; holds world record in 200m individual medley (long and short course) and 400m individual medley (short course); as part of US team, holds world record in 4×200m freestyle relay (long course); swims for Daytona Beach Swimming and Univ. of Florida; Golden Goggles Male Swimmer of the Year 2010, Male Race of the Year for 200m individual medley at Mutual of Omaha Pan Pacific Championships 2010, Swimmer of the Year 2010–11, American Swimmer of the Year 2010–11, FINA Swimmer of the Year 2010–11. *Leisure interests:* surfing, skate boarding, volleyball, basketball, drawing. *Telephone:* (407) 924-5516 (office). (954) 818-3796 (office). *E-mail:* erika@ wrighteas.com (office); shawnzenga@gmail.com (office). *Website:* ryanlochte.com.

LOCK, Margaret, PhD, FRSC; Canadian anthropologist and academic; *Marjorie Bronfman Professor Emerita in Social Studies in Medicine, McGill University;* m.; one s. one d.; ed Univ. of California, Berkeley; at McGill Univ., Montréal 1977–, Marjorie Bronfman Prof. in Social Studies in Medicine, affiliated with Dept of Social Studies of Medicine and Dept of Anthropology, now Prof. Emer.; mem. Canadian Inst. of Advanced Research, Population Programme 1993–2002; Officier, Ordre nat. du Québec; Canada Council Killam Fellowship 1993–95, Prix du Québec, domaine Sciences Humaines 1997, Molson Prize, Canada Council for the Arts 2002, Robert B. Textor Prize 2003, Killam Prize, Canada Council for the Arts 2005, Trudeau Foundation Fellowship 2005, named a Grande Montréalaise, Secteur Social 2005, Career Achievement Award, Soc. of Medical Anthropology, American Anthropological Asscn 2008. *Publications:* East Asian Medicine in Urban Japan: Varieties of Medical Experience 1980, Health and Medical Care in Japan: Cultural and Social Dimensions (co-ed.) 1987, Biomedicine Examined (co-ed.) 1988, La santé mentale et ses visages: Un Québec pluriethnique au quotidien (co-author) 1992, Knowledge, Power and Practice: The Anthropology of Medicine and Everyday Life (co-ed.) 1993, Encounters With Aging: Mythologies of Menopause in Japan and North America (six prizes, including Staley Prize, School of American Research, Canada-Japan Book Prize, Wellcome Medal, Royal Anthropological Soc. of GB 1997) 1993, Social Suffering (co-ed.) 1997, Pragmatic Women and Body Politics (co-ed.) 1998, Living and Working with the New Medical Technologies: Intersections of Inquiry (co-ed.) 2000, Remaking a World: Violence, Social Suffering, and Recovery (co-ed.) 2001, Twice Dead: Organ Transplants and the Reinvention of Death (several awards) 2002, New Horizons in Medical Anthropology: A Festschrift in Honor of Charles Leslie (co-ed.) 2002, Remaking Life and Death: Towards an Anthropology of the Biosciences (co-ed.) 2003, An Anthropology of Medicine (with Vinh-Kim Nguyen) (American Publishers Asscn PROSE Award for Archeology and Anthropology 2010) 2010, The Alzheimer Conundrum: Entanglements of Dementia and Aging 2013; numerous scholarly articles. *Address:* Department of Social Studies of Medicine, Room 103, 3647 Peel Street, Montréal, PQ H3A 1X1, Canada (office). *Telephone:* (514) 398-4982 (office). *Website:* www.mcgill.ca/ssom (office); www.mcgill.ca/anthropology (office).

LOCK, Thomas Graham, BSc, CEng, CBIM, FIMMM; British business executive; b. 19 Oct. 1931, Cardiff, Wales; s. of Robert H. Lock and Morfydd Lock (née Thomas); m. 1st Janice O B. Jones 1954 (divorced 1992); two d.; m. 2nd Judith Elizabeth Lucy 2004 (divorced 2010); ed Whitchurch Grammar School, Univ. Coll. of S. Wales, Monmouthshire Coll. of Advanced Tech. (Aston) and Harvard Business School, USA; Instructor Lt RN 1953–56; joined Lucas Industries Ltd 1956; Production Foreman, Lucas Electrical Ltd 1957–59, Factory Man. 1959–61; Dir Girling Bremsen GmbH 1961–66; Overseas Operations Dir Girling Ltd 1966–73; Gen. Man. and Dir Lucas Service Overseas Ltd 1973–79; Man. Dir Industrial Div. Amalgamated Metal Corpn PLC 1979–83, Chief Exec. 1983–91; Dir (non-exec.) Evode Group PLC 1985–91, Marshalls Universal PLC 1983–86; Liveryman Co. of Gold and Silver Wyre Drawers 1988–; Freeman, City of London. *Leisure interests:* sailing, music, skiing. *Address:* Parolas Villa, 4520 Pareklisia, nr Limassol, Cyprus (home). *Telephone:* (25) 634965 (home). *Fax:* (25) 634965 (home). *E-mail:* brython@cytanet.com.cy (home).

LOCKE, Gary F., BA, JD; American lawyer, diplomatist and fmr government official; b. 21 Jan. 1950; s. of James Locke and Julie Locke; m. Mona Lee 1994; one s. two d.; ed Yale Univ., Boston Univ.; Deputy Prosecuting Attorney, State of Washington, King Co.; mem. State House of Reps 1982–93; Chief Exec. King Co. 1994–97; Gov. of Washington 2005–2005; Pnr, Davis Wright Tremaine LLP (law firm), Seattle 2005–09; US Sec. of Commerce, Washington, DC 2009–11; Amb. to People's Repub. of China 2011–14; fmr mem. Bd of Dirs Digital Learning Commons, Pacific Health Summit Sr Advisory Group 2004, Fred Hutchinson Cancer Research Center, Safeco, Inc. *Address:* US Department of State, 2201 C Street NW, Washington, DC 20520, USA (office). *Telephone:* (202) 647-4000 (office). *Fax:* (202) 647-6738 (office). *Website:* www.state.gov (office).

LOCKHART, James, BMus, FRCM, FRCO (CHM); British conductor and music director; b. 16 Oct. 1930, Edinburgh, Scotland; s. of Archibald C. Lockhart and Mary B. Lawrence; m. Sheila Grogan 1954; two s. one d.; ed George Watson's Coll., Edin., Univ. of Edin. and Royal Coll. of Music; Asst Conductor, Yorkshire Symphony Orchestra 1954–55; Repetiteur and Asst Conductor, Städtische Bühnen Münster 1955–56, Bayerische Staatsoper, Munich 1956–57, Glyndebourne Festival Opera 1957–59; Dir Opera Workshop, Univ. of Texas 1957–59; Repetiteur and Asst Conductor, Royal Opera House, Covent Garden 1959–60, Conductor 1962–68; Asst Conductor, BBC Scottish Orchestra 1960–61; Conductor, Sadler's Wells Opera 1961–62; Prof. Royal Coll. of Music 1962–72; Musical Dir Welsh Nat. Opera 1968–73; Generalmusikdirektor, Staatstheater Kassel 1972–80, Koblenz and Theater der Stadt, Koblenz 1981–88, Rheinische Philharmonie 1981–91; Prin. Guest Conductor, BBC Concert Orchestra 1982–87; Dir of Opera, Royal Coll. of Music 1986–92, London Royal Schools' Vocal Faculty 1992–96, Opera Consultant 1996–98; Guest Prof. of Conducting, Tokyo Nat. Univ. of Fine Arts and Music (Tokyo Geidai) 1998–2001, Prof. Emer. 2001–; freelance conductor 2001–; Guest Prof. of Conducting, Sydney Conservatorium of Music 2005–; Hon. RAM 1993. *Leisure interests:* travel, swimming, hill-walking. *Address:* 5 The Coach House, Mill Street, Fontmell Magna, Shaftesbury, Dorset, SP7 0NU, England (home). *Telephone:* (1747) 811980 (home). *Fax:* (1747) 811980 (home). *E-mail:* lockgrog@zen.co.uk (home).

LOCKWOOD, David, CBE, PhD, FBA; British academic; *Professor Emeritus of Sociology, University of Essex;* b. 9 April 1929, Holmfirth, Yorks., England; s. of Herbert Lockwood and Edith Annie Lockwood (née Lockwood); m. Leonore Davidoff 1954; three s.; ed Honley Grammar School, London School of Econs; trainee, Victoria Textiles, Honley, Yorks. 1944–47; Nat. Service, Intelligence Corps, Austria 1947–49; Univ. of London Postgraduate Studentship in Econs 1952–53; Asst Lecturer and Lecturer in Sociology, LSE 1953–60; Rockefeller Fellow, Univ. of California, Berkeley, USA 1958–59; Univ. Lecturer, Faculty of Econs and Fellow of St John's Coll., Cambridge 1960–68; Visiting Prof., Dept of Sociology, Columbia Univ., USA 1966–67; Prof., Dept of Sociology, Univ. of Essex 1968–2001, Prof. Emer. 2001–; Pro-Vice-Chancellor 1989–92; Visiting Prof., Delhi School of Econs 1975, Stockholm Univ. 1989; Visiting Fellow, RSSS ANU 1993; mem. Social Science Research Council (Chair. Sociology and Social Admin. Cttee 1973–76), Academia Europaea 1990; Chair. Econ. and Social Research Council

Review of Govt Social Classifications 1994–98; Hon. DUniv (Essex) 2001, Hon. LittD (Cambridge) 2004; Lifetime Achievement Award, British Sociological Asscn 2012. *Publications include:* The Affluent Worker in the Class Structure (three vols) (jtly) 1968–69, The Blackcoated Worker 1958, (revised edn 1989), Solidarity and Schism 1992; numerous articles in journals and symposia. *Address:* 82 High Street, Wivenhoe, Essex, CO7 9AB, England (home). *Telephone:* (1206) 823530 (home). *E-mail:* lockd@essex.ac.uk (office).

LOCKYER, Darren; Australian rugby league player; *Captain, Brisbane Broncos, Queensland and Australia;* b. 24 March 1977, Brisbane, Queensland; s. of David and Sharon Lockyer; m. Loren Pollock 2007; ed ed Wandoan State School, Roma, Queensland; fullback, five-eighth; player for Brisbane Broncos 1995– (Capt. 2005–), Queensland Maroons 1998– (Capt. of Series Winning Sides 2001, 2006, 2007), Australia 1998– (Capt. 2003–), NRL All Stars 2010–; 333 appearances by June 2010 for Brisbane Broncos (121 tries, 1,175 points), 32 appearances for Queensland in State of Origin games, 54 appearances for Australia (36 as Capt.), 34 tries, 196 points; mem. Australian World Cup winning team 2000; mem. Australian Tri-Nations winning team 2004, 2006, 2009; has written a column for Queensland newspaper, The Courier Mail; Brisbane Broncos Rookie of the Year 1995, Clive Churchill Medal 2000, Brisbane Broncos Player of the Year 2002, 2003, Rugby League World Golden Boot Award 2003, 2006, Dally M. Medal Five-Eighth of the Year 2007, named in list of Australia's 100 Greatest Players (1908–2007) commissioned by NRL and ARL to celebrate the code's centenary year in Australia (only current player to make the list) 2008, chosen in Queensland Rugby League's Team of the Century at fullback 2008. *Address:* c/o Brisbane Broncos, Fulcher Road, Red Hill, Queensland 4059, Australia. *E-mail:* media@broncos.com.au. *Website:* www.broncos.com.au.

LODDER, Celsius Antônio, MSc; Brazilian economist and international administrator; b. 28 May 1944, Nova Lima, Minas Gerais; s. of Ary Lodder and Maria van Krimpen Lodder; m. Denise Lodder; three d.; ed Fed. Univ. of Minas Gerais, Belo Horizonte, Getúlio Vargas Foundation, Rio de Janeiro and Inst. of Social Studies, The Hague; researcher, Applied Econs Research Inst. Ministry of Econ., Finance and Planning 1970–80; subsequently held appointments with State of Minas Gerais and Fed. Govt of Brazil; Sec. for Commercial Policy, Ministry of Finance, later at Ministry of Industry, Commerce and Tourism; Supt Nat. Supply Authority, Ministry of Finance; Chief Adviser, State Bank of Minas Gerais 1983–84; Co-ordinator, Intergovernmental Relations Office, Civil Cabinet of Pres. of Brazil; Lecturer in Econs at various Brazilian univs; Exec. Dir Int. Coffee Org. 1994–2002; mem. Bd of Dirs American School of Brasília. *Publications:* books and reports on matters related to regional planning and devt. *Leisure interests:* reading, walking. *Address:* c/o Board of Directors, American School of Brasilia, SGAS 605, Bloco E, Lotes 34/37, 70200-650 Brasilia, DF, Brazil.

LODGE, David John, CBE, PhD, FRSL; British writer and academic; *Professor Emeritus of English Literature, University of Birmingham;* b. 28 Jan. 1935, London, England; s. of William F. Lodge and Rosalie M. Lodge (née Murphy); m. Mary Frances Jacob 1959; two s. one d.; ed St Joseph's Acad., Blackheath and Univ. Coll., London; asst, British Council, London 1959–60; Asst Lecturer in English, Univ. of Birmingham 1960–62, Lecturer 1963–71, Sr Lecturer 1971–73, Reader 1973–76, Prof. of English Literature 1976–87, Hon. Prof. 1987–2000, Prof. Emer. 2001–; Chair. Booker Prize Cttee 1989; Harkness Commonwealth Fellow, 1964–65; Visiting Assoc. Prof. Univ. of Calif. at Berkeley 1969; Henfield Writing Fellow, Univ. of E Anglia 1977; Fellow, Univ. Coll. London 1982, Goldsmith's Coll. 1992; Chevalier des Arts et des Lettres 1997; Yorkshire Post Fiction Prize 1975, Hawthornden Prize 1976, RTS Award for Best Drama Serial 1990. *Plays:* The Writing Game 1991, Home Truths 1999, Secret Thoughts 2011. *Publications:* fiction: The Picturegoers 1960, Ginger, You're Barmy 1962, The British Museum is Falling Down 1965, Out of the Shelter 1970, Changing Places: A Tale of Two Campuses 1975, How Far Can You Go? (aka Souls and Bodies) (Whitbread Book of Year) 1980, Small World: An Academic Romance 1984, Nice Work (Sunday Express Book of the Year) 1988, Paradise News 1991, Therapy 1995, Home Truths (novella) 1999, Thinks... (novel) 2001, Author, Author 2004, Deaf Sentence (novel) 2008, A Man of Parts 2011; non-fiction: Language of Fiction 1966, Graham Greene 1966, The Novelist at the Crossroads and Other Essays on Fiction and Criticism 1971, Evelyn Waugh 1971, Twentieth-Century Literary Criticism: A Reader (ed.) 1972, The Modes of Modern Writing: Metaphor, Metonymy and the Typology of Modern Literature 1977, Working with Structuralism: Essays and Reviews on Nineteenth- and Twentieth Century Literature 1981, Write On: Occasional Essays 1986, Modern Criticism and Theory: A Reader (ed.) 1988, After Bakhtin: Essays on Fiction and Criticism 1990, The Art of Fiction: Illustrated from Classic and Modern Texts 1992, The Practice of Writing: Essays, Lectures, Reviews, and a Diary 1996, Consciousness and the Novel 2002, The Year of Henry James 2006, Lives in Writing: Essays 2014. *Leisure interests:* television, cinema. *Address:* c/o Department of English, University of Birmingham, Birmingham, B15 2TT, England (office).

LODGE, Matthew James, BA (Hons); British diplomatist; b. 3 June 1968, Crosby, Lancs., England; s. of David James Lodge MBE and Helen Mary Lodge (née Hutchison); m. Alexia Lodge; two s.; ed Abingdon School, Oxon., Univ. of Birmingham; Desk Officer, Bosnia Section, FCO 1996–97, Entry Clearance Officer, Tbilisi and Yerevan Oct.–Dec. 1997, Second Sec., Embassy in Athens 1998–2000, Desk Officer, Czech Repub. and Slovakia, FCO Nov.–Dec. 2000, Second Sec., Embassy in Paris Jan.–Aug. 2001, Second Sec., Embassy in Brussels 2001–03, Head of Cyprus and Greece Section, Europe Directorate, FCO 2003–04, Pvt. Sec., Perm. UnderSec.'s Office 2004–07, Deputy Head of Mission, Embassy in Baghdad Mar.–Nov. 2007, Career Devt Attachment, UK Defence Acad., Shrivenham Jan.–April 2008, Head of Afghanistan Group, FCO 2008–10, Amb. to Finland 2010–13. *Address:* Foreign and Commonwealth Office, King Charles Street, London, SW1A 2AH, England (office). *Telephone:* (20) 7008-1500 (office). *E-mail:* fcocorrespondence@fco.gov.uk (office). *Website:* www.gov.uk/government/organisations/foreign-commonwealth-office (office).

LODHI, Maleeha, BSc, PhD; Pakistani diplomatist, journalist and academic; b. Lahore; m. (divorced); one s.; ed Univ. of Oxford, London School of Econs, UK; Lecturer in Politics and Sociology, LSE 1980–85; fmr Lecturer, Dept of Public Admin, Quaid-i-Azam Univ., Islamabad; Ed. The Muslim 1987–90; Ed. and Co-founder The News (daily newspaper) 1985–93, 1997–2000; Amb. to USA 1993–97, (with rank of Minister of State) 1999–2002, High Commr to UK 2003–08; Special International Affairs Adviser Jang Group, Geo Television Network 2010–; mem. UN Sec.-Gen.'s Advisory Bd on Disarmament; Fellow, Pakistan Inst. of Devt Econs, Kennedy School of Government, Harvard Univ.; Public Policy Scholar, Woodrow Wilson Center; award from All Pakistan Newspaper Soc. 1994, named by Time Magazine as one of 100 global pacesetters and leaders who would define the 21st century 1994, Hilal-e-Imtiaz Presidential Award for public service 2002. *Publications:* Pakistan's Encounter with Democracy, The External Dimension (ed) 1994; numerous contribs to int. journals. *Address:* Jang Group, Printing House, I.I. Chundrigar Road, Karachi 74200 (office); Geo Television Network, 7th Floor, Landmark Plaza, I. I. Chundrigarh Road, Karachi, Pakistan (office). *Telephone:* (21) 2626706 (Jang Group) (office); (11) 1436111 (Geo Television Network) (office). *Fax:* (21) 2629554 (Jang Group) (office). *Website:* www.jang.com.pk (office); www .geo.tv (office).

LODIN, Azizullah, BA, PhD; Afghan politician and government official; b. 1939, Herat; ed high school in Kabul, Kabul Univ., Univ. of Köln, Germany; Lecturer, Faculty of Econs, Kabul Univ. 1976–78; held as political prisoner and put in Pule-Charkhi for involvement with Anti-Communist activist group in Kabul 1978–80; joined mujahidin movt as political adviser to leadership of Harakat Inqlab Islami Afghanistan, Peshawar, Pakistan 1980; fmr Vice-Chair. Political Dept, Islamic Unity of Afghanistan, mem. Supreme Council 1983–85; worked on Afghan refugee affairs and liaisons with Govt of Pakistan and Int. Orgs; Founder Afghan's Doctor Union outside the country (first Afghan non-governmental org. in Pakistan); Founder Nahid-e-Shahid High School for Afghan refugee girls, Peshawar 1983; Chair. Afghan del. at Tribunal de peuple, Sorbonne, Paris, France 1981; Dir Political Dept, Islamic Revolutionary Party of Afghan mujahidin, Peshawar 1985–89; Econ. and Political Adviser to Pres. of Afghan Interim Govt chaired by Prof. Mujadidy; fmr mem. Bd of Dirs Reconstruction Authority for Afghanistan; fmr Pres. Task Force Cttee for Emergency Assistance Inside Afghanistan; Head of Afghan Consulting GmbH, Herat 1992–95; served as Pres. Afghan Econ. Council, SW Prov.; attached to resistance org. against Taliban in Iran 1995–2001; Founder Cyprus Peace Conf.; fmr Head of Political Affairs, Cyprus Del. to Bonn Conf. and a signing mem. of Bonn Agreement; Adviser to Pres. Karzai in SW Prov., Herat 2003; Pres. Gen. Admin of Anti-Bribery and Corruption, with rank of Minister 2003–04; Gen. Sec. Secr. of Nat. Ass. of Afghanistan 2004–07; Pres. Ind. Election Comm. of Afghanistan 2007–10. *Address:* c/o Independent Election Commission, PO Box 979, IEC Compound, Jalalabad Road, Paktia Kot, Kabul, Afghanistan. *Telephone:* 75-2035203 (mobile). *E-mail:* info@iec.org.af.

LOEAK, Christopher Jorebon; Marshall Islands politician and head of state; *President;* b. 11 Nov. 1952, Ailinglaplap Atoll; m. Anono Lieom Loeak; three c.; ed Hawaii Pacific Coll., Gonzaga Univ. School of Law, Spokane, USA; mem. Nitijela (Parl.) for Ailinglaplap constituency 1985–; Minister of Justice 1988–92, of Social Services 1992–96, of Educ. 1996–98, Minister for Ralik Islands 1998–99, Minister in Assistance to Pres. 1999, 2008–11; Pres. of the Marshall Islands 2012–. *Address:* Office of the President, Government of the Republic of the Marshall Islands, POB 2, Majuro, MH 96960, Marshall Islands (office). *Telephone:* (625) 3445 (office). *Fax:* (625) 4021 (office). *E-mail:* pressoff@ntamar.net (office). *Website:* www .rmigovernment.org (office).

LOEHNIS, Anthony David, CMG, MA; British banker; *Chairman, Alpha Bank London Limited;* b. 12 March 1936, London; s. of Sir Clive Loehnis and Rosemary Loehnis (née Ryder); m. Jennifer Forsyth Anderson 1965; three s. ed Eton Coll., New Coll. Oxford, Harvard School of Public Admin; in Diplomatic Service 1960–66; with J. Henry Schroder Wagg and Co. Ltd 1967–80 (seconded to Bank of England 1977–79); Assoc. Dir Bank of England 1980–81, Exec. Dir (Overseas Affairs) 1981–89; Group Exec. Dir, Vice-Chair. S. G. Warburg and Co. 1989–92; Exec. Dir UK–Japan 21st Century Group 1999–2002; Dir (non-exec.) St James's Place Capital PLC 1993–2005, Alpha Bank London Ltd 1994– (Chair. 2005–), Tokyo-Mitsubishi Int. PLC 1996–2007, AGCO Corpn (USA) 1997–2005, VTB Capital PLC 2007–13; Chair. Public Works Loan Bd 1997–2005. *Address:* Alpha Bank London, 66 Cannon Street, London, EC4N 6EP, England (office). *Telephone:* (20) 7332-6767 (office); (7595) 760424 (mobile). *Fax:* (20) 7332-0010 (office). *E-mail:* antloehnis@ gmail.com.

LÖFGREN, Lars, PhD; Swedish theatre, film and television director, playwright, poet and court official; *Lord Chamberlain;* b. 6 Sept. 1935, The Arctic Circle; m. Anna-Karin Gillberg 1963; one s. two d.; ed Gustavus Adolphus Coll., USA, Stanford Univ., USA, Sorbonne, France, Uppsala Univ., Sweden; Dir Royal Dramatic Theatre of Sweden 1985–97, Nordic Museum 1997–2001; Lord Chamberlain 1999–; Lord-in-Waiting to His Majesty the King; Commdr, Légion d'honneur 2001; Royal Prize of Swedish Acad. 1996. *Publications:* various plays, filmscripts, TV scripts, poetry, novels, Svensk Teater – Artistry of the Swedish Theater 2003. *Address:* The Office of the Marshal of the Court of the Royal Palace, 11130 Stockholm (office); Sjötullsbacken 27, 11525 Stockholm, Sweden (home). *Telephone:* (8) 402-6000 (office); (8) 855822 (home). *E-mail:* lars.lofgren@pof.se (home).

LOGAN, Lara, BCom; South African journalist and broadcaster; *Chief Foreign Affairs Correspondent, CBS News;* b. 1971, Durban; m. 1st Jason Siemon (divorced); m. 2nd Joseph Burckett 2008; one s.; ed Univ. of Natal, Univ. de l'Alliance Française, Paris, France; news reporter, Sunday Tribune, Durban 1988–89, then with Daily News, Durban 1990–92; Sr Producer, Reuters TV Africa 1992–96; freelance journalist 1996–2000, worked as reporter and ed./producer with ITN and Fox/SKY, CBS News, ABC News (London), NBC, European Broadcast Union; corresp., GMTV (breakfast show), London 2000–02; joined CBS News 2002, corresp. and contrib. to 60 Minutes II 2002–04, corresp. for 60 Minutes 2006–, Chief Foreign Affairs Corresp., CBS News 2006–; Emmy Award, Overseas Press Club Award, David Bloom Award 2008, Edward P. Murrow Awards 2008, 2010. *Address:* CBS News, 2020 M Street, NW, Washington, DC 20036, USA (office). *Website:* www.cbsnews.com (office).

LOGAN, Malcolm (Mal) Ian, AC, DipEd, PhD, MBA; Australian geographer, academic and fmr university administrator; b. 3 June 1931, Inverell, NSW; s. of A. J. Logan; m. Antoinette Lalich 1954; one d.; ed Tamworth High School, New England Univ. Coll., Sydney Teachers' Coll., Univ. of Sydney; Lecturer in Geography, Sydney Teachers' Coll. 1956–58; Lecturer in Geography, Univ. of

Sydney 1959–64; Sr Lecturer 1965–67; Prof. of Geography and Urban and Regional Planning, Univ. of Wisconsin, Madison, USA 1967–71; Prof. of Geography, Monash Univ. 1971–86, Pro-Vice-Chancellor 1982–85, Deputy Vice-Chancellor 1986, Vice-Chancellor 1987–96, also fmr Pres.; Deputy Chair. Int. Devt Program of Australian Univs 1991–93; Chair. Australian Centre for Contemporary Art 1990, Open Learning Agency of Australia 1993–96, Monash International Pty Ltd 1994–96 TENTAS Pty Ltd 1998–, Australia Educ. Gateway Pty Ltd 1998–; Dir Australia Communications Computing Inst. 1998–, Job Scene Pty Ltd 2000–; Chair. and Dir Pinnacle Pty Ltd 2000–; mem. Comm. for the Future 1995–; Visiting Prof., Univ. of Ibadan, Nigeria 1970–71, LSE, UK 1973, Nanyang Univ., Singapore 1979; Hon. DLitt (Monash) 1997. *Publications:* co-author: Studies in Australian Geography 1968, New Viewpoints in Urban and Industrial Geography 1971, Urban and Regional Australia 1975, Urbanisation, The Australian Experience 1980, The Brittle Rim 1989, Reconstructing Asia: The Economic Miracle That Never Was, The Future That Is 1998. *Leisure interests:* golf, reading. *Address:* 1/50 Bourke Street, Melbourne, Vic. 3000; c/o Monash University, Wellington Road, Clayton, Vic. 3168, Australia.

LOGSDAIL, Nicholas; British gallery owner; *Director, Lisson Gallery;* ed Slade School of Art; co-f., with Fiona Hildyard, the Lisson Gallery 1967, represents artists including Marina Abramović, Ai Weiwei, Allora and Calzadilla, Art & Language, Cory Arcangel, Daniel Buren, Gerard Byrne, James Casebere, Angela de la Cruz, Nathalie Djurberg & Hans Berg Spencer Finch, Ceal Floyer, Ryan Gander, Rodney Graham, Dan Graham, Carmen Herrera, Christian Jankowski, Peter Joseph, John Latham, Tim Lee, Lee Ufan, Sol LeWitt, Liu Xiaodong, Richard Long, Robert Mangold, Jason Martin, Haroon Mirza, Tatsuo Miyajima, Jonathan Monk, Tony Oursler, Giulio Paolini, Florian Pumhösl, Rashid Rana, Pedro Reyes, Fred Sandback, Santiago Sierra, Sean Snyder and Lawrence Weiner, exhibited many of the artists who came to be known under the term New British Sculptors, including Tony Cragg, Richard Deacon, Shirazeh Houshiary, Anish Kapoor, Julian Opie, Richard Wentworth and Bill Woodrow; opened gallery in Milan 2010, office in New York 2011, also galleries in New York and Singapore. *Address:* Lisson Gallery, 52–54 Bell Street, Lisson Grove, London, NW1 5DA, England (office). *Telephone:* (20) 7724-2739 (office). *Fax:* (20) 7724-7124 (office). *E-mail:* contact@ lissongallery.com (office). *Website:* www.lissongallery.com (office).

LOGUNOV, Anatoly Alekseyevich; Russian theoretical physicist; *Research Head, Institute for High Energy Research (IHEP);* b. 30 Dec. 1926, Obsharovka, Samara Region; s. of Aleksei Ivanovich Logunov and Agrippina Kuzminichna Logunova; m. Anna Nikolayevna Eshliman 1951 (died 1997); one s. (deceased) one d.; ed Moscow State Univ.; mem. CPSU 1960–91; mem. faculty staff Moscow State Univ. 1951–56; Deputy Dir for Research, Theoretical Physics Lab., Jt Inst. for Nuclear Research, Dubna 1956–63, Prof. 1961; Dir of Serpukhov Inst. for High Energy Physics (IHEP), Protvino, Moscow 1963–74, IHEP Research Head 1974–, Dir State Research Centre IHEP 1993–2003; Rector Moscow State Univ. 1977–92; mem. USSR (now Russian) Acad. of Sciences 1972–, Vice-Pres. 1974–91; Head, State Scientific-Tech. Programme of High Energy Physics 1987–91; mem. Acad. of Creative Endeavours 1992–; Full Prof., Inst. of Fundamental Research, Molise, Italy; mem. Editorial Bd Asia-Pacific Peace Forum 1995–; Chief Ed. annual publ. Science and Humankind 1977–91, journal Theoretical and Mathematical Physics 1989–; main research on quantum field theory, elementary particle physics, gravitation and relativity theory; Cand. mem. Cen. Cttee CPSU 1981–86, mem. 1986–90; Deputy, USSR Supreme Soviet 1978–89; four Orders of Lenin, Order of Honour, Order of Pole Star (Mongolia), Order of Yugoslavian Banner with Ribbon, Commdr Cross of Order of Merit (Poland), Order for Service to the Motherland (third and second classes) 1995, 2002; Dr hc (Belgrade, Berlin, Bratislava, Havana, Helsinki, Prague, Sofia Univs, several Japanese Univs; Lenin Prize 1970, USSR State Prizes 1973, 1984, Lyapunov Medal, Gibbs Medal, Hero of Socialist Labour 1980, Gold Medal Czech Acad. of Sciences. *Publications include:* The Updated Analysis of the Problem 1987, On Henri Poincaret's work On the Dynamics of the Electron 1988, The Third Irisated Bridge 1988, Relativistic Theory of Gravitation 1989, Principles of Quantum Field Theory 1990, Lectures in Relativity and Gravitation: A Modern Look 1991, Gravitational Field Theory 2000, The Theory of Gravity 2001, Poincaré and Relativity Theory 2005, Henri Poincaret's Relativistic Theory of Gravitation 2006; more than 350 contribs to scientific journals on high energy and elementary particle physics and on latest ideas about space-time and gravitation. *Address:* State Research Centre Institute for High Energy Physics, 142281 Protvino, Moscow Region, Russia (office). *Telephone:* (4967) 74-25-79 (office). *Fax:* (4967) 74-49-37 (office). *E-mail:* Anatoly.Logunov@ihep.ru (office).

LOHANI, Prakash Chandra, MBA, PhD; Nepalese politician and academic; b. 1944; ed Indiana Univ., Univ. of California, Los Angeles, USA; fmr Lecturer, Univ. of Calif.; fmr Minister of Foreign Affairs and of Finance; Minister of Finance, Interim Govt 2003–04; currently Jt Gen.-Sec. Rashtriya Jana Shakti Party (National People's Power Party); Adjunct Faculty and Chair. Bd of Regents, South Asian Inst. of Man. *Address:* South Asian Institute of Management, Lagankhel, Lalitpur, POBox 23955, Kathmandu; Rashtriya Jana Shakti Party (National People's Power Party), Ramalphokhari, Kathmandu, Nepal (office). *Telephone:* (1) 4437063 (office). *Fax:* (1) 4437064 (office). *E-mail:* pclohani@saim.edu.np; rjpnepal@info.com.np (office). *Website:* www.rjpnepal.org (office); www.saim.edu .np.

LOHIA, Aloke, BCom; Indian business executive; *Vice-Chairman and Group CEO, Indorama Ventures PCL;* b. 1958; m. Suchitra Lohia; three c.; ed Univ. of Delhi; Finance Dir PT Indo Rama Synthetics, Indonesia 1979–87; f. Indorama Ventures PCL, Thailand 1988, currently Vice-Chair. and Group CEO; Dr hc (Rajamangala Univ. of Technology Thanyaburi). *Address:* Indorama Ventures PCL, 75/102 Ocean Tower 2, 37th Floor, Soi Sukhumvit 19 (Wattana), Bangkok 10110, Thailand (office). *Telephone:* (2) 661-6661 (office). *Fax:* (2) 661-6664 (office). *Website:* www.indorama.net (office).

LOHIA, Ashok Kumar; Nepalese business executive; f. Mahashakti Soap and Chemical Industries Pvt. Ltd 1970, currently Chair. *Address:* Mahashakti Soap and Chemical Industries Pvt. Ltd, 534 Exhibition Rd, Kathmandu, Nepal (office). *Telephone:* (1) 4226638 (office). *Fax:* (1) 4225178 (office). *E-mail:* puja@msci.wlink .com.np (office).

LOHIA, Renagi Renagi, CBE, MA; Papua New Guinea broadcasting executive and fmr diplomatist; b. 15 Oct. 1945, Tubesereia; s. of Lohia and Koborei Lohia; m. Patty Lohia 1969; three s. two d.; ed Univ. of Papua New Guinea and Univ. of London, UK; Research Asst, Univ. of Papua New Guinea 1970–73; Sr Tutor 1973, Lecturer in Educ. 1974–82, Pro-Vice-Chancellor 1976, Deputy Vice-Chancellor 1977, Vice-Chancellor 1977–82, Chair. Educational Planning Cttee 1974–75, Educ. Faculty Rep. Jt Cttee on Teacher Educ. 1975–76; Chair. Public Services Comm. 1982–83; Amb. to USA and Mexico and High Commr in Canada 1983–89; Perm. Rep. to UN 1983–94; Chair. UN Decolonization Cttee; Special Asst Dept of Foreign Affairs 1986–87; Chief of Staff, Office of Prime Minister 1994–95; Chair. and CEO Nat. Broadcasting Comm. 1995–99; High Commr to Australia –2005. *Leisure interest:* sports. *Address:* c/o Department of Foreign Affairs, Central Government Offices, Kumul Ave, Post Office, Wards Strip, Waigani, NCD, Papua New Guinea.

LOHSE, Eduard, DTheol; German ecclesiastic; b. 19 Feb. 1924, Hamburg; s. of Dr Walther Lohse and Dr Wilhelmine Lohse (née Barrelet); m. Roswitha Flitner 1952; two s. one d.; ed Bethel/Bielefeld and Göttingen; Pastor, Hamburg 1952; Privatdozent, Faculty of Protestant Theology, Mainz 1953; Prof. of New Testament, Kiel 1956, Göttingen 1964; Bishop of Hanover 1971–88; Pres. of the Council of the Evangelical Church in Germany 1979–85; mem. Göttingen Akad. der Wissenschaften; Hon. DTheol (Mainz) 1961, (Glasgow) 1983. *Publications:* Märtyrer und Gottesknecht 1955, Die Offenbarung des Johannes 1960, Die Texte aus Qumran 1964, Die Geschichte des Leidens und Sterbens Jesu Christi 1964, Die Briefe an die Kolosser und an Philemon 1968, Umwelt des Neuen Testaments 1971, Entstehung des Neuen Testaments 1972, Die Einheit des Neuen Testaments 1973, Grundriss der neutestamentlichen Theologie 1974, Die Urkunde der Christen 1979, Die Vielfalt des Neuen Testaments 1982, Die Ethik der Bergpredigt 1984, Kleine Evangelische Pastoralethik 1985, Theologische Ethik des Neuen Testaments 1988, Erneuern und Bewahren Evangelische Kirche 1970–90 1993, Paulus – eine Biographie 1996, Der Brief an die Römar 2003, Vater Unser 2009. *Leisure interest:* music. *Address:* Ernst-Curtius-Weg 7, 37075 Göttingen, Germany. *Telephone:* (551) 42424 (home).

LOHSE, Martin J., DrMed; German pharmacologist and academic; *Professor and Chair, Institute for Pharmacology and Toxicology, Julius Maximilians University of Würzburg;* b. 26 Aug. 1956, Mainz; s. of Prof. Eduard Lohse and Roswitha Lohse; m. Friederike Lohse; three s.; ed Univ. of Göttingen, Univ. of London, UK and Univ. of Paris, France; worked at Pharmacological Insts in Bonn and Heidelberg; Asst Prof., Duke Univ., USA 1988–90; Group Leader, Gene Center, Univ. of Munich/Max-Planck Inst. for Biochemistry, Martinsried 1990–93; Prof. and Chair, Inst. for Pharmacology and Toxicology, Julius Maximilians Univ. of Würzburg 1993–, Chair. Graduate School 2003–, Vice-Pres. for Research 2009–; Chair. Rudolf-Virchow-DFG Research Center for Experimental Biomedicine 2001–; project man. several European research programmes; mem. Bavarian Acad. of Science 1998, Leopoldina German Acad. of Science 2000– (Vice-Pres. 2009), Northrhine-Westfalia Acad. of Science 2004, Nat. Ethics Council 2001–08, Senate and Excellence Comm., German Research Foundation 2001–10; mem. Editorial Bd Nature, Science, The EMBO Journal; mem. Advisory Bd numerous scientific foundations; Fed. Order of Merit (1st class) 2002, Bavarian Order of Merit 2006; Gerhard Hess Prize, FRG 1990, Research Prize, Fed. Dept of Health 1991, William Vaillant Prize 1996, Gottfried Wilhelm Leibniz Prize, Deutschen Forschungsgemeinschaft 1999, Ernst Jung Prize in Medicine 2000, Research Achievement Award, Int. Soc. of Heart Research 2007, Jakob Henle Medal 2010, Svedberg Lecturer, Univ. of Uppsala 2012, Visiting Professorship, Vallee Foundation, Harvard Medical School 2012. *Publications:* numerous articles in scientific journals. *Address:* Julius-Maximilians-Universität Würzburg, Institut für Pharmakologie und Toxikologie, Versbacher Straße 9, 97078 Würzburg, Germany (office). *Telephone:* (931) 201-48400 (office). *Fax:* (931) 201-48411 (office). *E-mail:* lohse@toxi.uni-wuerzburg.de (office). *Website:* www.pharmakologie.uni -wuerzburg.de (office).

LOIZAGA, Eladio, LLB; Paraguayan diplomatist, civil servant and politician; *Minister of Foreign Affairs;* b. 17 March 1949, Asunción; m.; two c.; ed Catholic Univ. and Nat. Univ., Asunción; joined Ministry of Foreign Affairs 1967, various posts with Dept of Int. Orgs Treaties and Instruments 1981, Dir of Dept 1983–88, Rep. to Yacyretá Binational Agency 1989–92, Adviser to Minister; elected to Nat. Chamber of Deputies 1989, mem. cttees concerning constitutional and legis. issues; Pvt. Sec. to Pres. of Paraguay and Minister Exec. Br. 1989–92; mem. Perm. Cttee of Congress 1992–93; Amb. and Perm. Rep. to UN, WTO and other specialized agencies, Geneva 1995–98; served with Embassy in Washington, DC and Alt. Rep. to OAS; Amb. and Perm. Rep. to UN, New York 2001–09, Pres. High-level Cttee of South–South Co-operation of UN Gen. Ass.; Minister of Foreign Affairs 2013–. *Address:* Ministry of Foreign Affairs, Edif. Benigno López, Palma, esq. 14 de Mayo, Asunción, Paraguay (office). *Telephone:* (21) 49-3872 (office). *Fax:* (21) 49-3910 (office). *E-mail:* sistemas@mre.gov.py (office). *Website:* www.mre.gov .py (office).

LOKHORST, Wim; Dutch business executive; ed Technische Universiteit Delft; Man. Dir Oiltanking GmbH –2003, mem. Bd of Dirs Marquard & Bahls AG (parent co.) 1996–, CEO 2003–10; mem. Asia Cttee, Hamburg Chamber of Commerce. *Address:* Marquard & Bahls AG, Admiralitaetstr. 55, 20459 Hamburg, Germany (office). *Telephone:* (40) 37004-0 (office). *Fax:* (40) 37004-141 (office). *E-mail:* office@ mbholding.de (office). *Website:* www.mbholding.com (office).

LOKUBANDARA, W(ijesinghe) J(ayaweera) M(udiyanselage), BA; Sri Lankan attorney, politician, poet and songwriter; *Governor of Sabaragamuwa Province;* b. 5 Aug. 1941, Haputale; s. of W. J. M. Gunesekara Bandara and R. M. Loku Manike; m. Malathi Lokubandara; three s.; ed Yahala-Bedda School, Bandarawela Cen. Coll., Univ. of Peradeniya, Univ. of London, UK (external degree); worked as an assistant legal draftsman; mem. Parl. (United Nat. Party) for Badulla 1977–, Chief Opposition Whip 1994–2001, Speaker of the Parl. 2004–10, mem. Cttee of Selection, House Cttee, Cttee on Standing Orders, Cttee on Parl. Business; fmr non-cabinet Minister of Indigenous Medicine; Minister of Cultural Affairs, Educ. and Media 1989–94; Minister for Justice, Law Reform and Nat. Integration and Minister for Buddha Sasana 2001–04; Gov. of Sabaragamuwa Prov. 2010–. *Publications:* The Mystique of Sigiriya, Sigiri Gee Siri, Rasadipani, Sastriya Vadalipi, Garu Kathanayakanumani: Mati Sabaye Kala

Kata. *Address:* Office of the Governor, Ratnapura, Sabaragamuwa Province (office); 14 Samagi Mawatha, Gangodawila, Nugegoda, Colombo, Sri Lanka (home). *Website:* www.sabaragamuwapc.com (office).

LOLLOBRIGIDA, Gina; Italian actress, photographer and sculptor; b. 4 July 1927, Sibiaco; d. of Giovanni Mercuri and Giuseppina Mercuri; m. 1st Milko Skofic 1949; one s.; ed Liceo Artistico, Rome; fmr model; first screen role in Pagliacci 1947; currently photographer and sculptor. *Films include:* Campane a Martello 1948, Cuori senza Frontiere 1949, Achtung, Banditi! 1951, Enrico Caruso 1951, Fanfan la Tulipe 1951, Altri Tempi 1952, The Wayward Wife 1952, Les belles de la nuit 1952, Pane, amore e fantasia 1953, La Provinciale 1953, Pane, amore e gelosia, La Romana 1954, Il Grande Gioco 1954, La Donna più bella del Mondo 1955, Trapeze 1956, Notre Dame de Paris 1956, Solomon and Sheba 1959, Never So Few 1960, Go Naked in the World 1961, She Got What She Asked For 1963, Woman of Straw 1964, Le Bambole 1965, Hotel Paradiso 1966, Les Sultans 1966, Le Piacevoli Notti 1966, Cervantes 1966, La Morte Fatto L'uovo (A Curious Way to Love) and (Death Laid an Egg) 1967, Stuntman 1968, Buona Sera Mrs Campbell 1968, Un Bellissimo Novembre (That Splendid November) 1968, The Private Navy of Sgt O'Farrell 1968, Peccato Mortale (Mortal Sin also known as The Lonely Woman also known as Roses and Green Peppers) 1972, King, Queen, Knave 1972, Le Avventure Di Pinocchio 1972, Bad Man's River 1972, The Bocce Showdown 1990, Les Cent et Une Nuits (A Hundred and One Nights) 1995, Plucked, XXL 1997. *Television:* Falcon Crest (series) 1984, Deceptions (TV film) 1985. *Publications:* Italia Mia (photography) 1974, The Philippines. *Leisure interest:* photography. *Address:* Via Appia Antica 223, 00178 Rome, Italy.

LOMAIA, Alexander, PhD; Georgian engineer, government official and diplomatist; *Permanent Representative, United Nations;* b. 1963, Tbilisi; m.; two s.; ed Georgian Tech. Univ., Moscow Construction Eng Inst.; engineer, Tbilhihroproekti Inst. 1985–87; fmr Ed., Argumenti Newspaper; mem., Georgian Community Hall, Moscow 1989–92; apptd Deputy Rep. of Govt to Moscow 1991, later Acting Rep.; Co-ordinator, Eurasia Fund Civil Public and Media Program 1995–2000; Dir, Georgia Representation to Eurasia Fund 2000–02; Regional Dir Democracy Coalition in post-Soviet states 2002–03; Exec. Dir Open Soc. Georgia 2003–; active in 'rose revolution' of 2003; Minister of Educ. and Sciences 2004–07; Nat. Security Adviser to Pres. 2007–09; Perm. Rep. to UN, New York 2009–. *Address:* Permanent Mission of Georgia to United Nations, One United Nations Plaza, 26th Floor, New York, NY 10021, USA (office). *Telephone:* (212) 759-1949 (office). *Fax:* (212) 759-1832 (office). *E-mail:* georgia@un.int (office); geomission.un@mfa.gov.ge (office). *Website:* www.un.int/georgia (office).

LOMAX, (Janis) Rachel, MA, MSc; British civil servant and economist; b. 15 July 1945; d. of William Salmon and Dilys Salmon; m. Michael Acworth Lomax 1967 (divorced 1990); two s.; ed Cheltenham Lady's Coll., Girton Coll., Cambridge, London School of Econs; Econ. Asst, HM Treasury 1968, Econ. Adviser 1972, Sr Econ. Adviser 1978, Prin. Pvt. Sec. to Chancellor of the Exchequer 1985–86, Under-Sec. 1986–90, Deputy Chief Econ. Adviser 1990–92, Deputy Sec. Financial Insts and Markets 1992–94, Deputy Sec. Cabinet Office 1994–95; Vice-Pres. and Chief of Staff, IBRD 1995–96; Perm. Sec. Welsh Office 1996–99, Dept of Social Security, then Dept for Work and Pensions 1999–2002; Perm. Sec. Dept for Transport 2002–; Deputy Gov. (responsible for monetary policy) Bank of England July 2003–08; Chair. UK Selection Cttee, Harkness Fellowships 1995–97; mem. Council Royal Econ. Soc. 1989–94; Gov. De Montfort Univ. 1997–2007, Henley Coll. of Man. 2000–03, LSE 2003–; Pres. Inst. of Fiscal Studies 2007–; mem. Bd of Dirs Royal Nat. Theatre 2002–, HSBC Holdings PLC 2008–, BAA Ltd 2010–, Arcus European Infrastructure Fund GP LLP, Scottish American Investment Co. PLC, Reinsurance Group of America Inc.; Trustee, Centre for Economic Policy Research; Dr hc (Univ. of Glasgow, City Univ., Univ. of Glamorgan). *Address:* c/o Board of Directors, HSBC Holdings PLC, 8 Canada Square, London, E14 5HQ, England.

LOMBARD, Didier; French telecommunications executive; *Chairman, France Telecom SA;* b. 1942; m.; three s.; ed École Polytechnique, École Nationale Supérieure des Télécommunications; with CNET (now Research and Devt Div., France Telecom) 1967; Scientific and Tech. Dir, Ministry of Research and Tech. 1988–90; Gen. Man. of Industrial Strategy, Ministry of Economy 1991–98; Founder, Chair. and Deputy Amb. for Int. Investment, Agency for Int. Investment 1999–2003; Exec. Vice-Pres., in charge of Technologies, Strategic Partnerships and New Usages, France Telecom SA 2003–, Chair. and CEO 2005–10, Chair. (non-exec.) 2010–, Chair. Strategy Cttee; mem. Bd of Dirs Thomson Reuters, Thales; mem. Supervisory Bd Radiall, ST Microelectronics. *Address:* France Telecom SA, 6 place d'Alleray, 75505 Paris Cedex 15, France (office). *Telephone:* 1-44-44-22-22 (office). *Fax:* 1-44-44-95-95 (office). *E-mail:* info@francetelecom.com (office). *Website:* www.francetelecom.com (office).

LOMBARD, Marie-Christine, MBA; French business executive; *CEO, Geodis;* b. 1958, Paris; m.; two c.; ed ESSEC Business School, Paris; began career at Lord & Taylor, New York, USA; fmr banking exec. with Chemical Bank, Paris, Paribas Bank, Lyon; Chief Financial Officer, Jet Services, France 1993–97, Man. Dir 1997–99, co. acquired by TNT Express (Dutch postal and logistics group) in 1999, Chair. and Man. Dir TNT Express France 1999–2004, Group Man. Dir TNT Express and mem. Bd of Man. 2004–12, Chair. and CEO TNT Express NV 2011–12 (resgnd); CEO Geodis 2012–; mem. Supervisory Bd Groupe Banques Populaire 2010–, Royal Wessanen NV 2006–09, Metro Group 2008–11; mem. Bd of Dirs Postnl NV; Chair. Lyon Ville de l'Entrepreneuriat; Chevalier, Légion d'honneur 2005; ranked by the Financial Times amongst Top 25 Businesswomen in Europe (23rd) 2005, (23rd) 2006, (23rd) 2007. *Address:* SNCF Geodis, Cap West, 7/9 allées de l'Europe, Clichy 92110, France (office). *Telephone:* 1-56-76-26-00 (office). *Website:* www.geodis.com (office).

LOMU, Jonah; New Zealand rugby union player; b. 12 May 1975, Auckland; m. Tanya Rutter 1996 (divorced); pnr Teina Stace; ed Wesley Coll., Auckland; bank officer ASB Bank of NZ; youngest ever capped All Black (at 19 years and 45 days); wing; int. debut NZ versus France 1994; semi-finalist at World Cup, 1995 and 1999; out of action for a year during 1996–97 with a rare kidney disorder, returned to int. side for All Blacks' UK tour end of 1997; gold medal rugby sevens, Kuala Lumpur Commonwealth Games 1998; missed World Cup of 2003 after kidney disorder recurred; 63 caps (185 Test points including 37 tries); ran 100m in 10.8 seconds; *Website:* www.jonahlomu.com

LONDOÑO PAREDES, Julio; Colombian politician and diplomatist; *Ambassador to Cuba;* b. 10 June 1938, Bogotá; m.; ed San Isidro Hermanos Maristas School, El Carmen Inst. and Mil. Cadet School, Bogotá; Prof. of Int. Politics, Univ. of Jorge Tadeo Lozano, Bogotá; Prof. of Int. Public Law, Univ. of El Rosario, Bogotá; served in army, retd 1981 with rank of Lt-Col; Head of Frontier Div., Ministry of Foreign Affairs 1968–79, Sec.-Gen. 1979–82, Vice-Minister 1982–83, Minister 1986–90; Amb. to Panama 1983–86; Perm. Rep. to UN 1994–99; currently Amb. to Cuba. *Publications:* History of the Colombo-Peruvian Conflict of 1932, Colombian Territorial Law, Colombian Border Issues. *Address:* Embassy of Colombia, Calle 14, No 515, entre 5 y 7, Miramar, Havana, Cuba (office). *Telephone:* (7) 24-1246 (office). *Fax:* (7) 24-1249 (office). *E-mail:* embacub@ cancilleria.gov.co (office).

LONFERNINI, Giovanni; San Marino lawyer and government official; *Secretary of State for Tourism and Relations with the Azienda Autonoma di Stato per i Servizi Pubblici;* b. 12 May 1976; Co-Capt.-Regent (Jt Head of State and Govt) of San Marino 2003–04, 2012–13; Sec. of State for Tourism and Relations with the Azienda Autonoma di Stato per i Servizi Pubblici 2013–; Sec.-Gen. San Marino Christian Democrat Party (Partito Democratico Cristiano Sammarinese). *Address:* Secretariat of State for Foreign and Political Affairs, Tourism and Relations with the Azienda Autonoma di Stato per i Servizi Pubblici (AASS), Palazzo Begni, Contrada Omerelli, 47890 San Marino (office); Partito Democratico Cristiano Sammarinese (PDCS), Via delle Scalette 6, 47890 San Marino (office). *Telephone:* (0549) 991193 (office). *Fax:* (0549) 992694 (office).

LONG, David H.; American business executive; *Chairman and CEO, Liberty Mutual Holding Company Inc.;* joined Liberty Mutual 1985, held various positions of increasing responsibility and authority principally in the Commercial Markets and Agency Markets business units –2005, Exec. Vice-Pres. and Man. Dir Commercial business unit 2005–06, Exec. Vice-Pres. Liberty Mutual Group Commercial Markets business unit 2006–09, Pres. Liberty International 2009–, Pres. Liberty Mutual Holding Co. Inc. 2010–, CEO 2011–, Chair. 2013–; Dir, QUINN Insurance Ltd 2011–; Trustee, Hartwick Coll. *Address:* Liberty Mutual Holding Co. Inc., 175 Berkeley Street, Boston, MA 02116, USA (office). *Telephone:* (617) 357-9500 (office). *Fax:* (617) 574-6688 (office). *E-mail:* info@libertymutual .com (office). *Website:* www.libertymutualgroup.com (office). www.libertymutual .com (office).

LONG, Malcolm William, LLB; Australian broadcasting executive; b. 13 April 1948, Fremantle, WA; s. of William Long and Dorothy Long; m. Helen Trotter 1973; two d.; ed Univ. of Western Australia; Dir Radio Talks and Documentaries, ABC 1978–82; Man. (Radio) Victorian ABC 1982–84; Dir ABC Radio 1985–92; Deputy Man. Dir Australian Broadcasting Corpn 1992–93; Dir PAN TV Ltd 1996–; Man. Dir SBS Corpn 1993–97; Man. Dir Malcolm Long Assocs Pty Ltd 1997–2003; Pres. Australian Museum Trust 1995–2000; Dir Macquarie Communications Infrastructure Group 2001–, Australian Film Television and Radio School 2003–07; fmr Chair. Exec. Cttee Int. Inst. of Communications; mem. Australian Broadcasting Authority 2000–05, Australian Communications and Media Authority 2005–. *Publications:* Marx & Beyond 1973, Beyond the Mechanical Mind (with P. Fry) 1977; numerous articles on broadcasting policy and culture. *Leisure interests:* music, reading, running. *Address:* Australian Communications and Media Authority, PO Box Q500, Queen Victoria Building, NSW 1230, Australia (office). *Telephone:* (2) 9334-7700 (office). *Fax:* (2) 9334-7799 (office). *E-mail:* ml@ mlongdigital.com (office). *Website:* www.acma.gov.au (office).

LONG, Marceau, LèsL, LenD; French civil servant; *President, Institut français des relations internationales;* b. 22 April 1926, Aix-en-Provence, Bouches-du-Rhône; s. of Lucien Long and Marcelle Seymard; m. Josette Niel 1949; two s. three d.; ed Lycée Mignet, Univ. of Aix-en-Provence, École nat. d'admin; Lecturer, Ecole nat. d'admin 1953–56, Inst. d'Etudes politiques 1953–56; seminars Ecole nat. d'admin 1963–68; at Council of State 1952–57, 1975–, Vice-Pres. 1987–95, apptd auditor 1952, master of petitions 1957, Sec.-Gen. to Govt 1975–82, Counsellor of State on long-term secondment 1976; apptd to Govt Comm. 1957, Tech. Counsellor to Cabinet, Sec. of State on Tunisian and Moroccan Affairs, then Foreign Affairs, then Judicial Counsellor to French Embassy, Morocco 1958, Dir-Gen. Admin. and Public Offices 1961–67, Sec. Gen. Admin, Ministry of Armies 1967–73, mem. Atomic Energy Cttee 1975–82; Chair. Organisation de la radio et de la télévision françaises (ORTF) 1973–74; Chair. Cie Air-Inter 1982–84; Chair. Cie Air France 1984–87; Chair. Cttee Inquiry on Law of Nationality 1987, Council of Admin. Tribunals and Courts of Appeal 1988–95; Lecturer Inst. d'études politiques de Paris, Ecole nat. d'admin 1963–68 (Chair. Bd of Govs 1987); Dir Crédit industriel et banque commerciale 1982–87, Soc. de Gestion de participations aéronautiques 1985; Vice-Pres. Conseil d'Etat 1987–95; apptd Pres. Admin. Council, Ecole nat. d'admin, Institut int. d'admin publique 1987, Inst. français des relations int. 1998–; Pres. Franco-American Foundation 1989–92, Hon. Pres. 1993–; Pres. Haut conseil à l'intégration 1989–93, 1994–95, Inst. des hautes études de la justice 1995–97, Inst. de la gestion déléguée 1996–2001; Pres. Soc. des amis des Archives de France; mem. Court of Arbitration, The Hague 1991–; mem. numerous admin. councils and cttees; Grand Officier, Légion d'honneur; Commdr Ordre nat. du Mérite; Officier des Palmes académiques. *Publications:* L'Economie de la Fonction Publique 1967, Les Services de Premier Ministre 1981, Les Grands Arrêts de la Jurisprudence Administrative (co-author) 1984, Etre Français aujourd'hui et demain, Rapport de la Commission de la Nationalité 1988, L'Esprit de justice: Portalis 1997, Les grands arrêts de la jurisprudence administrative (jtly) 2005; Mes regards sur l'Ecole nationale d'administration 1949–1995; d'Élève à Président 2009 and numerous contribs to magazines and books on public office and law. *Address:* Institut français des relations internationales, 27 rue de la Procession, 75015 Paris, France (office). *Telephone:* 1-40-61-60-00 (office). *Fax:* 1-40-61-60-60 (office). *E-mail:* lfri@ifri.org (office). *Website:* www.ifri.org (office).

LONG, Richard, CBE, RA; British artist; b. 2 June 1945, Bristol, England; s. of Maurice Long and Frances Carpenter; m. Denise Johnston 1969 (divorced 1999); two d.; pnr Denise Hooker; ed West of England Coll. of Art, Bristol and St Martin's School of Art, London; has exhibited widely since mid-1960s; work exhibited in Städtisches Museum, Mönchengladbach 1970, Museum of Modern Art, New York 1972, Stedelijk Museum, Amsterdam 1973, Scottish Museum of Modern Art, Edin. 1974, Kunsthalle, Berne 1977, Nat. Gallery of Canada, Ottawa 1982, Solomon R. Guggenheim Museum, New York 1986, Tate Gallery 1990, Hayward Gallery,

London (retrospective) 1991, ARC, Paris 1993, Palazzo delle Esposizioni, Rome 1994, São Paulo Bienal 1994, Nat. Modern Art Museum of Kyoto 1996, Kunstverein Hanover 1999, Guggenheim, Bilbao 2000, Museum Kurhaus Kleve 2001, Tate St Ives 2002, Galleria Lorcan O'Neill Roma 2003, Haunch of Venison 2003, 2006, Galeria Mário Sequeira, Braga 2004, Kulge Gallery, Seoul 2004, Sperone Westwater, New York 2004, Synagogue Stommeln 2004, Galerie Tschudi, Glarus 2005, Museum of Modern Art, San Francisco 2006, Lismore Castle, Waterford 2006, Scottish Nat. Gallery of Modern Art 2007; Chevalier des Arts et des Lettres 1990; Hon. DLit (Bristol) 1995; Turner Prize 1989, Wilhelm Lembruck Prize 1995, Praemium Imperiale 2009. *Publications include:* South America 1972, River Avon Book 1979, Twelve Works 1981, Countless Stones 1983, Stone Water Miles 1987, Old World New World 1988, Nile 1990, Walking in Circles 1991, Mountains and Waters 1992, River to River 1993, Mirage 1997, A Walk Across Across England 1997, From Time to time 1997, Every Grain of Sand 1999, Midday 2001, A Moving World 2002, Walking the Line 2002. *Address:* c/o James Cohan Gallery, 533 West 26th Street, New York, NY 10001, USA. *Telephone:* (212) 714-9500. *E-mail:* info@jamescohan.com. *Website:* www.richardlong.org.

LONG, Ziping; Chinese engineer and business executive; *Vice-Chairman and President, Jiangxi Copper Company Limited;* ed Jiangxi Inst. of Metallurgy, Central South Univ.; served at various operating and man. positions with Jiangxi Copper, including Deputy Chief and Factory Head of Guixi Smelter, Man. of JCC Guixi Smelter, Head of Smelting Dept in Guixi Smelter, Exec. Dir, Jiangxi Copper Co. Ltd 2007–09, Vice-Pres., Deputy Gen. and Chief Legal Adviser 2009–13, Gen. Man. 2013–, Exec. Dir, Vice-Chair. and Pres. 2013–; also Deputy Party Sec. *Address:* Jiangxi Copper Co. Ltd, 15 Yejin Avenue, Guixi 335424, People's Republic of China (office). *Telephone:* (701) 3777070 (office). *E-mail:* webmaster@ jxcc.com (office). *Website:* www.jxcc.com (office).

LONGO, Jeannie Michèle Alice; French cyclist; b. 31 Oct. 1958, Annecy; d. of Jean Longo and Yvette Longo; m. Patrice Ciprelli 1985; ed Inst. d'Etudes Commerciales (Grenoble), Univ. of Limoges; French cycling champion 1979–86; winner of over 13 world titles including world champion (road) 1979–89, 1992, 1995, 1998, 1999, 2000, runner up 1981, world champion (track) 1984, 1985, world champion (pursuit) 1986, 1988, 1989, world champion (against the clock) Spain 1997; winner Tour of Colorado 1986, 1987, Tour of Colombia 1987, 1988, Tour of Norway 1987, Tour de France 1987; silver medal World Track Race 1984, 1985, 1987; holder of several world records including world record for three km covered track, Grenoble 1992, five km uncovered track 1989; winner French Cycle Racing Championship 1992; silver medallist Olympic Games, Barcelona 1992, gold and silver medallist Road Race, Olympic Games, Atlanta 1996, bronze medallist, Olympic Games, Sydney 2000; achieved over 700 career wins, more than any other cyclist in history, setting 37 world records; winner French Road Race Championship 2006, 2008, French Time Trial Championship 2006, 2008, 2009, Trophée des Grimpeurs 2009, Chrono Des Nations 2009, 2010, French Elite Time-Trial Championship 2010, 2011; Consultant France Télévision 1999–; Officier, Légion d'Honneur, Commdr, Ordre Nat. du Mérite, Officier, Sovereign Order of Malta; Médaille d'Or, La Jeunesse et les Sports, Médaille d'Or, Acad. des Sports, Médaille du mérite et dévouement Français 2002. *Address:* Fédération Française de Cyclisme, 5 rue de Rome, 93561 Rosny-sous-Bois, France. *E-mail:* jeannielongo@ free.fr. *Website:* www.jeannielongo.com.

LONGORIA, Eva Jacqueline, BS; American actress and producer; b. 15 March 1975, Corpus Christi, Nueces Co., Tex.; d. of Enrique Longoria, Jr and Ella Eva Mireles; m. 1st Tyler Christopher 2002 (divorced 2004); m. 2nd Tony Parker 2007 (divorced 2011); ed Texas A&M Univ.-Kingsville, California State Univ., Northridge; won Miss Corpus Christi, USA title 1998; entered talent contest that led her to Los Angeles; later spotted and signed by a theatrical agent; guest starred in episode of Beverly Hills, 90210; began TV career in role of Isabella Braña on CBS soap opera The Young and the Restless 2001–03; has appeared on cover of Vogue, Marie Claire and Harper's Bazaar magazines; f. Eva's Heroes charity 2006; nat. spokesperson for PADRES Contra El Cancer; appointed to bi-partisan comm. given task of determining feasibility of creating Nat. Museum of the American Latino 2009; Co-Chair. Barack Obama's re-election campaign 2012; ALMA Award for Person of the Year 2006, named No. 14 in the FHM Sexiest Women poll 2008, named Philanthropist of the Year by the Hollywood Reporter 2009. *Films include:* Snitch'd (video) 2003, Señorita Justice (video) 2004, Carlita's Secret (video) (also co-producer) 2004, Hustler's Instinct (short) 2005, Harsh Times 2005, The Sentinel 2006, The Heartbreak Kid 2007, Over Her Dead Body 2008, Lower Learning 2008, Foodfight! (voice) 2009, Without Men 2011, Arthur Christmas (voice) 2011, For Greater Glory: The True Story of Cristiada 2012, Long Time Gone 2012, The Truth 2012, The Baytown Outlaws 2013; exec. producer: Hot Tamales Live: Spicy, Hot and Hilarious (video) (producer) 2003, Latinos Living the American Dream (documentary) (also writer and dir) 2010, The Harvest (documentary) 2011; dir: A Proper Send-Off (short) 2011. *Television includes:* The Young and the Restless (series) (ALMA Award for Outstanding Actress in a Daytime Drama 2002) 2001, Dragnet (series) 2003–04, The Dead Will Tell (film) 2004, Desperate Housewives (series) (Choice TV Breakout Performance – Female, Teen Choice Awards 2005, Outstanding Performance by an Ensemble in a Comedy Series, Screen Actors Guild Awards (shared with cast) 2005, 2006, Bambi Award for TV Series International 2007, Favorite Female TV Star, People's Choice Awards 2007) 2004–12, Children's Hospital (series) 2008; exec. producer: 2006 ALMA Awards (special) (producer) 2006, 2007 ALMA Awards (film) 2007, The Philanthropist (film) 2008, 2009 Alma Awards (film) 2009, 2011 ALMA Awards (film) 2011, Devious Maids (series) 2012, Ready for Love (series) 2012. *Address:* c/o Ron West, Thruline Entertainment, 9250 Wilshire Boulevard, Ground Floor, Beverly Hills, CA 90210, USA (office); Latin Hollywood Films, 153 San Vicente Boulevard, Suite 2-G, Santa Monica, CA 90402, USA (office). *Telephone:* (310) 595-1500 (office). (310) 451-2799 (office).

LONGRIGG, Anthony James, CMG; British diplomatist; b. 21 April 1944; m. Jane Rosa Cowlin 1968; three d.; joined FCO 1972, with Research Unit 1973; First Sec. Chancery, Moscow 1975–78; with E African Dept FCO 1978–80, Conf. for Security and Co-operation in Europe, FCO 1980–81; First Sec., Brasilia 1981–85; with Soviet Dept FCO 1985–87; Counsellor, Moscow 1987–91; Counsellor Econ./ EU Affairs, Madrid 1991–95; Head S Atlantic/Antarctic Dept FCO 1995–97;

Minister and Deputy Head of Mission, Moscow 1997–2000; Gov. of Montserrat 2001–04 (retd).

LONGUET, Gérard Edmond Jacques; French politician; b. 24 Feb. 1946, Neuilly-sur-Seine; s. of Jacques Longuet and Marie-Antoinette Laurent; m. Brigitte Fossorier 1967; four d.; ed Paris Univ., Ecole Nationale d'Admin; Pvt. Sec. to Prefect of Eure's Office 1973–74, to Prefect of Somme's Office 1974–76, to Sec. of State (attached to Prime Minister's Office) 1977–78; Deputy of Meuse 1978–81, 1988–93, Vice-Pres. Gen. Councillor's Office 1982–92; Gen. Councillor, Seuil d'Argonne 1979–92, Town Councillor 1983; Municipal Councillor, Bar-le-Duc 1983–89; mem. European Parl. 1984–86; Sec. of State March–Aug. 1986, then Minister at Ministry of Industry 1986–88; Minister of Industry, Posts and Telecommunications and Foreign Trade 1993–94, of Defence and Veterans' Affairs 2011–12; Sec.-Gen. Union pour la Démocratie Française (UDF) 1989; Regional Councillor of Lorraine 1992–2010 (resgnd), Pres. Regional Council 1992–2004; Pres. Republican Party 1990–95; Senateur de la Meuse 2001–11, Pres. of UMP Group in Senate 2009–11; Collection Dir, France Empire publrs; Pres. Sokrates Group, ETD 2003, Asscn des Régions de France. *Publications:* L'Epreuve de vérité 1995, L'Espoir industriel 1995. *Leisure interest:* skiing. *Address:* Sokrates Group, 56 rue de Chateaudun, 75009 Paris, France (office).

LONGUET-HIGGINS, Michael Selwyn, MA, PhD, FRS; British physicist and academic; *Senior Research Physicist Emeritus, Institute for Nonlinear Science, University of California, San Diego;* b. 8 Dec. 1925, Lenham, Kent; s. of the late Henry H. L. Longuet-Higgins and Albinia Cecil Bazeley; brother of Hugh Christopher Longuet-Higgins; m. Joan R. Tattersall 1958; two s. two d.; ed Winchester Coll., Trinity Coll., Cambridge Univ.; Research Fellow, Trinity Coll. Cambridge 1951–55, Commonwealth Fund Fellow, Scripps Inst., La Jolla, 1951–52; Research Scientist, Nat. Inst. of Oceanography 1954–67; Visiting Prof., MIT 1958, Inst. of Geophysics, Univ. of California 1961–62, Univ. of Adelaide 1963–64; Prof. of Oceanography, Oregon State Univ., Corvallis 1967–69; Royal Soc. Research Prof., Univ. of Cambridge (jt appointment with Inst. of Oceanographic Sciences) 1969–89; Sr Research Physicist, Inst. for Nonlinear Science, Univ. of California, San Diego 1989–, now Sr Research Physicist Emer.; Fellow, Trinity Coll. Cambridge 1969–; Foreign Assoc. NAS 1979; Hon. LLD (Glasgow) 1979; Hon. DTech (Tech. Univ. of Denmark) 1979; Sverdrup Gold Medal of American Meteorological Soc. 1983; Int. Coastal Eng Award, American Soc. of Civil Engineers 1984. *Publications:* contribs to scientific journals on physics and math. of the sea, especially ocean waves and currents. *Leisure interests:* music, gardening, mathematical toys. *Address:* Gage Farm, Comberton, Cambridge, CB3 7DH, England (home); Institute for Nonlinear Science, University of California San Diego, La Jolla, CA 92093, USA (office). *Telephone:* (858) 534-3936 (office); (1223) 262346 (home). *E-mail:* mlonguet@ucsd.edu (office). *Website:* inls.ucsd.edu (office).

LØNNING, Inge Johan, DTheol; Norwegian politician and theologian; b. 20 Feb. 1938, Bergen; s. of the late Per Lønning and of Anna Lønning (née Strømø); m. Kari Andersen 1962 (died 2008); two s. two d.; ed Univs of Bergen and Oslo and Pastoral Seminary of Church of Norway, Univ. of Tübingen, Germany; Naval Chaplain 1964–65; Asst Prof., Univ. of Oslo 1965–70; Research Fellow, Univ. of Tübingen 1967; Prof. of Systematic Theology, Univ. of Oslo 1971–, Dean, Faculty of Theology 1977–81, Rector, Univ. of Oslo 1985–92; mem. Oslo City Council 1972–76; Chair. Bd Norwegian Research Council for Science and Humanities 1980–84; Pres. Norsemen's Fed. 1989–2000, Nat. Rectors' Conf. 1989–92; Leader, European Movt in Norway 1993–95; mem. Parl. 1997–, Vice-Pres. Stortinget (Parl.) 2001–05, Pres. Lagtinget (Parl. of Aland) 2005–09; Vice-Pres. Høyre 1997–2002; Pres. Nordic Council 2003; Ed. Kirke og Kultur journal 1968–; mem. Norwegian Acad. of Science and Letters, Royal Norwegian Soc., Royal Soc. of Letters, Sweden; Commdr, Royal Norwegian Order of St Olav; Commdr with Star, Order of Merit of FRG; Hon. DD (Luther Coll. Decorah, USA, Abo Acad., Finland). *Publications:* Kanon im Kanon. Zum Dogmatischen Grundlagenproblem des Neutestamentlichen Kanons 1972, Martin Luther: Selected Writings (six vols, ed.) 1978–83, Fellesskap og frihet. Tid for idepolitikk 1997. *Leisure interests:* fishing, skiing. *Address:* Stortinget, Karl Johans Gate, 0026 Oslo (office); Skullerudstubben 22, 1188 Oslo, Norway (home). *Telephone:* 23-31-20-15 (office); 22-28-95-12 (home). *E-mail:* inge.lonning@stortinget.no (office). *Website:* www.stortinget.no (office).

LONSDALE, Anne M., CBE, BA LitHum, BA Or.Stud.; British university administrator (retd); b. 16 Feb. 1941, Huddersfield, Yorks.; d. of A. C. G. Menzies and Molly Menzies; m. 1st Geoffrey Griffin 1962 (died 1963); m. 2nd Roger Lonsdale 1964 (divorced 1994); one s. one d.; ed St Anne's Coll., Oxford; Lecturer in Classical Chinese, St Anne's Coll. Oxford 1965–73; Univ. Admin. 1973–86; Dir External Relations Office, Univ. of Oxford 1986–93; Sec.-Gen. Cen. European Univ. 1993–96; Pres. New Hall Cambridge 1996–2008, Pro-Vice-Chancellor, Univ. of Cambridge 1998–2004, Deputy Vice-Chancellor 2004–08, mem. Council of Senate 1997–2004; mem. Commonwealth Scholarship Comm. 1996–2003; Trustee, Moscow School of Social and Econ. Sciences, LEAD Int. UK, European Humanities Univ., Vilnius/Minsk; Hon. Sec. CARA (Cttee for Assistance to Refugee Academics); Chair. CAMFED Int; Cavaliere del'Ordine al Merito della Repubblica Italiana 1992, Officier des Palmes académiques 2003; Dr hc (Tashkent Oriental Studies Univ., Uzbekistan) 2001. *Publications:* publs on Chinese literature and univ. admin. *Leisure interests:* travel, film, contemporary art. *E-mail:* al213@cam.ac.uk (office).

LOOMBA, Baron (Life Peer), cr. 2011, of Moor Park in the County of Hertfordshire; **Raj Loomba,** CBE, FRSA; British business executive; *Executive Director, Rinku Group;* b. 13 Nov. 1943, Dhilwan, Punjab, British India; m. Veena Loomba; one s. two d.; ed D.A.V. Coll., Jalandhar, State Univ. of Iowa, USA; began in business on a market stall in Widnes, Cheshire 1964; Founder and Exec. Chair. Rinku Group (fashion and clothing co.), London, group designs and produces Tigi-Wear, Viz-A-Viz and iZ brands; longstanding supporter of business and cultural relations between India and UK; chaired Organizing Cttee for British Indian Golden Jubilee Banquet, Grosvenor House Hotel, London to celebrate 50th anniversary of India's independence 1997; Chair. British Indian Golden Jubilee Banquet Fund; Founder-Chair. and Trustee, Dr L.M. Singhvi Foundation; Chair. India First PLC; initiated Chatham House Prize (awarded annually to a world statesman) 2004; est. (with his wife) Shrimati Pushpa Wati Loomba Trust as a charitable trust to pioneer widows' rights 1997; launched 23 June as Int. Widows

Day 2005; Vice-Pres. for Europe, Global Org. of People of Indian Origin; Vice-Pres. Safer London Foundation, Barnardo's; Chair. Friends of the Three Faiths Forum, UK; mem. Bd London First 2000–04, Council of Royal Soc. of Int. Affairs (Chatham House) (first Indian) 2002–, Pres.'s Council 2004–06, Inst. of Int. of Dirs, Rotary Club of London, Bd of Govs Univ. of East London; Trustee, Maharajah Ranjit Singh Trust, India; Patron, RSA in India, Children In Need Inst.; Founding Patron, World Punjabi Org.; Vice-Patron, Gates; Paul Harris Fellow, Rotary International; Freeman of the City of London; Hind Rattan Award 1991, Int. Excellence Award 1991, Asian of the Year Award 1997, Pride of India Gold Medal 1998, Into Leadership Award 2000, Judges' Special Commendation, Worldaware Business Awards 2001, Highly Commended New Initiative, Beacon Prize 2004, Leadership Memento for The Loomba Trust, Prime Minister of India 2004, Neville Shulman Charity Cup, Life Time Achievers Award, Chief Minister of Punjab, Priyadarshni Acad. Global Award 2006, Charity of the Year Award, Asian Who's Who 2006, NRI Inst. of India Achievers Award, on behalf of Loomba Trust 2008, Distinguished Non-Resident Philanthropist (Forbes India Philanthropy Awards) 2012. *Address:* Rinku Group Ltd, 622 Western Avenue, London, W3 0TF (office); House of Lords, Westminster, London, SW1A 0PW, England. *Telephone:* (20) 8896-9922 (office); (20) 7219-5353. *Fax:* (20) 8896-9977 (office); (20) 7219-5979. *E-mail:* mail@rinku.co.uk (office). *Website:* www.rinku.co.uk (office); www.theloombatrust.org.

LOONE, Eero; Estonian philosopher and academic; *Senior Research Fellow, Tallinn University of Technology;* b. 26 May 1935, Tartu; s. of Nikolai Loone and Leida Loone (née Rebane); m. 1st Halliki Uibo 1965; m. 2nd Leiki Sikk 1971; two d.; ed Moscow Univ. and Acad. of Sciences, Moscow; mem. CPSU 1965–90; teacher, Univ. of Tartu 1963–, Prof. 1985–2000, Head, Dept of Philosophy 1986–89, 1993–94, 1998–2000, Head, Dept of Philosophy and Political Science 1989–93, Prof. Emer. 2000–; Prof. of Political Theory, Tallinn Univ. of Tech. 2008–09, Sr Research Fellow 2009=; Visiting Prof., British Acad. 1993, Ashby Lecturer 1994; Founding mem. ind. Estonian Union of Scientists 1989–2009, Estonia Foreign Policy Inst. 1991, Estonian Political Science Asscn 1993–; mem. Int. Political Science Asscn 1994–; NATO Democratic Insts Fellow 1993–94; Life mem. Clare Hall Cambridge, UK 1990–; Fulbright Scholar, Columbia Univ., New York, USA 1997. *Publications include:* Contemporary Philosophy of History 1980 (trans. into English as Soviet Marxism and Analytical Philosophies of History 1990). *Leisure interest:* science fiction. *Address:* Institute of Philosophy and Semiotics, University of Tartu, Ulikooli 18, 50090 Tartu (office); Vabaduse pst. 168-5, 10917 Tartu, Estonia (home). *Telephone:* (7) 375314 (office); (6) 778685 (home). *Fax:* (7) 375345 (office). *E-mail:* eero.loone@ut.ee (office). *Website:* www.fl.ut.ee (office).

LOOSLI, Hansueli; Swiss certified accountant and business executive; *Chairman, Coop Genossenschaft;* b. 1955; ed diploma in accounting and controlling; Controller, Deputy Dir, Mövenpick Produktions AG, Adliswil 1982–85; Man. Dir Waro AG, Volketswil 1985–92; Dir of Non-Food Product Procurement, Coop Switzerland, Wangen 1992–96, Man. Dir Coop Zurich, Zurich 1992–97, Chair. Exec. Cttee and Coop Group Exec. Cttee, Coop Switzerland, Basle 1997–2000, Chair. Exec. Cttee and CEO, Coop Genossenschaft, Basle 2001–11, Chair. Bd of Dirs 2011–; Chair. Coop Immobilien AG, Berne, Bell AG, Basel, Swisscom AG, Ittigen, Transgourmet Holding AG, Basel, Coop Mineraloel AG, Allschwil. *Address:* Coop Genossenschaft, Thiersteinerallee 12, Postfach 2550, 4002 Basel, Switzerland (office). *Telephone:* (61) 3366666 (office). *Fax:* (61) 3366040 (office). *E-mail:* info@coop.ch (office). *Website:* www.coop.ch (office).

LOOTAH, Wedad Nasser; United Arab Emirates writer and counsellor; b. 1964; began career as elementary school teacher; fmr educ. officer for Islamic endowment; Marriage Counsellor, Family Guidance Section, Dubai Courthouse 2001–. *Publications:* Top Secret: Sexual Guidance for Married Couples 2009. *Address:* c/o Dubai Courthouse, PO Box 4700, Dubai, United Arab Emirates (office). *E-mail:* info@dc.gov.ac (office). *Website:* www.dubaicourts.gov.ae (office).

LOPARDO, Frank; American singer (tenor); b. 23 Dec. 1957, New York; m. Carolyn J. Montalbano 1982; two s.; ed Queen's Coll. New York and Juilliard School of Music; studied with Dr Robert White Jr; professional debut as Tamino in The Magic Flute, St Louis 1984; debut at La Scala, Milan 1987, Glyndebourne Festival 1987, Metropolitan Opera as Almaviva in Il Barbiere di Siviglia 1989–90; now appears regularly at leading opera houses and music festivals around the world; roles include Alfredo in La Traviata, Lensky in Eugene Onegin, Edgardo in Lucia di Lammermoor, The Duke in Rigoletto, Ferrando in Così fan tutte, Don Giovanni, Lenski in Eugene Onegin, Rodolfo in La Bohème; also appears as soloist with leading orchestras and in recordings of such works as Mozart's Requiem, Carl Orff's Carmina Burana, Mozart's Don Giovanni and Così fan tutte, Verdi's Falstaff and La Traviata, as well as Rossini's Il Barbiere di Siviglia, Semiramide and L'Italiana in Algeri; Hon. DMus (Aaron Copland School of Music). *Leisure interest:* golf. *Address:* Columbia Artists Management Inc. 1790 Broadway, New York, NY 10019-1412, USA (office). *Telephone:* (212) 841 9500 (office). *Fax:* (212) 841 9744 (office). *E-mail:* info@cami.com (office); mail@franklopardo.com (office). *Website:* www.cami.com (office); www.franklopardo.com.

LOPATKIN, Nikolai Alekseyevich, DMed; Russian urologist; *Chairman, Research Institute of Urology;* b. 18 Feb. 1924; ed Second Moscow Medical Inst.; intern, Docent, Second Moscow Medical Inst. 1950–62; Prof., Head of Chair of Urology and Operative Nephrology 1963; Main Urologist of USSR Ministry of Public Health 1978–83; Dir and Prof., Research Inst. of Urology 1983–; Chair. All-Union (now Russian) Soc. of Urologists 1972–91, now Chair.; mem. Russian Acad. of Medical Sciences 1974; Chair. Scientific Council on Urology and Operative Nephrology, Russian Acad. of Sciences 1991; Ed.-in-Chief Urology and Nephrology; Hero of Socialist Labour and other decorations; USSR State Prize (three times). *Publications:* more than 250 works on urology, diagnostics and treatment of kidney insufficiency and kidney transplantation. *Address:* Research Institute of Urology, 3 Parkovaya ul. 51, 105425 Moscow, Russia (office). *Telephone:* (495) 164-66-20 (office). *E-mail:* lopatkin@uro.ru (office).

LOPATKINA, Ulyana Vyacheslavovna; Russian ballerina; b. 23 Oct. 1973, Kerch, Ukraine; ed Vaganova Acad. of Russian Ballet (studied with Natalya Dudinskaya); soloist, Kirov Ballet/Mariinsky Theatre 1991–95, Prin. Dancer 1995–; winner Int. Vaganova-prix Competition, St Petersburg 1991, Golden Sofit 1995, Golden Mask 1997, Baltika Prize 1997, 2001, State Prize of Russian Fed.

1999, Honoured Artist of Russia 2000, Peoplés Artist of Russia 2005,. *Repertoire includes:* leading roles in Giselle, Sleeping Beauty, Anna Karenina, Fountain of Bakhchisarai, Raimonda, Sheherazade, Swan Lake, Bayadera, Le Corsaire; performs in Goya-Divertissement; tours with Mariinsky Theatre in Europe, N and S America. *Address:* Mariinsky Theatre, 190000 St Petersburg, Teatralnaya pl. 1, Russia (office). *Telephone:* (812) 326-41-41 (office). *Website:* www.mariinsky .ru/en/company/ballet (office). www.uliana-lopatkina.com.

LOPES, Carlos, PhD; Guinea-Bissau economist, diplomatist and UN official; *Executive Secretary, United Nations Economic Commission for Africa;* b. 7 March 1960; ed Univ. of Geneva, Univ. of Paris 1 Panthéon-Sorbonne; taught at univs in Lisbon, Coimbra, Zurich, Uppsala, Mexico, São Paulo and Rio de Janeiro; fmr consultant for UNESCO, Swedish Int. Devt Cooperation Agency, UN Econ. Comm. for Africa, Research and Technological Exchange Group, Ruraltec Switzerland; Devt Economist, UNDP 1988, then Deputy Dir Office of Evaluation and Strategic Planning, Resident Rep. in Zimbabwe, Deputy, then Dir Bureau for Devt Policy, Asst Admin. UNDP, UN Resident Coordinator and UNDP Resident Rep. in Brazil 2003–05; apptd Dir Exec. Office of Sec.-Gen. in charge of Political, Peacekeeping and Humanitarian affairs 2005; Exec. Dir UNITAR 2007–12; Exec. Sec., UN Econ. Comm. for Africa 2012–; fmr Dir UN System Staff Coll.; elected to Lisbon Acad. of Sciences, Portugal 2008; mem. Instituto Ethos, Ecôle Polytechnique Fédérale de Lausanne, King Baudouin International Development Prize Selection Committee; mem. Advisory Bd Kofi Annan Foundation, UNESCO Int. Inst. for Educational Planning, Bonn Int. Center for Conversion, Swiss Network for Int. Studies; mem. Editorial Cttee Géopolitique Africaine, African Sociological Review, African Identities, Cooperation South Journal; Hon. PhD (Univ. of Cândido, Brazil). *Address:* United Nations Economic Commission for Africa, PO Box 3001, Addis Ababa, Ethiopia (office). *Telephone:* (11) 5443336 (office). *Fax:* (11) 5514416 (office). *E-mail:* ecaweb@un.org (office). *Website:* www.uneca.org (office).

LOPÈS, Henri Marie Joseph; Republic of the Congo author, politician and diplomatist; *Ambassador to France;* b. 12 Sept. 1937, Léopoldville, Belgian Congo (now Kinshasa, Democratic Repub. of the Congo); s. of Jean-Marie Lopès and Micheline Vulturi; m. Nirva Pasbeau 1961; one s. three d.; ed France; Minister of Nat. Educ. 1968–71, of Foreign Affairs 1971–73; mem. Political Bureau, Congolese Labour Party 1973; Prime Minister and Minister of Planning 1973–75, of Finance 1977–80; UNESCO Asst Dir-Gen. for Programme Support 1982–86, UNESCO Asst Dir-Gen. for Culture and Communication 1986–90, for Culture 1990–94, for Foreign Affairs 1994–95, Deputy Dir-Gen. 1996–98; Amb. to France (also accred to Portugal, Spain, UK and The Holy See (Vatican City)) 1998–; mem. Haut Conseil de la Francophonie; Chevalier, Légion d'honneur, Commdr du Mérite Congolais, etc.; Prix littéraire de l'Afrique noire 1972, Prix SIMBA de littérature 1978, Prix de littérature du Président (Congo), Prix de l'Acad. de Bretagne et des Pays de la Loire 1990, Grand Prix de la Francophonie de l'Acad. française 1993. *Publications:* Tribaliques (short stories), La Nouvelle Romance (novel), Learning to be (with others), Sans tam-tam (novel) 1977, Le Pleurer Rire (novel) 1982, Le Chercheur d'Afriques (novel) 1990, Sur l'autre Rive (novel) 1992, Le Lys et le flamboyant (novel) 1997. *Address:* Embassy of the Republic of the Congo, 37 bis rue Paul Valéry, 75116 Paris Cedex 16, France (office). *Telephone:* 1-45-00-60-57 (home). *Fax:* 1-40-67-17-33 (office). *E-mail:* ambacongo_france@yahoo.fr (office).

LÓPEZ, Carlos R. Henríquez; Panamanian banker; *President, Banco Nacional de Panamá;* fmr Vice-Pres., Banco Comercial de Panamá SA Bancomer; currently Pres., Banco Nacional de Panamá (govt-owned bank); fmr Dir FDR Investments Corpn. *Address:* Office of the President, Banco Nacional de Panamá, Casa Matriz, Vía España, Apdo 5220, Panamá 5, Panama (office). *Telephone:* 505-2000 (office). *Fax:* 269-0091 (office). *E-mail:* sugerencia@banconal.com.pa (office). *Website:* www .banconal.com.pa (office).

LOPEZ, Eugenio, III, BA, MBA; Philippine broadcasting executive; *Chairman and CEO, ABS-CBN Corporation;* b. 1952; s. of Eugenio Lopez Jr and Conchita La'O Lopez; ed Bowdoin Coll., Harvard Business School, USA; Dir of Finance, ABS-CBN Broadcasting Corpn 1986, Gen. Man. 1987, Pres. –1996, Chair. 1996–, currently also CEO (company renamed ABS-CBN Corpn 2010); Treas. Lopez Holdings Corpn (parent co., fmrly Benpres Holdings Corpn). *Address:* ABS-CBN Corporation, Sgt Esguerra Ave, corner Mother Ignacia St, Quezon City, Metro Manila, Philippines (office). *Telephone:* (2) 4152272 (office). *Fax:* (2) 4319368 (office). *Website:* www.abs-cbn.com (office).

LOPEZ, Jennifer, (J.Lo); American actress, singer, dancer and business executive; b. (Jennifer Lynn Lopez), 24 July 1969, Bronx, New York; m. 1st Ojani Noa 1997 (divorced 1998); m. 2nd Chris Judd 2001 (divorced 2003); m. 3rd Marc Anthony 2004; one s. one d. (twins); ed City Univ. of New York Baruch; began career as a Fly Girl on TV programme In Living Color and as a back-up dancer for Janet Jackson; gained recognition in film Money Train 1995; first leading role in biographical film Selena 1997; released debut album On the 6 1999; second album J.Lo reached No. 1 on Billboard 200 the same week her film The Wedding Planner led the box office 2001; released remix album J To Tha L-O! The Remixes 2002; released first full Spanish album Como Ama una Mujer 2007; seventh album Love? gave rise to her most successful career single On the Floor; collaborations with Ja Rule, Big Pun, Fat Joe; Dance Again World Tour 2012; est. clothing and lingerie lines and various perfumes with her celebrity endorsement; Golden Globe 1998, MTV Movie Award 1999, Billboard Latin Award for Hot Latin Track of the Year 2000, MTV Video Music Award for Best Dance Video 2000, VH1/Vogue Fashion Versace Award 2000, MTV Europe Music Award for Best Female Act 2001, MTV Award for Best Female 2002, American Music Award for Favorite Pop/Rock Female Artist 2003, American Music Award for Favorite Latin Artist 2007, 2011, ranked by Forbes magazine amongst The World's 100 Most Powerful Women (38th) 2012, Vanguard Award, Glaad Media Awards 2014. *Films include:* My Little Girl 1986, My Family, Mi Familia 1995, Money Train 1995, Jack 1996, Blood and Wine 1996, Selena (ALMA Award for Outstanding Actress) 1997, Anaconda 1997, U Turn 1997, Out of Sight (ALMA Award) 1998, Antz (voice) 1998, The Cell 2000, The Wedding Planner 2001, Angel Eyes 2001, Enough 2002, Maid in Manhattan 2002, Gigli 2003, Jersey Girl 2004, Shall We Dance? 2004, Monster-in-Law 2005, An Unfinished Life 2006, El Cantante 2006, Bordertown (Artists for Amnesty Prize 2007) 2006, The Back-Up Plan 2010, Scrat's Continental Crack-Up: Part 2 (short) (voice) 2011, What to Expect When You're Expecting 2012, Ice Age: Continental Drift (voice) 2012, Parker 2013. *Television includes:* In Living Color 1990, Nurses

on the Line: The Crash of Flight 7 1993, Second Chances (series) 1993–94, South Central (series) 1994, Hotel Malibu (series) 1994, How I Met Your Mother (series) 2010, judge, American Idol 2010–12. *Recordings include:* albums: On The 6 1999, J.Lo 2001, J To Tha L-O! (remixes) 2002, This Is Me… Then 2002, Rebirth 2005, Como Ama una Mujer 2007, Brave 2007, Love? 2011, Dance Again… The Hits 2012. *Address:* c/o WME Entertainment, 9601 Wilshire Boulevard, Beverly Hills, CA 90210, USA (office). *Telephone:* (310) 285-9000 (office). *Fax:* (310) 285-9010 (office). *Website:* www.wma.com (office); www.jenniferlopez.com.

LOPEZ, Oscar, MPA; Philippine business executive; *Chairman Emeritus, Lopez Group;* b. 1930, Manila; s. of Eugenio R. Lopez; m. Consuelo R. Lopez; three s. five d.; ed Littauer School of Public Admin (now Kennedy School of Govt), Harvard Univ., USA; began career as Publr, Manila Chronicle 1960–66; joined Meralco Securities Corpn (now First Philippine Holdings Corpn) 1965, CEO 1986; Chair. and CEO Benpres Holdings Corpn (now Lopez Holdings Corpn) 1999–2004, Chair. Lopez Group 1999, currently Chair. Emer., Chair. and Trustee Lopez Group Foundation Inc.; Chair. and CEO Metro Pacific Tollways Corpn 2007–08; Chair. Energy Devt Corpn 2007–, Bayan Telecommunications Holdings Corpn, Bayan Telecommunications Inc.; Dir ABS-CBN Corpn (formerly ABS-CBN Broadcasting) 1966–, Manila Electric Co. (Meralco), Maynilad Water Services Inc.; mem. Man. Asscn of the Philippines; Bundesverdienstkreuz (FRG) 2005; Man. of the Year, Man. Asscn of the Philippines 2000, Philippine Mil. Acad. Distinguished Citizen Award 2008, TOFIL Outstanding Filipino Award 2009. *Leisure interest:* mountain climbing. *Address:* Lopez Group Foundation Inc., 5/F Benpres Building, Meralco Avenue, corner Exchange Road, Ortigas Center, Pasig City 1600, Philippines (office). *Telephone:* (2) 4900779 (office). *Website:* www.lopezgroup.org (office).

LÓPEZ, Patxi; Spanish politician; *Lehendakari (President) of Basque Government;* b. 4 Oct. 1959, Portugalete; joined Young Basque Socialists 1975, Sec.-Gen. 1985–88; mem. Basque Socialist Party-Basque Left (PSE-EE/PSOE) 1977–, mem. Exec. Cttee 1988–, Sec. PSE-EE/PSOE 1991–95, Sec.-Gen. 1997–; mem. Basque Parl. 1991–; Lehendakari (Pres.) of Basque Govt 2009–. *Address:* Palacio de Ajuria-Enea, Paseo Fray Francisco 5, 01007 Vitoria-Gasteiz, Spain (office). *E-mail:* patxilopez@socialistasvascos.com. *Website:* www.patxilopez.com.

LÓPEZ AGRÀS, Pere; Andorran politician; Leader, l'Alternativa de la Massana; Minister of Finance 2009–11. *Address:* c/o Ministry of Finance, Carrer Prat de la Creu 62–64, Edif. Administratiu, Andorra la Vella AD500, Andorra (office).

LÓPEZ CHARRETON, Susana, BSc, MSc PhD; Mexican virologist and academic; *Professor of Developmental Genetics and Molecular Physiology, National Autonomous University of Mexico;* ed Nat. Autonomous Univ. of Mexico (UNAM); Asst Prof. of Molecular Biology, Centre for Research on Genetic Eng and Biotechnology, Cuernavaca 1989–93; Fogarty Fellow, Div. of Biology, California Inst. of Tech. 1992–93; currently Prof. of Developmental Genetics and Molecular Physiology, Dept of the Inst. of Biotechnology, UNAM; Howard Hughes Medical Inst. Int. Research Scholar 2005–10; Nat. Science Award, Mexican Acad. of Sciences 1993, Premio Bienal FUNSALUD en Infecciones Gastrointestinales Fundación Mexicana para la Salud 2000, Carlos J. Finlay Prize for Microbiology, UNESCO (co-recipient with her husband, Carlos Arias Ortiz) 2001, Premio Bienal Funsalud en Enfermedades Gastrointestinales (NADRO), Fundación Mexicana para la Salud 2002, Sor Juana Ines de la Cruz Medal, Nat. Autonomous Univ. of Mexico 2004, L'Oréal-UNESCO For Women in Science Award (Latin America) (for elucidating the mechanisms of rotavirus infections) 2012. *Publications:* numerous papers in professional journals. *Address:* Instituto de Biotecnología/UNAM, Avenida Universidad #2001, Col. Chamilpa CP 62210 Cuernavaca, Morelos Apdo Postal 510-3, CP 62250, Mexico (office). *Telephone:* (777) 329-1615 (office). *Fax:* (777) 331-14701 (office). *E-mail:* susana@ibt.unam.mx (office). *Website:* www .ibt.unam.mx (office).

LÓPEZ-COBOS, Jesús, DPhil; Spanish conductor; b. 25 Feb. 1940, Toro; s. of Lorenzo López and Gregoria Cobos; ed Madrid Univ. (philosophy), Madrid Conservatory (composition) and Vienna Acad. (conducting); worked with major orchestras including London Symphony, Royal Philharmonic, Philharmonia, Concertgebouw, Vienna Philharmonic, Vienna Symphony, Berlin Philharmonic, Hamburg NDR, Munich Philharmonic, Cleveland, Chicago Symphony, New York Philharmonic, Philadelphia, Pittsburgh Symphony; conducted new opera productions at La Scala, Milan, Covent Garden, London and Metropolitan Opera, New York; Gen. Musikdirektor, Deutsche Oper, Berlin 1981–90; Prin. Guest Conductor London Philharmonic Orchestra 1981–86, Orquesta Sinfonica de Galicia 2010–; Prin. Conductor and Artistic Dir Spanish Nat. Orchestra 1984–89; Music Dir, Cincinnati Symphony Orchestra 1986–2001 (now Music Dir Emer.), Music Dir Lausanne Chamber Orchestra 1990–2000, Orchestre Français des Jeunes 1998–2001, Teatro Real, Madrid 2002–10; Cross of Merit (First Class) (FRG) 1989, Officier des Arts et des Lettres 2001; Dr hc (Arts Univ. Cincinatti); First Prize, Besançon Int. Conductors' Competition 1969, Prince of Asturias Award (Spanish Govt) 1981, Founders Award, American Soc. of Composers, Authors and Publrs 1988, Fine Arts Medal (Spain) 2001. *Recordings include:* Bruckner symphonies, Haydn symphonies, Donizetti's Lucia di Lammermoor, Rossini's Otello and recital discs with José Carreras; works by Mahler, Respighi, Franck, de Falla, Villa-Lobos and Richard Strauss; Rossini's Il Barbiere di Siviglia and L'Italiana in Algeri; Il Comte Ory, Manon, Les Contes d'Hoffmann, Il Viaggio a Reims. *Address:* 8 Chemin de Bellerive, 1007 Lausanne, Switzerland.

LOPEZ-COLOMÉ, Ana Maria, PhD; Mexican neuroscientist, biochemist and academic; *Professor of Neuroscience and Biochemistry, Institute of Cellular Physiology, National Autonomous University (UNAM);* b. Mexico City; one s. one d.; ed Nat. Autonomous Univ. of Mexico (UNAM); fmr Lecturer, Faculty of Sciences, UNAM, Mexico City, currently Prof. of Neuroscience and Biochemistry, Inst. of Cellular Physiology; Univ. Councilor, UNAM; mem. Soc. for Neuroscience, Int. Soc. for Neurochemistry, American Soc. for Neurochemistry, ISDN, Mexican Soc. for Biochemistry, Mexican Soc. for Physiological Sciences, Academia de la Investigación Científica; Regional Ed. Molecules; works on retinal biochemistry in health and diseases leading to blindness; L'Oreal-UNESCO For Women in Science Award 2002. *Publications:* numerous articles in scientific journals. *Address:* Instituto de Fisiología Celular, UNAM, División de Neurociencias, Apartado postal 70-253, 04510 Mexico City, DF, Mexico (office). *Telephone:* (525) 622-5617 (office).

Fax: (525) 622-5607 (office). *E-mail:* acolome@ifc.unam.mx (office). *Website:* www .ifisiol.unam.mx (office).

LÓPEZ CONTRERAS, Carlos; Honduran lawyer, academic and politician; ed Nat. Univ. of Honduras, Univ. Complutense of Madrid, Spain; authorized as Attorney at Law and Notary Public by Supreme Court of Justice of Honduras 1974; Prof. of Law, Univ. of San Pedro Sula 1977–79, Nat. Univ. of Honduras 1981–85; Vice-Minister of Foreign Affairs 1979–80, Minister of Foreign Affairs 1986–90, 2009; Founding Pnr, ACZALAW (law firm), Sr Pnr 2002–; fmr Rep. for Honduras and mem. Perm. Court of Arbitration, Int. Court of Justice, The Hague, Netherlands; mem. Bd of Dirs for Honduras to Cen. American Bank for Econ. Integration 1990–91; consultant to Armed Forces and Ministry of Economy of Honduras; mem. Nat. Acad. of Law and Social Sciences; mem. Hispanic-Portuguese-American Inst. for Int. Law, El Escorial, Spain; mem. Partido Nacional. *Address:* c/o Ministry of Foreign Affairs, Centro Cívico Gubernamental, Antigua Casa Presidencial, Blvd Kuwait, Contiguo a la Corte Suprema de Justicia, Tegucigalpa, Honduras (office).

LÓPEZ GARCÍA, Antonio; Spanish painter, draughtsman and sculptor; b. 6 Jan. 1936, Tomelloso, La Mancha; m. María Moreno 1961; two d.; ed Escuela de Bellas Artes de San Fernando, Madrid; his art evolved from primitivist and surrealist influences to a strict realism; formed friendships with Francisco Lopez Hernandez, Amalia Avia and Isabel Quintanilla, out of which nucleus a realist group, the New Spanish Realists, was formed in Madrid; travelled to Italy on a scholarship with Francisco Lopez and studied Italian painting from the Renaissance 1955; gave classes at Escuela de Bellas Artes de San Fernando 1964–69; works in public collections including Museum of Fine Arts, Boston, Reina Sofia Nat. Museum, Madrid; Hon. mem. Acad. of Arts and Letters, New York 2004; Prize of Diputación de Jaén 1957, Prize of Fundación Rodríguez Acosta 1958, Molino de Oro Prize of Exposición Regional de Valdepeñas 1959, Darmstadt Prize 1974, Medalla de Oro, Castilla-La Mancha 1986, Medalla de Oro, Comunidad de Madrid 1990, Velázquez Prize for Fine Arts 2006. *Film:* his painting was the subject of the film El Sol del Membrillo (The Quince Tree Sun, directed by Victor Erice and written by both) 1992. *Address:* c/o Galería Marlborough SA, Orfila 5, 28010 Madrid (office); Poniente 3, 28036 Madrid, Spain (home). *Telephone:* (91) 3191414 (office). *Fax:* (91) 3084345 (office). *E-mail:* info@galeriamarlborough.com (office). *Website:* www.galeriamarlborough.com (office); www.artnet.com/artists/antonio -l%C3%B3pez+garc%C3%ADa.

LÓPEZ-IBOR, Juan José, MD, PhD; Spanish physician, psychiatrist and academic; *Professor Emeritus of Psychiatry, Madrid Complutense University;* b. 17 Dec. 1941, Madrid; s. of Juan J. López-Ibor Sr and Socorro Alino; four c.; ed Univ. of Madrid, Univ. of Frankfurt, Germany, St Bartholomew's Hosp., London, UK; Asst Prof. of Psychiatry, Madrid Univ. 1962–72; Head Prof. of Psychiatry, Oviedo Univ. 1972–73, Salamanca Univ. 1973–77, Alcalá de Henares Univ. 1982–; Head, Psychiatric Unit, Ramón y Cajal Hosp. 1977–; Dir Inst. of Psychiatry and Mental Health, San Carlos Clinical Hosp. and Prof. of Psychiatry, Madrid Complutense Univ. –2012, now Prof. Emer.; Pres. Spanish Psychiatry Soc. 1978–80, Int. Coll. of Psychosomatic Medicine 1985, World Psychiatric Asscn 1999–2002; Founder and Pres. Juan José López-Ibor Foundation; Temporary Adviser WHO 1984; mem. Real Academia Nacional de Medicina; Fellow, Royal Nat. Acad. of Medicine, Royal Coll. of Psychiatry; Hon. mem. World Psychiatric Asscn; Gran Cruz de la Sanidad de Madrid. *Publications:* author or co-author of more than 450 papers and 60 books including Los Equivalentes Depresivos 1972, 1978, El Cuerpo y la Corporalidad 1974, Las Depresiones 1976, Tratado de Psiquiatría 1982, 1984. *Leisure interests:* skiing, water skiing, sailing. *Address:* C/ Doctor Juan Jose López Ibor, nr. 2, 28035 Madrid, Spain. *Telephone:* (91) 3739199. *Fax:* (91) 3162749. *E-mail:* jli@lopez-ibor .com. *Website:* www.lopezibor.com.

LÓPEZ OBRADOR, Andrés Manuel; Mexican politician; b. 1953, Tepetitán, Tabasco; m. Rocio Beltran (died 2003); three s.; ed Universidad Nacional Autónoma de México; Dir Instituto Indigenista de Tabasco 1984; Dir of Social Promotion, Instituto Nacional del Consumidor 1985; joined Corriente Democrática 1986; joined Frente Democrático Nacional and stood for Gov. of Tabasco; joined Partido de la Revolución Democrática 1989 and led party in Tabasco, stood for Gov. and lost 1994; Pres. Partido de la Revolucíon Democrática 1996–99; Mayor of Mexico City 2000–05 (resgnd to work on his unsuccessful 2006 campaign for Pres.); runner-up in 2012 presidential election. *Address:* Partido de la Revolucíon Democrática (PRD), Col. Roma, Monterrey 50, 06700 Mexico (office). *Telephone:* (55) 5525-6059 (office). *Fax:* (55) 5208-7833 (office). *Website:* www.prd.org.mx (office).

LÓPEZ RODRIGUEZ, HE Cardinal Nicolás de Jesús, DScS; Dominican Republic ecclesiastic; *Archbishop of Santo Domingo;* b. 31 Oct. 1936, Barrancas; ed Pontifical Seminary 'Santo Tomas de Aquino', Santo Domingo, Int. Center for the Sociological Formation of the Clergy, Rome, Italy, Pontifical St Thomas Univ. and Pontifical Gregorian Univ., Rome; ordained priest 1961; pastoral work in diocese of La Vega 1961–64, 1966–68; Diocesan Counsellor, La Vega, 1969–78; Ecclesiastical Assessor Christian Family Movt and Cursillo Movt; Diocesan Vicar, later Pro-Vicar General, Gen. later Vicar Gen.; Rector of San Francisco de Macoris 1978; Rector Nordestana di San Francisco de Macorís Univ. 1979–84; Metropolitan and Primate of Santo Domingo 1981; cr. Cardinal (Cardinal-Priest of San Pio X alla Balduina) 1991; participated in Papal Conclave 2005, 2013; Grand Chancellor Catholic Univ. of Santo Domingo 1982; Mil. Ordinary for the Dominican Repub. 1982; Del. to Dominican Bishops' Conf. 1979–81, Pres. Bishops' Justice and Peace Comm., mem. (currently Pres.) Perm. Comm., Nat. Chaplain to the Christian Renewal of the Holy Spirit, Pres. Dominican Bishops' Conf. 1984–2002; attended Sixth Ordinary Ass. World Synod of Bishops, Vatican City 1983, Second Extraordinary Ass. World Synod of Bishops, Vatican City 1985; Pres. Latin American Episcopal Council 1991; Grand Cross of Isabella the Catholic (Spain) 1989; hon. degrees from Univ. of Santo Domingo and Creighton Univ., Neb., USA. *Address:* Calle Pellerano Alfau 1, Ciudad Colonial, Santo Domingo, Dominican Republic (office). *Telephone:* 221-8430 (office). *Fax:* 685-0227 (office).

LÓPEZ SUÁREZ, Guillermo; Salvadorean banker and politician; *Minister of Agriculture and Livestock;* ed Inst. of Tech. and Higher Studies, Monterrey, Mexico, N Dakota State School of Science, USA; Asst to Dir-Gen., Empresa Cocotera and Empresa Cafetalera Sol Mollet 1978–81; Head of Finance, Granjero

and Sello de Oro 1983–84; Dir-Gen. Grupo Lotisa, Maquilishuat, and Cumbres de Cuscatlán 1984–97; Financial Dir Grupo Avicola Salvadoreña and Grupo La Sultana 1987–95, Dir-Gen. 1995–; Dir-Gen. Grupo Pollo Campero 1994–2004; Minister of the Treasury 2004–06 (resgnd); Pres. Comisión Ejecutiva Portuaria Autónoma (CEPA) –2010; Minister of Agriculture and Livestock 2010–; fmr Adviser to Nat. Asscn of Pvt. Commerce, Asscn of Poultry Farmers of El Salvador, Fed. of Poultry Farmers of Cen. America and the Caribbean; fmr mem. Bd of Govs World Bank, IBRD, Int. Finance Corpn, IDA. *Address:* Ministry of Agriculture and Livestock, Final 1a, Avda Norte y Avda Manuel Gallardo, Santa Tecla, El Salvador (office). *Telephone:* 2241-1700 (office). *Fax:* 2229-9271 (office). *E-mail:* info@mag .gob.sv (office). *Website:* www.mag.gob.sv (office).

LORAN, Oleg Borisovich, DrMed; Russian surgeon and urologist; b. 24 June 1943, Moscow; s. of Boris Yulievich Loran and Irina Donatovna Loran; m. Irina Petrovna Grebennikova; one s. two d.; ed Moscow Sechenov Inst. of Medicine; surgeon, Salda City Hosp., Sverdlovsk Region 1966–69; intern, urologist, Moscow Botkin Hosp. of Urgent Medicine 1969–72; Asst, Head Div. of Urology, Prof., Moscow Medical Inst. of Stomatology (now Moscow State Medical and Stomatological Univ.) 1972–; Chief Urologist, Ministry of Public Health of Russian Fed.; Chief Scientific Sec., Russian Soc. of Urologists 1978; mem. Exec. Bd East European Soc. of Urologists, Bd Russian Asscn of Oncological Urology; mem. Editorial Bd journals Urology and Nephrology, Annals of Surgery; mem. Higher Attestation Comm. of Russian Fed.; mem. European Asscn of Urologists 1992; Diplomas of American Asscn of Urologists and American Urological Foundation. *Publications:* more than 230 scientific works including nine books on problems of urology, ten patents. *Leisure interests:* music, theatre. *Address:* Moscow State Medical Stomatological Institute, Delegatskaya str. 20/1, 127473 Moscow, Russia (office). *Telephone:* (495) 281-65-13 (office). *Website:* www.msmsu.ru (office).

LORCH, George A., BS; American business executive; *Lead Independent Director, Pfizer Inc.;* ed Virginia Polytechnic Inst. and State Univ.; joined Armstrong Holdings Inc. 1963, held various marketing positions 1963–83, Group Vice-Pres. for Carpet Operations 1983–88, Exec. Vice-Pres. 1988–93, Pres. and CEO 1993–94, Chair. May–Aug. 2000, mem. Bd of Dirs Armstrong World Industries Inc. (subsidiary) 1988–2000, Pres. and CEO 1993–2000, Chair. 1994–2000, Chair. Emer. Armstrong Holdings Inc. 2000–; mem. Bd of Dirs Pfizer Inc. 2000–, Chair. (non-exec.) 2010–11, Lead Ind. Dir 2011–; Ind. Dir, Autoliv Inc. 2003–, HSBC Finance Corpn 1994–, HSBC North America Holdings Inc., JPM Naples Event, Warner-Lambert Co. 1997–, RR Donnelley & Sons Co., The Williams Cos Inc. 2001–11, WPX Energy, Inc. 2011–, HSBC Finance Co., HSBC North America Holding Co., Masonite International, Inc. *Address:* Pfizer Inc., 235 East 42nd Street, New York, NY 10017-5755, USA (office). *Telephone:* (212) 733-2323 (office). *Fax:* (212) 573-7851 (office). *E-mail:* info@pfizer.com (office). *Website:* www.pfizer.com (office).

LORD, Hon. Bernard, BA; Canadian politician; b. 27 Sept. 1965; m. Diane Lord; two c.; ed Université de Moncton; Leader, Progressive Conservative Party of NB 1997; MLA for Moncton East (becoming Leader of the Official Opposition) 1998; Premier of NB 1999–2006, also Pres. of Exec. Council, Minister of Intergovernmental Affairs, Minister responsible for NB Advisory Council on Youth, Minister responsible for Premier's Council on Status of Disabled Persons; Grand Officier de l'Ordre de la Pléiade, Int. Asscn of Francophone Parliamentarians; Dr hc (Univ. of NB), (Université de Moncton); Alumni of the Year from the Université de Moncton. *Address:* c/o Office of the Premier, Centennial Building, POB 6000, Fredericton, NB E3B 5H1, Canada.

LORD, Winston, BA, MA; American civil servant and diplomatist; b. 14 Aug. 1937, New York; s. of Oswald Bates Lord and Mary Lord (née Pillsbury); m. Bette Bao 1963; one s. one d.; ed Yale Univ., Fletcher School of Law and Diplomacy; mem. Staff Congressional Relations, Politico-mil. and Econ. Affairs, US Dept of State, Washington 1961–65, Geneva 1965–67; mem. staff Int. Affairs, US Dept of Defense, Washington 1967–69; mem. staff Nat. Security Council, Washington 1969–73, Special Asst to Asst to Pres. on Security Affairs 1970–73; Dir Policy Planning Staff, US Dept of State, Washington 1973–77; Pres. Council on Foreign Relations 1977–85; Amb. to People's Repub. of China 1985–89; freelance lecturer, writer New York 1989–93; Asst Sec. of State for East Asian and Pacific Affairs 1993; Chair. Carnegie Endowment Nat. Comm. on America and the New World 1991–92, Nat. Endowment for Democracy 1992–93; Vice-Chair. Int. Rescue Cttee 1991–93, Co-Chair. 1997–2005, Chair. Emer. 2005–; fmr mem. Bd of Dirs Fletcher School of Law and Diplomacy, Int. Rescue Cttee, Nat. Cttee on US–China Relations, Nat. Endowment for Democracy, US–Japan Foundation; several hon. degrees. *Leisure interests:* sports, literature, arts. *Address:* c/o Board of Directors, International Rescue Committee, 122 East 42nd Street, New York, NY 10168, USA.

LORDKIPANIDZE, Vazha Giorgevich, DEcon; Georgian politician, sociologist and demographer; *Head of Demography Department, Tbilisi State University;* b. 29 Nov. 1949, Tbilisi; m. Irina Khomeriki; two d.; ed Tbilisi State Univ., Moscow Acad. of Social Sciences; Teacher Tbilisi State Univ. 1975–, Head Demography Dept 2000–; Sec., Second, First Secr. Cen. Comsomol Cttee of Georgia 1980–86; First Sec. Tbilisi Dist CP Cttee 1986–88; Head Dept of Culture and Ideology Cen. Cttee, CP of Georgia 1988–90; Sr Researcher, Inst. of Demography and Sociology, Georgian Acad. of Sciences 1991–92; Chief State Counsellor State Council of Georgia 1992; Head of Personnel, Eduard Shevardnadze Admin. 1992–95; Amb. to Russia 1995–98; Minister of State 1998–2000; mem. Parl. 2000–; Pres. Demographers' Asscn of Georgia 2000–; Vice-Pres. Int. Research Centre for East–West Relationships 2000–; mem. Georgian Acad. of Econs 1996–, UN Int. Acad. of Informatics; Pres. Special Olympic Cttee 2001; Head of Christian Democrat Party of Georgia 2002. *Publications:* various scientific articles, monographs and books. *Leisure Interest:* football. *Address:* Tbilisi State University, 1 Chavchavadze Avenue, 380079 Tbilisi (office); 5 Larsi Street, Flat 9, Tbilisi, Georgia (home). *Telephone:* (32) 25-12-38 (office); (32) 23-20-70 (home). *Fax:* (32) 25-12-39 (office); (32) 233259 (office); (32) 99-05-13 (home). *E-mail:* ikhomeriki@hotmail.com.

LOREN, Sophia; Italian actress; b. (Sofia Villani Scicolone), 20 Sept. 1934, Rome; d. of Riccardo Scicolone and Romilda Villani; m. 1st the late Carlo Ponti 1957 (marriage annulled 1962), m. again 1966 (died 2007); two s.; ed Scuole Magistrali Superiori; first screen appearance as extra in Quo Vadis; Chair. Nat. Alliance for

Prevention and Treatment of Child Abuse and Maltreatment; Goodwill Amb. for Refugees 1992; Chevalier, Légion d'honneur; numerous awards including Hon. Acad. Award for Lifetime Achievement 1990, Praemium Imperiale 2010. *Films include:* E Arrivato l'Accordatore 1951, Africa sotto i Mari (first leading role), La Tratta delle Bianche, La Favorita 1952, Aida 1953, Il Paese dei Campanelli, Miseria e Nobiltà, Il Segno di Venere 1953, Tempi Nostri 1953, Carosello Napoletano 1953, L'Oro di Napoli 1954, Attila 1954, Peccato che sia una canaglia, La Bella Mugnaia, La Donna del Fiume 1955, Boccaccio 1970, Matrimonio All'Italiana; and in the following American films: The Pride and the Passion 1955, Boy on a Dolphin, Legend of the Lost 1956, Desire Under the Elms 1957, That Kind of Woman 1958, Houseboat 1958, The Key 1958, The Black Orchid (Venice Festival Award 1958) 1958, It Started in Naples, Heller in Pink Tights 1960, The Millionairess 1961, Two Women (Cannes Film Festival Award for Best Actress 1961) 1961, El Cid 1961, Madame Sans Gêne 1962, Yesterday, Today and Tomorrow 1963, The Fall of the Roman Empire 1964, Lady L 1965, Operation Crossbow 1965, Judith 1965, A Countess from Hong Kong 1965, Arabesque 1966, More than a Miracle 1967, The Priest's Wife 1970, Sunflower 1970, Hot Autumn 1971, Man of La Mancha 1972, Brief Encounter (TV) 1974, The Verdict 1974, The Voyage 1974, The Cassandra Crossing 1977, A Special Day 1977, Firepower 1978, Brass Target 1979, Blood Feud 1981, Mother Courage 1986, Two Women 1989, Prêt à Porter 1994, Grumpier Old Men 1995, Between Strangers 2002, Peperoni ripieni e pesci in faccia 2004, Nine 2009, My House Is Full of Mirrors 2010. *Publications:* Eat with Me 1972, Sophia Loren on Women and Beauty 1984. *Address:* Case Postale 430, 1211 Geneva 12, Switzerland; William Morris Agency, 1 William Morris Place, Beverly Hills, CA 90212, USA.

LORENTZ, Francis; French business executive; *Executive Chairman, LD&A Jupiter;* b. 22 May 1942, Mulhouse; s. of Paul Lorentz and Lucienne Lorentz (née Biechy); m. Laure Doumenc; three c.; ed Lycée Kléber, Strasbourg, Ecole des Hautes Etudes Commerciales, Ecole Nat. d'Admin; with Ministry of Economy 1970–80; Exec. Vice-Pres. Société Lyonnaise des Eaux 1980–82; joined Honeywell-Bull as CEO 1982, Chair. and CEO Groupe Bull 1987–92; Chair. Dir-Gen. Régie autonome des transports parisiens (RATP) 1992–94; Prof., Univ. of Paris-Dauphine 1994–2000; Chair. Etablissement public de financement et de restructuration (EPFR) 1996–2000; Head of French Nat. e-Business Task Force 1997–2000; Dir Gen. Laser (groupe Galeries Lafayette) 2000–04; CEO e-LaSer and LaSer Informatique 2000–04; Chair. Institut de l'audiovisuel et des télécommunications en Europe (IDATE) 2000–11, Digiworld Inst. 2012–; Exec. Chair. Lorentz, Deschamps et Associés (now LD&A Jupiter) 2004–; Chevalier du mérite nat., Chevalier, légion d'honneur. *Publications:* several publs on devt admin, state-owned cos, industrial policy and future of e-commerce. *Leisure interests:* skiing, mountaineering, contemporary art, wine tasting, diving, tennis. *Address:* LD&A Jupiter, 8 rue Halévy, 75009 Paris, France (office). *Telephone:* 1-58-18-39-00 (office). *Fax:* 1-53-43-09-76 (office). *E-mail:* florentz@ldajupiter.com (office). *Website:* www.ldajupiter.com (office).

LORENZ, Hans-Walter, Dr rer. pol; German economist; *Professor of Economics, Friedrich Schiller University Jena;* b. 3 Aug. 1951, Bielefeld; s. of Walter Lorenz and Lieselotte Lorenz; m. Karin Hottmann 1987; ed Univ. of Göttingen; Research Asst, Univ. of Göttingen 1977–82, Asst Prof. 1984–91, Privatdozent 1991–94; Prof. of Econs, Friedrich Schiller Univ. 1994–; Visiting Scholar, Univ. of California, Berkeley, USA 1982–83; Visiting Prof., Univ. of Tech., Sydney, Australia 1999. *Publications include:* Business Cycle Theory (with G. Gabisch) 1987 (second edn 1989), Nonlinear Dynamical Economics and Chaotic Motion 1989 (second edn 1993, Japanese edn 2001), Determinismus, nicht-lineare Dynamik und wirtschaftliche Evolution 1990, Studien zur Evolutorischen Ökonomik III. Schriften des Vereins für Socialpolitik (co-ed.) 1995, Studien zur Evolutorischen Ökonomik IV. Schriften des Vereins für Socialpolitik (co-ed.) 2001; numerous articles in professional journals; several book reviews. *Address:* Room 4.149, Wirtschaftswissenschaftlichen Fakultät, Friedrich-Schiller-Universität, Carl-Zeiß-Str. 3, 07743 Jena (office); Hermann-Föge-Weg 1A, 37073 Göttingen, Germany (home). *Telephone:* (3641) 943210 (office); (551) 44317 (home). *Fax:* (3641) 943212 (office); (551) 44974 (home). *E-mail:* H.W.Lorenz@wiwi.uni-jena.de (office). *Website:* www .wiwi.uni-jena.de/Makro/index.html (office).

LORENZO ESTEFAN, Fernando, LicEcon, PhD; Uruguayan economist and politician; b. 31 Jan. 1960, Montevideo; ed Univ. de la República, Montevideo, Univ. de Paris IX-Dauphine, France, Univ. Carlos III de Madrid, Spain; Prof. of Econs, Univ. ORT, Montevideo 1998–, Univ. de la República 2001–; Researcher, Centro de Investigaciones Económicas (CINVE-Uruguay) 1995–97, Dir 1997–2004; fmr Dir, Commercial Policy Consultancy, Ministry of Economy and Finance, Dir Macroeconomic and Financial Consultancy 2005–08, Minister of Economy and Finance 2010–13; consultant on nat. and int. econ. affairs; Pres. Mercosur Econ. Investigation Network; mem. Asamblea Uruguay. *Publications include:* numerous research papers and publs on macroeconomic issues, int. trade and finance. *Address:* Asamblea Uruguay, Carlos Quijano 1273 Montevideo, Uruguay (office). *Telephone:* (2) 9032121 (office). *Fax:* (2) 9241147 (office). *E-mail:* info@2121.org.uy (office). *Website:* www.2121.org.uy (office).

LORGAT, Haroon, BCom; South African accountant, business executive and sports administrator; m. Farah Ebrahim; one s. one d.; ed Rhodes Univ.; qualified as Chartered Accountant 1985; worked briefly in man. at IBM before founding professional services firm, built large ind. firm through a series of mergers over 15 years before successfully merging with Ernst & Young; apptd Man. Pnr for Ernst & Young Western Cape and served on Nat. Exec. Cttee 2002–07; f. Kapela Investment Holdings pvt. equity firm, Cape Town and Johannesburg 2006; Chief Exec. Int. Cricket Council 2008–12; leading cricket all-rounder in SA, played in 76 First-class games 1977–91; has served in various capacities in South African cricket, including as Chair. Western Prov. Professional Cricket and as non-exec. Bd mem. Western Prov. Cricket Asscn; served as a non-exec. Dir for Cricket South Africa overseeing finance; Chair. Nat. Selectors for the South Africa cricket team 2004–07; mem. South African Inst. of Chartered Accountants. *Leisure interests:* golf, travel. *Address:* c/o International Cricket Council, Street 69, Dubai Sports City Emirates Road, PO Box 500 070, Dubai, United Arab Emirates. *E-mail:* enquiry@icc-cricket.com.

LORIMER, George Huntly, BSc, MS, PhD, FRS; British scientist and academic; *Distinguished University Professor, University of Maryland, College Park;* b. 14 Oct. 1942; s. of the late Gordon Lorimer and of Ellen Lorimer; m. Freia Schulz-Baldes 1970; one s. one d.; ed George Watson's Coll., Edinburgh, Univ. of St Andrews and Univ. of Illinois and Michigan State Univ., USA; scientist, Max-Planck Soc., Berlin 1972–74; Research Fellow, Inst. for Advanced Studies, Canberra 1974–77; Prin. Investigator, then Research Leader, Cen. Research Dept, E.I. Du Pont de Nemours & Co. 1978–91, Dupont Fellow 1991–97; currently Distinguished Univ. Prof., Univ. of Maryland, College Park; scientist, Soc. for Environmental Research, Munich 1977; mem. Editorial Bd Journal of Biological Chemistry 1998; mem. NAS 1997; Resident Scholar, Rockefeller Foundation Bellagio, Italy 1992, Research Award, Alexander von Humboldt Foundation 1997. *Publications include:* Osmotically Induced Water Movements in Corn Mitochondria 1969, The Role of Oxygen in Photorespiration 1972, Molecular Chaperones (Methods in Enzymology Vol. 290) 1998. *Leisure interests:* philately, music. *Address:* Department of Chemistry and Biochemistry, University of Maryland, 2121-Biomolecular Sciences Building, 2300 Symons Hall, College Park, MD 20742-3281 (office); 7705 Lake Glen Drive, Glen Dale, MD 20769, USA (home). *Telephone:* (301) 405-1828 (office). *Fax:* (301)314-9121 (office). *E-mail:* glorimer@umd.edu (office). *Website:* www.chem.umd.edu/george-lorimer (office); www.biochem.umd .edu/faculty/lorimer.htm (office).

LORING, Jeanne, BS, PhD; American biologist and academic; *Director, Center for Regenerative Medicine, Scripps Research Institute;* ed Univ. of Washington, Univ. of Oregon; Asst Prof. of Neurobiology, Univ. of Calif., Davis 1982–87; Sr Staff Scientist, Parkinson's Disease Research Program, HanaBiologics Inc. 1987–89; Sr Scientist, GenPharm Int. Inc. 1989–95; Sr Research Fellow, Molecular Dynamics Inc. 1995–97; Sr Dir (Transgenics and Neurobiology), Incyte Genomics Inc. 1997–2001; Founder and Chief Scientific Officer, Arcos BioScience Inc. 1997–2004; Adjunct Prof. of Stem Cells and Regenerative Medicine and Co-Dir NIH Exploratory Center for Human Embryonic Stem Cell Research, Burnham Inst. for Medical Research 2004–, also Dir Human Embryonic Stem Cell Training Course 2004–; Prof. of Developmental Neurobiology, Scripps Research Inst. 2007–, Dir Center for Regenerative Medicine 2008–, currently Prof., Kellogg School of Science and Tech.; currently also Adjunct Prof., Dept of Reproductive Medicine, School of Medicine, Univ. of California; mem. numerous scientific advisory bds; Educational Award, Clinical Research Professionals (San Diego chapter) 2006, Leadership Award, Burnham Inst. for Medical Research 2007, Stem Cell Research Award, Millipore Foundation 2008, 2009, Stem Cell Research Award, Esther O'Keefe Foundation 2009, 2010, Marie and Jimmy Mayer Award 2009. *Publications:* Human Stem Cell Manual: A Laboratory Guide 2007; numerous scientific papers. *Address:* Scripps Research Institute, 10550 North Torrey Pines Road, La Jolla, CA 92037, USA (office). *Telephone:* (858) 784-7767 (office). *E-mail:* jloring@ scripps.edu (office). *Website:* www.scripps.edu (office).

LORING, John Robbins, BA; American artist, designer and author; *Design Director, Tiffany & Co.;* b. 23 Nov. 1939, Chicago; s. of Edward D'Arcy and China Robbins Loring (née Logeman); ed Yale Univ., Ecole des Beaux Arts, Paris; Distinguished Visiting Prof., Univ. of Calif., Davis 1977; Bureau Chief Architectural Digest magazine, New York 1977–78; Design Dir Tiffany and Co., New York 1979–, Exec. Vice-Pres., 1981–84, Sr Vice-Pres. Design and Merchandising 1984–; mem. acquisitions comm. Dept of prints and illustrated books, Museum of Modern Art, New York 1990–; Contributing Ed. Arts magazine 1973–; work in perm. collections Museum of Modern Art, New York, Whitney Museum of American Art, Chicago Art Inst., Boston Museum of Fine Arts, RI School of Design, Baltimore Museum of Art, Yale Univ. Art Gallery, NY Historical Soc.; works commissioned by US Customhouse, New York, Prudential Insurance Co., Woodbridge, NJ, City of Scranton, Pa; Hon. DrArts (Pratt Inst.) 1996; Edith Wharton Award, Design and Art Soc. 1988, Pratt Inst. Legends Award 2002, Dallas Fashion Award 2004, Lifetime Achievement Award, Museum of Art and Design 2005. *Publications:* The New Tiffany Table Settings 1981, Tiffany Taste 1986, Tiffany's 150 Years 1987, The Tiffany Wedding 1988, Tiffany Parties 1989, The Tiffany Gourmet 1992, A Tiffany Christmas 1996, Tiffany's 20th Century 1997, Tiffany Jewels 1999, Paulding Farnham, Tiffany's Last Genius 2000, Magnificent Tiffany Silver 2001, Louis Comfort Tiffany at Tiffany & Co. 2002, Tiffany in Fashion 2003, Greetings from Andy Warhol 2004, Tiffany's Palm Beach 2005, Tiffany Diamonds 2005, Tiffany Colored Gems 2007, Tivoli Gardens 2007. *Leisure interests:* collecting 20th-century decorative arts, writing on design and lifestyle. *Address:* Tiffany & Co., 600 Madison Avenue, New York, NY 10022 (office); 621 Avon Road, West Palm Beach, FL 33401, USA (home). *Telephone:* (212) 230-5339 (office); (561) 659-3452 (home). *Fax:* (212) 230-5341 (office); (561) 651-7009 (home). *Website:* www.tiffany .com (office).

LORIUS, Claude, LèsSc, DèsSc; French glaciologist, academic and research institute director; *Director Emeritus of Research, Centre National de la Recherche Scientifique (CNRS);* b. 25 Feb. 1932, Besançon; ed Univ. of Besançon; joined CNRS, Grenoble 1953, Asst Dir Laboratoire de glaciologie et geophysique de l'environnement 1979–83, Dir 1983–88, currently Dir Emer. of Research, CNRS; responsibilities at Ministries of Research and the Environment, French Nat. Cttee on Antarctic Research 1987–94, French Inst. for Polar Research and Tech. (f. 1992); took part in 22 polar expeditions, mostly to Antarctica, led several French polar expeditions 1984–87; mem. World Climate Research Programme (OMM-ICSU) 1980–84, Exec. Cttee Past Global Changes (IGBP) 1989–98, European Cttee on Oceanography and Polar Sciences (European Science Foundation (ESF) and EC) 1989–97, Exec. Cttee Greenland Ice Core Project 1989–93; contributed to work of Scientific Cttee on Antarctic Research, Int. Council for Science (Pres. 1986–90), Int. Arctic Science Cttee 1991–98; led a working group on glaciology, ESF 1985–93; presided over European Program for Ice Coring in Antarctica project 1993–95; has helped organize many int. collaborations, notably the Vostok ice core; Corresp. mem. Acad. des Sciences (mem. 1994), Acad. des Technologies 2000; Foreign mem. Russian Acad. of Sciences 1994; mem. Academia Europaea 1989; Fellow, European Geophysical Soc. 1999; Officier, Légion d'honneur 1998; Humbolt Prize 1989, Belgica Medal 1989, Italgas Prize 1994, Tyler Prize for Environmental Achievement 1996, Balzan Prize for climatology (jtly with Jean Jouzel) 2001, Medaille d'or du CNRS 2002, Vernadsky Medal, European Geosciences Union 2006, Blue Planet Prize, Asahi Glass Foundation (co-recipient) 2008. *Achievements include:* was instrumental in discovery and interpretation of palaeo-atmosphere information within ice cores. *Publications:* Glaces de l'Antarctique: une mémoire, des passions 1991, L'Antarctique (with R. Gendrin) 1997; more than 100 scientific papers in professional journals. *Address:* CNRS, Campus Gérard Mégie, rue Michel-Ange, 16th arrondissement, Paris, France (office). *E-mail:* webcnrs@cnrs-dir.fr (office). *Website:* www.cnrs.fr (office).

LORTIE, Marc, BA; Canadian diplomatist; b. 1948, Beauport, Québec; m. Patricia Dunn; ed Séminaire de Québec, Laval Univ.; joined Dept of External Affairs 1971, overseas postings include in Tunisia 1973–75, in USA 1979–83; Head, Int. Media Relations, Office of Prime Minister, Ottawa 1985–87, Press Sec. 1987–89; Minister-Counsellor for Political Affairs, Embassy in Paris and Personal Rep. of Prime Minister for La Francophonie 1989–93; Sr Coordinator for Fed.-Prov. Relations, Dept of Foreign Affairs and Int. Trade 1998–2000, Asst Deputy Minister of Americas 2001; apptd Personal Rep. of Prime Minister, Third Summit of the Americas 2000; Amb. to Chile 1993–97, to Spain 2004–07, to France 2007–12; fmr Fellow, Centre for International Affairs, Harvard Univ. *Address:* Ministry of Foreign Affairs and International Trade, Lester B. Pearson Building, 125 Sussex Drive, Ottawa, ON K1A 0G2, Canada (office). *Telephone:* (613) 944-4000 (office). *Fax:* (613) 996-9709 (office). *E-mail:* enqserv@international.gc.ca (office). *Website:* www.international.gc.ca (office).

LÖSCHER, Peter, MA, MBA; Austrian business executive; b. 17 Sept. 1957, Villach; m.; four c.; ed Vienna Univ., Chinese Univ. of Hong Kong and Harvard Business School, USA; began career at Kienbaum and Partner (man. consultants), Germany 1985; mem. Strategic Planning Man. Team, Hoechst AG 1988–89, Dir Business Devt 1989–91, Man. Dir Hoechst Roussel Veterinaria AIE, Spain 1991–94, Vice-Pres. 1994–95, Project Leader 1996–97, Pres. and CEO Hoechst Marion Roussel Ltd, UK 1999; Chair., Pres. and CEO Aventis Pharma Ltd, Japan 2000–02; Pres. Amersham Health (life sciences co.), UK 2002–04, COO 2004; Pres. and CEO General Electric Healthcare Bio-Sciences and mem. Corp. Exec. Council 2004–05; Pres. Global Human Health Div. and mem. Exec. Cttee, Merck and Co. Inc. 2006–07; Pres. and CEO Siemens AG 2007–13, also Head of Corp. Devt; mem. Supervisory Bd Münchener Rückversicherungs-Gesellschaft AG; Chair. Asia-Pacific Cttee of German Business; Vice-Chair. European Round Table of Industrialists; Co-Chair. EU-Russia Industrialists' Round Table; Hon. Prof., Tongji Univ. 2011; Grand Decoration of Honour in Gold for Services to the Repub. of Austria 2010; Hon. DEng (Michigan State Univ.) 2008. *Address:* c/o Siemens AG, Wittelsbacherplatz 2, 80333 Munich, Germany. *E-mail:* contact@siemens.com.

LÖSCHNAK, Franz, DJur; Austrian jurist and politician; b. 4 March 1940, Vienna; m.; one s.; ed Univ. of Vienna; employed with Vienna City Council 1959–77, Dir of Personnel Affairs and Admin. Org. 1977; Under-Sec. Fed. Chancellery 1977; Minister, Fed. Chancellery 1985–87; Minister of Health and the Civil Service 1987–89; Minister of the Interior 1989–95; formed legal base of the Austrian Holocaust Memorial Service 1992; Pres. Vienna Athletic Sports Meeting 1982; Vice-Pres. Fed. Athletic Sports Meeting 1983, Pres. 1989; Pres. Austrian Sports Meeting 1995; Pres. Org. to Support the Austrian and Chinese Econ. Co-operation *c.* 2007; Decoration of Honour for Services to the Repub. of Austria; Order of Leopold II. *Publication:* Menschen aus der Fremde: Fluchtlinge, Vertriebene, Gastarbeiter (Themen der Zeit) 1993.

LØSETH, Øystein, MEng; Norwegian energy industry executive; *President and CEO, Vattenfall AB;* b. 1958; m.; three c.; ed Bedriftsøkonomisk Institutt, Oslo, Tech. Univ. of Trondheim; held various positions at Statoil 1984–93; Planning Man., Alliance Gas, London, UK 1993–94; Commercial Dir Naturkraft, Oslo 1994–97; Man. Dir Statkraft Energy Europe, Dir, Head of Strategy Div. and M&A, mem. Bd responsible for Production, Business Devt and R&D, Statkraft, Norway and the Netherlands 1997–2003; Man. Dir Nuon Energy Sourcing and CEO Nuon NV, Amsterdam, Netherlands 2003–09, mem. Bd of Dirs 2008–09; First Exec. Sr Vice-Pres. and Head of Business Group Benelux, Vattenfall AB 2009–10, Pres. and CEO Vattenfall AB 2010–. *Leisure interests:* trekking, cross-country skiing and mountain biking. *Address:* Vattenfall AB, Birger Jarlsgatan 33, Stockholm 162 87, Sweden (office). *Telephone:* (8) 739-50-00 (office). *Fax:* (8) 17-85-06 (office). *E-mail:* info@vattenfall.com (office). *Website:* www.vattenfall.com (office).

LOSHAK, Victor Grigoryevich; Russian journalist; *Editor-in-Chief, Ogoniok;* b. 20 April 1952, Zaporozhye, Ukraine; s. of Grigory Abramovich Loshak and Anna Davydovna Loshak; m. Marina Devovna Loshak; one d.; ed Odessa State Univ.; corresp. for various Odessa newspapers 1973–83; special corresp. Izvestia 1983–86; political observer Moskovskye Novosti 1986–91, First Deputy Ed. 1991–92, Ed.-in-Chief 1992–2003; Ed.-in-Chief Ogoniok (periodical) 2003–; Dir of Strategy, Kommersant Publishing House 2012–; broadcaster for Kultura (TV channel); mem. Int. Inst. of Press (Vice-Pres. Russian br.); Order of Honour 2000; Prize of Journalists' Union of Moscow. *Address:* Ogoniok, Krasnokazarmennaya str. pb. 14, 111250 Moscow (office); Kommersant Publishing House, 4 Vrubel Street, Building 1, 125080 Moscow, Russia (office). *Telephone:* (495) 540-47-10 (Ogoniok) (office); (495) 943-97-50 (Kommersant Publishing House) (office). *Fax:* (495) 775-41-06 (Ogoniok) (office); (495) 943-97-28 (Kommersant Publishing House) (office); www.kommersant.com (office). *E-mail:* pochta@ovarpress.ru (office). *Website:* www.ogoniok.com (office); www.kommersant.com (office).

LOSHCHININ, Valery Vassilyevich; Russian diplomatist; *Permanent Representative, United Nations, Geneva;* b. 11 Sept. 1940, Gomel Region, Byelorussia; m.; two s. two d.; ed Belarus State Univ., Diplomatic Acad. of USSR Ministry of Foreign Affairs; with Ministry of Foreign Affairs Belarus SSR, then USSR Ministry of Foreign Affairs 1965–77; with Perm. Mission to Russia 1977–89; Deputy Perm. Rep. to int. orgs, Geneva 1989–95, Perm. Rep. 2006–; Dir Second European Dept, Russian Ministry of Foreign Affairs 1995–96; Amb. to Belarus 1996–99; Perm. Rep. to int. orgs, Vienna 1999–2001; Deputy Minister of Foreign Affairs (responsible for relations with CIS countries) 2001–2002, First Deputy Minister of Foreign Affairs 2002–05. *Address:* Permanent Mission of the Russian Federation, 15 Avenue de la Paix, 1211 Geneva 20, Switzerland (office). *Telephone:* (22) 7331870 (office). *Fax:* (22) 7344044 (office). *E-mail:* mission.russian@vtxnet.ch (office). *Website:* www.geneva.mid.ru (office).

LOTHE, Jens, DPhil; Norwegian physicist and academic; *Professor Emeritus of Physics, University of Oslo;* b. 25 Nov. 1931, Oslo; s. of Jakob Lothe and Borghild Lothe; m. Solveig E. Seeberg 1960; two s. one d.; ed Univ. of Oslo; lecturer, Univ. of Oslo 1959–63, Assoc. Prof. 1963–72, Prof. of Physics 1972, now Prof. Emer.; mem. Norwegian Acad. of Science and Letters. *Publications:* The Theory of Dislocations (with J. P. Hirth) 1967; numerous papers on elastic waves. *Address:* Department of

Physics, University of Oslo, Blindern 0316 Oslo (office); Nedre Ringvolls 5, 1339 Voyenenga, Norway. *Telephone:* 22856491 (office); 67133076. *E-mail:* lothe@fys.uio.no (office). *Website:* www.fys.uio.no/english (office).

LOTT, (Chester) Trent, BPA, JD; American fmr politician; b. 9 Oct. 1941, Grenada, Miss.; s. of Chester P. Lott and Iona Lott (née Watson); m. Patricia E. Thompson 1964; one s. one d.; ed Univ. of Mississippi; called to Miss. Bar 1967; Assoc. Bryan & Gordon, Pascagoula, Miss. 1967; Admin. Asst to Congressman Colmer 1968–73; mem. 93rd–100th Congresses from 5th Dist Miss., Repub. Whip 97th and 98th Congresses; Senator from Miss. 1989–2007 (resgnd); Senate Majority Leader 1996–2001, Nov.–Dec. 2002, Minority Leader 2001–02; named as observer from House to Geneva Arms Control talks; mem. Senate Republican Policy Cttee; Co-founder Breaux Lott Leadership Group (lobbying firm) 2008–; mem. American Bar Asscn; Republican; Golden Bulldog Award, Guardian of Small Business Award. *Address:* Breaux Lott Leadership Group, 607 14th Street, NW, Washington, DC 20005, USA. *Telephone:* (202) 239-4747. *Fax:* (202) 239-4748. *Website:* breauxlott.com.

LOTT, Dame Felicity Ann Emwhyla, CBE, DBE, BA, LRAM, FRAM; British singer (soprano); b. 8 May 1947, Cheltenham, Glos., England; d. of John A. Lott and Whyla Lott (née Williams); m. 1st Robin Golding 1973 (divorced); m. 2nd Gabriel Woolf 1984; one d.; ed Pate's Grammar School for Girls, Cheltenham, Royal Holloway Coll., Univ. of London and Royal Acad. of Music; debut with ENO as Pamina in Die Zauberflöte 1975; prin. roles at Glyndebourne, Covent Garden, ENO, WNO, New York Metropolitan Opera, Vienna, La Scala, Paris Opéra, Brussels, Hamburg, Munich, Chicago, San Francisco, Dresden; wide recital repertoire; founder mem. Songmakers' Almanac; mem. Equity, Incorporated Soc. of Musicians; Hon. Fellow, Royal Holloway Coll., Hon. FRCM; Officier des Arts et des Lettres 2000, Chevalier, Légion d'honneur 2001; Dr hc (Sussex) 1990; Hon. DLitt (Loughborough) 1996; Hon. DMus (London) 1997, (Royal Scottish Acad. of Music and Drama) 1998, (Oxford) 2001, (Leicester) 2010, (Gloucester) 2010, (Paris Sorbonne) 2010; Kammersängerin, Bayerische Staatsoper, Munich 2003, Wigmore Medal. *Roles include:* Countess in Le Nozze di Figaro; Ellen Orford in Peter Grimes; Fiordiligi in Così fan Tutti; Elvira in Don Giovanni; Xiphares in Mitridate; Marschallin in Der Rosenkavalier; Countess in Capriccio (Richard Strauss); many recitals with Graham Johnson and duets with Ann Murray; DVD of Offenbach's Hélène in La Belle Hélène and La Grande Duchesse. *Leisure interests:* reading, gardening. *Address:* c/o Askonas Holt Ltd, Lincoln House, 300 High Holborn, London, WC1V 7JH, England (office). *Telephone:* (20) 7400-1700 (office). *Fax:* (20) 7400-1799 (office). *E-mail:* info@askonasholt.co.uk (office); mail@felicitylott.de (office). *Website:* www.askonasholt.co.uk (office); www.felicitylott.de.

LOU, Jiwei, BA, MEcon; Chinese politician and financial executive; *Minister of Finance;* b. Dec. 1950, Beijing; ed Tsinghua Univ., Chinese Acad. of Social Sciences; joined CCP 1973; following postgraduate studies, worked as Deputy Head of financial and banking office group of Gen. Office of State Council from 1982; Dir Inst. of Finance and Trade, Chinese Acad. of Social Sciences mid-1980s; apptd Deputy Dir Econ. System Reform Office, Beijing Municipality 1992; Dir Macro-Control Dept, State Comm. for Restructuring the Economy 1992–95; Vice-Gov. Guizhou Prov. 1995–98; Vice-Minister of Finance 1998–2007, Deputy Sec. CCP Leading Party Group 1998–2007; mem. Academic Affairs Cttee of State Council 1999–, Deputy Sec.-Gen. of State Council 2007; Chair. and CEO China Investment Corpn 2007–13; Minister of Finance 2013–; Alt. mem. 17th CCP Cen. Cttee 2007–12, mem. 18th CCP Cen. Cttee 2012–; considered by Time magazine as one of the 100 most influential people in the world 2008, ranked by Forbes magazine amongst The World's Most Powerful People (34th) 2009, (30th) 2010, (33rd) 2011, (39th) 2012. *Address:* Ministry of Finance, 3 Nansanxiang, Sanlihe, Xicheng Qu, Beijing 100820, People's Republic of China (office). *Telephone:* (10) 68551888 (office). *Fax:* (10) 68533635 (office). *E-mail:* webmaster@mof.gov.cn (office). *Website:* www.mof.gov.cn (office).

LOUBOUTIN, Christian; French footwear designer; b. 7 Jan. 1964, Paris 12th arrondissement; s. of Roger Louboutin and Irene Louboutin; apprenticeship at Folies Bergères 1980–86; worked freelance for Chanel, Yves Saint Laurent, Maud Frizon and other fashion houses 1986–89; turned to garden design 1989; cr. Christian Louboutin brand and opened first boutique in Paris 1992; opened first boutique in New York 1994; began contributing for couture and ready-to-wear seasons for Jean-Paul Gaultier, Chloé, Azzaro, Diane Von Furstenberg, Victor & Rolf, Givenchy and Lanvin 1995; partnership with landscape architect Louis Benech 1997–; collaborated with film dir David Lynch on exhbn 'Fetish' 2007; FFANY Award, Int. Fashion Group 1996, 2008, honoured by Fashion Inst. of Tech., New York including retrospective of his work 2008, Star Honouree, Int. Fashion Group 2008. *Publication:* Christian Louboutin. *Leisure interest:* trapeze flying. *Address:* 19 rue Jean-Jacques Rousseau, 75001 Paris, France (office). *Telephone:* 1-42-36-05-31 (office). *E-mail:* info@christianlouboutin.fr (office). *Website:* www.christianlouboutin.com (office).

LOUCKS, Vernon R., Jr, BA, MBA; American business executive; *Chairman, The Aethena Group, LLC;* b. 24 Oct. 1934, Evanston, Ill.; s. of Vernon Reece Loucks and Sue Burton; m. Linda Olson; six c.; ed Yale Univ. and Harvard Graduate School of Business Admin.; served as First Lt US Marine Corps; fmr Sr Man. Consultant, George Fry & Assocs; joined Baxter International Inc. 1966, mem. Bd of Dirs 1975, Pres. and COO 1976–80, CEO 1980–98, Chair. 1987–99, retd as Asst to the Pres. and the CEO; Chair. InLight, Inc. 1998–2000; Co-founder and Chair. The Aethena Group, LLC (pvt. equity group) 2000–; CEO Segway LLC Jan.–Nov. 2003; Chair. Proton Therapy Global Management; mem. Advisory Bd, PAX Scientific, Inc., Five9 Technologies, LLC, Metalmark Capital LLC, Pain Therapeutics Inc. 2007– (Dir 2003–07); fmr Special Advisor, NIH; mem. Bd of Dirs, Emerson Electric Co. 1979–2011, Quaker Oats Co. 1981–, Affymetrix, Inc. 1993–2009, GeneSoft Pharmaceuticals 1998–2004, Anheuser-Busch Cos 1998–, Edwards Lifesciences Corpn 2000–08, Oscient Pharmaceuticals Corpn 2004–05, MedAssets Inc. 2007–; mem. Business Advisory Bd, Bay City Capital LLC; Dir, Harvard Business School Bd of Assocs; Trustee, Rush Univ., Rush Univ. Medical Center, The Lawrenceville School; several awards, including Chicago Inst. of Medicine Citizen Fellowship Award 1982, Yale Medal 1997. *Address:* The Aethena Group LLC, 100 Woodbrook Lane, Baltimore, MD 21212, USA. *E-mail:* info@aethena.us. *Website:* aethena.us.

LOUDIYI, Abdellatif; Moroccan politician; *Minister-delegate to the Prime Minister, in charge of National Defence;* Dir of the Treasury and of External Finance, Ministry of Economy and Finance –2003, Sec.-Gen., Ministry of Economy and Finance 2003; Minister-del. to Prime Minister, in charge of Nat. Defence 2010–; Ind. *Address:* Office of the Prime Minister, Palais Royal, Touarga, Rabat, Morocco (office). *Telephone:* (53) 7219400 (office). *Fax:* (53) 7768656 (office). *E-mail:* courrier@pm.gov.ma (office). *Website:* www.pm.gov.ma (office).

LOUDON, Jonkheer Aarnout Alexander, LLM; Dutch fmr business executive; b. 10 Dec. 1936, The Hague; m. Talitha Adine Charlotte Boon 1962; two s.; ed Univ. of Utrecht; joined Bank Mees & Hope 1964, Head, New Issues Dept 1967; joined Akzo Group 1969, Dir Financial Affairs Akzo, Arnhem 1971; Finance Dir Akzo Coatings, France 1972; Pres. Akzo, Brazil 1975–77; mem. Man. Bd Akzo NV 1977, Deputy Chair. 1978, Chair. Bd 1982–94; Chair. Supervisory Bd Akzo Nobel NV 1994–2006; Chair. Supervisory Bd ABN AMRO Holding NV 1994–2006; mem. Supervisory Bd Royal Dutch Petroleum Co. 1997–2007; Sr Adviser Cinven PLC 2006–13; mem. Senate, Dutch Parl. 1995–99. *Leisure interest:* horse riding. *Address:* Houtweg 71, 2514 BN The Hague, Netherlands (home). *Telephone:* (70) 3463260 (home). *Fax:* (70) 3603825 (office). *E-mail:* aarnout@loudon.nu.

LOUDON, Rodney, DPhil, FRS; British theoretical physicist; *Professor Emeritus, Essex University;* b. 25 July 1934, Manchester; s. of Albert Loudon and Doris Helen Loudon (née Blane); m. Mary A. Philips 1960; one s. one d.; ed Bury Grammar School, Oxford Univ.; Postdoctoral Fellow, Univ. of California at Berkeley, USA 1959–60; Scientific Civil Servant, RRE, Malvern 1960–65; mem. Tech. Staff, Bell Laboratories, Murray Hill, NJ, USA 1965–66, 1970, RCA, Zürich, Switzerland 1975, British Telecom Research Labs 1984, 1989–95; Prof. of Theoretical Physics, Essex Univ. 1967–2007, Prof. Emeritus 2008–; Visiting Prof., Yale Univ. 1975, Univ. of Calif., Irvine 1980, Ecole Polytechnique, Lausanne 1985, Univ. of Rome 1987, 1996; Fellow, Optical Soc. of America 1994; Thomas Young Medal and Prize (Inst. of Physics) 1987, Max Born Award (Optical Soc. of America) 1992, Humboldt Award 1998. *Publications:* The Quantum Theory of Light 1973, 1983, 2000, Scattering of Light by Crystals (with W. Hayes) 1978, 2004, Surface Excitations (Ed. with V.M. Agranovich) 1984, An Introduction to the Properties of Condensed Matter (with D. Barber) 1989. *Leisure interest:* classical music. *Address:* 3 Gaston Street, East Bergholt, Colchester, Essex, CO7 6SD, England (home). *Telephone:* (1206) 298550 (home).

LOUEKOSKI, Matti Kalevi, LLM; Finnish politician, business executive and lawyer; b. 14 April 1941, Oulu; m. Pirjo Hiltunen 1969; one s. one d.; Sec.-Gen. Union of Finnish Student Corpns 1967–69; official at Ministry of Finance and Ministry of Interior 1969–70; Counsellor of Higher Educ. 1970–72; Special Adviser, Office of the Council of State 1975–76; established own law firm 1978; Dir Finnish Workers' Savings Bank 1979–83; mem. Parl. 1976–79, 1983–96; Minister of Educ. 1971–72; Minister without Portfolio Feb.–Sept. 1972; Minister of Justice 1972–75, of Justice and Nordic Co-operation 1987–90, of Finance 1990–91; Vice-Speaker of Parl. 1985–87, 1995–96; mem. Bd Bank of Finland 1996–2000, Deputy Gov. 2001–07, Alt. Gov. IMF 2000–07; mem. Financial Supervision Authority, Vice-Chair. 1996–97, Chair. 1998–2007; mem. Social Democratic Party.

LOUEMBÉ, Blaise; Gabonese government official; *Minister of the Digital Economy, Communication and Posts;* m.; six c.; ed Université des Sciences sociales de Grenoble, France; served in several positions at Treasury including Head of Customs Directorate 1988–90, Deputy Dir 1990–92, Gen-Man. Disbursement Services; Treasurer Paymaster Gen., Ministry of Economy, Finance, Budget and Privatization 2000–08, of the Budget, Public Accounts and the Civil Service, responsible for State Reform 2008–11, Minister of Housing, Town Planning, the Environment and Sustainable Devt 2011–12, Minister of the Digital Economy, Communication and Posts 2012–. *Address:* Ministry of Digital Economy, Communication and Posts, Libreville, Gabon (office).

LOUGHRAN, James, CBE, FRNCM, FRSAMD; British conductor; b. 30 June 1931, Glasgow, Scotland; s. of James Loughran and Agnes Loughran (née Fox); m. 1st Nancy Coggon 1961 (divorced 1983); two s.; m. 2nd Ludmila Navratil 1985; ed Glasgow, Bonn, Amsterdam and Milan; Assoc. Conductor, Bournemouth Symphony Orchestra 1962–65; debut Royal Opera House, Covent Garden 1964; Prin. Conductor BBC Scottish Symphony Orchestra 1965–71; Prin. Conductor and Musical Adviser, Hallé Orchestra 1971–83, Conductor Laureate 1983–91; debut New York Philharmonic with Westminster Choir 1972; Prin. Conductor Bamberg Symphony Orchestra 1979–83; Chief Guest Conductor BBC Welsh Symphony Orchestra 1987–90; Guest Conductor of prin. orchestras of Europe, America, Australasia and Japan, Guest Perm. Conductor, Japan Philharmonic Symphony Orchestra 1980, Hon. Conductor 2006–; Chief Conductor Århus Symphony Orchestra, Denmark 1996–2003, Chief Guest Conductor 2003–11; BBC Proms 1965–89 including The Last Night 5 times 1977–85; recorded complete Beethoven Symphonies with London Symphony Orchestra as contribution to European Broadcasting Union Beethoven Bicentenary Celebrations 1969–70; recordings with Hallé, London Philharmonic, Philharmonia, BBC Symphony, Århus Symphony, Scottish Chamber Orchestra, Japan Philharmonic; Liveryman, Worshipful Co. of Musicians 1992; Hon. DMus (Sheffield) 1983, (Royal Scottish Acad. of Music and Drama) 2005; First Prize, Philharmonia Orchestra Conducting Competition 1961, Mancunian of the Year 1981, Gold Disc, EMI 1983. *Leisure interests:* unwinding, golf. *Address:* 18 Hatfield Drive, Glasgow, G12 0YA, Scotland (home). *Telephone:* (141) 337-2091 (home). *E-mail:* jamesloughran@btinternet.com (home).

LOUIS, Jean-Victor, DenD; Belgian lawyer and academic; *Professor Emeritus, Université Libre de Bruxelles;* b. 10 Jan. 1938, Uccle; m. Maria Rosa Moya Benavent 1963; three s.; ed Univ. Libre de Bruxelles; Sec. Inst. d'Etudes Européennes, Univ. Libre de Bruxelles 1967–71, Dir of Research 1977–80, Pres. 1980–92; Lecturer, Univ. Libre de Bruxelles 1970–73, Prof. 1973–2003, Prof. Emer. 2003–; Prof. European Univ. Inst. 1998–2002; Adviser, Nat. Bank of Belgium 1972–80, Head, Legal Dept 1980–97, Adviser to Bd of Dirs 1990–97; Pres. Belgian Asscn for European Law 1983–85; legal expert, Institutional Cttee European Parl. 1992–94; Pres. Initiative Cttee 96, International European Movt 1995–98; mem., Monetary Cttee of International Law Asscn; Ed. Cahiers de Droit Européen 1977–; Exec. Dir Philippe Wiener-Maurice Anspach Foundation 1971–2002, Pres. 2002–; mem. European Constitutional Law Network; Francqui Chair 2007–08; Commdr, Order of Belgian Crown; Dr h.c (Univ.

Paris 2) 2001; Emile Bernheim Prize 1969, P.H. Spaak Prize 1979. *Publications include:* Les règlements de la Communauté économique européenne 1969, Le Droit de la Communauté économique européenne (dir and co-author), 15 vols 1970–, The European Community Legal Order 1979, Implementing the Tokyo Round (with J. Jackson and M. Matsushita) 1984, Vers un Système européen de banques centrales (ed.) 1989, From the EMS to the Monetary Union 1990, Banking Supervision in the EC (ed.) 1995, L'Union européenne et l'avenir de ses institutions 1996, The Euro and European Integration (ed.) 1999, The Euro in the National Context (ed.) 2002, The Euro: Law, Politics, Economics (co-ed. with A. Komninos), L'Ordre juridique de l'Union européenne (with T. Ronse) 2005, L'Europe, sortir du doute 2006, L'Union européenne et sa monnaie 2009; many articles on EC law, especially in field of monetary cooperation and integration. *Address:* 524 avenue Louise, Boîte 9, 1050 Brussels, Belgium.

LOUIS-DREYFUS, Margarita, LLB; Russian business executive; *Chairman, Louis Dreyfus and Louis Dreyfus SAS;* b. (Margarita Bogdanova), 1 June 1962, Leningrad (now St Petersburg); m. 2nd Robert Louis-Dreyfus 1992 (died 2009); three s.; ed Moscow State Univ.; Chair. Louis Dreyfus and Louis Dreyfus SAS 2009–; majority shareholder of Olympique de Marseille; Capitalist of the Year Award, Le Nouvel Economist 2011, ranked by Forbes magazine amongst The World's 100 Most Powerful Women (70th) 2013. *Address:* Louis Dreyfus SAS, 87 avenue de la Grande Armée, 75782 Paris, France (office). *Telephone:* 1-47-77-17-00 (office). *Fax:* 1-47-77–17-01 (office). *E-mail:* DRH-Paris@louisdreyfus.fr (office). *Website:* www.louisdreyfus.com (office).

LOUISY, Dame (Calliopa) Pearlette, GCMG, BA, MA, PhD; Saint Lucia government official and academic; *Governor-General;* b. 8 June 1946, Laborie, Saint Lucia; d. of Rita Louisy; ed St Joseph's Convent Secondary School, Univ. of the West Indies (UWI), Université Laval, Québec, Canada, Univ. of Bristol, UK; grad. teacher, St Joseph's Convent 1969–72, 1975–76; tutor, Saint Lucia 'A' Level Coll. 1976–1981, Prin. 1981–86; Dean Sir Arthur Lewis Community Coll. 1986–94, Vice-Prin. 1994–95, Prin. 1996–97; Gov.-Gen. of Saint Lucia 1997–; Commonwealth Scholar 1972; Hon. Distinguished Fellow, UWI 2003; Grand Cross, Order of St Lucia 1997, Dame of the Equestrian Order of St Gregory the Great 2002; Hon. LLD (Bristol) 1999, (Sheffield) 2003, (UWI) 2011; Int. Woman of the Year 1998, 2001, Paul Harris Fellow, Rotary International 2001–10, Caribbean Luminary, American Foundation of the Univ. of the West Indies 2007. *Publications:* A Guide to the Writing of Creole 1985, The Changing Role of the Small State in Higher Education 1993, Dilemmas of Insider Research in a Small Country Setting 1997, Higher Education in the Caribbean: Issues and Strategies 1999, Expanding the Horizons of Creole Research 1999, Globalisation and Comparative Education: A Caribbean Perspective 2001, Nation Languages and National Development in the Caribbean 2002, Whose Context for What Quality? – Informing Educational Strategies for the Caribbean 2004, Global Trends in Education – The Cultural Dimension 2007, Tertiary Education in Saint Lucia: Challenges and Priorities within the Evolving Global Environment 2011. *Leisure interests:* the performing arts, culture, gardening. *Address:* Government House, Morne Fortune, Castries, Saint Lucia, West Indies (office). *Telephone:* 452-2481 (office). *Fax:* 453-2731 (office). *E-mail:* govgenslu@candw.lc (office).

LOULY, Lt-Col Mohamed Mahmoud Ould Ahmed; Mauritanian army officer, politician and fmr head of state; b. 1943; Minister for Control and Investigation 1978–79, in charge of the Perm. Secr. of the Mil. Cttee for Nat. Recovery (CMRN) Jan.–March 1979, for the Civil Service and Higher, Tech. and Vocational Training March–May 1979; Pres. of Mauritania 1979–80. *Address:* c/o Office du Président, BP 184, Nouakchott, Mauritania.

LOURDUSAMY, HE Cardinal Simon, DCL; Indian ecclesiastic; *Prefect Emeritus, Congregation for the Eastern Churches;* b. 5 Feb. 1924, Kalleri, Pondicherry; ed Loyola Coll., Madras, Pontifical Urbaniana Univ., Rome, Italy; ordained priest 1951; diocesan chancellor and sec. to Archbishop of Pondicherry; Ed. weekly Catholic magazine Sava Viaby; Dir Catholic Doctors' Guild, Catholic Medical Students' Guild, Newman Asscns, catholic univ. students' union and of other ecclesiastical orgs; apptd Auxiliary Bishop of Bangalore, India 1962, Coadjutor Archbishop 1964, Archbishop 1968–71; consecrated Bishop (Titular Church of Sozusa, Libya) 1962; Titular Archbishop of Philippi 1964; Adjunct Sec. Congregation for the Evangelization of Peoples 1971–73, Sec. 1973–85; Pres. Pontifical Missionary Works 1973; Vice-Grand Chancellor Pontifical Urban Univ. 1973; cr. Cardinal-Deacon of S. Maria delle Grazie alle Fornaci fuori Porta Cavalleggeri (Deacony raised pro hac vice) 1985, Cardinal-Priest 1996; Prefect Congregation for the Eastern Churches 1985–91, Prefect Emer. 1991–; fmr Pres. Nat. Liturgical Comm. for India; Founder Nat. and Catechetical Centre, Bangalore; fmr mem. Bishops' Catechetics Comm.; del. to first ordinary ass. of Synod of Bishops 1967; Rep. of Bishops of India at Pan-Asiatic Catechetical-Liturgical Conf., Manila, Philippines 1967 (Vice-Pres. and Pres. Liturgy Section). *Address:* Congregation for the Eastern Churches, Palazzo del Bramante, Via della Conciliazione 34, 00193 Rome (office); Palazzo dei Convertendi, Via dei Corridori 64, 00193 Rome, Italy (home). *Telephone:* (06) 69884282 (office); (06) 69884796 (home). *Fax:* (06) 69884300 (office).

LOUSTEAU, Martín, BSc, MSc; Argentine economist, banker and government official; b. 8 Dec. 1970; ed Univ. of San Andres, London School of Econs, UK; worked at Ministry of Economy and Public Works 1996–97; Chief Economist and Dir, APL Economia (business consulting firm) 1997–2002; Adviser to Pres. of Cen. Bank and mem. Cttee on Inflation Targets 2003–04; Chief of Staff, Ministry of Production 2004–05, Minister of Production for Buenos Aires Prov. 2005; Pres. Banco de la Provincia de Buenos Aires 2005–07; Minister of the Economy 2007–08 (resgnd). *Address:* c/o Ministry of Economy and Production, Hipólito Yrigoyen 250, C1086AAB Buenos Aires, Argentina (office).

LOUTFY, Aly, PhD; Egyptian fmr politician and professor of economics; b. 6 Oct. 1935, Cairo; s. of Mahmoud Loutfy; m. Eglal Mabrouk 1966; one s.; ed Ain Shams and Louzan Univs; joined staff, Faculty of Commerce Ain Shams Univ. 1957, Prof. and Chair. Dept of Econs 1980; Prof., High Inst. of Co-operative and Admin. Studies; Part-time Prof., Inst. of Arab Research and Studies, Cairo; mem. Bd of Dirs Bank of Alexandria 1977–78, Bank of Commerce and Devt (Cairo) 1981–; mem. Legis., Political Science and Econ. Asscn 1977, Delta Sugar Co. 1978, Bank of Commerce and Devt 1980; Minister of Finance 1978–80; Prime Minister of Egypt

1985–86; Speaker of the Shoura Council 1985–89; Ideal Prof. Award, Egyptian Univs 1974, Gold Mercury Int. Award 1979. *Publications:* Economic Evolution, Economic Development, Economic Planning, Studies on Mathematical Economics and Econometrics, Financing Problems in Developing Countries, Industrialization Problems in Under-Developed Countries; 30 research papers in economics in Arabic, French and English. *Leisure interests:* tennis, reading, travel. *Address:* 29 Ahmed Heshmat Street, Zamalek, Cairo, Egypt (home).

LOUVIER, Alain; French composer, conductor and harpsichordist; b. 13 Sept. 1945, Paris; s. of René Louvier and Marthe Louvier (née Fournier); m. Marie-Paule Siruguet; one s. one d.; ed Centre Nat. de Télé-Enseignement, Conservatoire Nat. Supérieur de Musique, Paris; Dir Conservatoire Nat. de Région, Boulogne-Billancourt 1972–86, 2009–13; Dir Conservatoire Nat. Supérieur de Musique, Paris 1986–91, Prof. of Musical Analysis 1991–2010; Prix de Rome 1968, Arthur Honegger Award 1975, Paul Gilson Award 1981, Prix de la SACEM 2009. *Works include:* Chant des limbes for orchestra 1969, 3 Atmosphères for clarinet and orchestra 1974, Canto di Natale 1976, Le Clavecin non tempéré 1978, Messe des Apôtres 1978, Casta Diva (with Maurice Béjart) 1980, Poèmes de Ronsard for voice ensemble and chamber orchestra 1984, Envol d'écailles for flute, viola and harp 1986, Le Jeu des 7 Musiques for sax quartet 1986, Chant des aires for 25 flutes 1988, Agrexandrins pour piano 1992, L'Isola dei Numeri for piano 1992, Concerto for alto 1996, Météores for two pianos and orchestra 1998, String Quartet 1999, Eclipse for flute and string trio 2000, Une cloche de feu rose dans les nuages for piano and 11 voices 2000, Nuit de feu, Rumeur d'espace 2001, Herbier 2 for guitar, harp and mandolin 2004, Heptagone 2004, Solstices for children voices and piano 2005, Archimède for wind orchestra 2006, Etudes pour Agresseurs (six books for piano, clavecin, orgue) 1964–82, Etudes pour Agresseurs (book seven for piano, harpsichord, organ and orchestra) 2007, L'harpenteur étrange for harp 2009, Herbier 4 for piano and harpsichord 2011, Sonata for two violas 2013. *Publications:* L'Orchestre 1997, Louvier, Les claviers de lumière, par P.A. Castanet 2002, Messiaen et le Concert de la nature 2011. *Leisure interests:* botany and entomology. *Address:* 53 avenue Victor Hugo, 92100 Boulogne-Billancourt, France. *Telephone:* 6-85-41-53-59 (mobile). *E-mail:* alainlouvier@yahoo.fr. *Website:* alain-louvier-com.

LOUVRIER, Franck, DEng; French public relations officer and civil servant; *Director of Communications, Office of the President;* b. 30 May 1968, Nantes; ed Ecole Superieure de Gestion, Paris; Chief of Staff to Mayor of Neuilly, Nicolas Sarkozy 1999–2002; press and communications adviser to Sarkozy at Interior Ministry 2002–04, 2005–07, Finance Ministry 2004; Dir of Communications, Union pour un mouvement populaire (UMP) 2004–, presidential campaign of Nicolas Sarkozy 2005–06, Office of the Pres. of the Repub. 2007–. *Address:* Palais de l'Elysée, 55 rue du faubourg Saint-Honoré, 75008 Paris, France (office). *Telephone:* 1-42-92-81-00 (office). *E-mail:* franck.louvrier@elysee.fr (office). *Website:* www.elysee.fr (office).

LOUW, Eugene, BA, LLB; South African politician and lawyer; *Chairman and Senior Partner, Louw & Coetzee;* b. 15 July 1931, Cape Town; s. of Anath Louw and Johanna de Jager; m. Hantie Phyfer 1964; three s. one d.; ed Bellville High School and Univ. of Stellenbosch; Chair. Students' Council, Univ. of Stellenbosch 1957; attorney, pvt. practice, Durbanville 1964–79, 1993–; Mayor of Durbanville 1967–72; mem. Parl. for Durbanville 1974–79, Malmesbury 1972–74, Paarl 1989–94; Admin. of Cape Prov. 1979–89; Minister of Home Affairs 1989–92, of Defence and Public Works 1992–93; Chair. and Sr Partner Louw and Coetzee 1994–; Chair. Nat. Huguenot Tercentenary Festival Cttee 1988, Capab 1982–88, Nat. Dias Quincentenary Festival Cttee 1988, Constitutional Investigation Cttee into Regional Local Govt; Patron Western Prov. Rugby Union 1979–89; Abe Bailey Travel Bursary Holder; Alumnus of the Year Award (Stellenbosch Univ.) 1993; recipient of seven hon. citizenships; four public buildings named after him. *Leisure interests:* politics, legal profession, sport. *Address:* Louw & Coetzee, 35 Main Road, 7550 Durbanville (office); 10 Watsonia Close, Plattekloof, 7500 Parow (home); PO Box 15432, 7506 Panorama, South Africa. *Telephone:* (21) 9763180 (office); (21) 9305620 (home); (21) 9305620. *Fax:* (21) 9764288 (office); (21) 9305621 (home). *E-mail:* elouw@louwcoet.co.za (office). *Website:* www.louwcoet.co.za (office).

LOUW, Michael James Minnaar, BA; South African civil servant; b. 9 Nov. 1939; m.; three c.; ed Orange Free State Univ.; with Dept of Labour; with Directorate for Mil. Intelligence, South African Defence Force 1964–69; joined Bureau for State Security (became Nat. Intelligence Service) 1969, Special Adviser to Dir-Gen., Deputy Dir-Gen. 1988–92, Dir-Gen. 1992–94, Chief 1994–. *Address:* Private Bag X3, Hatfield 0028, South Africa.

LOUW, Raymond; South African media consultant; b. 13 Oct. 1926, Cape Town; s. of George K. E. Louw and Helen K. Louw (née Finlay); m. Jean Ramsay Byres 1950; two s. one d.; ed Parktown Boys' High School, Johannesburg, Univ. of Cape Town; reporter on Rand Daily Mail 1946–50, Worthing Herald 1951–52, North-Western Evening Mail (Barrow-in-Furness) 1953–54, Westminster Press Provincial Newspapers (London) 1955–56; Night News Ed. Rand Daily Mail 1958–59, News Ed. 1960–65, Ed. 1966–77; News Ed. Sunday Times 1959–60; Chair. SA Morning Newspaper Group 1975–77; Gen. Man. SA Associated Newspapers 1977–82, City Press, Johannesburg 1982–84; mem. Man. Cttee, South African Press Asscn 1977–82; Chair. South African Newspaper Press Conciliation Bd 1979–82; Ed. and Publr Southern Africa Report 1982–2011; Rapporteur, Five Freedoms Forum mission to Lusaka to meet banned African Nat. Congress leaders 1989; Chair. Media Defence Fund 1989–94, Campaign for Open Media 1985–94 (now merged as Freedom of Expression Inst., Chair. 1994–96); Chair. New Era Schools Trust 1988–2007, currently mem.; Co-chair. Campaign for Independent Broadcasting 1991–94; Dir Media Business Training Foundation 1992-4; Trustee, Inst. for Advancement of Journalism 1992–; Africa Consultant, World Press Freedom Cttee 2003–09; mem. Task Group on Govt Communications 1996; mem. Exec. Bd, International Press Inst., London, 1979–87, Fellow 1994; mem. Independent Media Comm. 1994; chosen by International Press Inst. to travel to Cameroon to make plea for release from jail of the late Pius Njawe (Ed. of Le Messager) 1998, Njawe freed six months later; mem. IPI delegations to the Pres. of Indonesia 2000, Zimbabwean Govt 2001, Israeli Govt 2003, Ethiopian Govt 2004 on media freedom issues; addressed UN Human Rights Comm. on need for press freedom to be declared a human right 1987; Founder and council mem. South African Nat. Editors' Forum 1996–; made numerous representations to parl. cttees

against proposed legislation that would restrict media freedom 2002–; Vice-Pres. South African PEN 2005–, South African PEN rep. at confs in Accra, Ghana, Dakar, Senegal 2007, Berlin, Germany 2008, Cairo, Egypt 2010; as mem. of FXI, described role of South African press between 1960 and 1994 to Truth and Reconciliation Comm. 1997; made representations on media issues to govt comms of inquiry; persuaded World Assocn of Newspapers to issue Declaration of Table Mountain at WAN annual conf., Cape Town 2007; as rep. of WAN, addressed Pan African Parl.'s Human Rights Cttee, Midrand on need to repeal "insult laws" in Africa 2011; Chair. SA Chapter Media Inst. of Southern Africa 2012–; Chair. Press Council of South Africa 2007–13; Hon. DLitt (Rhodes Univ.) 2012; Pringle Medal for services to journalism 1976, 1992, Media Freedom Award, Media Inst. of Southern Africa 2005, Wrottesley Award, South African Nat. Editors' Forum 2006, 2008, 2010, Mondi-Shanduka Newspaper Lifetime Achiever Award 2007, Vodacom Journalist of the Year Lifetime Achiever Award 2010, Award for Press Freedom Campaigning, Int. Press Inst. 2010, World Press Freedom Hero Award, Int. Press Inst. 2011. *Publications include:* Four Days in Lusaka – Whites from 'Home' in talks with the ANC 1989, Report on the media situation in South Africa (for UNESCO) 1994, narrative for Nelson Mandela, Man of Destiny – A Pictorial Biography (by Peter Magubane) 1996, Undue Restriction: Laws Impacting on Media Freedom in the SADC (ed.); numerous papers and articles on the media and press freedom. *Leisure interests:* sailing, walking, travel, wildlife. *Address:* 23 Duncombe Road, Forest Town, Johannesburg 2193, South Africa (home). *Telephone:* (11) 646-8790 (home). *Fax:* (11) 646-8790 (home). *E-mail:* rlouw@sn.apc.org (office).

LOVASZ, László, CandMathSci, Dr rer. nat, DrMathSci; Hungarian/American mathematician and computer scientist; *Professor, Mathematical Institute, Eötvös Loránd University;* b. 9 March 1948, Budapest; m.; four c.; ed Eötvös Loránd Univ., Budapest; Adjunct Prof., Univ. of Waterloo, Canada 1980–90; A.D. White Prof.-at-Large, Cornell Univ., Ithaca, NY 1982–87; John von Neumann Prof., Univ. of Bonn 1985; William K. Lanman Prof. of Computer Science and Math., Yale Univ., New Haven, Conn. 1993–2000; Sr Researcher, Theory Group, Microsoft Research, Redmond, Wash. 1999–2006; Dir Math. Inst., Eötvös Loránd Univ. 2006–11, Prof. 2011–; Pres. Int. Math. Union 2007–; Visiting Prof., Inst. for Advanced Study, Princeton, NJ 2011–12; mem. Exec. Cttee Int. Math. Union 1987–94, Abel Prize Cttee 2004–06; Ed.-in-Chief Combinatorica; Ed. 12 other journals; Corresp. mem. Hungarian Acad. of Sciences 1979 (Full mem. 1985, mem. Presidium 1990–93, 2008–), Rheinland-Westphalische Akad. der Wissenschaften 1993; mem. European Acad. of Sciences, Arts and Humanities 1981, Acadamia Europaea 1991, Deutsche Akad. der Naturforscher Leopoldina 2002, Russian Acad. of Sciences 2006. Royal Dutch Acad. of Science 2006, Royal Swedish Acad. of Sciences 2007, NAS 2012; affiliated with Budapest Semesters in Math. (programme in English for American and Canadian undergraduates); Hon. Prof., Univ. of Bonn 1984, Academia Sinica 1988; Hon. mem. London Math. Soc. 2009; Hungarian Nat. Order of Merit 1998; Dr hc (Univ. of Waterloo) 1992, (Univ. of Szeged, Hungary) 1999, (Budapest Univ. of Tech.) 2002, (Univ. of Calgary) 2006; Grünwald Geza Prize, Bolyai Soc. 1970 George Pólya Prize, Soc. for Industrial and Applied Math. 1979, Best Information Theory Paper Award, IEEE 1981, Ray D. Fulkerson Prize, American Math. Soc.-Math. Programming Soc. 1982, Hungarian State Prize 1985, Tibor Szele Medal, Bolyai Soc. 1992, Brouwer Medal, Dutch Math. Soc. 1993, Bolzano Medal, Czech Math. Soc. 1998, Wolf Prize (Israel) 1999, Knuth Prize, Asscn for Computing Machinery 1999, Corvin Chain Award (Hungary) 2001, Goedel Prize, Asscn for Computing Machinery-European Asscn for Theoretical Computer Science 2001, IEEE John von Neumann Medal 2005, John von Neumann Theory Prize, INFORMS 2006, Bolyai Prize (Hungary) 2007, Széchenyi Grand Prize (Hungary) 2008, Kyoto Prize, Inamori Foundation (co-recipient) 2010, Ray D. Fulkerson Prize, American Math. Soc.-Math. Prog. Soc. 2012. *Publications:* Combinatorial Problems and Exercises 1979, Algorithmic Theory of Numbers, Graphs, and Convexity 1986, Geometric Algorithms and Combinatorial Optimization 1993, Combinatorial Optimization: Papers from the Dimacs Special Year (co-author) 1995, Graph Theory and Combinatorial Biology (co-author) 1999, Computation Complexity (co-author) 2002, Discrete Mathematics: Elementary and Beyond (co-author) 2003, Handbook of Combinatorics (co-author) 2003, Discrete Mathematics and Computation 2004, Large Networks and Graph Limits 2012; more than 200 articles in math. journals and four monographs on discrete math., theory of computing and combinatorial optimization. *Address:* Eötvös Loránd Tudományegyetem, Számítógéptudományi Tanszék, Pázmány Péter sétány 1/C, 1117 Budapest, Hungary (office). *Telephone:* (1) 381-2183 (office); (1) 381-8083 (office). *E-mail:* lovasz@cs.elte.hu (office). *Website:* www.cs.elte.hu/~lovasz (office).

LOVE, Courtney; American rock musician, singer and actress; b. (Love Michelle Harrison), 9 July 1964, San Francisco, Calif.; d. of Hank Harrison and Linda Carroll; m. 1st James Moreland; m. 2nd Kurt Cobain (deceased); one s. one d.; began career as occasional actress and mem. of bands Faith No More and Babes in Toyland; Founding singer and guitarist, rock band Hole 1989–2002, 2010–12; solo artist 2003–. *Films:* Sid and Nancy 1986, Straight To Hell 1987, Tapeheads 1988, Basquiat 1996, Feeling Minnesota 1996, The People vs Larry Flynt 1996, 200 Cigarettes 1999, Man on the Moon 1999, Beat 2000, Julie Johnson 2001, Trapped 2002. *Recordings include:* albums with Hole: Retard Girl 1990, Pretty On The Inside 1991, Live Through This 1994, Celebrity Skin 1998; solo: America's Sweetheart 2004; singles: with Hole: Beautiful Son 1993, Doll Parts 1994, Ask for It 1995, Celebrity Skin 1998, Malibu 1998, Awful 1999; solo: Mono 2004, Nobody's Daughter 2009. *Publication:* Dirty Blonde (autobiog.) 2006. *Website:* www.courtneylove.com.

LOVE, Mike; American singer and songwriter; b. 15 March 1941, Baldwin Hills, Calif.; mem. Beach Boys 1961–; mem. own band, Endless Summer 1981; numerous tours, concerts and festival appearances; band est. Brother Records label 1967–; American Music Awards Special Award of Merit 1988, Grammy Lifetime Achievement Award 2001. *Recordings include:* albums: with The Beach Boys: Surfin' Safari 1962, Surfer Girl 1963, Little Deuce Coupe 1963, Shut Down Vol. 2, All Summer Long 1964, Christmas Album 1964, The Beach Boys Today! 1965, Summer Days (and Summer Nights) 1965, Beach Boys Party 1966, Pet Sounds 1966, Smiley Smile 1967, Wild Honey 1968, Friends 1968, 20/20 1969, Sunflower 1970, Surf's Up 1971, Carl and the Passions – So Tough 1972, Holland 1973, The Beach Boys in Concert 1973, Endless Summer 1974, 15 Big Ones 1976, The Beach Boys Love You 1977, M.I.U. 1978, LA (Light Album) 1979, Keepin' The Summer

Alive 1980, The Beach Boys 1985, Still Cruisin' 1989, Two Rooms 1991, Summer in Paradise 1992, The Sounds of Summer – The Very Best of The Beach Boys 2003, That's Why God Made the Radio 2012; solo: Looking Back With Love 1981. *Address:* c/o Elliott Lott, Boulder Creek Entertainment Corporation, 4860 San Jacinto Circle West, Fallbrook, CA 92028, USA (office); c/o Capitol Records, 1750 North Vine Street, Hollywood, CA 90028, USA. *Website:* www.thebeachboys.com.

LØVEID, Cecilie Meyer; Norwegian playwright and poet; b. 21 Aug. 1951, Mysen; d. of Erik Løveid and Ingrid Meyer; m. Bjørn H. Ianke 1978; one s. two d.; ed arts and crafts school in Bergen and studies in graphic design, theatre history and drama; mem. editorial staff, Profil (magazine) 1969; Sec. Norsk Forfattersentrum, Vestlandsardelingen 1974; Teacher, Writing Arts Centre, Bergen 1986; mem. Literary Council, Den norske Forfatterforening 1987; Prix Italia 1982, Aschehoug Prize 1984, Donbloug Prize (shared with Johannes Heggland) 1990, Ibsen Prize 1999, Gyldendal Prize 2001. *Publications:* poetry: Mørkets muligheter 1976, Fanget villrose 1977, Badehuset 1990, Mykt glass 1999, Spilt 2001, Gartnerløs 2007, Nye ritualer 2008, Svartere bunader 2010, Flytterester 2012, Straff (Punishment) 2013; prose: Most 1972, Sug 1979, Måkespisere (radio play) 1982; plays: Balansedame 1986, Maria Q. 1991, Rhindøtrene 1996, Osterrike 1998, Den riktige vind 1999, Visning 2005; children's books: Lille Pille og Lille Fille i Den dype skogs teater 1990, Hund får besøk 1992, Fars ansikt 2000. *Leisure interests:* old wooden toys, walking in the mountains, swimming. *Address:* c/o Colombine Theatre Agency, Gaffelgränd 1A, 11130 Stockholm, Sweden (office); Aller house, Elsesro 28A, 5095 Bergen, Norway (home). *Telephone:* (8) 411-70-85 (office). *E-mail:* info@colombine.se (office); cecilieloveid@gmail.com. *Website:* www .colombine.se (office); www.cecilieloveid.com.

LOVEJOY, Thomas Eugene, III, BS, PhD; American biologist, conservationist and academic; *Biodiversity Chair, H. John Heinz III Center for Science, Economics and the Environment;* b. 22 Aug. 1941, New York, NY; m. Charlotte Seymour 1966 (divorced 1978); three d.; ed Yale Univ.; has worked in Brazilian Amazon since 1965; directed conservation programme at World Wildlife Fund-US 1973–87; Asst Sec. for Environmental and External Affairs, Smithsonian Inst., Washington, DC 1987–98; apptd Counsellor to Sec. for Biodiversity and Environmental Affairs 1994; Chief Biodiversity Advisor to Pres. World Bank and Lead Specialist for Environment for Latin America and the Caribbean –2002; Sr Adviser to Pres. UN Foundation –2002; Pres. H. John Heinz III Center for Science, Econs, and the Environment 2002–08, Biodiversity Chair 2008–; Chair. Yale Inst. for Biospheric Studies; fmr Chair. US Man and Biosphere Program; Past Pres. American Inst. of Biological Sciences, Soc. for Conservation Biology; conceived idea for Minimum Critical Size of Ecosystems project (jt project between Smithsonian Inst. and Brazil's Instituto Nacional de Pesquisas da Amazônia); Fellow, AAAS, American Acad. of Arts and Sciences, American Philosophical Soc., Linnaean Soc. of London, American Ornithologists' Union; Order of Rio Branco (Brazil), Grand Cross of the Order of Scientific Merit (Brazil); Tyler Prize for Environmental Achievement 2001, Lindbergh Award 2002, BBVA Foundation Frontiers of Knowledge Award in the Ecology and Conservation Biology category (co-recipient) 2008. *Achievements include:* developed 'debt-for-nature swaps' for purchase of biologically sensitive tracts of land in debtor nations for purposes of environmental protection; has also supported Forests Now Declaration, calling for new market-based mechanisms to protect tropical forests; played key role in establishing conservation biology through First Int. Conf. on Research in Conservation Biology, La Jolla, Calif. Sept. 1978, introduced terms 'conservation biology' and 'biological diversity' to scientific community; serves on numerous scientific and conservation bds and advisory groups; drew up first projections of global extinction rates for Global 2000 Report to the President, predicted in 1980 extinction of 10%–20% of all species by 2020. *Television:* started public TV series Nature. *Publications:* numerous books and articles. *Address:* H. John Heinz III Center for Science, Economics and the Environment, 900 17th Street NW, Suite 700, Washington, DC 20006, USA (office). *Telephone:* (202) 737-6307 (office). *Fax:* (202) 737-6410 (office). *E-mail:* lovejoy@ heinzctr.org (office). *Website:* www.heinzctr.org (office).

LOVELL, Harold Earl Edmund, Jr, BA, MJ; Antiguan politician and barrister; *Minister of Finance, the Economy and Public Administration;* b. 27 Sept. 1955, St John's; ed Antigua Grammar School, Univ. of the West Indies, Thames Valley Univ., Middle Temple and Univ. of Birmingham, UK; fmr teacher, Antigua Grammar School, Antigua State Coll.; Minister of Foreign Affairs, Tourism, Int. Travel and Trade 2004–05, of Tourism, Civil Aviation, Culture and the Environment 2005–09, of Finance, the Economy and Public Admin 2009–; fmr Vice-Pres. Guild of Undergraduates, Univ. of the West Indies; fmr Gen. Sec., then Vice-Chair. Antigua Caribbean Liberation Movement; fmr Gen. Sec. Antigua and Barbuda Union of Teachers; Vice-Chair. United Progressive Party; mem. BBC Advisory Council for Leicestershire 1990–92. *Address:* Ministry of Finance and Economy, Government Office Complex, Parliament Drive, St John's, Antigua and Barbuda (office). *Telephone:* 462-5015 (office). *Fax:* 462-4860 (office). *E-mail:* minfinance@ antigua.gov.ag (office).

LOVELOCK, James Ephraim, CH, CBE, PhD, DSc, FRS; British scientist, inventor, writer and academic; *Honorary Visiting Fellow, Green College, Oxford;* b. 26 July 1919, Letchworth Garden City, Herts.; s. of Tom Arthur Lovelock and Nellie Ann Elizabeth Lovelock (née March); m. 1st Helen Mary Hyslop 1942 (died 1989); two s. two d.; m. 2nd Sandra Jean Orchard 1991; ed Strand School, Univ. of Manchester, London School of Hygiene and Tropical Medicine; staff scientist, Nat. Inst. for Medical Research, London 1941–61; Prof. of Chem., Baylor Univ. Coll. of Medicine, Tex., USA 1961–64; ind. scientist 1964–; Hon. Visiting Fellow, Green Coll., Oxford 2004–; Rockefeller Travelling Fellowship in Medicine, Harvard Univ., USA 1954; Visiting Scientist, Yale Univ. Medical School 1958–59; Visiting Prof., Univ. of Reading 1967–90; Pres. Marine Biology Asscn 1986–90; mem. Environmentalists for Nuclear Energy; Hon. DSc (Univ. of East Anglia) 1982, (Plymouth Polytechnic) 1988, (Univ. of Exeter) 1988, (Stockholm Univ.) 1991, (Univ. of Edinburgh) 1993, (Univ. of Kent) 1996, (Univ. of East London) 1996, (Univ. of Colorado) 1997; CIBA Foundation Award for Research in Ageing 1955, three NASA Certificates of Recognition for: Gas Chromatograph Interface System and Method, Vapor Phase Detectors, Combined Carrier Gas Separator and Generator for Gas Chromatography Systems 1972, Tswett Medal for Chromatography 1975, ACS Chromatography Award 1980, Stephen Dal Nogare Award 1985, Norbert Gerbier Prize, Silver Medal and Prize, Plymouth Marine Lab. 1986,

World Meteorological Asscn 1988, Dr A. H. Heineken Prize for the Environment, Royal Netherlands Acad. of Arts and Sciences 1990, Rosenstiel Award in Oceanographic Science 1990, Nonino Prize 1996, Volvo Environment Prize 1996, The Blue Planet Prize 1997, Goi Peace Prize 2000, Discovery Lifetime Award, Royal Geographical Soc. 2001, Wollaston Medal, Geological Soc. 2006. *Achievements include:* inventor of the electron capture detector (which made possible the detection of CFCs and other atmospheric nano-pollutants) and of the microwave oven; originator of the 'Gaia hypothesis' during 1960s as a result of work for NASA concerned with detecting life on Mars; hypothesis proposes that living and non-living parts of the Earth form a complex interacting system that can be thought of as a single organism; named after Greek goddess Gaia, hypothesis postulates that biosphere has a regulatory effect on the Earth's environment that acts to sustain life. *Publications:* Gaia: A New Look at Life on Earth 1979, The Great Extinction (co-author) 1983, The Greening of Mars (co-author) 1984, The Ages of Gaia 1988, Gaia: The Practical Science of Planetary Medicine 1991, Homage to Gaia: The Life of an Independent Scientist 2000, Gaia: Medicine for an Ailing Planet 2005, The Revenge of Gaia: Why the Earth is Fighting Back – and How We Can Still Save Humanity 2006, The Vanishing Face of Gaia 2009. *Leisure interests:* walking, reading novels, music. *Address:* Matthew Cottage, The Old Coastguards, Abbotsbury, Dorset, DT3 4LB, England. *Website:* www.jameslovelock.org.

LOVETT, Lyle; American singer, songwriter and actor; b. 1 Nov. 1957, Klein, Tex.; m. Julia Roberts 1993 (divorced 1995); backing singer for Nanci Griffith 1985; solo singer, songwriter 1986–; numerous TV appearances, regular tours; two Grammy Awards, four Country Music Awards. *Film appearances include:* The Player 1992, Short Cuts 1993, Prêt-à-Porter 1994, Bastard Out of Carolina 1996, Breast Men 1997, Fear and Loathing in Las Vegas 1998, The Opposite of Sex 1998, Cookie's Fortune 1999, The New Guy 2002, Three Days of Rain 2003, The Open Road 2009. *Recordings include:* albums: Lyle Lovett 1986, Pontiac 1988, Lyle Lovett and his Large Band 1989, Joshua Judges Ruth 1992, Leap of Faith (soundtrack) 1992, I Love Everybody 1994, Road to Ensenada 1996, Step Inside This House 1998, Live in Texas 1999, Can't Resist It 1999, Dr T and the Women 2000, My Baby Don't Tolerate 2003, It's Nor Large It's Big 2007, Natural Forces 2009, Release Me 2012. *Address:* Vector Management, PO Box 120479, Nashville, TN 37212, USA (office). *Telephone:* (615) 269-6600 (office). *E-mail:* info@ vectormgmt.com (office). *Website:* www.vectormgmt.com (office); www.lylelovett .com.

LOVINS, Amory B., MA, PhD, FRSA; American physicist, environmentalist and academic; *Chairman and Chief Scientist, Rocky Mountain Institute;* b. 13 Nov. 1947, Washington, DC; m. Hunter Lovins; ed Harvard Univ., Univ. of Oxford, UK; spent two years at Harvard Univ.; transferred to Univ. of Oxford; fmr spokesman for Friends of the Earth (UK); has been Regents' Lecturer in Energy and Resources and in Econs at Univ. of California; Grauer Lecturer, Univ. of British Columbia; Luce Visiting Prof., Dartmouth Coll.; Distinguished Visiting Prof., Univ. of Colorado; Oikos Visiting Prof., Business School, Univ. of St Gallen; an Eng Visiting Prof., Peking Univ.; MAP/Ming Prof., Stanford Univ. 2007; Co-founder (with his wife), Rocky Mountain Inst. (non-profit applied research centre), currently Chair. and Chief Scientist; co-f. and sold (to Financial Times Group 1999) E SOURCE (information source on advanced electric efficiency); Founder and Chair. RMI's fourth spinoff, Fiberforge, Inc. (eng firm); has briefed 19 heads of state and given expert testimony in eight countries and more than 20 states; served on US Dept of Energy's Sr Advisory Bd 1980–81, Defense Science Bd task force on mil. energy strategy 1999–2001, 2006–07; occasional adviser to Nat. Asscn of Regulatory Utility Commrs, World Business Council for Sustainable Devt, Kleiner Perkins Caufield & Byers; Fellow, AAAS 1984, World Acad. of Arts and Sciences 1988, World Business Acad. 2001; Hon. Mem. AIA 2007; Hon. Sr Fellow, Design Futures Council; 10 hon. doctorates; shared with Hunter Lovins: Mitchell Prize 1982, Right Livelihood Award 1983, Lindbergh Award 1999, Time magazine's Heroes for the Planet 2000; winner of first DELPHI Prize, Onassis Foundation 1989, MacArthur Fellowship 1993, Blue Planet Award, Shingo Prize, Jean Meyer Prize, Nissan Prize 1993, Heinz Award 1997, World Tech. Award (Environment) 1999, Happold Medal, Construction Industry Council (UK) 2000, Benjamin Franklin Medal, Royal Soc. of Arts 2005, named by The Wall Street Journal one of 39 people world-wide 'most likely to change the course of business in the '90s', honoured by Newsweek as 'one of the Western world's most influential energy thinkers', ranked by Car magazine amongst the Most Powerful People in the Global Automotive Industry (22nd), Volvo Environment Prize, Volvo Environment Foundation 2007. *Publications:* 29 books, including Soft Energy Paths: Towards a Durable Peace 1977, Non-Nuclear Futures: The Case for an Ethical Energy Strategy 1980, A Golden Thread: 2500 Years of Solar Architecture & Technology 1980, Energy/War, Breaking the Nuclear Link 1981, Least-Cost Energy: Solving the CO 2 Problem 1982, Brittle Power: Energy Strategy for National Security 1982, 2001, Energy Unbound: A Fable for America's Future 1986, Consumer Guide to Home Energy Savings 1991, Reinventing Electric Utilities: Competition, Citizen Action, and Clean Power 1996, Factor Four: Doubling Wealth – Halving Resource Use: A Report to the Club of Rome 1997, Natural Capitalism: Creating the Next Industrial Revolution 2000, Small is Profitable: The Hidden Economic Benefits of Making Electrical Resources the Right Size 2003, Winning the Oil Endgame: Innovation for Profit, Jobs and Security 2005; several hundred papers in professional journals as well as poetry, landscape photography, music (fmr pianist and composer) and an electronics patent. *Address:* Rocky Mountain Institute, 2317 Snowmass Creek Road, Snowmass, CO 81654 (office); Rocky Mountain Institute, 1820 Folsom Street, Boulder, CO 80302, USA (office). *Telephone:* (970) 927-3851 (Snowmass) (office); (303) 245-1003 (Boulder) (office). *E-mail:* info@rmi.org (office). *Website:* www.rmi.org (office); www.fiberforge.com (office).

LOVRIN, Ana, LLB; Croatian lawyer and politician; b. 2 Dec. 1953, Zagreb; m. Miodrag Lovrin; four d.; ed Faculty of Law, Univ. of Zagreb; legal officer in Tankerska plovidba, Zadar 1978–80; Man. Legal Staff, Zadar Airport 1980; mem. Zadar City Council, Zadar 1993; mem. Croatian Democratic Union (Hrvatska demokratska zajednica—HDZ) 1993–, Vice-Pres. 1999–2001, Pres. 2003–05, mem. Cen. Cttee 2002–; State Sec. of Zadar, in charge of legal affairs 1993–2001; Deputy Mayor of Zadar 2001–04, Mayor 2004–05; mem. Zadar local govt in charge of property rights and local govt matters 2005–06; Deputy in Sabor (Ass.) 2005–, Chair. Legislation Cttee, mem. Cttee for the Constitution, Rules of Procedure and Political System, Cttee for Tourism; Minister of Justice 2006–08. *Leisure interests:*

reading, classical music. *Address:* Hrvatska demokratska zajednica, 10000 Zagreb, trg Žrtava fašizma 4, Croatia (office). *Telephone:* (1) 4553000 (office). *Fax:* (1) 4552600 (office). *E-mail:* hdz@hdz.hr (office). *Website:* www.hdz.hr (office).

LOW, Tuck Kwong; Indonesian (b. Singaporean) coal mining executive; *President Commissioner, PT Bayan Resources;* b. 1948; s. of Low Sum; m.; one s. one d.; ed Japan Inst. of Energy; began working for father's building co. in Singapore; moved to Indonesia 1972; f. PT Jaya Supplies Indonesia 1973; f. PT Bayan Resources (coal mining co.) 1997, Pres. Dir 2004–08, Pres. Commr 2008–; fmr Pres. Dir PT Nirmala, PT Muji Inti Utama, PT Graha Balikpapan Pratama, PT Dinamika Energi Nusantara, PT Kaltim Kariangau Industry, PT Kariangau Power; fmr Dir Bayan Int., PT Kalimantan Citra Bara, Carbonic, Manhattan Investment Pte Ltd, Manhattan Kalimantan Investment Pte Ltd. *Address:* Bayan Resources Tbk, Floor 12, Graha Irama Building, Block X-1, HR Rasuna Said Road, Lot 1-2, Jakarta 12950, Indonesia (office). *Telephone:* (21) 5269868 (office). *Fax:* (21) 5269866 (office). *Website:* www.bayan.com.sg (office).

LOWASSA, Hon. Edward, MSc; Tanzanian politician; b. 1953; ed Univ. of Bath; Minister for Environment and Poverty 1988–2000; Man. Dir Arusha Int. Conference Centre 1989–90; Minister for Judiciary and Parliamentary Affairs 1990–93; Minister of Lands and Human Settlement Devt 1993–95; Minister of Water and Livestock Devt 2000–05; Prime Minister 2005–08 (resgnd). *Address:* c/o Office of the Prime Minister, POB 980, Dodoma, Tanzania (office).

LOWE, Hon. Douglas Ackley, AM; Australian fmr politician and administrator; b. 15 May 1942, Hobart, Tasmania; s. of Ackley Reginald Lowe and Dulcie Mary Lowe; m. Pamela June Grant 1963; two s. two d.; ed St Virgil's Coll.; worked as electrical fitter, Electrolytic Co.; State Sec. Tasmanian Section, Australian Labour Party 1965–69, State Pres. 1974–75; mem. Tasmania House of Ass. for Franklin 1969–81, Ind. 1981–86; Minister for Housing 1972–74; Chief Sec. 1974–76; Deputy Premier 1975–77; Minister for Planning and Reorganization 1975–76, for Industrial Relations 1976–79, for Planning and Environment 1976, for Health 1976–77; Premier of Tasmania 1977–81; Minister for Manpower Planning 1977–79, for Econ. Planning and Devt 1979–80, for Energy 1979, Treas. 1980–81; mem. Tasmanian Legis. Council 1986–92; Deputy Govt Leader Tasmanian Legis. Council 1989–92; Exec. Officer, Tasmanian Br., Australian Medical Asscn 1992–; Del. to Australian Constitutional Convention; State Pres., Tasmanian Swimming Inc. 1991–98, Life mem. 2000–; Queen's Silver Jubilee Medal 1977, Australian Sports Medal 2000, Centenary Medal 2000, President's Award, Australian Medical Asscn 2004. *Publications:* Directions for Future Development in Tasmania 1979, The Price of Power 1984. *Leisure interests:* swimming, tennis, fishing, football. *Address:* AMA Tasmania State Office, 147 Davey Street, Hobart, Tasmania 7000 (office); 1 Michele Court, Berriedale, Tasmania 7010, Australia (home). *Telephone:* (3) 6223-2047 (office). *Fax:* (3) 6223-6469 (office). *E-mail:* ama@amatas.com.au (office). *Website:* www.amatas.com.au (office).

LOWE, Sir Frank Budge, Kt, FRSA; British business executive; b. 23 Aug. 1941; s. of Stephen Lowe and Marion Lowe; m. Dawn Lowe 1991; two s. one d.; ed Westminster School; Man. Dir Collett Dickenson Pearce 1972–79; Founder and Chair. Lowe Agency 1981–2003 (retd), Emer. Chair. 2003–; Founder and Chair. Octagon 1997–2003; Dir Interpublic 1990–2003; Founder and Chair. The Red Brick Road 2006–09; Visiting Prof., Univ. Coll. London 1990–; The President's Award, Design and Art Dirs Asscn of London 1985. *Leisure interests:* tennis, skiing, shooting. *Address:* c/o The Red Brick Road, 50–54 Beak Street, London, W1F 9RN, England (office). *Website:* www.theredbrickroad.co.uk (office).

LOWRY, Glenn David, MA, PhD; American museum director; *Director, Museum of Modern Art;* b. 28 Sept. 1954, New York, NY; s. of Warren Lowry and Laure Lowry (née Lynn); m. Susan Chambers 1974; three s.; ed Williams Coll., Harvard Univ.; Asst Curator Fogg Art Museum, Harvard Univ. 1978–80; research asst in archaeological survey, Amalfi, Italy 1980; Curator (Oriental art) Museum of Art, Providence, RI 1981–82; Dir Joseph and Margaret Muscarelle Museum of Art, Williamsburg, Va 1982–84; Curator (Near Eastern Art) Freer Gallery, Smithsonian Inst., Washington 1984–90, Curatorial Co-ordinator 1987–89; Dir Art Gallery of Ont., Toronto 1990–95; Dir Museum of Modern Art, New York 1995–; Fellow, American Acad. of Arts and Sciences 2006; Chevalier, Ordre des Arts et des Lettres 1994, Officier 2004; Chevalier, Ordre nat. du Mérite 2000; Hon. DFA (Pennsylvania Acad. of Fine Arts) 2000, hon. degrees from Coll. of William and Mary 2009, Pratt Univ. 2010; Karl E. Weston Prize for Distinction in the Arts, Williams Coll. 1976, Travel Award, Inst. of Turkish Studies 1988, Scholarly Studies Award, Smithsonian Inst. 1990, Bicentennial Medal, Williams Coll. 2005;. *Publications include:* Fatehpursikri: A Source Book 1985, Akbar's India: Art from the Mughal City of Victory 1986, From Concept to Context: Approaches to Asian and Islamic Calligraphy 1986, Asian Art in the Arthur M. Sackler Gallery: The Inaugural Gift 1987, Jeweler's Eye: Islamic Arts of the Book from the Vever Collection 1988, Timur and the Princely Vision: Persian Art and Culture in the Fifteenth Century (Special Exhibitions Fund Award 1987) 1989, Governor Nelson A. Rockefeller Empire State Plaza Art Collection and Plaza Memorials 2002, (Introduction for) Duveen: The Story of the Most Spectacular Art Dealer of All Time 2003, Whose Muse?: Art Museums and the Public Trust 2003, The Museum of Modern Art in this Century 2009, Oil and Sugar: Contemporary Art and Islamic Culture 2009, Abodes of the Muses: Theorising the Modern Art Museum 2011, Design for the New Museum of Modern Art 2004; articles in ARTnews and The Economist. *Address:* Museum of Modern Art, 11 West 53rd Street, New York, NY 10019-5498, USA (office). *Website:* www.moma.org (office).

LOWY, Frank, AC; Australian business executive; *Chairman, Westfield Group;* b. 22 Oct. 1930, Czechoslovakia; m.; three s.; spent World War II years in Budapest, then moved to Palestine where he fought in underground Zionist army Haganah; immigrated to Australia 1952; Co-founder and Exec. Chair. Westfield Group (shopping centre co.) 1959–11, Chair. (non-exec. 2011–); Founder and Chair. Lowy Inst. for Int. Policy; mem. Int. Advisory Council, Brookings Inst.; Chair. Football Fed. Australia; fmr Pres. Art Gallery of New South Wales; mem. Bd of Dirs Reserve Bank of Australia 1995–2005; Dir Daily Mail and General Trust, UK; Dr hc (Univ. of New South Wales), (Tel-Aviv Univ.); Australian Grad. School of Man. Financial Times Global Business Leader Award 2005, Woodrow Wilson Award for Corp. Citizenship, Woodrow Wilson Int. Center for Scholars 2005, Henni Friedlander Award for the Common Good, Bowdoin Coll. 2007. *Address:* Westfield

Group, Westfield Towers, 100 William Street, Sydney 2011, Australia (office). *Telephone:* (2) 9358-7000 (office). *Fax:* (2) 9358-7079 (office). *Website:* www.westfield.com (office).

LOZOYA AUSTIN, Emilio Ricardo, BA (Econ), LLB, MPA; Mexican business executive; *CEO, Petróleos Mexicanos (PEMEX);* ed Instituto Tecnológico Autónomo de México (ITAM) and Universidad Nacional Autónoma de México, Mexico City, Harvard Univ., USA; analyst, office in charge of investing int. reserves in securities, Banco de México (Cen. Bank of Mexico) 1999–2001; mem. of several bds of dirs of cos in the infrastructure, concessions, financial and information tech. sectors, as well as of Qualitas Asscn 2003–06; Investment Officer, Inter-American Investment Corpn 2006–10; Dir and Head of Latin America, World Econ. Forum 2010–12; Exec. Dir and Co-founder JFH SA investment fund; responsible for int. affairs during the transition period of elected Pres. Enrique Peña Nieto 2012; CEO Petróleos Mexicanos (PEMEX) 2012–. *Address:* Petróleos Mexicanos (PEMEX), Avenida Marina Nacional 329, Col. Huasteca, 11311 México DF, Mexico (office). *Telephone:* (55) 1944-2500 (office). *Fax:* (55) 5531-6354 (office). *Website:* www.pemex.com (office).

LOZANČIĆ, Niko; Bosnia and Herzegovina politician and lawyer; b. 1957, Kakanj; mem. Croatian Democratic Union (HDZ), Leader 2001, Vice-Pres. 2001–; fmr municipal councillor, mem. House of Peoples and state-level House of Reps; Pres. Fed. of Bosnia and Herzegovina 2003–07. *Address:* c/o Office of the President, 71000 Sarajevo, Bosnia and Herzegovina (office).

LOZI, Salem al-; Sudanese international organization executive; *Director-General, Arab Organization for Agricultural Development;* fmr Dir-Gen. Agricultural Marketing Org.; currently Dir-Gen. Arab Org. for Agricultural Devt, Khartoum, Sudan. *Address:* Arab Organization for Agricultural Development, 7 al-Amarat Street, PO Box 474, Khartoum 11111, Sudan (office). *Telephone:* (1) 83472176 (office). *Fax:* (1) 83471402 (office). *E-mail:* info@aoad.org (office). *Website:* www.aoad.org (office).

LU, (Hsiu-lien) Annette; Taiwanese fmr politician; b. 7 June 1944, Taoyuan; ed Taiwan Prov. Taipei First Girls' High School, Nat. Taiwan Univ., Univ. of Illinois and Harvard Univ., USA; fmr Sr Specialist, Section Chief Exec. Law and Regulations Cttee of Exec. Yuan; participated in street demonstrations; sentenced to twelve years' imprisonment 1979, released after five years and four months on medical parole; f. North American Taiwanese Women's Asscn, Clean Election Coalition 1985–90; organized and led Alliance for the Promotion of UN Membership for Taiwan 1991; fmr mem. Legis. Yuan for Taoyuan (Democratic Progressive Party), mem. Foreign Affairs Cttee 1992–95; Nat. Policy Adviser to Pres. 1996; Magistrate for Taoyuan Co. 1996–99; Vice-Pres. of Taiwan 2000–08; Chair. Third Global Summit of Women, Taiwan 1994; f. Centre for Women's and Children's Safety; World Peace Prize 2001. *Publications:* novels: These Three Women, Empathy; non-fiction: New Feminism, I Love Taiwan, Viewing Taiwan from Abroad, Retrying the Formosa Case. *Address:* c/o Democratic Progressive Party, 10/F, 30 Beiping East Road, Taipei 10051, Taiwan.

LU, Daopei; Chinese medical scientist; b. Oct. 1931, Shanghai; ed Tongji Medical Coll.; doctor, Doctor-in-Charge, Chief Doctor, Prof. and Dir of Internal Medicine, People's Hosp. of Beijing Medical Coll. 1955–; Dir Blood Disease Research Inst., Beijing Medical Univ. of China; joined Chinese Peasants and Workers Democratic Party 1992, Chair. Beijing Municipal Cttee 1992–; Vice-Chair. CPPCC Beijing Municipal Cttee 1998–, mem. Standing Cttee 9th CPPCC Nat. Cttee 1998–2003; f. Daopei Hospitals Group; Vice-Chair. Chinese Medical Soc.; mem. Int. Bd of Marrow Transplantation Registration 1995–; Fellow, Chinese Acad. of Eng 1996–; initiator of bone-marrow transplants in China; Scientific and Technological Progress Award, Ho Leung Ho Lee Foundation 1997, Chen Jia-gen Prize for Promotion in Medicine & Pharmacy 1997, Tan Kah Kee Prize. *Address:* Beijing Medical University, 42 Bei Lishi Lu, Beijing 100044, People's Republic of China (office). *Telephone:* (10) 68314422 (office).

LU, Gongxun; Chinese party official; *Chairman, Standing Committee, Shanxi Provincial People's Congress;* b. 1933, Shuozhou City, Shanxi Prov.; joined CCP 1950; worker, Org. Dept, CCP Yanbei Prefectural Cttee, Shanxi Prov. 1956–57; Deputy Dir, Rural Work Dept, Shuoxian Co., Shanxi Prov. 1957–65; Deputy Sec. CCP Youyu Co. Cttee, Shanxi Prov. 1965–70; Deputy Sec. CCP Zuoyun Co. Cttee, Shanxi Prov. 1970–82, Sec. 1982–83; Head, Org. Dept, CCP Shanxi Prov. Cttee 1983–89; mem. Standing Cttee, CCP Shuozhou City Cttee, Shanxi Prov. 1983–89, Deputy Sec. 1988–93; Pres. Party School, CCP Shanxi Prov. Committee 1988–93; Chair. Standing Cttee of People's Congress, Shanxi Prov. 1993–; Alt. mem. 12th CCP Cen. Cttee 1982–87, 13th Cen. Cttee 1987–92; Del., 14th CCP Nat. Congress 1992–97, 15th CCP Nat. Congress 1997–2002; Deputy, 8th NPC 1993–98, 9th NPC 1998–2003. *Address:* Shanxi Provincial Chinese Communist Party, Taiyuan, Shanxi, People's Republic of China (office).

LU, Guanqiu; Chinese business executive; *Chairman, Wanxiang Group;* b. Dec. 1944, Xiaoshan, Zhejiang Prov.; m. Zhang Jinmei; Founder, Ningwei Commune Farm Machinery Plant 1969; Founder and Pres. Hangzhou Wanxiang Group (producer and exporter of cardan joints) –2003, currently Chair.; Del., 13th CCP Nat. Congress 1987–92, 14th CCP Nat. Congress 1992–97, Deputy 9th NPC 1998–2003. *Address:* Wanxiang Group, Wang Xiang Road, Xiao Shan District, Hangzhou, Zhejiang Province, 311215, People's Republic of China (office). *Telephone:* (571) 82832999 (office). *Fax:* (571) 82602132 (office). *Website:* www.wanxiang.com (office).

LU, Hao; Chinese politician; b. April 1947, Changli, Hebei Prov.; ed Shenyang School of Chemical Eng, Dalian Eng Coll., Lanzhou Univ.; technician, Research Inst., Group Army, PLA Services and Arms 1968–71; technician, No. 5266 Factory 1971–78, Personnel Sec. 1971–75; joined CCP 1981; teaching asst, political tutor, Lanzhou Univ. 1982; Deputy Dir then Dir, Gen. Office of CCP Gansu Prov. Cttee (Sec. Div.) 1982–85; Deputy Dir then Dir Org. Dept of CCP Gansu Prov. 1985–96; Sec. CCP Lanzhou City Cttee, Gansu Prov. 1996–2000; Gov. Gansu Prov. 2001–06; Deputy Sec. CCP Gansu Prov. Cttee 2002–; Deputy Dir, NPC Foreign Affairs Cttee 2011–; Alt. mem. 15th CCP Cen. Cttee 1997–2002, mem. 16th CCP Cen. Cttee 2002–07, 17th CCP Cen. Cttee 2007–12. *Address:* Foreign Affairs Committee, National People's Congress, Beijing, People's Republic of China (office).

LU, Lay Sreng; Cambodian politician; *Deputy Prime Minister and Minister of Rural Development;* b. 10 March 1937; ed California State Univ., Long Beach, USA; mem. resistance movt against Vietnamese occupation of Cambodia 1982–91; Minister of Information 1993–2003, Deputy Prime Minister and Minister of Rural Devt 2003–; First Vice-Pres. United Nat. Front for an Ind., Neutral, Peaceful and Co-operative Cambodia Party (Funcinpec). *Address:* Ministry of Rural Development, Jok Dimitrov, cnr rue 169, Phnom-Penh, Cambodia (office). *Telephone:* (23) 880007 (office). *E-mail:* mrd@cambodia.gov.kh (office). *Website:* www.mrd.gov.kh (office).

LU, Liangshu; Chinese agronomist; b. 3 Nov. 1924, Shanghai; s. of Lu Zezhi and Hu Lian; m. Yin Xueli 1950; three s.; deputy to 3rd NPC 1965, 5th NPC 1978; Deputy to 13th CCP 1988; Deputy Dir Science and Tech. Committee, Ministry of Agric. 1983; Pres. Chinese Acad. of Agricultural Sciences 1982–87; Pres. Chinese Assn of Agricultural Science Socs 1982–92, now Hon. Pres.; mem. Chinese Acad. of Eng (Vice-Pres. 1994). *Publications:* Food Composition and Development Strategy in China, Compilation on China's Agricultural Devt Strategy and the Progress of Science and Tech. *Leisure interests:* swimming, music. *Address:* Chinese Academy of Agricultural Sciences, 30 Baishiqiao Road, Beijing 100081, People's Republic of China (office). *Telephone:* (10) 68975516 (office). *Fax:* (10) 62174142 (office). *E-mail:* xujm@mail.caas.net.cn (office).

LU, Peijian; Chinese banking executive (retd); b. Aug. 1928, Hongze Co., Jiangsu Prov.; m. Sheng Lixia 1985; three c.; joined CCP 1944, New 4th Army 1944; accountant, Cen. China and E China Mil. Commands 1944–49; Section Chief, later Div. Chief, later Deputy Dir Gen. Office, Ministry of Finance 1949–78, Vice-Minister of Finance 1978–82; Pres. People's Bank of China 1982–85; Auditor-Gen. Nat. Audit Office of China 1985–94; Chair. Governing Bd ASOSAI (Asian Org. of Supreme Audit Insts) 1991–94; Chair. Bd of Supervisors, China Devt Bank 1994–2008; mem. 12th CCP Cen. Cttee 1982–87, 13th CCP Cen. Cttee 1987–92, 14th CCP Cen. Cttee 1992–97; mem. Standing Cttee 9th CPPCC Nat. Cttee 1998–2003. *Address:* c/o China Development Bank, No. 29 Fuchengmenwai Street, Xicheng District, Beijing 100037, People's Republic of China (office).

LU, Ping; Chinese civil servant; b. 7 Oct. 1927, Shanghai; m. Xi Liang 1949; one s. one d.; ed St John's Univ., Shanghai; Deputy Dir of Hong Kong and Macao Affairs Office, State Council 1987–90, Dir 1990–97; mem. 14th CCP Cen. Cttee 1992–97; Del. 15th CCP Nat. Congress; Vice-Chair. Preparatory Working Cttee for the Hong Kong Special Admin. Region 1993–95, Sec.-Gen. 1995; Dir Hong Kong Govt Admin. Dept 1994–97; Vice-Chair. China Welfare Inst. 1998–. *Address:* China Welfare Institute, Beijing, People's Republic of China (office).

LU, Qihui; Chinese sculptor; *Professor, Shanghai Oil Painting and Sculpture Institute;* b. 8 April 1936, Shanghai; d. of Ren Jin; m. Fang Zengxian 1960; one s. one d.; ed Sculpture Dept, Cen. Art Acad., E China Branch 1955–61; teacher, Shanghai Art College 1961–65; professional sculptor, Shanghai Oil Painting and Sculpture Inst. 1965–, Prof. 1988–; mem. Chinese Artists' Assn. *Works include:* Transplanting rice seedlings, workers group statues, Nat. Industrial Exhibition 1960, Statue of Child Labourers 1974, Sculpture for Chairman Mao Memorial Hall 1977, Statue of Lu Xun 1979, Angrily Seeking Verses against Reign of Terror 1980, Plateau in the Morning Sun 1986, Bada, an ancient Chinese Artist 1987 (exhibited New York in Contemporary Oil Painting from the PRC), The Emotion at Plateau 1989, Zhang Zhong-Jingi a Pioneer of Chinese Medical Science 1990 (bronze), Song Jie-Cai Rang of a Tibetan 1990 (stone), Hawk-dancing 1991 (statue), Wang Ge-Ji memorial (bronze) 1992, Magic painter Mar-Lang (bronze) 1993, Wu Chan-Shu memorial (bronze), one for Shanghai Memorial Hall 1994, one for Japanese Fakuoka 1995, Xia-Qiu-Son (bronze) 1995, Balzac Memorial (bronze), Garden of Famous People, Shanghai 1996, Sampan (bronze), for Shanghai Stadium 1997, Wu Fu-Zhi memorial (bronze) 1998, The Sound of Spring (forging) 2001, Liu Kai-Qu memorial (bronze) 2004. *Leisure interests:* Chinese painting, sport. *Address:* 278, 333 Alley, Chang-Dong Road, Xin-Qiao Town, Song Jiang, Shanghai, People's Republic of China (home). *Telephone:* (21) 67644032 (home).

LU, Qikeng; Chinese mathematician; b. 17 May 1927, Fushan City, Guangdong Prov.; m. Mulan Zhang 1962; one s. one d.; ed Zhongshan Univ.; Research Fellow, Math. Inst. Academia Sinica 1978–; Deputy Dir of Math. Inst. 1981–83; Research Prof., Shantou Univ. 1994–; mem. Dept Math. and Physics, Academia Sinica 1980–92, Chinese Math. Soc. 1952–, Chinese Acad. of Sciences 1980–, American Math Soc. 1992–, AAAS 1996–, New York Acad. of Sciences 1997–; Hua Loo Keng Prize 1992. *Publications:* Introduction to Several Complex Variables 1961, Differential Geometry and its Application to Physics 1983, The Classical Manifolds and Classical Domains 1994, New Results of Classical Manifolds and Classical Domains 1997. *Leisure interest:* classical music. *Address:* Institute of Mathematics, Shantou University, Beijing 515063, People's Republic of China (office). *Telephone:* (10) 6254-1841 (office); (10) 6255-5142 (home). *Fax:* (10) 6256-8356.

LU, Qizhou; Chinese engineer and business executive; *President and General Manager, China Power Investment Corporation;* fmr Vice-Gen. Man. and Party mem., Jiangsu Electric Power (co-ed.); later Vice-Gen. Man. State Grid; mem. Bd State Nuclear Power Technology Corpn; President, Gen. Man. and Party mem., China Power Investment Group Corporation. *Address:* China Power Investment Corporation, Building 3, 28 Financial Street, PO Box 2201, Xicheng District, Beijing 100140, People's Republic of China (office). *Telephone:* (10) 66298000 (office). *Fax:* (10) 66298095 (office). *E-mail:* info@cpicorp.com.cn (office). *Website:* www.cpicorp.com.cn (office).

LU, Rongjing; Chinese politician; b. 1933, Lujiang Co., Anhui Prov.; joined CCP 1954; Dir Tongguanshan Mine, Anhui Prov. 1968–76 (Sec. CCP Party Cttee 1968–76); fmr Deputy Sec. CCP Tongling City Cttee and Ma'anshan City Cttee, Anhui Prov.; Deputy Dir Industrial and Communications Office, Anhui Prov. 1978, Prov. Econ. Cttee 1979; Head, Org. Dept, CCP Anhui Prov. Cttee 1983–84, Deputy Sec. CCP Anhui Prov. Cttee 1985–88, Sec. 1988–98; Vice-Gov. Anhui Prov. 1987, Acting Gov. 1987–93; Chair. CPPCC Anhui Prov. Cttee 1996; mem. 13th CCP Cen. Cttee 1987–92, 14th CCP Cen. Cttee 1992–97, 15th CCP Cen. Cttee 1997–2002. *Address:* c/o Anhui Provincial Government, 1 Changjang Road, Hefei City, Anhui Province, People's Republic of China (office).

LU, Ruihua, MA; Chinese politician; b. Nov. 1938, Chaozhou City, Guangdong Prov.; ed Zhongshan Univ., Guangdong Prov.; joined CCP 1972; fmrly engineer,

Deputy Dir, Dir Foshan Analytical Instrument Factory; fmrly Mayor of Foshan, Vice-Chair. Foshan City Econ. Cttee, mem. Standing Cttee CCP Guangdong Prov. Cttee, mem. then Deputy Sec. Standing Cttee CCP Foshan City Cttee; Vice-Gov. Guangdong Prov. 1991–96, Gov. 1996–2003; Deputy Sec. CCP Guangdong Prov. Cttee 1996– (mem. Standing Cttee 2002–); Alt. mem. 14th CCP Cen. Cttee 1992–97, mem. 15th CCP Cen. Cttee 1997–2002; Deputy 7th NPC 1988–93, 8th NPC 1993–98, 9th NPC 1998–2003. *Address:* c/o People's Government of Guangdong, Guangzhou, Guangdong Province, People's Republic of China (office).

LU, Shengrong; Chinese sports official; b. 1940, Beijing; ed Beijing Foreign Languages Inst.; Vice-Pres. Int. Badminton Fed. 1984–93, Pres. 1993–2001; Chair. Int. Badminton Council; mem. IOC 1996–. *Address:* c/o State General Bureau for Physical Culture and Sports, 9 Tiyuguan Road, Chongwen District, Beijing, People's Republic of China.

LU, Shengzhong, MA; Chinese artist; b. 4 Jan. 1952, Pingdu Co., Shandong Prov.; s. of Lu Wanjin and Jiang Yongzhen; m. Liu Guangjun 1980; one s.; ed Cen. Acad. of Fine Arts; specializes in Chinese folk arts; Instructor at Cen. Acad. of Fine Arts; Deputy Sec.-Gen. Chinese Assn of Fine Artists. *Works include:* When Heaven and Earth are in Harmony, All Living Things, Thrive, Life, Solitary Walking, Magic and Acrobatics. *Publications include:* Chinese Folk Papercut, Chinese Folk New Year Paintings, Arts from My Mother, Solitary Walk on the Holy Road, Outline of Chinese Folk Woodcut Print, Words of Calling the Souls. *Address:* Central Academy of Fine Arts, No.8 Hua Jia Di Nan St., Chao Yang District, Beijing 100102, People's Republic of China (office). *Website:* www.cafa.edu .cn (office).

LU, Shih-Peng, BA; Taiwanese historian and academic; b. 16 Sept. 1928, Kao-yu, Chiang Su; s. of the late Lu Chun-tai and Lu Chia Chu-yin; m. Julia Wei-chun; one s. one d.; ed Nat. Taiwan Univ., Taipei, Harvard Univ., USA; Teaching Asst, Nat. Taiwan Univ., Taipei 1953–55; Research Asst, Academia Sinica, Taipei 1955–58; Lecturer, Tunghai Univ., Taichung 1958–63, Assoc. Prof. 1963–67, Prof. of History 1967–, Dir Evening School 1972–81, Chair. Dept of History 1981–87, Dean Coll. of Arts 1988–94; Visiting Scholar, Harvard Univ. 1961–63; Outstanding Youth, China Youth Corps 1952; Outstanding Prof., Ministry of Educ. 1992. *Publications:* Vietnam during the period of Chinese Rule 1964, The Modern History of China 1979, The Contemporary History of China 1992. *Address:* Tunghai University, 181 Tunghai Harbour Road, Sec. 3, Taichung, Taiwan (office). *Telephone:* (4) 3590121 (office). *Fax:* (4) 3590361 (office). *E-mail:* kpwang@mail.thu.edu.tw (office).

LU, Shumin; Chinese diplomatist; *Commissioner, Ministry of Foreign Affairs, Macao Special Administrative Region;* b. 24 Feb. 1950, Xi'an, Shanxi Province; m. Gao Shuqing; one d.; staff mem. Dept of N American and Oceanian Affairs, Ministry of Foreign Affairs 1976–77, Embassy in Canada 1977–79, Diplomatic Personnel Services Bureau, Beijing 1979–85; Third Sec., Embassy in Australia 1985; Second Sec. –1989; various staff positions at Ministry of Foreign Affairs including Deputy Div. Chief, Div. Chief, Counsellor –1993, Deputy Dir-Gen 1993–94, Counsellor, Embassy in USA 1994, Minister Counsellor –1998; Dir-Gen 1998–2002; Amb. to Indonesia 2002–05, to Canada 2005–08; Commr of Ministry of Foreign Affairs, Macao Special Admin. Region 2008–. *Address:* Office of the Commissioner of the Ministry of Foreign Affairs of the People's Republic of China, Macao Special Administrative Region, People's Republic of China (office). *E-mail:* fmco_mo@mfa.gov.cn (office). *Website:* www.fmcoprc.gov.mo (office).

LU, Yimin, BSc, MPA; Chinese engineer and business executive; *President and Vice-Chairman, China United Network Communications Group Company Limited (China Unicom);* ed Shanghai Jiao Tong Univ., John F. Kennedy School of Govt, Harvard Univ., USA; fmr mem. Sec. Bureau of Gen. Office of CCP Cen. Cttee, served as Deputy Dir and Dir Information Processing Office 1992–2001, Sec. at Deputy Dir-Gen. level 2001–05, Sec. at Dir-Gen. level 2005–07; Sr Man. and Exec. Dir, China Netcom Group Corpn (Hong Kong) Ltd (acquired by China Unicom 2008) 2007–09, Pres., Vice-Chair. and Deputy Sec. Party Leadership Group, China United Network Communications Group Co. Ltd (China Unicom) 2009–, mem. Bd of Dirs Nov. 2009–; Dir and Pres. A Share Co., CUCL; Dir (non-exec.) PCCW Ltd 2008–. *Address:* China Unicom Ltd 75th Floor, The Center, 99 Queen's Road Central, Hong Kong Special Administrative Region (office); China United Telecommunications Corpn Ltd, No. 133A, Xidan North Street, Xicheng District, Beijing 100032 (office); China United Telecommunications Corpn Ltd, 29/F, Lian Tong Tower, 1033 Chang Ning Road, Shanghai 200050, People's Republic of China (office). *Telephone:* 2126-2018 (Hong Kong) (office); (10) 66505588 (Beijing) (office); (21) 52732228 (Shanghai) (office). *Fax:* 2126-2016 (Hong Kong) (office); (21) 52732220 (Shanghai) (office). *E-mail:* info@chinaunicom.com.hk (office). *Website:* eng.chinaunicom.com (office); www.chinaunicom.com.hk (office); www .chinaunicom-a.com (office); www.chinaunicom.com.cn (office).

LU, Yongxiang; Chinese university professor and government official; *President, Chinese Academy of Sciences;* b. 28 April 1942, Ningbo City, Zhejiang Prov.; s. of Lu Zhau and Lee Feng; m. Diao Linlin 1966; one s. one d.; ed Zhejiang Univ., Tech. Univ. of Aachen, Germany; Asst Lecturer, Dept of Mechanical Eng, Zhejiang Univ. 1964–79, Assoc. Prof. 1981–83, Full Prof., Dir Inst. of Fluid Power Transmission and Control 1981–, Vice-Pres. Inst. of Science and Tech. 1985–88, Pres. and Deputy Dir 1988–95; Academician, Chinese Acad. of Sciences 1991, Vice-Pres. 1993–97, Pres. 1997–, mem. 4th Presidium of Depts 2000–; Vice-Chair. China Asscn for Science and Tech. 1986–96; mem. Academic Degrees Comm. of State Council 1986– (Vice-Chair. 1999), State Steering Group of Science, Tech. and Educ. 1998; mem. Third World Acad. of Sciences 1990 (Vice-Pres. 1998–), Chinese Acad. of Eng 1993, Nat. Natural Sciences Foundation of China; Del. NPC 1983–91; joined CCP 1964; mem. 14th CCP Cen. Cttee 1992–97, 15th CCP Cen. Cttee 1997–2002, 16th CCP Cen. Cttee 2002–07, 17th CCP Cen. Cttee 2007–12; Vice-Chair. 10th NPC Standing Cttee 2003–08, 11th NPC Standing Cttee 2008–13; Vice-Pres. First Council, China Overseas Friendship Assn 1997; Foreign mem. German Acad. of Natural Scientists Leopoldina 2005, Russian Acad. of Sciences 2006; Hon. DEng (The Hong Kong Univ. of Science and Tech.) 1996; Second Prize for Nat. Invention 1988, Third Prize 1989, Higher Eng Educ. Prize of Nation 1989, Gao Hua Super Prize 1993, Rudolf Diesel Gold Medal (Germany) 1997, Abdus Salam Medal, Acad. of Sciences for the Developing World 2006, Max-Planck-Gesellschaft Harnack-Medaille (Germany) 2006, and many other awards and prizes. *Publications:* Electrohydraulic Proportional Technique 1988; more than

160 published papers and over 20 patents. *Leisure interests:* model aeroplanes, playing football. *Address:* Chinese Academy of Sciences, 52 Sanlihe Road, Beijing 100864, People's Republic of China (office). *Telephone:* (10) 68597289 (office). *Fax:* (10) 68512458 (office). *E-mail:* engach@mail.cae.ac.cn (office). *Website:* english.cas .ac.cn (office).

LU, Youmei; Chinese hydraulic engineer; *Honorary Chairman, Chinese National Committee on Large Dams;* b. 1934, Taicang Co., Jiangsu Prov.; ed Hwa-Tung Water Resource Inst. (now Hohai Univ.); mem. CCP 1956–; engineer, Bureau for Construction of Liujia Gorge Hydropower Station of Yellow River –1970; posts in various bureaux of Ministry of Water Conservancy and Electric Power 1978–84; Vice-Minister of Water Conservancy and Electric Power 1984–88; Vice-Minister, Ministry of Energy Resources 1988–93; Pres. China Yangtze Three Gorges Project Construction; Vice Chair. Three Gorges Project Construction Cttee 1993–; Prof., Tsinghua Univ. and Hohai Univ.; fmr Chair. Chinese Nat. Cttee on Large Dams (CHINCOLD), currently Hon. Chair.; mem. Chinese Acad. of Engineering 2003–. *Address:* Chinese National Committee on Large Dams, No. 20 West Chegongzhuang Road, POB 366, Beijing 100044, People's Republic of China (office). *E-mail:* chincold@iwhr.com (office). *Website:* www.chincold.org.cn (office).

LU, Zhaoxi (Jonathan); Chinese business executive; *CEO, Alibaba Group;* b. 1969, Guangzhou; ed Guangzhou Univ.; began career in hotel industry, working as lobby man., room man. and restaurant man. –1997; joined Alibaba e-commerce group 2000, leading roles in several key divs including Dir Alibaba South China Sales Region 2000–04, Pres. Alipay (online payment service) 2004–08, Gen. Man. Taobao (online marketplace) 2008, CEO 2010, Chief Data Officer Aliyun (mobile operating service) and Head, Alibaba.com (business-to-business e-commerce platform) 2011, CEO Alibaba Group 2013–. *Address:* Alibaba.com, 6th Floor Chuangye Mansion, East Software Park, No. 99 Huaxing Road, Hangzou, Zhejiang Province, 310012 (office). Alibaba.com Technology Corpn Ltd, Room 408, Fanli Building, 22 Chaoyangwai Street, Chaoyang District, Beijing, 100020, People's Republic of China (office). *Telephone:* (571) 85022088 (Hangzhou) (office); (10) 6588-9698 (office). *Fax:* (571) 88157866 (Hangzhou) (office); (10) 6588-9699 (office). *Website:* www.alibaba.com (office).

LUBBERS, Ruud (Rudolphus) Frans Marie; Dutch politician and international organization official; b. 7 May 1939, Rotterdam; s. of Paulus J. Lubbers and Wilhelmine K. Van Laack; m. Maria E. J. Hoogeweegen 1962; two s. one d.; ed Erasmus Univ., Rotterdam; Sec. to Man. Bd, Lubbers Hollandia Eng Works 1963–65, Co-Dir 1965; mem. Bd Netherlands Christian Employers' Fed., Fed. of Mechanical and Electrical Eng Industries; mem. Programmes Advisory Council of Catholic Broadcasting Asscn; Minister of Econ. Affairs 1973–77; mem. Christian Democratic Appeal 1977, Parl. Leader 1978; mem. Second Chamber of States-Gen. (Parl.) 1977–2000; Prime Minister of the Netherlands 1982–94; Hon. Minister of State; taught Globalization Studies at Tilburg Univ. and John F. Kennedy School of Govt, Harvard Univ., USA 1995–2000; Chair. Globus, the Inst. for Globalization and Devt, Tilburg 1995–2000, now Hon. Chair.; Vice-Chair. Ind. World Comm. on the Oceans 1995–2000; UN High Commr for Refugees 2000–05 (resgnd); Dr hc (Radboud Univ., Nijmegen) 2004. *Address:* c/o Globus, Tilburg University, Warandelaan 2, Building E, PO Box 90153, 5000 LE Tilburg, Netherlands.

LUBCHENCO, Jane, BA, MS, PhD; American environmental scientist, academic and government official; *Mimi and Peter E. Haas Distinguished Visitor, Haas Center for Public Service, Stanford University;* b. 4 Dec. 1947, Denver; m.; two c.; ed Colorado Coll., Univ. of Washington, Harvard Univ.; Asst Prof. of Ecology, Harvard Univ. 1975–77; Research Assoc. Smithsonian Inst. 1978–84; Asst Prof., Oregon State Univ. 1977–82, Assoc. Prof. 1982–88, Prof. of Zoology 1988–, Distinguished Prof. of Zoology 1993–, Wayne and Gladys Valley Prof. of Marine Biology 1995–2008; US Under-Sec. of Commerce for Oceans and Atmosphere and Admin. Nat. Oceanic and Atmospheric Admin, Washington, DC 2009–13; Mimi and Peter E. Haas Distinguished Visitor, Haas Center for Public Service, Stanford Univ. 2013–; Fellow, AAAS, Pres. 1997–98, Ed.-in-Chief Science 1999–2000; Pres. Ecological Soc. of America 1992–94; mem. Bd of Trustees David and Lucile Packard Foundation, Environmental Defense, Monterey Bay Aquarium 2001–04, Trustee Emer. 2004–; Commr Pew Oceans Comm.; mem. Bd of Dirs Royal Swedish Acad. of Sciences' Beijer Inst. of Environmental Econs; mem. NAS 1996–, American Acad. of Arts and Sciences, American Philosophical Soc., Nat. Science Bd; MacArthur Fellow and Pew Scholar in Conservation and the Environment; Pres. ICSU 2001–05; Founder and Co-Chair. Aldo Leopold Leadership Program; Dr hc (Drexel Univ.) 1992, (Colorado Coll.) 1993, (Bates Coll.) 1997, (Unity Coll.) 1998, (Southampton Coll.) 1999, (Long Island Univ.) 1999, (Princeton Univ.) 2001, (Plymouth State Coll.) 2002, (Michigan State Univ.) 2003; numerous awards, including Scientist of the Year, Oregon Acad. of Sciences and American Philosophical Asscn 1994, David B. Stone Award 1999, Golden Plate Award 2001, Howard Vollun Award 2001, Heinz Award in the Environment 2002, Ed Ricketts Memorial Award, Monterey Bay Nat. Marine Sanctuary 2002, Nierenberg Prize for Science in the Public Interest, Scripps Inst. of Oceanography 2003, Distinguished Service Award, Soc. for Conservation Biology 2003, Distinguished Scientist Award, American Inst. of Biological Sciences 2004, Environmental Law Inst. Award 2004, Zayed Int. Prize for the Environment (Category 2) 2008. *Publications include:* 50 publs on ecology, biodiversity, climate change, sustainability science and the state of the oceans. *Address:* Haas Center for Public Service, Stanford University, 562 Salvatierra Walk, Stanford, CA 94305, USA (office). *Telephone:* (650) 723–0992 (office). *Website:* studentaffairs.stanford.edu/haas (office).

LUBIMOV, Alexey Borisovich; Russian pianist and academic; *Professor, Moscow Conservatory;* b. 16 Sept. 1944, Moscow; m. Aza Lubimova; one d.; ed Moscow State Conservatory; soloist, chamber musician, pianist, harpsichordist, organist; organizer and artistic dir of chamber ensembles and festivals of experimental character; well-known performer on historical keyboard instruments 1980–; teacher, Moscow Conservatory 1968–75, Prof. 1997–; Prof., Univ. Mozarteum, Salzburg 1999–2010; Honoured Artist of Russia 2003; winner, int. competitions in Rio de Janeiro (First Prize) 1965 and Montreal 1968. *Recordings:* more than 40 CDs (classical, Baroque and contemporary music) 1990–2004, Mozart Complete Sonatas on historical pianos 1991, Silvestrov: Metamusik 2003, Pärt's Lamentate 2005. *Leisure interests:* collecting ancient keyboard instruments. *Address:* c/o Helge R. Augstein, Artist Management Augstein & Hahn, 80331

Munich, Germany (office); Klimentovskiy per. 9, Apt 12, Moscow, Russia (home). *Telephone:* (89) 2602-4333 (office); (495) 951-62-51 (home). *Fax:* (89) 2602-4344 (office); (495) 629-51-45 (office); (495) 951-62-51 (home). *E-mail:* mail@augstein .info (office); alexeilubimov@mail.ru (home). *Website:* www.augstein.info (office).

LUBIN, Steven, BA, MS, PhD; American pianist and academic; *Professor, Conservatory of Music, Purchase College, State University of New York;* b. 22 Feb. 1942, New York, NY; s. of Jack Lubin and Sophie Lubin; m. Wendy Lubin 1974; two s.; ed Harvard Univ., Juilliard School, New York Univ.; piano studies with Lisa Grad, Nadia Reisenberg, Seymour Lipkin, Rosina Lhevinne, Beveridge Webster; recital and concert tours in USA, Canada, Mexico, UK, France, Netherlands, Spain, Italy, Germany, Austria, Finland, Australia, Taiwan, Japan and Ukraine; f. The Mozartean Players 1978–; mem. Faculty Juilliard School 1964–65, Aspen Music School 1967, Vassar Coll. 1970–71, Cornell Univ. 1971–75; Prof., Conservatory of Music, Purchase Coll., State Univ. of New York (SUNY) 1975–; Martha Baird Rockefeller Grant 1968, Stereo Review Recording of the Year Award 1988, Kempner Distinguished Professor Award, SUNY, Purchase 1999–2001. *Film:* soloist in Man and Music (British documentary) 1987. *Recordings include:* complete Beethoven Piano Concertos, Mozart and Schubert Trios, six Mozart Concertos as soloist and conductor and other solo and chamber music. *Publications:* articles in The New York Times, Keynote, Ovation, Keyboard Classics and Historical Performance, Brahms Soc. Newsletter 1999; contrib. to A Companion to Schubert's Schwanengesang 2000. *Leisure interests:* reading about relativity and quantum mechanics. *Address:* c/o C&K Artists, Postfach 760206, 22052 Hamburg, Germany (office); c/o John Gingrich Management, Inc., PO Box 1515, New York, NY 10023, USA (office); Conservatory of Music, School of the Arts, State University of New York, Purchase, NY 10577, USA (office). *Telephone:* (40) 33982610 (Hamburg) (office); (212) 799-5080 (New York) (office); (914) 251-6715 (office). *E-mail:* kwood@CKArtists.info (office); gingarts@verizon.net (office); steven.lubin@gmail.com (office). *Website:* www.c&kartists.info (office); www .gingarts.com (office); www.stevenlubin.com.

LUBINDA, Given; Zambian politician; mem. Nat. Ass. for Kabwata constituency, Lusaka; Minister of Information, Broadcasting and Tourism –2012, Minister of Foreign Affairs 2012–13; mem. Patriotic Front. *Address:* c/o Ministry of Foreign Affairs, POB RW50069, Lusaka, Zambia (office).

LUBOVITCH, Lar; American choreographer; *Artistic Director, Lar Lubovitch Dance Company;* b. 9 April 1943, Chicago, Ill.; ed Univ. of Iowa, Juilliard School; danced in numerous modern, ballet and jazz cos; Founder and Artistic Dir Lar Lubovitch Dance Co. 1968–; has choreographed more than 100 dances for the co.; his works are included in repertoires of most major int. dance cos including New York City Ballet, American Ballet Theater, Paris Opera Ballet, Royal Danish Ballet, Stuttgart Ballet, White Oak Dance Project and Netherlands Dance Theatre; has created dances for ice-skaters including John Curry; Distinguished Prof., Univ. of California, Irvine 2014; Guggenheim Fellowship 1971, Astaire Award 1994, Elan Award 2004, Prix Benois 2012. *Dances created include:* Whirligogs (music by Luciano Berio) 1969, The Time Before the Time After (After the Time Before) (Stravinsky) 1971, Les Noces (Stravinsky) 1976, Marimba (Steve Reich) 1976, Exultate, Jubilate (Mozart) 1977, Scriabin Dances (Scriabin) 1977, North Star (Philip Glass) 1978, Cavalcade (Reich) 1980, Beau Danube (Strauss) 1981, Big Shoulders (no music) 1983, A Brahms Symphony 1985, Concerto Six Twenty-Two (Mozart) 1986, Sleeping Beauty (Tchaikovsky; full-length televised ice-dancing version starring Robin Cousins and Rosalynn Sumners) 1987, Into the Woods (Sondheim) 1987, Musette (Poulenc) 1988, Rhapsody in Blue (Gershwin) 1988, Fandango (Ravel) 1989, Waiting for the Sunrise (Les Paul and Mary Ford) 1991, American Gesture (Charles Ives) 1992, The Red Shoes (Jule Styne; Astaire Award, Theater Devt Fund 1994) 1993, The Planets (Holst) (Emmy Award 1995, Grammy Award 1995) 1994, Oklahoma! (Rodgers and Hammerstein) 1994, The King and I (Rodgers and Hammerstein) 1996, Adagio (Bach) 1996, Othello (Goldenthal) 1997, Meadow (Schubert, etc.) 1999, The Hunchback of Notre Dame (Menken) 1999, Men's Stories (Marshall) 2000, My Funny Valentine (Rodgers) 2001, Smile With My Heart (Laird) 2002, Artemis (Chris Theofanidis) 2003, Pentimento (Richard Woodbury) 2004, Love Stories (Kurt Elling) 2005, Elemental Brubeck (Brubeck) 2005, Recordare (Goldenthal) 2005, Little Rhapsodies (Schumann; solo version) 2006, (trio version) 2007, Serenade (Dvorak) 2007, Cryptoglyph (Monk) 2007, Angel's Feet (montage) 2007, Jangle (Bartók) 2008, Coltrane's Favorite Things (Coltrane) 2010, Dogs of War (Prokofiev) 2010, Histoire du Soldat (Stravinsky) 2010, Lamentation Variation (Beethoven) 2010, The Legend of Ten (Brahms) 2010, Crisis Variations (Sharlat) 2011, Transparent Things (Debussy) 2012, As Sleep Befell (Prestini) 2013, Vez (Woolf) 2013, Crazy 8's (Woolf) 2013. *Film:* The Company (Robert Altman) 2003. *Television:* The Sleeping Beauty 1987, Concerto Six Twenty-Two and North Star/Dancemaker 1988, Fandango/Pictures From the Edge 1989, The Planets 1995, Othello 2003. *Address:* Lar Lubovitch Dance Company, 229 West 42nd Street, 8th Floor, New York, NY 10036, USA (office). *Telephone:* (212) 221-7909 (office). *Fax:* (212) 221-7938 (office). *E-mail:* lubovitch@aol.com (office). *Website:* www.lubovitch.org (office).

LUBRANI, Uri; Israeli diplomatist; *Adviser, Ministry for Strategic Affairs;* b. 7 Oct. 1926, Haifa; s. of Ahron Lubrani and Rose Lubrani; m. Sarah Levi 1953; four d.; ed Univ. of London, UK; fmr Head of Chancery, Office of Foreign Minister, Office of Prime Minister, Adviser to Prime Minister on Arab Affairs; later Amb. to Uganda, Rwanda, Burundi, Ethiopia and Iran; now Govt Co-ordinator for Lebanese Affairs; in charge of airlift of 18,000 Ethiopian Jews (Falashas) to Israel 1991; head Israeli team, negotiations on release of Israeli hostages in Lebanon and Shia Muslim prisoners in Israel; head Israeli del. to bilateral peace talks with Lebanon, Washington, DC 1992; now Adviser to the Minister for Strategic Affairs; Hon. DPhil (Ben-Gurion Univ.) 1991, (Beer) 1991; Jabotinsky Annual Award for Services to the Jewish People 1991, David Ben-Gurion Annual Award. *Address:* Office of the Adviser to the Minister for Strategic Affairs, Ministry of Defence, Hakirya, Tel-Aviv (office); Shamgar Street 34, Tzahala, Tel-Aviv, Israel (home). *Telephone:* (3) 6975157 (office); (3) 6474919 (home). *Fax:* (3) 6977358 (office); (3) 6493084 (home). *E-mail:* liban@mod.gov.il (office).

LUCAS, Sir Colin Renshaw, Kt, MA, DPhil, FRHistS; British academic; *Warden, Rhodes House Oxford;* b. 25 Aug. 1940; s. of the late Frank Renshaw Lucas and of Janine Charpentier; m. 1st Christiane Berchon de Fontaine Goubert 1964 (divorced 1975); one s.; m. 2nd Mary Louise Hume 1990; ed Sherborne School,

Lincoln Coll., Oxford; Asst Lecturer, then Lecturer, Univ. of Sheffield 1965–69; Visiting Asst Prof., Indiana Univ., USA 1969–70; Lecturer, Univ. of Manchester 1970–73; Fellow, Balliol Coll. Oxford and Lecturer in Modern History, Univ. of Oxford 1973–90; Prof., Chicago Univ., USA 1990–94, Dean Div. of Social Sciences 1993–94; Master of Balliol Coll. Oxford 1994–2001; Pro-Vice-Chancellor Univ. of Oxford 1995–97, Vice-Chancellor 1997–2004; Warden Rhodes House, Oxford 2004–; Chair. British Library 2006–10; Officier des Arts et des Lettres 1990, Chevalier, Ordre nat. du Mérite 1994, Chevalier, Légion d'honneur 1998, Officier 2005; Hon. DLitt (Lyon) 1989, (Sheffield) 2000, (Univ. of WA) 2000, (Glasgow) 2001, (Princeton) 2002, (Beijing) 2002, (Francis Xavier) 2003, (Oxford) 2003, (Oxford Brookes) 2004, (Warwick) 2006. *Publications:* The Structure of the Terror 1973, Beyond the Terror (with G. Lewis) 1983, The Political Culture of the French Revolution (ed.) 1988; contribs to academic journals. *Address:* Rhodes House, South Parks Road, Oxford, OX1 3RG, England. *Telephone:* (1865) 270902 (office). *Fax:* (1865) 270914 (office). *E-mail:* warden@rhodeshouse.ox.ac.uk (office).

LUCAS, Craig, BFA; American playwright and screenwriter; b. 30 April 1951, Atlanta, Georgia; s. of Charles Samuel Lucas and Eleanore Alltmont Lucas; ed Boston Univ.; mem. Dramatists' Guild, PEN, Writers' Guild of America; Sundance Audience Award, Obie and Outer Critics' Award, Los Angeles Drama Critics' Award. *Plays:* Missing Persons 1980, Reckless 1983, Blue Window (Los Angeles Drama Critics Circle Award 1986) 1984, Prelude to a Kiss 1987, The Scare 1989, God's Heart 1994, The Dying Gaul 1996, Savage Light (with David Schulner) 1996, The Singing Forest 2004, Prayer For My Enemy 2007. *Musicals:* Marry Me a Little (anthology of songs by Stephen Sondheim) 1981, Three Postcards (music and lyrics by Craig Carnelia) 1987, The Light in the Piazza 2004. *Films:* Longtime Companion 1990, Prelude to a Kiss 1991, Reckless 1995, Secret Lives of Dentists 2002, The Dying Gaul 2005, Birds of America 2008. *Address:* c/o Peter Franklin, William Morris Agency, 1325 Avenue of the Americas, New York, NY 10019, USA (office). *Telephone:* (212) 586-5100 (office). *Fax:* (212) 246-3583 (office). *E-mail:* craig.lucas@mac.com (office). *Website:* www.wma.com (office).

LUCAS, George Walton, Jr, BA; American screenwriter and film director and producer; *Creative Consultant, Lucasfilm Ltd;* b. 14 May 1944, Modesto, Calif.; s. of George Walton Lucas, Sr and Dorothy Ellinore Lucas (née Bomberger); m. 1st Marcia Lou Griffin 1969 (divorced 1983); one adopted s. two adopted d.; m. 2nd Mellody Hobson 2013; ed Univ. of Southern California School of Cinema-TV; apprenticeship at Warner Brothers Studios; Co-founder (with Francis Ford Coppola) American Zoetrope (film production co.) 1969; f. Lucasfilm Ltd 1971, currently Creative Consultant, group includes Lucasfilm Animation Ltd, Lucas Digital (Industrial Light & Magic and Skywalker Sound), LucasArts Entertainment Co., Lucas Licensing (Lucasfilm sold to Disney 2012); Founder and Chair. George Lucas Educational Foundation; mem. Bd of Councilors Univ. of Southern California School of Cinema-TV; Dr hc (Univ. of Southern California) 1994; Irving Thalberg Award 1991, American Film Inst. Lifetime Achievement Award 2005, Inaugural Filmmaker's Award from Motion Picture Sound Editors 2005, named amongst the 100 Greatest Americans by the Discovery Channel 2005, inducted into the Science Fiction Hall of Fame 2006, served as Grand Marshal for the Tournament of Roses Parade 2007, one of 13 California Hall of Fame inductees in The California Museum's yearlong exhibit 2009, Nat. Medal of Arts 2012. *Films include:* writer and dir: Look at Life 1965, Herbie 1966, Freiheit 1966, The Emperor 1967, Anyone Lived in a Pretty How Town 1967, Filmmaker 1968, American Graffiti 1973; producer: Kagemusha 1980, Body Heat 1981, Twice Upon a Time 1983, Howard the Duck 1986; writer and producer: Star Wars Episode V: The Empire Strikes Back 1980, Raiders of the Lost Ark 1981, Star Wars Episode VI: Return of the Jedi 1983, Indiana Jones and the Temple of Doom 1984, Captain Eo 1986, Willow 1988, Indiana Jones and the Last Crusade 1989, Radioland Murders 1994; writer, producer and dir: THX 1138 1971, Star Wars Episode IV: A New Hope 1977, Star Wars Episode I: The Phantom Menace 1999, Star Wars Episode II: Attack of the Clones 2002, Star Wars Episode III: Revenge of the Sith 2005; writer or producer or exec. producer: Indiana Jones and the Kingdom of the Crystal Skull 2008, Red Tails 2012. *Television includes:* the Adventures of Young Indiana Jones: The Perils of Cupid (film) 2007, Robot Chicken: Star Wars Episode II (film) 2008, Star Wars: The Clone Wars (series) 2008–12, Star Wars: Detours (series) 2012, Star Wars: Underworld (series) 2013. *Address:* Lucasfilm Ltd, 5858 Lucas Valley Road, Nicasio, CA 94946 (office); George Lucas Educational Foundation, PO Box 3494, San Rafael, CA 94912, USA. *Telephone:* (415) 662-1800 (office). *Fax:* (415) 448-2495 (office). *E-mail:* george.lucas@lucasfilm.com (office). *Website:* www.lucasfilm.com; www.edutopia.org.

LUCAS, Jonathan, BA, MA, PhD; Seychelles UN official; *Director, United Nations Interregional Crime and Justice Research Institute;* ed Univ. of Lyon, France, Univ. of Newcastle-upon-Tyne, UK, Acadia Univ., Canada, Grad. Inst. for Int. Studies, Switzerland; Consultant, ILO, Switzerland 1982; Assoc. Social Affairs Officer, Div. of Narcotic Drugs, UN 1984, later positions include Legal and First Officer, UN Int. Drug Control Programme; Sr Programme Man. Officer, Office of Exec. Dir, Dir-Gen., Office on Drug Control and Crime Prevention, UN, Vienna, Chief, Commissions Secr. Section 1998–2004, Rep. Regional Office for Southern Africa, UN Office on Drugs and Crime 2004–2010, Sec., Int. Narcotics Control Bd (INCB) and Chief, INCB Secr. 2010–11, Dir UN Interregional Crime and Justice Research Inst. 2011–. *Address:* United Nations Interregional Crime and Justice Research Institute, Viale Maestri del Lavoro, 10, 10127 Turin, Italy (office). *Telephone:* (11) 6537111 (office). *Fax:* (11) 6313 368 (office). *E-mail:* informationunicri.it (office). *Website:* www.unicri.it (office).

LUCAS, Michel; French banking executive; *President and Chairman of the Management Board, CIC Crédit Industriel & Commercial SA;* joined Confédération Nationale du Crédit Mutuel 1971, has held several exec. positions, currently CEO; Gen. Man. Banque Federative du Crédit Mutuel, Caisse Centrale du Crédit Mutuel, Crédit Mutuel Centre Est Europe; Pres. and Chair. Man. Bd CIC Crédit Industriel & Commercial SA 1998–; Pres. Assurances du Crédit Mutuel; Pres. Europay France SA –2004, Vice-Pres. 2004–; Dir Regional Bd MasterCard Europe 1992–, Vice-Chair. 2002–; Dir MasterCard International Inc. 2004–; mem. Bd of Dirs Banque de Luxembourg, Banque de Tunisie, Banque Marocaine du Commerce Extérieur, Caisses Desjardins, Banque Transatlantique. *Address:* CIC Crédit Industriel & Commercial SA, 6 avenue de Provence, 75452

Paris 9, France (office). *Telephone:* 1-45-96-96-96 (office). *Fax:* 1-45-96-96-66 (office). *E-mail:* filbass@cic.fr (office). *Website:* www.cic.fr/en (office).

LUCAS, Robert Emerson, BA, PhD; American economist and academic; *John Dewey Distinguished Service Professor, Department of Economics, University of Chicago;* b. 15 Sept. 1937, Yakima, Wash.; ed Univ. of Chicago; Asst Prof. of Econs, Carnegie Inst. of Tech. 1963–67; Assoc. Prof. of Econs, Carnegie-Mellon Univ. 1967–70, Prof. 1970–74; Ford Foundation Visiting Research Prof. of Econs, Univ. of Chicago 1974–75, Prof. of Econs 1975–80, John Dewey Distinguished Service Prof. of Econs 1980–, Vice-Chair. Dept of Econs 1975–83, Chair. 1986–88; Visiting Prof. of Econs, Northwestern Univ. 1981–82; Assoc. Ed. Journal of Monetary Economics 1977–; Ed. Journal of Political Economy 1988–; mem. American Econ. Asscn (mem. Exec. Cttee 1980–82, Vice-Pres. 1987, Pres.-Elect 2001, Pres. 2002), Econometric Soc. (Fellow, 1976, Pres. 1997); Fellow, AAAS 1980, Fellow, American Finance Asscn 2004; mem. NAS 1981–; Dr hc (Université Paris-Dauphine) 1992, (Athens Univ. of Econs and Business) 1994, (Univ. of Montreal) 1998; Nobel Prize for Econs 1995. *Publications:* Studies in Business-Cycle Theory 1981, Lectures in Economic Growth 2001. *Address:* Department of Economics, University of Chicago, 1126 E 59th Street, Chicago, IL 60637 (office); 460 West Barry Avenue, Chicago, IL 60657, USA (home). *E-mail:* relucas@uchicago.edu (office). *Website:* home.uchicago.edu/~sogrodow (office); economics.uchicago.edu (office).

LUCAS, Sarah, BA; British artist; b. 1962, London; d. of Irene Lucas; ed Working Men's Coll., London, London Coll. of Printmaking, Goldsmiths Coll., London; emerged as one of the major Young British Artists during the 1990s; works with a variety of materials and media, including photographs, sculpture and installations that use humour and visual puns to explore gender. *Dance:* Before and After: The Fall, The Michael Clark Co. (set design for a new work performed on tour) 2001. *Television:* Two Melons and a Stinking Fish (Illuminations for BBC TV/Arts Council) 1996, This Is Modern Art (Channel 4 six-part series) 1999, The History of Britart (BBC) 2001. *Address:* c/o Sadie Coles HQ, 69 South Audley Street, London, W1K 2QZ, England. *Telephone:* (20) 7493-8611. *Fax:* (20) 7499-4878. *E-mail:* info@sadiecoles.com. *Website:* www.sadiecoles.com.

LUCE, Baron (Life Peer), cr. 2000, of Adur in the County of West Sussex; **Richard Napier Luce,** Kt, KG, PC, GCVO, DL; British fmr politician; b. 14 Oct. 1936, London; s. of the late Sir William Luce, GBE, KCMG and of Lady Luce (née Margaret Napier); m. Rose Helen Nicholson 1961; two s.; ed Wellington Coll. and Christ's Coll., Cambridge, Wadham Coll. Oxford; Subaltern, Wilts. Regiment, Nat. Service 1955–57; Dist Officer, Kenya 1961–63; Marketing Man. Gallaher Ltd 1963–65; Marketing Man. Spirella Co. of GB 1965–67; Dir Nat. Innovation Centre 1967–71; mem. European Advisory Bd Corning Glass Int. 1976–79; Dir (non-exec.) Booker Tate 1991–96, Meridian Broadcasting 1991–97; MP for Arundel and Shoreham 1971–74, for Shoreham 1974–92; Opposition Whip 1974–75; Opposition Spokesman, Foreign and Commonwealth Affairs 1977–79; Parl. Under-Sec. of State 1979–81; Minister of State, FCO 1981–82, 1983–85; Minister of State (Minister for the Arts) and Minister of State for Civil Service, Privy Council Office 1985–90; Gov. and C-in-C Gibraltar 1997–2000; Lord Chamberlain of her Majesty's Household 2000–06; High Steward, Westminster Abbey 2011–; Vice-Chancellor Univ. of Buckingham 1992–96; Chair. Atlantic Council of UK 1991–96, Commonwealth Foundation 1992–96; mem. Royal Mint Advisory Cttee, Bd Trustees, Royal Collection Trust 2000–06; Pres. Voluntary Arts Network, Royal Overseas League, King George V Fund for Actors and Actresses 2006–11, Commonwealth Youth Orchestra 2010–13; Trustee Geographers' Map Trustees Ltd (A–Z); Trustee Emer. Royal Acad. of Arts; Vice-Patron Harambee and Langalanga Trusts; Parl. Crossbencher (Independent) in the House of Lords; Chair. Crown Nominations Comm. for the See of Canterbury 2012–; Hon. Vice-Pres. Overseas Pensioners' Asscn; Hon. Fellow, Christ's Coll. Cambridge; Hon. Fellow, Atlantic Council of the UK; KStJ. *Publications:* Ringing the Changes: A Memoir 2007. *Leisure interests:* walking, swimming, painting, reading, piano. *Address:* c/o House of Lords, Westminster, London, SW1A 0PW, England.

LUCIE-SMITH, (John) Edward (McKenzie), MA, FRSL; British art critic and poet; b. 27 Feb. 1933, Kingston, Jamaica; s. of John Dudley Lucie-Smith and Mary Lushington; ed King's School, Canterbury, Merton Coll., Oxford; officer in RAF 1954–56; fmrly worked in advertising and as freelance journalist and broadcaster; contributes to The Times, Sunday Times, Independent, Mail on Sunday, Spectator, New Statesman, Evening Standard, Encounter, London Magazine, Illustrated London News, La Vanguardia (Barcelona); now works as a freelance art historian and exhbn curator; John Llewellyn Rhys Memorial Prize. *Solo photographic exhibitions:* Zlato Oko, Novi Sad, Vojvoidina, Serbia 1998, Adonis Art, London 1998, Art Kiosk, Brussels 1999, Rivington Gallery, London 1999, Toni Berini Gallery, Barcelona 2000, Rosenfeld Gallery, Tel-Aviv 2001, Plus 1, Plus 2 Gallery, London 2001, Il Politicco, Rome 2002, D-137 Gallery, St Petersburg 2002, Butler Inst. of Art, Youngstown, Ohio 2003, Valentine Willie Fine Art, Kuala Lumpur 2003, Albemarle Gallery, London 2003, Art Gallery, Univ. of Buckingham 2003, Labiola Gallery, Ljubljana 2003, O'Connor, A Gallery, Toronto 2004, Museu de Arte Moderna, Rio de Janeiro 2004, Wunderkammer, Valencia 2005, Museum of Contemporary Art, Skopje, Macedonia 2005, Galerija Svetega Donalda, Piran, Slovenia 2006, O'Connor, A Gallery, Toronto 2007, City Art Museum, Helsinki 2007, Gallery Kontrast, Stockholm 2007, Piramid Sanat, Istanbul 2007, Galleria Forni, Bologna 2007, Grafiki Kolektiv, Belgrade 2008, Nat. Gallery, Kingston, Jamaica 2010. *Publications include:* A Tropical Childhood and Other Poems 1961, Confessions and Histories 1964, What is a Painting? 1966, Thinking About Art 1968, Towards Silence 1968, Movements in Art Since 1945 1969, Art in Britain 69–70 1970, A Concise History of French Painting 1971, Symbolist Art 1972, Eroticism in Western Art 1972, The First London Catalogue 1974, The Well Wishers 1974, The Burnt Child (autobiog.) 1975, The Invented Eye (early photography) 1975, World of the Makers 1975, Joan of Arc 1976, Fantin-Latour 1977, The Dark Pageant (novel) 1977, Art Today 1977, A Concise History of Furniture 1979, Super Realism 1979, Cultural Calendar of the Twentieth Century 1979, Art in the Seventies 1980, The Story of Craft 1981, The Body 1981, A History of Industrial Design 1983, Art Terms: An Illustrated Dictionary 1984, Art in the Thirties 1985, American Art Now 1985, Lives of the Great Twentieth Century Artists 1986, Sculpture Since 1945 1987, Art in the Eighties 1990, Art Deco Painting 1990, Fletcher Benton 1990, Jean Rustin 1991, Harry Holland 1992, Art and Civilisation 1992, Andres Nagel 1992, Wendy Taylor 1992, Alexander 1992,

British Art Now 1993, Race, Sex and Gender: Issues in Contemporary Art 1994, American Realism 1994, Art Today 1995, Visual Arts in the Twentieth Century 1996, Arts Erotica: an Arousing History of Erotic Art 1997, Adam 1998, Stone 1998, Zoo 1998, Sean Henry – The Centre Of The Universe (with Beatrice F. Buscaroli) 1999, Judy Chicago: an American Vision 2000, Flesh and Stone 2000, Changing Shape (poems) 2002, Censoring the Body 2008, Byzantium & Beyond: The Paintings of Dave Pearson (with Margaret Mytton) 2012; has edited numerous anthologies. *Leisure interest:* surfing the internet. *Address:* c/o Pat White, Rogers, Coleridge and White, 20 Powis Mews, London, W11 1JN, England (office). *Telephone:* (20) 7221-3717 (office). *Fax:* (20) 7229-9084 (office). *E-mail:* info@rcwlitagency.com (office); edward@edwardlucie-smith.co.uk (office). *Website:* www.rcwlitagency.com (office); www.edwardlucie-smith.co.uk.

LUCINSCHI, Petru, CandPhilSc, PhD; Moldovan fmr head of state and politician; *Head, Foundation for Strategic Studies and Development of International Relations;* b. 27 Jan. 1940, Floreşti; s. of Chiril Lucinschi and Parascovia Lucinschi; m. Antonina Georgievna Lucinschi 1965; two s.; ed Kishinev (Chişinău) Univ. and CPSU Cen. Cttee Higher Party School; served in Soviet Army 1962–63; Komsomol work for Cen. Cttee of Moldavian CP 1963–71; mem. CPSU 1964–91; First Sec. of Bălţi City Komsomol Cttee 1964–65; Head of Section, Second Sec., First Sec. of Cen. Cttee of Moldavian Komsomol 1965–71; Sec. of Cen. Cttee of Moldavian CP 1971–76, First Sec. Nov. 1989–91; First Sec. of Kishinev City Cttee 1976–78; Deputy Head, Propaganda Dept of CPSU Cen. Cttee 1978–86; Second Sec. of Cen. Cttee of Tadzhik CP 1986–89; Cand. mem. of CPSU Cen. Cttee 1986–89, mem. 1989–91, Sec. 1990–91; Deputy to USSR Supreme Soviet 1986–89; USSR People's Deputy 1989–91; mem. CPSU Politburo, 1990–91; Moldovan Amb. to Russia 1992–93; fmr Leader Agrarian Democratic Party; Chair. Moldovan Parl. 1993–2001; Pres. of Moldova 1996–2000; Head, Foundation for Strategic Studies and Devt of Int. Relations 2001–; mem., Russian Fed. Social Sciences Acad.; Chevalier, Légion d'honneur 1998, Order of Repub. of Moldova; Dr hc (Minsk, Baku); numerous awards, including Int. Pilgrim of Peace Award, Assisi (Italy). *Publications:* The Last Days of the USSR 1998, The Life and Death 2003, Moldova and Moldavians 2007. *Leisure interests:* sports, travelling, reading, theatre, hunting. *Address:* 76 Bucuresti str., Chişinău, Moldova (home). *Telephone:* (22) 237979 (office). *Fax:* (22) 237981 (office). *E-mail:* office@ipa.dnt.md (office).

LUCK, Edward C., BA, MA, MIA, MPhil, PhD; American political scientist, academic and UN official; *Dean and Professor, Joan B. Kroc School of Peace Studies, University of San Diego;* b. 17 Oct. 1948; m.; one d.; ed Dartmouth Coll., Columbia Univ.; Founder and Exec. Dir Center for the Study of Int. Org. (research centre jointly est. by School of Law, New York Univ. and Woodrow Wilson School of Public and Int. Affairs, Princeton Univ.) –2001; Prof. in the Professional Practice of Int. Affairs, School of Int. and Public Affairs, Columbia Univ. and Dir Center on Int. Org. 2001– (currently on public service leave); Vice-Pres. and Dir of Studies, Int. Peace Acad. 2008–09; Sr Consultant, Dept of Admin and Man., UN 1995–97, Staff Dir Gen. Ass.'s Open-ended High-level Working Group on the Strengthening of the United Nations System 1995–97, adviser to Pres. of Gen. Ass., Razali Ismail, on proposals for Security Council reform 1995–97, fmr sr consultant to Sec.-Gen.'s Special Rep. for Children and Armed Conflict, fmr mem. Sec.-Gen.'s Policy Working Group on the UN and Terrorism, Special Adviser at Asst Sec.-Gen. level to Sec.-Gen., UN 2008–12; served in several research and man. capacities, UNA of the USA 1974–84, Pres. and CEO 1984–94, Pres. Emer. 1994–98; Dean and Prof., Joan B. Kroc School of Peace Studies, Univ. of San Diego 2012–; fmr Visiting Prof., Sciences-Po, Paris; fmr consultant to numerous pvt. foundations and research centres. *Publications:* Mixed Messages: American Politics and International Organization, 1919–1999 1999, International Law and Organization: Closing the Compliance Gap (co-ed.) 2004, The UN Security Council: Practice and Promise 2006; has published numerous articles in Foreign Policy, Washington Quarterly, Current History, Disarmament, and other scholarly journals, as well as in the New York Times, Washington Post, Los Angeles Times, Christian Science Monitor, International Herald Tribune, USA Today, Newsday, and other newspapers. *Address:* Joan B. Kroc School of Peace Studies, 5998 Alcala Park, San Diego, CA 92110, USA (office). *Telephone:* (619) 260-4600 (office). *E-mail:* ecl2002@columbia.edu. *Website:* www.sandiego.edu/peacestudies.

ŁUCZAK, Aleksander Piotr, PhD; Polish politician and historian; *Vice-President, National Broadcasting Council;* b. 10 Sept. 1943, Legionowo; m. Janina Zakrzewska; one d.; ed Warsaw Univ. and Adam Mickiewicz Univ., Poznań; mem. United Peasants' Party (ZLS) 1966–91; mem. Polish Peasants' Party (PSL) 1991–; lecturer, Dept of History of the Peasant Movt Cen. Cttee ZSL until 1976; mem. Faculty, Univ. of Warsaw 1976–, Asst Prof. 1983–91, Prof. 1991; Adviser to Pres. of Cen. Cttee ZSL 1976–79; Head, Dept of Ideology, Press and Propaganda, Cen. Cttee PSL 1986, Vice-Chair., Head Council PSL 1991–97; Deputy Minister of Nat. Educ. 1986–87; Head, Office of Council of Ministers June–Oct. 1992; Deputy Prime Minister and Minister of Educ. 1993–94; Deputy Prime Minister, Minister and Head of Scientific Research Cttee 1994–96; Minister and Head of Scientific Research Cttee 1996–97; Deputy to Sejm (Parl.) 1989–2001; Chair. Polish Asscn of Adult Educ. 1995–2001; Pres. World Scout Parl. Union 1997–2000; mem. Nat. Broadcasting Council (KRRiT) 2001–, Vice-Pres. 2003–. *Publications:* more than 30 publs on recent history of Poland and the peasant movt. *Leisure interest:* tennis. *Address:* National Broadcasting Council, Skwer Ks. Kard. S. Wyszyńskiego 9, 01-015 Warsaw, Poland (office). *Telephone:* (22) 5973042 (office). *Fax:* (22) 5973180 (office). *E-mail:* luczak@krrit.gov.pl (office). *Website:* www.krrit.gov.pl (office).

LUDER, Owen (Harold), CBE, FRSA, PP RIBA; British architect, planner, environmentalist and writer; *Founder, Owen Luder Consultancy Ltd;* b. 7 Aug. 1928, London; s. of the late Edward Charles Luder and of Ellen Clara Luder; m. 1st Rose Dorothy (Doris) Broadstock 1951 (divorced 1988) (died); one s. (deceased) four d.; m. 2nd Jacqueline Ollerton 1989 (died 2008); ed Brixton School of Building, Regent St Polytechnic Evening School of Architecture (now Univ. of Westminster), Brixton School of Architecture; f. Owen Luder Partnership 1957, Sr Partner until 1978 (when partnership became unlimited co.), Chair. and Man. Dir 1978–87; f. Owen Luder Consultancy Communication in Construction 1988–2003; Dir (non-exec.) Jarvis PLC 1995–2003; Council mem. RIBA 1967–97, 2010–, Hon. Treas. 1975–78, Pres. 1981–83, Sr Vice-Pres. 1994–95, Pres. 1995–97, Architect mem. Architects' Registration Bd and Vice-Chair. 1997–2002, Chair. 2002–03; Pres. Norwood Soc. 1982–92; Sec.-Treas. Commonwealth Asscn of Architects 1985–87;

Pres. UIA Congress 1986; Vice-Pres. Membership Communications 1989–90; Dir Communication in Construction Ltd 1990; Consultant to Nat. Coal Bd for environmental, architectural and planning issues on Vale of Belvoir Coal Mining Project, UK 1975–87; Architect/Planner for revitalization schemes for British Rail Eng Works at Shildon, Co. Durham and Swindon; consultant for many commercial devt schemes, architectural consultant and qualified mediator; mem. Acad. of Experts 1992–, Vice-Chair. 1997–98; RIBA Architecture Bronze Medal 1963, Town Planning and Housing Council Silver Jubilee Award 'Housing in the 80s', Business Consultant of the Year 1985, and various other architectural, design and civic trust awards and commendations. *Publications:* Adventure in Architecture – A Portrait of the Owen Luder Partnership 1976, Promotion and Marketing for Building Professionals 1988, Sports Stadia After Hillsborough 1990, Keeping Out of Trouble 1999; frequent contribs to nat. and tech. publs. *Leisure interests:* photography, writing, Arsenal Football Club, swimming. *Address:* Owen Luder Consultancy Ltd, Apartment 702, Romney House, 47 Marsham Street, London, SW1P 3DS, England. *Telephone:* (20) 7222-0198. *E-mail:* owenluder@dsl.pipex.com.

LÜDERITZ, Alexander, DrIur; German professor of law; b. 19 March 1932, Göttingen; s. of Heinrich Lüderitz and Gertrud Lüderitz; m. Renate (née Wessling) Lüderitz 1960; one s. one d.; ed Cologne School of Law and Lausanne School of Law, Switzerland; mem. of the Bar 1961–65; Prof. of Law, Univ. of Frankfurt 1966–70, Dean, Faculty of Law 1969–70; Prof. of Law and Dir Inst. for Int. and Foreign Pvt. Law, Univ. of Cologne 1971–, Dean, Faculty of Law 1979–80; Visiting Prof., Univ. of California, Berkeley, USA 1982, Université d'Auvergne, France 1989, 1991, Univ. of Illinois, Urbana, USA 1995, Univ. of Toulouse, France 1995, 1996; Fellow, American Council of Learned Socs. *Publications:* Auslegung von Rechtsgeschäften 1966, International Sales 1991, International Privatrecht 1992, Commentary on German Conflicts Law (Corporation, Agency, Torts) 1996, Familienrecht 1997 (revised edn 2009); articles in learned journals. *Leisure interests:* hiking, stamp collecting. *Address:* Kellerhardtsweg 12, 51503 Roesrath, Germany. *Telephone:* (221) 470-2288; (2205) 3124. *Fax:* (221) 470 5129; (2205) 3124.

LUDEWIG, Johannes, PhD; German civil servant and business executive; *Executive Director, Community of European Railways and Infrastructure Companies;* b. 6 July 1945, Hamburg; m.; three c.; ed Univ. of Hamburg, Stanford Univ., USA, Ecole Nat. d'Admin., Paris, France; worked on energy, econ. and business policy, Fed. Ministry of Econs 1975–83; joined Office of the Fed. Chancellor 1983, Ministerial Dir, Dept of Econ. and Financial Policy 1991–94; fmr State Sec., Fed. Ministry of Econs; fmr Commr of Fed. Govt for New German Fed. States; mem. Exec. Bd Deutsche Bahn AG 1997–99, Chair. 1997–99; currently Exec. Dir Community of European Railways and Infrastructure Cos (CER). *Address:* CER, 53 Avenue des Arts, 1000 Brussels, Belgium (office). *Telephone:* (2) 213-08-71 (office). *Fax:* (2) 512-64-32 (office). *E-mail:* johannes.ludewig@cer.be (office). *Website:* www.cer.be (office).

LUDFORD, Baroness (Life Peer), cr. 1997, of Clerkenwell in the London Borough of Islington; **Sarah Ludford,** MSc; British politician; b. 14 March 1951, Halesworth; d. of Joseph Campbell Ludford and Valerie Kathleen Ludford (née Skinner); m. Steve Hitchins; ed Portsmouth High School for Girls, London School of Econs; barrister, called to the Bar Gray's Inn 1979; official, Secr.-Gen. and Directorate Gen. Competition, EC 1979–85; European and UK policy adviser, Lloyds of London 1985–87; Vice-Pres. Corp. External Affairs, American Express European 1987–90; freelance Euro consultant 1990–99; mem. Liberal Democrat Party; Councillor (Liberal Democrat) Islington Borough Council 1991–99; Vice-Chair. Liberal Democrat Federal Policy Cttee 1991–98; Vice-Pres. Gay and Lesbian Lib Dems (DELGA); MEP (Liberal Democrat) for London 1999–; mem. Council European Liberal Democrat and Reform (ELDR) Party; mem. Cttee on Citizens' Freedoms and Rights, Justice and Home Affairs, Human Rights, Common Security and Defence Policy; mem. Inter-Parl. dels: Cyprus, South-East Europe (also Vice-Pres.); ELDR spokeswoman on Justice and Home Affairs; rapporteur on Anti-Racism, European Parl. 2000, on Legal Rights for EU-resident foreign nationals 2001–02; Vice-Pres. European Parl. Inter-Group on Anti-Racism, co-ordinating European Parl. Kurdish Network; mem. Royal Inst. of Int. Affairs, European Movt. *Publications include:* The EU: From Economic Community to Human Rights Community (article); contrib. to To the Power of Ten 2000. *Leisure interests:* theatre, ballet, gardening. *Address:* European Parliament, Office 10G165, Rue Wiertz, 1047 Brussels, Belgium (office); Constituency Office, 36B St Peter's Street, London, N1 8JT, England (office). *Telephone:* (2) 284-71-04 (office); (20) 7288-2526 (office). *Fax:* (2) 284-91-04 (office); (20) 7288-2526 (office). *E-mail:* office@sarahludfordmep.org.uk (office); sarah.ludford@europarl.europa.eu (office). *Website:* www.europarl.europa.eu (office); www.sarahludfordmep.org.uk (office).

LUDWIG, Christa; Austrian/French singer (mezzo-soprano); b. 16 March 1928, Berlin, Germany; d. of Anton Ludwig and Eugenie Besalla-Ludwig; m. 1st Walter Berry 1957 (divorced 1970, died 2000); one s.; m. 2nd Paul-Emile Deiber 1972; opera debut at 18, guest appearance at the Athens Festival in Epidauros 1965; joined Vienna State Opera 1955, Hon. mem. 1981; appearances at festivals in Salzburg, Bayreuth, Lucerne, Holland, Prague, Saratoga, Stockholm; guest appearances in season in Vienna, New York, Chicago, Buenos Aires, Milan, Berlin, Munich; numerous recitals and soloist in concerts; Hon. mem. Vienna Konzerthaus, Vienna Philharmonic; Hon. Prof.; Commdr des Arts et des Lettres 1989, Grosses Ehrenzeichen 1994, Commdr, Ordre pour le Mérite 1997, Commdr, Légion d'honneur 2010; winner of Bach-Concours, record award for Fricka in Walküre and Des Knaben Wunderhorn, awarded title of Kammersängerin by Austrian Govt 1962, Prix des Affaires Culturelles for recording of Venus in Tannhäuser, Paris 1972, Silver Rose (Vienna Philharmonic) 1980, Golden Ring (Staatsoper, Vienna) 1980, Golden Gustav Mahler Medal 1980, Hugo Wolf Medal (Austria) 1980, Gold Medal (City of Vienna) 1988, Midem Classical Lifetime Achievement Award 2008, Hugo Wolf Medal (Germany) 2010. *Recordings include:* Lieder and complete operas including Norma (with Maria Callas), Lohengrin, Così fan tutte, Der Rosenkavalier, Carmen, Götterdämmerung, Die Walküre, Bluebeard's Castle, Don Giovanni, Die Zauberflöte, Le Nozze di Figaro, Capriccio, Fidelio. *Publication:* In My Own Voice (biog.) 1994. *Leisure interests:* music, archaeology, reading, home movie making, cooking, sewing, fashion, shopping, weaving, rug knitting and travelling. *Address:* c/o Ingpen & Williams, 7 St George's Court, 131 Putney Bridge Road, London, SW15 2PA, England.

LUERS, William Henry, MA, FAAS; American diplomatist and museum president; b. 15 May 1929, Springfield, Ill.; s. of Carl U. Luers and Ann L. Luers; m. Wendy Woods Turnbull 1979; three s. one d. by previous marriage and two step-d.; ed Hamilton Coll., Columbia and Northwestern Univs; Foreign Service Officer Dept of State 1957; Vice-Consul, Naples, Italy 1957–60; Second Sec. Embassy, Moscow 1963–65; Political Counsellor, Caracas, Venezuela 1969–73; Deputy Exec. Sec., Dept of State 1973–75; Deputy Asst Sec. for Inter-American Affairs, Washington 1975–77, Deputy Asst Sec. for Europe 1977–78; Amb. to Venezuela 1978–82, to Czechoslovakia 1983–86; Pres. Metropolitan Museum of Art, New York 1986–99; Pres. and CEO UN Asscn of USA 1999–2009; mem. Bd Rockefeller Brothers Fund, AOL-Latin America, Scudder Funds, Wickes Corpn; mem. Council on Foreign Relations, American Acad. of Arts and Sciences, American Acad. of Diplomacy; Hon. LLD (Hamilton Coll.) 1982; American Foreign Service Cup 1988. *Address:* 419 East 57th Street, Apt 14A, New York, NY 10022, USA (home). *Telephone:* (212) 593-0586 (home).

LUGANSKY, Nikolai L.; Russian pianist; b. 26 April 1972, Moscow; s. of Lev Borisovich Lugansky and Anna Nikolayevna Luganskaya; m. Lada Borisovna Luganskaya; one s. one d.; ed Moscow State Conservatory; wide repertoire comprises over 40 piano concertos and music from Bach to modern composers; ensemblist and interpreter of chamber music; performances in Russia and abroad in Australia, Austria, Belgium, Brazil, Canada, England, France, Germany Italy, Japan and elsewhere, including at the Royal Festival Hall and Wigmore Hall in London, the Gaveau and Louvre in Paris, Conservatoria Verdi in Milan, Gasteig in Munich, Concertgebouw in Amsterdam, Alte Oper in Frankfurt; first prize All-Union students' competition Tbilisi Georgia 1988, silver medal Bach Int. Competition, Leipzig, Germany 1988, second prize Rachmaninov Competition, Moscow 1990, first prize Tchaikovsky Int. Competition, Moscow 1994, Terence Judd award for the most promising pianist of a generation 1995. *Recordings:* some 25 albums including Rachmaninov piano concertos, Tchaikovsky's Piano Concerto No 1 2004, Liszt 2011. *Leisure interests:* chess, table tennis, reading. *Address:* Opus 3 Artists, 470 Park Avenue South, 9th Floor North, New York, NY 10016, USA (office); Kosygina str. 2, apt 2, Moscow 119334, Russia (home). *Telephone:* (212) 584-7500 (office); (495) 137-18-36 (home). *Fax:* (646) 300-8200 (office). *E-mail:* info@ opus3artists.com (office). *Website:* www.opus3artists.com (office).

LUGAR, Richard (Dick) Green, MA; American politician; b. 4 April 1932, Indianapolis, Ind.; s. of Marvin L. Lugar and Bertha Green Lugar; m. Charlene Smeltzer 1956; four s.; ed Shortridge High School, Denison Univ., Ohio, Pembroke Coll., Oxford Univ.; Rhodes Scholar, Pembroke Coll. Oxford 1956; served in USN 1957–60; Vice-Pres. and Treas. Thomas Green & Co. Inc. 1960–67, Sec.-Treas. 1968; Treas. Lugar Stock Farms Inc. 1960; mem. Bd of Trustees, Denison Univ. 1966, Advisory Bd, Ind. Univ., Purdue Univ. at Indianapolis 1969–75, Bd of Trustees of Indiana Cen. Univ. 1970; Vice-Chair. 1975, Visiting Prof. of Political Science, Dir of Public Affairs 1975–76; mem. Visiting Cttee of Harvard-MIT Jt Centre for Urban Studies 1973; mem. Bd of Dirs, Indianapolis Centre for Advanced Research 1973–76; mem. Indianapolis Bd of School Commrs 1964–67, Vice-Pres. 1965; Mayor of Indianapolis 1968–75; del. and keynote speaker, Ind. Republican Convention 1968, del. 1972; del. mem. Platform Cttee, Repub. Nat. Convention 1968, del., keynote speaker and mem. Platform Cttee 1972; cand. for US Senate 1974, Senator from Indiana 1977–2013, Chair. Nat. Republican Senatorial Cttee 1983–84, Foreign Relations Cttee 1985–87, 2003–07, Cttee on Agric. 1995–2001; mem. Advisory Comm. on Intergovernmental Relations 1969–75, Vice-Chair. 1970–75; mem. Advisory Bd of US Conf. of Mayors 1969–75; mem. Pres. Model Cities Advisory Task Force 1969–70, State and Local Govt Advisory Cttee of Office of Econ. Opportunity 1969–73, Nat. Advisory Comm. on Criminal Justice Standards and Goals 1971–73; mem. of Advisory Council, Nat. League of Cities 1971, mem. Council 1972–75; mem. Bd of Dirs Westview Osteopathic Hosp. 1969–76, Indianapolis Symphony Orchestra, Nat. Endowment for Democracy; mem. Nat. Acad. of Public Admin, Rotary Club of Indianapolis and other civic orgs; Trustee, Denison Univ., Indianapolis Univ.; Republican; hon. doctorates from 20 colls and univs in USA 1970–78; Exceptional Service Award, Office of Econ. Opportunity 1972, Fiorello La Guardia Award, New School of Social Research 1975. *Publication:* Letters to the Next President 1988. *Leisure interests:* music, reading, running, golf, tennis. *Address:* c/o 306 Hart Senate Office Building, Washington, DC 20510, USA.

LUGO MÉNDEZ, Fernando Armindo; Paraguayan politician, fmr ecclesiastic and fmr head of state; b. 30 May 1951, San Solano; one s.; ed Catholic Univ. of Our Lady of the Assumption, Pontifical Gregorian Univ., Rome; ordained priest of Soc. of the Divine Word 1977; moved to Ecuador as missionary in Bolivar prov., then studied in Rome; returned to Paraguay, apptd Bishop of San Pedro 1994–2005 (resgnd), resgnd from priesthood 2006; Leader, Movimiento Popular Tekojoja; Pres. of Paraguay 2008–12. *Address:* c/o Palacio de López, Asunción; Movimiento Popular Tekojoja, Asunción, Paraguay.

LUHABE, Wendy Y. Nomathemba, BA, BComm; South African business executive and university chancellor; *Chancellor, University of Johannesburg;* b. 29 May 1957, Daveyton, Gauteng Prov.; d. of Stanley Garfield Luhabe and Adelaide Boniwe Bulana; m. Mbhazima Shilowa; two s.; ed Univ. of Lesotho; marketing professional with Vanda Cosmetics, BMW South Africa & N America for 10 years; Founder Bridging the Gap 1992–2001; Founder Women Investment Portfolio Holdings 1994; social entrepreneur, Wendy Luhabe Foundation for the educ. and leadership devt of women, Women Pvt. Equity for women-owned enterprises, asset man. and advertising; Chair. Alliance Capital –2009, Vodacom Group –2009, Vendome SA, Industrial Devt Corpn, Int. Marketing Council; mem. Consultative Network of the Helsinki Process on Globalization and Democracy; Int. Trustee, The Duke of Edinburgh's Award Int. Foundation for Young People; Chancellor Univ. of Johannesburg 2006–; mem. Bd Johannesburg Securities Exchange, Cycad Financial Holdings; Dir (non-exec.) Women Pvt. Equity Fund, BMW SA; mem. Club of Rome 2006–; hon. degrees (Univ. of Fort Hare) 2005, (Stellenbosch Univ.) 2006; recognized by World Econ. Forum as a Global Leader for Tomorrow 1997, Leadership in Practice, Unisa Business Leadership School 1997, Outstanding Young Person, Osaka Jr Chamber of Commerce (Japan) 1997, one of 50 Leading Women Entrepreneurs of the World 1999, Award in Recognition of Championing

Women Empowerment, Black Management Forum 2004. *Publication:* Defining Moments 2002. *Leisure interests:* travel, metaphysics, decoupage, nature, culture, music. *Address:* PO Box 91413, Auckland Park, Johannesburg 2006, South Africa (office). *Telephone:* (11) 8807117 (office). *Fax:* (11) 8803767 (office). *E-mail:* wendy@ definingmoments.co.za (office). *Website:* www.definingmomentsworld.com (office).

LUHRMANN, Bazmark (Baz) Anthony; Australian writer, producer and director; b. 17 Sept. 1962, NSW; s. of Leonard Luhrmann and Barbara Luhrmann; m. Catherine Martin 1997; one d.; ed Narrabeen High School, Sydney; theatre work with Peter Brook (q.v.); owns Bazmark Inq. production co., Sydney; acting roles in films Winter of Our Dreams 1981, The Dark Room 1982; directed advertisement for Chanel No. 5 2004. *Recording:* Something for Everybody (concept album, including track Everybody's Free To Wear Sunscreen) (Platinum Album, Australia, Gold Album, USA). *Plays:* Strictly Ballroom, Haircut. *Operas directed:* La Bohème, Sydney 1990, New York 2002–03, San Francisco 2002, A Midsummer Night's Dream, Sydney 1993. *Films directed:* Strictly Ballroom (Cannes Film Festival Prix de la Jeunesse, Toronto Film Festival People's Choice Award, Chicago Film Festival Award for Best Feature Film) 1992, Romeo + Juliet (also producer) 1996, Moulin Rouge! (also producer) (numerous awards, including Golden Globe, Producers' Guild of America Film of the Year, Hollywood Film Festival Best Movie) 2001, Australia (also producer) 2008, Waist Up/Waist Down (short) 2012, Ugly Chic (short) 2012, The Surreal Body (short) 2012, The Exotic Body (short) 2012, The Classical Body (short) 2012, Schiaparelli & Prada: Impossible Conversations (short) 2012, Naïf Chic (short) 2012, Hard Chic (short) 2012, The Great Gatsby (also producer) 2013. *Screenplays:* Strictly Ballroom 1992, Romeo + Juliet 1996, Moulin Rouge (also story) 2001, Australia (also story) 2008, The Great Gatsby 2013. *Television includes:* A Country Practice (actor) 1981–82, La Bohème (film) 1993. *Address:* c/o Robert Newman, WME, 9601 Wilshire Blvd, 10th Floor, Beverly Hills, CA 90212, USA (office); Bazmark Inq., PO Box 430, Kings Cross, NSW 1340, Australia (office). *Website:* www.bazmark.com (office).

LÜHRMANN, Reinhard, Dr rer. nat; German biochemist and academic; *Director, Department of Cellular Biochemistry, Max Planck Institute of Biophysical Chemistry;* ed Univ. of Münster; Research Group Leader, Max Planck Inst. for Molecular Genetics, Berlin 1981–88; Prof. of Biochemistry and Molecular Biology, Univ. of Marburg 1988–99; Dir, Dept of Cellular Biochemistry, Max Planck Inst. for Biophysical Chem., Göttingen 1999–; Hon. Prof., Philipps Univ. of Marburg 2000–, Georg August Univ. of Göttingen 2007–; Max Planck Research Award 1990, Gottfried Wilhelm Leibniz Prize 1996, Feldberg Foundation Prize Lecturer 2002, Ernst Jung Prize 2003. *Publications:* numerous articles in scientific journals. *Address:* Max-Planck-Institut für biophysikalische Chemie, Abteilung Zelluläre Biochemie, Am Faßberg 11, 37077 Göttingen, Germany (office). *Telephone:* (551) 201-1407 (office). *Fax:* (551) 201-1197 (office). *E-mail:* reinhard .luehrmann@mpibpc.mpg.de (office). *Website:* www.mpibpc.mpg.de/luehrmann (office).

LUI, Frank Fakaotimanava, CNZM; Niuean politician; b. 1945, Alofi; m. Iris Lui; Premier of Niue 1993–99, also Minister for External Relations, Niueans Overseas, Police and Immigration, Civil Aviation and Public Service Comm.; Ind.; Companion, NZ Order of Merit 1999. *Address:* c/o Office of the Secretary to Government, PO Box 40, Alofi, Niue. *E-mail:* richard.hipa@mail.gov.nu.

LUIK, Jüri; Estonian diplomatist, politician and journalist; b. 17 Aug. 1966, Tallinn; m. Ruth Lausma Luik; one s.; ed Tallinn 7th High School, Tartu Univ. and postgraduate research, Carnegie, USA; Political Ed. Vikerkaar (monthly) 1988–90, Ed. 1990; specialist on Anglo-Saxon Countries, Estonian Inst. 1989–91; mem. Pro Patria (Isamaaliit) Party 1989–; attaché, Embassy of Estonia, UK 1991; Head, Political Dept, Ministry of Foreign Affairs 1991–92; mem. Riigikogu (Parl.) 1992–95; Minister without portfolio responsible for Estonian-Russian Negotiations 1992–93; Minister of Defence 1993–94, 1999–2001, of Foreign Affairs 1994–95; Sr Research Fellow, Carnegie Foundation 1995–96; Amb. to NATO and Benelux States, Brussels 1996–99; head of govt del. for accession talks with NATO 2002–03; Amb. to USA (also accred to Canada) 2003–07, Amb. and Perm. Rep. to NATO, Brussels 2007–12. *Leisure interests:* theatre, films, tennis. *Address:* Ministry of Foreign Affairs, Islandi Väljak 1, Tallinn 15049, Estonia (office). *Telephone:* 637-7092 (office). *Fax:* 637-7099 (office). *E-mail:* vminfo@vm.ee (office). *Website:* www.vm.ee (office).

LUKAS, D. Wayne, EdM; American race horse trainer; b. 2 Sept. 1935, Antigo, Wis.; s. of Ted Lukas and Bea Lukas; m. Laura Lukas; one s.; ed Univ. of Wisconsin; began career as Asst Basketball Coach, Univ. of Wisconsin, then Head Basketball Coach, LaCrosse High School; later spent more than ten years training quarter horses, with a record 150 wins; switched to training thoroughbreds 1978; six consecutive Triple Crown race wins: Tabasco Cat–Preakness 1994, Belmont 1994, Thunder Gulch–Derby 1995, Belmont 1995, Timber Country–Preakness 1995, Grindstone–Kentucky Derby 1996; total of 16 Breeder's Cup wins; all-time leading money winner (over US \$200 million); now makes guest appearances as motivational speaker; four-time Eclipse Award winner–Trainer of the Year, Nat . Museum of Racing's Hall of Fame 1999. *Address:* c/o Program Resources Professional Speakers Bureau, P.O. Box 22307, Louisville, KY 40252, USA (office).

LUKASHENKA, Alyaksandr Rygorovich; Belarusian politician, economist and head of state; *President;* b. 30 Aug. 1954, Kopys; m. Halyna Rodionovna Lukashena 1975 (estranged); two s.; one s. with Irina Abelskaya; ed Mogilev State Univ. and Belarus Agric. Acad.; served in Soviet Army 1975–77, 1980–82; Sec. Komsomol Cttee, Shklov, instructor Political Div. Komsomol Cttee W Border Dist 1975–77; Sec. Komsomol Cttee Mogilev City Food Dept; instructor regional Exec. Cttee 1977–80; Deputy Commdr of Co. 1980–82; Deputy Chair. Udarnik collective farm 1982–83; Deputy Dir Enterprise of Construction Materials 1983–85; Sec. CP Cttee Collective Farm of V.I. Lenin, Shklov Dist 1985–87; Dir Gorodets state farm 1987–94; elected Deputy, Supreme Council of Belarus SSR 1990–94; Chair. Parl. Comm. on Struggle against Corruption 1993–94; Pres. of Belarus 1994–; C-in-C Armed Forces of Belarus 1994–; Chair. Higher Council of Belarus and Russia Union 1997–; Chair. Supreme State Council of the Union State of Belarus and Russia 2000–; Hon. Academician, Russian Acad. of Sciences 1995, Hon. Citizen of Yerevan, Armenia 2001; Order of the Holy Cross of the Kts of the Holy Sepulchre 2000, José Martí Order (Cuba) 2000, Order of the Revolution (Libya) 2000, Order 'For Services to the Fatherland', (Second Class) (Russia) 2001,

Order of St Dmitry Donskoy (First Degree) 2005, Order of St Cyril (Belarusian Orthodox Church) 2006, Order of St Vladimir (First Class) (Russian Orthodox Church) 2007, Keys to the City of Caracas, Venezuela 2010, Order of Distinguished Citizen, Caracas 2010, Order of the Repub. of Serbia 2013; Honour Diploma of Eurasian Econ. Community 2006; Int. Prize of Andrey Pervozvanny 'For Faith and Loyalty' 1995, M. Sholokhov Int. Award 1997, Special Prize of IOC 'Gates of the Olymph' 2000, Medal of the Int. Fed. of Festival Orgs 2005. *Address:* Office of the President, 220016 Minsk, vul. K. Marksa 38, Dom Urada, Belarus (office). *Telephone:* (17) 222-35-03 (office). *Fax:* (17) 222-30-20 (office). *E-mail:* press@president.gov.by (office). *Website:* www.president.gov.by (office).

LUKE, Hon. Justice Desmond Edgar Fashole, BL, MA; Sierra Leonean chief justice (retd), diplomatist and politician; b. 6 Oct. 1935, Freetown; s. of Sir Emile Fashole-Luke and Lady Christina Fashole-Luke; one s. one d.; ed Prince of Wales School, Freetown, King's Coll., Taunton, UK, Keble Coll., Oxford, UK, Magdalene Coll., Cambridge, UK, Georgetown Univ., Washington, DC, USA; admitted to Bar of England and Wales 1962, of Sierra Leone 1963; in pvt. practice, barrister and solicitor 1963–69; Legal Adviser to Mobil Oil, British Petrol, Bata Shoe Co., Barclays Bank, Diamond Corpn, Allen & Elliot (SL) Ltd, Singer Sewing Machine Co. Ltd, Trade Marks Owners' Asscn, Adams and Adams Patent Attorneys and other industrial and commercial cos 1963–69; UN Human Rights Fellow, India 1964; Amb. to FRG (also accred to Netherlands, Belgium and Luxembourg 1970–73) 1969–73, to France, Italy and Perm. Rep. to EEC 1971–73; Deputy Leader Del. to Heads of State Summit of OAU, Addis Ababa, Non-Aligned Summit, Algeria 1969, Commonwealth Prime Minister's Conf., Ottawa 1973, Abidjan Peace Talks 1996, ECOWAS Conf., Abuja 1997, UN Gen. Ass., NY 1997; Leader Del. to IAEA Conf., Vienna 1970, to African Econ. Conf., Milan 1971, to Council of Ministers of OAU, Addis Ababa 1973–75, to UN Gen. Ass., NY 1973–74; Minister of Foreign Affairs 1973–75 (resgnd), of Health 1977–78; Man. Dir Africa Int. Ltd 1975; Chair. Comm. for Consolidation of Peace 1996–97; Chief Justice of Sierra Leone 1998–2002; Special Envoy of Pres. Kabbah to Pres. Kuffour of Ghana 2002; Grand Cross, Order of Merit (FRG) 1973; Grand Cordon, Order of Menelik II (Ethiopia) 1973; Oxford Blues Athletic Awards 1955–58, finalist (long jump), Commonwealth Games, Cardiff 1958, Oxford and Cambridge Freshman's Champion and Record Holder (high jump) 1954, Men in Action Certificate of Merit for Contrib. to Restoration of Democracy in Sierra Leone 1999, Jarwlee Lewis Meritorious Award for Services to State 2001. *Publications include:* Republican Constitution: What Form?. *Leisure interests:* sports, art, music. *Address:* c/o Office of the Chief Justice, Supreme Court, Freetown (office); Luke House, PO Box 214, Freetown, Sierra Leone (home). *Telephone:* (22) 231863 (office). *Fax:* (22) 225670 (office). *E-mail:* fasholeluke@yahoo.com (home).

LUKIANENKO, Levko (Hryhorovych); Ukrainian politician and lawyer; *Chairman, Ukrainian Republican Party;* b. 24 Aug. 1928, Chrypivka, Chernigiv Region; s. of Hryzko Lukianenko and Natalka Lukianenko; m. Nadia Oleyandrivna Lukianenko; two d.; ed Moscow M.V. Lomonosov State Univ.; mem. CPSU 1953–61; served in Soviet Army 1944–53; legal adviser, Lvov CPSU Regional Cttee 1958–59; barrister 1959–61; sentenced to death 1961 for formation of Ukrainian Workers' and Peasants' League, but sentence commuted to 15 years' imprisonment, released 1976; Co-Founder, on release, of Ukrainian Helsinki Group 1976, again arrested, sentenced to 10 years' imprisonment and 5 years' exile, returned to Ukraine 1989; mem. Verkhovna Rada (Parl.) 1990–92, 1995–98, 2002–06, 2006–07; Chair. Ukrainian Republican Party 1990–92, 2000–02, 2005–06, 2010–, Hon. Chair. 1992–; cand. in Ukrainian presidential elections 1991; Amb. to Canada 1992–93; Chair. Ukrainian Asscn of Researchers into Famine in Ukraine; Academician Acad. of Higher School of Ukraine 2002; Hero of Ukraine 2005; Hon. LLD (Alberta); Merit of Honour of Ukrainian Pres. *Publications:* Confession from the Condemned Cell 1991, For Ukraine 1991, I Believe in God and Ukraine 1991, I Do Not Permit Ukraine to Perish 1994, The Birth of a New Era 1997, In the Land of the Maple Leaf 1998, National Idea and National Will 2003, Indestructibility 2004, From the Time of Imprisonment 2005. *Leisure interests:* music, gardening. *Address:* 5 Hrushevsky Street, 01008, Kiev (office); 20 Sadova Street, v. khotiv, Kyivo-Sviatosh District, 08171 Kiev, Ukraine (home). *Telephone:* (44) 255-34-08 (office); (44) 255-16-84 (home). *Fax:* (44) 489-05-27 (office); (44) 989-33-25 (home). *E-mail:* urp@urp1990.com.ua (office). *Website:* urp1990.com.ua (office).

LUKIN, Vladimir Petrovich, PhD, DSc; Russian politician and diplomatist; *Commissioner for Human Rights (Federal Ombudsman);* b. 13 June 1937, Omsk; m.; two s.; ed Moscow State Pedagogical Inst., USSR Acad. of Sciences; researcher, Museum of Revolution, Inst. of World Econs and Int. Relations, USSR Acad. of Sciences 1959–65; on staff of journal World Review, Prague until Aug. 1968 when he was recalled to USSR for protesting against Soviet invasion of Czechoslovakia; Research Fellow, Inst. of US and Canadian Studies, USSR Acad. of Sciences 1969–87; Deputy Dir Dept of Assessment and Planning of the USSR Ministry of Foreign Affairs 1987–90; People's Deputy of RSFSR (now Russia) 1990–93; Chair. Foreign Affairs Cttee of the Russian Supreme Soviet 1990–92; Amb. to USA 1992–93; Co-Founder and Leader, pre-election bloc (later political movt) Yabloko (with G. Javlinsky) 1993, currently Deputy Chair.; mem. State Duma (Parl.) 1993–2003, Chair. Cttee for Foreign Affairs 1994–99, Deputy Chair. State Duma 2000–02; Commr for Human Rights of Russian Fed. (Fed. Ombudsman) 2004–; two decorative orders, one medal. *Publications include:* Centres of Power: Conceptions and Reality, China's Place in US Global Policy, With Concern and Hope: Russia and the West. *Leisure interests:* sport. *Address:* Office of the Commissioner for Human Rights in the Russian Federation, 103084 Moscow, Myasnitskaya str. 47 (office); c/o Yabloko Party, 121019 Moscow, Novy Arbat str. 21, 18th Floor, Russia (office). *Telephone:* (495) 207-39-69 (office). *Fax:* (495) 207-39-77 (office). *E-mail:* lukin@rodnet.ru (office).

LUKMAN, Rilwanu, BSc, CEng; Nigerian international civil servant, business executive and engineer; b. 26 Aug. 1938, Zaria, Kaduna State; s. of Qadi Lukman and Hajia Ramatu Lukman; m. 1966; two s. one d.; ed Govt Coll. Zaria (now Barewa), Nigerian Coll. of Arts, Science and Tech. (now Ahmadu Bello Univ.), Royal School of Mines, Imperial Coll. of Science and Tech., Univ. of London, Inst. of Prospecting and Mineral Deposits, Univ. of Mining and Metallurgy, Leoben, Austria, McGill Univ., Montreal, Canada; Asst Mining Engineer, A.G. Statagruvor, Sweden 1962–64; Inspector of Mines and Sr Inspector of Mines, Ministry of Mines and Power, Jos 1964–67, Acting Asst Chief Inspector of Mines 1968–70;

Gen. Man. Cement Co. of Northern Nigeria Ltd, Sokoto 1970–74; Gen. Man. and Chief Exec. Nigerian Mining Corpn, Jos 1974–84; Fed. Minister of Mines, Power and Steel, Lagos 1984–85, of Petroleum Resources, Lagos 1986–89, 2008–10, of Foreign Affairs 1989–90; Pres. OPEC Conf. 1986–89, Sec.-Gen. OPEC 1995–2000, Head Del. from Nigeria 2001, Alt. Pres. 2001–02; Fellow and Hon. Fellow Inst. of Mining and Metallurgy; Fellow Imperial Coll. London, Nigerian Mining and Geoscience Soc.; Past Vice-Pres. Asscn of Geoscientists for Int. Devt; mem. Soc. of Mining Engineers of AIME; Hon. KBE 1989; Officier Légion d'honneur 1990; Order of Liberator, First Class, Venezuela 1990; Hon. PhD (Bologna) 1988; Hon. DSc (Maiduguri) 1989, (Ahmadu Bello) 1991; Dr hc (Moore House Coll. Atlanta) 1989. *Leisure interests:* reading, walking.

LUKŠIĆ, Igor, MA, PhD; Montenegrin politician; *Deputy Prime Minister, responsible for European Integration and Minister of Foreign Affairs and European Integration;* b. 14 June 1976, Bar, Montenegrin SR, SFR Yugoslavia; m. Natasha Lukšić; two d.; ed Univ. of Montenegro, Podgorica; asst on implementation of assistance programmes of EC 'Obnova', Ministry of Foreign Affairs 1998–2000; Adviser on int. relations, Democratic Party of Socialists 2000–01; performed duties of Sec. in Ministry of Foreign Affairs Jan.–May 2001; elected mem. Parl. of Montenegro 2001, 2002, 2006, 2008; mem. Parl. of Serbia and Montenegro 2003–06; Adviser on Public Relations to the Prime Minister Jan.–April 2003; Deputy Minister of Foreign Affairs of Serbia and Montenegro 2003–04; Minister of Finance 2004–10, Gov. on behalf of Montenegro at World Bank and EBRD 2006; Deputy Prime Minister 2008–10; Prime Minister 2010–12; Deputy Prime Minister, responsible for European Integration and Minister of Foreign Affairs and European Integration 2012–; Assoc. Prof., Economy and Devt and Market Process, Faculty of Int. Econs, Finance and Business, Podgorica, Asst to course on Entrepreneurship, Faculty of Econs summer terms 2004, 2005, 2006; mem. Cttee for ECO Sciences, Montenegrin Acad. of Arts and Science; mem. Presidency of Democratic Party of Socialists, Presidency of Basketball Asscn of Montenegro 2010–11. *Publications include:* several academic works as well as a book of poetry and prose, Book of Laughter, Book of fear; publishes regular blogposts in both Montenegrin and English. *Address:* Ministry of Foreign Affairs and European Integration, 81000 Podgorica, Stanka Dragojevića 2, Montenegro (office). *Telephone:* (20) 246357 (office). *Fax:* (20) 224670 (office). *E-mail:* kabinet@mfa.gov.me (office). *Website:* www.mvpei.gov.me (office); igorluksic.wordpress.com.

LUKŠIĆ, Igor, PhD; Slovenian political scientist, academic and politician; *President, Social Democrats;* b. 3 Dec. 1961, Novo mesto, Slovenian SR, SFR Yugoslavia; ed Univ. of Ljubljana; Teaching Asst, Faculty of Social Sciences, Univ. of Ljubljana 1986, later Asst Prof., Prof. of Political Science 2003–, Chair. Dept of Political Science 1997–99, 2007–, Vice-Dean, Faculty of Social Sciences 1999–2001, Dean 2001–03, fmr Pres. Union of Slovenian Sports Socs; Ed.-in-Chief Teorija in praksa magazine 1995–2008; has lectured at several int. univs, including Michigan State Univ. and Univ. of California, Davis, USA and Univ. of Genoa, Italy; Vice-Pres. Social Democrats (Socialni demokrati—SD) 2005–09, Pres. 2012–; mem. Nat. Ass. (Parl.) 2008–; Minister of Educ. and Sport 2008–12. *Publications:* five books, including: Demokracija v pluralni družbi – Preverjanje veljavnosti konsociativne teorije (Democracy in a Plural Society) 1991, Liberalizem versus korporativizem (Liberalism versus Corporativism) 1994, Politični sistem Republike Slovenije (The Political System of the Republic of Slovenia) 2001; articles on political culture, the history of political ideas and political systems, and analysis of policies, published in Slovene, German, English, Czech and Serbo-Croatian. *Address:* Socialni demokrati, Levstikova 15, 1000 Ljubljana (office); Room C208, Faculty of Social Sciences, University of Ljubljana, Kardeljeva ploščad 5, PO Box 2547, 1001 Ljubljana, Slovenia (office). *Telephone:* (1) 2444100 (SD) (office); (1) 5805181 (Faculty) (office). *Fax:* (1) 2444111 (SD) (office). *E-mail:* info@socialnidemokrati.si (office); igor.luksic@fdv.uni-lj.si (office). *Website:* www.socialnidemokrati.si (office); www.fdv.uni-lj.si (office).

LUKYANOV, Anatoliy Ivanovich; Russian politician and poet; b. 7 May 1930; m.; one d.; ed Moscow Univ.; mem. CPSU 1955–91; Chief Consultant on Legal Comm. of USSR Council of Ministers 1956–61; Deputy Head of Dept of Presidium of USSR Supreme Soviet 1969–76, Head of Secr. 1977–83; mem. of editorial staff of Sovietskoe Gosudarstvo i Pravo 1978; mem. Cen. Auditing Comm. CPSU 1981–86, 1986–89; Deputy of RSFSR Supreme Soviet 1984–91; Head of Gen. Dept of Cen. Cttee CPSU 1985–87, Sec. of Cen. Cttee 1987–88; Cand. mem. Political Bureau 1988–90; First Vice-Chair. of Presidium, USSR Supreme Soviet 1988–90, Chair. 1990–91; Chief Adviser on Legal Reform in USSR 1986–89; mem. Cen. Cttee CPSU 1986–91; People's Deputy of USSR 1989–91; arrested 1991 following failed coup d'état; charged with conspiracy Jan. 1992; released on bail Dec. 1992, on trial 1993–94; mem. State Duma (Parl.) 1993–2003; mem. Cttee for Legis. and Judicial Reform 1994, Chair. 1996–99; Chair. Cttee for State Org. 2000–02; mem. Presidium, Cen. Exec. Cttee CP of Russian Fed.; Order of October Revolution. *Publications include:* many articles and books on Soviet legal system and Soviet constitution, three vols of poetry (under pseudonym A. Osenev). *Address:* c/o Communist Party of the Russian Federation, per. M. Sukharevskii 3/1, 103051 Moscow, Russia. *Telephone:* (495) 928-71-29. *Fax:* (495) 292-90-50.

LULA DA SILVA, Luiz Inácio; Brazilian trade union official, politician and fmr head of state; b. 27 Oct. 1945, Caetés (then a dist of Garanhuns), Pernambuco; s. of Aristides Inácio da Silva and Eurídice Ferreira de Mello; m. Marisa Leticia 1974; five c.; qualified as mechanic; started working at Indústrias Villares steelworks 1966; Assoc. mem. Exec. Cttee, São Bernardo do Campo and Diadema Metalworkers' Union 1969–72, First Sec. (responsible for social security) 1972–75, Pres. 1975–80; led steelworkers' strikes 1978, 1979; Pres. Partido dos Trabalhadores (Labour Party) 1980–87, 1993; a leader of the 'Elections Now' campaign for direct presidential elections 1984; a leader of campaign to impeach Pres. Collor de Mello 1992; Fed. Deputy 1986–; presidential cand. 1989, 1994, 2002; f. a 'Parallel Govt' (to prepare an alternative set of policies for the country) 1990; Councillor, Citizenship Inst. 1992–; Pres. of Brazil 2003–11; Brazilian Order of Merit, Brazilian Orders of Mil., Naval and Aeronautical Merit, Brazilian Order of Scientific Merit, Mexican Order of the Aztec Eagle, Norwegian Order of Royal Merit, First Class, Order of Prince Yaroslav the Wise (Ukraine) 2003, Order of Liberty (Ukraine) 2009; Dr hc (Inst. of Political Studies, Paris) 2011; Prince of Asturias Award for Int. Co-operation 2003, chief guest at India's Repub. Day celebration 2004, Jawaharlal Nehru Award 2006, ranked by the Financial Times amongst the 50 faces that shaped the 2000s, named by Newsweek magazine as 18th most important person in the world 2008, UNESCO Félix Houphouët-Boigny Peace Prize 2008, Chatham House Prize 2009, O.P. Dwivedi Public Service Award, Int. Asscn of Schools and Insts of Admin 2009, ranked 33rd by Forbes magazine amongst The World's Most Powerful People 2009, chosen as Man of the Year by El País and Le Monde newspapers 2009, Indira Gandhi Prize for Peace, Disarmament and Development 2010, Global Statesman, World Econ. Forum 2010, featured in TIME magazine's 100 Most Influential People in the World 2010, World Food Prize (co-recipient) 2011. *Address:* c/o Office of the President, Palácio do Planalto, Praça dos Três Poderes, 70150-900, Brasília, DF, Brazil.

LULLA, Kishore, BA; Indian film industry executive; *Chairman and CEO, Eros International;* b. 4 Sept. 1964; s. of Arjan Lulla; ed Mumbai Univ.; est. UK office of family-owned film distribution co. Eros Int. 1988, currently Chair. and CEO, has expanded co's operations into film production and financing; mem. BAFTA, Young Pres.'s Org.; BDO Stoy Hayward Business of the Year, Eastern Eye Asian Business Award 2007, India Splendour Award 2007. *Address:* Eros International Ltd, Unit 23, Sovereign Park, Coronation Road, London, NW10 7QP, England (office). *Telephone:* (20) 8963-8700 (office). *Fax:* (20) 8963-0154 (office). *E-mail:* UK -business@erosintl.co.uk (office). *Website:* www.erosplc.com (office).

LULU-BRIGGS, High Chief O.B.; Nigerian business executive; *Chairman, Moni Pulo Ltd;* b. 1930, Abonnema, Kalabari; m. Seinye Lulu Briggs; Founder-Chair. Moni Pulo Ltd (oil co.) 1992–; Dir (non-exec.) Transnational Corpn of Nigeria Plc 2007–, also mem. Nomination and Governance Cttee; Co-founder O.B Lulu-Briggs Foundation 2001–; Officer, Order of the Niger. *Address:* Moni Pulo Limited, 5, Odoni Street, Amadi Flats, Port Harcourt, Nigeria (office). *Telephone:* (8) 4462827 (office). *Fax:* (8) 4464017 (office). *E-mail:* info@monipulo.com (office). *Website:* www.monipulo.com (office).

LUM, Olivia, BSc; Malaysian business executive and fmr chemist; *Head of Research and Development, President and Group CEO, Hyflux Group;* b. Kampar, Perak; adopted at birth; ed Tiong Bahru Secondary School, Hwa Chong Jr Coll., Nat. Univ. of Singapore; chemist, Glaxo Pharmaceutical 1986–89; f. Hydrochem (now Hyflux Group) 1989, manufacturer of water filters and treatment chemicals, Head of Research and Devt, Pres. and Group CEO; mem. Parl. (nominated) 2002–05; mem. Bd of Dirs International Enterprise Singapore; Pres. Singapore Water Asscn; mem. Singapore-Tianjin Economic and Trade Council, Singapore-Jiangsu Cooperation Council, Singapore-Zhejiang Economic and Trade Council, Singapore-Oman Business Council, Singapore Business Federation Council; Ind. Dir (non-exec.) Singapore Exchange –2008 (resgnd); Int. Man. Action Award 2003, Global Female Invent and Innovate Award 2004, Ernst & Young World Entrepreneur Of The Year 2011, ranked by Fortune magazine amongst the 50 Most Powerful Women in Business outside the US (50th) 2010. *Address:* Hyflux Ltd, Hyflux Building, 202 Kallang Bahru, Singapore City, 339339, Singapore (office). *Telephone:* 6214-0777 (office). *Fax:* 6214-1211 (office). *E-mail:* contact_us@hyflux.com (office). *Website:* www.hyflux.com (office).

LUMLEY, Joanna Lamond, OBE, FRGS; British actress; b. 1 May 1946, Kashmir, India; d. of Maj. James Rutherford Lumley and Thyra Beatrice Rose Lumley; m. 1st Jeremy Lloyd (divorced); m. 2nd Stephen Barlow 1986; one s.; ed Army School, Malaysia, Mickledene, Kent, St Mary's St Leonards on Sea; Hon. DLitt (Kent) 1994; Hon. DUniv (Oxford Brookes) 2000; Dr hc (Queen's Univ. Belfast) 2008, (St Andrews) 2009; BAFTA Award 1992, 1994, Special BAFTA 2000. *Stage appearances include:* Noël Coward's Blithe Spirit 1986, Vanilla 1990, Revengers Comedies 1991, The Letter 1995, Hedda Gabler, Private Lives, An Ideal Husband, The Cherry Orchard 2007, La Bête (Broadway) 2010, The Lion in Winter 2011. *Films include:* Some Girls Do, Tam Lin, The Breaking of Bumbo, Games That Lovers Play, Don't Just Lie There Say Something, The Plank, On Her Majesty's Secret Service, Trail of the Pink Panther, Curse of the Pink Panther, Satanic Rites of Dracula 1978, Shirley Valentine, Innocent Lies 1995, James and the Giant Peach 1996, Cold Comfort Farm 1996, Prince Valiant 1997, Parting Shots 1998, The Tale of Sweeney Todd 1998, Mad Cows 1999, Maybe Baby 1999, The Cat's Meow 2000, EuroTrip 2004, Ella Enchanted 2004, The Magic Round-about (voice) 2005, The Corpse Bride (voice) 2005, Stories of Lost Souls 2006, Dolls 2006, Boogie Woogie 2009, Animals United (voice) 2010, The Snowman: The Live Stage Show (video) (narrator) 2010, Late Bloomers 2011, The Wolf of Wall Street 2013. *Television includes:* Release, Mark II Wife, Comedy Playhouse, It's Awfully Bad for Your Eyes Darling, Coronation Street, The Protectors, General Hospital 1974–75, The New Avengers 1976–77, Steptoe & Son, Are You Being Served?, The Cuckoo Waltz, Up The Workers, That was Tori, Sapphire and Steel 1978, Absolutely Fabulous (series) 1992–2012, Class Act 1994, Girl Friday (documen-tary) 1994, White Rajahs of Sarawak (documentary), Joanna Lumley in the Kingdom of the Thunder Dragon (documentary) 1997, Coming Home 1998, A Rather English Marriage 1998, Nancherrow, Dr Willoughby, MD, Mirrorball 1999, Absolutely Fabulous (series 4) 2001, Giraffes on the Move (documentary) 2001, Up in Town 2002, Absolutely Fabulous Special 2002, Agatha Christie's Marple 2004, Sensitive Skin 2005–07, Jam & Jerusalem 2006–08, In the Land of the Northern Lights 2007, Lewis (series) 2009, Mistresses 2010, Marple: The Mirror Crack'd from Side to Side 2010, Joanna Lumley's Nile 2010, Comic Relief: Uptown Downstairs Abbey (film) 2011, Joanna Lumley's Greek Odyssey 2011, three Absolutely Fabulous Specials (Identity 2011, Job 2012, Olympics 2012), Joanna Lumley: In Search of Noah's Ark 2012, Little Crackers (series) 2012, The Making of a Lady (film) 2012, Jonathan Creek 2013; co-producer The Cazalets (BBC 1) 2001. *Publications include:* Stare Back and Smile (autobiography) 1989, Forces' Sweethearts 1993, Girl Friday 1994, Joanna Lumley in the Kingdom of the Thunder Dragon 1997, No Room for Secrets (autobiog.) 2004, Joanna Lumley Absolutely 2009. *Leisure interests:* walking, gardening, collecting things, painting, music, travelling. *Address:* c/o John Grant, Conway van Gelder, 3rd Floor, 8/12 Broadwick Street, London, W1F 8HW, England (office). *Telephone:* (20) 7287-0077 (office). *E-mail:* john@conwayvg.co.uk (office).

LUMSDEN, Andrew Gino Sita, MA, PhD, FRS, FMedSci; British neurobiologist and academic; *Professor of Developmental Neurobiology, King's College London;* b. 22 Jan. 1947, Beaconsfield, Bucks., England; m. (divorced); two d.; ed Kingswood School, Bath, St Catharine's Coll., Cambridge, Yale Univ., USA, Univ. of London; Lecturer in Anatomy, Sr Lecturer, then Reader, Guy's Hosp. Medical School; Prof.

of Developmental Neurobiology, King's Coll. London 1989–, Dir MRC Centre for Developmental Neurobiology 2000–; Howard Hughes Int. Research Scholar 1993–98; Visiting Prof., Univ. of California, Berkeley 1994; mem. European Molecular Biology Org. 2008–; Fulbright Scholar 1968–70, W. Maxwell Cowan Prize for Developmental Neuroscience 2007. *Publications:* The Developing Brain (co-author) 2001; more than 150 scientific publs. *Leisure interests:* mechanical eng, natural history. *Address:* Medical Research Council Centre for Developmental Neurobiology, King's College London, New Hunts House, Guy's Campus, London, SE1 1UL (office); 16 Elephant Lane, London, SE16 4JD, England (home). *Telephone:* (20) 7848-6520 (office); (20) 7640-0187 (home). *Fax:* (20) 7848-6550 (office); (20) 7640-0189 (home). *E-mail:* andrew.lumsden@kcl.ac.uk (office). *Website:* www.kcl.ac.uk/devneuro/lumsden.php (office).

LUMSDEN, Sir David James, Kt, MusB, MA, DPhil; British musician (retd); b. 19 March 1928, Newcastle-upon-Tyne, England; s. of Albert Lumsden and Vera May Lumsden (née Tate); m. Sheila Daniels 1951; two s. two d.; ed Dame Allan's School, Newcastle-upon-Tyne, Selwyn Coll., Cambridge (Organ Scholar); Asst Organist, St John's Coll. Cambridge 1951–53; Organist and Choirmaster St Mary's, Nottingham and Univ. Organist 1954–56; Founder and Conductor Nottingham Bach Soc. 1954–59; Rector Chori Southwell Minster 1956–59; Dir of Music, Keele 1958–59; Prof. of Harmony, RAM 1959–61; Fellow and Organist, New Coll. Oxford and Lecturer, Faculty of Music, Univ. of Oxford 1959–76; Prin. Royal Scottish Acad. of Music and Drama, Glasgow 1976–82, RAM 1982–93; Conductor Oxford Harmonic Soc. 1961–63; Organist, Sheldonian Theatre 1964–76; Harpsi-chordist to the London Virtuosi 1972–75; Pres. Inc. Asscn of Organists 1966–68; Visiting Prof., Yale Univ., USA 1974–75; Conductor Oxford Sinfonia 1967–70; Choragus, Univ. of Oxford 1968–72; Pres. Inc. Soc. of Musicians 1984–85, Royal Coll. of Organists 1986–88; Chair. Nat. Youth Orchestra 1985–94, Nat. Early Music Asscn 1986–89; mem. Bd Scottish Opera 1978–83, ENO 1984–89; Hon. Fellow, Selwyn Coll. Cambridge, New Coll. Oxford, King's Coll., London; Hon. RAM; Hon. FRCO; Hon. GSMD; Hon. FRCM; Hon. FRSAMD; Hon. FRNCM; Hon. FTCL; Hon. FLCM; Hon. FRSCM; Hon. FGCM 2005; Hon. DLitt (Reading) 1989. *Music:* recordings of organ, choral and chamber music; recitals world-wide. *Publications:* An Anthology of English Lute Music 1954, Thomas Robinson's Schoole of Musicke 1603 1971, Music for the Lute (Gen. Ed.) 1965–82. *Leisure interests:* reading, walking, theatre, photography, travel. *Address:* 26 Wyke Mark, Dean Lane, Winchester, SO22 5DJ, England. *Telephone:* (1962) 877807. *E-mail:* lumsdendj@aol.com.

LUNA MENDOZA, Ricardo V., AB, MIA; Peruvian diplomatist; b. 19 Nov. 1940, Lima; s. of Ricardo Luna and Victoria Mendoza de Luna; m. Margarita Proaño 1969; one d.; ed Princeton Univ., NJ and Columbia Univ., USA, Diplomatic Acad. of Peru; joined Diplomatic Service 1967, posts held include Third Sec., Div. of Econ. Affairs, Foreign Ministry 1967, Third Sec., Embassy in UK 1968–70, Second Sec., Embassy in Israel 1970–71, First Sec., Perm. Mission of Peru to UN Office at Geneva, Head, UN Dept, Foreign Ministry 1975–77, Counsellor, Washington, DC 1978, Chef du Cabinet of Minister for Foreign Affairs 1979, Minister Counsellor, Mission of Peru to UNESCO 1980, Quito 1987, Minister, Perm. Mission to UN 1984, Under-Sec. for Multilateral Policy, Ministry of Foreign Affairs 1987–89, Perm. Rep. to UN 1989–92, Amb. to USA 1992–99, to UK 2006–10; Fellow, Center for Int. Affairs, Harvard Univ., USA 1980–81; Adjunct Prof. of Latin American Affairs, The Fletcher School, Tufts Univ. 1999–2006; fmr Lecturer, Woodrow Wilson School of Public and Int. Affairs, Princeton Univ.; Founding mem. Peruvian Centre for Int. Studies; mem. Peruvian Soc. of Int. Law; Order de Mayo (Argentina), Order Río Branco (Brazil), Panamerican Foundation Pan American Order. *Leisure interests:* art, art history, jazz, cinema, mountain climbing, hiking. *Address:* c/o Ministry of Foreign Affairs, Jirón Lampa 535, Lima 1, Peru (office).

LUND, Helge, MBA; Norwegian oil industry executive; *CEO, Statoil ASA;* b. 16 Oct. 1962; m.; two c.; ed Norwegian School of Econs and Business Admin (NHH), Bergen, Institut Européen d'Admin des Affaires (INSEAD), Fontainebleu, France; fmr Political Adviser to Conservative Parl. (Storting) Group; consultant with McKinsey & Co. –1993; joined Hafslund Nycomed 1993, Deputy Man.-Dir Nycomed Pharma AS 1997–99; Deputy Chief Exec. and COO Aker RGI Holding ASA 1999–2002; Deputy Chair. Aker Martitime 2001; apptd mem. Bd Kværner ASA 2001, CEO Aker Kværner ASA (following merger between Aker and Kværner) 2002–04; CEO Statoil ASA (renamed StatoilHydro in 2007 following merger between Statoil and Norsk Hydro's oil and gas business) 2004–, Statoil ASA 2009–; mem. Bd of Dirs Nokia Corpn. *Address:* Statoil ASA, Forusbeen 50, 4035 Stavanger, Norway (office). *Telephone:* 51-99-00-00 (office). *Fax:* 51-99-00-50 (office). *E-mail:* statoil@statoil.com (office). *Website:* www.statoil.com (office).

LUND, Henning, DrPhil; Danish chemist and academic; *Professor Emeritus of Chemistry, University of Aarhus;* b. 15 Sept. 1929, Copenhagen; s. of Prof. Hakon Lund and Bergljot I. G. Lund (née Dahl); m. Else Margrethe Thorup 1953; one s. three d.; ed Aarhus Katedralskole and Tech. Univ. of Copenhagen; Research Chemist, Leo Pharmaceutical Products 1952–60; Research Fellow, Harvard Univ. 1954–55; Asst Prof. of Chem., Univ. of Aarhus 1960, Prof. 1966–99, Prof. Emer. 1999–; Visiting Prof., Japan 1976, France 1981; Chair. UNESCO workshop for European Co-operation in Organic Electrochemistry 1976–81; Section Co-Chair. Int. Soc. of Electrochemistry 1973–78, 1986–90, Nat. Sec. 1986–90; Pres. Learned Soc., Univ. of Aarhus 1973–79; mem. Danish Research Council for Tech. Sciences 1977–82, Vice-Chair. 1980–82; mem. Royal Danish Acad. of Sciences and Letters 1979–; Dr hc (Rennes) 1998; Bjerrums Gold Medal 1969, M. M. Baizer Award (Electrochemical Soc.) 1996. *Publications:* Elektrodereaktioner i Organisk Polar-ografi og Voltammetri 1961, Encyclopaedia of Electrochemistry of the Elements, Vols 11–15 (co-ed.) 1978–84, Organic Electrochemistry (co-ed.) 1983, 1991, 2000; contrib. of about 300 papers to scientific journals. *Leisure interests:* music, literature, jogging. *Address:* Department of Chemistry, University of Aarhus, 8000 Aarhus (office); Vinkelvej 8A, 8240 Risskov, Denmark (home). *Telephone:* (45) 87-15-59-49 (office); (45) 86-17-90-27 (home). *Fax:* (45) 86-19-61-99 (office). *E-mail:* hlund@chem.au.dk (office). *Website:* www.chem.au.dk (office).

LUND, Kristin Skogen, BA, MBA; Norwegian business executive; *Executive Vice-President and Head of Digital Services, Telenor Group;* b. 1966; ed Univ. of Oregon, USA, Institut Européen d'Admin des Affaires (INSEAD), Fontainebleu, France; worked as man. in Lever Europe 1992–95; hired by Coca-Cola Co. 1995, Dir of Coca-Cola Beverages Sweden 1997–98; CEO Scandinavia Online

1998–2002, CEO Scanpix 2003–04; moved to Aftenposten AS (newspaper owned by Schibsted) 2004, CEO 2007–09, held various bd memberships within Schibsted Group; Dir of Nordic activities, Telenor Group 2009–10, Exec. Vice-Pres. and Head of Digital Services 2010–; mem. Bd Orkla Group, Norwegian Chamber Orchestra (Pres.); Vice-Pres. Confed. of Norwegian Enterprise (Næringslivets Hovedorganisasjon—NHO) 2008–10, Acting Pres. 2010–; mem. Council Civita (think tank); ranked by Fortune magazine amongst the 50 Most Powerful Women in Business outside the US (38th) 2011, (44th) 2012. *Address:* Telenor ASA, Snarøyveien 30, 1331 Fornebu, Norway (office). *Telephone:* 81-07-70-00 (office); 67-89-00-00 (office). *E-mail:* info@telenor.com (office). *Website:* www.telenor.com (office).

LUND, Peter Anthony; American broadcasting executive; *Chairman, EOS International Inc.;* b. 12 Jan. 1941, Minneapolis, Minn.; s. of Arthur H. Lund and Elizabeth Rohan; m. Theresa M. Kessel 1960; two s.; ed St Thomas Coll.; announcer, sales rep., Station KCCR, Pierce, SD 1961–62; sales rep., Station KELO TV, Sioux Falls, SD 1962–64; sales rep., sales man., Station WTTC, Minneapolis 1964–66; Gen. Sales Man. Westinghouse Broadcasting Co. 1966–71; Vice-Pres., Man. Station KSDO, San Diego, Calif. 1972–75, Station WTOP, Washington, DC 1976–77; Vice-Pres. CBS-owned AM Stations, New York 1977–80; Vice-Pres., Gen. Man. WBBM-TV, Chicago 1980–83, WCBS-TV, New York 1983–84; Exec. Vice-Pres. CBS Sports, New York 1984–85, Pres. 1985–87; Pres. Multimedia Entertainment 1987–90; Exec. Vice-Pres., Pres. Marketing, CBS 1990–94; Broadcast Group Pres. CBS Pres. 1995–97, Exec. Vice-Pres. CBS TV Network 1994–95, CEO CBS 1995–97, Pres. CEO CBS TV and Cable 1997; mem. Bd of Dirs DIRECTV Group Inc. 2000–, Crown Media Holdings, Inc., Emmis Communications Corpn; currently Chair. EOS International Inc. *Address:* EOS International Inc., 2292 Faraday Avenue, Carlsbad, CA 92008-7208, USA (office). *Telephone:* (760) 431-8400 (office). *Fax:* (760) 431-8448 (office). *E-mail:* info@eosintl .com (office). *Website:* www.eosintl.com (office).

LUNDGREEN-NIELSEN, Flemming Torkild Jacob, DPhil; Danish academic; b. 24 Jan. 1937, Hellerup; s. of Otto Nielsen and Edith Mortensen; ed Frederiksborg Statsskole and Univ. of Copenhagen; teaching posts at Univ. of Copenhagen 1965–2007, Lecturer 1972–88, Prof., DIS Study Div. 1970–90, Docent 1988–2007 (retd); mem. Danish Soc. of Language and Literature, Royal Acad. of Sciences and Letters. *Publications include:* Grundtvig. Skaebne og forsyn 1965, Den nordiske fortaelling i det 18. årh. 1968, Det handlende ord I-II 1980, CC Lyschanders digtning I-II 1989, Jens Bielke: Relation om Grønland 1990, Grundtvig og danskhed, in Dansk identitetshistorie 3 1992, På sporet af dansk identitet 1992, København laest og påskrevet 1997, Svøbt i mår. Dansk Folkevisekultur 1550–1700 I–IV (Ed. and Contrib.) 1999–2002, N.F.S. Grundtvig: Schriften in Auswahl !-III (Ed. and Contrib.) 2010; articles on Danish and Scandinavian literary subjects. *Address:* Upsalagade 22, 2100 Copenhagen Ø, Denmark. *E-mail:* fln@royalacademy.dk; fln@privat.tele.dk.

LUNDGREN, Dolph, MA; American (b. Swedish) actor, director and screenwriter; b. 3 Nov. 1959, Stockholm, Sweden; m. Anette Lundgren 1994; two d.; ed Washington State Univ., Massachusetts Inst. of Tech. and Royal Inst. of Tech. Stockholm; f. Thor Pictures (production co.) 1992. *Films include:* A View to a Kill 1985, Rocky IV 1985, Masters of the Universe 1987, Red Scorpion 1989, The Punisher 1989, Dark Angel 1990, Cover Up 1991, Showdown in Little Tokyo 1991, Universal Soldier 1992, The Joshua Tree 1993, Pentathlon (also producer) 1994, Men of War 1994, Johnny Mnemonic 1995, The Shooter 1995, Silent Trigger 1996, The Peacekeeper 1997, The Minion 1998, Sweepers 1998, Storm Catcher 1999, Bridge of Dragons 1999, Jill the Ripper 2000, The Last Patrol 2000, Agent Red 2000, Hidden Agenda 2001, Detention 2003, Direct Action 2004, Fat Slags 2004, Retrograde 2004, The Defender (also dir) 2004, The Mechanik (also writer and dir) 2005, The Inquiry 2006, Diamond Dogs (also exec. producer and dir) 2007, Missionary Man (also writer and dir) 2007, Direct Contact 2009, Command Performance (also writer and dir, performer: 'Breakdown', 'Girl') 2009, Universal Soldier: Regeneration 2009, Icarus (also dir) 2010, The Expendables 2010, The Expendables 2 2012. *Address:* c/o Jack Gilardi, ICM, 8942 Wilshire Blvd, Beverly Hills, CA 90211, USA (office); c/o 9595 Wilshire Blvd, Suite #1000, Beverly Hills, CA 90211, USA (office). *Telephone:* (310) 550-4135 (office); (310) 445-1601 (office). *E-mail:* jgilardi@icmtalent.com (office); craigbaumgarten@yahoo.com (office). *Website:* www.icmtalent.com (office); www.dolphlundgren.com. *Fax:* (310) 996-1892 (office).

LUNDGREN, Terry J., BA; American retail executive; *Chairman, President and CEO, Macy's, Inc.;* b. 1953, Long Beach, Calif.; m. Nancy Lundgren; two c.; ed Univ. of Arizona; joined Bullock Div., Federated Dept Stores Inc. (FDSI), LA 1975, Pres. Bullock Wilshire Security Operations –1988, Chair. and CEO Neiman Marcus 1988–94, Head, Federated Merchandising Group, New York 1994–95, COO and Chief Merchandising Officer, FDSI (renamed Macy's, Inc. 2007) 1997–2003, Pres. 1997–, CEO 2003–, Chair. 2004–. *Address:* Macy's Inc., 7 West Seventh Street, Cincinnati, OH 45202, USA (office). *Telephone:* (513) 579-7000 (office). *Fax:* (513) 579-7555 (office). *E-mail:* info@macysinc.com (office); info@fds .com (office). *Website:* www.macysinc.com (office); www.fds.com (office).

LUNDIN, Jan, BA; Swedish diplomatist and international organization official; *Director-General, Council of the Baltic Sea States Secretariat;* m.; two d.; ed Univ. of Uppsala, Univ. of Stockholm; several years with Swedish Ministry of Foreign Affairs (MFA), served at Embassy in Yugoslavia 1984–86, First Sec., Embassy in Lithuania 1992–94, Counsellor, Embassy in Russian Fed. 1994–96, Counsellor and Deputy Head of Mission, Embassy in Serbia, Deputy Head of Mission and Head of Political Dept, Embassy in Germany 1996–2000, Coordinator, Stability Pact for SE Europe, Ministry of Foreign Affairs 1999; Researcher, Stockholm Inst. for Soviet and E European Econs and Politics, Uppsala Univ. 1987–88; European Exec. Dir Russian–European Centre for Econ. Policy 1998–99; Dir-Gen., Council of the Baltic Sea States Secr. 2010–. *Address:* Council of the Baltic Sea States Secretariat, POB 2010, Slussplan 9, 103 11 Stockholm, Sweden (office). *Telephone:* (8) 440-19-20 (office). *Fax:* (8) 440-19-20 (office). *E-mail:* cbss@cbss.org (office). *Website:* www.cbss.org (office).

LUNDY, Victor Alfred, MArch, FAIA; American architect; b. 1 Feb. 1923, New York, NY; s. of Alfred Henry Lundy and Rachel Lundy; m. 1st Shirley Corwin 1947 (divorced 1959); one s. one d.; m. 2nd Anstis Manton Burwell 1960; one s.; ed New York Univ. Coll. of Architecture, Harvard Univ.; mil. service 1943–46; pvt.

practice, Sarasota, Fla 1951–59, New York 1960–75, projects include St Paul's Lutheran Church, Sarasota 1959, US Tax Court Bldg and Plaza, Washington, DC, US Embassy in Colombo, Sri Lanka, Recreation Shelters for Smithsonian Inst., travelling air-supported Exhbn Bldg and exhibit for US Atomic Energy Comm. and commercial, religious and govt bldgs throughout the USA and overseas; pvt. practice, Houston, Tex. 1976–87, Design Prin. and Vice-Pres. HKS Inc., Dallas, Tex. 1984–90, visiting professorships and lectureships, Harvard, Yale, Columbia, Calif. (Berkeley) and Houston Univs and Univ. of Rome, Italy; work included in many exhbns, including São Paulo Int. Biennial Exhbn of Architecture 1957, America Builds, Berlin 1957, Fifth Congress of Union Internationale des Architectes, Moscow 1958, Expo '70, Osaka, Japan 1970; Purple Heart Medal, US Combat Infantry Badge; numerous prizes and awards, honoured by the Smithsonian Inst. on his 90th birthday 2013. *Projects include:* GTE Telephone Operations World HQ, Irving, Tex., Greyhound Corp. (now Dial Corp.) Center, Phoenix, Ariz., Mack Center II, Tampa, Fla, Walnut Glen Tower (now Dr Pepper Bldg), Dallas, Tex. Austin Centre-Radisson Hotel and One Congress Plaza, Austin, Tex., Stahl Residence, Siesta Key, Fla 1953, Drive-In Church, Nokomis, Fla 1954, Greater Sarasota Chamber of Commerce (Pagoda Bldg) 1956, Alta Vista Elementary School, aka The Butterfly Wing 1957, 25 South Osprey Avenue 1957, Herron House, Venice, Fla 1957, Bee Ridge Presbyterian Church, Sarasota, Fla 1957, 533 S. US 301 1958, Warm Mineral Springs Motel, North Port 1958, St Paul's Lutheran Church, Sarasota 1958, Galloways Furniture Showroom, Sarasota (today, Visionworks), south of US 41 and 301 1959, Bubble Pavilions, for the New York World's Fair of 1964–65 (The Brass Rail Snack Bars), Church of the Resurrection, Harlem, New York City 1966 (now demolished), IBM branch office, Cranford, NJ, First Unitarian Church, Westport, Conn., US Tax Court Bldg, Washington, DC, Lundy home, Aspen, Colo 1972, The Sierra Blanca (NM) Ski Apache Ski Resort Lodge. *Film:* of his life and work: Victor Lundy: Sculptor of Space 2014. *Address:* HKS Inc., 1111 Plaza of the Americas North, Suite LB 307, Dallas, TX 75201 (office); 701 Mulberry Lane, Bellaire, TX 77401, USA (home). *Telephone:* (214) 969-3396.

LUNENFELD, Bruno, MD, FRCOG; Israeli endocrinologist; *President, International Society for the Study of the Aging Male;* b. 11 Feb. 1927, Vienna, Austria; s. of David Lunenfeld and Ernestine Lunenfeld; m. Pnina Buyanover 1996; two s.; ed British Inst. of Eng Tech., Medical School, Univ. of Geneva, Switzerland; Acting Chief, Endocrine Research and Devt, Tel-Hashomer 1962–64; Scientist, Weizman Inst. of Science 1961–66; Assoc. Prof. and Head Dept of Biology, Bar-Ilan Univ. 1964–69, Prof. Ordinarius and Head Dept of Life Sciences 1969–71, Prof. of Life Sciences 1971; Dir Inst. of Endocrinology, Sheba Medical Centre 1964–92, Chair. Div. of Labs 1977–81, Chair. Research and Ethical Cttee 1977–81; mem. Expert Cttee on Biological Standardization, WHO 1967–87; Counsellor, External Relations to Minister of Health and Head Dept of Int. Relations, Ministry of Health 1981–85; Acting Chief Scientist, Ministry of Health 1984–86; mem. Nat. Council for Research and Devt 1985–87; Visiting Prof., Yale School of Medicine, USA 1986–87; mem. Nat. Council for Health and Social Affairs 1985–87; Pres. Israel Fertility Asscn 1979–83, Israel Endocrine Soc. 1992–95; Founder and Pres., International Soc. for the Study of the Aging Male (ISSAM) 1997–; Medical Dir International Fertility Inst., Ranana 1996–99; Vice-Pres. Scientific Council of Israel Medical Asscn; mem. Exec. Bd Scientific Council, Exec. Council of Int. Cttee for Research in Reproduction, Exec. Council Medical Examination Bd, Exec. Council of International Andrology Soc., Exec. Council of International Soc. of Gynaecological Endocrinology (Treas. 1992–96); Ed.-in-Chief The Aging Male 1997–; Founder and Sec.-Gen. Asia Pacific Initiative on Reproduction 2004–; Hon. Fellow, American Coll. of Obstetricians and Gynaecologists, Hon. mem. Int. Fed. of Fertility Socs, European Soc. of Human Reproduction and Embryology, German Endocrine Soc. of Reproduction, Austrian Soc. of Fertility and Sterility, Asian Soc. of Andrology; Verdienstkreuz First Class (Germany) 1995; Pliskin Prize, Israel Trade Union Sick Fund 1962, Yaffeh Prize, Ministry of Health 1963, US Public Health Service Special Recognition Award 1983, Jacob Henle Medal (Georg Augustus Univ., Göttingen) 1993, Bertarelli Foundation Award 2002, World Fertility Awareness Month Lifetime Achievement Award 2005. *Achievements include:* discovered the clinical use of Human Menopausal Gonadotropin for the treatment of female and male infertility; pioneer in the study of gender-specific aging. *Publications include:* 21 books including, Infertility, Diagnosis and Treatment of Functional Infertility 1978, Ovulation Induction 1982, Diagnosis and Management of Male Infertility 1984, Ovulation Induction and In Vitro Fertilization 1986, Infertility in Male and Female 1986, 1993, Textbook of Men's Health 2002; 25 chapters in books; 495 papers in scientific journals; 120 published lectures and abstracts. *Leisure interests:* opera, sociology, photography. *Address:* 7 Rav Ashi Street, 69395 Tel-Aviv, Israel (home). *Telephone:* 3-6425434 (home). *Fax:* 3-6424454 (home). *E-mail:* blunenfeld@gmail.com. *Website:* www.issam.ch (office).

LUNGIN, Pavel Semenovich, (Pavel Loungine); Russian scriptwriter and director; b. 12 July 1949, Moscow; m. Yelena Lungina; ed Moscow State Univ.; debut as scriptwriter 1976, as film dir 1990; mem. Jury, Moscow Int. Film Festival 1993, Pres. 2009; People's Artist of Russia 2008; Special Prize, Cannes Film Festival. *Libretti:* librettist for Nikolai Karetnikov's opera Till Eulenspiegel (written 1983), Karetnikov's oratorio The Mystery of St Paul. *Films include:* The Problem is Brother 1976, The End of Taiga Emperor 1978, Invincible 1983, Fellow Traveller 1987, Oriental Romance 1992, Queen of Spades 2014; dir: Taxi-Blues (Best Dir Prize, Cannes Film Festival) 1990, Luna Park 1992, Lifeline 1996, The Wedding 2000, Tycoon 2002, Bednye Rodstvenniki 2005, The Island 2006, Lilacs 2007, Tsar 2009, The Conductor 2012. *Television includes:* Delo o myortvykh dushakh (mini-series) 2005, La maison haute (film documentary) 2005. *Address:* Novy Arbat str. 31, Apt 8, 121009 Moscow, Russia. *Telephone:* (495) 205-04-32. *E-mail:* info@lunginstudio.ru. *Website:* www.lunginstudio.ru.

LUNGU, Effron, BA; Zambian politician; b. 25 Dec. 1952; m.; fmr teacher; mem. Nat. Ass. (Parl.) for Chama South constituency 2011–; Deputy Minister of Foreign Affairs 2011–13, Minister Feb.–Aug. 2013; mem. Patriotic Front (PF). *Address:* c/o Ministry of Foreign Affairs and Tourism, POB RW50069, Lusaka, Zambia (office).

LUNN, Gary, BL; Canadian politician; b. 1957; m. Alexandra Lunn; two c.; ed Univ. of Victoria; fmr carpenter; fmr safety officer Crestbrook Forest Industries; lawyer 1995–97; mem. Parl. for Saanich—Gulf Islands 1997–2011, fmr Vice-Chair. Standing Cttee on Fisheries and Oceans; fmr Critic for Northern Devt, for Métis and Non-Status Indians, for Human Resources Devt, for Int. Trade, for Nat. Revenue and for Fisheries and Oceans, for Public Works and Govt Services and for the Privy Council; Minister of Natural Resources 2006–08, Sec. of State for Sport 2008–11; mem. BC Law Soc. *Address:* c/o Sport Canada, Canadian Heritage, 15 rue Eddy, Gatineau, QC K1A 0M5, Canada.

LUO, Gan, DipEng; Chinese state official, party official (retd) and engineer; b. 14 July 1935, Jinan, Shandong Prov.; m. He Zuozhi 1965; one s. one d.; ed Beijing Inst. of Iron and Steel Eng, Karl Marx Univ. and Freiburg Inst. of Mining and Metallurgy, Leipzig, GDR, May 7th Cadre School; worker, Leipzig Iron and Steel Plant and Leipzig Metal Casting Plant 1955–56; joined CCP 1960; Project Group Leader and Technician, Mechanical Eng Research Inst., First Ministry of Machine-Building Industry, Zhengzhou City, Henan Prov. 1962–69, Deputy Dir, later Dir Luohe Preparatory Office 1970–80; Chair. Science and Tech. Cttee, Henan Prov. 1980–81; Vice-Gov. Henan Prov. 1981–83; Sec. CCP Henan Prov. Cttee 1981–83; Minister of Labour and Social Services 1988; Sec.-Gen. of State Council 1988–98, State Councillor 1993–2003, Vice-Premier of State Council 1998–2003; Sec. Work Cttee for Cen. Govt Organs 1989–; Alt. mem. 12th CCP Cen. Cttee 1982–87, mem. 13th Cen. Cttee 1987–92, 14th Cen. Cttee 1992–97, 15th CCP Cen. Cttee 1997–2002, 16th CCP Cen. Cttee 2002–07; mem. CCP Politburo, Sec. Secr. CCP Cen. Cttee 1997–2002; mem. Standing Cttee, CCP Politburo 2002–07; Deputy Sec. Political and Legis. Affairs Cttee, Offices Under Cen. Cttee, 14th CCP Cen. Cttee 1993–98, Sec. 1998–07; mem. Secr. and Vice-Pres. All-China Fed. of Trade Unions 1983–88 (Deputy Sec. CCP Leading Party Group 1983–88). *Address:* c/o State Council, Zhong Nan Hai, Beijing, People's Republic of China (office).

LUO, Haocai; Chinese judge and politician; *President, Chinese Society for Human Rights Studies (CSHRS);* b. March 1934, Anxi Co., Fujian Prov.; ed Beijing Univ.; teaching asst, Lecturer, Assoc. Prof., Prof., Dept of Law, Beijing Univ. 1960–86; Vice-Pres. Beijing Univ. 1986–95; joined China Zhi Gong Party (Public Interest Party) 1992, Vice-Chair. Cen. Cttee 1992–97, Chair. Cen. Cttee 1997–2002; mem. Standing Cttee and Deputy Sec.-Gen. CPPCC 8th Nat. Cttee 1993–98, Vice-Chair. 9th Nat. Cttee 1998–2003, 10th Nat. Cttee 2003–; Chair. Beijing Fed. of Returned Overseas Chinese, Vice-Chair. All-China Fed. of Returned Overseas Chinese; adviser, Chinese Asscn for Int. Understanding 1999; fmr Vice-Chair. China Law Soc., Vice-Pres. 1986; Vice-Pres. and mem. Judicial Cttee Supreme People's Court 1995–2000; Pres. Chinese Soc. for Human Rights Studies (CSHRS) 2007–; mem. Exec. Council China Admin. Man. Asscn; mem. Govt Del., Macao Hand-Over Ceremony, Macao Special Admin. Region Preparatory Cttee 1999. *Address:* Chinese Society for Human Rights Studies, No. 22 Building, An Yuan Bei Li, Beijing 100029, Peoples Republic of China (office). *Website:* www.humanrights -china.org (office).

LUO, Jianchuan, PhD; Chinese mining executive; *Executive Director and President, Aluminum Corporation of China (CHALCO);* ed Kunming Univ. of Science and Tech., Cen. South Univ. of Industry; served as engineer with Lead and Zinc Bureau of China Non-ferrous Metals Industry Corpn; fmr Man. Haikou Nanxin Industry and Commerce Corpn; fmr Asst to Gen. Man. Jinpeng Mining Devt Corpn; fmr Vice-Pres. Beijing Xinquan Tech-trading Corpn; fmr Asst to Pres. of China Non-ferrous Metals Industry Trading Group Corpn; fmr Deputy Chief of Trading Div. of China Copper, Lead and Zinc Group Corpn; fmr Gen. Man. China Aluminum International Trading Corpn Ltd; joined Aluminum Corpn of China (CHALCO) 2001, later Gen. Man. Operations and Sales Div., later Vice-Pres. and Sr Vice-Pres., currently Exec. Dir and Pres. CHALCO, also Chair. Devt Planning Cttee. *Address:* Aluminum Corporation of China (CHALCO), 62 North Xizhimen Street, Haidian District, Beijing 100082, People's Republic of China (office). *Telephone:* (10) 8229-8103 (office). *Fax:* (10) 8229-8081 (office). *E-mail:* webmaster@chalco.com.cn (office); info@chinalco.com.cn (office). *Website:* www .chalco.com.cn (office); www.chinalco.com.cn (office).

LUO, Pingan; Chinese artist; b. 12 April 1945, Xian; s. of Luo Deyu and Tian Cuilan; m. Qi Juyan 1969; two s.; ed Xian Acad. of Fine Arts; mem. China Artists' Asscn, Shaanxi br.; Artist of Shaanxi Imperial Art Gallery (traditional Chinese painting); Vice-Pres. Changan Imperial Art Acad.; Dir Artistic Cttee of China Artistic Asscn, Shaanxi br.; Excellent Works Prize, Beijing 1988, Copper Medal of 7th Nat. Artistic Works-Exhbn 1989, Tabei City, Taiwan. *Publications:* The Collection of Luo Pingan's Painting, Collected Landscapes by Luo Pingan. *Leisure interests:* literature, folk art, countryside and music. *Address:* 32 North Street, Xian, Shaanxi Province, People's Republic of China. *Telephone:* 25333; 7251984 (home).

LUO, Tao; Chinese economist and business executive; *President and General Manager, China Nonferrous Metal Mining (Group);* ed Beijing Radio and Television Univ.; joined CCP 1973; fmr Vice-Dir and Vice-Sec. Party Cttee, Beijing Gen. Research Inst. for Nonferrous Metals; fmr Vice-Pres. and Sec. Comm. for Discipline Inspection, Vice-Chief of Dept of Personnel Educ., China Nonferrous Metal Industry Corpn; fmr Dir Dept of Personnel, Nat. Bureau for Nonferrous Metal Industry; Deputy Dean of Beijing Gen. Research Inst. for Non-ferrous Metals 1993–97; Deputy Dir Dept of Human Resources and Training, China Nonferrous Metal Industry Corpn 1997–98; Dir Dept of Human Resources, State Bureau of Non-ferrous Metals Industry 1998–2000; participated in establishment of Aluminium Corpn of China Ltd (Chinalco) 2000–01, Deputy Gen. Man. Aluminium Corpn of China Ltd 2001, fmr Chair. Bd of Supervisors; Dir, Ord River Resources Ltd 2004–12, Deputy Chair. (non-exec.) 2005–09, Chair. 2009–12; Chair. China Nonferrous Metals International Mining Co. Ltd and China Nonferrous Mining Corpn Ltd 2010–; Pres., Gen. Man. and Deputy Party Sec., China Nonferrous Metal Mining (Group) Co. Ltd 2012–; Chair. China Nonferrous Metal Industry's Foreign Engineering and Construction Co. Ltd, Zambia-China Economic and Trade Co-operation Zone Development Co. Ltd, China Nonferrous Metals Foreign Engineering and Construction Inc.; fmr Chair. (non-exec.) Kryso Resources PLC; Dir, Chaarat Gold Holdings Ltd, CNMIM. *Address:* China Nonferrous Metal Mining (Group), 10 Anding Road, Beijing 100029, People's Republic of China (office). *Telephone:* (10) 84426826 (office). *Fax:* (10) 84426699 (office). *E-mail:* webmaster@cnmc.com.cn (office). *Website:* www.cnmc.com.cn (office).

LUO, Xuejuan; Chinese swimmer; b. 26 Jan. 1984, Hangzhou; specialises in breaststroke; began swimming competitively in Hangzhou 1991; coached by Yadong Zhang 1996–; debut for China Team, World Championships, Fukuoka 2001; winner Gold Medal for 50m. breaststroke, World Championships, Fukuoka 2001, World Cup SC, Shanghai 2000, 2002, Melbourne 2000, NY 2001, Edmonton 2001, Barcelona 2003, Olympic Games, Athens 2004; winner Gold Medal for 100m. breaststroke, World Championships, Fukuoka 2001, Barcelona 2003, World Cup, Shanghai 2000, Melbourne 2000, Edmonton 2001, NY 2001, Shanghai 2001, Athens 2004; winner Gold Medal for 400m. medley relay, World Championships, Barcelona 2003; winner Silver Medal for 50m. breaststroke, World Championships SC, Moscow 2002, World Cup, Imperia 2002; winner Bronze Medal for 200m. breaststroke, World Championships, Fukuoka 2001, World Cup SC, Shanghai 2002; winner Bronze Medal for 100m. breaststroke, Pan Pacific Games 2002, World Championships SC, Moscow 2002; mem. Zhejiang Club; retired 2007; first Chinese torchbearer, Summer Olympics torch relay, Olympia, Greece 2008. *Leisure interest:* reading, music, fashion. *Address:* c/o International Association of Athletics Federations (IAAF), 17 rue Princesse Florestine, BP 359, MC98007, Monaco.

LÜPERTZ, Markus; German painter, sculptor, writer and academic; b. 25 April 1941, Reichenberg (now Liberec), Bohemia; ed Werkkunstschule, Krefeld, Kunstakademie, Düsseldorf, Villa Romana, Florence, Italy; worked mainly in Berlin 1960s; Prof., State Acad. of Fine Arts, Karlsruhe 1976; Prof. and Dir Kunstakademie Düsseldorf 1988–2009; works include The Fallen Warrior, Bonn 1994; Villa Romana Prize 1970, Prize of Deutschen Kritikerverband, Esslingen Artists' Guild 1990. *Publications:* Selected Poems 1961–83; editing own journal since 2003, called Frau und Hund of which two edns in other languages have appeared (Signora e cane, in Italian, and Femme et Chien, in French). *Address:* c/o Galerie Michael Werner, Gertrudenstrasse 24–28, 50667 Cologne, Germany. *Telephone:* (221) 77899950. *Fax:* (221) 77899952. *E-mail:* galeriewerner@ michaelwerner.de. *Website:* www.michaelwerner.de.

LUPOLIANSKI, Uri; Israeli politician; s. of Jacob Lupolianski and of the late Sarah Lupolianski; m.; twelve c.; school teacher, Jerusalem 1970s; Founder and Chair. Yad Sarah (charitable foundation) 1976–; Deputy Mayor of Jerusalem –2003, Acting Mayor, then Mayor 2003–08; mem. United Torah Judaism; The Israel Prize 1994. *Address:* Yad Sarah, 124 Herzl Boulevard, 96187 Jerusalem, Israel (office). *Telephone:* (2) 2644401/2/3 (office); (2) 6297997 (office). *Fax:* (2) 6444498 (office); (2) 6296014 (office). *E-mail:* UriL@yadsarah.org.il (office); LPUri@Jerusalem.muni.il (office). *Website:* www.yadsarah.org.il (office).

LUPU, Marian Ilie, PhD; Moldovan economist and politician; *Chairman, Democratic Party of Moldova;* b. 20 June 1966, Bălți; s. of Prof. Ilie Ion Lupu; m. 1992; one s. one d.; ed Gheorghe Asachi Lyceum, Chișinău, Moldova State Univ., Plekhanov Moscow Inst. of the Nat. Economy, Moscow, Int. Monetary Fund Inst., Washington, DC, USA, World Trade Org. Inst., Geneva, Switzerland; mem. Komsomol 1980–88; mem. CP Soviet Union 1988–91; worked in Dept for External Econ. Relations, Chișinău 1991–97, Dir 1997; Exec. Dir TACIS (EU aid programme) in Moldova 1992–2000; Deputy Minister of the Economy 2001–03, Minister of the Economy 2003–05; mem. Party of Communists of the Repub. of Moldova (PCRM) –2009, mem. Democratic Party of Moldova (PDM—Partidul Democrat din Moldova) 2009–, currently Chair.; mem. Parl. (PCRM) 2005–09, (PDM) 2009–, Chair. (Speaker) 2005–09, 2010–13; selected as Alliance for European Integration cand. for Pres. of Moldova 2009; Acting Pres. of Moldova 30 Dec. 2010–23 March 2012. *Address:* Parlamentul, 2073 Chișinău, bd Ștefan cel Mare 105 (office); Democratic Party of Moldova (PDM—Partidul Democrat din Moldova) 2001 Chișinău, str. Tighina 32, Moldova. *Telephone:* (22) 23-33-52 (office); (22) 27-82-29. *Fax:* (22) 23-30-12 (office); (22) 27-82-30. *E-mail:* inform@ parlament.md (office); pdm@mtc.md. *Website:* www.parliament.md (office); www .pdm.md.

LUPU, Radu, MA; Romanian pianist; b. 30 Nov. 1945, Galați; s. of Meyer Lupu and Ana Gabor; ed High School, Brașov, Moscow Conservatoire, USSR; first piano lessons 1951; won scholarship to Moscow 1961; entered Moscow Conservatoire 1963, graduated 1969; First Prize, Van Cliburn Competition 1966, Enescu Int. Competition, Bucharest 1967, Leeds Int. Competition 1969; a leading interpreter of the German classical composers; appears frequently with all the major orchestras; has toured Eastern Europe with London Symphony Orchestra; American debut 1972; gave world première of André Tchaikowsky Piano Concerto, London 1975; Grammy Award for Best Instrumental Record of Year (for Schubert record) 1995, Edison Award for Best Instrumental Record of Year (for Schumann record) 1995. *Recordings include:* complete Beethoven cycle (with Israel Philharmonic and Zubin Mehta), complete Mozart sonatas for violin and piano with Szymon Goldberg), Brahms piano concerto No. 1 (with Edo de Waart and London Philharmonic Orchestra), Mozart piano concerto K467 (with Uri Segal and English Chamber Orchestra), various Beethoven and Schubert sonatas, Mozart and Beethoven wind quintets in E flat, Mozart concerto for 2 pianos and concerto for 3 pianos transcribed for 2 pianos (with Murray Perahia and English Chamber Orchestra), Schubert Fantasie in F minor and Mozart sonata in D for 2 pianos (with Murray Perahia), Schubert Lieder (with Barbara Hendricks), Schubert Piano Duets (with Daniel Barenboim). *Leisure interests:* history, chess, bridge. *Address:* Opus 3 Artists, 470 Park Avenue South, 9th Floor North, New York, NY 10016, USA (office). *Telephone:* (212) 584-7500 (office). *Fax:* (646) 300-8200 (office). *E-mail:* info@opus3artists.com (office). *Website:* www.opus3artists.com (office).

LUQMAN, Ahmad Mohammad; Egyptian international organization executive; Dir-Gen. Arab Labour Org. (ALO). *Address:* Arab Labour Organization, PO Box 814, Cairo, Egypt (office). *Telephone:* (2) 3362721 (office). *Fax:* (2) 3484902 (office). *E-mail:* info@alolabor.org (office). *Website:* www.alolabor.org (office).

LURIE, Alison, AB; American novelist and academic; *Frederic J. Whiton Professor Emeritus of American Literature, Cornell University;* b. 3 Sept. 1926, Chicago; d. of Harry Lawrence Lurie and Bernice Stewart Lurie; m. 1st Jonathon Peale Bishop 1948 (divorced 1985); three s.; m. 2nd Edward Hower 1996; ed Radcliffe Coll.; Editorial Asst, Oxford Univ. Press 1946; worked as receptionist and sec.; Lecturer in English, Cornell Univ. 1969–73, Adjunct Assoc. Prof. 1973–76, Assoc. Prof. 1976–79, apptd Frederic J. Whiton Prof. of American Literature 1979, currently Frederic J. Whiton Prof. Emer. of American Literature; Fellow, Yaddo Foundation 1963, 1964, 1966, 1984, Rockefeller Foundation 1967, Guggenheim Fellow 1965; Dr hc (Univ. of Oxford) 2007, (Univ. of Nottingham) 2007; American

Acad. of Arts and Letters Literature Award 1978, Prix Femina Étranger 1989, Parents' Choice Foundation Award 1996. *Publications include:* V. R. Lang: a Memoir 1959, Love and Friendship 1962, The Nowhere City 1965, Imaginary Friends 1967, Real People 1969, The War Between the Tates 1974, Only Children 1979, Clever Gretchen and Other Forgotten Folktales (juvenile) 1980, The Heavenly Zoo (juvenile) 1980, Fabulous Beasts (juvenile) 1981, Foreign Affairs 1984 (Pulitzer Prize in Fiction 1985), The Man with a Shattered World 1987, The Truth about Lorin Jones 1988, Women and Ghosts 1994, The Last Resort 1998, Familiar Spirits 2001, Truth and Consequences 2005; non-fiction: The Language of Clothes 1981, Don't Tell the Grown Ups, Subversive Children's Literature (essays) 1990, Boys and Girls Forever: Reflections on Children's Classics (essays) 2003. *Leisure interests:* gardening, collecting of contemporary folklore and ghost stories. *Address:* Department of English, Cornell University, 250 Goldwin Smith Hall, Ithaca, New York, NY 14853-3201, USA (office). *Telephone:* (607) 255-6800 (office). *Fax:* (607) 255-6661 (office). *E-mail:* al28@cornell.edu (office). *Website:* www.arts.cornell.edu/english/people/?id=112 (office).

LURIE, Ranan Raymond; American/Israeli political cartoonist and journalist; *CEO, Lurie Studios LLC;* b. 26 May 1932, Port Said, Egypt; s. of Joseph Lurie and Rose Lurie (née Sam); m. Tamar Fletcher 1958; two s. two d.; ed Herzelia High School, Tel Aviv, Jerusalem Art Coll.; Israel Air Force intelligence officer and spokesman 1949–50; trained as Parachute Officer, French Foreign Legion 1955, British Paratroopers 1956, US 101 Airborne Div. 1962, served as Combat Paratroop Maj., Israeli Army Reserve 1950–67; Corresp. Maariv Daily 1950–52; Features Ed. Hador Daily 1953–54; Ed.-in-Chief Tavel (weekly news magazine) 1954; staff political cartoonist The Times of Cyprus 1954–56, Yedioth Aharonot Daily 1957–66; went to USA (invited by Life Magazine) 1968, naturalized 1974; political cartoonist, Life Magazine, New York 1968–73; Contrib. New York Times 1970–; weekly political cartoon page, Newsweek Int. 1974–77; Ed., political cartoonist, Vision Magazine of S America 1974–76, Honolulu Advertiser 1979; political cartoonist interviewer Die Welt, Bonn 1980–81; syndicated by United Features Syndicate 1971–73; syndicated nationally by Los Angeles Times and internationally by New York Times to over 260 newspapers 1973–75; syndicated nationally by King Features Syndicate, internationally by Editors Press Syndicate (345 newspapers) 1975–83, in USA by Universal Press Syndicate 1982–86; Lecturer, Univ. of Hawaii, American Program Bureau, Boston; political cartoonist, The Times, London 1981–83; Sr Political Analyst and cartoonist, The Asahi Shimbun, Tokyo 1983–84; Sr Analyst and political cartoonist, US News and World Report, Washington 1984–85; political cartoonist Time Magazine 1994–97; Ed.-in-Chief Cartoon News 1996–99; Chief Editorial Dir Editors' Press Service 1985; inventor of first animated electronic TV news cartoon; joined MacNeil/Lehrer News Hour as daily political cartoonist/analyst, appearing on 275 TV stations; Nightline (ABC TV network programme) and ZDF (German nat. TV); cr. Taiwan's official new nat. cartoon symbol 'Cousin Lee', Japan's nat. cartoon symbol 'Taro San'; Sr Adjunct Fellow, Center for Strategic and Int. Studies, Washington, DC; mem. Asscn of Editorial Cartoonists, Nat. Cartoonists' Soc. of America; syndicated internationally to 1,098 papers in 104 countries; listed in Guinness Book of World Records as 'most widely syndicated political cartoonist in the world' (Certificate of Merit for 20 years as consecutive title holder); Chief Judge Seoul Int. Cartoon Competition 1996; Hon. Assoc. mem. Asahi Shimbun; Sokolov Prize (highest Israeli journalism award – first recipient) 1954, US Headliners Award 1972, named Outstanding Editorial Cartoonist of Nat. Cartoonist Soc. 1972–78, Salon Award, Montréal Cartoon 1971, New York Front Page Award 1972, 1974, 1977, Certificate of Merit of US Publication Designers 1974, John Fischetti Political Cartoon Award 1982, Toastmasters' Int. and Leadership Award 1985, UN Soc. of Writers Award for Excellence 1995, Hubert H. Humphrey First Amendment Freedoms Prize 1996, Cartoon Award, UN 2000; Nat. Fed. of Hispanic-owned Papers est. Ranan R. Lurie Political Cartoon Award 1994, UN established an annual int. award in his honour (LurieUNaward.com) 1999. *Publications:* Among the Suns 1952, Lurie's Best Cartoons (Israel) 1961, Nixon Rated Cartoons (New York Times) 1973, Pardon Me, Mr President (New York Times) 1974, Lurie's Worlds (USA) 1980, So sieht es Lurie (Germany) 1981, Lurie's Almanac (UK) 1982, (USA) 1983, Taro's International Politics, Taro-San No Kokusai Seijigaku (Japan) 1984, Lurie's Middle East 1986, Lurie's Mideast Almanac (Israel) 1986, Lurie's Far East Views (China) 1987, The Cartoonist's Mask (novel) 2004; creator The Expandable Painting 1969, The Uniting Painting. *Leisure interests:* Tamar (wife), Rod, Barak (sons), Daphne, Danielle (daughters). *Address:* Cartoonews International, 375 Park Avenue, Suite 1301, New York, NY 10152, USA (home). *Telephone:* (212) 980-0855 (office). *Fax:* (212) 980-1664 (office). *Website:* cartoonews.com (home).

LUSCOMBE, David Edward, LittD, FBA, FSA, FRHistS; British historian and academic; *Professor Emeritus of Medieval History, University of Sheffield;* b. 22 July 1938, London, England; s. of Edward Dominic Luscombe and Nora Luscombe; m. Megan Phillips 1960; three s. one d.; ed St Michael's Convent School, Finchley Catholic Grammar School, London and King's Coll. Cambridge; Fellow, King's Coll. 1962–64, Churchill Coll. Cambridge 1964–72; Prof. of Medieval History, Univ. of Sheffield 1972–95, Leverhulme Personal Research Prof. of Medieval History 1995–2000, Research Prof. of Medieval History 2000–03, Prof. Emer. of Medieval History 2003–, Dean of Faculty of Arts 1985–87, Pro-Vice-Chancellor 1990–94, Chair. Humanities Research Inst. 1992–2003, Dir for Research in the Humanities Div. of Grad. School 1994–2003; mem. Governing Body, later the Asscn of St Edmund's House, Cambridge 1971–84; Visiting Prof., Royal Soc. of Canada 1991, Univ. of Conn. at Storrs 1993; Visiting Fellow, All Souls Coll. Oxford 1994; Raleigh Lecturer, British Acad. 1988; British Acad. Exchange Visitor to Japan Acad. 1996; mem. Council, British Acad. 1989–97, Chair. Publs Cttee 1990–97, Medieval Texts Editorial Cttee 1991–2004 (mem. 1982–91, 2004–), mem. Humanities Research Bd 1994–96; mem. Cttee, Soc. for Study of Medieval Languages and Literature 1991–96, Council, Royal Historical Soc. 1981–85, Cttee, Ecclesiastical History Soc. 1976–79, Supervisory Cttee British Acad./Oxford Univ. Press for New Dictionary of Nat. Biography 1992–99, Assoc. Ed. 1993–98; Vice-Pres. Soc. int. pour l'étude de la philosophie médiévale 1977–97, Pres. 1997–2002; mem. Commonwealth Scholarships Comm. in UK 1994–2000; Auditor, Higher Educ. Quality Council, Div. of Quality Audit 1994–97; mem. Council Worksop Coll. and Ranby House School 1996–2008; Fellow, Woodward Corpn 2000–08, Hon. Fellow 2008–. *Publications:* The School of Peter Abelard 1969, Peter Abelard's

Ethics 1971, Church and Government in the Middle Ages (co-ed.) 1976, Petrus Abaelardus (1079–1142): Person, Werk, und Wirkung (co-ed.) 1980, The Evolution of Medieval Thought by David Knowles (co-ed. revised edn with C. Brooke) 1988, David Knowles Remembered (co-author) 1991, Anselm, Aosta, Bec and Canterbury (co-ed.) 1996, Medieval Thought 1997; Cambridge Studies in Medieval Life and Thought, 4th series (Advisory Ed.) 1983–88, (Gen. Ed.) 1988–2004; The New Cambridge Medieval History, c. 1024– c. 1198, IV, 1–2 (co-ed.) 2004, Peter Abelard, Expositio in Hexameron (co-ed.) 2004, Peter Abelard, Sententie (co-ed.) 2006, Beauchief Abbey Cartulary (co-ed.) 2011; articles in learned journals. *Leisure interests:* family, using libraries, walking, cooking for two. *Address:* Department of History, University of Sheffield, Jessop West, 1 Upper Hanover Street, Sheffield, S3 7RA (office); 28 Endcliffe Hall Avenue, Sheffield, S10 3EL, England (home). *Telephone:* (114) 222-2555 (office). *Fax:* (114) 222-2576 (office). *E-mail:* d.luscombe@sheffield.ac.uk (office). *Website:* www.shef.ac.uk/history (office).

LUSCOMBE, Michael Gerard, BEc; Australian retail executive; *Chief Operating Officer, W-stores Company (Tanzania) Limited;* m. Karen Luscombe; three c.; ed Monash Univ., Monash Mount Eliza Business School; joined Woolworths in Vic. as trainee 1978, Store Man. 1980–94, Category Man., Buying and Marketing Dept 1994, later Merchandise Man., Operations Man., Vic. 1995–98, Nat. Man. Banking Dept, Sydney 1998–99, Gen. Man. Supply Chain 1999–2004, Dir of Supermarkets 2004–06, COO Woolworths Ltd June–Oct. 2006, CEO and Man. Dir 2006–11, COO W-stores Co. (Tanzania) Ltd 2011–; Chair. ALH Group; Dir and Past Chair. Australian Nat. Retailers Asscn; mem. or fmr mem. Bd of Dirs CIES – The Food Business Forum, The Consumer Goods Forum; Williamson Fellow, Vic. Community Leadership Program 1992. *Address:* W-stores Co. (Tanzania) Ltd, Infotech Place-Kawe Beach, Plot 565, Dar es Salaam, Tanzania (office). *Telephone:* (2) 8885-0000 (office). *E-mail:* info@w-stores.co.tz (office). *Website:* www.w-stores.co.tz (office).

LÜST, Reimar, Dr rer. nat; German physicist; *Professor of Physics, University of Hamburg;* b. 25 March 1923, Barmen; s. of Hero Lüst and Grete Lüst (née Strunck); m. 1st Dr Rhea Kulka 1953; two s.; 2nd Nina Grunenberg 1986; ed Univs of Frankfurt am Main and Göttingen; Research Physicist, Max Planck Inst. (MPI), Göttingen and Munich 1950–60, Enrico Fermi Inst., Univ. of Chicago 1955–56, Princeton Univ. 1956; Head, Dept for Extraterrestrial Physics, MPI for Physics and Astrophysics 1960, Dir Inst. of Extraterrestrial Physics 1963–72, later Scientific Mem. for Extraterrestrial Physics, MPI; Visiting Prof., Univ. of New York 1959, MIT 1961, Calif. Inst. of Tech. 1962, 1966; Chair. German Research Council 1969–72, Deutsche Gesellschaft für Luft- und Raumfahrt 1968–72; Pres. Max-Planck-Gesellschaft 1972–84; Dir-Gen. European Space Agency 1984–90; Prof. of Physics, Univ. of Hamburg 1992–; Pres. Alexander von Humboldt Foundation 1989–99, Hon. Pres. 1999; Chair. Bd Int. Univ. Bremen 1999–2004, Hon. Chair. 2005–; mem. Int. Acad. of Astronautics, Royal Astronomical Soc., Bavarian Acad. Sciences; Corresp. mem. Real Acad. de Ciencias Exactas, Físicas y Naturales de Madrid; Fellow, Imperial Coll. of Science and Tech., London; Hon. Prof., Inst. for Theoretical Physics, Chinese Acad. of Sciences, Beijing 1997, Beijing Univ. 1997; Hon. Foreign mem. American Acad. of Arts and Sciences, Austrian Acad. of Sciences; Hon. mem. Heidelberg Acad. of Sciences, Senat Max-Planck-Gesellschaft, Deutsche Gesellschaft für Luft- und Raumfahrt; Hon. Citizen of State of Texas 1999; Hon. Citizen of Freie Hansestadt Bremen 2001; Officier, Ordre des Palmes Académiques; Officier, Légion d'honneur; Bayerischer Maximiliansorden für Wissenschaft und Kunst; Grosses Verdienstkreuz mit Stern und Schulterband; Distinguished Service Cross (Poland) 1997; Dr hc (Sofia) 1991, (Birmingham) 1993, (Slovak Acad. of Sciences) 1995 and several other hon. degrees from int. univs; Planet 4386 named Lüst 1991; Daniel and Florence Guggenheim Int. Astronautics Award, Personality of the Year 1986, Tsiolkowsky Medal (USSR Fed. of Cosmonauts) 1987, Harnack Medal of Max Planck Soc. 1993 and numerous other awards; shared Adenauer-de Gaulle Prize 1994. *Publications:* articles on space research, astrophysics and plasmaphysics. *Leisure interests:* history, tennis, skiing. *Address:* Max-Planck-Institut für Meteorologie, Bundesstrasse 53, 20146 Hamburg (office); Bellevue 49, 22301 Hamburg, Germany (home). *Telephone:* (40) 41173300. *Fax:* (40) 41173390. *E-mail:* cornelia.sengbusch@mpimet.mpg.de (office).

LUSZTIG, George, MA, PhD, FRS; American mathematician and academic; *Abdun Nur Professor of Mathematics, Massachusetts Institute of Technology;* b. (Gheorghe Lusztig), 20 May 1946, Timişoara, Romania; m. 1st Michal-Nina Abraham 1972 (divorced 2000); two d.; m. 2nd Gongqin Li 2003; ed Univ. of Bucharest and Princeton Univ.; Visiting mem. Inst. for Advanced Study, Princeton, NJ 1969–71; Research Fellow, Dept of Math., Univ. of Warwick 1971–72, Lecturer 1972-74, Prof. 1974–78; Prof. of Math., MIT 1978–, Norbert Wiener Prof. 1999–2009, Abdun Nur Prof. 2009–; mem. NAS; Guggenheim Fellowship 1982; Cole Prize in Algebra, American Math. Soc. 1985, Brouwer Medal, Dutch Math. Soc. 1999, Steele Prize for Lifetime Achievement, American Math. Soc. 2008. *Publications:* The Discrete Series of GLn over a Finite Field, 1974, Characters of Reductive Groups over a Finite Field 1984, Introduction to Quantum Groups 1993, Hecke Algebras with Unequal Parameters 2003. *Leisure interest:* yoga. *Address:* Department of Mathematics, Massachusetts Institute of Technology, Room 2-276, 77 Massachusetts Avenue, Cambridge, MA 02139, USA (office). *Telephone:* (617) 253-4398 (office). *Fax:* (617) 253-4358 (office). *E-mail:* gyuri@math.mit.edu (office). *Website:* www-math.mit.edu/~gyuri (office).

LUTE, Jane Holl, PhD, JD; American government official, UN official and fmr army officer; *Deputy Secretary of Homeland Security;* m. Lt. Gen. Douglas Lute; two d.; ed Stanford Univ., Georgetown Univ.; career Officer, US Army (retd 1994); fmr teacher of Political Science, West Point Mil. Acad.; served in Europe, Persian Gulf during Operation Desert Storm 1991; mem. of Staff, Nat. Security Council, Dir of European Affairs 1991–94; Head of Carnegie Comm. on Preventing Deadly Conflict 1994–99; Sr Public Policy Fellow, Woodrow Wilson Centre for Int. Scholars 1994–99; Exec. Dir Asscn of US Army Project on role of American mil. power 2000; Exec. Vice-Pres. and COO UN Foundation and Better World Fund 2000–03; Asst Sec.-Gen. for Mission Support, UN Dept Peace-keeping Operations 2003–09; Deputy Sec., US Dept of Homeland Security, Washington, DC 2009–; mem. of Va Bar. *Address:* Office of the Deputy Secretary, Department of Homeland Security, Washington, DC 20528, USA. *Website:* www.dhs.gov.

LÜTKESTRATKÖTTER, Herbert Hermann, Dr-Ing; German business executive; b. 1950; ed Aachen Tech Univ. and its Inst. of Hydraulic Eng and Water Resources Man.; held planning and man. roles at Lahmeyer International 1978–99, becoming Man. Dir and also mem. Exec. Bd, Lahmeyer AG; Int. Business Man. Philipp Holzmann AG 1999, Labour Relations Dir 2000; fmr Chair. Exec. Bd Dussmann AG & Co. KGaA; joined Hochtief AG 2003, mem. Exec. Bd 2003–11, Deputy Chair. 2006–07, Chair. 2007–11, responsible for the Americas and Europe divs, for Corp. Devt, Corp. Communications and Corp. Governance; mem. Bd of Dirs Aecon Group Inc. 2005–; mem. Supervisory Bd ThyssenKrupp Elevator AG; Alt. Dir Leighton Holdings Ltd 2004–07, Dir (non-exec.) 2007–. *Address:* c/o Hochtief AG, Opernplatz 2, 45128 Essen, Germany.

LUTON, Jean-Marie; French engineer; *Honourary President, Starsem;* b. 4 Aug. 1942, Chamalières; s. of Pierre Luton and Marie Luton; m. Cécile Robine 1967; three s.; ed Lycée Blaise Pascal, Clermont-Ferrand, Lycée St Louis, Paris, Faculté des Sciences, Paris and Ecole Polytechnique; with CNRS 1964–71; Ministry of Industrial and Scientific Devt 1971–73; Head of Research, Centre Nat. d'Etudes Spatiales 1974–75, Head of Planning 1975–78, Dir of Programmes and Planning 1978–84, Deputy Dir-Gen. 1984–87, Dir-Gen. 1989–90; Dir of Space Programmes, Aérospatiale 1987–89; Dir-Gen. European Space Agency 1990–97; Pres., Dir-Gen., then Chair. Arianespace 1997–2006; Chair. and CEO Starsem 2002–06, Hon. Pres. 2006–; Chevalier, Légion d'honneur, Officier, Ordre nat. du Mérite; Prix de l'Astronautique; Prix de l'Innovateur industriel, Society of Satellite Professionals (USA) 1998. *Leisure interests:* tennis, sailing. *Address:* c/o Starsem, 2 rue François Truffaut, 91042 EVRY Cedex, France (office).

LUTSENKO, Yuriy Vitaliyovych; Ukrainian engineer and politician; b. 14 Dec. 1964, Rivne; s. of the late Vitaliy Ivanovych Lutsenko and Vira Mikhailivna Lutsenko; m. Irina Stepanivna; three s.; ed Lviv Polytechnical Inst.; mil. service in army 1984–86; Chief Constructor and Head, Tech. Workshop, Gazotron, Rivne 1989–94; Deputy Head, Rivne Oblast Council of People's Deputies 1994–96; Head, Rivne Oblast Admin Econs Cttee 1996–97; Deputy Minister of Science and Tech. 1997–98; adviser to Prime Minister 1998–99; adviser to Leader of Socialist Party of Ukraine 1999–2002; Deputy, Verkhovna Rada (Parl.) 2002–; Minister of Internal Affairs 2005–06, 2007–10, Acting Minister of Internal Affairs 2010; mem. Socialist Party of Ukraine 1996–2006, Sec., Political Council 1996, later held number of sr positions; mem. Construction, Transportation, Communal Services and Communications Cttee; active in Ukraine Without Kuchma! (UBK) campaign and 'Orange Revolution' of 2004; Founder Yuriy Lutsenko People's Self Defence movt 2007, registered as political party 2010; charged with abuse of office and forgery by Prosecutor Gen., arrested and held at Lukyanivska Prison from 26 Dec. 2010, went on hunger strike 22 April–24 May 2011, sentenced to four years' imprisonment for embezzlement and abuse of office Feb. 2012, protests against the sentence made by EU, US Dept of State, Canada and other Int. Orgs and human rights orgs, appealed against his sentence March 2012, lost appeal April 2013, pardoned and released from prison for health reasons 7 April 2013; closed People's Self-Defence 2013; f. new non-parl. org. Third Republic 2013; one of the organizers of Euromaidan (wave of demonstrations, civil unrest and revolution with public protests demanding closer European integration) Nov. 2013; hospitalized in intensive care ward following beating by police in street protests Jan. 2014; Commdr, Order of Prince Yaroslav the Wise, Fifth Class 2006. *Telephone:* 50-6563215 (mobile). *E-mail:* lutsenko_pressa@ukr.net (office); pressa@3republic.org .ua; 3respublik@gmail.com. *Website:* www.3republic.org.ua.

LUTTER, Marcus Michael, PhD; German professor of law; *Professor Emeritus and Dean, Zentrum für Europäisches Wirtschaftsrecht, University of Bonn;* b. 11 Dec. 1930, Munich; s. of Michael Lutter; m. Rebecca Garbe 1957; one s. two d.; ed Univs of Munich, Paris and Freiburg; notary, Rockenhausen 1957–60; research scholarship, Deutsche Forschungsgesellschaft, Brussels, Strasbourg, Paris, Rome, Utrecht 1961–63; notary, Rockenhausen and external lecturer, Univ. of Mainz 1964–65; Prof. Inst. for Civil Law, German and European Trade and Econ. Law, Univ. of Bochum 1966–79; fmr Prof. and Dir Inst. for Trade and Econ. Law, Univ. of Bonn, now Prof. Emer. and Dean of the Centre for European Econ. Law; Visiting Prof., Univ. of California, Berkeley 1972, Techno Univ., Tokyo 1982, Univ. of Oxford 1997; Publr Zeitschrift für Unternehmens-und Gesellschaftsrecht; Pres. German Lawyers' Asscn 1982–88; Hon. PhD (Vienna, Warsaw, Jena). *Publications:* Information and Confidentiality in the Supervisory Board 1984, 2006, European Company Law 1996, The Letter of Intent 1998, Duties and Rights of Board Members 2002; various monographs and treatises especially on participation, jt stock cos and supervisory bds. *Address:* Zentrum für Europäisches Wirtschaftsrecht der Universität Bonn, Adenauerallee 24–42, 53113 Bonn (office); Auf der Steige 6, 53129 Bonn, Germany (home). *Telephone:* (228) 739559 (office); (228) 231722 (home). *Fax:* (228) 737078 (office). *E-mail:* marcus.lutter@jura.uni -bonn.de (office). *Website:* www.jura.uni-bonn.de (office).

LUTTWAK, Edward Nicolae, PhD; American academic, international consultant and writer; *Senior Fellow, Center for Strategic and International Studies;* b. 4 Nov. 1942, Arad, Romania; s. of Joseph Luttwak and Clara Baruch; m. Dalya Iaari 1970; one s. one d.; ed elementary schools in Palermo and Milan, Carmel Coll., Wallingford, UK, London School of Econs and Johns Hopkins Univ.; Lecturer, Univ. of Bath, UK 1965–67; Consultant, Walter J. Levy SA (London) 1967–68; Visiting Prof., Johns Hopkins Univ. 1974–76; Sr Fellow, Center for Strategic and Int. Studies, Washington, DC 1977–87, Burke Chair. of Strategy 1987–92, Sr Fellow 1992–; Consultant to Office of US Sec. of Defense 1975, to Policy Planning Council, US Dept of State 1981, Nat. Security Council, The White House 1987, US Dept of Defense 1987, to Govts of Italy, Korea, Spain; Prin., Edward N. Luttwak Inc. Int. Consultants 1981–; Pres. Servicios Agricolas Tupinamba, Bolivia; Int. Assoc. Inst. of Fiscal and Monetary Policy, Japan Ministry of Finance (Okurasho); mem. editorial Bd The American Scholar, Journal of Strategic Studies, The National Interest, Géopolitique, The Washington Quarterly, Orbis; Hon. LLD (Bath) 2007; Nimitz Lectureship, Univ. of Calif. 1987, Tanner Lecturer, Yale Univ. 1989, Rosenstiel Lecturer, Grinner Coll. 1992. *Publications:* Coup d'Etat 1968, Dictionary of Modern War 1972, The Israeli Army 1975, The Political Uses of Sea Power 1976, The Grand Strategy of the Roman Empire 1978, Strategy and Politics: Collected Essays 1979, The Grand Strategy of the Soviet Union 1983, The Pentagon and the Art of War 1985, Strategy and History: collected essays 1985, International Security Yearbook 1984/85 (with Barry M. Brechman) 1985, On the

Meaning of Victory 1986, Strategy: The Logic of War and Peace 1987, The Dictionary of Modern War (with Stuart Koehl) 1991, The Endangered American Dream 1993, Il Fantasma della Povertà (co-author) 1996, Cose è davvero la Democrazia 1996, La Renaissance de la puissance aérienne stratégique 1998, Turbo-Capitalism 1999, Il Libro della Libertà 2000, Strategy: The Logic of War and Peace (ed.) 2002, The Grand Strategy of the Byzantine Empire 2010; books have been translated into 16 languages. *Leisure interest:* ranching in the Amazon. *Address:* Center for Strategic and International Studies, 1800 K Street, NW, Washington, DC 20006, USA (office). *Telephone:* (301) 656-1972 (office); (202) 775-3145 (office). *Fax:* (202) 775-3199 (office). *Website:* www.csis.org (office).

LUTZ, Robert (Bob) A., BS, MBA; American automotive industry executive; b. 12 Feb. 1932, Zürich, Switzerland; s. of Robert H. Lutz and Marguerite Lutz; m. 1st Betty D. Lutz 1956 (divorced 1979); m. 2nd Heide-Marie Schmid 1980 (divorced 1993); m. 3rd Denise Ford 1994; four d. from 1st marriage; ed Univ. of California, Berkeley; Capt. in US Marine Corps 1954–59; Research Assoc. IMEDE, Lausanne 1962–63; Sr Analyst, Forward Planning, General Motors Corpn (GM), New York 1963–65, Staff Asst, Man. Dir's Staff, Adam Opel AG (GM) 1965–66, various man. positions at GM France 1966–69, Asst Domestic Gen. Sales Man., Merchandising, Adam Opel AG 1969, Dir of Sales and mem. Man. Bd 1969–70; Vice-Pres. (Sales) and mem. Man. Bd, BMW AG 1970–74; Gen. Man. Ford of Germany 1974–76, Vice-Pres. (Truck Operations), Ford of Europe 1976–77; Pres. Ford of Europe 1977–79, Vice-Pres. Ford Motor Co. and Chair. of Bd Ford of Europe 1979–82; Exec. Vice-Pres. Ford Int. Automotive Operations, Dearborn, Mich. 1982–86, Exec. Vice-Pres. North American Truck Operations 1986; Head of, Int. Operations, Pres. and COO Chrysler Corpn 1988–96, Vice-Chair. 1996–98; Chair., CEO and Pres. Exide Corpn 1998–2001, Chair. 2001–02; Vice-Chair. of Product Devt, General Motors (GM) 2001–09, Chair. GM North America 2001–09, Vice Chair. and Sr Advisor to CEO 2009–10, Special Advisor 2010–; f. Lutz Communications (consultancy), Ann Arbor, Mich.; Chair. Silicon Graphics, ASCOM, Switzerland, New Common School Foundation; mem. Bd of Dirs Transonic Combustion, Inc. 2010–; Vice-Chair. Bd of Trustees, Marine Mil. Acad.; mem. Bd of Trustees, US Marine Corps Univ. Foundation. *Publications:* Guts: The Seven Laws of Business That Made Chrysler the World's Hottest Car Company 1999, Guts: 8 Laws of Business from One of the Most Innovative Business Leaders of Our Time 2003, Car Guys vs. Bean Counters 2011, Icons and Idiots: Straight Talk on Leadership 2013. *Address:* Lutz Communications, Ann Arbor, MI 48103-9628 (office); General Motors Corporation, 300 Renaissance Center, Detroit, MI 48265-3000, USA (office). *Telephone:* (866) 476-3931 (Lutz Communications) (office). *E-mail:* info@boblutzsez.com (office). *Website:* www.boblutzsez.com (office).

LUU, Jane, BS, PhD; Vietnamese/American astronomer and academic; *Senior Scientist, Lincoln Laboratory, Massachusetts Institute of Technology;* b. July 1963, Saigon, South Viet Nam; m. Ronnie Hoogerwerf; ed Stanford Univ., Univ. of California, Berkeley, Massachusetts Inst. of Tech.; emigrated to USA as a refugee 1975; Postdoctoral Fellow, Harvard-Smithsonian Center for Astrophysics, Univ. of California, Berkeley and Stanford Univ. 1990–94; Asst Prof., Harvard Univ. 1994–98; Prof., Leiden Univ., The Netherlands 1998–2001; Sr Scientist, Lincoln Laboratory, MIT 2001–; Annie J. Cannon Award in Astronomy, American Astronomical Soc. 1991, Hubble Fellowship, Space Telescope Science Inst., asteroid 5430 Luu named in her honour, Shaw Prize in Astronomy (co-recipient) 2012, Kavli Prize (co-recipient) 2012. *Publications:* numerous papers in professional journals. *Leisure interest:* playing the cello. *Address:* Lincoln Laboratory, Massachusetts Institute of Technology, 244 Wood Street, Lexington, MA 02420-9108, USA (office). *Telephone:* (781) 981-5500 (office). *E-mail:* llwebmaster@ll.mit .edu (office). *Website:* www.ll.mit.edu (office).

LUXON, Benjamin Matthew, CBE, FGSM; British singer (baritone); b. 24 March 1937, Redruth, Cornwall; s. of Maxwell Luxon and Lucille Grigg; m. Sheila Amit 1969; two s. one d.; ed Truro School, Westminster Training Coll., Guildhall School of Music and Drama; always a freelance artist; sang with English Opera Group 1963–70; has sung with Royal Opera House, Covent Garden and Glyndebourne Festival Opera 1971–96, Boston Symphony Orchestra 1975–96, Netherlands Opera 1976–96, Frankfurt Opera House 1977–96, Paris Opéra 1980, La Scala, Milan 1986; roles include Monteverdi's Ulisse, Janáček's Forester, Mozart's Don Giovanni and Papageno, Tchaikovsky's Onegin, Verdi's Posa and Falstaff, Wagner's Wolfram, Alban Berg's Wozzeck, Count Almaviva and Sherasmin in Oberon; performs as recitalist with piano accompanist David Willison; folk-singing partnership with Bill Grofut 1976–96; has recorded for all major record cos; retd from professional singing due to severe hearing loss 1996; vocal coach at Tanglewood, USA 1996; Hon. mem. RAM; Bard of Cornish Gorseth; Hon. DMus (Exeter), (RSA of Music and Drama) 1996, (Canterbury Christ Church Coll.) 1997. *Recordings include:* Mahler's 8th Symphony, Schubert's Song Cycles. *Leisure interests:* most sports, English watercolours of 18th and 19th centuries.

LUXTON, John, BAgrSc; New Zealand politician; *Spokesman for Tourism, Communications and Inward Investment, National Party;* m.; three c.; ed Massey Univ.; Nat. Party MP for Matamata 1987–96, for Karapiro 1996–99; Minister of Housing and Energy, Assoc. Minister of Educ. 1990–93, Assoc. Minister of Maori Affairs 1991–97; Minister of Maori Affairs, Police and Assoc. Minister of Educ. 1993–97, Minister of Commerce, Fisheries, Lands and Biosecurity, for Industry and Assoc. Minister for Agric. 1997–98; Minister of Food, Fibre, Biosecurity and Border Control, Assoc. Minister of Immigration and Assoc. Minister for Int. Trade 1998–99; Nat. Party Spokesperson on Int. Trade Negotiations and Inward Investment and Regional Devt, Assoc. Foreign Affairs 2000–01; Nat. Party Spokesman for Tourism, Communications, Inward Investment 2001–; fmr Chair. Tatua Industry Co-operative Dairy Co. Ltd, Deputy Chair. Wallford Meats Ltd; Dir Wallace Corpn Ltd, Tatua Co-operative Dairy Co., Asia 2000 Foundation; int. agric. consultant and farmer; AC Cameron Memorial Award 1987. *Address:* Parliament Buildings, Wellington, New Zealand. *Telephone:* (4) 471-9509 (office). *Fax:* (4) 473-0469 (office). *E-mail:* john.luxton@parliament.govt.nz (office).

LUZHKOV, Yurii Mikhailovich; Russian politician; b. 21 Sept. 1936, Moscow; m. Marina Bashilova 1958 (died 1989); two s.; m. 2nd Yelena Baturina 1991; two d.; ed Gubkin Inst. of Oil and Gas, Moscow; researcher, Research Inst. of Plastic Materials 1958–64; Head of Div. Ministry of Chemical Industry 1964–87; First Deputy Chair. Exec. Cttee, Moscow City Council and Chair. Moscow Agric. Industry Dept 1987–90; Chair. Exec. Cttee, Moscow City Council 1990–91; Vice-

Mayor of Moscow and Premier, Moscow City Govt 1991–92, Mayor and Head of City Govt 1992–2010, re-elected 1996, 1999, 2003, apptd 2007–10; mem. Russian Council of Fed. 1996–2001; Founder and Co-Chair. Fatherland (Otechestvo) Movt 1998–2001, formed alliance with All Russia party in 1999, subsequently merged with pro-Putin Unity party to create Unity and Fatherland-United Russia party (UF-UR) 2001, later simply United Russia (Yedinaya Rossiya); Co-Chair. Supreme Council, UF-UR; Chair. Int. Fund Assistance to Free Enterprise; Pres. Moscow Int. Business Asscn 2002; Hon. Prof., Acad. of Labour and Social Relations; Lenin Order, Red Banner Order, Order in the Name of Russia 2004; Hon. DSc (Lomonosov State Univ. Moscow); Golden Mask Prize for support of the arts. *Publications:* 72 Hours of Agony 1991, The Quietist Negotiations 1994, We Are Your Children, Moscow 1996. *Leisure interests:* football, tennis, skiing, equestrian sport, fishing, bee-keeping. *Address:* c/o Office of the Mayor and Prime Minister of the Government of Moscow City, 125032 Moscow, ul. Tverskaya 13, Russia (office). *Website:* www.luzhkov.ru (office).

LUZÓN LÓPEZ, Francisco; Spanish banker; b. 1 Jan. 1948, Cañavate, Cuenca; ed Univ. of Bilbao; trainee, Banco de Vizcaya 1972, Regional Man. Seville 1974, Man. of Planning and Man. Control, Bilbao 1975–78, Int. Div. Madrid 1978–80, Man. London 1980–81; mem. Bd and Gen. Man. Banco de Crédito Comercial 1981–82; mem. Bd and Gen. Man. Banco Occidental 1982–85; Gen. Man. Commercial Banking Network 1985–87; mem. Bd and Gen. Man. Banco de Vizcaya 1987–88, Banco Bilbao-Vizcaya 1988; Chair. Banco Exterior de España 1988–99; Vice-Pres. Banco Atlántico and mem. Bd Teneo 1991–94; Chair. and CEO Argentaria 1991–96; Chair. Caja Postal SA 1991–, Banco de Crédito Local 1994–99, Banco Hipotecario de España 1994–, Corporación Bancaria de España SA; mem. Bd of Dirs, Banco Santander Central Hispano 1997–2012, Exec. Vice-Pres. for Latin America 1999–2012; Worldwide Vice-Pres. Universia SA 1999–2012; Dir, Inditex-Zara SA 1997–2012, LATAM Airlines Group SA 2012–; adviser, IDB; Leader-Guest Prof., School of Business China-Europe (CEIBS), Shanghai; Lecturer, Univ. of Deusto, Bilbao. *Address:* c/o Ciudad Grupo Santander, Avenida de Cantabria s/n, 28660 Boadilla del Monte, Madrid (office); Paseo de Recoletos 10, 28001 Madrid, Spain; LATAM Airlines Group, Pdte. Riesco 5711, 20th Floor, Las Condes, Santiago, Chile. *Telephone:* (91) 2890000 (office). *E-mail:* investor.relations@lan.com. *Website:* www.santander.com (office).

LUZZATTO, Lucio, FRCPath, FRCP; Italian geneticist and haematologist; *Scientific Director, Istituto Toscano Tumori;* b. 28 Sept. 1936, Genoa; s. of the late Aldo Luzzatto and of Anna Luzzatto Gabrielli; m. Paola Caboara 1963; one s. one d.; ed Liceo D'Oria, Genoa, Univ. of Genoa Medical School, Univ. of Pavia; Sr Lecturer in charge of Sub-Dept of Haematology, Univ. of Ibadan, Nigeria 1967–68, Prof. of Haematology 1968–74, Consultant Haematologist, Univ. Coll. Hosp. Ibadan, Nigeria 1967–68; Dir Int. Inst. of Genetics and Biophysics, CNR, Naples 1974–81; Prof. of Haematology (Univ. of London) and Dir of Haematology Dept Royal Postgrad. Medical School, Consultant Haematologist Hammersmith Hosp., London, UK 1981–94, Hon. Dir MRC/LRF Leukaemia Unit, London 1987–93; Chair. Dept of Human Genetics, Courtney Steel Chair., Attending Physician in Genetics and Haematology, mem. Cell Biology Program, Memorial Sloan-Kettering Cancer Center, New York, Prof. of Medicine and Human Genetics, Cornell Univ. Medical Coll., New York 1994–2000; Scientific Dir Nat. Inst. of Cancer Research (IST), Genoa, Italy 2000–04, personal Chair of Haematology 2002–; currently Scientific Dir Istituto Toscano Tumori, Florence; Founding Pres. Nigerian Soc. for Haematology; fmr Pres. Italian Asscn of Genetics; fmr Chair. Ethics Cttee American Soc. for Gene Therapy; mem. European Molecular Biology Org. 1979, Human Genome Org. (HUGO) 1990, American Asscn of Physicians; Foreign mem. American Acad. of Arts and Sciences 2004; Hon. mem. American Soc. of Hematology; Hon. DSc (Ibadan) 1998; Dr hc of Pharmacy (Urbino) 1990; William Dameshek Medal 1975, Pius XI Medal 1976, Sanremo Int. Prize for Human Genetics 1982, Int. Chiron Award for Biomedical Research 1995, Premio Napoli 1995, Jose Carreras Medal 2002. *Publications:* more than 330 articles in scientific journals and scientific and medical textbooks. *Address:* Istituto Toscano Tumori, Via T. Alderotti 26N, 50139 Florence, Italy (office). *Telephone:* (55) 4385213 (office). *Fax:* (55) 4385252 (office). *E-mail:* lucio.luzzatto@regione.toscana.it (office). *Website:* www.ittumori.it (office).

LY, Oumar Tatam, MA; Malian economist and politician; b. 28 Sept. 1963, Paris, France; s. of Ibrahima Ly and Madina Tall Ly; m.; two c.; ed Ecole Normale Superieure de Lyon, Univ. Paris–1 (Sorbonne), Ecole supérieure des Sciences économiques et commerciales, Cergy-Pontoise, France; began career as economist, World Bank 1990; Project Man., Gen. Secr. of Pres. of Mali 1992–93, Technical Adviser 1993–94; Analyst, Central Man. Studies and Forecasting Dept, Banque centrale des États de l'Afrique de l'Ouest (BCEAO), Dakar 1994–96, Deputy Dir of Studies 1996, Chief Financial Officer 2000–06, Dir, Dept of Issue, Accounting and Finance 2007–09, Nat. Dir for Mali, BCEAO 2008, Special Adviser to Gov. –2013; Prime Minister 2013. *Leisure interests:* reading, cinema, tennis. *Address:* c/o Office of the Prime Minister, Quartier du Fleuve, BP 790, Bamako, Mali.

LYAKHOV, Col Vladimir Afanasyevich; Russian cosmonaut (retd); b. 20 July 1941, Antratsit, Voroshilovgrad Oblast, Ukrainian SSR; m.; two c.; ed Kharkov Aviation School for Pilots, Chuguyev, Kharkov Oblast, Gagarin Mil. Acad.; mem. CPSU 1963–91; served in fmr Soviet Air Force 1964–; mem. Cosmonaut team 1967–94; Commdr of space-ship Soyuz-32 1979 and Soyuz T-9 which connected up with orbital station Salyut-7; Commdr Soyuz TM-6 1988; space-walked 1983; spent 333 days, 7 hours, 47 minutes in space; worked in Yuri Gagarin Centre 1995–99; Hero of Soviet Union (twice), Pilot-Cosmonaut of the USSR, Order of Lenin (two), Order of the October Revolution, Medal 'For Merit in Space Exploration' (Russian Fed.), Order of Sukhbaatar (Mongolia), Order 'The Sun of Liberty' (Afghanistan), Order of Merit, Third Class (Ukraine); K. Tsiolkovski Gold Medal. *Leisure interest:* hockey. *Address:* c/o Yuri Gagarin Research & Test Training Centre, 141160 Star City, Moscow Region, Russian Federation. *Telephone:* (495) 526-34-07. *Fax:* (495) 526-26-12.

LYALL, John Adrian, RIBA, FRSA; British architect; *Managing Director, John Lyall Architects Ltd;* b. 12 Dec. 1949, Daws Heath, Essex; s. of Keith Lyall and Phyllis Lyall (née Sharps); m. Sallie Jean Davies 1991; one s. one d.; ed Southend High School for Boys, Essex, Architectural Asscn School of Architecture; worked for Cedric Price, Piano & Rogers, Bahr, Vermeer & Haecker, Rock Townsend 1996–79; Founder Multimatch Design Group 1970–73; in practice with Will Alsop

as Alsop & Lyall, later Alsop, Lyall & Störmer 1980–91; Man. Dir John Lyall Architects 1991–; RIBA Vice-Pres. of Cultural Affairs 1997, of Future Studies 1999–2000, Chair. of Validation Task Force, RIBA 2001; Bannister Fletcher Prof. Univ. Coll. London 1998; design teaching and lecturing at Architectural Asscn and Bartlett Schools, London and univs in USA, UK, Russia, Chile, Colombia and Ecuador; design adviser to Cardiff Bay Devt Corpn and English Partnerships; apptd as enabler for CABE 2001 and Chair. of RIBA's Educ. Validation Task Force 2001–02; Chair. Peterborough Design Panel 2009–; mem. CABE Design Review Panel 2008–; created Polyark II project 2009–10. *Television:* contrib. to Master-class – Denys Lasdun; panel mem. BBC Knowledge 2000–01. *Dance:* design collaborator with Rosemary Butcher Dance Co. on various performances 1990–96. *Music:* production designer for Opera 80 travelling opera 1980–83. *Achievements:* award-winning bldgs include: The Corn Exchange, Leeds (Ironbridge Award, British Archaeological Soc. 1990, 1998, Leeds Award for Architecture 1990, Europa Nostra Award, 1991, RIBA National Award, 1991, RIBA White Rose Award 1991, Civic Trust Commendation 1991, British Council of Shopping Centres Award 1991, Design Week Award 1991, Royal Inst. of Chartered Surveyors Urban Renewal Award 1995) 1991, White Cloth Hall, Leeds (Leeds Award for Architecture 1992, The Minerva Award 1993) 1992, Tottenham Hale Overground Station, London (Aluminium Imagination Award 1993) 1992 (Tottenham Hale London Underground Station and Station Forecourt 1999), Harry Ramsden's Restaurant, Cardiff Bay 1996, North Greenwich Jubilee Line Station, London (RIBA Regional Award 1999, RIBA Nat. Category Award 1999, Civic Trust Commendation 2000) 1999, Crystal Palace Park, London 2003, Silver House, Carnaby Street, London 2003–04, Regeneration of Cranfields Mills, Ipswich 2004–09, Hammersmith Pumping Station (residential conversion and new-build affordable housing block) 2004–08, Jerwood Dance House, Ipswich 2005, Goldsmiths Centre, Clerkenwell, London 2007–, Pumping Stations, Olympic site, London 2009–. *Publications:* John Lyall: Contexts and Catalysts 1999; contrib. to A Guide to Recent Architecture: London 1993, A Guide to Recent Architecture: England 1995, Context – New Buildings in Historic Settings 1998. *Leisure interest:* choral singing, gardening. *Address:* John Lyall Architects, 13–19 Curtain Road, London, EC2A 3LT (office); Newlands, Gandish Road, East Bergholt, Suffolk, CO7 6TP, England (home). *Telephone:* (20) 7375-3324 (office); (1206) 298368 (home). *Fax:* (20) 7375-3325 (office). *E-mail:* john.lyall@johnlyallarchitects.com (office). *Website:* www.johnlyallarchitects.com (office).

LYDON, Nicholas B., BSc, PhD, FRS; British/American biochemist, entrepreneur and academic; *CEO, Granite Bioppharma, LLC;* b. 27 Feb. 1957, England; ed Strathallan School, Perth, Scotland, Univs of Leeds and Dundee; researched interferon at Schering-Plough, Paris and Lyon, France 1982–85; Leader of Protein Kinase Inhibitor Programme, Ciba-Geigy Pharmaceuticals (now Novartis, cr. through merger with Sandoz 1996), Basel, Switzerland 1985–97; introduced to oncologist Brian J. Druker late 1980s, both scientists successful in developing the drug Gleevac at Novartis 1996; Founder, Pres. and CEO Kinetix Pharmaceuticals, Inc., Boston, Mass 1997–2000 (acquired by Amgen, Inc. 2000), Vice-Pres. for Small Molecule Drug Discovery 2000–02; Founder, Granite Biopharma, LLC (consulting co.), Jackson Hole, Wyo.; Co-founder and Dir AnaptysBio, San Diego, Calif., Blueprint Medicines, Cambridge, Mass; mem. Bd of Dirs and Scientific Advisory Bd Ambit Biosciences (Avalon VI), AnaptysBio, Inc. Biosciences (Avalon VII); Hon. LLD (Dundee) 2011; Warren Alpert Foundation Prize 2000, AACR-Bruce F. Cain Memorial Award 2002, Charles F. Kettering Prize, General Motors Cancer Research Foundation 2002, Lasker-DeBakey Clinical Medical Research Award (co-recipient) 2009, Japan Prize (co-recipient) 2012, GlaxoSmithKline Prize and Lecturer, Royal Soc. 2014. *Achievements include:* developed, with Brian J. Druker and Charles L. Sawyers, imatinib (or Gleevac) and dasatinib – targeted treatments for chronic myeloid leukemia. *Publications:* numerous papers in professional journals. *Address:* AnaptysBio, Inc., 10421 Pacific Center Court, Suite 200, San Diego, CA 92121, USA (office). *Telephone:* (858) 362-6295 (office). *Fax:* (858) 362-6296 (office). *E-mail:* corpdev@anaptysbio.com (office). *Website:* www.anaptysbio.com (office).

LYKKETOFT, Mogens; Danish politician; *Speaker of the Parliament;* b. 9 Jan. 1946, Copenhagen; s. of Axel and Martha Lykketoft; m. Mette Holm; two d.; ed Univ. of Copenhagen; worked at Econ. Council of the Labour Movt 1966–81, Head of Dept 1975–81; mem. Folketing (Parl.) 1981–, Political Spokesman for Social Democratic Party 1991–93, 2001–02, Leader 2002–05, Spokesman on Foreign Affairs 2005–09, Vice-Pres. of Parl. and Vice-Chair. Foreign Policy Cttee 2009–11, Speaker of the Parl. 2011–; Minister for Inland Revenue 1981–82, of Finance 1993–2000, of Foreign Affairs 2000–01. *Publications:* ed. of several books and numerous articles in magazines, periodicals and newspapers. *Address:* Folketinget, Christiansborg, 1240 Copenhagen (office); Trepilevej 1 B, 2930 Klampenborg, Denmark (home). *Telephone:* 33-37-40-34 (office). *E-mail:* smoly@ft.dk (office). *Website:* www.lykketoft.dk.

LYNAM, Desmond (Des) Michael, OBE, ACII; British sports broadcaster; b. 17 Sept. 1942, Ennis, Co. Clare, Repub. of Ireland; s. of Edward Lynam and Gertrude Veronica Malone; m. Susan Eleanor Skinner (divorced 1974); one s.; ed Varndean Grammar School, Brighton, Brighton Business Coll.; career in insurance –1967; freelance journalist and reporter local radio 1967–69; reporter, presenter and commentator BBC Radio 1969–78; presenter and commentator BBC TV Sport 1978–99 (including Grandstand, Sportsnight, Match of the Day, Commonwealth and Olympic Games and World Cup coverage); presenter, Holiday (BBC) 1988–89, How Do They Do That? (BBC) 1994–96, The Des Lynam Show (BBC Radio) 1998–99, ITV Sport 1999–2004, BAFTA TV Awards (ITV) 2000, The Premiership (ITV) 2001–04, Des Meets 2004, Countdown (Channel 4) 2005–06, Britain's Favourite View (ITV) 2007, Setanta Sports (Setanta) 2007–08, Sport Mastermind (BBC TV) 2008, Touchline Tales (BBC Radio 4) 2010–; columnist for The Daily Telegraph; Assoc., Chartered Insurance Inst.; TV Sports Presenter of the Year, TRIC 1985, 1987, 1988, 1993, 1997, Radio Times Male TV Personality 1989, RTS Sports Presenter of the Year 1994, 1998, Richard Dimbleby Award, BAFTA 1994, Variety Club of GB Media Award 1997. *Publications include:* Guide to the Commonwealth Games 1986, The 1988 Olympics 1988, The 1992 Olympics 1992, Sport Crazy 1998, I Should Have Been At Work! (autobiog.) 2005. *Leisure interests:* golf, tennis, Brighton and Hove Albion, reading, theatre. *Address:* c/o Jane Morgan Management, Elsinore House, 77 Fulham Palace Road, London, W6 8JA, England (office). *Telephone:* (20) 7478-7479 (office). *E-mail:* enquiries@janemorganmgt.com (office). *Website:* www.janemorganmgt.com (office).

LYNCH, Christopher S.; American business executive; *Non-Executive Chairman, Freddie Mac (Federal Home Loan Mortgage Corporation);* held several positions with KPMG LLP, including Nat. Partner in Charge – Financial Services, chaired KPMG's Americas Financial Services Leadership team, mem. of Global Financial Services Leadership and US Industries Leadership teams, led Banking & Finance practice, also served as a partner in Dept of Professional Practice and as Practice Fellow at Financial Accounting Standards Bd, retd 2007; Chair. (non-exec.) Freddie Mac (Fed. Home Loan Mortgage Corpn) 2011–; mem. Bd of Dirs American International Group, Inc.; mem. Nat. Audit Cttee Chair Advisory Council, Nat. Asscn of Corp. Dirs. *Address:* Freddie Mac, 8200 Jones Branch Drive, McLean, VA 22102-3110, USA (office). *Telephone:* (703) 903-2000 (office). *E-mail:* info@freddiemac.com (office). *Website:* www.freddiemac.com (office).

LYNCH, David; American film director; b. 20 Jan. 1946, Missoula, Mont.; m. 1st Peggy Reavey 1967 (divorced); one d.; m. 2nd Mary Fisk 1977 (divorced); one s.; m. 3rd Mary Sweeney 2006 (divorced); one s.; m. 4th Emily Stofle 2009; ed Hammond High School, Alexandria, Corcoran School of Art, School of Museum of Fine Arts, Boston and Pennsylvania Acad. of Fine Arts; Guest Artistic Dir AFI Fest 2010; Fellow, Center for Advanced Film Studies, American Film Inst. 1970; Founder and Chair. Bd of Trustees, David Lynch Foundation for Consciousness-Based Educ. and World Peace 2005–; Officier, Légion d'Honneur 2007; Dr hc (Royal Coll. of Art) 1991; Stockholm Int. Film Festival Lifetime Achievement Award 2003, Venice Film Festival Golden Lion 2006. *Films include:* The Grandmother 1970, Eraserhead 1977, The Elephant Man 1980, Dune 1984, Blue Velvet 1986 (Golden Palm, Cannes), Wild at Heart 1990 (Golden Palm, Cannes 1990), Storyville 1991, Twin Peaks: Fire Walk With Me 1992, Lost Highway 1997, Crumb (presenter), The Straight Stay 1999, Mullholland Drive (Best Dir, Cannes Film Festival) 2001, Darkened Room 2002, Rabbits 2002, Inland Empire 2006; numerous shorts and documentaries. *Television includes:* Twin Peaks (series) 1990–91. *Music includes:* album: Crazy Clown Time 2011. *Soundtracks include:* Twin Peaks 1990, Love Heritage 2002, Coachella 2006, Surveillance 2008, Psych 2010. *Website:* davidlynch.com; www.davidlynchfoundation.org.

LYNCH, John H., BA, MBA, JD; American politician, business executive and fmr state governor; b. 25 Nov. 1952, Waltham, Mass.; s. of William Lynch and Margaret Lynch; m. Dr Susan Lynch 1977; one s. two d.; ed Univ. of New Hampshire, Harvard Business School, Georgetown Univ. Law Center; fmr Dir Admisssions, Harvard Business School; fmr Pres. and CEO Knoll, Inc.; apptd to Univ. System of New Hampshire's Bd of Trustees 2000, Chair. 2001–04; Pres. The Lynch Group; Gov. of New Hampshire 2005–13; fmr Pres. Univ. of New Hampshire Alumni Asscn; mem. Bd Catholic Medical Center 1997–2003, Citizens' Bank of New Hampshire, Capitol Center for the Arts; Democrat. *Address:* c/o Office of the Governor, State House, 107 North Main Street, Concord, NH 03301, USA.

LYNCH, Michael Francis, AM, CBE; Australian arts administrator; *Chief Executive, South Bank Centre, London;* b. 6 Dec. 1950, Sydney; s. of Wilfred Brian Lynch and Joan Margaret Lynch; m. 1st Jane Scott 1967 (divorced 1987); one d.; m. 2nd Irene Hannan; two step s.; m. 3rd Christine Josephine Lynch; ed Marcellin Coll., Randwick, Univ. of Sydney; began career with Australian Council for the Arts 1973; fmr Gen. Man. King O'Malley Theatre Co., Australian Theatre for Young People; Admin. Australian Nat. Playwrights Conf.; Gen. Man. Nimrod Theatre 1976–78; Casting Dir and Man. Partner Forcast Pty Ltd 1981–89; Gen. Man. Sydney Theatre Co. 1989–94, Australia Council 1994–98; Chief Exec. Sydney Opera House 1998–2002; Chief Exec. South Bank Centre, London 2002–09; fmr Chair. Australia Asia Pacific Performing Arts Centres (AAPPAC); fmr mem. Performing Arts Centres Consortium (PACC) of N America. *Films:* Crocodile Dundee (Casting Dir) 1986, Raw Nerve (producer) 1988, Crocodile Dundee in Los Angeles (Casting Dir) 2001. *Leisure interests:* film, theatre, racing, beach. *Address:* South Bank Centre, South Bank, London, SE1 8XX, England (office). *Website:* www.sbc.org.uk (office).

LYNCH, Peter; American investor; *Vice Chairman, Fidelity Management and Research Company;* b. 19 Jan. 1944; m. Carolyn Lynch; three d.; intern Fidelity Investments 1966; Man. Fidelity Magellan Fund, Boston 1977–90; Trustee Fidelity Investments 1990–; currently Vice-Chair. Fidelity Man. and Research Co.; Chair. Inner-City Scholarship Fund; f. Lynch Foundation; Pres. Catholic Schools Foundation; mem. Univ. Bd of Trustees Boston Coll.; 14 hon. degrees; Hon. Chair. Boston Coll. Ever to Excel campaign; Mother Seton Award, Interfaith Relations Award. *Publications:* One Up on Wall Street 1989, Beating the Street 1993, Learn to Earn 1996 (all with John Rothchild). *Address:* Fidelity Investments Institutional Services Company Inc., 82 Devonshire Street, Boston, MA 02109, USA. *Telephone:* (617) 563-7000. *Fax:* (617) 476-3876. *Website:* www.401k.com.

LYNCH, Philip F., CBE; American business executive; *Founder, Stem Capital Partners;* ed Yale Univ.; fmrly with Lehman Brothers, held various man. positions in New York before moving to London in 1977 to become Br. Man., Sr Vice-Pres. and then Man. Dir 1987–2000, Co-head of Asia-Pacific Investment Banking 2000–02, Head of Global Finance, Europe, the Middle East and Africa 2002–06, Co-head of European Equities 2006–08, CEO Middle East and Africa, Nomura International plc (following acquisition of European and Asian arms of Lehman Brothers) 2008–10, CEO Asia (ex-Japan) and Middle East 2010–12; Founder Stem Capital Partners 2013–; Chair. (non-exec.), Int. Petroleum Exchange of London Ltd 1989–95; Chief Exec. Exchange Clearing House (ECHO) 1996–97, COO and Dir of Shareholder Affairs, CLS Services Ltd (after acquisition of ECHO) 1997–2000; Dir (non-exec.), Earthport plc 2006. *Address:* Stem Capital Partners, 2203–04, 22/F ManYee Building, 68 Des Voeux Road Central, Hong Kong Special Administrative Region, People's Republic of China (office). *Telephone:* 2503-5698 (office). *E-mail:* info@stemcapitalpartners.com (office). *Website:* www .stemcapitalpartners.com (office); stemcapital.net (office).

LYNDEN-BELL, Donald, CBE, MA, PhD, FRS; British astrophysicist and academic; *Professor of Astrophysics, Institute of Astronomy, University of Cambridge;* b. 5 April 1935, Dover, Kent, England; s. of the late Lt-Col L. A. Lynden-Bell and of M. R. Lynden-Bell; m. Ruth M. Truscott 1961; one s. one d.; ed Marlborough Coll. and Clare Coll. Cambridge; Harkness Fellow, Calif. Inst. of Tech. and Hale Observatories 1960–62, Visiting Assoc. 1969–70, Research Fellow,

then Fellow and Dir of Studies in Math., Clare Coll. Cambridge 1960–65; Asst Lecturer in Applied Math. Univ. of Cambridge 1962–65; Prin. Scientific Officer, later Sr Prin. Scientific Officer, Royal Greenwich Observatory, Herstmonceux 1965–72; Prof. of Astrophysics, Univ. of Cambridge 1972–2001; Dir Inst. of Astronomy, Cambridge 1972–77, 1982–87, 1992–94; Visiting Professorial Fellow, Queen's Univ. Belfast 1996–2003; Pres. Royal Astronomical Soc. 1985–87; Foreign Assoc., NAS 1993; Hon. mem. American Astronomical Soc. 2001; Hon. DSc (Sussex) 1987; Eddington Medal 1984, Gold Medal (Royal Astronomical Soc.) 1993, (Royal Soc. of SA), Catherine Wolf Bruce Medal of the Astronomical Soc. of the Pacific 1998, J. J. Carty Award, NAS 2000, Russell Lecturer, American Astronomical Soc. 2000, Kavli Prize 2008. *Publications:* article in journal Nature 1969 gave the theory of quasars predicting giant black holes in galactic nuclei (found 1995); contribs to Monthly Notices of Royal Astronomical Soc. *Leisure interest:* hill-walking. *Address:* Institute of Astronomy, OBS O13, The Observatories, Madingley Road, Cambridge, CB3 0HA, England (office). *Telephone:* (1223) 337525 (office). *E-mail:* dlb@ast.cam.ac.uk (office). *Website:* (office).

LYNE, Adrian; British film director; b. Peterborough; m. Samantha Lyne; one d.; ed Highgate School; joined J. Walter Thompson (advertising agency) in post room, later became asst producer of commercials; with two pnrs est. Jennie & Lyne 1971; dir of commercials; Palme d'Or, Cannes Commercial Film Festival 1976, 1978. *Films include:* Mr. Smith 1976, Foxes 1980, Flashdance 1983, $9^1/_2$ Weeks 1986, Fatal Attraction 1987, Jacob's Ladder (also co-writer) 1990, Indecent Proposal 1993, Lolita 1997, Unfaithful 2002. *Address:* c/o ICM, Oxford House, 76 Oxford Street, London, W1D 1BS, England. *Telephone:* (20) 7636-6565. *Fax:* (20) 7323-0101. *E-mail:* directors@icmlondon.co.uk.

LYNE, Rt Hon, Sir Roderic Michael John, KBE, CMG, BA; British diplomatist (retd) and business consultant; *Deputy Chairman, Council of the Royal Institute of International Affairs;* b. 31 March 1948; s. of the late Air Vice-Marshal Michael Lyne and Avril Joy Buckley; m. Amanda Mary Smith 1969; two s. one d.; ed Eton Coll., Univ. of Leeds; joined Diplomatic Service 1970, British Embassy, Moscow 1972–74, British Embassy, Senegal 1974–76; Eastern Europe and Soviet Dept, FCO 1976–78, Rhodesia Dept 1979, Asst Pvt. Sec. to Foreign and Commonwealth Sec. 1979–82; Perm. Mission to UN, New York 1982–86; Visiting Research Fellow, Royal Inst. of Int. Affairs (Chatham House) 1986–87, mem. Council 2008–; Head of Chancery and Political Section, Embassy, Moscow 1987–90; Head of Soviet Dept, FCO 1990–91, of Eastern Dept 1992–93; Pvt. Sec. to Prime Minister 1993–96; Dir of Policy Devt for CIS, Middle East and Africa, British Gas PLC 1996; Perm. Rep. to UN, Geneva 1997–2000; Amb. to Russia 2000–04; Special Adviser, BP plc 2004–09, HSBC Bank plc 2004–07; Chair. Int. Advisory Bd Altimo 2006–07; Deputy Chair. Council of the Royal Inst. of Int. Affairs 2009–; mem. Bd of Dirs Aricom 2006–09, Accor 2006–09, Russo-British Chamber of Commerce 2006–09, Petropavlovsk PLC 2009–; Sr Adviser, JPMorgan Chase Bank 2007–10; Visiting Prof., Kingston Univ. Business School 2005–10, mem. Bd of Govs Kingston Univ. 2007–, Chair. 2011–; cttee mem., The Iraq Inquiry 2009–; mem. Privy Council 2009; Hon. Prof., Moscow Higher School of Social and Econ. Studies 2001; Hon. PhD (Leeds) 2002, Hon. DBA (Kingston) 2004, Hon. DLitt (Heriot-Watt) 2004. *Publication:* Engaging with Russia: The Next Phase – Report to the Trilateral Commission (co-author) 2006 (updated edns in Japanese and Russian) 2007, The Imaginary Curtain in Russia: The Challenges of Transformation (co-eds Dutkiewicz and Trenin) 2011. *Leisure interests:* sport, grandchildren. *Address:* 39 Richmond Park Road, London, SW14 8JU, England (home). *E-mail:* Roderic .Lyne@btinternet.com (office).

LYNGSTAD, Anni-Frid (Frida); Norwegian singer; b. 15 Nov. 1945, Ballangen, Narvik, Norway; m. Benny Andersson 1978 (divorced 1981); one s. one d. (from previous relationship); leader of own dance band Anni-Frid Four; mem. pop group ABBA 1973–82; winner, Eurovision Song Contest 1974; world-wide tours; concerts include Royal Performance, Stockholm 1976, Royal Albert Hall, London 1977, UNICEF concert, New York 1979, Wembley Arena 1979; reunion with ABBA, Swedish TV This Is Your Life 1986; solo artist 1983–; World Music Award, Best Selling Swedish Artist 1993. *Film:* ABBA: The Movie 1977. *Recordings include:* albums: with ABBA: Waterloo 1974, ABBA 1976, Greatest Hits 1976, Arrival 1977, The Album 1978, Voulez-Vous 1979, Greatest Hits Vol. 2 1979, Super Trouper 1980, The Visitors 1981, The Singles: The First Ten Years 1982, Thank You For The Music 1983, Absolute ABBA 1988, ABBA Gold 1992, More ABBA Gold 1993, Forever Gold 1998, The Definitive Collection 2001; solo: Frida Alone 1976, Something's Going On 1982, Shine 1983, Djupa Andetag 1996, Frida 1967–72 1998, Frida: The Mixes 1998, Svenska Popfavoriter 1998; singles include: with ABBA: Ring Ring 1973, Waterloo 1974, Mamma Mia 1975, Dancing Queen 1976, Fernando 1976, Money Money Money 1976, Knowing Me Knowing You 1977, The Name Of The Game 1977, Take A Chance On Me 1978, Summer Night City 1978, Chiquitita 1979, Does Your Mother Know? 1979, Angel Eyes/Voulez-Vous 1979, Gimme Gimme Gimme (A Man After Midnight) 1979, I Have A Dream 1979, The Winner Takes It All 1980, Super Trouper 1980, On And On And On 1981, Lay All Your Love On Me 1981, One Of Us 1981, When All Is Said And Done 1982, Head Over Heels 1982, The Day Before You Came 1982, Under Attack 1982, Thank You For The Music 1983. *Website:* www.abbasite.com.

LYNTON, Michael, MBA; American media executive; *Chairman and CEO, Sony Pictures Entertainment;* b. 1 Jan. 1960, London, UK; s. of Mark O. L. Lynton and Marion Sonnenberg; m. Elizabeth Jane Alter; three d.; ed Harvard Coll., Harvard Business School; Assoc., The First Boston Corpn 1982–85; Sr Vice-Pres. Disney Publishing Group 1987–93, Pres. Hollywood Pictures, The Walt Disney Co. 1993–96; Chair. and CEO The Penguin Group 1996–2000; Pres. AOL International 2000–03, also Pres. for Int. Efforts and Exec. Vice-Pres. AOL Time Warner Inc. 2002–03; Chair. and CEO Sony Pictures Entertainment 2004–, CEO Sony Corpn of America 2012–, Sony Entertainment, Inc. 2012–; elected to Harvard Bd of Overseers by Harvard Alumni Asscn 2012–; mem. Bd of Dirs, Snapchat 2013–. *Address:* Sony Pictures Entertainment, 10202 West Washington Boulevard, Culver City, CA 90232, USA (office). *Telephone:* (310) 244-4000 (office). *Fax:* (310) 244-2626 (office). *E-mail:* info@@spe.sony.com (office). *Website:* www .sonypictures.com (office).

LYON, Mary Frances, BA, PhD, ScD, FRS, FIBiol; British geneticist; b. 15 May 1925, Norwich; d. of Clifford James Lyon and Louise Frances Lyon (née Kirby); ed Woking Grammar School, Girton Coll. Cambridge; on Medical Research Council

(MRC) Scientific Staff, Inst. of Animal Genetics Edin. 1950–55; Scientific Staff MRC Radiobiology Unit, Harwell 1955–90, Head of Genetics Section 1962–87; Clothworkers Visiting Research Fellow, Girton Coll. Cambridge 1970–71; Foreign Assoc. NAS 1979; Foreign Hon. mem. American Acad. of Arts and Sciences 1980; Francis Amory Prize, American Acad. of Arts and Sciences 1977, Royal Medal, Royal Soc. 1984, San Remo Int. Prize for Genetics 1985, Gairdner Int. Award 1985, William Allan Award, American Soc. of Human Genetics 1986, Wolf Prize in Medicine 1997, Mendel Medal, Genetics Soc. 2003, March of Dimes Prize in Developmental Biology 2004, Pearl Meisler Greengard Award 2006, Rosenstiel Award, Brandeis Univ. 2007. *Publications:* papers on genetics in scientific journals. *Address:* Medical Research Council Mammalian Genetics Unit, Harwell, Didcot, Oxon., OX11 0RD, England. *Telephone:* (1235) 841000. *Fax:* (1235) 841200. *E-mail:* m.lyon@har.mrc.ac.uk (office).

LYONS, Jenna; American fashion designer and retail executive; *President and Executive Creative Director, J. Crew Group, Inc.;* b. 1969, Boston, Mass; m. Robert Mazeau (divorced); one s.; ed Parsons The New School For Design; Intern, Donna Karan (designer womenswear label) 1990; Asst Designer, J. Crew Group, Inc. 1990–94, Designer 1994–95, Design Dir 1996–98, Sr Design Dir 1999, Vice-Pres. Women's Design 1999–2005, Sr Vice-Pres. 2005–07, Creative Dir 2007–10, Pres. and Exec. Creative Dir 2010–. *Address:* J Crew Group, Inc, 770 Broadway, New York, NY 10003, USA (office). *Telephone:* (203) 682-8200 (office). *E-mail:* jlyons@jcrew.com (office). *Website:* www.jcrew.com (office).

LYONS, Sir Michael, Kt, KBE, PhD; British economist, politician and television industry executive; b. 1950; m.; three c.; ed Stratford Grammar School, Middlesex Univ. and Queen Mary Coll., Univ. of London; worked as part-time street trader at Bell Street Market, London to fund higher educ.; furthered career as economist in public sector; fmr Lecturer in Econs, Univ. of Nottingham, Wallbrook Coll., London; mem. (Labour) Birmingham City Council 1980–83; Chief Exec. Wolverhampton Borough Council 1985–90, Notts. County Council 1990–94, Birmingham City Council 1994–2001; Prof. of Public Policy, Birmingham Univ. 2001–06; responsible for Lyons Inquiry into Local Govt, commissioned by Deputy Prime Minister and Chancellor of the Exchequer 2004–07; Chair. BBC Trust 2007–11; Chair. English Cities Fund 2002–, City of Birmingham Symphony Orchestra 2001–07, Regional Advisory Council, ITV –2006; Deputy Chair. and Acting Chair. The Audit Comm. 2003–06; mem. Bd of Dirs (non-exec.) Central Television 2003–06, MouchelParkman PLC, Wragge and Co., SQW Ltd. *Address:* c/o BBC Trust Unit, Room 211, 35 Marylebone High Street, London, W1U 4AA, England (office).

LYONS, Richard Kent, BS, PhD; American economist, academic and university administrator; *Bank of America Dean, Haas School of Business, University of California, Berkeley;* b. 10 Feb. 1961, Palo Alto, Calif.; s. of J. Richard Lyons and Ida P. Lyons; m.; two c.; ed Univ. of California, Berkeley, Massachusetts Inst. of Tech.; Research Analyst, Financial Industries Div., SRI Int., Menlo Park, Calif. 1983–84; Assoc. and Asst Prof., School of Business and School of Int. Affairs, Columbia Univ. 1987–93; Asst Prof., Haas School of Business, Univ. of California, Berkeley 1993–96, Assoc. Prof. 1996–2000, Prof. 2000–04, Acting Dean 2004–05, Exec. Assoc. Dean 2005–06, Bank of America Dean 2008–; Chief Learning Officer, Goldman Sachs, New York 2006–08; consultant to IMF, World Bank, US Fed. Reserve System, EC, UN, Citibank; mem. Council on Foreign Relations; Trustee, Matthews Asian Funds; fmr Trustee, iShares; NSF Grad. Fellowship 1984–87, Int. Affairs Fellowship, Council on Foreign Relations 1993, NSF grants 1994–97, 1997–2000, 2000–03; Distinguished Teaching Award, Univ. of Calif., Berkeley 1998. *Publications:* The Microstructure Approach to Exchange Rates 2001; numerous articles and papers. *Leisure interests:* guitar, skiing. *Address:* Office of the Dean, Haas School of Business, University of California, Berkeley, CA 94720-1900, USA (office). *Telephone:* (510) 643-2027 (office). *Fax:* (510) 642-5630 (office). *E-mail:* lyons@haas.berkeley.edu (office). *Website:* faculty.haas.berkeley.edu/lyons (office).

LYOVOCHKIN, Serhiy; Ukrainian government official; *Head of Presidential Secretariat;* b. 17 Aug. 1972; s. of Volodymyr Lyovochkin; m.; three c.; fmr police Col; adviser to Pres. Leonid Kuchma 1997–2002, First Aide to Pres. Kuchma 2002–05; head of Prime Minister Viktor Yanukovych's office 2006–07; Head of Presidential Secr. to Viktor Yanukovych 2010–; mem. Party of the Regions, currently Deputy Chair. *Address:* Office of the President, 01220 Kyiv, vul. Bankova 11, Ukraine (office). *Telephone:* (44) 255-71-40 (office). *Fax:* (44) 255-78-44 (office). *E-mail:* press@stpu.gov.ua (office). *Website:* www.president.gov.ua (office).

LYSSARIDES, Vassos, MD; Cypriot politician and physician; *Honorary President, Movement for Social Democracy;* b. 13 May 1920, Lefkara; s. of Michael Lyssarides and Eleni Lyssanides; m. Barbara Cornwall 1963; ed Univ. of Athens; mem. House of Reps 1960–, Pres. 1985–91; Pres. Socialist Party of Cyprus (originally founded as United Democratic Union of Centre—EDEK) (now Movt for Social Democracy) 1969–2002, Hon. Pres. 2002–; Sec.-Gen. Int. Cttee of Solidarity with the Struggle of the Peoples of Southern Africa; Vice-Pres. Presidium, Afro-Asian Peoples' Solidarity Org.; Hon. Citizen of numerous Greek municipalities; Hon. Pres. Nicosia Medical Asscn Hippocrates; Dr hc (Univ. of Athens), (Panteion Univ.); Highest Honour of Distinction, Palestinian Authorities. *Leisure interests:* poetry, painting. *Address:* PO Box 21064, 1096 Nicosia, Cyprus (home). *Telephone:* (22) 666763 (office); (22) 665385 (home). *Fax:* (22) 666762 (office). *E-mail:* edek@mtnmail.com.cy (office). *Website:* www.lyssarides.com.

LYSYSHYN, Ralph James, MA, PhD; Canadian diplomatist (retd); b. Canora, Sask.; ed Univ. of Alberta; served in various posts at Dept of Foreign Affairs and Int. Trade including Head of Section, Eastern European Div., Dir Arms Control and Disarmament Div.; fmr policy adviser to Prime Minister, Privy Council Office, Dir-Gen. Int. Security and Arms Control Bureau; fmr Pres. Forum of Feds; overseas postings include Third, then Second Sec., Embassy in Moscow 1974–76, Head of Chancery, Embassy in Lagos 1979–82, Counsellor, Embassy in Washington, DC 1982–86, Deputy Perm. Rep., Del. to NATO, Brussels 1990–94; Amb. to Poland 2002–05, to Russia (also accred to Armenia) 2006–10.

LYTH, Ragnar Vilhelm, BA; Swedish theatre director and academic; *Head of Theatre Directing, Swedish Dramatic Institute;* b. 2 April 1944, Karlstad; s. of Arne Lyth and Reidunn Eleonore; m. 1st Karin Falk 1967; m. 2nd Kerstin Österlin 1996; two s.; ed Nat. Film School, Swedish Dramatic Inst.; theatre and TV dir in Sweden,

Norway and Denmark; represented Sweden at int. TV festival 'INPUT', Philadelphia, Banff, Montreal 1985, 1989, 1993; Head of Stage Dirs, Swedish Dramatic Inst. 1984–86, currently Head of Theatre Directing; Chair. Swedish Dirs' Union; Prof. of Theatre Direction; Dir-in-Residence, Nat. Theatre, Oslo, Norway, Stockholm City Theatre; Sweden Art Award. *Plays directed include:* The Wild Duck 1997, Hedda Gabler 1998, Faust (I and II) 1999, Temperance 2000, The General Inspector 2001, Twelfth Night 2002, The Visit 2003, Endgame 2004, Tartuffe 2005. *Television:* Death Dance 1981, Hamlet 1985, Don Juan 1988, Maclean 1991. *Publications:* Theatre Life 2003. *Leisure interest:* nature. *Address:* Sjöbjörnsvägen 25, 11767 Stockholm, Sweden. *Telephone:* (8) 19-88-93. *E-mail:* ragnar.lyth@draminst.se (office); ragnar@ragnarlyth.se (home).

LYTVYN, Volodymyr Mykhaylovych, DrHis; Ukrainian academic and politician; b. 28 April 1956, Sloboda, Zhytomyr Oblast; s. of Mykhaylo Klymovych Lytvyn and Olga Andriivna Lytvyn; m. Tetyana Kostyantynivna; one s. one d.; ed Kyiv T. Shevchenko State (now Nat.) Univ.; researcher, Docent, Vice-Rector, Kyiv State Univ. 1978–86, Docent and Prof. 1991–94; Head of Dept, Ukrainian Ministry of Higher Educ. 1986–89; Lecturer, consultant, Asst to Sec., Cen. Cttee of Ukrainian Komsomol 1989–91; Adviser to Ukrainian Pres. 1994–2002, Deputy Head, Admin. to the Pres. 1995–96, Head Admin. 1999–2002; apptd to Nat. Security and Defence Council 1999; mem. Co-ordination Cttee on Problems of Foreign Policy 1996–; elected to Verkovna Rada (Parl.) 2002, Chair. 2002–06, 2008–12; currently Leader, People's Party (Narodna Partiya); mem. Ukrainian Acad. of Sciences 1997, Academician 2003. *Publications include:* Political Arena of Ukraine 1995; more than 200 articles on contemporary politics. *Leisure interests:* reading, football, taking care of Dalmatian dogs. *Address:* Verkhovna Rada, 01008 Kyiv, vul. M. Hrushevskoho 5 (office); People's Party (Narodna Partiya), 01034 Kyiv, vul. Reitarska 6a, Ukraine (office). *Telephone:* (44) 255-21-15 (Verkhovna Rada) (office); (44) 270-61-86 (Narodna Partiya) (office). *Fax:* (44) 253-32-17 (Verkhovna Rada) (office); (44) 270-65-91 (Narodna Partiya) (office). *E-mail:* umz@rada.gov.ua (office); info@narodna.org.ua (office). *Website:* www.rada.gov.ua (office); www.narodna.org.ua (office); www.lytvyn-v.org.ua.

LYU, Joseph Jye-Cherng; Taiwanese government official and banker; b. 1956; m. Cathie Lyu; one d.; ed Nat. Chengchi Univ., Kellogg Grad. School of Man., Northwestern Univ., USA; fmr Assoc. Prof., Nat. Chengchi Univ.; Vice-Pres. Bank of New York, Taipei Br. and New York Head Office –1981; fmr Vice-Pres. Banque Nationale de Paris, Taiwan; Pres. Land Bank of Taiwan –2004; Chair. Bank of Taiwan 2004–06; Minister of Finance 2006; Minister without Portfolio from 2006; fmr Chair. Bankers Asscn of Taiwan; fmr Man. Dir Bd Trust Asscn; fmr Dir Mega Financial Holding Co., Financial Information Service Co. Ltd, Taiwan Futures Exchange; Chair. Central Taiwan Theological Seminary; Dir, Hsu Wen-Lung Art & Culture Foundation. *Address:* c/o Ministry of Finance, 2 Ai Kuo West Road, Taipei 10066, Taiwan. *E-mail:* mof@mail.mof.gov.tu.

LYUBIMOV, Yuri Petrovich; Russian/Israeli/Hungarian theatrical director and actor; *Artistic Director, Moscow Taganka Theatre;* b. 30 Sept. 1917, Yaroslavl'; m. Katalin Koncz; one s.; ed Vakhtangov Theatre Studio; served in Soviet Army 1939–47; Teacher and Dir, Shukin Drama School (Vakhtangov Theatre) 1953–64; Founder and Artistic Dir, Moscow Theatre of Drama and Comedy (Taganka) 1964–84, 1989–; deprived of Soviet citizenship 1983, left Soviet Union 1984, acquired Israeli citizenship 1987, returned 1988, citizenship restored 1989, acquired Hungarian citizenship 1999; numerous decorations including Medal for the Defence of Leningrad 1943, for the Defence of Moscow 1944, State Prizes 1952, 1997, Order of the Labour Red Banner 1977, State Prize of Russia 1991, Order of the Great Patriotic War 1996, Services to the Motherland, 1st Class 1997, Golden Medal of Honour of the Pres. of Hungary 1997, Triumph Premium 1998, Nat. Order of the Repub. of Hungary 2002, Kt Commdr of Arts and Literature (France) 2002, Star of Italian Solidarity 2003, Estonian Order of the Cross of Terra Mariana 2003, Royal Order of the Polar Star (Sweden) 2004, Chevalier Cross Order of Honour of Poland 2004; numerous awards including Honoured Artist of the RSFSR 1954, Grand Prix, Int. Theatre Festival, Bonn 1998, Grand Prix, Int. Theatre Festival, Thessalonika 1999, Golden Mask Theatre Prize 2000, Diploma of American Acad. of Arts 2001, K. Stanislavsky Fund Prize 2003. *Roles include:* Oleg Koshevoy (The Young Guard, by Fadeyev), Shubin (On the Eve, by Turgenev), Chris (All My Sons, by Arthur Miller), Benedict (Much Ado About Nothing), Mozart (The Little Tragedies, by Pushkin); prominent in Soviet films 1947–, including Busy Stock, Robinson Crusoe, Cuban Cossacks. *Theatre productions include:* The Good Man from Szechuan 1963, Ten Days that Shook the World 1965, Mother (Gorky) 1969, Hamlet 1972, Boris Godunov (Moscow) 1982, Crime and Punishment (London) 1983, The Devils (London, Paris) 1985, Hamlet (London) 1987, Self-Murderer (Moscow) 1990, Electra (Moscow) 1992, Zhivago (Vienna) 1993, The Seagull (Athens) 1993, Creditors (Athens) 1994, Medea (Athens) 1995, The Brothers Karamazov (Moscow) 1997, Marat-Sade (Moscow) 1998, Sharashka (Moscow) 1998, Chronicles (Moscow) 2000, Eugene Onegin (Moscow) 2000, Theatrical Novel (Moscow) 2000, Socrates (Moscow) 2001, Faust (Moscow) 2002, Before and After 2003, Go and Stop the Progress (Moscow) 2004 and others (total of 104). *Opera productions include:* Al gran sole carico d'amore (La Scala) 1975, Boris Godunov (La Scala) 1981, Lulu (Turin, Chicago) 1983, Rigoletto (Florence) 1984, Hovancshina (La Scala) 1985, St Matthew's Passion (La Scala) 1985, Jenufa (London) 1986, Eugene Onegin (Bonn) 1987, The Queen of Spades (Karlsruhe) 1990, Lady Macbeth of Mtsensk (Hamburg) 1990, Love for Three Oranges (Munich) 1991, Nabucco (Bonn) 1997 and others. *Publications:* Le Feu Sacré 1985, Zapiski starego trepacha (Notes from an old Blabbermouth) 2000; several articles in the field of theatre. *Leisure interests:* music, cinema, gardening, poetry. *Address:* Taganka Theatre, Zemlanoy val 76, Moscow 109004, Russia (office). *Telephone:* (095) 915-10-37 (office); (095) 290-19-34 (home). *Fax:* (495) 764-92-24 (office); (095) 290-19-34 (home). *E-mail:* taganka-theatre@mtu-net.ru (office). *Website:* www.taganka-theatre.ru (office).

LYUBSHIN, Stanislav Andreyevich; Russian actor; b. 6 April 1933; m.; two s.; ed Shchepkin Theatre School; worked with various Moscow theatres: Sovremennik, Taganka, Yermolova, Malaya Bronnaya 1959–80; one of prin. actors with Moscow Arts Theatre 1980–, Anton Chekhov Arts Theatre 1987–; film debut 1959; RSFSR People's Artist 1981, People's Actor of Russia, Order of Service to Fatherland, Order of Friendship 2014. *Films include:* Segodnya uvolneniya ne budet (There Will Be No Leave Today) 1959, Tretya raketa (The Third Missile)

1963, Esli ty prav. . . 1963, Mne dvadtsat let (I am Twenty) 1964, Kakoe ono, more? 1964, Bolshaya ruda (The Big Ore) 1964, Alpiyskaya ballada 1965, Shchit i mech (The Shield and the Sword) 1968, Krasnaya ploshchad (Red Square) 1970, Pechki-lavochki (Happy Go Lucky, aka The Ship Crowd) 1972, Moya zhizn 1972, Monolog 1972, Slovo dlia zashchity (Speech for the Defence) 1976, Sentimentalnyy roman (Sentimental Romance) 1976, Pozovi menya v dal' svetluyu (Call Me from Afar) 1976, Step (The Steppe) 1977, Vstrecha (The Meeting) 1979, Tema (The Theme) 1979, Pyat vecherov (Five Evenings) 1979, My vesely, schastlivy, talantlivy! (We Are Cheerful, Happy, Talented!) 1986, Kin-Dza-Dza 1986, Zabavy molodykh (Joys of the Youth) 1987, Chyornyy monakh (The Black Monk) 1988, Vechnyy muzh 1989, Kanuvshee vremya 1989, Shkura (Skin) 1991, Nelyubov (No Love) 1991, Uvidet Parizh i umeret (To See Paris and Die) 1992, Bolshoy kapkan, ili solo dlya koshki pri polnoy lune (Big Trap, or Solo for Cat Under Full Moon) 1992, Tsar Ivan Groznyy (Tsar Ivan the Terrible) 1993, Mechty idiota (Idiot Dreams) 1993, Terra incognita 1994, Tsarevich Aleksei 1996, Kino pro kino 2002, The Country Estate 2004, Prodayotsya detektor lzhi 2005, Antikiller D.K: Lyubov bez pamyati 2009. *Television includes:* Pervaya lyubov (First Love) 1968, Ne strelyayte v belykh lebedey 1980, Dym (mini-series) 1992, The Country Estate (series) 2004, The Chess Player (series) 2004, Umnozhayushchiy pechal (mini-series) 2005, Rieltor (series) 2005, Kruzheva (series) 2008, Pyataya strazha (series) 2013. *Address:* 117571 Moscow, Vernadskogo prosp. 123, Apt 171, Russia. *Telephone:* (495) 433-35-14.

LŽICAR, Josef, DIur; Czech lawyer; b. 6 June 1944, Švábenice; s. of Josef Lžicar and Anna Lžicar; m. Zdenka; one s.; ed Charles Univ., Prague; lawyer and advocate 1967–; Chief of Office of Pres. of Czechoslovak Repub. 1989–1990; mem. Czech Chamber of Advocates 1990–, Czech Helsinki Cttee 1990–. *Leisure interest:* ornithology. *Address:* c/o Czech Helsinki Committee, Ostrovského 3, 150 00 Prague 5; Sokolovská 24–37, 18600 Prague 8, Czech Republic (office). *Telephone:* (2) 22325334 (office). *E-mail:* sekr@helcom.cz.

M

MA, Canrong; Chinese diplomatist; b. July 1945, Jiangsu Prov.; m. Zhu Yiping; ed Nanjing Univ.; joined Foreign Service 1972; with W European Affairs Dept, Ministry of Foreign Affairs 1972–73, Deputy Section Chief, then Section Chief 1981–87, Deputy Dir-Gen. 1993–96, Dir-Gen. 1996–99; Attaché, Embassy in Berlin 1973–81, Counsellor 1987–93; Asst Minister, Ministry of Foreign Affairs 1999–2001; Amb. to Germany 2002–09. *Address:* c/o Ministry of Foreign Affairs, 2 Chaoyangmen, Nandajie, Chao Yang Qu, Beijing 100701, People's Republic of China (office). *Telephone:* (10) 65961114 (office). *Fax:* (10) 65962146 (office). *E-mail:* webmaster@mfa.gov.cn (office). *Website:* www.fmprc.gov.cn (office).

MA, Chung-Ch'en (see MA, Zhongchen).

MA, Feng, (Ma Shuming); Chinese writer; b. 1922, Xiaoyi Co., Shanxi Prov.; ed Lu Xun Acad. of Literature and Art, Yan'an; joined 8th Route Army and CCP 1938; first short story (First Reconnaissance) published 1942; mem. China-Britain Friendship Asscn 1983–; Vice-Chair. CPPCC Prov. Cttee, Shanxi 1986–; Pres. Soc. of Chinese Folk Literature 1987–; Exec. Vice-Chair. Nat. Cttee China Fed. of Literary and Art Circles 1988–; Vice-Chair. Chinese Writers' Asscn 1990–; mem. Foreign Affairs Cttee. *Publications include:* Heroes of Lüliang (with Xi Rong), Liu Hulan (novel), The Young People of One Village (film script) and numerous short stories, including The Marriage Ceremony (Nat. Short Story Award Winner 1980). *Address:* China Federation of Literary and Art Circles, 10 Nong Zhan Guan Nanli, Beijing 100026, People's Republic of China (office). *Telephone:* 5005588.

MA, Fucai, BEng; Chinese oil industry executive; *Vice Director, State Energy Office;* b. 1947; ed Beijing Petroleum Inst.; Deputy Dir, later Dir Shengli Petroleum Admin Bureau 1990–96; Asst to Pres., China Nat. Petroleum Corpn (CNPC) Nov.-Dec. 1996, Vice-Pres. 1996–98, Pres. 1998–2004 (resgnd); Chair. PetroChina 1999–2004; Vice-Dir State Energy Office 2005–; Dir Daqing Petroleum Admin Bureau 1997–98; Alt. mem. 16th CCP Cen. Cttee 2002–07. *Address:* State Energy Office, Beijing, People's Republic of China (office).

MA, Jack, BA; Chinese business executive; *Executive Chairman, Alibaba Group;* b. Nov. 1964, Hangzhou, Zhejiang Prov.; ed Hangzhou Teacher's Inst.; began as English teacher, Hangzhou Electronics and Eng Inst.; f. China Pages (chinapages.com), regarded to be China's first internet-based co. 1995; Head, Information Dept China Int. Electronic Commerce Center (CIECC) 1998–99; f. Alibaba Group (China's largest e-commerce co.), Hangzhou, Chair. and CEO 1999–2013, Exec. Chair. 2013–, Pres. Rookie Network Technology div. 2013–; chosen by World Econ. Forum as one of Young Global Leaders; named 'one of the 25 Most Powerful Businesspeople in Asia' by Fortune Magazine 2005, a 'Businessperson of the Year' by BusinessWeek Magazine 2007, one of the 30 'World's Best CEOs' by Barron's 2008. *Address:* Alibaba.com, 6th Floor Chuangye Mansion, East Software Park, No. 99 Huaxing Road, Hangzou, Zhejiang Province, 310012 (office); Alibaba.com Technology Corpn Ltd, Room 408, Fanli Building, 22 Chaoyangwai Street, Chaoyang District, Beijing, 100020, People's Republic of China (office). *Telephone:* (571) 85022088 (Hangzhou) (office); (10) 6588-9698 (office). *Fax:* (571) 88157866 (Hangzhou) (office); (10) 6588-9699 (office). *Website:* www.alibaba.com (office).

MA, Kai; Chinese politician; *Vice-Premier;* b. June 1946, Shanghai, Jinshan; ed People's Univ. of China; fmr Deputy Dir State Comm. of Reform for Econ. Systems; Deputy Dir State Planning Comm. 1995–98; Minister of Nat. Devt and Reform Comm. (f. as State Planning Comm. 1952, renamed State Devt Planning Comm. 1998, merged with State Council Office for Restructuring the Econ. System and several offices under State Econ. and Trade Comm., renamed Nat. Devt and Reform Comm. 2003) 2003–08; mem. State Council 2008–, Sec.-Gen. 2008–13; Vice-Premier 2013–; mem. 16th CCP Cen. Cttee 2002–07, 17th CCP Cen. Cttee 2007–12; mem. 18th CCP Cen. Cttee 2012–, mem. 18th CCP Politburo 2012–; Dir State Council Leading Group for Migrant Workers 2013–; Pres. Nat. School of Admin 2007–. *Address:* State Council, Great Hall of the People, West Edge, Tiananmen Square, Beijing, People's Republic of China (office).

MA, Mary, BA; Chinese business executive; *Non-Executive Vice-Chair., Lenovo Group Holdings;* b. (Ma Xuezheng), Tianjin; ed Capital Normal Univ. and King's Coll., London, UK; began career as English trans. at Chinese Acad. of Sciences; Exec. Dir and Sr Vice-Pres. Legend Holdings Ltd (name changed to Lenovo Group Holdings 2003), Chief Financial Officer 2000–07, Non-Exec. Vice-Chair. 2007–; ind. Dir (non-exec.) Standard Chartered Bank (Hong Kong) Ltd, Sohu.com Inc. 2000–; mem. Hong Kong Dirs' Soc.; ranked by Fortune magazine amongst 50 Most Powerful Women in Business outside the US (3rd) 2001, (fifth) 2002, (fifth) 2003, (14th) 2004, (ninth) 2005, (10th) 2006, ranked by Forbes magazine amongst 100 Most Powerful Women (80th) 2004, (57th) 2005. *Address:* Lenovo Group Holdings, No. 6 Chuang Ye Road, Shangdi Information Industry Base, Haidan District, Beijing 100085, People's Republic of China (office). *Telephone:* (10) 58868888 (office). *E-mail:* cmk@lenovo.com (office). *Website:* www.lenovo.com (office).

MA, Mingzhe, PhD; Chinese business executive; *Chairman and CEO, Ping An Insurance (Group) Company of China Limited;* b. 1960; ed Zhongnan Univ. of Econs and Law; fmr Deputy Man. China Merchants Shekou Industrial Zone Social Insurance Co.; f. Shekou Ping An Insurance Co. (precursor to Ping An Insurance Group Co.) 1988, later Pres., Chair. Ping An Insurance (Group) Co. of China Ltd 1994–, CEO 2001–; mem. 11th CPPCC Nat. Cttee. *Address:* Ping An Insurance (Group) Co. of China Ltd, 15–18 Floors, Galaxy Development Centre, Fu Hua No. 3 Road, Fu Tian District, Shenzhen 518048, Guangdong (office); Ping An Insurance (Hong Kong) Co. Ltd, 11th Floor, Dah Sing Financial Centre, 108 Gloucester Road, Wanchai, Hong Kong Special Administrative Region, People's Republic of China (office). *Telephone:* (400) 8866338 (Shenzhen) (office); 28271883 (Hong Kong) (office). *Fax:* (755) 82431029 (Shenzhen) (office); 28020018 (Hong Kong) (office). *E-mail:* IR@paic.com.cn (office). *Website:* www.pingan (office); www.pingan.com.cn (office).

MA, Qingyu, MArch; Chinese architect and academic; *Dean, School of Architecture, University of Southern California;* b. 1965, Xi'an; ed Tsinghua Univ., Grad. School of Fine Arts, Univ. of Pennsylvania, USA; Architect, Kohn Pederson and Fox, New York 1991–95, Kling Lindquist 1997–99; Assoc. Prof. and Asst Dean of Architecture, Shenzhen Univ. 1995–96; f. MADA s.p.a.m., New York 1995–, Beijing and Shanghai 1999–; Lecturer, Architecture Dept, Univ. of Pennsylvania 1997–2000; Visiting Lecturer, Tongji Univ., Shanghai 2001–, Nanjing Univ. 2002–, Berlage Inst., Netherlands 2003, ETH 2004, Tech. Univ., Berlin 2004; Dean, School of Architecture, Univ. of Southern California 2007–, Della and Harry MacDonald's Dean Chair. in Architecture 2007–; fmr Visiting Prof., Harvard Univ., Columbia Univ., Universität Karlsruhe, Ecole Speciale d'Architecture, Paris; invited by Disney Headquarters to be a consultant for Shanghai Disney Project 2010; Frank Miles Day Memorial Prize, Design Vanguard Award, Architectural Record, Phaidon's Emerging Design Talents designation, New Trends of Architecture designation, Euro-Asia Foundation. *Buildings designed include:* Longyang Residential Complex, Shanghai, Silk Tower, Xi'an, Qingpu Community Island, Shanghai, Centennial TV and Radio Center, Xi'an, Tianyi City Plaza, Ningpo. *Address:* Dean's Office, School of Architecture, University of Southern California, Watt Hall, Suite 204, Los Angeles, CA 90089-0291, USA (office). *Telephone:* (213) 740-2723 (office). *Fax:* (213) 740-8884 (office). *E-mail:* archdean@usc.edu (office). *Website:* arch.usc.edu (office).

MA, Qizhi; Chinese politician; *Chairman, Ningxia Hui Autonomous Regional People's Government;* b. Nov. 1943, Jingyuan, Ningxia Hui Autonomous Region; ed Cen. Univ. for Nationalities; joined CCP 1972; teacher, Yucheng Middle School, Anshan Iron and Steel Works, Yinchuan City No. 2 Middle School, Ningxia Hui Autonomous Region; cadre of Communist Youth League, Ningxia Hui Autonomous Region Cttee; Vice-Sec. CCP Guyuan Pref. Cttee; Cttee Vice-Sec., now Dir-Gen. CCP Yinnan Pref.; Dir Propaganda Dept of CCP Ningxia Hui Autonomous Region Cttee 1969–93, Vice-Sec. 1993–98; Vice-Chair. Ningxia Hui Autonomous Regional People's Govt 1995–96, Chair. 1996–; Alt. mem. 14th CCP Cen. Cttee 1992–97, 15th CCP Cen. Cttee 1997–2002, mem. 16th CCP Cen. Cttee 2002–07. *Address:* c/o People's Government of Ningxia Hui Autonomous Region, Yinchuan, Ningxia, People's Republic of China.

MA, Wanfan, (Mayi); Chinese business executive; b. 1930, Longkou Co., Shandong Prov.; Chair. China Nat. Chemicals Corpn 1989; mem. 7th CPPCC Nat. Cttee 1987–92, 8th Nat. Cttee 1993–98, 9th Nat. Cttee 1998–2003. *Address:* c/o China National Chemicals Corporation, 16 Hepingli 7 District, Beijing 100013, People's Republic of China (office).

MA, Wanqi (Ma Man Kei); Chinese politician and business executive; b. 1919, Nanhai Co., Guandong Prov.; mem. 5th Nat. Cttee CPPCC 1978–82, Perm. mem. 6th Nat. Cttee CPPCC 1983–88, Vice-Chair. 8th Nat. Cttee CPPCC 1993–98, 9th Nat. Cttee 1998–2003, 10th Nat. Cttee 2003–08, Vice-Chair. 11th CPPCC Nat. Cttee 2008–13; mem. 6th Standing Cttee NPC 1986–88, 7th Standing Cttee 1988–92; Vice-Chair. Cttee for Drafting Basic LAw for Macao SAR, Vice-Chair. Macao SAR Preparatory Cttee 1998–99; Vice-Pres. All-China Sports Fed. *Address:* c/o National Committee of Chinese People's Political Consultative Conference, 23 Taiping Qiao Street, Beijing, People's Republic of China (office).

MA, Weihua, BA, PhD; Chinese economist and business executive; ed Jilin Univ., Southwest Finance and Economics Univ.; Deputy Section Dir and Deputy Sec.-Gen. Liaoning Prov. Planning Economy Comm. 1982–85, transferred to Gen. Office of Liaoning Prov. Govt 1985–86; worked in Gen. Office of Anhui Prov. Govt 1986–88; Deputy Dir Gen. Office, People's Bank of China 1988–90, Deputy Dir of Planning and Cash Dept 1990–92, Pres. Hainan Prov. Br., People's Bank of China and Dir of State Foreign Exchange Regulatory Bureaux, Hainan Br. 1992–98; Dir and CEO China Merchants Bank Co Ltd 1999–2013, Pres. 2004–13; Chair. Wing Lung Bank Ltd 2008–; Chair. CMB International Capital Corpn Ltd, China Merchants Cigna Life Insurance Co. Ltd; Chair. Shenzhen Domestic Bankers' Asscn; Ind. Dir (non-exec.) TOM Online Inc. 2003–, China Petrochemical International Co. 2010–, Fujian Petrochemical Co. Ltd 2010–, China Petroleum & Chemical Corpn 2010–, Winox Holdings Ltd 2011–; Ind. Dir Shenyang Dongruan Software Co. Ltd; Dir, Sinopec Corpn; mem. Standing Council of China Finance Acad., Shenzhen Soft Science Devt Foundation; Deputy Gov. China Industrialists Asscn; Trustee, China United Devt Research Inst.; Guest Prof., Peking Univ., Jilin Univ., Southwest Finance and Economics Univ., Yunnan Univ., Northwest Univ., Grad. School of the People's Bank of China; Rep. to 10th NPC; Standing Cttee mem. China Finance Insts, 8th Council of Red Cross Soc. of China; Dr hc (Univ. of Southern California, USA). *Address:* c/o China Merchants Bank Co. Ltd, 7088 Shen Nan Road, Futian District, Shenzhen 518040, Guangdong, People's Republic of China. *E-mail:* cmhk@cmhk.com.

MA, Wen; Chinese government official; b. 1948, Hebei Prov.; m. Yu Zhenqi; one d.; ed Nankai Univ.; sent to countryside during Cultural Revolution, Inner Mongolia Autonomous Region 1968; Deputy Head of commune brigade and of revolutionary cttee 1972–78; Teacher, Nankai Univ. 1982–87; Sec., Nat. Population and Family Planning Comm. CCP Cttee 1989–95, Deputy Dir, Publicity and Educ. Dept 1989–97; mem. 15th CCP Cen. Cttee Cen. Comm. for Discipline Inspection 1997–2002, 16th CCP Cen. Cttee Cen. Comm. for Discipline Inspection 2002–07, Deputy Sec. 2004–07, 2007–12; mem. 17th CCP Cen. Cttee 2007–12; Minister of Supervision 2007–13; Dir, Nat. Bureau of Corruption Prevention 2007–13; mem. CCP Cen. Cttee Public Security Comm. 2007–12. *Address:* c/o Chinese Communist Party Public Security Commission, Zhongnanhai, Beijing, People's Republic of China (office).

MA, Xinsheng; Chinese economist, engineer and business executive; *Chairman, Bailian Group Company Limited;* ed Univ. of Shanghai, Shanghai Nat. Accounting Inst.; Deputy Party Sec., then Party Sec. and Factory Man., Shanghai Rectifier Factory 1979–81; Deputy Gen. Man. Shanghai Electric Group Co. Ltd 1989–95; Gen. Man. and Party Sec., Shanghai Jidian Maoyi Building 1995–96; Chair. of Labour Union, Pres. and Deputy Party Sec., Shanghai Electric (Group) Corpn 1996–2003; Deputy Party Sec. Shanghai State-owned Assets Supervision and Admin Comm. 2003–07; Chair. Shanghai Friendship Group Inc. Co., Lianhua Supermarket Holdings Co. Ltd 2009–; currently Chair. and Party Sec., Bailian Group Co. Ltd; Chair. China Bailian (Hong Kong) Ltd; Dir, Shanghai Pudong Development Bank Co. Ltd 2008; CEO Award, Robert A. Mundel World Executive

Awards 2004. *Address:* Bailian Group, 315 South Zhongshan Road, Shanghai 200010, People's Republic of China (office). *Telephone:* (21) 63323636 (office). *Fax:* (21) 63322323 (office). *E-mail:* webmaster@bailiangroup.cn (office). *Website:* www .bailiangroup.cn (office).

MA, Ying-jeou, LLB, LLM, SJD; Taiwanese politician, academic and head of state; *President;* b. 13 July 1950, Hong Kong; m. Chow Mei-ching; two d.; ed Nat. Taiwan Univ., New York Univ. Law School, Harvard Univ. Law School, USA; with Marine Corps, Navy 1972–74; Legal Consultant, First Nat. Bank of Boston, USA 1980–81; Research Consultant, Univ. of Maryland Law School 1980–81; Assoc., Cole and Deitz (law firm), New York 1981; Deputy Dir First Bureau, Office of the Pres. of Taiwan 1981–88; Adjunct Assoc. Prof., Grad. School of Law, Nat. Chengchi Univ. 1981, Assoc. Prof. of Law, Nat. Chengchi Univ. Law School 1997–98; Deputy Sec.-Gen. Cen. Cttee, Kuomintang (KMT) 1984–88, Vice-Chair. 2004–05, Chair. 2005–07 (resgnd), 2009–; Chair. Research, Devt and Evaluation Comm., Exec. Yuan 1988–91, Sr Vice-Chair. Mainland Affairs Council 1991–93; Minister of Justice 1993–96; Minister of State without Portfolio 1996–97; Mayor of Taipei 1998–2006; Pres. of Taiwan 2008–. *Publications include:* Legal Problems of Seabed Boundary Delimitation in the East China Sea 1984, The Diauyutai (Senkaku) Islets and the Maritime Boundary Problems in the East China Sea (Chinese) 1986, Cross-Straits Relations at a Crossroad: Impasse of Breakthrough 2001; articles and 17 academic papers. *Leisure interests:* jogging, music, charity. *Address:* Office of the President, 122 Chungking South Rd, Sec. 1, 10048 Taipei (office); Kuomintang, 232 Sec. 2, Bade Rd., Taipei 10492, Taiwan (office). *Telephone:* (2) 23113731 (office); (2) 87711234 (office). *Fax:* (2) 23311604 (office); (2) 23434561 (office). *E-mail:* public@mail.oop.gov.tw (office). *Website:* www.president.gov.tw (office); www.kmt.org.tw (office).

MA, Yo-Yo, BA; American cellist; b. 7 Oct. 1955, Paris, France; of Chinese parentage; m. Jill A. Hornor 1978; one s. one d.; ed Harvard Univ. and cello studies with his father, with Leonard Rose and at Juilliard School of Music, New York; first public recital aged five; performed under many distinguished conductors with all major orchestras of the world, including Berlin Philharmonic, Boston Symphony, Chicago Symphony, Israel Philharmonic, London Symphony and New York Philharmonic; regularly participates in festivals of Tanglewood, Ravinia, Blossom, Salzburg and Edinburgh; also appears in chamber music ensembles with artists including Isaac Stern, Emanuel Ax, Leonard Rose, Pinchas Zukerman, Gidon Kremer and fmrly Yehudi Menuhin; premiered the Concerto by H. K. Gruber, Tanglewood 1989; recital tour with Emanuel Ax celebrating 20th anniversary of their partnership 1995–96; performed Bach's suites for solo cello at the Barbican Hall, London 1995; est. the Silk Road Project to promote study of cultural, artistic and intellectual traditions of the route 2001; Smithsonian Folklife Festival 2002; Judson and Joyce Green Creative Consultant, Chicago Symphony Orchestra 2010–; apptd Messenger of Peace by UN Sec.-Gen. 2006; mem. Pres.'s Cttee on the Arts and Humanities 2009–; Dr hc (Northeastern Univ.) 1985 and from other colls and univs, including Harvard, Yale, Tufts and Juilliard, Chinese Univ. of Hong Kong; Hon. DMA (Princeton) 2005; Avery Fisher Prize 1978, Glenn Gould Prize 1999, Nat. Medal of the Arts 2001, Dan David Prize 2006, Sonning Prize 2006, Award of Distinction, Int. Cello Festival 2007, World Econ. Forum Crystal Prize 2008, Musical America Award for Musician of the Year 2009, Presidential Medal of Freedom 2010, 15 Grammy Awards, two Emmy Awards, 19 Canadian Gemini Awards, Honoree, 34th Annual Kennedy Center Honors 2011, Polar Music Prize (Sweden) 2012. *Recordings include:* Portrait of Yo-Yo Ma 1989, The Japanese Album 1989, A Cocktail Party 1990, Hush 1992, Made in America 1993, The New York Album 1994, King Gesar 1996, From Ordinary Things 1997, Seven Years in Tibet 1997, Liberty! 1997, Piazzolla: Soul of the Tango 1997, The Protecting Veil and Wake Up...and Die 1998, John Williams Greatest Hits 1969–1999 1999, My First 79 Years 1999, Solo 1999, Brahms: Piano Concerto No.2, Cello Sonata Op. 78 1999, Lulie the Iceberg 1999, Songs and Dances 1999, Franz Joseph Haydn 1999, Simply Baroque 1999, Crouching Tiger, Hidden Dragon (film soundtrack) 2000, Corigliano: Phantasmagoria 2000, Simply Baroque II 2000, Appalachian Journey 2000, Dvorak: Piano Quartet No. 2, Sonatina in G, Romantic Pieces 2000, Classic Yo-Yo 2001, Classical Hits 2001, Heartland: An Appalachian Anthology 2001, Yo-Yo Ma Plays Bach 2002, Isaac Stern: In Tribute and Celebration 2002, Mozart: Piano Quartets 2002, Naqoyqatsi (film soundtrack) 2002, Yo-Yo Ma Plays the Music of John Williams 2002, Silk Road Journeys— When Strangers Meet 2002, Obrigado Brazil 2003, Classics for a New Century 2003, Paris—La Belle Époque 2003, Vivaldi's Cello 2004, The Dvorák Album 2004, Silk Road Journeys—Beyond the Horizon 2005, Essential Yo-Yo Ma 2005, R. Strauss: Don Quixote 2005, Memoirs of a Geisha (film soundtrack) 2005, Yo-Yo Ma plays Ennio Morricone 2006, Bach: Unaccompanied Piano Suites 2006, Appassionato 2007, Songs of Joy and Peace (Grammy Award for Best Classical Crossover Album 2010) 2008, 'Cinema Paradiso' on Chris Botti in Boston 2009, The Goat Rodeo Sessions 2011. *Address:* Opus 3 Artists, 470 Park Avenue South, 9th Floor North, New York, NY 10016, USA (office). *Telephone:* (212) 584-7500 (office). *Fax:* (646) 300-8200 (office). *E-mail:* info@opus3artists.com (office). *Website:* www .opus3artists.com (office); www.yo-yoma.com.

MA, Yongwei; Chinese banker; b. 1942, Rongcheng, Shandong Prov.; ed Liaoning Inst. of Finance and Econs; joined CCP 1965; fmr Gov. Agric. Bank of China (Sec. CCP Leading Party Group); Exec. mem. and Vice-Chair. Int. Confed. for Agricultural Credit 1993–98; mem. Monetary Policy Comm., People's Bank of China 2000; Chair., Pres. People's Insurance Co. of China 1994–95, Chair. and Pres. China Insurance Group Co. 1995–98; Chair. China Insurance Regulatory Comm. 1998–2003; Ind. Dir (non-exec.) China Life Insurance Co. 2006–12; Dir (non-exec.) Mingyuan Medicare Devt Co. Ltd 2008–12; Ind. Dir Cninsure Inc. 2008–12; Del., 13th CCP Nat. Congress 1987–92, 14th CCP Nat. Congress 1992–97, 15th CCP Nat. Congress 1997–2002; mem. Standing Cttee of Nat. Cttee of CPPCC 2003–08. *Address:* c/o China Life Insurance Company Limited, 16 Chaowai Ave., 23rd Fl. Chinalife Building, Chaoyang District, Beijing 100020, People's Republic of China. *E-mail:* info@chinalife.com.cn.

MA, Yuan; Chinese judge; b. 30 June 1930, Xinmin Co., Liaoning Prov.; two s.; ed Chinese People's Univ., Beijing; joined CCP 1953; teacher Dept of Law, Beijing Univ. and part-time lawyer 1955–62, part-time Prof. 1990–; Asst Judge, Judge Supreme People's Court 1963–82, Deputy Dir Civil Dept 1982–85, Vice-Pres. Supreme People's Court 1985–98; mem. Standing Cttee All China Women's Fed.;

Vice-Pres. China Marriage and Family Research Inst. 1983–; Pres. Chinese Asscn of Women Judges 1994–; Asst Sec.-Gen. Civil and Econ. Law Cttee, China Law Soc. 1983–; Hon. Prof., Renmin Univ. of China School of Law. *Address:* The School of Law, Renmin University of China, 59 Zhongguancun Ave, Beijing 100872, People's Republic of China (office). *Telephone:* (10) 82500352 (office).

MA, Zehua, MA; Chinese economist and business executive; *Chairman, China Ocean Shipping (Group) Company (COSCO);* ed Shanghai Maritime Univ.; successive positions as Exec. Vice-Pres. and Sec. CCP Party Cttee, China Shipping (Group) Co., Exec. Vice-Pres. China Ocean Shipping (Group) Co. (COSCO), Gen. Man. COSCO Qingdao, Deputy Gen. Man. COSCO Guangzhou, Pres. COSCO America Inc., Gen. Man. Devt Div. and Asst Pres. COSCO, Pres. COSCO (UK) Ltd –2011, mem. Bd of Dirs, Pres. and Deputy Sec. CCP Party Cttee COSCO 2011–13, Chair. and Sec. CCP Party Cttee. *Address:* China Ocean Shipping (Group) Company (COSCO), Ocean Plaza, 158 Fuxingmennei Street, Beijing 100031, People's Republic of China (office). *Telephone:* (10) 66493388 (office). *Fax:* (10) 66492266 (office). *E-mail:* info@cosco.com (office). *Website:* www.cosco.com (office).

MA, Zhengang; Chinese diplomatist; *President, China Institute of International Studies;* b. 9 Nov. 1940, Shandong; m. Chen Xiaodong; one s.; ed Beijing Foreign Languages Univ., Ealing Tech. Coll., London, LSE; staff mem., Attaché, Embassy in Yugoslavia 1970–74; Attaché N American and Oceanic Affairs Dept, Ministry of Foreign Affairs, Beijing 1974–81, Deputy Dir, then Dir N American and Oceanic Affairs Dept 1985–90, Deputy Dir-Gen., then Dir-Gen. N American and Oceanic Affairs Dept 1991–95; Vice-Consul, Consul, Consulate-Gen., Vancouver 1981–85; Counsellor, Embassy in Washington, DC 1990–91; Vice-Minister of Foreign Affairs 1995–97; Amb. to UK 1997–2002; Vice-Chair. 10th CPPCC Nat. Cttee 2003–; Amb., Ministry of Foreign Affairs 2002–04; Pres. China Inst. of Int. Studies (CIIS) 2004–, Chair. China Nat. Cttee, Council for Security Cooperation in Asia Pacific (CSCAP), Chair. editorial bd International Studies, Chair. of Academic Cttee. *Leisure interests:* literature, bridge, table tennis. *Address:* China Institute of International Studies, No.3, Toutiao, Taijichang, Beijing 100005, People's Republic of China (office). *Website:* www.ciis.org.cn (office).

MA, Zhongchen; Chinese party official; b. 1936, Tai'an, Shandong Prov.; joined CCP 1956; Deputy Sec. CCP Tai'an Co. Cttee, Shandong Prov. 1966–76, Sec. 1978–83; Sec. CCP Zhangqiu Co. Cttee, Shandong Prov. 1976–78; Sec. CCP Tai'an City Cttee, Shandong Prov. 1983–86; Vice-Gov. Shandong Prov. 1986–88; Sec.- Gen. People's Govt, Shandong Prov. 1986–88; Deputy Sec.-Gen. State Council 1987; Deputy Sec. CCP Shandong Prov. Cttee 1988–90; Vice-Minister of Agric. 1990–92; Vice-Gov. Henan Prov. 1992, Acting Gov. 1992–93, Gov. 1993–98; Deputy Sec. CCP Henan Prov. Cttee 1995–98, Sec. 1998–2000; Alt. mem. 12th CCP Cen. Cttee 1982–87, 13th Cen. Cttee 1987–92, 14th Cen. Cttee 1992–97, mem. 15th CCP Cen. Cttee 1997–2002. *Address:* c/o Office of the Governor, Zhengzhou City, Henan Province, People's Republic of China.

MA, Zonglin; Chinese business executive; *President, Power Construction Corporation of China (PowerChina);* mem. Bd of Dirs and Pres. Power Construction Corpn of China (PowerChina, state-owned corpn) 2011–. *Address:* Power Construction Corporation of China, No. 7 & 8 Building, Beijing Xiyuan Hotel, 1 Sanlihe Road, Haidian District, Beijing 100040, People's Republic of China (office). *Telephone:* (10) 58382266 (office); (10) 88358715 (office). *Fax:* (10) 58382888 (office). *E-mail:* infocenter@powerchin.com (office). *Website:* www.powerchin.com (office).

MA SI-HANG, Frederick, BA; Hong Kong government official; *Secretary for Financial Services and the Treasury;* b. 1952, Hong Kong; ed Univ. of Hong Kong; fmrly with J. P. Morgan Private Bank, Chase Manhattan Bank, Kumagai Gumi (HK) Ltd, RBC Dominion Securities Ltd, Hong Kong Exchanges and Clearing Ltd, Hong Kong Securities and Futures Comm.; Group Chief Financial Officer, Exec. Dir, mem. Exec. Cttee PCCW Ltd –2002; Sec. for Financial Services and the Treasury, Hong Kong Special Admin. Region 2002–. *Address:* c/o Government Secretariat, Central Government Offices, Lower Albert Road, Central, Hong Kong Special Administrative Region, People's Republic of China (office). *Telephone:* 28102900 (office). *Fax:* 28457895 (office). *Website:* www.fstb.gov.hk (office).

MA TAO-LI, Hon. Geoffrey, LLB, QC; Hong Kong barrister and judge; *Chief Justice, Court of Final Appeal of Hong Kong;* b. 11 Jan. 1956, Hong Kong; m. Madam Justice Maria Candace Yuen Ka-ning; one d.; ed in Altrincham and at Univ. of Birmingham, UK; called to the Bar, Gray's Inn, London, UK 1978, commenced practice as a barrister in England and Wales; called to the Bar in Hong Kong 1980, Vic., Australia 1983, Singapore 1990; QC 1993; fmr legal consultant to Messrs David Chong & Co., Singapore, Advocates & Solicitors; Head of Chambers, Temple Chambers, Hong Kong –2001; Recorder, Court of First Instance of the High Court 2000–01, Judge of the Court of First Instance of the High Court 2001–02, Justice of Appeal of the Court of Appeal of the High Court 2002–03, Chief Judge of the High Court 2003–10; Chief Justice of the Court of Final Appeal of Hong Kong 2010–; Chair. Appeal Tribunal Panel (Buildings) 1994–2001, Steering Cttee on Civil Justice Reform 2004–09, Monitoring Cttee on Civil Justice Reform 2009–; Deputy Chair. Bd of Review (Inland Revenue) 1997–2000, Securities and Futures Comm. (SFC) Appeals Panel 1999–2001, SFC Takeovers Appeal Cttee 1999–2001; mem. Bar Council of the Hong Kong Bar Asscn 1982–84, 1992–96; Adjudicator, Registration of Persons Tribunal, Hong Kong 1987–96; mem. Criminal and Law Enforcement Injuries Compensation Bd 1991–2001, Steering Cttee for the 11th Int. Congress of Maritime Arbitrators 1992–94, Civil Court Users Cttee of the Judiciary 1993–2001, Hong Kong Futures Exchange Disciplinary Appeal Tribunal 1994–2001, Man. Cttee of the Consumer Legal Action Fund 1994–98 (later Vice-Chair.), Appointment Advisory Bd of the Hong Kong Int. Arbitration Centre (HKIAC) 1997–, HKIAC Arbitration Ordinance Review Cttee 1998–, Working Party on Civil Justice Reform 2000–01; Hon. Lecturer, Dept of Professional Legal Educ., Univ. of Hong Kong 1987–; Hon. Bencher of Gray's Inn 2004; Hon. LLD (Birmingham) 2011. *Publications:* Hong Kong Civil Procedure (contributing ed.) 2002, Litigation in the Commercial List: 2002 Law Lectures for Practitioners (contrib.) 2002, Arbitration in Hong Kong: A Practical Guide (Ed.-in-Chief) 2003 (second edn 2011), Professional Conduct and Risk Management in Hong Kong (Ed.-in-Chief) 2007. *Address:* Court of Final Appeal of Hong Kong, 1 Battery Path, Central, Hong Kong Special Administrative Region, People's Republic of China (office). *Telephone:* 2123-0011 (office). *Fax:* 2121-0310 (office). *E-mail:* enquiry@judiciary.gov.hk (office). *Website:* www.judiciary.gov.hk (office).

MAALIM, Mahboub M., BSc, MSc; Kenyan engineer and international organization official; *Executive Secretary, Intergovernmental Authority on Development (IGAD);* b. Garissa; ed Univ. of Texas, USA; Dist Water Engineer, Ministry of Water 1985–94; Nat. Coordinator Arid Lands Resource Man. Project 1996–2004; Perm. Sec. Ministry of Water and Irrigation 2006–08; Exec. Sec. IGAD 2008–; Assoc. mem. American Soc. of Civil Engineers. *Address:* Office of the Executive Secretary, IGAD Secretariat, Avenue Georges Clemenceau, PO Box 2653, Djibouti, Republic of Djibouti (office). *Telephone:* 356452 (office). *Fax:* 353520 (office). *E-mail:* igad@igad.org (office). *Website:* www.igad.org (office).

MAALOUF, Amin, Maître en Sociologie; Lebanese/French writer; b. 25 Feb. 1949, Beirut, Lebanon; s. of the late Ruchdi Maalouf and of Odette Ghossein; m. Andrée Abouchdid 1971; three c.; ed Univ. Saint-Joseph, Beirut, Univ. de Lyon; journalist, an-Nahar 1971–76, Economia 1976–77; Ed. Jeune Afrique 1978–79, 1982–84; mem. Acad. française Fauteuil 29 2011–; Grand Cordon, Ordre du Cèdre (Lebanon); Officier, Ordre nat. du Mérite; Chevalier, Légion d'honneur; Commdr des Arts et des Lettres; Kt, Order of the Lion of Finland; hon. degrees from Univ. Catholique de Louvain, Belgium, American Univ. of Beirut, Lebanon, Tarragona Univ., Spain, Evora Univ., Portugal; Prix France-Liban 1986, Grand Prix de l'UNICEF 1991, Prix Goncourt 1993, Premio Nonino 1997, Premio Elio Vittorini 1997, Prix européen de l'essai 1998, Premio Grinzane Cavour 2001, Premio Antonio de Sancha 2003, Prix Méditerranée 2004, Premio Grupo de Compostela 2009, Prix du livre des Droits de l'Homme 2009, Premio Príncipe de Asturias 2010. *Publications:* Les Croisades vues par les Arabes 1983, Léon l'Africain 1986, Samarcande 1988, Les Jardins de lumière 1991, Le premier siècle après Béatrice 1992, Le Rocher de Tanios 1993, Les Echelles du Levant 1996, Les Identités meurtrières 1998, Le Périple de Baldassare 2000, L'Amour de Loin (opera libretto) 2001, Origines 2004, Adriana Mater (opera libretto) 2006, Le Dérèglement du monde 2009, Émilie (opera libretto) 2010, Les désorientés 2012. *Address:* c/o Académie française, 23 quai de Conti, 75006 Paris, France.

MAALOUF, Maria; Lebanese journalist, television presenter and media executive; ed Sainte Famille Maronites Coll., Univ. of Lebanon; presenter, Bila Rakib (Without Censorship) 2002–04, Maa Maria Maalouf (MBN TV) 2006–; Founder, Gulf Printing and Publishing Co.; Owner, Arrouwad (newspaper); mem. Syrian Nat. Soc. Party. *Publication:* A Woman Looking for a Homeland. *Address:* Maa Maria Maalouf, c/o National Broadcasting Network (NBN) Television, Adnan El Hakim Street, Jnah, Beirut, Lebanon (office). *Telephone:* 1841020 (office). *Fax:* 1841027 (office). *Website:* www.nbn.com.lb (office); www.mariamaalouf.com/maria (home).

MAAS, Heiko; German lawyer and politician; *Federal Minister of Justice and Consumer Protection;* b. 19 Sept. 1966, Saarlouis; m.; two c.; ed Univ. des Saarlandes; began career with Ford Werke GmbH, Saarlouis 1988; mem. Saarland Landtag (State Parl.) 1994–96, 1999–; Sec., Ministry of Environment, Energy and Transport 1996–98; Minister for Environment, Energy and Transport in Saarland 1998–99, Minister for Econs, Labour, Energy and Transport and Deputy Prime Minister in Saarland 2012–13; Fed. Minister of Justice and Consumer Protection 2013–; mem. Sozialdemokratische Partei Deutschlands (SPD), Chair. SPD Parl. Group 1999–2012, mem. SPD Party Exec. 2001–. *Address:* Federal Ministry of Justice and Consumer Protection, Mohrenstrasse 37, 10117 Berlin, Germany (office). *Telephone:* (30) 185800 (office). *Fax:* (30) 185809525 (office). *E-mail:* poststelle@bmj.bund.de (office). *Website:* www.bmj.de (office).

MAASIKAS, Matti; Estonian government official and diplomatist; *Permanent Representative, European Union;* b. 1967, Tallinn; m.; two c.; ed Tartu Univ.; Consultant, Ministry of Defence 1993–94; Int. Sec., Pro Patria Union (Estonian Conservative Party) 1994–96; Head of Foreign Relations Dept, Chancellery of Riigikogu (Parl.) 1996–99; Head of Prime Minister Mart Laar's Pvt. Office 1999–2001; Amb. to Finland 2001–05; Sec. Gen., Ministry of Foreign Affairs 2005–08; mem. of Cabinet, European Commr for Enlargement and Econ. and Monetary Affairs 2009–10; Adviser, Bureau of European Policy Advisers, EC 2010–11; Amb. and Perm. Rep. to EU 2011–. *Address:* Permanent Representation of Estonia to the EU, Rue Guimard 11/13, 1040 Brussels, Belgium (office). *Telephone:* (2) 227-39-10 (office). *Fax:* (2) 227-39-25 (office). *E-mail:* matti .maasikas@mfa.ee (office); permrep.eu@mfa.ee (office). *Website:* www.eu.estemb .be (office).

MAAZEL, Lorin, FRCM; American conductor and musician; *Chief Conductor, Munich Philharmonic Orchestra;* b. 6 March 1930, Neuilly, France; s. of Lincoln Maazel and Marie Varencove Maazel; m. 1st Miriam Sandbank (divorced), two d.; m. 2nd Israela Margalit (divorced), one s.; m. 3rd Dietlinde Turban 1986, two s. one d.; ed under Vladimir Bakaleinikoff and at Univ. of Pittsburgh; début as conductor 1938; Conductor, American Symphony Orchestras 1938–; violin recitalist; European début 1953; festivals include Bayreuth, Salzburg, Edin.; tours include S America, Australia, USSR and Japan; Artistic Dir, Deutsche Oper Berlin 1965–71; Musical Dir Radio Symphony Orchestra, Berlin 1965–75; Assoc. Prin. Conductor, New Philharmonia Orchestra, London 1970–72; Dir Cleveland Orchestra 1971–82, Conductor Emer. 1982–86; Prin. Guest Conductor London Philharmonia 1976–80; Dir Vienna State Opera 1982–84, Music Dir Pittsburgh Symphony Orchestra 1988–96; Music Dir Bavarian Radio Symphony Orchestra 1993–2001, NY Philharmonic 2002–09, Palau de les Arts Reina Sofía, Valencia 2005–12, Munich Philharmonic Orchestra 2011–; Music Dir Orchestre Nat. de France 1988–90; Commdr, Légion d'honneur 2009, Finnish Commdr of the Lion, Portuguese Commdr, Bundesverdienstkreuz (Germany); Hon. DMus (Pittsburgh) 1968, (Royal Coll. of Music) 1984; Hon. DHumLitt (Beaver Coll.) 1973; Hon. DCL (Univ. of S Sewanee) 1988; Dr hc (Ind.) 1988. *Composition:* 1984 (premiere Royal Opera House, London) 2005. *Leisure interests:* swimming, tennis, reading. *Address:* Munich Philharmonic Orchestra, Kellerstrasse 4, 81667 Munich, Germany (office). *Telephone:* (480) 98-51 00 (office). *Fax:* (480) 98-51 3 (office). *E-mail:* presse .philharmoniker@muenchen.de (office). *Website:* www.mphil.de (office); maestromaazel.com.

MABILANGAN, Felipe H., MA; Philippine diplomatist and international organization official; *Senior Foreign Affairs Adviser;* m. Ada Kalaw Ledesma; three c.; ed Univs of Oxford, UK and Geneva, Switzerland; various positions, Dept of Foreign Affairs 1971–79, Dir-Gen. for European Affairs 1988; Amb. to France (also accred to Portugal) 1979–87, to China (also accred to Mongolia) 1989–95;

Perm. Rep. to UN 1995–2001; currently Sr Foreign Affairs Adviser, Dept of Foreign Affairs; mem. UN Advisory Cttee on Admin. and Budgetary Questions 2001–04; del. to numerous int. confs; Chevalier Ordre nat. du Mérit (France), Gawad Mabini (Philippines). *Leisure interests:* golf, tennis. *Address:* Department of Foreign Affairs, DFA Building, 2330 Pasay City, Metro Manila, Philippines (office). *Telephone:* (2) 8189449 (office).

MABUS, Raymond Edwin, Jr, MA, JD; American fmr politician, lawyer and consultant; b. 11 Oct. 1948, Starkville, Miss.; s. of Raymond Edwin Mabus, Sr and Lucille C. Mabus; m. (divorced); two d.; ed Univ. of Mississippi, Johns Hopkins Univ., Harvard Univ.; called to Texas Bar 1976, Washington, DC 1978, Miss. 1982; Law Clerk US Circuit Court of Appeals, Montgomery, Ala 1976–77; Legal Counsel to House of Reps, DC 1977–78; Assoc. Fried, Frank et al., Washington, DC 1979–80; Gov.'s Legislative Aide, State of Miss., Jackson 1980–83; State Auditor, State of Miss. 1984–88; Gov. of Miss. 1988–92; Amb. to Saudi Arabia 1994–96; Counsel, Baker Donaldson Bearman & Caldwell 1996–; fmr Chair. Southern Govs' Asscn, Southern Regional Educ. Bd; Woodrow Wilson Scholarship, Johns Hopkins Univ. 1969; Democrat; King Abdul Aziz Award, Saudi Arabia 1996, Distinguished Public Service Award, US Dept of Defense. *Leisure interests:* spectator sports, walking, reading, photography, scuba diving. *Address:* 345 Richardson Road, Ridgelands, MS 39157, USA. *Telephone:* (601) 605-9400 (office); (601) 605-7400 (home). *Fax:* (601) 607-7104.

McADAM, Lowell C., BEng, MBA; American engineer and telecommunications industry executive; *Chairman and CEO, Verizon Communications Inc.;* ed Cornell Univ., Univ. of San Diego; spent six years in USN Civil Engineer Corps; held various exec. positions with Pacific Bell, including Area Vice-Pres. of Bay Area Marketing and Gen. Man. of South Bay Customer Services 1983–93; joined AirTouch as Exec. Dir of Int. Applications and Operations 1993, served as Vice-Pres. of Int. operations for AirTouch Communications and was Lead Tech. Partner for Cellular Ventures in Spain, Portugal, Sweden, Italy, Korea and Japan, later Pres. and CEO PrimeCo Personal Communications (jt venture owned by Bell Atlantic and Vodafone AirTouch), later COO; Exec. Vice-Pres. and COO Verizon Wireless 2000–07, Pres. and CEO 2007–10, Pres. and COO Verizon Communications Inc. 2010–11, Pres. and CEO Aug.–Dec. 2011, Chair. and CEO 2012–, Chair. Verizon Wireless Bd of Reps, mem. Bd of Dirs; past Chair. CTIA – The Wireless Asscn; Dir, Nat. Acad. Foundation. *Address:* Verizon Communications Inc., 140 West Street, New York, NY 10007, USA (office). *Telephone:* (212) 395-2121 (office). *Fax:* (212) 571-1897 (office). *E-mail:* info@verizon.com (office). *Website:* www .verizon.com (office).

McALEESE, Mary Patricia, LLB, MA, FRSA, MRIA; Irish academic, journalist and fmr head of state; b. 27 June 1951, Belfast, Northern Ireland; d. of Patrick J. Leneghan and Claire McManus; m. Martin McAleese 1976; one s. two d.; ed Queen's Univ. Belfast, Inn of Court of Northern Ireland, King's Inns, Dublin and Trinity Coll., Dublin; called to Northern Ireland Bar 1974; Reid Prof. of Criminal Law, Criminology and Penology, Trinity Coll., Dublin 1975–79, 1981–87; current affairs journalist and presenter, Radio Telefis Eireann 1979–85; Dir Inst. of Professional Legal Studies 1987–97; Pro-Vice-Chancellor, Queen's Univ., Belfast 1994–97; Pres. of Ireland 1997–2011; Dir (non-exec.) Northern Ireland Electricity 1992–97, Channel 4 TV 1993–97, fmr Dir Royal Group of Hosps Trust; Founder mem. Irish Comm. for Prisoners Overseas; mem. Catholic Church Episcopal Del. to the New Ireland Forum 1984, Catholic Church Del. to the North Comm. on Contentious Parades 1996; Del. to White House Conf. on Trade and Investment in Ireland 1995, and to the follow-up Pittsburg Conf. 1996; Hon. Fellow, Trinity Coll. Dublin, Inst. of Engineers of Ireland, Royal Coll. of Surgeons, Coll. of Anaesthetists, Liverpool John Moore's Univ., Royal Coll. of Physicians and Surgeons, Glasgow; Hon. Bencher, King's Inns, Inn of Court of Northern Ireland; Freeman, City of Kilkenny 2009; Hon. LLD (Nat. Univ. of Ireland, Vic. Univ. of Tech., Australia, Saint Mary's Univ., Canada, Loyola Law School, LA, Univ. of Aberdeen, Univ. of Surrey, Queen's, Belfast), (Nottingham) 1998, (Trinity Coll. Dublin, Metropolitan Univ., Manchester, Univ. of Delaware, Univ. of Bristol), (Univ. of Otago, NZ) 2007, (Mount Holyoke Coll., Mass) 2009, (Fordham Univ., NY) 2010, Hon. DHumLitt (Rochester Inst. of Tech., New York, USA), Hon. DLitt (Univ. of Ulster); Silver Jubilee Commemoration Medal, Charles Univ., Prague, Great Gold Medal, Comenius Univ., Bratislava, ranked by Forbes magazine amongst The World's 100 Most Powerful Women (33rd) 2004, (21st) 2005, (55th) 2006, (58th) 2007, (74th) 2008, (69th) 2009, (64th) 2010, The American Ireland Fund Humanitarian Award 2007. *Publications:* The Irish Martyrs 1995, Reconciled Being 1997. *Leisure interests:* hillwalking, theology. *Address:* c/o Áras an Uachtaráin, Phoenix Park, Dublin 8, Ireland.

McALLISTER, Sir Ian, Kt, CBE, BSc (Econs); British transport industry executive; b. 17 Aug. 1943, Glasgow; m. Susan Mitchell; three s. one d.; ed Thornleigh Salesian Coll., Bolton, Univ. Coll. London; grad. economist, Ford Motor Co. Ltd 1964, responsible for German Operations 1980s, Man. Dir Ford of Britain 1991, Chair. 1992–2002; Chair. (non-exec.) Network Rail Ltd 2002–09; Chair. Carbon Trust 2001–; Chair. Greater Essex Prosperity Forum 2007–; Dir (non-exec.) Scottish & Newcastle, Energy Saving Trust 2001–; Dir UCL Business 2007–. *Leisure interest:* Manchester United football club. *Address:* c/o Network Rail Ltd, Kings Place, 90 York Way, London, N1 9AG, England (office).

MACAN, Tom, BA; British diplomatist (retd); b. 14 Nov. 1946, Manchester, England; s. of Dr Thomas Townley Macan and Zaida Bindloss Macan (née Boddington); one s. one d.; ed Shrewsbury School, Univ. of Sussex; joined HM Diplomatic Service 1969, served in Bonn, Brasília and FCO; Press Sec. Embassy at Bonn 1981; Head Commonwealth Co-ordination Dept, FCO 1986–88, Head Training Dept 1988–90; Deputy Head of Mission at Lisbon 1990–95; Amb. to Lithuania 1995–98; seconded to BOC Group 1998–99; Minister at New Delhi 1999–2002; Gov. of the Virgin Islands 2002–06; mem. Inst. of Linguists. *Leisure interests:* sailing, steamboats, church architecture. *Address:* Stevney, Outgate, Ambleside, Cumbria, LA22 0NH, England (home). *Telephone:* (1539) 436978 (office). *E-mail:* ttm@mailcan.com (office).

McANUFF, Des; American/Canadian producer, director and writer; b. 19 June 1952, Princeton, Ill.; m. Bryna McAnuff; ed Woburn Collegiate; trained under drama coach Basya Hunter, Toronto; raised in Scarborough, Toronto; worked with Toronto Free Theatre as dir of several plays; moved to New York City, where he co-

f. Dodger Theatre Co. 1978, directed first production, Gimme Shelter; directed for American Repertory Theatre at Harvard, also Yale Rep; fmr faculty mem. Juilliard School; Artistic Dir La Jolla Playhouse (revived 1983)–2007, directed Romeo and Juliet, A Mad World, My Masters, Big River, As You Like It, The Seagull, The Matchmaker, A Walk in the Woods, Two Rooms, 80 Days, Macbeth, A Funny Thing Happened on the Way to the Forum, Twelfth Night, Three Sisters, Elmer Gantry, Much Ado About Nothing, The Who's Tommy, How to Succeed in Business Without Really Trying; Co-Artistic Dir Stratford Shakespeare Festival 2006–08, Artistic Dir 2008–12; also produced Tony award-winning revivals of Broadway classics, including Guys and Dolls, The Music Man, Into the Woods, 42nd Street, The King and I, and many others. Productions include: Big River (Tony Award for Best Dir—Musical) 1985, A Walk in the Woods 1988, The Gospel at Colonus 1988, Dangerous Games 1989, The Grapes of Wrath 1990, Prelude to a Kiss 1990, The Who's Tommy (Tony Award for Best Dir (Musical) 1993, Laurence Olivier Theatre Award for Best Dir of 1996 at Shaftesbury Theatre 1997) 1993, How to Succeed in Business Without Really Trying 1995, I Am My Own Wife 2003, Dracula, The Musical 2004, 700 Sundays 2004, Good Vibrations 2005, Jersey Boys 2005, The Farnsworth Invention 2007, Cry-Baby 2008. Films: Cousin Bette 1998, The Iron Giant (producer) 1999, The Adventures of Rocky and Bullwinkle 2000, Quills (exec. producer) 2000. Address: 375 Greenwich Street, New York, NY 10003, USA (office). Telephone: (212) 941-3867 (office). E-mail: mfrank@skunkincorporated.com (office).

MACAPAGAL ARROYO, Gloria, PhD; Philippine politician, economist, journalist and fmr head of state; b. 5 April 1947, San Juan; d. of the late Diosdado Pangan Macapagal (fmr Pres. of the Philippines) and Dr Evangelina Macaraeg Macapagal; m. Jose Miguel Tuason Arroyo 1968; two s. one d.; ed Assumption Convent, Georgetown Univ., Assumption Coll., Ateneo de Manila Univ., Univ. of the Philippines; Asst Prof., Ateneo de Manila Univ. 1977–87; Chair. Econs Dept, Assumption Coll. 1984–87; Prof., Univ. of the Philippines School of Econs 1977–87; Prof., Mary Knoll Coll., St Scholastica's Coll.; Asst Sec., Dept of Trade and Industry 1987–89, Under-Sec. 1989–92; Exec. Dir Garments and Textile Export Bd 1988–90; Senator 1992–98; Sec. Dept of Social Welfare and Devt 1998–2000; Vice-Pres. of Repub. 1998–2001, Pres. of the Philippines 2001–10 (re-elected 2004); Chair. and Pres. Univ. of the Philippines Health Maintenance Org. 1989–98; Exec. Dir Philippine Center for Econ. Devt 1994–98; Chair. Univ. of the Philippines Econ. Foundation 1994–98; mem. Presidential Task Force on Tax and Tariff Reforms 1994–98, Tech. Working Group of the Philippine Nat. Devt Plan for the 21st Century (Cttee on Nat. Framework for Regional Devt and Macroeconomics Framework for Devt Financing); mem. or fmr mem. Asscn for Philippines-China Understanding, Philippine Econs Soc., Georgetown Club of the Philippines, Concerned Women of the Philippines; arrested on corruption charges 2012, released on bail 2012, arrested on allegations of plunder 2012; Hon. LLD (La Trobe Univ.) 2000, (Waseda Univ.) 2002, (Fordham Univ.) 2003, (Old Dominion Univ.) 2003; Hon. DEcon (Tsinghua Univ.) 2001; Hon. DH (Mapua Inst. of Tech.) 2004; Hon. Community Coll. Assoc. Degree in Int. Relations (City Coll. of San Francisco) 2003; UPSE Fellowship 1970–71, Japan Foundation Grant 1976–77, Rockefeller Foundation Scholarship 1978–83, named Outstanding Senator and One of Asia's Most Powerful Women by Asiaweek, Woman of the Year by Catholic Educ. Asscn of the Philippines, Ulirang Ina, Ulirang Ina Awards Cttee 2001, Most Distinguished Alumna, Univ. of the Philippines Alumni Asscn 2001, Making a Difference for Women – Women of Distinction Award, Soroptimist International of the Philippines Region 2003, ranked by Forbes magazine amongst 100 Most Powerful Women (ninth) 2004, (fourth) 2005, (45th) 2006, (51st) 2007, (41st) 2008, (44th) 2009.

MacARTHUR, Dame Ellen Patricia, MBE, DBE; British yachtswoman; b. 8 July 1976, Whatstandwell, Derbyshire, England; d. of Ken MacArthur and Avril MacArthur; ed Anthony Gell School, Wirksworth; circumnavigated UK single-handed (youngest person to pass Yachtmaster Offshore Qualification) 1995; took part in Mini Transat race 1997; Class Winner Route du Rhum race 1999, 2002; second place in Vendée Globe Race (94 days' solo sailing, youngest woman to circumnavigate the globe single-handedly) 2001; set non-stop round the world record of 71 days, 14 hours, 18 minutes and 33 seconds 2005; f. Ellen MacArthur Cancer Trust 2003, Ellen MacArthur Foundation 2009; Chevalier, Légion d'honneur; BT/YJA Young Sailor of the Year 1995, Sailing's Young Hope (France) 1998, BT/YJA Yachtsman of the Year 1999, Cable Industry Outstanding Achievement Award, Women of the Year Awards 2001, Royal Geographical Soc. Discovery Award 2001, Walpole Medal of Excellence 2001, Pride of Britain Award 2001, Royal Inst. of Navigation Award 2001, Times Sportswoman of the Year 2001, Runner-up Sports Personality of the Year 2001, Int. Sailing Fed. World Sailor of the Year 2001. Publications: Taking on the World 2002, Race Against Time 2005, Full Circle 2010. Address: c/o Ellen MacArthur Foundation, The Sail Loft, 42 Medina Road, Cowes, Isle of Wight, PO31 7BX, England. E-mail: info@ellenmacarthur.com. Website: www.ellenmacarthurfoundation.org; www.ellenmacarthurcancertrust.org; www.ellenmacarthur.com

McASLAN, John Renwick, MA, RIBA, FRSA, FRIAS, FRICS, FICE; British architect; Executive Chairman, John McAslan + Partners; b. 16 Feb. 1954, Glasgow, Scotland; s. of Prof. T. Crawford and Jean Renwick McAslan; m. Dava Sagenkahn 1981; one s. two d.; ed Dunoon Grammar School, Dollar Acad., Univ. of Edin.; trained with Cambridge Seven Assocs, Boston, Mass. 1978–80; Richard Rogers and Partners, London 1980–84; Founding Partner and Dir Troughton McAslan (later John McAslan + Partners) 1984–96, Exec. Chair. 1996–; extensive int. teaching experience at architectural schools including Glasgow, Belfast, Cardiff, Dublin, Beijing, London, Edin., Mexico City, Sydney, Helsinki, Seoul, Tokyo 1990–; Chair. of numerous architectural award juries in UK 1990–; Visiting Prof., Univ. of Wales 1998–2001; Foundation Trustee, Whitechapel Art Gallery 1989–97; Founder John McAslan Family Trust, London 1997, Volubilis Foundation, Morocco 2001, RIBA/ICE McAslan Bursary 2004; External Examiner, various univs; Assoc. Int. mem. AIA; mem. Architectural Inst. of Japan; Architect of the Year Award, Civic Trust Award, RIBA Award for Architecture, Int. Brunel Award, Structural Steel Design Award, Royal Acad. of Arts Award, European Heritage Award, Architectural Inst. of Japan Award, AIA Merit Award. Publications include: more than 500 int. pubns on architectural work, including monographs and profiles. Leisure interests: travel, sport, jazz, blues and opera, spending time with family. Address: John McAslan + Partners, 7–9 William Road, London, NW1

3ER, England (office). Telephone: (20) 7313-6000 (office). Fax: (20) 7313-6001 (office). E-mail: j.mcaslan@mcaslan.co.uk (office). Website: www.mcaslan.co.uk (office).

McAULIFFE, Terence (Terry) Richard, JD; American lawyer and politician; Governor of Virginia; b. Syracuse, New York; m. Dorothy Swann; five c.; ed Catholic Univ. of America, Georgetown Law Center; mem. staff, Carter-Mondale Re-election Cttee; mem. Democratic Party, served in various positions including Finance Dir Democratic Nat. Cttee (DNC), Finance Dir Democratic Congressional Campaign Cttee, Nat. Finance Chair. Presidential Campaign of Dick Gephardt 1988, Nat. Co-Chair. Presidential Campaign Clinton–Gore 1996, Co-Chair. Presidential Inaugural Cttee 1997, Chair. DNC Convention, LA 2000, Chair. DNC 2001–05; Gov. of Virginia 2014–; cr. Hispanic Project, Women's Vote Center, Voting Rights Inst.; est. many cos in fields of banking, insurance, marketing and real estate; practising attorney. Publication: What a Party! My Life Among Democrats 2007. Address: Office of the Governor, Patrick Henry Building, 3rd Floor, 1111 East Broad Street, Richmond, VA 23219, USA (office). Telephone: (804) 786-2211 (office). Fax: (804) 371-6351 (office). E-mail: info@governor.virginia.gov (office). Website: www.governor.virginia.gov (office).

McAVOY, James; British actor; b. 21 April 1979, Glasgow, Scotland; s. of James McAvoy and Elizabeth McAvoy; m. Anne Marie Duff 2006; ed Royal Scottish Acad. of Music and Drama; BAFTA Orange Rising Star Award 2006. Films include: Regeneration 1997, Bright Young Things 2003, Inside I'm Dancing 2004 (Edinburgh Int. Festival Audience Award), Wimbledon 2004, Strings 2004, The Chronicles of Narnia: The Lion, the Witch and the Wardrobe 2005, The Last King of Scotland 2006, Penelope 2006, Burns 2006, Starter for Ten 2006, Becoming Jane 2007, Atonement 2007, Wanted 2008, The Last Station 2009, The Conspirator 2010, X-Men: First Class 2011, Welcome to the Punch 2013, Trance 2013, Filth (British Independent Film Award for Best Actor) 2013. Television includes: An Angel Passes By 1997, The Bill 1997, Lorna Doone 2000, Murder in Mind 2001, Band of Brothers 2001, Payment in Blood 2002, White Teeth 2002, Foyle's War 2002, Bollywood Queen 2002, Children of Dune 2003, State of Play 2003, Early Doors 2003, Shameless 2005, Macbeth 2005. Theatre includes: The Reel of the Hanged Man, Edinburgh 2000, Out in the Open, Hampstead Theatre 2001, Privates On Parade, Donmar Warehouse 2001–02, Breathing Corpses, Royal Court Theatre 2005, Three Days of Rain, Apollo Theatre 2009. Address: United Agents, 12–26 Lexington Street, London, W1F 0LE, England (office). Telephone: (20) 3214-0800 (office). Fax: (20) 3214-0801 (office). E-mail: info@unitedagents.co.uk (office). Website: unitedagents.co.uk (office).

McBRIDE, Christian; American jazz bass player; b. 31 May 1972, Philadelphia, Pa; s. of Lee Smith; ed High School for the Creative and Performing Arts, Philadelphia, Juilliard School, New York; began playing electric bass aged nine, followed by acoustic bass two years later; tour to Europe with Philadelphia Youth Orchestra 1989; travelling USA with classical jazz fusion group, Free Flight 1989; played with Bobby Watson, Freddie Hubbard 1990–93, Ray Brown and Jay Clayton 1991, Benny Green, Roy Hargrove, Joshua Redman, Diana Krall, Pat Metheny 1992, Joe Henderson, D'Angelo, Kathleen Battle, Herbie Hancock, Quincy Jones, Natalie Cole and Milt Jackson; signed to Verve Records 1994; joined George Duke's band 2002; f. own groups, including Christian McBride Band; soloist; Co-Dir The Jazz Museum, Harlem 2005–; Creative Chair for Jazz, Los Angeles Philharmonic Orchestra 2005–10; mem. Heaven on Earth 2009–; Scholarship to Juilliard School, named by Rolling Stone magazine "Hot Jazz Artist" of 1992, Jazz Journalists' Asscn Award for Bassist of the Year 2013. Commissions include: Bluesin' in Alphabet City by Jazz at Lincoln Center, performed by Wynton Marsalis with Lincoln Center Jazz Orchestra, The Movement, Revisited by the Portland (ME) Arts Soc. and Nat. Endowment for the Arts, written and arranged for quartet and 30-piece gospel choir 1998. Films include: Café Society 1995, Kansas City 1996. Recordings include: albums: Ray Brown's Super Bass 1989, Roy Hargrove's Public Eye 1990, Kenny Kirkland 1991, Joshua Redman 1993, Fingerpainting: The Music of Herbie Hancock 1997, Introducing Joshua Redman 1999, Bobby Hutcherson's Skyline 1999, Don Braden's Fire Within 1999, Sting's All This Time (CD, DVD and tour) 2001, George Duke's Face the Music 2002, The Good Feeling (Grammy Award for Best Large Jazz Ensemble Album 2012) 2011, People Music 2013, Out Here 2013; with Heaven on Earth: Heaven on Earth 2009; solo albums include: Gettin' To It 1994, Number Two Express 1996, A Family Affair 1998, Sci-Fi 2000, The Philadelphia Experiment 2001, Vertical Vision (with electrical quartet) 2003, Live at Tonic 2006, Conversations with Christian 2009, Kind of Brown (with Inside Straight) 2009. Address: c/o Andre Guess, GuessWorks, Inc., 89 Elm Street, Montclair, NJ 07042, USA (office). Telephone: (212) 863-9824 (office). Fax: (917) 591-5216 (office). E-mail: andre@guessworks.org (office); info@christianmcbride.com. Website: www.guessworksinc.com (office); www.christianmcbride.com.

McBRIDE, William Griffith, AO, CBE, MD, FRCOG, FRACOG, FRSM, MACT; Australian molecular biologist and medical practitioner; b. 25 May 1927, Sydney, NSW; s. of John McBride and Myrine Griffith; m. Patricia Glover 1957; two s. two d.; ed Canterbury Boys' High School, Sydney, Conservatorium of Music, Sydney, Univ. of London, UK, Univ. of Sydney; Medical Officer, St George Hosp. 1950, Consultant Obstetrician and Gynaecologist 1958; Medical Officer, Launceston Gen. Hosp. 1951; Medical Officer, Women's Hosp., Sydney 1952–53, Medical Supt 1955–57, Consultant Obstetrician 1966–83; Consultant Obstetrician, Bankstown Hosp., Sydney 1957–66; Consultant Obstetrician and Gynaecologist, Royal Hosp. for Women 1983–88; Consultant, L.B. Johnson Tropical Medicine Center, American Samoa 1998–; Govt of Solomon Islands Medical Services (for AUSAID) from 1999; Examiner in Obstetrics and Gynaecology, Univs of Sydney and New South Wales; Fellow of the Senate, Univ. of Sydney 1974–90, mem. Faculty of Medicine, Univ. of Sydney 1966–90; mem. WHO Cttee on Safety of Contraceptives 1971; Founding Dir Foundation 41 Research Lab. 1972–93; allegations of scientific fraud relating to anti-nausea drug, Debendox in 1987 led to his being struck off 1993, charges of misconduct in his obstetrics practice were dismissed and he was reinstated 1998; Dir Australian Opera 1979–82, mem. Australian Opera Council 1984–; Hereford cattle judge, West Midlands Show 1988; mem. AAAS American Coll. of Toxicologists, Soc. for Risk Analysis, New York Acad. of Sciences; Man of the Year 1962, Australian of the Year 1962, Gold Medal and BP Prize, L'Institut de la Vie 1971, Father of the Year 1972. Achievements include: discovered that thalidomide caused birth defects (Lancet 1961), that thalidomide is a mutagen (British Medical Journal 1994); showed that radioactive labelled thalidomide binds with DNA in rats 1997. *Publications:* Killing the Messenger 1994, Pharmacology & Toxicology 1999; more than 100 papers in medical and scientific journals. *Leisure interests:* surfing, tennis, riding, golf, breeder of Hereford cattle. *Address:* 11 Waratah Street, Mona Vale 2103; 95 Elizabeth Bay Road, Elizabeth Bay, NSW 2011, Australia. *Telephone:* (2) 9368-7808. *Fax:* (2) 9368-7807.

McBRIDE, William James (Willie-John), MBE; British fmr bank manager and fmr rugby union player; b. 6 June 1940, Toomebridge, Northern Ireland; s. of William James McBride and Irene Patterson; m. Penny Michael 1966; one s. one d.; ed Ballymena Acad.; first played rugby for Ireland against England 1962; six Lions tours, S. Africa 1962, NZ 1966, S. Africa 1968, NZ 1971, S. Africa 1974, Capt. unbeaten Lions 1974, Man. Lions 1983 NZ; holder of 63 int. caps; 17 Test appearances for Lions (record); toured Australia 1967 and Argentina 1970 for Ireland; fmr Bank Man.; Pres. Ballymena RFC; Pres. Wooden Spoon Soc. (Ulster); Vice-Pres. Northern Ireland Riding for Disabled; Freeman Borough of Newtownabbey; Int. Rugby Hall of Fame 1997; Dr hc (Nat. Univ. of Ireland) 2004. *Leisure interests:* golf, gardening, after-dinner speaking. *Address:* Gorse Lodge, 105 Ballycorr Road, Ballyclare, Co. Antrim, BT39 9DE, Northern Ireland. *Telephone:* (28) 9335-2710. *Fax:* (28) 9335-2710.

McBRIEN, Rev. Richard Peter, MA, STD; American theologian and academic; *Crowley-O'Brien Professor of Theology, University of Notre Dame;* b. 19 Aug. 1936, Hartford, Conn.; s. of the late Thomas H. McBrien and Catherine Botticelli; ed St Thomas Seminary, Bloomfield, Conn., St John Seminary, Brighton, Mass, Pontifical Gregorian Univ., Rome, Italy; Prof. of Theology and Dean of Studies Pope John XXIII Nat. Seminary, Weston, Mass 1965–70; Prof., Boston Coll., Newton, Mass 1970–80; Chair. Dept of Theology, Univ. of Notre Dame, Ind. 1980–91, Crowley-O'Brien Prof. of Theology 1980–; Hon. DLitt (Quincy Coll., Ill.) 1989, Hon. DD (Muhlenberg Coll., Pa) 1997, Hon. DHumLitt (Coll. of Liberal Arts & Sciences, DePaul Univ., Chicago) 2008; John Courtney Murray Award, Catholic Theology Soc. of America 1976. *Publications:* Do We Need the Church? 1969, Church: The Continuing Quest 1970, The Remaking of the Church 1973, Catholicism (two vols) (Christopher Award 1981) 1980, Caesar's Coin: Religion and Politics in America 1987, Report on the Church: Catholicism after Vatican II 1992, Catholicism (new edn) 1994, The HarperCollins Encyclopedia of Catholicism (Gen. Ed.) 1995, 101 Questions and Answers on the Church 1996, Lives of the Saints: From Mary and St Francis of Assisi to John XXIII and Mother Teresa 2001, Lives of the Popes: The Pontiffs from St Peter to Benedict XVI 2006, The Church: The Evolution of Catholicism 2008. *Leisure interests:* reading, films. *Address:* Department of Theology, University of Notre Dame, 130 Malloy Hall, Notre Dame, IN 46556, USA (office). *Telephone:* (574) 631-5151 (office). *Fax:* (574) 631-4169 (office). *E-mail:* rmcbrien@nd.edu (office). *Website:* theology.nd.edu/people/all/mcbrien-richard-p (office).

McCABE, Eamonn Patrick; British photographer; b. 28 July 1948; s. of James McCabe and Celia McCabe; m. 1st Ruth Calvert 1972 (divorced 1993); one s.; m. 2nd Rebecca Smithers 1997; one d.; ed Challoner School, Finchley and San Francisco State Coll., USA; began career as photographer with Physics Dept, Imperial Coll., London; fmr freelance photographer for local papers and The Guardian for one year; staff photographer, The Observer 1977–86, 1987–88; Official Photographer, Pope's Visit to Britain 1982; Picture Ed. Sportsweek 1986–87, The Guardian 1988–2001; freelance photographer 2001–; Dir Newscast 2001–; Fellow in Photography, Nat. Museum of Photography and TV, Bradford 1988; Hon. Prof., Thames Valley Univ. 1994; Sports Photographer of the Year, Royal Photographic Soc. and Sports Council 1978, 1979, 1981, 1984, News Photographer of the Year, British Press Awards 1985, Picture Ed. of the Year, Nikon Press Awards (six times from 1992). *Publications:* Sports Photographer 1981, Eamonn McCabe, Photographer 1987, Emerald Gems of Ireland 2001, Making of Great Photographs 2005, Artists and Their Studios 2008. *Leisure interests:* playing tennis, squash, cinema. *Address:* c/o The Guardian, Kings Place, 90 York Way, London, N1 9GU, England. *Telephone:* (20) 7278-2332. *Website:* www.guardian.co.uk.

McCABE, John, CBE, MusB, FRNCM, FLCM, FRCM, RAM, FTCL; British pianist and composer; b. 21 April 1939, Huyton, Lancs. (now Merseyside); s. of Frank McCabe and Elisabeth McCabe (née Herlitzius); m. 1st Hilary Tann 1968 (divorced 1974); m. 2nd Monica Smith 1974; ed Liverpool Inst. High School for Boys, Manchester Univ., Royal Manchester Coll. of Music, Staatliche Hochschule für Musik, Munich; pianist-in-residence, University Coll., Cardiff 1965–68; Pres. Inc. Soc. of Musicians 1983–84; Dir London Coll. of Music 1983–90; Chair. Asscn of Professional Composers 1985–86; travels world-wide as pianist-composer; Hon. DPhil (Thames Valley) 2001; Royal Manchester Inst. Medal 1962, Royal Philharmonic Prize 1962, Special Citation, Koussevitzky Recording Foundation 1974, Award for service to British music, Composers Guild 1975. *Compositions include:* The Chagall Windows, Variations on a theme of Hartmann, Notturni ed Alba, Concerto for Orchestra, Cloudcatcher Fells, Fire at Durilgai, Canyons, Edward II (ballet), Arthur, Part I: Arthur Pendragon, Arthur, Part II: Le Morte d'Arthur (ballets), plus other stage works, symphonies, concertos, much orchestral and chamber music, vocal works and keyboard music; numerous piano recordings including complete piano works of Haydn and Nielsen. *Publications:* Rachmaninov, Bartok's Orchestral Music, Haydn's Piano Sonatas, Alan Rawsthorne: Portrait of a Composer and numerous articles on music. *Leisure interests:* books, films, cricket, snooker. *Address:* c/o Novello and Co. Ltd, Music Sales, 8/9 Frith Street, London, W1V 5TZ, England (office). *Telephone:* (20) 7434-0066. *Fax:* (20) 7287-6329. *E-mail:* promotion@musicsales.co.uk. *Website:* www.johnmccabe.com.

McCABE, Patrick; Irish writer; b. 27 March 1955, Clones, Co. Monaghan; m. Margot Quinn 1981; two d.; ed St Patrick's Teacher Training Coll., Dublin; fmr teacher of disabled children; Irish Press Hennessy Award 1979, Sunday Independent Arts Award. *Play:* has written plays for BBC radio, Frank Pig Says Hello (stage play, based on novel The Butcher Boy). *Film screenplay:* The Butcher Boy (co-writer). *Publications include:* The Adventures of Shay Mouse 1985, Music on Clinton Street 1986, Carn 1989, The Butcher Boy (Irish Times/Aer Lingus Fiction Prize) 1992, Frank Pig Says Hello (play based on The Butcher Boy) 1992, The Dead School 1995, Breakfast on Pluto 1997, Mondo Desperado 1998, Emerald Gems of Ireland 2000, Call Me the Breeze 2003, Winterwood (Hughes and Hughes/Irish

Independent Irish Novel of the Year 2007) 2006, The Holy City 2009, The Stray Sod Country 2010; Contrib. to anthologies, periodicals. *Leisure interests:* cinema, music. *Address:* 11 Fermanagh Terrace, Clones, Co. Monaghan, Ireland.

McCAFFREY, Gen. (retd) Barry R., MA; American army officer (retd), academic, news analyst and consultant; *President, BR McCaffrey Associates LLC;* b. 17 Nov. 1942, Taunton, Mass.; m. Jill Ann Faulkner 1964; one s. two d.; ed Phillips Acad., Mass, US Mil. Acad., American Univ., Harvard Univ., Western Behavioral Science Inst., Nat. Defense Univ., Command and Gen. Staff Coll., Army War Coll.; commissioned into US Army 1964; served in Viet Nam 1966–67, 1968–69; Asst Prof. of Social Sciences, Dept of Social Sciences, US Mil. Acad. 1972–75, currently Adjunct Prof. of Int. Affairs; 3rd Infantry Div., Germany 1979–83; Div. Chief of Staff 9th Infantry Div. 1982–86; Asst Commandant US Army Infantry School 1986–88; US Deputy Mil. Rep. to NATO 1988–89; Prin. Staff Asst to Chair. of Jt Chiefs of Staff, Chief of Strategic Planning 1989–90; 24th Infantry Div. 1990–92; led div. into Iraq in Operation Desert Storm 1991; fmr Commdr-in-Chief US Armed Forces Southern Command; at retirement youngest four-star Gen. in Army and most highly decorated combat officer; Dir White House Office of Nat. Drug Control Policy 1996–2001; fmr mem. prin. negotiation team START II Nuclear Arms Control Treaty; mem. Nat. Security Council, Council on Foreign Relations, Nat. Asscn for Advancement of Colored People; Pres. B. R. McCaffrey Associates; currently NBC News analyst on terrorism; decorations from France, Brazil, Argentina, Colombia, Peru, and Venezuela; Distinguished Service Cross (twice), Silver Star (twice), Distinguished Service Medal, Combat Infantry Badge, US Health and Human Services Lifetime Achievement Award For Extraordinary Achievement in the Field of Substance Abuse Prevention 2004, recognized as one of the 500 Most Influential People in American Foreign Policy by World Affairs Councils of America 2004, US Dept of State Superior Honor Award for the Strategic Arms Limitation Talks, CIA Great Seal Medallion, US Coast Guard Distinguished Public Service Award, NAACP Roy Wilkins Renown Service Award, Norman E. Zinberg Award of the Harvard Medical School, Fed. Law Enforcement Foundation Nat. Service Award, Community Anti-Drug Coalitions of America Lifetime Achievement Award, Nat. Leadership Award by Community Anti-Drug Coalitions of America 2007, Golden Eagle, Soc. of American Mil. Engineers (SAME) 2007, inducted into US Army Ranger Hall of Fame 2007, American Red Cross Lifetime of Achievement Award, Air Force Asscn W. Stuart Symington Award. *Television:* appeared in over 6,000 TV interviews; media coverage includes Meet the Press, This Week, Fox Sunday News, Nightline, Today, Good Morning America, John McLaughlin's One on One, numerous feature interviews on CBS Evening News, NBC Nightly News, on World News, on PBS, on CNN, Montel Williams, Charlie Rose, Diane Rehm on NPR, C-Span Washington Journal. *Publications:* Proceedings of the Twenty-Fifth Student Conference on United States Affairs 1973, We Are Soldiers All: An Analysis of Possible Roles for Women in the Army 1973, numerous articles on mil. subjects, drugs law enforcement and money laundering. *Leisure interests:* hunting, reading military history. *Address:* BR McCaffrey Associates LLC, 2900 South Quincy Street, Suite 300A, Arlington, VA 22206, USA (office). *Telephone:* (703) 824-5160 (office). *Fax:* (703) 671-6318 (office). *E-mail:* brm@mccaffreyassociates.com (office). *Website:* www.mccaffreyassociates.com (office).

McCAIN, John Sidney, III, DFC; American politician and fmr naval officer; *Senator from Arizona;* b. 29 Aug. 1936, Panama Canal Zone, Panama; s. of John Sidney McCain, Jr and Roberta McCain (née Wright); m. 1st Carol Shepp 1965 (divorced 1980); one d. two adopted s.; m. 2nd Cindy Lou Hensley 1980; two s. one d. one adopted d.; ed US Naval Acad. and Nat. War Coll., Washington, DC; served in USN 1958–81, prisoner of war in Viet Nam 1967–73; promoted to Capt. 1977; Dir Navy Senate Liaison Office, Washington, DC 1977–81; mem. Bd of Dirs Community Assistance League, Phoenix 1981–82; mem. US House of Reps from 1st Ariz. Dist 1983–86; Senator from Arizona 1987–, Ranking Mem. Armed Services Cttee, mem. Health, Educ., Labor, and Pensions Cttee, Cttee on Homeland Security and Governmental Affairs, Cttee on Indian Affairs; unsuccessful campaign for Republican nomination for US Pres. 2000; unsuccessful Republican cand. for US Pres. 2008; f. Country First PAC 2009; Chair. Int. Republican Inst. 1993–; Republican; various decorations, including Legion of Merit, Silver Star, Purple Heart, Vietnamese Legion of Honour; Dr hc (Johns Hopkins Univ.) 1999, (Colgate Univ.) 2000, (Univ. of Pennsylvania) 2001, (Wake Forest Univ.) 2002, (Univ. of Southern California) 2004. *Publication:* Faith of My Fathers (with Mark Salter) 1999, Worth the Fighting For: A Memoir 2002, Why Courage Matters: The Way to a Braver Life 2004, Character is Destiny 2005, Hard Call (with Mark Salter) 2007. *Address:* 241 Russell Senate Office Building, Washington, DC 20510, USA (office). *Telephone:* (202) 224-2235 (office). *Fax:* (202) 228-2862 (office). *Website:* mccain.senate.gov (office); www.countryfirstpac.com.

McCALL, Carolyn, OBE, BA, MA; British business executive; *CEO, easyJet plc;* b. 13 Sept. 1961; m.; three c.; ed Univs of Kent and London; teacher, Holland Park School 1982–84; Risk Analyst, Costain Group PLC 1984–86; Planner, Guardian Newspapers Ltd (GNL) 1986–88, Advertisement Exec. 1988–89, Advertisement Man. 1989–91, Product Devt Man. 1991–92, Display Advertisement Man. 1992, Advertisement Dir Wired UK 1992–94, Deputy Advertisement Dir 1994–95, Advertisement Dir 1995–97, Commercial Dir 1997–98 (with responsibility for internet strategy – launched Guardian Unlimited 1999), Deputy Man. Dir 1998–2000, CEO of GNL 2000–06, and mem. Bd of Dirs Guardian Media Group PLC (GMG) 2000–10, Chief Exec. GMG 2006–10; CEO easyJet plc 2010–; Dir (nonexec.) New Look Group PLC 1999–2005, Tesco PLC 2005–08, Lloyds TSB 2008–09; Chair. Opportunity Now (gender equality and diversity org.) 2005–08; fmr Pres. Women in Advertising and Communications London; Trustee, Tools for Schools (educational charity) 2000–05; Veuve Clicquot Business Woman of the Year 2008, ranked by Fortune magazine amongst the 50 Most Powerful Women in Business outside the US (35th) 2012. *Address:* easyJet plc, Hanger 89, Luton Airport, Luton, Beds., LU2 9PF, England (office). *E-mail:* info@easyjet.com (office). *Website:* www.easyjet.com (office).

McCALL SMITH, Alexander, CBE; British writer and academic; *Professor Emeritus of Medical Law, University of Edinburgh;* b. 1948, Southern Rhodesia (now Zimbabwe); m. Elizabeth Parry; two d.; currently Emer. Prof. of Medical Law, Univ. of Edinburgh; fmr mem. Human Genetics Comm. (fmr Vice-Chair.), UNESCO Int. Bioethics Comm., British Medical Journal Ethics Cttee (fmr

Chair.), Roslin Inst. Ethics Cttee (fmr Chair.); Hon. DIur (Edinburgh) 2007; British Book Awards Author of the Year 2004, Booksellers' Asscn Author of the Year 2004, Waterstones Author of the Year 2004. *Publications:* fiction: The No. 1 Ladies' Detective Agency 1998, Tears of the Giraffe 2000, Morality for Beautiful Girls 2001, The Kalahari Typing School for Men 2002, The Full Cupboard of Life (Saga Award for Wit) 2003, At the Villa of Reduced Circumstances 2003, Portuguese Irregular Verbs 2003, In the Company of Cheerful Ladies 2004, 44 Scotland Street (serialized in The Scotsman) 2004, The Sunday Philosophy Club 2004, The 2½ Pillars of Wisdom 2004, Friends, Lovers, Chocolate 2005, Blue Shoes and Happiness 2006, Dream Angus: The Celtic God of Dreams 2006, Love Over Scotland 2007, The World According to Bertie 2007, The Right Attitude to Rain 2007, The Careful Use of Compliments 2007, The Miracle at Speedy Motors 2008, Corduroy Mansions 2008, Tea Time for the Traditionally Built 2009, The Unbearable Lightness of Scones 2009, La's Orchestra Saves the World 2009, The Comfort of Saturdays 2009, The Lost Art of Gratitude 2010, The Double Comfort Safari Club 2010, The Charming Quirks of Others 2010, The Forgotten Affairs of Youth 2011, The Dog Who Came in From the Cold 2012, The Great Cake Mystery 2012, The Limpopo Academy of Private Detection 2012; non-fiction: Law and Medical Ethics (with J. K. Mason) 1983, The Duty to Rescue: The Jurisprudence of Aid (with Michael A. Menlowe) 1993, Forensic Aspects of Sleep (with C. Shapiro) 1997, Justice and the Prosecution of Old Crimes: Balancing Legal, Psychological, and Moral Concerns (with Daniel W. Shuman) 2000, The Criminal Law of Botswana; children's fiction includes: White Hippo 1980, The Perfect Hamburger 1982, Jeffrey's Joke Machine 1990, The Five Lost Aunts of Harriet Bean 1990, Marzipan Max 1991, Uncle Gangster 1991, The Spaghetti Tangle 1992, Harriet Bean and the League of Cheats 1991, The Ice-Cream Bicycle 1992, Akimbo and the Lions 1992, The Doughnut Ring 1992, Springy Jane 1992, The Princess Trick 1992, The Cowgirl Aunt of Harriet Bean 1993, My Chameleon Uncle 1993, The Muscle Machine 1993, Paddy and the Ratcatcher 1994, The Banana Machine 1994, Akimbo and the Crocodile Man 1995, Billy Rubbish 1995, The Watermelon Boys 1996, Calculator Annie 1996, The Bubblegum Tree 1996, Bursting Balloons Mystery 1997, The Popcorn Pirates 1999, Chocolate Money Mystery 1999, Precious and the Puggles 2010; short story collections: Children of Wax: African Folk Tales 1991, Heavenly Date and Other Stories (revised edn as Heavenly Date: And Other Flirtations) 1995, The Girl Who Married a Lion (short stories) 2004, One City (contrib.) 2006. *Address:* c/o David Higham Associates, 5–8 Lower John Street, Golden Square, London, W1F 9HA, England (office). *Website:* www.alexandermccallsmith.co.uk.

McCALLISTER, Michael (Mike) B., BA, MBA; American business executive; *Chairman, Humana Incorporated;* b. 1952, Shreveport, La; ed Pepperdine Univ., Louisiana Tech. Univ.; joined Humana Inc. 1974, various positions including finance specialist, Vice-Pres. Health Plans and Hosps, Ariz. 1989–92, Vice-Pres. Health Plans and Hosps, Tex. 1992–96, Pres. Tex., Fla and Puerto Rico Div. 1996–97, Sr Vice-Pres. Health Plan Div. 1997–99, apptd to Office of the Chair. 1999–2000, Pres. and CEO 2000–10, Chair. and CEO 2010–12, Chair. 2013–; Founding Chair. World Wellness Alliance 2010–; mem. Bd Greater Louisville Health Enterprises Network, Louisville Fund for the Arts, Business Roundtable, American Asscn of Health Plans; mem. Advisory Bd Coll. of Admin and Business, Louisiana Tech. Univ.; Tower Medallion Award, Louisiana Tech. Univ. 2003. *Address:* Humana Inc., 500 West Main Street, Louisville, KY 40202, USA (office). *Telephone:* (502) 580-1000 (office). *Fax:* (502) 580-3677 (office). *E-mail:* info@humana.com (office). *Website:* www.humana.com (office).

McCALLUM, Martin, FRSA; British theatre producer; b. 6 April 1950, Blackpool, Lancs., England; s. of Raymond McCallum and Jessie McCallum; m. 1st Lesley Nunnerley 1971 (divorced); one s. one d.; m. 2nd Julie Edmett (divorced); one d.; m. 3rd Mary Ann Rolfe (divorced); two s.; ed Barfield School, Surrey, Frensham Heights School, Surrey; began career as student Asst Stage Man., Castle Theatre, Farnham Surrey 1967; worked as actor, stage man., lighting and sound technician; Production Man. Nat. Theatre at Old Vic (with Laurence Olivier and later Peter Hall) 1971–78; Founder Production Office West End 1978–84, productions included Filumena, Evita, Sweeney Todd; consultant to Glyndebourne Festival Opera, Arts Council's Regional Theatre Scheme; Man. Dir Cameron Mackintosh Ltd 1981–2000, Vice-Chair. 2000–03; Dir Donmar Warehouse Theatre 1992–2006, Chair. 1996–2004; initiated Wyndham Report 1998; est. New Writing Symposium 1999; Pres. Soc. of London Theatre 1999–2002; initiated inaugural jt Theatre Conf. of SOLT/TMA/ITC Theatre 2001 Future Directions; mem. League of American Theatres and Producers 1988–2010, Drama Panel, Arts Council of England 1999–2004, Cultural Strategy Group London 2000–04; mem. V&A Theatre Museum Cttee 1999–2004; consultant on design projects including Old Fire Station Theatre, Oxford (new build), Prince Edward Theatre (restoration) 1993, Musical Hall, Stuttgart (new build) 1994, Capital Theatre, Sydney (restoration) 1995, Musical Theatre, Duisberg (new build) 1996, Theatre Royal, Sydney (restoration) 1998, Wales Millennium Centre, Lyric Theatre (new build study) 1998, Auditorium Theatre, Chicago (restoration) 2001, Schaumburg Village Theatre, Illinois (new build) 2003, Fine Arts Building Theatre, Chicago (restoration study) 2003, Prince of Wales Theatre, London (restoration) 2003, Montecasino Theatre, Johannesburg, SA 2007 (new build scheme); Dir Sydney Theatre Co. 2005–; Co-Producer Matthew Bourne's dance production of Edward Scissorhands, London 2005; Exec. Producer Spider-Man Broadway 2010; New York Drama Desk Award 2007. *Leisure interests:* performing arts, music, art, gardens. *Telephone:* 401-279464 (mobile) (office). *E-mail:* martin@sunriseroad.com (office).

McCANDLESS, Bruce, II, BS, MS, MBA; American scientist, business executive and astronaut (retd); *Chief Scientist, Reusable Space Transportation Systems, Lockheed Martin Space Systems Company;* b. (Byron Willis McCandless), 8 June 1937, Boston, Mass; s. of Rear-Adm. Bruce McCandless and Sue W. B. McCandless Inman; m. Alfreda Bernice Doyle 1960; one s. one d.; ed Woodrow Wilson Senior High School, Long Beach, Calif., US Naval Acad., Stanford Univ., Univ. of Houston-Clear Lake; flight training, Pensacola, Fla and Kingsville, Tex.; weapons system and carrier landing training, Key West, Fla 1960; carrier duty, Fighter Squadron 102 1960–64; instrument flight instructor, Attack Squadron 43, Naval Air Station, Apollo Soucek Field, Oceana, Va; graduate studies in electrical eng, Stanford Univ. –1966; selected by NASA as astronaut April 1966; Co-investigator, Astronaut Manoeuvring Unit Experiment on Skylab 1968–74; back-up crew for first Skylab Mission 1973; Mission Specialist on STS-11, first flight of manned manoeuvring unit; Mission Specialist on STS-31, Hubble Space Telescope deployment; performed, with Col Robert L. Stewart, first untethered spacewalk during the STS-41B mission 7 Feb. 1984; retd from Navy as Capt. Aug. 1990; Man. Payload Systems and Tech., Lockheed Martin Astronautics Group and Vice-Pres. Lockheed Martin Overseas Corpn 1990–; Prin. Staff Engineer, Lockheed Martin Astronautics 1990–97; Chief Scientist, Reusable Space Transportation Systems 1997–; mem. US Naval Acad. Alumni Asscn (Class of 1958), US Naval Inst., IEEE, AIAA, Asscn for Computing Machinery, Nat. Audubon Soc. (fmr Pres. Houston Audubon Soc.); Fellow, American Astronautical Soc.; V.A. Prather Award, American Astronautical Soc. 1975, 1985, NASA Space Flight Medal 1984, 1991, Smithsonian Inst. Nat. Air and Space Museum Trophy 1985, Nat. Aeronautical Asscn Collier Trophy 1985, NASA Exceptional Eng Achievement Medal 1985, Defense Distinguished Service Medal 1985, Legion of Merit 1988, US Astronaut Hall of Fame 2005. *Television:* Horizon (series documentary) 1990, Max Q: Emergency Landing (film) (tech. adviser) 1998, When We Left Earth: The NASA Missions (mini-series documentary) 2008–09, NASA: Triumph and Tragedy (series documentary) 2009. *Leisure interests:* electronics, scuba diving, sailing, photography, cross country skiing. *Address:* Lockheed Martin Space Systems Company, 12257 South Wadsworth Blvd., Littleton, CO 80125-8500 (office); Mail Stop DC 3005, Lockheed Martin Astronautics, PO Box 179, Denver, CO 80201 (office); 21852 Pleasant Park Road, Conifer, CO 80433-6802, USA (home). *Telephone:* (303) 971-6308 (office). *Fax:* (303) 971-7698 (office). *E-mail:* brucemcc@logcabin.com (home); bruce.mccandless@lmco.com (office). *Website:* www.lockheedmartin.com (office).

McCANN, Renetta, BS; American advertising executive; *Chief Talent Officer (US), Leo Burnett Group;* b. 8 Dec. 1956, Chicago, Ill.; d. of Aditha Lorraine Collymore Walker; m.; two c.; ed Aquinas Dominican High School and Northwestern Univ.; joined Leo Burnett advertising agency as client service trainee 1978–79, Media Supervisor 1979–88, Vice-Pres. 1988–89, Media Dir 1989–95, Sr Vice-Pres. 1995–98, Man. Dir Starcom 1998, CEO Starcom MediaVest Group Americas (following merger with D'Arcy) –2005, CEO Starcom MediaVest Group Worldwide 2005–08, Head of Talent Devt Platform, VivaKi (subsidiary of Publicis Groupe) 2008, Chief Talent Officer (US), Leo Burnett Group 2012–; mem. Bd of Dirs Chicago Shakespeare Theater 2011–, Women's Initiative 2011–; mem. Advisory Bd Genius in Motion 2011–, Center for Excellence in Advertising 2011–; Trustee, Ancona School 2011; winner of numerous Effies and Cannes Lions, chosen as 'Media Maven' by Advertising Age 1991, selected as one of Ebony magazine's 57 Most Intriguing Blacks, named by Black Enterprise as Executive of the Year 2002, selected by Women's Advertising Club of Chicago as Advertising Woman of the Year 2002, named by Essence magazine as one of 50 Women Who Are Changing The World, ranked by Forbes magazine amongst Most Powerful Women (27th) 2006, (41st) 2007. *Address:* Leo Burnett Group, 35 West Wacker Drive, Chicago, IL, 60601, USA. *Telephone:* (312) 220-5959 (office). *Website:* www.leoburnett.us/chicago (office).

McCARRICK, HE Cardinal Theodore Edgar, BA, MA, DD, PhD; American ecclesiastic; *Archbishop Emeritus of Washington;* b. 7 July 1930, New York, NY; ed St Joseph's Seminary, Yonkers, New York, Catholic Univ. of America; ordained priest 1958; Auxiliary Bishop of New York 1977; Bishop of Metuchen 1981; Archbishop of Newark 1986–2000; Archbishop of Washington 2001–06, Archbishop Emer. 2006–; Cardinal Priest of the Titulus Ss Nerei et Achillei 2001; Pres. Papal Foundation 1997–; Chancellor The Catholic Univ. of America 2001–06; Pres. Bd of Trustees, Basilica of the Nat. Shrine of the Immaculate Conception; mem. US Sec. of State's Advisory Cttee on Religious Freedom Abroad 1996–99, US Comm. for Int. Religious Freedom 1999–2001; Distinguished Visiting Scholar, Library of Congress 2011–; Order of Cedars of Lebanon 2000; 35 hon. degrees 1976–2010; Eleanor Roosevelt Award for Human Rights 2000. *Address:* Archdiocese of Washington Pastoral Center, 5001 Eastern Avenue, PO Box 29260, Washington, DC 20017-0260, USA (office). *Telephone:* (301) 853-4500 (office). *Website:* www.adw.org (office).

McCARTHY, Sir Callum, PhD; British civil servant, economist and banker; b. 29 Feb. 1944, Brentwood, Essex; s. of Ralph McCarthy and Agnes Graham; m. Penelope Ann Gee 1966; two s. one d.; ed Univs of Oxford and Stirling, Business School, Stanford Univ., USA; econ. and operations researcher ICI 1965; Prin. Pvt. Sec. to Roy Hattersley (q.v.) and Norman Tebbit (q.v.), Dept of Trade and Industry 1972–85, also Under-Sec.; Dir of Corp. Finance, Kleinwort Benson 1985–89; Man. Dir, Head of Corp. Finance, BZW 1989–93; CEO Barclays Bank Group Japan and N America 1993–98; Dir-Gen. of UK Gas Supply 1998–2003; Dir-Gen. of UK Electricity Supply 1999–2003; Chair. Gas and Electricity Markets Authority 2000–03; Chief Exec. Ofgem 2000–03; Chair. Financial Services Authority 2003–08; Hon. Fellow, Merton Coll., Oxford 2006, Freeman, City of London 2008; Dr hc (Stirling Univ.) 2004. *Publication:* Introduction to Technological Economics (with D. S. Davies) 1967. *Leisure interests:* walking, reading, beekeeping. *Address:* c/o Financial Services Authority, 25 The North Colonnade, Canary Wharf, London, E14 5HS, England.

McCARTHY, Cormac; American writer; b. 20 July 1933, Rhode Island; s. of Charles Joseph McCarthy and Gladys McGrail; m. 1st Lee Holleman 1961 (divorced); one s.; m. 2nd Annie DeLisle (divorced); m. 3rd Jennifer Winkley 1998; ed Univ. of Tennessee; served in USAF 1953–57; MacArthur Fellowship 1981; Guggenheim Fellowship; Rockefeller Fellowship; PEN/Saul Bellow Award for Lifetime Achievement 2009. *Play:* The Stonemason 1994. *Film:* The Counselor (screenplay) 2013. *Publications:* novels: The Orchard Keeper 1965, Outer Dark 1968, Child of God 1973, Suttree 1979, Blood Meridian 1985, All the Pretty Horses (Vol. 1 of The Bouden Trilogy) 1992, The Crossing (Vol. 2 of The Bouden Trilogy) 1994, Cities of the Plain (Vol. 3 of The Bouden Trilogy) 1998, No Country for Old Men 2005, The Road (James Tait Black Memorial Prize for Fiction 2007, Pulitzer Prize for Fiction 2007, Quill Award for General Fiction 2007) 2006. *Address:* c/o Amanda Urban, International Creative Management, 730 Fifth Avenue, New York, NY 10019, USA (office); c/o Santa Fe Institute, 1399 Hyde Park Road, Santa Fe, NM 87501, USA.

McCARTHY, Gina, BA, MS; American government official; *Administrator, Environmental Protection Agency;* b. 1954, Massachusetts; m. Kenneth McCarey; one s. two d.; ed Univ. of Massachusetts, Tufts Univ.; mem. Hazardous Waste Facility Site Safety Council, Mass Exec. Office of Environmental Affairs 1985–90,

Council Chair. 1990–94, Exec. Dir, Admin. Council 1994–99, Asst Sec. for pollution prevention, environmental business and tech. 1999–2003, Under-Sec. for Policy 2003; Deputy Sec. for Operations, Mass Office of Commonwealth Devt 2003–04; Commr, Conn. Dept of Environmental Protection 2004–09; Asst Admin. for air and radiation, Environmental Protection Agency (EPA), Washington, DC 2009–13, Admin., EPA 2013–; Chair. The Climate Registry. *Address:* Environmental Protection Agency, 1200 Pennsylvania Avenue, NW, Washington, DC 20460, USA (office). *Telephone:* (202) 272-0167 (office). *Website:* www2.epa.gov/aboutepa/administrator-gina-mccarthy (office).

McCARTHY, James J., BS, PhD; American oceanographer and academic; *Professor of Biological Oceanography and Alexander Agassiz Professor of Biological Oceanography, Harvard University;* ed Gonzaga Univ., Scripps Inst. of Oceanography; Dir Museum of Comparative Zoology, Harvard Univ. 1982–2002, Acting Curator Malacology Dept, currently Prof. of Biological Oceanography and Alexander Agassiz Prof. of Biological Oceanography, holds faculty appointments in Dept of Organismic and Evolutionary Biology and Dept of Earth and Planetary Sciences, Head Tutor for degrees in Environmental Science and Public Policy, Master of Pforzheimer House; Chair. int. cttee that establishes research priorities and oversees implementation of Int. Geosphere – Biosphere Program 1986–93; has served and serves on numerous nat. and int. planning cttees, advisory panels and comms relating to oceanography, polar science and study of climate and global change; involved in two int. assessments on climate impacts; Co-Chair. Intergovernmental Panel on Climate Change (IPCC), Working Group II, for Third IPCC Assessment 2001; a lead author on Arctic Climate Impact Assessment; Vice-Chair. Northeast Climate Impacts Assessment 2007; Founding Ed. American Geophysical Union's Global Biogeochemical Cycles; Fellow, AAAS, Pres.-elect 2008–09, Pres. 2009–; Fellow, American Acad. of Arts and Sciences; Foreign mem. Royal Swedish Acad. of Sciences; David B. Stone Award, New England Aquarium. *Publications:* numerous scientific papers in professional journals on the regulation of plankton productivity in the sea. *Address:* 524 MCZ Labs, Museum of Natural History, Harvard University, 26 Oxford Street, Cambridge, MA 02138, USA (office). *Telephone:* (617) 495-2330 (office). *E-mail:* jmccarthy@oeb.harvard.edu (office). *Website:* www.oeb.harvard.edu/faculty/mccarthy/mccarthy-oeb.html (office); www.oeb.harvard.edu/faculty/mccarthy/McCarthyLab.html (office).

McCARTHY, John Philip, AO, MA, LLB; Australian lawyer and diplomatist; *National President, Australian Institute of International Affairs;* b. 29 Nov. 1942, Washington, DC, USA; s. of Edwin McCarthy and Marjorie McCarthy; two d.; ed Univ. of Cambridge, UK; practised as barrister in London, UK 1965–66; with Shearman and Sterling (law firm), New York, USA 1966–67; 1964; joined Dept of Foreign Affairs 1968; Second Sec., Vientiane 1969–72; First Sec., Washington, DC 1973–75; Chargé d'affaires a.i., Damascus 1977–78; Sr Pvt. Sec. to Minister for Foreign Affairs 1979–80; Amb. to Viet Nam 1981–83, to Mexico 1985–87, to Thailand 1992–94, to USA 1995–97, to Indonesia 1997–2000, to Japan 2001–05; High Commr in India and Amb. to Bhutan 2005–09, Special Rep. to Sri Lanka 2010; Deputy Sec. Dept of Foreign Affairs and Trade, Canberra 1994–95; Fellow, Australian Inst. of Int. Affairs 2009, Nat. Pres. 2010–. *Leisure interests:* skiing, Asian art, walking, travel. *Address:* Australian Institute of International Affairs, Stephen House, 32 Thesiger Court, Deakin, ACT 2600, Australia (office). *Telephone:* (2) 6282-2133 (office). *Fax:* (2) 6285-2334 (office). *E-mail:* ceo@aiia.asn.au (office). *Website:* www.aiia.asn.au (office).

McCARTHY, Paul; American artist; b. 1945, Salt Lake City; early work includes series of black paintings 1967–68; became known for visceral performances and film works 1970s; extended practice into stand-alone sculptural figures, installations and a series of large, inflatable sculptures 1990s; Tate Gallery Modern commissioned outdoor inflatable sculptures for North Landscape, London 2003. *Artistic Works include:* Blockhead, Tate Modern 2003, Daddies Bighead, Tate Modern 2003. *Recent Group Exhibitions include:* Stunt Videos, Tennis Palace City Art Museum, Helsinki (Finland) 2003, Spiritus, Magasin 3 Stockholm Konsthall (Sweden) 2003, Apparation, Kettle's Yard, Cambridge (UK) 2003, Spiritus, Douglas Hyde Gallery, Dublin (Ireland) 2003, Twilight, Gimpel Fils, London 2003, Sphere, Presentation House Gallery, Vancouver (Canada) 2003, From East to West, Gas Art Gallery, Torino (Italy) 2003, C'est arrive demain, Musée d'Art Contemporain, Lyon (France) 2004, Spiritus, Sundsvalls Museum, (Sweden) 2004, Partners, Haus der Kunst, Munich (Germany) 2004, Playlist, Palais de Tokyo, Paris (France) 2004, Point of View, Museum of Contemporary Art, NY 2004, Speaking with Hands, Guggenheim New York 2004, I am the Walrus, Chelm & Reid, NY 2004, Monument to Now, Deste Foundation Centre for Contemporary Art, Athina 2004. *Recent Solo Exhibitions include:* Retrospective, Museum of Contemporary Art, LA 2000, Retrospective, New Museum of Contemporary Art, NY 2001, Villa Arson (France) 2001, Tate Liverpool (UK) 2001, Stor retrospektiv, Museet for Samtidskunst, Oslo (Norway) 2003, Inaugural Show, Hauser & Wirth, London (UK) 2003, Painter 1995, Herzliya Museum of Art, Herzeliyya (Israel) 2004, Brain Box Dream Box, Stedelijk Van Abbemuseum (Netherlands) 2004. *Address:* c/o Luhring Augustine Gallery, 531 West 24th Street, New York, NY 10011, USA (office).

McCARTNEY, Rt Hon. Ian; British politician; b. 25 April 1951; s. of Hugh McCartney; m. 1st (divorced); two d. one s. (deceased); m. 2nd Ann Parkes; joined Labour Party 1966, Labour Party Organizer 1973–87; Councillor for Wigan Borough 1982–87; MP (Labour) for Makerfield 1987–2010; Opposition Spokesperson on NHS (Nat. Health Service) 1992–94, on Employment 1994–96, Chief Spokesperson on Employment 1996–97; Minister of State Dept of Trade and Industry 1997–99, Cabinet Office 1999–2001; Minister for Pensions Dept for Work and Pensions 2001–03; Minister without Portfolio, Chair. Labour Party 2003–06; Minister for Trade, FCO and Dept of Trade and Industry 2006–07; Minister to Watch, Spectator Awards 1999. *Leisure interests:* Rugby League (supports Wigan Warriors). *E-mail:* IanMcCartney@1makerfield.freeserve.co.uk.

McCARTNEY, Sir (James) Paul, Kt, MBE, FRCM; British singer, songwriter and musician (guitar, piano, organ); b. 18 June 1942, Liverpool, England; s. of James McCartney and Mary McCartney; m. 1st Linda Eastman 1969 (died 1998); one s. two d. one step-d.; m. 2nd Heather Mills 2002 (divorced 2008); one d.; m. 3rd Nancy Shevell 2011; ed Stockton Wood Road Primary School, Speke, Joseph Williams Primary School, Gateacre and Liverpool Inst.; wrote first song 1956, wrote numerous songs with John Lennon; joined pop group The Quarrymen 1956;

appeared under various titles until formation of The Beatles 1960; appeared with The Beatles for performances in Hamburg 1960, 1961, 1962, The Cavern, Liverpool 1960, 1961; worldwide tours 1963–66; attended Transcendental Meditation Course at Maharishi's Acad., Rishikesh, India Feb. 1968; formed Apple Ltd, parent org. of The Beatles Group of Cos 1968; left The Beatles after collapse of Apple Corpn Ltd 1970; formed MPL Group of Cos 1970; first solo album McCartney 1970; formed own pop group Wings 1971–81, tours of Britain and Europe 1972–73, UK and Australia 1975, Europe and USA 1976, UK 1979, World Tour 1989–90; also records as The Fireman, dance music duo with Youth 1994–; solo performances at Party at the Palace, Buckingham Palace 2002, Opening Ceremony, Summer Olympic Games, London 2012; Fellow, British Acad. of Composers and Songwriters 2000; Freeman of the City of Liverpool 1984, Hon. Fellow, Liverpool John Moores Univ. 1998; Dr hc (Sussex) 1988, Hon. DMus (Yale) 2008; two Grammy Awards for Band on the Run (including Best Pop Vocal Performance) 1975, Ivor Novello Award for Best Selling British Record 1977–78 for single Mull of Kintyre, for Int. Hit of the Year 1982 for single Ebony and Ivory, for Outstanding Services to British Music 1989, Guinness Book of Records Triple Superlative Award (43 songs each selling more than 1m copies, holder of 60 gold discs, estimated sales of 100m albums and 100m singles) 1979, Lifetime Achievement Award 1990, Polar Music Prize 1992, Lifetime Achievement Award People for the Ethical Treatment of Animals (with Linda McCartney) 1996, Radio Acad. Lifetime Achievement Award 2007, Q Icon Award 2007, BRIT Award for Outstanding Contribution to Music 2008, ASCAP Award for Songwriter of the Year 2009, Gershwin Prize for Popular Song, US Library of Congress 2010, Kennedy Center Honor 2010, Grammy Award for Best Rock Song (for Cut Me Some Slack, with Dave Grohl, Krist Novoselic and Pat Smear) 2014. *Recordings include:* albums: with The Beatles: Please Please Me 1963, A Hard Day's Night 1964, Beatles for Sale 1965, Help! 1965, Rubber Soul 1966, Revolver 1966, Sgt Pepper's Lonely Hearts Club Band 1967, Magical Mystery Tour 1967, The Beatles (White Album) 1968, Yellow Submarine 1969, Abbey Road 1969, Let It Be 1970, 1962–1966 (Red Album) 1973, 1967–1970 (Blue Album) 1973, Past Masters Vol. One 1988, Past Masters Vol. Two 1988, The Beatles Anthology: 1 1995, The Beatles Anthology: 2 1996, The Beatles Anthology: 3 1996, 1 2000; with Wings: Wild Life 1971, Red Rose Speedway 1973, Band On The Run (Grammy Award for Best Historical Album 2012) 1973, Venus and Mars 1975, Wings at the Speed of Sound 1976, Wings Over America 1976, London Town 1978, Wings Greatest 1978, Back To The Egg 1979, Wingspan 2001; solo: McCartney 1970, Ram 1971, McCartney II 1980, Tug of War 1982, Pipes of Peace 1983, Give My Regards to Broad Street 1984, Press To Play 1986, All the Best! 1987, CHOBA B CCCP 1988, Flowers in the Dirt 1989, Tripping the Live Fantastic 1990, Unplugged: The Official Bootleg 1991, Paul McCartney's Liverpool Oratorio (with Carl Davis) 1991, Off the Ground 1993, Paul is Live 1993, Flaming Pie 1997, Standing Stone (symphonic work) 1997, Run Devil Run 1999, Working Classical 1999, A Garland for Linda (with eight other composers for a cappella choir) 2000, Driving Rain 2001, Back in the US: Live 2002, Back in the World 2003, Chaos and Creation in the Back Yard 2005, Ecce Cor Meum (classical) (Classical BRIT Award for Best Album 2007) 2006, Memory Almost Full 2007, Kisses on the Bottom (Best Traditional Pop Vocal Album 2013) 2012, New 2013; with The Fireman: Strawberries Oceans Ships Forest 1994, Rushes 1998, Electric Arguments 2008; film soundtracks: The Family Way 1966, James Paul McCartney 1973, Live and Let Die 1973, The Zoo Gang (TV series) 1973. *Ballet:* Ocean's Kingdom (orchestral score, written for the New York City Ballet) 2011. *Films:* A Hard Day's Night 1964, Help! 1965, Magical Mystery Tour (TV film) 1967, Yellow Submarine (animated colour cartoon film) 1968, Let it Be 1970, Wings Over the World (TV) 1979, Rockshow 1981, Give My Regards to Broad Street (wrote and directed) 1984, Rupert and the Frog Song (wrote and produced) (BAFTA Award Best Animated Film) 1985, Press to Play 1986, Get Back (concert film) 1991, Live Kisses (concert film) (Grammy Award for Best Music Film 2014) 2012. *Radio:* (series) Routes of Rock (BBC) 1999. *Publications include:* Paintings 2000, The Beatles Anthology (with George Harrison and Ringo Starr) 2000, Sun Prints (with Linda McCartney) 2001, Many Years From Now (autobiography) 2001, Blackbird Singing: Poems and Lyrics 1965–1999 2001, High in the Clouds (juvenile, with Philip Ardagh and Geoff Dunbar) 2005. *Address:* c/o MPL Communications Ltd, 1 Soho Square, London, W1D 3BQ, England (office). *Website:* www.paulmccartney.com.

McCARTNEY, Stella, OBE, BA; British fashion designer; b. (Stella Nina McCartney), 13 Sept. 1971, Lambeth, London, England; d. of Sir Paul McCartney (q.v.) and the late Linda McCartney; m. Alasdhair Willis 2003; two s. one d.; ed Bexhill Coll., Central St Martin's Coll. of Art and Design; work with Christian Lacroix at age 15 and later with Betty Jackson; work experience in Fashion Dept, Vogue magazine; set up own clothing line, London 1995; Creative Dir Chloe, Paris 1997–2001; designed collection for Gucci 2001; est. own fashion house, in partnership with Gucci Group 2001–; launched first perfume, Stella 2003; designed costumes for film Sky Captain and the World of Tomorrow 2004; designed clothes for Madonna's Re-Invention Tour, Annie Lennox's summer tour 2004; launched a skincare line, CARE 2007; designed sportswear ranges for Adidas 2007–; launched a new lingerie line 2008; Stella McCartney Kids collection launched 2010; apptd Team GB's Creative Dir for the 2012 Olympics by Adidas 2010; designed costumes for the New York City Ballet's Ocean's Kingdom which premiered in New York 2011; VH1/Vogue Fashion and Music Designer of the Year 2000, Woman of Courage Award 2003, Glamour Award for Best Designer of the Year 2004, Designer of the Year, British Fashion Awards 2007, chosen by TIME magazine as amongst the 100 Most Influential People in the World 2009, Glamour magazine Woman of the Year 2009, Red Carpet Award, British Fashion Council 2011. *Address:* Peake House, 92 Golborne Road, London, W10 5PS, England (office). *Telephone:* (20) 7518-3111. *Fax:* (20) 7518-3112. *E-mail:* press@stellamccartney.com. *Website:* www.stellamccartney.com (office).

McCASKILL, Claire, BS; American lawyer and politician; *Senator from Missouri;* b. Rolla, Mo.; d. of William Y. McCaskill and Betty Anne McCaskill; m. 1st David Exposito (divorced 1995); one s. two d.; m. 2nd Joseph Shepard 2002; four step-c.; ed Hickman High School, Columbia, Univ. of Missouri-Columbia; has worked in public sector continuously since 1978; spent one year as a law clerk on Mo. Court of Appeals for Western Dist, Kansas City; fmr Asst Prosecutor, Jackson Co. Prosecutor's office, specializing in arson cases; attorney in pvt. practice 1989–91; mem. Mo. House of Reps for Brookside neighbourhood of Kansas City

1983–88; elected to Jackson Co. Legislature 1990–92; Jackson Co. Prosecutor (first woman) 1993–98; State Auditor 1999–2006; defeated Gov. Bob Holden in Democratic primary race 2004 (first person to defeat an incumbent gov. in state history); Senator from Missouri 2007–, mem. Armed Services, Commerce, Homeland Security Cttee, Indian Affairs Cttee, Special Cttee on Aging; Democrat. *Address:* 506 Hart Senate Office Building, Washington, DC 20510, USA (office). *Telephone:* (202) 224-6154 (office). *Fax:* (202) 228-6326 (office). *Website:* mccaskill .senate.gov (office); www.claireonline.com (office).

McCAW, Richard (Richie) Hugh; New Zealand professional rugby union player; *Captain, New Zealand National Rugby Union Team (All Blacks);* b. 31 Dec. 1980, Oamaru, North Otago; ed Otago Boys' High School, Dunedin, Lincoln Univ., Christchurch; plays as loose forward (openside flanker); began playing seriously at Otago Boys' High School 1994, selected in New Zealand Under 19 squad that won world championship in Wales 1999; selected in New Zealand Under 21 squad 2000, debut for Canterbury in Nat. Prov. Championship (NPC) against North Harbour 2000; Super Rugby debut with Crusaders against Hurricanes 2001; played full season with NPC champions Canterbury and captained New Zealand Under 21s; selected for New Zealand Nat. Rugby Team (All Blacks)'s end-of-year tour 2001, debut for All Blacks against Ireland (Man of the Match); selected as New Zealand's first choice open-side flanker for World Cup 2003; named Capt. of All Blacks 2004–, led team at World Cup 2007; captained All Blacks to victory in Rugby World Cup held in NZ defeating France 8–7 in final at Eden Park, Auckland 2011; with Canterbury, won NPC (later ITM Cup) five times and with Crusaders reached Super Rugby semifinals nine times, going on to win the final on four of these occasions; with All Blacks, won seven Tri Nations titles, completed three successful Grand Slam tours and won Bledisloe Cup eight times; played his 100th Super Rugby game, made a record-equalling 94th test appearance for NZ and became most capped All Black capt., leading the side in 57 test matches 2010; first All Black to reach 100 caps (in World Cup Pool game against France) 2011; plays for Canterbury 1999–; Hon. Squadron Leader, Royal NZ Air Force; New Zealand Under 21 Player of the Year 2001, Int. Rugby Board (IRB) Newcomer of the Year Award 2001, voted Newcomer of the Year by Int. Rugby Players Asscn 2002, Air New Zealand NPC Div. One Player of the Year 2002, 2004, Kelvin Tremain Memorial Trophy for Player of the Year 2003, 2006, New Zealand Player of the Year, Steinlager Rugby Awards 2003, 2006, 2009, IRB Int. Player of The Year 2006, 2009, 2010, New Zealand Sportsman of the Year 2010. *Leisure interest:* flying. *Address:* Crusaders, Level 1, PO Box 755, 5 Durham Street, Christchurch (office); c/o New Zealand Rugby Union, PO Box 2172, Wellington 6140, New Zealand. *Telephone:* (3) 379-8300 (office); (4) 499-4995. *Fax:* (3) 365-3565 (office); (4) 499-4224. *E-mail:* info@crfu.co.nz (office); info@nzrugby.co.nz. *Website:* www .crusaders.co.nz (office); www.nzru.co.nz; www.allblacks.com.

McCHRYSTAL, Gen. (retd) Stanley A., BS, MA, MS; American army officer (retd); *Senior Fellow, Jackson Institute for Global Affairs, Yale University;* b. 14 Aug. 1954; ed US Mil. Acad., West Point, NY, US Naval War Coll., Newport, RI, Salve Regina Univ., Newport, RI; commissioned as 2nd Lt in US Army 1976; initial assignment as Weapons Platoon Leader to C Co., 1st Bn, 504th Parachute Infantry Regt, 82d Airborne Div. 1976–78, as Rifle Platoon Leader Feb.–July 1978, as Exec. Officer July–Nov. 1978; enrolled as student in Special Forces Officer Course, Special Forces School, Fort Bragg, NC 1978–79, remained at Fort Bragg as Commdr Detachment A, A Co., 1st Bn, 7th Special Forces Group (Airborne) 1979–80; attended Infantry Officer Advanced Course, Infantry School, Fort Benning, Ga 1980–81; Intelligence and Operations Officer (S-2/S-3) for UN Command Support Group–Jt Security Area, S Korea 1981–82; serve as training officer in Directorate of Plans and Training, A Co., HQ Command, Fort Stewart, Ga March–Nov. 1982; Commdr A Co., 3rd Bn, 19th Infantry, 24th Infantry Div. (Mechanized) 1982–84, Bn Operations Officer (S-3) 1984–85, April 1988–June 1989, Bn Liaison Officer, 3rd Bn, 75th Ranger Regt Sept. 1985–Jan. 1986, May 1987–April 1988, Commdr A Co. Jan. 1986; student in Command and Staff Course, Naval War Coll. 1989–90; Army Special Operations Action Officer, J-3, Jt Special Operations Command 1990–93, deployed to Saudi Arabia for Operations Desert Shield and Desert Storm; Commdr 2nd Bn, 504th Parachute Infantry Regt, 82d Airborne Div. April 1993–Nov. 1994, 2nd Bn, 75th Ranger Regt Nov. 1994–June 1996; Sr Service Coll. Fellow, John F. Kennedy School of Govt, Harvard Univ. 1996–97; Commdr 75th Ranger Regt 1997–99; Mil. Fellow, Council on Foreign Relations 1999–2000; promoted to Brig. Gen. 2001; Asst Div. Commdr (Oper-ations), 82d Airborne Div., including duty as Commdr Coalition/Jt Task Force Kuwait, Camp Doha, Kuwait 2000–01; Chief of Staff, XVIII Airborne Corps, including duty as Chief of Staff of Combined Jt Task Force 180, HQ formation contributed by XVIII Airborne Corps to direct all Operation Enduring Freedom operations in Afghanistan 2001–02; Vice-Dir of Operations and mem. Jt Staff, J-3, Pentagon, Washington, DC 2002–03; selected to deliver nationally televised Pentagon briefings on US mil. operations in Iraq; Commdr Jt Special Operations Command 2003–08, served first as Commdg Gen. Jt Special Operations Command 2003–06, then as Commdr Jt Special Operations Command/Commdr Jt Special Operations Command Forward 2006–08; promoted to Lt-Gen. 2006; Dir Jt Staff and Commdr NATO operations 2008–09; promoted to Gen. 2009; Commdr Int. Security Assistance Force (ISAF), NATO 2009–10 (resgnd); Commdr US Forces Afghanistan (USFOR-A) 2009–10 (resgnd and retd); Sr Fellow, Jackson Inst. for Global Affairs, Yale Univ. 2010–; Co-Founder and Partner, McChrystal Group LLC, Alexandria, Va; Defense Distinguished Service Medal, Defense Superior Service Medal (with one Oak Leaf Cluster), Legion of Merit (with two Oak Leaf Clusters), Bronze Star, Defense Meritorious Service Medal, Meritorious Service Medal (with three Oak Leaf Clusters), Army Commendation Medal, Army Achievement Medal, Expert Infantryman Badge, Parachutist Badge (US), Ranger Tab, Special Forces Tab, Jt Chiefs of Staff Identification Badge. *Publication:* My Share of the Task: A Memoir 2013. *Address:* McChrystal Group LLC, 333 North Fairfax Street, Suite 100, Alexandria, VA 22314 (office); Jackson Institute for Global Affairs, Rosenkranz Hall, 115 Prospect Street, Yale University, New Haven, CT 06511, USA (office). *Telephone:* (203) 432-6253 (Yale) (office). *E-mail:* jackson.institute@yale.edu. *Website:* jackson.yale.edu (home); www .mcchrystalgroup.com (office).

McCLEAN, Maxine, BPA, MA, MBA; Barbadian management consultant and politician; *Minister of Foreign Affairs, Foreign Trade and International Business;* ed Univ. of the West Indies; fmr Lecturer in Man. Studies, Univ. of the West Indies;

Founder Strategic Interventions Inc. (consultancy firm) 1991; mem. Senate 2008–; Leader of Govt Business and Minister in the Prime Minister's Office Jan.–Dec. 2008; Minister of Foreign Affairs, Foreign Trade and Int. Business 2008–; fmr Pres., Vice-Pres. and mem. Supervisory Cttee City of Bridgetown Cooperative Credit Union Ltd; currently Pres. Univ. of the West Indies Cave Hill Campus Alumni Asscn; fmr Chair. Bd of Dirs Bridgetown Cruise Terminals Inc., Need Trust Fund of the Pinelands Creative Workshop, Dir Goddards Enterprises Ltd, RBTT Bank Barbados Ltd, Barbados Stock Exchange Inc.; OAS Fellowship, Univ. of Ohio 1979, Fulbright Fellowship, Louisiana State Univ. 1986. *Address:* Ministry of Foreign Affairs, Foreign Trade and International Business, 1 Culloden Road, St Michael, Barbados (office). *Telephone:* 431-2200 (office). *Fax:* 429-6652 (office). *E-mail:* info@foreign.gov.bb (office). *Website:* www.foreign.gov.bb (office).

McCLELLAN, Scott; American business executive and fmr government official; *Vice-President for Communications, Seattle University;* b. 14 Feb. 1968, Austin, Tex.; s. of Carole Keeton Strayhorn; m. Jill Martinez 2003; two s.; ed Univ. of Texas; Deputy Communications Dir for Texas Gov. George W. Bush 1999; served as Travelling Press Sec. during 2000 presidential campaign; Deputy Press Sec., The White House 2001–03, Press Sec. 2003–06; Sr Vice-Pres. for Corp. and Govt Affairs, HHB Inc. 2006; Vice-Pres. for Communications, Seattle Univ. 2012–; mem. APCO Worldwide Int. Advisory Council 2008. *Publication:* What Happened: Inside the Bush White House and Washington's Culture of Deception 2008. *Address:* Marketing Communications, Seattle University, 715 13th Avenue, Seattle, WA 98122, USA (office). *Telephone:* (206) 296-2104 (office). *E-mail:* mcclells@seattleu .edu (office). *Website:* www.seattleu.edu/marcom (office).

McCLELLAND, Robert, LLM; Australian lawyer and politician; *Attorney-General;* b. 26 Jan. 1958, Sydney; s. of Douglas McClelland; m. Michelle McClelland; one s. three d.; ed Univ. of NSW, Univ. of Sydney; worked as assoc. to Hon. Justice Philip Evatt, Fed. Court of Australia 1980–82; Solicitor, Turner Freeman Solicitors 1982–88, Pnr 1988–96; MP (Australia Labor Party) for Barton, NSW 1996–, Shadow Attorney-Gen. 1998–2001, Shadow Minister for Workplace Relations 2001–03, for Justice and Community Security 2003, for Homeland Security 2003, for Defence and Homeland Security 2004, for Defence 2005, for Foreign Affairs 2006–07, Attorney-Gen. 2007–. *Publications:* numerous legal essays. *Leisure interests:* Australian history, surfing, sailing, rugby league (St George). *Address:* PO Box 6022, House of Representatives, Parliament House, Canberra, ACT 2600, Australia (office). *Telephone:* (2) 6250-6666 (office). *Fax:* (2) 6250-5900 (office). *Website:* www.ag.gov.au (office); www.alp.org.au/people/nsw/ mcclelland_robert.php; www.attorneygeneral.gov.au (office).

McCLUNG, A(ndrew) Colin, BA, MS, PhD; American agronomist (retd); b. 1923; ed Univ. of West Virginia, Cornell Univ.; agronomy researcher, N Carolina State Coll. 1950–56; joined Int. Basic Econ. Corpn Research Inst. (later known as IRI Research Inst.) 1956, initiated research on soil degradation in central Brazil, including the 300 million-acre wasteland known as Cerrado, currently Washing-ton Rep. of IRI Research Inst.; fmr mem. Rockefeller Foundation, Winrock International; World Food Prize (co-recipient) 2006, recognized by Soil Science Soc. of America 2006. *Address:* c/o IRI Research Institute, Matão, São Paulo, Brazil.

McCLUSKEY, Leonard (Len) David; British trade unionist; *General Secretary, Unite;* b. 23 July 1950, Liverpool; s. of Leonard McCluskey and Margaret Fulton; m. 1st Ann P. Doyle (1969–97); one c.; ed Cardinal Godfrey School, Anfield; worked for Mersey Docks and Harbour Co. as a teenager and remained there for the next 11 years; trade unionist since 1968; became a shop steward aged 19; officer of Transport and Gen. Workers Union (TGWU) 1979, campaign organizer for TGWU in Merseyside during 1980s; supported Liverpool Militant during 1980s though not a mem.; mem. Labour Party (UK) 1970–; Nat. Sec. TGWU's Gen. Workers group 1990, moved to London to work in union HQ, TGWU's Nat. Organizer for the service industries 2004–10; Asst Gen. Sec. for Industrial Strategy, Unite –2010, Gen. Sec.-designate Unite Nov. 2010–Jan. 2011, Gen. Sec. Unite 2011–. *Address:* Unite, 128 Theobald's Road, Holborn, London, WC1X 8TN (office); Unite, 35 King Street, Covent Garden, London, WC2E 8JG, England (office). *Telephone:* (20) 7611-2500 (Holborn) (office); (20) 7420-8900 (Covent Garden) (office). *Fax:* (20) 7611-2555 (Holborn) (office); (20) 7420-8998 (Covent Garden) (office). *E-mail:* info@ unitetheunion.org (office). *Website:* www.unitetheunion.org (office).

McCOLGAN, Ellyn, BA, MBA, LLD; American business executive; *Executive Advisor, Aquiline Capital Partners LLC;* b. 16 Jan. 1954, Jersey City, NJ; ed Montclair State Coll.; with Shearson Lehman Brothers, New York 1983, later with Bank of New England; joined Fidelity 1990, fmrly with Fidelity Accounting and Custody Services, Pres. Fidelity Investments Tax-Exempt Services Co. 1996–2000, Fidelity Investments Institutional Retirement Group 2000–01, Fidelity Financial Intermediary Services (FFIS) 2001–02, Fidelity Brokerage Co. 2002–07 (resgnd); Pres. and COO Global Wealth Man. Group, Morgan Stanley 2008–09, mem. Man. Cttee; Exec. Advisor to Aquiline Capital Partners LLC, New York 2010–; mem. Bd of Dirs NASDAQ OMX Group, Inc 2012–, Primerica 2010–11; Trustee Museum of Fine Arts, Boston; mem. Boston Club; ranked by Fortune magazine amongst 50 Most Powerful Women in Business in the US (45th) 2005, (44th) 2006. *Address:* Aquiline Capital Partners LLC, 535 Madison Avenue, 24th Floor, New York, NY 10022 (office); 91 Central Park West, 8A, New York, NY 10023-4600, USA. *Website:* www.aquiline-llc.com (office).

McCOLL OF DULWICH, Baron (Life Peer), cr. 1989, of Bermondsey in the London Borough of Southwark; **Rt Hon Ian McColl,** CBE, MS, FRCS, FRCSE, FACS; British professor of surgery; *Part-Time Lecturer, Guy's Hospital;* b. 6 Jan. 1933; s. of the late Frederick George McColl and Winifred Edith McColl; m. Jean Lennox McNair 1960 (died 2012); one s. two d.; ed Hutchesons' Grammar School, Glasgow, St Paul's School, London, Guy's Hosp. Medical School, Univ. of London; Moynihan Fellowship, Asscn of Surgeons 1967; Reader in Surgery, St Bartholo-mew's Hosp., London 1967–71, Sub-Dean, St Bartholomew's Hosp. Medical Coll. 1969–71; Prof. of Surgery, Guy's Hosp., London 1971–98, Consultant Surgeon 1971–98, Dir of Surgery 1985–98, currently Part-time Lecturer; Chair. Dept of Surgery, United Medical and Dental Schools, St Thomas' Hosps 1985–92; Hon. Consultant to British Army 1976–98; Parl. Pvt. Sec. (Lords) to Prime Minister 1994–97; Deputy Speaker House of Lords 1994–2002; Chair. Bd Govs Mildmay Mission Hosp. 1984–; Vice-Chair. Disablement Services Authority for England 1987–91; Chair. Bd Dirs, Vice-Chair. Int. Bd Mercy Ships 1998–, Consultant

Surgeon 2000–; mem. Council, Royal Coll. of Surgeons 1986–94, Council, Imperial Cancer Research Fund 1986–94; Pres. Nat. Asscn of Limbless Disabled, Soc. of Minimally Invasive Surgery, Leprosy Mission; Vice-Pres. John Grooms Asscn for the Disabled; mem. Bd Govs American Coll. of Surgeons 1982–88; Fellow, King's Coll. London 2001; Hon. Fellow of Dental Surgery, Royal Coll. of Surgeons; George and Thomas Hutcheson's Award 2000, Nat. Maritime Historical Soc. Award 2002, Great Scot Award 2002. *Eponymous lectures:* Arris and Gale (2), Erasmus Wilson, Haig Gudenian Memorial, Colles, Letsomian, Lord Cohen Memorial. *Publications:* Intestinal Absorption in Man 1976, NHS Data Book 1984, Govt Report on supply of artificial legs and wheelchairs for England; articles on colonic diseases, medical audit and amputations. *Leisure interest:* forestry, ornithology. *Address:* House of Lords, Westminster, London, SW1A 0PW, England (office). *Telephone:* (20) 7219-5141 (office). *E-mail:* mccolli@parliament.uk (office).

McCOMB, Leonard William Joseph, RA, Dipl. Fine Art; British artist; b. 3 Aug. 1930, Glasgow, Scotland; s. of Archibald McComb and Delia McComb; m. 1st Elizabeth Henstock 1955 (divorced 1963); m. 2nd Joan Allwork 1966 (died 1967); m. 3rd Barbara Gittel 1973; ed Manchester Art School, Slade School of Fine Art, Univ. of London; teacher at art schools in Bristol, Oxford and London (RA schools, Slade, Goldsmiths', Sir John Cass) 1960–; Assoc. RA 1987, RA 1991, Keeper of the RA 1995–98; Judge, The Winsor & Newton Turner Watercolour Award 2005; Hon. mem. Royal Watercolour Soc. 1996, Royal Soc. of Printmakers 1996; Dr hc (Oxford Brookes Univ.) 2004; Jubilee Prize, RA 1986, Korn Ferry Award 1990, Times Watercolour Competition Prize 1992, 1993, Nordstern Printmaking Prize, RA 1992, Royal Watercolour Soc. Prize 1998, Sir Hugh Casson Drawing Prize, Royal Acad. Summer Exhbn 2005; Turner Medal, Royal Acad. Summer Exhbn 2006. *Works on display in public collections include:* Arts Council, British Council, ICA, Univ. of Cambridge, Tate Gallery, Victoria & Albert Museum, Ulster Museum, Cecil Higgins Art Gallery and Museum, Bedford, Birmingham City Art Gallery, British Museum, Manchester Art Gallery, National Portrait Gallery, Swindon Art Gallery, Towner Art Gallery, Eastbourne, Art Galleries of Worcester, Leicester and Belfast. *Radio:* Kaleidoscope (BBC Radio Four) 1984, Life's Little Luxuries (BBC Radio Four) 2001. *Television:* The South Bank Show – Royal Acad. Chat 1999. *Publication:* Leonard McComb: Drawings, Paintings and Sculptures 2004. *Leisure interests:* travelling, walking. *Address:* 4 Blenheim Studios, 29 Blenheim Gardens, London, SW2 5EU, England (home). *Telephone:* (20) 8671-5510 (home). *Fax:* (20) 8671-5510 (home).

McCOMB, William L., BA (Econ), MBA; American business executive; *CEO, Liz Claiborne, Inc.;* b. Columbia, Mo.; m.; three c.; ed Miami Univ., Ohio, Univ. of Chicago Grad. School of Business; held several positions with Leo Burnett advertising firm in Chicago, working on advertising for The Procter & Gamble Co. –1992; Asst Product Dir for Johnson & Johnson Consumer Products Co. 1992–95, joined Johnson & Johnson-Merck as Group Product Dir 1995–99, Vice-Pres., Marketing, McNeil Consumer Products Co. 1999–2001, Pres. McNeil Consumer Healthcare, with additional responsibilities as Pres. McNeil Consumer & Specialty Pharmaceuticals and Ortho Women's Health & Urology 2004–05, Co. Group Chair. Johnson & Johnson, responsible for the DePuy business 2005–06, mem. Medical Devices & Diagnostics Group Operating Cttee; CEO and mem. Bd of Dirs Liz Claiborne, Inc. 2006–; Vice-Chair. on Exec. Cttee and mem. Bd of Dirs Consumer Healthcare Products Asscn 2001–05; mem. Bd GS1, OREF, INROADS of Philadelphia. *Address:* Liz Claiborne, Inc., 1441 Broadway, New York, NY 10018, USA (office). *Telephone:* (212) 626-5200 (office). *E-mail:* info@lizclaiborneinc.com (office). *Website:* www.lizclaiborneinc.com (office).

McCONAUGHEY, Matthew; American actor; b. 4 Nov. 1969, Ulvade, Tex.; m. Camila Alves 2012; one s. one d.; ed Univ. of Texas at Austin. *Films include:* Dazed and Confused, The Return of the Texas Chainsaw Massacre, Boys on the Side, My Boyfriend's Back 1993, Angels in the Outfield 1994, Scorpion Spring, Submission 1995, Glory Daze, Lone Star, A Time to Kill 1996, Larger Than Life 1997, Amistad, Contact, Making Sandwiches, Last Flight of the Raven, Newton Boys, South Beach, EdTV 1999, U-571 2000, The Wedding Planner 2001, Frailty 2001, Reign of Fire 2002, How to Lose a Guy in Ten Days 2003, Tiptoes 2003, Sahara 2005, Two for the Money 2005, Failure to Launch 2006, We Are Marshall 2006, Fool's Gold 2008, Tropic Thunder 2008, Surfer, Dude 2008, Ghosts of Girlfriends Past 2009, The Lincoln Lawyer 2011, Bernie 2011, Killer Joe 2011, The Paperboy 2012, Magic Mike 2012, Mud 2013, Dallas Buyers Club (Golden Globe Award for Best Actor in a Motion Picture, Screen Actors Guild Award for Outstanding Performance by a Male Actor in a Leading Role, Academy Award for Best Actor in a Leading Role 2014) 2013, The Wolf of Wall Street 2013. *Television includes:* Freedom: A History of Us 2003, Eastbound & Down (series) 2012, True Detective 2014. *Address:* c/o Creative Artists Agency, 2000 Avenue of the Stars, Los Angeles, CA 90067, USA. *Telephone:* (424) 288-2000. *Fax:* (424) 288-2900. *Website:* www.caa.com.

McCONNELL, Addison Mitchell (Mitch), Jr, BA, JD; American politician and lawyer; *Senator from Kentucky;* b. 20 Feb. 1942, Tuscumbia, Ala; s. of Addison Charles McConnell and Julia McConnell (née Shockley); m. 1st Sherrill Redmon (divorced); m. 2nd Elaine L. Chao (q.v.) 1993; three d.; ed Univ. of Louisville Coll. of Arts and Sciences, Univ. of Kentucky Coll. of Law; served in US Army Reserve 1967; admitted to the Bar, Ky 1967; Chief Legis. Asst to Senator Marlow Cook, Washington, DC 1968–70; est. legal practice, Louisville 1970; Deputy Asst US Attorney-Gen. 1974–75; judge, Jefferson Co., Louisville 1978–85; Senator from Kentucky 1985–, Majority Whip 2003–07, Minority Leader 2007–, Chair. Ethics Cttee 1995–97, Rules Cttee 1999–2001, sr mem. Appropriations, Agric. and Rules Cttees; Chair. Nat. Republican Senatorial Cttee 1997–2001, Jefferson Co. Republican Cttee 1973–74; Co-Chair. Nat. Child Tragedies Coalition 1981; Founding Chair. Ky Task Force on Exploited and Missing Children 1982; mem. Pres.'s Partnership on Child Safety; mem. Ky Asscn of Co. Judge Execs (Pres. 1982), Nat. Inst. of Justice (mem. Advisory Bd 1982–84); Republican; Commendation, Nat. Trust in Historical Preservation in the US 1982, Conservationist of the Year Award, League of Ky Sportsmen 1983, Certificate of Appreciation, American Correctional Asscn 1985. *Leisure interests:* cooking, fishing. *Address:* 317 Russell Senate Office Building, Washington, DC 20510, USA (office). *Telephone:* (202) 224-2541 (office). *Fax:* (202) 224-2499 (office). *Website:* www.mcconnell.senate.gov (office).

McCONNELL, David John, PhD, MRIA; Irish geneticist and academic; *Professor of Genetics, Trinity College Dublin;* b. 15 May 1944, Dublin; s. of John

J. McConnell and Joan Warwick; m. Janet Overend 1966; two s.; ed Zion Nat. Schools, Rathgar, Dublin, Sandford Park School, Ranelagh, Dublin, Trinity Coll. Dublin and California Inst. of Tech.; Lecturer in Genetics, Trinity Coll. Dublin 1970–85, Fellow 1978, Assoc. Prof. of Genetics 1985–90, Head, Dept of Genetics 1987–98, Prof. of Genetics 1990–, Vice-Provost, Trinity Coll. 1990–91; Eleanor Roosevelt Fellow, Int. Union Against Cancer, Lab. of Prof. Wally Gilbert, Dept of Biochem. and Molecular Biology Harvard Univ. 1976–77; Visiting Prof., Univ. of California, Davis 1979; consultant in genetic eng and biotechnology, UNIDO 1982–; UNDP Star consultant, Beijing Agric. Univ. 1987; Chair. Adelaide Hosp. 1988–94, Pres. 1995–2001; Pres. Royal Zoological Soc. of Ireland 1992–96, Fellow; other professional appointments; Chair. Irish Times Trust 2001–10; Co-Vice-Chair. European Action on Global Life Sciences (EAGLES) 2004–; mem. Irish Council for Science, Tech. and Innovation 1997–2003; mem. Exec. Bd European Fed. of Biotechnology 2004–; mem. European Molecular Biological Org. (EMBO). *Publications:* more than 100 papers in scientific journals. *Leisure interests:* windsurfing, Kerry, gardening. *Address:* Department of Genetics, Smurfit Institute of Genetics, Trinity College, Dublin 2, Ireland (office). *Telephone:* (1) 702-2008 (office); (1) 702-1140 (office). *Fax:* (1) 671-4968 (office). *E-mail:* david.mcconnell@tcd.ie (office). *Website:* www.tcd.ie/Genetics (office).

McCONNELL, Harden M., PhD, FRSC; American chemist and academic; *Professor Emeritus, Department of Chemistry, Stanford University;* b. 18 July 1927, Richmond, Va; s. of Harry R. McConnell and Frances McConnell (née Coffee); m. Sofia Glogovac 1956; two s. one d.; ed George Washington Univ., California Inst. of Tech. and Univ. of Chicago; with Dept of Physics, Univ. of Chicago, Nat. Research Fellow 1950–52; Shell Devt Co., Emeryville, Calif. 1952–56; Asst Prof. of Chem., California Inst. of Tech. 1956–58, Assoc. Prof. of Chem. 1958–59, Prof. of Chem. 1959–63, Prof. of Chem. and Physics 1963–64; Prof. of Chem., Stanford Univ. 1964–79, apptd Robert Eckles Swain Prof. of Chem. 1979, now Prof. Emer., Chair. Dept of Chem. 1989–92; mem. several bds, Neuroscience Research Program, MIT; f. Molecular Devices Corpn 1983; Pres. Foundation for Basic Research in Chem. 1990–96; mem. ACS, NAS, Int. Acad. of Quantum Molecular Science; Foreign mem. Serbian Acad. of Sciences and Arts; Fellow, AAAS 1982, American Physical Soc., Biophysical Soc. 1999, American Soc. of Biological Chemists; Harkins Lecturer, Univ. of Chicago 1967, Falk-Plaut Lecturer, Columbia Univ. 1967, Renaud Foundation Lecturer 1971, Peter Debye Lecturer, Cornell Univ. 1973, Harvey Lecturer, Rockefeller Univ. 1977, A.L. Patterson Lecturer, Inst. for Cancer Research, Philadelphia 1978, Pauling Lecturer, Stanford Univ. 1981, Remsen Memorial Lecturer, Maryland Section ACS 1982, Prof. du Collège de France 1986, Le Bel Lecturer, Strasbourg 1986, Swift Lecturer, California Inst. of Tech. 1986, Venable Lecturer, Univ. of North Carolina 1987, Linus Pauling Distinguished Lecturer, Oregon State Univ. 1987, Davis Lecturer, Univ. of New Orleans 1994; Calif. Section Award of ACS 1961, Nat. ACS Award in Pure Chem. 1962, Harrison Howe Award 1968, Irving Langmuir Award in Chemical Physics 1971, Alumni Achievement Award, George Washington Univ. 1971, Dickson Prize for Science, Carnegie-Mellon Univ. 1982, Distinguished Alumni Award, California Inst. of Tech., 1982, Wolf Prize in Chem. 1983–84, ISCO Award 1984, Pauling Medal, Puget Sound and Oregon ACS Sections 1987, Wheland Medal, Univ. of Chicago 1988, NAS Award in Chemical Sciences 1988, Sherman Fairchild Distinguished Scholar, California Inst. of Tech. 1988, Nat. Medal of Science 1989, ACS Peter Debye Award, Physical Chem. 1990, RSC Bruker Prize 1995, ACS Award in Surface Science 1997, Gold Medal of Int. ESR Soc. 1997, Zavoisky Award 2000, Welch Award 2002. *Publications:* more than 400 scientific publs on chem., chemical physics, biophysics and immunology. *Leisure interest:* mathematics. *Address:* Department of Chemistry, Stanford University, Stanford, CA 94305, USA (office). *Telephone:* (650) 327-8695 (office). *E-mail:* harden@stanford.edu (office). *Website:* chemistry.stanford.edu (office).

McCONNELL, Vice Adm. John Michael (Mike); American consultant and naval officer (retd) and fmr government official; *Senior Vice-President, Booz Allen Hamilton Inc.;* b. 26 July 1943, Greenville, South Carolina; m. Terry McConnell; two c. two step-c.; ed Furman Univ.; commissioned as line officer in USN in 1967, served a tour in Vietnam and became intelligence officer, served as intelligence officer for Jt Chiefs Chair. Colin Powell during first Gulf War; Dir Nat. Security Agency 1992–96; Sr Vice-Pres. Booz Allen Hamilton Inc., McLean, Va 1996–2007, 2009–; Dir of Nat. Intelligence, Washington, DC 2007–09 (resgnd); mem. Pres.'s Intelligence Advisory Bd 2009–; mem. Bd of Dirs CompuDyne Corpn 2004–07. *Address:* Booz Allen Hamilton Inc., 8283 Greensboro Drive, McLean, VA 22102, USA (office). *Telephone:* (703) 902-5000 (office). *E-mail:* communications@bah.com (office). *Website:* www.boozallen.com (office).

McCONNELL OF GLENSCORRODALE, Baron (Life Peer), cr. 2010, of the Isle of Arran in Ayrshire and Arran; **Jack Wilson McConnell,** BSc, DipEd, MSP, PC; British politician, diplomatist and teacher; b. 30 June 1960, Irvine, Ayrshire, Scotland; s. of William Wilson McConnell and Elizabeth McEwan McConnell; m. Bridget Mary McLuckie 1990; one s. one d.; ed Arran High School, Isle of Arran, Stirling Univ.; math. teacher, Alloa 1983–92; Labour mem. Stirling Dist Council 1984–92, Treas. 1988–92, Leader 1990–92; Gen. Sec. Scottish Labour Party 1992–98, Leader 2001–07 (resgnd); co-ordinated Labour's Yes Yes Referendum Campaign 1997; mem. Scottish Constitutional Convention 1989–98; currently MSP for Motherwell and Wishaw; Minister for Finance, Scottish Exec. 1999–2000, for Educ. and External Affairs 2000–01; First Minister of Scotland 2001–07; Head, Clinton Hunter Devt Initiative on developing educ. in Malawi and Rwanda; Prime Minister's Special Rep. for Peacebuilding 2008–10; mem. Convention of Scottish Local Authorities (COSLA) 1988–92; mem. Amnesty International, Advisory Bd to Inst. of Cultural Diplomacy; Hon. DUniv (Stirling) 2008. *Leisure interests:* golf, music, watching football. *Address:* The House of Lords, Westminster, London, SW1A 0PW, England (office). *Website:* www.jackmcconnell.org.

MacCORMAC, Sir Richard Cornelius, Kt, CBE, BA, MA, PPRIBA, FRSA, RA; British architect and academic; *Chairman, MacCormac Jamieson Prichard Limited;* b. 3 Sept. 1938, Marylebone, London, England; s. of Dr Henry MacCormac CBE, FRCP and Marion Maud Broomhall; m. Susan Karin Landen 1964 (separated 1981); two s. (one deceased); partner, Jocasta Innes 1981 (died 2013); ed Westminster School, Trinity Coll. Cambridge, Bartlett School of Architecture, Univ. Coll., London; served in RN 1957–59; Project Architect, London Borough of Merton 1967–69; est. pvt. practice 1969; Partner, MacCormac, Jamieson, Prichard

Architects 1972–, Chair. 2002–; taught in Dept of Architecture, Univ. of Cambridge 1969–75, 1979–81, Univ. Lecturer 1976–79; Visiting Prof. of Architecture, Univ. of Edinburgh 1982–85, Univ. of Hull 1998–99; Studio Tutor, LSE City Policy and Eng 1998; Pres. RIBA 1991–93; London Forum of Amenity and Civic Socs 1997–; Dir Spitalfields Workspace 1981–; mem. Royal Fine Art Comm. 1983–93, mem. Architecture Cttee, Chair. Royal Acad. from 1998, Exhbns Cttee from 1999; Adviser, British Council 1993–; Co-founder Phoenix Initiative (Structural Steel Design Award 2004, RIBA Award 2004, Civic Trust Awards commendation 2004, Regeneration Award for Best Mixed-Use Regeneration Project 2004, English Partnerships Award for Partnership in Regeneration 2006, BURA Best Practice in Regeneration Award 2006); Trustee, Greenwich Foundation for the Royal Naval Coll. 1997–2002, Soane Museum; Hon. Fellow, Trinity Coll., Cambridge 2006; Hon. DSc 2008; Independent on Sunday Bldg of the Year 1994, Brick Award Supreme Winner 1996, Celebrating Construction Achievement, Regional Award for Greater London 2000, Royal Town Planning Inst. Planning Award, English Partnerships' Regeneration Award 2004. Major works include: Sainsbury Building for Worcester Coll., Oxford (Civic Trust Award 1984); Cable & Wireless training centre, Coventry (Royal Fine Arts Comm. (RFAC)/Sunday Times Bldg of the Year Award 1994); Garden Quadrangle, St John's Coll., Oxford; Bowra Bldg, Wadham Coll., Oxford; Burrell's Fields, Trinity Coll., Cambridge (RIBA Regional Award 1997, Civic Trust Award 1997; Ruskin Library, Lancaster Univ. (Independent on Sunday Building of the Year Award 1996, RFAC/BSkyB Building of the Year Univ. Winner 1998, Millennium Products status awarded by the Design Council 1999); designed a new home in Hampstead for then Arsenal Football Club striker Thierry Henry 1999; Southwark Station, Jubilee Line extension, London (Millennium Bldg of the Year, RFAC/BSkyB 2000); Wellcome Foundation Wing/Dana Centre at the Science Museum, London (Celebrating Construction Achievement Regional Award for Greater London 2000); Tesco supermarket in Ludlow (Civic Trust Award 2001); The Wellcome Wing Science Museum, London (Civic Trust Award 2002, Lighting Design Award 2002); Warwick Court (New City Architecture Award 2004); Friendship House (RIBA Award 2005, Housing Design Award 2005); Senior Common Room, St John's Coll., Oxford (RIBA Award 2006, Design Partnership Award, Nat. Asscn of Shopfitters 2006); The Learning Grid, Univ. of Warwick (Jason Farradane Award 2006); BBC Broadcasting House, Portland Place, Westminster (Natural Stone Award 2006, Natural Stone Craft Award 2007, Civic Trust Award – Regeneration 2008, Westminster Soc. Biennial Award for Urban Design 2011); Portelet Bay, Jersey (Daily Mail UK Property Award for Best Architecture – Multiple Units 2009, What House Award 2011); British Embassy Bangkok, Thailand; Kendrew Quadrangle, St John's Coll., Oxford (RIBA Award 2011, Oxford Preservation Trust Award 2011, Dedalo Minosse Award commendation 2011, Civic Trust Award 2012, David Steel Sustainable Bldg Award for Best Large Non-residential Devt 2012); Maggie's Cancer Care Centre Cheltenham (RIBA Award 2011, Cheltenham Civic Award for New Bldg 2011, Civic Trust Awards commendation 2012); Steampipe Bridge Birmingham (Univ. of Birmingham BUAFTA Awards for Tremendous Achievement – Idea of the Year 2012, Civic Trust Awards commendation 2013). Leisure interests: sailing, music, reading. Address: MJP Architects Ltd, 9 Heneage Street, Spitalfields, London, E1 5LJ, England (office). Telephone: (20) 7377-9262 (office). Fax: (20) 7247-7854 (office). E-mail: mjp@mjparchitects.co.uk (office). Website: www.mjparchitects.co.uk (office).

McCORMICK, Richard D., BS; American business executive; Chairman Emeritus, United States Council for International Business; b. Fort Dodge, Ia; s. of Elmo Eugene McCormick and Virgilla McCormick (née Lawler); m. Mary Patricia Smola 1963; four c.; ed Iowa State Univ.; engineer with AT&T, Kansas City, Mo. 1961–69, Northwestern Bell 1969–85, Pres. 1982–85; Exec. Vice-Pres. US West, Inc. (now part of Qwest Communications) 1985–86, Pres. and COO 1986–90, CEO 1990–98, Chair. 1992–98, Chair. (non-exec.) 1998–99, Chair. Emer. 1999–; Vice-Pres. ICC 1998–2000, Pres. 2001–03, Hon. Chair. 2003–; Chair. US Council for Int. Business 1995–2001, Vice-Chair. from 2001, now Chair. Emer. and Sr Trustee; mem. Bd United Airlines, Wells Fargo & Co. 1983–2010, Nortel Networks Corpn, United Technologies Corpn, Concept Five Technologies, Health Trio, Inc.; mem. Bd Creighton Univ., Omaha; mem. George W. Bush for President, Bush-Cheney '04, John McCain 2008, Freedom and Free Enterprise Political Action Cttee; Trustee, Denver Art Museum. Address: United States Council for International Business, 1212 Avenue of the Americas, New York, NY 10036, USA (office). Telephone: (212) 354-4480 (office). Fax: (212) 575-0327 (office). E-mail: info@uscib.org (office). Website: www.uscib.org (office).

McCORMICK, Richard Levis, BA, PhD; American historian, fmr university administrator and academic; President Emeritus, Rutgers University; b. 26 Dec. 1947, New Brunswick, NJ; m. 1st Suzanne Lebsock; one s. one d.; m. 2nd Joan Barry McCormick; one d.; ed Piscataway Township High School, NJ, Amherst Coll., Yale Univ.; Asst Prof. of History, Rutgers Univ. 1976–81, Assoc. Prof. 1981–85, Prof. 1985–92, Chair. Dept of History 1987–89, Founding Dir Rutgers Center for Historical Analysis 1988–89, Dean Faculty of Arts and Sciences 1989–92, Pres. Rutgers Univ. 2002–12, Pres. Emer. and Univ. Prof. 2012–; Exec. Vice-Chancellor, Provost and Vice-Chancellor for Academic Affairs, Univ. of North Carolina 1992–95; Pres. Univ. of Washington 1995–2002; Gov. James E. McGreevey's Comm. on Jobs, Growth, and Econ. Devt 2003–04, James E. McGreevey's Review, Planning, and Implementation Steering Cttee 2003–04, James E. McGreevey's Comm. to Support and Enhance New Jersey Mil. and Coast Guard Installations 2004–; mem. Asscn of American Univs 1995–, Business-Higher Educ. Forum 1999–, Council of Presidents, Asscn of Governing Bds of Univs and Colls 2001–, Interdisciplinary Task Force of Asscn of American Univs 2002–, Capital Planning Task Force of Comm. on Higher Educ. 2005–; mem. Bd of Dirs New Jersey Tech. Council 2003–, Robert Wood Johnson Univ. Hosp., New Brunswick, NJ 2003–; mem. Bd Overseers Robert Wood Johnson Medical School, Univ. of Medicine and Dentistry of NJ 2003–; mem. Bd Trustees State Theatre, New Brunswick 2003–, New Jersey Network Foundation 2003–, New Jersey Historical Soc. 2005–; George Washington Egleston Prize, Yale Univ. 1977, Visiting Fellowship, Shelby Cullom Davis Center for Historical Studies, Princeton Univ. 1981–82, John Simon Guggenheim Memorial Foundation Fellowship 1985, Woodrow Wilson Int. Center for Scholars Fellowship 1985. Publications: From Realignment to Reform: Political Change in New York State, 1893–1910 1981, Progressivism (co-author) 1983, The Party Period and Public Policy: American

Politics from the Age of Jackson to the Progressive Era 1986, Public Life in Industrial America, 1877–1917 1997, Raised at Rutgers: A President's Story 2014; numerous articles. Address: Executive Vice-President for Academic Affairs, The State University of New Jersey, 4 Huntington Street, New Brunswick, NJ 08901-1071, USA (office). Telephone: (848) 932-7705 (office). Fax: (732) 932-6185 (office). E-mail: rlm@rutgers.edu (office). Website: www.rutgers.edu (office).

McCOWEN, Alec, CBE; British actor; b. 26 May 1925, Tunbridge Wells; s. of Duncan McCowen and Mary Walkden; ed Skinners School, Tunbridge Wells and Royal Acad. of Dramatic Art; mem. Nat. Theatre; Variety Club Stage Actor 1970; Old Vic Theatre: played Touchstone, Ford, Richard II, Mercutio, Malvolio, Oberon 1959–60; with RSC: played Fool in King Lear 1964; Hadrian VII 1968, The Philanthropist 1970, The Misanthrope 1972, Dr Dysart in Equus 1972, Henry Higgins in Pygmalion 1974, Ben in The Family Dance 1976; with Prospect Co.: Antony in Antony and Cleopatra 1977; solo performance of St Mark's Gospel 1978, 1981; Frank in Tishoo 1979; Malvolio in Twelfth Night (TV) 1980; with Nat. Theatre: Crocker-Harris in The Browning Version, Arthur in Harlequinade; Capt. Corcoran in HMS Pinafore 1981, Adolf Hitler in The Portage to San Cristobal of AH 1982, solo performance in Kipling 1983, Reilly in The Cocktail Party 1986, Nicolai in Fathers and Sons 1987, Vladimir in Waiting for Godot 1987, Modern Love 1988, Dr Scoper in The Heiress 1989, Harry in Exclusive 1989, George in A Single Man 1990, Father Jack in Dancing at Lughnasa 1990, Caesar in Caesar and Cleopatra, Michael in Someone Who'll Watch Over Me 1992, Prospero in The Tempest 1993, Elgar in Elgar's Rondo, Gaev in The Cherry Orchard 1995, Clem in Tom and Clem 1997, Narrator in Peter Pan 1998; Dir: Definitely the Bahamas 1987; Evening Standard (now The Standard) Best Actor 1969, 1972, 1982. Films: Frenzy 1971, Travels with my Aunt 1973, Stevie 1978, The Assam Garden 1985, Personal Services 1986, Henry V 1989, Age of Innocence 1992, Gangs of New York 2000. Television: Private Lives 1976, Mr. Palfrey of Westminster 1984, Hunted Down 1989. Publications: Young Gemini 1979, Double Bill 1980, Personal Mark 1984. Leisure interests: music and gardening. Address: c/o Jeremy Conway, 8–12 Broadwick Street, London, W1F 8HW, England (office). Telephone: (20) 7287-0077 (office). Fax: (20) 7287-1940 (office).

McCOY, A(nthony) P(eter), OBE, MBE; Irish jockey; b. 4 May 1974, Moneyglass, Co. Antrim, NI; s. of Peadar McCoy; apprentice to Jim Bolger 1989; won first race riding Legal Steps at Thurles March 1992; Champion Hurdle Winner, Make a Stand 1997; Cheltenham Gold Cup Winner, Mr Mulligan 1997; 1,000th winner Majadou, Cheltenham 1999; 1,500th winner Celtic Nave, Exeter 2001; 2,000th winner Magical Bailiwick, Wincanton 2004; 3,000th winner Restless D'Artaix, Plumpton 2009; Champion Jump Jockey for 15 successive seasons 1995/96–2009/10; winners included Cheltenham Gold Cup, Champion Hurdle, Queen Mother Champion Chase, King George VI Chase and 2010 Grand National, riding Don't Push It on his 15th attempt; greatest number of career winners by any jockey 2002; greatest number of winners in any season by any jockey (289) 2001/02 (broke 55-year old record); has ridden more than 13,000 races (equivalent of 31,000 miles); Lester Awards: Conditional Jockey of the Year 1995, Jump Jockey of the Year 1996, 1997, 1998, 1999, 2000, 2001, 2002, 2003, 2004, 2005, 2006, 2007, 2008, 2009, 2010, 2011, 2012, 2013, Jockey of the Year 1997 (award discontinued after 1997), Jump Ride of the Year 2009, 2012; named Sportsman of the Year at British Sports Awards in London, voted for by Sports Journalists Asscn 2010, BBC Sports Personality of the Year (first jockey to win the award) 2010, 'Jump Off the Sofa Moment' Award, Jaguar Acad. of Sport Annual Awards 2010. Publications: Real McCoy: My Life So Far 1999, McCoy: The Autobiography 2003. Address: c/o Midas Public Relations, 7–8 Kendrick Mews, London, SW7 3HG, England.

McCOY, Sherilyn (Sheri) S., BS, MS, MBA; American cosmetics industry executive; CEO, Avon Products, Inc.; b. Quincy, Mass; m.; three s.; ed Univ. of Massachusetts, Princeton Univ., Rutgers Univ.; Assoc. Research Scientist, Personal Products Co., Johnson & Johnson 1982–96, Vice-Pres. Research and Devt, Personal Products Worldwide 1996–2000, Vice-Pres. for Marketing, Skin Care Franchise, Johnson & Johnson Consumer Cos Inc. 2000–02, Global Pres. Baby and Wound Franchise 2002–05, Co. Group Chair. and Worldwide Franchise Chair. Ethicon Inc. 2005–08, Worldwide Chair. Surgical Care Group 2008–09, Worldwide Chair. Pharmaceuticals Group 2009–11, mem. Exec. Cttee 2009–12, Vice-Chair. Exec. Cttee and mem. Office of the Chair., with responsibility for Pharmaceutical and Consumer business segments 2011–12; CEO Avon Products, Inc. 2012–; Vice-Pres. Montgomery Township Educ. Foundation; Bd mem. Bd FIRST (charity); mem. Rutgers Univ. Pres.'s Business Leaders Cabinet; ranked by Fortune magazine amongst the 50 Most Powerful Women in Business in the US (44th) 2008, (14th) 2009, (12th) 2010, (tenth) 2011, (17th) 2012, ranked by Forbes magazine amongst The World's 100 Most Powerful Women (66th) 2009, (84th) 2011, (39th) 2012, (27th) 2013. Publications: four US patents. Address: Avon Products, Inc., Global Headquarters, 777 Third Avenue, New York, NY 10017, USA (office). Telephone: (212) 282-7000 (office). E-mail: info@avoncompany.com (office). Website: www.avoncompany.com (office).

McCREEVY, Charlie, BComm, FCA; Irish accountant and politician; b. Sept. 1949, Sallins, Co. Kildare; m. Noeleen Halligan, three s., one s. three d. from previous m.; ed Univ. Coll. Dublin; Pnr, Tynan Dillon & Co. (chartered accountants), Dublin, Naas and Ballyhaunis; mem. Kildare Co. Council 1979–85; mem. Dáil 1977–; Minister for Social Welfare 1992–93, for Tourism and Trade 1993–94, for Finance 1997–2004; EU Commr for Internal Market and Services 2004–10; fmr Fianna Fáil Spokesperson on Finance. Address: Hillview House, Kilcullen Ross, Naas, Co. Kildare, Ireland. Telephone: (2) 299-11-11 (office). Fax: (2) 295-01-38 (office).

McCRORY, Patrick (Pat) Lloyd, BA, MA; American politician, state governor and business executive; Governor of North Carolina; b. 17 Oct. 1956, Columbus, Ohio; s. of Rollin 'Mac' McCrory and Audrey McCrory; m. Ann Gordon 1988; ed Ragsdale High School, Jamestown, Catawba Coll., Salisbury; received NC teaching certificate 1978; worked full-time for Duke Energy 1978–2008, first on man. training programme, later promoted to sr adviser with Business and Econ. Devt Group; mem. Bd of Trustees, Catawba Coll.; Partner, McCrory & Co. (sales consulting firm), Charlotte, NC 2009–12; Sr Dir of Strategic Initiatives, Moore & Van Allen PLLC law firm, Charlotte 2010–12; began political career in Charlotte when elected as an At-Large City Councilman 1989, re-elected 1991, 1993, served as Mayor Pro Tempore 1993–95; Mayor of Charlotte 1995–2009; apptd by Pres.

George W. Bush to US Homeland Security Advisory Council 2002–06; unsuccessful cand. for Gov. of NC 2008; paid adviser to transit tax campaigns 2008–12; Gov. of North Carolina 2013–; Republican; fmr Hon. Chair. Charlotte chapter of Alzheimer's Foundation and Arthritis Foundation; Dr hc (Catawba Coll.) 2001; nat. Home-ownership Hero Award 2003. *Address:* Office of the Governor, Constituent Services Office, 116 West Jones Street, Raleigh, NC 27603, USA (office). *Telephone:* (919) 733-2391 (office). *Fax:* (919) 733-2120 (office). *E-mail:* governor.office@nc.gov (office). *Website:* www.governor.state.nc.us (office).

McCRUM, (John) Robert, MA; British writer and newspaper editor; *Associate Editor, The Observer;* b. 7 July 1953; s. of the late Michael William McCrum and Christine Mary Kathleen fforde; m. 1st Olivia Timbs (divorced 1984); m. 2nd Sarah Lyall 1995; two d.; ed Sherborne School, Corpus Christi Coll., Cambridge and Univ. of Pennsylvania, USA; house reader, Chatto & Windus 1977–79; Editorial Dir Faber and Faber Ltd 1979–89, Ed.-in-Chief 1990–96; Literary Ed. The Observer (newspaper) 1996–2008, currently Assoc. Ed.; scriptwriter and co-producer The Story of English TV series 1980–86; Tony Godwin Prize 1979, Peabody Award 1986, Emmy Award 1987. *Publications include:* In the Secret State 1980, A Loss of Heart 1982, The Fabulous Englishman 1984, The Story of English 1986, The World is a Banana 1988, Mainland 1991, The Psychological Moment 1993, Suspicion 1996, My Year Off 1998, Wodehouse: A Life 2004, Globish: How the English Language Became the World's Language 2010. *Leisure interest:* the works of P. G. Wodehouse. *Address:* The Observer, Kings Place, 90 York Way, London, N1 9GU, England (office). *Website:* observer.guardian.co.uk (office).

McCULLAGH, Peter, PhD, FRS; Northern Irish statistician; *John D. MacArthur Distinguished Service Professor, University of Chicago;* b. 8 Jan. 1952, Plumbridge, Northern Ireland; s. of John A. McCullagh and Margaret B. McCullagh; m. Rosa Bogues 1977; one s. three d.; ed St Columb's Coll., Derry, Univ. of Birmingham, Imperial Coll., London; Asst Prof., Dept of Statistics, Univ. of Chicago 1977–79, Prof. 1985–, now John D. MacArthur Distinguished Service Prof.; Lecturer, Imperial Coll. London 1979–85; Fellow, American Acad. of Arts and Sciences 2002; Guy Medal (Bronze), Royal Statistical Soc. 1983, Presidents' Award, Cttee of Presidents of Statistical Socs (COPSS) 1990, Notable Alumni Award, St Columb's Coll. 2007. *Achievements include::* known for McCullagh's parametrization of the Cauchy distributions. *Publications:* Generalized Linear Models (with J. A. Nelder) 1983 (second edn 1989), Tensor Methods in Statistics 1987; more than 75 articles in professional journals and about 35 other publs. *Address:* Department of Statistics, University of Chicago, Eckhart 119, 5734 South University Avenue, Chicago, IL 60637 (office); 5039 Ellis Avenue, Chicago, IL 60615, USA (home). *Telephone:* (773) 702-8340 (office). *Fax:* (773) 702-9810 (office). *E-mail:* pmcc@galton.uchicago.edu (office). *Website:* galton.uchicago.edu/faculty/mccullagh.shtml (office); www.stat.uchicago.edu/~pmcc (office).

McCULLIN, Donald (Don), CBE; British photographer; b. 9 Oct. 1935, London; s. of Frederick and Jessica McCullin; m. 1st Christine Dent 1959 (divorced 1987); two s. one d. and one s. by Laraine Ashton; m. 2nd Marilyn Bridges 1995 (divorced 2001); m. 3rd Catherine Fairweather 2002; one s.; ed Tollington Park Secondary Modern, Hammersmith Art and Crafts School; RAF Nat. Service; photographer with Observer for four years; photographer with Sunday Times, London for eighteen years; freelance 1980–; has covered eight wars–Viet Nam, Cambodia, Biafra, Congo, Israel, Cyprus, Chad, Lebanon–and many famine areas; has travelled to 64 countries; Dr hc (Bradford) 1993, (Open) 1994, (Lincoln) 2005, (Gloucester) 2008, (Bath) 2011; World Press Photographer 1964, Warsaw Gold Medal 1964, Granada TV Award 1967, 1969, Designers and Art Directors Asscn Gold Award for Photography 1968, First Prize, World Press Photo Foundation 1969, 1977 Photokina Prize for Overall Achievement, Cologne 1972, American Soc. of Magazine Photographers Award 1978, German Soc. of Photography Erich Salomon Prize for Outstanding Use of Photography in Press, Berlin 1992, Two Gold, One Silver Art Director Awards, UK, Cornell Capa Award 2006. *Television:* films: Beautiful, Beautiful 1968, Just One More War 1977, Homefront 1986, The Redundant Warrior 1991, Contacts: Don McCullin 1992, Words Are Not Enough 2005. *Publications:* The Destruction Business 1971, The Concerned Photographer II 1972, Is Anyone Taking Notice? 1973, Hearts of Darkness 1980, Battle Beirut–A City in Crisis 1983, Perspectives 1987, Skulduggery 1987, Open Skies 1989, Unreasonable Behaviour (autobiog.) 1990, Sleeping with Ghosts 1995; A Life's Work in Photography 1995, India 1999, Don McCullin A Retrospective 2001, Don McCullin 2004, Don McCullin in Africa 2005, Don McCullin in England 2007, Southern Frontiers 2011, Shaped by War 2011. *Leisure interests:* walking, collecting Victorian children's books, antiques.

McCULLOUGH, Colleen; Australian author; b. 1 June 1937, Wellington, NSW; m. Ric Robinson 1984; ed Holy Cross Coll., Woollahra, Sydney Univ., Inst. of Child Health, London Univ.; trained as neuroscientist and worked in Sydney and English hospitals; Researcher and Lecturer, Dept of Neurology, Yale Univ. Medical School, USA 1967–77; moved to Norfolk Island, S Pacific 1979; mem. New York Acad. of Sciences, Bd of Visitors Int. Programs Center Dept of Political Science, Univ. of Oklahoma; Fellow, AAAS; fmr Patron, Gerontology Foundation of Australia; currently Patron, Macular Degeneration Foundation of Australia; Hon. Founding Gov. Prince of Wales Medical Research Inst.; Hon. DLitt (Macquarie) 1993; designated one of Australia's Living Nat. Treasures. *Publications include:* novels: Tim 1974, The Thorn Birds 1977, An Indecent Obsession 1981, A Creed for the Third Millennium 1985, The Ladies of Missalonghi 1987, The First Man in Rome 1990, The Grass Crown 1991, Fortune's Favourites 1993, Caesar's Women 1996, Caesar 1997, The Song of Troy 1998, Morgan's Run 2000, The October Horse 2002, The Touch 2003, Angel 2005, On, Off 2006, Antony and Cleopatra 2007, The Independence of Miss Mary Bennett 2008, Too Many Murders 2009; non-fiction: Cooking with Colleen McCullough and Jean Easthope 1982, Roden Cutler, VC – The Biography 1998 (aka The Courage and the Will 1999). *Address:* 'Out Yenna', Norfolk Island, Oceania (via Australia). *Fax:* (6723) 23313.

McCULLOUGH, David Gaub, BA; American historian and writer; b. 7 July 1933, Pittsburgh, Pa; m. Rosalee Ingram Barnes 1954; three s. two d.; ed Yale Univ.; Ed., Time Inc., New York 1956–61, United States Information Agency, Washington, DC 1961–64, American Heritage Publishing Co., New York 1964–70; Scholar-in-Residence, Univ. of New Mexico 1979, Wesleyan Univ. 1982, 1983; Visiting Prof., Cornell Univ. 1989; Marian McFadden Memorial Lecturer,

Indianapolis-Marion County Public Library 2002; mem. Jefferson Legacy Foundation, Nat. Trust for Historic Preservation, Soc. of American Historians, Harry S. Truman Library Inst.; several hon. doctorates. *Television:* host, Smithsonian World 1984–88, The American Experience 1988– (both PBS). *Publications include:* The Johnstown Flood 1968, The Great Bridge 1972, The Path Between the Seas (Nat. Book Award for History 1978, Samuel Eliot Morison Award 1978, Cornelius Ryan Award 1978, Francis Parkman Prize 1978) 1977, Mornings on Horseback (Nat. Book Award) 1981, Brave Companions 1991, Truman (Pulitzer Prize in Biography 1993, Harry S. Truman Public Service Award 1993) 1992, John Adams (Pulitzer Prize 2002) 2001, 1776 2005, The Course of Human Events 2005, In the Dark Streets Shineth: A 1941 Christmas Eve Story 2010, The Greater Journey 2011, Great Bridge 2012. *Address:* Janklow & Nesbit Associates, 445 Park Avenue, New York, NY 10022, USA (office). *Website:* www.davidmccullough.com.

McCULLUM, Brendon Barrie; New Zealand professional cricketer; b. 27 Sept. 1981, Dunedin, Otago; s. of S. J. McCullum (fmr first-class player for Otago); Ellissa Arthur; one s. one d.; ed King's High School, Dunedin; wicketkeeper batsman; right-handed batsman; plays for Otago 1999–2003, 2007–, New Zealand 2002–, Canterbury 2003–06, Glamorgan 2006, Kolkata Knight Riders 2008–10, 2012–, NSW 2009, Sussex 2010, Kochi Tuskers Kerala 2011, Brisbane Heat 2011–; First-class debut: 1999/2000; Test debut: NZ v S Africa, Hamilton 10–14 March 2004; One-Day Int. (ODI) debut: Australia v NZ, Sydney 17 Jan. 2002; T20I debut: NZ v Australia, Auckland 17 Feb. 2005. *Achievements include:* set new World Cup record by smashing 50 runs from 20 balls against Canada in Saint Lucia 21 March 2007; scored 158 not out in inaugural match of Indian Premier League (then the world highest score by a batsman in a Twenty20 match) 18 April 2008; first player to score 1000 T20I runs, playing against Zimbabwe in ICC World Twenty20 in Guyana 28 June 2010; scored 123 runs against Bangladesh at Pallekele, setting a new record for the highest T20I innings, and becoming the first player to score two T20I centuries Sept. 2012. *Address:* c/o Otago Cricket Association Inc., University Oval, Grandstand, Logan Park Drive, PO Box 1419, Dunedin, New Zealand. *Telephone:* (3) 477-9056. *Fax:* (3) 477-3056. *E-mail:* info@otagocricket.co.nz. *Website:* www.otagocricket.co.nz.

McCULLY, Murray, LLB; New Zealand politician; *Minister of Foreign Affairs and for Sport and Recreation;* b. 19 Feb. 1953, Whangarei; MP for East Coast Bays 1987–99, 2002–, for Albany 1999–2002; mem. Māori Affairs Select Cttee 2002–03, Foreign Affairs, Defence and Trade Cttee 2005–08; Minister of Customs 1991–96, of Housing 1993–96, of Tourism 1996–99, for Sport, Fitness and Leisure 1996–99, for Accident Rehabilitation and Compensation Insurance 1997–99, for Housing Corpn 1998–99, for Housing New Zealand 1998–99, for Accident Insurance 1999, of Foreign Affairs and for Sport and Recreation 2008–; Assoc. Minister of Tourism 1991–96, of Immigration 1998–99; Spokesman for Infrastructure 1999–2005, for Local Govt 1999–2002, for Sport, Fitness and Leisure 1999–2002, for Immigration 2002–03, for State Services 2002–05, for Conservation 2005–09; Parl. Asst to Leader of the Opposition 2003–05; mem. New Zealand Nat. Party. *Address:* Ministry of Foreign Affairs and Trade, Private Bag 18901, Wellington 5045, New Zealand (office). *Telephone:* (4) 439-8000 (office). *Fax:* (4) 472-9596 (office). *E-mail:* enquiries@mfat.govt.nz (office). *Website:* www.mfat.govt.nz (office).

McCUTCHEON, Stuart, BA (Hons), PhD; New Zealand physiologist, endocrinologist, academic and university administrator; *Vice-Chancellor, University of Auckland;* ed Massey Univ.; Lecturer, Massey Univ. while undertaking a PhD in metabolic physiology; Post-doctoral Fellow (Harkness Fellowship), Cornell Univ., USA 1982–84; Head of Dept of Animal Science, Massey Univ. 1990–94, Asst Vice-Chancellor (Research) 1994–99, Deputy Vice-Chancellor 1999–2001; Vice-Chancellor Victoria Univ. of Wellington 2001–05; Vice-Chancellor Univ. of Auckland 2005–; has served as adviser to several govt agencies and producer bds; fmr Dir or Bd mem. New Zealand Dairy Research Inst., Wellington Regional Econ. Devt Trust, Wellington Coll. of Educ., Malaghan Inst. of Medical Research, Universitas 21, U21 Global, Univ. of Auckland Foundation, UK and US Friends of Univ. of Auckland; Chair. NZ Vice-Chancellors' 2004–05, Universities NZ Research Cttee. *Publications:* numerous papers in professional journals on endocrinology and metabolic physiology. *Address:* Office of the Vice-Chancellor, The University of Auckland, Private Bag 92019, Auckland Mail Centre, Auckland 1142, New Zealand (office). *Telephone:* (9) 373-7599 (ext. 87751) (office). *Fax:* (9) 373-7591 (office). *E-mail:* s.mccutcheon@auckland.ac.nz (office). *Website:* www.auckland.ac.nz/uoa/professor-stuart-mccutcheon (office).

McDAID, James, MB, BCh, BAO; Irish politician and medical doctor; b. 3 Oct. 1949, Termon, Co. Donegal; m. Marguerite McLoughlin (separated); three s. one d.; ed St Eunan's Coll., Letterkenny, Nat. Univ. of Ireland, Galway; Sr Surgical House Officer, Letterkenny Gen. Hosp. 1974–79; Gen. Practitioner, Letterkenny 1979; Founder, Pres. Donegal Hospice Movt 1988; mem. Dáil Éireann for Donegal NE 1989–2010; Minister (desig.) for Defence 1991 (resgnd); mem. Dáil Cttee on Women's Rights 1992, Cttee of Public Accounts 1993, Cttee on Foreign Affairs and NI Sub-Cttee 1995; Spokesperson on North/South Devts 1995, for Equality and Law Reform 1996–97; Minister for Tourism, Sport and Recreation 1997–2002; Minister of State at the Dept of Transport (with special responsibility for road traffic including road haulage) 2002–04. *Leisure interests:* football, horse racing, golf. *Address:* Pearse Road, Letterkenny, Co. Donegal, Ireland (home). *Telephone:* (74) 25132 (home).

McDIARMID, Ian, MA; British actor and artistic director; b. 11 Aug. 1944, Carnoustie, Scotland; s. of the late Frederick McDiarmid and Hilda Emslie; ed Univ. of St Andrews, Royal Scottish Acad. of Music and Dramatic Art, Glasgow; Actor; Assoc. Dir Royal Exchange, Manchester; Jt Artistic Dir (with Jonathan Kent) Almeida Theatre 1990–2002; Gold Medal Royal Scottish Acad. of Music and Dramatic Art 1968. *Films include:* The Awakening 1980, Dragonslayer 1981, Gorky Park 1983, Return of the Jedi 1983, Dirty Rotten Scoundrels 1988, Restoration 1995, Little Orphan Annie 1995, Star Wars: Episode I: The Phantom Menace 1999, Sleepy Hollow 2000, Star Wars Episode II: Attack of the Clones, Star Wars Episode III: Revenge of the Sith 2005. *Plays include:* Almeida Theatre: Volpone, Ivanov, Tartuffe, School for Wives, Creditors, Kurt Weill Concerts, Government Inspector, The Jew of Malta, The Tempest, Faith Healer (Olivier Award for Best Actor, Critics Circle Award for Best Actor 2001), RSC: Henry V, The Merchant of Venice, The Party, Crimes in Hot Countries, The Castle; Royal Court: Hated Nightfall, Love of a Good Man, Insignificance; Barbican: The

Soldier's Tale; Royal Exchange, Manchester: Edward II, The Country Wife; Aldwych: The Black Prince; Oxford Playhouse: Peer Gynt, Mephisto; Booth Theater, New York: Faith Healer (Tony Award for Best Featured Actor) 2006; Donmar Warehouse: Pirandello's Henry IV 2005, Ibsen's John Gabriel Borkman 2007. *Plays directed include:* Almeida Theatre: Scenes from an Execution, Venice Preserved, Siren Song, A Hard Heart, Lulu, The Possibilities, The Rehearsal; Royal Exchange: Don Juan; Donmar Warehouse: Pirandello's Henry IV, Be Near Me 2009; Chichester Festival/Gielgud Theatre: Six characters in search of an author 2008. *Television includes:* Richard's Things 1981, Chernobyl: The Final Warning 1991, Heart of Darkness 1994, Hillsborough 1996, Rebecca, Karaoke, Creditors, The Nation's Health, The Professionals, Great Expectations 1999, All the King's Men 1999, Crime and Punishment 2001, Charles II 2004, Elizabeth I 2005, Our Hidden Lives 2005, City of Vice 2008, Margaret 2009. *Radio:* numerous plays and readings, including Volpone (title role), The Cocktail Party (as The Uninvited Guest). *Appearances:* Aldeburgh Festival, Scottish Chamber Orchestra, London Symphony Orchestra (The Soldier's Tale), Royal Opera House, Covent Garden (The King goes forth to France). *Publications:* Be Near Me (adapted from the novel by Andrew O'Hagan) 2009. *Address:* c/o Independent, Oxford House, London, W1D 1BS, England (office).

McDONAGH, Bobby, BA, MA; Irish diplomatist; *Ambassador to Italy;* b. 29 June 1954, Washington, DC, USA; m. Mary McDonagh; four d.; ed Gonzaga Coll., Dublin, Balliol Coll., Oxford, UK; joined Dept of Foreign Affairs 1977, has held numerous EU-related posts including mem. Secr. European Parl. 1983–85, based at Perm. Mission to EU 1987–90, joined Cabinet of Farm Commr 1990, served as Deputy Chef de Cabinet to Commr for Social Affairs, fmr Deputy to IGC Rep., Treaty of Amsterdam negotiations, Dir-Gen. EU Div., Dept of Foreign Affairs 2001–05, fmr Alt. mem. Convention on Future of Europe, Perm. Rep. to EU 2005–09, Amb. to UK 2009–13, to Italy 2013–. *Publication:* Original Sin in a Brave New World: The Paradox of Europe 1998. *Address:* Embassy of Ireland, Villa Spada, Via Giacomo Medici 1, 00153 Rome, Italy (office). *Telephone:* (06) 5852381 (office). *Fax:* (06) 5813336 (office). *E-mail:* romeembassy@dfa.ie (office). *Website:* www.embassyofireland.it (office); www.ambasciata-irlanda.it (office).

McDONAGH, Enda; Irish theologian and academic; *Professor of Moral Theology, St Patrick's College;* b. 27 June 1930, Co. Mayo; s. of Patrick McDonagh and Mary Kelly; ed St Jarlath's Coll., Tuam, St Patrick's Coll., Maynooth, Gregorian Univ., Rome and Univ. of Munich; Prof. of Moral Theology (and Canon Law), St Patrick's Coll. 1958–, Dir Postgraduate Studies in Theology 1970–76, Dean of Faculty of Theology 1973–79; Lecturer in Irish School of Ecumenics, Dublin 1970–; Husking Prof. of Theology, Univ. of Notre Dame, USA 1979–81; McKeever Prof. of Theology, New York 1990–92; Chair. Governing Body, Univ. Coll. Cork 1999–2007; Leverhulme Research Fellow, Univ. of Cambridge, UK 1978; Hon. LLD (Nat. Univ. of Ireland) 2000, Hon. DD (Trinity Coll. Dublin) 2001; Ferguson Lecturer, Univ. of Manchester 1978. *Publications:* Roman Catholics and Unity 1963, Religious Freedom 1967, Invitation and Response: Essays in Christian Moral Theology 1972, Gift and Call: Towards a Christian Theology of Morality 1975, Social Ethics and the Christian: Towards Freedom in Communion 1979, Doing the Truth: The Quest for Moral Theology (co-author) 1979, Church and Politics: From Theology to a Case History of Zimbabwe 1980, The Making of Disciples: Tasks of Moral Theology 1982, Between Chaos and New Creation 1985, Between Chaos and New Creation: Doing Theology at the Fringe (Theology and Life Series, No. 19) 1987, Small Hours of Belief 1989, The Gracing of Society 1989, Survival or Salvation?: A Second Mayo Book of Theology 1994, Faith in Fragments 1997, Religion and Politics in Ireland at the Turn of the Millennium: Essays in Honour of Garret Fitzgerald on the Occasion of His Seventy-Fifth Birthday (co-author) 2004, Vulnerable To The Holy: In Faith, Morality And Art 2005; ed. and contrib. The Meaning of Christian Marriage 1963, Moral Theology Renewed 1965, Truth and Life 1968, Faith and the Hungry Grass 1989, The Gracing of Society 1990, Salvation or Survival 1993, Faith in Fragments 1995, Vulnerable to the Holy 2005, Immersed in Mystery 2007. *Leisure interests:* theatre, poetry and the visual arts. *Address:* St Patrick's College, Maynooth, Co. Kildare, Ireland (office). *Telephone:* (1) 285222 (office). *Website:* www.maynoothcollege.ie (office).

McDONALD, Arthur B., OC, BSc, MSc, PhD, FRS, FRSC; Canadian astrophysicist and academic; *Gordon and Patricia Gray Chair in Particle Astrophysics, Queen's University;* b. 29 Aug. 1943; m.; four c.; ed California Inst. of Tech., Pasadena, Dalhousie Univ., Halifax, NS; Postdoctoral Fellow, Atomic Energy of Canada, Chalk River, Ont. 1969–70, Asst Research Officer 1970–75, Sr Research Officer 1980–82; Prof., Princeton Univ. 1982–89; Prof., Queen's Univ. 1989–, Univ. Research Chair 2002–06, Gordon and Patricia Gray Chair in Particle Astrophysics 2006–, Dir Sudbury Neutrino Observatory (SNOLAB) 1989–, Assoc. Dir SNOLAB Inst. 2009–; Visiting positions: Univ. of Washington, Seattle 1978, Los Alamos Nat. Lab. 1981, Queen's Univ. 1988, Univ. of Oxford, UK 2003, 2009, CERN, Geneva, Switzerland 2004, Univ. of Hawaii 2004, 2009, Affiliate Grad. Faculty, Univ. of Hawaii 2010; mem. Princeton Univ. Physics Dept Advisory Council 2009–, Scientific Advisory Bd Max-Planck-Institut für Kernphysik, Heidelberg, Germany 2010–; CIAR Cosmology and Gravity Program Assoc. 2000– (Chair. Advisory Bd 2000–05); mem. Canadian Assoc of Physicists 1964, American Physical Soc. 1969 (Fellow 1983), Professional Engineers of Ontario 2004; Certified mem. Professional Engineers of Ontario 2003; Hon. Life mem. Science North, Sudbury, Ont. 1997; Hon. LLD (Dalhousie) 1997, (Univ. Coll. of Cape Breton) 1999, (St Francis Xavier Univ.) 2009; Hon. DSc (Royal Mil. Coll.) 2001, (Univ. of Chicago), 2006, (Univ. of Alberta) 2011; numerous awards including Gov. Gen.'s Gold Medal, Dalhousie 1964, Rutherford Memorial Fellowship 1969–70, Killam Research Fellowship 1998, T.W. Bonner Prize in Nuclear Physics, American Physical Soc. 2003, Canadian Assoc of Physicists Medal for Lifetime Achievement in Physics 2003, Award of Excellence, Natural Sciences and Eng Research Council of Canada (NSERC) 2003, Gerhard Herzberg Canada Gold Medal for Science and Eng 2003, UK-Canada Rutherford Lecturer, Royal Soc. 2003, Bruno Pontecorvo Prize in Particle Physics, JINR, Dubna 2005, NSERC John C. Polanyi Award to SNO team 2006, Benjamin Franklin Medal in Physics (co-recipient) 2007, Donald R. Hamilton Lecturer, Princeton Univ. 2008, Huggins Science Lecturer, Acadia Univ. 2008, inducted into Canadian Science and Eng Hall of Fame 2009, Killam Prize in the Natural Sciences 2010, inducted into Nova Scotia Discovery Centre Hall of Fame 2010, E. Segre Lecturer, Univ. of California, Berkeley 2010, Royal Soc. of Canada Henry Marshall Tory Medal 2011. *Publications:* numerous papers

in professional journals. *Address:* Department of Physics, Engineering Physics and Astronomy, Queen's University, Kingston, ON K7L 3N6 (office); 830 Sandringham Place, Kingston, ON K7P 1N2, Canada (home). *Telephone:* (613) 533-2702 (office); (613) 533-2707 (office); (613) 541-1405 (mobile); (613) 389-9593 (home). *Fax:* (613) 533-6813 (office). *E-mail:* art@snolab.ca (office). *Website:* www .sno.phy.queensu.ca (office).

MacDONALD, Brian P., BS, MBA; American business executive; *Chairman, President and CEO, Sunoco Inc.;* ed Mount Allison Univ., McGill Univ., Canada; worked at General Motors Corpn and held a variety of positions in Financial Management, including Deputy Chief Financial Officer (CFO) for Isuzu Motors Ltd, Treas. GM Canada 1998–2000; Vice-Pres. and Treas. Dell International Inc. 2002–09, CFO Commercial Business Unit Dell, Inc. 2008–09, also Chair. Dell Financial Services; joined Sunoco Inc. 2009, Dir, Sunoco Partners LLC –Gen. Partner of Sunoco Logistics Partners LP 2009–, CFO and Sr Vice-Pres. Sunoco Inc. 2009–10, CFO and Sr Vice-Pres. Sunoco Partners LLC 2010–12, Vice-Pres. –2012, mem. Bd of Dirs, Chair., Pres. and CEO Sunoco Inc. 2012–; mem. Bd of Dirs Southeastern Pennsylvania Chapter of American Red Cross, SunCoke Energy Inc. 2010–12. *Address:* Sunoco Inc., 1735 Market Street, Suite LL, Philadelphia, PA 19103-7583, USA (office). *Telephone:* (215) 977-3000 (office). *Fax:* (215) 977-3409 (office). *E-mail:* info@sunocoinc.com (office). *Website:* www.sunocoinc.com (office).

McDONALD, Donald Benjamin, AO, BCom; Australian business executive; *Chairman, Australian Broadcasting Corporation;* b. 1 Sept. 1938, Sydney; s. of Benjamin McDonald and Maida Hands; m. Janet Isabel McDonald AO 1964; one s. one d.; ed Fort Street Boys' High School and Univ. of New South Wales; Finance Dir Vogue Publs 1965–68; with Australian Opera 1968–72 (Gen. Man. 1987–96), Musica Viva Australia 1972–78; Gen. Man. Sydney Theatre Co. 1980–86; Dir Australian Tourist Comm. 1993–96; Chair. State Opera Ring Corpn, S Australia 1996–98, Australian Broadcasting Corpn 1996–, Constitutional Centenary Foundation 1997–2000, The Really Useful Company (Aust) Pty Ltd; Dir Festival, Perth 1998–, Univ. of NSW Foundation 1998–, Focus Publishing Pty Ltd 1999–2000; fmr Dir Sydney 2000 Olympic Bid Ltd, Chair. Sydney 2000 Bid Cultural Cttee; fmr mem. Bd Sydney Organising Cttee for the Olympic Games (SOCOG), Chair. SOCOG's Cultural Comm.; mem. Bd Welsh Nat. Opera, Cardiff, UK 1997–2000, Opera Australia Capital Fund, Perth Int. Festival; Visiting Fellow, Univ. of Edin., UK 1992; Fellow, Senate of Univ., Sydney 1994–97. *Publication:* The Boyer Collection (ed.) 2001. *Leisure interests:* reading, swimming. *Address:* Australian Broadcasting Corporation, 700 Harris Street, Ultimo, NSW 2007, Australia (office). *Telephone:* (2) 9333-1500 (Radio) (office). *Fax:* (2) 9333-2603 (Radio) (office). *Website:* www.abc.net.au (office).

MacDONALD, Hon. Donald Stovel, PC, CC, BA, LLM; Canadian politician and lawyer; b. 1 March 1932, Ottawa, Ont.; s. of Donald A. Macdonald and Marjorie I. Stovel; m. 1st Ruth Hutchison 1961 (died 1987); four d.; m. 2nd Adrian Merchant Lang 1988; three step-s. three step-d.; ed Ottawa public schools, Ashbury Coll., Ottawa, Univs of Toronto and Cambridge and Osgoode Hall and Harvard Law Schools; with McCarthy and McCarthy, Barristers, Toronto 1957–62; MP 1962–78; Parl. Sec. to Minister of Justice 1963–65, to Minister of Finance 1965, to Sec. of State for External Affairs 1966–68, to Minister of Industry 1968; Minister without Portfolio 1968; Pres. Privy Council and Govt House Leader 1968; Minister of Nat. Defence 1970–72, of Energy, Mines and Resources 1972–75, of Finance 1975–77; partner, firm McCarthy & McCarthy, Toronto 1977–88; Counsel, McCarthy Tétrault, Toronto 1991–2000; High Commr in the UK 1988–91; Chair. Royal Comm. on the Econ. Union and Devt Prospects for Canada 1982–85, Inst. for Research and Public Policy, Montreal 1991–97; Chair. and Dir Siemens Canada Ltd, Dir Aber Diamond Corpn, Alberta Energy Co. Ltd, Sun Life Assurance Co. of Canada, Trans-Canada Pipelines Ltd, Boise Cascade Corpn 1996–, Chair. Atlantic Council of Canada, Special Advisory Cttee on competition in Ont.'s electricity system 1995–96, Design Exchange, Toronto 1993–96, Canadian Friends of Cambridge Univ. 1995–97; Sr Adviser UBS Bunting Warburg, Toronto 2000; Rowell Fellowship, Canadian Inst. of Int. Affairs 1956; Freeman City of London; Hon. Fellow, Trinity Hall, Cambridge, UK 1994; Hon. LLD (St Lawrence Univ., Univ. of New Brunswick), (Univ. of Toronto) 2000; Hon. DEng (Colo School of Mines). *Leisure interests:* cross-country skiing, tennis. *Address:* 27 Marlborough Avenue, Toronto, Ont., M5R 1X5, Canada (home). *Telephone:* (416) 964-6757 (home). *Fax:* (416) 964-8901 (home). *E-mail:* London@merchantmac.com.

MacDONALD, Hon. Flora Isabel, CC, PC; Canadian politician and consultant; *Secretary, Future Generations Canada;* b. 3 June 1926, North Sydney, NS; d. of George Frederick and Mary Isabel (née Royle) MacDonald; ed North Sydney High School, Empire Business Coll. and National Defence Coll., Kingston, Ont.; Exec. Dir Progressive Conservative HQ 1957–66; admin. officer and tutor, Dept of Political Studies, Queen's Univ. 1966–72; Nat. Sec. Progressive Conservative Assoc of Canada 1966–69; MP for Kingston and the Islands, Ont. 1972–88; Sec. of State for External Affairs 1979–80; Minister of Employment and Immigration 1984–86, of Communications 1986–88; host, weekly TV series North/South 1990–94; Chair. Int. Devt Research Centre 1992–97, Shastri Indo-Canada Advisory Council 1997–2004, HelpAge Int., London, UK 1997–2001; Co-Chair. Canadian Co-ordinating Cttee UN Year of Older Persons 1999; Pres. Future Generations, Franklin, W Va 1998–2007, Sec. Future Generations Canada 2007–; Partnership Africa-Canada 2002–04; mem. Carnegie Comm. on Preventing Deadly Conflict 1994–99; Visiting Fellow, Centre for Canadian Studies, Univ. of Edin. Sept.–Dec. 1989; Pres. Assoc of Canadian Clubs 1999–2003, World Federalist Movt—Canada (fmrly World Federalists of Canada) 2001–04, UNIFEM Canada; Patron, Commonwealth Human Rights Initiative; Hon. Patron for Canada of Nat. Museums of Scotland; Companion Order of Ont. 1995, Order of NS 2007; Padma Shri (India) 2004; 18 hon. degrees; Pearson Peace Medal, UN Assoc 2000, UNIFEM Canada Award 2002. *Leisure interests:* travel, reading, speedskating. *Address:* 1103 – 350 Queen Elizabeth Driveway, Ottawa, ON K1S 3N1, Canada (home). *Telephone:* (613) 238-1098 (home). *Fax:* (613) 238-6330 (home). *E-mail:* flora@intranet.ca (home).

McDONALD, Forrest, PhD; American academic and writer; b. 7 Jan. 1927, Orange, Texas; s. of John Forrest and Myra M. McGill; m. Ellen Shapiro 1963; five c.; ed Orange High School and Univ. of Tex. (Austin); State Historical Soc. of Wisconsin 1953–58; Assoc. Prof., Brown Univ. 1959–64, Prof. 1964–67; Prof., Wayne State Univ. 1967–76; Prof., Univ. of Alabama 1976–87, Distinguished

Research Prof. 1976, 1987–2002; J.P. Harrison Visiting Prof., Coll. of William and Mary 1986–87; Jefferson Lecturer Nat. Endowment for the Humanities 1987; Guggenheim Fellow 1962–63; mem. American Antiquarian Soc., Philadelphia Soc., The Historical Soc.; George Washington Medal (Freedom's Foundation) 1980, Frances Tavern Book Award 1980, American Revolution Round Table Book Award 1986, 16th Jefferson Lecturer in the Humanities (Nat. Endowment for the Humanities) 1987, Ingersoll Prize, Richard M. Weaver Award 1990, Salvatori Award for Academic Excellence 1992. *Publications include:* We The People: The Economic Origins of the Constitution 1958, Insull 1962, E Pluribus Unum: The Formation of the American Republic 1965, Presidency of George Washington 1974, The Phaeton Ride 1974, Presidency of Thomas Jefferson 1976, Alexander Hamilton: A Biography 1980, A Constitutional History of the United States 1982, Novus Ordo Seclorum: The Intellectual Origins of the Constitution 1985, Requiem: Variations on Eighteenth-Century Themes 1988, The American Presidency: An Intellectual History 1994, States' Rights and the Union 2000, Recovering the Past: A Historian's Memoir 2004. *Leisure interests:* gardening, tennis. *Address:* P.O. Box 155, Coker, AL 35452, USA. *Telephone:* (205) 339-0317.

McDONALD, Gabrielle Kirk, LLB; American judge and fmr professor of law; *Arbitrator, Iran-United States Claims Tribunal;* b. 12 April 1942, St Paul, Minn.; d. of James G. Kirk and Frances R. Kirk; one s. one d.; ed Boston Univ., Hunter Coll., Howard Univ. School of Law (First in Class Grad.); Counsel, Legal Defense and Educ. Fund, Nat. Asscn for the Advancement of Colored People; Partner and Attorney-at-Law, McDonald & McDonald, PC; Judge, US Dist Court for the Fed. Dist Court; Partner and Attorney-at-Law Matthews Branscomb PC; Of Counsel, Walker, Bright & Whittenton; Prof. of Law, Texas Southern Univ.; Thurgood Marshall School of Law, St Mary's Univ. School of Law; Int. Criminal Law Judge, Int. Criminal Tribunal for the Fmr Yugoslavia (ICTY), Pres. ICTY; Arbitrator, Iran-US Claims Tribunal; Special Counsel to the Chair. on Human Rights, Freeport-McMoRan Copper & Gold, Inc.; mem. Exec. Bd, ABA Center for Human Rights; mem. Bd of Dirs American Arbitration Asscn; mem. Bd, Int. Jury of the Félix Houphouët-Boigny Peace Prize, ABA Human Rights Center and Genocide Prevention Task Force; mem. Bd of Trustees, Howard Univ.; mem. American Acad. of Diplomacy, US Inst. of Peace, Horatio Alger Asscn of Distinguished Americans; Hon. Dr of Law (Georgetown Univ. Law Center), (Univ. of Notre Dame), (Howard Univ. School of Law), (Stetson Coll. of Law), (Jewish Theological Seminary), (Amherst Coll.), (Univ. of Hartford); Leadership Award, Cen. Eastern European Law Initiative, First Equal Justice and Ronald Brown Int. Law Awards, Nat. Bar Asscn, Goler Teal Butcher Award for Human Rights, American Soc. of Int. Law, Human Rights Award, Minnesota Advocates for Human Rights, Margaret Brent Women Lawyers of Achievement Award, ABA Comm. on Women in the Profession, Congressman Mickey Leland Legacy Award, First Women Ground Breakers in Int. Justice Award, Open Soc. Inst., Dorothy I. Height Lifetime Achievement Award, inducted into Texas Women's Hall of Fame. *Publications:* Substantive and Procedural Aspects of International Criminal Law, The Experience of International and National Courts (co-ed.) 2000; several published addresses and articles in int. law reviews. *Address:* Iran-United States Claims Tribunal, Parkweg 13, 2585 JH The Hague, Netherlands (office). *Telephone:* (70) 352-0064 (office). *Fax:* (70) 350-2456 (office). *E-mail:* e.deman@iusct.org (office). *Website:* www.iusct.org (office).

MACDONALD, (Hugh) Ian, OC, BCom, BPhil, LLD, MA; Canadian economist, academic and university administrator; *President Emeritus and Professor Emeritus of Economics and Policy, York University;* b. 27 June 1929, Toronto; five c.; ed Univ. of Toronto, Univ. of Oxford, UK; Chief Economist, Govt of Ontario 1965–67, Deputy Treas. 1967–68, Deputy Minister of Treasury and Econs 1968–72, Deputy Minister of Treasury, Econs and Intergovernmental Affairs 1972–74; Pres. York Univ., Toronto 1974–84, Pres. Emer. 1984–, Dir York International 1984–94, Prof. of Econs and Public Policy 1984–, currently Prof. Emer., Dir Master of Public Admin. Program 1994–; Chair. McGraw-Hill Ryerson 1985–; Chair. Commonwealth of Learning, Vancouver 1994–2003, Fellow 2004; mem. The AGF Funds 1979–; Hon. Life mem. Canadian Olympic Asscn 1997–, Hon. Prof. (Hunan Univ.) 2007; Kt of Grace, Order of St Lazarus of Jerusalem 1978, Southeastern Conf. Public Admin Senator Boorsma Medal, USA 2006; Hon. LLD (Toronto) 1974, DUniv (Open Univ., UK) 1998, Hon. DLitt (Open Univ., Sri Lanka) 1999, (The B.R. Ambedkar Open Univ., Hyderabad, India) 2002, (York Univ.) 2007; Gov.-Gen.'s Medal 1952, Centennial Medal 1967, Queen's Silver Jubilee Medal 1977, Canadian Confed. Medal for the 125th Anniversary 1992, Award of Merit, Canadian Bureau for Int. Educ. 1994, Vanier Medal 2000, Senator Boorsma Medal 2006, Queen's Golden Jubilee Medal 2002, Queen's Diamond Jubilee Medal 2012, honored as one of the eight 'Legends of the Ontario Public Service', Govt of Ontario 2013, honored as one of ten 'Alumni of Influence', Univ. Coll., Univ. of Toronto 2013. *Publications include:* numerous articles, essays and contribs to books. *Leisure interests:* ice hockey and tennis. *Address:* York University, Room N207, Schulich School of Business, 4700 Keele Street, Toronto, ON M3J 1P3, Canada (office). *Telephone:* (416) 736-5632 (office). *Fax:* (416) 736-5643 (office). *E-mail:* yorkmpa@yorku.ca (office). *Website:* www.schulich.yorku.ca (office).

McDONALD, John W., AB, JD; American diplomatist (retd), international organization executive and lawyer; *Chairman and CEO, Institute for Multi-Track Diplomacy;* b. 18 Feb. 1922, Koblenz, Germany; s. of John Warlick McDonald and Ethel Mae Raynor; m. 1st Barbara Jane Stewart 1943 (divorced); one s. three d.; m. 2nd Christel Meyer 1970; ed Univ. of Illinois, Nat. War Coll., Washington, DC; admitted to Ill. Supreme Court Bar 1946, to US Supreme Court 1951; Legal Div., US Office of Mil. Govt, Berlin 1947; Asst District Attorney, US Mil. Govt Courts, Frankfurt 1947–50; Sec. Law Cttee, Allied High Comm., Petersburg, Germany 1950–52; mem. Mission to NATO and OECD, Paris Marshal Plan 1952–54; Office of Exec. Sec. Dept of State 1954–55; Exec. Sec. to Dir of Int. Co-operation Admin. 1955–59; US Econ. Co-ordinator for CENTO Affairs, Ankara 1959–63; Chief, Econ. and Commercial Sections, Embassy in Cairo 1963–66; Deputy Dir Office of Econ. and Social Affairs, Dept of State 1967–68, Dir 1968–71; Co-ordinator, UN Multilateral Dev. Programmes, Dept of State 1971–74, Acting Deputy Asst Sec. of State for Econ. and Social Affairs 1971, 1973; Deputy Dir-Gen. ILO, Geneva, Switzerland 1974–78; Pres. Int. Telecommunications Satellite Org. (INTELSAT) Conf. on Privileges and Immunities 1978; Amb. to UN Conf. on TCDC 1978; Sec.-Gen. 27th Colombo Plan Ministerial Meeting 1978; US Co-ordinator for UN Decade on Drinking Water and Sanitation 1979; rep. to UN Confs with rank of

Amb. 1978–; Amb. to UNIDO III 1979–80; Chair. Fed. Cttee for UN Int. Year of Disabled Persons; Amb. to UN World Ass. on Ageing 1981–82; Co-ordinator for Multilateral Affairs, Center for the Study of Foreign Affairs, US Dept of State 1983–87; Pres. Iowa Peace Inst. 1988–92, People-to-People Cttee for the Handicapped, Countdown 2001, World Cttee: UN Decade of Disabled Persons; del. to many int. confs; Bd of Dirs Global Water 1982–; Chair. American Asscn for Int. Ageing 1983–; Law School Prof., George Washington Univ., Washington, DC 1987–88; Adjunct Prof. of Political Science, Grinnell Coll. 1989–92; Distinguished Visiting Prof., George Mason Univ., Fairfax, Va 1992–93; Adjunct Prof., Union Inst. 1995–98, George Mason Univ. 1998–2000; Co-founder, Chair. and CEO Inst. for Multi-Track Diplomacy, Washington, DC 1992–; mem. Cosmos Club, American Foreign Service Asscn, US Asscn for the Club of Rome, DKE; Hon. PhD (Mount Mercy Coll.) 1989, (Teiko Mary Crest Univ.) 1991, (Salisbury State Univ.) 1993; Hon. LLD (St John's Univ.) 2007; Superior Honour Award, Dept of State 1972, Presidential Meritorial Service Award 1984, Alumni Asscn Award, Univ. of Illinois School of Liberal Arts 2004, Alumni of the Year Award, Univ. of Illinois 2006, Amb. John W. McDonald Award for Leadership and Innovation in Global Governance and Conflict Resolution, Univ. of Massachusetts, Boston Campus 2011. *Publications:* The North-South Dialogue and the United Nations 1982, How To Be a Delegate 1984, International Negotiations 1985, Perspectives on Negotiation: Four Case Studies 1986, Conflict Resolution: Track Two Diplomacy 1987, US-Soviet Summitry 1987, US Base Rights Negotiations 1989, Multi-Track Diplomacy 1991, Defining a US Negotiating Style 1996, The Shifting Grounds of Conflict and Peacebuilding 2008. *Leisure interests:* reading, tennis, fencing, skiing. *Address:* Institute for Multi-Track Diplomacy, 1901 North Fort Myer Drive, Suite 405, Arlington, VA 22209, USA (office). *Telephone:* (703) 528-3863 (office); (703) 525-9755 (home). *Fax:* (703) 528-5776 (office). *E-mail:* jmcdonald@imtd.org (office). *Website:* www.imtd.org (office).

MacDONALD, Julien, OBE, MA; British fashion designer; b. 19 March 1972, Merthyr Tydfil, Wales; ed Cyfarthfa High School, Merthyr Tydfil, Faculty of Arts and Architecture, Brighton, Royal Coll. of Art; worked for Alexander McQueen and Koji Tatsuno as a student; knitwear designer for Chanel Ready-to-Wear, Chanel Couture and Karl Lagerfeld; has had four shows in his own right; Art Dir Max Factor Spring/Summer 1999 advertising campaign (including TV commercial); Chief Designer, Givenchy 2001–04; selected by British Airways to redesign their flight attendants' uniforms 2001; consultant, Boots PLC 2001–; creations have been worn by Joely Richardson, Dannii Minogue, Geri Halliwell, Dame Shirley Bassey, Carmen Electra, Naomi Campbell, Beyoncé Knowles, Bonnie Tyler and Selena Gomez; London Fashion Award for Glamour, named British Fashion Designer of the Year 2001. *Television:* judge on UK version of Project Runway, known as Project Catwalk (Sky One) 2008, judge on Britain & Ireland's Next Top Model 2010, celebrity contestant on Strictly Come Dancing 2013. *Telephone:* (20) 3542-0270 (office). *E-mail:* gemma@julienmacdonald.com (office). *Website:* www .julienmacdonald.com (office).

McDONALD, Robert A. (Bob), BS, MBA, FRSA; American business executive; b. 20 June 1953, Gary, Ind.; m. Diane McDonald; one s. one d.; ed US Mil. Acad., West Point, Univ. of Utah; Capt., US Army 1975–80; joined P&G 1980, Brand Asst, Solo, PS&D Advertising 1980–81, Sales Training, Oklahoma City Sales Dist 1981, Asst Brand Man., Dawn, PS&D Advertising 1981–82, Asst Brand Man., Cascade, PS&D Advertising 1982–83, Brand Man., Cascade 1983–84, Brand Man., Tide, PS&D Advertising 1984–86, Brand Man., Tide 1986–87, Assoc. Advertising Man., Laundry Products, PS&D Div. 1987–89, Man., Laundry Products, P&G Canada 1989–91, Gen. Man., Philippines, Asia/Pacific-South, P&G Far East 1991–94, Vice-Pres., Gen. Man.-Philippines, Asia/Pacific-South, P&G Far East 1994–95, Vice-Pres., Gen. Man., Laundry and Cleaning Products, P&G Asia, and Beauty Care Products-Japan, P&G Asia 1995–96, Regional Vice-Pres., Japan, Procter & Gamble Asia 1996–99, Vice-Pres., Northeast Asia 1999, Pres. Northeast Asia 1999–2001, Pres. Global Fabric Care 2001, Pres. Global Fabric & Home Care 2001–04, Vice-Pres. Global Operations, Procter & Gamble Co. 2004–07, COO Procter & Gamble Co. 2007–09, Pres. and CEO 2009–13, Chair. 2010–13; mem. Bd of Dirs Xerox Corpn, McKinsey Advisory Council; Chair. GS1, Fuqua Global Partnerships Cttee, Duke Univ.; Vice-Chair. US-China Business Council; Special Amb., Hyogo Pref. and Kobe City, Japan; mem. US Advisory Cttee for Trade Policy and Negotiations, Asscn of Grads, US Mil. Acad., West Point, Singapore Int. Advisory Council of Econ. Devt Bd; Mentor, Nat. Conf. on Ethics in America; mem. Advisory Bd Northwestern Integrated Marketing Communications, David Eccles School of Business, Univ. of Utah, Grad. School of Man., St Petersburg State Univ., Russia; mem. Bd of Visitors and Exec. Cttee, Fuqua School of Business, Duke Univ.; fmr Dir, Procter & Gamble and Clorox Jt Venture; fmr Chair. Soap and Detergent Asscn; fmr Gov. American Chamber of Commerce in Japan; fmr Moderator, Kobe Union Church Council; Inaugural Leadership Excellence Award, Stockdale Center for Ethical Leadership at US Naval Acad. and Harvard Business Review 2007, Pres.'s Leadership Award, Far East Council Boy Scouts. *Address:* c/o The Proctor & Gamble Co., 1 Procter & Gamble Plaza, Cincinnati, OH 43202-3315, USA. *E-mail:* info@pg.com.

MacDONALD, Roderick Alexander, BA, LLL, LLB, LLM, FRSC; Canadian professor of law; *F.R. Scott Professor of Constitutional and Public Law, Faculty of Law, McGill University;* b. 6 Aug. 1948, Markham, Ont.; ed Univ. of Toronto, Univ. of Ottawa, York Univ.; Asst Prof., Faculty of Law, Univ. of Windsor, Ont. 1975–77, Assoc. Prof. 1977–79; Assoc. Prof., Faculty of Law, McGill Univ. 1979–84, Prof. 1984–95, F. R. Scott Prof. of Constitutional and Public Law 1995–; visiting positions at Osgoode Hall Law School, Univ. of Toronto, Univ. of British Columbia, ANU, Univ. Blaise Pascal, Clermont-Ferrand, Univ. of Aix-Marseilles; Pres.-elect Royal Soc. of Canada 2008–09, Pres. 2009–; Dir, Law in Soc. Programme, Canadian Inst. for Advanced Research 1989–94; Pres. Law Comm. of Canada 1997–2000; consultant to World Bank, Ukraine 2002–04; Fellow, Trudeau Foundation 2004–; mem. Law Soc. of Upper Canada 1977–, Québec Bar 1983–, Int. Acad. of Comparative Law 1994–; Univ. of Ottawa Section Droit Civil Ordre du Mérite 2007; Royal Soc. of Canada Sir William Dawson Medal for Social Sciences 2007. *Publications:* more than 200 scholarly works. *Address:* Faculty of Law, 3674 Peel Street, Room 301, Montréal, PQ H3A 1W9, Canada (office). *Telephone:* (514) 398-8914 (office). *Fax:* (514) 398-3233 (office). *E-mail:* roderick.macdonald@mcgill .ca (office). *Website:* people.mcgill.ca/roderick.macdonald (office).

MacDONALD, Rodney, BS; Canadian politician; b. 2 Jan. 1972, Inverness, Nova Scotia; s. of Alex Angus and Elizabeth Ann MacDonald; m. Lori-Ann MacDonald; one s.; ed St. Francis Xavier Univ.; taught for Strait Regional School Board –1999; elected to Legislative Ass. as MLA for Inverness 1999, re-elected 2003; Leader Nova Scotia Progressive Conservative Party 2006–; Premier of Nova Scotia 2006–09; fmr Vice-Pres. GlennRod Music Inc. *Address:* c/o Nova Scotia Progressive Conservative Party, 801-1660 Hollis Street, Halifax, Nova Scotia B3J 1V7, Canada (office).

McDONALD, Sir Trevor, Kt, OBE; British broadcast journalist; b. 16 Aug. 1939, Trinidad; m.; two s. one d.; worked on newspapers, radio and TV, Trinidad 1960–69; Producer BBC Caribbean Service and World Service, London 1969–73; reporter Ind. TV News 1973–78, sports corresp. 1978–80, diplomatic corresp. 1980–87, newscaster 1982–87, Diplomatic Ed. Channel Four News 1987–89, newscaster News at 5.40 1989–90, News at Ten 1990–99, ITV Evening News 1999–2000, ITV News at Ten 2001–04, 2008, News at 10.30 2004–05; Chair. Better English Campaign 1995–97, Nuffield Language Inquiry 1998–2000; apptd Gov. English-Speaking Union of the Commonwealth 2000; Pres. European Year of Languages 2000; apptd Chancellor London South Bank Univ. 1999; Hon. Fellow, Liverpool John Moores Univ. 1998; Hon. DLitt (South Bank) 1994, (Plymouth) 1995, (Southampton Inst.) 1997, (Nottingham) 1997, Dr hc (Surrey) 1997, (Open Univ.) 1997, Hon. LLD (Univ. of West Indies) 1996; Newscaster of the Year TV and Radio Industries Club 1993, 1997, 1999; Gold Medal, Royal TV Soc. 1998, Richard Dimbleby Award for outstanding contrib. to TV, BAFTA 1999, Royal Television Soc. Lifetime Achievement Award 2005, BAFTA Fellowship, British Acad. Television Awards 2011. *Publications include:* Clive Lloyd: A Biography 1985, Vivian Richards: A Biography 1987, Queen and Commonwealth 1989, Fortunate Circumstances (autobiography) 1993, Favourite Poems 1997, World of Poetry 1999. *Leisure interests:* tennis, golf, cricket. *Address:* c/o ITN, 200 Gray's Inn Road, London, WC1X 8XZ, England.

MACDONALD OF RIVER GLAVEN, Baron (Life Peer), cr. 2010, of Cley-next-the-Sea in the County of Norfolk; **Ken Macdonald,** BA, QC; British barrister; *Founder-Member, Matrix Chambers;* b. 4 Jan. 1953; s. of Kenneth Macdonald and Maureen Sheridan Hacker; m. Linda Zuck 1980; two s., one d.; ed St Edmund Hall, Oxford; called to the Bar 1978, QC 1997; part-time judge, Crown Court 2001–; Dir of Public Prosecutions and Head of Crown Prosecution Service 2003–08; Chair. Criminal Bar Assn; Founder-mem. Matrix Chambers; Bencher of the Inner Temple 2003–; mem. Sentencing Guidelines Council 2003–08; mem. Criminal Procedure Rule Cttee 2003–08. *Leisure interests:* Arsenal Football Club, crime thrillers, film noir, 19th century history. *Address:* Matrix Chambers, Griffin Buildings, Gray's Inn, London, WC1R 5LN, England (office). *Telephone:* (20) 7404-3447 (office). *Website:* www.matrixlaw.co.uk (office).

McDONNELL, Robert Francis (Bob), BBA, MBA, MA, JD; American lawyer and politician; b. 15 June 1954, Philadelphia, Pa; s. of John McDonnell and Emma McDonnell; m. Maureen Patricia Gardner 1976; two s. three d.; ed Bishop Ireton High School, Alexandria, Va, Univ. of Notre Dame, Boston Univ., Regent Univ. School of Law; served as medical supply officer in US Army for four years, and in Army Reserve 1981–97 (retired with rank of Lt-Col), ran medical clinic in Germany 1976–79, in Newport News, Va 1979–81, various positions American Hosp. Supply Corpn 1981–85; policy intern, Republican Policy Cttee 1988; law clerk, Office of Commonwealth Attorney, Chesapeake, 1989, Asst Commonwealth Attorney, Virginia Beach 1990–91; represented 84th Dist in Virginia Beach in Virginia House of Dels 1992–2005, Co-Chair. Cttee on the Chesapeake and its Tributaries 2000–01, Chair. Courts of Justice Cttee 2003, also served on Rules Cttee 2000–05, Asst Majority Leader 2002–06; Pnr, Huff, Poole & Mahoney, Professional Corpn, Virginia Beach 1992–2006; Attorney Gen., State of Virginia 2006–09; Gov. of Virginia 2010–(14); Chair. Republican Govs Assn, Southern Growth Policies Bd, Southern Regional Educ. Bd, Legal Affairs Cttee of the Nat. Govs Assn; Republican; named Legislator of Year, Network of Victims of Crime 1996, Family Foundation 1998, 2001, Nat. Legislator of Year, Nat. Child Support Enforcement Assn 1998, Legislator of Year, Virginia Sheriff's Assn 2005. *Address:* Virginia Liaison Office, Commonwealth of Virginia, 444 North Capitol Street, Suite 214, Washington, DC 20001, USA (office). *Telephone:* (202) 783-1769 (office). *Fax:* (202) 783-7687 (office). *Website:* www.bobmcdonnell.com.

McDONOUGH, Denis R., BA, MSFS; American government official; *Chief of Staff to the President;* b. 2 Dec. 1969, Stillwater, Minn.; s. of William McDonough and Kathleen McDonough; ed St John's Univ., Collegeville, Minn., Edmund A. Walsh School of Foreign Service, Georgetown Univ., Washington, DC; following graduation, travelled extensively throughout Latin America and taught high school in Belize early 1990s; worked as an aide to Int. Relations Cttee, US House of Reps, Washington, DC 1996–99; Sr Foreign Policy Advisor to Senator Tom Daschle 1999–2004; Legis. Dir for Senator Ken Salazar 2004–05; Sr Fellow, Center for American Progress 2004; Chief Foreign Policy Advisor to Senator Barack Obama 2007–09; Head of Strategic Communication, Nat. Security Council 2009–10, also served as Nat. Security Council Chief of Staff; Deputy Nat. Security Advisor to Pres. Barack Obama 2010–13; Chief of Staff, The White House 2013–. *Address:* Office of the President, The White House, 1600 Pennsylvania Avenue, NW, Washington, DC 20500, USA (office). *Telephone:* (202) 456-1414 (office). *Fax:* (202) 456-2461 (office). *Website:* www.whitehouse.gov (office).

McDONOUGH, William Andrews; American architect and business executive; *Founding Principal, William McDonough + Partners;* b. 21 Feb. 1951, Tokyo, Japan; ed Dartmouth Coll., Yale Univ.; Founding Prin. William McDonough + Partners, New York City 1981– (moved to Charlottesville, Va 1994); first major comm. Environmental Defense Fund HQ 1985; Dean of School of Architecture, Univ. of Virginia 1994–99; several large corp. projects for The Gap, Nike and Herman Miller; commissioned in 1991 to write The Hannover Principles: Design for Sustainability as guidelines for the City of Hannover's EXPO 2000; commissioned for 20-year, US $2 billion environmental re-eng of Ford Motor Co.'s River Rouge Plant, Dearborn, Mich., including world's largest 'living roof'; Co-founder and Prin., MBDC; Venture Pnr and Sr Advisor, VantagePoint Venture Partners; first and only individual recipient of Presidential Award for Sustainable Devt 1996, named by TIME magazine as a Hero for the Planet 1999, Nat. Design Award, Smithsonian Cooper-Hewitt Nat. Design Museum 2004, Presidential Green Chem. Challenge Award. *Projects include:* Herman Miller 'GreenHouse' Factory and

Offices 1995, 901 Cherry, Offices for Gap Inc. 1997, Oberlin Coll.'s Adam Joseph Lewis Center for Environmental Studies 2000. *Publication:* Cradle to Cradle: Remaking the Way We Make Things (co-author) 2002. *Address:* William McDonough + Partners, 700 East Jefferson Street, Charlottesville, VA 22902, USA (office). *Telephone:* (434) 979-1111 (office). *Fax:* (434) 979-1112 (office). *E-mail:* info@mcdonoughpartners.com (office); media@mcdonough.com. *Website:* www.mcdonoughpartners.com (office); www.mcdonough.com.

McDONOUGH, William Joseph, BS, MA; American banker (retd); b. 21 April 1934, Chicago, Ill.; m. Suzanne Clarke 1985; three s. three d.; ed Holy Cross Coll., Worcester, Mass, Georgetown Univ., Washington, DC; USN 1956–61; US State Dept 1961–67; First Nat. Bank of Chicago 1967–89, Vice-Chair. and Dir holding co. 1986–89; subsequently served as adviser to IBRD and IFC; Special Advisor to Pres. of IDB; Chair. Illinois Comm. on Future of Public Service; Exec. Vice-Pres. and Head of Markets Group, Fed. Reserve Bank of New York and Man. Open Market Operations for Fed. Open Market Cttee 1992–93, Vice-Chair. Fed. Open Market Cttee, Pres. and CEO Fed. Reserve Bank of New York 1993–2003; Chair. Public Co. Accounting Oversight Bd 2003–05; fmr Vice-Chair. and Special Adviser to the Chair., Merrill Lynch & Co., Inc.; Chair. Investment Cttee for the UN Jt Staff Pension Fund; Co-Chair. UNA-USA; mem. Bd of Dirs New York Philharmonic Orchestra, Council on Foreign Relations 1995–; mem. Group of Thirty Consultative Group on Int. Econ. and Monetary Affairs, Inc. (G-30), Washington, DC, Inst. for Int. Econs; Yale Distinguished Leadership in Global Capital Markets Award 2001. *Address:* c/o Merrill Lynch & Co., Inc., 4 World Financial Center, 250 Vesey Street, New York, NY 10080, USA (office).

McDORMAND, Frances, MFA; American actress; b. 23 June 1957, Chicago, Ill.; d. of Veron McDormand and Noreen McDormand; m. Joel Coen (q.v.) 1994; one s.; ed Bethany Coll., Yale Univ. School of Drama; Screen Actors' Guild Award 1996, London Film Critics' Circle Award 1996, Ind. Spirit Award 1996, American Comedy Award 1997. *Films include:* Blood Simple 1984, Raising Arizona 1987, Mississippi Burning 1988, Chattahoochee 1990, Darkman 1990, Miller's Crossing 1990, Hidden Agenda 1990, The Butcher's Wife 1991, Passed Away 1992, Short Cuts 1993, Beyond Rangoon 1995, Fargo 1996 (Acad. Award for Best Actress), Primal Fear 1996, Lone Star 1996, Paradise Road 1997, Johnny Skidmarks 1997, Madeline 1998, Talk of Angels 1998, Wonder Boys (Best Supporting Actress, Broadcast Film Critics Assn, Florida Film Critics Circle, LA Film Critics Assn 2000) 1999, Almost Famous 2000, The Man Who Wasn't There 2001, Upheaval 2001, Laurel Canyon 2002, City By the Sea 2002, Something's Gotta Give 2003, North Country 2005, Friends with Money (Independent Spirit Award for Best Supporting Female) 2006, Miss Pettigrew Lives for a Day 2007, Burn After Reading 2008, Transformers: Dark of the Moon 2011, Moonrise Kingdom 2012, Promised Land 2012. *Stage appearances include:* Awake and Sing 1984, Painting Churches 1984, The Three Sisters 1985, All My Sons 1986, A Streetcar Named Desire 1988, Moon for the Misbegotten 1992, Sisters Rosensweig 1993, The Swan 1993, Good People (Tony Award for Best Actress in a Play) 2011. *Address:* c/o WME, 9601 Wilshire Blvd, Beverly Hills, CA 90212, USA. *Website:* www.wma.com.

McDOUGALL, Douglas; British business executive; *Chairman, Scottish Investment Trust PLC;* b. 1944; ed Univ. of Oxford; joined Baillie Gifford & Co. 1965, Pnr 1969–89, Jt Sr Pnr 1989–99; Chair. Scottish Investment Trust PLC 2003–; fmr Chair. Investment Man. Regulatory Org. Ltd (IMRO), Asscn of Investment Trust Cos, Institutional Fund Mans Assn; currently Chair. Law Debenture Corpn PLC, 3i Bioscience Investment Trust PLC, Foreign & Colonial Eurotrust PLC, The Independent Investment Trust PLC, Pacific Horizon Investment Trust PLC; Dir The Herald Investment Trust PLC, The Monks Investment Trust PLC. *Address:* The Scottish Investment Trust, 6 Albyn Place, Edinburgh, EH2 4NL, Scotland (office). *Telephone:* (131) 225-7781 (office). *Fax:* (131) 226-3663 (office). *Website:* www.sit.co.uk (office).

MacDOWELL, Andie; American actress; b. 21 April 1958, S. Carolina; d. of Marion MacDowell and the late Pauline MacDowell; m. 1st Paul Qualley; two d. one s.; m. 2nd Rhett DeCamp Hartzog 2001 (divorced 2004). *Television appearances include:* Secret of the Sahara 1987, Women and Men 2, In Love There Are No Rules 1991, Jo 2002, Riding the Bus with My Sister 2005, The Prince of Motor City 2008, Lone Star 2010, Jane by Design (series) 2012, Cedar Cove (series) 2013. *Films include:* Greystoke 1984, St Elmo's Fire 1985, Sex, Lies and Videotape 1989, Green Card 1990, Hudson Hawk 1991, The Object of Beauty 1991, The Player 1992, Ruby 1992, Groundhog Day 1993, Short Cuts 1993, Bad Girls 1994, Four Weddings and a Funeral 1994, Unstrung Heroes 1995, My Life and Me 1996, Multiplicity 1996, The End of Violence 1997, Town and Country 1998, Shadrack 1998, The Scalper 1998, Just the Ticket 1998, Muppets From Space 1999, The Music 2000, Town and Country 2001, Harrison's Flowers 2002, Crush 2002, Ginostra 2002, The Last Sign 2004, Beauty Shop 2005, Tara Road 2005, Barnyard (voice) 2006, Inconceivable 2008, The 5th Quarter 2009, Daydream Nation 2010, Monte Carlo 2011, Footloose 2011, Mighty Fine 2012, Breaking at the Edge 2013. *Address:* c/o ICM, 10250 Constellation Blvd, Los Angeles, CA 90067, USA.

McDOWELL, David Keith, MA; New Zealand diplomatist, conservationist and environmental consultant; b. 30 April 1937, Palmerston North; s. of Keith McDowell and Gwen McDowell; m. Jan Ingram 1960; one s. three d.; ed Victoria Univ. of Wellington; joined Ministry of Foreign Affairs 1959, seconded to Prime Minister's Dept, Western Samoa 1962–63, Head, UN and African and Middle East Divs 1973, Dir of External Aid 1973–76, Head, Econ. Div. 1980–81, Special Asst to Sec. Gen., Commonwealth Secr., London 1969–72; High Commr in Fiji 1977–80, in India, Nepal and Bangladesh 1983–85; Asst Sec. of Foreign Affairs for Asia, Australia and the Americas 1981–85; First Sec., Perm. Mission to UN 1964–68, Perm. Rep. 1985–88; Dir-Gen. Dept of Conservation 1988–89; CEO Dept of Prime Minister and Cabinet 1989–91; Amb. to Japan 1992–94; Dir-Gen. Int. Union for Conservation of Nature (IUCN—World Conservation Union), Switzerland 1994–99; pvt. consultant 1999–; mem. Review Panel, Environmental Performance of World Bank 2002, Ministerial Advisory Group on Oceans Policy 2002–03 (NZ), Strategic Advisory Group, Office of the Compliance Advisor/Ombudsman (CAO), Int. Finance Corpn 2003–; currently mem. Panel of Experts, Nam Theun Multi-Purpose Project, Ministry of Mines and Energy, Laos. *Leisure interests:* fishing, boating, tennis, conservation, gardening, music. *Address:* 86 Waerenga Road, Otaki, New Zealand (home). *Telephone:* (6) 364-6296 (office). *E-mail:* jan.david .mcdowell@xtra.co.nz (office).

McDOWELL, John Henry, MA, FBA, FAAS; British academic; *Distinguished University Professor, University of Pittsburgh*; b. 7 March 1942, Boksburg, South Africa; s. of Sir Henry McDowell and Norah McDowell (née Douthwaite); m. Andrea Lehrke 1977; ed St John's Coll. Johannesburg, Univ. Coll. of Rhodesia and Nyasaland, New Coll., Oxford; Fellow, Praelector in Philosophy, Univ. Coll., Oxford 1966–86; Prof. of Philosophy, Univ. of Pittsburgh 1986–88, Distinguished Univ. Prof. 1988–; Hon. DHumLitt (Chicago) 2008; Distinguished Achievement Award, Andrew W. Mellon Foundation 2010. *Publications include:* Ed. (with Gareth Evans) Truth and Meaning, Ed. (with Philip Pettit) Subject, Thought and Context, Mind and World, Mind, Value and Reality, Meaning, Knowledge and Reality, Having the World in View, The Engaged Intellect; trans of Plato, Theaetetus. *Leisure interests:* gardening, reading. *Address:* Department of Philosophy, University of Pittsburgh, Pittsburgh, PA 15260 (office); 947 Heberton Street, Pittsburgh, PA 15206, USA. *Telephone:* (412) 624-5792 (office); (412) 361-3784. *E-mail:* jmcdowel@pitt.edu (office). *Website:* www.philosophy.pitt.edu (office).

McDOWELL, Malcolm; British actor; b. (Malcolm Taylor), 13 June 1943, Leeds; m. 1st Mary Steenburgen 1980; one s. one d.; m. 2nd Kelley Kuhr 1992; began career with the RSC at Stratford 1965–66; early television appearances in such series as Dixon of Dock Green, Z Cars. *Stage appearances:* RSC, Stratford 1965–66, Entertaining Mr. Sloane, Royal Court 1975, Look Back in Anger, New York 1980, In Celebration, New York 1984, Holiday Old Vic 1987, Another Time, Old Vic 1993. *Films include:* If. . . 1969, Figures in a Landscape 1970, The Raging Moon 1971, A Clockwork Orange 1971, O Lucky Man 1973, Royal Flash 1975, Aces High 1976, Voyage of the Damned 1977, Caligula 1977, The Passage 1978, Time After Time 1979, Cat People 1981, Blue Thunder 1983, Get Crazy 1983, Britannia Hospital 1984, Gulag 1985, The Caller 1987, Sunset 1987, Sunrise 1988, Class of 1999, Il Maestro 1989, Moon 44, Double Game, Class of 1999, Snake Eyes, Schweitzer, Assassin of the Tsar 1991, The Player, Chain of Desire, East Wind, Night Train to Venice, Star Trek: Generations 1995, Tank Girl 1995, Kids of the Round Table, Where Truth Lies, Mr Magoo 1998, Gangster No 1 2000, Island of the Dead 2000, Just Visiting 2001, The Void 2001, Dorian 2001, The Barber 2001, Between Strangers 2002, Superman: Shadow of Apokolips 2002, I Spy 2002, I'll Sleep When I'm Dead 2003, Tempo 2003, Inhabited 2003, Red Roses and Petrol 2003, The Company 2003, Hidalgo 2004, Evilenko 2004, Bobby Jones, Stroke of Genius 2004, Tempesta 2004, Pinocchio 3000 (voice) 2004, Rag Tale 2005, Dinotopia: Quest for the Ruby Sunstone (voice) 2005, Cut Off 2006, Bye Bye Benjamin 2006, Exitz 2007, The List 2007, Halloween 2007, Doomsday 2008. *Television includes:* Our Friends in the North, Entourage, Heroes. *Address:* c/o Markham and Froggatt, 4 Windmill Street, London, W1P 1HF, England.

McDOWELL, Michelle, MBE, BSc, CEng, FREng, FICE, FConsE; British civil engineer; *Chair of Civil and Structural Engineering, BDP*; b. 6 April 1963, Co. Londonderry, Northern Ireland; d. of Ronald McDowell and Doris McDowell; pnr Jason Fox; one s.; ed Univ. of Bristol; joined BDP (design consultancy) 1997, currently Chair. Civil and Structural Eng; Vice-Chair. Asscn for Consultancy and Eng 2009, Chair. 2010; fmr Vice-Pres. Inst. of Civil Engineers; mem. British Council of Offices Nat. Judging Panel 2008–; Fellow, Royal Acad. of Eng 2010–, Asscn of Consulting Engineers; Hon. DEng (Bristol) 2012; First Woman of Property Award 2010, Veuve Clicquot Business Woman of Award 2011, ACE Eng Amb. of the Year 2012. *Projects include:* Royal Albert Hall, BBC Mailbox, Birmingham, Roche HQ, Chatham Historic Dockyard, Royal Alexandra Children's Hosp., All England Lawn Tennis Club, Wimbledon. *Address:* 16 Brewhouse Yard, London, EC1V 4LJ, England (office). *Telephone:* (20) 7812-8000 (office). *E-mail:* michellejmcdowell@gmail.com (home). *Website:* www.bdp.com (office).

MacEACHEN, Hon. Allan J., OC, PC, MA; Canadian politician; b. 6 July 1921, Inverness, NS; s. of Angus MacEachen and Annie Gillies; ed St Francis Xavier Univ., Univs of Toronto and Chicago and MIT; Prof. of Econs, St Francis Xavier Univ. 1946–48, later Head, Dept of Econs and Social Sciences; mem. House of Commons 1953–58, 1962–84; MP for Cape Breton Highlands-Cans., NS 1953–84; Special Asst and Consultant on Econ. Affairs to Lester Pearson 1958; Minister of Labour 1963–65; Minister of Nat. Health and Welfare 1965–68, of Manpower and Immigration 1968–70, of Finance 1980–82; Pres. Privy Council and Govt House Leader 1970–74; Sec. of State for External Affairs 1974–76; Pres. Privy Council 1976–77 and Deputy Prime Minister 1977–79; Deputy Leader of Opposition and Opposition House Leader 1979; Deputy Prime Minister and Minister of Finance 1980–82; Deputy Prime Minister and Sec. of State for External Affairs 1982–84; mem. Senate 1984–96, Leader of Govt in Senate June–Oct. 1984, Leader of Opposition in Senate 1984–91; Chair. Int. IMF Group of Ten 1980–81, Interim Cttee of IMF, Conf. on Int. Econ. Co-operation, 1982 Ministerial Meeting of the GATT, Int. Advisory Council of Bank of Montreal 1986–91; Canadian Chair. Atlantik-Brücke Annual Symposium (Canada-Germany Conf.) 1984–; Chair. Advisory Council Int. Ocean Inst. 1996–; Bd Dirs North-South Inst. 1996–; Trustee Royal Ottawa Health Care Group 1987–95; mem. Bd of Govs St Francis Xavier Univ.; Order of Merit, Germany. *Address:* R.R.1, Whycocomagh, Nova Scotia B0E 3M0, Canada (home).

MACEL, Christine; French gallery curator; *Chief Curator, Musée national d'art moderne – Centre Pompidou;* Chief Curator, Musée nat. d'art moderne – Centre Pompidou, Paris 2000–, Dir Département de création contemporaine et prospectif; has curated numerous exhbns, including Raymond Hains, Sophie Calle, Philippe Parreno, Gabriel Orozco, Dionysiac, Airs de Paris and The Promises of the Past; art critic for various magazines, including artpress, Flash Art and Artforum; mem. Jury, 54th Int. Art Exhbn of la Biennale di Venezia 2011. *Publications include:* 315 Livre: No. 3 (ed.) 2004, Time taken, the work of time in the world of art (essay on contemporary art) 2007, Airs de Paris (with Daniel Birnbaum) 2007, Damian Ortega: 315 Livre Numero 17 (with Anna Hiddleston and Sinziana Ravini) 2008, Promises of the Past – A Discontinuous History of Art in Former Eastern Europe, Parreno (co-ed.) 2009, Ralph Samuel Grossman (with Laurent Salomé and Ralph Samuel Grossmann) 2010, Gabriel Orozco 2010, Danser sa vie – Anthologie (with Emma Lavigne) 2011, Danser sa vie – Album (with Emma Lavigne, Anna Hiddleston and Florencia Chernajovsky) 2011, Danser sa vie: Art et danse de 1900 à nos jours (with Emma Lavigne and Alain Seban) 2011. *Address:* Musée national d'art moderne, Centre Pompidou, place Georges Pompidou, 75004 Paris, France

(office). *Telephone:* 1-44-78-12-33 (office). *E-mail:* info@centrepompidou.fr (office). *Website:* www.centrepompidou.fr (office).

McENERY, Peter Robert; British actor; b. 21 Feb. 1940; s. of the late Charles McEnery and of Ada Mary Brinson; m. 1978; one d.; Founder-mem. and Assoc. Artist with RSC. *Theatre roles include:* Eugene in Look Homeward Angel 1962, Rudge in Next Time I'll Sing to You 1963, Konstantin in The Seagull 1964, Edward Gover in Made in Bangkok 1986, Trigorin in The Seagull 1975, Frederick Treves in The Elephant Man (Royal Nat. Theatre) 1980, Fredrick in A Little Night Music 1990, Torvald in A Doll's House 1994, Hector in Heartbreak House 1997, Claudius in Hamlet (Royal Nat. Theatre) 2000–01, Laertes, Clarence, Tybalt, Silvius, Patroclus, Bassanio, Orlando, Pericles, Brutus, Antipholus, Albie Sachs, Lorenzaccio (with RSC). *Plays directed:* Richard III 1971, The Wound 1972. *TV:* Clayhanger 1976, The Aphrodite Inheritance 1979, The Jail Diary of Albie Sachs 1980, Japanese Style 1982, The Collectors 1986, The Mistress 1986, Witchcraft 1991, Reach for the Moon 2000. *Films:* Tunes of Glory 1961, Victim 1961, The Moonspinners 1963, Entertaining Mr Sloane 1970, La Curée, J'ai tué Raspoutine, Le Mur d'Atlantique, Le Montreur de Boxe. *Leisure interests:* steam railway preservation, skiing, American football. *Address:* United Agents, 12–26 Lexington Street, London, W1F 0LE, England. *Telephone:* (20) 3214-0800. *Fax:* (20) 7323-0101.

McENROE, John Patrick; American broadcaster and fmr professional tennis player; b. 16 Feb. 1959, Wiesbaden, then Fed. Repub. of Germany; s. of John P. McEnroe I and Katy McEnroe; brother of Patrick McEnroe, fmr professional tennis player; m. 1st Tatum O'Neal (q.v.) 1986; two s. one d.; 2nd Patty Smyth; two c.; one step-d.; ed Trinity High School, NJ and Stanford Univ.; amateur player 1976–78 (including NCAA singles championship 1978), professional 1978–93; winner of 77 singles titles during professional career, ranked world number one 1981–84; US Open Singles Champion 1979, 1980, 1981, 1984; US Open Doubles Champion 1979, 1981, 1989; Wimbledon Champion (doubles) 1979, 1981, 1983, 1984, 1992, (singles) 1981, 1983, 1984; WCT Champion 1979, 1981, 1983, 1984, 1989; Grand Prix Champion 1979, 1983, 1984; played Davis Cup for USA 1978–85, Capt. 1999–2000; only player to have reached the Wimbledon semifinals as pre-tournament qualifier 1977; tennis sportscaster, USA Network 1993–, CBS 1994–, ESPN; mem. Men's Sr Tours Circuits 1994–, winner numerous titles including Quality Challenge 1997, 1998, 1999, Honda Challenge 2003; returned to ATP Tour to play two doubles tournaments 2006; won at French Open with his brother Patrick for the over-45 legends doubles competition 2012; Owner John McEnroe Gallery, New York; coach, British Lawn Tennis Asscn 2003–; ATP Most Improved Player 1978, ITF World Champion 1981, 1983, 1984, ATP Player of the Year 1981, 1983, 1984, Nat. Father of the Year Award 1996, Int. Tennis Hall of Fame 1999, Davis Cup Commitment Award. *Television:* presenter The Chair (ABC game show) 2002, McEnroe (talk show) CNBC 2004–. *Publications:* You Cannot Be Serious (autobiog. with James Kaplan) 2002. *Leisure interest:* music. *Address:* The John McEnroe Gallery, 41 Greene Street, New York, NY 10013, USA. *Telephone:* (212) 219-0395. *Fax:* (212) 219-0399. *E-mail:* macgallery@earthlink.net. *Website:* johnmcenroegallery.com.

McENTEE, Andrew, BA, LLB, MA, LLM; British lawyer and international relations analyst; b. 2 July 1957, Glasgow, Scotland; s. of Shaun McEntee and Margaret McEntee (née O'Neill); ed Univ. of Stirling, Univ. of Wolverhampton, Univ. of North London, London Metropolitan Univ., School of Slavonic and East European Studies, Univ. Coll., London; Case Worker, Citizens' Advice Bureau 1982–83, Scottish Council for Civil Liberties (now Scottish Human Rights Centre) 1983–84; community care worker, Strathclyde Social Work Dept 1985–86; Gen. Sec. Chile Cttee for Human Rights/South American Human Rights Coordination 1986–91; Gen. Sec. Cen. America Human Rights Cttee 1993–96; UK-apptd Chair. Amnesty International Lawyers Network 1994–2001, Chair. Amnesty International UK 1998–2001; Sr Consultant, Atlantic Celtic Films Co. 1996–2002; Founder and UK Chair. Coalition for an Int. Criminal Court 1997–2002; adviser to Spanish and Chilean lawyers and victims and coordinator of Amnesty International case during extradition proceedings against Gen. Augusto Pinochet in London 1998–2000; Human Rights Adviser to OSCE mission to Serbia and Montenegro, Belgrade 2002–06; election observer in Latin America, Cen. and Eastern Europe, the Balkans, the Caucasus and Cen. Asia for FCO, OSCE and EU 2003–; Consultant/Assoc. Producer, Clover Films 2006–; Expert mem. UK Foreign Sec.'s Team of Experts for preventing sexual violence in armed conflict (Preventing Sexual Violence Initiative) 2012–; field worker, writer, lecturer and media commentator on human rights, security and int. relations; First Aid 'First Responder'. *Leisure interests:* gardening, hill walking, arts galleries, fmr Bellahouston Harrier. *Address:* Clover Films, 7 Alma Road, Windsor, Berks., SL4 3HU, England. *Telephone:* (1753) 850500 (office). *E-mail:* andrewmcentee@yahoo.com (office); info@clover-films.com (office). *Website:* www.clover-films.com (office); andrewmcentee.blogspot.com; andymcentee.wordpress.com.

McEWAN, Angus David, BE, MEngSc, PhD, FAA, FTSE; Australian (b. British) oceanographer; b. 20 July 1937, Alloa, Scotland; s. of David Nichol Rei McEwan and Anne Marion McEwan; m. Juliana R. Britten 1961 (divorced 1982); two d.; ed Upwey High School, Melbourne High School, Caulfield Tech. Coll., Melbourne Univ., Univ. of Cambridge; engineer, Aeronautical Research Labs, Melbourne 1956–58, Research Scientist 1961–62, 1966–69; Research Scientist, Program Leader, Chief Research Scientist, Div. of Atmospheric Research, CSIRO, Aspendale, Vic. 1972–81, Foundation Chief, Div. of Oceanography, Hobart 1981–95; Sr Scientific Adviser (Oceanographer) to CSIRO and Commonwealth Bureau of Meteorology 1995–2005; Australian Del. to UNESCO Intergovernmental Oceanographic Comm. (IOC) 1982–2004; mem. IOC Cttee on Climatic Changes and the Ocean 1982–90, Chair. 1987–90; Rep. of the Global Ocean Observing System (GOOS) Steering Cttee 1995–2003, Chair. Intergovernmental GOOS Cttee 1998–2001; Chair. Oceanographic Data Exchange Policy Group 2001–02; mem. numerous other nat. bodies and cttees concerning marine science; Rossby Fellow, Woods Hole Oceanographic Inst., USA 1975; Fellow, Australian Acad. of Technological Sciences and Eng; Hon. Research Prof. Univ. of Tasmania 1988–; Queen Elizabeth Fellow 1969–71, Australian Centenary Medal 2003. *Publications:* scientific articles on geophysical fluid dynamics. *Leisure interests:* sailing, sketching, woodwork. *Address:* 300 Sandy Bay Road, Sandy Bay, Tasmania

7005, Australia. *Telephone:* (3) 6221-2090. *Fax:* (3) 6221-2089. *E-mail:* oceans@iprimus.com.au.

McEWAN, Geraldine; British actress; b. 9 May 1932, Old Windsor, Berks.; d. of Donald McKeown and Norah McKeown; m. Hugh Cruttwell 1953; one s. one d.; ed Windsor County Girls' School. *Stage appearances:* first engagement with Theatre Royal, Windsor 1949; London appearances in Who Goes There? 1951, Sweet Madness, For Better, For Worse, Summertime; Shakespeare Memorial Theatre, Stratford on Avon 1956, 1958, 1961 playing Princess of France (Love's Labours Lost), Olivia (Twelfth Night), Ophelia (Hamlet), Marina (Pericles), Beatrice (Much Ado about Nothing); played in School for Scandal, USA 1962, The Private Ear and The Public Eye, USA 1963, in original cast of Loot 1965; appearances as mem. Nat. Theatre 1965–71: Armstrong's Last Goodnight, Love for Love, A Flea in Her Ear, The Dance of Death, Edward II, Home and Beauty, Rites, The Way of the World, The White Devil, Amphitryon 38; other theatre appearances include: Dear Love 1973, Chez Nous 1974, The Little Hut 1974, Oh Coward! (musical) 1975, On Approval 1975, Look After Lulu 1978, Geraldine McEwan's Jane Austen 1981; with Nat. Theatre: The Browning Version 1980, Harlequinade 1980, The Provoked Wife 1980–81, The Rivals (Evening Standard Drama Award for Best Actress), You Can't Take It With You 1983–84; A Lie of the Mind (Royal Court) 1987, Lettice and Lovage (Globe Theatre) 1988–89, Hamlet (Riverside Studios) 1992, The Bird Sanctuary (Abbey Theatre) 1994, The Way of the World (Nat. Theatre; Evening Standard Drama Award for Best Actress) 1995, Grace Note (Old Vic) 1997, The Chairs (Royal Court) 1997, (Golden Theater, New York) 1998, Hay Fever (Savoy) 1999; as dir: As You Like It 1988, Treats 1989, Waiting for Sir Larry 1990, Four Door Saloon 1991, Keyboard Skills 1993. *Films:* The Adventures of Tom Jones 1975, Escape from the Dark 1978, Foreign Body 1986, Henry V 1989, Robin Hood: Prince of Thieves 1991, Moses 1995, The Love Letter 1999, Titus 2000, Love's Labours Lost 2000, The Contaminated Man 2000, The Magdalene Sisters 2002, Food for Love 2002, Pure 2002, The Lazarus Child 2004, Vanity Fair 2004, The Lazarus Child 2005, The Curse of the Were-Rabbit (voice) 2005, Arrietty (voice) 2010. *Radio:* Arrived 2002. *Television:* The Prime of Miss Jean Brodie (TV Critics Best Actress Award) 1978, L'Elégance 1982, The Barchester Chronicles 1982, Come Into the Garden, Maude 1982, Mapp and Lucia 1985–86, Oranges Are Not The Only Fruit 1990 (BAFTA Best Actress Award), Mulberry 1992–93, Red Dwarf 1999, Thin Ice 2000, Victoria Wood's Christmas Special 2000, Carrie's War 2003, Agatha Christie's Marple (ITV) 2004–07. *Address:* c/o Independent Talent Group, Oxford House, 76 Oxford Street, London, W1D 1BS, England.

McEWAN, Ian Russell, CBE, MA, FRSL; British writer; b. 21 June 1948, Aldershot, Hants.; s. of the late David McEwan and Rose Moore; m. 1st Penny Allen 1982 (divorced 1995); two s. and two step-d.; m. 2nd Annalena McAfee 1997; ed Woolverstone Hall, Univs of Sussex and E Anglia; Hon. Fellow American Acad. of Arts and Sciences 1997; Hon. DPhil (Sussex) 1989, (E Anglia) 1993, (London) 1998; Primo Letterario, Prato 1982, Shakespeare Prize, Germany 1999, British Book Award for Author of the Year 2008, Jerusalem Prize 2011. *Screenplays:* The Imitation Game & Other Plays 1981, The Ploughman's Lunch 1985, Sour Sweet 1989. *Publications:* novels: The Cement Garden 1978, The Comfort of Strangers 1981, Rose Blanche (juvenile) 1985, The Child in Time (Whitbread Novel of the Year 1987, Prix Fémina Etranger 1993) 1987, The Innocent 1989, Black Dogs 1992, The Daydreamer (juvenile) 1994, Enduring Love 1997, Amsterdam (Booker Prize for Fiction 1998) 1998, Atonement (WHSmith Literary Award 2002, Nat. Book Critics Circle Fiction Award 2002, Los Angeles Times Prize for Fiction 2003, Santiago Prize for the European Novel 2004) 2001, Saturday (James Tait Black Memorial Prize 2006) 2005, On Chesil Beach (British Book Award for Book of the Year 2008) 2007, Solar (Bollinger Everyman Wodehouse Prize for Comic Fiction) 2010, Sweet Tooth 2012; short stories: First Love, Last Rites (Somerset Maugham Award 1976) 1975, In Between the Sheets 1978; librettos: Or Shall We Die? (oratorio) 1983, For You (opera) 2008. *Leisure interest:* hiking. *Address:* c/o Jonathan Cape, Random Century House, 20 Vauxhall Bridge Road, London, SW1V 2SA, England. *Website:* www.ianmcewan.com.

McEWAN, Ross, BBS; New Zealand banking executive; *Chief Executive, Royal Bank of Scotland Group;* m. Stephanie McEwan; two c.; ed Massey Univ., Stanford Univ., USA; began career in Personnel Dept at Unilever and Dunlop; later worked in both insurance and investment industries in Australia and NZ for more than 25 years; held sr positions at First NZ Capital Securities; fmr Chief Exec. National Mutual Life Asscn of Australasia/AXA NZ; Exec. Gen. Man., later Group Exec. for Retail Banking Services, Commonwealth Bank of Australia –2012; moved to UK as UK Retail CEO Royal Bank of Scotland 2012–13, Group Chief Exec. and Exec. Dir Royal Bank of Scotland Group plc 2013–. *Leisure interests:* water skiing, cycling, reading, spending time with his family. *Address:* Royal Bank of Scotland Group plc, Group Secretariat, Business House F Gogarburn, Edinburgh, EH12 1HQ, Scotland (office). *Telephone:* (131) 626-4117 (office). *Fax:* (131) 556-7468 (office). *E-mail:* info@rbs.com (office). *Website:* www.rbs.com (office).

McFADDEN, Daniel L., BS, PhD; American economist and academic; *E. Morris Cox Professor of Economics and Director, Econometrics Laboratory, University of California, Berkeley;* b. 29 July 1937, Raleigh, NC; m. Beverlee Tito Simboli McFadden; one d. two s.; ed Univ. of Minnesota; Instructor in Physics, Univ. of Minnesota 1957–58, Research Asst in Social Psychology 1959–60, Instructor in Econs 1961–62; Asst Prof. of Econs, Univ. of Pittsburgh 1963; Asst Prof. of Econs, Univ. of Calif., Berkeley 1963–66, Assoc. Prof. 1966–68, Prof. of Econs 1968–79, 1990–, E. Morris Cox Chair 1990–, Dir Econometrics Lab. 1991–95, 1996–, Chair. Dept of Econs 1995–96; Visiting Assoc. Prof., Univ. of Chicago 1966–67; Irving Fisher Research Prof., Yale Univ. 1977–78; Prof. of Econs, Mass Inst. of Tech. 1978–91, James R. Killian Chair, 1984–91, Dir Statistics Center 1986–88; Sherman Fairchild Distinguished Scholar, Calif. Inst. of Tech. 1990; Pres.-Elect American Econ. Asscn 2004–; mem. American Acad. of Arts and Sciences, NAS 1981–, American Philosophical Soc. 2006–; Dr hc (Univ. Coll. London) 2003, (North Carolina State Univ.) 2006; Econometrics Soc. Frisch Medal 1986, Nemmers Prize in Econs 2000, Nobel Prize for Econs (jt recipient) 2000, Richard Stone Prize in Applied Econometrics 2000. *Publications include:* Lectures on Longitudinal Analysis (Underground Classics in Economics) (jt author), Handbook of Econometrics IV (with R. Engle) 1994. *Address:* Department of Economics, University of California, 549 Evans Hall #3880, Berkeley, CA 94720-3880, USA (office). *Telephone:* (510) 643-8428 (office). *Fax:* (510) 642-0638 (office).

E-mail: mcfadden@econ.berkeley.edu (office). *Website:* emlab.berkeley.edu/users/mcfadden (office).

McFADDEN, Mary; American fashion designer; b. 1 Oct. 1938, New York; d. of Alexander Bloomfield McFadden and Mary Josephine Cutting; m. 1st Philip Harari 1964 (divorced); one d.; m. 2nd Frank McEwen 1968 (divorced); m. 3rd Armin Schmidt (divorced); m. 4th Kohle Yohannan (divorced); m. 5th Vasilios Calitsis 1996 (divorced); ed École Lubec, Univ. of Paris (Sorbonne), France, Traphagen School of Design, Columbia Univ., New School for Social Research; Dir of Public Relations, Christian Dior, New York 1962–64; Merchandising Ed. Vogue, SA 1964–65; political and travel columnist, Rand Daily Mail, SA 1965–68; Founder, Vukutu Sculpture Workshop, Rhodesia 1968–70; freelance ed. My Fair Lady, Cape Town and French Vogue 1968–70; Special Projects Ed. American Vogue 1970–73; fashion and jewellery designer (noted for tunics made from African and Chinese silks), New York 1973–; Chair. Mary McFadden Inc. 1976–; Partner, MMcC Collection by Mary McFadden 1991–; fmr Pres. Council of Fashion Designers of America; numerous awards, including Coty Award 1976, Neiman Marcus Award 1979, Best Dressed List Hall of Fame 1979, Coty American Fashion Critics' Hall of Fame Award 1979, Woman of the Year, Police Athletic League 1990, New York Landmarks Conservancy 1994, Designer of the Decade and Beyond, Fashion Group Int. and Philadelphia Breast Health Inst. 1997, Legends Award, Pratt Inst., Pres.'s Fellows Award, Rhode Island School of Design. *Films:* Zooni – The Last Chak Empress, Sufism in India. *Television:* QVC, Worldly Accessories. *Publications:* contribs to Vogue and House & Garden. *Leisure interests:* tennis, squash, travelling the world, lecturing. *Address:* Mary McFadden Inc., 240 West 35th Street, Floor 17, New York, NY 10001, USA (office). *Telephone:* (212) 736-4078 (office). *Fax:* (212) 239-7259 (office).

MACFADYEN, Air Marshal Ian David, CB, OBE, FRAeS; British government official and air force officer (retd); *Constable and Governor, Windsor Castle;* b. 19 Feb. 1942, Maidenhead, Berks., England; s. of Air Marshal Sir Douglas Macfadyen and Lady Macfadyen (now Rowan); m. Sally Harvey 1967; one s.; one d.; ed Marlborough, RAF Coll. Cranwell; joined RAF 1960, Cranwell cadet 1960–63, fighter pilot, 19 Squadron 1965–68, HQ, RAF Strike Command 1969; Flying Instructor RAF Coll. Cranwell 1970–73, RAF Staff Coll. 1973, 111 Squadron 1974–75; Flight Commdr 43 Squadron 1976, HQ 2ATAF RAF Germany 1976–79, Command 29 Squadron 1980–83, 23 Squadron 1983; with Ministry of Defence 1983–85, 1989–90; with Command RAF Leuchars, Fife 1985–87, Royal Coll. of Defence Studies 1988; Chief of Staff then Commdr HQ British Forces Middle East, Riyadh 1990–91, Asst Chief of Defence Staff, Operational Requirements (Air Systems) 1991–94; Dir-Gen. Saudi Arabia Armed Forces Project 1994–98; retd 1999; Lt-Gov. Isle of Man 2000–05; Nat. Pres. The Royal British Legion 2006–09; Constable and Gov. Windsor Castle 2009–; Chair. Bd of Trustees, Geoffrey de Havillan Flying Foundation; Trustee, RAF Museum 1999–2002; Hon. Air Cdre 606 (Chiltern) Squadron, Royal Auxiliary Air Force 2006–; Hon. Inspector Gen. Royal Auxiliary Air Force 2009; Trustee Bentley Priory Battle of Britain Trust 2006–; Pres. Windsor Festival 2010–, Dawn to Dusk Challenge 2010–; Patron Manx TT Riders Asscn 2005–, Alexander Devine Children's Hospice Service 2009–, Guillain-Barré Syndrome Asscn (GAIN) 2010–, Project Rainbow 2010–; Liveryman, Guild of Air Pilots and Navigators (GAPAN) 1999; Sword of Honour, Cranwell 1963; Queen's Commendation for Valuable Service in the Air (QCVSA) 1973; Officer, Order of St John of Jerusalem 2001. *Publication:* Gulf War contrib. to Imperial War Museum Book of Modern Warfare 1945–2000 2002. *Leisure interests:* golf, shooting, watercolour painting, gliding, history. *Address:* Collyns Mead, Hawkesbury Upton, Badminton, Glos., GL9 1BB, England (home). *Telephone:* (1753) 868286 (office). *E-mail:* poacher3@aol.com (home).

McFADYEN, Jock, RA, MA; British artist; b. 18 Sept. 1950, Paisley, Scotland; s. of James Lachlan McFadyen and Margaret McFadyen; m. 1st Carol Hambleton 1972 (divorced 1987); one s.; m. 2nd Susie Honeyman 1991; one s. one d.; ed Chelsea School of Art; has made works about London, New York, Belfast, Berlin, Orkney and France; represented in 30 public collections including Tate and in numerous pvt. and corp. collections; artist in residence Nat. Gallery, London 1981; part-time Lecturer Slade School of Fine Art 1985–2004; designed sets and costumes for The Judas Tree, Royal Opera House, Covent Garden 1992; Arts Council Major Award 1979, Prizewinner, John Moores Liverpool Exhbn 1991. *Publications:* numerous exhbn catalogues. *Leisure interests:* cycling, motorcycling, walking, swimming, greyhounds. *Address:* c/o The Grey Gallery (office). *Telephone:* (7910) 359087 (mobile) (office). *E-mail:* info@thegreygallery.com (office); info@jockmcfadyen.com (office). *Website:* www.jockmcfadyen.com (office).

McFARLAND, Susan R.; American business executive; *Executive Vice-President and Chief Financial Officer, Fannie Mae;* ed Texas A&M Univ., Stanford Univ. Exec. Program; Chief Financial Officer (CFO) of various lines of business, Capital One Financial Corpn –2004, Exec. Vice-Pres. and Controller 2004–11, Exec. Vice-Pres., Finance and Prin. Accounting Officer March–July 2011; Exec. Vice-Pres. and CFO Fannie Mae (fmrly the Fed. Nat. Mortgage Asscn), Washington, DC 2011–, mem. Exec. Cttee. *Address:* Fannie Mae, 3900 Wisconsin Avenue, NW, Washington, DC 20016-2892, USA (office). *Telephone:* (202) 752-7000 (office). *E-mail:* headquarters@fanniemae.com (office). *Website:* www.fanniemae.com (office).

MACFARLANE, Alan Donald James, MA, DPhil, PhD, FBA; British anthropologist and academic; *Professor of Anthropological Science, University of Cambridge;* b. 20 Dec. 1941, Assam, India; s. of Donald Macfarlane and Iris Macfarlane; m. 1st Gillian Jones 1965; m. 2nd Sarah Harrison 1981; one d.; ed Sedbergh School, Worcester Coll., Oxford, London School of Econs and School of Oriental and African Studies, London; Sr Research Fellow in History, King's Coll., Cambridge 1971–75, Fellow 1981–, Life Fellow 2008–, Lecturer in Social Anthropology, Univ. of Cambridge 1975–81, Reader in Historical Anthropology 1981–91, Prof. of Anthropological Science 1991–; Rivers Memorial Medal 1984, Radcliffe-Brown Memorial Lecturer, British Acad. 1992, Huxley Memorial Lecturer 2012. *Television series:* The Day the World Took Off (adviser and participant), Channel 4 2000. *Publications:* Witchcraft in Tudor and Stuart England 1970, Family Life of Ralph Josselin 1970, The Diary of Ralph Josselin (ed.) 1976, Resources and Population 1976, The Origins of English Individualism 1977, The Justice and the Mare's Ale 1981, Marriage and Love in England 1986, The Culture of Capitalism 1987, The Nagas: Hill Peoples of North India (co-author) 1990, The Cambridge Database

System Manual 1990, The Savage Wars of Peace 1997, The Riddle of the Modern World: Of Liberty, Wealth and Equality 2000; Ed. and trans. (with Sarah Harrison) of Bernard Pignède, The Gurungs of Nepal 1993, The Making of the Modern World: Visions from West and East 2002, The Glass Bathyscaphe: How Glass Changed the World (with Gerry Martin) 2002, Green Gold: The Empire of Tea (with Iris Macfarlane) 2003, Letters to Lily: On How the World Works 2005, Japan through the Looking Glass 2007, Reflections on Cambridge 2009, Dorset Days 2012, Dragon Days 2012, Invention of the Modern World 2012. *Leisure interests:* gardening, walking, music. *Address:* King's College, Cambridge, CB2 1ST, England (office). *Telephone:* (1223) 811976 (office). *Website:* www .alanmacfarlane.com.

MacFARLANE, Alistair George James, Kt, CBE, DSc, PhD, ScD, FRS, FEng, FRSE; British professor of engineering and vice-chancellor (retd); b. 9 May 1931, Edinburgh; s. of George R. MacFarlane and Mary MacFarlane; m. Nora Williams 1954 (died 2005); one s.; m. Anwen Tudor Davies 2008; ed Hamilton Acad., Univ. of Glasgow, Univ. of London, Univ. of Manchester; with Metropolitan-Vickers, Manchester 1953–58; Lecturer, Queen Mary Coll., Univ. of London 1959–65, Reader 1965–66; Reader in Control Eng, UMIST 1966–69, Prof. 1969–74; Prof. of Eng, Univ. of Cambridge 1974–89; Fellow, Selwyn Coll., Cambridge 1974–89, Vice-Master 1980–88; Prin. and Vice-Chancellor, Heriot-Watt Univ., Edin. 1989–96, Emer. Research Fellow 1997–99; Chair. Cambridge Control Ltd 1985–89; mem. Council Science and Eng Research Council (SERC) 1981–85, Computer Bd 1983–88; Chair. Scottish Council for Research in Educ. 1992–98, Scottish Library and Information Council 1994–98, Advisory Body on High Performance Computing 1994–98, BT Advisory Forum 1997–2000; Academic Adviser Univ. of Highlands and Islands Project 1997–2001; Trustee Scottish Library and Information System Council 1994–98; mem. Royal Soc. Council 1997–99, Vice-President Educ. Cttee 1997–99, Chair. 2000–04; Hon. Fellow, Selwyn Coll. 1989–; Hon. DEng (Glasgow) 1995, Hon. DUniv (Heriot-Watt) 1997, (Paisley) 1997, Hon. DSc (Abertay Dundee) 1998, Hon. DLitt (Lincolnshire and Humberside) 1999. *Publications:* Engineering Systems Analysis 1964, Dynamical System Models 1970, (with I. Postlethwaite) A Complex Variable Approach to the Analysis of Linear Multivariable Feedback Systems 1979, Frequency-Response Methods in Control Systems (ed.) 1979, Complex Variable Methods for Linear Multivariable Feedback Systems (ed.) 1980, (with S. Hung) Multivariable Feedback: a quasi-classical approach 1982, (with G. K. H. Pang) An Expert Systems Approach to Computer-Aided Design of Multivariable Systems 1987. *Leisure interest:* computing. *Address:* Tregarth, 2 Marine Parade, Barmouth, Gwynedd LL42 1NA, Wales (home). *Telephone:* (1341) 280445 (home). *E-mail:* alistair.macfarlane@btinternet.com (home).

MacFARLANE, Ian John, AC; Australian fmr central banker; b. 22 June 1946, Sydney; ed Monash Univ.; taught at Monash Univ.; with Inst. of Econs and Statistics, Univ. of Oxford, UK, then in various positions at OECD, Paris 1973–78; joined Reserve Bank of Australia (Research Dept) 1979, Head of Research 1988, Asst Gov. (Econ.) 1990–92, Deputy Gov. 1992–96, Gov. 1996–2006 (retd); Hon. DSc, Hon. DLitt.

McFARLANE, John, OBE, MA, MBA, FRSA; Australian/British financial services executive; *Non-Executive Chairman, Aviva plc;* b. 14 June 1947, Dumfries, Scotland; ed Dumfries Acad., Univ. of Edinburgh, Cranfield School of Man., London Business School; with Ford Motor Co. 1969–74; with Citibank 1975–93, including as Man. Dir Citicorp Investment Bank Ltd, Man. Dir Citicorp and Citibank UK; Group Exec. Dir Standard Chartered Bank plc 1993–97; CEO Australia and New Zealand Banking Group Ltd 1997–2007; Exec. Chair. Aviva plc July–Dec. 2012, Chair. (non-exec.) 2013–; Dir (non-exec.) Westfield Holdings 2008–, Old Oak Holdings 2008–; fmr Dir London Stock Exchange 1989–91, The Securities Asscn 1989–90, Auditing Practices Bd 1991–97, Capital Radio PLC 1995–98, Royal Bank of Scotland Group plc 2008–12; fmr Chair. Australian Bankers Asscn; fmr Pres. Int. Monetary Conf.; Fellow, Hong Kong Inst. of Bankers (FHKIB) 1995; Sr Fellow, Financial Services Inst. of Australasia (SFFIN) 1997; Fellow, Chartered Inst. for Securities and Investment (FCSI) 2009; Hon. DSc (Cranfield Univ.) 2012; MSI, The Securities Inst. (UK) 1993, Australian Centenary Medal 2003, inaugural Distinguished Alumnus Award, Cranfield 2003. *Address:* Aviva plc, St Helen's, 1 Undershaft, London, EC3P 3DQ, England (office). *Telephone:* (20) 7283-2000 (office). *Fax:* (20) 7662-7700 (Co. Sec.) (office). *E-mail:* aviva.info@aviva.com (office). *Website:* www.aviva.com (office).

McFARLANE, Hon. Robert Carl (Bud), MS; American fmr government official; *Principal, Energy and Communications Solutions LLC;* b. 12 July 1937, Washington, DC; s. of William McFarlane and Alma Carl; m. Jonda Riley 1959; one s. two d.; ed US Naval Acad. and Inst des Hautes Etudes, Geneva; US Marine Corps, Second Lt rising to Lt-Col 1959–79; White House Fellow, Exec. Asst Council to Pres. for Legis. Affairs 1971–72; Mil. Asst to Henry Kissinger (q.v.) 1973–75; Exec. Asst to Asst to Pres. for Nat. Security Affairs 1975–76; Special Asst to Pres. 1976–77; Research Fellow Nat. Defense Univ., Washington, DC 1977–78; mem. Professional Staff Senate Comm. on Armed Services 1979–81; Counselor Dept of State 1981–82; Deputy Asst to Pres., Nat. Security Affairs 1982–83; Personal Rep. of US Pres. in Middle East July–Oct. 1983; Asst to Pres. for Nat. Security Affairs 1983–85 (resgnd); pleaded guilty to four misdemeanour counts of withholding information from Congress as part of the Iran-Contra cover-up 1988, sentenced to two years' probation and a $20,000 fine, pardoned by Pres. George H. W. Bush Dec. 1992; Co-founder and fmr CEO Global Energy Investors; currently Prin., Energy and Communications Solutions LLC, Washington DC; mem. Bd of Dirs Aegis Defence Services; Chair. and CEO McFarlane Asscn 1986–; adviser to the John McCain presidential campaign 2008; Co-founder (with Henry Kissinger) and Vice-Chair. America-China Soc.; Co-founder US Energy Security Council 2011; mem. Bd of Advisors, Washington Inst. for Near East Policy, Set America Free Coalition (Founding mem.), Partnership for a Secure America; Pres. Inst. for the Analysis of Global Security; lobbyist for Macedonia 1992; has been working in southern region of Sudan and Darfur on inter-tribal relations and devt projects 2009–; Navy Distinguished Service Medal, Bronze Star with Valor device, Meritorious Service Medal, Navy Commendation Medal with Valor device, Army Commendation Medal, Combat Action Ribbon, Sec. of State Distinguished Service Award, Sec. of the Navy Medal for Distinguished Public Service, Presidential Service Badge; Alfred Thayer Mahan Award for Literary Achievement 1979, American-Swiss

Friendship Man of the Year Award 1985. *Publications:* At Sea Where We Belong 1971, Crisis Resolution (co-author) 1978, The Political Potential of Parity 1979. *Address:* Partnership for a Secure America, 1775 K Street NW, Suite 400, Washington, DC 20240, USA (office). *Telephone:* (202) 293-8580 (office). *E-mail:* info@psaonline.org (office); media@iags.org. *Website:* www.psaonline.org (office); www.usesc.org/energy_security.

MacFARLANE, Seth Woodbury, BFA; American actor, voice actor, animator and screenwriter, comedian, producer, director and singer; b. 26 Oct. 1973, Kent, Conn.; s. of Ronald Milton MacFarlane and Ann Perry MacFarlane (née Sager); ed Kent School, Rhode Island School of Design; began career as animator and writer for Hanna-Barbera TV shows, including Johnny Bravo, Cow and Chicken, Dexter's Laboratory and I Am Weasel; helped create Disney series Jungle Cubs; Exec. Producer of sitcom The Winner (Fox); cr. own YouTube series, Seth MacFarlane's Cavalcade of Cartoon Comedy 2008; has performed as a singer at Carnegie Hall, Royal Albert Hall, London; Webby Award for Film & Video Person of the Year 2009, Harvard Humanist of the Year 2011. *Films include:* Hellboy II: The Golden Army (voice) 2008, Futurama: Into the Wild Green Yonder (video) (singing voice) 2009, Tooth Fairy 2010, The Drawn Together Movie: The Movie! (video) (voice) 2010, Ted (voice) 2012. *Television includes:* The What a Cartoon Show (series) (voice) 1997, Family Guy (series) (Primetime Emmy Award 2000, 2002, Annie Award 2006, Teen Choice Award for Choice Animated Series 2010) 1999–, 3-South (series) (voice) 2002, Complete Savages (series) 2004, Star Trek: Enterprise (series) 2004–05, Robot Chicken (series) (voice) 2005–10, American Dad! (series) 2005–, The War at Home (series) 2006, Help Me Help You (series) 2007, Robot Chicken: Star Wars (film) (voice) 2007, Robot Chicken: Star Wars Episode II (film) (voice) 2008, Cavalcade of Cartoon Comedy (series) (voice) 2008–10, The Cleveland Show (series) 2009–, Phineas and Ferb (series) (voice) 2010, Robot Chicken: Star Wars Episode III (film) (voice) 2010, Lovin' Lakin (mini-series) 2012. *Recording:* debut album, Music Is Better Than Words 2011. *Address:* c/o WME Entertainment, 9601 Wilshire Boulevard, Beverley Hills, CA 90210-5213, USA (office). *Website:* www.wma.com (office).

MacFARLANE, (Stephen) Neil, MA, DPhil; Canadian political scientist and academic; *Lester B. Pearson Professor of International Relations, St Anne's College, Oxford;* b. 7 March 1954; ed Dartmouth Coll., NH, USA and Univ. of Oxford, UK; Research Assoc., IISS, London 1981–82; Postdoctoral Fellow, Centre for Int. Affairs, Harvard Univ. 1982–83; Research Assoc., Inst. for Int. Relations, Univ. of British Columbia 1983–84; Asst Prof. of Govt and Foreign Affairs, Univ. of Virginia 1984–87, Assoc. Prof. of Govt and Foreign Affairs 1987–91, Grad. Co-ordinator 1987–89, Dir Centre for Russian and East European Studies 1989–91; Research Assoc., Center for Slavic and East European Studies, Univ. of California, Berkeley 1986–87; Prof. of Politics, Queen's Univ., Kingston, Ont. 1991–96, Co-ordinator, Post-Soviet Studies Program, Centre for Int. Relations 1992–97, Grad. Admissions Co-ordinator, Dept of Political Studies 1993–94, Chair. Skelton Clark Cttee for Visiting Scholars, Dept of Political Studies 1993–96, Dir Centre for Int. Relations 1995–96; Lester B. Pearson Prof. of Int. Relations, Univ. of Oxford and Fellow, St Anne's Coll. 1996–, Dir Centre for Int. Studies 1997–, Head of Dept of Politics 2005–10, Deputy Head of Social Sciences Div. 2008–10; Adjunct Prof. of Political Science, Dalhousie Univ., Halifax, NS 1996–; Visiting Prof. in Int. Relations, Coll. of Europe, Bruges, Belgium 2007–08; Visiting Prof., S. Rajaratnam Prof. of Strategic Studies, Nanyang Technological Univ., Singapore 2008; Visiting Prof. of Int. Relations, Tbilisi State Univ., Georgia 2010–; mem. Bd Faculty of Social Studies, Univ. of Oxford 1997–, mem. Social Sciences Divisional Bd 2004–10; mem. Econ. and Social Research Council Research Grants Bd 2007–10. *Publications:* Western Engagement in the Caucasus and Central Asia 1999, Politics and Humanitarian Action 2000, Humanitarian Action: The Conflict Connection 2001, Intervention in Contemporary World Politics 2002, US Hegemony and International Organizations (co-author) 2003, The UN and Human Security: A Critical History (co-author) 2006. *Address:* St Anne's College, University of Oxford, Oxford, OX2 6HS, England (office). *Telephone:* (1865) 274891 (office). *Fax:* (1865) 274899 (office). *E-mail:* neil.macfarlane@politics.ox.ac .uk (office). *Website:* www.politics.ox.ac.uk (office).

MACFARLANE OF BEARSDEN, Baron (Life Peer), cr. 1991, in the District of Bearsden and Milngavie; **Norman Somerville Macfarlane,** KT, FRSE; British business executive; *Honorary Life President, United Distillers PLC;* b. 5 March 1926; s. of Daniel Robertson Macfarlane and Jessie Lindsay Somerville; m. Marguerite Mary Campbell 1953; one s. four d.; ed Glasgow High School; f. N. S. Macfarlane and Co. Ltd 1949, Chair. Macfarlane Group (Clansman) PLC 1973–98, Man. Dir 1973–90; Chair. Scottish Industrialists Council 1975–; Dir Glasgow Chamber of Commerce 1976–79; Chair. The Fine Art Soc. PLC 1976–98 (Hon. Pres. 1998); Underwriting mem. of Lloyds 1978–97; Dir American Trust PLC 1980–97, Chair. 1984–97; Dir Clydesdale Bank PLC 1980–96, Deputy Chair. 1993–96; Dir Edin. Fund Mans PLC 1980–98; Dir Gen. Accident Fire and Life Assurance Corpn PLC 1984–96; Chair. Guinness Co. 1987–89, Jt Deputy Chair. 1989–92; Chair. United Distillers PLC 1987–96, Hon. Life Pres. 1996–; Chair. Arthur Bell Distillers 1989; mem. Council CBI Scotland 1975–81; mem. Bd Scottish Devt Agency 1979–87; Chair. Glasgow Devt Agency 1985–92; Vice-Chair. Scottish Ballet 1983–87, (Dir 1975–87), Pres. 2001–; Pres. Stationers' Asscn of GB and Ireland 1965, Co. of Stationers of Glasgow 1968–70, Glasgow High School Club 1970–72, Royal Glasgow Inst. of the Fine Arts 1976–87; Hon. Pres. Charles Rennie Mackintosh Soc. 1988–; Regent Royal Coll. of Surgeons, Edin. 1997–; Dir Scottish Nat. Orchestra 1977–82, Third Eye Centre 1978–81; Gov. Glasgow School of Art 1976–87; Scottish Patron, Nat. Art Collection Fund 1978–; Patron Scottish Licensed Trade Asscn 1992–; Chair. Govs, High School of Glasgow 1979–92, Hon. Pres. 1992–; mem. Royal Fine Art Comm. for Scotland 1980–82; Lord High Commr Gen. Ass., Church of Scotland 1992, 1993, 1997; mem. Court, Glasgow Univ. 1979–87; Trustee, Nat. Heritage Memorial Fund 1984–97, Nat. Galleries of Scotland 1986–97; DL Dunbartonshire 1993; Vice-Pres. Professional Golfers Asscn; f. Scotvec.; Hon. Patron, Queen's Park F.C.; Hon. FRIAS, FRCPS (Glas); Hon. Fellow, Glasgow School of Art 1993; Hon. Patron Queen's Park Football Club; Freeman Dumfries & Galloway 2006, City of Glasgow 2007; Hon. LLD (Strathclyde) 1986, (Glasgow) 1988, (Glasgow Caledonian) 1993, (Aberdeen) 1995; Hon. DUniv (Stirling) 1992; Dr hc (Edin.) 1992; St Mungo Award 2005, Goodman Award for Art and Business 2007. *Leisure interests:* golf, cricket, theatre, art. *Address:* Macfarlane Group PLC, Clansman House, 21 Newton Place,

Glasgow, G3 7PY (office); 50 Manse Road, Bearsden, Glasgow, G61 3PN, Scotland. *Telephone:* (141) 333-9666 (office). *Fax:* (141) 333-1988 (office).

McFAUL, Michael Anthony, BA, MA, PhD; American political scientist, foreign policy analyst, academic and fmr diplomatist; *Professor of Political Science and Peter and Helen Bing Senior Fellow, Hoover Institution, Stanford University;* b. Mont.; ed Stanford Univ., Univ. of Oxford, UK; Research Fellow, Center for Int. Security and Arms Control, Stanford Univ. 1988–90, Research Assoc. 1992–94, Visiting Research Fellow, Hoover Inst. 1990–91, Research Fellow 1995–2003, Asst Prof., Dept of Political Science 1995–2001, Assoc. Prof. 2001–05, Prof. 2007–, Peter and Helen Bing Sr Fellow, Hoover Inst. 2003–, Dir Center on Democracy, Devt and Rule of Law, Freeman Spogli Inst. (FSI) for Int. Studies 2005–09, Deputy Dir FSI 2006–09 (Acting Dir 2007), Co-Dir FSI Iran Democracy Project 2003–; Visiting Scholar, Moscow State Univ. 1990–91; Sr Assoc., Carnegie Endowment for Int. Peace 1994–2009, Moscow Carnegie Center 1994–95, resident in Washington, DC 1998–2001; Sr Consultant and Commentator (Russian Parl. Elections), CBS News 1995, CNN 1996, 1999, 2000; Special Asst to the Pres. and Sr Dir, Russia and Eurasia Affairs, Nat. Security Council, The White House 2009–12; Amb. to Russia 2012–14; Research Assoc., Center for Int. Security and Arms Control; Sr Adviser to Nat. Democratic Inst.; mem. Bd of Dirs Eurasia Foundation, Firebird Fund, Freedom House, Int. Forum for Democratic Studies of Nat. Endowment for Democracy, Int. Research and Exchange Bd; mem. Steering Cttee Europe and Eurasia Div., Human Rights Watch; mem. Editorial Bd Current History, Journal of Democracy, Demokratizatsiya, Perspectives on European Politics and Society; consultant to several govt agencies and cos; mem. American Political Science Asscn, American Asscn for the Advancement of Slavic Studies, Council on Foreign Relations, Int. Forum for Democratic Studies, Pacific Council, Soc. for Comparative Research; Best Paper, Democratization Section of the American Political Science Asscn National Convention 2001, Dean's Award for Distinguished Teaching, Stanford Univ. 2005, Class Day Speaker, Stanford Univ. 2007. *Publications include:* The Troubled Birth of Russian Democracy: Political Parties, Programs and Profiles (co-author) 1993, Post-Communist Politics: Democratic Prospects in Russia and Eastern Europe 1993, Privatization, Conversion and Enterprise Reform in Russia (co-author) 1995, Russia's 1996 Presidential Election: The End of Bi-Polar Politics 1997, Rossiya v izbiratel'nom tsikle: 1999–2000 godov (Russia in the Electoral Cycle, 1999–2000) (co-ed.) 2000, Russia's Unfinished Revolution: Political Change from Gorbachev to Putin (Hon. Mention, Vucinich Prize for Best Book in Slavic Studies 2002) 2001, Popular Choice and Managed Democracy: The Russian Elections of 1999 and 2000 (co-author) 2003, Power and Purpose: American Policy toward Russia after the Cold War (co-author) (Lepgold Prize for Best Book in Int. Relations 2004) 2003, After the Collapse of Communism: Comparative Lessons of Transitions (co-ed.) 2004, Between Dictatorship and Democracy: Russian Postcommunist Political Reform (co-author) 2004, Revolution in Orange: The Origins of Ukraine's Democratic Breakthrough (co-ed.) 2006, Advancing Democracy Abroad: Why We Should and How We Can 2009, American Versus European Approaches to Democracy Promotion (co-ed.) 2009, Waves and Troughs of Democratization in the Post-communist World (co-ed.) 2009; contribs to New York Times, LA Times, Chicago Tribune, Moscow Times, Washington Post; numerous articles in professional journals. *Address:* Stanford University, Encina Hall West 307, Stanford, CA 94305-6055, USA (office). *Telephone:* (650) 723-1806 (office). *Fax:* (650) 723-1808 (office). *E-mail:* mcfaul@stanford.edu (office). *Website:* politicalscience.stanford.edu/faculty/michael-mcfaul (office); fsi.stanford.edu/mediaguide/michaelamcfaul (office).

McGAUCHIE, Donald G., AO; Australian telecommunications industry executive; b. 29 Jan. 1959, Sydney, NSW; Partner, C&E McGauchie-Terrick W Estate; Pres. Nat. Farmers' Fed. 1994–98; Chair. Woodstock Australia Ltd 1999–2002; apptd Dir Telstra Corpn Ltd 1998, Chair. 2004–09 (resgnd); Chair. Rural Finance Corpn 2003–04, Advisory Bd Telstra Country Wide; Deputy Chair. Ridley Corpn Ltd 1998–2004; mem. Bd Dirs Reserve Bank of Australia, Nat. Foods Ltd 2000–05, James Hardie Industries NV (Deputy Chair. Jt Bd and Supervisory Bd and mem. Remuneration Cttee), Nufarm Ltd, Sinclair Knight Merz (SKM) Consulting 2001–04; fmr mem. Foreign Affairs Council, Trade Policy Advisory Council; fmr Adviser to Prime Minister's Supermarket to Asia Council; fmr mem. Int. Trade Council on Agric., Food and Trade, Washington DC; Fellow, Australian Inst. of Co. Dirs. *Address:* James Hardie Industries, GPO Box 3935, Sydney, NSW 2001, Australia (office). *Telephone:* (2) 8274-5239 (office). *E-mail:* info@jameshardie.com .au (office). *Website:* www.jameshardie.com (office).

McGEE, Liam E., BA, MBA, JD; American (b. Irish) business executive; *Chairman, President and CEO, The Hartford Financial Services Group Inc.;* b. Co. Donegal, Ireland; ed Univ. of San Diego, Pepperdine Univ., Loyola Law School; held sr positions at Wells Fargo –1990; joined Bank of America 1990, Pres. Consumer and Small Business Bank for Bank of America Corpn –2010, also oversaw corpn's global tech. and delivery in more than 30 countries; mem. Bd of Dirs The Hartford Financial Services Group Inc. 2009, Chair., Pres. and CEO 2010–; mem. Business Roundtable, Bd of Catalyst, Bd of Andres H. Bechtler Arts Foundation, Nat. Urban League Bd of Trustees, Bd of Dirs Financial Services Roundtable; fmr Chair. Univ. of San Diego Bd of Trustees, United Way of Greater Los Angeles; served two terms as a Dir of Los Angeles Br. of Fed. Reserve Bank of San Francisco. *Address:* The Hartford Financial Services Group, Inc., Hartford Plaza, 690 Asylum Avenue, Hartford, CT 06115-1900, USA (office). *Telephone:* (860) 547-5000 (office). *Fax:* (860) 547-2680 (office). *E-mail:* info@thehartford.com (office). *Website:* www.thehartford.com (office).

MacGIBBON, Ross; British film director, producer, photographer and fmr ballet dancer; b. 29 Jan. 1955, Bromley, England; ed Royal Ballet School; dancer with Royal Ballet 1973–86; started working as dance filmmaker for TV 1986; only director to have directed four TV productions of The Nutcracker. *Films:* more than 75 films, including White Man Sleeps (Channel 4), Wyoming (1st Prize, IMZ DanceScreen competition) 1989, The Far End of the Garden 1991, Should Accidentally Fall (Special Jury Prize 1994, Video-Dance Grand Prix, Vancouver), Echo 1996 (Special Jury Prize), Swan Lake (Mariinsky Ballet) 1996, Exclusive Dance: Live from the Royal Albert Hall 1998, Maurice Béjart's der Nussknacker (Béjart Ballet Lausanne) 2000, La Belle Hélène (Theatre Musical de Paris) 2000, The Firebird & Les Noces 2001, Gianni Schicci (producer) 2004, Cloud Gate Dance Theatre of Taiwan: Cursive II 2005, Romeo & Juliet (The Royal Ballet) 2007, Swan

Lake (video) 2007, Spartacus: The Bolshoi Ballet (video) 2008, Swan Lake (The Royal Ballet) 2009, Mayerling (The Royal Ballet) 2009, La Bayadère (Royal Ballet) 2009, Ondine (The Royal Ballet) 2009, The Nutcracker (The Royal Ballet) 2009, Manon (The Royal Ballet) 2009, Three Ballets by Kenneth MacMillan: Elite Syncopations/The Judas Tree/Concerto 2010, Swan Lake 2012, Swan Lake 3D – Live from the Mariinsky Theatre 2013. *Television:* Dance for the Camera (series) 1994, Swinger (BBC 2) 1996, Peter and the Wolf (BBC 1) 1997, The Judas Tree (Channel 4) (Int. Emmy Award for Performing Arts 1998), Explosive Dance (special) 1998, A Midsummer Night's Dream (film) 1999, Coppélia, A Ballet in Three Acts (film) 2000, La belle Hélène (film) 2000, The Car Man (film) 2001, Great Performances (series) – The Nutcracker 2001, Bourne to Dance (film documentary) 2001, Swan Lake (Royal Swedish Ballet) (also exec. producer) 2002, est. Petersburg 300th Anniversary Gala (special) 2003, Nutcracker! (film) 2003, Faust (film) (exec. producer) 2004, Die Fledermaus (Glyndebourne Festival Opera) 2004, Riot at the Rite (film) (exec. producer) 2005, Giselle (film) 2006, Pinocchio (film) (exec. producer) 2006, The Sleeping Beauty (film) 2007, Sylvia (film) 2007, For Art's Sake: The Story of Ballets Russes (film documentary) 2009, Frederick Ashton: Les Patineurs/Divertissements/Scènes de Ballet 2011, The Most Incredible Thing (film) 2011, Peter and the Wolf (film) 2011, Matthew Bourne's Sleeping Beauty: A Gothic Romance 2012, Matthew Bourne's Swan Lake in 3D 2013, Matthew Bourne's Christmas (Channel 4) (Prix Italia 2013). *Telephone:* (20) 7821-1117; 7855-240617 (mobile). *E-mail:* rossmacgibbon@btinternet.com. *Website:* rossmacgibbon.com.

McGILLIS, Kelly; American actress; b. 9 July 1957, Newport Beach, Calif.; m. 1st Boyd Black 1979 (divorced 1981); m. 2nd Fred Tillman 1988 (divorced 2002); two d.; pnr Melanie Leis; ed Pacific School of Performing Arts and Juilliard School of Music, New York. *Films include:* Reuben, Reuben 1983, Witness 1985, Top Gun 1986, Ha-Holmim 1987, Made in Heaven 1987, The House on Carroll Street 1988, The Accused 1988, Winter People 1989, Cat Chaser 1989, Grand Isle 1991, The Babe 1992, North 1994, Painted Angels 1998, Ground Control 1998, The Settlement 1999, Morgan's Ferry 1999, At First Sight 1999, The Monkey's Mask 2000, No One Can Hear You 2001, 1 a Minute 2010, Stake Land 2010, The Innkeepers 2011. *Television includes:* In the Best of Families: Marriage, Pride & Madness 1994, Dark Eyes (series) 1995, Remember Me 1995, We the Jury 1996, The Third Twin 1997, Perfect Prey 1998, Storm Chasers: Revenge of the Twister 1998, Cold Shoulder 2006, Black Widower 2006, The L Word 2008. *Plays include:* The Graduate 2004. *Address:* c/o Chuck James, The Gersh Agency, 232 North Canon Drive, Suite 201, Beverly Hills, CA 90210, USA.

McGINN, Colin, MA, BPhil; British academic; *Professor, Department of Philosophy, University of Miami;* b. 10 March 1950; s. of Joseph McGinn and June McGinn; one s.; ed Manchester and Oxford Univs; lecturer, Univ. Coll. London 1974–85; Wilde Reader in Mental Philosophy, Oxford Univ. 1985–90; Prof., Rutgers Univ., USA 1990–2005; Prof., Dept of Philosophy, Univ. of Miami 2005–; John Locke Prize 1973. *Publications include:* The Character of Mind 1981, The Subjective View 1982, Wittgenstein on Meaning 1984, Mental Content 1989, The Problem of Consciousness 1991, Moral Literacy 1992, The Space Trap 1992, Problems in Philosophy 1993, Minds and Bodies: Philosophers and their Ideas 1997, Ethics, Evil and Fiction 1997, Knowledge and Reality 1998, The Mysterious Flame 1999, Logical Properties 2000, The Making of a Philosopher 2002, Consciousness and its Objects 2004, Mindsight: Image, Dream, Meaning 2004, The Power of Movies 2005, Shakespeare's Philosophy 2006, Mindfucking 2008, The Meaning of Disgust 2011. *Leisure interest:* fitness. *Address:* Department of Philosophy, University of Miami, Ashe Building, Room 705, PO Box 248054, Coral Gables, FL 33124-4670 (office); 270 West End Avenue, Apartment 9E, New York, NY 10023, USA. *Telephone:* (305) 284-4757 (office). *E-mail:* cmg124@aol.com (office). *Website:* www.as.miami.edu/phi (office).

McGINN, Richard A., BA; American telecommunications executive; *General Partner, RRE Ventures LLC;* b. 1947; m.; one d.; ed Grinnell Coll., Iowa; with Illinois Bell 1969; exec. positions, int. and computer systems groups, AT&T 1978, CEO network systems; CEO, Pres. Lucent Technologies 1997–2000, Chair. and CEO –2000; Gen. Partner, RRE Ventures LLC (investment advisory and venture capital firm) 2001–; Chair. (non-exec.) VeriFone Systems, Inc. 2012–March 2013, Interim CEO March–Sept. 2013; mem. Bd of Dirs American Express Co. 1998–, Viasystems Group, Inc., Roundbox Inc. 2005–, VeriFone Systems, Inc. 2008–14, Certeon Inc., Enpirion Inc., Taqua Systems Inc., VeriFone Inc., Mintera Corpn, Mountain Top Foundation; Ind. Dir, Nexsan Technologies Inc. 2003–; mem. Advisory Bd Roundbox Inc.; fmr mem. Bd of Dirs Lucent Technologies, Oracle Corpn; mem. Business Council. *Leisure interests:* adventure sports, deep-sea fishing. *Address:* RRE Ventures LLC, 130 East 59th Street, 17th Floor, New York, NY 10022, USA (office). *Telephone:* (212) 418-5100 (office). *E-mail:* info@rre.com (office). *Website:* www.rre.com (office).

McGLADE, Jacqueline M., BSc, MA, PhD, FLS, FRSA; British/Canadian environmental scientist, academic and international organization official; b. 1955; ed Univ. Coll. of North Wales, Univ. of Guelph, Canada, Univ. of Cambridge, UK; early career as Sr Research Scientist, Dept of Fisheries and Oceans, Canada; fmr academic positions include Prof. of Biological Sciences, Univ. of Warwick, England, Dir of Theoretical Ecology, Forschungszentrum Jülich, Germany, Prof. Aachen Univ., Germany, Adrian Fellow, Darwin Coll., Univ. of Cambridge, UK, Assoc. Prof., Int. Ecotechnology Research Centre, Cranfield Univ., UK; Dir NERC Centre for Coastal and Marine Sciences –2000; NERC Professorial Fellow in Environmental Informatics, Univ. Coll. London 2000–03. Prof. of Math. Biology 2003–; Exec. Dir, European Environment Agency 2003–13; fmr Chair., The Earth Centre; Bd mem. Environment Agency 1998–2003; Trustee, Natural History Museum; mem. UK-China Forum; holds full diplomatic status in Denmark; Hon. DSc (Kent) 2004; Swedish Jubileum Award 1990, Minerva Prize 1993, Masaryk Gold Medal 2005, Brno Univ. Gold Medal. *Radio:* The Ocean Planet (BBC Radio 4) 2000, King John's Treasure (BBC Radio 4) 2001, Learning from Nature (BBC Radio 4) 2002. *Television:* The Next Big Thing (BBC 2) 2000. *Publications include:* Integrated Fisheries Management: Understanding the Limits to Marine Resource Exploitation 1989, Governance of Fisheries and Aquaculture 1993, Ecology, Thermodynamics and Odum's Conjectures (co-author) 1993, Advanced Ecological Theory (ed.) 1999, Gulf of Guinea Ecosystem (co-ed.) 2002, The European Environment: State and Outlook 2005, Millennium Ecosystem Assessment, Vol. 2: Scenarios (co-ed.) 2005; more than 150 publs. *Address:* c/o European Environment Agency, Kongens Nytorv 6, 1050 Copenhagen, Denmark (office).

McGOUGH, Roger Joseph, CBE, MA, DLitt, FRSL; British poet and children's writer; *President, The Poetry Society;* b. 9 Nov. 1937, Liverpool; s. of Roger McGough and Mary McGarry; m. 1st Thelma Monaghan 1970 (divorced 1980); m. 2nd Hilary Clough 1986; three s. one d.; ed St Mary's Coll., Liverpool, Hull Univ.; Poetry Fellow Univ. of Loughborough 1973–75; writer-in-residence Western Australia Coll. of Educ., Perth 1986, Univ. of Hamburg 1994; Vice-Pres. The Poetry Society 1996–2011 (mem. Exec. Council 1989–93), Pres. 2012–; Fellow John Moores Univ. 1999; Trustee Chelsea Arts Club 1987–, fmr Chair.; Freeman City of Liverpool 2001; Hon. Prof. Thames Valley Univ. 1993; Hon. MA (Nene Coll.) 1998, Hon. DLitt (Hull Univ.) 2004, (Univ. of Surrey) 2006; Signal Award 1984, 1998, BAFTA Awards 1984, 1992, Cholmondeley Award 1998, Centre for Literacy in Primary Educ. Award for Best Book of Poetry for Children 2004, 2005. *Music:* wrote and performed Top Twenty hits Lily the Pink and Thank U Very Much 1968–69. *Plays include:* The Sound Collector and My Dad's a Fire-eater (for children); wrote lyrics for Broadway production of The Wind in the Willows 1984; adaptations of Molière's Tartuffe 2008, The Hypochondriac 2009, The Misanthrope 2012. *Plays for radio include:* Summer with Monika, FX, Walking the Dog. *Television:* Kurt, Mungo, B. P. and Me (Thames Television) 1985, The Elements (Channel 4) (Royal Television Soc. Award) 1993. *Publications:* The Mersey Sound (with Brian Patten and Adrian Henri) 1967, Watchwords 1969, After the Merrymaking 1971, Out of Sequence 1972, Gig 1972, Sporting Relations 1974, In the Glassroom 1976, Summer with Monika 1978, Holiday on Death Row 1979, Unlucky for Some 1981, Waving at Trains 1982, Melting into the Foreground 1986, Blazing Fruit: Selected Poems 1967–1987 1989, You at the Back 1991, Defying Gravity 1992, The Spotted Unicorn 1998, The Way Things Are 1999, Everyday Eclipses 2002, Collected Poems of Roger McGough 2003, Said and Done (memoir) 2005, Selected Poems 2006, That Awkward Age 2009, As Far As I Know 2012; for children: Mr Noselighter 1977, The Great Smile Robbery 1982, Sky in the Pie 1983, The Stowaways 1986, Noah's Ark 1986, Nailing the Shadow 1987, An Imaginary Menagerie 1988, Helen Highwater 1989, Counting by Numbers 1989, Pillow Talk 1990, The Lighthouse That Ran Away 1991, My Dad's a Fire-eater 1992, Another Custard Pie 1993, Lucky 1993, Stinkers Ahoy! 1995, The Magic Fountain 1995, The Kite and Caitlin 1996, Bad Bad Cats 1997, Until I Met Dudley 1998, Good Enough to Eat 2002, Moonthief 2002, The Bees' Knees 2002, Dotty Inventions 2002, What On Earth Can It Be? 2003; editor: Strictly Private 1981, The Kingfisher Book of Comic Verse 1986, The Kingfisher Book of Poems About Love 1997, The Ring of Words (anthology) 1998, Wicked Poems 2002, All the Best 2002, Sensational (anthology) 2004. *Address:* United Agents, 12–26 Lexington Street, London, W1F 0LE, England (office). *Telephone:* (20) 3214-0800 (office). *Fax:* (20) 3214-0801 (office). *E-mail:* info@unitedagents.co.uk (office); personal@ rogermcgough.org.uk (office). *Website:* unitedagents.co.uk (office); www .rogermcgough.org.uk.

McGOWAN, Kieran, BComm; Irish business executive; joined IDA Ireland (industrial devt agency f. as the Industrial Devt Authority) 1966, CEO 1990–98; mem. Bd of Dirs 1998–2012, Chair. 2007–12 (retd); mem. Bd of Dirs Elan Corpn plc, Enterprise Ireland 1998–, Irish Life & Permanent plc, United Drug plc, Charles Schwab Worldwide Funds plc; Chair. Governing Authority, Univ. Coll. Dublin 2004–09; Founder-mem. Inter Trade Ireland; fmr Pres. Irish Man. Inst., Dublin Molecular Medicine Centre. *Address:* c/o CRH plc, Belgard Castle, Clondalkin, Dublin 22, Ireland (office). *E-mail:* mail@crh.com.

McGRATH, Glenn Donald, AM; Australian professional cricketer; b. 9 Feb. 1970, Dubbo, NSW; ed Narromine High School, NSW; right-handed batsman, right-arm fast-medium bowler; teams: NSW 1992–2008, Australia 1993–2007 (retd), Worcs. 2000, Middx 2008, Delhi Daredevils 2008–; First-class debut: 1992/ 93; Test debut: Australia v NZ, Perth 12–16 Nov. 1993; One-Day Int. (ODI) debut: Australia v S Africa, Melbourne 9 Dec. 1993; T20I debut: NZ v Australia, Auckland 17 Feb. 2005; played in 124 Tests, scored 641 runs and took 563 wickets (average 21.64) with 29 five-wicket and three 10-wicket performances, best bowling 8/24 against Pakistan at the WACA 2004; ODIs: played in 250 matches, took 381 wickets (average 22.02), best bowling 7/15; First-class: scored 977 runs and took 835 wickets (average 20.85) with 42 five-wicket and seven 10-wicket performances; test hat-trick against West Indies at Perth 2001; 32 wickets in 2001 series against England; eighth to pass 400 wickets in test cricket (second Australian); included in NSW Team of the Millennium; first Australian fast bowler to play in 100 Test matches; highest score of 61 runs against NZ 2005 (third highest score in history for a No. 11 batsman); retd from Test cricket 23 Dec. 2006, from all int. cricket following World Cup 2007; Wisden Cricketer of the Year 1998, Wisden Australian Cricketer of the Year 1999, 2005–06, Allan Border Medal 2000, Test Player of the Year 2000, One-Day Int. Player of the Year 2001, World Cup Player of the Series 2007. *Publication:* World Cup Diary: Glenn McGrath. *Leisure interests:* time with family, golf. *Address:* c/o Titan Management, PO Box 6832, Silverwater, BC NSW 2128, Australia (office). *Telephone:* (2) 9746-6355 (office). *Fax:* (2) 9746-6366 (office). *E-mail:* sports@titanmanagement.com.au (office). *Website:* www.nswblues .com.au (office).

McGRATH, Harvey; British business executive; began career at Chase Manhattan Bank, London and New York; worked for the Man Group, first as Treas., then as Finance Dir, then as Pres. Man Inc., New York 1980–90, Chief Exec. Man Group plc, London 1990–2000, Chair. 2000–07; ind. Dir (non-exec.) Prudential plc 2008–12, Chair. 2009–12 (resgnd); Chair. Nomination Cttee; Chair. London Devt Agency; Vice-Chair. London Skills and Employment Bd 2006–11; Co-Chair. London Enterprise Partnership 2011–; fmr Chair. London First, East London Business Alliance; mem. Int. Advisory Bd, SOAS; Chair. Govs of Birkbeck Coll.; Trustee, New Philanthropy Capital, Royal Anniversary Trust, Children and Families Across Borders, icould (online careers resource), Prince's Teaching Inst. *Address:* c/o Prudential plc, Laurence Pountney Hill, London, EC4R 0HH, England. *E-mail:* info@prudential.co.uk.

McGRATH, John Brian, BSc, FRSA; British business executive; *Chairman, Cicely Saunders International;* b. 20 June 1938, Ruislip, Middlesex; m. Sandy Watson 1964; one s. one d.; ed Brunel Univ.; worked at UKAEA 1962–65; with NCB 1965–67; with Ford Motor Co. 1967–71; with Jaguar Cars 1971–75; with Stone-Platt 1976–82; Man. Dir Construction and Mining Div. and Chief Exec.

Compair 1982–83; joined Grand Metropolitan PLC 1985, Group Dir Watney Mann & Truman Brewers Ltd 1985, Chair. and Man. Dir Grand Metropolitan Brewing 1986–88, Jt Man. Dir Int. Distillers & Vintners 1988–91, Man. Dir and COO 1991–92, Chief Exec. 1992–93, Chair. and Chief Exec. 1993–96, Group Chief Exec. Grand Metropolitan PLC 1996–97; Dir (non-exec.) Cookson Group 1993–; Chair. Scotch Whisky Asscn 1995–2000; Chair. Guinness Ltd (now Diageo PLC) 1997–2000, CEO 1997–2000; Chair. Boots Co. PLC 2000–03 (Dir 1998–2003); Dir Carlton Communications PLC 2003, ITV PLC (formed by merger of Carlton Communications and Granada) 2004–07; Chair. Cicely Saunders Int. 2002–; Gov. Brunel Univ. 2004–;*Telephone:* (1249) 721589 (office). *E-mail:* jbmcgrath99@yahoo .co.uk (home).

McGREEVEY, James E., BA; American lawyer and fmr politician; b. 6 Aug. 1957, Jersey City; s. of John McGreevey and Veronica McGreevey; m. Dina Matos; two d.; ed St Joseph's High School, Columbia Univ., Georgetown Univ., Harvard Univ.; fmrly man. with Merck & Co.; fmr Asst Prosecutor for Middlesex Co.; Exec. Dir of State Parole Bd; mem. State Ass. of New Jersey 1990–91, State Senate 1994–97; Mayor of Woodbridge 1992–2002; Gov. of New Jersey 2002–04 (resgnd). *Address:* c/o Office of the Governor, POB 001, Trenton, NJ 08625, USA (office).

McGREGOR, Ewan Gordon, OBE; British actor; b. 31 March 1971, Perth, Scotland; s. of James McGregor and Carol McGregor; m. Eve Mavrakis 1995; three d. and one adopted d.; ed Guildhall School of Music and Drama, London; began career with Perth Repertory Theatre; has acted in mainstream, indie and art house films; Hon. DLitt (Univ. of Ulster). *Theatre includes:* What the Butler Saw, Little Malcolm and his Struggle against the Eunuchs (Hampstead Theatre Club) 1999 and Comedy Theatre, London, Guys and Dolls (Piccadilly Theatre, London) 2005, Othello (Donmar Warehouse, London) 2007–08. *Films include:* Being Human, Family Style, Shallow Grave (Best Actor Dinard Film Festival 1994), Blue Juice, The Pillow Book, Trainspotting, Emma, Brassed Off, Nightwatch, The Serpent's Kiss, A Life Less Ordinary, Velvet Goldmine, Star Wars Episode I: The Phantom Menace, Little Voice, Rogue Trader, Eye of the Beholder, Nora, Moulin Rouge (Best Actor, Berlin Film Festival, Empire Award, Variety Club Awards, Film Critics' Awards) 2001, Black Hawk Down 2002, Star Wars Episode II: Attack of the Clones 2002, Down with Love 2003, Young Adam (Scottish BAFTA Award for Best Actor 2004) 2003, Big Fish 2004, Stay 2004, Star Wars Episode III: Revenge of the Sith 2005, The Island 2005, Stay 2005, Stormbreaker 2006, Scenes of a Sexual Nature 2006, Miss Potter 2006, Cassandra's Dream 2007, Deception 2008, Incendiary 2008, I Love You Phillip Morris 2009, Angels and Demons 2009, The Men Who Stare At Goats 2009, Amelia 2009, The Ghost (European Film Award for Best Actor) 2010, Nanny McPhee and the Big Bang 2010, Jackboots on Whitehal (voice) 2010, Beginners 2010, Perfect Sense 2011, Salmon Fishing in the Yemen 2011, Haywire 2011, The Impossible 2012, Jack the Giant Slayer 2013, August: Osage County 2013. *Television includes:* Lipstick on Your Collar 1993, Scarlet and Black 1993, Kavanagh QC 1995, Doggin' Around, Tales From the Crypt 1996, ER 1997, Long Way Round 2004, Long Way Down 2007, The Corrections (film) 2012. *Publications:* Long Way Round (with Charley Boorman) 2005, Long Way Down (with Charley Boorman) 2007. *Leisure interest:* motor bikes. *Address:* c/o United Agents, 12–26 Lexington Street, London W1F 0LE, England (office); c/o Creative Artists Agency, 2000 Avenue of the Stars, Los Angeles, CA 90067, USA (office). *Website:* unitedagents.co.uk (office); www.caa.com (office). *Telephone:* (424) 288-2000 (office). *Fax:* (424) 288-2900 (office).

McGREGOR, Harvey, CBE, QC, MA, DCL, SJD; British barrister; b. 25 Feb. 1926, Aberdeen, Scotland; s. of the late William G. R. McGregor and Agnes Reid; ed Inverurie Acad., Scarborough Boys' High School, Queen's Coll. Oxford and Harvard Univ.; Bigelow Teaching Fellow, Univ. of Chicago 1950–51; called to the Bar, Inner Temple, London 1955, Bencher 1985; Fellow, New Coll. Oxford 1972–85, Warden 1985–96, Hon. Fellow 1996; Privilegiate, St Hilda's Coll. Oxford 2001; consultant to Law Comm. 1966–73; Deputy Ind. Chair. London and the Theatre Council 1971–92, Ind. Chair. 1992–; Visiting Prof., New York Univ. and Rutgers Univ. 1963–69; Fellow, Winchester Coll. 1985–96; mem. Editorial Bd Modern Law Review 1986–; mem. Acad. of European Pvt. Lawyers 1994–; Trustee Oxford Union 1977–2004 (Chair. 1994–2004); Trustee Migraine Trust 1999–; Assoc. mem. Soc. of Writers to the Signet 2002–; Founding Fellow Inst. of Contemporary Scotland 2002; Hon. Prof., Univ. of Edinburgh 1998–. *Publications:* A Contract Code 1993, McGregor on Damages (18th edn) 2009, European Contract Code (trans. from the French) 2004. *Leisure interests:* music, theatre, travel. *Address:* Hailsham Chambers, 4 Paper Buildings, Temple, London, EC4Y 7EX (office); 29 Howard Place, Edinburgh, EH3 5JY, Scotland (home). *Telephone:* (20) 7643-5000 (office); (131) 556-8680 (home). *Fax:* (20) 7353-5778 (office); (131) 556-8686 (home). *E-mail:* harvey.mcgregor@hailshamchambers.com (office). *Website:* www.hailshamchambers.com (office).

MacGREGOR, Joanna Clare, OBE, MA; British pianist, conductor, curator and academic; *Head of Piano, Royal Academy of Music;* b. 16 July 1959, London, England; d. of Alfred MacGregor and Angela Hughes; m. 1st Richard Williams 1986 (divorced 2002), remarried 2012; one d. (deceased); ed South Hampstead High School for Girls, New Hall, Cambridge, Royal Acad. of Music, London; Young Concert Artists Trust 1985–88; performances of classical, jazz and contemporary music in more than 80 countries at venues including Royal Albert Hall, Royal Festival Hall, Wigmore Hall, Lincoln Center and Carnegie Hall, New York, Sydney Opera House, Leipzig Gewandhaus, Opéra Bastille, Paris, Concertgebouw, Amsterdam; has performed with Rotterdam, Oslo and Netherlands Radio and Royal Philharmonic Orchestras, Sydney, Berlin, Chicago, BBC, RTÉ and London Symphony Orchestras, MDR Sinfonieorchester and Salzburg Camerata, New York and Hong Kong Philharmonics, Philharmonia, London Mozart Players, Manchester Camerata, Royal Scottish, Royal Liverpool, Hallé, English and Irish Chamber Orchestras; has worked with John Adams, Sir Harrison Birtwistle, Pierre Boulez, Sir Colin Davis, Sir Simon Rattle, Valery Gergiev, Lou Harrison, Arvo Pärt and numerous jazz artists, including Jason Yarde, Seb Rochford and Andy Sheppard; electronica artists and world music artists including Dhafer Youssef, Kuljit Bhamra, Brian Eno, Susanne Bishi, Moses Molelekwa and Sibongile Khumalo; numerous radio and TV appearances, including Last Night of the Proms 1997, South Bank Show 2002, Messiaen's Turangalila (BBC 4) 2012, Mozart/Gershwin (BBC 2) 2012; est. own record label SoundCircus 1998; Prof. of Music, Gresham Coll. 1998–2002; Prof. of Performance, Liverpool Hope Univ.; Head of Piano, RAM

2011–; mem. Arts Council of England 1998–2002; conducting debut on UK tour with Britten Sinfonia 2000, Assoc. Artistic Dir 2002–05; cr. Cross Border, multimedia work touring China with Jin Xing's Dance Theatre of Shanghai 2003; Artistic Dir Bath Int. Music Festival 2005–12; created On the Edge of Life examining social issues through music/multimedia 2006–12; performed complete Chopin Mazurkas 2010; curated Deloitte Ignite at Royal Opera House, Covent Garden 2011, Aventure at Luxembourg Philharmonique 2012–13; currently performing complete cycle of Mozart piano concertos; Goldberg Variations at Royal Albert Hall 2013; Hon. FRAM, Hon. Fellow, Trinity Coll. of Music, RSA, New Hall, Cambridge; Dr hc (Open Univ.) 2005, (Bath Univ.) 2008, (Bath Spa Univ.) 2011; European Encouragement Prize for Music 1995, NFMS Sir Charles Grove Award 1998, South Bank Show Award for Classical Music 2000, Royal Philharmonic Soc. Audience Development Award 2003. *Play:* Memoirs of an Amnesiac (radio play about Erik Satie). *Compositions include:* Lute Songs (orchestra), Lullaby for M (percussion), arrangements of Piazzolla tangos, Lost Highway: Gospel and Spirituals of the Deep South (orchestral), new arrangement of The Magic Flute (ensemble), settings of Angela Carter poems (voice and ensemble), Sidewalk Dances and Art of Fugue (Bach and Moondog, orchestral). *Recordings:* American contemporary music (Ives, Monk, Nancarrow, Copland, Barber, Cage, Lou Harrison), Britten Concerto, Satie, Gershwin recordings with LSO, and music by Bach (The Art of Fugue, French Suites, Goldberg Variations), Scarlatti, Bartók, Debussy, Ravel and Messaien (Vingt Regards, Harawi, Quartet for the End of Time), Deep River (music of the Deep South, with Andy Sheppard) 2006, orchestral arrangements of Moondog: Sidewalk Dances 2007, commissions and recordings of Harrison Birtwistle, Nitin Sawhney, Talvin Singh, Moses Molelekwa, Django Bates, Live in Buenos Aires (Piazzolla, Bach, Ginastera). *Publications:* wrote series of children's books for Faber Music 2001, Piano World (five vols) 2001, Art Not Chance 2001, Unbeaten Tracks 2006, Lowside Blues 2009. *Address:* c/o Ingpen & Williams, 7 St George's Court, 131 Putney Bridge Road, London, SW15 2PA, England (office). *Telephone:* (20) 8874-3222 (office). *Fax:* (20) 8877-3113 (office). *E-mail:* info@ingpen.co.uk (office); *Website:* www.ingpen.co.uk (office); www.warnerclassics.com/joanna-macgregor.

MacGREGOR, Baron (Life Peer), cr. 2001, of Pulham Market in the County of Norfolk; **John Roddick Russell MacGregor,** OBE, PC, MA, LLB; British politician and business executive; *Chairman, Select Committee on Economic Affairs, House of Lords;* b. 14 Feb. 1937, Glasgow; s. of the late Dr. N. S. R. MacGregor; m. Jean Mary Elizabeth Dungey 1962; one s. two d.; ed Merchiston Castle School, Edin., St Andrews Univ., King's Coll., London; Univ. Admin. 1961–62; Editorial Staff, New Society 1962–63; Special Asst to Prime Minister, Sir Alec Douglas-Home 1963–64; Conservative Research Dept 1964–65; Head of Pvt. Office of Rt Hon. Edward Heath (Leader of Opposition) 1965–68; Conservative MP for South Norfolk 1974–2001; an Opposition Whip 1977–79; a Lord Commr of HM Treasury 1979–81, Parl. Under-Sec. of State, Dept of Industry 1981–83; Minister of State, Minister of Agric., Fisheries and Food 1983–85, 1987–89; Chief Sec. to HM Treasury 1985–87; Sec. of State for Educ. and Science 1989–90; Lord Pres. of the Council and Leader of the House of Commons 1990–92; Sec. of State for Transport 1992–94; mem. House of Lords 2001–, Chair. Select Cttee on Econ. Affairs 2010–; with Hill Samuel & Co. Ltd 1968–79, Dir 1973–79, Deputy Chair. Hill Samuel Bank 1994–96, also Dir; Dir Slough Estates 1995–2006, Associated British Foods 1994–2007, Unigate (now Uniq) 1996–2005, London and Manchester Group 1997–98, Friends Provident 1998–2007, Supervisory Bd Daf Trucks NV 2000–08; Jt Chair. UK Food and Agriculture Advisory Bd, Rabobank International 1995–2011; Vice-Pres. Local Govt Asscn 1997–99; mem. Cttee on Standards in Public Life 1998–2003; Chair. Fed. of Univ. Conservative and Unionist Asscns 1959, Bow Group 1963–64; Chair. Pension Fund Trustees, SEGRO 2006–09, British Energy (now EDF) 2007–, Anglian Water Group 2009–12, Eggborough Power Ltd 2010–; First Pres. Conservative and Christian Democratic Youth Community 1963–65; mem. Magic Circle 1989, Inner Magic Circle 1999; mem. Council King's Coll. London 1996–2002, Inst. of Dirs 1996–2007, Norwich Cathedral Council 2002–, High Steward and Chair. of Council 2007–; Deputy Chair., Asscn of Governing Bodies of Ind. Schools 2001–06; Trustee Royal Norfolk Agricultural Asscn 2006–09; Hon. Fellow, King's Coll. London 1990; Hon. LLD (Westminster) 1995. *Leisure interests:* music, reading, travelling, gardening, conjuring. *Address:* House of Lords, London, SW1A 0PW, England. *Telephone:* (20) 7219-4439 (office).

MacGREGOR, (Robert) Neil; British museum director; *Director, British Museum;* b. 16 June 1946; s. of Alexander MacGregor and Anna MacGregor (née Neil); ed Glasgow Acad., New Coll., Oxford, Univ. of Edinburgh, Courtauld Inst. of Art; Lecturer, Univ. of Reading 1976; Ed. The Burlington Magazine 1981–86; Dir Nat. Gallery 1987–2002; Dir British Museum 2002–; Trustee Pilgrim Trust 1990–, Raad van Toezicht, Rijksmuseum, Amsterdam; Chair. Conf. of UK Nat. Museum Dirs 1991–97; Curator Cen. Inst. for Art History, Munich 1992–; mem. Supervisory Bd Rijksmuseum 1995–; mem. Bd of Electors Ashmolean Museum, Fitzwilliam Museum; mem. UNESCO; mem. Advisory Bd of the Hermitage, St Petersburg 1997–; mem. Visiting Cttee J. Paul Getty Museum, Malibu, Calif., USA; fmr Chair. Nat. Museums Dirs' Conf.; mem. Courtauld Inst. of Art 2002–; Fellow, New Coll. Oxford, Birkbeck Coll. London 2004; mem. Faculty of Advocates, Edin. 1972; Hon. mem. Royal Scottish Acad. 1995; Hon. Fellow, Ecole Normale Supérieure, Paris, British Acad.; Dr hc (York) 1992, (Edinburgh) 1994, (Reading) 1997, (Leicester) 1997, (Glasgow) 1998, (Strathclyde) 1998, (Oxford) 1998, (Exeter) 1998, (London) 1999. *Radio:* contributor to numerous radio programmes. *Television:* has presented two major series on art. *Video:* Making Masterpieces (three-video set; writer and presenter). *Publications:* A Victory of Anonymity 1994, Seeing Salvation 2000, Britain's Paintings: the story of art through masterpieces in British Collections 2003, A History of the World in 100 Objects 2010, Shakespeare's Restless World 2012; numerous articles in Apollo, The Burlington Magazine, Connoisseur, etc. *Address:* The British Museum, Great Russell Street, London, WC1B 3DG, England. *Telephone:* (20) 7323-8000 (office). *Website:* www.britishmuseum.org (office).

MacGREGOR, Susan (Sue) Katriona, CBE, FRSA; British broadcaster and journalist; b. 30 Aug. 1941, Oxford, England; d. of the late Dr James MacGregor and Margaret MacGregor; ed Herschel School, Cape, SA; announcer/producer, South African Broadcasting Corpn 1962–67; BBC Radio reporter World at One, World This Weekend, PM 1967–72; Presenter (BBC Radio 4) Woman's Hour

1972–87, Tuesday Call, Conversation Piece, Today 1984–2002, A Good Read 2003–10, The Reunion 2003–, (BBC TV) Around Westminster, Dateline London; Visiting Prof. of Journalism, Nottingham Trent Univ. 1995–2003; mem. Royal Coll. of Physicians Cttee on Ethical Issues in Medicine 1985–2000; mem. Bd Royal Nat. Theatre 1998–2003; Trustee, John Ellerman Foundation 2002–12, UNICEF UK 2004–13; Bd mem. Young Classical Artists' Trust 2003–12; Hon. MRCP 1995; Hon. DLitt (Nottingham) 1996; Hon. LLD (Dundee) 1997; Hon. DLitt (Nottingham Trent) 2000, (Staffordshire) 2001, (North London) 2002. *Publication:* Woman of Today 2002. *Leisure interests:* theatre, cinema, skiing. *Address:* c/o Knight Ayton Management, 35 Great James Street, London, WC1N 4HB, England (office). *Telephone:* (20) 7836-5333 (office).

McGREGOR, Wayne, CBE; British choreographer and director; *Resident Choreographer, Royal Ballet;* b. 12 March 1970, Stockport, Greater Manchester; ed Univ. Coll. Bretton Hall and José Limon School, NY, USA; originally trained in contemporary dance; cr. works for The Royal Ballet, Skindex, Stuttgart Ballet, English Nat. Ballet, San Francisco Ballet and Rambert Dance Co.; other work includes choreography for film Harry Potter and The Goblet of Fire and for Channel 4 (UK), BBC TV, The Old Vic, Nat. Theatre, Royal Court Theatre, ENO and Peter Hall Co.; Founder Random Dance 1992, became Resident Co. of Sadler's Wells Theatre 2001–; Resident Choreographer, Royal Ballet 2006–; Choreographer of Big Dance 2012 (Olympic-funded project); Hon. DSc (Plymouth Univ.) 2013; Outstanding Achievement in Dance Award, Time Out Live Awards 2001, Outstanding Choreography Award, Time Out Live Awards 2002, IMZ Dance Screen Award 2002, Laurence Olivier Award 2004. *Dances include:* Chroma, Engram, Qualia, Symbiont(s), NDT1 for Royal Ballet, over 30 pieces for Random Dance, Outlier, cr. two new ballets in celebration of Les Ballet Russes – Dyad 1909, for Wayne McGregor/Random Dance, and Dyad 1929, for Australian Ballet, Borderlands for San Francisco Ballet 2013, Raven Girl, Royal Ballet 2013. *Address:* Royal Opera House, Bow Street, Covent Garden, London, WC2E 9DD, England (office). *Website:* www.roh.org.uk/discover/artistdetail.aspx?id=535 (office).

McGUFFIN, Peter, MB ChB, PhD, FRCP, FRCPsych, FMedSci; British/Irish psychiatrist and geneticist; *Professor of Psychiatric Genetics, Medical Research Council Social, Genetic and Developmental Psychiatry Centre, Institute of Psychiatry, King's College London;* b. 4 Feb. 1949, Belfast, Northern Ireland; s. of Capt. William McGuffin and Melba M. Burnison; m. Prof. Anne Farmer 1972; one s. two d.; ed Univs of Leeds and London; MRC Fellow and Lecturer, Inst. of Psychiatry, London 1979–81; Visiting MRC Fellow, Washington Univ. Medical School, St Louis, Mo. 1981–82; MRC Sr Fellow, Hon. Consultant and Sr Lecturer, Inst. of Psychiatry, King's Coll. Hosp. London 1982–86; Prof. of Psychological Medicine, Univ. of Wales Coll. of Medicine 1987–98; Prof. of Psychiatric Genetics, MRC Social, Genetic and Developmental Psychiatry Centre, Inst. of Psychiatry, King's Coll. London 1998–, Dean and Head of School 2006–09, Dir MRC Social, Genetic and Developmental Psychiatry Centre 2010–12; Distinguished Fellow, Int. Soc. of Affective Disorders 2000; Fattorini Prize, Univ. of Leeds 1972, Foundation Fellow, Acad. of Medical Sciences (UK) 1998, Stromgren Medal, Danish Psychiatric Asscn 2004, Lifetime Achievement Award, Int. Soc. for Psychiatric Genetics 2007. *Publications include:* Scientific Principles of Psychopathology, The New Genetics of Mental Illness, Seminars on Psychiatric Genetics, Essentials of Postgraduate Psychiatry, Behavioural Genetics (4th edn), Measuring Psychopathology, Psychiatric Genetics and Genomics; many scientific papers and articles. *Leisure interests:* music (especially classical guitar), horse riding, running with my dogs. *Address:* MRC Social, Genetic and Developmental Psychiatry Centre, Institute of Psychiatry, Box P001, De Crespigny Park, London, SE5 8AF, England (office). *Telephone:* (20) 7848-0871 (office). *Fax:* (20) 7848-0866 (office). *E-mail:* p.mcguffin@iop.kcl.ac.uk (office). *Website:* www.iop.kcl.ac.uk (office).

McGUINNESS, Frank, BA, MPhil, DLit; Irish playwright and academic; *Professor, School of English, Drama and Film, University College Dublin;* b. 29 July 1953, Buncrana, Donegal; s. of Patrick McGuinness and Celine McGuinness; ed University Coll. Dublin; Lecturer in English, Univ. of Ulster, Coleraine 1977–79; Lecturer in English, Univ. Coll. Dublin 1979–80; Writer-in-Residence, School of English, Drama and Film 1997–; Prof. of Creative Writing 1997–; Lecturer in English, St Patrick's Coll., Maynooth 1984–97; Dir Abbey Theatre, Dublin 1992–96; Officier des Arts et Lettres; Hon. DLitt (Ulster) 2000; Harvey's Award, Evening Standard Drama Award, Ewart-Biggs Peace Prize, Cheltenham Literary Prize, Fringe First, Irish American Literary Prize 1992, Independent on Sunday Best Play 1992, New York Drama Critics' Award 1993, Writers' Guild Award 1993, Tony Award for Best Revival 1997, PEN Irish Writer Award 2014, London Theatre Offies Best Play Award 2014. *Publications include:* plays: The Factory Girls 1982, Observe the Sons of Ulster Marching towards the Somme 1985, Baglady 1985, Innocence 1986, Carthaginians 1988, Mary and Lizzie 1989, The Bread Man 1990, Someone Who'll Watch Over Me 1992, The Bird Sanctuary 1994, Mutabilitie 1997, Dolly West's Kitchen 1999, Gates of Gold 2002, Speaking Like Magpies 2005, There Came a Gypsy Riding 2007, Oedipus 2008, Greta Garbo Came to Donegal 2010, Ghosts 2011, The Match Box 2012, John Gabriel Borkman 2011, The Dead 2012, Damned by Despair 2012, The Hanging Gardens 2013, The Thebans: Libretto 2014, Electra 2014; poetry: Booterstown 1994, In Loving Memory 1989, The Sea with no Ships 1999, The Stone Jug 2003, Dulse 2007, In A Town of Five Thousand People 2012. *Leisure interests:* walking, painting, botany. *Address:* School of English, Drama and Film, University College Dublin, Belfield, Dublin 4, Ireland (office). *Telephone:* (1) 7168420 (office). *Fax:* (1)716-1174 (office). *E-mail:* pauline.slattery@ucd.ie (office). *Website:* www.ucd.ie/englishanddrama/staff/academicstaff/mcguinnessfrank (office).

McGUINNESS, Martin; Irish politician; *Deputy First Minister of Northern Ireland;* b. 23 May 1950, Derry; m.; four c.; took part in secret London talks between Sec. of State for NI and Irish Republican Army (IRA) July 1972; imprisoned for six months during 1973 in Irish Repub. after conviction for IRA membership; elected to NI Ass., refused seat; stood against John Hume (q.v.) in gen. elections of 1982, 1987, 1992; MP for Mid-Ulster, House of Commons 1997–; mem. Ulster-Mid, NI Ass. 1998–2000 (Ass. suspended Feb. 2000), 2000–02 (Ass. suspended Oct. 2002); Minister of Educ. 1999–2002; spokesman for Sinn Féin, also mem. Nat. Exec.; involved in peace negotiations with British Govt; Deputy First Minister of NI Ass. 2007–; Sinn Féin cand. for Irish presidential election 2011.

Leisure interest: fly-fishing. *Address:* Office of the Deputy First Minister, Parliament Buildings, Stormont Estate, Belfast, BT4 3XX (office); Sinn Féin, 51–55 Falls Road, Belfast, BT12 4PD, Northern Ireland (office). *Telephone:* (28) 9022-3000. *E-mail:* sinnfein@iol.ie (office). *Website:* www.irlnet.com/sinnfein (office).

McGUINTY, Hon. Dalton, JD; Canadian politician; b. 19 July 1955; s. of the late Dalton McGuinty, Sr and Elizabeth McGuinty; m. Terri McGuinty; three s. one d.; ed Univ. of Ottawa, McMaster Univ.; practised law Ottawa; mem. Ontario Legislature representing Ottawa South 1990–; Leader Ontario Liberal Party 1996–2013; Premier of Ont. 2003–13 (resgnd), also Minister of Intergovernmental Affairs 2003–13. *Address:* c/o Office of the Premier, Legislative Building, Queen's Park, Toronto, ON M7A 1A1, Canada.

McGUIRE, William W., MD; American business executive; practising physician specialising in cardiopulmonary medicine 1980–85; Pres. and CEO Peak Health Plan 1985–88; joined United HealthCare Corpn (renamed UnitedHealth Group) 1988, Pres. and COO 1989–91, CEO and Chair. 1991–2006; mem. Nat. Insts of Health Nat. Cancer Policy Bd; One of the 50 Best CEOs in America, Worth Magazine 2001. *Address:* c/o UnitedHealth Group, POB 1459, Minneapolis, MN 55440-1459, USA (office).

MACH, David Stefan, MA, RA; British sculptor; *Professor of Inspiration and Discovery, Dundee University;* b. 18 March 1956, Methil, Fife, Scotland; s. of Joseph Mach and Martha Cassidy; m. Lesley June White 1979; ed Buckhaven High School, Duncan of Jordanstone Coll. of Art, Dundee and Royal Coll. of Art; full-time sculptor 1982–; Prof. of Inspiration and Discovery, Univ. of Dundee 1994–; sculpture installation and collage exhibited at galleries and museums world-wide; Hon. Prof., Sculpture Dept, Edin. Coll. of Art 1999; Pat Holmes Memorial Prize 1975, Duncan of Drumfork Travelling Scholarship 1976, SED Minor Travelling Scholarship 1977, SED Major Travelling Scholarship 1978, RCA Drawing Prize 1982, City of Glasgow Lord Provost Prize 1992. *Publications:* David Mach 2002, David Mach – Precious Light 2011. *Leisure interests:* music (drumming), writing, travelling, driving, films, skiing. *Address:* 8 Havelock Walk, Forest Hill, London, SE23 3HG, England (office). *Telephone:* (20) 8699-5659 (office). *E-mail:* davidmach@davidmach.com (office). *Website:* www.davidmach.com (office).

MACHADO VENTURA, José Ramón; Cuban physician and politician; *Member, Council of State;* b. 26 Oct. 1930, San Antonio de las Vueltas, La Villas; ed Universidad de La Habana; served as guerrilla in Sierra Maestra mountains and cared for mems of rebel army during Cuban Revolution against Batista govt; Asst to the Pres. and Chief of Medical Services, City of Havana 1959; Minister of Health 1960–67; Politburo Del. to Matanzas Prov. 1968–71; First Sec. Havana Provincial Cttee, Partido Comunista de Cuba 1971–75, mem. Secr. of Cen. Cttee 1975–2008, mem. Politburo 1975–; Deputy, Asamblea Nacional del Poder Popular (Parl.) for Guantánamo 1976–2008; Vice-Pres. and Secr. Political Bureau 1976–2008, mem. Council of State 2008–, First Vice-Pres. 2008–13. *Address:* Oficina del Consejo de Estado, Havana, Cuba (office).

MACHAR TENY, Riek; South Sudanese politician and fmr resistance fighter; b. 1952; m. 1st Angelina Jany Teny; m. 2nd Emma McCune (died 1993); m. 3rd Becky Hagmann; ed Univ. of Bradford, UK; fmr mem. Sudan People's Liberation Army (SPLA), f. breakaway group SPLA-Nasir 1991–93, later SPLA-United 1993–94, Leader, South Sudan Defence Forces 1997–2002; Asst to Pres. of Repub. of Sudan 1997–2000; Pres. South Sudan Coordinating Council 1997–2000; Vice-Pres. of Southern Sudan (autonomous region) 2005–11; First Vice-Pres. of South Sudan following independence 2011–13 (dismissed); led opposition forces during conflict Dec. 2013–.

MACHARSKI, HE Cardinal Franciszek, DTheol; Polish ecclesiastic; *Archbishop Emeritus of Kraków;* b. 20 May 1927, Kraków; ed Jagiellonian Univ., Kraków, Fribourg Univ., Switzerland; ordained priest, Kraków 1950; engaged in pastoral work 1950–56; taught pastoral theology Pontifical Faculty of Theology, Kraków 1962–68; Rector, Kraków Seminary 1970–78; Archbishop of Kraków 1979–2005, Cardinal Emer. 2005–; High Chancellor, Pontifical Acad. of Theology, Kraków; cr. Cardinal (Cardinal-Priest of San Giovanni a Porta Latina) 1979; mem. Sacred Congregation for the Clergy 1979–, Sacred Congregation for Catholic Educ. 1979–, Sacred Congregation for Bishops 1983–, Sacred Congregation for Insts of Consecrated Life and Socs of Apostolic Life 1989–, Council for Public Affairs 1984–88; mem. Council of Cardinals and Bishops 1988–; mem. Secr. for Non-Believers 1981–86, Congregatation for the Clergy 1999–, Congregation for the Evangelization of Peoples 1999–; Vice-Pres. Episcopate of Poland, Conf. 1979–94; mem. Main Council Episcopate of Poland 1996–, Episcopate Cttee for Gen. Ministry 1989–; Vice-Chair. Scientific Council of Episcopate of Poland 1984–89, Episcopate Cttee for Ministry of Working People 1981; Chair. Episcopate Cttee for Laity 1979–91, Episcopate Cttee for Catholic Science 1981–94; mem. Episcopate Cttee for Ministry of Priesthood 1996–, Perm. Council of Episcopate of Poland 1996–2002; Chair. Second Ass. of Synod of Bishops of Europe 1999; Papal Legate to Int. Marian and Mariological Congress Kevelaer 1987, Nat. Eucharistic Congress, Bratislava 2000; participated in Papal Conclave 2005; Hon. Citizen of many Polish cities and towns; Order of Smile 1998; Dr hc (Fu Jen Catholic Univ., Taipei, Adamson Univ., Manila) 1989, (Acad. of Catholic Theology, Warsaw) 1992, (Pontifical Acad. of Theology, Kraków) 2000, (Jagiellonian Univ., Kraków) 2000. *Publications:* Collections: Sermons at the Calvary Shrine 1994, To Serve with Wisdom 1994, From the See of St Stanislaus 1995; more than 250 articles, sermons, speeches and pastoral letters. *Address:* Kuria Metropolitalna, ul. Franciszkańska 3, 31-004 Kraków, Poland (office). *Telephone:* (12) 6288100 (office); (12) 4294749 (office). *Fax:* (12) 4294405 (office). *E-mail:* kuria@diecezja .krakow.pl (office). *Website:* www.diecezja.krakow.pl (office).

MACHEL, Graça, DBE BA; Mozambican international organization official; *Chancellor, University of Cape Town;* b. 1945, southern Gaza Prov.; m. 1st Samora Machel 1975 (died 1986); two c.; m. 2nd Nelson Mandela 1998; ed Univ. of Lisbon, Portugal; worked underground for Front for Liberation of Mozambique (Frelimo) movt during country's war of independence from Portugal, Deputy Dir Frelimo Secondary School in Tanzania 1973; Minister for Educ. 1975–86; mem. Int. Steering Cttee, World Conf. on Educ. for All 1990; f. Foundation for Community Devt 1990; Chair. UNICEF study 1994, currently UNICEF Goodwill Amb., Pres.

UNESCO Mozambique Nat. Comm.; Chair. of Nat. Org. of Children of Mozambique; Chancellor Univ. of Cape Town 1999–; Founder, New Faces New Voices, Graça Machel Trust; Founding mem. The Elders, African Women's Foresight Network; mem. Africa Progress Panel; Hon. DBE (UK) 2007; hon. degree (Univ. of the Western Cape) 1992, (Univ. of Évora) 2008; Nansen Medal (for outstanding contrib. on behalf of refugee children) 1995, InterAction Humanitarian Award 1997, CARE Award, North-South Prize 1998. *Address:* Graça Machel Trust, 7 Eton Road, Block A, Sandhurst, 2196, South Africa. *E-mail:* info@gracamachel.org. *Website:* gracamacheltrust.org; awes.nfnv.org.

MACHEN, J. Bernard (Bernie), DDS, MS, PhD; American dental surgeon, educational psychologist and university administrator; *President, University of Florida;* b. Greenwood, Miss.; m. Chris Machen; two s. one d.; ed Vanderbilt Univ., St Louis Univ., Univ. of Iowa; Diplomate, American Bd of Pediatric Dentistry; veteran US Army Maj.; Prof. and Assoc. Dean, Univ. of North Carolina School of Dentistry 1983–89; Dean School of Dentistry, Univ. of Michigan 1989–95, Provost and Exec. Vice-Pres. for Academic Affairs, Univ. of Michigan 1995–97; Pres. Univ. of Utah 1997–2003; Pres. Univ. of Florida 2004–; mem. NAS Inst. of Medicine Cttee on Educating Dentists for the Future 1992–95; fmr Chief of Dept of Extension Services at US Army Inst. of Dental Research; Pres. American Asscn of Dental Schools 1987; mem. Bd of Trustees, Salt Lake Olympic Organizing Cttee for the 2002 Winter Olympics; Pres. Exec. Cttee Southeastern Conf. 2010–, Chair. Southeastern Conf. Academic Consortium 2010–; mem. Econ. Devt Transition Team of Gov.-elect Rick Scott 2010. *Address:* Office of the President, 226 Tigert Hall, PO Box 113150, Gainesville, FL 32611, USA (office). *Telephone:* (352) 392-1311 (office). *Fax:* (352) 392-9506 (office). *E-mail:* president@ufl.edu (office). *Website:* president.ufl.edu (office).

MACHETE, Rui, LLB; Portuguese lawyer and politician; *Minister of State and of Foreign Affairs;* b. 1940, Setúbal; ed Univ. of Lisbon; practised as lawyer 1964–; Head of Legal Services, Companhia Portuguesa de Eletricidade 1969–76; fmr adviser to Man. Bd, Energias de Portugal; fmr Prof., Inst. of Social Studies and Higher Inst. of Labour and Enterprise; fmr Visiting Prof., Univ. Católica Portuguesa; Sec. of State for Immigration 1975, Minister of Social Affairs 1976–79, of Justice 1983–85, Deputy Prime Minister and Minister of Nat. Defence 1985, Minister of State and of Foreign Affairs 2013–; Chair. Inst. for Financial Man. of Public Enterprises 1983; Dir Bank of Portugal 1981–89, Luso-American Devt Foundation 1985– (Chair. Exec. Bd 1988–2010); mem. Supreme Council, Portuguese Bar Asscn 2005–06; mem. Nat. Inst. of Dirs 1981–83; mem. Partido Social Democrata (PSD), Sec.-Gen. 1974–75, Vice-Pres. PSD Parl. Group 1979; Hon. DHumLitt (Univ. of Massachusetts, Dartmouth) 1997, Hon. LLD (Univ. Católica Portuguesa) 2007. *Address:* Ministry of Foreign Affairs, Palácio das Necessidades, Largo do Rilvas, 1399-030 Lisbon, Portugal (office). *Telephone:* (21) 3946000 (office). *Fax:* (21) 3946070 (office). *E-mail:* gabinete.ministro@mne.gov.pt (office).

MACHI, Sueo, PhD; Japanese atomic energy scientist; *National Co-ordinator, Forum for Nuclear Cooperation in Asia;* b. 15 Jan. 1934; s. of Yosaku Machi and Kichi Machi; m. 1964; one s. one d.; ed Univs of Shizuoka and Kyoto; employed in Japanese petrochemical industry 1959–63; joined Takasaki Radiation Chem. Research Establishment (TRCRE) of Japan Atomic Energy Research Inst. (JAERI) 1963, Gen. Man. Process Lab. II, TRCRE 1972–78, Gen. Man. Radiation Eng Section, TRCRE 1978–80; Section Head, Industrial Applications and Chem. Section and Co-ordinator of Regional Co-operative Agreement for Asia and Pacific, IAEA; Deputy Dir, Office of Planning, JAERI, Tokyo; Dir Dept of Research, TRCRE 1986, later Dir Dept of Devt, Dir-Gen. TRCRE 1989–91; Deputy Dir-Gen. and Head, Dept of Nuclear Science and Application, IAEA 1991–2000; Exec. Dir Japan Atomic Industrial Forum 2000–03; currently Nat. Co-ordinator, Forum for Nuclear Co-operation in Asia; Commr Atomic Energy Comm. of Japan 2004; Dr hc (Bucharest) 1995; Japan Chemical Soc. Prize 1969, The Iwatani Prize 1990, Minister of Science and Tech. Prize 1990. *Address:* Forum for Nuclear Cooperation in Asia, 5-18-7 Shimbashi, Minato-ku, Tokyo, 105-0004, Japan (office). *Telephone:* (3) 5470-1983 (office). *Fax:* (3) 5470-1991 (office). *E-mail:* fnca@fnca.mext.go.jp (office).

MACHIDA, Akira; Japanese judge; b. 16 Oct. 1936; ed Univ. of Tokyo; legal apprentice 1959; Asst Judge Tokyo Dist Family Court 1961, Sapporo Dist Muroran Br. Family Court and Civil Affairs Bureau, Gen. Secr. of Supreme Court 1961; Judge Sapporo Dist Family Court 1971; Chief Budget Div., Financial Affairs Bureau, Gen. Secr. of Supreme Court 1973, Gen. Affairs Div. 1975; Counsellor Cabinet Legislation Bureau 1977; Judge Tokyo Dist Court, Presiding Judge of Div. 1983; Dir Sec./Public Information Div., Gen. Secr. of Supreme Court 1984, Dir Financial Affairs Bureau 1986; Chief Judge Kofu Dist Court and Kofu Family Court 1991, Chiba Dist Court 1993; Judge Tokyo High Court, Presiding Judge of Div. 1994; Pres. Fukuoka High Court 1998, Tokyo High Court 1999; Justice Supreme Court 2000, Chief Justice 2002–06 (retd). *Address:* c/o Supreme Court of Japan, 4-2 Hayabusa-cho, Chiyoda-ku, Tokyo 102-8651, Japan (office).

MACHIDA, Katsuhiko; Japanese electronics industry executive; *Corporate Advisor, Sharp Corporation;* ed Kyoto Univ.; joined Sharp Corpn 1969, various positions in audio-visual and household appliance depts, with Dept of Int. Business 1992–97, Pres. and Chair. Man. Bd, Sharp Corpn 1998–2007, Chair. and CEO 2007–12, Dir and Corp. Advisor 2012–; Outside Dir, Sekisui House Ltd 2008–, Shionogi & Co. Ltd 2012–. *Address:* Sharp Corpn, 22-22 Nagaike-cho, Abeno-ku, Osaka 545-8522, Japan (office). *Telephone:* (6) 6621-1221 (office). *Fax:* (6) 6627-1759 (office). *E-mail:* info@sharp.co.jp (office). *Website:* www.sharp.co.jp (office); sharp-world.com (office).

MACHIMURA, Nobutaka; Japanese politician; b. 17 Oct. 1944; ed Faculty of Econs, Univ. of Tokyo, Wesleyan Univ., USA; joined Ministry of Int. Trade and Industry (MITI) 1969, seconded to Nat. Land Agency 1974, seconded to Japan External Trade Org., NY Trade Center 1979, Dir of Planning Div., Petroleum Dept, Agency of Natural Resources and Energy, MITI –1982; elected to House of Reps 1983–, Chair. Standing Cttee on Health and Welfare 1996–97; Parl. Vice-Minister, Ministry of Educ., Science, Sports and Culture 1989–90; Dir Cultural Affairs Div., Liberal Democratic Party (LDP) 1990–92, Dir Nat. Defence Div., Policy Research Council 1992, Acting Sec.-Gen. LDP 2001–02, Dir-Gen. Election Bureau 2002–04; Minister of Educ., Science, Sports and Culture 1997–98,

2000–01; State Sec. for Foreign Affairs 1998–2000; Special Adviser to Prime Minister 2000; Dir-Gen. Science and Tech. Agency 2000–01; Minister of Foreign Affairs 2004–05, 2007; Chief Cabinet Sec. and Minister of State for the Abduction Issue 2007–08 (resgnd). *Address:* Liberal-Democratic Party (LDP), 1-11-23, Nagata-cho, Chiyoda-ku, Tokyo 100-8910, Japan (office). *Telephone:* (3) 3581-6211 (office). *E-mail:* koho@ldp.jimin.or.jp (office). *Website:* www.jimin.jp (office).

MACHINEA, José Luis, PhD; Argentine economist; b. 5 Oct. 1946, Buenos Aires; s. of José Martin and Beatriz A. Rey; ed Univ. of Minnesota, USA; fmr Prof. of Macroeconomics, Catholic Univ. of Argentina; fmr Chief of Public Finance Dept and Chief of Research Dept at Argentine Cen. Bank, later Pres. Argentine Cen. Bank; Under-Sec. of Political Economy and Under-Sec. of Planning 1980s; consultant to World Bank and Inter-American Devt Bank 1990s; Dir of Research, Industrial Devt Inst. of the Argentine Industrial Union 1992–97; Pres. consultancy firm 1995–99; Pres. Argentine Foundation for Devt with Equity 1998–99; Minister of Economy 1999–2001; Exec. Sec. ECLAC 2003–08; Prebisch Chair, Univ. of Alcalá 2008–09; currently Prof. of Macroeconomics and Econ. Devt, Univ. Torcuato Di Tella, also Dean, School of Govt 2010–11. *Publications:* La Crisis de la Deuda, El Financiamiento Internacional y la Participacion del Sector Privado 2002, Economic Growth with Equity: Challenges for Latin America (co-author) 2007; numerous articles in books and journals on macroeconomics, monetary and financial issues. *Address:* Universidad Torcuato Di Tella, Miñones 2177, Buenos Aires, Argentina (office).

MACHT, Michael; German engineer and business executive; *Chairman of the Board of Management, Porsche AG;* b. 28 Aug. 1960, Stuttgart; ed Univ. of Stuttgart; worked at Fraunhofer Inst. for Industrial Eng IAO –1990; specialist in engine planning, Porsche AG 1990–91, Head of Labour Org. Dept 1991–92, Personal Asst to CEO 1992–98, Man. Dir Porsche Consulting GmbH 1994–98, Head of Production and Logistics and mem. Bd of Man. 1998–2009, oversaw construction and start of operation of Porsche's Leipzig factory, involved in devt of Cayenne SUV and four-door Panamera models, Chair. Bd of Man. (CEO) Porsche AG 2009–, mem. Bd of Man. Porsche SE in charge of tech. and products. *Address:* Porsche AG, Porscheplatz 1, 70435 Stuttgart, Germany (office). *Telephone:* (711) 911-11000 (office). *Fax:* (711) 911-26375 (office). *E-mail:* info@porsche-se.com (office). *Website:* www.porsche.com (office); www.porsche-se.com (office).

MACHULSKI, Juliusz; Polish film director, screenwriter, producer and actor; b. 10 March 1955, Olsztyn; s. of Jan Machulski and Halina Machulski; m. 1995; two c.; ed State Acad. of Film Television and Theatre, Łódź, California Inst. of Arts, Valencia, USA; CEO Studio Filmowe Zebra 1988–; acted in Personnel (Personel) by Krzysztof Kieslowski, The Index (Indeks) by Janusz Kijowski, and Kill Me, Cop (Zabij mnie, glino) by Jacek Bromski; lectured on film directing at Hunter Coll., New York 1993; producer of more than 30 films; Wyspianski Award 1985, Chair. of the Cttee of Cinematography Award 1990, Ministry of Culture and Art Award 1998. *Films directed include:* Vabank (Dir's Best Debut, Gdynia Film Festival) 1981, Sexmission (Golden Dollar, Gdańsk Film Festival) 1984, Vabank II czyli riposta 1985, King Size 1988, Déjà vu 1989, V.I.P. 1991, Szwadron 1992, Girl Guide 1995, Kiler (Golden Duck 1998) 1997, Kilerów 2-óch 1999, Money Is Not Everything 2001, Superprodukcja 2003, Vinci (Prize for Best Screenplay, Polish Film Festival, Gdynia 2004, Golden Lion 2004) 2004, Solidarnosc, Solidarnosc. . . (segment 'Sushi') 2005, How Much Does the Trojan Horse Weigh? 2008, Kolysanka 2010, Ambassada 2013. *Films produced include:* Kochankowie roku tygrysa 2005, Palimpsest 2006, The World Is Waiting for Us (co-producer) 2006, Saviour Square 2006, Hania 2007, All Will Be Well 2007, Twists of Fate 2007, The Last Action 2009, Projekt dziecko, czyli ojciec potrzebny od zaraz 2010, Uwiklanie 2011, In Darkness 2011, Bilet na ksiezyc (co-producer) 2013. *Television includes:* Goraczka mleka (short) 1977, Bezposrednie polaczenie (film) 1979, Matki, zony i kochanki (mini-series) 1996, Matki, zony i kochanki II (mini-series) 1998; plays: The Jury 1995, Meridian 19 2003. *Publications:* Vabank 1 and 2 (scripts) 1986, V.I.P. (script) 1990, Kiler (script) 1998, Kiler 2 1999, Sexmission 2001. *Leisure interest:* reading. *Address:* Studio Filmowe Zebra, ul. Puławska 61, 02-595 Warsaw, Poland (office). *Telephone:* (22) 8455484 (office).

MACHUNGO, Mário Fernandes da Graça; Mozambican politician; *President, Seguradora Internacional de Moçambique;* b. 1 Dec. 1940, Chicuque-Maxixe, Inhambane Prov.; m. Maria Eugénia Paiva Cruz; two d.; ed Inst. for Higher Learning in Econ. and Financial Sciences (ISCEF), Portugal; became underground mem. Mozambique Liberation Front (FRELIMO) 1962; Pres. Students' Union, ISCEF 1964–65; subsequently expelled from ISCEF; completed studies 1969; returned to Mozambique, worked as economist with Nat. Devt Bank; apptd. Minister for Econ. Co-operation in transitional Govt 1974; Minister for Trade and Industry 1975–76, for Industry and Energy 1976–78, for Agric. 1978–80, for Agric. and Planning 1980–83, for Planning 1983–94, Prime Minister of Mozambique 1986–94; elected to Cen. Cttee and Political Bureau of FRELIMO Party 1977, re-elected 1983, elected to Secr. and fmr Sec. for Econ. Policy 1986; Chair. Banco Internacional de Moçambique 1995; currently Pres. Seguradora Internacional de Moçambique (insurance co.). *Address:* Seguradora Internacional de Moçambique, Av 25 Setembro 1800, Maputo, Mozambique (office). *Telephone:* 21430959 (office). *Fax:* 21430241 (office). *E-mail:* simseg@zebra.uem.mz (office).

McILROY, Rory, MBE; British professional golfer; b. 4 May 1989, Holywood, Co. Down, Northern Ireland; s. of Gerry McIlroy and Rosie McIlroy; ed Sullivan Upper School; introduced to golf by his father who coached him from the age of 18 months; became youngest-ever mem. of Holywood Golf Club aged seven; played in his first professional European Tour event at The Forest of Arden aged 16; second person to top World Amateur Rankings 2007; represented Europe in winning Junior Ryder Cup team 2004; became youngest winner of West of Ireland and Irish Close Championships 2005, retained both Irish amateur titles 2006; won European Amateur Championship 2006; turned professional 2007; won the Silver Medal as leading amateur at British Open 2007; first professional event at Quinn Direct British Masters; finished third in his second professional event, the Alfred Dunhill Links Championship; entered the top 100 in the Official World Golf Rankings after making it to the Volvo Masters at Valderrama 2008; runner-up at UBS Hong Kong Open title 2009; maiden victory came in Dubai Desert Classic 2009; finished in second place in inaugural European Tour Race To Dubai; winner: Quail Hollow Championship 2010, UBS Hong Kong Open 2011, Lake Malaren Shanghai Masters 2011, The Honda Classic 2012, PGA Championship 2012, Deutsche Bank Championship 2012, BMW Championship 2012, Australian Open 2013; won his first major, US Open at Congressional Country Club, Md 2011; results in major championships: tied for tenth at US Open 2009, won US Open 2011, tied for third at PGA Championship 2009, 2010, tied for third at British Open 2010, tied for 15th at US Masters 2011; mem. Seve Trophy team representing GB & Ireland 2009 (winners), World Cup team representing Ireland 2009, Ryder Cup team representing Europe 2010 (winners), 2012 (winners); first became No. 1 in World Rankings 4 March 2012; Amb. for UNICEF Ireland 2011–; RTÉ Sports Person of the Year 2011, Mark H. McCormack Award 2012, Laureus World Breakthrough of the Year 2012. *Leisure interests:* Manchester United Football Club, cars, tennis, movies, music. *Address:* Holywood Golf Club, Nuns Walk, Demesne Road, Holywood, Co. Down, BT18 9LE, Northern Ireland. *Telephone:* (28) 9042-3135. *E-mail:* mail@holywoodgolfclub.co.uk. *Website:* www.holywoodgolfclub.co.uk; www.rorymcilroy.com.

MACINA, Stefano; San Marino politician; b. 23 Jan. 1956; m.; one d.; Sec. Fed. Industry, San Marino Labour Confed. –1980, Adjunct Gen. Sec. 1981–84, Gen. Sec. 1984–91; Sec. Partito Progressista Democratico Sammarinese (PPDS) 1992–96, mem. Grand and Gen. Council 1993, Pres. Group to advise PPDS-IM 1996; Sec. of State for Econ. Planning, Foreign Trade, Social Security, Labour and Co-operation 2000–01; Pres. Comm. on Foreign Policy, Emigration and Immigration, Information, Transport and Telecommunications, Security and Public Order 2002–03; Dir Centro Commerciale 'Azzurro' 2003–06; Sec. of State for Finance, the Budget, Post and Relations with the Azienda Autonoma di Stato Filatelica e Numismatica (AASFN) 2006–08; mem. several orgs and institutional comms, including Interparl. Group and Council of the XII; mem. Secr. Partito dei Socialisti e dei Democratici; Pres. San Marino Baseball Club. *Address:* c/o Secretariat of State for Finance, the Budget, Post and Relations with the Azienda Autonoma di Stato Filatelica e Numismatica (AASFN), Palazzo Begni, Contrada Omerelli, 47890 San Marino.

McINERNEY, Jay; American writer; b. 13 Jan. 1955; m. 1st Linda Rossiter; m. 2nd Merry Raymond; m. 3rd Helen Bransford 1991; m. 4th Anne Hearst; one s. one d.; ed Williams Univ.; fmr wine columnist, House & Garden Magazine; wine columnist, The Wall Street Journal. *Publications include:* Bright Lights, Big City 1984, Ransom 1986, Story of My Life 1988, Brightness Falls 1992, The Last of the Savages 1996, Model Behavior 1998, How It Ended 2000, The Good Life (novel) 2006, A Hedonist in the Cellar: Adventures in Wine 2006, The Last Bachelor 2009, How it Ended: New and Collected Stories 2009, The Juice: Vinous Veritas 2012. *Website:* www.jaymcinerney.com.

MacINNIS, Joseph Beverly, CM, MD; Canadian physician, marine research scientist and author; b. 2 March 1937, Barrie, Ont.; s. of Allistair MacInnis and Beverly Saunders; m. Deborah J. Ferris 1971; one s. three d.; ed Univs of Toronto and Pennsylvania; Pres. Undersea Research Ltd and has held consulting contracts for the USN, Smithsonian Inst., IBM, Canadian Ministry of State for Science and Tech. and Canadian Dept of Environment; est. SUBLIMNOS, Canada's first underwater manned station programme 1969; led 14 scientific expeditions into Arctic 1970–79 and during third expedition, SUB-IGLOO, world's first polar dive station established under ice; co-ordinated diving programme for ICE Station LOREX 1979; led team which discovered remains of English barque Breadalbane, sunk in 1853, 700 miles north of Arctic Circle in 340 feet of water; host, The New Wave (CBC television series) 1975–76, The Newfoundlanders: Voices from the Sea 1978; scientific consultant, Mysteries of the Sea (ABC) 1979; co-ordinator, Shot Point 260 (Texaco Canada film), Breakthrough (Dome Petroleum film) 1979; consultant Titanic Project 1985; first Canadian to dive to the Titanic 1987; Co-leader IMAX-Titanic Expedition 1991; has lectured and shown his films in all parts of world including Israel, Germany, Australia, the Philippines, USSR and Singapore; Pres. Undersea Research Ltd; mem. Canadian Environmental Advisory Council, Canadian Council of Fitness and Health, Pierre Elliott Trudeau Foundation; Fellow, Royal Canadian Geographical Soc.; Hon. FRCP; Queen's Anniversary Medal, The Admiral's Medal; Hon. LLD; Dr hc (Queen's) 1990; Hon. DSc (Lakehead Univ.) 2008, and three other hon. degrees. *Publications:* Underwater Images 1971, Underwater Man 1974, Coastline Canada 1982, Shipwreck Shores 1982, The Land that Devours Ships 1984, Titanic: In a New Light 1992, Saving the Oceans (gen. ed.) 1992, Fitzgerald's Storm: The Wreck of the Edmund Fitzgerald 1997, Surviving Terrorism: How to Protect Your Health, Wealth and Safety 2002, Titanic Dreams: Reflections on the Discovery, Exploration and Salvage of the World's Most Famous Shipwreck 2007, Breathing Underwater 2004, James Cameron's Aliens of the Deep 2004, Deep Leadership: Essential Insights from High-Risk Environments 2012; more than 30 scientific papers and articles in Scientific American, National Geographic Magazine etc. *Leisure interest:* jazz. *Address:* Undersea Research Ltd, 14 Dale Avenue, Toronto, ON M4W 1K4, Canada. *Telephone:* (416) 962-8258. *E-mail:* drjoemacinnis@sympatico .ca. *Website:* www.drjmacinnis.com.

McINTOSH, Toga Gayewea, BSc, MA, PhD; Liberian economist and politician; *Vice-President, ECOWAS;* m.; five c. (one d. deceased); ed Univ. of Ghana, Univ. of Colorado, USA, Univ. of Tennessee, Williams Coll., Williamstown, Mass, Univ. of Ife, Nigeria; Statistician, Bureau of Statistics, Ministry of Planning and Econ. Affairs 1969–74, becoming successively Dir for Manpower Planning, Sr Economist, Asst Minister, Deputy Minister, Minister of Planning and Econ. Affairs 1975–81; Sr Econ. Affairs Officer, UN Econ. Comm. for Africa, Ethiopia 1982–91; Sr Nat. Policy Adviser to Pres. of Liberia 1991–93; Man. Dir and Devt Consultant, Devt Man. Assocs, Gaborone, Botswana 1993–2004; Exec. Dir Governance Reform Comm., Monrovia 2004–05; Minister for Planning and Econ. Affairs 2006–08; Exec. Dir for Africa Constituency Group 1 2008–10; Minister of Foreign Affairs 2010–12; Vice-Pres. Econ. Community of West African States (ECOWAS) 2012–; fmr consultant to several African govts and int. agencies including World Bank Group, UNDP, African Devt Bank, African Union, USAID. *Publications include:* around 20 technical and professional articles on development issues. *Leisure interest:* football. *Address:* ECOWAS Executive Secretariat, 101 Yakubu Gowon Crescent, PMB 401, Asokoro, Abuja, Nigeria (office). *Telephone:* (9) 3147647 (office), (9) 3147646 (office). *E-mail:* info@ecowas.int (office). *Website:* www.ecowas .int (office).

McINTOSH OF HUDNALL, Baroness (Life Peer), cr. 1999, of Hampstead in the London Borough of Camden; **Genista Mary McIntosh,** BA, FRSA; British arts consultant; b. 23 Sept. 1946, London, England; d. of Geoffrey Tandy and Maire Tandy; m. Neil Scott Wishart McIntosh 1971 (divorced 1990); one s. one d.; ed Hemel Hempstead Grammar School, Univ. of York; Casting Dir, RSC 1972–77, Planning Controller 1977–84, Sr Admin. 1986–90, Assoc. Producer 1990; Dir Marmont Man. Ltd 1984–86; Exec. Dir Royal Nat. Theatre 1990–96, 1997–2002; Chief Exec. Royal Opera House Jan.–May 1997; mem. (Labour), House of Lords 1999–; Prin. The Guildhall School of Music and Drama 2002–03; mem. Bd RSC, The Roundhouse Trust, Southbank Sinfonia, Nat. Opera Studio; Patron, Helena Kennedy Bursary Scheme; Hon. Fellow, Goldsmiths Coll. 2003; Hon. DUniv. (York) 1998, (Middx) 2002, (City) 2002. *Leisure interests:* music, gardening, reading. *Address:* House of Lords, Westminster, London, SW1A 0PW, England (office). *E-mail:* mcintoshg@parliament.uk (office). *Website:* www.parliament.uk/biographies/lords/baroness-mcintosh-of-hudnall/2506 (office).

McINTYRE, Sir Donald Conroy, Kt, CBE, OBE; New Zealand singer (bass); b. 22 Oct. 1934, Auckland; s. of George Douglas and Hermyn McIntyre; m. Jill Redington 1961; three d.; ed Mt Albert Grammar School, Auckland, Auckland Teachers' Training Coll. and Guildhall School of Music, London; Prin. Bass, Sadler's Wells Opera 1960–67; with Royal Opera House, Covent Garden 1967–; annual appearances at Bayreuth Festival 1967–81; frequent int. guest appearances; Hon. DMus (Auckland) 1992; Fidelio Medal, AIDO 1989, NZ Award for Outstanding Contribs, Festival of the Arts 1990. *Roles include:* Wotan and Wanderer in Der Ring, Dutchman in Der Fliegende Holländer, Telramund in Lohengrin, Barak in Die Frau ohne Schatten, Pizzaro in Fidelio, Golaud in Pelléas et Mélisande, Kurwenal and King Marke in Tristan and Isolde, Gurnemanz, Klingsor and Amfortas in Parsifal, Heyst in Victory, Jochanaan in Salome, Macbeth, Scarpia in Tosca, the Count in Marriage of Figaro, Nick Shadow in The Rake's Progress, Hans Sachs in Die Meistersinger, Dr. Schöne in Woyzeck, Cardillac in Cardillac by Hindemith, Rocco in Fidelio, The Doctor in Der Freischütz, Prospero in Un Re In Asloto, Sarastro in The Magic Flute, Balstrode in Peter Grimes, Telramund in Lohengrin, Prus in The Makropoulos Case, Rheingold, The Ring (video). *Recordings include:* Pelléas et Mélisande, Oedipus Rex, Il Trovatore. *Leisure interests:* farm, tennis, walking. *Address:* Ingpen & Williams, 7 St George's Court, 131 Putney Bridge Road, London, SW15 2PA, England (office); Fox Hill Farm, Jackass Lane, Keston, Bromley, Kent BR2 6AN, England (home). *Telephone:* (1689) 855368 (home). *Fax:* (1689) 860724 (home).

MACK, Connie, III; American banker and fmr politician; *Senior Policy Advisor, Government Advocacy and Public Policy Practice Group, King and Spalding LLP;* b. (Cornelius McGillicuddy, III), 29 Oct. 1940, Philadelphia; s. of Cornelius M. McGillicuddy and Susan McGillicuddy (née Sheppard); m. Ludie Priscilla 1960; one s. one d.; ed Univ. of Fla; Vice-Pres. Business Devt First Nat. Bank, Ft Myers, Fla 1968–71; Sr Vice-Pres., Dir Sun Bank, Cape Coral, Fla 1971–75; Pres., Dir Fla Nat. Bank, Cape Coral 1972–82; mem. US House of Reps 1983–89, Senator from Fla 1989–2000; Republican Conf. Chair. 105th Congress 1996; Sr Policy Advisor, Shaw Pittman 2001; currently Sr Policy Advisor Govt Advocacy and Public Policy Practice Group, King and Spalding LLP, Washington, DC; Chair. Lee Moffitt Cancer Center and Research Inst., Tampa; mem. Bd of Dirs Darden Restaurants, Exact Sciences Corpn, Genzyme Corpn, Moody's Corpn, Mutual of America Life Insurance Co., American Momentum Bank, Spirit Aerosystems; Trustee Emer. American Cancer Soc. Foundation; mem. Pres's Advisory Panel for Fed. Tax Reform 2005; Republican;; Hon. DJur (Tampa Univ.); Hon. DHumLitt (St Thomas Univ.); Hon. Dr of Public Service (Miami Univ.); American Cancer Soc. Courage Award 1992, Nat. Coalition for Cancer Research Lifetime Achievement Award 1999, Susan G. Komen Breast Cancer Foundation Betty Ford Award. *Address:* King and Spalding LLP, 1700 Pennsylvania Avenue, NW, Washington, DC 20006, USA (office). *Telephone:* (202) 661-7952 (office). *Fax:* (202) 626-3737 (office). *E-mail:* cmack@kslaw.com (office). *Website:* www.kslaw.com (office).

MACK, James F., BA; American diplomatist and international organization executive; *Executive Secretary, Inter-American Drug Abuse Control Commission (Comisión Interamericana para el Control del Abuso de Drogas—CICAD);* b. 1941, Norwalk, Conn.; m. Sheila Marvin; four c.; ed Cornell Univ., Ithaca, NY; raised in Rye, NY; served as Peace Corps volunteer in Honduras; joined US Foreign Service 1966, first diplomatic postings were as political officer in Saigon and Nha Trang, S Viet Nam, and as Political Advisor to US Commdr of I Corps in Danang, served as S Viet Nam analyst in Bureau of Intelligence and Research, Dept of State 1969, as Political/Labor Officer, San José, Costa Rica, as Labor Officer, São Paulo, Brazil, as Prin. Officer, Ponta Delgada, Azores, Portugal, subsequent positions included Guatemala/Belize Desk Officer, Chief of Office of Labor/Man. Relations, Dept of State, Political Counselor at Embassy in San Salvador, Deputy Chief of Mission, Embassy in Asuncion, Dir Office of Andean Affairs, Dept of State 1990, Deputy Chief of Mission, Embassy in Quito, where also served as Chargé d'affaires for two years, Deputy Chief of Mission, Embassy in Lima 1994–97, additionally, while posted to US Embassies in Ecuador, Paraguay and Peru, coordinated US antinarcotics assistance to those countries, Amb. to Guyana 1997–2000, now retd career mem. Sr Foreign Service, US Dept of State, served as Prin. Deputy Asst Sec. in Bureau of Int. Narcotics and Law Enforcement Affairs; Co-ordinator Inter-American Observatory on Drugs, Inter-American Drug Abuse Control Comm. (Comisión Interamericana para el Control del Abuso de Drogas—CICAD), OAS 2002, Exec. Sec. CICAD 2004–; numerous State Dept awards for superior service. *Address:* Inter-American Drug Abuse Control Commission (CICAD), 1889 F Street, NW, Washington, DC 20006, USA (office). *Telephone:* (202) 458-3178 (office). *Fax:* (202) 458-3658 (office). *E-mail:* oidcicad@oas.org (office). *Website:* www.cicad.oas.org (office).

MACK, John J., BA; American financial services industry executive; *Senior Advisor, Morgan Stanley;* b. 17 Nov. 1944, Mooresville, NC; m. Christy King; two s. one d.; ed Duke Univ.; joined Morgan Stanley 1972, positions in bond dept 1972–76, Vice-Pres. 1976–77, Prin. 1977–79, Man. Dir 1979–85, Head Worldwide Taxable Fixed Income Div. 1985–92, apptd Dir 1987, Chair. Operating Cttee 1992–93, Pres. Morgan Stanley 1993–97; Pres., COO and Dir Morgan Stanley Dean Witter & Co. (later Morgan Stanley) 1997–2001, Chair. and CEO Morgan Stanley 2005–10, Chair. 2010–11, Sr Advisor 2012–; CEO Credit Suisse First Boston 2001–04, Co-CEO Credit Suisse Group 2003–04; mem. Bd of Dirs IMG, Catalyst Inc.; fmr Dir CICC (first investment bank in China), India Business School; mem. Int. Advisory Panel, Monetary Authority of Singapore, Chair's

Advisory Cttee Nat. Asscn of Securities Dealers (NASD); Vice-Chair. NYC 2012 (New York City bid for Olympic Games); mem. Business Council, Business Roundtable, Advisory Bd China Investment Corpn, Int. Business Leaders Advisory Council for the Mayor of Beijing, Int. Advisory Panel of The Monetary Authority of Singapore, Exec. Cttee of the Partnership for New York City, Financial Services Forum, Bd Bloomberg Family Foundation, Int. Business Council of World Econ. Forum, NYC Financial Services Advisory Cttee, Shanghai Int. Financial Advisory Council; Dir Business Cttee for the Arts; Chair. Bd of Trustees NY Presbyterian Hosp., Columbia and Cornell Univ. Hosps; mem. Bd of Trustees Duke Univ.; Trustee, Doris Duke Charitable Foundation. *Address:* Morgan Stanley, 1585 Broadway, New York, NY 10036, USA (office). *Telephone:* (212) 761-4000 (home). *Fax:* (212) 762-0575 (office). *E-mail:* mediainquiries@morganstanley.com (office). *Website:* www.morganstanley.com (office).

MACK, Timothy (Tim), BA; American athlete; b. 15 Sept. 1972, Cleveland, OH; ed Univ. of Tenn.; career as personal trainer; coached by Jim Bemiller; winner Gold Medal for pole vault, Golden League, Oslo 2002, Grand Prix, Rio de Janeiro 2001, Palo Alto 2002, Osaka 2002, 2004, Olympic Games, Athens (with performance of 19' 6.3") 2004; winner Bronze Medal for pole vault, Golden League, Zurich 2002; conducts pole vaulting clinics. *Address:* 2222 Bright Oak Way, Knoxville, TN 37931, USA (office). *Website:* www.timmack.com (office).

MACK SMITH, Denis, CBE, MA, FBA; British author and fmr professor of history; b. 3 March 1920, London; s. of Wilfrid Mack Smith and Altiora Gauntlett; m. Catharine Stevenson; two d.; ed St Paul's Cathedral Choir School, Haileybury Coll., Peterhouse, Cambridge; Fellow, Tutor, Peterhouse, Cambridge 1947, now Hon. Fellow; Sr Research Fellow, All Souls Coll., Oxford 1962, Emer. Fellow 1987–; Extraordinary Fellow, Wolfson Coll., Oxford 1987–2000, Hon. Fellow 2000–; Chair. Asscn for the Study of Modern Italy 1988–; Grande Ufficiale, Italian Order of Merit, Hon. Citizen of Santa Margherita Ligure. *Publications:* Cavour and Garibaldi in 1860 1954, Garibaldi 1957, Medieval and Modern Sicily 1968, The Making of Italy 1796–1866 1968, Italy: A Modern History 1969, Victor Emanuel, Cavour and the Risorgimento 1971, Mussolini's Roman Empire 1976, Cento Anni di Vita Italiana attraverso il Corriere della Sera 1978, Mussolini 1981, Cavour 1985, Italy and its Monarchy 1989, Mazzini 1993, Modern Italy 1997, La Storia Manipolata 1998. *Leisure interests:* music, travel. *Address:* White Lodge, Osler Road, Headington, Oxford, OX3 9BJ, England. *Telephone:* (1865) 762878.

MACKAY, Charles Dorsey, CBE, MA, MBA; British business executive; *Chairman, Historic Royal Palaces;* b. 14 April 1940, Congleton, Cheshire, England; s. of the late Brig. Kenneth Mackay CBE, DSO and Evelyn Mackay (née Ingram); m. Annmarie Joder-Pfeiffer 1964; two s. (one deceased) one d.; ed Cheltenham Coll., Queens' Coll. Cambridge, Institut Européen d'Admin des Affaires (INSEAD), Fontainebleau; with BP Co. 1957–69, McKinsey & Co. 1969–76, Pakhoed Holding NV, Rotterdam 1976–81 (Exec. Chair. Paktrans Div.); Dir Chloride Group PLC 1981–86, Chair. Overseas Div. 1981–85, Power Electronics Div. 1985–86; Dir Inchcape PLC 1986–96, Chair. and Chief Exec. Inchcape Pacific Ltd 1986–91, Chief Exec. 1991–96, Deputy Chair. 1995–96; mem. Bd of Dirs (non-exec.) Hongkong and Shanghai Banking Corpn Ltd 1986–92, HSBC Holdings 1992–98, Midland Bank 1992–93, British Airways 1993–96, Gucci Group NV 1997–2001, Johnson Matthey PLC (Sr Ind. Dir) 1999–2008, Eurotunnel Group 1997–2004 (Deputy Chair. 1999–2001, Chair. 2001–04); Deputy Chair. Thistle Hotels PLC 1996–2003; Chair. DSL Group Ltd 1996–97; Chair. TDG PLC 2000–08; Chair. Historic Royal Palaces 2006–; Chair. Production Services Network Ltd 2009–11; mem. Bd INSEAD 2000–11, mem. Advisory Council 2011–; mem. of Business Bd, House of Habib 2007–; Trustee, Development Trust (for the mentally handicapped) 1993–. *Leisure interests:* restoring old buildings, travel, fly fishing, tennis, skiing, classical music, opera. *Address:* Historic Royal Palaces, Kensington Palace, Kensington Gardens, London, W8 4PX, England (office). *Telephone:* (20) 3166-6130 (office). *Fax:* (20) 3166-6132 (office). *E-mail:* charles.mackay@hrp.org.uk (office). *Website:* www.hrp.org.uk (office).

MACKAY, David, BBA; Australian business executive; *President and CEO, Kellogg Company;* b. 16 Aug. 1955, Hamilton, New Zealand; m. Michelle Mackay; two c.; ed Charles Sturt Univ., NSW; joined Kellogg Australia as Group Product Man. 1985–87, Category Dir for ready-to-eat cereals, Kellogg HQ, USA 1987–91, Marketing and Sales Dir, Australia 1991–92, Man. Dir Sara Lee Bakery, Australia 1992–98, Man. Dir Australia 1998, UK and Ireland 1998–2000, Sr Vice-Pres. Kellogg Co. and Pres. Kellogg USA 2000, Exec. Vice-Pres. Kellogg Co. 2000–03, Pres. and COO 2003–06, Pres. and CEO 2006–; mem. Bd of Dirs Fortune Brands, Inc., Kalamazoo Inst. of Arts. *Address:* Kellogg Company, 1 Kellogg Square, Battle Creek, MI 49016-3599, USA (office). *Telephone:* (269) 961-2000 (office). *Fax:* (269) 961-6598 (office). *Website:* www.kelloggcompany.com (office).

MacKAY, Sir Donald Iain, Kt, MA, FRSE, FRSGS; British economist; b. 27 Feb. 1937, Kobe, Japan; s. of William MacKay and Rhona MacKay; m. Diana Marjory Raffan 1961; one s. two d.; ed Dollar Acad., Aberdeen Univ.; with English Electric Co. 1959–62; Lecturer, Aberdeen Univ. 1962–65, Prof. 1971–76; Lecturer, Glasgow Univ. 1965–68, Sr Lecturer 1968–71; Adviser to Sec. of State for Scotland 1971–1997; Chair. Pieda PLC 1974–97; Lecturer, BAAS 1974; Lister Prof., Heriot-Watt Univ. 1976–82, Hon. Prof. 1990–; Chair. Scottish Enterprise 1993–97, DTZ Pieda Consulting 1997, Scottish Science Trust 1997–99, Edinburgh Business School 1997, Scottish Mortgage Trust 2003–09; Dir Edinburgh Income and Value Trust, Grampian Holdings 1987–99 (fmr Chair.); mem. Scottish Econ. Council, Advisory Bd Reform Scotland; Dr hc (Stirling) 1994; Hon. DLitt (Aberdeen) 1994. *Publications:* Geographical Mobility and the Brain Drain 1969, Local Labour Markets and Wage Structures 1970, Labour Markets under Different Employment Conditions 1971, The Political Economy of North Sea Oil 1975, The Economics of Self-Government 1977; numerous articles in econ. and political journals. *Leisure interests:* bridge, golf, tennis. *Address:* c/o Reform Scotland, 7-9 North St David Street, Edinburgh, EH2 1AW, Scotland.

MacKAY, Donald James, BL; New Zealand diplomatist and lawyer; b. 1948; m.; two c.; ed Victoria Univ. of Wellington; solicitor and law clerk to Judges of Court of Appeal and High Court 1971–75; with Ministry of Foreign Affairs 1975–2001, positions include Head of Special Arbitration Unit, Dir of Disarmament and Int. Security Div., Amb. to Fiji and High Commr to Naura and Tuvalu 1991–95; Dir of Legal Div. 1995–96, Deputy Sec. Ministry of Foreign Affairs and Trade 1997–2001;

Amb. and Perm. Rep. to UN, New York 2001–05, to UN Office, Geneva and Amb. for Disarmament 2006–09.

MACKAY, Sir Francis H., Kt; British business executive; *Owner, Graysons Restaurants Ltd;* b. 24 Oct. 1944, London; m. Christine Mackay; one s., two d.; ed Bonaventure Grammar School; qualified as accountant, Appleby and Wood 1967; began career in financial positions with LCS Ltd, SGT PLC; fmr Finance Dir Global Ltd; Finance Dir Compass Group PLC 1986–91, CEO 1991–99, Chair. 1999–2006; Chair. (non-exec.) Kingfisher PLC 2001–06; Chair. Carlton Partners LLP 2006–09; Chair. ISS (Denmark) 2006–08; Founder and Owner Graysons Restaurants Ltd 2007–; Hon. DUniv (Oxford Brookes) 2002. *Leisure interests:* flying, opera, golf, family. *Address:* Graysons Restaurants Ltd, St Martin's House, 16 St Martin's Le Grand, London, EC1A 4EN, England (office). *Telephone:* (20) 7397-8702 (office). *E-mail:* jay.shaghaghi@graysonshospitality.com (office). *Website:* www.graysonsrestaurants.com (office).

MacKAY, The Hon. Peter Gordon, PC, QC; Canadian politician; *Minister of Justice and Attorney-General of Canada;* b. 27 Sept. 1965, New Glasgow, Nova Scotia; m. Nazanin Afshin-Jam; one s.; ed Acadia and Dalhousie Univs; called to the Bar, Nova Scotia 1991; Crown Attorney for Cen. Region, Nova Scotia 1993; mem. Parl. for Pictou-Antigonish-Guysborough 1997–2004, for Central Nova 2004–; Leader Progressive Conservative Party of Canada 2003–04, Deputy Leader Conservative Party of Canada 2004; fmr Critic for the Prime Minister, for the Solicitor Gen., for Public Security, for the Leader of the Govt in the House of Commons, for Justice, for Public Safety and Emergency Preparedness; fmr mem. Interim Cttee on Nat. Security and Intelligence; Minister of Foreign Affairs 2006–07, of Nat. Defence 2007–13, Minister of Justice and Attorney-Gen. of Canada 2013–. *Leisure interests:* rugby, baseball, football, hockey. *Address:* Department of Justice, East Memorial Building, 284 Wellington Street, Ottawa, ON K1A 0H8, Canada (office). *Telephone:* (613) 957-4222 (office). *Fax:* (613) 954-0811 (office). *E-mail:* webadmin@justice.gc.ca (office). *Website:* www.canada.justice.gc.ca (office).

MACKAY OF CLASHFERN, Baron (Life Peer), cr. 1979, of Eddrachillis in the District of Sutherland; *James Peter Hymers Mackay,* Kt, KT, PC, QC, LLB, MA, FRSE; British advocate and judge (retd); b. 2 July 1927, Scotland; s. of James Mackay and Janet Hymers; m. Elizabeth Gunn Hymers 1958; one s. two d.; ed George Heriot's School, Edin., Univ. of Edin., Trinity Coll., Cambridge; Lecturer in Math., Univ. of St Andrews 1948–50; Major Scholar, Trinity Coll., Cambridge 1947, Sr Scholar 1951; admitted to Faculty of Advocates 1955; QC 1965; Vice-Dean Faculty of Advocates 1973–76, Dean 1976–79, Lord Advocate 1979–84; Sheriff Prin., Renfrew and Argyll 1972–74; Commr Northern Lighthouses 1972–84; Dir Stenhouse Holdings Ltd 1976–78; mem. (Conservative) House of Lords 1979–; Senator of Coll. of Justice in Scotland 1984–85; Lord of Appeal in Ordinary 1985–87; Lord Chancellor 1987–97; Chancellor Heriot-Watt Univ. 1991–2005; Ed.-in-Chief Halsbury's Laws of England 1998–; Part-time mem. Scottish Law Comm. 1976–79; mem. Insurance Brokers' Registration Council 1978–79; Pres. Soc. of Conservative Lawyers; Vice-Pres. Family Mediators' Asscn, Carers Trust, High-landers' Museum Appeal Fund; Founding mem. World Prevention Alliance (eliminating disease in low-resource countries); mem. Int. Ethics Cttee, Int. Prevention Research Inst. (iPRI); Commissary, Univ. of Cambridge; Non-Voting Elder Brother of Trinity House; Lord Clerk Register (unremunerated post in Scottish system of govt); Fellow, Inst. of Taxation, American Coll. of Trial Lawyers, Int. Acad. of Trial Lawyers; Hon. FICE; Hon. FRCPE; Hon. FRCSE; Hon. FRCOG; Hon. Fellow Trinity Coll., Cambridge, Girton Coll., Cambridge; Hon. LLD (Edin., Dundee, Strathclyde, Aberdeen, St Andrews, Birmingham, Newcastle, Bath, Leicester, De Montfort, Glasgow, Cambridge, Robert Gordon Nat. Law School of India); Hon. DCL (Newcastle), (Oxford) 1998. *Publication:* Armour on Valuation for Rating (Sr Ed.) 1961, 1971. *Leisure interests:* walking, travel. *Address:* House of Lords, Westminster, London, SW1A 0PW, England (office). *E-mail:* mackayjp@parliament.uk (office). *Website:* www.parliament.uk/biographies/lords/lord-mackay-of-clashfern/1883 (office).

McKEE, J(ohn) Angus; Canadian business executive; b. 31 Aug. 1935, Toronto, Ont.; s. of John W. McKee and Margaret E. Phippen; m. Susan E. Harley 1970; one s. one d.; ed Trinity Coll. School, Port Hope, Ont. and Univ. of Toronto; joined Patiño Mining Corpn 1962, Asst to Pres. 1963, Vice-Pres. (Corp. Devt) 1966; Man. Dir Consolidated Tin Smelters Ltd 1968–71; Owner J. A. McKee and Assocs Ltd 1971–83; Pres. and CEO Canadian Occidental Petroleum Ltd 1983–93; Chair., Pres. and CEO Gulfstream Resources Canada 1993–2001; Dir, Stone & Webster Canada Ltd, Stone & Webster Inc. (USA) (both acquired by The Shaw Group 2000, then by Technip 2012), Teradyne Canada Ltd, CVI Ltd, Hardy Oil and Gas PLC 2000–01, Gulfstream Qatar Ltd 2001; mem. Bd of Govs, Trinity Coll. School, Port Hope. *Leisure interests:* skiing, shooting. *Address:* Stone & Webster, Inc., 100 Technology Center Drive, Stoughton, MA 02072-4705, USA. *Telephone:* (617) 589-5111. *Fax:* (617) 259-2156.

MacKELLAR, Hon. Michael John Randal, B.SCI.AGR., MA; Australian agricultural scientist, politician and business executive; b. 27 Oct. 1938, Sydney; s. of Geoffrey Neil and Colleen Randal MacKellar; m. Robin Morey Smith 1969; two s. one d.; ed Sydney Church of England Grammar School, Sydney Univ., Balliol Coll., Oxford; New South Wales Dept of Agric. 1961–69; mem. for Warringah, NSW, House of Reps. 1969–94; Parl. Sec. to Leader of Opposition 1973–74; Shadow Minister for Immigration 1974–75; Minister for Immigration and Ethnic Affairs 1975–79, Minister Assisting the Treas. 1978–79, Minister for Health 1979–82, Minister Assisting the Prime Minister 1979–80, Minister for Home Affairs and Environment Feb.–March 1981; Shadow Minister for Foreign Affairs 1983–84, for Science and Special Minister of State 1984–85; Deputy Opposition Leader of the House 1985; Opposition Whip 1989; mem. numerous House of Reps Cttees 1970–90; Chair. House of Reps Standing Cttee on Environment and Conservation 1982–83; mem. first Australian Parl. del. to People's Repub. of China 1973, Leader del. to UN Habitat Conf. 1976; mem. NSW Advisory Cttee for Australian Broadcasting Comm. 1973–75, Advisory Council of CSIRO 1984, Council of Australian Nat. Univ. 1970–76; CEO Plastics and Chemicals Industries Asscn 1994–97; COO Baker Medical Research Inst. 1997–; Bd mem. Sydney Paralympic Games Organizing Cttee 1997–2000; Chair. Australia/N.Z. Food Authority 1998–, Franchising Policy Council of Australia 1998–, FAO Centre for Excellence, Monash Univ. 1999–; Liberal Party. *Leisure interests:* tennis, cricket, golf, reading,

photography. *Address:* 19/158–160 Wattletree Road, Malvern, Vic. 3144, Australia.

McKELLEN, Sir Ian Murray, Kt, CBE, CH, BA; British actor; b. 25 May 1939, Burnley, Lancs.; s. of Denis Murray McKellen and Margery (Sutcliffe) McKellen; ed Bolton School, St Catharine's Coll., Cambridge; council mem. British Actors' Equity 1970–71; Cameron Mackintosh Prof. of Contemporary Theatre, Oxford Univ. 1991; Hon. DLitt (Nottingham) 1989, (Oxford) 1991; Clarence Derwent Award 1964, Variety and Plays and Players awards 1966, Actor of the Year (Plays and Players) 1976, Soc. of West End Theatres Award for Best Actor in Revival 1977, for Best Comedy Performance 1978, for Best Actor in a New Play 1979, Tony Award 1981, Drama Desk 1981, Outer Critics Circle Award 1981, Royal TV Soc. Performer of the Year 1983, Laurence Olivier Award 1984, 1991, Evening Standard Best Actor Award 1984, 1989, Screen Actor's Guild Award for best supporting Actor 2000, British Ind. Film Awards, Variety UK Personality Award 2003, Lifetime Achievement Award, San Sebastián Film Festival 2009. *Films include:* Alfred the Great 1969, The Promise 1969, A Touch of Love 1969, Priest of Love 1981, The Keep 1982, Plenty, Zina 1985, Scandal 1988, The Ballad of Little Jo 1992, I'll Do Anything 1992, Last Action Hero 1993, Six Degrees of Separation 1993, The Shadow 1994, Jack and Sarah 1994, Restoration 1994, Richard III 1995, Bent 1996, Swept from the Sea 1996, Apt Pupil 1997, Gods and Monsters 1998, X-Men 1999, Lord of the Rings: The Fellowship of the Ring 2001, Lord of the Rings: The Two Towers 2002, X-Men 2 2003, Emile 2003, Lord of the Rings: The Return of the King 2003, Asylum 2005, Neverwas 2005, Doogal (voice) 2006, The Da Vinci Code 2006, Flushed Away (voice) 2006, For the Love of God 2007, Stardust (voice) 2007, The Golden Compass (voice) 2007, The Hobbit: An Unexpected Journey 2012. *Stage appearances include:* first stage appearance as Roper (A Man for All Seasons), Belgrade Theatre, Coventry 1961; numerous other parts include title-roles in Henry V, Luther, Ipswich 1962–63; Aufidius (Coriolanus), Arthur Seaton (Saturday Night and Sunday Morning), title-role in Sir Thomas More, Nottingham Playhouse 1963–64; London début as Godfrey (A Scent of Flowers), Duke of York's Theatre 1964; Claudio (Much Ado About Nothing), Capt. de Foenix (Trelawny of the Wells), Nat. Theatre Co. 1965; Alvin (A Lily in Little India), Hampstead and St Martin's 1965–66; Andrew Cobham (Their Very Own and Golden City), Royal Court 1966; title-part in O'Flaherty, VC and Bonaparte (The Man of Destiny), Mermaid 1966; Leonidik (The Promise), Oxford Playhouse, Fortune and Henry Miller (Broadway début) 1966–67; Tom (The White Liars), Harold Gorringe (Black Comedy), Lyric 1968; Richard II (Edin. Festival 1969), Edward II, Hamlet, Prospect Theatre Co. 1968–71, British tour, Mermaid and Piccadilly Theatres; Darkly (Billy's Last Stand), Theatre Upstairs 1970; Capt. Plume (The Recruiting Officer), Corporal Hill (Chips With Everything), Cambridge Theatre Co. 1970; Svetlovidov (Swan Song), Crucible, Sheffield 1971; founder-mem. Actors' Co., Edin. Festival 1972 and touring as Giovanni ('Tis Pity She's A Whore), Prince Yoremitsu (The Three Arrows), title-role in Michael, the Wood Demon, Footman (The Way of The World), then Knots, Shaw Theatre, Edgar (King Lear), Brooklyn Acad. and Giovanni, Wimbledon 1973–74; début with RSC as Dr Faustus (Edin. Festival) 1974; title-role in The Marquis of Keith, Philip the Bastard (King John), Aldwych 1974–75; Colin (Ashes), Young Vic. 1975; Aubrey Bagot (Too True to Be Good), also at Globe, Romeo, Macbeth, Bernick (Pillars of the Community), Face (The Alchemist) Stratford season 1976; Langevin (Days of the Commune) 1976–78; organized RSC British tour of Twelfth Night (Toby Belch) and Three Sisters (Andrei); Max (Bent), Royal Court and Criterion 1979, Amadeus (New York) 1980, Short List (Hampstead Theatre Club), Cowardice (Ambassadors) 1983; int. tour of one-man show Acting Shakespeare (LA and Ritz Theatre, New York) 1984, (London) 1987; Assoc. Dir Nat. Theatre of Great Britain (also actor) 1984–86; Venice Preserv'd (Pierre), Coriolanus; Wild Honey (Platonov); McKellen/Pether-bridge Nat. Theatre Group: Duchess of Malfi (Bosola), Real Inspector Hound (Hound), The Critic (Mr Puff), The Cherry Orchard (Lopakhin); Wild Honey (Va Theatre, New York), USA Shakespeare tour 1987; Henceforward (Vaudeville Theatre) 1988–89; Othello (Iago) RSC 1989; Royal Nat. Theatre: Bent (Max), King Lear (Kent), Richard III 1990–92 (World Tour then US Tour), Napoli Milionaria 1991, Uncle Vanya 1992, An Enemy of the People 1997, Peter Pan 1997; Present Laughter, The Tempest (W Yorks. Playhouse) 1998–99, Dance of Death (Broad-hurst Theatre, NY) 2001, Aladdin (Mayne's Theatre, London) 2003, (Sydney Festival) 2004, The Seagull (RSC) 2007, King Lear (RSC) 2007, Waiting for Godot 2009–10. *TV appearances include:* David Copperfield 1965, Ross 1969, Richard II, Edward II and Hamlet 1970, Hedda Gabler 1974, Macbeth, Every Good Boy Deserves Favour, Dying Day 1979, Acting Shakespeare 1981, Walter, The Scarlet Pimpernel 1982, Walter and June 1983, Countdown to War 1989, Othello 1990, Tales of the City 1993, Cold Comfort Farm 1995, Rasputin 1996, Coronation Street 2005. *Publication:* William Shakespeare's Richard III (jtly) 1996. *Address:* c/o ICM, 76 Oxford Street, London, W1N 0AX, England. *Telephone:* (20) 7636-6565. *Fax:* (20) 7323-0101. *Website:* www.mckellen.com.

McKENNA, Andrew J., Sr, BA, LLB; American business executive; *Non-Executive Chairman, McDonald's Corporation;* b. 1930; ed Univ. of Notre Dame, DePaul Univ. School of Law; Chair. Chicago White Sox professional baseball team 1975–81, Chicago Cubs 1981–84; currently Chair. Schwarz Supply Source; mem. Bd of Dirs McDonald's Corpn 1991–, Chair. (non-exec.) 2004–; mem. Bd of Dirs Ryan Group 1970–82, Dean Foods 1982–2000, Tribune Co. 1982–2002, Aon Corpn 1982–, Bank One 1991–99, Chicago Bears Football Club Inc., Click Commerce Inc., Skyline Corpn; Founding Chair. Chicago Metropolis 2020 1999; fmr Chair. Econ. Club of Chicago, The Commercial Club of Chicago; Dir The American Ireland Fund, Children's Memorial Hosp. of Chicago, Lyric Opera, United Way of Metropolitan Chicago; Vice-Chair. Bd of Trustees, Univ. of Notre Dame 1986–92, Chair. 1992–2000, Chair. Emer. 2000–; Trustee and Chair. Emer., Museum of Science and Industry. *Address:* McDonald's Corporation, 2915 Jorie Blvd, Oak Brook, IL 60523, USA (office). *Telephone:* (630) 623-3000 (office). *Fax:* (630) 623-7056 (office). *Website:* www.mcdonalds.com (office).

McKENNA, Frank Joseph, LLB, PC, QC; Canadian diplomatist, politician, lawyer and business executive; *Deputy Chairman, Toronto-Dominion Bank;* b. 19 Jan. 1948, Apohaqui, Kings Co., NB; s. of Joseph McKenna and Olive Moody; m. Julie Friel 1972; two s. one d.; ed St Francis Xavier Univ., Queen's Univ. and Univ. of NB; Special Asst to Pres., Privy Council 1971; Research Asst Constitutional Law Unit, PMO 1973; Pnr, Martin, Lordon, McKenna, Martin & Bowes; Counsel, McInnes, Cooper 1998–; mem. NB Bar Asscn, Canadian Bar Asscn; mem. Legis.

Ass. 1982–97; Leader, NB Liberal Party 1985–97; Premier, Prov. of NB 1987–97; Amb. to USA 2005–06; Deputy Chair. Toronto-Dominion Bank 2006–; Chair. Bd of Dirs CanWest Global Communications Corpn –2005, mem. Bd of Dirs Gen. Motors of Canada Ltd –2005, Bank of Montreal –2005; Hon. LLD (Univ. of NB) 1988, (Mount Allison) 1991, (St Francis Xavier) 1994, (St Thomas) 1996, (Ryerson Polytechnic) 1999, (Royal Mil. Coll.) 2000; Vanier Award 1988, Econ. Developer of the Year, Econ. Developers' Asscn of Canada 1993, Distinction Award, Canadian Advanced Tech. Asscn 1996. *Leisure interests:* reading, sports and current affairs. *Address:* Toronto-Dominion Bank, Toronto-Dominion Centre, King Street West and Bay Street, Toronto, ON M5K 1A2, Canada. *Telephone:* (416) 982-8222. *Fax:* (416) 982-5671. *Website:* www.td.com.

McKENNA, Virginia, OBE; British actress and conservationist; *Founder and Trustee, Born Free Foundation;* b. 7 June 1931, London, England; d. of Terence McKenna and Anne Marie Dennis; m. Bill Travers (died 1994); three s. one d.; ed Herons Ghyll, Horsham, Sussex, Herschel, Cape Town, S Africa, Cen. School of Speech and Drama, London; f. Zoo Check Charitable Trust (now the Born Free Foundation) 1984; film debut in The Second Mrs Tanqueray 1951; speaker at numerous events; patron to numerous orgs; Belgian Prix Femina Award 1957, BAFTA SWET (Soc. of West End Theatres) Variety Club. *Stage appearances include:* The King and I 1979 (Soc. of West End Producers Award for Best Actress in a musical), Hamlet (RSC) 1985, Winnie 1988, A Little Night Music, The Devils (RSC), The Beggar's Opera (RSC), A Winter's Tale, As You Like It, The River Line, Penny for a Song, I Capture the Castle, A Personal Affair, The Bad Samaritan. *Films include:* Father's Doing Fine, The Cruel Sea 1953, Simba 1955, The Ship that Died of Shame, A Town Like Alice (BAFTA Best Actress Award) 1956, The Smallest Show on Earth 1957, The Barretts of Wimpole Street 1957, Carve Her Name With Pride (Prix Fémina Award, Belgium) 1957, Passionate Summer 1958, The Wreck of the Mary Deare 1959, Two Living, One Dead 1961, Born Free (Best Actress Award, Variety Club) 1966, Ring of Bright Water 1969, An Elephant Called Slowly 1969, Waterloo 1970, Swallows and Amazons 1974, The Disappearance 1977, Holocaust 2000 1977, Staggered 1994, Sliding Doors 1998, What Do You See? 2005, Home 2008. *Radio:* The Devils, The Flame Trees of Thika, A Town Like Alice, The Tempest. *Television includes:* Romeo and Juliet 1955 (BBC TV Best Actress Award, Guild of TV Producers and Dirs Award), Play of the Month: A Passage to India 1965, Play of the Month: Girls in Uniform 1967, The Lion at World's End (documentary) 1971, Play of the Month: The Deep Blue Sea 1974, The Gathering Storm 1974, Shades of Greene (episode Cheap in August) 1975, Peter Pan 1976, Waters of the Moon 1983, Puccini 1984, Lovejoy 1991, The Camomile Lawn (mini-series) 1992, Ruth Rendell Mysteries (episode The Speaker of Mandarin: Part One) 1992, September (mini-series) 1996, The Scold's Bridle 1998, Kavanagh QC (episode Time of Need) 1999, The Whistleblower 2001, Marple: A Murder is Announced 2005. *Publications:* On Playing with Lions (with Bill Travers), Some Of My Friends Have Tails, Into the Blue 1992, Journey to Freedom 1997; Co-Ed. and Contrib.: Beyond the Bars, Headlines from the Jungle (verse) 1990, Back to the Blue 1997, The Life in My Years 2009. *Leisure interests:* classical music, poetry, walking in the countryside, gardening. *Address:* c/o Aude Powell, Brunskill Management, The Courtyard, Edinhall, Penrith, Cumbria, CA11 8ST, England (office); Born Free Foundation, 3 Grove House, Foundry Lane, Horsham, West Sussex, RH13 5PL, England (office). *Telephone:* (1403) 240170 (office). *E-mail:* virginia@bornfree.org.uk (office). *Website:* www.bornfree.org.uk (office).

MACKENZIE, Andrew, BSc, PhD; Australian business executive; *CEO and Executive Director, BHP Billiton Ltd;* experienced in oil and gas, petrochemicals and minerals since 1980s; held several sr roles at BP, including Group Vice-Pres. for Tech. and Eng and Group Vice-Pres. for Chemicals; Chief Exec. of Diamonds and Minerals, Rio Tinto –2008; joined BHP Billiton as Chief Exec. of Non-Ferrous 2008, Dir, BHP Billiton Ltd and BHP Billiton Plc and CEO BHP Billiton 2013–; Dir (non-exec.) Centrica plc 2005–13. *Address:* BHP Billiton Ltd, BHP Billiton Centre, 180 Lonsdale Street, Melbourne, Vic. 3000, Australia (office). *Telephone:* 1300-55-4757 (office). *Fax:* (3) 9609-3015 (office). *E-mail:* webmaster@bhpbilliton.com (office). *Website:* www.bhpbilliton.com (office).

McKENZIE, Dan Peter, CH, MA, PhD, FRS; British geologist and academic; *Emeritus Royal Society Professor, Department of Earth Sciences, University of Cambridge;* b. 21 Feb. 1942, Cheltenham, Glos., England; s. of W. S. McKenzie and N. M. McKenzie (née Fairbrother); m. Indira M. Misra 1971; one s.; ed Westminster School and King's Coll., Cambridge; Fellow, King's Coll. 1965–73, 1977–, Sr Asst in Research, Dept of Earth Sciences, Univ. of Cambridge 1969–73, Asst Dir of Research 1973–79, Reader in Tectonics 1979–85, Prof. of Earth Sciences 1985–96, Royal Soc. Research Prof. 1996–2006, BP Prof. 2010–12, Emer. Royal Soc. Prof. 2012–; Foreign Assoc. NAS; Hon. DSc (Bristol) 2000; Balzan Prize 1981, Wollaston Medal, Geological Soc. of London 1983, Rutherford Memorial Lecturer 1988, Japan Prize (co-recipient) 1990, William Bowie Medal 2001, Crafoord Prize, Royal Swedish Acad. of Sciences 2002, Copley Medal, Royal Soc. 2011. *Publications:* numerous papers in professional journals. *Leisure interest:* gardening. *Address:* Bullard Laboratories, Madingley Rise, Madingley Road, Cambridge, CB3 0EZ, England (office). *Telephone:* (1223) 337177 (office). *Website:* www.esc.cam.ac.uk/people/academic-staff/dan-mckenzie (office).

MACKENZIE, Gen. Sir Jeremy John George, Kt, GCB, OBE, DL; British army officer; *Senior Military Adviser, Fabbrica d'Armi Pietro Beretta SpA;* b. 11 Feb. 1941, Nairobi, Kenya; s. of the late Lt-Col John William Elliot Mackenzie and of Valerie Mackenzie (née Dawes); m. Elizabeth Lyon (née Wertenbaker) 1969; one s. one d.; ed Duke of York School, Nairobi, Kenya, Staff Coll., Camberley; commissioned Queen's Own Highlanders 1961; Canadian Forces Staff Coll. 1974; Brigade Maj. 24 Airportable Brigade 1975–76; CO 1 Queen's Own Highlanders, NI and Hong Kong 1979–82; Instructor Staff Coll. 1982–83; Col Army Staff Duties 2 1983–84; Commdr 12th Armoured Brigade 1984–86; Service Fellowship King's Coll., Univ. of London 1987; Deputy Commdt 1987–89; Commdt 1989, Staff Coll. GOC 4th Armoured Div. BAOR 1989–91; Col Commdt WRAC 1990–92, AG Corps 1992–98, APTC 1997–; Col Highlanders 1994–2001; Commdr 1st (British) Corps 1991–92, NATO's ACE Rapid Reaction Corps (ARRC) 1992–94, Deputy Supreme Allied Commdr, Europe 1994–98, now consultant to NATO aspirant cos; ADC (Gen.) 1997–99; Gov. Royal Hosp. Chelsea 1999–2006; Sr Mil. Adviser, Fabbrica d'Armi Pietro Beretta SpA 2006–; Ensign Brig. Queen's Bodyguard of Scotland

(RCA); mem. Bd of Dirs Sirva plc 2003–08, Selex Communications 2003–; mem. Advisory Bd Blue Hackle Security 2006–; Commdr US Legion of Merit 1997 (second award 1999), Hungarian Presidential Order of Merit (1st Class) 1998, Czech Defence Minister's Order of Merit (1st Class) 1998, Bulgarian Order of the Madara Horseman (1st Class) 1999, Slovenian Gold Medal of the Armed Forces 2003; Officer, Order St John. *Publication:* The British Army and the Operational Level of War 1989. *Leisure interests:* shooting, fishing, painting.

MacKENZIE, Kelvin; British media executive; b. 22 Oct. 1946; m. Jacqueline M. Holland 1969; two s. one d.; joined The Sun newspaper, London, as sub-editor 1972, subsequently Night Ed.; apptd Man. Ed. New York Post 1978; rejoined The Sun as Night Ed. 1980; Night Ed. Daily Express Feb. 1981; rejoined The Sun, Ed. 1981–94; Man. Dir BSkyB Jan.–Oct. 1994 (resgnd); Dir Mirror Group PLC 1994–98, Deputy Chief Exec. and Group Man. Dir 1997–98; Chair. and CEO Talk Radio UK 1998–2000; Chair. and CEO The Wireless Group –2005; Exec. Chair. Highbury House Communications PLC Sept.–Dec. 2005 (resgnd); columnist, The Sun 2006–11; columnist, Daily Mail 2011–. *Address:* c/o Daily Mail, Northcliffe House, 2 Derry Street, London, W8 5TT, England (office). *Telephone:* (20) 7938-6000 (office). *Website:* www.dailymail.co.uk (office).

McKENZIE, Kevin; American ballet dancer, choreographer and director; *Artistic Director, American Ballet Theater;* b. 29 April 1954, Burlington, Vt; s. of Raymond James McKenzie and Ruth Davison; ed Acad. of Washington School of Ballet; soloist with Nat. Ballet of Washington 1972–74; Prin. Dancer, Joffrey Ballet 1974–78; Prin. Dancer, American Ballet Theater (ABT) 1979–91, Artistic Dir 1992–; Perm. Guest Artist, Washington Ballet 1990–91, Artistic Assoc. 1991–92; Assoc. Dir New Amsterdam Ballet 1984–; Hon. PhD (St Michael's Coll.); Silver Medal, Sixth Int. Ballet Competition, Varna 1972. *Principle roles include:* leading roles in all the major full-length classics, including Solor in La Bayadère, Don Jose in Carmen, the Prince in Cinderella, Franz in Coppélia, Gentleman With Her in Dim Lustre, Basil and Espada in Don Quixote (Kitri's Wedding), Albrecht in Giselle, a leading role in The Garden of Villandry, Her Lover in Jardin aux Lilas, leading role in The Leaves Are Fading, the Friend in Pillar of Fire, leading role in Raymonda (Grand Pas Hongrois), featured role in Requiem, Champion Roper in Rodeo, Romeo and Mercutio in Romeo and Juliet, Prince Desire in The Sleeping Beauty, Prince Siegfried in Swan Lake, James in La Sylphide and leading roles in Other Dances, Paquita, Les Sylphides, Sylvia Pas de Deux and Theme and Variations; cr. role of Amnon in Martine van Hamel's Amnon V'Tamar and a leading role in Clark Tippet's S.P.E.B.S.Q.S.A. *Directed:* Groupo Zamboria (New Amsterdam Ballet—NAB) 1984, Liszt Études (now called Transcendental Études) (NAB) 1991, Lucy and the Count (The Washington Ballet) 1992, The Nutcracker 1993; (with Susan Jones): Don Quixote (ABT) 1995, Swan Lake (ABT) 2000. *Address:* American Ballet Theater, 890 Broadway, New York, NY 10003, USA (office). *Telephone:* (212) 477-3030 (office). *Fax:* (212) 254-5938 (office). *Website:* www.abt.org (office).

McKENZIE SMITH, Ian, CBE, PRSA, PPRSW, RGI, FMA, FRSA, FRSE, FSA Scot, FSS, HRA, HRHA, HRUA, HRWA; British artist; b. 3 Aug. 1935, Montrose, Angus; s. of James McKenzie Smith and Mary Benzie; m. Mary Rodge Fotheringham 1963; two s. one d.; ed Robert Gordon's Coll., Aberdeen, Gray's School of Art, Aberdeen, Hospitalfield Coll. of Art, Arbroath, Aberdeen Coll. of Educ.; teacher of art, Fife 1960–63; educ. officer, Council of Industrial Design, Scottish Cttee 1963–68; Dir Aberdeen Art Gallery and Museums 1968–89; City Arts and Recreation Officer, Aberdeen 1989–96, Sec. Aberdeen Highland Games 1989–96; Deputy Pres. and Treas. RSA 1990–91, Sec. 1991–98, Pres. 1998–2007; Trustee Nat. Galleries of Scotland 1999–; mem. Scottish Arts Council 1970–77 (Chair. Art Cttee 1975–77), Scottish Museums Council 1980–87 (Chair. Industrial Cttee 1985–87); mem. Advisory Council on Export of Works of Art 1991–, Museums and Galleries Comm. 1997–2000; mem. Bd Friends of RSA 1972–, RSA Enterprises 1972–; trustee of numerous funds; Hon. RA 1999; Hon. LLD (Aberdeen) 1991; Hon. DArt (The Robert Gordon Univ., Aberdeen) 2000; RSA Guthrie Award 1971, RSA Gillies Award 1980, May Marshall Brown Award, Royal Scottish Soc. of Painters in Watercolours 1980.

McKERNAN, James, BA, PhD; American mathematician and academic; *Professor of Mathematics, Massachusetts Institute of Technology;* ed Trinity Coll., Cambridge, UK, Harvard Univ.; apptd instructor at Univ. of Utah 1991, later at Univ. of Texas –1995; Visiting Asst Prof., Oklahoma State Univ. 1994–95; faculty appointments at Univ. of California, Santa Barbara 1995–2007; Prof. of Math., MIT 2007–; Clay Research Award, Clay Math. Inst. 2007. *Publications:* numerous papers in professional journals on algebraic geometry. *Address:* Room 2-274, Department of Mathematics, Massachusetts Institute of Technology, 77 Massachusetts Avenue, Cambridge, MA 02139-4307, USA (office). *Telephone:* (617) 253-4391 (office). *Fax:* (617) 253-4358 (office). *E-mail:* mckernan@math.mit.edu (office). *Website:* www-math.mit.edu (office).

MACKEY, James Patrick, BA, LPh, BD, STL, DD, PhD; Irish philosopher, theologian and academic; *Thomas Chalmers Professor Emeritus of Theology, University of Edinburgh;* b. 9 Feb. 1934, Waterford; s. of Peter Mackey and Esther Morrissey; m. Noelle Quinlan 1973; one s. one d.; ed Mount St Joseph Coll., Nat. Univ. of Ireland, Pontifical Univ., Maynooth and Queen's Univ., Belfast, doctoral Research at Univ. of Oxford, UK and Univ. of Strasbourg, France; ordained priest 1958; Lecturer in Hebrew and Old Testament, Pontifical Univ., Maynooth 1959; Lecturer in Philosophy, Queen's Univ., Belfast 1960–66; Lecturer in Philosophy and Theology, St John's Coll., Waterford 1966–69; Assoc. Prof. of Philosophical and Systematic Theology, Univ. of San Francisco, USA 1969–73, Prof. 1973–79; Visiting Prof., Univ. of California, Berkeley, USA 1974–75; Thomas Chalmers Prof. of Theology, Univ. of Edin., UK 1979–99, Dean of Faculty of Divinity 1984–88, Dir Grad. School and Assoc. Dean 1995–98, Prof. Emer. 1999–, Fellow, Faculty of Divinity 1999–2002; Visiting Prof., Univ. of Dublin Trinity Coll. 2000–10; curricular consultant, Univ. Coll., Cork 2000–04; Visiting Prof., Dartmouth Coll., NH, USA 1989, Univ. of San Francisco 1990; mem. Ind. Assessment Panel and jt author of Report on NI Policing Bd 2005; Dir Derry City Int. Conf. on the Cultures of Europe 1992; mem. Consultative Group on the Past of N Ireland 2007–09; Assoc. Ed. Herder Correspondence 1966–69, Concilium 1965–73, Horizons 1973–79, Monograph Series: Biblical Foundations of Theology 1985–91; Founding Ed. Studies in World Christianity: the Edinburgh Review of Theology and Religion 1995–2001; British Acad. Research Scholarship, Univs of Oxford and

Strasbourg 1964–65, Lifetime Achievement Award, The Gerard Manley Hopkins Int. Soc. 2012. *Television:* scripted and presented two eight-part series on world religions for Channel 4, The Hall of Mirrors 1984, The Gods of War 1986, two six-part series for the BBC, Perspectives (on Northern Ireland) 1986, Perspectives II 1987, numerous other contribs to TV and radio. *Publications:* The Modern Theology of Tradition 1962, Life and Grace 1966 (American edn, The Grace of God, the Response of Man 1967, Spanish trans., Vida y Gracia 1969), Tradition and Change in the Church 1968 (French trans., Tradition et Evolution de la Foi 1969, Polish trans., Tradycja i Zmiana w Kosciele 1974), Morals, Law and Authority (ed.) 1969 (Italian trans., Il Magistero Morale; Compiti e Limite 1973), The Church: Its Credibility Today 1970, The Problems of Religious Faith 1972, Jesus, The Man and the Myth 1979 (German trans., Jesus der Mensch und der Mythos 1981, 1991), The Christian Experience of God as Trinity 1983, Religious Imagination (ed.) 1986, New Testament Theology in Dialogue (with J. D. G. Dunn) 1987, Modern Theology 1987, An Introduction to Celtic Christianity (ed.) 1989, Power and Christian Ethics 1994, The Cultures of Europe (ed.) 1994, The Critique of Theological Reason 2000, Religion and Politics in Ireland at the Turn of the Millennium (ed.) 2003, Christianity and Creation 2006, The Scientist and the Theologian 2007, Jesus of Nazareth 2008. *Leisure interest:* sailing. *Address:* 15 Glenville Park, Dunmore Road, Waterford, Ireland. *Telephone:* (51) 844624. *E-mail:* jpmackey_ie@yahoo.co.uk.

MACKI, Ahmad bin Abd an-Nabi; Omani government official; fmr Minister of Civil Service; Minister of Nat. Economy, Supervisor of Finance Ministry and Deputy Chair. Financial Affairs and Energy Resources Council –2011.

MACKIE, Robert (Bob) Gordon; American costume and fashion designer; b. 24 March 1940, Monterey Park, Calif.; s. of Charles Robert Smith and Mildred Agnes Mackie (née Smith); m. Marianne Wolford 1960 (divorced); one s.; ed Chouinard Art Inst.; mem. staff Edith Head 1962–63; designed costumes for film Divorce, American Style 1966; Co-Designer for films Divorce American Style 1967, Lady Sings the Blues 1972, Funny Lady 1975, The Villain 1979, Smokey and the Bandit II 1980, Encore! 1980, …All the Marbles 1981, Pennies from Heaven 1981, Fake-Out 1982, Butterfly 1982, Max Dugan Returns 1983, Staying Alive 1983, Brenda Starr 1989; designer for numerous TV shows including: Brigadoon 1966, Alice Through the Looking Glass 1966, Carousel 1967, Kismet 1967, Fred Astaire Show 1968, Diana Ross and The Supremes 1969, The Carol Burnett Show 1967–77, Sonny and Cher Comedy Hour 1971, Cher 1975, Donny and Marie 1976, Mitzi… Roarin' in the 20's 1976, The 48th Annual Academy Awards 1976, Diahann Carroll Summer Show 1976, Sonny and Cher Show 1976–77, An Evening with Diana Ross 1977, Mitzi… Zings Into Spring 1978, Mitzi… What's Hot, What's Not 1978, The Goldie Hawn Special 1978, The Grass Is Always Greener Over the Septic Tank 1978, The Star Wars Holiday Special 1978, The Captain & Tennille Songbook 1979, Goldie and Liza Together 1980, Ann-Margret: Hollywood Movie Girls 1980, Celebration 1981, The 54th Annual Academy Awards 1982, Fresno (mini-series) 1986, Plaza Suite 1987, Cher… at the Mirage 1990, The Carol Burnett Show (series) 1991, The Carol Burnett Show: A Reunion 1993, Gypsy 1993, Men, Movies & Carol 1994, Golden Anniversary 1995, Mrs. Santa Claus 1996, Blue Suede Shoes: Ballet Rocks! 1997, Bernadette Peters in Concert 1998, Cher: Live in Concert from Las Vegas 1999, Putting It Together 2000, Cher: The Farewell Tour 2003; Co-Designer theatrical productions On The Town 1971, Lorelei 1972, The Best Little Whorehouse Goes Public 1994; launched first ready-to-wear collection in 1982, line grew rapidly to include fragrances, eyewear, furs and various fashion accessories, added a line of knitwear, eveningwear, suits, a new fragrance, men's ties, handbags, scarves, watches, jewellery and stationery 1990s, launched made-to-order couture collection 1999; often called "the sultan of sequins, the rajah of rhinestones"; Emmy Award 1967 (co-recipient), 1969, 1976, 1983, Costume Designers' Guild Award 1968. *Publication:* Dressing for Glamour 1969. *Address:* Bob Mackie Studio, 1412 Broadway, New York, NY 10018, USA (office). *Telephone:* (212) 302-8200.

McKIERNAN, Gen. (retd) David D., MPA; American army officer (retd); ed The Coll. of William & Mary, Shippensburg Univ., Pa; received ROTC comm., entered US Army 1972, gained experience in the Balkans as a staff officer 1990s, joined Allied Command Europe Rapid Reaction Corps (ARRC) serving as Deputy Chief of Staff G-2/G-3 forward deployed in both Sarajevo, Bosnia-Herzegovina and Rheindahlen (Mönchengladbach), Germany 1996–98, Deputy Chief of Staff, Operations, HQ, US Army, Europe and Seventh Army during period of simultaneous operations in Bosnia, Albania and Kosovo 1998–99, assigned as G-3 (Operations), HQ, Dept of the Army 2001–02, assumed command of Third US Army and US Army Forces Cen. Command (ARCENT) 2002, became Coalition Forces Land Component Commdr for US Cen. Command in preparation for Operation Iraqi Freedom, led all coalition and US conventional ground forces that attacked Iraq March 2003, assigned as Deputy Commdg Gen./Chief of Staff for US Army Forces Command (largest major command in US Army), assumed command of 7th Army/US Army Europe, commands have included: 1st Bn, 35th Armor (Iron Knights), 1st Armored Div. 1988–90, 1st Brigade (Iron Horse), 1st Cavalry Div. 1993–95, 1st Cavalry Div. 1999–2001, 3rd US Army/Combined Forces Land Component Command 2002–04, Commdr CFLCC 2002–04, 7th US Army/US Army Europe 2005–, Commdg Gen. US Army, Europe 2004–08, Commdr Int. Security Assistance Force (ISAF), NATO 2008–09; awards and decorations include Ranger Tab, Parachutist Badge, Army Achievement Medal (with Oak Leaf Cluster), Army Commendation Medal (with 3 Oak Leaf Clusters), Meritorious Service Medal (with 3 Oak Leaf Clusters), Defense Meritorious Service Medal, Bronze Star, Legion of Merit (with 2 Oak Leaf Clusters), Defense Superior Service Medal, Army Distinguished Service Medal (with Oak Leaf Cluster), Defense Distinguished Service Medal,; hon. doctorate in Public Service (The Coll. of William & Mary). *Address:* c/o Media Operations Center, NATO Headquarters, Blvd Leopold III, 1110 Brussels, Belgium.

McKILLOP, Sir Thomas (Tom) Fulton Wilson, Kt, BSc, PhD; British business executive and chemist; b. 19 March 1943, Dreghorn, nr Irvine, Ayrshire; s. of Hugh McKillop and Annie McKillop (née Wilson); m. Elizabeth Kettle 1966; one s. two d.; ed Irvine Royal Acad., Univ. of Glasgow, Centre de Mécanique Ondulatoire Appliquée, Paris; research scientist, ICI Corp. Lab. 1969–75; Head of Natural Products Research, ICI Pharmaceuticals Ltd 1975–78, Dir of Research, France 1978–80, Chem. Man. 1980–84, Gen. Man. of Research 1984–85, Gen. Man. Devt

1985–89, Tech. Dir 1989–94; CEO AstraZeneca (fmrly Zeneca) 1994–2005, Dir 1996–2005; Deputy Chair. Royal Bank of Scotland Group 2005, Chair. 2006–08 (retd); Dir (non-exec.) Amersham Int. PLC 1992–97, Nycomed Amersham PLC 1997–2000, Lloyds TSB PLC 1999–, BP 2004–09; Dir Almirall 2007–; Pres. European Fed. of Pharmaceutical Industries and Asscns (EFPIA) 2002–05, Science Council 2007–; Pro-Chancellor Univ. of Leicester 1998–2008; mem. Soc. for Drug Research, ACS, Royal Inst.; Trustee, Darwin Trust of Edin. 1995–, Council for Industry & Higher Educ.; Hon. Fellow, Univ. of Lancashire 2004, ICHEME 2006; Hon. LLD (Manchester) 1999, (Dundee) 2003; Hon. DSc (Glasgow) 2000, (Leicester) 2000, (Huddersfield) 2000, (Nottingham) 2001, (St Andrews) 2004, (Salford) 2004, (Manchester) 2005, (Lancaster) 2007; Dr hc (Middlesex) 2000, (Paisley) 2006; Hon. DLit (Heriot-Watt) 2006. *Leisure interests:* carpentry, music, reading, walking. *Address:* c/o Royal Bank of Scotland Group, Gogarburn, Edinburgh, EH2 1HQ, Scotland.

MACKIN, Martin, MA; Irish politician; b. 23 Dec. 1963, Drogheda, Co. Louth; s. of Thomas Mackin and Josephine Mackin; ed Univ. Coll. Dublin, Coll. of Commerce, Dublin, Nat. Univ. of Ireland; press officer, Fianna Fáil 1992–95, Dir Fianna Fáil European Office 1995–98, Gen. Sec. Fianna Fáil 1998–2003. *Leisure interests:* music, current affairs, reading. *Address:* c/o Áras De Valera, 65–66 Lower Mount Street, Dublin 2, Ireland (office). *Telephone:* (1) 676-1551. *Fax:* (1) 678-5960. *E-mail:* martin@fiannafail.ie (office). *Website:* www.fiannafail.ie (office).

McKINLEY, Brunson, BA, MA; American diplomatist and international organization official; *Co-Chairman, Association for International Mobility;* b. 8 Feb. 1943, Fla; s. of Kenneth William McKinley and Lois Rebecca McKinley; m. Nancy Padlon (deceased); one s. one d.; ed Univ. of Chicago, Harvard Univ.; US Army 1965–70, with service in Viet Nam; joined diplomatic service, overseas postings include Italy, China, Vietnam, UK, Germany; Amb. to Haiti 1986–89, specialized in refugee and migration issues 1990–94, helped defuse Haitian-Cuban boat crisis 1994, developed trans-Atlantic dialogue on migration, successfully directed US participation in comprehensive action plan for Indo-Chinese refugees; US Bosnia Humanitarian Coordinator 1995–98; prin. compiler of refugee annex of Dayton Accords; Dir-Gen. Int. Org. for Migration, Geneva 1998–2008; Co-Chair. Asscn for Int. Mobility 2008–; several foreign decorations; Bronze Star, Air Medal, Award for Valor. *Publications:* numerous studies on migration subjects. *Address:* AIM, World Trade Center II, 29 route de Pré-Bois, PO Box 885, 1215 Geneva 15 (office); 15 Grand Rue, 1260 Nyon, Switzerland (home). *E-mail:* brunsonmick@gmail.com (office). *Website:* www.aim-international.org (office).

McKINNELL, Henry A. (Hank), Jr, BA, MBA, PhD; American pharmaceutical company executive; ed Univ. of British Columbia, Canada, Stanford Univ. Grad. School of Business; joined Pfizer Inc., Tokyo 1971, served in various exec. positions including Pres. Pfizer Asia, Hong Kong, Pres. Medical Technology Group, Chief Financial Officer, Pres. Pharmaceutical Group 1997, Pres. and COO Pfizer Inc. 1999–2000, Pres. 1999–2001, CEO 2001–06, Chair. 2001–07; Dir Chamber of Commerce, Business Council, Royal Shakespeare Co. America, Japan Soc.; mem. Bd of Dirs Moody's Corpn, ExxonMobil Corpn, John Wiley & Sons Inc., Business Roundtable (now Chair.), Business-Higher Educ. Forum (B-HEF); Chair. Advisory Council, Stanford Univ. Grad. School of Business; mem. Presidential Advisory Council on HIV/AIDS (PACHA); Fellow, New York City Public Library, New York City Police Foundation, Channel Thirteen/WNET, J. F. Kennedy Center for the Performing Arts; Trustee Memorial-Sloan Kettering Cancer Center, New York City Public Library, New York City Police Foundation; Dr hc (Polytechnic Univ.); Sitara-i-Eisaar Award (Pakistan), Global Leadership Award, UN Asscn of the USA, Woodrow Wilson Inst. Corp. Service Award, Cleveland E. Dodge Medal for Distinguished Service to Educ., Columbia Univ. Teachers Coll., Stanford Univ. Grad. School of Business/Excellence in Leadership Award. *Address:* Pfizer Inc., 235 East 42nd Street, New York, NY 10017-5755, USA (office).

McKINNON, Rt Hon. Donald (Don) Charles, PC, ONZ, GCVO; New Zealand politician and international organization official; *Director and CEO, Auckland War Memorial Museum;* b. 27 Feb. 1939; s. of Maj.-Gen. Walter McKinnon and Anna McKinnon (née Plimmer); m. 1st Patricia Maude Moore 1964 (divorced 1995); three s. one d.; m. 2nd Clare de Lore 1995; one s.; fmr estate agent and farm man. consultant; Nat. Party MP for Albany 1978–; fmr Jr and Sr Govt Whip, Opposition Spokesperson for Defence and Health; Sr Opposition Whip 1984–87; Deputy Prime Minister 1990–96; Leader of the House 1993–96; Minister of Foreign Affairs and Trade, of Pacific Island Affairs, 1990–99, for Disarmament and Arms Control 1996–99; Sec.-Gen. of the Commonwealth 2000–08; currently Dir and CEO Auckland War Memorial Museum; Hon. DComm (Lincoln, NZ), Dr hc (four Univs of Manchester) 2002, (Heriot-Watt Univ., Edinburgh), Hon. DJur (Univ. of Swaziland), Hon. DLitt (Univ. of Buea). *Leisure interests:* rugby, cricket, jogging, tennis, reading, riding. *Address:* 49 Dell Rd, Waiau Pa, RD4, Pukekohe, 2679, New Zealand (home). *Telephone:* (9) 232-0064. *E-mail:* deltamike41@hotmail.com.

McKINNON, Sir James, Kt, CA, FCMA; British public servant; b. 1929; ed Camphill School; Co. Sec. Macfarlane Lang & Co. Ltd, Glasgow 1955–65; Business Consultant, McLintock, Moores & Murray, Glasgow 1965–67; Finance Dir Imperial Group PLC, London 1967–86; Dir-Gen. Office of Gas Supply 1986–93; Chair. Ionica 1993–98; Chair. (non-exec.) Cowie Group 1994–, Trafficmaster plc –2004, Discovery Trust PLC 2004–05; Deputy Chair. (non-exec.) United Business Media plc –2000; mem. Bd Dirs Martin Currie Capital Return Trust plc (renamed F&C Private Equity Trust plc) 2005–; Pres. Inst. of Chartered Accountants of Scotland 1985–86; Dr hc (Paisley) 1995. *Publications:* articles in professional publs. *Leisure interest:* skiing. *Address:* F&C Asset Management plc, 80 George Street, Edinburgh, EH2 3BU, Scotland (office). *Telephone:* (131) 465-1000 (office). *E-mail:* enquiries@fandc.com (office). *Website:* www.fandc.com (office).

MacKINNON, Roderick, BA, MD; American physician, biophysicist and academic; *John D. Rockefeller Jr Professor, Laboratory of Molecular Neurobiology and Biophysics, The Rockefeller University;* b. 19 Feb. 1956, Burlington, Mass; ed Univ. of Massachusetts, Brandeis Univ., Tufts Univ. School of Medicine, Harvard Medical School; medical residency at Beth Israel Hosp., Harvard Medical School; postdoctoral work at Brandeis Univ. 1986–89, Asst Prof. of Physiology, Harvard Medical School 1989–92, Assoc. Prof. of Neurobiology 1992–95, Prof. of Neurobiology 1995–96; Prof. and Head of Lab. of Molecular Neurobiology and Biophysics, The Rockefeller Univ. 1996–, now John D. Rockefeller Jr Prof.; Investigator,

Howard Hughes Medical Inst. 1997–; Visiting Researcher, Brookhaven Nat. Lab.; mem. NAS 2000; Hon. DSc (Tufts) 2002; Newcomb Cleveland Prize 1997, W. Alden Spencer Award 1998, Albert Lasker Basic Medical Research Award 1999, Lewis S. Rosenstiel Award for Distinguished Work in Basic Medical Science 2000, Gairdner Foundation Int. Award 2001, Perl-UNC Neuroscience Prize 2001, Louisa Gross Horwitz Prize, Columbia Univ. 2003, Nobel Prize in Chem. (with Peter Agre) 2003. *Publications:* numerous papers in scientific journals on ion channels. *Address:* Laboratory of Molecular Neurobiology and Biophysics, The Rockefeller University, 1230 York Avenue, New York, NY 10021, USA (office). *Telephone:* (212) 327-7288 (office). *Fax:* (212) 327-7289 (office). *E-mail:* roderick.mackinnon@rockefeller.edu (office); mackinnon_admin@rockefeller.edu (office). *Website:* www.rockefeller.edu (office).

McKINSTRY, Nancy, BA, MBA; American publishing executive; *Chairman of the Executive Board and CEO, Wolters Kluwer NV;* b. 4 Jan. 1959, Conn.; ed Univ. of Rhode Island, Kingston and Columbia Univ., New York; held man. positions with Booz Allen Hamilton (int. man. consulting firm) 1980s; held a succession of man. positions with Wolters Kluwer cos in North America 1991–99, Vice-Pres. Product Man. and Sr Officer for CCH Inc. and Asst Vice-Pres. Electronic Products Div. for CCH –1996, Pres. and CEO CCH Legal Information Services 1996, CEO Wolters Kluwer's operations in North America –2001, mem. Exec. Bd Wolters Kluwer NV 2001–, Chair. Exec. Bd Wolters Kluwer NV, responsible for Wolters Kluwer's Divs, Business Devt, Strategy and Tech. 2001–03, Chair. Exec. Bd and CEO 2003–; CEO SCP Communications (medical information co.) 1999; mem. Bd of Dirs Ericsson 2004–, MortgageIT, American Chamber of Commerce in the Netherlands 2004–, TiasNimbas Business School; mem. Advisory Council of Amsterdam Inst. of Finance, Dutch Advisory Council of Institut Européen d'Admin des Affaires (INSEAD), Advisory Bd Univ. of Rhode Island, Bd of Overseers of Columbia Business School, University Club of New York City; Hon. LLD (Univ. of Rhode Island) 2005; ranked by Fortune magazine as one of the 50 Most Powerful Women in Business outside the US (10th) 2007, (13th) 2008–11, (15th) 2012, ranked by Forbes magazine amongst The World's 100 Most Powerful Women (53rd) 2007, (82nd) 2008, (43rd) 2009, (77th) 2010, ranked by the Financial Times amongst Top 25 Businesswomen in Europe (eighth) 2006, (14th) 2007, and 16th in Top 50 Women in World Business 2009; included in Wall Street Journal's 50 Women to Watch 2007. *Address:* Zuidpoolsingel 2, PO Box 1030, 2400 BA Alphen aan den Rijn, The Netherlands (office). *Telephone:* (172) 641400 (office). *Fax:* (172) 474889 (office). *E-mail:* info@wolterskluwer.com (office). *Website:* www.wolterskluwer.com (office).

MACKINTOSH, Sir Cameron Anthony, Kt; British theatre producer; b. 17 Oct. 1946, Enfield; s. of the late Ian Mackintosh and of Diana Mackintosh; ed Prior Park Coll. Bath; stage hand then Asst Stage Man. Theatre Royal, Drury Lane; worked with Emile Littler 1966, with Robin Alexander 1967; producer 1969–; Chair. Cameron Mackintosh 1981–; Dir Delfont Mackintosh 1991–; owns seven theatres in London's West End (Prince of Wales, Prince Edward, Novello, Wyndham's, Noël Coward, Queen's and Gielgud); Pres. Royal Scottish Acad. of Music and Drama 2004–; Hon. Fellow, St Catherine's Coll. Oxford 1990; Observer Award for Outstanding Achievement, Laurence Olivier Award 1991, Richard Rodgers Award 2002, Oscar Hammerstein Award 2002. *Productions:* Little Women 1967, Anything Goes 1969, Trelawny 1972, The Card 1973, Winnie the Pooh 1974, Owl and the Pussycat Went to See 1975, Godspell 1975, Side by Side by Sondheim 1976, Oliver! 1977, Diary of a Madam 1977, After Shave 1977, Gingerbread Man 1978, Out on a Limb 1978, My Fair Lady 1979, Oklahoma! 1980, Tomfoolery 1980, Jeeves Takes Charge 1981, Cats 1981, Song and Dance 1982, Blondel 1983, Little Shop of Horrors 1983, Abbacadabra 1983, The Boyfriend 1984, Les Misérables 1985, Café Puccini 1985, Phantom of the Opera 1986, Follies 1987, Miss Saigon 1989, Just So 1990, Five Guys Named Moe 1990, Moby Dick 1992, Putting it Together 1992, The Card 1992, Carousel 1993, Oliver! 1994, Martin Guerre 1996, The Fix 1997, Oklahoma! 1999, The Witches of Eastwick 2000, My Fair Lady 2001, Mary Poppins 2004, Avenue Q 2006. *Leisure interests:* cooking, taking holidays. *Address:* Cameron Mackintosh Ltd, 1 Bedford Square, London, WC1B 3RB, England. *Telephone:* (20) 7637-8866. *Fax:* (20) 7436-2683.

MACKINTOSH, Nicholas John, DPhil, FRS; British professor of experimental psychology; b. 9 July 1935; s. of Dr Ian Mackintosh and Daphne Mackintosh; m. 1st Janet Ann Scott 1960 (divorced 1978); one s. one d.; m. 2nd Bundy Wilson 1978 (divorced 1989); two s.; m. 3rd Leonora Caroline Brosan 1992; one s.; ed Winchester and Magdalen Coll., Oxford; lecturer, Univ. of Oxford 1964–67; Resident Prof., Dalhousie Univ. 1967–73; Prof., Univ. of Sussex 1973–81; Prof. of Experimental Psychology and Professorial Fellow of King's Coll., Cambridge 1981–2002; Resident Fellow, Lincoln Coll., Oxford 1966–67; Visiting Prof., Univ. of Pennsylvania 1965–66, Univ. of Hawaii 1972–73, Bryn Mawr Coll. 1977; Ed. Quality Journal of Experimental Psychology 1977–84. *Publications:* Fundamental Issues in Associative Learning (ed. with W. K. Honig) 1969, Mechanisms of Animal Discrimination Learning (with N. S. Sutherland) 1971, the Psychology of Animal Learning 1974, Conditioning and Associative Learning 1983, Animal Learning and Cognition 1994, Cyril Burt: Fraud or Framed? 1995, IQ and Human Intelligence 1998, papers in psychological journals. *Address:* c/o King's College, Cambridge, CB2 1ST, England. *Telephone:* (1223) 351386.

McKNIGHT, Hon. William (Bill) Hunter, PC; Canadian fmr politician; *Principal, McKnight & Associates;* b. 12 July 1940, Elrose, Sask.; m. Beverley Ogden; two s.; ed Wartime and Elrose, Sask.; fmr farmer and business exec.; MP for Kindersley-Lloydminster (Sask.) 1979–93, fmr Chair. House Standing Cttee on Agric., fmr mem. Transport Cttee, Man. and Mem.'s Services Cttee, Finance, Trade and Econ. Affairs Cttee, fmr Progressive Conservative Party spokesperson on Canadian Wheat Bd, on Int. Trade, fmr Deputy Opposition House Leader; Progressive Conservative Party Minister of Labour 1984–86, of Indian Affairs and Northern Devt 1986–89, of Defence 1989–91, of Agric. 1991–93, of Energy, Mines and Resources 1993; Chair. NAFTA Trade Consultants Inc. 1993; Founder, Dir and Chair. Anvil Range Mining Corpn 1994; Prin., McKnight & Assocs (int. trade and financial consultancy), Saskatchewan 1993–; Dir Gamblers Restaurant Inc. 1995–, Marvas Developments Ltd 1995–, Mid-North Resources Ltd 1995–, R.E.S. Int. Inc. 1995, Sci-Tec Instruments Inc. 1995–, Diadem Resources Ltd 2002–; Hon. Consul, Ecuador 1995.

McKUEN, Rod; American writer and composer; b. 29 April 1933, Oakland, California; has appeared in numerous films, concerts and on TV; composer of film scores and background music for TV shows; composer-lyricist of many songs; Pres. of numerous record and book cos; mem. Bd of Dirs American Nat. Theater of Ballet, Animal Concern; mem. Bd of Govs Nat. Acad. of Recording Arts and Sciences; mem. American Soc. of Composers, Authors and Publishers (ASCAP), Writers Guild, MPA; Pres. of American Guild of Variety Artists (AGVA); mem. Bd of Dirs California Music Theater; Grand Prix du Disque 1966, 1974, 1975, 1982, Golden Globe 1969, Motion Picture Daily Award 1969, Los Angeles Shrine Club Award 1975, Freedoms Foundation 1975, Horatio Alger Award 1976, Brandeis Univ. Literary Trust Award 1981, Freedoms Foundation Patriot Medal 1981, Salvation Army Man of the Year 1983, Rose d'Or, Cannes 1986, Myasthenia Gravis Community Service Award 1986. *Recordings include:* Symphony Number One, Concerto for Guitar and Orchestra, Concerto for Four Harpsichords, Seascapes for Piano and Orchestra, Adagio for Harp and Strings, Piano Variations, Concerto Number Three for Piano and Orchestra 1972, The Plains of My Country (ballet) 1972, The City (orchestral suite) 1973, Ballad of Distances (orchestral suite) 1973, Bicentennial Ballet 1975, Symphony Number Three 1975, over 200 record albums. *Film scores:* Joanna 1968, The Prime of Miss Jean Brodie 1969, Me, Natalie 1969, A Boy Named Charlie Brown 1970, Come to Your Senses 1971, Scandalous John 1971, Wildflowers 1971, The Borrowers 1973, Lisa Bright and Dark 1973, Awareness of Emily 1976, The Unknown War 1979, Man to Himself 1980, Portrait of Rod McKuen 1982, Death Rides this Trail 1983, The Living End 1983, The Beach 1984. *Publications include:* And Autumn Came 1954, Stanyan Street and Other Sorrows 1966, Listen to the Warm 1967, Twelve Years of Christmas 1968, In Someone's Shadow 1969, With Love 1970, Caught in the Quiet 1970, Fields of Wonder 1971, The Carols of Christmas 1971, And to Each Season 1972, Beyond the Boardwalk 1972, Come to Me in Silence 1973, America–An Affirmation 1974, Seasons in the Sun 1974, Alone, Moment to Moment 1974, The McKuen Omnibus 1975, Celebrations of the Heart 1975, My Country 200 1975, I'm Strong but I Like Roses, Sleep Warm, Beyond the Boardwalk 1976, The Sea Around Me... The Hills Above 1976, Coming Close to Earth 1977, Hand in Hand... 1977, Love's Been Good to Me 1979, We Touch the Sky 1979, Looking for a Friend 1980, The Power Bright and Shining 1980, Too Many Midnights 1981, Rod McKuen's Book of Days 1981, The Beautiful Strangers 1981, The Works of Rod McKuen, Vol. 1, Poetry 1982, Watch for the Wind... 1982, Rod McKuen – 1984 Book of Days 1983, The Sound of Solitude 1983, Suspension Bridge 1984, Another Beautiful Day 1985, Valentines 1985, Intervals 1986, Valentines 1986, A Safe Place to Land 2001, Rusting in the Rain 2004; prose: Finding My Father 1977, An Outstretched Hand 1980. *Address:* PO Box 2783, Los Angeles, CA 90028, USA. *E-mail:* rod@mckuen.com. *Website:* www.mckuen.com.

MacLACHLAN, Kyle, BFA; American actor; b. 22 Feb. 1959, Yakima, Wash.; m. Desiree Gruber; ed Univ. of Washington, Seattle; stage appearances in regional Shakespeare productions and off-Broadway in Palace of Amateurs. *Films include:* Dune 1984, Blue Velvet 1986, The Hidden 1988, Don't Tell Her It's Me 1990, The Doors 1991, Where the Day Takes You 1992, The Trial 1993, Twin Peaks: Fire Walk With Me 1992, Rich in Love 1993, Against the Wall 1994, The Flintstones 1994, Showgirls 1995, Trigger Effect 1996, Mad Dog Time 1996, One Night Stand 1997, X-Change 2000, Hamlet 2000, Timecode 2000, Perfume 2001, Me Without You 2001, Miranda 2002, Northfork 2003, Touch of Pink 2004, Free Jimmy (voice) 2006,. *Plays:* Palace of Amateurs, Minetta Lane Theatre (off Broadway), New York, On An Average Day, Comedy Theatre, London 2002. *Television includes:* Twin Peaks (series) 1990–91, Roswell 1994, Moonshine Highway 1996, Windsor Protocol 1996, The Invisible Man 1998, Thunder Point 1998, Route 9 1998, The Spring 2000, Sex and the City 2000–02, Jo 2002, The Librarian: Quest for the Spear 2004, Mysterious Island 2005, In Justice (series) 2006, Justice League: The New Frontier 2008, The Sisterhood of the Traveling Pants 2008, Desperate Housewives (series) 2006–12, Portlandia 2011–12, Muppets vs. Goldman Sachs 2012. *Website:* www.kylemaclachlan.com.

McLACHLIN, Beverley, MPh; Canadian lawyer and judge; *Chief Justice of Canada;* b. 7 Sept. 1943, Pincher Creek, Alberta; d. of Ernest Gietz and Eleanora Kruschell; m. 1st Roderick McLachlin (died 1988); one s.; m. 2nd Frank McArdle 1992; ed Univ. of Alberta; practised law with Wood, Moir, Hyde & Ross, Edmonton 1968–71; called to the Bar of BC; practised law with Bull, Housser and Tupper, Vancouver 1972–75; Assoc. Prof., Univ. of British Columbia 1974–81; named to Co. Court of Vancouver 1981, Supreme Court of BC 1981–85, BC Court of Appeal 1985–88; Chief Justice of the Supreme Court of BC 1988; Justice, Supreme Court of Canada 1989–, Chief Justice of Canada (first woman) 2000–; Chair. Canadian Judicial Council, Advisory Council of the Order of Canada, Bd of Govs of Nat. Judicial Inst.; mem. Privy Council of Canada; Hon. LLD (Toronto) 1995, (York) 1999, (Law Soc. Upper Canada) 2000, (Ottawa) 2000, (Calgary) 2000, (Brock Univ.) 2000, (Simon Fraser Univ.) 2000, (Victoria) 2000, (Alberta) 2000, (Lethbridge) 2001, (Bridgewater State Coll.) 2001, (Mount St Vincent Univ.) 2002, (PEI) 2002, (Montreal) 2003, (Manitoba) 2004, (Queen's Univ. Belfast) 2004, (Dalhousie) 2004, (Carleton) 2004, (Maine at Fort Kent) 2005. *Leisure interests:* hiking, swimming, cross-country skiing. *Address:* Supreme Court of Canada, Supreme Court Building, 301 Wellington Street, Ottawa, ON K1A 0J1, Canada (office). *Telephone:* (613) 992-6940 (office). *Fax:* (613) 952-3192 (office). *Website:* www.scc-csc.gc.ca (office).

McLAGLEN, Andrew V.; British film director; b. 28 July 1920, London; s. of Victor McLaglen; m. Veda Ann Borg 1946 (divorced 1958, died 1973); one s. one d.; ed Univ. of Virginia; acted in films Since You Went Away 1944, Paris Underground 1945; Unit Production Man. for Hondo 1953. *Films include:* as Asst Dir: Love, Honor and Goodbye 1945, Bullfighter and the Lady 1951, Wild Stallion (uncredited) 1952, Here Come the Marines 1952, The Quiet Man (second asst dir) 1952, Big Jim McLain 1952, Kansas Pacific 1953, Fort Vengeance 1953, Plunder of the Sun 1953, Island in the Sky 1953, The High and the Mighty 1954, Track of the Cat 1954, Blood Alley 1955; as Dir: Gun the Man Down 1956, Man in the Vault 1956, Seven Men from Now (producer) 1956, The Abductors 1957, Freckles 1960, The Little Shepherd of Kingdom Come 1961, McLintock! 1963, Shenandoah 1965, The Rare Breed 1966, Monkeys, Go Home! 1967, The Way West 1967, The Ballad of Josie 1968, The Devil's Brigade 1968, Bandolero! 1968, Hellfighters 1968, The Undefeated 1969, Chisum 1970, One More Train to Rob 1971, Something Big (also producer) 1971, Fools' Parade (also producer) 1971, Cahill, U.S. Marshal 1973, Mitchell 1975, The Last Hard Men 1976, Steiner – Das eiserne Kreuz, 2. Teil (aka Breakthrough) 1979, The Wild Geese 1978, North Sea Hijack 1980, The Sea Wolves: The Last Charge of the Calcutta Light Horse 1980, Deprisa, Deprisa 1981, Sweet Hours 1982, Antonieta 1982, Carmen 1983, Sahara 1983, Eye of the Widow 1989, Return from the River Kwai 1989. *Television includes:* Gunsmoke (series) 1956–65, Have Gun – Will Travel (series, 116 episodes) 1957, Perry Mason (series) 1957, Hotel de Paree (series) 1959, Rawhide (series) 1959, The Virginian (series) 1962, Banacek (series) 1972, Hec Ramsey (series) 1972, The Log of the Black Pearl 1975, Stowaway to the Moon 1975, Banjo Hackett: Roamin' Free 1976, Trail of Danger 1977, Code R (series) 1977, The Fantastic Journey (series) 1977, Murder at the World Series 1977, The Shadow Riders 1982, The Blue and the Gray (mini-series) 1982, Travis McGee 1983, The Dirty Dozen: The Next Mission 1985, On Wings of Eagles (mini-series) 1986.

MacLAINE, Shirley; American film actress, writer and film director; b. 24 April 1934, Richmond, Va; d. of Ira Beaty and Kathlyn MacLean; sister of Warren Bull Beatty (q.v.); m. Steve Parker 1954 (divorced 1982); one d.; ed grammar school and Lee High School, Washington; fmr chorus girl and ballet dancer; Theater Owners of America Star of the Year Award 1967, Berlin Film Festival Lifetime Achievement Award 1999, Malibu Film Festival Life Achievement Award 2001. *Films include:* The Trouble With Harry (Golden Globe Award for New Star of the Year) 1955, Artists and Models 1955, Around The World in 80 Days 1956, Hot Spell 1958, The Matchmaker 1958, Career 1959, Can-Can 1960, The Apartment 1960, The Children's Hour 1961, Two For The Seesaw 1962, Irma La Douce 1963, What A Way To Go 1964, The Yellow Rolls-Royce 1964, Gambit 1966, Woman Times Seven 1967, The Bliss of Mrs Blossom 1968, Sweet Charity 1969, Two Mules For Sister Sara 1970, Desperate Characters (Best Actress Award, Berlin Film Festival) 1971, The Possessions of Joel Delaney 1972, The Turning Point 1977, Being There 1979, Loving Couples 1980, The Change of Seasons 1981, Slapstick 1981, Terms of Endearment (Acad. Award for Best Actress) 1984, Out on a Limb 1987, Madame Sousatzka (Golden Globe Award for Best Actress) 1989, Steel Magnolias 1989, Waiting for the Light 1990, Postcards from the Edge 1990, Used People 1993, Wrestling Ernest Hemingway 1994, Guarding Tess 1994, Mrs Westbourne 1995, Mrs Winterbourne 1996, The Celluloid Closet, The Evening Star 1996, Looking for Lulu, Bet Bruce, Bruno (also dir), Joan of Arc 1999, The Dress Code 2000, Rumor Has It... 2005, In Her Shoes 2005, Bewitched 2005, Ant Bully 2006, Closing the Ring 2007, Valentine's Day 2010, Bernie 2011, The Secret Life of Walter Mitty 2013Elsa & Fred 2014. *Revues:* If My Friends Could See Me Now 1974, To London With Love 1976, London 1982, Out There Tonight 1990. *Television includes:* The West Side Waltz 1994, Joan of Arc, These Old Broads 2001, Downton Abbey (series) 2012–13. *Video:* Shirley MacLaine's Inner Workout 1989. *Produced and co-directed:* The Other Half of the Sky – A China Memoir 1973. *Publications include:* Don't Fall Off the Mountain 1971, The New Celebrity Cookbook 1973, You Can Get There From Here 1975 (Vols 1 and 2 of autobiog.), Out on a Limb (Vol. 3) 1983, Dancing in the Light 1985 (Vol. 4), It's All in the Playing (Vol. 5) 1987, Going Within (Vol. 6) 1989, Dance While You Can (Vol. 7) 1991, My Lucky Stars (Vol. 8) 1995, The Camino 2000, Out on a Leash 2003, Sage-ing While Age-ing 2007, I'm Over All That: And Other Confessions 2011. *Address:* MacLaine Enterprises Inc., 25200 Malibu Road, Suite 101, Santa Monica, CA 90265, USA (office). *Telephone:* (310) 317-8500. *Fax:* (310) 317-8504. *E-mail:* info@shirleymaclaine.com. *Website:* shirleymaclaine.com.

MacLAREN, Hon. Roy, PC, MA, MDiv; Canadian fmr diplomatist, politician and business executive; b. 26 Oct. 1934, Vancouver; s. of Wilbur MacLaren and Anne Bailey MacLaren; m. Alethea Mitchell 1959; two s. one d.; ed Univ. of British Columbia, Univ. of Cambridge, UK, Harvard Univ., USA, Univ. of Toronto; joined Dept of External Affairs 1957; served in Hanoi, Prague, Geneva, Ottawa, New York; Dir Public Affairs, Massey Ferguson Ltd 1969–73; Pres. Ogilvy and Mather (Canada) Ltd 1974–76; Chair. CB Media Ltd 1977–83, 1984–93; Dir Deutsche Bank (Canada), Royal LePage Ltd, London Insurance Group Inc.; elected Liberal MP for Etobicoke North 1979–96; Parl. Sec. to Minister of Energy, Mines & Resources 1980–82; Minister of State (Finance) 1983, Minister of Nat. Revenue 1984, for Int. Trade 1993–96; High Commr in UK 1996–2000; Commr Trilateral Comm.; Dir (non-exec.) Standard Life, Brascan, Patheon, Broadview Press, Pacific Safety Products, Amec N American Advisory Bd 2001–; Dir Canadian Opera Co.; Chair. Canada-India Business Council, Canadian Inst. of Int. Affairs, Canada-Europe Round Table; Hon. Col 7th Toronto Regt Royal Canadian Artillery 1997–2007; Hon. Dr Sacred Letters (Toronto); Hon. Dr Civil Letters (Univ. of N Alabama); Hon. LLD (Univ. of New Brunswick, Univ. of Prince Edward Island). *Publications:* Canadians in Russia, 1918–1919 1976, Canadians on the Nile, 1882–1898 1978, Canadians Behind Enemy Lines, 1939–1945 1981, Honourable Mentions 1986, African Exploits: The Diaries of William Grant Stairs 1997, Commissions High 2006, The Fundamental Things Apply 2011. *Leisure interests:* skiing, cross-country walking. *Address:* 425 Russell Hill Road, Toronto, Ont. M5P 2S4, Canada (home). *Telephone:* (416) 932-9255 (home). *Fax:* (416) 932-3571 (home).

McLARTY, Thomas F. (Mack), III; American business executive and fmr politician; *Chairman, McLarty Associates;* b. 1946, Hope, Ark.; m. Donna K. Cochran 1969; two s.; ed Univ. of Arkansas; worked in family automobile and transport business; elected to Ark. House of Reps 1969; Chair. Ark. State Democratic Party 1974–76; apptd mem. Bd Arkla Inc., La, subsequently joined staff, apptd Chair. 1983; Chief of Staff to Pres. Bill Clinton 1993–94, Presidential Counselor 1994–2001, Special Envoy for Americas 1997; Chair. Kissinger McLarty Assocs, Washington DC and New York City and Chair. McLarty Cos, Little Rock, Ark. 1998– (Kissinger McLarty Assocs separated to form Kissinger Assocs and McLarty Assocs 2008); Dir, Acxiom Corpn 1999–2010, Union Pacific Railroad; mem. Advisory Bd Leeds Equity Partners, Cato Inst./Inter-American Dialogue, Diligence Llc, New Democrat Network; Sr Advisor, The Carlyle Group 2003–; mem. Bd Council of Americas, Inter-American Dialogue, US-Mexico Binational Council, Council on Foreign Relations 2001; Trustee, Center for the Study of the Presidency; mem. Int. Council of Trustees, Religions for Peace; Democratic; Hon. LLD (Univ. of Arkansas) 2000; Sec. of State's Distinguished Service Medal, Order of Aztec Eagle (Mexico) and numerous other awards and honours. *Address:* McLarty Associates, 900 Seventeenth Street NW, Suite 800, Washington, DC 20006, USA. *Telephone:* (202) 419-1420. *E-mail:* info@maglobal.com. *Website:* www.maglobal.com.

McLAUGHLIN, Alden M., LLB, MBE, JP; Cayman Islands lawyer and politician; *Premier;* b. 6 Sept. 1961, George Town; m. Kim McLaughlin; two s.; ed Univ. of Liverpool, UK; joined Civil Service as Asst Labour Officer 1981, transferred to Judicial Dept, Deputy Clerk of the Court 1982–84; Articled Clerk, Charles Adams and Co. (law firm, now Charles Adams, Ritchie and Duckworth) 1984, Assoc. Attorney 1988, Partner 1993–2005; Founding mem. People's Progressive Movt, Gen. Sec. 2002–06, Leader 2011–; mem. Legis. Assembly for George Town 2000–; Minister of Educ., Training, Employment, Youth, Sports and Culture 2005–09; Leader of the Opposition 2011–13; Premier 2013–; fmr Pres. Cayman Islands Bar Asscn. *Address:* Office of the Premier, Government Administration Bldg, Elgin Avenue, George Town, Grand Cayman, Cayman Islands (office).

MacLAURIN OF KNEBWORTH, Baron (Life Peer), cr. 1996, of Knebworth in the County of Hertfordshire; **Ian Charter MacLaurin,** Kt, DL, FRSA; British business executive; b. 30 March 1937, Blackheath; s. of Arthur and Evelina MacLaurin; m. 1st Ann Margaret Collar 1962 (died 1999); one s. two d.; m. 2nd Paula Elizabeth Brooke 2001; ed Malvern Coll., Worcs.; joined Tesco as a Trainee Man. 1959; Dir Tesco Stores (Holdings) Ltd 1970, Man. Dir 1974–83, Deputy Chair. 1983–85, Chair. 1985–97; Chair. Vodafone 1998–99, Deputy Chair. 1999–2000, Chair. 2000–06, Adviser 2006–, Chair. Vodafone Group Foundation 2006–09; Chancellor, Univ. of Herts. 1996–; Chair. England and Wales Cricket Bd 1996–2002; Dir (non-exec.) Enterprise Oil 1984–91, Gleneagles Hotels PLC 1992–, Guinness PLC 1986–95, Nat. Westminster Bank PLC 1990–97, Whitbread PLC 1997–2001 (Deputy Chair. 1999–), Health Clinic 2001–02, Evolution 2004–10; Pres. Inst. of Grocery Distribution 1989–92; Fellow Inst. of Marketing 1987; Freeman of City of London 1981; Chair. Malvern Coll. Council 2003–; mem. MCC; mem. Lords Taverners and Worshipful Co. of Carmen; Hon. Fellow (Wales Cardiff) 1996; Hon. DUniv (Stirling) 1986, Dr hc (Hertfordshire). *Publication:* Tiger by the Tail (memoirs) 1999. *Leisure interests:* cricket, golf. *Address:* House of Lords, London, SW1A 0PW, England (office). *E-mail:* maclaurini@gmail.com (home).

MacLAVERTY, Bernard, BA, DipEd; Irish writer; b. 14 Sept. 1942, Belfast, Northern Ireland; s. of John MacLaverty and Mary MacLaverty; m. Madeline McGuckin 1967; one s. three d.; ed Queen's Univ., Belfast; fmrly medical lab. technician, English teacher; fmr Writer-in-Residence, Univ. of Aberdeen; mem. Aosdána; NI and Scottish Arts Councils Awards, Irish Sunday Independent Award 1983, Scottish Writer of the Year (co-recipient) 1988, Soc. of Authors Travelling Scholarship 1994, Stakis Scottish Writer of the Year, Creative Scotland Award 2003, Lord Provost of Glasgow's Award for Literature 2005. *Stage:* opera libretti: The King's Conjecture 2008, The Letter 2010, The Elephant Angel 2012. *Television:* plays: My Dear Palestrina 1980, Phonefun Limited 1982, The Daily Woman 1986, Sometime in August 1989; documentary: Hostages 1992; adaptation: The Real Charlotte, by Somerville and Ross 1989. *Screenplays:* Cal (London Evening Standard Award for Screenplay 1984) 1984, Lamb 1985, Bye-Child (short film, also Dir) (Best First Dir, BAFTA Scotland 2004) 2003. *Radio plays:* My Dear Palestrina 1980, Secrets 1981, No Joke 1983, The Break 1988, Some Surrender 1988, Lamb 1992, Grace Notes 2003, The Woman from the North 2007, Winter Storm 2009. *Publications:* novels: Lamb 1980, Cal 1983, Grace Notes (Saltire Scottish Book of the Year Award) 1997, The Anatomy School 2001; short story collections: Secrets and Other Stories 1977, A Time to Dance and Other Stories 1982, The Great Profundo and Other Stories 1987, Walking the Dog and Other Stories 1994, Matters of Life & Death and Other Stories 2006, Collected Stories 2013; juvenile fiction: A Man in Search of a Pet 1978, Andrew McAndrew 1988. *Address:* c/o Gill Coleridge, Rogers, Coleridge & White, 20 Powis Mews, London, W11 1JN, England (office). *Telephone:* (20) 7221-3717 (office). *Fax:* (20) 7229-9084 (office). *E-mail:* info@rcwlitagency.co.uk (office). *Website:* www.rcwlitagency.co.uk (office); www.bernardmaclaverty.com.

McLAY, James Kenneth (Jim), CNZM, QSO, LLB; New Zealand diplomatist, politician, lawyer and business consultant; *Permanent Representative, United Nations;* b. 21 Feb. 1945, Devonport, Auckland; s. of the late Robert McLay and Joyce Evelyn Dee; m. Marcy Farden 1983; one s.; ed King's Coll., Auckland, Univ. of Auckland; officer, Territorial Force 1967–70; barrister 1968–; Man. Ed. Recent Law 1969–70; MP for Birkenhead 1975–87; Attorney-Gen. and Minister of Justice 1978–84; Deputy Prime Minister 1984; Leader of Opposition 1984–86; Man. Dir J.K. McLay Ltd 1987–2009; Amb. and Perm. Rep. to UN, New York 2009–; Deputy Chair. TrustBank Auckland Ltd 1988–93; Chair. Macquarie New Zealand Ltd (Subsidiary of Macquarie Bank, Australia) 1994–, Unichem Chemist Ltd 1999–; mem. 1990 Comm. 1988–91; mem. Ministerial Working Party on Accident Compensation 1991; Chair. Review of Defence Funding and Man. 1991, Wholesale Electricity Market Study 1991–92, Wholesale Electricity Market Devt Group 1993–94; NZ Commr to Int. Whaling Comm. 1994–2002; Chair. Roading Advisory Group 1997, Project Marukav Audit Group 1998–, Council for Infrastructure Devt; mem. Bd Evergreen Forests Ltd 1995–, MotorRace NZ Ltd 1996–99, Neurouz Ltd 2001–, Generator Bonds Ltd 2003–, Metlifecare Ltd 2005–; mem. Advisory Bd Westfield New Zealand Ltd 1998–; Adviser to Building Industry Authority on revision to earthquake codes 1997; Trustee, Auckland Medical School Foundation 1993–99; Nat. Party; Companion of the NZ Order of Merit; NZ Suffrage Centennial Medal. *Publications:* numerous papers, articles, etc. on political, commercial and environmental issues. *Leisure interest:* trout fishing. *Address:* Permanent Mission of New Zealand to the United Nations, 600 Third Avenue, 14th Floor, New York, NY 10016, USA (office). *Telephone:* (212) 826-1960 (office). *Fax:* (212) 758-0827 (office). *E-mail:* nzmissionny@earthlink.net (office). *Website:* www.nzembassy.com/united-nations (office).

McLEAN, Alistair Murray, BA; Australian diplomatist; b. 1947, Melbourne, Vic.; s. of Rev John Alistair Kenneth McLean; m.; two c.; ed Geelong Coll., Univs of Melbourne and Hong Kong; joined Dept of Foreign Affairs 1970, Asst Sec. E Asia Br. 1992–96, First Asst Sec. N Asia Div. 2001–04, Deputy Sec. 2004; overseas posts in Hong Kong 1971–73, Beijing 1973–76, Counsellor, Embassy in Beijing 1979–83, in Washington, DC 1983–86, Consul-Gen. in Shanghai 1987–92, High Commr to Singapore 1997–2001, Amb. to Japan 2004–11; Order of Australia Medal 1991. *Leisure interests:* golf, tennis, classical music, Asian arts. *Address:* c/o Embassy of Australia, 2-1-14 Mita, Minato-ku, Tokyo 108-8361, Japan.

McLEAN, Angela, MA, PhD, FRS; British mathematician, biologist and academic; *Professor of Mathematical Biology and Senior Research Fellow in*

Theoretical Life Sciences, All Souls College, University of Oxford; ed Somerville Coll., Oxford, Univ. of California, Berkeley, Imperial Coll., London; brief period working in the City of London; joined Math. Biology Group at Nat. Inst. for Medical Research, Mill Hill, London; Royal Soc. Research Fellow, Univ. of Oxford 1990–98, secondment at Pasteur Inst., Paris 1994–98, Head of Math. Biology, Biotechnology and Biological Sciences Research Council's Inst. for Animal Health 1998–2000, Prof. of Math. Biology 2000–, Fellow of St Catherine's Coll., Oxford 2000–05, Dir Inst. for Emerging Infections of Humans, James Martin 21st Century School 2005–08, Co-Dir 2008–13, Sr Research Fellow in Theoretical Life Sciences, All Souls Coll., Oxford 2008–; mem. Science Advisory Council, Dept for Environment, Food and Rural Affairs, Nat. Expert Panel for New and Emerging Infections, Dept of Health; Prix Franco-britannnique, Acad. des sciences 1996, Gabor Medal, Royal Soc. 2011. *Publications:* numerous papers in professional journals on the use of mathematical models to aid our understanding of the evolution and spread of infectious agents. *Address:* Institute for Emerging Infections, Department of Zoology, University of Oxford, South Parks Road, Oxford, OX1 3PS, England (office). *Telephone:* (1865) 271210 (office); (1865) 279379 (All Soul's College) (office). *Fax:* (1865) 310447 (office). *E-mail:* angela.mclean@zoo.ox.ac.uk (office). *Website:* www.zoo.ox.ac.uk (office); www.emdis.ox.ac.uk (office).

MacLEAN, Brian W., BA, MA; American business executive; *President and Chief Operating Officer, The Travelers Companies Inc.;* ed Fordham Univ., Univ. of South Carolina; Audit Man., Peat Marwick (now KPMG LLP) –1988; joined Travelers 1988, served in several sr financial roles, Pres. of Select Accounts for Travelers Insurance Group Holdings, Inc. 1999–2002, Exec. Vice-Pres., Claim Services, The Travelers Companies Inc. 2002–05, Exec. Vice-Pres. and COO The Travelers Companies Inc. 2005–08, Pres. and COO 2008–. *Address:* The Travelers Companies Inc., 385 Washington Street, St Paul, MN 55102, USA (office). *Telephone:* (651) 310-7911 (office). *Fax:* (651) 310-3386 (office). *E-mail:* info@travelers.com (office). *Website:* www.travelers.com (office).

McLEAN, Don; American singer, instrumentalist and composer; b. (Donald Mclean), 2 Oct. 1945, New Rochelle, NY; s. of Donald McLean and Elizabeth Bucci; m. Patrisha Shnier 1987; one s. one d.; ed Iona Coll.; Pres. Benny Bird Publishing Corpn, Inc., Don McLean Music, Starry Night Music; mem. Hudson River Sloop Singers 1969; solo concert tours throughout USA, Canada, Australia, Europe, Far East etc.; numerous TV appearances; composer of film scores for Fraternity Row, Flight of Dragons; composer of over 200 songs including Prime Time, American Pie, Tapestry, Vincent (Starry, Starry Night), And I Love You So, Castles In the Air, etc.; mem. American Soc. of Composers, Authors and Publrs, BMI Broadcast Music, Inc. (BMI), Nat. Acad. of Recording Arts and Sciences, American Fed. of Television and Radio Artists, Lotos Club, Coffee House NYC, Groucho Club, London; Dr hc (Iona Coll.) 2001; recipient of many gold discs in USA, Australia, UK and Ireland; Israel Cultural Award 1981, American Pie inducted into Grammy Hall of Fame 2002, inaugurated into Songwriters Hall of Fame 2004, American Pie named by New York City radio station Q104.3 FM WAXQ No. 37 in their Top 1,043 Songs Of All Time 2008, Lifetime Achievement Award for Folk Music, BBC Radio 2 2012. *Recordings include:* albums: Tapestry 1970, American Pie 1971, Don McLean 1972, Playin' Favorites 1973, Homeless Brother 1974, Solo 1976, Prime Time 1977, Chain Lightning 1979, Believers 1982, Dominion 1983, Love Tracks 1988, Headroom 1991, Don McLean Christmas 1992, Favorites and Rarities (Box Set) 1993, The River of Love 1995, For the Memories Vols I and II 1996, Christmas Dreams 1997, Starry Starry Night 2000, Don McLean Sings Marty Robbins 2001, The Western Album 2003, You've Got to Share 2003, Christmastime! 2004, Rearview Mirror 2005, Addicted to Black 2009; singles include: The Mountains of Mourne 1973, Wonderful Baby 1975, Crying 1980, Since I Don't Have You 1981; hit cover versions: And I Love You So (Perry Como) 1973, American Pie (Madonna) 2000; compilation albums: The Very Best of Don McLean 1980, Don McLean's Greatest Hits – Then & Now 1987, The Best of Don McLean 1991, Favorites and Rarities 1992, Legendary Songs of Don McLean 2003, The Legendary Don McLean 2007, American Pie & Other Hits 2008. *Publications:* Songs of Don McLean 1972, The Songs of Don McLean (Vol. II) 1974. *Leisure interests:* antique furniture, film history, western horsemanship (trail riding). *Address:* c/o Steve Martin, The Agency Group, 1775 Broadway, Suite 515, New York, NY 10019, USA (office). *Telephone:* (212) 581-3100 (office). *E-mail:* stevemartin@theagencygroup.com (office). *Website:* www.theagencygroup.com (office); www.don-mclean.com.

McLEAN, Hon. Rev. Walter Franklin, PC, BA, LLD, MDiv, DD; Canadian politician, clergyman and business consultant; *Honorary Consul for Namibia in Canada;* b. 26 April 1936, Leamington, Ont.; s. of J. Lewis W. McLean and Frances Blair McLean; m. Barbara Scott 1961; four s.; ed Victoria Coll., Univ. of Victoria, Univ. of British Columbia, Knox Coll., Univ. of Toronto, Univ. of Edinburgh; Pres. Students' Admin. Council, Univ. of Toronto 1959-60; Pres. Nat. Fed. of Canadian Univ. Students 1961–62; Presbyterian mission staff, Nigeria 1962–67; Chaplain Univ. of Nigeria; Minister St Andrew's Presbyterian Church, Enugu; Co-ordinator CUSO 1963–67; Exec. Dir Man. Centennial Corpn 1969–71; Minister of Knox Presbyterian Church, Waterloo 1971–79; Alderman for City of Waterloo 1976–79; MP 1979–93; fmr mem. Standing Cttee on Communications and Culture, on External Affairs, on Nat. Defence; fmr mem. Special Sub-Cttee on Latin America and Caribbean; sworn to Privy Council 1984, Sec. of State of Canada 1984–85, Minister of State (Immigration) and Minister Responsible for the Status of Women 1984–86; mem. Canadian Del. to UN 1986–93; Prime Minister's Special Rep. on Southern Africa and Commonwealth Affairs 1989–93; Canadian Rep. at Southern Africa Devt Co-ordination Conf. (SADCC) 1987–93; at Commonwealth Foreign Ministers' Confs 1987, 1988, 1989, 1991; Chair. Parl. Sub-cttee on Devt and Human Rights 1990–93; Hon. Consul for Namibia in Canada 1993–; Pres. Franklin Consulting Services Ltd 1994–; Convenor Millennium Celebration, Presbyterian Church in Canada 2000; Prin. Osborne Group 2000–11; Pres. McLean and Associates 2004–; fmr Pres. Int. Council of Parliamentarians for Global Action; Chair. Canadian UNA Human Rights Cttee, Criminal Compensation Bd of Ontario 2000–03; Dir TAB/Ambit International, Calgary 2005–10; mem. Advisory Bd Royal Reads Univ., Victoria, BC 1995–2011, Bd Toronto School of Theology, Univ. of Toronto 2005–07; Hon. LLD (Wilfrid Laurier) 1995, Hon. DD (Knox Coll. Toronto) 2002; Paul Harris Fellow, Rotary International 1984, Canada's 125th Anniversary Medal 1992, Canadian Bureau for Int. Educ. Award of Merit 1994, Queen's 50th Anniversary Medal 2002, Distinguished Alumni Award (Univ. of Victoria) 2002. *Publication:* Parliamentary Report: Canada's

Relations With Southern Africa 1992. *Leisure interests:* golf, curling, music. *Address:* 122 Avondale Avenue S, Waterloo, Ont. N2L 2C3, Canada (office). *Telephone:* (519) 578-5932 (office). *Fax:* (519) 578-7799 (office). *E-mail:* walter@mcleanandassociates.ca (office). *Website:* www.mcleanandassociates.ca (office).

MACLEAN OF PENNYCROSS, Nicolas Lorne Wolfers, CMG, MA; British economist and strategic analyst; *Chief Executive, MWM (Strategy);* b. (Nicolas Lorne Maclean Wolfers), 3 Jan. 1946, London, England; s. of Marcel Wolfers and Audrey Wolfers (née Maclean of Pennycross); m. Qamar Sultan Aziz 22 Aug. 1978; two s.; ed Eton Coll., Oriel Coll., Oxford; fmrly with Samuel Montagu, Midland Bank Group; fmr Group Adviser, Prudential Corpn, and Exec. Dir Prudential Corpn Asia Ltd; Sr Fellow for Int. Affairs, IISS 2000–07; Chief Exec. MWM (Strategy) 2007–; mem. Chatham House Council, Dept. of Membership 1988–94; fmr mem. Jt Exec. British-American Project, Bd UK-Korea Forum for the Future; mem. Council, Canada-UK Colloquia, UK Adviser for colloquia 2009, 2011; Founder-mem. UK-Japan 21st Century Group; fmr Chair. Business-Europe (UNICE) Asia Cttee, Brussels; fmr Chair. Japan Festival Educ. Trust; Founder British English Teaching Programme, prototype for Japan Exchange and Teaching (JET) Programme; Coordinator for the Sponsors, 'The Great Japan Exhibition: Art of the Edo Period 1600–1868', Royal Acad. of Arts, London 1981–82; Special Adviser, 'Treasures from Korea: Two Thousand Years of Korean Civilization', British Museum 1983–84 (innovated with first ever Public Pvt. Partnership); Organiser, 'Visions from Vietnam', Royal Coll. of Art 1998; Gov., Sadler's Wells Theatre 1988–99; Pres. Clan Maclean Asscn of England and Wales 2009–; Special Millennium Award, Japan Soc. 2000; Fellow Emer., British Asscn of Japanese Studies 2003. *Publications:* Trading with China: A Practical Guide (co-author) 1979, Journey into Japan 1600–1868 (co-author) 1981, The Eurobond and Eurocurrency Markets (co-author) 1984, Mongolia Today (co-author) 1988; several articles. *Leisure interests:* reading, cinema, theatre, exhibitions, listening to music, travel, rowing, Scotland, Isle of Mull. *Address:* MWM (Strategy), 30 Malwood Road, London, SW12 8EN, England (office). *Telephone:* (20) 8675-6725 (office). *Fax:* (20) 8675-6886 (office). *E-mail:* nmatmwm@hotmail.com (office).

McLEISH, Rt Hon Henry, PC; British politician and academic; b. 15 June 1948, Methil, Fife; m. 1st (died 1995); one s. one d.; m. 2nd Julie McLeish 1998; ed Buckhaven High School, Methil, Heriot-Watt Univ.; fmr professional football for East Fife FC and Leeds United FC; began career as local govt research officer and planning officer; lecturer in Social Sciences, Heriot-Watt Univ. 1973–87; mem. Kirkcaldy Dist Council 1974–77; mem. Fife Regional Council 1978–87, Leader 1982–87; MSP for Fife Cen. 1999–2001, Opposition Spokesman on Social Security 1996–97; Minister for Enterprise and Lifelong Learning 1997–2000; First Minister of Scotland 2000–01; Consultant on Govt and Political Relations, Halogen Communications 2005–; mem. Scottish Broadcasting Comm. 2007–; Visiting Prof. Univ. of Arkansas, USA. *Publications:* Scotland First: Truth and Consequences 2004, Global Scots: Voices from Afar (with Kenny MacAskill) 2006, Wherever the Saltire Flies (with Kenny MacAskill) 2006, Scotland: The Road Divides (with Tom Brown) (2007). *Leisure interests:* reading, history, life and work of Robert Burns. *Address:* Halogen Communications, 4 Queen Street, Edinburgh, EH2 1JE, Scotland (office). *Telephone:* (131) 202-0120 (office). *Fax:* (131) 225-3757 (office). *E-mail:* info@halogencom.com (office). *Website:* www.halogencom.com (office).

McLELLAN, Rt Hon. Anne, PC, OC, BA, LLB, LLM; Canadian lawyer, academic and fmr politician; b. 31 Aug. 1950, Hants. Co., Nova Scotia; d. of Howard Gilmore McLellan and Joan Mary Pullan; ed Dalhousie Univ. and King's Coll. London, UK; Asst Prof. of Law, Univ. of New Brunswick 1976–80; Acting Assoc. Dean and Assoc. Prof. of Law, Univ. of Alberta 1980–89, Assoc. Dean 1985–87, Prof. 1989–93, Acting Dean 1991–92; MP for Edmonton W. 1993–2006; Minister of Natural Resources and Fed. Interlocutor for Métis and Non-Status Indians 1993–97; Minister of Justice and Attorney-Gen. 1997–2002; Minister of Health 2002–03; Deputy Prime Minister and Minister of Public Safety and Emergency Preparedness 2003–06; Chair. Social Union Cttee 1997–; Vice-Chair. Special Cttee of Council 1997–; Distinguished Scholar-in-Residence, Inst. for American Studies, Univ. of Alberta 2006; Counsel, Bennett Jones LLP 2006–; fmr Vice-Pres. Univ. of Alberta Faculty Asscn; mem. Econ. Union Cttee 1997–, Treasury Bd 1997–, Premier's Council for Econ. Strategy; fmr mem. Bd of Dirs Canadian Civil Liberties Asscn, Alberta Legal Aid; mem. Advisory Panel, Health Quality Council of Alberta 2011–; Hon. DrIur (Univ. of Alberta) 2007. *Address:* Alberta Institute for American Studies, 400 Arts & Convocation Hall, University of Alberta, Edmonton, AB T6G 2C9, Canada (office). *Telephone:* (780) 492-4648 (office). *E-mail:* anne.mclellan@ualberta.ca (office). *Website:* www.americanstudies.ualberta.ca (office); www.annemclellan.ca.

MacLENNAN, Murdoch; British newspaper executive; *CEO, Telegraph Media Group Limited;* began career as graduate trainee, The Scotsman newspaper; Production Dir Scottish Daily Record and Sunday Mail 1982–84; Dir of Production, Mirror Group 1984–85; Production and Tech. Dir, Express Newspapers 1985–89, Man. Dir 1989–92; Group Operations Dir, Mirror Group Newspapers and Man. Dir Scottish Daily Record and Sunday Mail 1992–94; Group Man. Dir, Associated Newspapers 1994–2004; CEO Telegraph Media Group Ltd 2004–; fmr Pres. IFRA (newspaper publrs' asscn); Chair. Press Asscn Remuneration Cttee; Vice-Pres. and Appeals Chair. Newspaper Press Fund; Chair. (non-exec.) PA Group 2010–; Vice-Chair. World Asscn of Newspapers; mem. Comm. on Scottish Devolution; Chancellor's Assessor, Univ. of Glasgow; Companion Inst. of Man.; Freeman of the City of London; Dr hc (Paisley); MacMillan Memorial Lecturer, Inst. of Engineers and Shipbuilders in Scotland 1998, ranked by MediaGuardian Media in its list of the 100 most powerful figures in the British Media (17th) 2010, (41st) 2011. *Address:* 111 Buckingham Palace Road, London, SW1W 0DT; Telegraph Media Group Ltd, 1 Canada Square, Canary Wharf, London, E14 5DT, England (office). *Telephone:* (20) 7538-5000 (office). *Fax:* (20) 7513-2512 (office). *Website:* www.pressoffice.telegraph.co.uk (office).

MACLENNAN OF ROGART, Baron (Life peer), cr. 2001, of Rogart Sutherland; **Rt Hon. Robert Adam Ross Maclennan,** PC, MA, LLB; British politician and barrister-at-law; b. 26 June 1936, Glasgow; s. of Sir Hector Maclennan and Lady Maclennan; m. Helen Cutter Noyes 1968; one s. one d. one step-s.; ed Glasgow Academy, Balliol Coll., Oxford, Trinity Coll., Cambridge, Columbia Univ., New York; MP for Caithness and Sutherland 1966–97, Caithness, Sutherland and

Easter Ross 1997–2001; Parl. Pvt. Sec. to Sec. of State for Commonwealth Affairs and Minister without portfolio 1967–70, Parl. Under-Sec. of State for Prices and Consumer Protection 1974–79; Opposition Spokesman on Scottish Affairs 1970–71, on Defence 1971–72, on Foreign Affairs 1980–81; resgnd from Labour Party 1981; Founder mem. SDP 1981; SDP Spokesman on Agriculture 1981–87, on Home and Legal Affairs 1983–87, on Econ. Affairs 1987; Leader SDP 1987–88; Jt Leader SLD 1988; Liberal Democrat convenor on Home Affairs 1988–94, Legal Affairs 1988–94, Nat. Heritage 1992–94; mem. Public Accounts Cttee 1979–2001; Liberal Democrat 1994–98, Spokesperson on Constitutional Affairs, Culture and Media 1994–2001; mem. Convention on Future of Europe 2002–03; Liberal Democrats Europe Spokesman on Europe 2001–04, European Constitution 2004–05, Scotland 2004–09, Cabinet Office 2005–10, Constitutional Affairs 2007–; Légion d'Honneur 2004. *Music:* wrote libretti of operas The Lie 1992 and Friend of the People 1999. *Leisure interests:* music, theatre and visual arts. *Address:* House of Lords, London, SW1A 0PW, England (office). *Telephone:* (20) 7219-4133 (office). *E-mail:* maclennanr@parliament.uk (office).

MACLEOD, Hugh Angus MacIntosh, BSc, DTech; American (b. British) professor of optical sciences and business executive; *President, Thin Film Center Inc.;* b. 20 June 1933, Glasgow, Scotland; s. of Dr John Macleod and Agnes Donaldson Macleod; m. Ann Turner 1957; four s. one d.; ed Lenzie Acad., Univ. of Glasgow; engineer, Sperry Gyroscope Co. Ltd 1954–60; Chief Engineer, Williamson Mfg Co. Ltd 1960–62; Sr Physicist, Mervyn Instruments Ltd 1963; Tech. Man. Sir Howard Grubb, Parsons and Co. Ltd 1963–70; Reader in Thin Film Physics, Newcastle upon Tyne Polytechnic 1971–79; Assoc. Prof., Univ. of Aix-Marseille III 1976, 1979; Prof. of Optical Sciences, Univ. of Arizona, USA 1979–95, Prof. Emer. of Optical Sciences 1995–; Dir-at-Large, Optical Soc. of America 1987–89; Pres. Thin Film Center Inc. 1992–; Dir OptoSigma Corpn 1995–98, Precision Optics Corpn 1997–2002; Dir Soc. of Vacuum Coaters 1998–2004, Vice-Pres. 2006–08, Pres. 2008–10; Fellow, Int. Soc. for Optical Eng (SPIE), Optical Soc. of America, Inst. of Physics (London); Dr hc (Aix-Marseille); Gold Medal SPIE 1987, Esther Hoffman Beller Medal, Optical Soc. of America 1997, John Matteuci Award 2000, Nathaniel H. Sugerman Award 2002, Life for Thin Film Award, Workshop of European Vacuum Coaters, Anzio 2004, Senator Award, Workshop of European Vacuum Coaters, Anzio 2008. *Publications:* Thin-Film Optical Filters 1969 (4th edn 2010); more than 200 articles, papers and book chapters on optics of thin films. *Leisure interests:* piano, computing. *Address:* Thin Film Center, Inc., 2745 East Via Rotonda, Tucson, AZ 85716-5227, USA (office). *Telephone:* (520) 322-6171 (office); (520) 795-5019 (home). *Fax:* (520) 325-8721 (office). *E-mail:* angus@thinfilmcenter.com (office). *Website:* www.thinfilmcenter.com (office).

McLEOD, James Graham, AO, MD, DPhil, DSc, FRACP, FRCP, FAA, FTSE; Australian professor of neurology and medicine; *Professor Emeritus of Neurology, University of Sydney;* b. 18 Jan. 1932, Sydney, NSW; s. of Hector R. McLeod and Dorothy S. McLeod (née Craig); m. Robyn E. Rule 1962; two s. two d.; ed Univ. of Sydney, Univs of Oxford and London, UK, Harvard Univ., USA; Sr Lecturer, Univ. of Sydney 1967–69, Assoc. Prof. 1970–72, Bushell Prof. of Medicine 1972–97, Bushell Prof. of Neurology 1978–97, Prof. Emer. 1997–; Visiting Medical Officer, Royal Prince Alfred Hosp., Sydney 1965–97, Head, Dept of Neurology 1978–94, Hon. Consultant Physician 1997–; mem. Bd Dirs Royal North Shore Hosp., Sydney (Vice-Chair.) 1978–86; Pres. Australian Asscn of Neurologists 1980–83; Rhodes Scholar 1953–56; Nuffield Travelling Fellow 1964–65; Sir Arthur Sims Travelling Prof. 1983–84; Commonwealth Sr Medical Fellowship 1989; mem. Australian Science and Tech. Council 1987–93; Fellow, Australian Acad. of Tech., Science and Eng, Australian Acad. of Science (Vice-Pres. 1987–88, Treas. 1993–97); Dr hc (Aix-Marseille) 1992; Rhodes Scholar 1953. *Publications:* A Physiological Approach to Clinical Neurology (with J. W. Lance q.v.), Introductory Neurology (with J. W. Lance q.v.) 1989, Peripheral Neuropathy in Childhood (with R. A. Ouvrier and J. D. Pollard) 1999, Inflammatory Neuropathies (ed.) 1994. *Leisure interests:* swimming, boating, music, literature. *Address:* 2 James Street, Woollahra, NSW 2025, Australia (home). *Telephone:* (2) 9362-8362 (home). *Fax:* (2) 9362-8348 (home). *E-mail:* james.mcleod@sydney.edu.au (home).

MACLEOD, Sir (Nathaniel William) Hamish, Kt, KBE, MA; British civil servant (retd); b. 6 Jan. 1940; s. of George Henry Torquil Macleod and Ruth Natalie Wade; m. Fionna Mary Campbell 1970; one s. one d.; ed Strathallan School, Perthshire, St Andrews Univ., Univ. of Bristol; commercial trainee Stewarts and Lloyds, Birmingham 1958–62; Admin. Officer Hong Kong Govt 1966, Dir of Trade and Chief Trade Negotiator 1983–87, Sec. for Trade and Industry 1987–89, Sec. for the Treasury 1989–91, Financial Sec. 1991–95; JP (Hong Kong) 1979–95; mem. Bd Scottish Oriental Smaller Cos Trust 1995–2011, Morgan Fleming Asian Investment Trust 1997–2003. *Leisure interests:* walking, golf. *Address:* 20 York Road, Edinburgh, EH5 3EH, Scotland (home). *Telephone:* (131) 552-5058 (home). *E-mail:* macleodhamish@hotmail.com (home).

McLOUGHLIN, Rt Hon. Patrick Allen; British politician; *Secretary of State for Transport;* b. 30 Nov. 1957, Stafford, Staffs.; m. Lynn Newman 1984; one s. one d.; ed Cardinal Griffin Roman Catholic School, Cannock, Staffordshire Coll. of Agric. at Rodbaston Coll.; farm worker 1974–79; miner at Littleton Colliery, Cannock from 1979; mem. Nat. Union of Mineworkers, became an industrial rep. for Nat. Coal Bd's Western Area Marketing Dept; Councillor, Cannock Chase Dist Council 1980–87, Staffordshire Co. Council 1981–87; contested Wolverhampton SE constituency 1983; MP for W Derbyshire (by-election) 1986–2010, for Derbyshire Dales 2010–, mem. (Select Cttees), Broadcasting 1994–95, Selection 1997–2001, Finance and Services 1998–2005, Accommodation and Works 2001–05, Modernization of the House of Commons 2004–05, Selection 2005, Admin 2005, Parl. and Political Service Honours 2012; Parl. Pvt. Sec. to Angela Rumbold as Minister of State, Dept of Educ. 1987–88, to Lord Young of Graffham as Sec. of State for Trade and Industry 1988–89; Parl. Under-Sec. of State, Dept of Transport (Minister for Aviation and Shipping) 1989–92; Jt Parl. Under-Sec. of State, Dept of Employment 1992–93; Parl. Under-Sec., Dept of Trade and Industry (Trade and Tech.) 1993–94; Asst Govt Whip 1995–96; Govt Whip 1996–97; Opposition: Pairing Whip 1997–98, Deputy Chief Whip 1998–2005, Chief Whip 2005–10; Parl. Sec. to the Treasury 2010–12; Chief Whip 2010–12; Sec. of State for Transport 2012–; Nat. Vice-Chair. Young Conservatives 1982–84; Conservative. *Leisure interests:* walking, gardening. *Address:* Department for Transport, Great Minster House, 76 Marsham Street, London, SW1P 4DR (office); House of Commons, Westminster, London,

SW1A 0AA, England (office). *Telephone:* (20) 7944-3011 (Ministry) (office); (20) 7219-3511 (Westminster) (office). *Fax:* (20) 7944-4399 (Ministry) (office). *E-mail:* patrick.mcloughlin@dft.gsi.gov.uk (office); patrick.mcloughlin.mp@parliament.uk (office). *Website:* www.dft.gov.uk (office); www.parliament.uk/biographies/commons/patrick-mcloughlin/25481 (office).

McMANUS, Sean J., BA; American broadcasting executive; *Chairman, CBS Sports;* b. 16 Feb. 1955; s. of Jim McKay; m.; c.; ed Fairfield Coll. Preparatory School, Conn., Duke Univ.; with ABC (American Broadcasting Corpn) Sports 1977–79, positions including Production Asst, Assoc. Producer; Assoc. Producer NBC Sports 1979, Vice-Pres. Program Planning and Devt 1982–87; joined Trans World International 1987, Sr Vice-Pres. US TV Sales and Programming –1996; Pres. CBS Sports 1996–2011, Chair. 2011–, Exec. Producer Nat. Football League (NFL) on CBS, Pres. CBS News 2005–11; ten-time Emmy Award-winner, inducted into the Broadcasting & Cable Hall of Fame 2010. *Address:* CBS Sports, 1401 West Cypress Creek Road, Fort Lauderdale, FL 33309, USA (office). *E-mail:* pr@cbssports.com (office). *Website:* www.cbssports.com/cbssports/team/smcmanus (office).

McMASTER, Sir Brian John, Kt, CBE, LLB; British arts administrator; b. 9 May 1943, Hitchin, Herts., England; ed Wellington Coll., Univ. of Bristol; with Int. Artists' Dept, EMI Ltd 1968–73; Controller of Opera Planning, ENO 1973–76; Gen. Admin., subsequently Man. Dir Welsh Nat. Opera 1976–91; Artistic Dir Vancouver Opera 1984–89; Festival Dir and CEO Edin. Int. Festival 1991–2006; mem. Bd Barbican Centre 2009–.

McMILLAN, C. Steven, MBA; American business executive; b. Troy, Ala; twice divorced; two d.; ed Auburn Univ., Ala, Harvard Business School (Baker Scholar); supply officer, USN 1970–73; man. consultant, McKinsey & Co., Chicago 1973–78; joined Sara Lee Corpn 1978, Pres. and CEO Aqualux Water Processing Co. 1978–79, Pres. and CEO Electrolux Canada 1979–82, Pres. and CEO Electrolux Corpn 1982–86, Sr Vice-Pres., Strategy Devt, Sara Lee Corpn 1986–90, Head of Packaged Meats, Bakery and Foodservices Businesses 1990–93, and Coffee & Grocery and Household & Bodycare Businesses 1993–97, Pres. and COO Sara Lee Corpn 1997–2000, Pres. and CEO 2000–01, Chair., Pres. and CEO 2001–04, Chair. and CEO 2004–05; mem. Bd of Dirs Monsanto 2000–; fmr Dir, Bank of America; mem. Advisory Bd J.L. Kellogg Grad. School of Man., Northwestern Univ.; mem. Bd Grocery Mfrs Asscn, Econ. Club of Chicago, Chicago Council on Foreign Relations, Catalyst; mem. Business Council, The Business Roundtable, G-100, Exec. Club of Chicago, Civic Cttee of Commercial Club of Chicago; serves on Bd of Steppenwolf Theatre Co.; Trustee, Chicago Symphony Orchestra; Dir Sara Lee Foundation, Charlie Trotter's Culinary Educ. Foundation. *Address:* c/o Monsanto Company, 800 North Lindbergh Blvd, St Louis, MO 63167, USA. *Telephone:* (314) 694-1000. *E-mail:* info@monsanto.com. *Website:* www.monsanto.com.

McMILLAN, David Loch, MA; British civil servant and international organization executive; *Director General, EUROCONTROL;* b. 16 Sept. 1954, Edinburgh, Scotland; ed Univ. of Edinburgh; began his career in FCO 1976, served in Morocco and Zimbabwe, also worked as Transport Sec.-Gen. at British Embassy in Washington, DC; held several posts in Dept of Transport (DfT), including Head of Information, Leader Div. responsible for air traffic control policy 1998–2001, DfT Dir of Rail Restructuring 2001–02, Dir of Strategy and Delivery, responsible for DfT's delivery agenda and for relations with the EU 2002–04, Dir-Gen. of Civil Aviation 2004–07; Dir Gen. EUROCONTROL (European Org. for the Safety of Air Navigation) 2008–; First Vice-Pres. European Civil Aviation Conf. and spokesman for Europe on aviation and environment at Int. Civil Aviation Org. 2005–07; participated in EU's High Level Group on the future of aviation regulation in Europe 2006, 2007. *Address:* c/o Ms Pauline Coady, Senior Personal Assistant to the Director General, EUROCONTROL, Rue de la Fusée 96, 1130 Brussels, Belgium (office). *Telephone:* (2) 729-35-01 (office). *Fax:* (2) 729-91-00 (office). *E-mail:* pauline.coady@eurocontrol.int (office). *Website:* www.eurocontrol.int (office).

MacMILLAN, Jake, PhD, DSc, FRS; British chemist and academic; *Professor Emeritus of Organic Chemistry and Senior Research Fellow, University of Bristol;* b. 13 Sept. 1924, Scotland; s. of John MacMillan and Barbara Lindsay; m. Anne Levy 1952; one s. two d.; ed Lanark Grammar School and Univ. of Glasgow; Assoc. Research Man., ICI 1962–63; Lecturer in Organic Chem., Bristol Univ. 1963–68, Reader 1968–78, Personal Chair. 1978–83, Head of Dept and Alfred Capper Pass Prof. of Organic Chem. 1983–90, Prof. Emer. 1990–, Sr Research Fellow 1996–; Foreign Assoc. NAS (USA) 1991–; Flintoff Medal 1978 and Hugo Muller Medal 1989, Royal Soc. of Chem., Research Medal, Int. Plant Growth Substance Asscn 1982, Charles Reid Barnes Award, American Soc. of Plant Physiology 1988, Pergamon Phytochemistry Prize 1995. *Publications:* over 290 papers and three books on organic chemistry and plant hormones. *Leisure interests:* gardening, theatre. *Address:* School of Chemistry, University of Bristol, Bristol, BS8 1TS (office); 7 Burrough Way, Winterbourne, S Glos., BS36 1LF, England (home). *Telephone:* (117) 331-7162 (office); (1454) 775244 (home). *Fax:* (117) 929-8611 (office). *E-mail:* jake.macmillan@bris.ac.uk (office). *Website:* (office).

MacMILLAN, Margaret Olwen, OC, BA, BPhil, DPhil, FRSL; Canadian university administrator, historian and writer; *Warden, St Antony's College Oxford;* b. Dec. 1943, Toronto, Ont.; ed Univ. of Toronto, St Antony's Coll., Oxford, UK; Prof. of History, Ryerson Univ., Toronto 1975–2002; Provost and Vice Chancellor, Trinity Coll., Univ. of Toronto 2002–07; Warden St Antony's Coll., Oxford 2007–; Ed. International Journal 1995–2003; Sr Fellow, Massey Coll., Univ. of Toronto; Hon. Fellow, St Antony's Coll. Oxford; Gov.-Gen.'s Literary Award 2003, BBC 4 Samuel Johnson Prize for Non-Fiction, Duff Cooper Award, Hessell-Tiltman Prize. *Publications:* Women of the Raj 1988, Canada and NATO: Uneasy Past, Uncertain Future 1990, Peacemakers: Six Months that Changed the World 2001, Paris 1919 2002, Parties Long Estranged: Canada and Australia in the 20th Century (co-ed.) 2003, Canada's House: Rideau Hall and the Invention of a Canadian Home (with Marjorie Harris and Anne L. Desjardins) 2004, Seize the Hour: When Nixon Met Mao 2006, Nixon and Mao 2007, Dangerous Games: The Uses and Abuses of History 2009. *Address:* Office of the Warden, St Antony's College, 62 Woodstock Road, Oxford, OX2 6JF, England (office). *Telephone:* (1865) 284717 (office). *Fax:* (1865) 274526 (office). *E-mail:* margaret.macmillan@sant.ox.ac.uk (office). *Website:* www.sant.ox.ac.uk (office).

McMURTRY, Larry Jeff; American writer; b. 3 June 1936, Wichita Falls, Tex.; s. of William Jefferson McMurtry and Hazel McIver; m. Josephine Ballard 1959 (divorced 1966); one s. *Television includes:* co-writer and co-producer with Diana Ossana of CBS mini-series Streets of Laredo and ABC mini-series Dead Man's Walk 1996. *Publications:* Horseman Pass By (aka Hud) 1961, Leaving Cheyenne 1963, The Last Picture Show 1966, In a Narrow Grave (essays) 1968, Moving On 1970, All My Friends Are Going to be Strangers 1972, It's Always We Rambled (essay) 1974, Terms of Endearment 1975, Somebody's Darling 1978, Cadillac Jack 1982, The Desert Rose 1983, Lonesome Dove 1985, Texasville 1987, Film Flam: Essay on Hollywood 1987, Anything for Billy 1988, Some Can Whistle 1989, Buffalo Girls 1990, The Evening Star 1992, Streets of Laredo 1993, Pretty Boy Floyd (with Diana Ossana) 1993, The Late Child 1995, Dead Man's Walk 1995, Zeke and Ned (novel, with Diana Ossana) 1996, Comanche Moon 1997, Duane's Depressed 1998, Walter Benjamin at the Dairy Queen 1999, Boone's Lick 2000, Sin Killer: The Berrybender Narratives, Book One 2002, The Wandering Hill: The Berrybender Narratives, Book Two 2003, Folly and Glory: The Berrybender Narratives, Book Three 2004, Loop Group 2004, When the Light Goes 2007, Books: A Memoir 2008, Rhino Ranch 2009, Literary Life: A Second Memoir 2010, Hollywood: A Third Memoir 2010. *Leisure interest:* antiquarian bookselling. *Address:* c/o Adam Shulman, Anonymous Content, 3532 Hayden Avenue, Culver City, CA 90232, USA (office); Saria Co. Inc., PO Box 552, Archer City, AZ 76351, USA (office). *Telephone:* (310) 558-6537 (office). *E-mail:* ashulman@ anonymouscontent.com (office). *Website:* www.flashandfiligree.com (office).

McNALLY, Alan G., BSc, MSc, MBA; Canadian business executive; b. 1945, Quebec City; m. Ruth McNally; two c.; ed Cornell Univ., York Univ. (including studies at Harvard Grad. School of Business, Oxford University Centre for Man. Studies and Institut Européen d'Admin des Affaires (INSEAD), France); spent six years with Aluminum Co. of Canada, in finance and other functions in Arvida, Quebec and Montreal head office 1984–90; Vice-Chair. Bank of Montreal 1990–2002; CEO Harris Trust and Savings Bank and Harris Bankcorp, Inc. 1993–2002, Chair. 1995–2004; Chair. Harris Financial Corpn (fmrly Bankmont Financial Corpn) 1998–2006, mem. Bd of Dirs May–Dec. 2006, Special Advisor 2007–; mem. Bd of Dirs Walgreen Co. 1999–, Chair. (non-exec.) 2009–12, Lead Dir Jan.–Oct. 2008, Acting CEO Oct. 2008–Feb. 2009; fmr Chair. MasterCard International Inc., New York; fmr Rep. of Fed. Reserve Bank of Chicago on Fed. Advisory Council to Bd Govs of Fed. Reserve, Washington, DC; Sr Advisor, TeleTech North America 2003–06; mem. Bd Chicago Clearing House Asscn, Econ. Club of Chicago, Commercial Club of Chicago; fmr mem. Bd of Evanston Northwestern Healthcare, Advisory Bd Northwestern Univ.'s Kellogg Grad. School of Man., Civic Cttee and Dir Chicago Club, Bd of Govs York Univ.; fmr Campaign Chair. for the Chicago United Way; fmr Dir Chicago Youth Centers, Kids' Help Phone, Canadian Council for Aboriginal Business; fmr Treas. Commercial Club of Chicago, Queen Elizabeth Hosp. Foundation; fmr Trustee, DePaul Univ., Kenyon Coll., Ohio; Hon. LLD (York Univ., Toronto); Daniel H. Burnham Award for outstanding efforts and involvement in Chicago's business, cultural, educational and philanthropic communities, Americanism Award, Anti-Defamation League, Community Builder Award, Christian Industrial League, Prime Movers Award honouring individuals and orgs that have created opportunities for minority and women-owned businesses in Chicago, Outstanding Exec. Leadership Award, York's Schulich School of Business. *Address:* c/o Walgreen Co., 200 Wilmot Road, Deerfield, IL 60015, USA. *E-mail:* info@walgreens.com.

McNALLY, Derek, PhD; British astronomer (retd); b. 28 Oct. 1934, Belfast, Northern Ireland; s. of David McNally and Sarah McNally (née Long); m. Shirley Allen 1959; one s. one d.; ed Royal Belfast Acad. Inst., Queen's Univ., Belfast and Royal Holloway Coll., London; Sec. Royal Astronomical Soc. 1966–72, Vice-Pres. 1972–73, Treas. 1996–2001; Asst Dir Univ. of London Observatory 1966–88, Dir 1988–97; Sr Lecturer in Astronomy, Univ. Coll., London 1970–99; Asst Gen. Sec. of Exec. Cttee, Int. Astronomical Union 1985–88, Gen. Sec. 1988–91, Chair. Resolutions Cttee 1997–2000, Finance Sub-cttee 1988–91, 2000–03, Advisor of Sec. of Exec. 1991–94, mem. Div. VI Interstellar Matter –2012, Div. XII Union-Wide Activities –2012, Div. B Facilities, Technologies and Data Science, Div. C Educ., Outreach and Heritage, Div. H Interstellar Matter and Local Universe, Div. B Comm. 5 Documentation & Astronomical Data, Div. H Comm. 34 Interstellar Matter, Div. C Comm. 46 Astronomy Educ. & Devt, Div. B Comm. 50 Protection of Existing & Potential Observatory Sites; Chair. ICSU Working Group on Adverse Environmental Impacts on Astronomy 1993–96; mem. Bd of Dirs Int. Dark-Sky Asscn; Hon. Research Fellow, Univ. of Hertfordshire 1999–2003. *Publications:* Positional Astronomy 1974, The Vanishing Universe (ed.) 1994, New Trends in Astronomy Teaching (ed.) 1998; numerous articles in astronomical journals. *Leisure interests:* natural history, music, travel. *Address:* 17 Greenfield, Hatfield, Herts., AL9 5HW, England. *Telephone:* (1707) 267145. *E-mail:* d.mcnally@herts.ac .uk (office). *Website:* www.iau.org/administration/ membership/individual/2081.

McNAMARA, Michael (Mike) M., BS, MBA; American electronics industry executive; *CEO, Flextronics International Limited;* ed Univ. of Cincinnati, Santa Clara Univ.; Prin., Pittiglio, Rabin, Todd & McGrath (consulting firm) 1987–92; Vice-Pres., Mfg Operations, Anthem Electronics 1992–93; Pres. and CEO Relevant Industries 1993–94, Vice-Pres. N America Operations, Flextronics Int. Ltd (after Flextronic acquisition of Relevant Industries) 1994–97, Pres. N America Operations 1997–2001, COO, Singapore 2002–05, mem. Bd of Dirs 2005–, CEO 2006–. *Address:* Flextronics International Ltd, 2 Changi South Lane, 486123, Singapore (office). *Telephone:* 6299-8888 (office). *Fax:* 6543-1888 (office). *E-mail:* board@ flextronics.com (office). *Website:* www.flextronics.com (office).

MacNAUGHTON, Sir Malcolm Campbell, Kt, MD, LLD, FRCOG, FRCP, FRSE, FFFP; British fmr medical scientist and academic; *Professor Emeritus of Obstetrics and Gynaecology, University of Glasgow;* b. 4 April 1925, Glasgow; s. of James Hay MacNaughton and Mary Robieson Hogarth; m. Margaret-Ann Galt 1955; two s. three d.; ed Glasgow Acad. and Glasgow Univ.; Sr Lecturer, Obstetrics and Gynaecology, Dundee and St Andrews Univs 1961–70; Muirhead Prof. of Obstetrics and Gynaecology, Univ. of Glasgow 1970–90, Prof. Emer. 1990–; Pres. Royal Coll. of Obstetricians and Gynaecologists, London 1984–87; Chair. Working Party on Accident and Emergency Services in Scotland (Scotmeg); Vice-Pres. Royal Coll. of Midwives 1992–; mem. Academic Bd St George's Univ. Medical School,

Grenada, West Indies; Hon. Fellow, Sri Lanka Coll. of Obstetricians and Gynaecologists, Royal Australian Coll. of Obstetricians and Gynaecologists, American Coll. of Obstetricians and Gynaecologists, Royal Coll. of Anaesthetists. *Publications:* Combined Textbook of Obstetrics and Gynaecology 1976, The Ovary 1976, Medical Gynaecology 1985. *Leisure interests:* walking, fishing. *Address:* 9 Glenburn Road, Bearsden, Glasgow, G61 4PT, Scotland (home). *Telephone:* (141) 942-1909 (home). *Fax:* (141) 942-1909 (home). *E-mail:* macnaughtonmalcolm@ hotmail.com (home).

McNEALY, Scott Glenn, BA, MBA; American computer industry executive; *Chairman, Sun Microsystems, Inc.;* b. 13 Nov. 1954, Columbus, Ind.; s. of Raymond William McNealy and Marmaline McNealy; m. Susan McNealy (née Ingemanson) 1994; four s.; ed Harvard and Stanford Univs; sales engineer, Rockwell Int. Corpn, Troy, Mich. 1976–78; staff engineer, FMC Corpn, Chicago 1980–81; Dir Operations, Onyx Systems, San José, Calif. 1981–82; Co-founder Sun Microsystems Inc., Mountain View, Calif. 1982, Vice Pres. of Operations 1982–84, Pres. and COO 1984, Chair., Pres. and CEO 1984–99, Chair. and CEO 1999–2002, Chair., Pres., CEO 2002–04, Chair. and CEO 2004–06, Chair. 2006–, also currently Chair. Sun Federal, Inc. (subsidiary); Distinguished Fellowship Award, British Computer Soc. 2007. *Leisure interest:* ice hockey, golf. *Address:* Sun Microsystems Inc., 4150 Network Circle, Santa Clara, CA 95054, USA (office). *Telephone:* (650) 960-1300 (office). *Fax:* (408) 276-3804 (office). *Website:* www.sun.com (office).

McNEE, Sir David Blackstock, Kt, QPM, FBIM, FRSA; British fmr police officer; b. 23 March 1925, Glasgow, Scotland; s. of John McNee and Mary McNee (née Blackstock); m. 1st Isabella Clayton Hopkins 1952 (died 1997); one d.; m. 2nd Lillian Bissland Campbell Bogie 2002; ed Woodside Senior Secondary School, Glasgow; Deputy Chief Constable, Dunbartonshire Constabulary 1968–71; Chief Constable, City of Glasgow Police 1971–75; Chief Constable, Strathclyde Police 1975–77; Commr Metropolitan Police 1977–82; Dir Fleet Holdings 1983–86; Chair. (non-exec.) Scottish Express Newspapers 1983; Orr Pollock & Co. Ltd (Greenock Telegraph), Craig M. Jeffrey Ltd (Helensburgh Advertiser), Integrated Security Services Ltd; Adviser Bd British Airways 1982–87; Dir (non-exec.), Clydesdale Bank PLC; Pres. Royal Life Saving Soc. 1982–90, Nat. Bible Soc. of Scotland 1983–96, Glasgow City Cttee, Cancer Relief 1987–93; CBIM 1980; Freeman, City of London 1977; Hon. Col 32 (Scottish) Signal Regt (Volunteers) 1988–92; KStJ 1974, Commdr 1977. *Publication:* McNee's Law: The Memoirs of Sir David McNee 1983. *Leisure interests:* fishing, golf, music.

McNEE, John, BA, MA; Canadian diplomatist; *Secretary-General, Global Centre for Pluralism;* m. Susan McNee; two c.; ed York Univ., Univ. of Cambridge, UK; joined Dept of External Affairs 1978, positions in Embassies in Madrid, London, Tel-Aviv, Amb. to Syria 1993–97 (also accred to Lebanon 1993–95); positions with Policy Devt Secr., Canada–US Transboundary Div., Ottawa, fmr Dir Personnel Div., Dir Gen., Middle East, North Africa and Gulf States Bureau; fmr mem. Prime Minister Trudeau's Task Force on Int. Peace and Security, Privy Council Office; Asst Deputy Minister, Africa and Middle East, Foreign Affairs, Ottawa 2001; Amb. to Belgium (also accred to Luxembourg) 2004–06, Amb. and Perm. Rep. to UN, New York 2006–11; inaugural Sec.-Gen. Global Centre for Pluralism, Ottawa 2011–. *Address:* Global Centre for Pluralism, c/o Delegation of the Ismaili Imamat, 199 Sussex Drive, Ottawa, ON K1N 1K6, Canada (office). *Telephone:* (613) 241-2532 (office). *Fax:* (613) 241-2533 (office). *E-mail:* info@pluralism.ca (office). *Website:* www.pluralism.ca (office).

McNEIL, General Dan K., BS; American military officer; *Commanding General, International Security Assistance Force, Afghanistan;* ed North Carolina State Univ., US Army Command and Gen. Staff Coll., Fort Leavenworth, Kan.; began mil. career 1968, command positions have included E Company, 2nd Bn (Airborne), 505th Infantry, 82nd Airborne Div. 1977–78, 1st Bn, 325th Infantry, 82nd Airborne Div. 1986–88, 3rd Brigade, 82nd Airborne Div. 1991–93, Asst Div. Commdr, 2nd Infantry Div., Eighth US Army, Korea 1995–96, Deputy Commanding Gen., I Corps and Fort Lewis 1997–98, Commanding Gen., 82nd Airborne Div. 1998–2000, Commanding Gen., XVIII Airborne Corps and Fort Bragg 2000–03, including duty as Commanding Gen., Combined Jt Task Force-180, Afghanistan, Deputy Commanding Gen./Chief of Staff, US Army Forces Command 2003–07, Commanding Gen., Int. Security Assistance Force, Afghanistan 2007–; Defense Distinguished Service Medal, Defense Superior Service Medal, Legion of Merit, Bronze Star Medal, Expert Infantryman Badge, Master Parachutist Badge (with Bronze Service Star), Army Aviator Badge, Special Forces Tab. *Address:* International Security Assistance Force, Afghanistan, NATO Headquarters, Blvd Leopold III, Brussels 1110, Belgium (office); c/o United States Army Forces Command, 1777 Hardee Avenue, Southwest, Fort McPherson, GA 30330-1062, USA (office). *E-mail:* moc.web@hq.nato.int (office).

MacNEILL, Brian F., BCom, CPA, CM; Canadian accountant and business executive; *Chairman, Petro Canada;* b. 1939, Calgary; m.; four c.; ed Montana State Univ.; began career as accounts clerk at oil and gas co., Calgary 1960; Accountant, Haskins & Sells, San Francisco 1967; Vice-Pres. and Treas. Hiram Walker Resources Ltd 1980–82; fmr Exec. Vice-Pres. and COO Enbridge Inc., becoming CEO 1990–2001; mem. Bd of Dirs Petro-Canada 1995–, currently Chair.; mem. Bd of Dirs Toronto Dominion Bank, Telus Corpn, West-Fraser Timber Co. Ltd; fmr mem. Bd of Dirs Dofasco Inc., Veritas DGC Inc., Legacy Hotels REIT, Sears Canada Inc., Western Oil Sands Inc.; Chair. Bd of Govs Univ. of Calgary; fmr Chair. United Way of Calgary; mem. Canadian Inst. of Chartered Accountants, Financial Execs Inst.; Fellow, Alberta Inst. of Chartered Accountants, Inst of Corp. Dirs. *Address:* Petro-Canada, 150 6th Avenue, SW, Calgary, Alberta, T2P 3E3, Canada (office). *Telephone:* (403) 296-8000 (office). *Fax:* (403) 296-3030 (office). *E-mail:* info@petro-canada.ca (office). *Website:* www.petro-canada.ca (office).

McNEISH, Sir James Henry Peter, Kt, KNZM, BA; New Zealand writer; b. 23 Oct. 1931, Auckland; s. of Arthur McNeish and Ina McNeish (née Bosworth); m. 1st Felicity Wily; one d.; m. 2nd Helen Schnitzer; one step-s.; ed Univ. of Auckland; Journalist, NZ Herald, Auckland, 1953–57; Theatre Workshop, Stratford East and teaching, London 1958–59; writer and documentary maker, BBC Home Service and Third Programme 1960–67; Katherine Mansfield Fellow, Menton, France 1973; Co-founder and Dir (with Helen McNeish) Bridge in NZ (educational trust) 1974–82; author, penal report for Justice Dept 1976; Visiting Writer, Berlin DAAD Kunstler-program 1983; Research Fellow, Nat. Library of NZ 1999; Berlin residency, Creative NZ 2009; Pres. of Honour, NZ Soc. of Authors 2012–13; Prime Minister's Award for Literary Achievement in Non-Fiction 2010. *Plays:* The Rocking Cave 1973, The Mouse Man 1975, Eighteen-Ninety-Five 1975, Thursday Bloody Thursday 1998. *Publications include:* Tavern in the Town 1957, Fire Under the Ashes: A Life of Danilo Dolci 1965, Mackenzie 1970, The Mackenzie Affair 1972, The Rocking Cave 1973, Larks in a Paradise (co-author) 1974, The Glass Zoo 1976, As for the Godwits 1977, Art of the Pacific (with Brian Brake) 1980, Belonging: Conversations in Israel 1980, Joy 1982, Walking on My Feet: Portrait of A.R.D. Fairburn 1983, Ahnungslos in Berlin: A Berlin Diary 1985, Lovelock 1986 (enlarged edn 2009), Penelope's Island 1990, The Man from Nowhere and Other Prose 1991, My Name is Paradiso 1995, Mr Halliday and the Circus Master 1996, The Mask of Sanity: The Bain Murders 1997, An Albatross Too Many 1998, Dance of the Peacocks: New Zealanders in Exile in the Time of Hitler and Mao Tse-tung 2003, The Sixth Man: The Extraordinary Life of Paddy Costello 2007, The Crime of Huey Dunstan 2010, Touchstones: A Memoir 2012. *Address:* c/o Andrew Hewson, Johnson & Alcock Ltd, Clerkenwell House, 45 Clerkenwell Green, London, EC1R 0HT, England (office); Michael Gifkins, PO Box 6496, Auckland 1, New Zealand (office). *Telephone:* (20) 7251-0125 (office); (9) 523-5032 (office). *E-mail:* andrew@johnsonandalcock.co.uk (office); michael.gifkins@xtra.co.nz (office). *Fax:* (9) 523-5033 (office).

McNERNEY, W. James (Jim), Jr, BA, MBA; American business executive; *Chairman, President and CEO, The Boeing Company;* b. 22 Aug. 1949, Providence, RI; m.; five c.; ed Yale and Harvard Univs; began career in brand man., Procter & Gamble; Sr Man. McKinsey & Co. –1982; Gen. Man. General Electric (GE) Mobile Communications 1982–86, Pres. GE Information Services 1988–89, Exec. Vice-Pres. GE Financial Services and GE Capital 1989–91, Pres. and CEO GE Electrical Distribution and Control 1991–92, Pres. GE Asia-Pacific, Hong Kong 1993–95, Pres. and CEO GE Lighting 1995–97, Pres. and CEO GE Aircraft Engines 1997–2000, Chair. and CEO 3M 2000–05; Chair., Pres. and CEO Boeing Co. 2005–, mem. Special Programs Cttee; mem. Bd Dirs Procter & Gamble, IBM; mem. The Field Museum Bd of Trustees, Chicago; Trustee, Northwestern Univ.; mem. Northwestern Memorial HealthCare Bd; mem. Exec. Cttee The Business Round-table; fmr Chair. The Business Council, US-China Business Council, American Soc. of Corp. Execs; Fellow, American Acad. of Arts and Sciences; Hon. FRAeS; Hon. DSc (Cranfield Univ., UK) 2009; Exec. of the Year, Nat. Man. Asscn 2008, John W. Dixon Award, Asscn of the US Army 2011, Semper Fidelis Award, Marine Corps Scholarship Foundation 2012, inaugural Turning Point Award, US Army War Coll. Foundation 2012. *Leisure interests:* skiing, golf, hiking, hockey. *Address:* The Boeing Co., 100 North Riverside Plaza, Chicago, IL 60606-1596, Cttee (office). *Telephone:* (312) 544-2000 (office). *Fax:* (312) 544-2082 (office). *E-mail:* info@boeing.com (office). *Website:* www.boeing.com (office).

McNICOL, Donald, PhD; Australian psychologist, academic and fmr university vice-chancellor; b. 18 April 1939, Adelaide, S Australia; s. of Ian Robertson McNicol and Sadie Isabelle Williams; m. Kathleen Margaret Wells 1963; one s. two d.; ed Unley High School, Univ. of Adelaide, Cambridge Univ.; Lecturer in Psychology, Univ. of Adelaide 1967–71; Sr Lecturer in Psychology, Univ. of NSW 1971–74, Assoc. Prof. 1975–81; Prof. of Psychology, Univ. of Tasmania 1981–86; Commr for Univs and Chair. Univs Advisory Council of Commonwealth Tertiary Educ. Comm. 1986–88; Vice-Chancellor Univ. of New England 1988–90, Univ. of Sydney 1990–96, Univ. of Tasmania 1996–2003; Deputy Pres. Australian Vice-Chancellors' Cttee 1993–94, Pres. 1994–96; Pres. Asscn of Univs of S Asia and the Pacific (AUAP) 1998–99; Pres. Australian Higher Educ. Industrial Asscn 2000–01; Fellow, Australian Psychological Soc. *Publication includes:* A Primer of Signal Detection Theory 1972, 2005. *Leisure interests:* walking, music, reading. *Address:* PO Box 1155, Sandy Bay, Tasmania 7006, Australia (home). *E-mail:* don.mcnicol@mcnicol.info (home).

McPEAK, Gen. Merrill Anthony, BA, MS; American air force officer (retd), investor and company director; *Chairman, American Battle Monuments Commission;* b. 9 Jan. 1936, Santa Rosa, Calif.; s. of Merrill Addison McPeak and Winifred Alice McPeak Bendall (née Stewart); m. Elynor Fay Moskowitz 1956; two s.; ed San Diego State Coll., Calif., George Washington Univ., Washington, DC; commissioned officer, USAF 1957, progressed through ranks to Gen. 1988; C-in-C Pacific Air Forces, Hickam, HI 1988–90; Chief of Staff USAF 1990–94; Chair. ECC Int. Corpn 1997–2002, Ethicspoint, Inc. 2003–12, Coast Plating, Inc. 2012–13; Chair. American Battle Monuments Comm.; DSM, Silver Star, Legion of Merit, DFC (two awards), Air Medal (13 awards); Thomas White Space Award, Oregon Aviation Hall of Honor, San Diego State Univ. Lifetime Achievement Award, George Washington Univ. 'George'. *Publications:* Hangar Flying 2012, Below the Zone 2013; op-eds in New York Times, Washington Post, Wall Street Journal. *Address:* 123 Furnace Street, Lake Oswego, OR 97034, USA (office). *Telephone:* (503) 699-2931 (office). *E-mail:* mamcpeak@comcast.net (office). *Website:* generalmcpeak.com.

McPHEE, John Angus, AB; American writer and academic; *Ferris Professor of Journalism, Princeton University;* b. 8 March 1931, Princeton, NJ; m. 1st Pryde Brown 1957; four d.; m. 2nd Yolanda Whitman 1972; two step-s. two step-d.; ed Princeton Univ., Univ. of Cambridge; dramatist, Robert Montgomery Presents television programme 1955–57; Assoc. Ed., Time magazine, New York 1957–64; staff writer, The New Yorker magazine 1965–; Ferris Prof. of Journalism, Princeton Univ. 1975–; Fellow, Geological Soc. of America; mem. American Acad. of Arts and Letters; various hon. doctorates; American Acad. and Inst. of Arts and Letters Award 1977, Princeton Univ. Woodrow Wilson Award 1982, American Asscn of Petroleum Geologists Journalism Award 1982, 1986, United States Geological Survey John Wesley Powell Award 1988, American Geophysical Union Walter Sullivan Award 1993, Pulitzer Prize for Non-Fiction 1999, Geological Soc. of America Public Service Award 2002, Acad. of Natural Sciences Gold Medal for Distinction in Natural History Art 2005, George Polk Career Award 2008. *Publications:* A Sense of Where You Are 1965, The Headmaster 1966, Oranges 1967, The Pine Barrens 1968, A Roomful of Hovings 1969, The Crofter and the Laird 1969, Levels of the Game 1970, Encounters with the Archdruid 1972, Wimbledon: A Celebration 1972, The Deltoid Pumpkin Seed 1973, The Curve of Binding Energy 1974, Pieces of the Frame 1975, The Survival of the Bark Canoe 1975, The John McPhee Reader 1977, Coming into the Country 1977, Giving Good Weight 1979, Alaska: Images of the Country (with Galen Rowell) 1981, Basin and

Range 1981, In Suspect Terrain 1983, La Place de la Concorde Suisse 1984, Table of Contents 1985, Rising from the Plains 1986, Outcroppings 1988, The Control of Nature 1989, Looking for a Ship 1990, Assembling California 1993, The Ransom of Russian Art 1994, The Second John McPhee Reader 1996, Irons in the Fire 1997, Annals of the Former World 1998, The Founding Fish 2002, Uncommon Carriers 2006, Silk Parachute 2010. *Address:* Joseph Henry House, Princeton University, Princeton, NJ 08544 (office); 475 Drake's Corner Road, Princeton, NJ 08540, USA (home).

McPHEE, Jonathan, LRAM, BM, MM; American music director and conductor; *Music Director and Principal Conductor, Boston Ballet;* b. Philadelphia, Pa; ed Royal Acad. of Music, London and Juilliard School of Music, New York, studied with Leonard Brain, David Diamond, Thomas Stacy, Rudolf Kempe, Sixten Ehrling, and participated in masterclasses with Sir Georg Solti and James Levine; affiliate, Martha Graham Dance Co., New York 1979–89, Joffrey Ballet, Chicago 1980–86, Dance Theater of Harlem 1980–86; now Music Dir and Prin. Conductor Boston Ballet; Music Dir Longwood Symphony Orchestra 2005–11, Lexington Symphony, Symphony New Hampshire; has conducted for numerous dance cos, including American Ballet Theater and New York City Ballet, Royal Ballet (UK), Martha Graham Dance Company, The Joffrey Ballet, Nat. Ballet of Canada, Australian Ballet, Den Norske Ballet (Norway), Royal Danish Ballet; has conducted Royal Philharmonic Orchestra, London, Nat. Arts Centre Orchestra, Ottawa, in guest engagements with Boston Ballet and Houston Ballet, Hamburg Philharmonic, Orquesta Sinfonica de Tenerife, Lithuanian Nat. Orchestra; invited to conduct Nashville Symphony as one of the conductors featured in Bruno Walter National Conductor Preview by the League of American Orchestras 2009; has also conducted dance music, musical theatre, operetta and grand opera (with Opera Boston, American Opera Center, New York, Boston Univ. Opera Inst.); works as arranger and composer are part of repertoires of orchestras and ballet companies world-wide, his edn of Stravinsky's Rite of Spring is the only reduced orchestration of this work authorized by the Stravinsky Trust; Naumburg Scholarship in Conducting and English Horn, Juilliard School of Music, Met-Life Award for Community Engagement, League of American Orchestras 2007, Commonwealth Award, State of Mass 2011. *Orchestral compositions:* Overture, Summer Day 1988, Trinity 1990, The Seduction 1992, Nightingale 1996, The Dream Whisperer 1997, Re:Marks 1998, Fantasy for two pianos and orchestra 2001, Images 2004. *Radio:* Kids Classical Hour (WCRB radio station) (Gabriel Award 1998). *Recordings include:* The Nutcracker, The Sleeping Beauty, Romeo & Juliet (all three with Boston Ballet Orchestra), Holiday in Boston, Michael Gandolfi's Caution to the Wind; conducted Danish Radio Symphony Orchestra and Aarhus Orchestra for the films of Martha Graham's works telecast by Dance In America that included Samuel Barber's Cave of the Heart, Gian Carlo Menotti's Errand into the Maze, and Edgard Varese' Integrales, Offrandes, and Octandre 2006. *Publications:* arrangements and compositions, including the reduced orchestration of Stravinsky's Rite of Spring and the complete Firebird. *Leisure interests:* skiing, scuba diving. *Address:* Boston Ballet, 19 Clarendon Street, Boston, MA 02116-6100, USA (office). *Telephone:* (617) 695-6950 (office). *E-mail:* jmcphee@bostonballet.org (office). *Website:* www.bostonballet.org (office); jonathanmcphee.com.

MacPHERSON, Elle; Australian model, actress and business executive; b. (Eleanor Nancy Gow), 29 March 1963, Cronulla, New South Wales; d. of Peter Gow and Frances Macpherson; m. 1st Gilles Bensimon 1986 (divorced 1989); two s. by Arpad Busson; m. 2nd Jeffrey Soffer 2013; Founder and Chief Exec. Elle Macpherson Inc.; f. Elle Macpherson sportswear, Elle Macpherson Intimates, The Body (beauty product line); Co-owner Fashion Cafe, New York; appeared in Sports Illustrated Swimsuit magazine edition 1986, 1987, 1988, 1989, 1990, 1991, 1992, 1993, 1994, 2004, 2006. *Films include:* Alice 1990, Sirens 1994, Jane Eyre 1996, If Lucy Fell 1996, The Mirror Has Two Faces 1996, Batman and Robin 1997, The Edge 1997, Beautopia 1998, With Friends Like These 1998, South Kensington 2001; video: Stretch and Strengthen, The Body Workout 1995. *Television includes:* H3O (series) 1995, Friends 1999–2000, 2004, A Girl Thing (mini-series) 2001, The Beautiful Life: TBL (series) 2009. *Address:* Artist Management, Penn House, B414 East 52nd Street, New York, NY 10022, USA (office). *Website:* www.ellemacpherson.com (office).

McPHERSON, James Munro, PhD; American historian, academic and writer; *George Henry Davis '86 Professor Emeritus of History, Princeton University;* b. 11 Oct. 1936, Valley City, ND; s. of James M. McPherson and Miriam O. McPherson; m. Patricia Rasche 1957; one d.; ed Gustavus Adolphus Coll. and Johns Hopkins Univ.; Instructor Princeton Univ. 1962–65, Asst Prof. 1965–66, Assoc. Prof. 1966–72, Prof. of History 1972–82, Edwards Prof. of American History 1982–91, George Henry Davis '86 Prof. of American History 1991, now Prof. Emer.; Pres. Soc. of American Historians 2000–01; Woodrow Wilson Fellow and Danforth Fellow 1958–62; Guggenheim Fellow 1967–68; Huntingdon Library-Nat. Endowment for the Humanities Fellowship 1977–78; Center for Advanced Study in the Behavioural Sciences Fellowship 1982–83; Huntington Seaver Fellow 1987–88; Pres. American Historical Asscn 2003; mem. American Philosophical Soc. 1991; Fellow, American Acad. of Arts and Sciences 2009; 10 hon. degrees from American colls and univs; Anisfield-Wolf Prize in Race Relations 1965, Pulitzer Prize in History 1989, Christopher Award 1989, Best Book Award, American Military Inst. 1989, Lincoln Prize 1998, Theodore and Franklin D. Roosevelt Prize in Naval History 1998, Jefferson Lecturer 2000, Pritzker Mil. Library Literature Award for lifetime achievement in mil. writing 2007, Lincoln Prize 2009. *Publications:* The Struggle for Equality: Abolitionists and the Negro in the Civil War and Reconstruction 1964, The Negro's Civil War 1965, Marching Toward Freedom 1968, The Anti-Slavery Crusade in America (co-ed, 59 vols) 1969, Blacks in America (essays) 1971, The Abolitionist Legacy 1975, Ordeal by Fire: The Civil War and Reconstruction 1982, Religion, Race and Reconstruction (essays, co-ed) 1982, Battle Cry of Freedom: The Civil War Era 1988, Battle Chronicles of the Civil War (ed, six vols) 1989, Abraham Lincoln and the Second American Revolution 1991, Images of the Civil War 1992, Gettysburg 1993, What They Fought For 1861–1865 1994, The Atlas of the Civil War 1994, Drawn With the Sword: Reflections on the American Civil War 1996, The American Heritage New History of the Civil War (ed) 1996, For Cause and Comrades: Why Men Fought in the Civil War 1997, Lamson of the Gettysburg: The Civil War Letters of Lt Roswell H. Lamson, US Navy 1997, Is Blood Thicker Than Water? Crises of Nationalism in the Modern World 1998, The Encyclopedia of Civil War Biographies (ed, three vols)

1999, To the Best of My Ability: The American Presidents (ed) 2000, Crossroads of Freedom: Antietam, The Battle That Changed the Course of the Civil War 2002, Hallowed Ground: A Walk at Gettysburg 2003, The Illustrated Battle Cry of Freedom 2003, Into the West (juvenile) 2006, Tried by War: Abraham Lincoln as Commander in Chief (Lincoln Prize, Gettysburg Coll. 2009) 2008, This Mighty Scourge: Perspectives on the Civil War 2009, Abraham Lincoln 2009; contrib. to reference works, scholarly books and professional journals. *Leisure interests:* tennis, bicycling, sailing. *Address:* c/o 41 William Street, Princeton, NJ 08540, USA (office); Department of History, 130 Dickinson Hall, Princeton University, Princeton, NJ 08544 (office); 15 Randall Road, Princeton, NJ 08540, USA (home). *Telephone:* (609) 258-4173 (office); (609) 924-9226 (home). *Fax:* (609) 258-5326 (office). *E-mail:* jmcphers@princeton.edu (office). *Website:* his.princeton.edu (office).

McPHERSON, M(elville) Peter, BA, MBA, JD; American lawyer, academic administrator and fmr government official; *President, Association of Public and Land-grant Universities;* b. 27 Oct. 1940, Lowell, Mich.; s. of Donald McPherson and Ellura E. McPherson (née Frost); m. Joanne Paddock 1989; four c.; ed Western Michigan Univ.; Peace Corps volunteer, Peru 1964–65; with Internal Revenue Service, Washington, DC 1969–75; Special Asst to the Pres. and Deputy Dir Presidential Personnel, White House, Washington, DC 1975–77; Partner Vorys, Sater, Seymour & Pease, Washington, DC 1977–80; Acting Counsel to the Pres., White House 1980–81; Admin. Agency for Int. Devt, Washington, DC 1981–87; Deputy Sec., Dept of Treasury 1987–89; Group Exec. Vice-Pres., Bank of America 1989–93; Pres. Michigan State Univ. 1993–2004, Pres. Emer. 2004–; Financial Co-ordinator, Office of Reconstruction and Humanitarian Assistance, Iraq 2003; Founding Co-Chair. Partnership to Cut Hunger and Poverty in Africa 2005–, now Chair.; Pres. Nat. Assocn of State Univs and Land-Grant Colls (now the Assocn of Public and Land-grant Univs) 2006–; Ind. Dir, Dow Jones & Co. 1998–, Chair. 2007; mem. Bd for Int. Food and Agric. Devt 1977–80; mem. Michigan Bar Assocn, DC Bar Assocn; UNICEF Award for "outstanding contribution to child survival", Humanitarian of the Year Award, American Lebanese League 1983, Jewish Nat. Fund Tree of Life Award 1998, Alexander Hamilton Award, Dept of Treasury, US Presidential Certificate of Outstanding Achievement, Secretary of State's Distinguished Service Award 2004. *Address:* Association of Public and Land-grant Universities, 1307 New York Avenue NW, Suite 400, Washington, DC, 20005-4722 (office); Partnership to Cut Hunger and Poverty in Africa, 499 South Capitol Street SW, Suite 500B, Washington, DC 20003, USA. *Telephone:* (202) 478-6060 (office). *Fax:* (202) 478-6046 (office). *E-mail:* pmcpherson@aplu.org (office). *Website:* www.aplu.org (office); www.partnership-africa.org.

McQUEEN, Steve Rodney, CBE; British artist, film director and producer; b. 9 Oct. 1969, London, England; ed Drayton Manor High School, Chelsea School of Art, Goldsmith's Coll., Tisch School of the Arts, New York Univ.; has exhibited widely in Europe and USA; major solo exhbn Inst. of Contemporary Art (ICA), London; works primarily in corp. film, photography and sculpture, apptd Official War Artist in response to the Iraq conflict, Imperial War Museum, London 2003; represented GB at Venice Biennale 2009; lives and works in London and Amsterdam; ICA Futures Award 1996, DAAD artist's scholarship 1998, Turner Prize 1999, London Critics Circle Film Award for Breakthrough British Filmmaker 2008, BAFTA Carl Foreman Award for Most Promising Newcomer 2009. *Films include:* Bear (silent) 1993, Deadpan (silent) 1997, Drumroll (short) 1998, Prey (short) 1999, Cold Breath (short) 2000, Illuminer (short) 2001, Girls, Tricky (short) 2001, 7th Nov. (short) 2001, Western Deep (short) 2002, Carib's Leap (short) 2002, Charlotte (short) 2004, Pursuit (short) 2005, Unexploded (short) 2007, Running Thunder (short) 2007, Gravesend (short) 2007, Hunger (writer and dir) (Caméra d'Or (first-time dir) Award, Cannes 2008, inaugural Sydney Film Festival Prize 2008, Diesel Discovery Award, Toronto Int. Film Festival 2008, Los Angeles Film Critics Assocn Award for a New Generation Film 2008, BAFTA Carl Foreman Award for Special Achievement by a British Dir 2009, Best Film Prize, London Evening Standard Film Awards 2009) 2008, Rayners Lane (short) 2008, Static (short) 2009, Giardini (short) 2009, Shame (writer and dir) 2011, 12 Years a Slave (writer and dir) (People's Choice Award, Toronto Int. Film Festival 2013, BAFTA Award for Best Picture, Golden Globe Award for Best Motion Picture, Drama, Academy Award for Best Picture 2014) 2013. *Address:* c/o Casarotto Marsh Ltd, Waverley House, 7–12 Noel Street, London, W1F 8GQ, England (office); c/o Thomas Dane Associates, First Floor, 11 Duke Street, St James's, London, SW1Y 6BN, England; c/o Marian Goodman Gallery, 24 West 57th Street, New York, NY 10019, USA. *E-mail:* jenne@casarotto.co.uk (office).

MACRI, Mauricio; Argentine politician; *Mayor of Buenos Aires;* b. 8 Feb. 1959, Tandil, Buenos Aires; divorced; three c.; ed Catholic Univ. of Argentina, Universidad del CEMA, Columbia Business School, Wharton Business School, USA; joined family business 1985 and served in various man. positions in cos including Sideco, SOCMA and Sevel; Pres. Boca Juniors football club 1995–; defeated in second round of election for Head of Govt of the Autonomous City of Buenos Aires 2003; serves as deputy representing city of Buenos Aires in Lower House of Congress 2005–; with Ricardo López Murphy created Propuesta Republicana (PRO) electoral front 2005–; Mayor of the Autonomous City of Buenos Aires 2007–; mem. Compromiso para el Cambio (Commitment to Change). *Address:* Compromiso para el Cambio, Edif. Anexo de la Cámara de Diputados, Riobamba 25, C 1025 ABA, Buenos Aires, Argentina (office). *Telephone:* (11) 6310-7710 (office). *E-mail:* ccambio@hcdn.gov.ar (office). *Website:* cpcambio.org.ar (office); www.ciudadpro.com; www.buenosaires.gov.ar.

McROBBIE, Michael A., BSc, MSc; Australian computer scientist, academic and university administrator; *President, Indiana University;* b. 11 Oct. 1950; m. Laurie Burns; three c., three step-c.; ed Univ. of Queensland, Australian Nat. Univ.; Prof. of Information Tech., Inst. of Advanced Study, ANU, also CEO Co-operative Research Centre for Advanced Computational Systems; Vice-Pres. for Information Tech., Indiana Univ., Bloomington, USA 1997–2006, also Vice-Pres. for Research 2003–06, Interim Provost and Vice-Pres. for Academic Affairs 2006–07, Pres. 2007–; Hon. mem. Alliance of Distinguished and Titled Profs; Dr hc (Queensland) 2007. *Publications:* several books, papers, and technical reports. *Leisure interests:* travel, reading, collecting art, theatre, opera. *Address:* Office of the President, Indiana University, Bryan Hall 200, 107 South Indiana Avenue, Bloomington, IN

47405, USA (office). *Telephone:* (812) 855-4613 (office). *E-mail:* iupres@indiana.edu (office). *Website:* www.indiana.edu/~pres (office).

MacSHANE, Denis, MA, PhD; British politician; b. 21 May 1948; s. of the late Jan Matyjaszec and of Isobel MacShane; m. Nathalie Pham 1987; one s. four d.; ed Merton Coll., Oxford, Birkbeck Coll., London; reporter, BBC 1969–77; Pres. Nat. Union of Journalists 1978–79; Policy Dir Int. Metalworkers Fed. 1980–92; Dir European Policy Inst. 1992–94; MP for Rotherham (Labour Party) 1994–; Parl. Pvt. Sec. to Ministers of Foreign Affairs 1997–2001; Parl. Under-Sec. of State, FCO 2001–02; Minister of State for Europe 2002–05; Visiting Fellow St Antony's Coll., Oxford 1998–99; mem. Council Royal Inst. of Int. Affairs 1999–, Council of Europe Parl. Ass. 2005–, NATO Parl. Ass. 2005–. *Publications include:* Solidarity: Poland's Independent Trade Union 1981, François Mitterrand: A Political Odyssey 1982, Black Workers, Unions and the Struggle for Democracy in South Africa 1984, International Labour and the Origins of the Cold War 1992, Britain's Steel Industry in the 21st Century 1996, Globalising Hatred: The New Anti-Semitism 2008. *Address:* House of Commons, London, SW1A 0AA, England (office). *E-mail:* macshaned@parliament.uk (office).

McSHARRY, Deirdre Mary; Irish journalist, editor and curator; b. 4 April 1932, London, England; d. of the late Dr John McSharry and Mary O'Brien; m. Ian Coulter Smyth; ed Dominican Convent, Wicklow, Trinity Coll., Dublin Univ.; actress at Gate Theatre, Dublin 1953–55; freelance with The Irish Times 1953; mem. staff Evening Herald, Dublin 1955–56; with bookshop Metropolitan Museum of Art, New York 1956; Reporter Women's Wear Daily, New York 1956–58; mem. staff Woman's Own 1959–62; Fashion Ed. Evening News 1962; Woman's Ed. Daily Express 1963–66; Fashion Ed. The Sun 1967–71; Fashion Ed. Cosmopolitan 1972, Ed. 1973–85; Ed.-in-Chief Country Living 1986–89; Consultant Nat. Magazine Co. and Magazine Div. The Hearst Corpn 1990–92; Ed. Countryside magazine, New York 1991–92; Chair. Bath Friends of The American Museum in Britain, Bath; mem. Council of the American Museum, Council of the Bath Festivals Trust 2002, The Costume Soc.; Trustee, The American Museum (in Britain) 2002–04; Ed. of the Year (Periodical Publrs Assocn) 1981, 1987, Mark Boxer Award: Editor's Ed. 1991. *Publication:* Inspirations: The Textile Tradition Then and Now (American Museum Catalogue) 2001. *Leisure interests:* architecture, textiles, decorative arts, literature. *Address:* Southfield House, 16 High Street, Rode, BA11 6NZ, England (home). *Telephone:* (1373) 831263 (home). *Fax:* (1373) 831263 (home). *E-mail:* Deirdre@DeirdreMcSharry.co.uk. *Website:* www.deirdremcsharry.co.uk.

MacSHARRY, Ray; Irish politician; b. 29 April 1938, Sligo; s. of Patrick McSharry and Annie Clarke; m. Elaine Neilan 1960; three s. three d.; ed Summerhill Coll., Sligo; fmr haulier, auctioneer, farm-owner; joined Sligo Jr Chamber of Commerce 1966 (past Pres.); mem. Sligo County Council, Sligo Borough Council and Sligo Town Vocational Educ. Cttee 1967–78; mem. Dáil 1969–89; Minister of State, Dept of Finance and Public Service 1977–79; Minister for Agriculture 1979–81; Tanaiste and Minister for Finance March–Nov. 1982; MEP for Connaught/Ulster 1984–87; Minister for Finance 1987–88; EC Commr with responsibility for Agric. and Rural Devt 1989–93; pvt. business 1993–; Chair. London City Airport, Irish Equine Centre 1995; Dir Ryanair, Bank of Ireland Group 1993–2005; Gov. E.I.B. 1982; Fianna Fáil; Freeman Borough of Sligo 1993; Grand-Croix, Order of Leopold II 1993; Hon. DEconSci (Limerick) 1994; Hon. LLD (Nat. Univ. of Ireland) 1994; Business and Finance Man. of the Year 1988, Marcora Prize, Italy 1991, European of the Year 1992. *Leisure interest:* sport. *Address:* Alcantara, Pearse Road, Sligo, Ireland. *Telephone:* (71) 69902. *Fax:* (71) 69902.

McSWEENEY, Barry, BSc, MSc; Irish biochemist; *Coordinator, National Knowledge Society Strategy, Department of Communications, Marine and Natural Resources;* b. Cork; ed Univ. Coll., Cork, Trinity Coll., Dublin; fmr Man. of European Product Devt, American Hosps Supply Corpn, Switzerland and Belgium; Dir of Medical Business, Biocon Biochemicals Ltd, Cork and Sees, France –1987; Founding Dir BioResearch Ireland 1987–95; Head of Unit, Research DG, EC, Brussels 1995–2000, Dir Inst. for Health and Consumer Protection, Jt Research Centre (JRC), Ispra, Italy 2000–01, Dir-Gen. JRC 2001–04; Chief Science Adviser to Irish Govt 2004–05; Research Coordinator, Dept of Communications, Marine and Natural Resources, currently Dir Nat. Knowledge Society Strategy; Chair. OECD Working Party on Biotechnology 1994–95, Sr Industry Advisory Group on Biotechnology (SAGB), Nat. Maritime Policy High Level Implementation Group, Exemplar Smart Communications Network Task Force; Co-Chair. World Tech. Forum 1990; mem. Advisory Cttee on Biotechnology, Science Foundation Ireland 2000; Irish Del. to i2010 (EU); Great Gold Medal, Cornelius Univ., Bratislava 2003, Alumni Achievement Award, Univ. Coll. Cork 2004. *Leisure interest:* horse-racing. *Address:* Department of Communications, Marine and Natural Resources, 29–31 Adelaide Road, Dublin 2, Ireland (office). *Telephone:* (1) 6782075 (office). *Fax:* (1) 6782449 (office). *E-mail:* barry.mcsweeney@dcmnr.gov.ie (office). *Website:* www.dcmnr.gov.ie (office).

McTIERNAN, John; American film director; b. 8 Jan. 1951, Albany, NY; m. 2nd Donna Dubrow 1988 (divorced 1997); m. 3rd Kate Harrington 2003; ed Juilliard School of Drama, State Univ. of New York, Old Westbury Filmmaking Coll.; pleaded guilty to making false statements to FBI during investigations into pvt. detective Anthony Pellicano in 2010, fined $100,000 and sentenced to one year in prison. *Films include:* Nomads (also screenplay) 1986, Predator 1987, Die Hard 1988, The Hunt for Red October 1990, Medicine Man 1992, Last Action Hero (also exec. producer) 1993, Die Hard: With a Vengeance (also producer) 1995, Amanda (1996) (producer) 1996, The 13th Warrior (also producer) 1999, The Thomas Crown Affair 1999, Rollerball (also producer) 2002, Basic 2003. *Television includes:* Robin Hood (exec. producer) 1991, The Right to Remain Silent (producer) 1996, Quicksilver Highway (exec. producer) 1997.

McVEIGH, Elliot R., BS, PhD; Canadian medical scientist and academic; *Massey Professor and Director, Department of Biomedical Engineering, School of Medicine, Johns Hopkins University;* ed Univ. of Toronto; joined Faculty of Radiology, Johns Hopkins Univ. School of Medicine 1988, Founder and Dir Medical Imaging Lab., Dept of Biomedical Eng 1991, Massey Prof. and Dir Dept of Biomedical Eng 2007–; apptd Sr Investigator, Lab. of Cardiac Energetics, NIH, Bethesda, Md 1999, later Prin. Investigator; Whitaker Development Award 1991. *Publications:* more than 150 peer-reviewed research papers in professional journals on cardiovascular MRI, image guided therapy and novel MRI methods. *Address:* Medical Imaging

Laboratory, Whitaker Biomedical Engineering Institute, Johns Hopkins University School of Medicine, 720 Rutland Avenue, Ross 720, Baltimore, MD 21205, USA (office). *Telephone:* (410) 502-7145 (office). *Fax:* (410) 502-9814 (office). *E-mail:* emcveigh@bme.jhu.edu (office). *Website:* www.bme.jhu.edu (office).

McVIE, John Gordon, BSc, MB, ChB, MD, PhD, DSc, FRCP, FRCPS, FRCPE, FRCSE, FMedSci; British doctor and cancer specialist; *Senior Consultant, Istituto Europea Oncologica, Milan;* b. 13 Jan. 1945, Glasgow, Scotland; s. of John McVie and Lindsaye Mair; m. 1st Evelyn Strang 1966 (divorced 1996); three s.; m. 2nd Claudia Joan Burke; one step-s. one step-d.; ed Royal High School, Edin. and Univ. of Edinburgh; House Officer, Royal Hosp. for Sick Children and Royal Infirmary, Edinburgh 1969–70; MRC Fellow, Univ. of Edinburgh 1970–71, Lecturer in Therapeutics 1971–76; Sr Lecturer in Clinical Oncology, Univ. of Glasgow 1976–80; Head, Clinical Research Unit, Netherlands Cancer Inst. Amsterdam 1980–84, Clinical Research Dir 1984–89; Scientific Dir, Cancer Research Campaign 1989–96; Dir Gen. Cancer Research UK 1996–2002; Sr Consultant, Istituto Europea Oncologica, Milan 2004–; Visiting Prof., Univ. of Sydney, Australia 1983, British Postgraduate Medical Fed., Univ. of London 1990–96, Univ. of Glasgow 1996–, Univ. of Wales 2004–; Pres. European Org. for Research and Treatment of Cancer 1994; European Ed., Journal of the National Cancer Institute 1995–2001; Founding Ed. ecancermedicalscience.com 2007; Dir, Beatson Inst. for Cancer Research 1989–96, Cancer Research Technology Ltd 1991–2002, Photo Therapeutics Group Ltd 1999–2001, 2001–02, Cancer Intelligence Ltd 2002–; mem. numerous advisory cttees etc.; Hon. DSc (Univ. of Abertay, Dundee) 1996, (Univ. of Nottingham) 1997, (Univ. of Portsmouth) 1999, (Edinburgh Napier Univ.) 2002, (Univ. of Ghent, Belgium) 2005; Gunning Victoria Jubilee Prize in Pathology, Univ. of Edinburgh, Honeyman Gillespie Lecturer in Oncology 1977. *Publications:* Cancer Assessment and Monitoring 1979, Autologous Bone Marrow Transplantation and Solid Tumours 1984, Microspheres and Drug Therapy 1984, Clinical and Experimental Pathology and Biology of Lung Cancer 1985; 35 chapters in books; 230 articles in books and journals. *Leisure interests:* opera, music in general, theatre, walking, rugby, cooking, Italian wine-tasting, family. *Address:* Istituto Europea Oncologica, Via Ripamonti 435, 20141 Milan, Italy (office). *Telephone:* (02574) 89946 (office). *Fax:* (02574) 89922 (office). *E-mail:* gordonmcvie@ieo.it (office); gordonmcvie@doctors.org.uk (home). *Website:* www.ieo.it (office); www .cancerintelligence.com (office).

McWHA, James Alexander, AO, BSc, BAgr (Hons), PhD; British/New Zealand university administrator (retd) and academic; b. 28 May 1947, Co. Down, Northern Ireland; s. of David McWha and Sarah Isabel Caughey; m. Jean Lindsay Ferries 1970; one s. two d.; ed Queen's Univ., Belfast, Univ. of Glasgow; Lecturer in Plant Physiology, Univ. of Canterbury, NZ 1973–79, Head of Dept of Plant and Microbial Sciences 1980–85; Prof. of Agricultural Botany, Queen's Univ. Belfast 1985–89; Deputy Chief Scientific Officer, Dept of Agric. for NI 1985–89, Council Nat. Inst. of Agricultural Botany 1985–89; Dir Dept of Scientific and Industrial Research Fruit Trees (NZ) 1989–92; CEO Horticulture and Food Research Inst. (NZ) 1992–95; Vice-Chancellor and Pres. Massey Univ. 1996–2002; Vice-Chancellor and Pres. Univ. of Adelaide 2002–12; PhD (ad eundem gradum) (Adelaide) 2002; Hon. DSc (Massey Univ.) 2004; Centenary Medal for services to educ. 2003. *Leisure interests:* classic and vintage cars, rugby union. *Telephone:* (8) 8344-2524. *E-mail:* james@ mcwha.org.

McWILLIAM, Candia Frances Juliet, BA; British writer; b. 1 July 1955, Edin.; d. of Colin McWilliam and Margaret McWilliam; m. 1st Quentin Gerard Carew Wallop (now Earl of Portsmouth) 1981; one s. one d.; m. 2nd Fram Dinshaw; one s.; ed Sherborne School, Dorset and Girton Coll., Cambridge. *Publications:* A Cast of Knives 1988, A Little Stranger 1989, Debatable Land 1994, Change of Use 1996, Wait till I Tell You 1997, Lady Rose and Mrs Memmary (with Ruby Ferguson) 2004, What to Look For in Winter 2010. *Leisure interest:* reading. *Address:* 62/5 Great King Street, Edinburgh, EH3 6QY, Scotland.

McWILLIAMS, Sir Francis, GBE, BSc, FREng, FCGI; British fmr lawyer, arbitrator and civil engineer; b. 8 Feb. 1926, Edin.; s. of John McWilliams and Mary McWilliams; m. Winifred Segger 1950; two s.; ed Holy Cross Acad., Edin., Univ. of Edin.; engineer with various local authorities and contractors in UK 1945–53; Town Engineer, Petaling Jaya Borc Corpn, Malaysia 1954–64; Consulting Civil and Structural Engineer, F. McWilliams & Assocs, Kuala Lumpur 1964–76; full-time student 1976–78; called to English bar at Lincoln's Inn 1978; pupil barrister 1978–79; Int. Arbitrator 1979–; magistrate, City of London Bench 1980–96; Chair. Centre for Econs and Business Research 1992–2002; Vice-Pres. and Chair. British/Malaysian Soc. 1994–2001; mem. Panel of Arbitrators of Inst. of Civil Engineers and other bodies; Sheriff City of London 1988–89, Lord Mayor of London 1992–93; Bencher of Lincoln's Inn 1993; fmr mem. Court of Aldermen, City of London; Master Worshipful Co. of Engineers 1990–91, Worshipful Co. of Loriners 1995; Hon. FICE, KStJ, Kt of St Gregory, Kt, Dato Sri Selera (Malaysia) 1973; Hon. DCL (City Univ.) 1992; Hon. DEng (Kingston); Dr hc (Edin.); several other awards and hons. *Publication:* Urban Regeneration and Environmental Challenge, Pray Silence for 'Jock' Whittington (From Building Sewers to Suing Builders). *Leisure interests:* golf, skiing. *Address:* Flat 7, Whittingehame House, Whittingehame, East Lothian, EH41 4QA, Scotland (home). *Telephone:* (1368) 850619 (home). *Fax:* (1368) 850619 (home).

MACY, William H.; American actor; b. 13 March 1950, Miami, Fla; m. Felicity Huffman; ed Goddard Coll., Vermont; co-f. St Nicholas Theater Co., Atlantic Theater Co. *Stage appearances include:* The Man in 605 1980, Twelfth Night, Bureaucrat, A Call From the East, The Dining Room, Speakeasy, Wild Life, Flirtations, Baby With the Bathwater, The Nice and the Nasty, Bodies Rest and Motion, Oh Hell!, Prairie du Chien, The Shawl, An Evening With Dorothy Parker, The Dining Room, A Call From the Sea, The Beaver Coat, Life During Wartime, Mr Gogol and Mr Preen, Oleanna, Our Town. *Play directed:* Boy's Life. *Films include:* Without a Trace, The Last Dragon, Radio Days, Somewhere in Time, Hello Again, House of Games, Things Change, Homicide, Shadows and Fog, Benny and Joon, Searching for Bobby Fischer, The Client, Oleanna, The Silence of the Lambs, Murder in the First, Mr Holland's Opus, Down Periscope, Fargo, Ghosts of Mississippi, Air Force One, Wag the Dog, Pleasantville 1998, A Civil Action, Psycho 1998, Magnolia 1999, State and Maine 2000, Panic 2000, Focus 2001, Jurassic Park III 2001, Welcome to Collinwood 2002, The Cooler 2003, Stealing Sinatra 2003, Out of Order (TV mini series) 2003, Seabiscuit 2004, Spartan 2004,

Cellular 2004, Sahara 2005, Edmond 2005, Thank You for Smoking 2005, Doogal (voice) 2006, Bobby 2006, Inland Empire 2006, Everyone's Hero (voice) 2006, Wild Hogs 2007, He was a Quiet Man 2007, The Sessions 2012. *Film directed:* Lip Service (TV) 1988. *Television appearances include:* Chicago Hope (series), The Murder of Mary Phagan (mini-series), Texan, A Murderous Affair, The Water Engine, Heart of Justice, A Private Matter, The Con, A Slight Case of Murder, Reversible Errors 2004, The Wool Cap 2004, The Unit 2007. *Address:* c/o Creative Artists Agency, 9830 Wilshire Blvd, Beverly Hills, CA 90212-1825, USA.

MĄDALSKI, Wojciech, MSc, MEng; Polish business executive; b. 2 May 1956, Wrocław; s. of Jozef Mądalski and Hanna Mądalska (née Machowska); m. Kasia Swiatek 1980; one d.; ed Tech. Univ. Wrocław, McMaster Univ., Hamilton, Ont., Canada; Teaching/Research Asst, McMaster Univ., Hamilton, Ont., Canada 1980–82; Research Engineer, Tech. Devt Div., Polysar Ltd, Sarnia, Ont. 1982–84, Marketing/Business Planning Analyst, Styrenics Div. 1984–86, Business Man., Adhesives and Sealants Div. 1986–88; Gen. Man., Silicone Business, Novacor Chemicals Inc., Akron, OH, USA 1988–91; Pres. and CEO, Shincor Silicones Inc. 1991–93; CEO, E. Wedel SA and Pres., PepsiCo Foods International (PFI), Poland 1993–95, Vice-Pres., PFI Europe Group, UK 1996–97, ECR Dir, Walkers Snack Foods Ltd 1998; CEO and Pres., Hortex Holding SA 1998–2001; Man. Dir, Carlsberg Breweries A/S, Poland 2002; CEO and Pres. of the Man. Bd, Netia Holdings SA 2002–06. *Address:* c/o Netia Holdings SA, ul. Poleczki 13, 02-822 Warsaw, Poland. *E-mail:* info@netia.pl.

MADANI, Iyad bin Amin; Saudi media executive and international organization official; *Secretary-General Designate, Organization of Islamic Cooperation;* b. April 1946, Mecca; ed Arizona State Univ., USA; Gen. Dir of admin. office, Saudi Airlines 1970; Gen. Dir Okaz Org. for Press and Publication –1993; Ed.-in-Chief Saudi Gazette (newspaper) –1999; mem. Shura Council –1999; Minister of Hajj 1999–2005, Minister of Information and Culture 2005–09; Head, Islamic Int. News Agency and Org. of Islamic Broadcasting 2007–09; Chair. Knowledge Econ. City, Madina 2012; currently Sec.-Gen. Designate, OIC (terms begins 2014); mem. Bd of Dirs Dept of Water and Sanitation; mem. King Abdulaziz and His Companions Foundation for Giftedness and Creativity; mem. Advisory Bd of Supreme Council, Gulf Cooperation Council; mem. Bd of Trustees, Gulf Univ., Bahrain; editorial consultant for Ahlan Wa Sahlan magazine; fmr Vice-Pres. King Abdullah bin Abdulaziz Foundation for Housing Devt; Darjah Kebesaran Panglima Setia Mahkota (Malaysia) 2009. *Address:* Organisation of Islamic Cooperation, PO Box 178, Jeddah 21411, Saudi Arabia. *Telephone:* (2) 651-5222. *Fax:* (2) 651-2288. *Website:* www.oic-oci.org.

MAD'ARIČ, Marek; Slovak politician; *Minister of Culture;* b. 23 March 1966, Bratislava; m.; ed Acad. of Musical and Dramatic Arts; Script Ed., Office of Literary and Dramatic Broadcasting, Slovak TV 1990–93, Ed.-in-Chief 1996–97, Script Ed., Slovak TV 1997–99, Deputy Pres. of the Council 2002–04; freelance scriptwriter 1993–96; copywriter, Istropolitana DArcy (advertising agency) 1999–2000; Head of Media and Press Dept, Social Democracy Party 2000–02, 2004–06; Minister of Culture 2006–10, 2012–. *Address:* Ministry of Culture, nám. SNP 33, 813 31 Bratislava, Slovakia (office). *Telephone:* (2) 2048-2111 (office). *Fax:* (2) 2048-2174 (office). *E-mail:* info@culture.gov.sk (office). *Website:* www.culture .gov.sk (office).

MADDEN, Sir David, KCMG, MA; British fmr diplomatist; b. 1946; m. Lady Penelope Anthea Madden; ed Univ. of Oxford, Courtauld Inst., London; joined British Diplomatic Service 1970; overseas assignments in Berlin, Moscow, Athens and Belgrade; various positions in FCO including Head of S European Dept –1994; High Commr to Cyprus 1994–99; Amb. to Greece 1999–2004 (retd); Political Adviser, EU Force in Bosnia and Herzegovina (EUFOR) 2004–05; Trustee, The Brooke (equine welfare charity) 2008–, mem. Finance and Governance Cttees. *Leisure interests:* music (especially opera), sport (especially tennis, cricket and rowing), reading, animal welfare. *Address:* The Brooke, 30 Farringdon Street, London, EC4A 4HH, England (office). *Telephone:* (20) 3012-3456 (office). *Fax:* (20) 3012-0156 (office). *Website:* www.thebrooke.org (office).

MADDEN, Francis J.; American engineer; key contrib. responsible for design, testing and production of Corona cameras for aerial photography; adapted techniques from motion-picture film, fabrics and other industries; served as Chief Engineer, Itek Corpn's Corona camera programme until retirement in 1975, collaborated with Physical Research Lab. at Boston Univ.; recognized for work on Corona by Dir of CIA 1995, named a Pioneer of Nat. Reconnaissance by Nat. Reconnaissance Office 2000, Charles Stark Draper Prize, Nat. Acad. of Eng (co-recipient) 2005. *Address:* c/o National Academy of Engineering, 500 Fifth Street, NW, Washington, DC 20001, USA. *Telephone:* (202) 334-3200. *E-mail:* NAEMembershipOffice@nae.edu.

MADDEN, John; British film director; b. 8 April 1949, Portsmouth, Hants. *Films include:* Golden Gate 1994, Mrs. Brown 1997, Shakespeare in Love (Acad. Award for Best Film, BAFTA Award for Best Film) 1998, Captain Corelli's Mandolin 2001, Proof 2004, Killshot 2006, The Debt 2011, The Best Exotic Marigold Hotel 2011. *Television includes:* Grown-Ups 1985, The Return of Sherlock Holmes (series; episode The Priory School) 1986, A Wreath of Roses 1987, Inspector Morse (series; episodes Dead on Time, The Infernal Serpent, Promised Land, The Way Through the Woods) 1987, After the War (mini-series) 1989, The Widowmaker 1990, The Storyteller: Greek Myths (mini-series; episode Theseus and the Minotaur) 1990, The Casebook of Sherlock Holmes (series; episode The Disappearance of Lady Frances Carfax) 1990, Ethan Frome 1993, Meat 1994, Prime Suspect 4: The Lost Child 1995, Truth or Dare 1996.

MADDOW, Rachel Anne, DPhil; American television presenter and political commentator; b. 1 April 1973, Castro Valley, Calif.; d. of Robert B. (Bob) Maddow and Elaine Maddow (née Gosse); pnr Susan Mikula 1999–; ed Castro Valley High School, Stanford Univ., Lincoln Coll., Oxford, UK (Rhodes Scholar); first radio hosting job at WRNX, Holyoke, Mass after winning contest to find new on-air personality; hired to co-host WRNX's morning show, The Dave in the Morning Show (first openly gay anchor to be hired to host a prime-time news programme in USA); went on to host Big Breakfast on WRSI, Northampton, Mass 2002–04; joined Air America 2004, hosted Unfiltered along with Chuck D (of the hip hop group Public Enemy) and Lizz Winstead (co-creator of The Daily Show) 2004–05; then The Rachel Maddow Show 2005–10; given position of MSNBC Political Analyst

2008, regular panellist on MSNBC's Race for the White House with David Gregory and MSNBC's election coverage, as well as frequent contrib. on Countdown with Keith Olbermann; substitute host for Countdown with Keith Olbermann April 2008 (first time hosting a programme on MSNBC); began hosting own nightly MSNBC TV show 2008–; Hon. LLD (Smith Coll., Northampton, Mass) 2010; John Gardner Fellowship, Stanford Univ., named in Out magazine's Out 100 list of the "gay men and women who moved culture" 2008, voted Lesbian/Bi Woman of the Year (American) in AfterEllen's Visibility Awards 2008, Gracie Award, American Women in Radio and Television 2009, Proclamation of Honor from Calif. State Senate 2009, listed fourth in Out magazine's Annual Power 50 List 2009, placed sixth in AfterEllen.com Hot 100 list (gay world), and third in its Hot 100: Out Women version 2009, included on list of openly gay media professionals in The Advocate's Forty under 40 issue June/July 2009, 21st Annual GLAAD Media Awards in category, Outstanding TV Journalism-Newsmagazine for her segment, Uganda Be Kidding Me 2010, Commencement Speaker, Smith Coll. 2010, Maggie Award for ongoing reporting of health-care reform, the murder of Dr George Tiller, and the anti-abortion movement 2010, Walter Cronkite Faith & Freedom Award, The Interfaith Alliance 2010, ranked by Forbes magazine amongst The World's 100 Most Powerful Women (50th) 2010. *Television includes:* host of The Rachel Maddow Show (TV series) on MSNBC 2008– (highest rated show on MSNBC on several occasions). *Publication:* Drift: the Unmooring of American Military Power 2012. *Address:* The Rachel Maddow Show, c/o MSNBC Interactive News LLC, 30 Rockefeller Plaza, New York, NY 10112, USA (office). *Telephone:* (212) 664-4444 (office). *Fax:* (212) 664-4085 (office). *Website:* www.msnbc.msn.com/id/26315908/ns/msnbc_tv-rachel_maddow_show (office); maddowblog.msnbc.msn.com (office).

MADDY, Penelope Jo, PhD; American academic; *Distinguished Professor of Logic and Philosophy of Science and of Mathematics, University of California, Irvine;* b. 4 July 1950, Tulsa, Okla; d. of the late Richard Parsons and of Suzanne Parsons; ed Univ. of California, Berkeley, Princeton Univ.; Lecturer then Asst Prof. of Philosophy, Univ. of Notre Dame 1978–83; Assoc. Prof. of Philosophy, Univ. of Illinois, Chicago 1983–87; Assoc. Prof. of Philosophy and Math., Univ., of California, Irvine 1987–89, Prof. 1989–98, Chair. Philosophy Dept 1991–95, Prof. of Logic and Philosophy of Science and of Math. 1998–2007, Distinguished Prof. of Logic and Philosophy of Science and of Math. 2007–; Founding Chair. Logic and Philosophy of Science 1998–2001; Westinghouse Science Scholarship 1968–72, Marshall Fellowship 1972–73, American Asscn of Univ. Women Fellowship 1982–83, NSF Fellowships 1986, 1988–89, 1990–91, 1994–95, Romanell Lecturer 2001, Gauss Lecturer 2006. *Publications:* Realism in Mathematics 1990, Naturalism in Mathematics (Lakatos Prize 2002) 1997, Second Philosophy 2007, Defending the Axioms 2011. *Address:* Department of Logic and Philosophy of Science, Office SST 759, School of Social Sciences, University of California, Irvine, CA 92697-5100, USA (office). *Telephone:* (949) 824-4133 (office). *E-mail:* pjmaddy@uci.edu (office). *Website:* www.lps.uci.edu/lps_bios/pjmaddy (office).

MADE, Joseph; Zimbabwean politician; *Minister of Agriculture, Mechanisation and Irrigation Development;* mem. Zimbabwe African Nat. Union-Patriotic Front (ZANU-PF); Minister for Lands, Agric. and Rural Devt –2007, of Agric., Mechanisation and Irrigation Devt 2007–; mem. Pres. Robert Mugabe's 'Gang of Four' politicians. *Address:* Ministry of Agriculture, Mechanisation and Irrigation Development, Ngungunyana Bldg, Private Bag 7701, Causeway, Harare, Zimbabwe (office). *Telephone:* (4) 700596 (office). *Fax:* (4) 734646 (office). *Website:* www.moa.gov.zw (office).

MADELIN, Alain, LenD; French lawyer and politician; *President, Cercles libéraux;* b. 26 March 1946, Paris; three c.; lawyer, Paris office, Fed. nat. des Républicains indépendants (FNRI) 1968–; mem. Nat. Secr. FNRI 1977; elected Deputy to Nat. Ass. (Union pour la démocratie française—UDF) 1978–86, 1988–93, 1995–2002, 2002–07 (UMP); co-organizer UDF 1989–93; Vice-Pres. UDF 1991–96; Minister of Industry, Posts and Telecommunications and Tourism 1986–88, of Enterprise and Econ. Devt 1993–95, of Econ. and Finance May–Aug. 1995; Sec.-Gen. Republican Party 1988–89, Vice-Pres. 1989–96; Pres. France-Corée Asscn 1991–93; Vice-Pres. Regional Council of Brittany 1992–98; Mayor of Redon 1995–2000; mem. European Parl. 1989–2002; Pres. Inst. Euro 92 1988–97, f., Pres. Idées Action 1993–97; Leader Démocratie libérale 1997–2002; mem. UMP 2002–; presidential cand. 2002; Pres. Cercles libéraux (think tank), Paris 2002–; Pres. Fonds mondial de solidarité numérique (Global Digital Solidarity Fund), Geneva 2008–. *Publications:* Pour libérer l'école 1984, Chers compatriotes 1994, Quand les autruches relèveront la tête 1995, Aux Sources du modèle libéral français 1997, Le Droit du plus faible 1999. *Address:* Cercles libéraux, 31 bd La Tour Maubourg, 75007 Paris, France (office); Fonds mondial de solidarité numérique, Villa La Concorde, Avenue de la Concorde 20, 1203 Geneva, Switzerland.

MADFAI, Husham H. Fahmi al-, BSc; Iraqi engineering consultant and government official; b. 28 Oct. 1928, Baghdad; s. of Hassan Fahmi al-Madfai and Wajiha Nouri al-Madfai; m. 1st Suad A. Mohloom (died 1984); one s. one d.; m. 2nd Suha M. A. Bakri 1993; ed Cen. High School, Baghdad, Eng Coll., Univ. of Baghdad, Hammersmith School of Art & Design, London and Inst. of Structural Engineers, London, UK; civil engineer, Basrah Petroleum Co. 1953–55; with Dept of Housing and Tourism Design and Policies, Devt Bd 1957–63; Head. Tech. Dept, Municipality of Baghdad 1963–68; own consulting firm (architects, planners and designers) 1968–80; Deputy Mayor (responsible for planning and man.), City of Baghdad 1980–88; own consulting firm (studies and eng) 1988–; Regional Consultant (feasibility, studies and design), Amman, Jordan 1994–; currently heading Dar Al Imara (DAI) for the Reconstruction Program of Iraq; mem. Iraqi Asscn of Philosophers and Scientists 1994. *Publications include:* Health Aspects in Town Planning 1968, Low-cost Prefabricated Housing 1975, Housing Programme for Iraq until the year 2000 1976, Environmental Problems in Arab Cities 1995. *Leisure interests:* archaeology, studying ancient cities, music, paintings, reading biographies, swimming, long walks. *Address:* PO Box 941021, Shmesan 1, Amman 11194, Jordan; Maghrib Street, Adhamiya 22/14/302, Baghdad, Iraq; MGTC LLC, ICON Tower, Unit 904, Tecom, Dubai UAE. *Telephone:* (6) 5688470 (Amman); (1) 4225021/2 (Baghdad); (4) 443-7330 (Dubai). *Fax:* (6) 5688498 (Amman); (4) 443-1937 (Dubai).

MADFAI, Kahtan al, BArch, PhD; Iraqi architect, town planner and author; b. 15 April 1926, Baghdad; s. of Hassan Fahmi al Madfai and Wajiha Shaikh Noori

Shirwai; m. Lily Vassiliki Vorré 1957; one d.; ed Central High School, Baghdad, Univ. of Wales Inst. of Science and Tech., Cardiff, UK; practised as architect in public housing sector 1957, planning and design 1961; co-f. Architectural School of Baghdad 1961; lecturer on theory of design 1955–69; f. architectural firm Dar al Imara 1954–79; Asst Man. Gen. Housing Iraq Project 1973–2000; designer and consultant architect; Chair. Pan-Arab Jury for awarding prizes for Arab Town Projects 1985–87; delivered papers and seminars Istanbul 1985, Oxford 1986, Tunis 1987, 1989, Bahrain 1994, Baghdad 1994, Univ. of South Georgia, USA 1996, AIA, Atlanta, USA 1996, Amman 1996; co-f. Soc. of Iraqi Artists; mem. S.P. Group of Artists, Baghdad; works in Baghdad include Ministry of Finance 1968, Bunniyd Mosque 1972, Museum of Natural History 1973, Burj Rubaya apartment building Abu Dhabi 1990, Fatiha Halls project 2003; mem Baghdad Union and Soc. of Engineers; several first prizes in architectural competitions, including Rohoon Bank Bldg, Baghdad 1955, Baghdad Cen. Commercial Zone 1970, Cen. PO 1975, Mohammedia Touristic Project, Basra 1977, Great Mosque Competition 1984. *Publications:* several books on architecture and town planning including Development of the Iraqi House 1956, Criteria for Baghdad's New Master Plan 1965, A Manifesto for Arabic Architecture 1986, Architecture and Language 1987, Allah and the Architect 1997; poetry: Fulool 1965, Zem Zem Zaman 1972, Reconstruction of the Sumerian God Abu 1990. *Leisure interests:* modern art, modern poetry, modern philosophy. *Address:* 11 Aristoxenov, Pangrati, Athens; 22 Vassileos Constantinou, 11635 Athens, Greece. *Telephone:* (210) 721-7189 (Athens) (home); (210) 751-4120 (Athens) (home); (1) 4225021 (Baghdad) (office); (210) 723-2836 (Athens) (office); (1) 4220680 (Baghdad) (home). *Fax:* (210) 724-9920 (Athens) (office).

MADIKIZELA-MANDELA, (Nomzano) Winnie; South African politician; b. (Nomzamo Winifred Zanyiwe Madikizela), 26 Sept. 1934, Bizana, Pondoland, Transkei; m. Nelson Mandela 1958 (divorced 1996); two d.; mem. of African Nat. Congress (ANC) until its banning in 1960; campaigned constantly on behalf of her husband gaoled for life for political activities 1964–90; held in solitary confinement 1969–70; named a "banned person" by S African authorities 1976; Head of ANC Social Welfare Operations 1990–92; sentenced to six years' imprisonment on four counts of kidnapping and of being an accessory to assault May 1991; sentence upheld on appeal, except charge of being an accessory to assault; prison term waived to suspended two-year term, fine imposed June 1993; suspended from ANC Women's League 1993, Head 1997; mem. ANC Nat. Exec. Cttee 1994, Deputy Minister for Arts, Culture, Science and Tech., Govt of Nat. Unity 1994–95; charged with fraud Oct. 2001, convicted of 43 counts of fraud and 25 of theft and sentenced to five years' imprisonment with one year suspended April 2003, Pretoria High Court overturned conviction for theft and upheld one for fraud and handed her a three years and six months suspended sentence; mem. ANC Exec. Cttee 2007–; Third World Prize 1985. *Publication:* Part of My Soul Went with Him 1985, 491 Days: Prisoner Number 1323/69 (journal) 2013. *Address:* c/o Executive Committee, African National Congress, 54 Sauer Street, Johannesburg 2001, South Africa. *Website:* www.anc.org.za.

MADKOUR, Nazli, MA; Egyptian artist and painter; b. 25 Feb. 1949, Cairo; d. of Mokhtar Madkour and Malak Salem; m. Mohamed Salmawy 1970; one s. one d.; ed Cairo Univ., American Univ., Cairo; fmrly econ. expert for Industrial Devt Centre for Arab States; professional artist 1981–; numerous solo and collective exhbns; represented in public and pvt. collections in Egypt and internationally. *Publication:* Egyptian Women and Artistic Creativity 1989. *Leisure interests:* travel, reading, music. *Address:* #40 Street 13, Maadi, Cairo 11431, Egypt. *Telephone:* (2) 3804446.

MADONNA; American singer, actress and fashion designer; b. (Madonna Louise Veronica Ciccone), 16 Aug. 1958, Bay City, Mich.; d. of Sylvio Ciccone and Madonna Ciccone; m. 1st Sean Penn 1985 (divorced 1989); one d. by Carlos Leon; m. 2nd Guy Ritchie 2000 (divorced 2008); two s. (one adopted); ed Rochester Adams High School, Mich., Univ. of Michigan, Alvin Ailey Dance School; moved to New York 1979, dancer 1979–, actress 1980–, solo singer 1983–; numerous worldwide concerts, tours, TV appearances; f. Maverick record label 1992 (sold to Warner Music Group 2004); Vice-Pres. ICA, London, UK; est. children's clothing line, Sweet Hearts 2004; launched Material Girl clothing line with daughter Lourdes 2010; numerous MTV Video Awards, including Vanguard Award 1986, American Music Awards for Favorite Female Video Artist 1987, Favorite Dance Single 1991, Academy Award for Best Song 1991, Juno Award for Int. Song of the Year 1991, Grammy Award for Best Longform Music Video 1992, BRIT Award for Best Int. Female 2001, 2006, numerous awards from Billboard, Vogue and Rolling Stone magazines, Echo Award for Best Int. Female Artist, Germany 2006, Ivor Novello Award for Int. Hit of the Year (for Sorry) 2007, ranked by Forbes magazine amongst The World's 100 Most Powerful Women (29th) 2010, Billboard Music Awards for Top Dance Artist 2013, for Top Touring Artist 2013. *Tours:* The Virgin Tour 1985, Who's That Girl World Tour 1987, Blond Ambition World Tour 1990, The Girlie Show World Tour 1993, Drowned World Tour 2001, Re-Invention World Tour 2004, Confessions Tour 2006, Sticky & Sweet Tour 2008–09, M.D.N.A. Tour 2012. *Plays:* Speed-the-Plow (Broadway) 1988, Up for Grabs (Wyndhams Theatre, London) 2002. *Films:* A Certain Sacrifice 1979, Vision Quest 1985, Desperately Seeking Susan 1985, Shanghai Surprise 1986, Who's That Girl? 1987, Bloodhounds on Broadway 1989, Dick Tracy 1990, Shadows and Fog 1991, Madonna: Truth or Dare (aka In Bed with Madonna) (documentary) 1991, A League of Their Own 1992, Body of Evidence 1993, Dangerous Game (aka Snake Eyes) 1993, Blue in the Face (aka Brooklyn Boogie) 1995, Four Rooms 1995, Girl 6 1996, Evita 1996, The Next Best Thing 2000, Star (short, uncredited) 2001, Swept Away 2002, Die Another Day (cameo) 2002, I'm Going to Tell You a Secret 2005, Arthur and the Minimoys (aka Arthur and the Invisibles) (voice) 2006, M by Madonna (H&M TV commercial, dir) 2007, Filth and Wisdom (writer and dir) 2008, I Am Because We Are (documentary, writer) 2008, Miu Miu (TV commercial, dir) 2010, W.E. (co-writer and dir) (Golden Globe Award for Best Original Song, 'Masterpiece' 2012) 2011. *Television includes:* Will & Grace (series) 2003. *Recordings include:* albums: Madonna 1983, Like A Virgin 1984, True Blue 1986, Who's That Girl? (film soundtrack) 1987, Like A Prayer 1989, I'm Breathless (soundtrack to film Dick Tracy) 1990, The Immaculate Collection 1990, Erotica 1992, Bedtime Stories 1994, Something To Remember 1995, Evita (film soundtrack) 1997, Ray Of Light (Grammy Award for Best Pop Album) 1998, Next Best Thing (film soundtrack) 2000, Music 2000, GHV2 2001, American Life 2003, Remixed and Revisited (EP)

2004, Confessions On A Dance Floor (Grammy Award for Best Electronic/Dance Album 2007) 2005, I'm Going to Tell You a Secret 2006, Hard Candy 2008, M.D.N.A. (Billboard Music Award for Top Dance Album 2013) 2012. *Publications:* Sex 1992, The English Roses (juvenile) 2003, Mr Peabody's Apples (juvenile) 2003, Yakov and the Seven Thieves (juvenile) 2004, The Adventures of Abdi (juvenile) 2004, Lotsa de Casha (juvenile) 2005. *Address:* Live Nation Inc., 9348 Civic Center Drive, Beverly Hills, CA 90210; 8491 West Sunset Boulevard, Suite 485, West Hollywood, CA 90069, USA. *Website:* www.madonna.com.

MADRAZO PINTADO, Roberto, LLB; Mexican politician and lawyer; b. 30 July 1952; s. of Carlos Madrazo Becerra y la Profra and Graciela Pintado Jiménez; m. Isabel de la Parra Trillo; two s. three d.; ed Universidad Nacional Autónoma, Mexico; entered civil service 1971; legal asst to Alvaro Obregón 1971–72; worked in office of Chief Justice 1972, adviser on social affairs 1979–81; Deputy Sec.-Gen. for Youth, Partido Revolucionario Institucional (PRI) 1975, Sec.-Gen. Nat. Movt of Revolutionary Youth 1977, Sec. of Public Relations and Man. 1984–87, Sec. of Org. 1988–, Pres. PRI 2002–06; elected Fed. Deputy, State of Tabasco 1976, State Gov. 1988–91; mem. 55th legislature, Fed. Govt 1991–93; Founder and Pres. Escuela Nacional de Cuadros; apptd Sec. of the Great Comm., Palace of San Lazaro; unsuccessful cand. for Pres. of Mexico 2006. *Publications:* Urbanism, Services and Public Security; numerous articles on social affairs, int. relations and devt. *Address:* c/o Partido Revolucionario Institucional, Insurgentes Norte 59, Edif. 2, subsótano, Col Buenavista, 06359 México, DF, Mexico (office).

MADSEN, Ib, PhD; Danish mathematician and academic; *Professor of Mathematics, Copenhagen University;* b. 12 April 1942, Copenhagen; s. of Hennig Madsen and Gudrun Madsen (née Davids-Thomsen); m. 1st Benedicte Rechnitzer 1963 (divorced 1982); m. 2nd Ulla Lykke Jorgensen 1984; two s.; ed Univ. of Copenhagen, Univ. of Chicago, USA; Research Stipend, Arhus Univ. 1965–70; Research Instructor, Univ. of Chicago 1971–72; Assoc. Prof., Arhus Univ. 1971–83, Prof. of Math. 1983–2009; Prof. of Math., Copenhagen Univ. 2009–; Ed Acta Mathematica 1988–; Asst Ed. Journal of the European Mathematical Society 2002–; mem. Royal Danish Acad. of Sciences 1978, Inst. for Advanced Study, Princeton 1986–87, Royal Swedish Acad. of Sciences 1998, Royal Norwegian Acad. 2002; Rigmor and Carl Holst-Knudsen Science Prize 1982, Humboldt Research Award 1992, Plenary Lecturer, Int. Congress of Mathematicians, Madrid 2006, ERC advanced grant 2009–13, Ostrowski Prize 2011. *Publications:* The Classifying Spaces for Surgery and Cobordism of Manifolds (with R. J. Milgram) 1979, From Calculus to Cohomology (with J. Tornehave) 1997; approx. 90 journal articles. *Address:* Department of Mathematics, Copenhagen University, Universitetsparken 5, 2100 Copenhagen Ø (office); Saabyesvej 10-2, 2100 Copenhagen Ø, Denmark (home). *Telephone:* 35-32-06-82 (office). *E-mail:* imadsen@math.ku.dk (office). *Website:* www.math.ku.dk (office).

MADSEN, Michael; American actor; b. 25 Sept. 1958, Chicago, Ill.; brother of Virginia Madsen; m. Jeannine Bisignano; one s.; began acting career at Steppenwolf Theater, Chicago, appearing in plays including Of Mice and Men, A Streetcar Named Desire; appeared in Broadway production of A Streetcar Named Desire 1992. *Films include:* Against All Hope 1982, WarGames 1983, Racing with the Moon 1984, The Natural 1984, The Killing Time 1987, Shadows in the Storm 1988, Iguana 1988, Kill Me Again 1989, Blood Red 1989, The End of Innocence 1990, Fatal Instinct 1991, The Doors 1991, Thelma and Louise 1991, Beyond the Law 1992, Almost Blue 1992, Reservoir Dogs 1992, Straight Talk 1992, Inside Edge 1993, A House in the Hills 1993, Trouble Bound 1993, Free Willy 1993, Money for Nothing 1993, Dead Connection 1994, Season of Change 1994, The Getaway 1994, Wyatt Earp 1994, Species 1995, Free Willy 2: The Adventure Home 1995, Man with a Gun 1995, Mulholland Falls 1996, The Winner 1996, Red Line 1996, Papertrail 1997, Surface to Air 1997, The Last Days of Frankie the Fly 1997, Donnie Brasco 1997, The Girl Gets Moe 1997, The Maker 1997, Catherine's Grove 1997, Executive Target 1997, Flat Out 1998, The Thief and the Stripper 1998, Ballad of the Nightingale 1998, Rough Draft 1998, Species II 1998, The Sender 1998, Fait Accompli 1998, The Florentine 1999, Detour 1999, Fall 2000, Bad Guys 2000, Ides of March 2000, The Stray 2000, Luck of the Draw 2000, The Alternate 2000, The Price of Air 2000, Outlaw 2001, Pressure Point 2001, The Ghost 2001, Choke 2001, L.A.P.D.: To Protect and to Serve 2001, Extreme Honor 2001, Welcome to America 2002, Love.com 2002, Die Another Day 2002, The Real Deal 2002, Where's Angelo? 2003, My Boss's Daughter 2003, Kill Bill: Vol. 1 2003, Vampires Anonymous 2003, Blueberry 2004, Kill Bill: Vol. 2 2004, Jacked$ 2004, Hoboken Hollow 2005, Firedog (voice) 2005, Sin City 2005, Chasing Ghosts 2005, The Last Drop 2005, L.A. Dicks 2005, Muzhskoy sezon. Barkhatnaya revolutsiya 2005, BloodRayne 2005, Living and Dying 2006, All In 2006, Last Hour 2006, Scary Movie 4 2006, Canes 2006, UKM: The Ultimate Killing Machine 2006. *Television includes:* War and Remembrance (miniseries) 1988, Vengeance Unlimited (series) 1998, Big Apple (series) 2001, 44 Minutes: The North Hollywood Shoot-Out 2003, Frankenstein 2004, Tilt (series) 2005. *Address:* c/o Michael Manchal, CAA, 9830 Wilshire Boulevard, Beverly Hills, CA 90212, USA. *Website:* www.michaelmadsen.com.

MADUEKWE, Chief Ojo, LLB, CFR; Nigerian politician and diplomatist; *High Commissioner to Canada;* b. 6 May 1945, Abia State; m. Ucha Maduekwe; ed Univ. of Nigeria; called to Nigerian Bar 1973; mem. House of Reps 1983, Constituent Ass. 1988; Adviser to Minister of Foreign Affairs 1993–95; mem. Nat. Constituent Conf. 1994–95; Tech. Adviser to Vision 2010 Cttee 1997; elected Senator 1998; Minister of Culture and Tourism 1999–2000, of Transport 2000–03; Legal Adviser to the Pres. 2003–05; Minister of Foreign Affairs 2007–10; High Commr to Canada 2012–; Nat. Sec., People's Democratic Party (PDP). *Address:* Nigerian High Commision, 295 Metcalfe Street, Ottawa, ON K2P 1R9, Canada (office). *Telephone:* (613) 565-1983 (office). *Fax:* (613) 236-0529 (office). *E-mail:* chancery@nigeriahcottawa (office). *Website:* www.nigeriahcottawa.com (office).

MADUNA, Penuell Mpapa, LLD; South African lawyer and politician; *Partner, Bowman Gilfillan;* b. 29 Dec. 1952; m. Nompumelelo Cheryl Maduna; three c.; ed Univ. of Zimbabwe, Univ. of Witwatersrand; worked in underground structures of ANC in 1970s, twice incarcerated and prosecuted; left SA 1980; fmr Regional Admin. Sec. Tanzania, Office of Treasurer-Gen. of ANC; fmr staff mem. and Legal Adviser, ANC HQ Lusaka, est. Dept of Legal and Constitutional Affairs 1985, Founder mem. Constitutional Cttee, participated in meetings with South African Govt and officials in 1980s and early 1990s leading to establishment of Convention

for a Democratic South Africa, mem. Negotiating Comm., now mem. Nat. Exec. Cttee; fmr MP Nat. Ass.; Minister of Mineral and Energy Affairs 1996–99, of Justice and Constitutional Devt 1999–2004; currently Pnr, Bowman Gilfillan (law firm), Johannesburg; Bd mem. Faculty of Law, Univ. of Witwatersrand 1996–. *Publication:* Fundamental Rights in the New Constitution 1994 (co-author). *Leisure interests:* soccer, reading, debating. *Address:* Bowman Gilfillan, 165 West Street, Sandton, Johannesburg, South Africa (office). *Telephone:* (11) 6699358 (office). *E-mail:* p.maduna@bowman.co.za (office). *Website:* www.bowman.co.za (office).

MADURO JOEST, Ricardo, BA; Honduran fmr central banker and fmr head of state; b. Panamá, Panama; m. Miriam Andreu; one s. (deceased) three d.; ed Stanford Univ., USA; mem. Partido Nacional (Nationalist Party), currently Chair. Cen. Cttee; Dir Rafael Callejas's election campaigns 1985, 1989; apptd Chair. Banco Cen. de Honduras 1990; fmr Co-ordinator of the Econ. Office; Pres. of Honduras 2002–05. *Address:* c/o Partido Nacional (PN), Paseo el Obelisco, Comayagüela, Tegucigalpa, Honduras (office).

MADURO MOROS, Nicolás; Venezuelan politician and head of state; *President;* b. 23 Nov. 1961, Caracas; m. Cilia Flores; two c.; worker on Caracas metro and founder of trade union for Caracas metro workers in 1980s; also mem. Movimiento Bolivariano Revolucionario 200 in 1980s, mem. Nat. Directorate 1994–97; Founding mem. Movimiento Quinta Republica 200 (MVR) 1997, elected to Asamblea Nacional 1998, Pres. Citizens' Participation Cttee 1999, Co-ordinator of MVR parl. team 2000–01, Co-ordinator of majority bloc parl. team 2001–05, Pres. Asamblea Nacional 2005–06; Minister of Foreign Affairs 2006–12; Vice-Pres. 2012–13, Pres. 2013–. *Address:* Central Information Office of the Presidency, Torre Oeste 18°, Parque Central, Caracas, 1010, Venezuela (office). *Telephone:* (2) 572-7110. *Fax:* (2) 572-2675. *Website:* www.presidencia.gob.ve.

MADY, Mohamed H. Al-, BS, MS; Saudi Arabian business executive and chemical engineer; *Vice-Chairman and CEO, Saudi Basic Industries Corporation (SABIC);* ed Univs of Colorado and Wyoming, USA; joined Saudi Basic Industries Corpn (SABIC) 1976, Dir-Gen. for Projects –1998, Vice-Chair. and CEO 1998–, Chair. R & T Exec. Cttee, SABIC EuroPetrochemicals Exec. Bd; Chair. and Man. Dir Saudi Arabian Fertilizer Co. (SAFCO); Chair. Gulf Petrochemicals & Chemicals Asscn; Co-Chair. US-Saudi Arabia Business Council; mem. Int. Business Council, World Econ. Forum, mem. Bd Boao Forum for Asia, World Sustainability Council, Int. Advisory Council King Abdullah Univ. of Science & Tech., Int. Advisory Bd, King Fahd Univ. of Petroleum and Minerals; mem. Bd of Trustees, Prince Mohammad bin Fahd Univ.; Chair. and Man. Dir Saudi Arabian Fertilizer Co.; Fellow, London Business School; Hon. DS (Univ. of Colorado) 2012 elected by Colorado Eng and Applied Sciences Coll. amongst the gifted students with global scientific and industrial contribs 2010, Int. Petrochemical Heritage Award 2009, ranked among the Top 40 Best Power Players in the Chemical Industry by ICIS Chemical Business in 2007, 2008, 2009, 2010. *Address:* Saudi Basic Industries Corporation, PO Box 5101, Riyadh 11422, Saudi Arabia (office). *Telephone:* (1) 2259655 (office); (1) 2258000. *Fax:* (1) 2259660 (office). *E-mail:* info@sabic.com. *Website:* www.sabic.com (office).

MAE, Vanessa; British violinist; b. (Vanessa-Mae Vanakorn Nicholson), 27 Oct. 1978, Singapore; ed Cen. Conservatoire, Beijing, People's Repub. of China, Royal Coll. of Music, London, UK; studied with Lin Yao Ji and Felix Andrievsky; concerto debut aged ten, Philharmonic Orchestra 1989; first nat. tour of UK with Tchaikovsky Concerto 1990; first int. tour with London Mozart Players 1990; released three classical recordings with orchestra (youngest artist to record both Tchaikovsky and Beethoven Violin Concertos) 1990–92; over 400 live performances in the Middle East, South Africa, China, SE Asia, Russia, Europe, Baltic States, Cen. Asia, USA, Cen. and S America; The Classical Tour 1997, Int. Red Hot Tour 1995, Storm on World Tour 1998; performed at Hong Kong to China Reunification Ceremony 1996, exclusively for HM The Queen, Buckingham Palace 1998, at 50th Anniversary of Geneva Conventions 1999; opened Classical Brit Awards, Royal Albert Hall 2000; collaborated on soundtrack for Walt Disney film Mulan; catwalk debut with Jean-Paul Gaultier; frequent TV appearances and participant in 'crossover' concerts; involved in work with ICRC, participated in TV Campaign Even Wars Have Limits; BAMBI Top Int. Classical Artist Award, Echo Klassik Award for Bestselling Album of the Year 1995, World Music Award for Best Selling Classical Artist 1996. *Recordings include:* Tchaikovsky and Beethoven Concertos 1990, The Violin Player (quadruple platinum) 1994, The Classical Album I 1996, China Girl: The Classical Album II 1997, Storm 1997, The Original Four Seasons 2000, Vanessa Mae: The Classical Collection Part I 2000, Subject to Change 2001, Choreography 2004. *Film:* Arabian Nights 2000. *Leisure interests:* snow skiing, dining out, academic studies, waterskiing, reading.

MAEDA, Terunobu, LLB; Japanese business executive; *Senior Adviser, Mizuho Financial Group, Inc.;* b. 2 Jan. 1945; ed Univ. of Tokyo; joined Fuji Bank Ltd 1968, Dir and Gen. Man. Credit Planning Div. 1995–96, Dir and Gen. Man. Corp. Planning Div. 1996–97, Man. Dir 1997–98, Man. Dir and Head of Public and Financial Insts Group 1998–99, Man. Dir and Chief Financial Officer (CFO) 1999–2001, Deputy Pres. and CFO 2001–02; mem. Bd Dirs Mizuho Holdings, Inc. (present Mizuho Financial Strategy Co. Ltd, subsidiary of Mizuho Asset Trust & Banking Co. Ltd (fmrly Mizuho Trust & Banking Co. Ltd)) 2002–07, Pres. and CEO Mizuho Financial Group 2002–07, Pres. and CEO Mizuho Financial Group, Inc. 2003–09, Chair. 2009–10, Sr Adviser 2010–; Vice-Chair. Nippon Keidanren. *Address:* Mizuho Financial Group, Inc., Marunouchi 2-chome Building, 2-5-1, Marunouchi, Chiyoda-ku, Tokyo 100-8333, Japan (office). *Telephone:* (3) 5224-1111 (office). *Fax:* (3) 3215-4616 (office). *E-mail:* info@mizuho-fg.co.jp (office). *Website:* www.mizuho-fg.co.jp (office).

MAEENA, Khaled al-; Saudi Arabian journalist and public relations consultant; *Editor-in-Chief, Arab News;* served as diplomat in China and Russia; Ed.-in-Chief, Arab News 1982–93, 1998–; Pres. and CEO Saudi Public Relations Co. (SPRC) 1993–2000; sr columnist for Gulf News, Urdu News, Asharq Al-Awsat, Al-Iqtisadiah, Times of Oman, China Post; joined Saudi Arabian Airlines (Saudia) 1982, held a variety of posts including public relations advisor and Editor-in-Chief of Saudia World (magazine); has hosted news and talk shows on Saudi TV; has represented Saudi Arabian media at several important Arab summit meetings including in Baghdad and Morocco. *Address:* Arab News, POB 10452, SRP Bldg,

Madinah Road, Jeddah 21433, Saudi Arabia (office). *Telephone:* (2) 639-1888 (office). *Fax:* (2) 639-3223 (office). *E-mail:* almaeena@arabnews.com (office). *Website:* www.arabnews.com (office).

MAEHARA, Seiji; Japanese politician; b. 30 April 1962, Kyoto; m. Airi Maehara; ed Matsushita Inst. of Govt and Man., Chigasaki; mem. Kyoto Prefectural Ass. 1991–93; mem. House of Reps for Kyoto No 2 constituency 1993–, Chair. Special Cttee on Okinawa and N Problems, mem. Cttee on Fundamental Nat. Policies; mem. Sakigake Party 1994–98, Japan New Party 1993–94; mem. Democratic Party of Japan 1998–, Pres. (youngest ever) 2005–06, Chair. Public Works Reform Project Team, Road-Related Special Corpn Working Team, New Public Works Research Cttee, Expressways Project Team; fmr Shadow Cabinet Dir-Gen., Defence Agency, fmr Shadow Cabinet Minister of State for Social Capital Devt; Minister of Land, Infrastructure, Transport and Tourism 2009–10, also Minister of State for Okinawa and N Territories and Disaster Man. 2009–10, Minister of Foreign Affairs 2010–11 (resgnd); Minister for Nat. Strategy and Econ. Policy Oct.–Dec. 2012. *Leisure interest:* photography. *Address:* Democratic Party of Japan, 1-11-1, Nagata-cho, Chiyoda-ku, Tokyo 100-0014, Japan (office). *Telephone:* (3) 3595-9988 (office). *Fax:* (3) 3595-9961 (office). *E-mail:* dpjenews@dpj.or.jp (office). *Website:* www.dpj.or.jp (office).

MAEHLER, Herwig Gustav Theodor, PhD, FBA; German papyrologist and academic; *Professor Emeritus, University College London;* b. 29 April 1935, Berlin; s. of Ludwig Maehler and Lisa Maehler; m. Margaret Anderson 1963; two d.; ed Katharineum, Lübeck and Univs of Hamburg, Tübingen and Basle; British Council Scholarship, Oxford 1961–62; Research Asst, Dept of Classics, Univ. of Hamburg 1962–63, Dept of Manuscripts, Hamburg Univ. Library 1963–64; Keeper of Greek Papyri, Egyptian Museum, West Berlin 1964–79; Lecturer in Classics, Freie Universität Berlin 1975–79; Reader in Papyrology, Univ. Coll. London 1979–81, Prof. 1981–2000, Prof. Emer. 2000–; Visiting Fellow, Inst. for Advanced Studies in the Humanities, Edin. 1977; Visiting Prof., Univs of Urbino 1984, Bologna 1986, Bari 1988, Basle 1990, Budapest 1998, 2001, 2004, Rome 1999, Venice 2004, Florence 2005, Graz 2011–12; Corresp. mem. German Archaeological Inst.; Fellow, Accad. Nazionale dei Lincei, Rome, Hungarian Acad. of Sciences, Budapest; Dr hc (Helsinki) 2000, (Budapest) 2001, (Rome II Tor Vergata) 2003. *Publications include:* Die Auffassung des Dichterberufs im frühen Griechentum bis zur Zeit Pindars 1963, Die Handschriften der S. Jacobi-Kirche Hamburg 1967, Urkunden römischer Zeit 1968, Papyri aus Hermoupolis 1974, Die Lieder des Bakchylides (two vols) 1982, 1997, Greek Bookhands of the Early Byzantine Period (with G. Cavallo) 1987, Bacchylides: A Selection 2004, Urkunden aus Hermupolis 2005, Hellenistic Bookhands (with G. Cavallo) 2008; editions of Bacchylides and Pindar. *Leisure interests:* chamber music (viola), horse riding (dressage). *Address:* Zeltgasse 6/12, 1080 Vienna, Austria. *Telephone:* (1) 408-3499. *E-mail:* hgt .maehler@virgin.net.

MAEMA, Lebohang Fine, KC, BA, LLB, LLM; Lesotho diplomatist and lawyer; *Clerk to the National Assembly;* b. 22 July 1957, Masery; three d.; ed Nat. Univ. of Lesotho, Univ. of Cambridge, UK; fmr mem. of Bd Cen. Bank of Lesotho; fmr Pres. Matlama Football Club; worked at Nat. Univ. of Lesotho; Crown Counsel, Attorney-Gen.'s Chambers 1982–83; Lecturer-in-Law, Nat. Univ. of Lesotho 1984–87; Deputy Pvt. Sec. to King of Lesotho, Royal Palace 1987–89, Pvt. Sec. 1989–90; Prin. Sec., Ministry of Justice and Prisons 1990–93; Attorney-Gen. 1993–2005; Amb. and Perm. Rep. to UN, New York 2005–09; Amb. to Ethiopia 2009–11, also Perm. Rep. African Union and High Commr to Kenya and Uganda; Clerk to the Nat. Ass. 2013–; Commdr of the Most Meritorious Order of Mohlomi; Cambridge Livingstone Scholar 1983. *Leisure interests:* listening to music, watching TV, soccer and movies. *Address:* Office of the Clerk to the National Assembly, POB 190, Maseru, Lesotho (office). *Telephone:* 22323035 (office). *Website:* www.parliament.ls (office).

MAESTRE CORTADELLA, Mireia; Andorran politician; b. 1971; Sec.-Gen. for Finance 1999–2001; Minister for Finance 2001–04; mem. Partit Liberal d'Andorra (Liberal Party of Andorra—PLA). *Address:* Partit Liberal d'Andorra, Carrer Babot Camp 13, 2°, Andorra la Vella, AD500, Andorra (office). *Telephone:* 807715 (office). *Fax:* 869728 (office). *E-mail:* pla@pla.ad (office). *Website:* www.pla.ad (office).

MAFFIA, Dante; Italian poet and author; b. 17 Jan. 1946, Roseto Capo Spulico (Cosenza); ed graduated in Rome; Founder-Ed. Il Policordo and Poetica magazines; contrib. to books of RAI and many periodicals, including Nuova Antologia, Misure critiche, Belfagor, Otto/Novecento, Cartolaria, Il Bel Paese, Hortus, Lunarionuovo, Idea, Poiesis; Ed. Rivista di Italianistica (S Africa), Il Belli; Corresp., La Nación; currently working at Univ. of Salerno; Calliope Award for literary fiction 1995. *Publications include:* poetry: Il leone non mangia l'erba (Premio Viareggio, Pino d'Oro) 1974, Le favole impudiche 1977, Passeggiate romane (Premio Trastevere) 1979, L'eredità infranta (Premio Brutium) 1981, Caro Baudelaire (Prizes: Tarquinia-Cardarelli, Martina Franca, Rhegium Julii) 1983, Il ritorno di Omero (Premio Alfonso Gatto) 1984, A vite i tutte i jùrne (Premio Acireale, Premio Lentini) 1987, U ddíje poverille (Premio Brutium del Presidente, Premio Lanciano) 1990, L'educazione permanente (Premio Città di Cariati, Premio Calliope, Premio Circe-Sabaudia) 1992, La castità del male (Premio Montale, Premio Città di Venezia) 1993, Confessione 1993, Racconto 1994, I rùspe cannarùte 1995, Possibili errori (Premio Anna Borra, Premio Contini-Bonacossi) 2000, Papaciòmme 2000, Canzoni d'amore (Premio D'Alessandro, Premio Anco Marzio, Premio Camaiore) 2002, Di Rosa e di rose, Firenze 2004, Ultimi versi d'amore 2004, Al macero dell'invisibile 2006, Poesie torinesi 2011, Sbarco clandestino 2011, Abitare la cecità 2011, La strada sconnessa 2011; prose: Corradino, La clessidra 1990, La danza del adiós (in Spanish) 1991, La barriera semantica (written in dialect poetry of the 20th century) 1996, Le donne di Courbet racconti (with a note by Alberto Moravia and a preface by Alberto Bevilacqua) 1996, Il romanzo di Tommaso Campanella (preface by Norberto Bobbio) (Premio Cirò Marina, Premio Stresa, Premio Palmi) 1996, Voci della scrittura calabrese 2003, Risalendo il Danubio – scritti su Claudio Magris 2005, Nel mondo di Antonio Tabucchi 2011, Sette donne per fare un uomo intero. Racconti di donne e sulle donne 2011, San Bettino Craxi e altri racconti 2011; other: exhbn catalogues and monographs of important painters and sculptors; works have been translated into many languages; ed.: Poesie alla Calabria, La narrativa calabrese dell'Otto/Novecento, Una simpatia di Giulio Carcano, Torquato Tasso di Carlo Goldoni, Torquato Tasso di Francesco De Sanctis (anthology). *Address:* P. le Caduti della Montagnola 50, 00142 Rome, Italy.

Telephone: (339) 6567133. *E-mail:* dantemaffia@libero.it (office). *Website:* www .dantemaffia.com (office).

MAGAN OF CASTLETOWN, Baron (Life Peer), cr. 2011, of Kensington in the Royal Borough of Kensington and Chelsea; **George Morgan Magan,** FCA; British merchant banker and politician; *Deputy Chairman, Conservative Party Foundation;* b. 14 Nov. 1945; with Peat Marwick Mitchell 1964–70, Kleinwort Benson Ltd 1971–74; Dir Morgan Grenfell & Co. Ltd 1974–88; Co-founder and Chair. J.O. Hambro Magan 1988–96, Chair. NatWest Markets Corp. Finance (upon sale of firm to NatWest 1996, assisted in creation and separation of firm to create Hawkpoint Partners, where he was Chair. 1997–2001); Chair. Mallett plc 2001–08, Morgan Shipley Ltd, Dubai 2001–, emuse, Dublin 2004–, Strategic Asset Management Solutions 2008–, Carlton Capital Partners (Deputy Chair. Carlton Corporate Finance); Dir Edmiston & Co. 2001–, Bank of Ireland 2003–09 (Deputy Gov. 2006–09), Allied Investment Partners, Abu Dhabi 2007–; Partner, Rhone Group LLC; Deputy Treas. Conservative Party 2002–03, Party Treas. and mem. Bd Conservative Party 2003, Dir Conservative Party Foundation 2003–, currently Deputy Chair.; Chair. St George's Chapel Windsor Castle Devt Appeal 2007–, Trustee, Foundation of The Coll. of St George, Windsor Castle 2008–; Trustee, London Philharmonic Orchestra 1992–2006 (Chair. 1997–2006), Royal Opera House, Covent Garden 1995–2001, British Museum Devt Trust 1999–2003. *Address:* Strategic Asset Management Solutions, 29th Floor, One Canada Square, Canary Wharf, London, E14 5DY (office); Conservative Party Foundation Ltd, 30 Millbank, London, SW1P 4DP (office); House of Lords, Westminster, London, SW1A 0PW, England (office). *Telephone:* (20) 8123-5083 (Canary Wharf) (office); (20) 7984-8037 (Millbank) (office); (20) 7219-5353 (House of Lords) (office). *Fax:* (20) 7219-5979 (House of Lords) (office). *E-mail:* info@strategicams.com (office); information@theconservativefoundation.co.uk (office). *Website:* www .theconservativefoundation.co.uk (office).

MAGANDE, Ng'andu Peter, BA, MSc; Zambian diplomatist, business executive and farmer; b. 5 July 1947, Namaila, Mazabuka; m.; two s. three d.; ed Univ. of Zambia, Makerere Univ., Uganda; joined Civil Service 1971; apptd Dir of Budget, Ministry of Finance 1981; Perm. Sec. in various govt depts 1983–94; Man. Dir Zambia Nat. Commercial Bank, Lima Bank; Exec. Dir Industrial Devt Corpn, Zambia Industrial and Mining Corpn 1986–94; technical assistance consultant to Govt 1994; Sec.-Gen. African, Caribbean and Pacific Secr. 1996; Minister of Finance and Nat. Planning 2003–08; mem. Movt for Multi-party Democracy; Commdr of the Order of the Repub. of Benin; Best Commercial Tobacco Farmer 1989.

MAGARIÑOS, Carlos Alfredo, MBA; Argentine government official, international organization official, consultant and business executive; *Chairman, Global Business Development Network, LLC;* b. 16 Aug. 1962, Buenos Aires; ed Nat. Univ. of Buenos Aires, Int. Devt Law Inst., Italy, Wharton School, Univ. of Pennsylvania, USA; Nat. Dir for Foreign Trade 1991; joined Ministry of Economy 1992, Under-Sec. of State for Industry 1992–93, Sec. of State for Mining and Industry 1993–96; Econ. and Trade Rep. of Argentina, Washington, DC, USA 1996–97; attained rank of Amb. 1996; Dir-Gen. UNIDO 1997–2005 (re-elected 2001); Sr Assoc. mem. St Antony's Coll., Oxford, UK 2006; currently Chair. Global Business Devt Network LLC (investment co.), Washington, DC; Dir Gen. Prospectiva/Foresight 2020 (consultancy), Buenos Aires, Lima, Vienna, Mumbai; Vice-Pres. Foro PAIS (think tank on agri-business); Chair. Global Alliance of SMEs (China-US); mem. Bd of Dirs Univ. San Ignacio of Loyola, Lima, Peru; fmr mem. Bd of Dirs Buenos Aires Province Bank; Order of San Carlos, Colombia 2000, Order of Quetzal, Guatemala 2001, Order of Merit, Gov. of Italy 2003, Order of Industrial Merit, Gov. of Colombia 2004, Nat. Order of Merit, Grand Cross, Gov. of Ecuador 2005, Friendship Medal, Gov. of Cuba 2006, Grand Decoration of Honour, Gov. of Austria 2006; Dr hc (Lomonosov, Moscow) 1999, (Econ. Sciences and Public Admin., Budapest) 2000, (Univ. of Social and Business Sciences of Argentina) 2001, (Nat. Tech. Univ. of Ukraine) 2002; Trophée des performances de l'année 2000, Inst. Supérieur de Gestion, Paris 2000; Peter the Great Int. Award, Russian Fed. 2002, Prix de la Fondation 2002, Crans Montana Forum, Monte Carlo 2002, Kennedy Cross, John F. Kennedy Univ. Argentina 2004, Priyadarshni Acad. Award, India 2004. *Publications:* El Rol del Estado en la Política Industrial de los 90 1995, China in the WTO: The Birth of a New Catching-Up Strategy 2002; articles on econ. and industrial issues: Gearing Up for a New Development Agenda 2000, Reforming the UN System: UNIDO's Need-Driven Model 2001, Updating and Fleshing Out the Development Agenda 2003, Economic Development and UN Reform: Towards a Common Agenda for Action 2005. *Address:* Prospectiva 2020, Tagle 2810, 1425 Buenos Aires, Argentina (office). *Telephone:* (11) 4809-3115 (office). *E-mail:* cmagarinos@gbdnetwork.com (office); carlos@carlosmagarinos .com. *Website:* www.gbdnetwork.com (office); www.carlosmagarinos.com.

MAGD, Ahmed Kamal Abul, LLD; Egyptian lawyer and diplomatist; *Ambassador to Canada;* ed Cairo Univ.; Prof. of Public Law, Cairo Univ. 1958–; fmr Minister of Youth, fmr Minister of Information; fmr Arab League Commr responsible for dialogue between civilizations; Vice-Pres. Nat. Council for Human Rights –2010; Amb. to Canada 2010–; fmr Legal and Constitutional Adviser to Crown Prince and Prime Minister of Kuwait; fmr Judge, Vice-Pres. and Pres. World Bank Admin. Tribunal; mem. Supreme Council of Research, Univ. of El-Azhar, Cairo; mem. Maghreb Acad., Egyptian Soc. of Human Rights, Egyptian Supreme Council for Women's Affairs and Rights. *Publications:* numerous articles in English and Arabic on constitutional and administrative law, including A Contemporary Islamic Point of View (pamphlet), Dialogue, Not Confrontation (book). *Address:* Embassy of the Arab Republic of Egypt, 454 Laurier Avenue East, Ottawa, ON K1N 6R3, Canada (office). *Telephone:* (613) 234-4931 (office). *Fax:* (613) 234-4398 (office). *E-mail:* egyptemb@sympatico.ca (office). *Website:* www.mfa .gov.eg (office).

MAGEE, Bryan, MA, DLitt; British author; b. 12 April 1930, London; s. of Frederick Magee and Sheila Lynch; m. Ingrid Söderlund 1954 (died 1986); one d.; ed Christ's Hosp., UK, Lycée Hôche, Versailles, France, Keble Coll. Oxford, UK, Yale Univ., USA; served with Army Intelligence Corps 1948–49; fmr TV reporter, This Week; music and theatre critic, Musical Times and The Listener; Lecturer in Philosophy, Balliol Coll., Oxford 1970–71; Visiting Fellow, All Souls Coll. Oxford 1973–74; MP for Leyton 1974–83; Pres. Critics Circle of GB 1983–84, Hon. mem. 2012–; Hon. Sr Research Fellow, King's Coll. London 1984–94, Visiting Prof.

1994–2000; Fellow, Queen Mary and Westfield Coll. London 1989–; Visiting Fellow, Wolfson Coll., Oxford 1991–94, New Coll. Oxford 1995, Merton Coll., Oxford 1998, St Catherine's Coll., Oxford 2000, Peterhouse, Cambridge 2001, Clare Hall, Cambridge (Life Mem.) 2004; Visiting Prof., Univ. of Otago, Dunedin, New Zealand 2006, 2009, 2012, also fmr Visiting Fellow at Yale Univ., Harvard Univ., Univ. of Sydney, LSE; newspaper columnist; mem. Arts Council of GB and Chair. Music Panel 1993–94; mem. Soc. of Authors; Hon. Fellow, Queen Mary Coll. London 1988–, Keble Coll. Oxford 1994–; Hon. DLitt (Univ. of Leicester) 2005; Silver Medal, Royal TV Soc. 1978. *Television:* Men of Ideas 1978, The Great Philosophers 1987. *Publications:* Crucifixion and Other Poems 1951, Go West Young Man 1958, The New Radicalism 1962, The Democratic Revolution 1964, Towards 2000 1965, One in Twenty 1966, The Television Interviewer 1966, Aspects of Wagner 1968 (revised edn 1988), Modern British Philosophy 1971, Popper 1973, Facing Death 1977, Men of Ideas 1978, The Philosophy of Schopenhauer 1983, 1997, The Great Philosophers 1987, On Blindness 1995 (re-issued as Sight Unseen 1998), Confessions of a Philosopher 1997, The Story of Philosophy 1998, Wagner and Philosophy 2000, Talking Philosophy 2001, Clouds of Glory: A Hoxton Childhood (J. R. Ackerley Prize for autobiog. 2004) 2003, Growing Up In a War 2007. *Leisure interests:* music, theatre. *Address:* Wolfson College, Oxford, OX2 6UD, England (office).

MAGEE, Jeff, MSc, PhD, CE; British computer scientist and academic; *Head of Computing Department, Imperial College London;* currently Prof. of Computing and Head of Computing Dept, Imperial Coll., London; Chair. Steering Cttee, Int. Conf. on Software Eng 2002–04; fmr Co-Ed. IEE Proceedings on Software Engineering; adviser or consultant to numerous cos, including BP, BT, NATS, Fujitsu, Barclays Capital, QinetiQ, Kodak, Philips; Chartered Fellow, British Computer Soc.; IEE Informatics Premium Prize 1999, British Computer Soc. Brendan Murphy Memorial Prize 1999, Asscn for Computing Machinery Outstanding Research Award 2005. *Publications:* over 100 refereed publs. *Address:* Distributed Software Engineering Section, Department of Computing, Imperial College London, Huxley Building, Room 572, 180 Queen's Gate, London, SW7 2BZ, England (office). *Telephone:* (20) 7594-8269 (office). *Fax:* (20) 7594-8024 (office). *E-mail:* j.magee@imperial.ac.uk (office). *Website:* www-dse.doc.ic.ac.uk/cgi-bin/moin.cgi/jnm (office).

MAGERS, Philomene; German gallery owner; Co-owner, with Monika Sprüth, of Sprüth Magers contemporary art galleries in Germany and UK, represents artists including Kenneth Anger, Siegfried Anzinger, Keith Arnatt, Richard Artschwager, John Baldessari, Bernd & Hilla Becher, Alighiero Boetti, George Condo, Walter Dahn, Thomas Demand, Philip-Lorca diCorcia, Thea Djordjadze, Robert Elfgen, Peter Fischli/David Weiss, Sylvie Fleury, Cyprien Gaillard, Andreas Gursky, Jenny Holzer, Gary Hume, Donald Judd, Axel Kasseböhmer, Karen Kilimnik, Astrid Klein, Joseph Kosuth, Kraftwerk, Barbara Kruger, David Lamelas, Louise Lawler, David Maljkovic, Anthony McCall, Robert Morris, Reinhard Mucha, Jean-luc Mylayne, Michail Pirgelis, Nina Pohl, Richard Prince, Sterling Ruby, Ed Ruscha, Analia Saban, Gerda Scheepers, Thomas Scheibitz, Frances Scholz, Andreas Schulze, Cindy Sherman, Stephen Shore, Alexandre Singh, Robert Therrien, Ryan Trecartin, Rosemarie Trockel, Marcel van Eeden, Andro Wekua and Andrea Zittel. *Address:* Sprüth Magers, Hebbelstraße 93, 50968 Cologne (office); Sprüth Magers Berlin, Oranienburger Straße 18, 10178 Berlin, Germany (office); Sprüth Magers London, 7A Grafton Street, London, W1S 4EJ, England (office). *Telephone:* (221) 93729750 (Cologne) (office); (30) 28884030 (Berlin) (office); (20) 7408-1613 (London) (office). *Fax:* (221) 937297517 (Cologne) (office); (30) 288840352 (Berlin) (office); (20) 7499-4531 (London) (office). *E-mail:* info@spruethmagers.com (office). *Website:* www.spruethmagers.com (office).

MAGGI, Blairo; Brazilian farmer, business executive and politician; *Governor of Mato Grosso;* b. 29 May 1956, São Miguel do Iguaçu, Paraná; Owner of André Maggi Group (harvests, processes and exports soybeans, world's largest soyabean producer), group also involved in infrastructure projects to sustain soy industry, notably soy terminals, highways and waterways; currently Gov. Mato Grosso state; Greenpeace Golden Chainsaw Award for being the Brazilian who most contributed to destruction of Amazon rainforest 2006, ranked 62nd by Forbes magazine amongst The World's Most Powerful People 2009. *Address:* Office of the Governor, Cuiabá, Mato Grosso, Brazil (office). *E-mail:* diretoria.grupomaggi@grupomaggi.com.br. *Website:* www.grupomaggi.com.br.

MAGGI, Maurren Higa; Brazilian athlete; b. 25 June 1976, São Carlos; m.; one d.; sprinter, hurdler and long jumper; S American record holder at 100m hurdles and long jump, with 12.71 seconds and 7.26m, respectively; has also jumped 14.53m in triple jump; first Brazilian woman to win Olympic gold medal in an individual sport; 100m hurdles titles: Silver Medal, South American Championships 1997; Gold Medal, South American Championships 1999; Silver Medal, Pan American Games 1999; Gold Medal, South American Championships 2001; Silver Medal, Universiade 2001; long jump titles: Gold Medal, South American Championships 1997, 1999 2001; Bronze Medal, Universiade 1999; Gold Medal, Pan American Games 1999; Gold Medal, Universiade 2001; Silver Medal, Int. Asscn of Athletics Feds (IAAF) World Cup 2002; Gold Medal, Ibero-American Championships 2002; Bronze Medal, IAAF World Indoor Championships 2003; suspended for two years, missed 2003 Pan American Games, gained a revocation 2004, missed Athens Olympics due to pregnancy; Gold Medal, Pan American Games 2007; Silver Medal, IAAF World Indoor Championships 2008; Gold Medal, Olympic Games, Beijing 2008; Brazilian Athlete of the Year 1999, 2008, Brazilian Athlete of the Decade 2001–10. *Address:* c/o Global Sports Communication, Snelliusstraat 10, 6533 NV Nijmegen, The Netherlands (office); Confederação Brasileira de Atletismo, 874 Av. Sete de Setembro, 69005-140 Manaus, Amazonas, Brazil (office). *Telephone:* (24) 3515077 (office); (92) 31823200 (office). *Fax:* (24) 3515088 (office). *E-mail:* gsc@global-sports-comm.nl (office); mmatletismo@uol.com.br (office). *Website:* www.globalsportscommunication.nl (office); colunistas.ig.com.br/maurrenmaggi (office).

MAGIDOR, Menachem, BSc, MSc, PhD; Israeli mathematician, university administrator and academic; *Professor of Mathematics and President Emeritus, Hebrew University of Jerusalem;* b. 24 Jan. 1946, Petah Tikva; m.; four d.; ed Hebrew Univ. of Jerusalem; served in Israeli Navy and reached rank of Lt Commdr; has conducted research in math. logic (mainly set theory), also in computer science, dealing with artificial intelligence and semantics of program-

ming languages; Prof. of Math., Hebrew Univ. of Jerusalem 1982–, Dean Faculty of Science 1992–96, Pres. Hebrew Univ. of Jerusalem 1997–2009, Pres. Emer. 2009–; Pres. Asscn of Symbolic Logic 1996–98. *Publications:* about 70 papers on set theory, model theory and computer science. *Address:* Institute of Mathematics, Hebrew University of Jerusalem, 91904 Jerusalem, Israel (office). *Telephone:* (2) 658-4143 (office). *Fax:* (2) 658-4784 (office). *E-mail:* mensara@savion.huji.ac.il (office).

MAGLOIRE, Paul Gustave; Haitian government official; b. 2 Dec. 1953; ed Ecole Normale Supérieure d'Haïti; fmr adviser to Prime Minister Gerard Latortue; Minister of the Interior and Nat. Security 2005–06; played a key role in the organization of legis. and presidential elections 2006; Founder and Pres. Foresight Company System International (PROSINT); influential amongst Haitian communities in USA for 18 years; worked at Information Agency of the US (USIA), Washington, DC for seven years, represented Haitian Govt in Oslo, Norway during UN Conf. on Integrated Missions May 2005; fmr CEO Soc. Agricole et de Production Agro-industrielle; fmr mem. Bd of Dirs Soc. Haïtienne de Filature (SAFICO); Co-founder Asscn Nationale des Artistes Haïtiens; fmr Special Advisor to industrialist Thomas Désulmé; mem. Parti Nat. du Travail (Nat. Labour Party). *Address:* c/o Ministry of the Interior and Territorial Collectivities, Palais des Ministères, Champs de Mars, Port-au-Prince, Haiti. *E-mail:* info@mict.gouv.ht.

MAGNAGNA, Christian; Gabonese engineer and politician; *Minister of Budget, Public Accounts and the Civil Service;* b. 31 Aug. 1961, Mounana; nine c.; ed École des Hautes Études d'Ingénieur, Lille, Inst. supérieur de Gestion de Paris, France; Financial Man., Groupe Société auxiliaire d'entreprises (SAE), Paris Region 1988–90, Chief Works Engineer 1991–92; Man. MEGE BETON SA, France 1992–95; Deputy Dir CARMO (SME), Mounana 1995–99; Sales and Marketing Dir, Société Nationale des Bois du Gabon 1999–2003; Dir-Gen., Fond d'entretien Routier (road maintenance fund) 2004–06, Man. Dir 2007–09; mem. Parti Démocratique Gabonais, mem. Central Cttee 1993–2002, mem. Nat. Council 2003–05, 2008–10, Dir of Campaign Cttee (for both legislative and presidential elections), mem. Political Bureau 2006–08; Minister-Del. to Minister of Budget, Public Accounts and Civil Service 2009, Minister of Water and Forests 2011, of Budget, Public Accounts and the Civil Service 2014–. *Leisure interests:* reading, tourism, golf, running, tennis. *Address:* Ministry of the Budget, Public Accounts and the Civil Service, BP 165, Libreville, Gabon (office). *Telephone:* 01-79-50-00 (office). *Fax:* 01-79-57-37 (office). *Website:* www.finances.gouv.ga (office).

MAGNER, Marjorie (Marge), BS, MSIA; American banker and business executive; *Managing Partner, Brysam Global Partners;* b. 1949, Brooklyn, New York; one s.; ed Brooklyn Coll., Krannert School of Man., Purdue Univ.; joined Chemical Bank 1973, Man. Dir Chemical Technologies Div. –1983, actuarial analyst, Equitable Life Insurance Co. 1983–87; with Commercial Credit (predecessor of Citigroup) 1987, COO Global Consumer Group, Citigroup Inc., New York 2002–03, Chair. and CEO 2003–05, mem. Man. Cttee and Global Consumer Planning Group, Citigroup 2003–05; Founding Mem. and Man. Pnr, Brysam Global Partners 2007–; mem. Bd of Dirs Accenture Ltd 2006–, Gannett Co., Inc. 2006–, Ally Financial, Inc. 2010–; Brooklyn Coll. Foundation; mem. Dean's Advisory Council, Krannert School of Man., Purdue Univ.; Hon. DMan (Purdue) 2004; ranked by Fortune magazine amongst 50 Most Powerful Women in Business in the US 2001, (22nd) 2002, (fifth) 2003, (fifth) 2004, ranked by Forbes magazine amongst 100 Most Powerful Women (19th) 2004, (34th) 2005, ranked by US Banker magazine amongst The 25 Most Powerful Women in Banking (first) 2004, (third) 2005, amongst Top 25 Non-Bank Women in Finance (11th) 2008, Distinguished Alumni Medal, Brooklyn Coll. 2005, The Marjorie Magner Lifetime Achievement Award named in her honour 2005. *Address:* Brysam Global Partners, 515 Madison Avenue, New York, NY 10022, USA (office). *Telephone:* (212) 297-2777 (office). *E-mail:* bgp@brysam.com (office). *Website:* www.brysam.com (office).

MAGNIEN, Agnès; French archivist and librarian; *Executive Director, Archives nationales;* trained archivist-palaeographer; Dir of Departmental Archives 1994–2000, Deputy Dir Gen. of Services, Gen. Council of Seine-Saint-Denis 2000–08; has worked at Archives nationales since 2006, Exec. Dir Archives nationales 2011–, also directs activities at Paris and Fontainebleau sites, responsible for Maison de l'Histoire de France from 2015. *Address:* Archives nationales, 59 rue Guynemer, 90001, 93383 Pierrefitte-sur-Seine Cedex, France (office). *Telephone:* 1-75-47-21-32 (office). *Fax:* 1-75-47-29-10 (office). *E-mail:* agnes.magnien@culture.gouv.fr (office). *Website:* www.archivesnationales.culture.gouv.fr (office).

MAGNO, Adaljíza Albertina Xavier Reis, (Ajiza Magno); Timor-Leste politician; b. 1975; mem. Parl. 2002–; Vice-Minister of Foreign Affairs and Cooperation 2005–, Acting Minister of Foreign Affairs 2007. *Address:* Ministry of Foreign Affairs and Cooperation, Av. de Portugal, Praia dos Coqueiros, Dili, Timor-Leste (office). *Telephone:* 3331234 (office). *Fax:* 3339025 (office). *E-mail:* administration@mnec.gov-tl.net (office).

MAGNUSSEN, James; Australian swimmer; b. 11 April 1991, Port Macquarie, NSW; s. of Robert Magnussen and Donna Magnussen; ed Australian Coll. of Physical Educ.; mem. Australian Trans-Tasman team vs New Zealand 2008; Telstra Australian Swimming Championships 2010: bronze medal, 100m freestyle (qualified for nat. team), gold medal, 100m freestyle 2011; Australian Short course championships 2011: gold medal, 100m freestyle, 200m freestyle; Commonwealth Games, Delhi 2010: gold medal, 4×100m freestyle; Pan Pacific Championships, Irvine 2010: silver medal, 4×100m freestyle; World Championships (long course), Shanghai 2011: gold medal, 100m freestyle, 4×100m freestyle, silver medal, 4×100m medley; Olympic Games, London 2012: silver medal, 100m freestyle, bronze medal, 4×100m medley relay; World Championships (long course), Barcelona 2013: gold medal, 100m freestyle, silver medal, 4×100m medley relay; swims for Sydney Olympic Park Aquatic Centre Swim Club; coach: Brant Best; Swimmer of the Year 2011, Swimmers' Swimmer of the Year 2011, People's Choice Award 2011. *Leisure interests:* Rugby League, surfing. *Address:* Sydney Olympic Park Aquatic Centre, Locked Bag 2127, Sydney Olympic Park, NSW 2127, Australia. *Telephone:* (2) 9752-3666. *Fax:* (2) 9752-3699. *E-mail:* aquaticcentre@sopa.nsw.gov.au. *Website:* www.aquaticcentre.com.au.

MAGNUSSON, Thor Eyfeld, BA; Icelandic state antiquary (retd); b. 18 Nov. 1937, Hvammstangi; s. of Magnus Richardson and Sigridur Thordardóttir; m.

Maria Vilhjalmsdottir 1964; two s. one d.; ed Univ. of Iceland, Univ. of Uppsala, Sweden; Asst Curator, Nat. Museum 1964, Dir 1968, State Antiquary 1968–2001; travel abroad includes numerous trips to Scandinavia and UK, group tour to Egypt, Lebanon, Jordan, Soviet Union, Bulgaria, Turkey, Greece and Italy 1965; visit to USA for pvt. programme at Carnegie Museum, Pittsburgh 1967. *Publications:* articles on archeology and ethnology in the Journal of the Icelandic Archaeological Society. *Address:* c/o National Museum, Suðurgata 41, 101 Reykjavik; Bauganes 26, 101 Reykjavik, Iceland (home). *Telephone:* 530-2200.

MAGOMEDOV, Magomedali Magomedovich; Russian/Dagestan politician; b. 15 June 1930, Levashi, Dagestan Autonomous Repub.; m.; six c.; ed Dagestan State Pedagogical Inst., Dagestan Inst. of Agric.; teacher, Dir Levashi secondary school, then Head Levashi Dept of Nat. Educ. 1949–57; Chair. Levashi Kolkhoz 1957–66; Head Agric. Production unit Levashi Dist 1966–69; Chair. Levashi Dist Exec. Cttee 1969–70; First Sec. Levashi Dist CP Cttee 1970–75; Head Div. of Agric. Dagestan Regional CP Cttee 1975–79; Deputy Chair., Chair. Council of Ministers Dagestan Autonomous Repub. 1979–87; Chair. Presidium Supreme Soviet Dagestan Autonomous Repub. 1987–94; Chair. State Council (Head Repub. of Dagestan) 1994–2006 (resgnd); mem. Russian Council of Fed. 1993–2001. *Address:* c/o House of Government, Lenina pl., 167005 Makhachkala, Dagestan, Russia (office).

MAGOWAN, Peter Alden, MA; American business executive; b. 5 April 1942, New York, NY; s. of Robert Anderson Magowan and Doris Magowan (née Merrill); m. 1st Jill Tarlau (divorced 1982); m. 2nd Deborah Johnston 1982; three d. from 1st marriage; ed Groton School, Stanford Univ., Univ. of Oxford, UK and Johns Hopkins School of Advanced Int. Studies; store man., Washington, DC, Safeway Stores 1968–70, Dist Man., Houston, Tex. 1970, Retail Operations Man., Phoenix, Ariz. 1971–72, Div. Man., Tulsa, Okla 1973–76, Man., Int. Div., Toronto, Canada 1976–78, Western Regional Man., San Francisco, Calif. 1978–79, Dir, Safeway Stores, Inc. 1979, Chair. 1980–98, CEO 1980–93, Pres. and COO 1988, also Chair. Exec. Cttee, retd 2005; Pres., Man. Gen. Partner, San Francisco Giants Major League Baseball franchise 1993–2008; fmr Dir of US Chamber of Commerce, The Hudson Inst., Pacific Gas and Electric Co., Food Marketing Inst.; Dir, Caterpillar, DaimlerChrysler, W5 Networks, Inc., Spring Group PLC; mem. Advisory Council, Johns Hopkins School of Advanced Int. Studies; Trustee, Johns Hopkins Univ.; Exec. of the Year 2000, Sports Business Journal. *Address:* c/o San Francisco Giants, AT&T Park, 24 Willie Mays Plaza, San Francisco, CA 94107, USA. *E-mail:* info@sfgiants.com.

MAGRIS, Claudio; Italian journalist, writer and academic; *Professor Emeritus of German Language and Literature, University of Trieste;* b. 10 April 1939, Trieste; s. of Duilio Magris and Pia de Grisogono Magris; m. Marisa Madieri 1964; two s.; ed Univ. of Turin; Lecturer in German Language and Literature, Univ. of Trieste 1968–70, Turin 1970–78, Trieste 1978–, now Prof. Emer.; mem. Deutsche Akad. für Sprache und Dichtung (Darmstadt), Österreichische Akad. der Wissenschaften, Accad. delle Scienze di Torino, Ateneo Veneto, Akad. der Wissenschaften (Göttingen); Decoration for Science and Art 2012, Cross of the Order of Merit (Germany) 2012; Debenedetti 1972, Val di Comino 1978, Goethe Medaille 1980, Aquileia 1983, Premiolino 1983, San Giusto d'Oro 1984, Musil Medaille der Stadt Klagenfurt 1984, Bagutta 1987, Accad. dei Lincei 1987, Marotta 1987, Città di Modena 1987, Antico Fattore 1988, Juan Carlos I 1989, Premio Strega 1997, Premio Chiara alla Carriera 1999, Premio Würth per la Cultura Europea 1999, Premio Grinzane Piemonte 1999, Medaglia d'Oro della Cultura della Scuola e dell'Arte 1999, Premio Sikken 2000, Premio Nietsche 2000, Premium Erasmianum 2001, Leipziger Buchpreis zur Europäischen Verständigung 2001, Österreichisches Ehrenkreuz für Wissenschaft und Kunst (First Class), Premio Principe de Asturias for Literature 2004, Österreichischem Staatspreis für Europäische literatur 2006, Friedenspreis des Deutschen Buchhandels 2009. *Plays:* Stadelmann 1988, Le Voci 1999, La Mostra 2001. *Publications include:* Il Mito absburgico nella letteratura austriaca moderna 1963, 1988, Wilhelm Heinse 1968, Tre studi su Hoffman 1969, Lontano da dove 1971, Joseph Roth e la tradizione ebraicoorientale 1971, L'altra ragione. Tre saggi su Hoffmann 1978, Dietro le parole 1978, Itaca e oltre 1982, Trieste. Un'identità di frontiera 1982, 1987, L'anello di Clarisse 1984, Illazioni su una sciabola 1984, Danubio 1986 (trans. in numerous languages), Stadelmann 1988, Un altro mare 1991, Microcosmi 1997, Utopia e disincanto 1999, Telling Tales (contrib. to charity anthology) 2004, Alla cieca 2005, L'infinito viaggiare 2005, Lei dunque capirà 2006, La storia non è finita 2006, Davanti alla legge. Due Saggi 2006, Alfabeti 2008; numerous essays and book reviews in Corriere della Sera and other European newspapers and periodicals; trans. Ibsen, Kleist, Schnitzler, Büchner. *Address:* Department of Anglo-German Literature, University of Trieste, Via Lazzaretto Vecchio 8, III Piano, Stanza 309, 34123 Trieste, Italy (office). *Telephone:* (040) 5587252 (office). *Fax:* (040) 6763093 (office).

MAGSI, Nawab Zulfikar Ali; Pakistani politician and government official; b. 14 Feb. 1954, Jhal Magsi, Balochistan; ed Aitchison Coll., Lahore; current Nawab (Chief) of Magsi Tribe; first came to politics in 1977, won seat in prov. ass. as ind. cand.; served in numerous prov. ministries, also worked in Home Ministry 1990s; mem. Pakistan People's Party; Chief Minister of Balochistan Prov. in Govt of Benazir Bhutto May–July 1993, Oct. 1993–96; stood as ind. cand. from his native PB-32 Jhal Magsi constituency and won without opposition Feb. 2008; Gov. of Balochistan 2008–13 (resgnd). *Address:* Pakistan Peoples Party, 8, Street 19, F-8/2, Islamabad, Pakistan (office). *Telephone:* (51) 2255264 (office). *Fax:* (51) 2282741 (office). *E-mail:* ppp@comsats.net.pk (office). *Website:* www.ppp.org.pk (office).

MAGUIRE, Adrian Edward, BPhil, MA, FSA; Irish fmr professional jockey; b. 29 April 1971; s. of Joseph Maguire and Philomena Maguire; m. Sabrina Maguire 1995; one d.; ed Kilmessan Nat. School, Trim Vocational School; champion pony race rider 1986, champion point-to-point rider 1990–91, champion conditional jockey 1991–92; wins include Cheltenham Gold Cup, Irish Grand Nat. (youngest ever winning jockey), Galway Plate, Imperial Cup, Greenalls Gold Cup, Queen Mother Champion Chase, King George VI Chase, Triumph Hurdle, Cathcart Chase 1994, Scottish National 1998, Whitbread Gold Cup 1998; holds records for most point-to-point winners in a season, most winners in a season for a conditional jockey (71) 1991–92; retd 2002 following neck injury, having won over 1,000 races. *Leisure interests:* squash, watching television. *Address:* 17 Willes Close, Faringdon, Oxon. SN7 7DU, England (home).

MAGUIRE, Joanne M., BEng, MEng; American aerospace industry executive; *Executive Vice-President, Lockheed Martin Space Systems Company;* d. of Mike Maguire; ed Michigan State Univ., Univ. of California, Los Angeles, Exec. Program in Man. at UCLA's Anderson School of Man., Harvard Program for Sr Execs in Nat. and Int. Security; joined TRW Space & Electronics (S&E) (now Northrop Grumman Space Tech.) 1975, held succession of increasingly responsible tech. and man. positions, later Program Man. for Defense Support Program, later Deputy Gen. Man. Defense Systems Div., later Vice-Pres. and Gen. Man. Space & Tech. Div., later Vice-Pres. and Gen. Man. Space & Laser Programs Div., later Deputy and Vice-Pres. Business Devt –2003; Vice-Pres. Special Programs, Lockheed Martin Space Systems Co. 2003, Vice-Pres. and Deputy of Lockheed Martin Space Systems Co. 2003–06, mem. Bd of Dirs 2004–, Exec. Vice-Pres. Lockheed Martin Space Systems Co. 2006–, officer of Lockheed Martin Corpn, also Chair. United Launch Alliance (Lockheed Martin jt venture); mem. Bd of Dirs Space Foundation, INROADS, Inc.; mem. AIAA, Soc. of Women Engineers; Outstanding Leadership Award, Women in Aerospace 1999, ranked by Fortune magazine amongst the 50 Most Powerful Women in Business in the US (35th) 2006, (38th) 2007, (31st) 2008, (35th) 2009, (31st) 2010, (29th) 2011, (31st) 2012, named by Corporate Board Member magazine as one of Top 50 Women in Technology 2008, honoured by Girls Inc. for achievements as a "leader and role model for young women" 2008. *Address:* Lockheed Martin Space Systems Company, 12257 South Wadsworth Blvd, Littleton, CO 80125-8500, USA (office). *Telephone:* (303) 977-3000 (office). *E-mail:* martha.a.hirschfield@lmco.com (office). *Website:* www.lockheedmartin.com (office).

MAGUIRE, Robert Francis, III, BA; American real estate executive; b. 18 April 1935, Portland, Ore.; s. of Robert Francis Maguire, Jr and Jean Maguire (née Shepard); ed Univ. of California, Los Angeles; Vice-Pres. Security Pacific Nat. Bank, Los Angeles 1960–64; Chair. Maguire Thomas Partners 1965, Chair. Maguire Properties Inc. (renamed MPG Office Trust 2010 Inc.) 2002–08, Chair. Emer. 2008–10, Co-CEO 2002–05, CEO June–Nov. 2002, 2006–08; mem. Exec. Bd Medical Sciences, UCLA; mem. Bd Dirs LA County Museum of Art, St John's Hosp., Santa Monica, Calif.; mem. Bd of Govs LA Music Center; Trustee, UCLA Foundation, Bard Coll., St John's Hosp., Santa Monica; mem. Bd Los Angeles County Museum of Art, Los Angeles Music Center. *Address:* c/o MPG Office Trust Inc., 333 South Grand Avenue, Suite 400, Los Angeles, CA 90071, USA.

MAGUIRE, Tobey; American actor; b. 27 June 1975, Santa Monica, Calif.; s. of Vincent Maguire and Wendy Maguire; m. Jennifer Meyer 2007; one d.; began career acting in commercials. *Television includes:* sitcoms: Blossom 1991, Roseanne 1991, Jake and the Fatman, Great Scott! 1992, This Boy's Life 1993; films: Spoils of War 1994, A Child's Cry for Help 1994. *Films include:* S.F.W. 1994, Revenge of the Red Baron 1994, Duke of Groove 1995, Seduced by Madness 1996, Joyride 1996, Deconstructing Harry 1997, The Ice Storm 1997, Pleasantville 1998, Fear and Loathing in Las Vegas 1998, Don's Plum 1998, Ride With the Devil 1999, The Cider House Rules 1999, Wonderboys 2000, Spider-Man 2002, Seabiscuit 2003, Spider-Man 2 2004, The Good German 2006, Spider-Man 3 2007, Tropic Thunder 2008, Brothers 2009, The Great Gatsby 2013. *Leisure interests:* boardgames, basketball, backgammon, yoga. *Address:* Creative Artists Agency, 9830 Wilshire Boulevard, Beverly Hills, CA 90212-1825, USA (office). *Telephone:* (310) 288-4545 (office). *Fax:* (310) 288-4800 (office). *Website:* www.caa.com (office).

MAGYAR, Bálint; Hungarian sociologist and politician; b. 1952, Budapest; m. Róza Hodosán; one d.; ed Eötvös Loránd Univ. of Budapest; Research Fellow, Inst. of World Econ., Hungarian Acad. of Sciences 1977–81, Inst. of Co-operation 1982–88; Financial Research Ltd 1988–90; involved in dissident political activities from 1979; Founding mem. Alliance of Free Democrats (SZDSZ), Pres. 1998–2000, mem. Exec. Bd 2001–; mem. Parl. 1990–; Minister of Culture and Educ. 1996–98, of Educ. 2002–06; State Sec. for Devt Policy, Prime Minister's Office 2007; János Neumann Prize 1998. *Film:* Dir Hungarian Stories (documentary) (Special Prize, Critics' Prize, Budapest Film Festival 1988). *Publication:* Dunaapáti 1944–1958 (sociography of a Hungarian village, three vols) (Ferenc Erdei Prize 1986). *Address:* c/o National Development Agency, Mozsár u. 16, 1066 Budapest (office); SZDSZ, Gizella u. 36, 1143 Budapest, Hungary.

MAH, Bow Tan, MSc; Singaporean politician; *Minister of National Development;* b. 12 Sept. 1948; m. Sheryn Kaye Von Senden; two s. two d.; ed St Joseph's Inst., Univ. of New South Wales, Australia; joined Singapore Bus Services 1974, Gen. Man. –1983; CEO Singapore Monitor, Singapore News and Publs Ltd (SNPL), later Group Gen. Man. SNPL, Group Gen. Man. (Co-ordination) Singapore Press Holdings Ltd 1985–88; Chair. Bd of Dirs NTUC Comfort 1983–86, Bd of Trustees 1988–93; Chair. Nat. Productivity Bd, Nat. Productivity Council, Skills Redevelopment Fund Advisory Council 1986–91; mem. Parl. 1988–; Minister of State for Trade and Industry and Minister of State for Communications and Information 1988, Minister of State for Trade and Industry and Minister of State for Communications 1990, Minister for Communications 1991–99, concurrently Minister for the Environment 1993–95, Minister for Nat. Devt 1999–; Chair. Service Improvement Unit, Political Supervisory Cttee 1991; Chair. Bd of Govs, Singapore Inst. of Labour Studies 1990–2002; Chair. Nat. Youth Achievement Award Advisory Bd 1994–, Singapore Labour Foundation 2001–; Adviser Football Asscn of Singapore (FAS) Council 1991–99, Pres. FAS 1999–2004, Adviser 2004–; Hon. DSc (Univ. of New South Wales) 2001; Nat. Trades Union Congress Medal of Honour 1991, Univ. of New South Wales Alumni Award for Achievement 1996. *Leisure interests:* golf, travelling, reading, football. *Address:* Ministry of National Development, 5 Maxwell Road, 21/22-00, Tower Block, MND Complex, 069110 Singapore (office). *Telephone:* 62221211 (office). *Fax:* 63257254 (office). *E-mail:* mnd_hq@mnd.gov.sg (office). *Website:* www.mnd.gov.sg (office).

MAHA VAJIRALONGKORN, HRH Crown Prince, BA, LLB; Thai; b. 28 July 1952, Bangkok; s. of HM King Bhumibol Adulyadej and Queen Sirikit; m. 1st Mom Luang Soamsawali Kitiyakara 1977 (divorced); one d.; fmr pnr Yuvadhida Polpraserth; four s. one d.; m. 2nd Mom Srirasmi Mahidol na Ayudhya (HRH Princess Srirasmi, The Royal Consort) 2001; one s.; ed Royal Mil. Coll. Duntroon and Univ. of New South Wales, Australia, Royal Thai Army Command and Gen. Staff Coll., Sukhothai Thammatirat Univ., Bangkok, Royal Coll. of Defence Studies, UK; conferred title Somdech Phra Boroma Orasadhiraj Chao Fah Maha Vajiralongkorn Sayam Makutrajakuman (heir to the throne) 28 Dec. 1972; Staff Officer Directorate of Army Intelligence 1975–78, Exec. Officer King's Own

Bodyguard 1978–80, Commdr 1980–84, Commanding Officer 1984–88, Commanding Gen. 1988–92, Commanding Gen. Royalty Security Command, Office of the Supreme Commander 1992–, Instructor Pilot, F-5 E/F fighter 1994, holds ranks of Gen. in Royal Thai Army, Adm. in Royal Thai Navy, Air Chief Marshal in Royal Thai Air Force. *Address:* c/o The Government Public Relations Department, Rama VI Road, Bangkok, Thailand (office). *Telephone:* 618-2373 (office). *Fax:* 618-2358 (office).

MAHAMA, Alhaji Aliu, BSc; Ghanaian politician; b. 3 March 1946, Yendi; ed Govt Secondary School, Tamale, Kwame Nkrumah Univ. of Science and Tech., Kumasi, Inst. in Project Planning and Man. and in Leadership; construction engineer, Bolgatanga Regional Office, State Construction Corpn 1972–75, Asst Regional Man., Koforidua Regional Office 1975–76, Regional Man. in charge of Northern Region 1976–82; Founder and Man. Dir LIDRA Ltd 1982–; Councillor, Yendi Dist Council 1978; mem. Tamale Municipal Assembly 1990; fmr Minister of Defence; Vice-Pres. of Ghana 2001–09; Chair. Northern Regional Contractors' Asscn 1996–2000; fmr Chair. Econ. Devt Cttee, Tamale-Louisville Sister State Cttee; fmr Bd mem. several secondary schools in Northern Region including Tamale Polytechnic; alumnus, Ghana Inst. of Man. and Public Admin; Founding mem. Real Tamale United Football Club; Fellow Inst. of Surveyors, Fellow Inst. of Administrators. *Leisure interests:* reading, football, badminton. *Address:* c/o New Patriotic Party, C912/2 Duade St, Kokomlemle, POB 3456, Accra -North, Ghana.

MAHAMA, John Dramani; Ghanaian politician and head of state; *President;* b. 29 Nov. 1958, Damongo; s. of Emmanuel Adama Mahama; m. Lordina Mahama; seven c.; ed Univ. of Ghana, Legon, Moscow Inst. of Social Sciences, USSR; Information, Culture and Research Officer, Embassy of Japan, Accra 1991–96; Int. Relations, Sponsorship Communications and Grants Man., PLAN International (non-govt org.) Ghana Country Office 1996; MP for Bole/Bamboi Constituency 1997–2009; Deputy Minister of Communications 1997–98, Minister of Communications 1998–2001; mem. Pan-African Parl., S Africa 2004–11, Chair. West African Caucus; Vice-Pres. of Ghana 2009–12, Pres. 2012–; mem. Nat. Democratic Congress, Dir of Communications 2002. *Publication:* My First Coup d'État and Other True Stories From the Lost Decades of Africa 2012. *Address:* Office of the President, POB 1627, Osu, Accra, Ghana (office). *Telephone:* (30) 2666997 (office). *Website:* www.oop.gov.gh (office).

MAHANTA, Prafulla Kumar, BSc, LLB; Indian politician; b. 23 Dec. 1952, Rupnarayan Satra; s. of Deva Kanta Mahanta and Lakshmi Prava Mahanta; m. Joyasree Goswami; one s. one d.; leader of Assam Movt 1979–85; f. Asom Gana Parishad (AGP) (regional political party) 1985, expelled 2005, f. AGP (Progressive) 2005, reinducted into AGP (after merger of AGP and AGP Progressive) 2008; Chief Minister of Assam 1985–90, 1996–2001; fmr Pres. All Assam Students Union. *Address:* Rupnarayan Satra, Kaliabor, Nagaon District (home); Asom Gana Parishad, Ambari, Guwahati 781 001, India (office). *Telephone:* (361) 562222 (office); (361) 561291. *Fax:* (361) 562069 (office). *Website:* www.asomganaparishad.in (office).

MAHAR, Sardar Ali Mohammad Khan; Pakistani politician; b. Khan Garh Mahar, Ghotki Dist, Sindh; s. of Haji Ali Anwar Khan Mahar; m.; Chief of Mahar tribe; Chief Minister of Sindh 2002–04 (resgnd); fmr mem. Nat. Security Council; mem. (Pakistan Peoples Party Parliamentarians) Nat. Ass. of Pakistan for NA-201(Ghotki-II) constituency 2013–. *Address:* Village Khangarh Sharif, Taluka Khangarh District, Ghotki; H. # E-27, Gizri Blueward Defence, Phase-IV, Karachi; H-212, Parliament Lodges, Islamabad, Pakistan. *Telephone:* (300) 2220222. *E-mail:* assembly@na.gov.pk. *Website:* www.na.gov.pk/en/profile.put?uid=17.

MAHARAJ, Mac (Sathyandranath Ragunanan), BA, MBA; South African politician and business executive; *Spokesperson for President of South Africa;* b. 27 April 1935, Newcastle, Natal (now KwaZulu-Natal); s. of N. R. Maharaj; m. Zarina Maharaj; two c.; ed St Oswald's High School and Univ. of Natal, Durban; Ed. New Age 1956; lived in UK where he worked as a teacher, rubbish collector and a canning factory and building site worker 1957–61, Founding mem. British Anti-Apartheid Movement; mem. Umkhonto Wesizwe (African Nat. Congress—ANC's armed wing) 1961, underwent mil. training in GDR 1961–62; returned to SA 1962; sentenced to 12 years' imprisonment Dec. 1964, served prison sentence on Robben Island 1965–76; left SA 1976; with ANC HQ, Lusaka, Zambia, Sec. Underground Section 1977; mem. Revolutionary Council 1978, Politico-Mil. Council 1985; mem. ANC Negotiation Cttee, Political Cttee 1984, Nat. Exec. Council 1985–90, 1991–, Nat. Working Cttee; Commdr Operation Vula, SA 1988–90; mem. Political Bureau and Cen. Cttee 1990; with Codesa Secr.; Jt Sec. Transitional Exec. Council 1994; Minister of Transport, Govt of Nat. Unity 1994–99; active in business 1999–; Dir (non-exec.), FirstRand Bank 1999–2003 (resgnd); Spokesperson, Pres. of South Africa, Jacob Zuma 2011–; mem. Faculty, Bennington Coll., Vt, USA 2005–. *Address:* Office of the Presidency, Private Bag X1000, Union Buildings, West Wing, Government Avenue, Pretoria 0001, South Africa. *Telephone:* (12) 3005200. *Fax:* (12) 3238246. *E-mail:* president@po.gov.za. *Website:* www.thepresidency.gov.za.

MAHARAJ, Pandit Birju; Indian dancer and choreographer; *Director, Kalashram;* b. 4 Feb. 1938, Lucknow; s. of Acchan Maharaj; m.; two s. three d.; Kathak teacher, Sangeet Bharti, Bharatiya Kala Kendra, Delhi; Head of Faculty and Dir Kathak Kendra, New Delhi –1998; Founder-Dir Kalashram (school for Kathak and associated disciplines) 1998–; Dr hc (Banaras Hindu Univ.), (Khairagarh Univ.); Padma Vibhushan 1986, Sangeet Natak Akademi Award, Kalidas Samman, Nritya Choodamani, Andhra Ratna, Nritya Vilas, Adharshila Shikhar Samman, Soviet Land Nehru Award, Shiromani Samman, Rajiv Gandhi Peace Award, Lata Mangeshkar Puraskaar 2002. *Films:* Shatranj Ke Khiladi 1977, Dil To Pagal Hai 1997, Gadar: Ek Prem Katha 2001, Devdas 2002, Vishwaroopam (Nat. Award for Best Choreography) 2013. *Leisure interests:* painting, poetry. *Address:* Kalashram, D-II/33, Shahjahan Road, New Delhi 110 011, India (office). *Telephone:* (11) 26277367 (office). *Fax:* (11) 23782889 (office). *E-mail:* admin@birjumaharaj-kalashram.com (office). *Website:* contact@birjumaharaj-kalashram.com (office); www.birjumaharaj-kalashram.com (office).

MAHAREY, Steve, BA, MA; New Zealand fmr politician and academic; m. Liz Mackay; two step-s.; taught business admin.; Sr Lecturer in Sociology, Massey Univ.; mem. Palmerston North City Council 1986–89, Chair. Palmerston North Labour Electorate Cttee, mem. Policy Council; Labour MP for Palmerston North

1990–; Opposition Spokesperson on Social Welfare and Employment, Broadcasting and Communications and Labour Relations 1994–97; Assoc. Spokesperson on Educ. with specific responsibility for Tertiary Educ., Educ. and Employment 1990–93, served on the Social Services, Educ. and Science, Commerce, Justice and Law Reform and Broadcasting Parl. Select Cttees; Minister for Social Devt and Employment 1999–2005, Assoc. Minister of Educ. (Tertiary Educ.) 1999–2004, Minister responsible for Community and Voluntary Sector 1999–2002, Minister of Broadcasting 2002–07, of Housing 2003–04, of Youth Affairs 2004, of Research, Science and Tech. 2004–07, Minister for Crown Research Insts. 2004–07, Minister of Educ. 2005–07, Minister responsible for the Educ. Review Office –2007; fmr Chair. Cabinet Social Devt Cttee; fmr mem. Cttees for Cabinet Policy, Appointments and Honours, Econ. Devt and Legislation; retd from politics 2007. *Publications:* numerous articles on media and cultural studies and social change. *Leisure interests:* mountain biking, swimming, music, social and political theory, travel, spectator sports. *Address:* c/o New Zealand Labour Party, Fraser House, POB 784, Wellington, New Zealand (office).

MAHASHER, Nasser al-, BS, MS; Saudi Arabian oil company executive; *Representative Director and CEO, S-Oil Corporation;* ed King Fahd Univ. of Petroleum and Minerals, Eastern Michigan Univ. and Wayne State Univ., USA; worked for Saudi Aramco (state-owned oil co.) for 22 years, including as Global Refining Co-ordinator, also Sr Vice-Pres.; fmr Pres. and CEO Saudi Petroleum International, Inc.; Pres. Saudi Petroleum Ltd, Tokyo 2008–12; Rep. Dir and CEO S-Oil Corpn 2012–. *Address:* S-Oil Corporation, 471 Gongduk-dong, Mapo-gu, Seoul 121-805, Republic of Korea (office). *Telephone:* (2) 3772-5151 (office). *E-mail:* info@s-oil.com (office). *Website:* www.s-oil.com (office).

MAHAT, Ram Sharan, MA, PhD; Nepalese politician; *Minister of Finance;* b. 1 Jan. 1951, Nuwakot; s. of Tol Kumari Mahat; m. Roshana Mahat; one s. one d.; ed Tribhuban Univ., Gokhale Inst. of Politics and Econs, Pune, India, School of Int. Service, American Univ.; Asst Resident Rep., UNDP, Islamabad 1989–90; econ. adviser to Prime Minister of Nepal 1991–92; Vice-Chair. Nat. Planning Comm. 1991–94; mem. Constituent Assembly (Parl.) from Nuwakot Dist 1994–; Minister of Finance 1995–99, 2001, 2006–07, 2014–; Minister of Foreign Affairs 1999; fmr Chair. Univ. Grants Comm.; mem. Bd of Trustees Asian Inst. of Technology, Bangkok 1993–94; Francis Humbert Humphrey Award for leadership role in the Public Service by USIA and t Inst. of International Education. *Publications include:* Industrial Financing in Nepal; numerous articles on nat. and int. econ. issues. *Leisure interests:* social service, reading books. *Address:* Bansbari, Kathmandu, Nepal (home). *E-mail:* ramsmahat@gmail.com. *Website:* www.ramsmahat.com.

MAHATHIR BIN MOHAMAD; Malaysian politician (retd); b. 20 Dec. 1925, Alur Setar, Kedah; m. Dr Siti Hasmah binti Haji Mohd Ali 1956; three s. two d.; ed Sultan Abdul Hamid Coll. and Univ. of Malaya in Singapore; Medical Officer, Kedah, Langkawi and Perlis 1953–57; private practice 1957–64; mem. UMNO (now Umno Baru) Supreme Council 1965–69, 1972–2008 (Pres. 1981), mem. Supreme Council 1972–2008; mem. House of Reps. for Kota Setar Selatan 1964–69, for Kubang Pasu 1974–; mem. Senate 1973; Chair. Food Industries of Malaysia Sdn. Bhd. 1973; Minister of Educ. 1974–77, of Trade and Industry 1977–81, of Defence 1981–86, of Home Affairs 1986–99, of Justice 1987, of Natural and Rural Devt; Deputy Prime Minister 1976–81, Prime Minister of Malaysia 1981–2003; Advisor, Petronas, Proton 2003–. *Publications:* The Malay Dilemma 1969, The Way Forward 1998. *Address:* c/o Petroliam Nasional Berhad (PETRONAS), Tower 1, Petronas Twin Towers, Kuala Lumpur City Centre, 50088 Kuala Lumpur, Malaysia (office). *E-mail:* webmaster@petronas.com.my (office). *Website:* www.petronas.com.my (office).

MAHATO, Rajendra; Nepalese politician; *Chairman, Sadbhavana Party;* Nepal Sadbhavana Party (NSP) cand. for Sarlahi-2 constituency in parl. election 1994, won seat 1999; broke away from NSP and formed own party, Sadbhavana Party 2007, Chair. 2007–; Minister for Industry, Commerce and Supply 2007–08; resgnd from interim Parl. Jan. 2008; won Sarlahi-4 seat in Constituent Ass. election April 2008; Minister of Health and Population 2011–13. *Address:* Sadbhavana Party, Kathmandu, Nepal (office).

MAHAVIR, Bhai, MA, LLB, PhD; Indian politician; b. 30 Oct. 1922, Lahore, Pakistan; s. of Bhai Parmanand and Bhagya Sudhi; m. Krishna Bhai Mahavir; two d.; Lecturer, Econs, D.A.V. Coll., Lahore 1944, Camp Coll., Karnal; fmr Man. Dir Akashvani Prakashan Ltd; fmr Vice-Chair. Punjabi Acad.; Founder mem. and first Gen. Sec. Bharatiya Jana Sangh; Pres. Delhi Pradesh Jana Sangh 1968–69; mem. Rajya Sabha 1968–74, 1978–84; Chair. Cttee on Subordinate Legislation of Rajya Sabha 1982–84; detained during Emergency Period; Chair. Governing Body, Rajdhani Coll., New Delhi; Dir Bhai Parmanand Vidya Mandir; Sec. Bhai Parmanand Smarak Samiti; mem. Nat. Exec. Bharatiya Janata Party, Chair. Cen. Disciplinary Cttee 1996–98; Gov. of Madhya Pradesh 1998–2003. *Address:* c/o Raj Bhavan, Bhopal (office); 389 D/S, New Rajendra Nagar, New Delhi 110 060, India (home).

MAHAYNI, Mohammad Khaled al-, PhD; Syrian economist and politician; b. 30 May 1943, Damascus; s. of Salim al-Mahayni and Weedad Araman; m. Falak Sakkal 1966; two s. two d.; ed Damascus Univ.; various public financial and econ. appointments 1961–70; auditor 1970–77; Dir of Debt Fund and Information, Ministry of Finance 1979–80, of Public Enterprises 1981–84; Deputy Minister of Finance 1984–87, Minister 1987–2001; Gov. IBRD 1987–2001, Arab Bank for Econ. Devt in Africa 1989; currently Dir Nat. Inst. of Admin, Damascus; Prof., Damascus Univ. 1992–. *Publications:* Methodology of the General Budget of the State in the Syrian Arab Republic 1984, Supplementary Policies for Financial Planning 1995, Government Accounting 1996, Public Finance and Tax Legislation 1999. *Leisure interests:* reading and computing. *Address:* National Institute of Administration, Damascus, Syria (office). *Telephone:* (11) 594827 (office). *Fax:* (11) 5948071 (office). *E-mail:* info@ina-syrie.com (office). *Website:* www.ina-syrie.com (office).

MAHDAVI KANI, Ayatollah Mohammad Reza; Iranian cleric and government official; *Chairman, Assembly of Experts;* b. 8 April 1931, Kan village, near Tehran; m. Soraya Mohammadian; ed seminaries in Borhan and Qom; fmr Head of Islamic Revolution Cttee; fmr mem. Guardian Council; Minister of the Interior 1980–81; Acting Prime Minister of Iran Sept.–Oct. 1981; Founder and Pres. Imam Sadiq

Univ., Tehran; fmr mem. Constitutional Amendment Council, Higher Council of Cultural Revolution; Chair. Majles-e Khobregan-e Rahbari (Ass. of Experts) 2011–; Sec.-Gen. Combatant Clergy Asscn 1979–. *Address:* Majles-e Khobregan-e Rahbari (Assembly of Experts), Tehran, Iran (office). *Website:* www .majlesekhobregan.ir (office).

MAHDI, Adil Abd al-, PhD; Iraqi economist and politician; *Vice-President;* b. 1942, Baghdad; m.; four c.; ed Coll. of Trade and Econs, Baghdad; moved to France 1969, worked for several think tanks; has also lived in Lebanon and Iran; Supreme Council for the Islamic Revolution in Iraq (SCIRI) rep. in Kurdistan 1992–96; returned to Iraq; interim Minister of Finance 2004–05, Vice-Pres. of Iraq 2005–. *Address:* c/o Office of the President, Baghdad, Iraq.

MAHDI, Sadiq al-, (since 1978 known as Sadiq Abdul Rahman), BSc, MSc; Sudanese politician; *President, Umma National Party;* b. 25 Dec. 1935, Al-Abasya, Omdurman; s. of the late Imam Al-Siddik Abdel-Rahman al-Mahdi and Sayeda Rahma Abdallah Jad-Allah; great grandson of Imam Abdul-Rahman El Mahdi; m. 1st Sayeda Hafya Mamoun Sharief 1960; m. 2nd Sayeda Sarrah al-Fadil Mahmoud 1962; ten c.; ed Comboni School, Victoria Coll., Gordon Memorial Coll., Khartoum, Univ. of Khartoum, St John's Coll., Oxford, UK; Pres. Unified Nat. Front 1961–64, Umma Mahdist (now Umma Nat. Party—Hizb al-Umma) from 1964, 1986–89, Pres. 2003–, Pres. Nat. Front 1972–77; Prime Minister 1966–67, 1986–89; arrested on a charge of high treason 1969; exiled April 1970; returned to Sudan and arrested Feb. 1972, released April 1974; exiled 1974–77; led unsuccessful coup against fmr Pres. Nimeri July 1976, returned to Sudan Sept. 1977; reconciliation with Pres. Nimeri 1977; led mediation mission over US hostages in Iran Crisis Jan. 1980; returned to prison Sept. 1983, released Dec. 1984; mem. Nat. Ass. 1986–89; Minister of Defence 1986–89; overthrown in coup June 1989, arrested July 1989, released and put under house arrest Nov. 1989; granted amnesty May 1991; arrested on charges of conspiring against mil. govt June 1994; re-arrested May 1995; escaped from house arrest Dec. 1996; in Eritrea 1996–2000, returned to Sudan Nov. 2000; unsuccessful cand. in presidential elections 2010; mem. Cttee, Sudanese Socialist Union 1978–79; mem. Club of Madrid, Arab Water Council (also mem. Bd of Trustees), Nat. Islamic Conf., Beirut; mem. Bd Arab Democracy Foundation; mem. Bd of Trustees, Org. for Democracy in the Arab World (Qatar); Visiting Fellow, St Antony's Coll., Oxford 1983; Imam of the Ansar (Sufi sect that pledges allegiance to Muhammad Ahmad) 2002–; selected by Inst. of Objective Studies, New Delhi as one of the great Muslim Leaders of the 20th Century in the realm of Leaders and Rulers 2006. *Publications include:* The Southern Question 1964, Speeches in Exile 1976, Questions on Mahadism 1979, Legitimate Penalties and Their Position in the Islamic Social System 1987, Democracy in Sudan: Will Return and Triumph 1990, Challenges of the Nineties 1991. *Leisure interests:* breeding and rearing horses, horse riding, polo, tennis, reading. *E-mail:* ralsadig@ hotmail.com; zakioffice@yahoo.com. *Website:* www.umma.org.

MAHDI, Salah al-, PhD; Tunisian flautist, composer, conductor, musicologist and music critic; b. (Mohamed Ibn Abderrahmane Ben Salah Mehdi Chérifi), 9 Feb. 1925, Tunis; ed Rashidia Inst., Zituna Univ., Inst. of Admin., Tunis and Univ. of Poitiers; teacher of music, Rashidiyya Inst. 1943; Dir Rashidiyya Inst. 1949; Judge, Law Courts of Tunis 1951; fmr Dir Dept of Fine Arts, Ministry of Educ.; participated in setting-up of Nat. Acad. of Music, Dance and Dramatic Art; Head of Direction of Music and Folk Art, Ministry of Culture 1961; later Pres. Nat. Cultural Cttee and Pres. Nat. Cttee of Music; f. Nat. Troupe of Popular Arts 1962; set up Tunisian Symphony Orchestra 1962, Nat. Soc. for Preservation of Koran, Nat. School of Koranic Intoned Psalms; Chair. Global Org. of Folk Art that falls within UNESCO; Vice-Chair. Int. Soc. of Music Educ., Int. Inst. of Music, Int. Folk Music Council; Founding mem. Int. Inst. of Comparative Music, Berlin; Pres. World Org. of Folk Arts and Traditions, Vienna; has held many other int. musical and cultural appointments; participant at numerous UNESCO and other int. congresses; mem. Soc. des Auteurs, Compositeurs et Editions de Musique (SACEM), now Hon. mem.; won contest to compose the music for the Tunisian nat. anthem 1958; Hon. Pres. Inter-Arab Acad. of Music. *Works include:* more than 600 compositions, including classical and folk songs, oriental and Western instrumental music, four nubas, several muwashahs, bashrafs, symphonic poems, chamber music and pieces for piano, flute, violin and harp. *Publications:* many musical, historical and literary works on Arab music including a compilation of Tunisian musical heritage; radio and stage plays. *Address:* 22 rue Brasil, Tunis, Tunisia.

MAHENDRA, Ranbir Singh, BA, LLB; Indian politician, sports organization administrator and lawyer; b. 7 Jan. 1944, Golagarh, Haryana; s. of Chaudhary Bansi Lal; m. Nirmal Kanta; one s. one d.; trained as lawyer; elected Jt Sec., Bd of Control for Cricket in India (BCCI), Kolkata 1980–85, Sec. 1985–89, mem. Finance Cttee, Pres. 2004–05; conducted first cricket World Cup outside of England 1987; fmr Sec. Haryana Cricket Asscn; Man. of Indian Cricket Team, World Cup, Australia 1992; fmr Vice-Pres. Nat. Cricket Acad.; mem. Indian Nat. Congress; MLA Haryana Vidhan Sabha 2005–; Hon. mem. Cricket Club of India, Karnataka State Cricket Club House and Delhi, Dist Cricket Asscn, Punjab Haryana High Court Bar Assn Ltd. *Address:* Haryana Vidhan Sabha Bhawan, Sector 1, Chandigarh 160 001 (office); 95, Sector 10 A, Chandigarh 160 011, India (home). *Telephone:* (172) 2741525 (office); (172) 2742885. *E-mail:* itcellvs@hry.nic.in (office). *Website:* haryanaassembly.gov.in (office).

MAHER, Terence Anthony, FCCA; British bookseller and publisher; b. 5 Dec. 1935, Manchester; s. of the late Herbert Maher and Lillian Maher; m. Barbara Grunbaum 1960; three s.; ed Xaverian Coll., Manchester; Controller, Carborundum Co. Ltd 1961–69; Dir Corp. Finance, First Nat. Finance Corpn 1969–72; f. Pentos PLC 1972, Chair. and CEO –1993; Chair. and CEO Dillons Bookstores 1977–93; Athena Int. 1980–93, Ryman 1987–93; Chair. The Chalford Publishing Co. Ltd 1994–98, Maher Booksellers Ltd 1995–2008, Race Dynamics Ltd 1998–2007; Founder Trustee, Liberal Democrats 1988–2001; mem. Advisory Council on Libraries 1997–98; Fellow, Chartered Asscn of Certified Accountants. *Achievements include:* led successful campaign to abolish price control on books in UK. *Publications:* Counterblast (co-author) 1965, Effective Politics (co-author) 1966, Against My Better Judgement (autobiog.) 1994, Unfinished Business (fiction) 2003, Grumpy Old Liberal – A Political Rant 2005, What would a Liberal Do? – A Polemic 2010. *Leisure interests:* skiing, tennis, walking, reading, bridge. *Address:* 33 Montagu Square, London, W1H 2LJ (home); The Old House,

Whichford, nr Shipston on Stour, Warwicks., CV36 5PG, England. *Telephone:* (20) 7723-4254 (London); (1608) 684-614 (Whichford).

MAHER ALI, Abdel Moneim, PhD; Egyptian biologist and business executive; *President, ARADIS Company SAE;* b. 9 March 1922, Dammanhour; s. of Ali Elsayed Shehata and Nagia M. Manaā; m. Fardous Abbas Abdelal 1948; two s.; ed Cairo Univ., Univ. Coll. London, UK and Ein Shams Univ.; Founder, Gen. Sec. Egyptian Youth Hostel Assoc. 1955–1970; Dir Cen. Agric. Pesticide Lab. UNDP Project 1963–69; Demonstrator, Dept of Plant Protection, Faculty of Agric., Assiut Univ. 1948–69, Assoc. Prof. 1969, Prof. 1969–82, Head, Dept of Plant Protection 1970, Prof. Emer. 1982–; Gen. Sec. Egyptian Zoological Soc., Egyptian Asscn for Conservation of Nature and Natural Resources, Egyptian Asscn for Environment Care, Egyptian Asscn for Medicinal Plants 1975–; Founder then Consultant, Wady Elassiuty Protected Area 1980–94; Pres. ARADIS Co. SAE, Arab Co. Environment Disinfection SAE Co. 1983–; now Chief Ed. Egyptian Journal for Natural Resources and Wildlife; Conservation Merit Award, World Wildlife Fund, Science and Arts 1st Class, Order of the Repub. 5th, 3rd and 2nd and other awards. *Publications include:* textbook on pest control, articles in scientific periodicals. *Leisure interests:* travel, sightseeing, archaeological tours. *Address:* 45 Jule Gamal Street, Agouza, Gizah (office); 50 Wizaret El Ziraā Street, 12th Floor, Dokki, Gizah (home); PO Box 318, Dokki Gizah, Egypt. *Telephone:* (2) 346-2029 (office); (2) 337-3988 (office); (2) 336-0846 (home). *Fax:* (2) 346-2029 (office). *E-mail:* medplantus@ yahoo.com (office).

MAHIGA, Augustine Philip, BA, MA, PhD; Tanzanian diplomatist and UN official; b. 28 Aug. 1945; m.; ed Univ. of East Africa, Dar-es-Salaam, Univ. of Toronto, Canada; Sr Lecturer in Int. Affairs and Regional Co-operation, Univ. of Dar-es-Salaam 1975–77; Dir of Research and Training, Office of the Pres. of Tanzania 1977–80, Acting Dir Gen. Office of the Pres. 1980–83; High Commr to Canada 1983–89; Amb. and Perm. Rep. to UN, Geneva 1989–92; on secondment to UNHCR 1993, UNHCR Chief of Mission, Monrovia, Liberia 1992–94, Deputy Dir and Co-ordinator Great Lakes Region of Africa Refugee Emergency Operation, Geneva 1994–98, UNHCR Chief of Mission, New Delhi 1998–2002, UNHCR Rep. to Italy (also accred to Malta and San Marino) 2002–03; Amb. and Perm. Rep. to UN, New York 2003–10, Head of del. to UN Security Council 2005, also Asst Sec.-Gen. for Peacebuilding Support for UN Peacebuilding Comm., Special Rep. for Somalia and Head of UN Political Office for Somalia (UNPOS) 2010–13; Lifetime Achievement Award, Miracle Corners of the World 2007. *Address:* c/o UN Political Office for Somalia (UNPOS), PO Box 48246-00100, Nairobi, Kenya.

MAHINDRA, Anand G., MBA; Indian business executive; *Chairman and Managing Director, Mahindra and Mahindra Limited;* b. 1 May 1955, Bombay (now Mumbai); m. Anuradha Mahindra; two d.; ed Harvard Coll., Harvard Business School, USA; Exec. Asst to Finance Dir, Mahindra Ugine Steel Co. Ltd 1981–89, Pres. and Deputy Man. Dir 1989–91; Deputy Man. Dir Mahindra and Mahindra Ltd 1991–97, apptd Man. Dir 1997, Vice-Chair. 2003–2012, Chair. and Man. Dir 2012–; Co-founder Harvard Business School Asscn of India; fmr Chair. Nat. Inst. of Industrial Eng, Mumbai; fmr Pres. Automotive Research Asscn of India; Co-promoter Kotak Mahindra Bank (fmrly Kotak Mahindra Finance Ltd); mem. Confed. of Indian Industry (Pres. 2003–04); mem. Advisory Cttee, Harvard Univ. Asia Centre, Exec. Cttee, The Nehru Centre, Mumbai, Advisory Council, Initiative on Corp. Governance, Harvard Business School, Harvard Global Advisory Council, Nat. Council of Applied Econ. Research, India Council for Sustainable Devt, Nehru Centre, Nat. Sports Devt Fund, Econ. Devt Bd of Rajasthan, Int. Advisory Council of Singapore's Econ. Devt Bd, Global Bd of Advisors of Council on Foreign Relations, New York; mem. Bd of Govs, Mahindra United World Coll. of India; Trustee, K. C. Mahindra Educ. Trust; Hon. Amb. of Foreign Investment Promotion for Repub. of Korea; Chevalier, l'Ordre du Mérite; Rajiv Gandhi Award 2004, Leadership Award, American India Foundation 2005, Person of the Year Award 2005, CNBC Asia Business Leader Award 2006, Most Inspiring Corp. Leader of the Year Award, NDTV Profit 2007, Business Man of the Year Award, Business India 2007, Harvard Business School Alumni Achievement Award 2008, Nat. Statesman for Excellence in Business Practices–Qimpro Platinum Standard Award 2008, CNBC TV18 Outstanding Business Leader of the Year Award 2009, Business Leader of the Year Award, Economic Times 2009, Ernst & Young Entrepreneur of the Year Award 2009, Business Leader of the Year, The Asian Awards 2011, named amongst Top 25 Most Powerful Business People in Asia by Fortune magazine 2011, Leadership Award (co-winner), US India Business Council 2012, Business Courage Award, Asia Business Leadership Forum 2012, Best Transformational Leader Award, Asian Centre for Corp. Governance and Sustainability 2012, Business Leader of the Year, NDTV 2012, Special Recognition for Creating a True Global Indian MNC, Zee Business – India's Best Market Analyst Awards 2013, Entrepreneur of the Year, Forbes India Leadership Awards 2013, Sustainability Devt Leadership Award, The Energy and Resources Inst. 2014. *Leisure interests:* playing tennis, sailing, photography. *Address:* Mahindra and Mahindra Ltd, Gateway Building, Apollo Bunder, Mumbai 400 001, India (office). *Telephone:* (22) 22895500 (office). *Fax:* (22) 22028980 (office). *Website:* www.mahindra.com (office).

MAHINDRA, Keshub, BSc; Indian business executive; *Chairman Emeritus, Mahindra and Mahindra Ltd.;* b. 9 Oct. 1923, Simla; s. of the late Kailash Chandra Mahindra and Savitri Mahindra; m. Sudha Y. Varde 1956; three d.; ed Wharton Business School, Univ. of Pennsylvania, USA; joined Mahindra and Mahindra Ltd 1947, Chair. 1963–2012, Chair. Emer. 2012–; Chair. Housing and Urban Devt Corpn Ltd 1971–75, Indian Inst. of Man., Ahmedabad 1975–85, India Nominating Cttee "Single Nation Programme", Eisenhower Exchange Fellowships, USA 1998–2005; Pres. Asscn of Indian Automobile Mfrs 1964–65, Bombay Chamber of Commerce and Industry 1966–67, Assoc. Chamber of Commerce and Industry 1969–70, MVIRDC, World Trade Center 1978–95, Employers' Fed. of India 1985–97, Indo-American Soc. 1991–92; Dir Bombay Dyeing and Mfg Co. Ltd, Bombay Burmah Trading Corpn Ltd, Housing Devt Finance Corpn Ltd, United World Coll. International Ltd, UK, Mahindra Ugine Steel Co. Ltd etc.; Dir Pratham India Educ. Initiative 2003–08; Pres. Centre for Research in Rural and Industrial Devt, Chandigarh, Governing Council, Univ. of Pennsylvania Inst. for Advanced Study of India, New Delhi; Chair. Mahindra Foundation, Health and Environment Cttee, Bd Trustees, Population First; Chair. and Trustee, K.C. Mahindra Educ. Trust; Pres. Emer. Employers' Fed. of India; mem. Apex Advisory

Council of Assoc. Chambers of Commerce and Industry of India, International Council Asia Soc. New York, USA 1983–97; Founding mem., Indo-Hellenic Friendship League, Governing Council, Integrated Research and Action for Devt (IRADe), New Delhi; mem. Foundation Bd, International Man. Inst., Geneva 1984–89, Prime Minister's Council on Trade and Industry; mem. Bd of Govs Mahindra United World Coll. of India; mem. Governing Body of HelpAge India 2000–04, Governing Body/Bd Govs of Bharat Shiksha Kosh 2002–05, Governing Bd United Way of Mumbai, Bombay First, International Advisory Bd Univ. of Pennsylvania Center for Advanced Study of India, Philadelphia; Hon. Fellow, All India Man. Asscn 1990, Hon. mem. Business Advisory Council, IFC, Washington, DC 1986–96, Rotary Club of Bombay 1984; Chevalier, Légion d'honneur 1987; numerous awards including Giants Int. Business Leadership Award 1972–82, Madras Man. Asscn Business Leadership Award 1983, Business India Indian Businessman of the Year 1989, Rotary Award for Vocational Excellence 1992, Shiromani Award 1992, Vikas Jyoti Award 1993, Sir Jengahir Ghandy Medal for Industrial Peace, XLRI, Jamshedpur 1994, Rotary Vocational Excellence Award in the Field of Industry 1996, IMC Diamond Jubilee Endowment Trust Award 1998, Motorindia Automan Award 2000, Dadabhai Naoroji Int. Award for Excellence and Lifetime Achievement Award 2000, All India Man. Asscn Lifetime Achievement Award for Man. 2003, Inst. of Co. Secs of India Lifetime Achievement Award for Excellence in Corp. Governance 2004, Qimpro Platinum Standard 'Statesman for Quality' Business Award 2005, Lakshya Business Visionary Award, NITIE 2006, Indian Business School Kolkata Lifetime Achievement Award 2007, Ernst and Young Entrepreneur of the Year Lifetime Achievement Award 2007, Soc. of Indian Automobile Manufacturers Award for Lifetime Contrib. to the Automotive Industry 2008, CNBC TV18 India Business Leaders Lifetime Achievement Award 2008. *Leisure interests:* golf, tennis, photography, reading. *Address:* Mahindra and Mahindra Ltd, Mahindra Towers, G M Bhosale Marg, Mumbai 400 018 (office); St Helen's Court, Pedder Road, Mumbai 400 026, India (home). *Telephone:* (22) 23514206 (home). *E-mail:* mahindra.keshub@mahindra.com (office). *Website:* www.mahindra.com (office).

MAHJOUB, Abdelmajid, BSc, MSc, PhD; Tunisian microbiologist, academic and international organization official; *Director General, Arab Atomic Energy Agency;* b. 5 Feb. 1950, Béni Hassen-Monastir; m.; four c.; ed High School of Radès & Tunis, Univ. of Tunis, Tulane Univ., New Orleans and Univ. of Nebraska-Lincoln, USA; high school teacher (Biology), La Marsa 1974–75; Asst Prof. and Head of Nutrition Educ. Section, Teaching and Man., Nat. Inst. of Nutrition, Tunis 1977–80, Assoc. Prof., Research and Teaching, Food Tech. and Microbiology, School of Food Industry, Univ. Tunis II 1985–92, Head of Dept of Food Tech. 1992–97; Dir Gen. Nat. Centre for Nuclear Sciences and Technologies 1997–2001; Programme Man. Officer, Africa Div., IAEA Dept of Tech. Co-operation 2001–08; Dir Gen. Arab Atomic Energy Agency 2009–. *Address:* Arab Atomic Energy Agency, PO Box 402, 7 Rue de l'assistance, Cité el Khadhra, 1003 Tunis, Tunisia (office). *Telephone:* (71) 808400 (office); 98-460711 (mobile). *Fax:* (71) 808450 (office). *E-mail:* amahjoub@aaea.org.tn (office); am.mahjoub@yahoo.fr. *Website:* www.aaea.org.tn (office).

MAHLAB, Ibrahim, BEng; Egyptian engineer and politician; *Prime Minister;* b. 1949; ed Cairo Univ.; several years with Arab Contracting Co., including as Dir of Bridges 1994, Vice-Chair. 1997, later Chair.; fmr mem. Shura Council (upper house of fmr Parl., abolished 2014); Minister of Housing 2013–14; Prime Minister 2014–; mem. Bd of Govs Arab Water Council; mem. Egyptian-French Business Asscn, American Chamber of Commerce in Egypt; mem. National Democratic Party, mem. Policy Cttee. *Address:* Office of the Prime Minister, 2 Sharia Majlis al-Sha'ab, Cairo, Egypt (office). *Telephone:* (2) 27935000 (office). *Fax:* (2) 27958048 (office). *E-mail:* questions@cabinet.gov.eg (office).

MAHMOUD, Lt-Gen. Ali Muhammad Habib; Syrian army officer and government official; b. 1939, Safita, Tartus; ed Military Acad., Damascus; joined Syrian Army 1959, regiment commdr 1971–75, Chief of Staff of mechanised infantry div. 1975–78, commdr of infantry brigade 1978–84, Commdr of mechanised infantry div. 1984–94, apptd Commdr of Special Forces 1994–2002, Deputy Chief of Staff 2002–04, Chief of Gen. Staff of Army and Armed Forces 2004–09; Minister of Defence 2009–11 (resgnd with rest of cabinet at Pres.'s request following popular protests), April–Aug. 2011; led Syrian forces in Lebanon 1982; mem. Baath Party. *Address:* c/o Ministry of Defence, place Omayad, Damascus, Syria.

MAHMOUD ABBAS, Badr al-Din, BA; Sudanese government official and fmr central banker; *Minister of Finance and National Economy;* ed Khartoum Univ.; fmr Deputy Gov., Central Bank of Sudan; Minister of Finance and Nat. Economy 2013–; mem. Bd of Dirs The Arab Investment Co.; Chair. Sudan Mems Panel, Asscn of Chartered Certified Accountants; over 20 years' experience in both internal and external consulting roles with several int. orgs. *Address:* Ministry of Finance and National Economy, POB 735, Khartoum, Sudan (office). *Telephone:* (183) 777563 (office). *Fax:* (183) 775630 (office). *E-mail:* info@mof-sudan.net (office). *Website:* www.mof.gov.sd (office).

MAHMUD, Aksa; Indonesian business executive; *Founder, Bosowa Group;* b. 16 July 1945, Barru; m. H. Siti Ramlah Aksa; five c.; ed Hasanuddin Univ.; f. CV Moneter 1973, PT Bosowa Berlian Motor 1978, later renamed Bosowa Group (conglomerate), associated cos include PT Asuransi Bosowa Periskop, Bosowa Taxis, PT Semen Bosowa Maros, PT Tuju Waliwali, PT Bosowa Cocoa Industries, PT Bumi Sawit Permai, PT Celebes Minahasa Suraya Adira; fmr mem. Regional Reps Council (Dewan Perwakilan Daerah, DPD) for S Sulawesi. *Address:* Bosowa Group, Menara Karya Lt 16, JL HR Rasuna Said (Kuningan), Blok X-5 Kav 1-2, Jakarta 12950, Indonesia (office). *Telephone:* (21) 57944344 (office). *Fax:* (21) 57944544 (office). *Website:* www.bosowa.co.id (office).

MAHMUD ALI, Abul Hasan, BA, MA; Bangladeshi politician and fmr diplomatist; *Minister of Foreign Affairs;* b. 2 June 1943, Dinajpur; two s.; ed Dhaka Univ.; Lecturer in Econs, Dhaka Univ. 1964–66; joined Pakistan Foreign Service 1966, Vice-Consul of Pakistan, New York 1968; joined Bangladesh Liberation Movt 1971, worked for independence of Bangladesh in USA as US Rep. of Provisional Govt of Bangladesh (in exile in Mujibnagar) 1971; Exec. Asst to Justice Abu Sayeed Chowdhury (Chief Overseas Rep. of Mujibnagar Govt and Leader, Bangladesh Del. to UN) 1971; following independence of Bangladesh 1971 served in various roles with Ministry of Foreign Affairs, including as First Sec. and Deputy High Commr, then High Comm. in Delhi 1977–79, Dir-Gen. for Admin, Int. Orgs, UN

and Econ. Affairs 1979–82, Deputy Chief of Mission with rank of Amb., Embassy in Beijing 1983–86, Amb. to Bhutan 1986–90, to Germany 1992–95, to Nepal Feb.–Oct. 1996, High Commr to UK 1996–2001; mem. Jatiya Sangsad (Parl.) for Dinajpur constituency 2009–13; Minister of Disaster Man. and Relief 2012–13, Minister of Foreign Affairs 2013–; mem. Bangladesh Awami League 2001–, mem. Party Cen. Election Comm. 2001. *Address:* Ministry of Foreign Affairs, Segunbagicha, Dhaka 1000, Bangladesh (office). *Telephone:* (2) 9562852 (office). *Fax:* (2) 9562188 (office). *E-mail:* info@mofabd.org (office). *Website:* www.mofa.gov.bd (office).

MAHMUDI, Al-Baghdadi Ali al-; Libyan politician; b. 1945, Az Zawiyah Dist of northwestern Libya; trained as a physician, has a medical degree specializing in obstetrics and gynaecology; Sec. of the Gen. People's Cttee for Health and Social Security 1992–97; Minister for the People's Cttees' Affairs 1997–2000; Deputy Prime Minister for Services Affairs March–Sept. 2000; Minister of Human Resources Affairs 2000–01, for Infrastructure, Urban Planning and Environment Affairs 2001; Deputy Prime Minister for Production Affairs 2001–06; Asst Sec. of the Gen. People's Cttee (Deputy Prime Minister) 2004–06, Sec. (Prime Minister) 2006–11; Chair. High Council for Oil and Gas 2006–, Libyan Investment Authority 2007–; subject of a travel ban issued by UN Security Council (Resolution 1970) 26 Feb. 2011; fled to Tunisia Aug. 2011.

MAHONEY, Rev. John Aloysius (Jack), SJ, MA, STD; British ecclesiastic and academic; b. 14 Jan. 1931, Coatbridge, Scotland; s. of Patrick Mahoney and Margaret Doris; ed Our Lady's High School, Motherwell, St Aloysius Coll., Glasgow, Univ. of Glasgow and Gregorian Univ., Rome; Lecturer in Moral and Pastoral Theology, Heythrop Coll., Oxon. 1967–70; Lecturer in Moral and Pastoral Theology, Heythrop Coll., Univ. of London 1970–86, Prin. 1976–81; F.D. Maurice Prof. of Moral and Social Theology, King's Coll. London 1986–93, Prof. Emer. 1999–; Founding Dir King's Coll. Business Ethics Research Centre 1987–93; Mercers' School Memorial Prof. of Commerce, Gresham Coll. City of London 1987–93, Prof. Emer. 1993–; Dixons Prof. of Business Ethics and Social Responsibility, London Business School 1993–98; Founder and Dir Lauriston Centre for Contemporary Belief and Action, Edin. 1998–2005; Lecturer in Theology, St Andrews Univ. 2004; Distinguished Prof., Dept of Theology, Georgetown Univ. 2008; Companion, Chartered Man. Asscn 1996; mem. Mount Street Jesuit Centre, London 2005–08, Mount Street Jesuit Community 2009–12, Lauriston Centre, Edinburgh 2012–; Hon. Fellow, Faculty of Divinity, Univ. of Edinburgh 1998–2003, Gresham Coll., London 1999–, St Mary's Univ. Coll. 1999–, Heythrop Coll., Univ. of London 2000–, Hon. Lecturer in Business Ethics, Glasgow Business School 2003–04; Hon. DD (Univ. of London) 2004; Pres.'s Medal, Georgetown Univ., Washington, DC 2003. *Publications:* Seeking the Spirit: Essays in Moral and Pastoral Theology 1981, Bioethics and Belief: Religion and Medicine in Dialogue 1984, The Making of Moral Theology: A Study of the Roman Catholic Tradition 1987, Teaching Business Ethics in the UK, Europe and the USA 1990, Business Ethics in a New Europe (ed.) 1992, The Challenge of Human Rights: Origin, Development and Significance 2007, Christianity in Evolution: An Exploration 2011. *Address:* 28 Lauriston Street, Edinburgh, EH3 9DJ, Scotland (home). *Telephone:* (131) 447-5700 (office). *E-mail:* jmlaur@aol.com (office).

MAHONY, HE Cardinal Roger Michael, STB, MA; American ecclesiastic; *Archbishop Emeritus of Los Angeles;* b. 27 Feb. 1936, Hollywood, Calif.; s. of the late Victor James Mahony and Loretta Marie Baron; ed St John's Seminary Coll., St John's Theologate, Calif., Catholic Univ. of America, Washington, DC; ordained RC Priest, Fresno, Calif. 1962; Bishop, Fresno, Calif. 1975; Bishop of Stockton, Calif. 1980; Archbishop of Los Angeles 1985–2011, Archbishop Emer. 2011–; cr. Cardinal (Cardinal-Priest of Santi Quattro Coronati) 1991; participated in Papal Conclave 2005, 2013; mem. numerous cttees of Nat. Confs of Catholic Bishops, USA 1976–; several Pontifical Councils, Vatican 1984–; Dr hc (Loyola Marymount, LA) 1986, (Portland, Ore.) 1988, (Notre Dame, Ind.) 1989, (St Patrick's Coll., Ireland) 1991, (Southern California) 2002. *Address:* 3424 Wilshire Boulevard, Los Angeles, CA 90010, USA (office). *Telephone:* (213) 637-7288 (office). *Fax:* (213) 637-6510 (office).

MAHUAD WITT, Jamil, PhD; Ecuadorean lawyer, politician and fmr head of state; b. 29 July 1949, Loja; s. of Jorge Antonio Mahuad Chalela and Rosa Witt García; m. Tatiana Calderón (divorced); one d.; ed Pontificia Universidad Católica del Ecuador, John F. Kennedy School of Govt, Harvard Univ., USA; legal assessor and dir of pvt. credit banks 1973–78; Pres. Federación de Estudiantes Universitarios Católicos del Ecuador 1974–75; Regional Sec. Federación de Estudiantes de las Universidades Católicas de América Latina 1975–81; mem. Democracia Popular 1981; Dir Empresa Nacional de Productos Vitales 1981–83; Minister of Labour 1981–83; Pres. Democracia Popular 1987–88, 1991–93; Vice-Pres. Demócrata Cristiano de América (ODCA), Andina Region 1991–97; Mayor of Quito 1992–98; Pres. of Ecuador 1998–2000 (deposed by armed forces). *Address:* c/o Democracia Popular, Calle Luis Saá 153 y Hnos Pazmiño, Casilla 17-01-2300, Quito, Ecuador.

MAIDA, HE Cardinal Adam Joseph, JD; American ecclesiastic; b. 18 March 1930, East Vandergrift, Pa; s. of Adam Maida and Sophie Maida (née Cieslak); ed Scott Township High School, St Mary's High School, Orchard Lake, Mich., St Vincent's Coll., Latrobe, Pa, St Mary's Univ., Baltimore, Md, Pontifical Lateran Univ., Rome, Italy, Duquesne Univ., Pittsburgh; admitted to practice law in Pa and before US Supreme Court; ordained priest 1956; further studies in Rome 1956–60; pastoral work in Diocese of Pittsburgh and as Asst Chancellor, Vice-Chancellor, Diocesan Gen. Consultor in the diocesan tribunal 1960–83; fmr Asst Prof. of Theology, La Roche Coll.; fmr Chaplain St Thomas More's Soc.; faculty mem. Duquesne Univ. 1971–83; consecrated Bishop of Green Bay, Wis. 1984; Archbishop of Detroit 1990–2008; cr. Cardinal (Cardinal Priest of SS Vitale, Valeria, Gervasio e Protasio) 1994; mem. Roman Curia Congregation for Catholic Educ., Congregation for the Clergy, Pontifical Council for the Interpretation of Legislative Texts, Pontifical Council for the Pastoral Care of Migrants and Itinerant Peoples, Cardinal Comm. for the Supervision of the Inst. for Works of Religion; served as Chair. US Conf. of Catholic Bishops Canonical Affairs Cttee, Washington, DC 1992, mem. Ad Hoc Cttee for Aid to the Church in Cen. and Eastern Europe, Bishops' Cttee on Evangelization, ex-officio mem. Int. Policy Cttee, Consultant to Cttee on Migration, Cttee on Pro-Life Activities, Episcopal Liaison Cttee for the Polish Apostolate; Chairman Bd of Trustees Mich. Catholic

Conf., Sacred Heart Major Seminary, Detroit, SS Cyril and Methodius Seminary, Orchard Lake; Ecclesiastical Protector Int. Order of Alhambra; mem. Bd of Govs Ave Maria School of Law, Ann Arbor, Mich.; Episcopal Moderator and Pres. John Paul II Cultural Foundation, USA; Pres. Pope John Paul II Cultural Center, Washington, DC; mem. Bd of Trustees Catholic Univ. of America, Washington, DC, Basilica of the Nat. Shrine of the Immaculate Conception, Washington, DC, The Papal Foundation, Phila, Pa, John Paul II Cultural Foundation, Rome; mem. Bd of Dirs Nat. Catholic Bioethics Center, Phila; Ecclesial Advisor, Nat. Fellowship of Catholic Men, Gaithersburg, Md; Papal Legate to 19th Int. Marian Congress, Czestochowa, Poland 1996; attended Special Ass. for America of World Synod of Bishops, Vatican City 1997, Special Ass. for Europe of World Synod of Bishops, Vatican City 1999; Superior of Mission sui iuris of Cayman Islands 2000. *Publications:* The Tribunal Reporter: A Casebook and Commentary on the Grounds for Annulment in the Catholic Church, Vol. 1 (ed.) 1970, Ownership, Control and Sponsorship of Catholic Institutions 1975, Issues in the Labor-Management Dialogue: Church Perspectives (ed.) 1982, Church Property, Church Finances and Church-Related Corporations, a Canon Law Handbook 1983. *Address:* c/o Archdiocese of Detroit, 305 Michigan Avenue, Detroit, MI 48226-2605, USA.

MAIDEN, Sir Colin James, Kt, MEng, DPhil; New Zealand fmr university vice-chancellor and company director; b. 5 May 1933, Auckland; s. of Henry A. Maiden and Lorna Richardson; m. Jenefor Mary Rowe 1957; one s. three d.; ed Univs of New Zealand and Oxford, UK; Head, Hypersonic Physics Section, Canadian Armament Research and Devt Establishment, Québec City, Canada 1958–60; Sr lecturer in Mechanical Eng Univ. of Auckland 1960–61; Head, Material Sciences Lab. Gen. Motors Corpn Defence Research Labs Santa Barbara, Calif. 1961–66; Man. of Process Eng Gen. Motors Corpn Tech. Centre, Warren, Mich. 1966–70; Vice-Chancellor, Univ. of Auckland 1971–94; Chair. New Zealand Energy Research and Devt Cttee 1974–81, New Zealand Vice-Chancellor's Cttee 1977–78, 1991, Liquid Fuels Trust Bd 1978–86, New Zealand Synthetic Fuels Corpn Ltd 1980–90, Tower Insurance Co. Ltd 1988–2002, Fisher & Paykel Ltd 1978–2001, Independent Newspapers Ltd 1989–2003; Dir Mason Industries Ltd 1971–78, Farmers Trading Co. Ltd 1973–86, Winstone Ltd 1978–88, Wilkins & Davies Ltd 1986–89, New Zealand Steel Ltd 1988–92, ANZ Banking Group (NZ) Ltd 1990–93, New Zealand Refining Co. Ltd 1991–2007, Progressive Enterprises Ltd 1992–2000, DB Breweries Ltd 1994–2008, Sedgwick (New Zealand) Ltd 1994–98, Transpower New Zealand Ltd 1994–2004, Tower Ltd 1995–2003, Foodland Associated Ltd 2000–05, Fisher and Paykel Healthcare Corpn Ltd 2001–11; various professional appointments; Hon. LLD (Auckland); Queen Elizabeth Silver Jubilee Medal 1977, Medal of Univ. of Bonn 1983, Thomson Medal, Royal Soc. of New Zealand 1986, Symons Award, Asscn of Commonwealth Univs 1999. *Publications include:* numerous scientific and tech. papers. *Leisure interest:* tennis. *Address:* Apartment 503, Oakridge, 10 Middleton Road, Remuera, Auckland, New Zealand (home). *Telephone:* (9) 524-7412 (home). *E-mail:* colinmaiden@xtra.co.nz.

MAIGA, Ousmane Issoufi; Malian politician; b. 1946, Gao; m.; four c.; ed Univ. of Kiev, Ukraine, American Univ., Washington, DC, USA; early internships at World Bank and French Ministry of Finance; fmr Deputy Dir Gen. Caisse Autonome d'Amortissement; Minister of Finance 2002–03; Minister of Equipment and Transport 2003–04; Prime Minister of Mali 2004–07. *Address:* c/o Office of the Prime Minister, quartier du Fleuve, BP 790, Bamako, Mali (office).

MAÏGA, Soumeylou Boubeye; Malian journalist and politician; *Minister of Defence and Veterans;* b. 8 June 1954, Gao; ed Centre d'études des sciences et techniques de l'information, Univ. Cheikh Anta Diop, Dakar, Senegal, Univ. Paris-Sud, France; began career as journalist with L'Essor (state-owned daily news-paper); Special Adviser to cabinet of Pres. Amadou Toumani Touré 1991–92; fmr mem. Parti malien du travail; Founder-mem. and Vice-Pres. Alliance pour la démocratie au Mali—Parti pan-africain pour la liberté, la solidarité et la justice (ADEMA) 1990; Chef de cabinet to Pres. Alpha Oumar Konaré 1992; Dir-Gen. Direction Générale de la Sécurité Extérieure (intelligence agency) 1993; unsuc-cessful cand. in presidential election 2002 (for ADEMA), 2007 (for Convergence); Minister of Foreign Affairs and Int. Co-operation 2011–12, of Defence and Veterans 2013–. *Address:* Ministry of Defence and Veterans, route de Koulouba, BP 2083, Bamako, Mali (office). *Telephone:* 2022-5021 (office). *Fax:* 2023-2318 (office).

MAILLOT, Jacques; French director and writer; b. 12 April 1962, Besançon; ed Institut d'Etudes Politiques de Lyon; worked as a graphic designer; hired at Cinémathèque Française as a conscientious objector; began his film career by directing four short films 1990; acted in Mille bornes (Milestones) 1999. *Films:* Des fleurs coupées (Cut Flowers) 1993, Corps inflammables (Flammable Material) (Prix Tournage, Avignon Film Festival 1995) 1995, 75 centilitres de prière (aka A Bottle of Wishes, USA) (Special Jury Award, Nat. Competition, Clermont-Ferrand Int. Short Film Festival 1994, Prix Jean Vigo for Short Film 1994) 1995, Entre ciel et terre (Between Heaven and Earth) 1996, Nos vies heureuses (Our Happy Lives) (Prix Tournage, Avignon Film Festival 1999) 1999, Froid comme l'été (Cold as Summer) (Prix Italia 2003) 2002, Les liens du sang (Rivals) 2008, Un singe sur le dos (Monkey on My Back) 2009. *Television:* Les prédateurs (screenplay) 2007. *Address:* c/o Delphine Gamory, Artmedia, 20 avenue Rapp, 75007 Paris, France. *Telephone:* 1-43-17-33-63. *E-mail:* d.gamory@artmedia.fr. *Website:* www .artemedia.fr.

MAINALI, Chandra Prakash; Nepalese politician; *Leader, Communist Party of Nepal (Marxist-Leninist) (CPN–ML);* b. 22 Aug. 1951, Chokpur; s. of Dhanpati Mainali and Chandrakumari Mainali; m.; one s. two d.; joined Communist Party of Nepal 1970, Gen.-Sec., Communist Party of Nepal (Marxist-Leninist) 1978, currently Leader; fmr Minister for Local Devt and Supply; fmr Leader United Left Front; joined interim Parl. 2007, mem. of Constituent Ass. 2008–. *Address:* Communist Party of Nepal (Marxist-Leninist) (CPN–ML), Maitidevi, Kathmandu, Nepal (office). *Telephone:* (1) 4443589 (office). *E-mail:* cpnml.cc@gmail.com (office). *Website:* www.cpnml.org.np (office).

MAINI, Sir Ravinder Nath, Kt, BA, MB, BChir, FRCP, FRCPE, FMedSci, FRS; British rheumatologist and academic; *Professor Emeritus of Rheumatology, Imperial College London;* b. 17 Nov. 1937, Ludhiana, Punjab, India; s. of Sir

Amar (Nath) Maini and Saheli Maini (née Mehra); m. 1st Marianne Gorm 1963 (divorced 1986); one s. one d. (and one s. deceased); m. 2nd Geraldine Room 1987; two s.; ed Sidney Sussex Coll., Cambridge; jr medical appointments at Guy's, Brompton and Charing Cross Hosps 1962–70; Consultant Physician, St Stephen's Hosp., London 1970–79, Rheumatology Dept, Charing Cross Hosp. 1970; Prof. of Immunology of Rheumatic Diseases, Charing Cross and Westminster Medical School 1981–89, Dir Kennedy Inst. of Rheumatology 1990–2000 (Head Clinical Immunology Div. 1979); Prof. of Rheumatology, Imperial Coll. School of Medicine at Charing Cross Hosp. Campus (fmrly Charing Cross and Westminster Medical School), Univ. of London 1989–2002, Prof. Emer. of Rheumatology 2002–, Head of Kennedy Inst. of Rheumatology Div. 2000–02; Visiting Prof., Univ. of Oxford 2011–; Pres. British Soc. for Rheumatology 1989–90 (Heberden Orator 1988), British League Against Rheumatism 1985–89; Chair. Research Sub-Cttee 1980–85 and mem. Scientific Coordinating Cttee, Arthritis and Rheumatism Council 1985–95; Chair. Standing Cttee for Investigative Rheumatology, European League Against Rheumatism 1990–97; mem. Exec. Cttee, Asscn of Physicians of GB and Ireland 1989–91; Chair. Rheumatology Cttee, Royal Coll. of Physicians 1992–96 (Croonian Lecturer 1995, Lumleian Lecturer 1999); mem. European Union of Medical Specialists 1994– (Pres. Section of Rheumatology 1996–99, Chair. European Bd of Rheumatology 1996–99); Samuel Hyde Lecturer, Royal Soc. of Medicine 1998; mem. Scientific Advisory Bd Nicholas Piramal India Ltd 2003–, Arana Therapeutics Ltd, Australia (previously known as Peptech) 2003–09; mem. Bd of Dirs Piramal Life Sciences, India 2008–11, Domantis, Cambridge 2003–07; mem. Council Medical Protection Soc. 2001–09; mem. Advisory Bd F-Star Biotechnologische Forschungs und Entwicklungsgesellschaft 2007–; mem. Bd of Trustees, Kennedy Inst. of Rheumatology Trust, Beit Memorial Fellowship, Sir Jules Thorn Trust, Graham Dixon Trust; Assoc. mem. NAS 2011; Hon. Consultant, Charing Cross Hosp., Hammersmith Hosps NHS Trust; Hon. mem. Australian Rheumatism Asscn 1977, Norwegian Soc. for Rheumatology 1988, American Coll. of Rheumatology 1988, Hellenic Rheumatology Soc. 1989, Hungarian Rheumatol-ogy Soc. 1990, Scandinavian Soc. for Immunology 1996, Mexican Soc. for Rheumatology 1996, Hon. Fellowship, Sidney Sussex Coll., Univ. of Cambridge 2004, Hon. Fellowship, Royal Soc. of Medicine 2004, Master, American Coll. of Rheumatology 2004; Dr hc (Univ. René Descartes, Paris) 1994; Hon. DSc (Glasgow) 2004; Carol Nachman Prize for Rheumatology (jtly), City of Wiesbaden 1999, Distinguished Investigator Award, American Coll. of Rheumatology 1999, Crafoord Prize (jtly), Royal Swedish Acad. of Sciences 2000, Courtin-Clarins Prize (jtly), Asscn de Recherche sur la Polyarthrite 2000, Albert Lasker Award for Clinical Medical Research 2003, Fothergillian Medal, Medical Soc. of London 2004, Cameron Prize (jtly), Univ. of Edin. 2004, Ambuj Nath Bose Prize, Royal Coll. of Physicians 2005, EULAR Meritorious Service Award in Rheumatology (jtly) 2005, Langdon Brown Lecture, Royal Coll. of Physicians 2005, Galen Medal, The Worshipful Soc. of Apothcaries of London 2006, Japan Rheumatism Foundation Int. RA Award (jtly) 2007, Dr Paul Janssen Award for Biomedical Research (jtly) 2008, Ernst Schering Prize (jtly) 2010, Canada Gairdner Int. Award (jtly) 2014. *Publications include:* Immunology of Rheumatic Diseases 1977, Modulation of Autoimmune Disease (ed.) 1981, Textbook of the Rheumatic Diseases, 6th edn (contrib.) 1986, T-Cell Activation in Health and Disease (ed.) 1989, Rheumatoid Arthritis (ed.) 1992, Oxford Textbook of Rheumatology (contrib.) 1993, Rheuma-tology (section ed.) 1993, Manual of Biological Markers of Disease (co-ed.: Section A, Methods of Autoantibody Detection 1993, Section B, Autoantigens 1994, Section C, Clinical Significance of Autoantibodies 1996), Oxford Textbook of Medicine (contrib.) 2001; 480 articles in scientific journals. *Leisure interests:* music appreciation, walking. *Address:* Kennedy Institute of Rheumatology, 65 Aspenlea Road, London, W6 8LH, England (office). *Telephone:* (20) 8383-4403 (office). *Fax:* (20) 8563-1585 (office). *E-mail:* r.maini@imperial.ac.uk (office). *Website:* wwwfom .sk.med.ic.ac.uk/medicine (office); www.kennedy.ox.ac.uk (office).

MAIRE, Edmond; French trade union official; *President, Société d'Investissement France Active;* b. 24 Jan. 1931, Epinay-sur-Seine; s. of Julien Maire and Marie-Thérèse Conchou; m. Raymonde Le Goff 1954; three c.; ed Conservatoire Nat. des Arts et Métiers; technician, chemical industry; Perm. Sec. Fed. of Chemical Industries of Confédération Française Démocratique du Travail (CFDT) 1958–70; mem. Exec. Cttee of CFDT, in charge of professional and social action; Sec.-Gen. of CFDT 1971–88; Pres. Villages-Vacances-Familles (VVF) 1989–99; Pres. de la Section Affaires Sociales du Conseil Nat. du Tourisme 1989–99; Pres. Société d'investissement France Active 1999–; mem. Conseil Economique et Social 1969–74. *Publications:* Demain l'autogestion 1976, Nouvelles frontières pour le syndicalisme 1987, L'Esprit libre 1999. *Address:* 120 rue Réaumur, 75002 Paris (office); 145 rue Pelleport, 75020 Paris, France (home). *Telephone:* 1-53-24-26-69 (office). *Fax:* 1-53-24-26-63 (office). *E-mail:* edmondm@franceactive.org (home).

MAISENBERG, Oleg; Austrian pianist; b. 29 April 1945, Odessa, USSR (now Ukraine); s. of Adel and Josef Maisenberg; two c.; ed Moscow Gnessin Inst. of Music (pupil of A. Yokheles); winner Franz Schubert Competition in Vienna 1967, 20th Century Music Competition, Vienna 1967; performed Rachmaninov's 1st Piano Concerto with Nat. Orchestra of Moldavia; emigrated to Austria 1981; concert performances world-wide as soloist and chamber musician; recordings of Schubert, Schuman, Liszt, Scriabin, Berg, Stravinsky, R. Strauss, Dvořák, Milhaud, Weber, Schönberg, Bartok, Rachmaninov and Prokofiev; Prof. Stuttgart Conservatory and Vienna Acad. of Music, Hon. mem. Konzerthaus Gesellschaft, Vienna. *Address:* c/o Matthias Dirnbacher, Künstleragentur Dr Raab and Dr Bohm, Plankengasse 7, 1010 Vienna, Austria (office). *Telephone:* (1) 5120501 (office). *Fax:* (1) 5127743 (office). *E-mail:* dirnbacher@rbartists.at (office). *Website:* www.rbartists.at (office).

MAISKY, Mischa (Michael); Belgian cellist; b. 10 Jan. 1948, Riga, Latvia (b. USSR); m. Maryanne Kay Lipman 1983; one s. one d.; ed Moscow Conservatory with Mstislav Rostropovich, Univ. of Southern Calif.; debut with Leningrad Philharmonic Orchestra 1965; emigrated to Israel 1972; debut with Pittsburgh Symphony Orchestra at Carnegie Hall 1973; debut at Royal Festival Hall 1976; debut at Berlin Philharmonic Hall 1978; numerous TV, film and video appearances all over the world; played Walton Concerto, London Festival Hall 1993, Shostakovich Concerto, London Proms, worldwide Bach tour including over 100 concerts 2000; All-Soviet prize-winner 1965, Int. Tchaikovsky Competition 1966, winner of Cassada Competition, Florence 1973 and Rostropovich Competition, Paris 1981, Grand Prix du Disque, Paris 1985, Record Acad. Prize, Tokyo 1985.

Recordings include: Six Suites for Solo Cello (Bach), Three Sonatas for Cello and Piano (Bach), Concerto in A minor Op. 102 for Violin, Cello and Orchestra (Brahms), Concerto for Cello and Orchestra in A Minor (Schumann). *Leisure interests:* music, chess, computing. *Address:* c/o Intermusica Artists Management Ltd, 36 Graham Street, Crystal Wharf, London, N1 8GJ, England (office); 138 Meerlaan, 1900 Overijse, Belgium. *Telephone:* (20) 7608-9900 (office). *Fax:* (20) 7490-3263 (office). *E-mail:* mail@intermusica.co.uk (office). *Website:* www .intermusica.co.uk (office); www.mischamaisky.com.

MAITLAND SMITH, Geoffrey, FCA; British business executive and accountant; b. 27 Feb. 1933, London, England; s. of the late Philip John Maitland Smith and of Kathleen Maitland Smith (née Goff); m. 3rd Lucinda Enid Whyte 1986; four s. two d.; ed Univ. Coll. School, London; Pnr, Thornton Baker & Co., Chartered Accountants 1960–70; Dir Sears PLC (fmrly Sears Holdings PLC) 1971–95, Chief Exec. 1978–88, Jt Chair. 1984–85, Chair. 1985–95; Chair. British Shoe Corpn 1984–92, Mallet PLC 1986–89, Selfridges Ltd 1985–93, Garrard & Co. 1985–90, Mappin & Webb Ltd 1985–90, Hammerson PLC 1993– 99 (Dir 1990–99), W. and F.C. Bonham and Sons Ltd 1996–2000, Fiske plc (non-exec.) 2000–05; Pres. Intercontinental Group of Dept Stores 1990–95; Deputy Chair. Midland Bank 1992–96 (Dir 1986–96); Dir Asprey PLC 1980–93, Cen. Ind. Television 1983–85, Courtaulds PLC 1983–90, Imperial Group PLC 1984–86, HSBC Holdings PLC 1992–96; Hon. Vice-Pres. Inst. of Marketing 1987–94; mem. Bd Financial Reporting Council 1990–98; Chair. Council, Univ. Coll. School 1987–96. *Leisure interest:* opera.

MAITLIS, Peter M., PhD, FRS, FRSC, FCIC; British chemist and academic; *Research Professor Emeritus, Department of Chemistry, University of Sheffield;* b. 15 Jan. 1933, Berlin, Germany; s. of Jacob Maitlis and Judith Maitlis; m. Marion Basco 1959; three d.; ed Univ. of Birmingham and Univ. of London; Asst Lecturer, Univ. of London 1956–60; Fulbright Fellow and Research Assoc., Harvard and Cornell Univs, USA, 1960–62; Asst Prof., Assoc. Prof. and Prof., McMaster Univ., Canada 1962–72; Prof. of Inorganic Chem., Sheffield Univ. 1972–94, Research Prof. 1994–2002, Research Prof. Emer. 2003–; Fellow, Alfred P. Sloan Foundation 1967–69; Chair. Chem. Cttee Science and Eng Research Council 1985–88; Pres. Dalton Div., RSC 1985–87; mem. Council Royal Soc. 1991–93; Foreign mem. Accad. dei Lincei (Italy) 1999; Steacie Prize in Natural Sciences 1970, RSC Medal 1981, Kurnakov Medal, Russian Acad. of Sciences 1998. *Lectures:* Sir Edward Frankland Lecturer, RSC 1985, Tilden Lecturer 1979, Ludwig Mond Lecturer 1999, David Craig Lecturer, ANU 2000, Stone Lecturer, Univ. of Bristol 2001, Paolo Chini Lecturer, Italian Chemical Soc. 2001, Glenn T. Seaborg Memorial Lecturer, Univ. of California, Berkeley 2004–05. *Publications:* The Organic Chemistry of Palladium (two vols) 1971, Metal-catalysis in Industrial Organic Processes (with G P Chiusoli) 2006; numerous research publs in scientific journals. *Leisure interests:* music, travel, reading, discussing politics, finance. *Address:* Department of Chemistry, Room C52, University of Sheffield, Sheffield, Yorks., S3 7HF, England (office). *Telephone:* (114) 222-9320 (office). *Fax:* (114) 222-9346 (office). *E-mail:* p.maitlis@sheffield.ac.uk (office).

MAJBRI, Ahmed; Libyan oil industry executive; *Chairman, Arabian Gulf Oil Co. (Agoco);* fmrly with Finance Dept, Arabian Gulf Oil Co. (Agoco), Benghazi, Chair. Agoco Feb. 2011–. *Address:* Arabian Gulf Oil Co. (Agoco), POB 2134, Benghazi, Libya (office). *Telephone:* (61) 222-8931 (office). *Website:* www.agoco.com.ly (office).

MAJEED, Gen. Tariq, MA; Pakistani army officer (retd); b. Aug. 1950, Lahore; ed Command and Staff Coll., Quetta, Malaysian Armed Forces Staff Coll., Kuala Lumpur, Asia-Pacific Center for Security Studies, Honolulu, Hawaii, Nat. Defence Coll., Islamabad; commissioned in Pakistan Army (Infantry, Baloch Regt) 1971, has commanded Light Anti-Tank Unit and an Infantry Bn, two Infantry Brigades, Infantry Div., participated in Indo-Pakistan War 1971, took part, as GOC Lahore in absence of Corps Commdr, in counter-coup launched by army high command against then govt of Mian Nawaz Sharif Oct. 1999, also led mil. operation on Jamia Hafsa, Dir Gen. Mil. Intelligence 2001–03, promoted to Lt-Gen. Dec. 2003, Chief of Gen. Staff 2003–06, Commdr 10 Corps, Rawalpindi 2006–07, in charge of armed forces who took down armed militias stationed inside mosque at Lal Masjid Siege 2007, promoted to four-star Gen. Oct. 2007, Chair. Jt Chiefs of Staff Cttee Oct. 2007–10; Hilal-e-Imtiaz (Mil.), Nishan-e-Imtiaz (Mil.). *Address:* c/o Joint Chiefs of Staff Committee, Joint Staff Headquarters, Chaklala, Rawalpindi, Pakistan.

MAJEWSKI, Tomasz; Polish athlete; b. 30 Aug. 1981, Nasielsk; m. Ani Majewski; one s.; ed Uniwersytet Kardynała Stefana Wyszyńskiego; winner Shot Put, Nat. Championships 2003, 2004, 2005, Nat. Indoor Championships 2004, 2005, 2006; fourth place, Shot Put, World Indoor Championships, Budapest 2004; gold medal, Shot Put, 23rd Summer Universiade, İzmir 2005; bronze medal, Shot Put, European Winter Throwing Cup, Tel-Aviv 2006, World Indoor Championships, Valencia 2008 (threw 20.93m); gold medal, Shot Put, Olympic Games, Beijing 2008 (achieved personal best throw of 21.51m during Olympic final on 15 Aug.), Poland's first Olympic medal in shot put since 1972); gold medal, IAAF World Athletics Final, Stuttgart 2008; silver medal, IAAF World Athletics Final, Thessaloniki 2009; silver medal, Shot Put, World Championships, Berlin 2009, European Championships, Barcelona 2010; bronze medal, Shot Put, World Indoor Championships, Valencia 2008, Istanbul 2012; gold medal, Shot Put, European Indoor Championships, Torino 2009; silver medal, Continental Cup, Split 2010; gold medal, Shot Put, Olympic Games, London 2012; coach Henryk Olszewski 2001–; Knight's Cross of the Order of Polonia Restituta (5th Class) 2008, Officer's Cross, Order of Polonia Restituta (4th Class) 2009. *Leisure interest:* basketball. *Address:* Polish Athletics Federation (Polski Zwiazek Lekkiej Atletyki), ul. Mysłowicka 4, 01-612 Warsaw, Poland. *E-mail:* pzla@pzla.pl. *Website:* www.pzla.pl.

MAJID, Choudhary Abdul, BA, LLB; Pakistani politician; *Prime Minister of Azad Jammu and Kashmir;* b. 14 Feb. 1946, Tangdev, Mirpur; ed Karachi Muslim Law School; mem. Azad Jammu and Kashmir (AJK) Legis. Ass., Speaker 1998–2001, Leader of the Opposition Feb.–July 2011; AJK Minister for Revenue, Agric. and Northern Resource Man. Project 1996; mem. Pakistan People's Party (PPP), mem. PPP Overseas Cttee, Chair. Social Action Programme, mem. Cen. Exec. Cttee 2006–, Vice-Pres. AJK PPP 1993, Sr Vice-Pres. 2005, currently Pres.; Prime Minister of Azad Jammu and Kashmir 2011–. *Address:* House No 167-G, Sector F/2, Mirpur, Azad Kashmir (home); Prime Minister's Secretariat, Muzaffarabad, Azad Jammu and Kashmir, Pakistan (office). *Telephone:* (5822)

921600 (office); (5822) 921601 (office). *Fax:* (5822) 921607 (office). *E-mail:* pm@ pmajk.gov.pk (office). *Website:* www.ajk.gov.pk (office); www.pmajk.gov.pk (office).

MAJKO, Pandeli Sotir, LLB; Albanian politician; b. 15 Nov. 1967; s. of Sotir and Janulla; m. Enkeleida Majko; one s., one d.; ed Univ. of Tirana; Rep. Dec. 1990 Movt; co-f. Democratic Party 1990, left party 1991; Jt Socialist Party of Albania 1991, Sec.-Gen. of Public Relations 1996–97, Sec. 1997–99, also leader of Parl. Group, Head of Del. to OSCE; Prime Minister of Albania 1998–99, Feb.–July 2002; Minister of Defence 2002–05; fmr Sec. Gen., Socialist Party of Albania; f. Forum of Euro-Socialist Youth 1991; Chair. Euro-Socialist Forum 1992–95; mem. Parl. 1992–; Torch of Democracy Award 1993. *Leisure interest:* reading. *Address:* Kuvendi Popullor (People's Assembly), Bulevardi Dëshmorët e Kombit 4, Tirana, Albania (office). *Telephone:* (4) 2264887 (office); (42) 251299 (home). *Fax:* (4) 2221764 (office). *E-mail:* marlind@parlament.al (office); pandelimajko@hotmail .com (home). *Website:* www.parlament.al (office).

MAJOR, Clarence, BS, PhD; American poet, painter, novelist and academic; *Professor Emeritus of English, University of California, Davis;* b. 31 Dec. 1936, Atlanta, Ga; s. of Clarence Major and Inez Huff; m. Pamela Ritter 1980; ed Union Inst. and Univ., Yellow Springs and Cincinnati, Ohio, State Univ. of NY, Albany; Prof. of English, Univ. of California, Davis 1989–2010, Prof. Emer. 2010–; various appointments at Sara Lawrence Coll., Brooklyn Coll., Queens Coll., New York Univ., Temple Univ., Washington Univ., Univ. of California, San Diego, State Univ. of NY, Binghamton; has given lectures in USA, Europe and in N and W Africa; Fulbright Fellowship, Pushcart Prize, Nat. Council on the Arts Award, Int. Writers' Hall of Fame, Gwendolyn Brooks Foundation Award, Chicago State Univ., Western States Book Award, Sister Circle Book Award, Stephen Henderson Poetry Award for Outstanding Achievement, Bronze Medal as Finalist for Nat. Book Award. *Publications:* novels: All-Night Visitors 1969, NO 1973, Reflex and Bone Structure 1975, Emergency Exit 1979, My Amputations (Western States Book Award for Fiction) 1986, Such Was the Season 1987, Painted Turtle: Woman with Guitar 1988; short stories: Fun and Games 1990, Calling the Wind: Twentieth Century African-American Short Stories 1993, Dirty Bird Blues 1996, All-Night Visitors (new version) 1998; poetry: Swallow the Lake 1970, Symptoms and Madness 1971, Private Line 1971, The Cotton Club 1972, The Syncopated Cakewalk 1974, Inside Diameter: The France Poems 1985, Surfaces and Masks 1987, Some Observations of a Stranger at Zuni in the Latter Part of the Century 1989, The Garden Thrives, Twentieth Century African-American Poetry 1995, Configurations: New and Selected Poems 1958–98, 1998, Waiting for Sweet Baby 2002; non-fiction: Dictionary of Afro-American Slang 1970, The Dark and Feeling: Black American Writers and their Work 1974, Juba to Jive: A Dictionary of African-American Slang 1994, Necessary Distance: Essays and Criticism 2001, Come by Here: My Mother's Life 2002, Conversations with Clarence Major, Clarence Major and His Art; numerous works in anthologies and periodicals. *Address:* Department of English, Voorhies Hall, University of California, Davis, CA 95616, USA (office). *E-mail:* clmajor@ucdavis.edu (office). *Website:* english .ucdavis.edu/people/directory/cmajor (office); www.clarencemajor.com.

MAJOR, Air Chief Marshal Fali Homi; Indian air force officer (retd); b. 29 May 1947, Secunderabad; m. Zareen Major; one s. one d.; ed Wesley High School, Secunderabad, Nat. Defence Coll., Army War Coll.; commissioned in Indian Air Force (IAF) 1967, has flown over 7,000 hours on Sentinel, T-6G, Mi-4, Mi-8 and Mi-17 helicopters, as Wing Commdr, commanded IAF's first Mi-17 Squadron, which operated at Siachen Glacier (world's highest battlefield), as Group Capt., commanded another Mi-17 Squadron, leading it during operations of Indian Peace Keeping Force in Sri Lanka, as Station Commdr of Air Force Station Sarsawa, led rescue of 11 passengers from stranded cable car at resort in Himachal Pradesh, has held several important staff and field appointments, including Jt Dir (Helicopter Operations) and Dir Operations (Transport & Helicopter), Air Officer Commdg Leh (Ladakh) following Kargil conflict 1999, promoted to rank of Air Vice-Marshal 2002, Asst Chief of the Air Staff (Personnel Airmen & Civilians) at Air HQ 2002–04, promoted to rank of Air Marshal 2004, Deputy Chief of Integrated Defence Staff (Operations), HQ Integrated Defence Staff 2004–05, directed relief, rescue and rehabilitation operations of Indian Armed Forces in India and abroad in aftermath of tsunami of Dec. 2004, Air Officer C-in-C Eastern Air Command 2005–07, Chief of the Air Staff 2007–09; Vayu Sena Medal (Gallantry), Shaurya Chakra for gallantry, Ati Vishist Seva Medal 2002, Param Vishisht Seva Medal 2006. *Leisure interests:* avid golfer and cricket fan. *Address:* c/o Public Relations Officer, Indian Air Force, Directorate of Public Relations, Ministry of Defence, Room No. 91, South Block, New Delhi, 110 011, India.

MAJOR, Jean-Louis, CM, LPh, MA, PhD, FRSC, OC; Canadian author and academic; *Professor Emeritus, University of Ottawa;* b. 16 July 1937, Cornwall, Ont.; s. of Joseph Major and Noella Daoust; m. Bibiane Landry 1960; one d.; ed Univ. of Ottawa, Ecole Pratique des Hautes Etudes, Paris, France; Lecturer, Dept of Philosophy, Univ. of Ottawa 1961–65, Prof. Dept des Lettres Françaises 1965, Titular Prof. 1971–99, Assoc. Dean (Research), Faculty of Arts 1991–97, Prof. Emer. 1999–; Visiting Prof., Dept of French, Univ. of Toronto 1970–71; Dir Corpus d'éditions critiques and Bibliothèque du nouveau monde 1981–; Chair. Academic Advisory Cttee of Ont. Council on Univ. Affairs 1991–93; Excellence in Research Award 1990, Lorne Pierce Medal, Royal Soc. of Canada 2000. *Publications include:* Saint-Exupéry, l'écriture et la pensée 1968, Anne Hébert et le miracle de la parole 1976, Le jeu en étoile 1978, Entre l'écriture et la parole 1984, a critical edn of Cocteau's Léone, Journal d'Henriette Dessaules 1989, Trente arpents de Ringuet 1991, Mailles à l'envers 1999, Québec Literature: From Collective Identity to Modernity and Back 1999, Contes par-ci par-là 2001, Antifables 2002, Appartenances 2010. *Address:* Département des Lettres Françaises, University of Ottawa, Ottawa, ON K1N 6N5, Canada (office).

MAJOR, Rt Hon., Sir John, KG, CH, AIB, FIB; British banker and fmr prime minister; b. 29 March 1943, Merton, London, England; s. of the late Thomas Major and Gwendolyn Minnie Coates; m. Norma Christina Elizabeth Johnson 1970; one s. one d.; ed Rutlish Grammar School, Merton; mem. Lambeth Borough Council 1968–71, Chair. Housing Cttee 1970–71; Sr Exec. Standard Chartered Bank PLC, various exec. posts in UK and overseas 1965–79; MP for Huntingdon 1983–2001 (Huntingdonshire 1979–83); Jt Sec., Conservative Parl. Party Environment Cttee 1979–81; Parl. Pvt. Sec. to Home Office Minister 1981–83; Asst Govt Whip 1983–84; Lord Commr of HM Treasury 1984–85; Parl. Under-Sec. of State for

Social Security 1985–86; Minister for Social Security and the Disabled 1986–87; Chief Sec. to Treasury 1987–89; Sec. of State for Foreign and Commonwealth Affairs July–Oct. 1989; Chancellor of the Exchequer 1989–90; Prime Minister, First Lord of the Treasury and Minister for the Civil Service 1990–97; Leader of the Conservative Party 1990–97; Pres. Eastern Area Young Conservatives 1983–85, mem. Int. Bd of Govs., Peres Centre for Peace, Israel 1997–; Chair. Emerson Electric Co. 1999–; mem. Baker Inst. 1998–2005, InterAction Council, Tokyo 1998–2008; Adviser to Carlyle Group 1998–2001, Chair. (European Bd) 2001–05; Pres. Surrey Co. Cricket Club 2000–02; Chair. Ditchley Council of Man. 2000–09, Advisory Bd Global Infrastructure Partners 2007–, Int. Advisory Bd Nat. Bank of Kuwait 2007–14; Dir (non-exec.) Mayflower Corpn 2000–03; Sr Adviser Credit Suisse 2001–; mem. European Bd, Siebel Systems Inc. 2001–03, Club de Madrid 2002–06; mem. Main Cttee Marylebone Cricket Club (MCC) 2001–04, 2005–08, 2009–11, Norfolk Cricket Umpires and Scorers Asscn 2002–; Pres. Asthma UK 1998–, Research Action Fund, Prostate Cancer UK 2009–, The Bow Group 2012–; Vice-Pres. Macmillan Cancer Relief, Inst. of Sports Sponsorship 2001–, Greater London Fund for the Blind 2005–; Chair. Queen Elizabeth Diamond Jubilee Trust 2011–; mem. British and Commonwealth Cricket Charitable Trust 2002–; Amb. Chance to Shine 2005–, Vision 2020; Patron of Mercy Ships, Support for Africa 2000, Atlantic Partnership 2001–, Foreign and Commonwealth Office Asscn 2001–, Professional Cricketers' Asscn 2001–, Deafblind UK 2002–, Consortium for Street Children 2002–, 21st Century Trust 2002–, Goodman Fund, Chicago 2002–, DEMAND 2002–, Wavemakers 2004–07, Foundation for Peace 2004–, Future Ireland 2004–, Dickie Bird Foundation 2004–, SeeAbility's Sight Pioneers 2006–, Margaret Thatcher Scholarship Trust 2012–, British Music Hall Soc. 2012–, Hoxton Hall 2012–; Vice-Patron, The Atlantic Council of the UK; Hon. Master of the Bench of the Middle Temple 1992, Hon. Bencher 1993–, Hon. Freeman, Merchant Taylors' Co. 2002–, Hon. Life Vice-Pres. Surrey Co. Cricket Club, Hon. Pres. Sight Savers Appeal 2001–, Hon. FCIB, Hon. Commr, Sir John A. Macdonald Bicentennial Comm. 2012–, Distinguished Elder Brother of the Court of Trinity House 2012, Hon. Patron, British Gymnastics 2013–; Grand Cordon, Order of the Rising Sun (Japan) 2012. *Publications include:* John Major: The Autobiography 1999, More Than A Game: The Story of Cricket's Early Years 2007, My Old Man: A Personal History of Music Hall 2012. *Leisure interests:* reading, travel, theatre, music, opera, football, cricket and other sports. *Address:* PO Box 38506, London, SW1P 1ZW, England.

MAJOR, Kendal, DDS; Bahamian dentist and politician; *Speaker, House of Assembly;* b. 9 Aug. 1961, Nassau; m. Monique Smith; two c. ; ed Tuskegee Univ., Howard Univ. Coll. of Dentistry, Washington DC, Univ. of Medicine and Dentistry of New Jersey, USA; began professional dental career as Sr Dental Officer, Princess Margaret Hosp., Nassau, becoming Dir of Dental Services; mem. House of Ass. (PLP) for Garden Hills 2012–, Speaker of; fmr Chair. Dental Council of The Bahamas; Founder and Dir Bahamas' First Study Club, Nassau; Dir Teen Challenge Bahamas; fmr mem. Nat. Comm. on Prison Reform; mem. Progressive Liberal Party (PLP), Vice-Chair. 2008–10. *Address:* House of Assembly, POB N 3003, Nassau, Bahamas (office). *Telephone:* (1242) 322 2041 (office). *Fax:* (1242) 322 1118 (office). *E-mail:* houseofassembly@bahamas.gov.bs (office). *Website:* www .bahamas.gov.bs (office).

MAJOR, Dame Malvina Lorraine, ONZ, GNZM, DBE; New Zealand operatic soprano; *Senior Fellow, Conservatorium of Music Faculty of Arts and Social Sciences, University of Waikato;* b. 28 Jan. 1943, Hamilton; d. of Vincent Major and Eva Major; m. Winston William Richard Fleming 1965 (died 1990); one s. two d.; ed Hamilton Tech. Coll. and London Opera Centre; debut as Rosina in The Barber of Seville, Salzburg Festival 1968; performances in Europe, UK, USA, Australia, Japan, Jordan, Egypt and NZ; concerts, opera and recording with NZ Symphony Orchestra, Auckland Philharmonia and Southern Symphony Orchestra; Founder Dame Malvina Major Foundation (for excellence in the performing arts) 1991; Amb. for the NZ Year of the Family 1994; fmr Prof. of Vocal Studies, Univ. of Canterbury; currently Sr Fellow, Conservatorium of Music Faculty of Arts and Social Sciences, Univ. of Waikato; fmr Chair. Diana, Princess of Wales Trust; Patron, Christchurch City Choir, Canterbury Opera, Nelson School of Music, Waikato Multiple Sclerosis; Hon. Life mem. NZ Horticultural Soc.; Dame Grand Companion, NZ Order of Merit 2007; Hon. DLitt (Massey Univ.); Dr hc (Waikato); NZ Winner, Mobil Song Quest 1963, Kathleen Ferrier Competition winner 1966, Outstanding Achievements in Music Award 1988, NZ Medal 1990, Entertainer and Int. Performer of the Year 1992, NZ Music Award—Classical Disc 1993, 1994, Benny Award, Variety Club of NZ 1998 and numerous other awards for services to music. *Leisure interests:* family, golf, sewing, gardening. *Address:* c/o James Bennett MNZM JP, 3 Featherstone Drive, Flagstaff, Hamilton 3210, New Zealand (office). *Telephone:* (7) 8543255 (office). *E-mail:* jimbennett@xtra.co.nz (office). *Website:* www.damemalvinamajor.co.nz; www.damemalvinamajorfoundation.co .nz.

MAK, Tak Wah, OC, BSc, MSc, PhD, FRSC; Canadian (b. Chinese) immunologist, molecular biologist and academic; *Professor, Department of Medical Biophysics and Department of Immunology and Director, Campbell Family Institute for Breast Cancer Research, University of Toronto;* b. 4 Oct. 1946, People's Repub. of China; s. of Kent Mak and Shu-tak Chan; m. Shirley Suet-Wan Lau (died 1998); two c.; ed Univ. of Wisconsin, Univ. of Alberta; Sr Scientist, Div. of Stem Cell and Developmental Biology, Advanced Medical Discovery Inst., Ont. Cancer Inst. 1974–, Head of Div. of Cellular and Molecular Biology 1991–93, currently Dir Advanced Medical Discovery Inst.; mem. Inst. of Medical Science, of Toronto 1979–, Assoc. Prof., Dept of Medical Biophysics 1979–84, Prof., Dept of Medical Biophysics and Dept of Immunology 1984–, Univ. Prof. 1997–, Grad. Sec., Dept of Medical Biophysics 1995–2001, Dir Advanced Medical Discovery Inst., Univ. Health Network, Toronto 2002–, Dir Campbell Family Inst. for Breast Cancer Research, Princess Margaret Hosp., Toronto 2004–; Founding Dir Amgen Inst. 1993–2002; mem. Bd Cancer Research Inc., New York 1989–; Ed. or Assoc. Ed. The International Journal of Immunology 1987–, The Immunologist 1994–, Current Opinion in Immunology 2001–, Cancer Cell 2002–, Proceedings of the National Academy of Sciences, USA 2003–; mem. numerous advisory bds of scientific journals and medical centres; Foreign Assoc., NAS 2002; mem. American Acad. of Arts and Sciences 2005; Hon. Prof., Cancer Inst., Chinese Acad. of Medical Sciences 1986, Beijing Union Medical Univ. 1986, Dept of Pathology, Univ. of Hong Kong 2004–07, Dept of Medicine Faculty, Univ. of Rome 'Tor Vergata', Italy 2007,

Dept of Biology and Chem., City Univ. of Hong Kong 2007; Hon. mem. Scandinavian Soc. of Immunology 1995; Order of Ont. 2008; Hon. DSc (Carleton Univ.) 1989, (Laurentian Univ.) 1992, (York Univ., Ont.) 2004, (Ryerson Univ., Ont.) 2004, (Univ. of Hong Kong) 2008; Hon. MD (Univ. of Zurich) 2001; Hon. MD in Surgery (Univ. of Rome) 2008; hon. degree (Georg August Univ., Germany) 2008; The Outstanding Award of the Year, Chinese Cultural Asscn of Canada 1984, E.W.R. Steacie Award, Nat. Sciences and Eng Research Council 1984, Ayerst Award, Canadian Biochemical Soc. 1985, Merit Award, Fed. of Chinese Professionals of Canada 1985, Stacie Prize, Stacie Trust Foundation 1986, Canadian Asscn of Mfrs of Medical Devices Award 1988, Emil von Behring Prize, Phillips-Universität Marburg (FRG) 1988, Univ. of Alberta 75th Anniversary Distinguished Scientist Award 1989, Gairdner Int. Award, Gairdner Foundation 1989, RSC McLaughlin Medal 1990, Canadian Foundation for AIDS Research Award 1991, Cinader Award 1994, Royal Soc. of London 1994, Sloan Prize, General Motors Cancer Foundation 1994, King Faisal Int. Prize for Medicine 1995, Sloan Prize, General Motors Cancer Research Foundation 1996, McLeans Magazine's Honour Roll 1996, Robert Noble Prize, Nat. Cancer Inst. of Canada 1997, Alumni of the Year, Univ. of Alberta 1997, McLaughlin Medal, University of Texas, Galveston, Texas 1997, Novartis Immunology Prizes, Novartis, Inc. Basel, Switzerland 1998, Killam Prize, Canada Council 2003, Paul Ehrlich and Ludwig Darmstaedter Prize 2004, Premier's Summit Awards in Medical Research, Ont. 2007, Alumni Recognition Award, Univ. of Alberta 2008, inducted into Canadian Medical Hall of Fame 2009. *Achievements include:* recognized world-wide for his discovery of T cell receptor (TCR), a key component of the immune system. *Publications:* more than 640 scientific papers in professional journals; more than 26 patents. *Leisure interests:* music, tennis, golf. *Address:* Department of Medical Biophysics, University of Toronto, Toronto Medical Discovery Tower, MaRS Centre, 101 College Street, Room 15-701, Toronto, ON M5G 1L7, Canada (office). *Telephone:* (416) 946-4501 (ext. 2234) (office). *E-mail:* tmak@uhnres.utoronto.ca (office). *Website:* medbio.utoronto.ca/faculty/mak.html (office).

MAKANIN, Vladimir Semenovich; Russian writer; b. 13 March 1937, Orsk, Orenburg Region; ed Moscow Univ., Higher Workshop for Scenario Writers and Film Dirs; started writing 1965; Pushkin Prize 1998, Penne Prize, Italy 1999, Russian State Prize 2000, European Prize for Literature 2012. *Publications include:* Straight Line 1965, Air-Vent, Portrait and Around (novel) 1976, Story about an Old Settlement (collection of short stories) 1974, Voices 1982, River with a Fast Current 1983, Where the Skies Meet the Hills 1987, One and One 1987, Subject of Averaging 1992, The Loss: A Novella and Two Stories (Writings from an Unbound Europe), Baize-Covered Table with Decanter (Russian Booker Prize) 1993, Quasi 1993, Captives 1996, Escape Hatch and The Long Road Ahead: Two Novellas 1998, Underground, or a Hero of Our Time 1998, Letter A 2000, A Good Love Story 2000, Asan (Big Book Award) 2008, Two Sisters and Kandinsky 2011. *Address:* c/o Okno Literary Agency, Solid Entertainment AB, S. Neptunig. 10C, 211 18 Malmo, Sweden; Novinski Boulevard 16, Apartment 14, 121069 Moscow, Russia (home). *E-mail:* info@okno-agency.com; vmakanin@hotmail.com. *Website:* www.okno-agency.com. *Telephone:* (495) 291-92-53 (home). *Fax:* (495) 781-01-82 (home).

MAKARCZYK, Jerzy, LLD; Polish judge and professor of law; *Professor of Legal Sciences, Polish Academy of Sciences;* b. 24 July 1938; s. of Zbigniew Makarczyk and Hanna Olszowska; ed Warsaw Univ. and Inst. of Legal Sciences, Polish Acad. of Sciences; Assoc. Prof. of Int. Public Law 1975, Prof. 1988; Deputy Dir Inst. of Legal Sciences, Polish Acad. of Sciences 1981–88, Prof. 1992–; Deputy Minister of Foreign Affairs 1989–90; Sec. of State, Ministry of Foreign Affairs 1990–92; in charge of negotiations with USSR and then Russia on withdrawal of troops from Polish territory 1990–2002; Judge, European Court of Human Rights 1992–; mem. ILO High Level Team to Myanmar 2001–; Adviser to Pres. of Repub. of Poland 2002–; Pres. Int. Law Asscn 1988–90; mem. Inst de Droit Int. 1993, Pres. 2003–; nominated cand.-judge to European Communities Court of Justice 2004; Commdr Légion d'honneur; Manfred Lachs Foundation Award 1998. *Publications:* Financing of Economic Development in the United Nations System 1974, Principles of a New International Economic Order 1988; ed. Collection of Essays in Honour of Judge Manfred Lachs 1984, Theory of International Law at the Threshold of the XXIst Century (ed.) 1996. *Leisure interests:* tennis, sailing. *Address:* Al. Przyjaciol 3 m. 14, 00-565 Warsaw, Poland. *Telephone:* (22) 6769135. *Fax:* (22) 6429540. *E-mail:* jmakarczyk@prezydent.pl.

MAKAREVICH, Andrei Vadimovich; Russian composer, singer and artist; b. 11 Dec. 1953, Moscow; one s. two d.; ed Moscow Inst. of Architecture; Founder, Artistic Dir, soloist, Time Machine (first professional rock group in Russia) 1969–; creator, presenter Smak (TV programme); Leader, Creol Tango Orchestra; drawings have been exhibited in Moscow, St Petersburg, Riga, Caserta (Italy), London, New York; Merited Artist of RSFSR, Order of Honour, Order of Contrib. to the Motherland. *Television:* presenter, Smak, Underwater World of Andrei Makarevich. *Recordings:* 26 albums, including music for nine films. *Publications:* nine books of poetry and prose. *Leisure interest:* spear hunting. *Address:* ORT (Russian Public TV), 127000 Moscow, Smak, Akademika Koroleva str. 12, Russia (office). *Telephone:* (495) 217-79-88 (office); (495) 367-63-09 (office). *Website:* www .mashina.ru (office); www.makar.info.

MAKAROV, Andrey Mikhailovich, CJur; Russian barrister; b. 22 July 1954, Moscow; ed Moscow State Univ.; worked in Research Inst., USSR Ministry of Internal Affairs 1976–83; mem. Moscow City Bd of Lawyers 1983–, acted as the defence lawyer in numerous major trials, including trial of fmr Deputy Minister of Internal Affairs V. Churbanov; Chief of Dept supervising activities of Comm. of Security Council in struggle against crime and corruption July–Oct. 1993; mem. State Duma (Parl.) 1993–, Vice-Chair. Budget and Taxation Cttee; Exec. Dir Russian br. of SOROS Foundation; Pres. Chess Fed. of Russia 1994–97; mem. Exec. Cttee Int. Chess Fed. (FIDE); Head, Barristers co. A. Makarov and A. Tobak 1998–; Chair. Council of Experts on Improving Tax System, State Duma 2000–. *Address:* Andrey Makarov and Aleksandr Tobak Barristers Bureau, 125167 Moscow, Leningradsky Prospect 39A, Russia (office). *Telephone:* (495) 213-86-94 (office).

MAKAROV, Gen. Nikolai Yegorovich; Russian army officer; b. 7 Oct. 1949, Glebovo, Ryazan Oblast; m.; one s.; ed Moscow Combined Arms Command School, Frunze Mil. Acad., Gen. Staff Acad., Moscow; began career as Commdr, Soviet

Platoon, German Democratic Repub., becoming Commdr of Co. and Bn; Deputy Regt Commdr, Baikal Mil. Dist (later Transbaikal Mil. Dist) 1979; Deputy Div. Commdr, Russian Jt Force, Tajikistan, becoming Commdr, Motorized Rifle Div., Chief of Staff 1993; Chief of Staff, Volga Mil. Dist –1998; Commdr of Ground and Shore Troops and Deputy Commdr of Baltic Fleet 1998–99; Chief of Staff and First Deputy Commdr, Moscow Mil. Dist 1999–2002; Commdr, Siberian Mil. Dist 2002; attained rank of Gen. 2005; Chief of Armaments for Russian Armed Forces and Deputy Minister of Defence 2007–08, Chief of Gen. Staff and First Deputy Minister of Defence 2008–12; mem. Historical Truth Comm. 2009–12; aide to Minister of Defence Sergei Shoigu 2013–; Order for Service in USSR Armed Forces (Third Class), Order for Distinguished Mil. Service, Order of St George (Second Class); 12 medals; Honoured Mil. Specialist of Russian Fed. *Address:* Ministry of Defence, 119169 Moscow, ul. Znamenka 19, Russia (office). *Telephone:* (495) 696-71-71 (office); (495) 696-86-73 (office). *Website:* mil.ru (office).

MAKAROV, Valery Leonidovich, PhD; Russian economist; *Director, Central Economics and Mathematics Institute, Russian Academy of Sciences;* b. 25 May 1937, Novosibirsk; s. of Leonid Makarov and Dina Yershov; m. Irena Nikolaev 1961; one s. one d.; ed Moscow Econ. Inst.; scientific worker, Inst. of Math., Siberian Div. USSR Acad. of Sciences 1961–67, Lab. Chief 1967–73, Deputy Dir 1973–80, Gen. Sec. Siberian Div. 1980–83; Prof. of Mathematical Econs Novosibirsk Univ. 1970–83; Dir Nat. Inst. of Industrial Man., Moscow 1983–85; Dir Central Econs and Math. Inst. 1985–; Prof. at Moscow Univ.; Founder and Rector, New Econ. School, Moscow 1992–; Ed.-in-Chief, Journal of Math. and Econ. Methods.; mem. Ed. Bd Econs of Planning, Econs of Transition, Econ. Systems Research; mem. Exec. Cttee, Int. Econ. Asscn 1995–; mem. several govt comms; Corresp. mem. USSR (now Russian) Acad. of Science 1979, mem. 1990; Fellow Econometric Soc.; Kantorovich Award (for contrib. to econ. theory) 1995. *Publications:* Mathematical Theory of Economic Dynamics and Equilibria (with A. Rubinov) 1977, Models and Computers in Economics 1979, Computer Simulation in Analysis of Regional Problems 1987, Mathematical Economic Theory: Pure and Mixed Types of Economic Mechanisms (with A. Rubinov and M. Levin) 1994. *Leisure interests:* tennis, skiing. *Address:* Central Economics and Mathematics Institute, Russian Academy of Sciences, 117418 Moscow, Nakhimouski Prospect 47, Russia. *Telephone:* (495) 129-10-11 (office); (495) 229-01-50 (home). *Fax:* (495) 310-70-15.

MAKAROVA, Inna Vladimirovna; Russian actress; b. 28 July 1926, Taiga, Kemerovo Dist; d. of Vladimir Makarov and Anna German; m. 1st S. Bondarchuk 1947; m. 2nd M. Perelman; one d.; ed All-Union Film Inst.; Order of Red Banner of Labour, Order of Merit RSFSR 1967; USSR State Prize 1949, People's Artist of USSR 1985. *Films include:* Molodaya gvardiya (The Young Guard) 1948, Selskiy vrach (The Village Doctor) 1951, Vozvrashcheniye Vasiliya Bortnikova (The Return of Vasili Bortnikov) 1952, Dimitrovgradtsy (People of Dimitrovgrad) 1956, Vysota (Height) 1957, Dorogoy moy chelovek (My Dear Fellow!) 1958, Nash korespondent 1959, Devchata (Girls) 1961, Bratya Komarovy 1961, Zhenitba Balzaminova (The Marriage of Balzaminov) 1964, Bolshaya ruda (The Big Ore) 1964, Zhenshchiny 1966, Malenkiy beglets (The Little Runaway) 1966, Urok literatury (A Literature Lesson) 1968, Novenkaya (The Rookie) 1968, Prestupleniye i nakazaniye (Crime and Punishment) 1969, Lyubov Yarovaya 1970, Russkoye pole (Russian Field) 1971, Neispravimyy lgun (Incorrigible Liar) 1973, Bezotvetnaya lyubov (Unanswered Love) 1979, Kontrolnaya po spetsialnosti 1981, Zhivaya raduga (Living Rainbow) 1982, Detstvo Bambi (Bambi's Childhood) 1985, Yunost Bambi (Bambi's Youth) 1986, Lermontov 1986, Ssuda na brak (Loan for a Marriage) 1987, Bolshaya lyubov 2006. *Television includes:* Vas vyzyvaet Taymyr (Taimyr Calls You) 1970, Harsnatsun hyusisits (A Bride from the North) 1975, Pechniki (Stove Builders) 1982, Myortvye dushi (Dead Souls) (mini-series) 1984, Maritsa 1985. *Leisure interest:* gardening. *Address:* 121059 Moscow, Ukrainian Blvd 11, Apt 14, Russia. *Telephone:* (495) 243-00-93.

MAKAROVA, Natalia Romanovna; Russian ballerina; b. 1940, Leningrad; m. 3rd Edward Karkar 1976; one s.; ed Vagonova Ballet School, Leningrad; mem. Kirov Ballet 1959–70; sought political asylum, London 1970; Prin. Dancer, American Ballet Theater 1970–92; appeared with Kirov Co. in London 1988, USSR 1989; f. Makarova and Co. 1980; Guest Artist, Royal Ballet 1972; Guest Artist, London Festival Ballet 1984; retd from dancing 1992; Dir Sleeping Beauty, Royal Ballet 2003; Honoured Artist of RSFSR, School of American Ballet Artistic Achievement Award 2004, Carina Ari Medal 2006, Kennedy Center Honor 2012. *Television:* In a Class of Her Own, Assoluta, Natasha 1985, Makarova Returns 1989, Great Railway Journeys: St Petersburg to Tashkent 1994. *Plays:* On Your Toes (musical), Broadway, New York (Tony Award for Best Actress in a Musical), West End, London (Laurence Olivier Award) 1984, Tovarich, Chichester Festival then West End, London 1991, Two for the Seesaw, Moscow 1992. *Publications:* A Dance Autobiography 1979, On Your Toes 1984.

MAKEI, Uladzimir U.; Belarusian politician; *Minister of Foreign Affairs;* b. 5 Aug. 1958, Grodno Oblast; ed Minsk State Teachers' Training Inst. of Foreign Languages, Diplomatic Acad., Austrian Ministry of Foreign Affairs; served in Soviet Army 1980–92, Col in Reserve; Third Sec., Information and Humanitarian Co-operation Dept, later Second Sec., Analysis and Forecasting Dept, later Second Sec., Secr. of the Ministry of Foreign Affairs 1993–95, Deputy Head of State Protocol Service 1995–96, Belarusian Rep. to Council of Europe, Counsellor, Embassy in Paris 1996–99, Head of All-European Co-operation Dept, Ministry of Foreign Affairs 1999–2000; Aide to the Pres. of Belarus 2000–08, Head of Presidential Exec. Office 2008–12; Minister of Foreign Affairs 2012–. *Address:* Ministry of Foreign Affairs, 220030 Minsk, vul. Lenina 19, Belarus (office). *Telephone:* (17) 327-29-22 (office). *Fax:* (17) 327-45-21 (office). *E-mail:* mail@mfa .gov.by (office). *Website:* mfa.gov.by (office).

MAKEN, Ajay, BA, BScl; Indian trade unionist and politician; b. 12 Jan. 1964, Delhi; s. of C. P. Maken and Santosh Maken; m. Radhika Maken; one s. two d.; ed St Xavier's School, Delhi, Univ. of Delhi; fmr leader, trade union movts of Delhi Transport Corpn and Delhi Electric Supply Undertaking; mem. Delhi Legis. Ass. 1993–2004, Speaker 2003–04; mem. Lok Sabha (lower house of Parl.) for New Delhi constituency 2004–; Gen.-Sec. Delhi Pradesh Congress Cttee 1993–97; Gen.-Sec. Indian Youth Congress 1997–98; Parl. Sec. to Chief Minister, Govt of Delhi 1998–2001; Minister of Transport, Power and Tourism, Govt of Delhi 2001–03; Union Cabinet Minister of State for Urban Devt 2006–09, for Home Affairs 2009–11, for Youth Affairs and Sports 2011–12, Union Cabinet Minister of Housing and Urban Poverty Alleviation 2012–13, Gen. Sec. and Head of Communication, Publicity and Publication, Indian Nat. Congress 2013–. *Leisure interests:* cricket and golf, surfing the net, watching science fiction movies, listening to old movie songs, ghazals (poetry) and reading non-fiction books. *Address:* Indian National Congress, 24 Akbar Road, New Delhi 110 011, India (office). *Telephone:* (11) 23019080. *Fax:* (11) 23017047. *E-mail:* aicc@congress.org .in. *Website:* www.aicc.org.in.

MAKGOBA, Archbishop Thabo Cecil, BSc, MA, PhD; South African ecclesiastic; *Anglican Archbishop of Cape Town;* b. 15 Dec. 1960, Johannesburg; m. Lungelwa Manona; ed Orlando High, Soweto, Univ. of the Witwatersrand, St Paul's Coll., Grahamstown, Univ. of Cape Town; ordained priest in Anglican Diocese of Johannesburg 1990, first as a curate at Cathedral, then as Chaplian of Univ. of the Witwatersrand; part-time Lecturer, Univ. of the Witwatersrand 1993–96; put in charge of St Alban's Church and later of Christ the King, Sophiatown, Archdeacon of Sophiatown 1999; consecrated Bishop of Queenstown (Suffragan Bishop of Grahamstown) 2002–04, Bishop of Grahamstown 2004–07; Archbishop of Cape Town and Metropolitan of the Anglican Church of Southern Africa 2007–; Procter Fellow, Episcopal Divinity School (USA) 2008; Chancellor Univ. of the Western Cape 2012–; Chair. Nat. Church Leaders' Consultation; Hon. DD (Gen. Theological Seminary) 2009, (Huron Univ. Coll.) 2013; Ernest Oppehheimer Memorial Trust Scholarship to study for his PhD. *Address:* Anglican Diocese of Cape Town, PO Box 1932, Zonnebloem Estate, Woodstock, Cape Town 8000, South Africa (office). *Telephone:* (21) 469-3760 (office). *Fax:* (21) 465-1571 (office). *E-mail:* goodhopeads@ctdiocese.org.za (office). *Website:* www.capetown .anglican.org (office).

MAKHALINA, Yulia Victorovna; Russian ballet dancer; b. 23 June 1968, St Petersburg; ed Vaganova Acad. of Russian Ballet under Prof. Marina Vasilyeva; joined Mariinsky Theatre 1985, Prin. Dancer 1989–; Gold Medal and Grand Prix, Fourth Int. Ballet Competition in Paris 1990, Prix de Lumière (Italy), Merited Artist of Russia 1995, Benois de la Dance Prize 1998. *Roles include:* Aurora and Lilac Fairy (Sleeping Beauty), Giselle and Myrtha (Giselle), Kitri (Don Quixote), Medora (Le Corsaire), Odette/Odile (Swan Lake), Nikiya and Gamzatti (La Bayadère), Mekhmene and Banu (Legend of Love), Raymonda (Raymonda), Sylphide (La Sylphide), Maria (Fountain of Bakhchisarai), Juliet (Romeo and Juliet), Zobeide (Sheherezade), Fire Bird (Firebird), Maria Taglioni (Pas de Quatre), (Dying Swan), Anna (Anna Karenina), Fairy (Cinderella), Carmen (Carmen), Duchess of Alba (Goya Divertissement), Terpsichore (Apollo), Second Movt (Symphony in C), Third Movt (In the Night), Manon (Manon), (Youth and Death), Soloist ("Paquita" Grand Pas), Soloist (Theme and Variations). *Address:* Mariinsky Theatre, St Petersburg, 190000, Teatralnaya pl. 1, Russia (office). *Telephone:* (812) 326-41-41 (office). *Website:* www.mariinsky.ru (office).

MAKHMALBAF, Mohsen; Iranian film director and novelist; b. 29 May 1957, Tehran; raised by his single mother; m. Marzieh Makhmalbaf; one s. two d.; 13 different jobs, including bellboy and plains worker aged 8–17; mem. of an underground Islamic militia group, shot and arrested while attempting to disarm a policeman aged 17; formed the Makhmalbaf Film House to teach film 1996; retrospective at Kerala Int. Film Festival, India; left Iran in 2005, then lived in Paris; mem. Jury, Venice Film Festival 2006; now lives in Kabul, Afghanistan with his family; Hon. Dr of Cinema (Univ. of Nanterre, France) 2010; Hon. DLitt (St Andrews Univ., UK) 2011; selected as the best filmmaker after the revolution by readers of cinema publs 1988, Federico Fellini Honour, UNESCO, Paris 2001, Sergei Parajanov Award, Yerevan Film Festival 2006, Freedom to Create Prize for his human right activity and promoting social justice through his art, Art Action (UK) 2009. *Films:* Towjeeh 1981, Hesar dar Hesar 1982, Marg Deegari 1982, Tobeh Nosuh (also writer) 1983, Do Cheshman Beesu (also actor) 1984, Este'aze 1984, Boycott 1985, Zangha 1985, The Cyclist (also production designer) 1987, The Pedlar (also writer) 1987, Arousi-ye Khouban (also writer) 1989, Rajayi School 1989, A Time for Love 1990, Farmandar 1990, The Nights of Zayandeh-Rood 1991, Nassereddin Shah, Actor-e Cinema 1992, The Unfinished Man 1992, The Actor (also writer) 1993, Images from the Ghajar Dynasty (short, also writer) 1993, Stone and Glass 1994, Salaam Cinema (documentary) 1995, Gabbeh 1996, A Moment of Innocence (also actor) (Among the Top Ten Films of the Decade, Int. Festival Dirs and Critics 1999) 1996, The Apple (also writer) 1998, The Silence (also writer and set designer) 1998, Madresei keh baad bord (short, also writer) 1998, Ghessé hayé kish (segment 'The Door') 1999, Blackboards (also producer) 2000, The Day I Became a Woman (also producer) 2000, Tales of an Island (segment 'Testing Democracy') (also actor and cinematographer) 2000, Kandahar (also producer) (Ecumenical Jury Prize, Cannes Int. Film Festival 2001, selected by TIME magazine as one of the top 100 films of all time 2005) 2001, The Afghan Alphabet (documentary) 2002, At Five in the Afternoon (novel) (also producer) 2003, Joy of Madness (documentary, also producer) 2003, Sex & Philosophy (also producer) 2005, Poet of the Wastes 2005, The Chair (short) 2005, Scream of the Ants (also producer) 2006, Two-Legged Horse (also writer and producer) 2008, The Man Who Came with the Snow (also screenplay) 2009, Mother's Paradise (also screenplay) 2011, The Gardener (documentary, also writer and producer) 2012, Ongoing Smile (documentary) 2013; Osama (exec. producer) 2003. *Publications:* Disgrace, Two Blind Eyes, The Sultan's Lake, The Crystal Graden, Death of Another, Divine Arrow, The Martyred Sheikh, The Dumb Man's Dream First Volume, The Dumb Man's Dream Second Volume, The Dumb Man's Dream Third Volume, Life is Color, Introduction on Islamic Art, Notes about Storywriting and Playwriting, The Buddha Was Not Demolished in Afghanistan, It Collapsed Out of Shame, The Bells, Mother, Legitimate Parliament, Rajayi's School, Birth of an Old Woman, The Cyclist, Marriage of the Blessed, Time of Love, Hail the Sun, Bread and the Vase, The Apple, Travel To Kandehar, To See and Not to See (some translated into 12 different languages). *Address:* Green Film House, 98 Mirdamad Boulevard, PO Box 19395/4866, Tehran, Iran (office); c/o MK2 Diffusion, 55 rue Traversière, 75012 Paris, France (office). *Telephone:* (21) 2225960 (Tehran) (office); 1-43-07-92-74 (Paris) (office). *Fax:* (21) 2270970 (Tehran) (office); 1-43-41-32-30 (Paris) (office). *Website:* www.makhmalbaf.com (office).

MAKHMUDOV, Lt-Gen. Eldar Akhmed oğlu; Azerbaijani government official and politician; *Minister of National Security;* b. 1956, Baku; m.; three c.; ed D. Bunyatzade Inst. of Economy, Baku State Univ.; career in mil. service; served

Organized Crime and Criminal Investigation Divs, Ministry of Interior 1980–2004, positions included Chief of Br, Drugs Suppression Unit 1993, Chief, Economic Crimes Dept, Chief of Branch, Drugs Suppression Dept 2004; Minister of Nat. Security 2004–; promoted to Maj.-Gen. 2004, to Lt-Gen. 2005. *Address:* Ministry of National Security, 1006 Baku, Parliament pr. 2, Azerbaijan (office). *Telephone:* (12) 493-76-22 (office). *E-mail:* cpr@mns.gov.az (office). *Website:* mns .gov.az (office).

MAKHULU, Most Rev. Walter Paul Khotso, CMG; British ecclesiastic; b. 2 July 1935, Johannesburg, SA; s. of Paul Makhulu; m. Rosemary Makhulu 1966; one s. one d.; ed Pimville Govt School, Johannesburg, Khaiso Secondary School, Coll. of the Resurrection and St Peter, SA, St Andrew's Coll., Birmingham; Area Sec. for Eastern Africa and African Refugees, Comm. on Inter-Church Aid Refugee and World Service, World Council of Churches 1975–79; Bishop of Botswana 1979–2000; Archbishop of Cen. Africa 1980–2000, Archbishop Emer. 2000–; Pres. All Africa Conf. of Churches 1981–86; Pres. World Council of Churches 1983–91; Hon. Curate Holy Trinity, Geneva; Presidential Order of Honour (Botswana) 2002, Officier, Ordre des Palmes académiques 1981; Hon. DD (Kent) 1988, (Gen. Theological Seminary, New York) 1990. *Leisure interests:* music, int. affairs. *Address:* Cheyne House, 10 Crondace Road, Fulham, London, SW6 4BB, England. *Telephone:* (20) 7371-9419 (office). *E-mail:* bishmak@makhulu.fsnet.co.uk (office).

MAKI, Fumihiko, MArch; Japanese architect; *Principal Partner, Maki and Associates;* b. 6 Sept. 1928, Tokyo; m.; two c.; ed Univ. of Tokyo, Cranbrook Acad. of Art, Harvard Univ. Grad. School of Design, USA; Assoc. Prof., Washington Univ. 1956–62, Harvard Univ. 1962–66; Lecturer, Dept of Urban Eng, Univ. of Tokyo 1964–79, Prof. of Architecture 1979–89; Prin. Pnr, Maki and Assocs 1964–; Hon. FAIA 1980, FRIBA; Hon. Fellow, German Inst. of Architects, French Acad. of Architecture, Czech Inst. of Architects, Mexican Inst. of Architects, Bund Deutscher Architekten, American Acad. of Arts & Sciences, Academia Scientiarum et Artium Europaea, Royal Australian Inst. of Architects, Royal Incorporation of Architects in Scotland, Taiwan Inst. of Architects; Officier, Ordre des Arts et Lettres 1998; Hon. Dr of Art and Architecture (Washington, USA); Wolf Foundation Prize in Arts 1988, Thomas Jefferson Medal for Architecture 1990, Int. Union of Architects (UIA) Gold Medal 1993, Pritzker Architecture Prize 1993, Prince of Wales Prize in Urban Design 1993, Arnold Brunner Memorial Prize in Architecture 1994, Praemium Imperiale 1999, AIA Gold Medal 2011. *Major works include:* Toyoda Memorial Hall, Nagoya Univ. 1960, Nat. Aquarium, Okinawa 1975, Hillside Terrace Housing Complex 1978–98, Iwasaki Art Museum 1979, Keio Univ. Library, Mita Campus 1981, Spiral 1985 (Reynolds Memorial Award 1987), Nat. Museum of Modern Art, Kyoto 1985, Tepia 1989, Nippon Convention Centre (Makuhari Messe) Stage 1 1989, Stage 2 1998, Tokyo Metropolitan Gymnasium 1990, Keio Univ. Fujisawa Campus 1992, YKK Research and Devt Centre 1993, Center for Arts Yerba Buena Gardens 1993, Isar Buropark 1995, Kaze-No-Oka Crematorium 1996, TV Asahi HQ 2003, Toki Messe 2003, Nat. Inst. for Japanese Language Tachikawa, Tokyo 2004, Sam Fox School of Design and Visual Arts, Washington Univ. 2006, Shimane Museum of Ancient Izumo 2007, Mihara Performing Arts Center 2007, Repub. Polytechnic Singapore 2007, Toyoda Memorial Hall Renovation, Nagoya, Aichi 2007, Univ. of Pennsylvania Annenberg Public Policy Center 2008, Novartis Campus, Basel, Switzerland 2009, MIT Media Lab., Massachusetts, USA 2009, WTC New York 2013. *Publications include:* Investigations in Collective Form 1964, Movement Systems in the City 1965, Metabolism 1960, Structure in Art and Science (contrib.) 1965, Miegakuresuru Toshi: A Morphological Analysis of the City of Edo-Tokyo 1979, Kioku no Keisho: A Collection of Essays 1992, Selected Passages on the City and Architecture 2000, Nurturing Dreams: Collected Essays on Architecture and the City 2008. *Address:* 13-4, Hachiyama-cho, Shibuya-ku, Tokyo 150-0035 (office); 16-22, 5-chome Higashi-Gotanda, Shinagawa-ku, Tokyo 141-0022, Japan (home). *Telephone:* (3) 3780-3880 (office). *Fax:* (3) 3780-3881 (office). *E-mail:* fmaki@maki-and-associates .co.jp (office). *Website:* www.maki-and-associates.co.jp (office).

MAKIHARA, Minoru, BA; Japanese business executive; *Senior Corporate Advisor, Mitsubishi Corporation;* b. 12 Jan. 1930, Hampstead, London, England; m. Kikuko Makihara; ed in UK, Japan, Harvard Univ.; joined Mitsubishi Corpn Marine Products Dept 1956–59, London Br. 1959–70, Rep. Mitsubishi Int. Seattle and Washington 1970–80, Gen. Man. Marine Products Dept, Tokyo 1980–87, Pres. Mitsubishi International, New York 1987–90, Sr Man. Dir Mitsubishi Corpn, also Chair. Mitsubishi International 1990–92, apptd Pres. Mitsubishi Corpn 1992, Chair. 1998–2004, now Sr Corp. Advisor; mem. Chair.'s Council, DaimlerChrysler AG (Daimler AG from 2007) 2001–07; mem. Bd of Dirs IBM Corpn 1997–2003, 2004–08, Ayala Corpn 1999–, Shinsei Bank Ltd 2000–, Tokio Marine Holdings Inc. 2002–; mem. Int. Advisory Council, Coca-Cola Co., J.P. Morgan Chase & Co., Inc.; Hon. KBE 2014. *Address:* Mitsubishi Corporation, 6-3, Marunouchi 2-chome, Chiyoda-ku, Tokyo, 100-8086, Japan (office).

MAKINE, Andreï, French/Russian writer; b. 10 Sept. 1957, Siberia; s. of Maria Stepanovna Dolina; worked as teacher of literature in Novgorod; emigrated from USSR to France 1987, writes in French; Priz de la Fondation Prince Pierre de Monaco 2005. *Play:* Le Monde selon Gabriel 2007. *Publications include:* fiction: La Fille d'un Héros (trans. as A Hero's Daughter) 1990, Confession d'un Porte-Drapeau Déchu (trans. as Confessions of a Fallen Standard-Bearer) 1992, Au Temps du Fleuve Amour (trans. as Once Upon the River Love) 1994, Le Testament Français (trans. as Dreams of My Russian Summers) (Prix Goncourt, Prix Médicis Étranger, Prix Goncourt des Lycéens, Eeva Joenpelto Prize, Finland) 1995, Le Crime d'Olga Arbelina (trans. as The Crime of Olga Arbelina) 1998, Requiem pour l'Est (trans. as Requiem for a Lost Empire) 2001, La Musique d'un Vie (trans. as A Life's Music) (Prix RTL-Lire) 2001, La Terre et le ciel de Jacques Dorme (trans. as The Earth and Sky of Jacques Dorme) 2003, La Femme qui Attendait (trans. as The Woman Who Waited) (Prix Lanterna Magica 2005) 2004, L'Amour Humain (trans. as Human Love) 2006, La Vie d'un Homme Inconnu (trans. as The Life of an Unknown Man) 2009, Le Livre des brèves amours éternelles 2011, Une Femme Aimée 2012, Brief Loves that Live Forever 2013; non-fiction: St Pétersbourg (with Ferrante Ferranti) 2002, Cette France qu'on oublie d'aimer 2006. *Address:* c/o Editions du Seuil, 25 boulevard Romain Rolland, 75993 Paris, France. *Website:* www.editionsduseuil.fr; andreimakine.com.

MÄKINEN, Tommi; Finnish entrepreneur and fmr rally driver; b. 26 June 1964, Puuppola, Jyväskylä; s. of Jukka Mäkinen; partner Eliisa Järvelä; two s.; first

competed on farm tractors, won jr Finnish nat. ploughing title 1982, 1985, sr title 1992; began rally car racing career in Finnish Championships 1985; Group N Finnish Champion 1988; won Arctic Rally 1989; with Nissan Motorsports Europe Team 1992; with Mitsubishi Ralliart Europe Team 1995–2001 (World Rally Champion 1996, 1997, 1998, 1999), set record for most world championship rally race wins (24 victories 1994–2002); record four consecutive wins at the Monte Carlo Rally –2002; with Subaru World Rally Team 2002–03; five time Rally Finland winner; est. Tommi Mäkinen Racing Oy Ltd 2004. *Leisure interests:* skiing, cycling, trial biking, hunting. *Address:* Tommi Mäkinen Racing Oy Ltd, Tervamaantie 9, 41120 Puuppola, Finland. *Telephone:* (20) 722-9750. *Fax:* (20) 722-9751. *E-mail:* info@tommimakinenracing.fi. *Website:* www.tommimakinen .net.

MAKK, Károly; Hungarian film director; *President, Széchenyi Academy of Literature and Arts;* b. 22 Dec. 1925; s. of Kálmán Makk and Emma Szmolka; m. Hanna Reichel Dömötör; one s. one d.; ed Budapest Univ. of Sciences, Univ. of Dramatic and Cinematic Arts; asst lecturer 1953, lecturer 1959–; mem. Univ. Council; worked as assistant Dir MAFILM Studio 1946–53, Dir 1954–; Guest Lecturer Istituto Centro Sperimentale per Film, Rome 1976 and German Film Acad., Munich 1973–74; mem. Széchenyi Acad. of Literature and Arts 1992–, Pres. 2011–; Golden Cross of Hungary 2006; Pres. 2011– Merited Artist and Eminent Artist titles, Balázs Béla Prize 1959, Kossuth Prize 1973, Outstanding Artist Prize 1982, Lifetime Achievement Award, Figueira da Foz, Portugal 1986, Life Achievement Award, Hungarian Film Festival 1994, Life Achievement Award, Karlovy Vary 2000, Master of Motion Picture, Hungary 2004. *Films directed include:* Liliomfi (Cannes selection) 1954, Ház a sziklák alatt (House under the Rocks) 1957 (San Francisco Grand Prix 1959), 39-es dandár (The Brigade No. 39) 1959, Megszállottak (The Fanatics) 1962, Elveszett paradicsom (The Lost Paradise) 1963, Az utolsó előtti ember (The Last but One) 1963, Isten és ember előtti (Before God and Man) 1968, Szerelem (Love) 1970 (1971 Int. Journalist Fed. Award and Jury's Special Award of Cannes), Macskajáték (Catsplay, nominated for Acad. Award) 1974, Egy erkölcsös éjszaka (A very moral night) 1977, Két történet a félmúltból (Two stories from the Recent Past), A téglafal mögött (Behind the Brick Wall), Philemon and Baucis, 1981, Egymásra nézve (Another Way) 1981 (1982 Int. Critiques Award and Best Female Performance of Cannes), Játszani kell (Playing for Keeps) 1984, Az utolsó kézirat (The Last Manuscript) 1987, Magyar rekviem (Hungarian Requiem) 1990, Magyar Pizza 1995, Játékos (The Gambler) 1997 (1998 Best Film, Pescara), Egy Hèt Pesten Es Budàn (A Long Weekend in Pest and Buda) 2003, Igy Ahogy Vagytok (As You Are) 2009. *Plays directed:* Enigma Variations 1998, Rebecaa 1999, WIT 2001, Egy Szerelem... 2009. *Leisure interests:* reading, writing, tennis, riding. *Address:* 1022 Budapest, Hankóczy Jenő utca 15, Hungary. *Telephone:* (1) 326-9314. *Fax:* (1) 326-9314 (home). *E-mail:* info@ makkkaroly.hu (office). *Website:* www.makkkaroly.hu (office).

MAKKAWI, Khalil, PhD; Lebanese diplomatist; *President of the Circle of Lebanese Ambassadors;* b. 15 Jan. 1930, Beirut; s. of Abdel Basset Makkawi and Rosa Makkawi; m. Zahira Sibaei 1958; one s. one d.; ed American Univ. of Beirut, Cairo Univ., Egypt, Columbia Univ., New York, USA; joined Foreign Ministry 1957, served in UN Section 1957–59, Deputy Perm. Rep. to UN, New York 1961–64, First Sec., Embassy in Washington, DC 1964–67, Chief of Int. Relations Dept, Foreign Ministry, Beirut 1967–70, Counsellor, Embassy in London 1970–71, Minister Plenipotentiary, London 1971–73, Amb. to GDR 1973–78, to UK and Repub. of Ireland 1978–83; Dir Political Dept, Foreign Ministry, Beirut, Chair. Preparatory Cttee of Lebanese Nat. Dialogue, mem. Lebanese Security Arrangement Cttee for South of Lebanon 1983–85, Amb. to Italy and Perm. Rep. to FAO 1985–90, Perm. Rep. to UN, New York 1990–94; Vice-Chair. Exec. Bd UNICEF 1993–95, Pres. 1995; Co-Chair. Int. Support Group for mine clearance in Lebanon (representing Ministry of Nat. Defence) 2002–05; fmr Pres. Lebanese-Palestinian Dialogue Cttee, Presidency of the Council of Ministers; Pres. Worldwide Alumni Asscn of American Univ. of Beirut 2005–09, President of the Circle of Lebanese Ambassadors; Chevalier, Nat. Order of the Cedar (Lebanon), Great Cross of Merit (Italy); Pres.'s Medal for Outstanding Voluntary Service, American Univ. of Beirut 2011. *Leisure interests:* music, swimming, reading, walking. *Address:* Bldg Al-Nada, 9th Floor, John Kennedy Street, Ain Mreisseh, Beirut, Lebanon. *Telephone:* (1) 362662; 3-774656 (mobile). *Fax:* (1) 372550. *E-mail:* khalil30@inco.com.lb.

MAKKI, Mohammed Hassan, DEcon; Yemeni politician and diplomatist; b. 22 Dec. 1933; ed Univs of Bologna and Rome, Italy; adviser, Ministry of the Economy 1960–62, Deputy Minister 1962, Minister 1963–64; Minister of Foreign Affairs April–Sept. 1966, 1967–68; Amb. to Italy 1968–70, 1977–79, to FRG 1970–72, Amb. and Perm. Rep. to UN, New York 1974–76, in Vienna 2000, Amb. to USA (also accred to Canada) 1975–76; Deputy Prime Minister 1972–74; Prime Minister of Yemen Arab Repub. March–June 1974; Deputy Prime Minister for Econ. Affairs June–Oct. 1974, 1980–84; Deputy Prime Minister of Yemen Arab Repub. 1985–90; First Deputy Prime Minister of Yemen 1990–93.

MAKLAKOVS, Maj.-Gen. Juris; Latvian military officer; *Commander, National Armed Forces;* b. 27 Oct. 1964, Ņukšu; m.; one s.; ed Mil. Aviation Eng School, US Army War Coll.; radio technician, Mil. Aviation Eng School 1985–87, Head of Radio Tech. Equipment Service Group 1987–88; Chief Engineer, Computer Centre, Nat. Defence Acad. 1993, Lecturer, Dept of Mil. Weapons and their Usage 1993–94, Dept of Eng 1994–95, Head of Dept of Eng 1995–97, Deputy Commdt in Academics 1997–2001, Commdt Nat. Defence Acad. 2001–04; Air Force Commdr 2004–06; Commdr Nat. Armed Forces 2006–; Button Award 1997, Honour Sign for contribs to devt of Latvian Nat. Armed Forces 2000, Honour Sign of Recognition Award 2001, Memorial Medal 2004. *Address:* Ministry of Defence, K. Valdemāra iela 10–12, Riga 1473, Latvia (office). *Telephone:* 6733-5300 (office). *Fax:* 6733-1021 (office). *E-mail:* kanceleja@mod.gov.lv (office). *Website:* www.mod.gov.lv (office).

MAKOGON, Yuri Fedorovich, PhD, DSc; Ukrainian physicist and engineer; *Visiting Professor/Research Associate, Texas A&M University;* b. 15 May 1930, Kherson; s. of Feodor Ivanovich Makogon and Efrosinia Dmitrievna Shevchenko; m. Inna Aleksandrovna Makogon 1961; one s. one d.; ed Krasnodar Tech. School, Gubkin Petroleum Inst., Moscow; worked at Shebelinskoe Gas-condensate Field, Ukraine 1956–58; Asst then Asst Prof., Gubkin Oil and Gas, Moscow Inst. 1961–74; Prof., Indian School of Mines, Dhanbad 1965–67, Freiberg Mining Acad., FRG 1967–68; Head, Gas-hydrate Lab., Cen. Gas Research Inst. of the USSR 1974–87; Dir Gas-hydrate Lab., Oil and Gas Research Inst., Russian Acad. of

Sciences 1990–95, Hydrocarbon and Environment Inst., Russian Acad. of Natural Sciences 1987–93; Co-founder Russian Acad. of Natural Sciences 1990, first Chair. Oil-Gas Consulate, Chair. Cttee on Data for Science and Tech. and Regional Sec. US Section; Co-founder and first Chair. Russian Section Int. Soc. of Petroleum Engineers (SPE) 1991–93; invited to join Texas A&M Univ., USA 1992, currently Visiting Prof./Research Assoc. and Head of Gas-hydrate Lab., Petroleum Eng Dept; recorded as scientific discoverer of gas hydrates in nature, State Register of USSR 1969; mem. Acad. of Sciences of Ukraine 2010; Hon. Diploma (Mendeleev Union Soc. of Russia) 1982; Dr hc (Nikolayev Inst. of Inorganic Chem., Russian Acad. of Sciences) 2005; Winner's Diploma, Ukraine Republican Inventors' Competition 1958, First Prize, Young Petroleum Scientist Conf. of Russia 1965, First Prize, Chess Tournament of Indian School of Mines 1967, Diploma of the Scientific Discovery Natural Gas Hydrates 1969, Golden Jubilee Medal of Russia 1970, Honour Diploma of Mendeleev Union Soc. Russia 1982, Gubkin State Prize 1989, Golden L. Kapitca Medal for Scientific Discovery 1997, V. Vernadsky Medal of Honour 2000, Albert Einstein Medal of Honour, Russian Acad. of Natural Sciences (US Section) 2002, Distinguished Lecturer Merit of SPE 2002–03, Golden Peter the Great Medal 2004, Hon. Merit in Science and Econs, Russian Acad. of Natural Sciences 2005, Certificate of Lifetime Achievement Awards of Honor, Sixth Int. Gas Hydrate Conf. 2008. *Publications:* eight monographs, 270 papers and 29 patents on gas hydrates. *Leisure interests:* painting, travelling, photography. *Address:* Harold Vance Department of Petroleum Engineering, 3116 TAMU - 721 Richardson Building, Texas A&M University, College Station, TX 77843-3116 (office); 1720 Purple Martin Cove, College Station, TX 77845, USA (home). *Telephone:* (979) 845-4066 (office); (979) 690-8871 (home). *E-mail:* makogon@tamu.edu (office). *Website:* www.pe.tamu.edu (office).

MAKONE, Theresa, BSc; Zimbabwean chemist, business executive and politician; b. 6 Oct. 1952, Mbare; d. of Titus Chigariro; m. Ian Makone; two d. (one deceased); ed Univ. of Rhodesia, Univ. of Nottingham, UK; in exile in UK 1973–78; Devt Chemist, Chibuku Breweries 1978–81; Quality Assurance Dir Sterling Winthrop Pharmaceuticals 1981; fmr Chief Technologist, Cairns Foods, later Research and Devt Man.; est. own beauty clinic and runs several businesses in Harare; mem. Movt for Democratic Change (MDC) 2000–, MDC Br. Treas. in Zviyambe West 2000, Prov. Chair. 2005–07, Chair. MDC Nat. Women's Ass. 2007–; MP for Harare North 2009–; Minister of Public Works 2009–10, Co-Minister of Home Affairs 2010–13. *Address:* c/o Ministry of Home Affairs, Private Bag 7703, Causeway, Harare, Zimbabwe (office).

MAKONI, Simba Herbert Stanley, BSc, PhD; Zimbabwean politician; b. 22 March 1950, Makoni; s. of Basil Kamunda and Clara Kamunda (née Matimba); m. Chipo Makoni (née Ususu) 1975; three s.; ed Univ. of Leeds and Leicester Polytechnic, UK; joined Zimbabwe African Nat. Union-Patriotic Front (ZANU-PF); ZANU Chief Rep. to W Europe 1977–80; mem. Nat. Ass. of Zimbabwe 1980–84; Deputy Minister of Agric. 1980; Minister of Industry and Energy Devt 1981–83, of Youth, Sport and Culture 1984, of Finance and Econ. Devt 2000–02; Exec. Sec., Southern African Devt Community 1984–93; Chief Exec. and Man. Dir Zimbabwe Newspapers Ltd, Zimpapers 1994–; Man. Pnr Makonsult Ltd; mem. UN Panel of Advisers on African Devt 1992–94, Inst. of Dirs, Zimbabwe 1994–, Zimbabwe Inst. of Man. 1994–, Council of Reps., South Centre 1994–, Nat. Blood Transfusion Service 1995–; mem. Nat. Council, Conf. of Zimbabwe Industries (CZI) 1996–, Chair. Econ. Affairs Cttee 1996–; mem. Nat. Econ. Consultative Forum 1998; Patron Nat. Council of Disabled Persons of Zimbabwe 1982–, Zimbabwe Inst. of Motor Industry 1995–; resgnd from ZANU-PF party 2008, ind. cand. for Pres. of Zimbabwe 2008. *Leisure interests:* gardening, reading, squash, health and fitness. *Address:* c/o Ministry of Finance and Economic Development, 2nd Floor, Munhumutapa Building, Samora Machel Avenue, Private Bag 7705, Causeway, Harare, Zimbabwe (office).

MAKOVETSKY, Sergey Vasilievich; Russian actor; b. 13 June 1958, Kiev, Ukrainian SSR, USSR; ed Moscow Shchukin Theatre School; with Moscow Vakhtangov Theatre 1980–; with Roman Viktyuk Theatre 1990–; Golden Aries Prize for Actor of the Year 1993, Nika Acad. of Cinema Award 1993. *Plays include:* The Master's Lessons, Madame Butterfly, Loika's Flat, Zoya's Apartment (Moscow Theatre Spring Prize 1989). *Films include:* Ekipazh mashiny boevoy (Battle Vehicle Crew) 1983, Polosa prepyatstviy (aka Stripe of Obstacles) 1984, Zaveshchaniye (Testament) 1986, Topinambury (American Artichokes) 1988, Posvyashchyonnyy (Initiated) 1989, Sukiny deti (Sons of Bitches) 1990, Chernov/Chernov 1990, Rebyonok k noyabryu (A Child by November) 1992, Patrioticheskaya komediya (Patriotic Comedy) 1992, Nash amerikanskiy Borya (Our American Borya) 1992, Prorva (Moscow Parade) 1992, Trotsky 1993, Malenkie chelovechki Bolshevistskogo pereulka, ili Khochu piva (Little People of the Bolshevik Lane, or I Want Beer) 1993, Makarov 1993, Khorovod (Round Dance) 1994, Pyesa dlya passazhira (A Play for a Passenger) 1995, Pribytiye poyezda (The Arrival of a Train) 1995, Letnie lyudi (Country Visitors) 1995, Chyornaya vual (The Black Veil) 1995, Le violon de Rothschild (Rothschild's Violin) 1996, Tri istorii (Three Stories) 1997, Sochineniye ko dnyu pobedy (Composition for Victory Day) 1998, Retro vtroyem 1998, Pro urodov i lyudey (Of Freaks and Men) 1998, Russkiy bunt (The Captain's Daughter) 2000, Brat 1 (The Brother 1) 2000, Brat 2 (The Brother 2) 2000, Mekhanicheskaya syuita 2001, Klyuch ot spalni 2003, Tretiy variant 2003, 72 metra (72 Meters) 2004, Alesha Popovich i Tugarin Zmey (voice) 2004, Zhmurki 2005, Blind Man's Bluff 2005, It Doesn't Hurt Me 2006, Karnavalnaya noch 2, ili 50 let spystya 2007, Nevalyashka 2007, Iskushenie 2007, 12 2007, The Russian Game 2007, Duska 2007, Ilya and the Robber (voice) 2007, Live and Remember 2008, The Priest 2009, The Miracle 2009, Utomlyonnye solntsem 2: Predstoyanie 2010, How Not to Rescue a Princess (voice) 2010, Samyy luchshiy film 3-DE 2011, Utomlennye solntsem 2 2011, The Girl and Death 2012, Eternal Homecoming 2012, Three Heroes on Distant Shores (voice) 2012. *Television includes:* Zhizn Klima Samgina (The Life of Klim Samgin) (series) 1986, Teatr imeni menya (voice) 1994, Operatsiya 'S novym godom' (Operation Happy New Year) 1996, Neudacha Poirot 2002, Gibel imperii (mini-series) 2005, S dnyom rozhdeniya, koroleva! (film) 2006, Nevernost (film) 2006, Liquidation (series) 2007, Isaev (series) 2009, Na solnechnoy storone ulitsy (film) 2011, Petr Pervyy. Zaveshchanie (mini-series) 2011, Delo Gastronoma No. 1 (mini-series) 2011, Utomlennye solntsem 2 (mini-series) 2011, Zhizn i sudba (series) 2012. *Address:* Vakhtangov Theatre, Arbat str. 26, 121007 Moscow, Russia. *Telephone:* (495) 241-01-28.

MAKRAM-EBEID, Mona, PhD; Egyptian professor of political science, international organization official and fmr politician; *Chairman, Association for the Advancement of Education;* b. Cairo; grand-d. of Makram Ebeid Pasha; m.; one s.; ed Univ. of Cairo and American Univ. in Cairo, Harvard Univ., USA; Prof. of Political Science and Political Sociology, American Univ. in Cairo 1983–; currently Distinguished Lecturer, Dept of Political Science; mem. People's Ass. (Parl.) 1990–95, mem. Foreign Affairs and Educ. Cttees; Pres. Parliamentarians for Global Action 1990–95; Founder-mem. Arab Org. for Human Rights; Adviser to World Bank for the Middle East and North Africa Region 1992–96; Founder and Chair. Asscn for the Advancement of Educ., Cairo 1995–; apptd Expert to UN Cttee for Policy Devt 2000–03; mem. Bd of Dirs British Univ. in Egypt, Jordan German Univ., Amman, Center for Political and Futuristic Studies, Cairo, Citadel Investment, Talal Abu Ghazalah Org.; Consultant to Search for Common Ground, Initiative for Peace and Co-operation in the Middle East, Washington, DC; Exec. mem. Club of Rome, Ibn Khaldum Centre for Developmental Studies, Nat. Centre for Middle Eastern Studies; mem. Int. Consultative Group for the Middle East Center for Strategic and Int. Studies, Washington, DC 1991, UNICEF Women for Devt Cttee, Women for Foreign Policy Group, Washington, DC, The Arab Thought Forum, Amman; several articles on politics in journals and magazines published in English, Arabic and French; Fulbright Scholar 1981, 1983; Chevalier de la Légion d'Honneur 1994, Commdr de la Pléiade, AIPLF (Int. Asscn for French-speaking Parliamentarians) 1995; Woman of the Year, Civil Soc. Review 1994. *Leisure interests:* tennis, theatre, ballet, swimming. *Address:* Department of Political Science, The American University in Cairo, PO Box 74, New Cairo 11835; Apt 16, 4th Floor, 14 Gue, Zamalek, Cairo, Egypt (home). *Telephone:* (2) 3407603. *Fax:* (2) 2608288. *Website:* www.aucegypt.edu/ACADEMICS/DEPT/POLS.

MAKSYMIUK, Jerzy; Polish conductor, composer and pianist; *Conductor Laureate, BBC Scottish Symphony Orchestra;* b. 9 April 1936, Grodno, Byelorussia (now Belarus); s. of Roman Maksymiuk and Bronisława Maksymiuk; m. Irena Kirjacka; ed Acad. of Music, Warsaw; Conductor, Great Theatre, Warsaw 1970–72; f. Polish Chamber Orchestra 1972–84; Prin. Conductor Polish Nat. Radio Symphony Orchestra, Katowice 1975–77; Prin. Conductor BBC Scottish Symphony Orchestra, Glasgow 1984–93, tours of Greece, Canada and Germany, Conductor Laureate 1993–; Guest Conductor Calgary Symphony, Nat. Arts Centre (Ottawa), BBC Welsh and Philharmonic Orchestras, English Chamber Orchestra, Scottish Chamber Orchestra, City of Birmingham Symphony, London Symphony, London Philharmonic, Philharmonia, Orchestre National de France, Rotterdam Philharmonic, Luxembourg Philharmonic, Hong Kong Philharmonic, Royal Liverpool Philharmonic, Bournemouth Sinfonietta, Ulster Orchestra, Tokyo Metropolitan Symphony, Israeli Chamber Orchestra, Los Angeles Chamber Orchestra, Staatskapelle, Sinfonia Varsovia and other orchestras; has toured Europe, USA, Canada, Japan, Israel and Australia with Polish Chamber Orchestra; collaborated with ENO (Mozart's Don Giovanni) 1990, (Johann Strauss' Die Fledermaus) 1993; regularly performs works of Penderecki, Lutoslawski, Gorecki, Szymanowski, as well as British composers including Peter Maxwell Davies and James MacMillan; Hon. DLitt (Strathclyde) 1990; First Prize, Paderewski Piano Competition 1964, Gold Medal, Elgar Society 1999. *Recordings include:* Paderewski: Symphony 'Polonia', The Romantic Piano Concerto, (Vols 1–4), Vivaldi Violin Concertos, Grieg: Pier Gynt Suites Nos. 1 & 2. *Address:* Gdańska 2 m. 14, 01-633 Warsaw, Poland (home). *Telephone:* (22) 8323021 (home).

MAKTOUM, Sheikh Ahmed bin Saeed al-, BA, FRAeS; United Arab Emirates government official and business executive; *Chairman and CEO, Emirates Airline and Group;* b. 22 Dec. 1958, Abu Dhabi; s. of fmr Ruler of Dubai Sheikh Saeed bin Maktoum al-Maktoum; brother of fmr Ruler of Dubai Sheikh Rashid bin Saeed al-Maktoum and uncle of current Ruler of Dubai Sheikh Muhammad bin Rashid al-Maktoum; ed Univ. of Denver, Colo, USA; Pres. Dubai Civil Aviation Authority 1985–; Chair. Emirates Airline and Group 1985–, later also CEO; also holds several other portfolios with Govt of Dubai, including Second Vice-Chair. Dubai Exec. Council; Chair. Dubai Airports, flydubai, Dubai Supreme Fiscal Cttee, Dept of Oil Affairs, Supreme Council for Energy, Dubai World DN, Econ. Devt Cttee, Dubai Power & Energy Cttee, Dubai Airport Free Zone Authority, Emirates Nat. Bank of Dubai, Noor Investment Group, Noor Takaful, Alliance Insurance Co., The British Univ. in Dubai, Dubai Air Wing, Dubai Aerospace Enterprises, Supreme Cttee– Dubai Events & Promotions Establishment (consisting of Dubai Shopping Festival and Dubai Summer Surprises), Exec. Authority for Expo 2020, Wasl Hospitality; Vice-Chair. Dubai World Trade Centre; mem. Bd of Dirs Investment Corpn of Dubai; mem. Bd Gen. Civil Aviation Authority of UAE, Dubai Council for Econ. Affairs; Patron, Emirates Foundation, Dubai Duty Free Foundation, Rotary Club of Dubai, Dubai Terry Fox Run, Rashid Therapy Centre; Int. Life Vice-Pres. Chelsea Football Club; Commdr, Légion d'honneur, Verfassungsportugaleser (Germany) for outstanding services to the City of Hamburg 2008; Ernst & Young Entrepreneur of the Year Award for the UAE 2011, Emirates Airline Festival of Literature Personality of the Year Award 2012, ranked by Arabian Business amongst the Power 500: The World's Most Influential Arabs (second) 2012–13. *Address:* Emirates, PO Box 686, Dubai, United Arab Emirates (office). *E-mail:* media.relations@emirates.com (office). *Website:* www.theemiratesgroup.com (office); www.emirates.com (office).

MAKTOUM, Hamdan bin Muhammad al-; United Arab Emirates politician; *Crown Prince of Dubai;* b. 14 Nov. 1982; s. of Sheikh Muhammad bin Rashid al-Maktoum and Sheikha Hind bint Maktoum bin Juma al-Maktoum; ed Rashid Private School, Sandhurst Mil. Acad., UK, London School of Econs, UK, Dubai School of Govt; Chair. Dubai Exec. Council 2006–; named Crown Prince of Dubai 2008–; Head of Sheikh Muhammad bin Rashid Establishment for Young Business Leaders; Pres. Dubai Sports Council. *Achievement:* won gold medal in equestrian event, Asian Games, Doha 2006. *Leisure interests:* horse riding, poetry. *Address:* Dubai Executive Council, Emirates Towers Building, 37th Floor, Sheikh Zayed Road, POB 73311, Dubai, United Arab Emirates (office). *Telephone:* (4) 330-2111 (office). *Fax:* (4) 330-3636 (office). *Website:* www.fazza3.com.

MAKTOUM, Sheikh Hamdan bin Rashid al-; United Arab Emirates politician; *Joint Deputy Ruler of Dubai and Minister of Finance and Industry;* b. 1945; s. of Rashid bin Said al-Maktoum; brother of the late Sheikh Maktoum Bin Rashid Al Maktoum; Deputy Prime Minister UAE 1971–73, Minister of Finance and Industry 1971–, also Jt Deputy Ruler of Dubai 1995–; Pres. Dubai Municipal

Council. *Address:* Ministry of Finance and Industry, PO Box 433, Abu Dhabi, United Arab Emirates. *Telephone:* (2) 6726000 (office). *Fax:* (2) 66663088 (office). *E-mail:* mofi@uae.gov.ae (office).

MAKTOUM, Maktoum bin Muhammad al-, BSc; United Arab Emirates politician; *Joint Deputy Ruler of Dubai;* b. 24 Nov. 1983; s. of Sheikh Muhammad bin Rashid al-Maktoum; ed Rashid School, American Univ. of Dubai; Chair. Dubai Tech. and Media Free Zone Authority (TECOM Investments); Chair. Dubai Media Inc.; Jt Deputy Ruler of Dubai 2008–; Vice-Pres. Al-Ahli Club (football club). *Leisure interest:* horse riding. *Address:* Office of the Chairman, Dubai Media Inc., POB 835, Dubai, United Arab Emirates (office). *Telephone:* (4) 336-9999 (office). *E-mail:* info@dmi.ae (office). *Website:* www.dmi.gov.ae (office).

MAKTOUM, Sheikh Muhammad bin Rashid al-; United Arab Emirates politician and race horse owner; *Ruler of Dubai; Vice-President, Prime Minister and Minister of Defence of UAE;* b. 1948; s. of the late Rashid bin Said al-Maktoum; m. 1st Sheikha Hind bint Maktoum bin Juma al-Maktoum 1979; m. 2nd Princess Haya bint al-Hussein 2004; ed Mons Officer Cadet Training Coll., Sandhurst Coll., Univ. of Cambridge, UK; trained in British army and RAF; Dir of Police and Public Security 1971; Minister of Defence 1972; Crown Prince of Dubai 1990–2006, succeeded his brother, Sheikh Maktoum bin Rashid al-Maktoum, as 6th Sheikh 2006, Vice-Pres. of Dubai 2006–, Prime Minister 2006–, currently also Minister of Defence; with brothers the late Sheikh Maktoum al-Maktoum, Sheikh Hamdan al-Maktoum and Sheikh Ahmed al-Maktoum, has had racing interests in UK 1976–; first winner, Hatta, Goodwood 1977; with brothers owns studs, stables, country houses and sporting estates in Newmarket and elsewhere in UK; worldwide racing interests based at Dalham Hall Stud, Newmarket; horses trained in England, Ireland and France; founder and Dir Godolphin Racing, Dubai 1994; f. Racing Post (daily) 1986; Owner, Balanchine, winner of Irish Derby 1994; winner, numerous classic races; leading owner 1985–89, 1991–93. *Publication:* My Vision: Challenges in the Race for Excellence 2006. *Address:* Ruler's Palace, Dubai (office); Office of the Prime Minister, POB 12848, Dubai, United Arab Emirates (office); c/o Warren Towers, Newmarket, Suffolk, England (office). *Telephone:* (4) 3534550 (office). *Fax:* (4) 3530111 (office). *Website:* www.sheikhmohammed.co.ae.

MAKUBUYA, (Edward) Khiddu, JSD; Ugandan lawyer, academic and politician; *Minister in charge of General Duties, Office of the Prime Minister;* b. 30 July 1949, Bulemezi; m.; ed Makerere Univ., Yale Univ. Law School, USA; advocate, Uganda High Court 1985; Lecturer, Faculty of Law, Makerere Univ. 1979–82, Sr Lecturer 1982–84, Assoc. Prof. 1985–95; mem. Uganda Constitutional Comm., participated in drawing up 1995 draft of Constitution of Repub. of Uganda; mem. Comm. of Inquiry into Violations of Human Rights; Pnr, Kasolo & Khiddu Advocates; MP for Katikamu South, Luwero Dist 1996–; State Minister for Foreign Affairs (Int. Cooperation) 1998–99, Minister of Educ. and Sports 1999–2005, of Justice and Constitutional Affairs and Attorney-Gen. 2005–11, Minister in charge of General Duties, Office of the Prime Minister 2011–; Ed.-in-Chief, Uganda Law Soc. Review 1984–87; Fellow, Inst. for the Study of Politics, New York, USA. *Address:* PO Box 2395, Kampala, Uganda (office). *Telephone:* (41) 285613 (office). *E-mail:* mekhiddu@parliament.go.ug (office).

MAKÚCH, Jozef; Slovak economist, academic and central banker; *Governor, National Bank of Slovakia;* b. 26 Aug. 1953, Podhájska; m.; three c.; ed Faculty of Nat. Economy, Univ. of Econs, Bratislava; Loan Inspector, Bratislava Br., Czechoslovak State Bank 1976–78; Asst Prof., Dept of Finance, Faculty of Nat. Economy, Univ. of Econs, Bratislava 1978–89, Assoc. Prof. 1989–94, Dean 1991–94; mem. Bd Národná banka Slovenska (Nat. Bank of Slovakia—NBS) 1993–96, 2006–, Exec. Dir Research Section 1994–2000, Exec. Dir NBS 2007–10, Gov. 2010–; Chair. Financial Market Authority (FMA) 2000–02, Chair. Bd of Dirs FMA 2002–05; Rep. of Slovakia in Cttee of European Securities Regulators; Rep. in Int. Asscn of Insurance Supervisors; mem. Governing Council of European Cen. Bank 2010–; Gov. IMF 2010–; Alt. Gov. EBRD 2010–; mem. Academic Council of Faculty of Nat. Economy, Univ. of Econs, Bratislava; mem. Editorial Bd BIATEC, Účtovníctvo, audítorstvo, danovníctvo (Accounting, Auditing, Taxation), scientific periodical of Faculty of Finance, Matej Bel Univ. *Publications include:* numerous textbooks, monographs, research papers and articles, published in Slovakia and abroad. *Address:* Národná banka Slovenska, Imricha Karvaša 1, 813 25 Bratislava, Slovakia (office). *Telephone:* (2) 5787-1111 (office). *Fax:* (2) 5787-1100 (office). *E-mail:* info@nbs.sk (office). *Website:* www.nbs.sk (office).

MAKUZA, Bernard; Rwandan politician and fmr diplomatist; b. 1961; m.; fmr mem. Mouvement démocratique républicain; fmr Amb. to Burundi, Amb. to Germany –2000; Prime Minister of Rwanda 2000–11; apptd to Senate 2011. *Address:* Senate, Kigali, Rwanda.

MAKWETU, Clarence Mlamli; South African politician; b. 6 Dec. 1928, Hoyita, Cofimvaba Dist, Transkei; s. of Minah Makwetu and Gqongo Makwetu; m. Mandisa Makwetu; two s.; ed Hoyita Primary School, Keilands Mission School, Nkwanca Sr Secondary School and Lovedale School; joined African Nat. Congress (ANC) Youth League 1954; instrumental in formation of ANC 1959; detained several times 1960–63; then served five years on Robben Island; subsequently returned to Transkei, working in construction and insurance; detained again 1977, 1979; banished by Chief Kaiser Matanzima to Libido Dist 1979–84; returned home and continued farming 1984; detained 1986; First Pres. Pan-Africanist Movt 1989–90; Deputy Pres. Pan-Africanist Congress of Azania (PAC) March–Dec. 1990; Pres. PAC 1990, expelled from PAC for bringing party into disrepute May 1997; MP Nat. Ass. 1994–97; claims lodged against his farm in Gwatyu, Cofimvaba Dist Sept. 2001; Order of Luthuli in Silver. *Address:* c/o PAC, PO Box 6010, Johannesburg 2000, South Africa. *E-mail:* admin@pac.org.za.

MALAJ, Arben; Albanian economist and politician; b. 19 Sept. 1961; m.; one c.; ed Univ. of Tirana; began career with Nat. Commercial Bank of Albania, Vlora; Dir Foundation of SME-s, Tirana –1997; Assoc. Prof. of Econ. Sciences, Univ. of Tirana 1997–; mem. Kuvendi Popullor (Parl.) for Kelmendi Dist (Socialist Party) 1997–; Minister of Finance and Gov. of Albania to the World Bank 1997–98; Chief of Parl. Comm. for the Economy and Econ. Table of the Stability Pact 1998–2000; Chief of Parl. Group of the Socialist Party 2000–02; Minister of Economy 2002–04, of Finance 2004–05; lecturer in numerous academic insts including Univ. of Bocconi, Italy, Univ. of Tetova, Macedonia, Univ. of Pristina, Kosova; mem. Int. Acad. of Emerging Markets, New York, USA. *Publications:* author or co-author of several

publications and scientific articles. *Address:* Kuvendi Popullor (People's Assembly), Bulevardi Dëshmorët e Kombit 4, Tirana, Albania (office). *Telephone:* (4) 2264887 (office). *Fax:* (4) 2221764 (office). *E-mail:* kontakto@arben-malaj.com. *Website:* www.arben-malaj.com.

MALAN, Pedro, PhD; Brazilian economist; *Chairman, Unibanco SA;* b. 19 Feb. 1943, Rio de Janeiro; s. of Elysio S. Malan and Regina S. Malan; m. 1st Ana María Toledo Piza Rudge; m. 2nd Catarina Gontijo Souza Lima 1980; two s. one d.; ed St Ignatius School, Rio de Janeiro, Polytechnic School of Catholic Univ. of Rio de Janeiro, School of Econs and Univ. of California, Berkeley; with Inst. of Applied Research, Brazilian Ministry of Planning 1966–69, 1973–83; Faculty of Econs, Catholic Univ. of Rio de Janeiro Jan.–Dec. 1979; Head Int. Trade and Finance Section, Inst. of Applied Econ. Research 1980–83; Dir Policy Analysis and Research Div. Centre of Transnat. Corpns, UN, New York 1983–84, Dept of Int. Econs and Social Affairs 1985–86; Exec. Dir World Bank, Washington, DC 1986–90; Exec. Dir Inter-American Devt Bank 1990–92; Pres. Cen. Bank of Brazil 1993–94; Minister of Finance 1994–2002; Vice-Chair. Bd of Dirs, Unibanco SA 2003–04, Chair. 2004–; Fed. of São Paulo Industries Prize for book External Economic Policy and Industrialization in Brazil 1980, Légion d'honneur 1996, Order of Mil. Merit 1998, Order of Naval Merit 1998. *Publications:* The Structure of Protection in Brazil (with J. Bergsman) 1971, The Brazilian Economy in the 1970s: Old and New Developments (with R. Bonelli) 1977, Brazilian External Debt and its Implications 1978, Structural Models of Inflation and Balance of Payments Disequilibria in Semi-Industrialized Economies (with John R. Wells) 1984, Financial Integration with the World Economy, The Brazilian Case 1983, Relações Econômicas Internacionais do Brasil no Período 1945–64 1984, Debt, Trade and Development: The Crucial Years Ahead 1985. *Leisure interests:* literature, classical music, diplomatic and financial history, swimming, tennis. *Address:* Unibanco Holdings SA, Avenida Eusébio Matoso 891, 22nd Floor, 05423-901 São Paolo, Brazil (office). *Telephone:* (11) 3047-1313 (office). *Fax:* (11) 3813-6182 (office). *Website:* www.unibanco.com.br (office).

MALAN, Wynand Charl, BA, LLB; South African politician, attorney, consultant and business executive; b. 25 May 1943, Port Elizabeth; s. of Dawid Johannes Malan and Annie Malan (née de Swardt); m. Judith Rousseau 1967; two s. one d.; ed Linden Hoërskool, Johannesburg and Univ. of Pretoria; attorney and Partner, van Wyk de Vries, Malan & Steyn, Johannesburg 1966–67, Leader Nat. Jeugbond, Transvaal 1972–74; mem. Rapportraad 1971–73, Nat. Chair. 1974–76; Randburg Town Councillor and Chair. Man. Cttee 1977; Nat. Party MP for Randburg 1977–87, Ind. MP for Randburg 1987–88, Democratic Party MP for Randburg 1989–90; fmr Leader Nat. Democratic Movt; fmr Co-Leader Democratic Party; mem. The Truth and Reconciliation Comm. 1995–2002; CEO Thebe Securities Ltd 2002–05; strategy consultant, pvt. practice 2006–; Eisenhower Fellowship 1980; ASPU Newsmaker of the Year Award 1987. *Leisure interests:* golf, chess, numismatics, clivia propagation. *Address:* PO Box 2075, Randburg 2125, South Africa (office). *Telephone:* (11) 7820119 (office). *Fax:* (11) 7820119 (office). *E-mail:* wcmalan@mweb.co.za (office).

MALASHENKO, Igor Yevgenyevich, PhD; Russian journalist; b. 2 Oct. 1954, Moscow; m. Yelena Pivovarova; two d.; ed Moscow State Univ.; jr, sr researcher, Inst. for US and Canadian Studies, USSR Acad. of Sciences 1980–89, research in problems of the concept of nuclear deterrence and public opinion; staff-mem. Int. Div. Cen. Cttee CPSU, admin. of Pres. Gorbachev March–Dec. 1991; Political Dir TV & Radio Co. Ostankino 1992–93; Co-founder, Pres. and Dir-Gen. Ind. TV Co. NTV 1993, Pres. NTV-Telemost Holding 1998; First Deputy Chair. Bd of Dirs Media-Most Co. 1998–2001; Adviser to Pres. of Russia on public relations problems, mem. election campaign staff of Boris Yeltsin 1996; Russian Union of Journalists' Prize 1994. *Leisure interests:* golf, photography. *Address:* NTV-Telemost, Academica Koroleva str. 19, 127427 Moscow, Russia (office). *Telephone:* (495) 215-15-88 (office).

MALAURIE, Jean, PhD; French anthropogeographer and writer; *Director Emeritus, Centre d'études arctiques (EHESS-CNRS);* b. 22 Dec. 1922, Mainz, Germany; s. of Albert Malaurie and Isabelle (Regnault) Malaurie; m. Monique Laporte 1951; one s. one d.; ed Lycée Condorcet, Faculté des Lettres de Paris, Inst. of Geography Univ. of Paris; Attaché then Research Fellow, CNRS 1948–56; mem. Nat. Comm. on Geography 1955–67, 1980–82; Prof. of Arctic Geomorphology and Anthropogeography, Ecole des Hautes Etudes en Sciences Sociales (EHESS), Paris 1957–, Founder and Dir Centre for Arctic Studies, EHESS-CNRS 1957, Dir Arctic Research, CNRS 1979–91, Dir Emer. EHESS–CNRS 1992–; Pres. Fondation Française d'études nordiques 1964–75, Soc. Arctique Française 1981–90; Founder and Dir Terre Humaine anthropological book series 1955–; Founder, Dir Inter-Nord int. journal of Arctic studies 1961 (21 vols); Chair. and organizer 14 int. Arctic confs and seminars; made 9 documentary films on the Inuit; led 31 Arctic scientific expeditions; first explorer to reach North geomagnetic pole by dog-sledge 29 May 1951; Chair. Cttee for the Defence of Arctic Minorities in Russia, Foundation for Culture, Moscow 1990–; Dir Acad. of Human Sciences of Russia 1997–; UNESCO Goodwill Amb. in charge of Arctic Polar issues 2007–; Pres. Uummannaq Polar Inst. (Greenland) 2009–; Hon. Pres. Fonds Polaire Jean Malaurie, Bibliothèque centrale, Nat. Museum of Natural History, Paris 1992–, State Polar Acad., St Petersburg 1994–; Hon. Dean Northern People's State Univ. Herzen, St Petersburg 1992 (and Gold Medal); Hon. Prof., Hautes études commerciales de Paris 2005; Commdr, Légion d'honneur, Ordre nat. du mérite, Ordre des Arts et Lettres, Order of the Dannebrog (Denmark) 2007; Hon. PhD (State Univ., St Petersburg) 2001; Dr hc (State Univ. of NY) 2007; Award of Acad. française 1968, Polar Medal, Soc. de Géographie, Paris 1953, 1961, Acad. des sciences Award 1967, Gold Medal, Soc. arctique française 1990, CNRS Medal 1992, Gold Medal, Soc. de Géographie Paris 1996, Grand Prix de la Ville de Paris 1999 Grand Prix Jules Verne 2000, Gold Medal of St Petersburg 2003, Patron's Gold Medal, Royal Geographical Soc., London 2005, Mungo Park Medal, Royal Scottish Geographical Soc. 2005, Gold Medal of Greenland 'Nersornaat' 2009, Gold Medal of Strasbourg 2013. *Films:* Les Derniers Rois de Thulé 1969, 2002, Inuit from Greenland to Siberia (seven films) 1980, Haïnak Inuit 1993, La Saga des Inuit (four films) 2007. *Music:* Chants et tambours inuit. De Thulé au Détroit de Béring 1987, Jean Malaurie. De la pierre à l'homme 2004. *Publications include:* Hoggar 1954, Les Derniers Rois de Thulé (translated into 22 languages) 1955, Thèmes de recherche géomorphologique dans le nord-ouest du Groenland 1968 (second edn 2012),

Ultima Thulé (second edn) 1990, Hummocks (second edn) 1999, L'appel du nord 2001, L'allée des baleines (second edn) 2003, Ot Kaminya K Tcheloveky 2003, Uummaa 2013. *Address:* Centre d'études arctiques (EHESS-CNRS), 27 rue Damesme, bureau 511, 75013 Paris, France (office). *E-mail:* jean.malaurie@ehess.fr (office). *Website:* www.jean-malaurie.fr.

MALCHÁREK, Jirko; Slovak politician; b. 28 June 1966, Jeseník; widowed; one s.; ed Secondary School of Mechanical Eng, Bratislava, Slovak Tech. Univ., Bratislava; Asst Dir Bratislava Transport Co. 1989–91; Office of Govt Commr for Automotive Industry and Conversion of Special Production 1991; Man. Dir, VSŽ Selecta Praha, Slovak branch 1993–98; Founder and head operational leasing co., Slovakia 1995–98; mem. Nat. Council of Slovak Repub. 1998–2005; Deputy Prime Minister and Minister of the Economy 2005–06. *Address:* c/o Ministry of the Economy, Mierová 19, 827 15 Bratislava, Slovakia (office).

MALCOLM, James Ian (Jim), OBE; British diplomatist (retd); b. 29 March 1946; s. of William Kenneth Malcolm and the late Jennie Malcolm; m. Sheila Nicholson Moore 1967; one s. one d.; ed Royal High School, Edinburgh; entered British Diplomatic Service in 1966, Attaché, UK Del. to NATO, Brussels 1969–72, Attaché, Embassy in Rangoon, Burma (Union of Myanmar) 1972–74, Third Sec., FCO, London 1974–77, Commercial Attaché, British High Comm., Nairobi, Kenya 1977–80, Consul, British Embassy, Damascus, Syria 1980–83, Second Sec. (Commercial), Embassy in Angola 1983–85, First Sec., FCO (dealing with Counter-Terrorism issues) 1985–87, First Sec. (Political/Econ.), Embassy in Jakarta, Indonesia 1987–94, First Sec., FCO (Head of BBC World Service Section) 1994–97, Deputy High Commr in Kingston, Jamaica and British Trade Commr to Cayman Islands 1997–2001, Amb. to Panama 2002–06 (retd). *Leisure interests:* reading and researching British history in Indonesia, Jamaica and Panama, playing golf, riding motorcycles, photography.

MALCOLM, Steven J., BCE; American energy industry executive; b. Sept. 1948, St Louis, Mo.; m. Gwen Malcolm; one d.; ed Univ. of Missouri-Rolla, Northwestern Univ.; began career in refining, marketing and transportation depts, Cities Gas Co.; joined Williams Cos Inc. 1984, Dir of Business Devt, Williams Natural Gas Co. 1984–86, Dir of Gas Man. 1986–89, Vice-Pres. of Gas Man. and Supply 1989–93, Sr Vice-Pres. and Gen. Man. Mid-Continent Region, Williams Field Services 1993–94, Sr Vice-Pres. and Gen. Man. Gathering and Processing 1994–96, Sr Vice-Pres. and Gen. Man. Midstream Gas and Liquids, Williams Energy Services 1996–98, Pres. and CEO Williams Energy Services 1998–2001, apptd Dir The Williams Cos Inc. 2001, Pres. and COO 2001–02, Pres. and CEO 2002–03, Chair., Pres. and CEO 2002–10; mem. Bd Tulsa Area United Way, Tulsa Community Foundation, YMCA, St John Medical Center, Boy Scouts of America Indian Nations Council; mem. Univ. of Tulsa Advancement and Athletics Cttees, YMCA Exec. Cttee; mem. Business Roundtable, Cttee to Encourage Corp. Philanthropy, Nat. Petroleum Council; fmr mem. Nat. Energy Services Asscn. *Address:* c/o The Williams Companies, Inc., 1 Williams Center, Tulsa, OK 74172, USA. *E-mail:* williams@int-env.ca. *Website:* co.williams.com.

MALCOMSON, James Martin, MA, PhD, FBA; British economist and academic; *Professor of Economics, University of Oxford;* b. 23 June 1946, Staunton-on-Wye, Herefords., England; s. of E. Watlock Malcomson and Madeline (Stuart) Malcomson; m. Sally Claire Richards 1979; one d. (deceased); ed Gonville and Caius Coll., Univ. of Cambridge, Harvard Univ., USA; Research Fellow, Lecturer, Sr Lecturer, Univ. of York 1971–85; Prof. of Econs, Univ. of Southampton 1985–98; Prof. of Econs, Univ. of Oxford 1999–; Fellow, All Souls Coll. Oxford 1999–; Fellow, Econometric Soc. 2005. *Publications:* numerous articles in scientific journals. *Leisure interests:* walking, music, film, theatre. *Address:* All Souls College, Oxford, OX1 4AL (office); Department of Economics, Manor Road Building, Manor Road, Oxford, OX1 3UQ, England (office). *Telephone:* (1865) 279379 (office). *Fax:* (1865) 279299 (office). *E-mail:* james.malcomson@economics.ox.ac.uk (office). *Website:* www.economics.ox.ac.uk (office).

MALCORRA, Susana; Argentine engineer and UN official; *Chef de Cabinet to the Executive Office, United Nations;* b. 1954; m.; one s.; ed Univ. of Rosario; grad. trainee with IBM, eventually becoming Dir of Public Sector, later assigned to IBM's corp. HQ in USA where she oversaw relations between HQ and Mexico and the Andean region of Latin America –1993; various admin. positions with Telecom Argentina 1993–2003, COO and Exec. Dir 1995–2001, CEO 2001–02; co-f. Vectis Management 2002; Deputy Exec. Dir (Admin) WFP 2004–07 (led initial phase of operational response to tsunami emergency Dec. 2004), Deputy Exec. Dir and COO Jan.–March 2008, Under-Sec.-Gen. and Head of Dept of Field Support, UN 2008–12, Chef de Cabinet to the Exec. Office 2012–; Founding mem. Argentine chapter, Int. Women's Forum; mem. Advisory Bd of Business School of Univ. of San Andres, Buenos Aires, Advisory Bd of Equidad. *Address:* United Nations, New York, NY 10017, USA. *Telephone:* (212) 963-1234 (office). *Fax:* (212) 963-4879 (office). *Website:* www.un.org (office).

MALECELA, Cigwiyemisi John Samwel, BCom; Tanzanian politician and diplomatist; b. 1934, Dodoma; m. Ezerina Mwaipopo; one s. three d.; ed Minaki Secondary School, Bombay Univ., India and Univ. of Cambridge, UK; admin. Officer, Civil Service 1960–61; Consul in USA and Third Sec. to the UN 1962; Regional Commr, Mwanza Region 1963; Amb. and Perm. Rep. to the UN, New York 1964–68; Amb. to Ethiopia 1968; E African Minister for Communications, Research and Social Services, E African Community 1969–72; Minister of Foreign Affairs 1972–75, of Agric. 1975–80, of Mines 1980–81, of Transport and Communications 1982–85; Regional Commr, Iringa 1987–89; High Commr to UK 1989–90; MP for Mtera 1990–2010; Prime Minister and First Vice-Pres. of Tanzania 1990–94; Minister without Portfolio 1995; Vice-Chair. Chama Cha Mapinduzi Party 1995–2007; Vice-Chair. Desert Locust Control Org. for East Africa; mem. Group of Eminent Persons of the Commonwealth on the South African situation 1985; Order of Merit of First Degree (Egypt), First Order of Independence (Equatorial Guinea); Hon. PhD (Univ. of Texas) 1977. *Leisure interests:* reading, sports. *Address:* c/o Office of the Prime Minister, PO Box 3021, Dar es Salaam, Tanzania. *E-mail:* ps@pmo.go.tz.

MALEENONT, Vichai; Thai business executive; *Chairman and CEO, BEC World Public Co. Ltd;* b. 1918; m.; seven c.; co-f. BEC World Public Co. Ltd (media group) 1970, currently Chair. and CEO. *Address:* BEC World Public Co. Ltd, 3199 Maleenont Tower, Rama 4 Rd, Klongton, Klongtoey, Bangkok 10110, Thailand

(office). *Telephone:* (2) 204-3333 (office). *Fax:* (2) 204-1384 (office). *E-mail:* ir@becworld.com (office). *Website:* www.becworld.com (office).

MALEK, Redha; Algerian politician and diplomatist; b. 21 Dec. 1931, Batna; s. of Malek Ahmed and Ladjouze Zoulikha; m. Rafida Cheriet 1963; two s. one d.; ed Univs of Algiers and Paris; Founding mem. General Union of Algerian Muslim Students (UGEMA) 1955, mem. Steering Cttee 1957; Ed.-in-Chief El-Moudjahid (weekly newspaper of FLN) 1957–62; mem. Algerian del. to negotiations of Evian 1961–62, Drafting Cttee of Program of Tripoli setting out FLN political programme 1962, mem. Cen. Cttee FLN 1979–; Drafting Cttee of Nat. Charter 1976; Amb. to Yugoslavia 1962–64, to France 1965–70, to USSR 1970–77, to USA 1979–82, to UK 1982–84; Minister of Information and Culture 1978–79; Pres. Conseil Nat. Consultatif 1992; Minister of Foreign Affairs 1992–93; mem. High Council of State 1992–94; Prime Minister of Algeria 1993–94 (removed by armed forces leaders); Pres. Alliance Nat. Républicaine 1995; involved in negotiations for release of 52 American hostages in Iran 1980–81; Harold Weill Medal, New York Univ. *Publications:* Tradition et Révolution 1993, Le véritable enjeu, l'enjeu de la modernité en Algérie et dans l'islam, L'Algérie à Evian 1995, Histoire des négociations secrètes (1956/1962).

MALENCHENKO, Col Yuri Ivanovich; Russian/Ukrainian cosmonaut; b. 22 Dec. 1961, Svetlovodsk, Kirovograd Oblast, Ukrainian SSR, USSR; m.; one s.; ed Kharkov Higher Mil. Aviation School, Zukovsky Mil. Aviation Eng Acad.; army service 1979–; Col, Russian Air Force; mil. pilot of 3rd class, flew more than 800 hours in fighters; served as a pilot, sr pilot and multi-ship flight lead in Odessa Region 1983–87, selected as a cosmonaut at Yu. A. Gagarin Research and Test Cosmonaut Training Centre 1987, underwent general space training 1987–89, qualified as a test-cosmonaut; took advanced training courses in preparation for spaceflight 1989–93; trained as Commdr of Mir-14 reserve crew Jan.–July 1993, completed training as a backup Commdr of Mir-15 crew 1993–94; trained for Mir-16 mission Feb.–June 1994; participant in flight to space station Mir Aug.–Sept. 1994; cosmonaut-explorer 1995–; missions include Soyuz TM-19, Mir EO-16, STS-106, Soyuz TMA-2, Expedition 7, Soyuz TMA-11, Expedition 16, Soyuz TMA-05M, Expedition 32, Expedition 33; carried out first and second career spacewalks during Mir-16 mission 9 and 14 Sept. 1994, third spacewalk during STS-106 mission to Int. Space Station (ISS) 11 Sept. 2000, fourth spacewalk 9 Nov. 2007, fifth spacewalk 20 Aug. 2012; became first person to marry in space when he married Ekaterina Dmitrieva, who was in Texas, while he was 240 miles over NZ on ISS 10 Aug. 2003; retired as cosmonaut 27 July 2009, return to the cosmonaut corps Feb. 2010; Hero of the Russian Fed., Nat. Hero of Kazakhstan Medal, Mil. Award of Excellence, Commendation Medal, Achievement Medal, Jubilee Medal '70 Years of the Armed Forces of the USSR', Meritorious Service Medals 1st, 2nd and 3rd Class. *Leisure interests:* sports and games, music, hunting. *Address:* Yu. A. Gagarin Research and Test Cosmonaut Training Centre, Star City, Moscow Region 141160, Russia. *Telephone:* (495) 526-34-07. *Fax:* (495) 526-26-12. *E-mail:* info@gctc.ru. *Website:* www.gctc.su.

MÄLER, Karl-Göran, PhD; Swedish economist and academic; *Professor and Director, Beijer International Institute of Ecological Economics;* b. 3 March 1939, Sollefteå; s. of Karl Markus Mäler and Henny Kristina Mäler; m. Sara Aniyar; two d.; ed Stockholm Univ.; Prof. of Econs, Stockholm School of Econs; Dir Beijer Int. Inst. of Ecological Econs, Royal Swedish Acad. of Sciences; Founding mem. European Asscn of Environmental and Resource Economists (EAERE); Co-organizer Ecological and Environmental Econs Research and Training Activity at Int. Centre for Theoretical Physics, Trieste, Italy; Dr hc (Haifa); Volvo Environment Prize 2002, EAERE European Lifetime Achievement Award in Environmental Econs (co-recipient) 2005, Older Linné Medal in Gold, Royal Swedish Acad. of Science. *Publications:* Environmental Economics: A Theoretical Inquiry 1974, Priskompensation Och Planeringsosakerhet I Forsvaret: Utredning Utford Pa Uppdrag Av 1978 ars Forsvarskommitte (co-author) 1981, Environmental Decision Making (co-author) 1984, Environment and Development: An Economic Approach (co-author) 1992, Economic Science, 1981–1990: The Sveriges Riksband (ed.) 1992, Poverty, Institutions, and the Environmental-Resource Base (co-author) 1994, Current Issues in Environmental Economics (co-ed.) 1995, Rights to Nature: Ecological, Economic, Cultural, and Political Principles of Institutions for the Environment (co-ed.) 1996, Biodiversity Loss: Economic and Ecological Issues (co-ed.) 1997, The Economics of Transnational Commons (co-ed.) 1997, The Environment and Emerging Development Issues (co-ed.) 2001, The Economics of Non-Convex Ecosystems (co-ed.) 2004. *Leisure interest:* bird watching. *Address:* Beijer Institute, Royal Swedish Academy of Sciences, Box 50005, 104 05 Stockholm, Sweden (office). *Telephone:* (8) 673-95-30 (office). *Fax:* (8) 15-24-64 (office). *E-mail:* karl@beijer.kva.se (office). *Website:* www.beijer.kva.se (office).

MALER, Leopoldo Mario, LLB, JD; Argentine artist and art foundation executive; b. 2 April 1937, Buenos Aires; s. of Abraham Maler and Esther Kraiselburd; m. 1st Silvia Oclander 1967; m. 2nd Joyce Pieck 1973 (divorced 1979); m. 3rd María Rosa Baquero 1988 (divorced 2003); one s.; ed New School for Social Research, New York, Univ. of Buenos Aires, Univ. Coll., London, UK, Int. Faculty of Comparative Law, Strasbourg, France (scholarship); worked for BBC World Service in the production of art and educ. programmes 1961–64; conducted a series of radio programmes on the theatre, Municipal Radio, Buenos Aires 1964–67; made TV programmes for Cen. of Information and radio programmes on arts and music for BBC World Service and BBC Radio 1 and 2, London 1967–74; conducted a four-hour daily radio show on current affairs and the arts, Radio Belgrano Network (23 radio stations), Buenos Aires 1974–75; consultant and producer for Latin American Radio Service of UN Dept of Public Information 1980–83; Co-founder Centre for Research and Studies of Latin American Art (CIEDAL), Santo Domingo, Dominican Repub. 1986; Co-founder and Admin. Dir, Design Center for Global Needs, San Francisco State Univ.; Ed. NACA Journal, Dept of Industry and Design 1988–93; Co-ordinator, Domus Acad. courses, Centro Cultural Borges, Buenos Aires 1997–99; Guest Lecturer, Architectural Asscn, London 1975; Lecturer, Leeds Polytechnic 1975, Hornsey Coll. of Art, London 1975; External Examiner Prof., Middlesex Polytechnic, London 1979–81; Guest Lecturer, Art Dept, Univ. of Iowa 1982, Univ. of Sydney 1982; Prof., Art Psychology, Parsons School of Design, Dominican Repub. 1983–85, First Dean, Parsons School of Design (Altos de Chavón/La Escuela de Diseño) 1983–85; Guest Lecturer, Universidad del Este, Dominican Repub. 1984, Miami Dade Community

Coll., Miami, Fla 1985, Art Dept, Sonoma State Univ., Calif. 1991, San Francisco Art Inst., Calif. 1992, Dept of Arts Practice, Univ. of California, Berkeley 1993, School of Fine Arts, Lamentin, Guadeloupe 1995, Univ. of Puerto Rico 1996, Santa Fe Art Inst., NM 1998, School of Fine Arts of Puerto Rico 2004; Dir Milan's Domus Acad. programme at Centro Cultural Borges, Buenos Aires 1997, 1999; Condecoracion Orden al Merito Artistico (Spain) 1992; Special Jury Prize, Leipzig Film Festival 1964, First Grand Prize, Int. Biennale of Art, São Paulo, Brazil 1977, Guggenheim Fellowship 1977, Special Jury Mention, Argentina 78, Buenos Aires 1978, General Motors Prize, First Biennale of Sports in the Arts, Montevideo, Argentina 1980, Premio Konex, Buenos Aires 1982, Gandhi Award for Social Communications, Buenos Aires 1983, Arawak Prize for the Best Foreign Art Show, Santo Domingo 1986, Medal from Mayor of Lamentin, Guadeloupe 1994, Gran Premio, competition for a monument at Universidad de San Juan, Puerto Rico 1996. *Works include:* monumental sculpture commissioned by IOC for the Olympic Park, Seoul, South Korea 1988; monumental sculpture commissioned by the City of Madrid to celebrate its designation as Cultural Capital of Europe, Parque Juan Carlos I 1992; Madona and Child, monumental sculpture entitled commissioned by the local French authorities of the island of Guadeloupe 1994; La Conciencia Empirica, monumental sculpture for the Botanical Gardens commissioned by the Universidad de San Juan 1996; monumental sculpture commissioned for Suwon (Folk Village), South Korea, celebrating the Football World Cup 2002; monumental sculpture commissioned for the city of Santo Tirso, Porto, Portugal 2003. *Works in public collections:* BEST Collection, Camara Municipal de Santo Tirso, Portugal, Hara Museum, Tokyo, Hess Collection, Napa, Calif., Jaragua Hotel Collection, Santo Domingo, Museum of Contemporary Art, Puerto Rico, Parque Ferial Juan Carlos I, Madrid, Seoul Olympic Park Collection, Seoul, Tamayo Museum, Mexico, Univ. of Puerto Rico, Victoria & Albert Museum, London, Watari Collection, Tokyo. *Ballets:* Ultrazoom (multimedia ballet, visual co-ordinator), Instituto Torcuato di Tella, Buenos Aires 1965, Wrote and directed Caperucita Rota, a scripted happening for a narrator and 14 Dancers, Centro de Experimentacion Audiovisual, Instituto Torcuato Di Tella, Buenos Aires 1966, X-IT (programme of six choreographic works with 14 dancers, fork-lift trucks and inflatable objects), The Place, London 1969. *Performance art:* Outrage, in commemoration of The Sharpville massacre, The Round House, London 1969, X-IT 2, a programme of choreographic works at The Place, London 1969, Playback 625, a play co-written with N. F. Sompson and directed at the Royal Court Theatre, London 1970, Crane Ballet, a ballet for three cranes and three acrobats, Camden Festival of Music, London 1971, Popol Vuh, a choreographic work, The Place, London 1972, Carnem et Cyclum (a medium rare event), Great Georges, Liverpool, UK 1972, Son et Lumière, Cathedral of Cuernavaca, Mexico 1978, Jurisdiction, Palazzo Grassi, Venice 1979, Three Easy Pieces, performance and video installations, Center Georges Pompidou, Paris 1979, 25HP, Trinity College, Dublin 1980, Fuoco-Forma-Forno, Vennice Biennale, Piazza San Marco and Furnace Segusso, Murano 1980, Pre-Esenciia, performance-installation, Palazzo Reale, Milan 1980, Dance Performance, Goldsmith Coll., London, from a workshop conducted by Merce Cunningham and John Cage 1980, From Amaru to Barthes, co-created with Marta Minujin at the bullfight ring of La Macarena, Medellin, Colombia 1981, You See I Eat, Gallery Watari, Tokyo 1982, Shadows and Exhumations, Hara Museum, Tokyo 1982, H2Ombre, Center for Inter-American Relations, New York 1982, Echoes and Reflection, installation, The Center for Inter-American Relations, New York 1982, Bookabulary, choreographic work and a monumental sculpture commissioned for Miami's International Book Fair 1985, Visiones del Bilinguismo, Center for Latin-American Arts and Studies, Miami 1985, Fifteen Weightless Answers, Voluntariado de las Casas Reales, Santo Domingo 1986, BA BE BI...linguism..., American-Dominican Cultural Center, Santo Domingo 1988, We bring food, in collaboration with Marta Minujin, Museum of Contemporary Art, Los Angeles 1998, Metrobolism, in celebration of the first centenary of the Univ. of Puerto Rico 2004. *Film:* Men in Silence (Best Short Film, London Film Festival) 1964. *Leisure interests:* scuba-diving, psychology, sailing, horseback riding, music. *Address:* c/o Nohra Haime Gallery, 730 Fifth Avenue, Suite 701, New York, NY 10019, USA; Apdo Postal 25320, Santo Domingo, Dominican Republic. *Telephone:* (212) 888-3550 (New York); (809) 696-0072 (Santo Domingo). *E-mail:* gallery@nohrahaimegallery.com; nohrahaime@aol.com. *Website:* www .nohrahaimegallery.com.

MALESKI, Denko, PhD; Macedonian diplomatist and professor of law; *Professor of Law, University of Saints Cyril and Methodius;* b. 14 Nov. 1946, Skopje; s. of Vlado Maleski and Maria Alivantova; m. Miriana Ivanskova 1970; three d.; ed Univs of London, Skopje and Ljubljana; Prof. of Int. Politics, Univ. of Sts Cyril and Methodius, Skopje 1981–91, currently Prof. of Law; Visiting Prof. (Fulbright Scholar), Bowling Green State Univ., Ohio, USA 1990; Minister of Foreign Affairs 1991–93; Amb. and Perm. Rep. to UN, New York 1993–97; Borjan Tanevski Foundation Award 2005. *Publications:* Contemporary Political Systems 1986, International Politics 2000, The Worlds of Thucydidies and Machiavelli 2001; numerous articles on democracy, political systems and int. relations. *Leisure interests:* reading, jogging. *Address:* University of Cyril & Methodius, PO Box 576, Bulevar Krste Misirkov b.b., 1000 Skopje, Macedonia.

MALEWEZI, Rt Hon. Justin Chimera, BA; Malawi teacher, educational administrator and politician; b. 23 Dec. 1944, Ntchisi; s. of the late Canon John Julius Malewezi and of Bartlet Rachel Malewezi; m. Felicity Rozina Chizalema 1970; two s. two d.; ed Columbia Univ., New York, USA; secondary school teacher 1967–69, headmaster 1969–74, educ. admin. 1974–78; mem. Nat. Ass., for Ntchisi North East; Deputy Sec., Ministry of Finance and Prin. Sec. in various ministries 1978–89; Head of Civil Service 1989–91; Vice-Pres. of Malawi 1994–99, 1999–2003; unsuccessful cand. during presidential election 2004; fmr mem. United Democratic Front (UDF), currently mem. People's Progressive Movement (PPM). *Leisure interests:* tennis, football. *Address:* National Assembly, Parliament Bldg, Private Bag B362, Lilongwe 3 (office); PO Box 30086, Lilongwe 3, Malawi (home). *Telephone:* 1773566 (office). *Fax:* 1774196 (office). *Website:* www.malawi.gov.mw/ parliament/parliament.htm (office).

MALHOTRA, Manish; Indian fashion designer; b. 1965; ed Elphinstone Coll., Mumbai; early career as a model; joined Equinox (boutique) 1989; designer, Reverie 1998–; designed team gear for Indian Premier League's Kolkata Knightriders; host The Manish Malhotra Show (TV talk show) 2005–; German Public Bollywood Award, Stylish Designer Of the Year, Elle Style Awards 1999,

Indira Priyadarshini Memorial Award, Int. Indian Film Acad. (IIFA) Award 2000, IIFA Award and Designer of the Year Award 2002, Rajiv Gandhi Award. *Films as costume designer include:* Dilwale Dulhaniya Le Jayenge 1995, Rangeela (Filmfare Award 1996) 1995, Khamoshi: The Musical 1996, Raja Hindustani (Showtime Opinion Poll Award 1998) 1997, Dil To Pagal Hai (Siemen's Viewer's Choice Award 1998) 1997, Kuch Kuch Hota Hai 1998, Dil Kya Kare 1999, Mohabbatein 2000, Kabhi Khushi Kabhie Gham 2001, Kal Ho Naa Ho 2003, Main Hoon Na 2004, Maine Pyaar Kyun Kiya 2005, Fanaa 2006, Kabhi Alvida Naa Kehna 2006, Sivaji: The Boss 2007, Om Shanti Om 2007, U Me Aur Hum 2008, Blue 2009, 3 Idiots 2009, My Name is Khan 2010, Robot 2010, Anjaana Anjaani 2010. *Leisure interests:* music, movies. *Address:* Shop 4/5 Vishnudham CHS, Corner of 14th Road, Linking Road, Khar (W), Mumbai 400 052, Maharashtra, India (office). *Telephone:* (22) 26050723 (office); 9987719978 (mobile) (office). *Fax:* (22) 26050724 (office). *Website:* www.manishmalhotra.in.

MALHOUTRA, Manmohan (Moni), MA; Indian international official and consultant; *Trustee, Indira Gandhi Memorial Trust and Jawaharlal Nehru Memorial Fund;* b. 15 Sept. 1937, Izatnagar; s. of Col Gopal Das Malhoutra and Shukla Malhoutra; m. Leela Nath 1963; two d.; ed Delhi Univ., Balliol Coll., Oxford, UK; entered Indian Admin. Service 1961; mem. Prime Minister's Secr. 1966–73; joined Commonwealth Secr. 1974; Dir Sec.-Gen.'s Office and Int. Affairs Div. 1977–82, Asst Commonwealth Sec.-Gen. 1982–93; Conf. Sec. to Commonwealth Heads of Govt Meetings, London 1977, Lusaka 1979, Melbourne 1981, also at Asia-Pacific Regional Heads of Govt Meetings; led Commonwealth Secr. team in Observer Group at pre-independence elections in Zimbabwe 1980; elections in Uganda 1980; Sec. Commonwealth Southern Africa Cttee; Head of Secr. of Commonwealth Group of Eminent Persons on South Africa 1986; Chef de Cabinet, Commonwealth Sec.-Gen.'s Office 1982–90, Head Commonwealth Secr. Human Resource Devt Group 1983–93; mem. Bd Dirs Int. Inst. for Democracy and Electoral Assistance, Stockholm 1996–2003; Sec.-Gen. Rajiv Gandhi Foundation, New Delhi 2001–07; mem. UK-India Round Table 2004–; Trustee, Indira Gandhi Memorial Trust, Jawaharlal Nehru Memorial Fund, Shiv Nadar Foundation, Ambuja Cement Foundation, Unltd. India Trust; Rhodes Scholar 1958. *Publications:* First Proof (contrib.) 2004, New Century: Whose Century (ed. and publr) 2000, India: The Next Decade (ed. and publr) 2006. *Leisure interests:* reading, music, theatre, travel. *Address:* 118 Golf Links, New Delhi 110 003, India. *Telephone:* (11) 24643630. *E-mail:* monimalhoutra@googlemail.com.

MALICK, Terrence; American film director; b. 30 Nov. 1943, Waco, Texas; ed Center for Advanced Film Studies, American Film Inst. *Films directed and written include:* Badlands (also producer) 1973, Days of Heaven 1978 (New York Film Critics Award, Nat. Soc. of Film Critics Award, Cannes Film Festival Award), The Thin Red Line (Golden Berlin Bear Award 1999, Chicago Film Critics Asscn Award 1999, Golden Satellite Award 1999) 1998, The New World (also producer) 2005, The Unforeseen (exec. producer) 2006, Tree of Life (Palme D'Or, Cannes Film Festival 2011). *Address:* c/o DGA, 7920 Sunset Boulevard, Los Angeles, CA 90046 (office); c/o Harley Williams, 1900 Avenue of the Stars, Floor 17, Los Angeles, CA 90067, USA.

MALIELEGAOI, Tuila'epa Sailele; Samoan politician; *Prime Minister and Minister of Foreign Affairs and Finance;* fmr Deputy Prime Minister and Minister of Finance, Trade, Industry and Commerce and Tourism; Prime Minister of Samoa 1998–, also Minister of Foreign Affairs, of Finance 2014–; mem. Human Rights Protection Party. *Address:* Prime Minister's Department, PO Box L 1861, Apia, Samoa. *Telephone:* 63122. *Fax:* 21339. *E-mail:* pmdept@ipasifika.net (office).

MALIK, Art; British (b. Pakistani) actor; b. (Athar-Ul-Haque Malik), 13 Nov. 1952, Bahawalpur, Pakistan; m. Gina Rowe; two d.; ed Guildhall School of Music and Drama, London. *Television:* The Jewel in the Crown, Chessgame, The Far Pavilions, The Black Tower, Death is Part of the Process, After the War, Shadow of the Cobra, Stolen, Cleopatra 1999, In the Beginning 2000, The Seventh Scroll 2001, Holby City (series) 2003–05, The English Harem 2005, The Path to 9/11 2006. *Films:* Richard's Things, A Passage to India, Underworld, Living Daylights, Side Streets, City of Joy 1992, Wimbledon Poisoner 1994, True Lies 1994, A Kid in King Arthur's Court 1995, Path to Paradise 1997, Booty Call 1997, Side Streets 1998, Tabloid 2001, Out Done 2002, Tempo 2003, Fakers 2004, Nina's Heavenly Delights 2006, Dean Spanley 2008, Franklyn 2008, Hotel (2009, The Wolfman 2010. *Theatre:* Othello (RSC), Cymbeline and Great Expectations (Royal Exchange, Manchester). *Address:* PFD, Drury House, 34/43 Russell Street, London, WC2B 5HA, England.

MALIK, Gunwantsingh Jaswantsingh, BSc, MA; Indian diplomatist; b. 29 May 1921, Karachi; s. of the late Jaswant Singh Malik and Balwant Kaur Malik (née Bhagat); m. Gurkirat Kaur 1948 (divorced 1982); two s.; ed Downing Coll., Cambridge, UK, Gujrat Coll., Ahmedabad; RAF 1943–46; Indian Foreign Service 1947–79, Second Sec., Indian Embassy, Brussels 1948–50, Addis Ababa 1950; Under-Sec. Ministry of External Affairs 1950–52; First Sec. and Chargé d'affaires Argentina 1952–56; in Japan 1956–59; Counsellor (Commercial) and Asst Commr Singapore 1959–63; Dir Ministry of Commerce 1963–64; Jt-Sec. Ministry of External Affairs 1964–65; Amb. to Philippines 1965–68, to Senegal, concurrently to Côte d'Ivoire, Mauritania, The Gambia and Upper Volta 1968–70, to Chile (also Accred to Peru, Ecuador and Colombia) 1970–74, to Thailand 1974–77, to Spain 1977–79; Leader trade del. to S. America 1964; mem. del. to ECAFE 1965, to Group of 77 in Lima 1971, to Gov. Body of UNDP 1971, to UNCTAD III 1972, to ESCAP 1975; Chair. Tech. and Drafting Cttee, ESCAP 1976; Deputy Chair. Cttee of the Whole 1977; Dir Indian Shaving Products 1986–88; Sec. Asscn Indian Diplomats 1983–84, 1989–91, Vice-Pres. 1985–86, Pres. 1986–87; Vice-Chair. Delhi Chapter Soc. for Int. Devt 1985–89; Chair. Ahluwalia Baradi Trusts 1988–93; Vice-Pres. Alliance Française de Delhi 1990–98, Pres. 2000–02; Chair. Maharani Voyages Pvt. Ltd 1999–2004. *Publications:* books: A Sikh Diplomat 2008, Susan's Tiger 2010; numerous literary, political and economic articles. *Leisure interests:* photography, writing, touring. *Address:* C224 Defence Colony, New Delhi 110 024, India (home). *Telephone:* (11) 40793410 (home). *Fax:* (11) 41550379 (home).

MALIK, Iftikhar Ali, BA; Pakistani business executive; *CEO, Guard Group of Industries;* b. 30 Dec. 1944, Lahore; s. of Muhammad Shafi Malik and Mumtaz Begum; m.; two s.; ed FC Coll., Lahore; currently CEO Guard Group (autofilter, brake lining and brake oil mfrs); Chair. Pakistan Automobile Spare Parts

Importers and Dealers Asscn 1985–86; mem. Exec. Cttee Lahore Chamber of Commerce and Industry 1980, Pres. 1990; Vice-Pres. and Zonal Chair. Fed. of Pakistan Chambers of Commerce and Industry 1994–97, Pres. and Life Mem. 2001–02; Life mem. SAARC Chamber of Commerce and Industry (currently Vice-Chair.), Indo-Pak Chamber of Commerce and Industry; mem. Man. Cttee, ECO Chamber of Commerce and Industry; Chair. Punjab Olympic Asscn; Vice-Chair. Mumtaz Bakhtawar Trust Hosps, Pakistan Olympic Asscn; Special Lifetime mem. Confed. of Asia Pacific Chambers of Commerce and Industry; Hon. mem. Islamic Chamber of Commerce and Industry. *Address:* Guard Group of Industries, 80 Badami Bagh, PO Box 465, Lahore (office); 57-FCC, Gulberg III, Lahore, Pakistan (home). *Telephone:* (42) 7725616 (office); (42) 5757996 (home). *Fax:* (42) 7722627 (office). *E-mail:* guard@brain.net.pk (office). *Website:* www.mbmt.org.

MALIK, Munir A.; Pakistani laywer and government official; *Attorney-General;* Leader of Lawyers' Movt in Pakistan; fmr Pres. Supreme Court Bar Asscn of Pakistan; leader of the legal defence team of Chief Justice Iftikhar Muhammad Chaudhry when the latter was dismissed by Gen. Pervez Musharraf; arrested following declaration of a state of emergency by Musharraf and kept in confinement at Attock jail 2007; Attorney-Gen. of Pakistan 2013–; Dorab Patel Rule of Law Award, Human Rights Comm. of Pakistan, Human Rights Defender Award, Asian Human Rights Comm. (co-recipient), Gwangju Prize for Human Rights 2008. *Address:* Office of the Attorney-General, Supreme Court of Pakistan, Constitution Avenue, Islamabad, Pakistan (office). *Telephone:* (51) 9220581 (office). *Fax:* (51) 9213452 (office). *E-mail:* mail@supremecourt.gov.pk (office). *Website:* www.supremecourt.gov.pk (office).

MALIK, Shoaib; Pakistani professional cricketer; b. 1 Feb. 1982, Sialkot, Punjab; m. 1st Ayesha Siddiqui 2008 (divorced 2010); m. 2nd Sania Mirza 2010; all-rounder; right-handed batsman; right-arm off-break bowler; plays for Gujranwala Cricket Asscn 1997–99, Pakistan Int. Airlines 1998–, Pakistan Reserves 1999–2000, Pakistan 1999– (Capt. 2007–09), Sialkot Cricket Asscn 2001–07, Glos. 2003–04, Sialkot Stallions 2004–07, Delhi Daredevils 2008, Asia XI; First-class debut: 1997/98; Test debut: Pakistan v Bangladesh, Multan 29–31 Aug. 2001; One-Day Int. (ODI) debut: Pakistan v West Indies, Sharjah 14 Oct. 1999; T20I debut: England v Pakistan, Bristol 28 Aug. 2006; fined Rs2m (£15,900) and banned for 12 months by Pakistan Cricket Bd from int. cricket following tour of Australia March 2010, ban overturned two months later; ranked second in ICC (Int. Cricket Council) ODI all-rounder rankings June 2008. *Address:* c/o Pakistan Cricket Board, Gaddafi Stadium, Lahore 54600, Pakistan. *Telephone:* (42) 571-7231. *Fax:* (42) 571-1860. *E-mail:* info@pcboard.com.pk. *Website:* www.pcboard.com.pk/home.html.

MALIKI, Nuri Kamal (Jawad) al-; Iraqi politician; *Prime Minister;* b. (Nouri Kamel al-Maliki), 1 July 1950, Hindiya; m.; four c.; ed Baghdad Univ.; official of Dawa party, fled Iraq to Syria 1980; returned to Iraq as one of Dawa leaders serving as spokesman and adviser to Dawa leader and Iraq interim Prime Minister Ibrahim al-Jaafari 2003; helped draft new constitution; mem. cttee tasked to purge Iraq Baathist legacy; Prime Minister of Iraq 2006–, also acting Minister of Defence and of the Interior 2010–. *Address:* Office of the Prime Minister, Baghdad, Iraq.

MALIKI, Riyad Najib al-, PhD; Palestinian politician; *Minister of Foreign Affairs and of Information;* b. 31 May 1955, Bethlehem; ed American Univ.; Prof., Coll. of Eng, Bir Zeit Univ. 1981–96; Founder and Dir-Gen. Panorama, the Palestinian Centre for the Dissemination of Democracy & Community Devt 1991–; Minister of Foreign Affairs and of Information 2007–; Coordinator Arab Program to Support and Develop Democracy; mem. Exec. Bd Pugwash (Conf. on Int. Affairs, Science and Nobel Peace Prize) 1995–, World Movt for Democracy 1997–; columnist, Al-Ayyam (weekly newspaper); European Peace Prize 2000, Italian Peace Prize 2005. *Address:* Ministry of Foreign Affairs, PO Box 1336, Ramallah; Ministry of Foreign Affairs, PO Box 4017, Gaza, Palestinian Autonomous Areas (office). *Telephone:* (2) 2405040 (office); (8) 2829260 (office). *Fax:* (2) 2403772 (office); (8) 2868971 (office). *E-mail:* info@mofa.gov.ps (office). *Website:* www.mofa.pna.ps (office).

MALINGA, Separamadu Lasith, (Separamadu Lasith Malinga Swarnajith); Sri Lankan professional cricketer; b. 28 Aug. 1983, Galle; ed Devapathiraja Coll., Mahinda Coll., Galle; right-arm fast pace bowler; right-handed batsman; specialist fast bowler with a rare round-arm action, plays for Galle Cricket Club 2001–04, Nondescripts Cricket Club 2004–, Sri Lanka (Vice-Capt. T20I team) 2004–, Kent 2007, Mumbai Indians 2008–, Tasmania 2009–11, Ruhuna Royals 2012–, Melbourne Stars 2012–, Dhaka Gladiators 2013–, BCCSL Acad. XI, Ruhuna; First-class debut: 2001/02; Test debut: Australia v Sri Lanka, Darwin 1–3 July 2004; One-Day Int. (ODI) debut: Sri Lanka v UAE, Dambulla 17 July 2004; T20I debut: England v Sri Lanka, Southampton 15 June 2006; played in 30 Tests, took 101 wickets (average 33.15) and scored 275 runs (one half-century), highest score 64, average 11.45, best bowling (innings) 5/50, (match) 9/210. *Achievements include:* became first ever player in int. cricket history to take four wickets in four consecutive balls against S Africa during Cricket World Cup (also only the fifth hat-trick in World Cup history, the third ODI hat-trick for Sri Lanka and the 24th in all ODI history) 28 March 2007; only bowler with two Cricket World Cup hat tricks, against S Africa 2007, against Kenya 2011; with Angelo Mathews, holds highest run partnership for the 9th wicket in an ODI (132 runs), against Australia in Melbourne 2010; holds the record for most wickets taken in a single IPL season, 28 in the Indian Premier League 4 2011; announced retirement from Test cricket April 2011. *Address:* c/o Cricket Tasmania, PO Box 495, Rosny Park, Tasmania 7018; c/o Cricket Tasmania, Bellerive Oval, 15 Derwent Street, Bellerive, Tasmania 7018, Australia. *Telephone:* (3) 6282-0400. *Fax:* (3) 6244-3924. *E-mail:* info@crickettas.com.au; events@crickettas.com.au. *Website:* www.tascricket.com.au.

MALINI, Hema; Indian actress, film director, dancer and politician; b. (Hema Malini Chakravarty), 16 Oct. 1948, Ammankudi, Tiruchirappalli district, Tamil Nadu; d. of V.S. Ramanujam Chakravarthy and Jaya Chakravarthy; m. Dharmendra 1980; two c.; ed Andhra Mahila Sabha, Chennai; trained as Bharatanatyam dance artist; film actress 1965–; mem. Bharatiya Janata Party (BJP) 2003–09, Gen. Sec. 2010–; MP (BJP) for Karnataka, Rajya Sabha 2011–; Owner, Natya Vihar Kalakendra dance school; Chair., Nat. Film Devt Corpn 2000–03; Padma Shri 2000; Filmfare Lifetime Achievement Award 2000, SaMapa

Vitasta Award 2006. *Television:* Jai Mata Ki 2003, Noopur. *Films:* as actress: Pandava Vanavasam 1965, Sapno Ka Saudagar 1968, Waris 1969, Jahan Pyar Mile 1969, Tum Haseen Main Jawaan 1970, Sharafat 1970, Abhinetri 1970, Aansoo Aur Muskan 1970, Johny Mera Naam 1970, Sri Krishna Vijayam 1971, Paraya Dhan 1971, Naya Zamana 1971, Lal Patthar 1971, Andaz 1971, Tere Mere Sapne 1971, Seeta Aur Geeta (Filmfare Award for Best Actress 1972) 1972, Raja Jani 1972, Gora Aur Kala 1972, Garam Masala 1972, Bhai Ho To Aisa 1972, Babul Ki Galiyaan 1972, Shareef Budmaash 1973, Prem Parvat 1973, Chhupa Rustam 1973, Gehri Chaal 1973, Jugnu 1973, Joshila 1973, Dulhan 1974, Amir Garib 1974, Dost 1974, Prem Nagar 1974, Kasauti 1974, Patthar Aur Payal 1974, Haath Ki Safai 1974, Sunehra Sansar 1975, Sanyasi 1975, Kahte Hain Mujhko Raja 1975, Do Thug 1975, Dharmatma 1975, Khushboo 1975, Pratigya 1975, Sholay 1975, Sharafat Chod Di Maine 1976, Naach Uthe Sansaar 1976, Maa 1976, Charas 1976, Aap Beati 1976, Dus Numbri 1976, Mehbooba 1976, Jaaneman 1976, Shirdi Ke Sai Baba 1977, Kinara 1977, Khel Khilari Ka 1977, Dream Girl 1977, Dhoop Chhaon 1977, Chacha Bhatija 1977, Palkon Ki Chhaon Mein 1977, Dillagi 1978, Azaad 1978, Apna Khoon 1978, Trishul 1978, Ratnadeep 1979, Janta Hawaldar 1979, Dil Kaa Heera 1979, Meera 1979, Hum Tere Aashiq Hain 1979, The Burning Train 1980, Bandish 1980, Do Aur Do Paanch 1980, Alibaba Aur 40 Chor 1980, Maan Gaye Ustad 1981, Jyothi 1981, Dard 1981, Aas Paas 1981, Krodhi 1981, Kranti 1981, Naseeb 1981, Kudrat 1981, Meri Aawaz Suno 1981, Samraat 1982, Farz Aur Kanoon 1982, Do Dishayen 1982, Bhagawat 1982, Satte Pe Satta 1982, Suraag 1982, Rajput 1982, Desh Premee 1982, Meharbaani 1982, Taqdeer 1983, Razia Sultan 1983, Andha Kanoon 1983, Nastik 1983, Justice Chaudhury 1983, Sharara 1984, Ram Tera Desh 1984, Raaj Tilak 1984, Qaidi 1984, Ek Naya Itihas 1984, Ek Nai Paheli 1984, Phaansi Ke Baad 1985, Durga 1985, Aandhi-Toofan 1985, Ramkali 1985, Yudh 1985, Hum Dono 1985, Babu 1985, Ek Chadar Maili Si 1986, Sitapur Ki Geeta 1987, Hirasat 1987, Apne Apne 1987, Anjaam 1987, Jaan Hatheli Pe 1987, Kudrat Ka Kanoon 1987, Vijay 1988, Mulzim 1988, Mohabbat Ke Dushman 1988, Rihaee 1988, Galiyon Ka Badshah 1989, Deshwasi 1989, Sachche Ka Bol-Bala 1989, Santosh 1989, Desh Ke Dushman 1989, Paap Ka Ant 1989, Lekin... 1990, Jamai Raja 1991, Hai Meri Jaan 1991, Vivekananda 1994, Param Vir Chakra 1995, Aatank 1996, Maahir 1996, Himalay Putra 1997, Hey Ram 2000, Censor 2001, Aman Ke Farishtey 2003, Baghban 2003, Veer-Zaara 2004, Bhagmati 2005, Ganga 2006, Baabul 2006, Laaga Chunari Mein Daag 2007, Gangotri 2007, Sadiyaan 2010, Bbuddah... Hoga Terra Baap 2011, Aarakshan 2011; as dir: Dil Aashna Hai 1992, Tell Me O Khuda 2011. *Address:* 17th Jai Hind Society, 12th Road, JBPD Scheme, Mumbai 49 (office); C-302, Swarna Jayanti Sadan, New Delhi, 110 001, India. *Telephone:* (22) 28402716 (Mumbai); (22) 28493319 (Mumbai); (11) 23739900 (New Delhi). *Fax:* (22) 28493320 (Mumbai). *E-mail:* hhemammalini@gmail.com.

MALINVAUD, Edmond, LenD; French economist and academic; *Honorary Professor, Collège de France;* b. 25 April 1923, Limoges; s. of Auguste Malinvaud and Andrée Ballet; m. Elisabeth Compagnon 1952; two d.; ed Lycée Gay-Lussac, Limoges, Lycée du Parc, Lyon, Univ. of Paris, Ecole polytechnique; with Inst nat. de statistique et des études économiques 1948–66, Insp.-Gen. 1966–74, Man. Dir 1974–87; Prof., Collège de France 1987–93, Hon. Prof. 1993–; Researcher, Cowles Foundation for Research in Econs, Chicago 1951; Prof., Ecole pratique des hautes études 1957–93; Prof., Univ. of Calif., Berkeley 1961, 1967; Dir Ecole nat. de la statistique et de l'admin. économique 1962–66; Chair. Int. Econometric Soc. 1963: Assoc. Prof., Law Faculty, Univ. of Paris 1969–71; Vice-Chair. Soc. de Statistique de Paris 1971–73, Chair. 1974; Dir of Econ. Projections, Ministry of Econ. and Finance 1972–74; mem. Bd Banque de France 1972–88; Dir Banque nat. de Paris 1973–81; Vice-Pres. Asscn française des sciences économiques 1985–87; Chair. Int. Econ. Asscn 1974–77; Chair. Int. Statistical Inst. 1979–81; Admin. Groupe des assurances nationales 1981–89; Pres. l'Acad. pontificale des sciences sociales 1994–2003; Hon. Prof., Coll. de France 1993; Dr hc (Basle, Louvain, Helsinki, Geneva, Lausanne, Montréal, Rome, Frankfurt, Milan, Lisbon, Athens, Santiago de Compostela, Bonn, Bielefeld); Commdr, Légion d'honneur, Palmes académiques, Grand Croix, Ordre nat. du mérite; Médaille d'argent, CNRS, Paolo Baffi Prize for Econs, Recktenwald Prize for Econs. *Publications:* Initiation à la compatibilité nationale 1957, Méthodes statistiques de l'économétrie 1964, Leçons de théorie micro-économique 1968, La croissance française 1972, Réexamen de la théorie du chômage 1980, Théorie macroéconomique 1981, Essais sur la théorie du chômage 1983, Voies de la recherche macroéconomique 1991, Equilibre général dans les économies de marché 1993, Diagnosing Unemployment 1994, Macroeconomic Theory, Vols A and B 1998, Vol. C 2000.

MALJERS, Floris Anton; Dutch business executive; b. 12 Aug. 1933, Middelburg; m. J. H. de Jongh 1958; two s. one d. (deceased); ed Univ. of Amsterdam; joined Unilever 1959, Man. Dir Unilever, Colombia 1964, Unilever, Turkey 1966, Man. Dir Vdberg & Jurgens, Netherlands 1970, mem. Parent Bd of Unilever and Head of Man. Edible Fats Group 1974, Chair. Unilever NV 1984–94, Vice-Chair. Unilever PLC 1984; Chair. Supervisory Bd Philips, Electronics NV 1994; Dir Amoco 1994–98, ABN/Amro Bank, KLM, Royal Dutch Airlines, Philips Electronics, Guinness 1994–98; Gov. European Policy Forum 1994; Chair. Bd of Trustees, Utrecht Univ. Hosp. 1994, Rotterdam School of Man., Erasmus Univ. 1999, now Prof. Emer.; Chair. Turkije Instituut (Turkey Institute); Hon. KBE 1992. *Address:* Turkije Instituut (Turkey Institute), Doelensteeg 16, 2311 VL Leiden, Netherlands. *Telephone:* (71) 527-2541. *E-mail:* info@turkije-instituut.nl. *Website:* www.turkije-instituut.nl.

MÄLK, Raul; Estonian diplomatist, economist and fmr journalist; *Special Diplomatic Representative for the Baltic Sea Region;* b. 14 May 1952, Parnu; ed Tartu Univ., Leningrad Inst. of Political Studies; economist and researcher, Inst. of Econs, Estonian Acad. of Sciences 1975–77; Sr Ed., Deputy Ed.-in-Chief, Ed.-in-Chief Estonian Radio 1977–90; Deputy Head Office of Chair. Supreme Soviet of Estonia 1990–92; Adviser to Minister of Foreign Affairs 1992–93; Head Office of Minister of Foreign Affairs 1993–94; Deputy Perm. Under-Sec. Ministry of Foreign Affairs 1994–96; Amb. to UK 1996–2001, also accred to Ireland 1996–2003 and to Portugal 2000–03; Minister of Foreign Affairs 1998–99; Head Estonian dels for negotiations with Russia, Finland, Latvia 1994–96; Dir-Gen. Policy Planning Dept, Ministry of Foreign Affairs 2001–07; Perm. Rep. of Estonia to EU 2007–11, Special Diplomatic Rep. for the Baltic Sea Region, Ministry of Foreign Affairs 2011–; Order of the White Star, Third Class (Estonia), also decorations from Portugal, Latvia, Malta and Poland; Estonian Journalists' Union Award 1990.

Leisure interests: theatre, music, attending sports events. *Address:* Ministry of Foreign Affairs, Islandi Square 1, 15049 Tallinn, Estonia (office). *Telephone:* 637-7000 (office). *Fax:* 637-7099 (office). *E-mail:* vminfo@mfa.ee (office). *Website:* www.vm.ee (office).

MALKIN, Evgeni Vladimirovich; Russian professional ice hockey player; b. 31 July 1986, Magnitogorsk, Chelyabinsk Oblast; s. of Vladimir Malkin and Tatiana Malkin; Russian Super League debut at age 17, 2003–04 season; first int. appearance with Russia at Int. Ice Hockey Fed. (IIHF) World Under-18 Championships, Yaroslavl 2003; played with Metallurg Magnitogorsk (Russian Super League) 2003–06, signed again for 2012–13 season; with Nat. Hockey League's Pittsburgh Penguins 2006–; mem. Team Russia, Winter Olympic Games, Turin 2006, Vancouver 2010; represented Russia at IIHF World Championships 2005, 2006, 2007, 2010, 2012; Nat. Hockey League awards include Calder Memorial Trophy (awarded to best rookie) 2006/07, Conn Smythe Trophy 2009, Art Ross Trophy 2009/10, 2011/12, Hart Memorial Trophy 2012, Kharlamov Trophy 2012; IIHF awards include Best Forward 2012, Most Valuable Player 2012. *Address:* c/ Pittsburgh Penguins, CONSOL Energy Center, 1001 Fifth Avenue, Pittsburgh, PA 15219, USA. *Website:* penguins.nhl.com.

MALKOVICH, John; American actor and producer; b. 9 Dec. 1953, Christopher, Ill.; s. of Dan Malkovich and Joe Anne Malkovich; m. Glenne Headley 1982 (divorced 1988); m. 2nd Nicoletta Peyran; one s. one d.; ed Eastern Illinois and Illinois State Univs; co-f. Steppenwolf Theatre, Chicago 1976; mem. Creative Bd of Dirs Artists Ind. Network; Co-founder Mr. Mudd (production co.) 1998; has directed three fashion shorts (Strap Hangings, Lady Behave, Hideous Man) for London-based designer Bella Freud; f. Mrs Mudd (clothing co.) 2002. *Theatre appearances include:* True West 1982, Death of a Salesman 1984, Burn This 1987; Dir Balm in Gilead 1984–85, Arms and the Man 1985, Coyote Ugly 1985, The Caretaker 1986, Burn This 1990, A Slip of the Tongue 1992, Libra 1994, Steppenwolf 1994. *Films include:* Places in the Heart 1984, The Killing Fields 1984, Eleni 1985, Making Mr. Right 1987, The Glass Menagerie 1987, Empire of the Sun 1987, Miles from Home 1988, The Accidental Tourist (exec. producer) 1988, Dangerous Liaisons 1989, Jane, La Putaine du roi 1989, Queen's Logic 1989, The Sheltering Sky 1989, The Object of Beauty 1991, Shadows and Fog 1992, Of Mice and Men 1992, Jennifer Eight, Alive, In the Line of Fire, Mary Reilly 1994, The Ogre 1995, Mulholland Falls 1996, Portrait of a Lady 1996, Con Air 1997, The Man in the Iron Mask 1997, Rounders 1998, Time Regained 1998, Being John Malkovich 1999, The Libertine 1999 (also dir), Ladies Room 1999, Joan of Arc 1999, Shadow of the Vampire 2000, Les Ames fortes 2001, Je Rentre à la Maison 2001, Hotel 2001, Knockaround Guys 2001, The Dancer Upstairs (dir and producer) 2002, Ripley's Game 2003, Johnny English 2003, Um Filme Falado 2003, The Libertine (also producer) 2004, The Hitchhiker's Guide to the Galaxy 2005, Colour Me Kubrick: A True...ish Story 2005, Art School Confidential (also producer) 2006, Klimt 2006, The Call 2006, Eragon 2006, Drunkboat 2007, In Tranzit 2008, Beowulf 2007, Gardens of the Night 2007, The Great Buck Howard 2008, Changeling 2008, The Mutant Chronicles 2008, Burn After Reading 2008, Disgrace 2008, Afterwards 2008, Jonah Hex 2010, Red 2010, Transformers: Dark of the Moon 2011. *Television includes:* Death of a Salesman 1985, RKO 281 1999, Les Misérables 2000, Napoleon (miniseries) 2002. *Address:* Mr. Mudd, 5225 Wilshire Boulevard, Suite 604, Los Angeles, CA 90036, USA; c/o Artists Independent Network, 32 Tavistock Street, London, WC2E 7PB, England (office). *Telephone:* (323) 932-5656 (Mr Mudd). *Fax:* (323) 932-5666 (Mr Mudd). *Website:* www.mrmudd.com.

MALLABY, Sir Christopher Leslie George, Kt, GCMG, GCVO, BA; British diplomatist and business executive; b. 7 July 1936, Camberley, Surrey, England; s. of Brig. A. W. S. Mallaby and M. C. Mallaby (née Jones); m. Pascale Thierry-Mieg 1961; one s. three d.; ed Eton Coll., King's Coll., Cambridge; diplomatic postings in Moscow 1961–63, Berlin 1966–69, New York 1974–74, Moscow 1974–77, Bonn 1982–85; Head of Arms Control, Soviet and E European and Planning Depts, FCO 1977–82; Deputy Sec. to Cabinet 1985–88; Amb. to FRG (now Germany) 1988–92, to France 1993–96; Man. Dir UBS Warburg (later UBS Investment Bank) 1996–2006; Chair. Primary Immunodeficiency Asscn 1996–2002, Advisory Bd Great Britain Centre, Humboldt Univ. Berlin 1998–2005, Advisory Bd German Studies Inst., Birmingham Univ. 1999–2006, European Org. for Research and Treatment of Cancer 2000–; Dir Charter European Investment Trust 1996–2007, Sun Life and Provincial Holdings PLC 1996–2000, EDF Trading 1999–2003, Vodafone Germany 2000–; Adviser to RMC 1996–2000, Herbert Smith 1997–2001; Trustee, Tate Gallery 1996–2002, Reuters (now Thomson-Reuters) 1998–; Founder Trustee, Entente Cordiale Scholarships 1996–2008 (Chair. 2001–08); Chair. Somerset House Trustees 2002–06; Hon. Fellow, GB Centre, Humboldt Univ. 2005; Dr hc (Univ. of Birmingham) 2004; Grand Cross, Order of Merit (Germany); Grand Officier, Légion d'honneur, Commdr, Ordre des Palmes académiques. *Leisure interests:* grandchildren. *E-mail:* christopher.mallaby@tiscali.co.uk (home).

MALLINCKRODT, Georg Wilhelm von; German banker; *President, Schroders PLC;* b. 19 Aug. 1930, Eichholz; s. of Arnold von Mallinckrodt and Valentine von Mallinckrodt (née von Joest); m. Charmaine Brenda Schroder 1958; two s. two d.; ed Schule Schloss Salem; with AGFA, Munich 1948–51; with Munchmeyer & Co., 1951–53; with Kleinwort & Co., London 1953–54; with J. Henry Schroder Bank Corp., NY 1954–55, 1957–, with J. Henry Schroder & Co. Ltd 1960, Dir Schroders PLC 1977, Chair. 1985–95, Pres. 1995–; Chair. J. Henry Schroder Bank AG, Zurich 1984–2003, Schroder Inc., NY 1984–; Dir Schroders Australia Holdings Ltd, Sydney 1984–2001, Schroder & Co. Inc., NY 1986–2000, Schroder Int. Merchant Bankers Ltd, Singapore 1988–2000, Siemens PLC 1989–2001; with Union Bank of Switzerland, Geneva 1956–57; Adviser, McGraw Hill 1986–89, Bain & Co.; Chair., Council of World Econ. Forum; Vice-Pres., German-British Chamber of Commerce, Trustee, Christian Responsibility in Public Affairs, Inst. of Business Ethics; Hon. DCL (Bishop's Univ., Québec) 1994, Hon. KBE 1997, Freeman of the City of London 2004; Cross of the Order of Merit 1990, Commdr's Cross, Order of Merit 2001, Kt Commdr, Order of St Gregory the Great 2012; Annual Sternberg Interfaith Award 2006. *Leisure interests:* opera, shooting. *Address:* Schroders PLC, 31 Gresham Street, London, EC2V 7QA, England (office). *Telephone:* (20) 7658-6370 (office). *Fax:* (20) 7658-2211 (office). *E-mail:* george.mallinckrodt@schroders.com (office). *Website:* www.schroders.com (office).

MALLOCH-BROWN, Baron (Life Peer), cr. 2007, of St Leonard's Forest in the County of West Sussex; **(George) Mark Malloch-Brown,** KCMG, MA, PC; British government minister, international organization official and fmr business executive; *Chairman of Global Affairs, FTI Consulting;* b. 16 Sept. 1953, London; m.; four c.; ed Magdalene Coll., Cambridge, Univ. of Michigan, USA; Political Corresp., Economist 1977–79; worked for UNHCR first in Thailand in charge of field operations for Cambodian refugees 1979–81, then in Geneva as Deputy Chief of Emergency Unit 1981–83; Founder Economist Devt Report 1983–86; lead int. partner, Sawyer Miller Group (communications management firm), advising govts political leaders and corpns 1986–94; mem. Soros Advisory Cttee on Bosnia and Herzegovina 1993–94; Dir of External Affairs, IBRD 1994–96, Vice-Pres. for External Affairs 1996–99, for UN Affairs 1996–99, Admin. UNDP 1999–2005, Chief of Staff in Exec. Office of UN Sec.-Gen. 2005–06, Deputy Sec.-Gen. April–Dec. 2006; Distinguished Visiting Fellow, Yale Center for the Study of Globalization 2007; Vice-Chair. Quantum Group of Funds (hedge fund group) 2007; Vice-Chair. Open Soc. Inst. 2007; Minister for Africa, Asia and UN 2007–09 (resgnd), also attended Cabinet; fmr Vice-Chair. World Econ. Forum, Davos, Switzerland; currently Chair. of Global Affairs, FTI Consulting, London; Adviser, SouthWest Energy (Ethiopia) 2010–; Chair. UN Devt Group; fmr Vice-Chair. Bd of Refugees Int., Washington, DC, USA; Dr hc (Michigan State) 2003, (Catholic Univ., Lima) 2004, (Pace Law School) 2005, (Walden Univ.) 2008; numerous awards including one of Time Magazine's 100 Most Influential People in the World 2005. *Publication:* The Unfinished Global Revolution. *Address:* FTI Consulting, 322 High Holborn, London, WC1V 7PB, England (office). *Telephone:* (20) 7979-7469 (office). *Fax:* (20) 3077-0599 (office). *E-mail:* camilla.decaires@fticonsulting.com (office). *Website:* www.fticonsulting.com (office).

MALLON, Séamus; Northern Irish politician, teacher and playwright; b. 17 Aug. 1936, Markethill, Co. Armagh, Northern Ireland; m.; one d.; ed Christian Bros; Grammar School, Newry, St Joseph's Coll. of Educ., Belfast; Chair. Social Democratic and Labour Party (SDLP) 1973–74, Deputy Leader 1979–2001; mem. Nat. Ass. 1973–74, Armagh Dist Councillor 1973–86; mem. Nat. Convention 1974–75; elected to Nat. Ass. 1982 but disqualified; mem. Irish Senate 1982, New Ireland Forum 1983–84, Forum for Peace and Reconciliation 1994–95, Nat. Forum and Talks 1996–98, British-Irish Inter-Parl. Body; MP, House of Commons for Newry and Armagh 1986–2005; mem. NI Ass. for Newry and Armagh 1998–2000; (Ass. suspended 11 Feb. 2000); Deputy First Minister (desig.) 1998–99, Deputy First Minister 1999–2000; Hon. LLD (Queen's Belfast) 1999, (NCEA) 2000, (Nat. Univ. Ireland) 2002. *Leisure interests:* golf, fishing, literature. *Address:* 5 Castleview, Markethill, Armagh, BT60 1QP, Northern Ireland (home). *Telephone:* (28) 3755-1411 (home).

MALLOY, Dannel Patrick (Dan), BA, LLB; American lawyer, politician and state governor; *Governor of Connecticut;* b. 21 July 1955, Stamford, Conn.; s. of William F. Malloy and Agnes Malloy (née Egan); m. Cathy Malloy 1982; three s.; ed Boston Coll. and Boston Coll. Law School; Asst Dist Attorney, Brooklyn, NY 1980–84; Partner, Abate & Fox law firm, Stamford 1984–95; mem. Stamford Bd of Finance 1983–94; Mayor of Stamford 1995–2009; Gov. of Connecticut 2011–; fmr Trustee and Vice-Chair. for Educ., Jobs, Educ. and Workforce Cttee, US Conf. of Mayors, Co-Chair. Small Business/Partner America Task Force; fmr mem. Mayors Against Illegal Guns Coalition; fmr mem. Exec. Cttee Democratic Nat. Cttee; fmr Pres. Conn. Conf. of Municipalities; Adjunct Prof., Univ. of Connecticut; mem. Bd of Trustees, Mitchell Coll., New London, Conn.; mem. ABA, Asscn of Trial Lawyers of America, Connecticut Trial Lawyers Assen, Connecticut Bar Assen, Nat. Trial Lawyers Assen; Democrat. *Address:* Executive Office of the Governor, State Capitol, 210 Capitol Avenue, Hartford CT 06106, USA (office); Washington Office of the Governor, State of Connecticut, 444 North Capitol Street, Suite 317, Washington, DC 20001, USA (office). *Telephone:* (860) 566-4840 (Hartford) (office); (202) 347-4535 (DC) (office). *Fax:* (860) 524-7395 (Hartford) (office); (202) 347-7151 (DC) (office). *Website:* www.governor.ct.gov (office); www.danmalloy.com.

MALLY, Komlan; Togolese politician; b. 12 Dec. 1960, Adiva; ed Ecole Nationale d'Administration, Univ. of Benin, Lomé; Prefect, Wawa Pref. 1996–99, Golfe Pref. 2002–06; mem. Parl. 2007–; Minister of Towns and Town Planning 2006–07; Prime Minister 2007–08 (resgnd); Minister of State and Minister of Health 2008–11; mem. Rassemblement du peuple togolais (RPT). *Address:* c/o Ministry of Health, rue Branly, BP 386, Lomé (office); Rassemblement du peuple togolais, place de l'Indépendance, BP 1208, Lomé, Togo (office).

MALLYA, Vijay, BCom; Indian business executive and fmr politician; *Chairman, United Breweries Group;* b. 18 Dec. 1955, Calcutta (now Kolkata); s. of the late Vittal Mallya and Lalitha Ramaiah; m. 1st Samira Mallya; m. 2nd Rekha Mallya; one s. two d.; ed La Martinière Boys Coll., St. Xavier's Coll., Univ. of Kolkata; fmrly with American Hoechst Corpn (now Aventis) USA, UK; Man. Brewing and Spirits Divs, United Breweries (UB) Group (mfr of Kingfisher Beer) 1980, Chair. 1983–; Founder and Chair. Kingfisher Airlines 2005–; Chair. Hoechst Marion Roussel India (Aventis), Aventis CropScience, Force India F1 Team, Royal Challengers Bangalore, East Bengal FC, Inst. of Econ. Studies of India, Fed. of Indian Chamber of Commerce and Industries, Motorsports Asscn of India; f. UBICS Inc. (software co.) 1993; f. Mallya Hospital, Bangalore; mem. Rajya Sabha (Parl.) for Karnataka 2002–08, 2010–; Nat. Working Pres. Janata Party; Officier, Légion d'honneur 2008; Dr hc (California Southern Univ.); Entrepreneur of the Year, Asian Awards 2010. *Leisure interests:* sports, yachting. *Address:* UB Group, UB Anchorage, 5th Floor, 100/1, Richmond Road, Bangalore 560 025, India (office). *E-mail:* cmo@ubmail.com (office). *Website:* www.theubgroup.com (office).

MALMSTRÖM, Cecilia, BA, PhD; Swedish academic, politician and international organization official; *Commissioner for Home Affairs, European Commission;* b. 15 May 1968, Stockholm; m.; two c.; ed Gothenburg Univ., Sorbonne, Paris; tech. asst and translator, SKF, Paris, Stuttgart, Barcelona 1986–89; psychiatric nurse, Lillhagen Hosp., Gothenburg 1989–92; social studies teacher, Lindholmen 1991–92; lay assessor, Gothenburg City Court 1991–94; Vice-Chair. Gothenburg Municipal Immigration Cttee 1994–98; Research Asst, Dept of Political Science, Gothenburg Univ. 1994–98, Sr Lecturer 1998–99; mem. Västra Götaland Regional Council 1998–2001; MEP 1999–2006, Vice-Chair. Dels to Hungary and Croatia Jt Parl. Cttees, served on Constitutional and Foreign Affairs cttees, Sub-cttee on Human Rights, substitute mem. Sub-cttee on Security and Defence 2004–06, Cttee on Internal Market and Consumer Protection 2004–06;

Minister for EU Affairs 2006–10; Commr for Home Affairs, EC, Brussels 2010–; mem. Liberal Party, mem. Bd 1997–, mem. Exec. 2001–. *Publications:* books and articles on European regionalism and politics, Spanish politics, terrorism and immigration. *Address:* European Commission, rue de la Loi 200, 1049 Brussels, Belgium (office). *Telephone:* (2) 299-11-11 (office). *Fax:* (2) 295-01-38 (office). *Website:* ec.europa.eu (office).

MALOFEEV, Anatoly Aleksandrovich; Belarusian politician; b. 14 May 1933, Gomel; one d.; ed Gomel Railway Coll., Belarus State Inst. of Nat. Econ., Higher Party School; worked as locksmith, Minsk, then Gomel and Minsk carriage repair plants 1949–62; mil. service; mem. CPSU 1954–91; various posts on CP cttees Gomel, at Dept of Chemical and Light Industries of Cen. Cttee of CP of Belarus, Chair. Gomel Regional Exec. Cttee of CP of Belarus, mem. Cen. CPSU Cttee 1986–91, Politburo 1990–91; USSR People's Deputy 1989–91; Deputy Supreme Soviet of Belorussia 1982–92; First Sec. Cen. Cttee of CP of Belorussia 1990–93; mem. Chamber of Reps 1996–2000, 2000–, Chair. 1997–2000; Chair. Parl. Comm. for Econ. Policies and Reforms 1996, Cttee on Int. Affairs and Ties with the CIS 2000–; Order Red Banner of Labour (twice), Award of the Fatherland (3rd degree) 1999, Hon. Charter of Council of Ministers, Hon. Charter of Nat. Ass. *Address:* Sovetskaya Str. 11, 220010 Minsk, Belarus (office). *Telephone:* (17) 222-63-98 (office); (17) 222-62-37 (office). *Fax:* (17) 222-6461 (office). *E-mail:* mizhn@house .gov.by (office).

MALONE, John C., BS, MS, PhD; American telecommunications industry executive; *Chairman, Liberty Media Corporation;* b. 7 March 1941, Milford, Conn.; m. Leslie Malone; ed Yale and Johns Hopkins Univs; fmr Pres. Jerrold Electronics Corpn; Pres. Tele-Communications Inc. (TCI), Denver 1973–96, Chair. and CEO (until merger with AT&T) 1996–99; mem. Bd Dirs and Chair. Liberty Media Corpn Denver 1999–, CEO Liberty Media International (formed by spinoff of Liberty Media's non-North American operations) 2004–, Chair. Liberty Global, Inc.; Chair. and CEO Discovery Holding Co.; Chair. The DIRECTV Group, Inc. 2008–; mem. Bd of Dirs Bank of New York, IAC/InterActiveCorp, Expedia, Inc.; mem. Bd of Dirs Nat. Cable TV Asscn (NCTA) 1974–77, 1980–93; Dr hc (Denver Univ.) 1992; NCTA Vanguard Award, TVC Magazine Man of the Year Award 1981, Wall Street Transcript's Gold Award for cable industry's best CEO 1982, 1985, 1986, 1987, Wall Street's Transcript Silver Award 1984, 1989, Women In Cable's Betsy Magness Fellowship Honoree, Univ. of Pennsylvania Wharton School Sol C. Snider Entrepreneurial Center Award of Merit for Distinguished Entrepreneurship, American Jewish Cttee Sherrill C. Corwin Human Relations Award, Communications Tech. Magazine Service and Tech. Award, Bronze Award 1993 Financial World CEO of the Year Competition, Hopkins Distinguished Alumnus Award 1994. *Address:* Liberty Media Corpn, 12300 Liberty Blvd, Englewood, CO 80112, USA (office). *Telephone:* (720) 875-5400 (office). *Fax:* (720) 875-7469 (office). *E-mail:* info@libertymedia.com (office); info@directv.com (office). *Website:* www .libertymedia.com (office); www.directv.com (office).

MALOSSE, Henri, DEA; French international organization official; *President, European Economic and Social Committee;* b. 6 Oct. 1954, Montpellier (Hérault); m.; one c.; ed Institut d'études politiques de Paris (Sciences Po), Diplomas from Univ of Munich, Germany and Univ of Warsaw, Poland; led French Chambers of Commerce and Industry Del. to EU 1979; cr. European Network of Euro Information Centres 1987; Founder and Pres. French Perm. Dels Circle (CDPF) bringing together 140 orgs represented in Brussels 1995–2003, Hon. mem. 2003–; mem. European Econ. and Social Cttee (EESC) Bureau 1995–, responsible for EESC's activities with cand. countries in connection with Convention on the Future of Europe 2001–03, Pres. ECO Section (Econ. and Monetary Union and Econ. and Social Cohesion) 2002–04, Pres. SOC Section (Employment, Social Affairs and Citizenship) 2004–06, Pres. Employers Group (Group I) 2006–13, Co-Pres. EU-Bulgaria Jt Cttee, Pres. EESC 2013–; Prof., Univ Kaunas Univ, Lituania, Wrocław Univ, Poland, Diplomatic Inst., Moscow, Russia; est. Masters/ DESS course on European Public Policies at Robert Schuman Univ, Strasbourg 1993; mem. Policy Bd Centre for European Studies, Strasbourg (CEES), École nat. d'admin, Strasbourg; mem. Steering Cttee Jean Monnet Asscn; Hon. Pres. Europe Defence Circle; Chevalier, Ordre nat. du Mérite. *Publications include:* Europe at Your Doorstep (l'Europe à votre porte), A Guide to EU Funding Mechanisms 1990, 1992, 1994, 1995, The European Institutions (Les institutions européennes) (with Pascal Fontaine) 1991, 1993, Towards a Greater Europe (Vers la Grande Europe 1996, Unifying the Greater Europe (Unifier la Grande Europe) (with Bernard Huchet) 2001, Europe from A to Z (with Pascal Fontaine) 2006, We Must Save the European Citizen! – A 'C plan' to a Citizen's Europe (Il faut sauver le citoyen européen ! – Un 'plan C' pour rendre l'Europe aux citoyens) (with Bruno Vever) 2008, Building Europe: The History and Future of a Europe of the People 2012. *Address:* European Economic and Social Committee, Rue Belliard 99, 1040 Brussels, Belgium (office). *Telephone:* (2) 546-8912 (Dir of Pres.'s Office) (office). *Fax:* (2) 513-48-93 (office). *E-mail:* PressEESC@eesc.europa.eu (office). *Website:* www.eesc.europa.eu/president (office).

MALOUF, David George Joseph, AO, BA; Australian writer and poet; b. 20 March 1934, Brisbane, Qld; s. of G. Malouf; ed Brisbane Grammar School and Univ. of Queensland; Hon. Fellow, Australian Acad. of the Humanities; Gold Medal, Australian Literature Soc. 1974, 1982, 2009, Age Book of the Year, NSW Premier's Award for Fiction, Vance Palmer Award, Pascal Prize, Commonwealth Writers' Prize and Prix Fémina Etranger, for The Great World 1991, inaugural IMPAC Dublin Literary Award 1993, Neustadt Int. Prize for Literature 2000, Criticos Prize 2010, many other awards. *Publications include:* poetry: Bicycle and other poems 1970, Neighbours in a Thicket 1974, First Things Last 1981, Selected Poems 1991, Poems 1959–89 1992, Typewriter Music 2007, Revolving Days: selected poems 2008; novels: Johnno 1975, An Imaginary Life 1978, Child's Play 1982, Fly Away Peter 1982, Harland's Half Acre 1984, 12 Edmondstone Street 1985, The Great World 1990, Remembering Babylon 1993, The Conversations at Curlow Creek 1996, Ransom 2009; short stories: Antipodes 1983, Dream Stuff 2000, Every Move You Make 2006, The Complete Stories 2007; play: Blood Relations 1987; opera librettos: Voss 1986, Mer de Glace 1991, Baa Baa Black Sheep 1993, Jane Eyre 2000. *Address:* c/o Rogers, Coleridge & White, 20 Powis Mews, London, W11 1JN, England (office); c/o Barbara Mobbs, 35A Sutherland Crescent, Darling Point, Sydney, NSW 2027 (office); 53 Myrtle Street, Chippen-

dale, NSW 2008, Australia (home). *Telephone:* (20) 7221-3717 (office). *Fax:* (20) 7229-9084 (office).

MALPAS, Sir Robert, Kt, CBE, BSc, FIMechE, FIChemE, FRSA; British business executive (retd); b. 9 Aug. 1927, Birkenhead, Merseyside, England; s. of the late Cheshyre Malpas and of Louise Marie Marcelle Boni; m. Joan Holloway; ed Taunton School, St George's Coll., Buenos Aires, Argentina, Univ. of Durham; joined ICI Ltd 1948, with ICI Europa, Brussels 1966–75, CEO ICI Europa Ltd 1973–75, Dir ICI 1975–78; Pres. Halcon Int. Inc., New York 1978–82; Man. Dir BP PLC 1983–89; Chair. Power Gen PLC 1989–90, Cookson Group PLC 1991–98; Dir (non-exec.) Bd BOC Group 1981–96, Eurotunnel 1987–2000 (Chair. 1996–98), Barings PLC 1989–95, Repsol SA (Spain) 1989–2002; mem. Advisory Bd SpecialChem Paris 1996–2000; Chair. Ferghana Pnrs 1998–2003, Evolution PLC 2000–05; Exec. Dir ENAGAS Spain 2002–06; fmr Chair. RL Capital; Pres. SCI 1988–89; Sr Vice-Pres. Royal Acad. of Eng 1989–92; Chair. LINK 1986–93, Natural Environment Research Council 1993–96; Hon. FRSC; Order of Civil Merit, Spain 1968; Hon. degrees from Loughborough, Newcastle, Surrey, Bath, Durham, Sheffield Hallam, Westminster Univs. *Leisure interests:* theatre, opera, reading, music, sports. *Address:* 2 Spencer Park, London, SW18 2SX, England (home). *Telephone:* (20) 8877-1147 (home). *Fax:* (20) 8877-1197 (office). *E-mail:* bobmalpas@aol.com (home).

MALTSEV, Col Gen. Leonid Semenovich, Cand. Sci., DrPolSci; Belarusian army general and government official; *State Secretary, Security Council of Belarus;* b. 29 Aug. 1949, Slonim Dist, Grodno Region; s. of Semen Danilovich Maltsev and Anna Vasilyevna Maltseva; m.; two s.; ed Minsk Suvorov Mil. High School, Belarus, Kiev Higher Combined Arms Command School, Ukraine, Frunze Mil. Acad., Moscow, Mil. Acad. of Gen. Staff of Russian Fed. Armed Forces, Moscow; commdr of platoon, co. and battalions in Grouping of Soviet Forces, Germany 1970s; Motorized Rifle Regt Deputy Commdr, Commdr, Chief of Staff, then Commdr of Motorized Rifle Div. in Far East Dist 1979–90; First Deputy Army Commdr in Belarus Armed Forces, 28th Arms Corps Commdr, Chief of Gen. Staff, First Deputy Minister of Defence then Minister of Defence of Repub. of Belarus 1992–96; First Deputy Chief, CIS Mil. Cooperation Coordination Staff 1997–2000; Deputy State Sec., Security Council of Belarus 2000–01, State Sec. 2009–; Minister of Defence 2001–09; Hon. Specialist of Ukraine; Hero Star, Order of Mil. Glory 2008, Order for Serving Motherland in USSR Armed Forces (Third Class) 1982, (Second Class) 1990, Order for Serving Motherland (First Class) 2003; 20 medals from USSR and Repub. of Belarus. *Publications:* four monographs, 25 scientific articles. *Address:* State Secretariat, Security Council of Belarus, K. Marx str. 38, Minsk, Belarus (office).

MALYSHEV, Andrey Borisovich, CandSocSci, CandEngSci; Russian nuclear engineer; b. 26 Sept. 1959, Moscow; m.; one d.; ed Moscow Power Eng Inst.; began career as engineer, Atomenergoproekt State Research and Devt Design Inst. 1982, apptd Dir-Gen. 1997; Deputy Minister, Ministry of Atomic Energy 2002–03; Head of Gosatomnadzor (State Atomic Inspection) of Russia (transformed into Fed. Nuclear Supervision Service 2004) 2003–06; Deputy Head, Fed. Agency for Nuclear Power 2006–07; mem. Man. Bd and Deputy Gen. Dir Russian State Corpn of Nanotechnologies (Rosnanotech) 2007–11, Deputy Chair. Man. Bd, JSC Rosnano (fmrly SC Rosnanotech) 2011–12; mem. Bd of Dirs, JSC Ruspolymet; Ind. Dir JSC RusHydro 2010–; Order of Honour 2005; Hon. Builder of Russia Award. *Publications:* reports, articles and conf. papers. *Leisure interest:* tennis. *Address:* RusHydro, 7 Malaya Dmitrovka Str., 127006 Moscow, Russia (office). *Telephone:* (495) 333-80-00 (office). *E-mail:* contact@rushydro.ru (office). *Website:* www.rushydro.ru (office).

MAŁYSZ, Adam Henryk; Polish fmr professional ski jumper; b. 3 Dec. 1977, Wisła; s. of Jan Małysz and Ewa Małysz; m. Izabela Polok 1997; one d.; ed Vocational School, Ustroń; coached by Heinz Kuttin (nat. coach) and by his uncle, Jan Szturc, Austria; debut for Poland in Czech Repub. 1994; World Champion, Normal Hill, Lahti, Finland 2001, runner-up, Large Hill 2001; Winner, World Cup in ski jumping 2001, 2002, 2003 (first ski jumper to win three consecutive overall World Cup titles); Four Ski-Jumps competition 2001; Winner, Polish Championships 2002; Silver and Bronze Medals, Olympic Games, Salt Lake City 2002; World Champion, Val di Fiemme, Italy 2003; Winner, Large Hill, World Cup: Lahti, 2003, Oslo, Norway 2003, Zakopane, Poland 2005, Harrachov, Czech Repub. 2005; Winner, Ski Flying, World Cup, Tauplitz, Austria 2005; Second Place, Large Hill, World Cup: Zakopane 2004, Titisee-Neustadt, Germany 2005, Innsbruck, Austria 2005; Third Place, Large Hill, Kuopio, Finland 2005; World Champion, Sapporo, Japan 2007; two Silver Medals, Olympic Games, Vancouver 2010; Bronze Medal, World Championships, Oslo 2011; announced retirement from competition 26 March 2011; mem. KS Wisla Ustronianka Ski Club, Wisla; Order of Polonia Restituta: Officer's Cross (4th Class) 2002, Commdr's Cross (3rd Class) 2007, Commdr's Cross with Star (2nd Class) 2010; Polish Sports Personality of the Year 2001, 2002, 2003, 2007. *Leisure interests:* football, cars. *Address:* ul. Kogpydło 59, 43-374 Wisła (office); c/o Polski Zwiazek Narciarski, ul. Mieszczanska 18/3, 30-313 Kraków, Poland. *Telephone:* (12) 260-99-70. *Fax:* (12) 269-71-12. *E-mail:* office@ pzn.pl. *Website:* www.pzn.pl.

MALYUTIN, Alexander; Russian journalist; b. 4 Feb. 1964, Novocherkassk, Rostov Oblast; ed AA Zhdanov State Univ., Leningrad, Mil. Acad. of Logistics and Transport; mil. service 1988–92; joined Kommersant publishing house 1992, initially as freelance, later joined staff, becoming Corresp., Special Corresp., Columnist; joined Russian edn of Forbes magazine 2003, Deputy Ed. 2011; First Deputy Chief Ed. Smart Money (business magazine) 2005–09; Ed.-in-Chief, Izvestiya (leading daily newspaper) 2011–12, Aug.–Dec. 2013; Co-founder Market.ru (internet portal). *Address:* c/o Izvestiya, 127994 Moscow, ul. Tverskaya 18/1, POB 4, Russia (office).

MAMATGELDIYEV, Maj.-Gen. Agageldy, MD; Turkmenistani army officer and politician; trained as physician; career in Turkmenistan Armed Forces, rank of Maj.-Gen.; fmr Head of Turkmen Border Guard Service; Minister of Defence 2003–09. *Address:* c/o Ministry of Defence, 744000 Aşgabat, ul. 1995 4, Turkmenistan.

MAMATSASHVILI, Teimuraz; Georgian engineer, economist and diplomatist; b. 10 Nov. 1942, Tbilisi; s. of David Mamatsashvili and Maria Robakidze; m. Irina Arkhangelskaya 1967; two d.; ed Georgian Ploytech. Inst., Tbilisi, Acad. of Foreign

Trade, Moscow; Sr Engineer, Inst. of Metrology, Tbilisi 1965–70; Sr Engineer, Trade Representation of USSR in Australia 1973–77; Sr Engineer, Deputy Dir, Dir Licensmash co. (part of Licensintorg Corpn), Moscow 1977–89; Trade Rep. to Tokyo, Japan 1989–92; Minister of Foreign Econ. Relations 1992–93; Amb. to UK 1995–2004, to Ireland 1998–2004; Perm. Rep. to Int. Maritime Org. 1995; Gov. EBRD 1996; two state Orders of USSR 1979, 1989. *Leisure interests:* hunting, video filming, gardening. *Address:* 4 Uznadze St., Appt. 31, Tbilisi, Georgia (home).

MAMBERTI, Archbishop Dominique François Joseph; French ecclesiastic and diplomatist; *Secretary for Relations with States, Roman Curia;* b. 7 March 1952, Marrakesh, Morocco; ordained priest 1981; traveled to Rome to study diplomacy at Pontifical Ecclesial Acad. 1984, joined Vatican diplomatic service 1986, has held posts in Algeria, Chile, UN, New York, Lebanon, has also worked in Secr. of State Section for Foreign Affairs, Apostolic Del. to Somalia 2002–04, Apostolic Nuncio (Amb.) to Sudan 2002–06, to Eritrea 2004–06, Sec. for Relations with States, Roman Curia 2006–; Titular Archbishop of Sagona 2002–. *Address:* Secretariat of State, Roman Curia, Palazzo Apostolico Vaticano, Citta del Vaticano 00120 Rome, Italy (office). *Telephone:* (06) 69883014 (office). *Fax:* (06) 69885364 (office). *E-mail:* vati032@relstat-segstat.va (office). *Website:* www.vatican.va/roman_curia/secretariat_state (office).

MAMEDOV, Etibar; Azerbaijani politician; *Chairman, National Independence Party (Istiklal);* led opposition movt against Popular Front of Azerbaijan (PFA); Founding Chair. Nat. Independence Party (Istiklal) 1992–; elected to Parl. 1995; cand. in Presidential elections 1998, 2003; formed new political alliance between Istiklal and Democratic Party of Azerbaijan to oppose Govt 2000. *Address:* National Independence Party (NIP–Milli Istiklal), Baku, Azadliq Avenue 179, Azerbaijan (office). *Website:* www.amip.info (office).

MAMEDOV, Georgiy Enverovich, PhD, CHisSc; Russian diplomatist; *Ambassador to Canada;* b. 9 Sept. 1947, Moscow; m.; one s. one d.; ed Moscow State Inst. of Int. Relations; researcher Inst. of USA and Canada 1970–77, mem. staff USSR Embassy in USA 1972–73, 1977–81, Sec., Counsellor, Deputy Chief, then Chief Dept of USA and Canada, USSR Ministry of Foreign Affairs 1981–91, Deputy Minister of Foreign Affairs of Russia 1991–2003; Amb. to Canada 2003–; mem. State Cttee on Defence Industry 1996–98. *Address:* Embassy of the Russian Federation, 285 Charlotte Street, Ottawa, ON K1N 8L5, Canada (office). *Telephone:* (613) 235-4341 (home). *Fax:* (613) 236-6342 (office). *E-mail:* rusemb@magma.ca (office). *Website:* (office).

MAMET, David Alan, BA; American playwright, screenwriter and director; b. 30 Nov. 1947, Chicago, Ill.; s. of Bernard Morris Mamet and Lenore June Mamet (née Silver); m. 1st Lindsay Crouse 1977 (divorced); m. 2nd Rebecca Pidgeon 1991; ed Goddard Coll.; Artist-in-Residence, Goddard Coll. 1971–73; Artistic Dir St Nicholas Theatre Co., Chicago 1973–75; Guest Lecturer, Univ. of Chicago 1975, 1979, New York Univ. 1981; Assoc. Artistic Dir Goodman Theatre, Chicago 1978; Assoc. Prof. of Film, Columbia Univ. 1988; Hon. DLitt (Dartmouth Coll.) 1996; Outer Critics Circle Award for contrib. to American theatre 1978, PEN/Laura Pels Foundation Award for Drama 2010. *Films directed:* House of Games 1986, Things Change 1987, Homicide 1991, Oleanna 1994, The Spanish Prisoner 1997, The Winslow Boy 1999, Catastrophe 2000, State and Main 2000, Heist 2001, Spartan 2004, Redbelt 2008. *Films written include:* The Postman Always Rings Twice 1981, The Verdict 1982, About Last Night 1986, The Untouchables 1987, House of Games 1987, Things Change 1988, We're No Angels 1989, Homicide 1991, Glengarry Glen Ross 1992, Hoffa 1992, Oleanna 1994, American Buffalo 1996, The Edge 1997, The Spanish Prisoner 1997, Wag the Dog 1997, Ronin 1998, State and Main 2000, Hannibal 2001, Heist 2001, Spartan 2004, Edmond 2005, Redbelt 2008. *Works include:* The Duck Variations 1971, Sexual Perversity in Chicago 1973 (Village Voice Obie Award 1976), The Reunion 1973, Squirrels 1974, American Buffalo (Village Voice Obie Award 1976) 1976, (New York Drama Critics Circle Award 1977), A Life in the Theatre 1976, The Water Engine 1976, The Woods 1977, Lone Canoe 1978, Prairie du Chien 1978, Lakeboat 1980, Donny March 1981, Edmond 1982 (Village Voice Obie Award 1983), The Disappearance of the Jews 1983, The Shawl 1985, Glengarry Glen Ross (Pulitzer Prize for Drama, New York Drama Critics Circle Award) 1984, Speed-the-Plow 1987, Bobby, Gould in Hell 1989, The Old Neighborhood 1991, Oleanna 1992, Ricky Jay and his 52 Assistants 1994, The Village (novel) 1994, Death Defying Acts 1996, Boston Marriage 1999, The Wicked Son 2006, Race 2009; screenplays: The Postman Always Rings Twice 1979, The Verdict 1980, The Untouchables 1986, House of Games 1986, Things Change (with Shel Silverstein) 1987, We're No Angels 1987, A Life in the Theatre (also dir) 1989, Oh Hell! 1991, Homicide 1991, Hoffa 1991, Glengarry Glen Ross 1992, The Rising Sun 1992, Oleanna 1994, The Edge 1996, The Spanish Prisoner 1996, Wag the Dog 1997, State and Main 2000, The Winslow Boy 1999, Boston Marriage 2001, Heist 2001, Hannibal 2001, Spartan 2004; children's books: Mr Warm and Cold 1985, The Owl (with Lindsay Crouse) 1987, The Winslow Boy 1999; essays: Writing in Restaurants 1986, Some Freaks 1989, On Directing Film 1990, The Hero Pony 1990, The Cabin 1992, A Whore's Profession (also screenplay adaptation) 1993, The Cryptogram 1994, Passover 1995, Make-Believe Town: Essays and Remembrances 1996, Plays 1996, Plays 2 1996, The Duck and the Goat 1996, The Old Religion 1996, True and False 1996, The Old Neighborhood 1998, Jafsie and John Henry 2000, Bambi vs Godzilla (non-fiction) 2007, The Secret Knowledge: On the Dismantling of American Culture 2012; Three Stories (fiction) 2013. *Address:* c/o ICM Partners, 10250 Constellation Boulevard, Los Angeles, CA 90067 (office); Abrams Artists Agency, 275 Seventh Avenue, 25th Floor, New York, NY 10001, USA (office). *E-mail:* vincent.devito@abramsart.com (office). *Website:* www.abramsartists.com (office).

MAMI, Cheb; Algerian rai singer, songwriter and actor; b. (Mohamed Khélifati), 11 July 1966, Graba-el-Oved, Saïda; signed to Disco Maghreb, after winning second prize in Ihan wa chabab contest on the radio 1982; numerous live performances at rai festivals, tours worldwide; military service, Algeria 1987–89; collaborations with Sting, K-Mel, Gordon Cyrus, Simon Law; imprisoned 2010, released 2011; World Music Award for Best Selling Arabic Artist 2007. *Recordings include:* albums: Douni El Bladi 1986, Prince Of Rai 1989, Let Me Rai 1990, Fatma Fatma, Saida 1994, Let Me Cry 1995, Douni El Bladi 1996, 100% Arabica (with Cheb Khaled) 1997, Meli Meli 1999, Dellali 2001, Lazrag Saani 2001, Du Sud au Nord 2004, Layali 2006. *Films include:* Automne... Octobre à Alger 1993, 100%

Arabica 1997. *Address:* c/o EMI Music France, 118 rue du Mont Cenis, 75891 Paris, Cedex 18, France.

MAMI, Kayrat Abdrazakovich; Kazakhstani lawyer and politician; *Chairman of the Senate;* b. 9 May 1954, Zhambyl dist, Alma-Ata Region; m.; three c.; ed Law Faculty of Kazakh State Univ.; held posts of Deputy Justice Minister, Deputy Head of the Presidential Admin and Chair. of the Supreme Court; Prosecutor Gen. of Kazakhstan 2009–11; Chair. of the Senate 2011–. *Address:* Office of the Chairman, Senat, Parliament House, 010000 Astana, Abay d-ly 33, Kazakhstan (office). *Telephone:* (7172) 15-33-76 (office). *Fax:* (7172) 33-31-18 (office). *E-mail:* smimazh@parlam.kz (office). *Website:* www.parlam.kz (office).

MÄMMÄDYAROV, Elmar Mähärräm oğlu, PhD; Azerbaijani diplomatist; *Minister of Foreign Affairs;* b. 2 July 1960, Baku; m.; two s.; ed Kyiv State Univ. School of Int. Relations and Int. Law, Ukrainian SSR, USSR Diplomatic Acad., Exchange Scholar at Center for Foreign Policy Devt, Brown Univ., USA; Second Sec. then First Sec., Ministry of Foreign Affairs 1982–88; Dir Div. of State Protocol 1991–92; First Sec. Perm. Mission to UN, New York 1992–95; Deputy Dir Dept of Int. Orgs, Ministry of Foreign Affairs 1995–98; Counsellor, Embassy in Washington, DC 1998–2003; Amb. to Italy 2003–04; Minister of Foreign Affairs 2004–. *Address:* Ministry of Foreign Affairs, 1009 Baku, S. Qurbanov küç. 4, Azerbaijan (office). *Telephone:* (12) 596-90-00 (office). *Fax:* (12) 498-84-80 (office); (12) 596-90-01 (office). *E-mail:* katiblik@mfa.gov.az (office); press-service@mfa.gov.az (office). *Website:* www.mfa.gov.az (office).

MAMUT, Alexander Leonidovich; Russian lawyer and business executive; b. 29 Jan. 1960, Moscow; s. of Leonid Mamut; widowed; three c.; ed Moscow State Univ.; lawyer 1985–; Founder and Head ALM Consulting Co. 1990–; business activities 1989–; Founder and mem. Bd of Dirs Bank Imperial 1990–; Founder and Chair. Exec. Bd Co. on Project Financing 1993–, later Jt Stock Interbanking Credit Org. Co. for Project Financing (COPF) 1996–2000; Chair. Troika-Dialog; mem. Council on Industrial Policy and Business of Russian Govt from 1994; adviser to Head of Admin. Russian Presidency from 1998; mem. Bd of Dirs Sobinbank 1999; mem. Observation Council Bank Moskovsky Delovoy Mir MDM-Bank from 1999, Chair. 1999–2001; bought LiveJournal (Russia's most popular blogging platform) 2007; bought UK bookshop chain Waterstone's 2011; sold stake in mobile phone chain Evroset to Alisher Usmanov and cellular operator Megafon 2012, gained stake in Internet co. SUP Media; merged SUP with another Internet co., Afisha-Rambler, owned by Vladimir Potanin to form Afisha-Rambler-SUP 2013, also owns Russian news sites Lenta.ru and Gazeta.ru; holds substantial stake in precious metals co. Polymetal; sold half his stake in fertilizer giant Uralkali 2013, and his stake in industrial warehouse real estate co. Multinational Logistic Partnership (MLP) 2013; bought stake in homebuilder PIK Group 2013; Co-founder Strelka Inst. for Media, Architecture and Design. *E-mail:* press@livejournalinc.com.

MANABE, Syukuro (Suki), BA, MA, DSc; American (b. Japanese) meteorologist and academic; *Senior Meteorologist, Atmospheric and Oceanic Science Program, Princeton University;* b. 21 Sept. 1931, Shingu, Shikoku-Chuo-Shi, Ehime Pref., Japan; s. of Seiichi Manabe and Sueko Manabe (née Akashi); m. Nobuko Nakamura 1962; two d.; ed Tokyo Univ., Japan; entered USA 1958, naturalized 1975; Research Meteorologist, Gen. Circulation Research Section, US Weather Bureau, Washington, DC 1958–63; Sr Research Meteorologist, Geophysical Fluid Dynamics Lab., Environmental Science Services Admin., Washington, DC 1963–68, Nat. Oceanic and Atmospheric Admin., Princeton, NJ 1968–97, mem. Sr Exec. Service, USA 1979–96, Sr Scientist 1996–97; Dir Global Warming Research Program, Frontier Research System for Global Change 1997–2001; Lecturer with rank of Prof., Atmospheric and Oceanic Sciences Program, Princeton Univ. 1968–1997; Visiting Research Collaborator, Atmospheric and Oceanic Science Program, Princeton Univ. 2002–03, Sr Meteorologist 2005–; Consultant, Japan Marine-Earth Science Tech. Org., Japan 2002–09; mem. NAS 1990; Foreign mem. Academia Europaea 1994, RSC 1995, Japan Acad. 2009; Fellow, American Geophysical Union 1967, AAAS 1997; Hon. mem. American Meteorological Soc. 1997, Japan Meteorological Soc. 2000, Royal Meteorological Soc. 2006; Hon. DS (McGill Univ.) 2004; Fujiwara Award, Japan Meteorological Soc. 1966, Meisinger Award, American Meteorological Soc. 1967 (2nd Half Century Award 1977, Rossby Research Medal 1992), Blue Planet Prize, Asahi Glass Foundation 1992, Revelle Medal, American Geophysical Union 1993 (Bowie Medal 2010), Asahi Prize (Asahi Shimbun Cultural Foundation) 1995, Volvo Environmental Prize, Volvo Environmental Foundation 1997, Milankovitch Medal, European Geophysical Soc. 1998, inducted into Earth Hall of Fame, Kyoto 2009 and many other awards. *Achievement:* pioneered prediction of global warming using computer simulations. *Publications:* more than 140 papers in scientific journals. *Leisure interests:* swimming, yoga. *Address:* Program in Atmospheric and Oceanic Sciences, Princeton University, 107 Sayre Hall, 300 Forrestal Road, Princeton, NJ 08540 (office); 6 Governors Lane, Princeton, NJ 08540-3666, USA (home). *Telephone:* (609) 258-2790 (office); (609) 924-0734 (home). *Fax:* (609) 258-2850 (office). *E-mail:* manabe@princeton.edu (office). *Website:* www.aos.princeton.edu (office).

MANAEV, Oleg T., MA, PhD; Belarusian research institute director and professor of media and communications studies; *Professor, Department of Media and Communication, European Humanities University;* b. 3 Feb. 1952, Vladivostok, USSR; ed Belarusian State Univ.; Jr Research Fellow, Scientific Centre for Sociological Research, Belarusian State Univ. 1976–78, Sr Research Fellow 1978–84, Head of Div. 1984–88, Prof., Dept of Sociology 1992–99, Founder and Prof., Dept of Social Communication 1999–2012; Visiting Prof., Slavic Research Centre, Hokkaido Univ., Japan June–Oct. 2013; Founding Dir Ind. Inst. of Socio-Econ. and Political Studies 1992–; Founding Chair. Belarusian Asscn of Think-Tanks (BTT), also Ed. BTT Analytical Bulletin; Chair. Belarusian Soros Foundation 1993–95; Fullbright Visiting Prof., Univ. of Southern California 2001; Prof., Dept of Media and Communication, European Humanities Univ., Vilnius, Lithuania 2012–; Visiting Lecturer and Fellow at univs and insts in USA, Canada, Brazil, UK, France, Sweden and Germany; dir several nat. and int. projects for UNESCO, OSCE, MacArthur Foundation, Westminster Foundation; Corresp. Ed. European Journal of Communication, London, Political Communication, Durham, NC; mem. International Assn for Media and Communications Research, World Assn for Public Opinion Research, American Political Science Assn; Scholar Rescue Fund Award, Inst. of Int. Educ., USA 2007. *Publications:* 20 authored and edited books, including: Effectiveness of Mass Media (co-ed.) 1981, Youth and the Democratization of Soviet Society (co-ed.) 1990, Interaction of Media, Public and Power in the Democratization Process (co-ed.) 1991, Media in Transition: From Totalitarianism to Democracy (co-ed.) 1993, Emerging Civil Society in Independent Belarus. Sociological Experience: 1991–2000 2000, Belarus on the Way to the Third Millennium (co-ed.) 2001, Mass Media in Belarus 2003, Independent Research in Independent Belarus: Fighting for Reality (ed.) 2004, Emerging Civil Society in Independent Belarus. Sociological Experience: 2001–2005 2005, Presidential Elections in Belarus: From Limited Democracy to Unlimited Authoritarianism (1994–2006) (ed.) 2006, Belarus and 'Wider Europe': Quest for Geopolitical Self-Identification (ed.) 2007, Emerging Civil Society in Independent Belarus. Sociological Experience: 2006–2010 2011, Youth and Civil Society in Belarus: New Generation 2011, Future of Belarus. Views of Independent Experts (ed) 2012; more than 200 scholarly articles and chapters in books. *Leisure interests:* sea travels, fishing. *Address:* Department of Media and Communication, European Humanities University, Valakupiu g. 5, Vilnius 10101, Lithuania (office). *Telephone:* (5) 274-0622 (office). *E-mail:* oleg.manaev@ehu.lt (office). *Website:* www.ehu.lt (office); www.iiseps.org (office).

MANAGADZE, Irakli; Georgian economist and fmr central banker; *Senior Policy Adviser, Financial Institutions Group, European Bank for Reconstruction and Development;* b. 27 Oct. 1967, Tbilisi; s. of Nodar Managadze and Manana Janelidze; m. Nino Simonia; one d.; ed State Univ., Tbilisi; Attaché, Ministry of Foreign Affairs 1991–92, Sr. Specialist, State Cttee. of External Econ. Relations 1992–93; Chief State Adviser, Econ. and Political Reform Comms., Georgian Cabinet of Ministers 1993–94; Asst. Exec. Dir. World Bank 1994–96, Institutional Specialist, Municipal and Social Infrastructure Div., European Dept. IV 1996–98; Pres. and Chair. Bd., Nat. Bank of Georgia 1998–2005; currently Sr Policy Adviser, Financial Institutions Group, EBRD. *Address:* European Bank for Reconstruction and Development, One Exchange Square, London, EC2A 2JN England (office). *Telephone:* (20) 7338-6000 (office). *Fax:* (20) 7338-6100 (office). *E-mail:* generalenquiries@ebrd.com (office). *Website:* www.ebrd.com (office).

MANANDHAR, Krishna Bahadur, MA; Nepalese fmr central banker; ed Tribhuvan Univ., Univ. of Manchester, UK; Research Officer, Centre for Econ. Devt and Admin, Kathmandu 1973; Section Officer, Planning Comm. 1973–74; served as Asst Research Officer, Nepal Rastra Bank (cen. bank), fmr Asst Controller, later Deputy Chief Controller, Exec. Dir Foreign Exchange Dept c. 2003, Deputy Gov. –2007, 2009–10, Chair., Acting Gov. and Chair. Man. Cttee 2007–09; mem. Bd of Dirs Rastriya Banijya Bank 1998–99, Nepal Arab Bank (now Nabil Bank Ltd) 1999–; Trustee and mem. Senate, Kathmandu Univ. *Address:* c/o Board of Directors, Nabil Bank Limited, Beena Marga, Durbar Marg, Kathmandu, Nepal.

MANANI MAGAYA, Gen. (retd) Alison; South Sudanese politician; b. W Equatoria; Minister of Labour, Khartoum 2002; Minister of Labour and Human Resources in Govt of Nat. Unity (under interim constitution) 2005; mem. Nat. Congress Party 1989–2010; joined Sudan People's Liberation Movt 2010; Minister of the Interior (first following independence 9 July 2011) 2011–13. *Address:* c/o Ministry of the Interior, Juba, South Sudan.

MANASIEVSKI, Jovan; Macedonian politician; *Chairman, Liberal-Democratic Party (Liberalno-Demokratska Partija);* b. 21 May 1968, Gostivar; ed Skopje Univ., St Cyril and Methodius; Counsellor to Mayor of Skopje, responsible for Communications and Co-ordination of Int. Co-operation 1997–2002; mem. Parl. 2002–, Minister of Labour and Social Policy 2004, Deputy Prime Minister and Minister of Defence –2006; mem. Liberal-Democratic Party (Liberalno-Demokratska Partija), Chair. 2006–. *Address:* Liberal-Democratic Party (Liberalno-Demokratska Partija), 1000 Skopje, Partizanski odredi 89, Macedonia (office). *Telephone:* (2) 3063675 (office). *E-mail:* contact@ldp.org.mk (office). *Website:* www.ldp.org.mk (office).

MANASSEH, Leonard Sulla, OBE, RA, AADipl, FRIBA, FCSD; British architect; b. 21 May 1916, Singapore; s. of the late Alan Manasseh and Esther Manasseh (née Elias); m. 1st 1947 (divorced 1956); two s.; m. 2nd Sarah Delaforce 1957; two s. one d. (deceased); ed Cheltenham Coll., The Architectural Asscn School of Architecture; Asst Architect, CREN London and Guy Morgan & Partners; teaching staff, Architectural Asscn and Kingston School of Art 1941–43; served Fleet Air Arm 1943–46; Asst Architect, Herts. County Council 1946–48; Sr Architect, Stevenage New Town Devt Corpn 1948–50; partner, Leonard Manasseh and Partners 1950–; teaching staff, Architectural Asscn 1951–59; opened office in Singapore and Malaysia with James Cubitt & Partners 1953–54; mem. Council, Architectural Asscn 1959–66, Pres. 1964–65, Council of Industrial Design 1965–68, Council RIBA 1968–70, 1976–82 (Hon. Sec. 1979–81), Council, Nat. Trust 1977–91, Ancient Monuments Bd 1978–84, Bd, Chatham Historic Dockyard Trust 1984–97; Pres. Franco-British Union of Architects 1978–79; RA Rep. Bd of Govs Dulwich Schools Foundation 1987–95; Surveyor to Dulwich Picture Gallery 1987–94, Chair. 1988–93; Pres. Royal West of England Acad. 1989–94; Past Pres. Royal Watercolour Asscn. *Radio:* The Reunion (BBC Radio 4 Festival of Britain) 2003. *Publications:* Office Buildings (with 3rd Baron Cunliffe) 1962, Snowdon Summit Report (Countryside Comm.) 1974, Eastbourne Harbour Study (Trustees, Chatsworth Settlement) 1976, Leonard Manasseh and Partners: 20th Century Architects 2011; planning reports and studies. *Leisure interests:* photography, travel, painting, watching aeroplanes, being optimistic. *Address:* 6 Bacon's Lane, Highgate, London, N6 6BL, England. *Telephone:* (20) 8340-5528. *Fax:* (20) 8347-6313.

MANAWI, Fazal Ahmad, MA; Afghan civil servant; *Chairman, Independent Election Commission of Afghanistan;* ed Islam Abad Int. Univ.; positions held include Deputy of Islamic Educ., Ministry of Educ., Instructor in Alberoni Univ., Deputy of Educ. in interlude of Resistance, Deputy Minister, Ministry of Educ., Deputy of Supreme Court, Deputy for Afghanistan's Scholars Council; has taken part in Jt Peace Jirga; currently Chair. Ind. Election Comm.; has participated in numerous nat. and int. seminars; *Website:* www.iec.org.af/eng.

MANCEL, Jean-François; French politician; b. 1948; s. of Michel Mancel and Renée Baque; six c.; ed Faculté de droit et Inst d'études politiques, École nationale d'administration, Paris; Pres. Conseil Général, Oise; Pres. Oise Departmental Ass. 1985–2004; Deputy to Nat. Ass. 1978– (RPR 1978–2002, UMP 2002–); mem.

Conseil Municipal of Beauvais 1977–89, of Novillers 1995–2001; Conseiller Général de L'Oise 1979–2004; Sec.-Gen. RPR 1995–97; mem. European Parl. 1984–86. *Leisure interests:* skiing, tennis. *Address:* Conseil Général de l'Oise, 1 rue Cambry, BP 941, 60024 Beauvais; Rassemblement pour la République, 123 rue de Lille, 75007 Paris, France. *Telephone:* 3-44-06-60-67 (office). *Fax:* 3-44-06-63-01 (office). *E-mail:* jfmancel@assemblee-nationale.fr (office).

MANCHAM, Sir James Richard Marie, Kt, FRSA; British politician, lawyer and international consultant; *Director, Mahé Publications Limited;* b. 11 Aug. 1939, Victoria, Mahé, Seychelles; s. of the late Richard and Evelyne (née Tirant) Mancham; m. 1st Heather Jean Evans 1963 (divorced 1974); one s. one d.; m. 2nd Catherine Olsen 1985; one s.; ed Univ. of Paris and Middle Temple, London; called to the Bar, Middle Temple 1961; mem. Legis. Council of the Seychelles 1961; mem. Govt Council 1967; Founder and Leader, SDP 1964, revived 1992–; mem. Legis. Ass. 1970–76, of Nat. Ass. 1976–77; Chief Minister 1970–75, Prime Minister 1975–76; Pres. of the Republic of Seychelles 1976–77 (deposed by coup); int. trade consultant 1981–; Chair. Mahé Publications Ltd 1984– (Dir 1993–), Airominor Ltd 1987–; Pres. Berlin-European Airways 1988–90; Founder and Chair. Crusade for the Restoration of Democracy in Seychelles 1990–; Leader of the Opposition, Pres. Democratic Party 1992–; Lecturer in Geopolitics of the Indian Ocean, Int. Univ. of Japan 1996; Hon. KBE 1976; Officier, Légion d'honneur, Grand Chevalier La Chaire de Rôtisseur and numerous medals and decorations; Int. Jurists Award for Contrib. to World Peace 2010. *Publications:* Reflections and Echoes from the Seychelles, Paradise Raped 1983, Galloo: The Undiscovered Paradise 1984, New York's Robin Island 1985, Peace of Mind 1989, Adages of An Exile 1991, Oh, Mighty America 1998, Who's Who in Seychelles 1999, Images of Yesterday 2001, Tel est mon destin – Je fais mon chemin 2003, The Future of Peace in the 21st Century 2010. *Leisure interests:* travel, water sports, tennis, writing. *Address:* PO Box 29, Mahé (office); Glacis-sur-Mer, Mahé, Seychelles (home). *Telephone:* 241717 (office); 241881 (home). *Fax:* 241545. *E-mail:* surmer@seychelles.net. *Website:* www.jamesmancham.com.

MANCHIN, Joseph (Joe), III, BS; American politician and business executive; *Senator from West Virginia;* b. 24 Aug. 1947, Farmington, Marion Co., W Va; s. of John Manchin and Mary Manchin (née Gouzd); m. Gayle Conelly 1967; one s. two d.; ed Farmington High School, West Virginia Univ.; Operator Manchin's Carpet Center, Marion Co. (chain of family-owned retail stores) 1970; Dir Enersystems –2004; elected to State House of Dels 1982, 1984, to State Senate 1986, 1988, 1992; unsuccessful cand. for Democratic gubernatorial nomination 1996; Sec. of State for W Va 2001–05; Gov. of W Va 2005–10; Senator from West Virginia 2010–, mem. Armed Services Cttee, Energy and Natural Resources Cttee, Select Cttee Aging; Chair. Nat. Govs Asscn 2010; mem. Nat. Rifle Asscn; Democrat; hon. degrees from Wheeling Jesuit Univ. 2006, Davis & Elkins Coll. 2010. *Leisure interests:* licensed pilot, the outdoors, hunting, angling, motorcycling. *Address:* 303 Hart Senate Office Building, Washington, DC 20510 (office); 300 Virginia Street East, Suite 2630, Charleston, WV 25301, USA (office). *Telephone:* (202) 224-3954 (DC) (office); (304) 342-5855 (Charleston) (office). *Fax:* (202) 228-0002 (DC) (office); (304) 343-7144 (Charleston) (office). *Website:* manchin.senate.gov (office).

MANCINI, Ange; French government official; Prefect of French Guiana 2002–06, of Martinique 2007–. *Address:* Préfecture, 82 rue Victor Sévère, BP 647–648, 97262 Fort-de-France Cédex, Martinique (office). *Telephone:* 5-96-39-36-00 (office). *Fax:* 5-96-71-40-29 (office). *E-mail:* contact.prefecture@martinique.pref.gouv.fr (office). *Website:* www.martinique.pref.gouv.fr (office).

MANCINO, Nicola; Italian politician and lawyer; b. 15 Oct. 1931, Montefalcione, Avellino; fmr communal, prov. and regional councillor, Chair. Campania Regional Exec. Council (twice), Christian Democrat (DC) Prov. Sec., Avellino, Regional Sec. Campania; elected Senator from Avellino 1976, 1979, 1983, 1987; Chair. DC Parl. Group 1984; Minister of Interior 1992–94, Pres. of Senate 1996–2001; Vice-Pres. Consiglio Superiore della Magistratura (Magistrates' Governing Body) 2006–. *Address:* Consiglio Superiore della Magistratura, Piazza Indipendenza 6, 00185 Rome, Italy (office). *Telephone:* (6) 444911 (office). *Fax:* (6) 4457175 (office). *E-mail:* seg-seggen@cosmag.it (office). *Website:* www.csm.it (office).

MANCUSO, Frank G.; American film industry executive; b. 25 July 1933, Buffalo, NY; m. Fay Mancuso; one s. one d.; ed State Univ. of NY; joined Paramount Pictures Corpn, Buffalo, NY 1962, Vice-Pres. and Gen. Sales Man. Paramount Pictures Corpn of Canada Ltd, Toronto 1970–72, Pres. and subsequently head of Paramount's Western Div., Los Angeles 1972–76, Vice-Pres., Gen. Sales Man., Paramount's Motion Picture Div., New York 1976–78, Sr Vice-Pres. 1978–79, Exec. Vice-Pres. in charge of Distribution and Marketing 1979–80, Pres. Paramount Distribution 1980–83, Pres. Motion Picture Group of Paramount Pictures Corpn 1983–84, Chair. and CEO Paramount Pictures Corpn 1984–91; Chair. and CEO MGM 1993–99; consultant, Santa Monica, Calif. 1999–; Chair. Motion Picture and Television Fund Corp. Bd of Dirs; Vice-Pres. Variety Clubs International and of Motion Picture Pioneers; Chair. Will Rogers Memorial Fund; Dir New York-Cornell Medical Center, Burke Rehabilitation Center, UCLA Medical Center, Museum of Broadcasting, Acad. of Motion Picture Arts and Sciences, Motion Picture Asscn and other orgs; Sherrill G. Corwin Human Relations Award, American Jewish Cttee 1985, received a star on the Italian Walk of Fame in Toronto, Canada 2010. *Address:* Motion Picture & Television Fund, The Wasserman Campus, 23388 Mulholland Drive, Woodland Hills, CA 91364, USA. *E-mail:* info@mptf.com. *Website:* www.mptf.com.

MANDAL, Badri Prasad; Nepalese politician; Deputy Prime Minister, Minister of Home Affairs, of Agric. and of Co-operatives and Local Devt 2002–03; Ministry of Forests and Soil Conservation Feb.–July 2005, of Agric. and Co-operatives July 2005–06; mem. Nepali Sadbhavana Party (NSP), Acting Pres. 2002, now leader of Mandal faction. *Address:* Nepali Sadbhavana Party (NSP) (Nepal Goodwill Party), Shantinagar, New Baneshwor, Kathmandu, Nepal (office). *Telephone:* (1) 4488068 (office). *Fax:* (1) 4470797 (office).

MANDELSON, Baron (Life Peer), cr. 2008, of Foy in the County of Herefordshire and Hartlepool in the County of Durham; **Rt Hon. Peter Benjamin Mandelson,** PC; British politician; b. 21 Oct. 1953, London, England; s. of the late George Mandelson and of Mary Mandelson (née Morrison); ed Hendon County Grammar School, St Catherine's Coll., Oxford; joined TUC Econ. Dept 1977–78; Chair. British Youth Council 1978–80; mem. Council, London Borough of Lambeth

1979–82; Producer, London Weekend TV 1982–85; Dir of Campaigns and Communications, Labour Party 1985–90; MP for Hartlepool 1992–2004; an Opposition Whip 1994–97, Shadow Frontbench Spokesman on Civil Service 1995–96, Dir Tony Blair's election campaign 1997; Minister without Portfolio 1997–98; Sec. of State for Trade and Industry July–Dec. 1998, for NI 1999–2001, for Business, Enterprise and Regulatory Reform 2008–10, First Sec. of State and Lord Pres. of the Council 2009–10; EU Commr for Trade 2004–08; Chair. Global Counsel LLP (consultancy) 2010–; Sr Adviser, Lazard Ltd (int. financial advisory firm) 2011–; Chair. UK-Japan 21st Century Group 2001–04; industrial consultant, SRU Group 1990–92; mem. Int. Advisory Cttee Centre for European Policy Studies 1993–; Pres. Hartlepool United Football Club. *Publications:* Youth Unemployment: Causes and Cures 1977, Broadcasting and Youth 1980, The Blair Revolution: Can New Labour Deliver? 1996, Pro-Europe, Pro-Reform: A Progressive Vision of the EU 2001, The European Union in the Global Age 2007, The Third Man (memoirs) 2010. *Leisure interests:* country walking, swimming, reading. *Address:* House of Lords, Westminster, London, SW1A 0PW, England (office). *Telephone:* (20) 7219-4893 (office). *E-mail:* info@global-counsel.co.uk (office). *Website:* www.parliament.uk/biographies/lords/peter-mandelson/35772 (office).

MANDELSTAM, Stanley, PhD, FRS; British physicist and academic; *Professor Emeritus of Physics, University of California, Berkeley;* b. 12 Dec. 1928, Johannesburg, S Africa; s. of Boris Mandelstam and Beatrice Mandelstam (née Liknaitzky); ed Univ. of Witwatersrand, S Africa, Univs of Cambridge and Birmingham; Boese Postdoctoral Fellow, Columbia Univ., USA 1957–58; Asst Research Physicist, Univ. of California, Berkeley 1958–60, Prof. of Physics 1963–94, Prof. Emer. 1994–; Prof. of Math. Physics, Univ. of Birmingham 1960–63; Prof. Associé, Univ. de Paris Sud 1979–80, 1984–85; Fellow, American Acad. of Arts and Sciences; Dirac Medal and Prize, Int. Centre for Theoretical Physics 1991, Dannie Heinemann Prize in Math. Physics 1992. *Publications:* papers on theoretical particle physics. *Leisure interests:* reading, music. *Address:* Department of Physics, 447 Birge Hall, University of California, Berkeley, CA 94720 (office); 1800 Spruce Street, Berkeley, CA 94720, USA (home). *Telephone:* (510) 642-6399 (office); (510) 540-5318 (home). *Fax:* (510) 643-8497 (office). *E-mail:* smandelstam@lbl.gov (office). *Website:* www.physics.berkeley.edu/research/faculty/mandelstam.html (office).

MANDIĆ, Andrija; Montenegrin metallurgical engineer, business executive and politician; *President, New Serbian Democracy;* b. 19 Jan. 1965, Šavnik; m.; two c.; ed Faculty of Tech. and Metallurgy, Veljko Vlahović Univ., Titograd (now Podgorica); owned a night club in Podgorica called The Scene; co-owner of smelting plant that produced aluminium alloys in Montenegro; mem. Union of Reform Forces of Yugoslavia (SRSJ) 1990–91, abandoned political life following dissolution of party after outbreak of civil wars in Yugoslavia; returned to pvt. business; joined People's Party (Narodna Stranka) mid-1990s; Co-founder Serb People's Party of Montenegro (Srpska Narodna Stranka Crne Gore) 1997, held numerous posts, originally as a Vice-Pres. of Municipal Bd for Podgorica and mem. Supreme Bd Board of the party, as well as mem. Exec. Bd, also served one term as Dir of the Party, Pres. 2002–09, Pres. New Serbian Democracy (Nova Srpska Demokratija—NOVA formed from merger of Serb People's Party and People's Socialist Party) 2009–; mem. Parl. of Montenegro, Head of NOVA Parl. club; fmr Deputy Minister for Industry. *Address:* New Serbian Democracy (Nova Srpska Demokratija—NOVA), 81000 Podgorica, Vojislava Grujića 4, Montenegro (office). *Telephone:* (20) 651903 (office). *Fax:* (20) 652147 (office). *E-mail:* centar@nova.org .me (office); pobjeda@andrijamandic.com. *Website:* www.nova.org.me (office); www .andrijamandic.com.

MANDIL, Claude; French administrative official, engineer and business executive; b. 9 Jan. 1942, Lyon; s. of Léon Mandil and Renée Mandil (née Mizraki); m. Annick Goubelle 1966; four s. one d.; ed Lycée Pasteur de Neuilly and Ecole Polytechnique; mining engineer, Metz 1967–71, Rennes 1971–74; Délégation à l'Aménagement du Territoire et à l'Action régionale (DATAR) 1974–77; Inter-Dept Dir and Regional Del. Agence nat. de Valorisation de la Recherche, Anvar 1978–81; Tech. Adviser to Prime Minister 1981–82; Dir-Gen. Inst. of Industrial Devt (IDI) 1983, Pres. 1984–88; Dir-Gen. Bureau des recherches géologiques et minières 1988; Dir-Gen. Energies et Matières Premières, Ministry of Industry and Land Devt 1990–98; Deputy Man. Dir Gaz de France 1998–2000; Pres. Institut français du pétrole 2000–03; Exec. Dir IEA 2003–07 (retd); Commdr, Ordre nat. du Mérite, Officier, Légion d'honneur, decorations from Germany, Norway, Japan and UK; Dr hc (Catholic Univ. of Louvain). *Leisure interest:* music. *Address:* 28 rue Sainte-Anne, 78000 Versailles, France. *E-mail:* claude.mandil@orange.fr.

MANDINGA, Vítor Fernando; Guinea-Bissau politician; fmr Leader, Democratic Convergence Party; Minister of Finance 2005–07, also mem. IMF Bd of Govs; Leader, Aliança Democrática 2008–. *Address:* Aliança Democrática, c/o Assembléia Nacional Popular, Bissau, Guinea Bissau (office).

MANDOKI, Luis; Mexican film director, writer and producer; b. 1954, Mexico City; m. Olivia Mandoki; one s. two d.; ed studied fine arts in Mexico and at San Francisco Art Inst., London Coll. of Printing, London Int. Film School; directed first short film Silent Music which won an award at Int. Amateur Film Festival of Cannes Film Festival 1976; directed short films and documentaries for Instituto Nacional Indigenista (Nat. Inst. for the Indigenous), Conacine (Nat. Comm. of Film) and Centro de Produccion de Cortometraje (Center for the Production of Short Films); film Motel selected to represent Mexico in film festivals world-wide 1984; film Voces inocentes selected to represent Mexico at Academy Awards for Best Foreign Film 2005. *Films directed:* Mundo mágico 1980, Campeche, un estado de animo (also producer) 1980, El secreto (Ariel Award, Mexican Acad. of Film 1980) 1980, Papaloapan 1982, Mundo mágico (segment La venganza de Carlos Mango) 1983, Motel (aka Murderer in the Hotel) 1984, Gaby: A True Story (also developer and co-producer) 1987, Noche de Califas (producer) 1987, White Palace 1990, Born Yesterday 1993, When a Man Loves a Woman (aka To Have and to Hold) 1994, Message in a Bottle 1999, Meeting Genevieve 2000, Amazing Grace 2000, Angel Eyes (Ojos de ángel) 2001, Trapped (aka 24 Stunden Angst) (also producer) 2002, Voces inocentes (Innocent Voices) (also screenplay and producer) (Glass Bear, 14plus: Best Feature Film, Berlin Int. Film Festival 2005, Jury Prize for Best Feature Film, RiverRun Int. Film Festival 2006) 2004, Fraude: México 2006 (aka Stolen) (documentary) (also producer) 2007. *Television:* The Edge 1989, Utopia (series) (exec. producer) 2003, ¿Quien es el Señor Lopez? (series) (also

producer) 2006. *Address:* c/o WME, 9601 Wilshire Blvd, Beverly Hills, CA 90210, USA (office).

MANDUCA, Paul; British business executive; *Chairman, Prudential plc;* Founding CEO Threadneedle Asset Management Ltd 1994–99; Global CEO Rothschild Asset Management 1999–2002; European CEO Deutsche Asset Management 2002–05; Chair. Bridgewell Group plc –2007; Dir (non-exec.) Wm Morrison Supermarkets Plc (Morrisons) 2005–11, chaired Audit Remuneration, later Sr Ind. Dir, mem. Nomination Cttee and Chair. Remuneration Cttee; Ind. Dir (non-exec.) Prudential 2010–, Sr Ind. Dir and mem. Nomination Cttee 2011–12, mem. Audit Cttee, Remuneration Cttee 2010–12, Chair. Prudential plc 2012–, also Chair. Nomination Cttee; Chair. Aon Ltd –2012; Dir (non-exec.) and Chair. Audit Cttee KazmunaiGas Exploration & Production Plc –2012; Chair. Henderson Diversified Income Ltd, JPM European Smaller Companies Investment Trust Plc –2012; Sr Ind. Dir and Chair. Audit Cttee, Development Securities plc –2010; Dir, Eagle Star 1994–99, Allied Dunbar 1994–99, Henderson Smaller Companies Investment Trust plc –2006; mem. Securities Inst. *Address:* Prudential plc, Laurence Pountney Hill, London, EC4R 0HH, England (office). *Telephone:* (20) 7548-3901 (office). *Fax:* (20) 7548-3631 (office). *E-mail:* info@prudential.co.uk (office). *Website:* www.prudential.co.uk (office).

MANDUR, László, BSc; Hungarian politician; *Deputy Speaker, Hungarian National Assembly;* b. 12 Feb. 1958, Csömör; m.; three c.; ed Coll. of Transport and Communication, Győr, Univ. of Econs, Budapest; clerk of works at Ferihegy II Airport; worked at Betonútépítő Construction Co. 1979–81; mem. of Hungarian Socialist Workers' Party 1979–89; mem. of staff, Young Communist League of Budapest Cttee, then Dist Sec. and later Budapest Sec. 1981–89; founding mem., Hungarian Socialist Party (MSZP) 1989, mem. of party exec. and faction leader, Budapest Dist III Ass. 1994–97, Co-Chair. MSZP Nat. Econs Section 1998–2000, mem. Budapest Party Council 1999–2000, MSZP Budapest Pres. 2000–04, mem. Nat. Exec. 2004–; Man. Dir Budapest Radio Kft. 1989–97; mem. Bd, then Chair., Hortobágy Fishery Rt. 1995–97; Chair. Antenna Hungaria Rt. 1996–98; mem. Supervisory Bd, Hajógyári Sziget Asset Man. Rt. 1996–99; Man. Dir Antel Invest Kft. 1997–98; Man. Dir Honline Kft. 1999; mem. Bd Budapest Waterworks Rt. 1999–2000; Man. Dir Trangon Bt. 2000–02; mem. Hungarian Nat. Ass. 2002–, Deputy Speaker 2002–; Commdr, Ordre Nat. du Mérite 2004. *Publications:* Mr. Producer (co-author) 1993. *Address:* Hungarian National Assembly, 1357 Budapest, Kossuth tér 1–3, Hungary (office). *Telephone:* (1) 441-4000 (office); (1) 441-4175 (office). *Fax:* (1) 441-4041 (office). *Website:* www.parlament.hu (office); www.mandur.hu.

MANDVIWALLA, Saleem; Pakistani politician; b. 25 Jan. 1959; s. of Hakim Mandviwalla; ed Fort Worth School of Aviation, Texas, USA; Chair. Bd of Investment 2008–13; Minister of State for Finance Div. 2008–13, Fed. Minister of Finance, Revenue, Planning and Devt, Econ. Affairs and Statistics Feb.–March 2013; Pres. Lasbela Chamber of Commerce and Industry, Balochistan; mem. Senate for Sindh (Pakistan People's Party) 2012–; mem. Man. Cttee Fed. of Chambers of Commerce and Industries (FPCCI). *Address:* c/o Ministry of Finance, Revenue and Planning and Development, Blk Q, Pakistan Secretariat, Islamabad, Pakistan (office).

MANFREDI, Valerio Massimo; Italian archaeologist, academic and writer; *Professor of Archaeology, Bocconi University;* b. 8 March 1943; specialist in topography of the ancient world; has taken part in many archaeological excavations in Italy and abroad; has taught at Università Cattolica, Milan, Venice Univ., Loyola Univ., Chicago and Ecole Pratique des Hautes Etudes, Paris, currently Prof. of Archaeology Bocconi Univ., Milan; corresp. on antiquities for pubs Panorama and Il Messaggero; Commendatore della Repubblica, Premio Rhegium Julii, Premio Hemingway 2004. *Television:* Stargate (LA7–TV). *Publications include:* Xenophon's Anabasis (translator), Lo Scudo di Talos, Palladion, Il Faraone delle Sabbie, L'Oracolo, Le Paludi di Hesperia, La Torre della Solitudine, Alexandros: Child of a Dream, Alexander: The Sands of Amon, Alexander: The Ends of the Earth, Chimaira Akropolis 2001, L'ultima legione (The Last Legion: Spartan) 2002, Il tiranno (trans. as Tyrant) 2003, L'impero del draghi 2005, Zeus e altro racconti 2006, L'armata perduta 2007, Idi di Marzo 2008, L'antica maledizione 2010, Otel Bruni 2011. *Leisure interest:* motorcycling. *Address:* Laura Grandi (Agent), Via Caradosso 12, 20123, Milan; Via delle Grazie 31, 41010, Piumazzo, Italy (home). *Telephone:* 059-931519 (home). *Fax:* 059-931519 (home). *E-mail:* toilos@tim.it (home).

MANGAL, Mohammad Gulab; Afghan politician; b. Laja Mangal, Paktika Prov.; ed Kabul Univ.; fmr mem. People's Democratic Party of Afghanistan; served as a Col in the Afghan Army; worked in Ministries of Interior and of Defence late 1970s; later joined the insurrection fighting the Soviet invasion of Afghanistan; fmr UN worker; apptd a Regional Co-ordinator of the Constitutional Loya Jirga (Grand Council) in Paktia Prov. 2001; Gov. of Paktika Prov. 2004–06, of Laghman Prov. 2006–08, of Helmand Prov. 2008–12. *Address:* c/o Office of the Governor, Lashkar Gah, Helmand Province, Afghanistan.

MANGALAZA, Eugène; Malagasy professor of anthropology and politician; b. 1950; three c.; ed Univ. Bordeaux III, France; Inspector of Higher Educ. in 1970s and 1980s; Deputy, Nat. People's Ass. 1975–1991; Dir of Human Resources, Port of Toamasina 1989; Prof. of Philosophy and Anthropology, Univ. of Toamasina, Rector 1989–2002; Visiting Prof., Toliara Univ., Univ. Bordeaux III, France, Univ. in Switzerland; mem. Asscn pour la renaissance de Madagascar; resident in La Reunion –Oct. 2009; Prime Minister Oct.–Dec. 2009. *Publications:* several publications in the field of anthropology. *Address:* c/o Office of the Prime Minister, BP 248, Palais d'Etat Mahazoarivo, 101 Antananarivo, Madagascar.

MANGANYI, Noel Chabani, BA, BA (Hons), MA, DLitt et Phil; South African psychologist, academic and fmr civil servant; *Council Professor, University of Pretoria;* b. 13 March 1940, Louis Trichardt dist; s. of Frans Manganyi and Sophie Manganyi; m. 1st Esmé Kakana (divorced); m. 2nd Dr Peggy Sekele 1990; two d.; ed Douglas Laing Smit Secondary School, Univ. of South Africa (UNISA); internship in clinical psychology, Baragwanath Hosp., Clinical Psychologist 1970–73; Postdoctoral Fellow, School of Medicine, Yale Univ., USA 1973–75; Prof. of Psychology Univ. of Transkei 1976–80; Prof., Sr Research Fellow, Univ. of the Witwatersrand 1981–90; in active forensic practice of psychology as expert witness for defence of anti-apartheid activists at Supreme Court, SA –1991; Vice-

Chancellor Univ. of the North, Pietersburg 1991–92; Exec. Dir PSI Jt Educ. Trust 1993–94; Dir-Gen. of Nat. Educ. 1994–99; Advisor to Vice-Chancellor and Prin. of Univ. of Pretoria 1999–2003, Vice-Prin. Univ. of Pretoria 2003–06, Council Prof. 2006–; Founder, Violence and Health Resources Project, Univ. of the Witwatersrand 1986, mem. Bd Wits University Press; mem. several psychology orgs; Hon. DLitt (Witwatersrand); Hon. DLitt et Phil (UNISA). *Publications:* published a series of monographs, including Being Black in the World 1973, Alienation and the Body in Racist Society 1977, Looking through the Keyhole 1981; Exiles and Homecomings: A Biography of Es'kia Mphahlele 1983, Bury Me at the Marketplace: Selected Letters of Es'kia Mphahlele, 1943–1980 1984, Political Violence and the Struggle in South Africa (co-ed.) 1990, Treachery and Innocence: Psychology and Racial Difference in South Africa 1991, A Black Man Called Sekoto 1996, Gerard Sekoto: I Mm an African 2004, On Becoming a Democracy: Transition and the Transformation of South African Society (ed.) 2004; several articles in scientific and professional journals. *Address:* Unit for Advanced Scholarship, University of Pretoria, PO Box 471, Wendywood, Johannesburg 2144, South Africa (office). *E-mail:* chabani@iafrica.com (office). *Website:* web.up.ac.za (office).

MANGESHKAR, Lata; Indian singer, actress and songwriter; b. (Hema Hardikar), 28 Sept. 1929, Indore; d. of actor and singer Dinanath Mangeshkar and Shudhhamati Mangeshkar; sister of Asha Bhosle; Indian film playback singer; first sang in Kiti Hasaal 1942; has recorded thousands of songs in 20 Indian languages; Hon. Citizenship of Republic of Suriname 1980, Hon. Citizenship of Houston, Texas, USA 1987; Hon. DLitt (Pune Univ.) 1990; Filmfare Awards 1958, 1962, 1965, 1969 (refused to be considered for this award after 1969 to encourage new talent), Filmfare Lifetime Achievement Award 1993, Filmfare Special Award 1994, National Awards, Best Female Playback Singer 1972, 1975, 1990, Maharashtra State Award, Best Playback Singer 1966, 1967, Bengal Film Journalist's Award, Padma Bhushan 1969, Best Female Playback Singer 1964, 1967, 1968, 1969, 1970, 1971, 1973, 1975, 1981, 1985, Key of the City of Georgetown, Guyana 1980, Dada Saheb Phalke Award 1989, Videocon Screen Lifetime Achievement Award 1996, Rajiv Gandhi Award 1997, Lux Zee Cine Lifetime Achievement Award 1998, Padma Vibhushan 1999, IIFA London, Lifetime Achievement Award 2000, Noorjehan Award 2001, Maharashtra Ratna 2001, Bharat Ratna 2001;,Noorjehan Award 2001, Maharashtra Ratna 2001, Hakim Khan Sur Award 2002, Asha Bhosle Award 2002, Swar Bharati Award, One Time Award for Lifetime Achievement 2008. *Films include:* Pahill Mangala Gaur 1942, Chimukla Sansaar 1943, Maakhe Baal 1943, Gajabhau 1944, Badi Maa 1945, Jeevan Yaatra 1946, Subhadra 1946, Mandir 1948, Chattapati Shivaji 1953, Pukar 2000. *Recordings include:* albums: soundtracks: Sargam 1979, Darr 1993, Hum Aapke Hain Koun. . .! 1994, Dilwale Dulhania Le Jayeng 1995, Dil To Pagal Hai 1997, Lagaan 2001; solo: Lata In Concert – An Era In An Evening 1997, Saadgi 2007. *Leisure interests:* photography, cooking. *Address:* Prabhu Kunj, 101 Peddar Road, Mumbai 400 026, India.

MANGLA, P. B., MA, MLibSc, MSLS, MInfSc, DLSc; Indian professor of library and information science; *Professor Emeritus, University of Delhi;* b. 5 July 1936, India; s. of Radha Krishan; m. Raj Mangla 1961; one s. one d.; ed Univ. of Punjab, Univ. of Delhi, Columbia Univ., New York and in London; Prof. and Head of Dept of Library Sciences, Univ. of Tabriz, Iran 1970–72, Visiting Prof. 1974–75; UNESCO expert, Guyana 1978–79; Prof. and Head of Dept of Library and Information Sciences, Univ. of Delhi 1972–, Dean Faculty of Arts 1976–78, 1984–88, Chair. Bd of Research Studies 1979–85; Library Consultant, Reserve Bank of India, Bombay 1992–93; Library Adviser, YMCA New Delhi 1992–; various other admin. posts in Delhi and numerous other univs 1972–; Chair. Manpower Devt Cttee of Nat. Information System in Science and Tech. 1977–; Sr Vice-Pres. and Founder-mem. Indian Assen of Academic Librarians 1981–83; mem. Bd Int. Fed. of Library Assens and Insts 1983– (Vice-Pres. 1987–89, 1989–91), Inst. of Information Scientists; Nat. Prof., UGC 1984–86; Chair. Bd of Eds Univ. of Delhi Annual Reports 1989–96; mem. Editorial Bd Third World Libraries (USA) 1989–, Journal of Library and Information Science, Education for Information, Amsterdam 1982–, Review in Library and Information Science, USA, LIBRI (Copenhagen), Third World Libraries (Chicago), Int. Journal of Information and Library Research (UK) 1989–; Special Adviser, IFLA Regional Section for Asia and Oceania 1991–; Chair. Programme Implementation Cttee, Nat. Service Scheme, Delhi Univ. 1989–, Governing Body Deshbandhu Coll., Delhi Univ. 1990–95, Dyal Singh Coll., Delhi Univ. 2001–04, Univ. Grants Cttee (UGC) Panel of Library and Information Science 1992–; Prof., Mangla Research Foundation 2001, Dyal Singh Coll., Delhi Univ. 2001–04 (Prof. Emer. 2004–); mem. Steering Cttee Inflibnet (UGC) 1990–99; mem. Planning Comm. (Govt of India) Working Group on Modernization of Libraries and Informatics for 7th, 8th and 9th Five-Year Plans; mem. Research Cttee INSDOC New Delhi 2000–02, Nat. Inst. of Science Communication and Information Resources 2002–; mem. Nat. Advisory Cttee Nat. Library 2002–, Expert Cttee Asiatic Soc. 2002–, Working Group on Libraries, Nat. Knowledge Comm. 2006, Search Cttee for Chair., Inflibnet (UGC) 2006; mem. Bd of Man., Nat. Library of India (Kolkata) 2004–; Fellow, Indian Library Assen; Rockefeller Foundation (New York) Merit Scholarship 1961–62, British Council sponsorship 1979, 1980, 1987, 1989, IDRC (Canada) sponsorship 1983, 1991, Int. Library Movt Award (India) 1984, Shiromani Award for Human Excellence 1991, IFLA Gold Medal 1991, Distinguished Services Award and Citation, Punjab Library Assen 1997, Library and Information Science: Parameters and Perspectives (two-vol. Festchrift) 1997, Certificate of Honour, IASLIC 2006; several memorial lectures; Hon. Fellow, Indian Library Assen. *Publications:* author/ed. of numerous books and specialist reviews in India and overseas. *Leisure interests:* travel, reading. *Address:* EB-210 Maya Enclave, New Delhi 110 064, India. *Telephone:* (11) 2512-0458; (11) 2512-0331 (home). *E-mail:* manglapb@yahoo.co.in (home).

MANGOAELA, Percy Metsing, BSc, BEd, LLB; Lesotho diplomatist and international civil servant; *Chairman, Lesotho Telecommunications Authority;* b. 26 Aug. 1942, Berea; m.; two d.; ed Memorial Univ. of Newfoundland, Dalhousie Univ., Canada, Makerere Univ., Kampala and Harvard Univ., USA; radio news reporter Dept of Information and Broadcasting 1966–68; joined Lesotho civil service 1968, Asst Sec., Ministry of Foreign Affairs, then Desk Officer, Int. Orgs and N America –1970; Dir of Civil Aviation 1973–76, Prin. Sec., Ministry of Transport and Communications 1976–79, 1990; Deputy Co-ordinator UN Trans-

port and Communications Decade for Africa, UN Econ. Comm. for Africa 1979–89; Prin. Sec., Depts of Trade and Industry and Consumer Affairs 1991–92.

MANGOLD, Klaus, DrIur; German business executive; *Chairman of the Supervisory Board, TUI AG;* b. 6 June 1943, Pforzheim; m.; two s.; ed Univs of Munich, Heidelberg and Mainz, Univ. of Geneva, Switzerland, Univ. of Paris, France, Univ. of London, UK; Asst Man. German-Mexican Chamber of Commerce, Mexico City 1972–73; Section Jr Barrister Thyssen 1973–75; Man. Union of German Textile Industry, Stuttgart 1976; mem. Bd of Dirs Rhodia AG (Rhone Poulenc Group) 1983–90, Chair. 1985–90; Chair. Quelle-Schickedanz AG, Fürth 1991–94; mem. Bd of Dirs DaimlerChrysler AG and CEO DaimlerChrysler Services AG 1995–2003, Exec. Adviser to Chair. DaimlerChrysler AG for Cen. and Eastern Europe and Cen. Asia 2003–07; Exec. Adviser to Chair. DaimlerChrysler AG for Cen. and Eastern Europe and Cen. Asia 2003–07; Vice-Chair. Rothschild Europe 2004–, Chair. Supervisory Bd Rothschild GmbH, TUI AG 2011–; Chair. Cttee on Eastern European Econ. Relations 2000–05; mem. of numerous supervisory and advisory bds including Rothschild & Cie, France and Germany, Chubb Corpn, USA, Rhodia, SA, Continental AG, Metro AG, Jenoptik AG, Magna International Inc., Canada; mem. Bd Alstom SA, Leipziger Messe GmbH, Universitätsklinikum Freiburg; Chevalier, Légion d'honneur. *Publications:* Die Zukunft der Dienstleistung (ed.) 1997, Die Welt der Dienstleistung (ed.) 1998. *Address:* TUI AG, Postfach 610209, 30602 Hanover (office); TUI AG, Karl-Wiechert-Allee 4, 30625 Hanover, Germany (office). *Telephone:* (511) 566-00 (office). *Fax:* (511) 566-1901 (office). *E-mail:* info@tui-group.com (office). *Website:* www.tui-group.com (office).

MANGOLD, Robert Peter, BFA, MFA; American artist; b. 12 Oct. 1937, N Tonawanda, NY; s. of Aloysius Mangold and Blanche Mangold; m. Sylvia Plimack 1961; ed Cleveland Inst. of Art and Yale Univ.; minimalist artist; Instructor, School of Visual Arts, New York 1963–, Hunter Coll. 1964–65, Cornell Univ. Skowhegan Summer Art School 1968; work represented in numerous public collections in USA, UK and Europe, including Museum of Modern Art, Solomon R. Guggenheim Museum and Whitney Museum of American Art, New York, San Francisco Museum of Modern Art, Tate Collection, London, Art Inst. of Chicago, Fundacío La Caixa, Barcelona, Hirshhorn Museum and Sculpture Garden, Washington, DC, J. Paul Getty Trust, Los Angeles, Kunstmuseum Basel, Switzerland, Los Angeles County Museum of Art, Museo Nacional de Arte Reina Sofia, Madrid, Tokyo Metropolitan Art Museum, Hallen für Neue Kunst, Schaffhausen, Switzerland; represented by The Pace Gallery, New York 1991–; Fellow, American Acad. of Arts and Letters; lives and works in upstate NY; Nat. Council on Arts Award 1966, Nat. Endowment for the Arts grant 1967, Guggenheim Fellowship 1969. *Address:* c/o The Pace Gallery, 32 East 57th Street, New York, NY 10022, USA. *Telephone:* (212) 421-3292. *Fax:* (212) 421-0835. *E-mail:* info@pacegallery.com. *Website:* www.pacegallery.com.

MANGOPE, Chief Lucas Manyane; South African politician and tribal chief; b. 27 Dec. 1923, Motswedi, Zeerust; s. of Manyane Mangope and Semakaleng Mangope; m. Leah Tscholofelo Dolo 1951; four s. three d.; ed St Peter's Coll. and Bethel Coll.; worked in the Dept of Bantu Admin and Devt, later taught at Motswedi; succeeded his father as Chief of the Bahurutshe-Boo-Manyane 1959; Vice-Chair. Tswana Territorial Authority 1961–68, Chief Councillor, Exec. Council 1968–72; Chief Minister of Bophuthatswana Homeland 1972–77; fmr Prime Minister, Minister of Finance, Minister of Law and order; Pres. 1977–94; Leader South African United Christian Democratic Party; mem. North-West Prov. legislature. *Leisure interests:* soccer, tennis, choral music. *Address:* PO Box 245, Buhrmannsdrif 2867, South Africa (office). *Telephone:* (18) 3814044 (office). *Fax:* (18) 3185979 (office).

MANGUEL, Alberto; Canadian (b. Argentine) writer, editor and translator; b. 13 March 1948, Buenos Aires, Argentina; Fellow, Simon Guggenheim Foundation, S. Fischer Stiftung; Officier, Ordre des Arts et des Lettres; Dr hc (Univ. of Liège, Anglia Ruskin Univ., Cambridge); Premio La Nacion 1971, Harbourfront Festival Prize 1992, Canadian Authors' Assen Prize 1992, Prix France-Culture 2000, Premio German Sánchez Ruiperez 2002, Prix Poitou-Charentes 2004, Prix Roger Caillois 2004, Premio Grinzane Cavour 2004. *Publications:* (in English) novels: News from a Foreign Country Came (McKitterick Prize 1992) 1991, Stevenson Under the Palm Trees 2002, The Return 2006, The Overdiscriminating Lover 2006, At the Mad Hatter's Table 2006, The Library at Night 2008, All Men Are Liars 2010; collections: In Another Part of the Forest: The Flamingo Anthology of Gay Literature (with Craig Stephenson) 1968, The Gates of Paradise: The Flamingo Anthology of Erotic Literature 1969, Black Water: The Flamingo Anthology of Fantastic Literature 1990; non-fiction: The Dictionary of Imaginary Places 1980, Into the Looking-Glass Wood: Essays on Books, Reading and the World 1985, A History of Reading (TLS Int. Book of the Year, Prix Médicis 1998) 1996, Reading Pictures 2001, A Reading Diary 2005, With Borges 2006, Homer's The Iliad and The Odyssey: A Biography 2007, The City of Words 2008, A Reader on Reading 2010; ed. of numerous anthologies, many trans. *Address:* c/o Guillermo Schavelzon Agency, Calle Muntaner 339 5, 08021 Barcelona, Spain (office). *Telephone:* (93) 2011310 (office). *Fax:* (93) 2006886 (office). *E-mail:* info@schavelzon.com (office). *Website:* www.schavelzon.com (office); www.alberto.manguel.com.

MANHIRE, William (Bill), BA, MLitt, MPhil; New Zealand poet, writer and academic; *Professor of Creative Writing and English Literature, Victoria University of Wellington;* b. 27 Dec. 1946, Invercargill; s. of Jack Manhire and Madeline Mary Manhire; m. Barbara Marion McLeod 1970; one s. one d.; ed S Otago Dist High School, Otago Boys' High School, Univ. of Otago at Dunedin, Univ. Coll., London, UK; Lecturer in English, Vic. Univ., Wellington 1973, f. creative writing programme 1976, Prof. of Creative Writing and English Literature 1997–; Dir Int. Inst. of Modern Letters 2001–; Fiction Ed. Victoria Univ. Press 1976–96; Fulbright Visiting Prof. in NZ Studies, Georgetown Univ., USA Jan.–June 1999; inaugural Te Mata Estate New Zealand Poet Laureate 1997–99; Nuffield Fellowship 1981; Companion NZ Order of Merit; Hon. DLitt (Otago); NZ Book Award 1977, 1984, 1992, 1996, Montana Book Award 1994, Katherine Mansfield Fellowship 2004, NZAF Arts Laureate 2005, Montana NZ Book Award 2006, Prime Minister's Award for Poetry. *Publications:* Malady 1970, The Elaboration 1972, Song Cycle 1975, How to Take Your Clothes Off at the Picnic 1977, Dawn/Water 1980, Good Looks 1982, Locating the Beloved and Other Stories 1983, Zoetropes: Poems

1972–82 1984, Maurice Gee 1986, The Brain of Katherine Mansfield 1988, The New Land: A Picture Book 1990, The Old Man's Example 1990, Milky Way Bar 1991, An Amazing Week in New Zealand 1993, Fault 1994, South Pacific 1994, Hoosh 1995, My Sunshine 1996, Songs of My Life 1996, Sheet Music: Poems 1967–1982 1996, Mutes and Earthquakes 1997, What to Call Your Child 1999, Doubtful Sounds: Essays and Interviews 2000, Collected Poems 2001, Under the Influence (memoir) 2003, Lifted (poems) 2005, Pine 2005, The Victims of Lightning 2010, Selected Poems 2012, These Rough Notes 2012; editor: New Zealand Listener Short Stories Vol. 1 1977, Vol. 2 1978, Some Other Country: New Zealand's Best Short Stories (with Marion McLeod) 1984, Six by Six 1989, Soho Square 1991, 100 New Zealand Poems 1994, Denis Glover: Selected Poems 1995, Spectacular Babies (with Karen Anderson) 2001, The Wide White Page: Writers Imagine Antarctica 2004, 121 New Zealand Poems 2006, The Goose Bath 2006, Still Shines When You Think of It (with Peter Whiteford) 2007, Ein Anderes Land 2012. *Leisure interest:* swimming. *Address:* Creative Writing Programme, International Institute of Modern Letters, Victoria University of Wellington, PO Box 600, Wellington, New Zealand (office). *Telephone:* (4) 463-6808 (office). *Fax:* (4) 463-6865 (office). *E-mail:* bill.manhire@vuw.ac.nz (office). *Website:* www.vuw.ac .nz/modernletters (office).

MANIATOPOULOS, Constantinos S.; Greek EU official and business executive; b. 1941; m. Theodora Hiou; one s.; ed Athens and Paris; fmrly employed in energy and industry sectors; Chair. and Man. Dir EKO Petroleum Co., Greece; Special Adviser to Minister of Energy; mem. Bd various nat. advisory bodies; Gen. Sec. Tech. Chamber of Greece; Dir-Gen. for Energy, EC (now EU) Comm. 1986–95. *Address:* 13 Makedonias Street, Kifissia, Athens, Greece; 10 Akti Miaouli, 18538 Piraeus (office).

MANIBE NGAI, Kosti; South Sudanese politician; b. W Equatoria; Minister of Cabinet Affairs in caretaker govt (between independence 9 July 2011 and appointment of new cabinet 26 August 2011); Minister of Finance and Econ. Planning Aug. 2011–13 (suspended June 2013). *Address:* c/o Ministry of Finance and Economic Planning, Juba, South Sudan.

MANIGAT, Leslie François; Haitian politician and academic; b. 16 Aug. 1930, Port-au-Prince; m. 2nd Mirlande Manigat 1970; f. School of Int. Studies at Univ. of Haiti, first Dir; fmr Research Assoc. Johns Hopkins Univ., Washington, DC; fmr Prof. Inst. of Political Studies, Paris; then with Univ. of West Indies, Trinidad and Tobago; with Simón Bolívar Univ., Caracas 1978; returned from 23 years in exile 1986; Pres. of Haiti Jan. 1988 (first democratically elected Pres. of Haiti), overthrown by Lt-Gen. Henri Namphy June 1988; Sec.-Gen. Rassemblement des Démocrates Nationalistes et Progressistes (RDNP) –2007; unsuccessful presidential cand. 2006. *Address:* c/o Rassemblement des Démocrates Nationalistes et Progressistes (RDNP), 234 route de Delmas, Delmas, Port-au-Prince, Haiti.

MANIGLIA FERREIRA, Adm. Ramón Orlando; Venezuelan government official and naval officer; commissioned into Venezuelan Navy, fmr Navy Commdr, C-in-C 2003, rank of Vice-Adm., then Three-Sun Adm. 2005; Inspector Gen. Nat. Armed Forces 2004–05; Minister of Nat. Defence 2005–06. *Address:* c/o Ministry of National Defence, Edif. 17 de Diciembre, planta baja, Base Aérea Francisco de Miranda, La Carlota, Caracas, Venezuela (office).

MANIK, Moosa (Reeko); Maldivian actor, politician and business executive; *Chairman, Maldivian Democratic Party;* fmr mem. People's Special Majlis, now mem. Parl.; Owner, Heavy Load Pvt. Ltd; Chair. Maldivian Democratic Party 2012–. *Address:* Maldivian Democratic Party, H. Sharasha, 2nd Floor, Sosun Magu, Malé 20-059, Maldives (office). *Telephone:* 3340044 (office). *Fax:* 3322960 (office). *E-mail:* secretariat@mdp.org.mv (office). *Website:* www.mdp.org.mv (office).

MANIKU, K. D. Ahmed; Maldivian government official; Deputy Minister of Environment and Construction –2005; Commr of Elections and Registrar of Political Parties 2005–08. *Address:* c/o Office of the Commissioner of Elections, PA Complex, 3rd Floor, Hilaalee Magu, Malé, Maldives. *Telephone:* 3324426. *E-mail:* info@elections.gov.mv.

MANIKU, M. U.; Maldivian business executive; Founder-Chair. Universal Enterprises Pvt. Ltd; fmr Special Econ. Adviser to the Pres.; Chair. Maldives Asscn of Tourism Industry. *Address:* Maldives Association of Tourism Industry, Gadhamoo Building, 3rd Floor, Henveyru, Malé, Maldives (office). *Telephone:* 3326640 (office). *Fax:* 3326641 (office). *E-mail:* mati@dhivehinet.net.mv (office).

MANILOV, Col-Gen. Valery Leonidovich, PhD; Russian civil servant and army officer; b. 10 Jan. 1939, Tulchin, Ukraine; m.; one d.; ed Odessa Higher Infantry School, Mil.-Political Acad., Gen. Staff Mil. Acad.; service in Odessa, Baikal mil. commands, S Group of armed forces, service in Afghanistan; on staff Ministry of Defence 1988–; Head Information Service of Jt Armed Forces of CIS 1992–93; Asst to Sec. Russian Security Council July–Oct. 1993, Deputy Sec. 1993–96; First Deputy Head of Gen. Staff. 1998–2000; mem. Acad. of Mil. Sciences, Russian Acad. of Natural Sciences, Int. Acad. of Informatization; mem. Council of Fed., Rep. Primorsky Territory 2001.

MANILOW, Barry; American singer, musician (piano) and songwriter; b. (Barry Alan Pincus), 17 June 1946, New York; s. of Harold Manilow and Edna Manilow; ed New York Coll. Music, Juilliard School of Music; worked in mailroom at CBS; film ed. WCBS-TV; Dir Music Ed Sullivan's Pilots; Music Dir, conductor and producer for Bette Midler; Amb. for Prince's Trust 1996; solo artist 1974–; f. Manilow Health and Hope Fund (nonprofit includes Manilow Music Project); Producer of the Year 1975, After Dark magazine Ruby Award 1976, Photoplay Gold Medal 1976, Grammy Award for Song of the Year (for I Write The Songs) 1977, Emmy Award (for The Barry Manilow Special) 1977, American Music Awards for Favorite Male Artist 1978–80, Grammy Award for Best Male Pop Vocal Performance (for At The Copa from Copacabana) 1979, Songwriters Hall of Fame Hitmaker Award 1991, Starlight Foundation Humanitarian of the Year 1991, Soc. of Singers Ella Award 2003. *Theatre:* Barry Manilow on Broadway (jt recipient Tony Award 1977) 1976, Barry Manilow at the Gershwin (Broadway) 1989, Copacabana (West End, London) 1994. *Television appearance:* Copacabana (film) 1985. *Recordings include:* albums: Barry Manilow I 1973, Barry Manilow II 1974, Tryin' To Get The Feelin' 1975, This One's For You 1976, Live 1977, Even Now 1978, One Voice 1979, Barry 1980, A Nice Boy Like Me 1980, If I Should Love

Again 1981, Live In Britain 1982, I Wanna Do It With You 1982, Here Comes The Night 1982, Oh, Julie! 1982, 2.00 AM Paradise Café 1984, Manilow 1985, Live On Broadway 1987, Swing Street 1987, Barry Manilow 1989, Songs To Make The Whole World Sing 1989, Because It's Christmas 1990, Showstoppers 1991, Hidden Treasures 1993, Singin' With The Big Bands 1994, Another Life 1995, Summer of '78 1996, Manilow Sings Sinatra 1998, Here At The Mayflower 2001, A Christmas Gift Of Love 2002, Two Nights Live 2004, Scores: Songs From Copacabana and Harmony 2004, The Greatest Songs of the Fifties 2006, The Greatest Songs of the Sixties 2006, The Greatest Songs of the Seventies 2007, In the Swing of Christmas 2007, Beautiful Ballads and Love Songs 2008, The Greatest Songs of the Eighties 2008, Happy Holiday! 2008, In the Swing of Christmas 2009, The Greatest Love Songs of All Time 2010, 15 Minutes 2011. *Publication:* Sweet Life: Adventures on the Way to Paradise 1987. *Address:* c/o William Morris Entertainment, 9601 Wilshire Blvd, Suite 300, Beverly Hills, CA 90210, USA (office). *Telephone:* (310) 285-9000 (office). *Fax:* (310) 285-9010 (office). *Website:* www.wma.com (office); www.barrymanilow.com.

MANIN, Yuri Ivanovich, BSc, PhD, DPhysMathSci (Habil.); Russian/German mathematician and academic; *Professor Emeritus, Max Planck Institute for Mathematics;* b. 16 Feb. 1937, Simferopol, Crimea, Ukrainian SSR, USSR; s. of Ivan Manin and Rebecca Miller; m. Xenia Semenova; one s.; ed Moscow State Univ.; Researcher, Steklov Math. Inst. Moscow 1960–, now Prin. Researcher; Prof. of Math., Moscow State Univ. 1965–91; Visiting Prof., several univs including Harvard Univ. and Columbia Univ., USA 1991–93; Prof., MIT, USA 1992–93; Scientific mem. Max Planck Inst. for Math., Bonn 1993–, Dir, Man. Dir 1995, now Prof. Emer.; Bd of Trustees Prof., Northwestern Univ., USA 2002–11, Bd of Trustees Prof. Emer. 2011–; mem. Academia Europaea, Pontifical Acad. of Science, Vatican, Acad. Leopoldina Germany, American Acad. of Arts and Sciences; Corresp. mem. Russian Acad. of Sciences, Göttingen Acad. of Sciences; Foreign mem. Royal Netherlands Acad. of Arts and Sciences, French Acad. des Sciences; Hon. mem. London Math. Soc. 2011; Order 'pour le Mérite' for Arts and Sciences (Germany) 2007, Grosses Verdienstkreuz mit Stern (Germany) 2008; Dr hc (Sorbonne, Univ. Pierre et Marie Curie, Paris VI) 1999, (Warwick) 2006; Abel Bicentennial DPhil hc (Oslo) 2002; Lenin Prize 1967, Brouwer Gold Medal 1987, Frederic Esser Nemmers Prize 1994, Rolf Schock Math. Prize (Royal Swedish Acad. of Sciences) 1999, King Faisal Prize for Science 2002, Georg Cantor Medal of German Math. Soc. 2002, Bolyai Int. Prize, Hungarian Acad. of Science 2010. *Publications:* Frobenius Manifolds, Quantum Cohomology and Moduli Spaces 1999; author, co-author of 11 monographs and more than 260 scientific papers. *Leisure interests:* literary criticism, linguistics, cultural studies. *Address:* Max Planck Institute for Mathematics, Vivatsgasse 7, 53111 Bonn, Germany (office). *Telephone:* (228) 402271 (office). *Fax:* (228) 402277 (office). *E-mail:* manin@mpim -bonn.mpg.de (office). *Website:* www.mpim-bonn.mpg.de (office).

MANITAKIS, Antonis, LLM, PhD; Greek lawyer, academic and politician; b. 1944, Thessaloniki; m. Kleopatra Theodorou; two s.; ed Université Libre de Bruxelles, Belgium; Prof. of Constitutional Law, Aristotle Univ. of Thessaloniki 1982–2011, taught Constitutional Law, Gen. Theory of the State, Human Rights and Judicial Review of Constitutionality for 35 years, later Dean of Faculty of Law and Econs and Head of Dept of Public Law and Political Science, as well as Dir of Postgraduate Studies Programme, Faculty of Law, Prof. Emer. 2012–; Visiting Prof., Univ. of Montpellier, Univ. of Paris X, Univ. of Rome 'La Sapienza', Univ. of Nantes; Visiting Research Fellow, Princeton Univ.; Alt. Chair. Nat. Council for Radio & Television 1997–99; fmr Pres. Nat. Comm. for Human Rights; active in the European Social Forum; served in caretaker govt between two elections under Prime Minister Panayiotis Pikrammenos May–June 2012; Minister of Admin. Reform and e-Governance following formation of coalition govt between New Democracy (Nea Demokratia), Panhellenic Socialist Movt (PASOK) and Democratic Left (Dimokratiki Aristera) 2012–13; honoured for his contrib. to academia by the Pres. of Greece 2007. *Publications include:* (in Greek): Constitutional Law, The Relation between Nation-State and Church, The Constitution of Europe Facing National and People's Sovereignty; Ti to kirion tis politias esti; three handbooks: What a State Is, What a Constitution Is, What a Political System Is; 16 monographs and 125 original research papers. *Address:* c/o Ministry of Administrative Reform and e-Governance, Vas Sofias 15, Athens 10674, Greece.

MANKELL, Henning; Swedish playwright and writer; b. 3 Feb. 1948, Stockholm; m. 3rd Eva Bergman 1998; four s.; merchant seaman 1964–66; Dir Teatro Avenida, Maputo, Mozambique 1987–; co-f. Leopard publishing house 2001–; Dr hc (Univ. of St Andrews) 2008; German Crime Prize 1999, Macallan CWA Golden Dagger Award 2001, Author of the Year, Germany 2002, Premio Pepe Carvalho, Spain 2007, Gumshoe Award 2005, Corine Literature Prize 2008. *Plays include:* The Amusement Park 1968, Tale on the Beach of Time 1997, Labyrinten (trans. as The Labyrinth) 2000, Italienska skor 2006, In Duisternis 2010, Politik 2010. *Publications include:* fiction: Bergsprängaren (trans. as The Rock Blaster) 1973, Vettvillingen (trans. as The Mad Man) 1978, Fångvårdskolonin som försvann (trans. as The Prison Colony that Disappeared) 1979, Dödsbrickan (trans. as The Death Badge) 1980, En seglares död (trans. as The Death of a Sailor) 1981, Daisy Sisters 1982, Sagan om Isidor (trans. as The Tale of Isidor) 1984, Leopardens Öga (trans. as The Eye of the Leopard) 1990, Comédia infantil 1995, Vindens Son (trans. as Daniel) 2000, Tea-bag 2001, Djup (trans. as Depth) 2004, Italienska Skor (trans. as Italian Shoes) 2006; crime fiction: Mördare utan ansikte (trans. as Faceless Killers (Acad. of Swedish Crime Writers' Prize 1991, Scandinavian Crime Soc. Prize 1991) 1991, Hundarna i Riga (trans. as The Dogs of Riga) 1992, Den vita lejoninnan (trans. as The White Lioness) 1993, Mannen som log (trans. as The Man Who Smiled) 1994, Villospår (trans. as Sidetracked) 1995, Den femte kvinnan (trans. as The Fifth Woman) 1996, Steget efter (trans. as One Step Behind) 1997, Brandvägg (trans. as Firewall) 1998, Pyramiden (trans. as The Pyramid) 1999, Danslärarens återkomst (trans. as The Return of the Dancing Master) 1999, Innan Frosten (trans. as Before the Frost) 2002, Kennedys Hjärna (trans. as Kennedy's Brain) 2005, Kinesen (trans. as The Man from Beijing) 2006, Den orolige mannen (trans. as The Troubled Man) 2009, A Treacherous Paradise 2011; juvenile fiction: Sandmålaren (trans. as The Sand Painter) 1974, Hunden som sprang mot en stjärna (trans. as The Dog that ran towards a star) 1990, Skuggorna Växer i Skymningen (trans. as The Shadows grow in the Dark) 1991, Katten som Älskade Regn 1992, Eldens Hemlighet (trans. as Secrets in the Fire) 1995, Pojken som sov med snö i sin säng (trans. as The Boy who slept with snow in his bed) 1996, A

Bridge to the Stars 1998; short stories: Anton och det Gripenstedtska sommarnöjet (trans. as Anton and the Summerhouse of Gripenstedtessays) 1974; essays: Jag dör, men minnet lever, I sand och i lera 1999. *Address:* c/o Leopard förlag AB, St Paulsgatan 11, 118 46 Stockholm, Sweden. *E-mail:* info@henningmankell.com. *Website:* www.henningmankell.com.

MANKIEWICZ, Frank, MS, AB, LLB; American lawyer and public affairs executive; b. 16 May 1924, New York; s. of Herman J. Mankiewicz and Sara Mankiewicz; m. 1st Holly Jolley 1952 (divorced); two s.; m. 2nd Patricia O'Brien 1988; ed Columbia Univ., Univ. of California, Berkeley, Univ. of California, Los Angeles; mem. Calif. and DC Bars; practised as lawyer, Los Angeles 1955–61; served with Peace Corps as Country Dir, Lima, Peru and later as Regional Dir for Latin America; Press Sec. to Senator Robert F. Kennedy 1966–68; syndicated columnist (with Tom Braden), Washington, DC and co-presenter, nightly newscast on CBS television affiliate 1968–71; Campaign Dir presidential campaign of George McGovern 1972; Pres. Nat. Public Radio 1977–83; Vice-Chair. Gray and Co. (now Hill & Knowlton) Washington, DC 1983–2009; Combat Infantryman's Badge, Bronze Star 1945; Hon. DHL (Lincoln Univ.) 1983; UCLA Public Service Award 1988. *Publications include:* Perfectly Clear: Nixon from Whittier to Watergate 1974, U.S. Richard Nixon: The Final Crisis 1976, With Fidel: A Portrait of Castro and Cuba 1977, Remote Control: Television and the Manipulation of American Life 1977. *Leisure interests:* baseball, literature, US political history. *Address:* Hill & Knowlton, 600 New Hampshire Avenue, NW, Suite 601, Washington, DC 20037 (office); 607 14th Street, NW, Washington, DC; 2022 Columbia Road, NW, Washington, DC 20009, USA (home). *Telephone:* (202) 944-5104 (office). *Fax:* (202) 944-1961 (office). *E-mail:* frank.mankiewicz@hillandknowlton.com (office). *Website:* www.hillandknowlton.com (office).

MAŃKO, Dariusz, PhD; Polish business executive; *President of the Management Board and CEO, Grupa Kęty SA;* b. 1968; ed Agricultural Univ., Poznań, Acad. of Econs, Katowice; sales rep. and later Head of Marketing and Devt, SAPA POLAND 1993–96; joined Grupa Kęty SA 1996, Man., ZML Kęty SA 1996–99, CEO and Gen. Dir, Metalplast-Bielsko SA 1999–2000, mem. Man. Bd Grupa Kęty SA 2000–, Pres. and CEO 2005–; Chair. Supervisory Bd ZRE Metalplast 1999–; mem. Supervisory Bd, Elektrobudowa SA 2002–03 (Chair. 2004–), Alupol Sp. Ltd (Chair. 2005–, Chair. Supervisory Bd Alupol Packaging SA 2010–). *Address:* Grupa Kęty SA, z siedzibą w Kętach, ul. Kościuszki 111, 32-650 Kęty, Poland (office). *Telephone:* (33) 8446000 (office). *Fax:* (33) 8446100 (office). *E-mail:* kety@grupakety.com (office). *Website:* www.grupakety.com (office).

MANLEY, John, OC, PC, BA, LLB; Canadian business executive, lawyer and fmr politician; *President and CEO, Canadian Council of Chief Executives;* b. 5 Jan. 1950, Ottawa; s. of John Joseph Manley and Mildred Charlotte Scharf; m. Judith Manley; one s. two d.; ed Carleton Univ., Univ. of Ottawa; fmrly practitioner in business and income tax law, Ottawa; law clerk to Chief Justice of Canada 1976–77; Chair. Ottawa-Carleton Bd of Trade 1985–86; mem. Parl. 1988–; Minister of Industry 1993–2000, also Minister responsible for Atlantic Canada Opportunities Agency, Canada Econ. Devt and Western Econ. Diversification 1996–97; Minister of Foreign Affairs 2000–02; Chair. Ad Hoc Cabinet Cttee on Public Security and Anti-terrorism; Deputy Prime Minister of Canada and Minister of Infastructure and Crown Corpn 2002–03; Minister of Finance 2002–03; Political Minister for Ont. 2002–03; Chair. Cabinet Cttees on Econ. Union and on Social Union 2002–03; retd from politics 2003; Sr Counsel, McCarthy Tétrault LLP, Ottawa 2003–; mem. Bd of Dirs Nortel Networks 2004–, CIBC 2005–; Chair. Ind. Task Force on the Future of North America, Council on Foreign Relations 2005; named Chair. of govt panel on future of Canada's presence in Afghanistan 2007; Pres. and CEO, Canadian Council of Chief Executives 2010–; Dr hc (Carleton Univ.) 1998, (Carleton Univ.), (Toronto Univ.), (Western Ontario Univ.); Internet Person of the Year 2000, Newsmaker of the Year, Time Canada 2001. *Leisure interest:* marathon runner. *Address:* Canadian Council of Chief Executives, 99 Bank Street, Suite 1001, Ottawa, ON K1P 6B9, Canada (office). *Telephone:* (613) 238-3727 (office). *Fax:* (613) 238-3247 (office). *E-mail:* info@ceocouncil.ca (office). *Website:* www.ceocouncil.ca (office).

MANN, Emily Betsy, BA, MFA; American writer, theatre director and playwright; *Artistic Director, McCarter Theatre;* b. 12 April 1952, Boston, Mass; d. of Arthur Mann and Sylvia Mann (née Blut); m. Gary Mailman; one s. from previous m.; ed Harvard Univ., Univ. of Minnesota; Resident Dir Guthrie Theater, Minneapolis 1976–79; Dir Brooklyn Acad. of Music Theater Co., Brooklyn, NY 1980–81; freelance writer and dir, New York 1981–90; Artistic Dir McCarter Theatre, Princeton, NJ 1990–; mem. Soc. of Stage Dirs and Choreographers, Theater Communications Group, New Dramatists, PEN, Writer's Guild; mem. Exec. Bd Dramatists' Guild; Dr hc (Princeton Univ.) 2002; BUSH Fellowship 1975–76, Obie Awards for Directing 1981, 2002, Obie Award for Playwriting 1981, New Drama Forum Asscn Rosamond Gilder Award 1983, Nat. Endowment for the Arts (NEA) Asscns Grant 1984, Tony Award for Outstanding Regional Theater 1984, Guggenheim Fellowship 1985, McKnight Fellowship 1985, CAPS Award 1985, NEA Playwrights Fellowship 1986, Brandeis Univ. Women of Achievement Award 1995, Douglass Coll. of NJ Woman of Achievement Award 1996, Rosamond Gilder Award for Outstanding Achievement in the Theater 1999, Harvard Univ. Alumnae Recognition Award 1999, Nat. Conf. for Community and Justice Award 2004, Leader of the Year Award, Princeton Regional Chamber of Commerce 2005, Person of the Year, Nat. Theatre Conf. 2011. *Publications include:* plays: Annulla Allen: The Autobiography of a Survivor 1977, Still Life (six Obie Awards 1981, Fringe First Award 1985) 1982, Execution of Justice (Helen Hayes Award, Bay Area Theater Critics Circle Award, HBO/USA Award, Playwriting Award Women's Cttee Dramatists Guild for Dramatizing Issues of Conscience) 1986, Having Our Say: The Delaney Sisters' First 100 Years (LA NAACP Award for Best Play) 1994, Greensboro: A Requiem 1996; musicals: Betsey Brown: A Rhythm and Blues Musical (co-author with Ntozake Shange); screenplays: Fanny Kelly (unproduced) 1981, You Strike a Woman, You Strike a Rock: The Story of Winnie Mandela (unproduced mini-series) 1988, The Greensboro Massacre (unproduced) 1992, Having Our Say (Christopher Award, Peabody Award) 1999, Political Stages (co-ed.) 2002. *Address:* McCarter Theatre, 91 University Place, Princeton, NJ 08540-5121, USA (office). *Telephone:* (609) 258-6502 (office). *Fax:* (609) 497-0369 (office). *E-mail:* emann@mccarter.org (office). *Website:* www.mccarter.org (office).

MANN, Matthias, BA, MA, Dr rer. nat; German chemist, biochemist and academic; *Director, Department of Proteomics and Signal Transduction, Max Planck Institute of Biochemistry;* b. 1959; ed Univ. of Göttingen; Postdoctoral Fellow, later Sr Scientist, Dept of Molecular Biology, Univ. of Southern Denmark 1989–92, Prof. of Bioinformatics, Dept of Biochemistry and Molecular Biology and Dir Centre for Experimental BioInformatics 1998–2007; Group Leader, Protein and Peptide Group, European Molecular Biology Lab., Heidelberg 1992–98; Dir Max Planck Inst. of Biochemistry, Martinsried 2005–; also Dir Dept of Proteomics, Novo Nordisk Foundation Centre for Protein Research, Faculty of Heath Sciences, Univ. of Copenhagen, Denmark 2007–; affiliated with NNF Centre for Protein Research; Visiting Prof., Harvard Medical School, USA 1999; mem. Editorial Bd, Journal of Proteome Research, Molecular and Cellular Proteomics, Cell, Carcinogenesis; mem. European Molecular Biology Org. 1999; Hon. Prof., Novo Nordisk Foundation Centre for Protein Research, Faculty of Health Sciences, Univ. of Copenhagen 2007; Dr hc (Utrecht) 2004; Malcom Award, Journal of Organic Mass Spectrometry 1991, Mattauch Herzog Prize in Mass Spectrometry 1996, Hewlett-Packard Prize for Strategic Research in Automation of Sample Preparation 1997, Edman Prize, Methods in Protein Structure Analysis Soc. 1998, Bieman Medal for Outstanding Achievement in Mass Spectrometry, American Soc. for Mass Spectrometry 1999, Bernhard and Matha Rasmussen's Memorial Award in Cancer Research 2001, Meyenburg Cancer Research Award 2001, Fesenius Prize for Analytical Chem., German Chemical Soc. 2001, Lundbeck Nordic Research Prize 2004, Novo-Nordisk Prize (co-recipient) 2004, Anfinsen Award, Protein Soc. 2005, Biochemical Analysis Prize, German Soc. for Clinical Chem. and Lab. Medicine 2006, HUPO Distinguished Achievement Award in Proteomic Sciences (co-recipient) 2008, Friedrich Wilhelm Joseph von Schelling Prize, Bavarian Acad. of Sciences 2010, Fyodor Lynen Lecture Medal, German Soc. of Biochemistry and Molecular Biology 2011, Leibniz Prize, German Research Soc. 2012, Ernst Schering Prize 2012, Louis-Jeantet Foundation Prize for Medicine 2012, Körber European Science Award 2012. *Publications:* more than 500 papers in professional journals. *Address:* Max Planck Institute of Biochemistry, Am Klopferspitz 18, 82152 Martinsried, Germany (office). *Telephone:* (89) 85782557 (office). *Fax:* (89) 85782219 (office). *E-mail:* mmann@biochem.mpg.de (office). *Website:* www.biochem.mpg.de/en/rd/mann (office).

MANN, Michael K.; American film producer, director and writer; b. 5 Feb. 1943, Chicago, Ill.; ed Univ. of Wisconsin, London Film School; Exec. Producer (TV) Miami Vice, Crime Story, Drug Wars: Camarena Story, Drug Wars: Cocaine Cartel, Police Story, Starsky and Hutch; mem. Writers Guild, Directors Guild; two Emmy Awards. *Films include:* The Jericho Mile (TV film, dir, scriptwriter) (Best Dir Award, Directors Guild) 1979, Thief (dir, exec. producer, scriptwriter) 1981, The Keep (dir, scriptwriter) 1981, Manhunter (dir, scriptwriter) 1986, Last of the Mohicans (dir, co-producer, scriptwriter) 1992, Heat (dir, co-producer, scriptwriter) 1995, The Insider (dir, producer) 1999, Ali 2001, Collateral (dir, producer) (Best Dir, Nat. Bd of Review) 2004, The Aviator (producer) (Best Film, BAFTA Awards 2005), Miami Vice 2006, The Kingdom 2007, Hancock 2008, Public Enemies 2009. *Address:* c/o Creative Artists Agency, 9830 Wilshire Boulevard, Beverly Hills, CA 90212, USA.

MANN, Yuri Vladimirovich; Russian literary scholar and historian; *Professor, Russian State Humanitarian University;* b. 9 June 1929, Moscow; s. of Vladimir Mann and Sonja Mann; m. Galina Mann 1956 (died 2007); two s.; ed Moscow Univ.; school teacher, Moscow 1952–56; Prof. of Russian Literature, Gorky Inst. of World Literature –1992; Prof., Russian State Humanitarian Univ. 1992–; Visiting Prof., Chicago Univ., USA 1991; Chief Ed. Complete Academic Works of N. V. Gogol (23 vols); mem. CPSU 1952–90, Russian PEN Centre 1995, Acad. of Natural Sciences 1996. *Publications include:* The Grotesque in Literature 1966, Russian Philosophical Aesthetics 1820's–1830's 1969, The Poetics of Russian Romanticism 1976, The Poetics of Gogol 1978, In Search of a Live Soul –Gogol's Dead Souls 1984, The Dialectics of Image 1987, The Aksakov Family 1992, Beyond the Mask of Laughter: The Life of Nikolai Gogol 1994, The Dynamics of Russian Romanticism 1995, The Poetics of Gogol: Variations on the Theme 1996, Russian Literature XIX Century. Romanticism 2001, Gogol: The Life and the Creation 1809–1845 2004, Exploring Gogol 2005, 19th Century Russian Literature (Romanticism) 2007, Creations of Gogol: Meaning and Form 2007, Turgenev and the Others 2008, Gogol: The End of the Road, 1845–1852 2009, Gogol: Fate and Creation 2009, Memory as Happiness as well as Memory as Pain… 2011. *Address:* Russian State Humanitarian University, Ul. Chayanov 15, Moscow 125267 (office); 3 Tverskaya-Yamskaya 44, Apartment 5, Moscow 125047, Russia (home). *Telephone:* (499) 250-66-92 (office); (499) 250-52-97 (home). *E-mail:* ymann@si.ru (home).

MANNAI, Jassim Abdullah al-, PhD; Bahraini business executive and international organization official; *Director-General and Chairman, Arab Monetary Fund;* b. 1948; ed Univ. of Paris (Sorbonne), France, Harvard Business School, USA; Exec. Vice-Pres. Gulf Investment Corpn, Kuwait 1987–94; CEO and Chair. Arab Trade Financing Program, Abu Dhabi 1994–; Dir-Gen. and Chair. Arab Monetary Fund, Abu Dhabi 1994–; Chair. Inter Arab Rating Co. EC (mem. Fitch IBCA Group) 1995–2001. *Publications:* numerous articles on economic and financial issues in various pubs. *Address:* Office of the Director-General, Arab Monetary Fund Building, Corniche Road, PO Box 2818, Abu Dhabi, United Arab Emirates (office). *Telephone:* (2) 6171701 (office). *Fax:* (2) 6332089 (office). *E-mail:* centralmail@amfad.org.ae (office). *Website:* www.amf.org.ae (office).

MANNHARDT, Thilo, MSc, MBA, PhD; German business executive; *CEO, Ultrapar Holdings;* ed Technische Universität Berlin; Sr Partner and Dir, McKinsey & Co. 1985–2012; mem. Bd of Dirs Ultrapar Holdings 2011–12, CEO 2013–. *Address:* Ultrapar Holdings, Avenida Brigadeiro Luiz Antônio 1343, São Paulo 01317-910, Brazil (office). *Telephone:* (11) 3177-7014 (office). *Fax:* (11) 3177-6107 (office). *E-mail:* info@ultra.com.br (office). *Website:* www.ultra.com.br (office).

MANNING, Sir David Geoffrey, Kt, GCMG, CVO, BA; British diplomatist; b. 5 Dec. 1949, Portsmouth, Hants.; s. of John Robert Manning and Joan Barbara Manning; m. Catherine Marjory Parkinson 1973; ed Ardingly Coll., Oriel Coll. Oxford, Johns Hopkins Univ., USA; Third Sec., FCO (Mexico, Cen. America Dept) 1972; Third, later Second Sec., Warsaw 1974–76; Second, later First Sec., New Delhi 1977–80; E European and Soviet Dept FCO 1980–82; Policy Planning Staff, FCO 1982–84; First Sec. (Political Internal), Paris 1984–88; Counsellor on loan to Cabinet Office 1988–90; Counsellor, Head of Political Section, Moscow 1990–93;

Head, Eastern Dept (fmrly Soviet Dept), FCO 1993–94; British mem. of ICFY Contact Group on Bosnia April–Nov. 1994; Head of Planning Staff 1994–95; Amb. to Israel 1995–98; Deputy Under-Sec. of State, FCO 1998–2000; Perm. Rep. to NATO Jan.–Aug. 2001; Foreign Policy Adviser to Prime Minister 2001–03; Head of Cabinet Office Defence and Overseas Secr. 2001–03; Amb. to USA 2003–07; apptd by HM The Queen to 'part-time, advisory role' in newly formed Household of HRH Prince William of Wales and HRH Prince Harry of Wales 2009; mem. Bd of Dirs Lloyds Banking Group plc 2008–09; Dir (non-exec.) BG Group plc (fmrly British Gas plc) 2008–, Lockheed Martin UK Holdings Ltd 2008–; mem. Advisory Bd Hakluyt & Co.; Trustee, Turner Contemporary. *Address:* c/o Board of Directors, BG Group plc, 100 Thames Valley Park, Reading, Berks., RG6 1PT, England (office). *Telephone:* (118) 935-3222 (office). *Fax:* (118) 935-3484 (office). *E-mail:* Box .info@bg-group.com (office).

MANNING, Jane, OBE, LRAM, FRAM, ARCM, FRCM, GRSM; British singer (soprano), lecturer and writer; *Visiting Professor, Royal College of Music;* b. 20 Sept. 1938, Norwich, Norfolk, England; d. of the late Gerald Manning and Lily Thompson; m. Anthony Payne 1966; ed Norwich High School for Girls, Royal Acad. of Music, London, Scuola di Canto, Cureglia, Switzerland; London debut concert 1964; since then active world-wide as freelance soprano soloist with special expertise in contemporary music; more than 350 BBC broadcasts; regular tours of USA since 1981 and of Australia since 1978; appearances at most leading European festivals and concert halls; New York debut 1983; more than 300 world premières including several operas; Founder/Artistic Dir Jane's Minstrels (ensemble) 1988; many recordings including complete vocal works of Messiaen and Satie; Vice-Pres. Soc. for Promotion of New Music 1996–2008; Visiting Prof., Mills Coll., Oakland, Calif. 1981, 1982, 1983, 1986, Royal Coll. of Music 1995–; Arts and Humanities Research Council Creative Arts Research Fellow, Kingston Univ. 2003–07, Visiting Prof. 2007–10; visiting lecturer, univs in UK, USA, Canada, Australia, NZ and Scandinavia; Chair. Eye Music Trust; Trustee, Musicians' Benevolent Fund; Hon. Prof., Keele Univ. 1996–2002; Hon. DUniv (York) 1988; Hon. DMus (Keele) 2004, (Dunelm) 2007; Special Award for Services to British Music, Composers' Guild of GB 1973. *Publications include:* New Vocal Repertory (Vol. I) 1986, (Vol. II) 1998; contrib. to A Messiaen Companion 1995, Voicing Pierrot (A Practical Guide) 2011; contrib. to History of Musical Performance; numerous articles in Tempo, etc. *Leisure interests:* cooking, ornithology, cinema, philosophy, theatre, reading. *Address:* 2 Wilton Square, London, N1 3DL, England. *Telephone:* (20) 7359-1593. *E-mail:* janetone@gmail.com. *Website:* www .classical-artists/janemanning.com.

MANNING, Patrick Augustus Mervyn, BSc; Trinidad and Tobago politician; b. 17 Aug. 1946, San Fernando, Trinidad; s. of Arnold Manning and Elaine Manning; m. Hazel Anne-Marie Kinsale 1972; two s.; ed Presentation Coll., San Fernando, Univ. of the West Indies; refinery operator, Texaco, Trinidad 1965–66; Parl. Sec. 1971–78, Minister 1978–86; Minister of Information and of Industry and Commerce 1981, of Energy 1981–86; Leader of the Opposition 1986–90; Prime Minister 1991–95, 2001–10, also Minister of Tobago Affairs; Minister of Finance 2001–07; fmr Minister of Nat. Security; Leader People's Nat. Movt 1987–. *Leisure interests:* table tennis, chess, reading. *Address:* c/o Office of the Prime Minister, Whitehall, Maraval Road, Port of Spain; People's National Movement, 1 Tranquillity Street, Port of Spain, Trinidad.

MANNING, Peyton Williams, BA; American professional football player; b. 24 March 1976, New Orleans, La; s. of Archie Manning and Olivia Manning; m. Ashley Thompson 2001; ed Isidore Newman High School, New Orleans, Univ. of Tennessee; quarterback; holds 42 Nat. Collegiate Athletic Asscn (NCAA), South Eastern Conf. (SEC) and Univ. of Tennessee records, including 33 Univ. of Tennessee single game, season and career records; first pick in 1998 Nat. Football League (NFL) draft by Indianapolis Colts 1998, holds numerous NFL passing records including most seasons (nine) with at least 4,000 passing yards 1999–2004, 2006–08, led Colts to Super Bowl XLI championship 2007, released by Colts 2012; signed with Denver Broncos 2012–; f. Peyback Foundation 1999; Gatorade Circle of Champions Nat. Player of the Year in high school, voted third-best quarterback in SEC history, named in SEC All-Decade Team, Maxwell Trophy (for coll. football's best player) 1997, Sullivan Award Winner 1997, named to Pro Bowl team 1999–2000, 2002–10, AFC Player of the Year 1999, 2003, 2004, 2005, 2008, 2009, Henry P. Iba Citizen Athlete Award 2002, USA Weekend's Most Caring Athlete Award 2002, First-team All-Pro 2003, 2004, 2005, 2008, 2009, Second-team All-Pro 1999, 2000, 2006, Associated Press (AP) Most Valuable Player of the NFL 2003 (jtly with Steve McNair) 2004, 2008, 2009, Bert Bell Award 2003, 2004, AP NFL Offensive Player of the Year 2004, John Wooden Trophy 2004, Walter Payton Man of the Year Award 2005, Pro Bowl Most Valuable Player 2005, Byron 'Whizzer' White Humanitarian Award 2005, AFC champion 2006, 2009, Super Bowl XLI Most Valuable Player 2007, Best Championship Performance ESPY Award 2007, Youthlinks Indiana Nat. Pathfinder Award 2010, NFL 2000s All-Decade Team. *Achievements include:* fastest player ever to reach 50,000 yards passing, fastest to 4,000 completions. *Publications:* Manning: A Father, His Sons and a Football Legacy (with Archie Manning) 2000. *Address:* c/o Brian Bishoff, IMG, 1360 East 9th Street, Suite 100, Cleveland, OH 44114 (office); Denver Broncos Football Club, Executive Offices and Training Facility, 13655 Broncos Parkway, Englewood, CO 80112, USA (office). *Telephone:* (216) 436-3571 (office); (303) 649-9000 (office). *Website:* www.imgfootball.com (office); www.denverbroncos.com (office); www .peytonmanning.com.

MANNINGHAM-BULLER, Baroness Eliza(beth) Lydia, DCB; British fmr government official; b. 14 July 1948; d. of Sir Reginald Manningham-Buller (later Viscount Dilhorne) and Lady Mary Lilian Lindsay; m. 1991; ed Northampton High School, Benenden School, Kent and Lady Margaret Hall, Univ. of Oxford; fmr English teacher; joined MI5 Security Service 1974, worked on case of KGB defector Oleg Gordievsky and on Lockerbie disaster, served as MI5 liaison officer at Embassy in Washington, DC, Dir for Surveillance and Tech. Operations 1993, Dir of Irish Counter-terrorism, Dir of Finance and Information Tech., Deputy Dir-Gen. 1997–2002, Dir-Gen. 2002–07 (retd); mem. House of Lords 2008–; Vice-Chair. Pollen Estate; mem. Bd of Dirs Ark Continuity Ltd, Genome Research Ltd; Sr Adviser to Inter Mediate Ltd; mem. Council, Imperial Coll. 2008–, Chair. 2011–; Gov. Wellcome Trust 2009–; Hon. Fellow, Lady Margaret Hall, Oxford 2003, Northampton Univ. 2008; Dr hc (Cranfield) 2003, (Open) 2005. *Address:* House of

Lords, London, SW1A 0PW, England (office). *Telephone:* (20) 7219-5353 (office). *Fax:* (20) 7219-5979 (office).

MANOLI, Mihail, PhD; Moldovan economist, diplomatist and politician; b. 20 Sept. 1954, Valea Mare; m.; one c.; ed Polytechnic Institute of Chisinau, M. Lomonosov Moscow State Univ.; Lecturer, Academy of Economic Studies, State Univ. of Moldova 1978–79, 1983–95; with Price Waterhouse 1993–95; Deputy Minister of Finance 1995–99, Minister of Finance 1999–2002; Amb. to USA (also accred to Canada) 2002–06; Deputy Pres. of Council of Experts, National Securities Comm. 2006–07; Counselor to Pres. of CB Universalbank 2007–08; Pres. Union of Insurers of Moldova 2008–10; Deputy Chair. Humanist Party of Moldova 2010–. *Address:* Humanist Party of Moldova (Partidul Umanist din Moldova), 2011 Chişinău, or. Codru, str. Sf. Gheorghe 12, Moldova (office). *Telephone:* (22) 23-41-51 (office). *E-mail:* presa.pasat@gmail.com (office). *Website:* www.pum.md (office).

MANOLIĆ, Josip, (Joža); Croatian politician and lawyer; b. 22 March 1920, Kalinovac; m. Marija Manolić (née Eker); three d.; ed Zagreb Univ.; mem. youth orgs and trade union activist 1938–; mem. anti-fascist movt; Sec., Dist Cttee League of Communist Youth of Croatia; Chief, Dept of Nat. Security in Bjelovar 1945–46 (dismissed); worked in Ministry of Internal Affairs of Croatia 1948–60; Interior Affairs Secr. in Zagreb 1960–65; mem. of Parl. Repub. of Croatia, Pres. Legis. Body of Constitutional Comm. 1965–71; mandate suspended because of nationalist activities; Co-founder Croatian Democratic Union (HDZ), first Chair. Exec. Cttee 1989, elected Vice-Pres. 1990; mem. of Croatian Parl. 1990–; Pres. Croatian Govt 1990–91, Vice-Pres. Presidency of Repub. of Croatia –1999; Pres. House of Counties of Croatian Parl. 1992–94; Pres. Emergency Bd of Croatia; Dir Bureau for the Protection of Constitutional Order 1991–93; Founder Croatian Ind. Democrats (HND), Pres. of HND; certificate for participation in anti-Fascist struggle 1941–45, certificate for participation in the defence of the homeland 1991–92. *Publication:* Manolić 1989–95 (collection of interviews). *Leisure interest:* chess. *Address:* Nazorova Str. 57, 41000 Zagreb, Croatia (office). *Telephone:* (1) 4848476 (office).

MANOOGIAN, Richard Alexander, BA; American business executive; *Chairman Emeritus, Masco Corporation;* b. 1936, Detroit, Mich.; s. of Alex Manoogian and Marie Manoogian; ed Yale Univ.; joined Masco Corpn 1958, apptd Dir 1964, Vice-Pres. 1964–68, Pres. 1968–85, Chair. and CEO 1985–2007, Exec. Chair. 2007–09, Chair. 2009–12, Chair. Emer. 2012–; CEO Metaldyne Corpn –1998; Chair. TriMas 1989–98; mem. Bd of Dirs JPMorgan Chase 1978–, Bank One Corpn 1978–, First Chicago NBD Corpn 1978–, Ford Motor Co. 2001–, Metaldyne Corpn 1984–2005, MSX International Inc. 1997–2004, Detroit Renaisssance, The American Business Conf., MSX Int.; Life Pres. Armenian Gen. Benevolent Union; Chair. Detroit Inst. of Arts, Alex and Marie Manoogian Foundation; Dir, Yale Univ. Art Gallery, Center for Creative Studies, The Fine Arts Cttee of the State Dept, Council of the Nat. Gallery of Art, Armenian Gen. Benevolent Union, Henry Ford Museum, Greenfield Village; mem. Henry Ford Museum, Michigan Business Roundtable, Mackinac Island State Park Comm., American Fed. of Arts, American Asscn of Museums, Museum Trustees Asscn, Chief Execs Org. (YPO); Trustee, Community Foundation of Southeastern Michigan, Archives of American Art (Smithsonian Inst.). *Address:* Masco Corporation, 21001 Van Born Road, Taylor, MI 48180-1300, USA (office). *Telephone:* (313) 274-7400 (office). *Fax:* (313) 792-4177 (office). *E-mail:* info@masco.com (office). *Website:* www.masco.com (office).

MANOROHANTA, Cécile; Malagasy politician, academic and university administrator; *President, Université Nord Madagascar;* mem. Faculty, Université Nord Madagascar, Antsiranana 2000–02, then Acting Rector and Pres., Pres. 2013–; Nat. Vice-Pres. ruling Tiako i Madagasikara (I Love Madagascar—TIM) party; Minister of Defence (first woman) 2007–09 (resgnd), Deputy Prime Minister, responsible for the Interior Sept.–Dec. 2009, apptd acting Prime Minister for two days 18–20 Dec. 2009; Commdr, Légion d'Honneur 2007. *Publications:* A Quantitative Study of Voice in Malagasy (UCLA Working Papers in Linguistics 6: Papers in African Linguistics 1) 2001; numerous papers on linguistics in professional journals. *Address:* Office of the President, Université Nord Madagascar, BP 0, 201 Antsiranana, Madagascar (office). *Telephone:* (20) 82-29-409 (office). *Fax:* (20) 82-29-409 (office). *E-mail:* presidence@univ-antsiranana.org (office). *Website:* www.univ-antsiranana.org (office).

MANSARAY, Binta, BA, MA; Sierra Leonean lawyer and UN official; *Registrar, Special Court for Sierra Leone, United Nations;* ed Fourah Bay Coll., Univ. of Sierra Leone, Fordham Univ., USA; fmr human rights advocate for victims and ex-combatants with several orgs; held post of Country Rep. for Women's Comm. for Refugee Women and Children in Sierra Leone, worked with Campaign for Good Governance, and served as consultant with UN Mission in Sierra Leone (UNAMSIL) and several civil soc. orgs; Outreach Coordinator, UN Special Court for Sierra Leone, Freetown 2003–07, Deputy Registrar, Special Court for Sierra Leone 2007–09, Acting Registrar 2009–10, Registrar 2010–. *Achievements include:* designed Court's grassroots programme to keep the people of Sierra Leone, and later Liberia, informed about the Court and the trials. *Address:* The Special Court for Sierra Leone, Jomo Kenyatta Road, New England, Freetown, Sierra Leone (office); The Special Court for Sierra Leone, PO Box 19536, 2500 CM The Hague, The Netherlands (office); The Special Court for Sierra Leone, Chrysler Building, 405 Lexington Avenue, 5th Floor, Room 5090, New York, NY 10074, USA (office). *Telephone:* (22) 297000 (Freetown) (office); (0831) 257000 (via Italy) (office); (212) 457-1293 (New York) (office); (70) 515-9750 (The Hague) (office). *Fax:* (22) 297001 (Freetown) (office); (0831) 257001 (via Italy) (office); (212) 457-4059 (New York) (office); (70) 322-2711 (The Hague) (office). *Website:* www.sc-sl.org (office).

MANSBRIDGE, Peter, OC; Canadian (b. British) broadcaster and journalist; *Chief Correspondent of CBC News and Anchor, The National, Canadian Broadcasting Corporation;* b. 6 July 1948, London, England, UK; s. of the late Stanley Harry Mansbridge and Brena Louise Mansbridge; m. 1st Parm Dhillon (divorced 1975); m. 2nd Wendy Mesley 1989 (divorced 1992); m. Cynthia Dale 1998; ed Glebe Collegiate Inst., Trinity Coll. School, Port Hope, Ont.; raised in Ottawa, Ont.; served in Royal Canadian Navy 1966–67; fmr airline freight man.; disc jockey and newscaster, CBC Radio, Churchill 1968, reporter, CBC Radio, Winnipeg 1971, reporter, CBC TV News 1972–85, reporter, The National, Saskatchewan 1975, with Parl. Bureau, Ottawa 1976–80, Co-Anchor, Quarterly Report, Anchor Sunday

Report 1985, Anchor, The National 1988–92, Anchor of news segment on The National 1992–, Anchor, Prime Time News 1992–, Chief Corresp. for CBC News; launched a new programme, Mansbridge One on One 1999–; Chancellor Mount Allison Univ., NB 2009–; Queen Elizabeth II Diamond Jubilee Medal 2012; Hon. LLD (Mount Allison Univ.) 1999, (Univ. of Manitoba, Winnipeg) 2001, (Univ. of Western Ontario) 2008, (Univ. of Windsor, Ont.) 2010; Hon. Dr of Journalism (Ryerson Univ., Toronto) 2005; 12 Gemini Awards for excellence in broadcast journalism. *Address:* Prime Time News, Canadian Broadcasting Corporation, 181 Queen Street, Ottawa, ON K1P 1K9, Canada (office). *Telephone:* (613) 288-6000 (office). *Fax:* (613) 724-5074 (office). *Website:* www.cbc.ca (office).

MANSELL, Kevin B.; American retail executive; *Chairman, President and CEO, Kohl's Department Stores;* b. St Louis, Mo.; ed Univ. of Missouri; various buying and merchandising roles, Venture Stores Div., May Dept Stores 1975; Divisional Merchandise Man. Kohl's Dept Stores 1982–87, Gen. Merchandise Man. 1987–96, Sr Exec. Vice-Pres. of Merchandising and Marketing 1998–99, Dir 1999–, Pres. 1999–, CEO 2008–, Chair. 2009–. *Address:* Kohl's Department Stores, N56 W17000 Ridgewood Drive, Menomonee Falls, WI 53051-5660, USA (office). *Telephone:* (262) 703-7000 (office). *Fax:* (262) 703-6143 (office). *E-mail:* info@kohls.com (office). *Website:* www.kohls.com (office).

MANSELL, Nigel Ernest James, CBE, OBE; British racing driver; b. 8 Aug. 1953, Upton-on-Severn, Worcs., England; s. of Eric Mansell and Joyce Mansell; m. Rosanne Perry; two s. one d.; ed Matthew Boulton Polytechnic, Solihull Tech. Coll.; began racing in karts; won 11 regional Championships 1969–76; Formula Ford and Formula Three 1976–79; Formula Two, later Formula One 1980; Lotus team 1981–84; Williams-Honda team 1985–87; Williams-Judd team 1988; Ferrari team 1989–90; Williams-Renault team 1991–92 and 1994 (part-time); McLaren team 1995; first competed in a Grand Prix, Austria 1980; won 31 Grand Prix races 1980–94, record since beaten by Michael Schumacher; Formula One World Drivers Champion 1992; American Newman-Haas Indy Car Team 1993; CART Indy Car World Series Champion 1993; Special Constable, Isle of Man –1995, Devon and Cornwall Constabulary; Owner Woodbury Park Golf and Country Club 1993–; Pres. UK Youth (charity); Hon. DEng (Birmingham) 1993; BBC Sports Personality of the Year 1986, 1992, CART Rookie of the Year 1993, inducted into Int. Motorsports Hall of Fame 2005. *Publications:* Mansell and Williams (with Derick Allsop) 1992, Nigel Mansell's IndyCar Racing (with Jeremy Shaw) 1993, My Autobiography (with James Allen) 1995, Driven to Win (with Derick Allsop). *Leisure interests:* golf, fishing, flying. *Address:* c/o Nicki Dance, Woodbury Park Golf and Country Club, Woodbury Castle, Woodbury, Exeter, Devon, EX5 1JJ, England. *Telephone:* (1395) 233382 (office). *Fax:* (1395) 232978 (office). *E-mail:* nickidance@woodburypark.co.uk. *Website:* www.woodburypark.co.uk; www .nigelmansell.co.uk.

MANSER, Michael John, CBE, RA, DIPL. ARCH., PRIBA, RWA; British architect; *Chairman (non-executive), The Manser Practice;* b. 23 March 1929, London; s. of the late Edmund G. and Augusta M. Manser; m. Dolores Josephine Bernini 1953; one s. one d.; ed School of Architecture, The Polytechnic of Cen. London; Chair. The Manser Practice (architects) 1961–; architectural corresp. the Observer 1964–66; wide variety of architectural projects including pvt. housing, industrial buildings, research labs, schools, swimming pools, commercial and domestic renovation and refurbishment, hotels, offices, air ferry terminals, London Underground stations, health bldgs, British embassies and British Council offices; Pres. RIBA 1983–85; Academician Royal Acad. 1994; RIBA Rep. RSA 1987–93 (Chair. Art for Architecture Award Scheme 1990–); mem. Council Nat. Trust 1991–93; Assessor Art in the Workplace Awards 1988–; Chair. Art and Work Awards 1996–; mem. Royal Acad. Council 1998–; Architectural Cttee 1998–, City of Westminster Public Art Panel 1999–, Works Cttee 1999–, Remuneration Cttee 2000–, Audit Cttee 2000–; Royal W of England Academician 1993–; City of Westminster Public Art Panel 2001; Chair. Nat. Homebuilder Design Awards 1998, RIBA Awards Cttee 1998–2002; Chair. British Architectural Library Trust 2008–; Hon. FRAIC; Civic Trust Award 1967, Civic Trust Commendation 1973, European Architectural Heritage Award 1975, Dept of Environment Good Design in Housing Award 1975, Structural Steel Design Award 1976, 1995, RIBA Award Commendation 1977; RIBA Award, RIBA Regional Award 1991, Royal Fine Art Comm. and Sunday Times Bldg of the Year Finalist 1991, Quarternario Int. Award for Innovative Tech. in Architecture Finalist 1993, Civic Trust Award 1993, RIBA Award and Regional Award 1995, Manser Medal RIBA Housing Award 2001, RIBA Award 2002 Buildings listed for Preservation in 2002. *Publications:* Planning Your Kitchen (co-author), Psychiatry in the Elderly (co-author), Companion to Contemporary Architectural Thought (co-author) 1993; contributions to nat. and tech. press. *Leisure interests:* architecture, music, books, gardening, boats. *Address:* The Manser Practice, Bridge Studios, Hammersmith Bridge, London, W6 9DA; 76 Whitehall Court, London, SW1A 2EL, England. *Telephone:* (20) 8741-4381 (office). *E-mail:* manser@manser.co.uk (office).

MANSFIELD, Eric Harold, MA, ScD, FIMA, FREng, FRAeS, FRS; British scientist and academic; b. 24 May 1923, Croydon, Surrey; s. of Harold G. Mansfield and Grace Pfundt Mansfield; m. 1st 1947 (divorced 1973); m. 2nd Eunice Shuttleworth-Parker 1974; two s. one d.; ed St Lawrence Coll., Ramsgate, Trinity Hall, Cambridge; various grades, Structures Dept, Royal Aircraft Est., Farnborough 1943–83, Chief Scientific Officer 1980–83; Visiting Prof., Univ. of Surrey 1984–90; mem. British Nat. Cttee for Theoretical and Applied Mechanics 1973–79, Gen. Ass. Int. Union of Theoretical and Applied Mechanics 1976–80; Bronze Medal, Royal Aeronautical Soc. 1967, James Alfred Ewing Gold Medal for Eng Research 1991, Royal Medal, Royal Soc. 1994. *Achievements include:* originator of Neutral Hole Theory, The Inextensional Theory for thin plates, Wrinkled Membrane Theory (modern version), Theory of Gravity-induced Wrinkles in Vertical Membranes, Theory for Objects Supported by Surface Tension, Theory for the Collapse of Rigid-Plastic Plates. *Publications:* Bending and Stretching of Plates 1964, Bridge: the Ultimate Limits 1986; articles in professional journals. *Leisure interests:* bridge, palaeontology, snorkelling, walking Poppy the dog. *Address:* Primrose Cottage, Alresford Road, Cheriton, Hants., SO24 0QJ, England (home). *Telephone:* (1962) 771280 (home).

MANSFIELD, Michael, QC, BA, FRSA; British barrister; *Professor of Law, Westminster University and City University;* b. 12 Oct. 1941, London; s. of Frank Mansfield and Marjorie Sayers; m. 1st Melian Mansfield 1967 (divorced 1992);

three s. two d.; m. 2nd Yvette Mansfield 1992; one s.; ed Highgate School and Keele Univ.; began practising 1967; est. Tooks Court chambers 1984; specialist in civil liberties work; Prof. of Law, Westminster Univ. 1997–, City Univ., London; Pres. Amicus, Haldane Soc., NCRM; Patron Acre Lane Neighbourhood Chambers, Brixton 1997–; Bencher, Gray's Inn 2008; Hon. Fellow, Kent Univ.; Hon. LLD (South Bank Univ.) 1994, (Univ. of Herts.) 1995, (Keele Univ.) 1995, (Westminster Univ.) 2005, (Ulster Univ.). *Radio:* Moral Maze, BBC Radio 4 1995–98, Today, BBC Radio 4. *Television:* Inside Story 1991, Presumed Guilty; contribution to Newsnight, BBC 2. *Publications:* Presumed Guilty 1994, Home Lawyer 2004, Memoirs of a Radical Lawyer 2010. *Leisure interests:* my children, drumming. *Address:* Tooks Chambers, 8 Warner Yard, London, EC1R 5EY, England (office). *Telephone:* (20) 7841-6100 (office). *Fax:* (20) 7841-6199 (office). *Website:* www.tooks.co.uk (office).

MANSFIELD, Sir Peter, Kt, BSc, PhD, FRS, PPL, PPLH; British physicist and academic; *Professor Emeritus in Residence, University of Nottingham;* b. 9 Oct. 1933, London, England; s. of the late S. G. Mansfield and R. L. Mansfield; m. Jean M. Kibble 1962; two d.; ed William Penn School, Peckham and Queen Mary Coll., London, Univ. of London; Research Assoc. Dept of Physics, Univ. of Ill. 1962; lecturer, Univ. of Nottingham 1964, Sr Lecturer 1967, Reader 1970, Prof. of Physics 1979–94, Prof. Emer. in Residence 1995–; MRC Professorial Fellow 1983–88; Sr Visitor, Max Planck Inst. for Medical Research, Heidelberg 1972–73; Fellow, Queen Mary Coll. 1985; Pres. Soc. of Magnetic Resonance in Medicine 1987–88; Hon. FRCR 1992; Hon. FInstP 1996; Hon. mem. British Inst. of Radiology (BIR) 1993; Hon. DrMed (Strasbourg) 1995; Hon. DSc (Univ. of Kent at Canterbury) 1996; Royal Soc. Wellcome Foundation Gold Medal and Prize 1985, Duddell Medal, Inst. of Physics 1988, Royal Soc. Mullard Medal 1990, ISMAR Prize 1992, Barclay Medal, BJR 1993, Gold Medal, European Asscn of Radiology 1995, Garmisch-Partenkirchen Prize for MRI 1995, Rank Prize 1997, Nobel Prize in Physiology or Medicine (jtly with Paul C. Lauterbur) 2003, several other awards. *Publications:* NMR Imaging in Biomedicine 1982, NMR Imaging (co-ed.) 1990, MRI in Medicine 1995, The Long Road to Stockholm 2013; some 200 scientific publs in learned journals. *Leisure interests:* reading, languages, flying. *Address:* Sir Peter Mansfield Magnetic Resonance Centre, Department of Physics and Astronomy, University of Nottingham, NG7 2RD, England (office). *Telephone:* (115) 951-4740 (office). *Fax:* (115) 951-5166 (office). *E-mail:* pamela.davies@nottingham.ac.uk (office). *Website:* www.magres.nottingham.ac.uk (office).

MANSFIELD, Terence Arthur, PhD, FRS, FSB; British biologist and academic; *Professor Emeritus and Honorary Fellow, Lancaster University;* b. 18 Jan. 1937, Ashby-de-la-Zouch, Leics., England; s. of Sydney W. Mansfield and Rose Mansfield (née Sinfield); m. Margaret M. James 1963; two s.; ed Univs of Nottingham and Reading; Research Fellow, Univ. of Reading 1961–65; Lecturer and Prof., Lancaster Univ. 1965–87, Dir Inst. of Environmental and Biological Sciences 1987–94, Provost of Science and Eng 1994–97, Research Prof. 1996–2001, Prof. Emer. and Hon. Fellow 2001–; mem. Agric. and Food Research Council 1989–93; Fellow, Soc. of Biology. *Publications:* Physiology of Stomata (co-author) 1968, Stomatal Physiology (co-ed.) 1981, Plant Adaptation to Environmental Stress (co-ed.) 1993, Disturbance of the Nitrogen Cycle (co-ed.) 1998, Glimpses of the Victorians at Church 2004; numerous chapters and journal articles on aspects of botanical science. *Leisure interests:* cricket, hill-walking, church history. *Address:* 25 Wallace Lane, Forton, Preston, Lancs., PR3 0BA, England. *Telephone:* (1524) 791338.

MANSHA, Mian Mohammad; Pakistani industrialist; *Chairman, Nishat Group;* s. of Mian Mohammad Yahya; Chair. Nishat Group, conglomerate with interests in banking, insurance, textiles and cement, including Muslim Commercial Bank, Nishat Mills, D. G. Khan Cement. *Address:* Nishat Chunian, 31-Q, Gulberg II, Lahore 54660, Pakistan (office). *Telephone:* (42) 5761730 (office). *Fax:* (42) 5878696 (office). *E-mail:* info@nctex.com (office). *Website:* www.nctex.com (office).

MANSHARD, Walther, Dr rer. nat; German geographer, academic and international civil servant; *Professor, Geographisches Institut, University of Freiburg;* b. 17 Nov. 1923, Hamburg; s. of Otto and Ida Manshard; m. Helga Koch 1951; one d.; ed Univ. of Hamburg; Asst lecturer, Univ. of Southampton, UK 1950–52; lecturer, Univ. of Ghana 1952–60; Dozent, Univ. of Cologne 1960–63; Prof. Univ. of Giessen 1963–70; Prin. Dir UNESCO Dept of Environmental Sciences 1970–73; Prof., Head of Dept Univ. of Freiburg 1973–77, 1980–; Vice-Rector, UN Univ., Tokyo 1977–80; Sec.-Gen. and Treas. Int. Geographical Union 1976–84; Sr Adviser UN Univ. 1990–93; Hon. DLitt 1991. *Publications:* Die geographischen Grundlagen der Wirtschaft Ghanas 1961, Tropisches Afrika 1963, Agrargeographie der Tropen 1968, Afrika–Südlich der Sahara 1970, Tropical Agriculture 1974, Die Städte des tropischen Afrika 1977, Renewable Natural Resources and the Environment 1981, Entwicklungsprobleme in Agrarräumen Tropen-Afrikas 1988, Umwelt v. Entwicklung in den Tropen 1995. *Address:* Geographisches Institut, University of Freiburg, Werderring 4, 79085 Freiburg i. Br.; Schwarzwaldstrasse 24, 79189 Bad Krozingen, Germany. *Telephone:* (761) 2033565 (office); (7633) 9888941 (home). *Fax:* (761) 2033575 (office); (7633) 3488 (home). *E-mail:* walther .manshard@geographie.uni-freiburg.de (office). *Website:* www.geographie.uni -freiburg.de (office).

MANSINGH, Lalit, MA; Indian diplomatist; *President, Forum for Strategic Initiatives;* b. 29 April 1941, Cuttack; s. of the late Mayadhar Mansingh and of Hemalata Mansingh (née Behura); m. Indira Singh 1976; one s. one d.; ed Utkal Univ., Orissa, Indian School of Int. Studies, Univ. of Delhi; lecturer in political science 1961–63; joined diplomatic service 1963, Deputy Chief of Mission to Kabul 1971–74, to Brussels 1976–80, to Washington, DC 1989–92, Amb. to UAE 1980–83; High Commr to Nigeria 1993–95, to London 1998–99; Jt Sec. Dept of Econ. Affairs, Ministry of Finance 1984–85; Dir Gen. Indian Council for Cultural Relations 1985–89; Dean, Foreign Service Inst. of India, New Delhi 1995, now Prof. Emer.; Foreign Sec., Ministry of External Affairs 1997–98; Amb. to USA 2001–04; Chair. World Cultural Forum India, Political Science Asscn, Ravenshaw Univ., Bd of Advisors, Mahatma Gandhi Inst. of Educ. for Peace and Sustainable Devt, UNESCO; Pres. India Strategic Forum, Forum for Strategic Initiatives; Vice-Pres. Indian Council for Cultural Relations; mem. Bd of Trustees, Int. Crisis Group, Brussels, Asia Pacific Leadership Network, Canberra, Int. Advisory Council, APCO Worldwide, Washington, DC, Governing Body of Devt Alternatives, New Delhi and Gram Vikas; Odisha Diplomatic Advisor, Fed. of Indian Chamber of

Commerce and Industry (FICCI), Chair. FICCI India-US Policy Group; mem. Non Official Group of Friends of Sri Lanka; participant of a Track II dialogue between India and Pakistan focusing on confidence building measures between the two nuclear-armed neighbours, Track II trilateral dialogue between India, Pakistan and Afghanistan; Global Envoy for Buddhism; Hon. LLD (Univ. of North Odisha) 2013; Univ. Gold Medals for top ranking graduate in History and Political Science, Kharavela Award, Govt of Orissa 2009. *Publications include:* Indian Foreign Policy: Agenda for the 21st Century (Ed.-in-Chief) 1998. *Leisure interests:* classical music, dance, fine arts, theatre. *Address:* N-38 Panchsheel Park, New Delhi 110 017, India (home). *E-mail:* lalitmansingh@yahoo.com (office).

MANSON, Marilyn; American singer and songwriter; b. (Brian Warner), 5 Jan. 1969, Canton, Ohio; m. Dita Von Teese 2005 (divorced 2007); fmr music journalist; Founder mem. Marilyn Manson & the Spooky Kids 1989–, later just Marilyn Manson; numerous TV appearances, tours; Kerrang! Icon Award 2005. *Recordings include:* albums: Portrait of an American Family 1994, Smells Like Children 1995, Antichrist Superstar 1996, Mechanical Animals 1998, The Last Tour on Earth 1999, Holy Wood (In the Shadow of the Valley of Death) 2000, Genesis of the Devil 2001, Live 2002, The Word According to Manson 2002, The Golden Age of Grotesque 2003, White Trash 2003, From Obscurity 2 Purgatory 2004, Eat Me, Drink Me 2007, The High End of Low 2009, Born Villain 2012. *Publication:* The Long Hard Road Out of Hell (autobiography) 1997. *Address:* c/o CAA, 162 Fifth Avenue, 6th Floor, New York, NY 10010, USA (office). *Telephone:* (212) 277-9000 (office). *Fax:* (212) 277-9099 (office). *Website:* www.caa.com (office); www .marilynmanson.com.

MANSOUR, Adly, LLB; Egyptian lawyer, judge and head of state; *Acting President;* b. 23 Dec. 1945, Cairo; m.; one s. two d.; ed Cairo Univ., postgraduate diplomas in Public Law and in Management; graduated from Faculty of Law 1967; joined State Council 1970, rose through the ranks to become Deputy Pres. of Supreme Constitutional Court (SCC) 1992–1 July 2013, Pres. SCC 1–3 July 2013; Acting Pres. of Egypt following ousting of Muhammad Mursi, sworn in 4 July 2013. *Address:* Ittehadeya Presidential Palace, Heliopolis, Cairo, Egypt (office). *E-mail:* president.adly@op.gov.eg (office). *Website:* www.presidency.gov.eg (office).

MANSOUR, Adnan; Lebanese diplomatist and government official; b. 1946, Bourj al-Barajneh; ed Saint Joseph Univ. Beirut; joined foreign service 1974, served as Consul in numerous countries, including Egypt, Athens, Australia, Oman, fmr mem. Del. to UN, New York, Amb. to Democratic Repub. of Congo 1990–94, to Iran 1999–2007, Perm. Rep. European Comm., Brussels 2008–11, Minister of Foreign Affairs and Emigrants 2011–14. *Address:* c/o Ministry of Foreign Affairs and Emigrants, al-Sultana Bldg, al-Jnah, Sultan Ibrahim, Beirut, Lebanon (office). *Website:* adnanmansour.net.

MANSOUR, Mohamed, MBA; Egyptian business executive and fmr government official; *Chairman, Al-Mansour Automotive Company;* b. 23 Jan. 1948, Sharkia; s. of Loutfy Mansour; brother of Yasseen Mansour and Youssef Mansour; m.; two s.; ed North Carolina State Univ., Auburn Univ., USA; taught at Auburn Univ., USA –1973; Minister of Transport 2005–08; currently Chair. Mansour Automotive Co., mem. Bd of Dirs Mansour Group; Chair. Man Capital LLP, Mantrac Group; Pres. Mansour Foundation for Development, Lead Foundation; fmr Chair. Unatrac, Crédit Agricole Bank Egypt, Egypt-US Business Council; fmr Pres. American Chamber of Commerce in Egypt; Bd mem. Centre for Contemporary Arab Studies, Georgetown Univ., USA; mem. Advisory Bd, George Washington School of Business, USA; fmr mem. Special Olympics of Egypt, Cairo, Alexandria Stock Exchanges, Social Fund for Development, Int. Advisory Bd, Coca Cola Co.; fmr Sec.-Gen. Egyptian Centre for Economic Studies. *Address:* Al-Mansour Automotive Company, 54, Sour Nadi Al Zamalek Street, Giza, Egypt (office). *Website:* www .almansour.com.eg (office).

MANSOUR, Yasseen, BSc; Egyptian business executive; *Chairman, Palm Hills Developments;* b. 1961; s. of Loutfy Mansour; brother of Mohamed Mansour and Youssef Mansour; m.; four c.; ed George Washington Univ., USA; started career at Mansour Automotive Co. 1986, Founder Manfoods (owner, operator of McDonald's franchise in Egypt), currently Chair. Palm Hills Developments (retail estate developer), mem. Bd of Dirs, Mansour Group; mem. Bd of Dirs Nat. Cancer Inst.; Co-founder Lead Foundation; Gen.-Sec. Mansour Foundation for Development; Sec.-Gen. Future Foundation. *Address:* Palm Hills Developments, Smart Village, A4 - B83, KM28, Cairo-Alexandria Desert Road, Abou Rawash, Egypt (office). *Telephone:* (2) 35351200 (office). *Fax:* (2) 35351208 (office). *Website:* www .palmhillsdevelopments.com (office).

MANSOUR, Youssef L., BSc, MBA; Egyptian business executive; *Chairman, Al Mansour Holding Company for Financial Investments;* b. 1945; s. of Loutfy Mansour; brother of Yasseen Mansour and Mohamed Mansour; m.; five c.; ed North Carolina State Univ., Auburn Univ., USA; CEO Loutfy Mansour Trading Co. 1976–81, Chair. Al Mansour Holding Co. for Financial Investments 1992–, Mansour Automotive Co. 2006–09, mem. Bd of Dirs Mansour Group; Chair. and CEO Mantrac –1992; launched Metro (first domestic supermarket chain) 1998, Kheir Zaman chain 2006; Vice-Pres. Mansour Foundation for Development; Founding mem. American Chamber of Commerce, Egypt. *Address:* Al Mansour Holding Company for Financial Investments, Zahraa El Maadi Industrial Zone, PO Box 97, New Maadi, Cairo, Egypt (office). *Telephone:* (2) 27548360 (office). *Fax:* (2) 27548385 (office). *Website:* www.mmd.mansourgroup.com (office).

MANSUROV, Tair Aimukhametovich, PhD; Kazakhstani construction engineer, politologist, diplomatist and regional governor; *Secretary-General, Eurasian Economic Community;* b. 1 Jan. 1948, Sarkand, Taldykorgan Region, Kazakhstan; s. of Aimukhamet Mansurov and Maken Tursynbekova; m. Saule Bakirova 1973; one s. two d.; ed Kazakh Politechnical Inst., Almaty, Higher Party School at Cen. Cttee of CP, Moscow; worked in construction orgs Alma-Ata, Chief Engineer Almaatacentrestroy 1965–79; Chief, Dept of Construction, Alma-Ata Regional CP Cttee 1979–87; First Sec. Leninskiy Dist CP Cttee, Alma-Ata 1979–87; Instructor, Dept of Construction, Cen. CP Cttee, Moscow 1988–91; Second Sec. Karaganda Region CP Cttee 1989–91; Chief of Section, Dept of Econs, Cen. CP Cttee, Moscow 1988–91; Deputy to Supreme Soviet of USSR 1988–91; Pres. Kazakhstan Devt Fund, Moscow 1991–93; Amb. to Russian Fed. 1994–2002, also accred to Finland 1996–2002; Amb. at Large and Advisor to Pres. of Kazakhstan 2002–03; Gov. N Kazakhstan Region 2003–07; Sec. Gen. Eurasian Econ. Community, Moscow

2007–; mem. Acad. of Creativity, Int. Acad. of High School, Acad. of Social Sciences; Kurmet Order 1996, Order of Dostyk 2001, Order of St Prince Daniel Moskovski (Russia) 2002, Order of Friendship (Russia) 2002, Order of St Segey Radonezhski (Russia) 2005, Order of Kazakhstan's First President Narsultan Nazarbeyev 2006; several medals. *Publications include:* Faces of Sovereignty: Sovereignty in the Prism of Social History 1994, Kazakhstan and Russia: Sovereignization, Integration, Experience of Strategic Partnership 1997, Kazakh–Russian Relations in the Epoch of Changes 2001, scientific and feature books about diplomatist N. Turiakulov 2004, Regulation of External Economic Activity of the Customs Union in Framework of EurAsEC (co-author) 2011, Eurasian Project of Nursultan Nazarbayev 2011, EurAsEC: From Economic Co-operation to Single Economic Space 2011. *Leisure interests:* political, historical and economic literature, sport. *Address:* Eurasian Economic Community, 105066 Moscow, 1st Basmanny pereulok 6/4, Russia (office). *Telephone:* (495) 223-90-00 (office). *Fax:* (495) 223-90-19 (office). *E-mail:* evrazes@evrazes.com (office). *Website:* www.evrazes.ru (office).

MANTASHE, Gwede, MA; South African trade union official and politician; *Secretary-General, African National Congress (ANC);* b. Transkei; ed Univ. of South Africa; Br. Chair. Matla Coal, Nat. Union of Mineworkers 1982–84, Regional Sec. Witbank 1985–88, Nat. Organizer 1988–93, Regional Co-ordinator 1993–94, Asst Gen. Sec. 1994–98, Gen. Sec. 1998–2006; mem. Cen. Cttee and Politburo SA Communist Party, Chair. 2007–; fmr mem. Exec. Cttee Congress of South African Trade Unions (COSATU); Sec.-Gen. African Nat. Congress 2007–; Dir Samancor 1995–; Exec. Dir Devt Bank of Southern Africa 2006–; Chair. Tech. Task Team, Jt Initiative for Priority Skills Acquisition. *Address:* African National Congress, 54 Sauer Street, Johannesburg 201, South Africa (office). *Telephone:* (11) 3761000 (office). *Fax:* (11) 3761134 (office). *E-mail:* nmtyelwa@anc.org.za (office). *Website:* www.anc.org.za (office).

MANTEGA, Guido, MA, PhD; Brazilian economist, academic and government official; *Minister of Finance;* b. 7 April 1949, Genoa, Italy; s. of Giuseppe Mantega and Anna Costa Mantega; m. Eliana Berger Mantega; ed Coll. of Econs and Business Admin, Univ. of São Paulo, Inst. of Devt Studies, Univ. of Sussex, UK; Prof. of Econs, School of Business Admin, Fundação Getúlio Vargas 1981–; Budget Dir and Head, Office of Municipal Dept of Planning, São Paulo 1982–92; Prof. of Econs, Pontifícia Universidade Católica de São Paulo-PUC-SP 1984–87; mem. Coordination of Econ. Program for Brazilian Labor Party (PT) in presidential elections 1984, 1989, 1998; Econ. Advisor to President Luiz Inácio Lula da Silva 1993–2002; coordinator PT's Econ. Program 2002; Minister of Planning, Budget, and Admin 2003–04; Pres. Banco Nacional de Desenvolvimento Econômico e Social (BNDES) 2004–06; Minister of Finance 2006–; mem. Bd of Dirs Petróleo Brasileiro SA (Petrobras) and Petrobras Distribuidora SA (BR) 2007–, currently Chair. *Publications:* numerous articles and books, including Acumulação Monopolista e Crises no Brasil 1981, A Economia Política Brasileira 1984, Custo Brasil: Mito ou Realidade 1997, Conversas com Economistas Brasileiros II 1999. *Address:* Ministry of Finance, Esplanada dos Ministérios, Bloco P, 5° andar, 70048-900 Brasília -DF, Brazil (office). *Telephone:* (61) 3412-2515 (office). *Fax:* (61) 3412-1721 (office). *E-mail:* gabinete.df.gmf@fazenda.gov.br (office). *Website:* www.fazenda .gov.br (office).

MANTEGAZZA, Sergio, Dipl. Bus. Admin; Swiss travel industry executive; *Owner, Globus brands;* b. 31 Oct. 1927, Mendrisio; s. of Antonio Mantegazza; m.; two s. one d.; ed Instituto Elvetico, Lugano, Gademann Handelsschule, Zurich; Man. Globus Gateway Tours, Lugano, Switzerland 1945–48, Gen. Man. 1948–52, Dir 1952–56, Man. Dir 1956–60, Pres. 1960–2008, CEO 2009–; Order of San Gregorio Magno 1992. *Address:* Globus Travel Services SA, Via alla Roggia, 6916 Grancia, Switzerland (office). *Telephone:* (91) 985-71-11 (office). *Fax:* (91) 985-73-78 (office). *E-mail:* smante@globuscosmos.ch (office). *Website:* www .globusandcosmos.com (office).

MANTEL, Hilary Mary, CBE, FRSL; British writer; b. 6 July 1952, Hadfield, Derbyshire; d. of Henry Thompson and Margaret Mary Thompson; m. Gerald McEwen 1973; ed London School of Econs, Univ. of Sheffield; Dr hc (Sheffield) 2002, (Sheffield Hallam) 2004, (Royal Holloway) 2009, (Bedford) 2009, (Kingston) 2010, (Exeter) 2011; David Cohen Prize 2013. *Radio:* The Giant, O'Brien (drama) 2002, Learning to Talk (5 plays) 2003, The Price of Light (drama) 2005. *Publications include:* Every Day is Mother's Day 1985, Vacant Possession 1986, Eight Months on Ghazzah Street 1988, Fludd (Winifred Holtby Memorial Award, Southern Arts Literature Prize, Cheltenham Festival Prize) 1989, A Place of Greater Safety (Sunday Express Book of the Year Award 1993) 1992, A Change of Climate 1994, An Experiment in Love (Hawthornden Prize 1996) 1995, The Giant, O'Brien 1998, Giving up the Ghost (MIND Book of the Year 2004) 2003, Learning to Talk 2003, Beyond Black (Yorkshire Post Fiction Award) 2005, Wolf Hall (Man Booker Prize 2009, Nat. Book Critics' Circle Award for Fiction 2009, Walter Scott Prize for Historical Fiction 2009, Galaxy Nat. Book Awards UK Author of the Year 2010, Ind. Booksellers' Book of the Year 2010) 2009, Bring Up the Bodies (Man Booker Prize 2012, Costa Book Award 2012, Author of the Year, Specsavers Nat. Book Awards) 2012. *Address:* c/o A. M. Heath & Co., 6 Warwick Court, Holborn, London, WC1R 5DJ, England (office). *Telephone:* (20) 7242-2811 (office). *Fax:* (20) 7242-2711 (office). *Website:* www.amheath.com (office).

MANTUROV, Denis; Russian business executive and government official; *Minister of Industry and Trade;* b. 23 Feb. 1969, Murmansk; ed Lomonosov Moscow State Univ., Presidential Acad. of Public Admin; Deputy Dir Gen. Ulan-Ude Aviation Plant 1998–2000; Business Dir Mil Moscow Helicopter Plant 2000–01; Deputy Chair. State Investment Corpn 2001–03; Dir Gen. Oboronprom (aerospace holding co.) 2003–07; Deputy Minister of Industry and Energy 2007–12, Minister of Industry and Trade 2012–. *Address:* Ministry of Industry and Trade, 109074 Moscow, Kitaigorodskii proyezd 7, Russia (office). *Telephone:* (495) 539-21-87 (office). *Fax:* (495) 539-21-72 (office). *E-mail:* info_admin@minprom.gov.ru (office). *Website:* www.minpromtorg.gov.ru (office).

MANUEL, Armando; Angolan politician; *Minister of Finance;* Dir of Treasury and Head of Research Dept and Treasury, Ministry of Finance –2012, Minister of Finance 2013–; Chair. Fundo Soberano de Angola (sovereign wealth fund) 2012–13; Econ. Adviser to Pres. José Eduardo dos Santos –2013. *Address:* Ministry of Finance, Largo da Mutamba, Luanda, Angola (office). *Telephone:*

22338548 (office). *Fax:* 22338548 (office). *E-mail:* geral@minfin.gov.ao (office). *Website:* www.minfin.gv.ao (office).

MANUEL, Trevor Andrew; South African politician; *Minister of the National Planning Commission;* b. 31 Jan. 1956, Cape Town; s. of Abraham J. Manuel and Philma van Söhnen; m. Lynn Matthews; three s.; ed Harold Cressy High School; mem. Labour Party Youth 1969–71, Policy Man. on Devt 1989–; construction technician 1974–81; Sec. Kensington Civic Assen 1977–82; Founding mem. Western Cape United Democratic Front (UDF) 1980s, Sec. Regional Exec. UDF 1983–90, mem. UDF Nat. Exec. Cttee 1983–86, 1989–90; Organizer CAHAC 1981–82; field worker Educational Resource and Information Centre 1982–84; in detention 1985, 1987–88, 1989, restricted 1985–86, 1986–90 (when not in detention); Publicity Sec. ANC Western Cape; mem. ANC Nat. Exec. Cttee 1991–; Minister of Trade and Industry, Govt of Nat. Unity 1994–96; Minister of Finance 1996–2009, Minister of the Nat. Planning Comm., Office of the Presidency 2009–. *Address:* National Planning Commission, Office of the Presidency, Union Buildings, West Wing, Government Avenue, Pretoria 0001, South Africa.

MANUELLA, Sir Tulaga, GCMG, MBE; Tuvaluan accountant and fmr Governor-General; b. 26 Aug. 1936; s. of Teuhu Manuella and Malesa Moevasa; m. Milikini Uinifaleti; two s. three d.; sub-accountant and ledger keeper 1953–55; clerical officer 1955–57; Sr Asst, then Asst Accountant, Treasury 1957–75; Asst Accountant, Tuvalu Govt; Accountant, then Acting Financial Sec., Ministry of Finance 1976–84; Financial Sec. Financial Div. Church of Tuvalu 1984–86; Pacific Conf. of Churches, Suva, Fiji 1987–91; Co-ordinator of Finance and Admin. Ekalesia Kelisiano 1992–94; Gov.-Gen. of Tuvalu 1994–1998; Chancellor Univ. of the S Pacific 1997–2000; Patron Pacific Islands Soc. in Britain and Ireland 1995. *Address:* c/o Office of the Governor-General, PO Box 50, Vaiaku, Funafuti, Tuvalu (office).

MANUKYAN, Vazgen, PhD; Armenian mathematician, academic and politician; *President, Public Council of Armenia;* b. 13 Feb. 1946, Leninakan (now Gyumri); s. of Mikael Manukyan and Astkhik Manukyan; m. Varduhi Ishkhanyan; three d.; ed Yerevan State Univ., Siberian Dept of USSR Acad. of Sciences; Prof., Yerevan State Univ. 1972–95; political activities since 1960s, one of the founders and leaders of Club of Armenian Culture 1967, mem. and co-ordinator Cttee Karabakh 1988; elected Head of the Bd Armenian Nat. Movt 1989; Prime Minister of Armenia 1990–91; Leader, Nat. Democratic Union 1991–; Deputy, Armenian Supreme Soviet 1990–91; Minister of Defence 1992–93; mem. Council of Nat. Security, Pres. 1992–93; Pres. Center for Strategic Studies 1993, Public Council of Armenia; Chair. Cttee on Econ. Reform, State Cttee on Land Reform and Privatization. *Publications include:* It is Time to Jump Off the Train 1990, Armenian Dream of a Deadlock of Survival 2002. *Address:* Public Council of Armenia, 26/1 Vazgen Sargsyan Street, 'Erebuni Plaza' Business Centre, 0010 Yerevan, Armenia (office). *Telephone:* (10) 523405 (office); (91) 428977 (home). *Fax:* (10) 523766 (home). *E-mail:* v_manukyan@publiccouncil.am (office); vazgenmanukian@gmail.com (home). *Website:* www.publiccouncil.am/en (office).

MANWANI, Harish, BA, MBA; Indian business executive; *Chairman, Hindustan Unilever Ltd;* b. 1954; m.; two d.; ed Mumbai Univ., Jamnalal Bajaj Inst. of Man. Studies, .Advanced Man. Program, Harvard Business School, USA; joined Hindustan Lever Ltd (HLL) in 1976, Div. Vice-Pres. Marketing, Detergents 1995, mem. Bd as Dir for Personal Products 1995, also held regional responsibility for Cen. Asia and Middle East Business Group, moved to UK as Sr Vice-Pres. (Global Hair Care and Oral Care) and Exec. Vice-Pres. Latin America Business Group 2000–01, Pres. (Home and Personal Care), Latin America Business Group 2001–04, also served as Chair. Unilever's Latin America Advisory Council, Pres. and CEO (Home and Personal Care), N America Business Group 2004–05, joined Unilever Exec. as Pres. Asia and Africa 2005–, also Chair. (non-exec.) Hindustan Unilever Ltd 2005–; mem. Exec. Bd Indian School of Business; India Business Leader Award CNBC-TV18 2007, Asia Business Leader of the Year Award, CNBC Asia 2008. *Leisure interests:* spending time with family, playing golf and bridge. *Address:* Hindustan Unilever Ltd, Unilever House, B. D. Sawant Marg, Chakala, Andheri (E), Mumbai 400 099, India (office). *Telephone:* (22) 39830000 (office). *Fax:* (22) 22871970 (office). *E-mail:* mediacentre.hul@unilever.com (office). *Website:* www.hul.co.in (office).

MANYANG JUUK, Kuol; South Sudanese politician; *Minister of Defence and Veteran Affairs;* m. Priscilla Nyankot Kuot; one s. two d.; fmr rebel commdr; fmr lecturer in Juba; Minister of Roads and Transport in govt of Nat. Unity of Sudan (prior to creation of South Sudan 2011); Gov. Jonglei State 2007–13; Minister of Defence and Veteran Affairs 2013–; mem. Sudan People's Liberation Movt (SPLM), Chair. Jonglei Br., mem. SPLM Higher Exec. Council. *Address:* Ministry of Defence, Juba, South Sudan (office). *Telephone:* (+249) 915485232 (mobile) (office). *E-mail:* kdeimkuol@yahoo.com (office). *Website:* www.splamilitary.net (office).

MANZ, Wolfgang; German pianist and academic; *Professor of Piano, Nürnberg University of Music;* b. 6 Aug. 1960, Düsseldorf; m. Julia Goldstein 1985; two s. one d.; studied with Drahomir Toman, Prague and Karlheinz Kämmerling, Hanover; teacher, High School of Music, Karlsruhe 1994–98; concert tours UK, Germany, Belgium and Japan; performed Promenade Concerts, London 1984, Gilels Memorial Concert, Düsseldorf 1986, Karajan Foundation, Paris 1987; currently Prof. of Piano, Nürnberg Univ. of Music; First Prize Mendelssohn Competition, Berlin 1981, Second Prize, Leeds Piano Competition 1981, Second Prize Brussels Queen Elizabeth Competition 1983, Van Cliburn Int. Piano Competition Award, Texas 1989. *Recordings include:* Chopin Studies, Beethoven Triple Concerto, with English Chamber Orchestra, solo recital Liszt, Schumann and Debussy, Dohnanyi Piano Quintet, Russian Music for Two Pianos (with Rolf Plagge). *Leisure interests:* composing, swimming, gardening. *Fax:* (9817) 808183 (office). *E-mail:* wolfgangmanz@t-online.de (home). *Website:* www.wolfgangmanz.de.

MANZONI, Giacomo, MusM; Italian composer; b. 26 Sept. 1932, Milan; m. Eugenia Tretti 1960; one s.; ed Bocconi Univ., Milan, Univ. of Tübingen and Conservatorio Verdi, Milan; Ed. Il Diapason (music review) 1956; music critic, l'Unità 1958–66; music ed. Prisma 1968; mem. editorial staff, Musica/Realtà 1980–; Prof., Conservatorio Verdi 1962–64, 1974–91, Conservatorio Martini, Bologna 1965–68, 1969–74, Scuola di Musica Fiesole 1988–2004, Accad. Musicale Pescarese 1993–96; mem. Accad. Nazionale di Santa Cecilia, Rome 1994–; has

given master classes in composition in Buenos Aires, Granada, Tokyo, Santiago, Beijing, etc.; Dr hc (Udine) and others; Premio Abbiati 1989, Golden Lion for musical career, Biennale Musica, Venice 2007, Premio Principe Gesualdo 2012. *Compositions include:* music theatre: La Sentenza 1960, Atomtod 1965, Per M. Robespierre 1975, Dr. Faustus—Scene dal romanzo di T. Mann 1989; with orchestra: Insiemi 1967, Ombre (alla memoria di Che Guevara) for chorus and orchestra 1968, Parole da Beckett 1971 for 2 choruses and orchestra, Masse: omaggio a E. Varèse, for piano and orch. 1977, Ode 1982, Scene Sinfoniche per il Dr Faustus 1984, Dedica (text by B. Maderna) 1985, 10 versi di E. Dickinson 1989, Malinamusik 1991, Finale e aria (I. Bachmann) 1991, Il deserto cresce (F. Nietzsche) 1992, Moi, Antonin A. (Artaud) 1997, Trame d'Ombre (da Zeami) 1998, O Europa! (A. József) 1999; Sul passaggio del tempo (R. Sanesi) 2001, Sembianti 2003, Studio da concerto for violin, winds and percussion 2005, Mercurio transita davanti al sole 2006, KOKIN b for two voices and orchestra 2008, Progetto Eliogabalo for narrator and orchestra 2009, Studio 2012 etc.; chamber music: Musica notturna 1966, Una voce chiama, for voice, viola and live electronics (F. Fortini) 1994, Quanto oscura selva trovai (Dante), for trombone, chorus and live electronics 1995, Oltre la soglia, for voice and string quartet 2000, Pensiero XX di G. Leopardi for narrator and string quartet 2001, Vergers for choir 2006, 6 Canti dal Kokin shū 2007, Il rumore del tempo for soprano and instruments 2010, 4° Rivolto for string sextet 2012, Per questo, for soprano and trumpet 2012 etc.; film and incidental music. *Publications:* A. Schoenberg 1975, Scritti 1991, Tradizione e Utopia 1994, Parole per musica 2007, Écrits 2007, Musica e progetto civile 2009; trans of Adorno and Schönberg. *Address:* Viale Papiniano 31, 20123 Milan, Italy (home). *Telephone:* (02) 4817955 (home). *E-mail:* gmanz@libero.it.

MAO, Chi-kuo, BEng, MEng, PhD; Taiwanese politician; *Vice-Premier, Executive Yuan;* b. Oct. 1948; ed Nat. Cheng Kung Univ., Asian Inst. of Tech., Bangkok, Thailand, Massachusetts Inst. of Tech., USA; Engineer and Div. Chief, Transportation Planning Bd, Ministry of Transportation and Communications (MOTC) 1976–78, Chief Sec., MOTC Secr. 1987–89, Dir-Gen., Tourism Bureau 1989–91, Dir-Gen., Provisional Eng Office of High Speed Rail 1991–93, Admin. Deputy Minister 1993–2000, also Dir-Gen., Civil Aeronautics Admin 1994, Minister of Transportation and Communications 2008–13; Chair. Chunghwa Telecom Co. Ltd 2000–03; Assoc. Prof., Nat. Cheng Kung Univ. 2003–06, Dean and Prof., Coll. of Man. 2006–08; Adviser to Exec. Yuan (Cabinet) 2003, Vice-Premier 2013–. *Address:* Executive Yuan, No.1, Sec. 1, Zhongxiao East Road, Zhongzheng District, Taipei 10058, Taiwan (office). *Telephone:* (2) 33566500 (office). *E-mail:* public@mail.oop.gov.tw (office). *Website:* www.ey.gov.tw (office).

MAO, Rubai; Chinese politician; b. 1938, Yangzhou City, Jiangsu Prov.; ed Nanjing Univ.; joined CCP 1959; Deputy Dir then Dir Meteorological Office of Tibet (Deputy Sec. CCP Party Cttee); Deputy Sec. CCP Tibet Autonomous Regional Cttee 1984, Vice-Chair. Tibet Autonomous Region 1986–93; Vice-Minister of State Construction Ministry 1993–97; Sec. CCP Ningxia Hui Autonomous Regional Cttee 1997–2002; Chair. People's Congress of Ningxia Hui Autonomous Region 1998–2002; mem. 15th CCP Cen. Cttee 1997–2002; Vice-Chair. Environment Protection and Resources Conservation Cttee of 10th Nat. People's Congress 2002, Chair. 2003; mem. Standing Cttee 10th Nat. People's Congress; Pres. Meteorology Soc. *Address:* Standing Committee, National People's Congress, Beijing, People's Republic of China (office). *Fax:* (10) 63098439 (office).

MAO, Zhiyong; Chinese party official; b. 1929, Yueyang Co., Hunan Prov.; joined CCP 1952; Sec. CCP Yueyang Co. Cttee 1964–66; Deputy CCP Sec. of Yueyang Pref. and Deputy CCP Sec. of Changde Pref., Hunan 1966–71; Deputy Sec.-Gen. CCP Hunan Prov. Cttee 1972–73, First Sec., Sec. 1977–88; mem. 5th NPC 1978–80; Sec. CCP Jiangxi Prov. Cttee 1988–95; Chair. Standing Cttee Jiangxi Prov. People's Congress 1993–98; mem. 11th CCP Cen. Cttee 1977–82, 12th CCP Cen. Cttee 1982–87, 13th CCP Cen. Cttee 1987–92, 14th CCP Cen. Cttee 1992–97; mem. 8th NPC 1993–98; Vice-Chair. 9th CPPCC Nat. Cttee 1998–2003. *Address:* National Committee of Chinese People's Political Consultative Conference, 23 Taipingqiao Street, Beijing, People's Republic of China (office).

MAOR, Galia, BA, MBA; Israeli economist and banker; b. 1943; m.; three c.; ed Hebrew Univ. of Jerusalem; joined Bank of Israel 1963, held numerous supervisory positions including Head of Open Market Operations, Supervisor of Banks 1982–89, Sr Dir Banking Systems, currently mem. Advisory Cttee; pvt. consultancy 1989–91; joined Bank Leumi as Deputy Gen. Man. 1991, Pres. and CEO 1995–2012; mem. Bd of Govs Hebrew Univ. of Jerusalem; Chair. Friends of Yeladim (Council for the Child in Placement), Friends of Acad. of the Hebrew Language, Israeli Cttee of INSEAD; Dr hc (Open Univ.), (Netanya Coll.); Recannati Award for Women's Excellence in Man. 2001, Women's Excellence Award, Hadassah 2001, Woman of the Year, Globes magazine 2008; ranked by Fortune magazine amongst 50 Most Powerful Women in Business outside the US (34th) 2002, (42nd) 2003, (36th) 2004, (32nd) 2005, (32nd) 2006, (35th) 2007, ranked by Forbes magazine amongst 100 Most Powerful Women (88th) 2006, (83rd) 2007. *Address:* c/o Bank Leumi le-Israel BM, PO Box 2, 24–32 Yehuda Halevi Street, Tel-Aviv 65546, Israel (office).

MAPFUMO, Thomas Tafirenyika Mukanya; Zimbabwean musician (mbira, guitar), singer and songwriter; b. 2 July 1945, Marondera; important figure in local Shona music 1970s–; singer in local bands, including The Cosmic Dots, the Springfields; f. Hallelujah Chicken Run Band 1973, Black Spirits 1976; performed with The Pied Pipers 1977; f. Acid Band 1977–, later banned from the radio, renamed Blacks Unlimited 1978; Mapfumo imprisoned for subversion 1977; currently lives in exile in Eugene, Ore., USA; researcher in traditional Zimbabwean folk music. *Recordings include:* albums: Hokoya! 1977, Mbira Music of Zimba 1980, Gwindingwe 1980, Mabesa 1983, Congress 1983, The Chimurenga Singles 1983, Ndangariro 1984, Corruption 1984, Mr Music 1985, Chimurenga For Justice 1986, Zimbabwe-Mozambique 1987, Nyamaropa Nhimutimu 1989, Shumba 1990, The Spirit of the Eagle 1991, Chimurenga Masterpis 1991, Hondo 1993, Chimurenga Int'l 1993, Vanhu Vatema 1994, Chimurenga: African Spirit Music 1997, Rise Up 2006, Exile 2009. *Address:* c/o Linda Rowan, Midnight Productions Hawaii/International, PO Box 853, Haleiwa, HI 96712, USA (office). *Telephone:* (808) 637-3139 (office). *E-mail:* lrowan39@yahoo.com (office). *Website:* www.thomasmapfumo.com.

MAPISA-NQAKULA, Nosiviwe; South African politician; *Minister of Defence and Military Veterans;* m. Charles Nqakula; one s.; Head African National Congress (ANC) Taskforce to relaunch Women's League 1990, Nat. Organizer 1991; mem. ANC Nat. Exec. Cttee; apptd Deputy Chair. ANC Parl. Political Cttee 2001; mem. SA Communist Party (SACP); MP, Chair. Intelligence Portfolio Cttee (Nat. Ass); apptd mem. Judicial Services Comm. 2001; Deputy Minister of Home Affairs 2002–04, Minister 2004–09, Minister of Correctional Services 2009–12, of Defence and Military Veterans 2012–. *Address:* Ministry of Defence and Military Veterans, Armscor Bldg, Block 5, Nossob Street, Erasmusrand 0181 (office); Private Bag X427, Pretoria 0001, South Africa (office). *Telephone:* (12) 3556101 (office). *Fax:* (12) 3470118 (office). *E-mail:* mil@mil.za (office). *Website:* www.dod .mil.za (office).

MAPLE, M. Brian, AB, MS, PhD; American physicist and academic; *Professor and Chairman, Department of Physics, University of California, San Diego;* ed San Diego State Univ., Univ. of California, San Diego; Asst Research Physicist, Univ. of California, San Diego 1969–75, Asst Prof. of Physics 1973–75, Assoc. Prof. 1975–81, Prof. 1981–90, Bernd T. Matthias Endowed Chair in Physics 1990–, Dir Center for Interface and Materials Science 1990–2009, Dir Inst. for Pure and Applied Physical Sciences 1995–2009, Chair. Dept of Physics 2009–; Visiting Scientist, Univ. of Chile, Santiago 1971–73; Visiting Prof., Instituto de Fisica José Balseiro, Argentina 1974; Assoc. Research Physicist, Univ. of Calif., Santa Barbara Inst. for Theoretical Physics 1980; Chair. Gordon Conf. on Superconductivity 1990, 2000; mem. Advisory Bd Superconductivity Review 1989–, CONNECT 1990–, Journal of Physics: Condensed Matter 1997–; mem. numerous int. advisory cttees; mem. American Physical Soc. 1977 (Fellow 1985), Calif. Catalysis Soc. 1977, American Vacuum Soc. 1977, Materials Research Soc. 1977; Fellow, AAAS 1997; Humboldt Research Award 1998, Frank H. Spedding Award 1999, American Physical Soc. James C. McGroddy Prize for New Materials 2000, Berndt T. Matthias Prize 2000. *Publications:* numerous papers on solid state physics and surface physics; Valence Fluctuations in Solids (co-ed.) 1982, Superconductivity in Ternary Compounds (Co-Ed.) 1982, Handbook on the Physics and Chemistry of Rare Earths (co-ed.) 2000. *Address:* Department of Physics, University of California, San Diego, 9500 Gilman Drive, MC 0319, La Jolla, CA 92093-3968, USA (office). *Telephone:* (858) 534-3968 (office); (858) 534-6832 (office). *Fax:* (858) 534-1241 (office). *E-mail:* mbmaple@ucsd.edu (office); chair@physics .ucsd.edu (office). *Website:* mbmlab.ucsd.edu (office).

MAPONYA, Richard John Pelwana, GCOB; South African entrepreneur and property developer; *CEO, Maponya Group;* b. 24 Dec. 1926, Lenyenye, Northern Transvaal (now Limpopo Prov.); s. of Godfrey Kgabane Maponya and Mary Machichane Maponya (née Mogashoa); m. Marina Nompinti Sondlo (died 1992); eight c.; ed Kagiso Teacher's Training Coll., Pietersburg; worked as an admin clerk after qualifying as a teacher; Propr Maponya's Supply Stores 1952, now CEO Maponya Group; Dir Maponya's Bus Services 1965, Maponya's Funeral Parlour (Pty) Ltd 1976, Afro Shopping Construction Enterprises (Pty) Ltd, Maponya's Discount Supermarket 1983–, Maponya's Bottle Store, Maponya's Motors (Pty) Ltd, Maponya Motors Property Holdings (Pty) Ltd, Maponya's Orlando Restaurant (Pty) Ltd, Maponya's Stud Farm, Lebowa Devt Corpn, numerous other cos; Man. Dir MA Africa (Pty) Ltd, Mountain Motors, Soweto 1978–; Propr BMW Agency, Soweto; opened Maponya Mall in Soweto 2007; Chair. Kilimanjaro Investments (East London-based bottler); racehorse owner; Founder and Pres. Nat. African Federated Chamber of Commerce and Industry 1965–; Chair. Trade and Transport Cttee, Soweto Council; mem. Urban Bantu Council 1965–77; Pres. Black Proprietors Garage Owners' Asscn; Founder and Trustee, The Nelson Mandela Children's Fund; Trustee, Baragwanath Hospital, SA Foundation, Urban Foundation; Grand Counsellor, Order of the Baobab in Gold 2007; Lifetime Achievement Award, Africa Awards for Entrepreneurship 2012. *Leisure interests:* racing, music. *Address:* PO Box 3302, Cramerview 2060; Maponya Developments, First Floor, Entrance 2, 32 Fricker Road, Illovo 2196, South Africa. *Telephone:* (861) 333264. *Fax:* (866) 852112. *E-mail:* info@mapdev.co.za. *Website:* www.mapdev.co .za.

MAPP, Wayne, LLB, LLM, PhD; New Zealand lawyer and politician; b. 12 March 1952, Te Kopuru; ed Auckland Univ., Univ. of Cambridge, UK; lawyer in pvt. practice 1978–82; Lecturer in Commercial Law, Auckland Univ. 1984–94, Assoc. Prof. 1994–96; mem. New Zealand Nat. Party 1982–, Divisional Policy Chair., Auckland 1993–96; MP for North Shore 1996–, mem. Select Cttees on Foreign Affairs, Defence and Trade 1997–99, on Justice and Law Reform 1997–2002, on Māori Affairs 1999–2001, 2003–04, on Social Services 2002, on Educ. and Science 2003–04, Transport and Industrial Relations 2005–06, on Privileges 2005–08; Spokesman for Defence 1999–2002, for Justice 1999–2002, for Disarmament and Arms Control 2002–03, for Foreign Affairs 2002–03, for Housing 2002–03, for Constitutional and Treaty of Waitangi Issues 2003–04, for Immigration 2003–04, for Labour and Industrial Relations 2004–06; Assoc. Spokesman for Treaty of Waitangi 1999–2002, for Constitutional and Treaty of Waitangi Issues 2004–05; Minister of Defence, of Research, Science and Tech., Assoc. Minister for Econ. Devt and for Tertiary Educ. 2008–11; Commr New Zealand Law Comm. 2012–. *Address:* New Zealand Law Commission, Level 19, 171 Featherston Street, Wellington 6011, New Zealand (office). *E-mail:* com@lawcom.govt.nz (office). *Website:* www .lawcom.govt.nz (office).

MAQBOOL, Lt-Gen. Khalid, MSc; Pakistani army officer (retd) and government administrator; b. 1948; ed Staff Coll., Quetta, Nat. Defence Coll., Rawalpindi, Naval Postgraduate Inst., Monterey, USA; commissioned in Pakistan Army 1966, saw action with infantry regt in Kashmir Sector 1971, Commdr of Corps, Infantry Div./Brigade, Chief Instructor, Nat. Defence Coll. and Command and Staff Coll., Quetta, Defence and Mil. Attaché to USA for two and half years; Chair. Nat. Accountability Bureau 2000–01; Gov. of Punjab Prov. 2001–08 (resgnd); Chancellor Univ. of Sargodha; Hilal-e-Imtiaz (Mil.), Hilal-e-Imtiaz. *Address:* c/o Office of the Governor, Lahore, Punjab, Pakistan.

MAQUEDA, Juan Carlos; Argentine politician, lawyer and university teacher; *Minister, Supreme Court of Justice;* b. 29 Dec. 1949, Río Tercero; m. María Belén Ferrer; ed La Salle Coll. and Catholic Univ. of Córdoba; Prof. of Law, Catholic Univ. of Córdoba 1977–80, Adjunct Prof. of Natural Law 1980, Prof. of History of Political Insts of Argentina 1981, Asst Prof. of Natural Law 1981–82, 1983–84, Prof. 1984–85, Adjunct Prof. of Constitutional Law 1985, Prof. of Political Theory

1986; Tech. Sec., Faculty of Law and Social Sciences, Univ. of Córdoba 1980–86; mem. Justicialista party; Prov. Deputy, Córdoba 1986–91; Deputy to Nat. Ass. 1991–99; Minister of Educ., Prov. of Córdoba 1999–2001; Pres. Constitutional Convention of Prov. of Córdoba Aug. 2001; Senator from Córdoba 2001–03, Vice-Pres. Nat. Senate 2001, Pres. 2002; Minister, Supreme Court Justice 2002–, Pres. Academic Council of the School of Justice 2005–; mem. Fed Council of Nat. Culture and Educ. 1999–2001; Vice-Pres. Argentine Group, Parliamentarians for Global Action. *Publications include:* El Pensamiento Político Español del Siglo XVI 1980, Los Partidos Políticos: Ordenamiento Legal 1985, Sistemas Electorales y los Sistemas de Partidos 1985, La Nueva Constitución de Córdoba: Labor Constituyente y Debates 1987, Labor Parlamentaria en la Cámara de Diputados de la Provincia de Córdoba y Debates 1988, 1989. *Address:* Corte Suprema de Justicia de la Nación, Talcahuano 550, Ciudad Autónoma de Buenos Aires, Argentina (office). *Telephone:* (11) 4370-4600. *E-mail:* jurisprudencia@csjn.gov.ar (office). *Website:* www.csjn.gov.ar (office).

MARA, Moussa; Malian accountant and politician; *Prime Minister;* b. 2 March 1975, Bamako; s. of Joseph Mara and Kadiatou Ly; m.; two c.; ed Intel de Paris; trained as accountant, mem. Asscn of Chartered Accountants 2000, Certified Public Accountant 2000; trainee accountant, Société d'Expertise Comptable Diarra (SECD), Bamako 1997, later becoming Assoc. Dir for Africa; Mayor, Dist IV, Bamako 2009–10, 2011; Founding Pres. Yéléma (political party) 2010–, cand. in presidential election 2013; Minister of Planning and Policy, Bamako City Council 2013–14; Prime Minister 2014–; fmr Sec.-Gen. Mali Asscn of Chartered Accountants; fmr Vice-Pres. West African Accounting Council; mem. Bd West African Accounting Diploma. *Address:* Office of the Prime Minister, Quartier du Fleuve, BP 790, Bamako, Mali (office). *Telephone:* 2022-4310 (office). *Fax:* 2023-9595 (office). *E-mail:* ecrireaupm@primature.gov.ml (office). *Website:* www.primature .gov.ml (office); www.moussamara.com.

MARADONA, Diego Armando; Argentine football manager and fmr professional footballer; b. 30 Oct. 1960, Lanús, Buenos Aires; s. of Diego Maradona and Dalma Salvadora Franco; m. Claudia Villafañe 1989 (divorced 2004); two d.; one s. with Cristina Sinagra; attacking midfielder/second striker; youth player, Argentinos Juniors 1969–76; sr career with Argentinos Juniors 1976–81, Boca Juniors 1981–82 (won Primera División 1981), FC Barcelona, Spain 1982–84 (won Copa del Rey 1983, Copa de la Liga 1983, Spanish Super Cup 1983), Napoli, Italy 1984–91 (won Serie A 1987, 1990, Coppa Italia 1987, UEFA Cup 1989, Italian Super Cup 1990), Sevilla, Spain 1992–93, Newell's Old Boys 1993, Boca Juniors 1995–97, Badajoz 1998; mem. Argentina nat. team 1977–94 (91 appearances, 34 goals, won Youth World Cup 1979, 75th anniversary FIFA Cup 1979, World Cup 1986 (Capt.), Artemio Franchi Trophy 1993), Head Coach 2008–10; Head Coach Al-Wasl, UAE 2011–12; f. Maradona Producciones; fmr Amb. for UNICEF; banned from football for 15 months after drugs test; convicted by Naples Court on charges of possession of cocaine, 14-month suspended sentence and fine of 4 million lire, Sept. 1991; Fed. Court in Buenos Aires ruled he had complied with the treatment; suspended for 15 months for taking performance-enhancing drug, ephedrine, in World Cup Finals June 1994; indicted for shooting an air rifle at journalists Aug. 1994; resgnd as coach of Deporto Mandiyu 1994; Man. Racing Club 1995; retd from playing 1997; host La Noche del Diez (talk show) 2005; Dir of Football Boca Juniors football club 2005–06; appointed Goodwill Amb. of Intergovernmental Inst. for use of Micro-algae Spirulina Against Malnutrition, IIMSAM 2006; South American Player of the Year 1979, World Footballer of the Year 1986, Footballer of the Century Award, Féd. Int. de Football Asscn (France) 2000. *Achievements include:* Golden Ball for Best Player of FIFA U-20 World Cup 1979, Argentine league Top Scorer 1979, 1980, 1981, Argentine Football Writers' Footballer of the Year 1979, 1980, 1981, 1986 South American Footballer of the Year, El Mundo, Caracas 1979, 1986, 1989, 1990, 1992, Italian Guerin d'Oro 1985, Argentine Sports Writers' Sportsman of the Year 1986, Golden Ball for Best Player of FIFA World Cup 1986, Best Footballer in the World Onze d'Or 1986, 1987, World Player of the Year, World Soccer Magazine 1986, United Press International Athlete of the Year 1986, Olimpia de Oro 1986, Capocannoniere (Serie A top scorer) 1987–88, Golden Ball for services to football, France Football 1996, Argentine Sports Writers' Sportsman of the Century 1999, 'FIFA Best Football Player of the Century', people's choice 2000, 'FIFA Goal of the Century' (1986 (2–1) vs England; second goal) 2002, Argentine Senate 'Domingo Faustino Sarmiento' recognition for lifetime achievement 2005. *Publication:* El Diego (autobiography) 2005. *Address:* c/o Asociación del Fútbol Argentino, Viamonte 1366, C1053ACB Buenos Aires, Argentina. *Website:* www .diegomaradona.com.

MARAFINO, Vincent Norman, MBA; American business executive; b. 8 June 1930, Boston, Mass; m. Doris M. Vernall 1958; three d.; ed San Jose State Coll. and Santa Clara Univ.; served with USAF 1953–55; Chief Accountant, American Standard Advance Tech. Lab., Mountain View, Calif. 1956–59; with Lockheed Missiles & Space Co., Sunnyvale, Calif. 1959–70, Asst Controller, Lockheed Corpn Burbank, Calif. 1970–71, Vice Pres., Controller 1971–77, Sr Vice-Pres. Finance 1977–83, Exec. Vice-Pres., Chief Financial and Admin. Officer 1983–88, Vice-Chair. and Chief Financial and Admin. Officer 1988–95, mem. Bd of Dirs Lockheed Missiles and Space Co., Inc., Chair. Lockheed Finance Corpn; mem. Bd of Trustees, Holy Cross Medical Center, Mission Hills; mem. Financial Execs Inst., American Inst. of CPAS. *Address:* c/o Lockheed Martin Corporation, 6801 Rockledge Drive, Bethesda, MD 20817, USA.

MARAGALL, Pasqual, PhD; Spanish civil servant and academic; b. 13 Jan. 1941, Barcelona; m.; three c.; ed Barcelona Univ., New School for Social Research, New York; lecturer in Econs Barcelona Univ.; Mayor of Barcelona 1982–97, organizer of 1992 Olympic Games in Barcelona; mem. Partit dels Socialistes de Catalunya, Pres. 2000–07; Pres. Council of Municipalities and Regions of Europe 1991–97, Cttee of the Regions of EU 1996–98; Pres. Govt of Catalonia 2003–06; Insignia Order of the Légion d'honneur 1993, Hon. OBE; Hon. DLitt (Winchester Art School, UK), Dr hc (Johns Hopkins USA) 1997, Laurea hc (Reggio Calabria Italy) 1998; Medal of the Council of Europe 1984, Olympic Golden Award 1992, Golden Medal Award Spanish Inst. New York 1993. *Address:* Catalan Socialist Party, Nicaragua 75, E-08029 Barcelona, Spain. *Telephone:* (934) 955400 (office). *Fax:* (934) 955430 (office). *E-mail:* pmaragall@psc.es (office). *Website:* www.psc.es (office).

MARAINI, Dacia; Italian writer and poet; b. 13 Nov. 1936, Fiesole; d. of Fosco Maraini and Alliata Topazia; m. 1st Lucio Pozzi; ed Collegio S.S. Annunziata, Florence and Rome. *Plays include:* La famiglia normale 1967, Centocelle gli anni del fascismo 1971, Dialogo di una prostituta con un solo cliente 1973, Da Roma a Milano 1975, Don Juan 1976, Due Donne di Provincia 1978, Erzbeth Bartory 1980, Donna Lionora giacubina 1981, I Sogni di Clitennestra 1981, Dramma d/amore al circo Bagno Balò 1981, Lezioni d'Amore 1982, Bianca Garofani 1982, Delitto 1987, Charlotte Corday 1989, Celia Carli 1990, Commedia Femminile 1994, Camille 1995. *Publications include:* La Vacanza 1962, L'Età del Malessere (The Age of Discontent, Prix Formentor) 1962, Crudeltà All'Aria Aperta 1966, A Memoria 1967, Mio Marito 1968, Memoirs of a Female Thief 1973, Donne mie 1974, Donna in Guerra 1975, Mangiami Pure 1978, Lettere a Marina 1981, Dimenticato di Dimenticare 1983, Il treno per Helsinki 1984, Isolina 1985, Devour me too 1987, La Bionda, la bruna e l'asino 1987, La Lunga Vita di Marianna Ucria 1990, L'Uomo tatuato 1990, Viaggiando con passo de volpe 1991, Bagheria 1993, Voci 1994, La ragazza con la treccia 1994, Mutino, Orlov e il gatto che si crede pantera 1995, Dolce per sé 1997, Se amando troppo 1998, Buio 1999, La nave per Kobe 2001, Colomba 2004, Il gioco dell'universo 2007, Il treno dell'ultima notte 2008, La Ragazza di via Maqueda 2009. *Address:* c/o Rizzoli, RCS Libri, Via Mecenate 91, 20138 Milan; Via Beccaria 18, 00196 Rome, Italy (home). *Telephone:* 3611795 (home). *Website:* www.rcslibri.it; www.daciamaraini.it.

MARAJ, Rashid Muhammad al-, BS; Bahraini central banker and fmr government official; *Governor, Central Bank of Bahrain;* ed Univ. of Houston, USA, Strathclyde Univ., UK; Engineer, Ministry of Industry and Devt 1979–80; Asst Under-Sec. for Econ. Affairs, Ministry of Finance and Nat. Economy 1981–95; Under-Sec., Ministry of Transport 1995–99; Gen. Man. and CEO, Arab Petroleum Investments Corpn, Saudi Arabia 1999–2005; Gov. Cen. Bank of Bahrain 2005–. *Address:* Central Bank of Bahrain, POB 27, Building 96, Block 317, Road 1702, Manama, Bahrain (office). *Telephone:* 17547777 (office); 17547500 (office). *Fax:* 17530399 (office); 17537799 (office). *E-mail:* governor@cbb.gov.bh (office); info@cbb .gov.bh. *Website:* www.cbb.gov.bh (office).

MARANDA, Pierre Jean, CM, MA, LPh, PhD, FRSC; Canadian anthropologist and academic; *Professor Emeritus, Laval University;* b. 27 March 1930, Québec; s. of Lucien Maranda and Marie-Alma Rochette; m. Elli-Kaija Köngäs 1962 (deceased); two s.; ed Laval Univ., Québec, Univ. of Montreal and Harvard Univ.; Asst Prof. of Classics, Univ. Laval 1955–58; Research Fellow, Harvard Univ. 1966–70; Dir of Research Ecole Pratique des Hautes Etudes, Paris 1968–69; Assoc. Prof. of Anthropology Univ. of BC 1969–71, Prof. 1971–75; Prof. Collège de France, Paris 1975; Research Prof. Laval Univ. 1974–96, Prof. Emer. 1996–; Pres. Steering Cttee of Cultural Hypermedia Encyclopedia of Oceania 1996–; Visiting Prof., Fed. Univ. of Rio de Janeiro 1983, Univ. of Toronto, ISISSS 1985, 1987, Univ. of British Columbia 1986, Université Omar Bongo, Libreville, Gabon 1991, 1992, Ecole des hautes études en sciences sociales, Paris 1994; Dr hc (Memorial Univ., Newfoundland) 1985; Médaille du Collège de France 1975, Canada Council Molson Prize in the Social Sciences and Humanities 1997. *Films:* Behind the Masks (with Claude Lévi-Strauss), Nat. Film Bd of Canada 1974, The Lau of Malaita, Solomon Islands (with Leslie Woodhead), Granada TV 1987. *Publications:* Structural Models in Folklore and Transformational Essays (with E. K. Köngäs) 1963, Echanges et communications (co-ed. with J. Pouillon) 1970, Structural Analysis of Oral Tradition (co-ed. with E. K. Köngäs) 1971, Introduction to Anthropology: A Self-Guide 1972, Mythology (ed.) 1972, French Kinship: Structure and History 1974, Mythology 1974, Soviet Structural Folkloristics 1974, Symbolic Production symbolique (ed.) 1977, L'Appropriation sociale de la logique (ed.) 1978, Imposer la bâtardise francophone (co-ed. with Eric Waddell) 1982, Automatic Text Reading: An Attempt at Artificially Intelligent Interpretation 1984, Dialogue conjugal 1985, DISCAN: A Computer Programme for Discourse Analysis 1989, L'unité dans la diversité culturelle: Une geste bantu, Vol. 1: Le sens des symboles fang, mbede, eshira 1993, Masques démasqués (co-ed. with Andrée Gendreau) 1993, Lo spazio semiotico dell'Andromaque di Racine 1994, Sémiotique de l'igname à Malaita, Iles Salomon 1995, A Semiotic Encyclopedia of the Lau People (Malaita, Solomon Islands) (computer diskette) 1997, Cultural Hypermedia Encyclopedia of Oceania (with Pierre Jordan and Christine Jourdan) (3rd edn) 1998, The Double Twist: From Ethnography to Morphodynamics (ed.) 2001, Peuples des eaux, gens des îles: l'Océanie (co-author) 2001, Voyage au pays des Lau. Le Déclin d'une gynécocratie, îles Salomon, début du XXIe siècles 2008; more than 90 articles in scientific journals. *Leisure interests:* skiing, swimming, tennis, bridge, music, art. *Address:* Département d'Anthropologie, Université Laval, Québec, QC G1K 7P4, Canada (office). *Telephone:* (418) 656-2131 (ext. 2168) (office); (418) 201-8109 (home); (418) 831-6542 (home). *Fax:* (418) 656-2831 (office). *E-mail:* pierre.maranda@ant.ulaval .ca (office); pmaranda@videotron.ca (home). *Website:* www.oceanie.org (office).

MARAPANE, Tilak Janaka; Sri Lankan politician; fmr Attorney-Gen.; Minister of Defence and of Transport, Highways and Aviation 2001–04. *Address:* c/o Ministry of Defence, 15/5 Baladaksha Mawatha, POB 572, Colombo 3, Sri Lanka.

MARAT, Allan, CBE, DPhil; Papua New Guinea politician; ed Univ. of Oxford; Leader People's Progress Party; Deputy Prime Minister, Minister for Trade and Industry 2002–03; Leader Melanesian Liberal Party 2007–; Attorney-Gen. and Minister of Justice 2007–10. *Leisure interests:* reading books on law, economics, business, politics. *Address:* c/o Department of the Attorney-General, POB 591, Waigani, NCD (office); POB 7431, Boroko, NCD, Papua New Guinea (home).

MARBER, Patrick; British writer and director; b. 19 Sept. 1964, London; s. of Brian Marber and Angela Benjamin; m. Debra Gillett 2002; three c.; ed Wadham Coll., Oxford; Cameron Mackintosh Prof. of Contemporary Theatre, Univ. of Oxford 2004. *Films:* screenplays: Old Street 2004, Asylum (co-screenwriter) 2005, Notes on a Scandal (sole screenwriter) 2006, Saturday 2008, Late One Night 2008. *Television:* The Day Today, Paul Calf Video Diary, Knowing Me Knowing You, 3 Fights 2 Weddings and a Funeral, The Curator, After Miss Julie. *Publications include:* Dealer's Choice (Evening Standard Award for Best Comedy, Writers' Guild Award for Best West End Play) 1995, After Miss Julie 1996, Closer (Evening Standard Award for Best Comedy, Critics' Circle Theatre Award, Laurence Olivier Award for Best New Play) 1997, Howard Katz 2001, The Musicians 2004, Don Juan in Soho 2006. *Address:* c/o Judy Daish Associates Ltd, 2 St Charles Place, London, W10 6EG, England (office). *Telephone:* (20) 8964-8811 (office). *Fax:* (20)

8964-8966 (office). *E-mail:* judy@judydaish.com (office); tracey@judydaish.com (office). *Website:* www.judydaish.com (office).

MARCEAU, Sophie; French actress; b. (Sophie Danièle Sylvie Maupu), 17 Nov. 1966, Paris; d. of Benoît Maupu and Simone Morisset; one s.; Meilleur Espoir Féminin (for César) 1982, (for Molière) 1991 and several foreign prizes. *Films include:* La Boum 1980, La Boum 2 1982 (César Award), Fort Saganne 1984, Joyeuses Pâques 1985, L'Amour Braque 1985, Police 1985, 'Round Midnight (uncredited) 1986, Descente aux Enfers 1986, Chouans! 1987, L'etudiante 1988, Mes nuits sont plus belles que vos jours 1989, Pacific Palisades 1989, Pour Sacha 1991, La note bleue 1991, Fanfan 1993, La fille de D'Artagnan 1994, Braveheart 1995, L'Aube à l'envers (Dir) 1995, Al di là delle nuvole (Beyond the Clouds) 1995, Firelight 1995, Anna Karenina 1997, Marquise 1997, The World is Not Enough 1998, Lost & Found 1999, A Midsummer Night's Dream 1999, La fidelité 2000 (Cabourg Romantic Film Festival Award), Belphégor – Le fantôme du Louvre (Belphecor: Curse of the Mummy) 2001, Parlez-moi d'amour (Dir) 2002 (Best Director, Montréal World Film Festival), Alex and Emma 2003, Je reste! 2003, Les clefs de bagnole (The Car Keys) 2003, A ce soir (aka Nelly) 2004, Anthony Zimmer 2005, Lezioni di volo 2006, La Disparue de Deauville 2007, Les Femmes de l'ombre 2008, LOL (Laughing Out Loud) 2008, De l'autre côté du lit 2008, Ne te retourne pas (Don't Look Back) 2009, L'homme de chevet 2009, With Love from the Age of Reason 2010, Happiness Never Comes Alone 2012, Arrêtez-moi 2013. *Stage appearances include:* Eurydice 1991, Pygmalion 1993. *Publication:* Menteuse 1996. *Leisure interests:* countryside, music, reading, travel. *Address:* c/o Artmédia, 20 avenue Rapp, 75007 Paris, France (office).

MARCHAND, Philippe, LenD; French politician and lawyer; b. 1 Sept. 1939, Angoulême, Charente; s. of Guy Marchand and Madeleine Bonat; m. Marie-Odile Filliau 1965; three s.; ed Collège de Parthenay, Univ. of Poitiers; lawyer at Saintes bar 1965–92; local councillor, Charente-Maritime 1976–2001, Saintes 1982–2001; Socialist Deputy for Charente-Maritime 1978–90, Vice-Pres. Assemblée Nationale 1985–86; Vice-Pres. Socialist Group in Parl. 1990–91; Titular Judge, High Court 1987; mem. Nat Comm. on Information Tech. and Freedom 1982–86, 1988–; Minister-del. in Ministry of the Interior 1990–91, Minister of the Interior 1991–92; regional councillor, Poitou-Charentes 1992–; mem. Comm. Nat. de Déontology de la Sécurité; Officier Légion d'honneur, Grand Cross of the Orden Isabel la Católica (Spain). *Address:* c/o Parti Socialiste, 10 rue de Solférino, 75333 Paris, France (office).

MARCHANT, Ian D.; British energy industry executive; *Chief Executive, Scottish and Southern Energy plc;* worked for Coopers & Lybrand including a two-year secondment to Dept of Energy working on electricity privatization; joined Southern Electric 1992, Finance Dir and mem. Bd of Dirs 1996–98, Finance Dir Scottish and Southern Energy plc (after merger of Southern Electric and Scottish Hydro Electric) 1998–2002, mem. Bd Dirs 1998–, Chief Exec. 2002–, lead Dir for Corp. Responsibility, mem. Nomination Cttee; Chair. UK Business Council for Sustainable Energy, Scottish Climate Change Business Delivery Group, 2020 Delivery Group, Eng Construction Forum 2009–; Dir (non-exec.) Maggie's Cancer Centres, John Wood Group plc 2006–; mem. Ofgem's Environmental Advisory Group, Energy Research Partnership. *Address:* Scottish and Southern Energy plc, Inveralmond House, 200 Dunkeld Road, Perth, PH1 3AQ, Scotland (office). *Telephone:* (1738) 456000 (office). *E-mail:* info@scottish-southern.co.uk (office). *Website:* www.scottish-southern.co.uk (office); www.hydro.co.uk (office).

MARCHENKO, Grigori Alexandrovich; Kazakhstani government official and central banker; *Governor, National Bank of Kazakhstan;* b. 26 Dec. 1959, Almaty; m.; ed Moscow State Inst. of Int. Relations, Georgetown Univ., USA; served in army 1979–81; engineer and acting Deputy Head, Dept of Sr Mans Ministry of Non-Ferrous Metals, Kazakh SSR 1984–85; Trans., Ed. and Leader Marketing Information Group, Kazakh Scientific Research Inst. 1986–88; acting head, Design Bureau of Semiconductor Machine Building, Chair. Scientific Production Co-operative Centre 1988–90; Asst to Vice-Pres. of Kazakhstan 1992–93; Deputy Gov. Nat. Bank of Kazakhstan 1994–96, Gov. 1999–2004, 2009–; Pres. Deutsche Bank-Securities (Kazakhstan) 1998–99; First Deputy Prime Minister of Kazakhstan 2004–06, Adviser to Pres. of Kazakhstan 2004–09; Chair. Halyk Bank 2005–09; Chair. Nat. Securities Comm. of Kazakhstan 1996–98; Pres. DB Securities of Kazakhstan 1998–99; Pew Fellow, Georgetown Univ. 1994. *Address:* National Bank of Kazakhstan, 050040 Almati, Koktem-3 21, Kazakhstan (office). *Telephone:* (727) 270-45-91 (office). *Fax:* (727) 250-60-90 (office). *E-mail:* hq@nationalbank.kz (office). *Website:* www.nationalbank.kz (office).

MARCHIONNE, Sergio, BA, BL, BComm, MBA; Italian/Canadian business executive; *Chairman, CNH Industrial NV; Chairman and CEO, Chrysler Group LLC;* b. 1952, Chieti, Italy; ed University of Toronto, York University, Toronto, University of Windsor; Chartered Accountant, Tax Specialist Deloitte & Touche 1983–85; Group Controller Lawson Mardon Group, Toronto 1985, later Dir of Corp. Devt; Exec. Vice-Pres. Glenex Industries 1989–90; Vice-Pres. of Finance and Chief Financial Officer Acklands Ltd 1990–92; Vice-Pres. for Legal and Corp. Devt, Chief Financial Officer and Sec. Lawson Group 1992–94; Exec. Vice-Pres. of Corp. Devt and Chief Financial Officer Algroup (following Algroup's acquisition of Lawson Group) 1994–96, CEO 1996–99, CEO Lonza Group Ltd (following demerger) 2000–01, Chair. 2002; CEO SGS Group Geneva 2002, Chair. SGS 2006–; mem. Bd Fiat SpA 2003–, CEO 2004–, CEO Fiat Auto 2005– (renamed Fiat Group Automobiles 2007), also Chair. CNH Case New Holland (Group co. operating in the agricultural and construction equipment business) 2006–, CEO Chrysler Group LLC 2009–, Chair. 2011–; mem. Bd of Dirs Exor SpA 2010–, Chair. Fiat Industrial SpA (co. cr. in Jan. 2011 through demerger of capital goods activities of Fiat SpA, including CNH, Iveco and FPT Industrial) 2011–; Chair., CNH Industrial NV 2013–; mem. Bd Dirs UBS AG 2007–10, Vice-Chair. 2008–10; mem. European Automobile Mfrs Asscn (ACEA), Pres. Bd 2012; mem. Bd Philip Morris International Inc.; Chair. Italian Br. of the Council for the United States and Italy; mem. Bd of Peterson Inst. for Int. Econs; Perm. mem. Fondazione Giovanni Agnelli; mem. Canadian Inst. of Chartered Accountants; Cavaliere del Lavoro; Hon. LLD (Univ. of Windsor), Hon. DBA (Univ. of Toledo, Ohio), hon. degree in Econs (Univ. of Cassino, Italy), Hon. MA (CUOA Foundation, Italy), degree ad honorem in Industrial Eng and Man. (Polytechnic Univ., Turin). *Address:* Fiat SpA, 250 Via Nizza, 10126 Turin, Italy (office); Chrysler Group LLC, PO Box 21-8004, Auburn Hills, MI 48321-8004, USA (office). *Telephone:* (011)

0061111 (Turin) (office); (248) 576-5741 (Auburn Hills) (office). *Website:* www
.fiatspa.com (office); www.cnhindustrial.com (office); www.chryslergroupllc.com
(office).

MARCHUK, Guri Ivanovich; Russian mathematician; b. 8 June 1925, Petro-
Khersonets Village, Orenburg Region; m.; three c.; ed Leningrad State Univ.; Sr
Research Assoc., Head of Dept, Inst. of Physics and Energetics, Obninsk 1953–62;
Inst. of Math., Siberian Br. of USSR Acad. of Sciences 1962–64, Deputy Chair.,
Chair. of Presidium 1964–79, Dir Computing Centre 1964–79; Prof., Novosibirsk
Univ. 1962–80; Deputy Chair. USSR Council of Ministers and Chair. State Cttee
for Science and Tech. 1980–86; Dir Dept of Computing Math. (now Inst.), Acad. of
Sciences 1980–, Adviser to Dir 1999–; Corresp. mem. USSR (now Russian) Acad. of
Sciences 1962–68, Academician 1968–, Vice-Pres. 1975–78, Pres. 1986–91, Chair.
Scientific Council on Medicine 1987–91; Deputy to USSR Supreme Soviet 1979–89;
Lenin Prize 1961, A. Karpinski Prize, Hamburg 1988; Order of Lenin (four times),
Keldysh Gold Medal 1981, Chebyshev Gold Medal 1996 and other decorations.
Publications: works on problems of computational math., earth sciences and
immunology. *Address:* Institute of Numerical Mathematics, Gubkin Str. 8, 117333
Moscow, Russian Federation. *Telephone:* (495) 938-17-69. *Fax:* (495) 938-18-21.
E-mail: guri@inm.ras.ru. *Website:* www.inm.ras.ru.

MARCHUK, Gen. Yevgen Kirilovich, CJur; Ukrainian politician; b. 28 Jan.
1941, Dolinivka, Kirovograd Region; m.; two s.; ed Kirovograd Pedagogical Inst.;
fmr school teacher of Ukrainian and German languages; with Ukrainian KGB
(State Security Cttee) 1963–91, Deputy Chair. 1990–91; Chair. Nat. Security
Service of Ukraine 1991; State Minister of Defence, Nat. Security and Emergencies
1991–94; Deputy Prime Minister July 1994, First Deputy Prime Minister 1994–95;
Prime Minister of Ukraine 1995–96; mem. Verkhovna Rada (United Social
Democratic Party faction) 1996–; Head of Cttee of Social Policy and Labour 1998–;
Sec., Ukrainian Nat. Security and Defence Council 2000–03; Minister of Defence
2003–04; Pres. Ukrainian Transport Union 1998; unsuccessful presidential cand.
1999. *Address:* c/o Ministry of Defence, 01021 Kyiv, vul. M. Hrushevskoho 30/1,
Ukraine.

MARCINKIEWICZ, Kazimierz; Polish politician; b. 20 Dec. 1959, Gorzów
Wielkopolski; ed Wrocław Univ., Adam Mickiewicz Univ., Poznan; worked as
teacher; mem. Solidarity Ind. Self-Governing Trade Union 1983–90; Founding
mem. Christian-Nat. Union party (ZChN) 1989; Supt Bd of Educ. in Gorzów
Wielkopolski 1990–92; Deputy Minister of Nat. Educ. 1992–93; consultant and
Deputy Dir Voivodship Methodological Centre in Gorzów 1993–95; mem. main Bd
of ZChN and head of bd in Gorzów Wielkopolski 1994; Deputy third Sejm
representing Electoral Action Solidarity-ZChN, later Deputy Chair. and Chair.,
Sejm Educ., Science and Youth Comm., also Deputy Chief, Special Comm. on
Admin. Reform; Head of Cabinet 1999–2000; left ZChN and f. Right Wing Alliance
2001, then head Parliamentary Club of Law and Justice party; Deputy fourth Sejm
and Chair. of State Treasury Comm.; Prime Minister of Poland 2005–06; ed and
publr ind. educational periodical Pokolenie; Co-founder, Ed. and Publr of Aspekty
(Catholic weekly); Cyberpolitician 2003. *Publications:* numerous articles on
economics. *Address:* c/o Law and Justice (Prawo i Sprawiedliwość—PiS), 02-018
Warsaw, ul. Nowogrodzka 84/86, Poland. *Telephone:* (22) 6215035. *Fax:* (22)
6216767. *E-mail:* biuro@pis.org.pl. *Website:* www.pis.org.pl.

MARCKER, Kjeld Adrian, PhD; Danish molecular biologist and academic (retd);
b. 27 Dec. 1932, Nyborg; s. of Kjeld A. C. Marcker and Minna C. Callesen; m. Anne
Birgit Hansen 1964; three d.; ed Nyborg Gymnasium and Univ. of Copenhagen;
Dept of Physical Chem., Univ. of Copenhagen 1958; Carlsberg-Wellcome Fellow,
MRC Lab. of Molecular Biology, Cambridge, UK 1962, mem. staff 1964, Fellow,
King's Coll., Cambridge 1968; Prof. in Molecular Biology, Århus Univ. 1970–2002;
mem. Royal Danish Acad., Danish Acad. of Tech. Science, Academia Europaea,
European Molecular Biology Org.; Novo Medical Prize 1971, Anders Jahre Medical
Prize 1973. *Publications:* articles in scientific journals. *Leisure interests:* soccer,
bird-watching, history. *Address:* Tjoernehegnet 32, 8541 Skoedstrup, Denmark.
Telephone: 86-22-01-18 (office); 51-92-71-23 (home). *E-mail:* KM@mb.au.dk.

MARCÓ DEL PONT, Mercedes; Argentine economist, politician and central
banker; b. 28 Aug. 1959, Buenos Aires; m. Jorge Cafferata; one s. two d.; ed Univ. of
Buenos Aires, Yale Univ., USA; Sr Researcher, Fundación de Investigaciones para
el Desarrollo (think-tank) 1982–87, Dir 1991–; teaching asst, Univ. of Buenos Aires
School of Econs 1984–85; Chief Adviser on petrochemical industry policy for
Ministry of Economy Planning Secr. 1989–91; consultant on econ. statistics, City of
Buenos Aires Statistical Dept 1999–2000; teacher, Center for Advanced Studies,
Nat. Univ. of Lomas de Zamora 1999–2002; cabinet adviser to Minister of
Production 2002; mem. Cámara de Diputados (parl.) for Buenos Aires (Front for
Victory, FPV) 2005–08, also Pres. Comm. for Small and Medium Enterprises; Pres.
Banco de la Nación Argentina 2008–10; Pres. Banco Central de la República
Argentina (central bank) 2010–13; mem. Plan Fénix (econ. think-tank), Univ. of
Buenos Aires 2001–; mem. Movimiento de Integración y Desarrollo. *Publication:*
Crisis y Reforma Económica 2004. *Address:* c/o Office of the President, Banco
Central de la República Argentina, Reconquista 266, C1003ABF, Buenos Aires,
Argentina.

MARCO TORRES, Gen. Rodolfo Clemente; Venezuelan politician and fmr
army officer; *Minister of Finance and of Public Banking;* b. 10 Sept. 1966; ed
Academia militar de Venezuela; took part in attempted coup against Pres. Carlos
Andres Perez Feb. 1992; has served in various capacities in govt insts including as
Pres. Agricultural Supply and Services Corpn 2008, Exec. Sec. Fondo Nacional
para el Desarrollo Nacional (FONDEN, nat. devt fund), sr position in Nat.
Treasury Office, Pres. Banco de Venezuela SA, Banco Bicentenario and Banco del
Tesoro (state-owned banks) 2005; Minister of State for Public Banking 2011–14,
Minister of Finance and of Public Banking 2014–, also Alt. Gov., World Bank, Sr
Gov., Inter-American Devt Bank, Sr mem. Bd for Venezuela, Devt Bank of Latin
America; Mil. Officer of Gen.-in-Chief Eleazar López Contreras. *Address:* Ministry
of Finance and Public Banking, Edif. Ministerio de Finanzas, esq. Carmelitas,
Avda Urdaneta, Caracas 1010, Venezuela (office). *Telephone:* (212) 802-1000
(office). *Website:* www.mppef.gob.ve (office).

MARCOS, Imelda Romualdez; Philippine politician and social leader; b. 2 July
1929, Tacloban City; d. of Vicente Orestes Romualdez and Remedios Trinidad; m.
Ferdinand E. Marcos 1954 (died 1989); one s. two d.; Gov. of Metro Manila

1975–86; visited Beijing 1976; took part in negotiations in Libya over self-govt for
southern provs 1977; Leader, Kilusan Bagong Lipunan (New Society Movt)
1978–81; mem. Batasang Pambansa (Interim Legis. Ass.) 1978–83; Minister of
Human Settlements 1978–79, 1984–86, of Human Settlements and Ecology
1979–83; mem. Cabinet Exec. Cttee 1982–84; Chair. Southern Philippines Devt
Authority 1980–86; indicted for embezzlement 1988, acquitted 1990; returned to
Philippines Nov. 1991; sentenced to 18–24 years' imprisonment for criminal graft
Sept. 1993; convicted of two charges of corruption, sentenced to 9–12 years on each
Sept. 1993; sentenced on appeal to Supreme Court; faced four charges of graft Sept.
1995; presidential cand. 1992, 1998; mem. Philippine House of Reps from first dist
of Leyte 1995–2001, from Ilocos Norte's 2nd district 2010–; opened Marikina City
Footwear Museum in Manila in which most of the exhibits are her own footwear
2001; arrested on charges of corruption and extortion committed during her
husband's presidency 2001; acquitted of 32 counts of graft 2008; voted 'Muse of
Manila' 1950. *Records include:* Imelda Papin featuring songs with Mrs Imelda
Romualdez Marcos 1989.

MARCUS, Claude, DrEcon; French fmr advertising executive; b. 28 Aug. 1924,
Paris; s. of Jack Marcus and Louise Bleustein; m. Claudine Pohl 1948; one s. three
d.; ed Faculté des Lettres, Aix and Faculté de Droit, Paris; fmr Vice-Chair.
Supervisory Bd, Man. Dir Publicis, Chair. Publicis Int.; fmr Chair. Perm. Comm.
Advertising Profession/Consumer Unions; Chevalier, Légion d'honneur, Officier,
Ordre nat. du Mérite, Médaille des Evadés, Chevalier, Ordre des Palmes
académiques et de l'Economie nationale. *Leisure interests:* antiques, tennis.
Address: 12 rue Félicien David, 75016 Paris, France. *Telephone:* 1-45-20-16-01.
Fax: 1-45-20-18-01. *E-mail:* claudius6@wanadoo.fr (home).

MARCUS, Gill, BCom; South African academic and central banker; *Governor,
South African Reserve Bank;* b. 10 Aug. 1949, Johannesburg; d. of Nathan Marcus
and Molly Marcus; ed Univ. of South Africa; mem. Nat. Exec. Cttee African Nat.
Congress (ANC) 1991–99; MP 1994–99, Chair. Jt Standing Cttee on Finance
1994–96, Deputy Minister of Finance 1996–99; apptd Deputy Gov. S African
Reserve Bank 1999–2004, Gov. 2009–; Prof., Policy, Leadership and Gender
Studies, Gordon Inst. of Business Science 2004–, now Extraordinary Prof.; Chair.
ABSA Group 2007–; Exec. Chair. Western Areas Ltd (gold mine) 2005–07; mem.
Bd Bidvest (BVT) 2005–, Gold Fields Ltd, Int. Marketing Council; mem. Advisory
Bd Auditor Gen. and Ind. Regulatory Bd for Auditors; Patron, Pretoria
Sungardens Hospice, Working on Fire Programme. *Leisure interests:* reading,
debating. *Address:* South African Reserve Bank, 370 Church St, PO Box 427,
Pretoria 0002, South Africa (office). *Telephone:* (12) 3133911 (office). *Fax:* (12)
3133197 (office). *E-mail:* info@resbank.co.za (office). *Website:* www.reservebank.co
.za (office).

MARCUS, Rudolph Arthur, BSc, PhD; American chemist and academic; *John
G. Kirkwood and Arthur A. Noyes Professor of Chemistry, California Institute of
Technology;* b. 21 July 1923, Montreal, Canada; s. of Myer Marcus and Esther
Marcus; m. Laura Hearne 1949 (died 2003); three s.; ed McGill Univ., Montreal;
worked for Nat. Research Council of Canada 1946–49; Univ. of N Carolina
1949–51; Asst Prof., Polytech. Inst. of Brooklyn 1951–54, Assoc. Prof. 1954–58,
Prof. 1958–64; Prof., Univ. of Ill. 1964–68; John G. Kirkwood and Arthur A. Noyes
Prof. of Chem., Calif. Inst. of Tech. 1978–; Visiting Prof. of Theoretical Chem.,
Univ. of Oxford, UK 1975–76; Visiting Linnett Prof. of Chem., Univ. of Cambridge,
UK 1996; mem. Courant Inst. of Math. Sciences, New York Univ. 1960–61,
Council, Gordon Research Confs 1965–68, Chair. Bd of Trustees and mem. Bd
1966–69; Chair. Div. of Physical Chem., ACS 1964–65; mem. Exec. Cttee American
Physical Soc. Div. of Chemical Physics 1970–72, Advisory Bd ACS Petroleum
Research Fund 1970–72, Review Cttee Argonne Nat. Lab. Chem. Dept 1966–72
(Chair. 1968–69), Brookhaven Nat. Lab. 1971–73, Radiation Lab., Univ. of Notre
Dame 1976–78, External Advisory Bd, NSF Center for Photoinduced Charge
Transfer 1990–, Nat. Research Council/NAS, Cttee on Climatic Impact; Chair.
numerous cttees including Cttee on Chemical Sciences 1977–79, Advisory Cttee for
Chem., NSF 1977–80, Review Cttee, Chem. Depts, Princeton Univ. 1972–78,
Polytech. Inst. of New York 1977–80, Calif. Inst. of Tech. 1977–78; Adviser, State
Key Lab. for Structural Chem. of Unstable and Stable Species, Beijing 1995,
Center for Molecular Sciences, Chinese Acad. of Sciences, Beijing 1995–; mem.
Editorial Bds numerous publs including Laser Chem. 1982–, Advances in
Chemical Physics 1984–, International Reviews in Physical Chemistry 1988–,
Progress in Physics, Chemistry and Mechanics (China) 1989–, Chemical Physics
Research (India) 1992–, Trends in Chemical Physical Research (India) 1992–; Hon.
Ed. International Journal of Quantum Chemistry 1996–; mem. NAS, American
Philosophical Soc., Int. Acad. of Quantum Molecular Science; Foreign mem. Royal
Society, London, Chinese Acad. of Sciences; Assoc. mem. Center for Advanced
Studies, Univ. of Ill. 1968–69; Fellow, American Acad. of Arts and Sciences; NSF Sr
Post-Doctoral Fellowship 1960–61; Alfred P. Sloan Fellowship 1960–63; Fulbright-
Hays Sr Scholar 1971–72; numerous lectureships; Hon. FRSC, Hon. Fellow, Univ.
Coll., Oxford 1995–, Hon. Prof., Fudan Univ., Shanghai 1994–, Inst. of Chem.,
Chinese Acad. of Sciences, Beijing 1995–, Hon. Visitor, Nat. Science Council,
Taiwan 1999, Hon. mem. American Philosophical Soc. 1990, Int. Soc. of
Electrochemistry, Korean Chemical Soc. 1996, Int. Soc. for Theoretical Chemical
Physics, Literary and Historical Soc., Univ. Coll., Dublin 2004, European Acad. of
Science 2004; Hon. DSc (Chicago) 1983, (Polytechnic Univ.) 1986, (Gothenburg)
1987, (McGill) 1988, (New Brunswick) 1993, (Queen's) 1993, (Oxford) 1995,
(Yokohama Nat. Univ.) 1996, (Univ. of NC) 1996, (Univ. of Ill.) 1997, (Technion–
Israel Inst. of Tech.) 1998, (Univ. Politécnica de Valencia, Spain) 1999, (North-
western Univ.) 2000, (Univ. of Waterloo, Canada) 2002, (Hyderabad, India) 2012;
many awards including Anne Molson Prize for Chem. 1943, Alexander von
Humboldt Foundation Sr US Scientist Award 1976, R. A. Robinson Medal,
Faraday Div., Royal Soc. of Chem. (RSC) 1982, C. F. Chandler Medal (Univ. of
Columbia) 1983, Wolf Prize 1985, ACS Peter Debye Award in Physical Chem. 1988,
Centenary Medal, Faraday Div., RSC 1988, Nat. Medal of Science 1989, ACS
Theodore William Richards Medal 1990, ACS Edgar Fahs Smith Award, ACS
Remsen Award, ACS Pauling Medal 1991, Nobel Prize in Chem. 1992,
Hirschfelder Prize in Theoretical Chem. (Univ. of Wisconsin) 1993, American
Acad. of Achievement Golden Plate Award 1993, Lavoisier Medal (Soc. Française
de Chimie) 1994, ACS Auburn-Kosolapoff Award 1996, ACS Award in Theoretical
Chem., ACS Oesper Award 1997, Top 75 Award, Chemical and Eng News, ACS
1998. *Achievements include:* devt of the Marcus Theory of electron transfer

reactions in chemical systems and RRKM Theory of unimolecular reactions. *Publications:* numerous articles in scientific journals, especially Journal of Chemical Physics and Journal of Physical Chem. *Leisure interests:* music, history, tennis and skiing. *Address:* Noyes Laboratory, Caltech Chemistry 127-72, California Institute of Technology, Pasadena, CA 91125 (office); 331 South Hill Avenue, Pasadena, CA 91106, USA (home). *Telephone:* (626) 395-6566 (office). *Fax:* (626) 792-8485 (office). *E-mail:* ram@caltech.edu (office). *Website:* www.cce.caltech.edu/faculty/marcus/index (office).

MARCY, Geoffrey W., BA, PhD; American astronomer and academic; *Professor of Astronomy and Director, Center for Integrative Planetary Science, University of California, Berkeley;* b. 29 Sept. 1954, Los Angeles, Calif.; s. of Robert Misrahi and Gloria Isaacs; m. Dr Susan Kegley 1994; ed Granada Hills High School, Los Angeles, Univ. of California, Los Angeles, Univ. of California, Santa Cruz; Carnegie Fellow, Carnegie Inst. of Washington 1982–84; Prof. of Physics and Astronomy, San Francisco State Univ. 1984–96, Distinguished Univ. Prof. 1997–99, Adjunct Prof. of Physics and Astronomy 1999–; Prof. of Astronomy, Univ. of California, Berkeley 1999–, Dir Center for Integrative Planetary Science 2000–; a Prin. Invesigator for NASA's Space Interferometry Mission 2001; mem. Cttee on the Status of Women in Astronomy (American Astronomical Soc.—AAS) 1994–97, Publs Bd, Publs of the Astronomical Soc. of the Pacific 1997–2002, Bd of Dirs, Astronomical Soc. of the Pacific 1997–99, Bd of Councillors, American Astronomical Soc. 1998–2000, NASA Working Group: Origins of Solar Systems 1998–2000, NASA Working Group: Terrestrial Planet Finder 1998–2001; mem. NAS 2002; Fellow, Calif. Acad. of Sciences 1996; ABC News Hour Person of the Week 26 Jan. 1996, Manne Siegbahn Award, Physics Cttee of Swedish Acad. 1996, Bunyan Lecturer, Stanford Univ. 1997, Alumnus of the Year, Univ. of California, Santa Cruz 1997, first Int. Astronomical Union Comm. 51 Bioastronomy Medal of Honor 1997, first Certificate of Recognition, Extrasolar Planetary Foundation 1999, UCLA Alumni Professional Achievement Award 1999, Invited Lecture and Exhibit, Centennial Meeting of American Physical Soc. 1999, G. Darwin Lecturer, Royal Astronomical Soc. 2000, California Scientist of the Year 2000, NSF Distinguished Lecturer 2000, NAS Henry Draper Medal 2001, Sackler Lecturer, Univ. of Leiden 2001, AAS Beatrice Tinsley Prize 2002, Carl Sagan Award, American Astronautical Soc. and Planetary Soc. 2002, NASA Medal for Exceptional Scientific Achievement 2003 Discover Magazine: Space Scientist of the Year 2003, Shaw Prize in Astronomy (Lecture) 2005, Niels Bohr Lecturer, Niels Bohr Inst. 2005, George Gamow Lecturer, Univ. of Colorado 2006, NASA Astrobiology Inst. 'Getting to the Core of Exoplanets: From Gas Giants to Ice Giants' 2007, Lecture: Nat. Air and Space Museum: New Worlds, Yellowstone, and Life in the Universe 2007. *Achievements include:* discovered 70 of first 100 known extrasolar planets; discovered first system of planets around a Sun-like star (Upsilon And), discovered first transiting planet around another star (HD209458), discovered first cand. Saturn-mass planets (HD46375, HD16141), discovered first extrasolar planet orbiting beyond 5 AU (55 Cancri d, co-discovered first Neptune-sized planets: Gliese 436b and 55 Cancri e. *Publications:* numerous scientific papers in professional journals. *Address:* 417 Campbell Hall, University of California, Berkeley, CA 94720, USA (office). *Telephone:* (510) 642-1952 (office). *Fax:* (510) 642-3411 (office). *E-mail:* gmarcy@astro.berkeley.edu (office). *Website:* astro.berkeley.edu/~gmarcy (office).

MARDADI, Abukar Abdi Osman; Somali politician; Minister of Defence 2010–. *Address:* Ministry of Defence, Mogadishu, Somalia (office). *Website:* www.mod.somaligov.net (office).

MÅRDH, Per-Anders, MD, PhD; Swedish university professor and physician; *Professor of Clinical Bacteriology, University of Uppsala;* b. 9 April 1941, Stockholm; s. of Gustav-Adolf Mårdh and Inga-Greta Mårdh (née Bodin); ed Univ. of Lund; Assoc. Prof., Univ. of Lund 1973; Dir WHO Collaboration Centre for Sexually Transmitted Diseases, Univ. of Lund 1980–85, then Uppsala Univ. 1985–; Prof. of Clinical Bacteriology, Univ. of Uppsala 1984–; Founder Scandinavian Asscn for Travel Medicine and Health 1990; Chair. Healthy Travel and Tourism Centre, Simrishamn; mem. Bd Int. Tourist Health Org., Osterlen Acad.; Assoc., Inst. of Clinical Sciences; Fernström's Award for young prominent research workers 1982. *Publications:* as ed.: Genital Infections and Their Complications 1975, Chlamydia trachomatis in Genital and Related Infections 1982, Chlamydial Infections 1982, International Perspectives on Neglected Sexually Transmitted Diseases 1983, Gas Chromatography/Mass Spectrometry in Applications in Microbiology 1984, Sexually Transmitted Diseases 1984, Bacterial Vaginosis 1984, Coagulase–negative Staphylococci 1986, Infections in Primary Health Care 1986, Genital Candida-infection 1990, Vaginitis/Vaginosis 1991, Travel and Migration Medicine 1997; Author: Chlamydia 1988, Swedish Red Houses 1991, Travel Well Travel Healthy 1992, Travel Medicine 1994, Women's Health 2013. *Leisure interests:* art, skiing. *Address:* Department of Obstetrics and Gynaecology, Lund University Hospital, 221 85 Lund, Sweden (office). *Telephone:* (46) 17-13-20 (office); (46) 17-10-00 (office); 73-611119 (mobile) (home). *E-mail:* per-anders.mardh@med.lu.se (office). *Website:* www.med.lu.se (office).

MAREE, John B., BComm, AMP; South African business executive; b. 13 Aug. 1924, Middelburg, Cape; s. of Dr John Maree; m. Joy du Plessis 1950; one s.; ed Univ. of the Witwatersrand and Harvard Business School, USA; Chair. Eskom Electricity Council 1985–97, Nedcor Group of Cos 1990–97, Denel Ltd 1992–95, Powertech Ltd 1997; Dir Devt Bank of SA, Old Mutual; Fellow, Inst. of Marketing Man.; Hon. DCom; Star of SA 1985, Order for Meritorious Service (Gold) 1989, Chevalier, Légion d'honneur, Order of Cloud and Banner, People's Repub. of China; one of top 5 Businessmen of the Year 1981. *Leisure interests:* golf, gardening. *Address:* 52 4th Road, Hyde Park, Sandton 2196, South Africa (home). *Telephone:* (11) 881-4363 (office); (11) 788-8812 (home). *Fax:* (11) 881-4799 (office). *E-mail:* drmaree@nedbank.co.za (office).

MARGA, Andrei, BA, PhD; Romanian philosopher, academic, writer and politician; b. 22 May 1946, Bucharest; m. Prof. Felicia-Delia Marga; Asst Lecturer, Babeş-Bolyai Univ., Cluj 1971–79, Lecturer 1979–90, Prof. of Contemporary Philosophy and Logic 1990–, Dean, Faculty of History and Philosophy 1990–92, Vice-Rector Babeş-Bolyai Univ. 1992–93, Rector 1993–2004, 2008–12, Pres. Academic Council 2004–08; Erich Voegelin Guest Prof., Ludwig Maximilians Univ., Munich, Germany 2004; Guest Prof., Univ. of Vienna, Austria 2004–05; Visiting Prof., Paul Valery Univ., Montpellier, France 2005, Prof., Hebrew Univ. of

Jerusalem, Israel 2012; Minister of Nat. Educ. 1997–2000; mem. Christian-Democratic Nat. Peasants' Party (PNȚCD) 1999–2001, Chair. Jan.–July 2001; formed the Popular Christian Party 2001; currently mem. Nat. Liberal Party (PNL); Minister of Foreign Affairs May–Aug. 2012; Vice-Chair. UNESCO-CEPES (European Centre for Higher Educ./Centre Européen pour l'Enseignement Supérieur) Bd 1998–; mem. Kuratorium of Institut für Kulturgeschichte Sud-Ost Europa, Munich 2001–, Collegium of the Journal of Law, Univ. of São Paulo, Brazil 2011–, Collegium of the Journal of Society and Economy, Corvinus Univ., Budapest, Hungary 2011–; Expert of the Agenzia per la Valutazione e la Promozione della Qualità delle Facoltà Ecclesiastiche (Vatican) 2011–, Hochschulrektorenkonferenz (HRK) (Germany) 2011–; Sr Consultant, Int. Network of Confucius Insts (HANBAN Foundation, Beijing, China) 2011–; mem. Academia Europaea (Jena) 2004–, Academia Europaea (Salzburg) 2005–, Uniunea Scriitorilor din România 2010–; Hon. Citizen, City of Bistrița 1999; Hon. Pres. Danubian Rectors Conf. 2006–10; Hon. Dignitary of Carmel City (Israel) 2008; numerous decorations including Grand Officier, Ordre nat. du Mérite 1999, Gra-Cruz da Ordem Nat. do Merito (Portugal) 2000, Ordinul Crucea Sfântului Apostol Andrei – Galaţi 2000, Ordinul Naţional Pentru Merit, rangul Mare Cruce 2000, Chevalier des Palmes académiques 2002, Das Grosse Verdienstkreuz 2003, Medaglia Pontificia. Anno XXVI. Joannes Paulus II (Vatican) 2005, Medaglia Pontificia. Anno I. Benedictus XVI (Vatican) 2006, Ordine della Stella della Solidarietà Italiana in grado di Cavaliere (Italy) 2009, Crucea Patriarhala – Patriarhia Română 2011; Dr hc ('Alexandru Ioan Cuza' Univ., Iași) 1999; Insigne Aureum (Univ. of Maribor, Slovenia) 2000; Dr hc (Univ. of Baia Mare) 2000, ('Ion Creangă' Univ. of Chișinău, Moldova) 2000, (Debrecen Univ., Hungary) 2003, (Paul Valery Univ.) 2008, ('Petru Maior' Univ. of Târgu-Mures) 2008, (Univ. of Oradea) 2009, (Corvinus Univ. of Budapest) 2010, ('Alecu Russo' Bălți State Univ., Moldova) 2010, ('1 Decembrie 1918' Univ. of Alba Iulia) 2010, (Baku Pedagogical State Univ., Azerbaijan) 2011, (Ştefan cel Mare Univ. of Suceava) 2011, (Constantin Brâncusi Univ. pf Târgu Jiu) 2011; Hon. DHumLitt (Plymouth State Univ., NH) 2006; Simion Bărnuțiu Award, Romanian Acad. 1985, România – Israel Award and The Medal of Jerusalem (Israel) 2002, Premiul Naţional 'Brătianu' 2003, Gold Medal, Univ. of Tübingen (Germany) 2003, Herder Prize (Austria/Germany) 2005, A Commendation of the Gov. of the State of NH (USA) 2006, Prize of Sara and Haim Ianculovici Foundation, Haifa (Israel) 2008, Medalia 'Prieten al Comunitatilor Evreiesti din România' – Federatia Comunitatilor Evreiesti din România (Fed. of Jewish Communities from Romania) 2009. *Publications include:* Herbert Marcuse. Studiu critic (Herbert Marcuse. A Critical Study) 1980, Cunoaștere și sens. Perspective critice asupra pozitivismului (Cognition and Sense. A Critical Approach of Positivism) 1984, Acţiune și raţiune in concepţia lui Jürgen Habermas (Action and Reason with Jürgen Habermas) 1985, Raţionalitate, comunicare, argumentare (Rationality, Communication, Argumentation) 1991, Introducere în metodologia și argumentarea filosofică (Introduction to Philosophical Methodology and Argumentation) 1992, Explorări în actualitate (Explorations into the Present Time) 1995, Filosofia unificării europene (The Philosophy of the European Unification) 1995 (second edn 1997), Academic Reform. A Case Study 1997, Reconstrucţia pragmatică a filosofiei (The Pragmatic Reconstruction of Philosophy) 1998, Educaţia in tranziţie (Education in Transition) 1999, Relativismul și consecinţele sale (Relativism and Its Consequences) 1999, Anii reformei: 1997–2000 (The Years of Reform: 1997–2000) 2001, Bildung und Modernisierung (Education and Modernization) 2001, Introducere în filosofia contemporană (Introduction to Contemporary Philosophy) 2002, Ieșirea din trecut (Documents and Reflections) 2002, Filosofia lui Habermas (The Philosophy of Habermas) 2006, Philosophia et Theologia Hodie 2008, La Sortie du Relativisme 2008, Fraţii mai mari. Intâlniri cu iudaismul (The Older brothers. Encounters with Judaism) 2009, Absolutul astăzi. Teologia și filosofia lui Joseph Ratzinger (Absolute today. Joseph Ratzinger's theology and philosophy) 2010, Criza and după criză (Crisis and after the crisis) 2010, Argumentarea (Argumentation) 2010, Challenges, Values and Vision 2011, Riflessioni italiane 2011, După cincisprezece ani. Fifteen Years after (1998–2004 și 2008–2012) 2011, România actuală (Diagnoză) 2011, The Destiny of Europe 2011, The Pragmatic Reconstruction of Philosophy 2012, Crizele Modernităţii Târzii 2012; numerous articles in learned journals. *Address:* Faculty of History and Philosophy, Babeş-Bolyai University, 400084 Cluj-Napoca, Str. Mihail Kogălniceanu 1, Romania (office). *Telephone:* (264) 405300 (office). *Fax:* (264) 405326 (office). *E-mail:* hiphi@hiphi.ubbcluj.ro (office). *Website:* hiphi.ubbcluj.ro (office).

MARGELISCH, Claude-Alain; Swiss lawyer and banking executive; *CEO, Swiss Bankers Association;* b. 1963; ed Univ. of Berne; qualified as an attorney-at-law and notary and worked in a law firm until 1993; joined Swiss Bankers Asscn 1993, Deputy CEO responsible for Int. Financial Markets –2010, CEO and Del. of Bd of Dirs 2010–. *Address:* Swiss Bankers Association, Aeschenplatz 7, PO Box 4182, 4002 Basel, Switzerland (office). *Telephone:* (61) 2959393 (office). *Fax:* (61) 2725382 (office). *E-mail:* office@sba.ch (office). *Website:* www.swissbanking.org (office).

MARGELOV, Mikhail Vitalyevich; Russian politician; b. 22 Dec. 1964, Moscow; m.; one s.; trans., Int. Dept, CPSU Cen. Cttee 1984–86; Arabic teacher, Higher KGB School 1986–89; Chief Ed. Arab Dept, ITAR-TASS 1989–90; with consulting cos World Resources, Boston Consulting Group, Ban & Co. 1990–95; with Video Int. 1995–; co-ordinator Boris Yeltsin Presidential election campaign; First Deputy Head Dept of Man., Russian Presidium 1996–97, Head of Dept of Public Relations 1997–98; Head of Advisory Group to the Chair., State Customs Cttee 1998; Head of Political Advisory Group, Novosti Information Agency 1999; Head of Russian Information Centre 1999–2000; Rep. for Pskov region, Russian Fed. Ass. 2000–, mem. Council of the Fed., Chair. Int. Affairs Cttee 2001–. *Address:* Nekrasov str. 23, Office 241, 180001 Pskov (office); Council of the Federation, Bolshaya Dmitrovka str. 26, Moscow, Russia (office). *Telephone:* (88112) 16-08-31 (office); (495) 292-13-58 (office).

MARGETTS, Sir Robert John, Kt, CBE, FREng, FIChemE; British insurance industry executive; *Deputy Chairman, Uralkali;* b. 10 Nov. 1946; ed Univ. of Cambridge; trained as chemical engineer; joined ICI PLC as process design 1969, Dir Agricultural Div. 1982–85, Petrochemicals & Plastics Div. 1985–87, Research & Operations Chemicals & Polymers Group 1987, ICI Eng 1987–89, Gen. Man. Personnel 1989–90, Chair. and Chief Exec. Tioxide Group 1991–92, Exec. Dir

1992–97, Vice-Chair. 1998–2000, Chair. ICI Pension Fund Trustee Ltd 1994–2000; Sr Ind. Dir and Deputy Chair. Uralkali (produces potash fertilisers) 2011–; Chair. Huntsman Corpn (Europe) 2000–10, Ensus PLC 2007–, Energy Technologies Inst. LLP 2007–, Ordnance Survey 2008–; Dir (non-exec.) English China Clays plc 1992–99, Legal & General Group plc 1996–2010 (Vice-Chair. 1998–2000, Chair. 2000–10), Anglo American plc 1999–2010 (Sr Ind. Dir 2003–08), BOC Group plc 2001–06 (Deputy Chair. 2001–02, Chair. 2002–06), Falck Renewables plc 2007–10, Neochimiki SA 2008–10, Wellstream plc 2010–11, Huntsman Corpn 2011–; Vice-Pres. Royal Acad. of Eng 1994–97; Chair. Action for Engineering 1995–97, UK Natural Environment Research Council (NERC) 2001–06, Govt Industry Forum Non-Food Uses of Crops 2001–04; Dir Foundation for Science and Tech.; Trustee, Council for Industry and Higher Educ. 2001–10 (mem. 1992–), Brain Research Trust 2002–; mem. CIA Council 1992–96, 2001–, Bd CEFIC 1993–95, 1998–2000, Council for Science and Tech. 1998–2007, Advisory Cttee on Business and the Environment 1999–2001, Technology Foresight Steering Group, Economy and Science and Tech. Honours Cttees 2005–, Advisory Bd Teijin Ltd (Japan) 2004–06; Gov. mem. Finance Cttee ICSTM 1991–2004; mem. Court Univ. of Surrey; Fellow, City & Guilds 2001; Hon. Fellow, Imperial Coll. 1999, Univ. of Cardiff 2007, Inst. of Energy 2008, Council for Industry and Higher Educ. 2011; Hon. Freeman, City of London 2004, Salters' Co. 2004; Hon. DEng (Sheffield) 1997, Hon. DSc (Cranfield) 2003. *Leisure interests:* sailing, skiing, tennis, watersports. *Address:* Uralkali Moscow Office, 119034 Moscow, Butikovsky per. 7, Russia (office). *Telephone:* (495) 730-23-71 (office). *Fax:* (495) 730-23-93 (office). *E-mail:* board@uralkali.com (office). *Website:* www.uralkali.com (office).

MARGRETHE II, HM, Queen of Denmark; b. 16 April 1940; d. of the late King Frederik IX and Queen Ingrid; m. Count Henri de Laborde de Monpezat (now Prince Consort Henrik of Denmark) 1967; two s., HRH Crown Prince Frederik and HRH Prince Joachim; ed Univs of Copenhagen, Århus and Cambridge, Sorbonne, Paris and London School of Econs, UK; succeeded to the throne 14 Jan. 1972; has undertaken many official visits abroad with her husband, travelling extensively in Europe, the Far East, N and S America; Hon. KG 1979; Hon. Freedom of City of London 2000; Hon. Bencher of the Middle Temple 1992; Hon. Fellow Lucy Cavendish Coll. Cambridge 1989, Girton Coll. Cambridge 1992; Order of the Elephant, Order of the Dannebrog, Order of the Cross of Terra Mariana (Estonia), Légion d'honneur, Order of the Redeemer (Greece) and numerous others; Hon. LLD (Cambridge) 1975; Dr hc (London) 1980, (Univ. of Iceland) 1986, (Oxford) 1992, (Edin.) 2000; Mother-Tongue Society's Prize 1987, Medal of the Head-mastership, Univ. of Paris 1987, Adeil Order 1990. *Achievements (miscellaneous):* illustrated J. R. R. Tolkien's Lord of the Rings 1977, Historierne om Regnar Lodbrog, Norse Legends as told by Jorgen Stegelmann 1979, Bjarkemaal 1982, Poul Oerum's Comedy in Florens 1990 and Cantabile poems by HRH the Prince Consort 2000, designed costumes for TV Theatre's The Shepherdess and the Chimney-sweep 1987, scenography and costumes for the ballet A Folk Tale, Royal Theatre 1991, découpages for TV film about the Hans Christian Andersen fairy tale Snedronningen 1999–2000, scenography and costumes for Tivoli pantomime ballet Kaerlighed i Skarnkassen 2001, illustrations for Karen Blixen's Seven Gothic Tales 2002. *Publications include:* (trans.) All Men are Mortal (with HRH the Prince Consort) 1981, The Valley 1988, The Fields 1989, The Forest (trans.) 1989. *Address:* Amalienborg, 1257 Copenhagen K; PO Box 2143, 1015 Copenhagen K, Denmark. *E-mail:* hofmarskallatet@kongehuset.dk (office). *Website:* www.kongehuset.dk (office).

MARGULIS, Grigoriy, DSc; American (b. Russian) researcher, academic and educator; *Professor of Mathematics, Yale University;* b. 24 Feb. 1946, Moscow, Russia; ed Moscow High School and Moscow Univ.; Jr Scientific Fellow, Inst. for Problems in Information Transmission, Moscow 1970–74, Sr Research Fellow 1974–86, Leading Research Fellow 1986–91; Prof. of Math., Yale Univ., New Haven, Conn. 1991–; Foreign Hon. mem. American Acad. of Arts and Science 1991, NAS 2001; Hon. Fellow, Tata Inst. of Fundamental Research 1996; Dr hc (Univ. of Bielefeld, Germany) 2000, (Ecole Normale Supérieure, Paris) 2010, (Univ. of York, UK) 2011, (Univ. of Lyon, France) 2013; Young Mathematicians' Prize, Moscow Math. Soc. 1968, Fields Medal, Int. Congress of Mathematicians, Helsinki 1978 (prevented by Soviet Govt from travelling to Helsinki to receive medal), Medal of Collège de France 1991, Humboldt Prize 1995, Lobachevski Prize 1996, Wolf Foundation Prize in Math. 2005, Dobrushin Int. Award 2011. *Publications:* numerous articles in math. journals on ergodic theory, dynamical systems, discrete subgroups of Lie groups, geometry, number theory, combinatorics. *Address:* Yale University, Department of Mathematics, 438 DL, PO Box 208283, New Haven, CT 06520-208283, USA (office). *Telephone:* (203) 432-4687 (office). *E-mail:* margulis@math.yale.edu (office). *Website:* www.math.yale.edu (office).

MARGVELASHVILI, Giorgi, PhD; Georgian philosopher, academic, politician and head of state; *President;* b. 4 Sept. 1969, Tbilisi; one d.; partner Maka Chichua; ed Tbilisi State Univ., Central European Univ., Hungary, Inst. of Philosophy, Georgian Acad. of Sciences; Mountain Guide and Group Leader, Caucasus Travel Ltd 1992–94; Jr Scientist, Psychological Lab. of Marginal Conditions 1993; Jr Scientist, Lab. of Georgian Culture 1993; Head, Dept of Advertising, Business Diary Ltd 1994–95; Lecturer in Philosophy and Cultural Studies, Tbilisi Independent Univ. 1996–97; Local Government Specialist/Program Consultant, Nat. Democratic Inst. for Int. Affairs, Tbilisi 1995–2000; Rector Georgian Inst. of Public Affairs (jt Georgian–USA establishment) 2000–06, 2010–12, Head of Research Dept 2006–10; became involved in politics 2003; Minister of Educ. and Science 2012–13; First Deputy Prime Minister 2013; named as Georgian Dream coalition presidential cand. for Oct. 2013 presidential election May 2013; Pres. of Georgia 2013–; Ind. *Publications include:* The Problem of Finality in Mythology 1993, Legislative Amendments to Local Government Training Manual #2 (ed.) 1998, Local Government Manual (co-author and ed.) 1998, Election Campaign and Training Manual (co-author) 1998, Philosophy of Individual Substance 1998, Legislative Amendments to Local Government Training Manual #1 (ed.) 1999, Our Generation's Privilege by Z. Zhvania (ed.) 2005; numerous articles and editorials on political, public, int. relations, culture and philosophy issues in newspapers and journals. *Leisure interest:* knitting. *Address:* Office of the President, 0103 Tbilisi, M. Abdushelishvili 1, Georgia (office). *Telephone:* (32) 228-27-36 (office). *Fax:* (32) 228-27-14 (office). *E-mail:* secretariat@admin.gov.ge (office). *Website:* www.president.gov.ge (office).

MARHELY, Daniel; French business executive; *Founder and Chief Technology Officer, Deezer;* left school aged 16; headed web dept of Agrafe communications agency 2001; focused exclusively on web devt from 2002; co-f. dating website Lovelee.com 2004; co-f. Aliza Medias 2006; started Blogmusik streaming music site which was not approved by SACEM (Soc. des auteurs, compositeurs et éditeurs de musique) music rights asscn, abandoned Blogmusik and dealt directly with rights owners; Blogmusik renamed Deezer.com as first legal music-on-demand website streaming service 2007, Chief Tech. Officer, now expanded globally into more than 160 countries with 20 million licensed music tracks, 32,000 radio channels, 26 million users and two million paid subscribers; mem. Conseil Nat. du Numérique. *E-mail:* pr@deezer.com (office). *Website:* www.deezer.com (office).

MARIAL BENJAMIN, Barnaba; South Sudanese politician; *Minister of Foreign Affairs and International Co-operation;* fmr Minister of Regional Cooperation, Govt and Minister of Information and Broadcasting –2013, Minister of Foreign Affairs and Int. Co-operation 2013–; mem. Sudan People's Liberation Movt. *Address:* Ministry of Foreign Affairs and International Co-operation, Juba, South Sudan (office).

MARIAM, Lt-Col Mengistu Haile; Ethiopian fmr head of state and army officer; b. 26 May 1937, Addis Ababa; m. Wubanchi Bishaw 1968; one s. two d.; ed Holeta Mil. Acad.; served in Army's Third Div., attaining rank of Maj.; mem. Armed Forces Co-ordinating Cttee (Derg) June 1974–; took leading part in overthrow of Emperor Haile Selassie Sept. 1974, Head of Derg Exec. Cttee Nov. 1974; First Vice-Chair. Provisional Mil. Admin. Council (PMAC) 1974–77, Chair. (Head of State) 1977–91; Pres. of Democratic Repub. of Ethiopia 1987–91 (overthrown in coup); Chair. PMAC Standing Cttee; Chair. Council of Ministers 1976–91, OAU 1983–84; Sec.-Gen. Workers' Party of Ethiopia 1984–91; accused of genocide in absentia; now living in Zimbabwe as political refugee; convicted of genocide 2006. *Leisure interests:* swimming, tennis, chess, reading, watching films. *Address:* PO Box 1536, Gunhill Enclave, Harare, Zimbabwe. *Telephone:* 745254.

MARIANI, Carlo Maria; Italian artist; b. 25 July 1935, Rome; s. of Anastasio Mariani and Anita de Angelis; m. 1st B. Brantsen 1959 (divorced 1983); m. 2nd Carol Lane 1990; one s. one d.; ed Accad. di Belle Arti, Rome; lives and works in Rome and New York; participated in Documenta 7, Kassel 1982, Venice Biennale 1982, 1984, 1990, Sydney Biennial 1986, Centre George Pompidou, Paris, Hirshorn Museum, Washington, DC, Museum of Modern Art, New York, San Francisco Museum of Modern Art, Mathildenhohe Darmstadt, Germany, Frank-furt Kunstverein, Germany, Museum of Modern Art, Rome, Palais des Beaux Art, Charleroi, France, Venice Bienniale, Italy, California Center for the Arts, Frye Museum, Seattle, Philadelphia Museum of Art, Museum of Palazzo Te Mantova, Italy, Smithsonian Nat. Portrait Gallery, Washington, DC and numerous other group exhbns in USA, Canada, UK, USSR, Europe and S America; lives and works in New York; Fetrinelli Prize, Accad. dei Lincei 1998.

MARIANI, Pierre; French business executive and fmr government official; *Chairman, Denizbank AŞ;* ed Ecole des hautes études commerciales, Ecole nationale d'admin; occupied various functions in Ministry of Economy and Finance 1982–92; Dir Cabinet of Budget Minister, Govt Spokesman and Head of Communication 1993–95; Man. Dir Soc. française d'investissements immobiliers et de gestion (real estate co. in Fimalac Group) 1995–96; Man. Dir and mem. Man. Bd Banque pour l'expansion industrielle (Banexi; commercial arm of BNP) 1996–97, Chair. Man. Bd 1997–99; Head of Int. Retail Banking, BNP Paribas Group 1999–2003, Head of Financial Services and Int. Retail Banking 2003–08, Deputy Man. Dir jtly responsible for Retail Banking activities and for Int. Retail Services of BNP Paribas 2008; Chair. Man. Bd and CEO Dexia SA 2008–11; Chair. Denizbank Anonim Şirketi 2011–; mem. Bd of Dirs Dexia Bank Belgium, Dexia Crédit Local, Dexia Banque Internationale à Luxembourg; mem. Exec. Cttee FBF; Vice-Chair. AFB; Dir and Chair. Audit Cttee, EDF SA 2009–. *Address:* Denizbank AŞ, Sancaktar Plazan. 128 K. 1/A, Evren Mah. Gulbahar Cad., Istanbul (Europe), Turkey (office). *E-mail:* info@denizbank.com (office). *Website:* www.denizbank.com (office).

MARIANI-DUCRAY, Francine, LenD; French state counsellor; *Member, Conseil Supérieur de l'Audiovisuel;* b. 7 Oct. 1954, Paris; m. Pierre Mariani; three c.; ed Ecole nationale d'administration (ENA) Paris, Inst. d'études politiques de Paris; joined Ministry of Culture 1979; Tech. Adviser to François Léotard, Minister of Culture and Communication 1986–88; a Dir Musée du Louvre 1988–91; Dir of Gen. Admin, Ministry of Culture 1993–98; Head of Gen. Inspections of Admin of Cultural Affairs, Ministry of Culture and Communication 1998–2001; Dir Musées de France 2001–08; Pres. Réunion des musées nationaux (RMN) 2001–03; Conseiller d'Etat 2008–; mem. Conseil Supérieur de l'Audiovisuel 2011–; Commdr, Ordre des Arts et des Lettres, Officier du mérite; Chevalier, Légion d'honneur 2005. *Address:* c/o Conseil Supérieur de l'Audiovisuel, Tour Mirabeau, 39–43, quai André-Citroën, 75739 cedex 15, Paris (office); 19 rue des Hauts Closeaux, 92310 Paris, France (home). *Telephone:* 1-40-58-36-04 (office); 1-45-34-04-32 (home). *Fax:* 1-40-58-36-88 (office). *E-mail:* francine.mariani-ducray@cda.fr (office). *Website:* www.cda.fr (office).

MARÍAS FRANCO, Javier; Spanish writer and translator; b. 20 Sept. 1951, Madrid; s. of Julián Marías Aguilera and the late Dolores Franco Manera; ed Institución Libre de Enseñanza, Colegio Estudio, Universidad Complutense de Madrid; trans. and writer of film screenplays 1969–; Ed. Alfaguara 1974; lecturer at various univs worldwide; mem. Int. Parliament of Writers (exec. council 2001–); Chevalier, Ordre des Arts et des Lettres, Premio Comunidad de Madrid 1998; Premio Nacional de Traducción (for translation of Tristram Shandy) 1979, Alberto Moravia Int. Prize, Rome 2000, Grinzane Cavour prize, Turin 2000. *Publications include:* novels: Los dominios del lobo 1971, Travesía del horizonte 1972, El Monarca del tiempo 1978, El hombre sentimental (Premio Herralde de Novela, Premio Ennio Flaiano 2000) 1986, El Siglo 1982, Todas las almas (Premio Ciudad de Barcelona) 1989, Corazón tan blanco (Premio de la Crítica 1993, Prix L'Oeil et la Lettre 1993, Int. IMPAC Prize 1997) 1992, Mañana en la batalla piensa en mí (Premio Fastenrath de la Real Academia Española de la Lengua 1995, Premio Internacional de Novela Rómulo Gallegos 1995, Prix Fémina Etranger, France 1996, Premio Arzobispo Juan de San Clemente 1995, Premio Letterario Internazionale Mondello-Città di Palermo 1998) 1994, Negra espalda del tiempo 1998, Tu rostro mañana 1. Fiebre y lanza (Premio Salambó 2003) 2002, Tu rostro mañana 2: Baile y sueño 2006, Tu rostro mañana 3. Veneno y sombra y adiós 2007; other fiction: Gospel (screenplay) 1969, Mientras ellas duermen (short stories) 1990, Cuando fui mortal (short stories) 1996, Mala índole (short story) 1998; non-fiction: Pasiones pasadas (articles and essays) 1991, Vidas escritas (articles) 1992, Literatura y fantasma (articles and essays) 1993, Vida del fantasma (articles) 1995, Si yo amaneciera otra vez (articles and poems) 1997, Miramientos (articles) 1997, Mano de sombra (articles) 1997, Desde que te vi morir (articles and poems) 1999, Seré amado cuando falte (articles) 1999, Salvajes y sentimentales (articles) 2000, A veces un caballero (articles) 2001, While the Women Are Sleeping (in trans., short stories) 2010; numerous translations; contrib. to anthologies, including Cuentos únicos 1989, El hombre que parecia no querer nada 1996; contrib. to journals and newspapers, including El País, El Diario de Barcelona, Hiperión, Revista de Occidente. *Address:* Mercedes Casanovas Agencia Literaria, Iradier 24, 08017 Barcelona, Spain. *E-mail:* webmaster@javiermarias.es. *Website:* www.javiermarias.es.

MARIĆ, Ljerka, BSc; Bosnia and Herzegovina economist and government official; *Director, Directorate for Economic Planning;* Minister of Finance, Canton of Fojnica 1998; Asst Minister of Finance and the Economy, Bosnian Fed. 2000; fmr Adviser to the Prime Minister; Minister of Finance and the Treasury of the Insts of Bosnia and Herzegovina 2003–07; currently Dir Directorate for Econ. Planning, Council of Ministers. *Address:* Directorate for Economic Planning, Ministry of Finance and the Treasury, 71000 Sarajevo, trg Bosne i Hercegovine 1, Bosnia and Herzegovina (office). *Telephone:* (33) 205345 (office). *Fax:* (33) 471822 (office). *E-mail:* trezorbih@trezorbih.gov.ba (office). *Website:* (office).

MARICAN, Tan Sri Dato' Mohamed (Mohd) Hassan, FCA; Malaysian petroleum industry executive; b. 18 Oct. 1952, Sungai Petani; m. Puan Sri Datin Sri Noraini Mohd Yusoff; ed Malay Coll., Kuala Kangsar; with Touche Ross & Co. 1972–80; Partner, Hanafiah Raslan and Mohamed 1980–89; Sr Vice-Pres. of Finance, Petroliam Nasional Berhad (PETRONAS) 1989–95, Pres. and CEO 1995–2010, Acting Chair. 2004–10, also mem. Bd of Dirs and Chair. PETRONAS subsidiaries PETRONAS Dagangan Berhad, PETRONAS Gas Berhad, Malaysia Int. Shipping Corpn Berhad, Engen Ltd SA; Chair. Perusahaan Otomobil Nasional Berhad (Proton) 2000–03; Dir, Int. Centre for Leadership in Finance; Ind. Dir, Sembcorp Industries Ltd 2010–; mem. Malaysian Inst. of Accountants, Malaysian Asscn of CPAs, Commonwealth Business Council; Dato' Setia Sultan Mahmud Terengganu, with title of Dato' 1992, Seri Paduka Mahkota Terengganu, with title of Dato' 1996, Panglima Setia Mahkota, with title Tan Sri 1997, Commdr, Légion d'honneur 2000, Friendship Medal (Viet Nam) 2001, Panglima Negara Bintang Sarawak, with title of Datuk Seri 2003; Dr hc (Univ. of Malaya). *Address:* Sembcorp Industries Ltd, 30 Hill Street, #05-04, Singapore 179360, Singapore (office). *Telephone:* 6723-3113 (office). *Fax:* 6822-3254 (office). *E-mail:* gcr@sembcorp.com (office). *Website:* www.sembcorp.com (office).

MARIN, Angel; Bulgarian army officer (retd) and politician; *Vice-President;* b. 8 Jan. 1942, Batak; m.; two c.; ed secondary school in Devin, Higher Mil. Artillery School, Shoumen, civilian degree in Radio Electronics Eng, Mil. Artillery Acad., Leningrad (now St Petersburg), USSR, univ. degree in mil. educ.; began mil. career as Lt-Engineer, held various positions in Missile Force, including Commdr Missile Launcher Unit, Commdr Start Platoon and Commdr Start Battery 1965–74, Commdr Separate Missile Div., Stara Zagora 1978–80, Commdr Artillery Regt, Stara Zagora 1980–82, Chief of Missile Force and Artillery, Second Div., Stara Zagora 1982–87, Chief of Missile Force and Artillery, Third Army, Sliven 1987–90, Commdr Missile Force and Artillery of the Ground Force of Bulgarian Armed Forces 1990–98, promoted to Maj.-Gen. 1991, dismissed from Army due to disagreement with the manner of army reform, retd 1998; Vice-Pres. of Bulgaria 2002–; graduated with distinction and a gold medal in 'Command of Chief of Staff HQ and Operative-Tactical', Mil. Artillery Acad., Leningrad. *Publication:* The Last War. *Address:* Office of the Vice-President, bul. Dondukov 2, 1123 Sofia, Bulgaria (office). *Telephone:* (2) 923-93-33 (office). *E-mail:* press@president.bg (office). *Website:* www.president.bg (office).

MARIN, Vice-Adm. Gheorghe, PhD; Romanian naval officer; *Chief of the General Staff;* b. 1 Jan. 1952, Negru-Vodă, Constanța dist; m. Elena Marin; one d.; ed Mircea cel Bătrân Naval Acad., Constanța, Faculty of Econ. Planning and Cybernetics, Econ. Studies Acad., Bucharest; Navigation and Communication Officer FPB (M) Squadron 1974–78; CO, Fast Patrol Boat 1980–81; Staff Officer, N3 1981–85; Chief Software Programming Section, Naval Informatics Centre 1985–89; Chief Naval Informatics Center 1989–95; CO Electronic Warfare Brigade within Naval Forces 1995–99; Supt, Mircea cel Bătrân Naval Acad. 1999–2003; Dir of Gen. Staff 2003–04, Chief of Naval Forces Staff 2004–06, Chief of Gen. Staff 2006–; Knight, Ordinul Național Steaua României, Grande Ufficiale, Ordine al Merito della Repubblica Italiana; Dr hc (Dunarea de Jos Univ.). *Publications:* more than 20 books and 70 articles. *Address:* Office of the Chief of the General Staff, Ministry of National Defence, 050561 Bucharest 5, Str. Izvor 13–15, Sector 5, Romania (office). *Telephone:* (21) 4023400 (office). *Fax:* (21) 3195698 (office). *E-mail:* sefsmg@mapn.ro (office). *Website:* www.defense.ro (office).

MARIN, Jean-Claude; French lawyer and judge; *Chief Public Prosecutor of Paris;* First Advocate Gen., Court of Cassation, Dir of Criminal Affairs and Pardons 2002–04, Solicitor and Chief Public Prosecutor of the Repub. of Paris 2004–. *Address:* Tribunal de Grande Instance de Paris, 4 blvd du Palais, 75055 Paris RP, France (office). *E-mail:* info@tgi-paris.justice.fr (office). *Website:* www.tgi-paris.justice.fr (office).

MARIN, Maguy; French choreographer and artistic director; b. 2 June 1951, Toulouse; s. of Antonio Marin and Luisa Calle; ed Conservatoire de Toulouse; joined Maurice Béjart's Ballet du XXème siècle; joined Ballet Théâtre de l'Arche (subsequently Compagnie Maguy Marin) 1979; Chevalier, Ordre des Arts et Lettres; Grand Prix Nat. de la chorégraphie 1983. *Choreographic works include:* May B 1981, Babel Babel 1982, Jaleo 1983, Hymen 1984, Calambre 1985, Cinderella 1985, Eden 1986, Leçons de Ténèbres 1987, Coups d'états 1988, Groosland 1989, Cortex 1991, Made in France 1992, Ay Dios 1993, Waterzooï 1993, Ramdam 1995, Aujourd'hui peut-être 1996, Pour ainsi dire 1999, Quoi qu'il en soit 1999, Points de fuite 2001, Les applaudissements ne se mangent pas (One Can't Eat Applause) 2002, Ça, quand même 2004, Umwelt 2005, Ha! Ha! 2006. *Address:*

Compagnie Maguy Marin, Centre Chorégraphique National de Rillieux-la-Pape, 30 Ter, avenue Général Leclerc, BP 106, 69143 Rillieux-la-Pape Cedex, France (office). *Telephone:* (4) 72-01-12-30 (office). *Fax:* (4) 72-01-12-31 (office). *E-mail:* info@compagnie-maguy-marin.fr (home). *Website:* www.compagnie-maguy-marin .fr (home).

MARIN GONZALEZ, Manuel, MA; Spanish politician and international organization official; b. 21 Oct. 1949, Ciudad Real; m. Carmen Ortiz; two c.; ed Madrid Univ., Coll. of Europe, Bruges and Univ. of Nancy; joined Spanish Socialist Party 1974; mem. Parl. for Ciudad Real, La Mancha 1977–86, 2000–; Sec. of State for Relations with the EEC 1982–85; EEC (now EU) Commr for Social Affairs, Employment, Educ. and Training 1986–89, for Co-operation and Devt 1989–94, for External Relations with the Mediterranean (South), Near and Middle East, Latin America and Asia (except Japan, People's Repub. of China, Repub. of Korea, Hong Kong, Macao, Taiwan) 1995–99, Vice-Pres. of Comm. 1993–99, Pres. (Acting) 1999; Spokesman, Foreign Affairs Cttee, Congress of Deputies 2001–04, Pres. Congress of Deputies 2004–08; Commr Global Comm. on Int. Migration; Grand Cross, Order of Isabel la Católica. *Address:* c/o Congress of Deputies, Carrera de San Jerónimo s/n, 28071 Madrid, Spain.

MARÍN ROMANO, Javier; Spanish banking executive; *CEO, Banco Santander SA;* b. 1966, Madrid; ed graduate in law and holds a degree in business admin; joined Santander Group in 1991, CEO Banif at Banco Santander SA (fmrly Banco Santander Central Hispano SA), also served as Deputy Sec. of Bd and Deputy Gen. Sec. of Banco Santander SA, Exec. Vice-Pres. of Global Pvt. Banking, Banco Santander SA 2007–10, Sr Exec. Vice-Pres. and Head of the Global Insurance, Asset Man. and Pvt. Banking Div. 2010–13, mem. Bd of Dirs 2013–, CEO Banco Santander SA 2013–. *Address:* Ciudad Grupo Santander, Edificio Pereda, 1st Floor, Avenida de Cantabria s/n, 28660 Boadilla del Monte, Madrid, Spain (office). *Telephone:* (91) 2890000 (office). *E-mail:* info@gruposantander.com (office). *Website:* www.santander.com (office).

MARINAC, Darko, BEng, PhD; Croatian business executive; *President of the Management Board, Podravka d.d.;* b. 1950, Zagreb; ed Zagreb Univ., Croatian Chamber of the Economy, Cologne Business School, Germany; joined Pliva (pharmaceutical group) 1975, Project Man. 1978, later Dir-Gen., penicillin plant, Dir, Veterinary and Agro-Chemical Div. 1984, Dir, Research and Devt Div. 1990–92, also Vice-Pres., Man. Bd 1996–99; Integration Dir, Polfa Krakow and Lachema Brno 1999–2000; Pres., Man. Bd, Podravka d.d. 2000–; Pres., Man. Bd, Croatian Employers' Asscn 2004–. *Address:* Podravka d.d., A. Starčevića 32, 48000 Koprivnica, Croatia (office). *Telephone:* (48) 6510 (office). *Fax:* (48) 622008 (office). *E-mail:* podravka@podravka.com (office). *Website:* www.podravka.com (office).

MARINHO, Roberto Irineu; Brazilian media executive; *President, Organizações Globo;* b. 13 Oct. 1947, Rio de Janeiro; s. of Roberto Marinho; m. 1st Aparecida Marinho; one s.; m. 2nd Karen Marinho; ed Getúlio Vargas Foundation; joined O Globo newspaper 1963; reporter ABC TV, New York 1969–70; Dir Rio Gráfica 1971–77; Vice-Pres. TV Globo 1978–98, Vice-Pres. Organizações Globo (media conglomerate) 1998–2003, CEO 2002–03, Pres. 2003–; Amigo do Livro Prize, Câmara Brasileira do Livro 2004. *Leisure interests:* coffee production. *Address:* Organizações Globo, Rua Irineu Marinho 70, Cidade Nova, 20230-901 Rio de Janeiro, Brazil. *Website:* www.globo.com.br.

MARINI, Franco; Italian politician; b. 9 April 1933, S. Pio; Sec.-Gen. Confed. of Workers' Trade Unions (CISL, trade union) 1985–91; Minister of Labour 1991–92; mem. Chamber of Deputies (lower house of parl.) 1992–2006, mem. Senato della Repubblica (upper house of parl.) 2006–13, Pres. 2006–08; mem. European Parl. (Italian Popular Party) 1999–2004; unsuccessful cand. in presidential election 2013; Sec. Partito Popolare Italiano 1997–99; mem. Partito Democratico 2007–. *Address:* Partito Democratico, Piazza Sant'Anastasia 7, 00186 Rome, Italy (office). *Telephone:* (06) 675471 (office). *Fax:* (06) 67547319 (office). *E-mail:* info@partitodemocratico.it (office). *Website:* www.partitodemocratico.it (office).

MARININA, Col. Aleksandra Borisovna, PhD; Russian writer and fmr criminologist; b. (Marina Anatolyevna Alekseyeva), 16 June 1957, Lviv, Ukraine; m. Col Sergey Zatochny; ed Moscow State Univ.; fmr mem. of staff, Acad. of Internal Affairs; began writing detective stories 1991–; mem. of staff, Moscow Inst. of Justice, Ministry of Internal Affairs 1994–97. *Films for television:* Kamenskaya (48 episodes). *Publications:* Death and Some Love, Ghost of Music, Stolen Dream, I Died Yesterday, Men's Game, Forced Murderer, Black List, Requiem, When Gods Laugh, He Who Knows (vols 1–2), and numerous others. *Leisure interests:* collecting hand bells, reading, Verdi operas, computer solitaire. *Address:* COP Literary Agency, Zhukovskogo str. 4, Apt 29, 103062 Moscow (office); Verhnaya Krasnoselskaya str. 9, Apt 44, 107140 Moscow, Russia (home). *Telephone:* (495) 628-84-56 (office); (495) 628-84-56 (home). *Fax:* (495) 628-84-56 (office). *E-mail:* alexandra@marinina.ru (office). *Website:* www.marinina.ru (home).

MARINO, Daniel Constantine (Dan), Jr; American sports commentator and fmr professional football player; b. 15 Sept. 1961, Pittsburgh; Pa; s. of the late Daniel Marino and of Veronica Marino; m. Claire Marino; three s. two d. (one adopted); ed Cen. Catholic High School, Univ. of Pittsburgh; quarterback; played coll. football at Univ. of Pittsburgh 1979–82; played for Miami Dolphins (Nat. Football League—NFL) 1983–99, retd 2000, returned to org. in Jan. 2004 as Sr Vice-Pres. of Football Operations but resgnd three weeks later; holds or held 25 NFL records and tied for five others, including most attempts (8,358), most passing yards (61,361), most completions (4,967), most passing touchdowns (420), most passing yards in a season (5,084 in 1984), most games, 400 or more yards passing (13); co-f. with his wife The Dan Marino Foundation 1992, The Dan Marino Center 1995; Dir Business Devt, Dreams Inc. 2000–; fmr studio analyst on HBO's weekly football programme 'Inside the NFL'; commentator, CBS's The NFL Today; Advisory Bd mem. 3Cinteractive, Fla; opened two restaurants in S Florida called Dan Marino's Town Tavern (later Dan Marino's Fine Food and Spirits) 2005, since closed, restaurant opened in other locations, in Miami, St Petersburg, Las Vegas, Nev. 2007; Dr hc in broadcast journalism (Univ. of Pittsburgh) 2008; 16-time winner of American Football Conf. (AFC) Offensive Player of the Week, AP NFL Most Valuable Player 1984, NFL Comeback Player of the Year Award 1994, NFL Man of the Year Award 1998, Walter Payton Man of the Year Award 1998, College Football Hall of Fame 2002, Pro Football Hall of Fame 2005. *Films include:* Ace Ventura: Pet Detective (as himself) 1994; cameo appearances in Holy Man 1998,

Little Nicky 2000, Bad Boys II 2003; Any Given Sunday (project consultant) 1999, featured in video by Hootie & the Blowfish. *Television includes:* guest-starred as himself in The Simpsons episode Sunday, Cruddy Sunday 1999. *Publications:* Marino – On the Record 1999, Dan Marino: My Life in Football 2005. *Address:* 1304 SW 160th Avenue, Suite 113, Sunrise, FL 33326, USA. *Website:* www.danmarino.com; www.danmarinofoundation.org.

MARINOS, Ioannis, (Kritovoulos, Popolaros, W.), BA; Greek journalist; *Columnist, To Vima*; b. 20 July 1930, Hermoupolis; ed School of Law, Univ. of Athens; journalist, To Vima (daily political journal) 1953–65, columnist 1992–; journalist, Economicos Tachydromos, Ed.-in-Chief 1956, Ed. and Dir 1964–96, consultant/columnist 1996–; political commentator in Ta Nea (daily) 1972–75; commentator for many radio and TV stations in Greece; mem. European Parl., European Popular Party 1999–2004; Chair., Structural Reforms Cttee, Ministry of Economy and Finance 2004–09; mem. Bd Music Hall of Athens, Red Cross, Amnesty Int; Hon. PhD (Aristotelian Univ. Salonika) 1999; more than 30 awards, including Best European Journalist of 1989 (EC Comm. and Asscn of European Journalists) and awards from UN and Athens Acad. *Publications include:* The Palestinian Problem and Cyprus 1975, For a Change Towards Better 1983, Greece in Crisis 1987, Common Sense 1993, Constitutional Reform: Ideas & Proposals (co-author) 2007, The Disincentives to Invest in Greece 2012, We Should Have Known Better 2013. *Leisure interests:* literature, history, classical music, fishing. *Address:* 26 Nikis Street, Athens 105 57 (office); 2 Kontziadon Street, Piraeus 185 37, Greece (home). *Telephone:* (210) 321-0280 (office); (210) 452-6823 (home). *Fax:* (210) 321-0281 (office); (210) 452-6723 (home). *E-mail:* jmarinos@dolnet.gr (office).

MARINUȚA, Vitalie, MA; Moldovan politician and fmr army officer; *Minister of Defence*; b. 16 June 1970, Holercani, Dubasari dist; m.; two c.; ed Airborne Command Mil. Acad., Reazani, Russia, US Army Command and Gen. Staff Coll., Fort Leavenworth, USA, Naval Postgraduate School, Monterey, USA, Int. Relations and Political Sciences Inst., Chisinau; held numerous positions in Moldovan Army including Platoon Leader, Company CO, Special Forces Officer 1992–99, CO 22nd Peacekeeping Bn 2000–02, Sr Staff Officer, Operations Directorate, Main Staff 2004–05; Mil. Policy Planning Staff Officer, US CENTCOM, Tampa, Fla USA 2005–06; Chief of Int. Cooperation and Euro-Atlantic Integration Section, Moldovan Ministry of Defence 2006–07; retd from active mil. service with rank of Lt-Col July 2007; Minister of Defence 2009–; Cherch 'Stefan cel Mare' Medal, 'Fraternity in Arms' Medal. *Address:* Ministry of Defence, 2021 Chișinău, șos. Hîncești 84, Moldova (office). *Telephone:* (22) 25-22-22 (office). *Fax:* (22) 25-24-00 (office). *E-mail:* ministru@army.md (office). *Website:* www.army.md (office).

MARIO, Ernest, BS, MS, PhD; American business executive and pharmacist; *Chairman and CEO, Capnia Inc.*; b. 12 June 1938, Clifton, New Jersey; s. of Jerry Mario and Edith Mario; m. Mildred Martha Daume 1961; three s.; ed Rutgers Coll. of Pharmacy, New Brunswick, New Jersey, Univ. of Rhode Island; Vice-Pres. Mfg Operations, Smith Kline 1974–77; joined E. R. Squibb & Sons 1977, Vice-Pres. Mfg for U.S. Pharmaceuticals Div. 1977–79, Vice-Pres. Gen. Man., Chemical Div. 1979–81, Pres. Chemical Eng Div. and Sr Vice-Pres. 1981–83, Pres. and CEO Squibb Medical Products 1983–86, mem. Bd 1984–85; Pres. Glaxo Inc. 1986–89, Chair. 1989–91, apptd to Bd of Glaxo Holdings PLC 1988, Chief Exec. 1989–93, Deputy Chair. 1992–93; Co-Chair. CEO ALZA Corpn 1993–97, Chair., CEO 1997–2001; Chair. and CEO Apothogen, Inc. 2002; Chair. IntraBiotics Pharmaceuticals, Inc. 2002–03; Chair. and CEO Reliant Pharmaceuticals Inc. 2003–07, Capnia Inc. 2007–; mem. Bd of Dirs Boston Scientific Corpn, Maxygen, Inc., Pharmaceutical Product Devt Inc., Vivus Pharmaceuticals 2010–, Delpor Inc. 2012–, XenoPort Inc. 2012–; Chair. American Foundation for Pharmaceutical Educ.; Trustee Duke Univ. 1989–2007, Rockefeller Univ., Univ. of Rhode Island Foundation; Remington Medal (American Pharmacists Asscn) 2007. *Leisure interests:* golf, swimming. *Address:* Capnia Inc., 2445 Faber Place, Suite 250, Palo Alto, CA 94303, USA (office). *Telephone:* (650) 213-8444 (office). *Fax:* (650) 213-8383 (office). *E-mail:* info@capnia.com (office). *Website:* www.capnia.com (office).

MARION, Jean-Luc, LèsL, PhD; French professor of philosophy; *Professor, University of Paris, Sorbonne*; b. 3 July 1946, Meudon; s. of the late Jean E. Marion and of Suzanne Roussey; m. Corinne Nicolas 1970; two s.; ed Lycée Int. de Sèvres, Ecole Normale Supérieure (Ulm), and Univ. of Paris, Sorbonne; Asst Prof., Univ. of Paris, Sorbonne 1973–81, Prof. 1995–, Dir Centre d'Etudes Cartésiennes 1995–; Dir Ecole Doctorale V 1998–95; Prof., Univ. of Poitiers 1981–88; Prof., Univ. of Paris X (Nanterre) 1988–95; John Nuveen Prof. of Chicago 1992–, Andrew Thomas Greeley Prof. 2010–; Visiting Prof., Washington Univ. 1990, Villanova Univ. 2000, Boston Coll. 2001–03; Assoc. Prof., Laval Univ., Canada 1993–96; Dir serie Epiméthée, Presses Universitaires de France, Paris 1981–; Co-Dir Les Études Philosophiques (journal); mem. Faculty Steering Cttee, Chicago Centre in Paris 2001–04; mem. Acad. Française 2008–, Accademia dei Lincei 2010–; Chevalier des Palmes académiques, Chevalier de la Légion d'honneur; Dr hc (Utrecht Univ.), (Univ. San Martin, Buenos Aires), (Haverford Coll., PA); Prix Charles Lambert, Acad. des Sciences Morales et Politiques 1978, Grand Prix de Philosophie, Acad. Française 1992, Karl-Jaspers Preis, Univ. of Heidelberg, Germany 2008. *Publications:* Sur l'ontologie grise de Descartes 1975, L'idole et la distance 1977, Sur la théologie blanche de Descartes 1981, Dieu sans l'être 1982, Sur le prisme métaphysique de Descartes 1986, Prolégomènes à la charité 1986, Réduction et Donation 1989, La croisée du visible 1991, Questions cartésiennes 1991, Questions cartésiennes II 1996, Hergé. Tintin le terrible 1996, Etant donné 1997, De surcroît 2001, Le phénomène érotique 2003, Le visible et le révélé 2005, Au lieu de soi, l'approche de saint Augustin 2007, Certitudes négatives, Le croire pour le voir 2010. *Leisure interest:* running. *Address:* Université de Paris Sorbonne, 1 rue Victor Cousin, 75005 Paris, France (office); University of Chicago, Swift Hall, 1025 East 58th Street, Chicago, IL 60637, USA (office); 80 rue Michel-Ange, 75016 Paris, France (home); 28 rue Serpente, #311, 75006 Paris. *Telephone:* (1) 53-10-58-58 (office); (1) 42-83-76-30 (home). *E-mail:* Jean-Luc.Marion@ens.fr (office); jmarion@uchicago.edu (office).

MARK, Sir Alan F., Kt, KNZM, CBE, PhD, FRSNZ; New Zealand botanist, ecologist and academic; *Professor Emeritus of Botany, University of Otago*; b. 19 June 1932, Dunedin, South Island; s. of Cyril L. Mark and Frances E. Marshall; m. Patricia K. Davie 1957; two s. two d.; ed Mosgiel District High School, Univ. of

Otago, Duke Univ., USA; Otago Catchment Bd, Dunedin 1959–61; Sr Research Fellow, Hellaby Indigenous Grasslands Research Trust 1961–65, Adviser in Research 1965–2000, Chair. Bd Govs 2000–09; Lecturer, Univ. of Otago 1960, Sr Lecturer 1966, Assoc. Prof. 1969, Prof. of Botany 1975–98, Prof. Emer. 1998–; Visiting Asst Prof., Duke Univ. 1966; Hon. mem. NZ Alpine Club 2002; Fulbright Travel Award 1955, James B. Duke Fellowship 1957, Loder Cup 1975, NZ 1990 Commemoration Medal, The Inaugural Awards of NZ (Conservation/Environment) 1994, Hutton Medal (Botanical/Conservation Research), Royal Soc. of NZ 1997, The Fleming Environmental Award, Royal Soc. of NZ 2010. *Publications:* New Zealand Alpine Plants (with N. M. Adams) 1973, Above the Treeline: A Nature Guide to Alpine New Zealand 2012; more than 190 scientific papers. *Leisure interests:* nature conservation, enjoying the outdoors. *Address:* Department of Botany, University of Otago, Box 56, Dunedin (office); 205 Wakari Road, Helensburgh, Dunedin, New Zealand (home). *Telephone:* (3) 479-75-73 (office); (3) 476-32-29 (home). *Fax:* (3) 479-75-83 (office). *E-mail:* alan.mark@otago.ac.nz (office). *Website:* www.otago.ac.nz/botany (office).

MARKELL, Jack, BA, MBA; American business executive, politician and state governor; *Governor of Delaware*; b. 26 Nov. 1960, Newark, Del.; s. of William Markell and Elaine 'Leni' Markell; m. Carla Markell; two c.; ed Brown Univ., Univ. of Chicago; fmr Sr Vice-Pres. for Corp. Devt, Nextel; fmr Consultant for McKinsey and Co. Inc.; Founder Del. Money School; State Treas. of Delaware 1999–2009; Gov. of Delaware 2009–; Chair. Information Services Task Force 2001, Del. Coll. Investment Plan Bd; Co-Chair. Gov.'s Task Force for Financial Independence 2002, Deferred Compensation Council, Common Core Standards Initiative; Chair. Nat. Govs Asscn (NGA) 2012–, Nat. Bd of Dirs for Jobs for America's Graduates; fmr Chair. Democratic Govs Asscn, Educ., Early Childhood and Workforce Cttee, NGA July–Dec. 2010; fmr Vice-Chair. NGA Econ. Devt and Commerce Cttee Jan.–July 2010; mem. Bd of Pardons, Cash Man. Policy Bd, Del. Econ. Financial Advisory Cttee, Employee Benefits Cttee, Strategic Econ. Devt Council; Democrat. *Address:* Office of the Governor, Legislative Hall, 150 William Penn Street, 2nd Floor, Dover, DE 19901 (office); Washington Office of the Governor, State of Delaware, 444 North Capitol Street, Suite 230, Washington, DC 20001, USA (office). *Telephone:* (302) 744-4101 (Dover) (office); (202) 624-7724 (DC) (office). *Fax:* (302) 739-2775 (Dover) (office); (202) 624-5495 (DC) (office). *Website:* governor.delaware.gov (office).

MARKER, Laurie; American zoologist and academic; *Executive Director, Cheetah Conservation Fund*; Co-owner, Jonicole Vineyards and Winery, Ore. 1973–88; Veterinary Clinic Asst, Wildlife Safari, Winston, Ore. 1974–76, Veterinary Clinic Supervisor 1976–80, Cheetah Curator 1977–88, Dir, Marketing and Educ. 1980–88; Exec. Dir Centre for New Opportunities in Animal Health Sciences Center, Nat. Zoo, Smithsonian Inst., Washington, DC 1988–91, Research Fellow 1991–; Founder and Exec. Dir Cheetah Conservation Fund, Namibia 1990–, Cheetah Conservation Fund; developed the Int. Cheetah Studbook 1988, currently Int. Studbook Keeper; Vice-Chair. World Conservation Union's (IUCN) Species Survival Comm.'s Cat Specialist Group 1988, mem. core management group; Andrew D. White Prof.-at-Large, Cornell Univ. 2013; Dr hc (Oxford) 2002; Conservationist of the Year, African Safari Club 1992, Burrows Conservation Award, Cincinnati Zoo 2000, Paul Harris Fellowship, Rotary Club International, Windhoek, Namibia 2001, Humanitarian of the Year, Marin Co. Humane Soc. 2001, Sandveld Conservancy's Certificate of Honour, Namibia 2002, Chevron-Texaco Conservationist of the Year 2003, Living Desert's Track's in the Sand – Conservationist of the Year 2005, Gold Medal, Soc. of Women Geographers 2008, Lifetime Achievement Award, San Diego Zoo 2008, Intel Environmental Award, Tech Museum 2008, Lifetime Achievement Award, Int. Wildlife Film Festival 2009, Tyler Prize for Environmental Achievement Recipient (co-recipient) 2010, Rainer Arnhold Fellow 2011–12, Distinguished Alumni, Eastern Oregon State Univ. 2011. *Publications:* numerous papers in professional journals. *Address:* Cheetah Conservation Fund, PO Box 2496, 2210 Mount Vernon Avenue, 2nd Floor, Alexandria, VA 22301-0496, USA (office). *Telephone:* (866) 909-3399 (office). *Fax:* (206) 338-2161 (office). *E-mail:* info@cheetah.org (office). *Website:* www.cheetah.org (office).

MARKHAM, Kenneth Ronald, PhD, FRSNZ, FNZIC; New Zealand research chemist (retd); *Research Associate, Industrial Research Ltd*; b. 19 June 1937, Christchurch; s. of Harold W. Markham and Alicia B. Markham; m. E. P. Eddy 1966; two d.; ed Victoria Univ. of Wellington, Melbourne Univ.; Tech. Trainee, Dominion Lab., Wellington 1955–62; Scientist, Chem. Div., Distinguished Scientist Industrial Research (DSIR) Ltd, Lower Hutt 1962–65, Scientist, Organic Chem. Section, Chem. Div., DSIR 1968–75, Section Leader, Natural Products Section 1976–92, Group Leader Chem. Div. 1980–87, Sr Research Fellow 1987, Plant Chem., Team Man. 1992–2004, Research Assoc. 2004–; Post-Doctoral Fellow, Botany Dept, Univ. of Texas 1965–66, Asst Prof. 1967; Monsanto Chemicals Research Fellow 1960; Hon. Research Assoc., Biological Sciences, Vic. Univ. of Wellington 1998–; mem. Ed. Advisory Bd int. journal Phytochemical Analysis 1990–, Int. Journal of Flavonoid Research 1998–; Int. Corresp., Groupe Polyphenols 1992–; Easterfield Award, Royal Inst. of Chem. 1971, NZ Govt Ministerial Award for Excellence in Science 1990, Science and Tech. Medal, Royal Soc. of NZ 1997, Pergamon Phytochemistry Prize 1999. *Publications:* The Systematic Identification of Flavonoids (with Mabry and Thomas) 1970, Techniques of Flavonoid Chemistry 1982, Flavonoids: Chemistry, Biochemistry and Applications (co-ed. with O. M. Andersen) 2006; 18 invited chapters on flavonoids, spectroscopy and Hebe, 255 scientific papers on phytochemistry and its interpretation in int. journals 1960–; one patent on UV screens. *Leisure interests:* philately, swimming, stock market, photography, world news, petanque, palms, genealogy. *Address:* Industrial Research Ltd (IRL), PO Box 31310, Lower Hutt (office); 160 Raumati Road, Paraparaumu, New Zealand (home). *Telephone:* (4) 931-3577 (office); (4) 905-5285 (home). *Fax:* (4) 569-0055 (office). *E-mail:* k.markham@irl.cri.nz (office); kpmarkham@paradise.net.nz (home). *Website:* www.irl.cri.nz (office).

MARKHAM, Richard J.; American business executive; *Partner, Care Capital LLC*; b. 26 Sept. 1950, Hornell, New York; ed Purdue Univ. School of Pharmacy; Dist Man. Merck Sharp & Dohme Div., Merck & Co. Inc., served successively as Product Man., Sr Product Man., Dir of Market Planning 1973–86, Exec. Dir of Marketing Planning 1986–87, Vice-Pres. of Marketing 1987–89, Vice-Pres. Merck Sharp & Dohme Int. 1989–91, Sr Vice-Pres. Merck & Co. 1993; mem. Bd of Dirs

Marion Merrell Dow Inc. 1993, Pres. and COO 1993–95; COO Hoechst Marion Roussel 1995–97, CEO 1997–99; CEO Aventis Pharma 1999–2002, Chair. Man. Bd Aventis Pharma AG 1999–2002, Vice-Chair. 2002–, COO 2002–05; Pnr Care Capital LLC 2004–; mem. Bd of Dirs Pharmaceutical Research and Mfrs Asscn; mem. Bd of Trustees Health Care Inst., NJ. *Address:* Care Capital, LLC, 47 Hulfish Street, Suite 310, Princeton, NJ 08542, USA (office). *Telephone:* (609) 683-8300 (office). *Fax:* (609) 683-5787 (office). *E-mail:* info@carecapital.com (office). *Website:* www.carecapital.com (office).

MARKL, Hubert, Dr rer. nat; German biologist and academic; b. 17 Aug. 1938, Regensburg; ed Univ. of Munich, Ludwig Maximilian Univ., Munich, Univ. of Frankfurt am Main; research internships, Harvard and Rockefeller Univs, USA 1965–66; Dozent, Univ. of Frankfurt am Main 1967–68; Full Prof. and Dir Zoological Inst., Tech. Univ. of Darmstadt 1968–74; Prof. of Biology, Univ. of Konstanz 1974–2003 (retd); Heinrich Hertz Visiting Prof., Univ. of Karlsruhe 1994–95; Vice-Pres. Deutsche Forschungsgemeinschaft (German Research Foundation) 1977–83, Pres. 1986–91; Pres. Berlin-Brandenburgische Akad. der Wissenschaften 1993; Chair. Gesellschaft Deutscher Naturforscher und Ärzte 1993–94; Pres. Max Planck Soc. 1996–2002; mem. German Acad. of Natural Scientists Leopoldina, Berlin-Brandenburg Acad. of Sciences, Bavarian Acad. of Sciences, Göttingen Acad. of Sciences, Heidelberg Acad. of Sciences, Rhine-Westphalian Acad. of Sciences, Academia Europaea, American Acad. of Arts and Sciences, AAAS, Indian Acad. of Sciences; Hon. Mem. Soc. of German Chemists 1997–; Bundesverdienstkreuz 1992, Order of Merit Star (Poland), Verdienstorden des Landes Baden-Württemberg 1997, Großes Verdienstkreuz mit Stern 1999, Bayerischer Verdienstorden 2001, Bayerische Verfassungsmedaille in Silber 2002; Hon. Dr rer. nat (Saarland) 1992, (Potsdam) 1999, Hon. PhD (Dublin) 1997, Hon. DHumLitt (Jewish Theological Seminary, New York) 2000, Hon. DrPhil (Tel-Aviv) 2001, (Hebrew Univ., Jerusalem) 2001, (Weizmann Inst. of Science, Rehovot) 2002; Lorenz Oken Medal, Gesellschaft Deutscher Naturforscher und Ärzte 1984, Karl Vossler Prize 1985, Arthur Burkhardt Prize 1989, Karl Winnacker Prize 1991, Ernst Robert Curtius Prize 1995, Prognos Prize 1997, Pro meritis scientiae et litterarum, Bayerischen Staatsministeriums für Wissenschaft, Forschung und Kunst 2002, Harnack Medal, Max-Planck-Gesellschaft 2004, Ehrenring der Eduard-Rhein-Stiftung 2004, Hanns Martin Schleyer Prize 2005. *Publications include:* Biophysik (co-ed.) 1977, 1982 (English: Biophysics 1983), Evolution of Social Behavior (ed.) 1980, Natur und Geschichte (co-ed.) 1983, Neuroethology and Behavioral Physiology (co-ed.) 1983, Evolution, Genetik und menschliches Verhalten 1986, Natur als Kulturaufgabe 1986, Wissenschaft: Zur Rede gestellt 1989, Wissenschaft im Widerstreit 1990, Die Fortschrittsdroge 1992, Wissenschaft gegen Zukunftsangst 1998, Schöner neuer Mensch? 2002; numerous scientific papers in professional journals on sensory physiology and social behaviour of animals, nature conservation and environmental protection, promotion and support of science and research. *Address:* Fachbereich Biologie, (Universität Konstanz, Postfach M 612, 78457 Konstanz, Germany (office). *Telephone:* (7531) 88-2725 (office); (7531) 43716 (home). *Fax:* (7531) 88-4345 (office). *E-mail:* hubert .markl@uni-konstanz.de (office). *Website:* www.uni-konstanz.de/FuF/Bio/forsch/ zoology/markl (office).

MARKÓ, Béla; Romanian/Hungarian politician and poet; b. 8 Sept. 1951, Târgul Secuiesc; m.; three c.; ed Faculty of Philology, Univ. of Babeş-Bolyai, Cluj-Napoca; poetry teacher, Santana de Mures Elementary School 1974–76; Ed. Igaz Szo Literary Magazine 1976–89; Ed.-in-Chief Lato Literary Magazine 1989; Sr mem. Democratic Alliance of Hungarians in Romania (DAHR) 1989, Vice-Pres. 1989–93, mem. Standing Cttee 1990–91, Pres. in Senate 1991–92, Pres. DAHR 1993–2011 (re-elected 1995, 1999, 2003); Senator for Mures 1990–, mem. Culture and Educ. Comms 1992, Foreign Policy and Culture Comms 1992–96; State Minister in charge of coordinating activities in fields of culture, educ. and European integration 2004–07; Deputy Prime Minister 2009–12; advocated autonomy for parts of Transylvania where ethnic Hungarians (Magyar) in a majority; signed cooperation agreement with Pres. Ion Iliescu's Social Democratic Party, leading to schism in DAHR 2000; mem. Writers' Union in Romania 1978–, Writers' Union in Hungary 1990–; Sec.-Gen. PEN Group of Hungarian Writers in Romania 1990–; Sec. Writers' Union Subsidiary in Târgu Mures 1990–96. *Publications:* poetry: 18 vols –1974, Notes on a Happy Pear Tree 1999, Comme un échiquier fermé 2001, Despre natura metaforelor, Timp canibal 1997; one vol. of Hungarian literature for 11th grade 1980–83, 1990–2002, two vols of essays and literary analysis, three vols of studies and political discourses, trans. into Hungarian of some plays by Lucian Blaga and Radu Stanca. *Address:* Democratic Alliance of Hungarians in Romania, 400489 Kolozsvár, Str. Majális 60, Romania (office). *Telephone:* (264) 590758 (office). *E-mail:* office@rmdsz.ro (office). *Website:* www.rmdsz.ro (office).

MARKOPOULOS, Christos, DSc; Greek politician and nuclear chemist; *President, Interbalkan Cooperation;* b. 25 Dec. 1925, Athens; s. of Antony Markopoulos and Paraskevi Vergopoulou; m. 1st Sapfo Mazaraki 1954 (divorced 1960); one s.; m. 2nd Kleopatra Papadopoulou 1974; two s.; ed Varvakios High School, Teachers' Acad., Athens, Univ. of Athens, Leicester Coll. of Tech., UK; Nat. State Chem. Lab. 1956–59; Group Leader, Greek Atomic Energy Comm. 1962–69, Dir Radio-immunochem. 1977–81; Asst Prof., Nat. Tech. Univ. of Athens 1965; Sr Researcher, Imperial Coll., London 1968; Visiting Scientist, Tech. Hochschule, Darmstadt, FRG; Visiting Prof., Univ. of Bologna 1973; Pres. Hellenic Nuclear Soc. 1975–81; mem. Steering Cttee, European Nuclear Soc. 1979–81; mem. Cen. Cttee, Panhellenic Socialist Movement (PASOK) 1975–93; mem. European Parl. 1981–84 (mem. Energy, Research and Tech. Comm.); Amb.-at-Large for West European Countries 1984–85; mem. Nat. Parl. of Greece 1985–89 (Pres. Foreign Affairs Cttee 1986–87); Head of Greek Parl. Del. in Council of Europe 1986–88 (Vice-Pres. Parl. Ass. 1987–88); Minister in charge of Int. Orgs 1988–89; Pres. Panhellenic Movt for Nat. Independence, World Peace and Disarmament 1981–90, Interbalkan Cooperation; Founder Int. Peace Olympiad Bureau, Co-ordinator First Peace Olympiad 1989; Founder and Pres. Movt for Peace, Human Rights and Nat. Independence 1991–2001 (Hon. Pres. 2001–), Fed. of Balkan Non-Governmental Orgs for Peace and Co-operation 1993; Pres. Int. Organizing Cttee, 2nd European Conf. on Peace, Democracy and Co-operation in Balkans 1996; Pro Merito Medal, Parl. Ass. Council of Europe 1986, Model of Council of Europe 1988, Medal of Civilization, UNESCO 1989, Diploma and Medal for Contrib. to Peace and Welfare of Humanity, Int. Peace Bureau 1992, Honour Award for Contrib. to Progress of Science of Chem., Asscn of Greek Chemists 1997, Honour Prize for

Participation in Nat. Resistance against German occupation 1999. *Publications:* Organic Chemistry (two vols) 1963 and 1971, Inorganic Chemistry (two vols) 1968 and 1971, Introduction to Modern Chemistry 1973, The Dominance of Prota and the Theory of Enforced Randomness 1991, Order and Anarchy 1996, Chance and Order 1997, Alexander and Diogenes 1999, Conjectures and Arpisms 1999, Order Anarchy Terrorism 2010; and numerous articles on nuclear disarmament, peace, int. affairs, European relations and human rights. *Leisure interests:* swimming, classical music. *Address:* 34 Eratous Street, 15561 Holargos, Athens, Greece (home). *Telephone:* (1) 6524687 (home). *E-mail:* ch_marko@hol.gr (home).

MARKOV, Sergey Aleksandrovich; Russian politician and academic; *Director, Institute of Political Studies;* b. 18 April 1958, Dubna, Moscow Region; s. of Aleksander Nikolayevich Markov and Anna Dmitriyevna Markova; m. Nina Leonidovna Markova; one d.; ed Moscow State Univ.; teacher, Moscow Inst. of Radio Electronics and Automatics, Moscow Inst. of Political Sciences; consultant, Security Council, Russian Fed.; Visiting Scholar, Univ. of Wisconsin-Madison; Sr Consultant, Nat. Democratic Inst. of Int. Relations 1997–; Dir Inst. of Political Studies 1997–; consulting expert, numerous nat. and int. orgs including Security Council at Russian Presidium, State Duma, Nat. Democratic Inst. of Int. Relations, Chase Manhattan Bank, ING Baring, Renaissance Capital 1990–; Exec. Dir Asscn of Consulting Centres, Russian Asscn of Political Sciences 1991–; Ed.-in-Chief, internet publr for strana.ru; Prof., Moscow State Univ.; Prof., Higher School of Econs 2000–; Co-Chair. Moscow Carnegie Centre 1994–97; Chair. Organizing Cttee Civil Forum 2001; Co-ordinator Nat. Civil Council on Foreign Policy 2002–. *Leisure interests:* tennis, swimming, cycling. *Address:* Institute of Political Studies, Zubovsky Boulevard 4, Entrance 8, 119021 Moscow Russia (office). *Telephone:* (495) 201-80-50 (office). *Fax:* (495) 201-81-70 (office). *E-mail:* markov@fep.ru (office). *Website:* www.fep.ru (office).

MARKOVIĆ, Duško; Montenegrin politician; *Deputy Prime Minister, responsible for the Political System, Internal and Foreign Affairs, and Minister of Justice;* b. 6 July 1958, Mojkovac; ed Faculty of Law in Kragujevac, Serbia; Legal Dept, 'Brskovo' Mine, Mojkovac 1983–86; Sec. of Municipal Ass., Mojkovac 1986–89, Pres. 1989–91; Sec. Gen. of the Govt 1991–98; mem. Parl. 1997–98; Deputy Minister of Internal Affairs and Head of State Security Service 1998–2005; Dir Nat. Security Agency 2005–10; Minister without Portfolio 2010; Deputy Prime Minister, responsible for the Political System, Internal and Foreign Affairs 2010–, also Minister of Justice 2011–. *Address:* Ministry of Justice, 81000 Podgorica, Vuka Karadžica 3, Montenegro (office). *Telephone:* (20) 407501 (office). *Fax:* (20) 407515 (office). *E-mail:* kabinet@mpa.gov.me (office). *Website:* www.pravda.gov .me (office).

MARKOVIĆ, Predrag; Serbian politician and publisher; b. 7 Dec. 1955, Cepure; ed Univ. of Belgrade; Ed. Student, Vreme (newspapers), Vidici (magazine); Owner Stubovi kulture (publishing house) 1993–; Pres. G17 PLUS Man. Bd 2000–01, Pres. Political Council, mem. Exec. Bd 2001–02, Vice-Pres. G17 PLUS party 2003–; Pres. Nat. Ass. of Serbia 2004–06; Acting Pres. of Serbia March–July 2004; Minister of Culture, Media and Information Soc. 2011–12; fmr Pres. Asscn of Publrs of Serbia and Montenegro; mem. PEN, Serbian Literary Soc. *Publications include:* Morali su doći nasmejani lavovi 1983, Otemenost duše 1989. *Address:* G17 PLUS, Trg Republike 5, 11000 Belgrade, Serbia (office). *Telephone:* (11) 3210355 (office). *Fax:* (11) 3284054 (office). *E-mail:* office@ujedinjeniregionisrbije.rs (office). *Website:* www.ujedinjeniregionisrbije.rs (office).

MARKOWITZ, Harry M., PhD; American economist, business executive and fmr professor of finance; *President, Harry Markowitz Company;* b. 24 Aug. 1927, Chicago, Ill.; s. of Morris Markowitz and Mildred Gruber; m. Barbara Gay; research staff, Rand Corpn, Santa Monica, Calif. 1952–60, 1961–63; Tech. Dir, Consolidated Analysis Centers, Ltd, Santa Monica 1963–68; Prof. of Finance, UCLA 1968–69; Pres. Arbitrage Man. Co., New York 1969–72; in pvt. practice as consultant, New York 1972–74; research staff, T. J. Watson Research Center, IBM, Yorktown Hills, NY 1974–83; Speiser Prof. of Finance, Baruch Coll., City Univ. of New York 1982–90, Vice-Pres. Inst. of Man. Science 1960–62; Pres. Harry Markowitz Co. 1984–; Dir Research Daiwa Securities Trust Co. 1990–2000; Fellow, Econometric Soc., American Acad. of Arts and Sciences; Pres. American Finance Asscn 1982; Nobel Prize in Econs (with W. F. Sharpe and M. H. Miller), 1990. *Publications:* Portfolio Selection: Efficient Diversification of Investments 1959, Mean-Variance Analysis in Portfolio Choice 1987; co-author, SIMSCRIPT Simulation Programming Language 1963; co-ed. Process Analysis of Economic Capabilities 1963. *Address:* 1010 Turquoise Street, Suite 245, San Diego, CA 92109, USA.

MARKS, David Joseph, MBE, FRSA, RIBA; British architect; b. 15 Dec. 1952, Stockholm, Sweden; s. of Melville Marks and Gunilla Marta Loven; m. Julia Barfield; one s. two d.; ed Int. School of Geneva, Switzerland, Kingston Polytech. School of Architecture, Architectural Asscn School of Architecture, London; fmrly with Tetra Ltd, Richard Rogers Partnership; co-f. Marks Barfield Architects with Julia Barfield 1989, London Eye Co. 1994, as Man. Dir raised the finance for Devt of the London Eye; Chair. Waterloo Project Bd 2002–07; lectures include The Prince's Foundation Urban Villages Forum 2000, Royal Inst. 2001, RIBA 2000, Royal Acad. of Arts 2000, 2001, British European Group Conf., Rome 2001, Berlin 2001; Royal Inst. of Chartered Surveyors Award, RIBA Award for Architecture 2000, London Tourism Awards 2000, London First Millennium Award, American Inst. of Architects Design Award 2000, European Award for Steel Structures 2001, Blueprint Award 2001, Prince Philip Designers Prize, Special Commendation 2001, Faculty of Bldg, Barbara Miller Trophy 2001, Pride of Britain Award for Innovation 2001, Design Week Special Award 2001, D&AD Awards, Silver and Gold 2001, Queen's Award for Enterprise (Innovation) 2003, Lambeth Civic Award 2011 and several other awards. *Leisure interests:* family pursuits. *Address:* Marks Barfield Architects, 50 Bromells Road, London, SW4 0BG, England (office). *Telephone:* (20) 7501-0180 (office). *Fax:* (20) 7498-7103 (office). *E-mail:* dmarks@ marksbarfield.com (office). *Website:* www.marksbarfield.com (office).

MARKS, Dennis Michael, BA; British music and arts executive, broadcaster, writer and film producer and director; b. 2 July 1948, London, England; s. of Samuel Marks and Kitty Ostrovsky; m. 1st Deborah Cranston 1972; one s. one d.; m. 2nd Sally Groves 1992; ed Haberdashers' Aske's School, Elstree, Trinity Coll., Cambridge; Dir and Producer BBC TV Music and Arts 1972–78; co-f. Bristol Arts

Unit 1978–81; f. Third Eye Productions 1981–85; Ed. Music Features BBC TV 1985–88, Asst Head of Music and Arts 1988–91, Head of Music BBC TV 1991–93; Gen. Dir ENO 1993–97; Pres. Int. Music Centre, Vienna 1989–92; ind. producer, dir, writer and broadcaster 1997–; Italia Prize 1989, Royal Philharmonic Soc. Award 1990, Int. Emmy 2008. *Radio:* Faultline, Appian Way, Composers' Days (BBC Radio 3) 2004, The Search for Sepharad, Turkey in Europe, Little Russia in Israel, Cultural Conchies. *Television:* producer and dir of several hundred documentaries and operas 1972–2010. *Publications:* Great Railway Journeys 1981, Repercussions (Afro-American Music) 1985, Wandering Jew – The Search for Joseph Roth 2011. *Leisure interests:* cookery, travel. *Address:* 12 Camden Square, London, NW1 9UY, England (office). *E-mail:* dennismarks@blueyonder.co .uk (office). *Website:* www.dennismarks.net.

MARKS, Matthew Stuart, BA; American art dealer and gallery owner; *Owner, Matthew Marks Gallery;* b. 14 Nov. 1962, New York, NY; s. of Dr Paul Marks; ed Bennington Coll.; consultant, Pace Editions Inc., New York 1982–86, Assoc., Pace Gallery 1985–87; Dir Anthony D'Offay Gallery, London 1987–89; opened first gallery 1989; moved to garage-door warehouse on 22nd Street in 1994. *Address:* Matthew Marks Gallery, 523 West 24th Street, New York, NY 10011, USA (office). *Telephone:* (212) 243-0200 (office). *E-mail:* info@matthewmarks.com (office). *Website:* www.matthewmarks.com (office).

MARKS, Michael, CBE; British business executive; *Founding Partner, NewSmith Capital Partners LLP;* b. 28 Dec. 1941, London; one s. two d.; ed St Paul's School, London; joined Smith Bros 1958, Dir 1975, Chief Exec. 1987, Chief Exec. and Exec. Chair. Smith New Court 1995; Co-Head Global Equities Group, Merrill Lynch 1995–98, Exec. Chair. Merrill Lynch Europe, Middle East & Africa 1997–2003, Exec. Vice-Pres. Merrill Lynch & Co. 2001–03, Chair. Merrill Lynch Investment Mans (MLIM) 2001–03, mem. Exec. Man. Cttee Merrill Lynch; mem. Int. Markets Advisory Bd, Nat. Asscn of Securities Dealers 1991–, Bd London Stock Exchange 1994–2004; Chair. London Investment Banking Asscn 1998–2002; Vice-Pres. British Bankers Asscn 1998–; Founding Pnr NewSmith Capital Partners LLP 2003–; Dir (non-exec. Old Mutual plc 2004–, RIT Capital Partners plc 2004–. *Address:* NewSmith Capital Partners LLP, Lansdowne House, 57 Berkeley Square, London, W1J 6ER, England (office). *Telephone:* (20) 7518-3700 (office). *Fax:* (20) 7518-3701 (office). *E-mail:* enquiries@newsmithcapital.com (office). *Website:* www.newsmithcapital.com (office).

MARKS, Michael E., MA, MBA; American business executive; *Managing Partner, Bigwood Capital, LLC;* ed Oberlin Coll., Harvard Business School; fmr Pres. and CEO Metcal, Inc. (precision heating instrument co.); mem. Bd of Dirs Flextronics Corpn (electronics mfg services provider) 1991–, Chair. 1993–2003, 2006–08, CEO 1994–2006, Pres. 2003; Founder and Man. Partner, Bigwood Capital, LLC (pvt. equity firm), Palo Alto, Calif. 2007–; mem. Kohlberg Kravis Roberts & Co. (pvt. equity firm), Menlo Park, Calif. 2006–07, Sr Advisor 2007–08; mem. Bd of Dirs SanDisk Corpn, Milpitas, Calif. 2003–, Schlumberger Ltd, Houston, Tex., Sun Microsystems, Inc., Santa Clara, Calif. *Address:* Bigwood Capital LLC, 245 Lytton Avenue, Suite 250, Palo Alto, CA 94301-1465 USA (office). *Telephone:* (650) 473-5465 (office).

MARKS, Paul Alan, AB, MD; American oncologist, cell biologist, academic and research institute director; b. 16 Aug. 1926, New York, NY; s. of Robert R. Marks and Sarah Marks (née Bohorad); m. Joan Harriet Rosen 1953; two s. one d.; ed Columbia Coll. and Columbia Univ.; Fellow, Columbia Coll. of Physicians and Surgeons 1952–53, Assoc. 1955–56, mem. of Faculty 1956–82, Dir Haematology Training 1961–74, Prof. of Medicine 1967–82, Dean Faculty of Medicine and Vice-Pres. Medical Affairs 1970–73, Dir Comprehensive Cancer Center 1972–80, Vice-Pres. Health Sciences 1973–80, Prof. of Human Genetics and Devt 1969–82, Frode Jensen Prof. of Medicine 1974–80; Prof. of Medicine and Genetics, Cornell Univ. Coll. of Medicine, New York 1982–, Prof., Cornell Univ. Grad. School in Medical Sciences 1983–; Attending Physician, Presbyterian Hosp., New York 1967–83; Pres. and CEO Memorial Sloan-Kettering Cancer Center 1980–99, Pres. Emer. 2000, mem. Sloan-Kettering Inst. for Cancer Research 1980–; Attending Physician, Memorial Hosp. for Cancer and Allied Diseases 1980–; Adjunct Prof., The Rockefeller Univ. 1980–, Visiting Physician, The Rockefeller Univ. Hosp. 1980–; Trustee, Hadassah Medical Centre, Jerusalem 1996–2000; mem. Advisory Cttee to Dir, NIH 1993–96, NIH External Advisory Cttee-Intramural Research Program Review 1993–94; mem. editorial bds of several scientific journals; Gov., Weizmann Inst. 1976–96; Dir Revson Foundation 1976–91; Master American Coll. of Physicians; mem. Inst. of Medicine, NAS; Fellow, American Acad. of Arts and Sciences, American Philosophical Soc., Royal Soc. of Medicine, London; Dr hc (Urbino) 1982, (Tel-Aviv) 1992, (Columbia Univ.) 2000; Hon. PhD (Hebrew Univ. of Jerusalem) 1987; Recognition for Acad. Accomplishments, Chinese Acad. of Medical Sciences 1982, Centenary Medal, Institut Pasteur 1987, Pres.'s Nat. Medal of Science 1991, Gold Medal for Distinguished Academic Accomplishments, Coll. of Physicians and Surgeons of Columbia Univ., New York, Japan Foundation for Cancer Research Award 1995, John Jay Award for Distinguished Professional Achievement, Columbia Coll. 1996, Lifetime Achievement Award, Greater NY Hosp. Asscn 1997, Humanitarian Award, Breast Cancer Foundation 2000, The John Stearns Award for Lifetime Achievement in Medicine, New York Acad. of Medicine 2002 and other awards; The Paul Marks Prize for Cancer Research cr. by Memorial Sloan Kettering Cancer Center's Bds of Overseers and Managers in his honour 2001. *Publications:* over 350 articles in scientific journals on histone deacetylase inhibitors, mechanism of action and potential as anti-cancer agents. *Leisure interest:* tennis. *Address:* Memorial Sloan-Kettering Cancer Center, 1275 York Avenue, New York, NY 10065 (office); PO Box 1485, Washington, CT 06793, USA (home). *Telephone:* (212) 639-6568 (office). *Fax:* (212) 639-2861 (office). *E-mail:* marksp@mskcc.org (office). *Website:* www.mskcc.org/research/lab/paul -marks (office).

MARKS, Peter Vincent, CBE; British retail executive; *Group Chief Executive, The Co-operative Group;* b. 27 Oct. 1949, Bradford, Yorks., England; m. Julia Law 1971; two d.; ed St Bede's Grammar School, Bradford High School, Heaton; left school aged 17 to stack shelves in what became Yorkshire Co-operatives (mem.-owned retailer) in Bradford, man. trainee in Food Div. 1967, Asst Personnel Man. 1974–76, Personnel Man. 1976–91, apptd Non-Food Trades Officer, responsible for Dept Stores, Funeral and Travel divs 1991, Food Div. 1996, Chief Gen. Man. (Retail) 1996–99, Deputy Chief Exec. 1999–2000, Chief Exec. 2000–02, Chief Exec.

United Co-operatives (following merger of Yorkshire and United Norwest Co-operatives) 2002–07, Group Chief Exec. The Co-operative Group (following merger of United Co-operatives with The Co-operative Group to create world's largest consumer co-operative) 2007–. *Leisure interests:* drumming (plays in Bradford band, Last Orders), working out, playing racquetball, supporting Bradford City Football Club, music, reading biographies. *Address:* The Co-operative Group (CWS) Ltd, New Century House, Manchester, M60 4ES, England (office). *Telephone:* (161) 834-1212 (office). *Fax:* (161) 834-4507 (office). *E-mail:* customer .relations@co-op.co.uk (office). *Website:* www.co-operative.coop (office).

MARKS, Tobin J., BS, PhD; American chemist and academic; *Vladimir N. Ipatieff Professor of Catalytic Chemistry, Northwestern University;* b. 25 Nov. 1944, Washington, DC; ed Univ. of Maryland, Massachusetts Inst. of Tech.; Asst Prof. of Chem., Northwestern Univ., Evanston, Ill. 1970–74, Assoc. Prof. 1974–78, Prof. 1978, Charles E. & Emma H. Morrison Prof. of Chem. 1986–, Prof. of Materials Science and Eng 1987–, Vladimir N. Ipatieff Prof. of Catalytic Chem. 1999–; mem. Editorial Bd several journals including Topics in Catalysis, Journal of Molecular Catalysis, Chemistry of Materials, Nouveau Journal de Chimie, Organometallics; mem. Corp. Tech. Advisory Bd, Dow Corning Corpn 1994–, Dow Chemical Co. 1995–; mem. AAAS, American Acad. of Arts and Sciences, NAS, ACS (Councillor, Inorganic Chem. Div. 1980–85), Materials Research Soc.; ACS Award in Organometallic Chem. 1989, ACS Award in Organic Chem. 1994, Royal Soc. of Chem. Centenary Medal 1997, Univ. of Pittsburgh Francis Clifford Phillips Award 1998, Italian Chemical Soc. Paolo Chini Award 1999, ACS Cotton Medal 2000, ACS Linus Pauling Medal 2001, ACS Willard Gibbs Medal 2001, Royal Soc. of Chem. Frankland Medal 2003, German Chemical Soc. Karl Ziegler Medal 2003. *Address:* WCAS Chemistry, Northwestern University, 2145 Sheridan Road, Evanston, IL 60208, USA (office). *Telephone:* (847) 491-5658 (office). *Fax:* (847) 491-7713 (office). *E-mail:* t-marks@northwestern.edu (office). *Website:* www.chem .northwestern.edu/brochure/marks.html (office).

MARKS OF HENLEY-ON-THAMES, Baron (Life Peer), cr. 2011, of Henley-on-Thames in the County of Oxfordshire; **Jonathan Marks,** QC, BA; British barrister; ed Univ. of Oxford; called to the Bar 1975; QC 1995; commercial and family law barrister with specialist interest in human rights and constitutional reform; TECBAR approved Adjudicator; trained mediator; Barrister, 4 Pump Court chambers. *Address:* 4 Pump Court, Temple, London, EC4Y 7AN (office); House of Lords, Westminster, London, SW1A 0PW, England. *Telephone:* (20) 7842-5555 (office); (20) 7219-5353. *Fax:* (20) 7583-2036 (office); (20) 7219-5979. *E-mail:* clerks@4pumpcourt.com (office). *Website:* www.4pumpcourt.com (office).

MARKUS, Alim; Indonesian business executive; *President Director, Maspion Group;* b. 24 Sept. 1951, Surabaya; s. of Alim Husin; m.; six c.; ed Nat. Univ. of Singapore; joined family co. Maspion (housewares and appliances mfr), becoming Pres. Dir PT Maspion and Maspion Group 1971–; Chair. Indonesia–China Asscn; Vice-Chair. East Java Indonesia Chamber of Commerce; Bintang Jasa Nararya 2013. *Address:* Maspion Group, Kembang Jepun 38–40, Surabaya 60162, Indonesia (office). *Telephone:* (31) 3530333 (office). *Fax:* (31) 3533055 (office). *E-mail:* info.hq@maspion.com (office). *Website:* www.maspion.com (office).

MARKWORT, Helmut; German journalist, publisher, editor and presenter; *Editor, FOCUS Magazine;* b. 8 Dec. 1936, Darmstadt; began in journalism 1956, various posts in local media –1964; Man. Ed. STERN in Düsseldorf 1964–66; founder and ed.-in-chief of several magazines and radio stations; Dir Hubert Burda Media Holding KG 1991–2010; Publr and Ed.-in-Chief FOCUS Magazine 1993–2010, Ed. 2010–, Man. FOCUS TV 1996–2010, Publr FOCUS Money 2000–, mem. Bd Tomorrow FOCUS AG 2001–11, Head of Bd Playboy Publishing Deutschland AG 2002–10, Publr FOCUS Schule 2004–13; Nat. Merit Cross (First Class) 1999; 'Horizont Mann der Medien' Award 1983, 1993, Advertising Age 'Marketing Superstar' 1994, Hildegard von Bingen Award for Journalism, BDS Mittelstandspreis, Bavarian Merit Medal 1996, Premio Capo Circeo 2004, Reinhold Maier Medal 2007, Karl Carstens Award 2007, Lifetime Achievement Award, Medium Magazine 2010, Wirtschaftspreis der Wirtschafts- und Mittel-standsunion 2010, Saumagen Medal 2011, Hessian Award for Journalism 2011, Medienmann Award 2011, Radio Regenbogen 2012, Thomas Dehler Award 2012. *Television:* presenter, Bookmark 2004–07, Der Sonntags Stammtisch panel show 2007–. *Leisure interests:* football, theatre. *Address:* FOCUS Magazine, Arabella str. 23, 81925 Munich, Germany (office). *Website:* www.focus.de (office).

MARLEY, Rita; Jamaican singer, songwriter and philanthropist; b. (Alpharita Constantia Anderson), 25 July 1946, Santiago de Cuba, Cuba; d. of Leroy Anderson and Cynthia 'Beda' Jarrett; m. Bob Marley 1966 (died 1981); two s. one d. and three d. from various relationships; grew up in upper level of Beachwood, Kingston, Jamaica; was singing with female ska trio named The Soulettes (later became the I-Threes), recording for Studio One, when she met her future husband mid-1960s; became involved in Rastafari Movt 1966, remains active mem. Ethiopian Orthodox Church; following her husband's death, recorded albums under her own name and looked after his estate; f. Rita Marley Foundation 2000; currently lives in Konkonuru, nr Aburi, Ghana; honoured by Clutch magazine as one of 21 International Women of Power 2008. *Films include:* The Mighty Quinn (actress and reggae music consultant) 1989, The Reggae Movie (special thanks) 1995, How High (writer and performer, One Draw) 2001, Africa Unite (exec. producer) 2008. *Albums include:* Pied Piper (single, on Club Ska '67) 1967, Rita Marley 1980, Who Feels It Knows It 1981, Harambe (Working Together for Freedom) 1988, We Must Carry on 1988, Beauty of God's 1990, Good Girls Cult 1990, One Draw 1990, Sings Bob Marley … and Friends 2003, Play Play 2004, Sunshine After Rain 2005, Gifted Fourteen Carnation 2006. *Publication:* No Woman No Cry (book). *Address:* c/o Rita Marley Foundation, PO Box 34, Aburi-Akwapim, Ghana.

MARLOWE, Hugh (see Patterson, Harry).

MARMOT, Sir Michael Gideon, PhD, FFPHM, FRCP; British academic and director of health research; *Director, International Institute for Society and Health and Professor of Epidemiology and Public Health, University College London;* b. 26 Jan. 1945; s. of Nathan Marmot and Alice Marmot (née Weiner); m. Alexandra Naomi Ferster 1971; two s. one d.; ed Univ. of Sydney, Australia, Univ. of California, Berkeley,USA; Resident Medical Officer, Royal Prince Alfred Hosp. 1969–70; Fellowship in Thoracic Medicine 1970–71; Resident Fellow and Lecturer Univ. of California, Berkeley 1971–76 (fellowships from Berkeley and American

Heart Asscn); Lecturer then Sr Lecturer in Epidemiology, London School of Hygiene and Tropical Medicine, Univ. Coll. London 1976–85, Prof. of Epidemiology and Public Health Medicine 1985–; Dir International Centre for Health and Soc., Univ. Coll. London 1994–; Visiting Prof., Royal Soc. of Medicine 1987; MRC Research Professorship 1995; Chair. Comm. on Social Determinants of Health, WHO 2005–08; est. Inst. of Health Equity, Univ. Coll. London 2011; mem. Faculty of Community Medicine; Foreign Assoc. mem. Inst. of Medicine (Nat. Acads of Sciences); Hon. Consultant in Public Health Medicine, Bloomsbury and Islington Dist Health Authority 1985–; Hon. MD (Univ. of Sydney) 2006, Dr hc (Université Libre de Bruxelles) 2008, (Universidad Peruana Cayetano Heredia) 2011, Hon. DSc (Northumbria Univ.) 2012; Balzan Prize for Epidemiology 2004, Harveian Oration 2006, William B. Graham Prize for Health Services Research 2008. *Publications include:* Mortality of Immigrants to England and Wales 1984, Coronary Heart Disease Epidemiology 1992, Stress and the Heart (with S. Stansfeld) 2002, Social Determinants of Health (with R. Wilkinson) 1999, Status Syndrome 2004, Calling Time: The Nation's Drinking as a Major Health Issue 2004, Coronary Heart Disease Epidemiology (co-author) 2005. *Leisure interests:* viola, tennis. *Address:* Department of Epidemiology and Public Health, University College London, 1–19 Torrington Place, London, WC1E 6BT (office); Wildwood Cottage, 17 North End, London, NW3 7HK, England (home). *Telephone:* (20) 7679-1694 (office). *Fax:* (20) 7419-6732 (office). *E-mail:* m.marmot@ucl.ac.uk (office). *Website:* www.ucl.ac.uk (office).

MAROIS, Pauline, MBA; Canadian politician; b. 29 March 1949; m. Claude Blanchet; four c.; ed Univ. of Laval, HEC Montréal; Dir-Gen., Centre local de services communautaires, Île-de-Hull 1973–74; press attaché to Minister of Finance, Québec 1978–79; Prof., Univ. du Québec en Outaouais 1988; mem. Nat. Assembly of Quebec for La Peltrie 1981–85, for Taillon 1989–2006, for Charlevoix 2007–14, Leader of the Official Opposition 2008–12; Minister for the Status of Women (Govt of Québec) 1981–83, Minister of Finance 1995–96, of Educ. 1996–98, of Health and Social Services 1998–2001, of Finance 2001–03; Deputy Premier of Québec 2001–03, Premier 2012–14; Leader Parti Québécois 2007–14. *Address:* c/o Office of the Premier, 885 Grande-Allée est, Edif. C, 3e étage, Québec, PQ G1A 1A2, Canada (office).

MARONI, Roberto; Italian politician; *President of Lombardy;* b. 15 March 1955, Varese; m.; two s.; graduated in law; worked in banks for 10 years, then head of legal office of a US multinational for eight years; entered politics 1979; co-f. Lega Lombarda party (subsequently Lega Nord), mem. Nat. Council, Political Sec. 2012–; mem. Chamber of Deputies 1992–94, 2006–08; elected Councillor, Varese; Minister of Internal Affairs 1994–95, 2008–11, of Labour and Social Affairs 2001–06; Pres. of Lombardy 2013–. *Leisure interests:* football, playing saxophone. *Address:* Office of the President, Piazza Città di Lombardia 1, 20124 Milan; Lega Nord, Via C. Bellerio 41, 20161 Milan, Italy (office). *E-mail:* webmaster@leganord .org (office). *Website:* www.leganord.org (office); www.regione.lombardia.it (office).

MAROONE, Michael E.; American automobile retail executive; *President and Chief Operating Officer, AutoNation Inc.;* b. 1953; fmr CEO and Pres. Maroone Group –1997, Pres. New Vehicle Dealer Div., AutoNation Inc. (after acquisition of Maroone Group by AutoNation) 1997–98, Group Pres. 1998–, COO 1999–, mem. Bd of Dirs 2005–; Partner Fla Panthers ice hockey team; Ford Motor Co. Chairman's Award, Time magazine Quality Dealer. *Address:* AutoNation Inc., 200 SW 1st Avenue, Fort Lauderdale, FL 33301, USA (office). *Telephone:* (954) 769-6000 (office). *Fax:* (954) 769-6537 (office). *Website:* corp.autonation.com (office).

MAROSI, Ernő, PhD; Hungarian art historian and academic; *Professor Emeritus of Art History, Eötvös Loránd University;* b. 18 April 1940, Miskolc; s. of Ferenc Marosi and Magdolna Kecskés; m. Julia Szabó (died 2004); two d.; ed Eötvös Loránd Univ.; Lecturer, Dept of Art History, Eötvös Loránd Univ. 1963, later Asst Prof., Deputy Head of Institute for Art History Research Group 1974, later Hon. Assoc. Prof., Prof. 1991–2000, now Prof. Emer.; mem. Research Group, Hungarian Acad. of Sciences, then Deputy Dir of Research Inst. 1974–91, Head of Dept 1974–91, Dir 1991–2000, Sr Fellow; mem. Int. Cttee of UNESCO on the History of Art 1991–; Sec. of TMB (Nat. Postgrad. Degree Granting Board), Special Cttee on the History of Art, Architecture and Archaeology; Ed. Acta Historiae Artium; Corresp. mem. of Hungarian Acad. of Sciences 1993–2001, mem. 2001–, Vice-Pres. 2002–08; mem. UNESCO Cttee for Art History 1991–96, Comm. Kossuth-Széchenyi Prize –1997, 2003–; Order of Merit Cross with the Star 2009; Shepherd Fellow, Univ. of Vienna 1968–69, Joseph Fitz Award 1991, Jeno Szucs Award 1995, Széchenyi Award 1997, Arnold Ipolyi Science Devt Award 2001, Deák Ferenc Research Award (Pro Cultura Renovanda Hungariae) 2007, Bonum ut pulchrum – Essays in Art History in Honour of Ernő Marosi on His Seventieth Birthday (Festschrift) presented to him 2010. *Publications:* A középkori művészet világa (The World of Arts of the Middle Ages) 1969, A román kor művészete (The Arts of the Romanesque Age) 1972, Bevezetés a művészettörténetbe (Introduction to the History of Arts) 1973, Magyar falusi templomok (Village Churches in Hungary) 1975, Emlék márványból vagy homokkőből (Relics from Marble or Sandstone) 1976, Die Anfänge der Gotik in Ungarn 1984, Magyarországi művészet 1300–1470 körül (Arts in Hungary 1300–1470) 1984, A budavári szoborlelet (co-author) 1989, Kép és hasonmás 1996, A középkor művészet I–II 1996–97, A középkori művészet történetének olvasókönyve (ed.) 1997, Az Árpád-kor művészeti emlékei 1997, A magyar művészettörténet-írás programjai 1999, Templomok Magyarországon 2002, A gótika Magyarországon 2008. *Address:* Institute of Art History, Faculty of Arts, Eötvös Loránd University, 1088 Budapest, Múzeum körút 6–8 (office); Hungarian Academy of Sciences, 1245 Budapest, PO Box 1000, Hungary. *Telephone:* (1) 4116500 (office). *E-mail:* isoram@arthist.mta.hu (office); info@ titkarsag.mta.hu. *Website:* arthist.elte.hu/index_en.php (office).

MAROVIĆ, Svetozar; Montenegrin lawyer, politician and fmr head of state; *Deputy Chairman, Democratic Party of Socialists of Montenegro (Demokratska Partija Socijalista Crne Gore);* b. 21 March 1955, Kotor, Montenegro; s. of Jovo Marović and Ivana Marović; m. Đurđina 'Đina' Prelević; one s. one d.; ed Faculty of Law, Veljko Vlahović Univ., Titograd, Univ. of Montenegro; Dir Municipal Public Accounting Dept in Budva; mem. Presidency of Cen. Cttee of League of Communists of Montenegro; Sec.-Gen. Democratic Party of Socialists of Montenegro (Demokratska Partija Socijalista Crne Gore), currently Deputy Chair.; mem. Parl. of Montenegro, Speaker 1998–2002; mem. Chamber of Citizens Parl. of Yugoslavia 1997; Pres. of Serbia and Montenegro 2003–06; Deputy Prime

Minister, responsible for the Political System and Domestic and Foreign Policy 2009–10; November's Award, Budva. *Leisure interest:* volleyball. *Address:* Demokratska Partija Socijalista Crne Gore, 81000 Podgorica, Jovana Tomaševića bb, Montenegro (office). *Telephone:* (20) 243952 (office). *Fax:* (20) 243347 (office). *E-mail:* office@dps.me (office). *Website:* www.dps.me (office).

MARQUAND, David Ian, FBA, FRHistS, FRSA; British academic, author and fmr politician; *Visiting Fellow, Department of Politics, University of Oxford;* b. 20 Sept. 1934, Cardiff, Wales; s. of Rt Hon. Hilary Marquand and Rachel Marquand; m. Judith M. Reed 1959; one s. one d.; ed Emanuel School, Magdalen Coll., Oxford, St Antony's Coll., Oxford, Univ. of California, Berkeley, USA; Sr Scholar, St Antony's Coll. Oxford 1957–58; Teaching Asst, Univ. of California 1958–59; editorial writer, The Guardian 1959–61; Research Fellow, St Antony's Coll. Oxford 1962–64, Hon. Fellow 2003–; Lecturer in Politics, Univ. of Sussex 1964–66; MP (Labour) for Ashfield, Notts. 1966–77; del. to Council of Europe and WEU assemblies 1970–73; Opposition Spokesman on Treasury Affairs 1971–72; Chief Adviser, Sec.-Gen. EC 1977–78; Prof. of Contemporary History and Politics, Univ. of Salford 1978–91; Prof. of Politics, Univ. of Sheffield 1991–96, Dir Political Economy Research Centre 1993–96, Hon. Prof. 1997–; Prin. Mansfield Coll. Oxford 1996–2002, Hon. Fellow; Visiting Fellow, Dept of Politics, Univ. of Oxford 2002–; Jt Ed. The Political Quarterly 1987–96; Hon. DLitt (Salford, Sheffield), Hon. Dr of Political Science (Bologna); George Orwell Memorial Prize 1979, Isaiah Berlin Prize for Lifetime Achievement in Political Studies. *Publications:* Ramsay Macdonald 1973, Parliament for Europe 1979, The Unprincipled Society 1988, The Progressive Dilemma 1991, The New Reckoning 1997, Religion and Democracy 2000, Decline of the Public 2004, Britain Since 1918 2008. *Leisure interest:* walking. *Address:* Department of Politics and International Relations, Manor Road, University of Oxford, Oxford, OX1 3UQ (office); Mansfield College, Oxford, OX1 3TF, England (office). *Telephone:* (1865) 751026 (office). *Fax:* (1865) 278725 (office). *E-mail:* david.marquand@politics.ox.ac.uk (office); david.marquand@ mansfield.ox.ac.uk (office). *Website:* www.politics.ox.ac.uk (office).

MARQUES AMADO, Luís Filipe; Portuguese economist and politician; b. 17 Sept. 1953; m.; two c.; ed Universidade Técnica de Lisboa, Inst. of Nat. Defense, Simon Fraser Univ., Canada; fmr Auditor, Court of Auditors; fmr mem. Regional Legis. Ass. of Madeira; mem. Assembléia da República (Ass. of the Repub.); Sec. of State for Internal Admin 1995–97, for Foreign Affairs and Co-operation 1997–99, 1999–2002; Minister of Nat. Defence and Maritime Affairs 2005–06, of Foreign Affairs 2006–11; fmr Visiting Prof., Georgetown Univ., USA. *Address:* c/o Ministry of Foreign Affairs, Palácio das Necessidades, Largo do Rilvas, 1399-030 Lisbon, Portugal (office).

MARR, Andrew William Stevenson, BA; British journalist; b. 31 July 1959, Glasgow, Scotland; s. of Donald Marr and Valerie Marr; m. Jackie Ashley 1987; one s. two d.; ed Dundee High School, Craigflower School, Loretto School, Trinity Hall, Cambridge; gen. reporter, business reporter The Scotsman 1982–84, Parl. Corresp. 1984–86, Political Ed. 1988; Political Ed. The Economist 1988–92; Political Corresp. The Independent 1986–88, Chief Commentator 1992–96, Ed. 1996–98, Ed.-in-Chief 1998; columnist The Express and The Observer 1998; Political Ed. BBC 2000–05; presenter Start the Week, BBC Radio 4 2002–; presenter morning interview programme, Sunday AM (BBC One) 2005–07, The Andrew Marr Show (BBC One) 2007–; Chair. Jury Bd Samuel Johnson Prize for Non-Fiction 2001; What The Papers Say Award for Columnist of the Year 1995, British Press Award for Columnist of the Year 1995, Creative Freedom Award for Journalist of the Year 2000, Channel 4 Political Awards Journalist Award 2001, Royal Television Soc. Television Journalism Award for specialist journalism 2001, Voice of the Listener and Viewer Award for Best Individual Contributor on TV 2002, BAFTA Richard Dimbleby Award 2004. *Publications:* The Battle for Scotland 1992, Ruling Britannia 1996, The Day Britain Died 2000, My Trade: A Short History of British Journalism 2004, A History of Modern Britain (also TV series; winner, British Documentary Award for Best Series 2008) 2007, The Making of Modern Britain (Galaxy Nat. Book Awards Non-Fiction Book of the Year 2010) 2009. *Leisure interests:* reading, wining and dining, painting. *Address:* Room 3200, BBC Television Centre, Wood Lane, London, W12 7RJ, England (office). *Website:* www.bbc.co.uk (office).

MARRA, Thomas M.; American business executive; *President and CEO, Symetra Financial Corporation;* ed St Bonaventure Univ.; joined Hartford Life Inc. as Assoc. Actuary 1980, Vice-Pres. and Dir, Individual Annuity Div. 1990–94, Sr Vice-Pres. and Dir 1994–96, Exec. Vice-Pres. 1996–2000, COO 2000–07, Pres. Hartford Life, Inc. 2002–07, Exec. Vice-Pres. Hartford Financial Services Group Inc. (The Hartford) 1990–2007, Dir Investment Products Div. 1998–2000, mem. Bd of Dirs 2002–09, Pres. and COO 2007–09; Sr Advisor, North America Financial Services Div., Boston Consulting Group 2009–; mem. Bd of Dirs, Pres. and CEO Symetra Financial Corpn 2010–; fmr Chair. American Council of Life Insurers, Nat. Asscn of Variable Annuities; mem. Bd of Trustees, St Bonaventure Univ., Bushnell Performing Arts Center, Hartford, Conn.; mem. American Acad. of Actuaries; Fellow, Soc. of Actuaries. *Address:* Symetra Financial Corpn, PO Box 34690, Seattle, WA 98124-1690 (office); Symetra Financial Corpn, 777 108th Avenue NE, Suite 1200, Bellevue, WA 98004-5135, USA (office). *Telephone:* (425) 256-8000 (office). *E-mail:* info@symetra.com (office). *Website:* www.symetra.com (office).

MARRACK, Philippa C., PhD, FRS; British/American immunologist and academic; *Professor of Immunology, Biochemistry and Molecular Biology and Medicine, School of Medicine, University of Colorado;* b. 28 June 1945, Ewell, Surrey; m. John W. Kappler; ed Univ. of Cambridge and Univ. of California, San Diego; Postdoctoral Fellow, MRC Lab. for Molecular Biology, Cambridge 1970–71; Research Bye Fellow, Girton Coll., Cambridge 1970–71; Postdoctoral Fellow, Damon Runyon Soc. for Cancer Research, Dept of Biology, Univ. of California, San Diego, La Jolla 1971–73; Postdoctoral Fellow, Dept of Microbiology, Univ. of Rochester, NY 1973–74, Assoc. 1974–75, Asst Prof. 1975–76, Asst Prof. of Oncology, Dept of Microbiology and James P. Wilmot Cancer Center, Univ. of Rochester School of Medicine and Dentistry 1976–79, Assoc. Prof. of Oncology 1979–82; Established Investigator, American Heart Asscn, Dallas, Tex. 1976–81; mem. Dept of Medicine, Nat. Jewish Hosp. and Research Center, Denver, Colo 1979–; Assoc. Prof., Depts of Biophysics, Biochemistry and Genetics and Dept of Medicine, Univ. of Colorado Health Sciences Center 1980–85, Prof., Dept of Biochemistry and Molecular Genetics and Dept of Medicine 1985–, Prof., Dept of

Microbiology and Immunology 1988–94, Prof., Dept of Immunology 1994–; Investigator, Howard Hughes Medical Inst., Denver 1986–; Head, Nat. Jewish Center for Immunology and Respiratory Medicine Denver 1988–90, Head, Div. of Basic Immunology, Nat. Jewish Medical and Research Center (now Nat. Jewish Health) 1998–99, currently Sr Faculty mem., Integrated Dept of Immunology; Distinguished Prof., Univ. of Colorado; mem. Laskar Award Selection Cttee 1993–; mem. Advisory Bd Cancer Research Inst. 1986–; mem. Council American Assen of Immunologists 1995–, Vice-Pres. 1999–2000, Pres. 2000–01; Charter Bd mem. Molecular Medicine Soc. 1995–; Sec.-Gen. Tri-Annual Meeting, Int. Union of Immunologists 1995–; Vice-Pres. Int. Union of Immunological Socs 1998–; mem. Trudeau Inst. 1997–, Scientific Advisory Bd Sandler Foundation 1999–; Advisory Ed. Journal of Experimental Medicine 1985–, Therapeutic Immunology 1992–; Assoc. Ed. Cell 1987–; Contributing Ed. Molecular Medicine 1995–; mem. Editorial Bd Cellular Immunology 1983–, Proceedings of the National Academy of Science 1997–, Journal of Autoimmunity 1997–; mem. NAS 1989–, British Soc. for Immunology, American Assen of Immunologists, American Heart Assen (Basic Science Council); Fellow, American Acad. of Arts and Sciences 1991–; Hon. mem. Scandinavian Soc. for Immunology 1990–; Hon. DSc (Univ. of Rochester) 1991, (Macalester Coll.) 1996; Arthur B. Lorber Award for Distinguished Service, Nat. Jewish Center for Immunology and Respiratory Medicine 1990, Prize Winner and Lecturer, Royal Soc. Wellcome Foundation 1990, Feodor Lynen Medal for Special Achievement and Distinguished Service Award 1990, Ernst W. Bertner Memorial Award, M. D. Anderson Cancer Center 1992, Christopher Columbus Discovery Award for Biomedical Research 1992, Paul Ehrlich and Ludwig Darmstädter Prize (Germany) 1993, William B. Coley Award for Distinguished Research in Fundamental Immunology, Cancer Research Inst. 1993, Dickson Prize in Medicine, Univ. of Pittsburgh 1995, Behring-Heidelberger Lecture Award 1995, FASEB Excellence in Science Award 1995, Louisa Gross Horwitz Prize, Columbia Univ. 1995, Rabbi Shai Schacknai Memorial Prize, Hadassah Univ. 1998, Howard Taylor Ricketts Prize, Univ. of Chicago 1999, Interscience Conf. on Antimicrobial Agents and Chemotherapy Award 1999, Irvington Inst. Scientific Leadership Award in Immunology 2001, Lifetime Achievement Award, American Assen of Immunologists 2003, L'Oréal-UNESCO For Women in Science Award 2004, Pearl Meister Greengard Prize, Rockefeller Univ. 2005. *Publications:* more than 250 articles in scientific journals on devt, specificity, activation and life history of T cells. *Address:* Kappler/Marrack Laboratory, Howard Hughes Medical Institute, National Jewish Health, 1400 Jackson Street, 5th Floor, Goodman Building, Denver, CO 80206, USA (office). *Telephone:* (303) 398-1322 (office). *Fax:* (303) 398-1396 (office). *E-mail:* marrackp@njhealth.org (office). *Website:* www.nationaljewish.org/ professionals/research/programs-depts/immunology/labs/kmlab (office).

MARRAH, Keifala, DEcon; Sierra Leonean civil servant and government official; *Minister of Finance and Economic Development;* m. Josephine Marrah; four c.; ed Fourah Bay Coll., Univ. of Hull, UK, State Univ. of New York, USA; fmr Nat. Pres. Kono Students Union; worked as Deputy Town Clerk, Koidu/New Sembehun Town Council; 18 years' experience in the public sector, with emphasis on local, central, parl., financial and econ. governance at int. levels; fmr adviser to int. insts including World Bank, IMF, Caribbean Devt Bank, Asian Devt Bank, Inst. of Public Admin, Canada, Commonwealth Assen of Tax Administrators, Commonwealth Auditors Gen.; fmr Budget Analyst, State Senate of New York; fmr Graduate Fellow, Centre for Int. Devt, New York; fmr Adviser on Public Expenditure Man., Commonwealth Secr., London; Chief of Staff in Office of the Pres., State House, Freetown 2010; Minister of Finance and Econ. Devt 2012–; African Leadership Network New Generation Leader for Africa 2012. *Address:* Ministry of Finance and Economic Development, The Treasury Building, George Street, Freetown, Sierra Leone (office). *Telephone:* (22) 222211 (office). *Website:* www.mofed.gov.sl (office).

MARRAKCHI, Ahmad, MSc, PhD; Tunisian university administrator; b. 9 Feb. 1935, Sfax; m.; four c.; ed Toulouse Univ., France; Assoc. Prof., then Prof., Univ. of Tunis; Scientific Advisor and Dir Tunis Nat. School of Eng (ENIT) 1975–85; est. Faculty of Tech. at Univ. of Qatar, Dean of Faculty and adviser to Pres. of Univ. 1990–99; mem. French Soc. of Electricians, European Soc. for Engineers Training; Founding mem. and Pres. Tunisian Soc. of Electronics Specialists; Founding Fellow, Islamic Acad. of Sciences 1986; elected Beit Al Hikma of the Tunisian Acad. 2012. *Address:* c/o Islamic World Academy of Sciences, PO Box 830036, Zahran, Amman 11183, Jordan. *Telephone:* 5522104. *Fax:* 5511803. *E-mail:* ias@go.com.jo. *Website:* www.iasworld.org/prof-ahmad-marrakchi.

MARRI, Helal Saeed Khalfan al-, BA, MBA, ACA; United Arab Emirates business executive; *Director General, Dubai World Trade Centre;* b. 1976; m.; three s.; ed Univ. of Kent and London Business School, UK; previously worked with KPMG, London; Strategy Consultant, McKinsey & Co. –2004; Dir Gen. Dubai World Trade Centre 2004–; Ind. Dir (non-exec.) Aramex, Depa United Group, Depa Ltd 2008–; Chair. Emirates NBD Asset Management, Emirates Financial Services, Hamdan bin Mohammed bin Rashid Sports Complex; mem. Bd Dubai Chamber of Commerce, Zabeel Investments, Taaleem PJSC; mem. Inst. of Chartered Accountants in England and Wales; ranked by Arabian Business amongst the Power 500: The World's Most Influential Arabs (74th) 2012. *Leisure interests:* fishing, volleyball, football. *Address:* Dubai World Trade Centre, PO Box 9292, Dubai, United Arab Emirates (office). *Telephone:* (4) 3321000 (office). *Fax:* (4) 3312173 (office). *E-mail:* info@dwtc.com (office). *Website:* www.dwtc.com (office).

MARRI, Maj.-Gen. Mohammed Ahmed al-; United Arab Emirates government official; *Director, General Directorate of Residency and Foreigners Affairs, Dubai;* ed Dubai Police Acad.; joined Dubai Police 1980, becoming Deputy Dir Dept of Criminal Evidence 2001–04, Deputy Dir Gen. of Inquiries and Criminal Investigation Dept 2004–06; Dir, Gen. Directorate of Residency and Foreigners Affairs, Dubai (fmrly Dubai Naturalisation and Residency Dept) 2007–; Chair. Labour Welfare Cttee; Head of Perm. Cttee of Labour Affairs; Bd Deputy, Community Devt Authority; mem. Higher Cttee for Crisis Man.; mem. Organizing Cttee Dubai Shopping Festival; honoured by the American Univ. in Dubai 2012, ranked by Arabian Business amongst the Power 500: The World's Most Influential Arabs (40th) 2012, (39th) 2013. *Address:* General Directorate of Residency and Foreigners Affairs-Dubai, Al Jaffliya area next to Bur Dubai Police Station, PO Box 4333, Dubai, United Arab Emirates (office). *Telephone:* (4) 313-9999 (office). *Fax:* (4) 501-1111 (office). *E-mail:* amer@dnrd.ae (office). *Website:* dnrd.ae (office).

MARRI, Mona Ghanem al-, BBA; United Arab Emirates public relations executive; *CEO, Brand Dubai;* b. 1979; m. Mohammad al-Gergawi; two c.; ed Dubai Higher Coll. of Tech.; Media and Public Relations Man., First Dubai Shopping Festival 1997; Project Man. Dubai Summer Surprises 1998; Founder and Man. Dir Dubai Press Club 1999; fmr CEO Jiwin (public relations co.); CEO Brand Dubai 2009–; Vice-Pres. Dubai Ladies' Club; Exec. Dir Arab Media Forum; Sec. Gen. Int. Assen of Press Clubs, Arab Journalism Award; Dir Dubai Media Inc., Young Arab Leaders; Outstanding Contribution to Community Outreach, Middle East Women's Achievement Awards 2008, named Outstanding Business Leader of the Middle East by World BPO Forum, New York. *Address:* Dubai Media Affairs Office, Dubai, United Arab Emirates (office).

MARRINER, Sir Neville, Kt, CBE, FRCM, FRAM; British music director and conductor; *Life President, Academy of St Martin in the Fields;* b. 15 April 1924, Lincoln; s. of Herbert H. Marriner and Ethel M. Marriner; m. Elizabeth M. Sims 1955; one s. (Andrew Stephen Marriner) one d.; ed Lincoln School, Royal Coll. of Music; Founder and Dir Acad. of St Martin-in-the-Fields, London 1956–, now Life Pres.; Musical Dir LA Chamber Orchestra 1969–78; Dir South Bank Festival of Music 1975–78, Dir Meadowbrook Festival, Detroit 1979–84; Music Dir Minn. Orchestra 1979–86, Stuttgart Radio Symphony Orchestra 1984–89, Barbican Summer Festival 1985–87; Hon. Conductor, I Culture Orchestra 2011–; Fellow, Trinity Coll. of Music, Hong Kong Acad. for Performing Arts; Kt of the Polar Star (Sweden) 1984, Officier, Ordre des Arts et Lettres (France) 1995; Hon. DMus (Hull) 1998, (Royal Scottish Acad.) 1999; Tagore Gold Medal, six Edison Awards (Netherlands), two Mozart Gemeinde Awards (Austria), three Grand Prix du Disque (France), two Grammy Awards (USA), Shakespeare Prize. *Recordings include:* Dvořák Serenades, Haydn Violin Concerto in C, Mozart Serenade K361, Il Barbiere di Siviglia, all Schubert's Symphonies, The English Connection (Vaughan Williams' The Lark Ascending, Elgar Serenade and Tippett Corelli Fantasia), Trumpet Concertos (with Hakan Hardenberger), Mendelssohn Piano Works (with Murray Perahia), Mozart Haffner Serenade, Bach Concertos, Suites and Die Kunst der Fuge, Vivaldi's The Four Seasons, Concerti Grossi by Corelli, Geminiani, Torelli, Locatelli and Manfredini, Mozart Symphonies, Concertos, Serenades and Divertimenti, Handel Messiah, Opera overtures and Water and Fireworks music, Die Zauberflöte 1980, Handel Arias (with Kathleen Battle), Il Turco in Italia and Don Giovanni, Verdi's Oberto 1997, Sylvia McNair: Love's Sweet Surrender 1998, Brahms Symphonies 1–4 1998, Schumann Symphonies 1–4 1998, complete Symphonies of Beethoven, Tchaikovsky, Weber, Gounod, Cantatas of Bach (with Fischer-Dieskau, Janet Baker), Haydn Symphonies. *Address:* Academy of St Martin in the Fields, Fourth Floor, 8 Baltic Street East, London, EC1Y 0UP, England (office). *Telephone:* (20) 7702-1377 (office). *Fax:* (20) 7481-0228 (office). *E-mail:* info@asmf.org (office). *Website:* www.asmf.org (office).

MARRIOTT, J. W. (Bill), Jr, BA; American business executive; *Chairman and CEO, Marriott International Inc.;* b. 25 March 1932, Washington, DC; s. of J. Willard Marriott and Alice Sheets Marriott; m. Donna Marriott; three s. one d.; ed Univ. of Utah; ship's service supply officer, USS Randolph 1954–56; joined The Hot Shoppes (family-owned restaurant chain, later renamed Marriott) 1956, various positions including Head of Hotels Div., Pres. Marriott Corpn 1964–97, Chair. and CEO Marriott Int. Inc. 1997–; mem. Bd of Trustees Nat. Geographic Soc., Naval Acad. Endowment Trust, Nat. Urban League; CEO of the Year Award, Chief Executive Magazine 1988. *Publications include:* The Spirit to Serve: Marriott's Way (co-author) 1997. *Address:* Marriott International Inc., Corporate Headquarters, One Marriott Drive, Washington, DC 20058, USA (office). *Telephone:* (301) 380-3000 (office). *Fax:* (301) 380-3969 (office). *Website:* www.marriottnewsroom.com (office).

MARRON, Donald Baird; American banker; b. 21 July 1934, Goshen, NY; m. Catherine D. Calligar; ed Bronx High School of Science, NY and Baruch School of Business; investment analyst, New York Trust Co. 1951–56, Lionel D. Edie Co. 1956–58; Man. Research Dept George O'Neill & Co. 1958–59; Pres. D. B. Marron & Co. Inc. 1959–65, Mitchell Hutchins & Co. Inc. (merger with D. B. Marron & Co. Inc.) 1965–69, Pres., CEO 1969–77; Pres. PaineWebber Inc. (merger with Mitchell Hutchins & Co. Inc.) 1977–88, CEO 1980, Chair. Bd 1981–2001; co-founder, fmr Chair. Data Resources Inc.; fmr Dir New York Stock Exchange; mem. Bd Fannie Mae; mem. Advisory Bd Carlyle Group 2005–; Vice-Pres. Bd of Trustees Museum of Modern Art, now Pres.; mem. Council on Foreign Relations Inc., Pres.'s Cttee on The Arts and the Humanities Inc.; Trustee Center for Strategic and Int. Studies, George Bush Presidential Library. *Address:* c/o Museum of Modern Art, 11 West 53rd Street, New York, NY 10019, USA (office).

MARS, Forrest Edward, Jr; American business executive; b. 1931; s. of the late Forrest Mars, Sr; brother of John Franklin Mars; m. 1st Virginia Cretella 1955 (divorced 1990); four d.; m. 2nd Deborah Adair Clarke (divorced 2010); ed Yale Univ.; CEO Mars, Inc. –2000, also Chair., Co-Pres. *Address:* c/o Mars Inc., 6885 Elm Street, McLean, VA 22101-3810, USA (office).

MARS, John Franklyn; American business executive; *Chairman, Mars Inc.;* b. 15 Oct. 1935; s. of the late Forrest Mars, Sr; brother of Forrest Edward Mars, Jr; m. Adrienne Bevis 1958; three c.; ed Yale Univ.; Chair. Kal Kan Foods, Inc.; Co-Pres. Mars, Inc. 1973–, CEO 2000, now Chair. *Address:* Mars, Inc., 6885 Elm Street, McLean, VA 22101-3810, USA (office). *Telephone:* (703) 821-4900 (office). *Fax:* (703) 448-9678 (office). *Website:* www.mars.com (office).

MARS-JONES, Adam, FRSL; British novelist and critic; b. 26 Oct. 1954, London, England; s. of the late Sir William Mars-Jones; partner Keith King; ed Westminster School, Trinity Hall, Cambridge and Univ. of Virginia, USA; film critic, The Independent 1989–97, The Times 1999–2001; regular contrib. since 1980 to Times Literary Supplement, Guardian, Observer and currently to London Review of Books; Hatchet Job of the Year Award 2012. *Publications:* Lantern Lecture (short stories) (Somerset Maugham Award 1982) 1981, Mae West is Dead 1983, The Darker Proof: Stories from a Crisis (with Edmund White) 1987, Monopolies of Loss 1992, The Waters of Thirst (novel) 1993, Blind Bitter Happiness (essays) 1997, Pilcrow (novel) 2008, Cedilla (novel) 2011, Noriko Smiling (film study) 2011. *Address:* 38 Oakbank Grove, Herne Hill, London, SE24 0AJ, England.

MARSALIS, Wynton; American musician (trumpet), music administrator and composer; b. 18 Oct. 1961, New Orleans; s. of Ellis Marsalis and Dolores Marsalis;

three c.; ed Berks. Music Center, Tanglewood, Juilliard School, New York; played with New Orleans Philharmonic age 14; joined Art Blakey and the Jazz Messengers 1980; toured with Herbie Hancock 1981; formed own group with brother Branford Marsalis 1982; leader Wynton Marsalis Septet; in addition to regular appearances in many countries with his own jazz quintet, he follows a classical career and has performed with the world's top orchestras; regularly conducts masterclasses in schools and holds private tuition; Artistic Dir Lincoln Center Jazz Dept, New York 1990–; numerous hon. doctorates; Edison Award, Netherlands, Grand Prix du Disque, eight Grammy Awards in both jazz and classical categories, Pulitzer Prize for Music 1997, Algur H. Meadows Award, Southern Methodist Univ. 1997, Ronnie Scott Award for Int. Trumpeter 2007, Nat. Endowment of the Arts Jazz Masters Award 2011. *Compositions:* Soul Gestures in Southern Blues 1988, Blood on the Fields (oratorio) 1994, Jazz/Syncopated Movements 1997. *Recordings include:* All American Hero 1980, Wynton 1980, Wynton Marsalis 1981, Think of One 1983, English Chamber Orchestra 1984, Hot House Flowers 1984, Baroque Music: Wynton Marsalis, Edita Gruberova, Raymond Leppard and the English Chamber 1985, Black Codes (From the Underground) 1985, J Mood 1985, Live at Blues Alley 1986, Tomasi/Jolivet: Trumpet Concertos 1986, Carnaval 1987, Baroque Music for Trumpets 1988, The Majesty of the Blues 1989, Crescent City Christmas Card 1989, Tune in Tomorrow (soundtrack) 1991, Quiet City 1989, 24 1990, Trumpet Concertos 1990, Blue Interlude 1992, Citi Movement 1992, In This House, On This Morning 1992, Hot Licks: Gypsy 1993, On the Twentieth Century 1993, Joe Cool's Blues 1994, Live in Swing Town 1994, In Gabriel's Garden 1996, Jump Start and Jazz 1996, Live at Bubba's 1996, One By One 1998, The Marcial Suite 1998, At the Octoroon Ball: String Quartet No. 1 1999, Big Train 1999, Fiddler's Tale 1999, Reeltime 1999, Sweet Release and Ghost Story 1999, Goin' Down Home 2000, Immortal Concerts: Jody 2000, The London Concert 2000, All Rise 2002, Angel Eyes 2002, The Magic Hour 2004, Two Men with the Blues (with Willie Nelson) 2008, He and She 2009. *Publications:* Sweet Swing Blues on the Road 1994, Marsalis on Music 1995, Requiem 1999. *Address:* c/o Laurel J. Wicks, Ted Kurland Associates, 173 Brighton Avenue, Boston, MA 02134, USA (office). *Telephone:* (617) 254-0007 (office). *Fax:* (617) 782-3577 (office). *E-mail:* laurel@tedkurland.com (office); info@wyntonmarsalis.org (office). *Website:* www.wyntonmarsalis.org.

MARSH, Rodney William, MBE; Australian professional cricket coach and fmr professional cricketer; b. 4 Nov. 1947, Armadale, WA; m.; three s.; ed Univ. of Western Australia; wicket-keeper; left-handed batsman; right-arm off-break bowler; played for Western Australia 1969–84, Australia 1970–84; played in 96 Test matches, scoring 3,633 runs (average 26.51, highest score 132) including three hundreds; played in 92 One-Day Ints, scoring 1,225 runs (average 20.08, highest score 66); scored 11,067 First-class runs (average 31.17, highest score 236) including 12 hundreds; Head Coach Commonwealth Bank Cricket Acad. 1990–2001; Dir England and Wales Cricket Bd Nat. Acad. 2002–05; England selector 2003–05; worked with Global Cricket Acad., Dubai; consultant, South Australian Cricket Asscn to undertake review of cricket throughout S Australia 2006–; Wisden Cricketer of the Year 1982, inducted into Australian Cricket Hall of Fame 2005. *Publication:* (with Jack Pollard) The Glovemen 1994. *Leisure interests:* golf, watching Aussie rules football. *Address:* The South Australian Cricket Association, ABN: 94 694 912 780, Adelaide Oval, War Memorial Drive, North Adelaide, South Australia 5006 (office); 4 Briar Avenue, Medindie, South Australia 5081, Australia (home). *Telephone:* (8) 8300-3800 (office). *Fax:* (8) 8231-4346 (office). *E-mail:* sacareception@saca.com.au (office); rmarsh@bettanet.net.au (home).

MARSHALL, Barry James, MB BS, FRACP, FAA, FRS; Australian gastro-enterologist and academic; *Co-Director, Marshall Centre for Infectious Diseases Research and Training, University of Western Australia;* b. 30 Sept. 1951, Kalgoorlie, WA; ed Univ. of Western Australia; physician, Royal Perth Hosp. 1974–83; Research Fellow, Gastroenterologist, Prof. of Medicine, Univ. of Virginia, USA 1986–96; currently Hon. Research Fellow, Helicobacter pylori Research Lab. and Co-Dir Marshall Centre for Infectious Diseases Research and Training, Univ. of Western Australia School of Biomedical and Chemical Sciences, Sir Charles Gairdner Hosp., Perth; Albert Lasker Award 1995, Dr A.H. Heineken Prize for Medicine 1998, Australian Achiever Award 1998, Florey Medal 1998, Buchanan Medal, Royal Soc. of Medicine, London 1998, Benjamin Franklin Award for Life Sciences 1999, Poppy Award, Australian Inst. of Political Sciences 2000, Nobel Prize for Medicine 2005, Western Australian of the Year 2007, Galen Medal, Soc. of Apothecaries 2009. *Research:* collaborated with Robin Warren on research leading to culture of Helicobacter pylori 1982 and recognition of asscn between H.pylori, gastritis, peptic ulcer and gastric cancer. *Leisure interests:* computers, electronics, photography. *Address:* University of Western Australia, M502, 35 Stirling Highway, Crawley, WA 6009, Australia (office). *Telephone:* (8) 9346-4815 (office). *Fax:* (8) 9346-4816 (office). *E-mail:* admin@hpylori.com.au (office). *Website:* www .hpylori.com.au (office).

MARSHALL, (Carole) Penny; American actress and director; b. 15 Oct. 1943, New York, NY; d. of Anthony Marshall and Marjorie Ward; m. 1st Michael Henry (divorced), one d.; m. 2nd Robert Reiner 1971 (divorced 1979); ed Univ. of New Mexico; Co-founder Parkway Productions. *Films include:* appeared in: How Sweet It Is 1967, The Savage Seven 1968, The Grasshopper 1979, '1941' 1979, Movers and Shakers 1985, She's Having a Baby 1988, The Hard Way 1991, Special Delivery 1999, Looking for Comedy in the Muslim World 2005, Everybody Wants to Be Italian 2007, Alice Upside Down 2007, Blonde Ambition 2007, New Year's Eve 2011; directed: Jumpin' Jack Flash 1986, Big 1988, Awakenings (also producer) 1990, A League of their Own (also producer) 1992, Renaissance Man (also producer) 1994, The Preacher's Wife 1996, The Time Tunnel: The Movie 1999, Jackie's Back 1999, Riding in Cars with Boys 2001; other produced: Calendar Girl 1993, Getting Away With Murder 1996, With Friends Like These 1998, Risk 2003, Cinderella Man 2005, Bewitched 2005. *Television includes:* The Odd Couple 1971–75, Laverne and Shirley 1976–83, Portlandia 2012, Sam & Cat 2013. *Address:* Parkway Productions, 7095 Hollywood Blvd, Suite 1009, Hollywood, CA 90028, USA (office). *Telephone:* (323) 874-6207 (office). *E-mail:* parkwayprods@aol .com (office).

MARSHALL, Hon. (Cedric) Russell, CNZM, BA, Dip Tchg; New Zealand politician and diplomatist (retd); b. 15 Feb. 1936, Nelson; s. of Cedric Thomas Marshall and Gladys Margaret Marshall (née Hopley); m. Barbara May Watson 1961; two s. one d.; ed Nelson Coll., Christchurch Teachers' Coll., Trinity Theological Coll., Auckland, Victoria Univ.; teacher at various schools 1955–56; Methodist Minister in Christchurch 1960–66, Masterton 1967–71; MP for Wanganui (Labour) 1972–90; Minister of Environment 1984–86, of Educ. 1984–87, of Conservation 1986–87, of Disarmament and Arms Control 1987–89, of Foreign Affairs 1987–90, of Pacific Island Affairs 1989–90; Sr Opposition Whip 1978–79; Chair. NZ Comm. for UNESCO 1990–99, NZ Rep., UNESCO Exec. Bd 1995–99; Chancellor, Victoria Univ. of Wellington 2000–01; High Commr to UK and Nigeria and Amb. to Ireland 2002–05; Chair. Africa Information Centre Trustees 1991–95, Commonwealth Observer Group, Seychelles 1993, Common-wealth Observer Mission to S Africa 1994, Cambodia Trust (Aotearoa-NZ) 1994–2001, Polytechnics Int. NZ 1994–2001, Educ. NZ 1994–2001, Tertiary Educ. Advisory Comm. 2000–01, Cambodia Trust (UK) 2002–05, Tertiary Educ. Comm. 2005–07; Pres. NZ Inst. of Int. Affairs 2007–11; Chair. Robson Hanan Trust – Rethinking Crime and Punishment 2010–11; Hunter Fellow, Victoria Univ. of Wellington 2009; mem. Commonwealth Observer Group, Lesotho 1993, Victoria Univ. of Wellington Council 1994–2002, Nelson Mandela Trustees 1995–2008; Labour. *Leisure interests:* classical music, genealogy. *Address:* 5 Whitianga View, Paremata, Porirua 5024, New Zealand. *Telephone:* (4) 233-6608. *E-mail:* russellmarshall@clear.net.nz.

MARSHALL, Garry Kent, BS; American actor, director and writer; b. 13 Nov. 1934, New York City; s. of Anthony Wallace Marsciarelli and Marjorie Irene Ward; m. Barbara Marshall; one s. two d.; ed Northwestern Univ., Evanston, Ill.; served in US Armed Forces during Korean War; writer for Stars and Stripes newspaper and Production Chief, Armed Forces Radio Network; copy boy then reporter, Daily News, NY 1956–59; joke writer for Joey Bishop and Phil Foster; career as stand-up comedian; began tv career as writer for The Tonight Show with Jack Parr 1959; Exec. Producer, American Broadcasting Co. (TV network), Paramount Studios 1970s; star on Hollywood Walk of Fame. *Film appearances include:* Toller Hecht auf krummer Tour 1961, Psych-Out 1968, Maryjane 1968, Goldfinger, Grand Theft Auto 1977, The Way They Were (TV) 1981, Lost in America 1985, Jumpin' Jack Flash 1986, But Seriously Folks (TV) 1986, Beaches 1988, Murphy Brown (TV) 1988, Pretty Woman 1990, Secret Agent 00 Soul 1990, Soapdish 1991, A League of Their Own 1992, Hocus Pocus 1993, The Last Shot (TV) 1993, Exit to Eden 1994, Statistically Speaking 1995, With Friends Like These 1998, Never Been Kissed 1999, Runaway Bride 1999, Can't Be Heaven 2000, This Space Between Us 2000, It's a Shame About Ray 2000, Tomcats 2001, The Hollywood Sign 2001, The Majestic 2001, Orange County 2002, Mother Ghost 2002, The Long Ride Home 2003, They Call Him Sasquatch 2003, Devil's Night 2003, Lucky 13 2005, Chicken Little (voice) 2005, Mute 2005, Keeping Up with the Steins 2006. *Films written, directed or produced:* Young Doctors in Love 1982, The Flamingo Kid 1984, Nothing in Common 1986, Overboard 1987, The Lottery 1987, Beaches 1988, Pretty Woman 1990, Frankie and Johnny 1991, Exit to Eden 1994, Dear God 1996, The Twilight of the Golds 1997, The Other Sister 1999, Runaway Bride 1999, The Princess Diaries 2001, Raising Helen 2004, Princess Diaries 2: The Royal Engagement 2004, Rogue Farm 2004, Georgia Rule 2007, New Year's Eve 2011. *Television shows written, directed or produced:* Make Room for Daddy 1953, The Jack Paar Show 1959–61, The Joey Bishop Show 1961–65, The Danny Thomas Show 1961–64, The Dick Van Dyke Show 1961–66, The Lucy Show 1962–68, Gomer Pyle, U.S.M.C. 1964, I Spy 1965–68, Hey Landlord 1966–67, Love American Style 1969, The Odd Couple 1970–75, The Little People 1972–74, Me and the Chimp 1972, Happy Days 1974–84, Laverne and Shirley 1976–83, Blansky's Beauties 1977, Mork & Mindy 1978–82, Angie 1979–80, Who's Watching the Kids 1978, Joanie Loves Chachi 1982–83, Herndon 1983, Nothing in Common 1987, Murphy Brown 1994. *Publications:* My Happy Days in Hollywood (memoir) 2012. *Address:* c/o Creative Artists Agency Inc., 9830 Wilshire Boulevard, Beverly Hills, CA 90212-1825, USA (office). *Telephone:* (310) 288-4800 (office). *Fax:* (310) 288-4800 (office). *Website:* www.caa.com (office).

MARSHALL, Margaret Anne, OBE; British singer (soprano); b. 4 Jan. 1949, Stirling, Scotland; d. of Robert Marshall and Margaret Marshall; m. Dr Graeme G. K. Davidson 1970; two d.; ed High School of Stirling and Royal Scottish Acad. of Music and Drama; first opera appearance in Orfeo ed Euridice, Florence 1977; has since sung at La Scala, Covent Garden, Glyndebourne, Scottish Opera, Barcelona, Hamburg, Cologne and Salzburg; concert performances in maj. European and US cities and festivals with maj. orchestras; numerous recordings; Hon. DMus (Univ. of St Andrew) 2009; first prize Munich Int. Competition 1974, James Gulliver Award for Performing Arts in Scotland. *Leisure interests:* squash, golf, cooking.

MARSHALL, Ray, PhD; American economist, academic and fmr government official; *Professor Emeritus and Audre and Bernard Rapoport Centennial Chair in Economics and Public Affairs, Lyndon B. Johnson School of Public Affairs, University of Texas;* b. 22 Aug. 1928, Oak Grove, La.; m. Patricia Williams 1946; one s. three d.; ed Millsaps Coll., Miss., Louisiana State Univ., Univ. of Calif. at Berkeley; Fulbright Research Scholar, Finland; post-doctoral research, Harvard Univ.; Instructor San Francisco State Coll.; Assoc. Prof. and Prof. Univs of Miss., Ky, La.; Prof. of Econs, Univ. of Texas 1962–67, Prof. of Econs 1969, Chair. Dept 1970–72, Prof. of Econs and Public Affairs, Lyndon B. Johnson School of Public Affairs 1981, Rapoport Prof. Econs and Public Affairs, Prof. Emer. 1998–, fmrly Dir Center for Study of Human Resources; US Sec. of Labor 1977–81; Co-Chair. Comm. on the Skills of the American Workforce; Trustee German Marshall Fund and Carnegie Corpn of NY 1982–90; mem. Comm. on Future of Labor/Man. Relations; Dr hc (Maryland, Cleveland State, Millaaps Coll., Bates Coll., Rutgers, Ind., Tulane, Utah State, St Edward's); Lifetime Achievement Award, Industrial Relations Research Asscn 2001. *Publications:* The Negro Worker 1967, The Negro and Apprenticeship 1967, Cooperatives and Rural Poverty in the South 1971, Human Resources and Labor Markets 1972, Anthology of Labor Economics 1972, Human Resources and Labor Markets 1975, Labor Economics: Wages, Employ-ment and Trade Unionism 1976, The Role of Unions in the American Economy 1976, An Economic Strategy for the 1980s 1981, Work and Women in the Eighties 1983, Unheard Voices: Labor and Economic Policy in a Competitive World 1987, Economics of Education 1988, Losing Direction: Families, Human Resource Development and Economic Performance 1991, Thinking for a Living (with Marc Tucker) 1992, Back to Shared Prosperity (ed.) 2000. *Address:* c/o University of Texas, L.B.J. School of Public Affairs, Drawer Y, University Station, Austin, TX

78713, USA. *Telephone:* (512) 471-6242 (office); (512) 345-1828 (home). *Fax:* (512) 345-8491 (home). *E-mail:* ray.marshall@mail.utexas.edu (office). *Website:* www.utexas.edu/lbj (office).

MARSHALL, Robin, BSc, PhD, FRS, FRAS, FInstP; British physicist and academic; *Research Professor of Particle Physics and Life Sciences, University of Manchester;* b. 5 Jan. 1940, Skipton, Yorks.; s. of the late Robert Marshall and Grace Eileen Marshall; m. 1963 (divorced 2002); two s. one d.; ed Ermysted's Grammar School, Skipton, Univ. of Manchester; Research Scientist, DESY, MIT, Daresbury Lab., Rutherford Appleton Lab. 1965–92; Sr Prin. Scientific Officer (Individual Merit) Rutherford Appleton Lab. 1985–92; Prof. of Experimental Physics and Head, Particle Physics Group, Univ. of Manchester 1992–2005, Research Prof. of Particle Physics and Life Sciences 2005–; Dir and Co. Sec. Frontiers Science and TV Ltd; mem. Council Royal Soc., Royal Soc. Rep. on Univ. of Manchester Ass., Chair. Royal Soc. Univ. Fellowship Cttee; Trustee, Museum of Science and Industry, Manchester; Max Born Medal and Prize, German Physical Soc. 1997. *Publications:* more than 200 scientific papers. *Leisure interests:* painting and drawing, movies. *Address:* Department of Physics and Astronomy, University of Manchester, Manchester, M13 9PL, England (office). *Telephone:* (161) 275-4170 (office); (161) 275-4175 (office). *Fax:* (161) 275-4246 (office). *E-mail:* R.Marshall@man.ac.uk (office); Robin.Marshall@manchester.ac.uk (office). *Website:* macnode1.hep.man.ac.uk/~robin (office).

MARSHALL, Ruth Ann, BBA, MBA; American business executive; ed Southern Methodist Univ.; began career at IBM, held numerous managerial and exec. positions over 18-year period; served as Group Exec. Vice-Pres. two Electronic Payment Service cos, MAC Regional Network and Buypass Corpn, Sr Exec. Vice-Pres. combined cos following acquisition by Concord EFS; Pres. MasterCard N America 1999, Pres., Americas, MasterCard Int. –2006 (retd); mem. Bd of Dirs Global Payments Inc. 2006–, American Standard Corpn, Pella Corpn, ConAgra Foods, Inc. 2007–, Regions Financial Corpn 2011–; mem. Bd several civic and academic orgs, including Citymeals-on-Wheels, The PGA First Tee, Cox School of Business at Southern Methodist Univ.; Credit Card Management's Leader of the New Millennium Award 1999, ranked by Fortune magazine amongst 50 Most Powerful Women in Business in the US 2003, ranked by Forbes magazine amongst 100 Most Powerful Women (88th) 2004, (41st) 2005. *Leisure interest:* competitive sports (especially golf), piano, travel. *Address:* 4923 Fisher Island Drive, Fisher Island, FL 33109, USA.

MARSHALL, Thomas (Tom) W., BCom, LLB, QC; Canadian lawyer and politician; *Premier of Newfoundland and Labrador;* s. of the late Jack Marshall and Sylvia Marshall; ed Memorial Univ. of Newfoundland, Dalhousie Univ.; began career as Assoc., Barry, Wells and Monaghan (law firm), Corner Brook 1972, Partner, Barry, Wells, Monaghan, Seaborn and Marshall 1975, Sr Partner, Monaghan, Marshall, Murphy and Watton –2003; mem. Newfoundland and Labrador House of Ass. for Humber East Dist 2003–; numerous portfolios in Newfoundland and Labrador Govt including Minister of Justice 2003–06, 2008–09, Jan.–Oct. 2013, also Attorney-Gen. 2003–05, 2008–09, 2012–, Minister of Finance and Pres. Treasury Bd 2006–08, 2009–13, 2013–14; Premier of Newfoundland and Labrador 2014–; mem. Progressive Conservative Party of Canada. *Address:* Office of the Premier, Confederation Bldg, East Block, POB 8700, St John's, Newfoundland and Labrador, A1B 4J6, Canada (office). *Telephone:* (709) 729-3570 (office). *Fax:* (709) 729-5875 (office). *E-mail:* premier@gov.nl.ca (office). *Website:* www.premier.gov.nl.ca/premier (office).

MARSHALL, Thurgood, Jr, BA, JD; American lawyer and business executive; *Partner, Bingham McCutchen LLP;* b. 1956; s. of the late Supreme Court Justice Thurgood Marshall, Sr; m. Teddi Levy; two s.; ed Univ. of Virginia; began legal career as law clerk to US Dist Court Judge Barrington D. Parker, US Dist Court for the Dist of Columbia; Partner, Bingham McCutchen LLP, Prin. with Bingham Consulting LLC; Dir of Legis. Affairs and Deputy Counsel for Vice-Pres. Al Gore and mem. congressional leadership staff –1997; Asst to Pres. Clinton and Cabinet Sec. 1997–2001, mem. President's Man. Council, served as sr mem. Continuity in Govt team and directed White House response to natural disasters and transportation emergencies, also Vice-Chair. White House Olympic Task Force for Winter Olympic and Paralympic Games, Salt Lake City 2002; Gov. US Postal Service (USPS) 2006–, Vice-Chair. Bd of Govs 2010–11, Chair. 2011–12; mem. Bd Ford Foundation; Sec. of Transportation's Award for Outstanding Public Service, US Coast Guard Distinguished Public Service Award, Fed. Govt Meritorious Service Medal, named by Washingtonian as one of Washington's top lawyers (Campaigns & Elections), named by Newsweek as one of the 100 people to watch in the new century, named by The Washington Post Magazine on its Best Lawyers List 2007, Leading Lawyer in Govt Affairs Law, The Best Lawyers in America 2008–09, 2011–14. *Address:* Bingham McCutchen LLP, 2020 K Street NW, Washington, DC 20006-1806, USA (office). *Telephone:* (202) 373-6598 (office). *Fax:* (202) 373-6001 (office). *E-mail:* tmarshall.jr@bingham.com (office). *Website:* www.bingham.com/People/Marshall-Thurgood (office).

MARSTERS, Tom John; Cook Islands politician; *Queen's Representative;* b. 4 Aug. 1945, Palmerston Island; m. Tuaine Tumupu; ed Avele Agric. Coll., Samoa, Grimsby Inst. of Tech., UK; began career as Agric. Officer; worked on Tuna Longline Feasibility Study, Island Foods Ltd; fmrly with Office of Sec. to Govt; fmr Clerk, House of Ariki (Parl.); fmr Dir of Fisheries, becoming Chief Admin Officer, Ministry of Agric. and Fisheries, later Deputy Sec. of Agric.; MP for Murienua 1991–2013; Deputy Prime Minister and Minister of Foreign Affairs, Immigration, Transport and Natural Resources 2010–13; Queen's Rep. 2013–mem. Cook Islands Party, Sec. Gen. 1968–99. *Achievements include:* has represented Cook Islands in boxing, rugby and golf. *Leisure interest:* golf. *Address:* Office of the Queen's Representative, Titikaveka, POB 134, Rarotonga, Cook Islands (office). *Telephone:* 29311 (office). *Fax:* 29311 (office). *E-mail:* queenrep@oyster.net.ck (office).

MARTA; Brazilian professional footballer; b. (Marta Vieira da Silva), 19 Feb. 1986, Dois Riachos, Alagoas; d. of Aldário da Silva and Tereza da Silva; forward; discovered by Brazilian female coach, Helena Pacheco, aged 14; player with Centro Sportivo Alagoano youth team 1999, Vasco da Gama club, Rio sr team 2000–02, Santa Cruz 2002–04, Umeå IK, Sweden 2004–08 (won Damallsvenskan 2005, 2006, 2007, 2008, Svenska Cupen 2007, UEFA Women's Cup 2004), Los Angeles Sol, USA 2009 (Women's Professional Soccer Regular Season Champion 2009), on

loan to Santos of Copa do Brasil 2009–10 (won Copa Libertadores de Fútbol Femenino 2009, Copa do Brasil de Futebol Feminino 2009), FC Gold Pride 2010, Santos 2011, Western New York Flash 2011–; mem. Brazilian Nat. Women's Team 2002–, won Sudamericano Femenino 2003, 2010, gold medal, Pan American Games 2003, 2007, silver medal at Olympic Games, Athens 2004, Beijing 2008, silver medal, FIFA Women's World Cup 2007, has made 55 appearances and scored 56 goals; top scorer in Damallsvenskan league (Sweden) 2004, 2005, 2006, 2008, Sudamericano Femenino 2010; UN Goodwill Amb. 2010–; U-20 World Cup Golden Ball 2004, Golden Ball (MVP) FIFA Under-19s Women's World Championship 2004, U-20 World Cup Golden Ball 2004, FIFA Women's World Player of the Year 2006, 2007, 2008, 2009, 2010, FIFA Women's World Cup Golden Ball 2007, FIFA Women's World Cup Golden Shoe 2007, Damallsvenskan Best Forward of the Year 2007, 2008, Women's Professional Soccer MVP 2009, 2010, Women's Professional Soccer Golden Boot 2009, 2010, Copa Libertadores de Fútbol Femenino Golden Ball 2009, Women's Professional Soccer Championship MVP 2010, Inaugural Winner of FIFA Ballon d'Or 2010. *Address:* Western New York Flash, 7070 Seneca Street, Elma, NY 14059, USA (office). *Telephone:* (716) 655-7529 (office). *Fax:* (716) 655-3615 (office). *E-mail:* contact@wnyflash.com (office); henrik@buffaloflashsoccer.com (office). *Website:* www.womensprosoccer.com/wny (office).

MARTEL, Yann, BA; Canadian writer; b. 1963, Salamanca, Spain; m. Alice Kuipers; two s. one d.; ed Trent Univ.; grew up in Alaska, BC, Costa Rica, France, Ont. and Mexico; fmr tree planter, dishwasher, security guard; became professional writer 1990. *Publications:* Facts Behind the Helsinki Roccamatios (short stories) (Journey Prize) 1993, Self (novel) 1996, Life of Pi (novel) (Hugh MacLennan Prize for Fiction 2001, Man Booker Prize 2002, Boeke Prize 2003) 2001, Beatrice and Virgil 2010, 101 Letters to a Prime Minister 2012. *Leisure interests:* visual arts, theatre, keeping fit. *Address:* c/o Knopf Canada, Random House of Canada Ltd, One Toronto Street, Unit 300, Toronto, ON M5C 2VC, Canada (office). *Telephone:* (416) 364-4449 (office). *Fax:* (416) 364-6863 (office). *Website:* www.randomhouse.ca (office).

MARTELLI, Claudio; Italian politician; b. 24 Sept. 1943, Milan; m.; four c.; mem. Italian Socialist Party (PSI) 1967–93, mem. Secr. 1973–75, Leader PSI Group, Milan Municipal Council 1975–79; elected Deputy 1979, 1983, 1987, 1992; Deputy Prime Minister 1989–92, Minister of Justice 1991–93; MEP for Italian Democratic Socialists (SDI) 1999–2004, mem. Cttee on Foreign Affairs, Human Rights, Common Security and Defence Policy, mem. Interparliamentary Del. for Relations with South-East Europe; Spokesman League of Socialists 2000–; Ed.-in-Chief La Sinistra Sociale socialist review. *Address:* c/o Socialisti Democratici Italiani (SDI) (Italian Democratic Socialists), Piazza S. Lorenzo in Lucina 26, 00186 Rome, Italy.

MARTELLY, Michel Joseph, (Sweet Mickey); Haitian musician, politician and head of state; *President;* b. 12 Feb. 1961, Port-au-Prince; m. Sophia Martelly; four c.; ed Saint-Louis de Gonzague High School; spent several years in Miami, Fla, USA employed as construction worker; successful career in Haiti as performing and recording artist, best known as pioneer of 'kompas' Haitian dance music; politically active for several years but held no political positions; Pres. of Haiti 2011–. *Recordings include:* Singles: Ooo La La 1988, Konpas Foret des Pins, Magouyè, 2008; Albums: 14 studio albums including Woule Woule 1989, Pa Manyen (Don't Touch) 1997, Dènye Okazyon 1999, SiSiSi 2001. *Address:* Office of the President, Palais National, rue de la République, Port-au-Prince, Haiti (office). *Telephone:* 2222-3024 (office). *E-mail:* webmestre@palaisnational.info (office).

MÅRTENSON, Jan; Swedish diplomatist; b. 14 Feb. 1933, Uppsala; m.; two s. two d.; ed Univ. of Uppsala; held various Foreign Ministry and diplomatic posts –1966; Head of Section, UN Dept Ministry for Foreign Affairs, Stockholm 1966–67, Head Information Dept 1973–75; Deputy Dir Stockholm Int. Peace Research Inst. 1968–69; Sec.-Gen. Swedish Prep. Cttee for UN Conf. on Human Environment 1970–72; Chef de Cabinet for King of Sweden 1975–79; Asst Sec.-Gen. Centre for Disarmament, UN Dept of Political and Security Council Affairs 1979–82, Under-Sec.-Gen. for Disarmament Affairs 1983–87; Chair. UN Appointments and Promotions Bd 1984–86; Sec.-Gen. Int. Conf. on Relationship between Disarmament and Devt 1987; Dir-Gen. UN Office, Geneva 1987–92, Under-Sec.-Gen. and Head UN Centre for Human Rights, Geneva 1987–92, Co-ordinator UN Second Decade Against Racism 1987; Amb. to Switzerland and Liechtenstein 1993–95; Amb.-at-Large, Ministry of Foreign Affairs 1996–98; Marshal of the Diplomatic Corps 1999–2004; Chair. Int. Club, Stockholm, Travellers' Club, Stockholm. *Publications include:* some 50 books; articles on disarmament and human rights. *Leisure interests:* gardening, fishing. *Address:* Karlaplan 14, 115 20 Stockholm, Sweden (home). *Telephone:* (8) 660-98-39 (home). *E-mail:* jm@swedishvision.se (office).

MÅRTENSSON, Arne, MBA; Swedish banker (retd); b. 10 Oct. 1951, Vänersborg; s. of Aldo Mårtensson and Ingrid Mårtensson; m. 2nd Heléne Melin-Mårtensson 1996; ed Stockholm School of Econs, Harvard Business School, USA; Industrial Devt Dept, Svenska Handelsbanken 1972–75, Vice-Pres. and Head Credit Dept, Regional Unit, Western Sweden 1975–77, Sr Vice-Pres. Admin., Cen. Sweden 1977–80, Sr Vice-Pres. and Area Man. Stockholm City 1980–84, Exec. Vice-Pres. and Gen. Man., Western Sweden, 1984–89, Pres. Stockholm 1989–91, Group Chief Exec. 1991–2001, Chair. 2001–06, Hon. Chair. 2006–; Deputy Chair. Telefonaktiebolaget LM Ericsson 2003–06; Dir (non-exec.) Holmen AB, Industrivärden AB, Sandvik AB, Skanska AB, V & S Vin & Spirit AB, Stockholm School of Econs Advisory Bd (Chair.), mem. Int. Business Council of World Econ. Forum –2006; following retirement, sailed round the world with his wife 2006; Hon. DEcon. *Publications:* Back at the Helm 2010, In the Wake of Cook 2011. *Leisure interests:* sailing, jogging, skiing. *Address:* c/o Svenska Handelsbanken, 106 70 Stockholm, Sweden. *Website:* hem.passagen.se/yaghan.

MARTIN, Carolyn (Biddy), PhD; American academic and university administrator; *Chancellor, University of Wisconsin;* b. Lynchburg, Va; ed Coll. of William and Mary, Middlebury Coll., Univ. of Wisconsin; Asst Prof., Dept of German Studies, Cornell Univ. 1985–91, Assoc. Prof. 1991–97, Prof. 1997–2008, Chair Dept of German Studies 1994–97, Sr Assoc. Dean, Coll. of Arts and Sciences 1996; Provost Cornell Univ. 2000–08; Chancellor Univ. of Wisconsin, Madison 2008–; Pres. Amherst Coll. *Address:* Office of the Chancellor, 161 Bascom Hall, 500 Lincoln Drive, University of Wisconsin, Madison, WI 53706, USA (office).

Telephone: (608) 262-9946 (office). E-mail: chancellor@news.wisc.edu (office). Website: www.chancellor.wisc.edu (office).

MARTIN, Chris; British singer, musician (guitar, piano) and songwriter; b. 2 March 1977, Devon, England; m. Gwyneth Paltrow 2003 (separated 2014); one s. one d.; ed University Coll., London; mem. Coldplay 1998–; BRIT Award for Best British Group 2001, 2003, 2012, MTV Award for Best UK and Ireland Act 2002, Billboard Group of the Year 2002, Ivor Novello Songwriters of the Year 2003, Grammy Awards for Record of the Year (for Clocks) 2004, for Best Rock Vocal Performance by a Duo or Group (for In My Place) 2004, for Song of the Year 2009, for Best Pop Performance by a Duo or Group (both for Viva la Vida) 2009, Q Award for Best Act in the World 2005, Digital Music People's Choice Award for best official site, for Best Digital Music Community (for Coldplay.com) 2005, MTV Europe Music Awards for Best UK & Ireland Act, for Best Song (for Speed of Sound) 2005, American Music Award for Favorite Alternative Music Artist 2005, BRIT Award for Best British Single (for Speed of Sound) 2006, Echo Award for Best Int. Group, Germany 2006, ASCAP Award for Song of the Year (for Speed of Sound) 2006, World Music Award for Best Rock Act 2008, Ivor Novello Award for Best British Song (for Viva la Vida) 2009. Recordings include: albums: Parachutes (BRIT Award for Best Album 2001, Grammy Award for Best Alternative Album 2002) 2000, A Rush of Blood To The Head (BRIT Award for Best British Album 2003, NME Award for Best Album 2003) 2002, X&Y (MasterCard British Album, BRIT Awards 2006, Juno Award for Int. Album of the Year 2006) 2005, Viva la Vida (Grammy Award for Best Rock Album 2009) 2008, Mylo Xyloto 2011. Address: c/o Dave Holmes, 3-D Management, 1901 Main Street, #3000, Los Angeles, CA 90405, USA (office); c/o Parlophone, Fifth Floor, EMI House, 43 Brook Green, London, W6 7EF, England (office). Telephone: (310) 314-1390 (office). Website: www.coldplay.com.

MARTIN, Hon. Clare, BA; Australian organization official, academic and fmr politician; Professorial Fellow, Northern Institute, Charles Darwin University; b. 15 June 1952, Sydney; d. of Prof. Noel Desmond Martin and Bernice Martin (née Downey); m. David Alderman; one s. one d.; ed Loreto Convent, Normanhurst, Sydney Univ.; Sr Political Journalist and Broadcaster ABC (TV and Radio) 1978–95; elected MLA (Australian Labour Party—ALP) for Fannie Bay NT 1995; Shadow Minister for Statehood, then Shadow Minister for the Arts 1995–96, Ethnic Affairs 1995–96, Correctional Services 1995–97, Lands, Planning and Environment 1995–97, Arts and Museums 1995–2001, Urban Devt 1996–97, Housing 1996–99, Asian Relations, Trade and Industry 1997–99, Racing and Gaming 1997–99, Young Territorians 1997–99; Leader ALP 1999–2007; Minister for Communications Science and Advanced Tech. 2001–02; Northern Territory Chief Minister 2001–07; Minister for Arts and Museums 2001–07, Young Territorians 2001–07, Women's Policy 2001–07, Sr Territorians 2001–07, Territory Devt 2002–07, Indigenous Affairs 2002–07; Treasurer 2001–07; CEO Australian Council of Social Service 2008–10; Professorial Fellow, Northern Inst., Charles Darwin Univ. 2010–; fmr Bd mem. YWCA NT; mem. Jt Ethics Cttee Menzies School Health Research, Royal Darwin Hosp. Leisure interests: being fit, reading, music, sport, family. Address: Northern Institute, Charles Darwin University, Darwin, NT 0909, Australia (office). Telephone: (8) 8946-7468 (office). Fax: (8) 8946-7175 (office). E-mail: thenortherninstitute@cdu.edu.au (office). Website: www.cdu.edu.au/the-northern-institute (office).

MARTIN, Claude Pierre Marcel; French diplomatist; b. 14 April 1944, Saint-Germain-en-Laye; m.; ed Lycée de Saint-Germain-en-Laye, Institut d'Etudes Politiques de Paris, Ecole Nationale des Langues Orientales; joined Ministry of Foreign Affairs 1968, Adviser to Cabinet on European Affairs 1974–78, Minister at Embassy in Beijing 1979–84, Perm. Rep. to EC 1984–86, Dir Asia/Oceania Div., Ministry of Foreign Affairs 1986–90, Amb. to China 1990–93, Assoc. Sec.-Gen. to Dir-Gen. European and Economic Affairs 1993–98, Amb. to Germany 1999–2007, Presidential Conseil des Affaires Etrangères, Ministry of Foreign Affairs; fmr Judge, Cour des comptes (audit court), Paris. Address: c/o Cour des comptes, 13 rue Cambon, 75001 Paris Cedex 01, France.

MARTIN, Sir Clive Haydn, Kt, OBE, TD, DL, FCMA, FCIS; British business executive; b. 20 March 1935; s. of Thomas Stanley Martin and Dorothy Gladys Martin; m. Linda Constance Basil Penn 1959; one s. three d.; ed St Alban's School, Haileybury and Imperial Service Coll., London School of Printing and Graphic Arts; nat. service in Germany 1956–58; Man. Dir Staples Printers Ltd (now MPG Ltd) 1972–85, Chair. 1972; ADC to The Queen 1982–86; Alderman, City of London 1985–2005, Sheriff 1996–97, Lord Mayor of London 1999–2000; Master, Stationers' and Newspaper Makers' Co. 1997–98; CO, Hon. Artillery Co. 1978–80, Regimental Col 1981–83, Master Gunner, Tower of London 1981–83; Master, Chartered Secretaries and Admins' Co. 2004–05; Fellow, Inst. of Paper, Printing and Publishing; Hon. DCL (City Univ.); Dr hc (London Inst.) 2001 Hon. Col, 135 Ind. Geographic Squadron, Royal Engineers 1999–2004; Hon. Col, The London Regiment 2001–. Leisure interests: ocean racing (owner and skipper, British Sardinia Cup Team 1984), walking, cycling.

MARTIN, G. Steven, PhD, FRS; American/British biochemist, biologist and academic; Dean of Biological Sciences and Professor of Cell and Developmental Biology, University of California, Berkeley; b. 19 Sept. 1943, Oxford, England; s. of Kurt Martin and Hanna Martin; m. Gail Zuckman 1969; one s.; ed Manchester Grammar School, Univ. of Cambridge; Postdoctoral Fellow, Virus Lab., Univ. of California, Berkeley 1968–71; mem. of staff, Imperial Cancer Research Fund, London 1971–75; Asst Prof. Dept of Zoology, Univ. of Calif., Berkeley 1975–79, Assoc. Prof. 1979–83, Prof. 1983–89, also Asst Research Virologist Cancer Research Lab. 1975–79, Assoc. Research Virologist 1979–83, Research Virologist 1983–, Prof. Dept of Molecular and Cell Biology 1989–, Richard and Rhoda Goldman Prof. of Cell and Developmental Biology 2002–07, Judy C. Webb Prof. of Cell and Developmental Biology 2007–12, Head, Div. of Cell and Developmental Biology 1999–2006, Dean of Molecular and Cell Biology 2007–11, Dean of Biological Sciences 2011–; NIH Merit Award 1989–97, 2002–11, John Simon Guggenheim Memorial Foundation Fellowship 1991–92, American Cancer Soc. Scholar Award in Cancer Research 1991–92. Publications: articles in various learned journals including Nature, Science, Cell. Leisure interests: hiking, bicycling, reading. Address: Department of Molecular and Cell Biology, University of California, Berkeley, 450 Li Ka Shing Center #3370, Berkeley, CA 94720-3370, USA (office). Telephone: (510) 642-1508 (office). Fax: (510) 642-7578 (office).

E-mail: gsm@berkeley.edu (office). Website: mcb.berkeley.edu/faculty/CDB/martins.html (office).

MARTIN, Sir George Henry, Kt, CBE; British music industry executive, producer and composer (retd); b. 3 Jan. 1926; s. of Henry Martin and Bertha Beatrice Martin; m. 1st Sheena Rose Chisholm 1948; one s. one d.; m. 2nd Judy Lockhart Smith 1966; one s. one d.; ed Bromley Co. School, Kent, Guildhall School of Music and Drama; Sub-Lt RNVR 1944–47; worked at BBC 1950; with EMI Records Ltd 1950–65, produced all records featuring The Beatles and numerous other artists; formed AIR Group of cos 1965, Chair. 1965–; built AIR Studios 1969; built AIR Studios, Montserrat 1979; completed new AIR Studios, Lyndhurst Hall, Hampstead 1992; co. merged with Chrysalis Group 1974, Dir 1978–; Chair. Heart of London Radio 1994–; scored the music for 15 films; Hon. Fellow, Guildhall School of Music, Hon. mem. Royal Acad. of Music; Hon. DMus (Berklee Coll. of Music) 1989, (Leeds Metropolitan Univ.) 2006, (Univ. of Oxford) 2011; Hon. MA (Salford) 1992; Grammy Awards 1964, 1967 (two), 1973, 1993, 1996, 2007, Ivor Novello Awards 1963, 1979, Lifetime Achievement Award (World Soundtrack Academy) 2002. Publications: All You Need Is Ears 1979, Making Music 1983, Summer of Love 1994. Leisure interests: boats, sculpture, tennis, snooker. Address: George Martin Music, AIR Studios, Lyndhurst Hall, Lyndhurst Road, Hampstead, London, NW3 5NG, England (office). Telephone: (20) 7794-0660 (office). Fax: (20) 7916-2784 (office). E-mail: info@georgemartinmusic.com (office). Website: www.georgemartinmusic.com.

MARTIN, George R. R.; American novelist and screenwriter; b. 20 Sept. 1948, Bayonne, NJ; s. of Raymond Collins and Margaret Martin; m. 1st Gale Burnick 1975 (divorced 1979); m. 2nd Parris McBride 2011; journalism intern, Medill News Service, Washington, DC 1971; sportswriter and public relations officer, NJ Dept of Parks, Bayonne 1971; Communications & Educ. Coordinator, Cook County Legal Assistance Foundation, Chicago 1972–74; Founder and Chair. Windy City Science Fiction Writers' Workshop, Chicago 1972–1976; Instructor in journalism, Clarke Coll. 1976–78, Writer-in-Residence 1978–79; mem. Writers' Guild of America West, Science Fiction & Fantasy Writers of America (Vice-Pres. 1996–98). Television includes: The Twilight Zone (writer) (TV series) 1986, Beauty and the Beast 1987–90, A Game of Thrones (TV adaptation of A Song of Ice and Fire books) 2011. Publications include: Dying of the Light 1977, Windhaven 1981, Fevre Dream 1982, The Armageddon Rag 1983, Jokers Wild 1987, Ace in the Hole 1990, Dealer's Choice 1992, Hunter's Run 2007, A Song of Ice and Fire series: A Game of Thrones 1996 (Locus Fantasy award 1997), A Clash of Kings 1998 (Locus Fantasy award 1999), A Storm of Swords 2000 (Locus Fantasy award 2001), A Feast for Crows 2005, A Dance with Dragons 2011, The Winds of Winter; collections: A Song for Lya 1976, Songs of Stars and Shadows 1977, Sandkings 1981, Songs the Dead Men Sing 1983, Nightflyers 1985, Tuf Voyaging 1987, Portraits of His Children 1987, Quartet 2001, GRRM: A RRetrospective 2003, Dreamsongs: A RRetrospective 2007. Website: www.georgerrmartin.com (office).

MARTIN, Harold; New Caledonian politician; President of the Government; b. 6 April 1954, Nouméa; Pres. Council on the Regulation and Establishment of Agricultural Prices 1991, 1993, 1994–95; Pres. Territorial Congress 1997–98, 2004–07, 2010–; Pres. of the Govt 2007–10, 2011–; Pres. L'Avenir Ensemble (Future Together Party) 2007–09; Mayor of Paita. Address: Congrès de la Nouvelle-Calédonie, 1 boulevard Vauban, BP. P3 98 851, Nouméa Cedex, New Caledonia (office). Telephone: 273129 (office); 270902 (office); 270217 (office). Fax: 277020 (office). E-mail: presidence@congres.nc (office). Website: www.congres.nc (office).

MARTIN, Ian; British UN official; b. 10 Aug. 1946; s. of Collin Martin and Betty Martin; Community Relations Officer, Redbridge Community Relations Council 1973–75, Councillor, London Borough of Redbridge 1978–82; Head of Asia Research Dept, Amnesty International 1985–86, Sec.-Gen. 1986–92; Sr Assoc., Carnegie Endowment for International Peace, Washington, DC 1993; Dir of Human Rights and Deputy Exec. Dir UN Mission to Haiti 1993–95, Chief of UN Human Rights Field Operation, Rwanda 1995–96, also served in Office of High Rep. in Bosnia, Deputy High Rep. Human Rights Field Operation in Bosnia and Herzegovina 1998–99, Dir Human Rights, International Civilian Mission in Haiti, Special Rep. for East Timor Popular Consultation 1999; Deputy Special Rep. of Sec.-Gen. UN Mission in Ethiopia and Eritrea 2000–01; Vice-Pres. International Centre for Transitional Justice 2002–05; UN human rights adviser during Sri Lankan peace process 2003–05, Rep. to UN High Commr for Human Rights, Nepal 2005–06, Special Envoy for Timor-Leste 2006, Special Rep. of Sec.-Gen. in Nepal 2006–09, Head of HQ Bd of Inquiry, Gaza Strip 2009, Special Adviser to Sec.-Gen. on Post-Conflict Planning for Libya –2011, Special Rep. of the Sec.-Gen. for Libya and Head, UN Support Mission in Libya (UNSMIL) 2011–12. Publications include: Immigration Law and Practice (co-author) 1982, Self-Determination in East Timor: the United Nations, the Ballot, and International Intervention 2001. Address: c/o United Nations Support Mission in Libya (UNSMIL), Department of Political Affairs, United Nations, New York, NY 10017, USA.

MARTIN, James Grubbs, PhD; American healthcare industry executive and fmr politician; Corporate Vice-President, Carolinas HealthCare System; b. 11 Dec. 1935, Savannah, Ga; s. of Arthur M. and Mary J. (Grubbs) Martin; m. Dorothy A. McAulay 1957; two s. one d.; ed Davidson (NC) Coll. and Princeton Univ.; Assoc. Prof. of Chem., Davidson Coll. 1960–72; mem. 93rd–98th Congresses from NC; Gov. of North Carolina 1985–93; Corp. Vice-Pres. Carolinas HealthCare System 1995–; mem. Bd of Dirs Duke Energy Co. 1994, Palomar Medical Technologies, Inc., aaiPharma Inc., Family Dollar Stores, Inc. 1997–; fmr mem. Bd of Dirs James G. Cannon Medical Research Center, J. A. Jones Construction 1993; mem. Bd of Visitors, McColl Graduate School of Business, Queens Univ. of Charlotte; Trustee Davidson Coll. 1998–; Dr hc Queens Univ. of Charlotte 1997; ACS Charles Lathrop Parsons Award 1983. Leisure interests: golf, sailing, music. Address: Carolinas HealthCare System, PO Box 32861, Charlotte, NC 28232-2861, USA (office). Telephone: (704) 355-5314 (office). Fax: (704) 355-0300 (office). E-mail: jgmartin@carolinas.org (office). Website: www.carolinashealthcare.org (office).

MARTIN, Kevin J., BA, MA, JD; American government official; Chairman, Federal Communications Commission; b. Charlotte, NC; m. Catherine Jurgensmeyer Martin; two s.; ed Univ. of NC, Duke Univ., Harvard Law School; fmr law clerk for US Court Dist Judge William M. Hoeveler; fmrly with Wiley, Rein &

Fielding; later with US Office of the Ind. Counsel; Legal Advisor to Fed. Communications Comm. (FCC) Commr 1997–99; Deputy Gen. Counsel to Bush campaign, Austin, Tex. 1999–2000; fmr Prin. Tech. and Telecommunications Advisor, Bush-Cheney Transition team, later Special Asst to the Pres. for Econ. Policy; fmr mem. staff Nat. Econ. Council; Commr FCC 2001–, Chair. 2005–; Chair. Fed.-State Jt Bd on Separations, Fed.-State Jt Conf. on Advanced Telecommunications Services, mem. Fed.-State Jt Bd on Universal Service. *Address:* Federal Communications Commission, 445 12th Street, SW, Washington, DC 20554, USA (office). *Telephone:* (202) 418-1000 (office). *Fax:* (202) 418-2801 (office). *E-mail:* Kevin.Martin@fcc.gov (office). *Website:* www.fcc.gov/commissioners/martin (office).

MARTIN, Sir Laurence Woodward, Kt, MA, PhD, DL; British academic; *Professor Emeritus, Newcastle University;* b. 30 July 1928, St Austell, Cornwall, England; s. of Leonard Martin and Florence Mary Woodward; m. Betty Parnall 1951; one s. one d.; ed St Austell Grammar School, Christ's Coll., Cambridge, Yale Univ., USA; RAF Flying Officer 1948–51; Asst Prof., MIT, USA 1956–61; Assoc. Prof., Johns Hopkins Univ., USA 1961–64; Prof., Univ. of Wales 1964–68; King's Coll. London 1968–78, Fellow, London 1984; Vice-Chancellor Newcastle Univ. 1978–90, Prof. Emer. 1991–; Arleigh Burke Chair in Strategy, Center for Strategic and Int. Studies, Washington, DC, USA 1998–2000; Visiting Prof., Univ. of Wales 1985–90; Dir Royal Inst. of Int. Affairs 1991–96; Bodichon Fellow, Girton Coll. Cambridge 2010; Hon. DCL (Newcastle) 1991; Lees Knowles Lecturer, Cambridge. *Radio:* Reith Lecturer (BBC) 1981. *Publications:* Peace Without Victory 1958, The Sea in Modern Strategy 1967, Arms and Strategy 1973, The Two Edged Sword 1982, The Changing Face of Nuclear War 1987, British Foreign Policy (co-author) 1997. *Leisure interests:* travel, walking, fishing. *Address:* 35 Witley Court, Coram Street, London, WC1N 1HP, England (home). *E-mail:* lw.martin@hirundo.co.uk (office).

MARTIN, Lynn; American academic, consultant and fmr politician; b. 26 Dec. 1939, Chicago, Ill.; m. Harry Leinenweber; two d.; ed Univ. of Illinois; mem. Winnebago Co. Bd 1972–76; mem. Ill. House of Reps 1977–79, Ill. Senate 1979–81; mem. US House of Reps 1981–91, mem. House Rules Cttee, House Budget Cttee, Cttee on Public Works and Transportation, Cttee on DC, Chair. House Repub. Conf. 1982–86, Vice- Co-Chair. Bi-partisan Ethics Task Force; US Sec. of Labor 1991–93; Prof., J.L. Kellogg Graduate School of Man., Northwestern Univ. 1993–99; Chair. Deloitte & Touche (now Deloitte LLP) Council on Advancement of Women 1993–2005; Pres. Martin Hall Group, LLC, Chicago 2005–; mem. Bd of Dirs Ameritech Corpn 1993–99, AT&T 1999–2012, Proctor & Gamble Co. 1994–2010, Constellation Energy Group Inc. 2003–09, Dreyfus Funds, Ryder System Inc.; fmr mem. Int. Advisory Council, Coco-Cola Co.; International ATHENA Award 2002.

MARTIN, Baron (Life Peer), cr. 2009, of Springburn, of Port Dundas in the City of Glasgow; **Rt Hon. Michael John Martin,** PC; British politician; b. 3 July 1945, Glasgow, Scotland; s. of Michael Martin and Mary Martin; m. Mary McLay 1966; one s. one d.; ed St Patrick's Boys' School, Glasgow; fmr sheet metal worker; AUEW Shop Steward, Rolls Royce, Hillington 1970–74, TU Organizer 1976–79; Councillor for Fairfield Ward, Glasgow Corpn 1973–74, for Balornock Ward, Glasgow Dist Council 1974–79; MP for Glasgow, Springburn 1979–2005, Parl. Pvt. Sec. to Rt Hon Denis Healey 1981–83, MP for Glasgow North East 2005–09 (resgnd), mem. Select Cttee for Trade and Industry 1983–86, Chair. Scottish Grand Cttee 1987–97, mem. Speaker's Panel of Chair. 1987–2000, Deputy Speaker of House of Commons 1997–2000, Speaker 2000–09 (resgnd); mem. House of Lords 2009–; mem. Coll. of Piping 1989–; Hon. Fellow of the Chartered Inst. of Bankers in Scotland 2003; Dr hc (Glasgow Univ.) 2003. *Leisure interests:* hill walking, local history, piping. *Address:* c/o House of Lords, Westminster, London, SW1A 0PW, England (office).

MARTIN, Micheál, MA; Irish politician; *Leader, Fianna Fáil;* b. 16 Aug. 1960, Cork; s. of Paddy Martin; m. Mary O'Shea; one s.; ed Colaiste Chríost Rí, Univ. Coll., Cork; fmr secondary school teacher; elected to Çork Corpn 1985, Alderman 1991; Lord Mayor of Cork 1992–93; mem. Dáil Éireann 1989–; fmr Chair. Oireachtas All Party Cttee on the Irish Language; fmr mem. Dail Cttee on Crime, Dail Cttee on Finance and Gen. Affairs; Minister for Educ. 1997–2000, for Health and Children 2000, for Enterprise, Trade and Employment –2008, of Foreign Affairs 2008–11 (resgnd); Nat. Chair. Fianna Fáil Nat. Exec. 1988–, Leader Fianna Fáil 2011–; Nat. Chair. Ogra Fianna Fáil; mem. Bd Cork Opera House, Graffiti Theatre Co., Nat. Sculpture Factory, Everyman Palace Theatre, Crawford Gallery, College of Commerce and several school bds; fmr mem. Governing Body Univ. Coll., Cork; won Cork Examiner Political Speaker of the Year Award 1987. *Address:* Fianna Fáil, 65–66 Lower Mount St, Dublin 2, Ireland (home). *Telephone:* (1) 6761551 (office). *Fax:* (1) 6785690 (office). *E-mail:* info@fiannafail.ie (office). *Website:* www.fiannafail.ie (office).

MARTIN, Rt Hon Paul, PC, BA, LLB; Canadian politician; b. 1938, Windsor, Ont.; s. of the late Paul Martin and Eleanor Martin; m. Sheila Ann Cowan 1965; three s.; ed Univs of Ottawa and Toronto; worked in legal branch of ECSC; called to Bar, Ont. 1966; with Power Corpn of Canada, Montreal; Chair. and CEO Canada Steamship Lines; Dir of seven major Canadian cos; MP for LaSalle-Émard, Montreal 1988–; cand. for leadership of Liberal Party 1990, Leader 2003–06; Co-Chair. Nat. Platform Cttee, Liberal Party of Canada 1993; Minister of Finance 1993–2002, also Minister Responsible for Fed. Office of Regional Devt 1993–95; Prime Minister of Canada 2003–06; Chair. G-20 (int. group) 1999–2002. *Publications:* Creating Opportunity: The Liberal Plan for Canada (jtly), Making History: The Politics of Achievement, Hell or High Water: My Life In and Out of Politics (auto-biog.) 2008. *Address:* Room 418-N Centre Block, House of Commons, Ottawa, ON K1H 7R3, Canada (office). *Telephone:* (613) 992-4284 (office). *Fax:* (613) 992-4291 (office). *E-mail:* martip@parl.gc.ca (office). *Website:* www.paulmartin.ca.

MARTIN, Ricky; Puerto Rican singer and actor; b. (Enrique Martin Morales), 24 Dec. 1971, San José, PR; two s.; mem. Latin pop band, Menudo 1984–89; solo artist 1989–; worked as actor and singer in Mexico; f. Ricky Martin Foundation 2000; American Music Award for Favorite Latin Artist 2000, Int. Humanitarian Award 2005. *Television:* Alcanzar una Estrella II (Mexican soap opera), played Miguel in General Hospital (US series). *Theatre:* Marius in Les Misérables (Broadway), Che in Evita (Broadway). *Film:* Hercules (voice in Spanish-language version). *Record-*

ings include: albums: Ricky Martin 1991, Me Amarás 1993, A Medio Vivir 1995, Vuelve (Grammy Award for Best Latin Pop Album) 1998, Ricky Martin 1999, Sound Loaded 2000, La Historia 2001, Almas de Silencio 2003, Life 2005, MTV Unplugged (Latin Grammy Awards for Best Male Pop Vocal Album and Best Long Form Music Video 2007) 2006. *Publication:* Me (autobiog.) 2010. *Address:* Columbia Records, Sony BMG Music Entertainment, 550 Madison Avenue, New York, NY 10022-3211, USA (office). *Telephone:* (212) 833-7100 (office). *Fax:* (212) 833-7416 (office). *Website:* www.sonybmg.com (office); www.rickymartin.com; www.rickymartinfoundation.org.

MARTIN, Steve; American actor, comedian, writer and musician (banjo); b. 14 Aug. 1945, Waco, Tex.; s. of Glenn Martin and Mary Lee Martin; m. 1st Victoria Tennant 1986 (divorced 1994); m. 2nd Anne Stringfield 2007; ed Long Beach State Coll., Univ. of California, Los Angeles; TV writer for several shows; nightclub comedian; TV special Steve Martin: A Wild and Crazy Guy 1978; Georgie Award, American Guild of Variety Artists 1977, 1978, American Cinematheque Career Achievement Honour 2004, John F. Kennedy Center for Performing Arts Mark Twain Prize for American Humor 2005, Kennedy Center Honor 2007, Academy Honorary Award 2013, Grammy Award for Best Roots Song (for Love Has Come for You, with Edie Brickell) 2014. *Recordings include:* Let's Get Small 1977 (Grammy Award), A Wild and Crazy Guy 1978 (Grammy Award), Comedy is Not Pretty 1979, The Steve Martin Bros, The Crow: New Songs for the Five-String Banjo (Grammy Award for Best Bluegrass Album 2010) 2009, Rare Bird Alert (with Steep Canyon Rangers) 2011, Love Has Come for You (with Edie Brickell) 2013. *Films include:* The Absent Minded Waiter 1977, Sgt Pepper's Lonely Hearts Club Band 1978, The Muppet Movie 1979, The Jerk 1979 (also screenwriter), Pennies from Heaven 1981, Dead Men Don't Wear Plaid (also writer) 1982, The Man With Two Brains (also writer) 1983, The Lonely Guy 1984, All of Me 1984 (Nat. Soc. of Film Critics Actor's Award), Three Amigos (also writer and exec. producer) 1986, Little Shop of Horrors 1986, Roxanne (also screenwriter and exec. producer) 1987, Planes, Trains and Automobiles 1987, Dirty Rotten Scoundrels 1988, Parenthood 1989, My Blue Heaven 1990, LA Story (also writer and exec. producer) 1991, Grand Canyon 1991, Father of the Bride 1991, Housesitter 1992, Leap of Faith 1992, A Simple Twist of Fate (also writer and exec. producer) 1994, Mixed Nuts 1994, Father of the Bride 2 1995, Sgt Bilko 1996, The Spanish Prisoner 1997, The Out of Towners 1999, Bowfinger (also writer) 1999, Joe Gould's Secret 2000, Novocaine 2001, Bringing Down the House 2003, Looney Tunes: Back in Action 2003, Cheaper by the Dozen 2003, Jiminy Glick in La La Wood 2004, Shopgirl (also screenplay and producer) 2005, Cheaper by the Dozen 2 2005, Pink Panther (also screenplay) 2006, It's Complicated 2009, Tangled (voice) 2010, The Big Year 2011. *Publications include:* The Pleasure of My Company 2003, Born Standing Up (autobiog.) 2007, An Object of Beauty 2010. *Website:* www.stevemartin.com.

MARTIN, Todd Christopher; American fmr professional tennis player; b. 8 July 1970, Hinsdale, Ill.; s. of Dale Martin and Lynn Martin; m. Amy Martin; one s.; ed Northwestern Univ.; winner, New Haven Challenger 1989; turned professional 1990; semi-finalist Stella Artois Grass Court Championships, London 1993, Champion 1994, Champion (doubles with Pete Sampras q.v.) 1995; finalist, Australian Open 1994, Grand Slam Cup, Munich 1995; semi-finalist, US Open 1994, Wimbledon 1994, 1996, Paris Open 1998; Champion, Scania Stockholm Open 1998; winner of 13 pro titles; mem. US Davis Cup Team 1994–99; Pres. ATP Players' Council 1995–97, 1998–99; est. Todd Martin Devt Fund, Lansing, Mich. 1994; Special Adviser, USA Tennis High Performance Program 2003–; announced retirement 2004; contrib. ESPN; mem. Bd of Dirs Tim and Tom Gullickson Foundation; currently coaching Mardy Fish; Adidas/ATP Tour Sportsmanship Award 1993, 1994, ATP Tour Most Improved Player 1993. *Address:* POB 4165, Vero Beach, FL 32963; c/o Todd Martin Development Fund, Court One North, 1609 Lake Lansing Road, Lansing, MI 48912, USA.

MARTIN, Tony; German professional road bicycle racer; b. 23 April 1985, Cottbus, East Germany; turned professional 2008, for Team High Road; rode for Köstritzer 2004, Gerolsteiner (stagiaire) 2005, Thüringer Energie Team 2006–07, Team High Road 2008–11, UCI ProTeam Omega Pharma-Quick Step 2012–; time trial specialist, three-time world champion 2011, 2012, 2013; part of two world championship-winning team time trial squads with Omega Pharma-Quick Step 2012, 2013; also won three Grand Tour individual time trial stages, two at the Tour de France 2011, 2013, one at Vuelta a España 2011; has also won several stage races, including the Eneco Tour 2010, Volta ao Algarve 2011, 2013, Paris–Nice 2011, Tour of Beijing 2011, 2012, Tour of Belgium 2012, 2013; silver medal, Summer Olympics, London 2012. *Address:* c/o Bund Deutscher Radfahrer e.V., Otto-Fleck-Schneise 4, 60528 Frankfurt am Main, Germany. *E-mail:* info@bdr-online.org. *Website:* www.rad-net.de.

MARTIN, Valerie; American writer and academic; *Professor of English, Mount Holyoke College;* b. 1948, Missouri; partner John Cullen; one d.; taught at Univ. of New Mexico, Univ. of Alabama Univ. of New Orleans, Univ. of Massachusetts, Sarah Lawrence Coll.; currently Prof. of English, Mount Holyoke Coll. *Publications include:* Love: Short Stories 1976, Set in Motion (novel) 1978, Alexandra (novel) 1980, A Recent Martyr (novel) 1987, The Consolation of Nature and Other Stories 1988, Mary Reilly (novel) 1990, The Great Divorce (novel) 1994, Italian Fever (novel) 1999, Salvation: Scenes from the Life of St Francis (biog.) 2001, Property (novel) (Orange Prize for Fiction) 2003, The Unfinished Novel and Other Stories 2006, Trespass 2007, The Confessions of Edward Day 2009, The Ghost of the Mary Celeste 2014. *Address:* The Friedrich Agency, 19 West 21st Street, Suite 201, New York, NY 10010, USA (office); Mount Holyoke College, 50 College Street, South Hadley, MA, 01075, USA (office). *E-mail:* mfriedrich@friedrichagency.com (office); valerie@valeriemartinonline.com. *Telephone:* (413) 538-2000 (office). *Website:* www.valeriemartinonline.com

MARTÍN DELGADO, José María, DenD; Spanish university rector; b. 26 June 1947, Málaga; s. of Rafael Martín Delgado and María Jesús Martín Delgado; m. Irene Martín Delgado 1973; one s. two d.; ed Univs of Granada and Bologna; Prof. of Fiscal and Tax Law, Univ. of Granada, Univ. Autónoma de Madrid, Univ. Autónoma de Barcelona, Univ. La Laguna and Univ. of Málaga (fmr Dean Faculty of Law) 1969–; Rector Univ. of Málaga 1984–94; Minister of Culture, Junta de Andalucía 1994–96; Rector Universidad Internacional de Andalucía 1996–; mem. Spanish Asscn of Fiscal Law, Int. Fiscal Asscn; Dr hc (Dickinson Coll., Pa). *Publications:* Análisis Jurídico del Fondo de Previsiones para Inversiones,

Ordenamiento Tributario Español 1977, Sistema Democrático y Derecho Tributario. *Leisure interests:* reading, music, fishing, tennis. *Address:* Universidad Internacional de Andalucía, Monasterio de Santa María de las Cuevas, Américo Vespucio nº2, Isla de la Cartuja, 41092 Seville, Spain (office). *Telephone:* (95) 446-2299 (office). *Fax:* (95) 446-2288 (office). *E-mail:* unia@uia.es (office). *Website:* www.unia.es (office).

MARTÍN FERNÁNDEZ, Miguel; Spanish banker; *President, Asociación Española de Banca;* b. 9 Nov. 1943, Jerez de la Frontera; m. Anne Catherine Cleary 1972; one s. two d.; ed Univ. Complutense, Madrid; Head Budget and Finance Sections, Ministry of Finance 1969–72, Deputy Dir 1972–76; Economist, World Bank, Latin American Region 1976–77, Alt. Exec. Dir for Spain, Italy and Portugal, World Bank 1977–78; Dir-Gen. Treasury, Ministry of Finance 1978–79; Under-Sec. for Budget and Public Expenditure 1979–81; Pres. Inst. for Official Credit 1982; Head Annual Accounts Centre, Banco de España 1983–84; Under-Sec. Economy and Finance 1984–86; Dir-Gen. Banco de España 1986–92, Deputy Gov. 1992–2000, Head Internal Audit Office 2000; Pres. Asociación Española de Banca 2006–; Gran Placa de la Orden del Mérito Postal, Encomienda del Mérito Agrícola. *Address:* Asociación Española de Banca, Velázquez 64–66, 28001 Madrid, Spain (office). *Telephone:* (91) 7891311 (office). *Fax:* (91) 7891310 (office). *Website:* www.aebanca.es (office).

MARTIN-LÖF, Per Erik Rutger, PhD; Swedish mathematician, philosopher and academic; *Professor Emeritus of Logic, Department of Mathematics, Stockholm University;* b. 8 May 1942, Stockholm; s. of Sverker Emil Bernhard Martin-Löf and Gertrud Cecilia Benedicks; m. Kerstin Maria Birgitta Forsell (died 2009); one s. two d.; ed Stockholm Univ.; Asst. Math. Statistics, Stockholm Univ. 1961–64, Doctoral Scholar, Faculty of Science 1965–66, 1967–68, Docent, Math. Statistics 1969–70, Prof. of Logic 1994–2009, Prof. Emer. 2009–; State Scholar of Swedish Inst., Moscow Univ. 1964–65; Amanuensis, Math. Inst., Århus Univ., Denmark 1966–67; Asst Prof., Dept of Math., Univ. of Ill., Chicago, USA 1968–69; Researcher in Math. Logic, Swedish Natural Science Research Council 1970–81, in Logic 1981–83, Prof. of Logic 1983–94; mem. Academia Europaea, Royal Swedish Acad. of Sciences; Dr hc (Leiden) 2004, (Marseilles) 2004. *Publications:* Notes on Constructive Mathematics 1970, Intuitionistic Type Theory 1984. *Leisure interest:* ornithology. *Address:* Department of Mathematics, Stockholm University, 106 91 Stockholm (office); Barnhusgatan 4, 111 23 Stockholm, Sweden (home). *Telephone:* (8) 20-05-83 (home). *Fax:* (8) 612-67-17 (office). *E-mail:* pml@math.su.se (office). *Website:* www.matematik.su.se (office).

MARTIN-LÖF, Sverker, MSc (Eng), DTech; Swedish construction industry executive; *Chairman, Skanska AB;* b. 1943, Stockholm; ed Royal Inst. of Tech., Stockholm; worked at Swedish Pulp and Paper Research Inst.; fmr Pres. MoDo Chemetics; fmr Tech. Dir Mo och Domsjö AB; fmr Pres. Sunds Defibrator AB; Pres. Svenska Cellulosa Aktiebolaget SCA 1988–2002, Chair. 2002–; Chair. Skanska AB 2001–, SSAB Svenskt Stål AB; Vice-Chair. AB Industrivärden, Telefonaktiebolaget LM Ericsson, Svenskt Näringsliv, Confed. of Swedish Enterprise; mem. Bd of Dirs LM Ericsson, Boliden 2002–, Svenska Handelsbanken AB; Hon. PhD (Mid-Sweden Univ., Sundsvall). *Address:* Skanska AB, Klarabergsviadukten 90, 111 91 Stockholm, Sweden (office). *Telephone:* (8) 753-88-00 (office). *Fax:* (8) 755-12-56 (office). *E-mail:* info@skanska.com (office). *Website:* www.skanska.com (office).

MARTIN MATEO, Ramón; Spanish professor of administrative law; b. 31 Aug. 1928, Valladolid; s. of Andrés Martín Mateo and Julia Martín Mateo; m. Clara Abad Lobejón 1966; four c.; Prof. of Admin. Law, Univs of País Vasco, Madrid, Valladolid and Alicante; Rector Universidad del País Vasco 1976–79, Univ. of Alicante 1986–94; UN Expert, Projects VEN 11-534 and Reform of the Regional Admin, Caracas 1974; mem. Council of State 1990–2003, Nat. Water Comm. 1991–98; Consultant to EEC for Uruguay 1991, Expert, EEC DG 1 Establishment of the Centre for Sustainable Devt, Buenos Aires 1992; Pres. Spanish Asscn of Environmental Law, Int. Asscn for Water Law; Dir Inst. of Water and Environmental Sciences; fmr Pres. Spanish Asscn of Regional Science; Chair. Editorial Bd Journal of Environmental Law; mem. Int. Council of Environmental Law, Club of Rome, Environment and Natural Resources Foundation; Corresp. mem. Venezuelan Acad. of Science Eng and Math. mem.; Hon. Prof., Universidad del Rosario, Bogotá, Nat. Univ. of San Marco, Lima; Hon. Pres. Inst. of Ecology of the Coast; Order Mérito Civil; Commdr, Order of Andrés Bello (Venezuela); Dr hc (Univ. of Mendoza, Argentina), (Univ. of León) 1995, (Univ. of the Basque Country) 2007, (Univ. Rovira i Virgili, Tarragona) 2007; Nat. Environmental Prize 1992, Jaime I Environment Prize 2000, Justice Prize 2001, Energy Prize of the Spanish Energy Club 2005, Prize of the Energy Agency of the City of Seville 2005. *Publications:* 40 books, including Aspectos Administrativos De La Planificación. El Sistema Venezolano (co-author) 1973, Derecho Administrativo Económico 1974, Ordenacion del sector publico en Espana (Monografias Civitas) 1974, Derecho ambienta 1977, Urbanismo Interdisciplinar – Santurce Dos 1977, Nuevo derecho energetico 1982, Manual de derecho autonomico 1984, Bioética y Derecho 1987, Liberalización de la Economía: Más Estado, menos Administración, La eficacia social de la jurisdicción contencioso-administrativa 1989, Tratado de Derecho Ambiental, Vol. I 1991, Vol. II 1992, Vol. III 1997, Vol. IV 2003, El hombre: una especie en peligro 1993, Nuevos instrumentos para la tutela ambiental 1994, La marca comunitaria: Derecho publico (Estudios Trivium comunitario) 1996, Nuevo ordenamiento de la basura 1998, El Marco Publico de la Economia de Mercado 1999 (revised edn) 2003, Memorias de un ingeniero social bienhumorado 2005, La gallina de los huevos de cemento 2007, Manual de Derecho Administrativo (revised edn 2008), La Verde Energía de la Biomasa 2008; numerous articles in professional journals. *Leisure interests:* mountaineering, music. *Address:* c/o Universidad de Alicante, Carretera de San Vicente del Raspeig, 03690 Alicante, Spain. *E-mail:* ramon.martin@ua.es. *Website:* web.ua.es/es/oficina-rector/biografias-de-los-rectores/ramon-martin-mateo.html.

MARTÍN VILLA, Rodolfo; Spanish politician and business executive; b. 3 Oct. 1934, Santa María del Páramo, León; m. María Pilar Pena Medina; two c.; ed Escuela Superior de Ingenieros Industriales, Madrid; Leader of Madrid Section, Sindicato Español Universitario, Nat. Leader 1962–64; Sec.-Gen. Syndical Org. 1969–74; mem. Council of the Realm; Nat. Econ. Adviser, Nat. Inst. of Industry; Nat. Econ. Adviser, Banco de Crédito Industrial, later Pres.; Civil Gov. of Barcelona and Prov. Head of Falangist Movement 1974–75; Minister for Relations with Trade Unions 1975–76, of the Interior 1976–79, of Territorial Admin.

1980–82; mem. Parl. (for Unión de Centro Democrático) 1977–83; First Deputy Prime Minister 1981–82; mem. Parl. (for Partido Popular) 1989–97 (resgnd); mem. Exec. Cttee, Partido Popular 1989–; apptd Chair. Sociedad Estatal de Participaciones Industriales 1997; Chair. Endesa (govt-controlled electricity group) 1997–2002, Hon. Chair. 2002–; Govt Commr for the Prestige oil-tanker disaster 2003; Chair. Sogecable (pay-TV provider) 2003–10; Dir, Sociedad de Gestión de Activos procedentes de la Reestructuración Bancaria (Sareb) 2012–; mem. Sr Corps of Inspectors of State Finance, Advisory Cttee FRIDE (think tank); fmr mem. special group of industrial engineers assisting Treasury, Bd Caja de Madrid. *Address:* Sareb, Paseo de la Castellana, 89-8A Planta, 28046 Madrid, Spain. *Telephone:* (91) 5563700. *E-mail:* info@sareb.es; atencion2@pp.es. *Website:* www.sareb.es/es-es/Paginas/web-Sareb.aspx.

MARTINA, Dominico (Don) F.; Curaçao politician; fmr finance officer, Govt of Curaçao; head, Govt social affairs Dept; f. Movimentu Antiyas Nobo 1979; MP 1979; Prime Minister of Netherlands Antilles 1979–84, 1985–88. *Address:* Movimentu Antiyas Nobo, Landhuis Morgenster, Willemstad, Curaçao. *Telephone:* (9) 468-4781.

MARTINDALE, Ken; American business executive; *President and Chief Operating Officer, Rite Aid Corporation;* began retail career with Smith's Food and Drug Centers 1975, rose from dist man. in store operations to Sr Vice-Pres. of Marketing and Sr Vice-Pres. of Sales and Merchandising; joined Fred Meyer, Inc. 1998, Exec. Vice-Pres., Sales and Procurement (following merger with Kroger Co.) 1998–99; f. and operated Orchard Street, Inc., Salt Lake City; consulted for nat. and regional food retailers on category management, marketing and strategic planning; fmr Chair., Pres. and CEO Intesource, Inc. (software co.); Co-Pres., Chief Merchandising and Marketing Officer, Pathmark Stores, Inc. (until co. sold to Great Atlantic & Pacific Tea Co.) –2007; Sr Exec. Vice-Pres. of Merchandising, Marketing and Logistics 2008–13, Sr Exec. Vice-Pres. and COO Rite Aid Corpn –2013, Pres. and COO Rite Aid Corpn 2013–; Pres. The Rite Aid Foundation; mem. Bd of Dirs Nat. Asscn of Chain Drug Stores. *Address:* Rite Aid Corpn, 30 Hunter Lane, Camp Hill, PA 17011, USA (office). *Telephone:* (717) 761-2633 (office). *Fax:* (717) 975-5871 (office). *E-mail:* contacttheboard@riteaid.com (office). *Website:* www.riteaid.com (office).

MARTINELLI BERROCAL, Ricardo, MA, MBA; Panamanian business executive, politician and head of state; *President;* b. 11 March 1952, Panama City; s. of Ricardo Martinelli Pardini and Gloria Berrocal de Martinelli; m. Marta Linares de Martinelli; three c.; ed Staunton Mil. Acad., USA, Univ. of Arkansas, INCAE Business School, Costa Rica; Dir Social Security Fund 1994–96; Chair. Bd of Dirs Panama Canal Authority and Minister for Canal Affairs 1999–2003; Pres. Cambio Democrático Party 1998–; Pres. of Panama 2009–; Chair. Importadora Ricamar SA, Supermercados 99; Chair. Bd of Dirs Central Azucarera La Victoria, Plastigol SA; Dir Gold Mills de Panamá, Global Bank, Panasal SA, Televisora Nacional de Panamá, Direct TV, Desarrollo Norte SA, Molino de Oro, AVIPAC, Calox Panameña. *Address:* Office of the President, Palacio Presidencial, Valija 50, Panamá 1; Cambio Democrático, Parque Lefevre, Plaza Carolina, arriba de la Juguetería del Super 99, Panamá, Panama (office). *Telephone:* 227-4062 (office); 217-2643 (office). *Fax:* 227-0076 (office); 217-2645 (office). *E-mail:* cambio.democratico@hotmail.com (office). *Website:* www.presidencia.gob.pa (office).

MARTINEZ, Arthur C., BSc, MBA,; American business executive; *Chairman, Abercrombie & Fitch Co.;* b. 25 Sept. 1939, New York; s. of Arthur F. Martinez and Agnes Martinez (née Caulfield); m. Elizabeth Rusch 1966; two c.; ed Polytechnic Univ., Harvard Univ.; joined Exxon Chemical Co. 1960; Int. Paper Co. 1967–69; Talley Industries 1969–70; exec. positions in int. finance, RCA Corpn New York 1970–80; Sr Vice-Pres. and Chief Financial Officer, Saks 1980–84, Exec. Vice-Pres. for Admin. 1984-87, Sr Vice-Pres. and Group Chief Exec. Retail Div. BATUS Inc. 1987–90, Vice-Chair. Saks Fifth Avenue 1990–92; Chair. and CEO Sears Merchandise Group, Sears, Roebuck & Co. 1992–95, Chair., CEO Sears, Roebuck & Co. 1995–2000, now Chair. and CEO Emer.; Chair. HSN, Inc. 2008–; Chair. Abercrombie & Fitch Co. 2014–; Chair. Supervisory Bd ABN AMRO Holding NV (now Royal Bank of Scotland) 2006; fmr Chair. Nat. Retail Fed.; mem. Bd of Dirs American International Group, Inc., IAC/InterActive Corpn, Kate Spade & Co., International Flavors & Fragrances, Inc. 2000– (Lead Dir 2006–), Northwestern Univ., Greenwich Hospital, Art Inst. of Chicago, Chicago Symphony Orchestra Asscn, Polytechnic Univ., Maine Coast Heritage Trust; fmr mem. Bd of Dirs Amoco Corpn, Ameritech Corpn, Fed. Reserve Bank of Chicago, PepsiCo, Inc. 1999–2012; Hon. JD (Notre Dame) 1997. *Leisure interests:* gardening, golf, tennis. *Address:* Office of the Chairman, Abercrombie & Fitch Company, 6301 Fitch Path, New Albany, OH 43054, USA (office). *Website:* www.abercrombie.com (office).

MARTÍNEZ, Chus, MA; Spanish curator and writer; *Head Curator, Museo del Barrio, New York;* b. 1972, Ponteceso (La Coruña); ed Bard School, New York; worked at Fundación La Caixa 2001–02; Artistic Dir, Sala Rekalde, Bilbao 2002–05; curated the Nat. Pavilion of Cyprus at 50th Biennale di Venezia 2005; Dir Frankfurter Kunstverein 2005–08; Chief Curator, Museo de Arte Contemporanea Barcelona 2008–10; Head of Dept, Artistic Direction, dOCUMENTA (13) (quinquennial exhibition), Kassel, Germany 2009–12; Curatorial Adviser, 29th Bienal de São Paulo 2010; Head Curator, Museo del Barrio, New York 2012–; Fulbright Scholarship. *Publications:* numerous critical essays. *Address:* Museo del Barrio, 1230 5th Avenue, New York, NY 10029, USA (office). *Telephone:* (212) 831-7272 (office). *E-mail:* info@elmuseo.org (office). *Website:* www.elmuseo.org (office).

MARTINEZ, Conchita; Spanish fmr professional tennis player; b. 16 April 1972, Monzón; d. of Cecilio Martínez and Conchita Martínez; turned professional 1988; reached last 16 French Open 1988, quarter-finals French Open 1989, 1990, 1991, 1992, 1993, semi-finals Italian Open 1991, French Open 1994, Australian, French and US Opens and Wimbledon 1995, French and US Opens 1996, quarter-finals Olympic Games 1992; with Arantxa Sanchez-Vicario won Olympic Doubles silver medal 1992 and bronze medal 1996; Wimbledon Singles Champion 1994 (first Spanish woman to win title); has won 43 WTA tour titles; Spanish Fed. Cup Team 1988–96, 1998, 2000–01; retd April 2006; currently commentator for Eurosport Spain, Canal+ and DirecTV in USA; Tournament Dir Andalucía Tennis Experience 2009; f. Conchita Martinez Sports Consultancy; currently Capt. Spain Fed Cup Team; WTA Tour Most Impressive Newcomer 1989, Most Improved Player, Tennis Magazine 1994, ITF Award of Excellence 2001, Int. Tennis Hall of Fame

2001. *Leisure interests:* golf, horse riding, music, soccer, cinema, beach volleyball, skiing. *Website:* www.conchitamartinez.com/en.

MARTÍNEZ, Diego Alfredo, BSc, MA; Ecuadorean economist and central banker; *President, Banco Central del Ecuador;* b. 31 Aug. 1978; ed Colegio San Gabriel, Pontificia Universidad Católica del Ecuador, Inst. of Social Studies, The Hague, Netherlands; Planning and Projects Man., Inst. for Regional Eco-Devt, Quito 2004; Research Asst, Econ. Devt Programme, Inst. of Social Studies, The Hague 2004–05; Researcher, Latin American School of Social Sciences, Quito 2006–07; Under-Sec. for Planning, Public Policy and Investment, Nat. Secr. for Planning and Devt, Quito 2007–08, Under-Sec. for Public Investment 2008–09, Under-Sec.-Gen. for Planning and Devt 2009–10, Under-Sec.-Gen. for Planning and Sec., Nat. Planning Bd 2011; Adviser to Nat. Sec. for Higher Educ., Science, Tech. and Innovation 2011–12, Under-Sec.-Gen. for Science, Tech. and Innovation 2012–13; Pres. Banco Central del Ecuador 2013–. *Address:* Banco Central del Ecuador, Avda 10 de Agosto N11-409 y Briceño, Casilla 339, Quito, Ecuador (office). *Telephone:* (2) 257-2522 (office). *Fax:* (2) 295-5458 (office). *Website:* www .bce.fin.ec (office).

MARTINEZ, Mel; American (b. Cuban) lawyer, politician and business executive; *Chairman, Southeast and Latin America, JPMorgan Chase & Company;* b. (Melquíades Rafael Martínez Ruiz), 23 Oct. 1946, Sagua La Grande, Cuba; m. Kitty Martinez; two s. one d.; ed Florida State Univ. Coll. of Law; lawyer, Orlando, Fla 1973–98; Chair. Orange Co., Fla 1998–2001, providing urban services to residents; US Sec. of Housing and Urban Devt 2001–03; Senator from Florida 2005–09; Chair. Republican Party 2006–07; lobbyist and Partner, DLA Piper 2009–10; Chair. Chase Bank Florida and its operations in Mexico, Central America and the Caribbean 2010–13, Chair., Southeast and Latin America, JPMorgan Chase & Co. 2013–; Co-Chair. Housing Comm., Bipartisan Policy Center; fmr Chair. of Gov. Jeb Bush's Growth Man. Study Comm., of Bd Greater Orlando Aviation Authority, of Bd Orlando/Orange Co. Expressway Authority; Republican. *Publication:* A Sense of Belonging: From Castro's Cuba to the U.S. Senate, One Man's Pursuit of the American Dream (autobiog., with Ed Breslin) 2008. *Address:* JPMorgan Chase & Co., 270 Park Avenue, New York, NY 10017-2070, USA (office). *Telephone:* (212) 270-6000 (office). *E-mail:* info@jpmchase.com (office). *Website:* www.jpmorganchase.com (office).

MARTINEZ, Susana, BA, JD; American lawyer, politician and state governor; *Governor of New Mexico;* b. 14 July 1959, El Paso, Tex.; d. of Jacobo 'Jake' Martinez and Paula Martinez (née Aguirre); m. Chuck Franco 1991; one step-s.; ed Riverside High School, El Paso, Univ. of Texas, El Paso, Univ. of Oklahoma Coll. of Law; moved to Las Cruces, NM mid-1980s; Asst Dist Attorney, Doña Ana Co. Dist Attorney's Office, Dist Attorney, Third Judicial Dist of NM 1997–2011 (re-elected three times); Special Prosecutor, New Mexico Children, Youth and Families Dept; Gov. of New Mexico 2011– (first female gov. and first Latina/Hispanic gov. in USA); Republican; named Woman of the Year by Heart Magazine 2008, Prosecutor of the Year, Prosecutors Section of State Bar of NM 2010. *Address:* Office of the Governor, 490 Old Santa Fe Trail, Room 400, Santa Fe, NM 87501 (office); Washington Office of the Governor, State of New Mexico, 444 North Capitol Street, Suite 400, Washington, DC 20001, USA (office). *Telephone:* (505) 476-2200 (Santa Fe) (office); (202) 220-1348 (DC) (office). *Fax:* (505) 476-2226 (Santa Fe) (office); (202) 220-1349 (DC) (office). *Website:* www.governor.state.nm.us (office).

MARTÍNEZ, Victor Hipólito, JD; Argentine politician, lawyer and academic; b. 21 Nov. 1924, Córdoba; m. Fanny Munte; three s.; ed Nat. Univ. of Córdoba; began teaching land law at Nat. Univ. of Córdoba 1956, Dean of Land Law Dept 1979; active in the centrist Unión Cívica Radical (UCR—Radical Civic Union); Rep. to the Prov. Ass. of Córdoba 1962; Mayor of Córdoba 1963–66; Dir of newspaper Los Principios 1970–72; unsuccessful cand. for Gov. of Córdoba Prov. 1973; served on govt panels on local, prov. and nat. levels on the subject of land law; est. Argentine Soc. of Natural Resource Law and Management; Vice-Pres. of Argentina 1983–89 (resgnd); Pres. of the Argentine Senate 1983–89; resumed his land law practice 1989; Hon. Citizen of Calif. 1985; Hon. mem. Inter-American Bar Asscn 1986; Grand Cross of the Crown of Italy 1989. *Address:* c/o Honorable Senado de la Nación Argentina, Hipólito Yrigoyen 1849, CP 1089, Ciudad Autónoma de Buenos Aires, Argentina.

MARTÍNEZ BONILLA, Hugo Roger; Salvadorean agronomist and politician; b. 2 Jan. 1968, Concepción de Oriente; m.; ed Univ. of El Salvador, Univ. of Toulouse, France, Cen. American Univ., Nicaragua, Latin American Univ. of Science and Tech., Costa Rica; Sec.-Gen., Soc. of Salvadorean Students of Agricultural Sciences 1988; fmr Asst to Sec.-Gen., Univ. Superior Council of Cen. America; fmr Dir of External Co-operation, Univ. of El Salvador; joined Frente Farabundo Martí para la Liberación Nacional (FMLN), Nat. Youth Co-ordinator 1993–95, Substitute Deputy to FMLN Group in Parl. 1994–97, mem. FMLN Political Comm. 1999–2001, MP for San Salvador 2003–, Assoc. Co-ordinator, FMLN Parl. Group 2008–09, Pres., Foreign Affairs, Cen. American Integration and Salvadoreans Overseas Parl. Comm., mem. Consultative Comm., Ministry of Foreign Relations 2000–09, Minister of Foreign Affairs 2009–13. *Address:* c/o Ministry of Foreign Affairs, Calle El Pedregal, Blvd Cancillería, Ciudad Merliot, Antiguo Cuscatlán, San Salvador, El Salvador (office).

MARTÍNEZ DE PERÓN, María Estela (Isabelita); Argentine politician and fmr dancer; b. 6 Feb. 1931, La Rioja Prov.; m. Gen. Juan Domingo Perón (Pres. of Argentina 1946–55, 1973–74) 1961 (died 1974); joined troupe of travelling folk dancers; danced in cabaret in several S American countries; met her future husband during his exile in Panama, lived in Spain 1960–73, returned to Argentina with Juan Perón, became Vice-Pres. of Argentina 1973–74, Pres. 1974–76 (deposed by mil. coup); Chair. Peronist Party 1974–85; detained under house arrest 1976–81; settled in Madrid, Spain 1985; arrested 2007 on Argentine warrant to testify about forced disappearances during her presidency, extradition denied by Spanish courts 2008.

MARTÍNEZ MARTÍNEZ, José Manuel; Spanish business executive; b. 15 July 1947, Murcia; ed Madrid Univ.; graduated as public works engineer, economist and actuary; began career at MAPFRE in 1972, first assigned to newly created dept of eng and construction risk insurance, acquired his first man. experience as Chief Exec. of re-insurance subsidiary, co. merged into holding co. Corporación MAPFRE 1985, Chief Exec. MAPFRE's listed holding co., Chair. MAPFRE VIDA

1996–2001, Chair. and CEO MAPFRE SA 2001–12, Chair. Fundación MAPFRE; mem. Bd of Dirs Consorcio Espafrol de Seguros, Consorcio de Compensacion de Seguros Fundación Carolina (Govt-sponsored foundation for Latin American scholarships); Hon. mem. Fundación Carlos III 2002, Alumni Asscn of ENAE Business School, Madrid 2006; Distinguished Service Award, Int. Insurance Soc. 1995, Los Mejores de 1997, La Verdad newspaper, Murcia 1997, Award International Character 2001, Academia Nacional de Seguros e Previdencia (Brazil) 2001, Dirigentes Award, Dirigentes Magazine 2002, Management Award, Confederación Española de Directivos y Ejecutivos 2006, Insurance Hall of Fame Award, Int. Insurance Soc. 2007, Gold Medal, Latin American Commerce Chambers (AICO) 2007, Tiepolo Award, Italian Chamber in Spain and Chamber of Commerce of Madrid 2007. *Address:* c/o MAPFRE SA, Carretera de Pozuelo-Majadahonda 52, 28220 Majadahonda, Madrid, Spain. *E-mail:* info@mapfre.com.

MARTÍNEZ SISTACH, HE Cardinal Lluís, DCL; Spanish ecclesiastic; *Archbishop of Barcelona;* b. 29 April 1937, Barcelona; s. of Joan Martínez Puig and Maria Sistach Masllorens; ed Pontifical Lateran Univ., Rome; ordained priest in Barcelona 1961; worked with Catholic Action and was notary on Barcelona's archdiocesan tribunal; elected pres. of Spain's asscn of canonists in 1983, and taught canon law for several years; Auxiliary Bishop of Barcelona and Titular Bishop of Aliezira 1987–91; Bishop of Tortosa 1991–97; Archbishop of Tarragona 1997–2004, of Barcelona 2004–; cr. Cardinal (Cardinal-Priest of San Sebastiano alle Catacombe) 2007; participated in Papal Conclave 2013; mem. Apostolic Signature (a Vatican court), Pontifical Council for Legis. Texts, Pontifical Council for the Laity, Prefecture for Econ. Affairs of the Holy See; apptd a Synod Father for the 13th Ordinary Gen. Ass. of the Synod of Bishops on the New Evangelization Oct. 2012; Gold Medal, Universitat Ramon Llull 2011. *Address:* Arzobispado, Carrer del Bisbe 5, 08002 Barcelona, Spain (office). *Telephone:* (93) 270-1012 (office). *Fax:* (93) 270-1303 (office). *E-mail:* webpalau@arqbcn.cat (office). *Website:* www.arqbcn.org (office).

MARTÍNEZ SOMALO, HE Cardinal Eduardo, DCL; Spanish ecclesiastic; *Chamberlain Emeritus of the Apostolic Chamber;* b. 31 March 1927, Baños de Río Tobía, La Rioja; ed diocesan seminary of Logroño, Pontifical Spanish Coll., Pontifical Gregorian Univ., Pontifical Ecclesiastical Acad., Pontifical Lateran Univ.; ordained 1950, pastoral and curial work in Calahorra; Prof., Pontifical Ecclesiastical Acad.; entered the Roman Curia, in the Secr. of State, later Head of Spanish section; elevated to rank of Mgr 1970; apptd Apostolic Nuncio to Colombia 1975; consecrated Archbishop of Thagora 1975; Substitute for Gen. Affairs 1979–88; cr. Cardinal (Cardinal-Deacon of Santissimo Nome di Gesù) 1988, Cardinal Protodeacon 1996–99, Cardinal-Priest of Santissimo Nome di Gesù 1999; Prefect Congregation for Divine Worship and the Discipline of the Sacraments 1988–92, Congregation for Insts of Consecrated Life and for Socs of Apostolic Life 1992–2004; Chamberlain (Camerlengo) of the Apostolic Chamber 1993–2007; mem. Pontifical Comm. for Latin America, Congregations for Evangelization of Peoples, for the Clergy, for Catholic Educ.; participated as a Cardinal-elector in the Papal Conclave 2005. *Address:* c/o Palazzo delle Congregazioni, Piazza Pio XII 3, 00193 Rome, Italy.

MARTINI-URDANETA, Alberto, Dr rer. pol, DScS; Venezuelan politician, lawyer and diplomatist; *Judge, Supreme Court;* b. 2 April 1930, Trujillo; m.; five c.; ed Cen. Univ. of Venezuela; clerk at Third Court of First Instance, Fed. Dist 1949–51, Sec. Labour Third Court of First Instance 1954–62; Substitute Judge, Labour Court of First Instance 1956, Judge 1957; Legal Counsellor to Ministry for Foreign Relations 1958; Founder-mem. (1956) and Sec.-Gen. Venezuelan Inst. of Social Legislation 1960–69; Pres. Venezuelan Industrial Bank 1971; Minister of Labour 1972–74; Dir-Gen. Venezuelan Inst. for Social Legis. 1978–79; Amb. and Perm. Rep. to UN and Other Int. Orgs, Geneva 1979–81, to UN, New York 1981–84; Supreme Court Judge July–Dec. 1999, Chief Justice of the Electoral Bd (Sala Electoral) 1999–2004; Chair. numerous int. cttees and orgs, including several ILO cttees and confs; mem. Venezuelan Inst. of Social Law, Asociación Iberoamericana de Juristas de Derecho del Trabajo y de la Seguridad Social Doctor Guillermo Cabanellas; Orden del Libertador en Grado de Gran Cordón, Orden al Mérito en el Trabajo en Primera Clase, Orden 27 de Junio en su Primera Clase, Ministry of Educ., Cruz de las Fuerzas Armadas de Co-operación en su Primera Clase, Orden de Mayo en el Grado de Gran Cruz, otorgada por la nación Argentina, Honor al Mérito, Consejo de la Judicatura, por labor de Juez 1988, Orden Francisco de Miranda en su Primera Clase, Orden al Mérito en la Función Judicia; Good Citizen Award, Libertador Municipality Council, Honour Medal of Merit Municipal Year, Municipal Council of Sucre 1997. *Publications:* Suspensión del Contrato de Trabajo, Regimenes Especiales de Trabajo, La Relación de Trabajo y El Hecho Social; numerous articles on labour and social matters. *Address:* c/o La Sede del Tribunal Supremo de Justicia, Prolongación de la Avenida Baralt, Esquina de Dos Pilitas, Foro Libertador, Caracas, Venezuela.

MARTINO, Antonio; Italian politician and university lecturer; b. 22 Dec. 1944, Messina, Sicily; s. of Gaetano Martino; Lecturer in Monetary History and Politics, Chair. Faculty of Political Science, mem. Bd of Dirs Libera Università Internazionale degli Studi Sociali (LUISS), Rome; fmr mem. Liberal Party (PLI); joined Forza Italia party 1994, Parl. Deputy 1994–; Minister for Foreign Affairs 1994–95, of Defence 2001–06. *Address:* Forza Italia, Via dell'Umiltà 36, 00187 Rome, Italy (office). *Telephone:* (06) 67311 (office). *Fax:* (06) 6788255 (office). *E-mail:* lettere@forza-italia.it (office). *Website:* www.forza-italia.it (office).

MARTINO, HE Cardinal Renato Raffaele, JCD; Italian ecclesiastic; *President Emeritus, Pontifical Council for Justice and Peace;* b. 23 Nov. 1932, Salerno; ordained priest 1957; entered Diplomatic Service of the Holy See, serving in Nicaragua, the Philippines, Lebanon and Brazil 1962–80; Titular Archbishop of Segermes 1980; Apostolic Pro-Nuncio to Thailand and Singapore and Apostolic Del. to Laos and Malaysia 1980, Apostolic Del. to Brunei Darussalam 1983; Perm. Observer of the Holy See to the UN 1986–2002, participated in Conf. of Sustainable Devt, Rio de Janeiro, Brazil 1992, Conf. on Population Devt, Cairo, Egypt 1994, Summit on Women, Beijing, China 1995, Conf. on Sustainable Devt, Johannesburg, SA 2002; Pres. Pontifical Council for Justice and Peace 2002–09 (currently Pres. Emer.), Pontifical Council for Pastoral Care of Migrants and Itinerant Peoples 2006–09; cr. Cardinal (Cardinal-Deacon of S. Francesco di Paola ai Monti) 2003; participated in Papal Conclave April 2005; Grand Prior, Sacred Military Constantinian Order of St George 2010–; mem. Congregation for the Evangelization of Peoples, Pontifical Council Cor Unum, Admin of the Patrimony of the Apostolic See, Pontifical Comm. for Vatican City State; decorations from govts of Italy, Portugal, Thailand, Argentina, Venezuela, Lebanon; eight hon. doctorates. *Address:* Pontifical Council for Justice and Peace, Piazza S. Calisto 16, 00153 Rome, Italy. *Telephone:* (06) 69879911. *Fax:* (06) 69887205. *E-mail:* pcjustpax@justpeace.va.

MARTINON, David, DEA; French civil servant; *Spokesman for the President;* b. 13 May 1971, Leiden, Netherlands; ed Institut d'études politiques, École nationale d'administration; began career as communications officer, États généraux de l'opposition 1990; communications adviser, Acte Public Communication 1991–94, Ministry of Defence 1995–98; Deputy Spokesman, Ministry of Foreign Affairs 1998–2001; Diplomatic Adviser to Minister of the Interior, Nicolas Sarkozy 2002–04, 2005–07; served as Dir of Int. Relations, Union pour un Mouvement Populaire (UMP); Chief of Staff, presidential campaign of Nicolas Sarkozy 2006–07; Spokesman for the Pres. 2007–. *Address:* Palais de l'Élysée, 55 rue du faubourg Saint-Honoré, 75008 Paris, France (office). *Telephone:* 1-42-92-81-00 (office). *E-mail:* dmartinon@u-m-p.org (office). *Website:* www.elysee.fr (office).

MARTINS, Peter; American ballet director, choreographer and former dancer; *Ballet Master-in-Chief, New York City Ballet;* b. 27 Oct. 1946, Copenhagen, Denmark; m. 1st Lise la Cour (divorced 1973); one c.; m. 2nd Darci Kistler 1991; one d.; pupil of Vera Volkova and Stanley Williams with Royal Danish Ballet; Dir NY City Ballet; Teacher, School of American Ballet 1975, NY Ballet 1975, Ballet Master 1981–83, Co-Ballet Master-in-Chief 1983–89, Ballet Master-in-Chief 1989–; Artistic Adviser, Pa Ballet 1982–; mem. Royal Danish Ballet 1965–67, Prin. Dancer (including Bournonville repertory) 1967; Guest Artist, NY Ballet 1967–70, Prin. Dancer 1970–83; Guest Artist Regional Ballet Cos, USA, also Nat. Ballet, Canada, Royal Ballet, London, Grand Theatre, Geneva, Paris Opera, Vienna State Opera, Munich State Opera, London Festival Ballet, Ballet Int., Royal Danish Ballet; Dance magazine Award 1977; Cue's Golden Apple Award 1977, Award of Merit, Phila Art Alliance 1985. *Choreographed Broadway musicals include:* Dream of the Twins (co-choreographer) 1982, On your Toes 1982, Song and Dance 1985. *Choreographed works include:* Calcium Light Night 1977, Tricolore (Pas de Basque Section) 1978, Rossini Pas de Deux 1978, Tango-Tango (ice ballet) 1978, Dido and Aeneas 1979, Sonate di Scarlatti 1979, Eight Easy Pieces 1980, Lille Suite 1980, Suite from L'Histoire du Soldat 1981, Capriccio Italien 1981, The Magic Flute 1981, Symphony No. 1 1981, Délibes Divertissement 1982, Piano-Rag-Music 1982, Concerto for Two Solo Pianos 1982, Waltzes 1983, Rossini Quartets 1983, Tango 1983, A Schubertiad 1984, Mozart Violin Concerto 1984, Poulenc Sonata 1985, La Sylphide 1985, Valse Triste 1985, Eight More 1985, We Are the World 1985, Eight Miniatures 1985, Ecstatic Orange, Tanzspiel 1988, Jazz 1993, Symphonic Dances 1994, Barber Violin Concerto 1994, Mozart Piano Concerto (No. 17) 1994, X-Ray 1995. *Publication:* Far From Denmark (autobiog.) 1982. *Address:* New York City Ballet, New York State Theater, 20 Lincoln Center Plaza, New York, NY 10023, USA. *Telephone:* (212) 870-5567. *Website:* www.nycballet.com.

MARTINSON, Ida Marie, PhD; American nurse; *Professor Emerita, School of Nursing, University of California, San Francisco;* b. 8 Nov. 1936, Mentor, Minn.; m. Paul Martinson 1962; one s. one d.; ed St Luke's Hosp. School of Nursing, Duluth, Minn. and Univs of Minnesota and Illinois; Instructor in Tuberculosis Nursing, St Luke's Hosp., Duluth 1957–58; Instructor in Nursing, Thornton Jr Coll., Harvey, Ill. 1967–69; Asst Prof. and Chair. of Research, Univ. of Minn. School of Nursing 1972–74, Assoc. Prof. and Dir of Research 1974–77, Prof. and Dir of Research 1977–82; Prof. Dept of Family Health Care Nursing, Univ. of Calif., San Francisco 1982–2003, now Prof. Emer., Chair. 1982–89; Carl Walter and Margaret Davis Walter Visiting Prof. at Payne Bolton School of Nursing, Case Western Reserve Univ., Cleveland, Ohio 1994–96; Chair. and Prof., Dept of Health Sciences, Hong Kong Polytechnic Univ. 1996–2000, now Advisor, Hong Kong Polytechnic Univ. Honor Soc. of Nursing; Fellow, American Acad. of Nursing; mem. Inst. of Medicine, NAS 1981–, mem. Governing Council 1984–86; Pres. Children's Hospice Int. 1986–88; Co-founder of Children's Cancer Foundation, Taiwan; f. East Asia Forum of Nursing Schools (EAFONS); Sigma Theta Tau Int. Soc. of Nursing 1999. *Publications:* Home Care: A manual for implementation of home care for children dying of cancer 1978, Home Care: A manual for parents (with D. Moldow) 1979, Family Nursing 1989, Home Care Health Nursing 1989; more than 100 articles in journals, 56 book chapters (1994) and one film; ed. of several books on home and family nursing. *Leisure interests:* skiing, walking, reading. *Address:* Department of Family Health Care Nursing, Box 0606, 521 Parnassus Ave, Nursing 431Y, University of California, San Francisco, San Francisco, CA 94143-0606, USA (office). *Telephone:* (415) 476-4668 (office). *Fax:* (415) 753-2161 (office). *E-mail:* ida.martinson@nursing.ucsf.edu (office). *Website:* nurseweb.ucsf.edu/www/ix-fd.shtml (office).

MARTIROSSIAN, Radick Martirosovich, PhD, DeS; Armenian scientist, fmr university rector and academic; *Head of Chair, Department of Microwave Radiophysics and Telecommunications, Yerevan State University;* b. 1 May 1936, Madagis, Nagorno Karabakh; s. of Martiros A. Martirossian and Astkhik G. Harutunian; m. Rena A. Kasparova 1965, two s.; ed Yerevan State Univ. and Lebedev Physics Inst. of Acad. of Sciences, Moscow; Assoc. Prof., Yerevan State Univ. 1966–82, Prof. 1982–, Rector 1993–2006; Corresp. mem. Nat. Acad. of Sciences of Armenia 1986, Academician 1990, Pres. 2006–, fmr Dir Inst. of Radiophysics and Electronics, Adviser to the Dir 2006–; Order of the St Mesrop Mashtots, several orders and medals of Armenia and USSR; Armenian State Prize in Science and Eng 1988, Ukrainian State Prize 1989, Gagarin Medal for Space Research, Laureate of Armenian and Ukrainian State Prizes. *Publications:* numerous papers on quantum electronics, applied problems of superconductivity, space research, radio astronomy, radio physics research methods of remote sensing of Earth. *Leisure interest:* chess. *Address:* Faculty of Radiophysics, Yerevan State University, 1 Alex Manoogian Street, 0025 Yerevan, Armenia. *Telephone:* (10) 55-52-40. *Fax:* (10) 55-46-41. *E-mail:* radiophys@ysu.am. *Website:* www.ysu.am/faculties/en/Radiophysics/section/staff/person/280.

MARTO, Michel Issa, BSc, MA, PhD; Jordanian economist, banker and fmr government official; *Chairman, Housing Bank for Trade and Finance;* b. 21 Aug. 1940, Jerusalem; s. of Issa Marto; m. Lucy Peridakis 1970; one s. two d.; ed Middle East Tech. Univ., Turkey, Univ. of Southern California, Stanford Univ., USA; Dir Econ. Research, Central Bank of Jordan 1969–70, Deputy Gov. 1989–97; Dir Econ. Research, Royal Scientific Soc. 1970–75; economist, World Bank, Washington, DC 1975–77; Deputy Gen. Man. Jordan Fertilizer Industry 1977–79; Deputy Gen. Man. Bank of Jordan 1979–86, Man. Dir 1986–89; Chair. Jordanian Securities Comm. 1997–98; Minister of Finance 1998–2003; Chair. Housing Bank for Trade and Finance, Amman 2004–; Chevalier, Ordre nat. du Mérite, Commdr, Légion d'honneur; Al-Hussein Distinguished Service Medal, Jordanian Star Medal (First Class), Jordanian Independence Medal (First Class), Jordan Star Medal (Second Order), Jordan Star Medal (First Order), Omicron Delta Epsilon (Honor Soc. in Econs), USA, Phi Kappa Phi (Top Univ. Grad.), USA. *Publications include:* various articles on economic topics in specialist journals. *Leisure interests:* reading, music, theatre. *Address:* Housing Bank for Trade and Finance, Parliament Street, PO Box 7693, Amman 11118 (office); PO Box 2927, Amman 11118, Jordan. *Telephone:* (6) 5926745 (home). *Fax:* (6) 5678121 (office); (6) 5930718 (home). *E-mail:* michelmarto1@yahoo.com (home); info@hbtf.com.jo (office). *Website:* www.hbtf.com (office).

MARTONYI, János, PhD; Hungarian politician and lawyer; *Minister of Foreign Affairs;* b. 5 April 1944, Kolozsvár (now Cluj-Napoca, Romania); m.; one s. one d.; ed József Attila Univ., Szeged, City of London Coll., Hague Acad. of Int. Law, The Netherlands, Hungarian Acad. of Sciences; corp. lawyer 1969–79; Trade Sec., Brussels 1979–84; Head of Dept then Sr Head of Dept, Ministries of Foreign Trade and Trade 1984–89; Commr for Privatization 1989–90; State Sec., Ministry of Int. Econ. Relations 1990–91, Ministry of Foreign Affairs 1991–94, Minister of Foreign Affairs 1998–2002, 2010–; Pres. Council of the EU Jan.–June 2011; Lecturer, Faculty of Law and Public Admin, Eötvös Loránd Univ., Budapest 1987–90, Prof. 1990–97; Head of Inst. for Int. Trade Law and Head of Dept, József Attila Univ., Szeged 1997–2002; Visiting Prof., Coll. of Europe, Bruges, Belgium and Natolin, Poland 1995–98, Cen. European Univ., Budapest 1996; full-time Prof. and Man. Partner, Martonyi és Kajtár, Baker & McKenzie (law firm), Budapest office 2002–09; Chair. Nézőpont Inst., Budapest; Pres. Free Europe Centre for European Integration of the Fidesz Hungarian Civic Union; Perm. Guest of Fidesz Presidium; mem. Bd Perm. Arbitration Court of Hungarian Chamber of Commerce and Industry Exec. Bd Centre for European Studies (foundation of European People's Party based in Brussels), Batthyány Soc. of Profs, Advisory Bd Heti Válasz (weekly), Budapest Chamber of Attorneys, Hungarian Lawyers' Soc., European Acad. of Sciences and Arts; Commdr, Légion d'honneur, Grosses Goldenes Ehrenzeichen (Austria) 2000. *Publications:* numerous articles and essays in various languages in the fields of int. trade law, competition policy and competition law, European integration and community (European) law, global regulations, co-operation in Cen. Europe and int. politics. *Address:* Ministry of Foreign Affairs, 1027 Budapest, Bem rakpart 47, Hungary (office). *Telephone:* (1) 458-1000 (office). *Fax:* (1) 375-37-66 (office). *E-mail:* iroda.konz@kum.hu (office). *Website:* www.mfa.gov.hu (office); www.kormany.hu (office).

MARTORE, Gracia, BA, MBA; American business executive; *President and CEO, Gannett Company;* ed Wellesley Coll.; worked in banking industry 1973–85; joined Gannett as Asst Treas. 1985, Vice-Pres. in Treasury group 1993–98, added Investor Relations duties 1995–98, Treas. 1998–2003, Vice-Pres., Investor Relations 1998–2001, Sr Vice-Pres. of Finance 2001–03, Sr Vice-Pres. and Chief Financial Officer (CFO) 2003–05, mem. Man. Cttee 2003–, Exec. Vice-Pres. and CFO 2005–10, Pres. and COO 2010–11, mem. Bd of Dirs, Pres. and CEO Gannett Co., Inc. 2011–; mem. Bd of Dirs FM Global, MeadWestvaco Corpn 2012–; named by Institutional Investor magazine as one of the best CFOs in America and as the Best CFO in America in the publishing and advertising agencies category 2004, 2005, 2006, named CFO of the Year by Virginia Business 2006, ranked by Fortune magazine amongst the 50 Most Powerful Women in Business in the US (45th) 2012. *Address:* Gannett Co., 7950 Jones Branch Drive, McLean, VA 22107-0150, USA (office). *Telephone:* (703) 854-6000 (office). *Fax:* (703) 854-2053 (office). *E-mail:* info@gannett.com (office). *Website:* www.gannett.com (office).

MARTOWARDOJO, Agus, BA; Indonesian central banker and government official; *Governor, Bank Indonesia;* b. 24 Jan. 1956, Amsterdam, Netherlands; m.; two c.; ed Univ. of Indonesia; Int. Loan Officer, Bank of America, Jakarta 1984–86; Vice-Pres., Corp. Banking Group, Bank Niaga, Jakarta 1986–94; Deputy CEO Empress Holding 1994; Pres. Dir Bank Bumiputera 1995–98; Pres. Dir Export Import Bank of Indonesia 1998–02; Man. Dir of Risk Man. and Credit Restructuring, Bank Mandiri 1999–2000, Man. Dir of Retail Banking and Operations Coordinator 2000–01, Man. Dir of Human Resources and Support Services 2001–02, Pres. Dir 2005–10; Pres. Dir Bank Permata 2002–05; Minister of Finance and State Enterprises Devt 2010–13; also worked with Indonesian Bank Restructuring Agency 2002–05; Gov. Bank Indonesia (central bank) 2013–; Chair. Asscn of Nat. Commercial Banks Pvt. 2003–06; Pres. Bankers Club Indonesia 2000–03, Indonesia Bankers Asscn 2005; Best Indonesian Exec., Asiamoney 2006, Leadership Achievement Award, Asia Banker 2006, Top Banker, Majalah Investor 2007, Best CEO Warta Ekonomi magazine 2008, Top Banking Exec., Majalah Investor 2008. *Address:* Bank Indonesia, Jalan M. H. Thamrin 2, Jakarta Pusat 10350, Jakarta 10350, Indonesia (office). *Telephone:* (21) 2310108 (office). *Fax:* (21) 3501867 (office). *E-mail:* humasbi@bi.go.id (office). *Website:* www.bi.go.id (office).

MARTRE, Henri Jean François; French telecommunications and space engineer; b. 6 Feb. 1928, Bélesta; s. of Marius Martre and Paule Maugard; m. Odette Coppier 1953; three d.; ed Ecole Polytechnique; telecommunications engineer 1952–59; Deputy Head of telecommunications service in the production of armaments 1961–64, Head of Bureau Département Electronique, then Head Industrial Bureau of the Cen. Service of Telecommunications to the Ministerial Del. for Armaments 1964–66, Deputy Dir Industrial Affairs 1966, Dir of Programmes and Industrial Aspects of Armaments 1971–74, Gen. Engineer First Class for Armaments 1974, Gen. Del. for Armaments 1977–83, State Admin. Société Nat. Industrielle Aérospatiale 1974–77, also SNECMA, Société Française d'Equipements pour la Navigation Aérienne; mem. Atomic Energy Cttee 1977–83; Pres. and Dir-Gen. Société Aérospatiale 1983–92; Vice-Pres. Surveillance Council for the Airbus Industry 1986–92; Pres. Club d'information et de reflexion sur l'économie mondiale (Cirem) 1987–98, Asscn européenne des constructeurs de matériel aérospatial 1988 (Hon. Pres. 1988), Groupement des industries françaises aéronautiques et spatiales (Gifas) 1990–93, France-Japan Cttee 1991–, Edifrance 1992–94, Asscn Française de Normalisation (AFNOR) 1993–2002, Supervisory Bd

ESL Network 1996–; Vice-Pres., Supervisory Bd KLM; mem. Bd of Dirs Siemens-France 1994–99, Renault 1996–2009, France Telecom 2003–; Vice-Pres. Conseil de Surveillance de Bertin & Cie 1996, Pres. 1997–99; mem. Conseil supérieur de l'aviation marchande 1998–; Trustee Sogepa-Advisory Council Banque de France; Grand-Croix Légion d'honneur, Commdr. Ordre nat. du Mérite, Médaille de l'Aéronautique, Grand Officer Order of Merit (Germany), Order of the Crown (Belgium), Order of the Pole Star (Sweden), Commdr Legion of Merit (USA), Commdr White Rose (Finland), Order of Mil. Merit (Brazil), Order of the Sacred Treasure (Japan). *Leisure interests:* skiing, sailing. *Address:* 13 rue du Clos Fenquières, 75015 Paris, France (home). *Telephone:* 1-45-33-08-82 (office). *E-mail:* henri.martre@orange.fr (office).

MARTY, Martin E., MDiv, PhD, STM; American academic and ecclesiastic; *Fairfax M. Cone Distinguished Service Professor Emeritus of the History of Modern Christianity, Divinity School, University of Chicago;* b. 5 Feb. 1928, West Point, Neb.; s. of Emil A. Marty and Anne Louise Wuerdemann Marty; m. 1st Elsa Schumacher 1952 (died 1981); seven c.; m. 2nd Harriet Lindemann 1982; ed Concordia Seminary, St Louis, Lutheran School of Theology, Chicago and Univ. of Chicago; Lutheran Minister 1952–63; Prof. of History of Modern Christianity, Univ. of Chicago 1963–, Fairfax M. Cone Distinguished Service Prof. 1978–98, now Prof. Emer.; Assoc. Ed. The Christian Century 1956–85, Sr Ed. 1985–98; Sr Scholar-in-Residence, Park Ridge Center 1985, Pres. 1985–89; Pres. American Soc. of Church History 1971, American Catholic History Asscn 1981, American Acad. of Religion 1988; Dir Fundamentalism project, American Acad. of Arts and Sciences 1988–, The Public Religion Project 1996–99; Fellow, AAAS, Soc. of American Historians; more than 70 hon. degrees; Nat. Book Award for Righteous Empire 1972, Nat. Medal Humanities 1997, Medal of AAAS, Univ. of Chicago Alumni Medal, Distinguished Service Medal, Order of Lincoln Medallion. *Publications include:* Modern American Religion 1997, The One and the Many: America's Search for the Common Good 1998, The Mystery of the Child, Building Cultures of Trust; The Christian World: A Global History, Dietrich Bonhoeffer's Letters and Papers from Prison: A Biography 2011; collaborated with photographer Micah Marty in producing Places Along the Way, Our Hope for Years to Come, The Promise of Winter, When True Simplicity is Gained. *Leisure interests:* good eating, baroque music, calligraphy. *Address:* The University of Chicago Divinity School, 1025 East 58th Street, Swift Hall Chicago, IL 60637 (office); 175 East Delaware #85081, Chicago, IL 60611, USA (home). *Telephone:* (773) 702-8200 (office). *Fax:* (773) 702-6048 (office). *E-mail:* memarty@aol.com (home). *Website:* divinity .uchicago.edu/faculty/marty.shtml (office); www.illuminos.com.

MARTYNAU, Syarhey Mikalayevich; Belarusian politician and diplomatist; b. 22 Feb. 1953, Leninakan (Gyumri), Armenian SSR, USSR; m.; two s.; ed Moscow State Inst. of Int. Econ. Relations, USSR; with Dept of Int. Econ. Orgs, Ministry of Foreign Affairs, USSR 1975–80, Asst to Minister of Foreign Affairs 1980–88, Deputy Head Dept of Int. Orgs 1988–91; Deputy Perm. Rep. of Repub. of Belarus to UN, New York, 1991–92; Chargé d'Affaires, Washington, DC, 1992–93; Amb. to USA 1993–97; First Deputy Minister of Foreign Affairs 1997–2001; Amb. to Belgium, Head of Mission to EC and Head of Mission to NATO 2001–03; Minister of Foreign Affairs 2003–12; Vice-Chair. First Cttee (Int. Security and Disarmament) of UN Gen. Ass. 1988–97; fmr Vice-Pres. Amendment Conf. of the State Parties to the (1963) Treaty Banning Nuclear Tests in the Atmosphere in Outer Space and Under Water; three-times Chair. Nuclear Disarmament Group of UN Disarmament Comm., several-times Vice-Chair. and Rapporteur UN Disarmament Comm., Chair. 1998; Pres. Conf. on Disarmament, Geneva 2000; mem. UN Cttee on Econ., Cultural and Social Rights, Geneva 2001–; mem. Minsk Int. Educational Centre. *Address:* c/o Ministry of Foreign Affairs, 220030 Minsk, vul. Lenina 19, Belarus. *E-mail:* mail@mfa.gov.by.

MARURAI, Jim; Cook Islands politician; b. 1947; m. Tuainekore Au Tamariki Marurai (died 2005); ed Tereora Coll., Rarotonga, Otago Univ., NZ; Prime Minister 2004–10, also Minister of Educ. 1999, Human Resources and Police, Head of State Telecommunications and Information Broadcasting 2004, Minister of Foreign Affairs and Finance 2009–10, of Educ., Police Dept, Public Service Comm. and Nat. Environment Service 2010; MP for Ivirua; mem. Democratic Party. *Address:* Office of the Prime Minister, Private Bag, Rarotonga, Cook Islands (office). *Telephone:* 29301 (office). *Fax:* 20856 (office). *E-mail:* jmarurai@oyster.net.ck (office); rosita@ oyster.net.ck (office). *Website:* www.cook-islands.gov.ck (office).

MARUSIN, Yury Mikhailovich; Russian singer (tenor); b. 8 Dec. 1945, Kizel, Perm Region; ed Leningrad State Conservatory; soloist, Maly Opera and Ballet Theatre, Leningrad 1972–80; soloist, Mariinsky Theatre 1980–90; guest soloist, Wiener Staatsoper 1986–91; USSR State Prize 1985, Best Foreign Singer Diploma (Italy) 1982, People's Artist of USSR 1983. *Repertoire includes:* over 50 parts in operas. *Address:* IMC Artists Management Inc., 51 MacDougal Street, Suite 300, New York, NY 10012, USA. *Telephone:* (212) 560-2221 (office). *E-mail:* imcartist@ onebox.com (office).

MARUSTE, Rait, PhD; Estonian judge and politician; b. 27 Sept. 1953, Pärnu; s. of Albert Maruste and Mare Maruste; m. 1st Mare Maruste (née Nurk) 1976; one s. one d.; m. 2nd Elisabet Fura'ga; ed Pärnu Jaagupi Secondary School, Tartu Univ., University of Leningrad; Lecturer, Faculty of Law, Tartu Univ. 1977–85, Docent 1985–92, Head of Dept of Criminal Law and Procedure 1991; cand. for doctorate 1991–93; studies abroad at HEUNI, Finland, 1991, Abo Akademi Univ., Finland 1991, Max Planck-Inst., Freiburg, Germany 1991, Univ. of Cambridge, UK 1992, Max Planck Inst., Heidelberg, Germany 1995, Centre For Advanced Studies, Oslo, Norway 2001; Chief Justice of Supreme Court 1992–98, Chair. (ex-officio) Constitutional Review Chamber 1998–; Judge (Section IV), European Court of Human Rights (ECHR) 1998–2010; mem. Estonian Reform Party 2010–; Chair. and Founding mem. Estonian Academic Law Soc., Bd of Estonian Law Centre Foundation, 1995–1998; mem. Int. Soc. for the Reform of Criminal Law, Estonian Working Group for Accession to ECHR, Editorial Bd of law journal Juridica 1993–1998, Comm. of Europe Drafting Cttee on Status of Judges in Europe 1998, Int. Justice in the World Prize Jury 2001–; Order of the White Star (Second Class) 1999. *Publications include:* (in Estonian): Human Rights and Principles of Fair Trial 1993, Constitution and Its Review 1997, Psychology (with Talis Bachmanniga) 2003, Constitutionalism and the Protection of Fundamental Rights and Freedoms 2004; more than 100 articles in journals. *Leisure interests:* sailing, skiing. *Address:* Estonian Reform Party, Tõnismägi 9, Tallinn 10119 (office); Pikk

Str. 94, Apt. 27, 2400 Tartu, Estonia (home). *Telephone:* 680-80-80 (office). *E-mail:* info@raitmaruste.ee; info@reform.ee. *Website:* www.reform.ee/search/gss/ Rait%20Maruste (office); www.raitmaruste.ee.

MARX, Anthony W., BA, MA, PhD; American political scientist, academic and university administrator; *President, Amherst College;* m. Karen Barkey; one s. one d.; ed Wesleyan, Yale and Princeton Univs; Co-founder Khanya Coll., SA 1984; Asst to Pres. of Univ. of Pennsylvania 1981–84; Prof. of Political Science, Columbia Univ., New York 1990–2003, Co-Dir Center for Historical Social Studies, Faculty Dir Masters of Int. Affairs, Dir Undergraduate Studies and of Dept's Honors Program, Co-founder Columbia Urban Educators Program 2001, Dir Mellon Foundation's Sawyer Seminar on Democracy and Inequality 2001–02; Pres. Amherst Coll. 2003–11; Pres. and CEO-elect New York Public Library 2011–; consultant to UNDP 1991; Fellow, US Inst. of Peace 1992–93, Nat. Humanities Center 1997–98, Howard Foundation, Harry Frank Guggenheim Foundation 1994, John Simon Guggenheim Fellow 1997; Ralph Bunche Award, American Political Science Asscn 1999, Barrington Moore Award, American Sociological Asscn 2000. *Publications include:* Lessons of Struggle: South African Internal Opposition 1960–1990 1992, Making Race and Nation: A Comparison of the United States, South Africa and Brazil 1998, Faith in Nation: Exclusionary Origins in Nationalism 2002; numerous articles. *Address:* Office of the President, Amherst College, 103 Converse Hall, AC #2208, PO Box 5000, Amherst, MA 01002-5000, USA (office). *Telephone:* (413) 542-2234 (office). *Fax:* (413) 542-2621 (office). *E-mail:* president@amherst.edu (office); cchavez@amherst.edu (office). *Website:* www.amherst.edu (office).

MARX, HE Cardinal Reinhard, DTh; German ecclesiastic; *Archbishop of Munich and Freising;* b. 21 Sept. 1953, Geseke, North Rhine-Westphalia; ordained priest, Diocese of Paderborn 1979; Auxiliary Bishop of Paderborn 1996–2001; Titular Bishop of Petina 1996–2001; Bishop of Trier 2001–07; Archbishop of Munich and Freising 2007–; Chair. Cttee for Social Issues at German Bishops' Conf.; cr. Cardinal (Cardinal-Priest of San Corbiniano) 2010; participated in Papal Conclave 2013. *Publication:* Das Kapital: A Plea for Man 2008. *Address:* Archdiocese of Munic and Freising, Postfach 330360, Rochusstrasse 5–7, 80063 Munich, Germany (office). *Telephone:* (89) 21370 (office). *Fax:* (89) 21371585 (office). *E-mail:* info@erzbistum-muenchen.de (office). *Website:* www.erzbistum -muenchen.de (office).

MARY, Sister Avelin, PhD, FIBR, FLS; Indian RC nun and marine biologist; *Director, Sacred Heart Marine Research Centre;* b. 5 May 1942, Sawyerpuram, Tuticorin dist, Tamil Nadu; d. of M. P. Raj and Annapooranam; ed Marathwada Univ., Aurangabad, postdoctoral research at NewYork Aquarium and Osborn Laboratories of Marine Science, New York, USA; Asst Prof. in Zoology 1977; postdoctoral position, New York Aquarium 1985; involved in bioactive marine natural products research 1986–; Reader, Zoology, St Mary's Coll., Tuticorin 1993–97, Prin. 1997–2000; research collaboration with Poseidon Ocean Sciences, New York 1994–; Visiting Scientist working on research projects in biofouling (biological coating acquired on ships during years at sea) at Duke Univ. Marine Lab., Univ. of Delaware, Fu Jen Univ., Taiwan, Tulane Univ., Univ. of Hawaii; Founder, Sacred Heart Marine Research Centre, Tuticorin, India 1991, Dir of Research 2000–; RC nun belonging to Congregation of Mother of Sorrows, Servants of Mary; Scientist of the Year, Nat. Environmental Science Acad. (NESA) 2002, Netaji Subhash Chandra Bose Nat. Award for Excellence, Jagruthi Kiran Foundation 2003, Best Citizen of India Award, International Publishing House, New Delhi 2009. *Achievements include:* has isolated 12 active compounds from Indian Ocean soft coral as non-toxic antifoulants. *Publications:* numerous scientific papers on marine biology. *Leisure interests:* reading, computer art design. *Address:* Office of the Director, Sacred Heart Marine Research Centre, St Mary's College Campus, Tuticorin 628 001, Tamil Nadu, India (office). *Telephone:* (461) 2325400 (office); 94-43323491 (mobile); (461) 2321896 (home). *E-mail:* info@poseidonsciences .com (office); avelinmary@yahoo.com (home). *Website:* www.poseidonsciences.com/ shmrc.html (office).

MARZOUKI, Moncef, PhD; Tunisian physician, academic, human rights activist and politician; *Interim President;* b. 7 July 1945, Grombalia; s. of Mohammed al-Badawi and Aziza Marzouki bin Karim; divorced; two d.; m. 2nd Beatrix Rhein 2011; ed Univ. of Strasbourg, France; f. Centre for Community Medicine, Sousse 1979; Prof. of Community Medicine, Sousse Univ. 1981–2000; mem. Ligue tunisienne des droits de l'homme (human rights org.) 1980, Vice-Pres. 1987, Pres. 1989–92 (org. banned); Founding mem. Nat. Cttee for the Defence of Prisoners of Conscience 1993 (resgnd), jailed for four months 1994, went into exile in France; Pres. Arab Comm. for Human Rights, Cairo 1996–2000; Lecturer, Univ. of Paris 2001; Leader, Congress for the Republic (opposition group) 2001–11 (banned 2002, legalized 2011); returned from exile after fall of Zine al-Abidine Ben Ali 2011; Interim Pres. of Tunisia Dec. 2011–. *Publications include:* Dictateurs en sursis: Une voie démocratique pour le monde arabe 2009. *Address:* Office of the President, Palais de Carthage, 2016 Carthage, Tunisia (office). *Website:* www .carthage.tn (office).

MAS-COLELL, Andreu, PhD; Spanish economist and academic; *Minister of Economy and Knowledge, Government of Catalonia;* b. 29 June 1944, Barcelona; m.; three c.; ed Univs of Barcelona and Valladolid, Univ. of Minnesota, USA; Profesor Ayudante, Univ. of Madrid 1966–68; Asst Research Economist, Univ. of California, Berkeley, USA 1972–75, Asst Prof. of Econs and Math. 1975–77, Assoc. Prof. 1975–78, Prof. 1979–81, Research Fellow, Math. Sciences Research Inst. and Ford Visiting Prof. 1985–86; Visiting Scholar, Univ. of Bonn, Germany 1976–77; Visiting Prof., Autonomous Univ. of Barcelona 1981–82; Visiting Prof., Pompeu Fabra Univ. 1993, Prof. of Econs 1995–, Head of Dept of Econs and Business 1997–; Prof. of Econs, Harvard Univ. 1981–95 (first Louis Berkman Prof. of Econs 1988); Commr for Univs and Research, Generalitat de Catalunya 1999–2000; Minister of Univs, Research and the Information Society, Generalitat de Catalunya 2000–03; Sec.-Gen. European Research Council 2009–10; Minister of Economy and Knowledge, Govt of Catalonia 2010–; mem. Council Econometric Soc. 1982–89, Exec. Cttee 1986–94, Second Vice-Pres. 1991, First Vice-Pres. 1992, Pres. 1993; Ed. Journal of Mathematical Economics 1985–89 (mem. Advisory Bd 1989–), Econometrica 1988–92; Assoc. Ed. Journal of Economic Theory 1975–80, SIAM Journal of Applied Mathematics 1977–80, Journal of Mathematical Economics 1977–85, Econometrica 1978–84, Revista Española de Economía 1984–90, Economic Theory 1990–94, Mathematics of Social Sciences 1990–97, Games and Economic Behavior 1993–95, Theoretical Economics 2006–08; mem. Advisory Council, Economic Notes 1990–94; mem. Advisory Bd, International Journal of Game Theory 1999–2003, Mathematics and Financial Economics 2006–09; mem. or chair. of numerous advisory panels and cttees; mem. Institut d'Estudis Catalans 2005, Real Academia de Ciencias Morales y Políticas 2007, Academia Europaea 2009; Foreign Assoc. NAS 1997; Fellow, American Acad. of Arts and Sciences 1985, Econometric Soc. 1978, Soc. for the Advancement of Econ. Theory 2011; Foreign Hon. mem. American Econ. Asscn 1997; Creu de Sant Jordi of the Generalitat de Catalunya, 2006; Dr hc (Alicante) 1992, (Toulouse) 2002, (HEC, Paris) 2005, (Universidad Nacional del Sur, Argentina) 2007 Sloan Fellow 1978–80, Guggenheim Fellow 1985–86, recipient of NSF grants 1978–79, 1981–84, 1985–87, 1992–95 and grants from Spanish Educ. Sec. 1996–99, Fisher-Schultz Lecturer, Cambridge World Meeting of the Econometric Soc. 1985, King Juan Carlos Prize in Econs 1988, Narcís Monturiol Medal for Scientific Merit, Generalitat de Catalunya 1990, Fundació Catalana per a la Recerca Science Prize (co-recipient) 1994, Walras-Bowley Lecturer, North American Summer Meeting of the Econometric Soc. 1997, Spanish Nat. Research Prize in Social Sciences Pascual Madoz 2006, Co-ordinator of Consolider Award, Ministry of Educ. and Science 2006, Cercle d'Economia Prize 2008, Reconeixement CECOT al Progrés Empresarial 2008, Prof. Luigi Tartufari Int. Prize for Econ. Sciences, Accad. Nazionale dei Lincei (co-recipient) 2009, Prize of Fundación BBVA Fronteras del Conocimiento en Economía, Finanzas y Gestión de Empresas (co-recipient) 2009. *Publications include:* trans. into Spanish of G. Debreu's Theory of Value (with J. Oliu) 1974, Non-cooperative Approaches to the Theory of Perfect Competition (ed.) 1982, The Theory of General Economic Equilibrium: A Differentiable Approach 1985, Contributions to Mathematical Economics, in Honor of Gérard Depardieu (co-ed.) 1986, Equilibrium Theory and Applications (co-ed.) 1991, Microeconomic Theory (with M. Whinston and J. Green) 1995, Cooperation: Game Theoretic Approaches (co-ed.) 1997, Nuevas Fronteras de la Política Económica (co-ed.) 1998, Higher Aspirations: An Agenda for Reforming European Universities (co-author) 2008; 128 articles in learned journals. *Address:* Department of Economics and Business, Pompeu Fabra University, Ramon Trias Fargas 25–27, 08005 Barcelona, Spain (office). *Telephone:* (93) 5422498 (office). *Fax:* (93) 5421223 (office). *E-mail:* andreu.mas-colell@upf.edu (office). *Website:* www.econ.upf.edu/~mcolell/ en (office).

MAS I GAVARRÓ, Artur; Spanish politician; *President, Government of Catalonia;* b. 1956, Barcelona; m.; three c.; ed Liceu Francès de Barcelona, L'Escola Aula, Faculties of Law and Econs, Univ. of Barcelona (degree in Econs and Business Science); Councillor, Barcelona City Council 1987–95, acted as Econ. Affairs Spokesman and Spokesman and Pres. Municipal Group of CiU; mem. Parl. of Catalonia 1995–; fmr Minister for Public Works, then Minister for Economy and Finance, then Chief Minister; Pres. Govt of Catalonia 2010–; Pres. Convergència Democràtica de Catalunya 1997–, Convergència i Unió 2000–. *Leisure interest:* French literature. *Address:* Palau de la Generalitat, Plaça St Jaume 4, 08002 Barcelona, Spain (office).

MASAKADZA, Hamilton; Zimbabwean professional cricketer; b. 9 Aug. 1983, Harare; right-handed batsman; occasional right-arm leg-break bowler; plays for Manicaland (Easterns) 1999–2001, 2007–, Zimbabwe 2001–, Mashonaland (Northerns) 2001–02, Matabeleland (Westerns) 2003–04, Mountaineers; First-class debut: 1999/2000; Test debut: Zimbabwe v West Indies, Harare 27–31 July 2001; One-Day Int. (ODI) debut: Zimbabwe v S Africa, Bulawayo 23 Sept. 2001; T20I debut: Bangladesh v Zimbabwe, Khulna 28 Nov. 2006. *Achievements include:* first black Zimbabwean to score a first-class century 2000; youngest player up until then to make a century (119 runs against the West Indies) on Test debut July 2001; first Zimbabwean to have two ODI scores of more than 150. *Address:* c/o Zimbabwe Cricket, Harare, Zimbabwe. *E-mail:* info@zimcricket.org. *Website:* www .zimcricket.org.

MASANGU MULONGO, Jean-Claude, BSc, MBA; Democratic Republic of the Congo economist and central banker; *Governor, Banque Centrale du Congo;* b. 8 Aug. 1953, Jadotville, Likasi, Katanga Prov.; s. of Jacques Masangu Mwanza and Antoinette Mwamba Monga; m. Irène Kayembe Maloba; ed Ecole Internationale, Geneva, Switzerland, Worcester Polytechnic Inst., USA, Louisiana State Univ.; began career as mechanical engineer with Consolidated Aluminum Corpn, USA; 17 years with Citibank, Kinshasa, positions include Sec.-Gen. responsible for Financial Man., Human Resources, Credit Admin and Legal Services 1988–91, Commercial Dir responsible for Man. of Multinationals, Deputy Gen. Man. 1992–93, Man. Dir 1993–97; Gov. Banque Centrale du Congo 1997–; Pres. Social Cttee, Asscn Congolaise des Banques (ACB) 1990, ACB Vice-Pres. 1993; Pres. Club Service Fifty-One Int. (non-profit org.). *Publication:* Pourquoi je crois au progrès de l'Afrique 2009. *Address:* Office of the Governor, Banque Centrale du Congo, 563 blvd Colonel Tshatshi au nord, BP 2697, Kinshasa, Democratic Republic of the Congo (office). *Telephone:* 818105970 (mobile) (office). *Fax:* (12) 8805152 (office). *E-mail:* webmaster@bcc.cd (office). *Website:* www.bcc.cd (office).

MASÁR, Vladimír, Ing.; Slovak fmr central banker; *Chairman, Deloitte Slovakia;* b. 2 May 1958, Partizánske; s. of Vladimír Masár and Jolana Masárová; m. Dagmar Glasová 1983; one s. two d.; ed Univ. of Econs Bratislava; State Bank of Czechoslovakia 1981–90; Deputy Dir City Br., Gen. Credit Bank 1990–91; Dir Credit Dept Tatra Bank-Slovakia 1992; State Sec. Ministry of Finance of Slovakia 1992; Gov. Nat. Bank of Slovakia 1993–99; Chair. Deloitte Slovakia 2000–. *Leisure interests:* swimming, tennis. *Address:* Deloitte Slovakia, Apollo BC, Prievozská 2/ B, 821 09 Bratislava, Slovakia (office). *Telephone:* (2) 5824-9130 (office). *Fax:* (2) 5824-9222 (office). *E-mail:* vmasar@deloittece.com (office). *Website:* www.deloitte .sk (office).

MASARSKY, Mark Veniaminovich, CandPhilSc; Russian business executive and journalist; b. 19 June 1940, Muryinskoye, Novgorod Region; m. Olga Yevgen'yevna Fedosova; one s. one d.; ed Rostov Univ.; teacher, Taganrog Radio-Tech. Inst. 1965–67, Rostov Univ. 1967–70, Khabarovsk Polytechnical Inst. 1970–75; Corresp. Young Communist 1977–82; f. and mem. Gold-diggers of Petchora co-operative 1982–87; f. and Chair. Volkhov Jt-stock co. 1987–, Russian Gold co.; one of founders of Moscow Commodity Exchange; Pres. Int. Asscn of Factory Leaders 1992–2001; Chair. Entrepreneurs Council, Moscow Govt 1996–; mem. Bd Dirs Russian Bank of Reconstruction and Devt, Novobank Volkhov-

Presnaya Investment Co., ITAR-TASS Co.; mem. Expert-Analytical Council to Pres. Yeltsin; mem. Conciliatory Comm. on Public Accord Agreement; mem. Bd Public Chamber, Pres.'s Admin. *Publications:* The Convincing, Time of Orders and Times of Troubles. *Address:* Entrepreneurs Council, Moscow Government, Novy Arbat 36, Moscow, Russia. *Telephone:* (495) 290-87-04.

MASCARENHAS GOMEZ MONTEIRO, António Manuel; Cape Verde politician and lawyer; m. Maria Monteiro 1967; one s. two d.; ed Univ. of Lisbon, Univ. of Coimbra, Catholic Univ. Louvain, Belgium; Asst and researcher, Inter-university Centre Public Law, Belgium 1974–77; Sec.-Gen. Nat. Ass. 1977–80; Judge of Supreme Court 1980–90; Pres. of Cape Verde 1991–2001; f. Asscns of Magistrates of Cape Verde 1977; Pres. Third Conference on Regional System of Human Rights Protection in Africa, America and Europe, Strasbourg 1992; mem. OAU Mission to Angola 1992; Pres. Colloquium on Constitutional Transition in Africa at Catholic Univ. Louvain 1993; Presidential Medal of Freedom 1991. *Publications:* Reflexions sur la compétence d'un gouvernement démissionaire 1977, La notion de l'expédition des affaires courantes 1977, La Charte Africaine des Droits de l'Homme et des Peuples 1991. *Address:* c/o Presidência da República, C.P. 100, Praia, Santiago, Cape Verde.

MASCHLER, Thomas Michael; British publisher; b. 16 Aug. 1933, Berlin, Germany; s. of Kurt Leo Maschler and Rita Masseron; m. 1st Fay Coventry 1970 (divorced 1987); one s. two d.; m. 2nd Regina Kulinicz 1988; ed Leighton Park School, Reading; Production Asst, André Deutsch 1955–56; Ed., MacGibbon and Kee 1956–58; Fiction Ed., Penguin Books 1958–60; Editorial Dir, Jonathan Cape Ltd 1960–70, Man. Dir 1960, Chair. 1970–91, Publr 1991; Dir Random House 1987. *Film:* The French Lieutenant's Woman (assoc. producer) 1981. *Publications include:* Declarations (ed.) 1957, New English Dramatists series (ed.) 1959–63, Publisher (memoir) 2005. *Address:* c/o Jonathan Cape Ltd, Random House, 20 Vauxhall Bridge Road, London, SW1V 2SA, England.

MASEFIELD, (John) Thorold, KStJ, CMG, MA; British diplomatist; b. 1 Oct. 1939, Kampala, Uganda; s. of Dr Geoffrey Bussell Masefield and Mildred Joy Thorold Rogers; m. Jennifer Mary Trowell MBE 1962; two s. one d. (and one d. deceased); ed Repton School, Derbyshire, St John's Coll. Cambridge; joined Commonwealth Relations Office 1962, Pvt. Sec. to Perm. Under-Sec. 1963–64, Second Sec. Kuala Lumpur 1964–65, Warsaw 1966–67, FCO 1967–69, First Sec. UK Del. to Disarmament Conf., Geneva 1970–74, Deputy Head Planning Staff. FCO 1974–77, Far Eastern Dept 1977–79, Counsellor, Head of Chancery, Consul-Gen. Islamabad 1979–82, Head Personnel Services Dept FCO 1982–85, Head Far Eastern Dept 1985–87, Fellow Center for Int. Affairs, Harvard Univ. 1987–88, Resident Chair. Civil Service Selection Bd 1988–89; High Commr in Tanzania 1989–92; Asst Under-Sec. of State for S and SE Asia and the Pacific, FCO 1992–94; High Commr in Nigeria 1994–97 (also Accred to Benin and Chad); Gov. and C-in-C of Bermuda 1997–2001; Chair. Brockenhurst Parish Council 2007–10. *Leisure interests:* fruit and vegetables. *Address:* c/o Foreign and Commonwealth Office, Whitehall, London, SW1A 2AH, England.

MASEKELA, Hugh; South African musician (trumpet); b. 1939, nr Johannesburg; ed Guildhall School of Music, London, Manhattan School of Music, New York; co-f. The Jazz Epistles 1959; fmrly in voluntary exile from early 1960s, in UK, USA, Ghana, Nigeria, Guinea and Botswana; f. Botswana Int. School of Music 1986; Musical Dir Graceland; Order of Ikhamanga 2010; Kora All African Music Award for Best Male Artist in Southern Africa 2005. *Compositions include:* wrote Sarafina (Broadway musical). *Recordings include:* Grrr 1966, The Promise of a Future 1968, Masekela 1968, Home is Where the Music Is (with Dudu Pukwana) 1972, The African Connection 1973, Techno Bush 1984, I Am Not Afraid (with Hedzoleh Soundz), Tomorrow 1987, Beatin' Aroun De Bush 1992, Stimela 1994, Reconstruction 1994, Black to the Future 1998, Boys Doin' It 1998, Sixty 2000, Time 2002, Still Grazing 2004, Revival 2005, Phola 2009, Jabulani 2010, Friends 2012. *Publication:* Still Grazing: The Musical Journey of Hugh Masekela 2003. *Address:* c/o John Cumming, Serious Ltd, 51 Kingsway Place, Sans Walk, Clerkenwell, London, EC1R 0LU, England (office). *Telephone:* (82) 8818565 (office); (20) 7324-1880 (office). *E-mail:* josh@88.co.za (office); john.cumming@ serious.org.uk (office). *Website:* www.hughmasekela.co.za (office); www.serious .org.uk (office).

MASEKO, Zola; South African film director; b. 1967; ed Nat. Film and TV School, Beaconsfield, England; born and raised in exile, Tanzania and Swaziland; joined Umkhonto We Sizwe (armed wing of African Nat. Congress) 1987; made first documentary Dear Sunshine 1992; returned to S Africa 1994; developed three-part tv series Homecoming 2005; joined Pistoleros Films 2005. *Films directed include:* The Foreigner (also writer) 1997, The Life and Times of Sarah Baartman 1998, The Return of Sarah Baartman 2002, Children of the Revolution 2002, A Drink in the Passage (Special Jury Award, Fespaco) 2002, Drum (also writer, Etalon d'Or de Yennenga Award Fespaco 2005) 2004. *Address:* Pistoleros Films, 5 Wandel Street Gardens, Cape Town 8001, South Africa (office). *Telephone:* (21) 4614336 (office). *Website:* www.pisoleros.co.za (office).

MASERA, Rainer Stefano, DPhil; Italian economist, academic and banker; *Dean of Economics Faculty and Professor of Political Economy, Università degli Studi Guglielmo Marconi;* b. 6 May 1944, Como; s. of Francesco Masera; m. Giovanna Aveta; two s. two d.; ed Univ. 'La Sapienza', Rome, Univ. of Oxford, UK; Exec. Officer, BIS, Basle 1971–75; mem. Bd 1975–88; mem. staff, then Head of Int. Dept, Research Dept, Bank of Italy 1975–77, Head of Research Dept 1982–84, Cen. Dir for Econs Research 1985–88; Alt. mem. EEC Monetary Cttee 1977–81; Man. Dir Istituto Mobiliare Italiano (IMI) SpA 1988–98; Minister for the Budget and Econ. Planning 1995–96; CEO Grupo SanPaolo IMI SpA, Turin 1998–2001, Chair. 2001–04; Chair. Banca Fideuram, Rome 2003–04; Chair. Rete Ferroviaria Italiana SpA 2004–07; Strategic Int. Advisor and Sr Dir, Mercer Oliver Wyman 2004–07; Chair. Advisory Cttee, SACE, Rome 2004–07; Man. Dir and Chair. Financial Inst. Group, Lehman Brothers (Italy), Rome 2007–08; Chief of Italian Del. of Frano-Italian Govt Cttee for the new Turin-Lyon railway link 2005–12; Expert mem. Bd, European Investment Bank 2001–13; Chair. Banca delle Marche SpA; mem. Bd of Dirs Colacem SpA; Chair. Advisory Cttee, Financial Man. of Fondazione Roma; Dean of Econs Faculty and Prof. of Political Economy, Università degli Studi Guglielmo Marconi, Rome; apptd one of the five 'wise men' for the review of the Lamfalussy process (IIMG) 2007; mem. de Larosière Group 2009; Cavaliere di

Gran Croce of the Italian Repub. 1996, Cavaliere del Lavoro 2002, Officier, Légion d'honneur 2003; Dr hc (Turin) 2001. *Publications:* L'Unificazione Monetaria e lo SME 1980, A European Central Bank 1989, International Monetary and Financial Integration 1988, Prospects for the European Monetary System 1990, Intermediari, Mercati e Finanza d'Impresa 1991. *Leisure interests:* tennis, skiing. *Address:* Department of Economic and Business Sciences, Università degli Studi Guglielmo Marconi, Via Plinio 44, 00193 Rome, Italy (office). *Telephone:* (06) 377251 (office). *Fax:* (06) 37725214 (office). *E-mail:* info@marconiuniversity.org (office). *Website:* www.marconiuniversity.org (office).

MASERI, Attilio, MD, FRCP; Italian cardiologist; *President, Heart Care Foundation;* b. 12 Nov. 1935, Udine; s. of Adriano Maseri and Antonietta Albini; m. Countess Francesca Maseri Florio di Santo Stefano Filippo 1960 (died 2000); one s.; ed Classical Lycée Cividale, Padua Univ. Medical School; Research Fellow Univ. of Pisa 1960–65, Columbia Univ., New York, USA 1965–66, Johns Hopkins Univ., Baltimore, USA 1966–67; Asst Prof., Univ. of Pisa 1967–70, Prof. of Internal Medicine 1970, Prof. of Cardiovascular Pathophysiology, Prof. of Medicine (Locum) 1972–79, Sir John McMichael Prof. of Cardiovascular Medicine, Royal Postgraduate Medical School, Hammersmith Hosp., Univ. of London 1979–91; Prof. of Cardiology and Dir Inst. of Cardiology, Catholic Univ. of Rome 1991–; Pres. Italian Fed of Cardiology 2004–07; Pres. Heart Care Foundation 2008–; Life mem. Johns Hopkins Soc. of Scholars; Fellow, American Coll. of Cardiology; Kt of Malta; Gold Medal Culture and Science from Pres. of the Italian Repub. 2004; Gold Medal of Merit for Public Health Service 2010; King Faisal Int. Prize 1992, Distinguished Scientist Award, American Coll. of Cardiology 1996, Invernizzi Prize for Medicine 1998, European Soc. of Cardiology Gold Medal Award 2002, Grand Prix Scientifique Fondation Lefoulon-Delalande, Institut de France 2004. *Publications:* Myocardial Blood Flow in Man 1972, Primary and Secondary Angina 1977, Perspectives on Coronary Care 1979, Ischaemic Heart Disease 1995; articles in major int. cardiological and medical journals. *Leisure interests:* skiing, tennis, sailing, wine. *Address:* Via Zandonai 9–11, 00194 Rome (home); Heart Care Foundation, Via La Marmora 36, 50121 Florence, Italy (office). *Telephone:* (055) 5101367 (office). *Fax:* (055) 5101360 (office). *E-mail:* amaseri@heartcarefound.org (office); heartcarefound@heartcarefound.org (office). *Website:* www.anmco.it/PerIlTuoCuore/ (office).

MASHEKE, Gen. Malimba; Zambian politician and army officer; b. 1941; fmr Army Commdr; Minister of Defence 1985–88, of Home Affairs 1988–89; Prime Minister of Zambia 1989–91; fmr Chair. United Nat. Independence Party (UNIP); currently Chair. Interreligious and Int. Fed. for World Peace (IIFWP), Zambia chapter; mem. Forum for Democracy and Devt. *Address:* c/o United National Independence Party (UNIP), POB 30302, Lusaka, Zambia.

MASHELKAR, Raghunath Anant, PhD, FRS; Indian research scientist and academic; *National Research Professor, National Chemical Laboratory;* b. 1 Jan. 1943, Mashel, Goa; m. Vaishali R. Mashelkar; one s. two d.; ed Univ. of Bombay; Dir Gen. Council of Scientific and Industrial Research 1995–2006; currently Nat. Research Prof., Nat. Chemical Lab.; Pres. Global Research Alliance; mem. Bd of Dirs Reliance Industries Ltd, GeneMedix Life Sciences Ltd, ICICI Knowledge Park, Thermax Ltd, Piramal Enterprises Ltd, KPIT Technologies Ltd, Tata Motors Ltd 2007–; Chair. Nat. Innovation Foundation, Reliance Innovation Council, Thermax Innovation Council, KPIT Innovation Council, Marico Innovation Foundation; Chair. Standing Cttee on Information Tech., WIPO; mem. Int. Intellectual Property Rights Comm. of UK Govt; Vice-Chair. WHO Comm. in Intellectual Property Rights, Innovation and Public Health (CIPIH); fmr mem. Scientific Advisory Council to the Prime Minister, Scientific Advisory Cttee to the Cabinet; has chaired 12 high-powered cttees set up to look into issues of higher educ., nat. auto fuel policy, overhauling the Indian drug regulatory system, dealing with the menace of spurious drugs, reforming Indian agriculture research system, etc.; consultant for restructuring publicly funded R&D insts world-wide, especially in S Africa, Indonesia and Croatia; fmr Pres. Indian Nat. Science Acad., Inst. of Chemical Engineers (UK); Foreign Assoc., NAS 2005; Assoc. Foreign mem. American Acad. of Arts and Sciences 2011; only the third Indian engineer to have been elected Fellow of the Royal Soc., London in 20th century 1998; Fellow, Royal Acad. of Eng (UK) 1996, World Acad. of Art and Science (USA) 2000; Foreign Fellow, US Nat. Acad. of Eng 2003, Australian Technological Science and Eng Acad. 2008; hon. doctorates from 30 univs, including Hon. DSc (Salford, UK) 1993, (Kanpur) 1995, (Indian School of Mines) 1997, (Bundelkhand Univ.) 2000, (Guwahati Univ.) 2000, (Anna Univ.) 2000, (Univ. of London) 2001, (Univ. of Wisconsin) 2002, (Banaras Hindu Univ.) 2002, (Allahabad Univ.) 2002, (MS Univ. of Baroda) 2003, (Kalyani Univ.) 2004), (Pretoria), (Delhi); more than 50 honours, awards and medals, including Shanti Swarup Bhatnagar Prize 1982, 2001, UDCT Outstanding Alumni Medal 1985, Fed. of Indian Chambers of Commerce and Industry Award 1987, Pandit Jawaharlal Nehru Tech. Award 1991, G.D. Birla Scientific Research Award 1993, Goyal Prize 1996, named by Business India as being among the "50 path-breakers in the post-independent India" 1997, JRD Tata Corp. Leadership Award (first scientist) 1998, appeared on cover of Business India as CEO of CSIR Inc. 1999, Padma Bhushan from Pres. of India 2000, Material Scientist of Year Award 2000, IMC Juran Quality Medal 2002, HRD Excellence Award 2002, Lal Bahadur Shastri Nat. Award for Excellence in Public Admin and Man. Sciences 2002, Medal of Eng Excellence, World Fed. of Eng Orgs, Paris 2003, Lifetime Achievement Award, Indian Science Congress 2004, Science Medal, Acad. of Science for the Developing World 2005, Ashutosh Mookherjee Memorial Award, Indian Science Congress 2005, Business Week (USA) Award of 'Stars of Asia' from George Bush, Sr (first Asian Scientist) 2005, Padma Vibhushan 2014. *Publications include:* books: Intellectual Property and Competitive Strategies in the 21st Century (with S.A. Khan) 2003, Advances in Transport Processes Vol. 1 1980, Vol. 2 1982, Vol. 3 1983, Vol. 4 1986, Transport Phenomena in Polymeric Systems Vol. 1 (ATP Vol. 5) 1987, Vol. 2 (ATP Vol. 6) 1989, Advances in Transport Phenomena in Fluidizing Systems (ATP Vol. 7) 1987, Vol. 8 1992, Vol. 9 1993, Frontiers in Chemical Reaction Engineering Vol. 1 1984, Vol. 2 1984, Recent Trends in Chemical Reaction Engineering Vol. 1 1987, Vol. 2 1987, Reactions and Reaction Engineering 1987, Heat Transfer Equipment Design 1988, Reading in Solid State Chemistry 1994, Dynamics of Complex Fluids 1998, Structure and Dynamics in the Mesophasic Domain 1999; author or co-author of 236 research papers on macromolecules in books and scientific journals since 1968; co-authored 28 patents 1988–2003. *Address:* National Chemical Laboratory, Dr Homi Bhabha Road, Pune

411 008 (office); 'Raghunath', D-4, Varsha Park, Baner, Pune 411 045, India (home). *Telephone:* (20) 25902605 (home); (20) 25902197 (home); (20) 27291268 (office). *Fax:* (20) 25902607 (office). *E-mail:* ram@ncl.res.in (office). *Website:* www.ncl-india.org (office).

MASHKOV, Vladimir Lvovich; Russian actor; b. 27 Nov. 1963, Tula; s. of Lev Petrovich Mashkov and Natalya Ivanovna Nikiforova; m. 1st Tatyana Lvovna Mashkova; one d.; 2nd Ksenia Borisovna Mashkova; ed Moscow Art Theatre School; actor and Stage Dir Oleg Tabakov Theatre-Studio 1988–; main roles in most productions; staged five productions; various film roles; numerous awards including K. Stanislavsky Prize for Best Direction 1994, Crystal Turandot Prize for Best Play 1995, Baltic Pearl for fast career growth 1997; various awards for best actor in film and theatre. *Plays (as stage director):* Star House by Local Time, Passions for Bumbarash, The Death-Defying Act, The Threepenny Opera, Number 13 2001. *Film roles include:* Zelyonyy ogon kozy (The Goat's Green Fire) 1989, Habi-assy 1990, Delay - raz! (aka Do It - One!) 1990, Lyubov na ostrove smerti (Love at the Death Island) 1991, Alyaska, ser! (Alaska, Sir!) 1992, Moi Ivan, toi Abraham (Me Ivan, You Abraham) 1993, Moscow Nights, Limita 1994, Katya Ismailova 1994, American Daughter 1995, Koroli i kapusta (Cabbages and Kings; voice) 1996, Noch pered Rozhdestvom (voice) 1997, Vor (The Thief) 1997, Sirota kazanskaya (Sympathy Seeker) (also dir) 1997, Sochineniye ko dnyu pobedy (Composition for Victory Day) 1998, Dve luny, tri solntsa (Two Moons, Three Suns) 1998, Mama (Mummy) 1999, Russkiy bunt (The Captain's Daughter) 2000, Dancing at the Blue Iguana 2000, 15 Minutes 2001, An American Rhapsody 2001, The Quickie 2001, Behind Enemy Lines 2001, Oligarkh 2002, Papa (also writer, dir and producer) 2004, Statski sovetnik 2005, The Good Shepherd 2006. *Television includes:* Casus Improvisus 1991, Dvadtsat minut s angelom 1996, Idiot (miniseries) 2003. *Address:* Oleg Tabakov Theatre-Studio, Chaplygina str. 12A, Moscow, Russia. *Telephone:* (495) 916-21-21 (Theatre); (495) 925-73-44 (Yelena Chukhrai Art Agency). *E-mail:* grtagent@mtu-net.ru (office); v_mashkoff@mtu-net.ru (home).

MASIKO, Kabakumba, (Princess Kabakumba Labwone Masiko), BSc; Ugandan economist and politician; *Minister of the Presidency;* b. 20 Oct. 1966, Masindi Dist; m. Major Masiko; ed Makerere Univ., Kampala; mobiliser, Nat. Resistance Movt Secr. 1986–96; MP for Masindi Dist 1996–2001, Bujenje Co. 2001–; Minister for Parl. Affairs and Govt Chief Whip 2006–09, Minister of Information and Nat. Guidance 2009–11, of the Presidency and for Kampala Capital City Authority 2011–. *Address:* POB 102, Masindi (office); President's Office, Kampala, Uganda. *Telephone:* (41) 222448 (office); (41) 234920 (office). *E-mail:* klmasiko@parliament.go.ug (office).

MASIRE, Quett Ketumile Joni, LLD, JP; Botswana fmr head of state; b. 23 July 1925, Kanye; s. of Joni Masire and Gabaipone Masire; m. Gladys Olebile Molefi 1957; three s. three d.; ed Kanye and Tiger Kloof; f. Seepapitso Secondary School 1950; reporter, later Dir, African Echo 1958; mem. Bangwaketse Tribal Council, Legis. Council; fmr mem. Exec. Council; Founder-mem. Botswana Democratic Party; mem. Legis. (now Nat.) Ass. March 1965; Deputy Prime Minister 1965–66; attended Independence Conf., London Feb. 1966; Vice-Pres. and Minister of Finance 1966–80 and of Devt Planning 1967–80, Pres. of Botswana 1980–98; Chair. Southern African Devt Community 1999, Congo Facilitator 2000-03; head of African Union Observer Mission to 2010 elections in Ethiopia; Chancellor Univ. of Botswana 1982–98; f. Sir Ketumile Masire Foundation 2007; mem. Bd of Dirs Mo Ibrahim Foundation; Hon. GCMG; Order of the Welwitschia 1995; Hon. LLD (Williams Coll.) 1980, (Sussex) 1986, (St John); Naledi Ya Botswana (Star of the Nation) 1986, Africa Prize for Leadership for the Sustainable End of Hunger 1989. *Leisure interests:* watching football. *Address:* PO Box 70, Gaborone, Botswana (home). *Telephone:* 353391 (home).

MASIRE-MWAMBA, Gabaipone Mmasekgoa, BSc, MBA, LLB; Botswana business executive and international organization official; *Deputy Secretary-General, Commonwealth Secretariat;* ed Univ. of London, UK, Univ. of Pittsburgh, USA; fmr Chief Exec. Investment Promotion Agency (BEDIA); fmr Group Man. of Corp. Business and Regulatory Affairs, Botswana Telecommunications Corpn; fmr UK Business Devt Man., Commonwealth Telecommunications Org.; Deputy Sec.-Gen. Commonwealth Secr. 2008–. *Address:* Commonwealth Secretariat, Marlborough House, Pall Mall, London, SW1Y 5HX, England (office). *Telephone:* (20) 7747-6385 (office). *Fax:* (20) 7839-9081 (office). *E-mail:* info@commonwealth.int (office). *Website:* (office).

MASISI, Motlhware Kgori James; Botswana diplomatist; m. Naledi T. Masisi; ed Ball State University, USA; accountant, Botswana Power Corpn 1976–79; joined Ministry of Commerce and Industry 1979, held various positions including Acting Dir Commerce and Consumer Affairs 1983–84; Dir Dept of Tourism 1987–90; Marketing Man. Shell Oil Botswana 1990–93; joined Foreign Service 1996, has held numerous posts including Charges d'affairs, Embassy in Tokyo, Minister-Counsellor, Embassy in Brussels, High Commr to South Africa 2004–06; Chief Trade Negotiator in Economic Partnership Agreement 2006–08; Chair. Citizen Entrepreneurial Development Agency (CEDA) 2008–09.

MASKAWA, Toshihide, PhD; Japanese physicist and academic; *Professor of Physics, Kyoto Sangyo University;* b. 7 Feb. 1940; ed Nagoya Univ.; Research Assoc., Nagoya Univ. 1967; Research Assoc., Kyoto Univ. 1970–76, Prof. 1980–2003, Prof. Emer. 2003–, Dir Yukawa Inst. for Theoretical Physics 1997–99; Assoc. Prof., Univ. of Tokyo 1976–80; Prof. of Physics, Kyoto Sangyo Univ. 2007–; mem. Japanese Science Council 1997–2000; Nishina Memorial Award 1979, JJ Sakurai Prize (American Inst. of Physics) 1985, Japan Acad. Award 1985, Asahi Award 1994, Sino-Japanese Cultural Award 1995, Nagoya Univ. Grad. School of Science Lecture Award 2002, European Physical Soc. High-energy Elementary Particle Physics Prize 2007, Nobel Prize for Physics (jtly) 2008. *Address:* Kyoto Sangyo University, Faculty of Science, Motoyama, Kamigamo, Kita-Ku, Kyoto 603-8555, Japan (office). *Website:* www.kyoto-su.ac.jp/department/sc/index.html (home).

MASKIN, Eric, AB, AM, PhD; American economist and academic; *Professor of Economics, Harvard University;* b. (Eric Stark Maskin), 12 Dec. 1950, New York City, NY; s. of Meyer Maskin and Bernice Rabkin Maskin; m. Gayle Sawtelle; one s. one d.; ed Harvard Univ.; Research Fellow, Jesus Coll., Cambridge, UK 1976–77, Visiting Overseas Fellow, St John's Coll., Cambridge 1987–88; Asst Prof. of Econs,

MIT 1977–80, Assoc. Prof. 1980–81, Prof. 1981–84, Visiting Prof. 1999–2000; Overseas Fellow, Churchill Coll., Cambridge 1980–82; Prof. of Econs, Harvard Univ. 1985–2000, Louis Berkman Prof. of Econs 1997–2000; Albert O. Hirschman Prof. of Social Science, Inst. for Advanced Study, Princeton, NJ 2000–11; Dir Summer School in Econ. Theory, Hebrew Univ. of Jerusalem 2008–; research areas have included game theory and mechanism design theory; mem. Educ. Advisory Bd, J.S. Guggenheim Foundation 2007–, Scientific Council, Toulouse School of Econs, Solvay School of Econs, Brussels, Higher School of Econs (Russia), Santa Fe Inst.; Ed. Quarterly Journal of Economics 1984–90, Economics Letters 1992–2011; mem. American Econ. Asscn, NAS, Econometric Soc. (Pres. 2003), Game Theory Soc. (Pres. 2010–12), European Econ. Asscn; Fellow, Econometric Soc. 1981, American Acad. of Arts and Sciences 1994, European Econ. Asscn 2004, Royal Spanish Acad. of Econ. Science and Finance 2008, Soc. for Advances of Econ. Theory 2010; Corresp. Fellow, British Acad. 2003; Hon. Prof., Wuhan Univ. 2004, Tsinghua Univ. 2007, Shenzhen Univ. 2008, Higher School of Econs, Russia 2009; Hon. Fellow, St John's Coll. Cambridge 2004, Jesus Coll. Cambridge 2009; Hon. MA, Univ. of Cambridge 1977, Hon. DHumLitt (Bard Coll.) 2008, Dr hc (Corvinus Univ., Budapest) 2008, (Univ. of Cambodia) 2010; Erik Kempe Award in Environmental Econs 2007, Nobel Prize in Econs (co-recipient with Leo Hurwicz and Roger B. Myerson) 2007, Centennial Medal, Harvard Univ. 2010, Cristobal Gabarron Foundation Int. Econs Award 2011. *Leisure interest:* music. *Address:* Department of Economics, Harvard University, Littauer Center 312, 1805 Cambridge Street, Cambridge, MA 02138, USA (office). *Telephone:* (617) 495-1746 (office). *E-mail:* emaskin@fas.harvard.edu (office). *Website:* www.economics .harvard.edu/faculty/maskin (office).

MASMANIDIS, Costas, BSc, PhD; Greek chemist, business executive and international organization executive; *Secretary-General, Black Sea Economic Cooperation (BSEC) Business Council;* b. 1946, Thessaloniki; ed Aristotelian Univ., Thessaloniki, Univ. of Cincinnati, USA; Post-doctoral Research Fellow, Rensselaer Polytechnic Inst., Troy, NY; 18-year career as Gen. Man. with Dow Chemical Co. in int. positions in USA, Switzerland, SA and Balkan countries and as Man. Dir of Greek subsidiary, and with int. positions as Country Man., Corp., sales and market Man.; currently Sec.-Gen. Black Sea Econ. Cooperation (BSEC) Business Council, Istanbul; Founding mem. and twice-elected Pres. Hellenic Asscn of Chemical Industries; mem. CEFIC; fmr Sec.-Gen. Athens-Piraeus Industry Asscn, Hellenic-Chinese Chamber of Commerce and Industry; fmr mem. Bd of Dirs Hellenic-American Chamber of Commerce and Industry; fmr mem. Gen. Council Fed. of Greek Industries. *Publications include:* Globalisation, Dematerialisation and the New Economy: The Transformation of Business and the Workplace at the Dawn of the 21st Century 2000, SME Innovation and Competitiveness (training manual), The Prospects of Business Cooperation in the Countries of the Mediterranean (study). *Address:* BSEC Business Council, Müsir Fuad Pasa Yalisi, Eski Tersane, 80860 Istinye, İstanbul, Turkey (office). *Telephone:* (212) 229-1144 (office). *Fax:* (212) 229-0332 (office). *E-mail:* info@bsec-business.org (office). *Website:* www.bsec-business.org (office).

MASOL, Vitaliy Andreyevich, PhD; Ukrainian politician (retd); b. 14 Nov. 1928, Olshivka, Chernigov Region; s. of Andrei Dmitrievich Masol and Lidiya Grigorievna Masol; m. Nina Vasilievna Masol 1978; one s.; ed Kiev Polytechnic Inst., Inst. of Econ. Man.; foreman, shop foreman, deputy chief engineer, Novokramatorsk machine-construction plant 1951–63, Dir 1963–71; mem. CPSU 1956–91, mem. Cen. Auditing Cttee 1981–86, Cen. Cttee 1989–91; Gen. Dir of production unit of heavy machine-construction factories in Kramatorsk, Ukraine 1971–72; First Deputy Chair. of Gosplan for Ukrainian SSR 1972–79; Deputy Chair. Ukrainian Council of Ministers 1979–87, Chair. (Prime Minister) 1987–90 (resgnd following mass student demonstrations), Prime Minister 1994–95; Chair. Planning and Budget Comm., USSR Supreme Soviet 1982–87; Deputy to USSR Supreme Soviet 1979–89, USSR People's Deputy 1989–91; mem. Parl. of Ukraine 1990–98, Higher Council of Pres. of Ukraine from 1997; adviser to Rostok bank; several orders, including Order of the Badge of Honour 1960, Order of Lenin 1966, 1986, Order of the October Revolution 1971, Order of the Red Banner of Labour 1978, Order of Merit, Third Class 1997, First Class 2008; Order of Prince Yaroslav the Wise, Fifth Class 1998, Fourth Class 2003; numerous awards. *Leisure interest:* tourism. *Address:* Desyatinnaya str. 8, Apt 8, Kiev 252025, Ukraine.

MASON, Sir (Basil) John, Kt, C.B., DSc, FRS; British meteorologist; b. 18 Aug. 1923, Docking, Norfolk; s. of the late John Robert Mason and Olive Mason; m. Doreen Sheila Jones 1948; two s.; ed Fakenham Grammar School and Univ. Coll., Nottingham; commissioned, Radar Branch, RAF 1944–46; Shirley Research Fellow, Univ. of Nottingham 1947; Asst lecturer in Meteorology, Imperial Coll., London 1948–49, lecturer 1949; Warren Research Fellow, Royal Soc. 1957; Visiting Prof. of Meteorology, Univ. of Calif. 1959–60; Prof. of Cloud Physics, Imperial Coll. of Science and Tech., Univ. of London 1961–65; Dir-Gen. Meteorological Office 1965–83, Pres. Royal Meteorological Soc. 1968–70; mem. Exec. Cttee World Meteorological Org. 1965–75, 1977–83; Chair. Council, Univ. of Surrey 1971–75; Pro-Chancellor Univ. of Surrey 1979–85; Pres. Inst. of Physics 1976–78; Treas. and Sr Vice-Pres. Royal Soc. 1976–86; Dir Fulmer Research Inst. 1976–78; Pres. BAAS 1982–83; Dir Royal Soc. Project on Acidification of Surface Waters 1983–90; mem. Advisory Bd Research Councils 1983–86; Pres. UMIST 1986–94, Chancellor 1994–96; Chair. Grad. School for Environment, Imperial Coll., London 1995–98; Chair. ICSU/WMO Scientific Cttee for World Climate Research Prog., Co-ordinating Cttee for Marine Science and Tech. 1987–89; Pres. Nat. Soc. for Clean Air 1989–91, Asscn for Science Educ. 1992–93, Nat. Soc. of Environmental Eng 1999–2003; Foreign mem. Norwegian Acad. of Science 1993; Bakerian Lecture, Royal Soc. 1971; Halley Lecture, Oxford Univ. 1977; Lecturer, Linacre Coll., Oxford 1990; Rutherford Lecture, Royal Soc. 1990; Hon. Fellow, Imperial Coll. of Science and Tech. 1974, UMIST 1979; Hon. DSc (Nottingham) 1966, (Durham) 1970, (Strathclyde) 1975, (City Univ.) 1980, (Sussex) 1983, (E Anglia) 1988, (Plymouth Polytechnic) 1990, (Heriot-Watt) 1991, (UMIST) 1994, (Reading) 1998; Hugh Robert Mill Medal, Royal Meteorological Soc. 1959, Charles Chree Medal and Prize, Physical Soc. 1965, Rumford Medal, Royal Soc. 1972, Glazebrook Medal and Prize, Inst. of Physics 1974, Symons Memorial Gold Medal, Royal Meteorological Soc. 1975, Naylor Prize and Lectureship, London Math. Soc. 1979, Royal Medal, Royal Soc. 1991. *Publications include:* The Physics of Clouds 1957, Clouds, Rain and Rain-making 1962, Acid Rain 1992. *Leisure interests:* music, foreign

travel, biography. *Address:* 64 Christchurch Road, East Sheen, London, SW14, England (home). *Telephone:* (20) 8876-2557 (home).

MASON, Dame Monica, DBE, OBE; British (b. South African) fmr ballet dancer and ballet company artistic director; b. 6 Sept. 1941, Johannesburg, SA; d. of Richard Mason and E. Fabian; m. Austin Bennett 1968; ed Johannesburg, Nesta Brooking School of Ballet, UK and Royal Ballet School, London; joined Royal Ballet in Corps de Ballet 1958, Soloist 1963, Prin. 1968, Sr Prin. –1989; selected by Kenneth MacMillan to create role of Chosen Maiden in Rite of Spring 1962; other roles created for her include: Diversions, Calliope Rag in Elite Syncopations, Electra, Mistress in Manon, Romeo and Juliet, Midwife in Rituals, Adieu 1980, Nursey in Isadora, Summer in The Four Seasons, The Ropes of Time; appeared in mime roles including Carabosse in The Sleeping Beauty and Lady Capulet in MacMillan's Romeo and Juliet; created role of Mrs Grose in William Tuckett's The Turn of the Screw; Répétiteur and Asst to Prin. Choreographer, Royal Ballet 1980–84, Prin. Répétiteur 1984–91, Asst Dir Royal Ballet 1991–2002, Dir 2002–12; Hon. DUniv (Surrey) 1996; Achievement in Dance Award 2003, Queen Elizabeth II Coronation Award 2011. *Repertory includes:* Odette/Odile in Swan Lake, Princess Aurora in The Sleeping Beauty, title role in Giselle, Prelude and Mazurka in Les Sylphides, leading role in Raymonda Act III, dramatic parts including Hostess in Les Biches and the Black Queen in Checkmate; other major roles performed include: leading role in MacMillan's Song of the Earth, Nijinska's Les Noces and Nureyev's Kingdom of the Shades scene from La Bayadère; appeared in first performances by Royal Ballet of Hans van Manen's Adagio Hammerklavier, Jerome Robbins' Dances at a Gathering and In the Night, Balanchine's Liebeslieder Walzer and Tudor's Dark Elegies; other roles include: the Lilac Fairy in The Sleeping Beauty, Empress Elisabeth and Mitzi Caspar in MacMillan's Mayerling, title role in The Firebird, Variations in Frederick Ashton's Birthday Offering, the Fairy Godmother and Winter Fairy in Cinderella, Lady Elgar in Enigma Variations, Queen of Denmark in Helpmann's Hamlet. *Address:* c/o Royal Opera House, Covent Garden, London, WC2E 9DD, England. *E-mail:* monica .mason@roh.org.uk.

MASON, Paul James, CB, PhD, FRS; British meteorologist (retd); *Professor Emeritus, University of Reading;* b. 16 March 1946, Southampton, Hants., England; s. of Charles Ernest Edward Mason and Phyllis Mary Mason (née Swan); m. Elizabeth Mary Slaney 1968; one s. one d.; ed Univs of Nottingham and Reading; Scientific Officer, then Prin. Scientific Officer, Meteorological Office 1967–79, Head Meteorological Research Unit, Cardington 1979–85, Asst Dir Boundary Layer Br., Meteorological Office 1985–89, Deputy Dir Physical Research, Meteorological Office 1989–91, Chief Scientist 1991–2003; Dir Univs Weather Research Network (UWERN), Univ. of Reading 2003–06, Prof. Emer. 2006–; mem. Council Royal Meteorological Soc. 1989–90, Pres. 1992–94; Chair. Steering Cttee Global Climate Observing System 2002–06; mem. Editorial Bd Boundary Layer Meteorology 1988–98; L.G. Groves Prize for Meteorology 1980, Buchan Prize, Royal Meteorological Soc. 1986, Mason Medal, Royal Meteorological Soc. 2006. *Publications:* scientific papers in meteorology and fluid dynamics journals. *Leisure interests:* walking, travel. *Address:* Department of Meteorology, University of Reading, PO Box 243, Earley Gate, Reading, Berks., RG66 6BB, England (office). *E-mail:* p.j.mason@reading.ac.uk (office).

MASON, Peter, BA, MBA; Australian investment banker; *Chairman, AMP Ltd;* Dir Mayne Group Ltd 1992–2005; fmr Deputy Chair. Children's Hosp. Sydney; fmr Chair. and CEO Schroders Australia Ltd, Group Man. Dir Schroders Asia Pacific; Chair. JP Morgan Chase Bank Australia 2000–05, Ord Minnett Holdings Pty 2004–05; mem. Bd AMP Ltd 2003–, Chair. 2005–, mem. Remuneration Cttee, Audit Cttee; fmr Chair. Children's Hosp. Fund; fmr Dir Lloyds Bank Australia, UK; Dir Australian Research Alliance for Children and Youth; Sr Adviser UBS Investment Bank Australasia; Govt Appointee, Univ. of NSW Council; Order of Australia. *Address:* AMP Ltd, Level 24, 33 Alfred Street, Sydney 2000, Australia (office). *Telephone:* (2) 9257-5000 (office). *Fax:* (2) 8275-0199 (office). *Website:* www .ampgroup.com (office).

MASON, Sir Ronald, Kt, KCB, DSc, FRS, CChem, FRSC, CEng, FIM; British professor of chemical physics (retd) and civil servant; *Chairman, Global Haps Communications Network;* b. 22 July 1930, Wales; s. of David John Mason and Olwen Mason (née James); m. 1st E. Pauline Pattinson 1953; m. 2nd E. Rosemary Grey-Edwards 1979; three d.; ed Quaker's Yard Grammar School and Univs of Wales and London; Research Assoc., Univ. Coll. London (UCL) 1953–60, Fellow 1995–; Lecturer, Imperial Coll. London 1960–63; Prof., Univ. of Sheffield 1963–70; Prof., Univ. of Sussex 1970–88; Chief Scientific Adviser, Ministry of Defence 1977–83; Pro-Vice-Chancellor, Univ. of Sussex 1977–78; many visiting professorships in Australia, Canada, France, Israel, NZ and USA 1965–83, Int. Relations, Univ. Coll. of Wales; Chair. Hunting Ltd 1986–87, British Ceramics Research Ltd 1990–98, UCL Hosps Nat. Health Service Trust 1993–2001, Science Applications Int. Corpn (UK) Ltd 1993–96; Pres. British Hydromechanics Research Asscn 1986–95, Inst. of Materials 1995–96; Chair. Council for Arms Control, London 1986–91; mem. UN Disarmament Studies Comm. 1983–91; Chair. UCL Hosps Charities 2004–08, Global Haps Communications Network 2009–; Hon. Fellow, Univ. of Glamorgan 1987; Hon. FIMechE 1993; Hon. DSc (Wales) 1986, (Keele) 1993; medals of various learned socs. *Publications:* many scientific research publs on structural chem. and chemical physics of surfaces, author/ed. of 10 monographs, papers on defence policies and tech. *Leisure interests:* gardening, travelling, music, opera. *E-mail:* mason.r@virgin.net (home).

MASON OF BARNSLEY, Baron (Life Peer), cr. 1987, of Barnsley in South Yorkshire; **Roy Mason,** PC, DL; British politician; b. 18 April 1924, Barnsley, Yorks; s. of Joseph and Mary Mason; m. Marjorie Sowden 1945; two d.; ed Carlton Junior School, Royston Sr School and London School of Econs (T.U.C. Course); mine worker 1938–53; branch official, Nat. Union of Mineworkers 1947–53; mem. Yorkshire Miners' Council 1949–53; MP for Barnsley (now Barnsley Cen.) 1953–87; Minister of State (Shipping), Bd of Trade 1964–67; Minister of Defence (Equipment) 1967–68; Postmaster-Gen. April–June 1968; Minister of Power 1968–69; Pres. Bd of Trade 1969–70; Sec. of State for Defence 1974–76, for Northern Ireland 1976–79; Opposition Spokesman for Agric., Fisheries and Food 1979–81; Hon. DUniv (Sheffield Hallam Univ.) 1993, Hon. DCL (Univ. of Northumbria) 2005. *Publication:* Paying the Price. *Leisure interests:* fly-fishing, philately, cravatology. *Address:* House of Lords, Westminster, London, SW1A 0PW (office); 12 Victoria Avenue, Barnsley, S. Yorks., S70 2BH, England (home).

MASORIN, Adm. Vladimir; Russian naval officer (retd); b. 24 Aug. 1947, Beloye, Tver region; m.; two s.; ed Black Sea Nakhimov Naval School, Naval Acad., Gen. Staff Acad.; Chief of Staff 1993–96, First Deputy Commdr Kola Flotilla 1993–96, Commdr Caspian Flotilla 1996–2002, Black Sea Fleet 2002–05, Chief of Navy Staff 2005, Navy C-in-C 2005–07; adviser to Ministry of Defence 2007–; Legion of Merit (USA) 2007. *Address:* c/o Ministry of Defence, 105175 Moscow, ul. Myasnitskaya 37, Russia (office). *Telephone:* (495) 293-38-54 (office). *Fax:* (495) 296-84-36 (office). *Website:* www.mil.ru (office).

MASOUD, Ahmad Wali, MA; Afghan diplomatist and politician; *Leader, Nizat-i Melli-i Afghanistan (National Movement of Afghanistan);* b. 1 Nov. 1964, Kabul; brother of the late Ahmed Shah Masoud, leader of Northern Alliance mil. forces in Afghanistan, and of Ahmad Zia Masoud; m. Beheshta Masoud; three d.; ed Muslim Public School, Peshawar, Pakistan, Mid-Cornwall Coll. of Further Educ., Polytechnic of Cen. London and Westminster Univ., UK; Foreign News Reporter, Times Newspaper 1989; Ed. Ariana News Bulletin 1989–1992; Rep. Jamiat-i Islami (Islamic Soc.), main political faction in Afghanistan, fighting Russian occupation 1989–92; Second Sec., Embassy of Afghanistan, London 1992, First Sec. and Chargé d'affaires a.i. 1993, Minister Counsellor and Chargé d'affaires a.i. 1993–2003, Amb. to UK 2003–07; currently Leader, Nizat-i Melli-i Afghanistan (Nat. Movt of Afghanistan), Kabul. *Address:* Nizat-i Melli-i Afghanistan, Taimani, St 1, Kabul, Afghanistan (office).

MASOUD, Ahmad Zia; Afghan diplomatist and politician; b. 1 May 1956, brother of the late Ahmad Shah Masoud and Ahmad Wali Masoud; m.; one s. three d.; ed Lycée Esteqlal and Kabul Polytechnic Inst.; mem. Shora-e-Nizar Movt; Amb. to Russian Fed. (non-resident Envoy to Moldova, Armenia, Azerbaijan, Georgia and Belarus), Moscow 2002–04; First Vice-Pres. 2004–09. *Address:* c/o Office of the President, Gul Khana Palace, Presidential Palace, Kabul, Afghanistan.

MASRI, Munib Rashid al-, MA; Palestinian business executive; *Chairman, Palestinian Development and Investment Company;* b. 1934, Nablus, British Mandate for Palestine; m. Angela Masri; four s. two d.; ed an-Najah School, Nablus, an-Najah Nat. Univ., Univ. of Texas, Austin, USA; fmr Jordanian cabinet minister; f. Edgo (eng services co.), London, UK; served as emissary of King Hussein of Jordan to Palestinian leader Yasser Arafat's HQ during fighting between Jordanian troops and Palestinian fighters 1970; acted as mediator between Israeli Prime Minister Benjamin Netanyahu and Yasser Arafat mid-1990s; first Palestinian businessman to return to Palestinian territories following Oslo agreements 1994; launched a political movement to rival Fatah and Hamas, called the Palestine Forum 2007; turned down an offer to become Prime Minister on three separate occasions; Founder and Chair. Palestine Devt and Investment Co. (Padico) 1994; f. Paltel phone co.; Deputy Chair. Palestine Investment Fund; mem. Palestinian Cen. Council; involved in education through the establishment of the Al Quds Univ. Investment Fund; Chair. Bd of Trustees, Sakakini Cultural Centre, Ramallah; helped set up the Eng and Tech. Coll. at an-Najah Univ. (named after him); mem. Bd of Trustees, American Univ. of Beirut; ranked by Arabian Business amongst the Power 500: The World's Most Influential Arabs (38th) 2012, (48th) 2013. *Address:* Padico Holding, PO Box 316, Nablus, Palestinian Autonomous Areas (office). *Telephone:* (9) 2384480 (office). *Fax:* (9) 2384355 (office). *E-mail:* padico@padico.com (office). *Website:* www.padico.com (office).

MASRI, Sabih Taher Darwish al-, BSc; Jordanian banking executive; *Chairman, Arab Bank;* b. 2 Dec. 1937; ed Univ. of Texas, Austin, USA; Founder Asra Group 1966–; Founder Palestine Securities Exchange, Chair. –2004; Chair. Sikon for Building Materials Co. (UAE) 1968–, Arab Supply & Trading Co. (Saudi Arabia) 1979–, Palestine Telecommunication Corpn (Palestine) 1998–, ZARA Holding Co. (Jordan) 1999–, ASTRA Industrial Group (Saudi Arabia) 2007–; Vice-Chair. Palestine Investment Fund 2002–; mem. Bd of Dirs Arab Bank 1998–, Deputy Chair.–Aug. 2012, Acting Chair. Aug.–Sept. 2012, Chair. Sept. 2012–; mem. Bd of Dirs Palestine Development & Investment Co. (Padico) 1994–, Cairo Amman Bank, VTEL Holdings Ltd, Al Masira Investment Co., Ayla Oasis Development Co., Rum Agricultural Co., Palestine Investment and Development Co. *Address:* Arab Bank Plc, PO Box 950545, Amman 11195, Jordan (office). *Telephone:* (6) 560-0000 (office). *Fax:* (6) 560-6793 (office). *E-mail:* info@arabbank .com (office). *Website:* www.arabbank.com (office).

MASRI, Taher Nashat, BBA; Jordanian politician and diplomatist; *Speaker, Jordanian Parliament (Upper House);* b. 5 March 1942, Nablus; s. of Nashat Masri and Hadiyah Solh; m. Samar Bitar 1968; one s. one d.; ed Al-Najah Nat. Coll., Nablus and North Texas State Univ., USA; with Cen. Bank of Jordan 1965–73; mem. Parl. (Lower House) 1973–74, 1984–88, 1989–97; Minister of State for Occupied Territories Affairs 1973–74; Amb. to Spain 1975–78, to France 1978–83, also accred to Belgium 1979–80, Rep. to EEC 1978–80; Perm. Del. to UNESCO 1978–83; Amb. to UK 1983–84; Minister of Foreign Affairs 1984–88, Jan.–June 1991; Deputy Prime Minister and Minister of State for Econ. Affairs April–Sept. 1989; Chair. Foreign Relations Cttee 1989–91, 1992–93; Prime Minister and Minister of Defence June–Nov. 1991; Speaker, Nat. Ass. 1993–94; Senator 1998–2001, 2005–, Deputy Speaker 2005–09, Speaker 2009–; fmr Rep. to Arab League; mem. and Rapporteur, Royal Comm. for Drafting the Nat. Charter 1990; Chair. Bd Princess Haya Cultural Centre for Children 1992–; Pres. Nat. Soc. for the Enhancement of Freedom and Democracy (JUND) 1993–97, Jordanian-Spanish Friendship Asscn 1998–, Bd of Trustees Jordan Univ. for Science and Tech., Irbid 1998–, Jordan British Soc. 2006–, Exec. Cttee Arab Thought Forum 2009–; Commr for Civic Socs with Arab League, Cairo (stationed in Amman) 2002; mem. and Head, Political Cttee of the Royal Comm. for Drafting the Nat. Agenda 2005–; mem. Alkuods Al-Sharif Defending Asscns 1996–2001, 2003–, Advisory Cttee Anna Lindh Euro-Mediterranean Foundation for the Dialogue between Cultures 2004–; Grand Cordon, Jewelled Al-Nahda (Order of the Renaissance) (Jordan), Order of Al-Nahda (1st Degree) (Jordan), Order of Al-Kawkab (Jordan) 1974, Gran Cruz de Mérito Civil (Spain) 1977, Order of Isabel la Católica (Spain) 1978, Commdr, Légion d'honneur 1981, Grand Officier, Ordre Nat. du Mérite, Order of Merit (Grand Cross, First Class, FRG), Kt Grand Cross (Italy); Hon. GBE; Grand Cordon, Ordre Nat. de Cedre (Lebanon), Grand Decoration of Honour in Gold with Sash for Services (Austria), Order of Diplomatic Service Merit and

Gwanghawa Medal (Repub. of Korea); numerous awards. *Address:* PO Box 5550, Amman 11183, Jordan. *Telephone:* (6) 4642227 (office); (6) 5920600 (home). *Fax:* (6) 4642226 (office). *E-mail:* t.n.masri@index.com.jo (office). *Website:* www.tahermasri .com.

MASSA, Sergio; Argentine politician and government official; b. 28 April 1972, Buenos Aires; m.; two c.; ed Belgrano Univ.; joined Unión del Centro Democrático 1989, then joined Partido Justicialista; Social Devt Adviser in Vice-Presidential campaign of Ramon Ortega 1999; Exec. Dir Nat. Agency for Social Security Admin (ANSES) 2002–07; elected mem. Chamber of Deputies 2005 but relinquished seat to stay at ANSES; Mayor of Tigre 2007– (currently on leave); Cabinet Chief 2008–; Lifetime Mem. Club Atlético Tigre 2007–09. *Address:* c/o Office of the Cabinet Chief, Julio A. Roca 782, C1067APB, Buenos Aires, Argentina (office).

MASSAD, Carlos, MA, PhD; Chilean banker, economist and academic; b. 29 Aug. 1932, Santiago; m.; five c.; ed Univ. of Chile, Univ. of Chicago, USA; Dir Dept of Econs, Univ. of Chile 1959–64; Vice-Gov. Cen. Bank of Chile 1964–67, Gov. 1967–70, 1996–2003 (resgnd); Exec. Dir IMF 1970–74; mem. Advisory Cttee, World Bank 1978–81; held various posts in Econ. Comm. for Latin America (CEPAL) 1970–92; Exec. Pres. Eduardo Frei Montalva Foundation 1993–94; Minister of Health 1994–96; Prof., Economics Faculty, Santiago Univ. 1982–90; Visiting Prof., UCLA 1988; Euromoney Best Cen. Banker of Latin America 1997, The Banker Cen. Bank Gov. For the Americas Region of the Year 2001. *Publications include:* Macroeconomics 1979, Rudiments of Economics 1980, Adjustment With Growth 1984; Economic Analysis: An Introduction to Microeconomics 1986, Internal Debt and Financial Stability (Vol. 1) 1987, (Vol. 2) 1988, The Financial System and Resource Distribution: Study based on Latin America and the Caribbean 1990, Elements of Economics: An Introduction to Economic Analysis 1993, On Public Health and Other Topics 1995, Macroeconomía en un mundo interdependiente (with Guillermo Patillo) 2000; and numerous articles. *Address:* c/o Central Bank of Chile, Agustinas 1180, Castilla 967, Santiago, Chile (office).

MASSE, Hon. Marcel; Canadian politician; *President, Société Héritage de Champlain;* b. 1936, Saint-Jean-de-Matha, Québec; s. of Rosaire Masse and Clermont; m. Cécile Martin 1960; one s. one d.; ed Ecole normale Jacques-Cartier, Univ. of Montreal, Sorbonne, City of London Coll., European Inst. of Business Admin.; fmr teacher of ancient history, Lanaudière Regional School Bd; Dir Lavalin (eng co.) 1974–84 (also Project Dir for UNDP, Vice-Pres., Vice-Pres. of Marketing and Commercial Devt); mem. Quebec Nat. Ass. 1966–73 (held portfolios of Minister of State for Educ., Minister responsible for Public Service, for Inter-Governmental Affairs, Minister of Planning and Devt); Minister of Communications 1984–85, 1985–86, of Energy, Mines and Resources 1986–89, of Communications 1989–90, responsible for La Francophonie 1990, of Defence 1991–93; Chief Consultant CFC (consultancy) 1994–95; Del.-Gen. of Québec to France 1996–97; Pres. Comm. franco-québécoise sur les lieux de mémoire communs 1997–2006, Comm. des biens culturels du Québec 1997–2000; f. Société Héritage de Champlain 2005, now Pres.; fmr Pres. Wilfrid Pelletier Foundation; Dir numerous orgs including Montreal Symphony Orchestra, Canadian Writers' Foundation, Canadian Refugee Foundation, Lanaudière Summer Festival, Club de Dakar, Jeunesses Musicales du Canada; Progressive Conservative; Officier, Légion d'honneur, Ordre du Québec. *Leisure interests:* reading, music, fishing, skiing. *Address:* CP 1030, Saint-Donat, PQ J0T 2C0, Canada (office).

MASSENGALE, Martin Andrew, BS, MS, PhD; American university administrator, agronomist and academic; *Director, Center for Grassland Studies, Foundation Distinguished Professor and President Emeritus, University of Nebraska;* b. 25 Oct. 1933, Monticello, Ky; s. of the late Elbert G. Massengale and Orpha Conn Massengale; m. Ruth A. Klingelhofer 1959; one s. one d.; ed W Kentucky Univ. and Univ. of Wis.; Asst Agronomist and Asst Prof., Univ. of Ariz., Tucson 1958–62, Assoc. Agronomist and Assoc. Prof. 1962–65, Agronomist and Prof. 1965–66, Agronomist, Prof. and Head of Dept 1966–74, Assoc. Dean, Coll. of Agric. and Assoc. Dir Agricultural Experiment Station 1974–76; Vice-Chancellor for Agric. and Natural Resources, Univ. of Nebraska, Lincoln 1976–81, Chancellor Univ. of Nebraska 1981–91, Interim Pres. 1989–91, Pres. 1991–94, Pres. Emer. 1994–, Dir Center for Grassland Studies and Foundation Distinguished Prof. 1994–; Pres. Crop Science Soc. of America 1973–74, Grazing Lands Forum 1997–98; Chair. Agronomic Science Foundation; mem. numerous cttees, nat. panels, advisory bds etc. including Chair., Exec. Comm. and Advisory Bd to US Sec. of Agric., US Senate and House of Reps Agric. and Appropriations Cttees; Fellow, AAAS, American Soc. of Agronomy, Crop Science Soc. of America and other professional socs; Hon. Lifetime Trustee, Neb. Council on Econ. Educ. 1999; Dr hc (Neb. Wesleyan Univ., Senshu Univ., Tokyo), Distinguished Alumni (Western Kentucky) 2002; numerous honours and awards, including Triumph of Agri Award 1999, Nebraska Agriculture Relations Co. Honoree 2000, Nebraska LEAD Alumni Asscn 'Friend of LEAD' Award 2001, Outstanding Pres.'s Award, All-American Football Foundation 2001, Alpha Gamma Rho Brothers of the Century Award 2004, US Dept of Agric. Charter Hall of Fame 2004, Nebraskaland Foundation Wagonmaster Award 2006, Gamma Sigma Delta Distinguished Achievement in Agric. Award 2008, Univ. of Nebraska Coll. of Agricultural Sciences and Natural Resources Alumni Asscn Service Award 2009. *Publications:* Renewable Resource Management for Forestry and Agriculture (co-ed.) 1978; numerous peer-reviewed articles in scientific journals. *Leisure interests:* reading, travel, golf, photography. *Address:* 203 Keim Hall, University of Nebraska, Lincoln, NE 68583-0953 (office); 3436 West Cape Charles Road, Lincoln, NE 68516, USA (home). *Telephone:* (402) 472-4101 (office); (402) 420-5350 (home). *Fax:* (402) 472-4104 (office). *E-mail:* mmassengale1@unl .edu (office). *Website:* www.grassland.unl.edu (office).

MASSERET, Jean-Pierre; French politician; b. 23 Aug. 1944, Cusset (Alliers); s. of Lucien Masseret and Claudia Rollet; m. Marie-Hélène Roddier 1967; three c.; ed Institut des Hautes Etudes de Défense Nationale; fmr Chief Insp., Inland Revenue; mem. staff of Minister for War Veterans 1981–86; Senator for Moselle 1983–, Vice-Chair. Senate Finance Cttee; Minister of State attached to Minister of Defence, with responsibility for War Veterans 1997–2001; Mayor of Havange (Moselle) 1995–97; Pres., Lorraine Regional Council 2004–, mem. Parti Socialiste Political Cttee; mem. Parl. Ass. of WEU, of Council of Europe, Socialist Party Nat. Office; fmr Chair. Lorraine Athletics League 1986–92; fmr regional champion runner. *Address:* Senat, Palais du Luxembourg, 75291 Paris Cedex 06, France (office). *Telephone:* 1-42-34-20-64 (office). *Fax:* 1-42-34-42-62 (office). *E-mail:* jp .masseret@senat.fr (office). *Website:* www.senat.fr (office).

MASSEY, Walter Eugene, BS, PhD; American physicist, academic and business executive; *Chairman, Bank of America Corporation;* b. 5 April 1938, Hattiesburg, Miss.; ed Morehouse Coll., Washington Univ. in St Louis, Mo.; served as Vice-Pres. for Research and Prof. of Physics, Univ. of Chicago; fmr Dir Argonne Nat. Lab.; fmr Dean of the Coll. and Prof. of Physics, Brown Univ.; fmr Asst Prof. of Physics, Univ. of Illinois; Dir NSF 1991–93; fmr Sr Provost of Univ. of California System; Pres. Morehouse Coll. 1995–2007; mem. Bd of Dirs Bank of America Corpn, Chair. 2009–; mem. or fmr mem. Bd of Dirs BP Oil, Motorola, McDonalds 1998–; mem. Bd Salzburg Global Seminar, Salzburg, Austria (with offices in Washington, DC) 1995–, Chair. 2007–; Trustee The Andrew W. Mellon Foundation. *Address:* Bank of America Corporate Center, 100 North Tryon Street, Charlotte, NC 28255, USA (office). *Telephone:* (704) 386-1845 (office). *Fax:* (704) 386-6699 (office). *E-mail:* info@bankofamerica.com (office). *Website:* www.bankofamerica.com (office).

MÄSİMOV, Kärım Qajimqanuli, DSc (Econ); Kazakhstani economist and politician; *Prime Minister;* b. 15 June 1965, Tselinograd (now Astana); ed Beijing Language and Culture Univ., Inst. of Int. Law, Wuhan Univ., China, Kazakh State Acad. of Man., Columbia Univ., USA; Chief Economist and Head of Dept, Ministry of Labour 1991–92; Sr Specialist, Rep. Office of Ministry of Foreign Econ. Relations in Urumqi, China 1992–93; Exec. Dir Trade House of Kazakhstan, Hong Kong 1994; Chair. Almaty Trade and Finance Bank 1995–97; Chair. People's Saving Bank of Kazakhstan 1997–2000; Minister of Transport and Communications 2000; Deputy Prime Minister 2001–03; Asst to the Pres. 2003–06; Deputy Prime Minister and Minister of Economy and Budget Planning April–Oct. 2006; Prime Minister of Kazakhstan 2007–12, 2014–; Head, Exec. Office of the Pres. 2012–14; Dr hc (Peoples' Friendship Univ., Russia) 2007. *Address:* Office of the Prime Minister, 010000 Astana, Beibitshilik kosh. 11, Kazakhstan (office). *Telephone:* (7172) 74-54-00 (office). *Fax:* (7172) 32-40-89 (office). *Website:* www.government.kz (office).

MASTELLA, Clemente; Italian journalist and politician; b. 5 Feb. 1947, Ceppaloni, Benevento; m. Sandra Lonardo; early career as journalist, RAI Naples; mem. Parl. 1976–; Mayor of San Giovanni di Ceppaloni 1987–1992, 2003; Co-founder Centro Cristiano Democratico party (after dissolution of Christian Democracy party) 1994; Minister of Labour 1994–95; Co-founder Cristiano Democratici per la Repubblica, then Unione Democratici per la Repubblica 1998; Sec. Popolari—UDEUR (Alleanza Popolare—Unione Democratici per l'Europa) (Union of Democrats for Europe) 1999–; Deputy Speaker of the House 2001–06; Minister of Justice 2006–08 (resgnd);*Website:* www.clementemastella.it.

MASTER, Simon Harcourt; British publisher; b. 10 April 1944, Caterham; s. of Humphrey R. Master and Rachel B. Plumbly; m. Georgina M. C. Batsford 1969; two s.; ed Ardingly Coll. Sussex; Publishing Dir Pan Books Ltd 1973–80, Man. Dir 1980–87; Chief Exec. Random House UK and Exec. Vice-Pres. Random House Int. Group 1987–89, Group Man. Dir Random Century Group 1989–90, Group Deputy Chair. 1989–2006, Chair., CEO Gen. Books Div., Random House UK 1992–2006; Chair., Arrow Books 1990–92 (non-exec.) HMSO 1990–95; mem. Council Publrs Asscn 1989–95 (Vice-Pres. 1995–96, 2000–2001, Pres. 1996–97, 2001–02); mem. Advisory Panel, London Book Fair 2008. *Leisure interests:* gardening, golf, classic cars, scuba diving.

MASTERSON, (Margaret) Valerie, CBE; British singer (soprano); b. Birken-head; d. of Edward Masterson and Rita McGrath; m. Andrew March; one s. one d.; Prof. of Singing, RAM, London 1992–97; Pres. British Youth Opera 1994–99, Vice-Pres. 2000–; has sung with D'Oyly Carte Opera, Glyndebourne, Royal Opera House, Covent Garden and English Nat. Opera and on TV and radio; also in major opera houses abroad including Paris, Aix-en-Provence, Toulouse, Munich, Geneva, Milan, San Francisco and Chicago; Hon. FRCM 1992; Hon. FRAM 1993; Hon. DLitt (South Bank Univ.) 1999; Award for Outstanding Individual Performance of the Year in a New Opera, Soc. of West End Theatre 1983. *Opera roles include:* La Traviata, Manon, Semele, Merry Widow, Louise, Lucia di Lammermoor, Mireille; other leading roles in Faust, Alcina, Die Entführung aus dem Serail, Le Nozze di Figaro, Così fan Tutte, La Bohème, Magic Flute, Julius Caesar, Rigoletto, Orlando, Der Rosenkavalier, Xerxes, The Pearl Fishers, Die Fledermaus. *Recordings include:* Julius Caesar, La Traviata, Elisabetta Regina d'Inghilterra, Bitter Sweet, Ring Cycle, recitals and various Gilbert and Sullivan discs. *Leisure interests:* enjoying life. *Address:* c/o Music International, 13 Ardilaun Road, London, N5 2QR, England (office). *Telephone:* (20) 7359-5183 (office). *Fax:* (20) 7226-9792 (office). *E-mail:* music@musicint.co.uk (office). *Website:* www.musicint.co.uk (office).

MASTERSON, Patrick, PhD, MRIA; Irish university professor; *President, European University Institute;* b. 19 Oct. 1936, Dublin; s. of Laurence Masterson and Violet Masterson; m. Frances Lenehan; one s. three d.; ed Belvedere Coll., Castlenock Coll., Univ. Coll., Dublin, Univ. of Louvain; mem. staff Dept of Metaphysics, Univ. Coll., Dublin 1963–72, Prof. Faculties of Arts, Philosophy and Sociology 1972–80, Dean of the Faculty of Philosophy and Sociology 1980–83, Registrar 1983–86, Pres. 1986–93; Pres. European Univ. Inst., Florence 1994–; Vice-Chancellor Nat. Univ. of Ireland 1987, 1988, 1993; Grande Oficial, Ordem do Mérito da República Portuguesa, Grande Ufficiale della Repubblica Italiana; Dr hc (Caen, Trinity Coll. Dublin, New York). *Publications:* Atheism and Alienation: A Study of the Philosophical Sources of Contemporary Atheism 1971, Images of Man in Ancient and Medieval Thought: (Studia Gerardo Verbeke ab amicis et collegis dictata) 1976. *Leisure interests:* modern art, reading, theatre, fishing. *Address:* Office of the President, European University Institute, Badia Fiesolana, Via dei Roccettini 9, 50016 San Domenico di Fiesole (FI), Italy. *Telephone:* (055) 4685310. *Fax:* (055) 4685312.

MASTIAUX, Frank, BSc, PhD; German business executive; *Chairman of the Board of Management and CEO, Energie Baden-Württemberg;* b. 24 March 1964, Essen; m.; three c.; management functions in areas of R&D and Supply & Trading, Asst to the CEO, Veba Oel AG, Gelsenkirchen 1993–99; Business Devt Man., CITGO Petroleum, Tulsa, Okla, USA 1998–99; Div. Head of Procurement and Sales, Veba Oel 1999–2000, Gen. Man. ARAL Mineralöl-Vertrieb GmbH (following merger with ARAL) 2000–01, Gen. Man. for Marketing Strategy and Planning as well as Market Research for entire BP group in London (following takeover of Veba

Oel/ARAL by BP) 2001–05, Head of Global Liquefied Petroleum Gas (LPG) business as CEO at BP 2005–07; CEO, Devt and Man. of Renewable Energies business, E.ON Climate & Renewables, Düsseldorf 2007–10, CEO E.ON International Energy 2010–12; Chair. Bd of Man. and CEO Energie Baden-Württemberg AG 2012–. *Address:* Energie Baden-Württemberg AG, Durlacher Allee 93, 76131 Karlsruhe, Germany (office). *Telephone:* (7) 21-63-00 (office). *Fax:* (7) 21-63-126-72 (office). *E-mail:* info@enbw.com (office). *Website:* www.enbw.com (office).

MASUDA, Hiroya; Japanese politician; b. 20 Dec. 1951; ed Univ. of Tokyo; began career at Ministry of Construction 1977; Dir Traffic Enforcement Div., Traffic Dept, Chiba Pref. Police HQ 1982–86; Dir Railway Traffic Div., Dept of Planning, Ibaraki Pref. 1986–93; Dir River Admin Policy Planning, Gen. Affairs Div., River Bureau, Ministry of Construction 1993–94, Dir Construction Disputes Settlement, Construction Industry Div., Econ. Affairs Bureau 1994–95; Gov. of Iwate Pref. 1995–2007; Minister for Internal Affairs and Communications, Minister of State for Decentralization Reform, Correcting Regional Disparities, Regional Govt (doshu-sei) and Privatization of the Postal Services 2007–08 (resgnd). *Address:* c/o Ministry of Internal Affairs and Communications, 2-1-2, Kasumigaseki, Chiyoda-ku, Tokyo 100-8926, Japan (office).

MASUI, Yoshio, PhD, FRS, OC, FRSC; Canadian (b. Japanese) biologist and academic; *Professor Emeritus, Department of Cell and System Biology, University of Toronto;* b. 1931, Kyoto; s. of Fusa-Jiro Masui and Toyoko Masui; m. Yuriko Masui 1959; one s. one d.; ed Kyoto Univ.; teacher of biology, Konan High School, Kobe; Research Asst, Biology Dept, Konan Univ. 1955–61, Lecturer 1961–65, Asst Prof. 1965–68, Prof. Emer. 1997–; Lecturer, Biology Dept, Yale Univ. 1969; Assoc. Prof., Zoology Dept, Univ. of Toronto 1969–78, Prof., Dept of Cell and System Biology 1978–97, Prof. Emer. 1997–; Visiting Prof. Tokyo Univ. 1999, Hiroshima Univ. 2000, Konan Univ. 2002–04; discovered Maturation Promoting Factor (MPF), cytostatic factor (CSF) proteins in the cytoplasm of cells that controls cell div.; Manning Award 1991, Gairdner Int. Award 1992, Albert Lasker Medical Research Award 1998. *Publications:* numerous scientific papers. *Address:* Department of Cell and System Biology, University of Toronto, 25 Harbord Street, Toronto, ON M5S 3G5 (office); 401-640 Sheppard Avenue East, North York, Toronto, ON M2K 1B8, Canada (home). *Telephone:* (416) 978-3493 (office); (647) 343-0497 (home). *Fax:* (416) 978-8532 (office). *E-mail:* yoshio.masui@utoronto.ca (office); masui@rogers.com (home). *Website:* www.csb.utoronto.ca (office).

MASUKO, Osamu; Japanese automotive industry executive; *Representative Director and President, Mitsubishi Motors Corporation;* ed Waseda Univ.; joined Mitsubishi Corpn 1972, Man. Korea Team, Motor Vehicle Dept 1990–91, Man. Indonesia Team 1991–95, Asst Gen. Man. Motor Vehicle Dept 1995–97, Chief Adviser, P.T. Krama Yudhi Tiga Berlian Motors, Jakarta 1997–2002, Gen. Man. Motor Vehicle Unit 2002–03, Sr Vice Pres. and Div. COO Motor Vehicle Business Div. 2003–04, Man. Dir and Head Overseas Operations 2004–05, Pres., COO, Chief Business Ethics Officer Mitsubishi Motors Corpn Jan.–April 2005, Rep. Dir, Pres. and Chief Business Ethics Officer April 2005–11, Rep. Dir and Pres. 2011–. *Address:* Mitsubishi Motors Corpn, 33-8, Shiba 5-chome, Minato-ku, Tokyo 108-8410, Japan (office). *Telephone:* (3) 6719-2111 (office). *Fax:* (3) 6719-0059 (office). *E-mail:* info@mitsubishi-motors.co.jp (office). *Website:* www.mitsubishi-motors.co .jp (office).

MASUR, Kurt; German conductor; b. 18 July 1927, Brieg, Silesia, Poland; ed Nat. Music School, Breslau, Hochschule für Musik, Leipzig; theatre conductor in Erfurt and Leipzig 1948–55, conductor, Dresden Philharmonic 1955–58, Chief Conductor 1967–72; Gen. Musical Dir, Mecklenburg State Theatre 1958–60; Prin. Musical Dir, Komische Oper in East Berlin 1960–64; Musical Dir Dresden Philharmonic 1967–72; Music Dir, Leipzig Gewandhaus Orchestra 1970–96, Conductor Laureate 1996–; UK début with New Philharmonia Orchestra 1973; début in USA with Cleveland Orchestra 1974; Music Dir Conductor New York Philharmonic 1991–2002; Prin. Conductor London Philharmonic Orchestra 1991–2007; Music Dir Orchestre Nat. de France 2002–08, Conductor Laureate 2008–; has toured extensively in Europe and the USA; Freeman of City of Leipzig; Hon. Pres. Kulturstiftung, Leipzig; Officier, Légion d'honneur, Bundesverdienstkreuz; Hon. Citizen of Brieg (Poland), Commdr Cross of Merit (Poland) 1999; hon. degrees from seven American univs and Univ. of Leipzig. *Address:* Masur Music International Inc., Ansonia PO Box 231478, New York, NY 10023, USA (office). *Telephone:* (646) 623-5803 (office). *Fax:* (212) 414-8276 (office). *E-mail:* info@kurtmasur.com (office). *Website:* www.kurtmasur.com (office).

MASUREL, Jean-Louis Antoine Nicolas, MBA; French industrialist and vintner; b. 18 Sept. 1940, Cannes; s. of Antoine and Anne-Marie Masurel (née Gallant); m. 1st 1964; two d.; m. 2nd Martine Fabrega 1987; ed Hautes Etudes Commerciales, Graduate School of Business Admin., Harvard Univ.; with Morgan Guaranty Trust Co., New York, last position Sr Vice-Pres. New York 1964–80; Sr Exec. Vice-Pres. Banque de Paris & des Pays Bas 1980–82; Deputy Pres. Banque Paribas 1982–83; Man. Dir Moët-Hennessy 1983–89, Vice-Chair. 1987; Man. Dir LVMH Moët-Hennessy Louis Vuitton 1987–89; Pres. Arcos Investissement SA 1989–, Hediard SA 1991–95; Hon. Pres. Harvard Business School Club de France 1993–96; mem. Supervisory Bd Peugeot SA 1987–, 21 Centrale Pnrs SA; Dir Soc. des Bains de Mer (SBM), Monaco 1994–; Sr Int. Adviser, BBL Investment Banking 1997–99, ING Barings 1999–2001; Dir Banque du Gothard SAM, Monaco 1998–, Oudart SA 1999–; Gov. American Hosp. in Paris; wine producer in Néoules (Domaine de Trians-Var); Chevalier des Arts et des Lettres 1996; Chevalier Légion d'honneur 2001. *Leisure interests:* hunting, skiing. *Address:* Arcos Investissement, 10a rue de la Paix, 75002 Paris; Domaine de Trians, 83136 Néoules, France (home). *Telephone:* 1-42-96-01-96. *Fax:* 1-42-96-01-70. *E-mail:* jlmasurel@wanadoo.fr (office). *Website:* www.trians.com (home).

MASUZOE, Yoichi, LLB; Japanese academic, politician and television commentator; *Governor of Tokyo;* b. 29 Nov. 1948, Fukuoka Pref.; ed Univ. of Tokyo; Research Fellow, Univ. of Tokyo 1971–73, Institut d'Histoire des Relations Internationales Contemporaines, Univ. of Paris, France 1973–75, Institut d'Hautes Etudes Internationales, Univ. of Geneva, Switzerland 1976–77; Assoc. Prof. of Political Science and History, Univ. of Tokyo 1979–89; Dir Masuzoe Inst. of Political Economy 1989–; mem. House of Councillors (Senator) 2001–13, fmr Dir Budget Cttee, Research Comm. on Constitution, Pres. Cttee on Foreign Affairs and

Defence 2005–07; Minister of Health, Labour and Welfare 2007–09; Gov. of Tokyo 2014–; mem. Liberal Democratic Party (LDP) –2010, Chair. Senate Policy Bd 2006–07; Ed.-in-Chief Cahiers Du Japon 1998–2001; Pres. The New Renaissance Party 2010–. *Publications include:* Akai bara wa saitaka (Politics in France) 1983, Sengyo to siteno seijika (Political Leadership) 1989, Sengo Nihon no Gen'ei (Dangerous Cult) 1995, 20 Seiki Enerugi Kakumei no Jidai (The Meaning of the 20th Century) 1998, Years of Trial: Japan in the 1990's 2000, Haha ni Mutsuki wo Aterutoki (Care for My Mother) 1998, Naikaku Soridaijin (Prime Minister) 2002, Nagata-cho vs. Kasumigaseki 2007, Watashi no Genten soshite Chikai (My History) 2008, Masuzoe Memo 2010, Nihon Shinsei Keikaku 2010. *Address:* Office of the Governor, 8-1 Nishi-Shinjuku 2-chome, Shinjuku-ku, Tokyo 163-8001 (office); Suite 323, Sangiingiinkaikan, 2-1-1, Nagata-cho, Chiyoda-ku, Tokyo 100-8962, Japan (office). *Telephone:* (3) 6550-0323 (office). *Fax:* (3) 6551-0323. *E-mail:* mipe@mipe.co.jp (office). *Website:* www.metro.tokyo.jp/ (office); shintokaikaku.jp (office).

MATA FIGUEROA, Gen.-in-Chief Carlos José; Venezuelan army officer and government official; Head of Mil. Affairs of Pres. 2009, Chief of Operational Strategic Command 2009–, also Minister of Defence 2010–12. *Address:* c/o Ministry of Defence, Edif. 17 de Diciembre, planta baja, Base Aérea Francisco de Miranda, La Carlota, Caracas, Venezuela (office).

MATACZYŃSKI, Maciej, LLD; Polish lawyer, business executive and academic; *Partner, Mataczyński Dybiński Krzemień;* ed Faculty of Law, Adam Mickiewicz Univ. (Fulbright Scholar), Poznań, T.M.C. Assera Inst., The Hague, Netherlands; tutor, European Law Professorship, Faculty of Law, Adam Mickiewicz Univ., Poznań 2003–; legal adviser on civil law contracts 2004–; Sec. and Ind. mem., subsequently Chair. Supervisory Bd PKN Orlen Jan.–Nov. 2006, Chair. Supervisory Bd 2008–13, Chair. Nomination and Remuneration Cttee, mem. Corp. Governance Cttee; Partner, Sowisło and Topolewski audit cttee, Poznań 2008–13, Mataczyński Dybiński Krzemień 2013–; Sec. Supervisory Bd TC Dębica SA and mem. Audit Cttee 2008–. *Publications:* numerous law publs in Poland and abroad. *Address:* Mataczyński Dybiński Krzemień, 00-872 Warsaw, ul. Chłodna 52, Poland (office). *Telephone:* (22) 6937572 (office). *Fax:* (22) 6937266 (office). *E-mail:* sekretariat@mataczynski.pl (office). *Website:* www.mataczynski.pl (office).

MATAKA, Elizabeth; Botswana social worker and UN official; b. 1946, Francistown; m.; four c.; ed Univ. of Zambia; several years' experience in the field of HIV/AIDS with govt insts, private sector and non-govt orgs in Zambia; Founder and Exec. Dir Family Health Trust, Lusaka 1990–2003; fmr Vice-Chair. Global Fund to Fight AIDS, Tuberculosis and Malaria; Exec. Dir Zambia Nat. AIDS Network 2003–07; Special Envoy of Sec.-Gen. for HIV/AIDS in Africa, UN 2007–12; mem. Advisory Bd UNESCO, North Star Foundation; mem. Reference Group, Swedish / Norwegian HIV/AIDS Team for Africa; Dir Centre for Infectious Disease Research, Zambia; Dir and Chair. Children Int. Zambia; Founder-mem. Southern African Network of AIDS Service Orgs; mem. Compact Working Group on Gender, Global Task Force on Women, Girls Gender Equality and HIV 2009–. *Address:* c/o UNAIDS Secretariat 20, Avenue Appia, 1211 Geneva 27, Switzerland.

MATAKI, Tateo; Japanese advertising industry executive; *Chairman, Dentsu Inc.;* Exec. Vice-Pres. Dentsu Inc. 1999–2002, Pres. and COO 2002–03, Pres. and CEO 2004–07, Chair. 2007–; Dir Japan Productivity Center for Socio-Econ. Devt (JPC-SED) 2003. *Address:* Dentsu Inc., 1-8-1 Higashi-shimbashi, Minato-ku, Tokyo 105-7001, Japan (office). *Telephone:* (3) 6216-5111 (office). *Fax:* (3) 5551-2013 (office). *Website:* www.dentsu.com (office).

MATANE, Sir Paulias Nguna, Kt, CMG, OBE, GCMG; Papua New Guinea diplomatist; b. 21 Sept. 1931, Viviran, Rabaul; s. of Ilias Matane and Elta Matane (née Toto); m. Kaludia Peril 1957; two s. two d.; worked in Dept of Educ. 1957–69; mem. Public Service Bd 1969; Head, Dept of Lands, Surveys and Mines 1969, of Business Devt 1970–75; Amb. to USA and Mexico 1975–80, Perm. Rep. to UN 1975–81, High Commr in Canada 1977–81; Sec., Dept of Foreign Affairs and Trade 1980–85; Chair. Cttee on the Philosophy of Educ. for Papua New Guinea 1986–88, Cocoa Industry Investigating Cttee of Cocoa Quality in Papua New Guinea 1986–88, Ocean Trading Co. Pty Ltd 1989–91, Newton Pacific (PNG) Pty Ltd 1989–; Censorship Bd of PNG 1990–93; Dir Treid Pacific (PNG) Pty Ltd 1987–96 (Chair. 1987–91); Presenter weekly radio programme Insait Long Komuniti 1998–, weekly programme on EMTV 1990–; columnist, The Time Traveller, in The National Newspaper 1999–; Dir Nat. Museum and Art Gallery (Bd of Trustees) 1995–99, Pres. 1999–; Dir Nat. Library and Archives 1996–; Chair. Community Consultative Cttee on East New Britain Provincial Govt of Autonomy –2004; Gov.-Gen. of Papua New Guinea 2004–11; mem. Nat. Investment and Devt Authority, Nat. Tourism Authority, Nat. Citizenship Advisory Cttee, Univ. of Papua New Guinea Council; Hon. DTech (Papua New Guinea) 1985, Hon. DPhil (Papua New Guinea) 1985; 10th Independence Anniversary Medal 1985, UN 40th Anniversary Medal, Silver Jubilee Medal 2001. *Publications include:* My Childhood in New Guinea, A New Guinean Travels through Africa, Two New Guineans Travel through South East Asia, What Good is Business?, Aimbe the Magician, Aimbe the Challenger, Aimbe the School Dropout, Aimbe the Pastor, Kum Tumun of Minj, Two Papua New Guineans Discover the Bible Lands (later retitled Travels Through the Bible Lands) 1987, To Serve with Love 1989, Chit-Chats 1991, East to West–The Longest Train Trip in the World 1991, Let's Do It PNG, Trekking through the New Worlds, Voyage to Antarctica 1996, Laughter Made in PNG 1996, Amazing Discoveries in 40 Years of Marriage 1996, The Word Power 1998, The Other Side of Port Moresby . . . In Pictures 1998, A Trip of a Lifetime 1998, Waliling Community United Church Then and Now 1998, Coach Adventures Down Under 1999, Some Answers to our Management Problems in the Public and Private Sectors 1999, More Answers to Our Management Problems 1999, Chit-Chats (vol. 3) 2000, Management for Excellence 2001, Exploring the Holy Lands 2001, Travels Through South-East Asia (vols 1 and 2) 2001, Humour: The Papua New Guinean Way, Ripples in the South Pacific Ocean, India: a Splendour in Cultural Diversity, Papua New Guinea: The Land of Natural Beauty, Diversity: The Time Traveller. *Leisure interests:* reading, squash, writing, travel, gardening, swimming. *Address:* Pauling Matane Foundation Inc., Government House, PO Box 79, Port Moresby, NCD (office); Newton Pacific and Associates Ltd, PO Box 3405, Kokopo, ENBP, Papua New Guinea. *Telephone:* 9829152 (office). *Fax:* 9829151 (office). *E-mail:* ggeneral@global.net.pg (office); pnggg9@gmail.com (office).

MATASKELEKELE, Kalkot; Ni-Vanuatu lawyer, judge and fmr head of state; b. 1949; ed Univ. of Papua New Guinea; fmr Judge, Supreme Court; fmr Solicitor-Gen.; mem. Nat. United Party; Pres. of Vanuatu 2004–09. *Address:* c/o Office of the President, Port Vila, Vanuatu (office).

MATATA PONYO, Augustin, BEcons; Democratic Republic of the Congo economist and politician; *Prime Minister;* b. 5 June 1964, Kindu, Maniema Prov.; Hortense Kachoko Mbonda; five c.; ed Univ. of Lubumbashi, Univ. of Kinshasa; began career as Asst, Econs Faculty, Univ. of Kinshasa; Econ. Researcher, Banque centrale du Congo 1988–2000; joined Ministry of Finance, becoming Econ. and Monetary Adviser, Macro-Econ. Adviser, responsible for Relations with IMF, World Bank and Int. Co-operation 2000–03, later Pres. Planning Dept, Bureau central de coordination internationale (BCECO) (procurement office under Ministry of Finance), Dir-Gen. BCECO 2003–10, Minister of Finance 2010–12; Prime Minister 2012–; mem. People's Party for Reconstruction and Democracy (Parti du Peuple pour la Reconstruction et la Démocratie). *Address:* Office of the Prime Minister, Kinshasa, Democratic Republic of the Congo (office). *Telephone:* 81-5555667 (mobile) (office). *E-mail:* cabinet@rimature.cd (office).

MATE, Dragutin; Slovenian politician, defence expert and fmr government official; *Member of Parliament;* b. 2 May 1963, Čakovec; ed Univ. of Ljubljana; teacher, Polanje Gymnasium, Ljubljana 1989–90; Deputy Sector Chief for Civil Defence and mem. Repub. Civil Defence Staff, Ministry of Defence 1990–91, worked in Counter-intelligence Dept 1991–92; Int. Co-operation Adviser, Office of Defence Minister 1992–96; Mil. and Air Force Attaché and Doyen, Mil. Diplomatic Corps, Bosnia and Herzegovina 1996; Deputy Dir Mil. Affairs Admin, Ministry of Defence, Dir Personnel Service then Dir Defence Admin 2000–04; Minister of Internal Affairs 2004–08; mem. Parl. 2011–; mem. City Council of Ljubljana; mem. Slovenian Democratic Party. *Address:* c/o Državni Zbor, Šubićeva Ulica 4, 1000 Ljubljana, Slovenia (office). *Telephone:* 1-478-9832 (office). *Fax:* 1-478-9836 (office). *E-mail:* dragutin-mate@dz-rs.si (office); dragutin-mate@sds.si (office). *Website:* www.sds.si (office).

MATENDA KYELU, Athanase; Democratic Republic of the Congo politician; Admin., Fed. of Businesses of the Democratic Repub. of Congo (FEC) –2003; mem. Parl. 2003–; Minister of Public Works and Infrastructure 2004–06, of Finance 2007–10; mem. People's Party for Reconstruction and Democracy (PPRD). *Address:* c/o Ministry of Finance, Boulevard du 30 juin, BP 12998, KIN I, Kinshasa–Gombe, Democratic Republic of the Congo (office).

MATEPARAE, Lt-Gen. Rt Hon. Sir Jeremiah (Jerry), GNZM, QSO, KStJ, MA (Hons); New Zealand army officer and government official; *Governor-General;* b. 14 Nov. 1954, Whanganui; m. Janine Mateparae; five c.; ed Officer Cadet School, Portsea, Australia, Univ. of Waikato; enlisted in Regular Force of NZ Army 1972; mem. Royal NZ Infantry Regt (RNZIR) 1976; appointments included command at platoon, co. and battalion level in NZ Infantry Bns, also served with NZ Special Air Service, commanded First Bn, RNZIR; other appointments included Chief Instructor NZ Army's Tactical School, Staff Officer Operations, NZ Army Training Group, Army Gen. Staff and Dir of Force Devt, HQ NZ Defence Force; apptd NZ Army's Land Commdr 1999; jt command of NZ forces in East Timor 1999–2001; re-apptd Land Component Commdr in HQ of Jt Forces NZ 2001; Chief of Army 2002–06; Chief NZ Defence Force (first Maori) 2006–11; Dir Govt Communication Security Bureau Feb.–July 2011; Gov.-Gen. of NZ 2011–; Fellow, NZ Inst. of Man.; Kt Grand Companion, NZ Order of Merit, Companion of the Queen's Service Order, Kt of Justice of the Order of St John, NZ Operational Service Medal, UNIFIL Medal, NZ General Service Medal (Non-Warlike) 1992, East Timor Medal, NZ Armed Forces Award with Clasp, Darjah Utama Bakti Cemerlang (Tentera); Hon. DLitt (Massey Univ.); Distinguished Alumni Award, Univ. of Waikato. *Address:* Office of the Governor-General, Government House, Private Bag 39995, Wellington Mail Centre, Lower Hutt 5045, New Zealand (office). *Telephone:* (4) 389-8055 (office). *Fax:* (4) 389-5536 (office). *E-mail:* info@govthouse.govt.nz (office). *Website:* www.gg.govt.nz (office).

MATER, Ahmed, MBBS; Saudi Arabian artist; b. 1979, Tabuk; s. of Mater Ahmed al-Ziad and Fatimah Hassan Abdullah Aseeri; m. Arwa Yahya al-Neimy; ed King Khalid Univ. Abha Coll. of Medicine; early career as physician at Aseer central hospital, before becoming artist; joined al-Miftaha Arts Village (part of King Fahd Culture Centre) 1999; works include painting, photography, installations, video and calligraphy; Founder Edge of Arabia (independent arts initiative), co-curator Edge of Arabia's first show, SOAS Brunei Gallery, London 2008; invited to participate in 53rd Venice Biennale 2009. *E-mail:* info@ahmedmater.com (office). *Website:* ahmedmater.com (office).

MATEŠA, Zlatko, PhD; Croatian politician, judge, academic and organization executive; *Assistant Dean, Zagreb School of Economics and Management;* b. 17 June 1949, Zagreb; divorced; two c.; ed Zagreb Univ., Henley Man. College, UK, J.F. Kennedy School of Govt, Harvard, USA, Beijing Sport Univ., People's Repub. of China; Asst Judge, Judge Zagreb Municipal Court 1978–; Asst Man., Man. Legal Dept INA-Trade (Industrija Nafte Asscn) 1978–82, Dir Legal and Personnel Dept 1982–85, Dir Joint Admin. Services 1985–89, mem. Man. Bd, Vice-Pres. 1989–90; Asst to Gen.-Man. INA-HQ 1990–92; mem. Croatian Democratic Union (HDZ); Dir Agency for Reconstruction and Devt of Govt of Croatia 1992–93; Minister without Portfolio 1993–95; Minister of Economy Sept.–Nov. 1995; Prime Minister of Croatia 1995–2000; currently Asst Dean Zagreb School of Econs and Man.; Pres. Croatian Olympic Cttee. *Leisure interests* flying, water polo. *Address:* Zagreb School of Economics and Management, Jordanovac 110, 10000 Zagreb, Croatia (office). *Telephone:* (1) 2354242 (office). *Fax:* (1) 2354243 (office). *E-mail:* zlatko.matesa@zsem.hr (office). *Website:* www.zsem.hr (office).

MATEU PI, Meritxell; Andorran diplomatist and politician; b. 19 Jan. 1966, Escaldes Engordany; three s. one d.; ed Paul Valéry Univ., Montpellier and Inst. of Int. Relations, Paris, France; Amb. to France 1995–99, also Perm. Rep. to Council of Europe and UNESCO, Amb. to EU, Belgium and Luxembourg 1997–98, to Netherlands 1998–99, to Denmark 1999, to Germany 1999–2004, to Slovenia 2001; Minister of Housing, Higher Educ. and Research 2001–07, of Foreign Affairs, Culture and Co-operation 2007–09; mem. Consell General (Parl.); mem. Parl. Ass., Council of Europe 2011–; mem. Demòcrates per Andorra; Officier, Ordre nat. du Mérite 1999. *Address:* Consell General del Principat d'Andorra, Carrer de la Vall s/

n, 500 Andorra la Vella, Andorra (office). *Telephone:* 877877 (office). *E-mail:* meritxellmateupi@gmail.com (home). *Website:* www.parlament.ad (office).

MATEV, Lachezar Nikolov, MA, MSc, PhD; Bulgarian diplomatist; b. 5 Aug. 1951, Sofia; m. Bisserka Mateva; two c.; ed Tech. Univ., Sofia, Sofia Univ., Moscow Diplomatic Acad.; mem. Bd, Higher Educ. Council, Ministry of Education 1977–82; Eastern European Countries Dept, Ministry of Foreign Affairs 1982; First Sec., Embassy in Prague 1982–89; Foreign Econ. Policy and Econ. Organisations Directorate 1992–93; Co-founder and Man. Dir Int. Business Devt magazine, 1992–93; Man. Dir VECCO Ltd; Head UN Agencies Section, Foreign Econ. Policy Dept 1993–95; mem., then Head, Bulgarian Del. to UNDP Exec. Bd 1994–95; Counsellor, Embassy in Madrid 1995–98; Head of Unit, European Integration Directorate, Ministry of Foreign Affairs, mem. Accession Negotiations Team, mem. Inter-Ministerial Cen. Coordination Unit for Nat. Plan for Econ. Devt, mem. Inter-Ministerial Cttee for Intellectual Rights' Protection, mem. Cttee on Use of Atomic Energy for Peaceful Purposes 1998–2002; Minister Plenipotentiary, Embassy in London 2002–05, Amb. to UK 2005–09, also Perm. Rep. to IMO 2007–09; Kt Commdr, Royal Order of St Francis 2006. *Leisure interests:* art, classical and opera music, theatre, tennis, swimming, karate, basketball, rowing, skiing, gardening, business and finance. *Address:* Ministry of Foreign Affairs, 1040 Sofia, ul. Al. Zhendov 2, Bulgaria (office). *Telephone:* (2) 971-14-08 (office). *Fax:* (2) 870-30-41 (office). *E-mail:* iprd@mfa.government.bg (office). *Website:* www.mfa.government .bg (office).

MATHAS, Theodore (Ted) A., AB, JD; American insurance executive; *Chairman, President and CEO, New York Life Insurance Company;* b. 1967, Norfolk, Va; m. Keryn Mathas; three c.; ed Stanford Univ., Univ. of Virginia; attorney, Debevoise & Plimpton –1995; joined Asset Man. Div., New York Life Insurance Co. 1995, Pres. Eagle Strategies Corpn (subsidiary co.) 1996–99, also Pres. NYLIFE Securities Inc. 1997–99, COO for career agency distribution system 1999–2001, COO Life & Annuity 2001–04, mem. Exec. Man. Cttee 2002–, mem. Bd Dirs and Vice-Chair. 2006–07, COO 2006–08, Pres. 2007–, CEO 2008–, Chair. 2009–; Dir Haier New York Life Insurance Ltd, Shanghai, Max New York Life Insurance Co. Ltd, New Delhi; mem. Bd American Council of Life Insurers. *Address:* New York Life Insurance Co., 51 Madison Avenue, Suite 3200, New York, NY 10010, USA (office). *Telephone:* (212) 576-7000 (office). *Fax:* (212) 576-8145 (office). *E-mail:* info@newyorklife.com (office). *Website:* www.newyorklife.com (office).

MATHER, Graham Christopher Spencer, MA; British politician, solicitor and *administrator; President, European Policy Forum;* b. 23 Oct. 1954, Preston, Lancs.; s. of Thomas Mather and Doreen Mather; m. 1st Fiona Marion McMillan Bell 1981 (divorced 1995); two s.; m. 2nd Geneviève Elizabeth Fairhurst 1997; ed Hutton Grammar School, New Coll., Oxford (Burnet Law Scholar); Asst to Dir-Gen. Inst. of Dirs 1980, est. Policy Unit 1983, Head of Policy Unit 1983–86; Deputy Dir Inst. of Econ. Affairs 1987, Gen. Dir 1987–92; Pres. European Policy Forum 1992–, European Media Forum 1997–, European Financial Forum 1999–, The Infrastructure Forum 2009–; MEP for Hampshire North and Oxford 1994–99; Visiting Fellow, Nuffield Coll. Oxford 1992–99; mem. Competition Appeals Tribunal 2000–11; mem. Monopolies and Mergers Comm. 1989–94, Westminster City Council 1982–86; Conservative parl. cand. for Blackburn 1983; Vice-Pres. Asscn of Dist Councils 1994–97; Consultant, Tudor Investment Corpn 1992–2012; Adviser, Elliott Assocs 2006–; Chair. World Free Zone Convention 2000–. *Publications:* Striking out Strikes (with C. G. Hanson) 1988; Europe's Constitutional Future (contrib.) 1990, Making Decisions in Britain 2000; papers and contribs to journals. *Address:* European Policy Forum, 49 Whitehall, London, SW1A 2BX, England (office). *Telephone:* (20) 7839-7565 (office). *Fax:* (20) 3137-2040 (office). *E-mail:* graham.mather@epfltd.org (office). *Website:* www.epfltd.org (office).

MATHER, John C., BA, PhD; American astrophysicist; *Senior Project Scientist, James Webb Space Telescope, Goddard Space Flight Center, National Aeronautics and Space Administration (NASA);* b. 7 Aug. 1946, Roanoke, Va; s. of Robert Eugene Mather and Martha Belle Cromwell Mather; m. Jane Anne Hauser; ed Swarthmore Coll., Pa, Univ. of California, Berkeley; began career as NAS Research Assoc., Goddard Inst. for Space Studies, NASA, becoming Study Scientist for Cosmic Background Explorer satellite (COBE), Goddard Space Flight Center 1976–88, then Project Scientist 1988–94, Head of Infrared Astrophysics Br. 1988–89, 1990–93, Study Scientist, James Webb Space Telescope (JWST) 1995–99, Sr Project Scientist 1999–; Chief Scientist, NASA HQ Science Mission Directorate 2007–08; mem. NAS 1997, American Acad. of Arts and Sciences 1998; Fellow, American Physical Soc. 1996, Int. Soc. for Optical Eng (SPIE) 2007, Optical Soc. of America 2009, AAAS; Hon. DSc (Swarthmore Coll.) 1994, (Maryland) 2008, (Notre Dame) 2011; Goddard Sr Fellow, holder of numerous awards, including John C. Lindsay Memorial Award 1990, NASA Exceptional Scientific Achievement Award 1991, Nat. Air and Space Museum Trophy 1991, American Inst. of Aeronautics and Astronautics Space Science Award 1993, American Acad. of Arts and Sciences Rumford Prize 1996, Univ. of Ariz. Marc Aaronson Memorial Prize 1998, George W. Goddard Award, Soc. of Photo-Optical Instrumentation Engineers 2005, Franklin Inst. Benjamin Franklin Medal 1999, Gruber Cosmology Prize 2006, Nobel Prize in Physics (with George F. Smoot) 2006, Antoinette de Vaucouleurs Medal, Univ. of Texas 2007, Robinson Prize in Cosmology, Univ. of Newcastle upon Tyne, UK 2008, Gold Medal from Prime Minister of India 2009, Chalonge Medal, Observatoire de Paris 2011. *Publication:* The Very First Light (with John Boslough) 1996, 2008. *Address:* Astrophysics Science Division, NASA/GSFC, Mail Code 443, Observational Cosmology, Greenbelt, MD 20771, USA (office). *Telephone:* (301) 286-6885 (office). *Fax:* (301) 286-5558 (office). *E-mail:* john.c .mather@nasa.gov (office). *Website:* astrophysics.gsfc.nasa.gov/staff/CVs/John .Mather (office).

MATHEWS, (Forrest) David, PhD; American educationalist and foundation executive; *President, CEO and Trustee, Charles F. Kettering Foundation;* b. 6 Dec. 1935, Grove Hill, Ala; s. of Forrest Lee and Doris Mathews; m. Mary Chapman 1960; two d.; ed Univ. of Alabama and Columbia Univ.; Infantry Officer US Army Reserves 1959–67; Pres. Univ. of Alabama 1969–80, Lecturer and Prof. of History 1969–80; Sec. of Health, Educ. and Welfare 1975–77; Chair. Nat. Council for Public Policy Educ. 1980–; Dir Acad. Educ. Devt 1975–2003; Pres., CEO and Trustee Charles F. Kettering Foundation 1981–; mem. Bd Dirs Nat. Civic League 1996–2005; mem. numerous advisory and other bds including Acad. for Educ. Devt, Nat. Civic League, Exec. Cttee of Public Agenda; Trustee Nat. March of

Dimes 1977–85, John F. Kennedy Center for Performing Arts 1975–77, Woodrow Wilson Int. Center for Scholars 1975–77, Miles Coll. 1978–, Teachers Coll., Columbia Univ. 1977–95, Gerald R. Ford Foundation 1988–; 16 hon. degrees; numerous awards. *Publications:* works on history of Southern USA, higher educ. in public policy, including The Changing Agenda for American Higher Education, The Promise of Democracy, Is There a Public for Public Schools? 1996, Politics for People: Finding a Responsible Voice 1999, Why Public Schools? Whose Public Schools? 2003, Reclaiming Public Education by Reclaiming Our Democracy 2006. *Leisure interest:* gardening. *Address:* The Charles F. Kettering Foundation, 200 Commons Road, Dayton, OH 45459 (office); 6050 Mad River Road, Dayton, OH 45459, USA. *Telephone:* (937) 434-7300 (office). *Fax:* (937) 428-5353 (office).

MATHEWSON, Sir George (Ross), Kt, CBE, MBA, PhD, FRSE, CEng, MIEE, CIMgt; British banking executive; b. 14 May 1940; s. of George Mathewson and Charlotte Gordon (née Ross); m. Sheila Alexandra Graham (née Bennett) 1966; two s.; ed Perth Acad., St Andrews Univ., Canisius Coll., Buffalo, NY, USA; Asst Lecturer, St Andrews Univ. 1964–67; various posts in Research and Devt, Avionics Engineer, Bell Aerospace, Buffalo, NY 1967–72; joined Industrial & Commercial Finance Corpn, Edinburgh 1972, Area Man., Aberdeen 1974, Asst Gen. Man. and Dir 1979; Chief Exec. and mem. Scottish Devt Agency 1981–87; Dir of Strategic Planning and Devt, Royal Bank of Scotland Group 1987–90, Deputy Group Chief Exec. 1990–92, Group Chief Exec. 1992–2000, Exec. Deputy Chair. 2000–01, Chair. 2001–06 (retd); Dir Scottish Investment Trust PLC (Chair. Nominations Cttee and Chair.'s Advisory Group) 1981–, IIF Inc. 2001–, Santander Central Hispano, SA 2001–; Pres. British Bankers' Asscn 2002–05; Fellow, Chartered Inst. of Bankers in Scotland 1994–; Hon. LLD (Dundee) 1983, (St Andrews) 2000; Hon. DUniv (Glasgow) 2001. *Publications include:* several articles on eng and finance. *Leisure interests:* rugby, tennis, business. *Address:* c/o The Royal Bank of Scotland PLC, 36 St Andrew Square, Edinburgh, EH2 2YB, Scotland (office).

MATHIAS, Peter, CBE, MA, DLitt, FBA, FRHistS; British fmr academic; b. 10 Jan. 1928, Somerset, England; s. of John Samuel Mathias and Marian Helen Love; m. Elizabeth Ann Blackmore 1958; two s. one d.; ed Colstons Hosp., Bristol, Jesus Coll. Cambridge, Harvard Univ., USA; Research Fellow, Jesus Coll. 1952–55; Lecturer, History Faculty, Cambridge Univ. 1955–68, Tutor and Dir of Studies, Queens' Coll., Sr Proctor, Cambridge Univ. 1965–66; Chichele Prof. of Econ. History, Oxford Univ., Fellow, All Souls Coll. 1969–87; Master of Downing Coll., Cambridge 1987–95; Pres. International Econ. History Asscn 1974–78, Hon. Pres. 1978–; Pres. Business Archive Council 1984–95, Vice-Pres. 1995–; Chair. British Library Advisory Council 1994–99; Vice-Pres. Royal Historical Soc. 1975–80 (Hon. Vice-Pres. 2001–), International Inst. of Econ. History Francesco Datini Prato 1987–99; Hon. Treas. British Acad. 1979–88, Econ. History Soc. 1967–88 (Pres. 1989–92, Vice-Pres. 1992–); Chair. Central European Univ. Press Advisory Bd 2002–; mem. Advisory Bd of the Research Councils 1983–88; Chair. History of Medicine Panel, Wellcome Trust 1980–88; Syndic Fitzwilliam Museum 1987–98; Chair. Fitzwilliam Museum Enterprises Ltd 1990–99, Bd of Continuing Educ., Cambridge Univ. 1991–95; Curator Bodleian Library, Oxford 1972–87; mem. Academia Europaea 1989, Beirat WissenschaftsKolleg, Berlin 1992–98, foreign mem. Royal Danish Acad., Royal Belgian Acad.; Trustee, GB-Sasakawa Foundation 1994–, Chair. 1997–2005, Pres. 2005–11, Hon. Pres. 2011–; Hon. Fellow, Jesus Coll., Queens' Coll., Downing Coll. Cambridge; Order of the Rising Sun (Japan) 2003; Hon. LittD (Buckingham, Birmingham, Hull, Warwick, de Montfort, East Anglia), Dr hc (Russian Acad. of Sciences) 2002, (Kansai Univ., Japan) 2006; Maria Theresa Medal, Univ. of Pavia 2002. *Publications include:* Brewing Industry in England 1700–1830 1959, Retailing Revolution 1967, Tradesmen's Tokens 1962, The First Industrial Nation 1969, 1983, The Transformation of England 1979, L'economia britannica dal 1815 al 1914 1994, Cinque lezioni di teoria e storia 2003, Gen. Ed. Cambridge Economic History of Europe 1968–90, History of Mankind Vol. 6 (UNESCO) 2007. *Leisure interests:* travel, New Hall porcelain. *Address:* 33 Church Street, Chesterton, Cambs., CB4 1DT, England (office). *Telephone:* (1223) 329824 (home). *E-mail:* pm314@cam.ac.uk (office).

MATHIES, Richard A., BS, MS, PhD, FRSC; American chemist and academic; *Gilbert Newton Lewis Professor and Dean, College of Chemistry, University of California, Berkeley;* b. 1946, Seattle, Wash.; m. JoAnne Mathies; two c.; ed Univ. of Washington, Cornell Univ.; Helen Hay Whitney Fellow, Yale Univ. 1974–76; Asst Prof., Coll. of Chem., Univ. of California, Berkeley 1976, Alfred P. Sloan Fellow 1979–81, Gilbert Newton Lewis Prof. 2008–, also Dean, Coll. of Chem. 2008–, Co-founder and Dir Center for Analytical Biotechnology 2003; mem. Scientific Advisory Bd IntegenX, Singule, NanoString, Inc., C8 Medisensors, Affymetrix; mem. American Optical Soc., American Soc. for Photobiology, AAAS; Fellow, Optical Soc. of America 2004, Soc. for Applied Spectroscopy 2008; Harold Lamport Award, New York Acad. of Sciences 1983, Research Award, American Soc. for Photobiology 1989, Frederick Conf. on Capillary Electrophoresis Award 1998, Research Award, Asscn for Lab. Automation 2001, Ellis R. Lippincott Award, Optical Soc. of America 2004, Instrumentation Award, Analytical Chem. Div., ACS 2010. *Achievements include:* work in developing energy transfer fluorescent labels that was critical to the early completion of the Human Genome Sequence. *Publications:* author of over 380 publs and 35 patents on photochemistry, photobiology, bioanalytical chemistry and genome analysis tech. *Address:* Office of the Dean, College of Chemistry, University of California, Berkeley, CA 94720-1776, USA (office). *Telephone:* (510) 642-4192 (office). *Fax:* (510) 642-3599 (office). *E-mail:* rich@zinc.cchem.berkeley.edu (office). *Website:* chem.berkeley.edu (office).

MATHIESEN, Árni M., MSc; Icelandic politician and UN official; *Assistant Director-General, Fisheries and Aquaculture Department, United Nations Food and Agriculture Organization;* b. 2 Oct. 1958, Reykjavík; s. of Matthías Á. Mathiesen and Sigrún Þorgilsdóttir Mathiesen; m. Steinunn Kristín Fridjónsdóttir 1991; three d.; ed Flensborgarskóli, Hafnarfjöður, Univs of Edin. and Stirling, Scotland, UK; qualified as veterinarian 1983, worked as veterinary officer for fish diseases 1985–95; Man.-Dir of Acquaculture, Faxalax hf. 1988–89; Chair. Flensborgarskóli Student Asscn 1977–78; Vice-Pres. Icelandic Asscn of Young Conservatives (SUS) 1985–87; Pres. Asscn of Young Conservatives (Stefnir), Hafnarfjöður 1986–88; elected mem. of Parl.; mem. Independence Party; Rep. of Iceland to Nordic Council 1991–95; mem. Parl. Cttee on EFTA and EEC 1995–99; Minister of Fisheries 1999–2005, of Finance 2005–09 (resgnd); currently Asst Dir-Gen., Fisheries and Aquaculture Dept, FAO; fmr Chair. Prevention of Cruelty to

Animals; mem. Bd Guarantee Div., Acquaculture Loans 1990–94, Bd Icelandic Veterinary Asscn 1986–87, Bd of Búnadarbanki Islands; mem. Salary Council, Confed. of Univ. Grads 1985–87; mem. Flensborgarskóli School Bd 1990–99; fmr mem. Bd of Búnadarbanki Islands, Agricultural Loan Fund. *Address:* Fisheries and Aquaculture Department, UN Food and Agriculture Organization, Viale delle Terme di Caracalla, 00100 Rome, Italy (office). *Telephone:* (06) 5705-1 (office). *Fax:* (06) 5705-3152 (office). *E-mail:* fao-hq@fao.org (office). *Website:* www.fao.org/fishery/en (office).

MATHIESEN, Matthias (Árnason), CandJuris; Icelandic politician and lawyer; b. 6 Aug. 1931, Hafnarfjörður; s. of Arni M. Mathiesen and Svava E. Mathiesen; m. Sigrún Thorgilsdóttir Mathiesen 1956; two s. one d.; ed Univ. of Iceland; Chief Exec. Hafnarfjörður Savings Bank 1958–67, Chair. 1967–2005; Advocate, Supreme Court 1967–74, 1991–; mem. Althing (Parl.) 1959–91, Speaker Lower Chamber 1970–71; Rep. of Althing to Nordic Council 1965–74, mem. Presidium 1970–71, 1973–74, Pres. 1970–71, 1980–81; Del. North Atlantic Ass., NATO 1963–69, 1972, Chair. Icelandic Del. 1964–67, Pres. of Ass. 1967–68; mem. Bd E Thorgilsson & Co. Ltd, Hafnarfjörður 1973–2001, Chair. 1982–2001; Dir Nat. Bank of Iceland 1961–74, 1980–83; Icelandic mem. of Bd of Govs World Bank Group (IBRD, IDA, IFC) 1983–85; Minister of Finance 1974–78, Minister of Commerce (including Banking) and of Nordic Co-operation 1983–85, for Foreign Affairs 1986–87, of Communications 1987–88; mem. Cen. Cttee, Independence Party 1965–91. *Address:* Hringbraut 59, Hafnarfjörður, Iceland (home). *Telephone:* (91) 5-02-76 (home).

MATHIESON, Peter William, MB BS (Hons), PhD, FRCP, FMedSci; British medical scientist, academic and university administrator; *Vice-Chancellor, The University of Hong Kong;* ed London Hosp. Coll., Univ. of Cambridge; held junior posts in and around West London; MRC Training Fellow, Univ. of Cambridge; held MRC-funded Fellowship in Lab. of Profs Peter Lachmann and Doug Fearon on complement/immunology; Foundation Prof. of Renal Medicine, Univ. of Bristol and Hon. Consultant Nephrologist, North Bristol NHS Trust 1995–2013, Head of Univ. Dept of Clinical Science at North Bristol and Dir of Research and Devt for North Bristol NHS Trust 2007, Dean of Faculty of Medicine and Dentistry 2008–13, now Hon. Prof. of Medicine and Dentistry; Vice-Chancellor The Univ. of Hong Kong 2013–; mem. Renal Asscn Clinical Trials Cttee 1996–2007, Chair. 2000–03, Pres. Renal Asscn 2007; Chair. Research Grants Cttee, Kidney Research UK (fmrly Nat. Kidney Research Fund) 2003–07. *Publications:* numerous papers in professional journals on human glomerular cell biology and regulation of glomerular permeability. *Leisure interests:* hill walking, travelling, spending time with family. *Address:* Vice-Chancellor's Office, The University of Hong Kong, 10/F Knowles Building, Pokfulam Road, Hong Kong Special Administrative Region, People's Republic of China (office). *Telephone:* 28592100 (office). *Fax:* 28589435 (office). *E-mail:* tsuilc@hku.hk (office). *Website:* www.hku.hk/vcoffice/home.html (office).

MATHIS-EDDY, Darlene, PhD; American poet and academic; *Professor Emerita, Ball State University;* b. 19 March 1937, Elkhart, Ind.; d. of the late William Eugene Mathis and Fern Roose Paulmer Mathis; m. Spencer Livingston Eddy, Jr 1964 (died 1971); ed Goshen Coll. and Rutgers Univ.; Instructor in English, Douglass Coll. 1962–64; Instructor in English, Rutgers Univ. 1964, 1965, Rutgers Univ. Coll. (Adult Educ.) 1967; Asst Prof. in English, Ball State Univ. 1967–71, Assoc. Prof. 1971–75, Prof. 1975–99, Poet-in-Residence 1989–93, Prof. Emer., English and Humanities 1999–, Ralph S. Whitinger Lecturer, Ball State Univ. Honors Coll. 1998–99; Adjunct Prof., Core Program and Coll. Seminar Program, Univ. of Notre Dame, South Bend, Ind. 2001–06; Consulting Ed. Blue Unicorn 1995–; Founding Ed. The Hedge Row Press 1995–; Docent, Midwest Museum of American Art 2010–; mem. Comm. on Women for the Nat. Council of Teachers of English 1976–79; Poetry Ed. BSU Forum; Vice-Pres. of Programs, American Asscn of Univ. Women, Elkhart Br.; Pres. American Asscn of Univ. Women 2008–; Woodrow Wilson Nat. Fellow 1959–62, Rutgers Univ. Grad. Honors and Honors Dissertation Fellow 1964–65, 1966–67, Notable Woodrow Wilson Nat. Fellow 1991; numerous creative arts, creative teaching, research grants and awards. *Publications:* Leaf Threads, Wind Rhymes 1986, The Worlds of King Lear 1971, Weathering 1992, Reflections: Studies in Light 1993; Contributing Ed. Snowy Egret 1988–90; numerous poems in literary reviews; book reviews and essays in numerous journals; articles in American Literature, English Language Notes, etc. *Leisure interests:* gardening, music, antiques, reading, sketching, photography, bird watching, cooking. *Address:* 1840 West Cobblestone Boulevard, Elkhart, IN 46514-4961, USA (home). *Telephone:* (574) 266-4394 (home).

MATHUR, Murari Lal, PhD; Indian mechanical engineer and academic; *Professor Emeritus, Faculty of Engineering, University of Jodhpur;* b. 10 July 1931, Masuda; s. of the late Dr S. D. Mathur and Lalti Devi; m. Vimla Mathur 1961; one s. three d.; ed Govt Coll., Ajmer, Birla Engineering Coll., Pilani, Glasgow Univ., UK; Asst Prof., MBM Eng Coll., Govt of Rajasthan 1952–57; Deputy Dir of Tech. Educ. and Sec. Bd of Tech. Educ., Govt of Rajasthan 1957–58; Prof. and Head Mechanical Eng Dept, Univ. of Jodhpur 1963–85, Prof., Dean Faculty of Eng 1966–68, 1974, 1977–80, Vice-Chancellor 1985–90, Prof. Emer. 1991–; Chair. Automotive Prime-Movers Sectional Cttee, Indian Bureau of Standards; Co-ordinator Solar Passive House Project; design consultant heat exchanger and heat recovery equipment; consultant Cen. Silk Bd and other industries; Fellow, Inst. of Engineers (India); Sri Chandra Prakash Memorial Gold Medal, Pres. of India's Prize, Inst. of Engineers Award. *Films:* has produced two educational films. *Publications:* books on thermal eng, internal combustion engines, gas turbines and jet propulsion, thermodynamics, fluid mechanics and machines, machine drawing and heat transfer; over 80 research papers. *Leisure interests:* reading, writing, lecturing on educational topics and topics concerning energy and environment, social service. *Address:* Alok Villa, 17-A, Shastri Nagar, Jodhpur 342 003, India (home). *Telephone:* 2433207 (home); (98) 29253207 (mobile) (home).

MATHYS, Adidjatou; Benin economist and government official; b. 1956, Porto-Novo; m.; three c.; ed Nat. Univ. of Benin; has held several posts at Directorate Gen. of Treasury and Public Accounting, including work with the Chief of Financial Affairs 1982, Asst Receiver, Recovery Center 1984–85, Deputy Head of Service for Expenditure 1985–86, Chief of Expenditure 1986–94, Receiver of Finance for Ouémé 1994–98, Deputy Gen. Man. 1998–99, Gen. Man. 1999–2003; Asst to Minister of the Economy and Finance 2004–06, Chief of Staff to Minister for the Budget 2007–07, Chief of Staff to Minister of the Economy and Finance

2007–11, Minister of the Economy and Finance 2011–12; campaign co-ordinator in presidential elections for Bruno Amoussou 2006, for Boni Yayi 2011; fmr mem. Bd of Dirs Banque Centrale des Etats de l'Afrique de l'Ouest, Continental Bank; mem. Parti Social-Démocrate; Knight of the Order of Merit of Benin. *Address:* c/o Ministry of the Economy and Finance, BP 302, Cotonou, Benin (office).

MATIBA, Kenneth; Kenyan politician; Chair. Kenya Breweries 1968–79; founder, Kenya Football League; fmr Chair. Kenya Football Fed.; entered Parl. 1979; resgnd from Govt over election-rigging 1988; imprisoned for 10 months for leading multi-party democracy movt July 1990; Chair. FORD-Asili Party; contested presidential election Dec. 1992; Founder and Chair. Alliance Hotels and Resorts; owner The People Daily newspaper. *Leisure interest:* mountain climbing. *Address:* Alliance Hotels and Resorts, POB 49839, 00100 Nairobi; c/o Forum for the Restoration of Democracy—Asili (FORD—Asili), Anyany Estate, POB 72595, Nairobi, Kenya. *E-mail:* alliance@africaonline.co.ke.

MATIN, Abdul, MA, PhD; Pakistani economist; b. 1 March 1932, Sawabi; s. of Dur Jamil Khan; m. Azra Matin 1959; three s.; ed Univ. of Peshawar and Univ. of Bonn, FRG; Chair. Dept of Econs, Univ. of Peshawar and Dir Bd of Econs, North-West Frontier Prov. (NWFP) 1959–70; Chief Economist, Govt of NWFP 1970–72; Minister and Deputy Perm. Rep., Mission to UN, New York 1973–76; Exec. Dir ADBP, Islamabad 1977–85; Vice-Chancellor Univ. of Peshawar 1987–89; Vice-Pres. and mem. of Cen. Cttee, Pakistan Tehrik-i-Insaaf (Movt for Justice) 1996–; Chair. of Task Forces to Regulate Pvt. Educational Insts in NWFP 1999–, to Reform Higher Secondary Govt Schools in NWFP 2000–; mem. Nat. Comm. on Manpower, Govt of Pakistan, Educ. Inquiry Cttee, NWFP, Prov. Finance Comm., NWFP 2002–, Health Regulatory Authority, NWFP 2003–, Higher Educ. Comm. of Pakistan 2003–, Econ. Reform Comm., NWFP 2004, Search Cttee for Vice-Chancellors, NWFP; Chair. Govt Working Group on Transport Policy 1991–92, Univs Services Reforms and Man. Cttee, Govt of NWFP 1998; mem. Bd of Man. Quaid-e-Azam Mazar 2000–, Pakistan Bait-ul-Mal; engaged in research project 'Revival and Reconstruction of Muslim World'; prepared policy draft for Nat. Centre for Rehabilitation of Child Labour 2001; Chair. Think Tank, Hamdard Shura, NWFP 1994–; Hamdard Foundation Award for Outstanding Services 1992, Khawaja Farid Sang, Lahore 2004. *Publications:* Industrialization of NWFP 1970; 95 articles on the problems, policies and pattern of econ. devt in professional journals. *Leisure interests:* extension lectures, public speeches, involvement in discourses on rectification of West-Ummah relations. *Address:* House No. 27, Street No. 9, Sector D-3, Phase I, Hayatabad, Peshawar, NWFP, Pakistan (home). *Telephone:* 5817144 (home). *Fax:* 5817144 (home).

MATIN, M. A., FRCS; Bangladeshi ophthalmologist and politician; b. 1 Dec. 1937, Pabna; ed Dhaka Medical Coll.; worked in Royal Eye Hosp. and King's Coll. Hosp., London 1964–67; Assoc. Prof. of Ophthalmology, Inst. of Postgraduate Medicine and Research, Dhaka 1967–72, Prof., then Head of Dept 1972–; Hon. Col and Consultant Ophthalmologist, Combined Mil. Hosp., Dhaka 1976; MP 1979–, re-elected MP (BNP) 2001–; Minister of Civil Aviation and Tourism 1979, Minister of Youth Devt and of Health and Population Control 1981, Minister of Home Affairs 1981–82, Minister of Commerce 1984, Minister of Works 1985, Deputy Prime Minister in charge of Ministry of Home Affairs 1986–88; Deputy Prime Minister 1988–89; Minister of Health and Family Planning 1988, 1989, of Home Affairs 1988–89; Adviser in charge of Home Affairs, of Shipping, and of Liberation War Affairs 2007–09; fmr Sec.-Gen. and Pres. Bangladesh Ophthalmological Soc. and Pres. Bangladesh Medical Services Asscn; Vice-Chair. Bangladesh Medical Research Council and Vice-Pres. Bangladesh Coll. of Physicians and Surgeons; Alim Memorial Gold Medal; Int. Award, Asian Pacific Acad. of Ophthalmology 1981. *Address:* c/o Ministry of Home Affairs, Bangladesh Secretariat, School Building, 2nd and 3rd Floors, Dhaka 1000; Shantinagar, Dhaka, Bangladesh (home).

MATLANYANE, Retšelisitsoe Adelaide, BA, MEconSc, PhD; Lesotho economist and central banker; *Governor, Central Bank of Lesotho;* ed Nat. Univ. of Lesotho, Univ. of Botswana, Univ. of Pretoria, South Africa; joined Central Bank of Lesotho 2006, Second Deputy Gov. 2006–07, First Deputy Gov. 2007–11, Acting Gov. 2011–12, Gov. 2012–. *Address:* Office of the Governor, Central Bank of Lesotho, cnr Airport and Moshoeshoe Roads, POB 1184, Maseru 100, Lesotho (office). *Telephone:* 22314281 (office). *Fax:* 22310051 (office). *E-mail:* cbl@centralbank.org.ls (office). *Website:* www.centralbank.org.ls (office).

MATLYUBOV, Lt-Gen. Bahodir Ahmedovich; Uzbekistani government official; b. 10 March 1952, Samarqand, Uzbek SSR, USSR; ed Samarqand State Univ.; held various positions at Samarqand Regional Internal Affairs Directorate 1978–94; Head, Buxoro Regional Internal Affairs Directorate 1994–97; held several sr positions in Ministry of Internal Affairs, including First Deputy Minister of Internal Affairs 1997–2004, Chair. State Cttee on Demonopolization and Competition and Business Support, Chair. State Customs Cttee 2004–06, Minister of Internal Affairs 2006–13; rank of Lt-Gen. 2001; mem. Security Council under the Pres. of Uzbekistan 2004–13; Shon-Saraf (Glory) Order (First and Second Degrees). *Address:* c/o Ministry of Internal Affairs, 100029 Tashkent, Yu. Rajaby ko'ch. 1, Uzbekistan. *E-mail:* info@mvd.uz.

MATOKA, Peter Wilfred, PhD; Zambian politician, international organization official, diplomatist and academic; *Senior Lecturer, Social Development Studies Department, University of Zambia;* b. 8 April 1930, Mwinilunga, NW Prov.; m. Grace J. Mukahlera 1957; two s. one d.; ed Rhodes Univ., S Africa, American Univ., Washington, DC, Univ. of Zambia, Univ. of Warwick, UK; civil servant, Northern Rhodesia Govt 1954–64; mem. of Parl. of Zambia 1964–78; Minister of Information and Postal Services 1964–65, of Health 1965–66, of Works and Housing 1967, of Power, Transport and Works 1968; mem. Cen. Cttee, United Nat. Independence Party (UNIP) 1967, 1971–78; Minister for Luapula Prov. 1969; High Commr of Zambia in UK 1969–70 (also accred to the Holy See); Minister for the S Prov. 1970, of Health 1971–72, of Local Govt and Housing 1972–77, of Devt Planning 1977, of Econ. and Tech. Co-operation 1977–78; Chief Whip, Nat. Ass. 1973–78; Sr Regional Adviser, UN Econ. Comm. for Africa, Addis Ababa 1979–83; High Commr in Zimbabwe 1984–88; Chair. Social and Cultural Sub-Cttee of Cen. Cttee of UNIP 1988–90, of Science and Tech. Sub-Cttee 1990–91; Sr Lecturer, Social Devt Studies Dept, Univ. of Zambia 1995–; Chair. WHO Africa Region 1966; Pres. Africa, Caribbean and Pacific Group of States 1977; Chair. Nat. Inst. of Scientific

Research 1977; Chair. Zambia-Kenya and Zambia-Yugoslavia Perm. Comms 1977; Chair. Lusaka MULPOC 1977; Chair. and Man. Dir FilZam Projects and Investments Services Centre Ltd 1992–; Vice-Chair. Nat. Tender Bd 1977; Life mem. CPA; mem. Perm. Human Rights Comm. of Zambia 1997–; Nat. Consultant on Child Labour Issues 1997–; Kt of St Gregory (Vatican) 1964; Kt, Egypt and Ethiopia, Grand Commdr of the Companion Order of Freedom 2006. *Leisure interests:* gardening, television, walking. *Address:* University of Zambia, PO Box 32379, Lusaka (office); Ibex Hill, PO Box 50101, Lusaka, Zambia (home). *Telephone:* (1) 291777 (office); (1) 260221 (home). *Fax:* (1) 253952 (office). *E-mail:* registra@unza.zm (office). *Website:* www.unza.zm (office).

MATOLCSY, György; Hungarian economist, politician and central banker; *Governor, Central Bank of Hungary;* b. 18 July 1955, Budapest; m.; two s.; ed Budapest Univ. of Economic Sciences; jr official, Industrial Org. Inst. 1977–78; mem. staff Ministry of Finance 1978–81, mem. Secr. 1981–85; Fellow, Finance Research Inst. 1985–90; Political State Sec., Prime Minister's Office 1990–91; Dir Privatization Research Inst. 1991; Dir EBRD, London 1991–94; Dir Property Foundation, Inst. for Privatization Studies 1995–99; Minister of Econ. Affairs 1999–2002, of Nat. Economy 2010–13; mem. Országgyűlés (Nat. Ass.) 2006–; EIB Gov. for Hungary 2010–; Gov. Cen. Bank of Hungary (Magyar Nemzeti Bank) 2013–; mem. and econ. strategist, Fidesz—Hungarian Civic Union. *Address:* Central Bank of Hungary (Magyar Nemzeti Bank), 1850 Budapest, Szabadság tér 8–9, Hungary (office). *Telephone:* (1) 428-2600 (office). *Fax:* (1) 428-2500 (office). *E-mail:* info@mnb.hu (office). *Website:* www.mnb.hu (office).

MATOMÄKI, Tauno Antero, MSc (Eng); Finnish business executive; *Chairman and CEO, Rosenlew RKW Finland Ltd;* b. 14 April 1937, Nakkila; s. of Niilo Matomäki and Martta Matomäki; m. Leena Matomäki (née Nilsson) 1963; one s. three d.; ed Tech. Univ., Helsinki; joined Rauma-Repola 1967, various positions, Pres. and CEO 1987–90, Pres. and CEO Repola Ltd 1991–96; Chair. and CEO Rosenlew RKW Finland Ltd; Chair. Rauma Ltd, United Paper Mills Ltd, Pohjolan Voima Ltd, Finnyards Ltd, UPM-Kymmene 1999–2001, Confed. of Finnish Industries, Finnish Employers' Confed.; mem. Bd of Dirs Effjohn AB; mem. Supervisory Bd Teollisuuden Voima Oy (Chair.), Kansallis-Osake-Pankki, Pohjola Insurance Co., Ilmarinen Pension Insurance Co., Polar Rakennusosakeyhtiö, Uusi Suomi Oy; Kt, Order of the White Rose of Finland (First Class). *Address:* Rosenlew RKW Finland Ltd, PL 22, Ulasoorintie 185, 28601 Pori, Finland. *Telephone:* (2) 517-8899. *Fax:* (2) 517-8890. *E-mail:* info@rosenlewrkw.com. *Website:* www.rosenlewrkw.com.

MATORI, Abdul Djalil; Indonesian politician; mem. PKB Party, Nahdlatul Ulama; Minister of Defence 2001–04; expelled from Muslim Clerics party; attended impeachment proceedings of Pres. Wahid May 2002. *Address:* c/o Ministry of Defence, Jalan Medan Merdeka Barat, 13–14, Jakarta Pusat, Indonesia (office).

MATORIN, Vladimir Anatolievich; Russian singer (bass); b. 2 May 1948, Moscow; s. of Anatoly Ivanovich Matorin and Maria Tarasovna Matorina; m. Svetlana Sergeyevna Matorina; one s.; ed Gnessin Pedagogical Inst. (now Acad.) of Music; soloist, Moscow Stanislavsky and Nemirovich-Danchenko Music Theatre 1974–91, Bolshoi Theatre 1991–; numerous int. tours; winner, All-Union Glinka Competition of vocalists and Int. Competition of Singers in Geneva, Merited Artist of Russia, People's Artist of Russia. *Opera roles include:* Boris Godunov, Ivan Susanin, King René (Iolanthe), Gremin (Eugene Onegin), Dosifei (Khovanshchina), Count Galitsky (Prince Igor), Don Basilio (Barber of Seville), Count (Invisible City of Kitezh) and more than 65 others. *Leisure interests:* poetry, sacred music, travelling by car. *Address:* Bolshoi Theatre of Russia, Teatralnaya pl. 1, 103009 Moscow (office); Periy Koptelskiy Pereulok 9/29, 129090 Moscow; Ulansky per. 21, korp. 1 apt. 53, 103045 Moscow, Russia (home). *Telephone:* (495) 692-38-86 (office); (495) 680-44-17 (home). *Fax:* (495) 680-44-17 (home).

MATOTO, 'Otenifi Afu'alo, BA, MA; Tongan civil servant and politician; m. Lavinia Matoto; two d.; ed Univ. of Auckland, New Zealand, Univ. of Durham, UK; Asst Teacher, Tonga High School 1968; joined Ministry of Finance as an Asst Sec. in 1971, twice acted as Devt Officer 1971–77, Sec. of Finance 1977–83; Man., Devt and Planning, Bank of Tonga 1983, held various managerial positions 1983–99; Man. Dir Tonga Devt Bank 1999–2006; Minister for Public Enterprises 2006–07, for Public Enterprises and Information 2007, for Finance and Information 2008–10; mem. bds or chair. numerous govt agencies, statutory bodies and cttees; mem. exec. cttees numerous professional and business asscns; Treas. Tonga Rugby Football Union (TRFU) 1975–82; Chair. TRFU Referees' Asscn early 1980s–early 1990s; mem. Nuku'alofa Rotary Club 1974–, served as Pres. for several years; ordained Minister of the Constitutional Free Church of Tonga. *Leisure interest:* sports, especially rugby. *Address:* c/o Ministry of Finance, Treasury Building, PO Box 87, Vuna Road, Kolofo'ou, Nuku'alofa, Tonga (office).

MATOVIČ, Igor; Slovak politician; *Leader, Ordinary People and Independent Personalities;* b. 11 May 1973, Trnava; m. Pavlina Matovičová; ed Comenius Univ., Bratislava; worked as a freelancer from 1997; f. regionPRESS publishing co. 2002, currently publishes 36 regional weeklies in Slovakia; elected to Nat. Council of the Slovak Repub. on the Freedom and Solidarity (SaS) list 2010; Leader, Ordinary People and Independent Personalities (Obyčajní Ludia a nezávislé osobnosti—OLaNO) party 2011–. *Address:* Ordinary People and Independent Personalities (Obyčajní Ludia a nezávislé osobnosti), Študentská 2, 91701 Trnava, Slovakia (office). *Telephone:* 90-7750558 (mobile). *E-mail:* igor.matovic@obycajniludia.sk (office). *Website:* www.obycajniludia.sk (office); matovic.blog.sme.sk.

MATSUDA, Iwao; Japanese politician; b. 19 May 1937; ed Univ. of Tokyo; elected mem. House of Reps 1986, 1990 1993; Parl. Vice Minister, Ministry of Educ., Science, Culture and Sports 1991–92; elected mem. House of Councillors 1998, 2004; Sr State Sec. for Int. Trade and Industry 2000–01; Sr Vice Minister of Economy, Trade and Industry 2001; Chief Dir Cttee on Economy and Industry 2002–04; Chair. Research Cttee on Int. Affairs 2004–05; Minister of State for Science and Tech. Policy, for Food Safety and for Information Tech. 2005–06. *Address:* Liberal-Democratic Party—LDP (Jiyu-Minshuto), 1-11-23, Nagata-cho, Chiyoda-ku, Tokyo 100-8910, Japan. *Telephone:* (3) 3581-6211. *E-mail:* koho@ldp.jimin.or.jp. *Website:* www.jimin.jp.

MATSUDA, Masatake; Japanese transport industry executive; *Director and Adviser, East Japan Railway Company;* b. 1936, Hokkaido; ed Hokkaido Univ.; began career with Japan Nat. Railway (JNR) 1961, held positions successively as Planning Man. Office of Planning Man., Planning Man. Hokkaido HQ, Dir-Gen. Reconstruction Promotion HQ, Man.-Dir and Gen. Man. Corp. Planning HQ E Japan Railway Co. (JR East–co. created following privatisation of JNR 1987), Vice-Pres., Pres. 1993, Chair. JR East –2006, Dir and Adviser 2006–; Dir Mizuho Holdings Inc.; Pres. World Exec. Council, Int. Union of Railways (UIC), Vice-Pres. UIC 2003–04; apptd mem. Prime Ministerial Advisory Panel tasked with overseeing Privatisation of Semigovernmental Expressway Corpns 2003, resgnd from panel in protest of privatisation scheme. *Address:* East Japan Railway Company, 2-2 Yoyogi 2-chome, Shibuya-ku, Tokyo 151-8578, Japan (office). *Telephone:* (3) 5334-1310 (office). *Fax:* (3) 5334-1297 (office). *Website:* www.jreast.co.jp (office).

MATSUDA, Seiko; Japanese singer and actress; b. (Noriko Kamachi), 10 March 1962, Fukuoka; m. 1st Masaki Kanda 1985 (divorced 1998); one c.; m. 2nd Hiroyuki Hatano 1998 (divorced 2000). *Films include:* Nogiku no haka 1981, Yume De Aetera 1982, Natsufuku no Ibu 1984, Karibu: Ai no shinfoni 1985, Final Vendetta 1996, Armageddon 1998, Drop Dead Gorgeous 1999, Partners 2000, Gedo 2000, Sennen no koi – Hikaru Genji monogatari 2002, Shanghai Baby 2007, Hotaru no Haka 2008, Yazima Beauty Salon The Movie 2010. *Television includes:* The Big Easy (series) 1996, Tattahitotsuno takaramono (film) 2004, Yo nimo kimyo na monogatari: Aki no tokubetsu hen 2005. *Recordings include:* albums: Squall 1980, North Wind 1980, Silhouette 1981, Kaze Tachi Nu 1981, Pineapple 1982, Candy 1982, Utopia 1983, Canary 1983, Tinkerbell 1984, Windy Shadow 1984, The Ninth Wave 1985, Sound of My Heart 1985, Supreme 1986, Strawberry Time 1987, Citron 1988, Precious Moment 1989, Seiko 1990, We Are Love 1990, Eternal 1991, Nouvelle Vague 1992, Sweet Memories 1992, A Time For Love 1993, Diamond Expression 1993, Glorious Revolution 1994, It's Style 1995, Was It The Future 1996, Guardian Angel 1996, Vanity Fair 1996, Sweetest Time 1997, My Story 1997, Forever 1998, Seiko Matsuda Remixes 1999, 20th Party 2000, Love & Emotion Vol. 1 2001, Love & Emotion Vol. 2 2001, Area 62 2002, Sunshine 2004, Fairy 2006, Baby's Breath 2007, My Pure Melody 2008, My Prelude 2010, Cherish 2011. *Publication:* Yume de Aetara 1982. *Address:* c/o Universal Music LLC, 8-5-30, Akasaka Minato-Ku, Tokyo 107-0052, Japan. *Telephone:* (3) 6406-3001. *E-mail:* office@seikomatsuda.jp (office). *Website:* www.seikomatsuda.net.

MATSUHISA, Nobuyuki (Nobu); Japanese chef and restaurateur; b. 10 March 1949, Saitama; m.; two d.; served apprenticeship in sushi bars in Tokyo, including Matsue Sushi, Shinjuku; opened sushi bar in Peru 1973, later moved to Argentina, Japan and Alaska, USA; opened Matsuhisa restaurant in Beverly Hills, Calif. 1987, Aspen, Colo 1999; opened Nobu restaurant in New York 1994, London 1997, Tokyo 1999, Milan, Greece, Dallas, Honolulu, Moscow, Dubai, Budapest, Hong Kong, Mumbai 2012, now manages 33 restaurants; Nobu Hotel Las Vegas opened 2013; Award from Japan Soc. 2009, Michelin One Star each for Nobu, New York, Nobu, London, Nobu Berkeley Street, London. *Film roles:* Casino 1995, Austin Powers in Goldmember 2002, Memoirs of a Geisha 2005, The Girl from Nagasaki 2013. *Publications:* Nobu: The Cookbook 2001, Nobu Now 2005, Nobu West 2007, Nobu Miami: The Party Cookbook 2008. *Address:* Matsuhisa Restaurant, 129 North La Cienega Blvd, Beverly Hills, CA 90211, USA (office). *Telephone:* (310) 659-9639 (office). *Fax:* (310) 659-0492 (office). *Website:* www.noburestaurants.com (office); www.nobumatsuhisa.com.

MATSUI, Hideki; Japanese professional baseball player; b. 12 June 1974, Kanazawa; ed Seiryo High School, Kanazawa; left fielder; drafted out of high school by Yomiuri Giants of Japanese Cen. League 1993 (number one selection), played 1993–2003, won three Japanese Series titles, hit Japan career 332 home runs with overall batting average of .308; left Japan to sign with NY Yankees 2003–09, Los Angeles Angels of Anaheim 2010, Oakland Athletics 2011–, major league debut 31 March 2003; operates Hideki Matsui House of Baseball, Neagari; nine times Japanese League All-Star; three Japanese League Most Valuable Player awards; American League All-Star Team 2003; runner-up American League Rookie of the Year 2003, Most Valuable Player, 2009 World Series. *Address:* c/o Oakland Athletics, 7000 Coliseum Way, Oakland, CA 94621, USA (office). *Telephone:* (510) 638-4900 (office). *Website:* oakland.athletics.mlb.com/index.jsp?c_id=oak (office).

MATSUMOTO, Hiroshi, BEng, MEng, PhD; Japanese engineer, academic and university administrator; *President, Kyoto University;* b. 17 Nov. 1942; ed Kyoto Univ.; Research Assoc., Dept of Electronics, Kyoto Univ. 1967–69, Research Assoc., Dept of Electrical Eng 1969–74, Assoc. Prof., Ionosphere Research Lab., Kyoto Univ. 1974–81, Assoc. Prof., Radio Atmospheric Science Centre 1981–87, Prof. 1987–2000, Centre Dir 1992–98, Prof., Radio Science Centre for Space and Atmosphere 2000–02, Prof. and Dir 2002–04, Prof. and Dir Research Inst. for Sustainable Humanosphere 2004–05, Exec. Vice-Pres. (Research, Finance), Kyoto Univ. 2005–08, Pres. Kyoto Univ. 2008–; Visiting Prof., Inst. for Space and Astronomical Sciences (JAXA/ISAS), Inst. for Fusion Sciences (NIFS) of Japan & Wuhan Univ., People's Repub. of China; AGU Fellow Award for Space Plasma Physics 1999, IEEE Fellow Award 2002, Assoc. Award, Royal Astronomical Soc., Science and Tech. Award, Ministry of Educ., Culture and Sports 2006, Russian Fed. of Cosmonautics Gagarin Medal 2006, Medal with Purple Ribbon 2007, Gold Booker Medal, Union Radio-Scientifique Internationale 2008, Hasegawa Nagata Award, Soc. of Geomagnetism and Earth, Planetary and Space Sciences (Japan) 2008. *Publications:* has authored and contributed to several books; approx. 300 scientific papers in English in int. journals and 133 scientific papers in Japanese. *Address:* Office of the President, Kyoto University, Yoshida-Honmachi, Sakyo-ku, Kyoto 606-8501, Japan (office). *Telephone:* (75) 753-7531 (office). *Fax:* (75) 753-2091 (office). *Website:* www.kyoto-u.ac.jp/en/profile/25president (office).

MATSUMOTO, Ken, MA; Japanese business executive; b. 2 Feb. 1935, Shanghai, China; s. of Shigeharu and Hanako Matsumoto; m. Junko Masuda 1969; one s.; ed Gakushuin High School, Swarthmore Coll., USA, Univ. of Tokyo; mem. Bd Dirs Auburn Steel Co. Inc., Auburn, NY 1973–77; Sr Man. Export Dept-I, Nippon Steel Corpn 1977–84; Dir Research Div., The Fair Trade Center 1984–90, Man. Dir 1990–; Bancroft Scholarship. *Leisure interests:* tennis, skiing. *Address:* 5-11-38, Miyazaki, Miyamae-ku, Kawasaki-shi, Kanagawa-ken, 216 Japan. *Telephone:* (44) 854-0693.

MATSUMOTO, Masayoshi; Japanese business executive; *President and CEO, Sumitomo Electric Industries;* mem. Bd of Dirs Sumitomo Electric Industries 1999–, fmr Sr Man. Dir, fmr Pres. and COO, now Pres. and CEO; Vice-Chair. Optoelectronic Industry and Tech. Devt Assen. *Address:* Sumitomo Electric Industries Ltd, 5-33 Kitahama 4-chome, Chuo-ku, Osaka 541-0041, Japan (office). *Telephone:* (6) 6220-4141 (office). *E-mail:* info@sei.co.jp (office). *Website:* global-sei .com (office); www.sei.co.jp (office).

MATSUMOTO, Masayuki; Japanese engineer and transport industry executive; *President, Central Japan Railway Company;* joined Japanese Nat. Railways (now Japan Railways–JR) 1972, Tech. Dir E Japan Railway Co. 2000, sr positions with Transport & Rolling Stock Dept 2001–02, Vice-Pres. Cen. Japan Railway Co. (JR Tokai) –2004, Pres. 2004–; Dir Ricoh Leasing Co. Ltd 2003; Exec. Man.-Dir Ricoh Co. Ltd 2004–; mem. Inst. of Electrical Engineers of Japan, Inst. of Electronics, Information and Communication Engineers, Information Processing Soc. of Japan. *Address:* Central Japan Railway Company, 1-1-4 Meieki, Nakamura-ku, Nagoya 450-6101, Japan (office). *Telephone:* (3) 3274-9727 (office). *Fax:* (3) 5255-6780 (office). *Website:* www.jr-central.co.jp (office).

MATSUMOTO, Takeaki; Japanese politician; b. 25 April 1959; s. of Juro Matsumoto; great great grand-s. of Itō Hirobumi (first Prime Minister of Japan); ed Univ. of Tokyo; began career at Corp. HQ and later Osaka br., Industrial Bank of Japan Ltd 1982; Special Asst to Minister of Defence 1989; Sec. for mem. House of Reps 1990; mem. House of Reps for Hyōgo 11th Dist 2000–05, 2009–, for Kinki proportional representation block 2005–09, mem. Cttee on Foreign Affairs; Sr Vice-Minister for Foreign Affairs 2010–11, Minister of Foreign Affairs March–Sept. 2011; mem. Democratic Party of Japan. *Address:* c/o Ministry of Foreign Affairs, 2-2-1, Kasumigaseki, Chiyoda-ku, Tokyo 100-8919, Japan. *Website:* www .m-takeaki.jp.

MATSUO, Kenji; Japanese insurance industry executive; *Senior Advisor, Meiji Yasuda Life Insurance Company;* Dir Meiji Life Insurance Co. –2003, mem. Bd of Dirs Meiji Yasuda Life Insurance Co. 2004– (after merger of Meiji Life Insurance Co. and Tasuda Mutual Life Insurance Co.), Man. Dir and Gen. Man. Real Estate Dept –2005, Pres. and Rep. Exec. Officer 2005–13, Rep. Exec. Officer 2–19 July 2013, Sr Advisor July 2013–; mem. Nominating Cttee, Compensation Cttee; mem. Bd of Dirs Life Insurance Assen of Japan, Nikon Corpn; Dir (non-voting) Société Generale Group 2006–. *Address:* Meiji Yasuda Life Insurance Co., 1-1, Marunouchi 2-chome, Chiyoda-ku, Tokyo 100-0005, Japan (office). *Telephone:* (3) 3283-8293 (office). *Fax:* (3) 3215-8123 (office). *E-mail:* info@meijiyasuda.co.jp (office). *Website:* www.meijiyasuda.co.jp (office).

MATSUO, Minoru, DEng; Japanese university administrator and professor of engineering; b. 4 July 1936, Kyoto; ed Kyoto Univ.; Asst Prof. School of Eng, Kyoto Univ. 1964–65, Assoc. Prof. 1965–72; Assoc. Prof. School of Eng, Nagoya Univ. 1972–78, Prof. 1978–98, Univ. Senator 1987–89, Dean 1989–92, Dir Center for Integrated Research in Science and Eng 1995–97, Pres. of Nagoya Univ. 1998–2004, currently Advisor, Nagoya Univ. Alumni Assen; with Nagoya Urban Devt Public Corpn, Supreme Advisor, Nagoya Urban Inst. *Publications include:* Reliability in Geotechnical Design 1984. *Address:* c/o Nagoya University Alumni Association Bureau, Nagoya University, Furo-cho, Chikusa-ku, Nagoya, 464–8601 (office); Nagoya Urban Development Public Corporation, 8 Iidamachi, Higashi-Ku Nagoya, Aichi 461-0013, Japan. *Telephone:* (52) 783-1920 (office). *E-mail:* nual -jimu@adm.nagoya-u.ac.jp (office). *Website:* www.nual.nagoya-u.ac.jp (office).

MATSUSHITA, Isao; Japanese business executive; *President and Representative Director, JX Holdings, Inc.;* ed Univ. of Tokyo; joined Nippon Mining Co. 1970; fmr Exec. Vice-Pres. and Man. Exec. Officer, Japan Energy Corpn, Pres. and Dir 2006–12; Exec. Vice-Pres. JX Nippon Oil & Energy Corpn 2010–12; Pres. and Rep. Dir JX Holdings, Inc. 2012–; Rep. Dir Japan Energy Devt 2007–; Dir, United Petroleum Devt Co. Ltd, JX Nippon Oil & Energy Corpn, JX Holdings, Inc. 2010–, Nippon Mining Holdings Inc. *Address:* JX Holdings, Inc., 2-6-3, Ote-machi, Chiyoda-ku, Tokyo 100-0004, Japan (office). *Telephone:* (3) 3502-1131 (office). *Fax:* (3) 3502-9352 (office). *E-mail:* info@hd.jx-group.co.jp (office). *Website:* www.hd.jx -group.co.jp (office).

MATSUSHITA, Yasuo, LLB; Japanese banker; b. 1 Jan. 1926; ed Univ. of Tokyo; joined Ministry of Finance 1950, Dir Commercial Banks Div., Banking Bureau 1971–72, Dir Secretarial Div., Minister's Secr. 1972–74, Dir-Gen. Kinki Finance Bureau 1974–75, Deputy Dir-Gen. Budget Bureau 1978, Deputy Vice-Minister 1978–80, Dir-Gen. Budget Bureau 1980–82, Admin. Vice-Minister of Finance 1982–86; Dir Taiyo Kobe Bank 1986–87, Pres. 1987–90; Chair. Mitsui Taiyo Kobe Bank 1990–92, renamed Sakura Bank 1992–94, Rep. Dir and Adviser, Sakura Bank June–Dec. 1994; Gov. Bank of Japan 1994–98, resgnd following arrest of sr bank official on bribery charges 12 March 1998. *Leisure interests:* reading, tennis.

MATSUYEV, Denis Leonidovich; Russian pianist; *Artistic Director, Crescendo;* b. 11 June 1975, Irkutsk; s. of Leonid Matsuyev and Irina Gomelskaya; ed Moscow State Conservatory (pupil of Prof. Sergei Dorensky); concerts 1993–; Soloist, Moscow State Academic Philharmonic Soc. 1995–; recitals in Paris, New York, Munich, Hamburg, Athens, Salzburg, Tokyo, Moscow and St Petersburg; played with State Symphony Orchestra of Russian Fed., Hon. Ensemble of Russia (St Petersburg), Tokyo Symphony, Budapest Philharmonic, Seoul Philharmonic; debut in London at Andrew Lloyd Webber Festival 1996; numerous tours in USA; Founder and Artistic Dir Crescendo (classical music and jazz festival) 2005–; Grand Prix Int. Piano Contest in SA 1993, 1st Prize, 11th Int. Tchaikovsky Competition, Moscow 1998. *Address:* Marshal Zhukov prosp. 13, Apt 4, 123308 Moscow, Russia (home). *Telephone:* (495) 290-17-04 (home).

MATTARELLA, Sergio; Italian lawyer, politician and lecturer in law; b. 23 July 1941, Palermo; m.; three c.; ed Palermo Univ.; fmr mem. Nat. Council and Cen. Leadership Christian Democrat Party, Deputy Political Sec. 1990–92; now mem. Italian Popular Party; Deputy for Palermo-Trapani-Agrigento-Caltanissetta 1983, for Sicilia 1 1994–2008; fmr Minister for Relations with Parl., Minister for Educ. –1990, Deputy Prime Minister 1998–2001, Minister for Defence 1999–2001; fmr Deputy Chair. Bicamerale; fmr Vice-Pres. Parl. Cttee on Terrorism; fmr mem. Parl. Inquiry Cttee on Mafia; mem. Third Standing Comm. on Foreign and EC Affairs; Political Ed. Il Popolo 1992–94; Prof. of Parl. Law, Univ. of Palermo.

Address: Faculty of Law, University of Palermo, Piazza Marina 61, 90133 Palermo, Italy (office). *Website:* www.giurisprudenza.unipa.it (office).

MATTHÄUS, Lothar Herbert (Loddar); German professional football manager and fmr professional footballer; *Coach, Bulgarian National Football Team;* b. 21 March 1961, Erlangen, Bavaria; m. 1st Silvia Matthäus 1981 (divorced 1992); two d.; m. 2nd Lolita Morena 1994 (divorced 1999); one s.; m. 3rd Marijana Kostić 2003 (divorced 2009); m. 4th Liliana Chudinova 2008; midfielder/defender/sweeper; youth player, FC Herzogenaurach; professional debut with Borussia Mönchengladbach 1979–84; played for Bayern Munich 1984–88, 1992–2000 (won Bundesliga 1984/85, 1985/86, 1986/87, 1993/94, 1996/97, 1998/99, 1999/2000, DFB-Pokal 1986, 1998, DFB-Ligapokal 1997, 1998, 1999, 2000, DFB-Supercup 1987, UEFA Cup 1996, Fuji-Cup 1987, 1988, 1994, 1995), Inter Milan 1988–92 (won Italian Championship (Serie A) 1989, Supercoppa Italiana 1989, UEFA Cup 1991), New York MetroStars March–Nov. 2000; mem. West German U-21 team 1979–83, West German B team 1979–81, West German/German nat. team 1980–96, 1998–2000 (won Euro 1980, Capt. 1988–94, won World Cup 1990, US Cup 1993), played in 25 World Cup matches, 150 appearances for nat. team, scored 23 goals; Sports Dir Rapid Vienna 2001–02; Man. Partizan Belgrade, Serbia and Montenegro 2002–03; Coach, Hungarian Nat. Team 2003–05, Atlético Paranaense, Brazil 2006, Red Bull Salzburg (fmrly Austria Salzburg) 2006–07, Maccabi Netanya, Israel 2008–09, Bulgarian Nat. Team 2010–; Ballon d'Or 1990, Onze d'Or 1990, FIFA World Player of the Year 1991, World Soccer Awards Player of the Year 1990, German Footballer of the Year 1990, 1999, named to FIFA 100. *Address:* c/o Bulgarian Football Union, Tsar Ivan Assen II No. 26, Sofia 1124, Bulgaria. *E-mail:* bfu@bfunion.bg. *Website:* www.bfunion.bg.

MATTHÄUS-MAIER, Ingrid; German banking executive and fmr politician; b. 9 Sept. 1945, Werlte, Aschendorf Co.; d. of Heinz-Günther Matthäus and Helmtraud Matthäus (née von Hagen); m. Robert Maier 1974; one s. one d.; ed studied law in Giessen and Münster; Research Asst, Münster Higher Admin. Court, then Admin. Court Judge in Münster; mem. Free Democratic Party (Freie Demokratische Partei—FDP) 1969, mem. North Rhine-Westphalian Exec. Cttee and of Fed. Exec. Cttee FDP; Fed. Chair. Young Democrats 1972; mem. Bundestag 1976, Chair. Finance Cttee 1979–82, resgnd all posts, left FDP and resgnd seat in Bundestag in protest at coalition change of FDP 1982; joined SPD 1982; re-elected to Bundestag 1983, Deputy Chair. SPD Parl. Group (in charge of fiscal, budgetary/borrowing, banking, stock exchange and monetary affairs) 1988, mem. Exec. Cttee SPD 1995–99, Titular mem. Mediation Cttee 1995, resgnd seat in Bundestag 1999; mem. Bd of Man. Dirs KfW Bankengruppe 1999–2006, Spokeswoman of Bd of Man. Dirs 2006–08, responsible for Secr. of Man. Affairs/Legal Affairs, Secr. of Domestic Credit Affairs, Communications and Internal Auditing, also responsible for Berlin Br.; Chair. mem. Supervisory Bd Deutsche Telekom AG, Deutsche Post AG, Bonn Deutsche Steinkohle AG, Herne 2007–, EVONIK Industries AG (fmrly, Essen –2009, RAG Aktiengesellschaft, Essen, Salzgitter Mannesmann Handel GmbH, Dusseldorf; ranked by Fortune magazine amongst 50 Most Powerful Women in Business outside the US (31st) 2007, ranked by the Financial Times amongst Top 25 Businesswomen in Europe (17th) 2006, (15th) 2007.

MATTHEI FORNET, Evelyn Rose, BA; Chilean economist and politician; b. 1953, Santiago; d. of Fernando Matthei and Elda Fornet; m. Jorge Desormeaux Jiménez; three c.; ed Colegio Alemán de Santiago, Pontificia Universidad Católica de Chile; began career with Research Dept, Forestry SA; Financial Analyst, later Head of Research Dept, Administradoras de Fondos de Pensiones (pension fund); fmr Deputy Dir Bancard SA; Deputy for Santiago Dist 23, Cámara de Diputados 1989–93, for San Antonio Dist 15 1993–97; mem. Senate for Coquimbo 1998–2011; mem. Finance and the Budget Cttees in both Chambers, also mem. Cttees on Health, Labour and Social Security, Senate Audit Cttee; Minister of Labour and Social Security 2011–13; cand. in presidential election Dec. 2013; mem. Unión Demócrata Independiente. *Address:* Unión Demócrata Independiente, Suecia 286, Providencia, Santiago, Chile (office). *Telephone:* (2) 2414200 (office). *E-mail:* udiweb@udi.cl (office). *Website:* www.udi.cl (office).

MATTHES, Ulrich; German actor; b. 9 May 1959, Berlin; s. of Günter Matthes and Else Matthes; with Düsseldorfer Schauspielhaus 1986–87, Bayerisches Staatstheater, Munich 1987–89, Kammerspiele, Munich 1989–92, Schaubühne, Berlin 1992–98, Deutsches Theater, Berlin; Förderpreis, Kunstpreis Berlin 1991, O.E. Hasse-Preis 1992, Bayerischer Filmpreis 1999. *Films:* Herr Ober! 1992, Ein falscher Schritt 1995, Winter Sleepers 1997, Feuerreiter 1998, Aimee & Jaguar 1999, Framed (short) 1999, The Farewell 2000, Traffic Affairs 2004, The Ninth Day 2004, Downfall 2004, Who Was Kafka? (voice) 2006, Vineta 2006, Novemberkind 2008, Die Unsichtbare 2011, Calm at Sea 2011, A Little Suicide (short, voice) 2012, Kunduz: The Incident at Hadji Ghafur 2012, The Notebook 2013. *Television:* An einem Tag im September (short) 1969, Die Wesenacks (film) (as Ulli Matthes) 1970, Artur, Peter und der Eskimo (film) 1973, Derrick (series) 1987–97, Wolff's Turf (series) 1995, Der Mörder und sein Kind (film) 1995, Nikolaikirche (film) 1995, The Old Fox (series) 1997, Todesspiel (film documentary) 1997, Polizeiruf 110 (series) 1997–99, Abgehauen (film) 1998, Der Hahn ist tot (film) 2000, A Case for Two (series) 2000, Mörderherz (film) 2002, The Bill (series) 2008, SOKO Leipzig (series) 2009, Neue Vahr Süd 2010, Tatort (series) 2011–14, Bornholmer Straße (film) 2014.

MATTHEW, Norman; Marshall Islands politician; b. 14 Jan. 1941; m. Rosalind Bien Matthew; seven c.; Co-Man., Ajidrik Wholesale 1961–86; Owner/Manager, RN Trading Co. 1986–95; mem. Nitijela (Parl.) for Aur Atoll 1995–; Minister of Internal Affairs 2008–12; fmr mem. United People's Party (UPP), now mem. Aelon Kein Ad (Our Islands) party; del. to Asia Pacific Parl. Forum. *Leisure interests:* fishing, sport, gardening. *Address:* c/o Ministry of Internal Affairs, POB 18, Majuro MH 96960, Marshall Islands (office).

MATTHEWS, Peter Hugoe, LittD, FBA; British professor of linguistics; *Professor Emeritus, Department of Theoretical and Applied Linguistics, University of Cambridge;* b. 10 March 1934, Oswestry, Shropshire, England; s. of John Hugo Matthews and Cecily Eileen Elmsley Hagarty; m. Lucienne Marie Jeanne Schleich 1984; one step-s. one step-d.; ed Montpellier School, Paignton, Clifton Coll.; St John's Coll., Cambridge; Lecturer, Univ. Coll. of North Wales, Bangor 1960–65, at Indiana Univ., Bloomington 1963–64; Lecturer, Reader and Prof., Univ. of Reading 1965–80; Visiting Prof., Deccan Coll., Pune 1969–70; Sr Research Fellow, King's

Coll., Cambridge 1970–71; Fellow, Nias Wassenaar, the Netherlands 1977–78; Prof. and Head of Dept of Linguistics, Univ. of Cambridge 1980–2001, Fellow, St John's Coll. 1980–, Praelector 1987–2001, Prof. Emer. 2001–; Pres. Philological Soc. 1992–96, Vice-Pres. 1996–; Hon. mem. Linguistics Soc. of America 1994. *Publications:* Inflectional Morphology: A Theoretical Study Based on Aspects of Latin Verb Conjugation 1972, Morphology 1974, Generative Grammar and Linguistic Competence 1979, Syntax 1981, Grammatical Theory in the United States from Bloomfield to Chomsky 1993, The Concise Oxford Dictionary of Linguistics 1997, A Short History of Structural Linguistics 2001, Linguistics: A Very Short Introduction 2003, The Concise Oxford Dictionary of Linguistics 2005, Syntactic Relations: A Critical Survey 2007. *Leisure interests:* cycling, gardening. *Address:* St John's College, Cambridge, CB2 1TP (office); 10 Fendon Close, Cambridge, CB1 7RU, England (home); 22 Rue Nina et Julien Lefevre, 1952 Luxembourg. *Telephone:* (1223) 338768 (office); (1223) 247553 (home). *Website:* www.mml.cam.ac.uk/dtal/staff/phm1000/index.html (office).

MATTHEWS, Sir Terence H. (Terry), Kt, OBE, BSc; British/Canadian telecommunications industry executive; *Chairman, Mitel Networks Corporation;* b. 1943, Newport, Wales; m.; four c.; ed Univ. of Wales, Swansea; emigrated to Ottawa, Canada 1969; co-f. Mitel Corpn (with Michael Cowpland) 1972, Chair. 1972–85, Chair. Mitel Networks Corpn (communications system div.) 2001–; f. Newbridge Networks Corpn 1986, Chair. and CEO 1986–2000; f. March Networks Corpn 2000, Chair. and CEO 2000–; f. Celtic House Int.; Founding Chair. Celtic Manor Resort (host of Ryder Cup 2010); Chair. Convedia Corpn, DragonWave, Tundra Semiconductor Corpn; Fellow Inst. of Electrical Engineers; mem. Royal Acad. of Eng; Hon. PhD (Univs of Wales, Glamorgan and Swansea, Carleton Univ., Ottawa). *Address:* Mitel Networks Corporation, 350 Legget Drive, POB 13089, Kanata, Ont. K2K 2W7, Canada (office). *Telephone:* (613) 592-2122 (office). *Fax:* (613) 592-4784 (office). *Website:* www.mitel.com (office).

MATTHIAS, Stefanos; Greek judge (retd); b. 27 May 1935, Athens; m.; one d.; ed Univ. of Athens, Univ. of Poitiers, France; judge 1961–2002; Pres. Supreme Civil and Penal Court 1996–2002; Dir Nat. School for Judges 1994–96; First Class Honour Cross. *Publications:* more than 40 studies and articles on pvt. law and on European Convention on Human Rights. *Leisure interest:* painting. *Address:* 26 Niriidon Str., 17561 Paleon Faliron, Greece (home). *Telephone:* (210) 9882632 (home); (210) 9827466 (home). *E-mail:* stefmatt@otenet.gr (home).

MATTHIESSEN, Poul Christian, MA, DSc (Econ); Danish demographer and academic; *Professor Emeritus of Demography, University of Copenhagen;* b. 1 Feb. 1933, Odense; s. of Jens P. E. Matthiessen and Laura E. Nielsen; m. Ulla Bay 1986; two d.; Research Asst, Copenhagen Telephone Co. 1958–63; Lecturer in Statistics and Demography, Univ. of Copenhagen 1963–70, Prof. of Demography 1971–95, Prof. Emer. 1995–; Pres. Carlsberg Foundation 1993–2002; Chair. Carlsberg's Bequest in Memory of Brewer J.C. Jacobsen 1993–2003; mem. Bd of Dirs Museum of Nat. History at Frederiksborg Castle 1993–2002, Den Berlingske Fond 1999–2008; mem. European Population Cttee 1972–2000; mem. Supervisory Bd Carlsberg A/S 1989–2003 (Chair. 1993–2003), Royal Scandinavia 1993–2001, Fredericia Bryggeri 1993–97, Falcon Bryggerier AB 1998–2001; mem. Royal Danish Acad. of Science and Letters 1982, Academia Europaea 1988; Chevalier, Ordre nat. du Mérite. *Publications:* Infant Mortality in Denmark 1931–60 1964, Growth of Population: Causes and Implications 1965, Demographic Methods (Vols I–III) 1970, Some Aspects of the Demographic Transition in Denmark 1970, The Limitation of Family Size in Denmark (Vols I–II) 1985, Immigration to Denmark 2009, Population and Society 2012. *Leisure interests:* literature, history, architecture. *Address:* Collstrups Foundation, Ny Kongensgade 20, 1553 Copenhagen, Denmark (office). *Telephone:* 21-65-50-78 (office). *E-mail:* pcm@post.tele.dk (office).

MATTHUS, Siegfried; German composer; b. 13 April 1934, Mallenuppen, E Prussia; s. of the late Franz Matthus and of Luise Perrey; m. Helga Spitzer 1958; one s.; ed Hochschule für Musik, Berlin, Acad. of Arts and Music, Berlin (masterclass with Hanns Eisler); composer and consultant, Komische Oper, Berlin 1964–2002; Prof. 1985–; Artistic Dir Chamber Opera Festival, Rheinsberg 1991; mem. Acad. of Arts of GDR, Acad. of Arts of W Berlin, Acad. of Arts, Munich; Nat. Prize 1972, 1984, Bundesverdienstkreuz (First Class) 2000. *Compositions include:* Te Deum, 10 operas, one oratorio, concertos, orchestral and chamber music, etc. *Leisure interests:* swimming, jogging, carpentry. *Address:* Elisabethweg 10, 13187 Berlin (home); Seepromenade 15, 16348 Stolzenhagen, Germany (home). *Telephone:* (30) 4857362 (Berlin) (home); (33397) 21736 (Stolzenhagen) (home). *Fax:* (30) 48096604 (Berlin) (home); (33397) 71400 (Stolzenhagen) (home). *E-mail:* smatthus@t-online.de (home). *Website:* www.siegfried-matthus.de.

MATTILA, Karita Marjatta; Finnish singer (soprano); b. Somero; d. of Arja Mattila and Erkki Mattila (née Somerikko); m. Tapio Kuneinen; ed Sibelius Acad., Finland and studied with Liisa Linko-Malmio, and Vera Rozsa in London; performs in all major opera houses and festivals world-wide and regularly with conductors including Levine, Abbado, Davis, Dohnanyi, Haitink, Pappano, Rattle, Salonen and Sawallisch; operatic repertoire encompasses works by Beethoven, Strauss, Tchaikovsky, Verdi, Puccini, Wagner and Janáček; has worked with prominent stage dirs, including Luc Bondy in his Don Carlos at Paris, London and Edinburgh Festival; collaborations with Lev Dodin in productions of Elektra for Salzburg Easter Festival and Pique Dame and Salome at Opéra Bastille, Peter Stein's productions of Simon Boccanegra in Salzburg and Don Giovanni in Chicago, and Jürgen Flimm's Fidelio in New York; influential artist in development of new music, regularly collaborating with contemporary composers in debut performances of modern works, including world premiere of Mirage by Kaija Saariaho with Orchestre de Paris led by Christoph Eschenbach in Paris, followed by performances in Berlin with Deutsche Symphony Orchestra led by Jukka-Pekka Saraste and in London with BBC Symphony Orchestra led by Jiri Belohlavek; season 2009–10 included performances of Tosca at the Metropolitan Opera and Bayerische Staatsoper, title role of Janacek's Katya Kabanova at Lyric Opera, Chicago and Emilie de Chatelet at Opera Nat. de Lyon; concert appearances included engagements with the Philadelphia Orchestra, Montreal Symphony Orchestra and performances of Richard Strauss's Four Last Songs with the Berlin Philharmonic led by Sir Simon Rattle; season 2010–11 included Emilia Marty in The Makropoulos Case at San Francisco Opera and Finnish Nat. Opera; Chevalier des Arts et des Lettres 2003; First Prize, Finnish Nat. Singing

Competition 1981, First Prize, BBC Singer of the World, Cardiff 1983, François Reichenbach Prize Orphée du Lyrique, Acad. du Disque Lyrique, Paris, Evening Standard Ballet, Opera and Classical Music Award for Outstanding Performance of the Year 1997, Acad. du Disque Lyrique Award 1997, Grammy Award for Best Opera 1998, chosen by the New York Times as the Best Singer of the Year for her performance in Fidelio at the Metropolitan Opera 2001, Pro Finlandia 2001, Musical America Musician of the Year 2005, Opera News Award for invaluable contrib. to opera 2011. *Recordings:* numerous solo and opera recordings, including 40th birthday concert, Helsinki (CD); other recordings include Strauss's Four Last Songs with Claudio Abbado, Arias & Scenes from the operas of Puccini, Verdi, Janacek, Tchaikovsky, Wagner and R. Strauss, German Romantic Arias by Beethoven, Mendelssohn and Weber with Sir Colin Davis, Grieg and Sibelius Songs with Sakari Oramo; complete recordings of Die Meistersinger von Nürnberg with the late Sir Georg Solti (Grammy Award for Opera 1998), Jenufa with Bernard Haitink (Grammy Award for Opera 2004), Schoenberg's Gurrelieder, Shostakovich's Symphony No. 14 with Sir Simon Rattle. *Leisure interests:* sport, yoga, golf, sailing. *Address:* c/o Bond House, Universal Music Classical Management & Productions Ltd, 347–353 Chiswick High Road, London, W4 4HS, England (office). *Telephone:* (20) 8742-5409 (office). *E-mail:* jeffrey.vanderveen@umusic .com (office). *Website:* www.umcmp.com (office).

MATTINGLY, Mack Francis, BS; American business executive, diplomatist and fmr politician; b. 7 Jan. 1931, Anderson, Ind.; s. of Joseph Hilbert Mattingly and Beatrice Wayts Mattingly; m. 1st Carolyn Longcamp 1957 (deceased); two d.; m. 2nd Leslie Ann Davisson 1998; ed Indiana Univ.; served in USAF 1951–55; Account Supervisor, Arvin Industries, Ind. 1957–59; Marketing, IBM Corpn 1959–79; Owner, M's Inc. 1975–80; Senator from Georgia 1981–87; Asst Sec.-Gen. for Defence Support, NATO, Brussels 1987–90; Amb. to Seychelles 1992–93; fmr Chair. Southeastern Legal Foundation, Georgia Ports Authority (now adviser); mem. Cumberland Island Asscn; mem. Bd of Dirs Novecon Tech., Atlanticus Corpn; US Trustee to Puerto Rico Conservation Trust; Trustee Emer., Kennesaw Univ.; Republican; Sec. of Defense Distinguished Service Medal for Outstanding Public Service 1988 and other awards for public service; also medals from USAF 1951–55. *Publications include:* numerous articles, speeches and book chapters. *Address:* 4315 10th Street, East Beach, St Simons Island, GA 31522, USA (home). *Telephone:* (912) 638-5430 (home). *E-mail:* mlmattingly@comcast.net (home).

MATTIS, Gen. James N.; American army officer; *Commander, US Central Command;* ed Cen. Washington State Univ., Amphibious Warfare School, Marine Corps Command and Staff Coll., Nat. War Coll.; entered US Marine Corps and commissioned as Second Lt 1972; as a Lt, served as rifle and weapons platoon commdr in 3rd Marine Div., as a Capt., commanded rifle co. and weapons co. in 1st Marine Brigade; as Maj., commanded Recruiting Station Portland; as Lt-Col, commanded 1st Bn, 7th Marines, one of Task Force Ripper's assault bns in Operation Desert Shield and Desert Storm; as Col, commanded 7th Marines (Reinforced); as Brig.-Gen., commanded 1st Marine Expeditionary Brigade and then Task Force 58, during Operation Enduring Freedom in southern Afghanistan; as Maj.-Gen., commanded 1st Marine Div. during initial attack (2003) and subsequent stability operations in Iraq during Operation Iraqi Freedom; in first tour as Lt-Gen., commanded Marine Corps Combat Devt Command and served as Deputy Commdt for combat Devt; commanded I Marine Expeditionary Force, Camp Pendleton, Calif. 2006–07; served as Commdr of US Marine Forces Cen. Command; rank of Gen. 2007; Supreme Allied Commdr Transformation, NATO 2007–09; Commdr US Jt Forces Command (USJFCOM), Norfolk, Va 2007–10; Commdr US Cen. Command 2010–; Kuwait Liberation Medal (Kuwait), Kuwait Liberation Medal (Saudi Arabia), Marine Corps Recruiting Service Ribbon (with Bronze Service Star), Sea Service Deployment Ribbon (with one Silver and two Bronze Service Stars), Humanitarian Service Medal, Global War on Terrorism Service Medal, Global War on Terrorism Expeditionary Medal, Iraq Campaign Medal, Afghanistan Campaign Medal, Southwest Asia Service Medal (with two Bronze Service Stars), Nat. Defense Service Medal (with two Bronze Service Stars), Marine Corps Expeditionary Medal, Navy and Marine Corps Meritorious Unit Commendation, Navy Unit Commendation, Jt Meritorious Unit Award, Presidential Unit Citation, Combat Action Ribbon, Navy and Marine Corps Achievement Medal, Meritorious Service Medal (with two Gold Award Stars), Bronze Star (with Combat Valor Device), Legion of Merit, Defense Superior Service Medal, Navy Distinguished Service Medal, Defense Distinguished Service Medal (with Oak Leaf Cluster). *Address:* US Central Command, 7115 South Boundary Boulevard, MacDill AFB, Tampa, FL 33621-5101, USA (office). *Telephone:* (813) 827-5895 (office). *Fax:* (813) 827-2211 (office). *E-mail:* pao@ centcom.mil (office). *Website:* www.centcom.mil (office).

MATTSON, Mark Paul, BS, MS, PhD; American neuroscientist and academic; *Chief, Laboratory of Neurosciences and Chief, Cellular and Molecular Neurosciences Section, Intramural Research Program, National Institute on Aging, Baltimore;* b. 1 April 1957, Rochester, Minn.; s. of DeWayne Paul Mattson and Martha Eileen Mattson (née Arvidson); m. Joanne Mattson (née Youngblood) 1983; one s. one d.; ed Iowa State Univ., North Texas State Univ., Univ. of Iowa; Postdoctoral Researcher in Developmental Neuroscience, Colorado State Univ. 1986–87; Asst Prof. of Anatomy and Neurobiology, Univ. of Kentucky 1989–93, joined faculty Sanders-Brown Research Center on Aging, Univ. of Kentucky Medical Center 1989, Assoc. Prof. 1993–97, Prof. 1997–2000; Chief, Lab. of Neurosciences, Nat. Inst. on Aging, Baltimore, Md, also Chief, Cellular and Molecular Neurosciences Section, Intramural Research Program 2000–; Prof. of Neuroscience, Johns Hopkins Univ. 2000–; Ed.-in-Chief Neuromolecular Medicine, Ageing Research Reviews; Assoc. Ed. Journal of Neuroscience, Neurobiology of Aging, Journal of Neurochemistry, Journal of Neuroscience Research; mem. Soc. for Neuroscience, New York Acad. of Sciences; Fellow, AAAS; numerous awards including Metropolitan Life Foundation Medical Research Award, Alzheimer's Asscn Zenith Award, Jordi Folch Pi Award, Santiago Grisolia Chair Prize, Tovi Comet-Wallerstein Award, Glenn Award, Alumni Fellow Award, Univ. of Iowa, several Grass Lectureships. *Publications include:* ed. of 12 books on topics in neuroscience, aging, neurological disorders, diet and adaptive stress responses; more than 500 original research articles and more than 100 review articles in peer-reviewed journals. *Leisure interests:* running, dirt bike riding, gardening, animal husbandry. *Address:* Laboratory of Neurosciences, Biomedical Research Center, 05C214, 251 Bayview Boulevard, Suite 100, Baltimore, MD 21224-6825, USA (office). *Telephone:* (410) 558-8463 (office). *Fax:* (410) 558-8465 (office). *E-mail:* mark.mattson@nih.gov (office). *Website:* www.grc.nia.nih.gov/branches/irp/mmattson.htm (office).

MATUBRAIMOV, Almambet Matubraimovich; Kyrgyzstani politician; b. 1952, Osh Oblast; ed Tashkent Inst. of Light and Textile Industry; worker in sovkhoz Kursheb Osh Oblast; master, sr master, textile factory KKSK 1977–80; army service 1980–82; head of workshop, head of production textile factory KKSK now Bishkek) 1982–84, Dir 1984–90; Chair. Exec. Cttee Sverdlov Region, Frunze (now Bishkek) 1990–91; First Deputy Minister of Industry Repub. of Kyrgyzstan 1991–93; First Deputy Prime Minister 1991–93; Chair. People's Council of Repub. of Kyrgyzstan (Uluk Kenesh) 1995–99; in opposition to Pres. Akayev 1999; worked in Mining Br. 1999–2005; Plenipotentiary of the Pres. for Southern Region 2005–06, Plenipotentiary on Econ. Cooperation with Eurasian Countries 2006; Deputy in Zhogorku Kenesh (Parl.) 2006–. *Address:* Uluk Kenesh, 720003 Bishkek, Kyrgyzstan.

MATUSCHKA, Mario, Graf von, DJur; German fmr diplomatist; b. 27 Feb. 1931, Oppeln, Silesia; s. of Michael, Graf von Matuschka and Pia, Gräfin Stillfried-Rattonitz; m. Eleonore, Gräfin von Waldburg-Wolfegg 1962; two s. two d.; ed St Matthias Gymnasium, Breslau, Domgymnasium, Fulda and Univs of Fribourg, Paris and Munich; entered foreign service 1961; Attaché, German Observer's Mission at UN, New York 1961–62; Vice-Consul, Consul, Salzburg 1963–66; Second Sec. Islamabad 1966–68; First Sec. Tokyo 1968–71; Foreign Office, Bonn 1971–75, 1978–80, 1982–88, 1990–93; Economic Counsellor, London 1975–78; Deputy Chief of Protocol, UN, New York 1980–82; State Sec., Chief of Protocol, Land Berlin 1988–90; Amb. and Perm. Rep. of Germany to OECD 1993–96; Diplomatic Adviser to Commr Gen., Expo 2000, Hanover 1996–97, Dir Holy See's Pavilion June–Oct. 2000; Sec. Gen. Internationaler Club La Redoute e.V. 1997–2000, mem. Bd 2000–02; Grand Officer's Cross of Merit, Sovereign Mil. Order of Malta 1961, Order of Merit (Germany) 1990, decorations from Japan 1972, Portugal 1989, Holy See 2002. *Publication:* 'Manuale' Prayer Book for German Asscn SMRO (co-ed.) 2005 (second edn 2011). *Address:* Godesberger Hof 14, 53173 Bonn, Germany. *Telephone:* (228) 71025578. *Fax:* (228) 71022579. *E-mail:* mario.matuschka@gmx.de.

MATUTE AUSEJO, Ana María; Spanish writer; b. 26 July 1926, Barcelona; d. of Facundo Matute and Mary Ausejo; m. 1952 (divorced 1963); one s.; ed Damas Negras French Nuns Coll., Hilversum International School, Netherlands; collaborated on literary magazine Destino; Visiting Lecturer, Indiana Univ. 1965–66, Univ. of Oklahoma 1969–; Writer-in-Residence, Univ. of Virginia 1978–79; mem. Real Academia Española de la Lengua 1996–; Hon. mem. Hispanic Soc. of America, American Asscn of Teachers of Spanish and Portuguese; Dr hc (Univ. of Leon); Highly Commended Author, Hans Christian Andersen Jury, Lisbon 1972, Gold Medal, Circulo de Bellas Artes de Madrid, 2006, Premio Nacional de las Letras Españolas 2007, Premio Cervantes 2010. *Children's books include:* El País de la Pizarra 1956, Paulina 1961, El Sal Tamontes Verde 1961, Caballito Loco 1961, El Aprendiz 1961, Carnavalito 1961, El Polizón del Ulises (Lazarillo Prize) 1965, Paulina 1984. *Publications include:* Los Abel 1948, Fiesta Al Noroeste (Café Gijón Prize) 1952, Pequeño Teatro (Planeta Prize) 1954, Los Niños Tontos 1956, Los Hijos Muertos (Nat. Literary Prize and Critics Prize) 1959, Primera Memoria (Nadal Prize) 1959, Tres y un sueño 1961, Historias de la Artamila 1961, El Río 1963, El Tiempo 1963, Los Soldados lloran de noche 1964 (Fastenrath Prize 1969), El Arrepentido y otras Narraciones 1967, Algunos Muchachos 1968, La Trampa 1969, La Torre Vigia 1971, Olvidado Rey Gudu 1974, Sólo un pie descalzo 1983, La virgen de Antioquía y otros relatos 1990, De ninguna parte 1993, La oveja negra 1994, El árbol de oro y otros relatos 1995, El verdadero final de la bella durmiente 1995, Todos mis cuentos 2000, Aranmanoth 2000, Paraíso inhabitado 2010. *Leisure interests:* painting, drawing, the cinema. *Website:* www.anamaria-matute.com.

MATUTES JUAN, Abel; Spanish international organization official and politician; b. 31 Oct. 1941, Ibiza; s. of Antonio and Carmen Matutes; m. Nieves Prats; one s. three d.; ed Univ. of Barcelona; studies in law and econs; fmr entrepreneur in tourism and property in island of Ibiza; fmr Lecturer in Econs and Public Finance, Univ. of Barcelona; Deputy Chair. Ibiza & Formentera Tourist Bd 1964–69; Mayor of Ibiza 1970–71; Senator for Ibiza and Formentera 1977–82; Deputy Alianza Popular 1982–85; Deputy Nat. Chair. Alianza Popular; mem. Community Comm. 1986–94; EC Commr for Credits and Investments, Small and Medium-Sized Enterprises and Financial Eng 1986–89, for American Policy, Latin American Relations 1989–93, for Energy and Euratom Supply Agency, Transport 1993–95; Nat. Vice-Pres., then mem. Exec. Cttee. political party Partido Popular (fmrly Alianza Popular) 1979–; mem. European Parl. 1994–96, Pres. Comm. for External Relations and Security of European Parl. 1994–96; Minister of Foreign Affairs 1996–2000; Pres. and Founder, Matutes Group of Companies; Pres. Foundation Empresa y Crecimiento; Exec. Vice-Pres. EXCELTUR (Hoteliers Asscn); mem. Eurogroup, Spanish Group of the Trilateral Comm.; mem. Bd of Dirs, BSCH, FCC, Insecc, Balearia, Assecurationi Internationali di Previdenza; mem. Royal Spanish Acad. of Econs and Financial Sciences; Dr hc (Complutense Univ., Madrid), (Univ. of Santiago, Chile) more than 40 nat. and foreign decorations and hons including Grand Cross of the Order of Merit (FRG), Grand Official Legion of Honor Order (France), Grand Gold Cross of Austrian Repub., Grand Cross Order of Merit (Italy), Grand Cross Order of Carlos III (Spain) Hon. Cttee Mem., Royal Inst. for European Studies. *Leisure interests:* tennis, sailing. *Address:* P.O. Box 416, Ibiza, Spain (office). *Telephone:* (971) 313811 (office). *Fax:* (971) 311864 (office). *E-mail:* matutes@fiesta-hotels.com (office).

MATVEYENKO, Valery P., DrTech; Russian physicist; *Director, Institute of Continuous Media Mechanics, Russian Academy of Sciences;* b. 9 Feb. 1948, Kizel, Perm region; m.; one d.; ed Perm State Polytechnic Inst.; Engineer, later Jr, then Sr Researcher, Urals Scientific Centre, Russian Acad. of Sciences 1972–79; Head of Lab., Scientific Sec., Deputy Dir, Inst. of Continuous Media Mechanics, Urals br. of Russian Acad. of Sciences 1979–93, Dir 1993–; mem. Russian Acad. of Sciences (corresp. mem. 1997–2003), academician 2003–; State Prize of Russian Fed. 1998; For Labour Valour Medal 1986, Order of Honour 1998, Order of Merit for the Motherland (fourth degree) 2008. *Publications include:* over 290 scientific works, five monographs. *Leisure interests:* fishing. *Address:* Institute of Continuous Media Mechanics, Urals branch of the Russian Academy of Sciences, Koroleva str.

1, Perm 614013, Russia (office). *Telephone:* 3422-37-84-61 (office). *Fax:* 3422-37-84-87 (office). *E-mail:* mvp@icmm.ru (office). *Website:* www.icmm.ru (office).

MATVEYEV, Victor A., Dr Phys., Math., Sciences; Russian physicist; *Director, Institute of Nuclear Research, Russian Academy of Sciences;* b. 11 Dec. 1941, Taiga, Novosibirsk region; m.; two c.; ed Leningrad State Univ.; Jr then Sr Researcher, Head of Sector, United Inst. of Nuclear Research 1965–78, Deputy Dir 1978–87, Dir 1987–; mem. Editorial Bd Yadernaya Fyzika (journal); mem. Russian Acad. of Sciences (corresp. mem. 1991–94); Lenin Prize. *Publications include:* Gravitation and Elementary Particle Physics 1980, Nonconservation of Barrion Numbers in Extreme Conditions 1988; numerous scientific papers on relativistic quark models of elementary particles, quantum field theory. *Address:* Institute of Nuclear Research, Russian Academy of Sciences, 60 let Okryabra prosp. 7a, Moscow 107312, Russia (office). *Telephone:* (495) 135-77-60 (office); (495) 334-00-71 (office). *Website:* www.inr.ac.ru (office).

MATVIYENKO, Valentina Ivanovna; Russian politician; *Chairman, Federation Council (Sovet Federatsii);* b. (Valentina Tyutina), 7 April 1949, Shepetivka, Khmelnytsky Oblast, Ukrainian SSR, USSR; m. Vladimir Vasilyevich Matviyenko; one s.; ed Leningrad Inst. of Chem. and Pharmaceuticals, Acad. of Social Sciences at CPSU Cen. Cttee, Acad. of Diplomacy USSR Ministry of Foreign Affairs; Komsomol work 1972–84; First Sec. Krasnogvardeisk Dist CP Cttee, Leningrad 1984–86; Deputy Chair. Exec. Cttee Leningrad City Council 1986–89; USSR Peoples' Deputy, mem. Supreme Soviet 1989–92; mem. of Presidium, Chair. Cttee on Family, Motherhood and Childhood Protection Affairs 1989–91; Russian Amb. to Malta 1991–94, to Greece 1997–98; rank of Amb. Extraordinary and Plenipotentiary; Dir Dept on Relations with Federal Subjects, Parl. and Public Orgs Ministry of Foreign Affairs 1995–97, Deputy Prime Minister responsible for social issues 1998–2003, Chair. Comm. on Int. Humanitarian Aid and Religious Orgs; Presidential Rep. in the North-Western Fed. Okrug March–Oct. 2003; Gov. of St Petersburg 2003–11; Deputy, St Petersburg City Authority 2011–; Chair. Fed. Council of the Russian Fed. (highest political office attained by a woman in Russia since the time of Empress Catherine the Great) 2011–; mem. Security Council of the Russian Fed. 2011–; placed under exec. sanction by US Pres. Barack Obama following the Crimean status referendum, freezing her assets in the USA and banning her from entering the USA March 2014; Hon. mem. Russian Acad. of Arts; Order of the Badge of Honour 1976, Order of the Red Banner of Labour 1981, Order of Honour 1996, Order of Merit for the Fatherland (Fourth Class) 1999, (Third Class) 2003, (Second Class) 2009; Decoration of Honour for Services to the Repub. of Austria 2001, Order Martyr Tryphon (Second Class) (Russian Orthodox Church) 2001, Order of St Princess Olga (Second Class) (Russian Orthodox Church) 2001, (First Class) 2006, Medal 'In Commemoration of the 300th Anniversary of St Petersburg' 2003, Grand Cross of the Order of Honour (Greece) 2007, Medal 'For outstanding contributions to the National Year of China and Russia' (China) 2008, Order of People's Friendship 2009, Grand Cross of Order of Lion (Finland) 2009, Order 'For the great love of independent Turkmenistan' (Turkmenistan) 2009, Order of Friendship of Peoples (Belarus) 2009, Kt's Cross, Order of the Lion of Finland 2009, Order of St Sergius (Second Class) (Russian Orthodox Church), (First Class) 2010; Gratitude of the Pres. of the Russian Fed. 1995, 2008, Pushkin Medal (MAPRYAL) 2003, ranked by Forbes magazine amongst the 100 Most Powerful Women (31st) 2008, Diploma of the Pres. of the Russian Fed. 2010, Prize of the Russian Fed. in Science and Tech. 2010, Badge of Honour 'For services to St Petersburg' 2011. *Address:* Office of the Chairman, Federation Council, 103426 Moscow, ul. B. Dmitrovka 26, Russia (office). *Telephone:* (495) 629-70-09 (office). *Fax:* (495) 629-67-43 (office). *E-mail:* post_sf@gov.ru (office). *Website:* www.council.gov.ru (office).

MATYJASZEWSKI, Krzysztof, PhD; Polish/American chemist and academic; *University Professor, Carnegie Mellon University;* b. 8 April 1950; s. of Henryk Matyjaszewski and Antonina Matyjaszewski; m. Malgorzata Matyjaszewska; one s. one d.; ed Technical Univ. of Moscow, USSR, Polish Acad. of Sciences, Polytechnical Univ. of Łódź; Post-doctoral Fellow, Univ. of Florida 1977–78; Research Assoc., Polish Acad. of Sciences 1978–84; Research Assoc., CNRS, France 1984–85; Invited Prof., Univ. of Paris, France 1985; Asst Prof., later Assoc. Prof., later Prof., Carnegie Mellon Univ., Pittsburg, Pa 1985–98, Head, Chem. Dept 1994–98, J.C. Warner Prof. of Natural Sciences 1998–, Univ. Prof. 2004–; Elf Chair, Acad. des sciences, Paris 1998; Adjunct Prof., Dept of Chemical and Petroleum Eng, Univ. of Pittsburgh 2000–, Polish Acad. of Sciences, Łódź 2000–; Visiting Prof., Univ. of Paris 1985, 1990, 1997, 1998, Univ. of Freiburg, Germany 1988, Univ. of Bayreuth, Germany 1991, Univ. of Strasbourg, France 1992, Univ. of Bordeaux, France 1996, Univ. of Ulm, Germany 1999, Univ, of Pisa, Italy 2000, Mich. Molecular Inst. 2004, Univ. of Paris, France 2005, École supérieure de physique et de chimie industrielles, Paris 2009, 2011, Pusan Nat. Univ., S Korea 2010; Ed. Progress in Polymer Science, Central European Journal of Chemistry; present or past mem. Editorial Bd numerous journals, including Macromolecules, Macromolecular Chemistry and Physics, Marcomolecular Rapid Communications, Journal of Polymer Science, Journal of Inorganic and Organometallic Polymers, Journal of Macromolecular Science, Pure and Applied Chemistry, International Journal of Polymeric Materials, Chinese Journal of Polymer Science, International Journal of Applied Chemistry, Chemistry Central Journal, Polymer, Polimery; ACS Polymeric Materials Science and Eng Fellow 2001; IUPAC Fellow 2002–, Corresp. mem. IUPAC Comm. on Polymer Nomenclature; Chair. ACS Polymer Curriculum Devt Award Cttee ACS, mem. Program Cttee, Polymer Chem. Div., Chair. Int. Cttee, Polymer Chem. Div.; mem. US Nat. Acad. of Eng, Polish Acad. of Sciences, Russian Acad. of Sciences; Hon. Fellow, Chinese Chemical Soc. 2012; Commdr's Cross, Order of Merit 2011; Dr hc (Ghent) 2002, (Russian Acad. of Sciences) 2006, (Tech. Univ. of Łódź) 2007, (Athens) 2009, (Institut Polytechnique, Toulouse) 2010, (Pusan Nat. Univ.) 2013, (Université Pierre et Marie Curie) 2013; Award of Scientific Sec. of Polish Acad. of Sciences 1974, Award of Polish Chemical Soc. 1980, Award of Polish Acad. of Sciences 1981, Award of Presidential Young Investigator, NSF 1989, ACS Carl S. Marvel-Creative Polymer Chem. Award 1995, Reed Lecturer, Rensellaer Polytechnic Inst. 1998, Milkovitch Lecturer, Univ. of Akron 1998, Humboldt Award for Sr US Scientists 1999, ACS Pittsburgh Award 2001, ACS Polymer Chem. Award 2002, ACS Cooperative Research Award in Polymer Science and Eng 2004, Award of Foundation for Polish Science 2004, Macro Group Medal (UK) 2005, ACS Hermann F. Mark Sr Scholar Award 2007, Presidential Green Chem. Challenge Award (USA) 2009, Gutenberg Award, Mainz

(Germany) 2010, Wolf Prize in Chem. 2011, ACS Applied Polymer Science Award 2011, Carnegie Science Award in Advanced Materials 2011, Japanese Soc. Polymer Science Award 2011, ACS Hermann F. Mark Award 2011, Maria Sklodowska-Curie Medal, Polish Chemical Soc. 2012, Dannie-Heineman Prize, Göttingen Acad. of Sciences 2012, Soc. Chimique de France Prize 2012, inaugural ACS AkzoNobel North America Science Award 2013. *Publications:* co-author/ed. 17 books, 83 book chapters, more than 800 scientific papers, 46 US and 130 int. patents. *Address:* Department of Chemistry, Carnegie Mellon University, 4400 Fifth Avenue, Pittsburgh, PA 15213, USA (office). *Telephone:* (412) 268-3209 (office). *Fax:* (412) 268-6897 (office). *E-mail:* km3b@andrew.cmu.edu (office). *Website:* www.cmu.edu/maty (office).

MATYUKHIN, Gen. Vladimir Georgyevich, DTechSci; Russian business executive and government official; *Head, Federal Information Technology Agency;* b. 4 Feb. 1945, Moscow; ed Moscow Inst. of Energy, Moscow State Univ.; mem. staff Moscow Pedagogical Inst. 1962–64; engineer Construction Bureau, Moscow Inst. of Energy 1964–73; service in state security organs 1969–; Deputy Dir-Gen. Fed. Agency of Govt Telecommunications and Information 1993–99, Dir-Gen. 1999–2003; First Deputy Minister of Defence –2004, Head of State Defence Procurements Cttee –2004; rank of Gen. (Army) 2004; Head, Fed. Information Tech. Agency 2004–; mem. Acad. of Cryptography, Acad. of Int. Communication; several medals including For Labour Valour 1986, For Services to the Motherland 1999, For Military Merit 2000, St Daniil of Moscow Second degree 2000, First degree 2007. *Publications:* numerous journal articles. *Leisure interests:* photography, floriculture. *Address:* c/o Ministry of Communications and Information Technology, ul. Tverskaya 7, 103375 Moscow, Russia (office). *Telephone:* (495) 771-80-71 (office). *Fax:* (499) 503-98-70 (office). *E-mail:* mvgpr@minsyaz.ru (office). *Website:* www.minsvyaz.ru (office).

MAU, Vladimir Alexandrovich, DrEcon, PhD; Russian politician and economist; *Rector, Academy of National Economy;* b. 29 Dec. 1959, Moscow; m. Dr Irina Starodoubrovskaia; one s.; ed Moscow Plekhanov Inst. of Nat. Econs, Inst. of Econs USSR Acad. of Sciences, Acad. de Grenoble, Université Pierre Mendès, France; with Inst. of Econs, USSR (now Russian) Acad. of Sciences 1981–91, Inst. for the Economy in Transition; Sr Lecturer, Econ. Dept, Moscow State Univ. 1988–92; Head of Dept, Inst. of Econ. Policy 1991; Adviser to Chair., Govt of Russian Fed. 1992; mem. Bd Dirs and Head of Dept, Inst. for the Economy in Transition 1993; Adviser to Deputy Mayor of Moscow 1993, to First Deputy Chair., Govt of Russian Fed. 1993–94; Prof., High School of Econs 1993–2002; Adviser to Leader of the Faction in the State Duma of Russia 1994–95; Deputy Dir, Inst. for the Economy in Transition and Head of Dept for Political Studies of Econ. Reforms 1994–97; Dir Working Centre for Econ. Reform, Govt of Russian Fed. 1997–2002; Lecturer, Stanford Univ. Overseas Dept 1997–; Rector Acad. of Nat. Economy (under Govt of Russian Fed.) 2002–; Fowler Hamilton Fellow, Christ Church, Univ. of Oxford 1997; mem. Editorial Bd Mir Rossii (Universe of Russia) Journal 1993–97, Otkrytaya Politika (Open Policy) Journal 1994–, Voprosy Ekonomiki (Problems of Economics) Journal, Vestnik Yevropy (Herald of Europe) Journal, Rossiyskoe Predprinimatelstvo (Russian Entrepreneurship) Journal Scientific Sec., Economic Heritage; mem. Editorial Council, Journal of Economic Transition, RAND Corpn; Ed.-in-Chief Ekonomicheskaya Politika (Economic Policy) journal 2006–; Hon. Economist of Russian Fed. 2000. *Publications:* 600 articles in books, scientific journals, magazines and newspapers in Russian, English, French, German, Italian on history of econ. thought, political economy, social and political issues of market reforms, econ. policy; 29 books including In The Quest of Planification 1990, The Laws of Revolution: Experience of Perestroika and Our Future (with Irina Starodubrovskaia) 1991, History of Economic Studies in the USSR: Outlines for Conception 1992, Reforms and Dogma: 1914–1929 1993, Economy and Power 1995, Political History of Economic Reform in Russia 1985–1994 1996, Economy and Law (Constitutional Problems of Economic Reforms in Russia) 1998, Economic Reform: Through the Prism of Constitution and Politics 1999, Russian Economic Reforms as Seen by an Insider: Success or Failure? 2000, Challenge of Revolution (with Irina Starodubrovskaia) 2001, Great Revolutions from Cromwell to Putin 2001, Constitutional Economics (with Peter Barenboimand and Vladimir Lafitsky) 2002, From Crisis to Growth 2005. *Leisure interest:* history, reading. *Address:* Academy of National Economy, Vernadskogo Prospekt 82, 119571, Moscow, Russia (office). *Telephone:* (495) 434-83-89 (office). *Fax:* (495) 433-24-85 (office). *E-mail:* rector@ane.ru (office). *Website:* www.ane.ru (office).

MAUCHER, Helmut Oswald, Diplom-Kaufmann; German business executive; *Honorary Chairman, Nestlé SA;* b. 9 Dec. 1927, Eisenharz (Allgäu); ed Frankfurt Univ.; completed commercial apprenticeship at Nestlé factory in Eisenharz, Germany, then transferred to Nestlé, Frankfurt; various man. positions within the Nestlé Co. in Germany 1964–80, Pres. and CEO Nestlé-Gruppe Deutschland, Frankfurt 1975–80, Exec. Vice-Pres. and mem. Exec. Cttee Nestlé SA, Vevey, Switzerland 1980–81, CEO 1981–97, Chair. 1990–2000, Hon. Chair. 2000–; Chair. Bd Trustees Stiftung Demoskopie Allensbach Germany; Chair. Universität Bayern e.V., Munich; mem Bd of Trustees Frankfurt Inst. for Advanced Studies; mem. Bd Koç Holding AS, Istanbul, Union Bancaire Privée, Geneva, Int. Course of Studies Bachelor and Master Philosophy and Econs, Bayreuth Univ.; mem. Bd of Trustees, Fondation Simón I. Patiño Geneva; mem. Advisory Council, Deutsche Vermögensberatung AG, Frankfurt; mem. Int. Advisory Cttee, Fitch Rating Agency, London and New York; Order El Aguila Azteca (Mexico) 1993, Grosses Goldenes Ehrenzeichen mit dem Stern für Verdienste um die Republik Oesterreich 1993, Das Grosse Verdienstkreuz des Verdienstordens mit Stern der Bundesrepublik Deutschland 1997, Das Osterreichische Ehrenkreuz für Wissenschaft und Kunst 1. Klasse 1999; Dr hc (Autonomous Univ. of Guadalajara, Mexico) 1989, (European Business School, Ostrich-Winkel, Germany) 1997, (Tech. Univ., Munich) 1998; Fortune Magazine Gold Medal 1984, Leadership Award for Corporate Statesmanship, International Institute for Management Development (IMD) 1993, IMD-Maucher Nestlé Chair 1993, Appeal of Conscience Foundation Award, New York 1995, INTERNORGA Prize, Hamburg 1996, Manager Magazine Business Hall of Fame 1997, Scopus Award, Hebrew Univ., Jerusalem 1999, Preis Soziale Marktwirtschaft, Konrad-Adenauer Stiftung e.V. 2004. *Publications:* Leadership in Action (translated from German 'Marketing ist Chefsache' into several languages), Management Breviary. *Address:* Nestlé SA, Avenue Nestlé 55, 1800 Vevey, Switzerland (office).

MAUD, Hon. Sir Humphrey John Hamilton, Kt, KCMG, MA, FRCM; British diplomatist (retd); *Chairman, Commonwealth Disaster Management Agency Ltd;* b. 17 April 1934, Oxford, England; s. of Lord and Lady Redcliffe-Maud; m. Maria Eugenia Gazitua 1963; three s.; ed Eton Coll., King's Coll., Cambridge, Nuffield Coll., Oxford; Instructor in Classics, Univ. of Minn., USA 1958–59; joined Diplomatic Service 1959, Third Sec., Madrid 1961–63, Third, later Second Sec., Havana 1963–65, at FCO 1966–68, Cabinet Office 1968–69, First Sec. Paris 1970–74, Sabbatical at Nuffield Coll., Oxford (Econs) 1974–75, Head of Financial Relations Dept, FCO 1975–79, Minister, Madrid 1979–82, Amb. to Luxembourg 1982–84; Asst Under-Sec. of State (Econ. and Commercial) 1985–88; High Commr in Cyprus 1988–89; Amb. to Argentina 1990–93 (reopened diplomatic relations between Britain and Argentina 1990 after the Falklands War); Commonwealth Deputy Sec.-Gen. 1993–99; currently Chair. Commonwealth Disaster Man. Agency Ltd; mem. Nat. Youth Orchestra 1949–52; Chair. Pall Mall Initiatives 2000–; Chair. Trustees, Musequality 2007–; mem. Council, Royal Coll. of Music 1997–2007, Queen's Medal for Music Advisory Cttee 2007–; Trustee, Cecil King Memorial Foundation 1997–, Dartington Int. Summer School Foundation 2008–. *Publications:* Round Table (various articles). *Leisure interests:* music, golf, bird-watching. *Address:* 31 Queen Anne's Grove, London, W4 1HW, England (home). *Telephone:* (20) 8994-2808 (home); 7803-721447 (mobile). *Fax:* (20) 8995-1165 (home). *E-mail:* hmaud@cdma.org.uk (office). *Website:* www.cdma.org.uk (office).

MAUDE, Rt Hon. Francis (Anthony Aylmer), PC, MA; British politician and business executive; *Minister for the Cabinet Office and Paymaster General;* b. 4 July 1953, Abingdon, Oxon., England; s. of Baron Maude of Stratford-upon-Avon; m. Christina Jane Hadfield 1984; two s. three d.; ed Abingdon School, Corpus Christi Coll., Cambridge, Coll. of Law; called to Bar, Inner Temple 1977 (Forster Boulton Prize); Councillor, Westminster City Council 1978–84; MP for Warwicks. N 1983–92, for Horsham 1997–; Parl. Pvt. Sec. to Minister of State for Employment 1984–85; as Asst Govt Whip 1985–87; Parl. Under-Sec. of State Dept of Trade and Industry 1987–89; Minister of State, FCO 1989–90; Financial Sec. to HM Treasury 1990–92; Chair. Govt's Deregulation Task Force 1994–97; Shadow Chancellor 1998–2000, Shadow Foreign Sec. 2000–01; Minister for the Cabinet Office 2010–; Paymaster Gen. 2010–; Chair. Prestbury Holdings, Jubilee Investment Trust, Incepta Group plc 2004–05; Chair., Conservative Party 2005–07; Dir Salomon Brothers 1992–93, Asda Group 1992–99, Utek 2006–; Man. Dir Morgan Stanley and Co. 1993–97; Deputy Chair. Benfield Group Ltd 2003–; Deputy Chair., Huntsworth plc. *Leisure interests:* skiing, cricket, reading, music. *Address:* House of Commons, Westminster, London, SW1A 0AA (office); Constituency Office, Gough House, Madeira Avenue, Horsham, RH12 1RL, England. *Telephone:* (20) 7219-2494 (office); (1403) 242000 (Horsham). *Fax:* (20) 7219-2990 (office); (1403) 210600 (Horsham). *E-mail:* francismaudemp@parliament.uk (office). *Website:* www.parliament.uk/biographies/commons/francis-maude/25444 (office); www .francismaude.com.

MAULDE, Bruno Guy André Jean de, LenD; French banker; b. 27 March 1934, Toulouse; s. of Guy de Maulde and Suzanna Mazars; m. Dominique Le Henaff 1958; three d.; ed Inst. of Political Studies, Toulouse, Nat. Coll. of Admin.; Insp. des Finances 1962; Adviser, External Econ. Relations Dept, Finance Ministry 1967–68; Alt. Exec. Dir IMF for France 1968–70; Financial attaché, Embassy, USA 1968–70, in New York 1970–71; French Treasury Adviser 1971–74, Asst Dir 1974–77, Deputy Dir 1977–78; Deputy Man. Dir Caisse Nat. de Crédit Agricole 1979–81; Financial Minister, Embassy of France and Exec. Dir IMF and IBRD, Washington 1981–85; Chair. and CEO Crédit du Nord 1986–93; Chair. Conseil des Bourses de Valeurs (CBV) 1990–94; Dir Compagnie Financière de Paribas 1993–94; Dir of various other corpns and public insts; mem. Council of Monetary Policy, Banque de France 1994–97; Chevalier, Légion d'honneur, Ordre nat. du Mérite, Croix de la Valeur militaire, Officier du Mérite agricole. *Leisure interest:* yachting. *Address:* Rozaven, 29930 Pont-Aven, France.

MAUMOON, Dunya, BA, MPhil; Maldivian politician; *Minister of Foreign Affairs;* b. 1970; d. of Maumoon Abdul Gayoom (fmr Pres. of Maldives) and Nasreena Ibrahim; m. Shuaib Shah; two s. one d.; ed Univ. of Cambridge, London School of Econs, UK; Asst Rep. Head, UN Population Fund (UNFPA), Maldives 1998–2007; Deputy Minister of Foreign Affairs 2007–08, Head of Multilateral Dept, later Minister of State, Ministry of Foreign Affairs 2012, Minister of Foreign Affairs 2013–; fmr mem. Dhivehi Raiyyithunge Party (DRP); mem. Progressive Party of Maldives (PPM), Pres. of Women's Wing 2013–. *Address:* Ministry of Foreign Affairs, Henveiru, Blk 77, Boduthakurufaanu Magu, Malé 20–077, Maldives (office). *Telephone:* 3323400 (office). *Fax:* 3323841 (office). *E-mail:* info@foreign.gov.mv (office). *Website:* www.foreign.gov.mv (office).

MAUNG, Deputy Sr Gen. Aye, BSc; Myanmar military officer; b. 25 Dec. 1937, Kon Balu; m.; ed Defence Services Acad.; joined Myanma Army 1959, C-in-C 1993–; Deputy C-in-C Defence Services; Vice-Chair. State Law and Order Restoration Council (SLORC) 1994–97, State Peace and Devt Council 1997–2011 (council dissolved). *Address:* c/o Office of the Chairman of the State Peace and Development Council, 15–16 Windermere Park, Yangon, Myanmar (office). *Telephone:* (1) 282445 (office).

MAUNG, Cynthia, MD; Myanma physician; *Director, Mae Tao Clinic;* b. 6 Dec. 1959, Rangoon; m. Kyaw Hein; two d.; ed Univ. of Rangoon; trained at North Okkalapa Gen. Hosp.; worked in rural clinic in Karen State; participated in nationwide anti-govt protests in 1988, fled to Thailand several months later; f. Mae Tao Clinic in Thailand to treat refugees fleeing from Myanmar; John Humphries Freedom Award 1999, American Women's Medical Asscn Pres.'s Award 1999, Jonathan Mann Award 1999, Van Hueven Goedhart Award, Foundation for Human Rights in Asia Special Award 2001, Ramon Magsaysay Award 2002, Global Concern for Human Life Award, Chou-Ta Kuan Foundation 2005, Unsung Heroes of Compassion Award 2005, World's Children's Hon. Award 2007, Asia Democracy and Human Rights Award 2007, Catalonia Int. Prize (jtly) 2008, Democracy Award, Nat. Endowment for Democracy (US) 2012. *Address:* Mae Tao Clinic, PO Box 67, Mae Sot, Tak 63110, Thailand (office). *Telephone:* (55) 563-644 (office). *Fax:* (55) 544-655 (office). *E-mail:* win7@loxinfo.co.th (office). *Website:* www .maetaoclinic.org (office).

MAUPIN, Armistead Jones, Jr; American writer; b. 13 May 1944; s. of Armistead Jones Maupin and the late Diana Jane Maupin (née Barton); ed Univ. of

North Carolina; reporter, News and Courier, Charleston, SC 1970–71, Associated Press, San Francisco 1971–72; Account Exec., Lowry Russom and Leeper Public Relations 1973; columnist, Pacific Sun Magazine 1974; publicist, San Francisco Opera 1975; serialist, San Francisco Chronicle 1976–77, 1981, 1983; Commentator, KRON-TV San Francisco 1979; serialist, San Francisco Examiner 1986; Exec. Producer, Armistead Maupin's Tales of the City 1993; contrib. to New York Times, Los Angeles Times and others; numerous awards, including: Freedom Leadership Award, Freedoms Foundation 1972, Communications Award, Metropolitan Elections Comm., LA 1989, Exceptional Achievement Award, American Libraries Asscn 1990, Outstanding Miniseries Award, Gay and Lesbian Alliance Against Defamation 1994. *Film:* The Night Listener (Exec. Producer, adapted from his book) 2006. *Publications include:* Tales of the City (Big Gay Read Award 2006) 1978, More Tales of the City 1980, Further Tales of the City 1982, Babycakes 1984, Significant Others 1987, Sure of You 1989, 28 Barbary Lane 1990, Back to Barbary Lane 1991, Maybe the Moon 1992, The Essential Clive Baker (co-author) 1999, The Night Listener 2000, Michael Tolliver Lives 2007, Mary Ann in Autumn 2010; as librettist: Heart's Desire 1990. *Address:* c/o Literary Bent, PO Box 4109990, Suite 528, San Francisco, CA 94141; c/o Amanda Urban, 40 West 57th Street, Floor 16, New York, NY 10019, USA. *E-mail:* inquiries@literarybent.cor. *Website:* www .armisteadmaupin.com.

MAURA, Carmen, BA; Spanish actress; b. 15 Sept. 1945, Madrid; d. of Antonio Maura; worked as a cabaret singer and translator; has appeared in numerous films including many of Pedro Almodóvar's works. *Other films include:* El espíritu 1969, Mantis 1971, El hombre oculto (The Man In Hiding) 1971, El asesino está entre los trece 1973, Un casto varón español 1973, Tanata 1974, Don Juan 1974, Vida íntima de un seductor cínico 1975, La encadenada (A Diary of a Murderess) 1975, El love feroz 1975, Leonor 1975, Pomporrutas imperiales 1976, La petición (The Request) 1976, Una pareja como las demás 1976, Ir por lana 1976, La mujer es cosa de hombres 1976, El libro del buen amor II (The Book of Good Love 2) 1976, Tigres de papel (Paper Tigers) 1977, ¿Qué hace una chica como tú en un sitio como éste? (What's a Girl Like You Doing in a Place Like This?) 1978, Mi blanca Varsovia 1978, Menos mi madre y mi hermana 1978, Folle… folle… fólleme Tim! 1978, De fresa, limón y menta (Strawberry, Lemon and Mint) 1978, Los ojos vendados (Blindfolded Eyes) 1978, Tal vez mañana… 1979, Café, amor y estereofonía 1979, La mano negra (The Black Hand) 1980, Aquella casa en las afueras (That House in the Outskirts) 1980, Pepi, Luci, Bom y otras chicas del montón (Pepi, Luci, Bom and Other Girls Like Mom) 1980, El hombre de moda (Man of Fashion) 1980, Gary Cooper, que estás en los cielos (Gary Cooper, Who Art in Heaven) 1980, Femenino singular 1982, Entre tinieblas (Dark Habits) 1983, El Cid cabreador 1983, ¿Qué he hecho yo para merecer esto!! (What Have I Done to Deserve This?) 1984, Extramuros (Beyond the Walls) 1985, Sé infiel y no mires con quién (Be Wanton and Tread No Shame) 1985, Matador 1986, Delirios de amor 1986, Tata mía (Dear Nanny) 1986, La ley del deseo (Law of Desire) 1987, 2.30 A.M. 1988, Mujeres al borde de un ataque de nervios (Women on the Verge of a Nervous Breakdown) (Best Actress, European Film Awards 1989) 1988, Bâton rouge 1988, ¡Ay, Carmela! (Best Actress, European Film Awards 1991) 1990, Cómo ser mujer y no morir en el intento (How to Be a Woman and Not Die Trying) 1991, Chatarra 1991, Sur la terre comme au ciel (In Heaven as on Earth) 1992, La reina anónima (The Anonymous Queen) 1992, Louis, enfant roi (Louis, the Child King) 1993, Sombras en una batalla (Shadows in a Conflict) 1993, Cómo ser infeliz y disfrutarlo (How to Be Miserable and Enjoy It) 1994, El rey del río 1995, Parella de tres 1995, El palomo cojo (The Lame Pigeon) 1995, Le bonheur est dans le pré (Happiness is in the Field) 1995, Amores que matan 1996, Vivir después 1997, Tortilla y cinema 1997, Alliance cherche oeuf 1997, Elles 1997, Alice et Martin 1998, El entusiasmo (Enthusiasm) 1998, El cometa (The Comet) 1999, Lisboa 1999, Superlove 1999, Carretera y manta (To the End of the Road) 2000, Le harem de Mme Osmane 2000, La comunidad 2000, Valentín 2002, 800 balas (800 Bullets) 2002, Le ventre de Juliette 2003, Le pacte du silence 2003, 25 degrés en hiver (25 Degrees in Winter) 2004, La promesa 2004, Al otro lado 2004, Entre vivir y soñar 2004, Reinas 2005, Free Zone 2005, Volver (Goya Award for Best Supporting Actress 2007) 2006, El Menor de los males 2007, La Virgen negra 2008, The Garden of Eden 2008, Que parezca un accidente 2008, Tetro 2009, Le mac 2010, Chicas 2010, The Women on the 6th Floor 2010, Escalade 2011, Let My People Go! 2011, Sofía y el Terco 2012, Paulette 2012. *Television includes:* Juan y Manuela (series) 1974, Suspiros de España (series) 1974, El coleccionismo y los coleccionistas (series) 1979, Cervantes (miniseries) 1980, La huella del crimen: El crimen de la calle Fuencarral 1984, Sal gorda (Coarse Salt) 1984, La mujer de tu vida: La mujer feliz 1988, Mieux vaut courir 1989, A las once en casa (series) 1998, Famosos y familia (series) 1999, Une mère en colère 2000, Arroz y tartana 2003, Mentir un peu 2004, Mentir un peu 2006, Círculo rojo (series) 2007, The War of the Saints 2009, Las chicas de oro (series) 2010, Carta a Eva (mini-series) 2012, Stamos okupa2 (series) 2012. *Address:* c/o VMA, 20, av Rapp, 75007 Paris, France.

MAURER, Peter, PhD; Swiss diplomatist; *President, International Committee of the Red Cross;* b. 20 Nov. 1956, Thun; m. Doris Maurer-Scheidegger; two d.; ed Univ. of Bern, Univ. of Perugia, Italy; joined Fed. Dept of Foreign Affairs 1987, served as Diplomatic Adviser, Political Secr. 1989–91, Pvt. Sec. to State Sec. for Foreign Affairs 1991–96; Deputy Perm. Observer to Observer Mission to UN, New York 1996–2000; Head, Political Affairs Div. IV (Human Security), Political Affairs Govt Directorate 2000–04; Amb. and Perm. Rep. to UN, New York 2004–10, Head of Fifth Comm. (overseeing budget and admin. matters); Sec. of State, Fed. Dept of Foreign Affairs 2010–12; Pres. International Cttee of the Red Cross 2012–. *Address:* International Committee of the Red Cross (ICRC), 19 ave de la Paix, 1202 Geneva, Switzerland (office). *Telephone:* 227346001 (office). *Fax:* 227332057 (office). *E-mail:* press.gva@icrc.org (office). *Website:* www.icrc.org (office).

MAURER, Ueli; Swiss communications consultant and politician; *Head of Federal Department of Defence, Civil Protection and Sports;* b. 1 Dec. 1950, Wetzikon; m.; six c.; Dir Zürich Farmers Asscn 1994–2008; mem. Zürich Cantonal Parl. 1978–86 (Pres. 1991); mem. House of Reps 1991; mem. Schweizerischen Volkspartei (Swiss People's Party), Pres. 1996–2008, Pres. Zürich Div. 2008; mem. Swiss Federal Council 2009–, Head of Fed. Dept of Defence, Civil Protection and Sports 2009–, Vice-Pres. for 2012, Pres. 2013; fmr Pres. Swiss Vegetable Farmers Asscn, Farmers Machinery Asscn (Maschinenring). *Address:* Federal Department

of Defence, Civil Protection and Sports, Bundeshaus Ost, 3003 Bern, Switzerland (office). *Telephone:* 313222111 (office). *Fax:* 313245104 (office). *E-mail:* postmaster .vbs@gs-vbs.admin.ch (office). *Website:* www.vbs.admin.ch (office).

MAURESMO, Amélie; French professional tennis player (retd); b. 5 July 1979, Saint-Germain-en-Laye; began to play tennis aged four; turned professional 1994; won both Jr French Open and Wimbledon titles 1996; finalist, Australian Open 1999; semi-finalist, US Open singles 2002, 2006; quarter-finalist, French Open singles 2003, 2004; silver medal, Olympic Games, Athens 2004; winner of two Grand Slam singles titles, Australian Open 2006, Wimbledon 2006; ranked World No. 1 Sept.–Oct. 2004; doubles finalist with Svetlana Kuznetsova, Wimbledon 2005; lives in Geneva, Switzerland; retd 2009; currently tennis commentator, EuroSport; Capt. l'Equipe de France de Fed-Cup; Int. Tennis Fed. Jr World Champion 1996. *E-mail:* agence@interactive-one.fr. *Website:* www .ameliemauresmo.fr (office).

MAURÍCIO, Armindo Cipriano; Cape Verde politician; *Secretary General, Partido Africano da Independência de Cabo Verde;* fmr Minister of Defence and Parl. Affairs; mem. Parl. for Ribeira Grande; Sec. Gen. Partido Africano da Independência de Cabo Verde. *Address:* Partido Africano da Independência de Cabo Verde, Av. Amílcar Cabral, CP 22, Praia, Santiago, Cape Verde (office). *Telephone:* 2608015 (extension 369); 2612720 (office). *Fax:* 2611410 (office). *Website:* www.paicv.cv (office).

MAURSTAD, Toralv; Norwegian actor and theatre director; b. 24 Nov. 1926, Oslo; s. of Alfred and Tordis Maurstad; m. Beate Eriksen; one s.; ed Universitet i Uppsala and Royal Acad. of Dramatic Art, London; debut in Trondheim 1947; Oslo/ Nye Teater 1951; Oslo Nat. Theatre 1954; Man. Dir Oslo Nye Teater (Oslo Municipal Theatre) 1967–78; Man. Dir Nat. Theatre 1978–86, actor/Dir Nat. Theatre 1987–; Norwegian Sr Golf Champion 1992; Kt First Class, Order of St Olav (Norway), Order of Oranian (Netherlands); Oslo Critics' Award, Ibsen Prize, Amanda, Aamot Statuette. *Plays acted in or directed include:* Young Woodley 1949, Pal Joey 1952, Peer Gynt 1954, Long Day's Journey 1962, Teenage Love 1963, Hamlet 1964, Arturo Ui (in Bremen, Germany) 1965, Brand (Ibsen) 1966, Of Love Remembered (New York) 1967, Cabaret 1968, Scapino 1975, Two Gentlemen of Verona 1976, The Moon of the Misbegotten 1976, Same Time Next Year 1977, Twigs 1977 (also TV production), Sly Fox 1978, Whose Life is it Anyway? 1979, Masquerade 1980, Amadeus 1980, Much Ado about Nothing 1981, Kennen Sie die Milchstrasse? 1982, Duet for One 1982, Hamlet 1983, Private Lives (with Liv Ullman) 1993, Dear Liar 1996, The Pretenders 1998, Copenhagen 2000, Enigma Variation 2001, Waiting for Godot 2005, Rigoletto (opera) 2005, Twelfth Night 2005. *Films:* Fant 1937, Trysil-Knut 1942, Kranes konditori 1951, Andrine og Kjell 1952, Cirkus Fandango 1954, Hjem går vi ikke 1955, Line 1961, Kalde Spor 1962, Om Tilla (About Tilla) 1963, Svarta palmkronor (Black Palm Trees) 1968, Hennes meget kongelige høyhet 1968, Song of Norway 1970, Flåklypa Grand Prix (voice) 1975, Glade vrinsk (writer) 1975, Etter Rubicon (After Rubicon) 1987, Det var en gang (voice) 1994, Jakten på nyresteinen (Chasing the Kidney Stone; voice) 1996, Solan, Ludvig og Gurin med reverompa (Gurin with the Foxtail; voice) 1998, Olsenbanden Junior på rocker'n 2004. *Radio plays:* Doll's House, Peer Gynt, Masquerade. *Television:* Gengangere 1962, Frydenberg 1965, Ett köpmanshus i skärgården (mini-series) 1972, Spyship (mini-series) 1983, The Last Place on Earth (mini-series) 1985, Konsultasjon eller helbredelsens kunst (dir) 1988, Olsenbandens første kupp (mini-series) 2001, Enigmavariasjoner 2002, Hotel Cesar (episode) 2004, Waiting for Godot 2006, Moon for the Misbegotten 2008. *Publication:* Du Store Min (autobiog.). *Leisure interests:* skiing, hunting, fishing, golf, tennis. *Address:* Nationaltheatret, Stortingsgt. 15, Oslo 1 (office); Box 58, Holmenkollen, 0712, Norway (home); Thorleif, Hangsvei 20, Voksenkollen 0712, Oslo, Norway. *Telephone:* 22-14-18-84 (home); 91370972 (mobile). *E-mail:* toral -ma@online.no (home).

MÁURTUA DE ROMAÑA, Oscar José Ricardo, BA, BL; Peruvian government minister, politician and diplomatist; b. 7 Feb. 1947, Lima; m.; three c.; ed Univ. Católica y San Marcos, Univ. of Oxford, Johns Hopkins Univ.; 2nd, then 1st Sec. Peruvian Embassy, USA; Counsellor in Belgium and at EU; Head Dept of Int. Political Econs/Econ.; Sec.-Gen. Presidency of the Repub.; Amb. to Canada, Bolivia; Dir-Gen. of Planning, of Judicial Affairs; Amb. to Thailand, concurrently to Viet Nam and Laos; Perm. Rep. ESCAP; Amb. to Ecuador; Dir Acad. of Diplomacy; Sub-Sec. for American Affairs, later Sec. for Foreign Affairs; Minister of Foreign Affairs 2005–06; OAS Rep. in Mexico 2007–; Del. to Confs of APEC, Asia Pacific Parl. Forum, Pacific Basin ECO Council, Pacific ECO Cooperation Council; Prof. of Int. Law Univ. Nacional de San Marcos y de Derecho; mem. Colegio de Abogados de Lima, Soc. Peruana de Derecho Int., Oxford Socs., Center of Int. Understanding; Hon. mem. Soc. Boliviana de Historia, Soc. de la Acad. Boliviana de Estudios Int., Siam Soc., Sociedad Fundadores de la Independencia; Hon. Prof., Univ. Andina Simon Bolivar, Quito; Hon. law doctorates (Winnipeg, Bangkok, Univ. Andina, Univ. Aquino); several decorations from Peruvian and foreign govts; Nat. Award of Culture, Nat. Award Journalism (Mexico) 2009. *Publications:* Derecho Internacional y Política Exterior 1995, Una Visión Latinoamericana del Asia Pacifico 1999, Las Nuevas Relaciones Bilaterales Perú-Ecuador 2000, Perú y Ecuador: Socios en el siglo XXI, Apuntes sobre la Agenda Interamericana México 2010. *Address:* CDM Polanco, Delegacion Miguel Hidalgo, Apartado Postal 11560, México, DF, Mexico (office). *Telephone:* (55) 280-1208 (office); (55) 280-1147 (office). *Fax:* (55) 281-7390 (office). *E-mail:* OMaurtua@oas.or (office); osjomar@hotmail .com (office). *Website:* www.oas.org (office).

MAVRIKOS, George; Greek trade union official and international organization executive; *General Secretary, World Federation of Trade Unions;* Deputy Pres. Gen. Confed. of Workers in Greece; Sec. All Workers Militant Front (PAME) (a CP of Greece-affiliated trade union); Vice-Pres. WFTU and Coordinator of its European Office –2005, Gen. Sec. WFTU 2005–. *Address:* World Federation of Trade Unions, 40 Zan Moreas Str., 117 45 Athens, Greece (office). *Telephone:* (21) 09236700 (office). *Fax:* (21) 09214517 (office). *E-mail:* info@wftucentral.org (office). *Website:* www.wftucentral.org (office).

MAVRONICOLAS, Kyriakos, FRCS; Cypriot ophthalmologist and politician; b. 1955, Paphos; m. Irene (Roula) Kokkinidou; two c.; ed First Gymnasium, Paphos, Nat. and Kapodistrian Univ. of Athens Medical School, Athens Law School; began career as ophthalmologist, Nicosia 1960, practised in UK 1981–87; fmr Gen. Sec.

Democratic Students' Movement (AGONAS); Sec. Athens Br., Socialist Party (EDEK), becoming EDEK Dist Sec., Nicosia 1989–93, later Party First Vice-Pres.; Deputy Pres. Social Democrat Movement (KISOS); Minister of Defence 2003–06. *Address:* c/o Ministry of Defence, 4 Emmanuel Roides Avenue, 1432 Nicosia, Cyprus (office).

MAVROYIANNIS, Andreas D., DipLaw; Cypriot diplomatist and politician; *Deputy Minister of European Affairs;* b. 20 July 1956, Agros; m. Calliopi Efthyvoulou; one s. one d.; ed Univ. of Thessalonica, Greece, Université de Droit et de Sciences Economique, Paris, Université de Paris X, Nanterre; joined Ministry of Foreign Affairs 1987; served at Embassy in Paris 1989–93, also in Political Div., Cyprus Question Div., EU Div., and as Assoc. European Correspondent; Dir, Office of Minister of Foreign Affairs 1995–97, 2002–03; Amb. to Ireland 1997–99, to France (also accred to Andorra, Tunisia and Morocco) 1999–2002; Acting Perm. Sec., Ministry of Foreign Affairs 2003; Amb. and Perm. Rep. to UN, New York 2003–, also accred as High Commr to St Lucia 2003–08 and Amb. to Brazil 2007–08; Chair. UN Cttee on Relations with Host Country 2003–; Amb. and Perm. Rep. to EU, Brussels 2008–11; Deputy Minister for European Affairs 2011–; Rep. at Cttee of Legal Advisers on Public Int. Law (CAHDI), Council of Europe 1988–92; Rep. Prep. Comm. for High Authority, Law of the Sea 1989; mem. Greek Cypriot negotiating team in bi-communal talks for solution of Cyprus issue 2002–03; Lecturer, Cyprus Mediterranean Inst. of Man., Cyprus Acad. for Public Admin, Law School of Univ. of Athens; Diploma of The Hague Acad. of Int. Law 1984. *Publications:* articles and reviews in scholarly journals and newspapers. *Address:* 56 Kyriakou Matsi Avenue, 1082 Nicosia, Cyprus (office). *Telephone:* (22) 400102 (office). *Fax:* (22) 400173 (office). *E-mail:* presidency@cy2012eu.gov.cy (office). *Website:* www.cy2012eu.gov.cy (office).

MAWER, Sir Philip John Courtney, Kt, MA, DPA; British parliamentary official and church official; *Chairman, All Churches Trust Ltd;* b. 30 July 1947; s. of Eric Douglas Mawer and Thora Constance Mawer; m. Mary Ann Moxon 1972; one s. two d.; ed Hull Grammar School, Univ. of Edinburgh, Univ. of London; Sr Pres. EU Student Rep. Council 1969–70; joined Home Office 1971; Pvt. Sec. to Minister of State 1974–76; Nuffield and Leverhulme Travelling Fellowship 1978–79; Sec. Lord Scarman Inquiry into Brixton Riots 1981; Asst Sec. Head of Industrial Relations, Prison Dept 1984–87; Prin. Pvt. Sec. to Home Sec. Douglas Hurd 1987–89; Under-Sec. Cabinet Office 1989–90; Sec.-Gen. Church of England Synod 1990–2002; Sec.-Gen. Archbishops' Council 1999–2002; Parl. Commr for Standards 2002–08, then ind. adviser to Prime Minister –2011; Chair. Professional Regulation Exec. Cttee of the Actuarial Profession 2009–13; Dir (non-exec.) Ecclesiastical Insurance Group 1996–2002, 2008–13 (Deputy Chair. 2009–13); Trustee All Churches Trust 1992– (Dir 2010–, Chair. 2013–); mem. Governing Body SPCK 1994–2002; Patron Church Housing Trust 1996–; Hon. Lay Canon of St Alban's Cathedral 2003–12; Hon. DLitt (Hull) 2006, Hon. LLD (Herts.) 2007. *Leisure interests:* family, friends. *Address:* All Churches Trust, Beaufort House, Brunswick Road, Gloucester, GL1 1JZ, England (office). *Telephone:* (1452) 423557 (office). *Website:* www.allchurches.uk (office).

MAWHINNEY, Baron (Life Peer), cr. 2005; **Brian Stanley Mawhinney,** Kt, PC, PhD; British parliamentarian and company director; b. 26 July 1940; s. of Frederick Stanley Arnot Mawhinney and Coralie Jean Mawhinney; m. Betty Louise Oja 1965; two s. one d.; ed Royal Belfast Academical Inst., Queen's Univ. Belfast, Univ. of Michigan, USA, Univ. of London; Asst Prof. of Radiation Research, Univ. of Iowa, USA 1968–70; lecturer, subsequently Sr Lecturer, Royal Free Hosp. School of Medicine 1970–84; mem. MRC 1980–83; MP for Peterborough 1979–97, for Cambridgeshire NW 1997–2005; Parl. Under-Sec. of State for Northern Ireland 1986–90; Minister of State, Northern Ireland Office 1990–92, Dept of Health 1992–94; Sec. of State for Transport 1994–95; Chair. Conservative Party 1995–97; Opposition Front Bench Spokesman on Home Affairs 1997–98; Pres. Conservative Trade Unionists 1987–90; mem. Gen. Synod of Church of England 1985–90; Chair. Football League 2003–10; Jt Deputy Chair. England 2018 World Cup Bid Co. 2008–10; Hon. Pres. Football League 2010–13; Hon. LLD (Queen's, Belfast) 2008; Freedom City of Peterborough 2008. *Publications:* Conflict and Christianity in Northern Ireland (co-author) 1976, In the Firing Line–Faith, Power, Politics, Forgiveness 1999. *Leisure interests:* sport, reading, business. *Address:* House of Lords, London, SW1A 0PW, England (office). *Telephone:* (1733) 261868 (office). *Fax:* (1733) 266887 (office). *E-mail:* judith5@waitrose.com (office). *Website:* www.parliament.uk (office).

MAXSTED, Lindsay, DipBus, FCA; Australian business executive; *Chairman, Westpac Banking Corporation;* ed Robert Gordon Univ.; Partner, KPMG 1984–2008, CEO 2001–07; mem. Bd Public Transport Corpn 1995–2001, Chair. 1997–2001; mem. Bd of Dirs Westpac Westpac Banking Corpn 2008–, Chair. 2011–; Chair. Transurban Group; Man. Dir Align Capital Pty Ltd; mem. Bd of Dirs BHP Billiton Ltd, BHP Billiton plc, Baker IDI Heart & Diabetes Inst. Holdings Ltd. *Address:* Westpac Banking Corporation, Level 20, Westpac Place, 275 Kent Street, Sydney, NSW 2000, Australia (office). *Telephone:* (2) 8253-0390 (office). *Fax:* (2) 8253-1888 (office). *E-mail:* info@westpac.com.au (office). *Website:* www .westpac.com.au (office).

MAXWELL, Ian, MA; British/French publisher; b. 15 June 1956, Maisons-Laffitte, France; s. of the late (Ian) Robert Maxwell and of Elisabeth Meynard; m. 1st Laura Plumb 1991 (divorced 1998); m. 2nd Tara Dudley Smith 1999; ed Marlborough Coll. and Balliol Coll., Oxford; Man. Dir Pergamon Press France 1980–81; Jt Man. Dir Pergamon Press GmbH 1980; Marketing Dir Pergamon Press Inc. 1982–83; Dir Sales Devt BPCC PLC 1985–86; Dir Group Marketing BPCC PLC (now Maxwell Communication Corpn PLC) 1986; Chair. Agence Centrale de Presse, Paris 1986–89; Dir TFI TV station, Paris 1987–89; CEO Maxwell Pergamon Publrs 1988–89; Jt Man. Dir Maxwell Communication Corpn 1988–91; Acting Chair. Mirror Group Newspapers 1991; Dir New York Daily News –1991, Telemonde Holdings 1997–; publishing consultant Westbourne Communications Ltd 1993; Publr Maximov Publs Ltd 1995; Chair. Derby Co. Football Club 1984–87, Vice-Chair. 1987–91; mem. Nat. Theatre Devt Council 1986; Pres. Club d'Investissement Média 1988. *Leisure interests:* skiing, water skiing, watching football.

MAXWELL DAVIES, Sir Peter, Kt, CH, CBE, MusB, FRCM, FRSAMD, FRNCM; British composer and conductor; *Master of the Queen's Music;* b. 8 Sept. 1934, Manchester, England; s. of Thomas Davies and Hilda Davies (née Howard); ed Leigh Grammar School, Royal Manchester Coll. of Music, Univ. of Manchester; studied with Goffredo Petrassi, Rome 1957 and with Roger Sessions, Milton Babbitt, Earl Kim, Princeton Univ., NJ, USA (Harkness Fellow) 1962–64; Dir of Music, Cirencester Grammar School 1959–62; Harkness Fellowship, Grad. School, Princeton Univ. 1962–64; lecture tours in Europe, Australia, USA, Canada, Brazil; Visiting Composer, Univ. of Adelaide 1966; Prof. of Composition, Royal Northern Coll. of Music, Manchester 1965–80 (Fellow 1978); Pres. Schools Music Asscn 1983–, Composers' Guild of GB 1986–, Nat. Fed. of Music Socs 1989–, Cheltenham Arts Festival 1994–96, Soc. for Promotion of New Music 1995–; Visiting Fromm Prof. of Composition, Harvard Univ. 1985; f. and Co-Dir (with Harrison Birtwistle q.v.) Pierrot Players 1967–71; f. and Artistic Dir The Fires of London 1971–87; f. and Artistic Dir St Magnus Festival, Orkney Islands 1977–86, Pres. 1986–; Artistic Dir Dartington Summer School of Music 1979–84; Assoc. Conductor and Composer Scottish Chamber Orchestra 1985–94, Composer Laureate 1994–; Conductor and Composer, BBC Philharmonic Orchestra (Manchester) 1992–2001; Assoc. Conductor and Composer Royal Philharmonic Orchestra 1992–2001; Master of the Queen's Music 2004–; Fellowship British Acad. of Composers and Songwriters 2005; mem. Accad. Filarmonica Romana 1979, Royal Swedish Acad. of Music 1993, Bayerische Akad. der Schönen Künste 1998, British Acad. of Songwriters, Composers and Authors; Hon. RAM 1979; Hon. mem. Guildhall School of Music and Drama 1981, Royal Philharmonic Soc. 1987, Royal Scottish Acad. 2001; Hon. Fellow, Royal Incorporation of Architects in Scotland 1994, Univ. of Highlands and Islands 2004; Freeman of the City of Salford; Officier des Arts et des Lettres 1988; several hon. degrees, including Hon. DMus (Edin.) 1979, (Manchester) 1981, (Bristol) 1984, (Open Univ.) 1986, (Glasgow) 1993, (Durham) 1994, (Hull) 2001, (Kingston) 2005; Hon. DLitt (Warwick) 1986, (Salford) 1999; Hon. DUniv (Heriot-Watt) 2002; Olivetti Prize 1959, Koussevitsky Award 1964, Koussevitsky Recording Award 1966, Cobbett Medal for services to chamber music 1989, First Award of Asscn of British Orchestras, for contribs to orchestras and orchestral life in UK 1991, Gulliver Award for Performing Arts in Scotland 1991, Nat. Fed. of Music Socs Charles Groves Award for outstanding contrib. to British Music 1995, Royal Philharmonic Soc. Award for Large-scale Composition (for Symphony No. 5) 1995, Inc. Soc. of Musicians Distinguished Musicians Award 2001, Ivor Novello Classical Music Award 2010. *Compositions include:* Sonata for trumpet and piano 1955, Alma redemptoris mater for ensemble 1957, St Michael sonata for 17 wind instruments 1957, Prolation for orchestra 1959, Five Klee Pictures for percussion, piano and strings 1959, Five Motets for soli, chorus and ensemble 1959, O Magnum Mysterium for chorus, instruments and organ 1960, Te Lucis ante Terminum 1961, String Quartet 1961, Frammenti di Leopardi for soprano, contralto and chamber ensemble 1962, First Fantasia on John Taverner's In Nomine for orchestra 1962, Veni Sancte Spiritus for soli, chorus and orchestra 1963, Second Fantasia on John Taverner's In Nomine 1964, Ecce Manus Tradentis for mixed chorus and instruments 1964, Shepherd's Calendar for young singers and instrumentalists 1965, Notre Dame des Fleurs 1966, Revelation and Fall for soprano and instrumental ensemble 1966, Antechrist for chamber ensemble 1967, Missa super L'Homme Armé for speaker and ensemble 1968, Stedman Caters for instruments 1968, Nocturnal Dances (ballet) 1969, St Thomas Wake-Foxtrot for orchestra 1969, Worldes Blis 1969, Eram quasi Agnus (instrumental motet) 1969, Eight Songs for a Mad King for male singer and ensemble 1969, Vesalii Icones for dancer and ensemble 1969, Taverner (opera) 1970, From Stone to Thorn for mezzo-soprano and instrumental ensemble 1971, Blind Man's Buff (masque) 1972, Hymn to Saint Magnus for chamber ensemble and mezzo-soprano 1972, Renaissance Scottish Dances 1973, Stone Litany for mezzo-soprano and orchestra 1973, Fiddlers at the Wedding 1974, Miss Donnithorne's Maggot for mezzo-soprano and chamber ensemble 1974, The Kestrel Paced Round the Sun 1975, Ave Maris Stella for chamber ensemble 1975, Three Studies for Percussion 1975, The Blind Fiddler for soprano and chamber ensemble 1975, Stevie's Ferry to Hoy (beginner's piano solo) 1975, Three Organ Voluntaries 1976, Kinloche His Fantasie (with Kinloch) 1976, Anakreontika (Greek songs for mezzo-soprano) 1976, Orchestral Symphony No. 1 1976, The Martyrdom of St Magnus (chamber opera) 1976, Runes from a Holy Island 1977, Westerlings (unaccompanied part songs) 1977, A Mirror of Whitening Light for chamber ensemble 1977, Le Jongleur de Notre Dame (Masque) 1978, The Two Fiddlers 1978, Salome (ballet) 1978, Black Pentecost (for voices and orchestra) 1979, Solstice of Light (for Tenor, Chorus and Organ) 1979, The Lighthouse (chamber opera) 1979, Cinderella (pantomime opera for young performers) 1979, A Welcome to Orkney (chamber ensemble) 1980, Orchestral Symphony No. 2 1980, Little Quartet (string quartet) 1980, The Yellow Cake Revue (for voice and piano) 1980, The Medium 1981, The Bairns of Brugh 1981, Piano Sonata 1981, Little Quartet No. 2 (for string quartet) 1981, Lullabye for Lucy 1981, Brass Quintet 1981, Songs of Hoy (Masque for children's voices and instruments) 1981, The Pole Star 1982, Sea Eagle (for horn solo) 1982, Image, Reflection, Shadow (for chamber ensemble) 1982, Sinfonia Concertante (for chamber orchestra) 1982, Into the Labyrinth (tenor and chamber orchestra) 1983, Sinfonietta Accademica (chamber orchestra) 1983, Unbroken Circle 1984, Guitar Sonata 1984, The No. 11 Bus 1984, One Star, At Last (carol) 1984, Orchestral Symphony No. 3 1984, The Peat Cutters 1985, Violin Concerto 1985, First Ferry to Hoy 1985, An Orkney Wedding, with Sunrise 1985, Sea Runes (vocal sextet) 1986, Jimmack the Postie (overture) 1986, Excuse Me 1986, House of Winter 1986, Trumpet Concerto 1987, Resurrection (opera in one act with prologue) 1987, Oboe Concerto 1988, Cello Concerto 1988, Mishkenot (chamber ensemble) 1988, The Great Bank Robbery 1989, Orchestral Symphony No. 4 1989, Hymn to the Word of God (for tenor and chorus) 1990, Concerto No. 4 for clarinet 1990, Caroline Mathilde (ballet) 1990, Tractus 1990, Dangerous Errand (for tenor soli and chorus) 1990, The Spiders' Revenge 1991, First Grace of Light 1991, Strathclyde Concerto No. 5 for violin and viola, No. 6 for flute 1991, Ojai Festival Overture 1991, A Selkie Tale (music-theatre work for performance by children) 1992, The Turn of the Tide (for orchestra and children's chorus and instrumental groups) 1992, Strathclyde Concerto No. 7 for double bass 1992, Sir Charles his Pavan 1992, Strathclyde Concerto No. 8 for bassoon 1993, A Spell for Green Corn: The MacDonald Dances 1993, Orchestral Symphony No. 5 (Royal Philharmonic Soc. Award for Large-Scale Composition 1995) 1994, Cross Lane Fair (for orchestra) 1994, Strathclyde Concerto No. 9 for six woodwind instruments 1994, The Three Kings (for chorus, orchestra and soloists) 1995, The Beltane Fire (choreographic poem) 1995, The Doctor of Myddfai (opera) 1995, Orchestral

Symphony No. 6 1996, Strathclyde Concerto No. 10 for orchestra 1996, Piccolo Concerto 1996, Job (oratorio for chorus, orchestra and soloists) 1997, Mavis in Las Vegas–Theme and Variations 1997, Orkney Saga I: Fifteen keels laid in Norway for Jerusalem-farers 1997, The Jacobite Rising (for chorus, orchestra and soloists) 1997, Piano Concerto 1997, Orkney Saga II: In Kirkwall, the first red Saint Magnus stones 1997, Sails in St Magnus I–III 1998, A Reel of Seven Fishermen 1998, Sea Elegy (for chorus, orchestra and soloists) 1998, Roma Amor Labyrinthus 1998, Reel with Northern Lights 1998, Swinton Jig 1998, Temenos with Mermaids and Angels (for flute and orchestra) 1998, Spinning Jenny 1999, Sails in Orkney Saga III: An Orkney Wintering (for alto saxophone and orchestra) 1999, Trumpet quintet (for string quartet and trumpet) 1999, Mr Emmet Takes a Walk 1999, Horn Concerto 1999, Orkney Saga IV: Westerly Gale in Biscay, Salt in the Bread Broken 2000, Orchestral Symphony No. 7 2000, Orchestral Symphony No. 8 (Antarctic Symphony) 2000, Canticum Canticorum 2001, De Assumtione Beatae Mariae Virginis 2001, Crossing Kings Reach 2001, Mass 2002, Missa Parvula 2002, Naxos Quartet No. 1 2002, Piano Trio 2002, Naxos Quartet No. 2 2003, No. 3 2003, No. 4 2004, No. 5 2004, Children's Games 2004, Judas Mercator for trombone solo 2004, Fanfare for Carinthia for four trumpets 2004, Tecum Principium for flute and marimba 2004, The Fall of the Leafe for string orchestra 2004, Lullay, my child and weep no more for SATB chorus 2004, Naxos Quartets No. 6 and No. 7 2005, O Verbum Patris for SATB chorus & organ 2005, The Golden Rule (anthem with lyrics by Andrew Motion, for the 80th birthday of HM Queen Elizabeth II) 2006, A Little Birthday Music (for the 80th birthday of HM Queen Elizabeth II) 2006, Liber Pulsationis Fabulatoris for chorus (dedicated to Sir Paul McCartney) 2008, A Birthday Card for Prince Charles (for the 60th birthday of HRH the Prince of Wales) 2008, The Sorcerer's Mirror (for 800th anniversary of Univ. of Cambridge) 2009, Violin Concerto No. 2 2009, The Last Island for string sextet 2009, Sea Orpheus 2010, Blake Dreaming for baritone and string quartet 2010, Homerton (for the choir of Homerton Coll., Cambridge) 2010, Kommilitonen! (opera) 2011, Symphony No. 9 2012, Symphony No. 10 2014; has written music for films: The Devils, The Boyfriend and many piano pieces, works for choir, instrumental works and realisations of 15th and 16th-century composers. *Recordings:* Naxos Quartets – Maggini Quartet (five-CD set); Missa parvula, two organ pieces, two motets; Magnificat and Nunc Dimittis and O Sacrum Convivium; Symphonies 1–6 (BBC Philharmonic, Scottish Chamber Orchestra, Philharmonia, Royal Philharmonic/composer); Ave Maris Stella, Image, Reflection, Shadow, Runes from a Holy Island – Fires of London/composer. *Address:* c/o Intermusica, Crystal Wharf, 36 Graham Street, London, N1 8GJ, England (office). *Telephone:* (20) 7608-9900 (office). *Fax:* (20) 7490-3263 (office). *E-mail:* mail@intermusica.co.uk (office). *Website:* www .intermusica.co.uk (office); www.maxopus.com.

MAY, Elaine; American actress, film director and screenwriter; b. 21 April 1932, Philadelphia; d. of Jack Berlin; m. 1st Marvin May (divorced); one d.; m. 2nd Sheldon Harnick 1962 (divorced 1963); appeared on radio and stage as child; performed Playwright's Theater, Chicago; appeared in student production Miss Julie, Univ. of Chicago; with Mike Nichols (q.v.) and others in improvisatory theatre group, The Compass (nightclub), Chicago 1954–57; improvised nightclub double-act with Mike Nichols, appeared New York Town Hall 1959; An Evening with Mike Nichols and Elaine May, Golden Theater, New York 1960–61; numerous TV and radio appearances; weekly appearance NBC radio show Nightline; Nat. Medal of Arts 2012. *Films:* Luv 1967, A New Leaf (also Dir) 1972, The Heartbreak Kid (Dir) 1973, Mikey and Nicky (Dir) 1976 (writer, Dir remake 1985), California Suite 1978, Heaven Can Wait (co-author screenplay) 1978, Ishtar (writer and Dir) 1987, In The Spirit 1990, The Birdcage 1996 (co-author screenplay), Primary Colors (co-author screenplay) 1998, The John Cassavetes Collection (director) 1999, Small Time Crooks 2000. *Publications:* Better Part of Valour (play) 1983, Hotline 1983, Mr. Gogol and Mr. Preen 1991, Death Defying Acts 1995.

MAY, Rt Hon. Theresa Mary, MA; British politician; *Secretary of State for the Home Department;* b. 1 Oct. 1956; d. of Rev. Hubert Brasier and Zaidee Brasier (née Barnes); m. Philip John May 1980; ed St Hugh's Coll., Oxford; worked for Bank of England 1977–83; with Inter-Bank Research Org. 1983–85; with Asscn for Payment Clearing Services 1985–97 (Head of European Affairs Unit 1989–96); mem. (Conservative Party) Merton London Borough Council 1986–94; contested (Conservative Party) Durham NW 1992, Barking June 1994; MP (Conservative) for Maidenhead 1997–; Opposition Frontbench Spokeswoman on Educ. and Employment 1998–99; Shadow Sec. of State for Educ. and Employment 1999–2001; Shadow Sec. for Transport, Local Govt and the Regions 2001–02; Chair. Conservative Party 2002–03; Shadow Sec. of State for Environment and Transport 2003–04, for the Family 2004–05, for the Family and Culture, Media and Sport 2005; Shadow Leader, House of Commons 2005–10, Shadow Minister for Women 2007–10; Sec. of State for the Home Dept 2010–, also Minister for Women and Equality 2010–12. *Publications:* articles Women in the House: The Continuing Challenge, in Parliamentary Affairs Vol. 57, No. 4 2004. *Leisure interests:* walking, cooking. *Address:* Home Office, 2 Marsham Street, London, SW1P 4DF (office); House of Commons, Westminster, London, SW1A 0AA; Constituency Office, c/o Maidenhead Conservative Association, 2 Castle End Farm, Ruscombe, RG10 9XQ, England. *Telephone:* (20) 7035-4848 (Home Office) (office); (20) 7219-5206 (Westminster); (118) 934-5433 (Ruscombe). *Fax:* (20) 7035-4745 (Home Office) (office); (20) 7219-1145 (Westminster). *E-mail:* mayt@parliament.uk (office); public.enquiries@homeoffice.gsi.gov.uk (office); office@maidenheadconservatives.com. *Website:* www.homeoffice.gov.uk (office); www .parliament.uk/biographies/commons/theresa-may/25452; www.tmay.co.uk.

MAY, Thomas; German university administrator; *Chancellor, Ludwig-Maximilians-Universität München;* b. 1958, Hildesheim; ed Univ. of Hamburg, Univ. Munich; Adviser, Deutsche Forschungsgemeinschaft (DFG, German Research Foundation) 1987–95; Deputy Sec.-Gen. German Council of Science and Humanities (Wissenschaftsrat) 1995–2003; Chancellor Ludwig-Maximilians-Universität München 2003–. *Address:* Office of the Chancellor, Ludwig-Maximilians-Universität München, Geschwister-Scholl-Platz 1, 80539 Munich, Germany (office). *Telephone:* (89) 2180-3269 (office). *Fax:* (89) 2180-6324 (office). *E-mail:* Kanzler@lmu.de (office). *Website:* www.uni-muenchen.de (office).

MAY OF OXFORD, Baron (Life Peer), cr. 2001, of Oxford in the County of Oxfordshire; **Robert McCredie May,** Kt, OM, AC, PhD, PRS, FAAS; Australian/British biologist and academic; *Professor, University of Oxford;* b. 1 Aug. 1936,

Sydney, NSW, Australia; s. of Henry W. May and Kathleen M. McCredie; m. Judith Feiner 1962; one d.; ed Sydney Boys' High School, Univ. of Sydney; Gordon MacKay Lecturer in Applied Math., Harvard Univ., USA 1959–61; at Univ. of Sydney 1962–73, Sr Lecturer in Theoretical Physics 1962–64, Reader 1964–69, Personal Chair 1969–73; Class of 1877 Prof. of Biology, Princeton Univ., USA 1973–88, Chair. Univ. Research Bd 1977–88; Royal Soc. Research Prof., Dept of Zoology, Univ. of Oxford and Imperial Coll., London, UK 1988–95, currently Prof. and Fellow, Merton Coll., Oxford 1988–; Chief Scientific Adviser to UK Govt and Head, Office of Science and Tech. 1995–2000; Pres. Royal Soc. 2000–05, British Ecological Soc. 2000–05; Crossbench Peer in House of Lords 2001–, mem. Science and Tech. Select Cttee 2006–, Science and Cttee Sub-cttees: I (Scientific Aspects of Ageing) 2005, I (Allergy/Waste Reduction) 2007–08, Systematics and Taxonomy Enquiry 2008, Draft Climate Change Bill Jt Cttee 2007; fmr Ind. mem. Jt Nature Conservancy Councils; Overseas mem. Australian Acad. of Sciences 1991–; Foreign mem. NAS 1992–; mem. Academia Europaea 1994–; Foreign mem. NAS 1992–; fmr Chair. Bd of Trustees, Natural History Museum, London; Trustee, British Museum 1989–, Royal Botanic Gardens, Kew 1991–95, WWF (UK) 1990–94, Nuffield Foundation (Exec. Trustee) 1993–, BAAS (now the British Science Asscn) 2006– (also Hon. Fellow, Pres.-Elect 2010); hon. degrees from univs including Uppsala (1990), Yale (1993), Sydney (1995), Princeton (1996), (ETH) 2003; Croonian Lecturer, Hitchcock Lecturer, John M. Prather Lecturer, Weldon Memorial Prize, Univ. of Oxford 1980, Medal of Linnean Soc. of London 1991, Marsh Christian Prize 1992, Frink Medal, Zoological Soc. of London 1995, Crafoord Prize 1996, Balzan Prize 1998, Blue Planet Prize 2001, Copley Medal, Royal Soc. 2007. *Publications:* Stability and Complexity in Model Ecosystems 1973, Exploitation of Marine Communities (ed.) 1974, Theoretical Ecology: Principles and Applications (ed.) 1976, Population Biology of Infectious Diseases (ed.) 1982, Exploitation of Marine Ecosystems (ed.) 1984, Perspectives in Ecological Theory (ed.) 1989, Population Regulation and Dynamics (ed.) 1990, Infectious Diseases of Humans: Transmission and Control (with R. M. Anderson) 1991, Large Scale Ecology and Conservation Biology 1994, Extinction Rates 1995, Evolution of Biological Diversity 1999, Virus Dynamics: the Mathematical Foundations of Immunology and Virology (with Martin Nowak) 2000. *Leisure interests:* tennis, running, hiking. *Address:* Department of Zoology, University of Oxford, The Tinbergen Building, South Parks Road, Oxford, OX1 3PS (office); House of Lords, Westminster, London, SW1A 0PW, England. *Telephone:* (1865) 271276 (office). *E-mail:* robert.may@zoo.ox.ac.uk (office). *Website:* www.zoo.ox.ac .uk/staff/academics/may_r.htm (office); www.parliament.uk/biographies/lords/robert-may/26570.

MAYAKI, Ibrahim Assane, PhD; Niger politician; *CEO, New Partnership for Africa's Development (NEPAD);* b. 24 Sept. 1951, Niamey; s. of Assane Adamou Mayaki and Marie Mosconi; m. Marly Perez Marin 1976; one s. one d.; ed Ecole nationale d'admin de Québec, Canada, Univ. of Paris II, France; fmr Prof. of Public Admin in Niger and Venezuela; worked in uranium sector in Niger at Soc. des mines de l'air (SOMAIR), subsidiary of COGEMA Group; Minister of Foreign Affairs and Co-operation 1996–97; Prime Minister of Niger 1997–2000; Guest Prof. of Int. Relations, Univ. of Paris XI 2000–04, researcher at Research Centre on Europe and the Contemporary World (CREMOC) 2000–04; Exec. Dir The Hub (initiative to coordinate agricultural devt in Western and Cen. Africa) 2004–09; CEO New Partnership for Africa's Devt (NEPAD) 2009–; Grand Officier, Ordre Nat. Niger; Commdr du Mérite agricole. *Publications:* several books on public affairs, planning and local devt; Quand la caravane passe… (autobiog.). *Leisure interest:* taekwondo (5th dan). *Address:* NEPAD Secretariat, Block B, Gateway Park Corner Challenger & Columbia Avenues Midridge Office Park, Midrand 1685, South Africa (office). *Telephone:* (11) 256-3600 (office). *E-mail:* ibrahimassanem@nepad.org (office). *Website:* www.nepad.org (office).

MAYALEH, Adib, PhD; Syrian central banker; *Governor, Central Bank of Syria;* b. 15 May 1955, Daraa; ed Univ. of Aix-en-Provence, France; Prof. of Econs, Damascus Univ.; Gov. Cen. Bank of Syria 2005–; Pres. Monetary and Credit Bd. *Address:* Central Bank of Syria, Al-Tajreddah Al-Maghrebiah Square, Damascus, Syria (office). *Telephone:* (11) 2220550 (office). *Fax:* (11) 2227109 (office). *E-mail:* a.mayaleh@bcs.gov.sy (office). *Website:* www.banquecentrale.gov.sy (office).

MAYALL, Richard (Rik) Michael; British comedian, actor and writer; b. 7 March 1958, Harlow, Essex, England; s. of John Mayall and Gillian Mayall; m. Barbara Robbin; one s. two d.; ed Univ. of Manchester; f. 20th Century Coyote theatre co.; Hon. MA (Worcester) 2007. *Theatre includes:* The Common Pursuit 1988, Waiting for Godot 1991–92, The Government Inspector, Cell Mates 1995, A Family Affair 2000, The New Statesman 2006, 2007, Alan B'Stard's Extremely Secret Weapon 2006, The New Statesman Episode 2006: The Blair B'Stard Project 2006, The New Statesman 2007. *Live Stand Up includes:* The Comic Strip 1981, Kevin Turvey and Bastard Squad 1983, Rik Mayall, Ben Elton, Andy De La Tour (UK tour & Edin. Fringe) 1983, Rik Mayall and Ben Elton 1984–85, (Australian tour) 1986, 1992, Rik Mayall and Andy De La Tour 1989–90, Rik Mayall and Adrian Edmondson (UK tours) 1993, 1995, 1997, 2001. *Films include:* Kevin Turvey Investigates (video) 1981, Eye of the Needle 1981, An American Werewolf in London 1981, Shock Treatment 1981, Couples and Robbers 1982, Whoops Apocalypse 1986, Dangerous Brothers Present: World of Danger (video) 1986, Eat the Rich 1987, Little Noises 1991, Drop Dead Fred 1991, Carry On Columbus 1992, Horse Opera 1993, Bottom Live (video) 1993, Bottom Live: The Big Number 2 Tour (video) 1995, Remember Me? 1997, Bring Me the Head of Mavis Davis (Best Actor, San Remo Film Festival 1997) 1997, Bottom Live 3: Hooligan's Island (video) 1997, Merlin – The Return 1999, Guest House Paradiso 1999, Blackadder Back and Forth 1999, Bottom 2001: An Arse Oddity 2001, Kevin of the North 2001, Day of the Sirens 2002, Oh Marbella! 2003, Cold Dark 2003, Chaos and Cadavers 2003, Sindy: The Fairy Princess (video) 2003, Bottom Live 2003: Weapons Grade Y-Fronts Tour (video) 2003, Churchill: The Hollywood Years 2004; provided voices for animations including Tom Thumb in The World of Peter Rabbit and Friends – The Tale of Two Bad Mice 1994, Toad in Willows in Winter (Emmy Award 1997) 1996, The Robber King in The Snow Queen 1995, Prince Froglip in The Princess and the Goblin 1993, Hero Baby in How to be a Little Sod 1995, Bud Tucker in Double Trouble (video game) 1996, Young William Tell in Oscar's Orchestra 1996, Le château des singes (A Monkey's Tale) 1999, Hogs of War (video game; voice) 2000, Peter & The Wolf – Carnival of the Animals 2003, Bottom Live 5 Tour 2003, Valiant (voice) 2005, Abba – The Last Music Video Ever 2004, Violent Nation 2004,

Snow White: The Sequel (voice) 2007, The Big Ugly Monster & The Little Stone Rabbit 2007, Just For The Record 2009, Eldorado 2009, This Side of the Afterlife (short; voice) 2010, Just for the Record 2010, Dog Judo 2010, The Legend of Harrow Woods (video) 2011, Evil Calls (video) 2011, The Itch of the Golden Nit (short) 2011, Highway to Hell (video) 2012, Errors of the Human Body 2012, One by One 2012, Don't Fear Death 2013. *Radio includes:* The Sound of Trumpets (BBC Radio 4) 1999, A Higher Education (BBC Radio 4) 2000. *Audio books:* Decline and Fall 2004, The Silver Spoon of Solomon Snow 2004, Dinosaurus and Spookyrumpus 2004, Children's Audio Books 2009, Cutey & The Sofaguard 2010, Tickety Books 2010, Children's Stories 2012, Me Books 2012, The Last Hurrah 2012. *Television includes:* A Kick Up the Eighties (series) 1981, Kevin Turvey: The Man Behind the Green Door 1982, The Young Ones (also creator and co-writer, two series, BBC) 1982, 1984, The Comic Strip Presents... (series) (Channel Four) 1983–84, 1992, George's Marvellous Medicine (five episodes, Jackanory, BBC) 1985, Saturday Live (series) 1986, Comic Relief 1986, Filthy Rich and Catflap (series) 1987, The New Statesman (four series, YTV) 1987–88, 1990, 1994 (Int. Emmy Award 1989, BAFTA Best New Comedy 1990, Special Craft Gold Medal Best Performer/ Narrator), Jake's Journey 1988, Grim Tales (two series, 1989, 1990), Bottom (three series, BBC) 1990, 1992, 1994 (British Comedy Awards Best New Comedy 1992), Rik Mayall Presents Briefest Encounter (Granada TV) (British Comedy Awards Best Comedy Actor 1993) 1993, Rik Mayall Presents Dancing Queen 1993, A. B'Stard Exposed 1994, Rik Mayall Presents The Big One 1995, Rik Mayall Presents Dirty Old Town 1995, Rik Mayall Presents Clair de lune 1995, Look at the State We're In! (mini-series) 1995, How to Be a Little Sod (series) 1995, The Wind in the Willows (voice) 1995, Wham Bam Strawberry Jam! (BBC) 1995, The Alan B'Stard Interview with Brian Walden 1995, The Canterville Ghost 1997, In the Red 1998, Jonathan Creek – Black Canary 1998, Watership Down (series; voice) 1999, Jellikins (series; voice) 1999, Tom and Vicky (series; voice) 1999, The Bill 1999, Jesus Christ Superstar 2000, The Knock (series) 2000, Murder Rooms 2000, Tales of Uplift and Moral Improvement (series) 2001, Believe Nothing (series) 2002, ABBA: Our Last Video Ever 2004, Shoebox Zoo (series; voice) 2004, King Arthur's Disasters (series; voice) 2005, All About George (series) 2005, King Arthur's Disasters (second series; voice) 2005–06, The Comic Strip Presents... (series) – Sex Actually 2005, SpongeBob SquarePants (series) 2006, Gina's Laughing Gear (series) 2007, Minder (series) 2009, Agatha Christie's Marple: Why Didn't They Ask Evans? (film) 2009, Minder – In Vino Veritas 2008, Midsomer Murders – The Creeper 2009, Who Let The Dogs Out (CBBC) (narrator) 2011–13, The Comic Strip Presents... (series) – The Hunt for Tony Blair 2011, – Five Go to Rehab 2012, Damo and Ivor 2013, Man Down 2013, Jonathan Creek – The Clue of the Savant's Thumb 2013. *Publication:* Bigger than Hitler, Better than Christ 2006. *Address:* c/o Aude Powell, Brunskill Management, Suite 8A, 169 Queen's Gate, London, SW7 5HE, England (office). *Telephone:* (20) 7581-3388 (office). *Fax:* (20) 7589-9460 (office).

MAYANJA, Rachel N., BL, LLM; Ugandan UN official; *Special Adviser to the Secretary-General on Gender Issues and Advancement of Women, United Nations;* three c.; ed Makarere Univ., Harvard Univ. Law School, USA; early career in UN Div. for Equal Rights for Women, Centre for Social Devt and Humanitarian Affairs; served in UN peacekeeping missions in Namibia (UNTAG) 1989–90 and Iraq/Kuwait (UNIKOM) 1992–94; sr positions in UN Office of Human Resources Man. including Chief of Common System, Specialist Services, Sec. to Sec.-Gen.'s Task Force on reform of Human Resources Man. 1999, Dir of Human Resources Man. Div., UN FAO 2000–04; Special Adviser to Sec.-Gen. on Gender Issues and Advancement of Women 2004–. *Address:* Office of the Special Adviser on Gender Issues and Advancement of Women (OSAGI), Department of Economic and Social Affairs, Two United Nations Plaza, 12th Floor, New York, NY 10017, USA (office). *Telephone:* (212) 963-5086 (office). *Fax:* (212) 963-1802 (office). *E-mail:* osagi@un .org (office).

MAYARD-PAUL, Thierry; Haitian lawyer and politician; s. of Constantin Mayard-Paul; ed St Louis De Gonzague High School, Port-au-Prince; pvt. practice as criminal lawyer with brother, Cabinet Constantin Mayard-Paul (family law firm); Chief of Staff for Pres. Michel Martelly 2011; Minister of the Interior and Territorial Collectivities 2011–12, also of Nat. Defence 2011–12. *Address:* c/o Ministry of the Interior and Territorial Collectivities, Palais des Ministères, rue Mgr Guilloux, Port-au-Prince, Haiti (office). *Telephone:* 2222-6490 (office). *Fax:* 2222-8057 (office).

MAYAWATI, BA, BEd, LLB; Indian lawyer and politician; *President, Bahujan Samaj Party;* b. (Mayawati Naina Kumari), 15 Jan. 1956, Badalpur, Gautam Budh Nagar Dist, UP; d. of Prabhu Das and Ram Rati; ed Univ. of Delhi, Meerut Univ.; mem. Lok Sabha (lower house of parl.) 1989–91, 1998–2004; Chief Minister of UP (first Dalit Chief Minister of an Indian state) June–Oct. 1995, March–Sept. 1997, 2002–03, 2007–12; mem. Rajya Sabha (upper house of parl.) 1994–96, 2004–07; mem. UP Legis. Ass. 1996–98, 2002–03; Pres. Bahujan Samaj Party 2003–; mem. UP Legis. Council 2007–; several honours and awards, ranked by Forbes magazine amongst 100 Most Powerful Women (59th) 2008. *Publications include:* Bahujan Samaj Aur Uski Rajniti (Hindi version) 2000 (English version) 2001, Mere Sangarshmai Jeevan Evam Bahujan Movement Ka Safarnama (four vols) (Hindi version) 2006 (English version) 2008. *Leisure interest:* Indian cuisine. *Address:* C-57, Indrapuri, New Delhi 110 012 (home); 13A Mall Avenue, Lucknow 226 001, India (home). *Telephone:* (11) 2621122 (New Delhi) (home).

MAYBERRY, John T., CM, BA; Canadian business executive; *Chairman, Bank of Nova Scotia (Scotiabank);* ed Univ. of Western Ontario, McMaster Univ.; fmr Chair. and CEO Dofasco Inc.; mem. Bd of Dirs Bank of Nova Scotia (Scotiabank) 1994–, currently Chair., mem. Exec. and Risk Cttee, Corp. Governance and Pension Cttee, ex-officio mem. Audit and Conduct Review Cttee, Human Resources Cttee; Lead Dir Fort Reliance Ltd (parent co. of Irving Oil Ltd); Dir or fmr Dir CFM Corpn, Decoma International Inc., Inco Ltd 2006–10, MDS Inc. (also Chair. (non-exec.)) 2006–10; mem. Order of Canada; Hon. LLD (McMaster Univ.). *Address:* Bank of Nova Scotia (Scotiabank), 44 King Street West, Toronto, ON M5H 1H1, Canada (office). *Telephone:* (416) 866-6161 (office). *Fax:* (416) 866-3750 (office). *E-mail:* info@scotiabank.ca (office). *Website:* www.scotiabank.ca (office).

MAYER, Colin Peter, BA, BPhil, DPhil, FBA, FRSA; British academic; *Peter Moores Professor of Management Studies, Saïd Business School, University of Oxford;* b. 12 May 1953, London, England; s. of the late Harold Charles Mayer and

of Anne Louise Mayer; m. Annette Patricia Haynes 1979; two d.; ed St Paul's School, London, Oriel Coll., Oxford, Wolfson Coll., Oxford, Harvard Univ., USA; HM Treasury, London 1976–78; Harkness Fellow, Harvard Univ. 1979–80; Fellow in Econs, St Anne's Coll. Oxford 1980–86, Price Waterhouse Prof. of Corp. Finance, City Univ. Business School 1987–92; Prof. of Econs and Finance, Univ. of Warwick 1992–94; Peter Moores Prof. of Man. Studies, Saïd Business School, Oxford 1994–, Peter Moores Dean 2006–11, Dir Oxford Financial Research Centre 1998–2006; del., Oxford University Press 1996–2006; Chair. OXERA Ltd 1987–2010; Assoc. Ed. Annals of Finance, European Financial Management Journal, Scottish Journal of Political Economy; mem. Exec. Cttee Royal Econ. Soc. 2002–06; Professorial Fellow, Wadham Coll. Oxford 1994–2006, 2011–, St Edmund Hall 2006–11; Gov. St Paul's School London 2002–11; Fellow, European Corp. Governance Inst.; Hon. Fellow, St Anne's Coll. Oxford, Oriel Coll. Oxford. *Publications:* Economic Analysis of Accounting Profitability (co-author) 1986, Risk, Regulation and Investor Protection (co-author) 1989, European Financial Integration (co-author) 1991, Capital Markets and Financial Intermediation (co-author) 1993, Hostile Takeovers (co-author) 1994, Asset Management and Investor Protection (co-author) 2002, Handbook of European Financial Markets and Institutions (co-author) 2008, Firm Commitment: Why the Corporation is Failing Us and How to Restore Trust in It 2013; contribs to academic journals and books. *Leisure interests:* piano, jogging, reading philosophy and science. *Address:* Saïd Business School, University of Oxford, Park End Street, Oxford, OX1 1HP (office); Wadham College, Oxford, OX1 3PN, England (office). *Telephone:* (1865) 288111 (office). *E-mail:* colin.mayer@sbs.ox.ac.uk (office). *Website:* www.sbs.ox.ac.uk (office).

MAYER, Marissa Ann, BS, MS; American computer scientist and business executive; *President and CEO, Yahoo! Inc.;* b. 30 May 1975, Wausau, Wis.; m. Zachary Bogue 2009; one s.; ed Wausau West High School, Nat. Youth Science Camp, W Va, Stanford Univ., Calif.; fmrly with UBS Research Lab. (Ubilab), Zürich, Switzerland and SRI Int., Menlo Park, Calif.; joined Google Inc. as software engineer (first female) 1999, Vice-Pres. Search Products and User Experience –2010, Vice-Pres. Local, Maps and Location Services 2010–12; Pres. and CEO Yahoo! Inc., Sunnyvale, Calif. 2012–; Lecturer in Computer Science, Stanford Univ.; mem. Bd of Dirs Walmart 2012–; Hon. DEng (Illinois Inst. of Tech.) 2009; named by Business Week magazine amongst the 25 Masters of Innovation 2006, named by PC World amongst the 50 Most Important People on the Web 2007, ranked by Fortune magazine amongst the 50 Most Powerful Women in Business in the US (50th) 2008 (youngest woman ever to make the list), (44th) 2009, (42nd) 2010, (38th) 2011, (14th) 2012, named by Fast Company magazine amongst the Most Influential Women in Technology 2009, ranked by Forbes magazine amongst The World's 100 Most Powerful Women (42nd) 2011, (21st) 2012, (32nd) 2013, Centennial Teaching Award, Stanford Univ., Forsythe Award, Stanford Univ. *Address:* Yahoo! Inc., 701 1st Avenue, Sunnyvale, CA 94089, USA (office). *Telephone:* (408) 349-330 (office). *Fax:* (408) 349-3301 (office). *Website:* www.yahoo.com (office).

MAYER, Peter, BA, MA; American/British book publisher; *President, Gerald Duckworth Publishers;* b. 28 March 1936, Hampstead, London, England; s. of Alfred Mayer and Lee Mayer; one d.; ed Columbia Univ., New York, Christ Church, Oxford; Grad. Fellow, Indiana Univ.; Fulbright Fellow, Freie Universität Berlin 1959; worked with Orion Press before joining Avon books for 14 years; Publr and Pres. Pocketbooks 1976–78; Chief. Exec. Penguin Books Ltd, London 1978–96, later Chair. Penguin USA; exec. positions with The Overlook Press (co-f. with his father 1971, currently Pres.) 1996–, acquired Ardis Publrs 2001, Duckworth Publrs (currently Pres.) 2003, Nonesuch Press 2005; mem. Bd Asscn of American Publrs –2003, Bd Frankfurt Bookfair Fellowship, Bd Nat. Book Foundation –2003), New York Univ. Publrs Advisory Bd, Scholastic Bd of Dirs, German Book Office; Officier, Ordre des Arts et des Lettres 1996; Most Distinguished Publr of the Year 1995, Foundation of Publrs' and Booksellers' Asscns in India Award for Outstanding Contrib. to Int. Publishing 1996, London Book Fair/Trilogy Lifetime Achievement Award 2008. *Publications include:* An Idea is Like a Bird 1963, The Pacifist Conscience (ed.) 1966. *Address:* Duckworth Publishers, 90–93 Cowcross Street, London, EC1M 6BF, England (office); The Overlook Press, 141 Wooster Street, New York, NY 10012, USA (office). *Telephone:* (20) 7490-7300 (London) (office); (212) 673-2223 (New York) (office). *Fax:* (20) 7490-0080 (London) (office); (212) 673-2296 (New York) (office). *E-mail:* info@duckworth-publishers.co.uk (office); sales@overlookpress.com (office). *Website:* www.ducknet.co.uk (office); www.overlookpress.com (office).

MAYER-KUCKUK, Theo, Dr rer. nat; German nuclear physicist; b. 10 May 1927, Rastatt; m. Irmgard Meyer 1965; two s.; ed Univ. of Heidelberg; Research Fellow, Max Planck Institut für Kernphysik, Heidelberg 1953–59, Scientific mem. 1964; Research Fellow, California Inst. of Tech., Pasadena 1960–61; Dozent, Univ. of Heidelberg 1962, Tech. Univ. Munich 1963; Prof. of Physics, Univ. of Bonn 1965–92, Dir Inst. of Nuclear and Radiation Physics 1965–92; Vice-Pres. IUPAP 1984–90; Pres. German Physical Soc. 1990–92, Vice-Pres. 1992–96; Scientific Dir Magnus-Haus Berlin 1994–2006; mem. Acad. of Sciences of Nordrhein-Westfalen 1982; Röntgenpreis, Univ. of Giessen 1964. *Publications:* Kernphysik, Atomphysik, Der gebrochene Spiegel 1989, Atomphysik. Eine Einführung 1997, Kernphysik. Eine Einführung 2002; research papers and review articles in physics journals. *Leisure interest:* sailing. *Address:* Institut für Strahlen- und Kernphysik der Universität Bonn, Nussallee 14, 53113 Bonn (office); Magnus-Haus, am Kupfergraben 7, 10117 Berlin; Dreiserstr. 26, 12587 Berlin, Germany (home). *Telephone:* (228) 732201 (office); (30) 6409-5993 (home). *Fax:* (30) 6495-8134 (home). *E-mail:* temka@web.de (home).

MAYFIELD, Rt Rev. Christopher John, MA, MSc; British ecclesiastic; b. 18 Dec. 1935, Plymouth, Devon; s. of Dr Roger Mayfield and Muriel Mayfield; m. Caroline Roberts 1962; two s. one d.; ed Sedbergh School, Gonville & Caius Coll. Cambridge, Linacre House, Oxford, Cranfield Univ.; ordained deacon 1963, priest 1964; curate, St Martin-in-the-Bull Ring, Birmingham 1963–67; Lecturer, St Martin's, Birmingham 1967–71; Vicar of Luton 1971–80; Archdeacon of Bedford 1979–85; Bishop Suffragan of Wolverhampton 1985–93; Bishop of Manchester 1993–2002; Lord Bishop of Manchester, House of Lords 1998–2002; Hon. Asst Bishop, Worcester; Dr hc (Manchester) 2002. *Leisure interests:* marriage, evangelism, walking, watching cricket and rugby. *Address:* Harewood House, 54

Primrose Crescent, St Peter's, Worcester, WR5 3HT, England (home). *Telephone:* (1905) 764822 (office); (1905) 764822 (home). *E-mail:* christopher@mayfield54 .orangehome.co.uk (home).

MAYHEW OF TWYSDEN, Baron (Life Peer), cr. 1997, of Kilndown in the County of Kent; **Patrick Barnabas Burke Mayhew,** Kt, PC, QC, MA; British politician and barrister; b. 11 Sept. 1929, Cookham, Berks.; s. of the late A. G. H. Mayhew and Sheila M. B. Roche; m. Rev. Jean Elizabeth Gurney OBE 1963; four s.; ed Tonbridge School and Balliol Coll., Oxford; Pres. Oxford Union Soc. 1952; called to Bar (Middle Temple) 1955; QC 1972; MP (Conservative) for Tunbridge Wells 1974–97; Parl. Sec., Dept of Employment 1979–81; Minister of State, Home Office 1981–83; Solicitor-Gen. 1983–87; Attorney-Gen. 1987–92; Sec. of State for Northern Ireland 1992–97; Dir (non-exec.) Western Provident Asscn 1998–2007, Vice-Chair. 2000–07; Chair. Prime Minister's Advisory Cttee on Business Appointments 1999–2008. *Leisure interest:* country pursuits. *Address:* House of Lords, Westminster, London, SW1A 0PW, England (office). *Telephone:* (20) 7219-3000 (office).

MAYHEW JONAS, Dame Judith, DBE, LLM; New Zealand politician, lawyer and academic; b. 18 Oct. 1948, Dunedin; m. 1976 (divorced 1986); m. 2nd Christopher Jonas 2003; ed Otago Girls' High School, Univ. of Otago; barrister and solicitor, NZ 1973, solicitor, England and Wales 1993; Lecturer in Law, Univ. of Otago 1970–73; Lecturer in Law and Sub-Dean, Univ. of Southampton, UK 1973–76, King's Coll., London 1976–89; Dir Anglo-French law degree, Sorbonne, Paris 1976–79; Dir of Training and Employment Law, Titmuss Sainer Dechert 1989–94; mem. Bd London Guildhall Univ. 1992–2002; mem. Court and Council Imperial Coll., London 2001–03; Dir of Educ. and Training, Wilde Sapte 1994–99; City and Business Adviser to Mayor of London 2000; mem. Court of Common Council Corpn of London 1986–2004, Chair. Policy and Resources Cttee 1997–2003; Special Adviser to Chair. of Clifford Chance 2000–03; Chair. Bd of Govs 1999–2003; Chair. Royal Opera House, London 2003–08, Ind. Schools' Council 2008–11, New West End Co. 2008–, London and Partners 2011–; Dir Gresham Coll. 1990, London First Centre 1996, Int. Financial Services London (fmrly British Invisibles) 1996, London First 1997, 4Ps 1997, London Devt Agency 2000 (Chair. Business and Skills Cttee –2004, Vice-Chair. 2003), Cross River Partnership; Trustee Natural History Museum 1998; Dir (non-exec.) Merrill Lynch 2006–; Gov. Birkbeck Coll. London 1993–; Provost King's Coll., Cambridge 2003–05; Trustee Natural History Museum, Imperial War Museum 2008–; Hon. LLD (Otago) 1998, (City Univ. London) 1999; named New Zealander of the Year in the UK 2004. *Leisure interests:* opera, theatre, old English roses, tennis. *Address:* New West End Company, 3rd Floor, Morley House, 320 Upper Regent Street, London W1B 3BE, England (office). *Telephone:* (20) 7462-0680 (office). *E-mail:* info@newwestend.com (office). *Website:* www.newwestend.com (office).

MAYIIK, Kornelio Koryom, BSc; South Sudanese economist and central banker; *Governor, Bank of South Sudan;* b. Warrap State; ed Khartoum Univ.; Minister for Coordination, High Exec. Council for S Sudan (govt of autonomous region) 1983; Minister of Finance for Greater Bahr el Ghazal State, S Sudan 1983–86; est. Ivory Bank, Khartoum 1991, Gen. Man. 1994–2000; Gen. Man. Central Bank of Sudan 2000–11; Deputy Gov. Bank of South Sudan (following establishment of separate S Sudan state) July–Aug. 2011, Gov. Aug. 2011–. *Address:* Office of the Governor, Bank of South Sudan, Juba, South Sudan (office). *Telephone:* 249811821111 (mobile) (office). *Fax:* 249811820211 (mobile) (office). *E-mail:* info@bankofsouthernsudan.org (office). *Website:* www .bankofsouthernsudan.org (office).

MAYNE, David Quinn, PhD, DSc, FRS, FREng, FIEEE, FIET; British engineer and academic; *Professor Emeritus and Senior Research Investigator, Imperial College London;* b. 23 April 1930, Germiston, S Africa; s. of Leslie Harper Mayne and Jane Quin; m. Josephine Mary Hess 1954; three d.; ed Christian Brothers' Coll., Boksburg and Univ. of the Witwatersrand, S Africa; Lecturer, Univ. of the Witwatersrand 1951–54, 1957–59; Research Engineer, British Thomson Houston Co. 1955–56; Lecturer, Imperial Coll. of Science, Tech. and Medicine 1959–66, Reader 1967–70, Prof. 1970–89, Prof. Emer. 1989–, Sr Research Investigator, Dept of Electrical and Electronic Eng 1996–, Fellow 2000–; Prof. of Electrical and Computer Eng, Univ. of California, Davis 1989–96, Prof. Emer. 1997–, Head Dept of Electrical Eng 1984–88, Sr Research Investigator Science Research Council 1979; Visiting Research Fellow, Harvard Univ., USA 1970; Visiting Prof., Univ. of California, Berkeley, Univ. of Newcastle, Australia, IIT, Delhi, Academia Sinica, Beijing, Univ. of California, Santa Barbara, Univ. of Wisconsin, Madison; Hon. Prof., Beihang Univ., Beijing 2008; Hon. DTech (Lund) 1995; Heaviside Premium 1979, 1984, Sir Harold Hartley Medal 1986, IEEE Control Systems Award 2009, IFAC High Impact Award 2011. *Publications:* Differential Dynamic Programming 1970, Model Predictive Control: Theory and Design 2009; 250 papers in professional journals on optimization, optimal control, adaptive control and optimization-based design. *Leisure interests:* walking, cross-country skiing, music. *Address:* Department of Electrical and Electronic Engineering, Imperial College London, London, SW7 2BT (office); 123 Elgin Crescent, London, W11 2JH, England (home). *Telephone:* (20) 7594-6287 (office); (20) 7792-0972 (home). *Fax:* (20) 7594-6282 (office). *E-mail:* d.mayne@imperial.ac.uk (office). *Website:* www3.imperial.ac.uk/ electricalengineering (office).

MAYNE, (David) Roger, BA; British photographer and artist; b. 5 May 1929, Cambridge; s. of A. B. Mayne and D. Mayne (née Watson); m. Ann Jellicoe 1962; one s. one d.; ed Balliol Coll., Oxford; self-taught in photography; photographs of London and other city street scenes 1955–61; photographed The British at Leisure 1962–63 for Milan Trienalle; taught at Bath Acad. of Art, Corsham 1966–69; works in Museum of Modern Art, New York, Metropolitan Museum of Art, New York, Art Inst. of Chicago, Bibliothèque Nationale, Paris, Nat. Gallery of Australia, Canberra, V & A Museum, London, Arts Council of GB; Lucie Award for Documentary Photography, New York 2006. *Publications:* Things Being Various (with others) 1967, The Shell Guide to Devon (with Ann Jellicoe) 1975, The Street Photographs of Roger Mayne 1986, 1993, Roger Mayne Photographs 2001, Roger Mayne at 80 2009. *Leisure interests:* listening to music, looking at art exhbns, watching sport, mountains. *Address:* Lindsay Stewart, Quaritch, 40 South Audley Street, London, W1K 2PR, England (office); Gitterman Gallery, 170 East 75th Street, New York, NY 10021, USA (office). *Telephone:* (20) 7297-4888 (office); (212) 734-0868 (office). *Website:* www.rogermayne.com (home).

MAYOPOULOS, Timothy J.; American lawyer and business executive; *President and CEO, Fannie Mae (Federal National Mortgage Association);* ed Cornell Univ., New York Univ. School of Law; fmrly in private practice; served in sr man. roles at Deutsche Bank AG, Credit Suisse First Boston, Donaldson, Lufkin & Jenrette, Inc.; Exec. Vice-Pres. and Gen. Counsel, Bank of America Corpn –2009; Exec. Vice-Pres., Gen. Counsel and Corp. Sec., Fannie Mae (Fed. Nat. Mortgage Asscn) 2009–10, Chief Admin. Officer 2010–12, Pres. and CEO 2012–. *Address:* Fannie Mae, 3900 Wisconsin Avenue NW, Washington, DC 20016-2892, USA (office). *Telephone:* (202) 752-7000 (office). *E-mail:* headquarters@fanniemae.com (office). *Website:* www.fanniemae.com (office).

MAYOR, Michel G. E., MPhys, PhD, DrAstron; Swiss astronomer and academic; *Professor, University of Geneva;* b. 12 Jan. 1942, Lausanne; m. Francoise Mayor-Pirolet; one s. two d.; ed Univs of Lausanne and Geneva; Researcher, Cambridge Observatory 1971; Pres. Int. Astronomical Union (IAU) Comm. on Galactic Structure 1988–91, Swiss Soc. for Astrophysics and Astronomy 1990–93; Researcher, Univ. of Hawaii 1994–95; currently Prof. of Astronomy, Univ. of Geneva; Dir Geneva Observatory 1998–2002; Foreign Assoc., Acad. Française des Sciences; Chevalier de la Légion d'honneur 2004; Dr hc (Catholic Univ. of Louvain, Belgium, Swiss Inst. of Tech., Lausanne, Fed. Univ. of Rio Grande del Norte, Brazil, Uppsala Univ.); Charles Louis de Saulces de Freycinet Prize, Acad. Française des Sciences 1983, IAU Comm. of Bioastronomy Medal 1997, Prix Marcel Benoist 1998, Astronomical Soc. of France Janssen Prize 1998, Observatory of the Côte d'Azur Adion Medal 1998, Balzan Prize for Physics, Natural Sciences and Medicine 2000 (jt recipient), Einstein Medal 2004, Shaw Prize for Astronomy 2005. *Achievements include:* discovered first extrasolar planet, "51 Peg b" 1995. *Publications:* New Worlds in the Cosmos: The Discovery of Exoplanets (with Pierre-Yves Frei) 2003; more than 300 scientific papers. *Address:* Observatoire de Genève, 51 chemin des Maillettes, 1290 Sauverny, Switzerland (office). *Telephone:* (22) 379-2460 (office). *Fax:* (22) 379-2205 (office). *E-mail:* Michel .Mayor@obs.unige.ch (office). *Website:* www.unige.ch/sciences/astro (office).

MAYOR ZARAGOZA, Federico, DrPhar; Spanish politician, biologist and university official; *President, Fundación Cultura de Paz;* b. 27 Jan. 1934, Barcelona; s. of Federico Mayor and Juana Zaragoza; m. María Angeles Menéndez 1956; two s. one d.; ed Univ. Complutense of Madrid; Prof. of Biochemistry, Faculty of Pharmacy, Granada Univ. 1963–73; Rector, Granada Univ. 1968–72; Prof. of Biochemistry, Autonomous Univ., Madrid 1973, Chair. Severo Ochoa Molecular Biology Centre (Higher Council of Scientific Research) 1974–78; Under-Sec. Ministry of Educ. and Science 1974–75; mem. Cortes (Parl.) for Granada 1977–78; Chair. Advisory Cttee for Scientific and Tech. Research 1974–78; Deputy Dir-Gen. UNESCO 1978–81, Dir-Gen. 1987–99; Minister for Educ. and Science 1981–82; Dir Inst. of the Sciences of Man, Madrid 1983–87; mem. European Parl. 1987; Pres. Scientific Council, Ramón Areces Foundation, Madrid 1989–, European Research Council Expert Group 2002–05; Founder and Pres. Fundación Cultura de Paz 1999–; Co-Chair. Alliance of Civilizations, UN 2005–06; Pres. Initiative for Science in Europe (ISE) 2007–11, Int. Comm. Against Death Penalty 2010–; mem. Club of Rome 1981–; Academician, Royal Acad. of Pharmacy, Royal Acad. of Medicine; mem. European Acad. of Arts, Sciences and Humanities, Int. Cell Research Org. (ICRO), AAAS, The Biochemical Soc. (UK), French Soc. of Biological Chem., ACS, Academia de Bellas Artes, and numerous other orgs; Grand Cross, Alfonso X El Sabio, Orden Civil de la Sanidad Carlos III, Caro y Cuervo (Colombia), Commdr Placa del Libertador (Venezuela), Grand Officier, Ordre Nat. du Mérite (France); Dr hc (Westminster) 1995; Press Freedom Prize, Int. Fed. of Newspaper Publrs. *Publications:* A contraviento (poems) 1987, Mañana siempre es tarde 1987 (English version: Tomorrow Is Always Too Late 1992), Aguafuertes (poems) 1991 (English version: Patterns 1994), La nueva página 1994, Memoria del futuro 1994, La paix demain? 1995, Science and Power 1995, UNESCO: Un idéal en action 1996, El fuego y la esperanza (poems) 1996, Terral (poems) 1998 (English version: Land Wind 1998), Un mundo nuevo (English version: The World Ahead: Our Future in the Making) 1999, Los nudos gordianos 1999, La fuerza de la palabra 2005, Un diálogo ibérico enel marco europeo y mundial 2006, Alzaré mi voz (poems) 2007, Voz de vida, voz debida 2007, Tiempo de acción 2008, En pie de paz (poems) 2008, Donde no habite el miedo 2011; numerous specialized works, trans., articles. *Leisure interests:* reading, writing, music. *Address:* Fundación Cultura de Paz, Velázquez 14, 3° D, 28001 Madrid (office); Mar Caribe 15, Majadahonda, 28220 Madrid, Spain (home). *Telephone:* (91) 4261555 (office). *Fax:* (91) 4316387 (office). *E-mail:* f.mayor@fmayor.e.telefonica.net (office). *Website:* www.fund -culturadepaz.org (office).

MAYORSKY, Boris Grigoryevich; Russian diplomatist; *Adviser, Ministry of Foreign Affairs;* b. 19 May 1937, Odessa, Ukraine; m.; two d.; ed Moscow Inst. of Int. Relations, UNO Translation Courses; with Africa Div. USSR Ministry of Foreign Affairs 1961; on staff USSR Embassy, Ghana 1961–64; attaché 1964–65; with UN European Secr., Geneva 1966–69, WHO, Geneva 1969–70; First Sec., Head of Sector Law Div. USSR Ministry of Foreign Affairs 1970–73, adviser, Comm. on Law Problems of Space 1973–89; First Deputy Head, Head Dept on Int. Scientific and Tech. Co-operation 1989–92; Amb. to Kenya 1992–2000, to Spain 2000–02; currently Adviser to Ministry of Foreign Affairs. *Address:* Ministry of Foreign Affairs, 119200 Moscow, Smolenskaya-Sennaya 32/34, Russia (office). *Telephone:* (495) 244-16-06 (office). *Fax:* (495) 230-21-30 (office). *E-mail:* ministry@ mid.ru (office). *Website:* www.mid.ru (office).

MAYRHUBER, Wolfgang; Austrian business executive; *Chairman of the Supervisory Board, Deutsche Lufthansa AG;* b. 22 March 1947, Waizenkirchen; ed Tech. Coll. of Steyr, Bloor Inst., Canada, Massachusetts Inst. of Tech., USA; joined Deutsche Lufthansa AG 1970, various positions including engineer, Engine Overhaul Facility, Hamburg, man. posts in Maintenance, Repair and Overhaul (MRO) Operation, Exec. Vice-Pres. and COO of Tech. Operations 1992–94, Chair. of Exec. Bd Lufthansa Technik AG 1994–2000, apptd to Exec. Bd Deutsche Lufthansa AG 2001–02, Deputy Chair. 2002–03, Chair. Exec. Bd and CEO 2003–10, Chair. Supervisory Bd 2013–, Chair. Supervisory Bd Lufthansa CityLine; Chair. Supervisory Bd Infineon Technologies AG 2011–; Vice-Chair. AMECO Corpn, Beijing, People's Repub. of China; mem. Supervisory Bd Fraport AG, Munich Re Group (Münchener Rückversicherungs-Gesellschaft AG), BMW Group, Austrian Airlines AG, Lufthansa Technik AG; mem. Bd of Dirs SN Airholding SA/NV (Belgium), HEICO Corpn, Fla, USA, UBS (Switzerland);

mem. Steering Cttee Asscn of European Airlines, Chair. 2006; Chair. Strategy and Policy Cttee IATA, mem. Bd Govs IATA. *Address:* Deutsche Lufthansa AG, Von-Gablenz-Strasse 2–6, 50679 Cologne, Germany (office). *Telephone:* (69) 6960 (office). *Fax:* (69) 6966818 (office). *Website:* www.lufthansa.com (office).

MAYS, Willie Howard, Jr; American fmr baseball player; b. 6 May 1931, Westfield, Ala; s. of William Howard Mays and Annie Mays (née Satterwhite); m. 1st Margherite Wendell Chapman 1956 (divorced 1962 or 1963, died 2010); one adopted s.; m. 2nd Mae Louise Allen 1971 (died 2013); ed Fairfield Industrial High School; played for the New York Giants 1951–57, San Francisco Giants (after team relocation) 1958–72, New York Mets 1972–73; career statistics include 3,283 hits and 660 home runs; hit 4 home runs in one game 30 April 1961; hit over 50 home runs in 1955 and 1965, representing the longest time span between 50-plus home run seasons for any player in Major League Baseball (MLB) history; played in a record-tying 24 All-Star games between 1954 and 1973; participated in four World Series, World Series champion 1954; retd, signed ten-year contract as Goodwill Amb. and part-time coach for the New York Mets; Special Asst to Team Pres., San Francisco Giants 1986–; nicknamed The Say Hey Kid; Hon. DHumLitt (Yale) 2004, (San Francisco State Univ.) 2009; Dr hc (Dartmouth Coll.) 2007; Nat. League Rookie of the Year 1951, Most Valuable Player 1954, 1965, Associated Press Athlete of the Year Award 1954, Gold Glove Award 1957, 1958, 1959, 1960, 1961, 1962, 1963, 1964, 1965, 1966, 1967, 1968, MLB All-Star Game MVP 1963, 1968, Roberto Clemente Award 1971, elected to Baseball Hall of Fame 1979, 100 Greatest World Athletes, ranked second on The Sporting News's List of the 100 Greatest Baseball Players 1999, elected to MLB All-Century Team 1999, MLB All-Time Team 1999, inducted into Caribbean Baseball Hall of Fame 2005, Lifetime Achievement Award, Bobby Bragan Youth Foundation 2005, Tee Ball Commr, White House Tee Ball Initiative 2006, inducted into California Hall of Fame 2007, service road in Harlem named Willie Mays Drive 2008, inducted into African-American Ethnic Sports Hall of Fame 2010, MLB Beacon of Life Award 2010. *Television:* appeared in several sitcoms, always as himself; performed Say Hey: The Willie Mays Song on episode 4.46 of The Colgate Comedy Hour 1954; appeared as the mystery guest in game show What's My Line?; appeared in three episodes of ABC's The Donna Reed Show 1964, 1966, Bewitched 1966, My Two Dads 1989. *Address:* c/o San Francisco Giants, AT&T Park, 24 Willie Mays Plaza, San Francisco, CA 94107, USA. *Telephone:* (415) 972-2000. *Website:* sanfrancisco .giants.mlb.com; baseballhall.org/hof/mays-willie.

MAYSTADT, Philippe, MA, PhD; Belgian politician and international finance executive; *President, European Investment Bank;* b. 14 March 1948, Verviers; three c.; ed Claremont Grad. School, Los Angeles, USA, Catholic Univ. of Louvain; Asst Prof., Catholic Univ. of Louvain 1970–77, Prof. 1989–2007; Adviser, Office of Minister for Regional Affairs 1974; Deputy for Charleroi 1977–91; Sec. of State for Regional Economy and Planning 1979–80; Minister of Civil Service and Scientific Policy 1980–81, for the Budget, Scientific Policy and Planning 1981–85, of Econ. Affairs 1985–88; Deputy Prime Minister 1986–88; Minister of Finance 1988–98, of Foreign Trade 1995–98; Deputy Prime Minister 1995–98; Pres. Parti Social Chrétien 1998–99; mem. Senate June–Dec. 1999; Pres. European Investment Bank 2000–; IMF Interim Cttee 1993–98; Finance Minister of the Year, Euromoney magazine 1990. *Publications:* Listen and then Decide 1988, Market and State in a Globalized Economy 1998, Comprendre l'économie: l'Etat et le marché à l'heure de la mondialisation 1998. *Address:* European Investment Bank, 100 Boulevard Konrad Adenauer, 2950 Luxembourg (office). *Telephone:* 4379-94464 (office). *Fax:* 4379-64474 (office). *E-mail:* p.maystadt@eib.org (office). *Website:* www.eib.org (office).

MAYWEATHER, Floyd Joy, Jr; American professional boxer; b. (Floyd Sinclair), 24 Feb. 1977, Grand Rapids, Mich.; s. of Floyd Mayweather, Sr and Deborah Sinclair; amateur record of 84 wins, 6 losses; won nat. Golden Gloves championships 1993, 1994, 1996, Michigan State Golden Gloves Champion 1994, 1996; US Nat. Amateur Featherweight Champion 1995; bronze medal, Featherweight (57 kg) Div., Summer Olympics, Atlanta 1996; first professional bout against Roberto Apodaca Oct. 1996; trained by his uncle, Roger Mayweather; major world titles: WBC Super Featherweight Champion 1998–2002 (vacated), WBC Lightweight Champion 2002–04 (vacated), WBC Light Welterweight Champion 2005–06 (vacated), IBF Welterweight Champion April–June 2006 (vacated), WBC Welterweight Champion 2006–08 (retd), WBC Light Middleweight Champion May–July 2007, (second) WBC Welterweight Champion 2011–, WBA Light Middleweight Champion 2012–; minor world titles: IBO Welterweight Champion, IBA Welterweight Champion; The Ring/Lineal Championship titles: Lineal Super Featherweight Champion 1998–2002, The Ring Lightweight Champion 2002–04, The Ring Welterweight Champion 2006–08; special titles: WBC Emer. Light Middleweight Champion, WBC Diamond Welterweight Champion; currently undefeated as a professional boxer; recipient of WBC Diamond Belt; appeared at World Wrestling Entertainment (WWE)'s No Way Out pay-per-view in Las Vegas, Nev. 2008; Int. Boxing Award Fighter of the Year 1998, 2007, The Ring 'Fighter of the Year' 1998, 2007, Nat. Golden Gloves Champion Outstanding Boxer Award 1994, Nat. PAL Champion Outstanding Boxer Award 1995, Yahoo! Sports, Best of the Decade 2000–09, World Boxing Hall of Fame Fighter of the Year 2002, World Boxing Council Boxer of the Year 2005, 2007, The Ring No. 1 pound for pound 2005–08, Boxing Writers Asscn of America Fighter of the Year 2007, ESPN Fighter of the Year 2007, New York Daily News Fighter of the Year 2007, World Boxing Council Event of the Year (The World Awaits) 2007, World Boxing Council Knockout of the Year (against Ricky Hatton) 2007, Best Fighter ESPY Award 2007, 2008, 2010, 2012, The Ring Magazine Event of the Year 2007, 2008, 2010, Sports Illustrated, The 50 Highest-Earning American Athletes (ranked 4th) 2008, Yahoo Sports, ranked No. 6 Most Powerful People in Boxing 2008, The Ring Magazine Comeback of the Year 2009, BoxRec, BBC Sport and Yahoo! Sports No. 1 pound for pound 2009–10, Yahoo! Sports Boxing's Most Influential (ranked 70th) 2010. *Television:* Dancing With the Stars 2007, guest host for WWE Raw in Las Vegas 2009. *Address:* c/o Marc Gerald, The Agency Group Ltd, 142 West 57th Street, Sixth Floor, New York, NY 10019, USA. *Telephone:* (212) 581-3100. *Fax:* (212) 581-0015. *E-mail:* marcgerald@theagencygroup.com. *Website:* www .theagencygroup.com; www.floydmayweather.com.

MAZAHERI, Tahmasb, MS; Iranian civil engineer, government official and banking official; b. 1953; ed Univ. of Tehran; fmr univ. lecturer; Head Bonyad

Mostazafan and Janbazan Foundation 1985–91; Sec.-Gen Bank Markazi Jomhouri Islami Iran (Cen. Bank) 1991–94, Gov. 2007–08; Minister of Econ. Affairs and Finance 2001–04, Deputy Minister of Econ. Affairs and Finance 2005–06; Man. Dir Export Devt Bank of Iran (EDBI) 2007–08. *Address:* c/o Bank Markazi Jomhouri Islami Iran, POB 15875-7177, 144 Mirdamad Blvd, Tehran, Iran (office).

MAZANKOWSKI, Rt Hon. Donald Frank, PC, OC; Canadian politician and business consultant; b. 27 July 1935, Viking, Alberta; s. of the late Frank Mazankowski and Dora Lonowski; m. Lorraine E. Poleschuk 1958; three s.; ed high school; MP 1968–93; Minister of Transport and Minister responsible for Canadian Wheat Board 1979; Minister of Transport 1984–86; Pres. Treasury Bd 1987–88; Minister responsible for Privatization, Regulatory Affairs and Operations 1988, of Agric. 1989–91, of Finance 1991–93; Deputy Prime Minister 1986–93, Pres. of the Queen's Privy Council for Canada 1989–91; business consultant 1993–; fmr Chair. Inst. of Health Econs, Canadian Genetics Diseases Network, Alberta Premier's Advisory Council on Health; Gov. Univ. of Alberta; dir numerous cos; Progressive Conservative Party; Alberta Order of Excellence 2003; Hon. DEng (Tech. Univ. of Nova Scotia) 1987, Hon. LLD (Univ. of Alberta) 1993, Hon. BA (Grant McEwan Univ.) 2009; Paul Harris Fellow, Rotary Int., Alberta Centennial Medal 2005. *Leisure interests:* fishing, golf. *Address:* 80 Nottingham Inlet, Sherwood Park, AB T8A 6N2, Canada. *Telephone:* (780) 410-0728. *Fax:* (780) 410-0748. *E-mail:* donmaz@shaw.ca.

MAZEAUD, Pierre, Docteur en droit; French politician; *President, Fondation Charles de Gaulle;* b. 24 Aug. 1929, Lyon; s. of Jean Mazeaud and Paulette Duirat; m. 1st Marie Prohom 1953 (divorced 1960); two d.; m. 2nd Sophie Hamel 1967; one s. one d.; ed Lycée Louis-le-Grand et Faculté de droit de Paris; Judge of Tribunal of Instance, Lamentin, Martinique 1961; in charge of conf., Faculty of Law, Paris 1955; Tech. Adviser to Prime Minister 1961; Judge of Tribunal of Great Instance, Versailles 1962; Tech. Adviser to Minister of Justice 1962; Tech. Adviser to Jean Foyer's Cabinet 1962–67; Tech. Adviser to Minister of Youth and Sports 1967–68; Deputy for Hauts-de-Seine 1968–73, for Haute-Savoie 1988–98, Vice-Pres. Assemblée Nationale 1992–93, 1997–98, Vice-Pres. Groupe des députés sportifs 1968; Minister responsible for Youth and Sport 1973–76; Councillor of State 1976; Pres. Law Comm. of Assemblée Nationale 1987–88, 1993–98; Vice-Pres. l'Assemblée Nationale 1992–93, 1997–98; Titular Judge, High Court 1987–97; Mayor, Saint-Julien-en-Genevois 1979–89; regional councillor, Rhône-Alpes 1992–98, Pres. Commission des finances de Rhône-Alpes; mem. Constitutional Council 1998, Pres. 2004–07; Pres. Fondation Charles de Gaulle 2007–; Vice-Pres. Cttee de réflexion sur la modernisation et le rééquilibrage des institutions 2007–; in charge of courses IEP (l'Institut d'études politiques) d'Aix-en-Provence; Professeur, IEP Paris 1999–; mem. Acad. des Sciences Morales et Politiques 2005–, Acad. des Sports; Officier, Légion d'honneur, Commdr de la Légion d'honneur, Officier du Mérite sportif. *Achievements include:* climbed Mount Everest 1978 (oldest man to do so). *Publications:* Montagne pour un homme nu 1971, Everest 78 1978, Sport et Liberté 1980, Nanga Parbat – montagne cruelle 1982, Des cailloux et des mouches ou l'échec à l'Himalaya 1985, Rappel au Règlement 1995. *Leisure interests:* mountaineering, skiing, swimming. *Address:* Fondation et Institut Charles de Gaulle, 5 rue de Solférino, 75007 Paris, France (office). *Telephone:* 1-44-18-66-77 (office). *Fax:* 1-44-18-66-99 (office). *E-mail:* contact@charles-de-gaulle.org (office). *Website:* www.charles-de-gaulle.org (office); r (office).

MAZOMBWE, HE Cardinal Medardo Joseph; Zambian ecclesiastic; *Archbishop Emeritus of Lusaka;* b. 24 Sept. 1931, Chundamira; ordained priest 1960; Bishop of Chipata 1970–96; Archbishop of Lusaka 1996–2006, Archbishop Emer. 2006–; apptd Cardinal-Priest of S. Emerenziana a Tor Fiorenza, cr. Cardinal 20 Nov. 2010. *Address:* Archdiocese of Lusaka, PO Box 32754, 41 Wamulwa Road, 10101 Lusaka, Zambia (office). *Telephone:* (1) 239257 (office). *Fax:* (1) 290631 (office).

MAZRUI, Ali A., MA, DPhil; Kenyan political scientist and academic; *Albert Schweitzer Professor in the Humanities and Director, Institute of Global Cultural Studies, State University of New York, Binghamton;* b. 24 Feb. 1933, Mombasa; s. of Al'Amin Ali Mazrui and Safia Suleiman Mazrui; m. 1st Molly Vickerman 1962 (divorced 1982); three s.; m. 2nd Pauline Ejima Uti-Mazrui 1991; two s.; ed Columbia Univ., USA, Univs of Manchester and Oxford, UK; Lecturer in Political Science, Makerere Univ., Uganda 1963–65, Prof. of Political Science 1965–72, Dean of Social Sciences 1967–69; Assoc. Ed. Transition Magazine 1964–73, Co-Ed. Mawazo Journal 1967–73; Visiting Prof., Univ. of Chicago 1965; Research Assoc. Harvard Univ. 1965–66; Dir African Section, World Order Models Project 1968–73; Visiting Prof., Northwestern Univ., USA 1969, McGill and Denver Univs 1969, London and Manchester Univs 1971, Dyason Lecture Tour of Australia 1972; Vice-Pres. Int. Political Science Asscn 1970–73, Int. Congress of Africanists 1967–73, Int. Congress of African Studies 1978–85, Int. African Inst. 1987–, World Congress of Black Intellectuals 1988–; Fellow, Center for Advanced Study in the Behavioral Sciences, Stanford 1972–73; Prof. of Political Science, Univ. of Michigan 1973–91; Sr Visiting Fellow, Hoover Inst. on War, Revolution and Peace, Stanford 1973–74; Dir Centre for Afro-American and African Studies 1979–81; Research Prof. Univ. of Jos, Nigeria 1981–86; Andrew D. White Prof.-at-Large, Cornell Univ. 1986–92, currently Sr Scholar in Africana Studies; Albert Schweitzer Prof. in the Humanities, State Univ. of New York, Binghamton 1989–, also Dir Inst. of Global Cultural Studies; Ibn Khaldun Prof.-at-Large School of Islamic and Social Sciences, Leesbury, Va 1997–; Walter Rodney Distinguished Prof., Univ. of Guyana, Georgetown 1997–98; Albert Luthuli Prof.-at-Large in the Humanities and Devt Studies, Univ. of Jos, Nigeria; Reith Lecturer 1979; Presenter, BBC TV series The Africans 1986; mem. World Bank's Council of African Advisers; Int. Org. Essay Prize 1964, Northwestern Univ. Book Prize 1969. *Publications:* Towards a Pax Africana 1967, On Heroes and Uhuru-Worship 1967, The Anglo-African Commonwealth 1967, Violence and Thought 1969, Protest and Power in Black Africa (co-ed.) 1970, The Trial of Christopher Okigbo 1971, Cultural Engineering and Nation Building in East Africa 1972, Africa in World Affairs: The Next Thirty Years (co-ed.) 1973, A World Federation of Cultures: An African Perspective 1976, Political Values and the Educated Class in Africa 1978, Africa's International Relations 1978, The African Condition (Reith Lectures) 1980, Nationalism and New States in Africa (co-author) 1984, The Africans: A Triple Heritage 1986, Cultural Forces in World Politics 1989, Africa Since 1935 (Vol. VIII of UNESCO General History of Africa; ed.) 1993, The Power of Babel: Language and

Governance in Africa's Experience 1998. *Leisure interests:* travel, dining out, swimming, reading thrillers and mystery novels. *Address:* State University of New York, Institute of Global Culture Studies, Office of Schweitzer Chair, P.O. Box 6000, Binghamton, NY 13902 (office); 313 Murray Hill Road, Vestal, NY 13850, USA (home). *Telephone:* (607) 777-4494 (office). *Website:* www.binghamton.edu/igcs (office).

MAZUKA, Michiyoshi; Japanese business executive; *Chairman and Representative Director, Fujitsu Ltd;* ed Gakushuin Univ.; joined Fujitsu Ltd 1971, has held several sr exec. positions including Chief Dir of Higashi Nihon Sales, Man. Exec. Officer, Sr Man. Dir and Vice-Pres., with fujitsureseller.com 2005, with Fujitsu America Inc. 2006–08, later Corp. Sr Vice-Pres. Fujitsu Ltd –2008, Chair. and Rep. Dir 2008–. *Address:* Fujitsu Headquarters, Shiodome City Centre, 1-5-2 Higashi-Shimbashi, Minato-ku, Tokyo 105-7123, Japan (office). *Telephone:* (3) 6252-2220 (office). *Fax:* (3) 6252-2783 (office). *E-mail:* info@fujitsu.com (office). *Website:* www.fujitsu.com (office).

MAZUMDAR-SHAW, Kiran, BSc; Indian business executive; *Chairman and Managing Director, Biocon India Ltd;* b. 23 March 1953, Bangalore; m. John Shaw 1997; ed Bishop Cotton Girls School, Mount Carmel Coll., Bangalore, Bangalore Univ., Ballarat Coll., Melbourne Univ., Australia; trainee Brewer, Carlton & United Breweries, Melbourne and trainee Maltster, Barrett Bros & Burston, Australia 1975–77; Brewery Consultant, Jupiter Breweries Ltd, Calcutta (now Kolkata) 1975–76; Tech. Man. Standard Malting Corpn, Baroda 1976; Trainee Man. Biocon Ltd, Cork, Repub. of Ireland 1978; Chair. and Man. Dir Biocon India Ltd 1978–; Dir Pharmacia United Ltd, Bangalore 1987–94; Chair. Syngene Int., Bangalore 1994–; Chair. Clinigene Int., Bangalore 2000–; mem. Bd Bio-Ventures for Global Health; Chair. and Mission Leader Confed. of Indian Industries Nat. Task Force on Biotechnology; Council mem. Basic Chemicals, Pharmaceuticals and Cosmetics Export Promotion Council 1983–; Vice-Pres. Asscn of Women Entrepreneurs of Karnataka (AWAKE) 1983–89, Indo-American Chamber of Commerce, Bangalore 1986–87; mem. Prime Minister's Council on Trade and Industry in India, Confed. of Indian Industries, Greater Mysore Chamber of Industries, Advisory Cttee, Dept of Biotechnology, Young Presidents' Org., Research Council, CFTRI, Bangalore Agenda Task Force, Bd of Science Foundation, Ireland; mem. Bd Govs Indian Inst. of Man. Bangalore; Trustee, Karnataka Chitrakala Parishat; Chair. All India Art Exhbn; Hon. DSc (Ballarat) 2004; Dr hc (Manipal Acad. of Higher Educ.) 2005; numerous awards including Gold Award for Best Woman Entrepreneur, Inst. of Marketing Man. 1982, AWAKE Outstanding Contrib. Award 1983, Int. Women's Asscn (Chennai) Woman of the Year 1998–99, Padma Shri 1989, Nat. Award for Best Small Industry, Sir M. Visveswaraya Memorial Award, Fed. of Karnataka Chambers of Commerce and Industry 2002, Rajyotsava Award 2002, Ernst & Young Entrepreneur of the Year Award in Healthcare and Life Sciences Category 2002, Australian Alumni High Achiever Award, IDP Australian Alumni Asscn 2003, The Economic Times Business Woman of the Year Award 2004, Padma Bhushan 2005, Indian Chamber of Commerce Lifetime Achievement Award 2005, Nikkei Asia Prize 2009, ranked by Fortune magazine amongst 50 Most Powerful Women in Business outside the US (44th) 2005, (48th) 2006, (50th) 2007, (49th) 2011, ranked by Forbes magazine amongst The World's 100 Most Powerful Women (99th) 2008, (92nd) 2009, (99th) 2011, (80th) 2012, (85th) 2013. *Publication:* Ale and Arty. *Leisure interests:* trekking, art collecting. *Address:* Biocon India Ltd, 20th K. M. Hosur Road, Electronic City, Bangalore 560 100, India (office). *Telephone:* (80) 28082808 (office). *Fax:* (80) 28523423 (office). *E-mail:* contact.us@biocon.com (office). *Website:* www.biocon.com (office).

MAZUROK, Yuri Antonovich; Ukrainian singer (baritone); b. 18 July 1931, Krasnik, Poland (now Ukraine); one s.; ed Lvov Inst. and Moscow Conservatoire; debut with Bolshoi Opera 1963, Prin. of the co. 1964–2001; has performed worldwide; retd from the stage 2001; awards include Prague Spring Vocal Competition 1960, Int. Enesco Singing Competition, Bucharest 1961, First Prize at World Fair, Montreal 1967, USSR People's Artist 1976. *Operatic roles include:* Eugene (Eugene Onegin), Prince Yeletsky (The Queen of Spades), Andrei (War and Peace), Figaro (The Barber of Seville), Scarpia (Tosca) and Escamillo (Carmen) and especially Verdi repertoire, including René (Un Ballo in Maschera), Rodrigo (Don Carlos), Germont (La Traviata). *Address:* c/o Bolshoi Theatre, Teatralnaya Pl. 1, 103009 Moscow, Russia (office).

MAZURSKY, Paul, BA; American film writer, director and actor; b. (Irwin Mazursky), 25 April 1930, Brooklyn, NY; s. of David Mazursky and Jean Gerson; m. Betsy Purdy 1953; two d.; ed Brooklyn Coll.; stage, TV and film actor 1951–; night club comedian 1954–60; writer, Danny Kaye Show 1963–67; co-writer, I Love You, Alice B. Toklas (film) 1968; mem. Bd of Govs Acad. of Motion Picture Arts and Sciences; Dr hc (Brooklyn Coll.). *Films include:* as writer and Dir, Bob & Carol & Ted & Alice 1969, Alex in Wonderland 1970, Blume in Love 1972, Harry & Tonto 1973, Next Stop, Greenwich Village 1976, An Unmarried Woman 1977–78, Willie & Phil 1979–80, Tempest 1982, Moscow on the Hudson 1984; as writer, producer and Dir, Down and Out in Beverly Hills 1986, Moon Over Parador 1988, Enemies A Love Story 1989, Scenes From a Mall 1991, The Pickle 1993, Faithful 1996, Yippee (documentary) 2006; as actor films include: Fear and Desire 1953, Blackboard Jungle 1955, Deathwatch 1966, Alex in Wonderland 1970, The Other Side of the Wind 1972, Blume in Love 1973, A Star Is Born 1976, An Unmarried Woman 1978, A Man, a Woman and a Bank 1979, History of the World: Part I 1981, Tempest 1982, Moscow on the Hudson 1984, Into the Night 1985, Down and Out in Beverly Hills 1986, Punchline 1988, Scenes from the Class Struggle in Beverly Hills 1989, Enemies: A Love Story 1989, Scenes from a Mall 1991, Man Trouble 1992, The Pickle 1993, Carlito's Way 1993, Love Affair 1994, Miami Rhapsody 1995, Faithful 1996, 2 Days in the Valley 1996, Touch 1997, Why Do Fools Fall in Love 1998, Antz (voice) 1998, Crazy in Alabama 1999, The Majestic (voice) 2001, Da wan 2001, Do It for Uncle Manny 2002, I Want Someone to Eat Cheese With 2006, Cattle Call 2006. *Television:* Winchell 1998, A Slight Case of Murder 1999, Once and Again (series) 1999–2002, The Sopranos (series) 2000–01, Coast to Coast 2004, Curb Your Enthusiasm (series) 2004. *Publications:* Show Me the Magic (autobiog.). *Address:* c/o Ken Kamins, 8942 Wilshire Boulevard, Beverly Hills, CA 92011, USA.

MAZZARELLA, David; American newspaper editor; b. 1938; with Assoc. Press, Lisbon, New York, Rome 1962–70; with Daily American, Rome 1971–75, Gannett News, Washington, DC 1976–77, The Bridgewater, Bridgewater, NJ 1977–83; Ed.,

Sr Vice-Pres. USA Today –1999; Ombudsman, Stars and Stripes (newspaper for American mil. services) 2000–01, 2007–, Ed. Dir 2001–07. *Publication:* Always Eat the Hard Crust of the Bread: Recollections and Recipes From My Centenarian Mother 2012. *Address:* Stars and Stripes, 529 14th Street, NW, Suite 350, Washington, DC 20450, USA (office). *Telephone:* (202) 761-0900 (office). *Fax:* (202) 761-089 (office). *E-mail:* mazzarellad@stripes.osd.mil (office); tdmazzarella@aol.com. *Website:* www.stripes.com (office); davidmazzarella.com.

MAZZONI DELLA STELLA, Vittorio; Italian banker; b. 21 May 1941, Siena; ed Univ. of Florence; joined Monte dei Paschi di Siena bank, Naples 1966, worked in Rome, then Siena brs, then in Market and Econ. Research Dept, apptd Man. 1976, mem. Bd of Dirs 1990, Deputy Chair. 1991–, Deputy Chair. Monte dei Paschi Banque, Paris 1991; mem. Bd of Dirs Sindibank, Barcelona 1991; Chair. ICLE (MPS banking group), Rome 1991; mem. Bd Dirs Centro Finanziaria SpA, Rome 1987–; mem. Bd Dirs and Exec. Cttee Deposit Protection Fund, Rome 1991–; mem. Bd Asscn of Italian Bankers (ABI) 1991–; elected Prov. Councillor, Siena 1980, Deputy Chair. Prov. Council 1980–82, Mayor 1983–90; Chair. Chigiana Foundation (music acad.), Siena 1991–. *Address:* Monte dei Paschi di Siena, Siena, Italy.

MBA, Paul Biyoghé; Gabonese politician; b. 18 April 1953, Donguila; ed Univ. of Rennes, France; Deputy Dir Banque Gabonaise de Développement 1977–83; Chargé des Affaires to Pres. of the Repub. 1980–83, Political Adviser to Pres. 1983–84, Jt Chief of Staff in Pres.'s Office 1984–89, Minister of Trade, Consumer Affairs and Technology Transfer 1989–90, Minister of State Control, Parastatal Reform and Privatization 1992–94, Minister of Small and Medium Enterprises 1999–2003, Minister of Trade and Industrial Devt, in charge of NEPAD 2003–08, Minister of Agric., Animal Husbandry and Rural Devt 2008–09; Prime Minister 2009–12 (resgnd); Deputy, Assemblée Nationale 1990–92, 1994–96, mem. Sénat 1997–99; Man. Dir Aban Br., Banque Internationale pour l'Afrique Occidentale 1986–92; Dir Société Nat. des Bois du Gabon 1987–90; mem. Parti démocratique gabonais (PDG); Hon. Pres., Gabonese Boxing Fed.; Grand Officier, Ordre Nat. de l'Etoile Equatoriale, Commdr, Ordre Nat. du Mérite, Commdr, Ordre du Mérite Maritime, Commdr, Ordre Nat. du Portugal, Chevalier, Légion d'Honneur. *Address:* c/o Office of the Prime Minister, BP 546, Libreville, Gabon.

MBA-ABESSOLE, Paul, PhD, DTheol; Gabonese ecclesiastic and government official; b. 9 Oct. 1939, Ngnung-Ako, Kango; ed Univ. de Paris, Inst. Catholique de Paris, France; teacher of French 1964–65; religious instructor 1965–73; curate 1973–76; political refugee in France 1983–89; typesetter 1984, 1986–87; returned to Gabon 1989; Founder and Leader Morena-bûcheron 1990, renamed Rassemblement nat. des bûcherons 1991, then Rassemblement pour le Gabon 2000; presidential cand. 1993, 1998; Mayor of Libreville 1996; Pres. of World Conf. of Mayors 1999; Minister of State for Human Rights and Missions 2002–03, later Deputy Prime Minister, also Minister of Agric., Livestock and Rural Devt, in charge of Human Rights 2003–07, of State in the Office of Pres. 2007, of Reform, Human Rights, the Fight against Poverty and Illicit Enrichment 2007, of Culture, the Arts, Educating the Population, Reconstruction Projects and Human Rights 2007–09. *Leisure interest:* reading. *Address:* c/o Office of the Prime Minister, PO Box 546, Libreville, Gabon (office). *Telephone:* 77-89-81 (office).

MBA MOKUY, Agapito; Equatorial Guinean politician; *Minister of Foreign Affairs and Co-operation;* fmr Chief of Admin and Finance, Social and Human Science, UNESCO and Sec., UNESCO Admin. Comm.; fmr Adviser to Pres. Obiang Nguema Mbasogo on matters related to Int. orgs.; Minister of Foreign Affairs and Co-operation 2012–. *Address:* Ministry of Foreign Affairs and Co-operation, Malabo, Equatorial Guinea (office). *Telephone:* 333093220 (office). *Fax:* 333093132 (office).

MBA NGUEMA, Gen. Antonio; Equatorial Guinean military officer and politician; *Minister of National Defence;* Minister of Nat. Defence 2004–. *Address:* Ministry of National Defence, Malabo, Equatorial Guinea. *Telephone:* (09) 27-94.

MBABAZI, Amama, LLB; Ugandan lawyer and politician; *Prime Minister;* b. 16 Jan. 1949, Mparo village, Rukiga Co.; m. Jacquleine Susan Mbabazi; three s. three d.; ed Makerere Univ., Law Devt Centre, Kampala; State Attorney in Attorney Gen.'s Chambers 1976–78; Sec., Uganda Law Council 1977–79; Prin. Asst to Yoweri Museveni 1978–79; Pnr Kategaya Mbabazi & Tumwesigye Advocates, Kampala 1981; in exile in Kenya and Sweden 1981–85; Dir-Gen. External Security Org. 1986–92; Minister of State for Defence 1992–98, for Foreign Affairs and Regional Co-operation 1998–2001, Minister of Defence 2001–09, also Attorney Gen. 2004–06, Minister for Security 2009–2011, Prime Minister 2011–; del. to Constitutional Ass. (responsible for drafting new Ugandan constitution) 1994–95; MP for Kinkizi West 2003–; mem. Nat. Resistance Movt (Sec. Gen. 2010–11); fmr head of Bd of Dirs of several state and pvt. cos; mem. Ugandan Law Soc. 1977–; Nalubaale Medal of Honour. *Address:* Office of the Prime Minister, Post Office Bldg, Yusuf Lule Rd, POB 341, Kampala, Uganda (office). *Telephone:* (41) 4236252 (office). *Fax:* (41) 4341139 (office). *E-mail:* ps@opm.go.ug (office). *Website:* www.opm.go.ug (office).

MBANEFO, Arthur Christopher Izuegbunam, FCA; Nigerian financial consultant and fmr diplomatist; b. 11 June 1930; m.; one s.; Minister for Commerce and Industries, Eastern Region of Nigeria (Repub. of Biafra) 1968–70; staff mem. Price Waterhouse & Co., London 1970–71; fmr Pnr, Akintola Williams & Co., Chartered Accountants; f. Arthur Mbanefo and Assocs (corp. and financial consulting co.) 1986; Pro-Chancellor and Chair. of Council, Univ. of Lagos 1984–86, Obafemi Awolowo Univ. 1986–90, Ahmadu Bello Univ. 1990–93; Perm. Rep. to UN, New York 1999–2003, Chair. G77 2000, Chair. Bd of Trustees UNITAR 2000–04; Dir Orient Petroleum Resources Ltd; Fellow, Inst of Chartered Accountants in England and Wales, Inst. of Chartered Accountants of Nigeria, Nigerian Inst. of Man. (mem. Council 1979–87); Pro-Chancellor and Chair. of Council Ahmadu Bello Univ. 1990–93, Obafemi Awolowo Univ. 1986–90, Univ. of Lagos 1984–86; f. Asscn of Accountancy Bodies of W Africa 1982, Pres. 1987; Hon. Yoruba Chieftaincy, Distinguished Order of Fed. Repub. of Nigeria 1981, Odu of Onitsha 1994, Commdr Order of the Niger 2002; several nat. and int. awards and medals, including from Govts of Italy and Brazil. *Address:* c/o Orient Petroleum Resources Ltd, Lion House, Abuja Estate, Enugu-Onitsha Express Way, Awka, Nigeria.

M'BAREK, Sghair Ould; Mauritanian politician; *President, Constitutional Council;* b. 1954, Néma; m.; four c.; ed Univ. of Nouakchott; Minister of Nat. Educ. 1992–93, 1997–98, 2000, of Rural Devt and the Environment 1994–95, of Health and Social Affairs 1995, of Commerce and Tourism 1998–99, of Equipment and Transport 1999, of Justice 2001–03; Prime Minister of Mauritania 2003–05; Mediator of the Repub. –2010; Pres. Constitutional Council 2010–. *Address:* Office of the President of the Constitutional Council, Nouakchott, Mauritania (office).

MBASOGO, Lt-Col Teodoro Obiang Nguema; Equatorial Guinean politician and army officer; *President and Supreme Commander of the Armed Forces;* fmr Deputy Minister of Defence; overthrew fmr Pres. Macias Nguema in coup; Pres. of Equatorial Guinea 1979–; Supreme Commdr of the Armed Forces 1979–; Minister of Defence 1986; Chair. African Union 2011–12. *Address:* Oficina del Presidente, Malabo, Equatorial Guinea (office).

MBEKI, Thabo Mvuyelwa, MA; South African politician and fmr head of state; b. 18 June 1942, Idutywa; s. of the late Govan Mbeki and of Epainette Mbeki; m. Zanele Dlamini 1974; ed Lovedale, Alice, St John's Umtata, Univs of London and Sussex; Leader African Students Org. 1961; Youth Organizer for African Nat. Congress (ANC), Johannesburg 1961–62; six weeks' detention, Byo 1962; left SA 1962; official, ANC offices, London, England 1967–70; mil. training, USSR 1970; Asst Sec. ANC Revolutionary Council 1971–72; Acting ANC Rep., Swaziland 1975–76; ANC Rep., Nigeria 1976–78, mem. ANC. Nat. Exec. Cttee 1975, re-elected 1985; Dir Information and Publicity, ANC 1984–89, Head of Dept of Int. Affairs 1989–93, Del. on Talks about Talks, with SA Govt 1990, Chair. ANC 1993; First Deputy Pres. of South Africa 1994–99; Pres. ANC 1997–2007; Pres. of South Africa 1999–2008 (resgnd); mem. Bd IOC 1993; Pres. African Union 2002–03; Hon. KCMG; KStJ. *Address:* ANC, 54 Sauer Street 2001, Johannesburg 2001, South Africa (office). *Telephone:* (11) 3761000 (office). *Fax:* (11) 3761134 (office). *E-mail:* nmtyelwa@anc.org.za (office). *Website:* www.anc.org.za (office).

MBETE, Baleka; South African politician; *National Chairperson, African National Congress;* b. 24 Sept. 1949, Durban; ed Inanda Seminary, Durban, Lovedale Teachers' Coll., King William's Town, E Cape; teacher, Isibonelo High School, KwaMashu, Durban 1975; went into exile, then teacher, Matter Dolorosa High School, Mbabane, Swaziland 1976–77; joined African Nat. Congress (ANC) 1976, worked in ANC Dept of Information and Publicity (Radio Freedom) and Women's Section, Dar es Salaam, Tanzania 1977–81, Public Relations work for ANC, Nairobi, Kenya 1981–83, worked in ANC underground political structures, Gaborone, Botswana 1983–86, mem. ANC Regional Women's Cttee and Regional Political Cttee, Harare, Zimbabwe 1986–87, Admin. Sec., Exec. Cttee, Lusaka, Zambia 1987–90, Sec.-Gen. ANC Women's League 1991–93, mem. ANC Nat. Exec. Cttee 1991, Chair. ANC Parl. Caucus 1995–, Nat. Chair. ANC 2007–; Deputy Speaker, Nat. Ass. 1996–2004, Speaker 2004–08; Deputy Pres. of South Africa 2008–09; apptd mem. Presidential Panel, Truth and Reconciliation Comm. 1995, African Peer Review Mechanism (APRM) Panel of Eminent Persons 2012–. *Address:* African National Congress, 54 Sauer Street, Johannesburg 201, South Africa (office). *Telephone:* (11) 3761000 (office). *Fax:* (11) 3761134 (office). *E-mail:* nmtyelwa@anc.org.za (office). *Website:* www.anc.org.za (office).

MBONJO, Pierre Moukoko; Cameroonian political scientist, business executive and politician; *Minister of External Relations;* b. 25 July 1954, Nkam; ed Institut d'études politiques, Paris; 25 years as lecturer in political science, Institut des Relations internationales du Cameroun (Iric); Special Adviser to Prime Minister and Govt Spokesman 1991–92, Chief of Cabinet in Prime Minister's Office 1996, Minister of Communications 2004–06, of External Relations 2011–; CEO Cimenteries du Cameroun (Cimencam) –2011; Dir Société Nationale d'Investissement du Cameroun 1996. *Publications include:* The Political Thought of Kwame Nkrumah 1998. *Address:* Ministry of External Relations, Yaoundé, Cameroon (office). *Telephone:* 2220-3850 (office). *Fax:* 2220-1133 (office). *Website:* www .diplocam.gov.cm (office).

MBOWENI, Tito, MA; South African politician, fmr central banker and business executive; *Chairman, AngloGold Ashanti Ltd;* b. 16 March 1959, Tzaneem, Nothern Prov.; ed Nat. Univ. of Lesotho and Univ. of E Anglia; mem. ANC 1980 (ANC, Zambia 1988); fmr Deputy Head Dept of Econ. Planning, Co-ordinator for Trade and Industry; Minister of Labour, Govt of Nat. Unity 1994–99; Gov. SA Reserve Bank 1999–2009; Chair. AngloGold Ashanti Ltd 2010–; Gov. Prof. Extraordinary in Economics, Univ. of Stellenbosch 2002–05; Hon. Prof. of Econs (Univ. of S Africa) 2002–03; Hon. DComm (Univ. of Natal) 2001. *Leisure interests:* fly-fishing, soccer. *Address:* Office of the Chairman, AngloGold Ashanti Ltd, 76 Jeppe Street, Newtown, Johannesburg 2001, South Africa (office). *Telephone:* (11) 6376000 (office). *E-mail:* jjones@anglogoldashanti.com (office). *Website:* www .anglogoldashanti.co.za (office).

MBUSA NYAMWISI, Antipas; Democratic Republic of the Congo politician; *Minister of Decentralization and Land Settlement;* b. 1959; fought with Rally for Congolese Democracy (RCD) against Govt 1998–99; Founder and Chair. RCD-Kisangani Party (later Forces du renouveau, Forces for Renewal Party) 1999–; Minister of Regional Co-ordination 2003–07, of Foreign Affairs and Int. Co-operation 2007–08, of Decentralization and Land Settlement 2008–; unsuccessful cand. in 2006 presidential election. *Address:* Ministry of Decentralization and Land Settlement, Kinshasa, Democratic Republic of the Congo (office).

MBYWANGI, Margarita; Paraguayan politician; b. 1962, Canindeyú; three c.; captured by settlers and sold into forced labour at age of four; Chief (cacique) of Aché Tribe 1992–; mem. Movimiento Popular Tekojojá (MPT); apptd Minister for Indigenous Affairs 2008. *E-mail:* joaquinbonett@gmail.com (office).

McTEER, Janet, OBE; British actress; b. 8 May 1961, Newcastle-upon-Tyne, England; d. of Alan McTeer and Jean McTeer; ed Royal Acad. of Dramatic Arts, London; Bancroft Gold Medal 1983. *Theatre includes:* Much Ado About Nothing, Uncle Vanya, Simpatico, Vivat! Vivat Regina, London 1995, A Doll's House, London (Tony Award 1997, Laurence Olivier Theatre Award for Best Actress 1997, London Critics' Circle Theatre Award for Best Actress 1997), New York 1996–97. *Films include:* Half Moon Street 1986, Hawks 1988, Sweet Nothing 1990, I Dreamt I Woke Up 1991, Prince 1991, Wuthering Heights 1992, Carrington 1995, Velvet Goldmine (voice) 1998, Populous: The Beginning (video game; voice) 1998, Tumbleweeds 1999, Waking the Dead 2000, Songcatcher 2000, The King is Alive

2000, The Intended (also co-writer) 2002, Romeo and Me 2004, Tideland 2005, As You Like It 2006, Cat Run 2011, Island 2011, Albert Nobbs 2011, The Woman in Black 2012. *Television appearances include:* Les Girls (series) 1988, Precious Bane 1989, Yellowbacks 1990, Portrait of a Marriage 1990, 102 Boulevard Haussmann 1990, The Black Velvet Gown 1991, A Masculine Ending 1992, Dead Romantic 1992, Don't Leave Me This Way 1993, The Governor (series) 1995, Marple: The Murder at the Vicarage 2004, Daphne 2007, Into the Storm 2009, Weekends at Bellevue 2011. *Leisure interests:* cooking, gardens. *Address:* c/o International Creative Management, 40 West 57th Street, Floor 16, New York, NY 10019-4098, USA (office); c/o Michael Foster, ARG, 46 Maddox Street, London, W1S 1QA, England (office). *Telephone:* (20) 7436-6400 (London) (office). *E-mail:* argtalent@ argtalent.com (office).

MDLALOSE, Frank Themba, BSc, UED, MB, CH.B.; South African politician and fmr diplomatist; b. 29 Nov. 1931, Nqutu Dist KwaZulu; s. of Jaconiah Zwelabo Mdlalose and Thabitha Mthembu; m. Eunice Nokuthula 1956; three s. two d.; ed Univ. of Fort Hare, Rhodes Univ. and Univ. of Natal; Intern, King Edward VII Hosp., Durban 1959; pvt. medical practice, Pretoria 1960–62, Steadville, Lady-smith, Natal, Atteridgeville 1962–70; medical practitioner, Madadeni 1970–78; Nat. Chair. Inkatha 1977; Minister of Health, KwaZulu 1983–90, Acting Minister of Educ. 1990, Minister without Portfolio 1991–94; Premier, KwaZulu-Natal 1994; Amb. to Egypt –2002 (retd); Hon. DrIur (Zululand) 1998. *Publication:* My Life (autobiog.) 2006. *Address:* PO Box 14110, Madadeni 2951, South Africa. *Telephone:* (34) 3291201.

MEACHER, Rt Hon. Michael Hugh, PC, MP; British politician; b. 4 Nov. 1939, Hemel Hempstead, Herts.; s. of late George H. and Doris M. (née Foxell) Meacher; m. 1st Molly C. (née Reid) 1962 (divorced 1985); two s. two d.; m. 2nd Lucianne Craven 1988; ed Berkhamsted School, New Coll., Oxford and London School of Econs; Lecturer in Social Admin., Univ. of York and LSE 1966–70; MP for Oldham West 1970–97, for Oldham West and Royton 1997–; Jr Minister, Dept of Industry 1974–75, Dept of Health and Social Security 1975–76, Dept of Trade 1976–79; mem. Nat. Exec. Cttee of Labour Party 1983–88, Shadow Cabinet 1983–97, Shadow Spokesman for Health and Social Security 1983–87, for Employment 1987–89, for Social Security 1989–92, for Overseas Devt 1992–93, for Citizens' Rights 1993–94, for Transport 1994–95, for Employment 1995–96, for Environmental Protection 1996–97; Minister of State for the Environment 1997–2003; mem. Treasury Select Cttee 1980–83; cand. for deputy leadership of Labour Party 1983; mem., parl. rep. for UNISON; mem. Child Poverty Action Group and other voluntary orgs. *Publications:* Taken for a Ride: Special Residential Homes for the Elderly Mentally Infirm: A Study of Separatism in Social Policy 1972, Socialism with a Human Face 1982, Diffusing Power 1992; over 1,000 articles on econ., industrial and social policy, regional devt, defence issues, the welfare state, media reform, civil service reform, the police, etc. *Leisure interests:* sport, music, reading. *Address:* House of Commons, Westminster, London, SW1A 0AA (office); 34 Kingscliffe Gardens, London, SW19 6NR, England (home). *Telephone:* (20) 7219-6461 (office). *Fax:* (20) 7219-5945 (office). *E-mail:* massonm@parliament.uk (office). *Website:* www.epolitix.com/webminster/michael-meacher (office).

MEAD, Carver Andress, MS, PhD; American computer scientist and academic; *Gordon and Betty Moore Professor of Engineering and Applied Science, Emeritus, California Institute of Technology;* b. 1 May 1934, Bakersfield, Calif.; ed Calif. Inst. of Tech.; began teaching at Calif. Inst. of Tech. 1957, est. Dept of Computer Science, currently Gordon and Betty Moore Emer. Prof. of Eng and Applied Science; pioneer of very-large-scale integrated (VSLI) circuit technology; developed first techniques for designing complex microchips, cr. gallium-arsenide (GaAs) transistor and first software compilation of a silicon chip; f. Actel Corpn, Silicon Compilers, Synaptics, Sonic Innovations, Foveon Inc., Silerity, Cascade Semiconductor Design; owns over 50 patents; Fellow American Physical Soc.; mem. Nat. Acad. of Eng; Hon. DSc (Univ. of Lund), D. Hon. (Univ. of Southern Calif.); Achievement Award, Electronics Magazine 1981, Harry Goode Memorial Award 1985, Phil Kaufman Award 1996, Lemelson-MIT Prize 1999, Computer Hisotyr Museum Fellow Award 2002, Nat. Medal of Tech. 2002. *Publications:* Introduction to VLSI Systems (co-author with Lynn Conway) 1980, Analog VLSI and Neural Systems 1989; over 100 articles in scientific journals. *Address:* California Institute of Technology, Computer Science Department, 1200 East California Boulevard, MC 256-80, Pasadena, CA 91125, USA (office). *Telephone:* (626) 395-2814 (office). *Website:* www.cs.caltech.edu (office).

MEAD, Matthew Hansen (Matt), JD; American lawyer, politician and state governor; *Governor of Wyoming;* b. 11 March 1962, Jackson, Teton Co., Wyo.; s. of Peter Bradford Mead and the late Mary Elisabeth Mead (née Hansen); grand-s. of the late Gov. and US Senator Clifford P. Hansen; m. Carol L. Mintzer; one s. one d.; ed Trinity Univ., Univ. of Wyoming Coll. of Law; Deputy Co. Attorney, Cambell Co. Attorney's Office, Wyo. 1987–90; Asst US Attorney, US Dept of Justice 1991–95; fmr Special Asst, Attorney Gen., State of Wyo.; fmr Prosecutor, Campbell Co.; pvt. law practice, Cheyenne 1995–97; Partner, Mead & Phillips 1997–2001; US Attorney for Dist of Wyoming, Cheyenne 2001–07; unsuccessful cand. in special election for Senate seat vacated by death of Craig L. Thomas; rancher, Albany/ Goshen Co.; Owner Mead Land & Livestock, LLC; Gov. of Wyoming 2011–; mem. Bd of Dirs Wyoming Bank & Trust, Wyoming Business Council; Lifetime mem. Nat. Rifle Asscn; Republican. *Address:* Office of the Governor, State Capitol Building, Room 124, 200 West 24th Street, Cheyenne, WY 82002-0010, USA (office). *Telephone:* (307) 777-7434 (office). *Fax:* (307) 632-3909 (office). *Website:* governor.wy.gov (office).

MEADE, Reuben T.; Montserratian economist and politician; *Premier;* b. 1954; ed Univ. of the West Indies; fmr Dir and Project Man., L&M Construction Inc.; fmr Dir of Devt, Govt of Montserrat; mem. Legis. Council, Leader of the Opposition 1997–2006; fmr Minister of Agric., Land, Housing and Environment; Chief Minister of Montserrat 1991–96, 2009–11, also Minister of Finance and Econ. Devt, Tourism and Sport 2009–; Premier 2011–; mem. Movt for Change and Prosperity; Pres. Montserrat Cricket Asscn; Montserrat Certificate and Medal of Honour. *Address:* c/o Office of the Chief Minister, Govt HQ, POB 292, Brades, Montserrat.

MEADE KURIBREÑA, José Antonio, PhD; Mexican economist, lawyer and government official; *Secretary of Foreign Affairs;* b. 27 Feb. 1969, Mexico City; ed

Instituto Tecnológico Autónomo de México (ITAM), Faculty of Law of Universidad Nacional Autónoma de Mexico, Yale Univ., USA; began career in Nat. Insurance and Finance; has served as Gen. Man. of Financial Planning of Nat. System of Savings for Retirement, Asst Sec. of Savings Protection Inst. of Bank Savings Protection, Gen. Dir Bank and Savings of the Ministry of Finance, Dir Gen. of Nat. Rural Credit Bank, Dir Financiera Rural; fmr Prof. of Econs, ITAM; Under-Sec. of Dependence 2010–11; Sec. of Energy Jan.–Sept. 2011, Sec. of Finance and Public Credit 2011–12; Chair. Petróleos Mexicanos (PEMEX) 2011; Sec. of Foreign Affairs 2012–. *Publications:* several articles on microeconomics and economic analysis of law. *Address:* Secretariat of State for Foreign Affairs, Avda Juárez 20, Col. Centro, Del. Cuauhtémoc, 06010 México, DF, Mexico (office). *Telephone:* (55) 3686-5100 (office). *Fax:* (55) 3686-5582 (office). *E-mail:* comentario@sre.gob.mx (office). *Website:* www.sre.gob.mx (office).

MEADOWS, Dennis L., BA, PhD; American scientist and academic; *Professor Emeritus of Systems Policy and Social Science Research, University of New Hampshire;* b. 7 June 1942; ed Carleton Coll., Sloan School of Man., Massachusetts Inst. of Tech.; mem. Faculty, MIT during late 1960s, Dir Club of Rome Project on the Predicament of Mankind 1970–72, later Prof. in Faculties of Man., Eng and Social Sciences, fmr Dir Grad. Program in business and engineering; fmr Dir of Research Inst. at Dartmouth Coll.; Prof. Emer. of Systems Policy and Social Science Research and fmr Dir Inst. for Policy and Social Science Research, Univ. of New Hampshire 1988–; Pres. Lab for Interactive Learning; Past Pres. Int. System Dynamics Soc., Int. Simulation and Games Asscn; co-f. Balaton Group (int. network of more than 300 professionals in more than 30 countries involved in systems science, public policy and sustainable devt); Hon. DHumLitt (Univ. of New Hampshire) 2009; Japan Prize (co-recipient) 2009. *Publications:* Dynamics of Commodity Production Cycles 1970, The Limits to Growth (co-author) 1972, Toward Global Equilibrium: Collected Papers (co-ed.) 1973, Dynamics of Growth in a Finite World 1974, Beyond Growth: Essays on Alternative Futures (co-ed.) 1975, Alternatives to Growth-I: A Search for Sustainable Futures: papers adapted from entries to the 1975 George and Cynthia Mitchell Prize and from presentations before the 1975 Alternatives to Growth Conference, held at the Woodlands 1977, Beyond the Limits: Confronting Global Collapse, Envisioning a Sustainable Future 1992, The Systems Thinking Playbook 1995, Limits to Growth: The 30-Year Update (co-author) 2004; numerous papers in scientific journals. *Address:* PO Box 844, Durham, NH 03824-0844, USA (home). *Telephone:* (603) 397-7442 (home). *E-mail:* dmeadows@cisunix.unh.edu (office).

MEAKINS, Ian K.; British business executive; *Group Chief Executive, Wolseley PLC;* fmrly with Bain & Co., Procter & Gamble; Founding Partner, Kalchas Group; joined United Distillers 1991, several int. man. positions with Diageo plc, including Pres. European Major Markets and Global Supply 2000–04; mem. Bd of Dirs and CEO Alliance UniChem plc (until merger with Boots PLC 2006) 2004–06; Chief Exec. Travelex Holdings Ltd 2006–09; Group Chief Exec. Wolseley PLC 2009–; Dir Impetus Trust. *Address:* Wolseley PLC, Parkview 1220, Arlington Business Park, Theale, West Berks., RG7 4GA, England (office). *Telephone:* (118) 929-8700 (office). *Fax:* (118) 929-8701 (office). *E-mail:* info@wolseley.com (office). *Website:* www.wolseley.com (office).

MEARSHEIMER, John J., BS, MA, PhD; American academic; *R. Wendell Harrison Distinguished Service Professor of Political Science, University of Chicago;* ed Univ. of Southern Calif., Cornell Univ., West Point Mil. Acad.; served as officer in USAF 1970–75; Research Fellow, Brookings Institution 1979–80; Research Assoc., Center for Int. Affairs, Harvard Univ. 1980–82; Asst Prof., Political Science Dept, Univ. of Chicago 1982–84, Assoc. Prof. 1984–87, Prof. 1987–96, R. Wendell Harrison Distinguished Service Prof. 1996–, also Co-Dir Program on Int. Security Policy; Visiting Scholar, Olin Inst. for Strategic Studies, Harvard Univ. 1992–93; mem. American Acad. of Arts and Sciences, IISS, Chicago Council on Global Affairs, Council on Foreign Relations; mem. or fmr mem. editorial bds International Security, Security Studies, International History Review, JFQ: Joint Forces Quarterly, Journal of Transatlantic Studies, Asian Security, China Security; Clark Award for Distinguished Teaching, Cornell Univ., Quantrell Award for Distinguished Teaching, Univ. of Chicago 1985, George Kistiakowsky Scholar, American Acad. of Arts and Sciences 1986–87, Distinguished Scholar Award, Int. Studies Asscn 2004. *Publications:* Conventional Deterrence (Edgar S. Furniss, Jr Book Award) 1983, Nuclear Deterrence: Ethics and Strategy (jt ed.) 1985, Liddell Hart and the Weight of History 1988, The Tragedy of Great Power Politics (Joseph Lepgold Book Prize) 2001, The Israel Lobby and US Foreign Policy (with Stephen M. Walt) 2007; contribs to Perspectives on International Relations, London Review of Books, Middle East Policy, Foreign Policy, International Relations, New Republic, International Security, New York Times, Chicago Tribune and numerous chapters in books. *Address:* Political Science Department, University of Chicago, 5828 South University Avenue, Chicago, IL 60637, USA (office). *Telephone:* (773) 702-8667 (office). *Fax:* (773) 702-1689 (office). *E-mail:* j-mearsheimer@uchicago.edu (office). *Website:* www.uchicago.edu (office).

MEBE N'GO, Edgar Alain; Cameroonian government official and politician; *Minister of Defence;* b. 22 Jan. 1957, Sangmélima; ed Ecole Nat. d'Admin et de Magistrature, Yaoundé; mem. Rassemblement démocratique du peuple camerounais (RDPC); Econ. Affairs Adviser to Gov. of E Prov. 1985–88; Sec.-Gen. N Prov. 1988–91; Préfet, Ocean Département 1991–95; Mefou and Afamba Département 1995–96, Mfoundi Département 1996–97; Dir Civil Cabinet of the Presidency 1997–2004; Del.-Gen. for Nat. Security (head of nat. police) 2004–09; Minister-Del. at the Presidency in charge of Defence (Minister of Defence) 2009–. *Address:* Ministry of Defence, Quartier Général, Yaoundé, Cameroon (office). *Telephone:* 2223-4055 (office).

MÉBIAME, Léon; Gabonese politician; b. 1 Sept. 1934, Libreville; ed Coll. Moderne, Libreville, Centre de Préparation aux Carrières Administratives, Brazzaville, Ecole Fédérale de Police, Ecole Nat. de Police, Lyon, France; posted to Chad 1957–59; Police Supt 1960; further studies at Sûreté Nat. Française, Paris; Deputy Dir Sûreté Nat., Gabon 1962–63, Dir 1963–67; successively Under-Sec. of State for the Interior, Minister Del. for the Interior and Minister of State in charge of Labour, Social Affairs and the Nat. Org. of Gabonese Women 1967; Vice-Pres. of the Govt, Keeper of the Seals and Minister of Justice Jan.–July 1968; Vice-Pres. of the Govt in charge of Co-ordination 1968–75, Pres. Nat. Consultative Council

1972; Prime Minister 1975–90; Minister of Co-ordination, Housing and Town Planning 1975–76, of Land Registry 1976–78, of Co-ordination, Agric., Rural Devt, Waters and Forests 1978–79, in Charge of State Corpns 1980–82, for Merchant Marine and Civil Service 1982–83, of Transport and Civil and Commercial Aviation 1989–90; Presidential Cand. Dec. 1993; Commdr Etoile Equatoriale; Grand Officier, Order nat. de Côte d'Ivoire, du Mérite Centrafricain; Chevalier, Etoile Noire du Bénin. *Address:* c/o Office du Premier Ministre, BP 546, Libreville, Gabon.

MEBOUTOU, Michel Meva'a; Cameroonian politician; b. Prov. du Sud. Francophone; Minister of Finance and the Budget –2004; mem. Bd of Govs IMF; mem. Bulu tribe. *Address:* c/o Ministry of Finance and the Budget, Quartier Administratif, Yaoundé, Cameroon (office).

MECHANIC, David, BA, MA, PhD; American sociologist and academic; *Rene Dubos University Professor of Behavioral Sciences, Rutgers University;* b. 21 Feb. 1936, New York; s. of Louis Mechanic and Tillie Mechanic (née Penn); m. Kate Mechanic; two s.; ed City Coll. of New York and Stanford Univ.; mem. Faculty, Univ. of Wisconsin 1960–79, Prof. of Sociology 1965–73, John Bascom Prof. 1973–79, Dir Center for Medical Sociology and Health Services Research 1971–79, Chair. Dept of Sociology 1968–70; Prof. of Social Work and Sociology, Rutgers Univ. 1979–, Univ. Prof. and Dean Faculty of Arts and Sciences 1981–84, Rene Dubos Univ. Prof. of Behavioral Sciences 1984–, Dir Inst. for Health, Health Care Policy and Aging Research 1985–2013; mem. various advisory panels etc.; mem. NAS; mem. Inst. of Medicine of NAS, American Acad. of Arts and Sciences; Guggenheim Fellowship 1977–78; numerous awards. *Publications include:* author of 12 books and about 400 papers and chapters and ed. of 11 books on sociological and health care subjects. *Address:* Rutgers University, 83 Somerset Street, New Brunswick, NJ 08901, USA (office). *Telephone:* (732) 445-4636 (office). *E-mail:* mechanic@rci.rutgers.edu (office). *Website:* www.rutgers.edu (office).

MECHANIC, William M. (Bill), PhD; American film industry executive; b. Detroit, Mich.; ed Michigan State Univ., Univ. of Southern California; Dir of Programming SelecTV 1978–80, Vice-Pres. Programming 1980–82; Vice-Pres. Pay TV, Paramount Pictures Corpn 1982–84; Vice-Pres. Pay TV Sales, Walt Disney Pictures and TV 1984–85; Sr Vice-Pres. Video 1985–87, Pres. Int. Theatrical Distribution and Worldwide Video 1987–93; Pres. and COO 20th Century Fox Film Entertainment 1993–96, Chair. and CEO 1996–2000; f. Pandemonium LLC (ind. production co.) 2000; mem. Bd of Councilors, School of Cinema Arts, Univ. of Southern Calif.; mem. Bd of Govs Acad. of Motion Picture Arts and Sciences (Execs Br) 2002–05. *Films include:* Dark Water (producer) 2005, The New World (exec. producer) 2005. *Address:* Pandemonium LLC, 100 North Crescent Drive, Suite 125, Beverly Hills, CA 90210-5449, USA.

MEČIAR, Vladimír, DrIur; Slovak politician; *Chairman, People's Party—Movement for a Democratic Slovakia;* b. 26 July 1942, Zvolen; s. of Jozef Mečiar and Anna (née Tomková) Mečiarová; m. Margita Mečiarová (née Bencková); two s. two d.; ed Comenius Univ., Bratislava; clerk 1959–69; various posts in Czechoslovak Union of Youth 1967–68; expelled from all posts and CP; employed as manual worker because of his attitude to Soviet occupation of Czechoslovakia at Heavy Engineering Works in Dubnica nad Váhom 1970–73; clerk, later commercial lawyer for Skloobal Nemšová 1973–90; politically active again after collapse of communist system 1989; Minister of Interior and Environment, Govt of Slovak (Fed.) Repub. 1990, Deputy to House of Nations, Fed. Ass. 1990–92; Chair. People's Party—Movement for a Democratic Slovakia (Ludová strana—Hnutie za Demokratické Slovensko—LS-HZDS) 1991–; Prime Minister of Slovakia 1990–91, 1992, 1994–98; Acting Pres. of Slovakia (served alongside Ivan Gašparovič) March–Oct. 1998; Opposition mem. Parl. 2002–; presidential cand. 2004 elections; Order of Maltese Cross 1995; Dr hc (Lomonosov Univ., Moscow) 1995, (Brača Karić Univ., Yugoslavia) 1996; Peutinger Award (Germany) 1995. *Publications:* Slovakia, Be Self-Confident!, Slovak Taboo. *Leisure interests:* sport, music, literature, hiking. *Address:* People's Party—Movement for a Democratic Slovakia (Ludová strana—Hnutie za Demokratické Slovensko), Tomášikova 32A, PO Box 49, 830 00 Bratislava, Slovakia (office). *Telephone:* (2) 4822-0203 (office). *Fax:* (2) 4822-0223 (office). *E-mail:* predseda@hzds.sk (office). *Website:* www.hzds.sk (office).

MECKSEPER, Friedrich; German painter and printmaker; b. 8 June 1936, Bremen; s. of Gustav Meckseper and Lily Ringel-Debatin; m. Barbara Müller 1962; one s. two d.; ed State Art Acad., Stuttgart, State Univ. for the Visual Arts, Berlin; apprentice mechanic, Robert Bosch GmbH, Stuttgart 1952–55; more than 100 solo and group exhbns of his prints, collages and paintings in Europe, USA, Australia and Japan; represented in many major museums of contemporary art and at print biennials world-wide; Prof. of Art, Int. Summer Acad., Salzburg 1977–79; Guest Lecturer, London 1968; German-Rome Prize 1963, Prize of the 7th Bienniale, Tokyo 1970, of the 6th Bienniale, Fredrikstad 1982, of the 1st Kochi Int. Print Triennial, Japan 1990. *Publications:* Friedrich Meckseper, Etchings 1956–1994; catalogue raisonné of the graphic work 1994. *Leisure interests:* locomotives, steamboats, ballooning, paintings, etchings, books. *Address:* Landhausstrasse 13, 10717 Berlin, Germany.

MEDAK, Peter; British/Hungarian/American film, theatre, opera and television director; b. 23 Dec. 1937, Budapest, Hungary; m. 1st Katherine La Kermance; m. 2nd Carolyn Seymour; m. 3rd Julia Migenes 1989; two s. four d.; worked with AB-Pathe, London 1956–63; Dir Universal Pictures 1963–, Paramount Pictures 1967–; has directed several operas, plays and series for US TV; Evening Standard Award for Best Director and Film: The Krays 1990. *Plays directed include:* Miss Julie. *Operas directed include:* Salome (Richard Strauss), La Voix Humaine (Poulenc), Schubert. *Films directed include:* Negatives 1968, A Day in the Death of Joe Egg 1970, The Ruling Class 1973, Third Girl From the Left 1973, Ghost in the Noonday Sun 1975, The Odd Job 1978, The Changeling 1979, Zorro, The Gay Blade 1981, Breaking Through 1984, The Men's Club 1986, The Krays 1990, La Voix Humaine 1991, Let Him Have It 1991, Romeo is Bleeding 1994, Pontiac Moon 1994, Hunchback of Notre Dame 1996, Species II 1997, David Copperfield 1998, Peter Gabriel: Play (video) 2004. *Television includes:* Court Marshall 1965, The Third Girl from the Left 1973, Space 1999 (two episodes) 1976–77, Alfred Nobel, The Babysitter 1980, Mistress of Paradise 1981, Hart to Hart (two episodes) 1982, Cry for the Strangers 1982, Remington Steele 1983, Faerie Tale Theatre (five episodes) 1984–87, Magnum, P.I. 1985, The Twilight Zone (seven episodes) 1985–87, Crime

Story 1987, Beauty and the Beast 1987, China Beach 1989, Nabokov 1989, Tales from the Crypt 1992, Homicide: Life on the Street (six episodes) 1994–98, Falls Road, Kindred 1996, The Hunchback 1997, Law & Order: Special Victims Unit 1999, David Copperfield 2000, Feasts of All Saints 2001, The Guardian 2001, The Wire 2002, South Beach 2002, Carnivale 2003, 7th Heaven 2004, House M.D. 2004, Marple: By The Pricking of My Thumbs 2006, In Justice 2006, Masters of Horror 2007, Sex and Lies in Sin City 2008, Breaking Bad 2009, Cold Case 2009. *Address:* c/o Sean Gasconie, United Agents Ltd, 12–26 Lexington Street, London, W1F 0LE, England (office); c/o Abram Nalibotsky, Amy Retzinger, Sean Barclay, The Gersh Agency, 9465 Wilshire Blvd, Suite 600, Beverly Hills, CA 90212, USA (office); c/o George Hayum, Hirsch Wallerstein Hayum Matlof & Fishman – Attorneys at Law, 10100 Santa Monica Blvd, Suite 1700, Los Angeles, CA 90067, USA. *Telephone:* (20) 3214-0800 (office); (310) 274-6611 (office); (310) 703-1777. *Fax:* (20) 3214-0801 (office); (310) 703-1799. *E-mail:* info@unitedagents.co.uk (office); info@gershla.com (office); ghayum@hwhmf.com. *Website:* unitedagents.co.uk (office); www .gershagency.com (office); www.hwhmf.com.

MEDELCI, Mourad, LèsSc, DèsSc; Algerian government official; b. 30 April 1943, Tlemcen; m.; five c.; ed Univ. of Algiers; began career working in Algerian energy industry 1970–80; Sec.-Gen., Ministry of Commerce 1980–88; Minister of Trade 1988–89, 1999–2001, of Finance 2001–02, 2005–07, of Foreign Affairs 2007–13; Minister Delegate of the Budget 1990–91; Adviser to Pres. of Algeria 2002–05; Gov. for Algeria, Islamic Devt Bank; Vice-Pres. Emir Abdelkader Foundation 1996; founding mem. Asscn for Int. Relations 1997; Founder and Pres. Asscn for Promotion of Eco-effectiveness and Quality in Enterprises (APEQUE) 1998; mem. African Peer Review (APR) Panel of Eminent Persons 2004. *Address:* c/o Ministry of Foreign Affairs, place Mohamed Seddik Benyahia, el-Mouradia, Algiers, Algeria (office).

MEDGYESSY, Péter, PhD; Hungarian politician, economist and diplomatist; b. 19 Oct. 1942, Budapest; m. 2nd Katalin Csaplár; one s. one d. (from previous marriage); ed Budapest Univ. of Econs (then Karl Marx Univ.); held several positions in Ministry of Finance, Dept of Finance, Dept of Prices, Dept of Int. Finances; fmr Dir-Gen. Dept of State Budget; Deputy Minister of Finance 1982–87; Minister of Finance 1987–88; Deputy Prime Minister in interim Govt of Miklós Németh (q.v.) 1988–89; Pres., Chief Exec. Magyar Paribas 1990–94; Pres. and CEO Hungarian Bank for Investment and Devt Ltd 1994–96; Minister of Finance 1996–98; Chair. Bd Dirs Inter-Europa Bank 1998–2001; Vice-Pres. Atlasz Insurance Co. 1998–2001; Prime Minister of Hungary 2002–04 (resgnd), Man. Prime Minister Aug.–Sept. 2004; Amb. at Large 2004–08; Prof., Coll. of Finance and Accounting, Budapest; Pres. Hungarian Econ. Soc.; Dir Int. Inst. of Public Finance, Saarbrücken; mem. Presidium Hungarian Bank Asscn 1996–, Council of World Econ. Forum; Commdr's Cross with Star, Order of Merit of Hungarian Repub. 1998, Chevalier de la Légion d'honneur 2000, Officer's Cross 2004, Order of Crown of Belgium 2002, Order of the Rising Sun – Gold and Silver Star (Japan) 2002, Grand Cross, Order of Merit (Chile) 2003, Grand Cross, Order of Merit (Norway) 2003, Grand Cross, Order of Merit (Germany) 2004; Medal of Irish Hungarian Econ. Asscn 2005. *Publications:* several articles on budgetary and exchange rate policies and monetary system in financial and econ. publs. *Leisure interests:* nature, music.

MEDINA, Cuauhtémoc, BA, PhD; Mexican art critic, historian and curator; *Chief Curator, Museo Universitario Arte Contemporáneo;* b. (Cuauhtémoc Medina González), 5 Dec. 1965, Mexico City; s. of José Humberto Medina Ortiz and Gladys González Alarcón; m. Danna Levin Rojo (divorced); one d.; partner Cristina Paoli Charles; ed Univ. Nacional Autónoma de Mexico, Mexico City, Univ. of Essex, England; Researcher, Instituto de Investigaciones Estéticas, Univ. Nacional Autónoma de Mexico 1992–, Chief Curator, Museo Universitario Arte Contemporáneo (MUAC), Mexico City 2013–; mem. Curare (Espacio Crítico para las Artes) 1992–97; columnist, Reforma newspaper 2000–13; First Curator, Latin American Art Collections, Tate London 2002–08; co-f. Teratoma, group of curators, critics and anthropologists, Mexico City 2003–09; Dir 7th Int. Symposium on Contemporary Art Theory, Mexico City 2009; has taught at Center for Curatorial Studies, Bard Coll., USA; Walter Hopps Award for Curatorial Achievement 2013. *Publications include:* Graciela Iturbide 55 2001, Francis Alÿs: Cuando la fe mueve montañas/When Faith Moves Mountains 2005, Francis Alÿs 2007, Manifesta 9: The Deep of the Modern (co-ed.) 2012; essays and articles in numerous publs. *Address:* Museo Universitario Arte Contemporáneo (MUAC), Universidad Nacional Autónoma de Mexico, Insurgentes Sur 3000, Ciudad Universitaria, Coyoacán, DF 04510 Mexico (office). *Telephone:* (55) 5622-6911 (office). *E-mail:* cuauhtemoc .medina@muac.unam.mx (office). *Website:* muac.unam.mx (office).

MEDINA, Danilo; Dominican Republic politician and head of state; *President;* b. Arroyo Cano, San Juan de la Maguana; s. of Juan Pablo Medina and Amelia Sánchez; m. Cándida Montilla; three d.; ed Universidad Autónoma de Santo Domingo (UASD), INTEC; f. San Juan de la Maguana br., Frente Revolucionario Estudiantil Nacionalista, UASD; joined Partido de la Liberación Dominicana 1973, mem. Cen. Cttee 1983; elected Deputy, Nat. Congress 1986, Pres. Chamber of Deputies 1990–94; Sec. of State to the Presidency 1996–2006; unsuccessful cand. for Pres. of Dominican Repub. 2000, 2006; President 2012–. *Address:* Office of the President, Palacio Nacional, Avda México, esq. Dr Delgado, Gazcue, Santo Domingo, Dominican Republic (office). *Telephone:* 695-8000 (office). *Fax:* 682-4558 (office). *Website:* www.presidencia.gob.do (office).

MEDINA ESTÉVEZ, HE Cardinal Jorge Arturo, DTheol, DCL; Chilean ecclesiastic; *Prefect Emeritus of Divine Worship and the Discipline of the Sacraments;* b. 23 Dec. 1926, Santiago de Chile; ed Major Seminary of Santiago; ordained priest 1954; mem. Major Seminary of Santiago, Theological Faculty of Santiago; attended Second Vatican Council early 1960s; Auxiliary Bishop of Rancagua and Titular Bishop of Tibili 1984–87, consecrated 1985, Bishop of Rancagua 1987–93, of Valparaíso 1993–96; Pro-Prefect Congregation for Divine Worship and the Discipline of the Sacraments 1996–98, Prefect 1998–2002, Prefect Emer. 2002–; cr. Cardinal (Cardinal-Deacon of San Saba) 1998, Cardinal Proto-Deacon –2007, Cardinal-Priest of San Saba 2008–; participated in Papal Conclave 2005, announced to the world the election of Pope Benedict XVI. *Address:* c/o Congregation for Divine Worship and the Discipline of the Sacraments, Palazzo delle Congregazioni, Piazza Pio XII 10, 00193 Rome, Italy. *Telephone:* (06) 69884005. *Website:* www.vatican.va/roman_curia/congregations/ccdds.

MEDINA-MORA ICAZA, Eduardo Tomas, LLB; Mexican politician and diplomatist; *Ambassador to USA;* b. 30 Jan. 1957, Mexico City; s. of Raúl Medina Mora Martin del Campo and Luisa Icaza Conrey; m. Laura Perez de Medina-Mora; three c.; ed Nat. Univ. of Mexico; fmr Asst Dir DESC, Corp. Strategic Planning Dir 1991–2000; fmr Co-ordinator of Advisers to Under-Secr. of Fisheries; fmr Head of Dept of Promotion and Market Research, Conasupo; fmr adviser to NAFTA Negotiating Team for Agric., Norms, Unfair Trading Practices, Investment and Rules of Origin; fmr legal adviser to Nat. Agric. and Fisheries Bd; fmr nat. adviser to Business Co-ordination Bd; fmr Dir Tech. Secr. Alliance for the Mexico-US Border; Gen. Dir Center for Research and Nat. Security (CISEN, civil intelligence agency) 2000–05; Sec. of State for Public Security 2005–06; Attorney Gen. 2006–09 (resgnd); Amb. to UK 2009–12, to USA 2013–; mem. and Nat. Tech. Sec., Nat. Security Cabinet; mem. Nat. Security Council; mem. Mexican Coll. of Lawyers, ABA; Orden del Mérito Civil, Reino de España; Medalla Blanca CNP España, Medalla de Honor Policía Nacional de Colombia. *Publications:* Las Pesquerías en la Zona Económica Exclusiva 1979, Uso Legítimo de la Fuerza 2008. *Address:* Embassy of Mexico, 1911 Pennsylvania Avenue NW, Washington, DC 20006, USA (office). *Telephone:* (202) 728-1600 (office). *Fax:* (202) 234-1698 (office). *E-mail:* mexembusa@sre.gob .mx (office). *Website:* embamex.sre.gob.mx/eua (office).

MEDINA QUIROGA, Cecilia, Licenciada en Ciencias Jurídicas y Sociale, DIur; Chilean jurist and academic; b. 17 Nov. 1935, Concepción; ed Univ. of Chile, Santiago, Univ. of Utrecht, Netherlands; Prof. of Int. Law of Human Rights, Faculty of Law, Univ. of Chile, Founder and Co-Dir Human Rights Centre; Visiting Prof., Harvard Law School, USA; has also taught at Lund Univ., Int. Inst. of Human Rights, Univ. of Toronto, UN Univ. for Peace, Univ. of Utrecht and in Sweden; mem. UN Human Rights Cttee 1995–2002, Chair. 1999–2000, author of General Comment 28 on the rights of men and women as set out in Article 3 of the Int. Covenant on Civil and Political Rights; Judge, Inter-American Court of Human Rights (Corte Interamericana de Derechos Humanos) 2004–09, Vice-Pres. 2007–08, Pres. 2008–09; mem. Int. Comm. of Jurists 2004–; selected by UN Human Rights Council for group of ind. experts assigned to investigate Nov. 2006 Beit Hanoun incident Dec. 2006; Commdr, Order of Orange Nassau (Netherlands); Gruber Prize for Women's Rights, Peter Gruber Foundation Int. Awards 2006. *Publications:* Nomenclature and Hierarchy: Basic Latin American Sources (co-author) 1979, Chile: La Nueva Constitución, Democracia y Derechos Humanos, Cuadernos ESIN, No. 18 1981, The Battle of Human Rights: Gross, Systematic Violations and the Inter-American System 1988, Derecho Internacional de los Derechos Humanos. Manual de Enseñanza (ed.) 1990, SIM Special No. 13, Training Course on International Human Rights Law: Selected Lectures, Peace Palace, The Hague, 16 Sept.–4 Oct. 1991 (ed.) 1992, Special Issue on The Americas, NQHR, Vol. 10, No. 2 (ed.) 1992, Constitución, Tratados y Derechos Esenciales Introducción y Selección de textos, Corporación Nacional de Reparación y Reconciliación 1994, Sistema Jurídico y Derechos Humanos. El derecho nacional y las obligaciones internacionales de Chile en materia de Derechos Humanos (co-ed.) 1996; numerous book chapters and articles in professional journals. *Address:* Centro de Derechos Humanos, Facultad de Derecho, Pio Nono 1, Santiago, Chile (office). *Telephone:* (2) 9785271 (office). *Fax:* (2) 9785366 (office). *E-mail:* diredh@ derecho.uchile.cl (office). *Website:* www.derecho.uchile.cl/cdh (office).

MEDINA VILLAVEIRÁN, Ernesto; Cuban economist and central banker; *President, Banco Central de Cuba;* has worked in Cuban banking sector since 1977; worked on int. mission in Angola; Pres. Banco Financiero Internacional SA –2009; Pres. Banco Central de Cuba 2009–. *Address:* Office of the President, Banco Central de Cuba, Cuba 410, Municipio Habana Viejo, Havana 10100, Cuba (office). *Telephone:* (7) 60-4811 (office). *Fax:* (7) 66-6601 (office). *E-mail:* chely@bc.gov.cu (office). *Website:* www.bc.gov.cu (office).

MEDIU, Fatmir; Albanian politician; *Minister of the Environment, Forestry and Water Administration;* b. 21 Jan. 1967, Durrës; m. Xhuljeta Mediu; two c.; ed Faculty of Geology and Mines, Tirana Univ.; engineer Albpetrol Enterprise, Fier 1990–91; joined Republican Party 1990, Chair. Fier Dist Br. 1991–92, Deputy Chair. Albanian Republican Party 1992–97, Chair. 1997–; elected mem. Parl. 2001, Chair. Republican Parl. Group 2001–05, Chair. Parl. Comm. on Stability Pact and European Integration 2001–05, mem. Comm. for Legislation and Foreign Affairs 2001–05, mem. Del. to European Parl. 2001–05; Minister of Defence 2005–08 (resgnd), of the Environment, Forestry and Water Admin 2009–; Pres. Building Democracy Foundation, Tirana 1998; mem. Int. Foundation, Washington DC, USA 1999, Exec. Cttee East–West Parliamentarian Practice, Amsterdam, Netherlands 2001, Parliamentarians for Global Action, New York 2002. *Address:* c/o Ministry of the Environment, Forestry and Water Administration, Rruga Durrësit 27, Tirana, Albania (office). *Telephone:* (4) 2270630 (office). *Fax:* (4) 2270627 (office). *E-mail:* info@moe.gov.al (office). *Website:* www.moe.gov.al (office).

MEDOJEVIĆ, Nebojša; Montenegrin politician; *President, Movement for Changes (Pokret za Promjene—PZP);* b. 13 June 1966, Pljevlja; m.; one s. one d.; ed Faculty of Electrical Eng., Univ. of Montenegro; Founder and Pres. Students Forum-Movt for Peace 1989; Founder Montenegrin Movt against Facism 1992; Co-founder Social-Democratic Party 1989, mem. of Presidency 1992–99; worked as Privatisation Man, Agency for Econ. Restructuring and Foreign Investments 1991–99; Leader Centre for Transition, Podgorica 1999–2002; Exec. Dir Group for Change 2002–06; Pres. and Leader, Movt for Changes (Pokret za Promjene—PZP); mem. Parl. 2006–; cand. for Pres. of Montenegro 2008. *Publications include:* Montenegrin Economy in Transition, Mass Voucher Privatisation, Public Procurements, Privatisation and Corruption, Conflict of Interests; has published more than 100 articles on problems of post-Communism transition. *Address:* Movement for Changes (Pokret za Promjene—PZP), 81000 Podgorica, bul. Ivana Crnojevica 107/1, Montenegro (office). *Telephone:* (81) 667010 (office). *E-mail:* gzpkotor@cg.yu (office); nm@nebojsamedojevic.org. *Website:* www.promjene.org (office); www.nebojsamedojevic.

MEDVEDCHUK, Viktor Volodymyrovich, DIur; Ukrainian politician, lawyer and business executive; *Chairman, Ukrainian Choice;* b. 7 Aug. 1954, Pochet Village, Aban Rayon, Krasnoyarsk Krai, Russian SFSR; s. of Volodymyr Nesterovych Medvedchuk and Faina Hryhorivna Hulko; m. Oksana Marchenko 1973; two d.; ed Nat. Taras Shevchenko Univ. of Kiev; lawyer, Kiev City Bar Asscn 1978–89; Head, Legal Advice Office, Shevchenko Dist, Kiev 1989–91; Pres. Union of Lawyers of Ukraine; fmr Head of the Supreme Board of Experts of the Ukrainian

Bar; Pres. Int. Law Co. B.I.M. 1991–; mem. Social Democratic Party of Ukraine (SDPU) (later Social Democratic Party of Ukraine (United)—SDPU(U)) 1994–, SDPU(U) Cen. Council 1995–98, Head, SDPU Comm. on Legal Reform 1995–96, mem. SDPU(U) Politburo 1995–, Deputy Chair. SDPU(U) 1996–98, Chair. 1998–2006, mem. SDPU(U) Parl. faction 2001–; Adviser to Pres. of Ukraine on Tax Policy Issues 1996–2000; Nat. Deputy of Ukraine to 2nd Verkhovna Rada 1997, mem. Cttee on Law and Order 1997–98, Co-ordinating Council on Legal Reforms affiliated to Pres. of Ukraine 1997–2000, Supreme Econ. Council affiliated to Pres. of Ukraine, State Comm. on Admin. Reforms in Ukraine, Nat. Deputy to 3rd Verkhovna Rada 1998, Deputy Chair. Verkhovna Rada 1998–2000, mem. Supreme Legal Council, Coordinating Council on Local Self-Govt, Deputy Chair. Co-ordinating Council on Internal Affairs, First Deputy Chair. Verkhovna Rada of Ukraine 2000–01, Nat. Deputy to 4th Verkhovna Rada, Head, SDPU(U) Parl. faction May–June 2002; Head, Admin of Pres. of Ukraine 2002–04; mem. Supreme Council of Justice from 2008; currently Chair. pro-Russian Ukrainian Choice which opposes Euromaidan protests supporting closer ties between Ukraine and the EU; Head, Nat. Council on Youth Policies affiliated to Pres. of Ukraine 1999–; Head, Comm. on State Awards and Heraldry 2002–, Organizing Cttee on Conduct of the Year of Ukraine in the Russian Fed. 2002–03, Working Group for putting forward suggestions on ensuring publicity and openness in work of public authorities 2002–; Chair. Comm. for guaranteeing smooth work of int. experts checking export of Kolchuga reconnaissance radio-electronic stations 2002–, Ukraina Nat. Palace Supervisory Bd 2002–, Organizing Cttee for carrying out the Year of the Russian Fed. in Ukraine 2002–, Public Service Coordinating Cttee under Pres. of Ukraine 2003–, Organizing Cttee for commemorating the Eastern (Crimean) War of 1853–1856 2003–, Coordinating Comm. for the reconstruction of the Zhashkiv-Chervonoznamyanka section of the Kiev-Odesa motorway 2003–, Organizing Cttee for celebrating the 150th anniversary of Ivan Franko's birthday 2003–, Supervisory Bd of Nat. Acad. of Public Admin under Pres. of Ukraine 2004–; Deputy Chair. Information Policy Council under Pres. of Ukraine 2002–; Co-Chair. Coordinating Cttee for charting and publishing the Nat. Atlas of Ukraine 2002–; mem. Bd USSR Union of Lawyers from Ukraine 1990–91, Coordinating Cttee on Struggle against Corruption and Organised Crime affiliated to Pres. of Ukraine 1994–99, Council of Employers and Producers affiliated to Pres. of Ukraine 1995–2000, Nat. Council for Security and Defence of Ukraine 2002–; mem. Ukrainian Acad. of Law, Int. Slavic Acad., Acad. of Econs; Honoured Lawyer of Ukraine 1992; Hon. Award of Ukrainian Pres.– Order 'For Merit' (3rd Class) 1996, (2nd Class) 1998, Order 'For Merit' 2000, Hon. Award of Ukrainian Pres.– Order of Prince Yaroslav the Wise (5th Class) 2004, Slovak Order of the White Cross (2nd Class) 2004. *E-mail:* info@medvedchuk.org.ua. *Website:* medvedchuk .org.ua.

MEDVEDEV, Armen Nikolayevich, Cand. of Arts; Russian film critic, film producer, journalist and civil servant; b. 28 May 1938, Moscow; m.; one d.; ed All-Union Inst. of Cinematography; mem. staff, Bureau of Propaganda of Soviet Cinema, USSR (now Russian) State Cttee on Cinematography 1959–, mem. Bd Dirs 1984–87, First Deputy Chair. 1987–89, Chair. 1992–99; Prof., All-Union Inst. of Cinematography; Ed.-in-Chief Soviet Film (magazine) 1966–72; Deputy Ed.-in-Chief Iskusstvo Kino (magazine) 1972–75, 1976–82, Ed.-in-Chief 1982–84; Ed.-in-Chief All-Union Co. Soyuzinformkino 1975–76; Head Dept of Culture and Public Educ., USSR Council of Ministers 1989–91; fmr consultant Govt of USSR 1991; Pres. Rolan Bykov Int. Fund of Devt of Cinema and TV for Children and Youth 1999–; Pres. 18th Int. Film Festival for Children and Young People 2001; Chair. Jury, Open Russian Film Festival, Sochi 2004; mem. Jury, XXVIth Moscow Int. Film Festival 2004; Hon. Worker of Arts; several decorations, including Order for Service to Motherland; numerous awards. *Films produced:* Velikiy polkovodets Georgiy Zhukov 1995, Khrustalyov, mashinu! Khrustalyov, My Car!) 1998. *Television role:* Krasnaya ploschad (Red Square) (mini-series) 2004. *Publications:* several books on cinema; articles and essays. *Address:* Koshtoyanz str. 6, Apt 225, 117454 Moscow, Russia. *Telephone:* (495) 133-12-19.

MEDVEDEV, Dmitrii Anatolyevich, PhD; Russian business executive, government official and fmr head of state; *Chairman of the Government;* b. 14 Sept. 1965, Leningrad (now St Petersburg); s. of Anatoly Afanasevich Medvedev and Yulia Veniaminovna Medvedeva (née Shaposhnikova); m. Svetlana Vladimirovna Linnik 1993; one s.; ed Leningrad State Univ.; Asst Prof., Leningrad State Univ. 1990–99; Adviser to Chair. Leningrad City Council and Expert Consultant, Cttee for External Relations, St Petersburg Mayor's Office 1990–95, mem. Exec. Cttee on Int. Relations 1991–95; Deputy Chief of Staff, Govt of Russian Fed. 1999–2000; Deputy Head, then First Deputy Head of Presidential Admin 2000–03, Head 2003–05; First Deputy Chair. of the Govt 2005–08; Pres. of Russian Fed. 2008–12; Chair. of the Govt 2012–; Chair. United Russia (Yedínaya Rossíya) 2012–; mem. Bd of Dirs OAO Gazprom 2000–08, Chair. 2000–01, 2002–08, Deputy Chair. 2001–02; Order in the Name of Russia 2004; ranked by Forbes magazine amongst The World's Most Powerful People (43rd) 2009, (12th) 2010, (59th) 2011, (61st) 2012, (53rd) 2013. *Publications include:* two short articles on the subject of his doctoral dissertation in Russian law journals, co-author of a textbook on civil law for univs first published 1991, Questions of Russia's National Development (textbook for univs) 2007, A Commentary on the Federal Law 'On the State Civil Service of the Russian Federation' (lead co-author) 2008. *Leisure interests:* British hard rock, including Deep Purple, Black Sabbath, Pink Floyd and Led Zeppelin, swimming, jogging, chess, yoga, reading the works of Mikhail Bulgakov and the Harry Potter books of J. K. Rowling, football (follows FC Zenit St Petersburg). *Address:* Office of the Chairman of the Government, 103274 Moscow, Krasnopresnenskaya nab. 2, Russia (office). *Telephone:* (495) 205-57-35 (office). *Fax:* (495) 205-42-19 (office). *Website:* www.government.ru (office), www.premier.gov.ru (office); er.ru (office).

MEDVEDEV, Nikolai Pavlovich; Russian politician; b. 26 Nov. 1952, Anayevo, Mordovia; m.; one s. one d.; ed Mordovian State Pedagogical Inst., Higher Comsomol School, Cen. Comsomol Cttee; with Saransk Professional Tech. School; worked in Comsomol orgs 1975–83; instructor, Saransk City CP Cttee, Sec. CP Cttee Saransk Machine-construction Factory 1983–90; Deputy Chair. Saransk City Soviet 1990–; RSFSR Peoples' Deputy; mem. Presidium, Supreme Soviet; mem. Comm. on Int. Relations at Soviet of Nationalities 1990–93; Head of Dept, Admin. of Russian Presidency 1993–94; Dir Inst. of Regional Policy 1995–97; Deputy Minister on Co-operation with CIS countries 1994–95; mem. State Duma

(Yabloko group) 1996–99; Dir Moscow Inst. of Regional Policy 2000–. *Publications:* several books including Establishment of Federalism in Russia, National Policy in Russia: From Unitarism to Federalism, International Conflicts and Political Stability. *Address:* Moscow Institute of Regional Policy, Moscow, Russia.

MEDVEDEV, Nikolai Yakovlevich, DrSc; Russian energy industry executive; *Chief Geologist and Deputy Director-General, OJSC Surgutneftegas;* b. 1943; Chief Geologist Neftyanaya Kompaniya Surgutneftegas 2000–03, Chief Geologist and Deputy Dir-Gen. OJSC Surgutneftegas 2000–, Chair. March–May 2006. *Address:* OJSC Surgutneftegas, 1 Kukuevitskogo Street, Surgut 628400, Tyumen, Russia (office). *Telephone:* (3462) 42-61-33 (office). *Fax:* (3462) 33-32-35 (office). *Website:* www.surgutneftegas.ru (office).

MEDVEDEV, Roy Aleksandrovich, PhD; Russian historian and sociologist; b. 14 Nov. 1925, Tbilisi; s. of Aleksandr Romanovich Medvedev and Yulia Medvedeva (née Reiman); twin brother of Zhores Medvedev (q.v.); m. Galina A. Gaidina 1956; one s.; ed Leningrad State Univ., Acad. of Pedagogical Sciences of USSR; mem. CPSU –1969, 1989–91; worker at mil. factory 1943–46; teacher of history, Ural Secondary School 1951–53; Dir of Secondary School in Leningrad region 1954–56; Deputy to Ed.-in-Chief of Publishing House of Pedagogical Literature, Moscow 1957–59; Head of Dept, Research Inst. of Vocational Educ., Acad. of Pedagogical Sciences of USSR 1960–70, Senior Scientist 1970–71; freelance author 1972–; People's Deputy of USSR, mem. Supreme Soviet of USSR 1989–91; mem. Cen. Cttee CPSU 1990–91; Co-Chair. Socialist Party of Labour 1991–2003. *Publications:* Vocational Education in Secondary School 1960, Faut-il réhabiliter Staline? 1969, A Question of Madness (with Zhores Medvedev) 1971, Let History Judge 1972, On Socialist Democracy 1975, Qui a écrit le 'Don Paisible'? 1975, La Révolution d'octobre était-elle inéluctable? 1975, Solschenizyn und die Sowjetische Linke 1976, Khrushchev–The Years in Power (with Zhores Medvedev) 1976, Political Essays 1976, Problems in the Literary Biography of Mikhail Sholokhov 1977, Samizdat Register 1978, Philip Mironov and the Russian Civil War (with S. Starikov) 1978, The October Revolution 1979, On Stalin and Stalinism 1979, On Soviet Dissent 1980, Nikolai Bukharin–The Last Years 1980, Leninism and Western Socialism 1981, An End to Silence 1982, Khrushchev 1983, All Stalin's Men 1984, China and Superpowers 1986, L'URSS che cambia (with G. Chiesa) 1987, Time of Change (with G. Chiesa) 1990, Brezhnev: A Political Biography 1991, Gensek s Lybianki: A Political Portrait of Andropov 1993, 1917. The Russian Revolution 1997, Capitalism in Russia? 1998, The Unknown Andropov 1998, Post-Soviet Russia 2000, The Unknown Stalin (with Zhores Medvedev) 2004, Putin 2004, Solzhenitsyn and Sakharov (with Zhores Medvedev) 2004, Moscow Model of Yuri Luzhkov 2005, Putin 2007, Divided Ukraine 2007, Nursaltan Nazarbayev 2008, The Soviet Union. The Last Years 2009, Boris Yeltsyn 2010; and over 400 professional and general articles. *Leisure interest:* allotment gardening. *Address:* c/o Z. A. Medvedev, 4 Osborn Gardens, London, NW7 1DY, England (home); Pos.Novo-Ivanovskoye 129, Post Box 16, P/O Nemchinovka, Odintsovky district, 143025 Moscow, Russia (home). *Telephone:* (495) 597-6120 (Moscow) (home).

MEDVEDEV, Zhores Aleksandrovich, PhD; British/Russian biologist (retd); b. 14 Nov. 1925, Tbilisi; s. of Aleksandr Romanovich Medvedev and Yulia Medvedeva (née Reiman); twin brother of Roy Medvedev (q.v.); m. Margarita Nikolayevna Buzina 1951; two s.; ed Timiriazev Acad. of Agricultural Sciences, Moscow, Inst. of Plant Physiology, USSR Acad. of Sciences; joined Soviet Army 1943, served at front as a pvt.; Scientist, later Sr Scientist, Dept of Agrochemistry and Biochemistry, Timiriazev Acad. 1951–62; Head of Lab., Molecular Radiobiology, Inst. of Medical Radiology, Obninsk 1963–69; Sr Scientist All-Union Scientific Research Inst. of Physiology and Biochemistry of Farm Animals, Borovsk 1970–72; Sr Scientist, Nat. Inst. for Medical Research, London 1973–92; mem. American Gerontological Soc., Biochemical Soc., Genetic Soc.; Soviet citizenship restored 1990; Book Award, Moscow Naturalist Soc. 1965, Aging Research Award of US Aging Asscn 1984, René Schubert Preis in Gerontology 1985. *Publications include:* Protein Biosynthesis and Problems of Heredity, Development and Ageing 1963, Molecular-Genetic Mechanisms of Development 1968, The Rise and Fall of T. D. Lysenko 1969, The Medvedev Papers 1970, A Question of Madness (with Roy Medvedev) 1971, Ten Years After 1973, Khrushchev – The Years in Power (with Roy Medvedev) 1976, Soviet Science 1978, The Nuclear Disaster in the Urals 1979, Andropov 1983, Gorbachev 1986, Soviet Agriculture 1987, The Legacy of Chernobyl 1990, The Unknown Stalin (with Roy Medvedev) 2001, Stalin and the Jewish Problem 2003, Solzhenitsyn and Sakharov (with Roy Medvedev) 2004, Nutrition and Longevity 2007, Polonii v Londone 2008; more than 400 papers and articles on gerontology, genetics, biochemistry, environment, history and other topics. *Leisure interests:* social research and writing, gardening. *Address:* 4 Osborn Gardens, London, NW7 1DY, England (home). *Telephone:* (20) 8346-4158 (home). *E-mail:* zhmedvedev@ yahoo.co.uk (home).

MEDZHITOV, Ruslan M., BSc, PhD; Uzbekistani immunologist, biochemist and academic; *David W. Wallace Professor of Immunobiology, School of Medicine, Yale University;* b. Tashkent; ed Tashkent State Univ., Moscow Univ.; postdoctoral studies at Yale Univ. Medical School, currently David W. Wallace Prof. of Immunobiology; Investigator, Howard Hughes Medical Inst.; mem. NAS 2010; Dr hc (Munich); MA Privatum (Yale Univ.); selected as Searle Scholar 2000, William B. Coley Award for Distinguished Research in Basic and Tumor Immunology, Cancer Research Inst., Emil von Behring Award, AAI-BD Biosciences Investigator Award, Blavatnik Award for Young Scientists, New York Acad. of Arts and Sciences, Howard Taylor Ricketts Award, Univ. of Chicago, Lewis S. Rosenstiel Award for Distinguished Work in Basic Medical Science, Brandeis Univ. 2010, Shaw Prize in Life Science and Medicine (co-recipient) 2012. *Publications:* numerous papers in professional journals. *Address:* Department of Immunobiology, Anlyan Center for Medical Research and Education, 300 Cedar Street, PO Box 208011, New Haven, CT 06520-8011, USA (office). *Telephone:* (203) 785-7541 (office). *E-mail:* ruslan.medzhitov@yale.edu (office). *Website:* immunobiology.yale .edu (office).

MEECE, Roger A., BS; American diplomatist and UN official; b. 1949, Indianapolis, Ind.; ed Michigan State Univ., Nat. Defence Coll. of Canada, US Foreign Service Inst.; Peace Corps volunteer in Sierra Leone 1971, several Peace Corps staff assignments, including Assoc. Dir for Peace Corps in Niger and Cameroon, Deputy Dir for Peace Corps, Brazzaville, Repub. of the Congo, Dir Peace Corps in Gabon; joined Foreign Service 1979, served in Embassies in

Cameroon and Malawi, worked in Bureau of Int. Narcotics Matters, Washington, DC, assigned to Office of Vice-Pres. of the USA 1986–88, Deputy Chief of Mission, Brazzaville, Consul-Gen., Halifax, Canada, Deputy Chief of Mission, Kinshasa 1995–98, Dir for Cen. African Affairs, State Dept 1998–2000, Amb. to Malawi 2000–03, Diplomat-in-Residence, Florida Int. Univ. 2003, served as Chargé d'affaires a.i., Embassy in Nigeria 2003, Amb. to Democratic Repub. of the Congo 2004–07, Chargé d'affaires a.i., Embassy in Ethiopia 2010; Special Rep. of the Sec.-Gen. and Head, UN Org. Stabilization Mission in the Democratic Repub. of the Congo (MONUSCO) 2010–13.

MEEK, Paul Derald, BS; American business executive; b. 15 Aug. 1930, McAllen, Tex.; s. of William Van Meek and Martha Mary Meek (née Sharp); m. Betty Catherine Robertson 1954; four d.; ed Univ. of Tex.; with Tech. Dept Humble Oil & Refining Co., Baytown, Tex. 1953–55; Cosden Oil & Chem. Co. 1955–76, Pres. 1968–76; Dir American Petrofina Inc. (now FINA), Dallas 1968–, Vice-Pres., COO 1976–83, Pres., CEO 1983–86, Chair. Bd, Pres., CEO 1984–86, Chair. Bd 1986–98; mem. Advisory Council Coll. Eng Foundation, Univ. of Tex. 1979–; Co-Chair. Industrial Div. United Way of Metropolitan Dallas 1981–82; Chair. Public Utilities Comm. of Tex. 1989–92; Trustee Southwest Research Inst.; mem. American Petroleum Inst., Dallas Wildcat Comm. (Chair. 1987–88). *Publication:* (contrib.) Advances in Petroleum Chemistry and Refining 1957. *Address:* c/o FINA Inc., PO Box 2159, 8350 North Central Expressway, Dallas, TX 75221, USA.

MEEKER, Mary, BA, MBA; American technical and investment analyst and author; *General Partner, Kleiner Perkins Caufield & Byers;* ed DePauw Univ., Cornell Univ.; began career as a securities analyst 1986; worked at Morgan Stanley 1991–2010, served as Man. Dir and Research Analyst; Gen. Partner, Kleiner Perkins Caufield & Byers 2011–; mem. Bd of Dirs Square, Lending Club, DocuSign, Quirky; Hon. DLitt (DePauw Univ.); ranked by Forbes magazine amongst The World's 100 Most Powerful Women (84th) 2012, (79th) 2013. *Publications include:* co-author: The Internet Report 1995, The Internet Advertising Report 1996, The Internet Retailing Report 1997, The Online Classified Advertising Report: It's About Search/Find/Obtain (SFO) 2002, The China Internet Report 2004, The Mobile Internet Report 2009, Internet Trend Report 2012, The Technology IPO Yearbooks; cr., with Liang Wu, USA, Inc. (award winning report/video about US Govt financial transactions) 2011. *Address:* Kleiner Perkins Caufield & Byers, 2750 Sand Hill Road, Menlo Park, CA 94025, USA (office). *Telephone:* (650) 233-2750 (office). *Fax:* (650) 233-0300 (office). *E-mail:* plans@kpcb.com (office). *Website:* www.kpcb.com (office).

MEESE, Edwin, III, BA, JD; American academic, lawyer and fmr government official; *Ronald Reagan Distinguished Fellow and Chairman, Center for Legal and Judicial Studies, The Heritage Foundation;* b. 1931; s. of Edwin Meese, Jr and Leone Meese; m. Ursula Meese; one s. one d.; ed Yale Univ. and Univ. of California, Berkeley; taught law at Univ. of San Diego Law School, Dir Center for Criminal Justice Policy and Man.; sr position under Gov. Reagan, State Capitol, Sacramento, Calif.; Reagan's Campaign Chief of Staff, presidential elections 1980, Dir Transition Org. 1980–81; Counsellor to Pres. Reagan and mem. Nat. Security Council, Domestic Policy Council and Cabinet 1981–85; US Attorney Gen. 1985–88; Ronald Reagan Distinguished Fellow and Chair. Center for Legal and Judicial Studies, The Heritage Foundation, Washington 1988–; Distinguished Visiting Fellow, Hoover Inst., Stanford Univ., Calif. 1988–; mem. Iraq Study Group, US Inst. of Peace 2006; Distinguished Sr Fellow, Inst. for United States Studies, Univ. of London 1996–2003; mem. Bd of Dirs Capital Research Center, Landmark Legal Foundation, Center for the Study of the Presidency, American Prosecutors Research Inst.; retd Col US Army Reserve; Harvard Univ. John F. Kennedy School of Govt Medal 1986. *Publications:* With Reagan: The Inside Story 1992, Making America Safer (co-ed.) 1997, Leadership, Ethics and Policing (co-author) 2004. *Leisure interest:* collecting models of police patrol cars. *Address:* The Heritage Foundation, 214 Massachusetts Avenue, NE, Washington, DC 20002, USA. *Telephone:* (202) 608-6180. *Fax:* (202) 547-0641. *E-mail:* staff@heritage.org. *Website:* www.heritage.org.

MEGAWATI, Sukarnoputri; Indonesian politician and fmr head of state; *Chairman, Partai Demokrasi Indonesia Perjuangan (Indonesian Democratic Struggle Party);* b. 23 Jan. 1947, Jogjakarta; d. of the late Achmed Sukarno (fmr Pres. of Indonesia) and Fatmawati; m. 1st Surendro (deceased); m. 2nd Hassan Gamal Ahmad Hassan; m. 3rd Taufik Kiemas; three c.; mem. House of Reps (Partai Demokrasi Indonesia–PDI) 1987; Leader PDI 1993–96 (deposed); Chair. Partai Demokrasi Indonesia Perjuangan (PDI-P) 1996–; Vice-Pres. of Indonesia 1999–2001, Pres. 2001–04; ranked by Forbes magazine amongst 100 Most Powerful Women (eighth) 2004. *Address:* Partai Demokrasi Indonesia Perjuangan (Indonesian Democratic Struggle Party), Jalan Lenteng Agung 99, Jakarta Selatan, Indonesia (office). *Telephone:* (21) 7806028 (office). *Fax:* (21) 7814472 (office). *Website:* www.pdiperjuangan.or.id (office).

MEGHJI, Hon. Zakia Hamdan; Tanzanian politician and teacher; b. 31 Dec. 1946; ed Univ. of Dar es Salaam; secondary school teacher 1971–72; tutor at women's training cooperative and at Moshi Cooperative Coll. 1972–78; tutor, World Cooperative Coll. 1978–86; Dist Commr 1988–90; Regional Commr 1990; Exec. Sec., Dept of Econs and Social Welfare 1991; Minister of Natural Resources and Tourism 1994–2006, of Finance 2006–08; mem. Chama Cha Mapinduzi party. *Address:* Chama Cha Mapinduzi, Kuu Street, PO Box 50, Dodoma, Tanzania (office). *Telephone:* 2180575 (office). *E-mail:* katibumkuu@ccmtz.org (office). *Website:* www.ccmtz.org (office).

MÉGRET, Bruno André Alexandre, MSc; French politician and engineer; *Leader, Mouvement national républicain;* b. 4 April 1949, Paris; s. of Jacques Mégret and Colette Constantinides; m. Catherine Rascovsky 1992; two s.; ed Lycée Louis-le-Grand, Paris, Univ. of California, Berkeley, École Polytechnique, Ecole nationale des Ponts et Chaussées; Head of Dept Nat. Devt Programme 1975–76; Dist Engineer, Eng Dept, Essonne Département 1977–79; tech. adviser, Office of Minister for Overseas Service 1979–81; Deputy Dir Infrastructure and Transport Ile-de-France Region 1981–86; Deputy, Front national d'Isère 1986–88, Vice-Pres. Front national Parl. Group 1987–98, left party Dec. 1998; Founder and Leader Mouvement nat. républicain (MNR) 1999–; mem. European Parl. 1989–99; Regional Councillor Provence-Côte d'Azur 1992–2004, Special Adviser to Mayor of Vitrolles 1997–2004; mem. and Hon. Pres. Comités d'action républicaine.

Publications: Demain le chêne 1982, L'Impératif du renouveau 1986, La Flamme 1990, L'Alternative nationale 1996, La Troisième voie 1997, La Nouvelle Europe 1998, Le Chagrin et l'espérance 1999, Pour que vive la France 2000, La France à l'endroit 2001, L'autre scénario 2006. *Address:* Mouvement national républicain, 15 rue de Cronstadt, 75015 Paris, France (office). *Telephone:* 9-51-45-84-93 (office). *Fax:* 1-56-56-52-47 (office). *E-mail:* presse@m-n-r.fr (office). *Website:* www.m-n-r.fr (office); www.bruno-megret.com (home).

MEGUID, Nagwa Abdel, PhD; Egyptian geneticist and academic; *Professor of Human Genetics, National Research Centre;* Clinical Researcher and Geneticist, Nat. Research Centre, Cairo, now Prof. of Human Genetics; L'Oreal-UNESCO For Women in Science Award 2002. *Publications:* numerous articles in scientific journals. *Address:* National Research Centre, El Buhoth Street, Dokki, Giza, 12311 Cairo, Egypt (office). *Telephone:* (2) 7617590 (office). *Fax:* (2) 3370597 (office). *E-mail:* meguid@nrc.org.eg (office). *Website:* www.nrc.sci.eg (office).

MÉHAIGNERIE, Pierre; French politician and engineer; b. 4 May 1939, Balazé, Ille et Vilaine; s. of Alexis Méhaignerie and Pauline Méhaignerie (née Boursier); m. Julie Harding 1965; one s. one d.; ed Lycée Saint-Louis, Paris, Ecole nationale supérieure agronomique, Rennes, Ecole nationale supérieure de sciences agronomiques appliquées, Paris; engineer, Génie Rural des Eaux et Forêts, Dept of Agric. 1965–67; technical counsellor, Ministry of Agric. 1969–71, Ministry of Cultural Affairs 1971–73; mem. Nat. Ass. for Ille-et-Vilaine 1973–76, 1981–86, 1988–93, 1995–; County Councillor for Vitré-Est 1976–2001, elected Mayor of Vitré April 1977–; Sec. of State to Minister of Agric. 1976–77; Minister of Agric. 1977–81, of Housing, Transport and Urban Affairs 1986–88, of Justice 1993–95; Pres. Finance Comm., Nat. Ass. 1995–97, 2002–07; mem. European Parl. 1979; Vice-Pres. Union pour la démocratie française 1988–2002; Pres. Conseil Gen. d'Ille et Vilaine 1982–2001, Pres. Centre des démocrates sociaux 1982–94; Secrétaire général Union pour une Majorité Populaire 2004–; Commdr du Mérite agricole. *Publications:* Aux Français qui ne veulent plus être gouvernés de haut 1995, Bretagne: désir d'avenir 1998. *Address:* Mairie, BP 70627, 35506 Vitré Cedex (office); Assemblée Nationale, 75355 Paris; 76 rue du Rachapt, 35500 Vitré, France (home). *Telephone:* 2-99-75-07-28 (office); 1-40-63-66-17 (office). *E-mail:* pmehaign@club-internet.fr (office). *Website:* www.pierre-mehaignerie.org (office).

MEHDORN, Hartmut; German transport industry executive; b. 31 July 1942, Berlin; m. Hélène Mehdorn (née Vuillequez); two s. one d.; ed studied mechanical eng in Berlin; began career as operating asst, Focke Wulf Bremen (renamed Fokker GmbH) 1966, led design and production of Airbus A 300 1974, Head of Production 1978–80; mem. Exec. Cttee and Head of Production, Planning and Purchase, Airbus Industrie AG 1980–84; Man. Dir Mfg, MBB (Messerschmidt Bölkow Blohm) 1984–86, mem. Bd 1986–89; Pres. German Airbus GmbH, Hamburg 1989–92; mem. Bd and Exec. Cttee Deutsche Aerospace AG (Daimler Benz Aerospace AG—DASA) 1992–95; CEO Heidelberger Druckmaschinen AG 1997–98; Chair. Man. Bd Deutsche Bahn (DB) AG 1999–2003, Chair. Man. Bd and CEO 2003–09 (resgnd); Chair. Supervisory Bd Vattenfalls Europe AG, DB Cargo AG, DB Wetz AG, DB Regio AG, DB Reise & Touristik AG; mem. Exec. Cttee SAP AG 2002–; mem. Bd of Dirs RWE AG 1998–99; Dir (non-exec.) Air Berlin PLC & Co. Luftverkehrs KG 2009–; mem. Advisory Bd Baden-Württemberg Commerzbank AG 2000–; mem. Supervisory Bd DEVK (Deutsche Eisenbahn Versicherung Lebensversicherung) AG, Lufthansa Technik AG, West LB AG; Hon. Senator, Ruprecht Karl Univ., Heidelberg 1999–; Cross of Order of Merit of FRG, Commdr, Légion d'honneur; Dr hc (Moscow State Univ. of Printing Arts) 1996, (Tech. Univ. of Hamburg-Harburg) 2000. *Address:* Air Berlin PLC & Co. Luftverkehrs KG, Saatwinkler Damm 42–43, 13627 Berlin, Germany (office). *Telephone:* (1805) 737800 (office). *Fax:* (30) 41021003 (office). *E-mail:* info@airberlin.com (office). *Website:* www.airberlin.com (office).

MEHEID, Minwer al-, BS, MA, PhD; Saudi Arabian civil engineer, architect and academic; *Professor, General Manager and Fellow, Royal Al-Albeit Institute for Islamic Thought;* b. 1 May 1957, Treif; ed California State Univ., USA, Prince's Foundation for the Built Environment, Wales and Univ. of London, UK; Founder Inst. of Traditional Islamic Arts and Architecture, World Islamic Sciences & Educ. (WISE) Univ.; currently Prof., Gen. Man. and Fellow, Royal Al-Albeit Inst. for Islamic Thought; winner of int. competition to restore fire-damaged Minbar (pulpit) of Saladin 1994, managed team of 20 craftsmen from Egypt, Jordan, Indonesia and Turkey during successful restoration; numerous exhbns locally and internationally; numerous TV interviews at home and abroad; First Prize in six local and int. competitions, chosen as one of the 500 Most Influential People in the Islamic World 2008–12, named by Business magazine as one of the 100 Most Powerful People in Dubai 2010, and one of the 500 Most Powerful People in Dubai 2010. *Film:* assisted in the making Stairway to Heaven (documentary about reconstruction of the Minbar of Saladin in the Al-Aqsa Mosque) 2008. *Publication:* book of translated articles on sacred art. *Address:* Institute of Traditional Islamic Arts and Architecture, World Islamic Sciences & Education University (WISE), PO Box 3644, 11953 Amman, Jordan (office). *Telephone:* (6) 5539496 (office). *Fax:* (6) 5539484 (office). *E-mail:* minwer1@gmail.com (home). *Website:* www.itiaa.edu.jo (office).

MEHMET, Alper (Alp), MVO; British diplomatist (retd); b. 28 Aug. 1948, Cyprus; s. of the late Bekir Mehmet and Leman Mehmet (née Yussuf); m. Elaine Mehmet; two d.; Immigration Officer 1970–79, seconded to British High Comm. from the Home Office, Lagos 1979–83, transferred to FCO 1983, Asst Pvt. Sec. to Parl. Under-Sec. of State 1983–85, Second Sec., Chancery/Information, Bucharest 1986–89, Deputy Head of Mission and Consul, Reykjavík 1989–93, Parl. Clerk, FCO 1993–95, FCO Spokesman for Asia, Press Office 1995–98, First Sec. and Head of Press and Public Affairs, Bonn Jan.–Sept. 1999, First Sec. and Head of Press and Public Affairs, Berlin 1999–2003, Amb. to Iceland 2004–08 (retd); Sr Special Adviser, Iceland for Fipra International 2008–; Vice-Chair. Migration Watch UK 2010–; UK Dir Aqua Omnis water co.; interviewer for Stabilisation Unit, UK; Foundation Gov. and Trustee, Parmiter's School; Treas., City and Hackney Alcohol Service; public speaking coach and adviser; regular interviewee and participant in discussions on UK and non-UK radio and TV. *Plays:* numerous roles, including Mosca in Volpone and Captain Cat in Under Milk Wood; numerous roles in musicals, including Fagin and Bill Sykes in Oliver and Todd in Sweeney Todd. *Achievements include:* first first-generation immigrant, mem. of HM Diplomatic Service and first Muslim to be appointed a UK Amb. *Publications:* articles for various newspapers and magazines. *Leisure interests:* football and cricket (played both, now watch), mem. Chingford Amateur Dramatic and Operatic Soc. *Telephone:* 7983-384734 (mobile) (office). *E-mail:* alp.mehmet@fipra.com (office); alp.mehmet@migrationwatchuk.com (office); alp.mehmet@aquaomnis.is (office). *Website:* www.fipra.com (office); www.migrationwatchuk.com (office); www.aquaomnis.is (office).

MEHRA, K. S.; Indian civil servant; *Commissioner, Municipal Corporation of Delhi;* m. Vimal Mehra 1978 (divorced 2008); various positions in Admin of Andaman and Nicobar Islands, Govt of Arunachal Pradesh, Govt of Delhi; Jt Sec. Ministry of Textiles –1999; Additional Commr Municipal Corpn of Delhi 1998–2000, Commr 2008–; Admin. Union Territory of Lakshadweep 2001–04; Prin. Sec. (Urban Devt), Delhi –2008; Chair. Lakshadweep Devt Corpn; ex-officio Insp.-Gen. of Police; Patron Lakshadweep Sahitya Kala Acad.; mem. New Delhi Municipal Council. *Address:* HQ Town Hall, Chandni Chowk, Delhi 110 006, India (office). *Telephone:* (11) 23961012 (office); (11) 23739363 (office); (11) 23312652 (home). *Fax:* (11) 23965016 (office). *Website:* www.mcdonline.gov.in (office).

MEHTA, Ajai Singh (Sonny); American (b. Indian) publishing company executive; *Chairman and Editor-in-Chief, Knopf Publishing Group;* b. 1942, India; m. Gita Mehta; one s.; ed Lawrence School, Sanawar, and St Catherine's Coll., Univ. of Cambridge; fmrly with Paladin, Pan and Picador Publs, UK; Pres. Alfred A. Knopf Div. of Random House (now Knopf Publishing Group, New York) 1987–, now Chair. and Ed.-in-Chief; Lifetime Achievement Award, Asian American Writers Workshop 2009. *Leisure interest:* music. *Address:* Alfred A. Knopf Inc., 1745 Broadway, New York, NY 10019, USA (office). *E-mail:* knopfpublicity@randomhouse.com (office). *Website:* www.randomhouse.com/knopf (office).

MEHTA, Aman, BA; Indian banker (retd); *General Manager of Medical, Tata Power Co. Ltd;* b. 1946, India; m.; two c.; ed Univ. of Delhi; with Mercantile Bank Ltd 1967–69; joined Hongkong and Shanghai Banking Corpn Ltd (HSBC) 1969, roles in various depts including Operations, Credit, Br. and Area Man., Merchant Banking, Man. Corp. Planning 1985, Chair. and Chief Exec. HSBC USA Inc. 1993–95, Deputy Chair. HSBC Bank Middle East 1995–98, Gen. Man. Int. and later Exec. Dir Int. HSBC 1998, CEO 1999–2004; Chair. HSBC Bank Malaysia Berhad 1999–2004, Dir HSBC Bank Australia, HSBC Investment Bank Asia Holdings Ltd, HSBC Holdings BV Netherlands; Man. Dir The Saudi British Bank 1988–91, Group Gen. Man. 1991–92; currently Gen. Man. of Medical, Tata Power Co. Ltd; mem. Bd of Dirs Tata Consultancy Services 2004–, Jet Airways Ltd 2004–, Raffles Holdings Ltd 2004–, PCCW Ltd 2004–, Vedanta Resources PLC 2004–, Wockhardt Ltd 2004–, Godrej Consumer Products Ltd 2006–, Cairn India Ltd 2007–, Emaar MGF Land Ltd 2007–, Max Healthcare Inst. Ltd; mem. Bd of Govs Indian School of Business; mem. Supervisory Bd ING Group 2008–; mem. Int. Advisory Council of INSEAD. *Address:* Tata Power Co. Ltd, Bombay House, Mumbai 400 001, India (office). *Telephone:* (22) 66658282 (office). *Fax:* (22) 66658801 (office).

MEHTA, Goverdhan, BSc, MSc, PhD, FRS; Indian organic chemist, academic and international organization official; b. 1943, Jodhpur; ed Univ. of Poona; Hon. Prof., Jawaharlal Nehru Centre for Advanced Scientific Research, Bangalore 1990–; Vice-Chancellor Univ. of Hyderabad 1994–98; Prof. of Organic Chemistry and fmr Indian Inst. of Science, Bangalore; Pres. Indian Nat. Science Acad. 1999–2001; mem. Exec. Bd Int. Council for Science (ICSU) 1999–2002, Pres. 2005–08, fmr Chair. ICSU Nat. Cttee; Co-Chair. Inter-Acad. Council 2001–05; Fellow, Int. Union of Pure and Applied Chem., fmr Chair. Int. Cttee; mem. Research Advisory Panel, Inst. of Life Sciences; Foreign mem. Russian Acad. of Sciences; Hon. FRSC; Officier dans l'Ordre Palmes Academiques, Chevalier de la Legion d'Honneur 2004; DSc hc (Univ. of Marseilles); Humboldt Research Prize, Germany, Third World Acad. of Sciences Medal, Padma Shri 2000, Shanti Swarup Bhatnagar Prize, Trieste Prize. *Publications:* more than 370 papers in int. journals. *Address:* Institute of Life Sciences, University of Hyderabad Campus, Gachibowli, Hyderabad 500 046, India (office). *Telephone:* (40) 66571500 (office). *Fax:* (40) 66571581 (office). *E-mail:* info@ilsresearch.org (office). *Website:* ilsresearch.org (office).

MEHTA, Adm. (retd) Sureesh; Indian naval officer (retd) and diplomatist; b. 18 Aug. 1947; m. Maria Teresa Mehta; two c.; ed Nat. Defence Acad., Defence Services Staff Coll., Wellington, Nat. Defence Coll., New Delhi; commissioned in Indian Navy 1967, joined Fleet Air Arm and flew Sea Hawk jet fighters from carrier INS Vikrant 1967, carried out instructional duties as Directing Staff in Defence Services Staff Coll., earlier appointments included command of frigate INS Beas and guided missile frigate INS Godavari, also commanded Naval Air Stations, INS Garuda, C-in-C Eastern Naval Command 2005–06, other operational Flag appointments have included Flag Officer Naval Aviation, Fleet Commdr Western Fleet during Kargil Crisis 1999, has held various staff appointments in Flag rank at New Delhi, including Asst Controller Carrier Projects, Asst Chief of Personnel (Human Resources Devt), Controller of Personnel Services, Chief of Personnel, Dir-Gen. Coast Guard, Deputy Chief of Naval Staff, Chief of Naval Staff 2006–09, Chair. Chiefs of Staff Cttee 2007–09; High Commr to New Zealand 2009–13; Ati Vishist Seva Medal 1995, Param Vishist Seva Medal 2005. *Address:* Ministry of External Affairs, South Block, New Delhi 110 011, India (office). *Telephone:* (11) 23011127 (office). *Fax:* (11) 23013254 (office). *E-mail:* eam@mea.gov.in (office). *Website:* www.mea.gov.in (office).

MEHTA, Tasneem Zakaria, MA; Indian art historian, writer and art critic; *Director and Managing Trustee, Dr Bhau Daji Lad Mumbai City Museum;* d. of the late Rafique Zakaria and of Fatma Zakaria; ed J. J. School of Art, Mumbai, Columbia Univ., USA, Univ. of Delhi; Dir and Man. Trustee, Dr Bhau Daji Lad Mumbai City Museum 2003–; Convenor (Mumbai chapter) Indian Nat. Trust for Art and Cultural Heritage, mem. Governing Council 1996–, currently also Vice-Chair.; mem. Advisory Bd Nat. Gallery of Modern Art; mem. Governing Council, Salar Jung Museum, Hyderabad, Nat. Inst. of Design, Ahmedabad; mem. Cen. Advisory Bd for Museums; fmr Sr Expert Adviser to UNESCO; Gov. Mumbai Metropolitan Regional Devt Authority, Heritage Soc. 1998–2009; Chair. The Skoda Prize. *Publication:* The Artful Pose (co-author). *Address:* Dr Bhau Daji Lad Mumbai City Museum, 91 A, Rani Baug, Veer Mata Jijbai Bhonsle Udyan, Dr Baba Saheb Ambedkar Marg, Byculla East, Mumbai 400 027, India (office).

Telephone: (22) 23731234 (office); (22) 65560394 (office). *Website:* www.bdlmuseum.org (office).

MEHTA, Ved (Parkash), MA, FRSL; American (naturalized) writer and academic; b. 21 March 1934, Lahore, British India; s. of Dr Amolak Ram and Shanti Mehta (née Mehra); m. Linn Cary 1983; two d.; ed Arkansas School for the Blind, Pomona Coll., Calif., Balliol Coll., Oxford, UK, Harvard Univ.; staff writer, New Yorker magazine 1961–94; Visiting Scholar, Case Western Reserve 1974; Visiting Prof. of Literature, Bard Coll. 1985, 1986; Noble Foundation Visiting Coll. of Art and Cultural History, Sarah Lawrence Coll. 1988; Fellow, New York Inst. for the Humanities 1988–92; Visiting Fellow (Literature), Balliol Coll., Oxford 1988–89; Visiting Prof. of English, New York Univ. 1989–90; Rosenkrantz Chair in Writing, Yale Univ. 1990–93, Lecturer in History 1990, 1991, 1992, Lecturer in English 1991–93; Assoc. Fellow, Berkeley Coll. (a constituent of Yale Coll.) 1988–89, Residential Fellow 1990–93; Arnold Bernhard Visiting Prof. of English and History, Williams Coll. 1994; Randolph Visiting Distinguished Prof. of English and History, Vassar Coll., New York 1994–96; Sr Fellow, Freedom Forum, Media Studies Center and Visiting Scholar, Columbia Univ., New York 1996–97; Fellow, Center for Advanced Study in Behavioral Sciences 1997–98; mem. Council on Foreign Relations 1979–, Usage Panel, American Heritage Dictionary 1982; Hon. Fellow, Balliol Coll. Oxford 1999; Hon. DLitrs (Pomona Coll.) 1972, (Williams Coll.) 1986; Hon. DLitt (Bard Coll.) 1982; Hon. DUniv (Stirling, Scotland) 1988; Hon. LHD (Bowdoin) 1995; Hazen Fellow 1956–59, Harvard Prize Fellow 1959–60, Residential Fellow, Eliot House 1959–61, Guggenheim Fellow 1971–72, 1977–78, Ford Foundation Travel and Study Grantee 1971–76, and Public Policy Grantee 1979–82, MacArthur Prize Fellow 1982–87, Asscn of Indians in America Award 1978, Signet Medal, Harvard Univ. 1983, Distinguished Service Award, Asian/Pacific American Library Asscn 1986, New York City Mayor's Liberty Medal 1986, Centenary Barrows Award, Pomona Coll. 1987, New York Public Library Literary Lion Medal 1990, and Literary Lion Centennial Medal 1996, New York State Asian-American Heritage Month Award 1991, South Asian Literary Asscn Lifetime Achievement Award 2004. *Television:* writer and narrator of documentary film, Chachaji: My Poor Relation (DuPont Columbia Award for Excellence in Broadcast Journalism 1977–78) (PBS) 1978, (BBC) 1980. *Publications:* Face to Face (Secondary Educ. Annual Book Award 1958, serial reading on BBC Light Programme 1958, dramatization on BBC Home Programme 1959) 1957, Walking the Indian Streets 1960, Fly and the Fly Bottle 1963, The New Theologian 1966, Delinquent Chacha (novel) 1967, Portrait of India 1970, John Is Easy to Please 1971, Mahatma Gandhi and His Apostles 1977, The New India 1978, Photographs of Chachaji 1980, A Family Affair: India Under Three Prime Ministers 1982, Three Stories of the Raj (fiction) 1986, Rajiv Gandhi and Rama's Kingdom 1995, A Ved Mehta Reader: The Craft of the Essay 1998; Continents of Exile (autobiography): Daddyji 1972, Mamaji 1979, Vedi 1982 (serial reading on BBC Book at Bedtime 1990), The Ledge Between the Streams 1984, Sound-Shadows of the New World 1986, The Stolen Light 1989, Up at Oxford 1993, Remembering Mr. Shawn's New Yorker 1998, All For Love 2001, Dark Harbor 2003, The Red Letters 2004, Veritas (concluding vol.) 2012, Ved Mehta's Collected Works 2013. *Leisure interest:* daydreaming. *Address:* 139 East 79th Street, New York, NY 10075, USA (home). *Fax:* (212) 472-7220 (home). *E-mail:* mehta.ved@gmail.com (home). *Website:* www.vedmehta.com.

MEHTA, Zarin, FCA; Indian arts administrator; *President and Executive Director, New York Philharmonic;* b. 28 Oct. 1938, Bombay; s. of the late Mehli Mehta and of Tehmina Daruvala Mehta; brother of Zubin Mehta (q.v.); m. Carmen Lasky 1966; one s. one d.; CA, London 1957, accountant Frederic B. Smart & Co., London 1957–62, Coopers & Lybrand, Montréal, Canada 1962–81; Dir Orchestre Symphonique de Montréal 1973–81, Man. Dir 1981–90; Exec. Dir and COO Ravinia Festival, Ill. 1990–99, CEO 1999–2000; Exec. Dir New York Philharmonic 2000–(12), Pres. 2004–(12); mem. Ordre de Comptables Agréés du Québec; Treas. Barenboim-Said Foundation; mem. Bd of Dirs WNYC Radio; Dr hc (Roosevelt Univ., Chicago) 1998; Bravo Award, Dominican Univ. 1996, Arts Entrepreneurship Award, Columbia Coll., Chicago, 1997, Dushkin Award, Music Inst. of Chicago 1998, Theodore L. Kesselman Award for Arts Educ., New York Youth Symphony 2007. *Address:* New York Philharmonic, Administrative Offices, Avery Fisher Hall, 10 Lincoln Center Plaza, New York, NY 10023, USA (office). *Telephone:* (212) 875-5900 (office). *E-mail:* pr@nyphil.org (office). *Website:* www.newyorkphilharmonic.org (office).

MEHTA, Zubin; Indian conductor; b. 29 April 1936, Bombay; s. of the late Mehli Mehta and of Tehmina Daruvala Mehta; m. 1st Carmen Lasky 1958 (divorced 1964); one s. one d.; m. 2nd Nancy Diane Kovack 1969; ed St Xavier's Coll., Mumbai, Vienna Acad. of Music, studied under Hans Swarowsky; first professional conducting in Belgium, Yugoslavia and UK (Liverpool); Music Dir Montreal Symphony 1961–67, Los Angeles Philharmonic Orchestra 1962–78; Music Dir New York Philharmonic Orchestra 1978–91; Music Dir Israel Philharmonic 1969–, appointed Dir for Life 1981; Music Dir Maggio Musicale, Florence 1969, 1986–, Chief Conductor 1985–; Gen. Music Dir Bavarian State Opera 1998–2006; conductor at festivals of Holland, Prague, Vienna, Salzburg and Spoleto; debut at La Scala, Milan 1969; conducts regularly with the Vienna and Berlin Orchestras; winner of Liverpool Int. Conductors' Competition 1958; Pres. Annual Festival del Mediterrani in Valencia 2006–; f. Mehli Mehta Music Foundation, Mumbai; Hon. mem. Vienna State Opera 1997, Hon. Conductor, Vienna Philharmonic Orchestra 2001, Hon. Conductor, Munich Philharmonic Orchestra 2004, Hon. Conductor, Los Angeles Philharmonic 2006, Hon. Conductor, Teatro del Maggio Musicale Fiorentino 2006, Hon. Conductor, Bavarian State Opera 2006, Hon. mem. Bavarian State Opera 2006, Hon. mem., Gesellschaft der Musikfreunde Wien 2007, Hon. citizenship Florence and Tel Aviv; Commendatore (Italy), Médaille d'Or Vermeil (City of Paris), Commdr, Ordre des Arts et des Lettres, Great Silver Medal of Service (Austria) 1997; Dr hc (Tel-Aviv Univ., Weizmann Inst. of Science, The Hebrew Univ. of Jerusalem, Jewish Theological Seminary, Westminster Choir Coll., Princeton, Brooklyn Coll., Colgate Univ.); winner of Liverpool Int. Conducting Competition 1958, Padma Bhushan 1966, co-winner Wolf Prize 1996, Lifetime Achievement Peace and Tolerance Award, UN 1999, Padma Vibhushan 2001, Kennedy Center Honor 2006, Bridgebuilder Award 2007, Dan David Prize 2007, Praemium Imperiale Award for Music, Tokyo 2008. *Leisure interest:* cricket. *Address:* c/o Natalia Ritzkowsky, Assistant to Zubin Mehta, Traubingerstr. 10 D, 82327 Tutzing, Germany (office). *Telephone:* (49) 8158906791 (office). *Fax:* (49) 8158906794 (office). *E-mail:* info@zubinmehta.net. *Website:* www .zubinmehta.net.

MEI, Baojiu; Chinese opera singer; b. Feb. 1934, Beijing; s. of Mei Lanfang; actor, Mei Lanfang Peking Opera Co. 1951–62, actor (First Class) Beijing Peking Opera Troupe 1962–; head, Mei Lanfang Peking Opera Troupe. *Plays:* Phoenix Returning to Its Nest, The Imperial Concubine Getting Drunk, Xiang Yu Bidding Farewell to Yu Ji, Yuzhoufeng. *Recordings include:* Masterpieces of Beijing Opera, Famous Arias from Beijing Opera. *Films:* A Great Master Recaptured 2006. *Address:* Peking Opera Troupe, Haihu West lane No. 30, Fengtai District, Beijing 100077, People's Republic of China (office).

MEIDANI, Rexhep Qemal, DèsSc; Albanian academic and fmr head of state; *Professor, University of New York Tirana;* b. 17 Aug. 1944, Tirana; m.; two c.; ed Univs of Caen and Paris XI, France, Univ. of Tirana; scientific collaborator, C.E.N., Saclay, France 1974–96; Asst, then Lecturer, then Docent, Univ. of Tirana and Univ. of Pristina, Kosova 1966–96, Prof. of Theoretical Physics 1987–, Dean of Faculty of Natural Sciences 1988–92; Visiting Scientist and Visiting Prof., Italy, France, Germany, UK, USA, Greece etc.; mem. Socialist Party of Albania 1996–97, 2002–, Gen. Sec. 1996–97; mem. Parl. 1997; Pres. of Albania 1997–2002; currently Prof., Univ. of New York Tirana, Univ. of Marlin Barleti; Chair. Bd Albanian Centre for Human Rights 1994–96, Ed.-in-Chief Human Rights quarterly 1994–96; Co-founder Citizens of Helsinki, Democratic Albania; mem. Albanian Cttee for Understanding and Cooperation in the Balkans 1986–90; Co-Ed. Bulletin of Natural Sciences 1978–89, Ed.-in-Chief 1989–94; Co-Ed. Balkan Physics Letters 1992–96; mem. Acad. of Sciences 2003, Club of Madrid, Int. Cttee for Democracy in Cuba, Int. Raoul Wallenberg Foundation, Editorial Advisory Bd World Leaders Magazine, European Asscn of Law Students (Elsa), Albania, War Invalids' Asscn against Nazism; Hon. Amb. of Millennium Goals, Amb. for Peace, Int. Hon. Citizen, New Orleans, USA 2002; Order 'Naim Frasheri', Third Class 1981, Nat. Order Golden Star of Romania 1999, Order of King Tomislav (Croatia) 2001, Nat. Order of Merit (Grade of Companion of Honour) (Malta) 2002; Hon. PhD (Istanbul Tech. Univ.) 1998, Dr hc (Aristotle Univ. of Thessaloniki) 1998, (Sofia Univ.) 1998, Hon. DHumLitt (American Univ., Rome) 1999, (Univ. of Bridgeport, Conn.) 2001, Preside d'Onore (Università Mediterranea René Cassin, Bari) 1999, Hon. DSc (Portsmouth, UK) 2002; Prize of the Repub., Second Class 1988, Gold Medal of Merit of the City of Athens 1998, Great Cross of Salvation (Greece) 1998, Médaille du Mérite (U.P. Universelle) 1998, Honorary Medal of the Centre Democritos (Greece) 1998, F. Lux Award, Clark Univ., Worcester, Mass, USA 2000, Golden Key of the City of Worcester 2000, Golden Key of the City of Prague, Czech Repub. 2001, Jan Masaryk Medal, Univ. of Economics, Prague 2001, Medal of the Robert Schumann Foundation, Paris 2001, Chancellor's Int. Medallion of Distinction, New Orleans Univ. 2002, Golden Key of the City of New Orleans 2002, Golden Medal of Freedom (Kosovo) 2010. *Publications:* President Meidani and Kosovo 2000, The Balkans – A General Outlook. Montenegro, Bosnia, Kosovo, FYR of Macedonia, Serbia: Near-Term Challenges 2001, Dall'Indipendenza verso L'Interdipendenza dell'Integrazione 2002, Globalization, Integration and the Albanian Nation 2002, Jus Gentium 2003, Politics, Moral and State 2003, Agreement with Myself 2004, The Traps of Nation-State 2005, Politics in Vivo-in Vitro 2006, Las trampas del Estado-nacion 2007, Is It Deterministic the Quantum Theory? 2007, On Space-Time 2008, Constitution: Bilan and Perspective 2009, On the Government (I) 2009, On the Government (II, III) 2010, Battle on the Voting Right 2010; numerous scientific monographs and books and hundreds of scientific and political articles published in Albania; many articles in int. scientific publs and numerous others on political and social problems. *Address:* IDM, Rr. Shenasi Dishnica, Nr 37, PO Box 8177, Tirana (office); Bulevardi Zogu I, Pallati 57, Shkalla 1, Apt 12, Tirana, Albania (home). *Telephone:* (4) 2400241 (office); (4) 2271887 (home); (4) 2271844 (home). *Fax:* (4) 2400640 (office). *E-mail:* rmeidani@hotmail.com (home); rmeidani@gmail.com (home); info@idmalbania.org (office); rmeidani@rmeidani .info (home). *Website:* www.idmalbania.org (office).

MEIER, Beat H., PhD; Swiss chemist and academic; *Head, Department of Chemistry and Applied Sciences, Eidgenössische Technische Hochschule Zürich (ETH Zürich);* b. 1954, Solothurn; ed Eidgenössische Technische Hochschule Zürich; Post-Doctoral Researcher, Los Alamos Nat. Labs, USA 1985–87; Staff Scientist, Eidgenössische Technische Hochschule Zürich (ETH Zürich) 1987, Prof. 1998–, also Head, Dept of Chem. and Applied Sciences; Prof. of Physical Chem., Nijmegen Univ., Netherlands 1994–98. *Address:* Laboratorium fur Physikalische Chemie, HCI D 225, Wolfgang-Pauli-Str. 10, 8093 Zürich, Switzerland (office). *Telephone:* (44) 632-44-01 (office). *Fax:* (1) 632-1621 (office). *E-mail:* beat.meier@ nmr.phys.chem.ethz.ch (office). *Website:* www.ethz.ch (office); www.nmr.ethz.ch/ ~beme (office).

MEIER, Richard Alan, BArch, FAIA; American architect; b. 12 Oct. 1934, Newark, NJ; s. of Jerome Meier and Carolyn Meier (née Kaltenbacher); m. Katherine Gormley 1978 (divorced); one s. one d.; ed Cornell Univ.; with Frank Grad & Sons, NJ 1957, Davis, Brody & Wisniewski, New York 1958–59, Skidmore, Owings & Merrill 1959–60, Marcel Breuer & Assocs 1961–63; Prof. Architectural Design Cooper Union 1962–73; Prin. Architect, Richard Meier & Assocs, New York 1963–80, Richard Meier & Partners 1980–; Visiting Critic, Pratt Inst. 1960–62, 1965, Princeton 1963, Syracuse Univ. 1964; Architect American Acad. in Rome 1973–74; Visiting Prof. of Architecture, Yale Univ. 1975, 1977, Harvard 1977; Eliot Noyes Visiting Critic in Architecture 1980–81; Visiting Prof., UCLA 1987, 1988, 1990, 2000; Univ. Professorship, Cornell Univ. 2000–04, mem. Advisory Council; mem. Jerusalem Comm.; mem. Bd of Dirs American Acad. and Inst. of Arts and Sciences; mem. Bd of Trustees, Cooper-Hewitt Museum; mem. Acad. Royale des Sciences, des lettres et des Beaux-Arts 1991; Fellow, American Acad. of Arts and Sciences; Hon. FRIBA; Dr hc (NJ Inst. of Tech.) 1987, (Universita di Napoli) 1991, (Parsons School of Deisgn) 1996, 1998, (Pratt School of Fine Arts) 1999, (Univ. of Bucharest) 2001, (NC State Univ.) 2004, (Mercy Coll.) 2004; Nat. AIA Awards: 1969, 1971, 1974, 1976, 1977, 1983–85, 1987, 1990, 1993, 2000, 2002, 2003, 2005, 2006, Regional AIA Awards: 1968, 1971, 1972, 1974, 1976, 1982, 1984–87, 1989 1990–93, 1996–2001, 2003–05, Progressive Architecture Award 1979, 1989–91, 1996, Architectural Record Award of Excellence for House Design 1964, 1968, 1969, 1977, Nat. Inst. of Arts and Letters Award in Architecture 1972, Pritzker Architecture Prize 1984, RIBA Gold Medal 1987, Progressive Architecture Gold Medal 1997, AIA Gold Medal 1998, Praemium Imperiale 1997; Commdr des Arts et

Lettres (France) 1992, Deutscher Architektur Preis 1993, 1995, AIA Twenty-Five Year Award 2000, World Architecture Award 2001, Pratt Legend Award 2004, American Acad. of Arts and Letters Gold Medal 2008, AIANY Pres.'s Award 2011, Sidney Strauss Award, New York Soc. of Architects 2011, Ellis Island Family Heritage Award 2012. *Major works:* Smith House, Darien, Conn. 1965–67, Westbeth Artists' Housing, New York 1967–70, Saltzman House, East Hampton, New York 1967–69, House in Old Westbury, Old Westbury, New York 1969–71, Bronx Devt Center 1970–77, Douglas House, Harbor Springs, Mich. 1971–76, Shamberg House, Chappaqua, New York 1972–77, The Atheneum, New Harmony, Ind. 1975–79, Hartford Seminary, Conn. 1978–81, Museum for Decorative Art, Frankfurt am Main, Germany 1979–85, High Museum of Art, Atlanta, Ga 1980–83, Renault HQ, France 1981, Museum für Kunsthandwerk, Germany 1984, Grotta House NJ 1984–89, The Getty Center, Los Angeles, Calif. 1985–97, Museum of Contemporary Art, Barcelona, Spain 1987–95, Canal+ Headquarters, Paris, France 1988–92, Rachofsky House, Dallas, Tex. 1991–96, US Courthouse, Islip, New York 1993–2000, Sandra Day O'Connor US Courthouse, Phoenix, Ariz. 1994–2000, City Hall and Cen. Library, The Hague 1995, Neugebauer House, Naples, Fla 1995–98, Int. Center for Possibility Thinking, Garden Grove, Calif. 1996–2003, Jubilee Church, Rome, Italy 1996–2003, J. Paul Getty Center 1997, San Jose Civic Center, San Jose, Calif. 1998–2005, 173/176 Perry Street Condominiums, New York 1999–2002, 66 Restaurant, New York 2002–03, Burda Collection Museum, Baden-Baden, Germany 2001–04, Charles Street Apartments, New York 2003–06, Italcementi i.lab, Bergamo 2005–12, OCT Shenzhen Clubhouse, Shenzhen 2008–12, and others. *Publications:* Richard Meier Museums, Building the Getty, Richard Meier, Richard Meier Architect 1–4, American Dream: The Houses at Sagaponac, Architecture in Detail: The Getty Center, Between Nature and Culture, Building the Getty/Richard Meier, Dives in Misericordia Church Rome: Project by Richard Meier Vols 1–3, Five Architects, Getty Center Design Process, Meier/Stella – Art and Architecture, Richard Meier, Richard Meier Architect (Monacelli Press), Richard Meier in Europe, Richard Meier Sculpture: 1992–1994, Richard Meier: The Architect as Designer and Artist, Richard Meier: Barcelona Museum of Contemporary Art, Richard Meier: Building for Art, Richard Meier: Collages, Richard Meier Details, Weishaupt Forum. *Address:* Richard Meier & Partners, 475 10th Avenue, Floor 6, New York, NY 10018, USA (office). *Telephone:* (212) 967-6060 (office). *Fax:* (212) 967-3207 (office). *E-mail:* mail@richardmeier.com (office). *Website:* www.richardmeier.com (office).

MEIMARAKIS, Evangelos-Vasileios (Vangelis); Greek lawyer and politician; *Speaker, Vouli (Parliament);* b. 14 Dec. 1953, Athens; m. Ioanna Kolokota; two d.; ed Athens Univ. Law School, Panteion Univ.; Founding mem. New Democracy youth group ONNED, fmr Pres.; mem. Nea Demokratia (New Democracy party) 1974–; mem. Parl. (New Democracy party) 1989–, New Democracy Political Planning and Programme Sec. 2000–01, Cen. Cttee Sec. 2001–06; Deputy Minister for Culture, responsible for sports 1992–1993; Minister of Nat. Defence 2006–09; Speaker of the Vouli (Parl.) 2012–. *Address:* Office of the President, Vouli, Parliament Building, Leoforos Vassilissis Sofias 2, 100 21 Athens (office); Solonos 113, 106 81 Athens (office); c/o New Democracy Party (Nea Demokratia), Odos Rhigillis 18, 106 74 Athens, Greece; Alkaiou 57, 157 71 Athens (home). *Telephone:* (210) 3708112 (Vouli) (office); (210) 3822024 (office); (210) 7798804 (home); (210) 3822024. *Fax:* (210) 3733566 (Vouli) (office); (210) 3845609. *E-mail:* meimarakis@ parliament.gr (office); info@meimarakis.gr. *Website:* www.hellenicparliament.gr (office); www.meimarakis.gr.

MEINWALD, Jerrold, MA, PhD, FAAS; American chemist and academic; *Goldwin Smith Professor Emeritus of Chemistry, Cornell University;* b. 16 Jan. 1927, New York, NY; s. of Dr Herman Meinwald and Sophie Baskind; m. 1st Dr Yvonne Chu 1955 (divorced 1979); two d.; m. 2nd Dr Charlotte Greenspan 1980; one d.; ed Brooklyn and Queen's Colls, Univ. of Chicago and Harvard Univ.; Instructor in Chem., Cornell Univ. 1952–54, Asst Prof. 1954–58, Assoc. Prof. 1958–61, Prof. 1961–72, Acting Chair. of Chem. 1968, Prof. of Chem. 1973–80, Goldwin Smith Prof. of Chem. 1980–2005, Andrew Mellon Foundation Prof. 1993–95, Goldwin Smith Prof. Emer. 2006–, Grad. School Prof. 2006–; Prof. of Chem., Univ. of California, San Diego 1972–73; Visiting Prof., Harvard Medical School 1997; Chemical Consultant, Schering-Plough Corpn 1957–2000, Procter & Gamble Pharmaceuticals 1958–96, Cambridge Neuroscience Research Inc. 1987–93; mem. Scientific Advisory Bd Entomed 2002–04; Consultant on Chemical Ecology, Max-Planck Soc. 1995–97; mem. of Visiting Cttee for Chem., Brookhaven Nat. Lab. 1969–73; numerous lectureships in USA, Canada, UK, Australia, NZ, France, Czechoslovakia, Switzerland, Belgium, China, Taiwan, Brazil, Japan; mem. Editorial Bd Organic Reactions 1967–78, Journal of Chemical Ecology 1974–, Insect Science and its Application 1979–91, Chemistry and Biochemistry 2004–, Proceedings of the National Academy of Science 2007–; Alfred P. Sloan Foundation Fellow 1958–62, Guggenheim Fellow 1960–61, 1976–77, NIH Special Postdoctoral Fellow 1967–68, Fogarty Int. Scholar 1983–84; Distinguished Scholar-in-Residence, Hope Coll., Holland, Mich. 1984; NAS Exchange Scholar to Czechoslovakia 1987; Fellow, Center for Advanced Study in the Behavioral Sciences (Stanford) 1990–91; Research Dir Int. Centre of Insect Physiology and Ecology, Nairobi 1970–77; mem. Advisory Bd Petroleum Research Fund 1970–73, Advisory Bd Research Corpn 1978–83, Advisory Council Dept of Chem., Princeton Univ. 1978–82, Advisory Bd (Chem. Section) NSF 1979–82, Scientific Advisory Bd Native Plants Inc. 1987–93; Organizing Chair. Sino-American Symposium on the Chem. of Natural Products, Shanghai 1980, UNESCO's Working Group on Co-operation in the Field of Natural Products Chem. 1982–87, Chem. Program Cttee Alfred P. Sloan Foundation 1985–91; mem. Bd Dirs Xerces Soc. 1994–, Scientific Cttee PROBEM/Amazonia 1996–2003; Pres. Int. Soc. of Chemical Ecology 1988–89; mem. NAS, American Philosophical Soc.; Fellow, American Acad. of Arts and Sciences (Sec. 2006–), Japan Soc. for the Promotion of Science; Hon. PhD (Göteborg) 1989; ACS Edgar Fah Smith Award 1977, ACS E. Guenther Award 1984, Distinguished Scientist-Lecturer Award, Kalamazoo Section of ACS 1985, ACS A.C. Cope Scholar Award 1989, Tyler Prize in Environmental Science 1990, ACS Gustavus John Esselen Award for Chem. in the Public Interest 1991, Silver Medal, Int. Soc. of Chemical Ecology 1991, J. Heyrovsky Medal, Czech Acad. of Sciences 1996, ACS Roger Adams Award in Organic Chem. 2005. *Publications:* Advances in Alicyclic Chemistry Vol. I (co-author) 1966, Explorations in Chemical Ecology (co-ed.) 1987, Pheromone Biochemistry (co-author) 1987, Chemical Ecology: The Chemistry of Biotic Interaction (co-ed.) 1995, Science and the

Educated American 2010; more than 400 research articles in major chemical journals. *Leisure interests:* playing flute, baroque flute and recorder. *Address:* Department of Chemistry and Chemical Biology, Cornell University, Ithaca, NY 14853 (office); 429 Warren Road, Ithaca, NY 14850, USA (home). *Telephone:* (607) 255-3301 (office); (607) 257-0035 (home). *Fax:* (607) 255-3407 (office). *E-mail:* circe@cornell.edu (office). *Website:* www.chem.cornell.edu (office).

MEIRELLES, Fernando; Brazilian film director; *Owner / Director, 02 Filmes;* b. (Fernando Ferreira Meirelles), 11 Sept. 1955, São Paulo; m. Ciça Meirelles; one s. one d.; ed Universidade de São Paulo; trained as architect; created experimental video productions at univ.; producer of TV programmes including Crig Rá, O Mundo no Ar, Ernesto Varella, TV Mix, Comédia da Vida Privada, Cidade dos Homens; Dir Rá-Tim-Bum (children's series, TV Cultura) 1989–90; Co-founder 02 Filmes Co. (largest commercial production co. in Brazil); debut as feature film director 1997; several awards for Rá-Tim-Bum including New York Film and TV Festival Gold Medal, Cannes Film Festival Lion and Clio Awards; over 20 other prizes. *Films include:* O Menino Maluquinho (Crazy Kid) 1997, E no Meio Passa um Trem (short film) 1998, Domesticas (Maids) 2000, Cidade de Deus (City of God) 2001, Palace II (short film) 2001, The Constant Gardener 2005, Blindness 2008, '360' 2012. *Address:* Rua Baumann 930, Vila Hamburguesa, São Paulo, SP 05318-000, Brazil (office). *Telephone:* (11) 38399410 (office). *Fax:* (11) 36410415 (office). *E-mail:* liane@o2filmes.com (office). *Website:* www.o2filmes.com (office).

MEIRELLES, Henrique de Campos, BCE, MBA; Brazilian banker; b. 31 Aug. 1945; m. Eva Missini; ed Univ. of São Paulo, Fed. Univ. of Rio de Janeiro and Harvard Business School, USA; Man. Dir BankBoston Leasing 1974, Vice-Pres., São Paulo 1978, Head Commercial Bank in Brazil 1980, Deputy Country Man. 1981, Pres. and Regional Man. in Brazil 1984, Pres. and COO BankBoston Corpn 1996, Pres. FleetBoston's Global and Wholesale Bank and mem. Bd of Dirs, also Office of the Chair. FleetBoston Financial 1999–2002; Fed. Dep. for Goiás state 2002; Gov. Cen. Bank of Brazil 2003–10; mem. Bd of Dirs Raytheon Corpn, New York, New England Conservatory, Inst. of Contemporary Art, Acción Int.; mem. Advisory Council Sloan School of Man., MIT, Harvard Business School Initiative on Global Corp. Governance, Boston Coll. Carroll School of Man., Center for Latin American Issues of the George Washington Univ., Brazilian-American Chamber of Commerce, New York, Adolfo Ibañez Univ., Santiago, Chile; Founding Pres. Latin American Leasing Fed.; Chair. Emer. Brazilian Asscn of Int. Banks; Chair. Soc. for the Revitalization of the City of São Paulo, Travessia Foundation; mem. Exec. Cttee US-Brazilian Business Council, American Chamber of Commerce, São Paulo; joined Partido do Movimento Democrático Brasileiro 2009. *Address:* c/o Banco Central do Brasil, SBS, Q.03, Bloco B, CP 08670, 70074-900 Brasília, DF, Brazil.

MEIRING, Gen. Georg Lodewyk, MSc; South African army officer; b. 18 Oct. 1939, Ladybrand; m. Anna Maria G. Brink; three s. two d.; ed Univ. of the Orange Free State; joined S African Army as a signals officer 1963, later Dir of Signals; Officer Commdg Witswatersrand Command, Johannesburg 1981–82; Chief of Army Staff, Logistics, S African Defence Force (SADF), Pretoria 1982–83; Gen. Officer Commdg SW Africa Territory Defence Forces, Windhoek 1987–89; Gen. Officer Commdg Far North, Pietersburg 1989–90; Deputy Chief, S African Army, SADF, Pretoria 1983–87, 1990–93, Chief S African Nat. Defence Force (SANDF) 1994–98; several mil. decorations, including Order of the Star of South Africa (Gold) 1998, Order of the Cloud and Banner, Fourth Class (Taiwan), Southern Cross Decoration, Southern Cross Medal, Mil. Merit Medal. *Leisure interests:* hunting, gardening, reading, walking. *Address:* Private Bag X414, Pretoria 0001, South Africa.

MEISEL, Steven; American fashion photographer; *Principal Photographer, Vogue;* b. 1955, New York City; ed High School of Art and Design, Parsons The New School for Design; began career as Lecturer at Parsons School of Design; work for fashion designer Halston as an illustrator; worked as illustrator for Women's Wear Daily; professional photographer 1980–; currently prin. photographer for American and Italian versions of Vogue magazine and for W magazine; photographer for advertising campaigns of designers Versace, Yves Saint Laurent, Prada, Dolce & Gabbana, Valentino, Louis Vuitton, Balenciaga and Calvin Klein; credited with discovering or promoting the careers of numerous successful models, including Linda Evangelista, Naomi Campbell, Nadège du Bospertus, Christy Turlington, Kristen McMenamy, Amber Valletta, Snejana Onopka, Iris Strubegger, Lara Stone, Coco Rocha, Caroline Trentini, Liya Kebede, Karen Elson, Doutzen Kroes and Raquel Zimmerman; exhbn of photography at White Cube2 Gallery, London 2001; has contributed photos for covers of albums including two RIAA Diamond-certified albums, Madonna's Like a Virgin 1984, Mariah Carey's Daydream 1995. *Publications include:* Sex. Erotic Fantasies. Madonna (with Madonna) 1992, Stern Portfolio No. 32: Steven Meisel 2003. *Address:* c/o Jim Moffat, Art+Commerce, 531 West 25th Street, 4th Floor New York, NY 10001, USA (office); c/o Vogue, Condé Nast Publications, 4 Times Square, New York, NY 10036, USA (office). *Telephone:* (212) 206-0737 (office); (212) 286-2860 (office). *Fax:* (212) 463-7267 (office). *E-mail:* artists@artandcommerce.com (office). *Website:* www.artandcommerce.com/artists/photographers/steven-meisel (office); www .vogue.com/magazine (office).

MEISNER, HE Cardinal Joachim; German ecclesiastic; *Archbishop of Cologne and Primate of Germany;* b. 25 Dec. 1933, Breslau; s. of Walter Meisner and Hedwig Meisner; ed Univ. of Erfurt, Pastoral Seminary at Neuzelle; ordained priest 1962; Chaplain of St Ägidien, Heiligenstadt 1963–66, St Crucis, Erfurt 1966; Caritas-Rector, Diocese of Erfurt 1966–75; Auxiliary Bishop of Erfurt-Meiningen and Titular Bishop of Vina 1975–80; Bishop of Berlin 1980–89; cr. Cardinal (Cardinal-Priest of Santa Pudenziana) 1983; Archbishop of Cologne and Primate of Germany 1988–; participated in Papal Conclave 2005, 2013; Hon. Citizen of Miguel Pereira, Brazil 1992; Hon. PhD (Jesuit Univ., Manila) 1990. *Publications:* Das Auditorium Coelicum am Dom zu Erfurt 1960, Nachreformatorische katholische Frömmigkeitsformen in Erfurt 1971, various articles in magazines. *Leisure interest:* Christian art. *Address:* Kardinal-Frings-Str. 10, 50668 Cologne, Germany (office). *Telephone:* (221) 16420 (office). *Fax:* (221) 16421700 (office). *E-mail:* erzbischof@erzbistum-koeln.de (office). *Website:* www.erzbistum-koeln.de (office).

MEJÍA, HE Cardinal Jorge María, DTheol; Argentine ecclesiastic; *Archivist Emeritus of Vatican Secret Archives;* b. 31 Jan. 1923, Buenos Aires; ed Pontifical

Univ. of St Thomas Aquinas (Angelicum), Pontifical Biblical Institute; ordained priest 1945; Titular Archbishop of Apollonia 1986; Official of Justice and Peace 1986–94; Sec. of Bishops 1994–98; Archivist of Vatican Secret Archives and Librarian of Vatican Library 1998–2003, Archivist Emer. 2003–; cr. Cardinal (Cardinal-Deacon of San Girolamo della Carità) 2001, Cardinal Priest of San Girolamo della Carità 2011; led del. from the Pontifical Comm. for Religious Relations with the Jews meeting for the Comm. for Dialogue between Jews and Catholics 2010; mem. Bd World Religious Leaders for the interfaith dialogue-based org. the Elijah Interfaith Inst. *Address:* c/o Palazzo Apostolico Vaticano, 00120 Città del Vaticano, Italy. *Telephone:* (06) 69883314. *Website:* www.vatican.va/ library_archives/vat_secret_archives/index.htm.

MEJÍA DOMÍNGUEZ, Rafael Hipólito; Dominican Republic politician; Pres. of the Dominican Repub. 2000–04. *Address:* c/o Administrative Secretariat of the Presidency, Palacio Nacional, Avda México, esq. Dr Delgado, Santo Domingo, D.N., Dominican Republic (office).

MEJÍA VÉLEZ, María Emma; Colombian journalist and politician; *Secretary-General, Union of South American Nations;* b. 27 Sept. 1953, Medellín; ed Universidad Pontificia Bolivariana, Medellín, Universidad del Valle, Cali; began career working for BBC Latin America division, London; Head, Focine (Colombian nat. film promotion co.) 1984–89; communications officer for presidential campaign of Liberal party leader Luis Carlos Galán 1985–89, campaign Sec.-Gen. for his successor César Gaviria (following assassination of Galán 1989) 1989–90; presidential councillor for Medellín (first political appointment) 1990–93; Amb. to Spain 1993–95; Minister of Educ. 1995–96, of Foreign Affairs 1996–98; Vice-Presidential Cand. (unsuccessful) 1998; apptd govt rep. to negotiations with FARC 1999; Cand. for Bogota Mayoral Elections 2000, 2003; investigative journalist at Caracol TV channel; host, 'Entérate con María Emma' (current affairs show), Caracol TV Internacional 2009–; Sec.-Gen., Union of South American Nations (UNASUR) 2011–; fmr mem. Partido Liberal Colombiano (PL); mem. Polo Democrático Alternativo (PDA) 2004–. *Address:* UNASUR, Edificio Río Amazonas, Av. Amazonas 477 y Roca 5to piso, Quito, Ecuador (office). *Telephone:* (5932) 250 2770 (office). *E-mail:* unasur@mmrree.gov.ec (office). *Website:* www.pptunasur .com (office).

MEKSI, Aleksandër Gabriel; Albanian politician and engineer; *Leader, Pole of Freedom (Polit të Lirisë);* b. 8 March 1939; fmr construction engineer and restorer of medieval architecture; mem. Democratic Party of Albania; Prime Minister of Albania 1992–97 (first following end of communist rule); Leader of Pole of Freedom (Polit të Lirisë—right-wing coalition between Christian Democratic Party, Movt for Nat. Devt and several asscns of landowners expropriated by the communist regime and victims of communist prosecution) 2009–. *E-mail:* info@ aleksandermeksi.com. *Website:* aleksandermeksi.com.

MEKSI, Ermelinda, DEcon, PhD; Albanian economist, academic and politician; b. 1957, Tirana; ed European Univ. of Tirana, Univ. La Sapienza, Italy; mem. of Faculty, Faculty of Econs, Univ. of Tirana 1975–80; Asst Prof. of Econs, Tirana Univ. 1981–87; co-f. Socialist Party 1991; mem. Parl. (Socialist Party) 1992–; Minister of State for Devt and Econ. Cooperation 1997–98; Minister of Econ. Cooperation and Trade 1998–2000; Head of Albanian Parl. Del. to European Parl. 2002–03; Deputy Prime Minister and State Minister of European Integration 2003, Minister of European Integration 2003–05; chief negotiator for Albanian WTO Accession 2000, Stability Pact and Stabilization and Asscn Agreement negotiations with EC 2004–06; mem. Parl. Cttee on Economy, Finances and Privatization; Visiting Prof., La Sapienza Univ., Rome 1992–93, Univ. of Bari, Univ. of Dublin, Kosovo Univ., Univ. La Signora del Buon Consiglio, Tirana, Marin Barleti Univ., Tirana, European Univ., Tirana; del. to several int. orgs including EC, World Bank, IMF, EBRD, UNDP, WTO, European Investment Bank; mem. Bd of Trustees, Marin Barleti Univ. *Publications:* author of several publications and co-author of several reference books and school texts. *Address:* Albanian Parliament, Tirana, Albania (office).

MELAMED, Leonid A., CandSci, PhD; Russian business executive; *Deputy Chairman, AFK Sistema;* b. 1967, Moscow; ed Sechenov Moscow Medical Acad.; worked at ROSNO 1991–2006, Dir Gen. and Chair. Man. Bd 2003–06; Chair. Expert Council on Insurance Legislation (part of Russian State Duma Cttee on Credit Orgs and Financial Markets) 2004–06; mem. Bd of Dirs Mobile TeleSystems OJSC 2006–, Pres. and CEO 2006–08; Pres. and CEO AFK Sistema 2008–11, Deputy Chair. 2011–; Chair. Russneft 2010–; mem. Bd of Dirs MTS Inc. 2006–, GSM Asscn 2008–, OJSC Rosno –2011, Bashneft Jt Stock Oil Co.; Exec. Dir Mobile Telesystems OJSC 2006–08; Chair. Expert Council in Insurance Legislation (part of Russian State Duma Cttee on Credit Orgs and Financial Markets) 2004–06; numerous awards in Russia, including being named Person of the Year in annual People of the Year project by internet holding co. Rambler 2004, Golden Salamander Russian Public Award in the insurance sector in the category of The Manager of Insurance Company, selected as one of the 250 Young Global Leaders by the World Econ. Forum 2007. *Address:* AFK Sistema, 125009 Moscow, 13 Mokhovaya Street, Russia (office). *Telephone:* (495) 228-15-01 (office). *Fax:* (495) 629-12-52 (office). *E-mail:* chairman@sistema.ru (office). *Website:* www.sistema.ru (office); www.sistema.com (office).

MELAMID, Aleksandr; Russian artist; b. 14 July 1945, Moscow; ed Stroganov School and Acad. of Art, Vilnius; initial artistic training at Moscow Art School; originator (with Vitaliy Komar) of 'Sots-art'; mem. of USSR Union of Artists, expelled for "distortion of Soviet reality and non-conformity with the principles of Socialist realism" 1972; moved to Israel 1977, to USA 1978. *Principal works include:* Young Marx 1976, Colour Writing 1972, Quotation 1972, Post Art 1973, Factory for Producing Blue Smoke 1975, Poster Series 1980. *Publications include:* Turkey (Around the world program) 1957, Painting by Numbers: Komar and Melamid's Scientific Guide to Art (co-ed.) 1999, When Elephants Paint: The Quest of Two Russian Artists to Save the Elephants of Thailand 2000.

MELANDRI, Giovanna, BEcons; Italian politician; b. 28 Jan. 1962, New York, USA; m.; one d.; ed Univ. of Rome; mem. Bd of Legambiente 1982–, Head of Int. Legambiente 1988–94; mem. Nat. Secr. of the Environment 1989–94, Nat. Direction of Partito Democratico della Sinistra 1991–2007 (mem. Exec. Cttee, in charge of Communication Policy 1996–98), Partito Democratico 2007–; mem. Camera dei Deputati (Chamber of Deputies) 1994–; mem. Young Progressive

Networks of Policy Network 2005–; Minister of Culture 1998–2001, for Youth and Sports 2006–08; Shadow Minister for Communication 2008–09; Head of Culture Dept, Democratic Party 2009–; promoter, Emily in Italia (initiative of 50 women active in politics and society promoting women in politics) 1998–; Officier, Légion d'honneur 2003; Hon. PhD (John Cabot Univ.) 2000. *Publications include*: (ed.): Ambiente Italia (annual environmental report of Legambiente) 1989–94, Italian World Watch Magazine 1986–91, Digitalia, l'ultima rivoluzione 1998, Cultura, paesaggio e turismo 2006), Come un chiodo: la moda, le ragazze, l'alimentazione 2007. *Address*: Partito Democratico, Piazza Saint'Anastasia 7, 00186 Rome, Italy (office). *Telephone*: (06) 675471 (office). *Fax*: (06) 67547319 (office). *E-mail*: info@partitodemocratico.it (office); melandri_g@camera.it (office). *Website*: www.partitodemocratico.it (office).

MELCHETT, 4th Baron, cr. 1928; **Peter Robert Henry Mond Melchett**, LLB, MA; British organic farmer, environmentalist and fmr politician; *Policy Director, Soil Association*; b. (Peter Mond), 24 Feb. 1948, Norfolk, England; s. of Lord Julian Melchett (died 1973) and Sonia Melchett; one s. one d.; ed Eton Coll., Univ. of Cambridge, Keele Univ., Staffs.; mem. Labour Party; House of Lords Peer 1973–99; Govt Minister, Depts of Environment and Industry 1975–77; Minister of State, NI Office 1977–79; Pres. Ramblers Asscn 1981–84; Chair. Community Industry 1979–86, Wildlife Link 1979–85; Special Lecturer School of Biological Sciences, Nottingham Univ. 1984–2002; joined Greenpeace UK 1985, Chair. and Exec. Dir (arrested and remanded in prison for two days after destroying six acres of genetically modified (GM) maize at farm in Lyng, cleared of causing criminal damage, Norfolk Crown Court 2000) 1989–2000; Chair. Greenpeace Japan 1995–2001; Consultant, Corp. Responsibility Dept, Burson-Marsteller UK (public relations co.) 2002–04; Policy Dir, Soil Asscn (organic foods certification body) 2002–; mem. BBC Rural Affairs Committee 2004–, Dept of Educ. School Meals Review Panel 2005; Patron Prisoners Abroad; Hon. DCL (Newcastle). *Address*: The Soil Association, South Plaza, Marlborough Street, Bristol, BS1 3NX, England (office). *Telephone*: (117) 987-4575 (office). *E-mail*: pmelchett@soilassociation.org (office). *Website*: www.soilassociation.org (office); www.courtyardfarm.co.uk (office).

MELCHIOR, Torben, LLM; Danish judge; *President, Supreme Court*; b. 19 Aug. 1940; ed Univ. of Copenhagen, Harvard Law School, USA; civil servant, Ministry of Justice 1966–81, Head, Directorate of Family Law 1982–86; High Court Judge 1986–90; Justice of Supreme Court 1991, Pres. Supreme Court 2004–. *Address*: Supreme Court, Prins Jørgens Gård 13, 1218 Copenhagen, Denmark (office). *Telephone*: 33-63-27-50 (office). *Fax*: 33-15-00-10 (office). *Website*: www.hoejesteret.dk (office).

MELÉNDEZ, Florentín, MA, PhD; Salvadorean academic, international organization official and udge; *Judge, Supreme Court of Justice*; ed Nat. Univ. of El Salvador, Complutense Univ. of Madrid, Spain; worked at UN and in public and pvt. insts in El Salvador on issues related to human rights; joined Inter-American Comm. on Human Rights (IACHR—Comisión Interamericana de Derechos Humanos), OAS 2004, Pres. 2004; currently Judge, Supreme Court of Justice; Special Rapporteur for rights of persons deprived of liberty in Americas; prepared Draft Declaration of Principles on Protection of Persons Deprived of Freedom; has also been Rapporteur for Argentina, Bolivia, Mexico and Dominican Repub.; del. on several occasions to Inter-American Court of Human Rights; visiting lecturer on human rights at several univs; Freedom Award, Marcelino Pan Y Vino/MAPAVI Foundation 2007. *Publications*: numerous books and compilations on human rights. *Address*: Supreme Court of Justice, Frente a Plaza José Simeón Cañas, Centro de Gobierno, San Salvador, El Salvador (office). *Telephone*: 2271-8888 (office). *Fax*: 2271-3767 (office). *Website*: www.csj.gob.sv (home).

MELÉNDEZ RIVAS, Adm.-in-Chief Carmen Teresa; Venezuelan naval officer and government official; *Minister of Defence;* b. 3 Nov. 1961; m. Orlando Maniglia; three c.; ed Catia La Mar Naval Acad., Vargas, Escuela Naval de Venezuela, Univ. José María Vargas; Cand. Platoon Commdr, Naval School of Venezuela 1984–85, Head of Payment Man. Dept, Finance Div. of Fuerza Armada Bolivariana (Navy) 1986–87, Women's Platoon Commdr, Naval School of Venezuela 1987–88, Head of Customs Dept of Chief of Navy Supply 1988–90, Head, Office of Planning and Budget Control Supply, Navy HQ 1990–92, Dir of Admin and Services, Planning and Budget Div., Ministry of Defence 1992–95, Head of Navy Financial Control Materials Div. 1995–96, Head of Control Div. (Navy Materials) 1996–97, Chief of Procurement Div. of Gen Admin Sector, Ministry of Defence 1997–99, Chief, Expenditure Control Div., Navy Finance Div. 1999–2000, Dir-Gen, Ministry of Admin. 2000–02; Internal Man. Dir of Office of Pres. 2002–03, Nat. Treasurer 2003–07; Dir Naval Budget and Financial Programming April–Sept. 2007, Dir of Naval Org. and Human Resource Devt 2010; Minister of Office of Presidency and Govt Man. 2012–13, Minister of Defence 2013–; rank of Vice-Adm. 2007, Adm. 2012, Adm.-in-Chief 2013. *Address*: Ministry of Defence, Edif. 17 de Diciembre, planta baja, Base Aérea Francisco de Miranda, La Carlota, Caracas, Venezuela (office). *Telephone*: (212) 908-1264 (office). *Fax*: (212) 237-4974 (office). *E-mail*: noiralith.gil@mindefensa.gov.ve (office). *Website*: www.mindefensa.gob.ve (office).

MELEȘCANU, Teodor Viorel, PhD; Romanian jurist and politician; b. 10 March 1941, Brad, Hunedoara Co.; m. Felicia Meleșcanu; one d.; ed Moise Nicoara High School, Arad, Bucharest Univ., Univ. Inst. for Higher Int. Studies, Geneva; with Ministry of Foreign Affairs 1966; mem. numerous dels to UN confs; First Sec. UN, Geneva; Sec., Ministry of Foreign Affairs, Minister of Foreign Affairs 1992–96, also Deputy Prime Minister; Senator (for Prahova constituency) 1996–2000, Minister of Defence 2007–08; Assoc. Prof. of Int. Law, Univ. of Bucharest 1996–; researcher, Romanian Inst. for Int. Studies 1996–; Founder and Pres. Alliance for Romania (social democratic party) 1997–2001, merged into Nat. Liberal Party (Partidul Național Liberal—PNL) 2001, First Vice-Pres. 2001–; presidential cand. 2000; mem. Asscn of Int. Law and Int. Relations (ADIRI), Int. Law Comm. (UN) (First Vice-Chair. 55th Session, Chair. 56th Session). *Publications*: Responsibility of States for the Peaceful Use of Nuclear Energy 1973, International Labour Organization Functioning and Activity, numerous studies and articles. *Leisure interests*: sports (tennis and ski), hunting and fishing. *Address*: National Liberal Party (NLP), 011866 Bucharest, Bd. Aviatorilor 86, Romania (office). *Telephone*: (21) 2310795 (office). *Fax*: (21) 2310796 (office). *E-mail*: dre@pnl.ro (office). *Website*: www.pnl.ro (office).

MELIANAS, Artūras, MA (Econ); Lithuanian politician; *Chairman, Liberal and Centre Union;* b. 25 June 1964, Panevėžys; s. of Joana Melianas and Teodor Melianas; m. Lina Melianas; three s.; ed Panevėžys Secondary School No. 3, Vilnius Coll., Vilnius Univ.; engineer at Vilnius Drill Plant 1985–90; Deputy Head of Social Security Div., Vilnius City Municipality 1990–97; mem. Vilnius City Municipality Council, Chair. Social Affairs Cttee 1997–2000; mem. Lithuanian Liberal Union from 1990, mem. Bd Liberal and Centre Union after consolidation of the Lithuanian Liberal, Lithuanian Centre and Modern Christian Democrats unions from 2003, Vice-Chair. Liberal and Centre Union 2009–; mem. Seimas (Parl.) 2000–04, elected in a multi-mandate electoral dist in accordance with the list of the Lithuanian Liberal and Centre Union, mem. Social Affairs and Labour Cttee (Chair. 2000–01) 2000–04; Adviser to the Mayor of Vilnius 2005; Head of Social Security Div. of Vilnius City Municipality 2005–06; Deputy Gov. Vilnius Co. 2006–08; mem. Seimas for Naujoji Vilnia electoral dist (No. 10), nominated by the Liberal and Centre Union 2008–12, mem. Social Affairs and Labour Cttee (Vice-Chair. 2008–12), mem. Comm. for Parl. Scrutiny of Operational Activities 2008–12; Minister of the Interior 2012; est. in co-operation with Vilnius foundation 'Children and World' free leasure club Debesėlis (Cloudlet) for young people in Naujininkai 1996; est. Naujininkų bendruomenė (Naujininkai Community) 2001, Day Centre in Pavilnys 2007; Co-founder and mem. Bd Dvarčionys Community 2008–; Vice-Chair. Lithuanian Red Cross 2003–04, Lithuanian Social Workers Asscn; Pres. Vilnius Capital LIONS club 2013–; mem. Viltis (Hope) Soc. *Leisure interests*: travelling, music, communication, socializing. *Address*: LiCS, Vilniaus g. 22/1, 01402 Vilnius (office); Raitininkų 8b-12, Vilnius 09232, Lithuania (home). *E-mail*: arturas.melianas@lics.lt (office). *Website*: www.lics.lt (office); www.melianas.lt.

MELINESCU, Gabriela; Romanian poet, editor, essayist and translator; b. 16 Aug. 1942, Bucharest; ed Univ. of Philology, Bucharest; began career as Ed. Femeia and Luceafarul magazines; based in Sweden 1975–; trans. of works by Swedenborg, Strindberg, Brigitta Trotzig, Goran Sonevi; Albert Bonniers Prize 2002, Nichita Stanescu Prize 2002, Inst. of Romanian Culture Prize 2004. *Publications include*: poetry: Ceremonie de iarna 1965, Fiintele abstracte 1967, Interiorul legii 1968, Boala de origine divina 1970, Juramantul de saracie, castitate si supunere (Writers' Union Prize) 1972, Inginarea lumiir 1972, Impotriva celui drag 1975, Zeul fecunditatii 1977, Oglinda femeii 1986, Lumina spre lumina 1993; prose: Jurnal suedez Vols I–III, Bobinocarii 1969, Catargul cu doua corabii (juvenile) 1969, Viata cere viata (jtly) (non-fiction) 1975, Copiii rabdarii 1979, Lupii urca in cer 1981, Vrajitorul din Gallipoli 1986, Regina strazii 1988, Omul pasare (Swedish Acad. De Nio Prize) 1991, Hemma utomlands (novel) 2003, Mamma som Gud (novel) 2010; contrib. to Crossing Boundaries: An International Anthology of Women's Experiences in Sport 1999. *Address*: c/o Editura Polirom, Board Copou nr. 4, 700506 Iași, Romania. *E-mail*: office@polirom.ro.

MELKERT, Adrianus (Ad) Petrus Wilhelmus, MA; Dutch politician, banker, independent adviser and UN official; b. 1956, Gouda; m. Mónica León Borquez; two d.; ed Univ. of Amsterdam; Pres., Council of European Nat. Youth Cttees 1979–81; Sec.-Gen. Youth Forum of the EC 1981–84; Pres. Nat. Cttee, UN Int. Youth Year 1984–85; Asst to Gen. Sec., Dir Internal Affairs, Netherlands Org. for Int. Devt Co-operation 1984–86; mem. Parl. 1986–; Minister of Social Affairs and Employment 1994–98; Parl. Leader Partij van de Arbeid (PvdA – Labour Party) 1998–2002, Party Leader 2001–02 (resgnd after 2002 election defeat); Exec. Dir for the Netherlands and 11 other mem. states, World Bank (IBRD) 2002–06; Under-Sec.-Gen. and Assoc. Admin., UNDP 2006–09; UN Sec.-Gen.'s Special Rep. for Iraq and Head, UN Assistance Mission for Iraq (UNAMI) 2009–11; Special Rapporteur, Global Child Labour Conf., The Netherlands 2010; Order of Oranje-Nassau 1998, Gran Cruz en la Orden de Bernardo O'Higgins (Chile) 1998, Das Grosse Verdienstkreuzmit Stern des Verdienstordens der Bundesrepublik Deutschland 2001. *E-mail*: adrianusmelkert@gmail.com.

MELLO, Craig C., BS, PhD; American geneticist and academic; *Howard Hughes Medical Investigator and Professor, Program in Molecular Medicine, University of Massachusetts Medical School;* b. 18 Oct. 1960, New Haven, Conn.; ed Fairfax High School, Va, Brown Univ., Harvard Univ.; Postdoctoral Fellow, Fred Hutchinson Cancer Research Center; joined faculty, Univ. of Massachusetts Medical School 1994, currently Prof. in Program in Molecular Medicine, Howard Hughes Medical Investigator 2000–; affiliated with Center for AIDS Research, Interdisciplinary Grad. Program, Cell Biology, Cancer Center, Program in Cell Dynamics; mem. NAS 2005; Warren Triennial Prize, Massachusetts Gen. Hosp., Wiley Prize in Biomedical Sciences (co-recipient), Rockefeller Univ. 2003, NAS Award in Molecular Biology (co-recipient) 2003, Lewis S. Rosenstiel Award for Distinguished Work in Medical Research (co-recipient), Brandeis Univ. 2005, Gairdner Foundation Int. Award 2005, Massry Prize (co-recipient) 2005, Paul Ehrlich and Ludwig Darmstaedter Prize (co-recipient) 2006, inaugural recipient Dr Paul Janssen Award for Biomedical Research, Johnson & Johnson 2006, Nobel Prize in Physiology or Medicine (co-recipient with Andrew Fire) for the discovery of RNA interference 2006. *Publications*: numerous scientific papers in professional journals. *Address*: Biotech Two, Suite 219, Program in Molecular Medicine, University of Massachusetts, 373 Plantation Street, Worcester, MA 01605, USA (office). *Telephone*: (508) 856-2254 (office). *E-mail*: Craig.Mello@umassmed.edu (office). *Website*: umassmed.edu (office); www.hhmi.org/research/investigators/mello.html (office).

MELLOR, Rt Hon. David, PC, QC, FZS; British lawyer, journalist, fmr politician and broadcaster; b. 12 March 1949, Wareham, Dorset, England; s. of Douglas H. Mellor; m. Judith Hall 1974 (divorced 1996); two s.; ed Swanage Grammar School, Christ's Coll., Cambridge, Inns of Court School of Law; called to the Bar (Inner Temple) 1972; apptd QC 1987; Chair. Cambridge Univ. Conservative Asscn 1970; fmr Vice-Chair. Chelsea Conservative Asscn; MP for Putney 1979–97; Parl. Under-Sec. of State, Dept of Energy 1981–83, Home Office 1983–86, Minister of State, Home Office 1986–87, FCO 1987–88; Minister for Health 1988–89; Minister of State, Home Office 1989–90; Minister for the Arts July–Nov. 1990; Chief Sec. to Treasury 1990–92; Sec. of State for Nat. Heritage April–Sept. 1992; Consultant Middle East Broadcasting Centre, Middle East Economic Digest, Abela Holdings, RACAL Tacticom, British Aerospace, Ernst & Young, G.K.N.; mem. Bd Amor Holdings, ENO 1993–95; Chair. Sports Aid Foundation 1993–97, Football Task

Force 1997–99; Deputy Chair. Trustees London Philharmonic Orchestra 1989–90; presenter Six-O-Six BBC Radio 5 1993–99, The Midnight Hour, BBC 2 1997–99, Across the Threshold (series) 1998–, Classic FM 1998–; sports columnist, Evening Standard 1997–2008; Exec. Dir Three Delta LLP 2006–; music critic, Mail on Sunday 2000–; fmr mem. Council Nat. Youth Orchestra; Special Trustee, Westminster Hosp. 1979–86; Hon. Assoc. British Veterinary Asscn (for work for animal welfare) 1986; Variety Club Award for BBC Radio Personality of the Year 1994. *Leisure interests:* classical music, football, reading. *Address:* 1st Floor, 14 Hay's Mews, London, W1J 5PT, England (office). *Telephone:* (20) 7514-5522 (office). *Fax:* (20) 7499-1811 (office).

MELLOR, David Hugh, MA, MEng, MS, PhD, ScD; British philosopher and academic; *Professor Emeritus of Philosophy, University of Cambridge;* b. 10 July 1938, London, England; s. of S. D. Mellor and E. N. Mellor (née Hughes); ed Newcastle Royal Grammar School, Manchester Grammar School and Pembroke Coll., Cambridge; Harkness Fellowship in Chem. Eng, Univ. of Minnesota, USA 1960–62, MIT School of Chem. Eng Practice 1962; Tech. Officer, ICI 1962–63; research student in philosophy 1963–68; Fellow, Pembroke Coll., Cambridge 1964–70; Fellow, Darwin Coll., Cambridge 1971–2005, Vice-Master 1983–87; Asst Lecturer in Philosophy, Univ. of Cambridge 1965–70, Lecturer 1970–83, Reader in Metaphysics 1983–86, Prof. of Philosophy 1986–99, Prof. Emer. 1999–, Pro-Vice-Chancellor 2000–01; Visiting Fellow in Philosophy, ANU 1975; Radcliffe Fellow in Philosophy 1978–80; Visiting Prof., Auckland Univ., NZ 1985; Pres. British Soc. for the Philosophy of Science 1985–87, Aristotelian Soc. 1992–93; Fellow, British Acad. 1983–2008; Hon. Prof. of Philosophy, Univ. of Keele 1989–92; Hon. PhD (Lund) 1997. *Publications:* The Matter of Chance 1971, Real Time 1981, Matters of Metaphysics 1991, The Facts of Causation 1995, Real Time II 1998, Probability: A Philosophical Introduction 2005, Mind, Meaning and Reality 2012; numerous articles on philosophy of science, metaphysics and philosophy of mind. *Leisure interest:* theatre. *Address:* 25 Orchard Street, Cambridge, CB1 1JS, England (home). *Telephone:* 7815-687505 (mobile). *E-mail:* dhm11@cam.ac.uk (home). *Website:* people.pwf.cam.ac.uk/dhm11 (office).

MELLOR, James R., BEE, MS; American business executive and electrical engineer; *Chairman, USEC Inc.;* b. 1931; m. Suzanne Mellor; three c.; ed Univ. of Michigan; Research Engineer, then Section Man. in charge of Electronics Systems Design, Hughes Aircraft Co. 1955–58; various eng and man. positions Litton Industries, including Corpn Vice-Pres., Pres. Data Systems Div., Vice-Pres. of Business Devt, Vice-Pres. of Eng, Dir of Advanced Devt, Sr Vice-Pres. Communications and Electronics Data Systems Group 1970–73, Exec. Vice-Pres. Defense Systems Group 1973–77; Dir AM Int. Inc. 1977–81, also Pres. and COO; joined Gen. Dynamics 1981, Exec. Vice-Pres. Marine, Land Systems and Int. 1986–91, Pres. and COO 1991–93, Pres. and CEO 1993–94, Chair. and CEO 1994–97, Consultant and mem. Bd of Dirs 1997; Chair. USEC Inc. 1998–; Chair. AmerisourceBergen Corpn 2004–06 (retd); Consultant to Dept of Defense 1972–75; fmr Chair. Shipbuilders Council of America, Computer and Business Equipment Mfrs Asscn; currently mem. Nat. Advisory Cttee, Univ. of Michigan, United States–Egypt Pres.'s Council; Officer, Order of the Crown (Belgium) 1987; Business Leader Recipient, Ellis Island Medals of Honour 1998. *Achievements include:* granted three patents relating to large screen display and digital computing tech. *Address:* Office of the Chairman, USEC Inc., 6903 Rockledge Drive, Bethesda, MD 20817, USA (office). *Website:* www.usec.com (office).

MELNIZKY, Walter, DJur; Austrian judge; b. 1 Nov. 1928, Vienna; s. of Ernst Melnizky and Maria Melnizky; m. Gertrude Melnizky 1953; one s.; ed Univ. of Vienna; judge 1954–57, 1962–69; Public Prosecutor 1957–62; Gen. Prosecutor 1969–86; Pres. Supreme Court 1987–93; Chair. Court of Arbitration Gen. Medical Council of Vienna from 1995; Pres. Austrian Automobile and Motorcycle Touring Club (ÖAMTC) 1981–2001; consultant, Syndicus Asscn of Public Experts 1988–; Komturkreuz des Landes Niederösterreich und Burgenlandes, Grosses Goldenes Ehrenzeichen am Bande (Austria), Grosses Verdienstkreuz mit Stern und Schulterband (Germany); received 'Der grosse Verein. Festschrift Walter Melnizky zum 85. Geburtstag' publ. on the occasion of his 85th birthday 2013. *Publications:* Österreichischer Juristentag (7.): Referate und Diskussionsbeiträge zu Zipf, Allgemeine Grundsätze des Strafgesetzbuches und die Rechtsprechung: TEILBD II/2 (co-author) 1980, Strafrecht, Strafprozessrecht und Kriminologie: Festschrift für Franz Pallin Zum 80. Geburtstag (co-author) 1989; numerous juridical essays, especially on traffic law and criminal law. *Leisure interests:* classical music, opera. *Address:* c/o ÖAMTC, Schubertring 1–3, 1010 Vienna; Hannplatz 4/14, 1190 Vienna, Austria (home). *Telephone:* (1) 711-99-702; (1) 368-73-74 (home). *Fax:* (1) 368-73-74 (home).

MELROSE, Donald Blair, DPhil, FAA; Australian physicist and academic; *Professor, University of Sydney;* b. 13 Sept. 1940, Hobart, Tasmania; s. of the late Andrew B. Melrose and of Isla L. Luff; m. Sara C. Knabe 1969; one s. one d.; ed N Sydney Boys' High School, John Curtin High School, Fremantle, Univs of Western Australia and Tasmania, Univ. of Oxford, UK; Research Fellow, Univ. of Sussex, UK 1965–66; Research Assoc., Belfer Grad. School of Science, Yeshiva Univ., New York, USA 1966–68; Research Fellow, Center for Theoretical Physics, Univ. of Maryland, USA 1968–69; Sr Lecturer in Theoretical Physics, ANU 1969–72, Reader 1972–79; Prof. of Theoretical Physics, Univ. of Sydney 1979–, Dir Research Centre for Theoretical Astrophysics 1991–99, Head of School 2001–02, Prof. of the Univ. 2000–; Australian Research Council Professorial Research Fellow 2003–07; Rhodes Scholar for Tasmania 1962, Pawsey Medal, Australian Acad. of Science 1974, Walter Boas Medal, Australian Inst. of Physics 1986, Thomas Ranken Lyle Medal, Australian Acad. of Science 1987, Harrie Massey Medal and Prize, Inst. of Physics 1998. *Publications:* Plasma Physics (two vols) 1980, Instabilities in Space and Laboratory Plasmas 1986, Electromagnetic Processes in Dispersive Media (with R. C. McPhedran) 1991, Plasma Astrophysics (with J. G. Kirk and E. R. Priest) 1994, Quantum Plasmadynamics 2008; more than 300 papers in scientific journals. *Leisure interests:* jogging, surfing, walking. *Address:* School of Physics, Room 110, H90, University of Sydney, Sydney, NSW 2006 (office); 8/84 Milray Avenue, Wollstonecraft, NSW 2065, Australia (home). *Telephone:* (2) 9351-4234 (office); (2) 9438-3635 (home). *Fax:* (2) 9351-7726 (office); (2) 9351-7726 (home). *E-mail:* melrose@physics.usyd.edu.au (office). *Website:* www.physics.usyd.edu.au/~melrose (office).

MELROY, Col (retd) Pamela Ann, MSc; American astronaut and air force officer (retd); *Deputy Director, Tactical Technology Office, Defense Advanced Research Projects Agency (DARPA);* b. 17 Sept. 1961, Palo Alto, Calif.; d. of David Melroy and Helen Melroy; m. Douglas W. Hollett; ed Wellesley Coll., Massachusetts Inst. of Tech.; participated in US Air Force ROTC program 1983; Undergraduate Pilot Training, Reese Air Force Base, Tex. 1985; flew KC-10 as Copilot, Aircraft Commdr and Instructor Pilot, Barksdale Air Force Base, La 1985–91; attended Air Force Test Pilot School, Edwards Air Force Base, Calif. 1991; Test Pilot, C-17 Combined Test Force 1991–94; logged over 5,000 hours in flight time in over 45 different aircraft; Astronaut Cand., NASA 1994; Shuttle Pilot training, Johnson Space Center 1995–96, has since served on Columbia Reconstruction Team, CAPCOM duties at mission control, as Pilot on STS-92 Discovery 2000, STS-112 Atlantis 2002, as Commdr STS-120 2007; logged over 38 days in space; Deputy Dir Orion Space Exploration Initiatives, Lockheed Martin Corpn 2009–11; Technical Advisor to the Assoc. Admin. and Dir of Field Operations, Office of Commercial Space Transportation, Federal Aviation Admin 2011–13, acting Deputy Assoc. Admin. 2013; Deputy Dir Tactical Technology Office, Defense Advanced Research Projects Agency (DARPA) 2013–; mem. Soc. of Experimental Test Pilots, Order of Daedalians, 99s (Int. Org. of Women Pilots); Air Force Meritorious Service Medal, First Oak Leaf Cluster; Air Medal, First Oak Leaf Cluster; Aerial Achievement Medal, First Oak Leaf Cluster; Expeditionary Medal, First Oak Leaf Cluster. *Address:* Defense Advanced Research Projects Agency, 675 North Randolph Street, Arlington, VA 22203-2114, USA (office). *Telephone:* (703) 526-6630 (office). *E-mail:* pamela.melroy@darpa.mil (office). *Website:* www.darpa.mil/Our_Work/TTO (office).

MELVILLE-ROSS, Timothy David, CBE, FCIS, FIOB, FRSA, CIMgt; British business executive; b. 3 Oct. 1944, Westward Ho, Devon; s. of the late Antony Melville-Ross and Anne Fane; m. Camilla Probert 1967; two s. one d.; ed Uppingham School and Portsmouth Coll. of Tech.; BP 1963–73; Rowe Swann & Co. (stockbrokers) 1973–74; Nationwide Bldg Soc. 1974–94, Dir and Chief Exec. 1985–94; Dir Monument Oil & Gas PLC 1992–99; Dir-Gen. Inst. of Dirs 1994–99; Deputy Chair. Monument Oil and Gas PLC 1997–99; Dir Bovis Homes Ltd 1997–2008 (Chair. 2005–08), DTZ Holdings PLC (Chair. 2000–11), Equity Trust SARL 2003–05; Chair. Investors in People UK 1999–2006; Chair. Supervisory Bd Bank Insinger de Beaufort NV 2000–05; Deputy Chair. Royal London Mutual Insurance 2003–05, Chair. 2006–; Chair. Manganese Bronze PLC 2003–; Chair. Higher Educ. Funding Council 2008–. *Leisure interests:* reading, music, bridge, sport, the countryside. *Address:* Little Bevills, Bures, Suffolk, CO8 5JN, England (home). *Telephone:* (1787) 227424 (home). *Fax:* (20) 7643-6062 (home).

MEMBE, Bernard Kamillius, MA; Tanzanian politician; *Minister of Foreign Affairs and International Relations;* b. 9 Nov. 1953; ed Univ. of Dar es Salaam and John Hopkins Univ., USA; Nat. Security Analyst, Office of the Pres. 1977–90; Ambassadorial Adviser, Ministry of Foreign Affairs 1992–2000; mem. Parl. (Chama Cha Mapinduzi Party—CCM) for Mtama 2000–; Deputy Minister of Home Affairs Jan.–Oct. 2006, of Energy and Minerals 2006–07; Minister of Foreign Affairs and Int. Relations 2007–. *Address:* Ministry of Foreign Affairs and International Relations, POB 9000, Dar es Salaam, Tanzania (office). *Telephone:* (22) 2111906 (office). *Fax:* (22) 2116600 (office). *E-mail:* bmembe@parliament.go.tz (office).

MEMMI, Albert; French writer; b. 15 Dec. 1920, Tunis; s. of François Memmi and Marguerite née Sarfati; m. Germaine Dubach 1946; three c.; ed Lycée Carnot, Tunis, Univ. of Algiers and Univ. de Paris à la Sorbonne; Teacher, Lycée Carnot, Tunis 1953, Teacher of Philosophy, Tunis 1955; Dir Psychological Centre, Tunis 1953–57; moved to France 1956; attached to Centre Nat. de la Recherche Scientifique (CNRS) 1957, Researcher, CNRS, Paris 1959–; Chargé de conférences, Ecole pratique des hautes études 1958, Asst Prof. 1959–66, Prof. 1966–70; Prof., Inst. de Psychanalyse, Paris 1968–; Prof., Univ. of Paris 1970–, Dir, Social Sciences Dept 1973–76, Dir, Anthropological Lab.; mem. Acad. des Sciences d'Outre-mer; Vice-Pres., Pen-Club 1976-79; Managing Agent, Syndicat des Ecrivains de Langue Française (SELF) 1981; Vice-Pres., Comité Nat. Laïcité-République 1991; mem. Comité de patronage du MRAP; mem. Ligue Internationale Contre le Racisme et l'Anti-sémitisme (LICRA); Hon. Cttee mem. l'Union Rationaliste, Comité Culturel Tunisien en France 1995; Scientific Cttee mem. Cahiers Francophones d'Europe Centre-Orientale 1996; Cttee mem. sponsoring Asscn des Anciens Elèves du Lycée Carnot de Tunis 1996; Advisory mem., Institut des Études Transrégionales du Centre d'Études, Int. Study Centre, Princeton Univ. 1995; mem. Acad. des Sciences d'Outremer, Accad. Internazionale, Acad. de la Méditerranée; Hon. Prof., Walker Aims Univ., Washington Univ., cole des Hautes Études Commerciales; Hon. mem. Asscn des Etudes Françaises en Afrique Australe 1996; Officier, Légion d'honneur; Commdr, Ordre de Nichan Iftikhar; Officier des Palmes académiques, des Arts et des Lettres, Ordre de la République Tunisienne; Chevalier des affaires culturelles du Burkina Faso; Dr hc (Ben Gurion) 1999, (Beer Schéba); Prix de Carthage 1953, Prix Fénéon 1953, Prix Simba 1978, Prix de l'Union Rationaliste 1994, Grand Prix Littéraire de l'Afrique du Nord, Grand Prix Littéraire du Maghreb 1995, Prix littéraire Tunisie-France 1999, Chalom du Crif 2000, Grand Prix de la ville de Bari 2000, Prix de l'Afrique méditerranéenne 2002, Prix de la Fondation Ignacio Silone 2003, Grand Prix de la Francophonie décerné par l'Acad. française 2004. *Publications include:* novels: Le Statue de Sel (trans. as The Pillar of Salt) 1953, Strangers 1955, Agar 1955, Le Scorpion 1969, Le Désert 1977, Le Pharaon 1988; poems: Le Mirliton du ciel 1990, short stories: Le nomade immobile 2000, Térésa et autre femmes 2004; non-fiction: Portrait du colonisé 1957, Portrait d'un Juif 1962, Anthologie des écrivains Maghrebins 1964, 1969, Anthologie des écrivains nord-africains 1965, Les français et le racisme 1965, The Liberation of the Jew 1966, Dominated Man 1968, Decolonisation 1970, Juifs et Arabes 1974, Entretien 1975, La terre intérieure 1976, La dependance 1979, Le racisme 1982, Ce que je crois 1984, Les écrivains francophones du Maghreb 1985, L'Écriture colorée 1986, Testament insolent 1990, Bonheurs 1992, A contre-courants 1993, Ah, quel bonheur 1995, Le Juif et l'autre 1995, L'Exercice du bonheur 1996, Le Buveur et l'amoureux 1996, Feu sur 40 idées recues 1999, Dictionnaire à l'usage des incrédules 2002, Portrait du décolonisé, arabo-musulman et de quelques autres 2004; contrib. to Le onde 1989–94, Le Figaro 1995, New York Times, L'Action. *Leisure interest:* writing. *Address:* 5 rue Saint Merri, 75004 Paris, France. *Telephone:* 1-40-29-08-31. *Fax:* 1-42-74-25-22. *E-mail:* albert.memmi@yahoo.fr.

MEN, Mikhail Aleksandrovich, CandSci; Russian politician; b. 12 Nov. 1960, Semkhoz, Moscow Region; s. of Aleksander Men; m.; three c.; ed Moscow Gubkin Inst. of Gas and Oil, Moscow State Inst. of Culture; Russian Acad. of State Service; fmr stage dir, amateur theatre and clubs of Moscow 1983–91; bass guitarist and singer for rock band Most 1986; mem. Moscow Region Duma 1993–95; mem. State Duma (Parl.) 1995–99; Deputy Chair. Cttee on Culture 1995–2005; Chair. All-Union Christian Union 1996–; Chair. Aleksander Men Foundation; elected Vice-Gov. Moscow Region 2000–02 (resgnd); Deputy Mayor of Moscow 2002–05; Gov. of Ivanovo Oblast 2005–13. *Publication:* Culture and Religion 2001. *Leisure interests:* music, sport. *Address:* c/o 153002 Ivanovo, ul. Pushkina 9, Russia (office). *Website:* www.menn.ru (home).

MENA KEYMER, Carlos Eduardo; Chilean lawyer, academic and fmr diplomatist; m.; two c.; fmr Under-Sec. of Navy; Amb. to Brazil 2000–03; Vice-Pres. Ejecutivo del Comité de Inversiones Extranjeras (Exec. Cttee on Foreign Investments) 2006–; Pres. Empresa Portuaria Arica (cargo handling co.). *Address:* Empresa Portuaria Arica, Máximo Lira 389, Arica, Chile (office). *Telephone:* (58) 25-5078 (office). *Fax:* (58) 23-2284 (office). *E-mail:* puertoarica@puertoarica.cl (office). *Website:* www.puertoarica.cl (office).

MÉNAGE, Gilles Marie Marcel; French government official and organization official; *Secretary-General, l'Institut François Mitterrand;* b. 5 July 1943, Bourg-la-Reine (Hauts-de-Seine); s. of Georges Ménage and Jeanne Paillottet; m. 1st Marie-France Beaussier (divorced); two d.; m. 2nd Doris Lenz; one s. one d.; ed Lycée Lakanal, Sceaux, Lycée Berthollet, Annecy, Inst. d'Études Politiques, Paris and Ecole Nat. d'Admin; civil admin., Ministry of Interior 1969; Deputy Prefect, Head of Staff for Prefect of Tarn-et-Garonne 1969–70, then for Prefect of Haute-Vienne and Limousin 1970–74; Tech. Adviser to Sec. of State for Posts and Telecommunications (PTT) 1974; Head of Staff for Pierre Lelong, Sec. for PTT 1974–76; Deputy Prefect and Special Adviser to Prefect of Paris 1976–77; Head of Staff for Prefect/Sec.-Gen. of Préfecture de Paris 1977–81; Sr Lecturer, Inst. d'Etudes Politiques, Paris 1976–77, Inst. Int. d'Admin. Publique 1980–81; Tech. Adviser, then Deputy Head of Staff for Pres. of France 1982–88, Chief of Staff 1988–92; Chair. Electricité de France 1992–95; working on energy project for Ministry of Industry 1996–97; Prefect 1997–; Chair. Int. Consortiums Consultants 1998–; Pres. 'Les florilèges du Château féodal de Madaillan' 2002; Sec. Gen. l'Institut François Mitterrand 2003–; Pres. 'Les Florilèges de Quercy, Gascogne, Guyenne' 2004; Chevalier, Ordre nat. du Mérite, Chevalier, Légion d'honneur. *Publications:* La France face aux dangers de guerre 1981, L'oeil du pouvoir: les Affaires de l'État (1981–1986) 1999, L'oeil du pouvoir: Face aux terrorismes (1981–1986) 2000, L'oeil du pouvoir: Face au terrorisme moyen oriental (1981–86) 2001. *Leisure interests:* skiing, music, organizing concerts for talented young musicians. *Address:* l'Institut François Mitterrand, 10 rue Charlot, 75003 Paris (office); EDF, 38 rue Jacques Ibert, 75177, Paris Cedex 17 (office); Château de Noilhac, 47140 Penne d'Agenais, France (home); International Consortiums, Château de Noilhac, 47140 Penne d'Agenais (office). *Telephone:* 1-40-42-82-85 (office); (5) 53-41-36-01 (home). *E-mail:* gilles.menage@libertysurf.fr (office). *Website:* www.mitterrand.org (office).

MENAGHARISHVILI, Irakli Afinogenovich; Georgian politician; *Director, Strategic Research Centre, Tbilisi;* b. 18 May 1951, Tbilisi; s. of Afinogen Menagarishvili and Ekaterine Jorbenadze; m. Manana Mikaberidze 1975; two s.; ed Tbilisi State Inst. of Medicine; leader Comsomol Orgs 1976–80; head of City Public Health Dept 1980–82; First Deputy Minister of Public Health 1982–86, Minister 1986–91, 1992–93; Dir Georgian Cen. of Strategic Studies; Co-ordinator of Humanitarian Aid of State Council of Georgia 1991–92; Deputy Prime Minister 1993–95; Minister of Foreign Affairs 1995–2004; Dir Strategic Research Centre, Tbilisi 2004–. *Address:* Strategic Research Center, 6 V. Beridze Street, 380008 Tbilisi, Georgia (office). *Telephone:* (32) 299-94-93 (office). *E-mail:* i.menagari@yahoo.com (office).

MENARD, John R., Jr, BA; American retail executive; *President and CEO, Menards Inc.;* m. (divorced); six c.; ed Univ. of Wis. at Eau Claire; opened his first home-improvement store in 1972; founder, Pres. and CEO Menards Inc. 1972–; mem. Bd of Dirs Polaris Industries Pnrs L.P. 2001–; sponsors Menards Racing team. *Address:* Menards Inc., 4777 Menard Drive, Eau Claire, WI 54703-9604, USA (office). *Telephone:* (715) 876-5911 (office). *Fax:* (715) 876-2868 (office). *Website:* www.menards.com (office); www.teammenard.net.

MENCHÚ TUM, Rigoberta; Guatemalan human rights activist; b. 9 Jan. 1959, San Miguel Uspantán; d. of the late Vicente Menchu and Juana Menchu; m. Angél Canil 1995; one c.; began campaigning for rights of Indians as teenager; fled to Mexico after parents and brother were killed by security forces 1980; co-ordinated protests in San Marcos against 500th anniversary of arrival of Columbus in Americas 1992; f. Rigoberta Menchú Tum Foundation, Guatemala City; Int. Goodwill Amb. UNESCO 1996–; Founding mem. Nobel Women's Initiative 2006; unsuccessful cand. for Pres. 2007; Pres. UN Indigenous Initiative for Peace 1999; Commdr, Légion d'honneur 1996; numerous hon. degrees; Nobel Peace Prize 1992. *Publications:* I, Rigoberta (trans. into 12 languages) 1983, Rigoberta: Grandchild of the Mayas (co-author) 1998. *Address:* Fundacion Rigoberta Menchú Tum, Avenida Simeón Cañas 4-04 Zona 2, Ciudad de Guatemala (office). *Telephone:* 2230-2431 (office). *Fax:* 2221-3999 (office). *E-mail:* guatemala@frmt.org (office). *Website:* www.frmt.org (office).

MENDELSOHN, John, BA, MD; American physician, medical researcher and administrator; b. 31 Aug. 1936, Cincinnati, Ohio; m. Anne Mendelsohn; three s.; ed Harvard Coll., Harvard Medical School; residency training in internal medicine at Brigham and Womans' Hosp., Boston; Research Fellow, NIH and Washington Univ. Medical School, St Louis; mem. faculty, later Asst Prof., then Prof., Univ. of Calif., San Diego 1970–85, est. National Cancer Inst.-designated cancer centre, Dir 1976–85; with Memorial Sloan-Kettering Cancer Center 1985–96, Chair. Dept of Medicine, held Winthrop Rockefeller Chair in Medical Oncology, also served for five years as Co-head of Program in Molecular Pharmacology and Therapeutics; Prof. and Vice-Chair. of Medicine, Cornell Univ. Medical Coll.; fmr Attending Physician at both Memorial and New York Hosps; Pres. Univ. of Texas M.D. Anderson Cancer Center, Houston, Tex. 1996–2011; Founding Ed. Clinical Cancer Research; fmr mem. editorial bds numerous leading scientific journals; Chair. Houston Grand Opera 2013–; Vice-Chair. BioHouston; mem. Bd Greater Houston Partnership, Bd Houston Tech. Center, Bd Center for Houston's Future, Houston

Forum; mem. NAS Inst. of Medicine 1997, American Acad. of Arts and Sciences 2013; Fulbright Scholar 1959, Raymond Bourgine Award 1997, Gold Medal of Paris 1997, Bristol-Myers Squibb Co. unrestricted grant for promising research 1997, Joseph H. Burchenal Clinical Research Award, American Asscn for Cancer Research 1999, Jill Rose Award, Breast Cancer Research Foundation 1999, Simon Shubitz Prize, Univ. of Chicago 2002, David A. Karnofsky Memorial Award, American Soc. of Clinical Oncology 2002, Bristol-Myers Squibb Freedom to Discover Award for Distinguished Achievement in Cancer Research 2004, jointly honoured with his wife for public service by Woodrow Wilson Int. Center for Scholars 2005, Fulbright Lifetime Achievement Medal 2005, Dan David Prize 2006, Landon Award, American Asscn for Cancer Research 2008, Medal of Honor, American Cancer Soc. 2011. *Publications:* The Molecular Basis of Cancer (Sr Ed.); more than 300 scientific papers and articles for journals and books. *Address:* The University of Texas M.D. Anderson Cancer Center, 1515 Holcombe Blvd, Box 0491, Houston, TX 77030, USA (office). *Telephone:* (713) 792-6670 (office). *Fax:* (713) 792-6671 (home). *E-mail:* jmendelsohn@mdanderson.org (office). *Website:* www .mdanderson.org (office).

MENDES, Gino; Guinea-Bissau politician; *Minister of Finance;* Sec. of Treasury and Fiscal Affairs –2013, Minister of Finance 2013–. *Address:* Ministry of Finance, Rua Justino Lopes 74a, CP 67, Bissau, Guinea-Bissau (office). *Telephone:* 3203670 (office). *Fax:* 3203496 (office). *E-mail:* info@mail.guine-bissau.com (office).

MENDES, Sam, CBE; British theatre director and film director; b. 1 Aug. 1965; s. of Valerie Mendes and Peter Mendes; m. Kate Winslet (q.v.) 2003; one s.; ed Magdalen Coll. School, Oxford and Peterhouse, Cambridge; fmr artistic Dir Minerva Studio Theatre, Chichester; Artistic Dir Donmar Warehouse 1992–2002; Co-Dir The Bridge Project (theatre Co. est. with Kevin Spacey at Old Vic Theatre, London and Brooklyn Acad. of Music, NY) 2007–; Critics' Circle Award 1989, 1993, 1996, Olivier Award for Best Dir 1996, Tony Award 1998, LA Critics' Award, Broadcast Critics' Award, Toronto People's Choice Award, Golden Globe Award (all 1999), Shakespeare Prize, Directors' Guild of Great Britain lifetime achievement award 2005. *Films:* American Beauty (Acad. Award for Best Dir, Best Film 2000) 1999, Road to Perdition 2002, Jarhead 2005, Revolutionary Road 2008, Away We Go 2009, Skyfall 2012. *Plays directed include:* London Assurance (Chichester), The Cherry Orchard (London), Kean (Old Vic, London), The Plough and the Stars (Young Vic, London) 1991, Troilus and Cressida (RSC) 1991, The Alchemist (RSC) 1991, Richard III (RSC) 1992, The Tempest (RSC) 1993; Nat. Theatre debut with The Sea 1991, The Rise and Fall of Little Voice (Nat. and Aldwych) 1992, The Birthday Party 1994, Othello (also world tour); Assassins, Translations, Cabaret, Glengarry Glen Ross, The Glass Menagerie, Company, Habeas Corpus, The Front Page, The Blue Room, To the Green Fields Beyond (all at Donmar Warehouse) 1992–2000; Uncle Vanya and Twelfth Night (Donmar Warehouse, Olivier Award for Best Dir 2003, Olivier Special Award 2003) 2002, Oliver! (London Palladium), Cabaret, The Blue Room (Broadway, NY). *Leisure interest:* cricket. *Address:* Creative Artists Agency, 2000 Avenue of the Stars, Los Angeles, CA 90067, USA (office). *Telephone:* (424) 288-2000 (office). *Fax:* (424) 288-2900 (office). *Website:* www.caa.com (office).

MENDES, Sérgio; Brazilian singer and songwriter; b. 11 Feb. 1941, Niterói; s. of Benedicto Mendes; m. Gracinha Leporace; ed Music Conservatory of Niterói; pioneered Bossa Nova movt in Brazil with Antonio Carlos Jobim, João Gilberto and Moacyr Santos; f. Bossa Rio Sextet in 1958, toured Brazil, Europe, Middle East and Japan; Bossa Nova Festival, New York 1962; moved to Calif., USA 1964; f. Brasil 64 band, toured USA, tour with Frank Sinatra 1967, tour of Japan 1968, Europe 1980; recorded albums with Black Eyed Peas 2006, 2008; continues to tour around the world. *Recordings include:* over 40 albums including Brasileiro (Grammy Award for Best World Music Album 1992) 1992, Timeless (Latin Grammy Award for Best Brazilian Pop Album 2006) 2006, Encanto 2008, Bom Tempo (Latin Grammy Award for Best Brazilian Contemporary Pop Album) 2010. *Address:* c/o Concord Music Group, Inc., 23307 Commerce Park Road, Cleveland, OH 44122 USA (office). *Website:* www.concordmusicgroup.com (office); www .sergiomendesmusic.com.

MENDES CABEÇADAS, Adm. José Manuel; Portuguese naval officer; b. 1943, Lisbon; m. Sibylle Ninette; two s. one d.; ed Naval Acad., Portuguese Naval War Coll.; began career in Portuguese Navy 1961; several sea duty tours with various ships, Commdr NRP Quanza and NRP Oliveira e Carmo; held positions successively as Dir Communication Centre, Lake Niassa and Ministry of Defence, Dir Naval Radio Station, Metangula, Mozambique, Staff Officer Personnel and Org. Div., Staff Officer Intelligence Div., Naval Command, Head of 1st Section Directorate of Personnel, Teacher of Man. Portuguese Naval War Coll.; assigned to Mil. Rep. to NATO, Brussels 1984, later Exec. Asst Iberian Atlantic Area, NATO HQ; Exec. Asst to Chief of Naval Command 1996–2000; Dir of Portuguese Naval War Coll. 2000–02; Chief of Naval Staff May–Nov. 2000; Chief of Defence 2002–06; apptd Vice Adm. 2000, Adm. 2002; Grand Officier Ordem Militar de Avis Distinguished Service Gold Medal, Distinguished Service Silver Medals, Mil. Merit Medals 1st, 2nd and 3rd Class, 2 Navy Cross Medals 2nd Class. *Address:* c/o Ministry of National Defence, Av. Ilha da Madeira, 1400-204 Lisbon, Portugal (office).

MENDES DA ROCHA, Paulo; Brazilian architect; b. 25 Oct. 1928, Vitória; ed Faculty of Architecture and Urban Planning, Mackenzie Univ., São Paulo; started pvt. practice 1955; Prof. Faculty of Architecture and Urban Planning, Univ. of São Paulo 1959–98; won nat. competition to design part of Paulistano Athletic Club in Sao Paulo; fmr Pres. Brazilian Inst. of Architects; Mies van der Rohe Award for Latin American Architecture, Barcelona, 2000, Pritzker Prize 2006. *Major works include:* Club Atletico Paulistano, Pinacoteca of São Paulo restoration project, Museu Brasileiro de Escultura (MuBE) project, Cultural Center FIESP, Pinacoteca de São Paulo, Poupatempo Itaquera, Urban Bus Terminal Parque D. Pedro II. *Publications include:* Paulo Mendes da Rocha: Projects 1967/2006 (with Rosa Artigas) 2007.

MÉNDEZ GUTIÉRREZ, Gonzalo; Bolivian government official and academic; b. Cochabamba; ed Universidad Mayor de San Simón, Univ. of Amberes, Catholic Univ. of Louvain, Belgium; fmr Nat. Dir of Academic Planning, Universidad Católica Boliviana; fmr Prof. Universidad Andina Simón Bolívar; fmr Dir of Finance and Planning, Municipality of Cochabamba; Minister of Nat. Defence

2005–06 (resgnd). *Address:* c/o Ministry of National Defence, Plaza Avaroa, esq. Pedro Salazar y 20 de Octubre 2502, La Paz, Bolivia (office).

MÉNDEZ ROMERO, Brig.-Gen. (retd) Arévalo Enrique; Venezuelan diplomatist, business executive and fmr army officer; *Chairman, Carbones del Zulia Sociedad Mercantil, SA;* ed Mil. Acad. of Venezuela, Inst. of Higher Defense Studies; Pvt. Sec. to Pres. and Vice Minister of Foreign Affairs 2000–05; Amb. to Spain 2005–07, to Argentina 2007–11; Chair. Carbones del Zulia Sociedad Mercantil, SA (nat. coal co.) 2011–; fmr Dir Banco de Desarrollo Económico y Social de Venezuela.

MENDILLO, Jane, BA, MBA; American investment manager and business executive; *President and CEO, Harvard Management Company, Inc.;* ed Yale Univ.; man. consultant with Bain & Co., Boston, Mass –1987; joined Harvard Management Co. (Harvard Univ.'s endowment arm) 1987, mem. Internal Equities Man. Team 1987–89, Vice-Pres. for Pvt. Equity 1989–91, Vice-Pres. for Trusts 1992–96, Vice-Pres. of External Investments 1997–2002, Pres. and CEO 2008–; Chief Investment Officer, Wellesley Coll. 2002–08; mem. Yale Univ. Investment Cttee 2002–08, Partners HealthCare System Investment Cttee (includes Massachusetts Gen. Hosp. and Brigham and Women's Hosp.), Harvard-Yenching Inst. Investment Cttee, Dimock Community Health Center Bd of Visitors, Roxbury; mem. Boston Security Analysts Soc., Inc., Boston Cttee on Foreign Relations, Boston Econ. Club; 100 Women in Hedge Funds Industry Leadership Award 2007, ranked by Forbes magazine amongst 100 Most Powerful Women (42nd) 2008, (37th) 2009. *Address:* Harvard Management Company, Inc., 600 Atlantic Avenue, Suite 15, Boston, MA 02210-2211, USA (office). *Telephone:* (617) 523-4400 (office). *E-mail:* general@hmc.harvard.edu (office). *Website:* www.hmc.harvard.edu (office).

MENDIS, Sunil; Sri Lankan business executive and banker; joined Hayleys Ltd 1962, mem. Bd of Dirs 1977–2004, Chair. and CEO 1993–2004; Gov. Central Bank of Sri Lanka 2004–06, Chair. Monetary Bd 2004–06; mem. Nat. Council for Econ. Devt 2004–06; mem. Bd of Govs South East Asian Central Banks (SEACEN) Research and Training Centre 2004–; fmr mem. Bd of Dirs Bank of Ceylon, US Educational Foundation in Sri Lanka, Private Sector Infrastructure Devt Co. Ltd, Export Devt Bd, Bd Investment, Presidential Salaries Comm. *Address:* c/o Central Bank of Sri Lanka, 30 Janadhipathi Mawatha, Colombo 1, Sri Lanka (office).

MENDONÇA BATISTA, Joesley; Brazilian business executive; *Chairman, JBS SA;* Partner, J&F Participações SA; has served in various capacities at JBS SA since 1988, including as Pres. Itaúsa JBS SpA, CEO JBS SA 2006–11, mem. Bd of Dirs 2009–, Chair. 2011–, mem. Bd of Dirs JBS USA Holdings, Inc. (also known as Swift & Co.), Pilgrim's Pride Corpn. *Address:* JBS SA, Avenida Marginal Direita do Tietê, 500 Vila Jaguará, São Paulo 05118-100, Brazil (office). *Telephone:* (11) 3144-4000 (office). *Fax:* (11) 3144-4279 (office). *E-mail:* info@jbs.com.br (office). *Website:* www.jbs.com.br (office).

MENDONÇA BATISTA, Wesley; Brazilian business executive; *President and CEO, JBS SA;* mem. JBS founding family and has served in various capacities at JBS since 1987, Pres. and CEO JBS USA 2007–11, Pres. and CEO JBS SA 2011–, Vice-Pres. Bd of Dirs 2011–, Pres. and CEO JBS USA Holdings Inc. (also known as Swift & Co.) 2007–; Chair. Pilgrim's Pride Corpn 2009–. *Address:* JBS SA, Avenida Marginal Direita do Tietê, 500 Vila Jaguará, São Paulo 05118-100, Brazil (office). *Telephone:* (11) 3144-4000 (office). *Fax:* (11) 3144-4279 (office). *E-mail:* info@jbs .com.br (office). *Website:* www.jbs.com.br (office).

MENDONÇA E MOURA, Álvaro; Portuguese politician and diplomatist; *Ambassador to Spain;* b. 17 March 1951, Oporto; m.; four c.; ed Univ. of Coimbra; Embassy Attaché 1975–78; Third Sec. 1978; Second Sec. 1978–82; First Sec. 1982–90; Counsellor 1990–93; Minister 1993–2002; Amb. 2002–; posted to Perm. Del. to EFTA, GATT, Geneva 1979, posted to Embassy, Pretoria, S Africa 1985, Chargé d'affaires a.i. 1988–89; Dir for African Affairs, Ministry of Foreign Affairs 1990–91; Chef de Cabinet, Sec. of State for Foreign Affairs and Co-operation 1991–92; Chef de Cabinet, Minister for Foreign Affairs 1992–95; Amb. in Vienna, Perm. Rep. to UN Office in Vienna 1995; non-resident Amb. in Ljubljana 1996; non-resident Amb. in Bratislava 1996; Amb., Perm. Rep. to UN Office and other Int. Orgs, Geneva 1999; Amb. and Perm. Rep. to EU 2002–08; Amb. to Spain 2008–; Head of Portuguese Del. to UN Comm. on Crime Prevention and Criminal Justice 1996, 1997, 1998, 1999; Chair. Preparatory Cttee, Cttee of Whole of UN Gen. Ass.'s Special Session on Narcotic Drugs 1997–98; Vice-Chair. UN Human Rights Comm. 2001–02; Chair. Gen. Ass., World Intellectual Property Org. 2001–02; Prof., Dept of Int. Relations, Lusiada Univ., Lisbon; mem. High-Level Group of Experts appointed by UN Sec. Gen. to review Int. Drug Control Programme, to strengthen UN machinery for Int. Drug Control, Vienna, New York 1998. *Address:* Embassy of Portugal, Calle Pinar 1, 28006 Madrid, Spain (office). *Telephone:* (91) 7824960 (office). *Fax:* (91) 7824972 (office). *E-mail:* embmadrid@ emb-portugal.es (office). *Website:* www.embajadaportugal-madrid.org (office).

MENDONÇA PREVIATO, Lucia, PhD; Brazilian biophysicist, parasitologist and academic; b. 17 Feb. 1949, Maceió, Alagoas; currently Prof. of Biophysics and Parasitology, Biophysics Inst., Fed. Univ. of Rio de Janeiro; Nat. Order for Scientific Merit 2002, L'Oréal-UNESCO for Women in Science Award 2004. *Publications:* numerous articles in scientific journals on the study of *Trypanosoma cruzi*, the protozoan parasite responsible for Chagas disease. *Address:* Biophysics Institute, Federal University of Rio de Janeiro, Rio de Janeiro 21944–170, Brazil (office). *E-mail:* luciamp@biof.ufrj.br (office). *Website:* www.biof.ufrj.br (office).

MENDOZA, June, AO, OBE, RP, ROI; British portrait painter; b. Melbourne, Australia; d. of John Morton and Dot Mendoza; m. Keith Mackrell; one s. three d.; ed Lauriston School for Girls, Melbourne, St Martin's School of Art, London; portraits include HM Queen Elizabeth II, HM Queen Elizabeth, the Queen Mother, HRH The Prince of Wales, Diana, Princess of Wales, Baroness Thatcher, Prime Ministers of Fiji, Australia, Philippines, Singapore, Pres. of Iceland, Philippines and many other govt, academic, industrial, regimental, theatrical and sporting personalities, series of internationally known musicians, large boardroom and family groups; large canvas for the House of Commons (440 portraits) of the House in session, for Australian House of Reps (170 portraits) for Parl., Canberra; has made numerous TV appearances and lectures regularly in UK and overseas; mem. Royal Soc. of Portrait Painters, Royal Inst. of Oil Painters; Freeman of City

of London 1997; Hon. mem. Soc. of Women Artists; Hon. DLitt (Bath, Loughborough); Dr hc (Open Univ.). *Leisure interests:* classical and jazz music, theatre. *Address:* 34 Inner Park Road, London, SW19 6DD, England (home). *Telephone:* (20) 8788-7826 (home). *Fax:* (20) 8780-0728 (home). *E-mail:* keithmackrell@btinternet.com (home); june@junemendoza.co.uk (home). *Website:* www.junemendoza.co.uk (home).

MENEM, Carlos Saul, DJur; Argentine politician; *President, Partido Justicialista, La Rioja Province;* b. 2 July 1935, Anillaco, La Rioja; s. of Saul Menem and Muhibe Akil; m. 1st Zulema Fátima Yoma 1966 (divorced); one s. (deceased) one d.; m. 2nd Cecilia Bolocco 2001; one s.; ed Córdoba Univ.; f. Juvenil Peronista (Peron Youth Group), La Rioja Prov. 1955; defended political prisoners following Sept. 1955 coup; Legal Adviser, Confederación General del Trabajo, La Rioja Prov. 1955–70; cand. Prov. Deputy 1958; Pres. Partido Justicialista, La Rioja Prov. 1963–; elected Gov. La Rioja 1973, re-elected 1983, 1987; imprisoned following mil. coup 1976–81; cand. for Pres. Argentine Repub. for Partido Justicialista 1989; Pres. of Argentina 1989–99; Vice-Pres. Conf. of Latin American Popular Parties (COPPAL) 1990–; arrested for alleged involvement in illegal arms sales during his presidency June 2001, charged July 2001, placed under house arrest for five months; Presidential Cand. 2003. *Publications:* Argentine, Now or Never, Argentina Year 2000, The Productive Revolution (with Eduardo Duhalde). *Leisure interests:* flying, tennis. *Address:* Partido Justicialista, Buenos Aires, Argentina.

MENENDEZ, Robert (Bob), BA, LLB; American politician; *Senator from New Jersey;* b. 1 Jan. 1954, New York, NY; m. Jane Jacobsen (divorced); one s. one d.; ed St Peter's Coll., Jersey City, Rutgers Univ., Newark; entered public service when he launched a successful petition drive to reform his local school bd 1973, elected to Union City Bd of Educ. 1974; admitted to NJ Bar 1980; Mayor of Union City 1986–92, simultaneously served in New Jersey Gen. Ass. 1987–91 and New Jersey Senate 1991–93; mem. US House of Reps for NJ 13th Congressional Dist 1993–2006, fmr Vice-Chair. House Democratic Caucus, Chair. 2002, Chair. Democratic Task Force on Educ. 2001–03, Democratic Task Force on Homeland Security 2001–03; Chair. Credentials Cttee, Democratic Nat. Convention 2004; highest-ranking Hispanic in Congressional history; Senator from New Jersey 2006–, mem. Finance Cttee, Banking, Housing and Urban Affairs Cttee, Foreign Relations Cttee (Chair. 2013–); Democrat. *Publication:* Growing American Roots. *Address:* 528 Hart Senate Office Building, Washington, DC 20510, USA (office). *Telephone:* (202) 224-4744 (office). *Fax:* (202) 228-2197 (office). *Website:* menendez .senate.gov (office).

MENEZES, Fradique Bandeira Melo de; São Tomé and Príncipe business executive and fmr head of state; b. 1942; m. (deceased); ed Instituto Superior de Psicologia Aplicada, Lisbon, Portugal and Univ. of Brussels, Belgium; fmr Minister for Foreign Trade; fmr Amb. to Belgium and Netherlands; mem. Acção Democrática Independente (ADI) Party; Pres. of São Tomé e Príncipe 2001–11, also C-in-C of Armed Forces. *Address:* c/o Office of the President, Palácio Presidencial, São Tomé, São Tomé e Príncipe (office).

MENG, Fengchao; Chinese engineer and business executive; *Chairman and General Manager, China Railway Construction Corporation;* ed Southwest Jiaotong Univ.; served in various positions at Ministry of Railways and its eng affiliates; Chair. China Zhongtie Major Bridge Eng Group Co. Ltd 1982–98; Vice-Pres. China Railway Eng Co. 2000–04; Pres. China Harbour Eng Co. (Group) 2005, mem. Bd of Dirs and Pres. China Communications Construction Group 2005–06, Exec. Vice-Chair. and Pres. China Communications Construction Co. Ltd 2006–10; Chair., Gen. Man. and Deputy Sec., CCP Cttee, China Railway Construction Corpn 2010–. *Address:* China Railway Construction Corporation, 40 Fuxing Road, Beijing 100855, People's Republic of China (office). *Telephone:* (10) 51888114 (office). *E-mail:* ir@crcc.cn (office). *Website:* www.crcc.cn (office).

MENG, Jianzhu; Chinese politician; *Secretary, CCP Central Committee Politics and Law Commission;* b. July 1947, Wuxian Co., Jiangsu Prov.; joined CCP 1968; Deputy Political Instructor and Deputy Leader of Boat Fleet, Supply Marketing and Transport Station, Qianwei Farm (also Sec. CCP Shanghai Communist Youth League) 1968–73, Sec. CCP Party Br. 1973–76, mem. CCP Qianwei Farm Party Cttee 1976–77 (also Leader, Publicity Dept), Sec. Cork Gen. Plant, Qianwei Farm, CCP Party Br. 1977–81, Dir Political Dept, Qianwei Farm 1977–81, Deputy Sec., later Dir CCP Party Cttee 1981–86; Sec. CCP Chuansha Co. Cttee, Shanghai 1986–90, Jiading Co. Cttee, Shanghai 1990–91; Sec. Rural Work Cttee, CCP Shanghai Municipal Cttee 1991–92; Deputy Sec.-Gen. Shanghai Municipal Govt 1992–93; Vice-Mayor and Chair. Shanghai Econ. Restructuring Comm. 1993–96; Deputy Sec. Shanghai Municipal Cttee 1996; Sec. Jiangxi Prov. Cttee 2001–07, Chair. Standing Cttee Jiangxi People's Congress 2001; Alt. mem. 15th CCP Cen. Cttee 1997–2002, mem. 16th CCP Cen. Cttee 2002–07, mem. 17th CCP Cen. Cttee 2007–12; mem. 18th CCP Cen. Cttee 2012–, mem. CCP Politburo 2012–; Minister of Public Security 2007–12; State Councillor 2008–13; Sec. CCP Cen. Cttee Politics and Law Comm. 2012–. *Address:* CCP Central Committee Politics and Law Commission, Beijing, People's Republic of China (office).

MENG, Weilin; Chinese business executive; *President, Zhejiang Materials Industry Group Corporation;* Chair. Logistics Cttee, Zhejiang Fed. of Logistics and Purchasing; currently Pres. Zhejiang Materials Industry Group Corpn. *Address:* Zhejiang Materials Industry Group Corporation, 56 West Huancheng Road, Hangzhou 310006, Zhejiang Prov., People's Republic of China (office). *Telephone:* (571) 87054509 (office). *Fax:* (571) 87054509 (office). *E-mail:* office@zjmi .com (office). *Website:* www.zjmi.com (office).

MENG, Xuenong, MSc; Chinese politician; b. 1949, Penglai, Shandong Prov.; ed Chinese Univ. of Science and Tech., Anhui Prov.; joined CCP 1972; worked in No. 2 Motor Vehicle Plant, Beijing 1969–71 (also Sec. CCP Communist Youth League 1971–74); Office Sec., Beijing Automobile Industry Co. 1971–74 (also Deputy Sec., later Sec. CCP Communist Youth League); Office Sec. Org. Dept CCP Zhejiang Prov. Cttee 1977–80, later Sec. of Gen. Office of Prov. Cttee; fmr Deputy Sec. CCP Communist Youth League Beijing Municipal Cttee; Gen. Man. Beijing Hotel Allied Co. 1986–87 (also Deputy Sec., later Sec. CCP Communist Youth League); Dir Admin for Industry and Commerce, Beijing 1987–93 (also Sec. CCP Leading Party Group); worked under Hu Jintao, Pres. of People's Repub. of China; Vice-Mayor of Beijing 1993–98, Exec. Vice-Mayor 1998–2002, Mayor 2003–04, mem. CCP Standing Cttee, Beijing Municipal Cttee; Deputy Dir Construction Comm. for

Project for Diverting Water from the South to the North 2003–07 (mem. CCP Leading Party Group 2004–07); mem. 16th CCP Cen. Cttee 2002–07, 17th CCP Cen. Cttee 2007–12, 18th CCP Cen. Cttee 2012–; Acting Gov. Shanxi Prov. 2007–08, Gov. 2008 (resgnd). *Address:* Chinese Communist Party, Quanguo Renmin Diabiao Dahui, Zhongguo Gongchan Dang, 1 Zhongnanhai, Beijing, People's Republic of China. *Website:* www.cppcc.gov.cn (office).

MENGES, Chris; British cinematographer and film director; b. 15 Sept. 1940, Kington, Herefordshire; m. 2nd Judy Freeman 1978; five c. from 1st marriage; TV cameraman on documentaries filmed in Africa, Asia and S America. *Films include:* camera operator: Poor Cow 1967, If. . .. 1968; cinematographer: Abel Gance: The Charm of Dynamite 1968, Loving Memory 1969, Kes 1969, Black Beauty (dir of photography) 1971, Gumshoe 1971, A Sense of Freedom 1979, Black Jack 1979, Bloody Kids 1979, Star Wars: Episode V – The Empire Strikes Back (dir of photography: studio second unit) 1980, The Gamekeeper 1980, Babylon 1980, East 103rd Street 1981, Looks and Smiles 1981, Warlords of the 21st Century 1982, Couples and Robbers 1982, Angel 1982, Local Hero 1983, Winter Flight 1984, Which Side Are You In? 1984, Comfort and Joy 1984, The Killing Fields (Acad. Award) 1984, Marie 1985, Fatherland 1986, The Mission (Acad. Award) 1986, Singing the Blues in Red, Shy People 1987, High Season 1987, Michael Collins (LA Film Critics Award 1997) 1996, The Boxer (dir of photography) 1997, The Pledge 2001, Dirty Pretty things 2002, The Good Thief 2002, Criminal (dir of photography) 2004, Tickets 2005, The Three Burials of Melquiades Estrada 2005, North Country 2005; Dir: East 103rd Street (also producer) 1981, A World Apart 1988, Criss-Cross 1992, The Life and Death of Chico Mendes, Second Best 1994, The Lost Son 1999, North Country 2005. *Television includes:* Auditions 1980, A Question of Leadership 1981, Tales Out of School: Made in Britain 1982, Walter 1982, Walter and June 1983, The Red and the Blue: Impressions of Two Political Conferences – Autumn 1982 1983, Concert for George 2003.

MENGISTU HAILE MARIAM (see MARIAM, Mengistu Haile).

MENKEN, Alan; American composer; b. 22 July 1949, New York; ed New York Univ.; began composing and performing Lehman Engel Musical Theater Workshop, BMI; Grammy Award for Best Song Written for Visual Media (for I See The Light) 2012. *Theatre music includes:* God Bless You Mr Rosewater 1979 (Off-Broadway debut), Little Shop of Horrors (with Howard Ashman), Kicks, The Apprenticeship of Duddy Kravitz, Diamonds, Personals, Let Freedom Sing, Weird Romance, Beauty and the Beast, A Christmas Carol. *Film music includes:* Little Shop of Horrors 1986, The Little Mermaid 1988 (two Acad. Awards 1989), Beauty and the Beast 1990 (two Acad. Awards 1991), Lincoln 1992, Newsies 1992, Aladdin 1992 (two Acad. Awards 1993), Life with Mikey 1993, Pocahontas (with Stephen Schwartz) 1995 (Golden Globe Award 1996, two Acad. Awards 1996), The Shaggy Dog 2006, Enchanted 2007, Tangled 2010, Mirror Mirror 2012. *Address:* The Shukat Company, 340 West 55th Street, Apartment 1A, New York, NY 10019, USA. *Telephone:* (212) 582-7614.

MENKERIOS, Haile, MA; South African (b. Eritrean) economist, diplomatist and UN official; *Special Representative of the Secretary-General and Head, United Nations Office to the African Union (UNOAU);* b. 1 Oct. 1946, Adi Felesti; s. of Drar Menkerios and Negusse Giorgis; m. Hebret Berhe 1979 (divorced); one s. one d.; ed Addis Ababa Univ., Brandeis and Harvard Univs, USA; Teaching Fellow, Harvard Univ. 1971–73; guerrilla fighter in Eritrean People's Liberation Army (EPLA) 1973–74; Head of Tigrigna Section, Dept of Information and Propaganda, Eritrean People's Liberation Front (EPLF) 1974–75, mem. Foreign Relations Cttee 1976–77, mem. Cen. Council 1977–2001, Deputy Head of Dept of Foreign Relations 1977–79, Head of Research Div., Political, Educ. and Culture Dept 1979–86; Dir Research and Information Centre of Eritrea 1986–87; Head, Research and Policy Div., Dept of Foreign Relations 1987–90; Gov. of East and South Zone of Eritrea 1990–91; mem. Eritrean Nat. Council 1991–2001; Rep. of Provisional Govt of Eritrea to Ethiopia 1991–93; Special Envoy of Pres. to Somalia 1991–96, to the Greater Lakes Region 1996–97; mem. High Level Horn of Africa Cttee on Somalia 1993–95; Amb. of State of Eritrea to Ethiopia and OAU 1993–96; Perm. Rep. of State of Eritrea to UN 1997–2001; Chair. UN Cttee of Experts re Sanctions on arms and terrorist camps, Afghanistan 2001; Sr Adviser to Special Envoy of Sec.-Gen. to the Inter-Congolese Dialogue 2002–03; Dir Africa Div., UN Dept of Political Affairs 2003–05; Deputy Special Rep. of the Sec.-Gen. for UN Mission in the Democratic Repub. of the Congo (MONUC) 2005–07; Asst Sec.-Gen. for Political Affairs, UN 2007–10; Special Rep. of the Sec.-Gen. for Sudan and Head of UN Mission in Sudan (UNMIS) 2010–11; Special Envoy of the Sec.-Gen. for Sudan and South Sudan, UN 2011–; Special Rep. of the Sec.-Gen. and Head, UN Office to the African Union (UNOAU) 2013–; mem. Advisory Bd, Conflict Prevention and Peace Forum; Fellow, Rift Valley Inst.; Medal of Honour for the fight against Genocide (Pres. of Rwanda), Medal of Recognition for support to the Liberation of Rwanda (Pres. of Rwanda). *Publications include:* various articles on African politics. *Leisure interests:* reading, sports. *Address:* Office of the Secretary-General, United Nations, New York, NY 10017 (office); 222 East 34th Street, Apt 1502, New York, NY 10016, USA (home). *Telephone:* (212) 963-1234 (office); (921) 9066032 (mobile). *Fax:* (212) 963-4879 (office). *E-mail:* menkerios@un.org (office). *Website:* www.un.org (office).

MENON, Anjolie Ela; Indian artist and muralist; b. 1940, West Bengal; m. Raja Menon; ed Sir J.J. Inst. of Applied Art, Mumbai, Univ. of Delhi, École des Beaux-Arts, Paris; mem. Advisory Cttee and Art Purchase Cttee, Nat. Gallery of Modern Art, New Delhi; mem. Bd of Trustees, Indira Gandhi Nat. Centre for Arts; represented India at Algeirs Biennale and Sao Paulo, Brazil; participated in several Int. shows; Padma Shri 2000. *E-mail:* anjolieelamenon@indianartcircle .com; a_menon@indianartcircle.com.

MENON, Mambillikalathil Govind Kumar, (Goku Menon), MSc, PhD, FRS; Indian physicist and academic; *Adviser, Department of Space, Indian Space Research Organization;* b. 28 Aug. 1928, Mangalore, Karnataka; s. of Shri Kizhekepat Sankara Menon and Mambillikalathil Narayaniamma; m. Indumati Menon 1955; one s. one d.; ed Jaswant Coll., Jodhpur, Royal Inst. of Science, Bombay, Univ. of Bristol, UK; Research Assoc., Univ. of Bristol 1952–53; Sr Award of Royal Comm. for Exhbn of 1851, Univ. of Bristol 1953–55; Reader, Tata Inst. of Fundamental Research, Bombay 1955–58; Assoc. Prof. 1958–60, Prof. and Dean of Physics Faculty 1960–64, Sr Prof. and Deputy Dir (Physics) 1964–66, Dir Tata

Inst. of Fundamental Research 1966–75; Sir C.V. Raman Prof., Indian Nat. Science Acad. 1986–91; M.N. Saha Distinguished Fellow 1994–99; Chair. Indian Space Research Org. 1972, Dr Vikram Sarabhai Distinguished Prof., 1999–2004, Adviser, Dept of Space 2004–; Chair. Electronics Comm. and Sec. to Govt of India Dept of Electronics 1971–78; Scientific Adviser to Minister of Defence, Dir-Gen. Defence Research and Devt Org. and Sec. for Defence Research 1974–78; Dir-Gen. Council of Scientific and Industrial Research 1978–81; Sec. to Govt of India, Dept of Science and Tech. 1978–82, Dept of Environment 1981–82; Chair. Comm. for Additional Sources of Energy; Chair. Science Advisory Cttee to Cabinet 1982–85; Scientific Adviser to Prime Minister 1986–89 and mem. Govt Planning Comm. (with rank of Minister of State) 1982–89; Minister of State for Science and Tech. and for Educ. 1989–90; MP 1990–96; Chair. Cosmic Ray Comm. ICSU/IUPAP 1973–75, Bharat Electronics Ltd, Bharat Dynamics Ltd (Missiles); Pres. Asia Electronics Union 1973–75, Indian Science Congress Asscn 1981–82, India Int. Centre, New Delhi 1983–88, 2007–11, Int. Council of Scientific Unions 1988–93, Indian Statistical Inst. 1990–2012; mem. Bd Dirs Escorts Ltd; Vice-Pres. IUPAP, Third World Acad. of Sciences 1983–88; mem. Pontifical Acad. of Sciences, Rome, Bd Inst. for Advanced Studies (UNU), Tokyo; Fellow, Indian Acad. of Sciences (Pres. 1974–76), Indian Nat. Science Acad. (Pres. 1981–82); Chair. Indian Inst. of Tech., Bombay 1997–2003, Indian Inst. of Information Tech., Allahabad 1999–2004, Indian Inst. of Tech., Delhi 2003–06; Hon. Pres. Asia Electronics Union; Hon. Fellow, Nat. Acad. of Sciences, India (Pres. 1987–88), Tata Inst. of Fundamental Research, Inst. of Electronics and Telecommunications Eng of India, Indian Inst. of Science, Bangalore, Nat. Inst. of Educ., Inst. of Physics (UK) 1997; Hon. mem. IEEE; Foreign Hon. mem. American Acad. of Arts and Sciences, Russian Acad. of Sciences; Hon. DEng (Stevens Inst. of Tech., USA); Hon. DSc (Jodhpur, Delhi, Sardar Patel, Roorkee, Banaras Hindu, Jadavpur, Sri Venkateswara, Allahabad, Andhra, Utkal, North Bengal, Aligarh Muslim, Guru Nanak Dev and Bristol Univs and Indian Inst. of Tech., Madras and Kharagpur); numerous awards including Shanti Swarup Bhatnagar Award for Physical Sciences, Council of Scientific and Industrial Research 1960, Padma Shri 1961, Padma Bhushan 1968, Repub. Day (Nat.) Awards, Khaitan Medal, Royal Asiatic Soc. 1973, Cecil Powell Medal, European Physical Soc. 1978, Pandit Jawaharlal Nehru Award for Sciences, Madhya Pradesh State Govt 1983, G.P. Chatterjee Award of Indian Science Congress Asscn 1984, Padma Vibhushan 1985, C.V. Raman Medal of Indian Nat. Science Acad. 1985, Abdus Salam Medal, Third World Acad. of Sciences 1997, Abdus Salam Award, asteroid 7564 Gokumenon named in his honour 2008. *Publications:* 160 papers on cosmic ray and elementary particle physics. *Leisure interests:* bird-watching, photography. *Address:* K-5 (rear side), Hauz Khas Enclave, New Delhi 110 016 (office); C-178 (First Floor), Sarvodaya Enclave, New Delhi 110 017, India (home). *Telephone:* (11) 26511454 (office); (11) 26966096 (home). *Fax:* (11) 26510825 (home). *E-mail:* mgkmenon@nic.in (office).

MENON, Raghu; Indian civil servant, government official and airline executive; *Secretary, Ministry of Information and Broadcasting;* officer of Indian Admin. Service of Assam-Nagaland cadre 1974, served in Ministry of Information and Broadcasting, apptd Jt Sec., Ministry of Civil Aviation 2002, Special Sec. and Financial Advisor –2008, Chair. and Man. Dir Air-India Ltd (state-owned airline merged with Indian airline under Nat. Aviation Co. of India Ltd) 2008–09; Sec. Ministry of Information and Broadcasting 2009–; Chair. Inter-Governmental Council of the Int. Programme for Devt of Communication 2010–. *Address:* Ministry of Information and Broadcasting, 'A' Wing, Room 552, Shastri Bhavan, New Delhi, 110 001, India (office). *Telephone:* (11) 23384453 (office). *E-mail:* jsp .onb@nic.in (office). *Website:* (office).

MENON, Shiv Shankar, MA; Indian diplomatist; *National Security Adviser;* b. 5 July 1949, Palakkad, Kerala; m. Mohini Sathe; one s. one d.; ed Univ. of Delhi; joined Indian Foreign Service 1972, Second Sec., Embassy in Beijing 1974–77; Under-Sec. in charge of Africa and then China 1977–79; First Sec., Embassy in Vienna 1979–83, also Alt. Gov. IAEA Bd and Deputy Perm. Rep. to UN Orgs; Dir Dept of Atomic Energy, Mumbai 1983–86; Counsellor and Deputy Chief of Mission, Embassy in Beijing 1986–89; Deputy Chief of Mission, Embassy in Tokyo 1989–92; Jt Sec. in charge of NE Div. 1992–95; Amb. to Israel 1995–97; High Commr to Sri Lanka 1997–2000; Amb. to China 2000–03; High Commr to Pakistan 2003–06; Foreign Sec. 2006–09; Nat. Security Adviser to the Prime Minister 2010–; Madhav Award, Scindia School Gwalior 2000. *Leisure interest:* classical music. *Address:* Ministry of External Affairs, South Block, New Delhi 110 011, India (office). *Telephone:* (11) 23011127 (office). *Fax:* (11) 23011463 (office). *Website:* meaindia .nic.in (office).

MENSAH, Joseph Henry, MSc; Ghanaian politician; b. 31 Oct. 1928; ed Achimota Coll., Univ. Coll. of Gold Coast (now Univ. of Ghana), London School of Econs, UK and Stanford Univ., USA; Asst Insp. of Taxes 1953; Research Fellow, Univ. Coll. of Gold Coast 1953–57; Lecturer in Econs, Univ. of Ghana 1957–58; Economist, UN HQ, New York 1958–61; Chief Economist, Prin. Sec. and Exec. Sec. of Nat. Planning Comm. Ghana 1961–65; Economist, UN, Div. of Trade and Econ. Co-operation and Econ. Comm. for Africa (ECA) 1965–69; Commr of Finance April–July 1969; mem. Parl. for Sunyani (Progress Party) 1969–72; Minister of Finance 1969–72, of Econ. Planning 1969–71; arrested Jan. 1972, released July 1973; re-arrested 1975; sentenced to eight years' imprisonment with hard labour Oct. 1975, released June 1978, in exile in London 1982; returned to Ghana Feb. 1995; mem. Parl. for Sunyani East (New Patriotic Party) 1997–2009; Minister in Charge of Govt Business 2001–03; Sr Minister, responsible for Public Sector Reform and the Nat. Institutional Renewal Programme 2003–06.

MENSHIKOV, Oleg Yevgenyevich; Russian actor; b. 8 Nov. 1960, Serpukhov, Moscow Region; ed Shchepkin Higher School of Theatre Art, Maly Theatre; Laurence Olivier Prize for Yesenin 1991, Film Critics' Prize for Best Actor of 1994, prizes for best men's role at Festivals Kinotaurus 1996, Baltic Pearl 1996, other awards. *Theatre roles include:* Ganya Ivolgin (Idiot after Dostoyevsky) 1981, Sergey (Sports Scenes of 1981) 1986, Caligula (Caligula) 1989, Yesenin (When She Danced) London 1991, Ikharev (Gamblers) London 1992, Nizhinsky (N. Nizhinsky) 1993. *Film roles include:* Rodnya (Kinfolk) 1981, Polyoty vo sne i nayavu (Flights in Dreams and in Reality) 1982, Kiss, Polosa prepyatstviy (Stripe of Obstacles) 1984, Mikhailo Lomonosov 1984, Po glavnoy ulitse s orkestrom (Through Main Street with an Orchestra) 1986, Moy lyubimyy kloun (My Favourite Clown) 1986, Moonzund (also singer) 1987, Bryzgi shampanskogo

(Splashes of Champagne) 1988, Zhizn po limitu (Limited Life) 1989, Lestnitsa (The Stairway) 1989, Yama (The Pit) 1990, Dyuba-Dyuba 1993, Utomlyonnye solntsem (Burnt by the Sun) 1994, Kavkazskiy plennik (Prisoner of the Caucasus) 1996, Sibirskiy tsiryulnik (The Barber of Siberia) 1998, Mama (Mummy) 1999, Est-Ouest (East-West) 1999, Statski sovetnik 2005; appeared in films of dirs N. Mikhalkov, A. Proshkin, A. Muratov, D. Khvan, S. Bodrov, R. Balayan, V. Kozakov, A. Sakharov. *Television includes:* Pokrovskiye vorota (Pokrov Gates) 1982, Potseluy (The Kiss) 1983, Volodya bolshoy, Volodya malenkiy (Big and Small Volodya) 1985, Prime Suspect 6 2003, Doctor Zhivago (mini-series) 2005, Zolotoy telenok (mini-series) 2006. *Address:* Maly Kozykhinsky per. 8/18, Apt 3, Moscow, Russia. *Telephone:* (495) 299-02-17 (home).

MENSHOV, Vladimir Valentinovich; Russian film director and actor; b. 17 Sept. 1939, Baku; m. Vera Alentova 1963; one d.; ed Moscow Arts Theatre Studio School, All-Union State Inst. of Cinema (VGIK) 1970; RSFSR State Prize 1978, Acad. Award for Moscow Does Not Believe in Tears 1980, USSR State Prize 1981, RSFSR Artist of Merit 1984, Prize of American Guild of Cinema Owners. *Leading roles in:* A Man in His Place 1973, Last Meeting 1974, Personal Opinions 1977, Time for Reflection 1983, The Intercept 1986, Where is Nofelet? 1987, The Town Zero 1988, Red Mob 1993, Russian Ragtime 1993. *Films include:* Loss (Rozygrysh) 1977, Moscow Does Not Believe in Tears 1980, Love and Doves 1984, Shirly-Myrly 1995, Envy of Gods 2000, Spartak i Kalashnikov 2002, Nochnoy dozor 2004, Vremya sobirat' kamni 2005, Dnevnoy dozor (Day Watch) 2006. *Address:* 3-d Tverskaya-Yamskaya 52, Apt. 29, 125047 Moscow, Russia. *Telephone:* (495) 250-85-43.

MENTRÉ, Paul; French civil servant and diplomatist; *Inspector-General of Finances;* b. 28 June 1935, Nancy; s. of Paul Mentré and Cécile de Loye; m. 1st Sabine Brundsaux 1958 (divorced 1975); two d.; m. 2nd Gaëlle Bretillot 1975; two s.; m. 3rd Jehanne Collard 1992; ed Ecole Polytechnique, Ecole Nat. d'Admin.; Insp. of Finance 1960; Special Asst, French Treas. 1965–70; Deputy Dir of the Cabinet of the Minister of Finance (V. Giscard d'Estaing) 1971–73; Under-Sec. Ministry of Economy and Finance 1971–72; Dir Crédit National 1973–75, Crédit Lyonnais 1973–75; Gen. Del. for Energy 1975–78; Financial Minister, French Embassy in Washington, DC 1978–82; Exec. Dir IMF and World Bank 1978–81; Insp.-Gen. of Finances 1981–; Man. Dir Banque Nationale de Paris 1986–87, Dir-Gen. 1987–90; Pres. Dir-Gen. Crédit Nat. 1987–90; Pres. Crédit sucrier 1990, technopole de Caen Synergia 1991–94, Valréal 1992–, Trouville-Deauville Dist 1995– (Communauté de communes Cœur Côte Fleurie from 2002); Exec. Sec. Cttee for the Monetary Union of Europe; Dir European Investment Bank 1987–91; Prof., Ecole des Hautes Etudes Commerciales; mem. Supervisory Council Crédit local de France 1987–90, French-German Council of Econ. Advisers; Dir Affine; Founder Victimes et Citoyens (support group for victims of road traffic accidents) 2001, Pres. 2004–; Chevalier, Ordre nat. du Mérite, des Arts et Lettres, Saudi Royal Order. *Publications:* Imaginer l'avenir, Gulliver enchaîné 1982, L'Amerique et nous, L'insoutenable légèreté du fort 1989, articles on economic issues in Le Figaro, Le Monde and Les Echos. *Leisure interests:* tennis, skiing. *Address:* Communauté de Communes Coeur Côte Fleurie, 12 Rue Robert Fossorier BP 30086, 14803 Deauville Cedex (office); c/o Ministry of the Economy, Finance and Industry, 139 rue de Bercy, 75572 Paris Cedex 12 (office); 18 rue de Bourgogne, 75007 Paris, France (home). *Telephone:* 2-31-88-54-49 (office); 1-40-04-04-04 (office). *Fax:* 2-31-88-19-76 (office); 1-43-43-75-97 (office). *E-mail:* info@coeurcotefleurie.org (office). *Website:* www.coeurcotefleurie.org (office); www.minefi.gouv.fr (office).

MENZEL, Jiří; Czech film and theatre director and actor; b. 23 Feb. 1938; s. of Josef Menzel and Božena Jindřichová; ed Film Acad. of Performing Arts, specialized in film directing, 1957–61; film Dir and actor 1962–89; Head of Dept of Film Directing, Film Acad. of Performing Arts, Prague 1990–92; Producer of Studio 89 1991–; Dir Vinohradské divadlo (theatre) 1997, 1998–, Artistic Dir 2000; mem. Supervisory Bd OPS, Prague, European City of Culture 2000 1999; Officier des Arts et des Lettres 1990, Medal of Merit 1996; Oscar Prize, Santa Monica 1968 for Closely Observed Trains, Akira Kurosawa Prize for Lifelong Merits in Cinematography, San Francisco 1990, Ennio Flaiano, Prize for Lifetime Achievement in Cinematography, Pescara, Italy 1996; Czech Lion Prize, Czech Film and TV Acad. (for lifetime career) 1997, Golden Seal Prize (Yugoslavia) 1997. *Plays directed:* Pré by J. Suchýs, Prague 1994, A Midsummer Night's Dream, Český Krumlov 2000. *Opera directed:* Dalibor by Smetana Cagliari 1999. *Recent film roles:* Jak si zaslouzit princeznu (How to Deserve a Princess) 1995, Ma je pomsta (Revenge is Mine) 1995, Truck Stop 1996, Une trop bruyante solitude (Too Loud a Solitude) 1996, Franciska vasárnapjai (Every Sunday) 1997, Vsichni moji blízcí (All My Loved Ones, USA) 1999, Ab ins Paradies (When Grandpa Loved Rita Hayworth) 2000, Potonulo groblje (The Sunken Cemetery) 2002, Útek do Budína 2002, Világszám! 2004, Rokonok 2006, Medvídek 2007, Operation Dunaj 2009, Signál 2012, The Door 2012. *Films directed include:* Ostre sledované vlaky (Closely Observed Trains) 1966, Vesnicko má stredisková (My Sweet Little Village) 1985, Konec starych casu (The End of the Good Old Days) (Grand Prize of the Int. Film Producers' Meeting, Cannes 1990) 1989, Skrivánci na niti (Skylarks on the String) 1990, The Beggar's Opera 1991, The Life and Extraordinary Adventures of Private Ivan Chonkin 1994, Ten Minutes Older: The Cello 2002, Obsluhoval jsem anglického krále (I Served the King of England) 2006, Jirí Menzel: 7 Questions (video documentary short) 2011, The Don Juans 2013. *Television includes:* Drákuluv svagr (mini-series) 1996, Hospoda (series) 1996–97, Zimni vila (film) 1999, A bárány utolsó megkísértése (film) 2007, Setkání v Praze, s vrazdou (film) 2009, Vyprávej (series) 2009. *Publication:* Tak nevím (novel) 1998. *Leisure interest:* literature. *Address:* Studio 89, Krátký film Praha a.s., Jindřišská 34, 112 07 Prague 1 (office); Divadlo na Vinchradech, Náměstí míru 7, 120 00 Prague 2, Czech Republic (home). *Telephone:* (2) 22520452 (office). *Fax:* (2) 22520452. *E-mail:* dnv@anet.cz.

MER, Francis Paul, LèsL (Econs); French business executive; b. 25 May 1939, Pau, Basses Pyrénées; s. of René Mer and Yvonne Casalta; m. Catherine Bonfils 1964; three d.; ed Lycée Montesquieu, Bordeaux, Ecole Nationale Supérieure des Mines, Paris and Ecole Polytechnique; mining engineer, Ministry of Industry 1966; tech. adviser, Abidjan 1967–68; Chair. Inter-ministerial Cttee on European Econ. Co-operation 1969–70; Head of Planning, Saint-Gobain Industries 1971; Dir of Planning, Compagnie Saint-Gobain-Pont-à-Mousson 1973; Dir of Planning, later Dir-Gen. Saint-Gobain Industries 1973; Dir Société des Maisons Phénix

1976–78; Asst Dir-Gen. Saint-Gobain-Pont-à-Mousson 1978–82, Pres.-Dir-Gen. de Pont-à-Mousson SA 1982–86; Pres.-Dir-Gen. Usinor-Sacilor 1986–2002, Chair. Usinor Group 2001–02; Pres. Chambre syndicale de la sidérurgie française 1988–, Conservatoire Nat. des Arts et Métiers 1989–, Eurofer 1990–97, Asscn nat. de Recherche Technique 1991–, Centre d'études prospectives et d'informations internationales 1995–2000; Pres. Int. Iron and Steel Inst. (INSI) 1997–98; Dir Crédit Lyonnais 1997–, Electricité de France 1997–, Air France 1997–; Minister of the Economy, Finance and Industry 2002–2004; Chair. Fondation pour L'Innovation Politique 2004; mem. Bd of Dirs Inco 2005–; Chair. Supervisory Bd Group Safran 2006–13; Commdr, Légion d'honneur, Ordre nat. du Mérite. *Address:* 9 rue Bobierre-de-Vallière, 92340 Bourg-la-Reine, France (home).

MERABISHVILI, Ivane; Georgian politician; *Secretary-General, United National Movement;* b. 15 April 1968, Ude, Adigeni Region; m. Tamar (Tako) Salaqaia; two s.; ed Tech. Univ. of Georgia; began career as Lab. Asst, Tech. Univ. of Georgia and Agrarian Univ., becoming Chief Lab. Asst, Asst, Jr Researcher 1992–95; Pres. Asscn for the Protection of Landowners' Rights 1995–; mem. Sakartvelos Parlamenti (Parl.) 1999–, Chair. Parl. Cttee for Econ. Policy and Reforms 2000–; Sec., Nat. Security Council Jan.–June 2004; Minister of State Security June–Dec. 2004, of Internal Affairs 2004–12; Prime Minister July–Oct. 2012; mem. Union of Citizens of Georgia –2002, United Nat. Movt 2002– (Sec.-Gen. 2012–); arrested along with Zurab Tchiaberashvili over alleged misspending of public funds by party activists during the 2012 election campaign May 2013, found guilty by Kutaisi City Court of abuse of office, bribery of voters and inefficient use of budget funds and sentenced to five years' imprisonment Feb. 2014, appealing the sentence. *Address:* United National Movement (Ertiani natsionaluri modzraoba), 0118 Tbilisi, Kakheti 45A, Georgia (office). *Telephone:* (32) 292-30-84 (office). *Fax:* (32) 292-30-91 (office). *E-mail:* info@unm.ge (office). *Website:* www .unm.ge (office).

MERAFHE, Lt-Gen. Mompati S., LLB; Botswana politician; b. 6 June 1936, Serowe; two s. three d.; ed Univ. of S Africa; police officer, later Deputy Commr of Police 1960–77; Commdr Botswana Defence Force, ranked Maj.-Gen. 1977, Lt-Gen. 1988; MP for Mahalapye; fmr Cabinet Minister for Public Admin; Minister of Foreign Affairs 1994, 1996–2008; Vice-Pres. 2008–12. *Address:* c/o Office of the President, Private Bag 001, Gaborone, Botswana.

MERALI, Naushad Noorali; Kenyan business executive; *Chairman, Sameer Group of Companies;* b. 1 Feb. 1951, Nairobi; m. Zarin Merali; launched Kencell Communications (with Vivendi Telecom) 2000 (later sold to Celtel and Bharti Airtel); Chair. Eveready East Africa Ltd –2008; currently Chair. Sameer Group of Cos; mem. Bd of Dirs W.P.H. Kenya Tea Co. –2005, Sameer Africa Ltd –2010, Sasini Ltd, Celtel International B.V, Ryce Motors, Zain Africa B.V; Co-founder Zarina and Naushad Merali Foundation; mem. Kenya Export Promotion Council, Nat. Investment Council, World Econ. Forum, Switzerland, Nat. Poverty Eradication Comm., Kenya Export Promotion Council, Nat. Econ. Social Council, Cttee to Review Terms and Conditions of Service for Civil Servants, Presidential Cttee on Employment; Chief of the Order of the Burning Spears. *Address:* Sameer Group of Companies, 49, Riverside Drive, PO Box 55358, Nairobi 00200, Kenya (office). *Telephone:* (20) 4204000 (office). *Fax:* (20) 4441492 (office). *E-mail:* info@sameer -group.co.ke (office). *Website:* www.sameer-group.com (office).

MERCADO RAMOS, Fernando, BA, JD; Puerto Rican politician, lawyer and poet; b. 18 June 1957, Lares; s. of Tomas Mercado-Estremere and Luz M. Ramos-Valez; m. Michelle Waters; two s.; ed Univ. of Puerto Rico, Univ. of Madrid, Spain; teacher of psychology and sociology, Colegio Nuestra Señora del Carmen Rió Piedras 1979–1981; legal counsel, Culture Comm., House of Reps 1982–84; Exec. Dir Comm. of the Govt 1985–88, Sec.-Gen. 1989–92; judge, Court of the First Instance 1992, Sec.-Gen. 1999; Sec.-Gen. Partido Popular Democrático 1999–2000; Sec. of State 2001–03; prominent political analyst for the Notiuno radio network in Puerto Rico; mem. American Acad. of Judicial Educ. 1996, American Judicature Soc., ABA Judicial Admin. Div., American Judges' Asscn, Colegio de Abogados de Puerto Rico 1981. *Publications include:* Grito a la Intimidad 1976, Un Pensamiento en Viaje 1990, Un Nuevo Lider: Esperanza de una Nueva Generación 1991. *Leisure interests:* reading, swimming, writing. *Address:* c/o Office of the Secretary of the State, Department of State, PO Box 9023271, San Juan, PR 00902-3271, Puerto Rico. *E-mail:* fmercado@estado.gobierno.pr.

MERCIECA, Mgr Joseph, BA, SThD, JUD; Maltese ecclesiastic; *Archbishop Emeritus of Malta;* b. 11 Nov. 1928, Victoria, Gozo; s. of Saverio Mercieca and Giovanna Vassallo; ed Gozo Seminary, Gregorian Univ. and Lateran Univ., Rome; ordained priest 1952; Rector Gozo Seminary 1952–69; Judge of Roman Rota 1969–74; ordained Titular Bishop of Gemellae in Numidia, apptd Auxiliary Bishop of Malta 1974; Vicar-Gen. 1975–76; Consultor, Congregation of the Sacraments and Congregation for the Doctrine of Faith, Vatican City 1976; Archbishop of Malta and Pres. Maltese Episcopal Conf. 1976–2006, Archbishop Emer. 2006–; mem. Apostolic Segnatura, Rome 1991. *Address:* c/o Archdiocese of Malta, PO Box 90, Head Office, Marsa MRS1000, Malta. *Telephone:* (21) 245350. *Fax:* (21) 242971. *E-mail:* info@maltadiocese.org. *Website:* www.maltadiocese.org.

MERCIER, Michel; French lawyer and politician; *Deputy Mayor of Thizy;* b. 7 March 1947, Bourg-de-Thizy (Rhône); ed Institut d'études politiques, Lyons; began career as Lecturer, Dept of Law, Univ. Lyon III; Municipal Councillor, Thizy 1971–, Mayor of Thizy 1977–2001, Deputy Mayor 2006–; Gen. Councillor, Rhône 1978–, Pres. Rhône Gen. Council 1990–; Vice-Pres. Rhône-Alpes Regional Council 1992–93 (resgnd), Regional Councillor 1992–93 (resgnd); mem. Court of Justice of the Repub. 1994–2009; mem. Assemblée nationale (Parl.) for Rhône 1993–95; Senator for Rhône 1995–2009, Pres. Senate Union Centriste Group 2002–09; Minister of Rural Areas and Spatial Planning 2009–10, of Justice and Freedoms and Keeper of the Seals 2010–12; Treas. Mouvement Démocrate 2007–09, Union pour la démocratie française 1998–2007; mem. Union pour un Mouvement Populaire (UMP) 2009–; Kt, Holy Order of Saint-Sépulcre. *Address:* Mairie de Thizy, Parc Charles Moncorgé, 69240 Thizy, France (office). *Telephone:* (4) 74-64-05-29 (office). *Fax:* (4) 74-64-30-22 (office). *E-mail:* info@thizy.fr (office). *Website:* www.thizy.fr (office).

MERCKX, Eddy; Belgian fmr cyclist; b. 17 June 1945, Meen, Brussels sel-Kiezegem; m. Claudine Merckx; one s. one d.; world amateur champion 1963, first professional race 1964, winner World Road Championships 1967, 1971, 1974,

Tours of Italy 1968, 1970, 1972, 1973, 1974, Tours de France 1969, 1970, 1971, 1972, 1974 (shares record for most wins, holds record (34) for most stage wins), Tours of Belgium 1970, 1971, Tour of Spain 1973, Tour of Switzerland 1974, 32 major classics; broke the then world hour record, Mexico City 1972; retd 1978 with 525 wins in 1,800 races; involved with manufacture of bicycles which bear his name 1980–; Belgian Sportsman of the Year 1969–74 (record), Belgian Athlete of the Century.

MEREDOV, Rashid Ovezgeldyyevich; Turkmenistani politician; *Deputy Chairman of the Government and Minister of Foreign Affairs;* b. 1960, Aşgabat, Turkmen SSR, USSR; ed Faculty of Law, Moscow Lomonosov State Univ.; teacher, Dept of Civil Law, Turkmen State Univ. 1982; Lecturer, then Sr Lecturer 1987–90; Chief Consultant and Head of Section, Head of Dept, Ministry of Justice, Turkmen SSR 1990–91; Head of law enforcement agencies under Pres. of Turkmenistan 1991–; Head of Law Dept, Office of the Pres. 1993–; Deputy Dir, Nat. Inst. for Democracy and Human Rights 1996–99, Dir 2001–05; First Deputy Minister of Foreign Affairs 1999–2001, Minister of Foregin Affairs 2001–; First Deputy Chair. of Majlis (Nat. Ass.) 1999–2001, Chair. 2001–; Deputy Chair. of the Govt 2003–05; Deputy Chair. of the Govt, responsible for the police and army 2007–; For the Love of Fatherland Medal, Gayrat Medal, Galkynyş Order. *Address:* Ministry of Foreign Affairs, 744000 Aşgabat, Arşabil şaýoly 108, Turkmenistan (office). *Telephone:* (12) 44-56-94 (office). *Fax:* (12) 21-86-75 (office). *E-mail:* fmatm@online.tm (office). *Website:* www.mfa.gov.tm (office).

MERENTES DÍAZ, Nelson José, PhD; Venezuelan politician and central banker; *President, Banco Central de Venezuela;* ed Central Univ. of Venezuela and Univ. of Budapest, Hungary; Minister of Science and Tech. Feb.–Nov. 2002, of State for Devt and Econs 2002–04, of State for Financial Devt Sept.–Dec. 2004, of Finance 2004–07, 2013–14; Pres. Nat. Bank for Econ. and Social Devt 2002–04; fmr Gov. for Venezuela World Bank, IMF, Caribbean Devt Bank; Head of Public Finance Office 2004–07; mem. Bd of Dirs Banco Central de Venezuela 2007–, apptd Pres. 2009, 2014–. *Address:* Banco Central de Venezuela, Avda Urdaneta, esq. de Carmelitas, Caracas 1010, Venezuela (office). *Telephone:* (212) 801-5111 (office). *Fax:* (212) 861-0048 (office). *E-mail:* info@bcv.org.ve (office). *Website:* www.bcv.org.ve (office).

MEREZHKO, Viktor Ivanovich; Russian scriptwriter; b. 28 July 1937, Olginfeld, Rostov-on-Don Region; m. (wife deceased); one s. one d.; ed Ukrainian Inst. of Polygraphy, Lvov, All-Union Inst. of Cinematography; engineer Molot Publrs, Rostov-on-Don 1961–64; freelance 1968–; TV broadcaster and Head of History Programming; Vice-Pres. TV-6 Ind. TV; Chair. Kinoshock Festival, Nika Prize Cttee; State Prize 1986. *Plays include:* I'm a Woman, Cry, Caucasian Roulette. *Films include:* over 45 film scripts, including Zdravstvuy i proshchay (Hello and Goodbye) 1972, Odinozhdy odin (One Once) 1974, Tryn-trava 1976, Zhuravl v nebe (Crane In the Sky) 1977, Vas ozhidayet grazhdanka Nikanorova (Citizen Nikanorova Waits for You) 1978, Ukhodya – ukhodi 1978, Tryasina (Quagmire) 1978, Kholostyaki 1980, Rodnya (Kinfolk) 1981, Otstavnoy kozy barabanshchik 1981, Polyoty vo sne i nayavu (Flights in Dreams and in Reality) 1983, Polosa vezeniya (Goldfishes) 1983, Osobyy sluchay 1983, Yesli mozhesh, prosti… (If You Can, Forgive…) 1984, Aplodismenty, aplodismenty… (Applause, Applause…) 1984, Prosti (Forgive Me) (also actor) 1986, Odinokaya zhenshchina zhelayet poznakomitsya (Lonely Woman Seeks Lifetime Companion) 1986, Zabavy molodykh (Joys of Youth) 1987, 9 maya 1987, Under the Blue Sky (Fipressi Prize, Venice Festival 1987), Shag (aka Message from the Future) 1988, Avtoportret neizvestnogo (Selfportrait of an Unknown Man) 1988, Martokhela monadire (Lonely Hunter) 1989, Sobachiy pir (Dogs' Feast) 1990, Nochnye zabavy (Night Fun) 1991, Yesli by znat… (If We'd Only Known) 1993, Kurochka Ryaba (Ryaba My Chicken) 1994, Greshnye apostoly lyubvi 1995, Ligne de vie (Line of Life) 1996, The Two from Big Road 1996, Kavkazskaya ruletka (Caucasus Roulette) 2002, Lisa Alisa (video) 2003; actor: Yesli yest parusa 1969, Pod nebom golubym 1989, Dikiy plyazh 1990, Russkiy roman (Russian Romance) 1993. *Television includes:* scriptwriter: Saga o kriminale (series) 2001, Provintsialy (series) (also actor) 2002. *Leisure interest:* collecting side-arms. *Address:* Usiyevicha str. 8, Apt 133, 125319 Moscow, Russia (home). *Telephone:* (495) 217-57-58; (495) 155-74-59 (home).

MERIDOR, Dan, LLB; Israeli lawyer and politician; *Deputy Prime Minister and Minister of Intelligence and Atomic Energy;* b. 23 April 1947, Jerusalem; m. Liora Meridor; four c.; ed Hebrew Univ.; served in Israel Defence Forces (IDF) as tank commander in 1967 Six Day War, continued to serve as captain in IDF reserves; practised law Jerusalem 1973–82; Cabinet Sec. of Govt 1982–84; mem. Knesset 1984–2003, 2009–; Minister of Justice 1988–92, of Finance 1996–97; Chair. Foreign Affairs and Defense Cttee 1997–2001; Minister without Portfolio responsible for Nat. and Diplomatic Strategy 2001–03; Leader Centre Party 2001; currently Deputy Prime Minister and Minister of Intelligence and Atomic Energy; mem. Likud Party 1984–99, 2009–; fmr Int. Chair Jerusalem Foundation. *Address:* Ministry of Intelligence and Atomic Energy, Jerusalem, Israel (office). *Telephone:* 2-6753800 (office). *E-mail:* dmeridor@knesset.gov.il (office).

MERIMÉE, Jean-Bernard, LenD; French diplomatist; b. 4 Dec. 1936, Toulouse (Haute-Garonne); s. of Jacques Merimée and Germaine Merimée (née Larrieu); m. Anna Mirams 1965; one s. two d.; ed Lycées Pasteur, Neuilly-sur-Seine and Louis-le-Grand, Paris, Institut d'Etudes Politiques de Paris, Ecole Nat. d'Admin, Paris; with Cen. Admin, Ministry of Foreign Affairs 1965, with Sec. 1972–75; Second then First Sec. to UK 1966–72; Chief of Mission of Co-operation, Côte d'Ivoire 1975–78, Chief of Protocol 1978–81; Amb. to Australia 1982–85, to India 1985–87, to Morocco, Rabat 1987–91; Amb. and Perm. Rep. to Security Council and Chief of Perm. Mission to UN, New York 1991–95; Amb. to Italy, Rome 1995–98, to Repub. of San Marino (resident in Rome) 1997–98, to Cen. Admin 1998–99; Perm. Rep. to UN 1999, Special Adviser to Sec.-Gen. on European Affairs with rank of Under-Sec.-Gen. 1999–2001; Dir Groupe Benjelloun (mobile telephone, banking and insurance cos), Morocco; mem. Advisory Bd BMCE Bank, France; Officier, Légion d'honneur, Officier, Ordre nat. du Mérite, Commdr of the Order of Christ (Portugal), Grand Officer of the Order of the Phoenix (Greece), Kt of the Dannebrog (Denmark), Officer of the Oak Crown (Luxembourg), Merit Commdr of the Supreme Order of Malta. *Address:* 21 bis rue Molière, 75001 Paris, France.

MÉRINDOL, Nicolas, BA, MBA; French certified public accountant and banking executive; *CEO, Caisse Nationale des Caisses d'Epargne;* ed Institut Supérieur de Gestion, Institut Nat. des Techniques Economiques et Comptables; began career with Renault in Argentina and France; later worked at Caisse des Dépôts; joined Exec. Cttee of Groupe Caisse d'Epargne 1988, moved to Caisse d'Epargne de Picardie 1991, served as Finance and Risk Man. Dir before joining Man. Bd of regional savings bank, apptd Dir for Org. 1996, later Dir of Financial Planning at Caisse Nationale des Caisses d'Epargne, mem. Man. Bd Caisse Nationale des Caisses d'Epargne with responsibility for banking operations and finance 2002–03, responsible for Commercial Banking Div. and Corp. Strategy 2003–06, CEO Caisse Nationale des Caisses d'Epargne 2006–; Chair. Crédit Foncier; Chair. Supervisory Bd Banque Palatine, Compagnie 1818; Chair. European Banking Industry Cttee 2006, Vice-Chair. 2007–; mem. Nat. Council for Sustainable Devt; mem. Bd Dirs Nat. Agency for Personal Care Services 2006–; mem. Bd Fund for Social Cohesion, Steering Cttee France Investissement. *Address:* Caisse Nationale des Caisses d'Epargne, 50 avenue Pierre Mendès, 75201 Paris Cedex 13, France (office). *Telephone:* 1-58-40-40-02 (office). *Fax:* 1-58-40-50-30 (office). *E-mail:* info@groupe.caisse-epargne.com (office). *Website:* www.groupe.caisse-epargne.com (office).

MERINO LUCERO, Beatriz, MA; Peruvian lawyer, politician and government official; b. 1949, Lima; ed Universidad Nacional Mayor de San Marcos, London School of Econs, UK, Harvard Univ. Law School, USA; lawyer fmrly specializing in tax and int. trade; elected Senator (Movimiento Libertad) 1990–92; mem. Congreso (Frente Independiente Moralizador) 1995–2000; Dir Master Tax and Fiscal Policy, Univ. of Lima 2000–01; elected Head of Sunat (tax agency) 2001–03; Pres. Council of Ministers (Prime Minister) June–Dec. 2003; member of the Inter-American Dialogue, Washington, DC –2005; Defensora del Pueblo (Ombudsman) 2005–11; Orden 'El Sol del Perú' en el Grado de Gran Cruz 2006; María Elena Moyano Prize, Ministry of Women and Social Devt, Vaso de Leche Award of the Women of Peru, Woman of the Year, OWIT Peru, Robert G. Storey Int. Award for Leadership, Center for American and Int. Law 2004. *Address:* c/o Defensoria del Pueblo, Jr. Ucayali N° 388, Lima, Peru.

MERKEL, Angela Dorothea, Dr rer. nat; German politician; *Chancellor;* b. 17 July 1954, Hamburg; d. of Horst Kasner and Herlind Kasner; m. 1st Ulrich Merkel (divorced 1982); m. 2nd Joachim Sauer 1998; ed Univ. of Leipzig; Research Assoc. in quantum chem., Zentralinstitut für physikalische Chemie, East Berlin 1978–90; joined Demokratischer Aufbruch (DA) 1989, Press Spokesperson 1990; Deputy Spokesman for Govt of Lothar de la Maizière, March–Oct. 1990; joined CDU (Christian Democratic Union) 1990, mem. Bundestag 1990–, Deputy Fed. Chair. 1991–98, CDU Chair. Fed. State of Mecklenburg-Vorpommern 1993–2000, Gen. Sec. CDU 1998–2000, Chair. 2000–, also Parl. Leader 2002–05; Fed. Minister for Women and Young People 1991–94, for Environment, Nature Conservation and Nuclear Safety 1994–98; Chancellor 2005–; Pres. European Council and Chair. G8 2007; mem. Council of Women World Leaders; Bundesverdienstkreuz 2008; Dr hc (Hebrew Univ. of Jerusalem) 2007, (Univ. of Leipzig) 2008, (Univ. of Tech., Wrocław) 2008; ranked by Forbes magazine amongst The World's 100 Most Powerful Women (first) 2006–09, (fourth) 2010, (first) 2011–13, named a Hero of the Environment 2007, Charlemagne Prize for distinguished services to European unity 2008, Presidential Medal of Freedom (US) 2011, ranked by Forbes magazine amongst The World's Most Powerful People (15th) 2009, (sixth) 2010, (fourth) 2011, (second) 2012, (fifth) 2013. *Publication:* Der Preis des Überlebens: Gedanken und Gespräche über zukünftige Aufgaben der Umweltpolitik (The Price of Survival: Ideas and Conversations about Future Tasks for Environmental Policy) 1997. *Leisure interests:* reading, hiking, gardening. *Address:* Office of the Federal Chancellery, Willy-Brandt str. 1, 10557 Berlin, Germany (office). *Telephone:* (30) 40000 (office). *Fax:* (30) 40002357 (office). *E-mail:* internetpost@bundeskanzler.de (office). *Website:* www.bundeskanzler.de (office); www.angela-merkel.de.

MERKIN, J. Ezra; American business executive; *Chairman, GMAC Financial Services;* ed Columbia Coll., New York, Harvard Univ. Law School, Cambridge, Mass; Man. Pnr, Gabriel Capital Group (and its predecessor) 1985–2008; Chair. GMAC Financial Services 2008–; Trustee and Chair. Investment Cttees Yeshiva Univ. and of UJA/Fed. of New York; Trustee, Carnegie Hall, New York, Beyeler Foundation and Museum, Basel, Switzerland, Gruss Foundation; mem. Bd of Visitors Columbia Coll.; Gov. Levy Econs Inst. of Bard Coll., Annandale-on-Hudson, NY; Pres. Fifth Avenue Synagogue, New York; Vice-Chair. Ramaz School, New York. *Address:* GMAC Financial Services, 200 Renaissance Center, Detroit, MI 48265-2000, USA (office). *Telephone:* (313) 556-5000 (office). *Fax:* (815) 282-6156 (office). *E-mail:* info@gmacfs.com (office). *Website:* www.gmacfs.com (office).

MERKLEY, Jeffery (Jeff) A., BA, MA; American politician; *Senator from Oregon;* b. 24 Oct. 1956, Myrtle Creek, Ore.; m. Mary Sorteberg 1992; one s. one d.; ed Stanford Univ., Princeton Univ.; Presidential Man. Fellow, Office of the US Sec. of Defense, Washington, DC 1982–91; Man. Pnr, Computer Medics 1989–91; Exec. Dir Portland Habitat for Humanity 1991–94; Dir of Housing Devt at Human Solutions 1995–96; Pres. World Affairs Council of Oregon 1996–2003, mem. Bd of Trustees 1991–; mem. Oregon State House of Reps 1998–2009, Speaker 2007–09; Senator from Oregon 2009–, mem. Health, Educ., Labor and Pensions Cttee, Banking, Housing and Urban Affairs Cttee, Environment and Public Works Cttee, Budget Cttee; Founder People's Investment Opportunity Program, Walk for Humanity; Democrat. *Address:* 313 Hart Senate Office Building, Washington, DC 20510, USA (office). *Telephone:* (202) 224-3753 (office). *Fax:* (202) 228-3997 (office). *Website:* merkley.senate.gov (office).

MERLINI, Cesare; Italian international affairs scholar and fmr professor of nuclear technologies; *Chair of Board of Trustees, Istituto Affari Internazionale;* b. 29 April 1933, Rome; m.; two s. two d.; ed Classical Licée, Turin, Turin Polytechnic; lecturer in Nuclear Technologies 1967–76; Prof. of Nuclear Technologies, Turin Polytechnic 1976–85; Dir Istituto Affari Internazionali, Rome 1970–79, Pres. 1979–2000, currently Pres. Bd of Trustees; Vice-Pres. Exec. Cttee Consiglio per le Relazioni fra Italia e Stati Uniti (Council for USA and Italy) 1983–2009; mem. Bd of Dirs and Exec. Cttee Unione Tipografico-Editrice Torinese publrs SpA, Turin, Chair. 1999–2002; mem. Trilateral Comm. 1973–2001, Council, Int. Inst. for Strategic Studies, London 1993–99; Non-resident Sr Fellow, Brookings Inst., Washington DC 2010–. *Publications:* Fine dell'atomo? Passato e futuro delle applicazioni civili e militari dell'energia nucleare 1987, L'Europa degli Anni Novanta: Scenari per un futuro imprevisto (co-author and ed.) 1991; co-author and ed. of numerous books on nuclear energy and int. strategy, author of numerous articles on European and int. affairs and of scientific pubs on nuclear reactors and related technological and eng problems. *Leisure interest:* horse riding. *Address:* c/o Istituto Affari Internazionali, Via Angelo Brunetti 9, 00186 Rome, Italy (office). *Telephone:* (6) 3224360 (office). *Fax:* (6) 3224363 (office). *E-mail:* iai@iai.it (office). *Website:* www.iai.it (office).

MERLO, Larry J.; American business executive; *President and CEO, CVS Caremark Corporation;* Exec. Vice-Pres.– Stores of CVS Pharmacy, Inc. 1998–2007, Exec. Vice-Pres.– Stores of CVS Corpn 2000–07, Exec. Vice-Pres. CVS Caremark Corpn 2007–10, Pres. CVS/pharmacy – Retail 2007–11, Pres. and COO 2010–11, Pres. and CEO CVS Caremark Corpn 2011–; mem. Bd of Dirs Nat. Asscn of Chain Drug Stores, Chair. 2010–11. *Address:* CVS Caremark Corpn, 1 CVS Drive, Woonsocket, RI 02895, USA (office). *Telephone:* (401) 765-1500 (office). *Fax:* (401) 766-2917 (office). *E-mail:* storecomments@cvs.com (office). *Website:* info .cvscaremark.com (office); www.cvs.com (office).

MERLONI, Andrea; Italian business executive; *Chairman, Fineldo SpA;* b. 1967, Rome; s. of Vittorio Merloni and Franca Carloni; Chair. Aermarche SpA 1992–96; bought Benelli SpA brand 1996, relaunched it in scooter and large motorbike industry, Chair. and CEO 1996–2005; Chair. and CEO WRAP SpA (part of Indesit group) 2000–07, Dir Indesit Co. SpA (fmrly Merloni Elettrodomestici SpA) 2006–, Deputy Chair. 2008–10, Chair. 2010–13; mem. Bd of Dirs Fineldo SpA (family holding co.), fmr Chair.; Chair. ISTAO – Adriano Olivetti Institute for the Study of Company Management; Chair. and CEO Alpha67 Srl,. *Address:* ISTAO – Adriano Olivetti Institute for the Study of Company Management, Villa Favorita, Via Zuccarini, 15, Ancona, Italy (office). *E-mail:* presidenza@istao.it (office). *Website:* istao.it (office).

MERLONI, Vittorio; Italian industrialist; *Honorary Chairman, Indesit Company;* b. 30 April 1933, Fabriano, Ancona; m. Franca Carloni; four c.; ed Univ. of Perugia; Chair. Merloni Elettrodomestici SpA 1970–2010 (renamed Indesit Co. 2005), Fineldo (family holding co. that controls Indesit Co. and other Group interests), Hon. Chair. 2010–; mem. Confederazione Generale dell'Industria Italiana (Confindustria) 1976–, Pres. 1980–84; mem. Bd Dirs Assocs of Harvard Business School 1981–94; Pres. Assonime (Asscn for Italy's limited liability cos) 2001–05; mem. Consiglio Nazionale dell'Economia e del Lavoro (Nat. Council of Economy and Labour); mem. two dels to China; honorary doctorate of Management Engineering (Politecnico University of Milan) 2001; Cavaliere di Gran Croce al merito della Repubblica, Cavaliere del Lavoro 1984; Hon. CBE (UK) 2003; Leonardo Award 2004, GEI Award 2005. *Leisure interests:* racing cars, boats. *Address:* Indesit Company SpA, Viale Aristide Merloni 47, 60044 Fabriano (AN), Italy (office). *Telephone:* (0732) 6611 (office). *Fax:* (0732) 662380 (office). *Website:* www.indesitcompany.com (office).

MERMAZ, Louis; French politician and professor of history; b. 20 Aug. 1931, Paris; m. Annie d'Arbigny; three c.; teacher Lycée le Mans, Lycée Lakanal, Sceaux; Jr Lecturer in Contemporary History, Univ. of Clermont-Ferrand; Sec.-Gen. Convention des institutions républicaines 1965–69; mem. Socialist Party Nat. Secr. 1974–79, 1987–; mem. Nat. Ass. for Isère 1967–68, 1973–90, 1997–2001; Mayor of Vienne 1971–2001; Conseiller Gén. Canton of Vienne-Nord 1973–79, Vienne-Sud 1979–88; Pres. Conseil gén. of Isère 1976–85; Chair. Socialist Party Exec. Cttee 1979; Minister of Transport May–June 1981, of Equipment and Transport May–June 1988, of Agric. and Forests 1990–92, for Relations with Parl. and Govt Spokesman 1992–93; Pres. Nat. Ass. 1981–86, Socialist Group in Nat. Ass. 1988–90, Asscn Mer du Nord-Méditerranée 1989–94; mem. Senate for Isère 2001–; Chevalier Légion d'honneur. *Publications:* Madame Sabatier, Les Hohenzollern, L'autre volonté 1984, Madame de Maintenon 1985, Les Geôles de la République 2001. *Address:* Sénat, Palais du Luxembourg, 15 rue du Vaugirard, 75005 Paris (office); Permanence Parlementaire, 2 rue des Célestes, 38200 Vienne, France. *Telephone:* 1-42-34-28-58 (office); 4-74-85-47-58. *E-mail:* l.mermaz@senat .fr (office). *Website:* www.senat.fr/senfic/mermaz_louis01020h.html (office).

MERNISSI, Fatema, PhD; Moroccan sociologist and writer; b. 1941, Fez; ed Univ. of Paris (Sorbonne) and in the USA; sociologist, feminist and author in the Koran; Prof., Univ. Mohammed V, Rabat. *Publications include:* The Veil and the Male Elite: A Feminist Interpretation of Women's Rights in Islam 1992, Islam and Democracy: Fear of the Modern World 1994, The Forgotten Queens of Islam 1994, Dreams of Trespass: Tales of a Harem Girlhood 1994, Fear of Modernity or The Political Harem, Women's Rebellion and Islamic Memory 1996, Dreams on the Threshold, Les Ait Débrouille 1997, Scheherazade Goes West 2001, Beyond the Veil: Male-Female Dynamics in Muslim Society 2003, Les Sindbads Marocains: Voyage dans le Maroc civique 2004. *E-mail:* fatema@mernissi.net (office). *Website:* www.mernissi.net.

MERO, Muhammad Mustafa, PhD; Syrian politician; b. 1940, Tal-Mineen, Damascus; m.; two s. three d.; ed Damascus Univ.; joined Arab Teachers' Union, becoming its Sec. Gen. for Cultural Affairs and Publs; Mayor of Daraa 1980–86, of Al-Hasaka 1986–93; Gov. of Aleppo Governorate 1993–2000; Prime Minister of Syria 2000–03 (resgnd), headed a ministerial and commercial del. to Iraq Aug. 2001 (first Syrian prime minister to visit Iraq since the Gulf War, also first Syrian prime minister to visit Turkey in 17 years 2003). *Address:* c/o Office of the Prime Minister, rue Chahbandar, Damascus, Syria (office).

MERON, Theodor, LLM, MJ, JSD; American judge and academic; *President, United Nations International Criminal Tribunal for the Former Yugoslavia;* b. 28 April 1930, Kalisz, Poland; ed Univ. of Jerusalem, Harvard Univ. Law School, Univ. of Cambridge, UK; fmr Legal Adviser, Israeli Foreign Ministry, fmr Amb. of Israel to Canada, later to UN in Geneva, resgnd 1977; US citizen 1984–; Visiting Prof. of Law, New York Univ. School of Law 1975, Prof. of Law 1977, Charles L. Denison Prof. of Int. Law 1994–2003, Charles L. Denison Prof. of Law Emer. and Judicial Fellow 2006–; Prof. of Int. Law, Grad. Inst. of Int. Studies, Geneva, Switzerland 1991–95; Ed.-in-Chief American Journal of Int. Law 1993–98; Judge UN Criminal Tribunal for the Fmr Yugoslavia (ICTY) 2001–, Pres. 2003–05, 2011–, also mem. Appeals Chamber (ICTY) and UN Criminal Tribunal for Rwanda (ICTR) 2001–; Pres. Int. Residual Mechanism for Criminal Tribunals 2012–; fmr Counsellor on Int. Law US Dept of State; mem. Council on Foreign Relations; Public mem. US Del. to CSCE Conf. on Human Dimension, Copenhagen; numerous visiting lectureships in univs in Europe and USA; mem. Inst. of Int. Law; Fellow, American Acad. of Arts and Sciences 2009–; Officier, Légion d'Honneur (France) 2007; Int. Bar Asscn Rule of Law Award, American Soc. of

Int. Law Hudson Medal 2006, American Council of Learned Soc. Haskins Prize 2008. *Publications include:* Investment Insurance in International Law, Henry's Wars and Shakespeare's Laws 1994, Bloody Constraint: War and Chivalry in Shakespeare 1998, War Crimes Law Comes of Age: Essays 1999, International Law in the Age of Human Rights 2003, The Humanization of International Law 2006, The Making of International Justice: A View from the Bench 2011; numerous articles and publs on int. law and human rights. *Address:* UN Criminal Tribunal for the Former Yugoslavia, Public Information Unit, PO Box 13888, 2501 The Hague, Netherlands (office); New York University School of Law, Vanderbilt Hall, 40 Washington Square South, Room 304, New York, NY 10012-1099, USA. *Telephone:* (70) 512-8840 (office); (212) 998-6191 (NY). *Fax:* (70) 512-5252 (office). *E-mail:* meront@juris.law.nyu.edu. *Website:* www.un.org/icty; its.law.nyu .edu/facultyprofiles/profile.cfm?personID=20122 (office).

MÉRORÈS, Léo, LLB, MA, PhD; Haitian diplomatist and UN official; b. 21 April 1943; ed State Univ. of Haiti, Ecole de Commerce Maurice Laroche, Port-au-Prince, New York Univ., USA; early career as salesman, Enterprises Gerard Theard, Port-au-Prince 1961; worked part-time as accountant and Asst to Head of Credit Dept, Shapiro & Sons Textile Corpn, New York, USA 1969–73; UNDP Deputy Resident Rep. in Togo and Madagascar 1978–84, worked in UNDP office in Rwanda 1974–78, UNDP Deputy Resident Rep. for Liberia, Mali and Cameroon 1984–92, responsible for UNDP offices in Gabon and Burundi 1989–92, Prin. Counsellor for UNDP working with Econ. Community of West African States (ECOWAS) countries 1992–2001, consultant on man. and econ. co-operation issues for several UN entities, including Dept of Econ. and Social Affairs, UN Office for Project Services (UNOPS) and UNDP 2001–04; Chargé d'affaires a.i., Perm. Mission to UN, New York 2004–05, Perm. Rep. to UN 2005–12; Vice-Pres. ECOSOC, representing Group of Latin America and Caribbean 2006–08, Pres. ECOSOC 2008–09. *Address:* Ministry of Foreign Affairs and Religion, Blvd Harry S Truman, Cité de l'Exposition, Port-au-Prince, Haiti (office). *Telephone:* 2222-8482 (office). *Fax:* 2223-1668 (office). *Website:* www.mae.gouv.ht (office).

MERRILL, Susan L., JD; American lawyer and securities industry executive; *Partner, Bingham McCutchen Law Firm;* b. 1957; m.; two c.; ed Univ. of Maryland, Brooklyn Law School; moved to New York to pursue acting career; judicial clerk for Hon. Francis Van Dusen, US Court of Appeals of the Third Circuit 1986–87; Assoc. Davis Polk & Wardell (law firm), New York 1987, Partner 1994–2004; Chief Enforcement Officer, NYSE Group Inc. (fmrly New York Stock Exchange) 2004–07, Exec. Vice Pres., Enforcement, Financial Industry Regulatory Authority, Inc. (formed after consolidation of NYSE Mem. Regulation with Nat. Asscn of Securities Dealers) 2007–10; Partner, Broker-Dealer Group, Bingham McCutchen Law Firm 2010–. *Address:* Bingham McCutchen, 399 Park Avenue, New York, NY 10022-4689, USA (office). *Telephone:* (212) 705-7000 (office). *Fax:* (212) 752-5378 (office). *E-mail:* info@bingham.com (office). *Website:* www.bingham.com (office).

MERSCH, Yves; Luxembourg central banker; *Member, Executive Board, European Central Bank;* b. 1 Oct. 1949; ed Univ. of Paris; called to the Bar, Luxembourg 1974; Public Law Asst, Univ. Paris XI 1974; Budget Asst, Ministry of Finance 1975; mem. staff IMF, Washington, DC, USA 1976–77; Ministry of Finance, Fiscal Affairs and Structural Policies 1977–80; Adviser, Ministry of Finance, Monetary Affairs and Int. Financial Relations 1981; Govt Commr Luxembourg Stock Exchange 1985; Dir Treasury 1989–98; Pres. Luxembourg Cen. Bank 1998–2012; Alt. Gov. for Luxembourg, IMF Bd Govs 1998–2012; mem. Governing Council and Gen. Council, European Cen. Bank 1998–, mem. Exec. Bd 2012–; Deputy Chair. Governing Bd, Int. Islamic Liquidity Management Corpn 2010–12; Co-Chair. Regional Consultative Group for Europe, Financial Stability Bd 2011–12; Pres. The Bridge Forum Dialogue a.s.b.l 2000–12, Fondation de la Banque centrale du Luxembourg 2011–12; mem. Bd Luxembourg School of Finance 2006–; Voting mem. Gen. Bd, European Systemic Risk Bd 2011–. *Address:* European Central Bank, Eurotower (Main building), Kaiserstrasse 29, Postfach 160319, 60311 Frankfurt am Main, Germany (office). *Telephone:* (69) 1344-0 (office). *Fax:* (69) 1344-6000 (office). *E-mail:* info@ecb.europa.eu (office). *Website:* www.ecb.europa .eu (office).

MERSON, Michael H., MD; American physician and academic; *Director, Center for Interdisciplinary Research on AIDS, Yale University;* b. 7 June 1945, New York; ed Amherst Coll., State Univ. of New York Downstate Medical Center, Johns Hopkins Univ.; joined Center for Disease Control, Atlanta 1972; worked in several countries including Brazil and Bangladesh; joined WHO 1978, Medical Officer Dir WHO Diarrhoeal Diseases Control Programme 1978–87, Dir Acute Respiratory Infections Control Programme 1987–90; Exec. Dir Global Programme on AIDS 1990–95; Dean and Chair Dept of Epidemiology and Public Health, Yale Univ. School of Medicine 1995–2005, Lauder Prof. of Public Health 2001–, Dir and Prin. Investigator Center for Interdisciplinary Research on AIDS (CIRA), also Dir of Admin. and Int. Research Cores 2005–; Prin. Investigator Yale's AIDS Int. Training and Research Program (AITRP), St. Petersburg, Russia and extension activities in China and South Africa, Prin. Investigator Int. Clinical, Operational and Health Services Research and Training Award (ICOHRTA) Program, Pretoria, South Africa; Co-investigator Bill and Melinda Gates Foundation, Global Health Program; Surgeon Gen. Exemplary Service Medal, S. Flemming Award, Frank Bobbott Alumni Award, Award for Outstanding Contribution to the Campaign Against HIV/AIDS (Russia). *Publications:* International Health: Diseases, Programs, Systems and Policies (co-ed.); over 150 articles on subjects from food-borne diseases to effectiveness of HIV interventions and numerous book chapters (jtly). *Address:* Yale Center for Interdisciplinary Research on AIDS, 40 Temple Street, Suite 1B, New Haven, CT 06510, USA (office). *Telephone:* (203) 764-8474 (office). *Fax:* (203) 764-4353 (office). *E-mail:* michael.merson@yale.edu (office). *Website:* cira.med.yale.edu (office).

MERTIN, Klaus, Dr rer. pol; German banker; b. 9 March 1922; fmr Chair. Supervisory Bd Deutsche Bank Berlin AG, Berlin, Dierig Holding AG, Augsburg; Deputy Chair. of Supervisory Bd Deutsche Centralbodenkredit AG, Berlin, Cologne; mem. or fmr mem. Supervisory Bd Aktiengesellschaft für Industrie und Verkehrswesen, Frankfurt, Badenwerk AG, Karlsruhe, Daimler-Benz AG, Stuttgart, Deutsche Bank Berlin AG 1971–88, Gerling-Konzern-Versicherungs-Beteiligungs AG, Cologne, Heidelberger Druckmaschinen AG, Heidelberg, Karstadt AG, Essen, Rheinmetall Berlin AG, Düsseldorf, Salamander AG, Kornwestheim, Schindler Aufzügefabrik GmbH, Berlin; mem. of Advisory Bd

Barmenia Versicherungen, Wuppertal; mem. of Admin. Council Deutsche Bank Compagnie Financière Luxembourg, Luxembourg; mem. of Exec. Council Schott Glaswerke, Mainz. *Address:* c/o Deutsche Bank AG, Taunusanlage 12, 60325 Frankfurt am Main, Germany.

MERTLÍK, Pavel, PhD, Hab. Dozent; Czech economist and fmr politician; *Chief Economist, Raiffeisenbank, Prague;* b. 7 May 1961, Havlíčkův Brod; m. Dana Mertlík; two s.; ed School of Econs, Prague, Charles Univ., Prague; Prof. of Econs, Prague School of Econs 1983–88; Research Fellow, Inst. of Forecasting of the Czech Repub. 1989–91; Prof. of Econs, Charles Univ. 1991–98, 2001–; Research Fellow, Czech Nat. Bank 1995–98; mem. Czech Social Democratic Party 1995–; Minister of Finance and Deputy Prime Minister 1998–2001; Chief Economist, Raiffeisen Bank, Prague 2001–; mem. Czech Econ. Soc., Pres. 2004–06; Visiting Prof. of Econs, Staffordshire Univ., UK 2008–; mem. Czech Acad. of Sciences, mem. Academic Ass. 2010–. *Publications:* numerous articles on price theory, monopolies, econ. transformation and privatization. *Leisure interests:* cycling, fishing, skiing. *Address:* Raiffeisenbank, Hvezdova 1716/2b, 14078, Prague 4, Czech Republic (office). *Telephone:* (2) 2114-1800 (office). *Fax:* (2) 2114-2800 (office). *E-mail:* pavel .mertlik@rb.cz (office). *Website:* www.rb.cz (office).

MERTON, Robert C., PhD; American economist and academic; *School of Management Distinguished Professor of Finance, A.P. Sloan School of Management, Massachusetts Institute of Technology;* b. 31 July 1944, New York, NY; s. of Robert K. Merton (q.v.) and Suzanne Merton; m. June Rose 1966 (separated 1996); two s. one d.; ed Columbia Univ., New York, California Inst. of Tech., Massachusetts Inst. of Tech.; Instructor in Econs, MIT 1969–70, Asst Prof. of Finance, Alfred P. Sloan School of Man. 1970–73, Assoc. Prof. 1973–74, Prof. 1974–80, J.C. Penney Prof. of Man. 1980–88, School of Man. Distinguished Prof. of Finance 2010–; Visiting Prof. of Finance, Harvard Univ. Business School 1987–88, George Fisher Baker Prof. of Business Admin. 1988–98, John and Natty McArthur Univ. Prof. 1998–2010, Univ. Prof. Emer. 2010–; Research Assoc. Nat. Bureau of Econ. Research 1979–; Sr Adviser, Office of Chair., Salomon Inc. 1988–93; Prin., Co-Founder Long-Term Capital Man. Greenwich, Conn. 1993–99; Sr Adviser, JP Morgan & Co. 1999–2001; Co-founder and Dir, Integrated Finance Ltd (IFL) 2002–07, Chief Science Officer and Dir, Trinsum Group (after merger of IFL and Marakon) 2007–08; Resident Scientist, Dimensional Holdings, Inc., Austin, Tex. 2010–; mem. numerous editorial bds; mem. NAS, American Finance Asscn (Dir 1982–84, Pres. 1986, Fellow 2000); Sr Fellow, Int. Asscn of Financial Engineers; Fellow, Econometric Soc., American Acad. of Arts and Sciences, Financial Man. Asscn 2000; Hon. Prof., HEC School of Man. (École des Hautes Études Commerciales), Paris 1995–, St Petersburg Univ. of Man. and Econs, Russia 2011; Hon. MA (Harvard) 1989; Hon. LLD (Chicago) 1991; Hon. DEconSc (Lausanne) 1996; Dr hc (Paris-Dauphiné) 1997, (Universidad Nacional Mayor de San Marcos, Lima, Peru) 2004; Hon. DrManSc (Nat. Sun Yat-sen Univ., Taiwan) 1998; Hon. DSc (Athens Univ. of Econs and Business) 2003, (Claremont Graduate Univ.) 2008; Leo Melamed Prize, Univ. of Chicago Business School 1983, Financial Engineer of the Year Award, Int. Asscn of Financial Engineers 1993, shared Nobel Prize for Econs 1997 for a new method for determining the value of derivatives, Michael Pupin Medal for Service to the Nation, Columbia Univ. 1998, Distinguished Alumni Award, Calif. Inst. of Tech. 1999, Distinguished Finance Educator Award, Financial Educ. Asscn 2008, Robert A. Muh Award in the Humanities, Arts, and Social Sciences, MIT 2009, Tjailing C. Koopmans Asset Award, Tilburg Univ. 2009, Kolmogorov Medal, Univ. of London 2010, Hamilton Medal, Royal Irish Acad. 2010, CME Group Fred Arditti Innovation Award 2011, numerous other awards. *Publications:* The Collected Scientific Papers of Paul A. Samuelson, Vol. III (Ed.) 1972, Continuous-Time Finance 1990, Casebook in Financial Engineering: Applied Studies in Financial Innovation (co-author) 1995, The Global Financial System: A Functional Perspective (co-author) 1995, Finance (co-author) 2000, numerous articles in professional journals. *Address:* Massachusetts Institute of Technology, E62-634, 77 Massachusetts Avenue, Cambridge, MA 02139, USA (office). *Telephone:* (617) 715-4866 (office). *Fax:* (617) 258-6855 (office). *E-mail:* rmerton@mit.edu (office). *Website:* mitsloan.mit.edu/faculty/detail .php?in_spseqno=41690 (home).

MERWIN, William Stanley (W.S.), AB; American poet, dramatist, writer and translator; b. 30 Sept. 1927, New York City; m. Paula Schwartz 1983; ed Princeton Univ.; Playwright-in-Residence, Poet's Theatre, Cambridge, Mass 1956–57; Poetry Ed. The Nation 1962; Assoc., Théâtre de la Cité, Lyons 1964–65; Special Consultant in Poetry, Library of Congress, Washington, DC 1999–2000; Poet Laureate of USA 2010–11; Acad. of American Poets Fellowship 1973; mem. Acad. of American Poets, American Acad. of Arts and Letters; Yale Series of Younger Poets Award 1952, Bess Hokin Prize 1962, Ford Foundation grant 1964, Harriet Monroe Memorial Prize 1967, PEN Translation Prize 1969, Rockefeller Foundation grant 1969, Pulitzer Prize in Poetry 1971, Shelley Memorial Award 1974, NEA grant 1978, Bollingen Prize 1979, Aiken Taylor Award 1990, Maurice English Award 1990, Dorothea Tanning Prize 1994, Lenore Marshall Award 1994, Ruth Lilly Poetry Prize 1998. *Publications:* poetry: A Mask for Janus 1952, The Dancing Bears 1954, Green with Beasts 1956, The Drunk in the Furnace 1960, The Moving Target 1963, The Lice 1967, Three Poems 1968, Animae 1969, The Carrier of Ladders 1970, Signs 1971, Writings to an Unfinished Accompaniment 1973, The First Four Books of Poems 1975, Three Poems 1975, The Compass Flower 1977, Feathers from the Hill 1978, Finding the Islands 1982, Opening the Hand 1983, The Rain in the Trees 1988, Selected Poems 1988, Travels 1993, The Vixen 1996, The Folding Cliffs 1998, Migration: New and Selected Poems (Nat. Book Award for Poetry) 2005, Present Company 2007, The Shadow of Sirius (Pulitzer Prize for Poetry 2009) 2008; plays: Darkling Child (with Dido Milroy) 1956, Favor Island 1957, The Gilded West 1961, adaptations of five other plays; other: A New Right Arm, West Wind: Supplement of American Poetry (ed.) 1961, The Miner's Pale Children 1970, Houses and Travellers 1977, Unframed Originals: Recollections 1982, Regions of Memory: Uncollected Prose 1949–1982 1987, The Essential Wyatt (ed.) 1989, The Lost Upland 1993, The Ends of the Earth (essays) 2005, Summer Doorways (memoir) 2005, The Book of Fables 2007; translator: Selected Translations 1948–1968 1968, Selected Translations 1968–1978 1979, Sir Gawain and the Green Knight: A New Verse Translation 2004. *Address:* Steven Barclay Agency, 12 Western Avenue, Petaluma, CA 94952, USA (office). *Telephone:* (707) 773-0654 (office). *Fax:* (707) 778-1868 (office). *Website:* www.barclayagency.com (office).

MERZ, Friedrich; German politician and lawyer; b. 11 Nov. 1955, Brilon; m. Charlotte Gass; one s. two d.; judge, Saarbrücken Dist Court 1985–86; lawyer 1986–, Asscn of Chemical Industry 1986–89, Regional Court of Appeal, Cologne 1992–; mem. European Parl. 1989–94; mem. Bundestag 1994–, Parl. Leader CDU 2000–02. *Address:* Bundeshaus, Platz der Republik, 11011 Berlin, Germany (office). *Telephone:* (30) 22772888 (office). *Fax:* (30) 22776436. *E-mail:* friedrich .merz@bundestag.de (office). *Website:* www.friedrich-merz.de (home).

MERZ, Hans-Rudolf, Dr rer. pol; Swiss management consultant and politician; b. 10 Nov. 1942, Herisau; m.; three s.; ed Univ. of St Gallen; Asst Lecturer, Univ. of St Gallen 1967–69; Sec., FDP St Gallen; Man. Appenzell Ausserhoden Industrial Asscn 1969–74; Deputy Dir UBS Wolfsberg training centre 1974–77; worked in pvt. practice as ind. consultant 1977–2003; Chair. Helvetia Patria Insurance Co., AG Cilander Textile Finishing, Anova Holding 1977–2003; elected Rep. Council of States 1997, served as Chair. Finance Cttee, mem. Foreign Affairs and Security Cttee; Vice-Pres. OCSE del.; mem. Fed. Council 2004–10, Head of Fed. Dept of Finance 2004–10, Vice-Pres. Fed. Council 2008, Pres. Swiss Confed. 2009. *Address:* c/o Federal Department of Finance, Bernerhof, Bundesgasse 3, 3003 Bern, Switzerland (office).

MESA GISBERT, Carlos Diego; Bolivian politician; b. 12 Aug. 1953; fmr historian and journalist; Vice-Pres. of Bolivia 2002–03, Pres. 2003–05 (resgnd); mem. Bolivian History Acad. *Address:* c/o Ministry of the Presidency, Palacio de Gobierno, Plaza Murillo, La Paz, Bolivia (office).

MESELSON, Matthew Stanley, PhD; American biologist and academic; *Thomas Dudley Cabot Professor of the Natural Sciences and Principle Investigator, Meselson Laboratory, Harvard University;* b. 24 May 1930, Denver, Colo; s. of Hymen Avram and Ann Swedlow Meselson; m. 1st Katherine Kaynis 1960; m. 2nd Sarah Leah Page 1969; two d.; m. 3rd Jeanne Guillemin 1986; ed Univ. of Chicago, Univ. of Calif. (Berkeley) and Calif. Inst. of Tech.; Research Fellow, Calif. Inst. of Tech. 1957–58, Asst Prof. of Physical Chem. 1958–59, Sr Research Fellow in Chemical Biology 1959–60; Assoc. Prof. of Biology, Harvard Univ. 1960–64, Prof. of Biology 1964–76, Thomas Dudley Cabot Prof. of Nat. Sciences 1976–; Chair. Fed. of American Scientists 1986–88; mem. NAS, Inst. of Medicine, American Acad. of Arts and Sciences, Acad. Santa Chiara, American Philosophical Soc., Council on Foreign Relations; Life Mem. New York Acad. of Sciences; Foreign mem. Royal Soc., Acad. des Sciences, Russian Acad. of Sciences; Fellow, AAAS; Hon. DSc (Oakland Coll.) 1966, (Columbia) 1971, (Chicago) 1975; Hon. ScD (Yale) 1987, (Northwestern) 2003; Dr hc (Princeton) 1988; Prize for Molecular Biology, NAS 1963, Eli Lilly Award in Microbiology and Immunology 1964, Public Service Award, Fed. of American Scientists 1972 Alumni Medal, Univ. of Chicago Alumni Asscn 1971, Alumni Distinguished Service Award, Calif. Inst. of Tech. 1975, Lehman Award of New York Acad. of Sciences 1975, Leo Szilard Award, American Physical Soc. 1978, Presidential Award of New York Acad. of Sciences 1983, MacArthur Fellow 1984–89, Scientific Freedom and Responsibility Award, AAAS 1990, Thomas Hunt Morgan Medal, Genetics Soc. of America 1995, Public Service Award, American Soc. for Cell Biology 2002, Linus Pauling Award 2004, Lasker Award for Special Achievement in Medical Science 2004, Mendel Medal, British Genetics Soc. 2008. *Publications:* numerous papers on the biochemistry and molecular biology of nucleic acids and on arms control of biological and chemical weapons, in various numbers of Proceedings of NAS and of Scientific American etc. *Address:* Biological Laboratories, Harvard University, 16 Divinity Avenue, Cambridge, MA 02138, USA (office). *Telephone:* (617) 495-5099 (office); (617) 495-2264 (office). *Fax:* (617) 496-2444 (office). *Website:* mcb.harvard.edu/meselson (office).

MESFIN, Seyoum; Ethiopian politician and diplomatist; *Ambassador to China;* b. 25 Jan. 1949, Tigray; m. four c.; ed Bahir Dar Polytechnic Inst., Addis Ababa Univ.; exec. mem. Tigray People's Liberation Front (TPLF); Chair. Foreign Affairs Cttee Ethiopian People's Revolutionary Democratic Front (EPRDF); Minister of Foreign Affairs 1991–2010; Amb. to China 2010–. *Address:* Ethiopian Embassy, 3 Xiu Shui Nan Jie, Jian Guo Men Wa, Beijing, 100600, People's Republic of China. *Telephone:* (10) 65325258. *Fax:* (10) 65325591. *E-mail:* ethchina@public3.bta.net .cn. *Website:* www.ethiopiaemb.org.cn.

MESGUICH, Daniel Elie Emile; French actor and theatre and opera director; b. 15 July 1952, Algiers; s. of William Mesguich and Jacqueline Boukabza; m. Danielle Barthélémy 1971; one s. three d.; ed Lycée Thiers, Marseille, Sorbonne, Paris and Conservatoire Nat. Supérieur d'Art Dramatique; actor 1969–; stage dir 1972–; f. Théâtre du Miroir 1974; Prof. Conservatoire Nat. Supérieur d'Art Dramatique 1983–; Dir Théâtre Gérard Philippe, Saint-Denis 1986–88, Théâtre de la Métaphore, Lille 1991–98; numerous appearances on stage, film and TV and dir of numerous stage plays and operas; Chevalier, Ordre Nat. du Mérite; Officier des Arts et des Lettres. *Films:* Molière 1977, La Fille de Prague avec un sac très lourd 1978, Dossier 51 1978, L'Amour en fuite 1978, Clair de femme 1979, La Banquière 1980, Allon-z'enfants 1980, La Chanson du mal-aimé 1981, Les Iles 1982, La Belle captive 1982, L'Araignée de satin 1982, Contes clandestins 1983, Les Mots pour le dire 1983, Paris vu par 20 ans après 1984, Le Radeau de la Méduse 1988, 1989, L'Autrichienne 1989, Toussaint Louverture 1989, La Femme fardée 1990, Jefferson in Paris 1994, Tiré à part 1997, Le divorce 2000, Le Tango des Rasherski 2003. *Plays directed:* Shakespeare: Hamlet, Le Roi Lear, Romeo et Juliet, Titus Andronicus, La Tempête, Antoine et Cleopâtre; Racine: Andromaque, Britannicus, Esther, Mithridate; Molière: Don Juan; Chekhov: Platonov. *Operas directed:* Le Grand Macabre (Ligeti), Le Ring (Wagner), Bal Masqué (Verdi), La Vie Parisienne (Offenbach), Wozzeck (Berg), Le Feu (Landowski), Eléphant Man (Laurent Petit Guard), Damnation de Faust (Berlioz). *TV roles include:* Kafka: la lettre au père 1975, Le Cardinal de Retz 1975, Lazare Carnot ou Le glaive de la révolution 1978, Joséphine ou la comédie des ambitions 1979, Aéroport: Charter 2020 1980, Médecins de nuit 1980, Dans quelques instants 1981, La Sorcière 1982, Napoléon, La Vie de Berlioz 1983, Le Château 1984, Grand hôtel 1986, La Garçonne 1988, Döende dandyn, Den 1989, Les Nuits révolutionnaires 1989, Mon dernier rêve sera pour vous 1989, L'Affaire Dreyfus 1995, L'Allée du roi 1996, Un pique-nique chez Osiris 2001. *Publications:* L'Eternel éphémère 1991, Le Passant composé 2004. *Address:* Agence A, Monita Derrieux, 34 rue Vivienne, 75002 Paris, France. *E-mail:* daniel.mesguich@wanadoo.fr (home).

MESHAAL, Khalid, BSc; Palestinian politician; *Head of Political Bureau, Hamas—Harakat al-Muqawama al-Islamiyya;* b. 1956, Silwad, West Bank; m.; four s. three d.; ed Kuwait Univ.; joined Muslim Brotherhood 1971; f. List of the Islamic Right (student org.), Kuwait Univ.; Physics Teacher, Kuwait 1978–84; Founding mem. Islamic Resistance Movt (Hamas—Harakat al-Muqawama al-Islamiyya) 1987, mem. Political Bureau, Chair. 1996–, Political Leader (in exile), Hamas 2004–. *Address:* Hamas Political Bureau, Damascus, Syria.

MESHKOV, Aleksey Yuryevich; Russian diplomatist and politician; *Ambassador to Italy;* b. 22 Aug. 1959, Moscow; m. Galina Ivanovna Meshkova; two s. two d.; ed Moscow State Inst. of Int. Relations; with diplomatic service 1981–; referent, Attaché then Third Sec., USSR Embassy, Spain 1981–86, First Sec., Counsellor then Sr Counsellor (Russian Embassy) 1992–97; Third, Second, First Sec. then Head of Div., Dept of Co-operation in Science and Tech., Ministry of Foreign Affairs 1986–92, Deputy Head, Dept of European Co-operation 1997–98, Head, Dept of Foreign Policy Planning 1999–2001, mem. Collegiate, Ministry of Foreign Affairs 2000–, Deputy Minister of Foreign Affairs 2001–04; Amb. to Italy 2004–; Order of Friendship. *Address:* Embassy of the Russian Federation, Via Gaeta 5, 00185 Rome, Italy (office). *Telephone:* (06) 4941680 (office). *Fax:* (06) 491031 (office). *E-mail:* rusembassy@libero.it (office). *Website:* www.ambrussia.com (office).

MESIĆ, Stjepan (Stipe); Croatian lawyer, politician and fmr head of state; b. 24 Dec. 1934, Orahovica; m. Milka Mesić (née Dudunić); two d.; ed gymnasium in Požega and Univ. of Zagreb; active in student politics; lawyer in Orahovica and Našice; compulsory mil. service; became a municipal judge after passing judicial exams; ind. cand. in municipal council elections 1966; Mayor of Orahovica 1967; mem. Parl. of Socialist Repub. of Croatia 1967; indicted for "acts of enemy propaganda", served one-year prison sentence in Stara Gradiška prison for participation in Croatian Spring Movt 1975; Sec. Croatian Democratic Union (Hrvatska demokratska zajednica—HDZ), later Chair. Exec. Council; Prime Minister first govt of Repub. of Croatia 1990; mem. Presidency of Socialist Fed. Repub. of Yugoslavia, subsequently Pres. until resgnd 1991; Speaker Croatian Parl. 1992–94; left HDZ and f. Croatian Ind. Democrats (Hrvatski Nezavisni Demokrati—HND) 1994, merged with Croatian People's Party (Hrvatska narodna stranka—HNS) 1997, later Exec. Vice-Pres.; Pres. Repub. of Croatia 2000–10; Hon. mem. Int. Foundation of Raoul Wallenberg 2002; Hon. Citizen of Podgorica, Montenegro 2007; State Order of the Star of Romania 2000, Grand Star of the Decoration of Honour for Merit (Austria) 2001, Golden Order Gjergj Kastrioti Skënderbeu (Albania) 2001, Grand Cross of the Order of Saviour (Greece) 2001, Order of St Michael and St George (UK), Kt of the Grand Cross with Grand Sash (Italy) 2001, Grand Order of the Crown of Malaysia 2002, Order of the Grand Cross with Chain (Hungary) 2002, Dostyk Medal of the First Degree (Kazakhstan) 2002, Medal for Merit (Chile) 2004, Grand Order of King Tomislav with Sash and Grand Star (Croatia) 2005; Charles Univ. Medal (Czech Repub.) 2001, Crans Montana Forum Award 2002, ABA Award 2002, Gold Medal of the Presidency of the Italian Repub. 2004, Raoul Wallenberg Award 2006, Int. League of Humanists Award 2007. *Publications:* The Break-up of Yugoslavia: Political Memoirs 1992, 1994. *Leisure interests:* nanbudo (martial art), swimming, golf. *Address:* c/o Office of the President, 10000 Zagreb, Pantovčak 241, Croatia.

MESSAGER, Annette; French artist; b. 30 Nov. 1943, Berck-sur-Mer; d. of André Messager and Marie L. Messager (née Chalessin); ed Ecole Nationale Supérieure des Arts Décoratifs; Chevalier des Arts et des Lettres, Légion d'honneur 2004; Officier, Ordre nat. du Mérite 2008; Prix Nat. de Sculpture 1996, Lion d'Or de la Biennale de Venice 2005. *Address:* c/o Marian Goodman, 79 rue du Temple, 75003 Paris; 146 blvd Camelinat, 92240 Malakoff, France (home). *Telephone:* 1-42-53-45-77.

MESSI, Lionel Andrés (Leo); Argentine professional football player; b. 24 June 1987, Santa Fe; s. of Jorge Horacio Messi and Celia María Messi (née Cuccitini); winger/striker; played football for Grandoli (local club coached by his father) aged five; as youth, played for Newell's Old Boys, Rosario 1995–2000, Barcelona, Spain 2000–04; sr career, played for Barcelona B 2004–05 (22 appearances, 6 goals), Barcelona 2004– (204 appearances, 232 goals (club record)), Argentina U20 2005 (7 appearances, 6 goals), Argentina U23 2008 (5 appearances, 2 goals), Argentina 2005– (67 appearances, 22 goals); winner, La Liga 2004–05, 2005–06, 2008–09, 2009–10, 2010–11, 2012–13, Copa del Rey 2008–09, 2011–12, Supercopa de España 2005, 2006, 2009, 2010, 2011, 2013, UEFA (Union of European Football Assncs) Champions League 2005–06, 2008–09, 2010–11, UEFA Super Cup 2009, 2011, FIFA Club World Cup 2009, 2011; FIFA U-20 World Cup 2005, Olympic Gold Medal, Beijing 2008; UNICEF Goodwill Amb. 2010–; appeared in court on tax fraud charges Sept. 2013; Tuttosport Golden Boy 2005, Olimpia de Plata 2005, 2007, 2008, 2009, 2010, 2011, FIFA U-20 World Cup Top Scorer 2005, FIFA U-20 World Cup Player of the Tournament 2005, U-21 European Footballer of the Year 2007, Copa América Young Player of the Tournament 2007, Player of the Year of Argentina 2005, 2007, FIFPro Special Young Player of the Year 2007, 2008, FIFPro World Young Player of the Year 2006, 2007, 2008, World Soccer Young Player of the Year 2006, 2007, 2008, Premio Don Balón (Best Foreign Player in La Liga) 2007, 2009, 2010, EFE Trophy (Best Ibero-American Player in La Liga) 2007, 2009, 2010, 2011, 2012, FIFA FIFPro World XI 2007, 2008, 2009, 2010, 2011, 2012, Bravo Award 2007, UEFA Team of the Year 2008, 2009, 2010, 2011, 2012, FIFA Team of the Year 2008, 2009, 2010, 2011, 2012, UEFA Champions League Top Goalscorer 2009, 2010, 2011, 2012, Trofeo Alfredo Di Stéfano 2009, UEFA Club Forward of the Year 2008–09, FIFPro World Player of the Year 2008–09, UEFA Club Footballer of the Year 2009, UEFA Champions League Forward of the Year 2009, LFP Best Player 2009, 2010, 2011, 2012, LFP Best Forward 2009, 2010, 2011, 2012, Onze d'Or 2009, 2010, 2012, La Liga Player of the Year 2009, 2010, 2011, FIFA Club World Cup Golden Ball 2009, 2011, Goal.com Player of the Year 2009, 2011, 2013, FIFA Ballon d'Or 2010, 2011, 2012, 2013, World Soccer Player of the Year 2009, 2011, 2012, FIFA Club World Cup Golden Ball 2009, Toyota Award 2009, FIFA World Player of the Year 2009, 2010, 2011, UEFA Champions League Final Fans' Man of the Match 2009, 2011, Marca Leyenda 2009, European Golden Shoe 2010, 2012, 2013, Copa del Rey top goalscorer 2011, UEFA Champions League Final Man of the Match 2011, UEFA Best Player in Europe Award 2011, Olimpia de Oro 2011, Male Best Athlete in Latin America 2011, L'Equipe Champion of Champions 2011, ESPY Best Int. Athlete 2012, World Soccer Greatest XI of All Time 2013, amongst

others. *Achievements include:* broke La Liga record for youngest footballer to play a league game; youngest to score a league goal; youngest Argentine to play in FIFA World Cup, Germany 2006. *Address:* FC Barcelona (Communication Department), Avenida Arístides Maillol s/n, 08028 Barcelona, Spain. *Telephone:* (93) 496-36-00; (93) 496-76-52 (Press); (902) 1899-00 (Gen. Club). *Fax:* (93) 496-37-67 (Press). *E-mail:* premsa@fcbarcelona.cat. *Website:* arxiu.fcbarcelona.cat/web/english/futbol/temporada_09-10/plantilla/jugadors/messi.html; www.leomessi.com.

MESSIER, Jean-Marie Raymond Pierre; French business executive; b. 13 Dec. 1956, Grenoble; s. of Pierre Messier and Janine Delapierre; m. Antoinette Fleisch 1983; three s. two d.; ed Lycée Champollion, Grenoble, Ecole polytechnique, Ecole Nat. d'Admin.; Inspecteur des Finances 1982; Dir Office of Minister in charge of privatization at Ministry of Econ., Finance and Privatization, then Tech. Adviser to Minister 1986–88; Man. Pnr, Lazard Frères et Cie 1989–94; Chair. Fonds Partenaires 1989–94; Dir, Gen. Man. and Chair. Exec. Comité Général des Eaux group (now Vivendi) 1994, Chair. and Man. Dir 1996–2002; Chair. and Man. Dir Cégétel 1996–2000, Cie Immobilière Phénix 1994–95, Cie Générale d'Immobilier et de Services (CGIS) 1995–96, SGE 1996–97; Dir Canal Plus 1995 (merged with Universal and Vivendi 2000 to form Vivendi Universal), Chair. and CEO 2000–02; fmr Dir LVMH, Strafor-Facom, Saint-Gobain, UGC, Daimler-Benz, New York Stock Exchange 2001–02; Founder and CEO Messier Pnrs LLC, NY 2003–; mem. Bd of Dirs Rentabiliweb 2007–. *Publication:* j6m.com: faut-il avoir peur de la nouvelle économie? 2000, My True Diary 2002. *Leisure interests:* flying, skiing, tennis. *Address:* Messier Partners LLC, One Rockefeller Plaza, 15th Floor, New York, NY 10001, USA (office).

MESSING, Joachim W., BSc, MSc, Dr rer. nat; German/American molecular biologist and academic; *University Professor of Molecular Biology, Selman A. Waksman Chair in Molecular Genetics and Director of the Waksman Institute of Microbiology, Rutgers University;* b. 1946; ed Univ. of Düsseldorf, Free Univ. of Berlin, Ludwig Maximilians Univ., Munich; Research Fellow, Max Planck Inst. of Biochemistry, Munich 1975–78; Research Assoc. in Bacteriology, Univ. of California, Davis, USA 1978–80; Asst Prof. of Biochemistry, Univ. of Minnesota, St Paul 1980–82, Assoc. Prof. of Biochemistry 1982–84, Prof. of Biochemistry 1984–85; Univ. Prof. of Molecular Biology, Rutgers Univ. 1985–, Founding Chair. Dept of Molecular Biology and Biochemistry and Dept of Genetics, first Selman A. Waksman Chair in Molecular Genetics 2009–, Dir Waksman Inst. of Microbiology 1988–; mem. German Acad. of Sciences Leopoldina 2007; Fellow, AAAS 2002; Honor Award, Sec. of US Dept of Agric. (US Rice Genome) 2004, Wolf Prize in Agric. (Israel) (co-recipient) 2013. *Achievements include:* co-developed the shotgun DNA sequencing method 1970s–1980s. *Publications:* numerous papers in professional journals. *Address:* Waksman Institute of Microbiology, Rutgers, The State University of New Jersey, 190 Frelinghuysen Road, Piscataway, NJ 08854-8020, USA (office). *Telephone:* (848) 445-4257 (office). *E-mail:* messing@waksman.rutgers.edu (office). *Website:* www.waksman.rutgers.edu/messing/home (office).

MESSNER, Hon. Anthony, AM, FCA; Australian government official and chartered accountant; b. 24 Sept. 1939, East Melbourne, Vic.; s. of Colin Thomas Messner and Thelma Luxford Messner; ed South Australia Inst. of Tech., Adelaide; practised as chartered accountant 1965–75, 1990–97; mem. Fed. Senate for S Australia 1975–90; Minister for Veterans' Affairs, Asst Treas. 1980–83, Shadow Minister for Social Security 1983–85, for Finance and Taxation 1985–87, for Communications 1987–88, for Public Admin 1988–89; Admin. Norfolk Island 1997–2003; consultant 2003–; Centennial Medal 2001. *Leisure interests:* rugby, reading biographies and history, music, cricket. *Address:* 59 Bride Road, Nowra, NSW 2541 (office); 100 Kanearoo Road, Berry, NSW 2535, Australia (home). *Telephone:* (2) 4422-1611 (office); (2) 4464-2768 (home). *Fax:* (2) 4464-2768 (home). *E-mail:* messnert@optusnet.com.au (office).

MESSNER, Reinhold; Italian mountaineer, lecturer and author; b. 17 Sept. 1944, Bressanone, South Tyrol; one s. three d.; ed Univ. of Padua; began climbing aged four with his father; joined expedition to Nanga Parbat (8,125m), Pakistan 1970; with partner, Peter Habeler, became first person to climb Mount Everest without supplementary oxygen; later climbed Everest alone by North Col route without oxygen; the first person to climb all the world's 8,000m peaks in Himalayas and adjoining ranges; made first crossing of Antarctica on foot (2,800km) since Shackleton 1989–90; collaborated with Dir Werner Herzog in filming his story Schrei aus Stein 1991; f. Messner Mountain Museum—MMM Juval (collections of Asiatica), MMM Dolomites/Monte Rite 2002, MMM Ortles/Sulden 2004, MMM Firmian/Bozen 2006, MMM Ripa/Bruneck 2011; mem. European Parl. (Green Party) 1999–2004; ITAS 1975, Primi Monti 1968, DAV 1976, 1979, Sachbuchpreis for Donauland 1995, Coni 1998, Bambi Lifetime Award 2000, Royal Geographical Soc.'s Gold Medal 2001, Piolet d'Or carrière 2010, Diners Club Magazine Award 2011. *Publications:* The Crystal Horizon 1989, Free Spirit: A Climber's Life 1991, Antarctica 1991, To the Top of the World 1992, Moving Mountains 2001, The Second Death of George Mallory 2001, The Naked Mountain 2003. *Address:* MMM Firmian, Sigmundskronerstr. 53, 39100 Bozen (office); Castle Juval, 39020 Kastelbell, Italy (home). *Telephone:* (0471) 631265 (office). *Fax:* (0471) 633890 (office). *E-mail:* info@reinholdmessner.it (office). *Website:* www.reinhold-messner.de (office).

MESTAN, Lyutvi Ahmed; Bulgarian politician and lecturer; *Chairman, Movement for Rights and Freedoms;* b. 24 Dec. 1960, Chorbadzhyisko; m.; mem. Parl. for Kardzhali 2001–09, for Stara Zagora 2009–, Deputy Chair. Parl. Group 2009–13, Chair. 2013–, mem. Culture, Civil Society and Media Cttee 2009–13, Educ., Science, Children, Youths and Sports Cttee 2009–13, Substitute mem. Del. to Parl. Ass. of OSCE 2012–13, mem. Friendship groups Bulgaria-India, -Kazakhstan, -Canada, -South Korea, -Norway, -Portugal, -Finland, -Croatia, -Japan 2009–13; Chair. Movement for Rights and Freedoms 2013–. *Address:* Movement for Rights and Freedoms (Dvizhenie za Prava i Svobodi), 1301 Sofia, bul. A. Stamboliyski 45A, Bulgaria (office). *Telephone:* (2) 811-44-52 (office). *Fax:* (2) 811-44-53 (office). *E-mail:* mestan@dps.bg (office); lyutvi.mestan@parliament.bg (office); press@dps.bg (office). *Website:* www.dps.bg (office).

MESTEL, Leon, BA, PhD, FRS; British astronomer and academic; *Professor Emeritus of Astronomy, University of Sussex;* b. 5 Aug. 1927, Melbourne, Australia; s. of Rabbi Solomon Mestel and Rachel née Brodetsky; m. Sylvia L. Cole 1951; two s. two d.; ed West Ham Secondary School, London and Trinity Coll., Cambridge;

ICI Research Fellow, Univ. of Leeds, 1951–54; Commonwealth Fund Fellow, Princeton Univ. Observatory, USA 1954–55; Univ. Asst Lecturer in Math., Univ. of Cambridge 1955–58, Univ. Lecturer 1958–66, Fellow, St John's Coll. Cambridge 1957–66; Visiting mem. Inst. for Advanced Study, Princeton 1961–62; J.F. Kennedy Fellow, Weizmann Inst. for Science, Israel 1966–67; Prof. of Applied Math., Univ. of Manchester 1967–73; Prof. of Astronomy, Univ. of Sussex 1973–93, Prof. Emer. 1993–; Eddington Medal 1993, Gold Medal, Royal Astronomical Soc. 2002. *Publications:* Stellar Magnetism 1999 (paperback 2003); papers, lecture notes, reviews, conf. reports on different branches of theoretical astrophysics. *Leisure interests:* reading, music. *Address:* 1 Highsett, Hills Road, Cambridge, CB2 1NX, England (home); Department of Applied Mathematics and Theoretical Physics, Centre for Mathematical Sciences, Wilberforce Road, Cambridge, CB3 0WA (office). *E-mail:* leon@mestel.fsnet.co.uk (home); L.Mestel@damtp.cam.ac.uk (office). *Telephone:* (1223) 337910 (office); (1223) 355233 (home). *Fax:* (1223) 765900 (office).

MESTERHÁZY, Attila, PhD; Hungarian politician; *Chairman, Hungarian Socialist Party;* b. 30 Jan. 1974, Pécs; m.; two c.; ed Lovassy László Gimnázium, Veszprém, Corvinus Univ. and Semmelweis Univ., Budapest; Fellow, Univ. of Valladolid, Spain 1995–96, Diplomatic Acad., Vienna 1996–98, Univ. of Groningen, the Netherlands 1997; worked in Prime Minister's Office as a specialist on econ. and European integration 1998; Man. Hill & Knowlton Strategies dealing with public relations 1999–2000; adviser to Prime Minister Péter Medgyessy 2000; State Sec. for Children, Youth and Sports, Office of the Prime Minister 2002–04; mem. Nat. Ass. 2004–; State Sec., Ministry of Youth, Family, Social Affairs and Equal Opportunities 2004–06; mem. Nat. Exec., Hungarian Socialist Party (Magyar Szocialista Párt—MSzP) 2003–, Chair. MSzP 2010–, a Vice-Pres. and apptd Chair. Parl. Caucus 2009; Socialist cand. for post of Prime Minister in parl. elections 2010; Hungarian Socialist Party and Together 2014 agreed to put forward a joint list for the 2014 parl. election Jan. 2014. *Address:* Hungarian Socialist Party (Magyar Szocialista Párt), 1066 Budapest, Jókai u. 6, Hungary (office). *Telephone:* (1) 459-7200 (office). *Fax:* (1) 210-0081 (office). *E-mail:* info@mszp.hu (office). *Website:* www.mszp.hu (office).

MESTIRI, Mohamed Said; Tunisian professor of medicine; b. 22 June 1919, Tunis; s. of Tahar Mestiri and Khedija Kassar; m. Zohra Chenik (d. of fmr Prime Minister Mohamed Chenik) 1950; four s. one d.; ed Lycée Carnot, Tunis, Faculty of Medicine, Algiers; Intern and Resident, Algiers Hosp. and Sadiki Hosp., Tunis 1947–51; Asst Surgeon, Sadiki Hosp. 1951–57; Chief Surgeon, H. Thameur Hosp. Tunis 1957–64; Chief, Dept of Gen. Surgery, La Rabta Hosp. 1965–85; Prof. of Surgery, Faculty of Medicine, Tunis 1970–85, Hon. Prof. 1985–; Founder and Pres. Tunisian Soc. of Surgery 1973–85; Foreign mem. French Acad. of Surgery; Foreign Corresp.; mem. Nat. Acad. of Medicine (France), mem. Assoc. 2011–; mem. Royal Belgian Acad. of Medicine; mem. Int. Soc. of Surgery; Hon. mem. Soc. Belge de Chirurgie; Commdr, Beylical Order Nichan Iftikhar 1957, Chevalier, Tunisian Ind., Commdr, Order of Tunisian Repub.; Medal of Bizerta 1962. *Publications include:* Moncef Bey: Le Règne 1988, Moncef Bey: L'Exil 1990, Le Ministère Chenik 1991, Le Métier et la Passion (memoirs) 1995, Abulcasis, grand Maître de la Chirurgie arabe 1997, La Chirurgie arabe ancienne et son Impact en Occident 1998, Le médicin dans la Cité 2006, Aux sources du Destour 2011. *Leisure interests:* swimming, bridge. *Address:* 5 avenue Ferhat Hached-Gammarth, 2070 La Marsa, Tunisia. *Telephone:* (1) 746-965. *Fax:* (1) 775-663 (office); (1) 746-905 (home). *E-mail:* said.mestiri@med.mail.com (home).

MESTRALLET, Gérard; French business executive; *Chairman and CEO, GDF Suez SA;* b. 1 April 1949, Paris; ed Ecole Polytechnique, Ecole Nationale d'Admin; joined Cie de Suez (provider of electricity, natural gas, water and waste man. services) 1984, Special Asst 1984–86, Deputy Chief Exec. for Industrial Affairs 1986–91, Chair. and CEO Suez 1995–97, Chair. Exec. Bd Suez Lyonnaise des Eaux (water treatment subsidiary co.) 1997–2001, Chair. and CEO Cie de Suez 2001–08, Chair. and CEO GDF Suez SA (formed by merger of Gaz de France and Suez SA) 2008–, Chair. Suez Énergie Services, Suez Environnement, Electrabel, Houlival, Suez-Tractebel (Belgium); Exec. Dir and Chair. Man. Cttee Société Générale de Belgique 1991–95; Chair. Hisusa (Spain); Vice-Chair. Aguas de Barcelona (Spain); mem. Bd of Dirs Saint-Gobain (France), Pargesa Holding SA (Switzerland), International Power (UK); mem. Supervisory Bd AXA; Chair. Paris EUROPLACE Asscn; mem. Institut Français des Administrateurs (French Inst. of Corp. Dirs); Rep. of Govt of France in negotiations with Walt Disney Co. to est. Euro Disney Theme Park 1995; mem. Advisory Bd CECIA (Council of Int. Advisers) 2000–08; Person of the Year Award, French-American Chamber of Commerce, NY Chapter 2001. *Leisure interest:* cycling. *Address:* GDF Suez SA, 1 place Samuel de Champlain, 92400 Courbevoie, France (office). *Telephone:* 1-44-22-00-00 (office). *E-mail:* info@gdfsuez.com (office). *Website:* www.gdfsuez.com (office); www.suez-environnement.com (office).

MESYATS, Gennady Andreyevich, DSc; Russian physicist and academic; *Vice-President, Russian Academy of Sciences;* b. 28 Feb. 1936, Kemerovo; s. of Andrei Mesyats and Anna Mesyats; m. Nina Alexandrovna (née Mashukova) Mesyats 1959; one s.; ed Tomsk Polytechnical Inst.; Sr Research Physicist, Research Inst. for Nuclear Physics, Tomsk Polytechnical Inst. 1961–64, Head of Lab. 1966–71; Deputy Dir Inst. of Atmospheric Optics, Tomsk 1971–76; Dir and Prof., Inst. of High Current Electronics, Tomsk 1976–86; Dir and Prof., Inst. of Electrophysics 1987–; Corresp. mem. USSR (now Russian) Acad. of Sciences 1979, mem. 1984–, Pres. Ural Div. 1986–99, Vice-Pres. of Acad. 1987–; Int. Chair. Supreme Attestation Comm. 1999–; Pres. Demidov Foundation; Vice-Pres. Int. Unit of Science and Eng Fellowships; mem. Russian Electrical Eng Acad.; Hon. Prof. Tomsk Polytechnic Univ. 1996, Russian Technological Univ. 2000; Dr hc (Urals State Technical Univ.) 1996; Order of Red Banner of Labour 1971, Badge of Honour 1981, Order of Lenin 1986, Order for Services to the Motherland 1996, 1999; Walter Dine Int. Prize 1990, Ervin Marx Award in Pulsed Power 1991, State Prize of USSR 1978, USSR Council of Ministers Prize 1990, A. G. Stoletov Prize 1996, State Prize of Russia 1999, Global Energy Prize 2003. *Publications:* Techniques for the Production of High-Voltage Nanosecond Pulses 1963, Generation of High-Power Nanosecond Pulses 1974, Field Emission and Explosive Processes in Gas Discharges 1982, High-Power Nanosecond X-Ray Pulses 1983, Pulsed Electrical Discharge in Vacuum 1989, Ectons 1994, About Our Science 1995, Pulsed Gas Lasers 1995, Explosive Electron Emission 1998, Physics of

Pulsed Breakdown in Gases 1998, Ectons in a Vacuum Discharge: Breakdown, the Spark and the Arc 2000. *Leisure interests:* reading fiction, studying Russian history, writing articles. *Address:* Russian Academy of Sciences, 14 Leninsky Prospekt, Moscow GSP-1 117901 (office); Apt 29, 3 Akademika Petrovskogo, Moscow 117900, Russia (home). *Telephone:* (495) 237-53-12 (office); (495) 952-50-81. *E-mail:* mesyats@pran.ru (office).

MÉSZÁROS, Márta; Hungarian film director and screenwriter; b. 19 Sept. 1931, Budapest; d. of László Mészáros; m. 2nd Jan Nowicki; ed Moscow Film School; emigrated with family to USSR 1936; now lives in Hungary; Golden Bear Award OCIC 1975, Béla Balázs Prize 1977, Artist of Merit 1989. *Films include:* End of September 1973, Free Breath 1973, Adopted Child 1975, Nine Months 1976, The Two of Them 1977, En Route 1979, Heritage 1980, Diary for my Children 1982, Fata Morgana Land 1983, Diary for my Loves 1986, Diary III 1989, Bye bye chaperon rouge 1989, Napló apámnak, anyámnak (Diary for My Father and Mother) 1990, A Magzat 1993, Siódmy pokój 1995, A Szerencse lányai 1999, Kisvilma: Az utolsó napló (Little Vilna: The Last Diary) 2000, Csodálatos mandarin (The Miraculous Mandarin) 2001, A Temetetlen halott 2004. *Address:* c/o MAFILM Studio, Lumumba utca 174, 1149 Budapest, Hungary. *Telephone:* (1) 183-1750.

META, Ilir Rexhep; Albanian politician and economist; *Speaker, Kuvendi Popullor (People's Assembly);* b. 24 March 1969, Skrapar; m. Monika Kryemadhi; one s. two d.; ed Tirana Univ.; Deputy, Kuvendi Popullor (People's Ass.) 1992–, Speaker 2013–; Co-founder Euro-Socialist Youth Forum of Albania (FRESSH) (Deputy Chair. 1992–95, Chair. 1995–2001); Deputy Chair. Parl. Comm. for Foreign Relations 1996–97; fmr Deputy Prime Minister 1998–99, Sec. of State for European Integration (Ministry of Foreign Affairs) and Minister of Govt Co-ordination March–Oct. 1998; Prime Minister of Albania 1999–2002; Deputy Prime Minister and Minister of Foreign Affairs 2002–03, 2009–10, Deputy Prime Minister and Minister of Economy, Trade and Energy 2010–11; mem. Socialist Party of Albania (Steering Council 1992–2004, Deputy Chair. and Int. Sec. 1993–96), left party 2004; Co-founder and Chair. Socialist Movt for Integration (Lëvizja Socialiste për Integrim—LSI) 2004–; mem. Socialist Youth International (Vice-Chair. 1993–96), Int. Comm. on the Balkans; Visiting Lecturer, Faculty of Econs, Tirana Univ.; Most Positive Personality of 2010 in Foreign Policy Award, Int. Inst. IFIMES, Ljubljana 2012. *Leisure interest:* sports. *Address:* Office of the Speaker, Kuvendi Popullor, Bulevardi Dëshmorët e Kombit 4, Tirana, Albania (office). *Telephone:* (4) 2228333 (office). *Fax:* (4) 2227673 (office). *E-mail:* speaker@parlament.al (office); imeta@ilirmeta.com (home); secretariat@lsi.al. *Website:* www.parlament.al (office); www.lsi.al.

METCALF, Donald, AC, BSc (Med), MD, FRS, FRACP, FRCPA, FAA; Australian immunologist, hematologist and academic; *Professor Emeritus, University of Melbourne;* b. 26 Feb. 1929, Mittagong, NSW; m. Josephine Metcalf; four d.; ed Univ. of Sydney; Demonstrator of Bacteriology, Univ. of Sydney 1950–51, Resident Medical Officer, Royal Prince Alfred Hosp., Sydney 1953–54; Carden Fellow in Cancer Research, The Walter and Eliza Hall Inst. of Medical Research, Melbourne 1954–56, Head, Cancer Research Lab., 1958–64, Head, Cancer Research Unit and Asst Dir 1965–96, Research Prof. of Cancer Biology, Univ. of Melbourne 1986–96, Prof. Emer. 1996–; Visiting Scientist, Harvard Medical School, Boston, USA, Roswell Park Memorial Inst., Buffalo, NY, USA, Swiss Inst. for Experimental Cancer Research, Lausanne, Radiobiological Inst., Rijswijk, Netherlands, Univ. of Cambridge, UK; Foreign Assoc. NAS; Hon. mem. Alpha Omega Alpha Medical Society (USA) 1998; Hon. DSc (Sydney); Hon. MD (Oslo); Syme Prize for Research, Univ. of Melbourne 1964, Britannica Australia Award for Medicine 1966, AMA-BMA Prize for Medical Research 1968, Mollison Prize for Research on Pathology, AMA 1968, Royal Soc. of Victoria Research Medal 1974, Gold Medal, Australian Cancer Soc. 1980, Wellcome Prize, Royal Soc. (shared) 1986, Bristol-Myers Award for Distinguished Achievement in Cancer Research, Hammer Prize for Cancer, Koch Prize (FRG), Gairdner Foundation Int. Award (Canada), Alfred P. Sloan Prize, General Motors Cancer Research Foundation (shared), Bertner Foundation Award, M.D. Anderson Cancer Center, Rabbi Shai Shacknai Prize, Hadassah Univ., Jerusalem, Albert Lasker Clinical Medical Research Award 1993, Louisa Gross Horwitz Prize, Columbia Univ., Jessie Stevenson Kovalenko Medal, NAS, Kantor Family Prize for Cancer Research Excellence, Hipple Cancer Research Center (inaugural recipient), Ernst Neumann Award, Int. Soc. for Experimental Hematology 1995, Royal Medal, Royal Soc., London 1995, Amgen Australia Prize (shared) 1996, The Warren Alpert Foundation Prize, Harvard Medical School 1996, Chiron Int. Award, Nat. Acad. of Medicine, Italy 2000, Prime Minister's Prize for Science 2001, honoured by Australia Post with issue of commemorative stamp 2002. *Publications:* Haemopoietic Cells 1971, Hemopoietic colonies: In Vitro Cloning of Normal and Leukemic Cells 1977, Clonal Culture of Hemopoietic Cells: Techniques and Applications 1984, The Hemopoietic Colony Stimulating Factors 1984, Molecular Control of Blood Cells 1988, Normal and Malignant Hematopoiesis: New Advances (Pezcoller Foundation Symposia, Vol. 6) 1995, Hemopoietic Colony-Stimulating Factors: From Biology to Clinical Applications (co-author) 1995, Summon up the Blood: In Dogged Pursuit of the Blood Cell Regulators 2000; more than 400 peer-reviewed scientific papers and 200 other scientific papers. *Address:* The Walter and Eliza Hall Institute of Medical Research, 1G Royal Parade, Parkville, Vic. 3050, Australia (office). *Telephone:* (3) 9345-2555 (office). *Website:* www.wehi.edu.au (office).

METCALF, John Wesley, BA, CM; Canadian author and editor; *Editor, Canadian Notes and Queries;* b. 12 Nov. 1938, Carlisle, UK; s. of Thomas Metcalf and Gladys Moore; m. Myrna Teitelbaum 1975; three s. three d.; ed Beckenham and Penge Grammar School and Univ. of Bristol; emigrated to Canada 1962; Writer-in-Residence, Univs of NB 1972–73, Loyola of Montreal 1976, Ottawa 1977, Concordia Univ. Montreal 1980–81, Univ. of Bologna 1985; Sr Ed. Porcupine's Quill Press 1989–, Ed. Canadian Notes and Queries (literary magazine) 1997–; Sr Ed. Biblioasis Press 2005–. *Publications:* The Lady Who Sold Furniture 1970, The Teeth of My Father 1975, Girl in Gingham 1978, Selected Stories 1982, Kicking Against the Pricks 1982, Adult Entertainment 1986, What is a Canadian Literature? 1988, Volleys 1990, How Stories Mean 1992, Shooting the Stars 1992, Freedom from Culture: Selected Essays 1982–1992 1994, Acts of Kindness and of Love (jtly) 1995, Forde Abroad 2003, An Aesthetic Underground 2003, Standing Stones: The Best Stories of John Metcalf 2004, Shut Up He Explained

2007. *Leisure interest:* collecting modern first editions. *Address:* 253 Botanica Private, Suite 5, Ottawa, ON K1Y 4P8, Canada. *Telephone:* (613) 761-6031 (office); (613) 761-6031 (home). *Website:* www.bibliosis.com.

METHENY, Patrick (Pat) Bruce; American jazz musician (guitar); b. 12 Aug. 1954, Lee's Summit, Mo.; ed Univ. of Miami; taught guitar at Univ. of Miami and Berklee Coll. of Music; fmrly guitarist with Gary Burton Quintet; has performed and recorded with musicians and composers, including Ornette Coleman, Herbie Hancock and Steve Reich; formed Pat Metheny Group 1978–; Boston Music Awards for Outstanding Jazz Album, Outstanding Guitarist, Outstanding Jazz Fusion Group 1986, Grammy Award for Best Instrumental Composition 1990, 1993, Best Contemporary Jazz Performance 1995, Best Rock Instrumental Performance 1996, Orville H. Gibson Award for Best Jazz Guitarist 1996, Best Guitarist (Jazz Times Magazine) 2000. *Recordings include:* albums: Bright Size Life 1976, Watercolours 1977, Pat Metheny Group 1978, New Chautauqua 1979, An Hour With Pat Metheny 1979, American Garage 1980, As Falls Wichita, So Falls Wichita Falls 1981, Offramp 1981, 80/81 1981, Travels 1983, Rejoicing 1983, Works 1984, First Circle 1984, Song X (with Ornette Coleman) 1985, Still Life (Talking) 1987, Works II 1988, Letter From Home 1989, Question And Answer (with Roy Haynes and Dave Holland) 1990, Secret Story 1992, Under Fire (film-score) 1992, Zero Tolerance For Silence 1992, I Can See Your House From Here 1993, The Road To You: Recorded Live In Europe 1993, Dream Teams 1994, Zero Tolerance for Silence 1994, We Live Here 1995, This World 1996, Quartet 1996, The Sign Of Four 1996, Imaginary Day 1997, Beyond the Missouri Sky 1997, Passaggio Per Il Paradiso (film-score) 1998, Like Minds 1998, All The Things You Are 1999, A Map Of The World (film-score) 1999, Last Train Home 1999, Jim Hall and Pat Metheny 1999, Trio 99>00 2000, Trio Live 2000, Move To The Groove 2001, Parallel Universe 2001, Sassy Samba 2001, Speaking Of Now 2002, One Quiet Night 2003, The Way Up (Grammy Award for Best Contemporary Jazz Album 2006) 2005, Metheny Mehldau 2006, Day Trip 2008, Orchestrion 2010, What's It All About (Grammy Award for Best New Age Album 2011) 2012, Unity Band (Grammy Award for Best Jazz Instrumental Album 2013) 2012. *Address:* Ted Kurland Associates, 173 Brighton Avenue, Boston, MA 02134-2003, USA (office). *Telephone:* (617) 254-0007 (office). *Fax:* (617) 782-3524 (office). *E-mail:* agents@tedkurland.com (office). *Website:* www.tedkurland.com (office); www .patmetheny.com.

METZ, Johann Baptist, DPhil, DTheol; German professor of theology; *Professor Emeritus of Theology, University of Münster;* b. 5 Aug. 1928, Auerbach; s. of Karl M. Metz and Sibylle Müller; ed Univs of Bamberg, Innsbrück and Munich; Prof. of Fundamental Theology, Univ. of Münster 1963–, currently Prof. Emer.; Prof. of Philosophy of Religion, Univ. of Vienna, Austria 1993–; mem. Founding Comm. of Univ. of Bielefeld 1966; consultant to Papal Secr. Pro Non Credendibus 1968–73; Adviser to German Diocesan Synod 1971–75; mem. Advisory Council, Inst. für die Wissenschaften vom Menschen (Vienna) 1982–; mem. Advisory Council Wissenschaftszentrum Nordrhein-Westfalen/Kulturwissenschaftliches Inst. 1989–2000; numerous guest professorships; Dr hc (Univ. of Vienna), (Jesuit School of Theology, Berkeley) 2009; awards from Univ. of Innsbrück and Boston Coll., Mass.; Buber-Rosenzweig-Medaille 2002, Preis de Salzburger Hochschulwochen 2007. *Publications:* books on theological and political themes in several languages, published in Europe, Russia, Repub. of China, Japan, N and S America. *Address:* Katholisch-Theologische Fakultät, Seminar für Fundamentaltheologie, Johannisstrasse 8–10, 4400 Münster (office); Kapitelstrasse 14, 48145 Münster, Germany. *Telephone:* (251) 83-2631 (office); (251) 36662 (home). *Fax:* (251) 36662 (home). *E-mail:* j.metz@uni-muenster.de.

METZGER, Henry, AB, MD, FAAS; American (b. German) scientific researcher; b. 23 March 1932, Mainz, Germany; s. of Paul Alfred Metzger and Anne (Daniel) Metzger; m. Deborah Stashower 1957; two s. one d.; ed Univ. of Rochester, Columbia Univ.; emigrated to USA 1938; Intern, then Asst Resident, Col-Presbyterian Medical Center 1957–59; Research Assoc., NIAMD, NIH 1959–61, Medical Officer, Arthritis and Rheumatism Branch, Bethesda, MD 1963–73, Chief, Section on Chemical Immunology 1973–, Chief, Arthritis and Rheumatism Branch, Nat. Inst. of Arthritis and Musculoskeletal and Skin Diseases 1983–94, Dir Intramural Research Program 1987–98; Fellow Helen Hay Whitney Foundation, Dept of Biology, Univ. of Calif., San Diego 1961–63; Pres. American Asscn of Immunologists 1991–92; Pres. Int. Union of Immunological Socs 1992–95; mem. Health Research Council BMFT, German Govt 1994–97; mem. NAS; Hon. mem. Chilean and French Socs of Immunology; several awards. *Publications:* over 200 scientific papers and contribs to scientific journals. *Address:* 3410 Taylor Street, Chevy Chase, MD 20815, USA (home).

MEXIA, António Luís Guerra Nunes; Portuguese economist, politician and business executive; *CEO, EDP – Energias de Portugal;* b. 12 July 1957, Lisbon; ed Univ. of Geneva, Switzerland; fmr Prof. in Econs, Univ. of Geneva, Universidade Católica Portuguesa, Lisbon, Universidade Nova de Lisboa; Asst to Sec. of State for Foreign Trade 1986–88; Vice-Chair. ICEP (Portuguese bd of external trade and foreign investment) 1988–90; joined Banco ESSI (investment bank of Espírito Santo group) 1990, served as mem. Exec. Bd of Dirs in charge of equity capital markets and project finance divs 1990–98; Chair. and CEO GDP (Gas de Portugal) and of Transgás 1998–2001; CEO GALP Energia 2001–04; mem. Partido Social Democrata; Minister of Public Works, Transport and Communications 2004–05; CEO EDP – Energias de Portugal SA 2006–; Vice-Pres. Portuguese Industrial Asscn. *Address:* EDP – Energias de Portugal, Praça Marquês de Pombal 12, 1250-162 Lisbon, Portugal (office). *Telephone:* (21) 001-2500 (office). *Fax:* (21) 002-1403 (office). *E-mail:* info@edp.pt (office). *Website:* www.edp.pt (office).

MEY, Alamine Ousmane; Cameroonian engineer, banker and politician; *Minister of Finance;* b. 1966; s. of Ousmane Mey; ed Rheinisch-Westfaelische Technische Hochschule Aachen, Germany, also studied in Belgium and Tunisia; trained as electronic engineer; two years as Asst Engineer with Asean Brown Boveri, Mannheim; Credit Analyst, CCEI Bank, Yaoundé 1994, Head, Industrial and Tourist Projects Div. 1996, Dir of Research and Devt 1999, Dir-Gen. Cenainvest, Dir-Gen. Afriland First Bank 2004–11; Minister of Finance 2011–; Chair. Vetagri (veterinary co.); fmr Dir Safar, Chad, Ccic (soap mfr), Saconets (telecommunications co.), Soil and Water (geotechnical research co.). *Address:* Ministry of Finance, BP 13750, Quartier Administratif, Yaoundé, Cameroon

(office). *Telephone:* 7723-2099 (office). *Website:* www.camnet.cm/investir/minfi (office).

MEYER, Sir Christopher John Rome, Kt, KCMG, MA; British diplomatist, broadcaster, commentator, author and academic and company director; *Chairman of the Advisory Board, Pagefield Communications;* b. 22 Feb. 1944, Beaconsfield, Bucks.; s. of the late Flight Lt R. H. R. Meyer and Mrs E. P. L. Landells; m. 1st Françoise Hedges 1976; two s. one step-s.; m. 2nd Catherine Laylle 1997; two step-s.; ed Lancing Coll., Lycée Henri IV, Paris, Peterhouse, Cambridge, Johns Hopkins School of Advanced Int. Studies, Bologna, Italy; Foreign Office 1966–67; Army School of Educ. 1967–68; Third Sec., later Second Sec. Moscow 1968–70; Second Sec. Madrid 1970–73; FCO 1973–78; First Sec. Perm. Representation of UK at EC 1978–82; Counsellor and Head of Chancery, Moscow 1982–84; Head of News Dept, FCO 1984–88; Visiting Fellow, Center for Int. Affairs, Harvard 1988–89; Minister (Commercial), Washington, DC 1989–92, Minister and Deputy Head of Mission 1992–93; Press Sec. to Prime Minister 1994–96; Amb. to Germany 1997, to USA 1997–2003; Chair. Press Complaints Comm. 2003–09; Morehead-Cain Visiting Prof., Univ. of North Carolina 2011; currently Dir (non-exec.) Arbuthnot Banking Group Plc; Chair. Advisory Bd, Pagefield Communications; mem. Int. Advisory Bd, British-American Business Inc.; Trustee, Parents and Abducted Children Together; Sr Assoc. Fellow, Royal United Services Inst.; Hon. Fellow, Peterhouse, Cambridge 2001; mem. Worshipful Co. of Stationers and Newspaper Makers 2009; Freeman of the City of London 2009. *Radio:* BBC Radio 4: presenter and scriptwriter of How to Succeed at Summits, Corridors of Power 2006, Lying Abroad 2007, The Watchdog and the Feral Beast 2009. *Television:* Mortgaged to the Yanks (BBC 2/4) (presenter, co-writer) 2006, Getting Our Way (BBC 4) (presenter, co-writer) 2010, Networks of Power (Sky Atlantic) (co-writer and presenter) 2012. *Publications:* DC Confidential 2005, Getting Our Way 2010, Only Child 2013; contrib. to The Huffington Post UK. *Leisure interests:* jazz, history, football. *Address:* 18 Marshall Street, London, W1F 7BE, England (office). *Telephone:* 7789-462199 (mobile) (office). *E-mail:* chrismeyer@btinternet.com (office).

MEYER, (Donatus) Laurenz (Karl); German politician; b. 2 Feb. 1948, Salzkotten; m.; four d.; ed Univ. of Münster; fmr mem. staff VEW AG, Dortmund; mem. Hamm City Council 1975–95; Parl. Group Chair. Christian Democratic Union (CDU), Hamm 1989–95; mem. Land Parl. of N Rhine-Westphalia (NRW) 1990–2002, Econ. Policy Spokesman of Land Parl. of NRW 1990–99, Vice-Chair. CDU Parl. Group of Land Parl. of NRW 1997–99, Chair. 1999–2000, Vice-Chair. Land Parl. of NRW 2000, Treas. CDU of NRW 1997–2001; mem. Fed. Party Exec., Sec.-Gen. CDU Germany 2000–04, currently Chair. Economy and Tech. Group; mem. Bundestag 2002–; Order of Merit (FRG). *Leisure interests:* tennis, golf. *Address:* Christlich-Demokratische Union, Konrad-Adenauer-Haus, Klingelhöferstrasse 8, 10785 Berlin, Germany (office). *Telephone:* (30) 220700 (office). *Fax:* (30) 22070111 (office). *E-mail:* laurenz.meyer@cdu.de (office). *Website:* www.laurenz-meyer.de; www.cdu.de (office).

MEYER, Edgar, BMus; American composer and double bassist; b. 24 Nov. 1960, Tulsa, Okla; s. of Edgar A. Meyer and Anna Mary Metzel; m. Cornelia (Connie) Heard 1988; one s.; ed Georgia Inst. of Tech., Atlanta, Indiana School of Music, Bloomington; began playing bass aged five under tutelage of father; began composing pop songs and classical pieces as a child; studied with Stuart Stanley at univ.; formed 'bluegrass' band Strength in Numbers, Nashville, Tenn. 1984; signed to MCA label; regular bass player, Santa Fe Chamber Music Festival 1985–93; appeared with concert artists Emanuel Ax (piano) and Yo-Yo Ma (cello); collaborated with Katty Mattea on album Where Have You Been (Grammy Award, Country Music Award, Acad. of Country Music Asscn Award) 1990; premiere of Concerto for Bass 1993; joined Chamber Music Soc., Lincoln Center, New York 1994; formed band Quintet for Bass and String Quartet, soloist debut performance 1995; premiere of Double Concerto for Bass and Cello 1995; premiere of Violin Concerto 2000; recitals with Amy Dorfman, Bela Fleck and Mike Marshall; performed at Aspen, Caramoor and Marlboro Festivals; debuted with Boston Symphony Orchestra, Tanglewood, Mass 2000; Visiting Prof., RAM, London, UK, Curtis Inst. of Music; winner, Zimmerman-Mingus Competition, Int. Soc. of Bassists 1981, Avery Fisher Prize 2000, Grammy Award for the Best Crossover Album 2001, MacArthur Award 2002. *Recordings include:* albums: Unfolding 1986, The Telluride Sessions (Strength in Numbers) 1989, Dreams of Flight 1987, Love of a Lifetime 1988, Appalachia Waltz 1996, Uncommon Ritual 1997, Short Trip Record 1999, Bach Unaccompanied Cello Suites Performed on a Double Bass 1999, Appalachian Journey (Grammy Award 2001) 2000, Perpetual Motion 2001, Edgar Meyer 2006. *Address:* c/o IMG Artists, The Light Box, 111 Power Road, London, W4 5PY, England (office). *Telephone:* (20) 7957-5800 (office). *Fax:* (20) 7957-5801 (office). *E-mail:* artistseurope@imgartists.com (office). *Website:* www.imgartists.com (office).

MEYER, Robert; Norwegian art photographer, photohistorian, academic and writer; b. 2 Oct. 1945, Oslo; s. of Robert Castberg Meyer and Edel Nielsen; m. Ingebjørg Ydstie 1985; one s. one d.; ed Fotoskolan, Univ. of Stockholm; photographer, Norwegian State Police 1963–64; advertising photographer 1964–; freelance photographer 1964–71; debut exhbn LYS, Oslo 1970; photojournalist, Norwegian Broadcasting, Oslo 1971–77; Ed. and Publr Ikaros 1976–80; full-time photohistorian engaged in research work 1977–; Prof., Nat. Coll. of Art, Bergen, f. Inst. of Photography (SHDK) 1990–; returned to Oslo 1998, est. a private coll. for photography; est. Forbundet Frie Fotografer (Asscn of Ind. Photographers) 1974, Norsk Fotohistorisk Forening (Norwegian Photohistorical Soc.) 1976; Chair. Fotogalleriet (Norwegian Photo Gallery Foundation) 1979; curator for several galleries and museums; Munch stipend 1981; art stipend 1988–90; two book prizes. *Publications:* Norsk fotohistorisk Journal 1976–78, Jim Bengston i Photographs 1981, Slow Motion 1985, Simulo 1987, Norsk Landskapsfotografi 1988, Den glemte tradisjonen 1989, Splint 1991. *Address:* c/o Fotogalleriet, Møllergata 34, 0179 Oslo; Professor Hansteens gate 68, 5006 Bergen, Norway (home). *Telephone:* 22-20-05-59; 22-20-21-20; 55-31-07-93 (home). *E-mail:* post@fotogalleriet.no; post@fffotografer.no.

MEYER, Robert B., BA PhD; American physicist and academic; *Professor, Department of Physics, Brandeis University;* ed Harvard Univ.; Sloan Foundation Research Fellow 1971–75; Researcher, Asst Prof., Assoc. Prof., Dept of Physics, Harvard Univ. 1970–78; fmr Nordita Visiting Prof., Chalmers Inst. of Tech., Göteborg, Sweden, Ecole Supérieure de Physique et de Chimie Industrielles de la

Ville de Paris, France; joined Dept of Physics, Brandeis Univ. 1978, Prof. of Physics 1985–, Dir Materials Research Science and Eng Center 2008–; Fellow, American Physical Soc. 1992; Joliot Curie Medal of City of Paris 1978, Special Recognition Award, Soc. for Information Display 1989, Second Prize, LVMH Science for Art Prize Vinci of Excellence 1993, Benjamin Franklin Medal in Physics 2004, Oliver Buckley Prize, American Physical Soc. 2006, George Gray Medal, British Liquid Crystal Soc. 2007. *Address:* Brandeis University, Department of Physics, MS 057, PO Box 549110, Waltham, MA 02454-9110, USA (office). *Telephone:* (781) 736-2870 (office). *Fax:* (781) 736-2915 (office). *E-mail:* meyer@brandeis.edu (office). *Website:* www.brandeis.edu/departments/physics (office).

MEYER, Roelof (Roelf) Petrus, BComm, LLB; South African fmr politician; b. 16 July 1947, Port Elizabeth; m. 1st Carené Lubbe 1971; two s. two d.; m. 2nd Michèle de la Rey 2002; ed Fickburg High School, Univ. of the Free State; practised as attorney, Pretoria and Johannesburg –1980; MP for Johannesburg West 1979–97; Deputy Minister of Law and Order 1986–88, of Constitutional Devt 1988–91 and of Information Services 1990–91; Minister of Defence and of Communication 1991–92, of Constitutional Devt and of Communication 1992–94, of Provincial Affairs and Constitutional Devt 1994–96; Sec.-Gen. Nat. Party 1996–97; Co-Founder United Democratic Movt 1997, Deputy Pres. 1998–2000; MP 1998–2000; Tip O'Neill Chair. in Peace Studies, Univ. of Ulster 2000–01; Chair. Civil Soc. Initiative 2000–; Chief Govt Negotiator at Multi-Party Negotiating Forum for new SA Constitution; Nat. Party, fmr Chair. Standing Cttee on Nat. Educ., fmr Chair. Standing Cttee on Constitutional Devt, fmr Parl. Whip. *Leisure interests:* reading, outdoor life, jogging. *Address:* PO Box 2271, Brooklyn Square, Pretoria 0075 (office); 732 Skukuza Street, Faerie Glen, 0043 Pretoria, South Africa (home). *Telephone:* (12) 3341826 (office); (82) 9900004. *Fax:* (12) 3341867 (office). *E-mail:* roelf.meyer@tilca.com (office); rmeyer@lantic.net (home). *Website:* www.tilca.com (office).

MEYER, Ron; American business executive; *Vice-Chairman, NBCUniversal;* b. 1944; m. Kelly Chapman; one s. three d.; served in US Marine Corps; messenger, Paul Kohner Agency 1964–70; TV agent, William Morris Agency 1970–75; Co-founder and Pres. Creative Artists Agency 1975–95; Pres., COO, Universal Studios 1995–13, Vice-Chair. NBCUniversal 2013–. *Address:* NBC Universal, 5750 Wilshire Blvd, Los Angeles, CA 90036, USA (office). *Website:* www.nbcuni.com (office).

MEYER, Stephenie, BA; American author; b. 24 Dec. 1973, Hartford, Conn.; d. of Stephen Morgan and Candy Morgan; m. Christian Meyer 1994; three s.; ed Chaparral High School, Scottsdale, Ariz., Brigham Young Univ., Provo, Utah; grew up in Phoenix, Ariz.; held only one job, as a receptionist in an Ariz. property co., before penning Twilight series, has sold more than 116 million copies world-wide in 37 languages; teamed up with skateboard and clothing co. Hobo Skate Company to produce own clothing line related to her science-fiction novel The Host 2009; named amongst one of Time magazine's Most Influential People 2007, (49th) 2008, ranked by Forbes magazine amongst The World's 100 Most Powerful Women (49th) 2010. *Publications include:* Twilight series: Twilight (Publishers Weekly Best Book of the Year, Amazon Best Book of the Decade… So Far, American Library Asscn Top Ten Best Book for Young Adults, New York Times Editor's Choice) 2005, New Moon 2006, Eclipse (British Book Award) 2007, Breaking Dawn 2008; other books: Prom Nights from Hell (section) 2007, The Host (science-fiction novel, spent 26 weeks as a best-seller) 2008, The Short Second Life of Bree Tanner (novella) 2010. *Address:* c/o Jodi Reamer, Writers House, 21 West 26th Street, New York, NY 10010, USA (office). *Telephone:* (212) 685-2400 (office). *Fax:* (212) 685-1781 (office). *Website:* www.writershouse.com (office); www.stepheniemeyer.com; www.thetwilightsaga.com.

MEYER, Thomas J., BS, PhD; American chemist and academic; *Kenan Professor of Chemistry, University of North Carolina and Associate Laboratory Director, Los Alamos National Laboratory;* ed OH Univ., Stanford Univ.; Woodrow Wilson Graduate Fellow, Stanford Univ. 1963–64, NSF Graduate Fellow 1965–66; NATO Postdoctoral Research Fellow, Univ. Coll., London, England 1967; Asst Prof. of Chemistry, Univ. of NC 1968–72, Assoc. Prof. 1972–75, Prof. 1975–82, M. A. Smith Prof. of Chemistry 1982–87, Kenan Prof. of Chemistry 1987–, Chair. Dept of Chemistry 1985–90, Vice-Provost for Graduate Studies and Research 1994–99; Visiting Prof., Sydney Univ., Australia 1976; Visiting Scientist, Xerox Webster Research Center, Webster, NY 1978; Visiting Scientist, Sandia Nat. Lab. 1981; Visiting Prof., Univ. Louis Pasteur, Strasbourg, France 1983; Visiting Scientist, Centre d'Etudes Nucleaires, Grenoble, France 1983; Visiting Prof., Univ. de Rennes, France 1986, Univ. di Ferrara, Italy 1992, Univ. of Buenos Aires, Argentina 1993; Assoc. Lab. Dir, Los Alamos Nat. Lab., NM 2000–; Dir Triangle Univs Licensing Consortium 1989–95, Triangle Univs Center for Advanced Studies Inc. 1994–, NC Biotechnology Center 1994–, Associated Univs Inc. 1995–97, NC Bd of Science and Tech. 1995–99, Research Triangle Inst. 1995–; mem. numerous socs including ACS, American Asscn of Univ. Profs, AAAS (Fellow 1981–), American Acad. of Arts and Sciences 1994–; mem. Editorial Bd Inorganic Chemistry 1983–87, Journal of the American Chemical Soc. 1983–87, Accounts of Chemical Research 1991–, Structure and Bonding 1997–, Journal of Photochemistry and Photobiology A 1998–; ACS Charles H. Stone Award 1982, ACS Award in Inorganic Chemistry 1990, ACS Southern Chemist of the Year Award 1992, Royal Australian Chemical Inst. Nyholm Award 1996, Inter-American Photochemical Soc. Award 1997, ACS Remsen Award 1999; numerous hon. lectures in USA and abroad. *Address:* Strategic and Supporting Research Directorate, Los Alamos National Laboratory, MS A127 ALDSSR, Los Alamos, NM 87545, USA (office). *Telephone:* (505) 667-8597 (office). *Fax:* (505) 667-5450 (office). *E-mail:* tjmeyer@lanl.gov (office). *Website:* www.lanl.gov/orgs/ssr/meyer.htm (office).

MEYER, Tobias; German art dealer; *Chairman of Worldwide Contemporary Art and Executive Vice-President of Contemporary Art, Sotheby's;* joined Sotheby's 1992, Worldwide Head of Contemporary Art 1997–, Prin. Auctioneer for Sotheby's sales of Contemporary Art and Impressionist and Modern Art in New York as well as for co.'s Contemporary Art sales in London, currently Chair. Worldwide Contemporary Art and Exec. Vice-Pres. Contemporary Art; has produced three of the four highest auction prices ever paid for post-war art, including Mark Rothko's White Center (Yellow, Pink and Lavender on Rose) for $72.8 million May 2007, Francis Bacon's Triptych 1976, which sold for $86.3 million May 2008, auction record for any work by a living artist at the time of the sale with Jeff Koons'

Hanging Heart ($23.6 million) November 2007, was also auctioneer for Sotheby's sales of Pablo Picasso's Garçon à la pipe ($104.2 million) and Dora Maar au chat ($95.2 million), currently Chair. Worldwide Contemporary Art and Exec. Vice-Pres. Contemporary Art. *Address:* Sotheby's, 1334 York Avenue at 72nd Street, New York, NY 10021, USA (office); Sotheby's, 34–35 New Bond Street, London, W1A 2AA, England (office). *Telephone:* (212) 606-7254 (New York) (office); (20) 7293-5000 (London) (office). *Fax:* (212) 606-7107 (New York) (office); (20) 7293-5989 (London) (office). *E-mail:* tobias.meyer@sothebys.com (office). *Website:* www.sothebys.com (office).

MEYER-LANDRUT, Andreas, PhD; German diplomatist; b. 31 May 1929, Tallinn, Estonia; s. of Bruno and Käthe Meyer-Landrut (née Winter); m. Hanna Karatsony von Hodos 1960; one s. one d.; m. 2nd Natali Somers (née Seferov); ed Univs of Göttingen and Zagreb; entered foreign service 1955, served in Moscow, Brussels and Tokyo 1956–68, Amb. to Congo (Brazzaville) 1969; in Foreign Office, Bonn 1971–80, Head of Sub-Dept for Policy towards Eastern Europe and GDR 1974–78, Dir Dept of Relations to Asia, Near and Middle East, Africa and Latin America 1978–80, Amb. to USSR 1980–83, 1987–89; State Sec. to Foreign Office 1983–87; Head of Fed. Pres.'s Office and State Sec. 1989–94; Man. Daimler Chrysler AG in Moscow 1994–2002; Adviser to German cos in Russia and CIS countries; Hon. Pres. German-Russian Forum Berlin; Hon. mem. German Equestrian Fed.; Grand Commdr Order of Merit. *Publications include:* Mit Gott und langen Unterhosen: Erlebnisse eines Diplomaten in der Zeit des Kalten Krieges 2003. *Address:* Malaja Bronnaja ul. 20A, 103104 Moscow, Russia (office); Auswärtiges Amt für BO, MOS 11013 Berlin PF 117, Germany. *Telephone:* (495) 290-4930 (office); (495) 200-6231 (office); (495) 200-62-31 (home). *Fax:* (495) 291-8605 (office); (495) 209-1672. *E-mail:* Andreas.Meyer-Landrut@gmx.net (office).

MEYEROWITZ, Elliot Martin, AB, MPhil, PhD, FAAS; American biologist and academic; *George W. Beadle Professor of Biology, California Institute of Technology;* b. 22 May 1951, Washington, DC; m. Joan Agnes Kobori; two c.; ed Columbia Univ., New York, Yale Univ., New Haven, Conn.; Jane Coffin Childs Memorial Fund Postdoctoral Fellow, Dept of Biochemistry, Stanford Univ. School of Medicine, Calif. 1977–79; Asst Prof. of Biology, California Inst. of Tech., Pasadena 1980–85, Assoc. Prof. 1985–89, Prof. of Biology 1989–2002, Exec. Officer for Biology 1995–2000, Chair. Div. of Biology 2000–10, George W. Beadle Prof. of Biology 2002–; Investigator, Howard Hughes Medical Inst.; Visiting A.F. Wood Prof., Univ. of Florida, Gainesville 2000; European Flying Fellowship in Plant Molecular Biology, Grad. School of Experimental Plant Sciences, Univ. of Ghent, Belgium, Institut des Sciences Vegetales, France, Max-Planck-Institut für Zuchtungsforschung, Germany 2001; Inaugural Dir Sainsbury Lab., Univ. of Cambridge 2011–12; mem. Editorial Bd Mechanisms of Development 1990–, Molecular Biology of the Cell 1991–, Cell 1991–, Trends in Genetics 1993–, Current Biology 1993–, Development 1994–, BioEssays 1996–, Current Opinion in Plant Biology 1997–, Genome Biology 1999–, Journal of Biology 2001–, Philosophical Transactions of the Royal Society B 2006–; mem. Scientific Advisory Bd Kumho Life and Environmental Science Lab. 1997–, Yale-Peking Univ. Jt Center for Plant Molecular Genetics 2001–, Temasek Life Sciences Lab. 2002–05; mem. Scientific Advisory Cttee, Inst. of Molecular Biology and Biotechnology, Heraklion, Crete 2001–07; mem. American Acad. of Arts and Sciences 1991–, NAS 1995–, American Philosophical Soc. 1998; Foreign Assoc. Acad. des sciences, France 2002–; Foreign mem. Royal Soc. (UK) 2004–; Assoc. mem. European Molecular Biology Org. 2008; Dr hc (Ecole Normale Supérieure, Lyon) 2007; Huebschman Prize in Biology, Columbia Univ. 1972, John S. Nicholas Award for Outstanding Biology Dissertation, Yale Univ. 1977, Sloan Foundation Research Fellowship, California Inst. of Tech. 1981, Pelton Award, Botanical Soc. of America and Conservation and Research Foundation 1994, Gibbs Medal, American Soc. of Plant Physiologists 1995, Genetics Soc. of America Medal 1996, Science pour l'Art Science Prize, LVMH Moët-Hennessy-Louis Vuitton 1996, Mendel Medal and Mendel Lecturer, Genetical Soc. of GB 1997, Int. Prize for Biology, Japan Soc. for the Promotion of Science 1997, Jean Weigle Memorial Lecturer, Univ. of Geneva 1998, Richard Lounsbery Award, NAS 1999, Annual Biology Lecturer, ETH, Zürich 2001, Wilbur Cross Medal, Yale Univ. 2001, Ross Harrison Prize, Int. Soc. of Developmental Biologists 2005, Balzan Prize 2006, Prix la Recherche 2009, Sibthorp Medal 2011, Dawson Prize in Genetics, Trinity Coll. Dublin 2013. *Publications:* more than 200 articles in scientific journals. *Address:* Division of Biology, California Institute of Technology, Mail Code 156-29, 1200 East California Boulevard, Pasadena, CA 91125, USA (office). *Telephone:* (626) 395-6889 (office). *Fax:* (626) 449-0756 (office). *E-mail:* meyerow@caltech.edu (office). *Website:* biology.caltech.edu/Members/Meyerowitz (office).

MEYEROWITZ, Joel; American photographer; b. 1938, Bronx, New York; s. of Hy Meyerowitz; one s.; fmr art dir in an advertising firm; began photographing career in 1962; early advocate of colour photography mid-1960s; gave lessons in colour photography at Cooper Union, New York 1971; commissioned by St Louis Art Museum, Missouri to photograph Eero Saarinen's Gateway Arch 1977; photographed Empire State Bldg 1978; produced and directed his first film, POP, an intimate diary of a three-week road trip made with his son and father 1998; cr. The World Trade Center Archive of more than 8,000 images, documenting destruction and recovery at Ground Zero and immediate neighbourhood following attacks on World Trade Center 2001; works in collection of ATT Collection, Boston Museum of Fine Art, Carnegie Inst. Museum of Art, Chicago Art Inst., George Eastman House, IBM Collection, Int. Center of Photography, New York, Merrill Lynch Collection, Metropolitan Museum of Art, Museum of Modern Art, New York, Miami Art Museum, Museum of Photographic Art, Philadelphia Museum of Art, San Francisco Museum of Modern Art, San Jose Museum of Art, Seagram Collection, St Louis Museum, Stedelijk Museum, Toledo Museum of Art, Virginia Museum, Whitney Museum of American Art, US Trust Company, Gund Collection, Hallmark Cards Collection; Guggenheim Fellow, NEA Award, NEH Award. *Publications:* Cape Light 1979, St Louis & the Arch 1981, A Summer's Day 1985, Wild Flowers 1986, The Arch 1988, Creating a Sense of Place 1990, Redheads 1991, Bay/Sky 1993, At the Water's Edge 1993, The Nutcracker 1993, Città e Destino (City and Destiny), La natura delle città (The Nature of Cities) 1995, Bystander: A History of Street Photography 1994, Joel Meyerowitz (Phaidon 55 series) 2001, Tuscany: Inside the Light 2003, Aftermath: The World Trade Center Archives 2006. *Website:* www.joelmeyerowitz.com.

MEYROWITZ, Carol M.; American business executive; *CEO, The TJX Companies, Inc.;* joined Hit or Miss div., The TJX Companies, Inc. 1983, later held sr man. positions with Hit or Miss and Chadwick's of Boston, Sr Exec. Vice-Pres. and Pres. The Marmaxx Group (co.'s largest div.) 2001–05, Pres. The TJX Companies, Inc. 2005–07, mem. Bd of Dirs and CEO 2007–, mem. Cttee of Exec. Man. 2007–; advisory consultant, Berkshire Partners LLC, Boston 2005–; ranked by Fortune magazine amongst 50 Most Powerful Women in Business in US (26th) 2006, (31st) 2007, (19th) 2008, (18th) 2009, (17th) 2010, (15th) 2011–12, ranked by Forbes magazine amongst The World's 100 Most Powerful Women (24th) 2009, (54th) 2010, (73rd) 2011, (68th) 2012, (82nd) 2013. *Address:* The TJX Companies, Inc., 770 Cochituate Road, Framingham, MA 01701, USA (office). *Telephone:* (508) 390-1000 (office). *Fax:* (508) 390-2828 (office). *E-mail:* info@tjx.com (office). *Website:* www.tjx.com (office).

MÉZARD, Marc, PhD; French physicist, academic and university administrator; *Director, École Normale Supérieure;* b. 29 Aug. 1957, Aurillac; ed École Normale Supérieure, Paris; joined CNRS 1981, worked at Lab. of Theoretical Physics, École Normale Supérieure, apptd to rank of Dir of Research at CNRS and assigned to Statistical Physics Lab. of École Normale Supérieure 1990; joined Lab. of Theoretical Physics and Statistical Models, Université Paris-Sud 2001, later Dir; Lecturer at École Polytechnique from 1987; also conducted research in La Sapienza Univ., Rome 1984–86, Kavli Inst., Univ. of California, Santa Barbara, Math. Sciences Research Inst., Univ. of California, Berkeley, USA; Pres. École Normale Supérieure 2012–; CNRS Bronze Medal 1985, CNRS Silver Medal 1990, Prix Ampère de l'Électricité de France, Acad. des sciences 1996, Humboldt Prize 2009. *Publications:* Information, Physics, and Computation (co-author), Spin Glass Theory and Beyond (co-author); numerous papers in professional journals on statistical physics, applied in particular to disordered systems. *Address:* Office of the Director, École normale supérieure, 45 rue d'Ulm, 75230 Paris Cedex 05 (office); Laboratory of Theoretical Physics and Statistics Models, Building 100, University of Paris Sud, 91405 Orsay, France (office). *Telephone:* 1-44-32-30-01 (office). *Fax:* 1-44-32-20-99 (office). *E-mail:* marc.mezard@ens.fr (office). *Website:* www.ens.fr (office); lptms.u-psud.fr/membres/mezard (office).

MEZOUAR, Salaheddine, MSc(Econ); Moroccan politician and business executive; *Minister of Foreign Affairs;* b. 11 Dec. 1953, Meknès; m.; two c.; ed Institut européen d'admin des affaires (INSEAD), Fontainebleau, France, Institut supérieur de commerce et d'admin des entreprises (ISCAE), Casablanca, Université des sciences sociales, Grenoble, France; held admin. and financial posts with Régies d'Eau et d'Électricité de Rabat et de Tanger early 1980s; Chief Financial Officer Franco-Tunisian electrical, plumbing, refrigeration and maintenance co. based in Tunis –1986; Chief of Div. and in charge of mission, Office d'exploitation des Ports (ODEP) 1986–91; joined Spanish co. specializing in manufacture of tissue where he served as Gen. Man. of subsidiary Settat and Commercial Dir of group for Morocco, Africa and Middle East 1991; Pres. Moroccan Asscn of Textile Industries and Clothing (AMITH) 2002; also served as Pres. Textile and Leather Fed. in Gen. Confed. of Moroccan Enterprises (CGEM); Minister of Industry, Trade and Upgrading of the Economy 2004–07, of the Economy and Finance 2007–11, of Foreign Affairs 2013–; mem. Cen. Cttee Rassemblement nat. des Indépendants; fmr Vice-Pres. Raja athletic club; fmr capt. nat. basketball team. *Address:* Ministry of Foreign Affairs and Co-operation, ave Franklin Roosevelt, Rabat Morocco (office). *Telephone:* (53) 7761583 (office). *Fax:* (53) 7765508 (office). *E-mail:* mail@maec.gov.ma (office). *Website:* www.maec.gov.ma.

MEZZOGIORNO, Giovanna; Italian actress; b. 9 Nov. 1974, Rome; d. of the late Vittorio Mezzogiorno and of Cecilia Sacchi; m. Alessio Federico Fugolo 2009; studied dancing for 13 years; moved to Paris aged 19 and attended the stages by Arianne Mnouchkine, worked for two years at the Peter Brook Workshop (Le Centre Int. de Créations Théatrales); stage debut with role of Ofelia in Qui est là, toured several European cities; film debut in Il viaggio della sposa 1997; Premio Coppola-Prati 1996, Targa d'Argento as the New Talent in Italian Cinema, Premio Flaiano as Best Actress of 1997–98. *Theatre includes:* 4.48 Psicosi (by Sarah Kane, directed by Piero Maccarinelli). *Films include:* Il viaggio della sposa (The Bride's Journey) 1997, Del perduto amore (Nastro d'Argento, Ciak d'Oro and Premio Pasinetti as Best Actress in a starring role) 1998, Asini 1999, Un uomo perbene 1999, Afrodita, el sabor del amor 2001, State zitti per favore 2001, L'ultimo bacio (Premio Flaiano) 2001, Malefemmene 2001, Nobel 2001, Tutta la conoscenza del mondo 2001, Ilaria Alpi – Il più crudele dei giorni 2002, La finestra di fronte (Facing Windows) (David di Donatello, Ciak d'Oro, Nastro d'Argento, Grolle d'Oro and Globo d'Oro, Foreign Press Asscn, Flaiano Award, Karlovy Vary Award as Best Actress in a Leading Role) 2003, L'amore ritorna 2004, Stai con me 2004, Last Chance Saloon 2004, Il club delle promesse (Au secours, j'ai trente ans!) 2004, La bestia nel cuore (The Beast in the Heart) 2005, Don't Tell 2005, Lezioni di volo 2006, AD Project (video) 2006, Flying Lessons 2007, Night Bus 2007, Love in the Time of Cholera 2007, Les murs porteurs 2007, L'amore non basta 2008, Piano Shooting 2008, Sono viva 2008, Vincere 2009, La Prima Linea 2009, Basilicata Coast to Coast 2010, Baciato dalla fortuna 2011; producer: In the Eyes (documentary) 2009. *Television includes:* Più leggero non basta (film for Italian Nat. TV Network, RaiDue) 1999, Les Misérables (mini-series) 2000, Entrusted (film) 2003, Virginia, la monaca di Monza (film) 2004.

MGALOBLISHVILI, Grigol, BA, MA; Georgian diplomatist and politician; *Permanent Representative, NATO;* b. 7 Oct. 1973; m.; two c.; ed Tbilisi State Univ., Istanbul Univ., Oxford Univ., UK; interpreter, Georgian Trade Mission in Turkey 1995–96, Attaché, Dept of Western European Countries, Ministry of Foreign Affairs 1996–98, First Sec., Embassy in Ankara 1998–2000, Political Counsellor 1998–2002, Deputy Dir Dept of US, Canada and Latin American Countries, Ministry of Foreign Affairs 2003–04, Dir Dept of European and Euro-integration 2004, Amb. to Turkey 2004–08; Prime Minister of Georgia Nov. 2008–Feb. 2009; currently Perm. Rep. to NATO, Brussels. *Address:* Permanent Mission of Georgia to NATO, blvd Léopold III, 1110 Brussels, Belgium (office). *Telephone:* (2) 707-41-11 (office). *Fax:* (2) 707-45-79 (office). *E-mail:* natodoc@hq.nato.int (office). *Website:* www.nato.int (office).

M'HENNI, Hedi; Tunisian physician and politician; b. 24 Dec. 1942, Sayada; m.; two c.; began career as physician specializing in preventive medicine; Dir Office national de la famille et de la population 1986; Minister of Public Health 1992–2001; Minister of Interior and Local Devt 2003–04, of Nat. Defence 2004–05;

Sec.-Gen. Rassemblement constitutionnel démocratique 2005–08. *Address:* c/o Rassemblement constitutionnel démocratique, ave Muhammad V, 1040 Tunis, Tunisia (office).

MIA, Mohammed Sidik; Malawi politician; *Minister of Transport and Public Infrastructure;* b. 1965; s. of the late Abdul Sidik Mia; m.; three c.; MP for Chikwawa Nkombezi 2004–; Deputy Minister of Agric., Irrigation and Food Security 2004–05, of Mines, Natural Resources and Environment 2005, of Transport and Public Works 2005, Minister for Irrigation and Water Devt 2005–09, Minister of Nat. Defence 2009–11, of Transport and Public Infrastructure 2011–. *Address:* Ministry of Transport and Public Infrastructure, Private Bag 322, Capital City, Lilongwe 3, Malawi (office). *Telephone:* 1789377 (office). *Fax:* 1789328 (office). *Website:* www.malawi.gov.mw/Transport/Home%20Transport.htm (office).

MIAO, Wei; Chinese politician; *Minister of Industry and Information Technology;* b. May 1955, Beijing; ed Hefei Univ. of Tech., CCP Cen. Cttee Central Party School; joined CCP 1984; Deputy Man., Sales Dept, China Nat. Automotive Industry Corpn 1985–89, Deputy Dir-Gen., Production Dept 1989–93; Deputy Dir, Automobile Dept, First Ministry of Machine-Building Industry 1993–95; Deputy Chief Engineer, Dongfeng Automobile Corpn 1995–97, Gen. Man. 1999–2005, also Sec., CCP Party Cttee 1997–2001; mem., CCP Provincial Cttee, Hubei Prov. 2003–05, mem. Standing Cttee 2005–08; Chair., City People's Congress, Wuhan City, Hubei Prov. 2007–08; Vice-Minister of Industry and Information Tech. 2008–10, Minister 2010–; Deputy, 10th NPC 2003–08, 11th NPC 2008–13; alt. mem. 17th CCP Cen. Cttee 2007–12, mem. 18th CCP Cen. Cttee 2012–. *Address:* Ministry of Industry and Information Technology, 13 Xichangan Dajie, Beijing 100804, People's Republic of China (office). *Telephone:* (10) 66014249 (office). *Fax:* (10) 66034248 (office). *E-mail:* mail@miit.gov.cn (office). *Website:* www.miit.gov.cn (office).

MICALI, Silvio, PhD; American/Italian electrical engineer and academic; *Ford Professor of Engineering, Massachusetts Institute of Technology;* b. 13 Oct. 1954, Palermo, Italy; ed Univ. of Rome, Univ. of California, Berkeley; Post-Doctoral Fellow, Univ. of Toronto, Canada 1982–83; Asst Prof., MIT 1983–86, Assoc. Prof. 1986–88, Tenured Assoc. Prof. 1988–91, Full Prof. 1991–, currently Ford Prof. of Eng, Electrical Eng and Computer Science Dept, also mem. Computer Science and Artificial Intelligence Lab.; mem. NAS 2007, Nat. Acad. of Eng, American Acad. of Arts and Sciences; Fellow, Int. Asscn for Cryptologic Research 2007; Gödel Prize 1993, RSA Prize in Cryptography, A.M. Turing Award, Asscn for Computing Machinery 2012. *Publications:* Randomness and Computation (ed.), 5th vol. of the series Advances in Computing Research 1989; more than 100 papers in scientific journals; 47 patents. *Address:* Room G644, The Stata Center, Massachusetts Institute of Technology, 32 Vassar Street, 32-G866, Cambridge, MA 02139, USA (office). *Telephone:* (617) 253-5949 (office); (617) 253-6090 (office). *Fax:* (617) 253-6652 (office). *E-mail:* silvio@csail.mit.edu (office). *Website:* people.csail.mit.edu/silvio (office).

MICELI, Felisa; Argentine economist and fmr government official; ed Univ. of Buenos Aires; Dir-Sec. Bank of the Province of Buenos Aires 1983–87; worked at Ecolatina consultancy firm in early 1990s; Rep. of Ministry of Economy at Cen. Bank 2002–03; Chair. Banco de la Nación Argentina 2003–05; Minister of the Economy 2005–07 (resgnd). *Address:* c/o Ministry of the Economy, Hipólito Yrigoyen 250, 1310 Buenos Aires, Argentina (office).

MICHAEL, Rt Hon. Alun Edward, BA; British politician; b. 22 Aug. 1943, Brynewran, Wales; s. of the late Leslie Charles Michael and Elizabeth (Betty) Michael; m.; two s. three d.; ed Keele Univ.; journalist South Wales Echo 1966–71; Youth and Community Worker, Cardiff 1972–84; Area Community Education Officer, Grangetown and Butetown 1984–87; mem. Cardiff City Council 1973–89 (fmr Chair. Finance, Planning, Performance Review and Econ. Devt, Chief Whip, Labour Group); mem. House of Commons (Labour and Co-op) for Cardiff S and Penarth 1987–; Opposition Whip 1987–88; Opposition Frontbench Spokesman on Welsh Affairs 1988–92, on Home Affairs and the Voluntary Sector 1992–97; Minister of State, Home Office 1997–98; Sec. of State for Wales 1998–99; First Sec. of Nat. Ass. for Wales 1999–2000; Minister of State for Rural Affairs and Local Environmental Quality, Dept for the Environment, Food and Rural Affairs 2001–05, Minister of State for Industry and Regions 2005–06; mem. Nat. Ass. for Wales for Mid and W Wales 1999–2001; mem. numerous parl. groups and cttees.; Vice-Pres. YHA. *Leisure interests:* opera, reading, long-distance running, mountain-walking, National Parks, classical music. *Address:* House of Commons, London, SW1A 0AA, England (office). *Telephone:* (20) 7219-5980 (office). *Fax:* (20) 7219-5930 (office). *E-mail:* alunmichaelmp@parliament.uk (office).

MICHAEL, George; British singer, songwriter and producer; b. (Georgios Kyriacos Panayiotou), 25 June 1963, Finchley, London; s. of Jack Kyriacus Panayiotou and the late Lesley Panayiotou; ed Bushey Meads School; debut in group The Executive 1979; formed (with Andrew Ridgeley) Wham! 1981–86, numerous consecutive hits; toured UK, France, USA, China, etc.; launched solo career 1986–; chose to release all further music free online 2004–; BRIT Awards for Best British Group 1985, Outstanding Contribution to British Music 1986, Best British Male Artist 1988, Best British Male Solo Artist 1997, Ivor Novello Awards for Songwriter 1985, 1989, Grammy Award (for I Knew You Were Waiting For Me, duet with Aretha Franklin) 1988, British Rock Industry Award for Best Male Artist 1988, Nordoff-Robbins Silver Clef Award 1989, American Music Awards for Favorite Pop/Rock Male Artist, Soul R&B Male Artist 1989, ASCAP Golden Note Award 1992. *Recordings include:* albums: with Wham!: Fantastic 1983, Make It Big 1984, Music From The Edge of Heaven 1986, The Final 1986; solo: Faith (Grammy Award for Best Album 1989, American Music Awards for Favorite Album 1989) 1987, Listen Without Prejudice: Vol. 1 (BRIT Award for Best British Album 1991) 1990, Older 1996, Older and Upper 1998, Ladies and Gentlemen: The Best of George Michael 1998, Songs from the Last Century 1999, Patience 2004, Twenty Five 2006, Symphonica 2014. *Publication:* George Michael: Bare (autobiography with Tony Parsons) 1990. *Address:* c/o Connie Filippello Publicity, 49 Portland Road, London, W11 4LJ, England (office). *Telephone:* (20) 7229-5400 (office). *Fax:* (20) 7229-4804 (office). *E-mail:* Cfpublicity@aol.com (office). *Website:* www.georgemichael.com.

MICHAEL, Ib; Danish novelist and poet; b. (Ib Michael Rasmussen), 17 Jan. 1945, Roskilde; ed Univ. of Copenhagen; Booksellers Club Golden Laurel for Author of the Year 1990, Danish Author Asscn Peace Prize 1991, Danish Acad. Prize 1994. *Publications include:* novels: En hidtil uset drøm om skibe (A Previously Unseen Dream of Ships) 1970, Den flyvende kalkundræber (The Flying Turkey Hunter) 1971, Hjortefod (Stag's Hoof) 1974, Rejsen tilbage (The Journey Back) 1977, Kejserfortællingen (The Tiger's Tale) 1981, Troubadurens læring (The Minstrel's Apprentice) 1984, Kilroy, Kilroy 1989, Vanillepigen (The Vanilla Girl) 1991, Den tolvte rytter (The Midnight Soldier) 1993, Brev til månen (Letter to the Moon) 1995, Prins (Prince) 1997, Kejserens atlas (The Emperor's Atlas) 2001, Paven af Indien (The Pope of India) 2003, Grill 2005, Orbit 2010; travelogue: Mayalandet (The Land of the Maya) 1973; poetry: Himmelbegravelse: Digte fra Tibet (Sky Burial: Poems from Tibet) 1986, Vinden i metroen (The Wind in the Metro) 1990; short stories: Atkinson's biograf (Atkinson's Cinema) 1998. *Address:* c/o Gyldendal Publishing, Klareboderne 3, 1001 Copenhagen, Denmark (office). *Telephone:* 58200115 (office). *Website:* www.gyldendal.dk/forfattere/ib-michael (office).

MICHAEL, HM King; Romanian fmr ruler; b. 25 Oct. 1921, Foishor Castle, Sinaïa; s. of the late King Carol II and Princess Helen of Greece; m. Princess Anne of Bourbon-Parma 1948; five d.; declared heir apparent, ratified by Parl. 4 Jan. 1926; proclaimed King 1927, deposed by his father 1930; succeeded to the throne of Romania following his father's abdication 1940; led coup d'état against pro-Nazi dictator, Ion Antonescu 1944; forced to abdicate following communist takeover of Romania 30 Dec. 1947; subsequently ran chicken farm in Herts., UK; went to Switzerland as test pilot 1956; has also worked for Lear Inc.; started electronics co. and worked as stockbroker; deported from Romania on first visit since exile Dec. 1990; returned to Romania 1992; Romanian citizenship and passport restored 1997; undertook official mission to Romania's integration into NATO and EU 1997; Collar and Grand Master, Order of Carol I of Romania, Order of Faithful Service, Order of Crown of Romania and Star of Romania, Grand Cross, Royal Victorian Order, Grand Cross, Légion d'honneur, Grand Cross, Order of Leopold (Belgium), Collar, Order of Annunciata, Grand Cross, Order of St Saviour (Greece), Marshal, Romanian Armed Forces. *Leisure interest:* restoring Second World War jeeps. *Address:* Palatul Elisabeta (Elisabeta Palace), Sos. Kiseleff 28, 011347 Bucharest, Romania (office). *E-mail:* office@princeradu.ro (office).

MICHAELIS, Peter; Austrian business executive; *Chairman of the Management Board and Managing Director, Österreichische Industrieholding AG;* b. 18 March 1946; ed Univ. of Salzburg, Univ. of Kiel, Germany; with Mannesmann Group 1975–2001; Speaker of the Bd, Österreichische Industrieholding AG (OIAG—govt holding co.) 2001–, Chair. Man. Bd and Man. Dir 2011–; Chair. or fmr Chair. Supervisory Bd Austrian Airlines (Österreichische Luftverkehrs) AG, Österreichische Post AG, Telekom Austria AG, APK Pensionskasse AG; mem. Supervisory Bd OMV (originally ÖMV for Österreichische Mineralölverwaltung meaning Austrian mineral oil authority) Group 2001–11, then Deputy Chair., Chair. –2011. *Address:* Österreichische Industrieholding AG (OIAG), Dresdner Strasse 87, 1201 Vienna, Austria (office). *Telephone:* (1) 71114-0 (office). *Fax:* (1) 71114-245 (office). *E-mail:* kommunikation@oiag.at (office). *Website:* www.oiag.at (office).

MICHAELS, Lorne; Canadian television and film producer; *Executive Producer, Saturday Night Live;* b. 17 Nov. 1944, Toronto; m. 1st Rosie Schuster (divorced); m. 2nd Susan Forristal (divorced); m. 3rd Alice Barry; three c.; ed Univ. of Toronto; fmr writer and producer CBC; fmr writer Rowan Martin's Laugh-In (TV show) NBC 1968, creator and Exec. Producer Saturday Night Live 1975–, Exec. Producer Late Night with Conan O'Brien; f. Broadway Video Inc. (production co.) 1975; ten Emmy Awards including Emmy Award for Best Writing in a Variety/Comedy Series 2002, Mark Twain Prize for American Humor 2004. *Films produced include:* Gilda Live (also writer) 1980, Three Amigos (also co-writer) 1986, Wayne's World 1992, Wayne's World II 1993, Lassie 1994, Tommy Boy 1995, Kids in the Hall: Brain Candy 1996, A Night at the Roxbury 1998, Superstar 1999, The Ladies Man 2000, Enigma 2001, Mean Girls 2004. *Television includes:* Things We Did Last Summer 1977, The Paul Simon Special (also writer) 1977, Steve Martin's Best Show Ever (also writer) 1981, The Coneheads 1983, The New Show 1984, The Kids in the Hall 1988, Sunday Night 1988, Frosty Returns 1992. *Address:* c/o Saturday Night Live, NBC Television Network, 30 Rockefeller Plaza, New York, NY 10112, USA (office). *Telephone:* (212) 664-4444 (office). *Fax:* (212) 664-4085 (office). *Website:* www.lornemichaels.com; www.nbc.com/Saturday_Night_Live (office).

MICHAELS-MOORE, Anthony, BA; British singer (baritone); b. (Anthony Michael Frederick Moore), 8 April 1957, Grays, Essex, England; s. of John Frederick Moore and Isabel Shephard; m. 1st Ewa Bozena Migocki 1980; one d.; m. 2nd Emily Doyle Schluter 2010; ed Gravesend School for Boys, Univ. of Newcastle, Royal Scottish Acad. of Music and Drama, Fenham Teacher Training Coll.; Prin. Baritone, Royal Opera House, Covent Garden 1987–97; roles in all British opera cos; debut La Scala, Milan (Licinius in La Vestale) 1993, Paris Bastille (Sharpless in Madama Butterfly) 1995, New York Metropolitan Opera (Marcello in La Bohème) 1996, Teatro Colón Buenos Aires (Andrea Chénier) 1996, Vienna Staatsoper (Lescaut in Manon) 1997, San Francisco Opera (Eugene Onegin) 1997, Santa Fe Opera (title role in Simon Boccanegra) 2004, Paris Théâtre des Champs-Elysées (title role in Falstaff) 2010, Opéra de Montréal (title role in Rigoletto) 2010, Opernhaus Zurich (title role in Falstaff) 2011, Seoul, Korea (Scarpia in Tosca) 2012, Oper Köln (Scarpia in Tosca) 2012; specialises in 19th-century baritone repertoire and English song; Winner Luciano Pavarotti/Opera Co. of Philadelphia Prize 1985, Royal Philharmonic Soc. Award Winner 1997. *Television appearances include:* BBC Proms (Beethoven's Missa Solemnis, Mahler's Symphony No. 8), Carmina Burana recorded at La Scala, Milan 1996. *Recordings include:* Carmina Burana, Lucia di Lammermoor, La Vestale, La Favorite, Falstaff and Il Tabarro, Aroldo. *Radio:* regular BBC Radio 3 broadcasts, Verdi operas from Royal Opera House, Met Opera relays from New York. *Leisure interests:* distance running, dog training, Indian cuisine. *Address:* c/o Julia Maynard, Intermusica Artists Management Ltd, 36 Graham Street, Crystal Wharf, London, N1 8GJ, England (office). *Telephone:* (20) 7608-9902 (office). *E-mail:* jmaynard@intermusica.co.uk (office); anthony@anthonymichaelsmoore.com (office). *Website:* www.intermusica.co.uk/michaels-moore (office) www.anthonymichaelsmoore.com (office).

MICHAL, Jiři, BSc; Czech business executive; *Chairman and CEO, Zentiva a.s.;* ed Univ. of Chem. and Tech., Prague; joined Zentiva a.s. 1974, various man. roles including Operational Dir, Chief Financial Officer, becoming CEO and Chair. 1993–; Vice-Pres. Czech Chemical Industry Asscn. *Address:* Zentiva a.s., U Kabelovny 130, 10237 Prague 10, Czech Republic (office). *Telephone:* (267) 241111 (office). *Fax:* (272) 702402 (office). *E-mail:* zentiva@zentiva.cz (office). *Website:* www.zentiva.eu (office).

MICHALCZEWSKI, Dariusz, (The Tiger); Polish/German fmr professional boxer; b. 5 May 1968, Gdańsk; m.; two s.; amateur boxer 1982–91, European Junior semifinalist in middleweight div. 1986, German Nat. Champion in light heavyweight div. 1990, European Champion in light heavyweight div. 1991; 133 wins in 150 amateur fights; defected from Polish amateur nat. team while competing in Germany 1988, gained citizenship and turned professional 1991; professional boxer 1991–2003, 2004–05; 48 wins (38 by knockout) in 50 professional fights; European champion, Göteborg 1991; became World Boxing Org. (WBO) light-heavyweight champion 1994 and defended the title 23 times; won WBO cruiserweight title in 1994 (abandoned 1995); won World Boxing Asscn (WBA), Int. Boxing Fed. (IBF) light-heavyweight titles in 1997; defeated by Julio César González Oct. 2003 (retd); came out of retirement to box Fabrice Tiozzo for WBA light heavyweight title in Hamburg Feb. 2005, stopped in six rounds, announced retirement May 2005. *Address:* Waldeweg 134B, 22393 Hamburg, Germany (office). *Telephone:* (40) 68912656 (office). *Website:* www.dariusz-tiger.de.

MICHALIK, Archbishop Józef, DTheol; Polish ecclesiastic; *Archbishop of Przemyśl and Chairman, Conference of Polish Episcopate;* b. 20 April 1941, Zambrów; ed Acad. of Catholic Theology, Warsaw, Angelicum, St Thomas Pontifical Univ., Rome; ordained priest, Łomża 1964; Vice-Chancellor Bishops' Curia, Łomża 1973–78; fmr lecturer Higher Theological Seminary, Łomża, Rector Pontifical Polish Coll., Rome 1978–86; staff mem. Pontifical Laity Council 1978–86; Bishop of Gorzów 1986–92; Chair. Episcopate Cttee for Academic Ministry 1986–95; Bishop Zielona Góra and Gorzów 1992–93; Archbishop of Przemyśl 1993–; Chair. Episcopate's Council for Poles Abroad, Councils of Episcopates of Europe Cttee for Laity; Vice-Chair. Consilium Conferentiarum Episcoporum Europea 2011–; mem. Main Council of Conf. of Polish Episcopate, (Chair. 2004–), Vatican Congregation for Bishops. *Publications:* My Talks with God 1976, La Chiesa e il suo rinnovamento secondo Andrea Frycz Modrzewski 1973, Brothers Look at Your Vocation 1991, Bóg i Ojczyzna, Wiara i Naród 1998, Mocą Twoją Panie 1998, Pan was potrzebuje 2000, Szukającym Prawdy 2002, Raport o stanie wiary w Polsce 2011. *Address:* Pl. Katedralny 4/A, 37-700 Przemyśl, Poland (office). *Telephone:* (16) 6786694 (office). *Fax:* (16) 6782674 (office). *E-mail:* michalik@episkopat.pl (office). *Website:* www.przemyska.pl (office).

MICHALOLIAKOS, Nikolaos G.; Greek politician; *General-Secretary, Golden Dawn;* b. 11 Dec. 1957, Athens; m. Eleni Zaroulia; one d.; ed Faculty of Maths., Nat. and Kapodistrian Univ. of Athens; joined nationalist 4th of August Party aged 16; participated in Athens local org. of EOKA-B; joined the Army's special forces, arrested after becoming mem. of a far-right extremist group July 1978, sentenced to one year's imprisonment for illegally carrying guns and explosives Jan. 1979, subsequently dismissed from the army; launched Chrysi Avgi (Golden Dawn) magazine 1980 (ceased publication April 1984); joined Nat. Political Union and became leader of youth section 1984; broke away from party and f. Popular Nat. Movt– Golden Dawn 1985, remained as leader until its disbandment 2005; continued political activity through the Patriotic Alliance 2005–07; Golden Dawn reformed under his leadership 2007, currently Gen.-Sec.; mem. Athens Council 2011–12; mem. Parl. 2012–; arrested along with four other Golden Dawn MPs and 15 others, charged with belonging to a criminal organization Sept. 2013. *Publications:* Enemies of the State 2000, For a Greater Greece in a Free Europe 2000, Against All 2001, The Last Loyals 2002, Pericles Giannopoulos: The Apollonian Speech 2006, The Confession of a Nationalist (reprinted) 2008, From the Ashes of Berlin to Globalisation 2008, Defending National Memory 2009. *Address:* Golden Dawn (Chrysi Avgi), Athens, Greece (office). *Telephone:* (210) 7521080 (office). *E-mail:* info@xryshaygh.com (office). *Website:* www.xryshaygh.com (office).

MICHAUD, Jean-Claude Georges; French broadcasting executive; b. 28 Oct. 1933; s. of Maurice Michaud and Suzanne Michaud; one s. one d. (from fmr marriage); ed Lycée Louis-le-Grand, Paris and Ecole Normale Supérieure, Paris; Counsellor, Ministry of Educ. 1961–62, Ministry of Information 1962–64; Asst Dir Television ORTF 1964–68, Counsellor to Dir-Gen. 1968–70; man. position, Librairie Hachette 1970–73; Deputy Dir for External Affairs and Co-operation, ORTF 1973–74; Dir of Int. Affairs and Co-operation, Télédiffusion France 1975–80, Dir of Commercial Affairs 1982–83, Overseas Dir 1983–85; Pres.-Dir-Gen. Soc. Française Radio-Télévision d'Outre-Mer (RFO) 1986–89; Pres. Dir-Gen. Sofratev 1989–98. *Publications:* Teoria e Storia nel Capitale di Marx 1960, Alain Peyrefitte 2002. *Leisure interests:* walking, skiing, reading. *Address:* 66 rue de la République, 69002 Lyon, France (home). *Telephone:* 4-78-68-20-32 (home). *E-mail:* michaud.jeanclaude@free.fr (home).

MICHEL, James Alix; Seychelles politician and head of state; *President;* b. 16 Aug. 1944; ed Teacher Training Coll., Seychelles; teacher 1960–61; with Cable & Wireless Telecommunications 1962–71; treas. and sec. staff union 1970–71; Accountant, Asst Man., then Man. Hotel des Seychelles 1971–74; mem. Exec. Cttee Seychelles People's United Party and Co-ordinator of Party Brs, also Ed. of The People 1974–77; Minister of State, Admin and Information 1977–79; mem. Cen. Exec. Cttee Seychelles People's Progressive Front 1978–, also Sec.; Chief of Staff Seychelles People's Defence Forces 1979–93; Minister of Educ., Information, Culture and Telecommunications 1979–86, of Educ., Information, Culture and Sports 1986–89, of Finance 1989–91, of Finance and Information 1991–93, of Finance, Information, Communications and Defence, also First Desig. Minister to discharge the functions of Pres. 1993–96; Vice-Pres. (retaining portfolios for Finance, Information and Communications) 1996; Vice-Pres. (with portfolios of Econ. Planning and Environment and Transport) 1998–2000; Vice-Pres. and Minister of Finance, Econ. Planning, Information Tech. and Communications 2001–04; Pres. of the Seychelles, with additional responsibility for Defence, Police, Information and Public Relations, Legal Affairs and Risk and Disaster Man. 2004–, and Minister of Finance 2005–06; Patron Seychelles Football Fed.; Foreign mem. Russian Acad. of Natural Sciences; Gran Croce dell'Ordine al Merito Melitense, Kt of Malta, Outstanding Civilian Service Medal, US Army Dept 1995. *Address:* Office of the President, State House, POB 55, Victoria, Mahé, Seychelles (office). *Telephone:* 224155 (office). *Fax:* 224985 (office). *Website:* www .virtualseychelles.sc.

MICHEL, Louis; Belgian politician; b. 2 Sept. 1947, Tirlemont; fmr lecturer at Inst. Supérieur de Commerce Saint-Louis; Prof. of Dutch, English and German Literature, Ecole Normale provinciale de Jodoigne 1968–78; Alderman of Jodoigne 1977–83, Mayor 1983–; Sec.-Gen. Parti Réformateur Libéral (PRL) 1980–82, Pres. 1982–90; Pres. Fed. of Local and Provincial PRL Office Holders 1990–92; Pres., parl. group in Council of Walloon Region 1991–92, in House of Reps 1992–95; MP 1978–99; Pres. PRL 1995–2001; Deputy Pres. of Liberal Int.; Deputy Prime Minister and Minister of Foreign Affairs 1999–2004; Rep. of Belgium to EU Special Convention on a European Constitution 2001–; Commr for Devt and Humanitarian Aid, EC 2004–09 (resgnd); MEP 2009–; mem. Parl. Comms on Finance, Budget, Institutional Reforms and Comm. charged with supervising electoral expenditures; mem. Benelux Inter parl. Consultative Council; Commdr Order of Leopold. *Address:* Mouvement Réformateur (MR), 84–86 ave de la Toison d'Or, 1060 Brussels, Belgium (office). *Telephone:* (2) 500-35-11 (office). *E-mail:* mr@mr.be (office). *Website:* www.mr.be (office).

MICHEL, Mohamedou Ould; Mauritanian government official and fmr diplomatist; fmr Minister of Planning; fmr Amb. to Australia, fmr Amb. to USA; fmr Sr Adviser to Pres. of Mauritania. *Address:* c/o Office of the President, BP 184, Nouakchott, Mauritania. *Telephone:* 525-26-36.

MICHEL, Pauline, Bacc. Pédagogie, LèsL; Canadian author, poet, screenwriter, songwriter and performer; b. 17 May 1944, Asbestos, PQ; ed École normale Marguerite Bourgeois, Univ. of Sherbrooke, Laval Univ., Québec City; fmr Prof., Cegep de Sherbrooke, Univ. du Québec à Montréal; numerous poetry and song tours and recitals in Canada, Africa, France; scenarist for TV and films; Parl. Poet Laureate of Canada 2004–06; mem. Union des écrivaines et des écrivains du Québec (UNEQ), Writers' Union of Canada, League of Canadian Poets, Soc. of Composers, Authors and Music Publrs of Canada (SOCAN), Soc. for Reproduction Rights of Authors, Composers and Publrs in Canada (SODRAC), Soc. des auteurs, compositeurs et éditeurs de musique (SACEM), Centre des auteurs dramatiques (CEAD) and others; Winner, Québec en chansons, Prix Adate, Ministry of Cultural Affairs grant, Canadian Embassy in Paris bursary 1980. *Plays:* Farfelu ou Les sens ensorceleurs, Au fil de l'autre, On perd la boule. *Films:* as co-screenwriter, actress, singer in La Caresse d'une ride (documentary), Les héritières d'Esther Blondin; consultant for Les Cheveux en quatre (documentary). *Recordings:* albums: Animagerie, Au coeur d'la vie 1979, Contrastes 1980, Hello moineau 1985, Le tour du monde 2000. *Music:* Sors de ta cage (comedy musical). *Radio:* À deux voix, Le jardin des ombres. *Writing for television:* screenwriter for L'animagerie, Youhou (Radio-Canada), Le Château des enfants, Télé-Métropole, Télé-Ressources, Passe-Partout (consultant) (Télé-Québec), A la Claire Fontaine (TV Ontario), Hello Moineau (coproduction for Francophone countries), La Maison de Ouimzie/Wimzie's House (broadcast in 100 countries), Dossi, Rémi et compagnie (France). *Publications include:* novels: Les yeux d'eau 1975, 2002, Mirage 1978, 2004, Le papillon de Vénus 1999, Eyes of Water 2006, Venus Butterfly 2010; short stories: Frissons d'enfants/Haunted Childhoods 2006; play: Au fil de l'autre 2004; poetry: L'oeil sauvage 1988, Funambule/Tightrope 2006; children's book: Cannelle et pruneau dans les feuilles de thé 1992; songbooks: Le tour du monde 2000, Hello Moineau 1985, Demeurez dans mon amour 1987, Voyez comme ils s'aiment 1988; contrib. of novellas and poems to numerous anthologies. *Leisure interests:* music, dance, cinema. *Address:* 1199 rue De Blois, Boucherville, QC J4B 7Z6, Canada. *Telephone:* (450) 906-3520. *E-mail:* pauline_michel@videotron.ca.

MICHELAKIS, Ioannis; Greek journalist and politician; *Minister of the Interior;* b. 10 April 1960, Kalymnos; m.; ed Grad. School of Industrial Studies, Univ. of Piraeus; worked as a journalist from 1979 before becoming New Democracy Rep.; fmr Chief Ed. MEGA Channel, fmr Dir MEGA Channel Cyprus; fmr Dir ANT1 TV; fmr Dir Eleftheros Typos newspaper; Spokesperson for New Democracy 2011–13; mem. Parl. 2012–; mem. Standing Cttee on Nat. Defence and Foreign Affairs, Cttee on Armament Programmes and Contracts, Special Perm. Cttee on Greeks Abroad; Minister of the Interior 2013–; Pres. Inst. for Democracy 'Konstantinos Karamanlis' 2013–. *Address:* Ministry of the Interior, Odos Stadiou 27, 101 83 Athens (office); Amerikis 10, 106 71 Athens, Greece. *Telephone:* (213) 1364000 (office); (210) 3388700. *Fax:* (213) 1364130 (office); (210) 3388704. *E-mail:* info@ypes.gr (office); johnmichelakis@parliament.gr (office). *Website:* www.ypes.gr (office).

MICHELBERGER, Pál, DSc; Hungarian engineer; b. 4 Feb. 1930, Vecsés; s. of Pál Michelberger and Mária Komáromy; m. Ilona Torma; one s. one d.; ed Technical Univ., Budapest; Assoc. Prof., Tech. Univ., Budapest 1963–68, Prof. 1968–, Rector 1990–94; mem. Bd of Mans, IKARUS Motor Coach Factory 1991–95, Hungarocamion Transport Co. 1992–94; Chair. Cttee for Machine Design, Scientific Soc. for Mechanical Eng, Co-Pres. 1976–90, Vice-Pres. 1990–93; Councillor, Fed. Int. des Techniques de l'Automobile 1974, Vice-Pres. 1978, Pres. 1992–94; Pres. (elect) Hungarian Rectors' Conf. 1994–95; mem. Perm. Cttee European Rectors' Conf. 1991–94; mem. Russian Acad. of Transportation 1992, Acad. Europaea 1993–, European Acad. of Science and Arts 1998–; Corresp. mem. Hungarian Acad. of Sciences 1982, mem. 1990 (Vice-Pres. 1993), Verein Deutscher Ingenieure 1983–; Hon. Pres. Hungarian Accreditation Cttee; A. G. Pattantyus Prize 1973, L. Eötvös Prize 1994, Széchenyi Prize 1995, O. Benedikt Prize 1998, Pázmány Prize 1999. *Publications:* seven books and numerous articles on vehicle dynamics. *Leisure interest:* music. *Address:* Szabadság út 141, 2040, Budaörs (office); c/o Technical University, Műegyetem rakpart 3-9, 1521 Budapest, Hungary. *Telephone:* (1) 463-1111 (office); (22) 422-668 (home). *Fax:* (1) 463-1783.

MICHELETTI BAÍN, Roberto; Honduran business executive, politician and fmr head of state; b. 13 Aug. 1948, El Progreso, Yoro; s. of Umberto Micheletti and Donatella Baín; m. Xiomara Girón 1993; three c.; mem. Honour Guard of Pres. Ramón Villeda Morales 1963; in exile in USA 1973–76; fmr Pres. Empresa de Transporte TUTSA, El Progreso; mem. Congreso Nacional (Parl.) 1982–, Pres. 2006–09; Dir Gen. Hondutel 1982–2002; mem. Partido Liberal de Honduras (PL), Pres. Yoro Regional PL Council, later Sec. PL Cen. Exec. Council, unsuccessful PL

cand. for Pres. of Honduras 2008; Acting Pres. of Honduras (following dismissal of Manuel Zelaya) 2009. *Address:* c/o Office of the President, Palacio José Cecilio del Valle, Blvd Juan Pablo II, Tegucigalpa, Honduras.

MICHELIN, François; French business executive; b. 15 June 1926, Clermont-Ferrand; s. of Etienne Michelin and Madeleine Michelin (née Calliès); m. Bernadette Montagne 1951; Man. Dir Compagnie Générale des Etablissements Michelin, Michelin & Cie 1959–66, Jt Man. Dir 1966–99; Man. Dir Cie Financière Michelin, Manufacture française des pneumatiques Michelin; Dir Peugeot SA; Conseiller d'Etat en service extraordinaire 1989; Chevalier, Légion d'honneur 2009. *Publication:* Et pourquoi pas? (jtly) (Prix de l'excellence, Maxim's Business Club 1999) 1998. *Leisure interest:* tennis.

MICHELIN, Nicolas; French architect and town planner; b. 1955, Paris; associate of Finn Geipel at Labfac (Laboratory for Architecture) 1990s; co-f., with Michel Delplace and Cyril Trétout, ANMA (Agence Nicolas Michelin & Associés), Paris 2000; Dir Ecole Nationale Superieure d'Architecture de Versailles 2000–09, est. Art Center 'La Maréchalerie'; Éd.-in-Chief Agora (biennial publ. on structure, town planning and design in Bordeaux) 2008; Grand Prix de l'Urbanisme 2007. *Film:* Nouveaux Paris: la ville et ses possibles (dir) 2005. *Publications include:* Attitudes 2010. *Address:* ANMA Agence Nicolas Michelin & Associés, 9 cour des Petites Écuries, 75010 Paris, France (office). *Telephone:* 1-53-34-00-01 (office). *Fax:* 1-53-34-09-99 (office). *E-mail:* agence@anma.fr (office); communication@anma.fr (office). *Website:* www.anma.fr (office).

MICHELL, Keith; Australian actor; b. 1 Dec. 1926, Adelaide, SA; s. of Joseph Michell and Maud Michell (née Aslat); m. Jeanette Sterk 1957; one s. one d.; ed Port Pirie High School, Adelaide Univ. Teacher's Coll. and School of Arts, Old Vic Theatre School; started career as art teacher; first stage appearance Playbox, Adelaide 1947; with Young Vic Theatre Co. 1950–51, first London appearance in And So To Bed 1951; Artistic Dir, Chichester Festival Theatre 1974–77; Top Actor Emmy Award 1971, British Film Award 1973, Logie Award 1974 and numerous others. *Stage appearances include:* Troilus and Cressida 1954, Romeo and Juliet 1954, Macbeth 1955, Don Juan 1956, Irma La Douce 1958, The Art of Seduction 1962, The Rehearsal 1963, Robert and Elizabeth 1964, The King's Mare 1966, Man of La Mancha 1968–69, Abelard and Heloise 1970, Hamlet 1972, Dear Love 1973, The Crucifer of Blood 1979, Captain Beaky Christmas Show 1981–82, The Tempest 1982, On the Rocks 1982, Amadeus 1983, La Cage aux Folles 1984–85, Jane Eyre 1986, Portraits 1987, The Royal Baccarat Scandal 1988, Henry VIII 1991, Aspects of Love 1992, Scrooge 1993–94, Monsieur Amilcar 1995, Brazilian Blue 1995, Family Matters 1998, All the World 2001, 2003, The Artisan's Angel (Ramazzini) (actor and dir) 2004. *Films include:* Dangerous Exile, The Hell Fire Club, Seven Seas to Calais, The Executioner, House of Cards, Prudence and the Pill, Henry VIII and His Six Wives, Moments, The Deceivers. *Television includes:* The Six Wives of Henry VIII 1972, Keith Michell in Concert at Chichester 1974, Captain Beaky and His Band, Captain Beaky, Vol. 2, The Story of the Marlboroughs, Jacob and Joseph, The Story of David, The Tenth Month, The Day Christ Died, My Brother Tom 1987, Capt. James Cook 1988, Murder She Wrote (series) 1988, The Prince and the Pauper 1996. *Television/video:* The Gondoliers, The Pirates of Penzance, Ruddigore, The Six Wives of Henry VIII. *Publications:* Shakespeare Sonnet series of lithographs 1974, Captain Beaky (illustrations for poems) 1975, Captain Beaky Vol. 2 1982, Alice in Wonderland 1982, Keith Michell's Practically Macrobiotic Cookbook 1987. *Leisure interests:* cooking, painting, writing.

MICHELL, Robert H., PhD, FRS, FMedSci; British biochemist and academic (retd); *Professor Emeritus of Biochemistry, University of Birmingham;* b. 16 April 1941, Yeovil, Somerset, England; s. of Rowland C. Michell and Elsie L. Michell (née Hall); m. 1st June Evans 1967 (divorced 1971); m. 2nd Esther Margaret Oppenheim 1992; two s. one d.; ed Crewkerne School, Univ. of Birmingham; Research Fellow, Univ. of Birmingham 1965–66, 1969–70, Harvard Medical School 1966–68; Lecturer, Univ. of Birmingham 1970–81, Sr Lecturer 1981–84, Reader 1984–86, Prof. of Biochemistry 1986–2006, Royal Soc. Research Prof. 1987–2005, Prof. Emer. 2005–; mem. European Molecular Biology Org. 1991, Council, Royal Soc. 1996–97; Hon. mem. Biochemical Soc. 2010; CIBA Medal, Biochemical Soc. 1988, Royal Soc. UK-Canada Rutherford Lecturer 1994, Biochemical Soc. Morton Lecturer 2002. *Publications include:* Membranes and their Cellular Functions (with J. B. Finean and R. Coleman) 1974, 1978, 1984, Membrane Structure (co-ed.) 1981, Inositol Lipids and Transmembrane Signalling (co-ed.) 1988, Inositol Lipids in Cell Signalling (co-ed.) 1989. *Leisure interests:* birdwatching, photography, modern literature, wildernesses, pottery. *Address:* School of Biosciences, University of Birmingham, Edgbaston, Birmingham, B12 2TT, England (office). *Telephone:* 7411-792640 (mobile) (home). *E-mail:* r.h.michell@bham.ac.uk (office).

MICHELS, Sir David Michael Charles, Kt; British leisure industry executive; *President, British Hospitality Association;* b. 1943; ed London Hotel School; various sales and marketing positions including Man.-Dir, Grand Metropolitan 1966–81; joined Ladbroke Group PLC 1981, Sales and Marketing Dir Ladbroke Hotels 1981–83, Man.-Dir Leisure Div. 1983–95, Man.-Dir Ladbroke Hotels 1985–97; Sr Vice-Pres. of Sales and Marketing, Hilton Int. (following acquisition of Ladbroke Group by Hilton Group PLC 1987) 1987–89, Deputy Chair. Hilton UK and Exec. Vice-Pres. Hilton Int. 1989–91, CEO Stakis PLC 1991–99, apptd mem. Bd Hilton Group PLC 1999 (after acquisition of Stakis by Hilton Group), CEO 1999–2000, Group CEO 2000–06 (after reunification of Hilton International with Hilton Hotel Corpn); mem. Bd of Dirs British Land Co. PLC 2003–, easyJet plc 2006–, Strategic Hotels & Resorts 2006–, Sr Ind. Dir Marks and Spencer Group plc 2006–08, Deputy Chair. 2008–; Pres. British Hospitality Asscn 2006–; fmr Dir Arcadia Group PLC, Hilton Hotel Corpn –2006; fmr Pres. Hilton in the Community Foundation; Trustee Anne Frank Trust; Hon. Fellow, Acad. of Food & Wine Service 2003. *Address:* British Hospitality Association, Queens House, 55-56 Lincoln's Inn Fields, London, WC2A 3BH, England (office). *Telephone:* (0845) 880-7744 (office). *Fax:* (20) 7404-7799 (office). *E-mail:* info@bha.org.uk (office). *Website:* www.bha.org.uk (office).

MICHELSEN, Axel, DPhil; Danish biologist and academic; *Professor Emeritus, University of Southern Denmark;* b. 1 March 1940, Haderslev; s. of Erik Michelsen and Vibeke Michelsen; m. Ulla West-Nielsen 1980 (died 2008); two s. one d.; ed Univ. of Copenhagen; Asst Prof. of Zoophysiology and Zoology, Univ. of

Copenhagen 1963–72; Prof. of Biology, Odense Univ. 1973–2005; Prof. Emer., Univ. of Southern Denmark; Chair. Danish Science Research Council 1975–78, Max-Planck Gesellschaft Fachbeirat 1977–81, Danish Nat. Cttee for Biophysics 1980–90, Danish Nat. Cttee for ICSU 1986–2000, 2004–06, Centre for Sound Communication 1994–2003, Carlsberg Lab. 2003–09; Dir Carlsberg Foundation 1986–2009; mem. Royal Danish Acad. of Sciences and Letters, Akad. der Naturforscher Leopoldina, Academia Europaea; Corresp. mem. Akad. der Wissenschaften und der Literatur (Mainz), Bayerische Akad. der Wissenschaften, Akad. der Wissenschaften zu Göttingen; Kt, Order of the Dannebrog (First Class) 1990; Alexander von Humboldt Prize 1990. *Publications:* The Physiology of the Locust Ear 1971, Sound and Life 1975, Time Resolution in Auditory Systems 1985, The Dance Language of Honeybees 1992. *Leisure interests:* wines, beekeeping, gardening. *Address:* Rosenvænget 74, 5250 Odense SV, Denmark (home). *Telephone:* 66-11-75-68 (home); 61-26-35-82 (home). *E-mail:* a.michelsen@biology .sdu.dk (office). *Website:* www.sdu.dk/ansat/a.michelsen.aspx (office).

MICHENER, Charles Duncan, BS, PhD, FAAS; American entomologist and academic; *Professor Emeritus of Entomology and Evolutionary Biology, University of Kansas;* b. 22 Sept. 1918, Pasadena, Calif.; s. of Harold Michener and Josephine Rigden Michener; m. Mary Hastings 1940; three s. one d.; ed Univ. of California, Berkeley; Tech. Asst in Entomology, Univ. of California 1939–42; Asst Curator, Lepidoptera and Hymenoptera, American Museum of Natural History, New York 1942–46, Assoc. Curator 1946–48, Research Assoc. 1949–; Curator, Snow Entomological Museum, Univ. of Kansas 1949–89, Dir 1974–83; Assoc. Prof. of Entomology, Univ. of Kansas 1948–49, Prof. 1949–89, Prof. Emer. 1989–, Chair. Dept of Entomology 1949–61, 1972–75, Watkins Dist Prof. of Entomology 1959–89, of Systematics and Ecology 1969–89; State Entomologist, S. Div. of Kansas 1949–61; Ed. Evolution 1962–64; American Ed. Insectes Sociaux (Paris), 1954–55, 1962–90; Assoc. Ed. Annual Review of Ecology and Systematics 1970–90; Pres. Soc. for the Study of Evolution 1967, Soc. of Systematic Zoology 1969, American Soc. of Naturalists 1978, Int. Union for the Study of Social Insects 1977–82 (Vice-Pres. Western Hemisphere Section 1979–80); mem. NAS, American Acad. of Arts and Sciences; Corresp. mem. Acad. Brasileira de Ciências; Guggenheim Fellow to Brazil 1955–56, Africa 1966–67; Fellow, Royal Entomological Soc. of London; Foreign Hon. mem. Russian Entomological Soc., Soc. of Systematic Biology, Netherlands Entomological Soc.; Morrison Prize, New York Acad. of Sciences 1943, Fulbright Scholar, Australia 1957–58, Founder's Award, American Entomological Soc. 1981, Thomas Say Award, Entomological Soc. of America 1997, C.V. Riley Award, Entomological Soc. of America 1999, Distinguished Research Medal, Int. Soc. of Hymenopterists 2002, Hamilton Award, Int. Union for Study of Social Insects 2010. *Publications:* Comparative External Morphology, Phylogeny and a Classification of the Bees (Hymenoptera) 1944, American Social Insects (with M. H. Michener) 1951, The Nest Architecture of the Sweat Bees (with S. F. Sakagami) 1962, A Classification of the Bees of the Australian and S. Pacific Regions 1965, The Social Behaviour of the Bees 1974, Kin Recognition in Animals (with D. Fletcher) 1987, The Bee Genera of North and Central America (with R. J. McGinley and B. N. Danforth) 1994, The Bees of the World 2000; 446 publs, mostly on bees. *Leisure interests:* travel, field work. *Address:* Entomology Division, Natural History Museum, University of Kansas, PSB, 1501 Crestline Drive, Lawrence, KS 66045 (office); 1706 West 2nd Street, Lawrence, KS 66044, USA (home). *Telephone:* (785) 864-4610 (office); (785) 843-4598 (home). *Fax:* (785) 864-5260 (office). *E-mail:* michener@ku.edu (office).

MICHIE, David Alan Redpath, OBE, FRSA; British painter and academic; *Professor Emeritus of Painting, Heriot Watt University;* b. 30 Nov. 1928, St Raphaël, France; s. of James Beattie Michie and Anne Redpath; m. Eileen Michie 1951 (died 2003); two d.; ed Hawick High School, Edinburgh Coll. of Art; Lecturer in Drawing and Painting, Gray's School of Art, Aberdeen 1957–61; Vice-Prin., Edinburgh Coll. of Art 1974–77, Head of School of Drawing and Painting 1982–90, Prof. of Painting 1988–90; Prof. Emer., Heriot Watt Univ. 1991–; Visiting Artist to Acad. of Fine Art, Belgrade 1979, to Art Studio Dept, Univ. of Calif. at Santa Barbara 1992; mem. Edinburgh Festival Soc. 1976–, Royal Scottish Acad. 1972, Royal Glasgow Inst. of Fine Art (RGI) 1983, Royal West of England Acad. (RWA) 1991–2000, Museums and Galleries Comm. 1991–96, Scottish Int. Trust 2004–; Founding Fellow, Inst. of Contemporary Scotland 2000; Hon. Fellow, Edinburgh Coll. of Art 2009; Guthrie Award, RSA 1964, David Cargill Award, R.G.I. 1977, Lothian Region Award 1977, Sir William Gillies Award, RSA 1980, Glasgow City of Culture Award, RGI 1990, Cornelissen Prize, RWA 1992. *Leisure interest:* music. *Address:* 17 Gilmour Road, Edinburgh, EH16 5NS, Scotland (home). *Telephone:* (131) 667-2684 (home).

MICHNIK, Adam; Polish journalist and historian; *Editor-in-Chief, Gazeta Wyborcza;* b. 17 Oct. 1946, Warsaw; m.; one s.; ed Adam Mickiewicz Univ., Poznań; active in anti-communist movt 1965–80, spent six years in prison; Co-Founder and mem. Cttee for the Defence of Workers (KOR) 1976–80; Biuletyn Informacyjny, Krytyka, Zapis (ind. periodicals); activist Solidarity Self-governing Ind. Trade Union in the 1980s; imprisoned 1985–86; participant Round Table plenary debates 1989; Deputy to Sejm (Parl.) 1989–91; Ed.-in-Chief Gazeta Wyborcza (daily) 1989–; mem. Int. Advisory Bd, Council on Foreign Relations; Officer's Cross of Merit (Hungary) 1998, Bernardo O'Higgins Commdr's Order (Chile) 1999, Order for Contrib. to Polish-German Reconciliation, European Univ. Viadriana, Frankfurt 2000, Grand Prince Gedymin Order (Lithuania) 2001, Grand Cross of Merit (Germany) 2001; Dr hc (New School for Social Research, New York, Univ. of Minnesota, Univ. of Michigan, Connecticut Coll.); French Pen Club Freedom Award 1982, Robert F. Kennedy Human Rights Award 1986, Alfred Jurzykowski Foundation Award, La Vie Man of the Year 1989, Shofar Award 1991, Brucke-Preis (Germany) 1995, Award of the European Journalists Asscn 1995, Medal of Imre Nagy 1995, OSCE Prize in Journalism and Democracy 1996, The Golden Pen (Bauer Verlag) 1998, The Francisco Cerecedo Journalist Prize 1999, Int. Press Inst. Freedom Hero 2000, Carl Bertelsmann Prize 2001, Erasmus Prize 2001, Dan David Prize 2006, Goethe Medal 2011. *Publications:* Cienie zapomnianych przodków (The Shadows of the Forgotten Ancestors) 1975, Kościół, lewica, Dialog (Church, The Left, Dialogue) 1977, Penser la Pologne 1983, Szanse polskiej Demokracji (Chances for Polish Democracy) 1984, Z dziejów honoru w Polsce. Wypisy więzienne (From the History of Honour in Poland. Prison Notes) 1985, Takie czasy: Rzecz o kompromisie (Such Other Times: Concerning Compromise) 1985, Listy z Białołęki (Letters from Białołęka), Polskie pytania (Polish Questions)

1987, Druga faza rewolucji 1990, Między Panem a Plebanem 1995, Diabeł naszego czasu 1995, Letters From Freedom 1998, Confessions of a Converted Dissident – Essay for the Erasmus Prize 2001; many articles in Gazeta Wyborcza, Der Spiegel, Le Monde, Libération, El País, Lettre Internationale, New York Review of Books, The Washington Post and others. *Address:* Gazeta Wyborcza, ul. Czerska 8/10, 00-732 Warsaw, Poland (office). *Telephone:* (22) 5504000 (office); (22) 5554002 (office). *Fax:* (22) 8416920 (office). *E-mail:* contact@agora.pl (office).

MICHON, John Albertus, MSc, PhD; Dutch psychologist and academic; *Professor Emeritus of Psychonomics, Leiden University;* b. 29 Oct. 1935, Utrecht; s. of J. J. Michon and S. A. de Ruijter; m. Hetty Sommer 1960; one s. one d. (deceased); ed Utrecht Mun. Gymnasium and Univs of Utrecht and Leiden; Research Assoc., Inst. for Perception, Soesterberg 1960–73, Head, Dept of Road User Studies 1969–73; Co-founder Netherlands Psychonomics Foundation 1968, Sec. 1968–72, Pres. 1975–80; Prof. of Experimental Psychology and Traffic Science, Univ. of Groningen 1971–92, Dir Inst. for Experimental Psychology 1971–92, Chair. Traffic Research Center 1977–92, Chair. Dept of Psychology 1978, 1983–86, Assoc. Dean, Faculty of Social Sciences 1983–86; mem. Bd Center for Behavioral, Cognitive and Neurosciences 1990–92, co-f. Dept of Cognitive Science 1990; Dir Netherlands Inst. for the Study of Criminality and Law Enforcement 1992–98; Prof. of Criminality Research, Leiden Univ. 1992–98, Sr Research Prof. of Psychonomics 1998–2002, Prof. Emer. 2002–; Pres. Int. Soc. for the Study of Time 1983–86, Hon. mem. 2004–; Co-founder and mem. Bd European Soc. for Cognitive Psychology 1984–90; Vice-Chair. Nat. Council for Road Safety 1977–86; Ed.-in-Chief, Acta Psychologica 1971–74; Visiting Prof. Carnegie Mellon Univ., Pittsburgh, Pa 1986–87; Co-ordinator EEC DRIVE Project Generic Intelligent Driver Support 1988–92; Chair. Advisory Cttee for Cognitive Science, 1995–97, Steering Cttee for the Cognitive Sciences, Netherlands Org. for Scientific Research (NWO) 2002–12; mem. Social Sciences Council (SWR) 1994–2003, Accreditation Cttee Research Schools 2000–07, Supervisory Cttee, Artificial Intelligence, Univ. of Groningen 2013–; mem. and Hon. Sec. Jury, Heineken Prize for Cognitive Science 2004–10; mem. Royal Netherlands Acad. of Arts and Sciences (KNAW) 1981 (Chair. Behavioral and Social Sciences Section 1988–98), Academia Europaea 1989, European Acad. of Sciences and Arts 1995–2010; Kt, Order of the Netherlands Lion 2002; Dr hc (Liège) 1995; NATO Science Fellowship 1965, NIAS Fellowship 1976, Honda Foundation Lecturing Award 1977, Medal of Honour, Netherlands Psychonomics Soc. 2005. *Publications:* Timing in Temporal Tracking 1967, Sociale Verkeerskunde 1976, Handboek der Psychonomie 1976, 1979, Beïnvloeding van Mobiliteit 1981, Time, Mind and Behaviour 1985, Guyau and the Idea of Time 1988, Handboek der Sociale Verkeerskunde 1989, Soar: A Cognitive Architecture in Perspective 1992, Generic Intelligent Driver Behaviour 1993, Nederlanders over Criminaliteit en Rechtshandhaving 1997; more than 270 articles and chapters in scientific journals and books. *Leisure interests:* visual arts (painting, drawing, cartoons), music. *Address:* Brigantynwal 7, 2317 GL Leiden, The Netherlands. *E-mail:* michonja@xs4all.nl (home). *Website:* www.jamichon.nl.

MICHOT, Yves Raoul; French aviation executive; b. 4 Nov. 1941, Nantes; s. of Raoul Michot and Lucienne Ruffel; m. Michèle Gouth 1964; two s. one d.; ed Ecole Polytechnique and Ecole Nationale Supérieure d'Aeronautique; Brétigny Flight Test Centre 1965–73; Govt Concorde Project Man. 1973–75; Tech. Adviser to Nat. Armament Dir 1975–78, to Minister of Defence 1978–80; Mirage 2000 Program Man., Ministry of Defence 1980–84; Mil. Programs Gen. Man. Aérospatiale 1984, Programs Gen. Man. 1985; Exec. Vice-Pres. Aérospatiale 1987, Exec. Vice-Pres. and COO 1989, Sr Exec. Vice-Pres. and COO and Pres. Aérospatiale 1995–99, Pres., Dir-Gen. 1996–99, Pres. Bd Dirs 1999; fmr Pres. European Asscn of Aerospace Industries (AECMA),; Pres. Club d'affaires franco-singapourien 1998–; Chair. Défense Conseil Int. –2007; Pres. Descartes Prize Grand Jury 2001, 2002; Officier, Légion d'Honneur, Commdr, Ordre Nat. du Mérite, Médaille de l'Aéronautique. *Address:* 3 rue Chabrier, 78370 Plaisir, France (home).

MICKELSON, Philip (Phil) Alfred, BS; American professional golfer; b. 16 June 1970, San Diego, Calif.; s. of Philip Mickelson and Mary Mickelson; m. Amy McBride 1996; one s. two d.; ed Arizona State Univ.; jr career won 34 San Diego County titles, three Nat. Collegiate Athletics Asscn (NCAA) Championships, three Jack Nicklaus Awards as Nat. Coll. Player of the Year, mem. Walker Cup team 1989, 1991, US Amateur Championships 1990, played in World Amateur Team Championship 1990, Tucson Chrysler Classic 1991; turned professional 1992; Professional Golf Asscn (PGA) titles Northern Telecom Open 1991 (last amateur player to win PGA event and first since 1985), 1995, 1996, Buick Invitational Calif. 1993, 2000, 2001, The International 1993, Mercedes Championships 1994, 1998, Phoenix Open 1996, GTE Byron Nelson Golf Classic 1996, NEC World Series of Golf 1996, Bay Hill Invitational 1997, Sprint International 1997, Pebble Beach Nat. Pro-Am, 1998, BellSouth Classic 2000, MasterCard Colonial 2000, The Tour Championship 2000, Canon Greater Hartford Open 2001, 2002, Bob Hope Chrysler Classic 2002, 2004, US Masters 2004, 2006, 2010, US PGA Championship 2005, Players Championship 2007, World Golf Championship–Calif. 2009, Shell Houston Open 2011, AT&T Pebble Beach Nat. Pro-Am 2012, The Open Championship, Muirfield 2013; mem. Presidents Cup team 1994 (winners), 1996 (winners), 1998, 2000 (winners), 2003 (tied), 2005 (winners), 2007 (winners), 2009 (winners), 2011 (winners), Alfred Dunhill Cup team 1996, Ryder Cup team 1995, 1997, 1999 (winners), 2002 (postponed from 2001), 2004, 2008 (winners), 2010, 2012; scored 59, lowest score in professional strokeplay history, at Grand Slam of Golf in Hawaii 2004 (only achieved on three other occasions on PGA tour); sponsored the Special Operations Warrior Project 2004 to support US troops; Co-Chair. American Jr Golf Asscn; involved in golf course design; Golf World Amateur of the Year 1991, Haskins Award 1990, 1991, 1992, ESPY Award Best Championship Performance 2004, ESPY Award Best Male Golfer 2004, elected into World Golf Hall of Fame 2011, inducted 2012. *Leisure interests:* football, flying. *Address:* c/o Steve Loy, Gaylord Sports Management, 13845 North Northsight Blvd, Suite 200, Scottsdale, AZ 85260, USA (office). *Telephone:* (480) 483-9500 (office). *E-mail:* sloy@gaylordsports.com (office). *Website:* www .gaylordsports.com (office); www.philmickelson.com.

MICKLETHWAIT, John; British journalist and writer; *Editor-in-Chief, The Economist;* ed Magdalen Coll., Oxford; fmrly with Chase Manhattan Bank; joined The Economist 1987, as Media Correspondent, then est. Los Angeles office 1990–93, Ed. business section 1993–97, New York Bureau Chief 1997–99, US Ed.

1999–2006, Ed.-in-Chief 2006–; Trustee, British Museum; Harold Wincott Press Award for Young Financial Journalist 1989, named Ed.'s Ed. by British Soc. of Magazine Eds 2010. *Publications include:* The Witch Doctors (with Adrian Wooldridge) (Financial Times/Booz Allen Global Business Book Award 1997) 1996, A Future Perfect: The Challenge and Hidden Promise of Globalisation (with Adrian Wooldridge) 2000, The Company: A Short History of a Revolutionary Idea (with Adrian Wooldridge) 2003, The Right Nation (with Adrian Wooldridge) 2004, God is Back (with Adrian Wooldridge) 2009; contrib. articles to the New York Times, Los Angeles Times, Wall Street Journal, Guardian, Spectator and the New Statesman, Boston Globe. *Address:* The Economist, 25 St James's Street, London, SW1A 1HG, England (office). *Telephone:* (20) 7830-7000 (office). *Website:* www.economist.com (office).

MICOSSI, Stefano; Italian economist and academic; *Director General, Assonime;* b. 27 Oct. 1946, Bologna; m. Daniela Zanotto; one s. one d.; ed Università Statale di Milano, Yale Univ., USA; economist, Bank of Italy Research Dept 1974–78, Head 1980–84, Asst Dir 1984–86, Dir Int. Div. 1986–88; seconded to IMF as Asst to Italy's Exec. Dir 1978–80; Dir of Econ. Research Confindustria (Confed. of Italian Industries) 1988–94; Prof. of Macroeconomic Policy Int. Free Univ. of Social Sciences 1989–94, Prof. of Monetary Theory and Policy 1993–94; Prof. of Int. Monetary Econs, Coll. of Europe, Bruges 1990–94, Prof. of European Integration 1999–; Dir-Gen. for Industry, EC 1994–99; Dir-Gen. Assonime (business asscn association and think tank), Rome 1999–. *Publications:* Jt Ed. Adjustment and Integration in the World Economy 1992, The Italian Economy 1993, Inflation in Europe 1997 and books on the European Monetary System 1988, numerous articles in professional journals. *Address:* Assonime, Piazza Venezia 11, 00187 Rome, Italy (office). *Telephone:* (06) 69529214 (office). *Fax:* (06) 69529219 (office). *E-mail:* eleonora.riccardi@assonime.it (office). *Website:* www.assonime.it (office).

MIĆUNOVIĆ, Branislav; Montenegrin theatre director and politician; *Minister of Culture, Sports and Media;* Prof. of Acting, Faculty of Dramatic Arts, Belgrade and Faculty of Dramatic Arts, Cetinje; fmr Theatre Dir at Yugoslav Drama Theatre, Belgrade, Serbian Nat. Theatre, Croatian Nat. Theatre, Nat. Theatre, Tuzla, Nat. Theatre, Nis, Zvezdara Theatre, Belgrade; directed works by Aleksandra Popovic, Velimir Lukic, Ljubomir Simovic, Veljko Radovic, Jordan Plevneša, Goran Stefanovskog, Iva Bresan, Gordan Mihic; Dir Montenegrin Nat. Theatre 2003–07; Minister of Culture, Sports and Media 2008–; mem. Cttee for the Arts Theatre, Montenegrin Acad. of Sciences and Arts. *Address:* Ministry of Culture, 81250 Cetinje, ul. Njegoševa, Montenegro (office). *Telephone:* (41) 232571 (office). *Fax:* (41) 232572 (office). *E-mail:* kabinet.kultura@mku.gov.me (office). *Website:* www.ministarstvokulture.gov.me (office).

MIDDELHOEK, André, PhD; Dutch civil servant; b. 13 Dec. 1931, Voorburg; s. of J. Middelhoek; m. Trudy van den Broek 1982; two d.; ed Univ. of Amsterdam; Cen. Planning Office, Govt of Netherlands 1958–69, Deputy Dir 1966–69; lecturer, Int. Inst. for Social Studies, The Hague 1960–69; Dir-Gen. of the Budget, Ministry of Finance 1969–77; mem. Court of Auditors of European Communities 1977–93; Pres. European Court of Auditors 1993–96; Pres. Cttee of Wise Men 1999–; Commdr, Order of Netherlands Lion; Grand Croix, Couronne de Chêne (Luxembourg). *Publications:* publs on econs, econ. planning, public finance, policy analysis, EU finance and audit. *Leisure interests:* swimming, tennis, genealogy, hiking. *Address:* Val des Seigneurs 32, #47, 1150 Brussels, Belgium (home). *Telephone:* (2) 687-55-53 (home). *E-mail:* andre.middelhoek@skynet.be (home).

MIDDELHOFF, Thomas, MBA, PhD; German business executive; *Chairman, Berger Lahnstein Middelhoff & Partners (BLM Partners);* b. 11 May 1953, Düsseldorf; m.; five c.; ed Univ. of Münster, Univ. des Saarlandes; fmr Lecturer in Marketing, Univ. of Münster; Head of Sales and Marketing, Middelhoff GmbH (family-owned textile co.) 1983; Man. Asst to CEO, Mohndruck Graphische Betriebe GmbH 1986–87, Man. Dir 1989–90, Chair. of Man. Bd 1990; Man. Dir Elsnerdruck GmbH, Berlin 1987–88; mem. Bd responsible for multimedia, Bertelsmann publishing 1990–94, Head of Corp. Devt and Coordinator for Multimedia 1994–97, Chair. and CEO Bertelsmann AG 1998–2004; Head of Europe Investcorp International Ltd 2003–05; Chair. Supervisory Bd Karstadt-Quelle AG 2004–05, of Bd of Man. 2005–09, also Chair. Supervisory Bd Arcandor AG (new name for holding group 2007) 2004–09, CEO 2005–09; Chair. Thomas Cook Group PLC 2005–09, Polestar Group Ltd 2004–06, 2007–, Moneybookers.com, London 2007–, Senator Entertainment AG 2006–; Founding Partner and Chair., Berger Lahnstein Middelhoff & Partners (BLM Partners) 2009–; mem. Bd of Dirs New York Times Co. 2003–; mem. Supervisory Bd Apcoa Parking 2003–; Vernon A. Walters Award 1998. *Address:* Berger Lahnstein Middelhoff & Partners, 10 Duke of York Square, London, SW3 4LY, England (office). *Telephone:* (20) 7259-8550 (office). *Fax:* (20) 7730-3144 (office). *E-mail:* info@blmpartners.com (office). *Website:* www.blmpartners.com (office).

MIDDENDORF, J. William, II, BS, MBA; American diplomatist, business executive and fmr government official; b. 22 Sept. 1924, Baltimore, Md; s. of the late Henry Stump and Sarah Boone Middendorf; m. Isabelle J. Paine 1953; two s. two d.; ed Holy Cross Coll., Harvard Univ. and New York Grad. School of Business Admin; USN service during World War II; in Credit Dept of Bank of Manhattan Co. (now Chase Manhattan Bank) 1947–52; Analyst, Wood Struthers and Co. Inc. (brokerage firm), New York 1952–58, Pnr 1958–62; Sr Pnr Middendorf, Colgate and Co. (investment firm), New York 1962–69; Amb. to Netherlands 1969–73; Under-Sec. of the Navy 1973–74, Sec. 1974–76; Pres. and CEO First American Bankshares, Washington, DC 1977–81; Pres. and CEO Middendorf & Co., Inc., Washington, DC 1989–; Chair. Middendorf SA 1989–; Amb. to OAS 1981–85, to EC 1985–87; Chair. Presidential Task Force on Project Econ. Justice 1985–86; mem. Bd of Dirs and Sec.-Treasurer, Int. Republican Inst.; Trustee Heritage Foundation 1989–; numerous hon. degrees; State Dept Superior Honor Award 1974, Dept of Defense Distinguished Public Service Award 1975, 1976, USN Public Service Award 1976, Ludwig Von Mises Inst. Free Market Award 1985, Arleigh Burke Award 1998; numerous other awards; Grand Master of Order of Naval Merit (Brazil) 1974, Grand Officer of the Order of Orange Nassau, Netherlands 1985,. *Athletic achievements:* US Nat. Sculling Champion in Masters Div. 1979, won a world masters championship in rowing at the 1985 Toronto Masters Games. *Compositions:* has composed seven symphonies, an opera and numerous marches and concertos. *Publications:* Investment Policies of Fire and Casualty Insurance Companies. *Address:* 565 West Main Road, Little Compton, RI 02837, USA.

MIDDLETON, (John) Christopher, MA, DPhil; British academic; *David J. Bruton Centennial Professor Emeritus of Modern Languages, University of Texas;* b. 10 June 1926, Truro; s. of Hubert S. Middleton and Dorothy M. Miller; m. 1953 (divorced); one s. two d.; ed Felsted School and Merton Coll. Oxford; Lektor in English, Univ. of Zürich 1952–55; Asst Lecturer in German, King's Coll. Univ. of London 1955–57, Lecturer 1957–66; Prof. of Germanic Languages and Literature Univ. of Texas 1966–98, David J. Bruton Centennial Emer. Prof. 1998–; Sir Geoffrey Faber Memorial Prize 1964, Guggenheim Poetry Fellowship 1974–75, Nat. Endowment for Humanities Poetry Fellowship 1980, Tieck-Schlegel Trans Prize 1985, Max Geilinger Stiftung Prize 1987, Soeurette Diehl Fraser Award for Trans, Texas Inst. of Letters 1993, Camargo Foundation Fellow 1999, American Acad. Berlin Fellow 2001, American Acad. of Arts and Letters Award for Literature 2012. *Publications:* Torse 3, poems 1948–61 1962, Nonsequences/Selfpoems 1965, Our Flowers and Nice Bones 1969, The Lonely Suppers of W.V. Balloon 1975, Carminalenia 1980, 111 Poems 1983, Two-Horse Wagon Going By 1986, Selected Writings 1989, The Balcony Tree 1992, Some Dogs 1993, Andalusian Poems 1993, Intimate Chronicles 1996, The Swallow Diver 1997, Twenty Tropes for Doctor Dark 2000, The Word Pavilion and Selected Poems 2001, Of the Mortal Fire 2003, The Anti-Basilisk 2005, The Tenor on Horseback 2007, Collected Poems 2008, Poems 2006–2009 2010, A Company of Ghosts 2011, Just Look at the Dancers 2012; prose: Pataxanadu and Other Prose 1977, Serpentine 1985, In the Mirror of the Eighth King 1999, Crypto-Topographia 2002, Depictions of Blaff 2010; trans: Ohne Hass und Fahne (with W. Deppe and H. Schönherr) 1958, Modern German Poetry 1910–60 (with M. Hamburger) 1962, Germany Writing Today 1967, Selected Poems, by Georg Trakl 1968, Selected Letters, by Friedrich Nietzsche 1969, Selected Poems, by Friedrich Hölderlin and Eduard Mörike 1972, Selected Poems of Goethe 1983, Selected Stories, by Robert Walser 1983, Andalusian Poems (with Leticia Garza-Falcón) 1993, Faint Harps and Silver Voices: Selected Translations 2000; essays and other writings. *Address:* The Summit, Apt 432, Austin, TX 78746 (home); Department of Germanic Studies, University of Texas, Austin, TX 78712, USA (office). *Telephone:* (512) 471-4123 (office); (512) 479-8569 (home). *Website:* www.utexas.edu/depts/german/faculty/middleton.html (office).

MIDDLETON, Sir Peter Edward, Kt, GCB, BA; British business executive and fmr civil servant; *Chancellor, University of Sheffield;* b. 23 April 1934; s. of Thomas Edward Middleton; m. 1st Valerie Ann Lindup 1964 (died 1987); one s. (deceased) one d.; m. 2nd Connie Owen 1990; ed Sheffield City Grammar School, Univs of Sheffield and Bristol; Sr Information Officer, HM Treasury 1962, Prin. 1964, Asst Dir, Centre for Admin. Studies 1967–69, Pvt. Sec. to Chancellor of Exchequer 1969–72, Treasury Press Sec. 1972–75, Head, Monetary Policy Div. 1975, Under-Sec. 1976, Deputy Sec. 1980–83, Perm. Sec. 1983–91; Deputy Chair., Barclays Group 1991–98, Chair. 1999–2004, Chair., BZW Div. 1991–98; Chair., Sheffield Urban Regeneration Co. Ltd 2001–06; mem. Council Univ. of Sheffield 1991–, Pro-Chancellor 1997–99, Chancellor 1999–; mem. Bd United Utilities Group PLC 1994–2007, Vice-Chair. 1998–99, Chair. 1999–2000, Deputy Chair. 2000–07; non-exec. mem. Bd Bass PLC/Six Continents 1992–2001, Dir 1992–2001, General Accident Fire and Life Assurance Corpn PLC (now CGU PLC) 1992–98; Chair., Camelot Group plc 2004–10; Chair., Marsh & McLennan UK 2005–; Chair., Reyniers & Co.; Sr Adviser, Fenchurch Advisory Pnrs 2005–; mem. Council Manchester Business School 1985–92; Gov. London Business School 1984–90, Ditchley Foundation 1985–; mem. Nat. Econ. Research Asscn 1991–2008; Chair. Inst. of Contemporary History 1993–2001, Dir 2001–; Chair. Centre for Effective Dispute Resolution 2004–; Pres. British Bankers' Asscn 2004–06; mem. Financial Reporting Council 1997–98; Dir Int. Monetary Conf. 2001–02; Vice-Chair. Bankers Benevolent Fund 2005–; Chair. Creative Sheffield 2006–; Chair. Bridge Int. Trust 2008–; Chair. Burford Advisors LLP 2008–; Chair. European Asscn for Banking & Financial History 2008; Visiting Fellow, Nuffield Coll., Oxford 1981–89; Hon. LittD (Sheffield) 1984. *Leisure interests:* music, walking, outdoor sports. *Address:* Office of the Chancellor, University of Sheffield, Western Bank, Sheffield, S10 2TN, England (office). *Telephone:* (114) 222-2000 (office). *Website:* www.sheffield.ac.uk (office).

MIDLER, Bette; American singer, entertainer and actress; b. 1 Dec. 1945, Honolulu, Hawaii; m. Martin von Haselberg 1984; one d.; ed Univ. of Hawaii; début as actress in film Hawaii 1965; mem. of cast in Fiddler on the Roof, New York 1966–69, Salvation, New York 1970, Tommy, Seattle Opera Co. 1971; night-club concert performer 1972–; After Dark Ruby Award 1973, Grammy Award 1973, Special Tony Award 1973, Emmy Award 1978. *Film appearances include:* The Rose (two Golden Globe Awards) 1979, Jinxed 1982, Down and Out in Beverly Hills 1986, Ruthless People 1986, Outrageous Fortune 1987, Big Business 1988, Beaches 1989, Stella 1990, For The Boys (Golden Globe Award) 1991, Hocus Pocus 1993, Gypsy (TV), The First Wives Club 1996, That Old Feeling 1997, Get Bruce 1999, Isn't She Great? 1999, Drowning Mona 2000, What Women Want 2001, Stepford Wives 2004, Then She Found Me 2007, The Women 2008, Parental Guidance 2012. *Recordings include:* The Divine Miss M. 1973, Bette Midler 1973, Broken Blossom 1977, Live at Last 1977, Thighs and Whispers 1979, New Depression 1979, Divine Madness 1980, No Frills 1984, Some People's Lives 1991, Best Of 1993, Bette of Roses 1995, Experience the Divine 1997, Bathhouse Betty 1998, From a Distance 1998, Bette 2000, Bette Midler Sings the Rosemary Clooney Songbook 2003, Bette Midler Sings the Peggy Lee Songbook 2005, Cool Yule 2006, Memories of You 2010. *Television includes:* The Tonight Show (Emmy Award) 1992, Gypsy 1993, Seinfeld 1996, Diva Las Vegas 1997, Murphy Brown 1998. *Publications include:* A View From A Broad 1980, The Saga of Baby Divine 1983. *Address:* c/o Creative Artists Agency, 2000 Avenue of the Stars, Los Angeles, CA 90067, USA (office). *Website:* www.bettemidler.com.

MIDORI, MSc; Japanese violinist and academic; *Jascha Heifetz Chair in Violin, University of Southern California;* b. (Midori Goto), 25 Oct. 1971, Osaka; d. of Setsu Goto; ed Professional Children's School, Juilliard School of Music, New York Univ.; began violin studies with mother aged four; moved to USA 1982; debut with New York Philharmonic 1982; recording debut 1986 aged 14; now makes worldwide concert appearances; Founder and Pres. Midori and Friends (foundation) 1992; faculty mem., Manhattan School of Music 2001–06; Jascha Heifetz

Chair in Violin, Univ. of Southern California 2006–; Dorothy B. Chandler Performing Arts Award, New York State Asian-American Heritage Month Award, Crystal Award (Japan), Suntory Award 1994, Kennedy Center Gold Medal in the Arts 2010. *Leisure interests:* cooking, reading, listening to music, art. *Address:* c/o Intermusica Artists Management Ltd, Crystal Wharf, 36 Graham Street, London, N1 8GJ, England (office); c/o Opus 3 Artists, 470 Park Avenue South, 9th Floor North, New York, NY 10016, USA (office); c/o Midori and Friends, 352 Seventh Avenue, Suite 301, New York, NY 10009, USA (office). *Telephone:* (20) 7608-9900 (office); (212) 584-7500 (office). *Fax:* (20) 7490-3263 (office); (646) 300-8200 (office). *E-mail:* mail@intermusica.co.uk (office); info@opus3artists.com (office); violin@gotomidori.com (office). *Website:* www.intermusica.co.uk (office); www.opus3artists.com (office); www.gotomidori.com; www.midoriandfriends.org.

MIDWINTER, John Edwin, OBE, BSc (Hons), PhD, DSc, FRS, FREng, FIET, FIEEE, FInstP; British professor of optoelectronics (retd); *Pender Professor Emeritus, University College London;* b. 8 March 1938, Newbury, Berks., England; s. of the late H. C. Midwinter and of V. J. Midwinter (née Rawlinson); m. Maureen A. Holt 1961; two s. two d.; ed King's Coll., London; Sr Scientific Officer, Royal Radar Establishment 1967–68; Sr Research Physicist, Perkin-Elmer Corpn, USA 1968–70; Head, Fibre Optic Devt, British Telecom Research Labs 1971–77, Head Optical Communications Technology 1977–84; British Telecom Prof. of Optoelectronics, Univ. Coll. London 1984–91, Head, Dept of Electronic and Electrical Eng 1988–98, Pender Prof. of Electronic Eng 1991–2004, Prof. Emer. 2004–, Vice-Provost 1994–99, Dir Univ. Coll. London Adastral Park Campus 2000–03; Vice-Pres. IEE 1994, Deputy Pres. 1998–2000, Pres. 2000–01; Dir Young Engineers 2004–05; Fellow, Inst. of Eng and Tech.; Hon. DSc (Nottingham) 2000, (Loughborough) 2001, (Queen's Univ. Belfast) 2004; IEE J.J. Thompson Medal 1987, Faraday Medal 1997, IEEE Eric Sumner Award and Medal 2002. *Publications:* Applied Non-Linear Optics 1972, Optical Fibers for Transmission 1977; more than 200 papers on lasers, non-linear optics and optical communications. *Leisure interests:* walking, skiing, writing, climate change, renewable energy.

MIELI, Paolo; Italian journalist; *Director, Corriere della Sera;* b. 25 Feb. 1949, Milan; two s.; ed classical lycée, La Sapienza Univ., Rome; Asst to Chair of History of Political Parties, Univ. of Rome; Corresp., Political Commentator at Home, Head of Cultural Desk and then Cen. Man. Ed., Espresso (weekly) 1967–85; worked for La Repubblica 1985–86; Leader Writer, La Stampa 1986–90, Ed.-in-Chief 1990–92; Ed. Corriere della Sera 1992–97, Dir 2004–; apptd Pres. RAI (Radiotelevisione Italiana) March 2003 (resgnd after five days); Prof. of Contemporary History, Univ. of Milan; mem. Bd Govs Storia Illustrata, Pagina and has collaborated with Tempi Moderni, Questi Istituzioni, Mondo operaio; Premio Spoleto 1990, Premio Mediterraneo 1991, Premio Alfio Russo 1995. *Publications include:* Litigo a Sinistra, Il Socialismo Diviso, Storia del Partito Socialista Negli Anni della Repubblica, Le Storie – La Storia 1999, Storia e Politica: Risorgimento, fascismo e comunismo 2001, La goccia cinese 2002. *Leisure interests:* ancient history, skiing. *Address:* Via Medaglie d'Oro 391, 00136 Rome (home); Corriere della Sera, Via Solferino 28, 20121 Milan, Italy (office). *Telephone:* (02) 2827979 (office). *Fax:* (02) 29009705 (office). *E-mail:* pmieli@corriere.it (office).

MIERS, Sir David, Kt, KBE, CMG, MA; British diplomatist (retd); b. 10 Jan. 1937, Liverpool, England; s. of the late Col R. Miers, DSO and Honor Bucknill; m. Imelda Wouters 1966; two s. one d.; ed Winchester Coll. and Univ. Coll., Oxford; joined diplomatic service 1961, served in Tokyo 1963, Vientiane 1966, Paris 1972, Tehran 1977, Amb. to Lebanon 1983–85, Asst Under-Sec. FCO 1986, Amb. to Greece 1989–93, to Netherlands 1993–96; Chair. Soc. of Pension Consultants 1998–2007, British Lebanese Asscn 1999–2011, The Anglo-Hellenic League 1999–; British Lebanese Asscn Lecturer, The Royal Thames Yacht Club 2012. *Leisure interest:* open air. *Address:* The Anglo-Hellenic League, The Hellenic Centre, 16–18 Paddington Street, London, W1U 5AS, England. *Telephone:* (20) 7486-9410 (voicemail). *E-mail:* info@anglohellenicleague.org. *Website:* www.anglohellenicleague.org.

MIFSUD BONNICI, Carmelo (Carm), LLD; Maltese lawyer, politician and academic; b. 17 Feb. 1960, Floriana; s. of fmr Pres. Ugo Mifsud Bonnici; m. Sandra Gatt; three s.; ed St Aloysius' Coll., Birkirkara, De La Salle Coll., Cottonera, Univ. of Malta; practised in criminal, civil and commercial fields; Sr Lecturer in Roman Law, Univ. of Malta; Pres. MKSU as univ. student; active in Partit Nazzjonalista (Nationalist Party) Youth Movt (MZPN) 1982–, held several posts in Exec.; mem. Parl. 1998–2013, perm. mem. several cttees, including Privileges and Laws; mem. Malta Environment and Planning Authority 2001–03; Parl. Sec., Ministry for Justice and Home Affairs 2003–08; apptd Minister for Justice and Home Affairs 2008; Minister for Home and Parliamentary Affairs Jan.–May 2012. *Publications:* Zewg Minuti Flimkien 1998, Il-Principji Hemm Jibqghu 2003, Sens u Sustanza 2008, Il-Politika tas-Sewwa 2013. *Address:* Partit Nazzjonalista, Herbert Ganado Street, Pietà 1541, Malta (office). *Telephone:* 21243641 (office). *Fax:* 21243640 (office). *E-mail:* admin@pn.org.mt (office). *Website:* www.pn.org.mt (office).

MIFSUD BONNICI, Ugo Enrico, BA, LLD; Maltese politician, lawyer and fmr head of state; b. 8 Nov. 1932, Cospicua; s. of Carmelo Mifsud Bonnici and Maria Mifsud Bonnici (née Ross); m. Gemma Bianco; two s. one d.; ed Royal Univ. of Malta; practising lawyer 1955–87; mem. Parl. 1966–94; Opposition Spokesman for Educ. 1972–87; Pres. Gen. Council and Admin. Council of Nationalist Party 1977–87; Minister of Educ. 1987, of Educ. and Interior 1990–92, of Educ. and Human Resources 1992–94; Pres. of Malta 1994–99; currently Lecturer on History of Law and Human Rights, Univ. of Malta, also Lecturer on Comparative Law, International Maritime Law Inst.; Chair. Cttee of Guarantee under the Law for the Protection of the Cultural Heritage; mem. Council of Europe Comm. for Democracy Through Law (Venice Comm.) 2002–; Hon. DLitt (Univ. of Malta) 1995, (Univ. of Paris IV) 1998. *Publications include:* Biex il-futur jerga' jibda 1976, Il-linja t-tajba 1981, Biex il-futur rega beda 1992, Il-Manwal tal-President 1997, Kif Sirna Republika 1999, Introduction to Comparative Law 2004, An Introduction to Cultural Heritage Law 2008, Il-Gross: Il-Kontribut Letterarju (ed) 2012, An Introduction to Education Law 2014; numerous newspaper articles. *Address:* 18 Erin Serracino Inglott Road, Cospicua, Malta (home). *Telephone:* 826975 (home). *E-mail:* ugomb@maltanet.net.

MIGAŠ, Jozef, DPhil, CSc; Slovak politician; b. 7 Jan. 1954, Pušovce; m. Alena Migašová; one s. one d.; ed Univ. of Kiev; fmrly with Acad. of Sciences, Košice,

Political Univ., Bratislava; f. Party of the Democratic Left, Chair. 1996–2001; diplomatist 1993–96; Chair. Nat. Council of the Slovak Repub. 1998–2002. *Address:* c/o National Council of the Slovak Republic, na'meste A. Dubčeka 1, 812 80 Bratislava (office); c/o Office of the Government of the Slovak Republic, nám. Slobody 1, 813 70 Bratislava 1, Slovakia. *Telephone:* (7) 593-41-201 (office); (7) 593-41-111. *Fax:* (7) 544-15-460 (office). *E-mail:* migajoze@nrsr.sk (office). *Website:* www.nrsr.sk (office).

MIGIRO, Asha-Rose Mtengeti, LLB, LLM, PhD; Tanzanian lawyer, politician, academic and UN official; b. 9 July 1956, Songea; m. Cleophas Migiro; two d.; ed Univ. of Dar-es-Salaam, Univ. of Konstanz, Germany; Head, Dept of Constitutional and Admin. Law, Univ. of Dar-es-Salaam 1992–94, fmr Sr Lecturer, Faculty of Law; mem. Parl. (Chama Cha Mapinduzi party) 1994–2000; mem. Regional Exec. Council 2000–05; Minister of Community Devt, Gender and Children's Affairs 2000–06, of Foreign Affairs and Int. Co-operation 2006–07; Deputy Sec.-Gen. UN 2007–12; Sec. for Politics and Foreign Relations, Chama Cha Mapinduzi party 2012–; Special Envoy of the Sec.-Gen. for HIV/AIDS in Africa, UN 2012–; mem. Advisory Bd UN Fund for Int. Partnerships; mem. UN Cttee on Elimination of Discrimination against Women. *Address:* Chama Cha Mapinduzi, Kuu St, POB 50, Dodoma, Tanzania (office). *Telephone:* 2180575 (office). *E-mail:* katibumkuu@ccmtz.org (office). *Website:* www.ccmtz.org (office).

MIGNON, Emmanuelle; French civil servant; b. 1968; ed École supérieure des sciences économiques et commerciales, Institut d'études politiques de Paris, École nationale d'administration; OSCE electoral observer, Bosnia and Herzegovina 1997; adviser to Minister of the Interior, Nicolas Sarkozy 2002–04; Educ. Dir, Union pour un Mouvement Populaire (UMP) 2004–06; Chief of Staff, Office of the Pres. 2007–08; French Rep. to Andorra 2007–08; adviser to the Pres. 2008–; Pres., Chambord Admin. Council 2007–; Nat. Commr, Scouts Unitaires de France 1990–; Gen. Sec. Strategy, Devt, Legal and Human Resources, EuropaCorp 2010–. *Address:* Élysée Palace, 55 rue du faubourg Saint-Honoré, 75008 Paris (office); EuropaCorp, 137 rue du Faubourg Saint-Honoré 75008 Paris, France (office). *Telephone:* 1-53-83-03-03 (EuropaCorp) (office); 1-42-92-81-00 (Elysée Palace) (office). *Fax:* 1-53-83-03-04 (EuropaCorp) (office). *E-mail:* emignon@u-m-p.org (office); contact@europacorp.com (office). *Website:* www.elysee.fr (office); www.europacorp.com (office).

MIGRANYAN, Andranik Movsesovich, MA, PhD; Russian/Armenian academic; *Director, Institute for Democracy and Cooperation;* b. 10 Feb. 1949, Yerevan; m.; one d.; ed Moscow State Inst. of Int. Relations, Inst. of Int. Workers' Movt USSR Acad. of Sciences; Prof., Moscow Inst. of Automobile Construction 1976–85; leading researcher, Inst. of Econ. and Political Studies Acad. of Sciences 1985–88; Head Cen. for Studies of Social-Political Problems and Interstate Relations of CIS 1992–93; mem. Pres.'s Council 1993–2000; Chief Expert Cttee on CIS countries of State Duma 1993–96; Chair. Bd Scientific Council on CIS Countries; Prof., Moscow State Inst. of Int. Relations (MGIMO) 1991–; Dir Inst. for Democracy and Cooperation, New York 2008–; co-f. Politika Fund; Vice-Pres. Reforma Fund 1994–2003; First Vice-Pres., Soglasie Fund 2004–; mem. Public Chamber of Russian Fed. 2005–. *Publications include:* Democracy and Morality 1989, Russia in Search for Identity 1997, Russia: From Chaos to Order? 2001; numerous book chapters and articles in newspapers and journals. *Address:* Institute for Democracy and Cooperation, 655 Third Avenue, Suite 2010, New York, NY 10017, USA (office). *Telephone:* (212) 922-0030 (office). *Fax:* (212) 922-1555 (office). *E-mail:* info@indemco.org (office). *Website:* www.indemco.org (office).

MIHAJLOVIĆ, Svetozar; Bosnia and Herzegovina politician; fmr Vice-Pres. of Serb Repub. of Bosnia and Herzegovina; co-Prime Minister of Bosnia and Herzegovina 1999–2000; Minister for Civil Affairs and Communications 2001–03. *Address:* c/o Ministry for Civil Affairs and Communications, Vojvode Putnika 3, 71000 Sarajevo, Bosnia and Herzegovina (office).

MIHÓCZA, Brig.-Gen. Zoltán, BA, MA; Hungarian military officer and diplomatist; b. 18 March 1963, Budapest; m. Erzsébet Bencze; one d.; ed Military Univ., Minsk, Byelorussian SSR, USSR, ADA Officers Advanced Course, El Paso, Texas and War Coll., Montgomery, Ala, USA; radio tech. engineer 1980–86; Deputy Commdr 11/7th Air Defence Bn (SA-2) 1986–89; Commdr Maintenance Co., 11th Air Defence Brigade 1989–92, Chief of Maintenance Service 1992–94, Chief of Missile Service 1995–96, Chief of Mil. Tech. 1997; Sr Officer, Meteorological Office, Hungarian Defence Force 1998; Sr Officer, Modernization Man. Office, J5 Defence Staff, Ministry of Defence 1999, 2002–03; Sr Officer, Logistics Br., J1/4 NATO HQ, JCS, Verona, Italy 1999–2002; MA Chief for Integration Defence Staff, Ministry of Defence 2003–04, MA Dir of Defence Staff 2005, Chief of NATO and Doctrines Br., Mil. Planning Directorate, Defence Staff 2005–06, Deputy Head of Operations and Training Dept 2006, Head of Force Planning Dept 2010–11; Mil. Rep. to NATO and EU, Brussels 2011–13; rank of 2nd Lt-Gen. 1986, 1st Lt-Gen. 1988, Capt. 1993, Maj. 1996, Lt-Col 2002, Col 2005, Brig.-Gen. 2010; Meritorious Service Medals Bronze and Gold, Distinguished Service Medals Third (10 years), 2nd (20 years) and 1st (30 years), NATO Meritorious Service Medal, NATO Kosovo Medal, Medal for Peacekeeping. *Address:* Ministry of Foreign Affairs, 1027 Budapest, Bem rakpart 47, Hungary (office). *Telephone:* (1) 458-1000 (office). *Fax:* (1) 212-5918 (office). *E-mail:* kozkapcsolat@kum.gov.hu (office). *Website:* www.kormany.hu/hu/kulugyminiszterium (office).

MIHÓK, Peter, PhD; Slovak business administrator and fmr diplomatist; *President, Slovak Chamber of Commerce and Industry (CCI);* b. 18 Jan. 1948, Topolčianky; s. of Augustin Mihók and Johanna Mihóková; m. Elena Skulová 1971; two d.; ed Econ. Univ., Bratislava; with Czechoslovak Chamber of Commerce 1971–78; Commercial Counsellor, Embassy, Morocco 1978–82; Dir Foreign Relations Dept; Incheba (Foreign Trade Co.) 1982–90; Dir Foreign Dept, Office of Govt of Slovakia 1990–91; Vice-Pres. Czechoslovak Chamber of Commerce and Industry (CCI) 1991–92; Dir Int. Politics Dept, Ministry of Foreign Affairs of Slovakia 1991; Plenipotentiary of Govt of Slovakia in EU, Head Negotiator in Brussels 1991–94; Pres. Slovak CCI 1992–; Vice-Chair. Supervisory Bd Heineken Slovakia 1998–; Globtel Orange Bratislava 2001–; Vice-Chair. World Chamber Fed. Paris 2001–; Pres. Ecosoc Slovakia 2000–; Deputy Pres. Eurochambers 2001–; mem. Supervisory Bd Incheba a.s. Bratislava 1999–, Chair. 2004–; mem. Presidency, European Econ. and Social Cttee, Brussels 2004–; mem. Advisory Body to Pres. of Slovakia; mem. Econ. Council of Govt of Slovakia, Chair. Govt

Pricing Cttee; mem. Council Slovak Electricity Works; Vice-Chair. Omnia Group, Kooperativa; mem. Scientific Council, Econ. Univ. Bratislava; Gold Medal of Hungarian CCI 1999, Officer, Order of Léopold II, Belgium 1995, Officier Ordre du Mérite, France 1996, Prominent of Economy, Slovakia 1997, Great Silver Order, Austria 1998, Commendatore Ordine, Stella della Solidarita Italiana 2003, Gold Medal, House of Europe 2003. *Publication:* Advertising in the Market Economy. *Leisure interests:* literature, philately, swimming. *Address:* Slovak Chamber of Commerce and Industry, Gorkého 9, 816 03 Bratislava, Slovakia (office). *Telephone:* (2) 5443-3291 (office). *Fax:* (2) 5413-1159 (office). *E-mail:* predseda@ scci.sk (office). *Website:* www.scci.sk (office).

MIHOV, Gen. Miho, MA; Bulgarian air force officer (retd) and fmr diplomatist; b. 1 Feb. 1949, Sennik; s. of Dimitar Mihov and Stanka Mihov; m. 1973; one s. one d.; ed Benkovski Air Force Acad., Dolna Mitropolia, Rakovski Nat. War Coll., Sofia, Gen. Staff Coll., Moscow, USAF Special Operations School; Training Flight Air Unit Deputy Commdr/Instructor; Air Squadron Deputy Commdr, Commdr, Air Regt, Deputy Commdr, Commdr; Air Corps Deputy Commdr; Air Defence Div. Commdr, Air Force Commdr; Chief of Gen. Staff of Bulgarian Armed Forces 1997–2002; Adviser to Pres. of Bulgaria 2002; Amb. to Macedonia 2005–09; Order of Merit and Valour, Medal for Service to the Bulgarian Armed Forces, Medal for the 40th Anniversary of the Victory over Hitler and Fascism, Medals and Orders of Distinguished Service, Order of Merit of Aviation (presented by King of Spain), Order presented by King of Sweden, Order presented by Pres. of Repub. of Bulgaria, Legion of Merit (USA). *Leisure interests:* hunting, skiing. *Address:* 18 T. Teznovski str., Sofia, Bulgaria (home). *Telephone:* (2) 963-01-81 (home). *E-mail:* mivanova@antimgroup.com (office). *Website:* http:/teremgb.bg/terem (office).

MIIKE, Takashi; Japanese film director and actor; b. 24 Aug. 1960, Yao, Osaka; ed Yokohama Film School; worked in TV for a decade before becoming Asst Dir to Shohei Imamura; directed first theatrically distributed film Shinjuku Triad Society 1995; int. debut with Audition 2000. *Films:* Toppuu! Minipato tai – Aikyacchi Jankushon (video) 1991, Red Hunter: Prelude to Kill (video) 1991, Ningen kyôki: Ai to ikari no ringu (video) 1992, Bodyguard Kiba (video) 1993, Oretachi wa tenshi ja nai (video) 1993, Oretachi wa tenshi ja nai 2 (video) 1993, Shinjuku autoroo (video) 1994, Bodyguard Kiba: Combat Apocalypse (video) 1994, The Third Gangster (video) 1995, Bodyguard Kiba: Combat Apocalypse 2 (video) 1995, Naniwa yuukyôden (video) 1995, Shinjuku kuroshakai: Chaina mafia sensô 1995, Shin daisan no gokudô – boppatsu Kansai gokudô sensô (video) 1996, Shin daisan no gokudô II (video) 1996, Jingi naki yabô (video) 1996, Rakkasei: Piinattsu (video) 1996, Kenka no hanamichi: Oosaka saikyô densetsu (video) 1996, Fudoh: The New Generation 1996, Young Thugs: Innocent Blood 1997, Jingi naki yabô 2 (video) 1997, Rainy Dog 1997, Full Metal gokudô (video) 1997, The Bird People in China 1998, Andromedia 1998, Blues Harp 1998, Kishiwada shônen gurentai: Bôkyô 1998, Nihon kuroshakai 1999, Silver – shirubaa (video) 1999, Audition 1999, Dead or Alive 1999, Sarariiman Kintarô 1999, The City of Lost Souls 2000, The Guys from Paradise 2000, Dead or Alive 2: Tôbôsha 2000, Tsukamoto Shin'ya ga Ranpo suru (video short documentary) 2000, Family 2001, Visitor Q (video) 2001, Ichi the Killer 2001, Agitator (also actor) 2001, The Happiness of the Katakuris 2001, Kikuchi-jô monogatari – sakimori-tachi no uta 2001, Zuiketsu gensô – Tonkararin yume densetsu 2001, Dead or Alive: Final 2002, Onna kunishuu ikki 2002, Shin Jingi no Hakaba (also actor) 2002, Shangri-La 2002, Pandoora (video) 2002, Deadly Outlaw: Rekka 2002, The Man in White 2003, Gozu 2003, Kikoku (video) 2003, One Missed Call 2003, The Man in White Part 2: Requiem for the Lion 2003, Zebraman 2004, Three… Extremes (segment 'Box') 2004, Izo 2004, Demon Pond (video) 2005, The Great Yokai War 2005, Big Bang Love, Juvenile A 2006, Waru 2006, Waru: kanketsu-hen (video) 2006, Sun Scarred 2006, Like a Dragon 2007, Sukiyaki Western Django 2007, Detective Story 2007, Crows Zero 2007, God's Puzzle 2008, Yatterman 2009, Crows Zero II 2009, Zebraman 2: Attack on Zebra City 2010, 13 Assassins 2010, Hara-Kiri: Death of a Samurai 2011, Ninja Kids!!! 2011, Ace Attorney 2012, For Love's Sake 2012, Lesson of the Evil 2012, Shield of Straw 2013, The Mole Song: Undercover Agent Reiji 2013, Kuime 2014. *Television:* Last Run: 100 Million Ten's Worth of Love & Betrayal (film) 1992, Tennen shôjo Man (mini-series) 1999, Tennen shôjo Man Next: Yokohama hyaku-ya hen (film) 1999, Multiple Personality Detective Psycho – Kazuhiko Amamiya Returns (mini-series) 2000, Sabu (film) 2002, Paato-taimu tantei (film) 2002, Negotiator (film) 2003, Paato-taimu tantei 2 (film) 2004, Ultraman Max (series) (multiple episodes) 2005, Masters of Horror (series, one episode) – Imprint (2006), Kêtai sôsakan 7 (series, one episode) – Ketai aruku!?/ Tsunagaru kizuna 2008, Q.P. (series, one episode) – Episode 1.1 2011.

MIKATI, Najib Azmi, MBA; Lebanese business executive and politician; b. 24 Nov. 1955, Tripoli; m.; three c.; ed American Univ. of Beirut, Harvard Univ., USA, Institut Européen d'Admin des Affaires (INSEAD), France; co-f. Investcom (telecommunications co.) with brother 1982; Minister of Public Works and Transport 1998–2000; mem. Majlis al-Nuab (Nat. Ass.) for Tripoli 2000–; Prime Minister April–July 2005, 2011–13 (resgnd); mem. Bd of Trustees American Univ. of Beirut; mem. Advisory Bd Harris School, Univ. of Chicago. *Address:* c/o Office of the President of the Council of Ministers, Grand Sérail, place Riad el-Solh, Beirut, Lebanon. *E-mail:* info@najib-mikati.net. *Website:* www.najib-mikati.net.

MIKEREVIĆ, Dragan, PhD, DSc; Bosnia and Herzegovina politician; b. 12 Feb. 1955, Doboj; m.; two c.; ed Univ. of Novi Sad; fmr Chief of Finance Dept, Municipality of Doboj, later Pres. Municipality Ass.; fmr Financial Dir Health Assurance Bureau, Republika Srpska; fmr Prof. of Econs, Univ. of Banja Luka, later Man. and mem. of research teams, Inst. for Economy, Univ. of Banja Luka; mem. Party of Democratic Progress 1999–, fmr Vice-Pres.; Chair. Council of Ministers (Prime Minister) of Bosnia and Herzegovina 2002, Minister for European Integration 2001–02; Prime Minister of Serb Repub. (Republika Srpska) of Bosnia and Herzegovina 2003–04 (resgnd). *Address:* c/o Party of Democratic Progress of Republika Srpska (Partija Demokratskog Progresa Republike Srpske), 78000 Banja Luka, ul. Prvog Krajiškog Korpusa 130, Bosnia and Herzegovina.

MIKHAILOV, Felix Trofimovich; Russian philosopher; b. 12 April 1930, Chimkent, Kazakhstan; ed Moscow State Univ.; researcher, Head of Chair 2nd Pirogov Moscow Inst. of Med. (now Russian State Med. Univ.) 1957–72; Head of Lab. Research Inst. of Methods of Teaching, USSR (now Russian) Acad. of Pedagogical Sciences 1972–74, Head of Lab. Research Inst. of Gen. and Pedagogical Psychology 1974–84; Chief Researcher, Head of Sector Inst. of

Philosophy, USSR (now Russian) Acad. of Sciences 1994–; visiting reader univs in USA, UK, Canada; mem. Russian Acad. of Educ. *Publications:* numerous books, papers and articles on problems of human self-consciousness, including The Mystery of Humans. *Address:* Institute of Philosophy, Russian Academy of Sciences (IF RAN), Volkhonka str. 14m building 5, 119842 Moscow, Russia (office). *Telephone:* (495) 203-91-09 (office).

MIKHAILOV, Nikolai Vasilyevich, DPhil; Russian politician; b. 14 May 1937, Sevsk, Bryansk Region; son of Vasiliy Mikhailov, Lyubov Mikhailova; m.; one s.; ed Moscow Bauman Higher School of Tech.; with defence industry enterprises 1961–96; Dir-Gen., Vympel Co. 1986–96; Deputy Sec. Security Council of Russian Fed. 1996–97; State Sec., First Deputy Minister of Defence of Russian Fed. 1997–2000; Co-Chair. Russian-American Comm. on Econ. and Tech. Co-operation 1998; Adviser to Chair. Bd of Dirs AFC Systema Co. 2001–13; adviser to Dir Gen. of Innovation Devt, Radiotechnical Inst. 2013–; USSR State Prize, State Prize of Russian Fed. 1997. *Publications:* (titles in trans.) Global World and Global Problems: Science and Labour in a Modern World; Military Defence Complex: Analyses and Challenges; Science and Knowledge: From Modern Times to the Future. *Leisure interests:* sports, music, classic literature. *Address:* 123060 Moscow, Raspletina str. 39, bied 14 (home); 127083 Moscow, 10, bild1, 8 Marta str. (office); Systema Financial Corporation, 103009 Moscow, Leont'yevsky per. 10, Russian Federation (office). *Telephone:* (495) 614-03-41 (office); (495) 598-04-34 (home); (495) 105-44-21 (home). *Fax:* (495) 614-38-22 (office). *E-mail:* nmikhailov@ sistema.ru (office), nmikhailov@mtu-net.ru (home). *Website:* www.sistema.ru (office); www.oaorti.ru (office).

MIKHAILOV, Viktor Nikitovich, DTechSc; Russian physicist and politician; *Director, Institute of Strategic Stability;* b. 12 Feb. 1934, Sopronovo, Moscow Region; m.; one s.; ed Moscow Inst. of Physics and Eng; on staff All-Union Research Inst., Arsamas; worked with group of nuclear bomb constructors; f. Scientific School of Explosive Nuclear Fission; Prof., Deputy, First Deputy Minister of Machine Construction of USSR (later USSR Ministry of Atomic Energy) 1988–1992; Minister of Atomic Energy Russian Fed. 1992–98; Scientific Leader Russian Fed. Nuclear Centre, VNII of Experimental Physics 1992–; Dir Inst. of Strategic Stability 1999–; Chair. Scientific Council 1998–; fmr mem. Security Council of Russia; mem. Russian Acad. of Sciences 1997–; Order of Honor 2005; Lenin Prize 1967, USSR State Prize 1992, Russian Fed. State Prize 1997. *Publication:* more than 200 works on nuclear energy problems. *Address:* ISS Minatom Russia, Luganskaya 9, 115304 Moscow, Russia (office). *Telephone:* (495) 321-35-47 (office); (495) 321-46-33 (office). *Fax:* (495) 321-40-56 (office). *E-mail:* mikhailov@niiit.ru (office). *Website:* www.iss.niiit.ru (office).

MIKHAILOV, Vyacheslav Aleksandrovich, DrHist; Russian politician; b. 13 April 1938, Dubovka, Volgograd Region; m.; two d.; ed Lvov State Univ.; teacher, secondary school, Lecturer, Lvov State Univ.; Head of Sector, Inst. of Marxism-Leninism at CPSU Cen. Cttee 1987–90; Head, Div. of Nat. Policy, CPSU Cen. Cttee 1990–91; scientific consultant, I and World (magazine), Head, Centre on Int. Problems and Protection of Human Rights 1991–93; Prof., Moscow Inst. of Int. Relations (MGIMO) 1992–93, 1999–; Deputy Chair. State Cttee on Problems of Fed. and Nationality 1993–95; First Deputy Minister on Problems of Nationality and Regional Policy Jan.–July 1995, Minister 1995–98, 1999–2000; First Deputy Sec. Security Council 1998–99; Chair. Expert Council on Nat., Migration Policy and Interaction with Religious Asscns under the Plenipotentiary Rep. of the Russian Pres. in the Cen. Fed. Dist 2003. *Publications:* three monographs on nat. problems and numerous articles. *Address:* MGIMO, Vernadskogo Prosp. 76, 117454 Moscow, Russia (office). *Telephone:* (495) 206-43-26 (office).

MIKHALKOV, Nikita Sergeyevich; Russian film director; b. 21 Oct. 1945, Moscow; s. of Sergey Vladimirovich Mikhalkov and Natalia Petrovna Koncha-lovskaya; m. 1st Anastasya Vertinskaya 1966; m. 2nd Tatyana Mikhalkova 1973; two s. two d.; ed Shchukin Theatre School, State Film Inst. under Mikhail Romm; mem. State Duma 1995 (resgnd); First Sec. Russian Union of Cinematographers 1997–98, Chair. 1998–; Artistic Dir TRITE Studio; first worked as actor in films: Strolling Around Moscow, A Nest of Gentlefolk, The Red Tent; mem. Bd of Dirs Pervyi Kanal; Chevalier, Légion d'honneur; RSFSR People's Artist 1984, Felix Prize for Best European Film 1993, State Prize of Russian Fed., Honoured Artist of Russia, Special Lion for Overall Work, Venice Film Festival 2007 and several other awards. *Films directed:* A Quiet Day at the End of the War, At Home Among Strangers, A Stranger at Home 1975, The Slave of Love 1976, An Unfinished Piece for Mechanical Piano 1977, Five Evenings 1978, Several Days in the Life of I. I. Oblomov 1979, Kinsfolk 1982, Without Witnesses 1983, Dark Eyes 1987, Urga 1990 (Prize at Venice Biennale 1991), Anna from 6 to 18 1994, Burned by the Sun (Acad. Award for Best Foreign Film) 1994. *Film appearance:* Persona non grata 2005. *Play:* An Unfinished Piece for Mechanical Piano, Rome 1987. *Leisure interests:* sport, hunting. *Address:* Maly Kozikhinsky per. 4, Apt. 16–17, 103001 Moscow, Russia.

MIKHALKOV-KONCHALOVSKY, Andrey Sergeyevich; Russian film dir-ector and scriptwriter; b. 20 Aug. 1937, Moscow; s. of Sergey Mikhalkov and Natalia Konchalovskaya; m. 1st Natalia Arinbasarova 1946; m. 2nd Irina Ivanova 1960; one s. two d.; ed Moscow State Inst. of Cinema, Moscow 1961–65; worked in Hollywood 1979–93; RSFSR People's Artist 1980. *Films include:* Roller and Violin (with A. Tarkovsky) 1959, Malchik i golub (The Boy and the Pigeon) 1961, Ivanovo detstvo (Ivan's Childhood) (actor) 1962, Mne dvadtsat let (I am Twenty) (actor) 1964, Pervyy uchitel (The First Teacher) 1965, Istoriya Asi Klyachinoy, kotoraya lyubila, da ne vyshla zamuzh (The Story of Asya Klyachina, Who Loved but Did Not Marry) 1966, Dvoryanskoe gnezdo (A Nest of Gentlefolk) 1969, Dyadya Vanya (Uncle Vanya) 1971, Romans o vlyublyonnykh (Romance of Lovers) 1974, Siberiada 1979, Split Cherry Tree 1982, Maria's Lovers (also composer of song Maria's Eyes) 1984, Runaway Train 1985, Duet for One 1986, Shy People 1987, Homer and Eddie 1988, Tango and Cash 1989, The Inner Circle 1991, Kurochka Ryaba (Ryaba My Chicken) (also producer) 1994, Lumière et compagnie (Lumière and Company) 1996, Dom durakov (House of Fools) (also producer) 2002, Moscow Chill (producer) 2005; scriptwriter (with Tarkovsky) Andrei Rublev 1969; also opera dir and theatre dir (productions at La Scala, Bastille, Mariinski Theatre). *Television includes:* The Odyssey (Odissea) 1997, The Lion in Winter 2003. *Address:* Mosfilmovskaya str. 1, Russkaya Ruletka, 119858 Moscow (Studio);

Malaya Gruzinskaya 28, Apt 130, 123557 Moscow, Russia (home). *Telephone:* (495) 143-93-09 (Studio); (495) 253-50-21 (home). *Fax:* (495) 143-91-89.

MIKHEEV, Vladimir Andreyevich, DrPhysSc, FInstP, FIMechE; Ukrainian physicist and engineer; *Consultant Engineer, Oxford Instruments NanoScience Ltd;* b. 5 Aug. 1942; m. Tatiana Mikheeva 1969; one s. one d.; ed Kharkov Polytechnic; researcher 1964–86; discovery of quantum diffusion 1972–77; Head of Lab. of Ultralow Temperatures, Inst. for Low Temperature Physics and Eng, Ukrainian Acad. of Science 1986–; Visiting Prof., Royal Holloway and Bedford New Coll. 1992; Consultant Engineer, Tech. Devt, Oxford Instruments NasnoScience Ltd 1994–; Ed. Research Matters –2004; Lenin Prize for Science and Tech. *Publications:* more than 120 articles published worldwide. *Address:* Oxford Instruments NanoScience Ltd, Tubney Woods, Abingdon, Oxon., OX13 5QX (office); 35 Browning Drive, Bicester, Oxon., OX26 2XN, England (home). *Telephone:* (1865) 393200 (office). *Fax:* (1865) 393333 (office). *E-mail:* vladimir.mikheev@oxinst.co.uk (office). *Website:* www.oxford-instruments.com (office).

MIKHELSON, Leonid Viktorovich; Russian engineer, business executive and art collector; *Chairman of Executive Management Board and CEO, OAO Novatek;* b. 11 Aug. 1955, Kaspiysk, Repub. of Dagestan, Russian SFSR, USSR; m.; one d.; ed Kuibyshev Inst. of Civil Eng; began career as foreman at construction and assembling co. in Surgut, Tyumen region, promoted to Chief Engineer; Chief Engineer, Ryazantruborovodstroy trust 1985–87; replaced his father as Head of Kuybyshevtruboprovodstroy 1987, co. privatized 1991, then turned into jt stock co. Samara nat. enterprise, Nova, head of it until 1994; CEO and Gen. Dir OJSC Novafininvest man. co. 1994–2000, Chair. 2000–02; Chair. OJSC Pur-Land Oil & Gas Co. 1998–2001, Gen. Dir 2001–; CEO OJSC Nordpayps 1998–2001; Chair. OJSC Tarkosaleneftegaz 1998, OJSC Yurharovneftegaz 2001, NGK Itera 2002, PJSC Stroytransgaz –2010; Chair. Exec. Man. Bd and CEO OAO Novatek 2003–; mem. Bd of Dirs OJSC CB Solidarity 1995, OJSC Rosneftegazstroy 1997–2001, OJSC Selkup Oil Co. 1998–2001, OJSC Polar Star 1998–2001, OJSC Mangazeya 1998, OJSC Truboizolyatsiya 1998, ZAO NOVA Bank 2000, OJSC Minley 2001, PJSC Stroytransgaz 2008–; mem. Supervisory Bd OJSC Novokuibyshevsk Television 1999–2001; Stock and Exchange Bd mem. Interregional Oil-and-Gas Exchange (non-profit partnership) 2004; supporter of the arts in Russia through his co. OAO Novatek; Founder and Pres. Victoria the Art of Being Contemporary foundation 2009–; Znak Pochyota Order (Order of Honour). *Leisure interests:* volleyball, fan of Wings of Soviets soccer team. *Address:* OAO Novatek, 22A Pobedy Street, 629850 Tarko-Sale, Yamalo-Nenets Autonomous, Tyumenskaya Oblast (office); Victoria — The Art of Being Contemporary, Olsufievsky pereulok 8, Bld 2, Moscow, Russia. *Telephone:* (34997) 24951 (office); (495) 6431976. *Fax:* (34997) 24479 (office). *E-mail:* novatek@novatek.ru (office); v-a-c@v-a-c.ru. *Website:* www.novatek.ru (office); www.v-a-c.ru.

MIKI, Shigemitsu; Japanese financial executive; *Senior Advisor, Bank of Tokyo-Mitsubishi UFJ Limited;* b. 1935; joined Mitsubishi Bank Ltd 1958, Pres. and Co-CEO Mitsubishi Tokyo Financial Group Inc. (later became Mitsubishi UFJ Trust and Banking Corpn) 2001–02, Pres. and CEO 2002–04, Man. Dir Bank of Tokyo-Mitsubishi 1989–94, Sr Man. Dir 1994–97, Rep. Dir 1996–, Deputy Pres. Bank of Tokyo-Mitsubishi UFJ Ltd 1997–2000, Pres. 2001–04, Chair. 2004–08, Sr Advisor 2008–; Standing Corp. Auditor, Tokio Marine Holdings Inc. 2000–02; Chair. Japanese Bankers Assen –2003; Counsellor, Policy Bd, Bank of Japan; Vice-Chair. Exec. Bd Nippon-Keidanren 2003–; mem. Bd of Dirs Mitsubishi Motors Corpn 2002–, Outside Statutory Auditor 2004–; Dir, UnionBanCal Corpn 2004–08, Japan Int. Medical Tech. Foundation; Trustee, Financial Accounting Standards Foundation, Accounting Standards Bd of Japan. *Address:* Bank of Tokyo-Mitsubishi UFJ Ltd, 2-7-1, Marunouchi, Chiyoda-ku, Tokyo 100-8388, Japan (office). *Telephone:* (3) 3240-8111 (office). *Fax:* (3) 3240-8203 (office). *E-mail:* info@bk.mufg.jp (office). *Website:* www.bk.mufg.jp/global (office).

MIKITA, Kunio; Japanese business executive; *Chairman, Mediceo Paltac Holdings Company Ltd;* b. 23 Oct. 1943; ed Kinki Univ.; joined Daisho Co. Ltd (named changed to Paltac 1976) 1966, mem. Bd of Dirs 1990–, Man. Dir 1995–96, Exec. Vice-Pres. 1996–98, Pres. 1998–2004, Rep. Dir and CEO 2004–, apptd Exec. Vice-Pres. Mediceo Paltac Holdings Co. Ltd (following acquisition of Paltac) 2005, later Vice-Pres. and Rep. Dir, Chair. 2008–. *Address:* Mediceo Paltac Holdings Co. Ltd, 7-15, Yaesu 2-chome, Chuo-ku, Tokyo 104-8464, Japan (office). *Telephone:* (3) 3517-5800 (office). *Fax:* (3) 3517-5011 (office). *E-mail:* info@mediceo-paltac.co.jp (office). *Website:* www.mediceo-paltac.co.jp (office).

MIKITANI, Hiroshi, BCom, MBA; Japanese business executive; *Chairman and CEO, Rakuten Inc.;* b. 11 March 1965, Kobe; m.; one c.; ed Hitotsubashi Univ., Harvard Business School, USA; began career as investment banker, Industrial Bank of Japan 1988–96; Founder and CEO Crimson Group (merger and acquisition consulting co.) 1995; f. MDM (Magical Digital Market) (online retail mall) 1997, renamed Rakuten Inc. 1999, Chair. and CEO 1997–; Chair. Japan Asscn of New Economy. *Publication:* Marketplace 3.0: Rewriting the Rules of Borderless Business 2013. *Leisure interest:* golf. *Address:* Rakuten Inc, Roppongi Hills, Mori Tower 6-10-1, Roppongi, Minato-ku, Tokyo 106-6138, Japan (office). *Telephone:* (3) 6387-0555 (office). *Website:* corp.rakuten.co.jp (office).

MIKKELSEN, Brian, MA; Danish politician; b. 31 Jan. 1966, Copenhagen; m. Eliane Wexøe Mikkelsen; four c.; ed Univ. of Copenhagen; Business Man. Conservative Secondary School Students 1985–86, Nat. and Scandinavian Chair. 1986–87; mem. Nat. Exec. Cttee, Conservative People's Party 1986–, Nat. Chair. 1989–90; mem. Exec. Cttee Christian Democratic Youth Org. 1989–90; mem. Nat. Exec. Conservative People's Party 1989–91, 1998–, Deputy Chair., Conservative People's Party Parl. Group 1999–; mem. Parl. 1994–; Minister for Culture 2001–08, of Justice 2008–10, of Econ. and Business Affairs 2010–11; Ed. The Conservative Season 2004; Exec. mem. Ledøje-Smørum FC 1983–84, FOF 1987–89, Tech. Council 1997–2001; mem. Danish Youth Council 1989–91, Holbæk Coll. of Educ. Council 1994–2001, Railway Council 1996–2001, Council for the Danish Centre for Human Rights 1998–2001, Danish Cultural Inst. Council 1998–2001, Danish Road Safety Council 2000–01, VL Group 7 2000–01, ARTE Council 2000–01; mem. World Anti-Doping Agency Foundation Bd 2002–03, Vice-Pres. 2004–06, mem. Exec. Cttee 2007–08. *Publications:* Nicaragua 1986, Namibia on the Road to Democracy 1988, The Conservative Breakthrough 1991, Land and

Small Businesses 1994. *Address:* c/o Ministry of Economic and Business Affairs, Slotsholmsgade 10–12, 1216 Copenhagen K, Denmark (office).

MIKKELSEN, Richard, MSc(Econ); Danish central banker (retd); b. 27 April 1920, Copenhagen; m. Ester Overgaard 1944 (died 1993); at Banken for Slagelse og Omegn 1937–45; apptd Asst Danmarks Nationalbank 1945, Head of Section 1954, Asst Head Dept 1961, Head Dept 1961, Dir 1966, Asst Gov. 1971, Gov. 1982–90; Attaché, Danish-OEEC Del., Paris 1955–57; mem. Bd European Monetary Agreement 1970–72; Industrial Mortgage Fund 1971–81; mem. Bd Mortgage Credit Council, Supervisor 1972–81; mem. Bd Export Finance Corpn 1975–90; mem. Steering Cttee and Bd Employees Capital Pension Fund 1980–91, Industrial Mortgage Credit Fund 1981–91, Monetary Cttee of EEC 1982–90; Nordic Financial Cttee 1982–90, Econ. Policy Cttee of OECD 1982–90; Chair. Financing Fund of 1992 1992–96; Commdr Order of Dannebrog. *Publication:* Monetary History of Denmark, 1960–90.

MIKL-LEITNER, Johanna, Mag. rer. soc. oec.; Austrian politician; *Federal Minister of the Interior;* b. (Johanna Leitner), 9 Feb. 1964, Hollabrunn; m.; two d.; ed Vienna Univ. of Economics and Business; teacher, Commercial Coll. of Laa an der Thaya 1989–90; business consultant 1989–90; trainee, Fed. of Austrian Industries 1990–93; Deputy Head, Signum Publishing House 1993–95; Marketing Dir Austrian People's Party (Lower Austrian br.) 1995–98, Exec. Dir 1998–2003, mem. Nat. Council 1999–2003; mem. Parl. (Austrian People's Party) 1999–2003; mem. Govt of Lower Austria with responsibility for Social Affairs, Labour and Family 2003–11; Vice-Pres. Ass. of European Regions 2008–11; Fed. Minister of the Interior 2011–. *Address:* Federal Ministry of the Interior, Herrengasse 7, Postfach 100, 1014 Vienna, Austria (office). *Telephone:* (1) 531-26-2452 (office). *Fax:* (1) 531-26-2191 (office). *E-mail:* johanna.mikl-leitner@bmi.gv.at (office). *Website:* www.bmi.gv.at (office).

MIKLOŠ, Ivan, DipEngEcon; Slovak politician and economist; b. 2 June 1960, Svídník; m.; two c.; ed Univ. of Econs, Bratislava, London School of Econs, UK; Asst, Univ. of Econs, Bratislava 1983–87, Chief Asst 1987–90; Adviser to Deputy Prime Minister responsible for Econ. Reform 1990; Dir Govt Dept of Econ. and Social Policy 1990–91; Minister of Privatization 1991–92; Exec. Dir and Pres. MESA 10 Org. 1992–98; Deputy Prime Minister for Econ. Affairs 1998–2002; Deputy Prime Minister and Minister of Finance 2002–06, 2010–12; mem. Parl. 2006–; First Deputy Chair. Civil Democratic Union 1992–93; Chair. Democratic Party 1993–2000; mem. Slovak Democratic and Christian Union-Democratic Party (SDKÚ-DS) 2001–, Vice-Chair. 2002–; First Vice-Pres. East-West Inst., New York 1998; mem. Windsor Group 1993–, Int. Advisory Bd, New Atlantic Initiative 1995–, World Econ. Forum – Global Leaders of Tomorrow 1999–, Int. Advisory Bd, BELA Foundation 2007–; Hon. PhD (Alma Coll., Mich., USA) 2000; named by Euromoney magazine Minister of Finance of the Year 2004. *Publications include:* numerous articles in specialized and popular press. *Leisure interests:* tennis, windsurfing, skiing, biking. *Address:* c/o Ministry of Finance, Štefanovičova 5, PO Box 82, 817 82 Bratislava, Slovakia.

MIKLOŠKO, Jozef, Doz., RNDr, DrSc; Slovak politician, mathematician, diplomatist, journalist and writer; b. 31 March 1939, Nitra; s. of Ondrej Mikloško and Marta Mikloško (née Kutliková); m. Mária Bitterová 1964; two s. two d.; ed Pedagogical Univ., Bratislava, Komenský Univ., Bratislava; teacher, Nové Zámky 1961–62; scientific worker, Inst. of Tech. Cybernetics, Slovak Acad. of Sciences, Bratislava 1963–90; Lecturer, Faculty of Mathematics and Physics, Komenský Univ., Bratislava 1969–89; Head of Int. Base Lab. for Artificial Intelligence 1985–90; Vice-Chair. Christian-Democratic Movt 1990; Deputy to Slovak Nat. Council 1990–91; Fed. Deputy Premier for Human Rights in Czechoslovak Fed. Repub. 1990–92; Deputy to House of the People, Fed. Ass. June–Dec. 1992; Adviser to Pres. of Slovakia 1993–95; Deputy to Town Council, Bratislava V 1994–2000; Deputy to the Nat. Council (Parl.) 2012–; Head of DACO publishing house 1995–2000, 2005–; Sec. Justice and Peace Comm. 1995–2000; Lecturer and Vice-Rector Trnava Univ. 1996–2000; Amb. to Italy, Malta and San Marino 2000–05; Chair. Solidarity Foundation 1993–97, Schiller Foundation for Protection of Life and Human Rights 1995–2000, Asscn of Slovak Catholic Publrs 2006–08, Asscn of Christian Seniors of Slovakia 2007–; mem. Govt Council for Seniors 2008–; mem. World Ecological Acad., Moscow 1994–, Int. Informatization Acad., Moscow 1995–, Slovak Asscn of Writers 1995– (mem. Presidium 2007–09), Slovak Asscn of Journalists 1997–2000; moderator, World Apostolate of Fatima 2011–; Grande Ufficiale d'Italia 2006; Laudis et Honoris Signum (Italy) 2001, Gold Star for European Culture 2005. *Publications:* Strong Secret: When We Were Young 1995, Farewell 1996, Very Top Secret: When We Were Free 1999, Top Secret: When We Were Italian 2006, Whom Maria Took To Heaven 2006, When We Were Young: After 60 Years 2007, Two Years Blogger 2010; five scientific books, 65 scientific publs, 250 newspaper articles, numerous blog posts. *Leisure interests:* literature, blogging, music, sport, history, church, politics. *Address:* Malokarpatská 22, 90021 Svätý Jur, Slovakia (home). *Telephone:* (2) 4497-0689 (home). *E-mail:* mikloskojozef@gmail.com (home); jozef.miklosko@nrsr.sk (office). *Website:* www.jozefmiklosko.sk; www.jozefmiklosko.blog.sme.sk.

MIKOLAJ, Ján, CSc; Slovak engineer, academic and politician; b. 19 Oct. 1953; ed Žilina Transport Univ.; Asst Prof., later Assoc. Prof., Road Construction Dept, Žilina Transport Univ. 1983–, mem. Scientific Council, Civil Eng Faculty 1992, Prof. and Head of Construction Implementation Dept, now the Dept of Construction Techs and Man. 1999–; Gen. Dir Slovak Road Admin 1995–98; elected to Nat. Council of Slovak Repub. (Slovak Nat. Party—Slovenská národná strana) 2002, 2006; Deputy Prime Minister and Minister of Educ. 2008–10. *Address:* c/o Ministry of Education, Stromová 1, 813 30 Bratislava, Slovakia (office).

MIKOSZ, Andrzej; Polish lawyer and politician; b. 17 Oct. 1965, Poznań; ed Adam Mickiewicz Univ., Poznań; Pnr Ziemski i Partnerzy (law firm), Poznań 1993–1996; co-f. Głowacki, Grynhoff, Hałaziński, Mikosz (law firm) 1996–1997; mem. Polish Securities and Exchanges Comm. and advisor to Minister of Agric. and Rural Devt 1998–2000; lawyer Weil, Gotshal and Manges, Warsaw 2000–02; Dir of Capital Markets practice, Lovells (law firm), Warsaw 2002–05; Minister of the Treasury 2005–2006. *Publications:* numerous papers on company law, capital markets and corporate governance. *Address:* c/o Ministry of the Treasury, ul. Krucza 36, 00–522 Warsaw, Poland (office).

MIKOV, Mihail Raikov; Bulgarian politician, academic and jurist; *Chairman, Narodno Sobraniye (National Assembly);* b. 16 June 1960, Kula; m.; two c.; ed Sofia Univ. 'St Kliment Ohridski'; Assoc. Prof. of Criminal Law, Sofia Univ. 'St Kliment Ohridski'; mem. Narodno Sobraniye (Nat. Ass.) for 5-Vidin 1997–, Chair. Parl. Group of leftist Coalition for Bulgaria 2005–, mem. Legal Matters Cttee, European Integration Cttee, Chair. Narodno Sobraniye 2013–; Minister of the Interior 2008–09. *Address:* Narodno Sobranie (National Assembly), 1169 Sofia, pl. Narodno Sobranie 2, Bulgaria (office). *Telephone:* (2) 939-39 (office). *Fax:* (2) 981-31-31 (office). *E-mail:* infocenter@parliament.bg (office). *Website:* www.parliament.bg (office).

MIKSER, Sven; Estonian politician; *President, Estonian Social Democratic Party;* b. 8 Nov. 1973, Tartu; one d.; ed Univ. of Tartu; Div. Asst, Dept of Romance-Germanic Philology, Univ. of Tartu 1996–99; mem. Estonian Centre Party 1995–2004, Political Sec. 1998–99; mem. Riigikogu (Parl.) for Tartu City constituency 1999–2002, 2003–; Minister of Defence 2002–03; mem. Estonian Social Democratic Party 2005–, Pres. 2010–; Chair. Sub-cttee, NATO Parl. Ass. of the Trans-Atlantic Defence and Security Cooperation; mem. Bd of Trustees, Univ. of Tartu. *Publications:* articles in nat. publs. *Address:* Estonian Social Democratic Party (Sotsiaaldemokraatlik Erakond), Ahtri 10A, 10151 Tallinn, Estonia (office). *Telephone:* 611-6040 (office); 631-6631. *Fax:* 611-6050 (office). *E-mail:* sven .mikser@riigikogu.ee (office); sven.mikser@sotsdem.ee (office); *Website:* www .sotsdem.ee (office); svenmikser.sotsdem.ee (office).

MIKULSKI, Barbara Ann, BA, MSW; American politician and fmr teacher; *Senator from Maryland;* b. 20 July 1936, Baltimore, Md; d. of William Mikulski and Christina Eleanor Kutz; ed Mount St Agnes Coll. and Univ. of Maryland; Baltimore Dept Social Services 1961–63, 1966–70; York Family Agency 1964; VISTA Teaching Center 1965–70; teacher, Mount St Agnes Coll. 1969; teacher, Community Coll., Baltimore 1970–71; Democratic nominee to US Senate 1974, 1976; mem. US House of Reps (96th–99th Congresses) from 3rd Md Dist 1977–87; Senator from Maryland 1987–, first woman Democrat elected to US Senate in her own right, became the longest serving woman in the history of the US Congress 17 March 2012, Dean of the Women; mem. Democratic Nat. Strategy Council; Adjunct Prof., Loyola Coll. 1972–76; mem. Nat. Bd of Dirs Urban Coalition; mem. Nat. Asscn of Social Workers; Democrat; Hon. Fellow, American Acad. of Nursing 2007; Polish Order of Merit 2001, Commdr's Cross and Star (Poland) 2001; Hon. LLD (Goucher Coll.) 1973, (Hood Coll.) 1978, (Bowie State Univ.) 1989, (Morgan State Univ.) 1990, (Massachusetts) 1991; Hon. DHL (Pratt Inst.) 1974. *Address:* 503 Hart Office Building, Washington, DC 20510, USA (office). *Telephone:* (202) 224-4654 (office). *Fax:* (202) 224-8858 (office). *Website:* mikulski.senate.gov (office).

MÍL, Jaroslav, MA, MBA; Czech business executive; b. 10 Aug. 1958, Prague; ed Electrotechnology Faculty, Czech Tech. Univ., Prague, Sheffield Business School, UK; various tech. positions, then Dir responsible for Procurement and Fuel Cycles, Czech Power Co. (ČEZ) 1985–2000, Chair. and CEO 2000–03; Chair. and CEO Elektrárny Opatovice (EOP) 2000; mem. Bd of Dirs Škoda-ÚJP Praha 1994–2000, Siberian Coal Energy Co. 2013–; apptd Pres. Confed. of Industry of the Czech Repub. 2003; Chair. Radioactive Waste Repository Authority 1997–2000, European Nuclear Council 2003–; mem. Bd of Govs World Nuclear Fuel Market, Atlanta, USA 1993–99; mem. Supervisory Bd Severočeské doly 1998–99, Bd Czech Asscn of Employers in Energy Sector 2000–; fmr Vice-Pres. BUSINESSEUROPE; fmr mem. ICC, Bd of Dirs EURELECTRIC, Slovenske elektrarne – ENEL SpA, Int. Advisory Cttee of Soc. for Strategic Man.; mem. Bd of Dirs Czech Tech. Univ. *Leisure interests:* family, skiing, golf, squash, cycling, hiking. *Address:* Siberian Coal Energy Co., 115054 Moscow, 53/7 Dubininskaya str., Russia. *Telephone:* (495) 795-2538. *Fax:* (495) 795-2542. *E-mail:* c/o@suek.ru. *Website:* www.suek.ru.

MILAKNIS, Valentinas Pranas; Lithuanian business executive and politician; b. 4 Oct. 1947, Rokiskis; m. Sofija Milakniene; one s. one d.; ed Kaunas Polytech. Inst.; fmr engineer, then Head of Group, Head of Sector, Deputy Chief Engineer Control System Planning and Design Construction Bureau, Municipal Econ. Planning Inst. 1970–89; apptd Man. Dir, then Dir-Gen. Alna AB Co. 1989, Chair. –2001; Minister of Nat. Economy 1999–2000; Dir-Gen. LRT (Lithuanian public TV and radio broadcaster) 2001–03. *Leisure interest:* shooting. *Address:* c/o Alna AB, A. Domaševiciaus 9, 2001 Vilnius, Lithuania (office).

MILANI, Cesare (Chez) Andrea, BA, LLB; South African trade union official and lawyer; b. 27 Nov. 1966, Cape Town; m.; one d.; ed Stellenbosch Univ., Univ. of South Africa School of Business Leadership; Nat. Legal Adviserm, Hospersa 1994–97; Gen. Sec. Fed. of Unions of SA (FEDUSA) 1997–2007; mem. Pres. Mbeki's Working Group, NEDLAC Exec. Cttee and Man. Cttee, CCMA Governing Body. *Leisure interests:* antiques, sailing. *Address:* c/o FEDUSA, PO Box 7779, Westgate 1734, South Africa. *E-mail:* info@fedusa.org.za.

MILANOVIĆ, Zoran; Croatian politician; *Prime Minister;* b. 30 Oct. 1966, Zagreb; s. of Stipe Milanović and Gina Milanović; m. Sanja Musić-Milanović 1994; two s.; ed Centre for Man. and Judiciary, Univ. of Zagreb; became an intern at Croatian Trade Court; joined Croatian Foreign Ministry 1993, went to Nagornyi Karabakh as part of UN peace mission 1994, adviser at Croatian Mission to EU and NATO, Brussels 1996–99, returned to Foreign Ministry 1999; enrolled in Social Democratic Party (SDP) of Croatia 1999, given responsibility for liaison with NATO 2000–03, elected to Chief Cttee of SDP 2004, Party Spokesman 2006, elected Co-ordinator for IVth election area for 2007 elections, Chair. SDP 2007–; Asst to Minister of Foreign Affairs 2003; Leader of the Opposition 2007–11; Prime Minister Dec. 2011–. *Address:* Office of the Prime Minister, 10000 Zagreb, Trg sv. Marka 2 (office); Social Democratic Party of Croatia (Socijaldemokratska partija Hrvatske), 10000 Zagreb, Iblerov trg 9, Croatia (office). *Telephone:* (1) 4569239 (Office of the PM) (office); (1) 4552055 (SDP) (office). *Fax:* (1) 6303022 (Office of the PM) (office); 1) 4557509 (SDP) (office). *E-mail:* press@vlada.hr (office); sdp@sdp.hr (office). *Website:* www.vlada.hr (office); www.sdp.hr (office); zoranmilanovic.sdp .hr.

MILBERG, Joachim, Dr-Ing; German automotive industry executive and engineer; *Chairman of the Supervisory Board, BMW AG;* b. 10 April 1943, Verl, Westphalia; ed Technische Universität Berlin; Research Asst, Inst. of Machine Tools and Production Tech., Berlin Tech. Univ. 1970–72; exec. employee, Werkzeugmaschinenfabrik Gildemeister AG (machine tools factory) 1972–78, Head of Automatic Tuning Machines division 1978–81; Prof. of Machine Tools and Man. Science, Munich Tech. Univ. 1981–93; mem. Bd of Man. Bayerische Motoren Werke (BMW) AG (Production) 1993–98, (Eng and Production) 1998–99, Chair. Bd of Man. 1999–2002, mem. Supervisory Bd 2002–04, Chair. 2004–; mem. Bd of Dirs Bertelsmann AG, Allianz SE, Munich, Festo AG, Esslingen, Leipziger Messe GmbH, Leipzig, MAN AG, Munich, SAP AG 2007–, Walldorf, ZF Friedrichshafen AG, John Deere & Co., USA 2003–; mem. Partner Cttee TÜV Süddeutschland, Munich; Pres. acatech – Deutsche Akad. der Technikwissenschaften 2003–09; Hon. Prof., Dept of Machine Tools and Industrial Eng, Tech. Univ. of Munich 1998, Univ. of Duisburg-Essen 2010; Verdienstkreuz am Bande des Verdienstordens der Bundesrepublik Deutschland 1994, Bayerischer Verdienstorden 2001, Bayerischer Maximiliansorden für Wissenschaft und Kunst 2010; Hon. Dr-Ing, Dr hc (Ljubljana, Slovenia) 1994, (Hanover) 1996, (Cranfield, UK) 2002, (Tech. Univ. of Berlin) 2004; Gottfried Wilhelm Leibniz Prize, German Research Foundation (DFG) 1989, Fritz Winter Prize 1991, Herwart Opitz Hon. Medal, VDI-Gesellschaft Produktionstechnik 1992, State Medal for outstanding service to the Bavarian economy 1999, Grashof Medal, Asscn of German Engineers (VDI) 2000, Gen. Pierre Nicolau Award, Collège Int. pour la Recherche en Productique Int. 2001, Hon. Award 'Golden Steering Wheel', Axel Springer Verlag 2001, Bavarian Environmental Medal for outstanding contribs to environmental protection and land devt 2002, Ernst Blickle Prize, SEW Euro Drive Foundation, Bruchsal 2003, Carl Friedrich Gauss Medal, Brunswick Scientific Soc. 2004, Arthur Burkhardt Prize 2005, Hanns Martin Schleyer Prize 2009. *Address:* BMW AG, Petuelring 130, 80788, Munich, Germany (office). *Telephone:* (89) 382-0 (office). *Fax:* (89) 382-244-18 (office). *E-mail:* info@bmwgroup.com (office). *Website:* www.bmwgroup.com (office); www.bmw.com (office).

MILBRADT, Georg, Dr rer pol; German politician and academic; b. 23 Feb. 1945, Eslohe, Sauerland; m. Angelika Meeth; two s.; ed Univ. of Münster; Asst, Inst. of Finance, Univ. of Münster 1970–80, Guest Prof. 1985–; Deputy Prof. of Finance and Econs, Univ. of Mainz 1980–83; Head, Dept of Finance, Münster 1983–90, later responsible for econ. devt and property man.; mem. CDU 1991–, Fed. Admin 2000–; Minister of Finance, Saxony State 1990–2001; mem. Bundesrates (Upper House of Parl.) Cttee on Mediation; mem. Saxony State Parl. 1994–; Minister-Pres. of Saxony April 2002–08 (resgnd); Regional Deputy Chair. Sächsischen Union 1999; Chair. Bd Sächsischen Aufbaubank, Dresden Airport, Sächsischen Landesbank; Deputy Chair. Bd Leipzig-Halle Airport; Chair. Tariff Community of German Länder (TdL); Bundesvierdienstkreuz 2005. *Leisure interests:* literature, computers. *Address:* CDU, Konrad-Adenauer-Haus, Klingelhöferstrasse 8, 10785 Berlin, Germany (office). *Telephone:* (30) 220700 (office). *Fax:* (30) 22070111 (office). *E-mail:* info@cdu.de (office). *Website:* www.cdu.de (office); www.georg -milbradt.de (office).

MILBURN, Rt Hon. Alan, PC, BA; British politician; b. 27 Jan. 1958; m. Mo O'Toole 1982 (divorced 1992); m. Ruth Briel; two s.; ed Stokesley Comprehensive School, Lancaster Univ.; co-ordinator Trade Union Studies Information Unit, Newcastle 1984–90; Sr Business Devt Officer N Tyneside Municipal Borough Council 1990–92; MP for Darlington 1992–2010; Opposition Front Bench Spokesman on Health 1995–96, on Treasury and Econ. Affairs 1996–97; Minister of State, Dept of Health 1997–98; Chief Sec. to Treasury 1998–99, Sec. of State for Health 1999–2003; Chancellor of the Duchy of Lancaster 2004–05; Chair. Parl. Labour Party Treasury Cttee 1992–95; mem. Public Accounts Cttee 1994–95; Chair. Charities Scrutiny Cttee 2004; Adviser Bridgepoint Capital 2007–, currently Chair. European Advisory Cttee; mem. Nutritional Advisory Bd, PepsiCo UK 2007–. *Address:* Bridgepoint Capital, 30 Warwick Street, London, W1B 5AL, England (office). *Telephone:* (20) 7432-3500 (office). *E-mail:* info@bridgepoint.eu (office). *Website:* www.bridgepoint.eu (office).

MILCHAN, Arnon; American film producer; b. 6 Dec. 1944, Tel-Aviv, Israel. *Plays produced:* Tomb, It's So Nice To Be Civilized, Amadeus (Paris production). *Films include:* Black Joy 1977, The Medusa Touch (exec. producer) 1978, Dizengoff 99 1979, The King of Comedy 1983, Can She Bake a Cherry Pie? (actor) 1983, Once Upon a Time in America (also actor) 1984, Brazil 1985, Legend 1985, Stripper (exec. producer) 1986, Man on Fire 1987, Big Man on Campus 1989, The Adventures of Baron Munchausen 1989, Who's Harry Crumb 1989, The War of the Roses 1989, Pretty Woman 1990, Q&A 1990, Guilty by Suspicion 1991, Switch (exec. producer) 1991, JFK (exec. producer) 1991, Memoirs of an Invisible Man (exec. producer) 1992, The Mambo Kings 1992, The Power of One 1992, Under Siege 1992, That Night 1992, Heaven and Earth 1993, Sommersby 1993, Falling Down 1993, Made in America 1993, Free Willy (exec. producer) 1993, Striking Distance 1993, The Nutcracker (exec. producer) 1993, Six Degrees of Separation 1993, The Client 1994, Natural Born Killers (exec. producer) 1994, Second Best 1994, The New Age 1994, Cobb (exec. producer) 1994, Boys on the Side 1995, Under Siege 2 1995, Free Willy 2: The Adventure Home 1995, Empire Records 1995, Copycat 1995, Heat (exec. producer) 1995, The Sunchaser 1996, A Time to Kill 1996, Tin Cup (exec. producer) 1996, Bogus 1996, The Mirror Has Two Faces 1996, Murder at 1600 1997, L.A. Confidential 1997, Free Willy 3: The Rescue (exec. producer) 1997, The Devil's Advocate 1997, Breaking Up (exec. producer) 1997, The Man Who Knew Too Little 1997, Dangerous Beauty 1998, City of Angels (exec. producer) 1998, Goodbye Lover (exec. producer) 1998, The Negotiator 1998, Simply Irresistible (exec. producer) 1999, A Midsummer Night's Dream (exec. producer) 1999, Entrapment (exec. producer) 1999, Fight Club (exec. producer) 1999, Up at the Villa (exec. producer) 2000, Big Momma's House (exec. producer) 2000, Tigerland 2000, Freddy Got Fingered (exec. producer) 2001, Joy Ride (exec. producer) 2001, Don't Say a Word 2001, Black Knight 2001, Joe Somebody (exec. producer) 2001, High Crimes 2002, Life or Something Like It 2002, Unfaithful (exec. producer) 2002, Daredevil 2003, Down with Love (exec. producer) 2003, Runaway Jury 2003, The Girl Next Door (exec. producer) 2004, Man on Fire 2004, First Daughter (exec. producer) 2004, Elektra 2005, Mr. & Mrs. Smith 2005, Bee Season (exec. producer) 2005, Stay (exec. producer) 2005, Just My Luck 2006, The Sentinel 2006, Meet the Spartans (exec. producer) 2008, What Happens in Vegas (exec. producer) 2008, Bride Wars (exec. producer) 2009, Knight and Day (exec. producer) 2010, Monte Carlo (producer) 2011, Broken City 2013, 12 Years a Slave (BAFTA Award for Best Picture, Golden Globe Award for Best Motion Picture, Drama 2014) 2013. *Television includes:* Masada (mini-series) (supervising producer) 1981, Free Willy (series; exec. producer), The Client (series; exec. producer) 1995, Michael Hayes (series; exec. producer) 1997, The Hunt for the Unicorn Killer 1999, Noriega: God's Favorite (exec. producer) 2000. *Address:* New Regency

Enterprises, 10201 West Pico Boulevard, Building 12, Los Angeles, CA 90035, USA (office). *Telephone:* (310) 369-8300 (office). *E-mail:* info@newregency.com (office). *Website:* www.newregency.com (office).

MILEDI, Ricardo, MD, FRS, FAAS, MRI; Mexican/American neurobiologist and academic; *Distinguished Professor, Neurobiology and Behavior, University of California, Irvine;* b. 15 Sept. 1927, Mexico DF; m. Ana Mela Garces 1955; one s.; ed Universidad Nacional Autónoma de Mexico; Research Fellow, Instituto Nacional de Cardiología, Mexico 1954–56; Visiting Fellow, John Curtin School of Medical Research, Canberra, Australia 1956–58; Hon. Research Assoc., Dept of Biophysics, Univ. Coll. London 1958–59, Lecturer 1959–62, Reader 1962–65, Prof. of Biophysics 1965–75, Foulerton Research Prof. of the Royal Soc. 1975–85, Foulerton Research Prof. and Head of Dept of Biophysics 1978–85; Distinguished Prof., Neurobiology and Behavior, Dept of Psychobiology, School of Biological Sciences, Univ. of California, Irvine 1984–; Fellow, Third World Acad. of Sciences, American Acad. of Arts and Sciences; mem. NAS 1989, European Acad. of Arts, Sciences and Humanities 1995, Mexican Acad. of Medicine 1995, Mexican Acad. of Sciences 1995; Hon. mem. Hungarian Acad. of Sciences; Dr hc (Univ. del País Vasco, Leioa, Spain) 1992, (Trieste Univ., Italy) 2000, (Univ. of Chihuahua, Mexico) 2000; King Faisal Foundation Int. Prize for Science, Principe de Asturias Prize (Spain) 1999, Royal Soc. Medal 1999, Univ. of California (Irvine) Medal, Ralph W. Gerard Prize, Society for Neuroscience 2010. *Publications:* more than 500 published papers. *Leisure interest:* hiking. *Address:* Department of Neurobiology and Behavior, University of California, 1215 Bio Sci II, Mail Code 4550, Irvine, CA 92697-4550 (office); 9 Gibbs Court, Irvine, CA 92616, USA (home). *Telephone:* (949) 824-4730 (office); (949) 856-2677 (home). *Fax:* (949) 824-6090 (office). *E-mail:* rmiledi@uci.edu (office). *Website:* faculty.sites.uci.edu/rmiledi (office).

MILES, (Henry) Michael (Pearson), OBE; British business executive; *Chairman, Schroders;* b. 19 April 1936; s. of the late Brig. H. G. P. Miles and Margaret Miles; m. Carol Jane Berg 1967; two s. one d.; ed Wellington Coll., Nat. Service, Duke of Wellington's Regt; joined John Swire & Sons 1958, Dir John Swire & Sons (HK) Ltd 1970–99, Chair. 1984–88; Man. Dir John Swire & Sons (Japan) Ltd 1973–76; Man. Dir Cathay Pacific Airways Ltd 1978–84, Chair. 1984–88; Chair. Swire Pacific 1984–88; Exec. Dir John Swire & Sons Ltd 1988–99, Adviser to Bd 1999–; Dir Johnson Matthey PLC 1990–2003, Chair. (non-exec.) 1998–2002; Chair. (non-exec.) Schroders 2003–; Dir (non-exec.) Baring PLC 1989–95 (Jt Deputy Chair. 1994–95), Portals Holdings 1990–95, BICC 1996–2002, HSBC Holdings 1984–88, ING Baring Holdings Ltd 1989–2002, BP PLC 1994–, Pacific Assets Trust PLC 1997–2003, Balfour Beatty 1996–2002; Chair. Hong Kong Tourist Asscn 1984–88, Korea-Europe Fund Ltd; Vice-Pres. China-Britain Business Group 1992–2000; Gov. Wellington Coll. 1988–. *Leisure interests:* golf, tennis. *Address:* Schroders, 31 Gresham Street, London, EC2V 7QA (office); Shalbourne House, Shalbourne, nr Marlborough, Wilts., SN8 3QH, England (home). *Telephone:* (20) 7658-6000 (office). *Website:* www.schroders.com (office).

MILES, Michael A., Jr., BA, MBA; American retail executive; *President and Chief Operating Officer, Staples Inc.;* ed Yale and Harvard Univs; began career at Bain & Company; joined PepsiCo Inc. as Dir of Strategic Planning, Restaurants 1993, Div. Vice Pres. Pizza Hut 1994, then Sr Vice-Pres. Concept Devt and Franchise, Pizza Hut (after Yum Brands Inc. spinoff from PepsiCo that included Pizza Hut) 1996–99, COO Pizza Hut Inc. 2000–03; COO Staples Inc. 2003–, Pres. 2006–. *Address:* Staples Inc., 500 Staples Drive, Framingham, MD 01702, USA (office). *Telephone:* (508) 253-5000 (office). *Fax:* (508) 253-8989 (office). *Website:* www.staples.com (office).

MILES, Roy Edward; British art dealer and writer; b. 9 Feb. 1935, Liverpool; s. of Edward Marsh and Elsa McKinley; m. Christine Rhodes 1970 (died 1997); ed Bembridge School, Isle of Wight, Sorbonne, Paris; dealer in British art and fine paintings; organizer of major exhbns of Victorian and Russian art; Gold Medal for Art 1943. *Television:* contribs to numerous art programmes. *Publications:* Priceless: Memoirs and Mysteries of Britain's No. 1 Art Dealer (autobiog.) 2003; articles in magazines, newspapers and journals. *Leisure interests:* classical music, history. *Address:* 10 Ennismore Gardens, London, SW7 1NP, England. *Telephone:* (20) 7581-7969 (home).

MILES, Sarah; British actress; b. 31 Dec. 1941, Ingatestone, Essex; m. Robert Bolt 1967 (divorced 1976), remarried 1988 (died 1995); ed Royal Acad. of Dramatic Art; with Nat. Theatre Co. 1964–65; Shakespeare stage season 1982–83; Assoc. mem. Royal Acad. of Dramatic Art. *Theatre appearances include:* Vivat! Vivat Regina!, Asylum 1988. *Films include:* Term of Trial 1962, The Servant 1963, The Ceremony 1963, Those Magnificent Men in Their Flying Machines 1965, I Was Happy Here 1965, Blowup 1966, Ryan's Daughter 1970, Lady Caroline Lamb 1972, The Hireling 1973, The Man Who Loved Cat Dancing 1973, Pepita Jiménez 1975, The Sailor Who Fell From Grace With the Sea 1976, The Big Sleep 1978, Priest of Love 1981, Venom 1982, Ordeal by Innocence 1984, Steaming 1985, Hope and Glory 1987, White Mischief 1987, Hope and glory 1987, Dotkniecie reki (The Silent Touch) 1992, Jurij 2001, I giorni dell'amore e dell'odio (Days of Grace) 2001, The Accidental Detective 2003. *Television includes:* Great Expectations 1974, James A. Michener's Dynasty 1976, Walter and June 1983, Harem 1986, Queenie 1987, A Ghost in Monte Carlo 1990, Dandelion Dead (mini-series) 1994, Ring Around the Moon, The Rehearsal, Poirot: The Hollow 2004. *Publications:* Charlemagne (play) 1992, A Right Royal Bastard (memoirs) 1993, Serves Me Right (memoirs) 1994, Bolt from the Blue (memoirs) 1996.

MILHAUD, Charles; French banking executive; b. 1943; science grad.; has spent entire career with Groupe Caisse d'Epargne, joined Caisse d'Epargne de Sète 1964, CEO 1967–80, CEO, then Chair. Man. Bd Caisse d'Epargne des Bouches du Rhône et de la Corse 1980–99, Chair. Man. Bd Centre Nat. des Caisses d'Epargne (thereafter Caisse Nationale des Caisses d'Epargne when it was cr. in Sept. 1999) 1999–2008 (resgnd), Chair. Caisses d'Epargne Foundation for Social Solidarity; Chair. Supervisory Bd Natixis, Financière OCEOR; Chair. French Banking Fed. 2006–07; Vice-Pres. Nexity; mem. Municipal Council of Marseille 2008–; Officier, Ordre nat. du Mérite 2001, Légion d'honneur 2005.

MILIBAND, Rt Hon. David Wright, PC, BA (Hons), SM; British politician and international organization official; *President and CEO-Designate, International Rescue Committee;* b. 15 July 1965, London; s. of the late Ralph Miliband and Marion Miliband (née Kozak); brother of Ed Miliband; m. Louise Shackleton 1998;

two adopted s.; ed Haverstock Comprehensive School, North London, Corpus Christi Coll., Oxford, Massachusetts Inst. of Tech., USA (Kennedy Scholar); Research Fellow, Inst. for Public Policy Research 1989–94; Sec. Comm. on Social Justice 1992–94; Head of Policy, Office of Leader of Opposition 1994–97; Head, Prime Minister's Policy Unit 1997–2001; MP (Labour) for South Shields 2001–13; Minister of State, Dept for Educ. and Skills 2002–04; Minister for the Cabinet Office 2004–05; Minister of Communities and Local Govt 2005–06; Sec. of State for the Environment, Food and Rural Affairs 2006–07, for Foreign and Commonwealth Affairs 2007–10; unsuccessful cand. in Labour Party leadership election Sept. 2010; Pres. and CEO Int. Rescue Cttee, New York Sept. 2013–; mem. Bd of Dirs, The Office of David Miliband Ltd 2010–; Vice-Chair. Sunderland AFC 2011–13 (resgnd). *Publications:* Publish and Still Not be Damned: A Guide for Voluntary Groups on the Provisions of the 1986 and 1988 Local Government Acts Regarding Political Publicity and the Promotion of Homosexuality, National Council for Voluntary Organisation (with Richard Gutch and Richard Percival) 1989, Beyond Economics: European Government after Maastricht. Discussion Paper, No. 12, Fabian Society (with Stephen Tindale) 1991, A More Perfect Union? Britain and the New Europe 1992, Reinventing the Left (ed.) 1994, Paying for Inequality: The Economic Cost of Social Injustice (co-ed.) 1994, Empowerment and the Deal for Devolution 2006. *Leisure interests:* supporting Arsenal Football Club, hoping for South Shields Football Club. *Address:* House of Commons, Westminster, London, SW1A 0AA (office); Ede House, 143 Westoe Road, South Shields, NE33 3PD, England (office); International Rescue Committee, 122 East 42nd Street, New York, NY 10168-1289, USA (office). *Telephone:* (20) 7219-3000 (House of Commons) (office); (191) 456-8910 (constituency office) (office); (212) 551-3000 (New York) (office). *Fax:* (191) 456-5842 (constituency office) (office); (212) 551-3179 (New York) (office). *E-mail:* milibandd@parliament.uk (office). *Website:* www .davidmiliband.info (office); www.rescue.org (office).

MILIBAND, Rt Hon. Edward Samuel (Ed), PC, BA, MSc; British politician; *Leader, Labour Party;* b. 24 Dec. 1969, London; s. of the late Ralph Miliband and Marion Kozak; brother of David Miliband; m. Justine Thornton 2011; two s.; ed London School of Econs, Corpus Christi Coll., Oxford; Special Adviser to Chancellor of Exchequer 1997, becoming Chair. Treasury Council of Econ. Advisers; MP (Labour) for Doncaster N 2005–; Parl. Sec. to Cabinet Office 2006, Chair. All-Party Group on Young People, Minister for Third Sector 2006–07, Minister for Cabinet Office and Chancellor, Duchy of Lancaster 2007–08; Sec. of State for Energy and Climate Change 2008–10; Leader of the Labour Party and Leader of the Opposition Sept. 2010–; Visiting Lecturer, Dept of Govt, Harvard Univ., USA 2003, also Visiting Scholar, Center for European Studies. *Address:* House of Commons, Westminster, London, SW1A 0AA (office); Labour Party, One Brewer's Green, London, SW1H 0RH (office); Hutton Business Centre, Bridge Works, Bentley, Doncaster, S Yorks., DN5 9QP, England (office). *Telephone:* (20) 7276-1234 (Westminster) (office); (20) 7219-4778 (Westminster) (office); (1302) 875462 (Doncaster) (office); (845) 092-2299 (Labour) (office). *Fax:* (20) 7802-1234 (Labour) (office). *E-mail:* ed.miliband.mp@parliament.uk (office). *Website:* www .parliament.uk/biographies/commons/edward-miliband/40791 (office); www .labour.org.uk (office).

MILIĆ, Srđan; Montenegrin (ethnic Serb) politician; *President, Socialist People's Party of Montenegro;* b. 17 Sept. 1965, Bar; m.; one s. two d.; ed Faculty for Foreign Trade and Tourism, Univ. of Dubrovnik, Croatia; moved to Budva following graduation; worked in tourism 1983–90; Asst, Faculty for Tourism, Kotor 1991–92; in pvt. commerce 1992–2002; joined reformed Socialist People's Party of Montenegro (SNP) 2002, researcher on EU and European integration of outside countries, mem. Main Bd and Main Bd's Exec. Cttee, Pres. SNP's Comm. for European and Euro-Atlantic integration, Pres. SNP 2006–; mem. Parl. (SNP-People's Party-Democratic Serb Party coalition's list) 2006–10, Leader of SNP Parl. Group 2006–10, mem. Parl. Comm. for European Integration; cand. in presidential election 2008; Pres. Nat. Council for European Integration 2008–09. *Address:* Socialist People's Party of Montenegro (Socijalistička Narodna Partija Crne Gore), 81000 Podgorica, Vaka Đurovića 5, Montenegro (office). *Telephone:* (20) 272421 (office). *Fax:* (20) 272420 (office). *E-mail:* snp@t-com.me (office). *Website:* www.snp.co.me (office).

MILINGO, Most Rev. Archbishop Emmanuel, DipEd; Zambian ecclesiastic; *Archbishop Emeritus of Lusaka;* b. 13 June 1930; s. of Yakobe Milingo and Tomaida Lumbiwe; m. Maria Sung 2001 (divorced); ed St Mary's Presbyterial School, Fort Jameson and Kasina Junior Seminary and Kachebere Major Seminary, Nyasaland (now Malawi); studied Pastoral Sociology (Diploma), Rome, Univ. Coll. Dublin, Ireland; curate, Minga Mission 1958–61; Parish Priest, St Ann's Mission, Chipata 1963–66; Sec. for Mass Media, Zambia Episcopal Conf. 1966–69; Archbishop of Lusaka 1969–83, Archbishop Emer. 1983–; Special Del. to Pontifical Comm. for Pastoral Care of Migrants, Refugees and Pilgrims 1983–; drew worldwide headlines in 2001 when he married a Korean woman in a large ceremony in New York organised by the Unification Church ('Moonies'), later expressed regret and contrition to Pope John Paul II, subsequently spent a year in seclusion, returning to Rome in 2002. *Publications:* Amake Joni, Demarcations, The World in Between, The Flower Garden of Jesus the Redeemer, My Prayers are Not Heard, Precautions in the Ministry of Deliverance, Against Satan, The World in Between: Christian Healing and the Struggle for Spiritual Survival, Confessions of an Excommunicated Catholic (auto-biog.); has produced his own CD. *Leisure interests:* writing and preaching to make Jesus Christ known and loved. *E-mail:* emmanuelmilingo@hotmail.com (home). *Website:* www.archbishopmilingo .org.

MILINKEVICH, Alyaksandr Uladzimeravich, PhD; Belarusian politician; *Leader, For Freedom Movement;* b. 25 July 1947, Grodno, Byelorussian SSR, USSR; m. 2nd Inna Kuley; two c. from first m.; ed Grodno Teacher Inst., USSR Acad. of Sciences, European Centre for Security Research, Garmisch-Partenkirchen, FRG; early career as teacher, Grodno 1969–72; Jr Researcher, USSR Acad. of Sciences (Belarus) 1972–78; Assoc. Prof., Grodno State Univ. 1978–80, 1984–90; Head, Dept of Physics, Univ. of Setif, Algeria 1980–84; Deputy Chair. Grodno Admin Exec. Cttee 1990–96; Leader, Ratusha (Town Hall) Org. 1996–2003; Pres. Grodno-93 football team; Founder and Head, Ratusha Resource Centre 1997 (closed by authorities 2003); headed presidential campaign of Syamyon Domash 2001; contested presidential election as cand. for coalition of

United Democratic Forces 2006; Founder and Leader, For Freedom Movt (Rukh 'Za Svabodu') (human rights group) 2008–; jailed by Govt for 15 days for taking part in an unsanctioned rally April 2006; Sakharov Prize, European Parl. 2006. *Address:* c/o United Civic Party (Abyadnanya Hramadzyanskaya Partya Belarusi), 220123 Minsk, vul. Khoruzhey 22/1701, Belarus (office). *Telephone:* (17) 289-50-09 (office). *Fax:* (17) 289-50-09 (office). *E-mail:* ucpb@ucpb.org (office); info@ milinkevich.org. *Website:* www.ucpb.org (office); www.milinkevich.org (office).

MILINTACHINDA, Piamsak; Thai international organization official; *Permanent Representative, Association of South East Asian Nations;* b. 1950, Bangkok; ed Chulalongkorn Univ. and Wayne State Univ., Detroit, USA; Attaché, Dept of Econ. Affairs, Ministry of Foreign Affairs 1977–80; Second Sec., Royal Thai Embassy, Singapore 1981–84; First Sec. Dept of ASEAN Affairs, Ministry of Foreign Affairs 1985–87, Deputy Dir-Gen. 1999; Counsellor, Perm. Mission to UN, New York 1988–91; Dir North American Div., Dept of American and South Pacific Affairs, Ministry of Foreign Affairs 1992–94; Minister, Deputy Perm. Rep. to WTO, Geneva 1995–99; Deputy Dir-Gen. Dept of European Affairs, Ministry of Foreign Affairs 2000–01; Deputy Exec. Dir APEC Secr. 2002, Exec. Dir 2003–05; Dir-Gen. Thailand Int. Devt Cooperation Agency 2004–06; Amb. to Hungary 2007–09; Perm. Rep. to ASEAN, Jakarta 2009–. *Address:* Office of the Permanent Representative of Thailand, c/o Association of Southeast Asian Nations Secretariat, 70a Jalan Sisingamangaraja, POB 2072, Jakarta 12110, Indonesia (office). *Telephone:* (21) 7262991 (office). *Fax:* (21) 7398234 (office). *Website:* www.aseansec .org (office).

MILIUS, John Frederick; American film writer, director and actor; b. 11 April 1944, St Louis; s. of William Styx Milius and Elizabeth Milius (née Roe); m. 1st Renée Fabri 1967; two s.; m. 2nd Celia K. Burkholder 1978; ed Univ. of Southern Calif.; Films include: The Devil's 8 1969, Evel Knievel 1971, Jeremiah Johnson 1972, The Life and Times of Judge Roy Bean 1973, Magnum Force 1973, Purvis FBI (for TV) 1974, The Wind and the Lion (also dir) 1975, Big Wednesday ((also dir), 1978, Apocalypse Now (Acad. Award for Best Screenplay 1980) 1979, 1941 (with Francis Ford Coppola q.v.) 1979, Conan the Barbarian (also dir) 1982, Red Dawn (also dir) 1984, Extreme Prejudice 1987, Farewell to the King (also dir) 1989, Flight of the Intruder (dir) 1991 Geronimo: An American Legend 1993, Clear and Present Danger 1994. *Address:* c/o Jeff Berg International Creative Management, 8942 Wilshire Boulevard, Beverly Hills, CA 90211, USA (office).

MILLAR, Sir Fergus Graham Burtholme, Kt, MA, DPhil, DLitt, FBA, FSA; British historian and academic (retd); *Camden Professor of Ancient History Emeritus, University of Oxford;* b. 5 July 1935, Edinburgh, Scotland; s. of J. S. L. Millar and J. B. Taylor; m. Susanna Friedmann 1959; two s. one d.; ed Edinburgh Acad., Loretto School, Trinity Coll., Oxford; Fellow, All Souls Coll., Oxford 1958–64; Fellow and Tutor in Ancient History, The Queen's Coll., Oxford 1964–76; Prof. of Ancient History, Univ. Coll., London 1976–84; Camden Prof. of Ancient History, Univ. of Oxford 1984–2002, currently Emer. Prof. of Ancient History; Fellow, Brasenose Coll. Oxford 1984–2002; Pres. Soc. for the Promotion of Roman Studies 1989–92 (Vice-Pres. 1977–89, 1992–2001, Hon. Vice-Pres. 2001–; Pres. Classical Asscn 1992–93; Publications Sec. British Acad. 1997–2002; Corresp. mem. German Archaeological Inst. 1977, Bavarian Acad. 1987, Finnish Acad. 1989, Russian Acad. 1999, American Acad. 2003; Hon. DPhil (Helsinki) 1994, Hon. DLitt (St Andrews Univ.) 2004; Premio Cultori di Roma 2005, Kenyon Medal for Classical Studies, British Acad. 2005. *Publications:* several historical studies, The Roman Near East 1993, The Crowd in Rome in the Late Republic 1998, The Roman Republic in Political Thought 2002. *Address:* Oriental Institute, Pusey Lane, Oxford, OX1 2LE (office); 80 Harpes Road, Oxford, OX2 7QL, England (home). *Telephone:* (1865) 288093 (office); (1865) 515782 (home). *Fax:* (1865) 278190 (office). *E-mail:* fergus.millar@bnc.ox.ac.uk (office).

MILLER, Aleksei Borisovich, PhD; Russian business executive; *Deputy Chairman of the Board of Directors and Chairman of the Management Committee (CEO), OAO Gazprom;* b. 31 Jan. 1962, Leningrad (now St Petersburg); m.; one s.; ed N.A. Voznesenskii Leningrad Inst. of Finance and Econs; engineer-economist, Gen. Planning Div., LenNIIProekt – Leningrad Civil Construction Research and Design Inst.; researcher, Leningrad Inst. of Finance and Econs 1990–91; mem. Cttee on Foreign Econ. Relations, Office of the Mayor of St Petersburg 1991–96; Dir of Devt and Investments, Morskoy Port of St Petersburg Open Jt Stock Co. 1996–99; Dir-Gen. Balttiiskaya Truboprovodnaya Sistema (Baltic Pipeline System) 1999–2000; Deputy Minister of Energy 2000–01; Chair. Man. Cttee (CEO) OAO Gazprom 2001–, Deputy Chair. Bd of Dirs 2002–; Order for the Services to the Fatherland, IV Class, Medal of Order for Services to the Fatherland, II Class, Order of Hungarian Repub. Cross, II Class, St Mesrop Mashtots Order (Armenia), Dostyk (Friendship) Order, II Class (Kazakhstan), Order of Honour (South Ossetia), Order of Merit of Italian Repub., Sergiy Radonezhsky Order of Russian Orthodox Church, II Class, Patriarchal Merit Certificate; named by Ekspert magazine (Russian business weekly) Person of the Year (jtly) 2005, ranked by Forbes magazine amongst The World's Most Powerful People (70th) 2012. *Address:* OAO Gazprom, 117997 Moscow, ul. Nametkina 16, V-420, GSP-7, Russia (office). *Telephone:* (495) 719-30-01 (office). *Fax:* (495) 719-83-33 (office). *E-mail:* gazprom@ gazprom.com (office). *Website:* www.gazprom.com (office).

MILLER, Andrew; British publishing executive; *CEO, Guardian Media Group;* gained accountancy qualifications with Price Waterhouse; held sr roles at Pepsi, Bass plc and Proctor & Gamble; Group Chief Financial Officer (CFO) Trader Media Group (jtly owned by Guardian Media Group (GMG) and Apax Partners pvt. equity group) –2009, mem. Bd of Dirs and CFO GMG 2009–10, Interim CEO April–July 2010, CEO July 2010–. *Address:* Guardian Media Group Headquarters, Kings Place, 90 York Way, London, N1 9GU, England (office). *Telephone:* (20) 3353-2000 (office). *E-mail:* contact@gmgplc.co.uk (office). *Website:* www.gmgplc.co.uk (office).

MILLER, Andrew, CBE, MA, PhD, FRSE; British academic; *Secretary and Treasurer, Carnegie Trust for the Universities of Scotland;* b. 15 Feb. 1936, Kelty, Fife; s. of William Hamilton Miller and Susan Anderson Miller (née Auld); m. Rosemary Singleton Hannah Fyvie 1962; one s. one d.; ed Beath High School, Univ. of Edinburgh; Asst Lecturer in Chem., Univ. of Edinburgh 1960–62; Post-Doctoral Fellow, CSIRO Div. of Protein Chem., Melbourne 1962–65; Staff Scientist, MRC Lab. of Molecular Biology, Cambridge 1965–66; Lecturer in Molecular Biophysics, Univ. of Oxford 1966–83; First Head, European Molecular Biology Lab., Grenoble

Antenne, France 1975–80; Prof. of Biochemistry, Univ. of Edinburgh 1984–94, Vice-Dean of Medicine 1991–93, Vice-Provost, Medicine and Veterinary Medicine 1992–93, Vice-Prin. 1993–94, Visiting Prof. 2001–03; Prin. and Vice-Chancellor, Univ. of Stirling 1994–2001, Prof. Emer. 2001–; Interim Chief Exec. Cancer Research, UK 2001–02; mem. Science and Eng Research Council Biological Sciences Cttee 1982–85; mem. Council Inst. Laue-Langevin, France 1981–85; mem. Univ. Grants Cttee, Biological Sciences Cttee 1985–88; Dir of Research, European Synchrotron Radiation Facility, Grenoble 1986–91; Fellow, Wolfson Coll., Oxford 1967–83, Hon. Fellow 1995–; mem. Univ. Funding Council-Biological Science Advisory Panel, Medical Advisory Panel 1989; mem. Council, Grenoble Univ. 1990–91, Royal Soc. of Edinburgh 1986 (Gen. Sec. 2001–05), Council Open Univ. 2001–05; mem. Minister of Educ.'s Action Group on Standards in Scottish Schools 1997–99, Scottish Exec. Science Strategy Group 1999–2000, UNESCO UK Science Cttee 2000–02; Adviser to Wellcome Trust on UK-French Synchrotron 1999–2000; Chair. Int. Centre for Math. Sciences, Edinburgh 2001–05; Leverhulme Emer. Fellow 2001–03; Bd mem. Food Standards Agency; Deputy Chair. Scottish Food Advisory Cttee 2003–05; Sec. and Treas., Carnegie Trust for the Univs of Scotland 2004–; Hon. DUniv (Stirling) 2002, (Open) 2006. *Publications:* Minerals in Biology (co-ed.) 1984; 180 research papers. *Leisure interests:* reading, walking, music. *Address:* Carnegie Trust for the Universities of Scotland, Andrew Carnegie House, Pittencrieff Street, Dunfermline, Fife, KY12 8AW, Scotland (office). *Telephone:* (1383) 724990 (office). *Fax:* (1383) 749799 (office). *E-mail:* amiller@carnegie-trust.org (office).

MILLER, Axel, LenD; Belgian banking executive; b. 20 Feb. 1965, Uccle; one s. three d.; ed Université Libre de Bruxelles; fmr Partner, Clifford Chance (law firm) for 14 years specializing in finance, mergers and acquisitions, int. commercial law; Gen. Counsel, Dexia Group 2001–02, mem. Man. Bd 2002–08, Man. Dir and Chair. Man. Bd 2003–08, CEO Dexia SA 2006–08, Group Head, Personal Financial Services 2003–08, mem. Strategy and Appointments Cttees, mem. Man. Bd Dexia Bank 2002–08, Dexia BIL, mem. Bd of Dirs Dexia Crédit Local; Vice-Pres. Financial Security Assurance Holdings; mem. Man. Bd Fédération des entreprises de Belgique; mem. Bd of Dirs Ethias, Crédit du Nord, LVI Holding (Carmeuse group). *Address:* c/o Dexia Group, Place Logier 11, Brussels 1210, Belgium.

MILLER, Hon. Dame Billie Antoinette; Barbadian politician and lawyer; b. 8 Jan. 1944; d. of the late Frederick Edward Miller; ed Queen's Coll., Barbados, King's Coll., Durham, UK; mem. Int. Fed. of Women Lawyers 1975–76; elected mem. Parl. for City of Bridgetown 1976, Mininster of Health and Nat. Insurance 1976–81, of Educ. 1981–85, of Educ. and Culture 1985–86; mem. Council Univ. of the West Indies 1981–86; apptd to Senate, Leader of Opposition Business 1986–91; re-elected mem. Parl. 1991, Deputy Leader of Opposition 1993–94; Sr Minister and Minister of Foreign Affairs and Foreign Trade 1994–2008; Chair. Exec. Cttee Commonwealth Parl. Assen 1991–99, NGO Planning Cttee for Int. Conf. on Population and Devt, Cairo, Egypt 1994, IDB's Advisory Council on Women in Devt, Washington, DC 1996–2002, Caribbean Tourism Org. 1997–98, Assen of Caribbean States' Ministerial Council 2000–01; Pres. Int. Planned Parenthood Fed., Western Hemisphere Region 1991–97, African, Caribbean and Pacific States Council of Ministers 1998, 32nd Regular Session of the Gen. Ass. of OAS 2002; Pres. Bd Dirs Interamerican Parl. Group on Population and Devt for the Caribbean and Latin America, New York; Co-ordinator of Caribbean Community (CARICOM) Ministerial Spokespersons with Responsibility for External Negotiations in Bilateral, African Caribbean and Pacific States-European Union (ACP-EU), WTO and Free Trade Area of the Americas (FTAA) Matters 2002–; Vice-Chair. Commonwealth Ministerial Action Group 2000–02, 6th WTO Ministerial Conf. 2005; mem. Int. Planned Parenthood Fed. Cen. Council, Planned Parenthood Fed. of America Inc., UN Population Fund's Advisory Panel for Activities Concerning Women, Inter-American Dialogue; Hon. Fellow, Honors Coll., Florida International Univ. 2001; Grand Officer, Nat. Order of Benin 2000, Nat. Order of Juan Mora Fernandez, Costa Rica 2001, Dame of St Andrew 2003, Order Bernardo O'Higgins (Chile) 2006; Queen's Silver Jubilee Medal 1977, Barbados Centennial Award 2000, Grantley Adams Award, Barbados Labour Party 2001, Woman of Great Esteem Award, Kingdom Ministries, USA 2002, Dame Elsie Payne Award of Excellence, Queen's Coll. Assen 2002, The Dame Billie Miller Lecture Series on Women in Govt in association with Medgar Evers Coll., CUNY 2004, Lifetime Achievement Award, Caribbean Tourism Org. 2006. *Publications:* numerous papers and articles on population and women's issues. *Leisure interests:* reading, interior design, Ikebana. *Address:* Ministry of Foreign Affairs and Foreign Trade, 1 Culloden Road, St Michael, Barbados (office).

MILLER, Bode; American professional skier; b. 12 Oct. 1977, Franconia, NH; s. of Jo Miller; ed Carrabassett Valley Acad., Me; World Cup debut: Park City, UT, USA 1996; mem. US Nat. Team 1996–; Gold Medals, Combined and Giant Slalom events, World Championships, St Moritz, Switzerland 2003, Silver Medal, Super-G; Silver Medals, Combined and Giant Slalom events, Winter Olympic Games, Salt Lake City, USA 2002, Bronze Medal, Winter Olympic Games, Vancouver, Canada 2010; 12 World Cup wins (six Giant Slalom, four Slalom, two Combined); won Alpine Skiing World Cup 2005, 2008; won Super G World Cup 2007; left US Ski Team 2007; f. Team America (ind. race team) 2007–09, rejoined US Ski Team 2009; f. SkiSpace.com (social networking and information site for skiers and snowboarders). *Leisure interest:* reggae and rap music. *Address:* c/o Lowell Taub, CAA Sports, 162 Fifth Avenue, 8th Floor, New York, NY 10010, USA. *Telephone:* (212) 277-9000. *Fax:* (212) 277-9099. *Website:* www.skispace.com/bode.

MILLER, David, LLB, MA; Canadian/American lawyer and politician; *President and CEO, WWF-Canada;* b. USA; m. Jill Arthur; two c.; ed Faculty of Law, Univ. of Toronto, Harvard Univ., USA; trained in employment and immigration law; fmr Partner, Aird & Berlis law firm, Toronto, Counsel –2013; cand. for New Democratic Party (NDP) in fed. elections, Parkdale-High Park constituency 1993, by-election in York S-Weston 1996; elected to Municipality of Metropolitan Toronto Council 1994–97, City of Toronto Council 1997–2003; Mayor of Toronto 2003–10; Pres. and CEO, World Wildlife Fund-Canada 2013–; mem. Bd Man. Bloor West Village Business Improvement Area, Colborne Lodge, Mackenzie House, Spadina House Community, Junction Gardens Business Improvement Area, Swansea Town Hall Community Centre; mem. Bd of Dirs Runnymede Hosp.; mem. Admin Cttee, Humber York Community Council, ABC Ad Hoc Cttee, Humber Watershed Alliance, Labour Relations Advisory Panel, Oak Ridges Moraine Steering Cttee,

Toronto Transit Comm.; mem. Law Soc. of Upper Canada. *Address:* WWF-Canada, 245 Eglinton Avenue, East Suite 410, Toronto, ON M4P 3J1, Canada (office). *Telephone:* (416) 489-8800 (office). *Fax:* (416) 489-0819 (office). *E-mail:* drmiller@wwfcanada.org (office). *Website:* www.wwf.ca (office).

MILLER, David A. B., BSc, PhD, FRS, FRSE; British physicist and academic; *Director, E.L. Ginzton Laboratory, Stanford University;* b. 19 Feb. 1954, Hamilton, South Lanarkshire, Scotland; ed Heriot-Watt Univ., St Andrews Univ.; Research Assoc., Heriot-Watt Univ. Dept of Physics 1979–80, Lecturer 1980–81; mem. Tech. Staff, AT&T Bell Laboratories, Holmdel, NJ, USA 1981–87, Head Photonics Switching Device Research Dept 1987–92, Head Photonics Research Dept 1996; Prof. of Electrical Eng, Stanford Univ. 1996, W. M. Keck Foundation Prof. of Electrical Eng 1997–, Prof. by Courtesy of Applied Physics 1997–, Dir Stanford Univ. Solid State and Photonics Lab. 1997–, Dir E.L. Ginzton Lab. 1997–, Co-Dir Stanford Photonics Research Center; Vice-Pres. Int. Comm. for Optics 1999–2002; Dir Optical Soc. of America 2000–03; mem. Editorial Bd Semiconductor Science and Technology 1987–90, Optical and Quantum Electronics 1988–, Applied Physics Reviews 1991–97; mem. NAS 2008, Nat. Acad. of Eng 2010; Fellow, Optical Soc. of America 1988, American Physical Soc. 1988, IEEE 1995; Dr hc (Vrije Universiteit) 1997, Hon. DEng (Heriot-Watt) 2003; Adolph Lomb Medal, Optical Soc. of America 1986, R.W. Wood Prize, Optical Soc. of America 1986, Int. Comm. for Optics Prize 1991, IEEE Third Millennium Medal 2000. *Achievement:* holder of 58 patents. *Publications:* over 200 papers on optics and optoelectronics. *Address:* E.L. Ginzton Laboratory, Stanford University, Center for Nanoscale Science and Engineering, 348 Via Pueblo Mall, Stanford, CA 94305-4088, USA (office). *Telephone:* (650) 723-0111 (office). *E-mail:* dabm@ee.stanford.edu (office). *Website:* engineering.stanford.edu/faculty/dabm (office); www.ee.stanford.edu/~dabm (office).

MILLER, David W., MS; American professor of aeronautics and space scientist; *Chief Technologist, NASA;* ed Massachusetts Inst. of Tech.; Research Assoc., MIT 1988–91, Prin. Research Scientist 1991–97, Asst Prof. 1997–2000, Assoc. Prof. 2000–06, Jerome C. Hunsaker Prof. of Aeronautics and Astronautics, Dir Space Systems Lab. –2014; held various positions on NASA projects, including Prin. Investigator for Regolith X-ray Imaging Spectrometer and for OSIRIS-REx asteroid sample return mission (planned for launch 2016), Prin. Investigator for Synchronized Position, Hold, Engage and Reorient Experimental Satellites (SPHERES) project on Int. Space Station, apptd Chief Technologist, NASA 2014–; fmr Vice-Chair. Air Force Scientific Advisory Bd; Sr Mem. American Inst. of Aeronautics and Astronautics; mem. American Soc. of Mechanical Engineers, American Astronautical Soc., Int. Soc. for Optical Eng. *Address:* NASA Headquarters, Suite 2R40, Washington, DC 20546, USA (office). *Telephone:* (202) 358-0001 (office). *Fax:* (202) 358-4338 (office). *Website:* www.nasa.gov (office).

MILLER, Edward A., PhD; American engineer; worked on USAF experimental RVX-1 and RVX-2 re-entry vehicles and MK III intercontinental ballistic missile (ICBM) Atlas launch vehicle; fmr Project Engineer and Program Man., General Electric, responsible for design, construction, deployment, operation and recovery of Corona's satellite recovery vehicle (first man-made object recovered from Earth orbit); fmr Leader, Itek Corpn's Viking Lander Program, helped obtain first imagery transmitted from surface of Mars in 1974; Asst Sec. of the Army 1975–77, led R&D programme that resulted in advanced weapons systems, including Apache and Blackhawk helicopters, Abrams M1 Tank, Patriot High Altitude Air Defense System; Army Distinguished Civilian Service Decoration; recognized as an Eminent Engineer by Nat. Eng Honor Soc. (Tau Beta Pi) 1976, named a Pioneer of Space Tech. 1985, honoured by Dir of CIA for his role as Corona Pioneer 1995, Charles Stark Draper Prize, Nat. Acad. of Eng (co-recipient) 2005. *Address:* c/o National Academy of Engineering, 500 Fifth Street, NW, Washington, DC 20001, USA. *E-mail:* NAEMembershipOffice@nae.edu.

MILLER, Edward D., MD, FRCP, FRCA; American anaesthesiologist, academic and university administrator; *Dean and CEO, Medical Faculty, School of Medicine, Johns Hopkins University;* b. 1 Feb. 1943, Rochester, NY; m. Lynne R. Miller; ed Ohio Wesleyan Univ., Univ. of Rochester School of Medicine and Dentistry; intern, Univ. Hosp., Boston 1968–69; Chief Resident in Anaesthesiology, Peter Bent Brigham Hosp., Boston 1969–71; Research Fellow in Physiology, Harvard Medical School 1971–73; Dir of Anaesthesia Research, Brooke Army Medical Center, Fort Sam Houston, Tex. 1973–75; Asst Prof. of Anaesthesiology, Univ. of Virginia 1975–79, Assoc. Prof. 1979–82, Prof. of Anaesthesiology 1982–83, Prof. of Anaesthesiology and Surgery 1983–86; E.M. Papper Prof. of Anaesthesiology and Chair., Dept of Anaesthesiology, Coll. of Physicians and Surgeons, Columbia Univ. 1986–94; Mark C. Rogers Prof. and Dir Dept of Anaesthesiology and Critical Care Medicine, Johns Hopkins Univ. 1994–, Interim Dean 1996–97, CEO 1997–, Vice-Pres. School of Medicine 1997–, Dean of Medical Faculty, Johns Hopkins Univ. School of Medicine 1997–, est. Center for Innovation in Quality Patient Care; mem. Asscn of Univ. Anaesthesiologists (Pres. 1990–92); Ed. Anesthesia and Analgesia 1982–92; fmr Ed. Critical Care Medicine; fmr Chair. Food and Drug Asscn Advisory Cttee on Anaesthesia and Life Support Drugs; mem., Inst. of Medicine, NAS, Maryland's Health Care Access and Cost Comm.; Bd mem. Greater Baltimore Cttee, Mercantile Safe Deposit and Trust Fund. *Address:* 100 SOM Administration, The Johns Hopkins University School of Medicine, 733 North Broadway, Baltimore, MD 21205, USA (office). *Telephone:* (410) 955-3180 (office). *Fax:* (410) 955-0889 (office). *E-mail:* emiller@jhmi.edu (office). *Website:* hopkinsmedicine.org (office).

MILLER, George H., BS, MS, PhD; American physicist and academic; *Laboratory Director and President, Lawrence Livermore National Security LLC;* ed Coll. of William and Mary; Physicist, Lawrence Livermore Nat. Lab., Univ. of California 1972–80, A-Div. Leader and Program Leader, Thermonuclear Design and Computational Physics Devt 1980–85, Assoc. Dir for Nuclear Design 1985–89, Assoc. Dir for Defense and Nuclear Techs 1990–, Assoc. Dir for Nat. Security 1996–2000, Assoc. Dir for Nat. Ignition Facility programs 2000–05, Interim Dir 2005–06, Lab. Dir and Pres. Lawrence Livermore Nat. Security LLC 2006–; Special Scientific Adviser on Weapon Activities, US Dept of Energy, Washington, DC 1989–90; mem. Sr Man. Group, Univ. of California; mem. American Physical Soc.; Fellowship Awards from NSF, Gulf Gen. Atomics. *Address:* Lawrence Livermore National Security LLC, 2300 First Street, Suite 204, Livermore, CA

94550, USA (office). *Telephone:* (925) 453-3580 (office). *Fax:* (925) 454-1447 (office). *Website:* www.llnsllc.com (office).

MILLER, George 'Kennedy', AO, MB, BS; Australian film director, producer, writer and physician; b. 3 March 1945, Chinchilla, Queensland; s. of James Miller and Angela Miller (née Balson); m. Sandy Gore 1985; one d.; ed Sydney Boys' High School, Univ. of New South Wales Medical School; Resident Medical Officer, St Vincent's Hosp., Sydney 1971–72; f. Kennedy Miller film co. with the late Byron Kennedy 1977, Chair. 1977–; Pres. Jury Avoriaz Film Festival 1984; mem. Jury Cannes Film Festival 1988; Chair. Byron Kennedy Memorial Trust 1984–; mem. Bd Dirs Museum of Contemporary Art, Sydney 1987–; Best Dir, Australian Film Inst. 1982, Best Dir TV Drama, Penguin Awards 1983, Grand Prix Avoriaz 1983, Best Foreign Film, LA Film Critics 1983 and numerous other prizes and awards. *Films include:* dir: Violence In the Cinema, Part 1 (also writer) 1971, Mad Max (also writer) 1979, Mad Max 2 (also writer) 1981, Twilight Zone: The Movie (segment 4) 1983, Mad Max Beyond Thunderdome (also producer and writer) 1985, The Witches of Eastwick 1987, Lorenzo's Oil (also producer and writer) 1992, 40,000 Years of Dreaming (also producer and writer) 1997, Babe: Pig in the City (also producer and writer) 1998, Happy Feet (also producer and writer) (BAFTA Award for Best Animated Film 2007) 2006; producer: The Chain Reaction (assoc. producer) 1980, The Year My Voice Broke 1987, Dead Calm 1989, Flirting 1991, Video Fool for Love 1995, Babe (also writer) (Golden Globe Award for Best Picture 1996) 1995, 40,000 Years of Dreaming 1997, Babe: Pig in the City 1998, Happy Feet (Acad. Award for Best Animated Feature Film 2007) 2006. *Television includes:* dir: Ryan (series) 1973, Bellamy (series; episode 1.02 The Carver Gang) 1981, The Dismissal (mini-series) (also exec. producer and writer) 1983, The Last Bastion (mini-series; co-dir) 1984; producer: Cowra Breakout (mini-series) 1984, Bodyline: It's Not Just Cricket (mini-series) 1984, The Riddle of the Stinson 1987, Vietnam (mini-series) 1987, The Dirtwater Dynasty (mini-series) 1988, The Clean Machine 1988, Fragments of War: The Story of Damien Parer 1988, Bangkok Hilton (mini-series) 1989. *Leisure interests:* art, music, sport. *Address:* 30 Orwell Street, King's Cross, NSW 2011, Australia. *Telephone:* (2) 357-2322.

MILLER, Heidi G., PhD; American investment banker; *President of International, JPMorgan Chase & Company;* b. 1953; m. Brian Miller; two c.; ed Princeton Univ., Yale Univ.; began career at Chemical Bank in 1979, Man. Dir and Group Head, Emerging Markets 1987–92; Vice-Pres. and Asst to Pres. Travelers Group Inc. 1992–98, later Chief Risk Officer of its Salomon Smith Barney unit, Chief Financial Officer Travelers Group Inc. 1995–98; Chief Financial Officer Citigroup Inc. 1998–2000; Sr Exec. Vice-Pres. Strategic Planning and Admin and mem. Bd of Dirs Priceline.com 2000–01; Vice-Chair. Marsh & McLennan Co. Inc. 2001–; Exec. Vice-Pres., Chief Financial Officer and mem. Bd Dirs Bank One, Chicago 2002–04, Exec. Vice-Pres. and CEO Treasury and Security Services, JPMorgan Chase & Co. (following merger with Bank One) 2004–10, Pres. of International 2010–; mem. Bd of Dirs General Mills Inc., Mead Corpn, Merck & Co. Inc., Progressive Corpn 2011–, Local Initiatives Support Corpn 2004–; Trustee Princeton Univ.; ranked by Fortune magazine amongst the 50 Most Powerful Women in Business in the US (50th) 2002, (29th) 2004, (28th) 2005, (25th) 2006, (27th) 2007, (17th) 2008–09, ranked by Forbes magazine amongst The World's 100 Most Powerful Women (99th) 2009, ranked by Fortune magazine amongst the 50 Most Powerful Women in Business outside the US (fifth) 2010, named by US Banker magazine amongst 25 Women to Watch 2004, also named amongst the 25 Most Powerful Women in Banking (fourth) 2005, (first) 2007–08, named by Global Finance magazine amongst Ones to Watch 2005. *Address:* JPMorgan Chase & Co., 270 Park Avenue, New York, NY 10017, USA (office). *Telephone:* (212) 270-6000 (office). *Fax:* (212) 270-1613 (office). *Website:* www.jpmorganchase.com (office).

MILLER, Jacques Francis, AC, BA, MD, PhD, DSc, FAA, FRS; Australian (b. French) medical research scientist and academic; *Professor Emeritus, University of Melbourne and Walter and Eliza Hall Institute of Medical Research;* b. (Jacques Francis Meunier), 2 April 1931, Nice, France; s. of the late Maurice Miller and Fernande Debarnot; m. Margaret D. Houen 1956; ed Univs of Sydney and London; received Australian citizenship 1955; Jr Resident Medical Officer, Royal Prince Alfred Hosp., Sydney 1956; pathological research, Univ. of Sydney 1957; cancer research, Chester Beatty Research Inst., London 1958–65; Head, Experimental Pathology and Thymus Biology Unit, Walter and Eliza Hall Inst. (WEHI), Melbourne 1966–, Prof. and Chair of Experimental Immunology, Univ. of Melbourne and WEHI 1990–97, Prof. Emer. 1997–; various other professional appointments; Foreign Assoc., NAS; Laureate Prof.; numerous awards and honours, including Esther Langer-Bertha Teplitz Memorial Prize 1965, Paul Ehrlich-Ludwig Darmstaedter Prize 1974, Inaugural Sandoz Prize for Immunology 1990, Florey-Faulding Medal and Prize 2000, Copley Medal, Royal Soc. 2001, Prime Minister's Prize for Science 2003. *Publications:* more than 400 papers in scientific journals, mostly on immunology and cancer research. *Leisure interests:* art, photography, music, literature. *Address:* Walter and Eliza Hall Institute of Medical Research, 1G Royal Parade, Parkville, Vic. 3050 (office); 5 Charteris Drive, East Ivanhoe, Vic. 3079, Australia (home). *Telephone:* (3) 9345-2555 (office); (3) 9499-3481 (home). *Fax:* (3) 9347-0852 (office). *Website:* www.wehi.edu.au (office).

MILLER, James Clifford, III, BBA, PhD; American business executive, academic and government official; *Senior Advisor, Husch Blackwell, LLP;* b. 25 June 1942, Atlanta, Ga; s. of James Clifford Miller, Jr and Annie Miller (née Moseley); m. Demaris Humphries 1961; one s. two d.; ed Univs of Georgia and Virginia; Asst Prof., Georgia State Univ., Atlanta 1968–69; Economist, US Dept of Transport 1969–72; Assoc. Prof. of Econs, Texas A&M Univ. 1972–74; Economist, US Council of Econ. Advisers, Washington, DC 1974–75; Asst Dir US Council of Wage and Price Stability 1975–77; Resident Scholar, American Enterprise Inst. 1977–81; Admin., Office of Information and Regulatory Affairs, Office of Man. and Budget and Exec. Dir Presidential Task Force on Regulatory Relief 1981; Chair. Fed. Trade Comm., Washington, DC 1981–85; Dir Office of Man. and Budget 1985–89; Adjunct Scholar, Center for Study of Public Choice, George Mason Univ. 1988–, Chair. Citizens for a Sound Econ. 1988–2003; Founder and Chair. The Cap Analysis Group (div. of int. law firm Howrey LLP) 2003–06; mem. Bd of Govs US Postal Service 2003–11, Chair. 2005–08; currently Sr Advisor to int. law firm Husch Blackwell LLP; chaired The Miller Comm. (ind. comm. apptd to address the fiscal and econ. health of the Cayman Islands) 2009; Thomas Jefferson Fellow

1965–66; DuPont Fellow 1966–67, Ford Foundation Fellow 1967–68; Distinguished Fellow, Center for Study of Public Choice, George Mason Univ. 1988–, Mercatus Center, George Mason Univ. 1997–; Sr Fellow (by courtesy), Hoover Inst., Stanford Univ. 1988–; mem. Bd of Dirs Washington Mutual Investors Fund 1992–, Independence Air 1995–99, Tax-Exempt Fund of Maryland 2000–, Tax-Exempt Fund of Virginia 2000–, Americans for Prosperity 2004–, Clean Energy Fuels Corpn 2006–; Chair. Exec. Cttee, Int. Tax and Investment Center; mem. American Econ. Asscn, Federalist Soc., Public Choice Soc., Southern Econ. Asscn. *Publications:* Why the Draft? The Case for a Volunteer Army 1968, Economic Regulation of Domestic Air Transport; Theory and Policy 1974, Perspectives on Federal Transportation Policy 1975, Benefit – Cost Analyses of Social Regulation 1979, Reforming Regulation 1980, The Federal Trade Commission: The Political Economy of Regulation 1987, The Economist as Reformer 1989, Fix the U.S. Budget! 1994, Monopoly Politics 1999; more than 100 articles in professional journals. *Leisure interests:* politics, econs. *Address:* Husch Blackwell LLP, 750 17th Street NW, Suite 1000, Washington, DC 20006, USA (office). *Telephone:* (202) 378-2302 (office). *Fax:* (202) 378-2319 (office). *E-mail:* jim.miller@huschblackwell .com (office). *Website:* www.huschblackwell.com (office).

MILLER, Jerzy; Polish politician and civil servant; b. 7 June 1952, Kraków; m.; ed Faculty of Electrical Eng, Electronics and Automatics, AGH Univ. of Science and Tech., Kraków; began career in public admin 1990, Dir Org. and Supervision Div. 1990–91, Dir Małopolskie Voivodship Office, Kraków 1991–92; Vice-Gov. fmr Krakow Voivodship 1993–98; Under-Sec. of State 1998–2000, Sec. of State, Ministry of Finance 2000–01; Govt Plenipotentiary for Decentralization of Public Finance under Prime Minister Jerzy Buzek 2001; Adviser to Pres. Nat. Bank of Poland 2001–03; Pres. Agency for Restructuring and Modernization of Agric. 2003; Dir Dept for Social Communication, Nat. Bank of Poland 2003–04, mem. Man. Bd 2004; Pres. Nat. Health Fund 2004–06; Deputy Mayor of Warsaw 2006–07; Gov. Małopolskie Voivodship 2007–09; Minister of Internal Affairs and Admin 2009–11. *Address:* c/o Ministry of the Interior, 02-591 Warsaw, ul. Stefana Batorego 5, Poland.

MILLER, Jonathan; American media executive; b. 1957; early career Vice-Pres. of Programming and NBA Entertainment with Nat. Basketball Asscn; CEO and Man. Dir Nickelodeon UK, then Man. Dir Int.; Pres. and CEO USA Broadcasting 1997–1999; Pres. and CEO USA Electronic Commerce Solutions 1999–2000; Pres. and CEO USA Information and Services (USAIS) 2000–2002; Chair. and CEO America Online Inc. (later AOL LLC) 2002–06. *Address:* c/o AOL LLC, 22000 AOL Way, Dulles, VA, 20166-9323, USA (office).

MILLER, Sir Jonathan Wolfe, Kt, CBE, MB, BCh, FRCP; British stage director, film director, physician and writer; b. 21 July 1934, London; s. of the late Emanuel Miller; m. Helen Rachel Collet 1956; two s. one d.; ed St Paul's School, St John's Coll., Cambridge and Univ. Coll. Hosp. Medical School, London; co-author of and appeared in Beyond the Fringe 1961–64; Dir John Osborne's Under Plain Cover, Royal Court Theatre 1962, Robert Lowell's The Old Glory, New York 1964 and Prometheus Bound, Yale Drama School 1967; Dir at Nottingham Playhouse 1968–69; Dir Oxford and Cambridge Shakespeare Co. production of Twelfth Night on tour in USA 1969; Research Fellow in the History of Medicine, Univ. Coll., London 1970–73; Assoc. Dir Nat. Theatre 1973–75; mem. Arts Council 1975–76; Visiting Prof. in Drama, Westfield Coll., Univ. of London 1977–; Exec. Producer Shakespeare TV series 1979–81; Artistic Dir Old Vic 1988–90; Research Fellow in Neuropsychology, Univ. of Sussex; Pres. Rationalist Soc. 2006–; Fellow, Univ. Coll. London 1981–, Royal Coll. of Physicians; mem. American Acad. of Arts and Sciences; Hon. Fellow, St John's Coll. Cambridge, Royal Coll. of Physicians (Edin.) 1998; Hon. Assoc., British Humanist Asscn, Nat. Secular Soc.; Dr hc (Open Univ.) 1983, Hon. DLitt (Leicester) 1981, (Kent) 1985, (Leeds) 1996, (Cambridge) 1996; Royal Television Soc. Silver Medal 1981, Royal Soc. of Arts Albert Medal 1992. *Productions include:* for Nat. Theatre, London: The Merchant of Venice 1970, Danton's Death 1971, The School for Scandal 1972, The Marriage of Figaro 1974; other productions The Tempest, London 1970, Prometheus Bound, London 1971, The Taming of the Shrew, Chichester 1972, The Seagull, Chichester 1973, The Malcontent, Nottingham 1973, Arden Must Die (opera) 1973, The Family in Love, Greenwich Season 1974, The Importance of Being Earnest 1975, The Cunning Little Vixen (opera) 1975, All's Well That Ends Well, Measure For Measure, Greenwich Season 1975, Three Sisters 1977, The Marriage of Figaro (ENO) 1978, Arabella (opera) 1980, Falstaff (opera) 1980, 1981, Otello (opera) 1982, Rigoletto (opera) 1982, 1984, Fidelio (opera) 1982, 1983, Don Giovanni (opera) 1985, The Mikado (opera) 1986, Tosca (opera) 1986, Long Day's Journey into Night 1986, Taming of the Shrew 1987, The Tempest 1988, Turn of the Screw 1989, King Lear 1989, The Liar 1989, La Fanciulla del West (opera) 1991, Marriage of Figaro (opera), Manon Lescaut (opera), Die Gezeichneten (opera) 1992, Maria Stuarda (opera), Capriccio (opera), Fedora (opera), Bach's St Matthew Passion 1993, Der Rosenkavalier (opera), Anna Bolena (opera), Falstaff (opera), L'Incoronazione di Poppea (opera), La Bohème (opera) 1994, Così fan tutte (opera) 1995, Carmen (opera) 1995, Pelléas et Mélisande (opera) 1995, She Stoops to Conquer, London 1995, A Midsummer Night's Dream, London 1996, The Rake's Progress, New York 1997, Ariadne auf Naxos, Maggio Musicale, Florence 1997, Falstaff, Berlin State Opera 1998, The Beggar's Opera 1999, Tamerlano, Sadler's Wells, Paris and Halle 2001, Jenůfa, Glimmerglass Opera 2006, The Cherry Orchard, Sheffield Crucible 2007, La Bohème, ENO, London 2009. *Films include:* Alice in Wonderland 1966, Take a Girl Like You 1969 and several films for television including Whistle and I'll Come to You 1967, The Body in Question (series) 1978, States of Mind (series) 1983, The Emperor 1987, Jonathan Miller's Opera Works (series) 1997, Brief History of Disbelief (series) 2005. *Publications include:* McLuhan 1971, Freud: The Man, his World, his Influence (ed.) 1972, The Body in Question 1978, Subsequent Performances 1986, The Don Giovanni Book: Myths of Seduction and Betrayal (ed.) 1990, On Reflection 1998, Nowhere in Particular 2001. *Leisure interest:* deep sleep.

MILLER, Karl Fergus Connor, BA, MA, FRSL; British academic, writer and editor; b. 2 Aug. 1931; s. of William Miller and Marion Miller; m. Jane Elisabeth Collet 1956; two s. one d.; ed Royal High School, Edinburgh and Downing Coll., Cambridge; Asst Prin., HM Treasury 1956–57; BBC TV producer 1957–58; Literary Ed., The Spectator 1958–61, New Statesman 1961–67; Ed., The Listener 1967–73; Lord Northcliffe Prof. of Modern English Literature, Univ. Coll., London

1974–92; Ed., London Review of Books 1979–89, Co-Ed. 1989–92; currently freelance; James Tait Black Prize 1975, Scottish Arts Council Book Award 1993. *Publications:* Poetry from Cambridge 1952–54 (ed.) 1955, Writing in England Today: The Last Fifteen Years (ed.) 1968, Memoirs of a Modern Scotland (ed.) 1970, A Listener Anthology, August 1967–June 1970 (ed.) 1970, A Second Listener Anthology (ed.) 1973, Cockburn's Millennium 1975, Robert Burns (ed.) 1981, Doubles: Studies in Literary History 1985, Authors 1989, Rebecca's Vest (autobiog.) 1993, Boswell and Hyde 1995, Dark Horses (autobiog.) 1998, Electric Shepherd: A Likeness of James Hogg 2003, Tretower to Clyro (selected essays) 2011. *Leisure interest:* football. *Address:* 26 Limerston Street, London, SW10 0HH, England (home). *Telephone:* (20) 7351-1994 (home).

MILLER, Lajos; Hungarian singer (baritone); b. 23 Jan. 1940, Szombathely; s. of Lajos Miller and Teréz Sebestyén; m. Zsuzsa Dobránszky; one s.; ed studied at Music Acad. of Budapest under Jenő Sipos; mem. Hungarian State Opera 1968–; roles include Verdi's Renato, Rodrigo, Simon Boccanegra, Don Carlos, Rolando in Battaglia di Legnano, Iago, Nabucco, Conte di Luna, Miller, Germont, Gluck's Orpheus, Orestes, Mozart's Don Giovanni, Guglielmo, Giordano's Carlo Gérard, Leoncavallo's Silvio, Rossini's Figaro, Guglielmo Tell, Tchaikovsky's Eugene Onegin, Yeletsky, Puccini's Scarpia, Bizet's Escamillo, Berio's Commandante Ivo, Donizetti's Enrico, Rimsky-Korsakov's Grasnoi, Puccini's Sharplesshas; sung with major cos in France, Germany, Italy, Monaco, Switzerland, Austria, UK, USA, Belgium, Venezuela, Canada, Chile, Japan, Argentina, Russia; Grand Prix, Fauré singing contest, Paris 1974, First Prize, Toti dal Monte singing contest, Treviso, Italy 1975, Liszt Prize 1975, Kossuth Prize 1980. *TV films:* Orfeusz Es Eurydike (Rainieri de Calzabigi and Christoph Willibald Gluck) 1985, Enrico (Lucia di Lammermoor), Marcello (Tabarro), Silvio (Pagliacci), Loth (Madarasz Loth), two portrait films 1995, Angelica (Ibert), L'elisir d'amore (Donizetti), Rigoletto (Verdi), Bank Ban 2002. *Leisure interests:* tennis, surfing, skiing, photography, making films. *E-mail:* info@lajosmiller.com (office). *Website:* www.lajosmiller.com.

MILLER, Leslie O.; Bahamian politician; fmr Minister of Trade and Industry. *Address:* c/o Ministry of Trade and Industry, Manx Building, West Bay Street, POB N-4849, Nassau, The Bahamas (office).

MILLER, Leszek Cezary, MPolSci; Polish politician; *Chairman, Democratic Left Alliance;* b. 3 July 1946, Żyrardów; m. Aleksandra Borowiec; one s.; ed Higher School of Social Sciences; electrician Enterprise of Linen Industry, Żyrardów 1963–70; mem. Polish United Workers' Party (PZPR) 1966–90, Staff mem. Cen. Cttee 1977–86; First Sec. Voivodeship's Cttee of Skierniewice 1986–89, mem. Cen. Cttee 1989–90, mem. Politburo Cen. Cttee 1989–90; participant in Round Table Talks 1989; Deputy to Sejm (Parl.) 1991–2005 (Chair. Left Alliance Caucus 1997–2001); Minister of Labour and Social Policy 1993–96, of Interior and Admin. Jan.–Oct. 1997; Minister, Head Council of Ministers Office 1996; mem. and Co-founder Social Democracy of Repub. of Poland 1990–99 (Gen. Sec. 1990–93, Vice-Chair. 1993–97, Chair. 1997–99); Chair. Democratic Left Alliance (SLD) 1999–2007, 2011–; Chair. Polish Left 2007–10; Prime Minister of Poland 2001–04 (resgnd); Kt's Cross of Polonia Restituta Order 1984, Golden Cross of Merit 1979, Chevalier of the Order of the Smile; Goodwill Amb., Polish Cttee of UNICEF 2000. *Leisure interests:* angling, literature. *Address:* Democratic Left Alliance (Sojusz Lewicy Demokratycznej), 00-419 Warsaw, ul. Rozbrat 44A, Poland (office). *Telephone:* (22) 6210341 (office). *Fax:* (22) 6216069 (office). *E-mail:* rk@sld.org.pl (office). *Website:* www.sld.org.pl (office).

MILLER, Rt Hon. Maria Frances Lewis, PC, BSc; British politician and marketing consultant; b. 24 March 1964, Wolverhampton, West Midlands; m. Iain Miller; two s. one d.; ed Brynteg Comprehensive School, Bridgend, London School of Econs; Advertising Exec., Greys Advertising Ltd 1985–90, Dir 1994–99; Marketing Man. with Texaco 1990–94; Dir, Rowland Group 1999–2003; joined Conservative Party 1983; contested Wolverhampton North East constituency in Gen. Election 2001; MP for Basingstoke 2005–10, for Basingstoke (revised boundary) 2010–, mem. Trade and Industry Cttee 2005–06, Children, Schools and Families Select Cttee 2007; Shadow Minister for Educ. 2005–06, for Family Welfare, including Child Support Agency 2006–07, for Families 2007–10; Parl. Under-Sec. of State (Minister for Disabled People), Dept for Work and Pensions 2010–12; Sec. of State for Culture, Media and Sport 2012–14, also Minister for Women and Equalities 2012–14; Pres. Wolverhampton North East Conservative Asscn 2001–07; Chair. Wimbledon Conservative Asscn 2002–03; Conservative. *Address:* House of Commons, Westminster, London, SW1A 0AA, England (office). *Telephone:* (20) 7219-5749 (office). *Fax:* (20) 7219-5722 (office). *E-mail:* maria .miller.mp@parliament.uk (office). *Website:* www.mariamiller.co.uk.

MILLER, Sir Peter North, Kt, MA, DSc; British insurance broker; b. 28 Sept. 1930, London, England; s. of Cyril T. Miller and Dorothy N. Miller; m. Jane Miller 1991; one s.; two s. one d. by previous m.; ed Rugby School and Lincoln Coll., Oxford; joined Thos. R. Miller & Son (Insurance) 1953, Partner 1959, Sr Partner 1971–, Chair. of Miller Insurance Group 1971–83, 1988–96; mem. Cttee Lloyds Insurance Brokers' Asscn 1973–77, Deputy Chair. 1974–75, Chair. 1976–77; mem. Cttee of Lloyds 1977–80, 1982–89, Chair. of Lloyds 1984–87; mem. Cttee on Invisible Exports 1975–77, Insurance Brokers' Registration Council 1977–81; Chair. British Cttee of Bureau Veritas 1980–2001; one of HM's Lts for City of London 1987–; Hon. Fellow, Lincoln Coll., Oxford 1992–; Commendatore, Ordine al Merito della Repubblica Italiana 1989. *Leisure interests:* all forms of sport (except cricket), particularly running, riding, tennis and sailing, wine, music. *Address:* Quinneys, Camilla Drive, Westhumble, Dorking, Surrey, RH5 6BU (home); c/o Miller Insurance Services LLP, Dawson House, 5 Jewry Street, London, EC3N 2PJ, England (office). *Telephone:* (20) 7488-2345 (office).

MILLER, Robert; Canadian electronics industry executive; f. Future Electronics 1968, now third-largest wholesale electronics distributor in world; supporter of Alcor Life Extension Foundation. *Address:* Future Electronics, 237 Hymus Boulevard, Pointe-Claire, PQ H9R 5C7, Canada (office). *Telephone:* (514) 694-7710 (office). *Fax:* (514) 695-3707 (office). *Website:* www.futureelectronics.com (office).

MILLER, Robert (Bob) G., BA, MBA; American business executive; ed Univ. of Missouri, Kansas City, Iowa State Univ.; joined Albertsons Inc. 1961, Sr Vice-Pres. and Regional Man. 1985–89, Exec. Vice-Pres. Retail Operations 1989–91; CEO Fred Meyer Stores Inc. 1991–99; Vice-Chair. and COO The Kroger Co. (following acquisition of Fred Meyer Stores Inc. by Kroger) 1999; Chair. and CEO Rite Aid Corpn 1999–2003, Chair. 1999–2007, Dir and mem. Exec. Cttee 1999–2011; Chair. Wild Oats Markets, Inc. 2004–06; mem. Bd of Dirs Harrah's Entertainment Inc. 1999–, Caesars Entertainment Corpn 1999–2008, Nordstrom, Inc. 2005–, The Jim Pattison Group, Inc., Food Marketing Inst. *Address:* c/o Rite Aid Corporation, 30 Hunter Lane, Camp Hill, PA 17011, USA. *E-mail:* contacttheboard@riteaid.com.

MILLER, Robert Joseph (Bob), BA, JD; American lawyer and politician; *Principal, Dutko Worldwide;* b. 30 March 1945, Evanston, Ill.; s. of Ross Wendell Miller and Coletta Jane Doyle; m. Sandra Ann Searles; one s. two d.; ed Santa Clara and Loyola Univs; First Legal Advisor, Las Vegas Metropolitan Police Dept 1973–75; JP 1975–78; Deputy Dist Attorney, Clark Co., Las Vegas 1971–73, Dist Attorney 1979–86; Lt Gov. of Nevada 1987–89, 1989–90, Gov. 1989–99; Chair. Nev. Comm. on Econ. Devt, Nev. Comm. on Tourism 1987–91; mem. Nat. Govs Asscn (Vice-Chair. Exec. Cttee 1995–96, Chair. 1996–97, fmr Chair. Cttee on Justice and Public Safety, Chair. Legal Affairs Cttee 1992–94, Lead Gov. on Transport 1992–); Sr Partner, Jones Vargas, Las Vegas 1999–2005; Prin., Dutko Worldwide, Las Vegas 2005–; Co-Chair. Russian Heritage Highway Foundation; Democrat; Hon. Consul Officer of Repub. of Bulgaria. *Address:* Dutko Worldwide, 900 South Pavilion Center, Las Vegas, NV 89133, USA (office). *Telephone:* (702) 240-0831 (office). *Fax:* (702) 240-0331 (office). *Website:* www.dutkoworldwide.com (office).

MILLER, Robert Stevens (Steve), Jr, AB, MBA, JD; American business executive; *Non-Executive Chairman, American International Group (AIG), Inc.;* b. 4 Nov. 1941, Portland, Ore.; s. of Robert Stevens Miller and Barbara Weston Miller; m. Margaret Rose Kyger 1966; three s.; ed Stanford Univ. and Harvard Law School; mem. financial staff, Ford Motor Co., Dearborn, Mich. 1968–71; Investment Man., Ford Motor de Mexico, Mexico City 1971–73; Dir of Finance, Ford Asia Pacific, Melbourne, Australia 1974–77; Vice-Pres. (Finance), Ford Motor de Venezuela, Caracas 1977–79; Vice-Pres.-Treas., Chrysler Corpn, Detroit, Mich. 1980–81, Exec. Vice-Pres. (Finance) 1981–85, 1985–88, Exec. Vice-Pres. 1988–92; Sr Partner, James D. Wolfensohn Inc. 1992–93; Chair. Morrison Knudson Corpn 1995–96; Chair. Waste Man. Inc. 1998–99, Pres. and CEO 1999, now Dir; Chair. and CEO Federal-Mogul Corpn 2000–05; Chair. and CEO Delphi Corpn 2005–07, Exec. Chair. 2007–09; Chair. (non-exec.) American International Group (AIG), Inc. 2009–; mem. Bd of Dirs Symantec Corpn 1994–, United Airlines, Reynolds American, Waste Management, Inc.; mem. Int. Advisory Bd, Creditanstalt Bankverein, Vienna, Austria. *Leisure interest:* model railroading. *Address:* American International Group, Inc., 180 Maiden Lane, New York, NY 10038, USA (office). *Telephone:* (212) 770-7000 (office). *Fax:* (212) 509-9705 (office). *E-mail:* boardofdirectors@aig.com (office); answercenter@aig.com (office). *Website:* www.aigcorporate.com (office).

MILLER, Steve; American business executive; *Chairman, American International Group (AIG), Inc.;* known as a turnaround expert who revived business including Bethlehem Steel Corpn and Delphi Corpn by restructuring them while they were under bankruptcy protection; Chair. Delphi Corpn –2009; mem. Bd of Dirs American International Group (AIG) Inc. 2009–, Chair. 2010–; Chair. MidOcean Partners (pvt. equity firm) 2009–; mem. Bd of Dirs Symantec Corpn, UAL Corpn. *Address:* American International Group, Inc., 70 Pine Street, New York, NY 10270, USA (office). *Telephone:* (212) 770-7000 (office). *Fax:* (212) 509-9705 (office). *E-mail:* AnswerCenter@AIG.com (office). *Website:* www.aigcorporate .com (office).

MILLER, Stuart A., BS, JD; American real estate executive; *CEO and President, Lennar Corporation;* b. 1957; s. of the late Leonard Miller and Susan Miller; m. Vicki Miller, four c.; ed Harvard Univ., Univ. of Miami; joined Lennar Corpn 1981, Vice-Pres. 1992–97, CEO and Pres. 1997–, Chair. LNR Property Corpn 1997–; mem. Jt Center for Housing Studies Policy Advisory Bd, Harvard Univ.; America's Most Powerful People, Forbes 2000. *Address:* Lennar Corporation, 700 NW 107th Avenue, Suite 400, Miami, FL 33172, USA (office). *Telephone:* (305) 559-4000 (office). *Fax:* (305) 229-6453 (office). *Website:* www.lennar.com (office).

MILLER, Thomas J., MA, PhD; American diplomatist; b. 1948, Chicago; ed Univ. of Michigan; mem. Sr Foreign Service at rank of Minister-Counselor; joined State Dept 1976; analyst for Vietnam, Laos and Cambodia 1976–77; Special Asst to Under-Sec. for Political Affairs 1977–79; Deputy Prin. Officer, US Consulate, Chiang Mai, Thailand 1979–81; served twice on Israeli Desk (once as Dir); Head Office of Maghreb Affairs; Acting Dir of an office on counter-terrorism; political section, Athens Embassy 1985–87, Deputy Chief of Mission, Athens 1994–97; Special Coordinator for Cyprus (with rank of Amb.) 1997–99; Amb. to Bosnia and Herzegovina 1999–2001, to Greece 2001–04; retd from US State Dept 2005; CEO Plan International (non-profit) –2009; CEO and Pres. United Nations Asscn 2009–10; Dir Washington, DC office, Independent Diplomat (advisory org.) 2010–; mem. Int. Advisory Bd Hellenic-American Heritage Council; Equal Opportunity Award (Dept. of State), Superior Honor Award (five times) (Dept of State), Meritorious Award (Dept of State) and many others. *Address:* c/o Independent Diplomat, 45 East 20th Street, 6th Floor, New York, NY 10003, USA. *Website:* www.independentdiplomat.org.

MILLER, Walter Geoffrey Thomas, AO; Australian diplomatist; *Vice-President, Australian Institute of International Affairs;* b. 25 Oct. 1934, Tasmania; s. of Walter T. Miller and Gertrude S. Galloway; m. Rachel C. Webb 1960; three s. one d.; ed Launceston High School, Univs of Tasmania and Oxford; served in Australian missions in Kuala Lumpur, Djakarta and at UN, New York; Deputy High Commr, India 1973–75; Amb. to Repub. of Korea 1978–80; Head, Int. Div. Dept of the Prime Minister and Cabinet, Canberra 1982; Deputy Sec. Dept of Foreign Affairs 1985–86; Amb. to Japan 1986–89; Dir-Gen. Office of Nat. Assessments Canberra 1989–95; High Commr to NZ 1996–2000; Vice-Pres. Australian Inst. of Int. Affairs 2005–; Rhodes Scholar 1956. *Leisure interests:* international relations, literature, ballet, tennis, reading, golf. *Address:* 124 Kent Street, Sydney, NSW 2000 (office); Australian Institute of International Affairs, Stephen House, 32 Thesiger Court, Deakin ACT 2600; 85 Union Street, McMahons Point, NSW 2060, Australia (home). *Telephone:* (2) 9247-2709 (office). *Website:* www.aiia.asn.au.

MILLER, William Hughes, BS, AM, PhD; American chemist and academic; *Kenneth S. Pitzer Distinguished Professor of Chemistry, University of California, Berkeley;* b. 16 March 1941, Kosciusko, Miss.; s. of Weldon Howard Miller and

Jewell Irene Miller (née Hughes); ed Georgia Inst. of Tech., Harvard Univ.; NATO Postdoctoral Fellow, Univ. of Freiburg, Germany 1967–68; Jr Fellow, Harvard Univ. 1967–69; Asst Prof., Dept of Chem., Univ. of Calif., Berkeley 1969–72, Assoc. Prof. 1972–74, Prof. 1974–, Miller Research Prof. 1978–79, 1998–99, Vice-Chair. Dept of Chem. 1984–88, Chair. 1989–93, Chancellor's Research Prof. 1998–2001, Kenneth S. Pitzer Distinguished Prof. 1999–; Sr Staff Scientist, Chemical Sciences Div., Lawrence Berkeley Nat. Lab. 1969–; mem. Editorial Bd Chemical Physics 1973–96, Nouveau Journal de Chimie 1977–87, International Journal of Quantum Chemistry 1979–89, Journal of Physical Chemistry 1983–89, Advances in Quantum Chemistry 1987–, Theoretical Chemistry Accounts 1997–; mem. ACS 1980–, Int. Acad. of Quantum Molecular Science 1985–, NAS 1987–; Fellow AAAS 1983–, American Physical Soc. 1984– (Vice-Chair. and later Chair., Div. of Chemical Physics 1997–2000), American Acad. of Arts and Sciences 1993–; Hon. Prof., Univ. of Shandong 1994; Int. Acad. of Quantum Molecular Science Annual Prize 1974, Humboldt Foundation Sr Scientist Award 1981, E.O. Lawrence Award 1985, ACS Irving Langmuir Award in Chemical Physics 1990, ACS Award in Theoretical Chem. 1994, J.O. Hirschfelder Prize in Theoretical Chem. 1996, ACS Ira Remsen Award 1997, Royal Soc. of Chem. Faraday Div. Spiers Medal 1998, ACS Peter Debye Award Award in Physical Chem. 2003, Welch Award in Chem. 2007, Herschbach Award in Chemical Dynamics 2007, Ahmed Zewail Award in Molecular Sciences 2011. *Publications:* more than 300 articles in scientific journals. *Leisure interest:* playing 'old time' banjo. *Address:* Department of Chemistry, University of California, Berkeley, CA 94720, USA (office). *Telephone:* (510) 642-0653 (office). *Fax:* (510) 642-6262 (office). *E-mail:* millerwh@berkeley .edu (office). *Website:* neon.cchem.berkeley.edu (office).

MILLER, Zell Bryan, MA; American fmr politician; b. 24 Feb. 1932, Young Harris, Ga; s. of Stephen G. Miller and Birdie Bryan; m. Shirley Carver 1954; two s.; ed Young Harris Coll., Univ. of Ga; Prof. of Political Science and History, Univ. of Ga, Young Harris Coll. 1959–64, 1999–; mem. Ga Senate 1960–64; Dir Ga Bd of Probation 1965–67; Deputy Dir Ga Dept of Corrections 1967–68; Exec. Sec. to Gov. of Ga 1968–71; Exec. Dir Democratic Cttee of Ga 1971–72; mem. State Bd of Pardons and Paroles, Atlanta 1973–75; Lt-Gov. of Ga 1975–90; Gov. of Ga 1990–98, Senator from Ga 2000–05; Pres. Council of State Govts 1991; Vice-Chair. Southern Gov.'s Asscn 1991; mem. American Battle Monuments Comm. 2005–; contrib. Fox News Channel 2005–. *Publications:* The Mountains Within Me, Great Georgians, They Heard Georgia Singing. *Address:* 1175 Peachtree Street, NE, #100–300, Atlanta, GA 30361, USA (office).

MILLER SMITH, Charles, MA; British business executive; *Chairman, Scottish Power PLC;* b. 7 Nov. 1939, Glasgow; s. of William Smith and Margaret Wardrope; m. Dorothy Adams 1964 (died 1999); one s. two d.; ed Glasgow Acad. and St Andrews Univ.; Financial Dir Vinyl Products, Unilever 1970–73, Head of Planning 1974; Finance Dir Walls Meat Co. 1976; Vice-Chair. Industan Lever 1979–81; Speciality Chemicals Group 1981; Chief Exec. PPF Int. 1983; Chief Exec. Quest Int. 1986; Financial Dir Unilever Bd 1989; Exec. Unilever Foods 1993–94; Exec. Dir ICI PLC 1994–95, Chief Exec. 1995–99, Chair. 1999–2001; Chair. (non-exec.) Scottish Power PLC 2000–; Dir HSBC Holdings PLC 1996–; Int. Adviser, Goldman Sachs 2001–05; currently European Adviser, Warburg Pincus LLC; mem. Defence Man. Bd, Ministry of Defence; Hon. LLD (St Andrews) 1995. *Leisure interests:* reading, walking. *Address:* Scottish Power PLC, Corporate Office, 1 Atlantic Quay, Glasgow, G2 8SP, Scotland (office). *Telephone:* (141) 248-8200 (office). *Fax:* (141) 248-8300 (office). *Website:* www.scottishpower.plc.uk (office).

MILLERON, Jean-Claude; French economist and international finance official; b. 8 Jan. 1937, Paris; s. of Pierre A. Milleron and Geneviève Hédouin; m. Marie-France Dannaud 1966; two s. one d.; ed Ecole Polytechnique, Paris, Ecole Supérieure des Sciences Econ., Paris; with Nat. Inst. of Statistics and Econ. Studies (INSEE), Paris 1963–70, Dir-Gen. 1987–92; Visiting Research Dept of Econs, Univ. of Calif., Berkeley 1970–71; Deputy Dir Nat. School of Statistics and Econ. Admin. (ENSAE), Paris 1971–78; Head of Dept of Econs, Planning Commissariat-Gen., Paris 1978–81; Dir of Forecasting, Ministry of Econ. and Finance 1982–87; Dir-Gen. INSEE 1986–92; Under-Sec.-Gen. Dept of Econ. and Social Information and Policy Analysis, UN, New York 1992–97; Special Adviser to French Minister of Econ., Finance and Industry 1997–98; apptd Exec. Dir of IMF and IBRD 1998; apptd Financial Minister, Embassy in Washington, DC 1998; Fellow, Econometric Soc. *Publications:* various books and articles on econ. theory and public econs. *Leisure interests:* jogging, hiking, opera. *Address:* c/o Ministry of the Economy, Finance and Industry, 139 rue de Bercy, 75572 Paris, France.

MILLETT, Baron (Life Peer), cr. 1998, of St Marylebone in the City of Westminster; **Peter Julian Millett,** MA (Cantab.); British judge (retd); b. 23 June 1932; s. of the late Dennis Millett and Adele Millett; m. Ann Harris 1958; three s. (one deceased); ed Harrow School and Univ. of Cambridge; called to Bar, Middle Temple 1955, Lincoln's Inn 1959, Singapore 1976, Hong Kong 1979; at Chancery Bar 1958–86; Lecturer in Practical Conveyancing and Examiner Council of Legal Educ. 1962–76; mem. Gen. Council of the Bar 1971–75; Judge, High Court of Justice, Chancery Div. 1986–94, Lord Justice of Appeal 1994–98, Lord of Appeal in Ordinary 1998–2004; mem. House of Lords 1998–; Non-Perm. Judge of the Court of Final Appeal, Hong Kong 2000–; Hon. Fellow, Trinity Hall, Cambridge; Hon. LLD (Queen Mary Coll. and Westfield Coll., London). *Address:* House of Lords, Westminster, London, SW1A 0PQ (office); Essex Court Chambers, 24 Lincoln's Inn Fields, London, WC2A 3EG, England (office). *Telephone:* (20) 7219-3202 (office); (20) 7813-8000 (office). *Fax:* (20) 7219-5979 (office); (20) 7813-8080 (office).

MILLIKEN, Hon. Peter Andrew Stewart, LLB, MA; Canadian politician and lawyer; *Special Advisor, Cunningham, Swan;* b. 12 Nov. 1946, Kingston, Ont.; s. of John Andrew Milliken and Catherine Margaret Milliken; ed Queen's Univ., Kingston, Wadham Coll., Oxford, UK, Dalhousie Univ., Halifax; Lecturer in Business Law, School of Business, Queen's Univ. 1973–81; called to Bar of Ont., Solicitor of Supreme Court of Ont. 1973; solicitor, Cunningham, Little, Kingston (law firm) 1973–78, PNR, Cunningham, Little, Bonham and Milliken 1978–89; MP for Kingston and the Islands 1988–2011; served as Asst House Leader, Vice-Chair. Standing Cttee on Privileges and Elections; Parl. Sec. to Leader of Govt in House of Commons 1993–96; Deputy Chair. Cttees of Whole House 1996, Deputy Speaker and Chair. Cttees of Whole House 1997, elected Speaker of House of Commons 2001–11; Special Advisor, Cunningham, Swan 2011–; Chair. Bd of Internal

Economy 2001–11; Fellow, School of Policy Studies, Queen's Univ. 2011–; Hon. Pres. United Empire Loyalists' Asscn of Canada; Hon. Patron Genealogical Soc. of Ont.; Hon. LLD (State Univ. of New York) 2001, (Queen's Univ.) 2012, (McGill Univ.) 2012. *Publications include:* Question Period: Developments from 1960 to 1967 1968. *Address:* School of Policy Studies, Robert Sutherland Hall, 138 Union Street, Queen's University, Kingston, ON K7L 3N6, Canada (office); Quaker Valley, R.R. No. 1, Elginburg, ON K0H 1M0, Canada (home). *Telephone:* (613) 533-3020 (office); (613) 548-7889 (home). *Fax:* (613) 533-2135 (office). *E-mail:* pasm@ rogers.com (home). *Website:* www.queensu.ca/sps (office).

MILLON, Charles, LèsScEcon; French politician and international organization official; *President, Unir Pour Lyon;* b. 12 Nov. 1945, Belley, Ain; s. of Gabriel Millon and Suzanne Gunet; m. Chantal Delsol 1970; three s. two d.; ed Ecole Sainte-Marie, Lyon, Faculté de Droit et de Sciences Economiques de Lyon; univ. tutor 1969; legal and taxation adviser 1970–; Mayor of Belley 1977–2001; Deputy 1981–86, 1988–93, First Vice-Pres. Ass. Nat. 1986–88, Leader Union pour la Démocratie Française in Nat. Ass. 1989; Minister of Defence 1995–97; Local Councillor, Ain 1985–88; Vice-Pres. Regional Council, Rhône-Alpes 1981–88, Pres. 1988–99, Pres. 1988–98; Founder and Pres. la Droite Movt 1998–99; Leader Droite Libérale Chrétienne 1999–2003; Municipal Councillor and Urban Community Councillor, Lyon 2001–; Pres. Unir Pour Lyon 2001–; Amb. to FAO 2003–07. *Publications:* L'Extravagante histoire des nationalisations 1984, L'Alternance-vérité 1986, La Tentation du Conservatisme 1995, La Paix civile 1998, Lettre d'un ami impertinent 2002. *Leisure interests:* reading, walking, mountaineering. *Address:* Groupe Unir Pour Lyon, 4 rue de la République, BP 1099, 69202 Lyon Cedex 01 (office); 11 bis rue des Barons, 01300 Belley, France (home). *Telephone:* 4-72-07-77-56 (office). *Fax:* 4-72-07-91-47 (office). *Website:* www.millon.org (office).

MILLS, Hayley Cathrine Rose Vivien; British actress; b. 18 April 1946, London; d. of the late Sir John Mills and Lady Mills (Mary Hayley Bell); m. Roy Boulting 1971 (divorced 1977); two s.; partner Firdous Bamji 1997–; ed Elmhurst Ballet School, Inst. Alpine Videmanette; first film appearance in Tiger Bay 1959; on contract to Walt Disney; first stage appearance as Peter Pan 1969; Silver Bear Award, Berlin Film Festival 1958, British Acad. Award; Special Oscar (USA), TV Best Actress Award 1982. *Stage appearances include:* The Wild Duck 1970, Trelawny 1972, The Three Sisters 1975, A Touch of Spring 1975, Rebecca 1977, My Fat Friend 1978, Hush and Hide 1979, The Importance of Being Earnest (Royal Festival Theatre, Chichester), The Summer Party 1980, Tally's Folly 1982, The Secretary Bird 1983, Dial M for Murder 1984, Toys in the Attic 1986, The Kidnap Game 1991, The King and I (Australian and NZ tour) 1991–92, The Card 1994, Fallen Angels 1994, Dead Guilty 1995–96, Brief Encounter 1997–98, The King and I (US tour) 1997–98, Suite in Two Keys (New York) 2001, A Little Night Music (USA) 2001, The Vagina Monologues (New York) 2001, Humble Boy (UK) 2004. *Films include:* Pollyanna 1960, The Parent Trap 1961, Whistle Down the Wind 1961, Summer Magic 1962, In Search of the Castaways 1963, The Chalk Garden 1964, The Moonspinners 1965, The Truth about Spring 1965, Sky West and Crooked 1966, The Trouble with Angels 1966, The Family Way 1966, Pretty Polly 1967, Twisted Nerve 1968, Take a Girl Like You 1970, Forbush and the Penguins 1971, Endless Night 1972, Deadly Strangers 1975, The Diamond Hunters 1975, What Changed Charley Farthing? 1975, The Kingfisher Caper 1975, Appointment with Death 1987, After Midnight 1990, 2BPerfectlyHonest 2004, Stricken 2005. *Television includes:* The Flame Trees of Thika 1981, Parent Trap II 1986, Good Morning Miss Bliss, Murder She Wrote, Back Home, Tales of the Unexpected, Walk of Life 1990, Parent Trap III, IV, Wild at Heart (series) 2007–09. *Publication:* My God (with Marcus Maclaine) 1988. *Leisure interests:* riding, reading, children, cooking, travel. *Address:* c/o Chatto and Linnit, 123A Kings Road, London, SW3 4PL, England. *Telephone:* (20) 7352-7722 (office). *Website:* www.hayleymills.com.

MILLS, Ian Mark, BSc, DPhil, FRS; British chemist and academic; *Professor Emeritus of Chemical Spectroscopy, University of Reading;* b. 9 June 1930; s. of John Mills and Marguerita Alice Gertrude Mills (née Gooding); m. Margaret Maynard 1957; one s. one d.; ed Leighton Park School, Univ. of Reading, St John's Coll. Oxford; Research Fellow, Univ. of Minn. 1954–56; Research Fellow in Theoretical Chem., Corpus Christi Coll., Cambridge 1956–57; Lecturer in Chem. Univ. of Reading 1957–64, Reader 1964–66, Prof. of Chemical Spectroscopy 1966–95, Prof. Emer. 1995–, Leverhulme Emer. Research Fellow 1996–98; Ed. Molecular Physics 1972–77, 1995–2004; mem. and Chair. of various cttees of IUPAC; Vice-Pres. Faraday Div. of RSC 1984–86; mem. British Nat. Cttee for IUPAC of RSC 1992–2000, Chair. 1998–2000; Pres., Consultative Cttee on Units of the Bureau Int. des Poids et Mesures 1995–; Chair. British Standards Inst. Cttee on Symbols and Units 1996–2004; mem. Council, Royal Inst. 2000–03; Lomb Medal 1960, Fellow 1974, Lippincott Medal of Optical Soc. of America 1982, RSC Spectroscopy Award 1990. *Publications:* Quantities, Units and Symbols in Physical Chemistry (co-author) 1988; various papers in learned journals on quantum mechanics and molecular spectroscopy. *Leisure interests:* sailing, walking. *Address:* Department of Chemistry, University of Reading, Reading, RG6 6AD (office); 57 Christchurch Road, Reading, RG2 7BD, England (home). *Telephone:* (118) 931-8456 (office); (118) 987-2335 (home). *Fax:* (118) 931-6331 (office). *E-mail:* i.m.mills@reading.ac.uk (office).

MILLS, Kyle David; New Zealand professional cricketer; b. 15 March 1979, Auckland; right-arm fast-medium pace bowler; right-handed batsman; plays for Auckland 1998–, New Zealand 2001–, Kings XI Punjab, Lincs. 2001, Kings XI Punjab 2008, Mumbai Indians 2009–10; First-class debut: 1998/99; Test debut: England v NZ, Nottingham 10–13 June 2004; One-Day Int. (ODI) debut: NZ v Pakistan, Sharjah 15 April 2001; T20I debut: NZ v Australia, Auckland 17 Feb. 2005; ranked first on Reliance Mobile ICC (Int. Cricket Council) ODI Bowling Rankings Oct. 2009. *Address:* c/o Auckland Cricket Association, Cricket House, Eden Park, 60 Walters Road, Mt Eden, PO Box 56906, Dominion Road, Auckland, New Zealand. *Telephone:* (9) 815-4855. *E-mail:* info@aucklandcricket.co.nz. *Website:* www.aucklandcricket.co.nz.

MILLS JONES, Joseph; Liberian economist and central banker; *Executive Governor, Central Bank of Liberia;* currently Exec. Gov. Central Bank of Liberia; Chair., Cttee of Govs, West African Monetary Zone 2012–. *Publications include:* A Macroeconometric Study of the Liberian Economy: A Short-run Analysis 1976. *Address:* Office of the Governor, Central Bank of Liberia, cnr Warren and Carey Streets, POB 2048, 1000 Monrovia, Liberia (office). *Telephone:* 6225685 (mobile)

(office). *Fax:* 6226114 (mobile) (office). *E-mail:* webmaster@cbl.org.lr (office). *Website:* www.cbl.org.lr (office).

MILNES, Sherrill, MMusEd; American singer; b. 10 Jan. 1935, Hinsdale, IL; s. of James Knowlton and Thelma Roe Milnes; m. 2nd Nancy Stokes 1969; one s.; one s. one d. by first marriage; m. 3rd Maria Zouves 1996; ed Drake Univ., Northwestern Univ.; studied with Boris Goldovsky, Rosa Ponselle, Andrew White, Hermanes Baer; with Goldovsky Opera Co. 1960–65, New York City Opera Co. 1964–67, debut with Metropolitan Opera Co., New York 1965, leading baritone 1965–; has performed with all American city opera cos and major American orchestras 1962–73; performed in Don Giovanni, Vespri Siciliani and all standard Italian repertory baritone roles, Metropolitan Opera and at San Francisco Opera, Hamburg Opera, Frankfurt Opera, La Scala, Milan, Covent Garden, London, Teatro Colón, Buenos Aires, Vienna State Opera, Paris Opera and Chicago Lyric Opera; founder and Artistic Dir VOICE (Vocal and Operatic Intensive Creative Experience) 2001–; Chair. of Bd Affiliate Artists Inc.; Order of Merit (Italy) 1984; three hon. degrees; three Grammy Awards, Sanford Medal, Yale Univ., Opera News Award 2008. *Recordings:* over 60 albums 1967–; most recorded American opera singer 1978. *Leisure interests:* table tennis, swimming, horse riding. *Address:* The VOICExperience Foundation, PO Box 1576, Plain Harbor, FL 34682-1576, USA (office). *E-mail:* voicexp@aol.com (office). *Website:* www .voicexperiencefoundation.com (office).

MILNOR, John Willard, AB, PhD; American mathematician and academic; *Distinguished Professor of Mathematics and Co-Director, Institute for Mathematical Sciences, State University of New York, Stony Brook;* b. 20 Feb. 1931, Orange, NJ; m. Prof. Dusa McDuff; ed Princeton Univ.; faculty, Princeton Univ. 1953–55, Alfred P. Sloan Fellow 1955–59, Prof. of Math. 1960–62, Henry Putman Prof. of Math. 1962; on staff, State Univ. of New York, Stony Brook 1988–, currently Distinguished Prof. of Math. and Co-Dir Inst. for Math. Sciences; Ed. Annals of Mathematics 1962–; mem. NAS 1963, American Acad. of Arts and Sciences, American Philosophy Soc.; Fellow, American Math. Soc. 2013; Hon. DSc (Syracuse Univ.) 1965, (Univ. of Chicago) 1967; Putnam Fellow, Princeton Univ. 1949–50, Fields Medal, Int. Congress of Mathematicians, Stockholm 1962, Nat. Medal of Science 1967, Leroy P. Steele Prize, American Math. Soc. 1982, 2004, 2011, Wolf Prize (Israel) 1989, Abel Prize, Norwegian Acad. of Science and Letters 2011. *Publications:* Morse Theory 1963, Lectures on the h-Cobordism Theorem 1965, Singular Points of Complex Hypersurfaces 1968, Introduction to Algebraic K-theory 1971, Symmetric Bilinear Forms (co-author), Characteristic Classes (co-author) 1974, Topology from the Differentiable Viewpoint 1997, Dynamics in One Complex Variable 1999; numerous articles in math. journals on differential topology, differential geometry and algebraic topology. *Address:* Institute for Mathematical Sciences, State University of New York, 5D-148 Math Tower, Stony Brook, NY 11794-3660, USA (office). *Telephone:* (516) 642-7307 (office); (516) 642-7318 (Sec.) (office). *Fax:* (516) 632-4774 (office). *E-mail:* jack@math.sunysb.edu (office). *Website:* www.math.sunysb.edu/~jack (office).

MILO, Paskal, PhD; Albanian politician; *Chairman, Social Democracy Party;* b. 22 Feb. 1949, Vlorë; s. of Koço Petromilo and Parashqevi Petromilo; m. Liliana Balla-Milo 1976; one s. two d.; ed Univ. of Tirana; journalist 1971–74; high school teacher 1975–80; Lecturer in History, Univ. of Tirana 1981–91, Dean Faculty of History and Philology 1991–92, Prof. 1996; Sec. of State for Educ. 1991; mem. Parl. (Social Democratic Party—SDP) 1992–96, Chair. Parl. Comm. for Educ. and Science 1992–96, Minister of Foreign Affairs 1997–2001, for European Integration 2001–02; left SDP to form Social Democracy Party (Partia Demokracia Sociale—PDS) 2003, Chair. 2003–; Chair. SE European Co-operation Process (SEECP); mem. Parl., Council of Europe 2006–. *Publications:* The End of an Injustice 1984, Albania and Yugoslavia 1918–27 1992, A Good Understanding and Cooperation in the Balkans, From Utopia to Necessity 1997, Albania and the Balkan Entente 1997, Constitutional Rights and Minorities in the Balkans: A Comparative Analysis 1997, The Soviet Union and Albania's Foreign Policy 1944–46 1997, Albania in East-West Relations 1944–45 1998, European Union: Identity, Integration, Future 2002, Diary of a Foreign Minister: Kosova Conflict 1997-2001 2009, Kosova from Rambouillet to Independence 2009. *Leisure interests:* football, music. *Address:* Partia Demokracia Sociale, Bulevardi 'Zogu i I', ish klinika dentare, Tirana, Albania (office). *Telephone:* (4) 274487 (office); (4) 250973 (home). *Fax:* (4) 274487 (office). *E-mail:* paskalmilo@yahoo.it (home).

MILOŠOSKI, Antonio, MA; Macedonian lawyer, politician, diplomatist and researcher; b. 29 Jan. 1976, Tetovo; m.; ed SS. Cyril and Methodius Univ., Skopje, Friedrich Wilhelm Univ., Bonn, Germany, Gerhard Merkator Univ. of Duisburg, Germany; mem. Exec. Cttee Youth Force Union of Internal Macedonian Revolutionary Org.—Democratic Party for Macedonian Nat. Unity 1995–97, Vice-Pres. 1997–98; Chair. Office of the Deputy Prime Minister of Fmr Yugoslav Repub. of Macedonia 1999–2000; Govt Spokesman 2000–01; Counsellor to the Prime Minister Jan.–May 2001; Research Fellow, Inst. for Political Science, Gerhard Merkator Univ., Duisburg 2005–06; Minister of Foreign Affairs 2006–11; Founder Youth Euro-Atlantic Forum (MEAF); columnist, Dnevnik newspaper 2000. *Address:* c/o Ministry of Foreign Affairs, 1000 Skopje, Dame Gruev 6, Former Yugoslav Republic of Macedonia.

MILOW, Keith; British artist; b. 29 Dec. 1945, London, England; s. of Geoffrey Keith Milow and the late Joan Ada; ed Camberwell School of Art and Royal Coll. of Art, London; experimental work at Royal Court Theatre, London 1968; teacher, Ealing School of Art 1968–70; Artist in Residence, Univ. of Leeds (Gregory Fellowship) 1970; worked in New York (Harkness Fellowship) 1972–74; teacher, Chelsea School of Art 1975, School of Visual Arts, New York City 1981–85; works in public collections in six countries, including Tate Modern and Victoria and Albert Museum, London, Guggenheim Museum and Museum of Modern Art, New York; lives and works in Amsterdam; Calouste Gulbenkian Foundation Visual Arts Award 1976; equal First Prize Tolly Cobbold/Eastern Arts 2nd Nation Exhbn 1979; Arts Council of GB Major Award. *Address:* Warmoesstraat 10, 1012 JD Amsterdam, Netherlands (home). *Telephone:* (20) 420-05-74 (home). *E-mail:* keithmilow@dds.nl (office). *Website:* www.keithmilow.com.

MILSOM, Stroud Francis Charles, QC, FBA; British academic; b. 2 May 1923, Merton, Surrey; s. of Harry Lincoln Milsom and Isobel Vida Collins; m. Irène Szereszewski 1955 (died 1998); ed Charterhouse School, Trinity Coll. Cambridge and Univ. of Pennsylvania Law School (as Commonwealth Fund Fellow); Fellow, Trinity Coll. 1948–55; Fellow, Tutor and Dean, New Coll. Oxford 1956–64; Prof. of Legal History, LSE 1964–76; Prof. of Law, Cambridge Univ. 1976–90, Fellow of St John's Coll. 1976–; called to Bar 1947, Hon. Bencher, Lincoln's Inn 1970, QC 1985; Literary Dir, Selden Soc. 1964–80, Pres. 1985–88; mem. Royal Comm. on Historical Manuscripts 1975–98; Foreign mem. American Philosophical Soc.; Hon. LLD (Glasgow) 1981, (Chicago) 1985, (Cambridge) 2003; Ames Prize, Harvard 1972, Swiney Prize, RSA 1974. *Publications:* Novae Narrationes 1963, Introduction to reissue of History of English Law (Pollock and Maitland) 1968, Historical Foundations of the Common Law 1969, 1981, Legal Framework of English Feudalism 1976, Studies in the History of the Common Law 1985, A Natural History of the Common Law 2003. *Address:* St John's College, Cambridge, CB2 1TP; 113 Grantchester Meadows, Cambridge, CB3 9JN, England (home). *Telephone:* (1223) 354100 (home).

MILUTINOVIĆ, Milan, LLM; Serbian lawyer, politician, diplomatist and fmr head of state; b. 19 Dec. 1942, Belgrade; s. of Aleksandar Milan Milutinović and Ljubica Vladimir Jokić; m. Olga Branko Spasojević; one s.; ed Univ. of Belgrade; mem. Presidency of Socialist Youth Union of Yugoslavia 1969–71; MP 1969–74; Sec. Communal Cttee of League of Communists 1972–74; Sec. for Ideology, City Cttee of League of Communists 1974–77; Minister of Science and Educ. of Serbian Repub. 1977–82; Dir Serbian Nat. Library 1983–87; Head of Sector for Press, Information and Culture, Sec. for Foreign Affairs 1987–89; Amb. to Greece 1989–95; Minister of Foreign Affairs, Fed. Repub. of Yugoslavia 1995–98; Pres. of Serbia 1997–2002; accused of crimes against humanity and violations of the customs of war by UN War Crimes Tribunal 2001, charged with crimes against humanity and war crimes by Int. Court of Justice 2003, found not guilty 2009; Order of Merit with Silver Star 1974, Medal for work with Gold Coronet 1980. *Publications include:* University – Eppur si muove! 1985. *Leisure interest:* philately.

MILYUKOV, Yuri Aleksandrovich, CandPhysMathSc; Russian banker; *Chairman, Managing Company Number One;* b. 29 April 1957; m.; two s.; ed Moscow Inst. of Physics Eng.; researcher, Lebedev Inst. of Physics USSR (now Russian Acad. of Sciences 1984–87; Chair. Council of Altair 1989–91; f. Moscow Commodity Exchange (MTB) 1990, Pres. 1993–97; mem. Council on Business, Govt of Russian Fed. 1992–; mem. Bd Dirs, Russian Industrialists and Entrepreneurs Union 1992–; mem. Presidium, All-Russian Movt Businessmen for New Russia 1993–94; mem. Co-ordination Council, Round Table of Russian Business 1994–; mem. Beer Lovers Party; mem. Cen. Cttee 1995–; mem. Political Consultative Council of Russian Presidency 1996; Chair. Rosmed; Chair. Russian Union of Stock Exchanges 1991–; Chair. Managing Company Number One; Chair. Stock Cttee, Moscow Stock Exchange 1996–; First Deputy Chair. Bd MDM Bank 1997–. *Leisure interest:* theatre. *Address:* Managing Company Number One, Romanov pereulok 3 building 1, office 68, 125009 Moscow, Russia (office). *Telephone:* (495) 234-0815 (office). *E-mail:* milyukov@yk1.ru (office).

MIMICA, Neven; Croatian politician and diplomatist; *Commissioner for Consumer Policy, European Commission;* b. 12 Oct. 1953, Split; m.; two c.; ed Univ. of Zagreb; held positions in various governmental bodies related to foreign relations and foreign trade policies, including several counselling positions at embassies in Cairo and Ankara 1979–97; apptd Asst to Minister of Economy 1997, served as Chief Negotiator during Croatia's accession to WTO and EU Asscn Agreement; Minister of European Integration 2001–03; mem. Parl. (Social Democratic Party) 2003–, Deputy Speaker 2008–11, Chair. Cttee for European Integration; Deputy Prime Minister, responsible for Interior, Foreign and European Affairs 2011–13; Commr for Consumer Policy, EC 2013–. *Address:* Commissioner for Consumer Policy, European Commission, Rue de la Loi 200, 1049 Brussels, Belgium (office). *Telephone:* (2) 295-34-30 (office). *Website:* ec.europa.eu/commission_2010-2014/ mimica/index_en.htm (office).

MIMURA, Akio, BS; Japanese business executive; b. 2 Nov. 1940; ed Tokyo Univ.; with Fuji Iron & Steel 1963–70 (remained with co. following merger with Yawata Steel to form Nippon Steel Corpn 1970), Man. Dir 1998–2000, Vice-Pres. 2000–03, Pres. and Rep. Dir 2003–08, Chair. and Rep. Dir 2008–12; Vice-Chair. (fmrly Chair.) Japan Iron and Steel Fed. Industry Asscn (JISF); Vice-Chair. Int. Iron and Steel Inst. (ISII) 2006–07. *Address:* c/o Nippon Steel & Sumitomo Metal Corpn, Marunouchi Park Building, 6-1, Marunouchi 2-chome, Chiyoda-ku, Tokyo 100-8071, Japan. *E-mail:* info@nssmc.com.

MIN, Huifen; Chinese musician and university professor; b. Nov. 1945, Yixing Co., Jiangsu Prov.; ed Shanghai Conservatory of Music; Prof., Shanghai Conservatory of Music 1993–; mem. 5th Nat. Cttee CPPCC 1978–83, 6th Nat. Cttee 1983–88, 7th Nat. Cttee 1988–93, 8th Nat. Cttee 1993–98; leading player of erhu (traditional instrument); First Prize, Nat. Erhu Playing Competition 1963, Shanghai Literature and Art Award 1988, Nat. Gold Record Award 1989. *Recordings include:* 15 albums including Erhu Solos, River of Sorrow, Yangguan Pass Melody, Wishes of the People of Honghu Lake. *Address:* Shanghai Conservatory of Music, Room 1101 Building 151, Weihai Road, Shanghai 200003, People's Republic of China.

MIN, Keh-sik, MS; South Korean business executive; b. 1941; ed Univ. of California, Berkeley, USA; fmr Man. Dir Daewoo Shipbuilding; fmr Pres. and COO, Research and Devt Centre, Hyundai Heavy Industries Co. Ltd, becoming Pres. 2001, Dir, Vice-Chair., Co-CEO and Chief Tech. Officer 2007–09, Chair. and Co-CEO 2009–; Pres., S Korea Br., Int. Conf. on Control, Automation and Systems (ICCAS), also mem. Advisory Council. *Address:* c/o Hyundai Heavy Industries Co. Ltd, 1, Jeonha-dong, Dong-gu, Gyeonsang nam-do, Ulsan 682-792, Republic of Korea. *E-mail:* ir@hhi.co.kr.

MINANI, Thomas; Burundian politician; fmr Dir-Gen. Coffee Office; Minister of Commerce and Industry 2003–05; mem. FRODEBU.

MINAYEV, Valery V., Dr Econ., Cand.His.; Russian economist and historian; *Pro-rector, Russian State University of Humanities;* b. 1949, Moscow region; ed Moscow State Inst. of Archives and History; teacher, Prof., Chair. Russian State Univ. of Humanities 1973–2002, Pro-rector 2002–; Deputy Chair. Scientific Council; mem. editorial bd of journals Novy Istorichesky Vestnik, Yurisprudentsya, Popular Economic Encyclopaedia; mem. Russian Academy of National

Sciences; medal of 850th anniversary of Moscow. *Publications include:* more than 70 scientific papers and monographs, including On Periodization of Demographic History 1995, The Formation of the Labour Market in Modern Russia: Population and Crises 2001, Problems of the Labour Market in Classical Theoretical Schools 2001, Tolerance and Polycultural Society 2002. *Address:* Russian State University of Humanities, Miusskaya pl. 6, Moscow 125267, Russia. *Telephone:* (4095) 250-61-31. *Fax:* (495) 250-62-11.

MIÑBAEV, Sawat Mukhametbayuly, CandEcon; Kazakhstani politician; b. 19 Nov. 1962, Taldy-Kurgan; s. of Mukhametbai Miñbaev and Oralbaeva Rakhima; m. Kaliyeva Janar Miñbaeva; one s. one d.; ed Moscow State Univ.; teacher, Almaty Inst. of Nat. Economy, later Assoc. Prof. 1989–91; Pres. Kazakhstan Construction Exchange 1991–92; First Deputy Chair. and Dir Kazkommerts Bank 1992–95; Deputy Minister of Finance and Dir of Treasury 1995–98, Minister of Finance 1998–99; Deputy Head of Pres.'s Admin. 1999; Minister of Agric. 1999–2001; Pres. Devt Bank of Kazakhstan 2001–02; head, Caspian Industrial Financial Group (man. consulting venture) 2002–03; Deputy Prime Minister of Kazakhstan 2003–06; Minister of Industry and Trade 2004–06, of Energy and Mineral Resources 2007–10, of Oil and Gas 2010–13; Chair. Samruk (state holding co.) 2006–07. *Address:* c/o Ministry of Oil and Gas, 010000 Astana, Kabanbai batyr kosh. 19, Kazakhstan. *E-mail:* ayan@memr.kz.

MINC BAUMFELD, Carlos, MSc, PhD; Brazilian geographer, academic and politician; *Minister of the Environment;* b. 12 July 1951, Rio de Janeiro; m.; two c.; ed Fed. Univ. of Rio de Janeiro, Tech. Univ. of Lisbon, Univ. of Paris I (Sorbonne); Co-founder Partido Verde 1986; now mem. Partido dos Trabalhadores; State Deputy for Rio de Janeiro 1986–; Asst Prof., Dept of Geography, Fed. Univ. of Rio de Janeiro; Sec. for the Environment, State Govt of Rio de Janeiro 2006–08; Minister of the Environment 2008–; UNEP Global Award 500 1989. *Publications:* Como Fazer Movimento Ecológico 1985, A Reconquista da Terra 1986, Ecologia e Política no Brasil 1987, Despoluindo a Política 1994, Ecologia e Cidadania 1997. *Address:* Ministry of the Environment, Esplanada dos Ministérios, Bloco B, 5° andar, 70068-900 Brasília, Brazil (office). *Telephone:* (61) 3317-1058 (office). *Fax:* (61) 3317-1755 (office). *E-mail:* carlos.minc@mma.gov.br (office). *Website:* www .mma.gov.br (office); www.minc.com.br.

MINCATO, Vittorio; Italian business executive; *Chairman, Fondazione CUOA;* b. 14 May 1936, Torrebelvicino, Vicenza; joined Ente Nazionale Idrocarburi (Eni) Group SpA (oil and gas co.) 1957, various positions including Admin. and Finance Man. Lanerossi (textile co.) 1957–77, Admin. Man. Eni SpA 1977–84, Asst to Chair. 1984–88, Man. Human Resources and Org. 1988–92, Chair. Savio (textile machinery) and Head of Fertilizers Section, EniChem 1990–92, Deputy Chair. and Man. Dir EniChem 1993–95, Chair. EniChem 1996–98, Man. Dir Eni SpA 1998–2005, CEO 2002–05, fmr Dir numerous other Eni cos including Agip, Lanerossi, Immobiliare Metanopoli, Sofid and Polimeri Europa; Chair. Poste Italiane SpA 2005–08, Fondazione CUOA (Centro Universitario Organizzazione Aziendale) 2007–; Pres. Camera di Commercio di Vicenza 2008–; mem. Bd of Dirs Il Sole 24 Ore SpA 2000–, Fondazione Eni Enrico Mattei, Exec. Bd Assonime (Asscn of Italian Ltd Liability Cos) 2001–, Bd Dirs Fondazione Teatro alla Scala, Man. Bd Assolombarda (industrialists' asscn); Cavaliere del Lavoro 2002. *Leisure interests:* classical music (especially Wagner), reading. *Address:* Fondazione CUOA, Villa Valmarana Morosini, Altavilla Vicentina, Italy (office). *Telephone:* (04) 44333711 (office). *Fax:* (04) 44333999 (office). *E-mail:* direzione@cuoa.it (office). *Website:* www.cuoa.it (office).

MINCHIN, Nicholas (Nick), BEcons, LLB; Australian politician; b. NSW; m. Kerry Minchin; two s. one d.; ed Australian Nat. Univ.; various positions with Liberal Party Fed. Secr. including Deputy Fed. Dir 1977–83; State Dir S Australian Liberal Party 1985–93; elected to Commonwealth Parl. as Liberal Senator for S Australia 1993; Parl. Sec. to Leader of the Opposition 1994–96, to the Prime Minister (upon election win) 1996–97; Special Minister of State and Minister Assisting the Prime Minister 1997–98; Minister for Industry, Science and Resources 1998–2001; Minister for Finance and Admin and Deputy Leader of the Govt in the Senate 2001–07. *Address:* 36 Grenfell Street, Kent Town, SA 5067, Australia (office). *Telephone:* (2) 6277-7400 (Parl.) (office). *Fax:* (2) 6273-4110 (Parl.) (office). *E-mail:* senator.minchin@aph.gov.au (office). *Website:* www.aph .gov.au/senator_minchin (office).

MINCKWITZ, Bernhard von; German business executive; b. 11 Aug. 1944, Göttingen; m. Cornelia Böhning; mem. Man. Bd Bertelsmann AG 1971–98; mem. Bd and Man. Dir Süddeutscher Verlag 1998–2003, Man. Dir Süddeutscher Verlag Hüthig Fachinformationen –2002; Chair. Supervisory Bd Softline AG 2006–13; mem. Sponsorship Foundation for Chinese Excellent Students from Poor Families from 2005. *Address:* c/o Softline AG, Lange Strasse 51, 77652 Offenburg, Germany. *E-mail:* info@softline-group.com.

MINDADZE, Aleksandr Anatol'yevich; Russian scriptwriter; b. 28 April 1949, Moscow; m. Galina Petrovna Orlova; two d.; ed All-Union State Inst. of Cinematography; screenplays since 1972; has worked with dir Vadim Abdrashitov since 2003; Merited Worker of Art of Russia, State Prize of Russia 1984, Silver Pegas Prize of Cultural Asscn Ennio Flaiano 1985, USSR State Prize 1991, co-recipient of Golden Ram Award with Vadim Abdrashitov for their contribution to Russian cinema 1994. *Film scripts include:* Vesenniy prizyv (Spring Selection) 1976, Slovo dlia zashchity (Speech for the Defence) (Prize of All-Union Film Festival, Prize of Lenin's Komsomol) 1976, Spring Mobilization (A. Dovzhenko Silver Medal) 1977, Povorot (The Turning Point) 1978, Okhota na lis (A Fox Hunt) 1980, Predel zhelaniy 1982, Ostanovilsya poyezd (The Train Has Stopped) 1982, Parad planet (Parade of the Planets) 1984, Plyumbum, ili opasnaya igra (Plumbum, or The Dangerous Game) 1986, Sluga (The Servant) 1988, Armavir 1991, Pyesa dlya passazhira (Play for a Passenger) (Silver Bear, Berlin Int. Film Festival) 1995, Vremya tantsora (Time of the Dancer) (Grand Prix, Kinotavr Film Festival, Sochi 1997 and several int. awards) 1998, Magnitnye buri (Magnetic Storms) 2003, Trio 2003, Kosmos kak predchuvstvie (Golden Eagle Award) 2005, Otryv (The Soar) (White Elephant Award, Munich Film Festival) 2007, Minnesota 2009. *Address:* Usiyevicha str. 8, Apt 89, 125319 Moscow, Russia (office). *Telephone:* (499) 155-75-34 (home). *E-mail:* mindadze@mail.ru (home).

MINDAOUDOU SOULEYMANE, Aïchatou, BA, MA, PhD; Niger politician, lawyer, academic and UN official; *Special Representative of the Secretary-General*

and Head, *United Nations Operation in Côte d'Ivoire (UNOCI)*; b. 1959; ed Univ. of Abidjan, Côte d'Ivoire, Univ. of the Sorbonne, Paris, France; Minister of Social Devt, Population and Women 1996–99, of Foreign Affairs 1999–2000, of Foreign Affairs, Co-operation and African Integration 2001–10; Deputy Jt Special Rep. for Political Affairs, African Union-UN Hybrid Operation, Darfur (UNAMID) 2011–12, Acting Jt Special Rep. 2012–13 and Acting Jt African Union-UN Chief Mediator for Darfur 2012–13; Special Rep. of the Sec.-Gen. and Head, UN Operation in Côte d'Ivoire (UNOCI) 2013–; fmr Sr Lecturer in Int. Law. *Address:* United Nations Operation in Côte d'Ivoire (UNOCI), Department of Peacekeeping Operations, United Nations, New York, NY 10017, USA (office); PO Box 11529, Niamey, Niger (home). *Telephone:* (212) 963-1234 (office); 72-35-15 (home). *Fax:* (212) 963-4879 (office). *E-mail:* indo-ai@ifrance.com. *Website:* www.un.org (office).

MINETA, Hon. Norman Yoshio (Norm), BS; American politician, transport industry executive, communications consultant and fmr government official; *Vice-Chairman, Hill Knowlton Strategies;* b. 12 Nov. 1931, San Jose, Calif.; s. of Kay Kunisaku Mineta and Kane Mineta (née Watanabe); m. Danealia Mineta; two s. two step-s.; ed Univ. of Calif., Berkeley; agent/broker Mineta Insurance Agency 1956–89; mem. Advisory Bd, Bank of Tokyo in Calif. 1961–75; mem. San Jose City Council 1967–71; Vice-Mayor, City of San Jose 1969–71, Mayor 1971–75; mem. House of Reps from 13th (now 15th) Calif. Dist 1975–95, Sub cttee on Surface Transportation 1989–92; Sr Vice-Pres. and Man. Dir Transportation Systems and Services, Lockheed Martin 1995–2001; US Sec. of Transportation, Washington, DC 2001–06 (resgnd); Vice-Chair. Hill Knowlton Strategies, Washington, DC 2006–; Chair. Nat. Civil Aviation Revenue Comm. 1997; Commr San Jose Human Relations Comm. 1962–64, San Jose Housing Authority 1966–; mem. Bd of Regents, Santa Clara Univ., Smithsonian Nat. Bd 1996–; Hon. PhD (Embry Riddle Aeronautical Univ.) 1991, (Univ. of Calif. at Berkeley) 2004, (UCLA) 2006, (Univ. of Wash.) 2008, Hon. DH (Rust Coll.) 1993; Hon Directorate (San Jose State Univ.) 2005; Presidential Medal of Freedom 2006. *Address:* Hill Knowlton Strategies, 607 14th Street, NW, Suite 500, Washington, DC 20005, USA (office). *Telephone:* (202) 944-1918 (office). *Fax:* (202) 354-8253 (office). *E-mail:* norm.mineta@hkstrategies .com. *Website:* www.hkstrategies.com (office).

MINFORD, (Anthony) Patrick (Leslie), CBE, PhD; British economist and academic; *Professor of Applied Economics, Cardiff Business School;* b. 17 May 1943; s. of Leslie Mackay Minford and Patricia Mary Sale; m. Rosemary Irene Allcorn 1970; two s. one d.; ed Horris Hill, Winchester Coll., Univ. of Oxford, London School of Econs; Econ. Asst, Ministry of Overseas Devt 1966; Economist, Ministry of Finance, Malawi 1967–69; Econ. Adviser Courtaulds Ltd 1970–71; HM Treasury 1971–73; HM Treasury Del. Washington, DC 1973–74; Visiting Hallsworth Fellow, Univ. of Manchester 1974–75; Edward Gonner Prof. of Applied Econs, Univ. of Liverpool 1976–97; Visiting Prof., Cardiff Business School 1993–97, Prof. of Applied Econs 1997–; Dir Merseyside Devt Corpn 1988–89; mem. Monopolies and Mergers Comm. 1990–96, Treasury Panel of Independent Econ. Forecasters 1993–96; Ed. Nat. Inst. for Econ. and Social Research Review 1975–76, Liverpool Quarterly Econ. Bulletin 1980–; Hon. DSc (Buckingham) 2002. *Publications:* Substitution Effects, Speculation and Exchange Rate Stability 1978, Unemployment – Cause and Cure 1983 (second edn 1985), Rational Expectations and the New Macroeconomics (with David Peel) 1983, The Housing Morass 1987, The Supply-Side Revolution in Britain 1991, The Cost of Europe (ed.) 1992, Rational Expectations Macroeconomics 1992, Markets not Stakes 1998, Britain and Europe: Choices for Change (with Bill Jamieson) 1999, Advanced Macroeconomics: A Primer (with David Peel) 2002, Money Matters: Essays in honour of Alan Walters 2004, Should Britain Leave the EU? – An Economic Analysis of a Troubled Relationship (co-author) 2005, An Agenda for Tax Reform 2006; articles in journals. *Address:* Cardiff Business School, Cardiff University, Colum Drive, Cardiff, CF10 3EU, Wales (office). *Telephone:* (29) 2087-5728 (office). *Fax:* (29) 2087-4419 (office). *E-mail:* minfordp@cardiff.ac.uk (office). *Website:* www.cf.ac.uk/carbs/faculty/minfordp/index.html (office).

MINGOS, (David) Michael Patrick, BSc, DPhil, FRS, FRSC; British scientist and academic; *Professor of Inorganic Chemistry, University of Oxford;* b. 6 Aug. 1944, Basra, Iraq; s. of Vasso Mingos and Rose Enid Billie Griffiths; m. Stacey Mary Hosken 1967; one s. one d.; ed Harvey Grammar School, Folkestone, King Edward VII School, Lytham, Univ. of Manchester, Univ. of Sussex; Fulbright Fellow, Northwestern Univ. Ill., USA 1968–70; ICI Fellow, Univ. of Sussex 1970–71; Lecturer, Queen Mary Coll. London 1971–76; Lecturer in Inorganic Chem., Univ. of Oxford 1976–90, Reader 1990–92, Prof. of Inorganic Chem. 2000–; Fellow, Keble Coll. Oxford 1976–92; Univ. Assessor 1991–92; Sir Edward Frankland BP Prof. of Inorganic Chem., Imperial Coll. London 1992–99, Visiting Prof. 1999–2002; Dean, Royal Coll. of Science 1996–99; Prin. St Edmund Hall, Oxford 1999–2009; visiting professorships in USA, Canada, France, Germany, Switzerland and consultant for various UK and US chemical cos; Gov. Harrow School; mem. numerous editorial bds; Hon. Fellow, Keble Coll., Oxford 2001, St Edmund Hall 2009, Univ. of Sussex 50th Anniversary Fellow 2011; Hon. DSc (UMIST) 2000, (Sussex) 2001; Corday Morgan Medal, Noble Metal Prize, Tilden Medal of RSC, Manchott Prize 1995, Michael Collins Award for Innovation in Microwave Chemistry 1996, Alexander von Humboldt Forschungs Prize 1999. *Publications include:* An Introduction to Cluster Chemistry 1989, Essentials of Inorganic Chemistry 1 1996, Essential Trends in Inorganic Chemistry 1998, Essentials of Inorganic Chemistry 2 1998, Regional Ed. Journal of Organometallic Chemistry 1997–2007, Series Ed. Structure and Bonding 2000. *Leisure interests:* cricket, tennis, walking, gardening, travel. *Address:* Inorganic Chemistry Laboratory, South Parks Road, Oxford, OX1 3QR, England (office). *Telephone:* (1865) 272600 (office). *Fax:* (1865) 279030 (office). *E-mail:* michael.mingos@seh.ox.ac.uk (office). *Website:* www.seh.ox.ac.uk (office).

MINKIN, Vladimir Isaakovich; Russian chemist; b. 4 March 1935; m.; one d.; ed Rostov State Univ.; Asst, Docent, Prof. Rostov State Univ.; Corresp. mem. USSR (now Russian) Acad. of Sciences 1990, mem. 1994; works on physical and organic chem., quantum chem. of organic compounds, organic photochemistry; mem. Comm. of IUPAC; USSR State Prize. *Publications include:* Dipole Moments in Organic Chemistry 1968, Quantum Chemistry of Organic Compounds 1986. *Leisure interests:* chess, literature. *Address:* Institute of Physical and Organic Chemistry, Stachki pr. 194/3, 344104 Rostov on Don, Russia. *Telephone:* (8632) 28-54-88 (office).

MINKS, Wilfried; German stage director, designer and professor of set design; b. 21 Feb. 1930, Binai, Czechoslovakia; twin s.; m. Ulrike Maack 1993; ed Bühnenbildstudium with Willi Schmidt at Hochschule für Bildende Künste, Hamburg; grew up in Bohemia, left as a 15-year-old refugee after World War II with his parents; theatre engagements in Ulm through Intendant Kurt Hübner (worked with Peter Zadek, Peter Palitzsch); Hübner (Intendant), Zadek, Minks, Bremen 1962–73; worked as stage designer with Luc Bondy, Dieter Dorn, Rainer Werner Fassbinder, Klaus Michael Grueber, Claus Peymann, Johannes Schaaf and Peter Stein; his work also led him to the Salzburg Festival Leonce and Lena by Georg Büchner, directed by Schaaf 1975, Vienna Burgtheater stage debut with The Merchant of Venice by William Shakespeare, directed by Zadek 1988, later as Dir at the Academy Theatre, including world premiere of Fernando Krapp Wrote Me a Letter by Tancred Dorst 1992; began working as theatre dir in Berlin, Hamburg, Munich, Bochum, Vienna, Zurich, etc. 1971, with main focus on recent drama, Schiller and Shakespeare, recent production Dennis Kelly, Orphan 2014; Prof. of Stage Design, Hochschule für Bildende Kunst, Hamburg 1970–95; cr. German Pavilion, Expo 1970, Osaka, Japan; screenplay and direction for film Die Geburt der Hexe 1980; mem. Free Acad. of the Arts, Hamburg 1973; Theaterpreis für Lebenswerk 'Der Faust' 2010, Bremen Town Musicians' Prize 2012. *Television production design:* Ein ungebetener Gast 1963, Der Spaßvogel 1964, Der Nebbich 1965, Die Unberatenen 1966, Der Kirschgarten 1966, Maß für Maß 1968, Rotmord (also writer) 1969, Das Kaffeehaus 1970, Die Jungfrau von Orleans (also dir and set designer) 1974, Die Geisel 1977. *Publications:* Catalogue, Wilfried Minks Bühnenbildner, Wilfried Minks Bühnenbau (with Ulrike Maack) 2011. *Address:* Wellingsbüttler Landstraße 166, 22337 Hamburg, Germany. *Telephone:* (40) 503600.

MINNELLI, Liza; American singer and actress; b. 12 March 1946, Los Angeles; d. of the late Vincente Minnelli and Judy Garland; m. 1st Peter Allen 1967 (divorced 1972); m. 2nd Jack Haley, Jr 1974 (divorced 1979); m. 3rd Mark Gero 1979 (divorced 1992); m. 4th David Gest 2002 (divorced 2007). *Films include:* Charlie Bubbles 1968, The Sterile Cuckoo 1969, Tell Me That You Love Me, Junie Moon 1971, Cabaret (played Sally Bowles) 1972 (Acad. Award for Best Actress, The Hollywood Foreign Press Golden Globe Award, the British Acad. Award and David di Donatello Award, Italy), Lucky Lady 1976, A Matter of Time 1976, New York, New York 1977, Arthur 1981, Rent-a-Cop 1988, Arthur 2: On the Rocks 1988, Sam Found Out 1988, Stepping Out 1991, Parallel Lives 1994, Sex and the City 2 2010. *Television includes:* Liza, Liza with a Z (Emmy Award) 1972, Goldie and Liza Together 1980, Baryshnikov on Broadway 1980 (Golden Globe Award), A Time to Live 1985 (Golden Globe Award), My Favourite Broadway: The Leading Ladies 1999. *Theatre:* Best Foot Forward 1963, Flora, the Red Menace 1965 (Tony Award), Chicago 1975, The Act 1977–78 (Tony Award), Liza at the Winter Garden 1973 (Special Tony Award), The Rink 1984, Victor-Victoria 1997, Liza's at the Palace 2008. *Recordings:* Liza with a Z, Liza Minnelli: The Singer, Liza Minnelli: Live at the Winter Garden, Tropical Nights, The Act, Liza Minnelli: Live at Carnegie Hall, The Rink, Liza Minnelli at Carnegie Hall, Results 1989, Maybe This Time 1996, Minnelli on Minnelli 2000, Liza's Back 2002, The Very Best of Liza Minnelli: Life is a Cabaret! 2002, Confessions 2010. *E-mail:* askliza@officiallizaminnelli.com (office). *Website:* www.officiallizaminnelli.com.

MINNER, Ruth Ann; American fmr politician; b. 17 Jan. 1935, Milford, Del.; m. 1st Frank Ingram (deceased); three s.; m. 2nd Roger Minner (died 1991); ed Delaware Tech. and Community Coll.; receptionist to Gov. of Del. 1972–74; mem. Del. House of Reps 1974–82, House Majority Whip; mem. Del. Senate, Del. to Gen. Ass. 1982–92; Lt-Gov. 1993–2001, Gov. of Del. 2001–09; mem. American Asscn for Single People; Democrat. *Leisure interest:* family.

MINNICK, Mary E., BS, MBA; American business executive and fmr beverage industry executive; *Partner, Lion Capital LLP;* b. 27 Nov. 1959, Evanston, Ill.; ed Bowling Green State Univ., Duke Univ.; joined The Coca-Cola Co. in 1983, later Pres. S Pacific Div., The Coca-Cola Co., later Pres. Coca-Cola Japan, Exec. Vice-Pres. The Coca-Cola Co. and Pres. and COO Coca-Cola Asia 2001–05, Exec. Vice-Pres. and Pres. Marketing, Strategy, and Innovation, Coca-Cola Co. 2005–07 (resgnd); Partner, Lion Capital LLP, London 2007–; mem. Bd of Dirs Target Corpn, Heineken; mem. Dean's Council, John F. Kennedy School of Govt, Harvard Univ.; mem. Bd Visitors, Fuqua School of Business, Duke Univ.; Alumni Wf360 (Womenfuture); ranked by Fortune magazine amongst 50 Most Powerful Women in Business in the US (30th) 2005, (31st) 2006, ranked by Forbes magazine amongst 100 Most Powerful Women (85th) 2005. *Address:* Lion Capital LLP, 21 Grosvenor Place, London, SW1X 7HF, England (office). *Telephone:* (20) 7201-2200 (office). *Fax:* (20) 7201-2222 (office). *Website:* www.lioncapital.com (office).

MINNIKHANOV, Rustam Nurgaliyevich; Russian mechanical engineer and politician; *President of Tatarstan;* b. 1 March 1957, Yaña Arış, Rybno-Slobodsky Dist; m.; two s.; ed Kazan Agricultural Inst., Correspondence Inst. of Soviet Trade; began career as engineer with Selkhoztekhnika (machinery mfrs), Sabinsky Dist Asscn 1978; fmr Sr Engineer and Chief Power Engineer with state timber enterprise; fmr Chair. Dist Consumer Soc., also Chair. Exec. Cttee of People's Deputies Dist Council and First Deputy Head of Dist Admin, Arsky Dist 1985–93; Head of Vysokogorsky Dist Admin 1993–96; Minister of Finance, Repub. of Tatarstan 1996–98, Prime Minister of Tatarstan 1998–2010, Pres. of Tatarstan 2010–; Chair. Tatneft (oil co.) 2005–06. *Leisure interest:* rally driving. *Address:* Office of the President, Kazan, Tatarstan, Russia (office). *Telephone:* (843) 567-89-01 (office). *Fax:* (843) 292-70-88 (office). *Website:* www.tatarstan.ru (office).

MINOGUE, Kylie Ann, OBE; Australian singer, actress, producer, fashion designer and entrepreneur and philanthropist; b. 28 May 1968, Melbourne, Vic.; started acting in Skyways 1980, The Sullivans 1981, The Henderson Kids 1984–85, then Neighbours 1986–88 (all TV series); solo artist 1988–, first female vocalist to have her first (released) five singles obtain silver discs in UK; numerous tours, concerts, TV and radio performances world-wide; launched own range of lingerie 2003; labels: PWL, Mushroom, Deconstruction, Parlophone, Warner Music Australia; Ordre des Arts et des Lettres 2008; Hon. Dr of Health Sciences (Anglia Ruskin Univ.) 2011; Woman of the Decade award 1989, nine Logies (Australian TV Industry awards), six Music Week Awards (UK), three Australian Record Industry Asscn Awards, three Japanese Music Awards, Irish Record Industry Award, Canadian Record Industry Award, World Music Award, Australian Variety Club Award, MO Award (Australia), Amplex Golden Reel Award,

Diamond Award (Belgium), MTV Video of the Year (for Did it Again) 1998, MTV Awards for Best Pop Act, Best Dance Act 2002, BRIT Award for Best Int. Female Solo Artist 2002, 2008, Grammy Award for Best Dance Recording (for Come into my World) 2004, Music Industry Trusts' Award 2007, Q Idol Award 2007, inducted into Australian Recording Industry Asscn (ARIA) Awards Hall of Fame 2011. *Tours:* Disco in Dream 1989, Enjoy Yourself Tour 1990, Rhythm of Love Tour 1991, Let's Get to It Tour 1991, Intimate and Live 1998, On a Night Like This 2001, KylieFever2002 2002, Showgirl: The Greatest Hits Tour 2005, Showgirl: The Homecoming Tour 2006–07, KylieX2008 2008–09, For You, For Me 2009, Aphrodite World Tour 2011, Anti Tour 2012, Kiss Me Once Tour 2014. *Play:* The Tempest 1999. *Films:* The Delinquents 1989, Streetfighter 1994, Biodome 1996, Sample People 1999, Cut 1999, Sample People 2000, Moulin Rouge 2001, Holy Motors 2012. *Television:* judge and mentor, The Voice UK (BBC 1) 2014. *Recordings include:* albums: Kylie 1988, Enjoy Yourself 1989, Rhythm of Love 1990, Let's Get To It 1991, Kylie – Greatest Hits 1992, Kylie Minogue 1994, Kylie Minogue (Impossible Princess) 1997, Intimate And Live 1998, Light Years 2000, Hits + 2000, Fever (BRIT Award for Best Int. Album 2002) 2001, Confide In Me (compilation) 2002, Body Language 2003, X 2007, Aphrodite 2010, Kiss Me Once 2014. *Publications:* Kylie 1999, Kylie La La La (with William Baker) 2003, The Showgirl Princess (juvenile) 2006. *Address:* Terry Blamey Management Pty Ltd, 329 Montague Street, Albert Park, Vic. 3206, Australia (office); Terry Blamey Management, PO Box 13196, London, SW6 4WF, England (office). *Telephone:* (20) 7371-7627 (London) (office). *Fax:* (20) 7731-7578 (London) (office). *E-mail:* info@ terryblamey.com (office). *Website:* www.kylie.com (office).

MINOVES TRIQUELL, Juli F., Lic. rel. pol., MA, MPhil, PhD; Andorran political scientist, economist, academic, politician and international organization official and fmr diplomatist; b. 15 Aug. 1969, Andorra la Vella; ed Lycée Comte de Foix, Andorra, Fribourg Univ., Switzerland, Yale Univ., USA; Teaching Asst, Constitutional Law and Political Economy, Dept of Political Science, Yale Univ. 1993; Counsellor, Perm. Mission of Andorra to the UN, New York 1993–94, Deputy Perm. Rep. and Chargé d'affaires a.i. 1994–95, Amb. and Perm. Rep. 1995–2001; Alt. Head of Andorran Del. to World Summit on Social Devt, Copenhagen; Special Plenipotentiary Rep. of Andorran Govt in negotiations to establish diplomatic relations with various govts 1994–98; Amb. to USA and Canada 1996; Vice-Pres. UN Gen. Ass. 1997; Head of Andorran del. to UN Special Ass. Rio+5 1997; Chief of Cabinet a.i. of the Minister of Foreign Affairs 1997–99; mem. special group of UN diplomats for inspections in Iraq 1998; Head of Andorran del. for the establishment of an Int. Criminal Court, Rome, 1998; Amb. to Spain 1998, to Finland and Switzerland 1999, to UK 2000; Minister of Foreign Affairs, Culture and Co-operation 2001–07, of Econ. Devt, Tourism, Culture, Univs, and Govt Spokesman 2007–09; Vice-Pres. and mem. of the Bureau, Liberal International, London 2005–09, Deputy Pres. Liberal International 2009–12; Council mem. CIDOB, Barcelona 2013; Asst Prof., Univ. of La Verne, Calif. 2012; Visiting Prof., Écoles des Affaires internationales, Institut d'Études Politiques de Paris (Sciences Po) 2012; Grand Cross, Order of Merit (Portugal) 1997, Grand Officer, First Class, Order of the Star of Italian Solidarity (Italy) 2009; Tristaina de periodisme journalism award 1986, Nat. Literature Award Fiter-i-Rosell 1988, El futur de les Valls Research Award 1989, Grad. Fellowship, Foundation Crèdit Andorrà 1991, Scholarship, Yale Univ. 1993, Departmental Distinction on Yale PhD dissertation. *Publications:* articles in Andorra 7 weekly magazine 1986–88, Segles de Memòria (novel) (Fiter i Rossell Award) 1989, Les Pedres del Diable (short stories) (Sant Carles Borromeu Award 1992). *Leisure interest:* running. *Address:* c/o Liberal International, 1 Whitehall Place, London, SW1A 2HD, England (office). *Telephone:* (20) 7839-5905 (office). *Fax:* (20) 7925-2685 (office). *E-mail:* jminoves@aya.yale.edu (office). *Website:* www.liberal-international.org (office).

MINOW, Newton N., JD; American lawyer; *Counsel, Sidley Austin LLP;* b. 17 Jan. 1926, Milwaukee, Wis.; s. of Jay A. Minow and Doris Minow (née Stein); m. Josephine Baskin 1949; three d.; ed Northwestern Univ.; Law Clerk to Supreme Court Chief Justice Vinson 1951; Admin. Asst to Gov. of Illinois 1952–53; served Stevenson's law firm 1955–57, Partner 1957–61; Chair. Fed. Communications Comm. 1961–63; Exec. Vice-Pres. Gen. Counsel Encyclopaedia Britannica, Chicago 1963–65; mem. Bd of Trustees, Rand Corpn 1965–75, 1976–86, 1987, Chair. 1970–72; Partner, Sidley Austin LLP (fmrly Leibman, Williams, Bennett, Baird & Minow and fmrly Sidley & Austin) 1965–91, Counsel 1991–; mem. Bd Trustees, Carnegie Corpn of New York 1987–97, Chair. 1993–97; Annenberg Univ. Prof., Northwestern Univ. 1987–; Dir The Annenberg Washington Program 1987–96; Trustee Northwestern Univ. 1975–87, Life Trustee 1987–; Life Trustee, Univ. of Notre Dame; Chair. Arthur Andersen & Co. Public Review Bd 1974–83, Public Broadcasting Service 1978–80; Democrat; Hon. Chair. and Dir Chicago Educational TV Asscn; Hon. LLD (Wisconsin) 1963, (Brandeis) 1963, (North-western Univ.) 1965, (Columbia Coll.) 1972, (Notre Dame) 1994, (Santa Clara) 1998, (Catholitic Theological Union) 2001, (John Marshall Law School) 2011, (Dominican Univ.) 2012. *Publications:* Equal Time: The Private Broadcaster and the Public Interest 1964, Presidential Television (co-author) 1973, Electronics and the Future (co-author) 1977, For Great Debates (co-author) 1987, Abandoned in the Wasteland: Children, Television and the First Amendment 1995, Inside the Presidential Debates: Their Improbable Past and Promising Future (co-author) 2008. *Leisure interest:* reading. *Address:* Sidley Austin LLP, 1 S Dearborn Street, Chicago, IL 60603 (office); 179 E Lake Shore Drive, Chicago, IL 60611, USA (home). *Telephone:* (312) 853-7555 (office). *Fax:* (312) 853-7036 (office). *E-mail:* nminow@sidley.com (office). *Website:* www.sidley.com (office).

MINT MOUKNASS, Naha; Mauritanian physician and politician; b. 1969; d. of Hamdi Ould Mouknass; Pres. Union pour la Démocratie et le Progrès; fmr MP for city of Nouadhibou; fmr mem. Foreign Affairs Comm.; Minister of Foreign Affairs and Co-operation 2009–11. *Address:* c/o Ministry of Foreign Affairs and Co-operation, BP 230, Nouakchott, Mauritania (office).

MINTER, Alan; British fmr professional boxer; b. 17 Aug. 1951, Penge, London, England; s. of Sidney Minter and Anne Minter; m. Lorraine Bidwell 1974; one s. one d.; ed Sarah Robinson School, Ifield; middleweight, southpaw; amateur boxer 1965–72; Amateur Boxing Asscn of England Middleweight Champion 1971; bronze medal, Olympic Games, Munich 1972; 145 amateur fights, 125 wins; professional boxer 1972–82; British Middleweight Champion 1975; won Lonsdale Belt outright 1976; won European Championship from Germano Valsecchi Feb. 1977, lost it to

Gratien Tonna Sept. 1977; forfeited British title Feb. 1977, regained it Nov. 1977; won vacant European title v. Angelo Jacopucci July 1978, retained it v. Tonna Nov. 1978; relinquished British title Nov. 1978; WBA Middleweight Champion and WBC Middleweight Champion v. Vito Antuofermo, Las Vegas March 1980 (first British boxer to win a world championship in USA for 63 years); retained titles v. Antuofermo June 1980, lost them to Marvin Hagler Sept. 1980; lost European title to Tony Sibson Sept. 1981; retd from boxing Feb. 1982, 39 wins (KO 23), 9 losses (KO 8), 1 no contest; nickname Boom Boom; lives in Littlehampton, West Sussex and tours UK in autograph and lecture shows, alongside fmr world boxing champion Jim Watt. *Publication:* Minter: An Autobiography 1980. *Leisure interest:* golf.

MINTON, Mark C., BA, MA; American diplomatist; *President, Korea Society;* ed Columbia Univ., Yale Univ.; served for three years in US Army; career mem. Foreign Service, began his career as a Political Officer in Tokyo 1977, served on Policy Planning Staff, Washington, DC, followed by assignment with Office of Soviet Union Affairs, Consul Gen. in Sapporo, Japan 1984, served in subsequent assignments with Dept of State's Exec. Secr., as Pearson Fellow with US Senate and as Deputy Dir (Japanese Affairs) at Dept of State, Minister-Counselor for Political Affairs, Embassy in Seoul 1992, returned to Washington, DC as Dir of Korean Affairs, Minister-Counselor for Political Affairs, US Mission to the UN, New York 1998, Deputy Chief of Mission, Embassy in Seoul –2006, served for over six months as Chargé d'affaires a.i., then Amb. to Mongolia 2006–09; fmr Diplomat-in-Residence, CUNY; Pres. Korea Soc. 2010–. *Address:* Korea Society, 950 Third Avenue, 8th Floor, New York, NY 10022, USA (office). *Telephone:* (212) 759-7525 (office). *Fax:* (212) 759-7530 (office). *Website:* www.koreasociety.org (office).

MINTON, Yvonne Fay, CBE; Australian singer (mezzo-soprano); b. 4 Dec. 1938, Sydney; d. of R. T. Minton; m. William Barclay 1965; one s. one d.; ed Sydney Conservatorium of Music, studied in London with H. Cummings and Joan Cross; sang with several opera groups in London; debut at Covent Garden 1965, prin. mezzo-soprano 1965–71; US debut at Lyric Opera, Chicago (Octavian in Der Rosenkavalier) 1972; guest artist, Cologne Opera 1969–, Australian Opera 1972–73, also with Hamburg State Opera and at Bayreuth, Paris, Salzburg, Metropolitan Opera, New York, Munich and San Francisco; many concert appearances; created role of Thea in Tippett's The Knot Garden 1970; Hon. ARAM. *Recordings include:* Der Rosenkavalier, Figaro, La Clemenza di Tito, Mozart's Requiem, Elgar's The Kingdom. *Leisure interests:* reading, gardening.

MINTZ, Shlomo; Israeli violinist; b. 30 Oct. 1957, Moscow, USSR; s. of Abraham Mintz and Eve (née Labko) Mintz; m. Corina Ciacci; two s.; ed Juilliard School of Music, New York, USA; went to Israel when very young; many concert tours; Premio Accad. Musicale Chigiana, Siena, Italy 1984; Music Dir, conductor, soloist Israel Chamber Orchestra 1989–93; Artistic Adviser Limburg Symphony Orchestra, Netherlands 1994; Principal Guest Conductor, Zagreb Philharmonic Orchestra 2008–; guest conductor and soloist for numerous orchestras world-wide; Premio Accademia Musicale Chigiana, Diapason D'Or, Grand Prix du Disque, Gramophone Award, Edison Award. *Recordings include:* Violin Concertos by Mendelssohn and Bruch (Grand Prix du Disque, Diapason d'Or) 1981, J. S. Bach Complete Sonatas and Partitas for Solo Violin, The Miraculous Mandarin by Bartok (with Chicago Symphony Orchestra, conducted by Abbado), Compositions and Arrangements by Kreisler (with Clifford Benson, piano), Twenty-four Caprices by Paganini, Two Violin Concertos by Prokofiev (with London Symphony Orchestra, conducted by Abbado), The Four Seasons by Vivaldi (with Stern, Perlman, Mehta). *Address:* Christa Morneweg Concert Management (office). *E-mail:* concert@ morneweg.ch (office). *Website:* www.morneweg.ch (office); www.shlomo-mintz .com.

MINUTO-RIZZO, Alessandro, LLD; Italian diplomatist, international organization official and academic; *Member of Faculty, School of Government, Libera Università Internazionale degli Studi Sociali 'Guido Carli';* b. 10 Sept. 1940, Rome; m.; two s.; mem. staff Directorate of Cultural Affairs, Ministry of Foreign Affairs, Rome 1969–72; First Sec. Washington, DC 1972–75; Counsellor, Brussels 1975–80; Head Eastern Europe Desk, Directorate for Econ. Affairs 1980–81, Head EEC External Relations Desk 1981–86; Minister Counsellor OECD, Paris 1986–92; Minister Plenipotentiary Jan. 1992; Diplomatic Counsellor of Minister for Budget and Econ. Planning 1992–96, of Minister for Co-ordination of European Policies (a.i.) 1995–96; Deputy Chief of Cabinet, Ministry of Foreign Affairs Jan.–Oct. 1996, Co-ordinator for EU Affairs 1996–97; Diplomatic Counsellor of Minister of Defence 1997–2000; Amb. to Cttee for Policy and Security of EU 2000–01; Deputy Sec.-Gen. NATO 2001–07, acting Sec.-Gen. 2003–04; currently mem. Faculty, School of Govt., Libera Università Internazionale degli Studi Sociali 'Guido Carli'; Del. to Council, ESA 1986–92; Chair. Admin. and Financial Cttee 1993–96; Chair. Ass. of Parties of Eutelsat 1989; mem. Man. Bd Italian Space Agency 1994–95; Chair. EU Cttee for Territorial Devt 1996. *Address:* School of Government, Libera Università Internazionale degli Studi Sociali 'Guido Carli', Via di Villa Emiliani, 14, 00197 Rome, Italy (office). *Telephone:* (06) 85225053 (office). *E-mail:* schoolofgovernment@luiss.it (office). *Website:* sog.luiss.it (office).

MIOT, Jean Louis Yves Marie; French journalist; b. 30 July 1939, Châteauroux (Indre); s. of René Miot and Madeleine Moreau; two s. three d.; ed Lycée Jean Giraudoux de Châteauroux and Univ. de Poitiers; Ed. Centre Presse, Poitiers 1964–68; journalist, French Antilles 1968–70; Ed.-in-Chief, later Political Dir Havre-Presse 1970–74; Man. Dir France Antilles Martinique Guadeloupe, launched France-Guyane (weekly) 1974–76; Head, Legis. Elections Service, Le Figaro 1977–78; Man. Dir Berry Républicain, Bourges 1978; Dir Groupe de Presse Robert Hersant 1978–79; Political corresp. L'Aurore 1979–80; mem. Man. Bd Société de Gestion and Assoc. Dir Le Figaro 1980–93; Pres. Advisory Bd Le Figaro 1993–96; Pres. Syndicat de la Presse Parisienne 1986–96; Pres. Fed. Nat. de la Presse Française 1993–96; Pres. Agence-France-Presse (AFP) 1996–99, Syndicat des agences de presse de nouvelles (SANOV) 1996–99; Pres. Dir Gen. Codalie, Financière-CDP and CD-Presse 1999–; mem. Conseil Econ. et Social 1993–96, Comm. de réflexion sur la justice 1997; Dir Société Financière de Radio-Diffusion (SOFIRAD) 1995; Chevalier, Légion d'honneur, Officier de l'Etoile Civique, Officer, Order of Lion (Senegal). *Address:* 10 rue Maître Albert, 75005 Paris, France (home). *E-mail:* janmio@wanadoo.fr (home).

MIOU-MIOU; French actress; b. (Sylvette Héry), 22 Feb. 1950, Paris; one d. by the late Patrick Dewaere; one d. by Julien Clerc; worked as child in Les Halles wholesale market; apprenticed in upholstery workshop; with comedian Coluche helped create Montparnasse café-theatre 1968; stage appearance in Marguerite Duras' La Musica 1985. *Films:* La cavale 1971, Themroc 1972, Quelques missions trop tranquilles 1972, Elle court la banlieue 1972, Les granges brûlées 1972, Les aventures de Rabbi Jacob 1972, Les valseuses 1973, La grande Vadrouille 1974, Lily aime-moi 1974, Pas de Problème 1974, Un génie, deux associés, une cloche 1975, La marche triomphale 1975, F. comme Fairbanks 1976, On aura tout vu 1976, Jonas qui aura vingt ans en l'an 2000 1976, Portrait de province en rouge 1977, Dites-lui que je l'aime 1977, Les routes du Sud 1978, Au revoir à lundi 1978, Le grand embouteillage 1978, La Dérobade 1978, La femme flic 1980, Est-ce bien raisonnable? 1980, La gueule du loup 1981, Josépha 1981, Guy de Maupassant 1982, Coup de foudre 1983, Attention, une femme peut en cacher une autre! 1983, Canicule 1983, Blanche et Marie 1984, Tenue de soirée 1986, Ménage, Les portes tournantes 1988, La lectrice 1988, Milou en mai 1990, Netchaiev est de retour 1991 La Totale! 1991, Le Bal des Casse-Pieds 1992, Tango 1993, Germinal 1993, Montparnasse–Pondichéry 1994, Un indien dans la ville 1994, Ma femme me quitte 1996, Le Huitiéme jour 1996, Nettoyage à sec 1997, Elles 1997, Hors jeu 1998, Tout va bien, on s'en va 2000, Mariages! 2004, L'Après-midi de monsieur Andesmas 2004, L'Un reste, l'autre part 2005, Riviera 2005, Les Murs porteurs 2005, The Science of Sleep 2006, Avril 2006, Family Hero 2006, Les Murs porteurs 2007, Affaire de famille 2008, Le Grand alibi 2008, Mia et le Migou (voice) 2008, Pour un fils 2009.

MIQDAD, Faisal al-; Syrian diplomatist; *Deputy Foreign Minister;* fmr Deputy, then Acting Amb. to UN, New York, Perm. Rep. 2002–05; Deputy Foreign Minister 2006–. *Address:* Ministry of Foreign Affairs, ave Shora, Muhajireen, Damascus, Syria (office). *Telephone:* (11) 3331200 (office). *Fax:* (11) 3320686 (office).

MIRABAUD, Pierre G.; Swiss banker and national organization official; b. 1948; ed Univ. of Geneva; past positions with Banque Rivaud SA, Morgan Guaranty Trust, Blunt Ellis & Loewi, Swiss Bank Corpn; joined Mirabaud & Cie 1976, Pnr 1979, Sr Pnr 1995–; Chair. Swiss Pvt. Bankers Asscn 1990–93, Swiss Bankers Asscn 2003–09; Vice-Chair. Avenir Suisse –2003; Founder and Chair. Pro Democratia Foundation; Chair. Quantum Endowment Fund NV; mem. Bd of Dirs Geneva Int. Airport. *Address:* c/o Swiss Bankers Association, PO Box 4182, 4002 Basel, Switzerland.

MIRAKHOR, Abbas, PhD; Iranian international banking executive, economist and academic; *Chair of Islamic Finance, International Centre for Education in Islamic Finance;* b. 1 July 1941, Tehran; m. Loretta Thomas 1965; two s.; ed Kansas State Univ., USA; Asst and Assoc. Prof. and Chair. Dept of Econs, Univ. of Alabama 1968–77, Prof. and Chair. Dept 1977–79, Vice-Chancellor 1979–80; fmr Prof., Az-Zahra Univ., Tehran; Prof. and Chair. Grad. Study Dept, Alabama A&M Univ. 1980–83; Prof. of Econs Fla Inst. of Tech. 1983–84; Economist, IMF 1984–87, Sr Economist 1987–90, Exec. Dir 1990–2008 (retd); Chair of Islamic Finance, Int. Centre for Educ. in Islamic Finance, Kuala Lumpur 2010–; Quaid-e-Azam Star for Service to Pakistan 1999, Order of Companion of Volta for Service to Ghana 2005; IEEE Eng Man. Soc. First Paper Prize 1972, Islamic Devt Bank Annual Prize for Research in Islamic Econs (jtly) 2003. *Publications:* numerous articles on econs. *Address:* International Centre for Education in Islamic Finance, Second Floor, Annexe Block, Menara Tun Razak (Menara Tradewinds), Jalan Raja Laut, 50350 Kuala Lumpur, Malaysia (office). *Telephone:* (3) 27814000 (office). *Fax:* (3) 26924094 (office). *E-mail:* info@inceif.org (office). *Website:* www.inceif.org (office).

MIRANDA FLAMENCO, Jaime, MA, MBA; Salvadorean politician; *Minister of Foreign Affairs;* b. 1955; ed Universidad Centroamericana José Simeón Cañas, Instituto Centroamericano de Administración de Empresas; fmr Programme Coordinator, Friedrich-Ebert-Stiftung, El Salvador; fmr Political Affairs Officer for UN Verification Mission in Guatemala; fmr Dir-Gen., Salvadorean Asscn for Integral Devt; fmr Deputy Minister of Devt Cooperation and Econ. Relations; Minister of Foreign Affairs 2013; Pres. Community of Democracies 2013–. *Address:* Ministry of Foreign Affairs, Calle El Pedregal, Blvd Cancillería, Ciudad Merliot, Antiguo Cuscatlán, El Salvador (office). *Telephone:* 2231-1000 (office). *Fax:* 2289-8016 (office). *E-mail:* webmaster@rree.gob.sv (office). *Website:* www.rree.gob.sv (office); www.community-democracies.org.

MIRANI, Aftab Shahban; Pakistani politician; b. Shikarpur; s. of Ghulam Kadir Shahban Mirani and Begum Sharfunisa Shahban Mirani; m.; one s. three d.; ed studies in farm man. and agric. in USA; fmr Pres. Shikarpur Municipality; mem. Sindh Prov. Ass. (Pakistan People's Party) 1977–90; Chief Minister of Sindh –1990; mem. Nat. Ass. 1990–; Minister of Defence 1993–96; Vice Chair. and Treasurer, Shaheed Zulfikar Ali Bhutto Institute of Science and Technology. *Leisure interests:* walking, swimming. *Address:* c/o Pakistan People's Party (PPP), 8, St 63, F-8/4, Islamabad, Pakistan.

MIRAPEIX LUCAS, Ferran, LenD, MBA; Andorran politician; b. 7 Sept. 1957; ed Univ. of Barcelona, Spain, LSE, UK, Northwestern Univ., USA; Finance Counselor of Comú de Sant Julià 2000–03, Chief Finance Counselor 2004–05; Minister of Finance 2006–09; Vice-Pres. Liberal Party of Andorra. *Address:* c/o Ministry of Finance, Carrer Prat de la Creu 62–64, Andorra la Vella Ad 500, Andorra.

MIRICIOIU, Nelly, Diploma of Bacalaureat (Piano) and Degree (Voice); Romanian/British singer (soprano); b. 31 March 1952, Adjud; d. of Voicu Miricioiu and Maria Miricioiu; m. Barry J Kirk; one s.; ed Octav Bancila Music School, Iasi, George Enescu Conservatoire; professional debut as Queen of the Night in The Magic Flute in Romania 1970; West European debut as Violetta in Scottish Opera production of La Traviata 1981; debut at Covent Garden as Nedda in I Pagliacci 1982, at La Scala as Lucia in Lucia di Lammermoor 1983; has since appeared at all major opera houses of the world and in int. recitals and concerts (Salzburg Festival, Concertgebouw, Royal Festival Hall); repertoire includes Mimi (La Bohème), Julietta (I Capuleti e I Montecchi), Gilda (Rigoletto), Elvira (Ernani), Marguerite and Elena (Mefistofele), Michaela (Carmen), Marguerite (Faust), Violetta (La Traviata), Roberto Devereux, Lucrezia Borgia and Maria Stuarda (Donizetti), Tancredi (Rossini), Elisabeth (Don Carlos), Il Pirata and Norma (Bellini), Emma d'Antiochia (Mercadante), Helena in I Vespri Siciliani (Verdi), Jerusalem (Verdi), Semiramide (Rossini), Desdemona in Othello, title roles in

Giovanna d'Arco, Tosca, Luisa Miller, Manon Lescaut, Anna Bolena, Lucia di Lammermoor and many more; has worked with many leading conductors and dirs, singing leading roles such as Tosca with José Carreras, José Cura, Neil Schicoff, Mimi in La Bohème with Plácido Domingo, Violetta in La Traviata with Franco Bonisolli, with Roberto Alagna, Renato Bruson, Alfredo Kraus, and many other leading artists; began 20-year series of Vara Matinee Concerts at Amsterdam Concertgebouw 1986; first recording, recital at Wigmore Hall, London 1986; master classes at Aldeburgh 2000, Vilar Young Artists scheme, Royal Opera House, Covent Garden 2000, London 2002, RAM, London 2003, 2005, 2009, 2010, 2011, Royal Coll. of Music, London 2006, Opera Studio, Israeli Opera 2004, Dutch IVC, 's-Hertogenbosch 2004, 2009, 2011, Grachten Festival, Amsterdam 2007, Verbier Festival 2010, Peter de Grote Festival 2011; jury mem. Maria Callas Grand Prix 2003, London Int. Music Festival 2003, Athens 2003, Dutch IVC 2004, 2010, 2012; Guest Prof., Acad. of Music, Maastricht 2010–; Cross Royal House of Romania, Comandor Meritul Cultural; winner of 10 int. competitions, including Second Prize, Francisco Viñas (First Prize not awarded) 1974, First Prize, Maria Callas Competition, Athens 1974, Second Prize, Paris 1975, Second Prize, Geneva 1976, Gold Medal, Katia Popova Competition 1977, First Prize, 's-Hertogenbosch Competition 1978, First Prize, Ostende 1980, American Biographical Insts Award 1994, Romanian Medal of Cultural Merit 2004. *Recordings include:* Puccini's Tosca, Mercadante's Orazi e Curiazi, Donizetti's Rosamunda d'Inghilterra (with Renée Fleming and Bruce Ford) and Maria de Rudenz (Maria), Rossini's Riccardo e Zoraide, Pacini's Maria Regina d'Inghilterra (Maria) 1998, Mascagni's Cavalleria Rusticana (Santuzza), a live recording in Rome of Respighi's La Fiamma (Silvana) and Nelly Miricioiu Live at the Concertgebouw, Nelly Miricioiu – A Rossini Gala 2000, Nelly Miricioiu – Bel Canto Portrait 2001, Roberto Devereux (Elisabetta) at Covent Garden 2003, Mercadante's Emma d'Antiochia 2005, Donizetti's Maria Padilla 2012. *Leisure interests:* literature, TV, cooking, socializing, movies. *Address:* c/o Zemsky/Green Artists Management, 104 West 73rd Street, New York, NY 10023, USA (office); c/o Royal Opera House (Contracts), Covent Garden, London, WC2E 9DD, England. *Telephone:* (212) 579-6700 (office); (20) 7240-1200; (1923) 829679 (home). *Fax:* (212) 579-4723 (office); (1923) 827487 (home). *E-mail:* agreen@zemskygreen.com (office); bzemsky@zemskygreen.com (office); info@roh.org.uk; ram36@dial.pipex.com (home); kirk@dial.pipex.com (home). *Website:* www.zemskygreen.com (office); www.royaloperahouse.org (office); www.nellymiricioiu.com (home).

MIRKAZEMI, Masoud Seyed, BS, MS, PhD; Iranian industrial engineer and politician; b. 1960, Tehran; ed Elm va San'at Univ.; joined Revolutionary Cttees after 1979 revolution; fmr Lecturer, Imam Hossein Univ., Elm va San'at (Science and Industry) Univ.; Head, Centre for Promotion of Productivity and System Evaluation 1989–2000; Head, Centre for Research and Logistic Studies, Ministry of Defence 2000, Adviser to Minister of Defence 2001–03; Dir Islamic Revolutionary Guard Corps Centre for Foundational Studies 2002–04; Pres. Shahed Univ. 2004–; Minister of Commerce 2005–09, Minister of Petroleum 2009–11; Man. Dir Etka Org., Tehran; Ed.-in-Chief Faramad (journal); f. Iran Logistics Asscn; mem. Univ. Scientific Bd. *Address:* c/o Ministry of Petroleum, Hafez Crossing, Taleghani Ave, Tehran, Iran (office).

MIRONOV, Oleg Orestovich, LLD; Russian lawyer; b. 5 June 1939, Pyatigorsk; m.; one s.; ed Saratov Inst. of Law; local investigator Pyatigorsk 1964; teacher, Prof. Constitutional Law Dept Saratov Inst. of Law; State Duma Deputy with CP of Russian Fed. 1993–95; mem., State Duma for Saratov Region 1995–98; mem. Cttee on Law and Legal Reform; mem. Central Cttee of CP of Russian Fed. –1998; Commr on Human Rights (Ombudsman) in Russian Fed. 1998–2003; mem. Interparl. Ass. of CIS, Acad. of Social Sciences, Russian Acad. of Lawyers; Honoured Jurist of Russian Fed. *Publications:* about 200 articles including monographs on problems of constitutional law, theory of state and law, politology. *Leisure interests:* mountain tourism, sports. *Address:* c/o Office of the Commissioner on Human Rights in the Russian Federation, Myasnitskaya str. 47, Moscow, Russia. *Telephone:* (495) 207-76-30 (office).

MIRONOV, Sergei Mikhailovich, CandJur; Russian engineer and politician; b. 14 Feb. 1953, Pushkin, Leningrad Oblast; m. Lyubov Ivanovna; one s. one d.; ed Leningrad (now St Petersburg) Plekhanov Mining Inst., St Petersburg State Tech. Univ., North-Western Acad. of Civil Service, St Petersburg State Univ.; army service 1971–73; engineer, Rusgeophysica (production co.) 1978–86; Sr Geophysicist, USSR Ministry of Geology, Mongolia 1987–91; Exec. Dir Russian Trade Chamber 1991–93, Construction Corpn– Restoration of St Petersburg 1994–95; mem., First Deputy Chair., then Chair. Legis. Ass. of St Petersburg 1995–2000; Head, Political Council, The Will of Petersburg (Volya Peterburga) regional political movt 2000–01; Rep. of St Petersburg Ass. to Sovet Federatsii (Fed. Council) June 2001, Chair. Fed. Council Dec. 2001–11; Founder and Chair. Russian Party of Life 2003, Chair. A Just Russia (Spravedlivaya Rossiya) (merger of Motherland, Russian Party of Life and Russian Pensioners' Party) 2006–11; Chair. Council of the House of A Just Russia Party Deputies 2011–; unsuccessful presidential cand. 2004, 2012; Order of Merit for the Fatherland (Third Degree) 2008. *Address:* A Just Russia (Spravedlivaya Rossiya), 107031 Moscow, ul. B. Dmitrovka 32/1, Russia (office). *Telephone:* (495) 650-38-80 (office). *E-mail:* VPParfenov@mironov.ru (home); info@spravedlivo.ru (office). *Website:* www.spravedlivo.ru (office); mironov.info; sergey-mironov.livejournal.com/profile; www.mironov.ru.

MIRONOV, Yevgeniy Vitalyevich; Russian actor; b. 29 Nov. 1966, Saratov; s. of Vitaly Sergeyevich Mironov and Tamara Petrovna Mironova; ed Saratov School of Theatre Art, Studio School of Moscow Art Theatre; actor, Oleg Tabakov Theatre-Studio 1990–; Merited Artist of Russia 1996. *Theatre roles include:* David Schwartz (Matrosskaya Tishina, A. Galich), Aleksander Aduyev (Common Story, Goncharov), Bumbarash (Passions over Bumbarash, Kim), Orestes (Oresteia, Aeschylus), Ivan Karamazov (The Brothers Karamazov and Hell, Dostoyevsky), Maratov (The Last Night of the Last Tsar, Radzinsky). *Films include:* roles in films by A. Kaidanovsky, A. Mitta, V. Todorovsky, Khotinenko, D. Yevstigneyev, N. Mikhalkov, S. Gazarov, including Zhena kerosinshchika (Kerosene Salesman's Wife) 1988, Pered rassvetom (Before Sunrise) 1989, Delay – raz! (Do It – One!) 1990, Lyubov (Love) (Prize for Best Kinotaurus Festival 1992, Constellation-92, Young Stars of Europe, Geneva 1992, Cinema Critics Prize-Best Actor of the Year 1992) 1991, Zateryannyy v Sibiri (Lost In Siberia) 1991, Kak zhivyote, karasi?

(How's Life, Crucians?) 1992, Ankor, eshchyo ankor! (Encore, Once More Encore!) (Prize of Cinema Critics, Best Actor of the Year 1993) 1992, Poslednyaya subbota (The Last Saturday) 1993, Limita (Nika Prize 1995) 1994, Utomlyonnye solntsem (Burnt by the Sun) (Prize for Supporting Actor, Constellation-95) 1994, Musulmanin (The Mussulman) (Cinema Critics Prize, Best Actor of the Year 1995) 1995, Revizor (Inspector) (Prize for Best Actor Role, Ural Festival 1996) 1996, Zmeinyy istochnik 1997, Mama (Mummy) 1999, Dnevnik ego zheny (His Wife's Diary) 2000, V avguste 44-go (In August of 1944) 2001, Dom durakov (House of Fools) 2002, Prevrashcheniye (Metamorphosis) 2002, Igra v modern 2003, Vecherniy zvon (video) 2004, Na Verkhney Maslovke 2005, Pobeg 2005, Kosmos kak predchuvstvie 2005. *Television includes:* Dvadtsat minut s angelom 1996, Idiot (mini-series) 2003. *Address:* Oleg Tabakov Theatre-Studio, Chaplygina str. 12A, Moscow, Russia. *Telephone:* (495) 916-21-21 (office); (495) 264-15-58 (home).

MIRONYUK, Svetlana; Russian media executive; *Editor-in-Chief, RIA Novosti;* b. 3 Jan. 1968, Moscow; m. S. A. Zverev; three c.; ed Lomonosov Moscow State Univ.; began career as Deputy Man. for Information Analysis and Public Relations, Media Post 1992–2000; Vice-Pres. Kros (public relations co.) 2000–03; joined RIA Novosti news agency 2003, Chair. 2003–, Dir Gen. 2004–, Ed.-in-Chief 2006–; mem. World Econ. Forum, Valdai Discussion Club, Russian Geographic Society, WWF; Media Manager of the Year 2007, Editor of the Year, Russian Fed. of Journalists 2011, C4F - Communction for Future Award, World Econ. Forum 2011. *Address:* Russian News and Information Agency RIA Novosti, 119021 Moscow, Zubovsky boulevard 4, Russia (office). *Telephone:* (495) 645-6470 (office). *Fax:* (495) 637-4545 (office). *E-mail:* press_service@rian.ru (office). *Website:* en.rian .ru (office).

MIROW, Thomas; German economist and banking executive; b. 6 Jan. 1953, Paris, France; m. Barbara Mirow; two d.; ed Univ. of Bonn; Asst and later Chef de Cabinet to fmr Chancellor Willy Brandt 1975–83; Dir Hamburg Press Office 1983–87; Political and Man. Consultant 1988–91; State Minister and Head of Chancellery, Hamburg State Admin 1991–93, State Minister for Urban Devt and Head of Chancellery 1993–97, State Minister for Econs 1997–2001; mem. EC High-Level Group on Lisbon Strategy 2004, Personal Rep. of Fed. Chancellor for Lisbon Strategy and Dir-Gen. for Econ. Policy, Fed. Chancellery 2005, State Sec. Fed. Finance Ministry 2005–08; Pres. EBRD 2008–12; Chair. Supervisory Bd Hamburger Hafen- und Lagerhaus AG (Hamburg Port) 1997–2001, Flughafen Hamburg GmbH 1997–2001; mem. Supervisory Bd Daimler Chrysler Luft- und Raumfahrtholding (Daimler Chrysler Aerospace Holding) 1997–2001; Man. Dir Alstertor Schienenlogistik Beteiligung GmbH 2002–05; mem. Admin. Council Hamburgische Landesbank 1997–2001; mem. Bd of Supervisory Dirs Kreditanstalt für Wiederaufbau 1997–2001; Sr Adviser Ernst & Young AG 2002–05; Adviser MM Warburg Bank 2002–05. *Address:* c/o European Bank for Reconstruction and Development, One Exchange Square, London, EC2A 2JN, England.

MIRRA, Dave; American professional BMX rider; b. 4 April 1974, Chittenango, NY; s. of Michael Mirra and Linda Mirra; brother of Tim Mirra; nicknamed 'Miracle Boy'; has won more medals (18) than any other BMX rider at X Games; subject of several video games about BMX riding. *E-mail:* mirrafan@davemirra .com. *Website:* www.davemirra.com.

MIRREN, Dame Helen Lydia, DBE; British actress; b. 26 July 1945, Chiswick, London; m. Taylor Hackford 1997; first experience with Nat. Youth Theatre culminating in appearance as Cleopatra in Antony and Cleopatra, Old Vic 1965; joined RSC 1967 to play Castiza in The Revenger's Tragedy and Diana in All's Well that Ends Well; Dr hc (St Andrews) 1999; Lifetime Achievement Award for her 'outstanding and lasting' contrib. to film and TV, Women In Film And TV Awards, London 2009. *Plays include:* ressida in Troilus and Cressida, Hero in Much Ado About Nothing, RSC, Stratford 1968; Win-the-Fight Littlewit in Bartholomew Fair, Aldwych 1969, Lady Anne in Richard III, Stratford, Ophelia in Hamlet, Julia in The Two Gentlemen of Verona, Stratford 1970 (the last part also at Aldwych), Tatyana in Enemies, Aldwych 1971; title role in Miss Julie, Elyane in The Balcony, The Place 1971; with Peter Brook's Centre Int. de Recherches Théâtrales, Africa and USA 1972–73; Lady Macbeth, RSC, Stratford 1974 and Aldwych 1975; Maggie in Teeth 'n' Smiles, Royal Court 1975; Nina in The Seagull and Ella in The Bed Before Yesterday, Lyric for Lyric Theatre Co. 1975; Margaret in Henry VI (Parts 1, 2 and 3), RSC 1977–78; Isabella in Measure for Measure, Riverside 1979; The Duchess of Malfi, Manchester Royal Exchange 1980 and Roundhouse 1981; The Faith Healer, Royal Court 1981; Antony and Cleopatra 1983, 1998, The Roaring Girl, RSC, Barbican 1983, Extremities (Evening Standard Award) 1984, Madame Bovary 1987, Two Way Mirror 1989; Sex Please, We're Italian, Young Vic 1991; The Writing Game, New Haven, Conn. 1993, The Gift of the Gorgon (New York) 1994; A Month in the Country 1994, Orpheus Descending 2001, Dance of Death (New York) 2001, Phèdre (London) 2009, The Audience (London) (Olivier Award for Best Actress in a Play 2014) 2013, WhatsOnStage Award for Best Actress in a Play 2014) 2013. *Films include:* Age of Consent 1969, Savage Messiah, O Lucky Man! 1973, Caligula 1977, The Long Good Friday, Excalibur 1981, Cal (Best Actress, Cannes) 1984, 2010 1985, White Nights 1986, Heavenly Pursuits 1986, The Mosquito Coast 1987, Pascali's Island 1988, When the Whales Came 1988, Bethune: The Making of a Hero 1989, The Cook, the Thief, His Wife and Her Lover 1989, The Comfort of Strangers 1989, Where Angels Fear to Tread 1990, The Hawk, The Prince of Jutland 1994, The Madness of King George 1995, Some Mother's Son 1996, Teaching Mrs Tingle 1998, The Pledge 2000, No Such Thing 2001, Greenfingery 2001, Gosford Park (Screen Actors' Guild Award for Best Supporting Actress) 2002, Calendar Girls 2003, The Clearing 2004, Raising Helen 2004, The Hitchhiker's Guide to the Galaxy (voice) 2005, Shadowboxer 2005, The Queen (Best Actress, Venice Film Festival, Nat. Bd of Review, Los Angeles Film Critics Asscn, Toronto Film Critics Asscn, Nat. Soc. of Film Critics 2006, Golden Globe for Best Actress (drama) 2006, Screen Actors' Guild Award for Outstanding Performance by a Female Actor in a Leading Role 2007, Best British Actress, London Film Critics' Circle Awards 2007, Best Int. Actress, Irish Film and TV Awards 2007, BAFTA Award for Best Actress 2007, Acad. Award for Best Actress 2007) 2006, National Treasure Book of Secrets 2007, Inkheart 2008, State of Play 2009, The Last Station 2009, Love Ranch 2009, The Debt 2010, The Tempest 2010, Brighton Rock 2010, Legend of the Guardians: The Owls of Ga'Hoole 2010, Red 2010, Arthur 2011, The Door 2012, Hitchcock 2012, Monsters University (voice) 2013, Red 2 2013. *Television includes:* Miss Julie, The Apple Cart, The Little Minister, As You

Like It, Mrs. Reinhardt, Soft Targets 1982, Blue Remembered Hills, Coming Through, Cause Celebre, Red King White Knight, Prime Suspect (BAFTA Award) 1991, Prime Suspect II 1992, Prime Suspect III 1993, Prime Suspect IV: Scent of Darkness 1995 (Emmy Award 1996), Prime Suspect V: Errors of Judgement 1996, Painted Lady 1997, The Passion of Ayn Rand 1998, Prime Suspect VI 2004, Elizabeth I (Golden Globe Award for Best Actress in a mini-series or film made for TV 2007, Screen Actors' Guild Award for Outstanding Performance by a Female Actor in a TV Movie or Mini-series 2007) 2005, Prime Suspect VII (Emmy Award for Best Actress in a Mini-series 2007) 2006, Nat. Theatre Live (series) – Phèdre 2009, Phil Spector (Screen Actors Guild Award for Outstanding Performance by a Female Actor in a TV Movie or Mini-Series 2013) 2013. *Publication includes:* In the Frame (autobiog.) 2007. *Address:* c/o Raj Raghavan, CAA, 4th Floor, Space One, 1 Beadon Road, London, W6 0EA, England (office). *Telephone:* (20) 8846-300 (office). *Fax:* (20) 8846-3090 (office). *Website:* www.caa.com (office); www.helenmirren.com; www.helenmirrenofficial.com.

MIRRLEES, Sir James Alexander, Kt, MA, PhD, FBA; British economist and academic; *Distinguished Professor at Large, Chinese University of Hong Kong;* b. 5 July 1936, Scotland; s. of the late George B. M. Mirrlees; m. 1st Gillian M. Hughes 1961 (died 1993); two d.; m. 2nd Patricia Wilson 2001; ed Univ. of Edinburgh and Trinity Coll., Cambridge; Adviser, MIT Center for Int. Studies, New Delhi 1962–63; Asst Lecturer in Econs and Fellow, Trinity Coll., Univ. of Cambridge 1963, Univ. Lecturer 1965; Research Assoc. Pakistan Inst. of Devt Econs 1966–67; Fellow, Nuffield Coll. and Edgeworth Prof. of Econs, Univ. of Oxford 1968–95; Prof. of Political Economy, Univ. of Cambridge 1995–2003; Distinguished Prof. at Large, Chinese Univ. of Hong Kong 2003–; Adviser to Govt of Swaziland 1963; Visiting Prof., MIT, USA 1968, 1970, 1976, 1987; Ford Visiting Prof., Univ. of California, Berkeley, USA 1986; Visiting Prof., Yale Univ., USA 1989; Laureate Prof., Univ. of Melbourne, Australia 2004–10; Distinguished Prof., Univ. of Macau 2004–10; mem. Treasury Cttee on Policy Optimization 1976–78; Pres. Econometric Soc. 1982, Royal Econ. Soc. 1989–92; European Econ. Asscn 2000; Hon. FRSE, Foreign Hon. mem. American Acad. of Arts and Sciences, NAS, Hon. mem. American Econ. Asscn; Hon. DLitt (Warwick) 1982, (Portsmouth) 1997, (Oxford) 1998, Hon. DScS (Brunel) 1997, Hon. DSc (Social Sciences) (Edin.) 1997, Dr hc (Peking, Chinese Univ. of Hong Kong, Macao, Liège, Helsinki School of Econs); Nobel Prize for Economics 1996, Royal Medal, Royal Soc. of Edinburgh 2009. *Publications:* co-author of four books; articles in academic journals. *Leisure interests:* music, travel, computing. *Address:* Chinese University of Hong Kong, Shatin, Hong Kong Special Administrative Region, People's Republic of China (office). *Telephone:* 2696-1400 (office). *Fax:* 2603-6159 (office). *E-mail:* jam28@cam.ac.uk (office).

MIRSAIDOV, Shukurulla Rakhmatovich, DEcon; Uzbekistani politician; b. 14 Feb. 1938, Leninabad; m.; four c.; ed Tashkent Finance and Econ. Inst.; mem. CPSU 1962–91; on staff State Planning Org. 1964–84; Head Cen. Statistical Dept, Uzbek SSR 1984–85; Chair. Tashkent City Council 1985–86; Head of Dept, CP of Uzbekistan 1988–89; Deputy Premier of Uzbekistan SSR 1989–90; Chair. Council of Ministers 1990–92; Vice-Pres. of Uzbekistan 1991–92; State Sec. for Pres. Karimov 1992; rep. Int. Fund for Privatization and Investments in Uzbekistan 1992–95; now in pvt. business. *Address:* International Fund for Privatization, Tashkent, Uzbekistan.

MIRVIS, Chief Rabbi Ephraim, BA; South African/British rabbi and Talmudic scholar; *Chief Rabbi, United Hebrew Congregations of the Commonwealth;* b. 1956, Johannesburg; s. of Rabbi Dr Lionel Mirvis and Freida Mirvis; m. Valerie Kaplan; four s. one d. (deceased); ed Herzlia High School, Cape Town, Yeshivat Kerem B'Yavneh, Yeshivat Har Etzion, Machon Ariel, Univ. of South Africa, Yaakov Herzog Teachers' Coll.; moved to Israel to study 1973; received his rabbinic ordination in Jerusalem; certified by Yaakov Herzog Teachers' Coll. as high school teacher in Israel; Rabbi of Adelaide Road Synagogue, Dublin, later Chief Rabbi of Ireland 1984–92; Rabbi of Western Marble Arch Synagogue, London 1992–96; Sr Rabbi at Finchley United Synagogue, also known as Kinloss, London 1996–2013; Founder Rabbi and Hon. Prin. of Morasha Jewish Primary School and Founder and Pres. Kinloss Community Kollel; Chief Rabbi of United Hebrew Congregations of Commonwealth 2013–; Chair. Bd Govs Stratford Jewish Schools, Dublin 1984–92; mem. Steering Cttee of Conf. of European Rabbis; Religious Advisor to Jewish Marriage Council 1997–; has served on Council of London School of Jewish Studies, on Steering Cttee of Encounter Conf., Singer's Prayer Book Publs Cttee; mem. Chief Rabbi's Cabinet 1996–; Chair. Rabbinical Council of United Synagogue 1999–2002; Pres. Irish Council of Christians and Jews 1985–92; Jerusalem Prize for Education in Diaspora, on behalf of Stratford Jewish Schools, from Pres. Chaim Herzog 1990. *Leisure interest:* supports Tottenham Hotspur Football Club. *Address:* Office of the Chief Rabbi, 305 Ballards Lane, London, N12 8GB, England (office). *Telephone:* (20) 8343-6301 (office). *Fax:* (20) 8343-6310 (office). *E-mail:* info@chiefrabbi.org (office). *Website:* www.chiefrabbi.org (office).

MIRVISH, David, CM; Canadian theatrical producer; b. 29 Aug. 1944; s. of the late Edwin Mirvish, CBE and Anne Macklin; producer and owner of the Old Vic Theatre, London and The Royal Alexandra and The Princess of Wales Theatres, Toronto; productions and co-productions include: Candide and Too Clever by Half (London), Into the Woods (London), Les Misérables (Canada), The Good Times Are Killing Me (New York), Miss Saigon, Crazy for You, Tommy (Toronto); Dir Williamstown Theatre Festival, USA –1992, Nat. Gallery of Canada, Nat. Theatre School of Canada 1989–91, Toronto French School; mem. Canadian Cultural Property Export Review Bd 1983–86; Rayne Award (Royal Nat. Theatre); Toronto Theatre Alliance (Dora) Humanitarian Award, Toronto Arts Award 1994. *Address:* Mirvish Productions, 284 King Street West, Suite 400, Toronto, Ont. M5V 1J2, Canada (office); The Old Vic, Waterloo Road, London, SE1 8NB, England (office). *Telephone:* (20) 7928-2651 (London) (office); (416) 593-0351 (Toronto) (office). *Fax:* (416) 593-9221 (office). *E-mail:* webmaster@mirvishproductions.com (office). *Website:* www.mirvishproductions.com (office).

MIRZA, Fehmida, BS, MD; Pakistani politician, physician and business executive; b. 20 Dec. 1956, Sialkot; d. of Qazi Abdul Majeed Abid; m. Zulfikar Ali Mirza; two s. two d.; ed Liaquat Medical Coll., Jamshoro; physician at MCH Centre, then School Health Centre 1983–89; Dir Mirza Sugar Mills 1989–99, CEO 1999–; mem. Nat. Ass. representing Badin 1997–, Speaker 2008–13; mem. Pakistan People's Party. *Address:* National Assembly of Pakistan, Parliament House, Islamabad (office); Deh Jakheji, Golarchi, Taluka S.F. Rahu, District Badin, Pakistan (home). *Website:* www.na.gov.pk (office).

MIRZA, Hamid Ali, BSc, LLB; Pakistani fmr judge; b. 14 Sept. 1940, Jacobabad, Sindh; ed Univ. of Sindh, Jamshoro, Nat. Inst. of Public Admin, Lahore; practised as an advocate 1961–73; Sr Civil Judge and Asst Sessions Judge, Prov. Judicial Service 1973–76; Additional Dist and Sessions Judge 1976–83, served at Karachi, Sukkur, Nawabshah and numerous other places of Prov. of Sindh, also served as OSD Law reforms, High Court of Sindh, Karachi for two years; Dist and Session Judge 1983–95, posted at Nawabshah July–Sept. 1985, at Karachi South 1990–91, 1992–94, also served as Judge, Small Causes Court, Karachi Jan.–March 1983, 1984–85; Registrar, High Court of Sindh 1983–84, 1994–95; Solicitor, Govt of Sindh 1985–90; Chair. Appellate Tribunal for Local Councils of Sindh 1991–92; Judge, High Court of Sindh 1995–2000; Judge, Supreme Court of Pakistan 2000–05 (retd); mem. Syndicate, Univ. of Sindh, Jamshoro 1995–97, 1998–2000; mem. Election Comm. of Pakistan, Chief Election Commr 2009–12 (retd); Trustee, Agha Khan Medical Univ. *Address:* c/o Election Commission of Pakistan Secretariat, Election House, Constitution Avenue G-5/2, Islamabad, Pakistan.

MIRZA, Jamil Ahmed; Pakistani artist and industrialist; b. 21 Feb. 1921, Delhi, India; s. of Mirza Noor Ahmed and of Sughra Begum; m.; three s. two d.; ed St. Joseph High School, Bombay (now Mumbai), India, Sir J.J. School of Art, Bombay; Film Art Dir, Calcutta (now Kolkata), India 1945–49; f. Elite Publishers Ltd, Karachi 1951, developed photo-offset printing, electronic colour scanning and invented computerised Urdu calligraphy 1981; Fellow, Sir J.J. School of Arts 1944; mem. Rotary Club 1965, Dist Gov. 1974; DLitt hc (Karachi) 1999; numerous art, civil and professional awards, including First Prize, Dolly Gursetji Mural Decoration 1942, three Best Entry Awards, All India Art in Industry 1943, Tamgha-I-Imtiaz (Medal of Distinction), Govt of Pakistan 1982, Rotary Int. Meritorious Services Award 1993, Lifetime Achievement Award, Pakistan Asscn of Printing and Graphics Art Industry 2001. *Exhibitions include:* Bombay Art Soc. 1928–43, The Children's Royal Acad., London, UK 1936, Royal Drawing Soc., London, UK 1936–37, All India Art Industry 1943–45. *Publications include:* Urdu Lexicon of Ligatures 1995. *Leisure interests:* painting, travelling, sports. *Address:* Elite Publishers Ltd, D-118, SITE, Karachi 75700 (office); Al-Noor, 23-B/6, PECHS, Karachi 75400, Pakistan (home). *Telephone:* (21) 2573435–39 (office); (21) 4547880 (home). *Fax:* (21) 2564720 (office); (21) 4559011 (home). *E-mail:* elite@elite.com.pk (office); amj@elite.com.pk (home). *Website:* www.elite.com.pk (office).

MIRZA, Sania; Indian professional tennis player; b. 15 Nov. 1986, Mumbai; d. of Imran Aziz Mirza and Nasima Mirza; m. Shoaib Malik 2010; ed Nasr School, St Mary's Coll.; winner, India Fed. Cup 2003, Wimbledon Championships (girls' doubles) 2003, Women's Tennis Asscn Title, Hyderabad Open 2005, Doha Asian Games (silver medal) (women's singles), (gold medal) (mixed doubles) 2006, Bank of the West Classic (women's doubles) 2007, Australian Open (mixed doubles) 2009, Commonwealth Games (silver medal) (women's singles), (bronze medal) (women's doubles), French Open (mixed doubles) 2012; Hon. DLit (MGR Educational and Research Inst. Univ., Chennai) 2008; Arjuna Award 2004. *Leisure interests:* cricket, music. *Website:* www.mysaniamirza.com.

MIRZAEV, Ruslan Erkinovich; Uzbekistani politician; Sec. Nat. Security Council –2005; Minister of Defence 2005–08. *Address:* c/o Ministry of Defence, 100000 Tashkent, Ak. Abdullayev k'och. 100, Uzbekistan (office).

MIRZIYOYEV, Shavkat Miromonovich; Uzbekistani politician; *Prime Minister;* b. 24 June 1957, Zaaminsky dist, Jizzax Oblast; ed Tashkent Inst. of Irrigation, Eng and Agric. Mechanization; worked in irrigation centres and establishments 1974–91; Sec. of Komsomol section, then lecturer, party organizer, Pro-Rector, Tashkent Inst. of Irrigation and Mechanization of Agric. –1996; Head of Admin, Mirzo-Ulugbeg dist, Tashkent 1992; Hokim (Gov.) Jizzax Viloyat 1996–2001, Samarqand Viloyat 2001–03; mem. Oly Majlis (Parl.) 1990–; Prime Minister 2003–; Head of the Agro-Industrial Complex 2005–. *Address:* Office of the Cabinet of Ministers, 100078 Tashkent, Mustaqillik maydoni 5, Uzbekistan (office). *Telephone:* (71) 139-82-95 (office). *Fax:* (71) 139-84-63 (office). *Website:* www.gov .uz (office).

MIRZO, Maj.-Gen. Sherali; Tajikistani army officer and government official; *Minister of Defence;* b. 1967, Hamadoni dist (fmrly Moskovskiy dist); ed Perm High Mil. Command Acad.; joined the newly ind. armed forces of Tajikistan 1994, commanded troops from the dist of Vose during the Tajikistani civil war, fought against opposition forces in Tavildara and Khovaling dists; later spent four years studying at the Mil. Acad. of the Gen. Staff of the Armed Forces of Russia; Deputy Minister of Defence 2005–06; Commdr, Border Guards Unit, State Cttee for Nat. Security (Tajikistani successor to the KGB) 2006–13; Minister of Defence 2013–. *Address:* Ministry of Defence, 734025 Dushanbe, Kuchai Bokhtar 59, Tajikistan (office). *Telephone:* (372) 21-69-83 (office). *Fax:* (372) 21-32-47 (office).

MIRZOEFF, Edward, CVO, CBE, MA; British television producer, director and executive producer; b. 11 April 1936, London, England; s. of Eliachar Mirzoeff and Penina Asherov; m. Judith Topper 1961; three s.; ed Hasmonean Grammar School, London, The Queen's Coll. Oxford; market researcher, Social Surveys (Gallup Poll) Ltd 1958–59, Public Relations Exec., Duncan McLeish & Assocs 1960–61; Asst Ed., Shoppers' Guide 1961–63; with BBC TV 1963–2000, Exec. Producer, Documentaries 1983–2000; Dir and producer of many film documentaries including: (with Sir John Betjeman) Metro-land 1973, A Passion for Churches 1973, The Queen's Realm 1977; Police – Harrow Road 1975, The Regiment 1977, The Front Garden 1979, The Ritz 1981, The Englishwoman and The Horse 1981, Elizabeth R (marking the Queen's 40th anniversary) 1992, Torvill and Dean – Facing the Music 1994, Treasures in Trust 1995, John Betjeman – The Last Laugh 2001; Ed. Bird's-Eye View 1969–72, 40 Minutes 1985–89; Exec. Producer, many documentary series including Real Lives 1985, Pandora's Box 1992, The Ark 1993, True Brits 1994, Situation Vacant 1995, The House 1995, Full Circle with Michael Palin 1997, The Fifty Years War: Israel and the Arabs 1998; Producer, Richard Dimbleby Lectures 1972–82, A.J.P. Taylor Lectures (three series); Exec. Producer, The Lord's Tale (Channel 4) 2002, A Very English Village 2005, The Lie of the Land (Channel 4) 2007; Chair. BAFTA 1995–97 (Vice-Chair., TV 1991–95); Trustee, BAFTA 1999–2011, Grierson Trust 1999–2009 (Vice-Chair. 2000–02, Chair. 2002–06, Patron 2010–); Vice-Pres. The Betjeman Soc. 2006–; mem. Bd of Dirs'

and Producers' Rights Soc. 1999–2007, Salisbury Cathedral Council 2002–10; BAFTA Awards: Best Documentary 1981, Best Factual Series 1985, 1989, Alan Clarke Award for outstanding creative contribution to TV 1995; Samuelson Award, Birmingham Festival 1988, BFI TV Award 1988, British Video Award 1992, Broadcasting Press Guild Award 1996, Royal Philharmonic Soc. Music Award 1996, Int. Emmy 1996. *Publications:* articles, now principally for The Oldie. *Leisure interests:* lunching with friends, opera. *Address:* 9 Westmoreland Road, London, SW13 9RZ, England.

MIRZOYEV, Gasan Borisovich; Russian lawyer; *President, Guild of Russian Lawyers;* b. 11 Dec. 1947, Baku, Azerbaijan; ed Azerbaijan State Univ., Moscow Inst. of Man.; State Arbiter of Moscow 1987–; Founder and Chair. Moscow State Centre on Legal Assistance, later Moscow Legal Centre 1993–, leading to creation of Russian Lawyers Guild; Rector and mem. Russian Bar Acad.; Vice-Pres. Russian Acad. of Natural Sciences; Pres. Human Rights Bd Int. Informatization Acad.; mem. Political Council, Union of Right Forces; Pres. Guild of Russian Lawyers 1994–; Deputy State Duma of Russian Fed. 1999–; Chair. Ed. Bd Rossiyskiy Advokat; Merited Lawyer of Russia. *Publications:* over 100 including monographs on problems of legal protection of business in Russia and protection of human rights; essays and articles. *Leisure interest:* chess. *Address:* Guild of Russian Lawyers, Maly Poluyaroslavsky per. 3/5, 107120 Moscow, Russia (office). *Telephone:* (495) 916-12-48 (office). *Fax:* (495) 975-24-16 (office). *E-mail:* grusadvocat@mtu-net.ru (office).

MIRZOYEV, Ramason Zarifovich; Tajikistani diplomatist and government official; *Director of the Resettlement Unit, Directorate of the Flooding Area of Rogun Hydro Power Project;* b. 15 Feb. 1945, Kulyab Region; m. Akobirova Sarvarbi; four s. one d.; ed Tadjik Inst. of Agric.; worked with construction teams Kulyab Region; in Afghanistan 1975–78; worked in CP bodies and orgs 1983–; USSR People's Deputy 1989–92; Deputy Chair. USSR Supreme Soviet 1989–91; Man. Council of Ministers Repub. of Tajikistan 1992–95; Amb. to Russian Fed. 1995–2001, to Iran 2001–11; Dir Resettlement Unit, Directorate of the Flooding Area, Rogun Hydro Power Project 2011–. *Address:* c/o Ministry of Foreign Affairs, Rudaki Prosp. 42, 73405 Dushanbe, Tajikistan.

MIRZOYEV, Vladimir V.; Russian stage director; b. 21 Oct. 1957; m.; one s. two d.; ed Moscow State Inst. of Theatre Arts; Artistic Dir Studio Domino of the Union of Theatre Workers 1987–89; lived and worked in Canada, f. theatre co. Horizontal Eight, Toronto 1989–93; Stage Dir Moscow Stanislavsky Drama Theatre 1994–; stage dir for productions at Moscow Vakhtangov Theatre, Lenkom Theatre, Vilnius Theatre of Russian Drama, Maryinsky Theatre and for television. *Plays include:* Possibilities, Feast Day (Studio Domino), Proposal, Bear, Caligula (studio Horizontal Eight, Toronto), Cyrano de Bergerac, Amphitrion (Moscow Vakhtangov Theatre), Two Women (Lenkom Theatre), Twelfth Night, Marriage, Khlestakov (Moscow Stanislavsky Drama Theatre), Tartuffe (Vilnius Theatre of Russian Drama). *Publications include:* contrib. to journal Sovietski Teatr 1981-87.

MISHIMA, Yoshinao, BEng, MEng, PhD, DEng; Japanese engineer, academic and university administrator; *President, Tokyo Institute of Technology;* ed Tokyo Inst. of Tech., Univ. of California, Berkeley, USA; Asst Research Engineer, Univ. of California, Berkeley 1979–81; Asst Prof., Precision and Intelligence Lab., Tokyo Inst. of Tech. 1981–89, Assoc. Prof., Precision and Intelligence Lab. 1989–97, Prof., Dept of Materials Science and Eng, Interdisciplinary Grad. School of Science and Eng 1997–, Dean, Interdisciplinary Grad. School of Science and Eng 2006–10, Dir Frontier Research Centre 2010–11, Dir Solutions Research Lab. 2011, Exec. Vice-Pres. for Educ. and Int. Affairs 2011–12, Pres. Tokyo Inst. of Tech. 2012–. *Publications:* numerous papers in professional journals. *Address:* Office of the President, Tokyo Institute of Technology, 4259 Nagatsuta-cho, Midori-ku, Yokohama, Kanagawa Prefecture, 226-0026, Japan (office). *Telephone:* (45) 924-5902 (office). *E-mail:* pr@jim.titech.ac.jp (office). *Website:* www.titech.ac.jp (office).

MIŠKOV, Juraj; Slovak politician and fmr advertising executive; *Minister of the Economy and Construction;* b. 15 April 1973, Bratislava; divorced; two c.; ed Comenius Univ., Bratislava; Ed. Slovak Radio, Bratislava 1991; Ed. SME (daily newspaper) 1992; Exec., Randolph, Young & Moore (advertising agency), Bratislava 1992–93; Exec., Burian, Miškov & Partners, Bratislava 1993–99; co-f. Miškov-Uličný-Weber (MUW, advertising agency) 1999, Gen. Dir MUW Saatchi & Saatchi, Bratislava 2000–09; mem. Nat. Council of the Slovak Repub. (Parl.) 2010–; Minister of the Economy and Construction 2010–; mem. Freedom and Solidarity Party, Deputy Chair. 2010–. *Address:* Ministry of the Economy and Construction, Mierová 19, 827 15 Bratislava, Slovakia (office). *Telephone:* (2) 4854-1111 (office). *Fax:* (2) 4333-7827 (office). *E-mail:* palkovicova@economy.gov.sk (office). *Website:* www.economy.gov.sk (office).

MISSONI, Angela; Italian fashion designer; *Creative Director, Missoni SpA;* b. 1958; d. of Ottavio (Tai) Missoni and Rosita Missoni; m.; two s. one d.; co. founded by her parents 1953, notable for its knitwear designs, made from a variety of fabrics in colourful patterns, including stripes, geometrics and abstract florals, Creative Dir 1996–, developed more than 25 sub-lines including M Missoni (lower-priced line owned by the Valentino Fashion Group), Missoni Home, Missoni menswear, fragrances (first launched 1980), and at one time, Missoni Sport (now discontinued); launched Hotel Missoni (Rezidor Hotel Group project) in Kuwait 2009, with others following in Paris, Miami and Dubai; clients include Margherita Missoni, Cameron Diaz, Demi Moore, Nicole Richie, Katie Holmes, Kim Kardashian, Nicole Kidman, Jennifer Lopez, Ashley Judd, Julia Roberts and Emilio Pucci; other product lines include beauty, eyewear, fragrances, home, handbags, jeans, lingerie, shoes, sneakers, underwear; collaborations with Margherita Missoni for ProKeds to benefit Orphan Aid Africa 2008, Estee Lauder 2005, Converse Spring 2010, Missoni for Target 2011. *Address:* Missoni SpA, Via Solferino 9, 20121 Milan, Italy (office). *Telephone:* (02) 8545821 (office). *E-mail:* press.info@missoni.it (office). *Website:* www.missoni.com (office); www .missonihome.it (office); www.m-missoni.com (office).

MISTRETTA, Charles A., PhD; American biomedical engineer, physicist and academic; *John R. Cameron Professor, Department of Biomedical Engineering, University of Wisconsin;* ed Univ. of Illinois and Harvard Univ.; James Picker Advanced Fellow in Academic Radiology 1972–74; apptd Prof., Depts of Medical Physics and Radiology, Univ. of Wisconsin, Madison, currently John R. Cameron Prof., Dept of Biomedical Eng, Coll. of Eng; Fellow, American Asscn of Physicists in

Medicine; Laufman-Greatbatch Prize, Assen for the Advancement of Medical Instrumentation 1983, J. Allyn Taylor Int. Prize in Medicine, Robarts Research Inst. and Univ. of Western Ontario (co-recipient) 1998. *Publications:* more than 120 articles in medical journals on investigations of non-invasive techniques for magnetic resonance imaging of cardiovascular system. *Address:* Clinical Science Center, University of Wisconsin, Box 3252, Module E3 E1/398, 600 Highland Avenue, Madison, WI 53792, USA (office). *Telephone:* (608) 263-8313 (office); (608) 265-9685 (office). *Fax:* (608) 263-0876 (office). *E-mail:* camistre@facstaff.wisc.edu (office); camistre@wisc.edu (office). *Website:* www.engr.wisc.edu/bme (office).

MISTRY, Cyrus Pallonji, BE, MSc; Irish business executive; *Chairman, Tata Group;* b. 4 July 1968; s. of Pallonji Mistry and Patsy Perin Dubash; m. Rohiqa Chagla; two s.; ed Cathedral and John Connon School, Mumbai, Imperial Coll., London, London Business School; Dir Tata Elxsi Ltd 1990–2009; Dir Shapoorji Pallonji and Co. 1991–94, Man. Dir Shapoorji Pallonji Group 1994, currently mem. Bd of Dirs; Dir Tata Power Co. Ltd –2006, Dir Tata Sons 2006–, Deputy Chair. and Chair.-Designate, Tata Group 2011–12, Chair. 2012–; mem. Bd of Dirs Forbes Gokak, Afcons Infrastructure, United Motors (India); Fellow, Inst. of Civil Engineers. *Address:* Tata Group, Bombay House, 24 Homi Mody Street, Mumbai, 400 001, India (office). *Telephone:* (22) 66658282 (office). *Website:* www.tata.com (office).

MISTRY, Dhruva, MA, RA, FRBS; Indian sculptor; b. 1 Jan. 1957, Kanjari, Gujarat; s. of Pramodray Mistry and Kantaben Mistry; ed Maharaja Sayajirao Univ. of Baroda, Royal Coll. of Art, London; British Council Scholar, RCA 1981–83; Artist in Residence in association with Arts Council of Britain at Kettle's Yard Gallery with Fellowship at Churchill Coll., Cambridge 1984–85; freelance Sculptor-Agent, Nigel Greenwood Gallery, London 1983–97; Sculptor in Residence, Victoria and Albert Museum, London 1988; Rep. GB for the Grand Rodin Prize Exhbn, Japan 1990; Prof., Head of Sculpture and Dean, Faculty of Fine Arts, Maharaja Sayajirao Univ. of Baroda 1999–2002; youngest Royal Academician since J.M.W. Turner when elected 1991; mem. Royal Acad. of Arts 1991; Fellow (first Indian), Royal Soc. of British Sculptors 1993; Prof., Head of Sculpture and Dean, Faculty of Fine Arts, Maharaja Sayajirao Univ. of Baroda 1998–2002; works in Vadodara; Hon. CBE 2001; Hon. DUniv (Univ. of Central England) 2007; Madame Tussaud's Award for Art, RCA 1983, Jack Goldhill Award, Royal Acad. of Arts 1991, Award for the Design of Humanities Prize Medal, London 1994, Design and Pres.'s Award for Victoria Square Sculptures 1995, The Landscape Inst. and Marsh Fountain of the Year Award 1995, Award of Excellence, Gujarat Gaurav Samiti 2006, Pride of Vadodara, Felicitation of top 20 by Divya Bhaskar 2009. *Major commissions include:* Mitchell Beazley 1982, Peter Moores Foundation, Liverpool 1983, Merseyside Devt Corpn, Liverpool 1984, Churchill Coll., Cambridge 1985, Nitchiman Corpn, Japan 1987, Glasgow Garden Festival 1988, British Art Medal Soc., London 1988, Nat. Museum of Wales, Cardiff 1989, Hunterian Art Gallery, Glasgow 1990, Victoria Square, The City Council, Birmingham 1992, Quaglino's, London 1993, Int. Classical Music Awards, London 1993, Tamano City Project, Uno, Japan 2002, Petronet LNG Ltd, Dahej 2004, Delhi Devt Authority, New Delhi for Delhi Univ. 2005. *Public collections include:* Arts Council, London, Birmingham Museum and Art Gallery, Birmingham Contemporary Art Soc., London, Churchill Coll., Cambridge, Cartwright Hall, Bradford, City Art Gallery, Manchester, City of Stoke-on-Trent, Dept of Fine Arts, Punjab Univ., Chandigarh, Fukuoka Art Museum and Asian Art Gallery, Fukuoka, Glynn Vivian Art Gallery, Swansea, Govt Museum and Art Gallery, Chandigarh, Hunterian Art Gallery, Glasgow, Harris Museum and Art Gallery, Preston, Jigyo-Chuo-Koen Park, Fukuoka, Lalit Kala Akademi, New Delhi, Leicestershire Educ. Authority, Laing Art Gallery, Newcastle-upon-Tyne, LNG Petronet Ltd, Dahej, Milton Keynes Devt Corpn, Merseyside Devt Corpn, Liverpool, Nat. Museum of Wales, Cardiff, Oriana, P&O Cruises, Osians Archive, New Delhi, Peter Moores Foundation, Liverpool, Roopankar Museum of Fine Art, Bhopal, RCA, London, Southampton Art Gallery, Sculpture at Goodwood, Tate Gallery, London, British Council, London, British Museum, London, British Library, London, Hakone Open Air Museum, Japan, Ulster Museum, Belfast, Victoria & Albert Museum, London, Walker Art Gallery, Liverpool, West Zone Culture Centre, Udaipur, Yorkshire Sculpture Park, West Bretton, Tamano City Council, Uno, Japan. *Publications include:* exhbn catalogues: Art Heritage, New Delhi, 1981, Sculpture and Drawings, Kettle's Yard Gallery, Univ. of Cambridge 1985, Cross-Sections, Sculpture and Drawings 1982–88, Collins Gallery, Univ. of Strathclyde, Glasgow 1988–89, Bronzes 1985–1990, Nigel Greenwood Gallery, London 1990, Asian Artist Today: Fukuoka Annual VII, Asian Art Museum, Fukuoka, Japan 1994, Work 1990–1995, Royal Acad., Friends Room in Association with Anthony Wilkinson Fine Art, London 1995, Prints 1988–1998, Gallery Espace, New Delhi 1989, Work 1997–2001, Sakshi Gallery, Mumbai 2001, Table Pieces 2003–2004, Sakshi Gallery, Mumbai 2005, Steel, Stainless Still, New Work 2004–2006, Coimbatore Palace, Bodhi Art, New Delhi 2007, Ink Jet, Canvas & Sculpture, Art Pilgrim, New Delhi 2007, Artist in Focus, Contemporary Works: India 2008, Harmony Show, Harmony Art Foundation, Mumbai 2008, Prisms 366°: Sounds & Echoes 1997–2007, Meru 2008, Bronzes 1987–1990, Grosvenor Vadehra, London 2011. *Leisure interests:* photography, reading, walking. *Address:* 76 Anushakti Nagar, Sama, Vadodara 390 024, India (office). *Telephone:* (265) 2712949 (office). *E-mail:* dhruva@dhruvamistry.com (home). *Website:* www.dhruvamistry.com.

MISTRY, Pallonji Shapoorji; Irish (b. Indian) construction industry executive; *Chairman, Shapoorji Pallonji Group;* b. 1 June 1929; m. Pat (Patsy) Perin Dubash 2003; two s. two d.; joined family business, Shapoorji Pallonji & Co. Ltd aged 18; mem. Bd of Dirs Union Bank of India, Bombay Dyeing & Manufacturing Co. Ltd, W. H. Brady Group of Cos, The Associated Cement Cos Ltd (Chair. 1977–79, 1997–2000); Chair. Forbes Gokak –2003; currently Chair. Shapoorji Pallonji Group, owns Shapoorji Pallonji Construction Ltd, Forbes Textiles and Eureka Forbes Ltd; largest individual shareholder in Tata Sons (holding co. of Tata Group which owns Corus Steel in UK and brands including Jaguar, Land Rover and Tetley tea); family owns a 200 acre (0.81 square km) stud farm in Pune; gave up Indian citizenship in order to obtain Irish citizenship as dual citizenship currently not allowed by Indian Govt 2003; Hon. mem. World Zarathushti Chamber of Commerce 2004. *Address:* Shapoorji Pallonji & Co. Ltd, Shapoorji Pallonji Centre, 41/44 Minoo Desai Marg, Colaba, Mumbai 400 005 (office); Deendayal Upadhyay Research Institute, 5th Floor, 7E, Jhandelwala Extension, New Delhi 110 035,

India (office). *Telephone:* (22) 67490263 (Mumbai) (office). *Fax:* (22) 66338176 (Mumbai) (office). *Website:* www.sp-group.co.in/keypersonnel.php (office); www.shapoorji.in (office).

MISTRY, Pranav, MS; India research scientist; b. 1981, Palanpur, Gujarat; ed Nirma Inst. of Tech., Ahmedabad, Indian Inst. of Tech., Bombay, Massachusetts Inst. of Tech., USA; Project Man. Microsoft India Devt Centre 2004, UX Researcher 2005–06; Research Intern with Global Connection Project (Carnegie Mellon Univ., NASA, Google and UNESCO); Teaching Asst Media Arts and Sciences, MIT 2007; Research Asst Ambient Intelligence, MIT Media Lab 2006–08, Researcher Microsoft Research, Visiting Researcher Japan Science and Tech. Agency; Research Asst Fluid Interfaces, MIT Media Lab 2008–; Inventor of SixthSense (interface using gestures) and Mouseless (invisible computer mouse); Pres. Zombie.labs, (research group); Lead Coordinator, HCI India; f. Sorotics (social robotics) group at Indian Inst. of Tech., Bombay; fmr Pres. Young Scientist Club, Palanpur; fmr coordinator Assen of Computer Eng Students; Young Indian Innovator Award, Digit Magazine 2009, Invention of the Year Award 2009, TR35 2009 Award, Tech. Review, Netexplorateurs of the Year Award 2010, Netexplorateurs Grand Prix 2010, France, listed among the 50 Most Creative People of the Year 2010. *Achievements include:* patents for digital user interface for inputting Indic scripts, radio frequency control of computing system, start menu display model, multi-mode multimedia device and computing system, task-oriented start menu, hardware control initiated task switching, single hardware control initiated switching between application and utilities. *Address:* Massachusetts Institute of Technology Media Lab, E14-548G75, Amherst Street, Cambridge, MA 02139, USA (office); Post Box 10, Palanpur 385 001, India (home). *Telephone:* (617) 835-4030 (office); (27) 42253536 (home). *E-mail:* pranav@mit.edu (office); pranavmistry@gmail.com. *Website:* www.media.mit.edu (office); www.pranavmistry.com.

MISTRY, Rohinton, BA, BSc, FRSL; Canadian author; b. 1952, Bombay (now Mumbai), India; m. Freny Elavia 1975; ed St Xavier's High School, Bombay, Univ. of Bombay, Univ. of Toronto and York Univ., Canada; moved to Canada 1975; bank clerk, Toronto 1975–85; began writing short stories 1982; writings have been translated into more than 30 languages; Hon. PhD (Ottawa) 1996, (Toronto) 1999, (York) 2003, (Ryerson Univ., Toronto) 2012; Gov.-Gen.'s Award for Fiction 1991, Commonwealth Writers' Prize for Best Book 1992, 1996, First Novel Award, W. H. Smith/Books in Canada 1992, Giller Prize 1995, Winifred Holtby Prize, RSL 1996, Los Angeles Times Fiction Prize 1997, ALOA Prize for Fiction (Denmark) 1997, Kiriyama Pacific Rim Book Prize for Fiction 2002, Canadian Authors' Assen Award for Fiction 2003, Guggenheim Fellowship 2005, Neustadt Int. Prize for Literature 2012. *Publications include:* Tales from Firozsha Baag (short stories) 1987, Such a Long Journey (novel) 1991, A Fine Balance (novel) 1995, Family Matters (novel) 2002, The Scream 2008; essays and articles in various languages and periodicals. *Address:* c/o Bruce Westwood, Westwood Creative Artists Ltd, 94 Harbord Street, Toronto, ON M5S 1G6, Canada (office). *Telephone:* (416) 964-3302 (office). *Fax:* (406) 975-9209 (office). *E-mail:* wca_office@wcaltd.com (office). *Website:* www.wcaltd.com (office).

MITA, Katsushige, BEE; Japanese business executive; *Chairman Emeritus, Hitachi Ltd;* b. 6 April 1924, Tokyo; s. of Yoshitaro Mita and Fuji Mita; m. Toriko Miyata 1957 (died 1989); two d.; ed Univ. of Tokyo; joined Hitachi Ltd 1949, Gen. Man. Omika Works Aug.–Nov. 1971, Kanagawa Works 1971–75, Dir 1975, Man. Computer Group 1976–78, Exec. Man. Dir 1977–79, Sr Exec. Man. Dir 1979–80, Exec. Vice-Pres. 1980–81, Pres. and Rep. Dir, Hitachi Ltd 1981–91, Chair. and Rep. Dir 1991–2000, Chair. Emer. 2000–, Hon. Chair. Advisory Bd The Hitachi Center for Tech. and Int. Affairs, Founder The Hitachi Foundation; Vice-Chair. Keidanren (Japan Fed. of Econ. Orgs) 1992–; mem. Int. Business Program Advisory Council, The Fletcher School, Tufts Univ., USA; Dr hc (Tufts Univ.) 1991; Blue Ribbon Medal (Japan) 1985, Officier, Légion d'honneur 1993, DSPN Dato (Malaysia) 1993; Will Rogers Award (USA) 1994. *Leisure interests:* golf, gardening. *Address:* c/o Hitachi Ltd, 6-6, Marunouchi, 1-Chome, Tokyo, Japan.

MITA, Toshio; Japanese energy industry executive; *Chairman, Chubu Electric Power Company, Inc.;* b. 12 Nov. 1946, Aichi Pref.; ed Seikei Univ.; joined Chubu Electric Power Co., Inc. 1969, served in various man. positions including Dir Hekinan Thermal Power Station 1995–97, Atsumi Thermal Power Station 1997–99, Kawagoe Thermal Power Station 1999–2001, Thermal Power Centre 2001–03, Tokyo Br. 2003–05, Man. Dir and Gen. Man. Sales Dept 2005–06, Pres. and Dir 2006–07, Pres. and Dir (Exec. Officer) 2007–10, Chair. 2010–, Chair. Chubu Econ. Fed. 2011–, Chair. Chubu Industrial and Regional Advancement Centre 2011–. *Address:* Chubu Electric Power Co., Inc., 1 Higashi-shincho, Higashi-ku, Nagoya 461-8680, Japan (office). *Telephone:* (52) 951-8211 (office). *Fax:* (52) 962-4624 (office). *E-mail:* info@chuden.co.jp (office). *Website:* www.chuden.co.jp (office).

MITARAI, Fujio, BA; Japanese business executive; *Chairman and CEO, Canon Inc.;* b. 23 Sept. 1935, Kamae, Oita (Kyushu); m. Chizuko Mitarai (died 2002); several c.; ed Chuo Univ.; joined Canon Camera Co. Inc. 1961, transferred to newly est. Canon USA 1966, Pres. and CEO Canon USA Inc. 1979–89, Vice-Pres. Canon Inc. –1995, Pres. and CEO 1995–2006, Chair. and CEO 2006–; Corp. Auditor Dai-ichi Mutual Life Insurance Co.; Vice-Chair. Nippon Keidanren (Japan Business Fed.) 2002–06, Chair. 2006–10, Chair. Emer. 2010–, Chair. Cttee on Corp. Governance 2000–; Person of the Year Award, Photographic Mfrs and Distributors Assen 1999, named by BusinessWeek one of the world's top 25 managers 2001, recipient Business Reformer Commendation from govt of Japan 2002, named to Barron's list of the World's 30 Best Chief Execs 2008–11, ranked 58th by Forbes magazine amongst The World's Most Powerful People 2009. *Leisure interest:* golf. *Address:* Canon Corporate Headquarters, 30-2 Shimomaruko 3-chome, Ohta-ku, Tokyo 146-8501, Japan (office). *Telephone:* (3) 3758-2111 (office). *Fax:* (3) 5482-5135 (office). *E-mail:* info@canon.com (office). *Website:* www.canon.com (office).

MITCHELL, Rt Hon. Andrew John Bower, PC, BA; British politician; b. 23 March 1956, Hampstead, London, England; s. of David Mitchell, MP; m.; two d.; ed Rugby School, Warwicks., Jesus Coll., Cambridge; Chair. Cambridge Univ. Conservative Assen Michaelmas 1977, Pres. Cambridge Union 1978; served as UN peacekeeper in Cyprus 1970s, went on to work abroad extensively in Africa and Asia; served in Royal Tank Regt of British Army; joined Lazard and worked with British cos seeking overseas contracts; fmr Sr Strategy Adviser for Accenture (man. consultancy firm); mem. (Conservative) Islington Health Authority, North London 1980s; contested Sunderland South constituency 1983; MP for Gedling 1987–97; contested Gedling 1997; MP for Sutton Coldfield 2001–10, for Sutton Coldfield (revised boundary) 2010–; Parl. Pvt. Sec. to William Waldegrave as Minister of State, FCO 1988–90, to John Wakeham as Sec. of State for Energy 1990–92; Asst Govt Whip 1992–93, Govt Whip 1993–95; Parl. Under-Sec. of State, Dept of Social Security 1995–97; Shadow Minister for Econ. Affairs 2003–04, Home Affairs 2004–05; Campaign Man. for David Davis in Conservative leadership contest 2005; Shadow Sec. of State for Int. Devt 2005–10; Sec. of State for Int. Devt 2010–12; Chief Whip in the House of Commons and Parl. Sec. to the Treasury Sept.–Oct. 2012 (resgnd), mem. Parl. and Political Service Honours Cttee Sept.–Oct. 2012; Sec. One Nation Group of Conservative MPs 1989–92, 2005–; Vice-Chair. Conservative Party (cands) 1992–93; mem. Work and Pensions Select Cttee 2001–03, Modernization of House of Commons Select Cttee 2002–04; Founder of Project Umubano (Conservative Party social action project in Rwanda and Sierra Leone) 2007; Trustee, E.M. Radiation Research Trust. *Achievements include*: Winner, Westminster Dog of the Year Award for his Welsh Springer Spaniel Molly 2009. *Address*: House of Commons, Westminster, London, SW1A 0AA (office); Constituency Office, Sutton Coldfield Conservative Association, 36 High Street, Sutton Coldfield, B72 1UP, England. *Telephone*: (20) 7219-8516 (London) (office); (121) 354-2229 (Sutton Coldfield). *Fax*: (20) 7219-1981 (London) (office); (121) 321-1762 (Sutton Coldfield). *E-mail*: andrew.mitchell.mp@ parliament.uk (office); info@sutton-coldfield-tories.org.uk. *Website*: www .parliament.uk/biographies/commons/andrew-mitchell/25190 (office); www .suttoncoldfieldconservatives.com; www.andrew-mitchell-mp.co.uk.

MITCHELL, Arthur; American dancer, choreographer and artistic director; b. 27 March 1934, New York; s. of Arthur Mitchell and Willie Mae Mitchell; ed School of American Ballet; with Ballet Theater Workshop 1954; with John Butler Co., 1955; Prin. Dancer, New York City Ballet 1955–72; dancer, choreographer and actor, Spoleto Festival of Two Worlds 1960; Founder and Artistic Dir American Negro Dance Co. 1966–; Founder, Choreographer and Artistic Dir Nat. Ballet Co., Brazil 1967; Founder, Dir and Choreographer Dance Theater of Harlem, New York City 1969–; Teacher of Dance, Karel Shook Studio, Melissa Hayden School, Cedarhurst, Long Island, Jones-Haywood School of Ballet, Washington; Choreographer (with Rod Alexander) Shinbone Alley; has appeared in numerous productions; Hon. Chair., USA Int. Ballet Competition 2010; hon. degrees include: Hon. DArts (Columbia Coll., Chicago) 1975; Hon. DFA (NC School of the Arts) 1981, (Fordham Univ.) 1983, (Princeton Univ., Williams Coll.) 1986, (Juilliard School) 1990; Hon. DA (Harvard) 1987; awards include: Ebony Magazine American Black Achievement Award 1983, Paul Robeson Award, Actors Equity Assocn, NAACP Image Awards Hall of Fame 1986, Arnold Gringrich Memorial Award 1987, Banquet of the Golden Plate 1989, Kennedy Center Honor for Lifetime Achievement 1993, Handel Medallion, City of New York, American Acad. of Arts and Letters Award for Distinguished Service to the Arts, Barnard Coll. Medal of Distinction, Zenith Award for Fine Arts 1994, Nat. Medal of Arts 1995. *Address*: Dance Theater of Harlem, 466 West 152nd Street, New York, NY 10031-1814, USA (office). *Telephone*: (212) 690-2800 (office). *Fax*: (212) 690-8736 (office). *Website*: www .dancetheatreofharlem.com.

MITCHELL, David, MA; British writer; b. Jan. 1969, Southport; m. Keiko Mitchell; one d.; ed Univ. of Kent; worked in Waterstone's, Canterbury 1990–91; taught English in Japan 1994–2002; one of Granta's Best of Young British Novelists 2003. *Publications*: Ghostwritten (Mail on Sunday/John Llewellyn Rhys Prize, James Tait Black Memorial Prize) 1999, Number9Dream 2001, Cloud Atlas (British Book Awards for Richard & Judy Best Read of the Year 2005, South Bank Show Literary Fiction Award, Geoffrey Faber Memorial Prize 2005) 2004, Black Swan Green 2006, The Thousand Autumns of Jacob de Zoet 2010. *Address*: c/o Sceptre, Hodder Headline Ltd, 338 Euston Road, London, NW1 3BH, England.

MITCHELL, Duncan, MSc, PhD, FRSSAf; South African professor of physiology; *Professor Emeritus, Brain Function Research Group, School of Physiology, University of Witwatersrand;* b. 10 May 1941, Germiston; s. of Thomas Mitchell and Maud K. (née Abercrombie) Mitchell; m. Lily May Austin 1966; one s. one d.; ed St John's Coll., Johannesburg, Univ. of Witwatersrand; mem. scientific staff, Research Org. of Chamber of Mines of SA 1964–72, Nat. Inst. for Medical Research, London 1973–75; Prof. of Physiology, Medical School, Univ. of Witwatersrand 1976–2006, Prof. Emer. 2007–; Gold Medal, Zoological Soc. of SA 2000. *Publications*: more than 200 papers in thermal, pain and sleep physiology. *Leisure interests*: nature conservation, ballet. *Address*: School of Physiology, University of the Witwatersrand, Medical School, 7 York Road, Parktown, 2193 Johannesburg (office); 73A Fourth Street, Linden, Johannesburg 2195, South Africa (home). *Telephone*: (11) 717-2359 (office); (11) 888-2671 (home); (83) 260-7205 (home). *Fax*: (11) 643-2765 (office). *E-mail*: Duncan.Mitchell@wits.ac.za (office); duncanmitch@gmail.com (home). *Website*: hermes.wits.ac.za/www/health/ physiology/staff/duncan.htm (office).

MITCHELL, Hon. Fred, JR, MPA, BA, LLB; Bahamian politician; *Minister of Foreign Affairs and Immigration;* b. 5 Oct. 1953, Nassau; s. of Fredrick A. Mitchell, Sr. and Lilla Angelina Mitchell (nee Forde); ed St Augustine's Coll., Antioch Univ., OH and John F. Kennedy School of Govt, Harvard Univ., USA, Univ. of Buckingham, UK; elected to Senate, fmr Chair. Senate Select Cttee on Culture; Public Relations Consultant, Al Dillette & Assocs; currently MP for Fox Hill, fmr Opposition Spokesman on Foreign Affairs, Labour and Immigration; Minister of Foreign Affairs and Public Service 2002–07; of Foreign Affairs and Immigration 2012–; Founding mem. Bahamas Cttee on S Africa; mem. Progressive Liberal Party; mem. New Providence Human Rights Assocn. *Address*: Ministry of Foreign Affairs, Goodman's Bay Corporate Centre, West Bay Street, POB N-3746, Nassau, Bahamas (office). *Telephone*: 322-7624 (office). *Fax*: 328-8212 (office). *E-mail*: mofa@bahamas.gov.bs (office). *Website*: www.bahamas.gov.bs (office).

MITCHELL, George John, BA, LLB; American business executive, lawyer, diplomatist and fmr politician; *Chairman Emeritus, DLA Piper;* b. 20 Aug. 1933, Waterville, Me; s. of George J. Mitchell and Mary Mitchell; m. Heather M. Mitchell; ed Bowdoin Coll., Brunswick, Me, Georgetown Univ., Washington, DC; served in US Army 1954–56; called to Bar 1960; trial attorney, US Dept of Justice, Washington, DC 1960–62; Exec. Asst to Senator Edmund Muskie 1962–65; Pnr, Jensen & Baird, Portland 1965–77; US Attorney for Maine 1977–79; US Dist

Judge 1979–80; US Senator from Maine (Democrat) 1980–95, Majority Leader, US Senate 1988–95; Chair. Maine Democratic Cttee 1966–68; mem. Nat. Cttee Maine 1968–77; Special Adviser to Pres. Clinton for Econ. Initiatives in Ireland 1995–2000; Chair. Cttee on NI 1995; Chancellor Queen's Univ., Belfast 1999–2009; Adviser Thames Water 1999–; mem. Bd of Dirs The Walt Disney Co. 1994–2006, Chair. 2004–06; with Verner, Liipfert, Bernhard McPherson & Hand (law firm) 1995–2002; Pnr, DLA Piper LLP, Washington, DC 2002–04, Chair. Global Bd, Co-Chair. Govt Controversies Practice Group 2005–, now Chair. Emer.; Special US Envoy to the Middle East 2009–11; Co-chair Housing Comm., Bipartisan Policy Center; mem. Bd of Dirs Staples Inc., Boston Red Sox (professional baseball team); headed investigation into alleged steroid use by major league baseball players 2007; Hon. KBE 1999; Hon. LLD (Queen's, Belfast) 1997; Philadelphia Liberty Medal 1998, Presidential Medal of Freedom 1999, Houphouët-Boigny Peace Prize (jtly) 1999, Tipperary Int. Peace Award 2000, Truman Inst. Peace Prize, German Peace Prize, UN Educational Peace Prize, Harry Hopkins Medal, Harry S. Truman Good Neighbor Award 2007. *Publications*: Men of Zeal (with William S. Cohen), World on Fire, Not for America Alone: The Triumph of Democracy and the Fall of Communism, Making Peace. *Address*: DLA Piper, 1251 Avenue of the Americas, New York, NY 10020-1104, USA (office). *Telephone*: (212) 335-4600 (office). *Fax*: (212) 335-4605 (office). *E-mail*: george .mitchell@dlapiper.com (office). *Website*: www.dlapiper.com (office); bipartisanpolicy.org.

MITCHELL, Rt Hon. Sir James Fitzallen, Kt, KCMG, PC, BSc, CBiol; Saint Vincent and the Grenadines politician, agronomist, biologist and hotelier; b. 15 May 1931, Bequia, Grenadines; s. of Reginald Mitchell and Lois Mitchell (née Baynes); m. Patricia Parker 1965 (divorced); four d.; ed St Vincent Grammar School, Imperial Coll. of Tropical Agric., Trinidad and Univ. of British Columbia; Agricultural Officer, Saint Vincent 1958–61; Ed. Pest Control Articles and News Summaries, Ministry of Overseas Devt, London 1964–65; MP for the Grenadines 1966–2001; Minister of Trade, Agric., Labour and Tourism 1967–72; MP (as an ind.) for the Grenadines 1972–79, re-elected in by-election 1979–2001; Premier of St Vincent 1972–74; Prime Minister of Saint Vincent and the Grenadines 1984–2000, also Minister of Finance and Planning and fmr Minister of Foreign Affairs; Founder New Democratic Party 1975, then Pres.; Chair. Caribbean Democrat Union 1991; Vice-Chair. Int. Democrat Union 1992–; Chair. Hotel Frangipani, Gingerbread, and several other cos; mem. Inst. of Biologists, London 1965–; Order of the Liberator (Venezuela) 1972, Grand Cross, Kts of Malta 1998, Order of Propitious Clouds, Grand Cross Don Infanta (Portugal), Chevalier d'honneur, Chaine de Rotisseur 1995, and other awards. *Publications include*: World Fungicide Usage 1965, Caribbean Crusade 1989, Guiding Change in the Islands 1996, A Season of Light 2001, Beyond the Islands (autobiog.) 2005. *Leisure interests*: sailing, farming. *Address*: Hotel Frangipani, Box One, Bequia, Saint Vincent (office). *Telephone*: (458) 3255 (office). *Fax*: (458) 3824 (office). *E-mail*: frangi@vincysurf.com (office).

MITCHELL, John; New Zealand professional rugby coach and fmr professional rugby union player; b. 23 March 1964, Hawera; made 134 appearances for Waikato Chiefs rugby team (86 as Capt.) and set record for most tries scored in a NZ season (21); made six mid-week appearances for NZ; Asst Coach England rugby team 1997–2000; returned to coach Waikato Chiefs 2001 season; All Blacks Coach 2001–03, team finished 3rd in World Cup 2003; Coach Waikato Nat. Provincial Championship Team 2003–4; Head Coach, Emirates Western Force, WA 2005–. *Address*: Emirates Western Force, PO Box 146, Floreat, WA 6014, Australia. *Telephone*: (8) 9383-7714. *Website*: www.rugbywa.com.au.

MITCHELL, Joni, CC; Canadian singer, songwriter, visual artist and poet; b. (Roberta Joan Anderson), 7 Nov. 1943, Fort Macleod, Alberta; d. of William A. Anderson and Myrtle Anderson (née McKee); m. 1st Chuck Mitchell 1965 (divorced); m. 2nd Larry Klein 1982; one d. by Brad McGrath; ed Alberta Coll.; Jazz Album of Year and Rock-Blues Album of Year for Mingus, Downbeat Magazine 1979, Juno Award 1981, Century Award, Billboard Magazine 1996, Polar Music Prize (Sweden) 1996, Gov. Gen.'s Performing Arts Award 1996, Nat. Acad. of Songwriters Lifetime Achievement Award 1996; inducted into Rock & Roll Hall of Fame 1997, into Nat. Acad. of Popular Music–Songwriters Hall of Fame 1997, into Canadian Songwriters Hall of Fame 2007, Grammy Award for Best Pop Instrumental Performance (for One Week Last Summer) 2008, Jack Richardson Producer of the Year Award 2008. *Recordings include*: albums: Song to a Seagull, Clouds, Ladies of the Canyon 1970, Blue 1971, For the Roses, Court and Spark 1974, Miles of Aisles, The Hissing of Summer Lawns 1975, Hejira 1976, Don Juan's Reckless Daughter, Mingus 1979, Shadows and Light 1980, Wild Things Run Fast 1982, Dog Eat Dog 1985, Chalk Mark in a Rain Storm 1988, Night Ride Home 1991, Turbulent Indigo (Grammy Awards for Best Pop Album, Best Art Direction 1996) 1994, Hits 1996, Misses 1996, Taming the Tiger 1998, Both Sides Now (Grammy Award for Best Traditional Pop Vocal Album 2001) 2000, Travelog 2002, Songs of a Prairie Girl 2005, Shine 2007. *Dance*: The Fiddle and the Drum (score for ballet with the Alberta Ballet) 2007. *Songs include*: Both Sides Now, Michael from Mountains, Urge for Going, Circle Game. *Television includes*: Joni Mitchell: Intimate and Interactive (Gemini Award 1996). *Publication*: Joni Mitchell: The Complete Poems and Lyrics. *Telephone*: (310) 288-6262 (office). *Fax*: (310) 288-6362 (office). *E-mail*: jtani@gtba.com (office). *Website*: www.jonimitchell.com.

MITCHELL, Julian, BA, MA, FRSL, FSA; British writer; b. 1 May 1935, Epping, Essex, England; s. of William Moncur Mitchell and Christine Mitchell (née Browne); partner Richard Rowson; ed Winchester and Wadham Coll., Oxford; mem. Literature Panel, Arts Council 1966–69, Welsh Arts Council 1988–92; John Llewellyn Rhys Prize 1965, Somerset Maugham Award 1966. *Films*: Arabesque (with Stanley Price) 1965, Another Country 1982, Vincent and Theo 1990, August 1996, Wilde 1997. *Television*: more than 50 TV plays and adaptations. *Publications*: novels: Imaginary Toys 1961, A Disturbing Influence 1962, As Far As You Can Go 1963, The White Father 1964, A Circle of Friends 1966, The Undiscovered Country 1968; biography: Jennie: Lady Randolph Churchill (with Peregrine Churchill), A Disgraceful Anomaly 2003; plays: Half Life 1977, Another Country 1981 (SWET Play of the Year 1982) 1981, Francis 1983, After Aida (or Verdi's Messiah) 1986, Falling over England 1994, August 1994 (adapted from Uncle Vanya), The Good Soldier (adapted from Ford Madox Ford) 2010, Family Business 2011, The Welsh Boy 2012. *Leisure interests*: fishing, local history. *Address*: 25

Rylett Road, London, W12 9SS, England. *Telephone:* (20) 8740-5036. *E-mail:* julian .mitchell606@btinternet.com.

MITCHELL, Katie, OBE; British theatre director; *Associate Director, Royal National Theatre;* b. 23 Sept. 1964; d. of Michael Mitchell and Sally Mitchell; m.; one d.; Pres. Oxford Univ. Dramatic Soc. 1984; awarded a Winston Churchill Memorial Trust Award to research Eastern European theatre in Russia, Lithuania, Georgia, Poland and Germany 1989; f. Classics on a Shoestring Theatre Co. 1990; Assoc. Dir, RSC 1997–98, Royal Court Theatre, London 2001–03, Abbey Theatre, Dublin 2000–02, Royal Nat. Theatre 2003–; Evening Standard Award for Best Dir 1996. *Plays directed:* Arden of Faversham, Vassa Zheleznova and Women of Troy (with Classics on a Shoestring) 1990–91, A Woman Killed with Kindness 1991, The Dybbuk 1992, Ghosts 1993, Henry VI 1994, Rutherford and Son 1994, The Machine Wreckers 1995, Easter 1995, The Phoenician Women 1996, Endgame (Donmar Warehouse) 1996, Don Giovanni 1996, The Last Ones 1996, The Mysteries 1997, The Beckett Shorts 1997, Uncle Vanya (RSC) 1998, Jenůfa 1998, The Oresteia 1999, Attempts on Her Life (Piccolo Theatre, Milan) 1999, The Maids (Young Vic, London) 1999, The Country 2000, Mountain Language Ashes to Ashes 2001, Katya Kabanova 2001, Iphigenia in Aulis (Abbey Theatre, Dublin) 2001, Nightsongs 2002, Ivanov 2002, Three Sisters 2003, Jephtha 2003, Iphigenia at Aulis 2004, Forty Winks (Royal Court) 2004, The Seagull 2006, The Waves 2006, Attempts on her Life 2006, The Sacrifice (Welsh Nat. Opera) 2007, The Jewish Wife/A Respectable Wedding (Young Vic) 2007, St Matthew Passion (Glyndebourne) 2007, The Idiot (Royal Nat. Theatre) 2008, The City 2008, The Maids (Sweden) 2008, Pains of Youth (Nat. Theatre) 2009, Royal Opera House: Parthenogenesis 2009, Clemency 2011, Die Wellen (Cologne, Germany) 2011, Wastewater (Royal Court Theatre, London) 2011. *TV work includes:* The Widowing of Mrs Holroyd 1995, The Stepdaughter 2000 (BBC), Turn of the Screw 2004. *Address:* c/o Leah Schmidt, The Agency, 24 Pottery Lane, London, W11 4LZ, England (office).

MITCHELL, Keith Claudius, MS, PhD; Grenadian politician; *Prime Minister;* b. 12 Nov. 1946, St Georg's; m. Marietta Mitchell; one s.; ed Presentation Coll., Grenada, Univ. of West Indies, Barbados, Howard Univ. and American Univ., Washington, DC; cand. for Grenada Nat. Party in 1972 elections; Gen. Sec. New Nat. Party 1984–89, Leader 1989–; Minister of Communication, Works, Public Utilities, Transportation, of Civil Aviation and Energy 1984–87, of Communications, Works, Public Utilities, Co-operatives, Community Devt, Women's Affairs and Civil Aviation 1988–89; Prime Minister and Minister of Finance, External Affairs, Mobilization, Trade and Industry, Information and Nat. Security 1995–99; Prime Minister and Minister of Nat. Security and Information 1999–2008, re-elected 2003, also Minister of Finance 2007–08; Prime Minister 2013–, also Minister of Finance, Energy, Nat. Security, Disaster Preparedness, Home Affairs, Public Affairs, Public Admin, Implementation and Information; Capt. Grenada Nat. Cricket Team 1971–74; Order of the Brilliant Star (Taiwan) 1995. *Leisure interest:* playing cricket. *Address:* Office of the Prime Minister, Ministerial Complex, 6th Floor Botanical Gardens, Tanteen, St. George's (office); New National Party (NNP), Upper Lucas Street, St. George's, Grenada (office). *Telephone:* 440-2255; 440-1875 (office). *Fax:* 440-4116; 440-1876 (office). *E-mail:* pmsec@gov.gd; nnpadmin@nnpnews.com (office). *Website:* www.gov.gd; www .nnpnews.com (office).

MITCHELL, Pat, MA; American broadcasting executive and television producer; *President and CEO, Paley Center for Media;* m. Scott Seydel; six c.; ed Univ. of Georgia; fmr news anchor and producer WBZ-TV Boston; first woman to host and produce her own nat. talk show, Woman to Woman 1980s; Co-Founder, developer of series, specials, documentaries, VU Productions –1992; has worked for NBC, CBS and ABC; Head CNN Productions, Time Inc. TV –2000; Pres. and CEO Public Broadcasting Service (PBS) 2000–06; Pres. and CEO Paley Center for Media (fmrly Museum of TV and Radio), New York 2006–; mem. Council on Foreign Relations, Women's Advisory Council of the Kennedy School of Govt, US–Afghan Women's Council; mem. Bd of Dirs Bank of America 2001–09, Participant Productions, Sun Microsystems 2005–10, Human Rights Watch; mem. Bd of Trustees Sundance Inst. (currently Vice-Chair.), Mayo Clinic; Founding mem. American chapter, Global Green USA; Dr hc (Emerson Coll., Hollins Univ., Bloomsburg Univ., Converse Coll.); Cable and Telecommunications Woman of the Year Award, CINE Golden Eagle for Lifetime Achievement, PROMAX Century Award, Sandra Day O'Connor Award for Leadership, Business Hall of Fame, Georgia State Univ. 2008, NATPE Brandon Tartikoff Legacy Award. *Television includes:* Woman to Woman (Emmy Award for Best Daytime Talk Program 1984), CNN Perspectives, Cold War (Peabody Award), Millennium: A Thousand Years of History. *Address:* Paley Center for Media, 25 West 52nd Street, New York, NY 10019, USA (office). *Telephone:* (212) 621-6800 (office). *Website:* www.paleycenter .org (office).

MITCHELL, Thomas Noel, PhD, LittD; Irish academic; b. 7 Dec. 1939; s. of Patrick Mitchell and Margaret Mitchell; m. Lynn S. Hunter 1965; three s. one d.; ed Nat. Univ. of Ireland, Trinity Coll. Dublin and Cornell Univ. NY; Instructor Cornell Univ. 1965–66; Asst Prof. Swarthmore Coll. 1966–73, Assoc. Prof. 1973–78, Prof. of Classics 1978–79; Prof. of Latin, Trinity Coll. Dublin 1979–91, Fellow 1980–, Sr Dean 1985–87, Sr Lecturer 1987–90, Provost 1991–2001; Cornell Visiting Prof. Swarthmore Coll. 1986; mem. Royal Irish Acad. (Vice-Pres. 1989); mem. American Philosophical Soc. 1996–; Distinguished Visiting Prof. Victoria Univ. Melbourne 2001–; Visiting Fellow, The Hoover Inst. Stanford Univ. Calif. 2002; Chair. Bd St James Hosp., Dublin, Press Council of Ireland 2007–; Hon. Fellow, RCPI 1992, R.C.S.I. 1993; Hon. LLD (Queen's Univ. Belfast) 1992, (Nat. Univ. of Ireland) 1992; Hon. D.Hum.Litt. (Swarthmore) 1992, (Lynn Univ., USA) 1998, (State Univ. of New York) 1998; Hon. PhD, (Charles Univ., Prague) 1998, (Dublin Inst. of Tech.) 1999; Hon. DLitt (Victoria Univ. of Tech.) 2000. *Publications:* Cicero, The Ascending Years 1979, Cicero, Verrines II.1. 1986, Cicero the Senior Statesman 1990; numerous articles and reviews on Cicero and Roman History. *Leisure interest:* gardening. *Address:* The Rubrics, Trinity College, Dublin 2 (office); Dodona, Blackwood Lane, Malahide, Co. Dublin, Ireland (home). *Telephone:* (1) 6081843 (office).

MITCHISON, (Nicholas) Avrion, DPhil, FRS; British professor of zoology and comparative anatomy; b. 5 May 1928, London; s. of the late Baron Mitchison and Naomi Mitchison; m. Lorna Margaret Martin 1957; two s. three d.; ed Leighton Park School and Univ. of Oxford; Lecturer, later Reader in Zoology, Univ. of Edin. 1956–62; Head, Div. of Experimental Biology, Nat. Inst. for Medical Research, Mill Hill 1962–71; Jodrell Prof. of Zoology and Comparative Anatomy, Univ. Coll. London 1970–89; Scientific Dir Deutsches Rheuma-Forschungszentrum, Berlin 1990–96; Sr Fellow, Dept of Immunology, Univ. Coll. London 1996–; Hon. Dir Imperial Cancer Research Fund, Tumour Immunology Unit, Univ. Coll. London; Hon. MD (Edin.); Paul Ehrlich Prize, Mitchison Prize for Rheumatology est. in his honour. *Address:* Department of Immunology, University College London, Wind-eyer Building, 46 Cleveland Street, London, W1P 6DB (office); 14 Belitha Villas, London, N1 1PD, England (home). *Telephone:* (20) 7380-9349. *Fax:* (20) 7380-9357. *E-mail:* n.mitchison@ucl.ac.uk (office).

MITHI, Mukut, BSc; Indian government official and politician; b. 1 Jan. 1952, Roing, Arunachal Pradesh; s. of Kumso Mithi and Anachi Mega; m. Pomaya Mithi; three s.; ed J.N. Coll., Pasighat; mem. Indian Nat. Congress (INC), later of Arunachal Congress, broke from later to form Arunachal Congress (Mithi)—AC(M) 1998, AC(M) later merged with INC 1999; Chief Minister of Arunachal Pradesh 1999–2003; Lt-Gov. Puducherry (fmrly Pondicherry) 2006–08 (resgnd); mem. Rajya Sabha (Parl.) 2008–; mem. Cen. Advisory Cttee for Nat. Cadet Corps, Governing Council, North-Eastern Indira Gandhi Regional Inst. of Health and Medical Sciences, Shillong 2008–. *Leisure interests:* basketball, jogging, singing, dancing, reading. *Address:* AB-8, Pandara Road, New Delhi 110 065; Ezengo, P.O.+P.S. - Roing, Lower Dibang Valley District, Arunachal Pradesh, India. *Telephone:* (3803) 222960; 9868181088. *E-mail:* mukut.mithi@sansad.nic.in.

MITRI, Tarek; Lebanese politician, academic and UN official; *Special Representative of the Secretary-General in Libya and Head, United Nations Support Mission in Libya (UNSMIL);* b. 1950, Tripoli; Dir Faith and Unity Bureau, WCC, Geneva mid-1980s, later Co-ordinator Islamic-Christian Dialogue; Programme Dir for Christian-Muslim Dialogue, Middle East Council of Churches 1984–91; Minister of Environment and Admin. Devt 2005–06, Minister of Culture 2006–08, Acting Minister of Foreign Affairs and Emigrants 2006–08, Minister of Information 2008–11; Co-founder Centre of Christian-Muslim Studies; Special Rep. of Sec.-Gen. and Head of UN Support Mission in Libya (UNSMIL), UN 2012–; fmr Prof., Harvard Univ., Amsterdam Free Univ., Univ. of Geneva, Univ. of Balamand; active mem. several groups and orgs concerning Muslim-Christian dialogue in Middle East and world-wide; fmr UNESCO Chair on Dialogue, St Joseph Univ., Beirut. *Address:* United Nations Support Mission in Libya (UNSMIL), Tripoli, Libya (office). *E-mail:* achouri@un.org (office). *Website:* unsmil.unmissions.org (office).

MITROFANOV, Aleksey Valentinovich; Russian politician and writer; b. 16 March 1962, Moscow; s. of Zoya Mitrofanova; m. Marina Lillevyali; ed Moscow Inst. of Int. Relations; with Ministry of Foreign Affairs 1985–88; researcher, Inst. of USA and Canada 1988–91; TV producer, Leisure Centre Sokol; mem. Higher Council, Liberal Democratic Party of Russia 1991–93; Minister of Foreign Affairs, Shadow Cabinet of Liberal Democratic Party 1992–96; mem. State Duma 1993–2008, Deputy Chair. Cttee on Int. Relations 1993–96, Chair. Cttee on Geopolitics 1996–99; Pres. Nat. Center of Geopolitics 2008–; mem. Cen. Council Spravedlivaya Rossiya (A Just Russia). *Films:* scriptwriter: Pchiojka (A Little Bee), Yuliya 2006; numerous documentaries including Yury Andropov 1993, Andrey Gromyko 1993. *Publications include:* Steps of New Geopolitics, Secret Visit of Professor Voland, t.A.T.u Come Back 2006. *Leisure interest:* chess. *Address:* c/o Central Council, A Just Russia (Spravedlivaya Rossiya), 123104 Moscow, ul. Tverskaya 13/1, Russia. *Telephone:* (495) 662-2616. *E-mail:* duma@ alexeymitrofanov.ru. *Website:* www.alexeymitrofanov.ru.

MITROFANOV, Alexandr; Czech political journalist; b. 27 June 1957, Rostov, Russia; m.; one s. one d.; ed Rostov State Univ., Russia; Ed. Škodovák, Škoda Plzeň 1980–88, Právo Lidu 1991–92; contrib. to Právo 1992–, Political Commentator; undertook sabbatical study in UK 1994, 1997; Křepelky Prize, Czech Literary Fund 1994, Ferdinand Peroutka Prize for Journalism 2001. *Publications:* Behind the Façade of Lidový dům, Czech Social Democracy, People and Events 1992–1998 1998, Politics Under Lid (with Markéta Maláčova) 2002, three chapters in Erratic Paths of Social Democracy 2005. *Leisure interests:* reading, writing books. *Address:* Právo, Slezská 13, 121 50 Prague 2, Czech Republic (office). *Telephone:* (2) 21001111 (office). *Fax:* (2) 21001276 (office). *E-mail:* alexandr.mitrofanov@pravo .cz (office). *Website:* pravo.novinky.cz (office).

MITROPOULOS, Efthimios E.; Greek academic and international organization official; b. 30 May 1939, Piraeus; m. Chantal Mitropoulos (née Byvoet); one s. one d.; ed Aspropyrgos Merchant Marine Acad., Hellenic Coast Guard Acad.; with Greek Merchant Navy 1959–62; Coast Guard Officer, Corfu and Piraeus 1964–65; mem. Greek Del. to IMO 1966–77, becoming Head; Harbour Master, Corfu 1977–79; joined IMO Secr. 1979, Head of Navigation Section 1985–89, Sr Deputy Dir for Navigation and Related Matters 1989–92, Dir Maritime Safety Div. 1992–2003, Asst Sec.-Gen. 2000–03, Sec.-Gen. 2004–11, Chair. Int. Maritime Law Inst. 2004–; Chancellor, World Maritime Univ., Malmo, Sweden 2004–; mem. Bd of Dirs Tsakos Energy Navigation Ltd 2012–; Gov. Royal Nat. Lifeboat Inst.; Fellow, Royal Inst. of Navigation; mem. Hellenic Inst. of Marine Tech., Shipmasters' Union of Greece, Royal Automobile Club; Hon. Citizen of Galaxidi, Greece, Hon. mem. Int. Asscn of Marine Aids to Navigation and Lighthouse Authorities, Int. Fed. of Shipmasters' Asscns, Propeller Club, Hon. Fellow, Nautical Inst., Inst. of Marine Eng, Science and Tech., Royal Inst. of Naval Architects, Hon. Life mem. Baltic Exchange; Officier, Orde du Mérite Maritime, Mil. Valour Medal and Phoenix Order (Hellenic Repub.), Commendatore, Order of Merit (Italy), St Marcus Cross, Patriarchate of Alexandria and All Africa, Grand Commdr, Order of the Phoenix (Hellenic Repub.), Medal for Valour & Honour (Hellenic Coast Guard), Grand'Ufficiale, Order of Merit (Italy), Medalla Blanca de Primera Clase (Guatemala), Medal of the Order of Naval Merit (Brazil), Order of Sikatuna, Rank of Datu (The Philippines), Grand Cross of Merit with Star and Sash Cross (Germany) 2012; hon. degrees from Nicola Vaptsarov Naval Acad., Bulgaria, Maritime Univ., Constanza, Romania, Schiller Int. Univ., Dalian Maritime Univ., China, Chung-Ang Univ., Seoul, Repub. of Korea, Univ. of Messina, Italy, City Univ., London, Univ. of the Aegean, Greece, Odessa Nat. Maritime Acad., Korea Maritime Univ., Busan, Univ. of Malta; numerous awards, including Coastguard Award (Grand Cross), Argentina, 15 November Medal, Uruguay, Medal of Naval Merit, Brazil, US Coast Guard Distinguished Public Service Award, Colombian

Navy Medal for 'Servicios Distinguidos a la Dirección General Marítima', Danish Shipowners' Asscn Maritime Award, Union of Greek Shipowners Environment Award 2006, Seatrade Personality of the Year 2008, Turkish Shipping Golden Anchor Lifetime Achievement Award 2008, Greek Personality of the Year, Lloyd's List 2008, Niki Award 2010. *Publications include:* Tankers: Evolution and Technical Issues 1969, Studies in Shipping Economics 1970, Safety of Navigation 1971, Categories and Types of Merchant Ships 1973, Collision Avoidance at Sea 1975, Separation of Traffic at Sea 1976, Shipping Economics and Policy 1981. *Leisure interests:* swimming, diving, fishing, football, classical music, naval history. *Address:* c/o Board of Directors, Tsakos Energy Navigation Ltd, 367 Syngrou Avenue, Athens 17564, Greece.

MITTA, Aleksander Naumovich; Russian film director; b. 29 March 1933, Moscow; ed Moscow Inst. of Construction Eng, All-Union Inst. of Cinematography; with Mosfilm studio 1961; Prof., Hamburg Univ. 1995–; Merited Worker of Arts of Russia 1974. *Films include:* The Fearless Ataman 1961, Drug moy Kolka (My Friend Kolka) 1961, Bez strakha i upryoka (No Fear, No Blame) 1962, Bolshoy fitil 1963, Zvonyat, otkroyte dver (Someone is Ringing, Open the Door) (Grand Prix Int. Festival in Venice) 1965, Gori, gori, moya zvezda (Twinkle, Twinkle, My Star) 1969, Tochka, tochka, zapyataya... (Period, Period, Comma...) 1972, Moskva, lyubov moya (Moscow, My Love) 1974, Skaz pro to, kak tsar Pyotr arapa zhenil (How Czar Peter the Great Married Off His Moor) 1976, Klouny i deti 1976, Ekipazh (The Crew) (Prize of All-Union Film Festival) 1980, Skazka stranstviy (The Story of the Voyages) 1982, Safety Margin 1988, Shag (A Step) 1988, Zateryannyy v Sibiri (Lost in Siberia) 1991, Raskalyonnaya subbota 2002, Chagall - Malevich 2013. *Television includes:* Alfred Schnittke and His Friends 1994, Border of the State (series) 1999–2000, Granitsa. Tayozhnyy roman (mini-series) 2000, Red-Hot Weekend 2003, Swan Paradise 2005. *Publication:* Cinema Between Hell and Paradise. *Leisure interest:* watching films on DVD. *Address:* Malaya Gruzinskaya str. 28, Apt 105, 123557 Moscow, Russia (home). *Telephone:* (495) 253-51-57 (Moscow) (home). *Fax:* (495) 253-73-20 (home).

MITTAL, Lakshmi Niwas, BCom; Indian steel industry executive; *Chairman and CEO, ArcelorMittal Steel Company NV;* b. 15 June 1950, Sadulpur, Rajasthan; s. of Mohan Lal Mittal and Geeta Mittal; m. Usha Mittal; one s. one d.; ed St Xavier's Coll., Calcutta; began career in family's steel-making business; Founder, Chair. and CEO LNM Group (later Mittal Steel Co.) 1976; f. Caribbean Ispat 1989; acquired Ispat Mexicana 1992, Ispat Sidbec, Canada 1994, Ispat Hamburger Stahlwerke, Germany 1995, Karmet, Kazakhstan 1995, Irish Ispat 1996, Thyssen's Long Product Div., Germany 1997, Ispat Unimetal Group 1999; Chair. and CEO of all mem. cos of LNM Group Inc., Ispat Int. NV, Ispat Karmet, Ispat Indo, Ispat Coal; Chair. and CEO Mittal Steel Co. NV (after merger with Int. Steel Group) 2004–06; Chair. and CEO ArcelorMittal Steel Co. NV (after merger with Arcelor) 2006–; Dir (non-exec.) ArcelorMittal South Africa; mem. Bd Dirs ICICI Bank Ltd, Goldman Sachs; mem. Exec. Cttee Int. Iron and Steel Inst., Foreign Investment Council in Kazakhstan, Int. Investment Council in South Africa, Investors' Council to Cabinet of Ministers, Ukraine, World Steel Asscn (fmr Chair.), Presidential Int. Advisory Bd, Mozambique, Int. Business Council, World Econ. Forum, Advisory Bd Kellogg School of Man., USA; Hon. Fellow, King's Coll., London 2007; Grand Cross of Civil Merit, Spain; Steelmaker of the Year Award 1996, Eighth Hon. Willy Korf Steel Vision Award 1998, Fortune European Businessman of the Year 2004, Wall Street Journal Entrepreneur of the Year 2004, Sunday Times Business Person of 2006, Financial Times Man of the Year 2006, Die Welt Gewinner 2006, Time magazine Int. Newsmaker of the Year 2006, Dwight D. Eisenhower Global Leadership Award 2007, Padma Vibhushan 2008, Forbes Lifetime Achievement Award 2008, ranked by Forbes magazine amongst The World's Most Powerful People (55th) 2009, (44th) 2010, (47th) 2011–12, (51st) 2013, World Steel Asscn Medal 2010. *Leisure interests:* swimming, yoga, golf. *Address:* ArcelorMittal, Hofplein 20, 3032 Rotterdam, Netherlands (office), ArcelorMittal, 7th Floor, Berkeley Square House, Berkeley Square, London, W1J 6DA, England (office); ArcelorMittal, 19 avenue de la Liberté, 2930 Luxembourg, Luxembourg (office). *Telephone:* (10) 217-88-00 (Rotterdam) (office); (20) 7629-7988 (London) (office); (4792-1 (Luxembourg) (office). *Fax:* (10) 217-88-50 (Rotterdam) (office); (20) 7629-7993 (London) (office); 4792-2675 (Luxembourg) (office). *E-mail:* contact@arcelormittal.com (office). *Website:* www.arcelormittal.com (office).

MITTAL, Som, BEng, MBA; Indian engineer and computer industry executive; *President, National Association of Software and Services Companies;* b. 7 Feb. 1952; ed Indian Inst. of Tech., Kanpur, Indian Inst. of Man., Ahmedabad; has worked for Larsen & Toubro, Escorts; fmr Managing Dir Compaq India Ltd; est. SRF Ltd (jt venture); worked for Wipro Infotech, CEO Business Solutions Div. 1993–94; fmr Pres. and CEO Digital Equipment (India) Ltd, Bangalore; Head of Services Business for Asia-Pacific and Japan region, Hewlett-Packard –2007; Chair. Nat. Asscn of Software and Services Cos (NASSCOM) 2003–04, Pres. 2008–; fmr Chair. Confed. of Indian Industry; mem. Exec. Council and fmr Pres. (South) Mfrs Asscn of Information Tech.; mem. Chief Minister's Task Force (Govt of Karnataka), Governing Council, Indian Inst. of Information Tech.; Founder-mem. Bd of Educ. Standards; Distinguished Alumnus Award, Indian Inst. of Tech., Kanpur 2000. *Address:* NASSCOM, 607, 5th Floor, Oxford Towers, Airport Road, Kodihalli, Bangalore 560 008 (office); International Youth Centre, Teen Murti Marg, Chanakyapuri, New Delhi 110 021, India. *Telephone:* (80) 41151705 (Bangalore) (office); (11) 23010199 (New Delhi) (office). *Fax:* (80) 41151707 (Bangalore) (office); (11) 23015452 (New Delhi) (office). *E-mail:* president@nasscom.in (office); info@nasscom.in (office). *Website:* www.nasscom.in (office).

MITTAL, Sunil Bharti; Indian telecommunications executive; *Chairman and Group CEO, Bharti Enterprises;* s. of Sat Paul Mittal; m.; two s. one d.; ed Punjab Univ., Harvard Univ., USA; Founder Bharti Enterprises 1976–, Dir 1995–, Chair. and Group CEO 2001–; Chair. Indo-US Jt Business Council; mem. Nat. Council of Confed. of Indian Industry (Pres. 2007–08); mem. Fed. of Indian Chambers of Commerce and Industry; fmr Co-Chair. World Econ. Forum 2007; mem. Int. Business Council, World Econ. Forum; mem. Indo-US CEOs Forum, Exec. Bd, Indian School of Business, Acad. of Distinguished Entrepreneurs, Babson Coll., Mass; mem. Leadership Council, Climate Group; mem. Bd of Trustees Carnegie Endowment for Int. Peace; mem. Int. Advisory Cttee, New York Stock Exchange Euronext Bd of Dirs; mem. Int. Business Advisory Council of London; mem.

Advisory Bd, Global Econ. Symposium; mem. Telecom Bd of Int. Telecommunication Union; Hon. Consul of Seychelles, Hon. Fellow, Inst. of Electronics and Telecommunication Engineers of India; Hon. DSc (Govind Ballabh Pant Univ. of Agric. and Tech.), Hon. LLD (Univ. of Leeds); Communication World Telecom Man of the Year 1997, Business India Businessman of the Year 2002, Padma Bhushan 2007, GSM Asscn Chair.'s Award 2008, Global Economy Prize, Kiel Inst. (Germany) 2009, Global Vision Award, US-India Business Council 2008, Lal Bahadur Shastri Nat. Award 2009. *Address:* Bharti Enterprises Ltd, Aravali Crescent 1, Nelson Mandela Road, Vasant Kunj, Phase II, New Delhi 110 070 (office); Bharti Tele-Ventures Ltd, Qutab Ambience (at Qutab Minar), Mehrauli Road, New Delhi 110 030, India (office). *Telephone:* (11) 41666000 (office); (11) 46666100 (office). *Fax:* (11) 41666011 (office); (11) 42666500 (office). *E-mail:* corpcomm@bharti.com (office). *Website:* www.airtel.in (office); www.bharti.com (office).

MITTER, Rajeet, MA; Indian diplomatist and civil servant; b. 1951, Calcutta (now Kolkata); m. Kavita Mitter; one s. one d.; ed Presidency Coll., Kolkata, Jesus Coll., Cambridge, UK; joined Foreign Service 1977, has served in various positions at Ministry of External Affairs and in Missions abroad, including Baghdad, London and Belgrade, fmr Jt Sec. (Gulf & Haj), Ministry of External Affairs; served in Ministry of Labour, Ministry of Finance, and as Jt Sec. (Trade Policy) in Dept of Commerce; Deputy High Commr to Singapore 1995–98, High Commr to Botswana 1998–2002, Amb. to the Philippines 2006–09, High Commr to Bangladesh 2009–11 (retd); fmr Chair. Governing Bd Colombo Plan Staff Coll. for Tech. Educ. *Address:* c/o Ministry of External Affairs, South Blk, New Delhi 110 011, India.

MITTERRAND, Frédéric; French/Tunisian writer, film and television producer and fmr government official; b. 21 Aug. 1947, Paris; s. of Robert Mitterrand and Edith Cahier; nephew of the late François Mitterrand; ed Univ. of Nanterre, Inst. d'études politiques, Paris; Dir Cinéma d'Art et Essai, Olympic Palace, Entrepôt and Olympic-Entrepôt 1971–86; Dir Comm. d'avances sur recettes du cinéma français (cinema funding comm.) 2000–03; Dir Gen. for Programming, Channel TV5 2003; Dir Acad. de France à Rome, Villa Médici 2008–09; Minister of Culture and Communication 2009–12; Chevalier, Légion d'honneur; Officier, Ordre nat. du Mérite; Commdr, Ordre des Arts et des Lettres; Officer, Order of Cultural Merit (Monaco) 2007. *Films:* as actor: Lettres d'amour en Somalie 1981, Madame Butterfly 1995, Mon copain Rachid 1997, Le Fabuleux Destin d'Amélie Poulain 2001, Folle de Rachid en transit sur Mars 2001, Bécassine - Le trésor viking 2001, The Car Keys (voice) 2003. *Television:* producer: Ne (assoc. producer) 1975, Les écrans déchirés (short) 1976, Étoiles et toiles 1981–86, Acteur Studio 1986–87, Ciné-Fêtes 1984, Permission de minuit 1987–88, Etoiles 1987–92, Destins 1987–88, Étoile Palace 1990, Du Côté de chez Fred 1988–91, C'est votre vie 1993, Les Amants du siècle 1993, Caravane de nuit 1994, Fairouz 1998, Je suis la Folle de Brejnev 2001; actor: Ça s'est passé comme ça (series, host) 2005. *Publications include:* Tous désirs confondus 1988 (new edn) 2009, Mémoires d'exill 1990, Destins d'étoiles, Vols 1, 2, 3, 4 1991–92, Monte Carlo: la légende 1993, Une saison tunisienne (under the direction of Frédéric Mitterrand and Soraya Elyes-Ferchichi) 1995, L'Ange bleu: un film de Joseph von Sternberg 1995, Madame Butterfly 1995, Les Aigles foudroyés – la fin des Romanov des Habsbourg et des Hohenzollern 1998, Un jour dans le siècle 2000, La Mauvaise Vie 2005, Lettres d'amour en Somalie 2006, Maroc, 1900–1960 Un certain regard (with Abdellah Taïa) 2007, Le Festival de Cannes 2007, Le désir et la chance 2012, La récréation 2013. *Address:* 104 rue de l'Université, 75007 Paris, France.

MITYUKOV, Mikhail Alekseyevich, CandJurSc; Russian politician, lawyer and academic; b. 7 Jan. 1942, Ust-Uda, Irkutsk Region; m. Ludmila Aleksandrovna Mityukova; two s. one d.; ed Irkutsk State Univ.; worked in Khakassia Autonomous Region (now Repub.), Deputy Chair. regional court 1968–87; Sr Teacher, Head of Chair of History and Law Abakan State Pedagogical Inst. 1987–90; Russian Fed. People's Deputy and mem. Supreme Soviet, Deputy Chair. then Chair. Cttee on Law 1990–93; First Deputy Minister of Justice 1993–94; mem. State Duma (Parl.) 1993–95, First Deputy Chair. 1994–95; participated in drafting new Russian Constitution; First Deputy Sec., Security Council of Russia 1996–98; Plenipotentiary Rep. of Russian Pres. in Constitutional Court 1998–2005; Prof., State Univ. (TSU) 1995–, State Univ. (MSLA) 2000–; Chair. Presidential Comm. for Rehabilitation of the Victims of Political Repression 2008–; Merited Jurist of the Russian Fed. award, several medals. *Publications:* more than 200 scientific works and monographs including Constitutional Courts on Post-Soviet Territory 1999, A History of Constitutional Justice in Russia 2002. *Address:* Ilinka str. 8/4, 103132 Moscow, Russia (office). *Telephone:* (495) 606-24-94 (office). *Fax:* (495) 606-34-53 (office). *E-mail:* rehabilitation@gov.ru (office).

MITZNA, Amram, MA; Israeli politician and army general (retd); b. 20 Feb. 1945, Kibbutz Dovrat; m.; three c.; ed Haifa Univ., Harvard Univ.; joined Israeli Armed Forces 1963; served as Brig. in Six-Day War 1967, Yom Kippur War 1973; resgnd in protest at Israeli treatment of Palestinians in Sabra and Shatila, Lebanon 1982; re-apptd Defence Force Commdr in West Bank during Palestinian uprising 1987–93, later Gen. of the Cen. Region Command, retd from army 1993, rank of Maj. Gen.; Mayor of Haifa 1993–2003; Chair. Israel Labour Party 2002–03; advocates removal of West Bank and Gaza settlements and direct negotiations with Palestinian leadership. *Address:* Knesset Residence, Kiryat Ben-Guryon, Jerusalem 91950, Israel (office). *Telephone:* (2) 6753810 (office). *Fax:* (2) 6753715 (office).

MIURA, Satoshi; Japanese telecommunications executive; *Chairman, Nippon Telegraph and Telephone Corporation (NTT);* b. 3 April 1944; joined Nippon Telegraph and Telephone Corpn 1967, held several exec. positions including Sr Vice-Pres. and Exec. Man., Personnel Dept 1996–97, Sr Vice-Pres. and Exec. Man. Personnel and Industrial Relations Dept 1997–98, Exec. Vice-Pres. and Exec. Man. Personnel and Industrial Relations 1998–99, Exec. Vice-Pres. and Deputy Sr Exec. Man. NTT East Provisional HQ 1999–2002, Sr Exec. Vice-Pres. NTT East 1999–2002, Pres. 2002–07, Sr Exec. Vice-Pres. NTT 2005–07, Pres. and CEO 2007–12, Chair. 2012–. *Address:* Nippon Telegraph and Telephone Corporation, 3-1, Otemachi 2-chome, Chiyoda-ku, Tokyo 100-8116 Japan (office). *Telephone:* (3) 5205-5581 (office). *Fax:* (3) 5205-5589 (office). *E-mail:* info@ntt.co.jp (office). *Website:* www.ntt.co.jp (office).

MIURA, Zenji; Japanese business executive; *Representative Director, President and CEO, Ricoh Company Limited;* joined Ricoh Co. Ltd 1976, Pres. Ricoh France SA Jan.–Aug. 1993, Chair. Aug. 1993, Deputy Gen. Man. Finance and Accounting Div., Ricoh Co. Ltd 1998–2000, Gen. Man. 2000–03, Exec. Vice-Pres. 2003–05, mem. Bd of Mans, Ricoh Production Print Solutions, LLC, Man. Dir Investor Relations and Man. Control, Internal Control, Finance and Accounting 2004–06, Corp. Exec. Vice-Pres., Ricoh Co. Ltd 2005–06, Rep. Dir, Ricoh Co. Ltd 2005–, Chief Financial Officer 2005–06, Gen. Man. Corp. Planning Div. and Chief Information Officer 2006–09, Chief Strategy Officer 2009–11, Gen. Man. Global Marketing Support Div. and Gen. Man. Trade Affairs and Export/Import Admin Div. 2009–11, Deputy Pres. 2011–13, Rep. Dir, Pres. and CEO Ricoh Co. Ltd 2013–; Audit and Supervisory Bd mem. Coca-Cola West Co. Ltd; Dir, Nippon Venture Capital Co. Ltd. *Address:* Ricoh Company Ltd, 8-13-1 Ginza, Chuo-ku, Tokyo 104-8222, Japan (office). *Telephone:* (3) 6278-2111 (office). *Fax:* (3) 3543-9329 (office). *E-mail:* www-admin@ricoh.co.jp (office). *Website:* www.ricoh.com (office).

MIYAHARA, Hideo, ME, DE; Japanese computer scientist, academic and fmr university administrator; *Professor, Department of Infomatics and Mathematical Science, Graduate School of Information Science and Technology, Osaka University;* ed Osaka Univ.; Asst Prof., Dept of Applied Math. and Physics, Faculty of Eng, Kyoto Univ. 1973–80; Assoc. Prof., Dept of Information and Computer Sciences, Faculty of Eng Science, Osaka Univ. 1980–86, Prof., Computation Centre 1986–89, Prof., Dept of Infomatics and Math. Science, Grad. School of Information Science and Tech. 1989–, Dir Computation Centre 1995–98, Dean Faculty of Eng Science 1998–2000, Dean Grad. School of Information Science and Tech. 2000–03, Pres. Osaka Univ. 2003–07; Visiting Scientist, IBM Thomas J. Watson Research Center, USA 1983–84; Pres. Nat. Inst. of Information and Communications Tech., Japan; Chair. Japan Cttee of Univs for Int. Exchange (JACUIE); Fellow, Information Processing Soc. of Japan, IEEE. *Publications:* numerous scientific papers in professional journals on performance evaluation of computer communication networks, broadband ISDN and multimedia systems. *Address:* Graduate School of Information Science and Technology, Osaka University, 1-1 Yamadaoka, Suita, Osaka 565-0871, Japan (office). *Telephone:* (6) 6850-6585 (office). *Fax:* (6) 6850-6589 (office). *E-mail:* miyahara@ist.osaka-u.ac.jp (office). *Website:* www.osaka-u.ac.jp (office).

MIYAHARA, Kenji, BA; Japanese business executive; *Senior Adviser, Sumitomo Corporation;* ed Kyoto Univ.; joined Sumitomo Shoji Kaisha 1958, Pres. and CEO Sumitomo Corpn of America 1990–96, Pres. and CEO Sumitomo Corpn 1996–2001, Chair. 2001–07, Sr Adviser 2007–; mem. Bd of Dirs NEC Corpn 2007–; Chair. Japan Foreign Trade Council Inc. 2000–04, Japan-Viet Nam Econ. Cttee 2003–, Japan Fed. of Trading Cos (JFTC) 2004–; Vice-Chair. Japan Fed. of Econ. Orgs (KEIDANREN) 2004; Counsellor, Bank of Japan 2004–; mem. Panel of Conciliators and Arbitrators, Int. Centre for the Settlement of Investment Disputes (ICSID); mem. US-Japan Pvt. Sector/Govt Comm. 2002–03; Hon. Chair. Japan Foreign Trade Council Inc. 2004–. *Address:* Sumitomo Corporation, 1-8-11 Harumi, Chuo-ku, Tokyo 104-8610, Japan (office). *Telephone:* (3) 5166-5000 (office). *Fax:* (3) 5166-6292 (office). *Website:* www.sumitomocorp.co.jp (office).

MIYAHARA, Koji; Japanese shipping industry executive; *Chairman and Chairman Corporate Officer, Nippon Yusen Kaisha (NYK) Line;* Sr Man. Dir Nippon Yusen Kaisha (NYK Line) –2004, Pres. 2004–09, Chair. 2009–, Chief Exec. CSR Man. HQ, Chair. Bulk/Energy Resources Transportation Strategy Cttee, Dir-Gen. NYK Cool Earth Project, Chair. Corp. Officer 2011–; Commdr, Ordre de la Couronne (Belgium) 2010. *Address:* Nippon Yusen Kabushiki Kaisha, 3-2, Marunouchi 2-chome, Chiyoda-ku, Tokyo 100-0005, Japan (office). *Telephone:* (3) 3284-5151 (office). *Fax:* (3) 3284-6359 (office). *E-mail:* info@nyk.com (office). *Website:* www.nyk.com (office).

MIYAKE, Issey; Japanese fashion designer; b. (Kazunaru Miyake), 22 April 1939, Hiroshima; ed Tama Art Univ. Tokyo and La Chambre Syndicale de la Couture Parisienne, Paris; Asst Designer to Guy Laroche, Paris 1966–68, to Hubert de Givenchy, Paris 1968–69; Designer, Geoffrey Beene (ready-to-wear firm), New York 1969–70; est. Miyake Design Studio, Tokyo 1970; Dir Issey Miyake Int., Issey Miyake & Assocs, Issey Miyake Europe, Issey Miyake USA and Issey Miyake On Limits (Tokyo); Exec. Adviser and Planner, First Japan Culture Conf., Yokohama 1980; developed Pleats Please universal form of contemporary clothing combining technology, functionality and beauty 1993, exhibited at Pompidou Centre, Paris; embarked upon A-POC (A Piece of Cloth) project with Dai Fujiwara and team of young designers 1998; est. Miyake Issey Foundation 2004; work has been exhibited in Paris, Tokyo and at MIT and appears in collections of Metropolitan Museum of Art, New York and Victoria & Albert Museum, London; Dr hc (RCA) 1993; Japan Fashion Editors' Club Awards, 1974, 1976, Mainichi Design Prize 1977, Pratt Inst. New York Award for Creative Design 1980, International Award, Council of America Fashion Designers 1984, Neiman-Marcus Award 1984, Award of Les Oscars 1985 de la Mode, Paris for Best Collection Presented by a Foreign Designer 1985, Award of the Japanese magazine for the textile industry Senken Shimbun 1986, Mainichi Newspaper Fashion Awards 1977, 1984, 1996, Kyoto Prize for Arts and Philosophy 2007. *Address:* Tokyo Headquarters, Miyake Design Studio, 1-23, Ohyama-cho, Shibuya-ku, Tokyo 151, Japan (office). *Telephone:* (3) 3481-6411 (office).

MIYAKE, Senji, BS; Japanese brewery executive; *Representative Director, President and CEO, Kirin Holdings Company Ltd;* b. 26 Jan. 1948; ed Keio Univ.; joined Kirin Brewery Co. Ltd 1970, Sales Man., Osaka Br. 1988–93, Pres. Kirin Brewery Co. Ltd (separated from Kirin Holdings Co. Ltd) 2007–09, Exec. Vice-Pres. Kirin Holdings Co. Ltd 2009–10, Rep. Dir, Pres. and CEO 2010–; Exec. Vice-Pres. Heineken Japan 1993–97, Sales Devt Man., Marketing Div. 1997–98, Sales Man., Sales and Marketing Div. 1998–2000, Nat. Chain Sales Man. Shutoken Regional Head Office 2000–01, Gen. Man. Tokai Regional Head Office 2001–02, Dir and Gen. Man. Tokai Regional Head Office 2002–03, Exec. Officer and Gen. Man. Tokai Regional Head Office 2003–04, Man. Exec. Officer and Gen. Man. Shutoken Regional Head Office 2004–06, Man. Exec. Officer and Pres. Beer, Wine and Spirits Div. 2006–07. *Address:* Kirin Holdings Co. Ltd, 10-1 Shinkawa 2-chome, Chuo-ku, Tokyo 104-8288, Japan (office). *Telephone:* (3) 5541-5321 (office). *Fax:* (3) 5540-3547 (office). *E-mail:* info@kirin.co.jp (office). *Website:* www.kirinholdings.co.jp (office).

MIYAKO, Harumi; Japanese singer; b. 22 Feb. 1948, Kyoto City; d. of the late Shoji Matsuda (Yi Jong Tack) and of Matsuyo Kitamura; m. Hiroomi Asatsuki 1978 (divorced 1982); Pnr Ikko Nakamura; ed pvt. music schools; began traditional Japanese dancing lessons aged 6, ballet lessons aged 9, joined a theatrical co. aged 11; winner Colombia Nationwide Popular Song Contest aged 15 1963; recording debut with release of Komaru kotoyo (You Upset Me) 1964; began career singing traditional enka (ethnic) music; appeared on every annual New Year's Eve Contest Kohaku uta gassen, NHK 1965–85; retd as singer 1984; worked as music producer and news commentator; special performance on music programme Kohaku uta gassen, NHK 1989; re-launched music career singing modern pop music 1990; annual concerts in Budo-Kan; regular appearances on TV music programmes; has released more than 115 records; Rookie of the Year Award 1964, Nihon Kayo Taisho (Japan Annual Pop Grand Prize) 1976, Nihon Record Taisho (Japan Record Annual Grand Prize) 1976. *Singles include:* Komaru kotoyo 1964, Anko tsubaki wa koi no hana (New Artist Award, Japanese Recording Industry) 1964, Namida no renraku fune 1965, Bakattcho debune 1965, Sukini natta hito 1968, Kita no shuka kara (Record of the Year, Japan Popular Music Award) 1976, I Want to Become an Everyday Woman 1984, Sennen No Koto 1990, Sakure Shigure 1993, Nana no ran 1994, Ajia Densetsu 1996, Jashu mon 1998, Ohara zessho 2000. *Address:* c/o Nippon Columbia Co. Ltd, 4-14-14 Akasaka, Minato-ku, Tokyo 107-8011, Japan (office). *Website:* miyakoharumi.net (office).

MIYAMOTO, Mikihiko; Japanese insurance executive; Pres. Yasuda Mutual Life Insurance Co. Ltd –2004; Chair. Meiji Yasuda Life Insurance Co. (cr. through merger of Yasuda Mutual and Meiji Life Insurance Cos 2004) Jan. 2004–06 (resgnd). *Address:* c/o Meiji Yasuda Life Insurance Company, 19-1 Nishi-Shinjuku, Shinjuku-ku, Tokyo 169-8701, Japan (office).

MIYAMOTO, Yoichi; Japanese business executive; *Representative Director and President, Shimizu Corporation;* joined Shimizu Corpn (contractor in eng and construction projects) 1971, positions held include Man. of Hokuriku Office, Exec. Officer, Man. of Kyushu Office, Man. Exec. Officer and Sr Man. Exec. Officer, Pres. and Rep. Dir 2007–; mem. Overseas Construction Asscn of Japan, Inc. *Address:* Shimizu Corpn, Seavans South, 1-2-3 Shibaura, Minato-ku, Tokyo 105-8007, Japan (office). *Telephone:* (3) 5441-1111 (office). *Fax:* (3) 5441-0526 (office). *E-mail:* info@shimz.co.jp (office). *Website:* www.shimz.co.jp (office).

MIYANAGA, Shunichi; Japanese business executive; *President and CEO, Mitsubishi Heavy Industries;* b. 27 April 1948; joined Mitsubishi Heavy Industries Ltd 1972, Sr Vice-Pres. and Deputy Head of Machinery HQ April–May 2006, Sr Vice-Pres. and Deputy Head of Machinery and Steel Structures HQ May 2006–08, Exec. Vice-Pres. and Head of Machinery and Steel Structures HQ April–June 2008, mem. Bd of Dirs 2008–, Exec. Vice-Pres. and Head of Machinery and Steel Structures HQ 2008–11, Sr Exec. Vice-Pres. and Head of Presidential Admin Office 2011–13, Pres. and CEO Mitsubishi Heavy Industries 2013–. *Address:* Mitsubishi Heavy Industries, 16-5, Konan 2-chome, Minato-ku, Tokyo 108-8215, Japan (office). *Telephone:* (3) 6716-3111 (office). *Fax:* (3) 6716-5800 (office). *E-mail:* info@mhi.co.jp (office). *Website:* www.mhi.co.jp (office).

MIYASHITA, Sohei; Japanese politician; mem. LDP; fmr civil servant in Finance Ministry; mem. for Nagano House of Reps 1979–2004; Dir-Gen. Defence Agency 1991–92, Environment Agency 1994–95; Minister of Health and Welfare 1998–99; Chair. Social Security Reform Study Group 2001–. *Address:* c/o Liberal Democratic Party, 1-11-23 Nagata-cho, Chiyoda-ku, Tokyo 100-8910, Japan (office).

MIYATA, Koichi; Japanese business executive; *President and Representative Director, Sumitomo Mitsui Financial Group, Inc.;* joined The Mitsui Bank Ltd 1976, mem. Bd of Dirs Sumitomo Mitsui Banking Corpn (subsidiary of Sumitomo Mitsui Financial Group, Inc.) 2003, 2009, 2011–, Man. Dir Sumitomo Mitsui Banking Corpn 2006–09, Sr Man. Dir 2009–10, mem. Bd of Dirs Sumitomo Mitsui Financial Group, Inc. 2010–, Gen. Man. Planning Dept and Treasury Unit, later Deputy Head of Treasury Unit and Sr Man. Dir 2010–11, Pres. and Rep. Dir Sumitomo Mitsui Financial Group, Inc. 2011–; Auditor, Japan Securities Depository Centre. *Address:* Sumitomo Mitsui Financial Group, Inc., 1-1-2, Marunouchi, Chiyoda-ku, Tokyo 100-0005, Japan (office). *Telephone:* (3) 3282-8111 (office). *Fax:* (3) 5512-4429 (office). *E-mail:* info@smfg.co.gp (office). *Website:* www.smfg.co.jp (office).

MIYATO, Naoteru, BA; Japanese insurance industry executive; *Chairman and Representative Director, T&D Holdings, Inc.;* b. 20 May 1943; ed Keio Univ.; joined Daido Life 1967, positions included Pres. Daido Int., New York and Gen. Man. Research Dept, Gen. Man. Gen. Marketing Dept 1994–99, mem. Bd of Dirs Daido Life 1994–, Man. Dir 1996–99, Sr Man. Dir March–July 1999, Pres. and Rep. Dir 1999–2004, Pres. and Rep. Dir T&D Holdings, Inc. (holding co.) 2004–11, Chair. and Rep. Dir 2011–, mem. Bd of Dirs Taiyo Life 2008–. *Address:* T&D Holdings Inc., 2-7-9 Nihonbashi, Chuo-Ku, Tokyo 103-0027, Japan (office). *Telephone:* (3) 3231-8685 (office). *Fax:* (3) 3231-8893 (office). *E-mail:* info@td-holdings.co.jp (office). *Website:* www.td-holdings.co.jp (office).

MIYAZAKI, Hayao; Japanese film producer, film director and animator; b. 5 Jan. 1941, Tokyo; ed Gakushuin Univ.; started career as animator Toei Douga Studios 1963; joined A Pro 1971, moved to Nippon Animation 1973; directed first TV series Mirai Shonen Conan 1978; moved to Tokyo Movie Shinsha 1979, directed first film Rupan Sansei: Kariosutoro no shiro 1979; f. Ghibli Studios with Isao Takahata 1981–; Mononoke Hime and Sen to Chihiro no Kamikakushi both set Japanese box office records; Venice Film Festival lifetime achievement award 2005. *Films:* as writer/dir: Rupan Sansei: Kariosutoro no Shiro (Lupin III: The Castle of Cagliostro) 1979, Kaze no tani no Nausicaa (Nausicaa of the Valley of the Wind) 1984, Tenku no Shiro no Laputa (Floating Island of Laputa) 1986, Tonari no Totoro (My Neighbour's Totoro) 1988, Majo no Takkyubin (Kiki's Delivery Service) 1989, Kurenai no Buta (The Red Pig) 1992, On Your Mark 1995, Mononoke Hime (Princess Mononoke) 1997, Tonari no Yamada-kun (My Neighbour Yamada) 1999, Sen to Chihiro no Kamikakushi (Spirited Away) (Japanese Acad. Award for Best Film 2002, Hong Kong Film Award for Best Asian Film 2002, Berlin Int. Film Festival Golden Bear Award 2002, Best Animation Acad. Award 2003) 2001, Kujira Tori 2001, Hauru no ugoku Shiro (Howl's Moving Castle) (Venice Film Festival Golden Osella, Nebula Award 2007) 2004, Yadosagashi 2006, Mizugumo monmon 2006, Hoshi wo katta hi 2006; as producer: Yanagawa horiwari monogatarai (The Story of Yanagawa's Canals) 1987, Omohide poro poro

(Memories of Yesterday) 1991, Heisei tanuki gassen pompoko (The Raccoon War) 1994, Mimi wo Sumaseba (Whisper of the Heart) 1995, Neko no ongaeshi (The Cat Returns) 2002. *Website:* www.studioghiblidvd.co.uk.

MIYOSHI, Toru, LLB; Japanese judge (retd); b. 31 Oct. 1927; ed Univ. of Tokyo; Asst Judge, Tokyo Dist Court and Tokyo Family Court 1955; Judge, Hakodate Dist Court and Hakodate Family Court 1965; Judge, Tokyo Dist Court (Presiding Judge of Div.) 1975; Pres. Research and Training Inst. for Court Clerks 1982; Pres. Oita Dist Court and Oita Family Court 1985; Pres. Nagano Dist Court and Nagano Family Court 1986; Chief Judicial Research Official of Supreme Court 1987; Pres. Sapporo High Court 1991, Tokyo High Court 1992; Justice of Supreme Court 1992; Chief Justice of Supreme Court 1995–97; mem. Advisory Council to Consider the Direct Election of the Prime Minister 2001; Head of Japan Conference (conservative pressure group) c. 2007.

MIZOTE, Kensei; Japanese politician; b. 13 Sept. 1942; ed Faculty of Law, Univ. of Tokyo; with Fuji Steel Co. (now Nippon Steel Corpn) 1966–71; Vice-Pres. Koyo Dockyard Co. Ltd 1971–79, Pres. 1979–87; Mayor of Mihara City, Hiroshima Pref. 1987–93; mem. House of Councillors for Hiroshima Pref. 1993–, Chair. Cttee on Gen. Affairs 2001, Cttee on Rules and Admin 2004, mem. Cttee on Budget and Finance 2001; Parl. Vice-Minister of Int. Trade and Industry 1997; Chair. Finance Sub-cttee, New Constitution Drafting Cttee, LDP 2005, Coastal Shipping Activation Sub-cttee, Special Cttee on Marine Transportation and Shipbuilding 2006; Minister of State, Chair. Nat. Public Safety Comm. and Minister of State for Disaster Man. 2006–07. *Address:* c/o National Public Safety Commission, 2-1-2, Kasumigaseki, Chiyoda-ku, Tokyo 100-8974, Japanese (office).

MIZRAHI, Isaac; American fashion designer, set and costume designer, television presenter and stage director; b. 14 Oct. 1961, Brooklyn, NY; s. of Zeke Mizrahi and Sarah Mizrahi; m. Arnold Germer 2011; ed Yeshiva of Flatbush, High School of Performing Arts, Manhattan, Parsons School of Design; apprenticed to Perry Ellis 1982, full-time post 1982–84; worked with Jeffrey Banks 1984–85, Calvin Klein 1985–87, Mark Morris, Twyla Tharp, Bill T. Jones and Mikhail Baryshnikov; started own design firm in partnership with Sarah Hadad Cheney 1987, first formal show 1988, first spring collection Nov. 1988, first menswear line launched April 1990, announced closure of firm Oct. 1998; partnered with Target Stores to launch a collection of women's sportswear and accessories 2002, cr. home collection for Target 2005; appeared off-Broadway in one-man show Les Mizrahi 1999; hosted The Isaac Mizrahi Show on Oxygen Network 1999; wrote and directed Supermodelhero, which first appeared online in 2005; designed for Claiborne 2009; launched label IsaacMizrahiLIVE! exclusively on QVC shopping channel 2010, sold to Xcel Brands, Inc. 2011, remains a shareholder, Creative Dir and media personality for his namesake brand under Xcel; costume designer for three Broadway revivals, including two plays, The Women (Drama Desk Award for Outstanding Costume Design 2002) 2001, Barefoot in the Park 2006, and one operetta, Threepenny Opera 2006, for Metropolitan Opera's production of Orfeo ed Euridice 2008; designed pro bono the Smithsonian American Art Museum and Nat. Portrait Gallery's conservators' denim work aprons 2006; designed sets and costumes and directed Stephen Sondheim's A Little Night Music for Opera Theatre of St Louis 2010; designed and directed Mozart's The Magic Flute for Opera Theatre of St Louis 2014; has appearances in numerous TV shows and films since the 1990s; narrated Peter and the Wolf at Guggenheim Museum's Works & Process performing arts series 2007, 2010; began co-hosting first season of The Fashion Show on Bravo TV with singer Kelly Rowland 2009, returned as co-host opposite supermodel Iman 2010; Womenswear Designer of the Year 1989, 1991, Drama Desk Award for Outstanding Costume Design 2002. *Film appearances:* Celebrity 1998, Small Time Crooks 2000, Hollywood Ending 2002. *Radio:* appeared on public radio game show Wait, Wait, Don't Tell Me 2006. *Television includes:* appearances on Sex and the City, Spin City, Ugly Betty, The Apprentice, Jeopardy! Million Dollar Celebrity Invitational, The Red Carpet Show for the Golden Globes (interviewer) 2006, Project Runway: All Stars (head judge) 2012, Live! With Kelly (red carpet corresp. during 84th Annual Academy Awards) 2012, The Big C 2013; co-wrote historical documentary Kingdom of David: The Saga of the Israelites for PBS. *Publications:* series of comic books called Isaac Mizrahi Presents the Adventures of Sandee the Supermodel. *Address:* c/o Xcel Brands, Inc., 475 10th Avenue #4, New York, NY 10018, USA. *Telephone:* (347) 727-2474. *E-mail:* info@xcelbrands.com. *Website:* www.xcelbrands.com/isaac_mizrahi.html; www.isaacmizrahiny.com.

MIZRAHI, Valerie, PhD; Zimbabwean biologist and academic; *Director, Institute of Infectious Disease and Molecular Medicine, University of Cape Town;* ed Univ. of Cape Town, South Africa; postdoctoral work at Pennsylvania State Univ., USA 1983–86; held positions with South African Council for Scientific and Industrial Research, Smith Kline & French Research & Devt; fmr Head of Molecular Biology Unit, South African Inst. for Medical Research –2000; Prin. Investigator and Dir Molecular Mycobacteriology Research Unit, South African Medical Research Council, Univ. of the Witwatersrand (fmrly South African Inst. for Medical Research) 2000–10; Prof. and Dir Inst. of Infectious Disease and Molecular Medicine, Univ. of Cape Town 2011–, also Dir Molecular Mycobacteriology Research Unit; Int. Research Scholar, Howard Hughes Medical Inst., Chevy Chase, Md 2000, 2005; Fellow, Royal Soc. of South Africa, American Acad. of Microbiology 2009; Assoc. Fellow, Acad. of Sciences of the Developing World; mem. Acad. of Science of South Africa; Order of the Mapungubwe in Silver 2007; L'Oréal-UNESCO For Women in Science Award 2000, DST Distinguished Woman Scientist Award 2006, Gold Medal of the South African Soc. for Biochemistry and Molecular Biology 2006. *Publications:* numerous articles in medical journals. *Address:* Institute of Infectious Disease and Molecular Medicine, Faculty of Health Sciences, University of Cape Town, Anzio Road, Observatory 7925, Cape Town 2050, South Africa (office). *Telephone:* (21) 4066098 (office). *Fax:* (21) 4066068 (office). *E-mail:* valerie.mizrahi@uct.ac.za (office). *Website:* www.iidmm.uct.ac.za (office).

MIZUKOSHI, Koshi; Japanese metal industry executive; *Advisor, Kobe Steel Ltd (KOBELCO);* b. 1 Sept. 1938, Seoul, S Korea; m.; two s.; ed Univ. of Tokyo; joined Planning and Business Admin Dept, Kobe Steel Ltd (KOBELCO) 1961, Inspection Section, Devt Dept 1965–73, Man. Corp. Planning Dept 1973–78, Asst to Pres. 1978–81, Gen. Man. Planning and Admin Dept, Iron and Steel Div.'s Production Group 1983–91, Man. Dir 1991–93, Sr Man. Dir 1993–96, mem. Bd of Dirs 1989–,

Rep. Dir 1996–, Exec. Vice-Pres. 1996–99, CEO and Pres. 1999–2004, Chair. 2004–09 (resgnd), Advisor 2009–; Vice-Chair. Kansai Econ. Fed.; mem. Bd of Dirs Foundation for Biomedical Research and Innovation, Kansai Int. Public Relations Promotion Office. *Address:* Kobe Steel Ltd, Shinko Building, 10-26 Wakinoha-macho 2-chome, Kobe 651-8585, Japan (office). *Telephone:* (78) 261-5111 (office). *Fax:* (78) 261-4123 (office). *E-mail:* info@kobelco.co.jp (office). *Website:* www.kobelco.co.jp (office).

MIZUNO, Akihisa, MCivilEng; Japanese business executive; *President, Chubu Electric Power Company, Inc.;* ed Univ. of Tokyo; joined Chubu Electric Power Co., Inc. 1978, Dir and Sr Man. Exec. Officer, Gen. Man. Corp. Planning and Strategy Div. 2008–09, Dir and Exec. Vice-Pres., Gen. Man. Corp. Planning and Strategy Div. and Affiliated Business Planning and Devt Dept 2009–10, Pres. and Dir Chubu Electric Power Co., Inc. 2010–. *Address:* Chubu Electric Power Co., Inc., 1 Higashi-shincho, Higashi-ku, Nagoya 461-8680, Japan (office). *Telephone:* (52) 951-8211 (office). *Fax:* (52) 962-4624 (office). *E-mail:* info@chuden.co.jp (office). *Website:* www.chuden.co.jp (office).

MKAPA, Benjamin William, BA; Tanzanian politician, journalist and diplomatist; b. 12 Nov. 1938, Masasi; s. of William Matwani and Stephania Nambanga; m. Anna Joseph Maro 1966; two s.; ed Makerere Univ. Coll.; Admin. Officer, Dist Officer 1962; Foreign Service Officer 1962; Man. Ed. Tanzania Nationalist and Uhuru 1966, The Daily News and The Sunday News 1972; Press Sec. to Pres. 1974; Founding Dir Tanzania News Agency 1976; High Commr in Nigeria 1976; Minister for Foreign Affairs 1977–80, for Information and Culture 1980–82; High Commr to Canada 1982–83; Amb. to USA 1983–84; Minister for Foreign Affairs 1984–90; MP for Nanyumbu 1985–95; Minister for Information and Broadcasting 1990–92, for Science, Tech. and Higher Educ. 1992–95; Pres. of Tanzania and C-in-C of Armed Forces 1995–2005; Chair. Chama Cha Mapinduzi (CCM) party 1996–2005; Chair. Southern African Devt Community 2003–04; Trustee, Aga Khan Univ., Karachi, Pakistan 2007–; Dr hc (Soka Univ., Tokyo) 1998; Hon. DHumLitt (Morehouse Coll., Atlanta, USA) 1999. *Leisure interest:* reading. *Address:* c/o Chama Cha Mapinduzi (Revolutionary Party of Tanzania), Kuu St, POB 50, Dodoma, Tanzania.

MKHATSHWA, Father Smangaliso, ThM, PhD; South African ecclesiastic and local government official; b. 26 June 1939, Barberton, Mpumalanga; s. of Elias Mkhatshwa and Maria Mkhatshwa (née Nkosi); ed Pax Coll., Pietersburg, St Peter's Seminary, KwaZulu Natal, Univ. of Leuven, Belgium; ordained RC priest 1965, worked as a pastor in Witbank until 1970, seconded to Church's Gen. Secr., Pretoria; detained for four months under Internal Security Act following Soweto uprising 1976, restricted by five-year banning order to Pretoria magisterial dist 1977–83, apptd Parish Priest of St Charles Lwanga, Soshanguve; Sec.-Gen. Southern African Catholic Bishops' Conf. 1981–88; Patron United Democratic Front 1983; detained in Ciskei Oct. 1983 and charged with subversion, incitement to public violence and addressing an unlawful meeting, found not guilty and released March 1984; detained under emergency regulations 1986, released and successfully sued the state for torture and assault; Sec.-Gen. Inst. for Contextual Theology 1988–94; mem. Parl. (African Nat. Congress—ANC) 1994–99, mem. Reconstruction and Devt Standing Cttee and Educ. Standing Cttee; Deputy Minister of Educ. 1996–99; mem. ANC Nat. Exec. Cttee 1997–99; Trustee, Kagiso Trust, Matla Trust; Pres. Cen. Transvaal Civics Asscn (later renamed SANCO Pretoria); Exec. Mayor of City of Tshwane 2000–06; Dr hc (Tübingen, Germany), (Georgetown Univ., USA), (Univ. Coll. of New Rochelle, USA); Steve Biko Human Rights Award, Indicator Newspaper Award. *Publications:* articles on theology and politics. *Leisure interests:* tennis, music, reading, theatre. *Address:* c/o Father Smangaliso Mkhatshwa Child and Youth Care Centre, Private Bag X73, Soshanguve 0164, South Africa. *Telephone:* (12) 7978300. *E-mail:* yaya@gauteng.gov.za.

MKRTUMYAN, Yuri Israelovich, CandHisSc; Armenian ethnographer; b. 1 Jan. 1939, Tbilisi; ed Moscow State Univ.; lab. asst, jr researcher Inst. of Archaeology and Ethnography, Armenian Acad. of Sciences 1962–71, Prof. 1996–; Sr Lecturer Yerevan State Univ. 1971–89; Head Chair of Ethnography, Yerevan State Univ. 1989–94; Sec. CP Cttee Yerevan State Univ.; mem. Cen. CPSU Cttee, mem. Bureau Cen. Cttee Armenian CP 1990–91; counsellor to Minister of Foreign Affairs, Repub. of Armenia April–June 1994; Amb. to Russia 1994–96; Dir Inst. of Ethnography and Archaeology 1997–. *Publications:* over 40 scientific works on theoretical and regional ethnography in Russian, Armenian and English. *Address:* Institute of Ethnography and Archaeology, Armenian Academy of Sciences, Charentsa Street 15, 375025 Yerevan, Armenia. *Telephone:* (10) 55-68-96 (office).

MKULO, Mustapha; Tanzanian politician; fmr Dir-Gen. Nat. Social Security Fund; Deputy Minister of Finance –2008, Minister of Finance, Planning, Economy and Empowerment 2008–12. *Address:* c/o Ministry of Finance and Economic Affairs, PO Box 9111, Dar es Salaam, Tanzania.

MKWEZALAMBA, Maxwell, MEcon, PhD; Malawi economist and politician; *Minister of Finance;* b. 2 Dec. 1959; m.; four c.; ed Chancellor Coll., Univ. of Malawi, Univ. of Manchester, UK, Univ. of Illinois at Urbana-Champaign, USA; Lecturer in Econs, Univ. of Malawi 1984–90, Lecturer and Head of Econs Dept, Chancellor Coll., Univ. of Malawi 1995–96; Research Fellow, Cornell Univ., USA 1995; Consultant Macroeconomist, Ministry of Econ. Planning and Devt 1996–97; Chief Economist and Coordinator for Advisory Services for Private Business Promotion, Malawi Chamber of Commerce and Industry 1997–98; Macroeconomist, World Bank, Malawi Country Office 1998–2000, 2003–04, Country Economist, World Bank, Washington, DC 1999; Commr for Econ Affairs, African Union Comm. 2004–13; Minister of Finance 2013–; Ed.-in-Chief, Malawi Chamber of Commerce and Industry Business Review 1997–98; Pres., Econs Asscn of Malawi 1998–2000; mem. Monetary Policy Cttee, Reserve Bank of Malawi 2000–03; Sec. to Cabinet Cttees on Economy and Budgetary and Financial Matters 2000–03; mem. Bd of Dirs several orgs including Nat. Roads Authority, Shire Bus Lines, David Whitehead and Sons, PFG Wright Insurance Brokers, Malawi Inst. of Man. 1997–2003; consultant on devt, financial and econ. man. issues for Malawi Govt, UNDP, UNICEF, German Agency for Tech. Cooperation. *Publications:* numerous papers and publications on macro-economic theory and policy, monetary econs, public finance, int. trade and finance and econs of devt. *Address:* Ministry of Finance, Capital Hill, POB 30049, Lilonge 3, Malawi (office). *Telephone:* 1789355 (office). *Fax:* 1789173 (office). *E-mail:* finance@finance.gov.mw (office). *Website:* www.finance.gov.mw (office).

MLADENOV, Nikolay Evtimov, BA, MA; Bulgarian politician and UN official; *Special Representative of the Secretary-General for Iraq and Head of Mission, United Nations Assistance Mission for Iraq (UNAMI);* b. 5 May 1972, Sofia; m.; one c.; ed Univ. of Nat. and World Economy, Sofia, King's Coll. London, UK; worked for Open Soc. Inst., Sofia 1996–98; Programme Coordinator, Social Dept for Bulgaria, World Bank 1998; Founder and Dir European Inst., Sofia 1999–2001; mem. Narodno Sobranie (Parl.) 2001–02; mem. Union of Democratic Forces (UDF), mem. Nat. Exec. Council 2002, Deputy Chair. European Integration Cttee, Vice-Pres. UDF 2004–05; Consultant to World Bank, Int. Republican Inst. and Nat. Democratic Inst. in Bulgaria, Afghanistan, Yemen and other Middle East countries 2005–07; Adviser to Defence and Foreign Policy Comms, Iraqi Parl. 2006; mem. European Parl. (Citizens for European Devt of Bulgaria—GERB— party, aligned with Group of the European People's Party–European Democrats) 2007–09, Chair. del. for relations with Iraq, mem. dels for Afghanistan and Israel; Minister of Defence 2009–10, of Foreign Affairs 2010–13; Special Rep. of the Sec.-Gen. for Iraq and Head of Mission, UN Assistance Mission for Iraq (UNAMI) 2013–; signatory of the Prague Declaration on European Conscience and Communism. *Address:* United Nations Assistance Mission for Iraq (UNAMI), Baghdad, Iraq (office). *E-mail:* unami-information@un.org (office). *Website:* unami .unmissions.org (office).

MLADIĆ, Gen. Ratko; Bosnia and Herzegovina fmr military leader; b. 12 March 1943, Kalinovik; m. Bosiljka 'Bosa' Mladić; one s. one d. (deceased); Serb nationalist; began mil. career as tank officer, Yugoslav People's Army (JNA), Bosnia and Herzegovina; gained popularity among Serb population for supporting their claim to enclave of Krajina during civil war in Croatia 1991; apptd CO JNA 1992; commanded siege of Sarajevo 1992–94; supported creation of a 'Greater Serbia' and opposed any peace settlement of Bosnian civil war, including Gen. Framework Agreement for Peace in Bosnia and Herzegovina 1995; indicted as war criminal 1995; given protection by Slobodan Milošević until his arrest by Yugoslav authorities and extradition to Int. Criminal Tribunal for the Fmr Yusoslavia (ICTY), The Hague 2001; went into hiding 2001; US Govt increased reward offered for information leading to his arrest to US $5m 2002; report issued by Netherlands Inst. for War Documentation held Mladić to be principally responsible for massacre of up to 8,000 Muslim men and boys in Srebrenica in 1995; arrested in Lazarevo, northern Serbia while living in hiding under assumed name of Milorad Komodić 26 May 2011, extradited to The Hague to stand trial for alleged war crimes and genocide, trial began 3 June 2011, trial adjourned, reconvened 15 May 2012.

MLAMBO-NGCUKA, Phumzile, BA, MPhil; South African politician; b. 3 Nov. 1955, KwaZulu Natal, Clermont Township; m. Bulelani Ngcuka; one s.; ed Nat. Univ. of Lesotho; teacher in KwaZulu Natal 1981–83; founder and Dir Young Women's Int. Programme, YWCA World Office, Geneva, Switzerland 1984–87; Dir TEAM (non-governmental org.), Cape Town 1987–89; Dir World Univ. Services 1990–92; est. Phumelela Services 1993–94; MP 1994–2008, Chair., Public Service Portfolio Cttee 1994–; Deputy Minister, Dept of Trade and Industry (DTI) 1996–99; Minister of Minerals and Energy 1999–2005; Deputy Pres. 2005–08 (resgnd); Chancellor Tshwane Univ. of Tech. 2007–; Founding mem., Guguletu Community Devt Corpn; mem. Nat. Exec. Cttee, African Nat. Congress 1997–. *Address:* African National Congress, 54 Sauer Street, Johannesburg 2001, South Africa (office). *Telephone:* (11) 3761000 (office). *Fax:* (11) 3761134 (office). *E-mail:* nmtyelwa@anc.org.za (office). *Website:* www.anc.org.za (office).

MLECHIN, Leonid M.; Russian journalist and writer; b. 12 June 1957; m.; one s.; ed Moscow State Univ.; staff, head of division, Deputy Ed.-in-Chief weekly Novoye Vremya 1979–93; Deputy Ed.-in-Chief newspaper Izvestia 1993–96; political reviewer All-Russian State Cttee on Radio and Television 1996–97; writer and narrator Particular Dossier (TV-Tsentr) 1997–. *Publications include:* more than 20 books, including detective stories, novels, historical non-fiction, and biographies of Yevgeny Primakov and the chairmen of the KGB. *Address:* TV-Tsentr, Moscow 113184, ul. B. Tatarskaya 33/1, Russia (office). *Telephone:* (495) 215-18-12 (office); (495) 217-75-50 (office).

MLECZKO, Andrzej; Polish graphic designer and illustrator; b. 5 Jan. 1949, Tarnobrzeg; one d.; ed Faculty of Architecture, Kraków Tech. Univ.; illustrator of books, paintings, drawings; contrib. to magazines in Poland and abroad 1971–; worked as theatre consultant for Kochanowski 1975–80, for Slowacki 1980–92; Andrzej Mleczko Author's Gallery, Kraków 1983–, Warsaw 2002–; has designed over 20,000 graphics, drawings and posters; mem. Polish Artists Soc. 1974–. *Film appearances:* Chłopaki nie płaczą (Boys Don't Cry) 2000, 'E=mc²' 2002. *Radio:* co-hosted (with Paweł Pawlik) Galeria Andrzeja Mleczki on RMF FM 2001, took part in Moja szkoła w Unii Europejskiej (My School in the European Union) 2003. *Publications:* Seks, mydło i powidło (Krakowska Książka Miesiąca (Cracovian Book of the Month Award) 2008); 46 books and albums. *Address:* Andrzej Mleczko Author's Gallery, ul. Św. Jana 14, 31-018 Kraków; ul. Marszatkowska 140, 00-061 Warsaw, Poland. *Telephone:* (12) 4217104 (Kraków); (22) 8295760 (Warsaw). *Fax:* (12) 4217104. *E-mail:* galeria@mleczko.pl. *Website:* mleczko.interia.pl.

MLINARIC, David, CBE; British interior designer; ed Bartlett School of Architecture, Univ. Coll., London; f. own co. David Mlinaric Ltd 1964, joined by Hugh Henry 1969, and by Tino Zervudachi 1983, now the int. interior design practice Mlinaric, Henry & Zervudachi Ltd 1989–, Tino Zervudachi moved to Paris to form Mlinaric, Henry & Zervudachi SA 1991, Mlinaric, Henry & Zervudachi, Inc., New York formed in 1998. *Publication:* Mlinaric on Decorating (illustrated) (with Mirabel Cecil) 2008. *Address:* Mlinaric, Henry & Zervudachi Ltd, 38 Bourne Street, London, SW1W 8JA, England (office); Mlinaric, Henry & Zervudachi S.A.S., 54 Galerie de Montpensier, Jardins du Palais Royal, 75001 Paris, France (office). *Telephone:* (20) 7730-9072 (London) (office); 1-42-96-08-62 (Paris) (office). *Fax:* (20) 7823-4756 (London) (office); 1-42-97-44-92 (Paris) (office). *E-mail:* jason@ mhzltd.com (office); antoine@mhzparis.com (office). *Website:* www.mlinaric-henry -zervudachi.com (office).

MMARI, Geoffrey Raphael Vehaeli, DipEd, PhD; Tanzanian university teacher and administrator; *Provost, Tumaini University, Dar es Salaam College;* b. 24 June 1934, Moshi; s. of the late Vehaeli Mmari and Luisia Mmari; m. Salome

Mmari 1959; one s. three d.; ed Univ. of E Africa, Univ. of N Iowa, USA, Univ. of Dar es Salaam; teacher and admin. 1966–69; univ. teacher 1969–; Vice-Chancellor Sokoine Univ. of Agric. 1984–88, Univ. of Dar es Salaam 1988–91; Co-ordinator Open Univ. Planning Office 1991–, Vice-Chancellor Open Univ. of Tanzania 1993–2005; Provost, Tumaini Univ., Dar es Salaam Coll. 2005–; Chair. Higher Educ. Accreditation Council, Nat. Examinations Council, Media Council of Tanzania, Tanzania Family Planning Asscn, Media Council of Tanzania; mem. Council Mzumbe Univ., Sokoine Univ. of Agric., State Univ. of Zanzibar, Math. Asscn of Tanzania; Drum Major for Justice Award 2003. *Publications:* Mwalimu: The Influence of Julius Nyerere (ed. with Colin Legum) 1995; ed. secondary math. books series; articles in journals and chapters in books 1960–. *Leisure interests:* reading, travelling, walking. *Address:* Tumaini University, Dar es Salaam College, PO Box 77588, Dar es Salaam, Tanzania (office). *Telephone:* (22) 276-0426 (office); (22) 276-0335 (office); (22) 260-2359 (home). *E-mail:* tudarco@yahoo.com (office).

MNANGAGWA, Emmerson; Zimbabwean politician; *Minister of Justice and Legal Affairs;* b. 15 Sept. 1946; fmr Admin. Sec. Zimbabwe African Nat. Union-Patriotic Front (ZANU-PF); Head Cen. Intelligence Org. 1980s; Minister of State Security; fmr Minister of Justice, Legal and Parl. Affairs 1989–2000; Speaker of Parl. 2000–05; Minister of Rural Housing 2005–09, of Defence 2009–13, of Justice and Legal Affairs 2013–. *Address:* Ministry of Justice and Legal Affairs, New Government Complex, cnr Samora Machel Ave and 4th St, Private Bag 7751, Causeway, Harare, Zimbabwe (office). *Telephone:* (4) 774620 (office). *Fax:* (4) 772999 (office). *Website:* www.justice.gov.zw (office).

MNUCHIN, Robert; American art dealer, gallery curator and fmr investment banker; *Co-Director, L&M Arts;* b. 5 Sept. 1933, New York, NY; m. 1st Elaine Terner Cooper; two s.; m. 2nd Adriana Mnuchin; one d.; ed Yale Univ.; joined Goldman Sachs 1957, became Pnr 1967, headed up trading and arbitrage div. during 1970s, served as mem. Man. Cttee 1980s, retd 1994; Co-founder (with Los Angeles dealer James Corcoran) C&M Arts, New York, later L&M when Corcoran left and merger with gallerist/art dealer Dominique Lévy 2005; artists exhibited include Willem de Kooning, Julian Schnabel and Cy Twombley. *Address:* L&M Arts, 45 East 78th Street, New York, NY 10075-0204, USA (office). *Telephone:* (212) 861-0020 (office). *Fax:* (212) 861-7858 (office). *E-mail:* mnuch@lmgallery.com (office). *Website:* www.lmgallery.com (office).

MO, Shaoping; Chinese lawyer; *Senior Partner, Beijing Mo Shaoping Law Firm;* b. 1958, Beijing; m.; one d.; ed Beijing Coll. of Politics and Law, Chinese Acad. of Social Sciences; China's leading advocate for political dissidents; in pvt. practice since 1992; f. Beijing Mo Shaoping Law Firm, Sr Partner 1995–; one of the initial signatories of Charter 08 manifesto calling for fundamental changes in China; Liberté, Egalité, Fraternité Human Rights Prize (France) 2007. *Address:* Beijing Mo Shaoping Law Firm, Waterside Pavilion, Inside Zhongshan Park, Dongcheng District, Beijing, People's Republic of China (office). *Telephone:* (10) 66055431 ext. 328-302 (office). *Fax:* (10) 66058311 (office). *E-mail:* shaoping@public.bta.net.cn (office).

MO, Timothy; British author; b. 30 Dec. 1950, Hong Kong; s. of Peter Mo Wan Lung and Barbara Helena Falkingham; ed Mill Hill School and St John's Coll., Univ. of Oxford; fmrly worked for Times Educational Supplement and New Statesman; fmr reporter for Boxing News and PAYE clerk; Hawthornden Prize 1983. *Publications include:* The Monkey King 1979 (Geoffrey Faber Memorial Prize 1979), Sour Sweet 1982, An Insular Possession 1986, The Redundancy of Courage 1991 (E. M. Forster Award 1992), Brownout on Breadfruit Boulevard 1995, Renegade or Halo 2 1999 (James Tait Black Memorial Prize 1999), Pure 2012. *Leisure interests:* weight training, scuba diving. *Website:* www.timothymo.co .uk.

MO, Yan; Chinese novelist and teacher; b. (Guan Moye), 17 Feb. 1955, Gaomi, Shandong Prov.; ed PLA Acad. of Arts, Beijing Normal Univ.; joined PLA 1976; Hon. Fellow, Modern Language Asscn 2010; Fukuoka Asian Culture Prize XVII 2006, Nobel Prize in Literature 2012. *Publications include:* Red Sorghum (adapted for film) 1987, Thirteen Steps, The Herbivora Family, Jiuguo, The Republic of Wine 1992, Garlic Ballads 1995, Big Breasts and Wide Hips (Kiriyama Prize 2005), 1996, Shifu You'll Do Anything for a Laugh (adapted for film as Happy Times) 2001, Life and Death Are Wearing Me Out 2008 (Newman Prize for Chinese Literature 2009), Frog (Mao Dun Literature Prize) 2011; other: White Dog Swing (adapted for film as Nuan 2003), Man and Beast, Soaring, Iron Child, The Cure, Love Story, Shen Garden and Abandoned Child. *Address:* c/o Arcade Publishing, 116 John Street, #2810, New York, NY 10038, USA. *Website:* www.arcadepub.com.

MOBERG, Anders C.; Swedish food retail executive; b. Almhult; with IKEA 1970–98, Chief Exec. 1986–98; Chief of Int. Affairs, Home Depot (US home improvements co.) 1998–2003; Pres. and CEO Royal Ahold NV, Netherlands 2003–07. *Address:* c/o Royal Ahold NV, Piet Heinkode 167–173, 1019 GM Amsterdam, Netherlands (office).

MOBY; American musician (guitar, drums, keyboards) and producer; b. (Richard Melville Hall), 11 Sept. 1965, Harlem, New York; s. of James Hall and Elizabeth Hall; ed Royle Grammar School, Darien, CT, Univ. of Connecticut; cr. first band 1979, new wave/punk rock band Vatican Commandos 1980, new wave band AWOL 1982; DJ The Beat, Port Chester, New York 1984, Mars, Palladium, Palace de Beauté, MK, New York 1989; production and remixes for Metallica, Smashing Pumpkins, Michael Jackson, Depeche Mode, Soundgarden, Blur, David Bowie, Orbital, Prodigy, Freddie Mercury, Brian Eno, B-52s, Ozzy Osbourne, John Lydon, Butthole Surfers, Erasure, Aerosmith, OMD, Pet Shop Boys, Jon Spencer Blues Explosion; numerous tours, festival appearances, TV and radio broadcasts; owner tea shop Teany, New York; mem. BMI, PMRS, AF of M, SAG, AFTRA; MTV Web Award 2002, Q Magazine Best Producer Award 2002, MTV Video Music Award for Best Cinematography in a Video (for We Are All Made Of Stars) 2002. *Compositions for film:* Double Tap (score) 1997, contrib. to numerous other film soundtracks. *Recordings include:* albums: Moby 1992, The Story So Far 1993, Ambient 1993, Early Underground 1993, Move (EP) 1994, Underwater 1995, Everything is Wrong (Spin Magazine Album of the Year) 1995, Voodoo Child: The End of Everything 1996, Animal Rights 1996, Rare: Collected B-Sides 1989–1993 1996, Everything is Wrong: Non-stop DJ Mix By Evil Ninja Moby 1996, I Like To Score 1997, Play 1999, Mobysongs 2000, 18 2002, Play: The B Sides 2004, Hotel 2005, Last Night 2008, Wait for Me 2009, Destroyed 2011, Innocents 2013.

Address: c/o DEF, 51 Lonsdale Road, Queen's Park, London, NW6 6RA, England (office); c/o Mute, 429 Harrow Road, London, W10 4RE, England. *Telephone:* (20) 7328-2922 (office). *Fax:* (20) 7328-2322 (office). *E-mail:* info@d-e-f.com (office). *Website:* www.moby.com.

MOCK, Alois, LLD; Austrian politician; *Honorary Chairman, Austrian People's Party;* b. 10 June 1934, Euratsfeld; s. of August Mock and Mathilde Mock; m. Dr Edith Mock (née Partik) 1963; ed Univ. of Vienna, Johns Hopkins Univ., Bologna and Free Univ., Brussels; mem. Austrian mission to OECD 1962–66; Pvt. Sec. to Fed. Chancellor 1966, Head of Private Office 1968; Minister of Educ. 1969–70; mem. Parl. 1970–99 (retd due to illness); Leader, Austrian People's Party (Österreichische Volkspartei—ÖVP) 1979–89, Hon. Chair. 1995–; Leader of Opposition 1979–87; Vice-Chancellor 1987–89; Minister of Foreign Affairs 1987–95; Pres. European Democratic Union, Vienna 1979–88; Pres. European Democratic Union 1979–98, Int. Democratic Union, London 1983–87; Co-founder Cen. European Cooperative (Pentagonale) 1989, later grew to 16 countries of Cen. European Initiative. *Publication:* Standpunkte 1983. *Address:* c/o Österreichische Volkspartei, Lichtenfelsgasse 7, 1010 Vienna, Austria.

MOCUMBI, Pascoal Manuel, MD; Mozambican medical doctor and fmr politician; *High Representative, European-Developing Countries Clinical Trials Programme;* b. 10 April 1941, Maputo; s. of Manuel Mocumbi Malume and Leta Alson Cuhle; m. Adelina Isabel Bernardino Paindane 1970; two s. two d.; ed Lausanne Univ. of Lausanne; Founding mem. Frente de Libertação de Moçambique (FRELIMO) 1962, Head, FRELIMO Information Dept, Dar-es-Salaam, Tanganyika 1963–65, Rep. FRELIMO Algeria 1965–67; Dir José Macamo Hosp., Maputo 1975–76; Prov. Health Dir, Chief Medical Officer, Clinical Doctor Beira Central Hosp., Sofala Prov. 1976–80; Clinical Doctor, Maputo Hosp. 1980–87; Asst Lecturer, Faculty of Medicine, Eduardo Mondlane Univ., Maputo 1984–87; mem. Nat. Ass., FRELIMO Political Cttee 1987–2005; Minister of Health 1980–87, of Foreign Affairs 1987–94; Prime Minister of Mozambique 1994–2004; High Rep., European-Developing Countries Clinical Trials Programme 2004–; mem. Medicines for Malaria Venture 2004–10, WHO Comm. on Social Determinants of Health 2005–08. *Leisure interests:* jogging, squash, reading. *Address:* 164 Av. Primeiro Dezembro, Matola, Maputo Province, Mozambique (home). *Telephone:* (21) 722918 (home). *Fax:* (21) 93880819 (office). *E-mail:* pascoal.mocumbi@tvcabo .co.mz (home); mocumbi@edctp.org (office). *Website:* www.edctp.org (office).

MOCZULSKI, Leszek Robert, LLM, DPolitSc, PhD; Polish historian, politician, lawyer, journalist and academic; *Professor of East European Studies, University of Warsaw;* b. 7 June 1930, Warsaw; s. of Stanisław Moczulski and Janina Moczulska (née Reimer); m. 1st Małgorzata Moczulska (née Smogorzewska) 1951 (deceased); m. 2nd Maria-Ludwika (née Różycka) Moczulska 1968; two d.; ed Acad. of Political Science, Warsaw, Law Faculty, Warsaw Univ.; reporter on Życie Warszawy (daily) 1950–53, on dailies and weeklies, including Dookoła Swiata, Warsaw 1955–57; imprisoned on charges of slandering Poland in foreign press 1957–58, acquitted; assoc. (pseud. Leszek Karpatowicz) Więź (monthly) 1959–62; Head History Section Stolica (weekly) 1961–77; ed. of underground journals Opinia 1977–78, Droga 1978–80, Gazeta Polska 1979–80; arrested Aug. 1980 and sentenced to seven years on charge of attempting to overthrow regime, amnestied Aug. 1984; sentenced to four years on charge of heading illegal org. March 1985, amnestied Sept. 1986; victim of reprisals 1946–89, including repeated 48-hour custody (250 times 1976–80), forbidden to publish, refused passport, prevented from finishing PhD; mem. Polish Journalists' Asscn 1951–, Theatre Authors and Composers' Union 1960– (mem. Bd 1972–77), Polish Historical Soc.; active in Movt for Rights of Man and Citizen (ROPCiO) 1977–80; Deputy to Sejm (Parl.) 1991–97; Hon. Chair. Parl. Club of Confed. of Independence of Poland (KPN) 1993–97; Chair. Parl. Cttee for Polish Connection Abroad 1993–97; mem. Confed. for an Independent Poland (KPN) 1979– (one of founders, temporary chair. 1979–80, Chair. 1980–2005, Hon. Chair. 2005–); mem. Polish del. to Parl. Ass., Council of Europe 1992–93, 1994–96; Prof. of East European Studies, Univ. of Warsaw; Prof., Dean of Law Dept and Pres. Coll. of Man., Legnica 2011–13; co-f. and mem. Ukraine Solidarity Cttee 2014; Gold Badge of Honour, Officer's Cross of Polonia Restituta Order (London) 1987. *Publications:* numerous contribs on history, politics and int. affairs, more than 20 books including Wojna polska (War) 1939 1972, Rewolucja bez rewolucji (Revolution Without Revolution) 1979, Trzecia Rzeczpospolita – zarys ustroju politycznego (A Constitutional System for Independent Poland) 1984, U progu niepodległości (Gateway to Independence) 1990, Bez wahania (Without Hesitation) 1992, Trzy drogi (Three Ways) 1993, Demokracja bez demokracji (Democracy Without Democracy) 1995, Geopolityka (Geopolitics) 1999, Investigation 2001, Narodziny Miedzymorza 2007, Wojna polska 1939 2009, Przerwane powstanie 1914 2010, Meloch: Paristwo jaho proedsignbionstinu, Spuiczenistwe jaho via roboca (Moloch: State as Company, Society as Manpower) 2013. *Leisure interests:* horse riding, old automobiles, sailing, old maps. *Address:* ul. Jaracza 3 m. 4, 00-378 Warsaw, Poland (home). *Telephone:* (22) 6252639 (home). *E-mail:* lmski@poczta .onet.pl (home).

MODI, Narendra Damodardas, MA; Indian politician; *Chief Minister of Gujarat;* b. 17 Sept. 1950, Vadnagar, Mehsana Dist; ed Gujarat Univ.; mem. Nava Nirman Andolan movt 1972–77; joined Bharatiya Janata Party 1986, Gen. Sec. for Gujarat 1988, elected to Ass. 1995, Nat. Sec., Delhi 1995, re-elected in Gujarat 1998, Gen. Sec. for Himachal Pradesh, the Punjab and Haryana 1998–2001, Nat. Gen. Sec. 1999–; Chief Minister of Gujarat 2001–03, 2003–; The Asian Winner, fDi Magazine Personality of the Year Award 2009. *Publications include:* Sangharsha ma Gujarat (Gujarat under Struggle), Setu Bandh, Patra Roop Guruji. *Address:* Office of the Chief Minister, Block No. 1, 5th Floor, New Sachivalaya, Ganghinagar, 382 010, India (office). *Telephone:* (79) 23232611 (office); (79) 23232601 (home). *Fax:* (79) 23222101 (office); (79) 23222020 (home). *E-mail:* cm@gujaratindia.com (office). *Website:* www.gujaratindia.com (office); www.narendramodi.in.

MODI, Vinay Kumar, BTechChemEng; Indian industrialist; b. 31 May 1943, Modinagar; s. of the late Rai Bahadur Gujar Mal Modi and Dayawati Modi; m. Chander Bala 1962; one s. one d.; ed Scindia School, Gwalior, Indian Inst. of Tech., Kanpur; Dir Modi Industries Ltd 1965–; Vice-Chair. and Man. Dir Modi Rubber Ltd 1976–; Chair. Gujarat Guardian Ltd, Modi Mirrlees Blackstone Ltd, Shree Acids and Chemicals Ltd; currently Chair. MAN Diesel India Ltd, Lombard Street Pvt. Ltd, Gujarat Acrylics Pvt. Ltd; fmr Pres. Steel Furnace Asscn of India; fmr Chair. Automobile Tyre Manufacturers Asscn; fmr Vice Chair. Chemical Allied Export Promotion Council, Calcutta; fmr Pres. All India Float Glass Manufacturing Asscn; mem. Bd Scindia School, Jaipuria Inst. of Man. and Tech., Inst. of Man. and Tech. Gaziabad; mem. Senate of Indian Inst. of Tech., Rourkee; Madhav Award 2007, Scindia School; various awards from govt for export performance; prizes from several asscns. *Publications:* various articles on steel, tyres and cement production. *Leisure interests:* golf, tennis, billiards. *Address:* Mody Industries (FC) Pvt. Ltd, 203, Bakshi, House, 40-41 Nehru Place, New Delhi 110 019; DDA Shopping Centre, New Friends Colony, New Delhi 110 065 (office); 55A, Friends Colony (East), New Delhi 110 065 (home); Modi Bhavan, Civil Lines, Modinagar 201 204, India (office). *Telephone:* (11) 6835766 (office); (11) 4444668 (office); (11) 6833633 (home); (11) 6833088 (home); (11) 6830703 (office). *Fax:* (11) 6830868 (office); (11) 6846175 (home); (11) 6464228 (office). *E-mail:* modivinay@ hotmail.com (office); modypump@vsnl.net (office). *Website:* www.modypumps.com (office).

MODIANO, Patrick Jean; French novelist; b. 30 July 1945, Boulogne-Billancourt; s. of Albert Modiano and Luisa Colpyn; m. Dominique Zehrfuss 1970; two d.; ed schools in Biarritz, Chamonix, Deauville, Thônes, Barbizon, coll. in Paris; Chevalier des Arts et des Lettres; Prix Roger Nimier 1968, Prix Felix Fénéon 1969, Grand Prix de l'Académie française 1972, Prix Goncourt 1978, Prix Pierre de Monaco 1984, Grand Prix du Roman de la Ville de Paris 1994, Grand Prix de Littérature Paul Morand de l'Académie française 2000, Austrian State Prize for European Literature 2012. *Publications include:* La place de l'étoile 1968, La ronde de nuit 1969, Les boulevards de ceinture 1972, Lacombe Lucien (screenplay) 1973, La polka (play) 1974, Villa triste (novel) 1975, Interrogatoire d'Emmanuel Berl 1976, Livret de famille (novel) 1977, Rue des boutiques obscures 1978, Une jeunesse 1981, Memory Lane 1981, De si braves garçons (novel) 1982, Poupée blonde 1983, Quartier perdu 1985, Dimanches d'août 1986, Une aventure de Choura 1986, La fiancée de Choura 1987, Remise de peine (novel) 1988, Catherine Certitude 1988, Vestiaire de l'enfance (novel) 1989, Voyage de noces 1990, Fleurs de ruine (novel) 1991, Un cirque passe (novel) 1992, Chien de printemps 1993, Du plus loin de l'oubli 1995, Dora Bruder 1997, Des inconnues 1999, La petite bijou 2001, Accident nocturne 2003, Un pedigree 2005, Dans le café de la jeunesse perdue 2007, L'Horizon 2010, L'Herbe de nuit 2012. *Address:* c/o Editions Gallimard, 5 rue Gaston-Gallimard, 75328 Paris Cedex 07, France.

MODINE, Matthew Avery; American actor, director and writer; b. 22 March 1959, Loma Linda, Calif.; s. of Mark Alexander Modine and Dolores Modine (née Warner); m. Caridad Rivera 1980; one s. one d.; ed Brigham Young Univ.; mem. Dramatic Jury, Sundance Film Festival 1994; Founder Bicycle For A Day; Golden Globe Award, Venice Film Festival Volpi Cup, Golden Lion. *Films include:* Private School 1983, Streamers 1983, Birdy 1984, The Hotel New Hampshire 1984, Mrs. Soffel 1984, Vision Quest 1985, Orphans 1987, Full Metal Jacket 1987, Married to the Mob 1988, The Gamble 1988, Gross Anatomy 1989, Memphis Belle 1990, Pacific Heights 1990, Wind 1992, Equinox 1992, Short Cuts 1993, And the Band Played On (HBO Cable) 1993, The Browning Version 1994, Jacob 1994, Cutthroat Island 1995, Bye Bye Love 1995, Fluke 1995, The Maker 1997, The Blackout 1997, The Real Blonde 1997, Any Given Sunday 1999, Notting Hill 1999, Bamboozled 2000, Very Mean Men 2000, In the Shadows 2001, Hitler: The Rise of Evil 2003, Le Divorce 2003, Funky Monkey 2004, Opa 2005, Transporter 2 2005, Kettle of Fish 2006, Mary 2006, Go Go Tales 2007, The Neighbor 2007, Have Dreams, Will Travel 2007, PoliWood 2009, The Trial 2010, Mia and the Migoo (English language version) 2011, Too Big to Fail (HBO) 2011, Jesus Was a Commie 2011, The Flying House 2011, Family Weekend 2012, Ansiedad (aka See If I Care) 2011, The Dark Knight Rises 2012, Girl in Progress 2012; dir: When I Was a Boy (short) 1993, Smoking (short) 1995, Ecce Pirate (short) 1997, I Think I Thought (short) 2008, To Kill an American (short) 2008. *Television includes:* What the Deaf Man Heard (film) 1996, Flowers for Algernon (film) 2000, The American (film) 2001, Jack and the Beanstalk: The Real Story (film) 2001, Redeemer (film) 2002, The Winning Season (film) 2004, Into The West (film) 2005, The Bedford Diaries (film) 2006, Weeds (film) 2007, Little Fish, Strange Pond (aka Frenemy) (film) 2009, Jobs (film) 2013. *Leisure interests:* painting, horticulture, carpentry. *Address:* c/o Untitled Entertainment, 8436 West 3rd Street, Los Angeles, CA 90048-4189, USA (office).

MOE, Thorvald, PhD; Norwegian economist, government official and international organization official; *Deputy Secretary General, Ministry of Finance;* b. 4 Oct. 1939, Oslo; s. of Thorvald Moe and Marie Cappelen Moe; m. Nina Kjeldsberg 1968; one s. one d.; ed Univ. of California, Los Angeles, Stanford Univ., USA; held various sr posts in Ministry of Finance, including Head of Division, Deputy Director and Deputy Director General in the Planning Department and the Budget Department 1970–79, Dir-Gen. Econ. Policy Dept 1978–86, Chief Econ. Adviser and Deputy Perm. Sec. 1989–97; Amb. to OECD 1986–89, Deputy Sec.-Gen. OECD 1998–2002; Deputy Sec. Gen. Ministry of Finance 2002–; Head of Norwegian Del. to Econ. Policy Cttee at OECD 2002–. *Leisure interests:* history, tennis. *Address:* Ministry of Finance, Akersgt. 40, POB 8008, Dep., 0030 Oslo, Norway (office). *Telephone:* 22-24-90-90 (office). *Fax:* 22-24-95-10 (office). *E-mail:* arkiv .postmottak@finans.dep.no (office). *Website:* odin.dep.no/fin (office).

MOELLER, Bernd, DTheol; German academic; *Professor Emeritus of Church History, University of Göttingen;* b. 19 May 1931, Berlin; s. of the late Max Moeller and Carola Bielitz; m. Irene Müller 1957; three d.; ed Univs of Erlangen, Mainz, Basle, Munich and Heidelberg; Research Asst Univ. of Heidelberg 1956–58, Privatdozent 1958–64; Prof. of Church History, Univ. of Göttingen 1964–now Emer., Rector 1971–72; Chair. Verein für Reformationsgeschichte, Heidelberg 1976–2001; mem. Akad. der Wissenschaften zu Göttingen, Academia Europaea; Dr hc (Zürich) 1998. *Publications:* Reichsstadt und Reformation 1962, Geschichte des Christentums in Grundzügen 1965, Spätmittelalter 1966, Oekumenische Kirchengeschichte (with R. Kottje) I-III 1970–74, Deutschland im Zeitalter der Reformation 1977, Die Reformation und das Mittelalter 1991, Kirchengeschichte. Deutsche Texte (1699–1927) 1994, Städtische Predigt in der Frühzeit der Reformation (with K. Stackmann) 1996, Luther – Rezeption 2001, Albrecht Dürer's Vier Apostel (with H. Arndt) 2003, Deutsche Biographische Enzyklopädie der Theologie und der Kirchen I–II 2005. *Address:* Herzberger Landstrasse 26, 37085 Göttingen, Germany. *Telephone:* (551) 42850.

MOERLAND, Piet Willem; Dutch banker, business executive and academic; b. 1949; ed Erasmus Univ., Rotterdam; Prof. for nearly 25 years at Univ. of

Groningen (Business Admin), then Univ. of Tilburg (Corp. Finance); mem. Bd of Supervision, Rabobank Nederland 1984–87, mem. Bd of Dirs 1987–2000, mem. Advisory Bd 2000–03, mem. Exec. Bd 2003–, Chair. Exec. Bd 2009–13 (resgnd); currently Supervisory Dir at Essent; mem. Advisory Bd Netherlands Order of Accountants and Admin Consultants; mem. Bd of Dirs Netherlands Bankers' Asscn (NVB), International Raiffeisen Union; Chair. European Asscn of Co-operative Banks (EACB/Groupement), Bd of Nat. Co-operative Council for Agric. and Horticulture of the Netherlands. *Address:* c/o Rabobank Group, PO Box 17100, 3500 HG Utrecht, The Netherlands.

MOERNER, W. E. (William Esco), BS, AB, MS, PhD; American physical chemist and academic; *Harry S. Mosher Professor in Chemistry and Professor, by courtesy, of Applied Physics, Stanford University;* b. 1953; ed Washington and Cornell Univs; Research Asst, Dept of Physics, Washington Univ., St Louis, Mo. 1972–75; Grad. Research Asst and NSF Grad. Fellow, Lab. for Atomic and Solid State Physics, Cornell Univ., Ithaca, NY 1975–81; research staff mem., IBM Almaden Research Center, San Jose, Calif. 1981–95, Man. Laser-Materials Interactions 1988–89, Project Leader 1989–95; Guest Prof. of Physical Chem., Swiss Fed. Inst. of Tech. (ETH Zurich) 1993–94; Prof. and Distinguished Chair in Physical Chem., Univ. of California, San Diego 1995–98; Robert Burns Woodward Visiting Prof., Harvard Univ. 1997–98; Prof. of Chem., Stanford Univ. 1998–2002, Harry S. Mosher Prof. of Chem. 2002–, Prof., by courtesy, of Applied Physics 2005–, Chair. Chem. Dept 2011–; Advisory Ed. Chemical Physics Letters 1998–, Chem-PhysChem 2004–, Single Molecules 2000–02; Sr mem. IEEE 1988–; mem. NAS 2007–; Fellow, American Physical Soc. 1992, Optical Soc. of America 1992, American Acad. of Arts and Sciences 2001, AAAS 2004; Geoffrey Frew Fellow, Australian Acad. of Sciences 2003; Roger I. Wilkinson Nat. Outstanding Young Electrical Engineer 1984, IBM Outstanding Tech. Achievement Awards for photon-gated spectral hole burning 1988, for single-molecule detection and spectroscopy 1992, Earle K. Plyler Prize for Molecular Spectroscopy, American Physical Soc. 2001, Wolf Prize in Chem. (with Allen Bard) 2008, Irving Langmuir Prize in Chemical Physics, American Physical Soc. 2009, Pittsburgh Spectroscopy Award 2012, Outstanding Alumni Achievement Award, Washington Univ. 2013, Kirkwood Award Medal, Yale Univ., New Haven Section of the ACS 2013. *Publications include:* numerous papers in professional journals on physical chemistry of single molecules, biophysics, nanoparticle trapping and nanophotonics; eight US patents, four patents pending. *Address:* Department of Chemistry, Stanford University, Stanford, CA 94305-5080, USA (office). *Telephone:* (650) 723-1727 (office). *Fax:* (650) 725-0259 (office). *E-mail:* moerner@stanford.edu (office); wmoerner@stanford.edu (office). *Website:* www.stanford.edu/group/moerner (office).

MOERSCH, Karl; German politician and journalist; b. 11 March 1926, Calw/Württemberg; s. of Karl F. Moersch; m. Waltraut Schweikle 1947; one s.; ed Univ. of Tübingen; journalist in Ludwigshafen, Bad Godesberg (Deutscher Forschungsdienst) and Frankfurt (Ed. of Die Gegenwart) 1956–58; Head of Press Dept, Freie Demokratische Partei (FDP) 1961–64; freelance journalist 1964–; fmr mem. Bundestag; Parl. Sec. of State, Minister of State, Ministry of Foreign Affairs 1970–76; mem. Exec. Bd of UNESCO 1980–85; Ludwig-Uhland Prize 1997. *Publications:* Kursrevision–Deutsche Politik nach Adenauer 1978, Europa für Anfänger 1979, Sind wir denn eine Nation? 1982, Bei uns im Staate Beutelsbach 1984, Geschichte der Pfalz 1987, Sueben, Württemberger und Franzosen 1991, Sperrige Landsleute 1996, Es geht seltsam zu – in Württemberg 1998, Immer wieder war's ein Abenteuer–Erinnerungen 2001, Kontrapunkt Baden-Württemberg 2002; contrib. numerous articles to newspapers, etc. *Address:* c/o MC Seniorenstift gGmbH, Thouretallee 3, 71638 Ludwigsburg (office); Gebhard-Müller-Allee 14, 71638 Ludwigsburg, Germany (home). *Telephone:* (7141) 957050 (office); (7141) 905745 (home). *Fax:* (7141) 905643 (home).

MOESER, James, BMus, MMus, DMus; American concert organist, university administrator and academic; *Professor of Music, University of North Carolina;* b. Colorado City, Tex.; m. Dr Susan Dickerson Moeser; one s. one d.; ed Univ. of Texas, Univ. of Michigan; Asst Prof. and Chair. Organ Dept, Univ. of Kansas 1966–75, Dean School of Fine Arts 1975–86, later Althaus Distinguished Prof. of Organ; Dean Coll. of Arts and Architecture and Exec. Dir Univ. Arts Services, Pennsylvania State Univ. 1986–92; Vice-Pres. for Academic Affairs and Provost Univ. of S Carolina 1992–96; Chancellor Univ. of Nebraska at Lincoln 1996–2000; Chancellor Univ. of N Carolina at Chapel Hill 2000–08, Prof. of Music 2009–; apptd by FBI to Nat. Security Higher Educ. Advisory Bd 2005; serves on Coll. Bd's Nat. Comm. on Writing and two Asscn of American Univs cttees; selected by Nat. Collegiate Athletic Asscn for its Presidential Task Force on the Future of Div. I Intercollegiate Athletics and its fiscal responsibility sub-cttee; mem. CEO Group of Six (group of pres and chancellors from major athletic confs); fmr mem. Bd of Dirs Nat. Asscn of State Univs and Land Grant Colls, Chair. Tech.-Transfer Coll. Comm.; fmr mem. Kellogg Comm. on the Future of State and Land-Grant Univs; Fulbright Scholar in Berlin and Paris, honoured by Grad. School at Texas with Outstanding Alumnus Award 2001. *Address:* Department of Music, University of North Carolina, 3320 Hill Hall, Chapel Hill, NC 27599-9100, USA (office). *Telephone:* (919) 962-1039 (office). *Website:* http://music.unc.edu (office).

MOFAZ, Lt-Gen. Shaul, BA, MBA; Israeli politician and fmr army officer; *Leader, Kadima Party;* b. 1948, Teheran, Iran; m. Orit Mofaz; four c.; ed Bar-Ilan Univ., US Marine Corps Command and Staff Coll., USA; immigrated to Israel 1957; paratrooper, Israel Defense Forces (IDF) 1966, served in Six-Day War 1967; command positions in Paratroop Brigade; Commdr Paratroop Reconnaissance Unit 1973; Deputy Commdr Paratroop Brigade; infantry brigade commdr 1982; Commdr IDF Officers' School 1984; Commdr Paratroop Brigade 1986–88; promoted Brig.-Gen. 1988; Commdr Reserve Armour Div. 1988–90; Commdr Galilee Div. 1990–92; Commdr IDF forces in Judea and Samaria 1993–94; promoted Maj.-Gen. 1994; GOC Southern Command 1994–96; Chief of Planning Directorate Gen. Staff 1996–97; Deputy Chief IDF Gen. Staff 1997; 16th Chief of Gen. Staff 1998–2002; Minister of Defence 2002–06; mem. Knesset 2006–; Deputy Prime Minister and Minister of Transport 2006–09; left Likud party to join newly formed Kadima party Dec. 2005, Leader 2012–. *Address:* Kadima Party, Petach Tikva, Tel-Aviv (office); Knesset, Jerusalem, Israel. *Telephone:* 3-9788000 (office); 2-6496116. *Fax:* 3-9788020 (office); 2-6496421. *E-mail:* shaulm@knesset.gov.il. *Website:* www.kadima.org.il (office); www.knesset.gov.il.

MOFFAT, Sir Brian Scott, Kt, OBE, FCA; British business executive; *Non-Executive Director, Macsteel Holdings Luxembourg SARL and Macsteel Global SARL;* b. 6 Jan. 1939; s. of Festus Moffat and Agnes Moffat; m. Jacqueline Cunliffe 1964; one s. (and one s. deceased) one d.; ed Hulme Grammar School; with Peat Marwick Mitchell & Co. 1961–68; joined British Steel Corpn (later British Steel PLC, now Corus Group PLC) 1968, Man. Dir Finance 1986–91, Chief Exec. 1991–99, Chair. 1993–2003; Dir (non-exec.) HSBC Holdings PLC 1998–2008, Deputy Chair. and Sr Ind. Dir (non-exec.) 2001–08; Dir (non-exec.) Enterprise Oil PLC 1995–2002, Bank of England 2000–06, Macsteel Global BV (fmrly Nosmas Holdings BV) 2003–10, Macsteel Global SARL BV 2010–, Macsteel Holdings Luxembourg SARL 2010–; Hon. DSc (Warwick) 1998, (Sheffield) 2001. *Leisure interests:* farming, fishing, shooting. *Address:* Springfield Farm, Earlswood, Chepstow, Monmouthshire, NP6 6AT, England (home). *Telephone:* (1291) 650959. *Fax:* (1291) 650747. *E-mail:* sirbmoffat@btinternet.com.

MOFFAT, Leslie Ernest Fraser, JP, BSc, MB, CH.B., MBA, FRCSE, FRCS (GLASG.), FRCPE; British urologist; b. 3 Nov. 1949; m.; three d.; ed Univs of Edinburgh and Stirling; Professorial House Officer posts City Hosp., Royal Infirmary, Edin. 1974–75; Sr House Officer Dept of Surgery, Royal Infirmary, Edin. 1976, Surgical Registrar 1977–79; Munro Prosector, Royal Coll. of Surgeons Edin. 1977–78; Research Registrar, Clinical Shock Study Group, Western Infirmary, Glasgow 1980–81; Urological Sr Registrar, Glasgow Teaching Hosps 1982–86; Clinical Sr Lecturer, Univ. of Aberdeen 1986–; Pres. Grampian Div. BMA 1994; Trustee Prostate Cancer charity, Hammersmith Hosp., London, Vice-Chair. –2010; Chair. Urological Cancer Working Party in Scotland; Founding Ed. UroOncology 1999–; Chair. Urological Cancer Working Party in Scotland 1999–; Medical and Specialist Adviser to Cancer BACUP; Urological Consultant to British Antarctic Survey; Medical mem., Employment and Support Allowance Trubunals; mem. Rates Appeal Tribunal; Hon. Consultant Royal Marsden Hosp. London; Burgess of Aberdeen 1999. *Publications:* Prostate Cancer – The Facts (co-author), Urological Cancer: A Practical Guide to Management; over 105 publs including 6 book chapters. *Leisure interests:* country life, opera. *Address:* UroOncology, Polwarth Building, Medical School, Foresterhill, Aberdeen, AB25 2ZD (office); Tillery House, Udny, Ellon, Aberdeenshire, Scotland (home). *Telephone:* (1224) 849136 (office); (1651) 842898 (home). *Fax:* (1224) 403618 (office). *E-mail:* lmoffat@aol.com (home).

MOFFATT, Henry Keith, ScD, FRS; British mathematician and academic; *Professor Emeritus of Mathematical Physics, University of Cambridge;* b. 12 April 1935, Edinburgh, Scotland; s. of the late Frederick Henry Moffatt and Emmeline Marchant Fleming; m. Katharine (Linty) Stiven 1960; two s. (one deceased) two d.; ed Univs of Edinburgh and Cambridge; Asst Lecturer, then Lecturer, Univ. of Cambridge 1961–76, Prof. of Math. Physics 1980–2005, Prof. Emer. 2005–; Fellow, Trinity Coll., Cambridge 1961–76, 1980–, Tutor 1971–74, Sr Tutor 1975; Prof. of Applied Math., Bristol Univ. 1977–80; Dir Isaac Newton Inst. for Math. Sciences 1996–2001; Pres. Int. Union of Theoretical and Applied Mechanics 2000–04, Vice-Pres. 2004–08; part-time Prof. Ecole Polytechnique, Paris 1992–99; Chair. Int. de Recherche Blaise Pascal 2002–03; Leverhulme Emer. Fellow 2003–05; Ed. Journal of Fluid Mechanics 1966–83; mem. Academia Europaea 1994; Foreign mem. Royal Netherlands Acad. of Arts and Sciences 1991, Acad. des Sciences, Paris 1998, Accad. Scienzia Lincei 2001, NAS 2008; Officier des Palmes académiques 1998; Dr hc (INPG Grenoble) 1987, (State Univ. of New York) 1990, (Edin.) 2001, (Eindhoven Tech. Univ.) 2006, (Glasgow) 2007; Smiths Prize 1960, Panetti-Ferrari Prize and Gold Medal 2001, Euromech Fluid Mechanics Prize 2003, Sr Whitehead Prize, London Math. Soc. 2005, Hughes Medal, Royal Soc. 2005, David Crighton Medal 2009. *Publications:* Magnetic Field Generation in Electrically Conducting Fluids 1978, Topological Fluid Mechanics (co-ed. with A. Tsinober) 1990, Topological Aspects of the Dynamics of Fluids and Plasmas (co-ed.) 1992. *Leisure interests:* French country cooking, hill walking. *Address:* DAMTP, Centre for Mathematical Sciences, Wilberforce Road, Cambridge, CB3 0WA (office); Trinity College, Cambridge, CB2 1TQ (office); 6 Banhams Close, Cambridge, CB4 1HX, England (home). *Telephone:* (1223) 363338 (home). *E-mail:* hkm2@damtp.cam.ac.uk (office). *Website:* www.damtp.cam.ac.uk (office).

MOFFETT, David McKenzie, BA, MBA; American mortgage executive; b. 22 Feb. 1952, Daytona Beach, Fla; s. of James Denny Jr and Dorothy McCall; m. 1st Cynthia Ann Daugherty 1973 (divorced 1977); m. 2nd Katherine Anne Martin 1979; three c.; ed Univ. of Oklahoma, Southern Methodist Univ.; planning analyst, First Nat. Bank & Trust Co. 1975–76, financial analyst 1978, Vice-Pres. 1978–80, Sr Vice-Pres. 1981–86, Exec. Vice-Pres. 1987–93; Chief Financial Officer Star Banc Corpn (merged with Firstar Corpn) 1993–98, Chief Financial Officer and Vice-Chair. Firstar Corpn 1998–2001, Chief Financial Officer, Vice-Chair. and Dir US Bancorp 2001–07 (after Firstar merger with US Bancorp 2001); CEO Fed. Home Loan Mortgage Corpn (Freddie Mac) Sept. 2008–March 2009; Sr Adviser The Carlyle Group 2007–08; fmr Chair. Chief Financial Officers' Council, Financial Services Roundtable; Chair. Bd of Dirs Ebay Inc. 2007–, MBIA Insurance Corpn 2007–, E.W. Scripps Inc. 2007–, Building Materials Holding Corpn 2007–; mem. Chief Financial Officers' Roundtable, Bank Admin Inst.; mem. Advisory Bd Price Coll. of Business, Univ. of Oklahoma; mem. Nat. Asset/Liability Man. Asscn, Bank Admin Inst.; Chair.'s Award, First Nat. Bank 1980. *Leisure interests:* running, golf, skiing, scuba diving, cycling. *Address:* c/o Freddie Mac, 8200 Jones Branch Drive, McLean, VA 22102, USA (office).

MOFFETT, James R., BS, MS; American geologist and mining executive; *Chairman, Freeport-McMoRan Copper & Gold;* ed Univ. of Texas at Austin, Tulane Univ.; consulting geologist 1964–69; Co-f. McMoRan Oil & Gas Co. 1969, merged with Freeport Minerals Co. to form Freeport-McMoRan Inc., Chair. and CEO 1984–97, mem. Bd of Dirs 1992–, currently Chair. Freeport-McMoRan Copper & Gold Inc. and Pres. Commr of PT Freeport Indonesia (mining unit), also Co-Chair. McMoRan Exploration Co.; serves on numerous boards; mem. Mining Foundation of the Southwest; Hon. DSc (Louisiana State Univ.); Hon. Dr of Financial Econs (Univ. of New Orleans); Horatio Alger Asscn of Distinguished Americans Award 1990, Norman Vincent Peale Award, Horatio Alger Asscn of Distinguished Americans 2000, mem. American Mining Hall of Fame. *Address:* Freeport-McMoRan Copper & Gold, One North Central Avenue, Phoenix, AZ 85004-4414, USA (office). *Telephone:* (602) 366-8100 (office). *E-mail:* info@fcx.com (office). *Website:* www.fcx.com (office).

MOGAE, Festus Gontebanye, MA; Botswana politician and fmr head of state; *Secretary-General's Special Envoy for Climate Change, United Nations*; b. 21 Aug. 1939, Serowe; s. of Ditlhabano and Dithunya Mogae; m. Barbara Gemma Modise 1968; three d.; ed Moeng Secondary School, North West London Polytechnic, Univs of Oxford and Sussex; Planning Officer, Ministry of Devt Planning 1968–69, Ministry of Finance and Devt Planning 1970, Sr Planning Officer 1971, Dir Econ Affairs 1972–74, Perm. Sec. 1975–76; Alt. Exec. Dir of IMF 1976–78, Exec. Dir 1978–80; Alt. Gov. for Botswana, IMF 1971–72, African Devt Bank 1971–76, IBRD 1973–76; Dir Botswana Devt Corpn 1971–74 (Chair. 1975–76), De Beers Botswana Mining Co. Ltd 1975–76, Bangwato Concessions Ltd 1975–76, BCL Sales Ltd 1975–76, Bank of Botswana 1975–76 (Gov. 1980–81); Gov. IMF 1981–82; Perm. Sec. to Pres. of Botswana 1982–89, Minister of Finance and Devt Planning 1989–98, Vice-Pres. 1992–98; Pres. of Botswana 1998–2008; UN Sec.-Gen.'s Special Envoy for Climate Change 2008–; Pres. Botswana Soc., Botswana Soc. of the Deaf; mem. Jt Devt Cttee of World Bank and IMF on the transfer of real resources to developing countries 1992–, Kalahari Conservation Soc., Commonwealth Parl. Assoc., Parliamentarians for Global Action, Global Coalition for Africa; Rep., Commonwealth Fund for Tech. Co-operation 1971–; est. Champions for an HIV-Free Generation; Hon. Fellowship, Botswana Inst. of Bankers 1999; Officier, Ordre Nat. Côte d'Ivoire 1979, Mali 1997, Presidential Order of Honour of Botswana 1989, Grand Cross, Légion d'honneur 2008; Hon. LLD (Botswana) 1998; Achievement Awards for AIDS Leadership (USA 2000, Gaborone 2001), Nat. Leadership Award, Africa-America Inst. 2002, Mo Ibrahim Prize 2008. *Leisure interests:* reading, tennis, music. *Address:* United Nations, New York, NY 10017, USA (office). *Telephone:* (212) 963-1234 (office). *Fax:* (212) 963-4879 (office). *Website:* www.un.org (office).

MOGAHED, Dalia, BEng, MBA; American (b. Egyptian) social scientist; *Executive Director, Gallup Center for Muslim Studies*; b. 1974, Cairo; m.; two s.; ed Univ. of Wisconsin, Univ. of Pittsburgh; began career as marketing products researcher for Procter & Gamble; currently Sr Analyst, Gallup Org. and Exec. Dir Gallup Center for Muslim Studies, New York; mem. Pres. Obama's Advisory Council on Faith-Based and Neighborhood Partnerships 2009–; fmr Dir Muslim–West Facts Initiative; mem. Women in Int. Security, Project on US Engagement with Global Muslim Community, Brookings Inst. Crisis in the Middle East Task Force. *Publications:* Who Speaks for Islam? What a Billion Muslims Really Think (with John Esposito) 2008; articles in numerous journals and newspapers including The Wall Street Journal, Harvard International Review, Middle East Policy. *Address:* Gallup Center for Muslim Studies, 1251 Avenue of the Americas, Suite 2350, New York, NY 10020-1104, USA (office). *Telephone:* (212) 548-2940 (office). *Fax:* (212) 548-2950 (office). *Website:* www.gallup.com/se/127907/Gallup-Center-Muslim-Studies.aspx (office).

MOGG, John Frederick; British civil servant and fmr EU official; *Chairman, Ofgem;* b. 5 Oct. 1943, Brighton; s. of Thomas W. Mogg and Cora M. Mogg; m. Anne Smith 1967; one d. one s.; ed Univ. of Birmingham; fmrly with Rediffusion group; First Sec. UK Perm. Representation at EC, Brussels 1979–82; various appointments in UK civil service 1982–89; Deputy Head, European Secr. Cabinet Office 1989–90; Deputy Dir-Gen. Internal Market and Industrial Affairs, European Comm. 1990–93, Dir-Gen. Internal Market (fmrly DG XV) Directorate-Gen. 1993–2002; mem. Gas and Electricity Markets Authority 2003; Chair. (non-exec.) Ofgem 2003–. *Address:* Ofgem, 9, Millbank, London, SW1P 3GE, England (office). *Telephone:* (20) 7901-7000 (office). *Fax:* (20) 7901-7066 (office). *E-mail:* enquiries@energywatch.org.uk (office). *Website:* www.ofgem.gov.uk (office).

MOGGACH, Deborah, BA, DipEd, FRSL; British writer; b. 28 June 1948, London, England; d. of Richard Hough and Helen Charlotte Hough; m. Anthony Moggach 1971 (divorced); one s. one d.; partner Mel Calman 1984 (died 1994); partner Csaba Pasztor 1994–2001; ed Camden School for Girls, Queen's Coll., London, Univs of Bristol and London; has lived in Pakistan and USA; trained as a teacher before going to work at Oxford University Press; has adapted many of her novels as TV dramas and has also written several film scripts; Chair. Soc. of Authors 1999–2001; mem. PEN; Hon. DLitt (Bristol) 2005. *Play:* Double Take. *Screenplay:* Pride and Prejudice 2005. *Television:* dramas: To Have and To Hold (mini-series) 1986, Stolen 1990, Goggle-Eyes (adaptation) (Writers' Guild Award for Best Adapted TV Serial) 1993, Seesaw (adaptation) 1998, Close Relations (adaptation) 1998, Love in a Cold Climate (adaptation) 2001, Final Demand (adaptation) 2003, The Diary of Anne Frank 2008. *Publications:* novels: You Must Be Sisters 1978, Close to Home 1979, A Quiet Drink 1980, Hot Water Man 1982, Porky 1983, To Have and To Hold 1986, Driving in the Dark 1988, Stolen 1990, The Stand-in 1991, The Ex-Wives 1993, Seesaw 1996, Close Relations 1997, Tulip Fever 1999, Final Demand 2001, These Foolish Things (adapted into film The Best Exotic Marigold Hotel 2012) 2004, In the Dark 2007, Heartbreak Hotel 2012; short stories: Smile and Other Stories 1987, Ta for the Memories 1994, Changing Babies and Other Stories 1995. *Leisure interests:* swimming in rivers, walking round cities. *Address:* c/o Curtis Brown Group Ltd, Haymarket House, 28–29 Haymarket, London, SW1Y 4SP, England (office). *Telephone:* (20) 7393-4400 (office). *Fax:* (20) 7393-4401 (office). *E-mail:* cb@curtisbrown.co.uk (office). *Website:* www.curtisbrown.co.uk (office).

MOGGIE, Datuk Leo, MA, MBA; Malaysian politician; b. 1 Oct. 1941, Kanowit, Sarawak; ed Univs of Otago and Pennsylvania State Univ.; Dist Officer, Kapit, Sarawak 1966–68; Dir Borneo Literature Bureau, Kuching, Sarawak 1968–69; attached to Office of Chief Minister, Kuching 1969–72; Deputy Gen. Man. Borneo Devt Corpn Kuching 1973–74; elected to Sarawak State Legis. Ass. and Parl.; Sec.-Gen. Sarawak Nat. Party (SNAP) 1976; Minister of Welfare Services, State Govt of Sarawak 1976–77, of Local Govt 1977–78; Minister of Energy, Telecommunications and Posts 1978–89, of Works and Public Utilities 1989–90, of Public Works 1990–95. *Address:* c/o Ministry of Public Works, Jalan Sultan Salahuddin, 50580 Kuala Lumpur, Malaysia.

MOGHERINI, Federica; Italian politician; *Minister of Foreign Affairs;* b. 1973, Rome; m.; two c.; ed Univ. La Sapienza, Rome; mem. Chamber of Deputies (Parl.) for Veneto I 2008–; mem. Italian Del. to Council of Europe; Pres. Italian Del. to NATO Parl. Ass. 2013; Minister of Foreign Affairs 2014–; mem. Istituto Affari Internazionali, Consiglio per le relazioni fra Italia e Stati Uniti; Fellow German Marshall Fund of the USA; fmr Dir European Youth Forum; fmr Vice-Pres. European Community Org. of Socialist Youth (Ecosy); mem. Partito Democratico

(PD); mem. Nat. Secr. 2007–08, 2009, 2013–. *Address:* Ministry of Foreign Affairs, Piazzale della Farnesina 1, 00194 Rome, Italy (office). *Telephone:* (06) 36911 (office). *Fax:* (06) 3236210 (office). *E-mail:* ministero.affariesteri@cert.esteri.it (office). *Website:* www.esteri.it (office).

MOGWE, Archibald Mooketsa, MBE, BA, PMS, PH; Botswana politician, diplomatist and teacher; b. 29 Aug. 1921, Kanye; s. of Rev. Morutwana T. Mogwe and Mary (née Leepo) Mogwe; m. Lena Mosele Senakhomo 1953; one s. two d.; ed schools in Bechuanaland Protectorate, teacher training in S Africa, Univs of Reading and Oxford; teacher 1944–57; Educ. Officer 1957–64; transferred to Secr. 1964, Perm. Sec. 1966; worked in Foreign Office 1966–, Sr Perm. Sec., Sec. to Cabinet and Head of Public Service 1968–74; Minister of Foreign Affairs 1974–84, of Mineral Resources and Water Affairs 1984–89, 1990–94; Amb. to USA 1996–2002. *Leisure interests:* soccer, classical music, shooting. *Address:* c/o Ministry of Foreign Affairs and International Co-operation, Government Enclave, Private Bag 00368, Gaborone, Botswana. *E-mail:* mofaic-admin@lists.gov.bw.

MOHAMAD, Goenawan; Indonesian poet, writer and journalist; b. 29 July 1941, Batang, Cen. Java; leader of Tempo magazine in Indonesia, forcibly closed twice by Suharto New Order admin; est. Inst. for Studies in the Free Flow of Information; mem. Int. Advisory Bd ARTICLE 19 human rights group; several awards for journalism, including Int. Ed. of the Year, World Press Review 1999, Dan David Prize 2006. *Publications include:* Potret Seorang Penyair Muda Sebagai Si Malin Kundang (The Portrait of A Young Poet as Malin Kundang) 1972, Seks, Sastra, Kita (Sex, Literature, Us) 1980, Pariksit dan Interlude 2001, Setelah Revolusi Tak Ada Lagi (Once the Revolution No Longer Exists) 2001, Kata, Waktu (Word, Time) 2001. *Address:* Tempo Interaktif, Kebayoran Center Blok A11–A15, Jl. Kebayoran Baru – Mayestik, Jakarta 12440, Indonesia (office). *Telephone:* (21) 725-5625 (office). *Fax:* (21) 720-6995 (office). *E-mail:* iklannews@tempo.co.id (office). *Website:* www.tempointeractive.com (office).

MOHAMED, Abdoulkader Kamil, MS; Djibouti water engineer, government official and politician; *Prime Minister;* b. 1951, Souali, Obock; ed Water Inst., Univ. of Limoges; Interim Dir Office National des Eaux de Djibouti (public water co.) 1978–79, Dir Gen. 1983–2005; Minister of Agric., Livestock and Water Resources 2005–11, Minister of Defence 2011–13, Prime Minister 2013–; mem. Assemblée Nationale 2008–; mem. Rassemblement populaire pour le progrès (in charge of party discipline). *Address:* Office of the Prime Minister, BP 2086, Djibouti (office). *Telephone:* 21351494 (office). *Fax:* 21355049 (office). *Website:* www.primature.dj (office).

MOHAMED, Amina C., LLM; Somali lawyer, diplomatist, international organization official and politician; *Secretary for Foreign Affairs;* b. 5 Oct. 1961, Kenya; m. Khalid Ahmed; two c.; ed Univ. of Kiev, Ukraine, Kenya School of Law, Univ. of Oxford, UK; began career as legal officer at Kenyan Ministry of Local Govt 1985; Legal Adviser, Ministry of Foreign Affairs 1986–90; Legal Adviser, Kenyan Mission to UN, Geneva 1990–93, Amb. and Perm. Rep. 2000–06; Chair., Int. Org. for Migration, London 2002–03; Chair., Gen. Council, WTO 2005–06; Dir Europe and Commonwealth Countries and Dir for Diaspora matters 2006–07, Chair. Task Force Sub-Cttee on Strengthening and Restructuring, Dept of Foreign Trade and Econ. Affairs; Perm. Sec., Kenyan Ministry of Justice, Nat. Cohesion and Constitutional Affairs 2008–11; Pres. UN Conf. on Transnational Crime, Vienna 2010–11; Asst Sec.-Gen. and Deputy Exec. Dir, UNEP 2011–13; Sec. (Minister) for Foreign Affairs 2013–; mem. Advisory Council, Life and Peace Inst., Advisory Bd, Strathmore Law School; Int. mem. World Econ. Forum Global Agenda Council on the Arctic; Life mem. Red Cross Soc.; UNITAR Fellow, Chief of the Order of the Burning Spear (Kenya), Kt, Order of the Star of Italian Solidarity. *Address:* Ministry of Foreign Affairs, Old Treasury Building, Harambee Avenue, PO Box 30551, 00100 Nairobi, Kenya (office). *Telephone:* (20) 318888 (office). *Fax:* (20) 240066 (office). *E-mail:* press@mfa.go.ke (office). *Website:* www.mfa.go.ke (office); www.aminamohamed.org.

MOHAMED, Caabi el Yachroutou; Comoran politician; Minister of Finance 1993–94; Prime Minister of Comoros April–Oct. 1995; Interim Pres. 1995–96; Vice-President with responsibility for Finance, the Budget, the Economy, Foreign Trade, Investments and Privatizations –2006; mem. Rally for Democracy and Renewal. *Address:* c/o Ministry of Finance, the Budget and Privatization, BP 324, Moroni, The Comoros.

MOHAMED, Mohamed Abdullahi, BA, MA; Somali/American diplomatist and politician; b. 1962, Mogadishu; m. Zeinab Moallim; two s. two d.; ed State Univ. of New York at Buffalo, USA; worked at Ministry of Foreign Affairs, Mogadishu, First Sec., Embassy in Washington, DC 1985–88; Commr and Finance Chair. Buffalo Municipal Housing Authority 1994–97, also case man. for lead abatement program 1995–99; Minority Business Co-ordinator, Erie Co. Div., US Equal Employment Opportunity Admin 2000–02; Commr for Equal Employment, New York State Dept of Transportation, Buffalo 2002–10; Prime Minister of Somalia 2010–11 (resgnd); fmr Chair. Buffalo Immigrant and Refugee Empowerment Coalition; fmr Pres. American Diversity of Buffalo; fmr teacher, Erie Community Coll. *Address:* c/o Office of the Prime Minister, 1 Villa Somalia, 2525 Mogadishu, Somalia.

MOHAMEDOU, Mohamed Mahmoud Ould, PhD; Mauritanian academic and politician; ed Univ. Panthéon-Sorbonne, Paris, City Univ. of New York; fmr Research Dir Int. Council on Human Rights, Geneva; fmr Prof. of Political Science, Harvard Univ., Assoc. Dir Program on Humanitarian Policy and Conflict Research, Harvard School of Public Health; Minister of Foreign Affairs and Co-operation 2008–09. *Publications:* Societal Transition to Democracy in Mauritania 1995, Iraq and the Second Gulf War, State-Building and Regime Security 1998, Contre-Croisade: Origines et Conséquences du 11 Septembre 2004. *Address:* c/o Ministry of Foreign Affairs and Co-operation, BP 230, Nouakchott, Mauritania (office).

MOHAMMAD, Haji Din; Afghan provincial governor and fmr rebel leader; s. of Amanullah Khan Jabbarkhail; m.; one s. (deceased); fmr mem. Yunus Khalis faction, Hizb-i Islami; fmr Mujahidin commdr; Minister of Nat. Security in Afghanistan's Interim Govt in Exile during the 1990s and as Minister of Educ. in the Mujahideen Govt est. after collapse of Communist govt; also served as Deputy Prime Minister in the same period, resgnd because of infighting among rival factions of Ahmad Shah Massoud and Gulbuddin Hekmatyar; during the Taliban era, lived in exile and later helped Abdul Haq in his efforts to establish a broad-based post-Taliban govt; Gov. Nangarhar Prov. 2002–04, Kabul Prov. 2005–09. *Address:* c/o Office of the Governor, Kabul, Afghanistan.

MOHAMMAD HUSSEINI, Khial; Afghan politician; Deputy Gov. of Ghazni Prov. –2004, Gov. 2004–05; lawmaker representing Ghazni Prov. in Afghan Parl. 2005–. *Address:* Wolasi Jirga (House of Representatives), Kabul, Afghanistan (office).

MOHAMMED, Amina J.; Nigerian UN official; *Special Adviser of the Secretary-General on Post-2015 Development Planning, United Nations;* b. 1961, Rosterman; d. of the late Djibril Mohammed; m.; four c.; ed Butere Girls High School; worked with Archcon Nigeria in association with Norman and Dawbarn UK 1981–91; Founder-Dir Afri-Projects Consortium 1991–2001; Coordinator of Task Force on Gender and Education, UN Millennium Project 2002–05; Sr Special Asst to Pres. of Nigeria on Millennium Devt Goals 2005–11; Special Adviser of the Sec.-Gen. on Post-2015 Devt Planning, UN 2012–; Founder-CEO Centre for Devt Policy Solutions; Chair. Advisory Bd, UNESCO Global Monitoring Report on Educ.; Adjunct Prof., Columbia Univ., New York; mem. Bd of Govs, International Devt Research Centre, Canada; serves on numerous int. advisory panels and bds, including those of Global Devt Program, Bill and Melinda Gates Foundation, UN Sec.-Gen.'s Global Sustainability Panel, African Population and Health Research Centre; Nat. Honours Award of the Order of the Fed. Repub. 2006; inducted into Nigerian Women's Hall of Fame 2007. *Address:* Office of the Secretary General, United Nations, New York, NY 10017, USA (office). *Telephone:* (212) 963-1234 (office). *Fax:* (212) 963-4879 (office). *E-mail:* kara.alaimo@post2015hlp.org (office). *Website:* www.un.org/sg (office); www.post2015hlp.org (office).

MOHAMMED, Bello Haliru; Nigerian veterinarian and politician; b. 9 Oct. 1945, Kebbi State; m.; six c.; ed Government Coll. (now Barewa Coll.), Zaria, Ahmadu Bello Univ.; fmr Lecturer, Ahmadu Bello Univ., Zaria; Commr for Agric., Sokoto State 1977, later Commr for Educ.; joined Great Nigeria People's Party (GNPP) 1979, GNPP Sec. for Sokoto State 1979–83; several years in private sector as Man. Dir Alpha & Beta Merchants Ltd (general merchandise co.); fmr Asst Gen. Man., later Gen. Man., Rima River Basin and Rural Devt Authority (govt agency); Comptroller Gen., Nigerian Customs Service 1988–94; Commr, Revenue Mobilization Allocation and Fiscal Comm. 1999; Minister of Communications 2001–03; Minister of Defence 2011–12; fmr Chair. Nigerian Railway Corpn; Founding mem. Democratic Party of Nigeria (DPN); Founding mem. People's Democratic Party (PDP), Nat. PDP Vice-Chair. for NW Zone 2004–08, Deputy Nat. Chair. 2008–11, Acting Nat. Chair. 2011; Fellow, Coll. of Veterinary Surgeons of Nigeria; Diamond Nigerian Telecoms Award 2008. *Address:* c/o Ministry of Defence, Ship House, Central Area, Abuja, Nigeria (office).

MOHAQQEQ, Haji Mohammad; Afghan politician and fmr rebel leader; *Founder and Leader, Hizb-i Wahdat-i Islami Mardum-i Afghanistan (People's Islamic Unity Party of Afghanistan);* b. Charkent Dist, Balkh Prov.; ed Mazar-e-Sharif; Chair. Political Cttee and Admin. of Northern Areas, Hizb-i-Wahdat-i Islami (Islamic Unity Party); fmr Minister of the Interior; led several attacks against Taliban Govt; Minister of Planning, Interim Govt 2001–04; presidential cand. 2004; Founder and Leader Hizb-i Wahdat-i Islami Mardum-i Afghanistan (People's Islamic Unity Party of Afghanistan); Deputy Chair. Jabahai Tafahim Millie (Nat. Understanding Front); mem. Hazara community. *Address:* Hizb-i Wahdat-i Islami Mardum-i Afghanistan, House 3, Mohammadia St, Tapa-i-Salaam, Karte Sakhi, Kabul, Afghanistan (office).

MOHIELDIN, Mahmoud, BS, MS, PhD; Egyptian economist, academic, government official and international organization official; *Special Envoy of the World Bank President on Millennium Development Goals;* b. 15 Jan. 1965; ed Cairo Univ., Univs of Warwick, York, UK; Asst. Dept of Econs, Cairo Univ. 1986–91, Asst Lecturer 1991–95, Lecturer in Financial Econs 1995–2001, Assoc. Prof. in Financial Econs 2001–06, Prof. of Econs 2006–; held several positions in Egyptian govt, including Econ. Adviser to Minister of State for Econ. Affairs, Sr Econ. Adviser to Minister of Economy and Foreign Trade, Sr Adviser to Minister of Foreign Trade; Minister of Investment 2004–10, also served as Gov. of Egypt to World Bank, Alt. Gov. to ADB, Alt. Gov. Islamic Development Bank; Man. Dir World Bank Group, Washington, DC 2010–12; Special Envoy of the World Bank Pres. on Millennium Development Goals 2013–; fmr mem. Bd of Dirs Central Bank of Egypt; mem. Bd of Trustees, British Univ. of Egypt; mem. Centre of European Studies, Arab Soc. for Econ. Research, Comm. on Growth and Devt. *Publications include:* Financial Development in Emerging Markets (co-ed). *Address:* World Bank Group, 1818 H Street, NW, Washington, DC 20433, USA (office). *Telephone:* (202) 473-1000 (office). *Fax:* (202) 477-6391 (office). *Website:* www.worldbank.org (office).

MOHILYOV, Maj.-Gen. Anatoliy Volodymyrovych; Ukrainian police officer and government official; b. 6 April 1955, Petropavlovsk-Kamchatskii, Kamchatka Oblast (now Kamchatka Krai), Russian SFSR, USSR; ed Slovyansk Pedagogical Inst., Donetsk, Ukrainian Acad. of Internal Affairs; mil. service in USSR 1979–81; physics teacher, Slovyansk secondary school No. 18, Donetsk 1981–82; joined Ministry of Internal Affairs as Dist Militia Officer for Minor Matters, Slovyansk Dist 1982, becoming Officer, Criminal Investigation Div., Head of Dist Militia Officers Unit, later Deputy Head of Operations, Slovyansk Dist; Sr Special Operative Authorized Officer, Inner Security Div. 1992–95, Artemivsk City Dept 1995–2000, Makiyivka City Dept 2000–05; Head of Internal Affairs Dept, Autonomous Repub. of Crimea 2007, later Deputy Minister and Head of Crimean Police, Chair. Council of Ministers (Prime Minister) 2011–14 (dismissed by Supreme Council amid ongoing protests in the region); Adviser to Minister of Internal Affairs of Ukraine 2007–10, Minister of Internal Affairs 2010–11. *Address:* c/o Council of Ministers, 95005 Crimea, Simferopol, ul. Kirova 13, Ukraine.

MOHL, Andrew, BEc (Hons); Australian financial services executive; *Chairman, Federal Government Export Finance and Insurance Corporation;* b. 1955; ed Monash Univ.; began career at Reserve Bank of Australia 1978, roles included Sr Economist and Deputy Head of Research, seconded to Fed. Reserve Bank of New York 1983–84; with ANZ Banking Group 1986–96, roles included Sr Economist, Group Chief Economist, Div. Chief Man. ANZ Retail Banking and Man. Dir ANZ

Funds Man.; Gen. Man. of Retail Distribution, AMP Financial Services 1996–99, Man. Dir AMP Asset Man., AMP Australian Financial Services 1999–2002, CEO AMP Group Ltd 2002–07, undertook a major restructuring of the group including demerger of AMP into Australian and UK-based cos; Dir AMP Foundation –2013, Commonwealth Bank of Australia 2008–; Chair. and Ind. non-exec. mem. Fed. Govt Export Finance and Insurance Corpn 2008–; mem. Advisory Council, Australian School of Business, Corp. Council, European Australian Business Council, Review Panel Selection Bd of the Banking Finance Oath; mem. Bd of Govs, Cttee for Econ. Devt of Australia; exec. coach to CEOs. *Address:* Federal Government Export Finance and Insurance Corporation, Level 10 Export House, 22 Pitt Street, Sydney, NSW 2000, Australia (office). *Telephone:* (2) 8273-5333 (office). *Fax:* (2) 9251-3851 (office). *E-mail:* info@efic.gov.au (office). *Website:* www.efic.gov.au (office).

MÖHLER, Hanns, BSc, MSc, PhD; German pharmacologist and academic; *Professor of Pharmacology, Eidgenössische Technische Hochschule Zürich and University of Zurich;* b. 8 March 1940, Ehingen; m.; two c.; ed Univs of Bonn, Tübingen and Freiburg; research work at Michigan State Univ., USA and MRC Labs, London, UK; apptd Vice-Dir (Science) Research Dept, Hoffmann-La Roche, Basel; qualified as Univ. Lecturer at Univ. of Freiburg, later promoted to Assoc. Prof.; Prof. of Pharmacology, Dept of Chem. and Applied Biosciences, ETH Zürich 1989–, Faculty of Medicine, Univ. of Zurich 1989–, Head of Inst. of Pharmacology; Co-ed. of numerous journals; mem. European Acad. of Sciences 1991–; Fellow, Collegium Helveticum 2004–; Golden Kraepelin Medal, German Inst. for Psychiatric Research 2003. *Publications:* a textbook on biochemistry, Pharmacology of GABA and Glycine Neurotransmission (Handbook of Experimental Pharmacology) 2000, The GABA Receptors (with by S. J. Enna) 2007; numerous scientific papers in professional journals on the neurobiology of the brain and molecular pharmacology of the action of drugs. *Address:* Institute of Pharmacology and Toxicology, Irchel Campus Y17, University of Zurich, Winterthurerstrasse 190, 8057 Zurich, Switzerland (office). *Telephone:* (44) 635-59-11 (office). *E-mail:* mohler@pharma.uzh.ch (office). *Website:* www.pharma.uzh.ch (office).

MOHN, Christoph; German media industry executive; *Chairman of the Supervisory Board, Bertelsmann SE & Co. KGaA;* b. 6 July 1965, Stuttgart; s. of Reinhard Mohn; great-great-grand s. of Carl Bertelsmann (f. Bertelsmann AG 1835); ed Westfälische Wilhelms-Universität; fmr intern, Bantam Doubleday Dell; with Bertelsmann Music Group (BMG), Hong Kong and New York, USA 1991–94; specialist in electronics and telecommunications, McKinsey & Co. Germany 1994–96; Vice-Pres. Telemedia (subsidiary of Bertelsmann AG) 1996–97; CEO Lycos Europe NV 1997–2009; mem. Supervisory Bd, Bertelsmann SE & Co. KGaA 2006–, Chair. 2013–; Chair. Exec. Bd Reinhard Mohn Foundation; Man. Dir Christoph Mohn Internet Holding GmbH. *Address:* Bertelsmann, Carl-Bertelsmann-Strasse 270, 33311 Gütersloh, Germany (office). *Telephone:* (5241) 80-0 (office). *Fax:* (5241) 80-62321 (office). *Website:* www.bertelsmann.com (office).

MOHN, Elisabeth (Liz); German media industry executive; *Chairwoman of the Executive Board, Bertelsmann Verwaltungsgesellschaft mbH;* b. 21 June 1941, Wiedenbrück; m. Reinhard Mohn 1982; three c.; joined Bertelsmann group's book club unit 1958, Chief Exec. Bertelsmann Admin Co. 2002–; Man. Dir and mem. Supervisory Bd Bertelsmann Trust 2002–, currently Chair. Exec. Bd Bertelsmann Verwaltungsgesellschaft, Vice-Chair. Exec. Bd Bertelsmann Stiftung, Deputy Chair. Bertelsmann Foundation; Founder and Pres. Assistance for Stroke Victims Foundation 1993–; f. Liz Mohn Foundation for Culture and Music 2005; Pres. Neue Stimmen (singing competition) 1987–; mem. European Acad. of Sciences, Salzburg 1997–, Club of Rome 1999–; Dr hc (Univ. of Tel-Aviv) 2005; Vernon A. Walters Award, Atlantik-Brucke 2008. *Address:* Bertelsmann AG, Carl-Bertelsmann-Strasse 270, 33311, Gütersloh, Germany. *Telephone:* (5241) 80-22 01 (office). *Fax:* (5241) 73611 (office). *E-mail:* liz.mohn@bertelsmann.de (office). *Website:* www.bertelsmann.com (office).

MOHOHLO, Linah Kelebogile, BEcons, MA; Botswana economist and central banker; *Governor, Bank of Botswana;* ed George Washington Univ., USA and Univ. of Exeter, UK; joined Bank of Botswana 1976, served in various positions including Deputy Dir of Research 1988, Dir Financial Markets Dept 1989, Deputy Gov. 1997–99, Gov. 1999–; worked with African Dept and Monetary and Exchange Affairs Dept, IMF, Washington, DC 1993–97; fmr Commr, Comm. of Africa; mem. Africa Emerging Markets Forum, Africa Progress Panel; mem. Advisory Bd Diamond Empowerment Fund; Cen. Bank Gov. of the Year for Africa and Middle East, Financial Times magazine 2001, Cen. Bank Gov. of the Year for Sub-Saharan Africa, Euromoney 2001, Presidential Order of Honour 2004, Africa's Banking Regulator of the Year 2007; apptd Eminent Person by UN Sec.-Gen. 2001. *Address:* Bank of Botswana, PO Box 712, Private Bag 154, 17938 Khama Crescent, Gaborone, Botswana (office). *Telephone:* 3606000 (office). *Fax:* 3913890 (office). *E-mail:* selwej@bob.bw (office). *Website:* www.bankofbotswana.bw (office).

MOHORITA, Vasil; Czech politician and business executive; *Head of External Relations, Zbrojovka;* b. 19 Sept. 1952, Prague; s. of Vasil Mohorita and Ludmila Mohoritová; m. Vlasta Mohoritová 1976; one s. one d.; ed Komsomol Coll., Moscow and CP of Czechoslovakia (CPCZ) Political Coll., Prague; joined CP of Czechoslovakia (Komunistická strana Československa—KSČ) 1970, mem. Cen. Cttee 1988–90, First Sec. Cen. Cttee 1989–90; Chair. Youth Union's Czechoslovak Cen. Cttee 1987–89; mem. Czechoslovak Nat. Front Presidium 1987; Deputy, Czechoslovak Nat. Council 1986–90; mem. Presidium Fed. Ass. Jan.–Oct. 1990, Deputy to Fed. Ass. House of People 1990–92; Chair. Communist Deputies Club Jan.–Nov. 1990; agent for Valemo, Parfia, Jamiko, CIS Group; Chair. Bd of Supervisors E.R. Tradings; Head of Sales, Frut Ovo (pvt. co.); mem. Party of Democratic Left 1993–97; Chair. Party of Democratic Socialism 1997–98; Head of External Relations, Zbrojovka, Brno 2000–. *Publications:* numerous articles. *Leisure interests:* reading historical and political literature, playing the guitar, basketball, tennis. *Address:* Zbrojovka, Lazaretni 7, 615 00, Brno, Czech Republic. *Website:* www.zbrojovkabrno.com.

MOHSENI, Saad; Afghan media executive; *Chairman, Moby Media Group;* b. 23 April 1966, London, UK; s. of Yassin Mohseni and Safia Mohseni; m. 1st (divorced), one d.; m. 2nd (divorced), two c.; m. 3rd Sarah Takesh; childhood in exile with family in Australia; began career with equities and corp. finance div. of Australian investment banking firm 1985; f. trading co. in Tashkent, Uzbekistan 1995; head of investment banking, Tricom Equities, Australia 1999; moved to Kabul following fall of Taliban, f. Moby Capital (now Moby Media Group), ventures include Arman Radio (Afghanistan's first privately-owned ind. FM radio station) 2003, Tolo TV network 2004, also owns music-recording co., advertising agency, TV and film production co., Afghan Scene magazine and two internet cafés; co-f. Farsi 1 TV channel (with Rupert Murdoch). *Address:* Moby Media Group, House #3, Street #12, Wazir Akbar Khan, PO Box 225, Kabul 1, Afghanistan (office). *Telephone:* (799) 321010 (office). *Fax:* (866) 2070812 (office). *E-mail:* info@mobygroup.com (office). *Website:* mobygroup.com (office).

MOHSIN, Selina; Bangladeshi educationalist, academic and diplomatist; ed various degrees and postgraduate diplomas and sr officer training from univs and int. insts in USA, France and UK; joined Educ. Service of the then East Pakistan 1970; Chief Educ. Officer, Commonwealth Secr., London, UK 1990s; Sr Educ. Adviser to Programme Support Unit, Canadian Int. Devt Agency –2008; High Commr to the Maldives 2008–10. *Address:* Ministry of Foreign Affairs, Segunbagicha, Dhaka 1000, Bangladesh (office); M. Dhaannaage, Third Floor, Orchid Magu, Malé, Maldives (home). *Telephone:* (2) 9562862 (office). *Fax:* (2) 9555283 (office). *E-mail:* info@mofabd.org (office). *Website:* www.mofa.gov.bd (office).

MOHTASHAMI, Ali Akbar, DTheol; Iranian politician; b. 30 Aug. 1946, Tehran; s. of Seyed Hossein and Fatemeh Mohtashami; m. Fatemeh Mohtashami 1968; two s. five d.; studied theology in Iran and Iraq; mil. training in Palestinian camps, Lebanon; went to Paris with Ayatollah Khomeini 1978; returned to Iran and took part in overthrow of monarchy 1979; mem. political advisory office of Ayatollah Khomeini; Dir of Ayatollah's representative delegation in Foundation of the Oppressed 1980; mem. IRIB Supervisory Council 1980–81; Amb. to Syria 1981–85; a founder of Hezbollah in Lebanon; Minister of the Interior 1985; mem. Parl. 1989–91; Chair. Parl. Cttee on Defence; Sec.-Gen. IPU Group of Iran (Chair. 1989–91); mem. Cttee to Protect the Islamic Revolution of Palestine, Cen. Council of Combatant Clergy; Sec.-Gen. of Int. Conf. on Intifada; Deputy Chair. Bd of Trustees Qods Inst.; Special Adviser to Pres. Mohammad Khatami; Man. Bayan newspaper (banned June 2000); currently Deputy to Majlis. *Publications include:* Plurality, From Iran to Iran (Memoirs) 1965–79. *Leisure interests:* study, sport (especially mountaineering and swimming). *Address:* General Secretariat of International Conference on Palestinian Intifada, 11 Khorshid Street, Pastor Avenue, Tehran (office); Islamic Consultative Assembly, Tehran (office); 11, Adib-ol-Mamalek Street, Ray Street, Tehran, Iran (home). *Telephone:* (21) 361892 (home).

MOI, Daniel Arap; Kenyan politician; b. 1924, Sacho, Baringo district; m. Lena Moi (died 2004); seven c.; ed African Mission School, Kabartonjo A.I.M. School and Govt African School, Kapsabet; teacher 1945–57; Head Teacher, Govt African School, Kabarnet 1946–48, 1955–57, teacher Tambach Teacher Training School, Kabarnet 1948–54; African Rep. mem., Legis. Council 1957–63; Chair. Kenya African Democratic Union (KADU) 1960–61; mem. House of Reps 1961–; Parl. Sec., Ministry of Educ. April–Dec. 1961; Minister of Educ. 1961–62, Local Govt 1962–64, Home Affairs 1964–67; Vice-Pres. of Kenya 1967–78, concurrently Minister of Home Affairs; Pres. of Kenya and C-in-C of the Armed Forces 1978–2002; Minister of Defence 1979–2002; Chair. KANU –2003; Chair. OAU 1981–82; mem. Rift Valley Educ. Bd, Kalenjin Language Cttee; Chair. Rift Valley Provincial Court; Kt of Grace, Order of St John 1980. *Address:* c/o Office of the President, Harambee House, Harambee Avenue, PO Box 30510, Nairobi, Kenya.

MOILY, Moodbidri Veerappa, BA, BL; Indian lawyer and politician; *Minister of Petroleum and Natural Gas;* b. 12 Jan. 1940, Marpadi Village, Moodibidri, Dakshina Kannada Dist, Karnataka; m. Malathi Moily; four c.; ed Govt Coll., Univ. Law Coll.; elected to Karnataka State Legis. Ass. from Udupi Dist constituency; Minister for Small-Scale Industries, Govt of Karnataka 1974–77, for Finance and Planning 1980–82; Leader of Opposition, Karnataka Ass. 1983–85; Minister for Law, Youth Service, Culture, Information, Parl. Affairs and Educ., Govt of Karnataka 1989–92; Chief Minister of Karnataka 1992–94; Chair. Tax Reforms Comm. 2000–02, Revenue Reforms Comm. 2002–04, Second Admin. Reform Comm. of India; Chair. Oversight Cttee apptd by Govt of India for Implementation of Reservations for Other Backward Classes (OBC) in cen. educational insts 2006–09; Minister of Law and Justice 2009–11, of Corp. Affairs 2011–12, of Power July–Oct. 2012, of Petroleum and Natural Gas 2012–; Pres. Media Wing of the Congress and Head Spokesperson –2009; MP for Chikkaballapur 2009–; apptd to various cttees by Indira Gandhi, one of which led to setting up of Nat. Bank for Agric. and Rural Devt (NABARD); Pnr, Moily Assocs law firm; practised law in courts of Karkala, Mangalore, High Court in Bangalore and at Supreme Court of India; regular columnist for print and electronic media, including The Hindu, Deccan Herald, Samyukta Karnataka; Dr hc (Mangalore Univ.) 2009, (Russian Acad.); Ameen Sadbhavana Award 2000, Devaraj Urs Prashasthi 2001, Aryabhatta Award 2001, Dr B.R Ambedkar Award 2002. *Publications include:* Sri Ramayana Mahanveshanam (epic poem) Vols I–IV 2001–04 (originally published in Kannada, now being translated into Hindi), Musings on India (collection of articles) 2001, Suligali, Sagardeepa, Kotta and Thembare (anthropological novels originally written in Kannada, now translated into Hindi, English and Tamil; Kotta has been telecast as a tele-film in Kannada and Hindi directed by M. S. Sathyu), Milana, Parajitha and Premavendare (dramas), Halu-Jenu Maththe, Nadeyali Samara and Yakshaprashne (poetry collection), Unleashing India: A Road Map for Agrarian Wealth Creation, Unleashing India: Water- Meeting our Nation's Needs. *Address:* Ministry of Petroleum and Natural Gas, Shastri Bhavan, Dr Rajendra Prasad Road, New Delhi 110 001, India (office). *Telephone:* (11) 23382889 (office). *Fax:* (11) 23382673 (office). *E-mail:* jse.png@nic.in (office). *Website:* www.petroleum.nic.in (office).

MOISEEV, Andrey Sergeyevich; Russian athlete; b. 3 June 1979, Rostov-na-Donu; competes in Modern Pentathlon, including shooting, fencing, swimming, showjumping and 3,000m run; coached by Audrey Tropin; winner Gold Medal (team), World Championships, Moscow 2004; winner Gold Medal (relay), World Championships, Moscow 2004; winner Gold Medal (individual), World Cup, Budapest 2004, Olympic Games, Athens 2004; winner Silver Medal (individual), World Cup Final, Moscow 2001, World Cup, Most 2003; winner Bronze Medal (individual), World Cup, Wahrendorf 2001; winner Bronze Medal (team), World Championships, Street 2001; winner Gold Medal (individual), Olympic Games,

Beijing 2008; mem. Dynamo Rostov Club. *Address:* c/o All-Russia Athletic Federation, 8, Luzhnetskaya nab., Moscow 119871, Russia. *Website:* eng.rusathletics.com.

MOISEIWITSCH, Benjamin Lawrence, PhD, MRIA; British mathematician and academic; *Professor Emeritus of Applied Mathematics, University of Belfast;* b. 6 Dec. 1927, London, England; s. of Jacob Moiseiwitsch and Chana Kotlerman; m. Sheelagh Mary Penrose McKeon 1953; two s. two d.; ed Royal Liberty School, Romford and Univ. Coll., London; Lecturer in Applied Math., Univ. of Belfast 1952–62, Reader in Applied Math. 1962–68, Prof. of Applied Math. 1968–93, Prof. Emer. 1993–, Head, Dept of Applied Math. and Theoretical Physics 1977–89, Dean Faculty of Science 1972–75. *Publications include:* Variational Principles 1966, Integral Equations 1977. *Leisure interest:* music. *Address:* Department of Applied Mathematics and Theoretical Physics, The Queen's University of Belfast, Belfast, BT7 1NN (office); 21 Knockfern Gardens, Belfast, BT4 3LZ, Northern Ireland (home). *Telephone:* (28) 9097-6040 (office); (28) 9065-8332 (home). *Fax:* (28) 9097-6061 (office). *E-mail:* b.moiseiwitsch@qub.ac.uk (office); bmoiseiwitsch@btinternet.com (home). *Website:* www.qub.ac.uk/mp/amtpt (office).

MOÏSI, Dominique; French professor of international relations; *Senior Advisor, Institut français des relations internationales;* b. 21 Oct. 1946, Neuilly-sur-Seine; s. of Jules Moïsi and Charlotte Tabakman; m. Diana Pinto-Moïsi 1977; two s.; ed Lycée Buffon, Paris, Institut d'études politiques, Paris, Faculté de droit de Paris, Harvard Univ., USA; Visiting Lecturer, Hebrew Univ. of Jerusalem 1973–75; Asst Lecturer, Univ. of Paris X 1975–89; Deputy Dir Inst français des relations internationales 1979–2006, Sr Advisor 2006–; Lecturer, Ecole Nationale d'Admin 1980–85, Ecole des hautes études en sciences sociales 1988–; Sec.-Gen. Groupe d'étude et de recherche des problèmes internationaux 1975–78; Assoc. Prof., Johns Hopkins Univ. European Centre, Bologna 1983–84; Visiting Prof., Collège d'Europe, Warsaw, Poland; Ed. Politique étrangère 1983–; Prof., Inst. d'études politiques, Paris; mem. Bd of Dirs Salzburg Seminar, Aspen Inst., Berlin; editorial writer for Financial Times and Die Zeit. *Publications include:* Crises et guerres au XXe siècle: analogies et différences 1981, Le nouveau continent: plaidoyer pour une Europe renaissante (with Jacques Rupnik) 1991, Les cartes de la France à l'heure de la mondialisation (jtly) 2000, Politique étrangère (jtly) 2003, Géopolitique de l'émotion 2008. *Leisure interests:* music, cinema, tennis, skiing. *Address:* Institut français des relations internationales (IFRI), 27 rue de la Procession, 75015 Paris (office); 4 rue Saint-Florentin, 75001 Paris, France (home). *Telephone:* 1-40-61-60-00 (office). *Fax:* 1-40-61-60-60 (office). *E-mail:* moisi@ifri.org (office). *Website:* www.ifri.org (home).

MOISIU, Alfred, DMilSc; Albanian fmr head of state; *Founder and Co-ordinator, Moisiu Foundation;* b. 1 Dec. 1929, Shkodër; s. of Spiro Moisiu; m. (deceased); one s. (deceased) three d.; ed High School of Tirana, mil. eng school in Leningrad (now St Petersburg) and Acad. of Mil. Eng, Moscow, USSR, Defence Acad. of Gen. Staff, Tirana, NATO Mil. Coll. Rome, Italy; participant in Nat. Liberation War 1943–45; platoon commdr, Jt Officers' School, Tirana 1948–49; Instructor, Skanderbeg Mil. Acad., Tirana 1949–51; assigned to Eng Directory, Ministry of Defence 1958–66; Commdr, Pontoon Brigade, Kavaja 1966–71; Head of Eng and Fortification Directory, Ministry of Defence 1971–81; Deputy Minister of Defence (discharged for political reasons) 1981–82; Co. Commdr, Burrel 1982–85; retd 1985–91; Minister of Defence 1991–92, Adviser on Defence 1992–94, Vice-Minister of Defence for Defence Policy 1994–97; Pres. of Albania 2002–07; Pres. Albanian Atlantic Asscn (pro-NATO non-governmental org.) 1994–2002; Founder and Co-ordinator, Moisiu Foundation and Civil Forum 2010–; Freeman of Bajram Curri, of Bari (Italy), of Vlora, of Martanesh Commune, of Lipljan (Kosovo), of Kavaje and Shengjin (Albania); Order of the Red Star, Order for Mil. Services, Skanderbeg Order (Second and Third Class), Hon. mem. (First Class) Kt Grand Cross of the Most Distinguished Order of St Michael (UK) and Order of St George (UK), Order of King Tomislav with Great Band (Croatia), Gold Medal of the League of Prizren (Kosovo), Great Cross of Merit (Poland), Great Order of King Vytautas the Great (Lithuania), Jubilee Medal for 50, 60 and 65 Years of the Victory in the Great Patriotic War 1941–45 (Russia); Dr of Mil. Sciences 1979; Gold Medal, Acad. of Mil. Eng, Moscow, Medal for Mil. Services, Medal of Liberation, Medal of the 10th Army Anniversary. *Publications:* Kosovo Between War and Peace (memoirs, three vols); has published many articles and studies in Albania and abroad on mil. affairs, defence and regional security policy, and about events in Kosovo. *Leisure interests:* scientific, military, historic and art literature. *Address:* Rr. Elbasanit, Pall. Amerikan 2, Nr 207, Tirana (office); Rr. Xhorxh W. Bush, Nd. 17, Hyrja 3, Ap. 1, 1017 Tirana, Albania (home). *Telephone:* (4) 2227757; (4) 2274834. *Fax:* (4) 2227757; (4) 2274834. *E-mail:* alfredmoisiu@yahoo.com. *Website:* www.forumicivil2010.al (office).

MOITINHO DE ALMEIDA, José Carlos de Carvalho, LenD; Portuguese judge (retd); b. 17 March 1936, Lisbon; m. Maria de Lourdes Saraiva De Menezes 1959; one s. one d.; Asst to Public Prosecutor 1963–68; Public Prosecutor, Court of Appeal, Lisbon 1962–72; Chef du Cabinet to Minister of Justice 1972–73; Deputy Attorney-Gen. 1974–79; Dir Office of European Law 1980–86; fmr Judge, Court of Justice of European Union and Pres. Third and Sixth Chambers; Judge, Supreme Court of Portugal 2000–11; Croix de Guerre, Ordre du Mérite (Luxembourg), Ordem de Merito (Portugal). *Publications:* Le contrat d'assurance dans le droit portugais et comparé, La publicité mensongère, Droit communautaire, ordre juridique communautaire, Les libertés fondamentales dans la CEE, Contrato de Seguro, Estudos. *Leisure interests:* swimming, gardening. *Address:* Vivenda Panorama, Av. do Monaco, 2675 Estoril, Portugal (home). *Telephone:* (21) 3218900 (office); (21) 4682997 (home). *Fax:* (21) 4647999 (home). *E-mail:* jcmoitinho@mail.telepac.pt (home).

MOJADDEDI, Sibghatullah; Afghan religious leader and politician; *Leader, Jebha-i-Nejat-i-Melli;* b. c. 1926; ed Al-Azhar Univ., Cairo, Egypt; imprisoned for involvement in plot to assassinate Soviet Prime Minister Nikita Krushchev 1959–64; f. Jami'at Ulamai Mohammadi (Org. of Muslim Clergy) 1972; f. Jebha-i-Nejat-i-Melli Afghanistan (Nat. Liberation Front of Afghanistan) 1979, Leader 1979–; acting Pres. Unity Govt April–June 1992; Head of Govt of Mujaheddin Council, Kabul 1992–94; Speaker, Meshrano Jirga (House of Elders) –2011; Chair. Nat. Comm. for Peace in Afghanistan. *Address:* Jebha-i-Nejat-i-Melli (National Liberation Front), Pashtun, Afghanistan (office).

MOLCHANOV, Vladimir Kyrillovich; Russian journalist and TV presenter; b. 7 Oct. 1950, Moscow; s. of Kyrill Molchanov; m. Consuella Segura; one d.; ed Moscow State Univ.; with Press Agency Novosti 1973–86; observer USSR State Cttee for TV and Radio 1987–91; artistic Dir studio of independent co. REN-TV 1991–, Observer Reuter-TV 1994–; regular appearances in his own TV programmes Before and After Midnight 1987–93, Before and After 1994–, Panorama 2000–, Longer than Age 2000–; academician, Acad. of Russian TV; Corresp. mem. Acad. of Natural Sciences; Prize of Journalists Union as the Best TV Journalist 1990 and other awards. *Publications include:* TV films: Remembrance, I, You, He and She, People and Years, Zone, I Still Have More Addresses, Tied with One Chain, August of 1991 (screenplays), Retribution Must Come (M. Gorky Prize 1982). *Leisure interest:* life in the country.

MOLDAZHANOVA, Gulzhan, MBA; Russian business executive; *CEO, Basic Element;* ed Kazakh State Univ., Lomonosov Moscow State Univ., Finance Acad. of Govt of Russian Fed., Antwerp Univ., Belgium; sr man. at Sibirsky Aluminium (Sibal, later renamed Basic Element—Basel) 1995–2000, Dir Sales and Marketing, Russian Aluminium Co. (RUSAL) 2000–02, Dir for Strategy and Corp. Devt 2002–04, mem. Bd of Dirs and Man. Dir Aluminium Business, Basic Element Co. (RUSAL's major shareholder) 2004–06, CEO Basic Element 2005–09, 2012–; CEO ESN Corpn 2009–11; named by The Wall Street Journal amongst Ten Managers to Watch In Top Firms in Europe 2004, ranked by Fortune magazine amongst 50 Most Powerful Women in Business outside the US (22nd) 2006, (20th) 2007, (10th) 2008, ranked by Forbes magazine amongst 100 Most Powerful Women (37th) 2008. *Address:* Basic Element, Moscow 123022, 30 ul. Rochdelskaya, Russia (office). *Telephone:* (495) 720-50-25 (office). *Fax:* (495) 720-53-95 (office). *E-mail:* info@basicelement.ru (office). *Website:* www.basicelement.ru (office).

MOLEFE, Popo Simon; South African politician; b. 26 April 1952, Sophiatown; m. 1st Olympia Molefe (divorced); three c.; m. 2nd Boitumelo Plaatje 1991; ed Naledi High School; microfilm machine operator, photographic printing machine operator 1976–78; mem. SASM 1973–76; mem. Black Peoples' Convention 1974, 1977; First Chair. Azanian People's Org. (AZAPO), Soweto Br. 1979–81; mem. Gen. and Allied Workers Union 1980–83; Sec. Transvaal Region, United Democratic Front 1983, Nat. Gen. Sec. 1983–91; mem. Nat. Exec. Cttee African Nat. Congress (ANC) 1991–; charged with treason and murder after detention in 1985, convicted at Delmas Treason Trial, sentenced to ten years' imprisonment after being held in custody for four years 1988, released 1989; Chair. ANC Nat. Elections Comm. 1992–94, ANC Alexandra Br. 1990; Vice-Chair. ANC PWV Region 1990–94; Premier NW Prov. Govt 1994–2004; Sec. Nat. Organizing Comm. of ANC. *Address:* Private Bag X2018, Mmabatho 8681; African National Congress, PO Box 61884, Marshalltown 2107, South Africa.

MOLELEKI, Monyane, MA; Lesotho politician; *Minister of Natural Resources;* b. 5 Jan. 1951, Mohlaka-oa-Tuka, Maseru Dist; m.; one s. two d.; ed Nazareth Primary School, Christ the King High School, Moscow State Univ.; Head Teacher, St Thomas Secondary School 1972–73; reporter and sub-ed., The Echo newspaper 1973–74; news reader, reporter and sub-ed., Radio Lesotho 1974–75; Extension Educator, Media Section, Inst. of Extra Mural Studies (IEMS), Nat. Univ. of Lesotho 1983–87, Admin. 1985–86; Public Relations Man. Lesotho Highlands Devt Authority (LHDA) 1988–91; mem. Parl. for Senqunyane Constituency 1993, later for Machache No. 38 Constituency; Minister of Natural Resources 1993–94, 1998, of Information and Broadcasting 1996–98, of Foreign Affairs 2004–07, of Natural Resources 2007–; Co-founder and Pres. Matela Multi-Purpose Co-Operative 1973–75; mem. Maseru Beautification Cttee 1984–91, Matlama Football Club Cttee 1984–91 (fmr Sec.-Gen.). *Address:* Ministry of Natural Resources, POB 772, Maseru 100, Lesotho (office). *Telephone:* 22322334 (office). *Fax:* 22313602 (office). *Website:* www.lesotho.gov.ls/natural (office).

MOLERO BELLAVIA, Adm. Diego Alfredo, BA, MA; Venezuelan army officer and government official; *Ambassador to Brazil;* ed Naval School of Venezuela, Central Univ. of Venezuela; performed duties as Chief of Intelligence Div. of the Security Unit Command; served in Honour Guard Regt of the Mil. 1989; Commdr Coast Guard Station School, Los Roques 1993–99; Commdr HQ of the Navy 1999–2007; Dir Basic School of the Bolivarian Nat. Armed Forces from 2007; Commdr Strategic Region of Integral Defence –2012; Minister of Defence 2012–13; Amb. to Brazil 2013–. *Address:* Embassy of Venezuela, SES, Avenue das Nações, Quadra 803, Lote 13, 70451-900 Brasília, DF, Brazil (office). *Telephone:* (61) 2101-1011 (office). *Fax:* (61) 2101-1011 (office).

MOLIGA, Lolo Letalu Matalasi, BA, MPA; American Samoan politician, state governor, business executive and fmr educator; *Governor of American Samoa;* b. Ta'u, American Samoa; s. of High Chief Moliga Sa'ena Auauna Moliga, and Soali'i Galea'i; ed Samoana High School, Manu'a High School, Chadron State Coll., Neb. and San Diego State Univ., Calif., USA; began career as teacher, later elementary school prin. before becoming Prin. of Manu'a High School in Manu'a Islands; later elementary and secondary educ. admin. within American Samoan Dept of Educ.; fmr Dir ASG Budget Office, as well as American Samoa's Chief Procurement Officer for two terms; Owner of construction firm; elected to American Samoa House of Reps for four terms; later Senator within American Samoa Senate, Senate Pres.; Pres. Devt Bank of American Samoa 2009–12; Gov. of American Samoa 2013–; Ind. *Address:* Office of the Governor, Executive Office Building, Third Floor, Utulei, Pago Pago, AS 96799, American Samoa (office). *Telephone:* (684) 633-4116 (office). *Fax:* (684) 633-2269 (office). *E-mail:* tupitosoliai@americansamoa.gov (office). *Website:* americansamoa.gov (office).

MOLIN, Yuri Nikolaevich; Russian chemist and physicist; *Advisor, Russian Academy of Sciences;* b. 3 Feb. 1934, USSR; s. of N. N. Molin and A. F. Kuramova; m. 1st N. G. Molina 1965; two d.; m. 2nd G. E. Iakovleva 2005; ed Moscow Inst. of Physics and Tech.; worked in USSR Acad. of Sciences Inst. of Chemical Physics 1957–59; various posts in USSR (now Russian) Acad. of Sciences Inst. of Chem. Kinetics and Combustion 1959–, Dir 1971–93, Head of Lab. 1993–2004, Advisor 2004–; teacher in Univ. of Novosibirsk 1966–, Prof. 1974–; mem. USSR (now Russian) Acad. of Sciences 1981; Fellow, Inst. Electron Paramagnetic Resonance Soc. 1998; Lenin Prize 1986, Mendeleev Lecturer 1992, N.N. Semenov Golden Medal, Russian Acad. of Sciences 2006. *Publications:* Spin Exchange 1980, Spin Polarization and Magnetic Effects in Radical Reactions 1984, Infrared Photochemistry 1985. *Leisure interest:* mountain walking. *Address:* Institute of Chem-

ical Kinetics and Combustion, Novosibirsk 630090, Russia (office). *Telephone:* (383) 333-16-07 (office); (383) 330-25-21 (home). *Fax:* (383) 330-73-50 (office). *E-mail:* molin@kinetics.nsc.ru (office). *Website:* www.kinetics.nsc.ru (office).

MOLINA, Alfred; British actor; b. 24 May 1953, London; m. Jill Gascoigne; ed Guildhall School of Music and Drama; on stage has appeared with RSC and at Nat. Theatre, Royal Court Theatre, Donmar Warehouse, Minskoff Theater, Broadway. *Films include:* Indiana Jones and the Raiders of the Lost Ark 1981, Anyone for Denis 1982, Number One 1984, Eleni 1985, Ladyhawke 1985, A Letter to Brezhnev 1985, Prick Up Your Ears 1987, Manifesto 1988, Not Without My Daughter 1991, American Friends 1991, Enchanted April 1991, When Pigs Fly 1993, The Trial 1993, American Friends 1993, White Fang 2: Myth of the White Wolf 1994, Maverick 1994, Hideaway 1995, The Perez Family 1995, A Night of Love 1995, The Steal, Species 1995, Before and After 1996, Dead Man 1996, Scorpion Spring 1996, Mojave Moon 1996, Anna Karenina 1997, The Odd Couple II 1997, Boogie Nights 1997, The Man Who Knew Too Little 1997, The Imposters 1998, Magnolia 1999, Dudley Do-Right 1999, The Trial 2000, Chocolat 2000, Texas Rangers 2001, Agatha Christie's Murder on the Orient Express 2001, Pete's Meteor 2002, Road to Perdition 2002, Frida 2003, My Life Without Me 2003, Coffee and Cigarettes 2003, Spider-Man II 2004, Steamboy 2004, Sian Ka'an (voice) 2005, The Da Vinci Code 2006, The Moon and the Stars 2006, As You Like It 2006, The Hoax 2006, Orchids 2006, The Moon and the Stars 2007, Silk 2007, The Ten Commandments 2007. *Television includes:* role of Blake in series El Cid, Year in Provence, Nervous Energy, Ladies Man (series), Loving Miss Hatto (film) 2012. *Website:* www.alfred-molina.com (office).

MOLINA, Mario J., PhD; American/Mexican chemist and academic; *Professor of Chemistry, University of California, San Diego;* b. 19 March 1943, Mexico City, Mexico; s. of Roberto Molina-Pasquel and Leonor Henriquez; m. Guadalupe Alvarez; one c.; ed Acad. Hispano Mexicana, Univ. Nacional Autónoma de Mexico (UNAM), Univ. of Freiburg and Univ. of California, Berkeley; Asst Prof., UNAM 1967–68; Research Assoc., Univ. of California, Berkeley 1972–73; Research Assoc., Univ. of California, Irvine 1973–75, Asst Prof. 1975–79, Assoc. Prof. 1979–82; Sr Research Scientist, Jet Propulsion Lab., Calif. 1983–89; Prof., Dept of Earth, Atmospheric and Planetary Sciences and Dept of Chem., MIT 1989–97, Inst. Prof. 1997–2003; Prof., Dept of Chem. and Biochemistry, Univ. of California, San Diego 2003–; Pres. Centro Mario Molina; mem. NAS, Inst. of Medicine; 30 hon. degrees; Max Planck Research Award 1994–96, UNEP Ozone Award 1995, Nobel Prize in Chem. 1995, Volvo Environment Prize 2004; many other awards and distinctions. *Publications:* numerous book chapters and articles in scientific journals. *Leisure interests:* music, reading, tennis. *Address:* University of California, San Diego, UHA 3050E, 9500 Gilman Drive #0356, La Jolla, CA 92093-0356 (office); 3535 Lebon Drive, Apt 2210, San Diego, CA 92122, USA (home). *Telephone:* (858) 534-1696 (office). *Fax:* (858) 534-1697 (office). *E-mail:* mjmolina@ucsd.edu (office). *Website:* www-chem.ucsd.edu/faculty/profiles/molina_mario_j.html (office); www .centromariomolina.org (office).

MOLINA BARRAZA, Col Arturo Armando; Salvadorean army officer and fmr head of state; b. 6 Aug. 1927, San Salvador; s. of Mariano Molina and Matilde Barraza de Molina; m. María Elena Contreras de Molina; four s. one d.; ed Instituto Nacional Gen. Francisco Menéndez, Escuela Militar, El Salvador, Escuela Superior de Guerra, Mexico, Escuela de Infanteria, Spain; Section and Co. Commdr, Escuela Militar; Artillery Garrison, Asst Dir Escuela de Armas, Section and Dept Chief, Staff HQ; Del. 6th Conf. of American Armed Forces, Peru 1965, 7th Conf. Buenos Aires; Gen. Co-ordinator, 2nd and 3rd Confs of Defence Council of Cen. American States; Dir Exec. Comm. for Shipping; Dir Nat. Cttee of Caritas, El Salvador; Pres. of El Salvador 1972–77; went into self-imposed exile, returning to El Salvador 1992.

MOLINA CONTRERAS, Gen. Jorge Alberto; Salvadorean army officer and politician; Del. to UN Conf. to Review Progress made in Implementation of Programme of Action to Prevent, Combat and Eradicate the Illicit Trade in Small Arms and Light Weapons in All Its Aspects, New York 2006; fmr Jt Chief of Staff of the Armed Forces; Minister of Nat. Defence 2008–09; rank of Brig.-Gen. 2005, Maj.-Gen. 2006, Gen. 2007. *Address:* c/o Ministry of National Defence, Alameda Dr Manuel E. Araújo, Km 5, Carretera a Santa Tecla, San Salvador, El Salvador.

MOLINA SÁNCHEZ, César Antonio, LicenDer; Spanish writer and politician; b. 1952, La Coruña; fmr Prof. of Literary Theory and Criticism, Complutense Univ., Prof. of Humanities and Journalism, Univ. Carlos III; worked for Cambio 16 (magazine) and Diario 16 (newspaper) 1985–96, becoming Deputy Dir; Man. Dir Círculo de Bellas Artes 1996–2004; Dir Cervantes Inst. 2004–07; Minister of Culture 2007–09; Deputy (Spanish Socialist Workers' Party–PSOE) for A Coruña 2008–09. *Publications include:* Épica 1974, Proyecto preliminar para una arqueología de campo (poetry) 1978, Últimas horas en Lisca Blanca 1979, La estancia saqueada (poetry) 1983, La revista Alfar y la prensa literaria de su época (1920-1930) 1984, Antología de la poesía Gallega contemporánea 1984, Gobierno de un jardín 1986, Derivas 1987, El fin de Finisterre 1988, Prensa literaria en Galicia (1809-1920) 1989, Prensa literaria en Galicia (1920-1960) 1989, Medio siglo de Prensa literaria española (1900-1950) 1990, Sobre el iberismo y otros escritos de literatura portuguesa 1990, Las ruinas del mundo 1991, El fin de Finisterre 1992, Para no ir a parte alguna 1994, Sobre la inutilidad de la poesía 1995, Nostalgia de la nada perdida; ensayo sobre narrativa contemporánea 1996, Vivir sin ser visto 2000, A fin de Fisterra (poetry) 2001, A Coruña, agua y luz 2001, Olas en la noche 2001, Regresar a donde no estuvimos 2003, Viaje a la Costa da morte 2003, En el mar de Anforas 2005, En honor de Hermes 2005, Fuga del amor 2005, El rumor del tiempo 2006, Custode delle antiche forme (poetry) 2007, Eume 2007, Esperando a los años que no vuelven 2007, Lugares donde se calma el dolor 2009, Cielo azar 2011, Donde la eternidad envejece 2012. *Address:* c/o Ministry of Culture, Plaza del Rey 1, 28071 Madrid, Spain.

MOLISA, Sela; Ni-Vanuatu politician and diplomatist; *Ambassador to People's Republic of China;* b. 15 Dec. 1952, Santo; s. of Mandei Rongtuhun and Ruth Rongtuhun; two s. one d.; ed Onesua High School, Malaba Coll., Efate, Univ. of the S Pacific, Fiji, Fifi School of Medicine; banker 1974–77; Gen. Man. Co-operative Fed. 1977–81; elected mem. Parl. 1982; Minister of Internal Affairs 1983, of Foreign Affairs 1983–87, of Finance 1987–91, 2002–04 (resgnd), 2008–10, of Trade, Commerce and Industry 1996, of Finance and Econ. Man. 1998–99, of Lands and

Natural Resources 2001–02; Amb. to People's Republic of China 2014–; apptd Govt Special Rep. to negotiate with rebels during attempted secession of Santo from Vanuatu 1980; involved in design and implementation of Vanuatu Comprehensive Reform Programme 1997–; mem. Vanua'aku Pati. *Leisure interests:* reading, swimming, listening to music, watching sports. *Address:* Embassy of Vanuatu, 3-1-11 San Li Tun Diplomatic Compound, Chao Yang Qu, Beijing 100600, People's Republic of China (office). *Telephone:* (10) 65320337 (office). *Fax:* (10) 65320336 (office).

MÖLK, Ulrich, DPhil; German academic; *Professor of Romance Literature, Akademie der Wissenschaften, University of Göttingen;* b. 29 March 1937, Hamburg; s. of Heinrich Mölk and Berta Mölk; m. Renate Mölk 1962; ed Univs of Hamburg and Heidelberg; Prof. of Romance Literature, Univ. of Giessen 1967; Prof. of Romance Literature, Akad. der Wissenschaften, Univ. of Göttingen 1974–, Dir Inst. für Lateinische und Romanische Philologie des Mittelalters 1974–2005; mem. Acad. of Göttingen, Vice-Pres. 1990–92, Pres. 1992–94. *Publications:* Guiraut Riquier, Las cansos 1962, Trobar clus 1968, Répertoire métrique de la poésie lyrique française 1972, Trotzki, Literaturkritik 1973, Trobadorlyrik 1982, Flaubert, Une Nuit de Don Juan, Edition 1984, Vita und Kult des hl. Metro von Verona 1987, Lohier et Malart 1988, Romanische Frauenlieder 1989, Die europäische Bedeutungsgeschichte von 'Motiv' 1992, Julien Sorel vor dem Schwurgericht 1994, Impressionistischer Stil 1995, Literatur und Recht 1996, Europäische Jahrhundertwende 1999, Albéric: le poème d'Alexandre 2000, Das älteste französische Kreuzlied 2001, Prousts Venedig 2002, Estetismo e decandentismo 2004. *Address:* Akademie der Wissenschaften, Theaterstrasse 7, 37073 Göttingen (office); Höltystr. 7, 37085 Göttingen, Germany (home). *Telephone:* (551) 395331 (office). *Fax:* (551) 395365 (office). *E-mail:* jhwroma@gwdg.de (office). *Website:* www.uni-goettingen.de/de/sh/1397 (office).

MOLL, Kurt; German singer (bass); b. 11 April 1938, Buir; m. Ursula Pade 1968; one s. two d.; ed Staatliche Hochschule für Musik, Cologne; operatic debut in Cologne; subsequently sang operatic roles at Aachen, Mainz, Wuppertal, Hamburg; appeared Bayreuth 1968, Salzburg 1970, La Scala, Milan 1972, Covent Garden, London 1975, Metropolitan Opera, New York 1978; Prof. Staatliche Hochschule für Musik, Cologne 1991–; mem. Hamburg, Bavarian and Vienna State Operas. *Address:* Voigtelstr. 22, 50933 Cologne, Germany.

MÖLLER, Erwin; German business executive; b. 23 Jan. 1939; m.; ed Tech. Univ. of Darmstadt; Chair. Supervisory Bd Metaleurop SA, Foutenay-sous-Bois, VTG Vereinigte Tanklager und Transportmittel GmbH, Hamburg; Chair. Exec. Bd Preussag AG; mem. Supervisory Bd Hannoversche Lebensversicherung AG, Hannover, Kabelmetal Electro GmbH, Hannover, Salzgitter Stahl GmbH, Düsseldorf; mem. Governing Council DSL Bank, Bonn; Chair. Bd and Dir Amalgamated Metal Corp. PLC, London; Hon. Consul Grand-Duchy of Luxembourg.

MOLLER, Gordon Desmond, ONZM, DipArch, FNZIA, PPNZIA; New Zealand architect; *Director, Moller Architects;* b. 26 July 1940, Hastings; s. of Oscar Carl Moller and Winifred Daisy Moller; m. Sylvia Anne Liebezeit 1962; one s. two d.; ed Wellington Coll., Hutt Valley High School, Univ. of Auckland; Dir Craig Craig Moller architectural practice 1969–2002, Moller Architects 2003–; Ed. New Zealand Architect Magazine 1976–83; Chair. Arts Marketing Bd, Aotearoa 1994, 1995, Site Safe NZ 2002, 2003, Construction Information Ltd 2006; Pres. Wellington Architectural Centre 1972, 1973; Professorial Teaching Fellow, Victoria Univ. School of Architecture 1990, 1991; Pres. NZ Inst. of Architects 2003–06; Co-convenor Auckland City Urban Design Panel 2003–10; mem. Design Consortium Wellington Civic Centre 1992, 1998, NZ Registered Architects Bd 2006–08, Tech. Advisory Group, Waterfront, Auckland; Chair. Auckland Theatre Co. 2011–; Chair. Judging Panel NZ Govt Starter Home Design Competition 2008–09; Trustee, Wellington City Gallery Foundation 1998–2006; mem. NZ Architectural Publications Trust 2003–; Hon. mem. Royal Australian Inst. of Architects; Officer, NZ Order of Merit 2006; Hon. DLitt (Victoria Univ. of Wellington) 2006; NZ Inst. of Architects Gold Medal 2006, 50 design awards 1970–2007. *Designs include:* School of Architecture, Wellington 1994, Sky Tower, Auckland 1994–97, numerous houses 1969–, Macau Tower and Entertainment Centre, Macau 1999–2001, Point Apartments, Auckland 2000, New Galleries, Te Papa, Wellington 2001, Viaduct Point Apartments, Auckland 2002, Sky City Conf. Centre 2002, Sky City Grand Hotel 2003, 67-storey Elliott Tower Project, Auckland 2006, new Houses of Parl., Muscat, Oman 2008–12, Viaduct Events Centre, Auckland Waterfront 2009–11, 30-storey commercial office bldg, Shortland Street Project, Auckland 2009, Hihiaua Cultural Centre, Whangarei 2009–11, various projects for Sky City 2011–12, new 600-seat drama theatre, Auckland Waterfront 2011–13. *Leisure interests:* photography, music, motoring, landscape gardening, design, travel, visual and performing arts. *Address:* 121 Customs Street West, Auckland (home); Level 13, West Plaza, 3 Albert Street, Auckland, New Zealand (office). *Telephone:* (9) 357-0686 (office); (9) 357-1140 (office); (21) 241-9237 (office). *Fax:* (9) 357-0689 (office). *E-mail:* gordon@mollerarchitects.com (office). *Website:* www.mollerarchitects.com (office).

MØLLER, Per Stig, MA, PhD; Danish politician; b. 1942; s. of Poul Møller and Lis Møller; ed Univ. of Copenhagen; Lecturer, Sorbonne Univ., Paris 1974–76; Cultural Ed. Radio Denmark 1973–74, Deputy Head, Culture and Soc. Dept 1976–79, Chief of Programmes 1979–84; Vice-Chair. Radio Council 1985–86, Chair. 1986–87; Commentator, Berlingske Tidende 1984–2001; Chair. Popular Educ. Asscn (FOF) 1983–89; mem. Parl. (Danish Conservative Party) 1984–, mem. Exec. Cttee 1985–89, 1993–98, Chair. 1997–98, Parl. Leader 1997–98, Foreign Policy Spokesman 1998–2001; mem. Council of Europe 1987–90, 1994–97, 1998–2001; Minister for the Environment 1990–93; Chair. Security Policy Cttee 1994–96, mem. Foreign Policy Cttee 1994–2001; Minister for Foreign Affairs 2001–10, of Culture 2010–11; Nat. Chair. Union of Conservative Gymnasium Students 1960–61, Vice-Chair. Conservative Students' Asscn 1961–62, Pres. Students' Union; Chevalier, Ordre Nat. du Lion 1975, Chevalier des Arts et des Lettres 1986, Grosskreuz des Verdienstordens der Bundesrepublik Deutschland 2002, Commdr (First Class), Order of the Dannebrog 2002, Commdr, Ordre Nat. du Benin 2003, Grand-Croix, Ordre de la Couronne de Chêne (Belgium) 2003, Order of Stara Planina (First Class) 2006, Commdr Grand Cross, Royal Order of the Polar Star (Sweden) 2007, Grand Cross, Order of the South Cross (Brazil) 2007, Grand Cross and Commdr, Order for Merits to Lithuania 2007, Grand Cross,

Order of the Phoenix (Greece) 2009, Order of the Cross of Terra Mariana (1st Class) 2011; Sound and Environment Award 1993, Georg Brandes Award 1996, Einer Hansen Research Fund Award 1997, G-1930s Politician of the Year 1997, Cultural Award of the Popular Educ. Asscn 1998, Raoul Wallenberg Medal 1998, Kaj Munk Award 2001, Rosenkjaer Award 2001, Robert Schumann Medal 2003, Nersornaat Medal of Merit in Gold 2005. *Publications include:* La Critique dramatique et littéraire de Malte-Brun 1971, Erotismen 1973, København-Paris (trans.) 1973, På Sporet af det forsvundne Menneske 1976, Livet I Gøgereden 1978, Fra Tid til Anden 1979, Tro, Håb og Faellesskab 1980, Midt I Redeligheden 1981, Orwells Håb og Frygt 1983, Nat uden Daggry 1985, Mulighedernes Samfund 1985, Stemmer fra Øst 1987, Historien om Estland, Letland og Litauen 1990, Kurs mod Katastrofer? 1993, Miljøproblemer 1995, Den naturlige Orden: Tolv år der flyttede Verden 1996, Spor: Udvalgte Skrifter om det åbne Samfund og dets Vaerdier 1997, Magt og Afmagt 1999, Munk 2000, Mere Munk 2003. *Address:* Folketinget, Palace of Christiansborg, 1240 Copenhagen K, Denmark.

MØLLER, Stig, LLM; Danish university administrator; *Director of Administration, University of Aarhus;* b. 29 Aug. 1939; ed Univ. of Copenhagen; Capt. of the Reserve 1963; Sec. Ministry of the Interior 1966–71, Ministry of Pollution Reduction 1971–73; Tutor in Admin. Law, Univ. of Copenhagen 1968–71; Teacher of Public Law, School of Admin 1968–79; Acting Head of Office, Dept of the Environment 1974–76, Head of Office 1976–79; Dir of Admin, Univ. of Aarhus 1979–; mem. Man. Group for Co-operation of Nordic Univ. Dirs of Admin (Chair. 1982–88) 1979–2000; mem. Bd of Dirs Ejendomsselskab AS, Aarhus Univ. Research Foundation. *Address:* University of Aarhus, Nordre Ringgade 1, 8000 Århus C, Denmark. *Telephone:* (89) 42-11-11 (office). *Fax:* (86) 19-70-29 (office). *E-mail:* au@au.dk (office). *Website:* www.au.dk/en/direktor (office).

MOLLOY, Patrick J.; Irish business executive; *Chairman, Blackrock Clinic;* b. 4 Jan. 1938; m. Ann Lynch; three s. two d.; ed Trinity Coll., Dublin, Harvard Business School, USA; Asst Gen. Man. Bank of Ireland 1975–78, Gen. Man. Area East 1978–83, Man. Dir 1983–91, Group CEO 1991–98; Dir (non-exec.) CRH plc 1997–2007, Chair. 2000–07; Chair. Blackrock Clinic, Enterprise Ireland –2009; mem. Bd of Dirs Waterford Wedgwood plc; Pro-Chancellor Trinity Coll. Dublin 2008–; Hon. LLD (Trinity Coll. Dublin) 1999. *Leisure interests:* fishing, shooting. *Address:* Blackrock Clinic, Rock Road, Blackrock, Co. Dublin, Ireland (office). *Telephone:* (1) 2832222 (office). *Fax:* (1) 2064314 (office). *E-mail:* info@blackrock-clinic.ie (office). *Website:* www.blackrock-clinic.ie (office).

MOLLOY, Robert M., BComm; Irish politician (retd); b. 6 July 1936, Salthill, Galway; s. of Michael Edward Molloy and Rita (Stanley) Molloy; m. Phyllis Barry 1972; two s. two d.; ed St Ignatius Coll., Univ. Coll., Galway; became mem. Dáil Eireann (House of Reps) 1965, retd 2002, House Cttee of Public Accounts 1965–69, House Cttee on Constitution 1967; Parl. Sec. to Minister for Educ. 1969–70; Minister for Local Govt 1970–73, for Defence 1977–79, of Energy 1989–92, of State to the Govt 1997–2002, and fmrly at the Dept of the Environment and Local Govt with special responsibility for Housing and Urban Renewal; mem. Galway Co. Council 1967–70, 1974–77, 1985–91, Galway Borough Council 1967–70, 1985–91; Mayor of Galway 1968–69; Chair., Galway Harbour Bd 1974–77, 1985–91, Lough Corril Navigation Trustees 1985–91; Chair., House Cttee on Bldg Land; mem., House Cttee on State-Sponsored Bodies 1982–87, 1994–, on the Irish Language 1992–, on Enterprise and Econ. Strategy 1994–; mem. Council of Europe 1996–, Governing Body, Univ. Coll. Galway 1977, Exec. Inter-Parl. Asscn; Dir, Salthill Failte Ltd 1985–91, Galway Harbour Co. 2003–12, Bord Iascaigh Mhara (Irish Sea Fisheries Board) 2007–11, Autism West Ltd 2009–. *Leisure interests:* swimming, sailing, golf. *Address:* St Mary's, Rockbarton, Salthill, Galway, Ireland (home). *Telephone:* (91) 521765 (home).

MÖLLRING, Hartmut; German politician and business executive; *Minister of Finance, Lower Saxony; Chairman of the Supervisory Board, Norddeutsche Landesbank (NORD/LB);* b. 31 Dec. 1951, Groß Ilsede, Kreis Peine; m.; three c.; ed Scharnhorstgymnasium, Hildesheim, studied law in Marburg and Göttingen; with Bundeswehr for two years; worked as trainee judge and prosecutor; mem. CDU and Junge Union 1972–, Chair. CDU Dist of Hildesheim; Councillor, City of Hildesheim 1974–2003, Chair. CDU Council Faction 1981–2003; budget officer and spokesperson, Ministry of Justice 1984–90; mem. Lower Saxony State Parl. 1990–, apptd Vice-Chair. CDU Parl. group, responsible for finance, economy, environment, leisure and tourism, spas, marinas and boat rides 1998; Minister of Finance, Lower Saxony 2003–; Chair. Supervisory Bd Norddeutsche Landesbank (NORD/LB); mem. Bd Bremer Landesbank, Deutsche Messe AG, German Bundesrat, Kreditanstalt für Wiederaufbau; mem. Advisory Bd Deutsche Bundesbank; Chair. Tarifgemeinschaft deutscher Länder 2003–; Pres. Eintracht Hildesheim sports club. *Address:* Hohnsen 51, 31134 Hildesheim; Norddeutsche Landesbank, Friedrichswall 10, 30159 Hanover, Germany (office). *Telephone:* (511) 361-24-10 (office). *Fax:* (511) 361-2506 (office). *E-mail:* info@nordlb.de (office). *Website:* www.nordlb.de (office).

MOLNÁR, József; Hungarian business executive; *Group CEO, MOL Group;* held various man. positions at BorsodChem Plc 1978–2001, Head of Pricing Dept 1982–87, Head of Controlling Dept 1987–91, Chief Financial Officer and first Deputy to CEO 1991–2001; CEO TVK (part of MOL Group) 2001–03, Group Planning and Controlling Dir, MOL Group 2003–04, Group Chief Financial Officer 2004–11, Group CEO 2011–, mem. Bd of Dirs TVK 2001–11, Slovnaft a.s. 2004–08. *Address:* MOL Hungarian Oil and Gas Plc, 1117 Budapest, Október huszonhar-madika u. 18, Hungary (office). *Telephone:* (1) 209-0000 (office). *E-mail:* info@mol.hu (office). *Website:* www.mol.hu (office).

MOLNÁR, Károly, PhD, DSc; Hungarian academic and politician; ed Tech. Univ. of Budapest; Asst, Dept of Chemical and Food Eng, Tech. Univ. of Budapest 1967–71, Sr Asst 1971–78, Assoc. Prof. 1978–91, Prof. 1991–, Head of Dept of Process Eng 1988–2008, Vice-Dean Faculty of Mechanical Eng 1992–94, Dean 1994–2001, Vice-Rector for Educ. 2000–04, Rector 2004–08; Minister without Portfolio responsible for Science, Research and Innovation 2008–10; Chair. Bd of Dirs Tisza Chemical Group PLC 1994–96, Deputy Chair. 1996–98; Chair. Hungarian Rectors Conf. 2006–08; Chair. Bd of Dirs Paks Nuclear Power Plant Ltd 2002–08; Chair. Complex Cttee on Chemical and Processing Eng, Hungarian Acad. of Sciences, Technological Scientific Council and Heat and Mass Transfer Cttee, Hungarian Scientific Soc. of Energy Econs; mem. European Fed. of

Chemical Eng, Int. Solar Energy Soc.; Commdr, Order of Merit 2005; János András Segner Award 1986, Gold Medal of Excellent Inventor 1986, 1991, Géza Szikla Award 1992, Lóránd Eötvös Award 1996, Pro Facultate Award 2002, Pro Universitate et Scientia Award 2002, Int. Socrates Award 2006, Széchenyi Award 2007, Arnold Ipolyi Award, Imre Szabó Award. *Address:* c/o Office of the Prime Minister, 1055 Budapest, Kossuth Lajos tér 1–3, Hungary (office).

MOLNÁR, Ľudovít, Dr rer. nat, DSc; Slovak computer scientist and fmr university administrator; *Dean, Faculty of Informatics and Information Technologies, Slovak Technical University;* b. 11 Oct. 1940, Komjatice Dist; m.; three c.; ed Comenius Univ., Bratislava; various teaching positions, Slovak Tech. Univ., Bratislava 1962–, Assoc. Prof. 1978–91, Prof. 1991–, Rector 2000–03, Co-founder and first Dean, Faculty of Informatics and Information Technologies; research periods in UK 1969–70, 1991, USSR 1974, Italy 1978, Cyprus 1983; mem. Asscn for Computing Machinery, IEEE Computer Soc.; IT Personality of the Year 2012. *Publications include:* numerous computer tech. manuals and textbooks; about 100 scientific papers in journals and proceedings of conferences at home and abroad. *Leisure interest:* literature. *Address:* Room 4.32, Faculty of Informatics and Information Technologies, Slovak University of Technology, Vazovova 5, 812 43 Bratislava 16, Slovakia (office). *Telephone:* (2) 21022432 (office). *E-mail:* ludovit .molnar@stuba.sk (office); molnar@fiit.stuba.sk (office); molnar@is.stuba.sk (office). *Website:* www.fiit.stuba.sk (office).

MOLONEY, Thomas Walter, MA, MBA, MPH; American academic, organization official and consultant; b. 8 Feb. 1946, New York; s. of Thomas Walter Moloney and Anne Heney; ed Colgate Univ., Columbia Univ.; Program Dir Nat. Center for the Deaf-Blind, New York 1971–72; Special Asst to Dir and Dean, Cornell Univ. Medical Center 1973–74; Asst Vice-Pres. Robert Wood John Foundation 1975–80; Visiting Lecturer, Princeton Univ. 1975–80; Sr Vice-Pres., The Commonwealth Fund, New York 1980–92; Dir of Public Policy and Health Programmes, Inst. for the Future 1992–99; Man. Pnr Futures Inc. (consulting firm) 1997–; mem. Bd Dirs New England Medical Center, Boston 1982–89; mem. Bd Grantmakers in Health, New York 1984–, Chair. 1984–88; Policy Scholar Eisenhower Center, Columbia Univ., New York 1992–, Inst. of Health Policy Studies, Univ. of California, San Francisco 1992–; mem. Nat. Bd of Medical Examiners 1986–90, Health Advisory Cttee, Gen. Accounting Office, Washington, DC 1987–; Bd, Foundation Health Services Research, Washington, DC 1989 and other bds; Fellow, American Acad. of Arts and Sciences; mem. Inst. of Medicine, NAS. *Publications:* Ed. New Approaches to the Medicaid Crisis 1983; numerous articles. *Address:* Futures Inc., Floor 8, 1170 North Ocean Boulevard, Palm Beach, FL 33480 (office); 72 Norwood Avenue, Upper Montclair, NJ 07043, USA.

MOLONEY, Tom; British publishing executive; b. 1959; joined Emap PLC (radio and magazines outfit) 1981, apptd Group Man. Dir Emap Metro and Elan 1989, Chief Exec. Consumer Magazines UK 1995–99, has overseen launch of magazines Heat, More, Q and Empire, mem. Exec. Bd 1995–2007, COO then Pres. and CEO Emap USA 1999–2001, Group COO 2001–03, CEO 2003–07.

MOLSON, Eric H., AB; Canadian brewing industry executive; b. 16 Sept. 1937, Montreal, PQ; s. of Thomas H. P. Molson and Celia F. Cantlie; m. Jane Mitchell 1966; three c.; ed Selwyn House School, Montreal, Bishop's Coll. School, Lennoxville, Le Rosey, Switzerland, Princeton and McGill Univs and US Brewers' Acad. New York; served as apprentice brewer with Molson Breweries of Canada Ltd, rising through various appointments to Pres., Chair. Molson Inc. (now Molson Coors Brewing Co.) 1988–2008, Vice-Chair. 2008–09 (retd). *Address:* Molson Coors Brewing Co., 1555 Notre Dame Street East, Montreal, PQ H2L 2R5, Canada (office). *Telephone:* (514) 597-1786 (office). *Fax:* (514) 598-6866 (office). *Website:* www.molson.com (office).

MOLTERER, Wilhelm, MSc; Austrian politician; b. 14 May 1955, Steyr; s. of Johann Kletzmayr and Anna Kletzmayr, Josef Molterer and Cäcilia Molterer (adoptive parents); m. Brigitte Molterer; two c.; ed Fed. Agricultural Coll., St Florian and Johannes Kepler Univ., Linz; Research Asst Dept of Agric. Policy, Univ. of Linz 1979–81; Head Econ. Policy Div., Austrian Farmers Fed. 1981–84, Dir 1989–93; Municipal Councillor, Sierning 1985–87; Sec. Office of Fed. Minister Dr. Josef Riegler 1987–89; mem. Nat. Council 1990–94; Sec.–Gen. Austria People's Party (ÖAP) 1993–94, Parl. Group Leader 2003–07, Chair. 2007–08; Fed. Minister of Agric. and Forestry 1994–2003 (and Environment and Water Man. 2000–03), of Finance 2007–08, Vice-Chancellor of Austria 2007–08. *Address:* Austrian People's Party, Lichtenfelsgasse 7, 1010 Vienna, Austria (office). *Telephone:* (1) 401-26-0 (office). *Fax:* (1) 401-26-10-9 (office). *E-mail:* email@oevp.at (office). *Website:* www .oevp.at (office).

MOLTMANN, Jürgen, DTheol; German theologian and academic; *Professor and Rector, Wuppertal Church University;* b. 8 April 1926, Hamburg; m. Dr. Elisabeth Moltmann-Wendel; four d.; POW during Second World War; with Dept of Theology, Univ. of Göttingen 1948–52, Prof. of Theology 1957–; fmr Minister, Bremen; Prof. and Rector Wuppertal Church Univ. 1958–; co-ed. Deutsch-Polnische Hefte 1959–68; Visiting Prof. in USA 1967–68; Dir Evangelische Theologie 1971–89; Dir CONCILIUM 1979–94; Dr hc (Duke Univ.), (Bethlehem Theological Seminary), (Kalamazoo Coll.), (Raday Kolleg, Budapest), (St Andrews Univ.), (Emory Univ.), (Univ. of Leuven), (Univ. of Iasi), (Nottingham Univ.), (Managua, Nicaragua), (Chung Yuan Univ., Taiwan), (Methodist Univ., São Paulo), (Univ. Alba Iulia, Romania); Italian Prize of Literature, Isle of Elba 1971, Amos Comenius Medal, Bethlehem, Pa 1992, Ernst Bloch Prize of the City of Ludwigshafen 1995, Grawemeyer Award on Religion, Louisville, Ky 2000, Robert Boyle Medal 2011. *Publications include:* Christliche Petzel und das Calvinismus in Bremen 1958, Prädestination und Perseveranz 1961, Anfänge Dialektische Theologie 1963, Theologie der Hoffnung (Theology of Hope) (Isle of Elba Literary Prize) 1964, Mensch 1971, Der gekreuzigte Gott (The Crucified God) 1972, Der Sprache der Befreiung 1972, Das Experiment Hoffnung 1974, Kirche in der Kraft des Geistes 1975, Zukunft der Schöpfung 1977, Trinität und Reich Gottes 1980, Gott in der Schöpfung (God in Creation) 1985, Das Weg Jesu Christi (The Way of Jesus Christ) 1989, Der Geist des Lebens (The Spirit of Life) 1991, Das Kommen Gottes (The Coming of God) (Grawemeyer Religion Award) 1995, Experiences in Theology 1999, Science and Wisdom 2002, In the End – the Beginning: The Life of Hope 2004, Sun of Righteousness, Arise! 2010, Ethics of Hope 2012. *Address:*

Liebermeister Strasse 12, 72076 Tübingen (office); Biesinger Strasse 25, 72070 Tübingen, Germany (home). *Telephone:* (7071) 41673 (home).

MOLYNEAUX OF KILLEAD, Baron (Life Peer), cr. 1997, of Killead in the County of Antrim; **James Henry Molyneaux,** KBE, PC; British politician; b. 27 Aug. 1920, Killead, Co. Antrim; s. of William Molyneaux and Sarah Gilmore; ed Aldergrove School, Co. Antrim; served in RAF 1941–46; mem. Antrim Co. Council 1964–73; Vice-Chair. Eastern Special Care Hosp. Man. Cttee 1966–73; Chair. Antrim Branch NI Asscn for Mental Health 1967–70; Hon. Sec., S Antrim Unionist Asscn 1964–70; MP for Antrim South 1970–83, for Lagan Valley 1983–97; Vice-Pres. Ulster Unionist Council 1974; Leader, Ulster Unionist Party, House of Commons 1974–97; Leader, Ulster Unionist Party 1979–95; mem. NI Ass. 1982–86; fmr JP (resgnd 1987); Deputy Grand Master of Orange Order and Hon. Past Grand Master of Canada; Sovereign Grand Master, Commonwealth Royal Black Inst. 1971–98. *Leisure interests:* music, gardening. *Address:* House of Lords, Westminster, London, SW1A 0PW, England (office); Aldergrove, Crumlin, BT29 4AR, Co. Antrim, Northern Ireland. *Telephone:* (28) 9442-2545 (Crumlin).

MOLYVIATIS, Petros; Greek diplomatist and politician; *Chairman, Board of Trustees, Konstantinos G. Karamanlis Foundation;* b. 12 June 1928, Lesvos; m. Niovi Christaki; one d. one s.; ed Univ. of Athens; Gen. Sec. Presidency of the Repub. 1980–85, 1990–95, fmr Diplomatic Adviser to the Pres.; mem. Parl. 1996–, fmr mem. Standing Cttees on Defence, Foreign Affairs, European Affairs; fmr mem. Greek dels to UN, NATO; fmr Amb.; Minister of Foreign Affairs 2004–06, May–June 2012; Pres. Greek Fire Relief Fund 2007–; currently Chair., Bd of Trustees, Konstantinos G. Karamanlis Foundation. *Address:* Konstantinos G. Karamanlis Foundation, 6 Karaiskaki and Eleftheriou Venizelou Streets, Filothei, 152 37 Athens, Greece (office). *Telephone:* (210) 6847990 (office). *Fax:* (210) 6847956 (office). *E-mail:* info@karamanlis-foundation.gr (office). *Website:* www .karamanlis-foundation.gr (office).

MOMEN, Abulkalam Abdul, BA (Hons), MA, LLB, MBA, MPA, PhD; Bangladeshi diplomatist, human rights activist, columnist and researcher; *Permanent Representative, United Nations;* m. Selina Momen; two s. three d.; ed Univ. of Dhaka, Harvard Univ. (Ford Foundation and Mason Fellow), Northeastern Univ., Boston, USA; captured by Pakistani occupation army 1971; worked in Bangladesh govt service 1970s–80s, forcibly retired under Martial Order No. 9 (since declared null and void) for opposing mil. rule 1982; mem. Democratic Nat. Cttee late 1980s, worked as South Asia Adviser for Michael Dukakis US presidential campaign 1988, also worked for John Kerry US presidential campaign 2004; worked for MIT, Cambridge, Mass and the World Bank, Washington, DC for two years; fmr Chair. Business Admin and Econs Dept, Framingham State Coll., USA; Faculty mem., Merrimack Coll., USA, Salem State Coll., USA, Northeastern Univ., USA, Univ. of Massachusetts, USA, Cambridge Coll., USA, Kennedy School of Govt, USA; US Expert (Econ. Adviser) under Saudi Arabian Ministry of Finance and Nat. Economy, Riyadh –2003; Amb. and Perm. Rep. to UN, New York 2009–; Pres. UNICEF Exec. Bd 2009–11; Coordinator for NAM Peacebuilding Caucus of the UN; apptd Facilitator for the UN Counter-Terrorism Strategy Review 2010; apptd Chair. Least Developed Country 2009, Second Cttee of UN Gen. Ass. 2012, Peacebuilding Comm. 2012; Vice-Pres., UN Econ. and Social Council 2011–12; Chair. Sub-cttee Kennedy School of Govt New England Alumni Council; Chair. 3rd FOBANA Convention, Boston 1989; fmr Pres. Women and Children International, Inc., Boston, Foundation for Eye Hosp., Bangladesh, Bangladesh Asscn of New England, Boston; Dir, American Anti-Slavery Org.; mem. Amnesty International; Life mem. New England Islamic Soc. (USA), Bangladesh Econ. Asscn, Jalalabad Asscn, Dhaka Univ. Alumni Asscn; Co-chair. Cttee for Democratic Bangladesh (USA) 1986–90; started movt to end trafficking of women and children early 1990s; launched campaign to have a SAARC Resolution and a SAARC Fund for the victims and to create public awareness of trafficking; testified before US Congress and US Labor Dept in 1993, 1994, 1995 and 1996 to end Asian slave trade, sexual exploitation, sexual mutilation of young girls, child labour; organized movt for restoration of multi-party democracy in Bangladesh; developed an admin. and political man. programme known as TGS to achieve accelerated devt of Bangladesh and developing countries; Home Town Hero, Eagle Tribune, Humanitarian Award, North America Bangladesh Medical Asscn, Friend of the Poor, Probani, Inc. of New York, Mukto-Gaaner Paki, Marupalash, Saudi Arabia, Our Pride citation, The Bangladesh-America Foundation, Inc., Washington, DC 2004, Gentleman of the Year Award, American Women Empowerment 2007. *Publications:* two books and more than 250 papers and articles in professional journals and elsewhere. *Address:* Permanent Mission of Bangladesh to United Nations, 820 Second Avenue, 4th Floor, New York, NY 10017, USA (office). *Telephone:* (212) 867-3434 (office). *Fax:* (212) 972-4038 (office). *E-mail:* bangladesh@un.int (office); bdpmny@gmail.com (office). *Website:* www.un.int/bangladesh (office).

MOMIS, John; Papua New Guinea politician; *President of Bougainville;* b. Salamaua; m. Elizabeth Momis; ed St Brendan's Coll., Queensland, Australia; ordained as Roman Catholic priest 1970, served as priest 1970–93; mem. Papua New Guinea (PNG) House of Ass. for N Solomons (now Bougainville) 1972–99, Deputy Leader of the Opposition 1985–87, 1987–88, 1994, Chair. Constitutional Planning Cttee 1972–75 (co-writer PNG Constitution); fmr Minister for Decentralization, Deputy Prime Minister and Minister for Public Service 1985, Minister for Provincial Affairs 1988–92, Shadow Minister for Bougainville Affairs 1992, Shadow Minister for Provincial Affairs 1993, Minister of Information and Communication 1994; Gov. of Bougainville 1999–2005; unsuccessful cand. in presidential election 2005; Amb. to People's Repub. of China –2010; co-f. Melanesian Alliance Party; mem. New Bougainville Party, Leader 2010–; Pres. of Bougainville 2010–. *Address:* Office of the President, Bougainville, Papua New Guinea (office).

MOMOTARO, Dennis, BA; Marshall Islands business executive and politician; *Minister of Finance;* b. 26 Oct. 1954; m. Daisy Momotaro; two s. two d.; ed Rockhurst Coll., Kansas City, Mo., USA; began career with Majuro Stevedoring and Terminal Co. 1969–73; teacher, Head Start Program, Majuro 1973; janitor, 9th Street Nursing Home, Kansas City 1977–78; worked in Mailing Dept, Federal Reserve Bank, Kansas City 1978–80; Asst Man., Momotaro Corpn, Majuro 1980–91, Gen. Man. 1991–2007; mem. Nitijela (Parl.) for Mejit 2007–; Minister of Transportation and Communication 2008, of Finance 2012–; fmr mem. Bd of Dirs of various businesses and orgs including Nat. Telecommunication Authority

1996–97, Marshall Islands Devt Authority 1997–2003, Marshall Islands Devt Bank 1999–2007, Majuro Stevedoring and Terminal Co. 2003–07. *Leisure interests:* fishing, tennis, baseball, basketball, volleyball, music. *Address:* Ministry of Finance, POB P, Majuro MH 96960, Marshall Islands (office). *Telephone:* (625) 3320 (office). *Fax:* (625) 3607 (office). *E-mail:* secfin@ntamar.net (office).

MOMPER, Walter; German politician; *President of Lower House, Berlin Chamber of Deputies;* b. 21 Feb. 1945, Sulingen; mem. Berlin Chamber of Deputies 1975–95, 1999–; party whip, SPD, Berlin 1985–89, Chair. –1992; Gov. Mayor of Berlin 1989–91; Vice-Pres. Lower House, Berlin 1999–2001, Pres. 2001–. *Address:* Abgeordnetenhauses, Seydelstrasse 28, 10117 Berlin, Germany. *Telephone:* 20623698.

MONAGENG, Sanji Mmasenono, LLB; Botswana judge; *First Vice-President, International Criminal Court;* b. 9 Aug. 1950, Serowe; m. Kopano Mmamotse; ed Univ. of Botswana, Court Adm. Course, RIPA International, London, UK, Int. Criminal Law Course, Grotius Centre for Int. Law Studies, Leiden Univ., The Hague, Netherlands; magistrate 1987–97; CEO and Exec. Sec. Law Soc. of Botswana 1997–2006; Judge of High Court of Repub. of the Gambia, under Commonwealth Fund for Tech. Cooperation Programme 2006–08; Judge of High Court of Kingdom of Swaziland 2008–; mem. and Commr African Comm. on Human and Peoples' Rights 2003–, Chair. 2007–09; Judge, Pre-Trial Div., Int. Criminal Court, The Hague, Netherlands 2009–, First Vice-Pres., ICC 2012–; secondment as Deputy Chief Adjudication Officer to UN Observer Mission to S Africa, Johannesburg March–May 1994, to Law Soc. of Zimbabwe Feb.–March 1998, to Law Soc. of England and Wales, London, UK Jan.–March 2005; Residency at Brandies Univ., Boston, USA Sept. 2005; Chair. Ethics, Law and Human Rights sector of Nat. AIDS Council in Botswana; sat on numerous bds, including Nat. Broadcasting Bd of Botswana, Open Soc. Initiative of Southern Africa, Human Rights Trust of Southern Africa; Co-founder Transparency International (Botswana Chapter), Dirs Inst. of Botswana; Commr, Int. Comm. of Jurists; mem. Int. Bar Asscn, Int. Soc. for the Reform of Criminal Law, Int. Asscn of Women Judges, Emang Basadi Women's Org., Women in Law and Devt in Africa (WILDAF), Media Inst. of Southern Africa (Botswana Chapter), Commonwealth Magistrates and Judges Asscn; Trustee, Southern Africa Litigation Centre; African Human Rights Consortium Award, Gaborone. *Publications:* Purpose of Sentencing, Role of Women in Promoting Peace. *Leisure interests:* farming, reading, walking. *Address:* International Criminal Court, PO Box 19519, 2500 CM The Hague, The Netherlands (office). *Telephone:* (70) 515-87-55 (office). *Fax:* (70) 515-87-89 (office). *E-mail:* sanji.monageng@icc-cpi.int (office). *Website:* www.icc-cpi.int (office).

MONCADA, Sir Salvador Enrique, Kt, MD, PhD, DSc, FRS, FRCP, FMedSci; British academic, physician and scientist; b. 3 Dec. 1944, Tegucigalpa, Honduras; s. of Salvador Moncada and Jenny Seidner; m. 1st 1966; one s. (deceased) one d.; m. 2nd HRH Princess Esmeralda of Belgium 1998; one s. one d.; ed Univ. of El Salvador; Assoc. Prof. of Pharmacology and Physiology, Univ. of Honduras 1974–75; Section Leader, Wellcome Research Laboratories, Beckenham, Kent 1975–77, Head of Prostaglandin Research 1977–84, Dir of Therapeutic Research 1984–86, Dir of Research 1986–95; Dir Wolfson Inst. for Biomedical Research, Univ. Coll. London 1996–2011; Foreign mem. NAS 1994; Hon. mem. Asscn of Physicians of GB and Ireland 1997, American Soc. of Hematology 1999; Hon. DMed (Universidad Complutense de Madrid) 1986, (Antwerp) 1997, Academico de Honor de la Real Academia Nacional de Medicina 1993; Hon. DSc (Sussex) 1994, (Mount Sinai School of Medicine New York), (Nottingham) 1995, (Univ. Pierre and Marie Curie, Paris) 1997, (Edin.) 2000; Prince of Asturias Prize for Science and Tech. 1990, Amsterdam Prize for Medicine 1992, First Roussel Uclaf Prize, Royal Medal 1994, Louis and Artur Lucian Award 1997, Galen Medal in Therapeutics, Dale Medal, Gold Medal of the Spanish Soc. of Cardiology 1999, Gold Medal of the Royal Soc. of Medicine 2000, Le Grand Prix Annuel Lefoulon-Delalande, Institut de France 2002, Croonian Lecturer, Royal Soc., London 2005, Dohme Lecturer, The Johns Hopkins Univ. School of Medicine, Baltimore 2010, Ernst Jung Gold Medal 2013. *Publications:* Nitric Oxide from L-Arginine: A Bioregulatory System (co-ed.) 1990, The Biology of Nitric Oxide (Vols 1–7) 1992–2000; more than 500 peer-reviewed papers and highly-cited review. *Leisure interests:* theatre, literature, music, walking, diving. *Address:* The Wolfson Institute for Biomedical Research, University College London, Gower Street, London, WC1E 6BT, England (office). *Telephone:* (20) 7679-6789 (office). *Fax:* (20) 7209-0470 (office). *E-mail:* s.moncada@ucl.ac.uk (office). *Website:* www.ucl.ac.uk/wibr (office).

MONCAYO GALLEGOS, Gen. Paco, MSc, PhD; Ecuadorean army officer (retd) and politician; *Mayor of Quito;* b. 1941; m. Marta de Moncayo; four c.; fmr Pres. of Rumiñahui Bank; fmr C-in-C of Armed Forces; fmr Head of the Ministry of Agric.; fmr Nat. Deputy; Mayor of Quito 2000–; currently Co-Pres. United Cities and Local Govts; mem. Acad. of Ecuadorian History; lectures in Geopolitics and Int. Law at Ecuador Cen. Univ. University; Simón Bolívar Medal, UNESCO 2004. *Address:* Alcaldía de Quito, Quito, Ecuador (office); c/o United Cities and Local Governments, Carrer Avinyó, 15, 08002 Barcelona, Spain. *E-mail:* info@cities -localgovernments.org. *Website:* www.cities-localgovernments.org.

MONDALE, Walter Frederick, LLB; American lawyer, diplomatist and fmr politician; *Senior Counsel, Dorsey and Whitney LLP;* b. 5 Jan. 1928, Ceylon, Minn.; s. of Rev. and Mrs Theodore Sigvaard Mondale; m. Joan Adams 1955; two s. one d.; ed Minnesota public schools, Macalester Coll., Univ. of Minnesota and Univ. of Minnesota Law School; admitted to Minn. Bar 1956, pvt. practice 1956–60; Attorney-Gen. of Minn. 1960–64; Senator from Minnesota 1964–77; Vice-Pres. of the US 1977–81, mem. Nat. Security Council 1977–81; unsuccessful Democratic Party cand. for US President 1984; Counsel, Winston and Strawn (law firm) 1981–87; Pnr, Dorsey and Whitney LLP (law firm) 1987–93, now Sr Counsel and Pnr, Int./Corp. Practice Group; Amb. to Japan 1993–96; Norway's Hon. Consul Gen. in Minneapolis 2008–; mem. Exec. Cttee Nobel Peace Prize Forum; fmr mem. Bd of Dirs Control Data, Columbia Pictures; fmr Regent, Smithsonian Inst.; mem. Democrat-Farm Labor Party;. *Publications:* The Accountability of Power: Towards a Responsible Presidency 1975, The Good Fight: A Life in Liberal Politics 2010. *Leisure interest:* fishing. *Address:* Dorsey and Whitney LLP, Suite 1500, 50 South Sixth Street, Minneapolis, MN 55402-1498, USA (office). *Telephone:* (612) 340-6307 (office). *Fax:* (952) 516-5673 (office). *E-mail:* mondale.walter@dorsey.com (office). *Website:* www.dorsey.com (office).

MONDJO, Charles Richard; Republic of Congo army officer and politician; *Minister at the Presidency for Defence;* b. 6 Aug. 1959, Brazzaville; s. of Nicolas Mondjo and Marguerite Konongo; m.; four c.; ed Prora Mil. Training Base, GDR; mem. Congolese Armed Forces, Head of Section, First Co., First Bn, Makola Training Centre 1979–80, Commdr 1980, Chief of Staff, 15th Bn, Mechanized Infantry, Pointe-Noire 1981–82, Chief of Staff, First Armoured Regt, Brazzaville 1986–87, Dir of Studies, Marien Ngouabi Mil. Acad., Brazzaville 1987–93, Commdr, Mil. Zone I 1997–2002, Chief of Staff of Congolese Armed Forces 2002–12; Minister at the Presidency for Defence 2012–. *Address:* Office of the Minister at the Presidency, Brazzaville, Republic of Congo (office). *Telephone:* 22-281-22-31 (office).

MONDLANE, Agostinho Salvador, BEcons; Mozambican economist and politician; *Minister of National Defence;* b. 21 Nov. 1959, Maputo; s. of Salvador Mondlane and Beatriz Rieza Alberto Nhaca; three c.; ed Eduardo Mondlane Univ., Univ. of London, UK; Prof., Commercial Inst. of Maputo 1982–83; Lecturer, Faculty of Econs, Eduardo Mondlane Univ. 1984; joined Ministry of Construction and Water 1988, Dir Urban Rehabilitation Project Implementation Unit –1990, Deputy Minister of Construction and Water 1990–94, of Public Works 1994–2000, of Defence 2007–14, Minister of Defence 2014–; mem. Frente de Libertação de Moçambique (Frelimo). *Address:* Ministry of National Defence, Av. Mártires de Mueda 280, CP 3216, Maputo, Mozambique (office). *Telephone:* 21492081 (office). *Fax:* 21491619 (office).

MONDRAGÓN DE VILLAR, María Elena, MEconSc; Honduran economist and central banker; *President, Banco Central de Honduras;* ed Univ. Nacional Autónoma de Honduras, Memphis State Univ., USA; 22 years with Banco Central de Honduras, various positions in Econs Dept, becoming Asst to Presidency, Pres. 2002–06, 2010–; Dir of Econs and Finance, Foundation for Promotion of Democracy and Social Welfare (FUNDEMOS) –2010; fmr Dir of Integration and Trade Policy, Ministry of Economy and Trade; Founding mem. National Identity Foundation; fmr Exec. Sec., later Pres., Foundation for Educ. Ricardo Ernesto Maduro Andreu; fmr Dir of Finance, Grupo Atlántida; fmr Project Man., Fundación Democracia y Desarrollo de Honduras. *Address:* Office of the President, Banco Central de Honduras, Avda Juan Ramón Molina, 7a Avda y 1a Calle, Apdo 3165, Tegucigalpa, Honduras (office). *Telephone:* 2237-2270 (office). *Fax:* 2237-1876 (office). *E-mail:* Carlos.Espinoza@bch.hn (office). *Website:* www.bch.hn (office).

MONEO, José Rafael, DArch; Spanish architect and academic; *Josep Lluis Sert Professor of Architecture, Harvard University;* b. 9 May 1937, Tudela, Navarra; s. of Rafael Moneo and Teresa Vallés; m. Belén Feduchi 1963; three d.; ed Madrid Univ. School of Architecture; Fellow, Acad. in Rome, Italy 1963–65; Asst Prof. Madrid School of Architecture 1966–70; Prof., Barcelona School of Architecture 1970–80; Visiting Fellow, Inst. for Architecture and Urban Studies, Cooper Union School of Architecture, New York, USA 1976–77; Chair. Dept of Architecture Harvard Univ. Grad. School of Design, USA 1985–90, Josep Lluís Sert Prof. 1992–; mem. American Acad. of Arts and Sciences, Accad. di San Luca di Roma, Real Academia de Bellas Artes de San Fernando of España; Hon. FAIA; Dr hc (Leuven) 1993; Premio di Roma 1962, Gold Medal for Achievement in Fine Arts, Govt of Spain 1992, Brunner Memorial Prize, American Acad. of Arts and Letters, Schock Prize in the Visual Arts 1993, Pritzker Award 1996, Int. Union of Architects Gold Medal 1996, Antonio Feltrinelli Prize 1998, RIBA Gold Medal 2003 and other distinctions. *Work includes:* Bankinter Bank, Madrid, Nat. Museum of Roman Art, Mérida, Thyssen Bornemisza Museum, San Pablo Airport, Seville, Manzana Diagonal, Barcelona, Davis Museum, Wellesley Coll., USA, City Hall Extension, Murcia 1998, Barcelona Concert Hall 1999, Kursaal Concert Hall, San Sebastian 1999, Audrey Jones Beck Building, Houston Museum of Fine Arts 2000, Cathedral of Our Lady of the Angels, Los Angeles, Calif., USA 2002, Chivite Winery, Arínzano, Navarra 2002, Arenberg Campus Library, Catholic Univ. of Louvain, Belgium 2002, Gen. and Royal Archive of Navarra, Pamplona 2003, Gregorio Marañón Mother's and Children's Hosp., Madrid 2003, Bank of Spain Extension, Madrid 2006, Contemporary Art Center of Aragon Beulas Foundation, Huesca 2004, Prado Museum Extension, Madrid 2007, Lab. for Integrated Science and Eng Bldg, Harvard Univ. 2007, Chace Center, Rhode Island School of Design 2008, Museum of the Roman Theater, Cartagena 2008, Library of Univ. of Deusto, Bilbao 2009, Lab. for Novartis Campus, Basel 2009, Commercial Center 'Aragoña', Zaragoza 2009. *Address:* Calle Cinca 5, 28002 Madrid, Spain (home). *Telephone:* (1) 564-2257 (office). *Fax:* (1) 563-5217 (office). *E-mail:* r.moneo@rafaelmoneo.com (office). *Website:* www.gsd.harvard.edu/people/faculty/moneo (office).

MONGE ÁLVAREZ, Luis Alberto; Costa Rican politician; b. 29 Dec. 1925, Palmares, Alajuela; s. of Gerardo Monge Quesada and Elisa Alvarez Vargas; ed Univ. of Costa Rica and Univ. of Geneva, Switzerland; mem. Cen. de Trabajadores Rerum Novarum 1947, subsequently Pres.; fmr Vice-Pres. Inter-American Labor Confed. (CIT); militant mem. Nat. Liberation Army 1948; mem. Nat. Constituent Ass. (Social Democrat) 1949; Co-founder Nat. Liberation Party 1951, Sec.-Gen. for 12 years; worked for ILO, Geneva for three years; Sec.-Gen. Interamerican Labor Org. (ORIT) for six years; served at Ministry of the Presidency, Govt of José Figueras 1955; mem. Legis. Ass. 1958, 1970, Pres. of Congress 1970–74; Prof. Inter-American School of Democratic Educ. and Dir Centre of Democratic Studies for Latin America (CEDAL); Pres. of Costa Rica 1982–86.

MONGELLA, Gertrude Ibengwe; Tanzanian international organization official; b. 1945; four c.; ed Univ. of Dar Es Salaam; fmr teacher; mem. Parl. 1980–93; Minister of State, Prime Minister's Office 1982–88, Minister of Lands, Tourism and Natural Resources 1985–87, Minister without Portfolio 1987–90; High Commr to India 1991–92; UN Asst Sec.-Gen. and Sec.-Gen., Fourth World Conf. on Women, Beijing 1993–95, UN Under-Sec. and Special Envoy to UN Sec.-Gen. on Women's Issues and Devt 1996–97; Sr Adviser to Exec. Sec. of Econ. Comm. for Africa (ECA) on Gender Issues 1997–; mem. Parl. for Ukerewe Constituency 2000–04; Pres. Pan African Parl. (consultative ass. of the African Union) 2004–08; Head of African Union's election monitoring team during Zimbabwe presidential election 2002; WHO Goodwill Amb. for Africa Region 2003–04; Chair. Int. Advisory Bd African Press Org. 2008–; Councillor, World Future Council, Johannesburg; Delta Prize for Global Understanding 2005, Guarini Inst. Global Leadership Award 2012. *Address:* World Future Council, 3 Second St, Melville, Johannesburg 2109, South Africa (office). *Telephone:* (11) 7261113 (office). *Fax:* (11) 5455136 (office). *E-mail:* africa@worldfuturecouncil.org (office). *Website:* www .worldfuturecouncil.org (office).

MONGIN, Pierre; French government official; *CEO, Régie Autonome des Transports Parisiens (RATP);* b. 9 Aug. 1954, Marseille; m. Danielle Charpin 1981; three c.; ed Ecole Nationale d'Admin; Dir Office of the Prefect of Ain 1980; Sec.-Gen. Pref. of Ariège 1981; Chief of Staff, Prefect of Yvelines 1982–84; Insp., Nat. Police, in charge of Gen. Inspectorate of Admin 1984–86; Chief of Staff, Office of Yves Galland, Minister of Local Govt 1987–88; Deputy Dir of the Budget, Police HQ 1988–93; Chief of Staff to Prime Minister Edouard Balladur 1993–95; Prefect of Eure-et-Loir 1995–99, of Vaucluse 1999, of Auvergne region and of Puy de Dome dépt 2002–04; Chief of Staff of Minister of Interior 2004–05, of the Prime Minister 2005–06; CEO RATP (Paris transport authority) 2006–; Chair. SYSTRA (SYSTRA is RATP firm specializing in urban and rail transport whose main shareholders are RATP and SNCF) 2010–. *Address:* RATP, LAC B916, 54 quai de la Rapée, 75599 Paris Cedex 12, France (office). *E-mail:* info@ratp.fr (office). *Website:* www.ratp.fr (office).

MONGUNO, Shettima Ali; Nigerian politician and educationist (retd); b. 1926, Monguno Dist, Borno Prov.; s. of Rahma Monguno and Fanna Monguno; m. 1st Ashe Monguno (divorced); m. 2nd Meta Monguno 1948 (died 1994); two s. five d.; m. 3rd Fatima Monguno 2001; ed Borno Middle School, Bauchi Teacher Training Coll., Katsina Higher Teachers' Coll., Univ. of Edinburgh, UK, Coll. of Arts, Science and Tech., Zaria, Moray House Coll. of Educ., Edinburgh; teacher, Yerwa Cen. Elementary School 1947–49, Borno Middle School 1952–56; MP (Kaga Marghi) 1959–66; Educ. Sec., Borno Native Admin 1952–58; Councillor for Educ., Borno Native Authority 1961–65; Fed. Minister of the Air Force 1965, of Internal Affairs 1965–66; Fed. Commr for Trade and Industry 1967–71, for Mines and Power, Petroleum and Energy 1971–75; Chair. Scholarship Bd, N Nigeria 1966–67; Chair. Borno Local Educ. Cttee 1966–67; Pres., OPEC 1972–73; Chair. Maiduguri Metropolitan Council 1976–79; Founding Pro-Chancellor, Calabar Univ. 1976–80, Univ. of Nigeria 1980–84; mem. Constituent Ass. 1978–79; Deputy Nat. Chair., Nat. Party of Nigeria (NPN) 1980–84; political detainee 1984–85 (cleared by mil. tribunal); del. to UN Gen. Ass., UNCTAD 1968, 1974 and many other int. confs; mem. Bd of Trustees, West African Examinations Council –1976; Chair. FRUCO Co. Nigeria Ltd 1987–2000; Chair. Bd of Trustees, Borno Educ. Endowment Fund 1986–87; Co-Pres. Provisional World Constitution and Parl. Asscn 1992–; mem. Bd of Trustees, World Environmental Movt for Africa (WEMFA) –1986; mem. Commonwealth Countries League Educ. Fund 1996–, Transparency International Nigeria 1997–; Life mem. Britain-Nigeria Asscn; Patron and Life mem. Nigeria-USA Council 1998; kidnapped by gunmen suspected of being mems of Islamic sect, Boko Haram, in Maiduguri, Borno State 3 May 2013, released three days later; Hon. Citizen, City of Oklahoma, Lima, Quito, Louisville; Hon. Mayor of Oklahoma City; Key to City of New York 1967; Distinguished Friend of Council, W African Exams Council 2002; numerous decorations including First Class Hons, Repub. of Egypt 1970, Order of the Two Niles (Sudan) 1970, First Class Nat. Honour (Cameroon) 1970, Honour of the Empire of Ethiopia 1970, Commdr, Order of Fed. Repub. (Nigeria) 1982; Hon. DLitt (Sokoto) 1984, (Maiduguri) 1996, (Univ. of Nigeria Nsuka) 2001; numerous awards including UNESCO Medal for Campaign against Illiteracy 1991, Borno State Merit Award. *Publication:* Corruption – Why It Thrives in Nigeria 1983. *Leisure interests:* gardening, reading, cycling, farming. *Address:* 5 Muhammed Monguno Road, Old Gra, Maiduguri, Borno State (office); PO Box 541, Maiduguri, Borno State, Nigeria (home). *Telephone:* (76) 231170; (76) 342140. *Fax:* (76) 231170; (76) 342140.

MONI, Dipu, MBBS, MPH, LLB, LLM; Bangladeshi politician; d. of the late M. A. Wadud; m. Tawfique Nawaz; one s. one d.; ed Dhaka Medical Coll., Johns Hopkins Univ. School of Public Health, USA, Univ. of London, UK; mem. Bangladesh Awami League, Sec. for Women's Affairs –2009, mem. Sub-cttee on Foreign Affairs; mem. Jatiya Sangsad (Parl.) for Chadnpur-3 2008–13; Minister of Foreign Affairs 2009–13; one of two Master Trainers for Women Political Activists. *Address:* c/o Bangladesh Awami League, 23 Bangabandhu Avenue, Dhaka, Bangladesh.

MONIÉ, Alain, MBA; French business executive; *President and CEO, Ingram Micro Inc.;* ed Ecole Nationale Supérieure d'Arts et Metiers, Institut Supérieur des Affaires, Jouy en Josas; began career in Mexico City as a civil construction engineer; held general man. positions with Sogitec Inc. (French aerospace simulation corpn); fmr controller for Renault; joined Allied Signals 1984, promoted from a regional sales man. to Head of Asia-Pacific operations, joined Honeywell through corpn's merger with Allied Signals Inc. 1999, Pres. Latin American Div. of Honeywell International 2001–03; Exec. Vice-Pres. Ingram Micro Inc. 2003–04, Pres. Asia-Pacific 2004–07, Pres. and COO Ingram Micro Inc. 2007–10, 2011–12, Pres. and CEO 2012–; CEO APRIL Management Pte, Singapore 2010–11; mem. Bd of Dirs Amazon.com, Inc. *Address:* Ingram Micro Inc., 1600 East St Andrew Place, PO Box 25125, Santa Ana, CA 92799-5125, USA (office). *Telephone:* (714) 566-1000 (office). *E-mail:* info@ingrammicro.com (office). *Website:* www.ingrammicro.com (office).

MONIZ, Ernest Jeffrey, BS, PhD; American nuclear physicist, academic and government official; *Secretary of Energy;* b. 22 Dec. 1944, Fall River, Mass; s. of Ernest Perry Moniz and Georgina Moniz (née Pavao); m. Naomi Hoki; one d.; ed Boston Coll., Stanford Univ., Univ. of Pennsylvania; Prof. of Physics, MIT 1973–97, Dir, Bates Linear Accelerator Center 1983–91, Head of Dept of Physics 1991–95, 1997, Prof. of Physics and Eng Systems 2001–, also Cecil & Ida Green Distinguished Prof. and Dir MIT Energy Initiative, Dir Lab. for Energy and the Environment; Assoc. Dir for Science, Office of Science and Tech. Policy, Exec. Office of the Pres. 1995–97; Under-Sec., US Dept of Energy 1997–2001, Sec. of Energy 2013–; Consultant, Los Alamos Nat. Lab. 1975–95; Dir American Science and Engineering, Inc. 1990–95, 2002–, ICF Int. Inc. 2011–; mem. Pres.'s Council of Advisors on Science and Tech. 2009–; Fellow, AAAS, American Physical Soc.; mem. Council on Foreign Relations. *Address:* US Department of Energy, Forrestal Bldg, 1000 Independence Avenue SW, Washington, DC 20585, USA (office). *Telephone:* (202) 586-5000 (office). *Fax:* (202) 586-4403 (office). *E-mail:* the.secretary@hq.doe .gov (office). *Website:* www.energy.gov (office).

MONK, Meredith Jane; American composer, singer, director and choreographer; b. 20 Nov. 1942, New York, NY; d. of Theodore G. Monk and Audrey Lois Monk (née Zellman); ed Sarah Lawrence Coll.; Founder and Artistic Dir House Foundation for the Arts 1968–; formed Meredith Monk & Vocal Ensemble 1978–; mem. American Acad. of Arts and Sciences 2006; Dr hc (Bard Coll.) 1988, (Univ. of the Arts) 1989, (Juilliard School of Music) 1998, (San Francisco Art Inst.) 1999, (Boston Conservatory) 2001; Golden Eagle Award 1981, Nat. Music Theatre Award 1986, German Critics' Award for Best Recording of the Year 1981, 1986, MacArthur Genius Award 1995, Samuel Scripps Award 1996, United States Artists Fellow 2006, Musical America Composer of the Year 2012, Doris Duke Artist 2012, NPR's 50 Great Voices 2012. *Films:* Book of Days, Ellis Island. *Compositions include:* Break 1964, 16 Millimeter Earrings 1966, Juice: A Theatre Cantata 1969, Key 1971, Vessel: An Opera Epic 1971, Paris 1972, Education of the Girlchild 1973, Quarry 1976, Songs from the Hill 1976, Dolmen Music 1979, Specimen Days: A Civil War Opera 1981, Ellis Island 1981, Turtle Dreams Cabaret 1983, The Games 1983, Acts from Under and Above 1986, Book of Days 1988, Facing North 1990, Three Heavens and Hells 1992, ATLAS: An Opera in Three Parts 1991, New York Requiem 1993, Volcano Songs 1994, American Archaeology 1994, The Politics of Quiet 1996, Steppe Music 1997, Magic Frequencies 1998, Micki Suite 2000, Eclipse Variations 2000, mercy 2001, Possible Sky 2003, impermanence 2004, Stringsongs 2005, Night 2005, Songs of Ascension 2008, Weave for two voices, chamber orchestra and chorus 2010, Realm Variations 2012, On Behalf of Nature 2013. *Leisure interests:* gardening, horseback riding. *Address:* The House Foundation, 260 West Broadway, Suite 2, New York, NY 10013, USA (office). *Telephone:* (212) 904-1330 (office). *Fax:* (212) 904-1305 (office). *E-mail:* monk@meredithmonk.org (office). *Website:* www.meredithmonk.org (office).

MÖNKH-ORGIL, Tsendiin; Mongolian politician; b. 1964, Sühbaatar prov.; ed Moscow Higher School of Int. Relations, Harvard Univ., USA; Attaché, Int. Orgs Dept, Ministry of Foreign Affairs 1998–91; Third, then Second Sec. for Political and Legal Affairs, Perm. Mission to UN, New York 1991–95; with int. law firm, Washington DC 1996; Dir-Gen. Mönh-Orgil, Idesh, Lynch 1997; apptd Deputy Minister of Law and Internal Affairs 2000; Minister of Foreign Affairs 2004–06 (resgnd); Minister of Justice and Home Affairs 2007–08. *Address:* c/o Ministry of Justice and Home Affairs, Government Building 5, Khudaldaany Gudamj 61A, Chingletei District, Ulan Bator, Mongolia (office).

MONKS, Baron (Life Peer), cr. 2010, of Blackley in the County of Greater Manchester; **John Stephen Monks,** BA; British trade union official; b. 5 Aug. 1945, Manchester, England; s. of Charles Edward Monks and Bessie Evelyn Monks; m. Francine Jacqueline Schenk 1970; two s. one d.; ed Univ. of Nottingham; joined TUC Org. Dept 1969, Asst Sec. Employment and Manpower Section 1974, Head Org., Employment Law and Industrial Relations Dept 1977–87, Deputy Gen.-Sec. 1987–93, Gen.-Sec. 1993–2003; Sec.-Gen. European Trade Union Confed. (ETUC) 2003–11; mem. Council Advisory, Conciliation and Arbitration Service (ACAS) 1979–95; mem. British Govt and EU Competitiveness Councils 1997; Visiting Prof., School of Man., Manchester Business School 1996–; mem. (Labour) House of Lords 2010–; Trustee, People's History Museum 1988–, Chair. 2005–; Dr hc (Nottingham, UMIST, Salford, Cranfield, Cardiff, Kingston, Southampton and Open Univs). *Leisure interests:* hiking, music, cycling. *Address:* House of Lords, Westminster, London, SW1A 0PW, England (office). *Telephone:* (20) 7219-6943 (office). *E-mail:* monksj@parliament.uk (office). *Website:* www .parliament.uk/biographies/lords/lord-monks/4186 (office).

MONNIER, Claude Michel, PhD; Swiss journalist (retd); b. 23 March 1938, Rwankéri, Rwanda; s. of Henri Monnier and Olga Pavlov; m. Estela Troncoso Balandrán 1958 (died 2005); two s.; ed Univs of Geneva and Mexico, Grad. Inst. of Int. Studies, Geneva; educational tour in Asia and America 1956–58; Research Fellow, Swiss Nat. Fund for Scientific Research, Tokyo 1963–66; Tokyo Corresp. Journal de Genève 1963–66, Foreign Ed. 1966–70, Ed.-in-Chief 1970–80; Ed. Le Temps Stratégique, Genève 1982–2001; mem. Bd French-speaking Swiss TV and radio 1989–2000; mem. Academic Council, Univ. of Lausanne 1998–2005, Bd Médias et Société Foundation, Geneva; Adviser to Gen. Man., Edipresse Suisse SA 2001–09. *Publications:* Les Américains et sa Majesté l'Empereur: Etude du conflit culturel d'où naquit la constitution japonaise de 1946 1967, Alerte, citoyens! 1989, L'année du Big-Bang 1990, La terre en a marre 1991, La déprime, ça suffit! 1992, Dieu, que la crise est jolie! 1993, Les Rouges nous manquent 1994, La bonté qui tue 1995, Envie de bouffer du lion 1996, Programme d'un agitateur 1997, Le temps des règlements de compte 1998, Le Culte suspect de l'action 1999, La trahison de l'an 2000 2000, Morts de trouille 2001, Il faut nous faire soigner! 2002, Où est ta victoire, George W.? 2003, La Suisse devient folle 2004, Et maintenant, on fait quoi? 2005, Les Helvètes auraient-ils la potion magique? 2006, Vous êtes viré? Bravo! 2007, Panique planétaire 2008, Ce coup-ci, les riches ont aussi la trouille 2009, Nous sommes gouvernés par des Martiens 2010. *Leisure interests:* walking, light aircraft flying. *Address:* Chemin de Saussac 2, 1256 Troinex, Geneva, Switzerland (home). *Telephone:* (22) 322-34-92 (office); (22) 343-95-55 (home). *E-mail:* claude.monnier@edipresse.ch (office).

MONOD, Jérôme; French business executive; b. 7 Sept. 1930, Paris; s. of Olivier Monod and Yvonne Monod (née Bruce); m. Françoise Gallot 1963; three s.; ed Wesleyan Univ., USA, Institut d'Etudes Politiques, Ecole Nat. d'Admin; Auditeur, Cour des Comptes 1957; Rapporteur, Study mission of Sec.-Gen. for Algerian Affairs 1958; Chargé de mission, Prime Minister's Office 1959–62; Conseiller Référendaire à la Cour des Comptes 1963; Chief Exec. Dél. à l'Aménagement du Territoire 1967–75; Special Asst to Prime Minister Jacques Chirac 1975–1976; Sec.-Gen. Rassemblement pour la République (RPR) 1976–78; Chair. Bd, Centre Français du Commerce Extérieur 1980–83; Pres. French Canadian Chamber of Commerce in Paris 1984–86; Vice-Pres. Société Lyonnaise des Eaux 1979–80, Chair. and CEO 1980–97; Vice-Chair. General Waterworks Corpn (USA) 1983–93; Vice-Chair., Compagnie de Suez 1995–97, Chair. Supervisory Bd, Suez Lyonnaise des Eaux 1997–2000, Chair. Lyonnaise des Eaux de Casablanca 1997–2000; Chair. Sino French Holding (China) 1996–; Adviser to Pres. of France 2000–02; mem. Bd of Dirs Total (Cie Française des Pétroles), Aguas de Barcelona (Spain), Dic-Degrémont (Japan), Lyonnaise American Holding (USA), Groupe GTM, GTM-Entrepose, Métropole Télévision; mem. Consultative Council Banque de France, Business Advisory Council, IFC (USA); mem. Int. Advisory Bd, NatWest Bank; mem. Steering Cttee, European Round Table 1995–2000; Commdr, Légion d'honneur, Officier des Arts et des Lettres, Chevalier des Palmes académiques. *Publications:* L'aménagement du territoire 1971, Transformation d'un pays: pour une géographie de la liberté 1975, Propositions pour la France 1977, Manifeste pour une Europe souveraine 1999, L'Aménagement du territoire 2002, Essai sur la Gouvernance publique 2004, L'aménagement du territoire 2006. *Leisure interests:* swimming, climbing. *Address:* 15, rue de Verneuil, 75007 Paris, France (home).

MONORY, Jacques; French painter; b. 25 June 1924, Paris; s. of Luis José Monory and Angèle Foucher; m. 2nd Sabine Monirys 1959 (divorced 1968); one s.; m. 3rd Paule Moninot 1993; ed Ecole des Beaux Arts de Paris, Ecole des Arts Appliqués, Paris; Diplomé de l'Ecole des Arts Appliqués; work represented in numerous public collections in Europe, USA and Japan. *Films:* Ex 1968, Brighton Belle 1973, La Voleuse (video) 1986, Le Moindre Geste peut faire signe 1986. *Publications:* Document bleu 1970, Diamondback 1979, Rien ne bouge assez vite au bord de la mort 1984, Quick 1985, Eldorado 1991, 3' 30" 1993, Angèle 2005. *Leisure interests:* shooting, swimming. *Address:* 9 Villa Carnot, 94230 Cachan, France (home). *Telephone:* 1-46-65-08-67 (home). *Fax:* 1-46-65-08-67 (home). *E-mail:* jacques.monory@wanadoo.fr (office). *Website:* www.jacquesmonory.com (office).

MONREAL LUQUE, Alberto, DEconSc; Spanish politician and economist; *President, Eurotabac;* b. 18 Nov. 1928, Madrid; s. of Federico Monreal and Irene Luque; m. María Elena Alfageme 1961; two s. one d.; ed Univ. de Madrid; mem. Cuerpo de Economistas del Estado 1957–; Prof., Faculty of Econ. Sciences, Univ. de Madrid 1957–68; Tech. Sec. Ministry of Public Works 1965–68; Sec. of State, Ministry of Educ. and Science 1968–69; Minister of Finance 1969–73; Pres. Tabacalera (Tobacco Monopoly Co.) 1974–82; Pres. Eurotabac 1994–; Econ. Consultant, Superior Council of Commerce, Ministry of the Economy; Deputy Chair. Grupo Anaya (publrs). *Address:* Eurotabac, Monte Esquinza 34, 28010, Madrid, Spain (office). *Telephone:* (91) 3104218 (office). *Fax:* (91) 3104286 (office). *E-mail:* eurotabac@retemail.es (office).

MONSENGWO PASINYA, HE Cardinal Laurent; Democratic Republic of the Congo ecclesiastic and academic; *Archbishop of Kinshasa;* b. 7 Oct. 1939, Mongobele, Inongo; ed Seminary of Bokoro, Major Seminary of Kabwe, Pontifical Urbaniana Univ. and Pontifical Biblical Inst., Rome, Pontifical Biblical Inst., Jerusalem, Israel; ordained priest, Diocese of Inongo 1963; carried out pastoral work and served as faculty mem. at Theological Faculty of Kinshasa for several years; Sec.-Gen. Congolese Episcopal Conf. 1976–80, Pres. 1980, 1992; Auxiliary Bishop of Inongo 1980–81; Titular Bishop of Aquae Novae in Proconsulari 1980–; Auxiliary Bishop of Kisangani 1981–88, Metropolitan Archbishop of Kisangani 1988–2007; Archbishop of Kinshasa 2007–; cr. Cardinal (Cardinal-Priest of Santa Maria 'Regina Pacis' in Ostia mare) 2010; participated in Papal Conclave 2013; Co-Pres. Pax Christi International 2007–. *Achievements include:* first African to obtain a doctorate in biblical studies. *Address:* Archeveche, Avenue de l'Universite, BP 8431, Kinshasa 1, Democratic Republic of the Congo (office). *Telephone:* (12) 3723546 (office).

MONSER, Edward L., BEng, BEduc; American business executive; *President and Chief Operating Officer, Emerson Electric Company;* ed Illinois Inst. of Tech., Eastern Michigan Univ., Exec. Educ. Program, Stanford Univ. Grad. School of Business; began career as sr engineer at Emerson's Rosemount div. 1981, served in several eng man. positions, Dir of Tech. 1987–89, apptd Dir of New Products and Tech. 1989, went on to hold Vice-Pres. positions before becoming Exec. Vice-Pres. and Gen. Man., Pres. Rosemount 1996–2001, COO Emerson Electric Co. 2001–, Pres. 2010–; mem. Bd of Trustees, Eisenhower Fellowships; Chair. Ranken Tech. Coll.; Trustee, St Louis Science Center; mem. Bd of Overseers Illinois Inst. of Tech.; mem. Bd of Dirs The Backstoppers, Inc.; mem. Econ. Devt Bd for China's Guangdong Prov.; fmr mem. Bd and fmr Vice-Chair. US-China Business Council. *Address:* Emerson Electric Co., PO Box 4100, 8000 West Florissant Avenue, PO Box 4100, St Louis, MO 63136-8506, USA (office). *Telephone:* (314) 553-2000 (office). *Fax:* (314) 553-3527 (office). *E-mail:* info@emerson.com (office). *Website:* www.emerson.com (office).

MONSUR, Hussain, MSc, DSc; Bangladeshi geologist, academic and oil industry executive; *Chairman, Bangladesh Oil, Gas and Mineral Corporation (PETRO-BANGLA);* b. 27 Jan. 1953, Kushabari, Sirajgonj; m. Rehana Akhtar; two d.; ed Rajshahi College, Moscow Geological Prospecting Institute, USSR, Free University of Brussels, Belgium, Kingston University, London; began career as lecturer, Dept of Geology, Univ. of Dhaka 1978, later becoming Prof., several other positions including Chair., Dept of Geology, Provost of Fazlul Haque Hall; Chair., Bangladesh Oil, Gas and Mineral Corpn (PETROBANGLA) (state-owned oil and gas exploration co.) 2001, 2009–. *Publications:* An Introduction to the Quaternary Geology of Bangladesh, Quaternary ebong Bangladesher Bhutattik Kramabikash; 28 scientific papers published in various nat. and int. journals. *Address:* PETROBANGLA, Petrocentre, 3 Kawran Bazar C/A, Dhaka 1215, Bangladesh (office). *Telephone:* (2) 8156655 (office). *Fax:* (2) 9120224 (office). *E-mail:* petchair@petrobangla.org.bd (office). *Website:* www.petrobangla.org.bd (office).

MONTAGNA, Gilberto Luis Humberto; Argentine civil engineer; b. 28 Jan. 1935; m.; four c.; ed Univ. of Buenos Aires; Sec. Chamber of Food Industrialists (CIPA) 1964–84, First Vice-Pres. 1984–94; Sec. Fed. of Food and Derivatives Industries (FIPAA) 1975–84, Pres. 1984–87; Sec. to Co-ordinator of Food and Derivates Industry (COPAL) 1975–79, Pres. 1979–88; Sec. Industrial Transitory Comm. (COTEI) of Unión Industrial Argentina (UIA) 1978–79, mem. Advising Exec. Comm. of UIA Comptrolling 1979–81, First Vice-Pres. UIA 1981–89, Third Vice-Pres. 1991–93; Tech. Adviser, ILO, Geneva 1978; Alt. Del. 1979–81; Founder, later Vice-Pres. Action for Pvt. Initiative; Vice-Pres. Establecimientos Modelo Terrabusi SAIC 1987–94; Dir Terra Garba Sacai y F, Atilena SCA; Commendatore della Repubblica Italiana 1992; Konex Business Leaders Award 1988. *Address:* c/o Unión Industrial Argentina, Avda Leandro N Arem 1067, 11°, 1001 Buenos Aires, Argentina.

MONTAGNIER, Luc Antoine, LèsL, DMed; French research scientist, academic and international organization official; *President, World Foundation for AIDS Research and Prevention;* b. 18 Aug. 1932, Chabris; s. of Antoine Montagnier and Marianne Rousselet; m. Dorothea Ackermann 1961; one s. two d.; ed Univs of Poitiers and Paris; Asst in Faculty of Science, Paris 1955–60, Attaché 1960, Head 1963, Head of Research 1967; Dir of Research, CNRS 1974–; Head of Lab., Inst. of Radium 1965–71; Head of Viral Oncology Unit, Pasteur Inst. 1972–, Prof., Pasteur Inst. 1985–; Univ. Chair Prof., Shanghai Jiaotong Univ. 2010–; Vice-Pres. Scientific Council AIDS Research Agency 1989–; Pres. World Foundation for

AIDS Research and Prevention (WFARP) 1993–; Prof., Queens Coll., New York 1997–2001; mem. Acad. nat. de Médecine 1989, Acad. des Sciences 1996; Commdr, Légion d'honneur 1994, Grand Officier 2009; Commdr, Ordre nat. du Mérite; Lauréat du CNRS 1964, 1973, Prix Rosen de Cancérologie 1971, Prix Galien 1985, Prix de la Fondation Louis-Jeantet 1986, Prix Lasker 1986, Prix Gairdner 1987, Japan Prize 1988, King Faisal Prize 1993, Warren Alpert Foundation Prize 1998, Prince of Asturias Prize for Science 2000, Nobel Prize in Physiology or Medicine (co-recipient) 2008 and many other prizes. *Publications include:* Vaincre le SIDA 1986, SIDA: les faits, l'espoir 1987, SIDA et infection par VIH (co-author) 1989, Des virus et des hommes 1994, Oxidative Stress in Cancer, AIDS and Neurodegenerative Diseases (co-author) 1997, New Concepts in Aids Pathogenesis (co-author), Virus (co-author) 2000, Les Combats de la Vie: Mieux que Guérir 2008, Le Nobel et le Moine 2009; numerous scientific papers. *Leisure interests:* piano playing, swimming. *Address:* World Foundation for AIDS Research and Prevention, UNESCO, 1 rue Miollis, 75732 Paris Cedex 15, France (office); Fondation Luc Montagnier, Rue du Mont-Blanc 16, 1201 Geneva, Switzerland. *Telephone:* 1-45-68-45-45 (office). *Fax:* 1-42-73-37-45 (office). *E-mail:* lucmontagnier@gmail.com (office). *Website:* montagnier.org (office).

MONTAGUE, Sir Adrian Alastair, Kt, CBE, KB, MA; British business executive; *Chairman, 3i Group plc;* b. 28 Feb. 1948; s. of the late Charles Edward Montague and Olive Montague (née Jones); m. 1st Pamela Evans 1970 (divorced 1982, died 2000); one s. two d.; m. 2nd Penelope Webb 1986; one s.; ed Trinity Hall, Cambridge; admitted solicitor 1973; with Linklater & Paines Solicitors, London 1971–94, Partner 1979; Dir Kleinwort Benson (subsequently Dresdner Kleinwort Benson) where he was Co-Head merged Global Project Finance businesses of Kleinwort Benson and Dresdner Bank 1994–97; Chief Exec. Pvt. Finance Initiative Taskforce, HM Treasury 1997–2000; Deputy Chair. Partnerships UK PLC 2000–01; Deputy Chair. Network Rail 2001–04; Chair. British Energy PLC 2002–09, Friends Provident PLC 2005–09, 3i Group 2010–; Dir Michael Page International PLC 2001–, Chair. (non-exec.) 2002–; Chair. (non-exec.) Partnerships for Health PLC; Chair. Infrastructure Investors Ltd 2005–; Dir CellMark AB, Gothenburg; Sr Int. Adviser to Société Générale, Paris 2001–04; mem. Strategic Rail Authority 2000–01; fmr Pvt. Finance Adviser to Deputy Prime Minister. *Address:* 3i Group plc, 16 Palace Street, London, SW1E 5JD, England (office). *Telephone:* (20) 7928-3131 (office). *Fax:* (20) 7928-0058 (office). *Website:* www.3i.com (office).

MONTANA, Claude; French fashion designer; b. 1949, Paris; m. Wallis Franken 1993; began career designing jewellery in London, then worked for leather and knitwear firms; first ready-to-wear show 1976; f. Claude Montana Co. 1979; opened boutiques in Paris 1983, 1986; f. Montana Fragrances Co. 1984; designer in charge of Haute Couture, House of Lanvin 1990-92; designed men's wear for Complice, Italy; mem. Chambre Syndicale du Pret-a-Porter.

MONTANA, Joseph Clifford (Joe), Jr, BBA; American fmr professional football player; b. 11 June 1956, New Eagle, Pa; s. of Joseph C. Montana, Sr and Theresa Montana; m. 1st Kim Moses 1974 (divorced 1977); m. 2nd Cass Castillo 1981 (divorced 1984); m. 3rd Jennifer Wallace 1985; two s. two d.; ed Univ. of Notre Dame; quarterback, San Francisco 49ers 1979–93, Kansas City Chiefs 1993–94, Nat. Football League (NFL); commentator NBC TV 1995–; career statistics include 3,409 completions, 40,551 passing yards, 273 touchdowns, 92.3 passer rating; mem. NFL Super Bowl championship teams 1982, 1985, 1989; played in Pro Bowl 1982–85; Pnr, Target-Chip Ganassi Racing Team 1995–; New Business Devt Dept, Viking Components Inc. 1999; owns horses and produces wine under the label Montagia; voted Most Valuable Player in NFL Super Bowl 1982, 1985, 1990 (record), NFL Comeback Player of the Year Award (jtly with Tommy Kramer) 1986, AP NFL Most Valuable Player 1989, 1990, Associated Press Male Athlete of the Year 1989, 1990, elected to Pro Football Hall of Fame 2000. *Television:* appeared as character 'Joe Clifford' (pseudonym derived from first and middle names) in NFL Network's Joe's Diner (TV short) television spots 2008. *Publication:* Cool Under Fire (with Alan Steinberg) 1989. *Address:* c/o IMG, 304 Park Avenue South, New York, NY 10010, USA. *Telephone:* (212) 774-6735. *E-mail:* speakers@imgworld.com. *Website:* www.imgspeakers.com.

MONTAÑO, Jorge, MPA, PhD; Mexican diplomatist and academic; *Permanent Representative, United Nations;* b. 16 Aug. 1945, Mexico City; s. of Jorge Montaño and Lucia Montaño; m. Luz María Valdes; one s. one d.; ed Nat. Autonomous Univ. of Mexico, London School of Econs, UK; posts with Nat. Inst. of Fine Arts, Ministry of Public Educ., Nat. Autonomous Univ. of Mexico; Dir-Gen., Office for UN Specialized Agencies, then Dir-in-Chief for Multilateral Affairs, Ministry of Foreign Affairs 1979–82; fmr Int. Affairs Adviser to Pres. Salinas de Gortari; fmr univ. lecturer, Mexico and UK; Amb. and Perm. Rep. to UN, New York 1989–93, 2013–; Amb. to USA 1993–95; Prof. and Research Assoc., Instituto Tecnológico Autónoma de México 1995–; Founder and Pres. Asesoria y Analisis (consulting firm) c. 1999, private consultant on the enforcement of N American Free Trade Agreement (NAFTA); Founder Foreign Affairs en Español y del Consejo Mexicano de Asuntos Internacionales (journal); mem. OAS Multilateral Evaluation Mechanism on Drugs 2001–03, Int. Narcotics Control Bd 2009–12. *Publication:* several books, including The United Nations and the World Order 1945–1992 1992; articles on sociological, political, human rights and foreign policy issues in Mexico; contrib. to La Jornada, Reforma, El Universal, El País. *Address:* Permanent Mission of Mexico to the United Nations, Two United Nations Plaza, 28th Floor, New York, NY 10017, USA (office). *Telephone:* (212) 752-0220 (office). *Fax:* (212) 752-0634 (office). *E-mail:* onuusr1@sre.gob.mx (office); montesco98@yahoo.com.mx. *Website:* mision.sre.gob.mx/onu (office).

MONTEALEGRE, Eduardo, ScB, MBA; Nicaraguan politician; b. 9 May 1955; ed Brown Univ., Harvard Univ., USA; early career as business exec. and dir of several financial insts, positions included Man. BANIC Corpn and Asst Dir Cen. Bank of Nicaragua; lived in exile in USA during Sandanista rule 1979–90 serving as Vice Pres. Banking Investment Group, Shearson Lehman Hutton before forming Montealegre & Co (pvt. financial advisory co.); Chief of Staff in the Presidency 1998, 2003, Minister of Foreign Affairs 1999–2000, of Treasury and Public Credit 2002–03; mem. Constitutionalist Liberal Party (PLC) –2005; co-f. Alianza Liberal Nicaragüense (ALN) 2005, presidential cand. 2006. *Address:* c/o Alianza Liberal Nicaragüense (ALN), Managua, Nicaragua.

MONTEBOURG, Arnaud, Maîtrise en droit; French lawyer and politician; *Minister of Economy and Industrial Renewal*; b. 30 Oct. 1962, Clamecy (Nièvre); s. of Michel Montebourg and Leïla Ould Cadi; ed Panthéon Sorbonne, Sciences Po, Paris; barrister, Appeal Court of Paris; Deputy (Parti Socialiste) for Fifth Dist of Saône-et-Loire to Nat. Ass. 1997–2012; co-f., with Prof. Bastien François, Convention pour la VIe République (C6R) calling for constitutional change and the founding of a 'Sixth Republic' 2001; Founding mem. Nouveau Parti Socialiste (New Socialist Party), left to create new movt within Socialist Party; apptd spokesman for Ségolène Royal's presidential campaign 2006; Gen. Councillor and Pres. Gen. Council of Saône-et-Loire 2008–; cand. in Socialist presidential primary 2011; Minister of Industrial Renewal 2012–14, of Economy and Industrial Renewal 2014–; Juge titulaire, Cour de justice de la République 2002–07. *Publications:* La machine à trahir 2001, Des idées et des rêves 2011, Votez pour la démondialisation 2011. *Address:* Ministère du Redressement productif, 139 rue de Bercy, 75572 Paris Cedex 12 (office); General Council of Saône-et-Loire, Space Duhesme, 18 rue de Flacé, 71026 Macon Cedex 09, France (office). *Telephone:* 1-40-04-04-04 (ministry) (office); (3) 85-39-66-00 (Macon) (office). *E-mail:* Sec-mrp-sp@cabinets .finances.gouv.fr (office). *Website:* www.industrie.gouv.fr (office); www .redressement-productif.gouv.fr (office); www.arnaudmontebourg.fr.

MONTEGRIFFO, Peter Cecil Patrick, LLB; British barrister; *Partner, Hassans*; b. 28 Feb. 1960, Gibraltar; s. of Dr Cecil Montegriffo and Lily Zammitt; m. Josephine Perera 1985; two s.; ed Bayside Comprehensive School, Univ. of Leeds and Lincoln's Inn/Council of Legal Educ.; called to the Bar 1982; practitioner in J.A. Hassan & Partners law firm (now Hassans), Partner 1988–; mem. Exec. Gibraltar Labour Party/Asscn for Advancement of Civil Rights 1982–88, Deputy Leader 1988–89; Leader Gibraltar Social Democrats 1989–91; Deputy Chief Minister and Minister for Trade and Industry 1996–2000. *Publications:* contribs to International Trust Laws, Practical Guide to Offshore Trusts, Offshore Materials, Asset Protection, Jordans (Changes and Development of Corporate Tax System). *Leisure interests:* literature, economics, music, travel. *Address:* Hassans, 57 Line Wall Road, Gibraltar (office); 14 Admiral's Place, Old Naval Hospital, Gibraltar (home). *Telephone:* 79000 (office); 79912 (home). *Fax:* 71966 (office); 42772 (home). *E-mail:* peter.montegriffo@hassans.gi (office); pcm@gibnet.gi (home). *Website:* www.gibraltarlaw.com/people_details.php?Person_ID=23 (office).

MONTEIRO DE BARROS, Patrick; Portuguese business executive; *Chairman, Petroplus Holdings*; Sr Vice-Pres. Philipp Brothers 1975–87; Pres. and CEO Sigmoil Resources 1987–88; Chair. and CEO Argus Resources Ltd (UK) 1988–2006; Vice-Chair. Petroplus Holdings 2006–11, Chair. 2011–; Chair. Monteiro de Barros Foundation, Lisbon, Protea Holdings, NY, USA; Dir (non-exec.) Espirito Santo Financial Group. *Address:* Petroplus Holdings, Industriestrasse 24, 6300 Zug, Switzerland (office). *Telephone:* (58) 580-11-00 (office). *E-mail:* info@petroplus.biz (office). *Website:* www.petroplusholdings.com (office).

MONTEIRO DE CASTRO, HE Cardinal Manuel; Portuguese ecclesiastic and diplomatist; *Major Penitentiary of the Apostolic Penitentiary*; b. 29 March 1938, S. Eufemia; ordained priest, Archdiocese of Braga 1961; apptd Titular Archbishop of Beneventum 1985; Apostolic Pro-Nuncio to The Bahamas (also accred to Barbados, Belize, Dominca, Grenada, Jamaica, Saint Lucia, and Trinidad and Tobago) and Apostolic Del. to Turks and Caicos Islands and Netherlands Antilles 1985–90, also accred as Apostolic Pro-Nuncio to Antigua and Barbuda 1987–90; Apostolic Nuncio to El Salvador 1990–98, to S Africa (also accred to Namibia, Swaziland and Lesotho) 1998–2000, to Spain (also accred to Andorra) 2000–09; Sec. of the Congregation for Bishops 2009–12; Major Penitentiary of the Apostolic Penitentiary 2012–; cr. Cardinal (Cardinal-Deacon of San Domenico di Guzman) 2012; participated in Papal Conclave 2013. *Address:* Paenitentiaria Apostolica, Palazzo della Cancelleria, Piazza della Cancelleria 1, 00186 Rome, Italy (office). *Telephone:* (06) 69887526 (office); (06) 69887523 (office). *Fax:* (06) 69887557 (office). *Website:* www.vatican.va/roman_curia/tribunals/apost_penit (office); www.penitenzieria .va (office); www2.fiu.edu/~mirandas/curia.htm#Penitentiary (office).

MONTENEGRO RIZZARDINI, Gloria, PhD; Chilean ecologist, botanist and academic; *Professor and Director of Botany, Faculty of Agronomy and Forestry Sciences, Pontificia Universidad Catolica de Chile*; b. 16 July 1941, Santiago; m.; two c.; ed Pontifical Catholic Univ. of Chile and Univ. of Texas, USA; currently Dir of Botany and of Research and Graduate Studies, Prof. of Botany and Phytochemistry, Faculty of Agronomy and Forestry Sciences, Pontificia Universidad Catolica de Chile; Visiting Prof., Univ. of Texas, Univ. of Arizona, USA; Pres. Advisory Bd COPEC-PUC Foundation for Science and Natural Resources, Fundación para la Investigación en Ciencia y Tecnología en Recursos Naturales; fmr Pres. Botanical Soc. of Chile, Latin-American Botany Asscn, Int. Soc. for Mediterranean Ecosystems; mem. Scientific Advisory Bd TWAS-TWNSO-Global Environmental Facility projects; mem. Exec. Cttee and Regional Co-ordinator of the Latin America Plant Science Network; mem. Int. Cooperative Biodiversity Group; Exec. mem. UNESCO Group 'Women, Science & Technology in Latin America'; mem. Bd 'Comunidad-Mujer in Chile Group' (for improvement of women's rights); Fellow, Latin American Acad. of Sciences, Third World Acad. of Sciences; Gold Medal of Providencia Co., L'Oréal-UNESCO Women in Science Award 1998, Pontificia Univ. Catolica de Chile Monseñor Carlos Casanueva Prize for Distinguished Prof. 2008, named one of the 100 Leading Women in Chile 2008. *Publications:* Landscape Disturbance and Biodiversity in Mediterranean-Type Ecosystems (co-ed.) 1998, Fire and Climatic Change in Temperate Ecosystems of the Western Americas (co-ed.) 2003; several patents and scientific publs. *Address:* Facultad de Agronomia e Ingenieria Forestal, Pontificia Universidad Católica de Chile, Av. Vicuña Mackenna 4860, Santiago, Chile (office). *Telephone:* 354-5726 (office). *Fax:* 354-5702 (office). *E-mail:* gmonten@uc.cl (office). *Website:* agronomia .uc.cl (office).

MONTERISI, HE Cardinal Francesco, DTheol, DCL; Italian ecclesiastic; *Archpriest Emeritus of the Basilica of San Paolo fuori le Mura*; b. 28 May 1934, Barletta; ed Pontifical Minor Seminary and Pontifical Major Seminary, Rome, Pontifical Lateran Univ., Rome, Pontifical Ecclesiastical Acad., Pontifical Lateran Univ.; ordained priest Trani e Barletta (e Nazareth e Bisceglie) 1957; Titular Archbishop of Alba Maritima 1982–; Pro-Nuncio to Korea 1982–93; Official of the Roman Curia 1987–; Apostolic Nuncio to Bosnia and Herzegovina 1993–98; Sec. Congregation for Bishops 1998–2009, served as Sec. of Papal Conclave that elected Pope Benedict XVI April 2005; Archpriest of Basilica di San Paolo fuori le Mura

2009–12, Archpriest Emer. 2012–; cr. Cardinal (Cardinal-Deacon of San Paolo alla Regola) 2010; participated in Papal Conclave 2013. *Address:* Basilica di San Paolo fuori le Mura, 00120 Città del Vaticano, Rome, Italy (office). *Telephone:* (06) 69880800 (office). *Fax:* (06) 69880803 (office). *E-mail:* info@annopaolino.org (office); spbasilica@org.va (office). *Website:* www.vatican.va/various/basiliche/ san_paolo/index_en.html (office).

MONTGOMERIE, Colin Stuart, OBE; British professional golfer; b. 23 June 1963, Glasgow, Scotland; s. of James Montgomerie; m. 1st Eimear Wilson 1990 (divorced 2004); one s. two d.; m. 2nd Gaynor Knowles 2008; ed Strathallan School, Leeds Grammar School, Houston Baptist Univ., Texas, USA; won Scottish Stroke Play Championship 1985, Scottish Amateur Championship 1987; turned professional 1987; won Portuguese Open 1989, Scandinavian Masters 1991, 1999, 2001, Heineken Dutch Open, Volvo Masters 1993, Peugeot Open de España, Murphy's English Open, Volvo German Open 1994, Volvo German Open, Trophée Lancôme, Alfred Dunhill Cup 1995, Dubai Desert Classic, Murphy's Irish Open 1996, 1997, 2001, Canon European Masters, Million Dollar Challenge 1996, World Cup (Individual), Andersen Consulting World Champion 1997, PGA Championship 1998, 1999, 2000, German Masters 1998, Compaq European Grand Prix 1997, King Hassan II Trophy 1997, British Masters 1998, Benson and Hedges Int. Open 1999, BMW Int. Open 1999, Cisco World Matchplay 1999, Loch Lomond Invitational 1999, Skins Game (US) 2000, Novotel Perrier Open de France 2000, Ericsson Australian Masters 2001, Volvo Masters Andalucia, TCL Classic 2002, Macao Open 2003; mem. European Ryder Cup team from 1991–2004 (undefeated in Ryder Cup singles); apptd Capt. European Ryder Cup team 2009, captained winning European team, Celtic Manor, Wales Oct. 2010; named Pres. Golf Foundation (English jr golf charity) 2011; named by Scotland's First Minister, Alex Salmond, as an Amb. for the Scottish jr golf programme, Clubgolf 2012; Hon. LLD (St Andrews); Sir Henry Cotton Rookie of the Year 1988, eight times winner of Volvo Order of Merit Trophy 1993–2005, European Tour Player of the Year 1995, 1996, 1997, 1999, BBC Sports Personality of the Year Coach Award 2010, named by the Golf Club Managers' Asscn's Golf Club Management magazine as the seventh most powerful person in British golf 2012, inducted into World Golf Hall of Fame 2013, Colin Montgomerie Golf Acad., Turnberry, Scotland named after him. *Publications:* Real Monty: The Autobiography of Colin Montgomerie, The Thinking Man's Guide to Golf. *Leisure interests:* music, cars, DIY, films. *Address:* c/o IMG, McCormack House, Burlington Lane, London, W4 2TH, England. *Website:* www.colinmontgomerie.com.

MONTGOMERY, David; American photographer; b. 8 Feb. 1937, Brooklyn, New York; m. 1st (divorced); two d.; m. 2nd Martine King 1983; one s. one d.; ed Midwood High School, Brooklyn Coll., Juilliard School of Music; toured USA as musician; British resident early 1960s–; freelance photographer/dir 1960–; regular contrib. to Sunday Times Colour Magazine, Vogue, Tatler, Rolling Stone, Esquire, Fortune, New York Sunday Times, House and Garden magazines; has contributed to many books on home style: four in association with Tricia Guild of Designers Guild, a definitive English flower book for Pulbrook & Gould and four books on New Age aromatherapy entitled 'Romance', 'Relaxation', 'Vitality' and 'Well Being'; did photography for Nicky Haslam's book 'Sheer Opulence'; commissioned by Royal Mail to do a special edition stamp for the Millennium issue; photographic commissions for several major retailers, including Harrods, John Lewis, The Body Shop; has also shot major advertising campaigns for Designers Guild, Colefax and Fowler, Jane Churchill, Sandersons; has worked on campaigns for brands including Rolex, Saab, Fiat; has photographed HM Queen Elizabeth II, HM Queen Elizabeth the Queen Mother, TRH Duke and Duchess of York, Rt Hon. Margaret Thatcher, Rt Hon Pierre Trudeau, Mick Jagger, Clint Eastwood, Lord Mountbatten, Lord Hume, HM King Hussein, HRH Queen Noor, Rt Hon Edward Heath, Rt Hon James Callaghan, Baron Thyssen-Bornemisza, Prince and Princess Thurn und Taxis, HE Cardinal Basil Hume, Jimi Hendrix, The Rolling Stones, Sir Paul McCartney, Chrissie Hynde, Pierce Brosnan, Barbra Streisand, S Club 7, Atomic Kitten; teacher and Prof., Univ. of East London 2006–08; Master Class courses at The Observer/Guardian 2011; gives private photography lessons; numerous awards for photography and advertising. *Publications:* contrib. to New York Times/Sunday Times, Vogue, Homes and Gardens, Rolling Stone. *Leisure interests:* flowers, photography, day-dreaming, jazz music. *Address:* c/o M+M Management, Studio B, 11 Edith Grove, London, SW10 0JZ, England (office). *Telephone:* (20) 7823-3723 (office). *E-mail:* photography@mmmanagement.com (office); davidmontgomeryphoto@gmail.com (home). *Website:* www .mmmanagement.com (office).

MONTGOMERY, David John, BA; British newspaper executive; *Chairman, Local World Ltd;* b. 6 Nov. 1948, Bangor, Co. Down, NI; s. of William John Montgomery and Margaret Jean Montgomery; m. 1st Susan Frances Buchanan Russell 1971 (divorced 1987); m. 2nd Heidi Kingstone 1989 (divorced 1997); m. 3rd Sophie, Countess of Woolton 1997; ed Queen's Univ., Belfast; Sub-Ed., Daily Mirror, London, 1973–76, Asst Chief Sub-Ed. 1976–80; Chief Sub-Ed. The Sun 1980; Asst Ed. Sunday People 1982; Asst Ed. News of the World 1984, Ed. 1985–87; Ed. Today 1987–91 (Newspaper of the Year 1988); Man. Dir News UK 1987–91; Chief Exec. London Live TV 1991–92, Dir 1991–92; Chief Exec. Mirror Group 1992–99; Dir Satellite Television PLC 1986–91, News Group Newspapers 1986–91, Donohue Inc. 1992–95, Newspaper Publishing 1994–98, Scottish Media Group 1995–99, Press Asscn 1996–99; Founder and Exec. Chair. Mecom Group plc 2000–09, CEO 2009–11; Chair. Tri-Mex Group PLC 1999–2008, Yava 2000–02, Africa Lakes PLC 2000–07, Integrated Educ. Fund Devt Bd, NI 2000–, Espresso 2001–07; f. Mecom Group (investment group), London, 2000, acquired Berliner Verlag (Berliner Zeitung and Berliner Kurier newspapers), Germany, 2005, sold in 2009; Chair. Local World Ltd (regional newspaper publr) 2012–. *Leisure interests:* music, family. *Address:* Local World Ltd, Northcliffe House, 2 Derry Street, London, W8 5TT (office); 15 Collingham Gardens, London, SW5 0HS, England (home). *Telephone:* (20) 3615-2824 (office); (20) 7373-1982 (home). *E-mail:* David .Montgomery@localworld.co.uk (office). *Website:* www.local-world.co.uk (office).

MONTGOMERY, R. Lawrence (Larry), BS; American retail executive; *Chairman, Kohl's Department Stores;* b. 1949; ed Ferris State Univ.; Pres., Block's Div., Allied Stores Corpn 1985–87; Sr Vice-Pres., L. S. Ayres Div., May Dept Stores 1987–88; Sr Vice-Pres. and Dir of Stores, Kohl's Dept Stores 1988–93, Exec. Vice-Pres. 1993–96, Vice-Chair. 1994–2000, mem. Bd of Dirs 1994–, CEO 1999–2002,

Chair. 2002–. *Address:* Kohl's Department Stores, N56 W17000 Ridgewood Drive, Menomonee Falls, WI 53051-5660, USA (office). *Telephone:* (262) 703-7000 (office). *Website:* www.kohls.com (office).

MONTGOMERY, Tim; American fmr athlete; b. 28 Jan. 1975, Gaffney, SC; pnr Marion Jones; one d.; ed Gaffney High School, Blinn Coll. JC, Norfolk State Coll.; fmrly American football and baseball player; ran 100m in 9.96 seconds age 19; world record holder (9.78 seconds 100m), Grand Prix Final, 2002; ran fastest 60m (6.48 seconds), Dortmund 2002; coached by Trevor Graham; runner-up: JUCO Indoor 1994, USA Championships 100m 1997, USA Indoors 60m 1997, USATF Outdoor Championship 100m 2002, Golden Gala 100m 2002, Norwich Union Grand Prix 100m 2002; winner: Bislett Golden Gala 100m 2001, Zurich 100m 2001, Sparkassen 100m 2002, Engen Grand Prix 100m 2002, Prefontaine 100m 2002, DN Galan 100m 2002, Weltklasse 100m 2002, Memorial Van Damme 100m 2002, Grand Prix Final 100m 2002; Bronze Medal: World Championships 100m 1997; Silver Medal: Olympics 4x100m relay 1996, 1999, Goodwill Games 100m 2001,World Indoors 60m 2001, World Championships 100m 2001; Gold Medal: World Championships 4x100m relay 1999, Olympics 4x100m relay 2000; arrested on fed. heroin distribution charges 2008. *Address:* c/o Vector Sports Management, 417 Keller Parkway, Keller, TX 76248, USA (office). *E-mail:* info@ vectorsportsmgmt.com (office). *Website:* www.vectorsportsmgmt.com (office).

MONTI, Mario; Italian international organization official, economist and government official; b. 19 March 1943, Varese; m. Elsa Antonioli; two c.; ed Bocconi Univ., Milan and Yale Univ., USA; Assoc. Prof., Univ. of Trento 1969–70; Prof., Univ. of Turin 1970–79; Prof. of Monetary Theory and Policy, Bocconi Univ. 1971–85, Prof. of Econs, Dir Inst. of Econs 1985–94, f. Paolo Baffi Centre for Monetary and Financial Econs 1985, f. Innocenzo Gasparini Inst. of Econ. Research 1989, Rector, Bocconi Univ. 1989–94, Pres. 2005–; Econ. Commentator, *Corriere della Sera* 1978–94; Rapporteur, Treasury Cttee on Savings Protection 1981, Chair. Treasury Cttee on Banking and Financial System 1981–82, mem. Competition Act Drafting Cttee 1987–88, mem. Treasury Cttee on Debt Man. 1988–89, on Banking Law Reform 1989–91; mem. working party preparing Italy for single market 1988–90; mem. Macroeconomic Policy Group, European Comm. and Centre for Econ. Policy Studies (CEPS) 1985–86; mem. EC responsible for Internal Market, Financial Services and Financial Integration, Customs, Taxation 1995–99, for Competition 1999–2004; Int. Adviser, Goldman Sachs Int. 2005–; first Chair. Breughel (European think tank) 2005–; European Chair. Trilateral Comm. (neoliberal think tank); mem. Bilderberg Group; named Senator for Life by Pres. Giorgio Napolitano 2011; Prime Minister of Italy (asked to lead new govt following resignation of Silvio Berlusconi) 2011–12 (resgnd), also Minister of Economy and Finance 2011–12; contested gen. election, Feb. 2013, as leader of centrist coalition, Civic Choice; remained on as caretaker Prime Minister until formation of new govt; ranked by Forbes magazine amongst The World's Most Powerful People (29th) 2012; Senator for Life (highest Italian honour). *Publications include:* Report on the Future of the Single Market 2010. *Address:* Senate, Piazza Madama, 00187 Rome, Italy (office). *Telephone:* (06) 67061 (office). *E-mail:* infopoint@senato.it (office). *Website:* www.senato.it (office).

MONTIEL, Eduardo Luis, DBA MS; Nicaraguan politician; b. San Sebastián, Managua; Eduardo Montiel Argüello; m. 1st; two c.; m. 2nd Eugenia Argeñal; ed Harvard Business School, MIT, USA; early career as industrial engineer; Dean, Instituto Centroamericano de Administración de Empresas (INCAE); Pres. Del. Comisión de Promoción de Inversiones; Adviser, govt enterprises in Latin America, USA, Europe; Minister of Finance and Public Credit 2004–05; mem. Editorial Council. *Publications include:* more than 70 publications. *Address:* Frente a la Asamblea Nacional, Apdo 2170, Managua, Nicaragua (office).

MONTILLA AGUILERA, José, LLB; Spanish politician; *President, Government of Catalonia;* b. 15 Jan. 1955, Iznájar, Cordoba; m.; five c.; ed Univ. of Barcelona; mem. Partit dels Socialistes de Catalunya (PSC) 1978–, mem. Exec. Comm. 1987–, Sec. 1994, First Sec. 2000; mem. City Council, Sant Joan Despí 1979–83; mem. Council and Mayor, Cornellá de Llobregat 1983–2004; Second Vice-Pres., Barcelona Del. 1987–95, First Vice-Pres. 1999; Deputy, Barcelona Congress 2004–; Minister of Industry, Tourism and Trade 2004–06; Pres. Govt of Catalonia 2006–. *Address:* Government of Catalonia, Plaça de Sant Jaume 4, 08002 Barcelona, Spain (office). *Telephone:* (93) 4024600 (office). *Fax:* (93) 3183488 (office). *E-mail:* gbpresident.presidencia@gencat.cat (office). *Website:* www.gencat .cat/president (office).

MONTKIEWICZ, Zdzislaw; Polish business executive; b. 28 June 1944, Sokolów Podlaski; ed Mil. Tech. Acad.; mem. staff Polish Acad. of Sciences 1972–74, Ministry of Foreign Affairs 1974–78, UN Security Council 1978–82; Dir-Gen. Dernan & Sental Manufacturing and Financial Group 1983–88; Dir-Gen. Poland office, IBM World Trade/Europe/Middle East/Africa Corpn 1988–91; Pres. Ciech SA 1994–97; Pres. Prudential/Prumerica Financial Poland 1997–2001; Pres. Man. Bd Powszechny Zaklad Ubezpieczen (PZU) SA (state-controlled insurer) 2002–03; Founder-mem. Polish Trade and Finance Union; mem. Zacheta Art Soc. *Leisure interest:* reading historical books. *Address:* c/o Powszechny Zaklad Ubezpieczen SA, al. Jana Pawla II 24, 00-133 Warsaw, Poland (office).

MONTORO ROMERO, Cristóbal Ricardo, DEcon; Spanish economist, academic and politician; *Minister for the Treasury and Public Administration Services;* b. 28 July 1950, Jaén; m.; two c.; ed Universidad Autónoma de Madrid; Deputy Dir of Studies, Banco Atlántico 1975–81; Dir of Studies, Inst. for Econ. Studies 1981–93; mem. Congreso de los Diputados (Parl.) for Madrid 1993–2000, for Jaén 2000–08, for Seville 2011–, Econ. Affairs Spokesperson for Partido Popular Parl. Group 2008–11; Sec. of State for the Economy 1996–2000, Minister for the Treasury 2000–04, for the Treasury and Public Admin Services 2011–; mem. European Parl. 2004–08; Full Prof. of Applied Econs, Univ. of Cantabria; mem. Partido Popular, mem. Nat. Exec. Cttee 1999–, Econ. and Labour Coordinator 2008–12; Grand Cross, Royal and Distinguished Order of Carlos III. *Address:* Ministry of the Treasury and Public Administration Services, Alcalá 9, Paseo de la Castellana 162, 28014 Madrid, Spain (office). *Telephone:* (91) 5958000 (office). *Fax:* (91) 5958486 (office). *E-mail:* informacion.alcala@meh.es (office). *Website:* www .meh.es (office).

MONTWILL, Alexander, PhD, DSc, MRIA, FInstP; Irish physicist and academic; *Professor Emeritus, Department of Physics, University College Dublin;* b. 28 Oct. 1935, Riga, Latvia; s. of Stanislaw Montwill and Jadwiga Huszcza; m. Ann O'Doherty 1966; one s. four d.; ed Belvedere Coll., Westland Row Christian Brothers' School, Dublin and Univ. Coll. Dublin; Lecturer, Univ. Coll. Dublin 1959–81, Assoc. Prof. 1981–85, Prof. of Experimental Physics 1985, Prof. Emer. 2002–, Head of Dept of Physics 1986–95; Visiting Assoc. Prof., City Coll. of New York 1966–68; Visiting Scientist, CERN, Geneva, Switzerland 1965–. *Radio includes:* 150 segments on physics for RTÉ. *Television includes:* Understanding the Universe (six-part series, RTÉ). *Publications:* Let There Be Light: The Story of Light from Atoms to Galaxies (with Ann Breslin) 2009, The Quantum Adventure – Does God Play Dice? (with Ann Breslin) 2011; numerous publs on high-energy physics in academic journals. *Leisure interests:* bridge, chess. *Address:* Department of Physics, University College, Belfield, Dublin 4, Ireland (office). *Telephone:* (1) 7162213 (office); (1) 2894763 (home). *Fax:* (1) 2837275 (office). *E-mail:* alex_montwill@hotmail.com (home).

MONTY, Jean Claude, CM, MA, MBA; Canadian business executive; b. 26 June 1947, Montreal; m. Jocelyne Monty; two s.; ed Coll. Sainte-Marie, Montreal and Univs of Western Ontario and Chicago, USA; Merrill Lynch, New York, Toronto and Montreal 1970–74; Bell Canada, Montreal 1974; Pres. Télébec Ltée. 1976; Nat. Defence Coll. Kingston, Ont. 1979–80; Bell Canada 1980–92, Pres. 1989, Pres. and CEO 1991–92; Pres. and COO Northern Telecom Ltd 1992, Pres. and CEO 1993–98; Chair. and CEO Bell Canada Enterprises (BCE) Inc. 1998–2002 (resgnd), Chair. BCE Emergis Inc. 2004–10; Dir Bombardier Inc. 1998–, Centria Inc., Fiera Capital Inc., Contramax Inc., Alcatel-Lucent 2008–; mem. Supervisory Bd Lagardère Group, Paris; fmr Special Advisor, General Atlantic LLC; Canada's Outstanding CEO of the Year 1997. *Leisure interest:* golf. *Address:* c/o Board of Directors, Bombardier Inc., 800 René-Lévesque Boulevard, West Montreal, PQ H3B 1Y8, Canada.

MONYAKE, Lengolo Bureng, MSc, UED; Lesotho fmr government official; b. 1 April 1930, Lesotho; s. of Bureng L. Monyake and Leomile Monyake; m. Molulela Mapetla 1957; two s. one d.; ed Fort Hare Univ. Coll., Univ. of Toronto, Carleton Univ., London School of Econs; Headmaster, Leabua High School 1952–61; Dir of Statistics, Govt of Lesotho 1968–74, Perm. Sec. 1974–76, Deputy Sr Perm. Sec. 1976–78; Amb. 1979–83; Man. Dir Lesotho Nat. Devt Corpn 1984–86; Minister for Foreign Affairs 1986–88, for Works 1988; Alt. Exec. Dir IMF 1988–90, Exec. Dir 1990–92; Deputy Exec. Sec. Southern African Devt Community 1993–98; currently with African Peer Review Mechanism (APRM), Lesotho; also currently Pres. Emer. Eighteenth Episcopal Dist, Connectional Lay Org., African Methodist Episcopal Church, Lesotho. *Leisure interests:* tennis, table tennis, music, photography. *Address:* PO Box 526, Maseruloo 100, Lesotho. *Telephone:* 22315995. *E-mail:* lengolob@leo.co.ls (home).

MOOD, Maj.-Gen. Robert; Norwegian army officer and UN official; *Inspector-General, Veteran Affairs, Armed Forces;* b. 8 Dec. 1958, Telemark; m. Eva Tverberg; one s.; ed United States Marine Corps Univ., NATO Defense Coll., Rome, Norwegian Army Staff Coll.; started mil. career 1977, Leader, Operations Officer, Norwegian Bn, UN Interim Force in Lebanon (UNIFIL) 1989–90, Lt Commdr, Telemark Bn 1993–94; achieved rank of Lt Colonel 1996; Operations Officer, 6th Div. –1998; Head of Telemark Bn 1999–2000, Chief of Planning Branch, High Command 2000–02, Chief of Hærens Kampvåpen 2002–04 Chief, Army Transformation and Doctrine Command (TRADOK) 2004–05, Chief of Staff 2005–09; Chief, Jt Implementation Comm., KFOR Command Group; Commanding Officer, Norwegian Army Transformation and Doctrine Command; Head of Mission and Chief of Staff, UN Truce Supervision Org. (UNTSO) 2009–11; Insp.-Gen. Veteran Affairs, Defence Veteran Services 2011–; Chief Mil. Observer and Head of Mission, UN Supervision Mission in Syria (UNSMIS) April–July 2012; Badge of Honour, Norwegian Veteran Asscn of Int. Operations; Defense Service Medal, Armed Forces Medal for Int. Operations, Army Nat. Service Medal, UN Medal for Truce Supervision Org., UN Medal for UN Interim Force in Lebanon, NATO Medal for Kosovo. *Leisure interests:* biking, hiking and fishing, mountaineering, traveling. *Address:* Defence Veteran Services, PO Box 800, Postmottak, 2617 Lillehammer, Norway (office). *Telephone:* 91-50-30-03 (office). *Website:* www .mil.no (office).

MOODY, Robert Vaughn, OC, BA, MA, PhD, FRSC; Canadian (b. British) mathematician and academic; *Professor Emeritus of Mathematics, Department of Mathematical and Statistical Sciences, University of Alberta; Adjunct Professor of Mathematics, University of Victoria;* b. 28 Nov. 1941; ed Univ. of Sask., Univ. of Toronto; Asst Prof., Dept of Math., Univ. of Sask. 1966–70, Assoc. Prof. 1970–76, Prof. 1976–89; Asst Prof., New Mexico State Univ., Las Cruces 1967–68; with Mathematisches Institüt, Universität Bonn 1973–74, Centre de Recherche de Mathematiques Appliquées, Montreal 1983–84; Prof., Concordia Univ., Montreal 1984–86; apptd Prof., Dept of Math., Univ. of Alberta 1989, Chair. Review Cttee, Dept of Math. and Statistics 1990, now Prof. Emer. of Math., Dept of Math. and Statistical Sciences; Scientific Dir Banff Int. Research Station for Math. Innovation and Discovery 2001–03; Guest Prof., Gesamthochschule Wuppertal Jan.–June 1979, Université de Paris VI Jan.–June 1979, Tata Inst. for Math., Bombay, India 1987; mem. Bd Fields Inst. for Research in Math. Sciences 1988–91, Council, Acad. of Science, RSC 1990–93; mem. Scientific Advisory Bd, Centre de Recherches de Mathematique, Université de Montréal 1993–96, Scientific Advisory Panel, Fields Inst. for Research in Math. Sciences 1993–98; mem. Editorial Bd Nova Journal of Algebra and Geometry1992–98, Canadian Journal of Mathematics, Canadian Mathematics Bulletin; mem. Publs Cttee, Canadian Math. Soc. 1982–85, 1988–90; mem. PIMS Scientific Review Panel 1997–; mem. Aspen Inst. for Physics 1982, 1983, 1984, 1986, 1987, 1990, 1997; co-discoverer of Kac-Moody algebra; Dr hc (Université de Montréal) 2000; Coxeter-James Lectureship, Canadian Math. Soc. 1978, Japan Soc. for the Promotion of Science Fellowship 1981, Eugene Wigner Medal (jtly with Victor Kac) for "work on affine Lie algebras that has influenced many areas of theoretical physics", Int. Cttee for Group Theoretical Methods in Math. and Physics 1994, Jeffrey-William Lectureship, Canadian Math. Soc. 1994, Ireland Lectureship, Univ. of New Brunswick 1995, Kaplan Award for Science, Univ. of Alberta 1995, Britten Lectureship, McMaster Univ. 1996, Alberta Science and Tech. Award for Outstanding Research 1996, Frontiers of Mathematics Lectureship, Texas A&M Univ. 1996, CRM/Fields Inst. Prize 1998, Killam Prize 2002, Lansdowne Professorship, Univ. of Victoria 2004, Golden Jubilee Professorship, Benares Hindu Univ., Varanasi 2004. *Publications:*

six books and more than 70 articles. *Address:* Department of Mathematical and Statistical Sciences, 632 Central Academic Building, University of Alberta, Edmonton, Alberta T6G 2G1, Canada (office). *Telephone:* (780) 492-3396 (office). *Fax:* (780) 492-6826 (office). *E-mail:* mathsci@math.ualberta.ca (office). *Website:* www.math.ualberta.ca/~rvmoody/rvm (office).

MOODY-STUART, Sir Mark, Kt, KCMG, MA, PhD, FGS, FRGS; British company director and geologist; *Chairman, Hermes Equity Ownership Services;* b. 15 Sept. 1940, Antigua, West Indies; s. of Sir Alexander Moody-Stuart and Judith Moody-Stuart (née Henzell); m. Judith McLeavy 1964; three s. one d.; ed Shrewsbury School and St John's Coll., Cambridge; with Shell Internationale Petroleum Mij. 1966–67, Koninklijke Shell E & P Lab. 1967–68, worked with Shell cos in Spain, Oman, Brunei 1968–72, Chief Geologist, Australia 1972–76, Shell UK 1977–78, Brunei Shell Services Man. 1978–79, Gen. Man. Shell 1978–79, Man. Western Div. Shell Nigeria 1979–82, Gen. Man. Shell Turkey 1982–86, Chair. and CEO Shell Malaysia 1986–89, Exploration and Production Co-ordinator, Royal Dutch/Shell 1990, Dir Shell Transport & Trading Co. PLC 1990–2005, Chair. 1997–2001, Man. Dir Royal Dutch/Shell Group 1991–2001, Chair. Cttee of Man. Dirs 1998–2001; Chair. (non-exec.) Anglo American plc 2002–09, mem. Remuner-ation, Safety and Sustainable Devt and Nomination Cttees; Jt Chair. G8 Task Force on Devt of Renewable Sources of Energy 2000; mem. Bd of Dirs Accenture 2001–, HSBC Holdings PLC 2001–10, Saudi Aramco 2007–; Chair. Business Action for Sustainable Devt 2001–02, Global Compact Foundation 2006–, Hermes Equity Ownership Services 2009–; Chair. Bd of Trustees, Innovative Vector Control Consortium 2008–; Pres. Liverpool School of Tropical Medicine 2001–08; Hon. Co-Chair. Int. Tax and Advisory Centre 2011–; mem. UN Sec.-Gen.'s Advisory Council for the Global Compact 2001–04, Bd UN Global Compact 2006–, Bd Global Reporting Initiative 2001–07, Bd Int. Inst. for Sustainable Devt 2002–10; Gov. Nuffield Hosps 2001–08; Fellow, Geological Soc. of London (Pres. 2002–04); Hon. FIChemE 1997; Hon. Fellow, St John's Coll., Cambridge 2001; Hon. DBA (Robert Gordon) 2000; Hon. LLD (Aberdeen) 2001; Hon. DSc (Royal Holloway, London); Cadman Medal Inst. of Petroleum 2002. *Publications:* papers in scientific and other journals. *Leisure interests:* sailing, travel, reading. *Website:* www.ivcc.com (office); www.hermes.co.uk/eos (office).

MOON, Kil-choo, BS, MS, PhD; South Korean engineer and research institute director; *President, Korea Institute of Science and Technology;* ed Univ. of Ottawa, Canada, Univ. of Minnesota, USA; Sr Project Man., Interpoll Inc., USA 1984–86, AeroVironment Inc., USA 1986–91; Man., Air Pollution Lab., Korea Inst. of Science and Tech. (KIST) 1991–92, Dir Environment Research Centre 1992–97, Dir Global Environmental Research Centre 1997–2001, Dir Tech. Transfer Div. 2003–04, Dir Gen. KIST, Gangneung 2004–06, Vice-Pres. KIST 2006–09, Pres. 2010–; Dir Directorate for Nat. Science and Eng Programs, Nat. Research Foundation of Korea Jan.–Nov. 2010; Exec. Vice-Pres. Int. Union of Air Pollution Prevention and Environmental Protection Asscns (IUAPPA) 2004–10; mem. Air and Waste Management Asscn, Chair. Korean Section 1997–2008; Pres. Korean Asscn for Aerosol and Particle Research (KAPAR) 1996–97, Korea Soc. for Atmospheric Environment (KOSAE) 2008–09; mem. Soc. of Automotive Eng, American Asscn for Aerosol Research, Nat. Acad. of Eng of Korea; Ministry Citation, Ministry of Environment 1994, Certification of Honour, IUAPPA, UK 2001, Scientific Award, KOSAE 2004, Ungbi Medal, Order of Science and Tech. Merit 2006. *Address:* Korea Institute of Science and Technology, 39-1 Hawolgok-dong, Wolsong-gil 5, Seongbuk-gu, Seoul 136-791, Republic of Korea (office). *Telephone:* (2) 958-5455 (office); *Fax:* (2) 958-5449 (office). *E-mail:* kcmoon@kist.re.kr (office). *Website:* www.kist.re.kr (office).

MOONEY, Beth E., BA, MBA; American banking executive; *Chairman and CEO, KeyCorp;* b. Midland, Mich.; ed Univ. of Texas, Southern Methodist Univ.; completed line assignments of increasing responsibility at Bank One Corpn, Citicorp Real Estate, Inc., Hall Financial Group and Republic Bank of Texas/First Republic; fmr Regional Pres., Bank One Corpn, Akron and Dayton, then Pres. Bank One Ohio; Sr Exec. Vice-Pres. and Chief Financial Officer, AmSouth Bancorporation (now Regions Financial Corpn), Ala, ran banking operations in Tenn. and northern La –2006; joined KeyCorp 2006, Vice-Chair. Key Community Banking, includes Retail Banking, Business Banking, Commercial Middle Market Banking, Wealth Management, Private Banking, Key Investment Services and KeyBank Mortgage –2010, Pres. and COO KeyCorp 2010–11, mem. Bd of Dirs, Chair. and CEO 2011–; mem. The Financial Services Roundtable; Trustee and Treas., Musical Arts Asscn (The Cleveland Orchestra); Trustee, Cleveland Clinic Foundation, Neighborhood Progress, Inc., United Way of Greater Cleveland; Distinguished Alumnus, Cox School of Business, Southern Methodist Univ. 2007–08; YWCA Women of Achievement Award 2008, ranked by Forbes magazine amongst The World's 100 Most Powerful Women (96th) 2011, ranked by Fortune magazine amongst the 50 Most Powerful Women in Business in the US (49th) 2011–12. *Address:* KeyCorp, 127 Public Square, Cleveland, OH 44114, USA (office). *Telephone:* (216) 689-3000 (office). *E-mail:* keyexpress@keybank.com (office). *Website:* www.keycorp.net (office).

MOONEY, Harold Alfred (Hal), MA, PhD; American biologist and academic; *Paul S. and Billie Achilles Professor Emeritus in Environmental Biology and Senior Fellow Emeritus, Woods Institute for the Environment, Stanford University;* b. 1 June 1932, Santa Rosa, Calif.; s. of Harold Walter Stefany and Sylvia A. Hart; m. Sherry L. Gulmon 1974; three d.; ed Univ. of California, Santa Barbara and Duke Univ.; Instructor to Assoc. Prof., UCLA 1960–68; Assoc. Prof., Stanford Univ. 1968–73, Prof. 1975–, Paul S. and Billie Achilles Prof. in Environmental Biology 1976–, now Emer., Sr Fellow Emer., Woods Inst. for the Environment; fmr Chair. US Nat. Research Council Cttee on Ecosystem Man. for Sustainable Marine Fisheries; served as Coordinator of UN Global Biodiversity Assessment 1995; fmr Pres. Ecological Soc. of America; mem. NAS, American Philosophical Soc.; Foreign mem. Russian Acad. of Sciences; Fellow, American Acad. of Arts and Sciences; Hon. mem. British Ecological Soc.; Mercer Award, Ecology Soc. of America 1961, Guggenheim Fellow 1974, Humboldt Award 1988, ECI Prize in Terrestrial Ecology, Inst. of Ecology Prize (Germany) 1990, Max Planck Research Award in Biosciences 1992, Eminent Ecologist Award (co-recipient), Ecological Soc. of America 1996, Ramon Margalef Prize in Ecology and Environmental Sciences 2007, Tyler Prize for Environmental Achievement 2008. *Publications:* 12 books. *Address:* Department of Biological Sciences, Room 477, Herrin Labs, Stanford

University, Stanford, CA 94305-5020 (office); 2625 Ramona Street, Palo Alto, CA 94306, USA (home). *Telephone:* (650) 723-1179 (office). *Fax:* (650) 723-9253 (office). *E-mail:* hmooney@stanford.edu (office). *Website:* med.stanford.edu/profiles/biologyprofiles/researcher/Harold_Mooney (office).

MOONVES, Leslie (Les); American television industry executive; *President and CEO, CBS Corporation;* b. 6 Oct. 1949, Valley Stream, Long Island, NY; m. Nancy Moonves 1979; two s. one d.; ed Bucknell Univ.; trained as actor at Neighbourhood Playhouse, NY; performed in numerous stage and tv productions; began to produce plays for Broadway and LA 1977; TV Exec., Twentieth Century Fox TV, Saul Ilson Productions and Catalina Productions 1978–85; Vice-Pres. Lorimar TV 1985–89, Pres. 1989–93; Pres. Warner Bros. TV 1993–95; Pres. CBS Entertainment and Group Exec. Vice-Pres., CBS TV 1995–98, Pres. and CEO CBS TV 1998–2003, elected to Corp. Bd of Dirs 1999, Chair. and CEO 2003–, oversees productions of UPN, CBS Enterprises, CBS News, CBS Sports, CBS Entertainment, King World Productions; Co-Pres. and Co-COO Viacom Inc. (after Viacom acquired CBS) 2000–05, Pres. and CEO CBS Corpn (after CBS split from Viacom) 2005–; Co-Chair. LA Bd of Govs, Museum of TV & Radio; mem. Nat. Collegiate Athletic Asscn (NCAA) Advisory Bd; mem. Bd of Dirs LA Free Clinic; mem. Bd of Trustees, Entertainment Industries Council; Trustee, American Film Inst., Nat. Council of Families and TV. *Address:* CBS Corporation, 51 West 52nd Street, New York, NY 10019, USA (office). *Telephone:* (212) 975-4321 (office); (212) 258-6000 (office). *Fax:* (212) 975-4516 (office); (212) 258-6464 (office). *Website:* www.cbscorporation.com (office).

MOORBATH, Stephen Erwin, DPhil, DSc, FRS; British scientist and academic; *Professor Emeritus, Department of Earth Sciences, University of Oxford;* b. 9 May 1929, Magdeburg, Germany; s. of Heinz Moorbath and Else Moorbath; m. Pauline Tessier-Varlêt 1962; one s. one d.; ed Lincoln Coll., Oxford; Asst Experimental Officer, Atomic Energy Research Est., Harwell 1948–51; Scientific Officer, AERE 1954–56; Research Fellow, Univ. of Oxford 1956–61, Sr Research Officer, 1962–78, Reader in Geology 1978–92, Prof. of Isotope Geology 1992–96, Prof. Emer. 1996–, Professorial Fellow, Linacre Coll. 1990–96, Fellow Emer. 1996; Research Fellow, MIT, USA 1961–62; several awards. *Publications:* numerous contribs to books and scientific journals. *Leisure interests:* music, philately, travel, linguistics. *Address:* Department of Earth Sciences, Oxford University, Parks Road, Oxford, OX1 3PR (office); 53 Bagley Wood Road, Kennington, Oxford, OX1 5LY, England (home). *Telephone:* (1865) 282147 (office); (1865) 739507 (home). *Fax:* (1865) 272072 (office). *E-mail:* stephen.moorbath@earth.ox.ac.uk (office). *Website:* www.earth.ox.ac.uk (office).

MOORCOCK, Michael John, (Edward P. Bradbury, Desmond Read); British novelist; b. 18 Dec. 1939, London, England; s. of Arthur Moorcock and June Moorcock; m. 1st Hilary Bailey 1963 (divorced 1978); one s. two d.; m. 2nd Jill Riches 1978 (divorced 1983); m. 3rd Linda M. Steele 1983; ed Michael Hall School, Sussex; worked as musician and journalist; Ed. Outlaws Own 1951–53, Tarzan Adventures 1957–59, Sexton Blake Library 1959–61, Current Topics 1961–62; Ed. New Worlds 1964–71, 1976–96, Consulting Ed. 1996–; British Fantasy Award 1993, World Fantasy Lifetime Achievement Award 2000, Science Fiction Hall of Fame 2002, Prix Utopia 2004, Bram Stoker Lifetime Achievement Award 2004, named Damon Knight Grand Master, Science Fiction and Fantasy Writers of America 2008. *Films:* The Final Programme 1973, The Land that Time Forgot 1975. *Records:* Warrior on the Edge of Time (Hawkwind) 1975, The New World's Fair 1975, The Brothel in Rosenstrasse 1982, Roller Coaster Holiday 2004. *Publications include:* The Eternal Champion sequence 1963–98, Behold the Man (Nebula Award 1967) 1966, The Knight of the Swords (August Derleth Fantasy Award 1972, 1973) 1971, The Jade Man's Eyes (British Fantasy Award) 1974, The Sword and the Stallion (August Derleth Fantasy Award 1975) 1974, The Hollow Lands (August Derleth Fantasy Award 1976) 1974, Condition of Muzak (Guardian Fiction Prize 1977) 1976, Gloriana (World Fantasy Award 1979) 1977, Gloriana (John W. Campbell Memorial Award, World Fantasy Award 1979) 1978, Byzantium Endures 1981, The Laughter of Carthage 1984, Mother London 1988, Jerusalem Commands 1992, Blood 1994, The War Amongst Angels 1996, Tales from the Texas Woods 1997, King of the City 2000, Silverheart (co-author) 2000, London Bone 2001, The Dreamthief's Daughter 2001, Firing the Cathedral 2002, The Skrayling Tree 2003, The Lives and Times of Jerry Cornelius 2004, Wizardry and Wild Romance 2004, The White Wolf's Son 2005, The Vengeance of Rome 2006, The Metatemporal Detective 2007, The Best of Michael Moorcock 2009, The Coming of the Terraphiles 2010, Modem Times 2.0 2011, The Sunday Books 2011, London Peculiar and Other Nonfiction (co-ed.) 2012. *Leisure interests:* climbing, travelling, walking, cats, birds. *Address:* c/o Howard Morhaim Literary Agency, 30 Pierrepont Street, Brooklyn, NY 11201, USA (office); PO Box 1230, Bastrop, TX 78602, USA (home). *Telephone:* (718) 222-8400 (office). *Fax:* (718) 222-5056 (office). *E-mail:* howard@morhaimliterary.com (office). *Website:* www.multiverse.org.

MOORE, Carole Irene, MS; Canadian librarian; b. 15 Aug. 1944, Berkeley, Calif., USA; ed Stanford and Columbia Univs; Reference Librarian, Columbia Univ. Libraries 1967–68; Reference Librarian, Univ. of Toronto Library 1968–73, Asst Head, Reference Dept 1973–74, Head 1974–80, Head, Bibliographic Process-ing Dept 1980–86, Assoc. Librarian, Tech. Services 1986–87, Chief Librarian, Univ. of Toronto Library 1986–2011, Research Libraries Group Dir 1994–96; mem. Preservation of Research Library Materials Cttee, Asscn of Research Libraries 2004–06; mem. Bd of Dirs Univ. of Toronto Press 1994–2011; Columbia Univ. School of Library Service Centenary Distinguished Alumni Award 1987. *Publications:* Labour Relations and the Librarian (ed.) 1974, Canadian Essays and Collections Index 1972–73 1976. *Leisure interest:* gardening. *Address:* Chief Librarian's Office, University of Toronto Libraries, 130 St George Street, Room 2015, Toronto, ON M5S 1A5, Canada (office). *Telephone:* (416) 978-2292 (office). *Fax:* (416) 971-2099 (office). *E-mail:* carole.moore@utoronto.ca (office). *Website:* www.library.utoronto.ca (office).

MOORE, Charles Hilary, MA; British journalist and writer; b. 31 Oct. 1956, Hastings; s. of Richard Moore and Ann Moore; m. Caroline Baxter 1981; twin s. and d.; ed Eton Coll. and Trinity Coll., Cambridge; mem. editorial staff, Daily Telegraph 1979–81, leader writer 1981–83; Asst Ed. and Political Columnist, The Spectator 1983–84, Ed. 1984–90, fortnightly columnist ('Another Voice') 1990–95; weekly columnist, Daily Express 1987–90; Deputy Ed. Daily Telegraph 1990–92, Ed. Sunday Telegraph 1992–95, Ed. Daily Telegraph 1995–2003, Group Consulting Ed. and columnist, Daily Telegraph 2003–; mem. Bd of Dirs Policy Exchange (think-tank) 2004–11 (Chairman –2011); Trustee, T. E. Utley Memorial Fund, Benenden Council, ShareGift. *Publications:* 1936 (co-ed. with C. Hawtree) 1986, The Church in Crisis (with A. N. Wilson and G. Stamp) 1986, A Tory Seer: The Selected Journalism of T. E. Utley (co-ed. with S. Heffer) 1986, Margaret Thatcher The Authorised Biography – Volume One: Not for Turning 2013. *Address:* c/o Daily Telegraph, 11 Buckingham Palace Road, London, SW1W 0DT, England (office).

MOORE, Demi; American actress; b. (Demi Gene Guynes), 11 Nov. 1962, Roswell, NM; d. of Charles Harmon and Virginia King (later Guynes); step-d. of Danny Guynes; m 1st Freddy Moore 1980 (divorced 1985); m. 2nd Bruce Willis (q.v.) 1987 (divorced 2000); three d.; m. 3rd Ashton Kutcher 2005 (divorced 2013); ed Fairfax High School, Hollywood; began acting with small part in TV series; worked as a model, Los Angeles; f. Moving Pictures (production co.); launched with her husband the Demi and Ashton Foundation (charity directed towards fighting child sexual slavery) 2011. *Theatre:* The Early Girl (Theater World Award). *Films include:* Choices 1981, Parasite 1982, Blame It on Rio 1984, No Small Affair 1984, St Elmo's Fire 1985, One Crazy Summer 1986, About Last Night 1986, Wisdom 1986, The Seventh Sign 1988, We're No Angels 1989, Ghost 1990, Nothing But Trouble 1991, Mortal Thoughts (also co-producer) 1991, The Butcher's Wife 1991, A Few Good Men 1992, Indecent Proposal 1993, Disclosure 1994, The Scarlet Letter 1995, Now and Then 1995, Striptease 1996, The Juror 1996, The Hunchback of Notre Dame (voice) 1996, Deconstructing Harry 1997, G.I. Jane (also producer) 1997, Passion of Mind 2000, The Hunchback of Notre Dame II (voice) 2002, Charlie's Angels: Full Throttle 2003, Half Light 2006, Bobby 2006, Flawless 2007, Mr Brooks 2007, The Joneses 2009, Happy Tears 2009, Bunraku 2010, Margin Call 2011, Another Happy Day 2011, LOL: Laughing Out Loud 2012, Very Good Girls 2013, Forsaken 2014; producer: Mortal Thoughts (co-producer) 1991, Now and Then 1995, Austin Powers: International Man of Mystery 1997, G.I. Jane 1997, Austin Powers: The Spy Who Shagged Me 1999, Austin Powers in Goldmember 2002. *Television includes:* General Hospital (series) 1982–83, The Master 1984, Bedroom 1984, Moonlighting 1989, Tales from the Crypt 1990, Master Ninja 1991, If These Walls Could Talk (also exec. producer) 1996, Ellen 1997, Will and Grace 2003, The Magic 7 (film) 2009; exec. producer: The Conversation (series) 2012. *Address:* c/o Moving Pictures, 1453 Third Street, Suite 420, Santa Monica, CA 90401, USA. *Telephone:* (310) 576-0577.

MOORE, Gillian, MBE, BMus, MA, FRCM; British music administrator; *Head of Contemporary Culture, Southbank Centre;* b. 20 Feb. 1959, Glasgow; d. of Charles Moore and Sara Queen; pnr Bruce Nockles; one s.; ed Univ. of Glasgow, Royal Scottish Acad. of Music and Drama, Univ. of York, Harvard Univ.; Educ. Dir London Sinfonietta 1983–93, Artistic Dir 1998–2006; Head of Educ., Southbank Centre, London 1993–98, also Music Audience Devt Man. 1996, Head of Contemporary Culture 2006–; Artistic Dir ISCM World Music Days, Manchester 1997–98; Visiting Prof., Royal Coll. of Music 1996–; Gov. Nat. Youth Orchestra of GB; mem. British Govt Nat. Curriculum Working Group on Music; Hon. Mem. Guildhall School of Music 1993; Dr hc (Brunel) 2006; Sir Charles Groves Award for Outstanding Contrib. to British Music 1992, Asscn of British Orchestras Award for Contrib. of Most Benefit to Orchestral Life in the UK 1999, Leslie Boosey Award 2008. *Address:* Southbank Centre, Belvedere Road, London, SE1 8XX, England (office). *Telephone:* (20) 7921-0897 (office). *Fax:* (20) 7639-6675 (home). *E-mail:* gillian.moore@southbankcentre.co.uk (office). *Website:* www.southbankcentre.co .uk (office).

MOORE, Gordon Earle, PhD, FIEEE, FRSEng; American fmr semiconductor executive; *Chairman Emeritus, Intel Corporation;* b. 3 Jan. 1929, San Francisco; m.; two c.; ed Univ. of Calif., Berkeley, Calif. Inst. of Tech.; with Fairchild Semiconductor –1968; Co-founder and Exec. Vice-Pres. Integrated Electronics (Intel, world's largest manufacturer of microprocessors) 1968–75, Pres. and CEO 1975–79, Chair. and CEO 1979–87, Chair. 1987–97, Chair. Emer. 1997–; Dir Gilead Sciences Inc.; mem. Nat. Acad. of Eng; mem. Bd Trustees Calif. Inst. of Tech.; Nat. Medal of Tech. 1990, Dan David Prize 2010. *Address:* Intel Corpn, 2200 Mission College Boulevard, Santa Clara, CA 95052-8119, USA (office). *Telephone:* (408) 765-8080 (office). *Fax:* (408) 765-9904 (office). *Website:* www.intel.com (office).

MOORE, The Hon. James, PC; Canadian politician; *Minister of Industry;* b. 10 June 1976, New Westminster; MP 2000–; Parl. Sec. to Minister Public Works and Govt Services 2006–07; Sec. of State for Official Languages, Pacific Gateway and the Vancouver-Whistler Olympics 2007–08; Minister of Canadian Heritage and Official Languages 2008–13, of Industry 2013–; mem. Canadian Alliance Party 2000–03, Conservative Party of Canada 2003–. *Address:* Department of Industry, C. D. Howe Building, 11th Floor, East Tower, 235 Queen Street, Ottawa, ON K1P 5G8, Canada (office). *Telephone:* (613) 954-5031 (office). *Fax:* (613) 954-2340 (office). *E-mail:* info@ic.gc.ca (office). *Website:* www.ic.gc.ca (office).

MOORE, Hon. John Colinton, AO, BCom, AASA; Australian fmr politician and company director; b. 16 Nov. 1936, Rockhampton; s. of T. R. Moore and D. S. Moore; m. 2nd Jacquelyn Moore; two s. one d. from previous m.; ed Armidale School, Queensland Univ.; stockbroker 1960; mem. Brisbane Stock Exchange 1962–74; Vice-Pres. and Treas. Queensland Liberal Party 1967–73, Pres. 1973–76, 1984–90; MP for Ryan 1975–2001; Minister for Business and Consumer Affairs 1980–82; Opposition Spokesman for Finance 1983–84, for Communications 1984–85, for Northern Devt and Local Govt 1985–87, for Transport and Aviation 1987, for Business and Consumer Affairs 1987–89, for Business Privatization and Consumer Affairs 1989–90; Shadow Minister for Privatization and Public Admin. 1994, for Privatization 1994–95, for Industry, Commerce and Public Admin. 1995–96; Minister for Industry, Science and Tourism 1996–97, of Industry, Science and Tech. 1997–98, for Defence 1998–2001; Vice-Pres. Exec. Council 1996–98; Dir William Brandt & Sons (Australia), Phillips, First City, Brandt Ltd, Merrill Lynch, Pierce, Fennell and Smith (Australia) Ltd, Citinat, Agricultural Investments Australia Ltd; mem. various int. dels, Council Order of Australia, Advisory Council General Motors, Australia. *Leisure interests:* tennis, cricket, reading, golf. *Address:* PO Box 2191, Toowong, Brisbane 4066; 47 Dennis Street, Indooroopilly, Brisbane, Australia (home). *Telephone:* 419 704764 (office); (7) 3217-7427 (home). *Fax:* (7) 3876-8088 (office). *E-mail:* john_moore1@bigpond.net.au (home).

MOORE, Julianne, BA; American actress; b. 3 Dec. 1961, Fayetteville, NC; m. 1st John Gould Rubin (divorced 1995); m. 2nd Bart Freundlich; one s. one d.; ed

Boston Univ. School for Arts; with the Guthrie Theater 1988–89. *Stage appearances include:* Serious Money 1987, Ice Cream with Hot Fudge 1990, Uncle Vanya, The Road to Nirvana, Hamlet, The Father, The Vertical Hour 2006. *Films include:* Tales from the Darkside 1990, The Hand That Rocks the Cradle 1992, The Gun in Betty Lou's Handbag 1992, Body of Evidence 1993, Benny and Joon 1993, The Fugitive 1993, Short Cuts 1993, Vanya on 42nd Street 1994, Roommates 1995, Safe 1995, Nine Months 1995, Assassins 1995, Surviving Picasso 1996, Jurassic Park: The Lost World 1997, The Myth of Fingerprints 1997, Hellcab 1997, Boogie Nights 1997, The Big Lebowski 1998, Eyes Wide Shut, The End of the Affair 1999, Map of the World 1999, Magnolia 1999, Cookie's Fortune 1999, An Ideal Husband 1999, Hannibal 2000, The Shipping News 2002, Far From Heaven (Best Actress, Venice Film Festival) 2002, The Hours 2002, Marie and Bruce 2004, Laws of Attraction 2004, The Forgotten 2004, Trust the Man 2005, Freedomland 2005, Children of Men 2006, Next 2007, I'm Not There 2007, Savage Grace 2007, Blindness 2008, Shelter 2009, The Private Lives of Pippa Lee 2009, A Single Man 2009, Chloe 2010, The Kids Are All Right 2010, Crazy, Stupid, Love 2011, Being Flynn 2012, What Maisie Knew 2012, The English Teacher 2012, Don Jon's Addiction 2013, Carrie 2013, The Seventh Son 2013. *Television includes:* The Edge of Night (series) 1984, As the World Turns (series) 1985–87, Money, Power Murder (film) 1989, B.L. Stryker (series) 1990, Lovecraft 1991, I'll Take Manhattan (miniseries) 1987, The Last to Go (film) 1991, Cast a Deadly Spell (film) 1991, 30 Rock (series) 2009–10, A Child's Garden of Poetry (film) (voice) 2011, Game Change (film) (Emmy Award for Best Lead Actress in a Miniseries or Movie 2012, Golden Globe Award for Best Performance by an Actress in a Mini-Series or Motion Picture Made for Television 2013) 2012. *Publication:* Freckleface Strawberry and the Dodgeball Bully (children's book) 2007. *Address:* c/o Kevin Huvane, Creative Artists Agency, 2000 Avenue of the Stars, Los Angeles, CA 90067, USA. *Telephone:* (424) 288-2000. *Fax:* (424) 288-2900. *Website:* www.caa.com.

MOORE, Michael Francis; American writer and filmmaker; b. 23 April 1954, Davison, Mich.; m. Kathleen Glynn 1991; ed Davison High School; elected to Davison, Mich. school bd aged 18; active in student politics; began career as journalist with The Flint Voice, later Ed., expanded into The Mich. Voice; Ed. Mother Jones magazine, San Francisco 1986–88; Founder and mem. bd of Dir Traverse City (Mich.) Film Festival. *Television includes:* Pets or Meat: The Return to Flint 1992, TV Nation (NBC series) 1994–95, 1997, And Justice for All (dir) 1998, The Awful Truth (series) 1999. *Films:* Roger and Me (writer, dir, producer) 1989, Canadian Bacon (writer, producer, dir) 1994, The Big One (dir) 1997, Bowling for Columbine (screenwriter, dir, producer; Jury Award, Cannes Film Festival 2003, Acad. Award for Best Documentary 2003) 2002, Fahrenheit 9/11 (dir; Palme d'Or, Cannes Film Festival, US People's Choice Award for Best Film 2005) 2004, Sicko 2007, Capitalism: A Love Story 2009. *Film appearances:* Lucky Number 1999, EdTV 1999. *Publications:* Downsize This!: Random Threats from an Unarmed America 1996, Stupid White Men (Book of the Year, British Book Awards 2003) 2001, Adventures in a TV Nation (with Kathleen Glynn) 2002, Dude, Where's My Country? 2003, Will They Ever Trust Us Again?: Letters from the War Zone 2004, The Official Fahrenheit 9/11 Reader 2004, Mike's Election Guide 2008 2008, Here Comes Trouble: Stories from My Life 2011, I Am Moore 2011. *Address:* c/o Random House Inc., 1745 Broadway, Suite B1, New York, NY 10019-4305, USA. *E-mail:* mike@michaelmoore.com. *Website:* www.michaelmoore.com.

MOORE, Rt Hon. Michael (Mike) Kenneth, ONZ, PC; New Zealand politician, international organization official and diplomatist; *Ambassador to USA;* b. 28 Jan. 1949, Whakatane; s. of the late Alan Moore and Audrey Moore; m. Yvonne Dereaney 1975; fmr social worker, printer; MP for Eden 1972–75, Papanui, Christchurch 1978–84, Christchurch N 1984–96, Waimakariri 1996–99; Minister of Overseas Trade and Marketing, also Minister of Tourism and Publicity and of Recreation and Sport 1984–87; Minister of Overseas Trade and Marketing and of Publicity 1987–88, 1989–90, of External Relations and Int. Trade 1988–90; Minister of Foreign Affairs Jan.–Oct. 1990; Prime Minister Sept.–Oct. 1990; Leader of the Opposition 1990–93; fmr Assoc. Minister of Finance; Dir-Gen. WTO 1999–2002; Amb. to USA 2010–; held numerous appointments and board memberships with global policy and commercial organisations, including UN Comm. on the Legal Empowerment of the Poor, Commr for UN Global Comm. on int. Migration, several pvt. sector bds; served on Econ. Devt Bd of South Australia; fmr adviser to other Govts; mem. Trilateral Comm.; fmr Adjunct Prof., Adelaide Univ., La Trobe Univ.; Founder School Aid (charity); Hon. Prof., Beijing Normal Univ., Zuhai, Chinese Univ. for Political Science and Int. Law, Beijing, Shanghai Customs Coll.; numerous honours from governments in Africa, Europe and South America; Dr hc (Lincoln Univ., People's Univ. of China, Beijing, Auckland Univ. of Tech., Canterbury Univ., La Trobe Univ.). *Publications include:* ten books, including A Pacific Parliament, Hard Labour, Fighting for New Zealand 1993, Children of the Poor 1996, A Brief History of the Future 1998, A World Without Walls 2007, Saving Globalisation 2009. *Address:* Embassy of New Zealand, 37 Observatory Circle NW, Washington, DC 20008, USA (office). *Telephone:* (202) 328-4800 (office). *Fax:* (202) 667-5227 (office). *E-mail:* wshinfo@mfat.govt.nz (office). *Website:* www.nzembassy.com/usa (office).

MOORE, Rt Hon. Michael Kevin, PC; British chartered accountant and politician; b. 3 June 1965, Dundonald, Co. Down, Northern Ireland; ed Jedburgh Grammar School, Univ. of Edinburgh; moved with family to Wishaw, Scotland 1970, then to Scottish Borders 1981; worked for a year as researcher for Liberal Democrat MP Archy Kirkwood before joining Edinburgh office of accountants Coopers & Lybrand, later Man. in office's corp. finance practice; worked as researcher for David Steel (Liberal Democrat politician); MP for Tweeddale, Ettrick and Lauderdale 1997–2005, for Berwickshire, Roxburgh and Selkirk 2005–, mem. Scottish Affairs Select Cttee 1997–99, Armed Forces Bill Select Cttee 2005–06; Liberal Democrat Spokesperson for Scotland 1997–99, 2001, for Transport 1999–2001; Shadow Minister for Foreign Affairs 2001–05; Shadow Sec. of State for Defence 2005–06, for Foreign and Commonwealth Affairs 2006–07, for Int. Devt 2007–08, for NI and Scotland 2008–10; Sec. of State for Scotland 2010–13; Campaign Chair. Scottish Parl. elections 1999, 2003; Parl. Group Convener 2000–01; Scottish MP Rep., Liberal Democrat Policy Cttee 2001–02; Deputy Leader Scottish Liberal Democrats 2002–10, Acting Leader July–Aug. 2008; mem. UK del. to NATO Parl. Ass. 2007–10; Liberal Democrat. *Address:* House of Commons, Westminster, London, SW1A 0AA, England (office); Constituency Office, 11 Island Street, Galashiels, TD1 1NZ, Scotland (office). *Telephone:*

(20) 7219-2236 (Westminster) (office); (1896) 663650 (Galashiels) (office). *Fax:* (20) 7219-0263 (Westminster) (office); (1896) 663655 (Galashiels) (office). *E-mail:* michaelmooremp@parliament.uk (office). *Website:* www.parliament.uk/ biographies/commons/michael-moore/638 (office).

MOORE, Michael Rodney Newton, CBE, MA, MBA; British lawyer and business executive; b. 15 March 1936; s. of Gen. Sir Rodney Moore and Olive Marion Robinson; m. Jan Moore; one s.; ed Eton Coll., Magdalen Coll., Oxford and Harvard Business School, USA; called to the Bar 1961; Chair. Tomkins PLC 1984–95, Quicks Group plc 1993–2002, Linx Printing Technologies plc 1993–2005, London International Group PLC 1994–, Status Holdings PLC 2000–; mem. Bd of Dirs, Clerical Medical & General Life Assurance Soc. 1993–, Deputy Chair. 1996–; Dir, Caledonian Stoneywood Ltd 1992–94, Gemvolk Ltd 1992–93, Brixton Estates plc 1997–2006, HBOS Insurance & Investment Group Ltd 1997–98, 2001–03, Warm Zones C.I.C. 2001–04, Which? Ltd 1993–2008 (Chair. 1997–2008); Chair. Nat. Soc. for Prevention of Cruelty to Children (NSPCC) 1992–95; Trustee, Public Concern at Work 1996–2003. *Leisure interests:* reading, music (especially opera), visiting ruins, tennis. *Address:* Peppering High Barn, Burpham, Arundel, West Sussex, BN18 9RN, England.

MOORE, Nicholas G., JD, BS; American business executive; *Senior Counselor, Bechtel Group Inc.;* m. Jo Anne Moore; four c.; ed St Mary's Coll., Calif., Hastings Coll. of Law, Univ. of Calif., Berkeley; joined Coopers & Lybrand 1968, Pnr 1974, Head of Tax Practice, San José office 1974–81, Man. Partner San José Office 1981, mem. firm council 1984, Exec. Cttee 1988, Vice-Chair. W Region 1991–92, Client Service Vice-Chair. 1992, Chair., CEO Coopers & Lybrand USA 1994, Chair. Coopers & Lybrand Int. 1997, Global Chair. and CEO PricewaterhouseCoopers LLP (formed from merger of Coopers & Lybrand Int. and Price Waterhouse) 1999–2001; currently Sr Counselor Bechtel Group Inc.; mem. Bd of Dirs, Network Appliance Inc. 2002–, Bechtel Group, Inc., Network Appliance Inc., Brocade Communications Systems, Inc., Hudson Highland Group, Inc., Gilead Sciences, Inc.; mem. Calif. Bar Asscn; Trustee Financial Accounting Foundation 1997–, St. Mary's Coll. of Calif.; Chair. Co-operation Ireland; mem. Bd of Trustees Cttee for Econ. Devt; Vice-Chair. Business Cttee, Metropolitan Museum of Art. *Address:* Bechtel Group, Inc., 50 Beale Street, San Francisco, CA 94105-1895, USA (office). *Telephone:* (415) 768-1234 (office). *Fax:* (415) 768-9038 (office). *Website:* www .bechtel.com (office).

MOORE, Sir Roger, Kt; British actor; b. 14 Oct. 1927, London; m. 1st Doorn van Steyn (divorced 1953); m. 2nd Dorothy Squires 1953 (divorced 1969, died 1998); m. 3rd Luisa Mattioli; two s. one d.; ed Royal Acad. of Dramatic Art; Special Amb. for UNICEF 1991–; Dag Hammarskjold Inspiration Award, UNICEF 2007. *Films include:* Crossplot 1969, The Man With the Golden Gun 1974, That Lucky Touch 1975, Save Us From Our Friends 1975, Shout At The Devil 1975, Sherlock Holmes in New York 1976, The Spy Who Loved Me 1976, The Wild Geese 1977, Escape To Athena 1978, Moonraker 1978, Esther, Ruth and Jennifer 1979, The Sea Wolves, 1980, Sunday Lovers 1980, For Your Eyes Only 1980, Octopussy 1983, The Naked Face 1983, A View to a Kill 1985, Bullseye! 1990, Fire, Ice and Dynamite 1990, Bed and Breakfast 1992, The Quest 1996, Spice World 1997, The Enemy 2001, Boat Trip 2002, The Fly Who Loved Me (voice) 2004, Here Comes Peter Cottontail: The Movie (voice) 2005. *Television appearances include:* The Alaskans (series) 1959, The Saint (series) 1962–69, The Persuaders (series) 1972–73, The Man Who Wouldn't Die 1992, Dream Team (series) 1999, Foley and McColl: This Way Up 2005. *Publications:* James Bond Diary 1973, My Word is My Bond (auto-biog.) 2008.

MOORE OF LOWER MARSH, Baron (Life Peer), cr. 1992, of Lower Marsh in the London Borough of Lambeth; **John Edward Michael Moore;** British politician; b. 26 Nov. 1937; s. of Edward O. Moore; m. Sheila S. Tillotson 1962; two s. one d.; ed London School of Econs; with Royal Sussex Regt Korea 1955–57; Pres. Students' Union LSE 1959–60; banking and stockbroking, Chicago 1962–65; Dir Dean Witter Int. Ltd 1968–79, Chair. 1975–79; underwriting mem. Lloyds 1978–92; Exec. Chair. Crédit Suisse Asset Man. 1991–, Energy Saving Trust Ltd 1992–95 (Pres. 1995–); mem. Parl. for Croydon Cen. 1974–92; Parl. Under-Sec. of State, Dept of Energy 1979–83; Econ. Sec. to HM Treasury June–Oct. 1983, Financial Sec. to HM Treasury Oct. 1983–86; Sec. of State for Transport 1986–87, for Dept of Health and Social Security 1987–88, for Social Security 1988–89; Dir Monitor Inc. 1990– (Chair. Monitor Europe 1990–), Blue Circle Industries 1993–, Camelot PLC 1994–96, Rolls-Royce PLC (Deputy Chair. 1996–2003, Acting Chair. 2003–05), Crédit Suisse Investment Man. Australia 1995–, Cen. European Growth Fund PLC 1995–, BEA Assocs USA 1996–98, TIG Inc. 1997–, Pvt. Client Partners, Zurich 1999–; mem. Court of Govs LSE 1977–. *Address:* House of Lords, Westminster, London, SW1A 0PW; Crédit Suisse Asset Management Ltd, Beaufort House, 15 St. Botolph Street, London, EC3A 7JJ, England (office). *Telephone:* (20) 7426-2626 (office). *Fax:* (20) 7426-2618 (office).

MOORMAN van KAPPEN, Olav, LLD; Dutch legal historian and academic; *Professor Emeritus of Legal History, Nijmegen University;* b. 11 March 1937, The Hague; s. of Karel S.O. van Kappen and Johanna J. Moorman; m. Froukje A. Bosma 1963; one s. one d.; ed Huygens Lyceum and Utrecht Univ.; Research Asst Faculty of Law, Utrecht Univ. 1961–64, Jr Lecturer 1965–68; Sr Lecturer Faculty of Law, Amsterdam Univ. 1968–71; Asst Prof. Faculty of Law, Leyden Univ. 1971–72; Prof. of Legal History, Nijmegen Univ. 1971–2000, Co. Dir Gerard Noodt Inst. for Legal History 1972–2000, Emer. Prof. 2000–; Visiting Prof. Munster Univ. 1982–83, Poitiers Univ. 1986, 1991 Düsseldorf Univ. 1989–90, Univ. René Descartes (Paris V) 1992, 1995, 1999; mem. Bd of Govs Netherlands School for Archivists 1979–81, Chair. 1981–95; mem. Netherlands Council of Archives 1979–89, Vice-Pres. 1986–89, Pres. 1990–95; mem. Nat. Council of Cultural Heritage 1990–95; mem. editorial Bd, Legal History Review 1983–2007; mem. Dutch Soc. of Sciences at Haarlem 1982, Royal Netherlands Acad. of Sciences 1986; Corresp. mem. Acad. of Sciences, Göttingen 1996; Dr hc (Univ. René Descartes (Paris V)); Cross of Merit 1st Class (FRG), Officier, Ordre des Palmes Académiques (France), Officier, Orde van Oranje-Nassau (Netherlands). *Publications:* over 360 books and articles on various aspects of legal history. *Address:* Institute of Legal Science of Nijmegen University, PO Box 9049, 6500 KK Nijmegen, Netherlands. *Telephone:* (24) 3612186. *Fax:* (24) 3616145.

MOOSA, Mohammed Valli, BSc; South African politician and international organization executive; *Chairman, Congress Steering Committee, International Union for the Conservation of Nature;* b. 9 Feb. 1957, Johannesburg; m. Elsabé Wessels; ed Lenasia State Indian High School, Univ. of Durban-Westville; active in South African Students' Org., Nat. Indian Congress and other political and trade-union activities; teacher 1979–82; involved in est. of Anti-South African Indian Council Cttee 1982, revival of Transvaal Indian Congress 1983; Founder mem. and fmr mem. Nat. Exec. Cttee United Democratic Front; fmr Leader Mass Democratic Movt; detained 1987, escaped 1988; planned Defiance Campaign; detained 1989; involved in Conf. for a Democratic Future 1989; mem. Nat. Reception Cttee for released African Nat. Congress (ANC) leaders 1989–90; with ANC 1990–, mem. Nat. Exec. Cttee 1991, fmr mem. Nat. Working Cttee, rep. of negotiating team Convention for a Democratic South Africa 1991–94; Deputy Minister of Prov. Affairs and Constitutional Devt 1994, Minister 1996–99, Minister of Environmental Affairs and Tourism 1999–2004; Pres. Int. Union for the Conservation of Nature 2004–08, Chair. Congress Steering Cttee. *Address:* IUCN Headquarters, Rue Mauverney 28, Gland 1196, Switzerland (office). *Telephone:* (22) 999-00-00 (office). *Fax:* (22) 999-00-02 (office). *E-mail:* webmaster@iucn.org (office). *Website:* www.iucn.org (office).

MOOSHAHARY, Ranjit Shekhar, BA; Indian government official and fmr police officer; b. 1 March 1946, Oldaguri, Kokrajhar Dist (now under Bodoland Territorial Area Dists of Assam); s. of the late Shikendra Mooshahary and Nandeswari Mooshahary; m. Rema Menon Mooshahary; one s. one d.; ed Union Christian Coll., Umiam, St Anthony's Coll., Shillong; joined Indian Police Service 1967, assigned to Kerala cadre, fmr Chief of Crime Br., Criminal Investigation Dept and Vigilance and Anti-Corruption Bureau, Kerala; Dir-Gen. Nat. Security Guards 2002–05, Border Security Force 2005–06; State Chief Information Commr, Assam 2006–08; Gov. of Meghalaya 2008–13; Hon. DLitt; Indian Police Medal for Meritorious Service, Pres.'s Police Medal for Distinguished Services, Man of the Year Award, Engkhong Trust Bijni 2008, Adivasi Ratna Award 2011. *E-mail:* mooshahary@gmail.com.

MOQBEL, Samir; Lebanese engineer and politician; *Deputy Prime Minister and Minister of Defence;* b. 1939; m. Joyce James; five c.; ed American Univ. of Beirut; CEO Samir Moqbel & Co. (real estate co.) 1965–; Minister of the Environment 1992–95, Deputy Prime Minister 2011–, also Minister of Defence 2014–; Pres. Alumni Asscn of the American Univ. of Beirut (Mount Lebanon) 1990–92; mem. Bd of Dirs Univ. of Balamand 1990–; mem. Chamber of Commerce and Industry of Beirut 1992–96. *Address:* Ministry of National Defence, Yarze, Beirut, Lebanon (office). *Telephone:* (5) 420000 (office). *Fax:* (5) 951036 (office). *E-mail:* cmd@army .gov.lb (office). *Website:* www.lebarmy.gov.lb (office).

MOQBEL OSMANI, Zarar Ahmad; Afghan fmr diplomatist and politician; *Minister of Foreign Affairs;* b. 1964, Parwan Prov.; ed Polytechnical Univ. of Kabul; Chief of Police, Parwan Prov. 1994; First Sec., later Amb. to Iran 1998–2002; Gov. Parwan Prov. 2004; Deputy Minister of Interior Affairs –Sept. 2005, Acting Minister of Interior Affairs Sept. 2005–March 2006, Minister of Interior Affairs 2006–08, of Refugees and Repatriation 2008, of Counter Narcotics 2009–13, of Foreign Affairs 2013–. *Address:* Ministry of Foreign Affairs, Malek Asghar Street, Kabul, Afghanistan (office). *Telephone:* (20) 2100372 (office). *Fax:* (20) 2100360 (office). *E-mail:* contact@mfa.gov.af (office). *Website:* mfa.gov.af (office).

MORA GRAMUNT, Gabriel; Spanish architect; *Partner, Mora-Sanvisens Arquitectes Associats;* b. 13 April 1941, Barcelona; s. of Evaristo Mora Gramunt and Josefa Mora Gramunt; m. Carmina Sanvisens Montón 1985; one s.; ed Tech. Univ. of Architecture, Barcelona (ETSAB); Assoc. Piñón-Viaplana 1967; tutor, ETSAB 1973; in partnership with Jaume Bach Nuñez, Bach/Mora Architects 1976, currently Mora-Sanvisens; Prof. of History of Modern Architecture, EINA School of Design 1978; Design Tutor, ETSAB 1978–; Visiting Prof., Univ. of Dublin 1993; has given numerous seminars and confs in Spain, Germany, France, Italy, the Netherlands, Austria, Slovenia, UK, Ireland, Finland and Latin America; various professional awards. *Works include:* Grass Hockey Olympic Stadium, Terrassa 1992, Edificio Central de Telefónica, Olympic Village, Barcelona 1992, Instituto IES Mollet del Vallès, Mollet del Vallès 1995, Escuela Ramon Fuster Cerdanyola del Vallès 1998–2002, Gimnasio y Sala de actos de la Escuela Tècnic Eulàlia, Barcelona, 2002, Estación de metro 'el Maresme Fòrum', Línia 4 de TMB, Barcelona 2004, Casa MPS, en la playa del Ros, Cadaqués 2004, Viviendas sociales Can Llong, Sabadell 2005, Casa VM en el Pasaje de S'Alqueria, Cadaqués 2007, Estación de Metro 'Alfons X', Línia L4 de TMB, Barcelona 2008, Escuela pública de Cadaqués 2008, Estación Metro 'La Sagrera', Línia 9 de TMB, Barcelona 2008–10, Biblioteca Municipal 'Esteve Paluzie', Barberà del Vallès 2009, Escuela pública 'CEIP de Palautordera', Palautordera 2010, Conjunto de viviendas sociales en la 'Mina', Sant Adrià del Besòs 2011, Estaciones Metro Hosp. Clíic –Hosp. Sant Pau, Línia 5 TMB, Barcelona 2011, Edificio Secundaria 'Ramón Fuster', Cerdanyola del Vallès 2012, apartment bldgs, agric. complex, health clinic etc. *Publications include:* Junge Architekten in Europa (co-author) 1983, Guía de arquitectura de Barcelona 1985, Young Spanish Architects (co-author) 1985, Arquitectura de Barcelona (co-author) 1990, Barcelona olímpica 1992, Bach Mora Arquitectos 1996. *Address:* Mora-Sanvisens Arquitectes Associats, C. Hercegovina 24, Pral. 1A, 08006 Barcelona, Spain. *Telephone:* (93) 4147720. *Fax:* (93) 4141627. *E-mail:* g.mora@coac.es. *Website:* www.morasanvisens.com

MORA RODAS, Nelson Alcides, Dr en Derecho; Paraguayan lawyer, politician and academic; b. 23 July 1956; m. Yolanda Peralta Alvarez; three c.; ed Nat. Coll. of the Capital, Faculty of Social Sciences, Nat. Univ. of Asunción, Catholic Univ. of Colombia, Bogotá, Univ. of Salamanca, Spain, Colegio Mayor de Nuestra Sra. del Rosario, Bogotá, Nat. War Coll., Asunción; Titular Prof. of Criminal Procedural Law, Catholic Univ., Villarrica; taught classes, courses and held confs at Nat. Univ. of Asunción, Visiting Prof., Faculty of Law and Social Sciences; fmr civil employee, Ministry of Justice and Labour; fmr Sec. of Court; fmr solicitor for Prosecutor Gen.; fmr Judge of First Instance in Penal and Civil Law; mem. Court of Criminal Appeal; Amb. to Colombia 1995–2003; Solicitor Gen. 2003–04; Minister of the Interior 2004–05, of Nat. Defence 2007–08; mem. Asoc. Nacional Republicana–Partido Colorado (Nat. Republican Asscn–Colorado Party); Degree of Grand Cross 'Academic Excellence', the Hispano-American Acad. of Sciences and Letters and Univ. Piloto of Colombia, Bogotá 1997, Grand Cross of Boyacá

(Colombia) 2003. *Publications:* Amarras fraternas, Colombia Paraguay 1999, Delincuencias Internacional Organizada. Drogas. Narcotráfico. Espacio Judicial Común 2000, Código Penal Paraguayo, Doctrina, Comentarios, Concordancias, Leyes Especiales 2000, Cerca del amanecer 2001. *Address:* Asociación Nacional Republicana–Partido Colorado, Casa de los Colorados, 25 de Mayo 842, Asunción, Paraguay (office). *Telephone:* (21) 44-4137 (office). *Fax:* (21) 49-7857 (office). *Website:* www.anr.org.py (office).

MORA WITT, Galo, PhD; Ecuadorean writer, musician and politician; *Minister of Culture;* b. 1957, Loja; ed Salesiana Univ.; guitarist and singer with Pueblo Nuevo 1978–; adviser to Casa de la Cultura Ecuatoriana 1996–2004; Minister of Culture 2008–. *Publications include:* Un pájaro redondo para jugar (Memoria y Fútbol) 2002, Memorial de una Lumbrera (biografía de Pío Jaramillo Alvarado); numerous essays and articles. *Address:* Ministry of Culture, Avda Portugal E9-138 y República del Salvador, Quito, Ecuador (office). *Website:* www.ministeriodecultura .gov.ec (office).

MORA ZEVALLOS, Daniel Emiliano; Peruvian politician; b. 18 Feb. 1945, Callao; ed Chorrillos Mil. School, Univ. of Lima, Int. Inst. of Humanitarian Law, San Remo, Italy; Prof., Political Acad. of Chile 1976–80; Founding mem. Perú Posible (PP) party 2000; Sec.-Gen., Ministry of Transport and Communication 2002–03, Head of advisory staff and Chair. Nat. Intelligence Council 2003–04; Presidential Adviser in Govt Palace 2005–06; mem. Congreso (Parl.) for Callao constituency 2011–; Minister of Defence July–Dec. 2011. *Address:* c/o Ministry of Defence, Edif. Quiñones, Avda de la Peruanidad s/n, Jesús María, Lima 1, Peru (office).

MORAGODA, (Asoka) Milinda, MBA; Sri Lankan politician; b. 4 June 1964; s. of Christopher Walter Pinto and Yasodha Neiliya Jayawardena; ed Royal Coll., Colombo, Int. Inst. for Man. Devt, Switzerland; Special Rep. for Sri Lankan Govt under Admin of Pres. Ranasinghe Premadasa early 1990s; fmr Special Advisor Ministry of Policy Planning and Implementation; fmr Special Advisor to Ministry of Industries, Science and Tech.; fmr Chair. Ceylon Inst. for Scientific and Industrial Research (now ITI); Founder-mem. Bd and Man. Cttee Janasaviya Trust Fund; Fellow, Centre for Int. Affairs, Harvard Univ., USA 1994–95; Founder-Chair. Mercantile Merchant Bank Ltd; also involved in creation of Colombo Stock Exchange, served as Alt. Dir on first Bd; mem. bd of dirs of several corp. bds; first entered Parl. as Nat. List MP 2000, contested from Colombo Dist as Organizer for Colombo East, elected 2001, re-elected (United Nat. Party—UNP) 2004; Minister for Econ. Reform, Science and Tech. and Deputy Minister of Policy Devt and Implementation 2002–04, played key role in establishing ceasefire and beginning peace talks between Govt and LTTE (Tamil Tigers), subsequently served as a prin. govt negotiator; apptd Chief UNP Organizer for Colombo West 2005; Minister of Tourism 2007–09, of Justice and Law Reforms 2009–10; Leader Sri Lanka Nat. Congress 2010–11 (disbanded); joined Sri Lanka Freedom Party 2011; currently Leader of the Opposition, Colombo Municipal Council; writes regular column in both Sunday Lankadeepa and in Sunday Thinakkural; mem. High Level Comm. on Legal Empowerment of the Poor (under UN Millennium Challenge Goals); mem. Young Global Leaders, World Econ. Forum, Geneva 2005–; Chair. Dayaka Sabawa of Amarapura Nikaya (one of three main Buddhist sects in Sri Lanka); Trustee, Soma Sadaham Sevana Trust (formed by Amarapura Dharmarakshitha Nikaya) 2005; also f. several non-profit orgs to engage in projects in areas of educ., social reform, social welfare, publishing, humanitarian services (including de-mining), culture and religion; Order of Rio Branco (Brazil) for services rendered as Hon. Consul for Brazil 1990–2004 1999; Global Leader of Tomorrow, World Econ. Forum 2000, Young Global Leader, World Econ. Forum 2009, www.milinda.org honoured in categories of Political and Personal Websites, Webby Awards 2007. *Radio:* weekly Sunday radio show on Sirasa FM, Sanvada (discusses relevant contemporary issues). *Television:* cr. and hosted series of talk shows, including: In Black and White, Obey Wedikawa (Your Forum), Gamin Gamata (Village to Village), Urumayaka Ulpath (Sources of Our Heritage). *Publications:* has contributed articles internationally to publs including The Washington Post and The Asian Wall Street Journal. *Address:* 8/30, Siddhartha Road, Colombo 6, Sri Lanka (office). *Telephone:* (11) 4020635 (office). *Fax:* (11) 4527111 (office). *E-mail:* email@milinda.org (office). *Website:* www.milinda.org (office).

MORAHAN, Christopher Thomas, CBE; British theatre, television and film director; b. 9 July 1929, London, England; s. of the late Thomas Morahan and Nancy Barker; m. 1st Joan Murray 1954 (died 1973); m. 2nd Anna Carteret 1974; two s. three d. (one deceased); ed Highgate School and Old Vic Theatre School; Dir Greenpoint Films and Head, plays, BBC TV 1972–76; Assoc. Dir Royal Nat. Theatre 1977–88; BAFTA Best TV Series 1984, Int. Emmy 1984, 1993, 1994, Evening Standard Best Dir 1984, Prix Italia 1987, and many other awards. *Stage productions include:* This Story of Yours, Royal Court 1968, Flint, Criterion Theatre 1970, The Caretaker, Mermaid Theatre 1972, State of Revolution, National Lyttelton 1977, Sir Is Winning, National Cottesloe 1977, The Lady from Maxim's, National Lyttelton 1977, Brand, National Olivier 1978, The Philanderer, National Lyttelton 1978, Strife, National Olivier 1978, The Fruits of Enlightenment, National Olivier 1979, Richard III, National Olivier 1979, The Wild Duck, Nartional Olivier 1979, Line 'Em, National Cottesloe 1980, Man and Superman, National Olivier 1980, Wild Honey, National Lyttelton (Evening Standard Best Director Award) 1984, New York 1986, Melon, Theatre Royal Haymarket, 1987, The Devil's Disciple, National Olivier, 1994, A Letter of Resignation, Comedy Theatre October 1997, Ugly Rumours, Tricycle Theatre, Kilburn 1998, Semi-Detached, Chichester Festival Theatre 1999, The Importance of Being Earnest, Chichester Festival Theatre and Theatre Royal Haymarket 1999, Quartet, Albery Theatre 1999, Heartbreak House, Chichester 2000, Naked Justice, West Yorkshire Playhouse and tour 2001, The Importance of Being Earnest, Savoy Theatre 2001, The Dwarfs (Pinter novel, adapted by Kerry Lee Crabbe), Tricycle 2003, The Linden Tree, Orange Tree Theatre 2006, Legal Fictions (double bill: The Dock Brief/Edwin, by John Mortimer) Richmond Theatre and touring 2007. *Films include:* Diamonds for Breakfast 1968, All Neat in Black Stockings 1969, Clockwise 1986, Paper Mask (also producer) 1990, Element of Doubt 1996. *Radio includes:* Art (BBC Radio 3). *Television includes:* Emergency-Ward 10 (series) 1957–59, Ghost Squad (series) 1961, The Hooded Terror (producer) 1963, The Road 1963, Malatesta 1964, Fable 1965, Coming Up for Air

1965, Nineteen Eighty Four 1965, A Game, Like, Only a Game 1966, Talking to a Stranger (BBC mini-series) 1966, The Ragged Trousered Philanthropists 1967, The Gorge 1968, The Letter 1969, Lay Down Your Arms 1970, Uncle Vanya 1970, Hearts and Flowers 1970, Lulie IV 1971, The Bankrupt 1972, The Common 1973, Pygmalion (producer) 1973, Fathers and Families (BBC series) 1977, The Jewel in the Crown (Granada mini-series) (also producer) 1984, In the Secret State 1985, After Pilkington (BBC) 1987, Troubles 1988, The Heat of the Day 1989, Can You Hear Me Thinking? 1990, Old Flames 1990, Ashenden (mini-series) 1991, Unnatural Pursuits (two-part play) 1992, Common Pursuit 1992, The Bullion Boys (also producer) 1993, Summer Days Dream 1994, It Could Be You 1995, The Peacock Spring 1996, Element of Doubt, A Dance to the Music of Time (two episodes) 1997. *Leisure interests:* photography, birdwatching. *Address:* c/o White-hall Artists, 10 Lower Common South, London, SW15 1BP (office); Highcombe Farmhouse, The Devil's Punchbowl, Thursley, Godalming, Surrey, GU8 6NS, England. *Telephone:* (20) 8785-3737 (office); (1428) 607031. *Fax:* (20) 8788-2340 (office); (1428) 607989. *E-mail:* chrismorahan@solutions-inc.co.uk (home).

MORAIS, José Pedro de; Angolan politician and economist; b. 20 Dec. 1955; ed in France; fmr Sec. of State for Construction Materials; Minister of Planning and Econ. Co-ordination 1992; Angola's nominee to Bd of IMF 1990s; Minister of Finance 2002–08. *Address:* c/o Ministry of Finance, Avda 4 de Fevereiro 127, CP 592, Luanda, Angola (office).

MORAIS, Marisa Helena do Nascimento; Cape Verde lawyer and politician; *Minister of Internal Administration;* b. 29 Sept. 1964, St Vincent; ed Univ. of Coimbra; lawyer in pvt. practice, then legal adviser to Minister of Justice; Minister of Justice 2009–11, of Internal Admin 2011–. *Address:* Ministry of Internal Administration, Praia, Santiago, Cape Verde (office). *Telephone:* (238) 615687 (office). *Fax:* (238) 614519 (office).

MORALES, Erik; Mexican boxer; b. Tijuana; s. of Jose Morales; brother of Diego Morales; m. America Morales; three c.; began boxing at age of five, had 114 amateur fights (108-6); trained by father in family boxing gym, Tijuana and by Fernando Fernandez; winner of 11 major amateur titles in Mexico; professional debut 1993; has had over 50 professional fights 2005; known as Erik "El Terrible" Morales; winner Mexican Super Bantamweight (SB) Title against Enrique Jupiter, Tijuana 1995, N American Boxing Fed. (NABF) SB Title against Juan Torres, Las Vegas, Nev. 1995, 1st NABF SB Defence against Alberto Martinez, Las Vegas 1995, 2nd NABF SB Defence against Kenny Mitchell, Tijuana 1995, 3rd NABF SB Defence against Rudy Bradley, Las Vegas 1996, 4th NABF SB Defence against Hector Acero-Sanchez, Las Vegas 1996, World Boxing Council (WBC) SB Title against Daniel Zaragoza, El Paso 1997, 1st WBC SB Defence against John Lowey, Tijuana 1997, 2nd WBC SB Defence against Remigio Molina, Tijuana 1998, 3rd WBC SB Defence against Jose Luis Bueno, Indio, Calif. 1998, 4th WBC SB Defence against Junior Jones, Tijuana 1998, 6th WBC SB Defence against Juan Carlos Ramirez, Las Vegas 1999, 7th WBC SB Defence against Reynante Jamiloi, Tijuana 1999, 8th WBC SB Defence against Wayne McCullough, Detroit, Mich. 1999, 9th WBC SB Defence against Marco Antonio Barerra, Las Vegas 2000, WBC Interim Featherweight Title against Kevin Kellery, El Paso, Tex. 2000, WBC Featherweight Title against Guty Espadas, Las Vegas 2001, 1st WBC Feather-weight Defense against Injin Chi, LA 2001, Defence of Title fights against Croft 2003, Velardez 2003, WBC Super Featherweight Title against Jesus Chavez 2004, Int. Boxing Asscn (IBA) Jr Lightweight Title against Carlos Hernandez 2004, IBA Super Featherweight Title and WBC Int. Super Featherweight Title against Manny Pacquiao, Las Vegas 2005; boxing promoter and man.; owner web boxing magazine box-latino.com; NABF Boxer of the Year 1996. *Leisure interests:* computer enthusiast. *Address:* c/o World Boxing Organization - Latino, Maza 557, Oficina 17, 1220 Buenos Aires, Argentina (office). *Telephone:* (11) 4931-7608 (office). *E-mail:* anaboxlatino@hotmail.com (office). *Website:* www.box-latino.com (office).

MORALES, Geraldo Rubén; Argentine politician; *President, Unión Cívica Radical;* b. 18 July 1959, Jujuy; m.; three s.; ed Universidad Nacional de Jujuy; began career at Instituto de Seguros, Dir Liquidation Dept 1980–89; Asst in Political Econs, Universidad Nacional de Jujuy 1985–92, Head of Macro econs 1992–93; Fed. Deputy for Jujuy state 1989–2000, Chair. Fed. Finance Cttee 1991–92, Leader Unión Cívica Radical (UCR) in Chamber of Deputies 1993; Minister for Social Devt 2000–01; Senator for Jujuy 2001–; Pres. Unión Cívica Radical (UCR) 2006–; unsuccessful cand. in governorship elections for Jujuy 1995, 1999. *Address:* Unión Cívica Radical, Alsina 1786, 1088 Buenos Aires (office); Hipólito Yrigoyen 1708, Piso 5, Of. 503, Buenos Aires, Argentina. *Telephone:* (11) 4375-2000 (UCR) (office); (11) 43795936. *E-mail:* morales@senado.gov.ar; presidencia@ucr.org.ar (office). *Website:* www.ucr.org.ar; morales.radicales.org.ar.

MORALES AIMA, Juan Evo; Bolivian politician and head of state; *President;* b. 29 Oct. 1959, Orinoca, Oruru; s. of Dionisio Morales Choque and Maria Mamani; fmr llama herder and trumpet player; farmed piece of land in Chapare for coca production 1980s; Founder and Leader, Movimiento al Socialismo (MAS) 1987; became leader of the 'cocaleros' (coca producers) following US attempts to eradicate cocaine production (Plan Dignity) 1998; expelled from govt after three policemen were killed in farmers' riots; mem. Congress; ran second in presidential elections 2002, succeeded in gaining resignation and exile of Pres. Gonzalo Sanchez de Lozada on issue of Bolivian gas exports 2003; Pres. of Bolivia 2006–. *Address:* Office of the President, Palacio de Gobierno, Plaza Murillo, La Paz; Movimiento al Socialismo, La Paz, Bolivia (office). *Telephone:* (2) 237-1082 (office). *Fax:* (2) 237-1388 (office). *E-mail:* despacho@presidencia.gov.bo (office). *Website:* www .presidencia.gov.bo (office); www.masbolivia.org (office).

MORALES ANAYA, Juan Antonio, PhD; Bolivian economist and social scientist; *President, Banco Central de Bolivia;* ed Catholic Univ. of Leuven, Belgium; Dir of Socio-Econs Research Inst. 1974–95; Catholic Univ. of Bolivia 1974–95; Dir Cen. Bank of Bolivia 1993–95, now Pres. *Address:* Banco Central de Bolivia, Avda Ayacucho esq. Mercado, Casilla Postal 3118, La Paz, Bolivia (office). *Telephone:* 37-4151 (office). *Fax:* 39-2398 (office). *E-mail:* jam@mail.bcb.gov.bo (office); vmarquez@mail.bcb.gov.bo. *Website:* www.bcb.gov.bo (office).

MORALES-BERMÚDEZ CERRUTI, Gen. Francisco; Peruvian politician and army officer; b. 4 Oct. 1921, Lima; grandson of the late Col Remigio Morales Bermúdez (Pres. of Peru 1890–94); m. Rosa Pedraglio de Morales Bermúdez; four

s. one d.; ed Colegio de la Inmaculada (Jesuit), Chorillos Mil. School; Founder-mem. Dept of Research and Devt, Army Gen. Staff; taught at School of Eng and at Army Acad. of War; Chief of Staff of First Light Div., Tumbes; Asst Dir of Logistics, Dir of Econ., War Ministry; advanced courses at Superior Acad. of War, Argentina and Centre for Higher Mil. Studies, Peru; apptd to reorganize electoral registration system 1962; Minister of Econ. and Finance 1968–74; Chief of Army Gen. Staff 1974–75: Prime Minister, Minister of War and Commdr-Gen. of Army Feb.–Aug. 1975; Pres. of Peru 1975–80; unsuccessful cand. in presidential elections 1985; being prosecuted by Italian judge Luisianna Figliolia for the presumed forced disappearance of 25 Italian citizens under Operation Condor (campaign of political oppression against leftists orchestrated by the right-wing dictatorships of South America 1970s) 2007–.

MORALES CARAZO, Jaime René; Nicaraguan business executive and politician; b. 10 Sept. 1936, Granada; s. of the late Carlos A. Morales and Anita Carazo Arellano; m. Amparo Vázquez Rovelo; two c.; f. Nicaraguan Devt Investments SA (INDES) in 1960s; mem. Nicaraguan Democratic Force 1983–93, Constitutional Liberal Party 1993–2002, Chair. Honour, Ethics and Justice Cttee 1993–2002, mem. Nat. Cttee 1993–2002; personal adviser (with rank of Minister) to Pres. of Nicaragua 1997–2001, Chair. Nat. Council on Sustainable Devt 1997–2001; Deputy in Nat. Ass. 2001–06; Vice-Pres. of Nicaragua 2007–12; mem. Central American Parliament (PARLACEN) 2012–. *Address:* Central American Parliament (Parlamento Centroamericano), 12 Avda 33-04, Zona 5, 01005 Guatemala City, Guatemala (office). *Website:* www.parlacen.int (office).

MORALES IBAÑEZ, Marisela, LLB; Mexican lawyer and government official; *Procurator-General;* b. 1 March 1970, Mexico City; ed Universidad Nacional Autónoma de México, Instituto Nacional de Ciencias Penales; began career as public defender in Eastern justice region 1988–93, Public Prosecutor in Procurator-Gen.'s Office, Mexico City 1993, Gen. Coordinator for Special Investigation of Federal Crimes 2000–05, Head, Office of Special Investigation on Organized Crime (SIEDO) 2008–11, Asst Procurator-Gen., then Procurator-Gen. of Mexico 2011–; Int. Women of Courage Award 2011. *Address:* Office of the Procurator-General, Avda Paseo de la Reforma 211–213, Col. Cuauhtémoc, Del. Cuauhtémoc, 06500 México DF, Mexico. *Telephone:* (55) 5346-0000 (office). *Fax:* (55) 5346-0908 (office). *E-mail:* ofproc@pgr.gob.mx (office). *Website:* www.pgr.gob .mx (office).

MORALES TRONCOSO, Carlos; Dominican Republic politician; *Secretary of State for Foreign Affairs;* b. 29 Sept. 1940; m. Luisa Alba de Morales; four d.; ed Louisiana State Univ.; several positions at Gulf & Western Americas Corpn 1976–84; Vice-Pres. of Dominican Repub. 1990–94; Sec. of State for Foreign Affairs 1994–96, 2004–; mem. Instituto Americano de Ingenieros Químicos (AICHE); Dr hc (Dominican Chamber of Commerce of New York) 1984; Gulf & Western Americas Industrialist of the Year 1982. *Publication:* De Lo Privado a Lo Público 2002. *Address:* Secretariat of State for Foreign Affairs, Avenida Independencia 752, Santo Domingo, DN, Dominican Republic (office). *Telephone:* 535-6280 (office). *Fax:* 535-5772 (office). *E-mail:* postmaster@serex.gov.do (office). *Website:* www.serex.gov.do (office).

MORAN, Jerry, BS, JD; American lawyer, politician and academic; *Senator from Kansas;* b. 29 May 1954, Great Bend, Barton Co., Kan.; m. Robba A. Moran; two d.; ed Fort Hays State Univ., Kan., Univ. of Kansas at Lawrence; early career as banker; est. law practice in Hays; returned to Fort Hays State Univ. as Adjunct Prof. of Political Science; Kansas State Special Asst Attorney Gen. 1982–85; Deputy Attorney, Rooks Co., Kan. 1987–95; mem. Kansas Senate 1989–97, Vice-Pres. 1993–95, Majority Leader 1995–97; mem. US House of Reps for 1st Congressional Dist of Kan. 1997–2010, mem. Cttee on Agric., Cttee on Transportation and Infrastructure, Cttee on Veterans Affairs, numerous sub-cttees, Co-Chair. House Hunger Caucus; Senator from Kan. 2011–, mem. Appropriations Cttee, Banking, Housing, and Urban Affairs Cttee, Small Business Cttee, Veterans' Affairs Cttee, Special Cttee on Aging; mem. Bd of Govs Univ. of Kansas School of Law 1990, Vice-Pres. 1993–94, Pres. 1994–95; mem. Bd of Dirs Kansas Chamber of Commerce and Industry 1996–97; Trustee, Eisenhower Foundation; mem. Bd of Trustees, Fort Hays State Univ. Endowment Assocn; mem. Exec. Cttee Coronado Area Council of the Boy Scouts of America; Republican; Hon. Bd mem. Special Olympics Kansas, Hon. Chair. Kansas Law Enforcement Torch Run 2008; named a Guardian of Small Business, Nat. Fed. of Ind. Business 2008, 2010, named Home Care Hero of the Year, Kansas Home Care Asscn 1998, Legis. Award, Nat. Rural Health Asscn 1999, Jim Edwards Alumnus of the Year Award, Leadership Kansas 2003, Intergovernmental Leadership Award, League of Kansas Municipalities 2003, Small Business Advocate Award, Small Business Survival Cttee 2004, Wheat Leader of the Year Award, Nat. Asscn of Wheat Growers & US Wheat Assocs 2004, Distinguished Leadership Award, American Asscn for Marriage & Family Therapy 2007. *Address:* 354 Russell Senate Office Building, Washington, DC 20510, USA (office). *Telephone:* (202) 224-6521 (office). *Fax:* (202) 228-6966 (office). *Website:* moran.senate.gov (office).

MORÁN LÓPEZ, Fernando; Spanish politician, diplomatist and author; b. 1926, Avilés; m. María Luz Calvo-Sotelo; one s. two d.; ed Institut des Hautes Etudes Internationales, Paris, London School of Econs, Madrid Univ.; began diplomatic career 1954; Asst Consul, Spanish Consulate-Gen., Buenos Aires 1956; Sec. Spanish Embassy, Pretoria; transferred to Ministry of Foreign Affairs 1963, specialized in African affairs, Asst Dir-Gen. for Africa, Near and Middle East, Political Dir Dept of Foreign Policy, later in charge of Africa, Near and Middle East 1971, Dir-Gen. of African Affairs 1975–77; First Sec. Spanish Embassy, Lisbon; Consul-Gen. Spanish Embassy, London 1974; Partido Socialista Popular cand. for elections to Congress of Deputies 1977; elected Partido Socialista Obrero Español Senator for Asturias, Socialist Spokesman for Foreign Affairs in Senate; Minister of Foreign Affairs 1982–85; Perm. Rep. to the UN 1985–87; MEP 1989–99; Légion d'honneur, Grand Cross of Carlos III, Grand Cross Order of Isabel la Católica 1985, Grand Cross of Christ (Portugal). *Publications:* También se muere el Mar 1984, Una política exterior para España, El día en que 1997, Palimpsesto 2002. *Leisure interests:* literature, theatre. *Address:* Alvárez de Baena 5, 28006 Madrid, Spain (home). *Telephone:* (91) 5643719 (home).

MORANO, Nadine; French politician; b. (Nadine Pucelle (change by Presidential Decret to Nadine Pugelle 1976), 6 Nov. 1963, Nancy; elected mem. of Nat. Ass. for

Meurthe-et-Moselle constituency 2002–08, Vice-Pres. working groups on Nat. Security and Youth, Integration and Citizenship, mem. Comm. on Family, Social and Cultural Affairs; Regional Councillor for Lorraine 2004–; mem. Union pour un Mouvement Populaire (UMP), Spokesperson 2007–, also serves as Gen. Del. for Employment; Sec. of State for Family 2008–09, for the Family and Solidarity 2009–10, Minister in the Ministry of Labour, Employment and Health, responsible for Learning and Vocational Training 2010–12; mem. Génération Entreprise. *Address:* 1 rue St Waast, BP 158, 54206 Toul (office); Conseil Régional de Lorraine, Place Gabriel Hocquard, 57036 Metz Cedex 01, France. *Telephone:* (3) 83-64-24-43 (office); (3) 87-33-60-00. *Fax:* (3) 83-63-13-95 (office); (3) 87-32-89-33. *E-mail:* deputee@nadine-morano.com (office). *Website:* www.lorraine.eu.

MORAUTA, Sir Mekere, Kt, KCMG, BEcons; Papua New Guinea politician and banker; b. 12 June 1946; s. of Morauta Hasu and Morikoai Elavo; m. Roslyn Morauta; two s.; ed Univ. of Papua New Guinea, Flinders Univ. of South Australia; research officer, Dept of Labour 1971; economist, Office of the Econ. Adviser 1972; Sec. for Finance, Govt of Papua New Guinea 1973–82; Man. Dir Papua New Guinea Banking Corpn 1983–92; Chair. Nat. Airline Comm. 1992–94; Gov. Bank of Papua New Guinea 1993–94; Exec. Chair. Morauta Investments Ltd 1994–97; MP for Moresby NW 1997–, Leader of the Opposition 2007–; Minister for Planning and Implementation 1997, for Fisheries 1998–99, for Public Enterprise 2011–12; Prime Minister and Treas. of Papua New Guinea 1999–2002; Leader, Papua New Guinea Party 2007–; fmr Chair. Nat. Capital Dist Comm.; mem. Bd of Dirs Angco; Hon. DTech (Univ. of Tech., Lae) 1987. *Publications:* numerous econs-related papers. *Address:* c/o Ministry of Public Enterprise, Waigani, NCD, Papua New Guinea (office).

MORAVČÍK, Jozef, LLD, CSc; Slovak politician; b. 19 March 1945, Očová Zvolen Dist; m.; two d.; ed Charles Univ., Komenský Univ.; clerk with Chemapol (trade co.) Bratislava; lecturer Law Faculty, Komenský Univ., Bratislava 1972–85, Head of Dept of Business Law 1985–90; Dean, Law Faculty 1990–91; Deputy to Slovak Nat. Council 1991–92; mem. Movt for Democratic Slovakia (MDS) 1991–94; Minister of Foreign Affairs of ČSFR July–Dec. 1992; Chair. Council of Ministers of CSCE July–Dec. 1992; Minister of Foreign Affairs, Slovak Repub. 1993–94; Prime Minister of Slovakia March–Dec. 1994; Chair. Democratic Union of Slovakia 1994–97; Chair. Policy Planning Council 1997–; Mayor of Bratislava 1998–2002. *Address:* Magistrát hlavného mesta SR Bratislavy, Primaciálne hám. 1, PO Box 192, 814 22 Bratislava, Slovakia (office). *Telephone:* (7) 5443-5324 (office). *Fax:* (7) 5443-5405 (office). *E-mail:* primator@bratislava.sk (office). *Website:* www .bratislava.sk (office).

MORAVEC, Ivan; Czech pianist and academic; b. 9 Nov. 1930, Prague; m. 1st (deceased); m. 2nd; one s., one d.; ed Conservatoire, Prague 1946–51; teacher, Acad. of Musical Arts, Prague 1969–, Prof. 2000–; soloist with Czech Philharmonic Orchestra; concert tours Europe, USA, Japan; festivals in Salzburg, Edinburgh, Aldeburgh, Prague Spring, Schleswig-Holstein, Tanglewood, etc.; recitals in London 2007, Toulouse 2007, Munich 2007, Denver 2007, New York 2007, Salzburg 2008, Prague 2009, 2012; Cannes Classical Award 1999, Charles IV Prize 2000, Platinum Disc Award, Supraphon 2000, Medal of Merit 2000, Int. Prize Charles Univ. 2000, Harmonie Prize 2001, Cannes Classical Award for Lifetime Achievement 2002. *Recordings include:* Chopin: Nocturnes, Vol. 1 1965 (selected by the New York Times as one of five representative works to showcase their celebration of the bicentennial of Chopin's birth 2010) (remastered and reissued 2012), Debussy: Preludes, Children's Corners Suite 1967, Moravec Plays Chopin 1969, Ivan Moravec Live in Brussels 1983, Brahms Piano Concertos 1989, Chopin Scherzi, Etudes, Mazurkas 1991, Schumann Piano Concerto, Brahms Piano Concerto No. 1 1993, Mozart: Piano Concertos K 466, 488, 491, 503 1996, 1997, two-CD compilation of his recordings published as part of the Philips series, Great Pianists of the 20th Century 1998, Ivan Moravec Plays Mozart 2001, Ivan Moravec/Chopin 2003, Beethoven Piano Concerto No. 4, Ravel, Franck 2004, numerous record of the year listings in High Fidelity, Stereo Review, New York Times, Time Magazine, Newsweek. *Leisure interest:* culture. *Address:* c/o Linda Marder, 127 West 96th Street, #13B, New York, NY 10025, USA (office); Pod Vyhlídkou 520, 160 00 Prague 6, Czech Republic. *Telephone:* (212) 864-1005 (office); (2) 23123696. *Fax:* (212) 864-1066 (office); (2) 33343696. *E-mail:* lymarder@ aol.com (office). *Website:* www.cramermarderartists.com/moravec.htm (office); www.ivanmoravec.net.

MORCELI, Noureddine; Algerian middle-distance runner; b. 28 Feb. 1970, Ténès; coached by his brother Abderrahmane Morceli; World Champion, 1,500m Tokyo 1991, Stuttgart 1993, Gothenburg 1995; fmr world record-holder at 1,500m, one mile, 2,000m, 3,000m; gold medal, Olympic Games, Atlanta 1996; announced intention to compete in 2003 over 5,000m and 10,000m but did not race 2003–04; IAAF Athlete of the Year 1994. *Address:* c/o Ministry of Youth and Sports, 3 rue Mohamed Belouizdad, Algiers, Algeria. *Website:* www.iaaf.org/athletes/ biographies/athcode=1936/index.html.

MORCHIO, Giuseppe; Italian automobile industry executive; b. 20 Nov. 1947, Rapallo, Genoa; m.; two c.; ed Genoa Polytechnic Univ.; began career in cable sector of Manuli Group; Dir of Logistics, Pirelli Group 1980, then Vice-Pres. Mfg, Quality and Logistics, Pirelli Group Worldwide, then Corp. Exec. Vice-Pres., Pirelli SpA; Chair. and CEO Pirelli Neumáticos, Barcelona; Pres. and CEO Pirelli Tyre North America; CEO Pirelli Cavi SpA Holding 1993–95; Chair. and CEO Pirelli Cavi e Sistemi SpA 1995–2003, Dir 1999–2003; CEO Fiat SpA 2003–04 (resgnd), Chair. Fiat Auto, Iveco, Magneti Marelli, Coamu, Teksid (all with Fiat Group) 2003–04; mem. Bd CNH, Ferrari, Banco di Desio e della Brianza; mem. Exec. Cttee Bd Dirs Confindustria (business asscn). *Leisure interest:* sailing. *Address:* c/o Fiat SpA, Corporate Headquarters, Via Nizza 250, 10126 Turin, Italy.

MORDACQ, Patrick; French fmr government official and international consultant; b. 20 May 1934, Bordeaux; m. Marie Thérèse de Yturbe 1967; one s. one d.; ed Ecole Nat. d'Admin; Commissariat Gen. du Plan d'Equipement et de la Productivité 1963–67, Head, Finance Service 1967; Office of Minister of Equipment and Housing 1968; Head, Office of Foreign Investment, Treasury 1969; Deputy Chair. Comm. of Industry for VIth Plan 1970; Head, Office of Loans, Aid and Guarantees to Business, Treasury 1971–74; Finance Dir Groupe Jacques Borel Int. 1974–77; Financial Counsellor, French Embassy, Bonn 1979; Head, Regulation of Finance, Treasury 1984–86; Govt Commr Centre Nat. des Caisses d'Epargne et de Prévoyance 1984–86; CEO Comm. des Opérations de Bourse 1986–91; Dir for France, EBRD (London) and Financial Counsellor, French Embassies, Poland, Romania and Bulgaria 1991–96; Conseiller-Maître, Cour des Comptes 1996–2002; Chair. Bd of Auditors, OECD 2002–07; consultant, institutional building projects (public finance man.) 2002–; Chevalier, Légion d'honneur, Officier, Ordre nat. du Mérite, Commdr, Bundesverdienstkreuz (Germany). *Address:* 5 rue Pierre le Grand, 75008 Paris, France. *E-mail:* mordacqpatrick@gmail.com.

MORDASHOV, Alexey A., MBA; Russian business executive; *CEO, Severstal' OAO;* ed Leningrad Inst. of Eng and Econs, Newcastle Business School, Northumbria Univ., Newcastle, UK; has worked for Severstal' OAO since 1988, started career as sr shop economist, Chief Financial Officer 1992–96, CEO 1996–2002, 2006–, Chair. and CEO 2002–06, mem. Remuneration Cttee, Human Resources Cttee; Chair. Silovye mashiny OAO, Severstal'-Holding OOO, Alyans-1420 ZAO, SVEZA OAO; Gen. Dir (CEO) Terrsprof OOO, Laguna-Delta ZAO, Algoritm OOO; fmr Gen. Dir Finkom OOO, Prima-Invest OOO, Severstal' Garant ZAO; Head of Russian Union of Industrialists and Entrepreneurs (RSPP) Cttee on Trade Policy; mem. Entrepreneurs Council, Govt of Russian Fed., EU-Russia Business Co-operation Council 2006–, Atlantic Council Pres.'s Int. Advisory Bd, Russian-German work group responsible for strategic econ. and finance issues; Dr hc (St Petersburg State Univ. of Eng and Econs) 2001, (Univ. of Northumbria) 2003. *Address:* Severstal' OAO, Moscow 127299, 2–3 Klara Tsetkin Street, Russia (office). *Telephone:* (495) 926-7766 (office). *Fax:* (495) 926-7766 (office). *E-mail:* antonova@severstal.com (office). *Website:* www.severstal.com (office).

MOREAU, Jeanne, FBA; French actress; b. 23 Jan. 1928, Paris; d. of Anatole-Désiré Moreau and Katherine Buckley; m. 1st Jean-Louis Richard 1949 (divorced); one s.; m. 2nd William Friedkin 1977 (divorced); ed Collège Edgar-Quinet, Conservatoire national d'art dramatique; stage actress with Comédie Française 1948–52; Théâtre Nat. Populaire 1953; Pres. Cannes Film Festival July 1975; Paris Int. Film Festival 1975; Pres. Acad. des Arts et Techniques du Cinéma 1986–88; Pres. Comm. des avances sur recettes 1993–94; mem. Acad. des Beaux-Arts, Inst. de France (Acad. of Modern Art) 2000–, jury of December Prize 2001–; Fellow, BAFTA; Hon. Acad. 1998; Officier, Légion d'honneur, Officier Ordre nat. du Mérite, Commdr des Arts et Lettres; Molière Award 1988, European Cinema Prize, Berlin 1997, Golden Bear, Int. Film Festival, Berlin 2000. *Plays include:* L'heure éblouissante, La machine infernale, Pygmalion, La chatte sur un toit brûlant, La bonne soupe, La chevauchée sur le lac de Constance, Lulu, L'intoxe, Night of the Iguana, Le récit de la Servante Zerline 1986, La Célestine 1989, Un trait de l'espirit 2000. *Films include:* Dernier amour (Last Love) 1949, Pigalle-Saint-Germain-des-Prés 1950, L'homme de ma vie (The Man in My Life) 1952, Il est minuit, docteur Schweitzer (aka Dr. Schweitzer) 1952, Dortoir des grandes (Girls' Dormitory) 1953, Julietta 1953, Touchez pas au grisbi (Hands Off the Loot) 1954, Les intrigantes (The Plotters) 1954, Secrets d'alcove 1954, La Reine Margot (Queen Margot) 1955, M'sieur la Caille 1955, Les hommes en blanc (Men in White) 1955, Gas-Oil 1955, Le salaire du péché (The Wages of Sin) 1956, Jusqu'au dernier (Until the Last One) 1957, Les louves (The She-Wolves) 1957, L'étrange Monsieur Steve 1957, Trois jours à vivre (Three Days to Live) 1957, Échec au porteur (Not Delivered) 1958, Ascenseur pour l'échafaud (Lift to the Scaffold) 1958, Le dos au mur (Back to the Wall) 1958, Les amants (The Lovers) 1958, Les quatre cents coups (The Four Hundred Blows) 1959, Les liaisons dangereuses (Dangerous Liaisons) 1959, Matisse ou Le talent de bonheur (voice) 1960, 5 Branded Women 1960, Moderato cantabile 1960, Le dialogue des Carmélites 1960, La notte 1961, Une femme et une femme (A Woman Is a Woman) (uncredited) 1961, Jules et Jim 1962, Eve 1962, Le procès (The Trial) 1962, La baie des anges (Bay of Angels) 1963, Peau de banane (Banana Peel) 1963, Le feu follet (Will o' the Wisp) 1963, The Victors 1963, Le journal d'une femme de chambre (The Diary of a Chambermaid) 1964, The Train 1964, The Yellow Rolls-Royce 1964, Mata-Hari 1964, Viva Maria! 1965, Campanadas a medianoche (Chimes at Midnight) 1965, Mademoiselle 1966, L'amour à travers les âges 1967, Le plus vieux métier du monde (The Oldest Profession in the World) 1967, The Sailor from Gibraltar 1967, La mariée était en noir (The Bride Wore Black) 1968, The Immortal Story (Une histoire immortelle) 1968, Great Catherine 1968, Le corps de Diane (Diana's Body) 1969, The Deep 1970, Monte Walsh 1970, Comptes rebours (aka Reckonings Against the Grain) 1971, L'humeur vagabonde (Vagabond Humour) 1972, Chère Louise (Dear Louise) 1972, Nathalie Granger 1972, Joanna Francesa 1972, Les valseuses (Going Places, USA) 1973, Le jardin qui bascule (The Garden That Tilts) 1974, Je t'aime 1974, La race des 'seigneurs' (aka Elite Group) 1974, Pleurs 1974, Hu-Man 1975, Souvenirs d'en France 1975, Lumière (also writer and dir) 1976, Monsieur Klein 1976, The Last Tycoon 1976, Le petit théâtre de Jean Renoir 1976, L'adolescente (also writer) 1978, Madame Rosa 1978, Your Ticket Is No Longer Valid 1981, Plein Sud 1981, Mille milliards de dollars (A Thousand Billion Dollars) 1982, Querelle 1982, Au-delà de cette limite votre billet n'est plus valable 1982, La truite (The Trout) 1982, Lillian Gish (producer and dir), Le paltoquet 1986, Sauve-toi Lola 1986, Le miraculé 1987, Jour après jour (Day After Day) 1989, Nikita 1990, Alberto Express 1990, La femme fardée 1990, Anna Karamazova 1991, La Vieille qui marchait dans la Mer (The Old Lady Who Walked in the Sea) 1991, To Meteoro vima tou pelargou (The Suspended Step of the Stork) 1991, Bis ans Ende der Welt (Till the End of the World) 1991, L'amant (The Lover) (voice) 1992, La nuit de l'océan 1992, À demain 1992, L'absence (The Absence) 1993, Map of the Human Heart 1993, Je m'appelle Victor (My Name Is Victor) 1993, A Foreign Field 1993, The Summer House 1994, Les cent et une nuits de Simon Cinéma (A Hundred and One Nights of Simon Cinema) 1995, Al di là delle nuvole (Beyond the Clouds) 1995, I Love You, I Love You Not 1996, The Proprietor 1996, Amour et confusions (Love and Confusions) 1997, Un amour de sorcière (Witch Way Love) 1997, Ever After 1998, Il manoscritto del principe (The Prince's Manuscript) 2000, Genesys (video game) 2001, Lisa 2001, Cet amour-là 2001, The Will to Resist 2002, La petite prairie aux bouleaux (The Birch-Tree Meadow) (writer) 2003, Akoibon 2005, Le temps qui reste 2005, Go West (also assoc. producer) 2005, Sortie de Clown 2006, Roméo et Juliette 2006, Disengagement 2007, Plus tard 2008, Visage 2009. *Television includes:* Le petit théâtre de Jean Renoir (The Little Theatre of Jean Renoir) 1970, Saint, martyr et poète 1975, L'arbre 1982, L'intoxe 1983, Vicious Circle 1985, The Last Seance 1986, Le tiroir secret (mini-series) 1986, L'ami Giono: Ennemonde 1990, Clothes in the Wardrobe 1992, Catherine the Great 1995, Belle Époque (mini-series; voice) 1995, Balzac 1999, Les Misérables (mini-series) 2000, Zaïde, un

petit air de vengeance 2001, Les parents terribles 2003, La Contessa di Castiglione 2005, Les rois maudits (mini-series) 2005, Sous les Vents de Neptune 2008. *Leisure interest:* reading. *Address:* c/o Spica Productions, 4 Square du Roule, 75008 Paris, France.

MOREL, Pierre Jean Louis Achille; French diplomatist; *Special Representative for Central Asia, European Union;* b. 27 June 1944, Romans (Drôme); s. of André Morel and Janine Vallernaud; m. Olga Bazanoff 1978; three c.; ed Lycée du Parc, Lyon, Paris, Ecole nat. d'admin; Europe Dept, Ministry of Foreign Affairs 1971–73, Policy Planning Centre 1973–76, First Sec. then Second Counsellor, Embassy, Moscow 1976–79, Ministerial Rep., Gen. Secr. Interministerial Cttee on European Econ. Co-operation 1979–81, Office of Pres. of Repub., Technical Adviser to Gen. Secr. 1981–85, Dir Political Affairs, Ministry of Foreign Affairs 1985–86, Amb. and France's Rep. to Disarmament Conf., Geneva 1989, Head of French Del. Preparatory Cttee to CSCE 1990, Diplomatic Adviser, Office of Pres. of Repub. 1991–92; Amb. to Georgia 1992–93, to Russia (also accred to Moldova, Turkmenistan, Mongolia, Tajikistan and Kyrgyzstan) 1992–96, to China 1996–2002, to The Holy See 2002–05; Adviser to Policy Planning Centre, Ministry of Foreign Affairs 2005–06; EU Special Rep. for Cen. Asia 2006–, for the crisis in Georgia 2008–11; Officier, Légion d'honneur, Commdr, Ordre nat. du Mérite. *Publications:* trans. Mantrana 1984, Sauts de Temps 1989, Serpentara 1998 by Ernst Jünger. *Address:* c/o Council of the European Union, Rue de la Loi 175, 1048 Brussels, Belgium (office). *Telephone:* (2) 281-64-51 (office); (2) 281-74-30 (office). *Fax:* (2) 281-51-46 (office). *E-mail:* pierre.morel@ext.eeas.europa.eu (office). *Website:* www.eeas .europa.eu (office).

MORELLET, François Charles Alexis Albert; French painter and sculptor; b. 30 April 1926, Cholet, Maine-et-Loire; s. of Charles Morellet and Madeleine Guérineau; m. Danielle Marchand 1946; three s.; ed Lycée Charlemagne, Institut Nat. des Langues et Civilisations Orientales, Paris; Commercial Dir then Man. Dir Morellet-Guérineau 1948–76; artist 1942–; Commdr des Arts et des Lettres 2012; Grand prix nat. de sculpture 1987, Preis Peter C. Ruppert für Konkrete Kunst in Europa 2008. *Works include:* mural at 22 Reade Street, Lower Manhattan, New York 1988, neon piece, Grande halle de la Villette, Paris 1988, steel sculpture, La Défense, Paris 1991, neon piece, Debis-Haus, Potsdamerplatz, Berlin 1998, transparent films on glass, Obayashi Corpn, Tokyo 1998, neon pieces, Bundestag, Berlin 2000, marble piece, Jardin des Tuileries, Paris 2000, Gold Leaves, French Embassy, Berlin 2003, Musée des Beaux-Arts, Angers 2006, Musée d'Orsay, Paris 2006, Bundestag Elisabeth Lüders-Haus, Berlin 2003, Cité Internationale de Lyon, Palais des Congrès, Lyon 2006, Villa Pisani, Bagnolo di Lonigo 2008, Musée du Louvre, Paris 2010, Kunstmuseum Bochum 2011, Immeuble Louvre/Saint-Honoré, Paris (Place du Palais Royal, rue de Rivoli, rue Saint-Honoré, rue Marengo) 2013. *Publication:* Mais comment taire mes commentaires 1999–2011. *Leisure interests:* travel, underwater fishing. *Address:* 83 rue Porte Baron, 49300 Cholet, France (home). *Telephone:* (2) 41-62-23-81 (office). *Fax:* (2) 41-71-04-74 (office). *E-mail:* f.morellet@wanadoo.fr (office).

MORENÉS EULATE, Pedro, LLB; Spanish lawyer, business executive, politician and academic; *Minister of Defence;* b. 17 Sept. 1948, Las Arenas, Vizcaya; s. of Don José María de Morenés y Carvajal, 4th Viscount of Alesón and Doña Ana Sofía Alvarez de Eulate y Mac-Mahón; m.; three c.; ed Univ. of Navarre, INSIDE Inst., Deusto Commercial Univ., Bremen Inst. of Shipping Econs; began career as lawyer 1979; worked in pvt. law firms; Head of Legal Services br., Shipbuilding Div., Nat. Industry Inst. (INI) 1991–94, Man. Dir Commercial br., Shipbuilding Div. and mem. Steering Cttee 1994–96; fmr Prof. of Vessel Chartering and Shipping Freight, Spanish Maritime Inst., Madrid and in European Inst. for Maritime Studies; Sec. of State for Defence, Ministry of Defence 1996–2000, Sec. of State for Security, Ministry of Home Affairs 2000–02, Sec. of State for Science and Tech. Policy, Ministry of Science and Tech. 2002–05, Minister of Defence 2011–; Gen.-Sec. Círculo de Empresarios Business Circle 2005–10; Chair. Construcciones Navales del Norte SL 2009–11, MBDA Spain (missile systems firm) 2010–11, Segur Iberica 2011; mem. Bd of Dirs Telefónica SA, Tabacalera SA 1996–98; Great Cross, Order of Isabella the Catholic, Silver Cross of the Civil Guard, Medal for Police Merit. *Address:* Ministry of Defence, Paseo de la Castellana 109, 28071 Madrid, Spain (office). *Telephone:* (1) 3955000 (office). *E-mail:* secretaria .ministro@minisdef.es (office). *Website:* www.mde.es (office).

MORENO, Glen, BA, JD; American/British business executive; *Chairman, Pearson plc;* b. 1943, Calif., USA; ed Stanford Univ., Univ. of Delhi, India, Harvard Law School; sr positions at Citigroup in Europe and Asia 1969–87; CEO Fidelity International 1987–91, mem. Bd of Dirs; Sr Ind. Dir, Man Group plc, Dir (non-exec.) 1994–2009; Chair. Pearson plc 2005–; Acting Chair. UK Financial Investments 2009; Sr Ind. Dir, Lloyds Banking Group 2010–12; Gov., Ditchley Foundation; Dir, Royal Acad. of Dramatic Art. *Address:* Pearson plc, 80 Strand, London, WC2R 0RL, England (office). *Telephone:* (20) 7010-2304 (office). *Fax:* (20) 7010-6601 (office). *Website:* www.pearson.com (office).

MORENO BARBER, Javier, Licenciado en Ciencias Químicas, Master of Journalism; Spanish journalist and editor; *Director, El País;* b. 1963, Paris, France; ed Univ. of Valencia, Autonomous Univ. of Madrid; worked in Germany –1992; worked for econs section of El País 1992–94, Man. Ed. Mexican edn of newspaper 1994, returned to to Spain and co-ordinated Latin American edn, served as special envoy to several int. events, Head of Econs section 1999–2002, corresp. in Berlin 2002–03, Dir econ. daily Cinco Dias 2003–06, Dir El País 2006–, apptd cttee to undertake extensive redesign of newspaper Feb. 2007, completed Oct. 2007. *Address:* El País, Miguel Yuste 40, 28037 Madrid, Spain (office). *Telephone:* (91) 337-8200 (office). *Fax:* (91) 337-7758 (office). *E-mail:* redaccion@elpais.com (office). *Website:* www.elpais.com (office).

MORENO BARBERA, Admiral Antonio; Spanish naval officer; b. 17 April 1940, Madrid; m. Pepa Deckler Andreu; four c.; ed Naval War Coll.; began career in Spanish Navy 1956; apptd Lt JG 1961; served on board destroyer Alava, submarines Almirante García de los Reyes S-31, Delfín S-61, Marsopa S-63, Submarine Flotilla Staff; Commdr submarines Tonina S-62 and Galerna S-71 1975–83; Commdg Officer frigate Asturias F-74 1983–89; Commdr Submarine Flotilla 1988–92; shore assignments include Leading Lecturer on Logistics, Naval Warfare Coll., Lecturer on Tactics, Submarine School, Chief of Tactical Studies, Dept at Naval Staff, Exec. Asst to Chief of Naval Staff; Commdr of Fleet of

Amphibious Force (Delta Group) 1992–94; Chief of Rota Naval Base 1994–95; Chief of the Jt Defence Staff 1995–97; Chief of Naval Staff 1997–99; Chief of Defence Staff 1999–2004; apptd Vice-Admiral 1994, Admiral 1997; Grand Cross of St Hermenegildo, Commdr US Legion of Merit; four Naval Merit Crosses, Sahara Medal (Combat Zone), Brazilian Naval Merit Medal, Naval Merit Grand Cross, Mil. Merit Grand Cross, Chilean Great Star Mil. Merit Cross, Brazilian Naval Merit Grand Cross. *Address:* c/o Ministry of Defence, Paseo de la Castellana 109, 28071 Madrid, Spain (office).

MORENO CHARME, Alfredo, BEng, MBA; Chilean civil engineer, business executive and politician; b. 1957, Santiago; m. Ana María Echeverría; four c.; ed Univ. Católica de Chile, Univ. of Chicago, USA; fmr Prof., School of Admin, Univ. Católica de Chile; Minister of Foreign Affairs 2010–14; Chair. Teletón Chile Foundation, Telemercadoes Europa SA, Telemercados Europa, Editorial Santiago; fmr Chair. ICARE, Ladeco, Banco de Chile, Fondos Mutuos BanChile, Radio Minería, Editorial Ercilla, Provida; mem. Bd of Dirs SACI Falabella SA 2004–, CMR Falabella y Mall Plaza, Empresas Conosur SA, Sodimac SA, Penta SA, Derco SA; Vice Chair. Banco Penta, Empresas Dersa SA; Vice-Pres. Organización Internacional de Teletones; Dir Federación de Criadores de Caballos Chilenos; mem. Int. Cabinet, Dom Cabral Foundation, Brazil; mem. Global Advisory Bd, Grad. School of Business, Univ. of Chicago. *Address:* c/o Ministry of Foreign Affairs, Teatinos 180, Santiago, Chile (office).

MORENO FERNÁNDEZ, Abelardo; Cuban diplomatist; m.; one d.; joined Ministry of Foreign Affairs 1961; Perm. Sec. to UN, Geneva 1964–68, Deputy Rep. to UN Security Council, New York 1990–91, Minister Counsellor to UN 1992–95; Deputy Dir for Political Affairs, Ministry of Foreign Affairs 1995, Dir for Multilateral Affairs 1995–2000, Deputy Minister for Foreign Affairs 2000–09; Perm. Rep. to UN, New York Jan.–Aug. 2009; Prof., Higher Inst. for Int. Relations, Cuba; Visiting Lecturer, Columbia Univ., New York, Higher Inst. for Int. Relations, Geneva, Indian Inst. for Non-Aligned Studies. *Address:* c/o Ministry of Foreign Affairs, Calzada 360, esq. G, Vedado, Plaza de la Revolución, Havana, Cuba (office). *Telephone:* (7) 836-4500 (office). *E-mail:* cubaminrex@minrex.gov.cu (office). *Website:* www.cubaminrex.cu (office).

MORENO GARCÉS, Lenín, Licenció en Administración Pública; Ecuadorean politician and organization executive; *Vice-President;* b. 19 March 1953, Nuevo Rocafuerte; s. of Senator Prof. Servio Moreno; m. Rocío Gonzalez; three d.; ed Instituto Nacional Mejía, Colegio Nacional Sebastián Benalcázar, Universidad Cen. del Ecuador; Dir Centro de Formación Profesional Continental 1976–78; Sales Man., Satho 1982–84; Marketing Man., Zitro 1985–86; Dir OMC Publigerencia Andina 1986–92; Admin. Dir Ministry of Govt 1996–97; Exec. Dir Cámara de Turismo de Pichincha 1997–99, Exec. Dir Federación Nacional de Cámaras de Turismo 1997–99; Exec. Dir Cámara de Turismo de Pichincha 1997–99; Dir Nat. Council on Disabilities (CONADIS) 2001–04; Academic Dir Eventa Foundation 2004–06; Vice-Pres. of Ecuador 2007–. *Publications:* several books, including Filosofía para la vida y el trabajo, Teoría y Práctica del Humor, Ser Feliz es Fácil y Divertido, Los Mejores Chistes del Mundo, Humor de los Famosos, Trompabulario, Ríase no sea enfermo, Cuentos no Ecológicos. *Address:* Palacio de Carondelet, Quito, Ecuador (office). *Telephone:* (2) 258-4000 (office). *E-mail:* info@presidencia .gov.ec (office). *Website:* www.presidencia.gov.ec/modulos.asp?id=26 (office); www .leninmoreno.com.

MORENO-MEJÍA, Luis Alberto, BA, MBA; Colombian journalist, diplomatist and international organization official; *President, Inter-American Development Bank;* b. 3 May 1953, Philadelphia, USA; m. Gabriela Febres-Cordero 1970; one s. one d.; ed Florida Int. Univ., Thunderbird Univ., Phoenix, Ariz. and Harvard Univ.; Div. Man. Praco 1977–82; exec. producer of nationwide nightly news programme and other entertainment and children's programmes 1982–90; Neiman Fellow, Harvard Univ. 1990–91; Pres. Inst. de Foment Industrial 1991–92; Minister of Econ. Devt 1992–94; telecommunications adviser and pvt. consultant, Luis Carlos Sarmiento Org., Bogotá 1994–97; Pnr, Westsphere Andean Advisers 1997–98; Campaign Man. of Andrés Pastrana 1994; Amb. to USA 1998–2005; Pres. IDB, Washington, DC 2005–; Orden al Mérito Civil Ciudad de Bogotá, en el Grado de Gran Cruz, awarded by Mayor of Bogotá 1990, Orden al Mérito Industrial – José Gutiérrez Gómez, Colombian Nat. Business Asscn 2002, Orden de Boyacá en el Grado de Gran Cruz awarded by the Pres. of Colombia 2002; King of Spain Prize for journalistic excellence. *Publications include:* articles on Colombian and int. politics and econs for publs in Colombia and USA; writings have appeared in New York Times, Boston Globe, Miami Herald, El Tiempo, Foreign Affairs en Español and Semana. *Address:* Inter-American Development Bank, 1300 New York Avenue, NW, Washington, DC 20577, USA (office). *Telephone:* (202) 623-1000 (office). *Fax:* (202) 623-3096 (office). *E-mail:* pic@iadb .org (office). *Website:* www.iadb.org (office).

MORENO OCAMPO, Luis; Argentine lawyer and academic; b. 4 June 1952, Buenos Aires; ed Univ. of Buenos Aires; Deputy Public Prosecutor in trials against mil. junta 1985–87; Dist Attorney, Fed. Circuit, City of Buenos Aires 1987–92; in pvt. practice (specializing in corruption control programmes and ethical advice for large cos) 1992–; Chief Prosecutor (first in position), Int. Criminal Court, The Hague 2003–12; Sub-Dir Research Centre, Univ. of Buenos Aires Law School 1984, also Adjunct Prof. of Penal Law; Visiting Prof. of Law, Harvard Univ., USA; co-f. Poder Ciudadano; mem. Advisory Cttee Transparency Int., Pres. for Latin America and the Caribbean. *Film appearance:* (as himself) The Devil Came on Horseback 2006. *Publications include:* In Self Defense: How to Avoid Corruption 1993, When Power Lost the Trial: How to Explain the Dictatorship to Our Children 1996. *Address:* c/o International Criminal Court, Maanweg 174, 2516 AB, The Hague, The Netherlands.

MORENO-RAZO, Alma Rosa, BA, MA, PhD; Mexican economist, financial officer and fmr diplomatist; *Partner, ITG Consultores;* ed Instituto Tecnológico Autónomo de México, El Colegio de México, New York Univ., USA; fmr Deputy Dir for Planning, Promotion and Tech. Assistance, Nat. Bank of Public Works and Services (Banobras); fmr Exec. Dir Reconstruction and Syndicated Loans Multibanco Comermex; held various positions at Ministry of Finance and Public Credit, Gen. Co-ordinator for Income and Tax Policies 1998–99, Pres. Nat. Service for Tax Admin (SAT) 1999–2000, Head of Liaison Unit with Mexican Congress, Special Adviser to Sec. of Finance on Income Policies and Federalism, Dir-Gen. for Income

Policies; Visiting Researcher, Centre for Econ. Investigation and Educ. in Mexico 2000–01; Amb. to UK 2001–2004; Chief Admin. Officer, Grupo Financiero Banorte SAB de CV 2004–08; Partner, ITG Consultores 2009–; Adviser to Dir-Gen. of PEMEX (petroleum co.), Mexico City; Fellow, Center on Emerging and Pacific Economies, Univ. of California, San Diego 2010.

MORETTI, Nanni; Italian actor and filmmaker; b. (Giovanni Moretti), 19 Aug. 1953, Brunico, Bolzano; m.; one c.; co-f. Sacher Film S.r.l. (film production co.) 1986; est. Cinema Nuovo Sacher 1991; founder and artistic Dir Sacher Film Festival 1996; co-f. Tandem (film distribution co.) 1997; jury mem., Cannes Int. Film Festival 1997; jury Pres., Venice Int. Film Festival 2001, Cannes Film Festival 2012. *Films include:* as actor, dir and writer: Io sono un autarchico (I am Self Sufficient, also producer) 1976, Ecce Bombo 1978, Sogni d'oro (Sweet Dreams, Special Prize Venice Int. Film Festival) 1981, Bianca 1983, La Messa è finita (The Mass is Ended, Silver Bear Berlin Int. Film Festival 1986) 1985, Palombella rossa (Red Wood-Pigeon, also producer) 1989, Aprile (also producer) 1998, La Stanza del figlio (The Son's Room, also producer, Palme d'Or Cannes Film Festival) 2001; as dir: La Cosa (the Thing, also producer, writer) 1990, Caro diario (Dear Diary, also producer, writer, three David di Donatello Awards, Best Dir Cannes Int. Film Festival) 1994, L'unico paese al mondo 1994, Il Giorno della prima di Close Up (Opening Day of Close Up) 1996, The Last Customer (also producer) 2003, Il caimano (David di Donatello Awards for Best Film, Best Dir, Best Producer 2006, Silver Ribbon Best Producer 2007) 2006, We Have a Pope (Habemus Papam) (also actor) (Globi d'Oro Best Film Award 2011, Ciak d'Oro Awards for Best Film and Screenplay 2011, Silver Ribbon awards for Best Film, Best Story and Best Producer 2011) 2011; also actor in: Domani accadrà (It's Happening Tomorrow) 1988, Il Portaborse 1991, La Seconda Volta (The Second Time) 1996, Trois vies & une seule mort (Three Lives and Only One Death) 1996, Quiet Chaos 2008. *Address:* Sacher Film S.r.l., Via Piramide Cestia 1, 00153 Rome (office); Via Pindemonte 22, 00152 Rome, Italy (home). *Telephone:* (06) 5745353 (office). *Fax:* (06) 5740483 (office).

MORGAN, Most Rev. Dr Barry, PhD; British ecclesiastic; *Archbishop of Wales;* b. 31 Jan. 1947, Neath, Wales; m. Hilary Morgan 1969; one s. one d.; ed Ystalyfera Grammar School, Swansea Valley, Univ. Coll., London, Selwyn Coll., Cambridge, Westcott House, Cambridge, Univ. of Wales; ordained deacon 1972, priest 1973; subsequently curate in parish of St Andrews Major, Michaelston-le-Pit, Glam.; Chaplain and Lecturer, St Michael's Coll. and Univ. of Wales, Cardiff; Warden of Church Hostel, Bangor; Chaplain and Lecturer in Theology, Univ. of Wales, Bangor; Dir of Ordinands and In-service Training Adviser, Diocese of Bangor; Rector of Wrexham; Archdeacon of Meironnydd and Rector of Criccieth with Treflys 1986; elected and consecrated Bishop of Bangor 1993–99; Bishop of Llandaff 1999–2003; Archbishop of Wales 2003–; led Clergy School, Diocese of Kerala, India 2002; rep. Church in Wales on WCC; has served on several comms and working parties; Pres. Welsh Centre for Int. Affairs 2004–10; Pro Chancellor Univ. of Wales 2006; mem. Anglican Communion Standing Cttee 2003–11; Fellow, Bangor Univ. 1994, Cardiff Metropolitan Univ. 2003, Cardiff Univ. 2004, Univ. of Wales, Lampeter 2004, Trinity Univ., Carmarthen 2009, Swansea Univ. 2009, Learned Soc. of Wales 2013. *Publications include:* O Ddydd i Ddydd 1980, The History of the Church Hostel and Anglican Chaplaincy at the University College of North Wales, Bangor 1986, Concepts of Mission and Ministry in Anglican Chaplaincy Work 1988, Ministry in the Church in Wales – The Shape of Things to Come? 2002, Strangely Orthodox – R.S. Thomas and his Poetry of Faith 2006. *Leisure interest:* golf. *Address:* Llys Esgob, The Cathedral Green, Llandaff, Cardiff, CF5 2YE, Wales (office). *Telephone:* (29) 2056-2400 (office). *Fax:* (29) 2056-8410 (office). *E-mail:* archbishop@churchinwales.org.uk (office). *Website:* www .churchinwales.org.uk (office).

MORGAN, David Raymond, AO, BEcons, MSc, PhD; Australian banking executive; b. 14 March 1947, Melbourne, Vic.; s. of Raymond K. Morgan and Verna Morgan; m. Roslyn Joan Kelly; two c.; ed La Trobe Univ., Univ. of London, UK, Harvard Univ., USA; Sr Economist Dept of Fiscal Affairs, IMF, Washington, DC 1976–79; Asst Sec. Foreign Investment Br., Fed. Treasury 1980–81, Fiscal and Monetary Policy Br. 1982–83, mem. Taxation Policy Div., Treasury Dept Canberra 1983–85; First Asst Sec.-Gen. Financial and Econ. Policy, Commonwealth Treasury 1986–87; Deputy Sec. of Finance 1987, of Econs 1989; Deputy Man. Dir Westpac Financial Services Group 1990, Chief Gen. Man. Asia Pacific Div., Westpac, Sydney 1990, Man. Dir Westpac Financial Services Group 1990–91, Group Exec. Retail Banking, Westpac Banking Corpn 1992–94, Group Exec. Institutional and Int. Banking 1994–97, Exec. Dir Westpac Banking Corpn 1997–2008, Man. Dir and CEO 1999–2008 (retd); moved to London to head up J.C. Flowers (private equity group); Dir, BHP Billiton; Dir (non-exec.) Castle Trust; mem. Union Club. *Leisure interests:* wine, tennis, classical music. *Address:* J.C. Flowers & Co. UK LLP, 125 Old Broad Street, 24th Floor, London, EC2N 1AR, England (office). *Telephone:* (20) 7710-0500 (office). *Fax:* (20) 7710-0519 (office). *E-mail:* info@jcfco.com (office). *Website:* www.jcfco.com (office).

MORGAN, Gwyn, BSc (MechEng), PEng; Canadian business executive; b. 4 Nov. 1945, Carstairs, Alberta; s. of Ian Morgan and Margaret Morgan; ed Univ. of Alberta and Cornell Univ., NY; Petroleum Engineer, Alberta Energy Resources Conservation Bd –1970; Man. Operations and Eng, Consolidated Natural Gas Ltd, Consolidated Pipelines Ltd, Norlands Petroleums Ltd 1970–75; joined Alberta Energy Co. Ltd 1975, positions including Pres. and CEO, Founding Pres. and CEO EnCana Corpn (following merger of Alberta Energy Co. Ltd and Pan Canadian Energy Corpn) 2002–05, Exec. Vice-Chair. 2005–09; Dir HSBC Bank North America, SNC-Lavalin Inc., Alcan Inc., American Petroleum Inst., Inst. of the Americas; Founding mem. Canadian Asscn of Petroleum Producers Bd of Govs; mem. Advisory Bd Accenture Energy; Past Pres. Ind. Petroleum Asscn of Canada; fmr Vice-Chair. Canadian Council of Chief Execs (fmrly Business Council on Nat. Issues); fmr Dir Public Policy Forum; fmr mem. Bd of Man. Calgary Foothills Gen. Hosp.; Trustee Fraser Inst.; Hon. Col (retd) 410 Tactical Fighter Squadron, Canadian Air Force; Univ. of Western Ont. Ivey Business Leader Award 2002, Alberta Business Hall of Fame, Univ. of Alberta Canadian Business Leader Award 2002, Canadian CEO of the Year 2005. *Leisure interests:* hiking, skiing, cycling, ocean sailing, physical fitness. *Address:* c/o EnCana Corporation, Suite 1800, 855 2nd Street SW, PO Box 2850, Calgary, Alberta T2P 2S5, Canada. *Telephone:* (403) 645-2000. *Fax:* (403) 645-4644. *Website:* www.encana.com.

MORGAN, Howard James, MFA; British artist; b. 21 April 1949, N Wales; s. of Thomas James Morgan and Olive Victoria Morgan (née Oldnall); m. Susan Ann Sandilands 1977 (divorced 1998); two s. one d.; two s. one d. (with Sarah Milligan); ed Fairfax High School, Sutton Coldfield, Univ. of Newcastle-upon-Tyne; career artist; comms by HM The Queen, HM The Queen of The Netherlands, HRH Prince Michael of Kent, TRH The Prince & Princess of Hanover, Tom Stoppard, Philip Larkin, Francis Crick, Paul Maurice Dirac, Dame Antoinette Sibley (Nat. Portrait Gallery, London); Mr & Mrs Neil McConnell; perm. display of work at Nat. Portrait Gallery, London; mem. Royal Soc. of Portrait Painters 1986–; Royal Soc. of Portrait Painters Prize 2004. *Leisure interests:* riding, 1938 Citroën, books. *Address:* Studio 401½, Wandsworth Road, Battersea, London, SW8 6JP; 12 Rectory Grove, Clapham Old Town, London, SW4 0EA, England (home). *Telephone:* (7892) 773870 (mobile). *E-mail:* howard@howard-morgan.co.uk (office). *Website:* www .howard-morgan.co.uk (office).

MORGAN, Rt Hon. (Hywel) Rhodri, PC, MA; British politician; b. 29 Sept. 1939; s. of the late Thomas John Morgan and of Huana Morgan; m. Julie Edwards 1967; one s. two d.; ed St John's Coll. Oxford, Harvard Univ., USA; Research Officer, Cardiff City Council, Welsh Office and Dept of Environment 1965–71; Econ. Adviser, Dept of Trade and Industry 1972–74; Industrial Devt Officer, S Glamorgan Co. Council 1974–80; Head of Bureau for Press and Information, European Comm. Office for Wales 1980–87; Labour MP for Cardiff W, House of Commons 1987–2001; Opposition Spokesman on Energy 1988–92, Welsh Affairs 1992–97; Sec. for Econ. Devt, Nat. Ass. for Wales 1999–2000; First Minister, Nat. Ass. for Wales 2000–09. *Publication:* Cardiff: Half and Half a Capital 1994. *Leisure interests:* long-distance running, wood carving, marine wildlife. *Address:* 4th Floor, Transport House, 1 Cathedral Road, Cardiff, CF11 9SD (office); Lower House, Michaelston-le-Pit, Dinas Powys, South Glamorgan, CF64 4HE, Wales (home). *Telephone:* (29) 2022-3207 (office); (29) 2051-4262 (home). *Fax:* (29) 2023-0422 (office). *E-mail:* rhodri.morgan@wales.gov.uk (office).

MORGAN, James N., PhD; American economist and academic; *Senior Research Scientist Emeritus, Institute for Social Research, University of Michigan;* b. 1 March 1918, Corydon, Ind.; s. of John Jacob Brooke and Rose Ann Davis Morgan; m. Gladys Lucille Hassler 1945; three s. one d.; ed Northwestern Univ. and Harvard Univ.; Asst Prof. of Econs, Brown Univ. 1947–49; Carnegie Research Fellow, Inst. for Social Research, Univ. of Michigan 1949–51, Fellow, Center for Advanced Study in the Behavioral Sciences 1955–56, Program Dir Survey Research Center, Inst. for Social Research 1956–88, Prof. of Econs 1957–88, Prof. Emer. 1988–, Sr Research Scientist Emer., Inst. for Social Research 2005–; Fellow, Wissenschaftskolleg zu Berlin 1983–84, American Statistical Asscn, American Gerontological Asscn; mem. NAS, American Acad. of Arts and Sciences; Distinguished Faculty Award 1997, Woytinsky Lecture 1999. *Publications include:* Income and Welfare in the United States 1962, Economic Behavior of the Affluent 1965, Economic Survey Methods 1971, Five Thousand American Families (ed.) (10 vols) 1972–84, Economics of Personal Choice 1980, Household Survey of Grenada 1985; numerous articles in scientific journals. *Leisure interests:* travel, photography. *Address:* Institute for Social Research, University of Michigan, 426 Thompson Street, Ann Arbor, MI 48104 (office); 1217 Bydding Road, Ann Arbor, MI 48103, USA (home). *Telephone:* (734) 764-8388 (office); (734) 668-8304 (home). *Fax:* (734) 647-4575 (office). *E-mail:* jnmorgan@umich.edu (office). *Website:* www.isr.umich.edu (office).

MORGAN, Baron (Life Peer), cr. 2000, of Aberdyfi in the County of Gwynedd; **Kenneth Owen Morgan,** DPhil, DLitt (Oxon.), FBA, FRHistS; British historian and academic; *Professor Emeritus, University of Wales;* b. 16 May 1934, Wood Green, London, England; s. of David James Morgan and Margaret Morgan (née Owen); m. 1st Jane Keeler 1973 (died 1992); one s. one d.; m. 2nd Elizabeth Gibson 2009; ed Univ. Coll. School, London, Oriel Coll., Univ. of Oxford; Lecturer, History Dept, Univ. Coll., Swansea 1958–66, Sr Lecturer 1965–66; Fellow and Praelector, Modern History and Politics, The Queen's Coll., Univ. of Oxford 1966–89; Prin., Univ. Coll. of Wales, Aberystwyth 1989–95; Pro-Vice-Chancellor, Univ. of Wales 1989–93, Vice-Chancellor 1993–95, Prof. 1989–99, Emer. Prof. 1999–; Ed. Welsh History Review 1961–2003; Jt Ed. 20th Century British History 1994–99; mem. House of Lords Constitutional Cttee 2001–04; Election Commentator BBC Wales 1964–79; Fellow, American Council of Learned Socs Columbia Univ. 1962–63; Visiting Prof. 1965; Visiting Prof., Univ. of Witwatersrand 1997–2000, Univ. of Bristol 2000, Univ. of Rouen 2003, King's Coll., London 2011–; mem. (Labour) House of Lords 2000–; Hon. Fellow, Univ. Coll., Swansea 1985, Hon. Prof. 1995–; Hon. Fellow, The Queen's Coll., Oxford 1992, Univ. of Wales, Cardiff 1997, Trinity Coll., Carmarthen 1998, Oriel Coll. Oxford 2003; Supernumerary Fellow, Jesus Coll., Oxford 1991–92; Hon. DLitt (Wales), (Glamorgan) 1997, (Greenwich) 2004; Druid, Nat. Eisteddfod of Wales 2008, Gold Medal for Lifetime Achievement, Hon. Soc. of Cymmrodorion 2009. *Radio:* regular commentator (also on TV) on politics and modern history 1964–. *Publications:* Wales in British Politics 1963, David Lloyd George 1963, Freedom or Sacrilege? 1966, Keir Hardie 1967, The Age of Lloyd George 1971, Lloyd George: Family Letters (ed.) 1973, Lloyd George 1974, Keir Hardie: Radical and Socialist 1975, Consensus and Disunity 1979, Portrait of a Progressive (with Jane Morgan) 1980, Rebirth of a Nation: Wales 1880–1980 1981, David Lloyd George 1981, Labour in Power 1945–51 1984, The Oxford Illustrated History of Britain (ed.) 1984, Labour People 1987, The Oxford History of Britain (ed.) 1988, The Red Dragon and The Red Flag 1989, Academic Leadership 1991, The People's Peace: British History 1945–90 1992, Modern Wales: Politics, Places and People 1995, Young Oxford History of Britain and Ireland (Gen. Ed.), 1996, Callaghan: A Life 1997, Crime, Protest and Police in Modern British Society (ed.) 1999, The Great Reform Act of 1832 2001, The Twentieth Century 2001, Universities and the State 2002, Michael Foot: A Life 2007, Ages of Reform 2010, David Lloyd George (ed.) 2013. *Leisure interests:* music, sport, travel, architecture. *Address:* House of Lords, Westminster, London, SW1A 0PW (office); The Croft, 63 Millwood End, Long Hanborough, Witney, Oxon., OX29 8BP, England. *Telephone:* (20) 7219-8616 (office); (1993) 881341 (home). *E-mail:* kenneth.morgan@hotmail.co.uk (home).

MORGAN, Michèle, (pseudonym of Simone Roussel); French actress; b. 29 Feb. 1920; d. of Louis Roussel; m. 1st Bill Marshall; one s.; m. 2nd Henri Vidal (deceased); studied with R. Simon, Paris; actress 1936–; mem. Jury, Cannes Festival 1972, Pres. 1971; Grand Officier, Légion d'honneur, Officier, Ordre nat. du Mérite, Commdr des Arts et des Lettres; Hon. César 1992, Career Golden Lion, Venice Film Festival, 1996, Victoire (France) for Best Actress 1946, 1948, 1950, 1952, 1955, Médaille de vermeil, Paris 1967. *Plays include:* Le tout pour le tout 1979, Chéri 1981, Les monstres sacrés 1993. *Films include:* Le Mioche 1936, Mes tantes et moi 1936, Gigolette 1936, Gribouille 1937, Le Récif de corail 1938, Orage 1938, Quai des brumes 1938, La Loi du nord 1939, L'Entraîneuse 1940, Les Musiciens du ciel 1940, My Life with Caroline 1941, Remorques 1941, Joan of Paris 1942, Untel père et fils 1943, Two Tickets to London 1943, Higher and Higher 1943, Passage to Marseille 1944, Symphonie pastorale 1946 (Cannes Festival Prize for Best Actress), The Chase 1946, The Fallen Idol 1948, Aux yeux du souvenir 1948, Fabiola 1948, La Belle que voilà 1950, Maria Chapdelaine 1950, Le Château de verre 1950, L'Étrange Madame X 1951, Les sept péchés capitaux 1952, Minute de vérité 1952, Les orgueilleux 1953, Obsession 1954, Oasis 1955, Napoléon 1955, Les grandes manoeuvres 1955, Marguerite de la nuit 1955, Marie Antoinette 1956, Si Paris nous était conté 1956, The Vintage 1957, Retour de manivelle 1957, Le miroir à deux faces 1958, Femmes d'un été 1959, Pourquoi viens-tu si tard? 1959, Les scélérats 1959, Fortunat 1960, Le puits aux trois vérités 1961, Les lions sont lâches 1961, Rencontres 1962, Le crime ne paie pas 1962, Landru 1963, Constance aux Enfers 1963, Il Fornaretto di Venezia 1963, Méfiez-vous, mesdames 1963, Les yeux cernés 1964, Dis-moi qui tuer 1965, Les centurions 1966, Benjamin 1968, Le chat et la souris 1975, Robert et Robert (cameo) (uncredited) 1978, Un homme et une femme, 20 ans déjà (uncredited) 1986, Ils vont tous bien 1990. *Television includes:* Studio One (series) – Silent the Song 1953, – Camille 1953, La bien-aimée (film) 1967, Le tout pour le tout (film) 1981, Emmenez-moi au théâtre: Chéri (film) 1984, Le tiroir secret (mini-series) 1986, La veuve de l'architecte (film) 1995, Des gens si bien élevés (film) 1997, La rivale (film) 1999. *Publications:* Mes yeux ont vu 1965, Avec ces yeux-là 1977, Le fil bleu 1993. *Address:* c/o Agents Associés, 201 rue du Faubourg Saint-Honoré, 75008 Paris, France (office).

MORGAN, Nicky, PC; British lawyer and politician; *Minister for Women and Financial Secretary to the Treasury;* b. 1972; m. Jonathan Morgan; one s.; ed St Hugh's Coll., Oxford; began career as solicitor specialising in corp. law with several private and public cos 1994–2010; MP for Loughborough 2010–; Parl. Private Sec. to Cabinet Minister for Univs and Science 2010–12; Asst Govt Whip 2012–13; Econ. Sec. to the Treasury 2013–14; Minister for Women and Financial Sec. to the Treasury 2014–; mem. Conservative Party. *Address:* House of Commons, London, SW1A 0AA, England (office). *Telephone:* (20) 7219-7224 (office). *E-mail:* nicky .morgan.mp@parliament.uk (office). *Website:* www.nickymorgan.org (office).

MORGAN, Peter William Lloyd, MBE, MA; British business executive; b. 9 May 1936, Neath; s. of the late Matthew Morgan and of Margaret Gwynneth (née Lloyd) Morgan; m. Elisabeth Susanne Davis 1964; three d.; ed Llandovery Coll., Trinity Hall, Cambridge; served Royal Signals 1954–56; joined IBM UK Ltd 1959, Data Processing Sales Dir 1971–74, Group Dir of Data Processing Marketing, IBM Europe, Paris 1975–90, Dir IBM UK Ltd 1980–87, IBM UK Holdings Ltd 1987–89; Dir Gen. Inst. of Dirs 1989–94; Dir South Wales Electricity PLC 1989–95, Chair. 1996; Dir Nat. Provident Inst. 1990–95, Chair. 1996–99; Dir Firth Holdings PLC (now Hyder Consulting PLC) 1994–, Zergo Holdings PLC (now Baltimore Technologies PLC) 1994–, (Chair. 2000–), Oxford Instruments PLC 1999–; Chair. Pace Micro Tech. PLC 1996–99, KSCL Ltd 1999–2000, Technetix PLC 2002–; Dir IDP SA (Paris) 2000–02; Dir Asscn of Lloyds' Mems 1997–, Council mem. Lloyds of London 2000–, Dir Lloyds.com 2001–; mem. Econ. and Social Cttee, EU 1994–2002, Advisory Cttee Business and the Environment 2001–; Master, Co. of Information Technologists; Radical of the Year, Radical Soc. 1990. *Leisure interests:* music, history, gardening, skiing, wine, dog walking. *Address:* Baltimore Technologies PLC, Innovation House, Mark Road, Hemel Hempstead, Herts., HP2 7DN, England (office). *Telephone:* (118) 903-8905 (office); (1428) 642757 (home). *Fax:* (1653) 600066 (office); (1428) 643684 (home). *E-mail:* petermorgan@baltimore .com (home). *Website:* www.baltimore.com (office).

MORGAN, Piers Stefan; British broadcaster, writer and fmr journalist; b. (Piers Stefan O'Meara), 30 March 1965, Guildford; s. of Anthony Pughe-Morgan and Gabrielle Oliver; m. 1st Marion E. Shalloe 1991 (divorced); three s.; m. 2nd Celia Walden 2010; one d.; ed Cumnor House Preparatory School, Chailey School, Sussex, Lewes Priory Sixth Form Coll. and Harlow Journalism Coll.; reporter, Surrey and S London newspapers 1987–89; Showbusiness Ed. The Sun newspaper 1989–94; Ed. The News of the World newspaper 1994–95, Daily Mirror (later The Mirror) 1995–2004; Co-founder Press Gazette Ltd, Owner, Press Gazette 2005–07; Editorial Dir First News (newspaper for children) 2006; Atex Award for Nat. Newspaper Ed. of Year 1994, What the Papers Say Newspaper of the Year Award 2001, GQ Ed. of the Year 2002, British Press Awards Newspaper of the Year 2002, Magazine Design and Journalism Awards Columnist of the Year Award (Live Magazine) 2007. *Television:* presenter, The Importance of Being Famous (Channel 4) 2004, Morgan & Platell (Channel 4) 2005–06, You Can't Fire Me, I'm Famous (BBC1) 2006–07, Piers Morgan on Sandbanks (ITV 1) 2008, Piers Morgan's Life Stories 2009–10; judge: America's Got Talent (NBC) 2006–08, Britain's Got Talent (ITV 1) 2007–09, Piers Morgan's Life Stories 2009–, Piers Morgan On 2010, Piers Morgan Tonight (CNN) 2011–. *Publications include:* Private Lives of the Stars 1990, Secret Lives of the Stars 1991, Phillip Schofield, To Dream a Dream 1992, Take That, Our Story 1993, Take That: On the Road 1994, The Insider (memoir) 2005, Don't You Know Who I Am? 2007, God Bless America 2009. *Leisure interests:* cricket, Arsenal Football Club. *Address:* c/o James Grant Media, 94 Strand on the Green, Chiswick, London, W4 3NN, England (office). *Telephone:* (20) 8742-4950 (office). *Fax:* (20) 8742-4951 (office). *E-mail:* tracey@jamesgrant.co.uk (office). *Website:* www.jamesgrantmedia.co.uk (office).

MORGAN, William Newton, MArch, FAIA; American architect; *President, William Morgan Architects;* b. 14 Dec. 1930, Jacksonville, Fla; s. of Thomas Morgan and Kathleen Fisk Morgan; m. Bernice Leimback 1954; two s.; ed Duncan U. Fletcher High School, Harvard Coll., Harvard Grad. School of Design, Università degli Studi per Stranieri, Perugia and Univ. of Rome, Italy; USN 1952–55; Lehman Fellow, Harvard Univ. 1956–57; Fulbright Grantee, Italy 1958–59; Pres. William Morgan Architects, P.A. 1961–; Wheelwright Fellow, Harvard Grad. School of Design 1964–65, Visiting Critic 1981–82; AIA Fellowship 1978; Nat. Endowment of the Arts Fellow 1980; Adjunct Prof. of Art History, Jacksonville Univ. 1995–, Univ. of N Florida 1997, Univ. of Florida 1998; Beineke-Reeves Distinguished Prof. of Architecture, Univ. of Florida 1998–2000; mem.

Savannah Coll. of Art and Design Advisory Bd 2003–06; mem. Soc. of American Archaeology Presentation, Vancouver, BC 2008; numerous awards and distinctions, including AIA Honor for Design Excellence 1974, AIA Honor for Research and Recording Ancient American Architecture 1998, Gibbons Eminent Scholar of Architecture and Urban Design, Univ. of S Florida 1990. *Architectural designs include:* Florida State Museum, Gainsville 1969–70, Jacksonville Police Admin. Bldg 1971–75, Pyramid Condominium, Ocean City, Md 1972–74, First Dist Court of Appeal, Tallahassee 1983–85, Westinghouse HQ, Orlando 1984–86, US Embassy, Khartoum 1987–91, US Courthouses, Fort Lauderdale 1976–78, Tallahassee 1992–98, Neiman-Marcus, Fort Lauderdale 1980–82. *Publications:* Prehistoric Architecture in the Eastern United States 1980, Prehistoric Architecture in Micronesia 1988, Ancient Architecture of the Southwest 1994, Pre-Columbian Architecture in Eastern North America 1999, Earth Architecture: From Ancient to Modern 2008; numerous articles. *Leisure interest:* furniture design and building. *Address:* 1945 Beach Avenue, Atlantic Beach, FL 32233, USA (home). *E-mail:* wnmorgan@aol.com (office). *Website:* www .williammorganarchitects.com (office).

MORGAN OF ELY, Baroness (Life Peer), cr. 2011, of the City of Cardiff 2011; **(Mair) Eluned Morgan;** British political scientist, academic and fmr politician; *Honorary Distinguished Professor, School of European Studies, Cardiff University;* b. 16 Feb. 1967, Cardiff; d. of Rev. Bob Morgan and Elaine Morgan; m. Dr Rhys Jenkins; one s. one d.; ed United World Coll. of the Atlantic, Univ. of Hull; worked as researcher for S4C and BBC; worked as a Stagiaire in European Parl. 1990; MEP (Labour) for Mid and West Wales 1994–99, for Wales 1999–2009, Labour European Spokesperson on Energy Industry and Science, mem. Budgetary Control Cttee 1999–2009, Substitute mem. 2004–07, mem. Mashreq and Gulf States Del. 2002–04, Substitute mem. Environment, Public Health and Consumer Policy Cttee 2002–04, mem. Industry, Research and Energy Cttee 2004–09, EU-Bulgaria Jt Parl. Cttee 2004–06, Euro-Mediterranean Parl. Ass. Del. 2004–07, Substitute mem. Regional Devt Cttee 2004–07, ACP-EU Jt Parl. Ass. Del. 2004–09, mem. People's Repub. of China Del. 2007–08, Substitute mem. Climate Change Temporary Cttee 2007–09, Environment, Public Health and Food Safety Cttee 2007–09, mem. Russia Del. 2008–09; fmr mem. Nat. Ass. Advisory Group (est. Rules of Welsh Ass.), Yes For Wales cross-party group campaigning for Welsh Ass.; currently employed by SWALEC; Hon. Distinguished Prof., School of European Studies, Cardiff Univ. *Publication:* European Parliament Position on the Energy Green Paper and the Electricity Directive. *Address:* Cardiff School of European Studies, Cardiff University, 65–68 Park Place, Cardiff, CF10 3AS, Wales (office); House of Lords, Westminster, London, SW1A 0PW, England. *Telephone:* (29) 2087-4889 (office); (20) 7219-5353. *Fax:* (29) 2087-4946 (office); (20) 7219-5979. *E-mail:* euros@cardiff.ac.uk (office). *Website:* www.cardiff.ac.uk (office).

MORGAN OF HUYTON, Baroness (Life Peer), cr. 2001, of Huyton in the County of Merseyside; **Sally Morgan,** MA; British politician; *Chairman, Ofsted;* b. 28 June 1959, Liverpool, England; d. of Albert Edward Morgan and Margaret Morgan; m. John Lyons 1984; two s.; ed Belvedere Girls' School, Univs of Liverpool, Durham and London; secondary school teacher 1981–85; Labour Party Student Organizer 1985–87, Sr Targeting Officer 1987–93, Dir of Campaigns and Elections 1993–95, Head of Party Liaison for Leader of Opposition 1995–97; Political Sec. to Prime Minister 1997–2001; Minister of State for Women June–Nov. 2001; Dir of Govt Relations 2001–05; mem. (Labour) House of Lords 2001–; Chair. Ofsted 2011–; mem. Bd of Dirs Olympic Delivery Authority; Dir (non-exec.) Carphone Warehouse PLC; adviser to Bd, ARK; mem. Advisory Bd, The Foundation (business consultants), Centre for Human Rights, Inst. of Educ., Univ. of London; mem. Advisory Cttee, Virgin Group Holdings Ltd; Chair. Future Leaders (charity); mem. Bd, Teaching Leaders; Trustee, Mayor's Fund for London. *Leisure interests:* relaxing with friends, cooking, gardening, walking. *Address:* House of Lords, Westminster, London, SW1A 0PW, England (office). *Telephone:* (20) 7219-3000 (office). *E-mail:* morgan@parliament.uk (office). *Website:* www .parliament.uk/biographies/lords/sally-morgan/26954 (office); www.ofsted.gov.uk (office).

MORGENTHAU, Robert Morris, BA, LLB; American lawyer and fmr government official; *Of Counsel, Wachtell, Lipton, Rosen & Katz;* b. 31 July 1919, New York; s. of Henry Morgenthau, Jr and Elinor Morgenthau (née Fatman); m. 1st Martha Pattridge (deceased); one s. four d.; m. 2nd Lucinda Franks 1977; one s. one d.; ed Deerfield Acad., Amherst Coll., Yale Univ.; barrister, New York 1949; Assoc., Patterson, Belknap & Webb, New York 1948–53, Pnr 1954–61; US Attorney for Southern Dist of New York 1961–62, 1962–70; Dist Attorney, New York Co. (Manhattan) 1975–2009 (retd); currently Of Counsel, Wachtell, Lipton, Rosen & Katz, New York; mem. New York Exec. Cttee State of Israel Bonds; Democratic cand. for Gov. of New York 1962; mem. Bd of Dirs P.R. Legal Defense and Educ. Fund; Trustee, Baron de Hirsch Fund, Fed. of Jewish Philanthropies; Co. Chair. New York Holocaust Memorial Comm.; Pres. Police Athletic League 1962; mem. Bar Asscn of City of New York; Democrat; Dr hc (New York Law School) 1968, (Syracuse Law School) 1976, (Union Univ., Albany Law School) 1982, (Colgate Univ.) 1988; Frank Hogan Award, NY State Dist Attorney's Assocn 2000, Lone Sailor Award, USN Memorial Foundation 2000, Award for Excellence in Public Service, NY State Bar Assocn 2001. *Address:* Wachtell, Lipton, Rosen & Katz, 51 West 52nd Street, New York, NY 10019, USA. *Telephone:* (212) 403-1223 (office). *E-mail:* RMMorgenthau@wlrk.com (office). *Website:* www.wlrk .com (office).

MORGRIDGE, John P., MBA; American computer industry executive; *Chairman, Cisco Systems Inc.;* ed Univ. of Wis., Stanford Univ.; Capt. USAF 1957–60; Vice-Pres. Honeywell Inc. 1960–80; Vice-Pres. Stratus Computer 1980–86; Pres. and COO Grid Systems 1987–88; Pres. and CEO Cisco Systems Inc. 1988–95, Chair. 1995–; Lecturer (part-time), Grad. School of Business, Stanford Univ. 1997–; mem. Bd of Dirs American Leadership Forum for Silicon Valley, The Nature Conservancy, Cisco Foundation, Cisco Learning Inst., CARE, Interplast; mem. Tech. Advisory Bd Milwaukee Public Schools, Advisory Council Stanford Business School; Hon. DSc (Univ. of Wis.) 1994, Hon. LHD (Lesley Coll.), Hon. PhD (Northern Ill. Univ., The American Int. Univ. in London, Carleton Univ.) Ernest C. Arbuckle Award, Stanford Univ. 1996. *Address:* Cisco Systems Inc., 170 West Tasman Drive, San Jose, CA 95134-1706, USA (office). *Telephone:* (408) 526-4000 (office). *Fax:* (408) 526-4100 (office). *Website:* www.cisco.com (office).

MORI, Akira; Japanese business executive; *President and CEO, Mori Trust Co. Ltd;* b. 1936, Tokyo; s. of Taikichiro Mori; m.; two s. one d.; began career as banker; joined Mori Building Co. (family real estate business) 1972, CEO Mori Building Development Co. Ltd 1993–99, Pres. and CEO Mori Trust Co. Ltd (following reorganization of business) 1999–. *Address:* Mori Trust Co. Ltd, Toranomon 2-chome, Tower 2-3-17, Toranomon, Minato-ku, Tokyo 105-0001, Japan (office). *E-mail:* koho@mori-trust.co.jp (office). *Website:* www.mori-trust.co.jp (office).

MORI, Hanae; Japanese fashion designer; b. 8 Jan. 1926, Shimane; m.; two s.; graduate in Japanese literature; began career as costume designer for films in 1950s and has designed for over 500 films; opened first shop in Shinjuku, Tokyo 1951; now has 67 Hanae Mori shops in Japan, a store in New York, three shops in Paris and one in Monaco; first overseas show New York 1965; couture business and ready-to-wear; mem. Chambre Syndicale de la Haute Couture, Paris (first Asian mem.) 1977–; retrospective exhbn at The Space, Hanae Mori Bldg Tokyo 1989; Co-Founder Asscn for 100 Japanese books; launched Hanae Mori perfume brand 1995; Order of Cultural Merit 'Bunka Koro Sho' (Japan), Chevalier Légion d'honneur, Ordre des Arts et Lettres; numerous awards and prizes, including Neiman Marcus Award 1973. *Address:* Hanae Mori Haute Couture, 5 place de l'Alma, 75008 Paris, France (office). *Telephone:* 1-47-23-52-03 (office). *Fax:* 1-47-23-62-82 (office). *Website:* www.hanaemori.com (office); www.hanaemoriusa.com (office).

MORI, Hideo, BA; Japanese business executive; b. 1 April 1925, Osaka City; s. of Shigekazu Mori and Ikue Mori; m. Masako (née Okano) Mori; two s.; ed Kyoto Univ. 1947; joined Sumitomo Chemical Co. Ltd 1947, Dir 1977, Man. Dir 1980, Sr Man. Dir 1982, Pres. 1985–93, Chair. 1993–2000, later Counsellor; Chair. Sumitomo Pharmaceuticals Co. Ltd, ICI-Pharma Ltd, Japan Upjohn Ltd, Nippon Wellcome KK; Dir and Counsellor Japan Petrochemical Ind. Asscn; Exec. Dir Japan Fed. of Employers' Asscns; Dir Japan Tariff Asscn, Nihon Singapore Polyolefin Co. Ltd; Pres. Japan Chemical Industry Asscn 1990; mem. Bd of Exec. Dirs Fed. of Econ. Orgs (Keidanren); Blue Ribbon Medal 1987. *Leisure interest:* golf. *Address:* c/o Sumitomo Chemical Co. Ltd, 2-27-1, Shinkawa 2-chome, Chuo-ku, Tokyo 104-8260, Japan.

MORI, Immanuel (Manny), BA; Micronesian politician and head of state; *President;* b. 25 Dec. 1948, Fefan Island, Chuuk State; m. 1st Elina Ekiek (deceased); four d.; m. 2nd Emma Mori; ed Xavier High School, Chuuk and Univ. of Guam; began career at Citicorp Credit-Guam Bank 1973, Asst Man., Saipan Branch 1974–76; Asst Admin. Trust Territory Social Security Admin 1976–79; Nat. Revenue Officer, State of Chuuk 1979–81; Controller, Federated States of Micronesia Devt Bank 1981–84, Pres. and CEO 1984–97; Exec. Vice-Pres. Bank of Federated States of Micronesia 1997–99; mem. Micronesian Congress 1999–2003, 2004–, Vice-Chair. Judiciary and Govt Operations Cttee 1999–2003, Health Educ. and Social Affairs Cttee 1999–2003, Chair. Ways and Means Cttee 2001–03, Vice-Chair. External Affairs Cttee 2004–05, Chair. Resources and Devt Cttee 2005–07; Gen.-Man. and CEO Chuuk Public Utility Corpn 2004–07; Pres. of Federated States of Micronesia 2007–. *Address:* Office of the President, PO Box PS-53 Palikir, Pohnpei FM 96941, Federated States of Micronesia (office). *Telephone:* 320-2228 (office). *Fax:* 320-2785 (office). *E-mail:* ppetrus@mail.fm (office). *Website:* www .fsmpio.fm (office).

MORI, Shigefumi, MA, DrSci; Japanese mathematician and academic; *Professor, Research Institute of Mathematical Sciences, Kyoto University;* b. 23 Feb. 1951, Nagoya; ed Kyoto Univ.; Asst, Kyoto Univ. 1975, Prof., Research Inst. of Mathematical Sciences 1990–; Lecturer in Math., Univ. of Nagoya 1980, Asst Prof. 1982–88, Prof. 1988–90; Visiting Prof., Harvard Univ. 1977–80, Inst. for Advanced Study, Princeton, Univ. 1981–82, Columbia Univ., New York 1985–87, Univ. of Utah, USA 1987–89, 1991–92; mem. Japan Acad. 1999–; Iyanaga Prize, Japan Math. Soc. 1983, Chunichi Culture Prize 1984, Japan Math. Soc. Autumn Prize (co-recipient) 1988, Inoue Science Prize 1989, Cole Prize in Algebra, American Math. Soc. 1990, Japan Acad. Prize (co-recipient) 1990, Fields Medal, Int. Congress of Mathematicians, Kyoto 1990, Japanese Govt Prize (Person of Cultural Merits) 1990, Fujiwara Award, Fujiwara Foundation of Science 2004. *Publications:* numerous articles in math. journals on algebraic geometry. *Address:* Research Institute of Mathematical Sciences, Kyoto University, Kyoto 606-8502, Japan (office). *Telephone:* (75) 753-7227 (office). *Fax:* (75) 753-7276 (office). *E-mail:* mori@kurims.kyoto-u.ac.jp (office). *Website:* www.kurims.kyoto-u.ac.jp (office).

MORI, Shosuke; Japanese energy industry executive; *Chairman and Representative Director, Kansai Electric Power Company Inc.;* ed Kyoto Univ.; joined Kansai Electric Power Co. Inc. 1963, Gen. Man., Systems Eng Div. 1989–94, Exec. Officer and Gen. Man., Corporate Planning Office 1994–97, mem. Bd of Dirs and Man., Power Systems Div. 1997–99, Man. Dir 1999–2001, Exec. Vice-Pres. 2001–05, Pres. and Dir 2005–10, Chair. and Rep. Dir 2010–; Dir, The Japan Atomic Power Co.; External Dir, All Nippon Airways Co. Ltd 2006–. *Address:* Kansai Electric Power Co. Inc., 6-16 Nakanoshima 3-chome, Kita-ku, Osaka 530-8270, Japan (office). *Telephone:* (6) 6441-8821 (office). *Fax:* (6) 6447-7174 (office). *E-mail:* info@kepco.co.jp (office). *Website:* www.kepco.co.jp (office).

MORI, Yoshiro; Japanese politician; b. 14 July 1937; m. Chieko Mori; one s. one d.; ed Waseda Univ.; with Sankei Newspapers, Tokyo 1960–62; mem. House of Reps, for Ishikawa Pref. Dist 1 1969–96, Dist 2 1996–; Deputy Dir-Gen. Prime Minister's Office 1975–76; Deputy Chief Cabinet Sec. 1977–78; Dir Educ. Div., Policy Research Council, Liberal Democratic Party (LDP) 1978–81, Deputy Sec.-Gen. LDP 1978–79, 1984–85, Chair. Special Cttee on Educational Reform, Policy Research Council 1984–87, Acting Chair. Policy Research Council 1986, Acting Chair. Gen. Council 1986–87, Chair. Nat. Org. Cttee 1987–88, Chair. Research Comm. on Educational System, Policy Research Council 1989–91, Chair. Policy Research Council 1991–92, Sec.-Gen. LDP 1993–95, Chair. Gen. Council 1996–98, Sec.-Gen. LDP 1998–2001; Chair. Standing Cttee on Finance, House of Reps 1981–82, on Rules and Admin. 1991; Minister of Educ. 1983–84, of Int. Trade and Ind. 1992–93, of Construction 1995–96; Prime Minister of Japan 2000–01. *Address:* c/o Liberal Democratic Party, 1-11-23 Nagata-cho, Chiyoda-ku, Tokyo, 100-8910, Japan.

MORIKAWA, Keizo; Japanese oil company executive; *Representative Director, President and CEO, Cosmo Oil Company Ltd;* joined Cosmo Oil Co. Ltd 1971, Pres. Singaporean subsidiary, Cosmo Oil International Pte Ltd 1994–97, Dir for the Corp. Planning Dept 1997–2002, Sr Exec. Officer and Dir 2002–08, Exec. Vice-Pres. and Rep. Dir Cosmo Oil Co. Ltd 2008–12, Rep. Dir, Pres. and CEO 2012–. *Address:* Cosmo Oil Co. Ltd, 1-1-1, Shibaura, Minato-ku, Tokyo 105-8528, Japan (office). *Telephone:* (3) 3798-3211 (office). *Fax:* (3) 3798-3841 (office). *E-mail:* info@ cosmo-oil.co.jp (office). *Website:* www.cosmo-oil.co.jp (office).

MORIKAWA, Kosuke, PhD; Japanese scientist and academic; *Research Director, Biomolecular Engineering Research Institute (BERI);* b. 28 Sept. 1942, Tokyo; m. Keiko Tanaka 1966; ed Koyamadai High School, Tokyo Univ.; instructor Tokyo Univ. 1971–75, research assoc. Arhus Univ., Denmark 1975–77, MRC Lab. of Molecular Biology, Cambridge, UK 1978–80; instructor Kyoto Univ. 1980–86, Dir First Dept Protein Eng Research Inst. 1986–, Research Dir Biomolecular Eng Research Inst. (BERI) 1996–. *Leisure interest:* listening to classical music, particularly by Bach and Mozart. *Address:* Department of Structural Biology, Biomolecular Engineering Research Institute, 6-2-3 Furuedai, Suita, Osaka 565-0874 (office); 1-22-16 Hiyoshidai, Takatsuki, Osaka 569-1022, Japan. *Telephone:* (726) 89-0519 (home); (6) 6872-8211 (office). *Fax:* (6) 6872-8219. *E-mail:* morikawa@beri.or.jp (office). *Website:* www.beri.or.jp (office).

MORIKAWA, Toshio, LLB; Japanese banker; b. 3 March 1933, Tokyo; m. Sawako Morikawa; two d.; ed Univ. of Tokyo; joined Sumitomo Banking Corpn (now Sumitomo Mitsui Banking Corpn) 1955, Dir 1980–84, Man. Dir 1984–85, Sr Man. Dir 1985–90, Deputy Pres. 1990–93, Pres. 1993–97, Chair. 1997–2001, Advisor 2001–; mem. Bd Dirs NEC Corpn 2000–; Chair. Fed. of Bankers' Asscns 1994–95. *Leisure interests:* golf, driving. *Address:* c/o Sumitomo Mitsui Financial Group Inc., 1-2, Yurakucho 1-Chome, Chiyoda-ku, Tokyo 100-0006, Japan. *Telephone:* (3) 5512-3411 (office). *Fax:* (3) 5512-4429 (office). *Website:* www.smbc .co.jp (office); www.smfg.co.jp (office).

MORILLON, Gen. Philippe; French army officer (retd) and politician; b. 24 Oct. 1935, Casablanca, Morocco; m. 1st Anne Appert 1958 (deceased); three d.; m. 2nd Christine Gaudry 1998; ed Ecole Militaire de Saint-Cyr, Ecole Supérieure, Army Staff Coll.; platoon leader, French Foreign Legion during Algerian war of independence; fmr Div. Commdr of French units stationed in Germany; mil. expert, Assemblée Nationale 1984–86; Deputy Under-Sec. for Int. Relations, Ministry of Defence 1988–90; Deputy Commdr, then Commdr UN Protection Force (UNPROFOR) in Bosnia-Herzegovina 1992–93; Adviser on Defence to Govt of France 1993; Commdr Force d'Action Rapide 1994–96; mem. European Parl. (Union pour la démocratie française, mem. Group of the Alliance of Liberals and Democrats for Europe) 1999–2009, Chair. Cttee on Fisheries 2004–09; EU Chief Observer to Constitutional Referendum of Congo 2005, Legis. and Presidential Elections in Congo 2006, Elections in Afghanistan 2009; Pres. Asscn L'envol pour les enfants européens; fmr Pres. French Inter-ministerial Coordinating Cttee for the 12th World Youth Day, Paris 1997; Commdr Ordre nat. du Mérit 1988, Grand Officier de la Légion d'honneur 1993; Servitor Pacis Award, Path to Peace Foundation 1999. *Publications:* Croire et Oser 1993, Paroles de Soldat 1996, Mon Credo 1999, Le Testament de Massoud 2005. *Leisure interest:* reading.

MORIN, Edgar, Lic. en Hist. et Géog., Lic. en Droit et Sciences écon.; French scientific researcher and philosopher; *Director Emeritus, Centre national de la recherche scientifique (CNRS);* b. 8 July 1921, Paris; s. of Vidal Nahoum and Luna Beressi; m. Edwige Lannegrace; two d.; resistance fighter 1942–44; Head of Propaganda Dept, French mil. govt, Germany 1945; Ed.-in-Chief Paris newspaper 1947–50; Researcher, CNRS 1950–, Dir of Research 1970–93, Dir Emer. 1993–; Dir Review Arguments 1957–62, Communications 1972–; Dir Centre d'études transdisciplinaires (sociologie, anthropologie, politique), Ecole des hautes études en sciences sociales 1977–93; Commdr, Légion d'honneur, des Arts et des Lettres, Grande Croix, Ordre de Santiago de l'Espada (Portugal), Officier, Ordre du mérite (Spain); Dr hc (Brussels, Perugia, Palermo, Geneva, Natal, João Pessoa, Odense, Porto-Alegre, Milan, Guadalajara); Prix européen de l'Essai Charles Veillon 1987, Prix média de l'Asscn des Journalistes Européens 1992, Prix Internacional Catalunya 1994, Prix int. Nonino 2004. *Publications include:* L'Homme et la mort 1951, Le Cinéma ou l'homme imaginaire 1956, Autocritique 1959, Le Vif du sujet 1969, Le Paradigme perdu: la nature humaine 1973, La méthode (six vols) 1977–2004, De la nature de l'URSS 1983, Penser l'Europe 1987, Vidal et les siens 1989, Terre-Patrie 1993, Mes démons 1994, Amour, poésie, sagesse 1998, Vers l'Abîme 2007, La Voie 2011; numerous other publs. *Leisure interests:* music, theatre, movies, literature. *Address:* 7 rue Saint-Claude, 75003 Paris, France (home). *Telephone:* 1-42-78-90-99 (home). *Fax:* 1-48-04-86-35 (home). *E-mail:* lafaye@ehess.fr (office).

MORIN, Hervé; French politician; b. 17 Aug. 1961, Pont-Audemer; m. Catherine Broussot; two s. one d.; ed Deauville Lycée, Ecole Jeanne d'Arc, Caen, Univ. of Caen, Univ. of Paris II, Inst. of Political Studies, Paris; Dir of Services, Nat. Ass. 1987–93, 1998; Lecturer, Univ. of Paris V 1989–95; Municipal Councillor 1989–95; mem. Gen. Council of Eure 1992–2004; Tech. Adviser on Nat. Affairs and the Environment, Office of the Minister of Defence 1993–95; Mayor of Epaignes 1995–; Pres. Cormeilles Town Community 1995–; mem. Union pour la Démocratie Française (UDF) 1998–2007, Leader Parl. Group 2002–07; mem. Nouveau Centre 2007–, Leader 2008–; Deputy for Eure 1998–; Spokesperson for François Bayrou during presidential campaign 2002; Regional Councillor for Haute-Normandie 2004–; Minister of Defence 2007–10; Pres. France-Niger Group, Nat. Ass.; Pres. Asscn for the Reunification of Normandy 1999–. *Address:* c/o Ministry of Defence, 14 rue Saint Dominique, 75007 Paris, France (office). *Website:* www.herve-morin .net.

MORIN, Roland Louis, LenD; French public servant; *Vice-President, Commission Nationale des Comptes de Campagne et des Financements Politiques;* b. 6 Sept. 1932, Taza, Morocco; s. Fernand Morin and Emilienne Morin (née Carisio); m. Catherine Roussy 1961; one s. one d.; ed Lycée Gouraud, Rabat, Faculty of Law and Humanities, Bordeaux and Ecole Nat. d'Admin; auditor, Audit Office 1960; Asst to Prime Minister and Chargé de Mission, Algeria 1960–61; Pvt. Recorder Comm. for Verification of Public Accounts, Asst to Recorder-Gen. 1964; Tech. Counsellor Louis Joxe Cabinet (Minister of State for Admin. Reform) 1966–67, Edmond Michelet Cabinet (Minister of State for Public Affairs) 1967–68;

Referendary Counsellor Audit Office 1967; Asst to Prime Minister, Departmental Head for Econ. and Financial Programmes and Affairs 1968; Dir of Financial Affairs, Gen. Del. for Scientific and Tech. Research 1969, Asst to Del.-Gen. 1970, Asst Del.-Gen. 1974, Dir 1978; rejoined Audit Office 1980; Prof. Inst. d'Etudes Politiques de Paris 1965–90; Chargé de Mission with Jean-Pierre Chevènement (Minister of State, Minister for Research and Tech.) 1981–82, Dir Gen. Research and Tech., Ministry of Research and Industry 1982–86; Conseiller maître, Cour des comptes 1986, Pres. 1993–2000, Hon. Pres. 2000–; mem. Comité nat. d'évaluation de la recherche (CNER) 1989–94, Commission nationale des comptes de campagne et des financements politiques (CNCCFP) 1997–2000 (Vice-Pres. 2000–); Officier, Légion d'honneur, Ordre nat. de Mérite, Chevalier des Palmes académiques, Mérite agricole. *Publications:* Les sociétés locales d'économie mixte et leur contrôle 1964, Théorie des grands problèmes économiques contemporains. *Leisure interest:* tennis. *Address:* 24 Résidence des Gros-Chênes, 91370 Verrières-le-Buisson (home); Villa Ej-Jemaïa, 903 rocade des Playes, 83140 Six-Fours-les-Plages, France. *E-mail:* Service-juridique@cnccfp.fr. *Website:* www.cnccfp.fr.

MORISHITA, Yoichi; Japanese electronics executive; *Executive Advisor, Matsushita Electric Industrial Company Ltd;* ed Kwansei Gakuin Univ.; joined Matsushita Electric Industrial Co. Ltd 1957, Man. Electric Motor Osaka Sales Office, Electric Motor Dept 1971–87, apptd mem. Bd of Dirs 1987, Man.-Dir and Dir Living Sales Div. 1989–90, Sr Man.-Dir 1990–91, Head Consumer Products Business Group 1991–92, Exec. Vice-Pres. 1992–93, Pres. 1993–2000, Chair. 2000–06, Exec. Advisor 2006–; Chair. Kansai Electric Industry Devt Centre 1993, Telecommunications Council 1998, Japan Security Systems Asscn 1998; Acting Chair. Japan Electronics and Information Tech. Industries Asscn (JEITA) 2001; Vice-Chair. Electric Industries Asscn of Japan 1993, Japan Fed. of Econ. Orgs (Keidanren) 1999; Commr Tax Comm. 1997, Industrial Structure Council 1999; mem. Keidanren Cttee on China. *Address:* Matsushita Electric Industrial Company Ltd, 1006 Oaza Kadoma, Kadoma, Osaka 571-8501, Japan (office). *Telephone:* (6) 6908-1121 (office). *Fax:* (6) 6908-2351 (office). *Website:* matsushita .co.jp (office).

MORISSETTE, Alanis Nadine; Canadian rock singer, songwriter and actor; b. 1 June 1974, Ottawa; m. Mario Treadway 2010; one s.; signed contract as songwriter with MCA Publishing aged 14, recorded two albums for MCA's recording div.; moved to Toronto, later to LA, USA; BRIT Award for Best Int. Newcomer 1996, four Grammy Awards, including Album of the Year and Best Rock Album, MTV European Music Award for Best Female Artist 1996. *Recordings include:* albums: Alanis 1991, Now Is The Time 1992, Jagged Little Pill 1995, Space Cakes (live) 1998, Supposed Former Infatuation Junkie 1998, Alanis Unplugged (live) 1999, Under Rug Swept 2002, Feast On Scraps: Inside Under Rug Swept 2002, So-called Chaos 2004, Jagged Little Pill Acoustic 2005, Flavors of Entanglement (Juno Award for Pop Album of the Year 2009) 2008, Havoc and Bright Lights 2012. *Film appearances:* Anything for Love 1993, Dogma 1999, Jay and Silent Bob Strike Back 2001, De-Lovely 2004, Radio Free Albemuth 2010. *Television appearances:* as actor: You Can't Do That on Television 1986, Degrassi: the Next Generation 2005, Lovespring International 2006, Nip/Tuck 2006, Weeds 2009–10, Up All Night 2012; host of Music Works series 1994. *Address:* c/o Creative Artists Agency, 2000 Avenue of the Stars, Los Angeles, CA 90067, USA. *Website:* www.alanis.com.

MORITA, Tomijiro; Japanese insurance executive; b. 1941; m.; ed Univ. of Tokyo; joined Dai-ichi Mutual Life Insurance Co. Ltd 1960, Vice-Pres. 1996–97, Pres. 1997–2004, Chair. Dai-ichi Life Insurance Co. Ltd 2004–11; fmr Chair. Seiko Holdings Corpn, currently Corp. Auditor; Exec. Dir Hotel Okura Co. Ltd; mem. Rep. Bd Japan Finance Org. for Municipal Enterprises, Advisory Cttee Japan Tobacco Inc.; Chair. Japan's Life Insurance Asscn; mem. Bd of Dirs Japan Productivity Centre for Socio-Econ. Devt (JPC-SED), Odakyu Group; mem. Exec. Cttee Japan-US Business Council 2003–. *Address:* c/o Dai-ichi Life Insurance Co. Ltd, 13-1, Yurakucho 1-chome, Chiyoda-ku, Tokyo 100-8411, Japan. *E-mail:* info@ dai-ichi-life.co.jp.

MORITS, Yunna Petrovna; Russian poet; b. 2 June 1937, Kiev, Ukraine; m. Yuri Grigor'yevich Vasil'yev; one s.; ed Gorky Literary Inst.; began publishing poetry 1954; has participated in int. poetry festivals London, Cambridge, Toronto, Rotterdam, other locations; has made recordings of recitations of her poetry; mem. Russian PEN, Exec. Cttee, Russian Acad. of Natural Sciences; Golden Rose, Italy 1996, Triumph Prize, Russia 2000, A. D. Sakharov Prize for Civil Courage of Writer 2004. *Publications include:* eleven collections of poetry (trans. in many languages), including The Vine 1970, With Unbleached Thread 1974, By Light of Life 1977, The Third Eye 1980, Selected Poems 1982, The Blue Flame 1985, On This High Shore 1987, In the Den of Vice 1990, The Face 2000, In This Way 2000, By the Law to the Postman Hello 2005, and six books for children including The Great Secret for a Small Company 1987, A Bunch of Cats 1997, Move Your Ears 2003; poems appeared in journal Oktyabr 1993–97; also short stories, essays, scripts for animated cartoons. *Leisure interests:* painting and drawing (more than 300 works published). *Address:* 129010 Moscow, Astrakhansky per. 5, Apartment 76, Russia (home). *Telephone:* (495) 680-08-16 (home). *E-mail:* morits@owl.ru (home). *Website:* morits.ru.

MORITZ, Sir Michael Jonathan, Kt, KBE, MA, MBA; British/American investment industry executive; *Chairman, Sequoia Capital;* b. 1954, Cardiff, Wales; m.; two c.; ed Howardian High School, Cardiff, Christ Church, Oxford, Wharton School, Univ. of Pennsylvania; worked as a reporter for Time 1984–86; Co-founder Technologic Pnrs (tech. newsletter and conf. co.) 1984–86; joined Sequoia Capital, Menlo Park, California as Man. Dir Partner 1986–, Chair. 2012–; mem. Bd of Dirs Flextronics 1993–2005, Yahoo! 1995–2003, PayPal 1999–2002, Google Inc. 1999–2007, 24/7 Customer 2003–, Green Dot Corpn 2003–, Kayak.com 2005–, Sugar Inc. 2007–, Klarna AB 2010–, LinkedIn 2011–; internet co. investments include Google, Yahoo!, PayPal, eBay, Apple Computer, Cisco, Webvan, YouTube, eToys; Hon. Student, Christ Church, Oxford 2005; listed first in Forbes' Midas List of the top dealmakers in the technology industry 2006, 2007, ranked amongst TIME 100 2007. *Publications:* Going For Broke: The Chrysler Story (with Barry Seaman) 1981, The Little Kingdom: The Private Story of Apple Computer 1984. *Address:* Sequoia Capital, 3000 Sand Hill Road, Building 4, Suite 180, Menlo Park, CA 94025, USA (office). *Telephone:* (650) 854-3927 (office). *Fax:* (650) 854-2977 (office). *E-mail:* moritz@sequoiacap.com (office). *Website:* www .sequoiacap.com (office).

MORIYAMA, Raymond, OC, MArch, FRAIC, RCA, FRSA, FAIA; Canadian architect and planner; *Principal, Moriyama and Teshima Architects;* b. 11 Oct. 1929, Vancouver; s. of John Michi Moriyama and Nobuko Moriyama; m. Sachiko Miyauchi 1954; three s. two d.; ed Univ. of Toronto, McGill Univ.; Raymond Moriyama Architects and Planners 1958–70; Partner, Moriyama and Teshima Architects 1970–, Prin. 1980–; Design Tutor, Univ. of Toronto 1961–63; Chair. Ecological Research Ltd 1970; Chair. Mid-Canada Conf., Task Force on Environmental and Ecological Factors 1969–70; mem. Bd and Life mem. Royal Canadian Inst.; Dir Canadian Guild of Crafts 1973–75; mem. of Council, Ont. Coll. of Arts 1972–73; mem. Advisory Cttee, MBA Programme in Arts Admin, York Univ. 1982; Founding mem. Asia Pacific Foundation of Canada 1982; mem. Bd, Multilingual TV; mem. Bd of Trustees, Royal Ont. Museum; mem. Council's Advisory Cttee, N York Gen. Hosp.; Chancellor Brock Univ. 2001–07; Fellow, Toronto Soc. of Architects 1998; Int. FRIBA; several exhbns of architectural work of office; numerous TV documentaries; Regeneration Suite dedicated to work of Raymond Moriyama; Order of Ontario 1992, Order of Rising Sun Gold Rays with Rosette 2004; 10 hon. doctorates, including from Univ. of Toronto, McGill Univ., York Univ.; Civic Awards of Merit (Toronto and Scarborough), Gov.-Gen.'s Medal for Architecture (four times), P.A. Award 1989, Toronto Arts Award 1990, Winner, int. competition for Nat. Saudi Arabian Museum, Riyadh 1996–99, Gold Medal, Royal Architectural Inst. of Canada 1997, Best Architect in Toronto Award 1997, 1998, Governor General's Medal in Architecture 2009, Aga Khan Award of Excellence in Architecture 2010 and many other awards. *Works include:* Japanese Canadian Cultural Centre/Noor Cultural Centre, Toronto 1954–2005, Ontario Science Centre, Toronto 1964–69, Scarborough Civic Centre 1968–74, Niagara Falls and River 100 Year Plan, and Work with 16 univs 1968–, Toronto Reference Library 1973–77, Meewasin Valley 100 Year Plan, Saskatoon 1974–76, Science North, Sudbury 1980–84, Ottawa City Hall 1987–91, Canadian Embassy, Tokyo, Japan 1988–92, Canadian War Museum, Ottawa 2001–05, 124 km Wadi Hanifa Reclamation/Bioremediation, Riyadh, Saudi Arabia 2003. *Publications:* Great American Goose Egg Co. (Canada) Ltd, The Global Living System and Mid-Canada Task Force Committee on Ecological and Environmental Factors 1970, Can Your Life Become a Work of Art 1975, The Satisfactory City: The Survival of Urbanity 1975, Into God's Temple of Eternity, Drive a Nail of Gold, TANT – Time, Appropriateness, Nature and Transition 1982, Architect as Nature's Collaborator (lecture at McGill Univ.) 1996, In Search of a Soul (documentary on the concept and realization of the new Canadian War Museum in Ottawa). *Leisure interests:* fishing, sailing. *Address:* 32 Davenport Road, Toronto, ON M5R 1H3, Canada (home). *Telephone:* (416) 925-4484 (home). *Fax:* (416) 925-4736 (home). *E-mail:* rm@mtarch.com (office). *Website:* www.mtarch.com (office).

MORJANE, Kamel; Tunisian international organization official, diplomatist and government official; b. 9 May 1948, Hammam-Sousse; m. Dorra Ben Ali,; two c.; ed Faculty of Law and Nat. School of Admin, Univ. of Tunis, Graduate Inst. of Int. and Devt Studies, Univ. of Geneva, Switzerland; worked as journalist; fmr Asst Prof. Univ. of Geneva; joined staff UNHCR 1977, Dir, Human Resources 1988–89, SW Asia, Middle East and N Africa Div. 1990–94, Africa Div. 1994–96, Asst High Commr 2001–05; apptd Perm. Rep. to UN, Geneva 1996, later UN Sec.-Gen.'s Special Rep. for Democratic Repub. of Congo 1999–2001; Minister of Defence 2005–10, of Foreign Affairs 2010–11; Grand Officier, Ordre Sept Novembre, Grand Officier, Ordre de la République, Médaille de la Jeunesse (Tunisia), Commander, Ordre Mano (Togo). *Address:* c/o Ministry of Foreign Affairs, ave de la Ligue des états arabes, 1030 Tunis, Tunisia (office).

MØRK, Truls; Norwegian cellist; b. 25 April 1961, Bergen; s. of John Mørk and Turid Otterbech; two s. one d.; ed studied under his father, with Frans Helmerson at Swedish Radio Music School, in Austria with Heinrich Schiff and in Moscow with Natalia Shakovskaya; debut, BBC Promenade Concerts 1989; has since appeared with leading European, American and Australian orchestras, including the Berlin Philharmonic, New York Philharmonic, Philadelphia Symphony, Cincinnati Philharmonic, Rotterdam Philharmonic, London Philharmonic, Pittsburgh Symphony, City of Birmingham Symphony, Orchestre de Paris, NHK Symphony, Royal Concertgebouw and Cleveland, Los Angeles and Gewandhaus Symphony Orchestras; regular appearances at int. chamber music festivals; founder Int. Chamber Music Festival in Stavanger, Artistic Dir –2012; prizewinner Moscow Tchaikovsky Competititon 1982, first prize Cassadó Cello Competition, Florence 1983, UNESCO Prize European Radio-Union Competition, Bratislava 1983, W. Naumburg Competition, New York 1986, Norwegian Critics' Prize 2011, Sibelius Prize 2011. *Recordings include:* Schumann, Elgar and Saint-Saëns concertos, Tchaikovsky Rococo Variations, recitals of cello works by Grieg, Sibelius, Brahms, Rachmaninov and Myaskovksy, Dvořák and Shostakovich cello concertos, Haydn cello concertos with Norwegian Chamber Orchestra, Britten Cello Symphony and Elgar Cello Concerto with Sir Simon Rattle and the City of Birmingham Symphony Orchestra, Britten Cello Suites (Grammy Award 2002), Schumann Cello Concerto with Paavo Järvi and Orchestre Philharmonique de Radio France 2005, C.P.E. Bach Cello Concerti with Bernard Labadie and Les Violons du Roy (ECHO Klassik Award) 2011, Rautavaara Percussion Concerto/ Cello Concerto No. 2 (Gramophone Award for Best Contemporary Recording 2012) 2011. *Address:* Harrison Parrott, 5–6 Albion Court, London, W6 0QT, England (office). *Telephone:* (20) 7229-9166 (office). *Fax:* (20) 7221-5042 (office). *E-mail:* info@harrisonparrott.co.uk (office). *Website:* www.harrisonparrott.com (office).

MORLEY, Malcolm, ARCA; British artist; b. 7 June 1931, London; ed Royal Coll. of Art and Camberwell School of Arts and Crafts, London; discovered art serving a three-year term in Wormwood Scrubs prison; began to produce paintings in an abstract expressionist style from 1956; moved to New York 1958; influenced by Barnett Newman, Andy Warhol and Roy Lichtenstein; began to be more expressionist and to incorporate collage into his work 1970s; returned to a more precise photo-realist style 1990s; Fellow, American Acad. of Arts and Sciences 2009–; 1st Annual Turner Prize, The Tate Gallery, London 1984, 1991, Skowhegan School of Painting and Sculpture Award 1992. *Address:* c/o Sperone Westwater, 415 West 13 Street, New York, NY 10014, USA. *Telephone:* (212) 999-7337. *Fax:* (212) 999-7338. *E-mail:* info@speronewestwater.com. *Website:* www .speronewestwater.com.

MOROSS, Manfred David, BSc, MBA; British business executive; b. 30 Aug. 1931; s. of Dr H. Moross and A. Moross; m. Edna Fay Jacobson 1956; three s. one d.; ed Univ. of Witwatersrand and Harvard Univ.; joined ICI in UK 1953 then returned to South Africa to join Anglo-Transvaal Consolidated Investments; joined Schlesinger Org., Johannesburg, Chair. Int. Group –1974; fmr mem. Bd of Dirs Rand Selection Trust, Whitehall Financial Group, New York, Whitehall Investment Corpn, New York, Siem Industries Inc., Bermuda; mem. Bd of Govs Weizmann Inst. of Science 1982, Chair. Int. Bd 2005–; f. Manfred D. Moross Foundation; Dr hc Weizmann Inst. of Science. *Leisure interests:* tennis, reading. *Address:* 7 Princes Gate, London, SW7 1GL, England (home).

MOROZ, Oleksandr Oleksandrovych; Ukrainian politician; b. 29 Feb. 1944, Buda, Kyiv Oblast; m. Valentina Andriyivna Lavrinenko; two d.; ed Ukrainian Agric. Acad., Higher CP School; trained as engineer in Kyiv; engineer and mechanic in state farm professional school, dist and regional enterprises of Selkhoztekhnika 1965–76; sec. regional trade union, First Sec. Dist CP Cttee; Head of Agric. Div. Regional CP Cttee; Co-founder and Chair. Socialist Party of Ukraine 1991–2010, 2011–12; People's Deputy of Ukrainian SSR, then mem. Verkhovna Rada (Parl.) 1994–2007, Chair. 1994–98, 2006–07; presidential cand. 1994, 1999, 2004, 2010. *Publications:* author or co-author of a number of legal projects including Code on Land: Where Are We Going?, Choice, Subjects for Meditation; several articles. *Address:* Socialist Party of Ukraine, 02100 Kyiv, vul. Bazhova 12, Ukraine (office). *Telephone:* (44) 573-58-97 (office). *E-mail:* pr@spu.in .ua (office). *Website:* www.spu.in.ua (office).

MOROZOV, Oleg Viktorovich, CPhilSc; Russian politician; *Head of Department, Presidential Administration of the Russian Federation;* b. 5 Nov. 1953, Kazan; m.; one d.; ed Kazan State Univ.; docent, Kazan State Univ.; Head of Div. Tatar Regional CP Cttee 1987–89; instructor, Asst to Sec., CPSU Cen. Cttee 1989–91; consultant, Office of USSR Pres. 1991–92; Deputy Dir-Gen. Biotekhnologiya; mem. State Duma 1993– (re-elected as mem. Otechestvo—Vsya Russia Movt 1999), fmrly Head, Regions of Russia Deputy Group and Deputy Speaker State Duma –2012; Head of the Presidential Administration 2012–; mem. Deputies' group New Regional Politics 1994–96; Chair. Deputies' Group Russian Regions 1997–; joined Yedinstvo Party 2001. *Leisure interests:* collecting toy hippopotamuses, serious classical music. *Address:* Administration of the President, 4 Staraya Square, 103132 Moscow, Russia. *Telephone:* (495) 292-83-52 (office). *Fax:* (495) 292-91-69 (office); (495) 606-43-40 (office). *E-mail:* pr_morozov@gov.ru (office). *Website:* www.duma.gov.ru.

MOROZOV, Vladimir Mikhailovich; Russian singer (bass); *Head of Vocal Training Department, Herzen State Pedagogical University;* b. 12 Feb. 1933, Leningrad; m.; one s.; ed Leningrad State Conservatory; soloist with Kirov (now Mariinsky) Opera 1959–; Prof. and Head of Vocal Training Dept, Herzen State Pedagogical Univ. of Russia; mem. CPSU 1965–91; Glinka Prize 1974, USSR State Prize 1976, RSFSR People's Artist 1976, USSR People's Artist 1981. *Roles include:* Varlaam (Boris Godunov), Ivan the Terrible (The Women from Pskov), Grigory (Quiet Flows the Don), Peter the Great (Peter I), Dosifey (Khovanshchina). *Address:* Herzen State Pedagogical University of Russia, St Petersburg, 48 Moika Emb., St Petersburg 191186, Russia.

MORPARIA, Kalpana, BSc, LLB; Indian banker; *CEO, J.P. Morgan, India;* b. 1949; ed Univ. of Mumbai; Sr Legal Officer, ICICI Bank Ltd 1975–96, Gen. Man. in charge of Legal, Planning, Treasury and Corp. Communications Depts 1996–98, Sr Gen. Man. in charge also of Human Resources Devt, Planning and Strategic Support Group and Special Projects Dept 1998–2001, apptd Exec. Dir 2001, later Head, Corp. Center and Official Spokesperson, ICICI Bank Ltd, Deputy Man. Dir 2004–06, Jt Man. Dir 2006–07, Chief Strategy and Communications Officer, ICICI Group 2007–08, currently Dir ICICI Home Finance Co. Ltd, ICICI Lombard Gen. Insurance Co. Ltd, ICICI Prudential Life Insurance Co. Ltd, ICICI Venture Funds Man. Co. Ltd, ICICI Securities and Finance Co. Ltd, ICICI Capital Services Ltd, ICICI Infotech Services Ltd, ICICI Personal Financial Services Ltd, ICICI Web Trade Ltd, ICICI Investment Man. Co. Ltd; Ind. Dir Dr Reddy's Laboratories Ltd 2007–, CMC Ltd 2008–; CEO J.P. Morgan, India 2008–; mem. Fraud Monitoring Cttee, Share Transfer and Shareholders'/Investors' Grievance Cttee, Asset-Liability Man. Cttee, Cttee of Dirs; Women Achievers Award in the Field of Finance and Banking, Indian Merchants' Chamber (Ladies Wing) 1999, named amongst 25 Most Powerful Women in Indian Business by Business Today 2004, 2005, 2006, ranked jt 93rd by Forbes magazine amongst 100 Most Powerful Women 2006, ranked by Fortune magazine amongst 50 Most Powerful Women in Business outside the US (44th) 2008. *Address:* JPMorgan Asset Management India Private Ltd, Kalpataru Synergy, 3rd Floor, West Wing, Santacruz - East, Mumbai 400 055 (office); CMC Ltd, PTI Building, 5th Floor, 4 Sansad Marg, New Delhi 110 001, India (office). *Telephone:* (22) 67837000 (Mumbai) (office); (11) 23736151 (New Delhi) (office). *Fax:* (22) 26531167 (Mumbai) (office); (11) 23736159 (New Delhi) (office). *Website:* www.jpmorganmf.com (office); www.cmcltd.com (office).

MORPURGO, Michael, OBE; British writer; b. 5 Oct. 1943, St Albans, Herts.; m. Clare Morpurgo; co-f. Farms for City Children project; Children's Laureate 2003–05; Writer-in-Residence, The Savoy Hotel, London 2007; Whitbread Children's Book Award 1995, Smarties Book Prize 1996, Bronze Prize in 6–8 years group 2003, Children's Book Awards 1996, 2000, 2002. *Publications include:* Beyond the Rainbow Warrior, Billy the Kid, Black Queen, Colly's Barn, Conker, Dear Olly, Escape from Shangri-La, Farm Boy, Friend or Foe, From Hearabout Hill, Grania O'Malley, Joan of Arc, Kensuke's Kingdom, King of the Cloud Forests, Long Way Home, Marble Crusher, Mr Nobody's Eyes, My Friend Walter, Out of the Ashes, Red Eyes at Night, Sam's Duck, Snakes and Ladders, The Butterfly Lion, The Nine Lives of Montezuma, The Rainbow Bear, The Sleeping Sword, The War of Jenkins' Ear, The White Horse of Zennor, The Wreck of the Zanzibar, Toro! Toro!, Twist of Gold, Waiting for Anya, War Horse, Wartman, Who's a Big Bully Then?, Why the Whales Came, Wombat Goes Walkabout, The Last Wolf 2002, Private Peaceful (Prix Sorcières for children's novel, France, Blue Peter Book Award 2005, California Young Reader Medal 2008) 2003, The Amazing Story of Adolphus Tips 2005, Alone on a Wide Wide Sea 2006, On Angel Wings 2006, Born to Run 2007, Kaspar Prince of Cats 2008, Running Wild 2009, Not Bad for a Bad Lad 2010, An Elephant in the Garden 2010, Shadow 2010, Little Manfred 2011, The Pied Piper of Hamelin 2011, Sparrow: The True Story of Joan of Arc 2012, Outlaw: The Story of Robin Hood 2012, Homecoming 2012, A Medal For Leroy 2012. *Address:* c/o Laura West, David Higham Associates, 5–8 Lower John Street,

Golden Square, London, W1R 4HA, England (office). *E-mail:* laurawest@ davidhigham.co.uk (office). *Website:* www.davidhigham.co.uk (office); www .michaelmorpurgo.com.

MORRICONE, Ennio; Italian composer; b. 10 Nov. 1928, Rome; s. of Mario Morricone and Libera Morricone; m. Maria Travia; three s. two d.; ed Accad. of Santa Cecilia, Rome; began career in field of classical composition and arrangement; has composed and arranged scores for more than 500 film and TV productions; best known film scores include The Good, the Bad and the Ugly, Once Upon a Time in the West, The Mission, Le Professionnel; numerous awards including Hon. Acad. Award 2007, Royal Swedish Acad. of the Arts Polar Music Prize 2010; Grand Official, Ordine al merito della Repubblica Italiana 2006, Chevalier, Ordre nat. de la Légion d'honneur 2008. *Film scores include:* Il Federale 1961, La Voglia matta 1962, Diciottenni al sole 1962, La Cuccagna 1962, Il Successo 1963, Le Monachine 1963, I Basilischi 1963, Duello nel Texas (as Dan Savio) 1963, La Scoperta dell'America 1964, I Motorizzati 1964, ...e la donna creò l'uomo 1964, I Maniaci 1964, Prima della rivoluzione 1964, Per un pugno di dollari (For A Fistful of Dollars, as Leo Nichols) 1964, Le Pistole non discutono 1964, I Malamondo 1964, Thrilling 1965, Slalom 1965, Menage all'italiana 1965, Idoli controluce 1965, La Battaglia di Algeri 1965, Gli Amanti d'oltretomba 1965, Altissima pressione 1965, I Pugni in tasca 1965, Centomila dollari per Ringo 1965, Il Ritorno di Ringo 1965, Per qualche dollaro in più (For a Few Dollars More) 1965, La Ragazza del bersagliere 1966, Per Firenze 1966, Navajo Joe (as Leo Nichols) 1966, Mi vedrai tornare 1966, Matchless 1966, I Lunghi giorni della vendetta 1966, Un Fiume di dollari 1966, Uccellacci e uccellini 1966, El Greco 1966, Un Uomo a metà 1966, La Resa dei conti 1966, Il Buono, il brutto, il cattivo (The Good, the Bad and the Ugly) 1966, Sette donne per i MacGregor 1967, Pedro Páramo 1967, Il Giardino delle delizie 1967, Dalle Ardenne all'inferno 1967, L'Avventuriero 1967, Le Streghe 1967, OK Connery 1967, I Crudeli (as Leo Nichols) 1967, Per pochi dollari ancora (theme) 1967, Arabella 1967, Il Mercenario 1968, Italia vista dal cielo 1968, Grazie, zia 1968, Il Grande silenzio 1968, Ecce Homo 1968, Diabolik 1968, Da uomo a uomo 1968, La Bataille de San Sebastian 1968, Roma come Chicago 1968, C'era una volta il West (Once Upon a Time in the West) 1968, Vergogna schifosi 1969, Giotto 1969, La Donna invisibile 1969, L'Assoluto naturale 1969, Cuore di mamma 1969, L'Alibi 1969, Galileo 1969, Un Bellissimo novembre 1969, Ruba al prossimo tuo 1969, Un Tranquillo posto di campagna 1969, Una Breve stagione 1969, Le Clan des Siciliens 1969, Zenabel 1969, Uccidete il vitello grasso e arrostitelo 1970, Metello 1970, Giochi particolari 1970, La Califfa 1970, Two Mules for Sister Sara 1970, La Moglie più bella 1970, Indagine su un cittadino al di sopra di ogni sospetto 1970, Hornets' Nest 1970, Vamos a matar, compañeros 1970, Oceano 1971, Gli Occhi freddi della paura 1971, Incontro 1971, Forza 'G' 1971, Una Lucertola con la pelle di donna 1971, Veruschka 1971, Il Decameron 1971, La Tarantola dal ventre nero 1971, Giornata nera per l'ariete 1971, Il Giorno del giudizio 1971, Sacco e Vanzetti 1971, L'Istruttoria è chiusa: dimentichi 1971, Malastrana 1971, Giù la testa 1971, Maddalena 1971, ¡Viva la muerte... tua! 1971, La Violenza: Quinto potere 1972, Questa specie d'amore 1972, Quando la preda è l'uomo 1972, Perché? 1972, Il Maestro e Margherita 1972, Lui per lei 1972, Guttoso e il 'Marat morto' di David 1972, Les Deux saisons de la vie 1972, D'amore si muore 1972, Crescete e moltiplicatevi 1972, La Cosa buffa 1972, Chi l'ha vista morire? 1972, Bianchi bandinelli e la Colonna Traiana 1972, Anche se volessi lavorare, che faccio? 1972, Le Tueur 1972, Cosa avete fatto a Solange? 1972, Bluebeard 1972, J. and S. – storia criminale del far west 1972, L'Attentat 1972, Sbatti il mostro in prima pagina 1972, Un Uomo da rispettare 1972, Il Ritorno di Clint il solitario 1972, Quando le donne persero la coda 1972, La Vita, a volte, è molto dura, vero Provvidenza? 1972, Vaarwel 1973, Allonsanfan 1973, Le Serpent 1973, Le Moine 1973, La Proprietà non è più un furto 1973, Revolver 1973, Rappresaglia 1973, Il Mio nome è Nessuno 1973, Il Giro del mondo degli innamorati di Peynet 1974, Fatti di gente per bene 1974, La Cugina 1974, L'Anticristo 1974, Spasmo 1974, Mussolini: Ultimo atto 1974, Sesso in confessionale 1974, Le Trio infernal 1974, Le Secret 1974, Labbra di lurido blu 1975, Gente di rispetto 1975, Peur sur la ville 1975, Leonor 1975, Der Richter und sein Henker 1975, The Human Factor 1975, Una Vita venduta 1976, Todo modo 1976, René la canne 1976, Per amore 1976, Film 1976, Il Deserto dei Tartari 1976, L'Arriviste 1976, Ariel Limon 1976, L'Agnese va a morire 1976, Der Dritte Grad 1976, Divina creatura 1976, 1900 1976, L'Eredità Ferramonti 1976, Stato interessante 1977, Il Mostro 1977, The Dragon, the Odds 1977, Corleone 1977, Le Ricain 1977, Exorcist II: The Heretic 1977, Orca 1977, Holocaust 2000 1977, L'Immoralità 1978, Forza Italia! 1978, Il Gatto 1978, One, Two, Two: 122, rue de Provence 1978, Così come sei 1978, La Cage aux folles 1978, Ten to Survive 1979, Il Prato 1979, Il Ladrone 1979, Dedicato al mare Egeo 1979, L'Umanoide 1979, Bloodline 1979, La Luna 1979, I... comme Icare 1979, Uomini e no 1980, The Fantastic World of M.C. Escher 1980, Windows 1980, Un Sacco bello 1980, The Island 1980, L'Oeil 1980, La Banquière 1980, La Cage aux folles II 1980, La Dame aux camélias 1980, Il Pianeta azzurro 1981, Bianco, rosso e Verdone 1981, So Fine 1981, Le Professionnel 1981, La Tragedia di un uomo ridicolo 1981, Porca vacca 1982, Nana 1982, A Time to Die 1982, The Thing 1982, White Dog 1982, Blood Link 1982, Maja Plisetskaja 1982, Hundra 1983, Le Ruffian 1983, Le Marginal 1983, Sahara 1983, Pelota 1984, Once Upon a Time in America 1984, Les Voleurs de la nuit 1984, Code Name: Wild Geese 1984, Red Sonja 1985, Kommando Leopard 1985, Il Pentito 1985, La Cage aux folles 3 – 'Elles' se marient 1985, La Venexiana 1986, La Gabbia 1986, The Mission 1986, Quartiere 1987, Mosca addio 1987, Il Giorno prima 1987, The Untouchables 1987, Gli Occhiali d'oro 1987, Il Cuore di mamma 1988, Frantic 1988, A Time of Destiny 1988, Rampage 1988, Cinema Paradiso 1989, Casualties of War 1989, Fat Man and Little Boy 1989, Tre colonne in cronaca 1990, Tempo di uccidere 1990, ¡Átame! 1990, Stanno tutti bene 1990, The Big Man 1990, Tracce di vita amorosa 1990, State of Grace 1990, Hamlet 1990, Money 1991, La Domenica specialmente 1991, Bugsy 1991, A Csalás gyönyöre 1992, Beyond Justice 1992, City of Joy 1992, La Villa del venerdì 1992, Love Potion No. 9 1992, Roma imago urbis 1993, In the Line of Fire 1993, Il Lungo silenzio 1993, La Scorta 1993, Jona che visse nella balena 1994, Wolf 1994, Love Affair 1994, Disclosure 1994, The Night and the Moment 1995, Pasolini, un delitto italiano 1995, L'Uomo delle stelle 1995, I Magi randagi 1996, Vite strozzate 1996, La Lupa 1996, Cartoni animati 1997, Marianna Ucrìa 1997, U Turn 1997, Lolita 1997, Il Fantasma dell'opera 1998, Lucignolo 1999, In the Line of Fire: The Ultimate Sacrifice 2000, Canone inverso – making love 2000, Mission to Mars 2000, Malèna 2000, La Ragion pura 2001, Cowboys Don't Kiss in Public 2001, Threnody 2002, Senso '45 2002, Ripley's Game 2002, Il Diario di

Matilde Manzoni 2002, L'Ultimo pistolero 2002, Arena Concerto 2003, La Luz prodigiosa 2003, The Wages of Sin 2003, 72 metra 2004, Kill Bill: Vol. 2 2004, Guardiani delle nuvole 2004, Sorstalanság 2005, Karol, un uomo diventato papa 2005, Libertas 2005, Fateless 2005, E ridendo l'uccise 2005, Adolfo Celi, un uomo per due culture 2006, A Crime 2006, La Sconosciuta 2006, The Weatherman 2007, Ultrasordine 2007, I demoni di San Pietroburgo 2008, Baaria – La porta del vento 2009, Spider Dance 2010. *Television scores include:* The Virginian (series theme) 1962, Lo Squarciagola 1966, 1943: un incontro 1969, La Sciantosa 1970, Nessuno deve sapere (series) 1971, Correva l'anno di grazia 1870 1971, L'Uomo e la magia 1972, L'Automobile 1972, Moses the Lawgiver 1975, Drammi gotici 1976, Noi lazzaroni (series) 1978, Le Mani sporche 1978, Invito allo sport (series) 1978, Orient-Express (series) 1979, The Life and Times of David Lloyd George (series) 1981, Marco Polo (series) 1982, The Scarlet and the Black 1983, Wer war Edgar Allan? 1984, Die Försterbuben 1984, Via Mala (series) 1985, C.A.T. Squad 1986, I Promessi sposi (series) 1988, Gli Indifferenti (series) 1988, Camillo Castiglioni oder die Moral der Haifische 1988, Gli Angeli del potere 1988, C.A.T. Squad: Python Wolf 1988, Il Principe del deserto (series) 1989, The Endless Game 1990, Cacciatori di navi 1990, Una Storia italiana 1992, Piazza di Spagna (series) 1993, Missus 1993, La Piovra series 1–10 1984–99, Genesi: La creazione e il diluvio 1994, Abraham 1994, Jacob 1994, Joseph 1995, Moses (title music) 1996, Il Barone (series) 1996, Samson and Delilah 1996, In fondo al cuore 1997, Nostromo (series) 1997, David (theme) 1997, Ultimo 1998, I Guardiani del cielo 1998, Il Quarto re 1998, La Casa bruciata 1998, Ultimo 2 – La sfida 1999, Nanà 1999, Esther 1999, Padre Pio – Tra cielo e terra 2000, Un Difetto di famiglia 2002, Il Papa buono 2003, Musashi (series) 2003, Charlie Chaplin – Les années suisses 2003, Il Cuore nel pozzo 2005, Cefalonia 2005, Karol, un umono divetato Papa 2005, Lucia 2005, La Provinciale 2006, Giovanni Falcone, l'uomo che sfido Cosa Nostra 2006, L'ultimo de Corleonesi 2007, Résolution 819 2008, Pane e libertà 2009, Quatraro mysteriet 2009, Mi ricordo Anna Frank 2009. *Classical compositions:* more than 15 piano concertos, 30 symphonic pieces, choral music and one opera. *Address:* c/o Gorfaine/ Schwartz Agency Inc., 4111 West Alameda Avenue, Suite 509, Burbank, CA 91505, USA (office). *Telephone:* (818) 260-8500 (office).

MORRILL, Rev. John Stephen, DPhil, FBA; British historian and academic; *Professor of British and Irish History, University of Cambridge;* b. 12 June 1946, Manchester; s. of William Henry Morrill and Marjorie Morrill (née Ashton); m. Frances Mead 1968 (died 2007); four d.; ed Altrincham Grammar School, Trinity Coll., Oxford; Research Fellow, Trinity Coll. Oxford 1974–74, Hon. Fellow 2006–; Lecturer in History, Univ. of Stirling 1974–75; Fellow, Selwyn Coll. Cambridge 1975–, Sr Tutor 1989–92, Vice-Master 1994–2005; Lecturer in History, Cambridge Univ. 1975–92, Reader in Early Modern History 1992–98, Prof. of British and Irish History 1998–; mem. Council, Royal Historical Soc. 1988–92, Vice-Pres. 1992–96; Chair. Communications and Activities Cttee, British Acad. 1998–, mem. Council 1998–, Vice-Pres. 2000–02; mem. and Trustee Arts and Humanities Research Council 2000–04, Chair. Rescue Cttee 2001–04; ordained Perm. Deacon, RC Diocese of East Anglia 1996; mem. Acad. of Finland 2001; Hon. DLitt (Univ. of East Anglia) 2001; Hon. DUniv (Surrey) 2001. *Publications:* Cheshire 1630–1660 1974, The Revolt of the Provinces 1976, Reactions to the English Civil War 1981, Oliver Cromwell and the English Revolution 1989, The Impact of the English Civil War 1991, Revolution and Restoration 1992, The Nature of the English Revolution 1992, The British Problem 1534–1707 1996, The Oxford Illustrated History of Tudor and Stuart Britain 1996, Revolt in the Provinces 1998, Soldiers and Statesmen of the English Revolution (co-author) 1998; 40 articles in learned journals. *Leisure interests:* music, theology, whisky, cricket. *Address:* Selwyn College, Cambridge, CB3 9DQ (office); 1 Bradford's Close, Bottisham, Cambridge, CB25 9DW, England (home). *Telephone:* (1223) 335895 (office); (1223) 811822 (home). *Fax:* (1223) 335837 (office). *E-mail:* jsm1000@cam.ac.uk (office).

MORRIS, Christopher, FCA; British chartered accountant; *Partner, Begbies Traynor;* b. 28 April 1942; s. of Richard Archibald Sutton Morris, MC and Josephine Fanny Mary Morris (née Galliano); m. Isabel Ramsden (divorced); two s.; qualified 1967; Pnr, Head of UK insolvency arm Touche Ross & Co. (later Deloitte) 1972–2000; Sr Partner Corp. Recovery; Pnr Begbies Traynor 2004–; cases have included liquidation of Laker Airways 1982, British Island Airways, British Air Ferries, Rush & Tompkins, London & County Securities, Polly Peck Int., Banco Ambrosiano, Bank of Credit and Commerce International (BCCI); Fellow Soc. of Practitioners of Insolvency. *Leisure interests:* racing, wine, the countryside. *Address:* Begbies Traynor, 32 Cornhill, London, EC3V 3BT, England (office). *Telephone:* (20) 7398-3800 (office). *Fax:* (20) 7398-3799 (office). *Website:* www .begbies-traynor.com (office).

MORRIS, Sir Derek James, Kt, MA, DPhil; British economist and academic; *Provost, Oriel College, University of Oxford;* b. 23 Dec. 1945, Harrow, Middx, England; s. of Denis William Morris and Olive Margaret Morris; m. Susan Mary Whittles 1975; two s.; ed Harrow Co. Grammar School, St Edmund Hall and Nuffield Coll., Oxford; Research Fellow, Univ. of Warwick 1969–70; Fellow and Tutor of Econs Oriel Coll., Oxford 1970–98, now Provost; Econ. Dir Nat. Econ. Devt Office 1981–84; Chair. Oxford Econ. Forecasting Ltd 1984–98; mem. Monopolies and Mergers Comm. 1991–95, Deputy Chair. 1995–98, Chair. Competition (fmrly Monopolies and Mergers) Comm. 1998–2004; Chair. Morris Review of Actuarial Profession 2004; Hon. Fellow, St Edmund Hall, Oxford 2002, Trinity Coll., Dublin 2004; Dr hc (Univ. Coll., Dublin) 2004, (Univ. of East Anglia) 2006. *Publications include:* The Economic System in the UK (ed.) 1971, Industrial Economics and Organisation (with D. Hay) 1985, Chinese State-Owned Enterprises and Economic Reform 1994; numerous journal articles on econs. *Leisure interests:* skiing, rugby, history. *Address:* Oriel College, Oxford, OX1 4EW, England (office). *Telephone:* (1865) 276543 (office). *E-mail:* lodge@oriel.ox.ac.uk (office). *Website:* www.oriel.ox .ac.uk (office).

MORRIS, Desmond John, BSc, DPhil; British zoologist; b. 24 Jan. 1928, Purton, Wilts., England; s. of Capt. Harry Howe Morris and Marjorie Morris (née Hunt); m. Ramona Joy Baulch 1952; one s.; ed Dauntsey's School, Wilts., Univs of Birmingham and Oxford; zoological research worker Univ. of Oxford 1954–56; Head of Granada TV/Film Unit Zoological Soc. of London 1956–59, Curator of Mammals 1959–67; Dir Inst. of Contemporary Arts, London 1967–68; Research Fellow, Wolfson Coll., Oxford 1973–81; privately engaged in writing books on animal and human behaviour 1968–73, 1981–2011 and making TV programmes;

artist; Scientific Fellow, Zoological Soc. of London; Hon. FLS; Hon. DSc (Reading) 1998. *Television:* Zootime (Granada) 1956–67, Life in the Animal World (BBC) 1965–67, The Human Race (Thames TV) 1982, The Animals Roadshow (BBC) 1987–89, The Animal Contract 1989, Animal Country 1991–95, The Human Animal 1994, The Human Sexes 1997. *Publications include:* The Reproductive Behaviour of the Ten-spined Stickleback 1958, The Story of Congo 1958, Curious Creatures 1961, The Biology of Art 1962, Apes and Monkeys 1964, The Mammals: A Guide to the Living Species 1965, The Big Cats 1965, Men and Snakes (with Ramona Morris) 1965, Zootime 1966, Men and Apes (with Ramona Morris) 1966, Men and Pandas (with Ramona Morris) 1966, Primate Ethology (Ed.) 1967, The Naked Ape 1967, The Human Zoo 1969, Intimate Behaviour 1971, Manwatching: A Field-Guide to Human Behaviour 1977, Gestures, Their Origins and Distribution 1979, Animal Days (autobiography) 1979, The Giant Panda 1981, The Soccer Tribe 1981, Inrock (fiction) 1983, Bodywatching 1985, The Illustrated Naked Ape 1986, Dogwatching 1986, Catwatching 1986, The Secret Surrealist 1987, The Human Nestbuilders 1988, The Animals Roadshow 1988, Horsewatching 1988, The Animal Contract 1990, Animal-Watching 1990, Babywatching 1991, Christmas Watching 1992, The World of Animals 1993, The Naked Ape Trilogy 1994, The Human Animal 1994, Body Talk: A World Guide to Gestures 1994, The Illustrated Catwatching 1994, Illustrated Babywatching 1995, Catworld: A Feline Encyclopedia 1996, Illustrated Dogwatching 1996, The Human Sexes 1997, Illustrated Horsewatching 1998, Cool Cats: The 100 Cat Breeds of the World 1999, Cosmetic Behaviour and the Naked Ape 1999, The Naked Eye 2000, Dogs, a Dictionary of Dog Breeds 2001, People-Watching 2002, The Silent Language 2004, The Nature of Happiness 2004, The Naked Woman: A Study of the Female Body 2004, Watching: Encounters with Humans and Other Animals (autobiography) 2006, The Naked Man 2008, Baby, The Story of a Baby's First Two Years 2008, Planet Ape (with Steve Parker) 2009. *Leisure interest:* archaeology. *Address:* c/o Jonathan Cape, 20 Vauxhall Bridge Road, London, SW1V 2SA, England. *Fax:* (1865) 512103 (home). *E-mail:* dmorris@ukstudio.org (office). *Website:* www.desmond-morris.com (home).

MORRIS, Doug; American record company executive, producer and songwriter; *Chairman, Universal Music Group;* b. Nov. 1938; ed Columbia Univ.; fmr songwriter music publisher Robert Mellin Inc.; writer and prod. Laurie Records from 1965, later Vice-Pres. and Gen. Man.; f. Big Tree label (sold to Atlantic Records 1978); Pres. ATCO Records (part of Warner Music) 1978–80, Pres. Atlantic Records 1980–90, Co-Chair. and Co-CEO Atlantic Recording Group 1990–94, Pres. and COO, then Warner Music USA 1994; co-cr. Interscope Records; Chair. MCA Music Entertainment Group (now Universal Music Group) 1995–, CEO 1995–2010, f. Universal Records, apptd to Vivendi Universal Management Bd 2005; co-f. (with Jimmy Iovine q.v.) Jimmy and Doug's Farm Club project, comprising a record label, website and cable TV show 1999–; jt owner Pressplay subscription-based music download website; bd mem. The Robin Hood Foundation, The Cold Spring Harbor Laboratory; Dir Rock and Roll Hall of Fame; NARAS President's Merit Award 2003. *Compositions include:* Sweet Talkin' Guy, The Chiffons 1966. *Address:* Universal Music Group, 2200 Colorado Avenue, Santa Monica, CA 90404, USA (office). *Website:* www.umusic.com (office); www.farmclub.com (office).

MORRIS, Errol Mark, BA; American film director; b. 5 Feb. 1948, Hewlett, NY; m. Julia Sheehan 1984; one s.; ed Univ. of Wisconsin, Princeton Univ., Univ. of California, Berkeley; documentary film dir; mem. American Acad. of Arts and Sciences; MacArthur Fellowship, Guggenheim Fellowship. *Films include:* Gates of Heaven 1980, Vernon, Florida 1982, The Thin Blue Line 1988, The Dark Wind 1991, A Brief History of Time 1991, Fast, Cheap and Out of Control 1997, Mr. Death: The Rise and Fall of Fred A. Leuchter, Jr. 1999, The Fog of War: Eleven Lessons from the Life of Robert S. McNamara (Academy Award for Best Documentary Feature) 2003, Standard Operating Procedure (Grand Jury Silver Bear, Berlin Film Festival) 2008, Tabloid 2010. *Publications:* Standard Operating Procedure (with Philip Gourevitch) 2008, Believing is Seeing: Observations on the Mysteries of Photography 2011, A Wilderness of Error: The Trials of Jeffrey MacDonald 2012. *Address:* Fourth Floor Productions Inc., 650 Cambridge Street, Cambridge, MA 02141, USA (office). *Telephone:* (617) 225-0012 (office). *Fax:* (617) 225-0016 (office). *E-mail:* info@errolmorris.com (office). *Website:* www.errolmorris.com (office).

MORRIS, Baroness (Life Peer), cr. 2005, of Yardley in the County of West Midlands; **Estelle Morris,** BEd; British politician; b. 17 June 1952; d. of Charles Richard Morris and Pauline Morris; ed Whalley Range High School, Manchester, Coventry Coll. of Educ., Warwick Univ.; teacher 1974–92; Councillor, Warwick Dist Council 1979–91, Labour Group Leader 1981–89; MP for Birmingham, Yardley 1992–; Opposition Whip 1994–95, Opposition Front-bench Spokeswoman on Educ. 1995–97; Parl. Under-Sec. of State, Dept for Educ. and Employment (DfEE) 1997–98, Minister of State 1998–2001, Sec. of State for Educ. and Skills 2001–02; Minister of State for the Arts, Dept for Culture, Media and Sport 2003–05; Privy Councillor; Pro Vice-Chancellor Sunderland Univ. 2005–08; Chair. Strategy Bd Inst. of Effective Educ., Univ. of York; Hon. Degrees (Warwick) 2003, (Wolverhampton) 2004, (Leeds Metropolitan) 2004, (Bradford) 2005, (Birmingham) 2006, (Manchester Metropolitan, Cumbria) 2007, (Sunderland) 2008. *Address:* House of Lords, London, SW1A 0PW, England (office). *Telephone:* (20) 7219-3000 (office). *Website:* www.parliament.uk (office).

MORRIS, Rev. Floyd Emerson, MPhil; Jamaican politician; *President of the Senate;* b. 23 July 1969, Bailey's Vale, Port Maria; s. of Lloyd Morris and Jemita Pryce; m. Shelley-Ann Morris 2011; ed Univ. of the West Indies; began career as consultant, Nat. Youth Service; fmr Politics Lecturer, Dept of Govt, Univ. of the West Indies (UWI); fmr coordinator, UWI Centre for Disability Studies; Founder and CEO F.E. Morris International Consultancy Services; Minister of State in the Ministry of Labour and Social Security 2001–07; apptd to Senate 1998–2007, 2012–, elected Pres. 2013–; host of radio programme 'Seeing from a Different Perspective' 2011–; mem. Nat. Advisory Bd for Persons with Disabilities 1995–. *Leisure interests:* sports, dominoes. *Address:* The Senate, Gordon House, 81 Duke Street, Kingston, Jamaica (office). *Telephone:* 922-0200-7 (office). *Fax:* 967-0064/ 967-1708 (office). *Website:* www.japarliament.gov.jm (office).

MORRIS, James Humphry (see Morris, Jan).

MORRIS, James Peppler; American singer (bass-baritone); b. 10 Jan. 1947; s. of James Morris and Geraldine Peppler; m. 1st Joanne F. Vitali 1971; one d.; m. 2nd Susan Quittmeyer 1987; one s. one d. (twins); ed Univ. of Maryland, Peabody Conservatory and Acad. of Vocal Arts; debut at Metropolitan Opera, New York 1970; opera and concert appearances throughout USA, Canada, S. America, Europe, Japan and Australia. *Recordings include:* Wotan in the New Ring Cycles, The Flying Dutchman, operas by Wagner, Offenbach, Mozart, Verdi, Donizetti, Bellini. *Title roles include:* The Flying Dutchman, Don Giovanni, Le Nozze di Figaro, Macbeth, Boris Godunov, Faust, Billy Budd, Otello. *Address:* Columbia Artists' Management Inc., 1790 Broadway, New York, NY 10019-1412, USA (office). *Telephone:* (212) 841 9500 (office). *Fax:* (212) 841 9744 (office). *E-mail:* info@cami.com (office). *Website:* www.cami.com (office).

MORRIS, James T., BA, MBA; American international organization official and business executive; b. 18 April 1943, Terre Haute, Ind.; m. Jacqueline Harrell Morris; three c.; ed Indiana Univ., Butler Univ.; Chief of Staff to Mayor of Indianapolis 1967–73; Dir of Community Devt, Lilly Endowment 1973, Vice-Pres., Pres. 1984–89; Chair. and CEO IWC Resources Corpn, Ind. Water Co. 1989–; Exec. Dir UN WFP 2002–07; Chair. NCAA Foundation; Chair. Bd of Trustees Ind. Univ.; Treas. US Olympic Cttee; mem. Bd Govs American Red Cross; Inductee, Ind. Acad.; Dr hc (Butler Univ.), (Ind. Univ.), (Vincennes Univ.), (Rose Hufman Inst. of Tech.), (Univ. of Southern Ind.), (Martin Univ.), (Franklin Coll.), (Marian Coll.), (Wabash Coll.), (Univ. of Notre Dame); Medal of Freedom, Ellis Island, New York, Whitney Young Award, Indianapolis Urban League, Charles L. Whistler Award, Int. Citizen of the Year, Int. Center of Indianapolis and numerous other awards. *Address:* c/o World Food Programme, Via Cesare Giulio Viola 68, Parco dei Medici, 00148 Rome, Italy. *Telephone:* (06) 6513-3030.

MORRIS, Jan, (James Humphry Morris), CBE, MA, FRSL; British writer; b. 2 Oct. 1926, Somerset, England; ed Christ Church Coll., Oxford; editorial staff, The Times 1951–56, The Guardian 1957–62; Commonwealth Fellowship, USA 1954; mem. Yr Academi Gymreig, Gorsedd of Bards, Welsh Nat. Eisteddfod; Hon. Fellow, Univ. Coll. Wales, Univ. of Wales, Bangor; Hon. FRIBA; Hon. Student, Christ Church Oxon.; Dr hc (Univ. of Wales) 1993, (Univ. of Glamorgan) 1996. *Publications:* as James Morris: Coast to Coast (aka I Saw the USA) 1956, Sultan in Oman 1957, The Market of Seleukia (aka Islam Inflamed: A Middle East Picture) 1957, Coronation Everest 1958, South African Winter 1958, The Hashemite Kings 1959, Venice 1960, South America 1961, The Upstairs Donkey (juvenile) 1962, The World Bank: A Prospect (aka The Road to Huddersfield: A Journey to Five Continents) 1963, Cities 1963, The Outriders: A Liberal View of Britain 1963, The Presence of Spain 1964, Oxford 1965, Pax Britannica: The Climax of an Empire 1968, The Great Port: A Passage through New York 1969, Places 1972, Heaven's Command: An Imperial Progress 1973, Farewell the Trumpets: An Imperial Retreat 1978; as Jan Morris: Conundrum 1974, Travels 1976, The Oxford Book of Oxford 1978, Destinations: Essays from 'Rolling Stone' 1980, The Venetian Empire: A Sea Voyage 1980, My Favourite Stories of Wales 1980, The Small Oxford Book of Wales, Wales The First Place, A Venetian Bestiary 1982, The Spectacle of Empire 1982, Stones of Empire: The Buildings of the Raj 1983, Journeys 1984, The Matter of Wales: Epic Views of a Small Country 1984, Among the Cities 1985, Last Letters from Hav: Notes from a Lost City 1985, Stones of Empire: The Buildings of the Raj 1986, Scotland, The Place of Visions 1986, Manhattan, '45 1987, Hong Kong: Xianggang 1988, Pleasures of a Tangled Life 1989, Ireland Your Only Place 1990, City to City 1990, O Canada 1992, Sydney 1992, Locations 1992, Travels with Virginia Woolf (ed.) 1993, A Machynlleth Triad 1994, Fisher's Face 1995, The Princeship of Wales 1995, The World of Venice 1995, 50 Years of Europe 1997, Hong Kong: Epilogue to an Empire 1997, Lincoln: A Foreigner's Quest 1999, Our First Leader 2000, A Writer's House in Wales 2001, Trieste and the Meaning of Nowhere 2001, A Writer's World: Travels 1950–2000 2003, Portmeirion (with others) 2006, Contact! A Book of Glimpses 2009, Hav 2011. *Address:* c/o AP Watt at United Agents LLP, 12–26 Lexington Street, London, W1F 0LE, England (office); Trefan Morys, Llanystumdwy, Gwynedd, LL52 0LP, Wales (home). *Telephone:* (20) 3214-0800 (office); (1766) 522222 (home). *Fax:* (20) 3214-0801 (office). *E-mail:* info@unitedagents.co.uk (office); janmorris1@ msn.com (home). *Website:* www.apwatt.co.uk (office).

MORRIS, Mark William; American choreographer and dancer; *Artistic Director, Mark Morris Dance Group;* b. 29 Aug. 1956, Seattle, Wash.; s. of William Morris and Maxine Crittenden Morris; Artistic Dir Mark Morris Dance Group 1980–, Founder and Artistic Dir Mark Morris Dance Center, Brooklyn, NY 2001–; Dir of Dance, Théâtre Royal de la Monnaie, Brussels 1988–91; Co-founder White Oak Dance Project (with Mikhail Baryshnikov q.v.) 1990; performed with various dance cos including Lar Lubovitch Dance Co., Hannah Kahn Dance Co., Laura Dean Dancers and Musicians, Eliot Feld Ballet, Koleda Balkan Dance Ensemble; cr. over 120 works for Mark Morris Dance Group, including Gloria 1981, Mythologies 1986, Falling Down Stairs 1987, L'Allegro, il Penseroso ed il Moderato 1988, Dido and Aeneas 1989, The Hard Nut 1991, Grand Duo 1993, Lucky Charms 1994, The Office 1994, I Don't Want to Love 1996, Peccadillos 2000, V 2001, All Fours 2004, Mozart Dances 2006, Festival Dance 2011; has cr. dances for many ballet cos, including eight for San Francisco Ballet, and for Paris Opera Ballet, American Ballet Theatre, Boston Ballet and others; cr. Platee (for Edinburgh Festival) 1996, King Arthur (for ENO) 2006, Orfeo ed Euridice (for Metropolitan Opera) 2007; numerous tours abroad including performance at Guangzhou Opera House, People's Repub. of China 2012; 11 hon. doctorates; New York Dance and Performance Award 1984, 1990, Guggenheim Fellowship 1986, MacArthur Foundation 'Genius' Award 1991, Leonard Bernstein Lifetime Achievement Award for the Elevation of Music in Society 2010. *Films:* WNET presents Mark Morris Dance Group in The Hard Nut, Dido and Aeneas (A Rhombus Media Production). *Television:* Great Performances presents Dance in America: Mark Morris 1986, South Bank Show (UK): Hidden Soul of Harmony 1990, Four Saints in Three Acts 2000. *Address:* Mark Morris Dance Group, 3 Lafayette Avenue, Brooklyn, NY 11217, USA (office). *Telephone:* (718) 624-8400 (office). *Fax:* (718) 624-8900 (office). *E-mail:* info@mmdg.org (office). *Website:* www.mmdg.org (office).

MORRIS, Michael G., MSc, LLB; American energy industry executive; b. 1946, Fremont, Ohio; m. Linda Morris; two s.; ed Detroit Coll. of Law, East Michigan Univ.; f. and fmr Pres. ANR Gathering Co.; fmr Pres. Colorado Interstate Gas; fmr Exec. Vice-Pres. ANR Pipeline Co.; fmr Pres. CMS Marketing, Services and

Trading; Pres. and CEO Consumers Energy –1997; Chair., Pres. and CEO Northeast Utilities System 1997–2003; Chair., Pres. and CEO American Electric Power 2004–11, mem. Bd of Dirs 2004–; Dir, St Francis Care Inc., Nuclear Electric Insurance Ltd, American Gas Asscn, Spinnaker Exploration, Flink Ink Corpn, Webster Financial Corpn, Cincinnati Bell; Second Vice-Chair. Edison Electrical Inst.; mem. US Dept of Energy Electricity Advisory Bd, Nat. Govs Asscn Task Force on Electricity Infrastructure, CT Gov.'s Council on Econ. Competitiveness and Tech.; fmr Chair. Connnecticut Business and Industry Asscn; fmr mem. Bd Detroit Coll. of Law, Inst. of Gas Tech., East Michigan Univ. Foundation, Olivet Coll. Leadership Advisory Council, Library of Michigan Foundation; mem. Michigan Bar Asscn; Trustee, Bushnell Overseers. *Address:* American Electric Power Company Inc., 28th Floor, 1 Riverside Plaza, Columbus, OH 43215-2373, USA (office). *Telephone:* (614) 716-1000 (office). *Fax:* (614) 223-1823 (office). *E-mail:* info@aep.com (office). *Website:* www.aep.com (office).

MORRIS, Michael Jeremy, MBE, MA; British performing arts producer; *Co-Director, Artangel;* b. 30 March 1958, London, England; s. of Lawrence Morris and Monica Morris; m. Sarah Culshaw 1991; one s. one d.; ed Oundle School, Keble Coll. Oxford and City Univ., London; Assoc. Dir of Theatre, Inst. of Contemporary Arts 1981–84, Dir of Performing Arts 1984–87; mem. Drama and Dance Panel, British Council 1984–90; Founding Dir Cultural Industry Ltd (presenting and producing contemporary theatre, music and dance) 1987–; Co.-Dir Artangel (commissioning outstanding artists to create new work) 1991–, Artangel Media 2000–; Dir first production and co-author of libretto of Michael Nyman's opera The Man Who Mistook His Wife for a Hat 1986; Dir first production and author of libretto of Mike Westbrook's opera Coming Through Slaughter 1994; has commissioned and produced projects by Robert Wilson, Michael Clark, William Forsythe, Brian Eno and Laurie Anderson, John Berger and Simon McBurney, amongst many others; Dir Cultural Industry Ltd. *Leisure interests:* world music, fine wine, foreign food, popular art. *Address:* Artangel, 31 Eyre Street Hill, London, EC1R 5EW, England (office). *Telephone:* (20) 7713-1400 (office). *Fax:* (20) 7713-1401 (office). *E-mail:* info@artangel.org.uk (office). *Website:* www.artangel.org.uk (office).

MORRIS, Sir Peter John, Kt, AC, MB, BS, PhD, FRCS, FMedSci, FRS; Australian surgeon and academic; *Chairman, British Heart Foundation;* b. 17 April 1934, Horsham, Vic.; s. of Stanley Henry Morris and Mary Lois (née Hennessy) Morris; m. Jocelyn Mary Gorman 1960; three s. two d.; ed Univ. of Melbourne; Resident Surgical Officer, St Vincent's Hosp. 1958–61; Surgical Registrar, Southampton Gen. Hosp., UK 1963–64; Clinical Assoc. and Fellow, Mass. Gen. Hosp., Boston, USA 1964–66; Asst Prof. of Surgery, Medical Coll., Richmond, Va, USA 1967; Dir Tissue Transplantation Labs, Univ. of Melbourne, Australia 1968–74, Reader in Surgery 1971–74; Consultant Surgeon, Lymphona Clinic, Cancer Inst., Melbourne 1969–74; Nuffield Prof. of Surgery, Univ. of Oxford, UK 1974–2002 (now Prof. Emer.), Dir Oxford Transplant Centre; Pres. The Transplantation Soc. 1984–86, European Surgical Asscn 1996–98, Int. Surgical Soc. 2001–; Vice-Chair. Clinical Medicine Bd, Univ. of Oxford 1982–84; Vice-Pres. Royal Coll. of Surgeons of England 2000–01, then Pres.; Chair. Council, Inst. of Health Sciences, Univ. of Oxford 2000–; Council mem. MRC, London 1983–87; Ed. Transplantation 1979–; Fellow, Balliol Coll., Univ. of Oxford 1974–; mem. UFC 1989–92; Gov. Health Foundation 1998–2003; Pres. Royal Coll. of Surgeons of England 2001–04, Medical Protection Soc.; currently Chair. British Heart Foundation, Dir Centre for Evidence in Transplantation; Hon. FRCSE, FACS 1986, FRACS 1996, FRCP, FRCPE; Hon. Fellow, American Coll. of Surgeons, American Surgical Asscn, Royal Australasian Coll. of Surgeons, Japan Surgical Soc., German Surgical Soc., Coll. of Physicians and Surgeons of Glasgow; Hon. Prof., Univ. of London; Hon. DSc (Hong Kong) 2000, (Imperial Coll.) 2003; Selwyn Smith Prize (Australia), Lister Medal (UK) 1998, Hamilton Fairley Medal, Royal Coll. of Physicians 2005; Medawar Prize, TTS 2006. *Publications:* Kidney Transplantation 1978 (revised sixth edn) 2008, Tissue Transplantation 1982, Transient Ischaemic Attacks 1982, Progress in Transplantation 1984, Oxford Textbook of Surgery (with R. Malt) 1993, (second edn with W. Wood) 2001. *Leisure interests:* golf, tennis, cricket. *Address:* Royal College of Surgeons, 35–43 Lincoln's Inn Fields, London, WC2A 3PE (office); 19 Lucerne Road, Oxford, OX2 7QB, England (home). *Telephone:* (20) 7869-6604 (office). *Fax:* (20) 7869-6644 (office). *E-mail:* ntalawila@rceng.ac.uk (office); pmorris@rcseng.ac.uk (office); peterj.morris@virgin.net (home). *Website:* www.transplantevidence.com (office).

MORRIS, Richard Graham Michael, CBE, MA, DPhil, FRS, FRSE, FMedSci; British neuroscientist and academic; *Royal Society/Wolfson Professor of Neuroscience, University of Edinburgh;* b. 27 June 1948, Worthing, Sussex, England; s. of Robert Morris and Edith Morris; m. Hilary Ann Lewis 1985 (divorced); two d.; partner Monica Muñoz-Lopez; one s.; ed Univs of Cambridge and Sussex; Lecturer in Psychology, Univ. of St Andrews 1977–86, MRC Research Fellow 1983–86; Reader, then Prof. of Neuroscience, Univ. of Edin. 1986–, Dir Centre for Neuroscience 1993–97, Chair. Dept of Neuroscience 1998, currently Dir Centre for Cognitive and Neural Systems, Royal Soc./Wolfson Prof. of Neuroscience 2006–; Sec. Experimental Psychology Soc. 1983–87; Chair. UK Brain Research Asscn 1990–94; mem. MRC Neuroscience Research Grants Cttee 1983–87, Neuroscience and Mental Health Bd 1993–97, Innovation Bd 1998–2000, MRC Strategy Group 2000–02; Forum Fellow, World Econ. Forum 2000; Life Sciences Co-ordinate OST Foresight Project on Cognitive Systems 2002–04; Pres. Fed. of European Neuroscience Socs 2006–08; Head, Neuroscience and Mental Health, The Wellcome Trust, London 2007–10; mem. various editorial bds, including Bd of Reviewing Eds, Science magazine 2007–; Decade of the Brain Lecturer 1998, Zotterman Lecturer 1999, Yngve Zotterman Prize, Karolinska Inst. 1999, Henry Dryerre Prize, Royal Soc. of Edin. 2000, BNA Outstanding Contrib. to Neuroscience 2002, EJN European Neuroscience Award 2004, Feldberg Prize 2006, Santiago Grisola Award 2007, Presidential Lecturer, Soc. for Neuroscience 2009, Ipsen Neuronal Plasticity Prize 2013. *Publications:* Parallel Distributed Processing (ed.) 1988, Neuroscience: Science of the Brain, 1994, 2003, Long-Term Potentiation (co-ed. with T. V. P. Bliss and G. L. Collingridge) 2004, The Hippocampus Book (co-author and ed.) 2007; more than 150 scientific papers on neural mechanisms of memory. *Leisure interest:* sailing. *Address:* Centre for Cognitive and Neural Systems, University of Edinburgh, 1 George Square, Edinburgh, EH8 9JZ, Scotland (office). *Telephone:* (131) 650-3520 (office); 7736-477190 (mobile) (office); (131) 441-5501 (home). *Fax:* (131) 651-1835 (office).

E-mail: r.g.m.morris@ed.ac.uk (office); ccns@ed.ac.uk (office). *Website:* www.ccns.sbms.mvm.ed.ac.uk/people/academic/morris.html (office).

MORRIS, Richard Keith, OBE, BPhil, MA, FSA; British writer, archaeologist and composer; *Director, Institute for Medieval Studies, University of Leeds;* b. 8 Oct. 1947, Birmingham; s. of John Richard Morris and Elsie Myra Wearne; m. Jane Whiteley 1972; two s. one d.; ed Denstone Coll., Staffs., Pembroke Coll., Oxford and Univ. of York; musician, writer 1971–; Research Asst, York Minster Archaeological Office 1972–75; Churches Officer, Council for British Archaeology 1975–77, Research Officer, 1978–88, Dir 1991–99; Hon. Lecturer, School of History, Univ. of Leeds 1986–88, Dir Inst. for Medieval Studies 2003–; Lecturer, Dept of Archaeology, Univ. of York 1988–91; Commr, English Heritage 1996–, Chair. Advisory Cttee 2003–; Chair. Ancient Monuments Advisory Cttee for England 1996–2001, Historic Settlements and Landscapes Cttee 2001–03, Bede's World 2001–; mem. Heritage Lottery Fund Expert Panel 2005–; Trustee, Nat. Coal Mining Museum for England 2003–08; Hon. Visiting Prof., Univ. of York 1995; Hon. Vice-Pres. Council for British Archaeology; Frend Medal, Soc. of Antiquaries 1992. *Opera:* Lord Flame (jtly). *Music:* Five Auden Songs. *Film:* Nothing but Names (screenplay). *Publications:* Cathedrals and Abbeys of England and Wales 1979, The Church in British Archaeology 1983, Churches in the Landscape 1989, Guy Gibson (jtly) 1994, Cheshire: The Biography of Leonard Cheshire, VC, OM 2000, The Triumph of Time 2008. *Leisure interests:* aviation history, natural history, 20th-century music and opera. *Address:* Institute for Medieval Studies, Parkinson Building, University of Leeds, Leeds, LS2 9JT (office); 13 Hollins Road, Harrogate, N Yorks., HG1 2JF, England (home). *Telephone:* (113) 343-3617 (office); (1423) 50429 (home). *Fax:* (113) 343-3616 (office). *E-mail:* r.k.morris@leeds.ac.uk (office); r.k.morris@dsl.pipex.com (home). *Website:* www.leeds.ac.uk/ims/about/staffdetails.html#morris (office).

MORRIS, Sarah, BA; American (b. British) artist and film maker; b. 1967, London; ed Jesus Coll., Cambridge, Brown Univ.; works held in numerous int. collections including Victoria and Albert Museum, Saatchi Gallery, Tate Modern, London, Palm Springs Art Museum, Musée d'Art Moderne de la Ville de Paris, Dallas Museum of Art, Deste Foundation, Athens, Museum of Modern Art, New York, and others; American Acad. Philip Morris Award/Berlin Prize Fellow 1999, Joan Mitchell Foundation Painting Award 2001. *Films:* Midtown (New York) 1998, AM/PM (Las Vegas) 2000, Capital (Washington, DC) 2001, Miami 2002, Los Angeles 2008, Beijing 2008. *Address:* c/o Friedrich Petzel Gallery, 537 West 22nd Street, New York, NY 10011, USA (office).

MORRIS, Warwick; British consultant on Asia and fmr diplomatist; b. 10 Aug. 1948; m. Pamela Morris, MBE; one s. two d.; joined FCO 1969, Information Dept 1969–71, Third Sec. (Information), Embassy in Paris 1972–74, full-time language training, Seoul 1975–76, Second Sec. (Political), Embassy in Seoul 1977–79, Pvt. Sec. to Deputy Perm. Under-Sec., FCO 1979–80, Personnel Operations Dept 1980–82, Head of Section, Hong Kong Dept 1982–84, First Sec. (Commercial), Embassy in Mexico City 1984–87, First Sec., Head of Chancery, Seoul 1988–91, Deputy Head, Far Eastern Dept, FCO 1992–93, Counsellor, later Head of Perm. Under-Sec.'s Dept 1993–94, Counsellor (Econ. and Commercial), New Delhi 1995–98; at Royal Coll. of Defence Studies, London 1999; Amb. to Viet Nam 2000–03, to Repub. of Korea 2003–08 (retd); Chair. Anglo-Korean Soc. (UK) 2011–; consultant on Korean and Vietnamese affairs; Chair. Locate in Kent 2012–; Vice-Chair. Vietnam-UK Network 2013–; Hon. PhD (Soonchunyang Univ.) 2006; Hon. Fellow, Robinson Coll., Univ. of Cambridge 2011. *Address:* Rosewood, Stonewall Park Road, Langton Green, Kent, TN3 0HD, England (home).

MORRIS OF HANDSWORTH, Baron (Life Peer), cr. 2006, of Handsworth in the County of West Midlands; **William (Bill) Morris,** FRSA, OJ; British trade union official (retd); b. 19 Oct. 1938, Jamaica; s. of William Morris and Una Morris; m. Minetta Morris 1957 (died 1990); two s.; ed Mizpah School, Manchester, Jamaica; Dist Officer, Transport & Gen. Workers' Union (TGWU), Nottingham 1973, Dist Sec. Northampton 1977, Nat. Sec. Passenger Services 1979–85, Deputy Gen. Sec. TGWU 1986–92, Gen. Sec. 1992–2003; mem. TUC Gen. Council 1988–2003; mem. Comm. for Racial Equality 1977–87, IBA Gen. Advisory Council 1981–86, ITF Exec. Bd 1986–2003, Prince of Wales Youth Business Trust 1987–90, BBC Gen. Advisory Council 1987–88, Employment Appeals Tribunal 1988–2008, Royal Comm. on Lords Reform 1999, Bd of Govs South Bank Univ. 1997, Comm. for Integrated Transport 1999–2005; Dir (non-exec.) Court of the Bank of England 1998–2006; Dir Unity Trust Bank 1994–2003; Chancellor Univ. of Tech., Jamaica 2000–10, Staffordshire Univ. 2004–11; Chair. Morris Enquiry 2003–04; mem. (Labour) House of Lords 2006–; Chair. Midland Heart Housing Asscn 2007–, Bd of Trustees Performance Birmingham Ltd 2008–; Vice-Chair. Jamaica Nat. Money Services 2007–; mem. Cricket Bd for England and Wales 2005–, Mergers and Take Over Panel 2005–; Adviser to Voice newspaper 2006–; Hon. Fellow, City & Guilds 1992, Royal Soc. of Arts; Dr hc (South Bank Univ.) 1994, (Open Univ.) 1995; Hon. DLitt (Westminster) 1998 and several other hon. degrees; Public Figure of the Year, Ethnic Multicultural Media Awards (EMMA) 2002. *Leisure interests:* walking, gardening, watching sports, jazz concerts. *Address:* House of Lords, Westminster, London, SW1A 0PW, England (office). *E-mail:* morrisw@parliament.uk (office). *Website:* www.parliament.uk/biographies/lords/lord-morris-of-handsworth/3796 (office).

MORRIS OF ABERAVON, Baron (life Peer), cr. 2001, of Aberavon in the County of West Glamorgan and of Ceredigion in the County of Dyfed; **John Morris,** KG, PC, QC, LLD; British politician and barrister; b. 5 Nov. 1931, Aberystwyth; s. of the late D. W. Morris and of Mary Olwen Ann Morris; m. Margaret M. Lewis JP 1959; three d.; ed Ardwyn, Aberystwyth, Univ. Coll. of Wales, Aberystwyth, Gonville and Caius Coll., Cambridge and Acad. of Int. Law, The Hague; commissioned Royal Welch Fusiliers and Welch Regt; called to Bar, Gray's Inn 1954, Bencher 1985; Labour MP for Aberavon 1959–2001; Parl. Sec. Ministry of Power 1964–66; Jt Parl. Sec. Ministry of Transport 1966–68; Minister of Defence Equipment 1968–70; Sec. of State for Wales 1974–79; a Recorder, Crown Court 1982–97; Legal Affairs and Shadow Attorney-Gen. 1983–97; Attorney-Gen. 1997–99; Chancellor Univ. of Glamorgan; fmr Deputy Gen. Sec. and Legal Adviser, Farmers' Union of Wales; mem. UK Del., Consultative Ass., Council of Europe and WEU 1963–64; mem. Cttee of Privileges 1994–97, Select Cttee on Implementation of the Nolan Report 1995–97; Chair. Nat. Pneumoconiosis Jt Cttee 1964–66, Nat. Road Safety Advisory Council 1967–68, Jt Review of Finances and Man. British Railways 1966–67; mem. N Atlantic Ass. 1970–74; HM Lord Lt for Dyfed; Pres. London Welsh Asscn; Hon. Fellow, Univ. Coll. of Wales, Aberystwyth and Swansea, Trinity Coll., Carmarthen, Gonville and Caius Coll. Cambridge; Hon. LLD (Wales). *Address:* House of Lords, London, SW1A 0PW, England (office). *Telephone:* (20) 7219-3470 (office).

MORRISON, Denise M., BS; American business executive; *President and CEO, Campbell Soup Company;* ed Boston Coll.; began career in sales at Procter & Gamble, Boston, Mass; later joined Pepsi-Cola in Trade and Business Devt; spent most of 1980s at Nestlé USA, held sr marketing and sales positions, including Business Dir for Confections Marketing, Nat. Sales Man. Frozen/Chilled, and Vice-Pres. of Marketing and Sales for Nestlé Ice Cream Co.; moved to Nabisco Inc. 1995, served as Sr Vice-Pres. and led Nabisco Food Co.'s sales org. and was Gen. Man. for the Down the Street div.; Exec. Vice-Pres. and Gen. Man. Kraft Foods' Snacks and Confections divs –2003; Pres. Global Sales and Chief Customer Officer, Campbell Soup Co. 2003–05, Pres. Campbell USA 2005–07, Sr Vice-Pres. and Pres. North America Soup, Sauces and Beverages 2007–10, Exec. Vice-Pres., mem. Bd of Dirs and COO 2010–11, Pres. and CEO Campbell Soup Co. 2011–; fmr Dir The Goodyear Tire & Rubber Co., Ballard Power Systems Inc.; Founding mem. and mem. Bd Healthy Weight Commitment Foundation; mem. GMA Industry Affairs Council, NJ Econ. Advisory Council for the Gov.; mem. Bd Students In Free Enterprise; fmr Chair. Catalyst's Advisory Bd; fmr Pres. NJ Women's Forum; fmr mem. Bd Food Industry Crusade Against Hunger and Leadership California; New York YWCA Acad. of Women Achievers 2001, New Jersey Woman of Influence, NJBIZ magazine 2003, Althea Gibson Beacon Award for Business Leadership 2003, Exec. of the Year, Snack Food & Bakery magazine 2003, Salute to Policy Makers Award, Exec. Women of New Jersey 2007, Garden State Woman of the Year for Corpns, Garden State Women magazine 2007, Aiming High Award, Legal Momentum 2007, One of the Top 50 Women to Watch, Wall Street Journal 2007, One of the Top 50 Women in Business in the State of NJ, NJBIZ magazine 2008, Top Woman in Grocery, Progressive Grocer magazine 2008, 2009, 2010, Trail-blazer Award, Philadelphia Magazine 2010, One of the 50 Most Influential Irish Women, Irish Voice 2010, Woman of Distinction, American Heart Asscn of NJ 2010, ranked by Forbes magazine amongst The World's 100 Most Powerful Women (80th) 2011, (81st) 2013, ranked by Fortune magazine amongst the 50 Most Powerful Women in Business in the US (21st) 2011, (20th) 2012. *Address:* Campbell Soup Company, 1 Campbell Place, Camden, NJ 08103-1701, USA (office). *Telephone:* (856) 342-4800 (office). *Fax:* (856) 342-3878 (office). *E-mail:* info@campbellsoupcompany.com (office). *Website:* www.campbellsoupcompany .com (office).

MORRISON, Graham, MA, DipArch, RIBA; British architect; *Partner, Allies and Morrison;* b. 2 Feb. 1951, Kilmarnock, Scotland; s. of Robert Morrison and Robina S. Morrison; divorced; one s. one d.; ed Brighton Coll., Jesus Coll., Cambridge; in partnership with Bob Allies, formed Allies and Morrison Architects 1983, Partner 1983–; mem. RIBA Council 1992–95; Royal Fine Arts Commr 1998–99; mem. Architecture Advisory Cttee, Arts Council 1996–97, Design Review Cttee, Comm. on Architecture and the Built Environment (CABE) 2000–04, London Advisory Cttee of English Heritage 2001–13, English Heritage's CABE and Urban Panel 2009–12, English Heritage Advisory Cttee 2013–; Commr with English Heritage 2011–; External Examiner, Univ. of Cambridge 1994–97, Univ. of Portsmouth 2003–05, Bartlett School of Architecture 2010–11; Special Prof. of Architecture, Univ. of Nottingham 2004–05; 32 RIBA Awards and 12 Civic Trust Awards. *Projects include:* restoration of the Royal Festival Hall, BBC Media Village at White City, master plans for King's Cross and the London 2012 Olympics and legacy. *Exhibitions include:* New British Architecture, Japan 1994, Allies and Morrison Retrospective, USA Schools of Architecture 1996–98; also exhbns in Helsinki, Delft, Strasbourg 1999. *Publications:* Allies and Morrison 1996, Allies and Morrison Vol. 1 2012. *Address:* Allies and Morrison, 85 Southwark Street, London, SE1 0HX, England (office). *Telephone:* (20) 7921-0100 (office). *Fax:* (20) 7921-0101 (office). *E-mail:* gmorrison@alliesandmorrison.com (office); gm@ gmorrison.plus.com (home). *Website:* www.alliesandmorrison.com (office).

MORRISON, James Douglas, AO, PhD, DSc, FAA, FRSE; Australian mass spectrometrist; *Foundation Professor Emeritus of Chemistry, La Trobe University;* b. 9 Nov. 1924, Glasgow, Scotland; s. of James K. Morrison and Rose Ann Wheeler; m. Christine B. Mayer 1947; three s.; ed Lenzie Acad., Scotland and Univ. of Glasgow; Instructor, Dept of Chem., Univ. of Glasgow 1946–48; Research Officer, CSIRO 1949, Chief Research Officer 1965–67; Foundation Prof. of Chem., La Trobe Univ. 1967–90, Prof. Emer. 1990–; Resident Head, Chisholm Coll. 1972–77; Adjunct Prof., Univ. of Utah 1975–, Univ. of Delaware 1987–; Commonwealth Fund Fellow, Chicago Univ. 1956–57; Visiting Prof., Princeton Univ. 1964, Univ. of Utah 1971; mem. Council, Royal Soc. of Victoria, Pres. 1975–76; mem. Council, Australian Acad. of Science, Vice-Pres. 1986–87; Fellow, Royal Australian Chemical Inst.; Rennie and Smith Medals, Royal Australian Chemical Inst., ANZSMS Medal 2009. *Publications:* articles in scientific journals. *Leisure interests:* fossil hunting, Byzantine studies, travel. *Address:* 40 Central Avenue, Mooroolbark, Vic. 3138, Australia. *Telephone:* (3) 9725-7525. *E-mail:* J.D .Morrison@latrobe.edu.au (office).

MORRISON, Sir Kenneth Duncan, Kt, CBE; British retail industry executive (retd); joined Wm Morrison Supermarkets PLC 1952, Chair. and Man. Dir 1956–97, Exec. Chair. 1997–2008 (retd). *Address:* c/o Wm Morrison Supermarkets PLC, Hilmore House, Thornton Road, Bradford, West Yorkshire BD8 9AX, England (office).

MORRISON, Robert S., BA, MBA; American business executive; *Operating Partner, Z Capital Management LLC;* b. 4 April 1942, Chicago, Ill.; s. of Forrest John Morrison and Grayce Morrison Scheck Hopkins; m. Susan E. Brennan 1988; five c.; ed Coll. of the Holy Cross, Univ. of Pennsylvania; served in the United States Marine Corps from 1963 to 1967, rising to the rank of captain; Asst Brand Man. Procter & Gamble 1969–72, Brand Man. 1972–75, Assoc. Advertising Man. 1975–81, Div. Man. 1981–83; Vice-Pres. Marketing Kraft Inc. 1983–85, Group Vice-Pres., Pres. Refrigerated Products Group 1985–89, Pres. Kraft Gen. Foods Canada 1989–91, Gen. Foods USA 1991–95, Chair. and CEO Kraft Foods Inc. 1994–97; Chair., CEO and Pres. Quaker Oats Co. 1997–2001; Vice-Chair. Pepsi Co. Inc. 2001–03; currently Operating Partner, Z Capital Management LLC; mem. Bd of Dirs Aon Corpn, Illinois Tool Works Inc., 3M Co. (Interim Chair. and CEO

June–Dec. 2005), Mrs. Fields Famous Brands, Chicago Club, Lyric Opera, Rush-Presbyterian-St. Luke's Medical Center, Museum of Science and Industry (Chair.); Trustee, Holy Cross Coll.; Decorated Silver Star, Purple Heart, Semper Fidelis Award, Marine Corps Scholarship Foundation 1997. *Leisure interests:* golf, tennis, skiing. *Address:* Z Capital Management LLC, Two Conway Park, 150 Field Drive, Suite 300, Lake Forest, IL 60045, USA (office). *Website:* www.zcap.net (office).

MORRISON, Toni, MA; American novelist and academic; *Goheen Professor in the Humanities Emerita, Princeton University;* b. (Chloe Anthony Wofford), 18 Feb. 1931, Lorain, Ohio; d. of George Wofford and Ella Ramah (Willis) Wofford; m. Harold Morrison 1958 (divorced 1964); two c.; ed Lorain High School, Howard Univ., Cornell Univ.; taught English and Humanities, Tex. Southern Univ. 1955–57, Howard Univ. 1957–64; Ed., then Sr Ed. Random House, New York 1965–85; Assoc. Prof. of English, State Univ. of New York 1971–72, Schweitzer Prof. of the Humanities 1984–89; Robert F. Goheen Prof. of the Humanities, Princeton Univ. 1989–, now Emer.; Visiting Lecturer Yale Univ. 1976–77, Bard Coll. 1986–88; Clark Lecturer Trinity Cambridge 1990; Massey Lecturer Harvard Univ. 1990; mem. Council, Authors Guild, American Acad. of Arts and Sciences, American Acad. of Arts and Letters, Authors League of America, Nat. Council on the Arts; Commdr Ordre des Arts et des Lettres; Ohioana Book Award 1975, American Acad. and Inst. of Arts and Letters Award 1977, Nat. Book Critics Circle Awards 1977, 1997, NY State Gov.'s Arts Award 1987, Nobel Prize for Literature 1993, Nat. Book Foundation Medal 1995, Nat. Humanities Medal 2000, Presidential Medal of Freedom 2012. *Publications:* The Bluest Eye 1970, Sula 1974, The Black Book (ed) 1974, Song of Solomon 1977, Tar Baby 1983, Dreaming Emmett (play) 1986, Beloved 1987 (Pulitzer Prize and Robert F. Kennedy Book Award 1988), Jazz 1992, Playing in the Dark: Whiteness and the Literary Imagination (lectures) 1992, Race-ing Justice, En-gendering Power (ed, essays) 1992, Honey and Rue (song cycle) 1993, Nobel Prize Speech 1994, Birth of a Nation'hood: Gaze, Script and Spectacle in the O. J. Simpson Trial 1997, Paradise 1998, Collected Essays of James Baldwin (ed) 1998, Love 2003, A Mercy 2008, Home 2011; co-author, for children: The Big Box (poems) 1999, The Book of Mean People 2002, The Ant or the Grasshopper, The Lion or the Mouse 2003, Beloved 2004, Sula 2004, Peeny Butter Fudge 2009, Little Cloud and Lady Wind 2010, Home 2012. *Address:* Program in Creative Writing, Princeton University, Room 305, 185 Nassau Street, Princeton, NJ 08544, USA (office). *Telephone:* (609) 258-1071 (office). *Fax:* (609) 258-1454 (office). *Website:* www.princeton.edu (office).

MORRISON, Van, OBE; British singer, songwriter and musician; b. (George Ivan Morrison), 31 Aug. 1945, Belfast, Northern Ireland; one d.; left school aged 15; joined The Monarchs, playing in Germany; founder and lead singer, Them 1964–67; solo artist 1967–; BRIT Award for Outstanding Contribution to British Music 1994, Q Award for Best Songwriter 1995, Grammy Award for Best Pop Collaboration with Vocals 1995, BMI Icon Award 2004, Ronnie Scott Award for Int. Male Singer 2007. *Recordings include:* albums: Blowin' Your Mind 1967, Astral Weeks 1968, Moondance 1970, His Band and Street Choir 1970, Tupelo Honey 1971, Saint Dominic's Preview 1972, Hardnose the Highway 1973, It's Too Late To Stop Now 1974, Veedon Fleece 1974, This Is Where I Came In 1977, A Period of Transition 1977, Wavelength 1978, Into the Music 1979, Common One 1980, Beautiful Vision 1982, Inarticulate Speech of the Heart 1983, Live At The Royal Opera House, Belfast 1984, A Sense of Wonder 1984, No Guru, No Method, No Teacher 1986, Poetics Champion Compose 1987, Irish Heartbeat 1988, Avalon Sunset 1989, Enlightenment 1990, Bang Masters 1990, Hymns to the Silence 1991, The Best of Van Morrison 1993, Too Long in Exile 1993, A Night in San Francisco 1994, Days Like This 1995, Songs of the Mose Allison: Tell Me Something 1996, The Healing Game 1997, Brown Eyed Girl 1998, The Masters 1999, Super Hits 1999, Back On Top 1999, The Skiffle Sessions: Live in Belfast 1998 2000, You Win Again 2000, Down The Road 2002, What's Wrong With This Picture? 2003, Magic Time 2005, Pay the Devil 2006, Keep it Simple 2008, Born to Sing: No Plan B 2012. *Address:* c/o Polydor Ltd, Black Lion House, 72–80 Black Lion Lane, Hammer-smith, London, W6 9BE, England. *Website:* www.vanmorrison.co.uk.

MORRITT, Rt Hon. Sir (Robert) Andrew, Kt, PC, CVO, QC; British fmr judge; *Arbitrator, One Essex Court;* b. 5 Feb. 1938, London; s. of Robert Augustus Morritt and Margaret Mary Morritt (née Tyldesley Jones); m. Sarah Simonetta Merton 1962; two s.; ed Eton Coll., Magdalene Coll., Cambridge; 2nd Lt Scots Guards 1956–58; called to Bar, Lincoln's Inn 1962, QC 1977, Bencher 1984, Treas. 2005; Jr Counsel to Sec. of State for Trade in Chancery Matters 1970–77, to Attorney-Gen. in Charity Matters 1972–77; Attorney-Gen. to HRH The Prince of Wales 1978–88; a Judge of High Court of Justice, Chancery Div. 1988–94; a Lord Justice of Appeal 1994–2000; Vice-Chancellor, Co. Palatine of Lancaster 1991–94; Chancellor of The High Court 2000–13 (retd); currently Arbitrator One Essex Court; Pres. Council of the Inns of Court 1997–2000; mem. Gen. Council of Bar 1969–73, Advisory Cttee on Legal Educ. 1972–76, Top Salaries Review Body 1982–87. *Leisure interests:* fishing, shooting. *Address:* One Essex Court, Temple, London, EC4Y 9AR, England (office). *Telephone:* (20) 7583-2000 (office). *Fax:* (20) 7583-0118 (office). *Website:* www.oeclaw.co.uk (office).

MORSCHAKOVA, Tamara Georgyevna, DJurSc; Russian judge; b. 28 March 1938, Moscow; m.; one d.; ed Moscow State Univ.; jr researcher, Inst. of State and Law, USSR Acad. of Sciences 1958–71; Sr Researcher, Chief, then Leading Researcher, All-Union Research Inst. of Soviet Construction and Law 1971–91; mem. Scientific-Consultative Council, Supreme Court of Russian Fed. 1985; Prof., Moscow State Juridical Acad. 1987–; Justice, Constitutional Court of Russian Fed. 1991–95, Deputy Chair. 1995–2002, Councillor 2002; Head of Chair, State Univ. Higher School of Economics 2001–; mem. Independent Legal Expert Council, Independent Human Rights Council 2012–; Honoured Jurist of Russian Fed.; Honoured Scientist of Russian Fed. *Publications:* books include Efficiency of Justice 1975, Reform of Justice 1990, Commentary to Legislation on Judiciary 2003, Criminal Procedure Law 2003. *Address:* Independent Human Rights Council, Moscow, Pokrovsky Boulevard 4/17, p. 1, office D, Russia (office). *Telephone:* (915) 437-64-87 (office). *E-mail:* info@nspch.ru (office). *Website:* nspch .ru/en (office).

MORSCHEL, John P.; Australian business executive; *Chairman, Australia and New Zealand Banking Group Ltd (ANZ);* ed Diploma in Quantity Surveying; Chair. Leighton Holdings Ltd 2001–04, Rinker Group Ltd 2003–07; mem. Bd of Dirs CSR Ltd 1996–2003, Chair. 2001–03; Ind. Dir (non-exec.) Australia and New

Zealand Banking Group Ltd (ANZ) 2004–, Chair. 2010–, Chair. Governance Cttee and ex-officio mem. all other Bd Cttees; mem. Bd of Dirs Lend Lease Corpn Ltd 1983–95, Westpac Banking Corpn 1993–2001, Rio Tinto Plc 1998–2005, Rio Tinto Ltd 1998–2005, Tenix Pty Ltd 1998–2008, Gifford Communications Pty Ltd 2000–, Capitaland Ltd 2010–, Singapore Telecommunications Ltd 2001–10, Tenix Group Pty Ltd 2008–; Fellow, Australian Inst. of Co. Dirs. *Address:* ANZ Centre, Level 9, 833 Collins Street, Docklands, Vic. 3008, Australia (office). *Telephone:* (3) 9683-9999 (office). *Fax:* (3) 9273-4875 (office). *E-mail:* media.relations@anz.com (office). *Website:* www.anz.com.au (office).

MORSE, Sir (Christopher) Jeremy, Kt, KCMG; British banker; b. 10 Dec. 1928, London; s. of the late Francis J. Morse and Kinbarra Morse (née Armfield-Marrow); m. Belinda M. Mills 1955; three s. one d.; ed Winchester Coll. and New Coll., Oxford; fmrly with Glyn, Mills & Co., Dir 1964; Dir, Legal and Gen. Assurance Soc. Ltd 1963–64, 1975–87; Exec. Dir, Bank of England 1965–72, Dir (non-exec.) 1993–97; Alt. Gov., IMF 1966–72; Chair. of Deputies of 'Cttee of Twenty', IMF 1972–74; Deputy Chair., Lloyds Bank Ltd 1975–77, Chair. 1977–93; Chair., Lloyds Merchant Bank Holdings 1985–88; Dir (non-exec.) ICI 1981–93, Zeneca 1993–99; Chair. Cttee of London Clearing Bankers 1980–82, City Communications Centre 1985–87; mem. Council, Lloyd's 1987–98; mem. NEDC 1977–81; Pres., Inst. Int. d'Études Bancaires 1982–83, Int. Monetary Conf. 1985–86, Banking Fed. of EC 1988–90, Chartered Inst. of Bankers 1992–93; Vice-Pres. Business in the Community 1986–98; Chair. City Arts Trust 1977–79, Per Jacobsson Foundation 1987–99, Governing Bodies Asscn 1994–99; Chancellor, Bristol Univ. 1988–2003; Pres. Classical Asscn 1989–90; Fellow, All Souls Coll., Oxford 1953–68, 1983–, Sub-Warden 2004–06; Chair. Trustees, Beit Memorial Fellowships for Medical Research 1976–2003; Fellow, Winchester Coll. 1966–83, Warden 1987–97; Hon. Life mem. British Chess Fed. 1988–, Hon. Master of Chess Composition, FIDE 2006–; Hon. DLitt (City) 1977, Hon. DSc (Aston) 1984, Hon. LLD (Bristol) 1989. *Publication:* Chess Problems: Tasks and Records 1995. *Leisure interests:* poetry, golf, problems and puzzles, coarse gardening. *Address:* 102A Drayton Gardens, London, SW10 9RJ, England (home). *Telephone:* (20) 7370-2265 (home).

MORTADA, Hani; Syrian government official, academic and paediatrician; *Minister of Higher Education;* b. 1939, Damascus; m.; three c.; ed Damascus Univ.; Head Paediatrics Dept, Faculty of Medicine, Damascus Univ. 1987–92, Dean Faculty of Medicine 1991–2000, Pres. Damascus Univ. 2000–03; Minister of Higher Educ. 2003–. *Address:* Ministry of Higher Education, ave Kasem Amin, ar-Rawda, Damascus, Syria (office). *Telephone:* (11) 2129870 (office). *Fax:* (11) 3327719 (office). *E-mail:* mhe@scs-net.org (office). *Website:* www.moufadaleh.org (office).

MORTAZA, Mashrafe Bin; Bangladeshi professional cricketer; *Captain, Bangladesh National Cricket Team;* b. 5 Oct. 1983, Norail Dist, Jessore; m. Sumona Haque Shumi 2008; ed Victoria Coll.; right-arm fast-medium pace bowler; right-handed lower-middle order batsman; plays for Bangladesh 2001– (Vice-Capt. 2007–09, Capt. Test side 2009, ODI side 2009, 2010), Asia XI, Khulna Div. 2002–, Kolkata Knight Riders 2009, Dhaka Gladiators 2012–; First-class debut: 2001/02; Test debut: Bangladesh v Zimbabwe, Dhaka 8–12 Nov. 2001; One-Day Int. (ODI) debut: Bangladesh v Zimbabwe, Chittagong (MAA) 23 Nov. 2001; T20I debut: Bangladesh v Zimbabwe, Khulna 28 Nov. 2006; has played in 36 Tests, taken 78 wickets and scored 797 runs (3 half-centuries), highest score 79, average 12.85, best bowling (innings) 4/60, (match) 5/88; ODIs: 128 matches, took 162 wickets and scored 1,220 runs, highest score 51 (not out), average 15.25, best bowling (innings) 6/26, (match) 6/26; T20Is: 20 matches, took 19 wickete and scored 196 runs, highest score 36, average 16.33, best bowling (innings) 4/19, (match) 4/19. *Leisure interest:* motorcycling. *Address:* c/o Bangladesh Cricket Board, Sher-e-Bangla National Cricket Stadium, Mirpur, Dhaka 1216, Bangladesh. *E-mail:* pd@tigercricket.com. *Website:* www.tigercricket.com.

MORTELL, Michael Philip, MSc, MS, PhD; Irish mathematician and university administrator; b. 9 Feb. 1941, Cork; m. Patricia Yule 1967; two d.; ed Charleville Christian Bros School, Univ. Coll., Cork and California Inst. of Tech., USA; Asst Prof. and Assoc. Prof., Center for Application of Math., Lehigh Univ., USA 1967–72; Lecturer in Math. and Physics, Univ. Coll. Cork 1972–89, Registrar 1979–89, Pres. 1989–99, Prof. Applied Math. 1999–2006; Visiting Prof., Univ. of British Columbia, Canada 1976–77, Univ. of Queensland, Australia 1979; Visiting Assoc., California Inst. of Tech. and New York Univ. 1999–2000; Foundation Fellow, Univ. of Auckland, NZ 2003; Vice-Chancellor Nat. Univ. of Ireland; Chair. Conf. of Heads of Irish Univs; Hon. LLD (Univ. of Dublin, Queen's Univ. Belfast, Limerick Univ.), Hon. DSc (Lehigh Univ.). *Publications:* some 50 papers on nonlinear waves and perturbation methods. *Leisure interests:* reading, art, gardening, sport. *Address:* Department of Applied Mathematics, University College, Cork, Ireland (office). *Telephone:* (21) 4205827 (office); (21) 0857543219 (home). *Fax:* (21) 4270813 (office). *E-mail:* m.mortell@ucc.ie (office). *Website:* euclid .ucc.ie (office).

MORTENSEN, Viggo Peter, Jr, BA; American/Danish actor, poet, photographer, painter and jazz musician; b. 20 Oct. 1958, New York City; s. of Viggo P. Mortensen (Danish) and Grace Mortensen (American); m. Exene Cervenka 1987 (divorced 1998); one s.; ed St Lawrence Univ., Canton, NY; spent early childhood in Manhattan, family travelled widely and spent several years living in Venezuela, Argentina and Denmark (where he worked as a truck driver); worked as trans. for Swedish ice hockey team during Winter Olympics, Lake Placid 1980; began acting in New York, studying with Warren Robertson; appeared in several plays and movies, eventually moved to Los Angeles; Owner Perceval Press (publishing co.). *Stage appearances:* Tybalt in Romeo and Juliet, Indiana Repertory Theatre, Indianapolis 1985–86, Nazi capt. in Bent, Coast Playhouse, West Hollywood, Calif. 1987, Live at Beyond Baroque, Beyond Baroque, Venice, Calif. 1999, Beyond Baroque Live 2, Beyond Baroque 2004. *Films:* Witness 1985, Salvation! 1987, Prison 1988, Fresh Horses 1988, The Reflecting Skin 1990, Tripwire 1990, Leatherface: Texas Chainsaw Massacre III 1990, Young Guns II 1990, The Indian Runner 1991, Boiling Point 1993, Deception 1993, Carlito's Way 1993, The Young Americans 1993, American Yakuza 1993, The Crew 1994, Floundering 1994, Ewangelia wedlug Harry'ego 1994, Gimlet 1995, Crimson Tide 1995, The Passion of Darkly Noon 1995, Black Velvet Pantsuit 1995, The Prophecy 1995, The Portrait of a Lady 1996, Albino Alligator 1996, Daylight 1996, G.I. Jane 1997, La Pistola de

mi hermano 1997, A Perfect Murder 1998, Psycho 1998, A Walk on the Moon 1999, 28 Days 2000, The Lord of the Rings: The Fellowship of the Ring 2001, The Lord of the Rings: The Two Towers 2002, The Lord of the Rings: The Return of the King 2003, Hidalgo 2004, A History of Violence 2005, Alatriste 2006, Eastern Promises (British Independent Film Award for Best Actor, Sant Jordi Award for Best Foreign Actor, Satellite Award for Best Actor, Toronto Film Critics Asscn Award for Best Actor, Vancouver Film Critics Circle Award for Best Actor) 2007, Appaloosa 2008, Good 2008, The Road 2009. *Television:* George Washington (miniseries) 1984, Search for Tomorrow (series) 1985, Once in a Blue Moon 1990, Vanishing Point 1997. *Achievements:* painted the large murals in his artist's studio in film A Perfect Murder 1998. *Albums:* 1991 (poetry) 1991, Don't Tell Me What to Do (music and poetry) 1994, One Less Thing to Worry About (music and poetry; with others) 1997, Live at Beyond Baroque (with others) 1999, One Man's Meat 1999, The Other Parade (music and poetry; with others) 1999, Pandemonium-fromamerica (with Buckethead) 2003, Beyond Baroque Live 2 (with others) 2004, Please Tomorrow (with Buckethead) 2004, This That and the Other (with Buckethead) 2004, Intelligence Failure (with Buckethead) 2005. *Publications:* Ten Last Night (poetry) 1993, Recent Forgeries (also illustrator, with accompanying CD) 1998, Coincidence of Memory (also illustrator) 2002, Sign Language (also photographer) 2002, Un hueco en el sol 2003; audiobooks: Myth: Dreams of the World 1996, The New Yorker Out Loud (contrib.) 1998; non-fiction: The Horse Is Good (also photographer) 2004, Twilight of Empire: Responses to Occupation (co-author) 2004, Strange Familiar: The Work of Georg Gudni (co-author) 2005; photography: Hole in the Sun 2002, 45301 2003, Miyelo (with Mike Davis, James Mooney, and Sonny Richards) 2004, Mo Te Upoko-o-te-ika/For Wellington 2004, Linger 2005, I Forget You For Ever 2006, Skovbo 2008, Sådanset 2008, Winter Songs 2010. *Leisure interests:* horse riding, San Lorenzo football club (Buenos Aires), New York Mets professional baseball team, Montréal Canadiens professional ice hockey team. *Address:* c/o Jenny Rawlings, Creative Artists Agency, 9830 Wilshire Blvd, Beverly Hills, CA 90212-1825, USA (office). *Telephone:* (310) 288-4545 (office). *Fax:* (310) 288-4800 (office). *Website:* www.caa.com (office).

MORTIER, Roland F. J., DPhil; Belgian academic; *Professor Emeritus, Université Libre de Bruxelles;* b. 21 Dec. 1920, Ghent; s. of the late Arthur Mortier and Berthe Baudson; m. Loyse Triffaux 1948; one s.; ed Antwerp Atheneum, Univ. Libre de Bruxelles and Univ. of Ghent; Prof., Univ. Libre de Bruxelles 1955–85, Prof. Emer. 1990–; Visiting Prof., Univs of Toronto, Stanford, Yale, Paris, Cologne, Jerusalem, London, Cleveland, Maryland, Duisburg, Pisa; Vice-Pres. Inst. des Hautes Etudes de Belgique; Past Pres. Soc. Diderot, FCLA, ISECS; mem. Acad. Royale de Langue et de Littérature Françaises, Belgium, Inst de France 1993; Foreign mem. Hungarian Acad. of Sciences; Corresp. Fellow, British Acad., Academia Europaea; other professional appointments and affiliations; Hon. mem. of the Acad. of Japan 2003; Chevalier, Légion d'honneur 2001; Dr hc (Montpellier, Göttingen, Jerusalem); Prix Francqui 1965, Prix Montaigne 1983, Prix Counson 1985, Prix de l'Union rationaliste de France 1993, Giltsilver Medal of the Acad. Française 2001, Grand Prix de la Francophonie de l'Acad. Française 2006. *Publications:* Diderot en Allemagne 1954, Clartés et Ombres du Siècle des Lumières 1969, Le Tableau littéraire de la France au XVIIIe Siècle 1972, La Poétique des Ruines en France 1974, L'Originalité, une nouvelle catégorie esthétique 1982, Le coeur et la raison 1990, Anacharsis Cloots, ou l'Utopie Foudroyée 1995, Les combats des lumières 2000, Le prince d'Albanie 2000; critical edns of Voltaire and Diderot, of Prince de Ligne 2001, Le 18e siècle français au quotidien 2002, Selected Works of the Prince de Ligne (3 vols) 2006. *Leisure interests:* reading, walking. *Address:* 10 avenue Général de Longueville, BP 12, 1150 Brussels, Belgium (home). *Telephone:* (2) 772-01-94 (home). *Fax:* (2) 772-01-94 (home).

MORTON, Donald Charles, PhD, FAA; Canadian astronomer; *Researcher Emeritus, National Research Council of Canada;* b. 12 June 1933; s. of Charles O. Morton and Irene M. Wightman; m. Winifred Austin 1970; one s. one d.; ed Univ. of Toronto, Princeton Univ., USA; astronomer, US Naval Research Lab. 1959–61; from Research Assoc. to Sr Research Astronomer (with rank of Prof.), Princeton Univ. 1961–76; Dir Anglo-Australian Observatory (Epping and Coonabarabran, NSW) 1976–86; Dir-Gen. Herzberg Inst. of Astrophysics, Nat. Research Council of Canada 1986–2000, Researcher Emer. 2001–; mem. Int. Astronomical Union, Royal Astronomical Soc. (Assoc. 1980), Astronomical Soc. of Australia (Pres. 1981–83, Hon. mem. 1986), Canadian Astronomical Soc., Canadian Asscn of Physicists; Fellow, Australian Acad. of Science 1984–. *Publications:* research papers in professional journals. *Leisure interests:* mountaineering, running. *Address:* National Research Council of Canada, 5071 West Saanich Road, Victoria, BC V9E 2E7, Canada (office). *Fax:* (250) 363-0045 (office). *E-mail:* don.morton@nrc -cnrc.gc.ca (office).

MOSA, Markus; German business executive; *Chairman of the Management Board and CEO, Edeka Zentrale AG & Co. KG;* b. 1967, Brühl bei Köln; m.; two d.; ed Univ. of Cologne; joined Spar Handels AG 1994, Schenefeld 1994, held several positions –1999, joined Netto Marken-Discount 1999, Man. Dir Netto Marken-Discount AG & Co. KG (fmrly Michael Schels & Sohn GmbH & Co. oHG) 2001–07, fmr Spokesman of Exec. Bd, Edeka AG (acquired Netto), Hamburg, Chief Financial Officer Edeka Zentrale AG & Co. KG –2008, Chair. Man. Bd and CEO 2008–. *Address:* Edeka Zentrale AG & Co. KG, New York Ring 6, 22297 Hamburg, Germany (office). *Telephone:* (40) 63-77-0 (office). *Fax:* (40) 63-77-22-31 (office). *E-mail:* info@edeka.de (office). *Website:* www.edeka.de (office).

MOSBAKK, Kurt; Norwegian politician; b. 21 Nov. 1934, Orkdal; s. of Henrik Mosbakk and Jenny Mosbakk; m. Grete Tidemandsen 1975; two s. one d.; ed Norwegian Coll. Econs and Business Admin; Pvt. Sec. to Minister of Defence 1964–65; Minister of Trade and Shipping 1986–88; County Exec. of Østford 1988–; Deputy Chair. Norwegian Defence Comm. 1990–92; fmr Deputy Mayor Lørenskog; Chair. Akershus Co. Labour Party 1969–74; Chief Co. Exec. Finnmark Co. 1976; Chair. Bd Norwegian State Housing Bank 1978–86; Chair. Norwegian Tourist Bd 1990. *Leisure interest:* literature. *Address:* c/o NORTRA, Drammensvn 40, PO Box 2893 Solli, 0230 Oslo, Norway.

MOSCA, Bertrand; French television executive; *Director, France 2;* began as public relations officer at Centre Georges Pompidou 1977; began career as journalist for Première 1987, for C'est pas juste 1988; held several asst positions within France Télévisions group, Dir Youth Programmes for France 3, responsible for buying fiction 1996, Program Dir, France 3 2000–05, cr. Plus belle la vie drama series, Exec. Head of Innovation, Diversity and New Cultures Feb.–Sept. 2011, other programmes include C'est mon choix and les Minikeums; Dir France 2 2011–. *Film:* Manège (short) 1986. *Television:* Les histoires du Père Castor (series) (unit programmer) 1993, Molly (film) (exec. producer) 1999. *Address:* France 2, Relations Téléspectateurs, 86982 Futuroscope Cedex, France (office). *Telephone:* (8) 90-71-02-02 (office). *E-mail:* info@france2.fr (office). *Website:* www.france2.fr (office).

MOSCOSO DE GRUBER, Mireya Elisa; Panamanian politician and fmr head of state; b. 1 July 1946, Panama; d. of Plinio Antonio Moscoso and Elisa Rodríguez de Moscoso; m. Arnulfo Arias (died 1988); one s.; ed Colegio Comercial María Inmaculada, Miami Dade Community Coll., USA; fmr Exec. Sec. Social Security Agency; fmr Sales Man., Deputy Man. and Gen. Man. Arkapal SA (coffee co.); Govt rep. on numerous int. missions; spent ten years in exile in USA; Pres. Partido Arnulfista; Pres. of Panama 1999–2004; fmr Pres. Arias Foundation, Madrid; fmr mem. Asscn of Boquete Coffee Growers, Asscn of Milk Producers, Nat. Asscn of Ranchers. *Address:* c/o Partido Panameñista, Avda Perú y Calle 38e, No 37–41, al lado de Casa la Esperanza, Apdo 9610, Panamá 4, Panama (office).

MOSCOVICI, Pierre; French politician; b. 16 Sept. 1957; s. of Serge Moscovici and Marie Bromberg; ed Univ. of Paris X, I, IV, Institut d'études politiques, Paris, Ecole nat. d'admin, Strasbourg; official, Cour des Comptes 1984–88; Adviser, pvt. office of Minister of Nat. Educ., Youth and Sport 1988–89, Special Adviser to Minister 1989–90; Head. Gen. Planning Comm.'s Public Sector Modernization and Finance Dept 1990; mem. Parti Socialiste (PS) Nat. Council and Nat. Bureau 1990, Nat. Sec. responsible for policy research and devt 1990–92, 1995–97, Nat. Treas. 1992–94; mem. Doubs Gen. Council, Sochaux-Grand-Charmont canton 1994–2001; Municipal Councillor, Montbéliard 1995–2008, Pres. Agglomeration community of the Pays de Montbéliard 2008–; Gen. Councillor, Doubs 1994–2001; Regional Councillor, Franche-Comté 1998–2004; Municipal Councillor, Valen-tigney 2008–; mem. European Parl. 1994–97, 2004–07, Vice-Pres. 2004–07; Nat. Ass. Deputy for 4th Doubs constituency 1997, 2007–12; Minister Del. attached to Minister for Foreign Affairs, with responsibility for European Affairs 1997–2002; Minister of the Economy, Finances and Foreign Trade 2012–14; Rep. Chairman on the Future of Europe 2002. *Publications include:* A la recherche de la gauche perdue 1994, L'urgence, plaidoyer pour une autre politique 1997, Au coeur de l'Europe 1999, L'Europe, une puissance dans la mondialisation 2001, Les 10 questions qui fâchent les Européens 2004, L'Europe est morte, vive l'Europe 2006. *Leisure interests:* tennis, skiing. *Address:* 51 avenue des Alliés, 25200 Montbéliard (office); Assemblée Nationale, 126 rue de la Université, 75355 Paris 07 SP, France. *Telephone:* 3-81-32-31-69 (office). *Fax:* 3-81-32-31-67 (office). *E-mail:* pmoscovici@ assemblee-national.fr (office). *Website:* www.assemblee-nationale.fr.

MØSE, Erik; Norwegian judge; *Judge, International Criminal Tribunal for Rwanda;* b. 1950; ed Univ. of Oslo, postgraduate studies in Geneva, Switzerland; Lecturer, Univ. of Oslo 1981–; Head of Div., Ministry of Justice –1986; fmr Deputy Judge; Supreme Court Advocate at Solicitor Gen.'s Office 1986–93; Judge, Court of Appeals, Oslo 1993–99; Vice-Pres. Int. Criminal Tribunal for Rwanda 1999–2003, Pres. 2003–07, Judge 2007–; fmr Chair. Council of Europe's Steering Cttee for Human Rights, Cttee for drafting European Convention for the Prevention of Torture, and several other cttees; Fellow Univ. of Essex, UK; Commdr, Royal Norwegian Order of Merit; Dr hc (Essex). *Publications:* numerous books and publs on human rights. *Address:* International Criminal Tribunal for Rwanda, Arusha International Conference Centre, PO Box 6016, Arusha, Tanzania (office). *Telephone:* (212) 963-2850 (UN, New York) (office); (27) 250-4369 (Arusha) (office); (27) 250-4372 (Arusha) (office). *Fax:* (212) 963-2848 (UN, New York) (office); (27) 250-4000 (Arusha) (office); (27) 250-4373 (Arusha) (office). *E-mail:* ictr-press@un .org (office). *Website:* www.ictr.org (office).

MOSER, Baron (Life Peer), cr. 2001, of Regents Park in the London Borough of Camden; **Claus Adolf Moser,** KCB, CBE, FBA; British statistician and academic; b. 24 Nov. 1922, Berlin; s. of the late Dr. Ernest Moser and Lotte Moser; m. Mary Oxlin 1949; one s. two d.; ed Frensham Heights School, London School of Econs; RAF 1943–46; Asst Lecturer in Statistics, LSE 1946–49, Lecturer 1949–55, Reader in Social Statistics 1955–61, Prof. of Social Statistics 1961–70; Statistical Adviser Cttee on Higher Educ. 1961–64; Dir LSE Higher Educ. Research Unit 1964–; Dir Royal Opera House Covent Garden 1965–87, Chair. 1974–87; Dir Cen. Statistical Office, Head of Govt Statistical Service 1967–78; Visiting Fellow, Nuffield Coll. 1972–80; Vice-Chair. N. M. Rothschild and Sons 1978–84, Dir 1978–90; Dir The Economist 1979–93, Chair. Economist Intelligence Unit 1978–84; Warden of Wadham Coll., Oxford 1984–93, Pres. 1989–90; Chair. Askonas Holt Ltd 1990–2002, British Museum Devt Trust 1993–2004, Basic Skills Agency 1997–2002; Dir Equity & Law Life Assurance Soc. 1980–87, Int. Medical Statistics Inc. 1982–88, Octopus Publishing Group 1982–87, Property and Reversionary Investments 1986–87; Chancellor Univ. of Keele 1986–2002, Open Univ. of Israel 1994–2004; Pres. British Asscn 1989–95; Pro-Vice-Chancellor Oxford Univ. 1991–93; Trustee Soros Foundation 1993–1997; Gov. Royal Shakespeare Theatre 1982–93, British American Arts Asscn 1982–, Pilgrim Trust 1982–99, Nat. Comm. on Educ. 1991–95; mem. Gov. Body, Royal Ballet School 1974–87; Hon. Fellow RAM 1970, LSE 1976, Inst. of Educ., Univ. of London 1997, RIBA 2005; Commdr Ordre nat. du Mérite 1976, Commdr's Cross, Order of Merit (FRG) 1986; Hon. DScS (Southampton) 1975, (Leeds, Surrey, Keele, York, Sussex, City Univs) 1977, Hon. DTech (Brunel) 1981, Hon. DSc (Wales) 1990, (Liverpool) 1991, Hon. DScEcon (London) 1991, Dr hc (Brighton) 1994. *Publications:* Measurement of Levels of Living 1957, Survey Methods in Social Investigation 1958, Social Conditions in England and Wales (co-author) 1958, British Towns (co-author) 1961 and papers in statistical journals. *Leisure interest:* music. *Address:* 3 Regents Park Terrace, London, NW1 7EE, England (home). *Telephone:* (20) 7485-1619 (home).

MOSES, Edwin (Ed) Corley, BSc, MBA; American sports administrator and fmr athlete; b. 31 Aug. 1955, Dayton, Ohio; m. Myrella Bordt Moses 1982; one s.; ed Fairview High School and Morehouse Coll., Atlanta, Ga, Pepperdine Univ.; won gold medals for 400m hurdles, Olympic Games, Montreal 1976 (in world record time), Los Angeles 1984, bronze medal, Seoul 1988; one of only three men to break 48 seconds for 400m hurdles; holds record for greatest number of wins consecu-tively in any event; winner 122 consecutive races (107 finals) 1977–87, lost to Danny Harris June 1987; won three World Cup titles and two World Champion-

ships; set world record in his event four times; at one time held 13 fastest times ever recorded; retd 1989, comeback 1991, second comeback 2003; competed int. for USA in bobsleigh and two- and four-man sleds; US Rep. to Int. Amateur Athletic Fed. from 1984; mem. Jt Olympic Cttee Athletes Comm., Exec. Bd of US Olympic Cttee, Bd of Dirs Jesse Owens Foundation, IOC Ethics Comm. 2000–; Pres. Int. Amateur Athletics Asscn; elected as inaugural Chair. Laureus World Sports Acad. 2000; Vice-Chair. US Olympic Foundation; fmr Chair. US Olympic Cttee Substance Abuse Cttee; Founding Partner Platinum Group (representing athletes' business interests); Dr hc (Univ. of Massachusetts, Boston) 2009; Track & Field News Athlete of the Year 1980, Jesse Owens Int. Award 1981, James E. Sullivan Award, Amateur Athletic Union 1983, ABC Wide World of Sports Athlete of the Year 1984, Sports Illustrated Sportsman of the Year (shared) 1984, Speaker of the Athletes' Oath at Olympic Games 1984, Miami Boulevard West and Sunrise Avenue in Dayton, Ohio renamed Edwin C. Moses Boulevard 1984, inducted into Nat. Track and Field Hall of Fame 1994, ranked 47th on ESPN's SportCentury 50 Greatest Athletes 1999. *Leisure interests:* aviation, scientific breakthroughs in athletics, scuba diving. *Address:* c/o Laureus World Sports Academy, 460 Fulham Road, London, SW6 1BZ, England.

MOSHAHED, Ahmad; Afghan diplomatist and government official; *Chairman, Independent Administrative Reform and Civil Service Commission;* Amb. to Iran in Transitional Govt 2004; Minister of Educ. 2004; currently Chair. Ind. Admin. Reform and Civil Service Comm., Kabul. *Address:* Independent Administrative Reform and Civil Service Commission, Shah Mahmood Khan Ghazi Watt, Prime Minister's Compound Opposite the Vice President's Office, Kabul, Afghanistan (office). *Website:* iarcsc.gov.af/en.

MOSHER, Gregory Dean, BFA; American theatre producer, director and academic; *Director of University Arts Initiatives and Adjunct Assistant Professor of Theatre Arts, Columbia University;* b. 15 Jan. 1949, New York; s. of Thomas Edward Mosher and Florence Christine Mosher; ed Oberlin Coll., Ithaca Coll., Juilliard School; Dir Stage 2 Goodman Theatre, Chicago 1974–77, Artistic Dir 1978–85; Artistic Dir Lincoln Center Theater 1985–92, Resident Dir 1992–2004; Dir Univ. Arts Initiatives and Adjunct Asst Prof. of Theatre Arts, Columbia Univ., New York 2004–; Chevalier, Ordre des Arts et des Lettres; two Tony Awards (as producer of revivals: Anything Goes, Our Town), Obie Award, Margo Jefferson, Outer Critics. *Productions include:* new works by Tennessee Williams, Studs Terkel, David Mamet, John Guare, Michael Weller, Wole Soyinka, Elaine May, David Rabe, Mbongeni Ngema, Edward Albee, Spalding Gray, Arthur Miller, Leonard Bernstein, Stephen Sondheim, Richard Nelson, Jerome Robbins; produ-cer: Samuel Beckett's first directing work in US, Krapp's Last Tape 1979, Bosoms and Neglect 1979, Endgame 1980, The Man Who Had Three Arms 1983, Hurlyburly 1984, The Flying Karamazov Brothers "Juggling and Cheap Theatrics" 1986, The House of Blue Leaves 1986, The Front Page 1987, Death and the King's Horseman 1987, The Regard of Flight 1987, The Comedy of Errors 1987, Anything Goes 1987, Sarafina! 1988, Speed-the-Plow (Broadway and RNT) 1988, Our Town 1988, The Tenth Man 1989, Some Americans Abroad 1990, Six Degrees of Separation 1990, Monster in a Box 1991, Mule Bone 1991, Two Shakespearean Actors 1992, A Streetcar Named Desire 1992, Freak 1998, James Joyce's The Dead 2000. *Plays directed:* Glengarry Glen Ross (David Mamet), Broadway 1984–85, American Buffalo 1975, A Life in the Theater 1977, Edmond 1982, Glengarry Glen Ross 1984, Speed-the-Plow (David Mamet), Danger: Memory (Miller premiere) 1987, Broadway 1988, London 1989, Our Town (50th anniversary production, Thornton Wilder), Broadway 1988, Oh Hell, Lincoln Center Theater 1989, Uncle Vanya 1990, Mr Gogol and Mr Preen 1991, A Streetcar Named Desire 1992, Stanley (producing dir) 1997. *Films:* American Buffalo 1996 (producer), The Prime Gig 2000 (dir). *Television includes:* King Lear (actor) 1974, The Comedy of Errors (dir) 1987, Uncle Vanya (dir) 1991, A Life in the Theatre (dir) 1993, The House of Blue Leaves (exec. producer) 1987. *Address:* Arts Initiative at Columbia University, 206 Prentis Hall, 632 West 125th Street, Mail Code 5011, New York, NY 10027, USA (office). *Telephone:* (212) 851-1872 (office). *E-mail:* gm2127@columbia.edu (office). *Website:* www.cuarts.com (office).

MOSHINSKY, Elijah, BA; British opera director; b. 8 Jan. 1946; s. of Abraham Moshinsky and Eva Moshinsky; m. Ruth Dyttman 1970; two s.; ed Melbourne Univ. and St Antony's Coll. Oxford; apptd to Royal Opera House 1973, Assoc. Producer 1979–; work for Royal Opera includes original productions of Peter Grimes 1975, Lohengrin 1978, The Rake's Progress 1979, Un Ballo in Maschera 1980; Macbeth 1981, Samson et Dalila 1981, Tannhäuser 1984, Otello 1987, Die Entführung aus dem Serail 1987, Attila 1990, Simon Boccanegra 1991, Stiffelio 1993, Aida 1994, Otello 1994, The Makropoulos Case 1996, The Queen of Spades 1998; has also produced work for ENO, Australian Opera, Metropolitan Opera, New York, Holland Festival, Maggio Musicale, Florence etc. *Theatre productions include:* Troilus and Cressida (Nat. Theatre) 1976, The Force of Habit (Nat. Theatre) 1976, Three Sisters (Albery) 1987, Light Up the Sky (Globe) 1987, Ivanov (Strand) 1989, Much Ado About Nothing (Strand) 1989, Another Time (Wynd-ham's) 1989, Shadowlands (Queen's) 1989, Cyrano de Bergerac 1992, Genghis Cohn 1993, Danton 1994; Dir Matador (Queen's) 1991, Becket (Haymarket) 1991, Reflected Glory (Vaudeville) 1992, Richard III 1998, The Female Odd Couple (Apollo) 2001; productions for BBC TV of works by Shakespeare, Ibsen and Sheridan. *Leisure interests:* painting, telephone conversation.

MOSIER, Frank Eugene; American business executive; b. 15 July 1930, Kersey, Pa; s. of Clarence Mosier and Helen Mosier; m. Julia M. Fife 1961; one s. one d.; ed Univ. of Pittsburgh; joined Standard Oil Co. Cleveland 1953, Vice-Pres. (supply and distribution) 1972–76, (supply and transport) 1976–77, Sr Vice-Pres. (mar-keting and refining) 1977–78, (supply and transport) 1978–82, (downstream petroleum dept) 1982–85, Exec. Vice-Pres. 1985–86, Pres. and COO 1986–88, BP America Inc. (following 1987 merger of BP and Standard Oil), Cleveland, Pres. 1987–88, Vice-Chair. 1988–91 (retd), Vice-Chair. Advisory Bd 1991–93; mem. Bd of Dirs Associated Estates Realty Corpn 1993–; fmr mem. Bd of Dirs Boykin Lodging Co. *Address:* c/o Board of Directors, Associated Estates Realty Corporation, 5025 Swetland Court, Richmond Heights, OH 44143-1467, USA.

MOSIMANN, Anton, OBE; Swiss chef and restaurateur; *Chairman, Mosimann's Limited;* b. 23 Feb. 1947, Solothurn; s. of Otto Mosimann and Olga Mosimann; m. Kathrin Roth 1973; two s.; ed pvt. school in Switzerland; apprentice, Hotel Baeren, Twann; worked in Canada, France, Italy, Sweden, Japan, Belgium, Switzerland

1962–; cuisinier at Villa Lorraine, Brussels, Les Prés d'Eugénie, Eugénie-les-Bains, Les Frères Troisgros, Roanne, Paul Bocuse, Collonges au Mont d'Or, Moulin de Mougins; joined Dorchester Hotel, London 1975, Maître Chef des Cuisines 1975–88; Owner Mosimann's (fmr Belfry Club) 1988–, Mosimann's Party Service 1990–, The Mosimann Acad. 1995–, Creative Chefs 1996–; World Pres. Les Toques Blanches Internationales 1989–93; Visiting Prof., Univ. of Strathclyde 2003; Pres. Royal Warrant Holders' Asscn 2006–07; DL Greater London 2011; Hon. mem. Chefs' Asscns of Canada, Japan, Switzerland, SA, World Asscn of Chefs Socs 2008; Freedom of the City of London 1999; Royal Warrant of Appointment to HRH The Prince of Wales 2000; Hon. Prof., Thames Valley Univ. 2004; Croix de Chevalier du Mérite agricole, Ordre du Mérite agricole 2006; Hon. Dr of Culinary Arts (Johnson and Wales Univ., USA); Hon. DSc (Bournemouth) 1998; Personalité de l'Année Award 1986, Swiss Culinary Amb. of the Year 1995, Restauranteur of the Year, Int. Food and Beverage Forum, Rhode Island 2000, Lifetime Achievement Award (Hotel & Caterer) 2004, Lifetime Achievement Award, Davos Tourism for World Econ. Forum 2010, Carl-Freidrich von Rumohr Prize, Gastronomic Acad. Deutschlands for lifetime achievement 2013, numerous awards in int. cookery competitions. *Television includes:* Anton Goes to Sheffield (Glenfiddich Award 1986) 1986, Cooking with Mosimann (series) 1990, Anton Mosimann Naturally (series) 1991–92, Natürlich, Leichtes Kochen (Swiss TV) 1997, Mosimann's Culinary Switzerland (Swiss TV) 1998. *Publications:* Cuisine à la Carte 1981, A New Style of Cooking: The Art of Anton Mosimann 1983, Cuisine Naturelle 1985, Anton Mosimann's Fish Cuisine 1988, The Art of Mosimann 1989, Cooking with Mosimann 1989, Anton Mosimann – Naturally 1991, The Essential Mosimann 1993, Mosimann's World 1996, Mosimann's Fresh 2006, 25 Years of Mosimann's 2013. *Leisure interests:* classic cars and int. car rallies, collecting antiquarian cookery books, enjoying fine wine, passionate about food and travelling, especially to food markets of the Far East. *Address:* Mosimann's, 11B West Halkin Street, London, SW1X 8JL, England (office). *Telephone:* (20) 7235-9625 (office). *Fax:* (20) 7245-7847 (office). *E-mail:* amosimann@mosimann.com (office). *Website:* www .mosimann.com (office).

MOSISILI, Bethuel Pakalitha, BA; Lesotho politician; b. 14 March 1945, Waterfall; m.; two s. two d.; ed Univs of Botswana, Lesotho and Swaziland, Univ. of Wisconsin, USA, Univ. of South Africa, Simon Fraser Univ., Canada; joined Basutoland Congress Party 1967; Deputy Headmaster Bereng High School 1972–73; Asst Lecturer in African Languages, Univs of Botswana, Lesotho and Swaziland 1973–76; Lecturer in African Languages, Nat. Univ. of Lesotho 1976–83; Sr Lecturer, Univ. of Fort Hare, South Africa 1983–84, Univ. of Transkei 1985–88, Univ. of Zululand 1989–92; mem. Parl. 1993–; Minister of Educ. and Training, Sports, Culture and Youth Affairs 1993–95; apptd Deputy Prime Minister 1995; Minister of Home Affairs and Local Govt 1995–98; Prime Minister of Lesotho and Minister of Defence and Nat. Security 1998–2012; fmr Deputy Leader, Lesotho Congress for Democracy, apptd Leader 1998; mem. Lesotho Educational Research Asscn, African Languages Asscn of South Africa, South African Pedagogical Soc. *Address:* c/o Office of the Prime Minister, PO Box 527, Maseru 100, Lesotho.

MOSKOVSKY, Col-Gen. Aleksey Mikhailovich; Russian army officer; b. 1947, Smolensk; ed Kiev Higher Mil. Engineering Radio Technical School, Novosibirsk State Univ.; worked in devt and testing of armaments and mil. tech.; Deputy State Mil. Insp. of Russia, Sec. Council of Defence 1997–98; Deputy Sec. Russian Council of Security 1998–2001, supervised security in defence, tech. and scientific areas; Deputy Minister of Defence, Head of Armaments 2001–07; State Prize of Russian Fed., Prize of Council of Ministers for devt of new weapons. *Address:* c/o Ministry of Defence, 105175 Moscow, ul. Myasnitskaya 37, Russia (office).

MOSLEY, Max Rufus; British fmr racing driver and lawyer; b. 13 April 1940, London, England; s. of the late Sir Oswald Mosley and of the Hon. Lady Diana Mosley (née Freeman-Mitford); m. Jean Marjorie Taylor 1960; two s.; ed Christ Church Oxford; called to Bar (Gray's Inn) 1964; fmr Dir March Cars Ltd, Legal Adviser to Formula One Constructors Asscn, fmr Formula Two racing driver, Co-founder March Grand Prix Team; Pres. Fed. Int. du Sport Automobile (FISA) 1991–93, Fed. Int. de l'Automobile (FIA) 1993–2009 (mem. FIA Senate 2009–); Chair. Mfrs Comm. 1986–91; Hon. Pres. European Parl. Automobile Users Group 1994–99; Chair. European New Car Assessment Programme 1997–2004; Chair. Global New Car Assessment Programme 2011–; Vice-Chair. Supervisory Bd ERTICO Intelligence Transport Systems Europe 1999–2001, Chair. 2001–04, Pres. and Spokesperson 2004–06; Founder-mem. Institut du Cerveau et de la Moelle Epiniere 2005, EC CARS 21 High Level Group 2005–09; Patron EU eSafety Aware Communications Platform 2006–09; Hon. Pres. Nat. Road Safety Council of Armenia 2006, Fed. Int. de l'Automobile 2009–; Order of Merit (Italy) 1994, Order of Madarksi Kannik, First Degree (Bulgaria) 2000, Castrol/Inst. of the Motor Industry Gold Medal 2000, Quattroruote Premio Speciale per la Sicurezza Stradale (Italy) Gold Medal 2001, Goldene VdM-Dieselring (Germany) 2001, Order of Merit (Romania) 2004, Visitante Ilustre de la Ciudad de Asuncion (Ecuador) 2004, Chevalier, Légion d'honneur 2006, Comandr, Ordre de Saint Charles (Monaco) 2006; Hon. DCL (Northumbria) 2005. *Leisure interests:* walking, snowboarding. *Address:* 7 Blvd des Moulins, Monte Carlo 98000, Monaco (office); 60 Trafalgar Square, London, WC2N 5DS, England (office). *E-mail:* tozerp8@gmail .com; callierflorence@gmail.com.

MOSLEY, Nicholas (see Ravensdale, 3rd Baron).

MOSLEY, Walter; American writer; b. 12 Jan. 1952, Los Angeles; s. of Leroy Mosley and Ella Mosley (née Slatkin); m. Joy Kellman 1987 (divorced); ed Goddard Coll., Johnson State Coll., City Coll. CUNY; Artist-in-Residence, Africana Studies Inst., New York Univ. 1996; mem. Bd of Dirs Nat. Book Awards, Poetry Soc. of America –2007; Past Pres. Mystery Writers of America; Dr hc (City Coll. of New York); American Library Asscn Literary Award 1996, O. Henry Award 1996, Anisfield Wolf Award 1996, TransAfrica Int. Literary Prize 1998. *Publications include:* Devil in a Blue Dress (Shamus Award) 1990, A Red Death 1991, White Butterfly 1992, Black Betty 1994, RL's Dream 1995, A Little Yellow Dog 1996, Gone Fishin' 1997, Always Outnumbered, Always Outgunned 1997, Blue Light 1998, Walkin' the Dog 1999, Fearless Jones 2001, Futureland: Nine Stories of an Imminent Future 2001, Bad Boy Brawly Brown 2002, Fear Itself 2003, Six Easy Pieces (short stories) 2003, What Next: An African American Initiative Toward World Peace 2003, The Man in My Basement 2004, Little Scarlet 2004, Cinnamon

Kiss 2005, 47 (for young adults) (Carl Brandon Society Parallax Award 2006) 2006, Fortunate Son 2006, Killing Johnny Fry 2007, This Year You Write Your Novel 2007, Blonde Faith 2007, Diablerie 2008, The Long Fall 2009, Known to Evil 2010, The Last Days of Ptolemy Grey 2010, Twelve Steps to Political Revelation 2011, When the Thrill Is Gone 2011, All I Did Was Shoot My Man 2012, Parishioner 2012; contribs to New York Times, Library of Contemporary Thought, New Yorker, GQ, Esquire, USA Weekend, Los Angeles Times Magazine, Savoy. *Address:* c/o Gloria Loomis Watkins/Loomis Literary Agency, PO Box 20925, New York, NY 10025, USA (office). *Telephone:* (212) 532-0080 (office). *Website:* www.waltermosley .com.

MOSMANN, Timothy R., BS, BSc, MD, FRSC; South African/Canadian micro-biologist, immunologist and academic; *Professor, Department of Microbiology and Immunology, and Michael and Angela Pichichero Director in the David H. Smith Center for Vaccine Biology and Immunology, University of Rochester Medical Center, University of Rochester;* ed Univ. of Natal, Rhodes Univ., Univ. of British Columbia, Canada; emigrated to Canada; fmr Research Fellow, Univ. of Toronto, Canada, Univ. of Glasgow, UK; apptd Asst Prof., Univ. of Alberta, Canada, later Chair. Dept of Immunology; in between, spent eight years in industry, as a research scientist at DNAX Research Inst., Palo Alto, Calif., USA; recruited to Univ. of Rochester, NY, USA 1998, currently Prof., Dept of Microbiology and Immunology, and Michael and Angela Pichichero Dir in the David H. Smith Center for Vaccine Biology and Immunology, Univ. of Rochester Medical Center; Int. Research Scholar, Howard Hughes Medical Inst. 1991–96, 1997–2001; numerous honours and awards, including Centennial Fellow, MRC of Canada 1975–77, Bernhard Cinader Lectureship, Canadian Soc. for Immunology 1993, Avery-Landsteiner Prize, German Soc. for Immunology 1994, NIH Fogarty Scholar-in-Residence 1996–99, William B. Coley Award, Cancer Research Inst. (USA) 1997, ASTECH Award for Outstanding Leadership in Alberta Science 1997, William S. Coley Award for Research in Immunology (jtly) 1997, Paul Ehrlich and Ludwig Darmstaedter Prize (Germany) 2008. *Achievements include:* made funda-mental discoveries about the regulation of immune responses in allergic and infectious diseases including, with Dr Robert L. Coffman of the Univ. of Rochester, the discovery of the TH1 and TH2 subsets of T-lymphocytes, the two major types of T-cells that control immune responses. *Publications:* numerous papers in profes-sional journals. *Address:* University of Rochester School of Medicine and Dentis-try, 601 Elmwood Avenue, Box 609, Rochester, NY 14642, USA (office). *Telephone:* (585) 275-8762 (office); (585) 273-1400 (office). *Fax:* (585) 273-2452 (office). *E-mail:* Joyce_Feltz@urmc.rochester.edu (office). *Website:* www.urmc.rochester.edu (office).

MOSONYI, György, DipEng; Hungarian business executive; *Chairman of the Supervisory Board, MOL Group;* b. 1949; ed Veszprém Univ.; joined Shell Int. Petroleum Co. (SIPC) as Lubricant Sales Rep. 1974, Commercial Dir 1986–92, worked at Shell HQ, London, UK 1991, Man. Dir Shell-Interag Ltd 1992–93, Chair. and CEO Shell Hungary Rt. 1994–99, also Chair. Cen. European Region and Gen. Man. Shell Czech Repub. 1998; mem. Bd of Dirs and Group CEO MOL Group 1999–2011, Chair. Supervisory Bd MOL Group 2011–, Chair. Sustainable Devt Cttee; Chair. TVK Plc; Chair. Supervisory Bd SLOVNAFT a.s.; mem. Bd of Dirs Hungarian Telekom Plc 2012–; Vice-Pres. Supervisory Bd INA d.d.; Vice-Chair. Hungarian Chamber of Commerce and Industry; Vice-Pres. Confed. of Hungarian Employers and Industrialists; mem. Jt Venture Asscn's Presidium; Pres. Hungarian Nat. Cttee of World Petroleum Council. *Address:* MOL Group, Október huszonharmadika u.18, 1502 Budapest, Hungary (office). *Telephone:* (1) 209-0000 (office). *Fax:* (1) 464-1335 (office). *Website:* www.mol.hu (office).

MOSS, Andrew, LLB, CA; British chartered accountant and insurance executive; b. March 1958; m. 1st Susan Moss; four c.; m. 2nd Deirdre Galvin 2012; ed Christ Church Coll., Oxford; accountancy training, Coopers & Lybrand; Vice-Pres. and Head of Fiduciary Compliance, Citibank NA 1988–89; Asst Dir Group Treasury, Midland Montagu/HSBC Markets 1989–95, Head of Group Asset and Liability Man. HSBC Group 1995–97, Chief Financial Officer, Investment Banking and Markets, HSBC Group 1997–2000; Dir Finance, Risk Man. and Operations, Lloyd's of London 2000–04; Group Finance Dir Aviva plc 2004–07, Group Chief Exec. 2007–12 (resgnd); Co-Chair. Insurance Industry Working Group with the Chancellor of the Exchequer 2009; mem. Bd and Appointments Cttee of the Asscn of British Insurers, Pan European Insurance Forum, European Financial Services Round Table; Treas. Geneva Asscn. *Leisure interests:* golf, rugby, gardening. *Address:* c/o Aviva PLC, St Helen's, 1 Undershaft, London, EC3P 3DQ, England.

MOSS, Bernard K., MD, PhD, FAAS; American virologist and academic; *Genetic Engineering Section Chief and Chief, Laboratory of Viral Diseases, National Institute of Allergy and Infectious Diseases;* b. 26 July 1937, New York; ed New York Univ., New York Univ. School of Medicine and Massachusetts Inst. of Tech.; Intern, Children's Hosp. Medical Center, Boston, Mass 1961–62; Investigator, Lab. of Biology of Viruses, Nat. Inst. of Allergy and Infectious Diseases, NIH, Bethesda, Md 1966–70, Head, Macromolecular Biology Section 1971–84, Chief, Lab. of Viral Diseases 1984–, currently Chief, Genetic Eng Section; Foundation for Microbiology Lectureship 1980–81; Wellcome Visiting Prof. in Microbiology, American Soc. of Microbiology 1987; Adjunct Prof., George Washington Univ. Grad. Genetics Program, Washington, DC 1994–; Adjunct mem. Inst. for Biomedical Science 1996–; Adjunct Prof., Univ. of Maryland; Head, WHO Collaborating Center for Research on Viral Vectors for Vaccines 1988–2001; mem. Vaccinia Sub-cttee of Nat. Vaccine Program Interagency Group 1988–, Poxvirus Subgroup of Int. Cttee on Taxonomy of Viruses 1992–95, 1997–, WHO Advisory Cttee on Variola Virus 1999–, Fellowship Recruitment Cttee of AAAS 2000–; Ed. Virology 1992–; mem. Editorial Bd Journal of Virology 1972–, AIDS Research and Human Retroviruses 1989–, Current Opinion in Biotechnology 1990–; mem. Editorial Advisory Bd Advances in Virus Research 1984–, NIH Catalyst 1993–; mem. American Soc. for Microbiology, American Soc. of Biological Chemists, NAS 1987–, American Soc. for Virology 1994– (currently Pres.), American Acad. of Microbiology 1996–; NSF Research Fellowship 1958, US Public Health Service (PHS) Postdoctoral Fellow-ship 1963–66, PHS Commendation Medal 1979, PHS Meritorious Service Medal 1984, Science Digest magazine 100 Most Innovative Scientists of 1985, PHS Distinguished Service Medal 1986, Solomon A. Berson Medical Alumni Achieve-ment Award, New York Univ. 1987, Dickson Prize for Medical Research, Univ. of Pittsburgh 1988, Invitrogen Eukaryotic Expression Award 1991, ICN Int. Prize in

Virology, ICN Pharmaceuticals Research 1994, Sackler Scholarship, Univ. of Tel-Aviv 1996, J. Allyn Taylor Int. Prize in Medicine, Robarts Research Inst. 1997, Cancer Research Campaign Lecturer, Univ. of Glasgow, UK 1999, Bristol-Myers Squibb Award for Distinguished Achievement in Infectious Disease Research 2000. *Publications:* more than 560 articles in scientific journals. *Address:* Laboratory of Viral Diseases, National Institute of Allergy and Infectious Diseases, NIH, Building 33, Room 1E13C.1, 33 North Drive, Bethesda, MD 20892-3210, USA (office). *Telephone:* (301) 496-9869 (office). *Fax:* (301) 480-1535 (office). *E-mail:* bmoss@nih.gov (office); bmoss@niaid.nih.gov (office). *Website:* www.niaid.nih.gov/LabsAndResources/labs/aboutlabs/lvd/geneticEngineeringSection/Pages/moss.aspx (office).

MOSS, Kate; British model; b. 16 Jan. 1974, Addiscombe, Croydon, London, England; d. of Peter Edward Moss and Linda Rosina (Shepherd); one d. with fmr pnr Jefferson Hack; engaged to Pete Doherty 2007; m. Jamie Hince 2011; ed Riddlesdown High School, Purley; discovered at age 14 by Sarah Doukas, founder of Storm Model Management, at JFK Airport, New York 1988; has modelled for Face, Harpers and Queen, Vogue, Dolce & Gabbana, Katherine Hamnett, Versace (q.v.), Yves Saint Laurent; exclusive contract world-wide with Calvin Klein (q.v.) 1992–; designed Kate Moss collection for Topshop 2007; named Female Model of the Year VH-1 Awards 1996. *Films:* Inferno (TV film) 1992, Unzipped 1996, Blackadder Back & Forth (short) 1999, The 4 Dreams of Miss X (video short) 2007. *Publication:* Kate 1994. *Address:* c/o Storm Model Management, 1st Floor, 5 Jubilee Place, London, SW3 3TD, England (office). *Telephone:* (20) 7376-7764 (office). *Fax:* (20) 7376-5145 (office). *Website:* www.stormmodels.com (office).

MOSS, Sir Stirling, Kt, OBE; British fmr racing driver and business executive; *Managing Director, Stirling Moss Limited;* b. 17 Sept. 1929, London, England; s. of Alfred Moss and Nora Aileen Moss; m. 1st Katherine Stuart Molson 1957 (divorced 1960); m. 2nd Elaine Barbarino 1964 (divorced 1968); one d.; m. 3rd Susie Paine 1980; one s.; ed Haileybury and Imperial Service Coll.; bought his first racing car, a Cooper 500, with prize money from show-jumping 1947; British Champion 1951; built his own car, the Cooper-Alta 1953; drove in H.W.M. Formula II Grand Prix team 1950, 1951, Jaguar team 1950, 1951; Leader of Maserati Grand Prix team 1954; mem. Mercedes team 1955; leader of Maserati Sports and Grand Prix teams 1956, Aston Martin team 1956; mem. Vanwall, Aston Martin, Maserati teams 1958; winner of Tourist Trophy (TT) race, UK 1950, 1951, 1953, 1955, 1958, 1959, 1960, 1961, Gold Coupe des Alpes (three rallies without loss of marks) 1954, Italian Mille Miglia 1955, Sicilian Targa Florio 1955, eight int. events including NZ, Monaco Grand Prix, Nurburgring 1,000 km (FRG) 1956, Argentine 1,000 km UK, Pescara (Italy), Moroccan Grand Prix 1957, 11 events including Argentine, Netherlands, Italian Grand Prix and Nurburgring 1,000 km 1958, 19 events including NZ, Portuguese, US Grand Prix 1959, 19 events including Cuban, Monaco, Austrian, S African Grand Prix 1960, 27 events including Monaco, German, Pacific Grand Prix, Nassau Tourist Trophy 1961; competed in 529 events, finishing in 387, winning 211, during motor racing career 1947–62; retd from racing after accident at Goodwood, UK April 1962, made comeback 1980, subsequently taking part in numerous vintage car races; many business ventures, consultancy work on vehicle evaluation, property conversion, design; Man. Dir Stirling Moss Ltd; Dir 28 cos; also journalism and lecturing; Pres. or Patron of 28 car clubs; Hon. FIE 1959; Gold Star, British Racing Drivers' Club 10 times 1950–61, Driver of the Year (Guild of Motoring Writers') (twice), Sir Malcolm Campbell Memorial Award 1957. *Publications include:* Stirling Moss 1953, In the Track of Speed 1957, Le Mans '59 1959, Design and Behaviour of the Racing Car 1963, All But My Life 1963, How to Watch Motor Racing 1975, Motor Racing and All That 1980, My Cars, My Career 1987, Stirling Moss: Great Drives in the Lakes and Dales 1993, Motor Racing Masterpieces 1995, Stirling Moss (a biog.) 2001, Stirling Moss Scrapbook 1955 2005, Stirling Moss Scrapbook 1956–1960 2009, Stirling Moss: All My Races 2009. *Leisure interests:* theatre and cinema, designing houses, model making, motor trials, historic racing, interior decorating, woodwork. *Address:* c/o Stirling Moss Ltd, 46 Shepherd Street, Mayfair, London, W1J 7JN (office); 44 Shepherd Street, London, W1J 7JN, England (home). *Telephone:* (20) 7499-3272. *E-mail:* stirlingmossltd@aol.com (office). *Website:* www.stirlingmoss.com.

MOSTAFAVI, Mohsen, Diploma in Architecture; Iranian architect and academic; *Dean, Graduate School of Design, Harvard University;* m. Homa Farjadi; ed Architectural Asscn School of Architecture, London, Univ. of Essex, Univ. of Cambridge, UK; fmr Design Critic, Univ. of Cambridge; fmr Visiting Prof., Frankfurt Acad. of Arts (Stadelschule); fmrly taught at Univ. of Pennsylvania School of Design; Assoc. Prof. of Architecture, Grad. School of Design, Harvard Univ. 1990–95, Dir MArch I Program 1992–95, Dean 2008–; Chair. Architectural Asscn, School of Architecture, London 1995–2004; fmr Arthur L. and Isabel B. Wiesenberger Prof. in Architecture, Cornell Univ. –2007, Gale and Ira Drukier Dean, Coll. of Architecture, Art and Planning, Cornell Univ. 2004–07; mem. Steering Cttee Aga Khan Award for Architecture; jury mem. Holcim Foundation for Sustainable Construction; fmr mem. Design Cttee, London Devt Agency; winner of Pritzker Prize 2000. *Publications:* Architecture and Continuity (co-author) 1983, On Weathering: the Life of Buildings in Time (co-author, American Inst. of Architects Prize) 1993, Delayed Space (co-author) 1994 Approximations 2002, Surface Architecture 2002 (CICA Bruno Zevi Book Award), Logique Visuelle 2003, Landscape Urbanism: a Manual for the Machinic Landscape 2004, Structure as Space 2006; contribs to The Architectural Review, AAFiles, Arquitectura, Bauwelt, Casabella, Centre, Daidalos. *Address:* Office of the Dean, Graduate School of Design, Harvard University, 48 Quincy Street, Gund Hall, Cambridge, MA 02138, USA (office). *Telephone:* (617) 495-4364 (office). *Website:* www.gsd.harvard.edu (office).

MOTANYANE, Sephiri Enoch; Lesotho politician; *Speaker, National Assembly;* b. 1935; began political career as youth cadre of Basutoland Congress Party (BCP) early 1960s; over 40 years as mem. Nat. Ass.; Deputy Speaker Nat. Ass. –2012, Speaker 2012–; held several govt portfolios including Minister of the Crown, Minister for Justice and Human Rights, Minister of Law, Constitutional Affairs and Rehabilitation, Minister in the Prime Minister's Office; mem. Lesotho Congress for Democracy, fmr Sec.-Gen. *Address:* Office of the Speaker, National Assembly, PO Box 190, Maseru 100, Lesotho (office). *Telephone:* 22323035 (office). *Fax:* 22310438 (office). *Website:* www.parliament.ls (office).

MOTE, Clayton Daniel (Dan), Jr, MS, DSc; American university administrator and professor of mechanical engineering; *President, University of Maryland;* m. Patricia Mote; one d. one s.; ed Univ. of Calif., Berkeley; mem. Faculty, Dept of Mechanical Eng, Univ. of Calif., Berkeley 1967–98, Vice-Chancellor, Chair in Mechanical Systems and Pres. UC Berkeley Foundation 1991–98; Glenn L. Martin Inst. Prof. of Mechanical Eng and Pres. Univ. of Maryland, College Park 1998–; consultant to US Congress on educational issues; Pres. Atlantic Coast Conf. 2004–05; fmr Vice-Chair., Basic Research Cttee, US Dept of Defense; mem. Nat. Acads Cttee, Senate Energy Sub-Cttee, US Senate Energy and Natural Resources Cttee; mem. Leadership Council, Nat. Innovation Initiative, Council on Competitiveness; mem. Council, Nat. Acad. of Eng; Fellow AAAS, Int. Acad. of Wood Science, Acoustical Soc. of America; holds patents in USA, Norway, Finland and Sweden; Hon. mem. ASME Int.; two hon. doctorates; Humboldt Prize, FRG, Berkeley Citation, UC Berkeley Distinguished Eng Alumnus, J.P. Den Hartog Award, ASME Int. Tech. Cttee on Vibration and Sound 2005. *Publications:* over 300 articles, books and chapters in books on dynamics of gyroscopic systems and biomechanics. *Address:* Office of the President, University of Maryland, Main Administration Building, College Park, MD 20742-5025, USA (office). *Telephone:* (301) 405-5803 (office). *E-mail:* president@umd.edu (office). *Website:* www.umd.edu (office).

MOTEGI, Toshimitsu; Japanese politician; *Minister of Economy, Trade and Industry;* b. 7 Oct. 1955; ed Faculty of Econs, Univ. of Tokyo, John F. Kennedy School of Govt, Harvard Univ., USA; joined Marubeni Corpn 1978; political journalist, Yomiuri Shimbun 1983–84; Man. Consultant, Mckinsey & Co. 1984–93; mem. House of Reps (Tochigi Pref. 5th Dist) 1993–, Dir Cttee on Foreign Affairs 1997, Cttee on the Budget 2004–07, Chair. Cttee on Health, Labour and Welfare 2007–; Vice-Minister for Int. Trade and Industry 1999–2002; Sr Vice-Minister for Foreign Affairs 2002–03; Minister of State for Okinawa and Northern Territories Affairs, Science and Tech. Policy, and Information Tech. 2003–08; apptd Minister of State for Financial Services and Admin. Reform 2008, Minister of Economy, Trade and Industry 2012–, also currently Minister of State for Corpn in support of Compensation for Nuclear Damage, Minister in charge of Nuclear Incident Econ. Countermeasures, Minister in Charge of Industrial Competitiveness; Deputy Sec. Gen., LDP 1998–2006, Chief Deputy Sec. Gen. 2006–. *Address:* Ministry of Economy, Trade and Industry 1-3-1, Kasumigaseki, Chiyoda-ku, Tokyo 100-8901, Japan (office). *Telephone:* (3) 3501-1511 (office); (3) 3506-6000 (office). *Fax:* (3) 3501-6942 (office). *E-mail:* webmail@meti.go.jp (office). *Website:* www.meti.go.jp (office); www.kantei.go.jp (office).

MOTION, Sir Andrew Peter, Kt, MLitt, FRSA; British biographer and poet; b. 26 Oct. 1952, London, England; s. of Andrew R. Motion and Catherine G. Motion; m. 1st Joanna J. Powell 1973 (divorced 1983); m. 2nd Janet Elisabeth Dalley 1985; two s. one d.; ed Radley Coll. and Univ. Coll., Oxford; Lecturer in English, Univ. of Hull 1977–81; Ed. Poetry Review 1981–83; Poetry Ed. Chatto & Windus 1983–89, Editorial Dir 1985–87; Prof. of Creative Writing Univ. of E Anglia, Norwich 1995–2003; Chair. Literature Advisory Panel Arts Council of England 1986–98; Poet Laureate 1999–2009; Chair of Creative Writing, Royal Holloway Coll., Univ. Coll. London 2003–; Chair., Museums, Libraries and Archives Council 2008–; Chair. Man Booker Prize jury 2010; mem. Poetry Soc. (Vice-Pres.); Hon. DLitt (Hull) 1996, (Exeter) 1999, (Brunel) 2000, (A.P.U.) 2001, (Open Univ.) 2002; Arvon/Observer Prize 1982, Dylan Thomas Award 1987, Whitbread Biography Award 1993. *Publications:* poetry collections: The Pleasure Steamers 1978, Independence 1981, The Penguin Book of Contemporary British Poetry (ed., anthology) 1982, Secret Narratives 1983, Dangerous Play (Rhys Memorial Prize) 1984, Natural Causes 1987, Love in a Life 1991, The Price of Everything 1994, Salt Water 1997, Selected Poems 1996–97 1998, Public Property 2001, Here to Eternity: An Anthology of Poetry (ed.) 2001, The Cinder Path 2009; poems as Poet Laureate: Remember This: An Elegy on the Death of HM Queen Elizabeth The Queen Mother 2002, A Hymn for the Golden Jubilee 2002, On the Record (for Prince William's 21st birthday) 2003, Spring Wedding (for the wedding of Prince Charles and Camilla Parker Bowles) 2005, The Golden Rule (anthem for 80th birthday of HM Queen Elizabeth II, with music by Sir Peter Maxwell-Davies) 2006, Diamond Wedding (for the Diamond Wedding Anniversary of HM Queen Elizabeth II and HR Duke of Edinburgh) 2007; non-fiction: The Poetry of Edward Thomas 1981, Philip Larkin 1982, The Lamberts (Somerset Maugham Award 1987) 1986, Philip Larkin: A Writer's Life 1993, William Barnes Selected Poems (ed.) 1994, Keats 1997, Wainewright the Poisoner 2000, In the Blood: A Memoir of my Childhood 2006, Ways of Life: Selected Essays and Reviews, 1994–2006 2008; fiction: The Pale Companion 1989, Famous for the Creatures 1991, The Invention of Dr Cake 2003, Silver: Return to Treasure Island 2012; other: additional texts for a performance of Haydn's Seven Last Words of Our Saviour on the Cross 2003. *Leisure interest:* fishing. *Address:* c/o Faber & Faber, Bloomsbury House, 74–77 Great Russell Street, London, WC1B 3DA, England. *Website:* www.faber.co.uk.

MOTLANTHE, Kgalema; South African trade union official, politician and fmr head of state; *Deputy President;* b. 19 July 1949, Johannesburg; three c.; mem. UmKhonto we Sizwe (ANC mil wing), detained during student protests 1976, arrested again 1977, spent 10 years in detention at Robben Island 1977–87; Educ. Officer Nat. Union of Mineworkers 1987–92, Sec.-Gen. 1992–97; Sec.-Gen. ANC 1997–2007, Deputy Pres. Dec. 2007–; mem. Parl. July 2008–; Minister without Portfolio July–Sept. 2008; Acting Pres. of South Africa Sept. 2008–May 2009, Deputy Pres. 2009–. *Address:* c/o The Presidency, Union Bldgs, West Wing, Government Avenue, Pretoria 0001 (office); African National Congress, 54 Sauer Street, Johannesburg 2001, South Africa (office). *Telephone:* (12) 3005200 (office); (11) 3761000 (office). *Fax:* (12) 3238246 (office); (11) 3761134 (office). *E-mail:* president@po.gov.za (office); nmtyelwa@anc.org.za (office). *Website:* www.gov.za/president/index.html (office); www.anc.org.za (office).

MOTSEPE, Patrice, BA, LLB; South African lawyer and business executive; *Chairman, African Rainbow Minerals Ltd;* b. 28 Jan. 1962, Soweto; s. of Augustine Motsepe; m. Precious Makgosi Moloi; three s.; ed Univ. of Swaziland, Univ. of Witwatersrand; Visiting Attorney, McGuire Woods Battle and Boothe 1991–92; Assoc. Partner, Bowman Gilfillan Attorneys, Johannesburg 1994–95, Partner 1995–96; Founder-Chair. Future Mining (Pty) Ltd 1995–; f. African Rainbow Minerals Ltd (ARMgold) 1997, mem. Bd of Dirs 2003–, Chair. 2004–; Chair. Naledi Mining 1997–, Teal Exploration and Mining Inc. 2005–, Ubuntu-Botho Investments; Chair. (non-exec.) Harmony Gold Mining Co. Ltd 2003–; Dir (non-exec.) Absa Group Ltd 2004–, Absa Bank Ltd 2004–, Sanlam Ltd (also Deputy Chair.) 2004–, Sanlam Life Insurance Ltd (also Deputy Chair.) 2006–; Pres. Nat. African Federated Chamber of Commerce 2002, Business Unity South Africa 2004–08; Vice-Pres. South African Chamber of Mines; mem. Gauteng Law Soc.; mem. Bd of Dirs African Fashion International; Owner, Mamelodi Sundowns Football Club; South Africa's Business Leader of the Year, Ernst & Young 2002, South Africa's Best Entrepreneur Award 2002. *Achievements include:* first African to join Giving Pledge (campaign by Bill Gates and Warren Buffett to encourage wealthy people to give at least half of their wealth to philanthropic causes). *Address:* African Rainbow Minerals Ltd., PO Box 786136, Sandton 2146, South Africa (office). *E-mail:* ir.admin@arm.co.za (office). *Website:* www.arm.co.za (office).

MOTSUENYANE, Samuel Mokgethi, BSc (Agric.); South African business executive and diplomatist; b. 11 Feb. 1927, Potchefstroom; s. of the late Solomon P. Motsuenyane and Christina D. Motsuenyane; m. Jocelyn Mashinini 1954; six s.; ed North Carolina State Univ., USA, Jan Hofmeyr School of Social Work; Nat. Organizing Sec. African Nat. Soil Conservation Asscn 1952–59; NC State Univ., USA 1960–62; Pres. NAFCOC 1968–92; Chair. African Business Publications, African Business Holdings, NAFCOC Permanent, Venda Nat. Devt Corpn, New-Real African Investments; Dir African Devt and Construction Holdings, NAFCOC Nat. Trust, Barlow Rand, Blackchain Ltd, numerous other cos; Chancellor, Univ. of the North (SA) 1985–90; Pres. Motsuenyane Comm. to investigate torture and disappearances in ANC detention camps 1992–93; Amb. to Saudi Arabia (also accred to Yemen, Kuwait and Oman) 1996–2000; Leader South African Observer Mission to the Presidential Elections in Zimbabwe 2002; Pres. Boy Scouts of SA 1976–81; Leader of Senate 1994–96; Dr hc (Univ. of Witwatersrand) 1983; Hon. DEconSc (Cape Town) 1986; Harvard Business Award 1977. *Publications:* numerous articles. *Leisure interests:* gardening, reading. *Address:* c/o Ministry of Foreign Affairs, Private Bag X152, Pretoria 0001, South Africa.

MOTTAKI, Manouchehr, MA; Iranian diplomatist and politician; b. 1953, Bandar Gaz, Golestan; ed Bangalore Univ., India, Tehran Univ.; joined Islamic Revolutionary Guards Corps (IRGC) 1979, IRGC Liaison Officer to Ministry of Foreign Affairs (MOF) 1979–80; Deputy of Islamic Consultative Ass. (Majlis) 1980–84, 2004–; Head of Political Bureau, MOF 1984–85; Amb. to Turkey 1985–89, to Japan 1994–99; Dir-Gen. of W European Affairs, MOF 1989; Deputy Foreign Minister for Int. Affairs 1989–92, for Consular and Parl. Affairs 1992–94; Adviser to Minister of Foreign Affairs 1999–2001; Vice-Pres. Islamic Culture and Communications Org. 2001–04; Campaign Man. for Presidential cand. Ali Larijani 2005; Minister of Foreign Affairs 2005–10. *Address:* c/o Ministry of Foreign Affairs, Shahid Abd al-Hamid Mesri Street, Ferdowsi Avenue, Tehran, Iran.

MOTTLEY, Mia Amor, QC; Barbadian lawyer and politician; b. 1 Oct. 1965; ed Merryvale Private School, The UN Int. School, Queen's Coll., London School of Econs, UK; called to the Bar of England and Wales, Inner Bar of Barbados 2002; Opposition Senator, Senate of Barbados and Shadow Minister of Culture and Community Devt 1991–94, served on several Jt Select Cttees including on Praedial Larceny and Domestic Violence; MP 1994–; Minister of Educ., Youth Affairs and Culture 1994–2001; Gen. Sec. Barbados Labour Party 1996–2008, Leader 2008–; Chair. Caribbean Community (CARICOM) Standing Cttee of Ministers of Educ. 1996, 1997; Deputy Prime Minister, Attorney-Gen., Leader of Govt Business in House of Ass. and Minister of Home Affairs 2001–06; Deputy Prime Minister, Leader of Govt Business in House of Ass. and Minister of Econ. Affairs and Devt 2006–08; Leader of the Opposition 2008–10; mem. Nat. Security Council of Barbados, Barbados Defence Bd, Privy Council of Barbados 2002. *Address:* Barbados Labour Party, Grantley Adams House, 111 Roebuck Street, Bridgetown, Barbados (office). *Telephone:* 429-1990 (office). *Fax:* 427-8792 (office). *E-mail:* will99@caribsurf.com (office). *Website:* labourparty.wordpress.com (office).

MOTTRAM, Sir Richard Clive, KCB, GCB, BA; British civil servant; b. 23 April 1946; s. of John Mottram and Florence Yates; m. Fiona Margaret Erskine 1971; three s. one d.; ed King Edward VI Camp Hill School, Birmingham, Univ. of Keele; joined Civil Service 1968, assigned to Ministry of Defence, Asst Pvt. Sec. to Sec. of State for Defence 1971–72, Prin. Naval Programme and Budget 1973, Cabinet Office 1975–77, Pvt. Sec. to Perm. Under-Sec., Ministry of Defence 1979–81, Pvt. Sec. to Sec. of State for Defence 1982–86, Asst Under-Sec. of State (programmes) 1986–89, Deputy Under-Sec. of State (Policy) 1989–92, Perm. Sec. Office of Public Service and Science, Cabinet Office 1992–95, Ministry of Defence 1995–98, Dept of the Environment, Transport and the Regions 1998–2001, Dept for Transport, Local Govt and the Regions 2001, for Work and Pensions 2002–05, Intelligence, Security and Resilience, Cabinet Office 2005–07 (retd); Hon. DLitt (Keele) 1996. *Leisure interests:* cinema, theatre, tennis. *Address:* c/o Cabinet Office, 70 White-hall, London, SW1A 2AS, England (office).

MOTULSKY, Arno G., BS, MD; American medical geneticist and academic; *Professor Emeritus of Medicine and Genome Sciences, University of Washington;* b. 1923, Germany; s. of Herman Motulsky and Rena Motulsky (née Sass); m. Gretel Stern 1945 (died 2009); one s. two d.; ed Cen. YMCA Coll., Chicago, Yale Univ., Univ. of Illinois Medical School; Intern, Fellow, Asst and Sr Resident (Internal Medicine) Michael Reese Hosp., Chicago 1947–51; Staff mem. in charge of Clinical Investigation, Dept of Hematology, Army Medical Service Graduate School, Walter Reed Army Medical Center; Research Assoc. in Internal Medicine, George Washington Univ. School of Medicine, Washington 1952–53, Instructor 1953–55, Asst Prof. 1955–58, Assoc. Prof. 1958–61, Prof., Dept of Medicine 1961–, Prof. Dept of Genetics 1961–, Dir Medical Genetics Training Program 1961–89, Dir Center for Inherited Diseases 1972–89, Prof. Emer. of Medicine and Genome Sciences 1994–; Pres. Int. Congress of Human Genetics 1986; Ed. American Journal of Human Genetics 1969–75, Human Genetics 1969–98; mem. American Soc. of Human Genetics, NAS 1976, American Acad. of Arts and Sciences 1978, American Philosophical Soc.; Hon. DSc (Illinois) 1982, Hon. MD (Würzburg) 1991; William Allan Memorial Award 1970, Alexander von Humboldt Award 1984, San Remo Int. Prize for Genetic Research 1988, Excellence in Educ. Award 1999, Lifetime Achievement Award, American Coll. of Medical Genetics 2009, Victor A. McKusick Leadership Award, American Soc. of Human Genetics 2009. *Publications:* Human Genetics – Problems and Approaches (with F. Vogel) 1996 (fourth edn with M. Speicher and S. Antonarakis 2010); more than 400 medical and scientific articles. *Leisure interests:* reading, collecting African art, antique maps. *Address:* Univer-

sity of Washington, Department of Genome Sciences, PO Box 355065, Seattle, WA 98195-5065, USA (office). *Telephone:* (206) 543-3593 (office). *Fax:* (206) 685-7301 (office). *E-mail:* agmot@u.washington.edu (office). *Website:* depts.washington.edu/medgen/faculty/motulsky.html (office).

MOTZFELDT, Josef, (Tuusi), Higher Diploma (Teaching); Greenlandic politician; *President, Inatsisartut (Parliament);* b. 24 Nov. 1941, Igaliko; ed Hjørring Coll. (Hjørring Statsseminarium); trained as a teacher; Minister for Trade, Traffic and Vocational Training 1984–88; mem. Inatsisartut (Parl.) 1987–, Pres. 2009–; Chair. Inuit Ataqatigiit Party 1994–2007; Minister of Economy 1999–2001, Minister of Economy (Greenland Home Rule Govt) 2002–03; Minister of Finance and Foreign Affairs, Vice-Premier and Minister for Nordic Cooperation 2003–07; Chair. for the West-Nordic Council 2009–10, 2012–; Chair. Nat. Gallery of Arts of Greenland; Greenland Homerule Silver Award. *Film:* Tukuma (co-dir) 1984. *Leisure interests:* literature, the arts. *Address:* Inatsisartut, PO Box 1060, 3900 Nuuk, Greenland (office). *Telephone:* 346118 (office). *Fax:* 324606 (office). *E-mail:* tuusi@ina.gl (office). *Website:* www.inatsisartut.gl (office); ia.gl (office).

MOUALLEM, Walid; Syrian diplomatist and politician; *Deputy Prime Minister and Minister of Foreign Affairs and Expatriates;* b. 1941; ed Cairo Univ., Egypt; joined diplomatic corps 1964; held positions at missions in Saudi Arabia and Spain; fmr Chargé d'affaires a.i., London; Amb. to Romania 1975–80; Head, Foreign Ministry Bureau, Damascus 1984–90; Amb. to USA 1990–2000; Deputy Minister of Foreign Affairs 2005–06, Minister of Foreign Affairs 2006–11 (resgnd with rest of cabinet at Pres.'s request following popular protests), Minister of Foreign Affairs and Expatriates April 2011–; Deputy Prime Minister 2012–. *Address:* Ministry of Foreign Affairs and Expatriates, rue ar-Rashid, Damascus, Syria (office). *Telephone:* (11) 3331200 (office). *E-mail:* syr-mofa@scs-net.org (office).

MOUALLIMI, Abdallah Yahya Al-, BS, MS; Saudi Arabian diplomatist and business executive; *Permanent Representative, United Nations;* b. 5 May 1952; m. Sahar Haider O. Hajjar; four c.; ed Oregon State Univ., Stanford Univ., USA; Vice-Chair. Olayan Financing Co. 1991–98, now Adviser; Founder-Pres. Dar al-Mouallimi Consulting Co. 1995–; mem. of Shoura Council (Parl.) 1997–2001; Mayor of Jeddah 2001–05; Co-Founder and Chair. HBG Holdings Ltd 2006–; Perm. Rep. to EU, Brussels (also accred as Amb. to Luxembourg) 2007–11, Perm. Rep. to UN, New York 2011–; Chair. (non-exec.) European Islamic Investment Bank PLC 2011–; fmr Chair. Jeddah Chamber of Commerce, Egyptian Finance Co.; mem. Bd of Dirs Allujain Corpn –2008, Majid Bin Abdulaziz Soc. for Devt and Social Services, Sanad Insurance Co., Coca-Cola Bottling Co. Saudi Arabia, Jeddah Provincial Council, Alumni Soc. of Modern Capital Inst., Consulting Comm. to Supreme Council of Gulf Cooperation Council; Bd mem. Gen. Org. for Mil. Industries, Saudi Nat. Commercial Bank, Egypt Finance Co., Assir Establishment for Press, Saudi Telecom; mem. Consultative Council of Saudi Arabia 1997–2001; Grand Cross, Order of the Crown (Belgium) 2011. *Address:* Permanent Mission of Saudi Arabia to United Nations, 809 United Nations Plaza, 10th and 11th Floors, New York, NY 10017, USA (office). *Telephone:* (212) 557-1525 (office). *Fax:* (212) 983-4895 (office). *E-mail:* saudi-mission@un.int (office). *Website:* www.saudimission.org (office).

MOUFTAKIR, Mohammed; Moroccan film director and screenwriter; b. 1965, Casablanca; ed Univ. Hassan II, Aïn Chock; worked as asst dir on various int. productions for five years; achieved int. recognition with debut feature film Pegase. *Films include:* L'Ombre de la Mort (short) 2003, La Danse du Foetus (short) (Grand Jury Prize, Tangier Nat. Film Festival) 2005, Fin du Mois (short) (Grand Jury Prize, Tangier Nat. Film Festival) 2007, Chant Funèbre (short) 2008, Terminus des Anges 2009, Pegase (Golden Stallion, Pan African Film Festival, Burkina Faso 2011) 2009. *Address:* c/o Centre Cinématographique Marocain, BP 421, Avenue El Majd, Quartier Industriel, Rabat, Morocco (office).

MOUGEOTTE, Etienne Pierre Albert; French journalist; *Editor-in-Chief, Le Figaro Magazine;* b. 1 March 1940, La Rochefoucauld; s. of Jean Mougeotte and Marcelle Thonon; m. Françoise Duprilot 1972; one s. two d.; ed Lycée Buffon, Lycée Henri-IV, Paris, Inst. d'études politiques de Paris, Inst. Français de presse; reporter, France-Inter 1965-66, Beirut Corresp. 1966–67; Ed. Europe Numéro 1 1968–69; Chief Reporter, Asst Ed.-in-Chief Information Première (TV) 1969–72; Producer l'Actualité en question 1972; journalist Radio-Télé Luxembourg 1972–73; Ed.-in-Chief Europe 1 1973, News Dir 1974–81; monthly contrib. Paradoxes 1974–; Editorial Dir Journal du Dimanche 1981–83, Télé 7 Jours 1983–87; Dir Gen. Broadcasting TF1 1987–89, Dir Gen. 1987–89, Vice-Pres. Broadcasting 1989–; Vice-Pres. French Fed. of Press Agencies 1975–81; mem. Interprofessional communication group (Gic) 1985–87; Pres. Nat. Videocommunication Syndicate 1982–87, TF1 Films, Tricom; Dir TF1 1991–2007; Pres. TF1 Films Productions; Dir TF1 Films 1991–2007, Pres. TF1 Films and TF1 Digital 2000–07; Assoc. Prof. École de Journalisme, Univ. of Paris Sciences Po 2004–; Ed.-in-Chief Le Figaro Magazine 2007–; Officier Légion d'honneur, Ordre nat. du Mérite. *Leisure interests:* tennis, golf. *Address:* Société du Figaro SA, 14 boulevard Haussman, 75009 Paris, France (office). *Website:* www.lefigaro.fr/lefigaromagazine (office).

MOUKHTAR, Gamal ed-Din; Egyptian institute director and academic; *President, Arab Academy for Science, Technology and Maritime Transport;* fmr Chair. Egyptian Antiquities Org.; currently Pres. Arab Acad. for Science, Tech. and Maritime Transport, Alexandria. *Publications include:* Cairo: The Site and the History (co-author) 1988, Alexandria: The Site and the History (co-author) 1993, Sinai: The Site and the History (co-author) 1998. *Address:* Arab Academy for Science, Technology and Maritime Transport, PO Box 1029, Alexandria, Egypt (office). *Telephone:* (3) 5565429 (office). *Fax:* (3) 5622525 (office). *E-mail:* info@aast .edu (office). *Website:* www.aast.edu (office).

MOULAERT, Jacques, LLD, MPA; Belgian banker; *Honorary Chairman, ING Bank Belgium SA;* b. 23 Oct. 1930, Ostend; s. of the late Albert Moulaert and of Marie Magdeleine de Neckere; m. Christiane Laloux 1957; four d.; ed St Barbara Coll. Ghent, Univ. of Ghent and Harvard Univ., USA; Gen. Sec. Aleurope SA 1961; Asst Man. Compagnie Lambert 1967; Man. Compagnie Bruxelles Lambert (CBL) 1972; Man. Dir Groupe Bruxelles Lambert 1979; Chair. Bd Bank Brussels Lambert (BBL) 1993–2001; Hon. Chair., ING Bank Belgium SA; fmr mem. Bd of Dirs Tractebel, Cockerill-Sambre, Royale Belge, Sabena, Viohalco; fmr Visiting Prof., Université Catholique de Louvain; Officier, Ordre de la Couronne; Commdr, Ordre de Léopold, Ordre de St-Sylvestre. *Address:* 2 Tailleur de Pierre, 1380

Lasne, Belgium (home). *Telephone:* (2) 633-10-52 (home). *Fax:* (2) 633-64-15 (home). *E-mail:* jacques.moulaert@skynet.be.

MOULAYE, Mohamed, DSc; Mauritanian politician and public official; b. 1 Oct. 1936, Ouagadougou, Burkina Faso; s. of El Hassan Moulaye and Maimouna Dem; m. Ginette Marcin 1962; three s. five d.; Founder-mem. Asscn de la Jeunesse de Mauritanie 1956; Sec.-Gen. Section PRM Boutilimit 1960; mem. Nat. Ass. 1965–75; Directeur des finances 1966; Contrôleur financier 1967–75; Minister of Finance 1975–77, 1979; Parl. rapporteur to Comm. des Finances; fmr mem. IPU; Dir Office of Pres. of Mauritania 1979–80; Conseiller Econ. et Financier du Chef de l'Etat, Président de la Comm. Centrale des Marchés Publics; Pres. Parti du Centre démocratique mauritanien 1992, now Democratic Centre Party; First Vice-Pres. Action pour le Changement; mem. Conseil général, Banque Centrale de Mauritanie 1980–; Dir Personnel Air Afrique, Financial Dir 1985–; Chair. and Man. Dir Arrachad, Nouackchott 1990; Chevalier, Ordre nat. du Mérite. *Leisure interests:* reading, cinema. *Address:* BP 289, Nouackchott, Mauritania.

MOULD, Jeremy R., PhD; Australian (b. American) astronomer and academic; *Professor, Centre for Astrophysics and Supercomputing, Swinburne University of Technology;* b. 31 July 1949, USA; ed Univ. of Melbourne, Australian Nat. Univ.; emigrated to Australia 1963; fmr Research Fellow, Kitt Peak Nat. Observatory; fmr Prof., California Inst. of Tech.; fmr Dir Research School of Astronomy and Astrophysics, ANU and American Nat. Optical Astronomy Observatory; currently Prof., Centre for Astrophysics and Supercomputing, Swinburne Univ. of Tech.; Asteroid 18240 Mould named in his honour, George Van Biesbroeck Prize (co-recipient) 1981, Newton Lacy Pierce Prize in Astronomy (co-recipient) 1984, Cosmology Prize, Gruber Foundation (co-recipient) 2009. *Publications:* numerous papers in professional journals. *Address:* Room SA 117, Centre for Astrophysics and Supercomputing, Swinburne University of Technology, PO Box 218, Hawthorn, Vic. 3122, Australia (office); National Optical Astronomy Observatory, Tucson, AZ 85726-6732, USA (office). *Telephone:* (3) 9214-4921 (Hawthorn) (office); (520) 318-8281 (Tucson) (office). *Fax:* (3) 9214-8797 (Hawthorn) (office); (520) 318-8170 (Tucson) (office). *E-mail:* jrm@noao.edu (office). *Website:* www.noao.edu/noao/staff/jrm (office); astronomy.swin.edu.au/staff/jmould.html (office); astronomy.swin.edu.au/~jmould (office).

MOULINE, Larbi; Moroccan business executive, diplomatist and consultant; b. 10 Nov. 1934, Rabat; s. of Mohamed Mouline and Habiba Balafrej; m. Naima Mouline 1959; three s. one d.; ed Ecole Nat. Supérieure des Mines, St Etienne, France; Man. Dir O.C.P. (phosphate co.) 1959–74, Pres. Amicale des Hors-Cadres; Gen. Man. Sonasid (steel co.) 1975–83; Amb. to India 1984–86, to Greece 1987–88; Adviser to Minister of Privatization and Econ. Affairs, Minister of Agric. 1989–94; now pvt. consultant; Sec.-Gen. Asscn des Intervenants Scientifiques (ASSIST), Rabat; Kt of the Throne (Morocco), Order of Phoenix (Greece). *Publications:* A Study on Economic Development Linked to a Steel Complex in Morocco 1977, A Study on Mechanization in Phosphate Mines. *Leisure interests:* reading, music, golf, travel. *Address:* 27 rue Cadi Sanhaji, Souissi, Rabat, Morocco. *Telephone:* (37) 750282. *Fax:* (37) 639501. *E-mail:* imouline@iam.net.ma (home).

MOUNGAR, Fidèle, Chadian physician and politician; b. Logone Region; fmr head of surgery, Peronne Hosp., Somme, France; Prime Minister of Chad 1993; Chair. Action tchadienne pour l'unité et le socialisme (ACTUS), Collectif des partis pour le changement (COPAC). *Address:* Action tchadienne pour l'unité et le socialisme, N'Djamena, Chad (office). *E-mail:* actus@club-internet.fr (office).

MOUNT, Sir (William Robert) Ferdinand, MA, FRSL, FSA; British writer and journalist; b. 2 July 1939, London; s. of the late Robert Mount and Julia Mount; m. Julia Margaret Lucas 1968; two s. (one deceased), one d.; ed Eton Coll., Christ Church, Oxford; Political Ed., The Spectator 1977–82, 1985, Literary Ed. 1984–85; Head, Prime Minister Margaret Thatcher's Policy Unit 1982–84; Dir, Centre for Policy Studies 1984–91; Political Columnist, The Standard 1980–82, The Times 1984–85, Daily Telegraph 1985–90; Ed., Times Literary Supplement 1991–2002; Sr Columnist, The Sunday Times 2002–04; Vice-Chair., Power Comm. 2004–05; mem. RSL (mem. of Council 2002–05); Hon. Fellow (Univ. of Wales, Lampeter) 2002. *Publications include:* Very Like a Whale 1967, The Theatre of Politics 1972, The Man Who Rode Ampersand 1975, The Clique 1978, The Subversive Family 1982, The Selkirk Strip 1987, Of Love and Asthma 1991 (Hawthornden Prize 1992), The British Constitution Now 1992, Communism 1992, Umbrella 1994, The Liquidator 1995, Jem (and Sam) 1998, Fairness 2001, Mind the Gap: The New Class Divide in Britain 2004, Heads You Win 2004, The Condor's Head 2007, Cold Cream: My Early Life and Other Mistakes 2008, Full Circle: How the Classical World Came Back to Us 2010, The New Few: A Very British Oligarchy 2012. *Address:* 17 Ripplevale Grove, London, N1 1HS, England (home). *Telephone:* (20) 7607-5398 (home).

MOUNTAIN, Ross Stewart; New Zealand international organization official and fmr UN official; *Director General, DARA;* b. 13 Nov. 1944, Christchurch; s. of Noel Stewart Mountain and Frida Thekla Monrad; m.; three d.; ed Victoria Univ., Wellington; Inter-Agency Youth Liaison Officer, Div. of Social Affairs, UN, Geneva 1973–75, Coordinator UN Non-Governmental Liaison Service 1975–83; Chief of Information Section, UNDP European Office 1976–85; Deputy Resident Rep. in S Pacific, Fiji 1985–88; UNDP Resident Rep. ad interim and Dir UN Information Centre, Kabul, Afghanistan 1988–91; UN Special Coordinator for Emergency Relief Operations, UNDP Resident Rep., World Food Programme and UN Population Fund (UNFPA) Rep. in Liberia 1991–93; UNDP Rep. and UN Humanitarian Affairs Coordinator, Haiti, on secondment from UN Resident Coordinator and UNDP Resident Coordinator for Eastern Caribbean, Barbados 1993–95; UN Resident Coordinator in Lebanon and Resident Rep. of UNDP and UNFPA 1995–98; Asst Emergency Relief Coordinator and Dir Geneva Office, Office for the Coordination of Humanitarian Affairs (OCHA) 1998–2003; Special Rep. of UN Sec.-Gen. for Iraq, also UN Humanitarian Coordinator and UNDP Resident Rep. 2003–04; Deputy Special Rep. of UN Sec.-Gen. in the Democratic Repub. of the Congo 2004–09; Dir Gen. DARA (int. aid and devt org.), Madrid 2010–; fmr Humanitarian Coordinator ad interim for E Timor Crisis, Special Humanitarian Envoy for floods in Mozambique, Special Humanitarian Coordinator for Liberia, Head OCHA Crisis Task Team for Iraq. *Address:* DARA, Felipe IV, 9, 28014 Madrid, Spain (office). *Telephone:* (91) 5310372 (office). *E-mail:* mountain@daraint.org (office). *Website:* www.daraint.org (office).

MOUNTCASTLE, Vernon Benjamin, Jr, MD; American neurophysiologist (retd) and academic; *Professor Emeritus, Krieger Mind-Brain Institute, Johns Hopkins University;* b. 15 July 1918, Shelbyville, Ky.; s. of Vernon B. Mountcastle and Anna-Francis Marguerite Waugh; m. Nancy Clayton Pierpont 1945; two s. one d.; ed Roanoke Coll., Johns Hopkins Univ. School of Medicine; House Officer, Surgery, The Johns Hopkins Hosp. Baltimore, Md 1943; with USN Amphibious Forces 1943–46; through jr ranks, The Johns Hopkins Univ. School of Medicine 1948–59, Prof. of Physiology 1959, Dir of Dept of Physiology 1964–80, Univ. Prof. of Neuroscience 1980–92, Prof. Emer. 1992–; Dir Bard Labs of Neurophysiology, Johns Hopkins Univ. 1981–91; Pres. Neurosciences Research Foundation 1981–85; Dir Neuroscience Research Program 1981–84; Penfield Lecturer, American Univ., Beirut 1971; Sherrington Lecturer, Liverpool Univ. 1974; Sherrington Lecturer, Royal Soc. of Medicine, London, Mellon Lecturer, Univ. of Pittsburgh 1976, Visiting Prof., Collège de France, Paris 1980 and numerous other hon. lectureships; Nat. Pres. Soc. for Neuroscience 1971–72; mem. NAS, American Acad. of Arts and Sciences, American Phil. Soc.; Foreign Fellow, Royal Soc. (UK); Hon. DSc (Pennsylvania) 1976, (Roanoke) 1968, (Northwestern) 1985; Hon. MD (Zurich) 1983, (Siena) 1984; Lashley Prize, American Philosophical Soc. 1974, F. O. Schmitt Prize and Medal, MIT 1975, Gold Medal, Royal Soc. of Medicine 1976, Horwitz Prize, Columbia 1978, Gerard Prize, Soc. for Neuroscience 1980, Int. Prize, Fyssen Foundation Paris 1983, Lasker Award 1983, Nat. Medal of Sciences 1986, McGovern Prize and Medal, AAAS 1990, Neuroscience Award Fidia Fed. 1990, Australia Prize 1993, Neuroscience Prize, NAS 1998. *Publications:* The Mindful Brain (with G. M. Edelman) 1978, Medical Physiology (two vols) (ed. and major contrib.) 14th edn 1980, Perceptual Neuroscience: The Cerebral Cortex 1998, The Sensory Hand 2005; more than 50 articles in scientific journals on the physiology of the central nervous system, especially on the neuronal mechanisms in sensation and perception. *Leisure interests:* gardening. *Address:* 15601 Carroll Road, Monkton, MD 21111, USA (home). *Telephone:* (410) 472-2514 (home). *E-mail:* mountcastle@mbi.mb.jhu.edu (office).

MOUNTER, Julian D'Arcy, QM, MA; British journalist, television director, producer and broadcasting executive; *Chairman and CEO, Media Consultants and Investments;* b. 2 Nov. 1944, Cornwall, England; s. of Francis Mounter and Elizabeth Moore; m. Patricia A. Kelsall-Spurr 1983; two s.; ed Skinners Grammar School, Tunbridge Wells, Grenville Coll., Univ. of Leicester; reporter with various local newspapers 1961–65; journalist, The Times 1966–71; Weekend World, London Weekend TV 1971–73; Head of Current Affairs and Documentaries, Westward TV 1973–74; Reporter/Dir Panorama and Midweek, BBC TV 1974–78; Producer Inside Business, Thames TV 1978–79, Exec. Producer, Current Affairs 1979–81, Controller, Children's and Young Adults' Dept 1981–84; Dir Programmes and Production, Thorn-EMI Satellite and Cable 1984–86; Dir Cosgrove Hall Ltd 1981–84, JRA Ltd 1980–85, Cameralink Ltd 1980–85, Blackwell Videotec Ltd 1980–85; Dir-Gen. and CEO Television New Zealand 1986–91; Chair. South Pacific Pictures Ltd, Broadcast Communications Ltd 1988–91; Dir The Listener, Visnews (UK) Ltd 1987–89, Reuters TV Ltd 1989–91; Chief Exec. and Pres. Star TV Ltd Hutchvision Ltd, Media Assets Ltd, Asia News Ltd 1992–93; Chair. New Media Investments 1994–98, Majestic Films and TV Ltd 1993–95, Swoffers Ltd 1995–96, Renown Leisure Group Ltd 1995–2000; CEO and Man. Dir Seven Network Ltd, Australia 1998–2000; Dir, Deputy Chair. and Chair. Channel Television Ltd 1994–99; Chair. and CEO Media Consultants and Investments 2001–; Dir Int. Council of Nat. Acad. of Television Arts and Sciences, New York 1993–2005 (Assoc. Dir 2005–08), Diverse Productions Ltd, FBC Media and various others 2002–09; Chair. Steering Bd; mem. Advisory Bd Pax Mondial 2008–12; Trustee, Int. Inst. of Communications 1988–95; Hon. Visiting Fellow, Univ. of Leicester 2005; Queen's Medal for Services to NZ 1990; various press and TV awards. *Leisure interests:* ocean sailing, naval history, music, flying. *Address:* Media Consultants and Investments, 2 Clifton, St Peter Port, GY1 2PH, Guernsey, Channel Islands (office). *E-mail:* executive@mediahelp.tv (office).

MOUREAUX, Philippe; Belgian politician; b. 12 April 1939, Etterbeek; m.; four c.; secondary school teacher 1961–62; Asst, subsequently Prof., Université Libre de Bruxelles 1967–; Adviser, Deputy Prime Minister's Office 1972–73, on staff Prime Minister's Office 1973–74, Chef de cabinet to Deputy Prime Minister 1977–80, Minister of the Interior and Institutional Reforms 1980, of Justice and Institutional Reforms 1980–81, Minister and Chair. Exec. of French Community, responsible for cultural affairs, budget and foreign affairs 1981–85, Feb.–May 1988, Deputy Prime Minister and Minister for the Brussels Region and Institutional Reforms 1988–89, 1990–92, of Social Affairs 1992–93; Minister of State 1995–; Co-Pres. Conférence intergouvernementale et interparlementaire pour le renouveau institutionnel 1999-2000; mem. Parti Socialiste. *Address:* Administration communale, Rue du Comte de Flandre, 20, 1080 Brussels, Belgium. *Telephone:* (2) 412-37-00. *Fax:* (2) 412-37-02. *E-mail:* pmoureaux@molenbeek.irisnet.be.

MOURINHO, José; Portuguese football manager; *Manager, Chelsea Football Club;* b. (José Mário Dos Santos Mourinho Félix), 26 Jan. 1963, Setubal; s. of José Mourinho Félix and Maria Júlia Dos Santos; m. Matilde 'Tami' Faria 1989; one s. one d.; completed UEFA coaching course after studying in Britain 1987; worked as fitness trainer at various clubs and coached jr team Vitoria Setubal then asst Estrela Amadora 1990–92; interpreter, Sporting Lisbon 1992–1993; interpreter and Asst Coach Porto 1993–1996; Asst Coach Barcelona, Spain 1996–2000; Coach Benfica 2000, Uniao de Leiria 2000–01, Porto 2002–04 (won UEFA Cup 2003, Portuguese Championship 2003, 2004, Taça de Portugal 2002/03, SuperCup Cândido de Oliveira 2003, Champions League 2004); Man. and First Team Coach, Chelsea Football Club, England 2004–07, 2013– (won FA Premier League 2004/05, 2005/06, FA Cup 2007, Football League Cup 2005, 2007, FA Community Shield 2005); Man. FC Internazionale Milano 2008–10 (won Supercoppa Italiana 2008, Serie A title 2008/09, 2009/10, Coppa Italia 2009/10, UEFA Champions League 2009/10), Real Madrid Club de Fútbol 2010–13 (won Copa del Rey 2010/11, La Liga 2011/12, Supercopa de España 2012); univ. degree in Physical Educ. specializing in Football Methodology; Officer, Order of Infante Dom Henrique; Dr hc (Tech. Univ. of Lisbon) 2009; UEFA Champions League Man. of the Year 2002/03, 2003/04, Portuguese Liga Manager of the Year 2002/03, 2003/04, World Soccer Magazine Coach of the Year 2003/04, 2004/05, UEFA Team of the Year Coach of the Year 2003, 2004, 2005, FA Premier League Man. of the Year 2004/05, 2005/06, IFFHS World Man. of the Year 2004, 2005, FA Premier League Man. of the Month 11/

2004, 01/2005, 03/2007, BBC Sports Personality of the Year Coach Award 2005, Onze d'Or European Coach 2005, selected as the New Statesman Man of the Year 2005, Serie A Man. in the Year 2009, Int. Sports Press Asscn Best Man. in the World 2010, Football Extravaganza's League of Legends 2011, Prémio Prestígio Fernando Soromenho 2012. *Address:* Chelsea Football Club, Stamford Bridge, Fulham Road, London, SW6 1HS, England (office). *Telephone:* (20) 7835-6000 (office). *Fax:* (20) 7381-4831 (office). *E-mail:* info@chelseafc.com (office). *Website:* www.chelseafc.com (office).

MOUSA, Ali bin Muhammad bin; Omani economist, central banker and fmr politician; *Deputy Chairman, Central Bank of Oman;* fmr Minister of Health; Chair. Oman Tender Bd 2010–; currently Deputy Chair. Bd of Govs, Central Bank of Oman. *Address:* Central Bank of Oman, POB 1161, 44 Mutrah Commercial Centre, Ruwi 112, Oman (office). *Telephone:* 24777777 (office). *Fax:* 24788995 (office). *E-mail:* cboccr@omantel.net.om (office). *Website:* www.cbo-oman.org (office).

MOUSAWI, Faisal Radhi al-, MB, BCh, FRCSE; Bahraini government official and orthopaedic surgeon; b. 6 April 1944, Bahrain; one s. three d.; ed Univ. of Cairo, Egypt; fmr Rotary Intern, Cairo Univ. Hosp.; House Officer, Sr House Officer, Dept of Surgery, Govt Hosp., Bahrain; Sr House Officer, Accident and Orthopaedic Surgery, Cen. Middx Hosp., London; Orthopaedic Surgery, St Helier Hosp., Carshalton, Surrey; Gen. Surgery, Nelson Hosp., London, St Bartholomew's Hosp., London; Registrar, Orthopaedic Surgery, Whittington Hosp., London, Gen. and Traumatic Surgery, Wexford Co. Hosp., Ireland; locum consultant, Whittington Hosp. 1983–84; Consultant Orthopaedic Surgeon, Salmaniya Medical Centre, Bahrain 1976–, Chair. Dept of Surgery 1982–84, Chief of Medical Staff June–Aug. 1982, Chair. Dept of Orthopaedic Surgery; Asst Prof., Coll. of Medicine and Medical Sciences, Arabian Gulf Univ.; Asst Under-Sec., Ministry of Health 1982–85, Minister of Health 1995–2002; Chair. Shura Council 2002–06; mem. Scientific Council, Arab Bd for Surgery 1979–; Chair. Arab Bd Cttee for Sub-specialities in Surgery, Arab Bd for Orthopaedic Surgery 1990–, Chair. Training Cttee 1988–; Chair. Nat. Arab Bd Cttee and Co-ordinator, Arab Bd Programme in Surgery, Bahrain; Examiner, Ministry of Health Qualification Examination 1982–, Royal Coll. of Surgeons, Ireland, Part B Fellowship Examination; mem. Editorial Bd Bahrain Medical Bulletin; Founding mem. and Pres. Gulf Orthopaedic Asscn; mem. European Soc. for Sport Medicine, Knee Surgery and Arthroscopy; Fellow, British Orthopaedic Asscn, Royal Coll. of Surgeons, Ireland. *Publications:* numerous papers and articles. *Leisure interest:* tennis. *Address:* c/o Shura Council, PO Box: 2991, Shaikh Duaij Road, Ghudaibiya, Bahrain (office). *Website:* www.shura.gov.bh (office).

MOUSKOURI, Ioanna (Nana); Greek singer and fmr politician; b. 13 Oct. 1934, Athens; d. of Constantin Mouskouri and Alice Mouskouri; m. 1st George Petsilas; one s. one d.; m. 2nd Andre Chapelle; ed Athens Nat. Conservatory; singer 1956–; living in Paris 1962–; has given concerts world-wide; has sold more than 300 million records world-wide; recorded more than 1,500 songs in Greek, French, English, German, Dutch, Italian and Spanish; numerous TV appearances, including Numéro 1 1979 and Nana Mouskouri à Athènes 1984; UNICEF Amb. 1993–, Special Rep. for the Performing Arts and Hon. Spokesperson; mem. European Parl. 1994–99; Founder and Pres. Foundation 'Nana Mouskouri-Focus on Hope'; Gran Cruz Placa de Plata (Dominican Repub.) 2006, Officier, Légion d'honneur 2007, Grand Commdr, Order of Benefaction (Greece) 2007, Officier, Ordre Nat. du Québec 2013; 300 Gold and Platinum Discs world-wide, Greek Broadcasting Festival Award 1959, Barcelona Festival Award, No. 1 French Female Singer 1979, No. 1 Female Singer World-wide, Canada 1980, IFPI Multiplatinum Music Award 1996, UNICEF World of Children Award 1997 and numerous other awards and prizes. *Songs include:* L'enfant au tambour, Les parapluies de Cherbourg, C'est bon la vie, Plaisir d'amour, Ave Maria, L'amour en héritage, Only Love, White Rose of Athens, Je chante avec toi Liberté. *Publications:* Chanter ma vie 1989, Memoirs 2007, My Name is Nana 2007, Itinéraire intime 2013. *Leisure interest:* collecting antique jewellery, antiques and paintings. *Address:* c/o Nema Productions SA, 12 Robert de Traz, 1206 Geneva, Switzerland (office). *Telephone:* (22) 3460130 (home). *Fax:* (22) 7522293 (home). *E-mail:* nemaprod@bluewin.ch (home); nemaprod@mac.com (office). *Website:* www.nanamouskouri.net.

MOUSSA, Abou; Chadian UN official; b. 1950; m.; three c.; ed Univ. of Lagos, Nigeria, Advanced School of Journalism, France, Univ. of Paris 1 Panthéon-Sorbonne, France; joined UNHCR 1980, served in several duty stations, including Democratic Repub. of Congo, Switzerland, Ethiopia, Zambia fmr Regional Dir for West Africa; Rep. of Sec.-Gen. and Head of UN Peacebuilding Support Office in Liberia (UNOL) 2002–03, Deputy Special Rep. of Sec.-Gen., Humanitarian Coordinator and UN Devt Programme Resident, Rep. for Liberia 2003–05, Prin. Deputy Rep. of Sec.-Gen. in Côte d'Ivoire 2005–11, Special Rep. of Sec.-Gen. and Head, UN Regional Office for Central Africa (UNOCA) 2011–14. *Address:* c/o United Nations Regional Office for Central Africa (UNOCA), 23773, Cité de la Démocratie, Villas 55–57, Libreville Gabon.

MOUSSA, Amre Mahmoud, LLB; Egyptian politician, diplomatist and international organisation official; b. 3 Oct. 1936, Cairo; ed Cairo Univ.; joined Ministry of Foreign Affairs 1957; served in several diplomatic posts abroad, including Amb. to India 1983–86; Perm. Rep. to the UN 1990–91; Minister of Foreign Affairs 1991–2001; Sec.-Gen., League of Arab States (Arab League) 2001–11. *Address:* c/o League of Arab States, POB 11642, Tahrir Square, Cairo, Egypt.

MOUSSA DAWALEH, Ilyas, BEcons; Djibouti business executive and politician; *Minister of the Economy and Finance;* b. 1966; ed Univ. Rabelais, Tours, Institut Portuaire du Havre, France, Washington State Inst. of Public Policy, USA, Int. Maritime Org. Inst., UK; Head, Private Sector Dept, Nat. Planning Directorate, attached to Presidency of the Repub. 1992–93; Head of Gen. Man.'s Office, Port Autonome Int. de Djibouti 1993–94, Project Man. 1994–96, Dir of Operations 1996–2004; Minister of the Economy and Finance, in charge of Industry and Planning 2011–; Chair. Tamamoul Motors; fmr Chair. Bureau Main d'œuvres des Dockers (trade union); Dir of electoral campaign of Pres. Ismaïl Omar Guelleh 2011; co-f. Club des jeunes Entrepreneurs, Djibouti; mem. COMESA Nat. Cttee, Djibouti-Ethiopia Jt Comm., Djibouti Chamber of Commerce Nat. Reform Comm.; mem. Rassemblement populaire pour le progrès. *Address:* Ministry of the

Economy, Finance and Planning, BP 13, Djibouti (office). *Telephone:* 353331 (office). *Fax:* 356501 (office). *E-mail:* sg_mefpp@intnet.dj (office). *Website:* www.ministere-finances.dj (office).

MOUSSAVI, Farshid, BSc, DipArch, MArch II (Harvard); British (b. Iranian) architect and academic; *Professor in Practice of Architecture, Harvard University;* b. 17 Aug. 1965, Shiraz, Iran; d. of M. Mosavi and F. Kargozari-Moussavi; one d.; ed Univ. Coll., London, Bartlett School of Architecture, Harvard Univ., USA, Dundee Univ., RIBA; moved to London with family 1979; worked with Renzo Piano workshop, Genoa; with Office for Metropolitan Architecture, Rotterdam 1991–93; Co-founder and Owner (with Alejandro Zaera-Polo) Foreign Office Architects Ltd, London 1995–2011; Founder Farshid Moussavi Architecture, London 2011–; Unit Master, Architectural Asscn School of Architecture 1993–2000; Visiting Prof., Princeton Univ., UCLA, Columbia Univ., Berlage Inst., Amsterdam, Hoger Architecture Inst., Belgium; Prof. and Head of Architecture Inst., Acad. of Fine Arts, Vienna 2002–05; Kenzo Tange Visiting Design Critic, Harvard Univ. Grad. Design School 2005, currently Prof. in Practice of Architecture; represented UK at Architecture Biennale, Venice, Italy 2002; mem. Int. Design Cttee, London 2003, Design and Architecture Advisory Group to British Council, Aga Khan Award for Architecture Steering Cttee 2005– (Chair. Jury 2004); Bd Strelka Inst. for Architecture, Media and Design, Moscow 2011–; mem. Jury, RIBA Gold Medal, RIBA Pres.'s Medal, Stirling Prize for Architecture, 11th Architecture Biennale; columnist, Architecture Review 2011–; Trustee, Whitechapel Art Gallery, Architecture Foundation; numerous awards, including RIBA Int. Awards 2005, 2006, 2011, Special Award for Topography, 9th Venice Architecture Biennale 2004, Enric Miralles Prize for Architecture 2004, Charles Jencks Award for Architecture 2005, Architect of the Year Award, Architectural Digest, Madrid 2007, ELLE Award for Architecture 2008, Condé Nast Traveller Innovation and Design Award 2009, Green Good Design Award 2011. *Architectural works include:* Yokohama Int. Ferry Terminal, Japan (Kanagawa Architecture Prize 2003, Eric Miralles Prize for Architecture 2004, RIBA Worldwide Award 2005) 1996–2002, Belgo Restaurant, Notting Hill Br., London 1998, Bristol 1999, New York 1999, Bluemoon Hotel, Groningen, Netherlands, Municipal Police HQ, La Villajoyosa, Spain 2000–04, Public Square and Theatre, nr Alicante 2001–06, Coastal Park, nr Barcelona 2002–04, T'Raboes Harbour Facilities, Amersfoort, Netherlands 2002–, Meydan retail complex and multiplex, Istanbul, Turkey (Building Design's Retail Architect of the Year Award 2008, European Business Award for the Environment, Urban Land Inst. Award for Excellence, Prime Property Award, ArkiPARC Award 2009) 2007, Carabanchel social housing complex, Madrid, Spain (RIBA European Award 2008, Int. Architecture Award 2010), John Lewis dept store and cineplex, Leicester (RIBA Award 2009, Civic Trust Award and Special Award 2010) 2008, Museum of Contemporary Art, Cleveland, Ohio, USA 2006–12, residential complex in La Défense dist of Paris, France 2011–, 13th Venice Architecture Biennale installation, 'Architecture and its Affects' 2012, l'Îlot 'Citroën' development, Nantes 2013–, Jardins de la Lironde residential complex, Montpellier 2013–. *Publications include:* FOA Recent Projects 2001, The Yokohama Project 2002, El Croquis (monograph) 2003, Phylogenesis: FOA's Ark 2003, FOA's Ark Evolving Container for the Proliferating Singularities 2004, The Function of Ornament 2006, The Function of Form 2009. *Address:* Farshid Moussavi Architecture, 66 Warwick Square, London, SW1V 2AP, England (office). *Telephone:* (20) 7033-6490 (home). *E-mail:* office@farshidmoussavi.com (office). *Website:* www.farshidmoussavi.com (office).

MOUSSAVI, Mir Hussein; Iranian politician; b. 29 Sept. 1941, Khameneh, Iran; m. Zahra Rahnavard; ed Nat. Univ., Tehran; trained as an architect; joined Islamic Soc. at univ. in Tehran and active in Islamic socs since; imprisoned briefly for opposition to the Shah 1973; a Founder-mem. Islamic Republican Party (IRP) 1979; apptd Chief Ed. Jomhouri-e Eslami (Islamic Republic) newspaper 1979; Foreign Minister Aug.–Oct. 1981; elected Prime Minister by Majlis (consultative ass.) 1981–89, Adviser to the Pres. 1997–2005; currently mem. Shura-ye Tashkhis-e Maslahat-e Nezam—Council to Determine the Expediency of the Islamic Order, High Council of Cultural Revolution; Co-founder and Pres. Iranian Acad. of Arts, Tehran 1999–2009; cand. for Pres. of Tehran 2009. *Address:* c/o Iranian Academy of Arts, No. 23, Bouzarjmehr alley, Loqman-ul-Doleh Adham alley, South Palestine Street, Tehran, Iran (office). *E-mail:* honar@honar.ac.ir (office).

MOUSTIERS, Pierre Jean (Rossi), LenD; French author and producer; b. 13 Aug. 1924, La Seyne (Var); ed Univs of Aix-Marseilles and Neuchâtel; Attaché, Office des Changes, French zone in Germany 1947–49; Chief of Information Services, Nat. Information and Protection Centre for Construction (CNIP) 1950–60; medical lab., pharmaceutical lab. Merck, Darmstadt 1961, later regional insp.; Literary Critic, Nice-Matin 1970, Radio-Marseille; Officier des Arts et Lettres, Médaille des Combattants de la Résistance; Hommes et Lectures Prize 1962, Grand Prix de littérature sportive, Prix Jean Giono, Italy 1986. *Play:* Les Trois Chaînes (Théâtre de Boulogne-Billancourt) 1976. *Television:* L'hiver d'un gentilhomme 1973, La mort du Pantin 1975, Une place forte 1976, Un crime de notre temps 1977, La ronde de nuit (Grand Prix du Scénario) 1978, Le Coq de Bruyère 1980, Le Curé de Tours (Prix Acad. Balzac for TV adaptation 1980) 1980, Antoine et Julie 1981, Bel Ami 1983, L'Affaire Caillaux (Sceptre d'Or) 1985, Le Coeur du Voyage 1986, L'Eté de la Révolution 1989, Les Grandes Familles 1989, L'Interdiction 1992, Pris au piège 1993, Eugénie Grandet 1993, Un si bel orage 1995. *Publications:* Le journal d'un geôlier 1957, La mort du Pantin 1961, Le pharisien 1962, La paroi (Grand Prix du Roman, Acad. française 1969) 1969, L'hiver d'un gentilhomme (Prix des Maisons de la Presse 1972) 1971, Une place forte (Grand Prix littéraire de Provence 1975, Prix Louis Philippe Kammans) 1974, Un crime de notre temps (Prix des libraires 1977) 1976, Prima Donna 1978, Le Coeur du voyage 1981, La grenade 1984, Un Aristocrate à la lanterne 1986, L'Eclat 1990, Un si bel orage 1991, La Flambée 1993, L'Or du torrent 1995, A l'Abri du Monde (Prix Chateaubriant) 1997, Saskia 1999, Ce fils unique 2000; Hervé Bazin ou le romancier en mouvement (essay) 1973, Ce Fils Unique 2000, De Rêve et de Glace 2001, Le Dernier Mot d'un Roi (Prix du roman historique) 2003, Demain, dès l'Aube 2005, L'avenir ne s'oublie pas 2006. *Leisure interests:* mountaineering, reading, painting and drawing, taxidermy. *Address:* Campagne Sainte Anne, boulevard des Acacias, 83100 Toulon, France. *E-mail:* pierremoustiers@wanadoo.fr. *Website:* www.pierremoustier.com.

MOUT, Marianne Elisabeth Henriette Nicolette, PhD; Dutch historian and professor of history; *Professor Emeritus of Modern History and of Central European Studies, Leiden University;* b. 31 May 1945, Wassenaar; d. of Arie Mout and Maria Helena van Tooren; m. 1st Robbert Salomon van Santen (divorced 1979); m. 2nd Peter Felix Ganz 1987; ed Rijnlands Lyceum, Wassenaar, Univ. of Amsterdam, Charles Univ., Prague; research student, Czechoslovakia 1966, 1967; Asst Keeper, Jewish Historical Museum, Amsterdam 1969; Ed., Martinus Nijhoff publrs 1970; Lecturer in Modern History, Utrecht Univ. 1975–76; Sr Lecturer in Dutch History, Leiden Univ. 1976–94, Prof. of Central European Studies 1990–2010, Prof. Emer. 2010–, Prof. of Modern History 1994–2010, Prof. Emer. 2010–; Man. Ed. Tijdschrift voor Geschiedenis 1981–86; Fellow, Netherlands Inst. for Advanced Studies, Wassenaar 1987–88, 1993–94; Pres. Conseil Int. pour l'édition des oeuvres complètes d'Erasme 1998–; Pres. Soc. for Netherlandish Literature 1999–2003; Pres. Royal Netherlands Historical Soc. 2004–07; mem. Bd Inst. of Netherlands History 1989–2009; mem. Royal Netherlands Acad. of Arts and Sciences, Academia Europaea; Corresp. mem. Austrian Acad. of Sciences; Österreichisches Ehrenkreuz für Wissenschaft und Kunst 1. Klasse (Austria). *Publications:* Komenský v Amsterodamu (with J. Polišenský) 1970, Bohemen en de Nederlanden in de zestiende eeuw 1975, Plakkaat van Verlatinge 1581 1979, Die Kultur des Humanismus 1998; numerous articles, mainly on 16th–17th century Dutch and Cen. European history of ideas and cultural history and 19th–20th century historiography; ed. and co-ed. of several books, including Gerhard Oestreich, Antiker Geist und moderner Staat bei Justus Lipsius 1989, Erasmianism Idea and Reality 1997, The World of Emperor Charles V 2004, Truth in Science, the Humanities, and Religion 2010. *Address:* Oranje Nassaulaan 27, 2361 LB Warmond, The Netherlands (home). *Telephone:* (71) 301-1407 (home). *Fax:* (71) 301-1407 (home). *Website:* www.hum.leiden.edu/history/staff/mout.html (office).

MOUTAWAKIL, Nawal el-; Moroccan sports administrator, politician and fmr athlete; b. 15 April 1962, Casablanca; m.; two c.; ed Iowa State Univ., USA; gold medallist, 400m hurdles, Olympic Games, Los Angeles 1988 (first Moroccan, African and Muslim woman to win Olympic Gold); Asst Coach, Iowa State Univ.; Dir Nat. School of Track and Field, Casablanca br. 1991; Vice-Pres. Moroccan Track and Field Fed. 1992; mem. Moroccan Nat. Olympic Cttee; Sec. of State for Sport and Youth 1997; Minister of Youth and Sports 2007–09; Sr Exec., Fondation Banque Marocaine du Commerce Exterieur; mem. Athletes' Comm., Int. Asscn Athletics Feds 1989–, mem. Council 1995–, mem. Devt Sub-Comm. for Women; mem. IOC (first Muslim woman) 1998–, mem. Electoral Coll., mem. IOC Exec. Bd 2008–, Pres. Coordination Cttee for Games of XXXI Olympiad in 2016 in Rio de Janeiro, Brazil 2010–; mem. Comité Int. des Jeux Mediterranéens, Comité Int. des Jeux de la Francophonie, Laureus World Sports Acad.; mem. Rassemblement national des indépendants; Chevalier, Ordre nat. du Mérite Exceptionnel (Morocco) 1983, Chevalier, Ordre nat. du Lion (Senegal) 1988; named as one of Outstanding Arab Women 2008. *Address:* c/o Morocco Olympic Committee, p.a. Siège des Sports, Boulevard Ibn Sina Aguedal 51, B.P. 134, Rabat, Morocco.

MOUTINOT, Laurent; Swiss lawyer and politician; b. 2 March 1953, Geneva; m. Suzanne Moutinot (deceased); three c.; advocate, Geneva Bar 1978–97; Pres. Asloca romande 1990–93, Vice-Pres. Asloca suisse 1990–97; Deputy, Grand Council of Geneva 1993–97, Leader of Parl. Group 1994–96; elected (Parti socialiste) to Council of State of Geneva, Head, Dept of Works and Housing 1997–2005, Head, Dept of Institutions 2005, Vice-Pres. 2001–02, Pres. 2002–03, 2007–08. *Address:* c/o Conseil d'Etat, Rue David-Dufour 5, case postale, 1211 Geneva 8, Switzerland (office). *Website:* www.laurentmoutinot.ch (office).

MOUTON, Jacques; French banker; *Honorary Chairman, Caisse Nationale des Caisses d'Epargne;* b. 1937; Chair. Supervisory Bd and Chair. Remuneration and Selection Cttee, Caisse Nationale des Caisses d'Epargne 2003–07, Hon. Chair. 2007–. *Address:* Caisse Nationale des Caisses d'Epargne, 50 avenue Pierre-Mendès, 75201 Paris Cedex 13, France (office). *Telephone:* 1-58-40-41-42 (office). *Fax:* 1-58-40-48-00 (office). *E-mail:* info@caisse-epargne.fr (office). *Website:* www .caisse-epargne.fr (office).

MOUTON, Jannie, BComm, CA; South African business executive; *Chairman, PSG Group Ltd;* b. 2 Oct. 1946, Carnavon; m. (deceased); two c.; ed Univ. of Stellenbosch; started career as Financial Man., Federale Volksbeleggings Ltd; Finance Dir, Kanhym 1981–82; Co-founder and Man. Dir Senekal Mouton & Kitshoff Inc. 1982–95; f. PSG Group Ltd (fmrly PAG Ltd) 1995, currently Chair.; currently Chair. (non-exec.) Paladin Capital Ltd, Zeder Investments Ltd; Founder-Chair. Capitec Bank 2001–07; Dir (non-exec.) Steinhoff International Holdings 2002–, Pioneer Food Group Ltd 2009–; Entrepreneur of The Year Award 2012. *Address:* PSG Group Limited, Ou Kollege, 35 Kerk Street, PO Box 7403, Stellenbosch, South Africa (office). *Telephone:* (21) 8879602 (office). *E-mail:* driesm@psggroup.co.za (office). *Website:* www.psggroup.co.za (office).

MOXLEY, John Howard, III, MD, FACP; American physician and business executive; *Managing Director, North American Health Care Division, Korn/Ferry International;* b. 10 Jan. 1935, Elizabeth, NJ; s. of John Howard Moxley, Jr and Cleopatra Mundy Moxley; m. Doris Banchik; three s.; ed Williams Coll. and Univ. of Colorado School of Medicine; hosp. posts 1961–63; Clinical Assoc., Nat. Cancer Inst., Solid Tumor Branch 1963–65; Sr Resident Physician, Peter Bent Brigham Hosp. 1965–66; mem. Lymphoma Task Force Nat. Cancer Inst. 1965–77; Instructor in Medicine and Asst to the Dean, Harvard Medical School 1966–69; Dean Univ. of Md School of Medicine and Assoc. Prof. of Medicine 1969–73; Vice-Chancellor for Health Sciences and Dean of School of Medicine, Univ. of Calif., San Diego and Assoc. Prof. of Medicine 1973–80; Asst Sec. of Defense for Health Affairs, Dept of Defense, Washington, DC 1979–81; Sr Vice-Pres., Corp. Planning and Alternative Services, American Medical Int. Inc. 1981–87; Pres. and CEO MetaMedical Inc., Beverly Hills, Calif. 1987–89; Man. Dir, N American Health Care Div., Korn/Ferry Int. 1989–; Dir Henry M. Jackson Foundation for the Advancement of Mil. Medicine 1983, Naval Studies Bd; Dir Nat. Fund for Medical Educ. 1986–, Chair. 1993–; Fellow, American Fed. for Clinical Research; mem. Inst. of Medicine (NAS), American Soc. of Clinical Oncology, American Medical Asscn; Sec. of Defense Medal for Distinguished Public Service and other awards. *Publications:* numerous papers in scientific journals. *Address:* Korn/Ferry International, 1900 Avenue of the Stars, Suite 2600, Los Angeles, CA 90067 (office); 2408 Latigo Drive, Solvang, CA 93463, USA (home). *Telephone:* (310) 200-1296

(office). *E-mail:* moxleyj@kornferry.com (office). *Website:* www.kornferry.com (office).

MOXON, (Edward) Richard, MB, BChir, FRS, FRCP, FMedSci; British medical doctor and academic; *Professor Emeritus, Medical Sciences Division, University of Oxford;* b. 16 July 1941, Leeds; s. of the late Gerald Richard Moxon and Margaret Forster Mohun; m. Marianne Graham 1973; two s. one d.; ed Shrewsbury School, St John's Coll., Cambridge and St Thomas' Hosp. Medical School, London; with Hosp. for Sick Children, Great Ormond St, London 1969; Research Fellow in Infectious Diseases, Children's Hosp. Medical Center, Boston, Mass, USA 1971–74; Asst Prof. of Pediatrics, Johns Hopkins Hosp., Baltimore, Md, USA 1974–80, Dir Eudowood Pediatric Infectious Diseases Unit 1982–84; Action Research Prof. of Paediatrics, Univ. of Oxford 1984–; Group Leader, Molecular Infectious Diseases Group (Pathogenic Bacteria), The Weatherall Inst. of Molecular Medicine, John Radcliffe Hosp. 1988–; Visiting Scientist, Dept of Molecular Biology, Washington Univ., St Louis, Mo. 1990–91; Fellow, Jesus Coll. Oxford 1984–; Founder and Chair. Oxford Vaccine Group 1994–; mem. Steering Group, Encapsulated Bacteria, WHO 1987–93; Chair. MRC Sub-cttee Polysaccharide Vaccines 1986–90; Convenor, BPA Immunology and Infectious Diseases Group 1984–89; mem. American Soc. Clinical Investigation; Founding Fellow, Acad. of Medical Sciences, UK 1998; Fellow, Infectious Diseases Soc. of America, American Soc. Pediatric Research; Mitchell Lecturer, Royal Coll. of Physicians 1992, Bazely Oration, Annual Gen. Meeting of Australian Soc. for Microbiology, Perth 1993, Blackfan Lecturer, Boston Children's Hosp. 1994, Blackfan Lecturer, Children's Hosp. Medical Alumni Council 125th Anniversary Celebration, Boston, Mass 1994, Bob Deich Memorial Lecturer, Univ. of Rochester, NY 1995, ASM Div. Lecturer, Gen. Meeting 1997, Teale Lecturer, Royal Coll. of Physicians 1998, Burroughs-Wellcome Lecturer, Univ. of Pennsylvania 1998, Dolman Lecturer, Univ. of British Columbia 1999, J.H.P. Jonxis Lecturer, Beatrix Children's Hosp., Groningen, Netherlands 2001, Anthony Dawson Lecturer, St Bartholomew's and London Hosp. 2003, Bill Marshall Award Lecturer, European Soc. of Paediatric Research, Tampere, Finland 2004, Hattie Alexander Memorial Lecturer, Columbia Univ., New York 2005, Excellence Award, European Soc. for Clinical Microbiology and Infectious Diseases, Munich 2007, Fred Griffith Review Lecturer, Soc. for Gen. Microbiology, Edinburgh 2007. *Publications:* Neonatal Infections (with D. Isaacs) 1991, A Practical Approach to Paediatric Infectious Diseases (with D. Isaacs) 1996, Longman Handbook of Neonatal Infections (with D. Isaacs) 1999; Modern Vaccines (editorial adviser) 1990, Progress in Vaccinology (ed.) 2000; more than 400 scientific articles on infections, molecular basis of bacterial virulence and vaccines published in major peer-reviewed journals. *Leisure interests:* music, literature, wine, sports. *Address:* Department of Paediatrics, The Weatherall Institute of Molecular Medicine, University of Oxford, John Radcliffe Hospital, Headington, Oxford, OX3 9DS (office); 9A North Parade Avenue, Oxford, OX2 6LX, England (home). *Telephone:* (1865) 222307 (office). *Fax:* (1865) 222444 (office). *E-mail:* richard.moxon@paediatrics.ox.ac.uk (office). *Website:* www.imm.ox.ac.uk (office).

MOYANA, Kombo James, MA, MPhil, PhD; Zimbabwean banker; b. 4 July 1942, Chipinge; m.; one s. three d.; ed Columbia Univ., New York, USA; Research Fellow, Inst. de Développement Economique et de Planification, Dakar 1972; Fellow, UNITAR, New York 1973; int. finance economist, Div. of Money, Finance and Devt UNCTAD, New York and Geneva 1974–80; seconded to Ministry of Econ. Planning and Devt of Govt of Zimbabwe 1980; Deputy Gov. Reserve Bank of Zimbabwe 1980, Gov. 1983; Alt. Gov. IMF 1983; Pres. Inst. of Bankers (Zimbabwe) 1985–86; Exec. Sec. Preferential Trading Area of Eastern, Cen. and Southern African States –1991; CEO Trade & Investment Bank Ltd; Chair. Asscn of African Cen. Banks 1991–93. *Leisure interest:* farming. *Address:* PO Box 1283, Harare, Zimbabwe. *Telephone:* 790731; 7910721.

MOYANO, Hugo; Argentine trade union official; *Secretary-General, Confederación General del Trabajo (CGT);* b. 9 Jan. 1944, La Plata; Rep., Mar del Plata Div., Sindicato de Choferes de Camiones (trade union) 1962, Sec.-Gen. 1962–72, Sec.-Gen. Sindicato de Choferes de Camiones, Buenos Aires 1987–91, 1991–2003; Sec.-Gen. Mar del Plata Br., Partido Justicialista (PJ) 1983, becoming Sec. and Vice-Pres. Parl. Transport Comm.; Global Vice-Pres. Road Transport Div., Int. Fed. of Transport Workers 1998–; Sec.-Gen. Confederación Argentina de Trabajadores del Transporte 2003–05; Sec.-Gen. Confederación General del Trabajo (CGT) 2005–. *Address:* Confederación General del Trabajo, Azopardo 802, C1107ADN Buenos Aires, Argentina (office). *Telephone:* (11) 4343-1883 (office). *Website:* www.cgtra .org.ar (office).

MOYERS, William (Bill) D., FAAS; American journalist and broadcaster; *Executive Editor, Public Affairs Television, Inc.;* b. 5 June 1934, Hugo, Okla; s. of Henry Moyers and Ruby Johnson; m. Judith Davidson 1954; two s. one d.; ed Univ. of Texas, Edinburgh Univ. and Southwestern Baptist Theological Seminary; Exec. Asst to Senator Lyndon Johnson 1959–60; Assoc. Dir US Peace Corps 1961–63, Deputy Dir 1963; Special Asst to Pres. Johnson 1963–66, Press Sec. to Pres. 1965–66; Publr of Newsday, Long Island, NY 1966–70; host of This Week, weekly current affairs TV programme 1970; Ed.-in-Chief Bill Moyers Journal, Public Broadcasting Service 1971–76, 1978–81; Contrib. Newsweek 1974–76; Chief Corresp. CBS Reports 1976–78, Sr News Analyst, CBS News 1981–86; Exec. Ed. Public Affairs TV Inc. 1987–; news analyst, NBC News 1995–; Pres. Florence and John Schumann Foundation 1991–; mem. American Philosophical Soc.; Emmy Awards 1983–90, Gold Baton Award 1991, 1999, American Jewish Cttee Religious Liberty Award 1995, Walter Cronkite Award 1995, Fred Friendly First Amendment Award 1995, Charles Frankel Prize 1997, George Peabody Award 2000. *Publications include:* Listening to America 1971, The Secret Government 1988, Joseph Campbell and the Power of Myth 1988, A World of Ideas 1989, Healing and the Mind 1993, Genesis: A Living Conversion 1996, Fooling with Words 1999, Moyers on America 2004, Moyers on Democracy 2008, Bill Moyers Journal: The Conversation Continues 2011. *Address:* Public Affairs Television Inc., 250 West 57th Street, Suite 718, New York, NY 10107, USA. *Website:* www.billmoyers.com.

MOYES, David William; British football manager and fmr professional football player; b. 25 April 1963, Bearsden, East Dunbartonshire, Scotland; s. of David Moyes, Sr and Joan Moyes; one s. one d.; centre-back; youth career with IBV Vestmannaeyjar 1978, Drumchapel Amateurs 1978–80; sr career with Glasgow Celtic 1980–83 (won Scottish League Div. 1981/82), Cambridge United 1983–85, Bristol City 1985–87 (won Assoc. Members' Cup 1986), Shrewsbury

Town 1987–90, Dunfermline Athletic 1990–93, Hamilton Academical 1993, Preston North End 1993–99 (won Football League Third Div. 1995/96); played for Scotland U-18 1980; Man. Preston North End 1998–2002 (won Football League Second Div. 1999–2000), Everton 2002–13, Manchester United 2013–14; Co-owner of racehorse Desert Cry, trained by Donald McCain; League Managers Asscn Manager of the Year 2002/03, 2004/05, 2008/09. *Address:* c/o Manchester United FC, Sir Matt Busby Way, Old Trafford, Manchester, M16 0RA, England.

MOYNIHAN, Brian Thomas, JD; American lawyer and banking executive; *CEO, Bank of America;* b. 9 Oct. 1959, Marietta, Ohio; s. of; m. Susan E. Berry; three c.; ed Brown Univ., Univ. of Notre Dame Law School; with Edwards & Angell LLP, Providence, RI –1993; joined FleetBoston Financial as Deputy Gen. Counsel 1993, Exec. Vice-Pres. 1999–2004, with responsibility for brokerage and wealth man. divs 2000–04, joined Bank of America following co.'s merger with Fleet-Boston Financial 2004, led several lines of business, including Consumer and Small Business Banking, Pres. Global Wealth and Investment Man. 2004–08, Pres. Global Corp. and Investment Banking 2007–08, CEO Merrill Lynch after its sale to Bank of America 2008, Gen. Counsel, Bank of America 2008–09, mem. Bd of Dirs and CEO 2010–, Chair. Global Diversity and Inclusion Council; fmr Chair. Travelers Aid Soc. of Rhode Island, Providence Haitian Project, Inc.; Trustee, Corpn of Brown Univ. 2010–. *Address:* Bank of America Corporate Center, 100 North Tryon Street, Charlotte, NC 28255, USA (office). *Telephone:* (704) 386-1845 (office). *Fax:* (704) 386-6699 (office). *E-mail:* info@bankofamerica.com (office). *Website:* www.bankofamerica.com (office).

MOYNIHAN, 4th Baron, cr. 1929; Colin Berkeley Moynihan, MA; British business executive and organization official; b. 13 Sept. 1955; m. Gaynor-Louise Metcalf 1992; two s. one d.; ed Monmouth School, Univ. Coll., Oxford; World Gold Medal for Lightweight Rowing, Int. Rowing Fed. 1978, World Silver Medal for Rowing 1981, Silver Medal for Rowing, Olympics 1980; Personal asst to Chair. Tate and Lyle Ltd 1978–80, Man. Tate and Lyle Agribusiness 1980–82; CEO Ridgways Tea and Coffee Merchants 1982–83, Chair. 1983–87; Minister for Sport 1987–90; Chair. CMA Consultants 1993–; Man. Dir Ind. Power Corpn plc 1996–2001; Chair. and CEO Consort Resources Group 2000–03; Exec. Chair. Clipper Windpower Europe Ltd 2004–, Dir Clipper Windpower PLC 2005–; Dir Energreen AS, Zeropex AS, Rowan Companies Inc. 1996–; Chair. British Olympic Asscn 2005–12; Gov. Sports Aid Foundation (London and SE) 1980–82; mem. Court of Assistants, Worshipful Co. of Haberdashers; mem. Advisory Bd Conservative Friends of Int. Devt, British Expertise; Pres. Welsh Amateur Rowing Asscn; Vice-Pres. British Wind Energy Asscn; Dir, Int. Inspiration Bd; Chair. British Ski & Snowboarding; mem. Bd London Community Sports; Trustee, Canoeing Foundation, British Olympic Foundation; Freeman City of London 1978. *Leisure interests:* reading, sport, music. *Address:* House of Lords, Westminster, London, SW1A 0PW, England (office). *Telephone:* (20) 7219-5879 (office); (20) 7820-1978 (home). *Fax:* (20) 7820-7808 (home). *E-mail:* c.moynihan@cmagroup.org.uk (office). *Website:* www.parliament.uk/biographies/lords/colin-moynihan/27082 (office).

MOYO, Jonathan, MPA, PhD; Zimbabwean politician; *Minister of Information and Communications Technology;* b. 12 Jan. 1957; m.; fmr mem. Zimbabwe African Nat. Union-Patriotic Front (ZANU-PF); Minister of State for Information and Publicity 2000–05; fmr mem. Pres. Robert Mugabe's 'Gang of Four' politicians; architect of Zimbabwe's highly controlled press regime; mem. Parl. (ind.) for Tsholotsho; Minister of Information and Communications Technology 2013–. *Leisure interests:* philosophy, classics, music, composition, tennis, scriptwriting. *Address:* Ministry of Information and Communications Technology, Linquenda House, Baker Ave, POB CY825, Causeway, Harare, Zimbabwe (office). *Telephone:* (4) 703894 (office). *Fax:* (4) 707213 (office).

MOYO, S(imon) K(haya); Zimbabwean politician and diplomatist; *National Chairman, Zimbabwe African National Union-Patriotic Front (ZANU—PF);* b. 1945; fmr mem. of Parl. (ZANU—PF) for Bulilima-mangwe South, fmr ZANU (PF) Politburo Deputy-Sec. for Legal Affairs, currently Nat. Chair. ZANU—PF;;Minister of Transport and Energy 1996, of Mines, Environment and Tourism 1998, Sr Minister of State 2013–; Amb. to South Africa 2000–11. *Address:* Zimbabwe African National Union-Patriotic Front (ZANU—PF), Corner Rotten Row and Samora Machel Avenue, POB 4530, Harare, Zimbabwe (office). *Telephone:* (4) 753329 (office). *Fax:* (4) 774146 (office). *Website:* www.zanupf.org.zw (office).

MOZILO, Angelo R., BSc; American financial services industry executive; b. 1938, New York, NY; ed Fordham Univ.; Co-founder Countrywide Financial Corpn 1969, Chair. and CEO –2008 (following takeover by Bank of America); Co-founder IndyMac Bank (f. as Countrywide Mortgage Investment, spun off as ind. bank 1997, collapsed and seized by fed. regulators July 2008); Chair. Countrywide Home Loans Inc.; Pres. Mortgage Bankers Asscn of America (MBA) 1991–92, mem. Bd of Dirs 1992–; mem. Bd of Dirs Jt Center for Housing Studies, Harvard Univ., The Home Depot 2006–; mem. Bd of Trustees Nat. Housing Endowment, Fordham Univ., Gonzaga Univ., St Francis High School, Calif.; Hon. LLD (Pepperdine Univ.); Ellis Island Medal of Honor, Albert Schweitzer Award, Boy Scouts of America James E. West Fellowship Award, Jane Wyman Humanitarian Service Award, Arthritis Foundation, Special Achievement Award for Humanitarian Service, Nat. Italian American Foundation, Housing Person of the Year Award 2004; inducted into Hall of Fame, Nat. Asscn of Home Builders. *Address:* 2816 Ladbrook Way, Westlake Village, CA 91361, USA.

MPAHLWA, Mandisi Bongani Mabuto; South African politician and diplomatist; *Ambassador to Russia;* b. 21 Aug. 1960; ed Mangosuthu Univ. of Tech., Univ. of London; went into exile 1985, did voluntary work for ANC; returned to SA 1990; Deputy Minister of Finance 1999–2004; Minister of Trade and Industry 2004–09; Amb. to Russia 2011–. *Address:* South African Embassy, 123001 Moscow, Granatnyi per. 1, str. 9, Russia (office). *Telephone:* (495) 926-11-77 (office). *Fax:* (495) 926-11-78 (office). *E-mail:* moscow.ambassador@foreign.gov.za (office). *Website:* saembassy.ru (home).

MPALANYI-NKOYOYO, Rt Rev. Livingstone, DD; Ugandan ecclesiastic; *Archbishop Emeritus of Uganda and Bishop Emeritus of Kampala;* b. 4 Oct. 1939, Namukozi Village, Ssingo Co., Mityana Dist; s. of the late Erisa Wamala Nkoyoyo; m. Ruth Nkoyoyo; three s. two d.; ed Bishop Lutaaya Theological Coll., Buwalasi Theological Coll., Legoni Trinity Coll. Ghana, Cranmer Theological

House; worked as a mechanic 1959–62; lay reader, Church of Uganda 1962; curate, Kasubi Parish 1970, priest 1971–74; Parish Priest, Nsangi Parish 1975–76; Archdeacon, Namirembe Archdeaconry 1977; Asst Bishop, Namirembe Diocese 1980; Suffragan Bishop, Mukono Area 1982; Bishop, Mukono Diocese 1984; Archbishop of Uganda and Bishop of Kampala 1995–2004, Archbishop Emer. of Uganda and Bishop Emer. of Kampala 2004–. *Address:* c/o Church of Uganda, PO Box 14123, Willis Road, Namirembe, Kampala, Uganda. *Telephone:* (41) 270218. *Fax:* (41) 4251925. *E-mail:* COUOffice@gmail.com. *Website:* churchofuganda.org.

MPOMBO, George W.; Zambian politician; mem. Nat. Ass. (Movt for Multi-party Democracy—MMD) 2001–, Minister of Energy and Water Devt 2003-05, Minister for Copperbelt Prov. 2005-06, Minister of Defence 2006–09 (resgnd). *Address:* c/o Ministry of Defence, PO Box 31931, Lusaka, Zambia (office).

MPOUHO-EPIGAT, Ernest; Gabonese politician and fmr diplomatist; *Minister of National Defence;* b. 1967; s. of the late Julien Mpouho-Epigat (fmr Minister of Nat. Defence); nephew of Ali Bongo (Pres. of Gabon); ed Université Paris-1 Hautes Etudes Politiques, Tolbiac, France; fmr Chair. Société gabonaise de services (pvt. security firm); mem. Nat. Ass. (Parl.) for Bongoville; Minister of Nat. Defence 2014–; mem. Parti Démocratique Gabonais. *Address:* Ministry of National Defence, BP 13493, Libreville, Gabon (office). *Telephone:* 01-77-86-96 (office). *Fax:* 01-77-86-96 (office).

MQULWANA, Koleka, BA, Higher Dip in Ed; South African politician and diplomatist; *High Commissioner to Australia;* ed Univ. of the Western Cape, courses in Australia and NZ (Certificate in Int. Governance, Man. Skills, Basic Financial Skills, Procurement Policy, Risk Man. and Governance); mem. Western Cape Prov. Parl. –2011, mem. Standing Cttee on Finance 1999–2002, Standing Cttee on Public Accounts 1999–2004, Chair. Standing Cttee on Local Govt, Environmental Affairs and Devt Planning 2001–04, mem. Exec. Council (MEC) for Social Devt 2004–08, MEC for Public Works and Transport 2008–09, Spokesperson on Public Works and Transport 2009–10; High Commr to Australia 2011–. *Address:* South African High Commission, corner State Circle and Rhodes Place, Yarralumla, ACT 2600, Australia (office). *Telephone:* (2) 6272-7344 (office). *Fax:* (2) 6273-3203 (office). *E-mail:* info@sahc.org.au (office). *Website:* www.sahc.org.au (office).

MRAD, Abd ar-Rahim; Lebanese politician; fmr Minister of Educ.; Minister of National Defence 2004–05. *Address:* c/o Ministry of National Defence, Yarze, Beirut, Lebanon (office).

MRAMBA, Basil; Tanzanian politician; ed Makerere Univ., City Univ. Grad. School, London, UK, Harvard Grad. School of Business, USA; Man. Asst, Williamson Diamond Mwadui 1964–69; Manpower Devt Dir Nat. Development Corpn 1969–72; Dir Gen. Small Scale Industries Org-SIDO 1973–80; mem. Parl. 1980–95; Minister of Trade and Industry 1995–2000, 2006–08; Minister of Finance 2000–06; Minister of Infrastructure Devt 2006. *Address:* c/o Ministry of Industry, Trade and Marketing, POB 9503, Dar es Salaam, Tanzania (office).

MRAMOR, Dušan, PhD; Slovenian economist and academic; *Professor of Finance, University of Ljubljana;* b. 1 Nov. 1953, Ljubljana; s. of Ivan Mramor and Marija Mramor; m. Dr Nezka Mramor Kosta; one s. one d.; ed Univ. of Ljubljana; fmr Visiting Prof., Indiana Univ., USA, Cen. European Univ., Budapest, Wirtschaftuniversität, Vienna; fmr Assoc. Dean and Dean, Faculty of Econs, Univ. of Ljubljana, fmr Chair. Bd, Prof. of Finance 2000–, Pres. Human Resources Cttee; fmr mem. Prime Minister's Strategic Econ. Council; Minister of Finance 2002–04; fmr Pres. Expert Council Agency for the Securities Market; fmr Vice-Pres. Bd of Dirs SKB bank; fmr mem. Expert Council Slovenian Inst. of Auditing, Co-ordinating Cttee Slovenian Asscn of Economists, Slovenian Asscn of Accountants, EIASM; Vice-Pres. Bd Initial Accreditation Cttee Asscn to Advance Collegiate Schools of Business; fmr Vice-Pres. European Finance Asscn; fmr mem. Strategic Council of the Pres. of Slovenia; Vice-Pres. Prime Minister's Cttee for Devt; Best Financial Expert 2003 (award by Kapital) Best Financial Expert 2004 (Kapital), Second Place, Best Paper, Faculty of Econs, Univ. of Ljubljana 2010. *Publications:* several articles in financial journals. *Leisure interests:* skiing, basketball, mountaineering. *Address:* Faculty of Economics, University of Ljubljana, Kardeljeva ploscad 17, Ljubljana 1000, Slovenia (office). *Telephone:* (1) 5892400 (office). *Fax:* (1) 5892698 (office). *E-mail:* dusan.mramor@ef.uni-lj.si (office). *Website:* www.ef.uni-lj.si (office).

MRKIĆ, Ivan; Serbian diplomatist; *Minister of Foreign Affairs;* b. 30 May 1953, Belgrade; m. Ivona Mrkić; two s.; ed Univ. of Belgrade; joined Fed. Secr. for Foreign Affairs 1978, Officer, Directorate for Int. Orgs 1979–82, Attaché (political affairs), Mission of the Socialist Fed. Repub. (SFR) of Yugoslavia to UN 1982–86, Adviser and later Asst Chief of Directorate, Sector for Multilateral Activities 1990–92, also Minister-Counsellor, Mission of SFR Yugoslavia to EC, Brussels 1990–92; Chef de Cabinet of Dobrica Ćosić (first Pres. of Fed. Repub. of Yugoslavia) 1992–93; Chargé d'affaires a.i., later Amb. to Cyprus 1993–99, Deputy Head of Sector for Bilateral Relations 1999, Asst Fed. Minister for Foreign Affairs and Head of Sector for Bilateral Relations 2000–01, Amb. at Fed. Ministry of Foreign Affairs 2001–03, at Ministry of Foreign Affairs of Serbia-Montenegro 2003–04, mem. Group of Ambs for special and ad hoc affairs 2004; Pres. Nat. Comm. for implementation of the Chemical Weapons Convention 2005; Amb. of Serbia to Japan 2006–11, Sec. of State, Ministry of Foreign Affairs 2011–12, Minister of Foreign Affairs 2012–. *Address:* Ministry of Foreign Affairs, 11000 Belgrade, Kneza Miloša 24–26, Serbia (office). *Telephone:* (11) 3616333 (office). *Fax:* (11) 3618366 (office). *E-mail:* msp@mfa.rs (office). *Website:* www.mfa.gov.rs (office).

MROCZKOWSKI, Marek, MEconSc; Polish business executive; *CEO, Unipetrol a.s.;* ed Warsaw School of Econs; with Polski Koncern Naftowy ORLEN SA 1994–2001; Pres. and CEO, POLKOMTEL SA 2001–02; Pres. and CEO, ELANA SA, Torun 2003–04; currently CEO, Unipetrol a.s., also Vice-Chair., Bd of Dirs. *Address:* Unipetrol a.s., 110 05 Prague, Czech Republic (office). *Website:* www.unipetrol.cz (office).

MROUDJAÉ, Ali; Comoran politician; *Leader, Parti Comorien pour la Démocratie et le Progrès;* b. 2 Aug. 1939, Moroni; s. of Chohezi Mroudjae and Charif Zahara; m. Nourdine Batouli 1967; three s. five d.; Minister of Foreign Affairs and Co-operation 1979–82; Prime Minister of the Comoros 1982–85; Minister of State for Internal and Social Affairs Jan.–Sept. 1985; numerous other portfolios; currently

Leader Parti Comorien pour la Démocratie et le Progrès. *Leisure interests:* reading, swimming, travelling. *Address:* Parti Comorien pour la Démocratie et le Progrès, Route Djivani, BP 179, Moroni; BP 58, Rond Point Gobadjou, Moroni, Comoros (office). *Telephone:* 7731733. *Fax:* 7730650.

MSUYA, Cleopa David, BA; Tanzanian politician and civil servant (retd); b. 4 Jan. 1931, Chomvu Usangi, Mwanga Dist; s. of David Kilenga and Maria Ngido; m. Rhoda Christopher 1959; four s. two d.; ed Old Moshi and Tabora Secondary Schools, Makerere Univ. Coll., Uganda; Civil Service, Community Devt Officer 1956–61, Commr for Community Devt 1961–64, Prin. Sec. to Ministry of Community Devt and Nat. Culture 1964, to Ministries of Land Settlement and Water Devt 1965–67, to Ministry of Econ. Affairs and Devt Planning 1967–70 and to Treas. 1970–72; Minister of Finance 1972–75, 1983–85, for Finance, Econ. Affairs and Planning 1985–89, for Industries 1975–80, for Industries and Trade 1990–95; Prime Minister 1980–83, 1994–95; First Vice-Pres. 1994–95; mem. Nat. Ass. 1995–2000; Gov. ADB, IMF; mem. Bd Dirs of several public corpns. *Address:* c/o Office of the Prime Minister and First Vice-President, PO Box 980, Dodoma, Tanzania.

MSWATI III, HM The King of Swaziland; Makhosetive; b. 19 April 1968; s. of the late King Sobhuza II and Queen Ntombi Laftwala; m. to 14 wives (Emakhosikati); 23 c.; ed Sherborne School, UK; crowned King of Swaziland 25 April 1986. *Leisure interests:* swimming, rugby. *Address:* Lozitha Palace, Mbabane, Swaziland.

MTETWA, Beatrice, LLB; Zimbabwean lawyer; ed Univ. of Botswana; lawyer, Kantor and Immerman (law firm), Harare; Dir The Zimbabwe Independent newspaper; lawyer for Foreign Corresps Asscn of Zimbabwe; Council mem. Law Soc. of Zimbabwe, currently Pres.; mem. Zimbabwe Lawyers for Human Rights; arrested for allegedly 'obstructing the course of justice' March 2013, released on bail; Human Rights Lawyer of the Year 2003, Cttee to Protect Journalists Int. Press Freedom Award 2005, Bindmans Law and Campaigning Award 2006, Burton Benjamin Award 2008, International Human Rights Award, ABA 2010, Inamori Ethics Prize, Case Western Reserve Univ. 2011. *Address:* c/o Zimbabwe Lawyers for Human Rights, 6th Floor Beverly Court, 100 Nelson Mandela Avenue, Harare; Kantor and Immerman, MacDonald House, 10 Selous Avenue, Harare (office); c/o The Zimbabwean Independent, Zimind Publishers (Private) Limited, Suites 23 and 24, One Union Avenue, Harare, Zimbabwe. *Telephone:* (4) 7043512 (office). *Fax:* (4) 704436 (office). *E-mail:* kanim@ecoweb.co.zw (office).

MU'ALLA, HH Sheikh Saud bin Rashid al-, (Ruler of Umm al-Qaiwain); United Arab Emirates ruler; b. 1 Oct. 1952; s. of the late Rashid bin Ahmed Al Mu'alla (Ruler of Umm al-Qaiwain); ed Cairo Univ., Egypt; apptd Third Sec., Ministry of Foreign Affairs 1973; apptd Commdr Umm al-Qaiwain Nat. Guard as Col; apptd Head of Emiri Court (Diwani) 1979; apptd by father as Crown Prince 1982; succeeded to the throne upon the death of his father 2009, mem. Supreme Council of the Union 2009–; has served as Chair. of numerous cos including National Bank of Umm al-Qaiwain, Umm al-Qaiwain Gas Co., Umm al-Qaiwain Cement Co.

MUASHER, Marwan Jamil, MS, PhD; Jordanian politician and diplomatist; *Vice-President for Studies, Carnegie Endowment for International Peace;* b. 14 June 1956, Amman; two c.; ed American Univ. of Beirut, Lebanon, Purdue Univ., USA; Asst Research Engineer, Univ. of Petroleum and Minerals, Saudi Arabia 1983–84; Dir Computer Centre, Jordan Electric Power Co. 1984; Sr Consultant Special System Co. 1984–85; Head, Computer Unit and Monitory System, Ministry of Planning 1985–87, Dir Socio-Econ. Information Centre, Nat. Information System 1987–90; Press Adviser to Prime Minister 1990–91; Head, Jordan Information Bureau, USA 1991–94; Amb. to Israel 1995–96, to USA and Mexico 1997–2002; Minister of Information 1996, of Foreign Affairs 2002–04; Deputy Prime Minister and Minister of State for Prime Ministry Affairs and Govt Performance 2004–05; Senator 2006–07; Sr Vice-Pres. for External Affairs, Communications and UN Affairs, World Bank, Washington, DC 2007–10; Vice-Pres. for Studies, Carnegie Endowment for Int. Peace 2010–; Sr Fellow, Jackson Inst. for Global Affairs, Yale Univ.; political columnist, Jordan Times 1983–90; Al-Kawkab Medal, First Order (Jordan) 2000, Dr hc (Purdue Univ.) 1999, Independence Medal 2000, Diplomat of the Year Award, LA Int. Affairs Council 2000. *Publications:* The Arab Center: The Promise of Moderation 2008. *Address:* Carnegie Endowment for International Peace, 1779 Massachusetts Ave, NW, Washington, DC 20036-2103, USA (office). *Telephone:* (202) 483-7600 (office). *Fax:* (202) 483-1840 (office). *Website:* www.carnegieendowment.org (office).

MUBARAK, Fahd ibn Abdullah al-, BSc, MBA, PhD; Saudi Arabian academic and central banker; *Governor, Saudi Arabian Monetary Agency;* b. Eastern Prov.; ed Univ. of Houston, USA; began career as Asst Prof., King Fahd Univ. of Petroleum and Minerals; six years as mem. Saudi Arabian Consultative Council (Shoura Council), fmr Vice-Chair. Econ. and Energy Cttee; fmr Gen. Man. Rana Investment Co.; Chair. Bd of Dirs Saudi Stock Exchange (Tadawul); Co-founder and shareholder Amwal Al Khaleej (alternative investment firm); fmr Chair. and Man. Dir Morgan Stanley Saudi Arabia; Gov. Saudi Arabian Monetary Agency 2011–; fmr Dir Mobily (telecommunications co.), Majid Al Futtaim Holding LLC (also known as Majid Al Futtaim Group LLC); Ind. Dir, Saudi Hollandi Bank –2011; mem. numerous nat., econ. and charitable cttees; ranked by Arabian Business amongst the Power 500: The World's Most Influential Arabs (17th) 2012, (20th) 2013. *Address:* Saudi Arabian Monetary Agency, PO Box 2992, Riyadh 11169, Saudi Arabia (office). *Telephone:* (1) 463-3000 (office). *Fax:* (1) 466-2966 (office). *E-mail:* info@sama.gov.sa (office). *Website:* www.sama.gov.sa (office).

MUBARAK, Gamal, MBA; Egyptian politician and business executive; b. 1963; s. of fmr Pres. Hosni Mubarak and Suzanne Mubarak; m. Khadija El-Gammal 2007; ed American Univ., Cairo; started career with Bank of America, served as investment banker for six years in London, est. Medinvest Associates (pvt. equity fund); returned to Egypt 2000; joined Nat. Democratic Party 2000, fmr Sec. Policies Cttee, also fmr mem. Gen. Secr.; fmr Chair. Future Generation Foundation; fmr spokesman for US-Egyptian Business Advisory Body. *Address:* c/o National Democratic Party, Cairo, Egypt (office).

MUBARAK, Khaldoon Khalifa al-, BEcons; United Arab Emirates business executive; *Managing Director and CEO, Mubadala Development Company;* b.

1975, Abu Dhabi; ed Tufts Univ., Boston, USA; began career as Sales Exec., Abu Dhabi Nat. Oil Co.; currently Man. Dir and CEO Mubadala Devt Co.; mem. Abu Dhabi Exec. Council, Chair. Abu Dhabi Exec. Affairs Authority 2006–; Chair. Emirates Nuclear Energy Corpn, Abu Dhabi Motor Sport Man. Co., Abu Dhabi Media Zone Authority, Emirates Aluminium; Chair. hester City Football Club, UK 2008–; Deputy Chair. Urban Planning Council 2007–; mem. Abu Dhabi Council for Econ. Devt; Dir First Gulf Bank, Ferrari SpA, Aldar Properties; Co-Chair. US Chamber of Commerce's US-UAE Business Council 2007–; mem. Bd of Trustees, New York Univ.; Commdr, Ordine della Stella della solidarietà italiana 2007; ranked by Arabian Business amongst the Power 500: The World's Most Influential Arabs (11th) 2010, (20th) 2012, (16th) 2013. *Address:* Mubadala Development Company, PO Box 45005, Abu Dhabi, United Arab Emirates (office). *Telephone:* (2) 4130000 (office). *Fax:* (2) 4130001 (office). *E-mail:* info@mubadala.ae (office). *Website:* www.mubadala.ae (office).

MUBARAK, (Muhammad) Hosni, BMilSci, BA; Egyptian air force officer and fmr head of state; b. 4 May 1928, Kafr El-Moseilha, Minuffya Governorate; m. Suzanne Sabet; two s.; ed Mil. Acad., Air Acad.; joined Air Force 1950, Lecturer Air Force Acad. 1952–59; Commdr Cairo West Air Base 1964; Dir-Gen. Air Acad. 1967–69; Air Force Chief of Staff 1969–72; C-in-C 1972–75; promoted to Lt-Gen. 1974; Vice-Pres. of Egypt 1975–81; Pres. 1981–2011 (stepped down following popular protests); Vice-Pres. Nat. Democratic Party (NDP) 1979, Pres. 1982; mem. Higher Council for Nuclear Energy 1975–; Sec.-Gen. NDP and Political Bureau 1981–82, Chair. 1982–; Chair. OAU 1989–90, 1993–94, Arab Summit 1996–, GI5 1998, 2000; Pres. Emergency Arab Summit 2000, D-8 Summit 2001, COMESA Summit 2001; Order of Star of Honour 1964, 1974, Medal of the Star of Sinai of the First Order 1983 and numerous other foreign decorations; Dr hc (Bulgaria) 1998, (Beijing) 1999, (St Johns) 1999, (George Washington) 1999; Louise Michel Prize 1990, Prize of Democratic Human Rights, Social and Political Studies Centre, Paris 1990, UN Prize of Population 1994 and numerous other awards and honours. *Leisure interest:* squash. *Address:* c/o Presidential Palace, Abdeen, Cairo, Egypt.

MUBARAK, HE Suzanne, BA, MA; Egyptian sociologist and national organization official; b. 28 Feb. 1941, Menya; m. Pres. Hosni Said Mubarak; two s.; ed St Claire School, Heliopolis, Cairo, American Univ. in Cairo (AUC); Founder and Chair., Integrated Care Soc. 1977; First Lady of Egypt 1981–2011; Pres. First and Second Nat. Conf. on Women 1994–96; f. Suzanne Mubarak Museum for Children 1996; initiated Unified Law on Children 1996; Pres., Nat. Council for Women 2000–11; Founder and Chair. Egyptian Soc. for Childhood and Devt; f. Egyptian Children's Literature Centre for Documentation, Research and Information; fmr Pres. of Advisory Bd to Nat. Council for Childhood and Motherhood; fmr Pres. Egyptian Nat. Women Cttee; fmr Pres. of Egyptian Section, Int. Bd of Books for Young People (IBBY); fmr Pres. Egyptian Red Crescent Soc.; initiated Nat. Campaign for Safe Blood Transfusion; fmr Vice-Pres. Comm. on Ethics of Scientific Knowledge and Tech. (COMEST); Head of Egyptian Del. to UN World Conf. to Review and Appraise the Achievements of UN Decade for Women, Equality, Devt and Peace, Nairobi, Kenya 1985; Hon. Chair., Int. Symposium on Children's Books, UNICEF, Cairo 1986; Paul Harris Fellow, Rotary Foundation, Rotary Int. 1992; Dr hc (Iwa Univ., Seoul, South Korea) 1999, (American Univ. in Cairo) 2000, (American Univ. in Spain) 2000; DIur, Westminster Coll., New Wilmington, Pa, USA, Degree of Prof. Counsellor, Shanghai Univ., People's Republic of China 1999; Maurice Pate Award, UNICEF Exec. Bd 1989, Highest Award, Rehabilitation Int. Centre 1989, Enrique de la Mata Int. Prize for Peace, Together for Peace Foundation 1992, Health for All Gold Medal, WHO 1994, Int. Book Award, Int. Book Cttee 1995, Award of Highest Honour, Soka Univ. 1995, American World Book Asscn Award for Publ., Award of Arab Publrs Fed. 1996, Avicenne Medal, UNESCO 1997, Prize of Tolerance, European Acad. of Sciences and Arts 1998, Rotary Award 1999. *Publications:* Social Action Research in Urban Egypt: A Case Study of Primary School Upgrading in Bulaq (thesis) 1982. *Address:* c/o The National Council for Women, 1113 Corniche El-Nil, 1st Floor, PO Box 11625, Cairo, Egypt (office).

MUBEEN, Gen. Mohammad Abdul; Bangladeshi fmr army officer; m. Syeda Sharifa Khanom; two s. one d.; ed Y Cadet in Mirzapur Cadet Coll., Defence Services Command and Staff Coll., Nat. Defence Coll., Mirpur, Dhaka; commissioned in Regt of Infantry of Bangladesh Army 1976; served in various capacities at bn level, commanded two infantry bns and an infantry brigade; served as Brigade Maj. (Operation Staff) in an Ind. Infantry Brigade HQ, Gen. Staff Officer First Grade (Operation Staff) in Infantry Div. HQ and in Bangladesh Mil. Acad., Pvt. Sec. to Chief of Army Staff and Dir of Mil. Training Directorate at Army HQ; served as Commdt of Defence Services Command and Staff Coll.; also held appointments of Dir Gen. Bangladesh Inst. of Int. and Strategic Studies and Prin. Staff Officer, Prime Minister's Office, Armed Forces Div. 2008–09; Chief of Army Staff 2009–12 (retd); promoted to rank of Gen. 2009; commanded two Infantry Divs as GOC in Jessore and Chittagong; served as Chief of Staff (Northern Region), UN Operations in Mozambique (ONUMUZ); mem. Army Hockey team. *Leisure interests:* playing golf, keen interest in all games and sports. *Address:* c/o Office of the Chief of Army Staff, Army Headquarters, GS Branch, Dhaka, Bangladesh.

MUCCIOLI, Anna Maria, LLB; San Marino lawyer and politician; b. 15 Aug. 1964, San Leo; m.; two s.; ed Y Cadet in Mirzapur Cadet Coll., Defence Capitano di Castello (Mayor) of Chiesanuova 2003–08; legal adviser to Sec. of State for Land, Environment and Agric. 2008–12; mem. Consiglio Grande e Generale (Great and Gen. Council, Parl.) 2011–, mem. Finance and Budget Comm.; mem. and Pres. San Marino Antimafia Comm. 2012–13; Co-Captain Regent (jt head of state) 2013–14; mem. Partito Democratico Cristiano Sammarinese (San Marino Christian Democrat Party) 2008–. *Address:* c/o Office of the Captains-Regent, Contrada Omerelli, 47890 San Marino, San Marino (office).

MUDASSIR HUSAIN, Justice Syed J. R., BA, LLB; Bangladeshi judge (retd); b. 1 March 1940, Hobigonj; s. of the late Advocate Syed Md. Mumidul Husain and Syeda Honse-Ara-Akther Khatun; m. Syeda Mazida Khatun; three d. one s.; ed Dhaka Univ.; enrolled as Advocate of High Court of E Pakistan 1965; part-time Lecturer, Central Law Coll. Dhaka 1966–78; Examiner and Question Setter, Dept of Law, Univ. of Dhaka; reporter, Bangladesh Law Reports 1973–77; apptd Asst Attorney Gen. 1977; enrolled as Advocate of Appellate Div. 1980; apptd Deputy Attorney Gen. 1984; apptd Judge, High Court Div. 1992, Judge of the Appellate Div. 2002; Chief Justice, Supreme Court 2004–07 (retd); rep. World Intellectual Property Org. 2003. *Leisure interest:* reading books, watching world television, watching cricket and football. *Address:* c/o Supreme Court, Dhaka 1000; Flat 1 – BA-RC Tower, 74 Elephant Road, Dhaka 1205, Bangladesh (home). *Telephone:* (2) 8652523 (home).

MUDAVADI, Wycliffe Musalia; Kenyan economist and politician; *Deputy Prime Minister;* b. 21 Sept. 1960, Vihiga Dist; m.; three c.; fmr employee Tysons Ltd (property consultants firm) –1989; land economist, Nat. Housing Corpn 1984–89; mem. Parl. for Sabatia 1989–; Minister of Supplies and Marketing 1989–92, of Finance 1992–97, of Agric. 1997–99, of Transport and Communications 1999–2002, Deputy Prime Minister 2008–, also Minister of Local Govt 2008–12; Vice-Pres. of Kenya Nov.–Dec. 2002; Nat. Vice-Chair. Kenya African Nat. Union 2002–; cand. in presidential election 2013; Founder Rainbow Alliance; mem. Inst. of Surveyors. *Address:* Office of the Deputy Prime Minister, Jogoo House 'A', Taifa Rd, POB 30004, Nairobi (home); Kenya African National Union, KICC POB 72394, Nairobi, Kenya (office). *Telephone:* (20) 217475 (office). *Website:* www .localgovernment.go.ke (office).

MUDD, Daniel H., BA, MPA; American business executive; b. 1959; s. of Roger Mudd; m.; four c.; ed Univ. of Virginia, John F. Kennedy School of Govt at Harvard Univ.; served as officer in US Marine Corps, including combat service in Beirut, Lebanon; Robert Bosch Foundation Fellowship, Germany 1989; Vice-Pres. of Business Devt, GE Capital 1991–93, Man. Dir Int. Financing 1993–95, Pres. and CEO European Fleet Services, Brussels 1995–96, Pres. Asia Pacific 1996–99, Pres. and CEO Japan 1999–2000; Vice-Chair. and COO Fannie Mae, Washington, DC 2000–04, interim CEO 2004–05, Pres. and CEO 2005–08, mem. Bd of Dirs 2000–08; mem. Bd of Dirs Fortress Investment Group LLC, Center for the Study of the Presidency, Homes for Working Families, Hampton Univ.; mem. Bd of Mans Univ. of Virginia. *Address:* c/o Fannie Mae, 3900 Wisconsin Avenue, NW, Washington, DC 20016-2892, USA. *Telephone:* (202) 752-7000. *E-mail:* headquarters@fanniemae.com. *Website:* www.fanniemae.com.

MUDGE, Dirk; Namibian politician; b. 16 Jan. 1928, Otjiwarongo; m. Stienie Jacobs; two s. three d.; mem. Nat. Legis. Ass. 1965–; Chair. of Turnhalle Constitutional Conf. 1977; Vice-Chair. of Nat. Party and mem. SW Africa Exec. Council Sept. 1977; formed Republican Party of SW Africa 1977; Chair. Democratic Turnhalle Alliance (now DTA of Namibia) 1977; mem. Constituent Ass. 1978–79, Nat. Ass. 1979–83; Pres. Ministers' Council 1980–83, Minister for Finance and Governmental Affairs 1985–89; mem. Nat. Ass. 1991–93; Founding Trustee, Democratic Media Trust (now Dirk Mudge Trust) 1992–2013. *Address:* c/o Dirk Mudge Trust, P.O. Box 86908, Eros, Windhoek 9000, Namibia. *Website:* dirkmudgetrust.com.

MUDIMBE, Valentin-Yves, (Hermano Mateo); American academic and writer; *Newman Ivey White Professor of Literature, Duke University;* b. 8 Dec. 1941, Likasi Jadotville, Belgian Congo (now the Democratic Repub. of the Congo); ed Univ. of Lovanium, Belgian Congo, Catholic Univ. of Louvain, Belgium, Univ. of Besançon and Univ. of Paris, France; specialist in phenomenology and structuralism; fmr Lecturer, Univs of Louvain, Paris-Nanterre, Zaïre, Haverford Coll., Stanford Univ.; Assoc. Dir of Studies, Ecole des Hautes-Etudes, Paris 1988–99; Louis H. Jordan Lecturer, SOAS, Univ. of London, UK; Samuel Fischer Prof., Free Univ. of Berlin, Germany; Commonwealth Prof., Univ. of Cambridge, UK; currently Newman Ivey White Prof. of Literature, Duke Univ., NC; Visiting Prof., El Colegio de Mexico, Univ. of Antioquia, Colombia, Univ. of Cologne, Germany, Univ. of Warwick, UK; Gen.-Sec. Soc. for African Philosophy in N America (SAPINA) 1988–99; Chair. Int. African Inst., Univ. of London; Corresp. mem. Belgian Acad. of Overseas Sciences 1978–2006, Hon. Corresp. mem. 2006–; Chevalier de la Pléiade, Ordre de la Francophonie et du Dialogue des Cultures 1997; Dr hc (Université de Paris VII-Denis Diderot), (La Chancellerie des Universités de Paris, Sorbonne) 1997, (Katholieke Universiteit Leuven) 2006. *Publications include:* L'odeur du père 1982, The Invention of Africa 1988, Parables and Fables 1991, Le corps glorieux des mots et des êtres 1994, The Idea of Africa 1994, Tales of Faith 1997; editor: The Surreptitious Speech 1992, Nations, Identities, Cultures 1997, Diaspora and Immigration (with Sabine Engel) 1999, Cheminements 1999, The Normal & Its Orders (with Gode Iwele and Laura Kerr) 2006; co-editor: Africa and the Disciplines (with Robert H. Bates and Jean O'Barr) 1993; 70 articles; three collections of poetry, four novels. *Address:* Duke University, Literature Program, 101 Friedl Bldg, Box 90670, Durham, NC 27708, USA (office). *Telephone:* (919) 684-4240 (office). *Fax:* (919) 684-3598 (office). *E-mail:* mwr079@gmail.com (office).

MUDRINIĆ, Ivica, BASc; Croatian business executive; *Senior Vice-President for Strategic Support, Deutsche Telekom AG;* b. 1955; ed Univ. of Toronto, Canada; began career in Product Devt Dept, Motorola Communications –1985; f. MX Engineering Inc. 1985; returned to Croatia 1990, becoming Adviser for Communications to Croatian Pres., Asst Minister for Maritime Affairs, Transport and Communications 1991–92, Minister 1992–94; Pres., Telecommunications Council 1994–96; Pres. Man. Bd, Hrvatska Radiotelevizija 1996–98; CEO, Hrvatska pošta i telekomunikacije 1998–99, Pres., T-Hrvatski Telekom (following liberalisation) 1999–, then Pres. and CEO –2013, Sr Vice-Pres. for Strategic Support, Deutsche Telekom AG (parent co.) 2013–. *Address:* Deutsche Telekom AG, Friedrich-Ebert-Allee 140, 53113 Bonn, Germany (office). *Website:* www.telekom.com (office).

MUELLER, Edward A., BS, MBA; American telecommunications industry executive; *CEO, Qwest Communications International, Inc.;* b. St Louis; ed Univ. of Missouri, Washington Univ.; joined Southwestern Bell 1968, held several sr positions including Pres. and CEO Southwestern Bell, Pres. and CEO Pacific Bell 1997–99, Pres. SBC Int. Operations 1999–2000; Pres. and CEO Ameritech 2000–02; CEO Williams-Sonoma, Inc. 2003–07; mem. Bd of Dirs 2005–; CEO Qwest Communications Int., Inc., Denver 2007–. *Address:* Qwest Communications International, Inc., 1801 California Street, Denver, CO 80202, USA (office). *Telephone:* (303) 992-1400 (office). *Fax:* (303) 992-1724 (office). *Website:* www .qwest.com (office).

MÜLLER, Gerd; German politician; *Federal Minister of Economic Co-operation and Development;* b. 25 Aug. 1955, Krumbach/Schwaben; m.; two c.; ed Regensburg Univ.; fmr teacher and Deputy Head, Inst. of Int. Relations, Hanns-Seidel-Stiftung, Munich; mem. European Parl. 1989–94; mem. Bundestag (Parl.) 1994–; Parl. State Sec., Fed. Ministry of Food, Agric. and Consumer Protection 2005–13; Fed. Minister of Econ. Co-operation and Devt 2013–; mem.

Christlich-Soziale Union; Bayerischer Verdienstorden 2007. *Address:* Federal Ministry of Economic Co-operation and Development, Dahlmannstrasse 4, 53113 Bonn, Germany (office). *Telephone:* (228) 995350 (office). *Fax:* (228) 995353500 (office). *E-mail:* info@bmz.bund.de (office). *Website:* www.bmz.de (office); www .gerd-mueller-waehlen.de.

MUELLER, Robert Swan, III, MA, JD; American lawyer and fmr government official; b. 7 Aug. 1944, New York City; s. of Robert Swan Mueller, Jr and Alice Mueller (née Truesdale); m. Ann Standish 1966; two d.; ed Princeton Univ., New York Univ. and Univ. of Virginia; Capt., US Marine Corps 1967–70; Assoc., Pillsbury, Madison & Sutro, San Francisco 1973–76; Asst US Attorney, US Attorney's Office, Northern Dist Calif., San Francisco 1976–80, Chief, Special Prosecutions Unit 1980–81, Criminal Div. 1981–82; Chief, Criminal Div. Mass. Dist, US Attorney's Office, Boston 1982–85, First Asst US Attorney in Boston 1985, US Attorney for Mass Dist 1986–87, Deputy US Attorney for Mass Dist 1987–88; Pnr, Hill & Barlow, Boston 1988–89; Asst to Attorney Gen. for criminal matters, US Dept of Justice, Washington, DC 1989–90, Asst Attorney Gen. for Criminal Div. 1990–93; lawyer, Hale & Dorr, Washington, DC 1993; Interim US Attorney, Northern Dist Calif. 1998–2001; Dir FBI 2001–13; Bronze Star, Purple Heart, Vietnamese Cross of Gallantry. *Address:* c/o Department of Justice, Federal Bureau of Investigation, J. Edgar Hoover Building, 950 Pennsylvania Avenue NW, Washington, DC 20530, USA.

MUELLER-STAHL, Armin; German actor; b. 17 Dec. 1930, Tilsit, East Prussia (now Sovetsk, Russia); ed Berlin Conservatory; began career with music studies (violin), subsequently became actor; moved to FRG 1980; Hon. DHumLitt (Chicago); Bundesfilmpreis 1981, Silver Bar Award 1992. *Films include:* Heimliche Ehen 1956, Königskinder (Royal Children) 1962, ...und Deine Liebe auch 1962, Christine 1963, Nackt unter Wölfen (Naked Among Wolves) 1963, Preludio 11 1964, Alaskafüchse 1964, Tödlicher Irrtum 1970, Der Dritte (The Third) 1972, Januskopf 1972, Die Hosen des Ritters Bredow 1973, Kit & Co. 1974, Jakob, der Lügner (Jacob the Liar) 1975, Nelken in Aspik 1976, Die Flucht (The Flight) 1977, Lola 1981, Die Flügel der Nacht 1982, Die Sehnsucht der Veronika Voss 1982, Der Westen leuchtet 1982, Trauma 1983, Viadukt (aka The Train Killer) 1983, Un dimanche de flic (A Cop's Sunday) 1983, L'homme blessé (The Wounded Man) 1983, Eine Liebe in Deutschland (A Love in Germany) 1983, Tausend Augen (Thousand Eyes) 1984, Rita Ritter 1984, Glut (Embers) 1984, Oberst Redl (Colonel Redl) 1985, Die Mitläufer 1985, Vergeßt Mozart (Forget Mozart) 1986, Bittere Ernte (Angry Harvest) 1986, Momo 1986, Der Joker (Lethal Obsession) 1987, Killing Blue (Midnight Cop) 1988, Das Spinnennetz (Spider's Web) 1989, Schweinegeld (aka C*A*S*H: A Political Fairy Tale, UK) 1989, A Hecc 1989, Music Box 1989, Avalon 1990, Kafka 1991, Bronsteins Kinder (Bronstein's Children) 1991, Night on Earth 1991, Utz 1992, The Power of One 1992, Far from Berlin 1992, Red Hot 1993, Der Kinoerzähler (The Film Narrator) 1993, The House of the Spirits 1993, Taxandria 1994, The Last Good Time 1994, Holy Matrimony 1994, A Pyromaniac's Love Story 1995, Theodore Rex (video) 1995, Shine (Australian Film Prize 1996), Conversation with the Beast 1996, Der Unhold (The Ogre) 1996, The Assistant 1997, The Game 1997, The Peacemaker 1997, The Commissioner 1998, The X-Files 1998, The Thirteenth Floor 1999, The Third Miracle 1999, Jakob the Liar 1999, The Long Run 2000, Mission to Mars (uncredited) 2000, Pilgrim 2000, The Story of an African Farm 2004, The Dust Factory 2004, Local Color 2006, Ich bin die Andere 2006, Eastern Promises 2007, Leningrad 2007. *Television includes:* Fünf Patronenhülsen (Five Cartridges) 1960, Flucht aus der Hölle (mini-series) 1960, Die Letzte Chance 1962, Der Andere neben dir 1963, Wolf unter Wölfen (mini-series) 1964, Ein Lord am Alexanderplatz 1967, Columbus 64 1966, Wege übers Land (mini-series) 1968, Die Dame aus Genua 1969, Kein Mann für Camp Detrick 1970, Die Verschworenen (mini-series) 1971, Die Sieben Affären der Dona Juanita (mini-series) 1973, Das Unsichtbare Visier (series) 1973, Stülpner-Legende (series; uncredited) 1973, Die Eigene Haut 1974, Geschlossene Gesellschaft 1978, Die Längste Sekunde 1980, Collin (mini-series) 1981, Ferry oder Wie es war 1981, Ja und Nein 1981, Die Gartenlaube 1982, Ich werde warten 1982, An uns glaubt Gott nicht mehr (God Does Not Believe in Us Anymore) 1982, Ausgestoßen 1982, Der Fall Sylvester Matuska 1982, Flucht aus Pommern 1982, Ruhe sanft, Bruno 1983, Tatort - Freiwild 1984, Hautnah 1985, Gauner im Paradies 1986, Auf den Tag genau 1986, Unser Mann im Dschungel (aka Amazonas Mission) 1987, Amerika (mini-series) 1987, Franza 1987, Jokehnen oder Wie lange fährt man von Ostpreußen nach Deutschland? (mini-series) 1987, Tagebuch für einen Mörder 1988, In the Presence of Mine Enemies 1997, 12 Angry Men 1997, Jesus 1999, Crociati (Crusaders) (mini-series) 2001, Die Manns - Ein Jahrhundertroman (mini-series) 2001, The Power of Knowledge (series) 2005. *Publications:* Verordneter Sonntag (Lost Sunday), Drehtage, Unterwegs Nach Hause (On the Way Home).

MUFAMADI, Fholisani Sydney, MSc; South African politician; b. 28 Feb. 1959, Alexandra, Johannesburg; m. Nomusa Kumalo; one s. two d.; ed Univ. of London, UK; pvt. teacher, Lamula Secondary School 1980; Gen. Sec. Gen. and Allied Workers' Union 1982; Publicity Sec. United Democratic Front (UDF); Asst Gen. Sec. Congress of South African Trade Unions 1985; mem. Nat. Peace Cttee, helped draft Nat. Peace Accord 1991; mem. African Nat. Congress (ANC) Nat. Exec. Cttee, ANC Working Cttee, Cen. Cttee of South African Communist Party, Political Bureau; ANC Rep. at Transitional Exec. Council on Law and Order, Safety and Stability 1993–94; Minister of Safety and Security, Govt of Nat. Unity 1994–99, of Prov. Affairs and Local Govt 1999–2008 (resgnd); Hon. DSc (Igbinedion Univ., Okada). *Leisure interest:* reading. *Address:* African National Congress, 54 Sauer Street, Johannesburg 2001, South Africa (office). *Telephone:* (11) 3761000 (office). *Fax:* (11) 3761134 (office). *E-mail:* nmtyelwa@anc.org.za (office). *Website:* www.anc .org.za (office).

MUFTI, Hania, MSc; Jordanian lawyer and international organization executive; b. Amman; ed in Jordan and Lebanon and Univ. of Bath, UK; more than 20 years' professional experience in human rights research and advocacy; Researcher, Middle East Research Dept, Amnesty International's Secr., London, UK 1981–97; Dir Middle East and North Africa Div., Human Rights Watch, London 2000–07; UN Chief of Human Rights Office with UN Assistance Mission for Iraq 2007–08; has continued to investigate human rights standards maintained by troops in Iraq during occupation of the country; also gathers evidence for the trials of fmr Iraqi leaders; named by TIME magazine as one of the 100 most influential people in

2005. *Publications include:* author of numerous reports for Amnesty International, including Iraq: The World Would Not Listen 1994, Kuwait: Three Years of Unfair Trials 1994, Iraq: Human Rights Abuses in Iraqi Kurdistan Since 1991 1995, Bahrain: A Human Rights Crisis 1995. *Address:* c/o Human Rights Watch, First Floor, Audrey House, 16–20 Ely Place, London, EC1N 6SN, England. *Telephone:* 7980-540036 (mobile). *E-mail:* hrwuk@hrw.org. *Website:* www.hrw.org/london.

MUGABE, Robert Gabriel, BA, BAdmin, BEd, MSc (Econ), LLM; Zimbabwean politician, head of state and fmr teacher; *President;* b. 21 Feb. 1924, Kutama; m. 1st Sarah Mugabe (died 1992); one s. (deceased); m. 2nd Grace Marufu 1996; ed Kutama and Empandeni Mission School, Fort Hare Univ. Coll., S Africa, Univs of S Africa and London; teacher, at Drifontein Roman Catholic School, Umvuma 1952, Salisbury S Primary School 1953, in Gwelo 1954, Chalimbana Teacher Training Coll. 1955, in Accra, Ghana 1958–60; entered politics 1960; Publicity Sec. of Nat. Dem. Party 1960–61; Publicity Sec. Zimbabwe African People's Union 1961; detained Sept.–Dec. 1962, March–April 1963; escaped to Tanzania April 1963; Co-Founder of Zimbabwe African Nat. Union (ZANU) Aug. 1963; Sec.-Gen. Aug. 1963; in detention in Rhodesia 1964–74; Pres. ZANU; mem. Politburo ZANU 1984–; Jt Leader of Patriotic Front (with Joshua Nkomo) 1976–79; contested Feb. 1980 elections as Leader of ZANU (PF) (name changed to ZANU 1984) Party, Pres. 1988–; Minister of Defence 1980–87, also fmrly of Public Works, Industry and Tech.; Prime Minister of Zimbabwe 1980–87; Pres. of Zimbabwe 1988–; Chancellor Univ. of Zimbabwe; apptd Amb. for southern Africa, African Union 2003; Dr hc (Ahmadu Bello Univ., Nigeria) 1980; Newsmaker of the Year Award (S African Soc. of Journalists) 1980, Africa Prize 1988; Int. Human Rights Award (Howard Univ., Washington, DC) 1981, Jawarhalal Nehru Award 1992. *Address:* Office of the President, Munhumutapa Building, Samora Machel Avenue, Private Bag 7700, Causeway, Harare, Zimbabwe. *Telephone:* (4) 707091 (office).

MUGLER, Thierry; French fashion designer; b. 1946, Strasbourg; ed in Strasbourg; fmr ballet dancer, Opéra du Rhin, Strasbourg; later window-dresser and clothing designer, Gudule boutique, Paris; designer of fashion collection for André Peters, London; subsequently began career as freelance clothing designer in Amsterdam, later in Paris where he launched Café de Paris collection; designer of menswear and fashion accessories; launched own Thierry Mugler fashion label, Paris 1973; launched Thierry Mugler Diffusion fashion co.; opened own boutique, Place des Victoires, Paris; clothing also sold in dept stores in USA and Japan; launched range of perfumes. *Address:* Thierry Mugler Parfums, 10 Cavendish Place, London, W1G 9DN, England. *Telephone:* (20) 7307-6700 (office). *Fax:* (20) 7307-6705 (office). *Website:* www.thierrymugler.com (office).

MUHAMMAD VI, HM The King of Morocco; b. 21 Aug. 1963, Rabat; s. of the late King Hassan II; m. Lalla Salma Bennani 2002; one s. (Crown Prince Moulay Hassan, b. 2003) one d. (b. 2007); ed Collège Royal, Université Mohammed V, Faculté des Sciences Juridiques, Economiques et Sociales de Rabat; Head of Moroccan del., 7th Summit of Non-Aligned Nations, New Delhi 1983, 10th Franco–African Conf., Vittel 1983; apptd Co-ordinator Admin. and Services, Armed Forces 1985; rank of Gén. de Div. 1994; Hon. Pres. Asscn Socio–Culturelle du Bassin Méditerranéen 1979–; Chair. Org. Cttee 9th Mediterranean Games, Casablanca 1982; succeeded to the throne on the death of his father 23 July 1999. *Address:* Royal Palace, Rabat, Morocco.

MUHAMMAD, Ali Nasser; Yemeni politician; b. 1939, Dathina Rural District; active mem. of Nat. Liberation Front (NLF) 1963–67; Gov. of the Islands 1967, of Second Prov. 1968; mem. Nat. Front Gen. Command March 1968; Minister of Local Govt 1969, of Defence 1969–77, of Educ. 1974–75; mem. Front Exec. Cttee 1970; mem. Presidential Council of People's Democratic Repub. of Yemen 1971–78, Chair. June–Dec. 1978; Chair. Council of Ministers (Prime Minister) 1971–85; mem. Supreme People's Council (SPC) 1971, Chair. Presidium of SPC (Head of State) 1980–86 (overthrown in coup Jan. 1986); mem. Political Bureau of Nat. Front 1972–75, of United Political Org. Nat. Front 1975–78, of Yemen Socialist Party (YSP) 1978–86, Sec.-Gen. of YSP 1980–86.

MUHAMMED, Magaji, BA; Nigerian government official and diplomatist; b. 31 Dec. 1940, Dutsinma, Katsina State; ed Ahmadu Bello Univ.; Dist Officer Idoma, Wukari and Tiv Div., Prin. Asst Sec. Mil. Gov.'s Office, Kaduna 1965–75; fmr Admin., Kaduna Capital Territory, Perm. Sec. 1975; joined Civil Service 1980, Dir Project Implementation, Ministry of Industries, Dir Commercial and Industrial Incentives, Ministry of Trade and Industries; Amb. to Saudi Arabia 2000–03; Minister of Industry –2005, of Internal Affairs 2005–06 (resgnd). *Address:* c/o Ministry of Internal Affairs, Area 1, Secretariat Complex, Garki, Abuja, Nigeria (office).

MUHAMMEDOV, Hojamuhammet; Turkmenistani economist and politician; *Deputy Chairman of the Council of Ministers, responsible for Textile Industry, Trade and the Chamber of Commerce and Industry;* b. 1966, Aşgabat; ed Turkmen Nat. Econ. Inst.; early career as forwarding agent, Turkmenengilazyksenagat 1983; fmr Construction Engineer, Supplies Dept, Turkmenhimsnabbyt; fmr stock-keeper, State Cttee for Logistics of Turkmenistan; Deputy Dir, later Dir, Kharytimpeks Co., also Dir Gulistan State Trading Centre 1998–2005; Deputy Chair. State Commodity and Raw Materials Exchange 2005–06, Chair. 2006; Chair. Supreme Supervisory Chamber of Turkmenistan July–Nov. 2007; Deputy Chair., Council of Ministers, responsible for Textile Industry, Trade and Chamber of Commerce and Industry 2007–; Acting Presidential Chief of Staff March 2009–. *Address:* Office of the President and the Council of Ministers, 744000 Aşgabat, Presidential Palace, Turkmenistan. *Telephone:* (12) 35-45-34 (office). *Fax:* (12) 35-51-12 (office). *Website:* www.turkmenistan.gov.tm (office).

MUHITH, Abul Maal Abdul, BA (Hons), MA, MPA; Bangladeshi economist, civil servant, diplomatist and politician; *Minister of Finance;* b. 1934, Sylhet; s. of Abu Ahmad Abdul Hafiz and Sayed Shahar Banu Chowdhury; m. Sayed Sabia Muhith; two s. one d.; ed Sylhet MC Coll., Dhaka Univ., Univ. of Oxford, UK, Harvard Univ., USA; joined Pakistan Civil Service 1956, served in different depts of East Pakistan, Cen. Pakistan and later Bangladesh, Sec. of Planning 1972–77, Sec. of External Resource Dept, Ministry of Finance and Planning 1977–81, served as Deputy and Chief Sec. Pakistan Planning Comm.; served as diplomat, Embassy in Washington, DC, USA; retd 1981; emerged from retirement as econs and devt specialist in Ford Foundation and IFAD; Minister of Finance and Planning 1982–83; then worked as specialist of different insts of World Bank and UN;

Visiting Fellow, Princeton Univ., USA 1984–85; Minister of Finance 2009–; early proponent of Bangladesh Environment Movt; Founder-Pres. BAPA. *Publications include:* 21 books on various subjects, including admin. and liberation war affairs. *Address:* Ministry of Finance, Bangladesh Secretariat, Bhaban 7, 1st 9-Storey Bldg, 3rd Floor, Dhaka 1000, Bangladesh (office). *Telephone:* (2) 8690202 (office). *Fax:* (2) 865581 (office). *E-mail:* info@mof.gov.bd (office). *Website:* www.mof.gov.bd (office).

MÜHLEMANN, Lukas, MBA; Swiss business executive; b. 1950; ed Univ. of St Gallen and Harvard Univ.; fmr systems engineer IBM; man. consultant McKinsey & Co. 1977–94, Prin. 1982, Dir 1986, Man. Dir McKinsey's Swiss offices 1989, mem. Bd Dirs McKinsey & Co., Inc., New York 1990; CEO Swiss Re 1994, Man. Dir 1994, Deputy Chair. 1996; CEO Credit Suisse Group 1997–2002, Chair. Bd Dirs 2000–02, mem. Bd Dirs Credit Suisse, Credit Suisse First Boston; mem. Bd Tonhalle Foundation, Zurich, Zurich Opera House, Banco Gen. de Negocios; Pres. Harvard Club of Switzerland. *Address:* c/o Credit Suisse Group, Paradeplatz 8, P.O. Box 1, CH 8070 Zurich, Switzerland.

MUHYIDDIN, Tan Sri Dato' Haji Mohd Yassin bin; Malaysian politician; *Minister of International Trade and Industry;* b. 1947; Chief Minister of Johor 1982–95; Minister of Youth and Sports 1995–99, of Domestic Trade and Consumer Affairs 1999–2004, of Agric. and Agro-Based Industry 2004–08, of Int. Trade and Industry 2008–; currently Vice-Pres. United Malays Nat. Org. *Address:* Ministry of International Trade and Industry, Blok 10, Kompleks Pejabat Kerajaan, Jalan Duta, 50622 Kuala Lumpur, Malaysia (office). *Telephone:* (3) 62033022 (office). *Fax:* (3) 62012337 (office). *E-mail:* webmiti@miti.gov.my (office). *Website:* www .miti.gov.my (office).

MUIR, Richard John Sutherland, CMG, BA; British consultant and diplomatist (retd); *Senior Consultant, MEC International Ltd;* b. 25 Aug. 1942, London; s. of John Muir and Edna Hodges; m. Caroline Simpson 1965; one s. one d; ed Stationers' Co. School and Univs of Reading and Strasbourg; joined FCO 1966, Second Sec., Embassy in Jeddah 1967–70, Embassy in Tunis 1970–72, at FCO 1972–75, First Sec., Embassy in Washington, DC 1975–79, Prin. Dept of Energy, FCO 1979–81, Counsellor, Embassy in Jeddah 1981–85, at FCO 1985–91, Under-Sec. and Chief Insp. Diplomatic Service 1991–94, Amb. to Oman 1994–98, to Kuwait 1999–2002 (retd); joined MEC Int. 2003, currently Sr Consultant; fmr Dir (non-exec.) Mott Macdonald Int.; mem. Next Century Foundation. *Leisure interests:* walking, sailing, fishing, opera. *Address:* MEC International Ltd, Granville House, 132-135 Sloane Street, London, SW1X 9AX, England (office). *Telephone:* (20) 7591-4816 (office). *Fax:* (20) 7591-4801 (office). *E-mail:* mec@ meconsult.co.uk (office). *Website:* www.meconsult.co.uk (office).

MUIR, William (Bill) F., BEng, MBA; American business executive; *President, GMAC Financial Services;* b. 28 Dec. 1954, Freeport, NY; ed Cornell Univ., Harvard Univ.; joined General Motors (GM) at Treas.'s Office, New York 1983, Dir of Foreign Exchange and Int. Cash Man. 1986–87, Dir of Overseas Borrowings 1987–89, Dir of Corp. Finance and Investor Relations 1989–90, Gen. Dir of Business Devt 1990–92, Vice-Pres. of Nat. Accounts, GMAC Financial Services 1992–95, Vice-Pres. of Eastern US Operations 1995–96, Exec.-in-Charge of Operations, later Exec. Dir of Planning, GM's Delphi Automotive Systems 1996, Exec. Vice-Pres. and Chief Financial Officer GMAC Financial Services Feb. 1998–2004, Chair. GMAC's Insurance Group 1999–, Pres. GMAC Financial Services 2004–, mem. Bd of Dirs GMAC Commercial Finance, GMAC Bank. *Address:* GMAC Financial Services, 200 Renaissance Center, Detroit, MI 48265-2000, USA (office). *Telephone:* (313) 556-5000 (office). *Fax:* (815) 282-6156 (office). *E-mail:* info@gmacfs.com (office). *Website:* www.gmacfs.com (office).

MUIZ, Abdulla; Maldivian government official; fmr Deputy Attorney-Gen., then Attorney-Gen. 2011–12; mem. Nat. Crime Prevention Cttee 2011–. *Address:* c/o Attorney-General's Office, Huravee Building, 3rd Floor, Ameer Ahmed Magu, Malé 20-05, Maldives.

MUIZZU, Uz Ahmed, LLB, LLM; Maldivian lawyer and judge; *Prosecutor General;* ed Malaysiage Int. Islamic Univ., Int. Maritime Org. Law Inst.; fmr judge, Criminal Court of Maldives; mem. Special Majlis for Haa Alifu constituency; Sr Pnr, Muizzu, Suoodh & Co. (law firm); Prosecutor Gen. 2009–; mem. Bd of Dirs Maldives Tourism Devt Corpn Plc. *Address:* Office of the Prosecutor General, Supreme Court of the Maldives, Malé (office); Muizzu, Suoodh & Co., Second Floor, H. Orchidmaage, Ameeru Ahmed Magu, Malé 20-206, Maldives. *Telephone:* 3323092 (office); 3344911. *Fax:* 3316471 (office); 3344922. *E-mail:* info@msc.com .mv. *Website:* msc.com.mv.

MUJAHID, Jamila; Afghan journalist and broadcaster; b. Kabul; m. Sayed Amin; five c.; ed in Afghanistan; broadcaster with Radio-Television Afghanistan from 1980, evening news broadcaster on TV and radio 1985–96; worked for NGOs during Taleban regime; first female broadcaster to appear on Radio-Television Afghanistan announcing the departure of the Taliban 2001; Pres. Afghanistan Women in Media Network, Kabul 2002–; f. Voice of Afghan Women Radio (Dir of radio station 2003, relaunched 2005–); Ed., Malalai women's magazine 2003–. *E-mail:* sayedmobinsadat@yahoo.com (office).

MUJAMMEDOV, Hojamuhammed; Turkmenistani economist and politician; b. 1966, Aşgabat; ed Turkmen Inst. of Nat. Economy; began career 1983; worked as forwarding agent of Turkmenengilazyksenagat Asscn, Ministry of Trade and Consumers' Co-operation; various positions, including as construction engineer, as engineer of Supplies Dept of Turkmenhimsnabbyt, as stock keeper of Dept of State Cttee for Logistics; Deputy Dir and Dir, Harytimpeks Co., Ministry of Trade and Foreign Econ. Relations 1998–2005, Dir of State Trade Centre Gulistan; Deputy Chair. State commodity and Raw Materials Exchange 2005–06, Chair. 2006–07; Chair. Supreme Supervisory Chamber of Turkmenistan 2007; apptd Deputy Chair. Council of Ministers in charge of Trade and the Textile Industry 2007; Deputy Chair., Chief of the Govt and Presidential Staff 2012–13. *Address:* c/o Office of the President and the Council of Ministers, 744000 Aşgabat, Presidential Palace, Turkmenistan. *E-mail:* nt@online.tm.

MUJAWAR, Ali Muhammad, BA, MA, PhD; Yemeni academic and politician; b. 1953, Shabwa; ed Algiers Univ., Algeria and Grenoble Univ., France; mem. Higher Studies Cttee, Business Dept, Univ. of Aden 1990–2000, Head, Business Man. Dept, Faculty of Econs 1994–96, Dean of Faculty of Oil and Minerals 1996–99,

Dean, Faculty of Man. Studies 2001–03; Gen. Man. Al-Barah Cement Factory 1999–2000; fmr Deputy Minister of Civil Service and Insurance, Minister of Fisheries 2003–06, of Electricity and Water 2006–07, Prime Minister 2007–11. *Address:* c/o Office of the Prime Minister, San'a, Yemen (office).

MUJEZINOVIĆ, Mustafa; Bosnia and Herzegovina politician, diplomatist and fmr electrical engineer; *Ambassador to UK;* b. 27 Dec. 1954, Sarajevo; m. Emina Mujezinović; ed First Gen. High School, Sarajevo, Faculty of Electrical Eng, Sarajevo Univ.; Constructor, then Quality Engineer, Factory of Transformer Stations and Switchgear Plants, TTS 'Energoinvest', Sarajevo 1978–83, Head of Tech. Group, Sales Dept 1983–90, Sales Man. and mem. Man. Bd 1990–92; Pres. Municipality Stari Grad (Old Town), Sarajevo 1994–95, Mayor of Municipality Stari Grad, Sarajevo 1995–96; first Prime Minister of Sarajevo Canton 1996–98, Gov. of Sarajevo Canton 1998–2000; Amb. of Bosnia and Herzegovina to OSCE 2000–01; Dir of Privatization Fund 'Prevent Invest' 2002–04; Amb. of Bosnia and Herzegovina to Malaysia 2004–08; Advisor to Man. of Devt Bank of Fed. of Bosnia and Herzegovina 2008–09; Prime Minister of Fed. of Bosnia and Herzegovina 2009–11; Amb. to UK 2012–; mem. Party of Democratic Action (Stranka Demokratske Akcije—SDA). *Address:* Embassy of Bosnia and Herzegovina, 5–7 Lexham Gardens, London, W8 5JJ, England (office). *Telephone:* (20) 7373-0867 (office). *Fax:* (20) 7373-0871 (office). *E-mail:* embassy@bhembassy.co.uk (office). *Website:* bhembassy.co.uk (office).

MUJICA CORDANO, José (Pepe) Alberto; Uruguayan farmer, politician and head of state; *President;* b. 20 May 1935, Montevideo; m. Lucía Topolansky; fmr mem. Movimiento de Liberación Nacional–Tupamaros guerrilla movt; fmr mem. Partido Nacional; imprisoned for 14 years during dictatorship, granted amnesty with return of democracy 1985; Founding mem. and leader Movimiento de Participación Popular (part of Frente Amplio); mem. Cámara de Senadores (parl.) –2005, 2008–; Minister of Livestock, Agric. and Fisheries 2004–08; Frente Amplio presidential cand. 2009; Pres., Eastern Repub. of Uruguay 2010–. *Address:* Frente Amplio, Colonia 1367, 2°, 11100 Montevideo, Uruguay (office). *Telephone:* (2) 9022176 (office). *E-mail:* comunicacion@frenteamplio.org.uy (office). *Website:* www .frenteamplio.org.uy (office).

MUJOTA, Fehmi; Kosovo politician; *Minister of Infrastructure;* ed Univ. of Prishtina; fmr mem. Kosovo Liberation Army; fmr Mayor Shtime Municipality; mem. Democratic Party of Kosovo; mem. Kosovo Ass., First Vice Chair. Cttee for Public Services, Local Admin and Media; Minister of the Kosovo Security Force 2008–11, of Infrastructure 2011–. *Address:* Ministry of Infrastructure, 10000 Prishtina (office); Democratic Party of Kosovo, Rruga Nënë Terezë 20, 10000 Prishtina, Kosovo (office). *Telephone:* (38) 211202 (office). *E-mail:* pdk@pdk-ks.org (office). *Website:* www.pdk-ks.org (office).

MUJURU, Joyce Teurai-Ropa; Zimbabwean politician; *Vice-President;* b. 15 April 1955, Mount Darwin; m. Tapfumanei Ruzambu Solomon Mujuru (Nhongo) 1977 (died 2011); four d.; ed Women's Univ. in Africa; Minister of Youth, Sport and Recreation 1980–81, of Community Devt and Women's Affairs 1981–88, of Community and Co-operative Devt 1989–92, of Rural Resources and Water Devt 1996–2004; Vice-Pres. of Zimbabwe 2004–; Second Sec. and Vice-Pres. ZANU (PF) party 2004–; Gov. and Resident Minister of Mashonaland Cen. Prov. 1993–96; Fellow, Inst. of Engineers 2000–; Liberation Medal, War Veteran Order of Merit, Pride of Africa Women, Women Advancement for Economic and Leadership Empowerment in Africa 2010. *Leisure interests:* church and women's meetings, knitting, sewing, cooking, outdoor life. *Address:* Office of the Vice-President, Munhumutapa Building, Samora Machel Avenue, Private Bag 7700, Causeway, Harare (office); No. 9 Tara Township, Ruwa (home); Box 57, Ruwa, Zimbabwe (home). *Telephone:* (4) 707091 (office). *Website:* www.vpmujuruoffice.gov.zw.

MUKAI, Chiaki, MD, PhD; Japanese astronaut, surgeon and academic; *Director, Center for Applied Space Medicine and Human Research, Japan Aerospace Exploration Agency;* b. 6 May 1952, Tatebayashi, Gunma Pref.; m. Makio Mukai; ed Keio Girls' High School, Tokyo, Keio Univ. School of Medicine; science astronaut, NASDA (renamed JAXA–Japan Aerospace Exploration Agency 2003) 1983–, first Japanese woman in space having logged 566 hours, Dir Space Biomedical Research Office, Human Space Technology and Astronaut Dept, Human Space System and Utilization Mission Directorate,JAXA 2007–11, Sr Adviser to JAXA Exec. Dir 2011–, Dir JAXA Center for Applied Space Medicine and Human Research (J-CASMHR) 2012–; NASA experience includes Japanese Payload Specialist, First Material Processing Test (Spacelab-J), STS-47 1985, back-up Payload Specialist, Neurolab (STS-90) Mission, flew aboard STS-65 1994, STS-95 Discovery 1998, Deputy Mission Scientist for STS-107; bd certified for medicine 1977, as cardiovascular surgeon 1989; Resident in Gen. Surgery, Keio Univ. Hosp. 1977–78; mem. Medical Staff, Shimizu Gen. Hosp., Shizuoka Pref. 1978–79, Emergency Surgery Staff, Saiseikai Kanagawa Hosp., Kanagawa Pref. 1979–80; Resident in Cardiovascular Surgery, Keio Univ. Hosp. 1980–82, Chief Resident 1982–83; mem. Medical Staff in Cardiovascular Surgery, Saiseikai Utsunomiya Hosp., Tochigi Pref. 1982–83; Asst Prof., Dept of Cardiovascular Surgery, Keio Univ. 1983–87, Visiting Assoc. Prof., Dept of Surgery 1992–98, Visiting Prof. 1999–; Visiting Scientist, Div. of Cardiovascular Physiology, Space Biomedical Research Inst., NASA Johnson Space Center 1987–88; Research Instructor, Dept of Surgery, Baylor Coll. of Medicine, Houston, Tex. 1992–; Visiting Prof., Int. Space Univ. Strasbourg, France 2004–07; mem. American Aerospace Medical Asscn, Japan Soc. of Microgravity Applications, Japan Soc. of Aerospace and Environmental Medicine, Japanese Soc. for Cardiovascular and Thoracic Surgery, Japan Surgical Soc. *Leisure interests:* snow skiing, Alpine competitive skiing, bass fishing, scuba diving, tennis, golf, photography, American literature, travel. *Address:* JAXA Center for Applied Space Medicine and Human Research, Japan Aerospace Exploration Agency, 7-44-1 Jindaiji, Higashi-Machi, Chofu-shi, Tokyo 182-8522, Japan (office). *Telephone:* (281) 483-0123 (office). *Website:* www.jaxa.jp/index_e.html (office).

MUKAMBAYEV, Usup Mukambayevich; Kyrgyzstani politician and lawyer; b. 28 Jan. 1941, Dzholgolot, Kyrgyzia; m. Prof. Galina Mukumbayeva; two d.; ed Kyrgyz State Univ., higher courses at State Security Cttee of USSR; shepherd, Kolkhoz Ak-Suy Region; army service; Sec. CP Cttee of State Security Cttee 1974–78; Deputy Head of Admin, State Security Cttee, Osh Oblast 1978–80, Head of Admin, State Security Cttee, Talas and Osh Oblasts 1980–86; First Deputy

Chair. State Security Cttee, Kyrgyz Repub. 1986–91; Minister of Justice 1991–93; mem. Parl. (Zhogorku Kenesh) of Kyrgyzstan 1987–2000, Chair. Legis. Ass. 1996–2000, Pres.'s Rep. in Parl. 2001; Academician, Int. Acad. of Turk Nations, Moscow 1997; Honoured Lawyer of the Kyrgyz Repub. 1993; Order of the Red Star 1985; Dank Medal 2000. *Publications:* Constitutional Development of Kyrgyzstan 1999, About the Activity of the Legislative Assembly of Zhogorku Kenesh of the Kyrgyz Republic 2000. *Leisure interest:* walking on mountain routes. *Address:* 176 Kurenkeeva str. 720040 Bishkek, Kyrgyzstan (home). *Telephone:* (312) 67-00-37 (home).

MUKASA, Shinji; Japanese construction industry executive; Exec. Vice-Pres. Obayashi Corpn –1997, apptd Pres. 1997, Pres. and CEO –2007; Pres. and Dir Overseas Construction Asscn of Japan Inc. (OCAJI); Dir Global Infrastructure Fund Research Foundation. *Address:* Obayashi Corporation, Shinagawa Intercity Tower B, 2-15-2 Konan, Minato-ku, Tokyo 108-8502, Japan. *E-mail:* info@obayashi .co.jp.

MUKASEY, Michael Bernard, BA, LLB; American lawyer, government official and fmr judge; *Partner, Debevoise & Plimpton LLP;* b. 1941, Bronx, New York; m. Susan Mukasey 1974; one s. one d.; ed Columbia Univ., Yale Law School; Assoc., Webster Sheffield Fleischmann Hithcock & Brookfield (law firm), New York City 1967–72; Asst US Attorney, US Dist Court for the Southern Dist of New York 1972–76, Chief Judge, Chief Official Corruption Unit 1975–76; Assoc. then Pnr, Patterson Belknap Webb & Tyler 1976–87, 2006–07; Judge, US Dist Court for the Southern Dist of New York 1988–2006, Chief Judge 2000–06 (retd); US Attorney Gen., Dept of Justice, Washington, DC 2007–09; advisor to Rudy Giuliani Republican presidential nomination campaign 2007; Pnr, Debevoise & Plimpton LLP, New York 2009–; Dr hc (Brooklyn Law School) 2002; numerous awards including Learned Hand Medal, Fed. Bar Council. *Address:* Debevoise & Plimpton LLP, 919 Third Avenue, New York, NY 10022, USA (office). *Telephone:* (212) 909-6589 (office). *Website:* www.debevoise.com (office).

MUKERJEA, Pratim (Peter), MBA; British/Indian broadcasting executive; b. London; s. of Khrishna Mukerjea and Baloram Mukerjea; m. Indrani Mukerjea; two s. one d.; ed business studies, Hatfield, Herts.; began career with Heinz (UK), later with British Store House and advertising agency O&M (UK office); fmr Regional Group Account Dir, DDB Needham Advertising, Hong Kong; fmr Account Dir, Ogilvy & Mather, New Delhi and London; Sales Dir (Hong Kong, later India and Middle East) Star TV 1993–97, Exec. Vice-Pres. 1997–99, CEO Star India 1999–2007; Co-founder (with his wife), Chief Strategy Officer and Chair. INX Media Pvt. Ltd 2007–09; mem. Bd of Dirs ESPN STAR Sports, Hathway, Media Content and Communications Services (India) for Star News. *Address:* c/o INX Media Pvt. Ltd, Urmi Corporate Park, 1st Floor, Solaris – D, Opp. L & T Gate No. 6, Saki Vihar Road, Powai, Mumbai 400 072, India.

MUKHAMEDOV, Irek Javdatovich, OBE; Russian/Tatar ballet dancer; *Guest Artist, Royal Ballet;* b. 8 Feb. 1960; m. Maria Zubkova; one s. one d.; ed Moscow Choreographic Inst.; joined Moscow Classical Co.; debut with Bolshoi Ballet in title role of Grigorovich's Spartacus 1981; other roles include Ivan IV in Ivan the Terrible, Jean de Brienne in Raymonda, Basil in Don Quixote, Romeo in Grigorovich's Romeo and Juliet, Boris in Grigorovich's The Golden Age; toured extensively with Bolshoi Ballet and made worldwide guest appearances; joined The Royal Ballet 1990; Covent Garden debut in MacMillan's pas de deux Farewell (with Darcey Bussell) 1990; f. Irek Mukhamedov & Co. 1991–; appeared in musical The King and I, London 1995. *Address:* c/o Knight Ayton Management, 114 St Martin's Lane, London, WC2N 4BE, England (office). *Telephone:* (20) 7836-5333 (office). *Fax:* (20) 7836-8333 (office). *E-mail:* info@knightayton.co.uk (office). *Website:* www.knightayton.co.uk (office).

MUKHAMEJANOV, Baurzhan A., PhD; Kazakhstani politician; b. 1960; ed Kirov Kazakh State Univ.; fmr Deputy Head of Presidential Admin; Minister of Justice 1997–2000, of Internal Affairs 2005–09. *Address:* c/o Ministry of Internal Affairs, 010000 Astana, Manasa 4, Kazakhstan (office).

MUKHAMEJANOV, Ural; Kazakhstani politician; b. Nov. 1948, Kustanai; ed Novosibirsk Inst. of Cooperative Trade; fmr Inspector, Personnel Policy Dept of Presidential Admin; mem. Majlis (Ass.) from Kustanai district, Chair. (Speaker) of Majlis 2004–07; mem. Fatherland Republican Political Party (Otan); Order of Kurmet. *Address:* 010000 Astana, Parliament House, Kazakhstan (office). *Telephone:* (7172) 15-30-19 (office). *Fax:* (7172) 33-30-99 (office). *E-mail:* Smimazh@ parlam.kz (office). *Website:* www.parlam.kz (office).

MUKHAMETSHIN, Farid Khairullovich, DScS; Russian/Tatar politician; *Chairman, State Council of Tatarstan;* b. 22 May 1947, Almetyevsk, Tatarstan; m.; two c.; ed Almetyevak Higher Professional Tech. School, Ufa Inst. of Oil; metal turner in factories; CP functionary; Sec. Almetyevsk City CP Cttee; Chair. Exec. Cttee, Almetyevsk City Soviet; Deputy Chair. Council of Ministers, Minister of Trade of Tatar ASSR 1970–91; Chair. Supreme Soviet of Tatarstan Repub. 1991–94; mem. Council of Fed. 1991–94, 1998–; Prime Minister of Tatarstan Repub. 1995–98; Chair. State Council of Tatarstan 1998–; del. to Council of Europe, Chair. Regional Comm.; Leader Tatarstan New Age political movt 1999–. *Address:* Parliament Buildings, 420060 Tartarstan, Kazan, pl. Svobody 1, Russia (office). *Telephone:* (843) 267-63-00 (office). *Fax:* (843) 267-64-89 (office). *E-mail:* gossov@gossov.tatarstan.ru (office). *Website:* www.gossov.tatarstan.ru (office).

MUKHANOV, Viatcheslav F., PhD; Russian theoretical physicist and academic; *Professor, Arnold Sommerfeld Center for Theoretical Physics, Ludwig-Maximilians-Universität;* b. 2 Oct. 1956, Kanash, Chuvash ASSR, Russian SFSR; ed Moscow Inst. of Physics and Tech.; worked with G. Chibisov at Lebedev Physical Inst., Moscow 1980–81; currently Prof., Arnold Sommerfeld Center for Theoretical Physics, Ludwig-Maximilians-Universität, Germany; Oskar Klein Medal, Stockholm Univ., Sweden 2006), Tomalla Prize (Switzerland) 2009, Blaise Pascal Chair, École Normale Supérieure, Paris 2011, Amaldi Medal 2012, Cosmology Prize, Gruber Foundation (co-recipient) 2013. *Achievements include:* best known for the theory of Quantum Origin of the Universe Structure. *Publications:* Theory of Cosmological Perturbations (co-author) 1992, Physical Foundations of Cosmology 2005, Introduction to Quantum Effects in Gravity 2007; numerous papers in professional journals. *Address:* Arnold Sommerfeld Center for Theoretical Physics, Chair on Cosmology, Theresienstr. 37, 80333 Munich,

Germany (office). *Telephone:* (89) 21804543 (office). *Fax:* (89) 21804153 (office). *E-mail:* viatcheslav.mukhanov@physik.lmu.de (office). *Website:* www.theorie .physik.uni-muenchen.de/cosmology (office).

MUKHERJEE, Bharati, BA, MA, MFA, PhD; American (b. Indian) academic and writer; *Professor, English Department, University of California, Berkeley;* b. 27 July 1940, Kolkata; d. of Sudhir Lal Mukherjee and Bina Banerjee; m. Clark Blaise 1963; two s.; ed Univs of Calcutta, Baroda and Iowa; fmr Prof. of English, McGill Univ., Montréal, Lecturer, Skidmore Coll.; Lecturer in Literature and Creative Writing, Queen's Coll., New York; Prof., Univ. of Calif., Berkeley 1990–. *Publications include:* The Tiger's Daughter 1971, The Tiger's Daughter and Wife 1975, Days and Nights in Calcutta (with Clark Blaise) 1977, Darkness 1985, The Sorrow and the Terror (with Clark Blaise) 1987, The Middleman and Other Stories (Nat. Book Critics Circle Award for Fiction 1988) 1988, Jasmine 1989, The Holder of the World 1993, Leave it to Me 1996, Desirable Daughters 2002, The Tree Bride 2004, Miss New India 2011. *Address:* 334 Wheeler Hall, English Department, University of California, Berkeley, CA 94720, USA (office). *Telephone:* (510) 642-2765 (office). *E-mail:* mukhster@aol.com. *Website:* english.berkeley.edu (office).

MUKHERJEE, Pranab Kumar, LLB, MA; Indian politician and head of state; *President;* b. 11 Dec. 1935, Kirnahar, Birbhum Dist, W Bengal; s. of Kamada Kinkar Mukherjee and Rajlakshmi Mukherjee; m. Suvra Mukherjee; two s. one d.; ed Vidyasagar Coll., Univ. of Calcutta; started career as lecturer; Ed. Palli-O-Panchayat Sambad (Bengali monthly); Founder-Ed. Desher Dak (Bengali weekly) 1967–71; mem. Rajya Sabha 1969–2004, Leader 1980–88; Deputy Minister of Industrial Devt, Govt of India 1973; Deputy Minister for Shipping and Transport Jan.–Oct. 1974; Minister of State, Ministry of Finance 1974–75; Minister for Revenue and Banking 1975–77; Minister of Commerce 1980–82, 1993–95, of Finance Jan.–Sept. 1982, 1982–85, 2009–12, of External Affairs 1995–96, 2006–09, of Defence 2004–06; Pres. of India 2012–; Deputy Chair. Planning Comm. with Cabinet rank; f. Rashtriya Samajwadi Congress 1987–; mem. Exec. Cttee Congress (I) Party 1972–73, All India Congress Cttee 1986; Treas. Congress (I) Party, mem. Working Cttee, Deputy Leader in Rajya Sabha; Pres. W Bengal Pradesh Congress Cttee 1985–2000, Nikhil Bharat Banga Sahitya Sammelan 1995–2001, 2004–12; Leader of the House, Lok Sabha 2004–12; Trustee, Bangiya Sahitya Parishad 1984–1990, Bidhan Memorial Trust Kolkata 1998–; Chair. Econ. Advisory Cell 1987–89, Group 24 (ministerial group attached to IMF and World Bank) 1984, Planning Bd Asiatic Soc., Kolkata 1984–86, 1992–96, 2004–07, Cen. Election Coordination Cttee 1999–12; mem. Cen. Parl. Bd 1978–86, Bd of Govs IMF 1982–85, World Bank 1982–85, Asian Devt Bank 1982–85, African Devt Bank 1982–85, Cen. Election Cttee 2001–12; Hon. DLitt; Best Parliamentarian Award 1997, Padma Vibhushan 2008. *Publications include:* Bangla Congress: An Aspect of Constitutional Problems in Bengal 1967, Mid-term Poll 1969, Beyond Survival: Emerging Dimensions of Indian Economy 1984, Off the Track 1987, Challenges Before the Nation 1992, Saga of Struggle and Sacrifice 1992. *Leisure interests:* reading, gardening, music. *Address:* Office of the President, Rashtrapati Bhavan, New Delhi 110 004, India (office). *Telephone:* (11) 23015321 (office). *Fax:* (11) 23017290 (office). *E-mail:* presidentofindia@rb.nic.in (office). *Website:* www .presidentofindia.nic.in (office).

MUKHTAR, Chaudhry Ahmed; Pakistani politician and business executive; Owner Service Shoe business and several other cos in Pakistan; sr leader of Pakistan People's Party (PPP), Gujrat Dist; Minister of Commerce in Govt of Benazir Bhutto 1993–96; mem. Parl. for Gujrat-II 2008–; Minister of Defence 2008–12; Minister of Water and Power 4–19 June 2012; Chair. Pakistan International Airlines. *Address:* c/o Ministry of Defence, Pakistan Secretariat, No. II, Rawalpindi 46000, Pakistan.

MUKHTAR, Mansur, BSc, MPhil, PhD; Nigerian economist, academic and politician; b. 21 Sept. 1959; ed Ahmadu Bello Univ., Univs of Cambridge and Sussex, UK; economist, Central Bank of Nigeria 1980–81; Asst Lecturer, Bayero Univ. 1981–82, Lecturer and Head Dept of Econs 1988–90; special adviser to Minister of Agric. and Natural Resources 1990–92; economist, World Bank, Washington, DC 1992–97, Admin. Young Professionals Program 1997–2000; Deputy Gen. Man. of Strategic Man. and Econs Div., United Bank for Africa PLC 2000–01; Dir Portfolio Man. and Strategy, Debt Man. Office, Ministry of Finance 2001–03, Dir Gen. 2003–07; Exec. Dir African Devt Bank, Tunis 2007–09; Minister of Finance 2009–10; mem. Program Implementation Monitoring Cttee 1998–99, Sub-Cttee on Economy and Finance, Presidential Policy Advisory 1999; Officer of the Fed. Repub. of Nigeria; several prizes, grants and awards. *Address:* c/o Ministry of Finance, Ahmadu Bello Way, Central Area, PMB 14, Garki, Abuja, Nigeria (office).

MULALLY, Alan Roger, BS, MS, MA; American automotive industry executive; *President and CEO, Ford Motor Company;* b. 4 Aug. 1945, Oakland, Calif.; m. Jane Connell; three s. two d.; ed Univ. of Kan., Sloan School of Man., Massachusetts Inst. of Tech.; joined The Boeing Co. 1969, numerous eng and program man. positions including contribs on 727, 737, 747, 757, 767 aeroplanes, Vice-Pres. of Eng, Vice-Pres. and Gen. Man. 777 program, Sr Vice-Pres. of Airplane Devt, Boeing Commercial Airplanes Group 1994–97, Sr Vice-Pres. The Boeing Co. and Pres. Boeing Information, Space and Defense Systems 1997–98, Exec. Vice-Pres. The Boeing Co. and Pres. Boeing Commercial Airplanes 1998–2006, CEO 2001–06; Pres. and CEO Ford Motor Co. 2006–; fmr Chair. Bd of Govs Aerospace Industries Asscn; fmr Co-Chair. Washington Competitive Council; fmr mem. Advisory Bds NASA, Univ. of Washington, Univ. of Kansas, MIT; fmr mem. Scientific Advisory Bd USAF; mem. Nat. Acad. of Eng; Fellow, AIAA 1995 (Pres. –2006), Royal Acad. of Eng; Hon. FRAeS 1999; Hon. DSc (Univ. of Kansas) 2012; Industry Engineer of the Year, Nat. Soc. of Professional Engineers 1978, Tech. Man. Award, American Inst. of Aeronautics and Astronautics 1986, Univ. of Kan. Eng School Distinguished Eng Service Award 1994, Reed Aeronautics Award, American Inst. of Aeronautics and Astronautics 1996, Engineer of the Year, Design News magazine 1996, named Person of the Year by The Financial Times ArcelorMittal Boldness in Business Awards 2011, named CEO of the Year by Chief Executive magazine 2011. *Leisure interests:* tennis and golf. *Address:* Ford Motor Company, 1 American Road, Dearborn, MI 48126-2798, USA (office). *Telephone:* (313) 322-3000 (office). *Fax:* (313) 845-6073 (office). *E-mail:* info@ford.com (office). *Website:* corporate.ford.com (office).

MULAMBA NYUNYI WA KADIMA, Gen. (Léonard); Democratic Republic of the Congo politician, army officer and diplomatist; b. 1928, Luluabourg (now Kananga); s. of Kadima Mulamba and Ngalula Mulamba; m. Adolphine N'galula 1956; six s. two d.; ed Mil. School, Luluabourg; commissioned 1954; Maj. and Deputy Dir of Cabinet, Ministry of Defence 1961–64; Lt-Col 1962; Col, Chief of Staff and Commr of Eastern Prov. (now Haut Zaïre) after re-occupation of Kivu Province 1964–65; Prime Minister 1965–66; Pres. Soc. nationale d'Assurances (SONAS) 1966; Amb. to India 1967–69; Amb. to Japan 1969–76, also accred to Repub. of Korea 1971–76; Amb. to Brazil 1976–79; Général de Division, Général de Corps d'Armée 1979; Mil. Medal, Cross of Bravery, Commdr Ordre de la Couronne (Belgium), Grand Officier Ordre nat. du Léopard (Zaïre), Ordre du Mérite (Cen. African Republic), Compagnon de la Révolution. *Leisure interests:* hunting, reading. *Address:* c/o Chancellerie des Ordres Nationaux, BP 2014, Kinshasa, Democratic Republic of Congo.

MULARONI, Antonella; San Marino lawyer, judge and politician; b. 27 Sept. 1961; ed Univ. of Bologna, Italy; qualified as lawyer and notary public 1987; Political Sec. to Sec. of State for Finance, Budget and Econ. Planning 1986–87, Dir Office for Relations with San Marino Communities Abroad, Dept of Foreign Affairs 1987–90; Deputy Perm. Rep. of Repub. of San Marino to Council of Europe 1989–90; served as lawyer and notary public 1991–2001; mem. (People's Alliance) Great and Gen. Council (Parl.) 1993–2001, 2008–; Judge European Court of Human Rights 2001–08; Sec. of State for Foreign and Political Affairs, Telecommunications and Transport 2008; Co-Captain Regent (jt head of state) April–Oct. 2013; fmr mem. San Marino Christian Democratic Party Cen. Cttee; Founding mem. People's Alliance of San Marino Democrats 1993, Co-ordinator Jan.–June 1993, Pres. of Ass. 1998–99. *Address:* c/o Office of the Captains-Regent, Contrada Omerelli, 47890 San Marino, San Marino (office).

MULARONI, Pier Marino; San Marino politician; b. 6 Sept. 1962; Capitano (mayor) of Castello di Faetano 1986–93; mem. Consiglio Grande e Generale (Parl.) 1993–; co-Capt.-Regent April–Oct. 1997; Sec. of State for Labour 2001–02, for Finance, Transport, the Budget and Relations with Azienda Autonoma di Stato Filatelica e Numismatica (AASFN) and Azienda Autonoma di Stato per i Servizi Pubblici (AASS) 2002–06, for Labour, Co-operation and Youth Policies 2007–08; founding mem. Unione per la Repubblica 2011. *Address:* c/o Secretariat of State for Labour, Co-operation and Youth Policies, Palazzo Mercuri, Contrada del Collegio 38, 47890 San Marino (office).

MULAY, Dnyaneshwar M., MA; Indian diplomatist, academic and author; *High Commissioner to the Maldives;* b. 5 Nov. 1958; m. Sadhna Mulay; two s. one d.; joined Foreign Service 1983, has held several positions in missions in Damascus, Mauritius, Japan and Russia, has also worked extensively in Indian Govt, Jt Sec. (HQ), Ministry of External Affairs –2009, High Commr to the Maldives 2009–; Chief Patron India Club, Maldives 2009–; writes regular columns in Marathi dailies including Lokmat and Loksatta, and weekly Sadhana, published in Pune. *Publications:* Maati Pankh Aaani Aakas (autobiography; in Marathi), Russia Navya Dishanche Amantran, Swatahteel Awakash (poetry collection) (State Literary Award, Govt of Maharashtra). *Address:* Indian High Commission, H. Athireege Aage, Ameeru Ahmed Magu, Henveiru, Malé 20-25, Maldives (office). *Telephone:* 3323015 (office). *Fax:* 3324778 (office). *E-mail:* hc@hicomindia.com.mv (office); maldives_hc_india@hotmail.com (office). *Website:* www.hcimaldives.com (office).

MULCAHY, Anne M., BA; American business executive; b. 21 Oct. 1952, Rockville Centre, NY; ed Marymount Coll., Tarrytown, NY; joined Xerox Corpn, Stamford, Conn. 1976, held various sales and sr man. positions 1976–92, Vice-Pres. Human Resources 1992–95, Vice-Pres. and Staff Officer Customer Relations 1995–97, Chief Staff Officer 1997–99, Corp. Sr Vice-Pres. 1998–99, Pres. Gen. Markets Operations 1999–2000, Pres. and COO 2000–01, CEO 2001–09, also Chair. 2002–10; Chair. Bd of Trustees Save The Children Federation, Inc. 2009–; mem. Bd Dirs Johnson & Johnson, Target Corpn, The Washington Post Co., LPL Financial 2013–; Chair. Corp. Governance Task Force of the Business Roundtable; mem. Business Council; ranked by Fortune magazine amongst 50 Most Powerful Women in Business (fourth) 2003, (fourth) 2004, (second) 2005, (second) 2006, (second) 2007, (fourth) 2008, ranked by Forbes magazine amongst 100 Most Powerful Women (42nd) 2004, (sixth) 2005, (fifth) 2006, (13th) 2007, (10th) 2008, (15th) 2009, named by The Wall Street Journal one of 50 Women to Watch 2005. *Address:* c/o Save the Children US Headquarters, 54 Wilton Road, Westport, CT 06880, USA.

MULCAHY, Sir Geoffrey John, Kt, BSc, MBA; British business executive; *Chairman, Javelin Group;* b. 7 Feb. 1942, Sunderland, England; s. of Maurice Mulcahy and Kathleen Mulcahy (née Blenkinsop); m. Valerie Elizabeth Mulcahy 1965; one s. one d.; ed King's School, Worcester, Univ. of Manchester, Harvard Univ.; started career in labour relations, marketing and planning with Esso Corpn; Finance Dir Norton Abrasives' European Div., then with British Sugar; joined Woolworth Holdings (now Kingfisher PLC) 1983, first as Group Financial Dir, then Group Man. Dir 1984–86, CEO 1986–93, Chair. 1990–95, Group CEO Kingfisher Group 1995–2003; Chair. Javelin Group Ltd 2003–; Dir (non-exec.), Brown & Jackson 2005–. *Leisure interest:* sailing, squash. *Address:* Javelin Group Ltd, 200 Aldersgate Street, London EC1A 4HD, England (office). *Telephone:* (20) 7961-3200 (office). *Fax:* (20) 7961-3299 (office). *E-mail:* info@javelingroup.com (office). *Website:* www.javelingroup.com (office).

MULDOON, Paul Benedict, BA, FRSL; Irish/American poet, academic and editor; *Howard G. B. Clark '21 University Professor in the Humanities and Professor of Creative Writing, Princeton University;* b. 20 June 1951, Portadown, Northern Ireland; s. of Patrick Muldoon and Brigid Regan; m. Jean Hanff Korelitz 1987; one s. one d.; ed St Patrick's Coll., Armagh, Queen's Univ., Belfast; radio and TV producer, BBC NI 1973–86; has taught at Univs of Cambridge, East Anglia, Columbia Univ., Univ. of California, Berkeley, Univ. of Massachusetts, Univ. of St Andrews, Univ. of Ulster; Lecturer, Princeton Univ. 1987–88, 1990–95, Dir Creative Writing Program 19932–2002, Prof. 1995–, Howard G. B. Clark '21 Prof. in the Humanities and Prof. of Creative Writing 1998–, Founding Chair. Lewis Center for the Arts 2006–12; Founder Princeton Poetry Festival 2009–; Visiting Prof., Bread Loaf School of English 1997–2010; Poetry Ed. The New Yorker 2007–; mem. Aosdána, American Acad. of Arts and Sciences 2000–, American Acad. of

Arts and Letters 2008–; Hon. Prof. of Poetry, Univ. of Oxford 1999–2004; Eric Gregory Award 1972, Sir Geoffrey Faber Memorial Awards 1980, 1991, Guggenheim Fellowship 1990, American Acad. of Arts and Letters Award for Literature 1996, Irish Times Poetry Prize 1997, Pulitzer Prize for Poetry 2003, Griffin Prize 2003, American Ireland Fund Literary Award 2004, Shakespeare Prize 2004, Aspen Prize for Poetry 2005, European Prize for Poetry 2006, John William Corrington Award 2009. *Publications include:* poetry: Knowing My Place 1971, New Weather 1973, Spirit of Dawn 1975, Mules 1977, Names and Addresses 1978, Immram 1980, Why Brownlee Left 1980, Out of Siberia 1982, Quoof 1983, The Wishbone 1984, Selected Poems 1968–83 1986, Meeting the British 1987, Madoc: A Mystery 1990, Incantata 1994, The Prince of the Quotidian 1994, The Annals of Chile (T. S. Eliot Prize) 1995, Kerry Slides 1996, New Selected Poems 1968–1994 1996, Hopewell Haiku 1997, The Bangle (Slight Return) 1998, Hay (poems) 1999, Poems 1968–1998 2001, Horse Latitudes 2006, Plan B (with Norman McBeath) 2009, Wayside Shrines 2009, Maggot 2010, The Word on the Street 2013, One Thousand Things Worth Knowing 2014; for children: The O-O's Party 1981, The Last Thesaurus 1995, The Noctuary of Narcissus Batt 1997; other: Monkeys (TV play) 1989, Shining Brow (opera libretto) 1993, Six Honest Serving Men (play) 1995, Bandanna (opera libretto) 1999, To Ireland, I (essays) 2000; ed.: The Scrake of Dawn 1979, The Faber Book of Contemporary Irish Poetry 1986, The Essential Byron 1989, Moy Sand and Gravel (Pulitzer Prize for Poetry) 2002; trans.: The Astrakhan Cloak, by Nuala Ni Dhomhnaill 1993, The Birds, by Aristophanes (with Richard Martin) 1999. *Leisure interests:* electric guitar, English longbow. *Address:* Creative Writing Program, Room 122, Lewis Center for the Arts, 185 Nassau Street, Princeton University, Princeton, NJ 08544, USA (office). *Telephone:* (609) 258-4708 (office). *E-mail:* muldoon@princeton.edu (office). *Website:* www .paulmuldoon.net.

MULDOWNEY, Dominic John, BPhil; British composer; b. 19 July 1952, Southampton; s. of William Muldowney and Barbara Muldowney (née Lavender); m. Diane Ellen Trevis 1986; one d.; ed Taunton's Grammar School, Southampton and Univ. of York; Composer-in-Residence, Southern Arts Asscn 1974–76; Music Dir Royal Nat. Theatre 1976–97; Prof. of Composition, RAM 1999–; has composed music for British and int. festivals, for many films and TV and over 50 scores for the theatre; Prix Italia 1993, 1997, Sony Award 1997. *Compositions include:* Piano Concerto 1983, Saxophone Concerto 1984, Sinfonietta 1986, Ars Subtilior 1987, Lonely Hearts 1988, Violin Concerto 1989, Three Pieces for Orchestra 1990, Percussion Concerto 1991, Oboe Concerto 1992, Trumpet Concerto 1993, Concerto for 4 Violins 1994 The Brontës (ballet) 1995, Trombone Concerto 1996, Clarinet Concerto 1997, The Fall of Jerusalem (oratorio) 1998, God's Plenty (ballet) 1999, Red Razzmatazz (opera) 2005, War Oratorio 2007, The Last Confession 2007, Tsunami 2008. *Leisure interest:* driving through France and across America. *Address:* c/o Carlin Music, 3 Bridge Approach, Chalk Farm, London, NW1 8BD, England (office). *E-mail:* info@carlinmusic (office). *Website:* www.carlinmusic .com (office).

MULET, Edmond; Guatemalan lawyer, politician, diplomatist and UN official; *Assistant Secretary-General for Peace-keeping Operations, United Nations;* b. 13 March 1951, Guatemala City; s. of Augusto Mulet Descamps and Simone Lesieur; m. Karen Lind; five s.; ed Universidad Mariano Galvez; notary public; elected to Nat. Congress 1982, cand. to Nat. Constituent Ass. 1984, elected to Congress 1986–91, re-elected 1991–96; elected Sec.-Gen. Union del Centro Nacional party 1996; mem. Guatemalan-Belize Comm., first as Rep. of Congress and later as Del. from Exec. Br.; Amb. to USA 1993 (resgnd following coup d'état in Guatemala) resumed duties 1994–96, Amb. to EU, Belgium and Luxembourg 2000–06; Special Rep. of UN Sec.-Gen. in Haiti and Head of UN Stabilization Mission in Haiti (MINUSTAH) 2006–07, 2010–11 (following death of Hédi Annabi in earthquake of 12 Jan. 2010); Asst Sec.-Gen. for Peace-keeping Operations, UN 2007–10, 2011–. *Address:* Department of Peace-keeping Operations, United Nations, New York, NY 10017, USA (office). *Telephone:* (212) 963-1234 (office). *Fax:* (212) 963-4879 (office). *Website:* www.un.org/en/peacekeeping/about/dpko (office).

MULFORD, David Campbell, BA, MA, DPhil; American economist, investment banker and fmr diplomatist; *Vice-Chairman International, Credit Suisse Group;* m. Jeannie Simmons; two c.; ed Lawrence Univ., Boston Univ., Univ. of Oxford, UK; served as Special Asst to Sec. of Treasury as White House Fellow 1965–66; Man. Dir and Head of Int. Finance, White, Weld & Co. (investment bank) 1966–74; Sr Investment Advisor, Saudi Arabia Monetary Agency 1974–83; Under-Sec. and Asst Sec. for Int. Affairs, US Treasury Dept 1984–92; Int. Chair. Credit Suisse First Boston (now Credit Suisse Group), London 1992–2003, currently Vice-Chair. Int.; Amb. to India 2004–09; mem. Council on Foreign Relations; affil. with Center for Strategic and Int. Studies, Washington, DC; Chevalier, Légion d'honneur 1990, Order of May for Merit (Argentina) 1993, Officer's Cross Medal for Merit (Poland) 1995; Dr hc (Lawrence Univ.) 1984; Alexander Hamilton Award, US Treasury Dept 1992, Distinguished Alumni Award, Boston Univ. 1992. *Address:* Credit Suisse Group, Eleven Madison Avenue, New York, NY 10010, USA (office). *Telephone:* (212) 325-2000 (office). *Fax:* (212) 325-8057 (office). *Website:* www .credit-suisse.com (office).

MULIKOV, Iskander; Turkmenistani police officer and government official; *Minister of Internal Affairs;* b. 1975, Aşgabat; ed Turkmen Interior Ministry School; began career in state law enforcement system and held several posts within Ministry of Internal Affairs; Chief, Daşoguz Dist Police Feb.–June 2009; Minister of Internal Affairs June 2009–. *Address:* Ministry of Internal Affairs, 744000 Aşgabat, Magtymguly Şayoly 85, Turkmenistan (office). *Telephone:* (12) 35-13-28 (office). *Fax:* (12) 39-19-44 (office).

MULINO, José Raúl, LLL; Panamanian lawyer and politician; *Minister of Public Security;* b. 13 June 1959; ed Univ. Santa Maria La Antigua, Tulane Univ., New Orleans, USA; Vice-Minister of Foreign Affairs 1990–93, Minister of Foreign Affairs 1993–94; mem. Nat. Council for Foreign Affairs 1994–95; Deputy Magistrate, Corte Suprema de Justicia 1994–95; Minister of the Interior and Justice 2009–10, of Public Security 2010–; mem. Asociación Panameña de Ejecutivos de Empresa (Pres. 1989–90), Asociación Panameña de Derecho Marítimo, American Soc. of Int. Law; Hon. mem. Consejo Nacional de la Empresa Privada (Vice-Pres. 1989–90). *Address:* Ministry of Public Security, Avda Central, entre calle 2 y 3, San Felipe, Apdo 1628, Panamá 1, Panama (office). *Telephone:* 512-2000 (office). *Fax:*

512-2126 (office). *E-mail:* informa@gobiernoyjusticia.gob.pa (office). *Website:* www .gobiernoyjusticia.gob.pa (office).

MULIOKELA, Wamundila; Zambian politician and business executive; *Chairman, ZESCO Ltd;* mem. Parl. 2001–06; fmr Deputy Minister of Mines and Minerals; Deputy Minister of Defence –2005, Minister of Defence 2005–06; Chair. ZESCO Ltd (power utility) 2006–. *Address:* ZESCO Ltd, Great East Road, Stand No 6949, 10101 Lusaka, Zambia. *Website:* www.zesco.co.zm.

MULJADI, Kartini; Indonesian lawyer and fmr judge; *Founder and Senior Partner, Kartini Muljadi & Rekan;* b. 1930; widowed; three c.; ed Univ. of Indonesia; judge, Special Court of Jakarta 1958–70 (retd); f. Kartini Muljadi & Rekan (law firm), Jakarta 1990, currently Sr Pnr; adviser to Indonesian Govt, Indonesian Bank Restructuring Agency, World Bank, Int. Finance Corpn; major shareholder, PT Tempo Scan (pharmaceutical co.); Trustee, Indonesian Chamber of Commerce and Industry, Indonesian Inst. of Commrs and Dirs, Indonesian AIDS Foundation; Hon. mem. Indonesian Bar Asscn, Indonesian Capital Market Arbitration Bd; Capital Markets Lifetime Achievement Award 2004. *Address:* Kartini Muljadi & Rekan, Jalan Gunawarman No. 18, Kebayoran Baru, Jakarta 12110, Indonesia (office). *Telephone:* (21) 72794535 (office). *Fax:* (21) 72794551 (office). *E-mail:* kartini.muljadi@kmuljadilaw.com (office). *Website:* www .kmuljadilaw.com (office).

MULLA, Habib al-, LLB, LLM, PhD; United Arab Emirates lawyer and business executive; *Founder and Executive Chairman, Habib Al Mulla & Company;* ed UAE Univ., Harvard Law School, USA, Univ. of Cambridge, UK; has held numerous prominent govt positions, including as mem. UAE Fed. Nat. Council 2000–02 and Fed. Parl. of the UAE, as mem. Legis. Cttee, in charge of reviewing federal legislation, as mem. Econ. Cttee, in charge of reviewing fiscal and economic policy of the federation, as Dir Inst. of Advanced Legal and Judicial Studies, in charge of training judges and prosecutors in Emirate of Dubai, as Chair. UAE Jurists Asscn; Founder and Exec. Chair. Habib Al Mulla & Co.; Vice-Chair. Bd of Trustees, Dubai Int. Arbitration Centre; Chair. Chartered Inst. of Arbitrators UAE Cttee; designed the legal framework establishing the Dubai Int. Financial Centre; Chair. Legis. Cttee, Dubai Financial Services Authority 2003–06; mem. ICC Inst., UAE ICC Nat. Cttee, Panel of Experts of the Broadcasting and Publs Standards Tribunal of the Tech., Electronic Commerce and Media Free Zone Authority (TECOM) in Dubai; Dir Supervisory Bd of Rasmala (Regional Investment Banking Group); Vice-Pres. Bd Govs, American Univ. in Dubai; mem. Bd of Trustees, Dubai School of Govt; Fellow Mem., Chartered Inst. of Arbitrators; ranked by Arabian Business amongst the Power 500: The World's Most Influential Arabs (75th) 2012. *Publications:* numerous books and articles on UAE law and economy, including a two-part book on his life's work entitled Life's Harvest. *Address:* Habib Al Mulla & Co., Level 14, O14 Tower, Al Khail Road, Business Bay, PO Box 2268, Dubai, United Arab Emirates (office). *Telephone:* (4) 423-0000 (office). *Fax:* (4) 447-9777 (office). *E-mail:* habib.almulla@habibalmulla.com (office). *Website:* www .habibalmulla.com (office).

MULLAJONOV, Faizulla Maksudjonovich; Uzbekistani economist and central banker; *Chairman, Central Bank of the Republic of Uzbekistan;* b. 10 March 1950, Sirdarya region; m.; five c.; ed Tashkent Inst. of State Economy; Credit Inspector, later Sr Credit Inspector, Sirdarya Regional Br., State Bank of USSR 1971–72, Head, Credit Group, Verhnevolinskiy Br. 1972–73, Man., Krestyanskiy Br. 1973–76, Man., Golodnosteppskiy Br. 1976–86, Deputy Gov., Sirdarya Regional Br., State Bank of USSR 1986–87, Gov. 1987, 1990–91; Head, Sirdarya Regional Br., Agroprombank 1987–90; Chair. Cen. Bank of the Repub. of Uzbekistan 1991–; Hon. Economist, Repub. of Uzbekistan 1995–; Independence Jubilee Breastplates 1991, 2001, 2006, Order of Labour Glory 2000, Distinguished Services Order 2010. *Address:* Central Bank of the Republic of Uzbekistan, 100001 Tashkent, O'zbekiston shox ko'ch. 6, Uzbekistan (office). *Telephone:* (871) 212-61-10 (office). *Fax:* (871) 233-35-09 (office). *E-mail:* hidirova@cbu.uz (office). *Website:* www.cbu .uz (office).

MULLAN, Peter, BSc; British actor and film director; b. 1954, Glasgow; ed Univ. of Glasgow; debut with Wildcat Theatre Co. 1988; Hon. MA (Caledonian Univ., Glasgow) 2000. *Film appearances include:* Riff-Raff 1990, The Bid Man 1991, Shallow Grave 1994, Braveheart 1995, Ruffian Hearts 1995, Good Day for the Bad Guys 1995, Trainspotting 1996, Fairytale: A True Story, My Name is Joe (Best Actor Award, Cannes Film Festival 1998) 1998, Duck 1998, Miss Julie 1999, Mauvaise passe 1999, Ordinary Decent Criminal 2000, The Claim 2000, Session 9 2001, The Magdalene Sisters 2002, Entering Blue Zone 2002, Young Adam 2002, Kiss of Life 2003, Kono yo no sotoe–Club Shinchugun 2004, Criminal 2004, Blinded 2004, Waves 2004, On a Clear Day 2005, Cargo 2006, Children of Men 2006, True North 2006, The Last Legion 2007, Dog Altogether 2007, Boy A 2007, Tyrannosaur 2011. *Films written and directed include:* Good Day for the Bay Guys 1995, Fridge 1996, Orphans (Golden Lion Award, Venice Film Festival 1998) 1997, The Magdalene Sisters (Golden Lion Award, Venice Film Festival 2002) 2002. *Films produced include:* Caesar 2000. *Television includes:* Rab C. Nesbitt (series) 1990, Jute City (film) 1991, Nightlife (film) 1996, Cardiac Arrest (series) 1996–97, Bogwoman (film) 1997.

MULLEN, Larry, Jr; Irish musician (drums) and actor; b. 31 Oct. 1961, Dublin; ed Mount Temple School, Dublin; Founder-mem. and drummer with the Feedback 1976, renamed the Hype, finally renamed U2 1978–; major concerts include Live Aid Wembley 1985, Self Aid Dublin, A Conspiracy of Hope (Amnesty Int. Tour) 1986, Smile Jamaica (hurricane relief fundraiser) 1988, Very Special Arts Festival, White House, Washington, DC 1988; numerous tours world-wide; U2 have won 22 Grammy Awards, including Best Rock Performance by a Duo or Group with Vocal (for Desire) 1988, BRIT Awards for Best Int. Act 1988–90, 1992, 1998, 2001, Best Live Act 1993, Outstanding Contribution to the British Music Industry 2001, JUNO Award 1993, World Music Award 1993, Grammy Award for Song of the Year, Record of the Year, Best Rock Performance by a Duo or Group with Vocal (all for Beautiful Day) 2000, Grammy Awards for Best Pop Performance by a Duo or Group with Vocal (for Stuck In A Moment You Can't Get Out Of), for Record of the Year (for Walk On), for Best Rock Performance by a Duo or Group with Vocal (for Elevation) 2001, American Music Award for Favorite Internet Artist of the Year 2002, Ivor Novello Award for Best Song Musically and Lyrically (for Walk On) 2002, Golden Globe for Best Original Song (for The Hands That Built America, from film Gangs of New York) 2003, Grammy Awards for Best Rock Performance by a Duo or Group with Vocal, Best Rock Song, Best Short Form Music Video (all for Vertigo) 2004, Nordoff-Robbins Silver Clef Award for lifetime achievement 2005, Q Award for Best Live Act 2005, Digital Music Award for Favourite Download Single (for Vertigo) 2005, Meteor Ireland Music Award for Best Irish Band, Best Live Performance 2006, Grammy Awards for Song of the Year, for Best Rock Performance by a Duo or Group with Vocal (both for Sometimes You Can't Make it on Your Own), for Best Rock Song (for City of Blinding Lights) 2006, Amnesty International Ambassadors of Conscience Award 2006, Golden Globe Award for Best Original Score, Motion Picture (Ordinary Love in Mandela: Long Walk to Freedom) 2014, Palm Springs Film Festival Sonny Bono Visionary Award 2014; Portuguese Order of Liberty 2005. *Films include:* Rattle and Hum 1988, Man on the Train 2011, A Thousand Times Good Night 2013. *Recordings include:* albums: Boy 1980, October 1981, War 1983, Under a Blood Red Sky 1983, The Unforgettable Fire 1984, Wide Awake In America 1985, The Joshua Tree (Grammy Award for Album of the Year, Best Rock Performance by a Duo or Group with Vocal) 1987, Rattle and Hum 1988, Achtung Baby (Grammy Award for Best Rock Performance by a Duo or Group with Vocal 1992) 1991, Zooropa (Grammy Award for Best Alternative Music Album) 1993, Passengers (film soundtrack with Brian Eno) 1995, Pop 1997, The Best Of 1980–90 1998, All That You Can't Leave Behind (Grammy Award for Best Rock Album 2001) 2000, The Best Of 1990–2000 2002, How To Dismantle An Atomic Bomb (Meteor Ireland Music Award for Best Irish Album 2006, Grammy Awards for Album of the Year, for Best Rock Album 2006) 2004, No Line on the Horizon 2009. *Address:* c/o Principle Management, 30–32 Sir John Rogersons Quay, Dublin 2, Ireland (office). *E-mail:* nadine@numb.ie (office). *Website:* www.u2.com.

MULLEN, Adm. Michael (Mike) Glenn, MSc; American naval officer; b. 4 Oct. 1946, Los Angeles, Calif.; m. Deborah Mullen; two s.; ed Naval Postgraduate School, Monterey, Calif., Harvard Business School; served as jr officer aboard USS Collett, USS Blandy, USS Fox, USS Sterrett, held command posts aboard USS Noxubee, USS Goldsborough, USS Yorktown, as Flag Officer commanded Cruiser-Destroyer Group Two and George Washington Battle Group, fmr Commdr US Second Fleet/NATO Striking Fleet Atlantic; non-operational posts have included Co. Officer and Exec. Asst to Commdt of Midshipmen, US Naval Acad., Annapolis, Dir Surface Officer Distribution, Bureau of Naval Personnel; posts with Chief of Naval Operations include Deputy Dir and Dir of Surface Warfare, Deputy Chief of Naval Operations for Resources, Requirements and Assessments, 32nd Vice-Chief of Naval Operations 2003–04; served as Commdr Allied Jt Force Command Naples, Chief of Naval Operations 2004–07; Chair. Jt Chiefs of Staff 2007–11; Jt Chiefs of Staff Identification Badge, Navy Surface Warfare Badge (Officer), Defense Distinguished Service Medal, Navy Distinguished Service Medal (2), Defense Superior Service Medal, Legion of Merit Decoration (6), Meritorious Service Medal, Navy and Marine Corps Commendation Medal, Navy and Marine Corps Achievement Medal, Navy Unit Commendation Ribbon, Navy Meritorious Unit Commendation Ribbon, Navy 'E' Ribbon, Navy Expeditionary Medal, Nat. Defense Service Medal (3), Armed Forces Expeditionary Medal, Viet Nam Service Medal, Global War on Terrorism Service Medal, Humanitarian Service Medal (2), Navy Overseas Service Ribbon (4), Navy Sea Service Deployment Ribbon (2), Repub. of Viet Nam Gallantry Cross Unit Citation Medal, Repub. of Viet Nam Civil Actions Unit Citation Ribbon. *Address:* c/o Office of the Chairman of the Joint Chiefs of Staff, 9999 Joint Staff Pentagon, Washington, DC 20318-9999, USA.

MÜLLER, Gerhard, Dr rer. nat; German chemist and academic; *Professor of Chemistry, University of Konstanz;* b. 7 March 1953, Rehren, Lower Saxony; ed Tech. Univ. of Munich; Postdoctoral Assoc., Univ. of California, Berkeley 1980–81; Postdoctoral Assoc., Max-Planck-Inst. für Kohlenforschung, Mulheim 1982–83; Research Assoc., Tech. Univ. of Munich 1983–89, Lecturer 1989; Prof. of Chem., Univ. of Konstanz 1990–, Vice-Dean, Dept of Chem. 1992–93, 1995–96, Dean 1993–95, 2003–05, 2009, Vice-Pres. of Research 1998–2000; mem. German Nat. Cttee, Int. Union of Crystallography 1994–2000, Chair. Div. of Molecular Compounds 1992–2000; Asst Ed. Zeitschrift für Naturforschung B 1986–; mem. German Chemical Soc., German Crystallographic Soc., Nat. Geographic Soc. *Publications:* more than 290 scientific papers in professional journals on organometallic chemistry. *Address:* Fachbereich Chemie, Universität Konstanz, Postfach 5560-M723, Room L703, Universitaetsstrasse 10, 78457 Konstanz, Germany (office). *Telephone:* (7531) 88-3735 (office). *Fax:* (7531) 88-3140 (office). *E-mail:* gerhard.mueller@uni-konstanz.de (office). *Website:* cms.uni-konstanz.de/mueller (office).

MÜLLER, Herta; German (b. Romanian) writer; b. 17 Aug. 1953, Nitzkydorf, Banat, Romania; m. Richard Wagner; ed Univ. of Timişoara; as a student, involved with Aktionsgruppe Banat (authors' group opposed to Nicolae Ceauşescu's rule of Romania); worked as translator in a machine factory 1977–79; emigrated to Germany 1987; Heiner-Müller Guest Prof., Freie Universität Berlin 2005; has lectured in Germany, UK and USA; mem. German Acad. for Language and Poetry 1995–; Kleist Preis 1994, Aristeion Prize 1995, Int. IMPAC Dublin Literary Award 1998, Franz Kafka Preis 1999, Literature Prize, Konrad Adenauer Foundation 2004, Berliner Literaturpreis 2005, Würth Preis 2005, Nobel Prize for Literature 2009, Hoffmann-von-Fallersleben-Preis 2010. *Publications:* Niederungen 1982, Drückender Tango: Erzählungen 1984, Der Mensch ist ein grosser Fasan auf der Welt 1986, Barfüssiger Februar: Prosa 1987, Reisende auf einem Bein 1989, Der Teufel sitzt im Spiegel 1991, Der Fuchs war damals schon der Jäger 1992, Eine warme Kartoffel ist ein warmes Bett 1992, Der Wächter nimmt seinen Kamm: vom Weggehen und Ausscheren 1993, Herztier: Roman 1994, Hunger und Seide: Essays 1995, In der Falle 1996, Heute wär ich mir lieber nicht begegnet 1997, Der fremde Blick oder Das Leben ist ein Furz in der Laterne 1999, Im Haarknoten wohnt eine Dame 2000, Heimat ist das, was gesprochen wird 2001, Der König verneigt sich und tötet 2003, Die blassen Herren mit den Mokkatassen 2005, Atemschaukel 2009 (translated as The Hunger Angel 2012). *Address:* c/o Carl Hanser Verlag, Kolbergerstrasse 22, 81679 Munich, Germany (office). *E-mail:* info@hanser.de (office). *Website:* www.hanser-literaturverlage.de (office).

MÜLLER, K. Alex, PhD; Swiss physicist and academic; *Professor Emeritus, Physics Institute, University of Zurich;* b. 20 April 1927, Basel; ed Swiss Fed. Inst. of Tech.; Project Man., Battelle Inst., Geneva 1958–62; Lecturer, Univ. of Zurich 1962, Titular Prof. 1970, Prof. 1987–2009, Prof. Emer. 2009–; joined IBM Zurich

Research Lab., Rüschlikon 1963, Man. Dept of Physics and Fellow 1973–92, Researcher 1985–, Fellow Emer. 1992–98; Fellow, American Physical Soc.; mem. European Physics Soc.; Foreign Assoc. mem. NAS, Russian, Slovenian, Polish and Sachsen Acads of Sciences; Hon. mem. Swiss Physical Soc., Zurich Physical Soc., Acad. of Ceramics; Hon. DSc (Geneva) 1987, (Tech. Univ. of Munich) 1987, (Università degli Studi di Pavia) 1987, (Leuven) 1988, (Boston) 1988, (Tel-Aviv) 1988, (Tech. Univ. of Darmstadt) 1988, (Nice) 1989, (Universidad Politecnica, Madrid) 1989, (Bochum) 1990, (Università degli Studi di Roma) 1990, (Trondheim) 1992, (Metz) 1995, (Salzburg) 1995, (Regensburg) 1996, (Cottbus, Germany) 1997, (Leipzig) 2000, (Bar Ilan) 2006, (Tbilisi) 2007; with G. Bednorz: Marcel-Benoist Prize 1986, Nobel Prize for Physics (with G. Bednorz) for discovery of new superconducting materials 1987, 13th Fritz London Memorial Award, UCLA 1987, Dannie Heineman Prize, Minna James Heineman Stiftung, Acad. of Sciences, Gottingen, Germany 1987, Robert Wichard Pohl Prize, German Physical Soc. 1987, Hewlett-Packard Europhysics Prize 1988, Int. Prize for New Materials Research, American Physical Soc. 1988, Minnie Rosen Award, Ross Univ., New York 1989, Special Tsukuba Award (Japan) 1989, Int. 'Aldo Villa' Prize, Italian Ceramic Soc. 1991. *Publications:* more than 400 publs on structural phase transitions, critical and multicritical phenomena, the behaviour of ferroelectrica at low temperatures and superconductivity in cuprates. *Address:* University of Zürich, Physik-Institut, Winterthurerstr. 190, 8057 Zürich (office); Haldenstr. 54, 8909 Hedingen, Switzerland (home). *Telephone:* (44) 6355749 (office). *Fax:* (44) 6355704 (office). *Website:* www.physik.uzh.ch (office).

MÜLLER, Klaus-Peter; German banker; *Chairman of the Supervisory Board, Commerzbank AG;* b. 16 Sept. 1944, Duppach; m.; one d.; apprenticeship in banking, Bankhaus Friedrich Simon KGaA, Düsseldorf 1962–64; with Düsseldorf Br., Commerzbank AG 1966–68, New York Rep. Office and Br. 1968–73, Jt Man. Düsseldorf and Duisburg Br. 1973–82, Jt Man. New York Br. 1982–86, Exec. Vice-Pres. 1986–90, Head of Corp. Banking Dept 1990–2001, Head, East German Operations 1990–, mem. Bd of Man. Dirs 1990–, Chair. Commerzbank AG 2001–08, Chair. Supervisory Bd 2008–; mem. Bd Fraport AG (Frankfurt Airport Services Worldwide) –2010, Fresenius SE, Fresenius Management SE 2010–, Linde AG, MaschmeyerRürup AG (ind. int. consultancy) 2010–, Landwirtschaftliche Rentenbank, Parker Hannifin Corpn; Pres. Asscn of German Banks, Berlin 2005–; Hon. Prof., Frankfurt School of Finance and Man. 2007; Dr hc (Finance Acad. of Russian Fed.) 2004. *Address:* Commerzbank AG, 60261 Frankfurt/Main, Germany (office). *Telephone:* (69) 13620 (office). *Fax:* (69) 285389 (office). *E-mail:* info@commerzbank.com (office). *Website:* www.commerzbank.com (office).

MÜLLER, Peter; German lawyer and politician; b. 25 Sept. 1955, Illingen; m. Astrid Gercke-Müller; three s.; ed Lebach Grammar School, Univs of Bonn and Saarbrücken; trainee lawyer 1983–86; Asst Lecturer, Univ. of Saarland 1983–86, later Chair. Constitutional and Admin. Law; Judge, Saarbrücken Regional Court –1990; mem. CDU Parl. Party, Saarland Parl. 1990–; Minister Pres. of Saarland 1999–2011; Dr hc (Tokyo) 2001. *Publication:* Nach dem Pisa-Shock. Plädoyers für eine Bildungreform (co-ed.) 2002, Bevölkerungsentwicklung und Grundgesetz, Ein Festschrift für Georg Ress 2005. *Leisure interests:* active footballer, plays chess and skat, clarinet and saxophone. *Address:* Landtag des Saarlandes, Postfach 101833, 66081 Saarbrücken, Germany (office).

MULLER, Phillip Henry; Marshall Islands diplomatist and politician; b. 2 Jan. 1956; m. Yolenda deBrum; four c.; ed Rockhurst Coll., Kansas City, Mo., USA; Deputy Minister of Foreign Affairs 1982–84, Minister-in-Assistance to Pres. 1984–86, Minister of Educ. 1986–94, of Foreign Affairs 1994–99, 2012–14; mem. Nitijela (parl.) 1984–99; Public Relations and Govt Relations Consultant, GMP Assocs Inc. (eng and architectural co.) 2000–08; Amb. and Perm. Rep. to UN, New York 2008–12. *Leisure interests:* tennis, bowling, fishing. *Address:* c/o Ministry of Foreign Affairs, POB 1349, Majuro MH 96960, Marshall Islands (office).

MULLER, Steven, PhD; American academic and university administrator; *Distinguished Professorial Lecturer and FPI Fellow, Paul H. Nitze School of Advanced International Studies (SAIS) and President Emeritus, Johns Hopkins University;* b. 22 Nov. 1927, Hamburg, Germany; s. of Werner A. Muller and Marianne Muller (née Hartstein); m. 1st Margie Hellman 1951; two d.; m. 2nd Jill E. McGovern 2000; ed Hollywood High School, Los Angeles, Univ. of Calif., Los Angeles, Univ. of Oxford, UK, Cornell Univ.; Instructor in Political Science, Wells Coll. 1953; US Army 1954–55; Research Fellow in Social Science, Cornell Univ. 1955–56; Asst Prof. of Political Science, Haverford Coll. 1956–58; Asst Prof. of Govt, Cornell Univ. 1958–61, Assoc. Prof. and Dir Center for Int. Studies 1961–66, Vice-Pres. for Public Affairs 1966–71; Provost, Johns Hopkins Univ. 1971–72, Pres. 1972–90, Pres. Emer. 1990–, Distinguished Professorial Lecturer and FPI Fellow, Paul H. Nitze School of Advanced Int. Studies 1993–; Pres. Johns Hopkins Hosp. 1972–83; Chair. 21st Century Foundation 1990–96; Chair. of Bd St Mary's Coll. of Maryland; Co-Chair. American Inst. for Contemporary German Studies; Dir Law/Gibb Corpn, Org. Resources Counselors, Inc., Atlantic Council of the US, German Marshall Fund of the US; fmr mem. Bd of Dirs, CSX Corpn, Millipore Corpn, Beneficial Corpn, Alex. Brown & Sons Inc., Van Kampen Closed End Funds; Commdr's Cross of the Order of Merit (FRG). *Publications:* Documents on European Government 1963, From Occupation to Cooperation 1992 (co-ed.), In Search of Germany 1996 (co-ed.), Universities in the Twenty-First Century 1996; articles in learned journals. *Leisure interest:* philately. *Address:* Johns Hopkins University, Paul H. Nitze School of Advanced International Studies, 1619 Massachusetts Avenue, NW, Suite 406, Washington, DC 20036 (office); 2315 Bancroft Place, NW, Washington, DC 20008-4005, USA (home). *Telephone:* (202) 663-5821 (office); (202) 387-2777 (home). *Fax:* (202) 663-5822 (office); (202) 387-6777 (home). *E-mail:* kareese@jhu.edu (office); catalina53@juno.com (home). *Website:* www.sais-jhu.edu (office).

MÜLLER, Werner, PhD; German politician and business executive; *Chairman of the Supervisory Board, Deutsche Bahn AG;* b. 1 June 1946, Essen; m.; two c.; ed Univs of Mannheim, Duisberg and Bremen; Lecturer, Univ. of Applied Sciences, Ludwigshafen 1970–72; part-time Lectureships, Univs of Mannheim and Regensburg 1970–73; Head of Market Research, Rheinisch-Westfälische electricity co. (RWE) 1973–80; Gen. Rep. and Chief Exec. VEBA AG (power co.) 1980–92, mem. Exec. Bd VEBA Kraftwerke Ruhr AG, Gelsenkirchen 1992–97; ind. industrial consultant 1997–98; apptd Adviser to Gerhard Schroder, Minister-Pres. of Lower Saxony 1991; Fed. Minister of Econ. and Tech. 1998–2002; Chair. Exec. Bd RAG

AG, Essen 2003–07, also Chair. Exec. Bd RAG Beteiligungs-AG (renamed Evonik Industries AG 2007), Essen 2006–08; Chair. Supervisory Bd, Deutsche Bahn AG 2005–. *Address:* Deutsche Bahn AG, Potsdamer Platz 2, 10785 Berlin, Germany (office). *Telephone:* (30) 297-0 (office). *Fax:* (30) 29761919 (office). *E-mail:* info@db.de (office). *Website:* www.db.de (office).

MULLIEZ, Vianney; French retail executive; *Chairman, Board of Directors and Chairman, Executive Committee, Groupe Auchan;* b. 5 March 1963, Roubaix; m.; three c.; ed Ecole des Hautes Etudes Commerciales, Paris; worked eight years with PricewaterhouseCoopers; f. MBV & Associés (accountancy firm); Dir of Finance, Auchan France 1998–2000, Dir for Int. Devt 2000–04, Pres. Immochan International (subsidiary co.) 2004, Chair. Supervisory Bd Groupe Auchan 2006–10, Chair. Bd of Dirs and Chair. Exec. Cttee 2010–; Pres. Supervisory Bd Asscn Familiale Mulliez 2006–. *Leisure interest:* golf. *Address:* Groupe Auchan, 40 avenue de Flandre, PO Box 139, 59964 Croix Cedex, France (office). *Telephone:* (3) 20-81-68-00 (office). *Fax:* (3) 20-81-69-09 (office). *E-mail:* info@groupe-auchan.com (office). *Website:* www.groupe-auchan.com (office).

MULLIGAN, Deanna M., BS, MBA; American business executive; *President and CEO, The Guardian Life Insurance Company of America;* ed Univ. of Nebraska, Stanford Univ. Grad. School of Business; held roles of Sr Vice-Pres. at New York Life, Exec. Vice-Pres. at AXA Financial and Prin., McKinsey & Co., New York; est. and ran own consulting firm, DMM Management Solutions, LLC, advising insurance cos on strategic and operational issues; Exec. Vice-Pres., Individual Life and Disability business, The Guardian Life Insurance Co. of America 2008–10, Pres. and COO 2010–11, mem. Bd of Dirs, Pres. and CEO 2011–; Dir and Chair. RS Investment Management Co., LLC, Trustee, RS Investment Trust and RS Variable Products Trust; mem. Bd of Dirs American Council of Life Insurers, Life Insurance Council of New York; Trustee, The American Coll.; Co-Pres. and Trustee, North Salem Open Land Foundation; fmr mem. Bd Project Renewal, Red Cross of Greater New York; mem. Partnership for New York City, The Economic Club of New York; ranked by Fortune magazine amongst the 50 Most Powerful Women in Business in the US (47th) 2011, featured in Crain's New York Business as one of "The 50 Most Powerful Women in NY.". *Address:* The Guardian Life Insurance Co. of America, 7 Hanover Square, New York, NY 10004, USA (office). *Telephone:* (212) 598-8000 (office). *Fax:* (212) 919-2170 (office). *E-mail:* info@guardianlife.com (office). *Website:* www.guardianlife.com (office).

MULLIN, Leo F., BS, MBA; American business executive; m. Leah Mullin; one s. one d.; ed Harvard Univ., Harvard School of Arts and Sciences, Harvard Business School; began career as man. consultant McKinsey & Co. 1967, Pnr 1973–76; Sr Vice-Pres. Strategic Planning, Consolidated Rail Corpn (Conrail), Phila 1976–81; sr man. positions First Chicago 1981–93, Pres. and COO 1993–95; Vice-Chair. Unicorn Corpn and Commonwealth Edison 1995–97; Chair. and CEO Delta Air Lines Inc. 1997–2004 (resgnd); mem. Bd of Dirs Bellsouth Corpn, Johnson & Johnson, Juvenile Diabetes Research Foundation; fmr mem. Bd of Dirs Air Transport Asscn of American, Int. Air Transport Asscn (IATA); mem. Business Council, Atlanta Chamber of Commerce, Robert W. Woodruff Arts Center; mem. Bd of Trustees GA Research Alliance. *Address:* c/o Board of Directors, Johnson & Johnson, One Johnson & Johnson Plaza, New Brunswick, NJ 08933, USA.

MULLIS, Kary Banks, BS, PhD; American biochemist and academic; b. 28 Dec. 1944, Lenoir, NC; s. of Cecil Banks Mullis and Bernice Alberta Barker Fredericks Mullis; m. 4th Nancy Cosgrove Mullis; two s. one d. from two previous marriages; ed Dreher High School, Georgia Inst. of Tech., Atlanta, Univ. of California, Berkeley; Lecturer in Biochemistry, Univ. of California, Berkeley 1972; Post-doctoral Fellow, Univ. of Kansas Medical School 1973–76, Univ. of California, San Francisco 1977–79; researcher, Cetus Corp., Emeryville, Calif. 1979–86; Dir Molecular Biology Xytronyx, Inc., San Diego 1986–88; consultant on nucleic acid chemistry for more than a dozen corpns, including Angenics, Cytometrics, Eastman Kodak, Abbott Laboratories, Milligen/Biosearch, Specialty Laboratories 1987–96; Distinguished Researcher, Children's Hosp. Oakland Research Inst., Calif.; Chair. StarGene, Inc.; Vice-Pres. Histotec, Inc., Vyrex Inc.; Visiting Prof., Univ. of South Carolina; Partner in Questar International 1998; mem. Advisory Bd USA Science and Eng Festival; mem. Bd of Scientific Advisors of several cos, provides expert advice in legal matters involving DNA and frequent lecturer at colls and univs, corpns and academic meetings world-wide; known for his opposition to the HIV/AIDS hypothesis, to climate change and for his belief in astrology; Hon. DSc (Univ. of South Carolina) 1994; Dr hc in Pharmaceutical Biotechnology (Univ. of Bologna, Italy) 2004; Preis Biochemische Analytik Award 1990, William Allan Memorial Award, American Soc. of Human Genetics 1990, Preis Biochemische Analytik, German Soc. of Clinical Chem. and Boehringer Mannheim 1990, Gairdner Foundation Award 1991, Nat. Biotechnology Award 1991, R&D Magazine Scientist of the Year 1991, John Scott Award, City Trusts of Philadelphia (co-recipient) 1991, Koch Award 1992, Chiron Corpn Award 1992, Japan Prize 1992, Calif. Scientist of the Year 1992, Thomas A. Edison Award 1993, shared Nobel Prize for Chem. devising the polymerase chain reaction (PCR) technique 1993, Japanese Science and Tech. Foundation Award 1993, inducted into Nat. Inventors Hall of Fame 1998, Ronald H. Brown American Innovator Award 1998. *Publications:* Specific Enzymatic Amplification of DNA In Vitro: The Polymerase Chain Reaction 1986, The Unusual Origin of the Polymerase Chain Reaction 1990, The Polymerase Chain Reaction (co-ed.) 1994, Dancing Naked in the Mind Field (autobiog.) 1998; numerous articles in scientific journals; several major patents. *Leisure interest:* surfing. *E-mail:* lectures@karymullis.com. *Website:* www.karymullis.com.

MULLOVA, Viktoria, Russian violinist; b. 27 Nov. 1959, Moscow; d. of Yuri Mullov and Raissa Mullova; one s. two d.; ed studied in Moscow at Cen. Music School and Moscow Conservatory under Leonid Kogan; left USSR 1983; has appeared with most major orchestras and conductors and at int. festivals; lives in London; First Prize, Sibelius Competition, Helsinki 1980, Gold Medal, Tchaikovsky Competition, Moscow 1982. *Recordings include:* more than 20 discs including Beethoven Violin Concerto, Mendelssohn Violin Concerto with the Orchestre Revolutionnaire et Romantique, John Eliot Gardiner, Mozart Violin Concertos Nos 1, 3 & 4, Orchestra of the Age of Enlightenment; on Onyx Classics: Vivaldi Violin Concertos 2005, Recital (with Katia Labèque) 2006, Bach's Six Solo Sonatas and Partitas 2009, The Peasant Girl 2011, Bach: Concertos 2013. *E-mail:* paul.moseley@onyxclassics.com (office); info@onyxclassics.com (office); info@

viktoriamullova.com (office). *Website:* www.onyxclassics.com (office); www.viktoriamullova.com.

MULONI, Irene Nafuna, BSc, MBA; Ugandan electrical engineer and politician; *Minister of Energy and Mineral Development;* b. 18 Nov. 1960, Bulambuli Dist; m. Felix Muloni; one s. three d.; ed Makerere Univ., Capella Univ., USA; Man. Dir Uganda Electricity Distribution Co. Ltd 2002–11; mem. Parl. (Nat. Resistance Movt) for Bulambuli Dist 2011–; Minister of Energy and Mineral Development 2011–; Founder mem. Asscn of Women Engineers, Technicians and Scientists in Uganda. *Address:* Ministry of Energy and Mineral Development, Amber House, Kampala Road, Kampala, Uganda (office). *Telephone:* (41) 4311111 (office). *Fax:* (41) 4234732 (office). *E-mail:* imuloni@parliament.go.ug (office). *Website:* www.energyandminerals.go.ug (office).

MULRONEY, David, BA; Canadian public servant and diplomatist; b. Nov. 1954; ed Univ. of Toronto; Asst Trade Commr, St John's Regional Office, Industry Trade and Commerce 1981–82; joined Dept of Foreign Affairs and Int. Trade 1982, Trade Commr, Embassy in Seoul 1982–85, Consul, Consulate Gen. in Shanghai 1985–88, Deputy Dir, East Asia Trade Div. 1988–90, Exec. Asst, Deputy Minister for Int. Trade 1990–92, Commercial Counsellor, High Comm. in Kuala Lumpur 1992–95, Exec. Dir Canada-China Business Council 1995–98, Exec. Dir Canadian Trade Office in Taipei 1998–2001, Asst Deputy Minister, Asia-Pacific 2001–05, Asst Deputy Minister, Bilateral Relations, Foreign Affairs Canada 2005–06; Foreign and Defence Policy Advisor to the Prime Minister in Privy Council Office 2006–07, Assoc. Deputy Minister of Foreign Affairs 2007–08, Deputy Minister of Afghanistan Task Force 2008–09; Amb. to People's Repub. of China (also accred to Mongolia) 2009–12. *Address:* c/o Foreign Affairs and International Trade Canada, Lester B. Pearson Bldg, 125 Sussex Drive, Ottawa, ON K1A 0G2, Canada.

MULRONEY, Rt Hon. (Martin) Brian, PC, CC, LLD; Canadian fmr politician, business executive and lawyer; *Senior Partner, Ogilvy Renault;* b. 20 March 1939, Baie Comeau, Québec.; s. of Benedict Mulroney and Irene Mulroney (née O'Shea); m. Mila Pivnicki 1973; three s. one d.; ed St Thomas Coll. High School, Chatham, St Francis Xavier Univ., Antigonish, NS, Université Laval, Québec; called to Bar of Québec 1965; Partner, Ogilvy, Cope, Porteous, Montgomery, Renault, Clarke & Kirkpatrick, Montreal 1965–76, Sr Partner, Ogilvy Renault 1993–; Exec. Vice-Pres. (Corp. Affairs), Iron Ore Co. of Canada 1976–77, Pres. and Dir 1977–83; Leader, Progressive Party of Canada 1983–93; mem. Parl. 1983–93; Leader of Opposition 1983–84; Prime Minister of Canada 1984–93 (resgnd); Co-Chairman of the United Nations Summit on Children; Chair. Forbes Global (New York), Int. Advisory Bd Barrick Gold Corpn, Toronto, Bd Quebecor World Inc.; Chair. and Dir Persona Communications, Inc., St John's; Dir Barrick Gold Corpn, Archer Daniels Midland Co., Cendant Corpn, Trizec Properties Inc., AOL Latin America, Quebecor Inc., Quebecor World Inc., Quebecor Media, Montreal, Lion Capital LLP, London, Said Holdings Ltd, Bermuda; mem. Int. Advisory Council, JP Morgan Chase & Co., New York, China Int. Trust and Investment Corpn, Beijing, Independent News and Media PLC, Dublin, Magna International, Toronto; Sr Counsellor to Hicks, Muse, Tate & Furst, Dallas; Trustee Montreal Heart Inst. Foundation, Freedom Forum, Int. Advisory Council Les Hautes Etudes Commerciales Univ. of Montreal, World Trade Center Memorial Foundation, Council on Foreign Relations; Grand Officier Ordre nat. du Québec; several hon. degrees; numerous awards. *Publication:* Where I Stand 1983. *Leisure interests:* tennis, swimming. *Address:* Ogilvy Renault, 1981 McGill College Avenue, Suite 1100, Montreal, PQ H3A 3C1 (office); 47 Forden Crescent, Westmount, PQ H3Y 2Y5, Canada (home). *Telephone:* (514) 847-4779 (office). *Fax:* (514) 286-1238 (office). *E-mail:* bmulroney@ogilvyrenault.com (office). *Website:* www.ogilvyrenault.com (office).

MULUZI, Bakili; Malawi politician, business executive and fmr head of state; b. 17 March 1943, Machinga; m. Patricia Shanil; seven c.; ed Huddersfield Tech. Coll., Thirsted Tech. Coll. and coll. in Denmark; clerk, colonial civil service of Nyasaland; fmr Sec.-Gen. Malawi Congress Party (resgnd 1982); mem. Parl. 1975; held various Cabinet portfolios including Educ. and Minister without Portfolio; business interests in transport, merchandise distribution and real estate; Leader, United Democratic Front 1992–; Pres. of Malawi 1994–2004; arrested on fraud and corruption charges 2006, on trial 2011–; Hon. DJur (Lincoln, MO, Glasgow); Hon. Dr rer. pol (Nat. Chengchi, Taipei). *Publications:* Democracy with a Price 2000, Mau Anga: The Voice of a Democrat 2002. *Leisure interests:* reading, watching football, assisting the needy. *Address:* c/o United Democratic Front, POB 5446, Limbe, Malawi.

MULVA, James (Jim) J., MBA; American oil industry executive (retd); b. 19 June 1946, Oshkosh, Wis.; m. Miriam Mulva; two c.; ed Univ. of Texas, Austin; served as US Navy Officer 1969–73; joined Phillips Petroleum Co. 1973, Chief Financial Officer 1990–93, Sr Vice-Pres. 1993–94, Exec. Vice-Pres. 1994, Pres. and COO 1994–99, Chair., Pres. and CEO 1999–2002, Pres. and CEO ConocoPhillips Co. (cr. following merger of Phillips Petroleum Co. and Conoco Co.) 2002–04, Chair. and CEO 2004–12; Chair. American Petroleum Inst. 2006; mem. Bd of Dirs General Electric, M.D. Anderson Cancer Center, General Motors Co. 2012–; mem. The Business Council, The Business Roundtable; Trustee, Boys and Girls Clubs of America; Hon. DEng (Colorado School of Mines) 2010; Petroleum Exec. of the Year 2002. *Address:* c/o Corporate Secretary, ConocoPhillips, PO Box 4783, Houston, TX 77210-4783 (office); General Motors Co., PO Box 33170, Detroit, MI 48232-5170, USA (office). *E-mail:* info@gm.com (office). *Website:* www.conocophillips.com; www.gm.com (office).

MUMBA, Rev. Nevers, MPP; Zambian politician, evangelist and diplomatist; *High Commissioner to Canada;* b. 18 May 1960, Chinsali; s. of Sunday Mumba; m. Florence Mumba; five c.; ed Christ for the Nations Inst., Dallas, Tex., Regent Univ., Virginia, USA; fmr TV evangelist; Founder and fmr Pres. Victory Ministries International, Chair. Bd Victory Coll.; Co-founder and Nat. Chair. Nat. Citizen's Coalition (NCC); presidential cand. 2001; disbanded NCC and joined ruling Movt for Multiparty Democracy 2003; Vice-Pres. of Zambia 2003–04; Amb. to Canada 2009–, also accred to Cuba and the Bahamas; Dr hc (Univ. of Mich., Flint, USA); Ghandi, King, Ikeda Award, Morehouse Coll., Atlanta, Ga. *Television:* presenter, Zambia Shall be Saved. *Publications:* Integrity With Fire, Zambia Shall be Saved. *Leisure interest:* boxing. *Address:* Zambian High Commission, 151 Slater St, Suite 205, Ottawa, ON K1P 5H3 (office); 9 Mission Inn Grove, Nepean, ON K2R 1C2,

Canada (home). *Telephone:* (613) 232-4400 (office); (613) 823-8789 (home). *Fax:* (613) 232-4410 (office). *E-mail:* zhc.ottawa@bellnet.ca (office). *Website:* www .zambiahighcommission.ca (office); www.neversmumbaglobal.com.

MUMBENGEGWI, Simbarashe Simbanenduku, BA, DipEd; Zimbabwean diplomatist, politician and public servant; *Minister of Foreign Affairs;* b. 20 July 1945, Chivi Dist; s. of the late Chivandire Davis Mumbengegwi and Dzivaidzo Shuvai Chimbambo; m. Emily Charasika 1983; one s. four d.; ed Monash Univ., Melbourne, Australia, Univ. of Zimbabwe; active in Zimbabwe African Nat. Union (ZANU) Party 1963–, in exile, Australia 1966–72, Deputy Chief Rep. in Australia and Far East 1973–76, Chief Rep. 1976–78, Chief Rep. in Zambia 1978–80, mem. Cen. Cttee 1984–94, Patriotic Front Nat. Consultative Ass. 1994–2006, Patriotic Front Cen. Cttee 2006–; elected MP 1980, 1985; Deputy Minister of Foreign Affairs 1981–82, Minister of Water Resources and Devt 1982, of Housing 1982–84, of Public Construction and Nat. Housing 1984–88, of Transport 1988–90; Perm. Rep. to UN 1990–95; Amb. to Belgium, the Netherlands and Luxembourg, Perm. Rep. to EU 1995–99; Perm. Rep. to Org. for the Prohibition of Chemical Weapons (OPCW) 1997–99, Chair. Conf. of the State Parties 1997–98, mem. Exec. Council 1997–99; Amb. to the UK and Ireland 1999–2005; Minister of Foreign Affairs 2005–. *Leisure interests:* reading, photography, jogging, tennis, golf. *Address:* Ministry of Foreign Affairs, Munhumutapa Building, Samora Machel Avenue, POB 4240, Causeway, Harare, Zimbabwe (office). *Telephone:* (4) 727005 (office); (4) 705420 (office). *Fax:* (4) 705161 (office); (4) 727175 (office). *Website:* www.zimfa.gov.zw (office).

MUMFORD, David Bryant, PhD; American mathematician and academic; *University Professor Emeritus, Brown University;* b. 11 June 1937, Three Bridges, Sussex, England; s. of William Bryant Mumford and Grace Schiott; m. 1st Erika Jentsch 1959 (died 1988); three s. one d.; m. 2nd Jenifer Moore 1989; ed Harvard Univ.; Jr Fellow, Harvard Univ. 1958–61, Prof. of Math. 1967–77, Higgins Prof. 1977–97, Prof. Emer. 1997–, Chair. Math. Dept 1981–84, MacArthur Fellow 1987–92; Univ. Prof. of Math., Div. of Applied Math., Brown Univ. 1996–, now Emer.; Pres. Int. Math. Union 1995–98; mem. NAS 1975, American Acad. of Arts and Sciences, American Philosophical Soc. 1997; Foreign mem. Accad. Nazionale dei Lincei 1991, Royal Soc. 2008, Norwegian Acad. of Sciences and Letters; Hon. Fellow, Tata Inst. of Fundamental Research 1978; Hon. mem. London Math. Soc. 1995; Hon. DSc (Warwick) 1983, (Norwegian Univ. Science and Tech.) 2000, (Rockefeller Univ.) 2001, (Brown) 2011, (Turin) 2012, (Hyderabad) 2012; Fields Medal 1974, Longuet-Higgins Prize 2005, 2009, Shaw Prize 2006, Steele Prize2007, Wolf Prize in Math. 2008, Nat. Medal of Science 2010, BBVA Foundation Frontiers of Knowledge Award in the Basic Sciences category (with Ingrid Daubechies) 2012. *Publications:* Geometric Invariant Theory 1965, Abelian Varieties 1970, Algebraic Geometry I 1976, Two and Three Dimensional Patterns of the Face 1999, Indra's Pearls: The Vision of Felix Klein (co-author) 2002, Pattern Theory: The Stochastic Analysis of Real-World Signals (co-author) 2010. *Leisure interest:* sailing. *Address:* Brown University, Division of Applied Mathematics, Room 210, 182 George Street, Providence, RI 02912 (office); 15 Sleeper Street, #505, Boston, MA 02210, USA (home). *Telephone:* (401) 863-3441 (office); (617) 670-2989 (home). *Fax:* (401) 863-1355 (office). *E-mail:* david_mumford@brown.edu (office). *Website:* www.dam.brown.edu/people/mumford (office).

MUMUNI, Alhaji Muhammad, LLB, LLM, BL; Ghanaian politician; *Minister of Foreign Affairs, Regional Integration and NEPAD;* b. 28 July 1949; ed Univ. of Ghana, Ghana Law School; fmr Nat. Service Coordinator for the North; fmr Legal Officer, Bank for Housing and Construction; fmr Dist Magistrate; mem. Parl. for Kumbungu 1997–2004, mem. Judiciary Cttee, Standing Orders Cttee; Minister of Employment and Social Welfare 1997–2000, of Foreign Affairs, Regional Integration and NEPAD 2009–; Vice-Pres. 86th Session, Institutional Labour Congress, Geneva 1998. *Address:* Ministry of Foreign Affairs, Treasury Road, POB M53, Accra, Ghana (office). *Telephone:* (21) 664951 (office). *Fax:* (21) 680017 (office). *E-mail:* ghmaf00@ghana.com (office).

MUN, Il-bong; North Korean politician; mem. Supreme People's Ass.; Minister of Finance 2000–05. *Address:* c/o Ministry of Finance, Pyongyang, Democratic People's Republic of Korea (office).

MUNASINGHE, Gamini Surath; Sri Lankan fmr diplomatist; ed Univ. of Ceylon, Peradeniya; Deputy High Commr to UK 1991–97, High Commr to South Africa (also accred to Namibia, Seychelles and Mauritius) 1998–2001, to Zambia 2001–03, Additional Sec., Ministry of Foreign Affairs 2002–03,) High Commr to Bangladesh 2003–06; mem. Bd of Dirs Environmental Resources Investment PLC (fmrly Walker and Greig Ltd) 2007–; mem. Admin. Council Rajarata Univ. of Sri Lanka. *Address:* c/o Board of Directors, Environmental Resources Investment PLC, No.450, Taj Samudra Hotel, 25 Galle Face Centre Road, Colombo 01, Sri Lanka (office).

MUNAVVAR, Mohamed, LLM; Maldivian politician and lawyer; b. 20 Dec. 1961, Meedhoo; m.; one s. two d.; ed Majeedhiyya School, Patrice Lumumba People's Friendship Univ., Moscow, Russia, Bureau of Parl. Studies and Training, Lok Sabha Secr., New Delhi, India, Dalhousie Univ., Halifax, NS, Canada; Attorney-Gen., Repub. of the Maldives 1993–2003; MP for Addu constituency for several years; arrested Aug. 2004, transferred to house arrest Oct.–Dec. 2004 (charges withdrawn); legal adviser to Maldivian Democratic Party –2007, Pres. 2007–08 (resgnd); applied to Election Comm. for a party registration 2010. *Address:* c/o Maldivian Democratic Party (MDP), H. Sharasha, 2nd Floor, Sosun Magu, Malé 20-059, Maldives (office). *Telephone:* 3340044 (office). *Fax:* 3322960 (office). *E-mail:* secretariat@mdp.org.mv (office). *Website:* mdp.org.mv (office).

MUNDA, Arjun; Indian politician; b. 5 Jan. 1968, Jamshedpur; s. of the late Ganesh Munda and of Saira Munda; m. Meera Munda; three s.; Chief Minister of Jharkhand 2003–05 (resgnd), reappointed March 2005–Sept. 2006 (resgnd), 2010–13; Welfare Minister, Govt of Jharkhand 2000–06, mem. Bharatiya Janata Party (Gen. Sec. 2010–), Bihar Vidhan Sabha 1995–2000, Jharkhand Vidhan Sabha 2000–2009, Cttee on Energy 2009; Chair. Rural Integrated Devt Center, Jamshedpur, All Jharkhand Yoga Asscn, Shaheed Smarak Smati, Kharswan, Beenapari High School, Jamshedpur, Jharkhand Deaf and Dumb Asscn; MP 2009–. *Leisure interests:* golf, archery, music, reading, travelling, social work. *Address:* Ghorabandha, Luabasa, East Singhbhum, India (home). *Telephone:* (657) 2268292. *Fax:* (657) 2200805 (home). *E-mail:* arjun.munda@gmail.com.

MUNDELL, Robert Alexander, PhD; Canadian economist and academic; *University Professor of Economics, Columbia University;* b. 24 Oct. 1932, Kingston, Ont.; s. of William Campbell Mundell and Lila Teresa Mundell; m. 1st Barbara Sheff 1957 (divorced 1972); two s. one d.; m. 2nd Valerie Natsios 1998; one s.; ed Univ. of British Columbia, Univ. of Washington, Massachusetts Inst. of Tech., London School of Econs, Univ. of Chicago; Instructor, Univ. of BC 1957–58; economist, Royal Comm. on Price Spreads of Food Products, Ottawa 1958; Asst Prof. of Econs, Stanford Univ., USA 1958–59; Prof. of Econs, Johns Hopkins Univ., School of Advanced Int. Studies, Bologna, Italy 1959–61; Sr Economist, IMF 1961–63; Visiting Prof. of Econs, McGill Univ. 1963–64, 1989–90; Prof. of Int. Econs, Grad. Inst. of Int. Studies, Geneva, Switzerland 1965–75; Prof. of Econs Univ. of Chicago 1966–71; Prof. of Econs and Chair. Dept of Econs, Univ. of Waterloo, Ont. 1972–74; Univ. Prof. of Econs, Columbia Univ., New York 1974–; Ed. Journal of Political Economy 1966–71; Annenburg Distinguished Scholar in Residence, Univ. of Southern Calif. 1980; Richard Fox Visiting Prof. of Econs, Univ. of Pa 1990–91; First Rockefeller Visiting Research Prof. of Int. Econs, Brookings Inst. 1964–65; Guggenheim Fellow 1971; Marshall Lectures, Cambridge Univ. 1974; Distinguished Lecturer, Ching-Hua Inst., Taipei, Taiwan 1985; Pres. N American Econ. and Financial Asscn 1974–78; Dr hc (Univ. of Paris) 1992, (People's Univ. of China) 1995; Jacques Rueff Prize and Medal 1983, Nobel Prize for Econs 1999. *Publications:* The International Monetary System: Conflict and Reform 1965, Man and Economics 1968, International Economics 1968, Monetary Theory: Interest, Inflation and Growth in the World Economy 1971, Global Disequilibrium in the Lloyd Economy (co-author) 1989, Building the New Europe (co-author) 1991, Inflation and Growth in China (co-author) 1996; numerous papers and articles in journals. *Leisure interests:* painting, tennis, hockey, skiing, art history. *Address:* Department of Economics, Columbia University, 1031 International Affairs Building, MC 3308, 420 West 118th Street, New York, NY 10027, USA (office). *Telephone:* (212) 854-3669 (office). *Fax:* (212) 854-8059 (office). *E-mail:* ram15@columbia.edu (office). *Website:* www.columbia.edu/cu/economics (office).

MUNDIE, Craig James, BS, MS; American computer software industry executive; *Chief Research and Strategy Officer, Microsoft Corporation;* b. 1949, Cleveland; m.; one d.; ed Georgia Inst. of Tech.; Software Developer, Systems Equipment Corpn (SEC), then at Data Gen. Corpn (which acquired SEC) 1972; Co-founder and CEO Alliant Computer Systems Corpn 1982–92; Gen. Man. Advanced Consumer Tech., Microsoft Corpn, Redmond, Wash. 1992–93, Vice Pres. Advanced Consumer Tech. Group 1993–96, Sr Vice Pres. Consumer Platforms Div. 1996–2001, Sr Vice-Pres. Advanced Strategies and Policies 2001–06, Chief Research and Strategy Officer 2006–; mem. Nat. Security Telecommunications Advisory Cttee 2000–, Markle Foundation Task Force on Nat. Security in the Information Age 2002–, Council on Foreign Relations 2002–; Trustee Fred Hutchinson Cancer Research Center, Seattle; mem. Advisory Bd Coll. of Computing, Ga Inst. of Tech. *Address:* Microsoft Corporation, 1 Microsoft Way, Redmond, WA 98052-6399, USA (office). *Telephone:* (425) 882-8080 (office). *Fax:* (425) 936-7329 (office). *Website:* www.microsoft.com (office).

MUNEKUNI, Yoshihide, BA; Japanese automobile executive; b. Hiroshima; ed Hosei Univ.; joined Honda Motor Co. Ltd 1966, career assignments include Dir then Exec. Vice-Pres. America Honda Motor Co. Inc., Pres. and Dir Honda N America Inc. 1989–90, Chair. Honda N America Inc. 1990–95, COO Automobile Sales Operations Honda Motor Co. Ltd 1995–97, Chair. and Rep. Dir 1997; Chair. Japan Automobile Mfrs Asscn (JAMA) 2002–04; mem. Japan–USA Govt-Business Forum 2002.

MUNEOKA, Shoji; Japanese steel industry executive; *Representative Director, Chairman and CEO, Nippon Steel & Sumitomo Metal Corporation;* joined Nippon Steel Corpn in 1970, served as Dir of Sec., later Man. Dir and Vice-Pres. –2008, Rep. Dir and Pres. Nippon Steel Corpn 2008–12 (merged with Sumitomo Metal Industries Ltd to become Nippon Steel & Sumitomo Metal Corpn 2012), Rep. Dir, Chair. and CEO 2012–, also Chair. associated co. based in Shanghai; Chair. Japanese Iron and Steel Fed. *Address:* Nippon Steel & Sumitomo Metal Corpn, Marunouchi Park Building, 6-1, Marunouchi 2-chome, Chiyoda-ku, Tokyo 100-8071, Japan (office). *Telephone:* (3) 6867-4111 (office). *Fax:* (3) 6867-5607 (office). *E-mail:* info@nssmc.com (office). *Website:* www.nssmc.com (office).

MUNGAN, Zeren, MEconSc; Turkish-Cypriot economist and politician; *Minister of Finance;* b. 1956; began career as Under-Sec. of Finance, State Planning Org. 1984, held various positions including Chair., Prevention of Proceeds of Crime Comm.; Lecturer in Law and Public Finance, Anadolu Univ. 1991–2004; consultancy work as specialist in public finance; fmr CEO Turkish Cypriot Chamber of Commerce; Minister of Finance 2013–. *Address:* Ministry of Finance, Lefkoşa, Mersin 10, Turkey (office). *Telephone:* 2283116 (office). *Fax:* 2278230 (office). *E-mail:* bim@kktcmaliye.com (office). *Website:* www.kktcmaliye.com (office).

MUNGIU, Cristian; Romanian film director and producer; b. 27 April 1968, Iaşi; ed Univ. of Iaşi, Univ. of Film, Bucharest; fmr teacher and jurnalist; directed eight short films at film school, including The Hand of Paulista that was Romania's entry in the 1999 Student Acad. Awards, graduated from film school 1998; made several short films, then his first feature film, Occident 2002, which won prizes in several film festivals and was featured in Director's Fortnight at Cannes Film Festival 2002; formed Mobrafilms production co. 2006. *Films:* writer and dir: Zapping 2000, Nici o întâmplare 2000, Corul pompierilor 2000, Occident (aka West) 2002, Lost and Found (segment 'Turkey Girl') 2005, 4 luni, 3 săptămâni şi 2 zile (4 Months, 3 Weeks & 2 Days; also producer) (Palme d'Or, Cannes Film Festival (first Romanian dir) 2007) 2007; producer: Bucuresti-Berlin 2005, Offset (exec. producer) 2006; other: Teen Knight (first asst dir) 1998, Train de vie (Train of Life; second asst dir) 1998.

MUNGOSHI, Charles Muzuva; Zimbabwean writer, poet and playwright; b. 2 Dec. 1947, Chivhu; m. Jesesi Jaboon 1976; four s. one d.; ed secondary school; clerk in bookshop, Harare 1969–74; Ed. with the Literature Bureau 1974–81; Dir and Ed. publisher in Zimbabwe 1981–88; Writer-in-Residence, Univ. of Zimbabwe 1985–87; Visiting Arts Fellow, Univ. of Durham 1990; Writer-in-Residence, Univ. of Florida, Gainesville, USA 2000; Hon. DLitt (Zimbabwe) 2004; Noma Award for Publishing in Africa, Book Centre/PEN Award, Commonwealth Writers Award (Africa Region). *Film:* The Axe (writer and Dir) 1999. *Publications include:* (novels)

Makunun'unu Maodzamwoyo (in Shona) 1970, Waiting for the Rain 1975, Ndiko Kupindana Kwamazuva (in Shona) 1975, Kunyarara Hakusi Kutaura? (in Shona) 1983; (short stories) Coming of the Dry Season 1972, Some Kinds of Wounds 1980, Setting Sun and Rolling World 1987, One Day Long Ago: Tales from a Shona Childhood (folk tales) 1991, Walking Still 1997; (poetry) The Milkman Doesn't Only Deliver Milk 1981. *Leisure interests:* travelling reading, acting. *Address:* P.O. Box 1688, Harare (office); 47/6156 Uta Crescent, Zengeza 1, Chitungwiza, Zimbabwe. *E-mail:* muzuva47@yahoo.com.

MUNGUÍA PAYÉS, David; Salvadorean army officer (retd) and government official; *Minister of Justice and Public Security;* s. of Mariano Munguía; ed Univ. of El Salvador; fmr adviser to Christian Democratic Pres. José Napoleón Duarte; fmr army officer, rank of Col (retd); fmr Co-ordinator, Nat. Unity Movt; Minister of Nat. Defence 2009–11, of Justice and Public Security 2011–. *Address:* Ministry of Justice and Public Security, Centro de Gobierno, Complejo Plan Maestro, Edifs B1, B2 y B3, Alameda Juan Pablo II y 17 Avda Norte, San Salvador, El Salvador (office). *Telephone:* 2526-3000 (office). *Fax:* 2526-3105 (office). *Website:* www .seguridad.gob.sv (office).

MUNITZ, Barry, PhD; American foundation administrator, academic and university administrator; b. 26 July 1941, Brooklyn, New York; s. of Raymond J. Munitz and Vivian LeVoff Munitz; m. Anne Tomfohrde 1987; ed Brooklyn Coll., Princeton Univ., Univ. of Leiden, Netherlands; Asst Prof. of Literature and Drama, Univ. of Calif., Berkeley 1966–68; Staff Assoc., Carnegie Comm. on Higher Educ. 1968–70; mem. Presidential staff, then Assoc. Provost Univ. of Ill. 1970–72, Academic Vice-Pres. 1972–76; Vice-Pres., Dean of Faculties, Cen. Campus Univ. of Houston 1976–77, Chancellor 1977–82; Pres., COO Federated Devt Co. 1982–91; Vice-Chair. Maxxam Inc., LA 1982–91; Chancellor Calif. State Univ., Long Beach 1991–98, Prof. of English Literature, UCLA 1991–; Pres., CEO J. Paul Getty Trust, LA 1998–2006 (resgnd); Woodrow Wilson Fellow 1963; mem. Bd of Advisors Leeds Weld and Co. *Publications:* The Assessment of Institutional Leadership 1977; articles and monographs. *Address:* c/o J. Paul Getty Trust, Suite 400, 1200 Getty Center Drive, Los Angeles, CA 90049, USA (office).

MUNJAL, Brij Mohan Lall; Indian business executive; *Chairman and Managing Director, Hero Group;* b. 1923, Kamalia, Pakistan; m.; three s. one d.; started career making bicycle parts; Chair., Man. Dir Hero Group (bicycle manufacturer), Hero Honda Motors Ltd (Honda partner for making motorcycles), Hero Cycles Ltd, Hero Honda Finlease Ltd, Munjal Showa Ltd, Sunbeam Auto Ltd; Dir Easy Bill Ltd, Hero Financial Services Ltd, Munjal Auto Industries Ltd, Shivam Autotech Ltd; fmr Pres. Confed. of Indian Industry, Soc. of Indian Automobile Mfrs; fmr mem. Regional Bd, Reserve Bank of India; Hon. Fellow, Indian Inst. of Industrial Eng; Dr hc (Banaras Hindu Univ.) 2004; Businessman of the Year Award 1994, NSIC Award 1995, Distinguished Entrepreneurship Award, PHD Chamber of Commerce and Industry 1997, Most Admired CEO Award, Business Baron 1999, Sir Jehangir Ghandy Medal for Industrial Peace, Xavier Labour Relations Inst. 2000, Ernst & Young Entrepreneur of the Year Award 2001, Madras Man. Asscn Business Leadership Award 2002, Lifetime Achievement Award, All India Man. Asscn 2003, Lifetime Achievement Award, Amity Business School 2004, Lifetime Achievement Award, HT Power Jobs 2004, Padma Bhushan 2005. *Address:* Hero Honda Motors Ltd, 34 Community Centre, Basant Lok, Vasant Vihar, New Delhi 110 057, India (office). *Telephone:* (11) 26142451 (office). *Fax:* (11) 26143321 (office). *Website:* www.herohonda.com (office).

MUNK, Walter Heinrich, BS, MS, PhD; American (b. Austrian) geophysicist and academic; *Professor of Geophysics Emeritus and Secretary of the Navy/Chief of Naval Operations Oceanography Chair, Scripps Institution of Oceanography;* b. 19 Oct. 1917, Vienna, Austria-Hungary; s. of Dr Hans Munk and Rega Brunner; m. 1st Judith Horton 1953 (died 2009); m. 2nd Mary Coakley 2011; ed Columbia Univ., California Inst. of Tech., Univ. of California, Los Angeles; Asst Prof. of Geophysics, Scripps Inst. of Oceanography, La Jolla, Calif. 1947–54, apptd Prof. of Geophysics 1954, now Prof. Emer. and Sec. of Navy/Chief of Naval Operations Oceanography Chair, mem. Univ. of California's Inst. of Geophysics, est. br. of inst. at Scripps in La Jolla 1960, Dir Scripps Div. 1963–82, Assoc. Dir of univ.-wide inst. (renamed the Inst. of Geophysics and Planetary Physics); mem. JASON (panel of scientists advising the US govt) 1968; mem. NAS 1956, Royal Soc. of London 1976; Guggenheim Fellow (three times), Fulbright Fellow, named California Scientist of the Year by California Museum of Science and Industry 1969, Arthur L. Day Medal, Geological Soc. of America 1965, Sverdrup Gold Medal, American Meteorological Soc. 1966, Gold Medal, Royal Astronomical Soc. 1968, first Maurice Ewing Medal, American Geophysical Union and USN 1976, NAS Alexander Agassiz Medal 1977, Capt. Robert Dexter Conrad Award, USN 1978, Nat. Medal of Science 1983, William Bowie Medal, American Geophysical Union 1989, first recipient of Walter Munk Award, Oceanography Soc., Office of Naval Research and US Dept of Defense Naval Oceanographic Office 1993, Vetlesen Prize 1993, Kyoto Prize 1999, first Prince Albert I Medal 2001, Crafoord Prize, Royal Swedish Acad. of Sciences 2010, Roger Revelle Medal 2012. *Achievements include:* first to show rigorously why one side of the moon always faces the earth 1960. *Publications:* The Rotation of the Earth: A Geophysical Discussion (with G. J. F. MacDonald) 1960, Ocean Acoustic Tomography (co-author) 1995; numerous papers in professional journals. *Address:* Institute of Geophysics and Planetary Physics, Scripps Institution of Oceanography, University of California, San Diego, 9500 Gilman Drive, MC 0225, La Jolla, CA 92093-0225, USA (office). *Telephone:* (858) 534-2877 (office). *Fax:* (858) 534-6251 (office). *E-mail:* wmunk@ucsd.edu (office). *Website:* scripps.ucsd.edu (office).

MUNK OLSEN, Birger, DLitt; Danish professor of medieval culture and philology; *Professor, Saxo Institute, University of Copenhagen;* b. 26 June 1935, Copenhagen; m. 1st Annalise Bliddal 1964 (divorced 1988); m. 2nd Gudrun Haastrup 1994; two d.; ed Ecole Normale Supérieure, Sorbonne, Paris and Pontificia Univ. Gregoriana, Rome; Assoc. Prof. of Romance Philology, Univ. of Copenhagen 1961–68; Lecturer Univ. Paris-Sorbonne 1968–74; Prof. of Romance Philology, Univ. of Copenhagen 1974–83, Prof. of Medieval Culture and Philology 1983–; Chair. Danish Nat. Research Council for the Humanities 1987–90; Danish Rep. Standing Cttee for the Humanities, European Science Foundation 1988–92; mem. Royal Danish Acad. 1985– (Vice-Pres., Chair. Humanities Section 1989–95, Pres. 1996–2004), Danish Council for Research Planning and Policy 1987–89, Academia Europaea 1988– (Exec. Council 1989–92); Corresp. mem. Acad. des

Inscriptions et Belles Lettres (Inst. de France) 1996, mem. 1998–; Vice-Pres. Soc. Int. de Bibliographie Classique 1994–99, Pres. 1999–2004; Hon. mem. Academia Româna 2000; mem. European Science and Tech. Asscn 1997–2000, Corresp. FRSE 2001; Kt, Order of the Dannebrog, Officier, Légion d'honneur, Ordre nat. du Mérite, Commandor, Ordinul Naţional Pentru Merit (Romania); Dr hc (Paris) 2003; Prix Brunet 1984. *Publications:* Les 'Dits' de Jehan de Saint-Quentin 1978, L'étude des auteurs classiques latins aux XI[e]et XII[e]siècles, Vols I–IV 1982–89, I classici nel canone scolastico altomedievale 1991, L'atteggiamento medievale di fronte alla cultura classica 1994, La réception de la littérature classique au Moyen Age 1995. *Address:* Ny Kongensgade 20, 1557 Copenhagen V, Denmark; 51 rue de Tolbiac, 75013 Paris, France; Torshoj 1, Veddinge, 4540 Faarevejle, Denmark. *Telephone:* 33-91-91-81 (Copenhagen); 1-45-84-27-18 (Paris); 20-21-72-17 (Faarevejle). *Fax:* 35-32-81-55 (office). *E-mail:* bmo@hum.ku.dk (office).

MUÑOZ LEOS, Raúl; Mexican business executive and chemical engineer; b. 14 Oct. 1939, México; ed Nat. Univ. of Mexico (UNAM); joined Du Pont SA 1964, various sr positions in production, sales, market research, planning and admin, Exec. Vice-Pres. Du Pont Mexico –1988, Pres. (first Mexican to head co.) 1988–2000; Dir Gen. Pemex (Petróleos Mexicanos) 2000–04; mem. Bd of Dirs, Química Flúor SA, Nylon de México, Sears Roebuck and Co., Mexican Foundation for Rural Devt, Mexican Health Foundation; Nat. Vice-Pres. COPARMEX; Pres. Grupo Diálogo Inversión; fmr Pres. Mexican Inst. of Chemical Engineers; mem. Editorial Bd, El Economista; mem. Diálogo México, American Chamber of Commerce of Mexico; Trustee, UNAM Faculty of Chem., Museum of the City of Mexico, Antiguo Colegio de San Ildefonso. *Address:* c/o Petróleos Mexicanos (Pemex), Avenida Marina Nacional 329, Colonia Huasteca, 11311 México, DF, Mexico.

MUÑOZ VALENZUELA, Heraldo, BA, PhD; Chilean diplomatist and politician; *Minister of Foreign Affairs;* b. 22 July 1948, Santiago; m. Pamela Quick; one d.; ed State Univ. of New York, USA, Harvard Univ., USA, Catholic Univ. of Chile, Univ. of Denver, USA; Nat. Supervisor, People's Stores (Almacenes del Pueblo) 1973; Co-founder Party for Democracy (PPD); mem. Political Comm. Sec. of Int. Relations, Socialist Party 1983–85; Chair. Metropolitan Santiago Region of PPD 1988–90; Jt Rep. of Socialist Party and PPD, Exec. Cttee, NO Campaign to defeat Gen. Pinochet 1988; Campaign Chief, Ricardo Lagos' senatorial race 1989; Amb. to OAS 1990–94, Pres. Environment Comm. 1991–92, Pres., Perm. Council 1993; Amb. to Brazil 1994–98; Pres., Economist Confs 1998–99; Int. Coordinator, Presidential Campaign of Ricardo Lagos 1999; Head of Int. and Defence Comm. 1999; Deputy Foreign Minister 2000–02; Minister Sec. Gen. of Govt 2002–03; Perm. Rep. to UN, New York 2003–10, mem. UN Security Council 2003–04, Pres. 2004; Asst Sec.-Gen., Asst Admin. and Regional Dir for Latin America and the Caribbean, UNDP 2010–14; Minister of Foreign Affairs 2014–; Founder-Dir, Programa de Seguimento de las Politicas Exteriores Latinoamericanas (PROSPEL, foreign policy Inst.), Santiago 1983–90; fmr Pres. Latinanalyst Consultores; currently Prof., Inst. of International Studies, Univ. of Chile; Fellowships from Resources for the Future, Ford Foundation, Tinker Foundation, Twentieth Century Fund, MacArthur Foundation; PhD Fellow, Brookings Inst., Washington, DC 1977; Dr hc (State Univ. of New York) 1996; Distinguished Alumnus Award, Grad. School of International Studies, Univ. of Denver 1991. *Publications:* more than 20 books, including Latin American Nations in World Politics (co-ed.) 1998, Globalización XXI 2000, A Solitary War: A Diplomat's Chronicle of the Iraq War and Its Lessons (also in Spanish) 2008, The Dictator's Shadow: Life under Augusto Pinochet 2008; numerous essays in published academic journals including: Foreign Policy, Journal of Democracy, Journal of Interamerican and World Affairs, Latin American Research Review; contrib. to newspapers including El Mercurio, Folha de São Paulo, Los Angeles Times, Miami Herald, Página 12. *Address:* Ministry of Foreign Affairs, Teatinos 180, Santiago, Chile (office). *Telephone:* (2) 2827-4200 (office). *Website:* www.minrel.gov.cl (office).

MUNRO, Alice, BA; Canadian writer; b. 10 July 1931, Wingham, Ont.; d. of Robert E. Laidlaw and Anne Chamney; m. 1st James A. Munro 1951 (divorced 1976); three d.; m. 2nd Gerald Fremlin 1976 (died 2013); ed Univ. of Western Ontario; Foreign Hon. mem. American Acad. of Arts and Letters; Chevalier, Ordre des Arts et des Lettres 2010; Gov.-Gen.'s Award for Literature 1978, 1986, Canadian Booksellers' Award 1972, Marian Engel Award 1986, Canada-Australia Literary Prize 1994, Lannan Literary Award 1995, WH Smith Literary Award 1996, Fiction Prize, Nat. Book Critics Circle 1999, Giller Prize 1999, O. Henry Award 2001, Man Booker Int. Prize 2009, Nobel Prize for Literature 2013. *Publications include:* Dance of the Happy Shades (Gov.-Gen.'s Award for Literature) 1968, A Place for Everything 1970, Lives of Girls and Women 1971, Something I've Been Meaning to Tell You 1974, Who Do You Think You Are? (aka The Beggar Maid) 1978, The Moons of Jupiter 1982, The Progress of Love 1986, Friend of My Youth 1990, Open Secrets 1994, Selected Stories 1996, The Love of A Good Woman 1998, Hateship, Friendship, Courtship, Loveship, Marriage 2001, Runaway (short stories) 2005, The View from Castle Rock 2006, Too Much Happiness 2009, Dear Life 2012. *Address:* PO Box 1133, Clinton, ON N0M 1L0, Canada.

MUNS ALBUIXECH, Joaquín, PhD; Spanish economist, academic and international civil servant; *Professor Emeritus, University of Barcelona;* b. 25 June 1935, Barcelona; m. M. Tardà; one s. two d.; ed Univ. of Barcelona and London School of Econs; Economist, Nat. Studies Div. of OECD 1962–63; Asst Prof. of Econs Univ. of Barcelona 1963–65, Prof. of Econs, Univ. of Barcelona 1968–73, Sr Prof. of Int. Econ. Org. 1973–2005, Jean Monnet Prof. of European Integration 1991–2005, Prof. Emer. 2005–; Economist, Western Hemisphere Dept of IMF 1965–68, Exec. Dir IMF 1978–80; Exec. Dir IBRD 1980–82; Econ. Adviser to Barcelona City Council 1968–73; Econ. Adviser to Govt of Spain and to various public and pvt. insts 1973–78; Adjunct Prof., SIS American Univ. 1982; mem. European Parl. (Liberal Group) 1987–89; mem. Vatican Council of Econ. Advisers 1988–94; mem. Governing Council Bank of Spain 1994–2004; economic journalist; Cross of St George (Catalonia) 1984; Outstanding Researcher Catalan Foundation for Research and Innovation (FCRI) 1995, King Juan Carlos Prize for Econs 2008, Prize for Academic Career, Inst. of Financial Studies 2010, Godó Prize for Journalism 2010. *Publications:* (in English): Adjustment, Conditionality and International Financing (ed.) 1984; (in Spanish): Industrialization and Growth in the Developing Countries 1972, The European Option for the Spanish Economy

1973, The International Economic Crisis: Thoughts and Proposals 1975, Crisis and Reform of the International Monetary System 1978, History of the Relations between Spain and the IMF 1958–82, Twenty-five Years of the Spanish Economy 1986, The EMU and its Future 1992, Radiography of the Crisis 1993, Spain and the World Bank 1994, Spain and the Euro: Risks and Opportunities (ed.) 1997, The Culture of Stability and the Consensus of Washington (with M. Guitián) 1999, Readings on Economic Integration: The European Union (ed.) 2005, Compilation of the Principal Documents of the Relations Spain-IMF 1958–2007 (comp., 16 vols) 2008. *Leisure interests:* travel, music. *Address:* Diagonal 690, 08034 Barcelona (office); C. Muntaner, 268, 08021 Barcelona, Spain (home). *Telephone:* (93) 4021939 (office); (93) 2094534 (home). *Fax:* (93) 4021934 (office); (93) 4140697 (home). *E-mail:* jmuns@ub.edu (office). *Website:* www.ub.edu/muns/personal.html (office).

MUNTEAN, Mihail; Moldovan singer (tenor); b. 15 Aug. 1943, Kriva, Briceni; s. of Ion Muntean and Elizaveta Muntean; m. Rosentul Galina Andrian 1969; one s. one d.; ed Kishinev Inst. of Arts, La Scala, Milan; Prin. Tenor with Moldovan State Acad. Theatre of Opera and Ballet 1971–, Gen. Dir 1996–97; Prof. Chair of Vocal Arts, Music Acad. of Moldova 1993–; Provost Art Inst., Mil. Acad. Stefan Cel Mare 1996–; Pres. Centre for Devt and Support of Culture Mihai Munteanu 1998–; Hon. Prof., Modern Humanitarian Inst. Moscow 1997–; Dr hc (Univ. of Arts, Iasi, Romania, Univ. Ovidius Constanţa, Romania; Verdi Award 1978, USSR People's Artist 1986, Moldovan State Award 1984, Award of the Republic 1993. *Opera roles include:* Lensky in Eugene Onegin, Riccardo in Un Ballo in Maschera, Don Carlo in Don Carlo, Cavaradossi in Tosca, Calaf in Turandot, Hermann in The Queen of Spades, Radames in Aida, Turiddu in Cavalleria Rusticana, Otello in Otello, Canio in Pagliacci, Manrico in Il Trovatore, Samson in Samson et Dalila, Ismael in Nabucco, Don José in Carmen, Don Alvaro in La Forza del Destino, Pinkerton in Madame Butterfly; performances and concerts throughout the world. *Leisure interests:* collecting books, family, children, music. *Address:* 16 N. Iorga str., Apt 13, 2012 Chişinău, Moldova (office). *Telephone:* 911-7577 (office); (2) 23-75-19. *Fax:* (2) 23-75-19. *E-mail:* mihai.muntean@mail.ru (home).

MÜNTEFERING, Franz; German politician; b. 16 Jan. 1940, Neheim; s. of Franz Müntefering and Anna Schlinkmann; m. Ankepetra Rettich 1995; two d.; apprenticeship in industrial admin. 1954–57; industrial admin. in eng firm 1957–61; mil. training 1961–62; mem. Social Democratic Party of Germany (SPD) 1966–, sub-Dist Chair. Hochsauerland 1984–88, mem. Dist Exec. W Westphalia 1984–, Dist Chair. 1992–98, mem. Exec. Cttee 1991–, Fed. Business Man. 1995–99, Chair. state org. North Rhine Westphalia 1998–2001, Gen. Sec. 1999, Chair. SPD 2002–05; mem. Sudern City Council 1969–79; mem. Bundestag 1975–92, Parl. Business Man. SPD Bundestag Parl. Group 1991–92; mem. North Rhine Westphalia Landtag 1996–98; Fed. Minister of Transport, Construction and Housing 1998–99, Vice-Chancellor and Minister of Labour and Social Affairs 2005–07 (resgnd); mem. IG Metall (Eng TU) 1967–. *Address:* c/o Sozialdemokratische Partei Deutschlands (SPD) (Social Democratic Party of Germany), Willy-Brandt-Haus, Wilhelmstr. 141, 10963 Berlin, Germany.

MUNTIANAS, Viktoras; Lithuanian engineer and politician; b. 11 Nov. 1951, Marijampolė; ed Marijampolė Secondary School No 3, Vilnius Civil Eng Inst. (now Vilnius Gediminas Tech. Univ.), Vilnius Higher School for Party Studies; Jr Research Fellow, Lithuanian Construction and Architecture Research Inst. 1978–79; construction site man., later Chief Engineer, Kaunas Construction Plant 1979–85; Deputy Chair., Exec. Cttee of Kėdainiai Dist 1986–90; Gov., Kėdainiai Dist 1990–93; Gov. AB Ūkio Bankas, Kėdainiai Br. 1994–96; Vice-Pres., Trust Vikonda 1996–97; mem., Municipal Bd, later Mayor, Kėdainiai Dist 1997–2004; mem. Seimas 2004–; Deputy Chair. Bd of Seimas 2004–06, Speaker 2006–08, mem. Cttee on Budget and Finance 2004–06, Comm. on Anti-corruption 2006–; mem. Labour Party Group 2004–06, Ass. of Elders, Parl. Group for Relations with France, Seimo Delegacija Lietuvos ir Ukrainos Aukščiausiosios Rados Asamblėjoje; mem. CPSU –1989; mem. and Deputy Chair., Labour Party 2003–06; mem. and Chair. Civil Democracy Party 2006–. *Leisure interests:* hunting, sports, angling. *Address:* c/o Seimas, Gedimino pr. 53, Vilnius 01109, Lithuania. *Telephone:* (5) 239-6559. *E-mail:* viktoras.muntianas@lrs.lt (office). *Website:* www.lrs.lt (office).

MURAD, Ferid, BA, MD, PhD; American pharmacologist and academic; *John S. Dunn Distinguished Chair Physiology and Medicine Director, Institute of Molecular Medicine, University of Texas;* b. 14 Sept. 1936, Whiting, Indiana; s. of John and Henrietta Josephine Murad; m. Carol A. Leopold 1958; one s. four d.; ed DePauw Univ., Ind. and Western Reserve Univ., Cleveland, Ohio; Dir Clinical Research Center, School of Medicine, Univ. of Va 1971–81, Div. of Clinical Pharmacology 1973–81, Prof. Depts of Internal Medicine and Pharmacology 1975–81; Prof. Depts. of Internal Medicine and Pharmacology, Stanford Univ. 1981–89, Acting Chair. Dept of Medicine 1986–88; Chief of Medicine Palo Alto Veterans Admin. Medical Center, Calif. 1981–86; Adjunct Prof. Dept of Pharmacology, Northwestern Univ., Chicago 1988–96; Chair. Dept of Integrative Biology and Pharmacology, Univ. of Texas Medical School, Houston 1997– also Prof., now John S. Dunn Distinguished Chair in Physiology, Dir Depts of Pharmacology and Physiology, Medicine Dir Inst. of Molecular Medicine 1999–; Vice-Pres. Pharmaceutical Research and Devt, Abbott Laboratories 1988–92; CEO and Pres. Molecular Geriatrics Corpn, Lake Bluff, Ill. 1993–95; Ciba Award 1988, Albert and Mary Lasker Award for Basic Research 1996, Nobel Prize in Medicine or Physiology 1998, AAMC Research Award 2002, Grisalin Award 2005. *Publications:* more than 405 publs and books, including Discovery of Some of the Biological Effects of Nitric Oxide and its Role in Cellular Signaling (Nobel Lecture 1998) 1999. *Leisure interests:* golf, carpentry. *Address:* Imm, University of Texas, 1825 Pressler, Suite 530, Houston, TX 77030, USA (office). *Telephone:* (713) 500-2433 (office). *Fax:* (713) 500-2498 (office). *E-mail:* ferid.murad@uth.tmc.edu (office). *Website:* www.uth.tmc.edu/uth_orgs/imm/centers/cellsignal.html (office).

MURAKAMI, Haruki, BA; Japanese writer; b. 12 Jan. 1949, Kyoto; m. Yoko Takahashi 1971; ed Kobe High School, Waseda Univ.; Owner, Peter Cat jazz club, Tokyo 1974–81; began writing in 1978, lived in Europe 1986–89, USA 1991–95; Visiting Scholar, Princeton Univ. 1991–93; Una's Lecturer in the Humanities, Univ. of Calif., Berkeley 1992; Writer-in-Residence, Tufts Univ. 1993–95, Harvard Univ. 2005–06; Franz Kafka Prize 2006, Jerusalem Prize 2009. *Publications:* fiction: Hear the Wind Sing (Gunzo Literature Prize) 1979, Pinball 1980, A Wild Sheep Chase (Noma Literary Award for New Writers) 1982, Hard-Boiled Wonderland and The End of the World (Junichi Tanizaki Award) 1985, Norwegian Wood 1987, Dance Dance Dance 1988, South of the Border, West of the Sun 1992, Wind-Up Bird Chronicle (Yomiuri Literary Award 1996) 1994–95, Sputnik Sweetheart 1999, Kafka on the Shore 2002, After Dark 2004, 1Q84 2009, Colourless Tsukuru Tazaki and His Years of Pilgrimage 2013; short stories: Slow Boat to China 1983, A Perfect day for Kangaloos 1983, Dead Heat 1985, The Elephant Vanishes 1986, TV People 1990, Phantoms of Lexington 1998, After the Quake 2000, Blind Willow, Sleeping Woman (Frank O'Connor Int. Short Story Award, Kiriyama Prize 2007) 2006; non-fiction: Underground 1997, The Place That was Promised (Kuwahara Takeo Award) 1998, What I Talk About When I Talk About Running 2008; essays: A Young Reader's Guide to Short Fiction 1997; has translated works by F. Scott Fitzgerald, Raymond Carver, Truman Capote, Paul Theroux, John Irving, J. D. Salinger. *Leisure interests:* running marathons, music, jazz, classical etc. *Address:* ICM, 40 West 57th Street, New York, NY 10019, USA (office). *Telephone:* (212) 556-5600 (office). *Website:* www.icmtalent.com (office); www.randomhouse.com/features/murakami/site.php (office).

MURAKAMI, Kenji; Japanese business executive; *Vice-Chairman, Daiwa House Industry Company Ltd;* b. 1947; ed Ritsumeikan Univ.; joined Daiwa House Industry Co. Ltd 1970, held positions including Man. Hiroshima Pref. Dist, Exec. Officer, Man. Dir, Sr Man. Dir, Chief Man. Tokyo Store and Pres. Tokyo Office, Rep. Dir 1997–, Pres. and COO Daiwa House Industry Co. Ltd 2004–11, Vice-Chair. 2011–; Dir Nippon Venture Capital Co. Ltd; Pres. The Machinami Foundation 2009–. *Address:* Daiwa House Industry Co. Ltd, 3-3-5 Umeda, Kita-ku, Osaka 530-8241, Japan (office). *Telephone:* (6) 6346-2111 (office). *Fax:* (6) 6342-1419 (office). *E-mail:* info@daiwahouse.com (office). *Website:* www.daiwahouse .com (office); www.daiwahouse.co.jp (office).

MURAKAMI, Ryunosuke (Ryū); Japanese writer and film director; b. 19 Feb. 1952, Sasebo City, Nagasaki; m. Tazuko Takahashi 1976; fmr rock band drummer, TV talk show host; writer and film-maker 1976–. *Films include:* adaptations of many of his novels, including Almost Transparent Blue (writer and dir) 1978, Daijôbu, mai furendo (writer and dir) 1983, Raffles Hotel (writer and dir) 1989, Topâzu (writer and dir) 1992, Ôdishon (writer) 1999, Kyoko (writer and dir) 2000, Hashire! Ichiro (from novel Hashire! Takahashi) 2001, Shôwa kayô daizenshū 2003, Shikusutinain 2004, Popular! 2006, Koinrokkā Beibīzu 2008. *Publications include:* novels: Kagirinaku tōmei ni chikai burrū (trans. as Almost Transparent Blue) (Akutagawa Prize, Gunzou Prize) 1976, Hashire! Takahashi, Ōdishon, Topâzu (trans. as Tokyo Decadence), Raffles Hotel, Daijôbu, mai furendo (trans. as All Right, My Friend), Kyoko (trans. as Because of You), 69 1987, Coin Locker Babies 1995, In the Miso Soup (Yomiuri Literary Award 1998) 1997, Exodus (serialised) 1998–99, Piercing 2007, Audition 2009, Popular Hits of the Showa Era 2011; non-fiction: Ano kane de nani ga kaeta ka 2003. *Address:* c/o Kodansha International Ltd, Otowa YK Building, 1-17-14 Otowa, Bunkyo-ku, Tokyo 112-8652, Japan.

MURAKAMI, Seiichiro, BA; Japanese politician; b. 11 May 1952; ed Tokyo Univ.; elected to House of Reps for Ehime Pref. 1986–; Sec. of State for Finance 1992–93, Chair. Parl. Cttee on Coal Problems 1994–95, on Finance 1997–98, Deputy Chair. Japan-Albania Parl. Friendship Asscn, Chief Sec. Japan-Cyprus Parl. Friendship Asscn; Deputy Sec.-Gen. LDP 1995–, Commr Policy Research Council 1999, Chair. Dist Affairs Cttee; Sr Vice-Minister on Finance 2000–02; Minister of State for Regulatory Reform, for Industrial Revitalization Corpn of Japan, for Admin. Reform, for Special Zones of Structural Reform and for Regional Revitalization 2004–05; Chair. Deliberative Council on Political Ethics. *Address:* c/o Liberal-Democratic Party (Jiyu-Minshuto), 1-11-23, Nagata-cho, Chiyoda-ku, Tokyo 100-8910, Japan. *Telephone:* (3) 3581-6211. *E-mail:* info@jimin.jp. *Website:* www.jimin.jp/english/profile/members/114716.html.

MURAKAMI, Takashi, MA, PhD; Japanese artist and designer; b. 1963, Tokyo; ed Univ. of Fine Arts, Tokyo; trained in classical Nihon-gah style of Japanese traditional painting; pop artist whose style fuses historic Japanese painting with contemporary cartoons; made debut as modern artist with solo exhbn Takashi, Tamiya 1991; invited to participate in PS1 Int. Studio Program on Rockefeller Foundation Asian Cultural Council fellowship grant, NY 1994; f. Hirpon Factory (Kaikai Kiki—production studio) Asaka City, Saitama 1994; Guest Prof., Dept of Art, UCLA, Calif. 1998; worked for French fashion house Louis Vuitton (LV) and cr. LV 'Murakami bag' 2003; his recurring character, Mr DOB, appears on t-shirts, posters, key-chains and mugs worldwide; work has been exhibited in Asia, America and Europe; curator Super Flat exhbn (showcase of contemporary Japanese artists), Little Boy exhbn; directed artwork for Kanye West's album, Graduation, 2007; has participated in numerous group exhbns in Japan, Korea, USA, Italy, Denmark, Norway, Sweden, Finland, Austria, Australia, France, New Caledonia, Philippines 1991–. *Solo Exhibitions include:* Gallery Ginza Surugadai, Tokyo 1989, Art Gallery at Tokyo Nat. Univ. of Fine Arts and Music 1991, Aoi Gallery, Osaka 1991, Rontgen Kunst Inst. 1992, Nasubi Gallery, Tokyo 1993, Gallery Koto, Okayama 1994, Emmanuel Perrotin, Paris (France) 1995, Yngtingagatan, Stockholm (Sweden) 1995, Feature Inc., NY 1996, Gavin Brown Enterprize, NY 1996, Ginza Komatsu, Tokyo 1996, Univ. of Buffalo Art Gallery, NY 1997, Blum & Poe, Santa Monica, CA 1998, Tomio Koyama Gallery, Tokyo 1998, Marianne Boesky Gallery, NY 1999, Bard Coll. Museum of Art 1999, Issey Miyake Men, Aoyama, Tokyo 2000, Grand Cen. Terminal, NY 2001, Museum of Fine Arts, Boston, 2001, Galerie Emmanuel Perrotin, Paris 2001, Museum of Contemporary Art, Tokyo 2001, Cartier Foundation, Paris 2002, Pacifico Yokohama Exhibition Hall 2003, 2004, Museum of Contemporary Art, Los Angeles 2007, Brooklyn Museum, NY 2008. *Address:* c/o Kaikai Kiki New York, 5–17 46th Road, Long Island City, NY 11101, USA (office). *Telephone:* (718) 706-2213 (office). *Fax:* (718) 706-2218 (office). *E-mail:* info@kaikaikikiny.net (office). *Website:* english.kaikaikiki.co.jp (office).

MURALITHARAN, Muttiah; Sri Lankan fmr professional cricketer; b. 17 April 1972, Kandy; s. of Muttiah Sinnasamy; ed St Anthony's Coll., Kandy; right-arm off-break bowler, lower-order right-hand batsman; teams: Tamil Union Cricket and Athletic Club 1991–, Sri Lanka 1992–, Lancs. 1999, 2001, 2005, 2007, Kent 2003, Chennai Super Kings 2008–10, Victorian Bushrangers 2009–, Kochi Tuskers Kerala 2011, Glos. 2011–, Wellington Firebirds 2011, Royal Challengers Bangalore 2012–, Melbourne Renegades 2012–; First-class debut: 1989/90; Test debut: Sri Lanka v Australia, Colombo (RPS) 28 Aug.–2 Sept. 1992; One-Day Int. (ODI) debut: Sri Lanka v India, Colombo (RPS) 12 Aug. 1993; T20I debut: NZ v Sri Lanka, Wellington 22 Dec. 2006; played in 133 Tests, scored 1,261 runs (highest score 67) and taken 800 wickets (average 22.72), best bowling (innings) 9/51, (match) 16/220; ODIs: 350 matches, 534 wickets (average 23.08), best bowling 7/30; First-class: 232 matches, 1,374 wickets (average 19.64), best bowling (innings) 9/51, (match) 16/220; numerous records, including quickest and youngest player to reach 400 Test wickets (in 72 matches) and 500 Test wickets (in 87 matches); world's highest wicket-taker 2000, 2001; became highest wicket-taker in Test cricket when he surpassed Courtney Walsh's 519 wickets in 2004, overtook Shane Warne's 708 wickets 3 Dec. 2007; first player to take 800 Test wickets, against India, Galle 22 July 2010, announced retirement from Test cricket; most ODI wickets (534); announced retirement from int. cricket following defeat by India in Cricket World Cup final, Mumbai 2 April 2011; has stated his surname should be romanized as 'Muralidaran'; Wisden Cricketer of the Year 1999, CEAT Int. Cricketer of the Year 2000, rated Best Ever Test Bowler by Wisden Dec. 2002. *Address:* c/o Sri Lanka Cricket, A.P.B. Tennekoon, 35 Maitland Place, Colombo 7, Sri Lanka. *Telephone:* (1) 691439. *E-mail:* cricket@sri.lanka.net; info@ srilankacricket.lk. *Website:* www.srilankacricket.lk.

MURALITHARAN, Vinayagamoorthy, (ColKaruna Amman); Sri Lankan politician and fmr rebel leader; *Deputy Minister of Resettlement;* b. 7 Nov. 1966, Kiran, Batticaloa Dist; m. Vidyawathi Muralitharan; one s. two d.; ed Central Coll. of Batticaloa; selected for Medical Faculty of Eastern Univ. of Sri Lanka; joined Liberation Tigers of Tamil Eelam 1983, commdr in charge of Batticaloa and Amparai Dists, Eastern Prov. 1987–2004; Founder and Leader, Tamil Makkal Viduthalai Pulikal breakaway group after defection to govt 2004 (recognized as political party 2007); apptd mem. Parl. for United People's Freedom Alliance (UPFA) 2008–; Minister of Nat. Integration 2009–10; Deputy Minister of Resettlement 2010–; Award from Mass Communicators Asscn of Sri Lanka for his special involvement in bringing peace to Sri Lanka. *Leisure interests:* listening to music, playing the guitar, playing football, reading and studying law-related books, cooking, hanging around in his home town with the people. *Address:* Ministry of Resettlement, 189 Galle Road, Colombo 03, Sri Lanka (home). *Telephone:* (11) 2585857 (office); (77) 3667457 (mobile); (11) 2395273 (office). *Fax:* (11) 2395276 (office). *E-mail:* muraliv25@yahoo.com (office); ministryofresettlement@gmail.com (office); resettlementmin@yahoo.com (office). *Website:* www.resettlementmin.gov.lk (office).

MURALIYEV, Amangeldy Mursadykovich; Kyrgyzstani politician; b. 7 Aug. 1947, Kum-Aryk; ed Frunze (Bishkek) Polytechnical Inst., USSR Govt Acad. of Nat. Econ.; engineer, Frunze (Bishkek) factories 1970–80; Dir heavy machine construction factory 1980–82, Kyrgizavtomash factory 1982–88; Chair., Frunze City Council (Mayor) 1988–91; Chair. State Cttee on Economy, State Sec. 1991–92; Min. Chair. Fund of State Property 1994–96; Deputy Prime Minister 1996; Gov. Osh Oblast 1996–99; Prime Minister 1999–2000; Minister of Econ. Devt, Industry and Trade (acting) 2004–06; First Deputy Prime Minister 2010; Co-ordinator Political Bd Union Party of Kyrgyzstan 2001–; Pres. Kyrgyzstan Stock Exchange 2001–04; Chair. Kyrgyz Altyn (gold co.) 2010–; mem. Kyrgyzstan Eng Acad.; Hon. Pres. Kyrgyzstan Football Fed. 1991–2008. *Address:* c/o Office of the Government, 720003 Bishkek, Dom Pravitelstva, Kyrgyzstan.

MURANO, Elsa Alina, BSc, MSc, DrSc; American food scientist, academic, university administrator and fmr government official; *Professor of Nutrition and Food Science, Texas A&M University;* b. (Elsa Casales), 14 Aug. 1959, Havana, Cuba; m. Dr Peter S. Murano; ed Miami Dade Coll., Florida Int. Univ., Virginia Tech Univ.; Asst Prof., Dept of Microbiology, Immunology and Preventative Medicine, Iowa State Univ. 1990–95; Assoc. Prof., Dept of Animal Science, Texas A&M Univ. 1995–97, becoming Sadie Hatfield Prof. in Agric., also Assoc. Dir Center for Food Safety, Inst. for Food Science and Eng 1995–97, Dir 1997–2001, Vice-Chancellor and Dean Coll. of Agric. and Life Sciences 2005–07, also Dir Tex. Agricultural Experiment Station (now Tex. AgriLife Research) 2005–07, Pres. Texas A&M Univ. 2008–09 (resgnd), Pres. Emer. and Prof. of Nutrition and Food Science 2009–; US Under-Sec. of Agric. for Food Safety, Washington, DC 2001–04. *Publications:* author or co-author of seven books, book chapters and monographs, numerous scholarly papers, abstracts and related materials. *Address:* Texas A&M University, Department of Nutrition & Food Science, 2254 TAMU, College Station, TX 77843-2254, USA (office). *Telephone:* (979) 845-0834 (office). *Fax:* (979) 845-5027 (office). *E-mail:* eamurano@tamu.edu (office). *Website:* nfs.tamu.edu (office).

MURAOKA, Takamitsu, PhD, FAHA; Japanese academic; *Professor Emeritus of Hebrew, University of Leiden;* b. 9 Feb. 1938, Hiroshima; s. of Yoshie Muraoka and Sachi Muraoka; m. Keiko Kageyama 1965; two s. one d.; ed Tokyo Kyoiku, The Hebrew Univ., Jerusalem; Lecturer in Semitic Languages, Dept of Near Eastern Studies, Univ. of Manchester, UK 1970–80; Prof. of Middle Eastern Studies, Chair. Dept, Melbourne Univ. 1980–91; Prof. of Hebrew, Univ. of Leiden 1991–2003, Prof. Emer. 2003–; Ed. Abr-Nahrain (Leiden) 1980–92; Visiting Prof., Univ. of Göttingen, Germany 2001–02; Research Fellow, Netherlands Inst. of Near Eastern Studies 2004–06; Assoc. Research Fellow, Kirchliche Hochschule, Wuppertal, Germany 2011–; Hon. Prof. in Semitic Languages, Presbyterian Coll. and Theological Seminary, Seoul 2006–07; Hon. Fellow, Acad. of the Hebrew Language 2006–; Alexander von Humboldt Research Award 2001–02. *Publications:* A Greek-Hebrew/Aramaic Index to I Esdras 1982, Emphatic Words and Structures in Biblical Hebrew 1985, Classical Syriac for Hebraists 1987, A Grammar of Biblical Hebrew (with P. Joüon) 1991, 2006, Studies in Qumran Aramaic (ed.) 1992, A Greek-English Lexicon of the Septuagint (Twelve Prophets) 1993, Studies on the Hebrew of the Dead Sea Scrolls and Ben Sira (co-ed.) 1997, A Grammar of Egyptian Aramaic (with B. Porten) 1998, 2003, Classical Syriac – A Basic Grammar with a Chrestomathy 1997, 2005, Hebrew/Aramaic Index to the Septuagint Keyed to the Hatch-Redpath Concordance 1998, A Greek-English Lexicon of the Septuagint – Chiefly of the Pentateuch and the Twelve Prophets 2002, A Greek-English Lexicon of the Septuagint 2009, A Greek-Hebrew/Aramaic Two-way Index to the Septuagint 2010, A Grammar of Qumran Aramaic 2011. *Leisure interest:* angling. *Address:* Wijttenbachweg 57, 2343 XW Oegstgeest, Netherlands.

MURATA, Ryohei, LLB; Japanese diplomatist; b. 2 Nov. 1929, Kyoto; s. of Tahei Murata and Yoshiko Murata; m. Reiko Akama 1958; one d.; ed Kyoto Univ.; joined Ministry of Foreign Affairs 1952; Deputy Dir-Gen. Middle Eastern and African Affairs Bureau 1974–76, Treaties Bureau 1976–78; Amb. to UAE 1978–80; Dir-Gen. Middle Eastern and African Affairs Bureau 1980–82, Econ. Affairs Bureau 1982–84; Amb. to Austria 1985–87; Deputy Minister for Foreign Affairs 1987, Vice-Minister 1987–89; Amb. to USA 1989–91, to Germany 1992–94; Adviser to the Foreign Minister 1994–2002, to Sanwa Bank and to Hotel Okura 1995–2001, to The Nippon Foundation 2000–. *Publications:* Between Friends 1985, OECD 2000, Ocean, World and Japan 2001, Why Has the Quality of the Foreign Ministry Deteriorated? 2002, Japanese Foreign Policy in Perspective 1952–2002 2003. *Leisure interest:* contract bridge. *Address:* The Nippon Foundation, 1-2-2, Akasaka, Minato-ku, Tokyo (office); No. 1003 Sakaimachi-Nishiki, 514 Kikuyacho, Nakagyo-ku, Kyoto 604-8127, Japan (home). *Telephone:* (3) 6229-5209 (office); (75) 212-4807 (home). *Fax:* (3) 6229-5120 (office); (75) 212-4807 (home). *E-mail:* r_murata@ps.nippon-foundation.or.jp (office).

MURATA, Yoshitaka; Japanese politician and government official; b. 30 July 1944, Shizuoka City; ed Univ. of Tokyo for Foreign Studies, Kyoto Univ., Univ. of Grenoble and Ecole Nat. d'Admin, France; joined Ministry of Finance 1968, seconded as Sec., Embassy in Beijing, People's Repub. of China 1974–76, Sec. to Minister of Labour 1978; Dir Office of Public Relations 1985–88, Dir Local Taxation Agency in Capital Area 1986–87, Dir Research Div., Int. Finance Bureau 1987–89; elected to House of Reps for Okayama Constituency 1990–; various positions in House include Dir Cttee on Rules and Admin, Cttee on Transport, Cttee on Finance and Monetary Affairs, Cttee on Audit and Oversight of Admin, Chair. Standing Cttee on Economy, Trade and Industry 1990–2004; various positions in Cabinet include Parl. Sec. of Econ. Planning, of Finance and of Monetary Affairs Agency 1990–2004; Chair. of Nat. Public Safety Comm. and Minister of State for Disaster Man. and for Nat. Emergency Legislation 2004–05; fmr Deputy Sec.-Gen. and Dir of Transportation Div., Policy Research Council, Liberal Democratic Party (LDP). *Address:* c/o Liberal-Democratic Party–LDP (Jiyu-Minshuto), 1-11-23, Nagata-cho, Chiyoda-ku, Tokyo 100-8910, Japan (office).

MURAYAMA, Tomiichi; Japanese politician (retd); b. 3 March 1924, Oita Pref.; m. Yoshie Murayama; two d.; ed School of Political Science and Econs, Meiji Univ.; fmr sec. of a trade union of Oita Pref. Govt employees; entered local govt 1955; mem. Japanese Socialist Party (JSP), now Social Democratic Party of Japan (SDPJ), renamed Democratic League 1995, renamed Shakai Minshuto (Social Democratic Party); Chair. Oita Pref. of JSP, Chair. Diet Affairs Cttee 1991–93, Chair. SDPJ 1993–96; mem. House of Reps 1972–2000; Prime Minister of Japan 1994–96; mem. House's Cttee on Social and Labour Affairs; retd from politics 2000; Grand Cordon of the Order of the Paulownia Flowers 2006. *Publications:* several books on social and labour affairs. *Leisure interest:* drama appreciation. *Address:* Social Democratic Party, 2-4-3, 7F Nagatacho Building, Nagata-cho, Chiyoda-ku, Tokyo 100-0014 (office); 3-2-2 Chiyomachi, Oita, Oita 870, Japan (home). *Telephone:* (3) 3580-1171 (office); (975) 32-0033 (home). *Fax:* (3) 3580-0691. *E-mail:* sdpjmail@omnics.co.jp (office). *Website:* www.omnics.co.jp (office).

MURCH, Walter; American film editor and sound designer; b. 12 July 1943, New York City; m. Muriel Murch; two c.; ed Johns Hopkins Univ., Univ. of Southern California; worked with George Lucas, Francis Ford Coppola and Anthony Minghella as film ed. and sound designer; Acad. Award for Best Sound (Apocalypse Now), BAFTA Award and two Acad. Awards (The English Patient). *Films include:* The Godfather (sound-effects ed.) 1972, American Graffiti (sound designer) 1973, The Godfather, Part II (sound designer) 1974, The Conversation (ed. and sound designer) 1974, Julia (ed.) 1977, Apocalypse Now (and sound designer) 1979, Return to Oz (Dir) 1985, The Unbearable Lightness of Being (ed.) 1988, The English Patient (ed. and sound mixer) 1996, The Talented Mr Ripley (ed.) 1999, K-19: Widowmaker (sound and ed.) 2002, Cold Mountain (sound and ed.) 2003. *Publication:* In the Blink of an Eye: A Perspective on Film Editing (with Francis Ford Coppola q.v.) 1995.

MURDOCH, Elisabeth, BA; British media executive; *Chair and CEO, Shine Ltd;* b. 22 Aug. 1968; d. of Rupert Murdoch (q.v.) and Anna Maria Murdoch (née Torv); m. 1st Elkin Kwesi Pianim (divorced); two d.; m. 2nd Matthew Freud 2001; one d.; ed Vassar Coll., Poughkeepsie, New York; presentation and promotions asst, Nine Network Australia 1990–91, researcher and producer 1991–93, Man. of Programming and Promotion Fox TV LA 1993, Programme Dir KSTU Fox 13 Salt Lake City 1993–94, Dir of Programme Acquisitions FX Cable Network LA 1994–95, Pres., CEO, EP Communications 1995–96 (Peabody Award for Broadcast Excellence 1995); Gen. Man. Broadcasting Dept, BSkyB Ltd 1996, Dir of Programming 1996–98, Man. Dir Sky Networks 1998–2000; Dir Future Publishing 2000–; Co-Founder Shine Ltd 2001, Chair. and CEO 2001–. *Address:* Shine Ltd, Primrose Studios, 109 Regent's Park Road, London, NW1 8UR, England (office). *Telephone:* (20) 7985-7013 (office). *Fax:* (20) 7985-7191 (office). *E-mail:* nichola.kemp@ shinelimited.com (office). *Website:* www.shinelimited.com (office).

MURDOCH, James Rupert Jacob; British/American media executive; *Deputy Chief Operating Officer, Chairman and CEO, International, 21st Century Fox;* b. 13 Dec. 1972, Wimbledon, London, England; s. of Rupert Murdoch (q.v.) and Anna Maria Torv; m. Kathryn Hufschmid 2000; one s. one d.; ed Horace Mann High School, New York, Harvard Univ.; f. record label Rawkus Entertainment 1995; joined News Corpn 1996, Pres. News Digital Media 1997–99, Exec. Vice-Pres. News Corpn 1999–, mem. Exec. Cttee News Digital systems; CEO and Chair. Star TV 2000–03; Dir (non-exec.) BSkyB 2003, CEO 2003–07, Chair. (non-exec.) 2007–12 (resgnd); Chair. and CEO Europe and Asia, News Corporation 2007–, Deputy COO 2011–13 (co. restructured with News Corporation's publishing assets spun off into similarly named News Corp while existing News Corporation renamed 21st Century Fox and its legal successor 2013), Deputy COO and Chair. and CEO, International, 21st Century Fox 2013–; Exec. Chair. News International 2009–12 (resgnd), Dir, News Group Newspapers Ltd –2011, News International Holdings –2011; mem. Bd of Dirs GlaxoSmithKline 2009–12, Sotheby's 2010–12, YankeeNets, Inner City Scholarship Fund, Jump Start, Harvard Lampoon Trustees. *Leisure interests:* reading, painting. *Address:* 21st Century Fox, 1211 Avenue of the Americas, New York, NY 10036, USA (office). *Telephone:* (212) 852-7000 (office). *Fax:* (212) 852-7145 (office). *Website:* www.21cf.com (office).

MURDOCH, Lachlan Keith, BA; American (b. British) media executive; *Executive Chairman, Illyria Pty Ltd;* b. 8 Sept. 1971, London, England; s. of Rupert Murdoch (q.v.) and Anna Maria Murdoch Mann; m. Sarah O'Hare 1999; two s. one d.; ed Trinity School, Manhattan, Aspen Country Day School, Andover, Mass, Princeton Univ.; with News Corporation 1994–2005, mem. Bd of Dirs 1996–, Publr The Australian 1995, Gen. Man. Queensland Newspapers Ltd 1994–95, Sr Exec. Vice-Pres. 1999–2000, Head of US Print Operations 1999–2005, Deputy COO News Corporation 2000–05, Publr New York Post 2002–05, Deputy CEO News Limited 1995–97, Chair. and CEO 1997–2008; Dir Beijing PDN Xinren Information Technology Co. Ltd (People's Repub. of China) 1995; Deputy Chair. Star TV Ltd 1995–; Exec. Chair. Illyria Pty Ltd 2005–; Acting CEO Ten Network Holdings Ltd Feb.–April 2011, Chair. 2012–; Exec. Chair. DMG Radio Australia 2009–; Deputy Chair. Prime Media Group Ltd Oct.–Nov. 2010; Dir, Queensland Press Ltd 1994–, Foxtel Management Pty Ltd 1995– (Exec. Dir 1998–), Beijing PDN Xiren Information Technology Co. Ltd 1996–, The Herald & Weekly Times Ltd 1996–, OneTel Ltd 1999–, Sky Global Networks Inc. 2000–, The Partnership for New York City, Inc., NYC2012, Inc., OmniSky Corpn 2000–, Rovi Guides, Inc. (alternatively Gemstar-TV Guide International Inc.) 2001–04, New Newscorp LLC 2013–; Dir (non-exec.) NDS Group Ltd 2002–05; mem. Bd Robin Hood Foundation, New York 1999–; Cannes Lions Media Person of the Year 2005. *Leisure interest:* rock climbing. *Address:* Illyria Pty Ltd, 33 Nickson Street, Surry Hills, NSW 2010, Australia (office). *Telephone:* (2) 9690-4611 (office). *Fax:* (2) 9690-4699 (office). *E-mail:* info@illyria.com.au (office). *Website:* www.illyria.com.au (office).

MURDOCH, (Keith) Rupert, AC; American (b. Australian) publisher, broadcaster and media business developer; *Executive Chairman, News Corp;* b. 11 March 1931, Melbourne, Vic., Australia; s. of the late Sir Keith Murdoch and of Dame Elisabeth Murdoch; m. 1st Patricia Booker (divorced); one d.; m. 2nd Anna Maria Torv 1967 (divorced); two s. one d.; m. 3rd Wendi Deng 1999 (divorced 2013); two d.; ed Geelong Grammar School, Vic., Worcester Coll., Oxford, UK; inherited Adelaide News 1954; built up News Corporation (Group CEO (prior to co.'s separation into two publicly traded cos in 2013) 1979–2013, Chair. 1991–2013 (co. restructured with News Corporation's publishing assets spun off into similarly named News Corp while existing News Corporation renamed 21st Century Fox and its legal successor 2013), Exec. Chair. News Corp 2013–, Chair. and CEO 21st Century Fox 2013–); has acquired newspapers, broadcasting and other interests in Australia, UK, USA, Latin America, Europe and Asia, including: Australia – newspapers: The Australian (nat.), Daily Telegraph, Sunday Telegraph, Daily Mirror (Sydney), Sunday Sun (Brisbane), The News and Sunday Mail (Adelaide), The Sunday Times (Perth); USA– New York Post; UK– newspapers: Sun, News of the World (nat., acquired 1969); acquired Times Newspapers Ltd 1981, group includes The Times, The Sunday Times, The Times Literary Supplement, The Times Educational Supplement, The Times Higher Education Supplement; Dir, Times Newspapers Holdings 1981–2012 (Chair. 1982–90, 1994–2012), News International Group Ltd –2012; magazines: Weekly Standard (US politics); film: Fox Film Entertainment; TV: British Sky Broadcasting (UK), STAR (Asia), Fox Broadcasting Co., Fox Cable Networks; other interests include lifestyle portal MySpace.com, book publr HarperCollins and ownership of 35 US TV stations; Chair. and CEO Fox Entertainment Group 1992–; mem. Bd of Dirs Associated Press 2008–; Commdr of the White Rose (First Class) 1985, Kt, Order of St Gregory the Great 1998; ranked by Forbes magazine amongst The World's Most Powerful People (seventh) 2009, (13th) 2010, (24th) 2011, (26th) 2012, (33rd) 2013. *Leisure interests:* sailing, skiing. *Address:* News Corp, 1211 Avenue of the Americas, New York, NY 10036, USA (office); News Corp Australia, 2 Holt Street, Surry Hills, Sydney, NSW 2010, Australia (office). *Telephone:* (212) 852-7017 (New York) (office); (2) 9288-3000 (Sydney) (office). *Fax:* (212) 852-7145 (New York) (office); (2) 9288-3292 (Sydney) (office). *Website:* newscorp.com (office).

MURDOCH, Tom; I-Kiribati politician; *Minister of Finance and Economic Development;* mem. Maneaba Ni Maungatabu (House of Ass.) for Kuria; Minister of Finance and Economic Devt 2012–. *Address:* Ministry of Finance and Economic Development, POB 67, Bairiki, Tarawa 248 001, Kiribati (office). *Telephone:* 21801 (office). *Fax:* 21307 (office). *E-mail:* account@mfep.gov.ki (office). *Website:* www .mfep.gov.ki (office).

MURDOCH, Wendi Deng; American (b. Chinese) media executive; b. (Deng Wenge), 1968, Xuzhou, Jiangsu Prov.; m. 1st Jake Cherry (divorced); m. 2nd Rupert Murdoch 1999 (divorced 2013); two d.; ed California State Univ., Northridge, Yale Univ.; began career with internship at Star TV (subsidiary of News Corpn) Hong Kong, eventually becoming Vice-Pres.; Chief of Strategy, MySpace China (social networking website) 2007–11; Co-CEO Big Feet Productions (film production co.), Los Angeles 2008–; mem. Bd of Advisors, Yale School of Man., Fund for Public Schools (New York), Art.sy, AdChina, Myspace China. *Film:* Snow Flower and the Secret Fan (co-producer).

MURERWA, Herbert; Zimbabwean politician; *Minister of Lands and Rural Resettlement;* m.; mem. Zimbabwe African Nat. Union-Patriotic Front (ZANU-PF); High Commr to UK 1984–1990; Minister of Environment and Tourism 1990–95, of Industry and Commerce 1995–96, of Finance and Econ. Devt 1996–2000, 2002, of Higher Educ. and Tech. 2000–01, of Int. Trade and Tech. 2001–02; Minister of Higher Educ. and Tech. and Acting Minister of Finance and Econ. Devt –2005, Minister of Finance and Econ. Devt 2005–07, of Lands and Rural Resettlement 2009–. *Address:* c/o 321 Ard-na-lea Close, Glen Lorne, Chisepiti, Harare, Zimbabwe.

MUREŞAN, HE Cardinal Lucian; Romanian ecclesiastic; *Major Archbishop of Făgăraş şi Alba Iulia (Romanian);* b. 23 May 1931, Firiza (now the Ferneziu dist of Baia Mare); s. of Peter Mureşan and Maria Mureşan; ordained priest, Diocese of Maramureş 1964, Bishop of Maramureş 1990–94; Archbishop of Făgăraş şi Alba Iulia 1994–2005, Major Archbishop of Făgăraş şi Alba Iulia 2005–; Head of the Romanian Church United with Rome, Greek-Catholic; cr. Cardinal (non-voting) (Cardinal-Priest of Sant'Atanasio) 2012. *Address:* Archdiocese of Făgăraş şi Alba Iulia, Str. Petru Pavel Aron 2, 515400 Blaj AB, Romania (office). *Telephone:* (258) 712057 (office); (258) 710608 (office). *Fax:* (258) 713602 (office). *E-mail:* mitropolia@bru.ro (office). *Website:* www.bru.ro/blaj (office).

MURIGANDE, Charles, PhD; Rwandan politician and diplomatist; *Ambassador to Japan;* b. 15 Aug. 1958, Butare; ed Facultés Universitaires Notre Dame de la Paix, Namur; Scientific Adviser to Dir-Gen., Geographical Inst. of Burundi 1986–88, also Head of Computing Center, Geographical Inst. of Burundi 1986–88; Post-doctoral Fellow, Howard Univ., Washington, DC, USA 1989, later Asst Prof. and Head of Biostatistical Div., Coll. of Medicine; Spokesperson, Rwandan Patriotic Front USA; Adviser to Pres. on Foreign Affairs 1994–95; Minister of Transport and Communications 1995–97; Rector, Nat. Univ. of Rwanda 1997–98; Gen.-Sec. Rwandese Patriotic Front (RPF) 1998–2002; Minister of Foreign Affairs and Regional Co-operation 2002–08, for Cabinet Affairs 2008–09, of Education 2009–11; Amb. to Japan (also accred as High Commr to New Zealand) 2011–. *Address:* Embassy of Rwanda, Annex Fukazawa, 1-17-17, Fukazawa, Setagaya-ku, Tokyo, 158-0081, Japan (office). *Telephone:* (3) 5752-4255 (office). *Fax:* (3) 3703-0342 (office). *Website:* www.rwandaembassy-japan.org (office).

MURILLO JORGE, Marino Alberto, BEcons; Cuban politician; *Chairman, Economic Policy Commission;* ed Coll. of Nat. Defence; fmr Dir of Audits and Econs, Ministry of Food; fmr Vice-Minister of Econs and Planning –2009; Minister for Internal Trade; Minister of Economy and Planning 2009–11, Vice-Pres. Council of Ministers 2009–; Chair. Economic Policy Comm. 2011–; mem Partido Comunista de Cuba. *Address:* c/o Ministry of Economy and Planning, 20 de Mayo, entre Territorial y Ayestarán, Plaza de la Revolución, Havana, Cuba (office).

MURKOWSKI, Frank Hughes, BA; American banker and fmr state official; b. 28 March 1933, Seattle, Wash.; s. of Frank Michael and Helen (Hughes) Murkowski; m. Nancy R. Gore 1954; two s. four d. including Lisa Murkowski; ed Ketchikan High School, Santa Clara Univ., Seattle Univ.; service with US Coast Guard 1955–57; with Pacific Nat. Bank of Seattle 1957–59, Nat. Bank of Alaska, Anchorage 1959–67, Vice-Pres. in Charge of Business Devt, Anchorage 1965–67; Commr, Dept of Econ. Devt, Alaska State, Juneau 1967–70; Pres. Alaska Nat. Bank of the North, Fairbanks 1971–80; Pres. Alaska State Chamber of Commerce 1977; Senator from Alaska 1981–2002, Chair. Cttee on Energy and Natural Resources 1995–2001; Gov. of Alaska 2002–07; Vice-Pres. Bd of Trade, BC (Canada) and Alaska; mem. American Bankers Asscn, Alaska Bankers Asscn (fmr Pres.); Republican. *Leisure interests:* hunting, fishing, skiing, tennis, golf. *Address:* c/o Office of the Governor, State Capitol, PO Box 110001, Juneau, Alaska 99811-0001, USA.

MURKOWSKI, Lisa, BA, LLB; American politician and lawyer; *Senator from Alaska;* d. of Frank Hughes Murkowski; m. Verne Martell; two s.; ed Georgetown Univ., Williamette Coll. of Law; worked in pvt. law practice for eight years; served as Anchorage Dist Court Attorney for two years; elected to Alaska State House of Reps 1998, 2000, 2002, served as House Majority Leader 2003; apptd Senator from Alaska 2002–04, elected 2004–, apptd Deputy Whip and Chair. Class of New Senators, sr mem. Energy and Natural Resources Cttee, mem. Appropriations Cttee (Ranking Republican mem. Interior and Environment Sub-cttee), mem. Health, Educ., Labor and Pensions Cttee, sr mem. Indian Affairs Cttee; mem. Alaska Fed. of Republican Women, Midnight Sun Republican Women, Anchorage Republican Women's Club; Republican. *Leisure interests:* skiing, fishing, camping. *Address:* 709 Hart Senate Building, Washington, DC 20510 (office); 510 L Street, Suite 600, Anchorage, AK 99501, USA. *Telephone:* (202) 224-6665 (DC) (office); (907) 271-3735 (Anchorage) (office). *Fax:* (202) 224-5301 (DC) (office); (907) 276-4081 (Anchorage) (office). *Website:* murkowski.senate.gov (office).

MÜRNIECE, Linda; Latvian politician and fmr police officer; b. 28 Jan. 1970, Dobele; m. Raimonds Mürnieks; ed Jūrmala Secondary School No. 1, Univ. of Latvia; Insp., State Police 1992–93; Chief Insp. and Asst to Head, State Econ. Sovereignty Protection Dept, Security Police 1993–95; Chief Insp., Press Centre, Ministry of the Interior 1995–97; Head of Advertising, VEF Bank 1997–2001; New Era Party Project Man. May–July 2002; mem. Saeima 2002–, Deputy Chair. Defence and Internal Affairs Cttee 2002–, Deputy Chair. New Era Party Parl. Group March–Oct. 2004, Chair. Cttee on Supervising Prevention and Combating of Corruption, Contraband and Organized Crime 2004–; Sec. Nat. Security Cttee 2002–04; Parl. Sec., Ministry of the Interior 2002–04, Ministry of Defence Jan.–Dec. 2005; Minister of Defence Jan.–April 2006, of the Interior 2009–11 (resgnd). *Address:* c/o Ministry of the Interior, Ciekurkalna 1, līnija 1, korp. 2, Rīga, 1026, Latvia.

MUROFUSHI, Minoru (Jack), BA; Japanese business executive; ed Tokyo Univ.; joined C Itoh 1956, Gen. Man. Coal Dept, New York 1963–71, Vice-Pres. C Itoh (America) (now ITOCHU) 1971, mem. Bd 1985, Chief Exec. 1990–98, also Chair. Bd 1999, now Counselor; CEO Development Bank of Japan 2008–11; fmr Vice-Chair. Tokyo Chamber of Commerce and Industry; mem. Bd of Dirs HSBC Holdings 1992–2002; mem. Exec. Cttee, Trilateral Comm. Pacific Asia Group 1999–2000; mem. Competitiveness Comm. organized by Prime Minister Obuchi 2000–01.

MUROMACHI, Kaneo; Japanese banking executive; *President, Mitsubishi UFJ Environment Foundation;* Sr Man.-Dir Sanwa Bank 1997–99, Pres. 1999–2001, Pres. and CEO 2001–02; Sr Adviser to UFJ Bank (created by merger of Sanwa Bank and Tokai Bank) 2004; Chair. UFJ Holdings Inc. 2004–05 (acquired by Mitsubishi UFJ Financial Group, Inc.), now Hon. Advisor, Bank of Tokyo Mitsubishi UFJ; Special mem. The Tax Comm. 2002; Dir Inamori Foundation, Foundation for Advanced Studies on Int. Devt (FASTID) 2003–; Councillor, Grad. School of Int. Man., IUJ Business School, Japan; Pres. Mitsubishi UFJ Environment Foundation. *Address:* Mitsubishi UFJ Environment Foundation, 2-4-3 Tokyo-Mitsubishi UFJ Bank Shiba Building 2F, Shiba, Minato-ku, Tokyo 105-0014, Japan (office). *Telephone:* (3) 5730-0337 (office). *Fax:* (3) 5232-0312 (office). *Website:* www.bk.mufg.jp/global/csr/contribution/foundation/eco.html (office).

MURPHY, Catherine J., BS, PhD; American chemist and academic; *Peter C. and Gretchen Miller Markunas Professor of Chemistry, University of Illinois, Urbana-Champaign;* ed Univ. of Illinois, Urbana-Champaign, Univ. of Wisconsin; NSF Postdoctoral Fellow, California Inst. of Tech. 1990–92; NIH Postdoctoral Fellow 1993; Asst Prof., Dept of Chem. and Biochemistry, Univ. of South Carolina 1993–98, Assoc. Prof. 1998–2002, Prof. 2002–09, Guy F. Lipscomb Prof. of Chem. 2003–09; Peter C. and Gretchen Miller Markunas Prof. of Chem., Univ. of Illinois, Urbana-Champaign 2009–, Affiliate, Dept of Materials Science and Eng 2010–, Micro and Nanotechnology Lab. 2010–; Visiting Researcher, Dept of Chem., Univ. of Bristol, UK 2000; Harold McMaster Visiting Scientist, Coll. of Arts and Sciences, Bowling Green State Univ. 2010; Sr Ed. Journal of Physical Chemistry 2006–;

mem. Editorial Advisory Bd Journal of Inorganic Biochemistry 1996–2007, Journal of Cluster Science 1997–, Langmuir 2002–, Inorganic Chemistry 2004–06, Chemistry of Materials 2004–09, NanoLetters 2005–, Chemical Communications 2005–, Journal of Colloid and Interface Science 2006–08, ACS Nano 2007–, Nanoscale 2009–; Fellow, AAAS 2008; Merck Award in Biochemistry, Univ. of Illinois 1986, Bronze Tablet, Univ. of Illinois 1986, McElvain Scholar, Univ. of Wisconsin 1986–87, Wisconsin Alumni Research Foundation Fellow 1986–87, Summer Energy Research Fellow, Electrochemical Soc. 1989, W.R. Grace & Co. Fellow, Univ. of Wisconsin 1989–90, NSF CAREER Award 1995–98, Cottrell Scholar Award 1996–2001, Alfred P. Sloan Foundation Research Fellow 1997–99, Camille Dreyfus Teacher-Scholar Award 1998–2000, Golden Key Faculty Award for the Integration of Research and Undergraduate Teaching 1998, Michael J. Mungo Award for Excellence in Undergraduate Teaching, Univ. of South Carolina 2001, Outstanding Undergraduate Research Mentor Award, Univ. of South Carolina 2003, Russell Award for Research in Science, Math. and Eng, Univ. of South Carolina 2005, Nanotech Briefs Nano 50 Award, Innovator Category 2008, Kolthoff Lectureship in Chem., Univ. of Minnesota 2009. *Publications:* Nanoparticles and Nanostructured Surfaces: Novel Reporters with Biological Applications, Proceedings of SPIE, Vol. 4258 (ed.) 2001, Biomedical Nanotechnology Architectures and Applications, Progress in Biomedical Optics and Imaging: Proceedings of SPIE, Vol. 4626 (co-ed.) 2002, Chemistry: The Central Science (12th edn) (co-author) 2012; more than 150 scientific papers in professional journals. *Address:* Department of Chemistry, University of Illinois at Urbana-Champaign, A512 Chemical & Life Sciences Laboratory, 600 South Mathews Avenue, Mail Code 712, Box 59-6, Urbana, IL 61801, USA (office). *Telephone:* (217) 333-7680 (office). *Fax:* (217) 244-3186 (office). *E-mail:* murphycj@illinois.edu (office). *Website:* www .chemistry.illinois.edu/faculty/Catherine_Murphy.html (office); www.scs.illinois .edu/murphy (office).

MURPHY, Christopher (Chris) Scott; American politician; *Senator from Connecticut;* b. 3 Aug. 1973, White Plains, NY; s. of Scott L. Murphy and Catherine Murphy (née Lewczyk); m. Catherine Holahan; two c.; ed Wethersfield High School, Williams Coll., Univ. of Connecticut School of Law, Hartford, Exeter College, Coll., UK; interned for US Senator Chris Dodd; campaign manager for Charlotte Koskoff's campaign against Nancy Johnson 1996; worked for Connecticut State Senate Majority Leader George Jepsen 1997–98; elected to Planning and Zoning Comm., Southington 1997; mem. Connecticut House of Reps from 81st Dist 1999–2003; practised real estate and banking law 2002–06; mem. Connecticut Senate from 16th Dist 2003–07; mem. US House of Reps for 5th Congressional Dist of Conn. 2007–13, mem. Cttee on Foreign Affairs, Cttee on Oversight and Govt Reform; Senator from Connecticut 2013–; Democrat. *Address:* United States Senate, Washington, DC 20510, USA (office). *Telephone:* (202) 224-3121 (office). *Website:* www.senate.gov (office).

MURPHY, Dervla Mary; Irish author and critic; b. 28 Nov. 1931, Cappoquin; d. of Fergus Murphy and Kathleen Rochfort-Dowling; one d.; ed Ursuline Convent, Waterford; American Irish Foundation Literary Award 1975, Ewart-Biggs Memorial Prize 1978, Irish American Cultural Inst. Literary Award 1985. *Publications:* Full Tilt 1965, Tibetan Foothold 1966, The Waiting Land 1967, In Ethiopia with a Mule 1968, On a Shoestring to Coorg 1976, Where the Indus is Young 1977, A Place Apart 1978, Wheels Within Wheels 1979, Race to the Finish? 1981, Eight Feet in the Andes 1983, Muddling Through in Madagascar 1985, Ireland 1985, Tales from Two Cities 1987, Cameroon with Egbert 1989, Transylvania and Beyond 1992, The Ukimwi Road 1993, South from the Limpopo 1997, Visiting Rwanda 1998, One Foot in Laos 1999, Through the Embers of Chaos: Balkan Journeys 2002, Through Siberia by Accident 2005, Silverland: A Winter Journey Beyond the Urals 2006, The Island That Dared 2008, A Month by the Sea: Encounters in Gaza 2013, Other Encounters 2014. *Leisure interests:* reading, music, cycling, swimming, walking. *Address:* Lismore, Co. Waterford, Ireland.

MURPHY, Edward (Eddie) Regan; American comedian and actor; b. 3 April 1951, Brooklyn, New York; s. of Vernon Lynch (stepfather) and Lillian Lynch; m. 2nd Nicole Mitchell 1993 (divorced 2006); five c.; feature player in Saturday Night Live TV show 1980–84; film debut in 48 Hours 1982; tours with own comedy show; comedy albums: Eddie Murphy 1982, Eddie Murphy: Comedian 1983, How Could It Be 1984, So Happy 1989; has also released seven record albums of comedy and songs; f. Eddie Murphy Productions (production co.) 1996; recipient of numerous awards and nominations. *Films include:* 48 Hours 1982, Trading Places 1983, Delirious 1983, Best Defence 1984, Beverly Hills Cop 1984, The Golden Child 1986, Beverly Hills Cop II 1987, Eddie Murphy Raw 1987, Coming to America 1988, Harlem Nights 1989, 48 Hours 2 1990, Boomerang 1992, Distinguished Gentleman 1992, Beverly Hills Cop III 1994, The Nutty Professor 1996, Dr. Dolittle 1998, Holy Man 1998, Life 1998, Bowfinger 1999, Toddlers 1999, Pluto Nash 1999, Nutty Professor II: The Klumps 2000, Shrek 2001 (voice), Dr Dolittle 2 2001, Showtime 2002, I Spy 2002, Daddy Day Care 2003, Shrek 4–D 2003 (voice), Haunted Mansion 2003, Shrek 2 (voice) 2004, Dreamgirls (Golden Globe for Best Supporting Actor 2007, Screen Actors' Guild Award for Outstanding Performance by a Male Actor in a Supporting Role 2007) 2006, Norbit 2007, Shrek the Third (voice) 2007, Meet Dave 2008, Imagine That 2009, Shrek Forever After (voice) 2010, Tower Heist 2011, A Thousand Words 2012. *Address:* Eddie Murphy Productions, 152 West 57th Street, 47th Floor, New York, NY 10019, USA. *Telephone:* (212) 399-9900.

MURPHY, Gerry, MBS, PhD, FInstD, CCMI; Irish business executive; b. 1955; m.; two s.; ed Univ. Coll. Cork, Univ. Coll. Dublin; fmrly with Grand Metropolitan PLC (now Diageo), Ireland, UK and USA 1978–91; CEO Greencore Group PLC, Dublin 1991–95, Exel PLC (fmrly NFC) 1995–2000, Carlton Communications PLC 2000–03, Kingfisher PLC 2003–08; Dir (non-exec.) Abbey Nat. 2004, Reckitt Benckiser 2005–. *Address:* c/o Kingfisher PLC, 3 Sheldon Square, London, W2 6PX, England (office).

MURPHY, Glenn K., BA; Canadian retail executive; *Chairman and CEO, Gap Inc.;* b. Montreal; ed Univ. of Western Ont.; began career with A.C. Nielsen; 14 years in category man., marketing, procurement and operations, Loblaw Cos Ltd, becoming Exec. Vice-Pres. Loblaws Supermarkets 1997–2000; Pres. and CEO Chapters Inc. 2000; Chair. and CEO Shoppers Drug Mart 2001–07; mem. Bd of Dirs Gap Inc. 2007–, Chair. and CEO 2007–. *Address:* Gap Inc., Two Folsom

Street, San Francisco, CA 94105, USA (office). *Telephone:* (650) 952-4400 (office). *Fax:* (415) 427-2553 (office). *Website:* www.gap.com (office).

MURPHY, Rt Hon. James (Jim) Francis; British politician; *Shadow Secretary of State for Defence;* b. 23 Aug. 1967, Glasgow, Scotland; m. Claire Murphy; two s. one d.; Pres. Nat. Union of Students, Scotland 1992–94, Nat. Union of Students, UK 1994–96; Dir Endsleigh Insurance 1994–96; Project Man. Scottish Labour Party 1996–97; MP for Eastwood constituency (now E Renfrewshire) 1997–, mem. Public Accounts Cttee 2000–01, Parl. Pvt. Sec. to Sec. of State for Scotland 2001–02, Govt whip 2002–05, Parl. Sec. at Cabinet Office 2005–06, Minister of State for Employment and Welfare Reform 2006–07, for Europe 2007–08; Sec. of State for Scotland 2008–10; Shadow Sec. of State for Scotland May–Oct. 2010, for Defence 2010–; Minister of the Year, awarded by the House Magazine following vote by MPs and Lords of all parties 2008. *Leisure interest:* supports Glasgow Celtic Football Club. *Address:* House of Commons, Westminster, London, SW1A 0AA, England (office); East Renfrewshire Parliamentary Office, Suite 4/5, 1 Spiersbridge Way, Thornliebank, G46 8NG, Scotland. *Telephone:* (20) 7219-4615 (London) (office); (141) 6206310 (Thornliebank). *Fax:* (20) 7219-5657 (London) (office); (141) 6206311 (Thornliebank). *E-mail:* jimmurphymp@parliament.uk (office). *Website:* www.parliament.uk/biographies/commons/jim-murphy/25192 (office); www.jimmurphymp.com (office); jimmurphymp.org.

MURPHY, John Michael; British artist; b. 7 Sept. 1945, St Albans; s. of James Murphy and Maureen (née Tarrant) Murphy; ed St Michael's Coll., Hitchin, Luton and Chelsea Schools of Art; has participated in several group exhbns in Britain, Europe and USA; Arts Council of GB Award 1980. *Address:* c/o Lisson Gallery, 52–54 Bell Street, London, NW1 5DA, England (office).

MURPHY, Kathleen A., BA, JD; American lawyer and financial services industry executive; *President, Fidelity Personal Investing, Fidelity Investments;* b. 27 Jan. 1963, Wallingford, Conn.; m. George Hornyak; one s.; ed Fairfield Univ., Univ. of Connecticut School of Law; with Aetna Financial Services 1985–2000, positions included Gen. Counsel and Chief Compliance Officer; with ING Groep NV (after acquisition of Aetna by ING) 2000–09, positions included Gen. Counsel and Chief Admin. Officer, ING US Financial Services, Group Pres. ING US Worksite and Institutional Financial Services, ING N America Insurance Corpn, Dir ING Canada Inc. 2006–08, ING Life Insurance and Annuity Co., ING USA Life Insurance and Annuity Co., ING US Foundation Bd, ING Insurance Co. of America, CEO ING US Wealth Man. 2007–09; Pres. Fidelity Personal Investing, Fidelity Investments 2009–; fmr Chair. Conn. Children's Trust Fund; mem. Bd of Dirs Nat. Conf. for Civil Justice in the Northeast, Conn. Business and Industry Asscn, Metro Hartford Alliance, American Benefits Council, Gov. of Conn.'s Prevention Partnership Program, America's Promise Alliance (also mem. Exec. Cttee), Univ. of Connecticut Foundation; Trustee, Wheeler Clinic, Boys & Girls Club of America; mem. Bd Michael Smurfit School of Business, Univ. Coll. Dublin, Ireland; ranked by Fortune magazine amongst the 50 Most Powerful Women in Business in the US (40th) 2007, (41st) 2008–09, (36th) 2010, (32nd) 2011–12, named by Irish America Magazine to their Wall Street 50 and Business 100 lists 2007, profiled by Fortune magazine as one of their Women of Power 2009, named by U.S. Banker magazine as one of the 25 Most Powerful Women in Banking 2008 and as one of the Top 25 Nonbank Women in Finance 2009. *Address:* Fidelity Investments, PO Box 770001, Cincinnati, OH 45277-0003, USA (office). *Website:* www.fidelity.com (office).

MURPHY, Rt Hon Paul Peter, PC, MA; British politician; *Vice-Chairman, British-Irish Parliamentary Assembly;* b. 25 Nov. 1948; s. of the late Ronald Murphy and Marjorie Murphy; ed Oriel Coll., Oxford; man. trainee Co-operative Wholesale Soc. 1970–71; Lecturer in History and Govt, Ebbw Vale Coll. of Further Educ. 1971–87; mem. Torfaen Borough Council 1973–87 (Chair. Finance Cttee 1976–86); Sec. Torfaen Constituency Labour Party 1974–87; MP for Torfaen 1987–; Opposition Front Bench Spokesman for Wales 1988–94, on NI 1994, on Foreign Affairs 1994–95, on Defence 1995–97; Minister of State, NI Office 1997–99; Sec. of State for Wales 1999–02, 2008–09, for NI 2002–05; Chair. Intelligence and Security Cttee 2005–07; Co-Chair. British-Irish Parl. Ass. 2006–07, 2009–10, Vice-Chair. 2010–; mem. Jt Cttee on Nat. Security Strategy 2010–; Hon. Fellow, Oriel Coll. Oxford, Glyndwr Univ., Wrexham; Kt of St Gregory 1997, Kt Commdr of the Constantinian Order of St George. *Leisure interest:* music. *Address:* House of Commons, London SW1A 0AA, England (office). *Telephone:* (20) 7219-3000 (office); (1495) 750078 (constituency office) (office). *Website:* www .parliament.uk (office).

MURPHY, Philip Dunton, AB, MBA; American business executive and fmr diplomatist; b. 16 Aug. 1957, Boston, Mass; m. Tammy Murphy; three s. one d.; ed Harvard Univ., The Wharton School, Univ. of Pennsylvania; spent 23 years at Goldman Sachs, headed Goldman Sachs' Frankfurt office, with oversight responsibility for activities in Germany, Switzerland and Austria, as well countries of Cen. Europe 1993–97, Pres. Goldman Sachs (Asia) 1997–99, held several sr positions before becoming a Sr Dir 2003–06 (retd); Dir Murphy Endeavors, LLC, Red Bank, NJ 2006–; Nat. Finance Chair. Democratic Nat. Cttee 2006–09; Amb. to Germany 2009–13; has served on bds and/or cttees of NAACP, Local Initiatives Support Corpn, Center for American Progress, 180 Turning Lives Around and several programmes of Univ. of Pennsylvania, amongst others; Co-chaired nat. task force on 21st century public educ.; chaired task force on public sector employee benefits in NJ; fmr mem. Bd US Soccer Foundation, US Soccer Fed. World Cup Bid Cttee. *Leisure interest:* soccer. *Address:* Murphy Endeavors, LLC, 21 East Front Street, Red Bank, NJ 07701 USA (office). *Telephone:* (732) 933-9988 (office).

MURPHY, Thomas (Tom); Irish playwright and theatre director; b. 23 Feb. 1935, Tuam, Co. Galway; s. of John (Jack) Murphy and Winifred Shaughnessy; m. Jane Brennan; ed Tuam Vocational School, Vocational Teachers' Training Coll., Dublin; metalwork teacher 1957–62; playwright and theatre Dir 1962–; Writer-in-Asscn Druid Theatre Co., Galway 1983–86, Abbey Theatre 1986–89; Tom Murphy at the Abbey (Irish Nat. Theatre), six-play season 2001; mem. Irish Acad. of Letters, Aosdána; Hon. DLitt (Trinity Coll., Dublin) 1998, (Nat. Univ. of Ireland, Galway) 2000; Irish Acad. of Letters Award 1972, Harveys Award 1983, 1985, Sunday Tribune Arts Award 1985, Independent Newspapers Award 1983, 1989, Drama-Logue Critics' Award 1995, Irish Times ESB Theatre Awards Special

Tribute 1997, 2000, Irish Times Theatre Award for Best Play 2005, Ulysses Medal, Univ. Coll. Dublin 2013. *Stage plays:* On the Outside 1959, A Whistle in the Dark 1961, A Crucial Week in the Life of a Grocer's Assistant 1966, The Orphans 1968, Famine 1968, The Morning After Optimism 1971, The White House 1972, The Vicar of Wakefield (adaptation) 1974, On the Inside 1974, The Sanctuary Lamp 1975, The J. Arthur Maginnis Story 1976, The Blue Macushla 1980, The Informer (adaptation) 1981, The Gigli Concert 1983, Conversations on a Homecoming 1985, Bailegangaire 1985, A Thief of a Christmas 1986, Too Late for Logic 1989, The Patriot Game 1991, She Stoops to Folly 1995, The Wake 1998, The House 2000, The Cherry Orchard 2003, The Drunkard 2003, Alice Trilogy 2005, The Last Days of a Reluctant Tyrant 2009. *Publication:* The Seduction of Morality (novel) 1994. *Leisure interests:* music, gardening. *Address:* c/o Alexandra Cann Representation, Box 116, 4 Montpelier Street, London, SW7 1EE, England (office). *Telephone:* 7796-954969 (mobile) (office). *E-mail:* alex@alexandracann.co.uk (office).

MURPHY, William P., Jr, MD; American physician, biomedical engineer and business executive; *CEO, Small Parts Inc.;* b. 1923, Boston, Mass; s. of William Parry Murphy; m.; ed Harvard Univ., Univ. of Ill. School of Medicine, MIT; cr. first invention, a residential snow blower, at high school; practised medicine at St Francis Hosp., Honolulu, Hawaii and Peter Bent Brigham Hosp., Boston; medical consultant to US Army during Korean War, cr. first dialysis machines for use during war and flexible sealed blood bags for transfusions with colleague Dr. Carl Walter; f. Medical Devt Corpn (renamed Cordis Corpn 1959) 1957, purchased by Johnson & Johnson 1996; cr. first motor-driven angiographic injectors, disposable vascular diagnostic catheters, hollow-fiber artificial kidneys, medical procedural trays, physiologic cardiac pacemakers, externally programmable and dual chamber demand pacemakers; f. Small Parts Inc. 1963, currently CEO; mem. Bd of Dirs Bioheart Inc.; co-founder and CEO Hyperion Inc., Miami 1986–2003; est. FIRST (Fore Inspiration and Recognition of Science and Tech.) 1989; Founding Fellow, American Soc. for Artificial Internal Organs and American Inst. for Medical and Biological Eng 1993; holds 17 US patents; numerous awards including Distinguished Service Award, Int. Soc. for Artificial Organs 1981, Distinguished Service Award, N American Soc. of Pacing and Electrophysiology 1985, Jay Malina Award, Beacon Council 2003, Lemelson-MIT Lifetime Achievement Award 2003. *Publications:* over 30 medical papers. *Leisure interests:* sailing his antique steampowered tugboat. *Address:* Small Parts, Inc, 13980 N.W. 58th Court, POB 4650, Miami Lakes, FL 33014-0650, USA (office). *Telephone:* (800) 220-4242. *E-mail:* parts@smallparts.com (office). *Website:* www.smallparts.com (office).

MURPHY-O'CONNOR, HE Cardinal Cormac, STL, PhL; British ecclesiastic; *Archbishop Emeritus of Westminster;* b. 24 Aug. 1932, Reading, Berks.; s. of the late Dr Patrick George Murphy-O'Connor and Ellen Theresa Cuddigan; ed Prior Park Coll., Bath, The Venerable English Coll., Rome and Gregorian Univ., Rome; ordained Priest 1956; Asst Priest, Corpus Christi Parish, Portsmouth 1956–63, Sacred Heart Parish, Fareham 1963–66; Pvt. Sec. Chaplain to Bishop of Portsmouth 1966–70; Parish Priest, Portswood, Southampton 1970–71; Rector Venerable English Coll., Rome 1971–77; Bishop of Arundel and Brighton 1977–2000; Archbishop of Westminster 2000–09, Archbishop Emer. 2009–; cr. Cardinal 2001; First Chair. Bishops' Cttee for Europe 1980–83; Jt Chair. Anglo-RC Int. Comm. 1983–2000; Chair. TVS Religious Advisers Panel 1985–90; Pres. Catholic Bishops' Conf. of England and Wales 2000– (Dept for Mission and Unity 1993–); Vice-Pres. Council of the Episcopal Confs of Europe 2001–; mem. Presidential Cttee of Pontifical Council for the Family 2001–, Congregation for Divine Worship and the Discipline of the Sacraments 2001–, Admin of Patrimony of the Holy See 2001–, Council for the Study of Org. and Econ. Problems of the Holy See 2001–, Pontifical Council for Culture 2002–, Pontifical Comm. for Cultural Heritage of the Church 2002–, Pontifical Council for Promoting Christian Unity 2002–, Congregation for Bishops 2009–, Congregation for Evangelization of Peoples 2009–; Hon. Bencher of the Inner Temple 2001, Freeman of the City of London 2001, Prior of British and Irish Del. of Constantinian Order 2002; Bailiff Grand Cross of Sovereign Mil. Order of Malta 2002; Hon. DD (Lambeth) 1999. *Publications:* The Family of the Church 1984, At the Heart of the World 2004. *Leisure interests:* music, walking, reading, sport. *Address:* 7 Dukes Avenue, Chiswick, London, W4 2AA, England (home). *Telephone:* (20) 8747-6922 (home). *Fax:* (20) 8742-1145 (office). *E-mail:* cardinal@rcdow.org.uk. *Website:* www.rcdow .org.uk (office).

MURR, Elias; Lebanese government official, lawyer and business executive; b. 1962, Bteghrin; s. of Michel Murr; m. Karine Lahoud 1992; three c.; fmr Ed.-in-Chief Al-Jumhouriyah newspaper; business interests in finance and real estate; Minister of the Interior 2000–04; Deputy Prime Minister and Minister of Nat. Defence 2005–11. *Address:* c/o Ministry of National Defence, Yarze, Beirut, Lebanon (office).

MURR, Muhammad Ahmad al-; United Arab Emirates editor and government official; *Speaker, Federal National Council;* b. 1955, Dubai; ed Syracuse Univ., USA; worked in the field of banking man. during 1980s; fmr Ed.-in-Chief, Khaleej Times (daily newspaper); fmr Exec. Ed.-in-Chief Al Bayan (Arabic daily newspaper); fmr Deputy Chair. Dubai Cultural Council (now Dubai Culture & Arts Authority); Founder-mem. Science and Culture Symposium, Dubai, Pres. 1987–2001; fmr Dir Emirates Media Inc.; apptd to 15th Chapter of Fed. Nat. Council (Parl.) as rep. of Dubai 2011, Speaker, Fed. Nat. Council 2011–; Emirates Appreciation Award in the field of Literature 2006. *Publications include:* numerous articles and essays, including weekly columns Awraq Al Ahad (Al Khaleej newspaper), Hadeeth Al Ethnain (Al Bayan newspaper) and Muntasaf Al Osbou (Al Reyada Wa Al Shabab magazine); around 15 collections of short stories, including Dubai Tales and The Wink of the Mona Lisa (published in English); other publs include The Wink of an Eye, Bleeding Heart, Two Neighbours, National Hopes, Wonders of the World, Kalam Al Nass: A Study of the Local Dialects, Emirates in Austrian Eyes, Around the World in 22 Days. *Address:* Office of the Speaker, Federal National Council, POB 836, Abu Dhabi, United Arab Emirates (office). *Telephone:* (2) 6812000 (office). *Fax:* (2) 6812846 (office). *E-mail:* fncuae@emirates.net.ae (office). *Website:* www.almajles.gov.ae (office).

MURRAY, Andrew (Andy) Barron, OBE; British professional tennis player; b. 15 May 1987, Dunblane, Scotland; s. of William Murray and Judy Murray (née Erskine); ed Dunblane High School, Schiller Int. School, Barcelona, Spain; righthanded (two-handed backhand); began playing tennis aged three; declined invitation to train with Rangers Football Club at their School of Excellence aged 15; moved to Barcelona to train on clay courts of Sánchez-Casal Acad. aged 15; won his first senior title at Glasgow Futures event 2003; won Jr US Open beating Sergiy Stakhovsky 2004; youngest Briton ever to play in Davis Cup 2005; turned professional 2005; played his first Asscn of Tennis Professionals (ATP) tournament with wild card to Open SEAT clay-court tournament, Barcelona 2005; advanced to doubles semifinal (with brother Jamie Murray) 2004; semifinalist, Jr Roland Garros 2005; achieved a top-10 ATP ranking for first time 16 April 2007; winner, San Jose 2006, 2007, St Petersburg 2007, 2008, ATP Masters Series: Madrid 2008, Cincinnati 2008, 2011; winner, Marseille 2008, Doha 2008, 2009, Valencia 2009, ATP World Tour Masters 1000: Canada 2009, 2010, Miami 2009, 2013, Rotterdam 2009, Aegon Championships, London Queen's Club 2009, 2011, 2013, Shanghai Masters 2010, 2011, Tokyo 2011, Bangkok 2011, Brisbane Int. Title 2012, 2013, finalist Shanghai Masters 2012; Grand Slam results: winner, US Open 2012, Wimbledon 2013, finalist, US Open 2008, Australian Open 2010, 2011, 2013, Wimbledon 2012, semifinalist, Wimbledon 2009, 2010, 2011, French Open 2011; other tournaments: semifinalist, ATP World Tour Finals 2008, 2010; US Open Series Champion 2010; competed at Olympic Games, Beijing 2008; won gold medal, Olympic Games, London 2012; two doubles titles (with brother Jamie), Valencia 2010, Tokyo 2011; coaches: Leon Smith 1998–2002, Emilio Sánchez 2002–05, Mark Petchey 2005–06, Brad Gilbert 2006–07, Miles Maclagan 2007–10, Alex Corretja 2010–11, Ivan Lendl 2012–14; bought Cromlix House Feb. 2013, opened as a 15-room five-star hotel April 2014; Freeman of the City of Stirling 2014; Hon. DUniv (Stirling) 2014; BBC Young Sports Personality of the Year 2004, twice named LTA's Young Player of the Year, Best ATP World Tour Match of the Year 2010, 2011, 2012, Laureus World Breakthrough of the Year Award 2013, Glenfiddich Spirit of Scotland Award for Top Scot 2013, Glenfiddich Spirit of Scotland Award for Sport 2013, BBC Sports Personality of the Year 2013, Award from Tennis Scotland 2014. *Address:* XIX Entertainment, 33 Ransomes Dock, 35–37 Parkgate Road, London, SW11 4NP, England (office). *E-mail:* info@xixentertainment.com (office). *Website:* www.andymurray.com

MURRAY, Bill; American actor and writer; b. 21 Sept. 1950, Evanston, Ill.; m. 1st Margaret Kelly 1980 (divorced 1996); four s.; m. 2nd Jennifer Butler 1997 (divorced 2008); ed Loyola Acad., Regis Coll., Second City Workshop, Chicago; performer off-Broadway Nat. Lampoon Radio Hour; appeared in radio series Marvel Comics' Fantastic Four; Emmy Award for best writing for comedy series 1977. *Films include:* Meatballs 1977, Mr Mike's Mondo Video 1979, Where the Buffalo Roam 1980, Caddyshack 1980, Stripes 1981, Tootsie 1982, Ghostbusters 1984, The Razor's Edge 1984, Nothing Lasts Forever 1984, Little Shop of Horrors 1986, Scrooged 1988, Ghostbusters II 1989, What About Bob? 1991, Mad Dog and Glory 1993, Groundhog Day 1993, Ed Wood 1994, Kingpin 1996, Larger Than Life 1996, Space Jam 1996, The Man Who Knew Too Little 1997, With Friends Like These 1998, Veeck as in Wreck 1998, Rushmore 1998, Wild Things 1998, The Cradle Will Rock 1999, Hamlet 1999, Company Man 1999, Charlie's Angels 2000, The Royal Tenenbaums 2001, Osmosis Jones 2001, Lost in Translation (Golden Globe, Best Actor Musical or Comedy 2004, BAFTA Award, Best Actor in a Leading Role) 2003, Coffee and Cigarettes 2003, Garfield: The Movie (voice) 2004, The Life Aquatic with Steve Zissou 2004, Broken Flowers 2005, The Lost City 2005, Garfield 2 (voice) 2006, The Darjeeling Limited 2007, Get Smart 2008, City of Ember 2008, The Limits of Control 2009, Fantastic Mr Fox (voice) 2009, Get Low 2009, Moonrise Kingdom 2012, Hyde Park on Hudson 2012, A Glimpse Inside the Mind of Charles Swan III 2012, The Monuments Men 2014, The Grand Budapest Hotel 2014; co-producer, dir, actor film Quick Change 1990. *Television:* writer and regular appearances TV series Saturday Night Live 1977–80; Olive Kitteridge (mini-series) 2014. *Publications:* Cinderella Story: My Life in Golf 1999. *Leisure interest:* golf. *Address:* c/o Jessica Tuchinsky, Creative Artists Agency, 9830 Wilshire Boulevard, Beverly Hills, CA 90212, USA.

MURRAY, John Loyola, BL, SC; Irish judge; *Chief Justice, Supreme Court;* b. 27 June 1943, Limerick; s. of John C. Murray and Catherine Casey; m. Gabrielle Walsh 1969; one s. one d.; ed Crescent Coll., Rockwell Coll., Univ. Coll. Dublin and King's Inns, Dublin; Pres. Union of Students of Ireland 1964–66; barrister-at-law 1967; Bencher, King's Inns 1986; SC, Bar of Ireland 1981; Attorney-Gen. Aug.–Dec. 1982, 1987–91; mem. Council of State 1987–91; Judge, Court of Justice of European Communities 1991–99; Judge, Supreme Court 1999–, Chief Justice 2004–; Hon. LLD (Limerick). *Leisure interests:* yachting, travel, art. *Address:* Supreme Court, Four Courts, Inns Quay, Dublin 7, Ireland (office). *Website:* www .courts.ie (office).

MURRAY, Leslie (Les) Allan, BA, AO; Australian poet; b. 17 Oct. 1938, Nabiac, NSW; s. of the late Cecil Allan Murray and Miriam Pauline Murray (née Arnall); m. Valerie Gina Morelli 1962; three s. two d.; ed Univ. of Sydney; translator, ANU 1963–67; in Prime Minister's Dept 1970–71; Acting Ed., Poetry Australia 1973–80; Ed., New Oxford Book of Australian Verse 1985–97; Literary Ed., Quadrant 1989–; Petrarca Prize (Germany) 1995, T. S. Eliot Prize 1997, Queen's Gold Medal for Poetry 1999, Mondello Prize (Italy) 2004. *Publications include:* The Ilex Tree (with Geoffrey Lehmann) 1965, The Weatherboard Cathedral 1969, Poems Against Economics 1972, Collected Poems 1976, Selected Poems: The Vernacular Republic 1979, The Boys Who Stole the Funeral (verse novel) 1980, Selected Poems 1986, Dog Fox Field 1990, The Paperbark Tree (selected prose) 1991, Translations from the Natural World 1992, Fivefathers (ed.) 1995, Subhuman Redneck Poems 1996, A Working Forest (prose) 1997, Fredy Neptune (verse novel) 1998, Conscious & Verbal 1999, Learning Human – New Selected Poems 2001, Poems the Size of Photographs 2002, New Collected Poems 2003, The Best Australian Poems (ed.) 2004, The Biplane Houses 2006, Taller When Prone 2010, Killing the Black Dog: A Memoir of Depression 2011. *Leisure interests:* cinema, gossip, ruminative driving. *Address:* Margaret Connolly & Associates, 16 Winton Street, Warrawee, NSW 2074, Australia (office). *Website:* www.lesmurray.org (office).

MURRAY, Hon. Lowell, PC, BA, MA, LLD; Canadian politician; b. 26 Sept. 1936, New Waterford, Nova Scotia; s. of the late Daniel Murray and Evelyn Young; m. Colleen Elaine MacDonald 1981; two s.; ed St Francis Xavier Univ., NS, Queen's Univ., Ont.; fmr Chief of Staff to Minister of Justice and Minister of Public Works; Progressive Conservative Nat. Campaign Chair. in gen. Election 1977–79, 1981–83; Senator 1979–, Co-Chair. Jt Senate-House of Commons Cttee on Official Languages 1980–84; Chair. Standing Cttee on Banking, Trade and Commerce

1984–86; Chair. Standing Senate Cttee on Nat. Finance 1995–96, 1999–2004, Chair. Standing Senate Cttee on Social Affairs, Science and Tech. 1997–99; Leader of Govt in the Senate 1986–93 and Minister of State for Fed.-Provincial Relations 1986–91; Minister responsible for Atlantic Canada Opportunities Agency 1987–88; Acting Minister for Communications 1988–89; mem. Bd Dirs Sony of Canada 1995–; mem. Bd Trustees Inst. for Research on Public Policy 1984–86, Trilateral Cttee 1985–86, Council of the Fed. Advisory Panel on Fiscal Imbalance 2005–06; Progressive Conservative. *Address:* The Senate, Room 502, Victoria Building, Ottawa, ON K1A 0A4, Canada (home). *Telephone:* (613) 995-2407 (office). *Fax:* (613) 947-4730 (office). *E-mail:* murral@sen.parl.gc.ca (office).

MURRAY, Patty, BA; American politician; *Senator from Washington;* b. 11 Oct. 1950, Bothell, Wash.; d. of David L. Johns and Beverly A. Johns (née McLaughlin); m. Robert R. Murray 1972; one s. one d.; ed Washington State Univ.; teacher, Shoreline Community Coll. 1984–87; campaigned against proposed closure of Wash. State Parent Educ. Programme 1980; fmr mem. Wash. State Senate; instructor Shoreline Community Coll. Seattle 1984–88; Senator from Wash. 1993–, Chair. Veterans Affairs Cttee, Vice-Chair. Senate Democratic Policy Cttee, sr mem. Budget Cttee, Appropriations Cttee, Co-Chair. Jt Select Cttee on Deficit Reduction 2010; Democrat. *Leisure interests:* fishing, exploring Washington state's great outdoors, spending time with her family. *Address:* 448 Russell Senate Office Buidling, Washington, DC 20510, USA (office). *Telephone:* (202) 224-2621 (office). *Fax:* (202) 224-0238 (office). *Website:* murray.senate.gov (office).

MURRAY, Sir Robin MacGregor, Kt, MD, DSc, FRS, FRCP, FRCPsych, FMedSci; British psychiatrist, institute director and academic; *Professor of Psychiatric Research, Institute of Psychiatry, King's College London;* b. 31 Jan. 1944, Glasgow, Scotland; s. of James. A. C. Murray and Helen MacGregor; m. Shelagh Harris 1970; one s. one d.; ed Univs of Glasgow and London; jr posts with Dept of Medicine, Univ. of Glasgow 1970–72, with Maudsley Hosp. 1972–75; Sr Lecturer, Inst. of Psychiatry, King's Coll., London 1978–82, Dean 1982–89, Prof. of Psychological Medicine 1989–99, Prof. of Psychiatric Research, Inst. of Psychiatry 1999–; Hon. Consultant, South London and Maudsley NHS Foundation Trust; Lilly Int. Fellow, Nat. Inst. for Mental Health, Bethesda, Md, USA 1976–77; Pres. Asscn of European Psychiatrists (now European Psychiatric Asscn) 1995–96; Fellow, Royal Coll. of Psychiatrists; Hon. mem. Asscn of European Psychiatry 2002; Gaskell Gold Medal and Research Prize, Royal Coll. of Psychiatrists 1976, Sr Leverhulme Research Fellow, Royal Soc. 1993, Kurt Schneider Award 1994, Adolf Meyer Award 1997, Paul Hoch Award 1998, Stanley Dean Award 1999, Hilton Distinguished Investigator Award of the Nat. Alliance for Research into Schizophrenia and Depression (NARSAD) 1999, Fifth Castilla del Pino Award for Achievement in Psychiatry 2002, Psykiatriyhdistys Suomen Medal, Finnish Psychiatric Soc. 2003, ranked eighth most influential researcher in psychiatry by Thomson Reuters' Science Watch and third in schizophrenia research 1997–2007. *Publications:* Schizophrenia 1996, Psychosis in the Inner City 1998, First Episode Psychosis (co-author) 1999; publs on schizophrenia, depression, psychiatric genetics and epidemiology, alcoholism and analgesic abuse. *Leisure interests:* Scottish and Jamaican music, swimming. *Address:* Institute of Psychiatry, King's College London, De Crespigny Park, London, SE5 8AF, England (office). *Telephone:* (20) 7703-6091. *Fax:* (20) 7701-9044. *Website:* www.iop.kcl.ac.uk (office).

MURRAY, Simon, CBE; British banker, business executive and author; *Independent Non-Executive Chairman, Glencore International plc;* b. 25 March 1940, Leicester; s. of Patrick G. Murray and Maxine M. K. Murray; m. Jennifer A. Leila Mather 1966; one s. two d.; ed Bedford School (Sr Exec. Programme) and Stanford Business School 9Stanford Exec. Program), USA; joined French Foreign Legion 1960, served for five years in 2nd Foreign Parachute Regt (2ème REP), fought in Algerian War of Independence against guerrillas of Front de Libération Nationale; Jardine Matheson & Co., Ltd 1966–73; Dir Matheson & Co., London 1973–75; Man. Dir Jardine Eng Corpn 1975–80; Founder and Man. Dir Davenham Investments Ltd 1980–84; Group Man. Dir Hutchison Whampoa Ltd 1984–93, mem. Bd Dirs –2007; pioneered mobile phones in Hong Kong and developed in the UK the mobile phone system now know as Orange; Exec. Chair. (Asia/Pacific) Deutsche Bank 1994–97; Founder and Chair. Simon Murray & Assocs; mem. Bd of Dirs and Ind. Non-Exec. Chair. Glencore International plc 2011–; Founder and current Chair. GEMS Ltd (pvt. equity investment group); Chair. Gleacher Partners Asia, Hong Kong; advisor, Bain & Co. (Asia), Inc., N.M. Rothschild & Sons Ltd, UK, China Nat. Offshore Oil Corpn; mem. Bd of Dirs IRC, Essar Energy, Orient Overseas, Wing Tai Properties, Greenheart, Compagnie Financière Richemont; Dir (non-exec.) Vodafone 2007–10; Officier, Ordre nat. du Mérite; Chevalier, Légion d'honneur; Hon. BA (Law) (Bath Univ.) 2005. *Achievement:* oldest man, aged 63, to walk unsupported to the South Pole 2004. *Publication:* Legionnaire: An Englishman in the French Foreign Legion 1978 (made into a film called Simon: An English Legionnaire 2002). *Leisure interests:* flying helicopters with his wife Jennifer (first woman to fly solo round the world in a helicopter), squash, jogging, reading. *Address:* Glencore International AG, Baarermattstrasse 3, 6340 Baar, Switzerland (office). *Telephone:* (41) 7092000 (office). *Fax:* (41) 7093000 (office). *E-mail:* info@glencore.com (office). *Website:* www.glencore.com (office).

MURRAY, Stuart, FRAIA, RIBA, DipArch, ASTC; Australian fmr architect and planner; b. 27 Oct. 1926, Sydney; s. of Cyril Hargreaves Murray and Daphne Williams; m. 1st Elizabeth Grime 1952 (divorced 1965); two s. two d.; m. 2nd Adrienne Solti 1982; ed Fort Street High School, Sydney, Sydney Tech. Coll. School of Architecture and Univ. of Sydney; Office of Burley Griffin 1944–46; Office of Sydney Ancher 1947–49; Office of Denis Clarke Hall, London 1950–52; partner, Ancher Mortlock & Murray 1953–64; Dir Ancher Mortlock Murray & Woolley, Architects 1965–75; Stuart Murray & Assocs, Architects & Planners 1976–; Dir N Sydney Planning Consultants 1968–72; work includes: Canberra Housing, Nat. Heritage List 1960, Elizabeth Bay Apartments, RAIA Heritage List 1967, Great Hall, Univ. of Newcastle (winner, Limited Competition 1968) 1971, Aeronautics School, Univ. of Sydney 1974, North Sydney Devt Control Plan 1974, Polo Club, Forbes, NSW 1977, school and univ. bldgs, homes and apts etc.; winner, Nat. Competition, Town Hall, Waverley, Sydney: Winner, 1957 (unbuilt), Great Hall, Univ. of Newcastle 1968. *Publications:* papers on civic design and urban environment. *Leisure interests:* architecture, art, music, literature, philosophy,

cooking, travel. *Address:* Stuart Murray & Associates, Suite 1, 144 High Street, North Sydney, NSW 2060, Australia (office). *Telephone:* (2) 9955-4779 (office); (2) 9929-0990 (home). *Fax:* (2) 9955-3653 (office).

MURSHED, Yasmeen, BA, MA; Bangladeshi educationalist, business executive and diplomatist; b. 19 May 1945, Calcutta (now Kolkata), India; d. of Khwaja Zakiuddin and Begum Binoo Zakiuddin; grand-d. of Khwaja Shahabuddin, fmr Prime Minister of Pakistan; m. Syed Tanweer Murshed (died 1988); one s. one d.; ed Viqarunnisa Noon School, Dhaka, Univ. of the Punjab, Pakistan; began career in educ. as a teacher in various insts, including Karachi Grammar School, Islamabad Model School for Girls, Govt Coll. for Women, Islamabad 1967–71; returned to Bangladesh after Liberation and began teaching small groups of students at home 1971; est. Scholastica Tutorial 1977 (later known as Scholastica), Chair. Bd of Man. –2007; fmr Chair. Etcetera Bangladesh (Pvt.) Ltd, Office and Home Solutions (Pvt.) Ltd, Scholastica Transport Services (Pvt.) Ltd, Printcraft Co. Ltd, Services for Professional Educ. and Enterprise Devt; mem. Bd of Dirs United Insurance Co. Ltd, Chittagong Stock Exchange; undertook role in Centre for Analysis and Choice early 1990s; has represented Bangladesh at several int. confs and meetings, participated in Sixth Int. Conf. of the Asscn for Women in Devt, Washington, DC, USA 1993; Founding mem. and first Pres. Asia/Pacific Women in Politics Network; del. to Muslim Women's Conf., Beijing and Beyond: Implementing the Platform for Action in Muslim Societies, Washington, DC 1996, Asscn for Women in Devt Forum, Washington, DC 1996, Nat. Democratic Inst. Conf. on Consolidating the Third Wave Democracies: Trends and Challenges, Taiwan 1995, Global Best Practices with Cambridge, Delhi 2006 and others; apptd Minister of Women and Children's Affairs, Minister of Primary and Mass Educ., Minister of Social Welfare 2006; High Commr to Pakistan 2008–12; writes column on books and writers for The Daily Star; mem. Ascent Educ. Devt Trust (Founder-mem.), Educ., Science, Tech. and Cultural Devt Trust, Standard Chartered-Financial Express Corp. Social Responsibility Trust, Int. Chamber of Commerce (Bangladesh), Commonwealth Soc. of Bangladesh; mem. Jury Bd The Daily Star and DHL Business Awards 2004, DCCI Business Awards 2005. *Publications include:* several textbooks on econs and Islamic studies and articles for journals, newspapers and magazines.

MURSI, Muhammad, BSc, MSc, PhD; Egyptian politician and fmr head of state; b. (Muhammad Mursi Isa al-Ayyat), 8 Aug. 1951, Sharqia Governorate, northern Egypt; m. Naglaa Ali Mahmoud 1979; five c.; ed Cairo Univ., Univ. of Southern California, USA; Asst Prof., California State Univ., Northridge 1982–85; returned to Egypt to teach at Zagazig Univ. 1985, fmr Chair. Dept of Materials Science, Faculty of Eng; mem. Parl. in People's Ass. of Egypt 2000–05; arrested several times under Pres. Hosni Mubarak's regime, spent seven months in jail; a leading figure in the Muslim Brotherhood 1991–2012, mem. Guidance Office until 2011; Chair. Freedom and Justice Party (FJP) following its founding by the Muslim Brotherhood in the wake of the Egyptian revolution 2011–12 (resgnd); stood as FJP's cand. in presidential election May–June 2012; Pres. of Egypt 2012–13; Sec. Gen. Non-Aligned Movement 2012–; ousted by the Army and placed under house arrest following mass protests calling for his resignation 3 July 2013.

MURTAGH, Peter, BA; Irish journalist; *Reporter, The Irish Times;* b. 9 April 1953, Dublin; s. of Thomas Murtagh and Olive de Lacy; m. Moira Gutteridge 1988; one s. one d.; ed The High School, Dublin, Trinity Coll., Dublin, Scandinavian Int. Man. Inst., Copenhagen, Denmark; reporter, The Irish Times 1981–84, Foreign Ed., Opinion Ed., Managing Ed. 1997–; Ed. Insight, The Sunday Times, London 1985; reporter, Deputy Foreign Ed. and News Ed. The Guardian, London 1986–94; Ed. The Sunday Tribune, Dublin 1994–96; apptd Duty Ed. and Man. Ed. The Irish Times 1996, later Foreign Ed., Opinion Ed., currently Reporter; Journalist of the Year, Ireland 1983, Reporter of the Year, UK 1986. *Publications:* The Boss: Charles J. Haughey in Government (with J. Joyce) 1983, Blind Justice – The Sallins Mail Train Robbery (with J. Joyce) 1984, The Rape of Greece – The King, the Colonels and the Resistance 1994, The Irish Times Book of the Year (ed., annually) 1999–2012, Buen Camino! – A Father/Daughter Journey from Croagh Patrick to Santiago de Compostela (with Natasha Murtagh) 2011. *Leisure interests:* family, newspapers, Ireland, motorcycling, Camino do Santiago. *Address:* The Irish Times, Tara Street, Dublin 2 (office); Penharbour, Somerby Road, Greystones, Co. Wicklow, Ireland (home). *Telephone:* (1) 6758000 (office). *Fax:* (1) 6615302 (office). *E-mail:* pmurtagh@irishtimes.com (office). *Website:* www.irishtimes.com (office).

MURTEIRA NABO, Francisco Luís, MBA; Portuguese economist and business executive; *Chairman, Galp Energia SGPS SA;* b. 1939, Evora; ed Instituto Superior de Economia e Gestao, Escola de Direccao e Negocios-AESE; Chief Alderman, City Hall, Lisbon 1976–81; Chair. Portuguese Radio Marconi Co. 1978–82; Vice-Pres. Sorefame 1982–83; Sec. of State for Transport 1983–85; Admin. Companhia Industrial de Portugal e Colónias 1986–87; Deputy Sec. for Educ., Health and Social Affairs, Office of Macao 1987–89, Deputy Sec. for Econ. Affairs, Admin of Macao 1989–90, Head of Govt of Territory of Macao 1990–91; Minister of Social Equipment (Public Works) 1995–96; Chair. Portugal Telecom, SGPS, SA 1996–2003 (also Chair. Exec. Cttee); Chair. Galp Energia SGPS SA 2005–; Pres. Câmara do Comércio e Indústria Luso-Chinesa (Portuguese-Chinese Chamber of Commerce and Industry); mem. Direcção da Associação Comercial de Lisboa (Directorate of Commercial Asscn of Lisbon), Institut Européen d'Admin des Affaires (INSEAD); Chair. Proforum (Asscn for the Devt of Eng); fmr Dir (non-exec.) BPG (Banco Portugues de Gestao, SA), Companhia de Seguros Sagres, SA, Holdomnis – Gestao e Investimentos, SA, Templo – Gestao e Investimentos, SA, Seng Heng Bank, BES – Banco Espirito Santo, SA; Pres. Portuguese Economists Asscn; fmr Pres. COTEC Portugal (Asscn for Business Innovation); mem. Conselho Superior de Ciência, Tecnologia e Inovação (Supreme Council for Science, Tech. and Innovation); Trustee, Fundação Oriente. *Address:* GALP – Petróleos e Gás de Portugal SGPS SA, Rua Tomás da Fonseca, Torre C, Edificio Galp Energia, 1600-209 Lisbon, Portugal (office). *Telephone:* (21) 724-25-00 (office); (21) 724-08-66 (office). *Fax:* (21) 724-29-65 (office); (21) 724-05-73 (office). *E-mail:* investor.relations@galpenergia.com (office). *Website:* www.galpenergia.com (office).

MURTHY, N(agavara) R(amarao) Narayana, CBE, BE; Indian business executive and software engineer; *Executive Chairman, Infosys Technologies Limited;* b. 20 Aug. 1946, Mysore, Karnataka; s. of R. H. Kulkarni and Vimala Kulkarni; m Sudha Murthy; one s. one d.; ed Nat. Inst. of Eng, Univ. of Mysore,

Indian Inst. of Tech., Kanpur; began career as Chief Systems Programmer, Indian Inst. of Man., Ahmedabad; joined Patni Computer Systems, Pune; co-f. Infosys Technologies Ltd 1981, Chair. 1981–2006, CEO 1981–2002, Exec. Chair. and Chief Mentor 2002–06, Chair. (non-exec.) and Chief Mentor 2006–11, Chair. Emer. 2011–13, Additional Dir and Exec. Chair. 2013–; Pres. Nat. Asscn of Software and Service Cos (NASSCOM), India 1992–94; Chair. Governing Body, Int. Inst. of Information Tech., Bangalore, Bd of Mems of School of Man., Asian Inst. of Tech., Bangkok, Thailand, Asia Business Council, Hong Kong; fmr Chair. Governing Body, Indian Inst. of Man., Ahmedabad; mem. Bd of Dirs Institut Européen d'Admin des Affaires (INSEAD), Bd of Overseers Univ. of Pennsylvania's Wharton School, Bd of Trustees Cornell Univ., Business Advisory Council of Great Lakes Inst. of Man., Chennai, Bd of Trustees Singapore Man. Univ., Bd of Advisors William F. Achtmeyer Center for Global Leadership at Tuck School of Business, Bd of Govs Asian Inst. of Man. (Philippines); mem. Advisory Bds and Councils of several Univs, including Stanford Grad. School of Business, Corp. Governance Initiative at Harvard Business School, Yale Univ., Univ. of Tokyo's President's Council; mem. Bd Dirs Cen. Bd of Reserve Bank of India; Ind. mem. Bd Dirs DBS Bank of Singapore, Unilever, HSBC; Co-Chair. Indo-British Partnership; mem. Prime Minister's Council on Trade and Industry, Asia Advisory Bd of British Telecommunications plc, Bd of NDTV, India; IT adviser to several Asian countries; Foreign Fellow, American Nat. Acad. of Engineers 2010; Hon. Fellow, Inst. of Electrical and Electronics Engineers, USA 2010 Padma Shri 2000, Chevalier, Légion d'honneur 2008, Padma Vibushan 2008; Dr hc from several univs in India and abroad; numerous awards, including Nikkei Asia Award, Wharton School Dean's Medal, JRD Tata Corp. Leadership Award 1996–97, Distinguished Alumnus Award, Indian Inst. of Tech., Kanpur 1998, featured in BusinessWeek's The Stars of Asia 1998, 1999, 2000, 1998, named by BusinessWeek as one of the nine Entrepreneurs of the Year 1999, named by TIME/CNN as one of the 25 Most Influential Global Executives 2001, Indo-French Forum Medal (first recipient) 2003, Ernst & Young Global World Entrepreneur of the Year 2003, one of two people named Fortune magazine as Asia's Businessmen of the Year 2003, named by TIME magazine's Global Tech Influentials list as one of 10 leaders who are helping shape the future of technology 2004, ranked first in Economic Times Corp. Dossier list of India's Most Powerful CEOs 2004, 2005, voted seventh Most Admired CEO/Chair. in the World in global study conducted by Burson-Marsteller with Economist Intelligence Unit 2005, ranked eighth by The Economist amongst the top 15 Most Admired Global Leaders 2005, ranked 28th by the Financial Times amongst the World's Most Respected Business Leaders 2005, voted by TIME magazine as one of the Asian heroes who have brought about revolutionary changes in Asia in the last 60 years 2006, Ernst Weber Leadership Medal 2007, rated as Global Leader of 2009, ASME Hoover Medal 2012, Philanthropist of the Year, The Asian Awards 2013, Sayaji Ratna Award, Baroda Man. Asscn 2013. Publication: A Better India: A Better World (lectures) 2009. Address: Infosys Technologies Ltd, Corporate Headquarters, Plot Nos 44 & 97A, 3rd Cross, Electronic City, Hosur Rd, Bangalore 560 100, India (office). Telephone: (80) 28520261 (office). Fax: (80) 28520362 (office). E-mail: infosys@infosys.com (office). Website: www.infosys.com (office).

MUSA, Said, LLB; Belizean politician and attorney-at-law; b. 19 March 1944, San Ignacio; s. of Hamid Musa and Aurora Musa (née Gibbs); ed St John's Coll., Belize City, Manchester Univ., England; called to the Bar London 1966; worked as barrister, Gray's Inn, London 1966–67; circuit magistrate Belize 1967–68, Crown Counsel 1968–70; lawyer pvt. practice 1970–79, 1984–89, 1993–98 (Sr Counsel 1983–); Pres. Public Service Union 1969; f. People's Action Cttee, Soc. for Promotion of Educ. and Research (SPEAR) 1969; obliged to leave public service because of political activities; joined People's United Party (PUP); Chair. Fort George Div. PUP 1974–; Chair. PUP 1986–94, Deputy Leader 1994–96, Leader 1996–; Co-Founder Journal of Belizean Affairs 1972; apptd Senator to Nat. Ass. by George Price 1974; negotiator in talks to safeguard territorial integrity of Belize on independence 1975–81; mem. House of Reps for Fort George constituency 1979–84, 1993–98, 2012–; Attorney-Gen. and Minister for Educ., Sports and Culture 1979–84; Minister of Foreign Affairs, Econ. Devt and Educ. 1989–93 (negotiated recognition of Belizean sovereignty by Guatemala 1991); Leader of the Opposition 1996–98; Prime Minister of Belize 1998–2008, concurrently Minister of Finance and Foreign Affairs, then Minister of Finance and Econ. Devt 1998–2003, of Nat. Devt and the Public Service 2004–08, of Finance 2005–08; mem. Privy Council. Publications: People's Assemblies, People's Government; articles in nat. press. Leisure interests: reading, int. affairs, human rights, music, tennis. Address: People's United Party, 3 Queen Street, Belize City (office); 91 North Front Street, Belize City (home); 7 E Street, Belize City, Belize (home). Telephone: 223-2940 (office). Fax: 223-1149 (office). E-mail: mandb@btl.net (home); sahootoo@yahoo .com (home).

MUSCAT, Joseph, MA, PhD; Maltese journalist and politician; Prime Minister; b. 22 Jan. 1974; m. Michelle Tanti; two d.; ed Univ. of Malta, Univ. of Bristol, UK; began career as journalist with Labour Party radio station, Super One Radio; moved to Super One TV, becoming Asst Head of News 1996; Ed. maltastar.com (Labour Party online newspaper) 2001–04; columnist, l-Orizzont (Maltese-language newspaper published by Gen. Workers' Union) and it-Torca (sister Sunday title); regular contributor to The Times (English-language newspaper); mem. European Parl. (Party of European Socialists) 2004–08; mem. House of Reps (Parl.) 2008–, Leader of the Opposition 2008–13; Prime Minister 2013–; mem. Partit Laburista (PL, Labour Party), Leader 2008–; Companion of Honour, Nat. Order of Merit 2013. Address: Office of the Prime Minister, 55a, Transcontinental House, Zachary Street, Valletta VLT 1210, Malta (office). Telephone: 22001852 (office). Fax: 22001851 (office). E-mail: lawrence.gonzi@gov.mt (office). Website: www.opm.gov.mt (office).

MUSCATELLI, Anton, PhD, FRSE; British economist, academic and university administrator; Principal and Vice-Chancellor, University of Glasgow; Prin. and Vice-Chancellor Heriot-Watt Univ. 2007–09; Prin. and Vice-Chancellor Univ. of Glasgow 2009–; mem. RAE Panels for Econs and Econometrics 2001, 2008; fmr mem. Research Grants Bd of ESRC and its Int. Advisory Cttee, Council of Royal Econ. Soc.; special advisor on monetary policy to House of Commons Treasury Select Cttee 2007–10; fmr consultant to EC and World Bank; Convenor of Universities Scotland 2008–10, Chair. Research and Knowledge Exchange Cttee; Vice-Pres. Universities UK 2008–10; Co-Chair. Steering Bd for creation of Nat.

Centre for Univs and Business; mem. Bd Scottish Funding Council; Academician, Learned Socs of Social Sciences. Publications: numerous papers in professional journals on monetary econs, central bank independence, fiscal policy, int. finance and macroeconomics. Address: University of Glasgow, Glasgow, G12 8QQ, Scotland (office). Telephone: (141) 330-5995 (office). E-mail: principal@glasgow .ac.uk (office). Website: www.gla.ac.uk (office).

MUSEVENI, Gen. Yoweri Kaguta; Ugandan head of state; President and Commander-in-Chief of Armed Forces; b. 1944, Ntungamo, Mbarara; s. of Amos Kaguta and Esteri Kokundeka; m. Janet Kataaha; four c.; ed Mbarara High School, Ntare School, Univ. Coll. of Dar es Salaam; Research Asst Office of fmr Pres. Milton Obote 1971; in Tanzania planning overthrow of regime of Idi Amin 1971–79; f. Front for Nat. Salvation (FRONASA) 1972; taught at Moshi Co-operative Coll., Tanzania 1972; participated in Tanzanian invasion of Uganda 1979; Defence Minister in interim Govt of Uganda Nat. Liberation Front (UNLF) following overthrow of Amin 1979–80; following election of Dr Obote, amid allegations of ballot-rigging, in 1980, spent five years as leader of Nat. Resistance Army (NRA) waging a guerrilla war 1981–86; Pres. of Uganda (following overthrow of Govt by NRA forces) and Minister of Defence, then Pres. and C-in-C of Armed Forces 1986–; Chair. Preferential Trade Area (PTA) 1987–88, 1992–93, OAU 1990–91. Publications: Selected Essays 1985, Selection of Speeches and Writings, Vol. I: What is Africa's Problem? 1992, Vol. II 1997, Sowing the Mustard Seed – The Struggle for Freedom and Democracy 1997. Leisure interest: football. Address: Office of the President, Parliament Building, P.O. Box 7168, Kampala, Uganda. Telephone: (41) 258441. Fax: (41) 256143. E-mail: info@gouexecutive.net (office). Website: www.gouexecutive.net (office).

MUSGRAVE, Thea, CBE, MusDoc; British composer; b. 27 May 1928, Edinburgh, Scotland; d. of James Musgrave and Joan Musgrave (née Hacking); m. Peter Mark 1971; ed Univ. of Edinburgh and Paris Conservatoire (under Nadia Boulanger); Lecturer, Extra-Mural Dept, Univ. of London 1958–65; Visiting Prof., Univ. of California, Santa Barbara, USA 1970; Guggenheim Fellow 1974–75, 1982–83; Distinguished Prof., Queen's Coll., CUNY, USA 1987–2002; Hon. DMus (CNAA, Smith Coll., Old Dominion Univ.); Koussevitzky Award 1972, 2000. Works include: Chamber Concertos 1, 2 & 3 1966, Concerto for Orchestra 1967, Clarinet Concerto 1968, Beauty and the Beast (ballet) 1969, Night Music 1969, Horn Concerto 1971, The Voice of Ariadne (chamber opera) 1972–73, Viola Concerto 1973, Space Play 1974, Mary, Queen of Scots (opera) 1976–77, A Christmas Carol (opera) 1978–79, Harriet, A Woman Called Moses 1980–84, An Occurrence at Owl Creek Bridge (radio opera) 1981, Black Tambourine for women's chorus and piano 1985, Pierrot 1985, For the Time Being for chorus 1986, The Golden Echo 1987, Narcissus 1988, The Seasons (orchestral) 1988, Rainbow (orchestral) 1990, Simón Bolívar (opera) 1993, Autumn Sonata 1993, Journey through a Japanese Landscape (marimba concerto) 1993, On the Underground (vocal) 1994, Helios (oboe concerto) 1995, Phoenix Rising (orchestral) 1997, Canta, Canta for clarinet and ensemble 1997, Lamenting with Ariadne 1999, The Mocking Bird for baritone and ensemble 2000, Pontalba (opera) 2003, Turbulent Landscapes (orchestral) 2004, Wood, Metal, Skin (concerto for percussion and orchestra) 2004, Journey into Light for soprano and orchestra 2005, Two's Company (duet for oboe and percussion) 2005, Green for string ensemble 2008, Snapshots for piano 2009, Ithaca (SATB chorus) 2010, Towards the Blue (wind quartet and string quartet) 2010; chamber music, songs, choral music, orchestral music. Leisure interests: cooking, cinema, reading. Address: c/o Chester Novello, 14–15 Berners Street, London, W1T 3LJ, England (office). Telephone: (20) 7612-7400 (office). Website: www.chesternovello.com (office); www.theamusgrave.com (home).

MUSGROVE, David Ronald (Ronnie), AA, BBA, JD; American lawyer, politician and fmr state governor; Of Counsel, Copeland, Cook, Taylor & Bush; b. 29 July 1956, Tocowa, Miss.; m. 1st Melanie Ballard 1977 (divorced 2001); m. 2nd Dr Melody Bounds 2007; four c.; ed Northwest Junior Coll., Univ. of Mississippi and Univ. of Mississippi School of Law; called to the Bar, Miss. State Courts, US Dist Court for the Northern and Southern Dists of Miss.; Partner, Smith, Musgrove & McCord, Miss.; a two-term State Senator and Lt Gov. under Kirk Fordice; Lt Gov. State of Miss. 1996–2000, Gov. of Miss. 2000–04; unsuccessful cand. in special election for one of Miss.'s seats in US Senate 2008; currently a practising attorney at Copeland, Cook, Taylor & Bush, Ridgeland, Mo.; Distinguished Visiting Lecturer, Univ. of Mississippi; Adjunct Prof., Mississippi Coll. School of Law, Jackson; Chair. Nat. Assessment Governing Bd's NAEP 12th Grade Preparedness Comm., Nat. Advisory Cttee on Rural Health and Human Services; Co-Chair. Biomass Research and Devt Tech. Advisory Cttee; fmr Chair. Southern Regional Educ. Bd, Southern States Energy Bd, Southern Growth Policy Bd, Southern Govs Asscn; fmr Vice-Chair. Nat. Govs Asscn; mem. Bd of Dirs Mississippi Sports Hall and Fame Museum; mem. ABA, The Mississippi Bar, Mississippi Bar Foundation, Madison Co. Bar Asscn, Hinds Co. Bar Asscn, Capital Area Bar Asscn; Fellow, Miss. Bar Foundation; mem. Rotary Club; Paul Harris Fellow; Distinguished Service Award, Nat. Guard Bureau, Washington, DC. Address: Copeland, Cook, Taylor & Bush, 1076 Highland Colony, Concourse 600 Suite 100, Ridgeland, MS 39157, USA (office). Telephone: (601) 856-7200 (office). Fax: (601) 707-2999 (office). E-mail: rmusgrove@cctb.com (office). Website: www .copelandcook.com (office).

MUSHARRAF, Gen. (retd) Pervez; Pakistani politician, fmr head of state and fmr army officer; President, All Pakistan Muslim League; b. 11 Aug. 1943, Delhi, India; s. of Syed Musharraf Uddin; m. Sehba Farid 1968; one s. one d.; ed St Patrick's High School, Karachi, Forman Christian Coll., Lahore, Command and Staff Coll., Quetta, Nat. Defence Coll., Rawalpindi, Royal Coll. of Defence Studies, UK; spent early childhood in Turkey 1949–56; joined Pakistan Mil. Acad. 1961; commd in Artillery Regt 1964; fought in 1965 war with India (Imtiazi Sanad Gallantry Award); spent much of mil. career in Special Services Group; Company Commdr Commando Battalion Indo-Pakistan War 1971; Dir-Gen. Mil. Operations, Gen. HQ 1993–95; apptd C-in-C of Pakistani Army Oct. 1998, Chair. Jt Chiefs of Staff Cttee 1999, led mil. coup 1999, Chief of Staff 1999–2007; Chief Exec. Nat. Security Council of Pakistan 1999–2002; Pres. of Pakistan 2001–08 (resgnd); mem. Pakistan Muslim League (Quaid e Azam Group) –2010; lived in self-imposed exile in London, UK 2008–13, returned to Pakistan March 2013; Founder and Pres. All Pakistan Muslim League 2010–; arrest warrant issued by Anti Terrorism Court and was charged with conspiracy to commit murder of Benazir Bhutto Feb. 2011;

treason charges against him registered by Sindh High Court March 2011; disqualified by High Court judges from taking part in the upcoming general election and his arrest ordered by the court over an attempt to impose house arrest on judges in March 2007 April 2013. *Publication:* In the Line of Fire: A Memoir 2006. *Leisure interests:* squash, tennis, golf, reading, mil. history, rock music. *Address:* APML Central Secretariat, House No, 01, Street No. 37, F-6/1, Islamabad, Pakistan (office). *Telephone:* (51) 2814270 (office). *Fax:* (51) 2814276 (office). *E-mail:* info@apmlpak.com (office). *Website:* www.apmlpak.com (office).

MUSHIKIWABO, Louise, MA; Rwandan politician; *Minister of Foreign Affairs and Co-operation;* b. Kigali; m.; ed Nat. Univ. of Rwanda, Univ. of Delaware, USA; English teacher, Lycée de Kigali 1985; worked as public relations consultant, Washington, DC, USA; fmr Ed., Africa Dept, IMF; Communications Dir African Devt Bank 2006–08; Minister of Information 2008–09, of Foreign Affairs and Co-operation 2009–; Co-founder and Pres. The Rwanda Children's Fund, Washington, DC. *Publication:* Rwanda Means the Universe 2006. *Address:* Ministry of Foreign Affairs, blvd de la Révolution, BP 179, Kigali, Rwanda (office). *Telephone:* 575386 (office). *Fax:* 573797 (office). *E-mail:* info@minaffet.gov.rw (office). *Website:* www .minaffet.gov.rw (office).

MUSHKETIK, Yuri Mikhailovich; Ukrainian writer; b. 21 March 1929, Verkiivka, Chernigiv Region; s. of Mikhail Petrovich Mushketik and Uliana Onufriivna Mushketik; m. Lina Sergiivna Mushketik (née Lushnikova); two d.; ed Kiev State Univ.; mem. CPSU 1951–91; Chair. Bd Union of Writers of Ukraine 1987–; Ed.-in- Chief Dripro journal; Chair. Nat. Cttee of UNESCO; first works published 1952; T. Shevchenko Ukrainian State Prize 1980. *Publications include:* Fires in the Middle of the Night 1959, Black Bread 1960, The Heart and the Stone 1961, Drop of Blood 1964, A Bridge Across the Night 1975, White Shadow 1975, Position 1979, Pain 1981, The Boundary 1987, Selected Works (2 vols) 1989, Hetman's Treasure (novel) 1993, Brother Against Brother (novel) 1995. *Leisure interests:* reading American literature, history of Ukrainian Cossacks. *Address:* Suvorova Str. 3, Apt. 10, 252010 Kiev, Ukraine. *Telephone:* (44) 290-80-04.

MUSIN, Aslan Yespulayevich; Kazakhstani government official; b. 2 Jan. 1954; ed Almaty Inst. of Econs; fmr Akim (Gov.) Aktobe and Atyrau Oblasts; Minister of Econ. Affairs and Budget Planning 2006–07; Deputy Prime Minister Jan.–Sept. 2007; Chair. Majlis (Parl.) 2007. *Address:* c/o Majlis, 010000 Astana, Parliament House, Kazakhstan (office).

MUSK, Elon, BA, BS; Canadian/American (b. South African) engineer and business executive; *CEO and Chief Technology Officer, SpaceX;* b. 28 June 1971; m. 1st Justine Musk 2000 (divorced 2008); five s.; m. 2nd Talulah Riley 2010 (divorced 2012); ed Pretoria Boys High School, Univ. of Pennsylvania and Univ. of Pennsylvania Wharton School; bought first computer and taught himself to program aged ten; sold first commercial software for space game aged 12; left home aged 17; emigrated to Regina, Sask., Canada 1989; left Canada to study business and physics in USA 1992; dropped out of grad. programme in applied physics and materials science at Stanford Univ. to co-found (with brother Kimbal Musk) Zip2 1995, acquired by Compaq's AltaVista div. 1999; co-f. X.com (online financial services and e-mail payment co.) 1999, merged with Confinity, operator of the then largest auction payments service, PayPal, under X.com as corp. name 2000, changed name to PayPal Inc. Feb. 2001, acquired by eBay Oct. 2002; f. Space Exploration Technologies (SpaceX), Hawthorne, Calif. June 2002, currently CEO and Chief Technology Officer, co. develops and manufactures space launch vehicles, including the Falcon 1 and Falcon 9 rockets and first spacecraft the Dragon, awarded NASA contract for 12 flights of Falcon 9 rocket and Dragon spacecraft to Int. Space Station 2008, Falcon 1 rocket became first privately-funded liquid-fuelled vehicle to put a satellite into Earth orbit Sept. 2009; Co-founder and Head of Product Design, Tesla Motors, led devt of Tesla Roadster electric sports car, CEO 2008–, Model X unveiled 2011, four-door Model S sedan in production 2012; primary investor and Chair. SolarCity (photovoltaics products and services startup co.) 2006–; mem. Bd of Dirs Halcyon Molecular (biotechnology co.) 2008–; Chair. Musk Foundation; Trustee, X Prize Foundation; mem. or fmr mem. Bd The Space Foundation, Nat. Acads Aeronautics and Space Eng Bd, The Planetary Soc., Stanford Eng Advisory Bd, Bd of Trustees California Inst. of Tech. (Caltech) 2010–; Hon. DUniv (Univ. of Surrey, UK) 2009; Dr hc in Design (Art Center Coll. of Design, Pasadena, Calif.) 2010; Global Green Product Design Award 2006, Index Design Award 2007, Inc Magazine Entrepreneur of the Year Award 2007, R&D Magazine Innovator of the Year 2007, AIAA George Low Award for the most outstanding contrib. in the field of space transportation in 2007–08, named by Esquire magazine as one of the 75 most influential people of the 21st century 2008, Nat. Conservation Achievement Award, Nat. Wildlife Fed. for Tesla Motors and SolarCity 2008, Aviation Week Laureate for the most significant achievement world-wide in the space industry 2008, Von Braun Trophy, Nat. Space Soc. 2009, World Technology Award (co-recipient) 2009, recognized as Living Legend in Aviation by the Kitty Hawk Foundation for creating the successor to the Space Shuttle (Falcon 9 rocket and Dragon spacecraft) 2010, listed as one of TIME magazine's 100 people who most affect the world 2010, Gold Space Medal, Fédération Aéronautique Internationale for designing the first privately developed rocket to reach orbit 2010, Automotive Exec. of the Year (world-wide) 2010, ranked tenth most popular space hero (tied with rocketry pioneer and scientist Wernher von Braun) in a Space Foundation survey 2010, named by Forbes magazine as one of America's 20 Most Powerful CEOs 40 And Under 2011, Heinlein Prize for Advances in Space Commercialization 2011, honoured as a Legendary Leader at the Churchill Club Awards 2011, Gold Medal, Royal Aeronautical Soc. 2012, ranked by Forbes magazine amongst The World's Most Powerful People (66th) 2012, (47th) 2013. *Address:* Space Exploration Technologies (SpaceX), 1 Rocket Road, Hawthorne, CA 90250, USA (office). *Telephone:* (310) 363-6000 (office). *E-mail:* media@spacex.com (office). *Website:* www.spacex.com (office); www.teslamotors.com (office); www.muskfoundation.org.

MUSLERA, Graciela; Uruguayan architect and politician; *Minister of Housing, Territorial Regulation and the Environment;* b. 1963, Montevideo; four c.; ed Universidad de la República; Technical Adviser, Banco República 1998–2006, Man. responsible for Coordination of Maintenance and Construction Sites 2006–07; Sec. to Senator Lucia Topolansky 2001–05; Vice-Pres. Nat. Housing Agency 2007–10; Minister of Housing, Territorial Regulation and the Environment 2010–; mem. Movimiento de Participación Popular. *Address:* Ministry of

Housing, Territorial Regulation and the Environment, Zabala 1432, esq. 25 de Mayo, 11000 Montevideo, Uruguay (office). *Telephone:* (2) 9170710 (home). *Fax:* (2) 9163914 (home). *E-mail:* ministro@mvotma.gub.uy (office). *Website:* www.mvotma .gub.uy (home).

MUSLIMYAR, Fazl Hadi; Afghan politician; *Speaker, Meshrano Jirga;* m.; five s. two d.; ed Univ. of Jalalabad; local commdr in Nangahar Prov. during Soviet occupation; .elected to Nangarhar Prov. Council 2005, Chair. 2005–09; elected Senator, Meshrano Jirga (House of Elders) 2009, First Deputy Speaker 2010, Acting Speaker 2010–11, Speaker 2011–; Dir Dawat Islami Party, Nangarhar 2010–; *Website:* mj.parliament.af.

MUSOKE, Rt Hon Kintu; Ugandan politician, journalist and publisher; b. Masaka; Minister of Information 1989–91; Minister for Presidency 1991–94; Minister of State for Security; Prime Minister of Uganda 1994–2000; currently Sr Adviser to Pres. of Uganda; Chair. Advisory Cttee, USA Presidential Emergency Fund for Aids Relief (PEPFAR). *Address:* c/o Office of the Prime Minister, PO Box 341, Kampala (office); PO Box 15025, Kampala, Uganda (home). *Telephone:* (41) 4257370 (home). *Fax:* (41) 4235459 (office). *E-mail:* kintumusoke@hotmail.com (home).

MUSOKOTWANE, Situmbeko; Zambian economist and government official; b. 25 May 1956, Kalabo District, Western Province; m. Mate Musokotwane; two c.; ed Univ. of Zambia, Univ. of Dar es Salaam, Tanzania, Univ. of Konstanz, Germany; joined Bank of Zambia as economist 1991, later becoming Deputy Gov.; Gov. Central Bank of Swaziland (contracted by IMF) 1997–2000; held several cabinet positions including Adviser to Minister of Finance 2000–03, Sec. to the Treasury and Deputy Sec. to the Cabinet, Minister of Finance and Nat. Planning 2008–11; econ. adviser to Pres. of Zambia –2008; MP for Liuwa constituency; fmr Prof., Univ. of Zambia; fmr Dir ZCCM Investments Holdings plc; mem. Movement for Multi-party Democracy (MMD). *Address:* Movement for Multi-party Democracy, POB 30708, Lusaka, Zambia (office). *Telephone:* (21) 1250177 (office). *Fax:* (21) 1252329 (office). *E-mail:* mmd@zamtel.zm (office). *Website:* www.mmdzam.org (office).

MUSONGE, Peter Mafany, BSc, MSc; Cameroonian civil engineer and politician; *Grand Chancellor of National Orders;* b. 3 Dec. 1942, Muea-Buea; s. of John Musonge and Frida Nduma Woko; m. Anne Mojoko Mbongo 1970; three s., one d.; ed Stanford Univ., Drexel Univ., USA; Gen. Man. Nat. Civil Eng Lab. 1980–84; Gen. Man. Nat. Civil Eng Equipment Pool 1984–87; Gen. Man. Cameroon Devt Corpn (CDC) 1988–96; Prime Minister and Head of Govt of Cameroon 1996–2004; Grand Chancellor of Nat. Orders, Office of the Presidency 2007–; mem. Rassemblement démocratique du peuple camerounais (RDPC); Grand Officier de la Légion d'honneur 1999; Grand Officer, Cameroon Order of Valour 2003. *Leisure interests:* reading, sport, music. *Address:* Grand Chancellery, Presidency, Yaoundé, Cameroon (office). *Telephone:* 2220-0711 (office).

MUSONI, James; Rwandan politician; Commr Gen., Rwanda Revenue Authority –2005; Minister for Commerce, Industry, Investment Promotion, Tourism and Cooperatives 2005–06, of Finance and Economic Planning 2006–09; mem. Front Patriotique Rwandais. *Address:* c/o Ministry of Finance and Economic Planning, BP 158, Kigali, Rwanda.

MUSSELWHITE, Charlie, (Memphis Charlie, Charlie Kelly, Mussels); American blues-harp player; b. (Charles Douglas Musselwhite III); 31 Jan. 1944, Kosciusko, Miss.; s. of the late Charles Douglas Musselwhite, Jr and Ruth Maxine Musselwhite; m. Henrietta Musselwhite; one s. one d.; ed Memphis Tech. High School; concerts tours in USA; performed on albums with Bonnie Raitt, The Blind Boys of Alabama, Tom Waits, Mickey Hart and INXS; Presenter, weekly radio show Charlie's Back Room (KRSH); 24 W.C. Handy Awards, Lifetime Achievement Awards (Monterey Blues Festival, San Javier Jazz Festival, Spain), Mississippi Gov.'s Award for Excellence in the Arts, Pete Pedersen Lifetime Achievement Award, Howlin' Wolf Award, Trophées France Blues 2000, 2002, Blues Music Hall of Fame 2010. *Recordings include:* Stand Back! 1967, Louisiana Fog 1968, Stone Blues 1968, Tennessee Woman 1968, Memphis, Tennessee 1970, The Harmonica According to Charlie Musselwhite 1979, Curtain Call Cocktails 1982, Mellow-Dee 1986, Ace of Harps 1990, Signature 1991, Where Have All the Good Times Gone? 1992, In My Time 1993, Memphis Charlie 1993, The Blues Never Die 1994, Takin' Care of Business 1995, Rough News 1997, Continental Drifter 1999, Best of the Vanguard Years 2000, One Night in America 2002, Sanctuary 2004, Delta Hardware 2006, Rough Dried 2007, Get Up! (with Ben Harper) (Grammy Award for Best Blues Album 2014) 2013. *Address:* c/o Morrow Management, 5003 Westpark Drive, Suite 102, Valley Village, CA 91601, USA (office); c/o The Rosebud Music Booking Agency, PO Box 170429, San Francisco, CA 94117, USA (office); c/o Real World Studios, Box Mill, Mill Lane, Box, Wilts., SN13 8PL, England. *Telephone:* (818) 642-9217 (office); (415) 386-3456 (office). *E-mail:* JParker@morrowmanagement.com (office); henri@sonic.net (office); info@rosebudus.com (office). *Website:* www.morrowmanagement.com (office); www.rosebudus.com (office); www.realworldrecords.com; www.charliemusselwhite.com. *Fax:* (415) 386-0599 (office); (1225) 743787.

MUSTAFA, Isa, BA, MA, PhD; Kosovo politician; b. 15 May 1951, Prapashticë, Prishtina, Kosovo, Serbian SR, SFR Yugoslavia (now Kosovo); m.; two s. one d.; ed Univ. of Prishtina; began career as an examiner at Univ. of Prishtina 1974; Head of Municipal Govt of Pristina 1984–88; Minister of Economy and Finance, Govt of Repub. of Kosovo, in exile, headed by Bujar Bukoshi 1991–99; warrant for his arrest issued by Serbian regime, lived in Western Europe as a political refugee, mainly in Germany, Switzerland, Albania, Slovenia and Croatia –1999; following Kosovo War returned home in 1999, returned to politics in 2006 as a High Political Adviser of Pres. Fatmir Sejdiu; Mayor of Prishtina 2007–13; Chair. Democratic League of Kosovo (LDK) 2010–. *Address:* Democratic League of Kosovo (Lidhja Demokratike e Kosovës), 10000 Prishtina, Kompleksi Qafa, Kosovo (office). *Telephone:* (38) 242242 (office). *Fax:* (38) 245305 (office). *E-mail:* ildk@ldk-ks.eu (office). *Website:* www.ldk-ks.eu (office).

MUSTAFAJ, Besnik; Albanian writer, academic, politician and diplomatist; b. 23 Sept. 1958, Bajram Curri City; m.; two c.; ed Univ. of Tirana; Prof. of Foreign Literature, Faculty of History and Philology, Univ. of Tirana 1983–91; Founding mem. Democratic Party of Albania 1990–, Sec. for Int. Relations 1999–2005;

elected MP 1991, Deputy Chair. Foreign Relations Comm. 2001–05, Deputy Chair. of Perm. Del. to European Parl. 2001–05; Amb. to France and Perm. Rep. to UNESCO, Paris 1992–97; Minister of Foreign Affairs 2005–07 (resgnd); Co-founder Albanian Helsinki Cttee 1990; Founding Chair. Albanian Writers' Pen Club. *Publications include:* Vera pa kthim (The Summer of no Return) 1989, Gjinkallat e vapës (The Cicadas of the Heat) 1994, Një sagë e vogël (A Little Saga) 1995, Daullja prej letre (The Paper Drum) 1996, Boshti (The Void) 1998; several books and papers on poetry and aesthetics. *Address:* c/o Democratic Party of Albania, Rruga Punëtorët e Rilindjes 1, 1001 Tirana, Albania.

MUSTAPHA, Faisz, PC, LLB, HE; Sri Lankan lawyer and diplomatist; m. Ameena Mustapha; fmr lawyer; mem. Perm. Court of Arbitration 1993–; Chair. Sri Lanka Comm. on Elimination Discrimination and Monitoring Fundamental Rights; fmr Chair. and mem. Finance Comm.; mem. Sri Lanka Law Comm.; Deputy-Pres. Bar Asscn; fmr Chair. Sri Lanka Human Rights Comm.; Trustee Lt-Gen. Denzil Kobbekaduwa Trust; High Commr to UK 2002–05 (also accred as Amb. to Ireland 2003–05); currently Pres.'s Counsel, mem. Presidential Panel of Legal/Constitutional Experts 2006–, Presidential Comm. of Inquiry into failed finance cos 2007–. *Address:* c/o President's Secretariat, Republic Sq., Colombo 1, Sri Lanka. *Telephone:* (911) 2324801. *Fax:* (11) 2331246. *E-mail:* gosl@presidentsl.org. *Website:* www.presidentsl.org.

MUSTAPHA, Shettima, BSc, PhD; Nigerian politician; b. 26 Nov. 1939, Nguru; ed Ahmadu Bello Univ., Zaria, Univ. of Cambridge, UK, Purdue Univ., USA; Commr, Borno State 1979–83; cand. for Vice-Pres. in 1983 election; held as political prisoner 1983–85; Regional Head of Jos Office, Fed. Agric. Coordinating Unit, Fed. Ministry of Agric. 1985–89, Head of Agric. Projects Monitoring and Evaluation Unit 1989–90, Minister of Agric. and Natural Resources 1990–92; Nat. Treas. People's Democratic Party 1998–2001; fmr Chair. Savannah Bank of Nigeria plc; Minister of Defence 2008–09, of the Interior 09–10; fmr consultant to World Bank, IFAD, FAO, UNDP; Fellow, Genetics Soc. of Nigeria; mem. American Soc. of Agronomy, Agricultural Soc. of Nigeria; Hon. Fellow, Entomological Soc. of Nigeria; Officer, Order of the Fed. Repub. *Address:* c/o Ministry of the Interior Area 1, Secretariat Complex, Garki, PMB 16, Abuja, Nigeria (office).

MUSTILL, Baron (Life Peer), cr. 1992, of Pateley Bridge in the County of North Yorkshire; **Michael John Mustill,** Kt, PC, FBA; British judge, author and arbitrator (retd); b. 10 May 1931; s. of Clement Mustill and the late Marion Mustill; m. 1st Beryl R. Davies (divorced); m. 2nd Caroline Phillips; two s. one step d.; ed Oundle School and St John's Coll., Cambridge; called to Bar, Gray's Inn 1955, Bencher 1976, QC 1968; Deputy Chair. Hants. Quarter Sessions 1971; Recorder, Crown Court 1972–78; Judge, High Court, Queen's Bench Div. 1978–85; Presiding Judge, NE Circuit 1981–84; a Lord Justice of Appeal 1985–92; Lord of Appeal in Ordinary 1992–97; Pres. British Maritime Law Asscn 1995–, Chartered Inst. of Arbitrators 1995–98, Asscn of Average Adjusters 1996–97, Seldon Soc. 1997–2000; Yorke Distinguished Visiting Fellow, Univ. of Cambridge 1996–; mem. Comité Maritime Arbitration 1996–, Indian Council of Arbitration; Hon. Prof. of Law, Univ. of Birmingham 1995–. *Publications:* The Law and Practice of Commercial Arbitration in England (with S.C. Boyd) 1982, Anticipatory Breach of Contract 1990; articles in legal journals. *Address:* Essex Court Chambers, 24 Lincoln's Inn Fields, London, WC2A 3ED (office); House of Lords, Westminster, London, SW1A 0PW; 42 Laurier Road, London, NW5 1SJ, England (home). *Telephone:* (20) 7813-8000 (office); (20) 7485-3726 (home). *Fax:* (20) 7813-8080 (office).

MUSTONEN, Olli; Finnish pianist, composer and conductor; b. 7 June 1967, Helsinki; s. of Seppo Mustonen and Marja-Liisa Mustonen; m. Sole Mustonen; began studies with harpsichord, studied piano with Ralf Gothóni and Eero Heinonen, composition with Einojuhani Rautavaara; has played with many of the world's leading orchestras; has appeared at festivals including Berlin, Hollywood Bowl, BBC Proms and Salzburg; Artistic Dir Turku Music Festival 1990–92, Ludus Mustonalis concert series; co-founder and Dir, Helsinki Festival Orchestra; Conductor, Tapiola Sinfonietta 2003–; Edison Award 1992, Gramophone Award for Best Instrumental Recording 1992. *Major compositions:* Fantasia (for piano and strings) 1985, Toccata (for piano, string quartet and double bass) 1989, two Nonets (for two string quartets and double bass) 1995, 2000, Triple Concerto (for three violins and orchestra) 1998, Jehkin Iivana Sonata for piano 2006, Sinuhe Sonata for solo oboe 2005–06. *Leisure interests:* mathematics, nature, politics, sports. *Address:* c/o Van Walsum Management Ltd, 11 York Road, London, SE1 7NX, England. *Telephone:* (20) 7902-0520 (office). *Fax:* (20) 7902-0520 (office). *E-mail:* vwm@vanwalsum.com (office). *Website:* www.vanwalsum.co.uk (office).

MUSYOKA, (Stephen) Kalonzo, LLB; Kenyan lawyer and politician; b. 24 Dec. 1953, Tseikuru village, Mwingi Dist; m. Pauline Musyoka; four c.; ed Univ. of Nairobi; lawyer with Kaplan & Stratton Advocates; Sr Pnr, Musyoka & Wambua Advocates; mem. Parl. 1985, Deputy Speaker, Nat. Ass. 1988–93; Sec. Kitui branch, Kenya African Nat. Union (KANU) Party 1985–88, fmr Nat. Organizing Sec. 1988, Vice-Chair. 2002; Asst Minister for Work, Housing and Planning 1986–88; Minister of Foreign Affairs 1992–98, 2002–04; fmr Minister of Educ., Tourism and Information; Minister of the Environment and Natural Resources 2004–05; defected from KANU to launch Liberal Democratic Party just before Dec. 2002 presidential elections, Leader, Orange Democratic Movt—Kenya 2007–; unsuccessful cand. in presidential elections 2007; Vice-Pres. of Kenya and Minister of Home Affairs 2008–13. *Address:* Kenya National Assembly, Parliament Buildings, PO Box 41842, Nairobi (office). *Telephone:* (20) 221291 (office). *Fax:* (20) 336589 (office).

MUTA, Taizo, BSc, MSc, DSc; Japanese theoretical physicist, university administrator and academic; b. 1 June 1937; ed Kyushu Univ., Tokyo Univ.; Research Assoc., Faculty of Science, Kyoto Univ. 1965–71, Asst Prof., Research Inst. for Fundamental Physics 1971–82; Prof., Faculty of Science, Hiroshima Univ. 1982–, mem. Senate 1991, Presidential Aide 1993–95, Dean Faculty of Science 1995–99, Vice-Pres. 1999–2001, Prof., Grad. School of Science 2000–, Pres. 2001–07; Dir Mazda Motor Corpn. *Publications include:* Foundations of Quantum Chromodynamics: An Introduction to Perturbative Methods in Gauge Theories (World Scientific Lecture Notes in Physics, Vol. 5) 1984, 1990 International Workshop of Strong Coupling Gauge Theories and Beyond, July 28–31, 1990, Nagoya, Japan 1991, International Workshop on Electroweak Symmetry Breaking: November

12–15, 1991 Hiroshima (co-author) 1992; numerous scientific papers in professional journals on the theory of elementary particles, quantum chromodynamics and dynamical symmetry breaking in quantum field theory. *Leisure interests:* astronomy, fishing, skiing. *Address:* c/o Board of Directors, Mazda Motor Corp, 3-1 Shinchi, Fuchu-cho, Aki-gun, Hiroshima, 730-8670, Japan (office).

MUTABOBA, Joseph, MPhil; Rwandan diplomatist and UN official; *Deputy Joint Special Representative for Political Affairs, UNAMID, United Nations;* b. 21 Dec. 1949; m.; three c.; ed North London Univ., UK; served as Sec.-Gen. in Ministries of Foreign Affairs and of Internal Affairs, as Deputy Nat. Co-ordinator for Rwanda and Head of Peace and Security thematic group in Int. Conf. on Great Lakes Region, and as sr diplomat in Addis Ababa and Washington, DC; Perm. Rep. to UN, New York 1999–2001; Pres. of Rwanda's Special Envoy to Great Lakes Region –2009; Special Rep. of UN Sec.-Gen. for Guinea-Bissau and Head of UN Integrated Peace-building Office in Guinea-Bissau (UNIOGBIS) 2009–13, Deputy Jt Special Rep. for Political Affairs, AU-UN Hybrid Operation in Darfur (UNAMID) 2013–. *Address:* UNAMID, El Fasher, POB 5041, Grand Central Station, NewYork, NY 10163-5041, USA. *E-mail:* unamid-enquiries@un.org.

MUTALOV, Abdulkhashim Mutalovich, PhD; Uzbekistani politician and business executive; b. 27 April 1947, Telyau, Tashkent Region; s. of Abdurahmonov Mutal and Abdurahmonova Turihon; m. Mutalova Hurinisa; one s.; ed All-Union Inst. of Food Industry; worker, Tashkent Factory of Bread Products; army service 1965–79; Dir Akhangaran Enterprise of Bread Products 1979–86; Deputy Minister of Bread Products Uzbek SSR 1986–87, Minister 1987–91; Deputy Chair. Cabinet of Ministers 1991–92; Prime Minister of Uzbekistan 1992–96; Chair. State grain co. Uzdon Makhsulot 1996–; Orden Znak Pochota 1986. *Publications:* Main Directions in Formation of Free-Market Relations in Grain-Processing Enterprises of the Republic of Uzbekistan 1993. *Leisure interests:* tennis. *Address:* Tegirmon Novvovhona Jihozlari LLC (Bakery Equipment Co.), Tashkent (office); Turob Tula Street 28–57, Chilanzar District, Tashkent, Uzbekistan (home). *Telephone:* (712) 984652 (office); (712) 1394184 (home). *Fax:* (712) 984656 (office). *E-mail:* gulnaz@corp.uzreport.com (home).

MUTAMBARA, Arthur, BSc, MSc, PhD; Zimbabwean politician; b. 25 May 1966; ed Univ. of Zimbabwe, Univ. of Oxford, UK, Massachusetts Inst. of Tech., USA; active in student politics in 1980s; worked as man. consultant, McKinsey and Co.; fmr Prof. of Business Strategy, Kellogg Business School, Northwestern Univ., USA; Man. Dir Africa Tech. and Business Inst. 2003–; Leader of pro-Senate faction Movement for Democratic Change—Mutambara (MDC—M) 2006–; arrested for political activities, released without charge, March and May 2006; Deputy Prime Minister 2009–13. *Address:* Movement for Democratic Change, Harare, Zimbabwe (office). *E-mail:* a.mutambara@mdczim.com (office). *Website:* www.mdczim.com (office).

MUTASA, Didymus Noel Edwin; Zimbabwean politician; *Minister of State for Presidential Affairs;* b. 27 July 1935, Rusape; ed Goromonzi Govt School, Univ. of Birmingham, UK; began career as clerk and admin. officer in civil service; Co-founder Southern Region Fed. Services Asscn 1960; Co-founder Cold Comfort Soc. (multi-racial farming co-operative) 1964–70; arrested 1970, held in solitary confinement, Sinoia Prison 1970–72; in exile 1972–79; Founder mem. Zimbabwe African Nat. Union (ZANU) Br., Birmingham, UK and Dist Chair. ZANU UK 1975; joined ZANU HQ, Maputo, Mozambique 1977, Deputy Sec. for Finance, ZANU Cen. Cttee 1978; mem. Parl. for Manicaland 1980–, Speaker of Parl. 1980–90, Sec. for Transport and Welfare 1984–, Minister for Political Affairs 1990, Anti-Corruption and Anti-Monopolies Programme Minister 2003–05, Minister of State for Nat. Security 2005–09, for Presidential Affairs 2009–. *Address:* c/o Office of the President, Munhumutapa Bldg, Samora Machel Ave, Private Bag 7700, Harare (office); Zimbabwe African National Union—Patriotic Front, corner of Rotten Row and Samora Machel Avenue, POB 4530, Harare, Zimbabwe. *Telephone:* (4) 753329 (ZANU—PF) (office). *Fax:* (4) 774146 (ZANU—PF) (office). *Website:* www.zanupfpub.co.zw (office).

MUTAWAKIL, Wakil Ahmad; Afghan politician; served as spokesman and personal sec. to Taliban leader Mullah Mohammad Omar –1999; Foreign Minister in Taliban Govt of Islamic Emirate of Afghanistan 1999–2002; surrendered in Kandahar to govt troops following ousting of regime Feb. 2002, held for three years under house arrest in Kabul 2002–05; now part of present govt under admin of Hamid Karzai; cand. in parl. elections Sept. 2005.

MUTEBI II, HM Kabaka of Buganda; (Ronald Muwenda Mutebi); b. 13 April 1955, Mmengo; s. of the late Kabaka Sir Edward Fredrick Walugembe Mutesa II (King Freddy) and Lady Sarah Nalule Kisosonkole; m. Lady Sylvia Nagginda 1999; ed Kingsmead Preparatory School, Sussex, Bradford Public School, Reading, Magdalene Coll., Cambridge, UK; lived in exile in England following overthrow of his father Mutesa II by fmr Pres. of Uganda Milton Obote 1966–86; Assoc. Ed. African Concord; returned to Uganda 1986; crowned 37th Kabaka (King) of Buganda, marking restoration of ancient kingdom of Buganda, 31 July 1993. *Leisure interest:* squash. *Address:* Mmengo Palace, PO Box 58, Kampala, Uganda.

MUTHARIKA, Arthur Peter, LLB, LLM, JSD; Malawi lawyer, academic and politician; *Minister of Foreign Affairs and International Co-operation;* b. 1940, brother of Bingu wa Mutharika, Pres. of Malawi; m. (deceased); one s. two d.; ed Univ. of London, UK, Yale Univ., USA; magistrate, Dar es Salaam, Tanzania 1965; admitted to Tanzanian bar 1971; Prof. of Law, Univ. of Dar es Salaam 1968–71, UN Inst. for Training and Research Program for Foreign Service Officers from Africa and Asia, Makerere Univ., Uganda 1969, Haile Selassie Univ., Ethiopia 1970, Rutgers Univ., USA 1972; Asst Prof. of Law, Washington Univ., St Louis, USA 1972–74, Assoc. Prof. 1974–77, Prof. 1997–; Academic Visitor, London School of Econs 1980; MP for Thyolo-East constituency 2009–; fmr Minister of Justice and Constitutional Affairs, of Educ., Science and Tech., Minister of Foreign Affairs and Int. Co-operation 2011–; mem. Democratic Progressive Party (DPP), adopted as DPP cand. for presidential election 2011. *Address:* Ministry of Foreign Affairs and International Co-operation, POB 30315, Lilongwe 3, Malawi (office). *Telephone:* 1789323 (office). *Fax:* 1788482 (office). *E-mail:* foreign@malawi.net (office). *Website:* www.foreignaffairs.gov.mw (office).

MUTHURAMAN, Balasubramanian, BTech, MBA; Indian steel industry executive; *Vice-Chairman, Tata Steel;* b. 26 Sept. 1944; ed Indian Inst. of Tech.

(IIT), Madras, Xavier's Labour Research Inst., Jamshedpur, Advanced Man. Programme, Centre Européen d'Éducation Permanente (CEDEP)/Institut Européen d'Admin des Affaires (INSEAD), France; joined Tata Steel as grad. trainee 1966, worked in areas of Iron-making and Eng Devt for 10 years, spent 19 years in Marketing and Sales Div. rising to Vice-Pres., selected to head Cold Rolling Mill Project 1995, Exec. Dir (Special Projects) 2000–01, Man. Dir Tata Steel 2001, currently Vice-Chair.; Chair. Tata Sponge Iron Ltd, Tata Steel KZN (Pty) Ltd, SA, TM International Logistics Ltd, The Tinplate Co. of India Ltd, Natsteel Asia Pte Ltd, Natsteel Asia (S) Pte Ltd, Singapore, Millennium Steel Public Co. Ltd, Bangkok; mem. Bd Dirs Tata Inc., New York, Tata Int. Ltd, Tata Industries Ltd, Mumbai, The Dhamra Port Co. Ltd; Chair. Bd of Govs Xavier Labour Relations Inst., Jamshedpur, Nat. Inst. of Tech., Jamshedpur, Research Council of Nat. Metallurgical Lab., Jamshedpur; Pres. Indian Inst. of Metals; mem. Bd of Dirs Int. Iron and Steel Inst., Brussels (mem. Exec. Cttee), West Bengal Industrial Devt Corpn Ltd, CEDEP; mem. UN Global Compact Bd, Nat. Council of Confed. of Indian Industries; mem. Bd Govs IIT, Kharagpur; Hon. Rotarian, Jamshedpur Rotary Club (East and West), Hon. Fellow, All India Man. Asscn 2007; Distinguished Alumnus Award, IIT, Madras 1997, Tata Gold Medal, Indian Inst. of Metals 2002, CEO of the Year Award, Indian Inst. of Materials Man. 2002, Nat. HRD Network Pathfinders Award in the CEO Category 2004, CEO of the Year, Business Standard 2005, CEO with Human Resources Orientation Award, World HRD Congress at Mumbai 2005, Management Man of the Year 2006–2007 Award, Bombay Man. Asscn 2007. *Leisure interests:* playing cricket and golf, reading literature on general management, finance, marketing and business. *Address:* The Tata Iron and Steel Co. Ltd, Bombay House, 24 Homi Mody Street, Mumbai 400 001, India. *Telephone:* (22) 66658282 (office). *Fax:* (22) 66658113 (office). (22) 66657725 (office). *E-mail:* muthuraman@tatasteel.com (office). *Website:* www .tatasteel.com (office).

MUTI, Riccardo; Italian conductor; *Music Director, Chicago Symphony Orchestra;* b. 28 July 1941, Naples; s. of Domenico Muti and Gilda Sellitto; m. Cristina Mazzavillani 1969; two s. one d.; ed San Pietro Conservatory, Majella, Naples and Milan Conservatory of Music; Prin. Conductor, Maggio Musicale, Florence 1969–81; Prin. Conductor, Philharmonia Orchestra, London 1973–82, Music Dir 1979–82, Conductor Laureate 1982–; Prin. Guest Conductor, Philadelphia Orchestra 1977–80, Prin. Conductor and Music Dir 1980–92, Conductor Laureate 1992–; Music Dir, La Scala, Milan 1986–2005; Prin. Conductor, Filarmonica della Scala 1988–2005; Prin. Guest Conductor Designate, New York Philharmonic; Music Dir, Chicago Symphony Orchestra 2010–; Hon. Dir for Life, Teatro dell'Opera di Roma 2010–; concert tours in USA with Boston, Chicago and Philadelphia Orchestras; concerts at Salzburg, Edinburgh, Lucerne, Flanders and Vienna festivals; also conducted Berlin Philharmonic, Bayerische Rundfunk Sinfonie Orchester, Vienna Philharmonic, New York Philharmonic and Concertgebouw Amsterdam; opera: Florence, Munich, Covent Garden, La Scala, Ravenna, Vienna, Accad. di Santa Cecilia (Rome), Accademico Dell'Accademia Cherubini (Florence); Grand Golden Medal of the City of Monaco, Grand Silver Ehrenkreuz Medal (Austria), Officer Order of Merit (Germany), Verdienstkreuz (First Class, Germany) 1976, Cavaliere Gran Croce (Italy) 1991, Légion d'honneur (France), Hon. KBE 2000, Russian Order of Friendship 2001, Silver Medal of the Salzburg Mozarteum 2001; Hon. mem. American Acad. of Arts & Sciences; Hon. PhD (Weizmann Inst. of Science), Dr hc (Pennsylvania, Philadelphia, Bologna, Urbino, Milan, Cremona, Lecce); Guido Cantelli Award 1967, Diapason d'Oro, Premio Critica Discografia Italiana, Prix Académie nat. du disque 1977, Deutscher Schallplatten Preis, 'Bellini d'Oro', Abbiati Prize, Grand Prix du disque for La Traviata (Verdi), Requiem in C minor (Cherubini) 1982, Disco d' Oro for Music for Films, Wolf Prize 2000, Musical America Award for Musician of the Year 2010, Grammy Award for Best Classical Album (for Verdi: Requiem) 2011. *Address:* c/o Chicago Symphony Orchestra, Symphony Center, 220 South Michigan Avenue, Chicago, IL 60604, USA (office). *E-mail:* info@riccardomuti.com (office). *Website:* www.riccardomuti.com (office).

MUTKO, Vitalii Leontyevich, CandEconSci; Russian mechanical engineer and politician; *Minister of Sport, Tourism and Youth Policy;* b. 8 Dec. 1958, Kurinskaya, nr Tuapse, Krasnodar Territory; m.; two d.; ed Leningrad (now St Petersburg) Construction Vocational School No. 226, Petrokrepost (now Shlisselburg) Nautical School, Leningrad Region, Leningrad River Vocational Coll., Leningrad Inst. of Water Transport, Faculty of Law, St Petersburg State Univ., St Petersburg State Univ. of Econs and Finance; served as seaman on ships from NW River Steam Navigation and Leningrad sea port 1977–78, originally worked on Vladimir Ilich river steamship, later transferred to work on river-sea dry cargo ship, also worked in port of Hamburg; Komsomol activist during his studies 1978, headed coll.; Komsomol org., headed local trade union coll. cttee; joined CPSU 1979; following graduation, worked at Exec. Cttee of Kirov Dist Soviet of People's Deputies in Leningrad 1983, worked as an instructor and Head of Dept for Social Issues, Sec., later Chair. Exec. Cttee 1990, set up Council of Chairmen 1990; Deputy, Kirov Regional Council 1990, Head of Admin of Kirov Dist 1991; organized meetings of workers from Kirov factory against Aug. putsch conspirators 1991; Deputy Mayor of St Petersburg and Chair. of Mayor's Cttee on Social Issues 1992–95; Curator of Zenit St Petersburg Football Club 1992–95, Pres. 1995–2003; authorized rep. of Vladimir Putin in presidential elections 2000; headed electoral staff of St Petersburg Gov. cand. Valentina Matviyenko 2000; Pres. Russian Football Premier League 2001–03; Fed. Council rep. from St Petersburg Govt 2003–08, Chair. Comm. on Youth and Sport Affairs, mem. Cttee on Fed. and Regional Policy Issues, Comm. on Control of Maintenance of Activity of Fed. Council; Pres. Russian Football Union 2005; mem. Tech. and Devt Cttee of FIFA 2006–; Senator for St Petersburg (for second time) 2007–; mem. presidential cttee on devt of physical culture and sport, highest standard sport, and on preparation and direction of 2014 XXII Winter Olympic Games and XI Winter Paralympics in Sochi 2007–; Minister of Sport, Tourism and Youth Policy 2008–; Pres. Special Olympics Cttee for St Petersburg, Golden Pelican (charity); Order of Honour 1994, Order of Friendship 2002; medals dedicated 'In Commemoration of the 300th Anniversary of St Petersburg', 'In Commemoration of the 1000th Anniversary of Kazan'. *Address:* Federal Agency for Physical Culture and Sport, 105064 Moscow, 18 ulitsa Kazakova (office); Federal Agency for Tourism, 103084 Moscow, 47 ulitsa Myasnitskaya, Russia (office). *Telephone:* (495) 263-08-40 (Sport) (office); (495) 105-72-56 (Sport) (office); (495) 208-29-37 (Tourism) (office); (495) 207-79-07

(Tourism) (office). *Fax:* (495) 263-07-61 (Sport) (office). *E-mail:* info@rossport.ru (office); rustourism@ropnet.ru (office). *Website:* www.rossport.ru (office); www .russiatourism.ru (office).

MUTOLA, Maria Lurdes; Mozambican athlete; b. 27 Oct. 1972, Maputo; d. of João Mutola and Catarina Mutola; ed Eugene High School, Ore., USA; gold medallist, 800m, World Indoor Championships 1993, 1995, 1997, 2001, 2003, 2004; winner 800m World Cup 1992, 1994, 1998, 2002; winner 800m Grand Prix Final 1993, 1995, 1999, 2001; gold medallist, 800m, World Championships 1995, 2001, 2003; bronze medallist, 800m, Olympic Games, Atlanta 1996, gold medallist 800m, Sydney 2000; winner 800m World Athletics Final 2003; world record holder at 1,000m indoor; African record holder at 800m and 1,000m (outdoor); between 1992 and 1995 she won 42 consecutive races; won all six Golden League races 2003 winning US$1 million prize; f. Lurdes Mutola Foundation 2001; Hon. UN Amb. 2003–. *Address:* c/o Lurdes Mutola Foundation, 25th of September Avenue, Times Square Building, Block II, 1st Floor, Door 12, Maputo, Mozambique. *Website:* www .flmutola.org.mz.

MUTTER, Anne-Sophie; German violinist; b. 29 June 1963, Rheinfelden/Baden; m. 1st Dithelf Wunderlich 1989 (deceased); m. 2nd André Previn 2002 (divorced 2006); studied with Prof. Aida Stucki, Winterthur, Switzerland; began musical career playing piano and violin 1969; played in the Int. Music Festival, Lucerne 1976; début with Herbert von Karajan at Pfingstfestspiele, Salzburg 1977; soloist with major orchestras of the world; also plays with string trio and quartet; Guest Teacher RAM, London 1985; est. foundation promoting gifted young string players throughout the world; Hon. Pres. Mozart Soc., Univ. of Oxford 1983; Order of Merit (Germany and Bavaria); Hon. doctorate (Norwegian Univ. of Science and Tech. (NTNU), Trondheim) 2012; Youth Music Prize (FRG) for violin 1970, for piano 1970, for violin 1974, Artist of the Year, Deutscher Schallplattenpreis, Grand Prix Int. du Disque, Record Acad. Prize, Tokyo 1982, Internationaler Schallplattenpreis 1993, Herbert von Karajan Award 2003, Musical America Award for Instrumentalist of the Year 2011, Atlantic Council's Distinguished Artistic Leadership Award 2012. *Recordings include:* Mozart: Five Violin Concertos 2005, Bach, Gubaidulina: Violin Concertos (with the Trondheim Soloists) 2008, Mendelssohn's Violin Concerto 2009, Brahms: The Violin Sonatas 2010, Rihm/Currier (ECHO Klassik Award for Concerto Recording of the Year/Violin – 20th/21st Century 2012) 2011. *Leisure interests:* graphic arts, sport. *Address:* Kaye Artists Management, Barratt House, 7 Chertsey Road, Woking, GU21 5AB, England (office); Effnerstrasse 48, 81925 Munich, Germany; c/o London Symphony Orchestra, Barbican Hall, The Barbican Centre, London, EC2Y 8DS, England. *Telephone:* (89) 984418 (Germany). *Fax:* (89) 9827186 (Germany).

MUXAMEJANOV, Oral B.; Kazakhstani politician; b. 11 Nov. 1948, Qostanay; m.; one s. two d.; ed Novosibirsk Inst. of Soviet Co-operative Trade, Russia, Almaty Higher Party School; worked in Oblast Consumer Products Union and Worsted Cloth Factory, Qostanay 1971–75; various positions with Komsomol (Communist Youth League) and party organs, and in regional Soviet of People's Deputies, Torgai Oblast (now Qostanay Oblast) 1975–92; Head of Regional Admin, Amangeldinsky Dist, Torgai Oblast 1992–94; Deputy, Supreme Soviet of Kazakhstan (Parl.) 1994–95 (dissolved under new constitution 1995); Head of Dept of Social-Cultural Devt, Office of the Pres. 1995–97; Inspector, Presidential Admin, becoming Head of Dept of Organizational-Control Work 1997–2004; Deputy, Majlis (Parl.) from electoral dist No 49, Qostanay Oblast 2004–07, 2007–, Chair. Majlis 2004–07, 2008–12; mem. Light of the Fatherland People's Democratic Party (Nur Otan), Leader, Parl. Fraction 2008–. *Leisure interests:* literature, poetry, fishing, billiards. *Address:* c/o Office of the Chairman, Majlis, 010000 Astana, Parliament House, Kazakhstan.

MUZAFFAR, Chandra, PhD; Malaysian political scientist, academic and international organization executive; *President, International Movement for a Just World;* b. 10 March 1947, Bedong, Kedah; m.; two d.; ed Univ. of Singapore; Lecturer, Science Univ. of Malaysia 1970–83, Sr Research Fellow 1992–97; Prof. and first Dir Centre for Civilizational Dialogue, Univ. of Malaya 1997–99; Founder-Pres. multi-ethnic social reform group Aliran Kesedaran Negara (Nat. Consciousness Movt) 1977–91; mem. Exec. Cttee Asian Comm. on Human Rights 1985; arrested by Malaysian Govt under Internal Security Act Oct. 1987, released without conditions Dec. 1987; nominated as monitor by Human Rights Watch 1988; Pres. Int. Movt for a Just World (JUST), Kuala Lumpur 1997–; Deputy Pres. Kealidan (Nat. Justice Party) 1999–2001; Chair. Bd of Trustees, 1Malaysia Foundation; mem. Bd Dirs Integrity Inst., Malaysia 2004–, and several int. NGOs; Weigand Distinguished Visitor Fellowship, Duke Univ., USA 2000; Prof. of Global Studies, Science Univ. of Malaysia 2007–12; Hon. Prof., Universidad Nacional Experimental Politecnica de la Fuerza Armada, Caracas, Venezuela 2009; Harry J. Benda Prize for distinguished scholarship on SE Asia, Asscn of Asian Studies, North America 1989, Juliet Hollister Award 'Interfaith Visionary', Temple of Understanding, New York, USA 2010. *Publications:* author or ed. of 27 books on religion, human rights, Malaysian politics, and int. relations, including Rights, Religion, and Reform 2002, Subverting Greed 2002, Muslims, Dialogue, Terror 2003, Global Ethic or Global Hegemony? 2005, Hegemony: Justice; Peace 2008, Religion and Governance 2009, Plea for Empathy 2010, Religion Seeking Justice and Peace 2010, Exploring Religion in Our Time 2011, Muslims Today 2011. *Leisure interest:* reading. *Address:* International Movement for a Just World, PO Box 288, 46730 Petaling Jaya, Selangor (office); No. 1258, Jalan Telok, Section 5, Petaling Jaya 46000 Selangor, Malaysia (office). *Telephone:* (3) 7781-2494 (office); (3) 6201-5170 (home). *Fax:* (3) 7781-3245 (office). *E-mail:* cmuzaffar@just -international.org (office). *Website:* www.just-international.org (office).

MUZITO, Adolphe; Democratic Republic of the Congo economist and politician; b. 1957; ed Univ. of Kinshasa; Regional Finance Insp., Finance Inspectorate Gen. 2007; Minister of the Budget 2007–08; Prime Minister 2008–12 (resgnd); Sec.-Gen. Parti Lumumbiste Unifie 2007–. *Address:* c/o Office of the Prime Minister, Kinshasa, Democratic Republic of the Congo.

MVOUBA, Isidore; Republic of the Congo politician; *Minister of State, Co-ordinator of Basic Infrastructures, and Minister of Civil Aviation and of Maritime Trade;* b. 1954, Kindamba; with Chemin de fer Congo Océan 1977; mem. Parti Congolais du Travail (PCT); Presidential Campaign Dir for Denis Sassou Nguesso 1992, 2002; Minister of Youth and Sports 1992–93; Prin. Pvt. Sec. for Head of State

1997–99; Minister for Transport, Civil Aviation and the Merchant Navy 1999–2005; Minister of State for Transport and Privatization in charge of Co-ordination of Govt Action 2002–05, concurrently Prime Minister 2005–09 (post abolished), Minister of State, Co-ordinator of Basic Infrastructures, and Minister of Civil Aviation and of Maritime Trade 2009–; mem. Assemblée nationale (Parl.) as PCT MP for Kindamba constituency 2007–. *Address:* Ministry of Maritime Transport and the Merchant Navy, Brazzaville, Republic of the Congo (office). *Website:* www.congo-site.net (office).

MWAKWERE, Chirau Ali; Kenyan politician and diplomatist; *Minister of the Environment and Mineral Resources;* b. 1945, Golini, Ziwani, Kwale Dist; m. Rose Batsigira; Amb. to Zimbabwe –2004; mem. Nat. Ass. (Parl.) for Matuga; Minister of Foreign Affairs June 2004–05, of Transport 2005–10, of the Environment and Mineral Resources 2012–. *Address:* Ministry of the Environment and Mineral Resources, NHIF Bldg, Ragati Rd, POB 30126, 00100 Nairobi, Kenya (office). *Telephone:* (20) 2730808 (office). *Fax:* (20) 2725707 (office). *Website:* www.environment.go.ke.

MWAMBA, Alexis Thambwe, LenD; Democratic Republic of the Congo lawyer and politician; *Minister of Foreign Affairs;* ed Univ. of Burundi, Univ. Libre de Bruxelles, Belgium; lawyer, Kinshasa Bar; fmr mem. Movt for the Liberation of Congo (resistance group); fmr Pres. Union des Démocrates Indépendants; Founding mem. Rassemblement congolais pour la Démocratie; fmr Man. Dir Société Minière du Kivu (Sominki); fmr Amb. of Zaire (now Democratic Repub. of Congo) to Italy; fmr Dir Office des Douanes et Accises (customs office); fmr Minister of Public Works, of External Trade, and of Transport; in exile in Brussels 1997; Minister of Planning and Reconstruction 2003–06; mem. Nat. Assembly (Ind.) for Kindu constituency 2006–; Minister of Foreign Affairs 2008–. *Address:* Ministry of Foreign Affairs, Kinshasa, Democratic Republic of the Congo (office).

MWAMBA, Geoffrey Bwalya; Zambian business executive and politician; *Minister of Defence;* b. 15 March 1959; m. Chama Mwamba; mem. Nat. Ass. for Kasama Central; Minister of Defence 2011–; f. GBM Group, GBM Trucking and Milling Co., GBM Milling Co. Ltd; mem. Patriotic Front. *Address:* Ministry of Defence, POB 31931, Lusaka, Zambia (office). *Telephone:* (21) 1252366 (office).

MWANDO SIMBA, Charles; Democratic Republic of the Congo politician; *Minister of National Defence and War Veterans;* b. 12 Oct. 1936, Katanga; ed Univ. of Antwerp, Belgium; mem. Assemblée nationale (Parl.) for Moba constituency 1965, 1970–80, 2006–; Gov. Kivu Prov. 1980–87; several ministerial posts since 1987, including Minister of Planning, of Public Works, of Transport and Communication, of Rural Devt 2007–08, of Nat. Defence and War Veterans 2008–; mem. UNADEF. *Address:* Ministry of National Defence and War Veterans, BP 4111, Kinshasa-Gombe, Democratic Republic of the Congo (office). *Telephone:* (12) 59375 (office).

MWANSA, Kalombo T., LLB, LLM, MPhil, PhD; Zambian politician and professor of law; *Minister of Home Affairs;* b. 9 Sept. 1955, Nchelenge; m. 1983; two s. two d.; ed Univ. of Zambia, Harvard Univ., USA, Univs of Cambridge and London, UK; Tutor in Law, Univ. of Zambia 1979–80, Lecturer in Law and Criminology 1983–88, Acting Dean of Law School 1992–93; Perm. Sec. Ministry of Home Affairs 1993–98; Acting Chair. Police and Prisons Service Comm. 1994–96; Perm. Sec. of Admin, Cabinet Office 1998–99; Deputy Sec. to Cabinet 1999–2002, Acting Sec. 2001, 2002; Minister of Foreign Affairs 2002–04, of Home Affairs 2004–05, 2008–, of Mines and Mineral Devt 2005–08; nominated mem. Parl. 2002–; Livingstone Scholar, Jesus Coll. Cambridge 1982–83; Commonwealth Scholar, SOAS 1988–92; awards from Lusaka Hindu Asscn, Law Asscn of Zambia. *Publications include:* Property Crime in Zambia, Death Penalty in Zambia, Zambia Police and Crime Prevention, Juvenile Delinquency in Zambia. *Leisure interests:* reading, vegetable gardening, soccer. *Address:* Ministry of Home Affairs, POB 32862, Lusaka, Zambia (office). *Telephone:* (21) 1213505 (office).

MWAPE, Lupando Augustine Festus K.; Zambian politician and diplomatist; fmr engineer, teacher; mem. Parl. for Lukashya constituency; Minister of Communications and Transport –2003; Deputy Minister of Northern Prov. –2004; Vice-Pres. of Zambia 2004–06; Amb. to People's Repub. of China 2007–12; Spontaneous Award, Ngoma Awards. *Address:* c/o Embassy of Zambia, 5 Dong Si Jie, San Li Tun, Chao Yang District, Beijing 100600, People's Republic of China (office).

MWEMWENIKARAWA, Nabuti; I-Kiribati politician; *Secretary, Maurin Kiribati Party;* mem. Parl. for North Tarawa 1998–2002; Minister for Finance and Econ. Devt 2003–07; currently Sec., Maurin Kiribati Party; unsuccessful cand. in 2007 presidential elections. *Address:* Maurin Kiribati Party, c/o Maneaba Ni Maungatabu, Tarawa, Kiribati (office).

MWENCHA, Erastus Jarnalese Onkundi, BA, MA, MBS; Kenyan economist and international finance official; *Deputy Chairperson, African Union Commission;* b. 15 Nov. 1947, Kisii; m.; three s.; ed Univ. of Nairobi, York Univ., Canada; entered civil service as an economist in Industrial Survey and Promotion Centre, Ministry of Commerce and Industry 1974, Prin. Industrial Devt Officer 1980; Dir of several public enterprises 1979–83, including Kenya Medical Research Inst., Kenya Industrial Research and Devt Inst.; also served as Head of Dept of Industry and as a Sr Economist in Ministry of Commerce and Industry; apptd Sec. Industrial Sciences Advisory Council 1979; Sr Industrial Expert, Econ. Comm. for Africa 1983; Dir of Industry, Energy and Environment, Preferential Trade Area for Eastern and Southern Africa 1987–97; Acting Sec.-Gen. Common Market for Eastern and Southern Africa (COMESA) 1997–98, Sec.-Gen. 1998–2008; Deputy Chair. African Union Comm. 2008–; fmr mem. Research Council of Nat. Council for Science and Tech.; Order of the Moran of the Burning Spear 1998. *Publications:* contrib. to The Free Trade Area of the Common Market for Eastern and Southern Africa. *Leisure interests:* playing golf, ardent Christian. *Address:* African Union Commission, PO Box 3243, Addis Ababa, Ethiopia (office). *Telephone:* (115) 514555 (office); (115) 517700 (ext. 236) (office). *Fax:* (115) 511299 (office). *E-mail:* dinfo@africa-union.org (office). *Website:* www.africa-union.org (office).

MWINYI, Ali Hassan; Tanzanian teacher, diplomatist and fmr head of state; b. 8 May 1925, Kivure, Mkuranga Dist, Tanganyika; m. Siti A. Mwinyi 1960; five s. four d.; ed secondary school, Dole, Zanzibar, Zanzibar Teachers' Training Coll., Durban Univ. Inst. of Educ. and Hall Univ., UK; moved to Zanzibar as a child;

primary schoolteacher at Mangapwani, Zanzibar 1945–50; Headteacher, Bumbwini Primary School 1950–54; Tutor, Zanzibar Teachers' Training Coll. 1956–61, later Prin.; joined Shiraz Party (ASP) 1964; Prin. Perm. Sec. of Educ. Zanzibar 1964–65; Asst Gen. Man. Zanzibar State Trading Corpn 1965–70; Asst Treasurer Makadara ASP Br., Zanzibar 1966–70; Chair. E African Currency Bd 1964–70, Nat. Kiswahili Council (BAKITA) 1964–77, Zanzibar Censorship Board 1964–65, Tanzania Food and Nutrition Council (LISHE); Minister of State, Office of Pres., Tanzania 1970; Minister for Health 1972–75, for Home Affairs 1975–77; Amb. to Egypt 1977–82; Minister of Natural Resources and Tourism 1982–83, of State in Vice-Pres.'s Office 1983–84; interim Pres. of Zanzibar Feb.–April 1984, Pres. April 1984; Vice-Pres. of Tanzania 1984–85, Pres. 1985–95, also fmr Minister of Defence and Nat. Service; fmr C-in-C of Armed Forces; mem. Chama Cha Mapinduzi (CCM or Revolutionary Party), Vice-Chair. 1984–90, Chair. 1990–96; Chair. Commonwealth Observer Mission to Regional and Gen. Elections in Guyana 6–19th Dec. 1997, OAU Mission to Regional and Gen. Elections in Nigeria Feb.–March 1998, Nat. Advisory Bd on the Control of HIV/AIDS; mem. Tanzania-Britain Soc.; fmr mem. Council Univ. of Dar es Salaam; Patron Tanzania Union Govt and Health Employees, Dar es Salaam Islamic Club, Tanzania Railway Workers Union, Muslims' Asscn for the Revertees, Shinyanga Orphanage Centre, Union of Tanzania Press Club, Tanzania Heralds for Youth Services, Publishers' Asscn of Tanzania, Tanga Muslim Org., Tanzania Muslim Hajj Trust; Hon. Life mem. Tanzania Law Soc.

MWINYI, Hussein Ali, MD; Tanzanian physician and politician; b. 23 Dec. 1966; ed Azania Secondary School, Tambaza High School, Marmara Univ., Turkey, Hammersmith Hosp., UK; doctor, Ministry of Health 1993–97, specialist doctor 1997–98; Lecturer in Medicine, Hubert Kairuki Memorial Univ. 1998–2000; Deputy Minister of Health 2000–05; MP for Kwahani 2005–; Minister of State for Union Affairs 2006–08; Minister of Defence and Nat. Service 2008–12; mem. Chama Cha Mapinduzi (CCM—Revolutionary Party of Tanzania). *Address:* c/o Ministry of Defence and National Service, PO Box 9544, Dar es Salaam, Tanzania.

MWIRARIA, Daudi; Kenyan politician; b. 3 Sept. 1938, Meru; ed Univ. of London, UK and Univ. of E Africa; statistician for E African Common services org. 1962, then Dir E African Statistical Dept; Sec., Common Market, E African Community; Perm. Sec. in various ministries 1977–88; retd from Civil Service to enter politics 1992, MP (Democratic Party–DP) for N Imenti 1992–; Minister of Finance 2003–06 (resgnd); founder mem. and Leader Cen. Kenya Parl. Group; Deputy Chair. DP. *Leisure interests:* reading, farming, photography, golfing. *Address:* c/o Democratic Party of Kenya (DP), Continental House, POB 56396, Nairobi 30007 Kenya (office).

MYAGKOV, Andrei Vasilyevich; Russian actor; b. 8 July 1938, Leningrad; ed Leningrad Inst. of Chemical Tech., Studio-School, Moscow Art Theatre; began acting in Sovremennik Theatre 1965–77, with Moscow Art Theatre 1977–; USSR State Prize, RSFSR State Prize, RSFSR People's Artist. *Theatre includes:* Aduyev in Ordinary Story, Trubetskoy in Decembrists, Repetilov in Trouble from Intelligence, Misail in Boris Godunov. *Films include:* Pokhozhdeniya zubnogo vracha (Adventures of a Dentist) 1965, Staryy dom (The Old House) 1969, Bratya Karamazovy (The Brothers Karamazov) 1969, Moya sudba 1970, Nezhdannyy gost (The Uninvited Guest) 1972, Grossmeyster 1972, Nadezhda (Hope) 1973, Utrenniy obkhod (Morning Round) 1974, Strakh vysoty (Fear of the Height) 1975, Vy mne pisali. . . 1976, Sluzhebnyy roman (Office Romance) 1977, Primite telegrammu v dolg 1979, Garazh 1979, Rassledovaniye 1980, 4:0 v polzu Tanechki (4:0 for Tanechka) 1982, Poslesloviye (Epilogue) 1983, Oglyanis!. . . (Turn Back!. . .) 1983, Letargiya 1983, Polosa prepyatstviy (Stripe of Obstacles) 1984, Zhestokiy romans (A Cruel Romance) 1984, Poslednyaya doroga (The Last Road) 1986, Ot zarplaty do zarplaty (From Pay to Pay) 1986, Chelovek, kotoryy bral intervyu 1986, Svobodnoye padeniye 1987, Silnee vsekh inykh veleniy (Above All Else) 1987, Kuvyrok cherez golovu 1987, Mat (Mother) 1989, Vinovata li ya. . . (Am I Guilty. . .) 1992, Na Deribasovskoy khoroshaya pogoda, ili na Brayton Bich opyat idut dozhdi (There's Good Weather in Deribasovskaya, It's Raining Again in Brighton Beach) 1992, Osenniye soblazny (Autumn Temptations) 1993, Iskusstvo umirat (The Art of Dying) 1995, Privet, duralei! (Hello, Fools!) (voice) 1996, Kontrakt so smertyu 1998, Skaz pro Fedota-streltsa (The Tale of Fedot, the Shooter) 2002. *Television includes:* Ironiya sudby, ili S lyogkim parom! (Irony of Fate) 1975, Dni Turbinykh 1976, Iz zapisok Lopakhina (From Lopakhin's Notes) 1977, Aktivnaya zona (Active Zone) 1979, Gonki po vertikali (Vertical Races) 1983, 32oe dekabrya 2004. *Address:* General Yermolov str. 6, Apt 42, 121293 Moscow, Russia. *Telephone:* (495) 148-93-64.

MYAING, U Linn, BSc; Myanma diplomatist; b. 15 Oct. 1947, Yangon; m. Daw Thi Thi Ta; two d.; ed Defence Studies Acad.; commissioned as officer in Myanmar Navy 1967–93; Deputy Dir Americas Div., Political Dept, Ministry of Foreign Affairs 1993–94, served first as Counsellor, then as Minister Counsellor, Perm. Mission to UN and other Int. Orgs, Geneva 1994–97, Deputy Dir Gen. Ministry of Foreign Affairs, also attached as Minister, Deputy Perm. Rep. to Perm. Mission of Myanmar, Geneva 1998–99, Amb. to France (also accred to UNESCO) 1999–2001 (also accred to Belgium, the Netherlands, Switzerland and EU) 2000–01, Amb. to USA 2001–07; Adviser to Bd, Serge Pun and Assocs (Myanmar) Ltd 2006–. *Address:* Serge Pun & Associates (Myanmar) Ltd, 10th & 11th floors, FMI Centre, No. 380, Bogyoke Aung San Road, Pabedan Tsp, Yangon, Myanmar (office). *Website:* www.spa-myanmar.com (office).

MYASNIKOV, Vladimir Stepanovich, DrHist; Russian historian and sinologist; *Head, Centre for Chinese and Russian Relations and Deputy Director, Institute of Far East, Russian Academy of Sciences;* b. 15 May 1931, Moscow; ed Moscow State Inst. of Int. Relations; researcher Inst. of Sinology 1956–60, Inst. of Peoples of Asia 1963–64, Inst. of Econs of World Socialist System 1964–66; researcher, Scientific Sec., Head of Div. Inst. of Far East, Russian Acad. of Sciences 1966–85, Deputy Dir 1985–, Head Centre for Chinese and Russian Relations 1992–; Corresp. mem. Russian Acad. of Sciences 1990, mem. 1997. *Publications:* over 150 published works, books, monographs. *Address:* Institute of Far East, Russian Academy of Sciences, Nakhimovsky prosp. 32, 117218 Moscow (office); Novocheremoushkinskaya str. 49, 160 Moscow, Russia (home). *Telephone:* (495) 124-07-22 (office). *Fax:* (495) 718-96-56 (office). *E-mail:* ifes@cemi.rssi.ru (office).

MYASNIKOVICH, Mikhail Vladimirovich, DSc; Belarusian engineer and politician; *Prime Minister*; b. 6 May 1950, Novy Snov; m.; one s. one d.; ed Brest State Tech. Univ.; began career as Engineer, Tech. Dept, Minskproject Design Inst. 1972; Chief Engineer, Minskvodokanal Production Asscn 1973–77; Chief Engineer, Directorate for Public Service Enterprises, Minsk City Exec. Cttee 1977, Chief of Directorate 1979; Chair. Exec. Cttee, Sovietsky Dist Soviet of People's Deputies, Minsk City 1983, Deputy Chair. Minsk City Exec. Cttee 1984, Sec., Minsk City Cttee of Communist Party of Belarus 1985–86; Minister of Housing and Communal Services, Belarusian SSR (BSSR) 1986, Vice-Chair. BSSR Council of Ministers 1990, also Chair. BSSR State Cttee for Economy and Planning; Deputy Prime Minister, Repub. of Belarus (following independence) 1994–95; Head of Presidential Admin 1995–2001; Prime Minister 2010–; mem. Nat. Acad. of Sciences of Belarus, Chair. Presidium 2001–10. *Address:* Office of the Council of Ministers, 220010 Minsk, vul. Savetskaya 11, Belarus (office). *Telephone:* (17) 222-41-73 (office). *Fax:* (17) 222-66-65 (office). *E-mail:* contact@government.by (office). *Website:* government.by (office).

MYASOYEDOV, Boris Fedorovich; Russian chemist; b. 2 Oct. 1930; m.; one s.; ed Moscow I. Mendeleyev Inst. of Chem. and Tech.; Jr, Sr Researcher, Head of Lab, Deputy Dir V. Vernadsky Inst. of Geochem. and Analytical Chem.; Corresp. mem. USSR (now Russian) Acad. of Sciences 1990, mem. 1994; research in chem. of radioactive elements, radionucleides, creation and application of chem. sensors and analysers; USSR State Prize, V. Khlopin Prize Acad. of Sciences. *Publications:* Chemical Sensors: Possibilities and Perspectives 1990. *Leisure interests:* music, stamp collecting. *Address:* Institute of Geochemistry and Analytical Chemistry, Kosygin str. 19, 117975 Moscow, Russia. *Telephone:* (495) 137-41-47 (office); (495) 420-90-81 (home). *Fax:* (495) 938-20-54.

MYERS, Barton, MArch, FAIA; American/Canadian architect, planner and academic; *President, Barton Myers Associates Inc.*; b. 6 Nov. 1934, Norfolk, Va; s. of Barton Myers and Meeta Myers (née Burrage); m. Victoria George 1959; one d.; ed Norfolk Acad., U.S. Naval Acad. and Univ. of Pennsylvania; Partner, A.J. Diamond & Barton Myers, Toronto 1968–75; Founder and Prin. Barton Myers Assocs Inc., Toronto 1975–86, Barton Myers Assocs Inc., LA 1981–; Asst Prof. of Architecture Univ. of Toronto 1968–70; mem. Advisory Cttee Nat. Capital Comm., Ottawa 1968–74; Founder and Pres. Bd of Dirs, Trace Magazine 1980–82; Visiting Prof., Harvard Grad. School of Design 1981; Sr Prof., School of Architecture and Urban Design, UCLA 1981–; mem. AIA, Soc. of Architectural Historians, GSA Nat. Register of Peer Professionals; numerous design awards, including Royal Architectural Inst. of Canada Gold Medal 1994, several AIA awards including Los Angeles Gold Medal 2002. *Major works by Diamond & Myers Assocs include:* York Square, Toronto; Ont. Medical Asscn, Toronto; Myers & Wolf Residences, Toronto; Housing Union Bldg, Univ. of Alberta Citadel Theatre, Edmonton; Dundas-Sherborne Housing, Toronto. *Major works by Barton Myers Assocs Inc. include:* Seagram Museum, Waterloo, Ont.; Howard Hughes Center, LA; Wang Tower, LA; Performing Arts Center, Portland, Ore.; Pasadena City Center; Music Center Expansion, LA; CBC Network HQ, Toronto; Cerritos Center for the Performing Arts, Calif.; Woodsworth Coll., Univ. of Toronto; NW Campus Housing, UCLA; Art Gallery of Ont. expansion (competition winner); York Univ. Fine Arts Bldg expansion, Toronto; New Jersey Performing Arts Center, Newark (New Jersey Golden Trowel Award, Int. Masonry Inst., Chicago Athenaeum Award 1998); The Ice House Renovation, Beverly Hills, Calif.; UCSD/Scripps Ocean Atmosphere Research Facility, La Jolla, Calif.; Univ. of New Mexico, Albuquerque (Master Devt Plan); Hall of Justice, Sacramento, Calif. (Historical Preservation Award Calif. Preservation Foundation 2002); House and studio at Toro Canyon, Montecito, Calif. (CCAIA Honor Award in Design 2000, AIA PIA Housing Award for Innovation in Housing Design 2002); 421 South Beverly Drive, Beverly Hills, Calif. (Beverly Hills Architectural Design Award 2002); Tempe Center for the Arts, Tempe, Ariz. 2006. *Publications:* Barton Myers Selected and Current Works (in The Master Architect series) 1994, New Stage for a City (monograph) 1998, Barton Myers: 3 Steel Houses (House Design series) 2004. *Leisure interests:* travel, reading. *Address:* Barton Myers Associates Inc., 1025 Westwood Boulevard, Los Angeles, CA 90024, USA (office). *Telephone:* (310) 208-2227 (office). *Fax:* (310) 208-2207 (office). *E-mail:* b_myers@bartonmyers.com (office). *Website:* bartonmyers.com (office).

MYERS, Dale Dehaven, BSAE; American engineer, business executive and consultant; b. 8 Jan. 1922, Kansas City, Mo.; s. of Wilson A. Myers and Ruth Myers; m. Marjorie Williams 1943; two d.; ed Univ. of Washington, Seattle; Aerophysics Dept, N American 1946, Chief Engineer, Missile Div. 1954, Vice-Pres. and Program Man. Hound Dog Air-Launched Missile Program 1957; Vice-Pres. and Program Man., Apollo Command and Service Modules, N American 1964; Assoc. Admin. for Manned Space Flight, NASA Headquarters 1970–74, Deputy Admin., NASA 1986–89; US Govt Rep. to AGARD 1988–89; Pres. N American Aircraft Operations, Rockwell Int. Corpn 1974–77, Corp. Vice-Pres. 1974–77; Under-Sec., US Dept of Energy, Washington, DC 1977–79; Pres. and COO Jacobs Eng Group Inc., Pasadena 1979–84; Pres. Dale Myers and Assocs, Leucadia, 1984–86, 1989–; mem. Bd of Dirs Ducommun Inc., 1982–86, Jacob's Eng Group 1979–86, MacNeal Schwendler Corpn 1990–98, SYS 1984–86, SAIC's GSC 1993–97, San Diego Aerospace Museum 1992–2004; mem. NASA Advisory Comm. 1984–86, NASA Aero Comm. 1994–97; Fellow, American Astronautical Soc.; mem. Nat. Acad. of Engineers 1974, Int. Acad. of Astronautics 1991; Hon. Fellow, AIAA; Hon. PhD (Whitworth Coll.); NASA Public Service Award 1969, NASA Distinguished Service Medal 1971, 1974, DSM (Dept of Energy) 1979. *Leisure interests:* golf, old cars. *Address:* PO Box 232518, Encinitas, CA 92023, USA. *Telephone:* (760) 753-4043 (office); (760) 753-5770 (home).

MYERS, (Margaret Jane) Dee Dee, BS; American business executive, consultant and fmr government official; *Executive Vice-President, Worldwide Corporate Communications and Public Affairs, Warner Bros. Entertainment Inc.*; b. 1 Sept. 1961, Quonset Point, RI; d. of Stephen George Myers and Judith Ann Burleigh; m. Todd S. Purdum; two d.; ed Univ. of Santa Clara; Press Asst, Mondale for Pres. Campaign, LA 1984, for Senator Art Torres, LA 1985; Deputy Press Sec. for LA Mayor Tom Bradley 1985–87, for Tom Bradley for Gov. Campaign 1986; Calif. Press Sec., Dukakis for Pres. Campaign, LA 1988; Press Sec., Feinstein for Gov. Campaign, LA and San Francisco 1989–90; Campaign Dir Jordan for Mayor Campaign, San Francisco 1991; Press Sec., Clinton for Pres. Campaign, Little

Rock, Ark. 1991–92; Press Sec., The White House, Washington, DC 1993–94; Co-Host Equal Time, CNBC, Washington, DC 1995–97; Contributing Ed. Vanity Fair magazine, Washington, DC 1995–; Founder and Pres. Dee Dee Myers & Associates; Man. Dir The Glover Park Group (communications consultancy) 2010–14; Exec. Vice-Pres. Worldwide Corporate Communications and Public Affairs, Warner Bros. Entertainment Inc. 2014–; mem. Bd Trustees, Calif. State Univ. 1999–2004 (Vice-Chair. 2000–01); consultant to NBC TV drama The West Wing; Robert F. Kennedy Award, Emerson Coll., Boston 1993. *Film:* Contact 1997. *Publication:* Why Women Should Rule the World 2008. *Leisure interests:* running, cycling, music, major league baseball. *Address:* Warner Bros. Entertainment Inc., 4000 Warner Blvd, Burbank, CA 91522, USA. *Telephone:* (818) 954-6000 (office). *Website:* www.warnerbros.com (office).

MYERS, Mike; Canadian actor and writer; b. 25 May 1963, Toronto, Ont.; s. of Eric Myers and Bunny (née Hind) Myers; m. Robin Ruzan 1993 (divorced 2005); Canadian Comedy Award 2000. *Stage appearances:* The Second City, Toronto 1986–88, Chicago 1988–89; actor and writer: Mullarkey & Myers 1984–86. *Television includes:* John and Yoko (TV film) 1985, Saturday Night Live 1989–94 (Emmy Award for Outstanding Writing in a Comedy or Variety Series 1989), Russell Gilbert Show 1998, Dir The Bacchae (TV Film) 1999. *Films:* Wayne's World 1992, So I Married an Axe Murderer 1992, Wayne's World II 1993, Austin Powers: International Man of Mystery 1997, Meteor 1998, McClintock's Peach 1998, Just Like Me 1998, It's A Dog's Life 1998, 54 1998, Austin Powers: The Spy Who Shagged Me 1998, Pete's Meteor 1999, Shrek (voice) 2001, Austin Powers in Goldmember 2002, View from the Top 2003, Shrek 4–D (voice) 2003, Nobody Knows Anything 2003, Cat in the Hat 2003, Shrek 2 (voice) 2004, Shrek the Third (voice) 2007, The Love Guru 2008, Inglourious Basterds 2009, Shrek Forever After (vocie) 2010. *Address:* c/o David O'Connor, Creative Artists Agency, 9830 Wilshire Boulevard, Beverly Hills, CA 90212, USA.

MYERS, Norman, CMG, BA, MA, PhD, FLS, FRSA; British scientist; *Fellow, Green College, Oxford*; b. 24 Aug. 1934, Whitewell, Yorks.; s. of John Myers and Gladys Myers (née Haworth); m. Dorothy Mary Halliman 1965 (separated 1992); two d.; ed Clitheroe Royal Grammar School, Lancs., Keble Coll., Oxford, Univ. of California, Berkeley, USA; Dist Officer, Kenya Admin 1958–61; taught French and English at Delamere School for Boys, Nairobi 1961–65; freelance author and journalist, professional photographer, lecturer and broadcaster on African wildlife 1966–69; ind. scientist and consultant in Environment and Devt with focus on the tropics 1972–; has worked for many int. orgs and govt agencies; Man. Dir Norman Myers Scientific Consultancy Ltd 1982–; mem. Editorial Bd Global Environmental Change, Biodiversity and Conservation, Ecological Economics, The Environmentalist, Environmental Conservation; Environment, Development and Sustainability; Ecoscience, World Forest Resource Management, Forest Ecology and Management, Futures; Fellow, Green Coll. Oxford 2000–; Adjunct Prof. of Environmental Science, Nicholas School of the Environment, Duke Univ., USA; Visiting Prof., Harvard Univ., Cornell Univ., Stanford Univ., Univ. of Califonia, Berkeley, USA; Amb. to World Wide Fund (WWF) for Nature UK; Foreign Assoc., NAS; mem. American Asscn of Environmental and Resource Economists, American Inst. of Biological Sciences; Fellow, AAAS, World Acad. of Art and Science; Hon. Visiting Fellow, Green Coll., Oxford; Order of the Golden Ark (Netherlands) 1983, Kt of the Golden Ark (Netherlands) 1992; hon. science degree (Univ. of Kent) 2003; Gold Medal, WWF Int. 1983, Gold Medal, New York Zoological Soc. (now the Wildlife Conservation Soc.) 1986, Volvo Environment Prize 1992, UNEP Sasakawa Environment Prize 1995, Blue Planet Prize 2001 (one of only two people worldwide to receive all three leading environmental prizes), Pew Fellow in Environment, Liveable City Award, City of London, Haas Int. Alumnus Award, Univ. of California, Berkeley. *Publications:* The Long African Day 1972, The Sinking Ark (five scientific/literary awards) 1979, Conversion of Tropical Moist Forests (report to NAS) 1980, A Wealth of Wild Species (four book clubs and two science awards) 1983, The Primary Source: Tropical Forests and Our Future 1984, Economics of Ecosystem Management (co-ed.) 1985, The Gaia Atlas of Planet Management 1985, The Gaia Atlas of Future Worlds: Challenge and Opportunity in an Age of Change 1990, Population, Resources and the Environment: The Critical Challenges (for UN Population Fund) 1991, Tropical Forests and Climate (ed.) 1992, Ultimate Security: The International Basis of Political Stability 1993, Scarcity or Abundance: A Debate on the Environment (co-author) 1994, Environmental Exodus: An Emergent Crisis in the Global Arena (co-author) 1995, Perverse Subsidies (co-author) 1998, Hotspots: Earth's Biologically Richest and Most Endangered Terrestrial Ecoregions (co-author) 1999, Towards a New Green Print for Business and Society (in Japanese) 1999, Perverse Subsidies: How Tax Dollars Undercut the Environment and the Economy (co-author) 2001, New Consumers: The Influence of Affluence on the Environment (co-author) 2004, The New Gaia Atlas of Planet Management (co-author) 2005, Institutional Roadblocks: Why Policy Processes Often Fail to Deliver (co-author) 2008; more than 300 scientific papers in professional journals on ecology, conservation biology, energy, population growth, environmental policy, environmental sociology and anthropology. *Leisure interests:* marathon running, mountaineering, professional photography. *Address:* Upper Meadow, 2 Douglas Downes Close, Quarry Road, Headington, Oxford, OX3 8FS, England. *Telephone:* (1865) 750387. *Fax:* (1865) 741538. *E-mail:* myers1n@aol.com (office).

MYERS, Gen. (retd) Richard B., BS, MBA; American air force officer (retd), business executive and academic; *Colin L. Powell Chair for National Security, Leadership, Character and Ethics, National Defense University*; b. 1942, Kansas City, Mo.; m.; two d. one s.; ed Kansas State Univ., Auburn Univ., Air Command/Staff Coll., Ala, US Army War Coll., Pa and Harvard Univ.; commissioned 2nd Lt, USAF 1965; fighter pilot, Vietnam 1969; various assignments to Commdr US Forces, Japan and 5th Air Force, Yakota Air Base, Japan 1993–96; Asst to Chair. Jt Chiefs of Staff, The Pentagon, 1996–97; rank of Gen. 1997; Commdr Pacific Air Forces, Hickam Air Force Base, Hawaii 1997–98; C-in-C N American Aerospace Defense Command/US Space Command, Peterson Air Force Base, Colo 1998–2000; Vice-Chair. Jt Chiefs of Staff 2000–01, Chair. 2001–05 (retd); fmr mem. NATO Mil. Cttee; Colin L. Powell Chair for Nat. Security, Leadership, Character and Ethics, Nat. Defense Univ., Washington, DC 2006–; Foundation Prof. of Mil. History, Kansas State Univ. (part-time) 2006–; mem. Bd of Dirs Northrop Grumman Corpn 2006–, Aon Corpn 2006–, Deere & Co. 2006–, United Technologies Corpn 2006–, Rivada Networks, MRI Global; Chair. Bd of Govs United Service Org.; mem.

Defense Health Bd-Fed. Advisory Cttee to the Sec. of Defense, Office of the Sec. of Defense Policy Bd; Defense Distinguished Service Medal with Oak Leaf Cluster, Distinguished Service Medal, Legion of Merit, Distinguished Flying Cross with Oak Leaf Cluster, Meritorious Service Medal with Three Oak Leaf Clusters, Air Medal with 18 Oak Leaf Clusters, Air Force Commendation Medal, Presidential Medal of Freedom 2005. *Address:* Institute for National Security Ethics and Leadership, National Defense University, 300 5th Avenue SW, Fort Lesley J. McNair, Washington, DC 20319, USA (office). *E-mail:* insel@ndu.edu (office). *Website:* www.ndu.edu/INSEL (office); www.generalrichardmyers.com.

MYERSON, Jacob M., MA; American economist and diplomatist; b. 11 June 1926, Rock Hill, SC; s. of Solomon Myerson and Lena Myerson (née Clein); m. 1st Nicole Neuray 1965 (died 1968); one d. (deceased); m. 2nd Helen Hayashi 1974 (died 1995); ed Washington, DC, Pennsylvania State Coll., George Washington Univ.; entered US Foreign Service 1950; Economic Analyst for the Office of the US High Commr, Berlin 1950–52, mem. US Regional Mission for the OEEC and Marshall Plan, Paris 1953–56; State Dept Desk Officer for EC and European Free Trade Area Affairs 1956–60; Chief of Political Section of US Mission to the European Communities, Brussels 1960; Special Asst to the Under-Sec. of State, Officer in Charge of NATO Political Affairs, State Dept, then Deputy Political Adviser and Counsellor to the US Mission to NATO, Brussels 1965–68, Adviser to the US del. at several ministerial sessions of the N Atlantic Council 1966–70; Econ. Counsellor US Mission to the European Communities, Brussels, then Deputy Chief and Minister Counsellor 1970–75; Amb. to UN Econ. and Social Council, New York 1975–77; Minister Counsellor for Econ. and Commercial Affairs, US Embassy, Paris 1977–80; Deputy Sec.-Gen. of the OECD 1980–88; Order of the Sacred Treasure (Japan) 1990; Rivkin Award American Foreign Service Assoc. 1969. *Leisure interest:* modern and contemporary art. *Address:* 2 rue Lucien-Gaulard, 75018 Paris, France.

MYERSON, Roger B., AB, SM, PhD; American economist and academic; *Glen A. Lloyd Distinguished Service Professor of Economics, University of Chicago;* b. 29 March 1951, Boston, Mass; m. Regina Weber Myerson; two c.; ed Harvard Univ.; Asst Prof. of Managerial Econs and Decision Sciences, Northwestern Univ. 1976–79, Assoc. Prof. 1979–82, Prof. 1982–2001; Visiting Researcher, Universität Bielefeld, Germany 1978–79; Visiting Prof. of Econs, Univ. of Chicago 1985–86, 2000–01, Prof. of Econs 2001–07, Glen A. Lloyd Distinguished Service Prof. of Econs 2007–; Assoc. Ed. Journal of Economic Theory 1983–93; mem. Editorial Bd International Journal of Game Theory 1982–92, Games and Economic Behavior 1989–97; Fellow, Econometric Soc. 1983, American Acad. of Arts and Sciences 1993, NAS 2009; Dr hc (Universität Basel, Switzerland) 2002; Nobel Prize in Econs (with Leo Hurwicz and Eric S. Maskin) 2007. *Publications:* Game Theory: Analysis of Conflict 1991, Probability Models for Economic Decisions 2005; more than 80 articles in academic journals. *Address:* Department of Economics, University of Chicago, 1126 East 59th Street, Chicago, IL 60637, USA (office). *Telephone:* (773) 834-9071 (office). *Fax:* (773) 702-8490 (office). *Website:* home.uchicago.edu/rmyerson (office).

MYHRVOLD, Nathan P., BSc, MSc, MA, PhD; American business executive; *Founder and CEO, Intellectual Ventures;* b. 3 Aug. 1959, Seattle, Wash.; ed Univ. of California, Los Angeles, Princeton Univ., Santa Monica Coll., Calif.; Postdoctoral Fellow, Dept of Applied Math. and Theoretical Physics, Univ. of Cambridge, UK –1986, worked with Prof. Stephen Hawking on research in cosmology, quantum field theory in curved space-time and quantum theories of gravitation; left Cambridge to co-found Dynamical Systems Research Inc., Oakland, Calif. to produce Mondrian (clone of IBM's TopView multitasking environment for DOS), co. acquired by Microsoft 1986; with Microsoft Corpn 1986–2000, held various positions within co., f. Microsoft Research 1991 and numerous tech. groups, rose to become Chief Strategist and Chief Tech. Officer; Founder and CEO Intellectual Ventures (patent portfolio developer and broker) 2000, holds large number of patents in areas of tech. and energy; mem. Advisory Bd Dept of Physics, Univ. of Washington; Affiliate Research Assoc. of Paleontology, Museum of the Rockies, Bozeman, Mont., funds and participates in palaeontological research and yearly expeditions; mem. United Way's Million Dollar Roundtable, USA Science and Eng Festival's Advisory Bd; worked for two years as a stagier at Rover's French restaurant, Seattle, completed culinary training with chef Anne Willan at Ecole De La Varenne; has worked as Chief Gastronomic Officer for Zagat Survey (publr of Zagat restaurant guide books); Hertz Foundation Fellowship for grad. study 1984, James Madison Medal, Princeton Univ. 2005, named by Foreign Policy magazine to its list of top global thinkers 2010. *Achievements include:* master French chef who competed on team that won first place in several categories at World Championship of Barbecue, Memphis, Tenn. 1991. *Publications:* America 24/7 2003, Washington 24/7 2003 (wildlife photography), Modernist Cuisine: The Art and Science of Cooking 2011; research has been published in scientific journals including Science, Nature, Paleobiology, Journal of Vertebrate Paleontology and the Physical Review; contrib. of articles to magazines including Harvard Business Review, The Wall Street Journal, Fortune, Time and National Geographic Traveler. *Leisure interests:* nature and wildlife photography, cuisine. *Address:* Intellectual Ventures, 3150 139th Avenue SE, Building 4, Bellevue, WA 98005, USA (office). *Telephone:* (425) 467-2300 (office). *E-mail:* info@intellectualventures.com (office). *Website:* www.intellectualventures.com (office); www.modernistcuisine.com.

MYINT MAUNG, U; Myanma diplomatist and administrator; b. 10 March 1921, Magwe; m.; three c.; ed Univ. of Rangoon; joined Army 1942; has held the following positions: Head of Co-operative Dept; Chief of Admin. Div. of Burma Socialist Programme Party, also mem. Party Inspection Cttee; mem. Pyithu Hluttaw (People's Congress) for Magwe Constituency; mem. Bd of Dirs People's Bank of the Union of Burma, Exec. Cttee of Burma Sports and Physical Fitness Cttee, Cen. Cttee of Burma Red Cross Soc.; Chair. Resettlement Cttee of Cen. Security and Admin. Cttee, Independence Award Cttee; Amb. and Perm. Rep. to UN, New York 1975–77; Minister of Foreign Affairs 1977–79; Amb. to China –1989; mem. State Council and Attorney-Gen. 1988. *Address:* c/o Ministry of Foreign Affairs, Building 9, Nay Pyi Tawt, Myanmar. *E-mail:* mofa.aung@mptmail.net.mm.

MYNERS, Baron (Life Peer), cr. 2008, of Truro in the County of Cornwall; **Paul Myners,** CBE, FRSA; British publishing executive and government official; b. 1 April 1948, adopted by a Cornish family; m. Alison Macleod; one s. four d.; ed Univ.

of London; teacher with Inner London Educ. Authority 1971–72; finance writer, Daily Telegraph 1972–75; with N. M. Rothschild (merchant bank) 1974–85; CEO Gartmore Investment Man. 1985–87, Chair. 1987–2001; Deputy Chair. Powergen 1999–2001; Exec. Dir Nat. Westminster Bank 1999–2000; Chair. Guardian Media Group 2001–08, also Publisher The Guardian and The Observer newspapers; Financial Services Sec. and Minister for the City, HM Treasury 2008–10, also Govt Spokesperson for HM Treasury in House of Lords, Chair. All Party Parl. Group on Corp. Governance 2010; mem. Financial Reporting Council 1995–2004, Company Law Review Consultative Cttee 1998–2000; Court of Dirs of Bank of England 2005–; Chair. Low Pay Comm. 2006–; Chair. Aspen Insurance Holdings, Bermuda 2002–07, Liberty Ermitage 2006–08, Autonomous Research LLP 2011– (also Partner), Cevian Capital (UK) LLP 2011– (also Partner), Platform Acquisition Holdings Ltd 2013–; Dir (non-exec.), mmO₂2001, Bank of New York, Marks & Spencer 2002 (interim Chair. 2004); Dir RIT Capital Partners PLC 2010–, OJSC MegaFon 2013–; Sr Ind. Dir Co-operative Group (resgnd Labour Whip in House of Lords and is non-affiliated) 2013–14 (resgnd); Chair. Tate Galleries –2009; Pres. Howard League for Penal Reform 2012–; Visiting Fellow, Nuffield Coll., Oxford; Exec. Fellow, London Business School; mem. Royal Acad. Trust, United Response; Trustee, ARK (charity); Hon. Fellow, Asscn of Corp. Treasurers 2010; Dr hc (Univ. of Exeter) 2008. *Leisure interest:* London Symphony Orchestra. *Address:* House of Lords, Westminster, London, SW1A 0PW, England (office). *Telephone:* (20) 7219-5353 (office); (20) 7219-5979 (office). *E-mail:* contactholmember@parliament.uk (office). *Website:* www.parliament.uk/biographies/lords/lord-myners/3869 (office).

MYRATGULYEV, Amandurdy; Turkmenistani government official; Head of Main State Tax Service 2004–05; Deputy Prime Minister and Minister of the Economy and Finance 2005–07. *Address:* c/o Ministry of the Economy and Finance, ul. 2008 4, 744000 Asgabat, Turkmenistan (office).

MYRDAL, Jan; Swedish writer; b. 19 July 1927, Stockholm; s. of the late Gunnar Myrdal and Alva Reimer; m. 1st Nadja Wiking 1948; m. 2nd Maj Lidberg 1953; m. 3rd Gun Kessle 1956 (died 2007); m. 4th Andrea Gaytan Vega 2008; one s. one d.; Sunday columnist (politics, culture) Stockholms-Tidningen 1963–66, Aftonbladet 1966–72; Chair. and Publr Folket i Bild/Kulturfront 1971–72, columnist 1972–; Hon. DLit (Upsala Coll., NJ) 1980; Hon. PhD (Nankai Univ., China) 1993. *Works include:* films: Myglaren 1966, Hjalparen 1968, Balzac or The Triumphs of Realism 1975, Mexico: Art and Revolution 1991; TV documentaries: Democratic Kampuchea 1978–79, Guerilla Base Area of Democratic Kampuchea 1979, China 1979, 20 films on history of political caricature and posters 1975–87. *Publications include:* (in Swedish) novels: Hemkomst 1954, Jubelvår 1955, Att bli och vara 1956, Badrumskranen 1957, Karriär 1975, Barndom 1982, En annan värld 1984; drama: Folkets Hus 1953, Moraliteter 1967, Garderingar 1969, B. Olsen 1972; travel: Resa i Afghanistan 1960, Bortom berg och öknar 1962, Turkmenistan 1966, Sidenvägen 1977, Indien väntar 1980; politics: Kina: Revolutionen går vidare 1970, Albansk utmaning 1970, Ett 50-tal 1972, lag utan ordning, Kinesiska frågor, Tyska frågor 1976, Kina efter Mao Tse-tung 1977, Kampuchea och kriget 1978, Kampuchea hösten 1979, Den albanska utmaningen 1968–86, 1987, Mexico, Dröm och längtan 1996; essays: Söndagsmorgon 1965, Skriftställning 1968, Skriftställning II 1969, III 1970, IV 1973, V 1975, Klartexter 1978, Skriftställning X 1978, Balzac und der Realismus (in German) 1978, Strindberg och Balzac 1981, Ord och Avsikt 1986, Det nya Stor, Tyskland 1992, När Västerlandet trädde fram 1992, Inför nedräkningen 1993, När morgondagarna sjöng 1994, En fest i Liu Lin 1994, När morgondagarna sjöng 1994, Rölvag as an example 1995, Maj, en kärlek 1998, Om vin 1999, Det odelbara ordet 2002, Gubbsjuka 2002, Meccano 2005, Sälja krig som margarin 2005; autobiography: Rescontra 1962, Samtida bekännelser 1964, Inför nedräkningen 1993, När morgondagarna sjöng 1994, En kärlek 1998, Maj: En kärlek 1998; art: Ansikte av sten, Angkor 1968, Ondskan tar form 1976; Dussinet fullt 1981, Den trettonde 1983, Franska revolutionens bilder 1989, 5 ar av frihet 1830–35 1991, När Västerlandet tradde fram 1992, André Gill 1995, Drömmen om det goda samhallet; Kinesiska affischer 1966–1976 1996; wine: Jan Myrdal on vin 1999; biography: August Strindberg and Ole Edvart Roelvag 1997, Johan August Strindberg 2000; (in English) Report from a Chinese Village 1965, Chinese Journey 1965, Confessions of a Disloyal European 1968, Angkor: an essay on art and imperialism 1970, Gates to Asia 1971, Albania Defiant 1976, The Silk Road 1979, China Notebook 1975–78 1979, Return to a Chinese Village 1984, India Waits 1984, Childhood 1991, Another World 1993, 12 Going on 13 1995. *Leisure interests:* collecting Meccano, computing for fun. *Address:* Kalvängen 70 D, 739 91 Skinnskatteberg, Sweden (home). *Telephone:* (223) 51-012 (home). *Fax:* (223) 51-007 (home). *E-mail:* myrdal@myrdal.pp.se (home). *Website:* www.myrdal-kessle.se (home).

MYRZAKMATOV, Melisbek Jooshbayevich; Kyrgyzstani politician; b. 18 April 1969, Papan village, Kara-Suu dist, Osh Oblast; ed Osh Technological Univ.; began working as Insp., State Tax Inspectorate, Osh 1996; Deputy Dir for Commerce, Koopsnab Co. 1997–99; Pres. Eldik (charitable foundation) 2004–07; Dir Osh migrant service 2007; Deputy to Jogorku Kenesh (Ak Jol party) 2007–09; Acting Mayor then Mayor of Osh 2009–13 (dismissed), defeated in subsequent mayoral election Jan. 2014; Owner of Oomat Market (more than 1,500 traders) in Kara-Suu; Dir Yug Keramzitstroi brick factory and other construction materials cos; began construction of Taatan-Osh trading centre (4,000 workplaces); Hero of the Kyrgyz People Award 2010. *Address:* c/o Office of the Mayor, 732500 Osh, Lenina 221, Kyrgyzstan. *E-mail:* admin@oshcity.kg.

MYSEN, Bjorn O., BSc, MA, PhD; American (b. Norwegian) research scientist; *Senior Staff Scientist, Geophysical Laboratory, Carnegie Institution of Washington;* b. 20 Dec. 1947, Oslo, Norway; s. of Martin Mysen and Randi Mysen; m. Susanna Laya 1975; two c.; ed Univ. of Oslo, Pennsylvania State Univ.; Carnegie Foundation Fellow 1974–77; Sr Staff Scientist, Experimental Geochemist, Carnegie Inst., Washington, DC 1977–; Visiting Scientist, Bayerisches Geoinstitut, Germany 1988; Research Assoc., CNRS-Orléans, France 1994; Visiting Prof., Institut de Physique du Globe, Paris, France 2001, 2004, Inst. for Study of the Earth's Interior, Univ. of Okayama at Misasa, Japan 2006–09; mem. Royal Norwegian Acad. of Science and Letters 1985; Fellow, Mineralogy Soc. of America 1991; Geochemistry Fellow, Geochemical Soc. 2008, European Geochemical Soc. 2008; F. W. Clarke Medal 1977, Reusch Medal 1978, ISI Highly Cited 2001, George W. Morey Award, American Ceramical Soc. 2006. *Publications:* Structure and Properties of Silicate Melts 1988, Silicate Glasses and Melts – Properties and

Structure 2005; seven edited books and more than 270 other peer-reviewed scientific publs. *Address:* Geophysical Laboratory, Carnegie Institution of Washington, 5251 Broad Branch Road NW, Washington, DC 20015, USA (office). *Telephone:* (202) 478-8975 (office). *Fax:* (202) 478-8901 (office). *E-mail:* mysen@gl .ciw.edu (office); bmysen@ciw.edu (office). *Website:* people.gl.ciw.edu/bmysen/ MysenB/Research_Interests_%26_CV.html (office).

MYŚLIWSKI, Wiesław; Polish writer; b. 25 March 1932, Dwikozy, nr Sando-mierz; m. Wacława Stec; one s.; ed Catholic Univ. of Lublin; worked at People's Publishing Cooperative until 1976, Ed., quarterly magazine Regiony 1994–99; Ed., fortnightly Sycyna 1994–99; numerous awards include Stanisław Piętak Prize 1968, 1973, Prize of Ministry of Culture and Art 1971, State Prize 1985, Władysław S. Reymont Prize 1997, Alfred Jurzykowski Foundation Award, New York 1998, Bogumił S. Linde Prize, Toruń-Göttingen, Polish Culture Foundation Gold Sceptre Prize 2011. *Publications include:* novels: Nagi sad (Naked Orchard) 1967, Pałac (Palace) 1970 (screenplay 1980), Kamień na kamieniu (Stone upon Stone) (Best Translated Book Award – with Bill Johnston, USA 2012) 1984, Widnokrąg (Horizon) (Nike Literary Prize 1997) 1996, Traktat o łuskaniu fasoli (Treatise on Shelling Beans) (Nike Literary Prize, Gdynia Literary Prize 2007, Grand Prix Littéraire de St Emilion, France 2011) 2006, Ostatnie rozdanie (Final Deal) 2013; screenplays: Przez dziewięć mostów (Across Nine Bridges) 1972, Klucznik (Steward) (TV) 1979, Droga (The Road) (TV) 1981, Kamień na kamieniu (Stone upon Stone) 1995; plays: Złodziej (Thief) 1973, Klucznik (Steward) 1978, Drzewo (Tree) 1988, Requiem dla gospodyni (Requiem for the Housewife) 2000. *Address:* ul. Nowoursynowska 119C, 02-797 Warsaw, Poland (home).

MYTARAS, Dimitris; Greek artist; b. 1934, Chalkis; s. of Basilis Mytaras and Efrosini Mytaras; m. Chariklia Mytaras 1961; one s.; ed Athens School of Fine Arts and Ecole des Arts Décoratifs, Paris; Prof., Athens School of Fine Arts; has exhibited in many of the world's capitals and has participated in most important Biennales; assoc. with Kreonidis Gallery, Athens, Metropolis Art Galleries, New York, the Inter Art Group, Tokyo and Galerie Flak, Paris; main periods of his painting are: Mirrors 1960–64, Dictatorship 1966–70, Epitaphs 1971–76, Portraits 1977–87, Theatre Scenes 1988–91. *Publications:* D. Mytaras: Peinture 1982, D. Mytaras: Peinture 1990, D. Mytaras: Drawings 1994, D. Mytaras: Parepiptonda. *Address:* Kamariotou 15, 115–24 N Filothei, Athens, Greece. *Telephone:* 6913658. *Fax:* 6928327.

MYTTON, Graham Lambert, PhD, FRSA, MMRS; British consultant; b. 21 Oct. 1942, Sanderstead, Croydon, England; s. of Peter Mytton and Joan Jackson; m. Janet Codd 1966; two d.; ed Trinity School, Croydon, Purley Grammar School and Univs of Liverpool, Manchester and Dar es Salaam; Man. BBC Radio studio 1964–66; Research Fellow, Zambia Broadcasting 1970–73; radio producer, BBC African Service 1973–75; current affairs producer, BBC Radio Four 1976; Head, Hausa Language Section, BBC African Service 1976–82; Head, Int. Broadcasting Audience Research, BBC World Service 1982–91, Head, Audience Research and Correspondence 1991–96, Controller, Marketing 1996–98; ind. consultant and trainer in audience, opinion and market research 1998–; Dir Intermedia, Washington, DC 2001–10; Chair. InterMedia UK 2009–12; AT&T Guest Lecturer,

George Washington Univ. 1995; Faculty mem., Oxford Centre for Mission Studies 2000–; various training and research projects with UNICEF, Internews, BBC Media Action, Thomson Foundation, Fondation Hirondelle, Press Now, Press Unlimited, OSCE, UN Office for the Coordination of Humanitarian Affairs and other agencies and businesses 2000–; External Examiner, Univ. of Westminster and others; Hon. Fellow, Bangladesh Marketing and Social Research Soc. 2011; Silver Medal, Market Research Soc. 1997, Wally Langschmidt Memorial Lecturer, SABC, Johannesburg 1999, Piet Smit PAMRO Achiever of the Year Award 2012. *Publications include:* Mass Communications in Africa 1983, Global Audiences (ed.) 1993, Handbook on Radio and TV Audience Research 1993, 1999, Manuel de recherche sur l'audience de la radio et de la télévision 2000; several articles in academic journals on audience research, broadcasting and devt development issues. *Leisure interests:* stamp collecting, singing, bird watching. *Address:* Roffeys, Coldharbour, Dorking, Surrey, RH5 6HE, England (office). *Telephone:* (1306) 712122 (office). *Fax:* (1306) 712958 (office). *E-mail:* gmytton@gn.apc.org (office).

MZIMELA, Rev. Sipo E., MA, PhD; South African ecclesiastic, civil servant and politician; b. 1937, Durban; m.; three d.; ed General Theological Seminary and New York Univ., USA; in exile 1961, W Germany 1964–74, USA 1974, African Nat. Congress (ANC) Rep. to USA and UN 1974–80; ordained Episopal Priest New York 1976; worked with SA refugees; Rector Episcopal Church of the Epiphany, Ventnor, NJ and Adjunct Prof., New York Univ. 1981–83; Head, Dept of Religion and Lecturer, St Paul's United Theological Coll., Limuru, Kenya 1984–87; Founder SA Educ. Fund 1987; Assoc. Priest, St Bartholomew's Episcopal Church, Atlanta 1988–94, Assisting Priest 2005–; Inkatha Freedom Party Rep. to USA 1990; fmr Minister of Works, KwaZulu Govt 1994; Minister of Correctional Services, Govt of Nat. Unity 1994–99; mem. Parl. for Inkatha Freedom Party, later mem. Parl. and Chief Whip United Democratic Movt; returned to USA 2002; Asst Prof. of Religious Studies, Agnes Scott Coll. 2004. *Publications include:* Apartheid – South African Nazism, Whither South Africa Now?, Marching to Slavery – South Africa's Descent to Communism 1983. *Address:* St Bartholomew's Episcopal Church, 1790 LaVista Road NE, Atlanta GA 30329, USA. *Telephone:* (404) 634-3336. *E-mail:* babs@stbartsatlanta.org.

MZIMELA, Sizakele (Siza) Petunia, BA; South African airline industry executive; *CEO, South African Airways (Pty) Ltd;* b. 1967; m.; two c.; ed Univ. of Swaziland, Gordon Inst. of Business Science; worked in Small Business and Retail Div., Standard Bank 1991–94; Corp. Planning Analyst, Total SA 1994–96; Research Analyst, South African Airways (Pty) Ltd 1996, later Man. Market Devt, Sr Man., Alliances, Regional Gen. Man. Africa and the Middle East 2000–01, Exec. Vice-Pres. for Global Passenger Services 2001–02, for Global Sales and Voyager 2002–03, CEO South African Airways 2010–, CEO South African Express Airways 2003–10; mem. Bd of Dirs IATA 2011–, South Africa Tourism, Oprah Winfrey Leadership Acad. for Girls. *Address:* South African Airways (Pty) Ltd, Airways Park, Jones Road, Johannesburg, Gauteng 1627, South Africa (office). *Telephone:* (11) 978-2888 (office). *Fax:* (11) 978-1795 (office). *Website:* www.flysaa .com (office).

NA-RANONG, Kittiratt, BEcons, MBA; Thai financial services industry executive and government official; b. 3 Aug. 1958; ed Assumption Coll., Chulalongkorn Univ., Sasin Graduate Inst. of Business Admin; began career in corp. lending div., Thai Farmers' Bank (now Kasikorn Bank); worked in trading, research and asset man. divs of Securities One (broker), Bangkok 1987; five years as Pres. Stock Exchange of Thailand; Deputy Prime Minister and Minister of Commerce 2011–12, Deputy Prime Minister and Minister of Finance 2012–14; fmr Chief Investment Officer, Univentures Pcl; fmr Chair. Cathay Asset Management; fmr Pres. First Asia Securities Pcl and One Asset Management; fmr Chair. Nat. Econs Research Council; Chancellor Shinawatra Univ.; fmr Deputy Dir for Academic Affairs, Sasin Graduate Inst. of Business Admin; managed Thai nat. football team for Asian Cup 2007; Dir Mass Rapid Transit Authority of Thailand, State Enterprises Capital Policy Cttee, Vayupak Fund Cttee; mem. Securities and Exchange Comm. of Thailand; Knight Grand Cordon (First Class), Most Noble Order of the Crown of Thailand 2011. *Address:* c/o Ministry of Finance, Thanon Rama VI, Samsennai, Phaya Thai, Rajatevi, Bangkok 10400, Thailand.

NÄÄTÄNEN, Risto Kalervo, PhD; Finnish psychologist and academic; *Professor of Cognitive Neuroscience, University of Tartu;* b. 14 June 1939, Helsinki; s. of Prof. Esko K. Näätänen and Rauni Näätänen (née Raudanjoki); m. Marjatta Kerola 1960; three s.; ed Univ. of Helsinki; Asst Dept of Psychology, Univ. of Helsinki 1965–69, Prof. of Psychology 1975–, Dir Cognitive Brain Research Unit 1991–2007; Researcher Acad. of Finland 1969–75, Research Prof. 1983–95, Acad. Prof. 1995–2007; Prof. of Cognitive Neuroscience, Univ. of Tartu, Estonia 2010–; Visiting Prof., Århus Univ., Denmark; Scientific Organizer (with Prof. G. Rizzolatti) of European Science Foundation Winter School 1990; Fellowships, Dept of Psychology, UCLA, USA 1965–66, Univ. of Dundee, UK 1979–80, Univ. of Marburg, Germany 1980–81, The Neurosciences Inst., New York 1985–86, Inst. for Advanced Study, Berlin 1988–89; Vice-Pres. Fed. of European Psychophysiology 1994–96, Pres. 1996–2000; mem. Brain Research Soc. of Finland (Pres. 1983–91), Int. Brain Research Org. (Governing Council 1985–91), Nordic Psychophysiology Soc. (Pres. 1992–95), Advisory Council, Int. Asscn for the Study of Attention and Performance; mem. Finnish Acad. of Science and Letters 1980–, Academia Europaea 1991– (Council 2000–); Foreign mem. Russian Acad. of Sciences 1994, Royal Swedish Acad. of Sciences 2008; Kt (First Class), Order of the White Rose of Finland, Commdr; Dr hc (Jyväskylä) 2000, (Tartu) 2000, (Barcelona) 2007, (St Petersburg) 2008, (Helsinki) 2010; Purkinje Medal (Prague) 1988, Finnish Cultural Foundation Prize 1990, State Traffic Safety Medal 1992, Distinguished Contributions Award, Soc. of Psychophysiological Research, Washington, DC 1995, First Science Prize (Finland) 1997, 20th Anniversary Award, Int. Soc. of Psychophysiology, Montreal, Canada 2002. *Publications:* Selective Attention and Evoked Potentials 1967, Road-User Behaviour and Traffic Accidents (with H. Summala) 1976, Attention and Brain Function 1992, The Orienting Response in Information Processing (with E.N. Sokolov, J.A. Spinks & H. Lyytinen; numerous articles. *Leisure interests:* sports, the Green Movement, traffic safety. *Address:* Cognitive Brain Research Unit, The Department of Psychology, PO Box 9, Siltavuorenpenger 20 C, University of Helsinki, 00014 Helsinki (office); Mäkipellontie 12 D, 00320 Helsinki, Finland (home). *Telephone:* (9) 19129445 (office). *E-mail:* risto.naatanen@helsinki.fi (office). *Website:* www .cbru.helsinki.fi (office).

NABARRO, David, BA, MA, MSc, CBE, FRCP; British physician, public health official and UN official; *Special Representative of the Secretary-General on Food Security and Nutrition, United Nations;* b. 26 Aug. 1949, London, England; s. of Sir John David Nunes Nabarro and Lady Joan Nabarro; m. Gillian Frances Holmes 2002; one s. one d.; two s. one d. from previous relationship; ed Worcester Coll., Oxford, Univ. Coll. Hosp., Univ. of London; began career as Medical Officer, Save the Children Fund, later postings include Relief Expedition, N Iraq 1974–75, Dist Medical Officer, Dhankuta, E Nepal 1977–79, Regional Medical Adviser, S Asia, Kathmandu, Nepal 1982–85; House Officer, later Sr House Officer with Nat. Health Service 1975–77; Lecturer in Nutrition and Public Health, London Univ. 1980–82; Sr Lecturer in Int. Health, Liverpool Univ. Medical School 1985–89, also Hon. Consultant, Mersey Regional Health Authority; Regional Health and Population Adviser, E Africa, British Govt Overseas Devt Admin (ODA) 1989–90, Chief Health and Population Adviser and Head of Health and Population Div., ODA 1990–97 (renamed British Govt Dept for Int. Devt, DFID 1997) 1997–99; Project Man., Roll Back Malaria, WHO, Geneva 1999–2000, Exec. Dir Office of the Dir-Gen., WHO 2000–02, Exec. Dir Sustainable Devt and Sr Policy Adviser to Dir-Gen. 2002–03, Rep. of Dir-Gen. for Health Action in Crises 2003–05; Sr Co-ordinator for Avian and Human Influenza, UN Devt Group, New York 2005–; Deputy UN System Co-ordinator for Global Food Security Crisis 2008; Special Rep. of Sec.-Gen. on Food Security and Nutrition, UN 2009–. *Address:* Office of the Secretary-General, UN Headquarters, First Avenue at 46th Street, New York, NY 10017, USA (office). *Website:* www.un.org (office); www .davidnabarro.com (office).

NABÉ, Louceny; Guinean central banker and fmr politician; *Governor, Banque Centrale de la République de Guinée;* fmr Contracts Man., AU Metals Co. sarl; Minister of Mines 2008–09; Gov. Banque Centrale de la République de Guinée 2010–. *Address:* Office of the Governor, Banque Centrale de la République de Guinée, 12 blvd du Commerce, BP 692, Kaloum, Conakry, Guinea (office). *Telephone:* 30-41-26-51 (office). *Fax:* 30-41-48-98 (office). *E-mail:* gouv.bcrg@eti -bull.net (office). *Website:* www.bcrg-guinee.org (office).

NABIULLINA, Elvira Sakhipzadovna, PhD; Russian economist, government official and central banker; *Governor, Bank Rossii—Central Bank of the Russian Federation;* b. 29 Oct. 1963, Ufa, Bashkir ASSR; ed M.V. Lomonosov Moscow State Univ.; Chief Specialist, Russian Union of Industrialists and Businessmen on econ. policy 1992–94; Deputy Head, Dept of Econ. Reform 1994–96, Head of Dept 1996–97; Deputy Minister of the Economy 1997–98; Vice-Pres. Bd of Dirs Promtorgbank 1998–99; Exec. Dir Euroasian (rating service) 1999; First Deputy Minister of Econ. Devt and Trade 2000–07, Minister of Econ. Devt 2007–12; Econ. Adviser to Pres. Putin 2012–13; Gov. Bank Rossii—Cen. Bank of the Russian Fed.

2013–; Vice-Pres. Fund Centre of Strategic Devt 1999–2000, Pres. 2003–05, Head of Research Group 2005–07; Head of Advisory Council of Organizing Cttee on Preparation and Maintenance of Presidency of the Russian Fed. in G8 2005–06; fmr mem. Pres.'s Expert Council on Priority Nat. Projects and Demography; World Fellow, Yale Univ., USA 2007. *Address:* Bank Rossii—Central Bank of the Russian Federation, 107016 Moscow, ul. Neglinnaya 12, Russia (office). *Telephone:* (495) 771-91-00 (office). *Fax:* (495) 621-64-65 (office). *E-mail:* webmaster@cbr.ru (office). *Website:* www.cbr.ru (office).

NACHTWEY, James, FRPS; American photojournalist and war photographer; b. 1948, Syracuse, NY; ed Leominster High School and Dartmouth Coll.; influenced by imagery from Viet Nam War and American Civil Rights Movt; became self-taught photographer; held a series of odd jobs, including as a truck driver; also worked on merchant ships; started work as newspaper photographer, NM 1976; moved to New York and began working as freelance photographer 1980; worked for Black Star 1980–85; contract photographer, Time magazine 1984–; covered first overseas assignment in NI 1981; worked in SA, Latin America, Middle East, Russia, Eastern Europe, fmr Soviet Union shooting pictures of war, conflict and famine, and images of sociopolitical issues (pollution, crime and punishment) in Western Europe and USA; covered elections in SA 1994, invasion of Iraq 2003, tsunami in SE Asia 26 Dec. 2004; made series of photographs about attacks on World Trade Center 11 Sept. 2001; compiled a photo essay on effects of Sudan conflict on civilians; has worked on extensive photographic essays in El Salvador, Nicaragua, Guatemala, Lebanon, West Bank and Gaza, Israel, Indonesia, Thailand, India, Sri Lanka, Afghanistan, the Philippines, South Korea, Somalia, Sudan, Rwanda, SA, Russia, Bosnia, Chechnya, Kosovo, Romania, Brazil and USA; mem. Magnum Photos 1986–2001; Co-founding mem. VII Photo Agency 2001; Hon. DFA (Massachusetts Coll. of Art); numerous honours and awards, including Common Wealth Award, Martin Luther King Award, Dr Jean Mayer Global Citizenship Award, Henry Luce Award, Robert Capa Gold Medal (five times), World Press Photo Award (twice), Magazine Photographer of the Year (seven times), Int. Center of Photography Infinity Award (three times), Leica Award (twice), Bayeaux Award for War Corresps (twice), Alfred Eisenstaedt Award, Canon Photo Essayist Award, W. Eugene Smith Memorial Grant in Humanistic Photography, Dan David Prize, Dan David Foundation and Tel-Aviv Univ. 2003, Heinz Foundation Achievement Award 2006, TED (Tech. Entertainment Design) Prize (co-recipient) 2007. *Address:* c/o TIME magazine, 1271 Avenue of the Americas, New York, NY 10020-1393, USA (office). *Telephone:* 212-522-1212 (office). *Fax:* 212-522-0602 (office). *Website:* www.time.com (office); www .jamesnachtwey.com.

NADAL PARERA, Rafael (Rafa); Spanish professional tennis player; b. 3 June 1986, Manacor, Majorca; s. of Sebastian Nadal and Ana Maria Parera; ed coached by Toni Nadal; began playing tennis aged four; turned professional 2001; played his only jr Grand Slam event at Wimbledon in 2002 and reached semi-finals; won first ATP match defeating Ramon Delgado in Majorca to become the ninth player in open era to win an ATP match before 16th birthday; became second-youngest player to be ranked among world's top 100 singles players 2003; reached fourth round at Australian Open 2005, semi-finalist 2008, winner 2009, finalist 2012, 2014; winner, French Open 2005, 2006, 2007, 2008, 2010, 2011, 2012 (beating Bjorn Borg's previous record of six titles), 2013 (first male player to win eight titles at the same Grand Slam tournament); runner-up, Wimbledon 2006, 2007, 2011, winner 2008, 2010; quarter-finalist, US Open 2006, semi-finalist 2008, 2009, winner 2010, 2013, runner-up 2011; semi-finalist, Masters Cup 2006, 2007; gold medal, men's singles, Olympic Games, Beijing 2008; runner-up, Barclays ATP World Tour Finals, London 2010, 2013; clay-court winning streak of 81 matches (longest among male players in open era) April 2005–May 2007; World No. 1 18 Aug. 2008–5 July 2009, 7 June 2010–3 July 2011, 7 Oct. 2013–; winner, Monte-Carlo Rolex Masters 2012, Barcelona Open 2012, 2013, Internazionali BNL d'Italia, Rome 2012, 2013, Brasil Open 2013, Abierto Mexicano Telcel, Acapulco 2013, BNP Paribas Open, Indian Wells 2013, Mutua Madrid Open 2013,2014, Coupe Rogers, Montreal 2013, Western & Southern Open, Cincinnati 2013, Qatar ExxonMobil Open, Doha 2014, Rio Open presented by Claro hdtv Rio de Janeiro 2014; youngest player in history to win Davis Cup at first attempt; became seventh man to complete a Career Grand Slam after winning US Open 13 Sept. 2010; 13 Grand Slam singles titles; ATP Newcomer of the Year 2003, ATP Most Improved Player 2005, Laureus World Newcomer of the Year 2006, Prince of Asturias Award 2008, BBC Overseas Sports Personality of the Year 2010, Laureus Sportsman of the Year Award 2011. *Achievements include:* asteroid 128036 Rafaelnadal named in his honour. *Publication:* Rafa (with John Carlin) 2012. *Leisure interests:* playing PSP, soccer and golf, fishing, going out with friends in Majorca. *Address:* c/o Carlos Costa, IMG, Via Augusta, 200 4th Floor, 08021 Barcelona, Spain (office). *Telephone:* (93) 2003455 (office). *Fax:* (93) 2005924 (office). *E-mail:* kc@ rafaelnadal.com. *Website:* www.rafaelnadal.com.

NADAR, Shiv; Indian business executive, engineer and philanthropist; *Chairman and Chief Strategy Officer, HCL Technologies;* b. 18 July 1945, Tamil Nadu; s. of Sivasubramaniya Nadar and Vamasundari Devi; m. Kiran Nadar; one d.; ed Madurai American Coll., P.S.G. Coll. of Tech.; Systems Analyst, Cooper Eng; Sr Man. Trainee, DCM Ltd 1968; f. Hindustan Computers Ltd (later HCL) 1976, CEO HCL Technologies Ltd 1991, currently Chair. and Chief Strategy Officer; mem. Exec. Bd Indian School of Business, Hyderabad; mem. Public Health Foundation of India, Global Charter The Indus Entrepreneurs; Founder S.S.N. Coll. of Eng, Chennai 1996; Hon. Fellow, All India Man. Asscn 2006; Dr hc (Madras) 2007; CNBC Business Excellence Award 2005, Ernst & Young Entrepreneur of the Year Award 2007, Padma Bhushan 2008, featured by Forbes magazine amongst 48 Heroes of Philanthropy 2009. *Address:* HCL Technologies Ltd, A10/11, Sector 3, Noida 201 301, India (office). *Telephone:* (120) 2520917 (office). *Fax:* (120) 2526907 (office). *E-mail:* webhost@hcl.in (office). *Website:* www.hcl.in (office).

NADELLA, Satya, BS, MSCS, MBA; American (b. Indian) computer industry executive; *CEO, Microsoft Corporation;* b. (Satyanarayana Nadella), 1967, Hyderabad, AP, India; s. of B. N. Yugandhar; m. Anupama Venugopal 1992; one

s. two d.; ed Hyderabad Public School, Begumpet, Manipal Inst. of Tech., Karnataka (then affiliated to Mangalore Univ.), Univ. of Wisconsin-Milwaukee, Univ. of Chicago Booth School of Business; mem. tech. staff, Sun Microsystems –1992; joined Microsoft 1992, later Vice-Pres. Microsoft Business Div., Sr Vice-Pres., Research and Devt, for Online Services Div. 2007–11, Pres. Server and Tools Business 2011–14, Exec. Vice-Pres. Cloud and Enterprise Group 2011–14, CEO Microsoft Corpn 2014–. *Leisure interests:* cricket, poetry. *Address:* Microsoft Corporation, 1 Microsoft Way, Redmond, WA 98052-8300, USA (office). *Telephone:* (425) 882-8080 (office). *Fax:* (425) 936-7329 (office). *E-mail:* info@microsoft.com (office). *Website:* www.microsoft.com (office).

NADER, Ralph, AB, LLB; American lawyer, author and consumer advocate; b. 27 Feb. 1934, Winsted, Conn.; s. of Nadra Nader and Rose Bouziane; ed Princeton and Harvard Univs; admitted to Conn. Bar 1958, Mass Bar 1959, also US Supreme Court; US Army 1959; law practice in Hartford, Conn. 1959–; Lecturer in History and Govt, Univ. of Hartford 1961–63; Founder and fmr Head of Public Citizen Inc. 1980; Lecturer, Princeton Univ. 1967–68; Co-founder Princeton Project 55 1989; launched political movt Democracy Rising 2001; Green Party cand. for presidential election 1996, 2000, ind. cand. 2004, 2008; mem. ABA; f. Clean Water Action Project, Disability Rights Center, Public Interest Research Groups (PIRGs), Center for Study of Responsive Law, Center for Auto Safety, Pension Rights Center, Project for Corp. Responsibility; Contributing Ed. Ladies Home Journal 1973–81, syndicated columnist, In the Public Interest 1972–; f. The Multinational Monitor (monthly magazine); Nieman Fellows Award 1965–66, named one of ten Outstanding Young Men of Year by the US Jr Chamber of Commerce 1967, Woodrow Wilson Award, Princeton Univ. 1972. *Film appearance:* (as himself) Fun with Dick and Jane 2005. *Publications include:* Unsafe at Any Speed 1965, Who Runs Congress? 1972, The Consumer and Corporate Accountability 1974, Taming the Giant Corporation (co-author) 1976, The Menace of Atomic Energy (with John Abbotts) 1979, The Lemon Book 1980, Who's Poisoning America? 1981, The Big Boys 1986, Winning the Insurance Game (co-author) 1990, Good Works 1993, No Contest: Corporate Lawyers and the Perversion of Justice in America 1996, The Ralph Nader Reader 2000, Crashing the Party 2002, Civic Arousal 2004, It Happened in the Kitchen: Recipes for Food and Thought, Why Women Pay More (with Frances Cerra Whittelsley), Children First! A Parent's Guide to Fighting Corporate Predators, The Seventeen Traditions 2007, Only the Super-Rich Can Save Us! 2009. *Address:* Democracy Rising, PO Box 18485, Washington, DC 20036; PO Box 19312, Washington, DC 20036, USA. *E-mail:* info@nader.org. *Website:* www.democracyrising.us; www.nader.org.

NADINGAR, Emmanuel; Chadian politician; Deputy Chief of Staff, Govt of Chad –2004; Minister of Nat. Defence, Veterans and Victims of War 2004–07, of Petroleum 2007–08, Minister-del. to the Prime Minister, responsible for Decentralization 2008–10; Prime Minister of Chad 2010–13. *Address:* c/o Office of the Prime Minister, BP 463, N'Djamena, Chad.

NAEEM, Mohamed Monaza; Maldivian business executive and politician; f. Monaza Contracting Co. Pvt. Ltd 1978; MP for Laamu Atoll, Chair. Business Cttee of Special Majlis 2007; Founder and Leader Maldivian Nat. Congress 2007–10; apptd Minister of State for Home Affairs 2011; sr mem. People's Asscn. *Address:* Naeem & Sons Trading Pvt. Ltd, 1/7, First Floor, M. Velidhooge, Dhambu Goalhi, Malé, Maldives (office). *Telephone:* 3316921 (office). *Fax:* 3316922 (office). *E-mail:* info@monaza.mv (office). *Website:* www.monaza.mv (office).

NAEGLE, Sue; American television executive; *President, HBO Entertainment;* b. Rockaway, NJ; m. Dana Gould; three adopted d. from China; ed Indiana Univ.; began career in post room of United Talent Agency, LA 1991, became agent 1994, Co-head of TV Dept and Partner 1999; Pres. Entertainment Div., HBO (Time Warner co.) 2011–, oversees all series programming and specials; ranked by Forbes magazine amongst The World's 100 Most Powerful Women (88th) 2011, (46th) 2012, (76th) 2013. *Address:* Home Box Office, Inc., 1100 Avenue of the Americas, New York, NY 10036, USA (office). *Telephone:* (212) 512-1000 (office). *Fax:* (212) 512-1182 (office). *E-mail:* info@hbo.com (office). *Website:* www.hbo.com (office).

NAEK, Farooq Hamid, LLB, MA; Pakistani lawyer and politician; *Minister of Law and Justice;* ed Univ. of Karachi, Sindh Muslim Law Coll.; enrolled as advocate 1970, as advocate of Supreme Court 1976, as advocate of High Court 1976; fmr Asst Dir, Directorate of Labour and Social Welfare, Govt of Sindh; Civil Judge and First Class Magistrate 1971–75; resigned from judicial service after serving as civil judge for two years and became active mem. Pakistan People's Party mid-1970s; Deputy Attorney Gen. 1994–96; Senator from Karachi 2003–, Chair. of Senate 2009–12; Fed. Minister of Law, Justice, Parl. Affairs and Human Rights 2008–09, of Law and Justice 2012–; successfully defended fmr Prime Minister Benazir Bhutto and her husband Asif Ali Zardari in numerous cases filed by earlier govts in courts in Pakistan, UK, Switzerland and Spain; arrested leading demonstration against rule of Gen. Zia Ul Haq 1983, remained in Cen. Prison, Karachi for six months along with ten other lawyers, declared Prisoner of Conscience by Amnesty International; elected Gen. Sec. Karachi Bar Asscn 1983, elected Pres. 1989; mem. Sindh Bar Council 1984–89 (re-elected 1990–94), twice elected Vice-Chair. 1986, 1993; mem. Pakistan Bar Council 1997–. *Address:* Ministry of Law and Justice, Block R, Pakistan Secretariat, Islamabad (office); House 8, Street-19, F-8/2, Islamabad (home); 60/A/1, 3rd Sunset Street, Phase-III Extension, DHA Karachi, Pakistan (home). *Telephone:* (51) 9211278 (office); (51) 9212710 (home); (21) 5897581 (home). *Fax:* (51) 9201722 (office). *E-mail:* contact@molaw.gov.pk (office). *Website:* www.molaw.gov.pk (office).

NAFISI, Azar, PhD; Iranian writer and academic; *Executive Director, Dialogue Project, School of Advanced International Studies, Johns Hopkins University;* b. 1 Dec. 1955; d. of Ahmad Nafisi; m.; one d.; ed Univ. of Oklahoma, USA; fmrly teacher, Tehran Univ., Allemeh Tabatabai Univ.; fmrly Visiting Fellow, Univ. of Oxford; currently Visiting Prof. and Exec. Dir Dialogue Project, School of Advanced Int. Studies, Johns Hopkins Univ., Washington, DC. *Publications include:* Anti-Terra: A Study of Vladimir Nabokov's Novels 1994, Reading 'Lolita' in Tehran: A Memoir in Books 2003, La Voce Verde 2006, Things I've Been Silent About 2009; contrib. numerous chapters and articles on promotion of democracy, human rights in Muslim societies, women's rights, literature, culture. *Address:* Paul H. Nitze School of Advanced International Studies, Johns Hopkins University, The Rome Building, Room 731, 1619 Massachusetts Avenue NW, Washing-

ton, DC 20036, USA (office). *Telephone:* (202) 663-5785 (office). *E-mail:* anafisi@jhu.edu (office); info@azarnafisi.com (office). *Website:* www.sais-jhu.edu (office); www.azarnafisi.com.

NAG, Rajat Mohan, BTech, MSc, MBA, MSc; Canadian engineer, economist and financial analyst; *Managing Director General, Asian Development Bank;* b. 12 Sept. 1948, Sylhet, Bangladesh; s. of Rohini Mohan Nag and Asha Lata Nag; m. Shikha Nag; one s. one d.; ed Indian Inst. of Tech., Delhi, Univ. of Saskatchewan, London School of Econs, UK; worked as Supervising Engineer, later Economist, later Chief Economist in an eng firm in Canada for agricultural, water, energy and mining projects; fmr Sr Financial Analyst for Bank of Canada; fmr Visiting Lecturer in Financial and Econ. Analysis, Carleton Univ., McGill Univ., Concordia Univ.; joined Asian Devt Bank (ADB) as Project Economist in Agric. Dept 1986, assigned to ADB's Nepal Resident Mission 1991–94, held various sr positions in ADB's Programs Dept (West) and in Financial Sector and Industry Div., Infrastructure Dept (West), mem. man. cttee that formulated proposals for re-organization of ADB operations 2001, Deputy Dir Programs Dept (West) 2000–02, Dir Gen. for SE Asia and Mekong Depts 2002–06, Special Advisor to ADB Pres. on Regional Econ. Co-operation and Integration 2005–06, Dir Gen. newly amalgamated SE Asia Dept 2006, Man. Dir Gen. ADB 2006–. *Leisure interest:* involved with various community and charitable orgs. *Address:* Asian Development Bank, 6 ADB Avenue, 1500 Mandaluyong City, Philippines (office). *Telephone:* (2) 632-5416 (office). *Fax:* (2) 636-2683 (office). *E-mail:* rnag@adb.org (office). *Website:* www.adb.org (office).

NAGAE, Shusaku; Japanese business executive; *Chairman, Panasonic Corporation;* served as Dir of Project Sales Operations, Tokyo HQ, Panasonic Corpn, Dir of Electrical Construction Materials Marketing Business Unit and Sr Man. Dir, Exec. Vice-Pres. Panasonic Electric Works Co. Ltd April–June 2010, Pres. in charge of Lighting Co. and Panasonic Ecology Systems Co. Ltd 2010–11, Sr Man. Exec. Officer, Panasonic Corpn 2011–12, Pres. Eco Solutions Co. Jan. 2012–, Exec. Vice-Pres., Panasonic Corpn June 2012–13, Chair. 2013–. *Address:* Panasonic Corporation, Corporate Headquarters, 1006 Oaza Kadoma, Kadoma-shi, Osaka 571-8501, Japan (office). *Telephone:* (6) 6908-1121 (office). *Fax:* (6) 6908-2351 (office). *E-mail:* info@panasonic.net (office). *Website:* panasonic.net (office).

NAGAI, Kiyoshi, PhD, FRS; Japanese biologist and academic; *Senior Research Scientist, Structural Studies Division, Medical Research Council Laboratory of Molecular Biology;* b. 25 June 1949, Osaka; s. of Otoji Nagai and Naoko Nagai; m. Yoshiko Majima 1974; one s. one d.; ed Osaka Univ. Morimoto Lab.; Research Scientist, MRC Lab. of Molecular Biology 1981–, Jt Head of Structural Studies 2001–10, Sr Research Scientist 2010–; Research Group Leader, Nagai Group (molecular mechanism of pre-mRNA splicing); Fellow, Darwin Coll. Cambridge 1993–; Novartis Medal and Prize, Biochemical Soc. 2000. *Publications:* RNA-Protein Interaction (co-ed. with Iain Mattaj) 1995); numerous publs in scientific journals. *Leisure interests:* reading, playing cello in chamber groups. *Address:* Structural Studies Division, MRC Laboratory of Molecular Biology, Hills Road, Cambridge, CB2 0QH, England (office). *Telephone:* (1223) 402292 (office). *Fax:* (1223) 213556 (office). *E-mail:* kn@mrc-lmb.cam.ac.uk (office). *Website:* www2.mrc-lmb.cam.ac.uk (office).

NAGAI, Koji, BA; Japanese financial services executive; *Group CEO, Nomura Holdings, Inc.;* ed Chuo Univ.; joined Nomura 1981, later Deputy Pres. of domestic unit, Pres. Nomura's domestic brokerage –2012, Pres. Nomura Securities Co. April 2012–, Group CEO Nomura Holdings, Inc. Aug. 2012–. *Address:* Nomura Holdings, Inc., 1-9-1, Nihonbashi, Chuo-ku, Tokyo 103-8645, Japan (office). *Telephone:* (3) 3211-1811 (office). *E-mail:* info@nomura.co.jp (office). *Website:* www.nomura.co.jp (office).

NAGANO, Kent; American conductor; *Music Director, Montreal Symphony Orchestra and Bayerische Staatsoper;* b. 22 Nov. 1951, Berkeley, Calif.; ed studied under Ozawa, Boulez and Bernstein; first achieved int. recognition when he conducted Boston Symphony Orchestra in performance of Mahler's Symphony No. 9 1984; conducted US premiere of Messiaen's The Transfiguration; debut at Paris Opera conducting world premiere of Messiaen's St François d'Assise; debut, Metropolitan Opera, New York conducting Poulenc's Dialogues des Carmélites 1994; Music Dir, Berkeley Symphony Orchestra, Calif. 1978–2009, Opéra de Lyon 1988–99, Hallé Orchestra 1991–2000; Artistic Dir, Deutsches Symphonie-Orchester Berlin 2000–07; Prin. Conductor and Music Dir, Los Angeles Opera 2001–06; Music Dir, Montreal Symphony Orchestra 2006–, Bayerische Staatsoper 2006–13; Prin. Guest Conductor and Artistic Adviser, Gothenburg Symphony Orchestra 2013–; Prin. Music Dir and Conductor, Hamburg State Opera and Philharmonic Orchestra (2015–20); Officier, Ordre des Arts et des Lettres 1992, Order of the Rising Sun, Gold Rays 2009; Grammy Awards for Busoni's Dr Faust with Opéra Nat. de Lyon, Prokofiev's Peter and the Wolf with the Russian Nat. Orchestra, Saariaho's L'Amour de Loin with Deutsches Symphonie-Orchester Berlin (Best Opera Recording 2011). *Address:* c/o Janet Marsden, International Classical Artists, Dunstan House, 14A St Cross Street, London, EC1N 8XA, England (office). *Telephone:* (20) 7902-0520 (office). *Fax:* (20) 7902-0150 (office). *E-mail:* info@icartists.co.uk (office). *Website:* www.osm.ca; www.bayerische.staatsoper.de; www.kentnagano.com.

NAGANO, Tsuyoshi; Japanese business executive; *President and CEO, Tokio Marine Holdings, Inc.;* joined Tokio Marine 1975, Exec. Officer and Gen. Man. Nagoya Production Dept III, Tokai Div., Tokio Marine 2003–04, Exec. Officer and Gen. Man. Nagoya Production Dept III, Tokio Marine & Nichido 2004–06, Man. Exec. Officer, Tokio Marine & Nichido 2006–08, Man. Dir and Gen. Man. Corp. Planning Dept, Tokio Marine & Nichido 2008–09, Dir, Tokio Marine Holdings, Inc. 2008–09, Sr Man. Dir Tokio Marine & Nichido 2010–11, Sr Man. Dir Tokio Marine Holdings, Inc. 2011–12, Sr Man. Dir and Gen. Man. Int. Business Devt Dept 2012–13, Exec. Vice-Pres., Tokio Marine & Nichido 2012–13, Exec. Vice-Pres. and Gen. Man. Int. Business Devt Dept, Tokio Marine Holdings, Inc. 2012–13, Pres. and CEO Tokio Marine & Nichido 2013–, Tokio Marine Holdings, Inc. 2013–. *Address:* Tokio Marine Holdings Inc., Nichido Building Shinkan, 1-2-1 Marunouchi, Chiyoda-ku, Tokyo, 100-0005, Japan (office). *Telephone:* (3) 6212-3333 (office). *E-mail:* ir@tokiomarinehd.com (office). *Website:* www.tokiomarinehd.com (office).

NAGAO, Makoto, MEng, PhD; Japanese academic and engineer; *President, National Institute of Information and Communications Technology (NICT);* b. 4

Oct. 1936; ed Kyoto Univ.; pioneer of natural language processing and intelligent image processing tech.; led research developing first machine translation systems and digital library systems; Asst Prof., Faculty of Eng, Kyoto Univ. 1961–67, Lecturer 1967–68, Assoc. Prof. 1968–73, Prof. 1973–, Dir Data Processing Centre 1986–90, Dean Faculty of Eng 1997, Pres. Kyoto Univ. 1997–2003; Visiting Assoc. Prof., Dept of Informatics, Grenoble Univ. 1969–70; Pres. Japan Asscn of Nat. Univs 2001–03; Pres. Nat. Inst. of Information and Communications Tech. (NICT) 2004–; Pres. Japanese Cognitive Science Soc. 1988–90, Int. Asscn for Machine Tech. (IAMT) 1991–93, Asia-Pacific Asscn for Machine Tech. 1992–96, Asscn for Nat. Language Training 1994–96, Inst. of Electronics, Information and Communication Engineers (IEICE) 1998–99, Information Processing Soc. of Japan (IPSJ) 1999–2000, Japan Library Asscn 2002–; mem. Science Council of Japan 2000–03; Fellow, IEEE 1999; Hon. DSc (Univ. of Nottingham, UK) 1999; IEEE Emmanuel R. Piore Award 1993, Bunka-shou Culture Prize 1994, IEICE Distinguished Achievement and Contribs Award 1997, IPSJ Contribs Award 1997, IAMT Medal of Honour 1997, Japanese Govt Purple Ribbon Medal 1997, JSAI Achievement Award 1998, NHK Broadcast Cultural Award 1998, C&C Prize 1999, Takayanagi Kinen-shou Memorial Award 2000, Asscn for Computational Linguistics Lifetime Achievement Award 2003, Japan Prize for Information and Media Tech. 2005. *Publications:* in English: A Structural Analysis of Complex Aerial Photographs 1980, Machine Translation: How Far Can It Go? 1989, Knowledge and Inference 1990; in Japanese: Engineering for Pattern Recognition and Language Understanding 1989, Artificial and Human Intelligence 1992, Digital Library 1994, Natural Language Processing (co-author) 1996, What Is Understanding? 2001. *Address:* National Institute of Information and Communications Technology (NICT), Incorporated Administrative Agency, 4-2-1 Nukui-Kitamachi, Koganei, Tokyo 184-8795 (office); 39-1 Kitaikeda, Iwakura, Sakyo, Kyoto, Japan (home). *Telephone:* (42) 327-7523 (office). *Fax:* (42) 327-7586 (office). *E-mail:* nagao-sec@ nict.go.jp (office). *Website:* www.nict.go.jp (office).

NAGARE, Masayuki; Japanese sculptor; b. 1923, Nagasaki; m. (divorced; one d.; ed Ritsumeikan Univ.; enrolled in Zen Temple; apprentice to a sword maker; fighter pilot volunteer, World War II; several solo exhbns. *Works include:* Cloud Fortress, New York, Nagare Park, Okushiri, as well as over 2,000 other pieces. *Address:* c/o Jason McCoy Gallery, 41 East 57th Street, New York, NY 10022, USA. *Website:* www.nagaremasayuki.com.

NAGASE, Jinen; Japanese politician; b. 3 Oct. 1943; joined Ministry of Labour 1966, Sec. to Minister of Labour 1982–84, Dir Employment Security Bureau, Measures for the Aged Dept, Employment Measures Div. 1984–86, Dir Labour Relations Bureau, Labour Legislation Div. 1986–88 (resgnd from Ministry); mem. House of Reps for Toyama Pref. 1st Dist (LDP) 1990–, Deputy Chair. LDP Diet Affairs Cttee 1994, State Sec. for Health and Welfare 1995–96, Dir LDP Environment Div. 1996, Chair. LDP Social Affairs Div. 1996, Dir LDP Labour Admin Div. 1997, Deputy Sec.-Gen. LDP and Chief Dir House Cttee on Health and Welfare 1998, Sr State Sec. for Labour 1999–2000, Chair. House Standing Cttee on Judicial Affairs 2000, Sr State Sec. for Justice 2000–01, Sr Vice-Minister of Justice 2001–02, Chief Dir House Cttee on Health, Labour and Welfare 2002–03, Chief Deputy Chair. Policy Research Council 2004, Dir Jt Meeting of Both Houses on the Reform of Pension and Other Social Security Systems 2005, Deputy Chief Cabinet Sec. 2005–06, Minister of Justice 2006–07. *Address:* c/o Ministry of Justice, 1-1-1, Kasumigaseki, Chiyoda-ku, Tokyo 100-8977, Japan.

NAGASHIMA, Shigeo, BA; Japanese professional baseball player and manager (retd); b. 20 Feb. 1936, Chiba Pref.; s. of Toshi Nagashima and Chiyo Nagashima; m. Akiko Nishimura 1965; two s. two d.; ed St Paul's Univ., Tokyo; professional baseball player, Tokyo Yomiuri Giants 1958–74, Man. 1975–81, 1993–2001; Rookie of the Year 1958, Most Valuable Player of the Year (five times), Best Average Hitter of the Year (six times), Most Home-run Hitter of the Year (twice), Most Runs batted in Hitter of the Year (five times), Man. of Champion Team of the Year three times. *Leisure interest:* golf.

NAGATSUMA, Akira, LLB; Japanese lawyer and politician; b. 14 June 1960, Nerima, Tokyo; ed Keio Univ., Tokyo; began career with NEC Corpn; fmr reporter, Nikkei Business magazine; mem. House of Reps for Tokyo No. 7 constituency 2000–, fmr mem. Parl. Cttee on Health, Labour and Welfare; mem. Democratic Party of Japan (DPJ), Deputy Chair. DPJ Policy Research Cttee; fmr Next (Shadow) Cabinet Minister of State for Pensions and Deputy Chief Cabinet Sec.; Minister of Health, Labour and Welfare, also Minister of State for Pension Reform 2009–10. *Address:* c/o Ministry of Health, Labour and Welfare, 1-2-2, Kasumigaseki, Chiyoda-ku, Tokyo 100-8916, Japan.

NAGAYAMA, Osamu; Japanese business executive; *Chairman, Sony Corporation;* b. 1947; ed Faculty of Business and Commerce, Keio Univ.; joined Long-Term Credit Bank of Japan 1971, worked at London Br. 1975–78; joined Chugai Pharmaceutical Co. Ltd 1978, Dir, Pharmaceutical Sales and Marketing Div. and Int. Business Div. 1983–85, Deputy Gen. Man. Pharmaceutical Research and Devt Div. and mem. Bd of Dirs 1985–86, Deputy Gen. Man. Personal Healthcare Div. 1986–87, Sr Vice-Pres. 1987–89, Deputy Pres. 1989–92, Pres. Chugai Pharmaceutical Co. Ltd 1992–2012, COO –2012, Chair., Pres. and CEO 2012–; Dir, Sony Corpn 2010–, Vice-Chair. 2012–13, Chair. 2013–; Ind. Dir, Nomura Partners Funds, Inc.– The Japan Fund 2005–; mem. Exec. Cttee Roche. *Address:* Sony Corporation, 1-7-1 Konan, Minato-ku, Tokyo 108-0075, Japan (office). *Telephone:* (3) 6748-2111 (office). *Fax:* (3) 6748-2244 (office). *E-mail:* info@sony.net (office). *Website:* www.sony.net (office).

NAGAYASU, Katsunori; Japanese business executive; *Chairman, Bank of Tokyo-Mitsubishi UFJ Limited;* ed Univ. of Tokyo; joined Mitsubishi Bank in Kyoto br. 1970, Deputy Gen. Man., Planning Dept 1992–96, became part of Planning Dept of Bank of Tokyo-Mitsubishi (following merger with Bank of Tokyo) 1996; Man. Dir Nippon Trust Bank Ltd 2000–01; Man. Dir Mitsubishi Trust & Banking Corpn and its Bank 2001–02; served as Gen. Man. Trust Business Planning Div. and Co-Gen. Man. Corp. Business Planning Div. of Integrated Corp. Banking Business Group of Mitsubishi Trust & Banking Corpn, Dir, Bank of Tokyo-Mitsubishi UFJ Ltd (subsidiary of Mitsubishi UFJ Financial Group, Inc.) 1997–2000, Rep. Dir 2000; Man. Dir 2002–04, Chief Exec. Commercial Banking Business Unit 2004–05, Sr Man. Dir Bank of Tokyo-Mitsubishi UFJ Ltd Jan.–May 2005, Deputy Pres. Business & Systems Integration Div. 2005–08, Pres. 2008–10,

Dir, Mitsubishi UFJ Financial Group, Inc. 2001–04, 2008–, Group Head of Integrated Corp. Banking Business Group 2004–06, Chief Planning Officer and Deputy Pres. Mitsubishi UFJ Financial Group, Inc. 2006–07, Chief Compliance Officer 2007–08, Pres., CEO and Rep. Dir Mitsubishi UFJ Financial Group, Inc. 2010–13, Chair. Bank of Tokyo-Mitsubishi UFJ Ltd 2012–; Dir Mitsubishi Tokyo Financial Group, Inc. (subsidiary of Mitsubishi UFJ Financial Group, Inc. and holding co. of Mitsubishi Trust & Banking Corpn) 2001–04, Man. Officer 2004–06; Dir, Acom Co. Ltd 2006–, UnionBanCal Corpn 2012–; External Audit and Supervisory Bd mem., Nippon Steel & Sumitomo Metal Corpn; Chair. Japanese Bankers Asscn 2009. *Address:* Bank of Tokyo-Mitsubishi UFJ, 7-1, Marunouchi 2-chome, Chiyoda-ku, Tokyo 100-8388, Japan (office). *E-mail:* info@bk.mufg.jp (office). *Website:* www.bk.mufg.jp/global (office).

NAGEL, Andrés; Spanish artist; b. 15 Aug. 1947, San Sebastián; qualified as an architect; subject of books 'Nagel' by Edward Lucie-Smith 1992 and 'Una Decada' by Lluisa Borrás 2003. *Address:* Caserío Parada 36, 20015 San Sebastián, Guipúzcoa, Spain (office). *Website:* www.andresnagel.com.

NAGEL, Günter; German landscape architect; b. 2 Feb. 1936, Dresden; s. of Heinrich Nagel and Erna Nagel (née Hempel); m. Helga Jähnig 1962; one c.; ed Dresden, Humboldt Univ., Berlin and Berlin Tech. Univ.; Scientific Asst, Garden and Landscape Design, Berlin Tech. Univ. 1962–70, lectureship in Design, Garden and Landscape; freelance landscape architect; lectureships at Fine Arts Univ., Berlin (Prof. 1974) and Tech. Univ. Brunswick 1970–74; Prof. and Dir Inst. for Park Planning and Garden Architecture, Univ. of Hanover 1977–2000, Vice-Pres. of the Univ. 1986–88; mem. German Soc. for Garden Design and Preservation of Natural Resources; mem. Deutscher Werkbund; mem. Bd of Trustees, Fritz Schumacher Foundation, Karl Foerster Foundation; Dir Acad. of Arts, Berlin, German Acad. of Town and Country Planning. *Publications:* Gärten in Cornwall 1975, Freiräume in der Stadtentwicklung 1978, Erholungsraum Stadtlandschaft 1980, Stadtumbau Grunfunktionen im Hamburger Hafen 1983, Gestaltung und Nutzung des Freiraums Strasse 1985, Verbesserung des Wohnumfeldes 1985, Qualität öffentlicher Freiräume 1986. *Address:* c/o Institut für Grünplanung und Gartenarchitektur, Universität Hannover, Herrenhäuser Strasse 2, 30419 Hannover, Germany.

NAGEL, Ivan, PhD; German professor of aesthetics and history of performing arts; *Professor Emeritus, Universität der Künste, Berlin;* b. 28 June 1931, Budapest, Hungary; ed Univ. of Heidelberg, Univ. of Paris, France, Univ. of Frankfurt and Univ. of Durham, UK; Theatre and Music Critic, Deutsche Zeitung 1959–61, Süddeutsche Zeitung 1969–71; Artistic Adviser, Münchner Kammerspiele 1962–69; Gen. Man. Deutsches Schauspielhaus, Hamburg 1972–79; Pres. Int. Theatre Inst. 1972–79; Cultural Corresp. Frankfurter Allgemeine, New York 1980–83; Fellow, Wissenschaftkolleg, Berlin 1983–84, 1988–89; Dir State Theatre, Stuttgart 1985–88; Prof. of Aesthetics and History of the Performing Arts, Universität der Künste, Berlin 1988–96, now Prof. Emer.; Dir Drama Section Salzburg Festival 1997–98; Founder and Pres. Theater der Welt (int. theatre festival), Hamburg 1979, 1989, Cologne 1981, Stuttgart 1987; mem. Akad. der Künste, Berlin, Akad. für Sprache und Dichtung, Darmstadt and Akad. der Darstellenden Künste, Frankfurt; Hon. PhD 2008; Berlin Merit Order 2002, Fed. Merit Order 2003; Merck Award 1988, Kortner Award 1998, Moses Mendelssohn Award 2000, Ernst Bloch Award 2003, Heinrich Mann Award 2005. *Publications:* Autonomie und Gnade: Über Mozarts Opern 1985 (English trans. Autonomy and Mercy 1991), Gedankengänge als Lebensläufe: Versuche über das 18. Jahrhundert 1987, Kortner Zadek Stein 1989, Danneckers Ariadne auf dem Panther 1993, Vier Regisseure: Bondy, Castorf, Sellars, Wilson 1996, Der Künstler als Kuppler: Goyas Nackte und Bekleidete Maja 1997, Streitschriften 2001, Falschwörterbuch 2004, Drama und Theater: Von Shakespeare bis Jelinek 2006, Gemälde und Drama: Giotto, Masaccio, Leonardo 2009, Schriften zur Kunst 2010, Schriften zum Drama 2010, Schriften zum Theater 2011. *Leisure interest:* music. *Address:* Keithstr. 10, 10787 Berlin, Germany (home). *Telephone:* (30) 2114710 (home). *Fax:* (30) 2114710 (home). *E-mail:* ivannagel@gmx.de (office).

NAGEL, Thomas, BA, BPhil, PhD, FBA; American academic; *Professor of Philosophy and Law, School of Law, New York University;* b. 4 July 1937, Belgrade, Serbia; s. of Walter Nagel and Carolyn Baer Nagel; m. 1st Doris Blum 1968 (divorced 1972); m. 2nd Anne Hollander 1979; ed Cornell and Harvard Univs and Univ. of Oxford, UK; Asst Prof. of Philosophy, Univ. of California, Berkeley 1963–66; Asst Prof. of Philosophy, Princeton Univ. 1966–69, Assoc. Prof. 1969–72, Prof. 1972–80; Prof. of Philosophy, New York Univ. 1980–, Prof. of Philosophy and Law 1986–, Fiorello LaGuardia Prof. of Law 2001–03, Univ. Prof. 2002–; Fellow, American Acad. of Arts and Sciences; Hon. DLitt (Oxford) 2008, Hon. DrIur (Harvard) 2010; Dr hc (Bucharest) 2010; Mellon Distinguished Achievement Award, Andrew Mellon Foundation 2006, Rolf Schock Prize in Logic and Philosophy, Royal Swedish Acad. of Sciences 2008, Balzan Prize in Moral Philosophy 2008. *Publications include:* The Possibility of Altruism 1970, Mortal Questions 1979, The View from Nowhere 1986, What Does It All Mean? 1987, Equality and Partiality 1991, Other Minds 1995, The Last Word 1997, The Myth of Ownership (with Liam Murphy) 2002, Concealment and Exposure & Other Essays 2002, Secular Philosophy and the Religious Temperament: Essays 2002–08, Mind and Cosmos 2012. *Address:* School of Law, New York University, 40 Washington Square South, 418, New York, NY 10012, USA (office). *Telephone:* (212) 998-6225 (office). *Fax:* (212) 995-4179 (office). *E-mail:* thomas.nagel@nyu.edu (office). *Website:* philosophy.fas.nyu.edu (office).

NAGGAR, Zaghloul Raghib an-, PhD; geologist and academic; *Chairman, Committee of Scientific Notions in the Quran;* b. 17 Nov. 1933; ed Cairo Univ., Univ. of Wales, UK; taught at Ain Shams Univ., Cairo, King Saud Univ., Riyadh, Univ. Coll. of Wales, Aberystwyth, Kuwait Univ., Univ. of Qatar, Doha; fmr Prof. of Geology, King Fahd Univ. of Petroleum and Minerals, Dhahran; now at Arab Devt Inst.; Chair., Cttee of Scientific Notions in the Quran (part of Egyptian Supreme Council of Islamic Affairs); mem. Geological Soc., London, Geological Soc. of Egypt, American Soc. of Petroleum Geologists, Tulsa; Fellow, Inst. of Petroleum, London, Islamic Acad. of Sciences, mem. Council 1994; Secondary Educ. Award (Egypt), Best Papers Award (Arab Petroleum Congress) 1970. *Publications:* more than 150 scientific articles, 45 books in Arabic, French and English. *Address:* c/o Islamic Academy of Sciences, PO Box 830036, Amman, Jordan (office). *Telephone:* 5522104 (office). *Fax:* 5511803 (office). *Website:* www.elnaggarzr.com.

NAGUIB, Patriarch Antonios; Egyptian ecclesiastic and academic; *Patriarch Emeritus of Alexandria (Coptic);* b. 7 March 1935, Minya; ed interritual seminary of Maadi, Cairo, Pontifical Urbanian Coll., Rome; ordained to Coptic Catholic priesthood 1960; served as pastor for a year at Fikryak, Minya; returned to Rome and obtained a licentiate in theology 1962 and in scripture 1964; Prof. of Sacred Scripture in Maadi seminary from 1964; worked with group of Protestant and Orthodox specialists preparing Arabic trans. of the Bible; Bishop of Minya, Egypt 1977–2002 (resgnd); Patriarch of Alexandria of the Copts 2006–13, Patriarch Emer. 2013–; named Relator Gen. (Recording Sec.) of Special Ass. of Synod of Bishops for the Middle East, held at the Vatican Oct. 2010; cr. Cardinal 2010; participated in Papal Conclave (one of four cardinal-electors from outside the Latin Church) 2013. *Address:* Patriarcat Copte Catholique, BP 69, 34 Rue Ibn Sandar, Saray El Koubbeh, 11712 Cairo, Egypt (office). *Telephone:* (2) 2571740 (office). *Fax:* (2) 4545766 (office).

NAGY, Peter Alan, BFA; American artist, curator and gallery owner; *Founder and Director, Nature Morte Gallery;* b. 11 Nov. 1959, Bridgeport, Conn.; s. of Paul Louis Nagy and Kathleen Marie Furdon Nagy; Co-founder Nature Morte Gallery, New York 1982–88; moved to Delhi, India 1992, re-opened Nature Morte, Delhi 1997, opened Nature Morte, Berlin 2008. *Address:* Gallery Nature Morte, A1 Neeti Bagh, New Delhi 110 049, India (office). *Telephone:* (11) 41740215 (office). *Fax:* (11) 41764608 (office). *E-mail:* info@naturemorte.com (office). *Website:* www .naturemorte.com (office).

NAHLES, Andrea Maria, MA; German politician; *Federal Minister of Labour and Social Affairs;* b. 20 June 1970, Mendig, Rhineland-Pfalz; m. Marcus Frings; one d.; ed Univ. of Bonn; mem. Bundestag (Parl.) 1998–2002, 2005–; Fed. Minister of Labour and Social Affairs 2013–; mem. SPD, State Chair. Young Socialists, Rhineland-Pfalz 1993, Nat. Chair., Young Socialists 1995–99, mem. SPD Party Exec. 1997–, mem. SPD Präsidium 2003–, Deputy Chair. SPD 2007–09, Sec.-Gen. 2009–13; co-f. Forum Demokratische Linke 21 2000; mem. IG Metall (trade union); mem. Euro Solar (European Asscn for Renewable Energy). *Address:* Federal Ministry of Labour and Social Affairs, Wilhelmstrasse 49, 10117 Berlin, Germany (office). *Telephone:* (30) 185270 (office). *Fax:* (30) 185271830 (office). *E-mail:* info@ bmas.bund.de (office). *Website:* www.bmas.de (office); www.andrea-nahles.de.

NAHM, Werner, PhD, FRS, MRIA; German mathematical physicist and academic; *Director and Senior Professor, School of Theoretical Physics, Dublin Institute for Advanced Studies;* b. 21 March 1949, Münster; ed Johann Wolfgang Goethe Univ., Frankfurt am Main, Ludwig Maximilian Univ., Munich, Univ. of Bonn; Postdoctoral Researcher, Univ. of Bonn 1972–75, Heisenberg Fellow 1982–86, Prof. 1989–2002; Fellow and mem. staff, CERN 1976–82; Assoc. Prof., Univ. of California, Davis, USA 1986–89; Sr Prof., Dublin Inst. for Advanced Studies, Ireland 2002–, Dir School of Theoretical Physics; External Scientific mem. Max Planck Inst. for Math., Bonn; mem. Acad. of Sciences and Literature, Mainz; Gothenburg Lise Meitner Prize, Chalmers Univ. of Tech. 2012, Max Planck Medal, Deutsche Physikalische Gesellschaft 2013. *Publications:* numerous papers in professional journals. *Address:* Room 403, School of Theoretical Physics, Dublin Institute for Advanced Studies, 10 Burlington Road, Dublin 4, Ireland (office). *Telephone:* (1) 6140143 (office). *Fax:* (1) 6680561 (office). *E-mail:* nahm@mpim -bonn.mpg.de (office). *Website:* www.dias.ie (office); www.mpim-bonn.mpg.de (office).

NAHODHA, Shamsi Vuai, BA; Tanzanian politician; b. 20 Nov. 1962; ed Dar es Salaam Univ.; Chief Minister, Supreme Revolutionary Council of Zanzibar 2000–10 (post abolished); Minister of Home Affairs 2010–12; Minister of Defence and Nat. Service 2012–13; Branch Vice-Pres., Commonwealth Parl. Asscn; mem. Chama Cha Mapinduzi (CCM). *Address:* c/o Ministry of Defence and National Service, POB 9544, Dar es Salaam, Tanzania (office).

NAHORNY, Włodzimierz; Polish pianist and composer; b. 5 Nov. 1941, Radzyń Podlaski; m. Anna Woźniakowska; ed Gdansk Acad. of Music; has performed in numerous concerts in Europe 1964–, including Int. Jazz Workshop, Hamburg 1965–69, Jazz Festival, Edin. 2000, Shanghai Music Festival 2001, Algiers 2002, Novosibirsk 2003, Sarajevo 2004, Kowno 2004, Rome 2004, Paris 2004, Expo Nagoya, Japan 2005, Brussels 2007, Stockholm, Moscow, Periu (Russia) Jazz Festival 2008, Petersburg 2009, Brussels 2010, 2011, Düsseldorf Jazz Festival 2010; teaches at Gdansk Acad. of Music 2006–; Commdr's Cross with Star, Order of Rebirth of Poland 2011; First Prize, Jazz nad Odrą, Int. Jazz Festival, Vienna 1967, Musician of the Year, Jazz Forum magazine 1967, First Prize, Polish Song Festival, Opole 1972, 1973, Meritorious Activist of Culture 1974, 1986, Grand Prix Jazz Melomani, Łódź 1997, Fryderyk Polish Music Award 2000, Bronze Medal, Meritorius of Culture Gloria Artist 2005. *Compositions:* soundtracks: Rondo, Pełnia; for theatre: Medea, Księżniczka Turandot; songs: Her Portrait, Chianti, Śpiewnik Nahornego (Nahorny's Songbook) 2003. *Recordings:* Nahorny-Chopin Polish Fantasy, Nahorny-Szymanowski Myths, Nahorny-Karłowicz Concerto Dolce Far Niente, Ballet 'Polish Fantasy', Baltics Opera, Gdansk, Nahorny-Loebl New Christmas Songs 2007, Nahorny-Mtynarski Talk with Me 2008, Tucoim-Kwiaty Polskie (Polish Flowers) 2009, Nahorny Sextet Chopin Genius Loci 2010; for theatre: Lanie Robertson, I Love O'Keeffe, Dir Cristoff Kolberger. *Leisure interests:* books, garden, theatre. *Address:* ul. Nałęczowska 62/14, 02-922 Warsaw, Poland (office). *Telephone:* (22) 642-76-81 (home). *Fax:* (22) 642-76-81 (home). *E-mail:* nahorny@nahorny.pl (home).

NAHYAN, Sheikh Abdullah bin Zayed an-; United Arab Emirates government official and diplomatist; *Minister of Foreign Affairs;* b. 30 April 1972; s. of Zayed bin Sultan an-Nahyan; ed United Arab Emirates Univ.; Under-Sec., Ministry of Information and Culture 1995–97, Minister of Information and Culture 1997–2006, Minister of Foreign Affairs 2006–; mem. Council of Ministers; Chair. Emirates Media Inc. 1999–; Chair. Nat. Media Council 2006–; Deputy Chair. Abu Dhabi Fund for Devt 2005–. *Address:* Ministry of Foreign Affairs, POB 1, Abu Dhabi, United Arab Emirates (office). *Telephone:* (2) 4444488 (office). *Fax:* (2) 4449100 (office). *E-mail:* mofa@mofa.gov.ae (office). *Website:* www.mofa.gov.ae (office).

NAHYAN, Sheikh Hamdan bin Zayed bin Sultan an-, BA; United Arab Emirates politician; *Ruler's Representative in Western Region of Abu Dhabi;* b. 1063, Al Ain; s. of the late Pres. Sheikh Zayed bin Sultan an-Nahyan (founder of UAE) and Sheikha Fatima bint Mubarak Al Ketbi; m. Shamsa bint Hamdan bin

Mohammed an-Nahyan; six s.; ed United Arab Emirates Univ.; Minister of State for Foreign Affairs 1990–2006; Deputy Prime Minister and Minister of Public Works 1997–2009; Ruler's Rep. in Western Region of Abu Dhabi 2009–; Chair. Emirati German Friendship Soc., Red Crescent Authority, Emirates Camel Racing Fed.; Pres. Abu Dhabi Univ. Bd of Trustees; fmr Pres. UAE Football League; Hon. Chair. Al-Jazira Club, Chair. Hon. Panel. *Address:* Office of the President of the United Arab Emirates and Ruler of Abu Dhabi, Manhal Palace, PO Box 280, Abu Dhabi, United Arab Emirates (office). *Telephone:* (2) 6652000 (office). *Fax:* (2) 6651962 (office).

NAHYAN, HH Sheikh Hamed bin Zayed an-; United Arab Emirates royal and government official; *Managing Director, Abu Dhabi Investment Authority;* third s. of Sheikha Mouza, one of several wives of UAE's late founder, Sheikh Zayed bin Sultan an-Nahyan; half brother of HH Sheikh Khalifa bin Zayed an-Nahyan, Pres. of UAE, younger brother of the late Sheikh Ahmed bin Zayed an-Nahyan; currently Chair. Abu Dhabi Crown Prince's Court and Chair. Higher Corpn of Specialized Economy Zones (ZonesCorp); Man. Dir Abu Dhabi Investment Authority 2010–. *Address:* Abu Dhabi Investment Authority, 211 Corniche, PO Box 3600, Abu Dhabi, United Arab Emirates (office). *Telephone:* (2) 415-0000 (office). *Fax:* (2) 415-1000 (office). *E-mail:* info@adia.ae (office). *Website:* www.adia .ae (office).

NAHYAN, HH Sheikh Khalifa bin Zayed an-, (Ruler of Abu Dhabi); United Arab Emirates; *President;* b. 25 Jan. 1948, al-Ain; s. of the late HH Sheikh Zayed bin Sultan an-Nahyan; apptd Rep. of Ruler of Abu Dhabi in Eastern Region of Abu Dhabi and Head of Courts Dept in Al-Ain on his father's accession as Ruler of Abu Dhabi 1966, Crown Prince of Abu Dhabi and Head of Abu Dhabi Defence Force 1969; Prime Minister of Abu Dhabi and Minister of Defence and Finance 1971–74, first Chair. Abu Dhabi Exec. Council 1974; Deputy Prime Minister of UAE 1973; Supreme Commdr UAE Armed Forces 1976; Chair. Supreme Petroleum Council late 1980s–, Abu Dhabi Fund for Devt, Abu Dhabi Investment Authority, Research and Wildlife Devt Agency; Pres. of UAE and Ruler of Emirate of Abu Dhabi 2004–; ranked by Forbes magazine amongst The World's Most Powerful People (56th) 2010, (53rd) 2011, (33rd) 2012, (34th) 2013. *Leisure interests:* falconry, fishing, reading history and poetry. *Address:* Office of the President of the United Arab Emirates and Ruler of Abu Dhabi, Manhal Palace, PO Box 280, Abu Dhabi, United Arab Emirates (office). *Telephone:* (2) 6652000 (office). *Fax:* (2) 6651962 (office).

NAHYAN, HH Sheikh Mansour bin Zayed bin Sultan an-, BA; United Arab Emirates royal, government official and business executive; *Chairman, International Petroleum Investment Company;* b. 20 Nov. 1970, Trucial States, Abu Dhabi; s. of the late HH Sheikh Zayed bin Sultan an-Nahyan and of his wife Sheikha Fatima; half brother of Pres. of UAE and Emir of Abu Dhabi, Khalifa bin Zayed an-Nahyan; m. Sheikha Alia bint Mohammed bin Butti al-Hamed mid-1990s; one s.; m. Sheikha Manal bint Mohammed bin Rashid al-Maktoum 2005; three c.; mem. of ruling family of Abu Dhabi; apptd Chair. Presidential Office for UAE 1997, apptd by his half brother as First Minister of Presidential Affairs following merger of Presidential Office and Presidential Court; apptd Chair. Ministerial Council for Services; Deputy Prime Minister 2009–; apptd Chair. Nat. Centre for Documentation and Research 2000; apptd Deputy Chair. Abu Dhabi Educ. Council 2005; apptd Chair. Emirates Foundation 2005, Abu Dhabi Food Control Authority 2005, Abu Dhabi Fund for Devt 2005, First Gulf Bank –2006, Abu Dhabi Judicial Dept 2006, Khalifa bin Zayed Charity Foundation 2007, Emirates Investment Authority 2007–, Emirates Horse Racing Authority; mem. Supreme Petroleum Council 2005–; Chair. International Petroleum Investment Co. 2005–; mem. Bd of Dirs Abu Dhabi Investment Council 2005–; Owner of Manchester City Football Club 2008–; mem. Bd of Trustees, Zayed Charitable and Humanitarian Foundation. *Achievements:* an accomplished horse rider, has won several Endurance Racing tournaments held in the Middle East. *Address:* International Petroleum Investment Company, PO Box 7528, Sheikh Zayed the 1st Street, Al Muhairy Centre, Office Tower, 10th Floor, Abu Dhabi, United Arab Emirates (office). *Telephone:* (2) 6336555 (office). *Fax:* (2) 6330111 (office). *E-mail:* info@ipic.ae (office). *Website:* www.ipic.ae (office).

NAHYAN, HH Sheikh Mohammed bin Zayed an-, (Crown Prince of Abu Dhabi); United Arab Emirates government official; *Deputy Supreme Commander of the UAE Armed Forces;* b. 1961; s. of Zayed bin Sultan an-Nahyan and Fatima bint Mubarak al-Ketbi; m.; nine c.; ed Royal Mil. Acad. Sandhurst, UK; Deputy Crown Prince of Abu Dhabi 2003–04, Crown Prince of Abu Dhabi 2004–; Chief of Staff of Armed Forces of UAE 1993–2005, Deputy Supreme Commdr UAE Armed Forces 2005–; Chair. Exec. Bd 2004–; mem. Abu Dhabi Exec. Council, Deputy Chair. 2004–; mem. Supreme Petroleum Council; Chair. Abu Dhabi Council for Econ. Devt, Abu Dhabi Educ. Council 2005–; Head of Mubadala Devt Co. 2002–, UAE Offsets Group; Pres. Emirates Centre for Strategic Studies and Research; Special Adviser to his brother Sheikh Khalifa bin Zayed an-Nahyan; numerous decorations. *Address:* Abu Dhabi Council for Economic Development, PO Box 44484, Abu Dhabi, United Arab Emirates (office). *Telephone:* (2) 6913300 (office). *Fax:* (2) 6913400 (office). *E-mail:* info@adced.ae (office). *Website:* www.adced.ae (office).

NAHYAN, HE Sheikh Nahyan bin Mubarak an-; United Arab Emirates university chancellor and politician; *Minister of Culture, Youth and Community Development;* b. 1948; Chancellor, United Arab Emirates Univ. 1976–, Higher Colls of Tech. 1988, Abu Dhabi Petroleum Univ., Zayed Univ.; Minister of Higher Educ. and Scientific Research 1990–2004, of Educ. 2004–13, of Culture, Youth and Community Devt 2013–; Chair. Union Nat. Bank, Abu Dhabi Group (construction co.), Bank Alfalah Ltd; Hilal-i-Pakistan Award, Pres. of Pakistan. *Address:* Ministry of Culture, Youth and Community Development, PO Box 17, Abu Dhabi (office); United Arab Emirates University, PO Box 15551 Al-Ain, United Arab Emirates (office). *Telephone:* (2) 6213800 (office); (3) 7544375 (office). *Fax:* (2) 6313778 (office); (3) 7540555 (office). *E-mail:* moe@uae.gov.ae (office); chancellor@ uaeu.ac.ae (office). *Website:* www.moe.gov.ae (office); www.uaeu.ac.ae (office).

NAHYAN, Sheikh Sultan bin Zayed an-; United Arab Emirates government official and army officer; b. 1955; s. of Zayed bin Sultan an-Nahyan; m. Shamsa bint Mohammed bin Khalifa an-Nahyan; ed in Abu Dhabi, Lebanon, Sandhurst Mil. Acad., UK; Commdr Western Mil. Dist 1976; Gen. Commdr UAE Armed Forces 1978; now Deputy Commdr Abu Dhabi Defence Forces; Deputy Prime

Minister 1990–99; mem. Supreme Petroleum Council, Abu Dhabi Investment Authority. *Address:* PO Box 831, Abu Dhabi, United Arab Emirates. *Telephone:* (2) 651881.

NAIDENOV, Angel Petrov; Bulgarian politician and fmr merchant seaman; *Minister of Defence;* b. 28 Sept. 1958, Kardzhali; m. Nina Naidenova (divorced); ed Nikola Vaptsarov Naval Acad., Varna, G. S. Rakovski Nat. Defence Acad., Sofia; worked for shipping cos Parahodstvo Bulgarski Morski Flot AD, Varna and Navigation Maritime Bulgare (NAVIBULGAR); fmr Ship's Mate and specialist, Darzhavno Stopansko Obedinenie Voden Transport, Varna (state-owned shipping group); fmr specialist, Deputy Dir and Dir, Darzhavno Stopansko Predpriyatie Despred, Haskovo (Despred State Econ. Enterprise); Mayor of Dimitrovgrad 1990–94; Gov. of Haskovo Region 1995–97; mem. Narodno Sobranie (Nat. Ass., parl.) for Constituency No 14 (Pernik) (BSP) 1995–, fmr Deputy Chair. Parl. Cttees on Nat. Security, Foreign Affairs and Defence, Chair. Parl. Cttee on Defence 2005–09, Chair. Parl. Group of Coalition for Bulgaria 2005–09, Deputy Chair. 2009–; Minister of Defence 2013–; mem. Bulgarian Socialist Party (BSP), mem. Exec. Office of BSP Nat. Council, also Party Spokesperson. *Address:* Ministry of Defence, 1092 Sofia, ul. Dyakon Ignatiy 3, Bulgaria (office). *Telephone:* (2) 922-09-22 (office). *Fax:* (2) 987-96-93 (office). *E-mail:* vtcherneva@gmail.com (office). *Website:* www.mod.bg (office).

NAIDOO, Beverley, BA (Hons), PGCE, PhD; South African/British author; b. (Beverley Trewhela), 21 May 1943, Johannesburg, South Africa; d. of Ralph Henry Trewhela and Evelyn Levison; m. Nandhagopaul Naidoo 1969; one s. one d.; ed Univs of Witwatersrand, York and Southampton; NGO worker, SA 1964; detained without trial, SA 1964; teacher, London then Dorset, UK 1969–89; educ. adviser on English and cultural diversity, Dorset 1990–97; writer 1985–; int. writers' workshops, talks and readings 1991–; Hon. Visiting Fellow, School of Educ., Univ. of Southampton 1992–2006; Hon. DLitt (Southampton) 2002, (Exeter) 2007; Hon. DUniv (Open Univ.) 2003; The Other Award (UK) 1985, Child Study Children's Book Cttee Award (USA) 1986, 1998, Vlag en Wimpel Award (Netherlands) 1991, African Studies Asscn Africana Children's Book Award (USA) 1998, 2004, 2010, 2011, Arts Council Writer's Award (UK) 1999, Smarties Silver Medal for Children's Books (UK) 2000, Carnegie Medal for Children's Literature (UK) 2000, Jane Addams Book Award (USA) 2002, 2004, Sankei Children's Book Award (Japan) 2003, Parents' Choice Silver Award (USA) 2011. *Play:* The Playground, Polka Theatre, London 2004. *Radio:* The Other Side of Truth (BBC) 2003. *Publications:* Censoring Reality: An Examination of Non-fiction Books on South Africa 1985, Journey to Jo'burg 1985, Chain of Fire 1989, Through Whose Eyes? Exploring Racism: Reader, Text and Context 1992, Letang and Julie (series – illustrator Petra Rohr-Rouendaal) 1994, No Turning Back 1995, Where Is Zami? (illustrator Petra Rohr-Rouendaal) 1998, The Other Side of Truth 2000, Out of Bounds 2001, Baba's Gift (with Maya Naidoo, illustrator Karin Littlewood) 2003, The Great Tug of War and Other Stories 2003, Web of Lies 2004, Burn My Heart 2007, Call of the Deep 2008, S is for South Africa (with photographer Prodeepta Das) 2011, Aesop's Fables (illustrator Piet Grobler), Death of an Idealist: In Search of Neil Aggett 2012. *Leisure interests:* reading, theatre, walking. *Address:* c/o Hilary Delamere, The Agency, 24 Pottery Lane, London, W11 4LZ, England (office). *Telephone:* (20) 7727-1346 (office). *Fax:* (20) 7727-9037 (office). *E-mail:* info@theagency.co.uk (office). *Website:* www.theagency.co.uk (office); www.beverleynaidoo.com.

NAIDOO, Jayaseelan (Jay); South African trade union official, banker and business executive; *Chairman, Global Alliance for Improved Nutrition;* b. 20 Dec. 1954, Durban; m. Lucie Pagé 1992; two s. one d.; ed Sastri Coll., Durban and Univ. of Durban-Westville; mem. SASO 1977; involved in community orgs, Natal 1976–79; studies interrupted by political events 1978; Organizer Fed. of South African Trade Unions (FOSATU) 1980; Gen. Sec. Sweet Food & Allied Workers Union 1982, Congress of South African Trade Unions (COSATU) 1985–93; Minister, Office of the Pres., Govt of Nat. Unity 1994–96; Minister of Posts and Telecommunications and Broadcasting 1996–99; Chair. Devt Bank of Southern Africa 2000–10, Global Alliance for Improved Nutrition (GAIN) 2003–; mem. Bd Dirs J&J Group 2000–, ITU Telecom 2007–; mem. Health Advisory Comm. Clinton Global Initiative 2007–; Chevalier, Légion d'honneur 2006. *Leisure interests:* jazz, skiing cross-country, family, cuisine. *Address:* c/o Development Bank of Southern Africa, PO Box 1234, Halfway House, Midrand 1685, South Africa (office). *E-mail:* jay@jandjgroup.com (office). *Website:* www.jandjgroup.com (office); www.gainhealth.org (office).

NAIDU, K. Muppavarapu Venkaiah, BA, BL; Indian politician; b. 1 July 1949, Chavatapalem, Nellore Dist, Andhra Pradesh; s. of the late Rangaiah Naidu and Ramanamma Naidu; m. M. Usha; one s. one d.; fmr agriculturalist; political activist, imprisoned during Nat. Emergency 1975–77; Pres. Youth Wing of Janata Party, Andhra Pradesh (AP) 1977–80, State Univ. of Bharatiya Janata Party (BJP—Indian People's Party) 1988–93, Student Union, Andhra Univ. 1973–74; Vice-Pres. Youth Wing of All-India BJP 1980–83, Leader of BJP Legis. Party, AP 1980–85, Gen. Sec. All-India BJP 1993–2002, Pres. BJP 2002–04; mem. Legis. Ass., AP 1978–83, 1983–85; elected to Rakya Sabha 1998; Minister of Rural Devt 2000–02. *Address:* c/o Bharatiya Janata Party (BJP), 11 Ashok Road, New Delhi 110 001, India.

NAIDU, Nara Chandrababu, MA; Indian politician; b. 20 April 1951, Chittoor; s. of N. K. Naidu and Smt. Ammanamma Naidu; m. Nara Bhuvaneswari Naidu; one s.; ed Sri Venkateswara Univ., Tirupathi; MLA Andhra Pradesh Legis. Ass. 1978; fmr Dir A. P. Small Scale Industries Devt Corpn; Minister 1978–83; fmr Chair. State Karshak Parishad; re-elected to Assembly 1989, 1994; Gen. Sec. and Co-ordinator Telugu Desam Party 1989–94; Minister of Finance and Revenue 1994–95; Chief Minister of Andhra Pradesh 1995–2004; Pres. Telugu Desam Party (Telugu Nation); f. Heritage Foods; Co-chairperson Nat. Task Force on Information Tech.; Businessperson of the Year Award, The Economic Times 1998, IT Man of the Year Award, Computer World 1999, named South Asian of the Year, Time Asia magazine 1999. *Address:* Telugudesam State Party Office, N. T. R. Trust, Bhavanam Road, Number 2, Banjara Hills, Hyderabad 500 034, India (office). *Telephone:* (40) 30699999 (office). *Fax:* (40) 23542108 (office).

NAIK, A(nil) M(anibhai); Indian business executive; *Chairman and Managing Director, Larsen & Toubro Limited;* b. Ambabari, now in Daman, Maharashtra; ed Birla Vishwakarma Mahavidhyalaya Eng Coll., Vallabh Vidyanagar, Gujarat; joined Larsen & Toubro Ltd (eng co. and one of India's largest cos) as a jr engineer 1965, Gen. Man. 1985–89, Vice-Pres. (Operations) and mem. Bd of Dirs 1989–95, Pres. (Operations) 1995–99, Man. Dir and CEO 1999–2003, Chair. and Man. Dir 2003–; Chair. and Pres. Kharel Educ. Soc.; led Indian industry's del. to 17th Congress of World Energy Council, Houston, USA 1998; mem. del. led by Prime Minister Atal Behari Vajpayee, along with key Cabinet colleagues; participated in India-EU Summit, Copenhagen Oct. 2002, Sixth India-EU Business Summit, New Delhi Sept. 2005; Sr mem. Confed. of Indian Industry Nat. Council; mem. Bd of Trade, Ministry of Commerce, Govt of India; mem. Bd of Govs Indian Inst. of Man., Ahmedabad; mem. Bd of Trustees Indian Business Trust for HIV/AIDS; Fellow, Indian Nat. Acad. of Engineers; Hon. Consul Gen. for Denmark; Kt, Order of the Dannebrog (Denmark) 2008; JRD Tata Corp. Leadership Award, All India Man. Asscn 2004, Exec. of the Year Award, Indian Asscn of Secs & Admin. Professionals 2004, Lifetime Achievement Excellence Award for Best Corp. Man. of the Decade, Foundation of Indian Industry & Economists 2004, Sankara Ratna Award, Sankara Nethralaya 2005, Man. Man of the Year Award, Bombay Man. Asscn 2005, Outstanding Chief Exec. Award, Indian Inst. of Industrial Eng 2005, IEI Eng Personality Trophy, Inst. of Engineers India 2008, featured among 'India's 50 Most Powerful People' by Business Week 2008, Distinguished Alumnus, Birla Vishwakarma Mahavidyalaya (also known as BVM Eng Coll.), Vallabh Vidyana-gar, Gujarat 2008, V. Krishnamurthy Award for Excellence, Centre for Org. Devt, Hyderabad 2008, Entrepreneur of the Year Award (Professional Category), Ernst & Young 2008, Transformational Leader Award, Indian Merchants' Chamber and Asian Centre for Corp. Governance & Sustainability 2008, Gujarat Garima (Pride of Gujarat) Award, Govt of Gujarat 2009, Business Leader of the Year, The Economic Times 2009, Gujarat Garima Award 2009, Lakshya Business Visionary Award, Nat. Inst. of Industrial Eng, Mumbai 2009, Padma Bhushan 2009. *Achievements include:* instrumental in setting up Larsen & Toubro Public Charitable Trust (conducts skill training at Mumbai, Lonavala, Aurangabad, Latur and Kharel). *Address:* Larsen & Toubro Ltd, L&T House, Ballard Estate, PO Box 278, Mumbai 400 001, India (office). *Telephone:* (22) 67525856 (office). *Fax:* (22) 67525858 (office). *E-mail:* ccd@lth.ltindia.com (office). *Website:* www.larsentoubro.com (office).

NAIK, Air Chief Marshal (retd) Pradeep Vasant; Indian fmr air force officer; b. 22 July 1949, Nagpur; m. Madhubaala Naik; two s.; ed Sainik School Satara, Nat. Defence Acad., Defence Services Staff Coll., Nat. Defence Coll., Coll. of Defence Man.; commissioned into Indian Air Force (IAF) 1969; initial training on HT-2 trainer aircraft, has flown Vampire and Hunter aircraft, extensive operational experience on all variants of MiG-21; Qualified Flying Instructor with considerable instructional experience; also Fighter Combat Leader, Tactics and Air Combat Devt Establishment (TACDE); selected as one of first eight pilots to convert to MiG-23 BN in fmr USSR, responsible for its induction into IAF; commanded front line fighter squadron and fighter base and Air Force Station Bidar; fmr Dir of Staff at TACDE and Defence Services Staff Coll.; has held numerous staff appointments, including Sr Air Staff Officer at HQ Western Air Command, Air Officer Commdg-in-Chief of Cen. Air Command, Vice-Chief of Air Staff –2009, Chief of the Air Staff 2009–11; Hon. ADC to Pres. of India; Param Vishisht Seva Medal, Vishisht Seva Medal. *Leisure interests:* cricket, golf, volleyball, Indian classical music. *Address:* c/o Public Relations Officer, Indian Air Force, Directorate of Public Relations, Ministry of Defence, Room Number 91, South Block, New Delhi, 110 011, India.

NAILATIKAU, Ratu Epeli, OBE; Fijian government official, diplomatist, army officer and head of state; *President;* b. 5 July 1941, Levuka, Ovalau; s. of Ratu Edward Cakobau and Vasemaca Tuiburelevu; m. Adi Koila Mara; one s. one d.; ed Levuka Public School and Queen Victoria School; completed mil. training in New Zealand, seconded to 1st Bn, Royal New Zealand Infantry Regt in Sarawak, Malaysia 1966, Brig.-Gen., Fiji Infantry Regt 1987–88, Commdr of Armed Forces 1982–88; fmr High Commr to UK; Amb. to Denmark, Egypt, Germany, Israel and Holy See, to the Pacific 1998–99; Perm. Sec. for Foreign Affairs and External Trade 1999–2000; Deputy Prime Minister 2000–01; Minister for Fijian Affairs 2000–01; Speaker of House of Reps 2001–06, Chair. Parl. Appropriations and House Cttees 2001–06; Minister of Foreign Affairs and Trade 2007 (in Cdre Josaia Bainimar-ama's interim govt), Minister of Foreign Affairs, International Co-operation and Civil Aviation 2007–08, of Prov. Devt and Multi-Ethnic Affairs 2008–09; Vice-Pres. of Fiji April–July 2009, Acting Pres. July–Nov. 2009, Pres. 2009–; LVO, Meritorious Service Decoration, Venerable Order of the Hosp. of St John of Jerusalem. *Address:* Office of the President, Government House, Berkley Crescent, Government Buildings, POB 2513 Suva, Fiji (office). *Telephone:* 3314244 (office). *Fax:* 3301645 (office).

NA'IM, Abdullahi Ahmed An-, LLB, Dip.Crim., PhD; Sudanese/American academic; *Charles Howard Candler Chaired Professor of Law, Emory University;* b. 19 Nov. 1946, Shendi, Sudan; ed Khartoum, Univs of Cambridge and Edinburgh, UK; Lecturer and Assoc. Prof. of Law, Univ. of Khartoum 1976–85; Rockefeller Fellow, Columbia Univ. Center for Study of Human Rights 1981–82; Visiting Prof., UCLA 1985–87; Fellow, Woodrow Wilson Int. Center for Scholars 1987–88; Ariel F. Sallows Prof. of Human Rights, Univ. of Saskatchewan, Canada 1988–91; Olof Palme Visiting Prof., Uppsala Univ., Sweden 1991–92; Visiting Fellow, Harvard Law School Human Rights Program 1991; Scholar-in-Residence, Ford Foundation Office for Middle East and N Africa, Cairo, Egypt 1992–93; Prof. of Law and Sr Fellow of Law and Religion Program, Emory Univ., Atlanta 1995–, Charles Howard Candler Chaired Prof. of Law 1999–; Visiting Prof., Utrecht Univ. 1999, Harvard Law School 2003; Wiarda Chair, Faculty of Law, Utrecht Univ. 2005–06; Global Legal Scholar, Univ. 0f Warwick School of Law, UK 2007–09; Scholar-in-Residence, Ford Foundation, New York May–Dec. 2007; Extraordinary Prof., Human Rights Centre, Univ. of Pretoria, South Africa 2009; Exec. Dir Human Rights Watch/Africa, Washington, DC 1993–95; Commr Int. Comm. of Jurists; mem. Bd Urban Morgan Inst. for Human Rights, Cairo Inst. for Human Rights Studies, Int. Council on Human Rights Policy, Geneva, Global Rights, Washington, DC 2009–; mem. Editorial Bd Human Rights Quarterly, International Politics; Dr hc (Univ. catholique de Louvain) 2009; Dr J.P. van Praag Award of Dutch Humanist Ethical Soc. 1999, Marion Creekmore Award for Internationalization, Emory Univ. *Publications:* Sudanese Criminal Law: The General Principles of Criminal Responsibility 1985, The Second Message of Islam by Ustadh Mahmoud Mohamed Taha (English trans.) 1987, Toward an Islamic Reformation: Civil Liberties, Human Rights and International Law 1990, Human Rights in Africa: Cross-Cultural Perspectives (co-ed.) 1990, Cry of the Owl by Francis Deng (Arabic trans.) 1991, Human Rights in Cross Cultural Perspectives: Quest for Consensus (ed.) 1992, Human Rights and Religious Values (co-ed.) 1995, Proselytization and Communal Self-Determination in Africa (ed.) 1999, The Politics of Memory: Truth, Healing and Social Justice (ed.) 2002, Cultural Transformation and Human Rights in Africa (ed.) 2002, Human Rights Under African Constitutions (ed.) 2003, African Constitutionalism and the Role of Islam 2006, Islam and the Secular State 2008; numerous writings, including 60 articles and 28 short articles and book reviews. *Address:* School of Law, Emory University, 1301 Clifton Road, Atlanta, GA 30322, USA (office). *Telephone:* (404) 727-1198 (office). *E-mail:* Abduh46@law.emory.edu (office). *Website:* www.law.emory.edu/aannaim (office).

NAIPAUL, Sir V(idiadhar) S(urajprasad), Kt, CLit, BA, FRSL; Trinidadian/British writer; b. 17 Aug. 1932, Chaguanas; m. 1st Patricia Ann Hale 1955 (died 1996); m. 2nd Nadira Khannum Alvi 1996; one d. (adopted); ed Queen's Royal Coll., Port-of-Spain and Univ. Coll. Oxford; for two years freelance broadcaster with BBC, producing programmes for the Caribbean area; fiction reviewer on New Statesman 1958–61; grant from Trinidad Govt to travel in Caribbean and S America 1961; in India 1962–63, 1975, 1988–89, in Uganda 1965–66, in USA 1969, 1978–79, 1987–88, in Argentina 1972, 1973–74, 1977, 1991, in Venezuela 1977, 1985, in Iran, Pakistan, Malaysia and Indonesia 1979–80, 1995; mem. Soc. of Authors; Hon. DLitt (Univ. of the West Indies, St Augustine) 1975, (St Andrews) 1979, (Columbia) 1981, (Cambridge) 1983, (London) 1988, (Oxford) 1992; John Llewellyn Rhys Memorial Prize 1958, Somerset Maugham Award 1961, Phoenix Trust Award 1962, Hawthornden Prize 1964, W. H. Smith Award 1968, Booker Prize 1971, Jerusalem Prize 1983, Ingersoll Prize 1986, David Cohen British Literature Prize 1993, Nobel Prize for Literature 2001. *Publications:* The Mystic Masseur 1957, The Suffrage of Elvira 1958, Miguel Street 1959, A House for Mr Biswas 1961, The Middle Passage 1962, Mr Stone and the Knights Companion 1963, An Area of Darkness 1964, The Mimic Men 1967, A Flag on the Island 1967 (collection of short stories), The Loss of El Dorado 1969, In a Free State 1971, The Overcrowded Barracoon (essays) 1972, Guerrillas 1975, India: A Wounded Civilization 1977, A Bend in the River 1979, A Congo Diary 1980, The Return of Eva Perón 1980, Among the Believers 1981, Finding the Centre 1984, The Enigma of Arrival 1987, A Turn in the South 1989, India: A Million Mutinies Now 1990, A Way in the World 1994, Beyond Belief 1998, Letters between a Father and Son 1999, Reading and Writing: A Personal Account 2000, Half a Life 2001, Literary Occasions 2004, Magic Seeds 2004, A Writer's People 2007, The Masque of Africa: Glimpses of African Belief 2010. *Address:* c/o The Wylie Agency, 17 Bedford Square, London, WC1B 3JA, England (office). *Telephone:* (20) 7908-5900 (office). *Fax:* (20) 7908-5901 (office). *E-mail:* mail@wylieagency.co.uk (office). *Website:* www.wylieagency.com (office).

NAIR, Dileep, BMechEng, MPA; Singaporean banker, diplomatist and fmr UN official; *Ambassador to Laos;* ed McGill Univ., Montreal, Canada, Kennedy School of Govt, Harvard Univ., USA; with Housing and Devt Bd 1974–79; joined Admin. Service 1979, various posts including Dir in charge of expenditure control, Deputy Sec. Ministry of Trade and Industry 1986–89, Ministry of Defence 1989–97; CEO Post Office Savings Bank of Singapore 1997–98, Man. Dir Devt Bank of Singapore 1998–2000; Under-Sec.-Gen. for Internal Oversight Services, UN 2000–05; Consul-Gen. in Dubai 2005–11; Amb. to Laos 2011–; fmr Vice-Pres. Singapore Indian Devt Asscn; mem. Hindu Advisory Bd; mem. Bd of Govs Raffles Inst.; Colombo Plan Scholar 1969–73. *Address:* Embassy of Singapore, Unit 4, rue Thadeua, Ban Wat Nak, Km 3, Sisattanak, Vientiane, Laos (office). *Telephone:* (21) 353939 (office). *Fax:* (21) 353938 (office). *E-mail:* singemb_vte@sgmfa.gov.sg (office). *Website:* www.mfa.gov.sg/vientiane (office).

NAIR, G. Madhavan, BSc; Indian engineer; *President, International Academy of Astronautics;* b. 31 Oct. 1943, Thiruvanathapuram; ed Coll. of Eng, Univ. of Kerala; Head of Payload Integration Section, Thumba Equatorial Rocket Launching Station, Trivandrum 1967–72; Project Man. Telecommand System, Vikram Sarabhai Space Centre (VSSC), Trivandrum 1972–74, Head, Electronics Systems 1980–84, Project Engineer, SLV-3 Project 1974–80, Assoc. Project Dir Polar Satellite Launch Vehicle 1984–88, Project Dir 1988–95, Programme Dir ILVP, VSSC, Trivandrum 1994–96, Dir Liquid Propulsion Systems Centre, Trivandrum 1995–99, Dir VSSC 1999–2003; Chair. Indian Space Research Org. 2003–09; Sec. to Dept of Space, Govt of India 2003–09; Chair. Space Comm. 2003–09, Chair. Governing Body, Nat. Remote Sensing Agency, Hyderabad 2003–08; Chair. Antrix Corpn, Bangalore 2003–09; Pres. Astronautical Soc. of India 2004, Aeronautical Soc. of India 2005; Vice-Pres., Scientific Activities Cttee, Int. Acad. of Astronautics 2006–07, Pres. 2009–; Gen. Pres. 97th Indian Science Congress 2009–10; Fellow, Indian Nat. Acad. of Eng 2009–10, Astronautical Soc. of India, Nat. Acad. of Sciences; mem. System Soc. of India, Working Cttee of Current Science Asscn 2004–06, Int. Acad. of Astronautics 2004; Sr Assoc. Nat. Inst. of Advanced Studies 2004–07; Pres. Intersputnik Bd 2005; Chair. Research Council of Nat. Aerospace Laboratories 2007–10; currently Chair. Bd of Govs Indian Inst. of Tech., Patna; Hon. Fellow, Aeronautical Soc. of India 2007, Indian Soc. for Non-Destruction Testing; Hon. DPhil (Punjab Technical Univ.) 2003; Dr hc (Indian Inst. of Tech., Delhi) 2004, (Univ. of Mysore, G.J. Univ., Hissar) 2006; Hon. DSc (Sri Venkateswara Univ., Indian Inst. of Tech., Delhi) 2004, (Rani Durgavati Vishwavidyalaya, Indira Gandhi Nat. Open Univ., Delhi, Rani Durgavati Vishwavidyalaya, Jabalpur) 2005, (Cochin Univ. of Science and Tech., Kochi) 2006, (Univ. of Kerala, Rajiv Gandhi Technical Univ., Bhopal) 2007, (SRM Univ., Chennai) 2008, (Pandit Ravishankar Shukla Univ., Raipur, Karnatak Univ., Dharwad, Indian Inst. of Tech., Bombay, Indian Inst. of Tech., Kharagpur) 2009; Nat. Aeronautical Award 1994, FIE Foundation Award 1994, Shri Om Prakash Bhasin Award 1995, Swadeshi Sastra Puraskar Award 1995, Padma Bhushan 1998, Vikram Sarabhai Memorial Gold Medal 2003, Personality of the Decade Award 2004, Melpadom Attumail Georgekutty Award 2004, Raja Sir Muthiah Chettiar Endowment Award 2004, 10th Science and Tech. Award 2003–04, Sathyabama Deemed Univ. 2005, Benedict Mar Gregorios Award, Asscn of Mar Ivanios Coll. Old Students 2005, Dr. Yelavarthy Nayudamma Memorial Award 2004 2005, H.K. Firodia Award 2005, Shri Balvantbhai Parekh Award, Indian Planetary Soc. 2006, Best R&D Man of the Year, Corporate Excellence Award 2005

2006, Lokmanya Tilak Award 2006, Sree Chithira Thirunal Award, Sasthra Ratna Purskara 2006, Gold Medal from the Prime Minister 2007, 9th Sri Chandrasekarendra Saraswathi Nat. Eminence Award 2006, Dr A.S.G. Jayakar Award, Science India Forum, Muscat and Indian Inst. of Scientific Heritage, Oman Chapter 2007, Shankar Ratna Award 2007, Bharat Shiromani Award 2006, 2007, M. M. Chugani Award 2006, 2008, Raja Rammohan Puraskar Award 2008, NDTV Indian of the Year Award 2009, Kururamma Award 2009, Yashwantrao Chavan Nat. Award 2008, 2009, Chanakya Award 2009, A.V. Rama Rao Tech. Award 2009, M.P. Birla Memorial Award 2009, Padma Vibhushan 2009. *Address:* International Academy of Astronautics, 6 rue Galilee, 75116 Paris, France (office). *Telephone:* 1-47-23-82-15 (office). *Fax:* 1-47-23-82-16 (office). *Website:* iaaweb.org (office).

NAIR, Mira; Indian film director and producer; b. 15 Oct. 1957, Bhubaneswar, Orissa; m. 1st Mitch Epstein; m. 2nd Mahmood Mamdan; one s.; ed Irish Catholic boarding school, Simla, Univ. of Delhi and Harvard Univ., USA; performed with experimental theatre co., Calcutta (now Kolkata); began career as documentary and feature film maker at Harvard Univ.; currently Asst Prof., School of the Arts, Columbia Univ., New York; Govt of India Padma Bhushan 2012; New Generation Award, Los Angeles Film Critics' Asscn 1988, Asian Media Award 1992, India Abroad Person of the Year 2007, Faith Hubley Web of Life Award, Rochester-High Falls Int. Film Festival 2004. *Films:* Jama Masjid Street Journal 1979, So Far from India 1983, India Cabaret (American Film Festival Award for Best Documentary of 1985) 1985, Children of Desired Sex (documentary), Salaam Bombay! (Cannes Film Festival Camera d'Or Award for Best First Feature by a New Dir, Prix du Publique, Lilian Gish Award, Los Angeles Women in Film Festival 1988, three awards at Montreal World Film Festival 1988, Nat. Film Award 1989) 1988, Mississippi Masala (three awards at Venice Film Festival, Critics Special Award, São Paulo Int. Film Festival 1991, Golden Osella Award 1991) 1991, Buddha, The Day the Mercedes Became a Hat 1993, The Perez Family 1996, Kama Sutra 1996, My Own Country 1998, The Laughing Club of India 1999, Monsoon Wedding (Golden Lion Award, Venice Film Festival, Audience Award, Canberra Short Film Festival 2001, Zee Cine Award 2002) 2001, Hysterical Blindness 2002, 11'09"01–September 11 2002 (UNESCO Award 2002), Vanity Fair 2005, The Namesake (Golden Aphrodite Award 2006) 2006, Migration 2007, 8 2008, New York I Love You 2009, Amelia 2009, The Reluctant Fundamentalist 2012. *Address:* Film Department, School of the Arts, Columbia University, 513 Dodge Hall, 2960 Broadway, New York, NY 10027, USA (office). *Telephone:* (212) 854-2815 (office). *E-mail:* film@columbia.edu (office). *Website:* wwwapp.cc.columbia.edu/art/app/arts/index.jsp (office).

NAJDER, Zdzisław Marian, PhD; Polish civic leader and author; b. 31 Oct. 1930, Warsaw; s. of Franciszek Najder and Józefa Najder (née Kowalska); m. Halina Paschalska 1965; one s.; ed Warsaw Univ., Univ. of Oxford, UK; Asst Inst. for Literary Research of Polish Acad. of Sciences 1952–57; Sr Asst Aesthetics, Warsaw Univ. 1958–59; on staff, Twórczość (monthly) 1957–81; taught Polish literature at Columbia and Yale Univs, USA 1966 and Univ. of California, Berkeley, USA 1966–67; Prof. of Philosophy, Univ. of California, Davis 1967–68, Regents' Prof. 1968–69; Prof. of English Literature, Northern Illinois Univ., USA 1971–72; Visiting Scholar, Stanford Univ., Calif. 1974–75; adviser to Solidarity Trade Union 1980–90; Visiting Fellow, St Antony's Coll., Oxford, UK 1981, 1988; Head, Polish section of Radio Free Europe, Munich 1982–87; charged with spying, sentenced to death in absentia by Warsaw Mil. Tribunal 1983, stripped of Polish citizenship 1985, sentence revoked 1989, case dismissed 1990; mem. editorial staff, Kontakt, Paris 1988–91; Chair. Nat. Civic Cttee 1990–92; Chief Adviser to the Prime Minister 1992; Pres. Civic Inst. 1991–97, Atlantic Club 1991–93; Chair. Joseph Conrad Soc. (Poland) 1994–; Prof. of English Literature, Univ. of Opole 1997–2003; Adviser to Chair. Cttee for European Integration 1998–2001; Prof., European Acad., Kraków 2005–; mem. Polish Writers' Union 1956–83, PEN Club 1957–, Nat. Council for European Integration 1999–2003; f. Polish Agreement for Independence 1976; Founder and Pres. Club of Weimar 2005–; Commdr's Cross, Order of Polonia Restituta 1983, Commdr, Ordre nat. du Mérite 1991, Chevalier, légion d'honneur 2004; Juliusz Mieroszewski Award 1982, Prize of Modern Language Asscn 1984, Polish PEN Club Prize 1988. *Publications:* studies and essays including Conrad's Polish Background 1964, Nad Conradem 1965, Values and Evaluations 1975, Życie Conrada-Korzeniowskiego 1981, Ile jest dróg? 1982, Wymiary polskich spraw 1990, Jaka Polska 1993, Z Polski do Polski poprzez PRL 1995, Conrad in Perspective: Essays on Art and Fidelity 1997, W sercu Europy 1998, Sztuka i wierność 2000. *Leisure interests:* travel, walks in forest, 12th-century Romanesque art. *Telephone:* (22) 8448536 (home). *Fax:* (22) 8448536 (home). *E-mail:* zdzislaw.najder@list.pl (home).

NAJEEB, Fazeel, BA (Econs), MA; Maldivian economist, lawyer and central banker; b. Fuahmulah; ed Univs of Sunderland, Hull and London, UK; Investment Promotion Officer, then Ass. Dir Investment, then Deputy Dir Investment, then Deputy Dir Int. Co-operation, then Dir Int. Co-operation, Ministry of Trade –2008; pursued PhD studies in intellectual property law in UK 2008; Gov. and Chair. Maldives Monetary Authority 2008–13. *Address:* c/o Maldives Monetary Authority, Boduthakurufaanu Magu, Malé 20182, Maldives.

NAJJAR, Iyyad Ibrahim; Syrian film producer and trade union official; b. 1972; Founder Clacket Productions, Damascus (TV and film production co.); also First Deputy Chief, Arab Union for Goods Freight and Logistics (trade union), Syrian Regional Office. *Address:* Clacket Productions, POB 5894, Mezze Highway, Farabi Street, Building 4, Damascus, Syria (office). *Telephone:* (11) 6124446 (office). *E-mail:* info@clacketproductions.com (office). *Website:* www.clacketproductions.com (office).

NAJJAR, Mohammad Mostafa, MEng; Iranian politician; b. 1956, Tehran; ed Khajeh Nasir Toosi Univ., Industrial Man. Univ.; joined Revolutionary Cttees (Revolutionary Police) 1979 and Islamic Revolutionary Guard Corps 1979; Deputy Man. Dir Sasad (defence industry eng.) 1976–2007; Minister of Defence 2005–09, Minister of the Interior 2009–13. *Address:* c/o Ministry of the Interior, Jahad Sq., Fatemi St, Tehran, Iran (office).

NAJMIDDINOV, Safarali Mahsudinovich; Tajikistani politician; ed Tajik State Univ.; fmr Chief Accountant and Head of Dept of Finance, State Cttee of Statistics; Head of Trade Dept, Municipality of Dushanbe 1982–92; Deputy

Minister of Trade 1991–2000; Minister of Finance 2000–13. *Address:* c/o Ministry of Finance, 734067 Dushanbe, Nazarov 64/14, Tajikistan.

NAKADAI, Tatsuya; Japanese actor; b. 13 Dec. 1932, Tokyo; m. Tomoye Ryu 1957 (died 1996); ed Haiyuza Actors' Training School; worked with Masaki Kobayashi and Akira Kurosawa; stage work comprises both shingeki (modern theatre) featuring a highly acclaimed Hamlet and roles in other Shakespeare, Gorky, Ibsen and Chekhov adaptations, and avant-garde, including work with Kobo Abe's theatre group. *Films:* Kabe atsuki heya (The Thick-Walled Room) 1953, Shichinin no samurai (The Seven Samurai) 1954, Hi no tori 1956, Fukuaki no seishun 1956, Sazae-san 1956, Oshidori no mon (Lovebirds' Gate) 1956, Ôban 1957, Arakure (Untamed) 1957, Hikage no musume 1957, Zoku Ôban: Fû unhen 1957, Kiken na eiyu (A Dangerous Hero) 1957, Zokuzoku Ôban: Dôto uhen 1957, Sazae-san no seishun (Sazae's Youth) 1957, Kuroi kawa (Black River) 1957, Haha sannin (A Boy and Three Mothers, USA) 1958, Kekkon no subete (All About Marriage) 1958, Buttuke honban (Go and Get It) 1958, Enjo (Conflagration) 1958, Hadaka no taiyo (Naked Sun) 1958, Yajû shisubeshi 1959, Kagi (The Key) 1959, Ginza no onéchan (Three Dolls in Ginza, USA) 1959, Anyakôro 1959, Ningen no joken I (No Greater Love) 1959, Ningen no joken II (The Road to Eternity) 1959, Musume tsuma haha (Daughters, Wives and a Mother) 1960, Aoi yaju (The Blue Beast, USA 1965) 1960, 'Minagoroshi no uta' yori kenjû-yo saraba! (Get 'em All, USA 1961) 1960, Qnna ga kaidan o agaru toki (When a Woman Ascends the Stairs) 1960, Qginsama (Love Under the Crucifix, USA 1965) 1960, Yojimbo (The Bodyguard) 1961, Tsuma to shita onna to shite (As a Wife, As a Woman) 1961, Ningen no joken III (A Soldier's Prayer) 1961, Eien no hito (Immortal Love) 1961, Tsubaki Sanjûrô 1962, Karami-ai (The Inheritance, USA 1964) 1962, Yushu heiya (Madame Aki) 1963, Tengoku to jigoku (Heaven and Hell) 1963, Shiro to kuro (Pressure of Guilt) 1963, Gojuman-nin no isan (Legacy of the 500,000) 1963, Miren 1963, Onna no rekishi (A Woman's Life) 1963, Seppuku (Harakiri, USA) 1964, Jigoku sakusen 1964, Kaidan (Ghost Story) 1964, Chi to suna (Fort Graveyard) 1965, Saigô no shinpan 1965, Dai-bosatsu tôge (The Sword of Doom, USA) 1966, Tanin no kao (The Face of Another) 1966), Jinchoge (Daphne) 1966, Yotsuya kaidan 1966 (Illusion of Blood) 1966, Gohiki no shinshi (Cash Calls Hell) 1966, Satsujin kyo jidai (The Age of Assassins) 1967, Kojiro 1967, Jôi-uchi: Hairyô tsuma shimatsu (Samurai Rebellion) 1967, Tabiji 1967, Oggi a me. . . domani a te! (Today We Kill, Tomorrow We Die!) 1968, Kiru (Kill!, USA) 1969, Rengo kantai shirei chôkan: Yamamoto Isoroku (Admiral Yamamoto) (narrator) 1968, Nikudan (The Human Bullet) 1968, Goyokin (Official Gold) 1969, Eiko e no 5,000 kiro (5,000 Kilometres to Glory) 1969, Nihonkai daikasen (Battle of the Japan Sea) 1969, Hitokiri (Tenchu!, USA 1970) 1969, Tengu-to (Blood End) 1969, Jigokuhen (Portrait of Hell) 1969, Ezo yakata no ketto (Duel at Ezo) 1970, Bakumatsu (The Ambitious) 1970, Buraikan (Outlaws) 1970, Zatôichi abare-himatsuri (Blind Swordsman's Fire Festival) 1970, Tenkan no abarembo (Will to Conquer, USA 1971) 1970, Inochi bonifuro (At the Risk of My Life) 1971, Gekido no showashi: Okinawa kessen (The Battle of Okinawa) 1971, Shussho Iwai (Prison Release Celebration) 1972, Ôshô 1973, Kanashimi no Belladonna (Belladonna) (voice) 1973, Ningen kakumei (The Human Revolution, USA) 1973, Asayake no uta (Rise, Fair Sun, USA 1975) 1973, Karei-naru ichizoku 1974, Seishun no mon (The Gate of Youth, USA 1976) 1975, Tokkan (Battle Cry) 1975, Wagahai wa neko de aru (I Am a Cat) 1975, Kinkanshoku 1975, Banka 1976, Fumô chitai 1976, Sugata Sanshiro 1977, Jo-oh-bachi (Queen Bee) 1978, Kumokiri nizaemon (Bandit vs. Samurai Squad) 1978, Hi no tori (The Firebird) 1978, Buru kurisumasu (Blue Christmas) 1978, Yami no karyudo (Hunter in Darkness) 1979, Kagemusha (Kagemusha the Shadow Warrior), 203 kochi (The Battle of Port Arthur) 1980, Nihon no atsui hibi bôsatsu: Shimoyama shigen (Willful Murder) 1981, Kirûin Hanako no shôgai (Onimasa) 1982, Uchû senkan Yamato: Kanketsuhen (Final Yamato) (narrator) 1983, Ran (Chaos) 1985, Shokutaku no nai ie (The Empty Table) 1985, Atami satsujin jiken 1986, Hachiko monogatari 1987, Yushun (Oracion, USA) 1988, Return From the River Kwai 1988, Ni-ni-roku (Four Days of Snow and Blood, USA 1989, Kagerô 1991, Goh-hime (Basara – The Princess Goh) 1992, Toki rakujitsu (The Distant Setting Sun) 1992, Yao shou du shi (The Wicked City) 1992, Kozure Ôkami: Sono chîsaki te ni 1993, Gekko no natsu (Summer of the Moonlight Sonata 1993, East Meets West 1995, Miyazawa Kenji son ai 1996, "Hideyoshi" (TV series) 1996, Ame agaru (After the Rain) 1999, Kin'yû fushoku rettô: Jubaku (Jubaku: Spellbound) 1999, Sukedachiya sukeroku (Vengeance for Sale) 2001, Shiroi inu to Waltz wo (To Dance with the White Dog) 2002, Hi wa mata noboru 2002, Ashura no gotoku (Like Asura) 2003.

NAKAE, Toshitada; Japanese journalist; b. 4 Oct. 1929, Chiba City; m. Yohko Nakae 1959; three s.; ed Tokyo Univ.; local reporter, Asahi Shimbun 1953–58, econ. reporter 1958–72, Econ. Ed. 1972–76, Asst Man. Ed. 1976–78, Man. Ed. 1978–83, Dir 1982–97, Pres. 1989–96, Special Adviser 1996–; Pres. Japan Newspaper Publrs and Eds Asscn 1991–95; Commdr des Arts et des Lettres 1994; Newspaper Culture Award 2007. *Publications:* (in English trans.) Cities 1966, The Pulitzer Prize Story 1970, The News Media 1971, The Economy of Cities 1971. *Leisure interests:* driving, listening to music, karaoke. *Address:* 1-11-1-401 Hamadayama, Suginami-ku, Tokyo, Japan. *Telephone:* (3) 3302-7087. *Fax:* (3) 3302-7087.

NAKAE, Yosuke; Japanese diplomatist; *Honorary President, Institute for Japan–China Relations;* b. 30 Dec. 1922, Osaka; s. of Yasuzo Nakae and Itsu Kawase; m. Yasuko Takakura 1959; one s. one d.; ed Kyoto Univ.; Dir-Gen. Asian Affairs Bureau, Ministry of Foreign Affairs 1975; Amb. to Yugoslavia 1978–82, to Egypt 1982–84, to People's Repub. of China 1984–87; Commr, Japan Atomic Energy Comm. 1987–91; Pres.'s Adviser, Mitsubishi Heavy Industries Co. Ltd 1991–99; Pres., Inst. for Japan–China Relations 1992–2004, Hon. Pres. 2004–; Grand Cordon of the Order of the Sacred Treasure 1995. *Ballet scenarios performed include:* Creature 1975, Mobile et Immobile 1983, Friendship Across the Strait 1987, Magpies' Bridge 1998. *Publications:* ballet scenarios: Creature 1975, Mobile et Immobile – Mirage à l'Abu-Simbel 1983, Friendship Across the Strait 1987, Magpies' Bridge 1998; books: Future of China 1991, An Unbefitting Ambassador Talks 1993, Memoirs of Sino-Japanese Diplomacy 2008, Diplomacy for Asia, Mobile et immobile 2010. *Leisure interest:* writing scenarios for ballet. *Address:* 3-21-5, Eifuku, Suginami, Tokyo 168-0064, Japan. *Telephone:* (3) 3325-7359. *Fax:* (3) 3325-7359.

NAKAGAWA, Junko; Japanese business executive; *Executive Managing Director and Chief Financial Officer, Nomura Holdings, Inc.;* ed Kobe Univ.; joined Nomura Securities Co. 1988, held various sr positions in underwriting and finance divs, led several key projects, including Nomura's listing on New York Stock Exchange 2001, left co. to accompany her husband overseas 2004, returned as Pres. Nomura Healthcare Support and Advisory 2008–10, Co-Deputy Chief Financial Officer (CFO), Nomura Holdings, Inc. 2010–11, Exec. Man. Dir and CFO (first woman) 2011–; ranked by Fortune magazine amongst the 50 Most Powerful Women in Business outside the US (34th) 2011. *Address:* Nomura Holdings, Inc., 9-1 Nihonbashi 1-chome, Tokyo 103-8645, Japan (office). *Telephone:* (3) 5255-1000 (office). *Fax:* (3) 3274-4496 (office). *E-mail:* info@nomura.com (office). *Website:* www.nomura.com (office).

NAKAGOME, Kenji; Japanese insurance industry executive; *President and Representative Director, T&D Holdings, Inc.;* b. 1954; joined Taiyo Life 1976, Gen. Man. Gen. Affairs Dept March–July 2001, Dir of Taiyo Life 2001–, Man. Dir Taiyo Life 2003–04, Man. Dir T&D Holdings 2004–06, Dir and Man. Exec. Officer Taiyo Life and T&D Holdings, Inc. 2006–07, Dir and Sr Exec. Officer Taiyo Life and T&D Holdings, Inc. 2007–08, Rep. Dir and Sr Exec. Officer Taiyo Life 2008–09, Dir of T&D Holdings, Inc., Pres. and Rep. Dir Taiyo Life 2009–11, Pres. and Rep. Dir T&D Holdings, Inc. 2011–. *Address:* T&D Holdings Inc., 2-7-9 Nihonbashi, Chuo-Ku, Tokyo 103-0027, Japan (office). *Telephone:* (3) 3231-8685 (office). *Fax:* (3) 3231-8893 (office). *E-mail:* info@td-holdings.co.jp (office). *Website:* www.td-holdings.co.jp (office).

NAKAI, Hiroshi; Japanese politician; b. 10 June 1942, Jilin, China; ed Keio Univ.; mem. House of Reps for Tokai constituency 1976–, mem. Parl. Judicial Cttee; fmr mem. Democratic Socialist Party, fmr mem. Shinshinto (New Frontier Party), fmr mem. Liberal Party, mem. Democratic Party of Japan (DPJ) 2003–, fmr Vice-Pres., Chair. DPJ Standing Officers Council, fmr Dir DPJ Abduction Issue Strategy HQ; Minister of Justice 1994; Chair. Nat. Public Safety Comm. (State Minister) and Minister of State for the Abduction Issue 2009–10. *Address:* c/o National Public Safety Commission, 2-1-2, Kasumigaseki, Chiyoda-ku, Tokyo 100-8974, Japan (office). *Website:* www.nakai-hiroshi.net (office).

NAKAJIMA, Shigehiro; Japanese business executive; *Representative Director, President and Chief Operating Officer, Fujifilm Holdings Corporation;* fmr Sr Vice-Pres. and Corp. Vice-Pres., Fujifilm Corpn, Dir, Fujifilm Holdings Corpn 2010–, Exec. Vice-Pres. 2011–, Pres. and COO 2012–, Dir, Pres. and COO Fujifilm USA, Inc., Dir, Fuji Xerox Co. Ltd. *Address:* Fujifilm Holdings Corpn, 26–30 Nishiazabu 2-chome, Minato-ku, Tokyo 106-8620, Japan (office). *Telephone:* (3) 3406-2111 (office). *Fax:* (3) 3406-2173 (office). *E-mail:* info@fujifilm.com (office). *Website:* www.fujifilm.com (office).

NAKAMURA, Kenzo, PhD; Japanese physicist and academic; *Head, Physics Division 3, Institute of Particle and Nuclear Studies, High Energy Accelerator Research Organization (KEK);* ed Univ. of Tokyo; Research Assoc., Physics Dept, Univ. of Tokyo 1973–84, Inst. for Cosmic Ray Research 1988–95; Assoc. Prof., Nat. Lab. for High Energy Physics (KEK) 1984–88, Head, Experimental Planning and Program Coordination Div. 1995, currently Head, Physics Div. 3, Inst. of Particle and Nuclear Studies, High Energy Accelerator Research Org. (KEK); mem. Kamiokande Collaboration and Super-Kamiokande Collaboration 1987–; Asahi Prize (Super-Kamiokande Group) for discovery of neutrino mass 1998. *Publications:* numerous articles in scientific journals. *Address:* KEK-IPNS, Room No. 4-307 (Building No. 4), 1-1 Oho, Tsukuba, Ibaraki 305-0801, Japan (office). *Telephone:* (29) 864-5435 (office). *Fax:* (29) 864-2580 (office). *E-mail:* kenzo.nakamura@kek.jp (office). *Website:* legacy.kek.jp (office).

NAKAMURA, Kuniharu; Japanese business executive; *Representative Director, President and CEO, Sumitomo Corporation;* joined Sumitomo Corpn 1974, Gen. Man. Motor Vehicles Dept No. 1, Motor Vehicles Dept No. 3, Motor Vehicles Business Planning and Co-ordination Dept, Planning and Admin Dept, Transportation and Construction Systems Business Unit, Exec. Officer and Gen. Man. Corp. Planning and Co-ordination Dept 2005–07, Man. Exec. Officer and Gen. Man. 2007–08, Man. Exec. Officer and Gen. Man. Corp. Planning and Co-ordination 2008–09, Sr Man. Exec. Officer and Gen. Man. Mineral Resources, Energy, Chemical and Electronics Business Unit April–June 2009, Rep. Dir, Sr Man. Exec. Officer and Gen. Man. 2009–12, Rep. Dir, Exec. Vice-Pres. and Gen. Man. April–June 2012, Rep. Dir, Pres. and CEO Sumitomo Corpn June 2012–. *Address:* Sumitomo Corporation, 8-11 Harumi 1-chome, Chuo-ku, Tokyo 104-8610, Japan (office). *Telephone:* (3) 5166-5000 (office). *Fax:* (3) 5166-6292 (office). *E-mail:* info@sumitomocorp.co.jp (office). *Website:* www.sumitomocorp.co.jp (office).

NAKAMURA, Kunio; Japanese electronics industry executive; b. 5 July 1939, Shiga; ed Osaka Univ.; joined Matsushita Electric Industrial Co. Ltd 1962, Dir Tokyo Special Sales Office, Corp. Consumer Sales Div. 1985–89, Dir Corp. Man. Div. for the Americas and Chair. Matsushita Electric Corpn of America 1993–97, Man. Dir 1996–97, Sr Man. Dir 1997–2000, Pres. Matsushita Electric Industrial Co. Ltd 2000–06, Chair. 2006–12 (renamed Panasonic Corpn Oct. 2008), Pres. Panasonic Co. 1989–92, Pres. Panasonic UK Ltd 1992–93; Pres. AVC Co. 1997–2000. *Address:* Panasonic Corpn, Corporate Headquarters, 1006 Oaza Kadoma, Kadoma City, Osaka 571-8501, Japan (office). *Telephone:* (6) 6908-1121 (office). *Fax:* (6) 6908-2351 (office). *E-mail:* info@panasonic.net (office). *Website:* panasonic.net (office).

NAKAMURA, Kuniwo; Palauan former head of state; *Leader, Ta Belau Party; Vice-Pres. of Palau 1989–92; Pres. of Palau 1993–2001; Leader Ta Belau Party. Address:* Ta Belau, c/o Olbiil era Kelulau, Koror, PW 96940, Palau (office).

NAKAMURA, Mitsuyoshi; Japanese business executive; *President and Representative Director, Kajima Corporation;* has spent most of career as marketer involved in business devt with Kajima Corpn, Sr Man. Dir –2005, Pres. and Rep. Dir 2005–. *Address:* Kajima Corpn, 3-1 Motoakasaka 1-chome, Minatu-ku, Tokyo 107-8388, Japan (office). *Telephone:* (3) 3403-3311 (office). *Fax:* (3) 3470-1444 (office). *E-mail:* info@kajima.co.jp (office). *Website:* www.kajima.co.jp (office).

NAKAMURA, Mutsuo, LLB, LLM, LLD; Japanese university administrator and academic; *President, Hokkaido University;* b. 7 Feb. 1939; ed Hokkaido Univ.; Instructor of Law, Hokkaido Univ. 1963–70, Assoc. Prof. 1970–74, Prof. 1974–2001, mem. Senate 1984–88, Dean Faculty of Law 1988–90, Vice-Pres.

Hokkaido Univ. 1997–99, Pres. 2001–. *Address:* Office of the President, Hokkaido University, Kita 8, Nishi 5, Kita-ku, Sapporo 060-0808, Japan (office). *Telephone:* (11) 706-2111 (2000) (office). *Fax:* (11) 706-4885 (office). *E-mail:* nakamura@general.hokudai.ac.jp (office). *Website:* www.hokudai.ac.jp (office).

NAKAMURA, Shozaburo; Japanese politician; fmr businessman; mem. LDP; mem. for Minami Kanto bloc, House of Reps; fmr Dir-Gen. Environment Agency, Parl. Vice-Minister of Finance (three times); Minister of Justice 1998–99 (resgnd). *Leisure interests:* skiing, scuba diving. *Address:* c/o Ministry of Justice, 1-1-1, Kasumigaseki, Chiyoda-ku, Tokyo 100-8977, Japan. *E-mail:* webmaster@moj.go.jp.

NAKAMURA, Shuji, BE, MS, PhD; Japanese physicist and academic; *Professor of Materials Science, University of California, Santa Barbara;* b. 22 May 1954, Ehime; ed Univ. of Tokushima; Research and Devt (R&D) Dept, Nichia Chemical Industries Ltd 1979–84, Group Head, R&D 1st Section 1985–88, Group Head, R&D 2nd Section 1989–93, Sr Researcher, Dept of Devt 1993–99; Visiting Research Assoc., Dept of Electronic Eng, Univ. of Florida 1988–89; Prof., Materials Science Dept, Univ. of California, Santa Barbara 1999–, also Research Dir Solid State Lighting & Energy Center; mem. Nat. Acad. of Eng 2003; numerous awards, including Sakurai Award 1995, Nishina Memorial Award 1996, Okochi Memorial Award 1997, Julius-Springer Prize for Applied Physics 1999, Takayanagi Award 2000, Carl Zeiss Research Award 2000, Honda Award 2000, Crystal Growth and Crystal Technology Award 2000, Asahi Award 2001, Optical Soc. of America Nick Holonyak Award 2001, Franklin Institute Medal in Eng 2002, Millennium Tech. Prize 2006, Harvey Prize, Technion, Israel (co-recipient) 2009, Technology & Engineering Emmy Award, Nat. Acad. of Television Arts & Sciences 2012, named Silicon Valley Intellectual Property Law Asscn Inventor of the Year 2012. *Achievement:* inventor of solid-state white lights made from LEDs. *Publications:* more than 400 papers in scientific journals; more than 100 Japanese and US patents. *Address:* Materials Science Department, University of California, Santa Barbara, CA 93106-5055, USA (office). *Telephone:* (805) 893-5552 (office). *Fax:* (805) 893-8983 (office). *E-mail:* shuji@engineering.ucsb.edu (office); *Website:* engineering.ucsb.edu/faculty/profile/82 (office); www.sslec.ucsb.edu/nakamura (office).

NAKAMURA, Toshikazu, PhD; Japanese clinical professor of medicine; *Professor and Chairman, Division of Molecular Regenerative Medicine, Osaka University Graduate School of Medicine;* ed Osaka Univ. Grad. School of Science; Assoc. Prof., School of Medicine, Univ. of Tokushima 1980–88; Prof., Faculty of Science, Kyushu Univ. 1988–93; Prof., Biomedical Research Centre, Osaka Univ. Medical School 1993–2001, Prof., Div. of Molecular Regenerative Medicine, Osaka Univ. Grad. School of Medicine 2001–; Princess Takamatsu Cancer Research Award, Academic Award, Mochida Memorial Foundation, Osaka Science Award, Inoue Prize for Science, and other awards. *Publications:* numerous articles in scientific and medical journals. *Address:* Division of Molecular Regenerative Medicine, Course of Advanced Medicine, B7, Osaka University Graduate School of Medicine, Suita, Osaka 565-0871, Japan (office). *Telephone:* (6) 6879-3783 (office). *Fax:* (6) 6879-3789 (office). *E-mail:* nakamura@onbich.med.osaka-u.ac.jp (office). *Website:* www.med.osaka-u.ac.jp (office).

NAKAMURA, Yuji; Japanese diplomatist; b. Sept. 1944, Tokyo; m. Kazuko Nakamura; ed Tokyo Univ.; joined Ministry of Foreign Affairs 1966, Counsellor, Third Dept, Cabinet Legislation Bureau 1981–83, Dir Cen. and Eastern Europe Div., European and Oceanian Affairs Bureau 1983–85; posted to Germany 1985, Minister, Embassy in Bonn 1990–91, Minister, Embassy in Vienna 1991, fmr Consul-Gen. in Sydney; Amb. to Switzerland 2002–05 (also accred to Liechtenstein 2003–05), to Italy (also accred to Albania) 2006–08. *Address:* Ministry of Foreign Affairs, Kasumigaseki 2-2-1, Chiyoda-ku, Tokyo 100-8919, Japan (office). *Telephone:* (3) 3580-3311 (office). *Fax:* (3) 3581-2667 (office). *E-mail:* webmaster@mofa.go.jp (office). *Website:* www.mofa.go.jp (office).

NAKANE, Chie; Japanese social anthropologist and academic; *Professor Emerita, University of Tokyo;* b. 30 Nov. 1926, Tokyo; d. of Minoru Nakane and Chiyo Nakane; ed Univ. of Tokyo; lived in China in 1940s; embarked on career investigating Asian societies including Japan, India, China and Tibet; Prof. of Social Anthropology, Inst. of Oriental Culture, Univ. of Tokyo (first woman prof.) 1979–87, Dir Inst. 1980–82, Prof. Emer. 1987–; Visiting Prof., Univ. of Chicago, USA, SOAS, London, UK; Prof.-at-Large, Cornell Univ., USA; mem. Japan Acad. (first and only woman mem.) 1995; Dir, Oriental Library and Art Museum of Seikado, Tokyo 2010–; Fellow, Center for Advanced Studies in Behavioral Sciences USA 1973–74; Hon. Fellow, Royal Anthropological Inst. of Britain and Ireland 1975; Foreign mem. American Philosophical Soc. 1977; mem. UNESCO World Comm. on Culture and Devt 1993–95, Pres. Japan Nat. Comm. of UNESCO 1995–96; mem. Jury, Rolex Awards for Enterprise 1980, 2002; Hon. mem., Royal Anthropological Inst. of GB and Ireland 1975, Gold Medal of Int. Union for Anthropological and Ethnological Sciences 2005; Imperial Order of Culture 2001; Japan Foundation Award 1987. *Publications:* Garo and Khasi – A Comparative Study in Matrilineal Systems 1967, Kinship and Economic Organization in Rural Japan 1967, Japanese Society 1970, Social Anthropology – A Comparative Study of Asian Societies 1987, Recent Trends in Mongolian, Tibetan and Vietnamese Studies (ed.), Acta Asiatica 76 1999, Caste, Its Diversity and Fluidity (article) 2002, Development Processes of Tibet Politico-Religious Systems (article) 2007. *Leisure interest:* oil painting. *Address:* The Japan Academy, 7–32 Ueno Park, Tokyo 110-0007, (office); 1404 Takanawa, 4-24-55, Minato-ku, Tokyo 108–0074, Japan (home). *Telephone:* (3) 3822-2101 (office); (3) 3473-4321 (home). *Fax:* (3) 3822-2105 (office). *Website:* www.japan-acad.go.jp (office).

NAKANISHI, Hiroaki, BSc, MSc; Japanese business executive; *Representative Executive Officer and President, Hitachi Ltd;* ed School of Eng, Tokyo Univ., Dept of Computer Science, Stanford Univ., USA; joined Hitachi as engineer in Computer Control Design Dept, Omika Works 1970, served in increasingly responsible man. and eng positions in Information and Telecommunications Systems Group, as well as Chief Exec. for Europe, Gen. Man. Global Business 2003, Vice-Pres. 2003–04, Sr Vice-Pres. Hitachi Ltd 2004–09, Chief Exec. for North America 2005–06, Exec. Vice-Pres. 2006–09, Exec. Chair. Hitachi Global Storage Technologies Inc. 2007–10, Exec. Dir 2010–, Exec. Vice-Pres. Hitachi America Ltd, Chair. –2007, CEO Hitachi Global Storage Technologies, Inc. of Hitachi America Ltd and Hitachi

Ltd 2006–09, Rep. Exec. Officer, in charge of Power Systems Business, Industrial Systems Business, Automotive Systems Business and Production Tech. and Gen. Man. Supervisory Office of Monozukuri, Supervisory Office for Transportation Systems and Corp. Quality Assurance Div., Hitachi Ltd 2009–, Pres. 2010–, also Exec. Vice-Pres. and Exec. Officer, Hitachi America Ltd; Sr Vice-Pres., Exec. Officer and Gen. Dir North America and Exec. Officer, Hitachi China Ltd, Exec. Vice-Pres. Babcock-Hitachi K.K. *Address:* Hitachi Ltd, 6-6 Marunouchi 1-chome, Chiyoda-ku, Tokyo 100-8280, Japan (office). *Telephone:* (3) 3258-1111 (office). *Fax:* (3) 3258-2375 (office). *E-mail:* service@cm.hbi.co.jp (office). *Website:* www.hitachi.com (office).

NAKANISHI, Koji, BSc, PhD; Japanese chemist and academic; *Centennial Professor of Chemistry Emeritus, Columbia University;* b. 11 May 1925, Hong Kong; s. of Yuzo and Yoshiko Nakanishi; m. Yasuko Nakanishi (deceased); one s. one d.; ed Nagoya Univ., Harvard Univ., USA; Asst Prof., Dept of Chem., Nagoya Univ. 1955–58, Prof. 1958–63; Prof., Dept of Chem., Tohoku Univ. 1963–69; Dir of Research, Int. Centre for Insect Physiology and Ecology, Nairobi, Kenya 1969–77; Prof., Dept of Chem., Columbia Univ., USA 1969–80, Centennial Prof. 1981–2007, Prof. Emer. 2007–, Chair., Dept of Chem. 1987–90, Dir of Research, Chem. Unit, Biosphere 2 Center, Univ. of Arizona 2001–; Dir Suntory Inst. for Bio-organic Research, Osaka 1979–81; mem. American Acad. of Arts and Sciences 1973–; Fellow, New York Acad. of Sciences 1980, Accad. Nazionale delle Scienze (Italy) 1993, AAAS 1996; Hon. mem. Pharmaceutical Soc. of Japan 1991 (mem. 2002), Chemical Soc. of Japan 1997; Order of Culture 2007; numerous awards, including Chemical Soc. of Japan Award in Pure Chem. 1954, Asahi Cultural Prize 1968, ACS Guenther Award 1978, Royal Soc. of Chem. Centenary Medal 1979, Japan Acad. Prize 1990, Swedish Acad. of Pharmaceutical Sciences Scheele Award 1992, Czech Acad. of Sciences Heyrovsky Gold Medal 1995, Nakanishi Prize awarded in alternate years by ACS and Chemical Soc. of Japan 1996, King Faisal Int. Prize (Saudi Arabia) 2003, Tetrahedron Prize 2005, Nagoya Gold Medal 2005, Silver Medal, Int. Soc. of Chemical Ecology 2007, Kosolapof Award, ACS Auburn Section 2009, Burton Kallman Scientific Award, Natural Products Asscn 2009. *Publications include:* author, co-author or ed. of nine books; co-ed nine-vol. series on natural products; more than 800 articles in scientific journals. *Leisure interest:* magic. *Address:* Department of Chemistry, Columbia University, 3000 Broadway, Mail Code 3114, New York, NY 10027 (office); 560 Riverside Drive, NY 10027, USA (home). *Telephone:* (212) 663-7605 (office). *Fax:* (212) 932-1289 (office). *E-mail:* kn5@columbia.edu (office). *Website:* www.columbia.edu/cu/chemistry (office).

NAKANISHI, Shigetada, PhD; Japanese biochemist and academic; *Director, Osaka Bioscience Institute;* b. Ogaki; ed Kyoto Univ.; earned degree in medicine; Post-doctoral Fellow, Nat. Cancer Inst., NIH, Bethesda, Md, USA 1971; returned to Kyoto Univ. 1974; currently Dir Osaka Bioscience Inst.; mem. NAS 2000–; Person of Cultural Merit 2006; Bristol-Myers Squibb Award for Distinguished Achievement in Neuroscience Research 1995, Keio Medical Science Prize (co-recipient) 1996, Gruber Neuroscience Prize, The Peter and Patricia Gruber Foundation 2007. *Achievements include:* pioneered research into communication between nerve cells in the brain; with research team unravelled molecular detail of information transfer and processing, and provided pharmacologists with many new possibilities for drug design. *Publications:* Systems Biology: The Challenge of Complexity (co-ed.) 2009; numerous scientific papers in professional journals. *Address:* Osaka Bioscience Institute, 6-2-4 Furuedai, Suita, Osaka 565-0874, Japan (office). *Telephone:* (6) 6872-4850 (office). *Fax:* (6) 6871-6686 (office). *E-mail:* nakanishi@obi.or.jp (office). *Website:* www.obi.or.jp (office).

NAKANO, Kazuhisa, BA; Japanese business executive; *Chairman and Representative Director, Idemitsu Kosan Company Limited;* ed Waseda Univ.; joined Idemitsu Kosan Co. Ltd 1971, served as Pres. Idemitsu Oil & Gas Co. Ltd (subsidiary), Vice-Pres. and Rep. Dir Idemitsu Kosan Co. Ltd 2007–09, Pres. and Rep. Dir 2009–13, Chair. and Rep. Dir 2013–. *Address:* Idemitsu Kosan Co. Ltd, 1-1, Marunouchi 3-chome, Chiyoda-ku, Tokyo 100-8321, Japan (office). *Telephone:* (3) 3213-3115 (office). *Fax:* (3) 3213-9354 (office). *E-mail:* info@idemitsu.com (office). *Website:* www.idemitsu.com (office).

NAKAO, Takehiko, BA, MBA; Japanese international organization official; *Chairman and President, Asian Development Bank;* b. 5 March 1956, Osaka; m. Asako Ishibashi; two s.; ed Univ. of Tokyo, Univ. of California, Berkeley; joined Ministry of Finance 1978, with Research Div., Int. Finance Bureau 1978–80, Research Div., Tax Bureau 1982–84, Dir Izumiotsu Local Tax Office 1984–85; Loan Officer, Export-Import Bank of Japan 1985–87, Deputy Dir, Investment Advisory Div., Security Bureau 1987, Deputy Dir, Int. Taxation Div. 1987–89, First Tax Div. 1989–90, Research Div. 1990–91, Int. Org. Div. 1991–93; Adviser, Policy Devt and Review Dept, IMF 1994–97; Deputy Dir Coordination Div., Ministry of Finance 1993–94, Special Officer in charge of Asian monetary cooperation 1997–98, Dir Int. Org. Div., Int. Bureau 1998–2000, Budget Examiner, Budget Bureau 2000–02, Devt Policy Div. 2002–04, Coordination Div. 2004–05; Minister, Embassy in Washington, DC 2005–07; Vice-Minister of Finance for International Affairs, Ministry of Finance 2011–13; Chair. and Pres. Asian Devt Bank 2013–; Visiting Prof., Univ. of Tokyo 2010–11; Rep. at G-7 and G-20 summits 2012. *Publications include:* International Taxation System 1989, America's Economic Policy: Can it Sustain its Strength? 2008. *Address:* Asian Development Bank, 6 ADB Avenue, 1550, Mandaluyong City, Philippines (office). *Telephone:* (2) 6324444 (office). *Fax:* (2) 6362444 (office). *Website:* www.adb.org (office).

NAKASONE, Hirofumi; Japanese politician; b. 28 Nov. 1945; s. of Yasuhiro Nakasone (fmr Prime Minister of Japan); ed Keio Univ.; with Asahi Chemical Industry Co. Ltd 1968; Sec. to Prime Minister Yasuhiro Nakasone 1983; mem. House of Councillors (Liberal Democratic Party—LDP) 1986–; Parl. Vice-Minister, Ministry of Int. Trade and Industry 1990; Chair. Standing Cttee on Commerce and Industry, House of Councillors 1993, Cttee on Orgs Involved with Women's Issues, Social Educ. and Religion, LDP 1995; Head Deputy Chair. LDP Diet Affairs Cttee, House of Councillors 1996; Chair. Standing Cttee on Rules and Administration, House of Councillors 1997; Chair. LDP Policy Bd, House of Councillors 1998, Special Cttee on Managing Debts of Japan Nat. Railway Settlement Corpn and Reform of Nat. Forestry Services 1998; Minister of Educ., Science, Sports and Culture and Minister of State for Science and Tech. 1999–2000; Minister of Foreign Affairs 2008–09. *Address:* c/o Liberal Democratic Party, 1-11-23, Nagata-cho, Chiyyoda-ku, Tokyo 100-8910, Japan (office). *Telephone:* (3) 3581-6211 (office). *E-mail:* koho@ldp.jimin.or.jp (office). *Website:* www.jimin.jp (office).

NAKASONE, Yasuhiro; Japanese politician; b. 27 May 1918, Takasaki, Gunma Prov.; s. of Matsugoroh Nakasone and Yuku Nakasone; m. Tsutako Kobayashi 1945; one s. (Hirofumi Nakasone) two d.; ed Tokyo Imperial Univ.; fmr mem. House of Reps; fmr Minister of State, Dir-Gen. of Science and Tech. Agency; Chair. Nat. Org. LDP, Jt Cttee on Atomic Energy, Special Cttee on Scientific Tech., Chair. LDP Exec. Council 1971–72, Sec.-Gen. LDP 1974–76, Chair. 1977–80; Minister of Transport 1967–68; Minister of State and Dir-Gen. Defence Agency 1970–71; Minister of Int. Trade and Industry 1972–74; Minister of State and Dir-Gen. of Admin. Man. Agency 1980–82; Prime Minister of Japan 1982–87; Chair. and Pres. Int. Inst. for Global Peace 1988–89, Inst. for Int. Policy Studies 1988–; after involvement in Recruit affair resigned from LDP, rejoined April 1991. *Publications include:* Ideal of Youth, Frontier in Japan, The New Conservatism, Human Cities – A Proposal for the 21st Century 1980, Tenchiyujou (autobiog.) 1996. *Leisure interests:* golf, swimming, painting. *Address:* 3-22-7, Kamikitazawa, Setagaya-ku, Tokyo, Japan (home). *Telephone:* (3) 3304-7000 (home).

NAKATA, Hideo; Japanese film director; b. 19 July 1961, Okayama; ed Univ. of Tokyo; began career as Asst Dir, Nikkatsu Studios; worked under supervision of Masaru Konuma; directorial debut with God's Hand (TV film) 1992; adapted horror novel Ringu by Suzuki Koji into feature film 1998. *Films directed include:* God's Hand (TV) 1992, Don't Look Up/Ghost Actress (also writer) 1996, Ringu 1998, Chaos 1999, Ringu 2 (also writer) 1999, Sadistic and Masochistic 2000, Sleeping Bride 2000, Dark Water (also writer) 2002, Last Scene 2002, Samara: The Ring 2 2005, The Eye 2006, Out 2006, The Entity 2006. *Address:* c/o United Talent Agency Inc., 9560 Wilshire Boulevard, Suite 500, Beverly Hills, CA 90212, USA (office). *Telephone:* (310) 273-6700 (office). *Fax:* (310) 247-1111 (office).

NAKAYAMA, Kyoko, BA; Japanese politician and diplomatist; *Minister of State for Social Affairs and Gender Equality, Minister of Public Records Management and National Archives and Minister of State for the Abduction Issue;* b. 26 Jan. 1940; ed Univ. of Tokyo; with Ministry of Foreign Affairs 1964–66; Ministry of Finance 1966–75, 1978–93, Deputy Dir-Gen. Minister's Secr.) 1993; with IMF, Washington, DC 1975–78; Exec. Vice-Pres. The Japan Foundation 1993–99; Amb. to Uzbekistan 1999–2002; Councillor of Cabinet Secr. (for the Abduction Issue) 2002–04; Special Advisor to Prime Minister (for Abduction Issue) 2006–08; mem. House of Councillors 2007–; Minister of State for Social Affairs and Gender Equality, Minister of Public Records Man. and Nat. Archives, and Minister of State for the Abduction Issue 2008–. *Address:* Cabinet Office, 1-6-1, Nagata-cho, Chiyoda-ku, Tokyo 100-8914, Japan (office). *Telephone:* (3) 5253-2111 (office). *E-mail:* info@cao.go.jp (office). *Website:* www.cao.go.jp (office).

NAKAYAMA, Nariaki; Japanese politician; b. 7 June 1943; ed Univ. of Tokyo; entered Ministry of Finance 1966, Chief of Ebara Tax Office 1971, Head of Budget Bureau 1978, Dir Tokai Local Finance Bureau 1980, Dir for Minister's Secr. 1982; with World Bank, Washington, DC, USA 1975; mem. House of Reps for Miyazaki Pref. 1986–, Chair. Cttee on Commerce and Industry 1999, Special Cttee on Disasters 2000, Cttee on Health, Labour and Welfare 2003; Parl. Vice-Minister for Educ. 1990; Dir Environment Div., LDP 1992, Commerce and Industry Div. 1996, Deputy Chair. Research Comms 2002, Deputy Sec.-Gen. 2003; Vice-Minister of Int. Trade and Industry 2000–01, of Economy, Trade and Industry 2001–04; Minister of Educ., Culture, Sports, Science and Tech. 2004–05; Minister of Land, Infrastructure and Transport Sept. 2008 (resgnd). *Address:* c/o Liberal-Democratic Party–LDP (Jiyu-Minshuto), 1-11-23, Nagata-cho, Chiyoda-ku, Tokyo 100-8910, Japan (office).

NAKAYAMA, Taro, MD, PhD; Japanese politician; b. 27 Aug. 1924, Osaka; ed Osaka Medical Coll.; mem. Osaka Pref. Ass. 1955–68; mem. House of Councillors 1968–86, Parl. Vice-Pres. Labour Party 1971; Chair. Cttee on Cabinet 1976, Chair. Cttee on Rules and Admin 1979; Dir-Gen. Prime Minister's Office 1980; Chief Okinawa Devt Agency 1980; Chair. Parl. Affairs Cttee of LDP 1982, LDP Financial Cttee 1988, LDP Political Reform HQ 1998, LDP Research Comm. on Foreign Affairs 1999; mem. Gen. Council of LDP 1998–; mem. House of Reps 1986–; Minister of Foreign Affairs 1989–91; Chair. Research Comm. on Constitution of House of Reps 2000–; Chair. Asian Population and Devt Asscn and Chair. or Pres. numerous int. parliamentarians' friendship leagues including Japan–India Parliamentarians' Friendship League; Grand Cordon, First Order of Rising Sun, 1997. *Publications:* five books including Scientific Strategy for the Post-Oil Age 1979. *Address:* 1-7-1 Nagata-Cho, Chiyoda-ku, Tokyo, Japan.

NAKIB, Falah an-; Iraqi civil engineer and politician; b. Samarra; s. of Gen. Hassan al-Naqib; fmr mem. Iraqi Nat. Congress, Iraq Nat. Movt; apptd Gov. Salahaddin Prov. by US-led admin; Interim Minister of the Interior 2004–05. *Address:* c/o Office of the Minister of the Interior, Green Zone, Baghdad, Iraq.

NALBANDIAN, Edvard, PhD; Armenian diplomatist; *Minister of Foreign Affairs;* b. 16 July 1956, Kirovakan (now Vanadzor); s. of the late Vardanush Nalbandian; m.; one d.; ed Moscow State Inst. of Int. Relations, Inst. of Oriental Studies, USSR Nat. Acad. of Sciences; worked at USSR Embassy in Beirut 1978–83; at USSR Ministry of Foreign Affairs, Moscow 1983–86; Counsellor of USSR Embassy (then Russian Fed. Embassy) in Egypt 1986–92; Chargé d'affaires a.i. in Cairo 1992–93, Amb. to Egypt 1994–98 (also accred Morocco and Oman), to France 1999–2008 (also accred to Israel, the Holy See and Andorra) 2004–08; Special Rep. of the Pres. of Armenia to Int. Org. of Francophony 2006; Minister of Foreign Affairs 2008–; Commdr, Légion d'honneur 2001, Grand Officier 2011; Grand Cross of St Gregory (Holy See) 2003, Second Degree Medal 'For Services Contributed to the Motherland' 2012; Award of Friendship of Nations (USSR) 1982, Mkhitar Gosh Medal 2001. *Address:* Ministry of Foreign Affairs, 0010 Yerevan, Republic Square, Government Building 2, Armenia (office). *Telephone:* (10) 62-00-00 (office). *Fax:* (10) 62-00-62 (office). *E-mail:* info@mfa.am (office). *Website:* www.mfa.am (office).

NALLET, Henri Pierre; French politician; *Vice-President, Fondation Jean Jaurès;* b. 6 Jan. 1939, Bergerac (Dordogne); s. of Jean Nallet and France Lafon; m. Thérèse Leconte 1963; one s.; ed Inst. d'Etudes Politiques, Bordeaux; Sec.-Gen. Jeunesse Étudiante Catholique 1963–64; Inst. de Formation des Cadres Paysans 1965–66; Féd. Nat. des Syndicats d'Exploitants Agricoles (FNSEA) 1966–70; Dir of

Research, Dept of Econ. and Rural Sociology, Inst. Nat. de Recherche Agronomique (INRA) 1970–81; agricultural adviser, Secr. Gen. of Presidency of Republic 1981–85; Minister of Agric. 1985–86; Socialist Deputy to Nat. Ass. 1986–88; Minister of Agric. and Forestry 1988–90, Garde des Sceaux, Minister of Justice 1990–92; Conseiller-Gen. of Yonne 1988–2001; Mayor of Tonnerre 1989–2000; Conseiller d'état 1992–; Deputy for Yonne 1997–99; Pres. Del. of Nat. Ass. to EU; mem. Parl. Ass. of Council of Europe and of WEU; Consultant IBRD 1992–, EU 1992–; Vice-Chair. European Socialist Party 1997–2003; Nat. Sec. for Int. Affairs of Socialist Party 1999–2003; Directeur Général Relations Extérieures Groupe de Recherche Servier; Pres. World Council of Nutrition 1985–87; Vice-Pres. Fondation Jean Jaurès 1997–; Officier Légion d'honneur 2001. *Publications:* Tempête sur la justice 1992, Les Réseaux multidisciplinaires. La Documentation française 1999, Le multilateralisme: une réforme possible 2004. *Address:* 22 rue Garnier, 92578 Neuilly-sur-Seine Cedex, France. *E-mail:* fondation@jean-jaures .org (office). *Website:* www.jean-jaures.org (office).

NAM, Joong-soo, BBA, MBA, PhD; South Korean telecommunications executive; *President and CEO, KT Corporation;* ed Seoul Nat. Univ., Univ. of Massachusetts and Duke Univ. Fuqua School of Business, USA; joined KT Corpn 1981, Vice-Pres. IMT-2000 Business Group –2001, Chief Financial Officer 2001–03, Pres. and CEO KT Freetel Co. (mobile affiliate) 2003–05, Pres. and CEO KT Corpn 2005–. *Address:* KT Corporation, 206 Jungja-dong, Bundang-gu Songnam, Kyonggi 463-711, Republic of Korea (office). *Telephone:* (31) 727-0114 (office). *Fax:* (31) 727-0949 (office). *E-mail:* info@kt.co.kr (office). *Website:* www.kt.co.kr (office).

NAM, Young-sun, BA; South Korean business executive; *Co-CEO, Representative Director, Explosives Division and Treasury Team, Hanwha Chemical Corporation;* b. 2 April 1953; ed Yonsei Univ.; joined Korea Plastics 1978; Dir for Planning and Co-ordination, Planning Team, Hanwha Gen. Explosives 1997–99, Div. Man., Floor Covering Business Div., Hanwha L&C, Hanwha Gen. Explosives 1999–2003, Man. Dir, Marketing Team, Hanwha Restructuring HQ 2003–04, Officer in Charge, Hanwha Corpn/Explosives Div. 2004–05, Rep. Dir, Hanwha Corpn/ Explosives Div. and Treasury Team 2005–. *Address:* Hanwha Chemical Corpn, Hanwha Building, 1 Changgyo-dong, Chung-ku, Seoul 100-797, Republic of Korea (office). *Telephone:* (2) 729-2700 (office); (2) 729-1114 (office). *Fax:* (2) 729-1762 (office). *E-mail:* hanwhacorp@hanwha.co.kr (office). *Website:* english.hanwhacorp .co.kr (office).

NAMALIU, Rt Hon. Sir Rabbie Langanai, KCMG, PC, BA, MA; Papua New Guinea politician; b. 3 April 1947, Raluana, E New Britain Prov.; s. of Darius Namaliu and Utul Ioan Namaliu; m. 1st Margaret Nakikus 1978 (died 1993); two s. one step-d.; m. 2nd Kelina Tavul 1999; one s.; ed Keravat High School, Univ. of Papua New Guinea, Univ. of Victoria, BC, Canada; fmr Tutor, Lecturer in History and Fellow, Univ. of Papua New Guinea; Prin. Pvt. Sec. to Chief Minister 1974; fmr Prov. Commr, E New Britain and Chair. Public Services Comm.; held sr positions in Office of Prime Minister and Leader of Opposition under Mr Somare; MP (Pangu Pati) for Kokopo Open 1982–2007, Speaker 1994–97; Minister for Foreign Affairs and Trade 1982–84, for Primary Industry 1984–85; Prime Minister 1988–92; Sr Minister for State 1997–98, for Petroleum and Energy 1998–99; Minister of Foreign Affairs and Immigration 2002–06, of Finance 2006–07, of the Treasury 2007; Deputy Leader, Pangu Pati 1985–88, Leader 1988–92; Pres. African Caribbean Pacific Council of Ministers 1984; Co-Pres. ACP/EEC Jt Council of Ministers 1984; Vacation Scholar, ANU 1968; Visiting Fellow, Center for Pacific Studies, Univ. of Califoria, Santa Cruz, USA 1976; Hon. MA, LLD (Victoria, BC) 1983; Independence Medal 1975, Queen's Silver Jubilee Medal 1977, Pacific Man of the Year 1988. *Leisure interests:* reading, fishing, walking, golf. *Address:* c/o Pangu Pati (Papua New Guinea Unity), PO Box 289, Waigani, NCD, Papua New Guinea.

NAMBIAR, Vijay K., MA; Indian diplomatist and UN official; *Special Adviser to the Secretary General on Myanmar, United Nations;* b. aug. 1943, Poona (now Pune); m. Malini Nambiar; two d.; ed Univ. of Bombay; joined Foreign Service 1967, early years specializing in Chinese language and serving in Hong Kong and Beijing; subsequent posts included Belgrade, Yugoslavia in mid-1970s; numerous bilateral and multilateral postings in Beijing, Belgrade and New York in 1970s and 1980s, also Jt Sec. (Dir Gen.) for E Asia 1988 and multilateral affairs at New Delhi HQ 1980s; Amb. to Algeria 1985–88, to Afghanistan 1990–92, to Malaysia 1993–96, to China 1996–2000, to Pakistan 2000–01; Perm. Rep. to UN, New York 2002–04; Deputy Nat. Security Adviser (DNSA) and Head, Nat. Security Council Secr. 2005–06; Under-Sec.-Gen. and Special Adviser to UN Sec.-Gen., New York 2006–07, Chef de Cabinet (Chief of Staff), UN Sec.-Gen. 2007–12, Special Adviser to the UN Sec.-Gen. on Myanmar 2010–, also Acting Special Rep. of the Sec.-Gen. on Sexual Violence in Conflict 2012; Chancellor's Gold Medal, Univ. of Bombay 1965. *Address:* Office of the Secretary-General, United Nations, New York, NY 10017, USA (office). *Telephone:* (212) 963-1234 (office). *Fax:* (212) 963-4879 (office). *Website:* www.un.org (office).

NAMBU, Yoichiro, ScD; American (b. Japanese) physicist and academic; *Harry Pratt Judson Distinguished Service Professor Emeritus, Department of Physics and Enrico Fermi Institute, University of Chicago;* b. 18 Jan. 1921, Tokyo; s. of Kichiro Nambu; ed Univ. of Tokyo; Prof., Osaka City Univ. 1950–56; Researcher, Inst. for Advanced Study, Princeton, NJ, USA 1952–54; Research Assoc., Dept of Physics and Enrico Fermi Inst., Univ. of Chicago 1954–56, Assoc. Prof. 1956–58, Prof. 1958–77, Harry Pratt Judson Distinguished Service Prof. 1977–91, Emer. 1991–, Chair. Dept of Physics 1974–77; mem. NAS 1971, American Acad. of Arts and Sciences 1971; Hon. mem. Japan Acad. 1984–; Govt of Japan Order of Culture 1978; Hon. DSc (Osaka City Univ.) 1980, (Northwestern Univ.) 1987, (Osaka Univ.) 1996; Nat. Medal of Science, American Physical Soc., Dannie Heineman Prize for Math. Physics 1970, J. Robert Oppenheimer Prize 1976, Max Planck Medal 1985, Dirac Medal, Int. Centre for Theoretical Physics 1986, Sakurai Prize, American Physical Soc. 1994, Wolf Prize in Physics 1994, Gian Carlo Wick Medal, World Fed. of Scientists 1996, Bogoliubov Prize, Jt Inst. for Nuclear Research 2003, Benjamin Franklin Medal in Physics, Franklin Inst. 2005, Pomeranchuk Prize, Inst. of Theoretical and Experimental Physics, Russia 2007, Nobel Prize for Physics (jtly) 2008. *Address:* Enrico Fermi Institute, University of Chicago, 5640 South Ellis Avenue, Chicago, IL 60637, USA (office). *Telephone:* (773) 702-7286 (office). *Fax:* (773) 834-2222 (office). *E-mail:* nambu@theory.uchicago.edu (office). *Website:* www.physics.uchicago.edu (office).

NAMGYEL, Maj.-Gen. Vetsop; Bhutanese diplomatist, army officer and government official; *Ambassador to India;* ADC to King Jigme Singye Wangchuk for 35 years; Amb. to India 2009–. *Address:* Embassy of Bhutan, Chandragupta Marg, Chanakyapuri, New Delhi 110 021, India (office). *Telephone:* (11) 26889807 (office). *Fax:* (11) 26876710 (office). *E-mail:* bhutan@vsnl.com (office).

NAMI, Özdil, BA, MBA; Turkish-Cypriot politician; *Minister of Foreign Affairs;* b. 23 May 1967, London, UK; m.; one c.; ed Boğaziçi Univ., Univ. of California, Berkeley, USA; Lecturer in Econs, Eastern Mediterranean Univ. 1993–97, Near East Univ., European Univ. of Lefke; mem. Legis. Ass. (Parl.) 2003 –; Minister of Foreign Affairs 2013–; mem. Turkish Cypriot Chamber of Commerce 2000–01; Chair. Cyprus Asscn of Businessmen 2001–03; mem. Parl. Ass., Council of Europe 2005; mem. Cumhuriyetçi Türk Partisi (Republican Turkish Party). *Address:* Ministry of Foreign Affairs, Selçuklu Road, Lefkoşa, Mersin 10, Turkey (office). *Telephone:* 2283241 (office). *Fax:* 2284290 (office). *E-mail:* bakanlik@trncinfo.org (office). *Website:* www.trncinfo.org (office).

NAMOLOH, Maj.-Gen. (retd) Charles Dickson Ndaxu Phillip; Namibian military officer, diplomatist and politician; *Minister of Regional and Local Government, Housing and Rural Development;* b. 28 Feb. 1950, Odibo; s. of Phillip Hidishange Namoloh and Fransiska Kaimba Nghihangakenwa; ed St Mary's Mission Anglican School, Indira Gandhi Univ., Delhi, Nasser High Mil. Acad., Egypt, Vystrel Field Acad., Moscow, Naval Post Graduate School, Monterey, USA; fighter with People's Liberation Army of Namibia (Plan) 1975–77, Plan Chief of Staff for NE front 1977–79, Plan Chief of Staff 1979–89; Chief of Staff, Namibian Defence Force 1990–95; Amb. to Angola 1995–2003; High Commr to India 2003–05; Minister of Defence 2005–12; Minister of Regional and Local Govt, Housing and Rural Devt 2012–; mem. Nat. Ass. 2005–; Head of Politics, Security and Defence Cttee, South African Devt Community; Swapo Highest Medal of Ongulumbashe 1989, Order of the Eagle 2004. *Address:* Ministry of Regional and Local Government and Housing and Rural Development, PMB 13289, Windhoek, Namibia (office). *Telephone:* (61) 2975111 (office). *Fax:* (61) 226049 (office). *Website:* www.mrlgh.gov.na (office).

NAMPHY, Lt-Gen. Henri; Haitian army officer and fmr head of state; b. 2 Nov. 1932, Cap-Haïtien; fmr Chief of Haitian Gen. Staff; Pres. (Head of State), Nat. Governing Council (formed after overthrow of Jean-Claude Duvalier q.v., in coup) 1986–88, Head of State June–Sept. 1988 (deposed in coup d'état); Vice-Chair. Legislature 1987–88; now living in exile in Dominica.

NAN, Zhenzhong; Chinese journalist and politician; b. May 1942, Lingbao, He'nan Prov.; ed Zhengzhou Univ.; joined Xinhua News Agency 1964, fmrly Vice-Chief, then Chief Shandong Br., Xinhua News Agency, Assoc. Ed. then Ed.-in-Chief, Office of Gen. Editing 1986, Vice-Pres. Xinhua News Agency 1993–2000, Ed.-in-Chief 2000–07 (retd); Vice-Chair. All-China Journalists' Asscn; joined CCP 1978; Del., 13th CCP Nat. Congress 1987–92, 14th CCP Nat. Congress 1992–97, 15th CCP Nat. Congress 1997–2002, 16th CCP Nat. Congress 2002–07; Deputy, 9th NPC 1998–2003, 10th NPC 2003–08, mem. 11th NPC Standing Cttee 2008–13; Vice-Chair. 11th NPC Foreign Affairs Cttee 2008–13; awarded title China's Prominent Journalist of the Year 1984, winner, first Fan Chanjiang News Awards 1991. *Publications:* The Responsibility System of Agricultural Production in China 1981, I Learn to Be a Journalist 1985, The Eyes of a Correspondent 1988, The Reflections of a Correspondent 1993, Selected Works by Nan Zhenzhong 1996, The Ability to Discover 1999, The Strategic View of a Correspondent 1999, On Success – A Discussion with Young Journalists 2003. *Address:* c/o Xinhua (New China) News Agency, 57 Xuanwumen Xidajie, Beijing 100803, People's Republic of China (office).

NANDAN, Rohit, MA; Indian civil servant and airline industry executive; *Chairman and Managing Director, Air India Limited;* b. 27 Jan. 1957, Uttar Pradesh; joined the Admin. Service 1982, Exec. Magistrate, Land Revenue Man. and Dist Admin 1984–85, Additional Dist Magistrate 1985–86, Project Dir 1986–88, Collector and Dist Magistrate, Farukhabad 1990–91, Collector and Dist Magistrate, Mainpuri 1991–93; Jt Sec., Ministry of Home Affairs 1988–90, Special Sec. 1994–95; Dir Personnel and Gen. Admin March–July 1991, Staff Officer 2001–02; Special Sec., Ministry of Information and Broadcasting 1995–96, March–June 1997, Sec. June–Sept. 1997, Dir and Sec., Information Tech. Dept 2002–03; Dir Ministry of Culture 1996–97; Sec., Industries 1997–2000; Sec., Disabled Welfare Dept, Ministry of Social Justice and Empowerment 2003–07; Personal Sec. to Chief Minister of UP Handicapped Welfare Dept June–Nov. 2007; Personal Sec., Rural Devt Dept, Ministry of Rural Devt 2007–09; Jt Sec., Ministry of Civil Aviation 2009–11, Chief Man. Dir 2011; Chair. and Man. Dir Air India Ltd 2011–. *Address:* Office of the Chairman, Air India Ltd, 3rd Floor, Tower-II, Jeevan Bharati 124, Connaught Circus, New Delhi 110 001 (office); Air India Building, Nariman Point, Mumbai 400 021, India (office). *Telephone:* (11) 24624074 (New Delhi) (office); (22) 22023031 (Mumbai) (office). *Fax:* (11) 24694171 (New Delhi) (office); (22) 22021096 (office). *Website:* www.airindia.in (office).

NANDI-NDEITWAH, Neitumbo; Namibian politician; *Minister of Foreign Affairs;* b. 29 Oct. 1952, Onamutai, Oshana region; m. Epaphras Denga Ndeitwah; ed Keele Univ., UK, Glasgow Coll. of Tech.; joined SWAPO 1966, Deputy Sec.-Gen. 1996, mem. Politburo 1996, later Sec. for Information and Mobilisation; went into exile in Zambia 1974, worked at SWAPO HQ, Lusaka 1974–75, SWAPO Deputy Rep. in Zambia 1976–78, Chief Rep. in Zambia 1978–80; returned to Namibia 1989; mem. Nat. Ass. (SWAPO) 1990–; Deputy Minister of Foreign Affairs 1990–96, Dir Gen. of Women's Affairs in Office of the Pres. 1996, Minister of Women's Affairs and Child Welfare 2000, Minister of Information and Broadcasting 2005, of Environment and Tourism 2010–12, of Foreign Affairs 2012–; Pres. Namibian Nat. Women's Org. 1991–94; mem. Bd Namibian Econ. Policy Research Unit 1998–. *Address:* Ministry of Foreign Affairs, Government Bldgs, Robert Mugabe Avenue, PMB 13347, Windhoek, Namibia (office). *Telephone:* (61) 2829111 (office). *Fax:* (61) 223937 (office). *E-mail:* headquarters@mfa.gov.na (office). *Website:* www.mfa.gov.na (office).

NANO, Fatos Thanas, PhD; Albanian politician and economist; b. 16 Sept. 1952, Tirana; m. Xhoana Nano; three c.; ed Tirana Univ.; Lecturer in Political Economy, Faculty of Econs, Tirana Univ. 1978–; mem. Parl. 1991–2005; Sec.-Gen., Council of Ministers 1990, Deputy Chair. Jan.–Feb. 1991, Chair. (Prime Minister) Feb.–June 1991; Chair. Socialist Party of Albania (Partia Socialiste e Shqipërisë) 1991–2005;

stripped of immunity from prosecution to face charges of embezzlement July 1993; convicted of misappropriation of state funds, of dereliction of duty and of falsifying state documents April 1994; sentenced to 12 years' imprisonment; declared political prisoner of conscience by Amnesty International, Int. Parl. Union and Council of Europe Parl. Ass.; released and pardoned March 1997, found non-guilty by Tirana Court 2001; Prime Minister of Albania 1997–98, 2002–05; Founder Movt for Solidarity 2007; unsuccessful cand. in presidential elections 2007; Dr hc. *Address:* c/o Partia Socialiste e Shqipërisë, Tirana, Albania.

NANTERME, Pierre; French business executive; *Chairman and CEO, Accenture Ltd;* ed École Supérieure des Sciences Économiques et Commerciales, Paris; joined Accenture 1983, Partner 1993, leadership roles included Man. Dir Strategy Group in West Europe and Man. Dir of client group in France, Belgium, Luxembourg and the Netherlands, spent most of his career with Accenture in Financial Services Operating Group, serving as Man. Dir for Europe, Africa and Latin America, also served as Man. Dir Core Europe operating unit and Global Man. Dir Accenture's Insurance industry group, Chief Leadership Officer 2006–07, also served as country Man. Dir for France 2005–07, Group Chief Exec. Financial Services Operating Group –2010, mem. Bd of Dirs and CEO Accenture Ltd 2011–, Chair. 2013–, Head of Global Man. Cttee; Chair. French Consulting Asscn (SYNTEC), French Employers Asscn's Comm. for Econ. Affairs (MEDEF) 2005–; Chevalier, Légion d'honneur 2010. *Address:* Accenture Ltd, 1 Grand Canal Square, Grand Canal Harbour, Dublin 2, Ireland (office). *Telephone:* (1) 6462000 (office). *Fax:* (1) 6462020 (office). *E-mail:* info@accenture.com (office). *Website:* www.accenture.com (office).

NAOSHIMA, Masayuki; Japanese politician; b. 23 Oct. 1945, Osaka Pref.; ed Kobe Univ.; began career with Toyota Motor Corpn; fmr Vice-Chair. Confed. of Japan Automobile Workers Unions; mem. House of Councillors 1992–, Chair. Parl. Cttee on Land and Transport; fmr mem. Democratic Socialist Party; mem. Democratic Party of Japan (DPJ) 1998–, Chair. DPJ Policy Research Cttee, Sec.-Gen. DPJ Parl. Caucus; fmr Next (Shadow) Chief Cabinet Sec.; Minister of Economy, Trade and Industry 2009–10. *Leisure interests:* reading, swimming. *Address:* c/o Ministry of Economy, Trade and Industry, 1-3-1, Kasumigaseki, Chiyoda-ku, Tokyo 100-8901, Japan.

NAOURI, Jean-Charles; French financier and business executive; *Chairman, President and CEO, Groupe Rallye;* b. 8 March 1949, Algeria; served as Sr Adviser to Finance Minister Pierre Beregovoy 1982–86; Founder and Chair. Foncière Euris (pvt. equity fund), has roles in several cos by Euris including Censor, Fimalac 2002–, Chair. Casino Group 2003–, CEO 2005–, Man. SCI Penthièvre 2003–, Chair., Pres. and CEO Groupe Rallye, Chair. Finatis; Caisse Nationale des Caisses d'Epargne 2004–; mem. Bd of Dirs HSBC France; mem. Supervisory Bd Groupe Marc de Lacharrière; Man. Pnr, Rothschild et Compagnie Banque. *Address:* Groupe Rallye, 83 rue du Faubourg Saint Honoré, Paris 75008 (office); Groupe Casino, 24 rue de la Montat, Saint Etienne 42100, France (office). *Telephone:* 1-44-71-13-62 (Paris) (office); 4-77-45-31-31 (Saint Etienne) (office). *Fax:* 1-44-71-13-60 (Paris) (office). *E-mail:* info@rallye.fr (office). *Website:* www.rallye.fr (office); www .groupe-casino.fr (office).

NAPE, Jeffery, CMG; Papua New Guinea politician; b. 1951; Speaker, Nat. Parl. 2004–12, Acting Gov.-Gen. of Papua New Guinea May–June 2004, Dec. 2010–May 2011; mem. Nat. Alliance party. *Address:* c/o Parliament House, Waigani, NCD, Papua New Guinea (office).

NAPIER, Iain J. G., FCMA; British business executive; *Chairman, Imperial Tobacco Group PLC;* fmr mem. Bd of Dirs Bass PLC, Chief Exec. Bass Leisure and then of Bass Brewers and Bass International Brewers; Vice-Pres., UK and Ireland, Interbrew SA –2001; Chief Exec. Taylor Woodrow Int. Housing and Devt 2001–05; Dir (non-exec.) Imperial Tobacco Group PLC 2000–, Chair. 2007–, Chair. Nominations Cttee; Chair. (non-exec.) McBride PLC 2007–, John Menzies plc; Dir (non-exec.) John Menzies plc 2007–, Molson Coors Brewing Co. 2008–, William Grant & Sons Holdings Ltd; mem. Bd of Dirs Collins Stewart PLC –2001. *Address:* Imperial Tobacco Group PLC, PO Box 244, Upton Road, Bristol, BS99 7UJ, England (office). *Telephone:* (117) 963-6636 (office). *Fax:* (117) 966-7405 (office). *E-mail:* info@imperial-tobacco.com (office). *Website:* www.imperial-tobacco.com (office).

NAPIER, John; British stage designer; b. 1 March 1944; s. of James Edward Thomas Napier and Florence Napier (née Godbold); m. 1st Andreanne Neofitou; one s. one d.; m. 2nd Donna King; one s. one d.; ed Hornsey Coll. of Art, Cen. School of Arts and Crafts; production designs include: A Penny for a Song, Fortune and Men's Eyes, The Ruling Class, The Fun War, Muzeeka, George Frederick (ballet), La Turista, Cancer, Isabel's a Jezebel, Mister, The Foursome, The Lovers of Viorne, Lear, Jump, Sam Sam, Big Wolf, The Devils (ENO), The Party, Knuckle, Kings and Clowns, Lohengrin (Covent Garden), Macbeth, Richard III, Hedda Gabler, Twelfth Night, The Greeks, Nicholas Nickleby, Cats, Starlight Express, Time, Les Misérables, Miss Saigon, Sunset Boulevard, Burning Blue, Jesus Christ Superstar, Idomeneo (Glyndebourne), Who's Afraid of Virginia Woolf?, An Enemy of the People, Peter Pan, Martin Guerre, Candide, Jane Eyre, Nabucco (Metro-politan Opera), South Pacific, Skellig 2003, Aladdin (Old Vic), Equus 2007 (and New York transfer 2008), Disconnect, Birdsong, Don Giovanni (Welsh Nat. Opera) 2011; Designer, Co-Dir Siegfried & Roy Show, Las Vegas 1990; film designs include Hook 1991; numerous stage and TV set designs world-wide; Hon. Fellow, London Inst. 2001; Royal Designer for Industry, Royal Soc. of Arts 1996, five Tony Awards. *Leisure interest:* photography. *Address:* c/o Macnaughton Lord Representation, Unit 10, The Bromhouse Studios, 50 Sullivan Road, London, SW6 3DX, England (office). *Telephone:* (20) 7499-1411 (office). *E-mail:* info@mlrep.com (office).

NAPIER, John Alan, MA (Econ); British business executive; b. 22 Aug. 1942; s. of the late William Napier and Barbara Napier (née Chatten); m. 1st Gillian Reed 1961; two s. one d.; m. 2nd Caroline Denning 1992; one d. two step-s. one step-d.; ed Colchester Royal Grammar School and Emmanuel Coll., Cambridge; jr and middle man. positions, Int. Publishing Corpn and Reed International 1960–69; Man. Dir Index Printers 1969–72; Man. Dir QB Newspapers 1972–76; Exec. Dir (Australia) James Hardie Industries 1976–86; Group Man. Dir AGB PLC 1986–90; Group Man. Dir Hays PLC 1991–98; Chair. Booker PLC 1998–2000; Exec. Chair. Kelda Group PLC 2000–02, Chair. (non-exec.) 2002–; Chair. Yorkshire and Humber Rural Affairs Forum 2002–; Chair. Royal & Sun Alliance Insurance Group (RSA) plc 2003–12. *Leisure interests:* rural matters, outdoor activities, people, philosophy. *Address:* c/o Royal & Sun Alliance Insurance Group plc, 9th Floor, One Plantation Place, 30 Fenchurch Street, London, EC3M 3BD, England.

NAPIER, HE Cardinal Wilfrid Fox, OFM, BPh, BTh, MA; South African ecclesiastic; *Archbishop of Durban;* b. 8 March 1941, Swartberg; s. of Thomas D. Napier and Mary Davey; ed Little Flower School, Ixopo, Natal, Nat. Univ. of Ireland, Galway and Catholic Univ., Louvain, Belgium; ordained priest of Order of Friars Minor 1970; Asst Pastor, St Anthony's Parish, Lusikisiki 1971; Parish Priest, St Francis Parish, Tabankulu 1973; Apostolic Admin., Diocese of Kokstad 1978; Bishop of Kokstad 1981–92; Archbishop of Durban 1992–; cr. Cardinal (Cardinal-Priest of San Francesco d'Assisi ad Acilia) 2001; participated in Papal Conclave 2005, 2013; Vice-Pres. S African Catholic Bishops' Conf. 1984, Pres. 1988–94, 2003–06, First Vice-Pres. 1994, Chair. Dept for Finance; mem. Pontifical Council for the Pastoral Care of Health Care Workers 2012–; Hon. LLD (Nat. Univ. of Ireland, Galway) 1995. *Leisure interests:* gardening, tennis, golf, DIY mechanics, fishing. *Address:* Archbishop's House, 154 Gordon Road, Durban 4001 (office); PO Box 47489, Greyville 4023, South Africa. *Telephone:* (31) 3031417 (office). *Fax:* (31) 231848 (office). *E-mail:* chancery@durban-archdiocese.co.za (office).

NAPIERALSKI, Grzegorz Bernard, MA; Polish politician; b. 18 March 1974, Szczecin; m. Małgorzata Juras; two d.; ed Mechanics School, Szczecin, Univ. of Szczecin; Sec. of Szczecin br. of Social Democracy of the Repub. of Poland (later became Democratic Left Alliance—SLD) 1995–99, Vice-Chair. 2004–05, Sec. Gen. 2005–08, Chair. 2008–11; became aide to Voivod in Zachodniopomorskie Voivodship 2002; mem. Sejm (Parl.) 2004–, Chair. SLD Parl. group 2009–; unsuccessful cand. in presidential election 2010. *Address:* Democratic Left Alliance (Sojusz Lewicy Demokratycznej), ul. Wiejska 4/6/8, 00-902 Warsaw, Poland (office). *Telephone:* (22) 6210341 (office). *Fax:* (22) 6216069 (office). *E-mail:* rk@sld.org.pl (office). *Website:* www.sld.org.pl (office); www.napieralski.com.pl.

NAPOLITANO, Giorgio; Italian politician and head of state; *President;* b. 29 June 1925, Naples; m. Clio Maria Bittoni; two s.; ed Univ. of Naples Frederico II; joined Italian Communist Party (PCI) 1945, mem. Nat. Cttee, subsequently responsible for Comm. for Southern Italy 1956, then Sec. for Naples and Caserta, coordinator of Party Sec.'s Office and Political Office 1966–69, responsible for culture and later econ. policy and int. relations during 1970s and 80s; joined Democratic Party of the Left (later Democrats of the Left) following dissolution of PCI, 1981; elected to Chamber of Deputies 1953, Pres. 1992–94; Minister of the Interior 1996–98; MEP 1999–2004; Senator for Life 2005–; Pres. of Italy 2006–; Dr hc (Università degli Studi di Bari) 2004; Dan David Prize 2010. *Publications:* Movimento Operaio e Industria di Stato 1962, Intervista sul PCI (jtly) 1975, In Mezzo al Guado 1979, Oltre i Vecchi Confini 1988, Europa e America dopo l'89 1992, Dove va la Repubblica – Una Transizione Incompiuta 1994, Europa Politica 2002, Dal PCI al Socialismo Europeo: Un'Autobiografia Politica 2005. *Address:* Office of the President, Palazzo del Quirinale, 00187 Rome, Italy (office). *Telephone:* (06) 46991 (office). *Fax:* (06) 46993125 (office). *E-mail:* presidenza .repubblica@quirinale.it (office). *Website:* www.quirinale.it (office).

NAPOLITANO, Janet Ann, BS, JD; American lawyer, university administrator and fmr government official; *President, University of California;* b. 29 Nov. 1957, New York, NY; d. of Leonard Michael Napolitano and Jane Marie Napolitano (née Winer); ed Santa Clara Univ., Univ. of Virginia Law School; grew up in Pittsburgh, Pa and Albuquerque, NM; served as a clerk for Judge Mary M. Schroeder on US Court of Appeals for the Ninth Circuit; Assoc., Lewis & Roca (law firm), Phoenix, Ariz. 1984–89, Partner 1989–93, attorney 1997–98; US Attorney, Phoenix 1993–97; Attorney-Gen. of Ariz. 1999–2002; Gov. of Ariz. (first woman) 2003–09; Sec. of Homeland Security, Washington, DC 2009–13 (resgnd); Pres. Univ. of California (system of 10 campuses) 2013–; mem. Ariz. Bar Assen, Maricopa Co. Bar Assen, American Judicature Soc., Ariz. Women Lawyers' Assen, Ariz. Women's Forum, Charter 100; Fellow, Ariz. Bar Foundation; Democrat; Truman Scholar from NM, Santa Clara Univ. 1977, Leader of Distinction, Anti-Defamation League, Woman of Distinction, Crohns and Colitis Disease Foundation, Women Making History Award, Nat. Museum of Women's History, ranked by Forbes magazine amongst The World's 100 Most Powerful Women (51st) 2009, (13th) 2010, (15th) 2011, (ninth) 2012, (eighth) 2013. *Publications:* numerous contribs to legal journals. *Leisure interests:* hiking, trekking, whitewater rafting, travel, reading, film, sports including basketball, tennis and softball. *Address:* Office of the President, University of California, Franklin Building, 1111 Franklin Street, Oakland, CA 94607-5200, USA (office). *E-mail:* president@ucop.edu (office). *Website:* www.universityofcalifornia.edu (office).

NAQI, Abbas Ali, BComm; Kuwaiti government official and international organization official; *Secretary General, Organization of Arab Petroleum Exporting Countries;* b. 1947; ed Kuwait Univ., Univ. of Southern California, USA; Financial Accountant, State Budget, Ministry of Finance and Oil 1971–75, Controller, Oil and Gas Marketing, Ministry of Oil 1975–81, Controller, Int. Relations and Orgs Dept 1981–84, Dir Econ. Planning and Analysis Dept 1984–89, Dir Oil Accounting and Financial Analysis Dept 1989–94, Asst Under-Sec. for Econ. Affairs 1994–2007, Under-Sec. 2007–08; Sec. Gen. Org. of Arab Petroleum Exporting Countries (OAPEC) 2008–, mem. Exec. Bd representing Kuwait 2000–08; Chair. Kuwaiti Nat. Cttee for UN Convention on Climate Change 1994–; Vice-Pres. representing Asia, Second UN Convention on Climate Change 1996; Head of Jt Exec. Cttee, Aramco Overseas Co. 2000–02; mem. Bd of Dirs Arab Maritime Petroleum Transport Co. 1977–96, Kuwait Nat. Petroleum Co. 1995–98, Kuwait Oil Co. 1998–2002, Arab Petroleum Investments Corpn 1996–, Kuwait Gulf Oil Co. 2004–07, Kuwait Nat. Petroleum Corpn 2007–; mem. UN Cttee for Sustainable Devt, Kuwait Accountant Soc. *Address:* Organization of Arab Petroleum Exporting Countries, PO Box 20501, Safat 13066, Kuwait (office). *Telephone:* 24959000 (office). *Fax:* 24959755 (office). *E-mail:* oateefa@oapecorg.org (office). *Website:* www .oapecorg.org (office).

NARANG, Gopi Chand, MA, PhD; Indian academic and writer; *Professor Emeritus, University of Delhi;* b. 11 Feb. 1931, Dukki, Baluchistan, British India; s. of Dharam Chand Narang and Tekan Bai; m. Manorma Narang; two s.; ed Univ. of Delhi, Indiana Univ., USA; Urdu writer; Lecturer, St Stephen's Coll., Delhi 1957–58; Lecturer, Univ. of Delhi 1959–61, Reader of Urdu 1961–73, Prof. of Urdu 1985–2005, Prof. Emer. 2005–; Prof. and Head, Jamia Millia Islamia Univ.

1974–85, Acting Vice-Chancellor 1981–82; Visiting Prof., Univ. of Wisconsin at Madison, USA 1963–65, Univ. of Minnesota 1968–70, Univ. of Oslo, Norway 1997; Chair Prof., Central Univ., Hyderabad 2011–; Vice-Pres. Sahitya Akademi 1998–2002, Pres. 2003–07, Fellow 2007–; mem. Nat. Book Trust 1997–2007; mem. Advisory Bd T.V. Urdu Channel, Doordarshan 2008–; mem. Advisory Cttee on Culture, Govt of India 2008–; mem. Cen. Advisory Bd of Educ., Govt of India 2009–; Fellow, Royal Asiatic Soc., London, UK 1963–72; Hon. DLitt (Central Univ. of Hyderabad) 2007, (Aligarh Muslim Univ.) 2009, (Manulana Azad Nat. Urdu Univ.) 2009; Ghalib Award 1962, 1985, Nat. Award 1977, Iqbal Centenary Gold Medal 1977, Mir Award 1977, Urdu-Hindi Sahitya Cttee Award 1985, Amir Khusrau Award 1987, Canadian Acad. of Urdu Language and Literature Award 1987, Padma Shri 1991, Rajiv Gandhi Award 1994, Sahitya Akademi Award 1995, Rockefeller Foundation Fellowship 1997, Khwaja Ashkar Husain Award 2000, Indira Gandhi Memorial Fellowship 2002–04, Bapu Reddy Jaatheeya Sahiti Puraskaram 2003, Zainabia Trust Award 2003, Padma Bhushan 2004, Mazzini Gold Medal, Italian Govt 2005, Sahir Ludhianvi Award 2005, Bahadurshah Zafar Award 2010, Iqbal Samman 2012, Moortidevi Award of Jnanpith 2012, Sitara-e Imtiaz, Govt of Pakistan 2012, Kusumanjali Sahitya Samman 2013. *Publications:* in Urdu: Hindustani Qisson se Makhuz Urdu Mansnawiyan 1959, 2002, Imla Nama 1974, Puranon ki Kahaniyan 1976, Wazahati Kitabiyat 1976, Safar Ashna 1982, Iqbal ka Fan 1983, Usloobiyat-e-Mir 1985, Naya Urdu Afsana 1986, Saniha-e-Karbala bataur She'ri Isti'ara 1986, Amir Khusrau ka Hindavi Kalaam 1987, Urdu ki Nai Kitab 1989, Adabi Tanqeed aur Usloobiyaat 1989, Qaari Asaas Tanqeed 1992, Saakhtiyaat, Pas-Saakhtiyaat aur Mashriqi She'riyaat 1995, Urdu Maba'd-e-Jadidiyat par Mukalama 1998, Urdu Ghazal aur Hindustani Zehn-o-Tahzib 2002, Hindustan ki Tehreek-e-Azadi aur Urdu Shairi 2004, Taraqqi Pasandi Jadidiyat Ma'bad Jadidiyat 2004, Jadidiat ke Baad 2005, Anis-o-Dabir 2005, Wali Dakni 2005, Urdu Zaban aur Lisaniyaat 2006, Sheriyat Tashkeel o Tanqeed 2009, Dekhna Taqreer ki Lazzat 2010, Khwaja Ahmad Faruqi ke Khutoot Gopi Chand Narang ke Naam 2010, Kaghaz-e Atish Zadah 2011, Tapishnama-e Tamanna 2012, Ghalib: Maani-afrini, Jadliyati Waza', Shunyata aur Sheriyat 2013; in English: as ed.: Karkhandari Dialect of Delhi 1961, Readings in Literary Urdu Prose 1967, Anthology of Modern Urdu Poetry 1981, Contribution of Writers to Indian Freedom Movement 1985, Rajinder Singh Bedi: Selected Short Stories 1989, Krishnan Chander: Selected Short Stories 1990, Balwant Singh: Selected Short Stories 1996, Urdu Language and Literature: Critical Perspectives 1991, Encyclopedia of Indian Literature (four vols) 1987–94, Masterpieces of Indian Literature (three vols) 1997, Let's Learn Urdu 2000. *Address:* D-252 Sarvodaya Enclave, New Delhi 110 017, India. *Telephone:* (11) 26511460; (11) 26568956. *E-mail:* narang_5@yahoo.co.in. *Website:* gopichandnarang.com.

NARASIMHAN, Maidavolu; Indian government official; b. 3 June 1927, Bangalore; s. of M. Seshachelapati; m. Shanthy Sundaresan; one s.; ed Presidency Coll., Madras and St John's Coll., Cambridge, UK; joined Reserve Bank of India, Bombay 1950, Sec. 1967, Gov. May–Nov. 1977; Chief of S Asia Div., IMF 1960–63, Exec. Dir of IMF for India, Bangladesh and Sri Lanka 1980–82; Exec. Dir IBRD 1978–80; Additional Sec. Ministry of Finance 1972, Sec. Banking Dept 1976–78, Sec. Dept of Econ. Affairs 1982; Finance Sec., Govt of India 1983; Prin. Admin. Staff Coll. of India, Hyderabad 1983–85, Chair. 1991–; Vice-Pres. Asian Devt Bank, Manila 1985–88; Norton Prize, Madras Univ., Padma Vibhushan 2000, Telugu Talli Award 2001, Lifetime Achievement Award 2001. *Publications include:* World Economic Environment and Prospects for India 1988, Economic Reforms: Development and Finance 2002, From Reserve Bank to Finance Ministry and Beyond: Some Reminiscences 2002. *Leisure interests:* reading, music. *Address:* 'Sukruti', 8-2-681/7, Road No. 12, Banjara Hills, Hyderabad 500 034, India (home). *Telephone:* (40) 23310994 (office); (40) 23396511 (home). *Fax:* (40) 23310994 (office); (40) 23312954.

NARASIMHAN, Ekkadu Srinivasan Lakshmi, BSc, LLB, MA; Indian lawyer, diplomatist and politician; *Governor of Andhra Pradesh;* b. 1946; m. Vimala Narasimhan; ed Madras Univ., Madras Law Univ., Nat. Defence Coll., Delhi; joined Indian Police Service in 1968, served in various capacities in Police and Intelligence Bureau services, Head of Intelligence Bureau –2006; served in Ministry of External Affairs, first Sec., Embassy in Moscow 1981–84; fmr Dir-Gen. of Police in Chhattisgarh; Gov. of Chhattisgarh 2007–10, of Andhra Pradesh 2009–. *Address:* Office of the Governor, Raj Bhavan Rd, Hyderabad, Andhra Pradesh, India (office). *Telephone:* (40) 23310521 (office). *Fax:* (40) 23312650 (office). *E-mail:* governor@ap.nic.in (office).

NARASIMHAN, Mudumbai Seshachalu, PhD, FRS; Indian mathematician and academic; *Honorary Fellow, Tata Institute of Fundamental Research;* b. 1932, Thandarai, Tamil Nadu; ed Loyola Coll., Chennai, Univ. of Bombay; fmr Prof. at Tata Inst. of Fundamental Research, Mumbai mid-1960s–1992, now Hon. Fellow; Head of Research Group in Math., Int. Centre for Theoretical Physics, Trieste 1992; pioneer of study of moduli spaces of holomorphic vector bundles on projective varieties; Shanti Swarup Bhatnagar Prize for Math. 1975, Third World Acad. Award for Math. 1987, Padma Bhushan 1990, King Faisal Int. Prize for Science, King Faisal Foundation (co-recipient) 2006. *Address:* Tata Institute of Fundamental Research, Homi Bhabha Road, Mumbai 400 005, India (office). *Telephone:* (22) 22782000 (office). *Fax:* (22) 22804610 (office). *E-mail:* webmaster@tifr.res.in (office). *Website:* www.tifr.res.in (office).

NARAYAN, Shovana, MA; Indian dancer and government official; m. Dr Herbert Traxl; ed Miranda House, Univ. of Delhi; officer, Indian Audits and Accounts Service 1976–; f. Asavari Centre of Dance; fmr Deputy Dir-Gen. Bharat Sanchar Nigam Ltd; fmr Special Dir Gen. Organising Cttee Commonwealth Games 2010; Visiting Lecturer, Univ. of Vienna, Austria; holds two annual dance festivals; mem. Delhi Public School Soc. 1998–; Padma Shri 1992, Sangeet Natak Akademi Award 1999–2000, Parishad Samman, Govt of Delhi, Indira Priyadarshini Award, Rajiv Gandhi Puraskar, Rajdhani Ratna Award, Bihar Gaurav Puraskar, Oisca Award, Dadabhai Naoroji Award, IMM Award for Excellence. *Dance performances include:* Festival of Arts of India, Théatre de la ville, Paris 1973, Sanskritik Festival of Arts of India, UK 1976, 1978, 1986, Festival of Arts of India, Switzerland 1976, 1980, Reykjavik Icelandic Arts Festival 1982, India Festival, Festival of Arts of India 1987–88, Salzburg Landestheatre, Austria, 1987, Carinthian Summer Festival, Villach, Austria, Finkenstein Summer Festival, Programmes in Sweden, Netherlands, Belgium, Germany and Poland 1999, World

Hindi Conf., London, Manchester, Netherlands 1999, int. festivals in Africa (Algeria, Ghana, Zambia, Kenya, Namibia), in Europe (Germany, Austria, Netherlands, Slovenia, Sweden, Belgium, Poland, Italy, Hungary, Czech Repub.), in SE Asia (Singapore, Thailand, Indonesia, Malaysia), in Middle East (Syria, Abu Dhabi, Dubai), in Cen. Asia (Uzbekistan: Tashkent, Bukhara, Kazakhstan: Almaty, Kyrgyzstan: Bishkek, Frunze, Turkmenistan: Ashgabat), in South Asia (Nepal, Sri Lanka and Bangladesh) during the period 1976–2000, Thailand 2003, Asian Alaskan Dance Festival 2003, Nepal, Bangladesh 2006. *Publications include:* Indian Classical Dances, Performing Arts in India: A Policy Perspective, Indian Theatre and Dance Traditions, Kathak: Rhythmic Echoes and Reflections, The Dance Legacy of Patliputra, Kathak, Sterling Book of Indian Classical Dances, Folk Dance Traditions of India, Meandering Pastures of Memories 2006. *Leisure interest:* charity work. *Address:* D-II-301, Pandara Road, New Delhi 110 003, India. *Telephone:* (11) 23387686. *E-mail:* shov2@hotmail.com. *Website:* www.shovananarayan.com.

NARAYANAN, Mayankote Kelath, BA (Econs); Indian government official; *Governor of West Bengal;* b. 10 March 1934, New Delhi; s. of the late C. B. Nair and M. K. Kallianikvity Amma; m. Padmini Narayanan; one s. one d.; Head of Indian Intelligence Bureau 1987–90, 1991–92; Special Adviser to Prime Minister Manmohan Singh with rank of Minister of State 2004–; Nat. Security Adviser to the Prime Minister 2005–10; Gov. of West Bengal 2010–, acting Gov. of Sikkim 2010; Padmashree Award 1992. *Address:* Office of the Governor, Raj Bhavan, Kolkata 700 001, West Bengal (office); 10 Teen Murti Lane, New Delhi 110 011, India (home). *Telephone:* (33) 22001641 (office); (11) 23019856 (home). *Fax:* (33) 22002444 (office). *E-mail:* mk.narayanan@pmo.nic.in (office). *Website:* www.pmindia.nic.in (office).

NARDELLI, Robert L., BS, MBA; American business executive; b. 17 May 1948, Old Forge, Pa; m. Sue Nardelli 1971; four c.; ed Western Illinois Univ., Univ. of Louisville; with General Electric (GE) Corpn 1971–88; Exec. Vice-Pres. and Gen. Man. Case Corpn, Racine, Wis. 1988–91; returned to GE and served in various exec. positions, including CEO Canadian Appliance Mfg Co., Toronto 1991–92, GE Transportation Systems, Erie, Pa 1992–95, GE Power Systems 1995–2000, Sr Vice-Pres. GE and mem. Bd of Dirs GE Capital Corpn; Pres. Home Depot Inc. 2000–02, Pres. and Chair. 2002–07 (resgnd); Chair. and CEO Chrysler LLC, Auburn Hills, Mich. 2007–09; mem. Bd of Dirs The Coca-Cola Co. 2002–05; mem. Pres.'s Council on Service and Civic Participation 2003; mem. Advisory Bd Univ. of Louisville Grad. School of Business; Dr hc (Univ. of Louisville) 2001, (Siena Coll.) 2001, (Western Illinois Univ.) 2002. *Address:* c/o Chrysler LLC, 1000 Chrysler Drive, Auburn Hills, MI 48326-2766, USA.

NAREV, Ian M., BA, LLB (Hons), LLM, LLM; New Zealand business executive; *Managing Director and CEO, Commonwealth Bank Group;* m.; several d.; ed Univ. of Auckland, Univ. of Cambridge, UK, New York Univ. (Hauser Scholar), USA; fmr Ed.-in-Chief Univ. of Auckland Law Review; lawyer specializing in mergers and acquisitions –1998; Partner, McKinsey & Co., worked in New York, Sydney and Auckland offices 1998–2007, Global Partner 2003–07, Head of New Zealand office 2005–07, joined Commonwealth Bank Group 2007, Group Head of Strategy 2007–09, Group Exec., Business and Pvt. Banking 2009–11, Man. Dir and CEO 2011–; mem. Bd of Dirs Commonwealth Bank Foundation (Chair.), Financial Markets Foundation for Children; Chair. Springboard Trust; Trustee, Louise Perkins Foundation; Amb. for Australian Indigenous Educ. Foundation. *Address:* Commonwealth Bank of Australia, Level 7, 48 Martin Place, Sydney 1155, Australia (office). *Telephone:* (2) 9378-2000 (office). *Fax:* (2) 9378-3317 (office). *E-mail:* info@commbank.com.au (office). *Website:* www.commbank.com.au (office).

NARIMAN, Fali Sam, BA, LLB; Indian lawyer and politician; *President, Bar Association of India;* b. 10 Jan. 1929, Rangoon, Burma (now Myanmar); m. Bapsi F. Nariman 1955; one s. one d.; ed St Xavier's Coll., Bombay, Govt Law Coll., Bombay; advocate, High Court of Bombay 1950; Sr Advocate, Supreme Court of India 1971–; Additional Solicitor Gen. of India 1972–75; mem. Rajya Sabha (Parl.) 1999–2005 (mem. Rules Cttee, Ethics Cttee, Consultative Cttee for Ministry of External Affairs, Standing Cttee of Parl. on External Affairs); Founder Chair. Law Asscn for Asia and the Pacific (LAWASIA) Standing Cttee on Human Rights 1979, Pres. LAWASIA 1985–87; Pres. Bar Asscn of India 1991–, Int. Council for Commercial Arbitration 1994–2002; Chair. Exec. Cttee Int. Comm. of Jurists, Geneva 1995–97; Co-Chair. Int. Bar Asscn Human Rights Inst. 2001–03; Vice-Chair. Int. Court of Arbitration of the ICC, Paris 1989–2002; mem. Delhi Legal Aid and Advice Bd 1981–, London Court of Int. Arbitration 1988–2005, Advisory Council of Jurists of the Asia-Pacific Forum of Nat. Human Rights Insts 1999–, Press Comm. of India, Advisory Bd of UNCTAD, Governing Council Body of Nat. Law School Univ., Bangalore, Gen. Council of West Bengal Nat. Univ. of Judicial Sciences, Kolkata; Founding mem. People's Union for Civil Liberties; Leader, Indian Del. of Lawyers to 59th Int. Law Asscn Conf., Belgrade, Serbia and to Int. Bar Asscn Conf., Berlin, Germany; Hon. mem. Int. Comm. of Jurists, Geneva 1998–; several nat. and int. awards, including Kinlock Forbes Gold Medal and Prize for Roman Law and Jurisprudence 1950, Padma Bhushan 1991, named a Living Legend of the Law by the Int. Bar Asscn 1995, Global Medal Laurel 1998, Peter Gruber Foundation Justice Prize 2002, Padma Vibhushan 2007. *Publications include:* India's Legal System: Can It Be Saved? 2006; numerous articles on politics, religion, the constitution and human rights. *Address:* Bar Association of India, 93 Lawyers Chambers, Supreme Court of India, New Delhi 110 001, India (office). *Telephone:* (11) 3385902 (office). *Fax:* (11) 3329273 (office).

NARITA, Yoriaki, DJur; Japanese professor of law; *Advisor, Japan Energy Law Institute;* b. 20 Jan. 1928, Tokyo; s. of Masaji Narita and Masako Narita; m. Akiko Narita 1956; two d.; ed Tokyo Univ.; Lecturer, Faculty of Econs, Yokohama Nat. Univ. 1929, Asst Prof. 1933, Prof. 1943, Dean of Econs 1982–86, Dir and Prof., Grad. School of Int. and Business Law 1990–93; Advisor, Japan Energy Law Inst. 1993–. *Publications:* Introduction to Modern Administrative Law, Legal Theories and Reform of Local Self-government, Land Policy and Law. *Leisure interest:* gardening. *Address:* Japan Energy Law Institute, Tanakayama Bldg, 7F, 4-1-20, Toranomon Minato-ku, Tokyo 105-0001, Japan (office). *Telephone:* (3) 3434-7701 (office). *Fax:* (3) 3434-7703 (office). *Website:* www.jeli.gr.jp (office).

NARLIKAR, Jayant Vishnu, PhD, ScD (Cantab.); Indian cosmologist and academic; *Professor Emeritus, Inter-University Centre for Astronomy and Astro-*

physics; b. 19 July 1938, Kolhapur; s. of Prof. Vishnu Vasudeva Narlikar and Sumati Narlikar; m. Mangala S. Rajwade 1966; three d.; ed Banaras Hindu Univ. and Fitzwilliam Coll., Cambridge, UK; Berry Ramsey Fellow, King's Coll., Cambridge 1963–69, Sr Research Fellow 1969–72, Grad. Staff mem., Inst. of Theoretical Astronomy, Univ. of Cambridge 1966–72, Prof., Tata Inst. of Fundamental Research 1972–89; mem. Science Advisory Council to the Prime Minister 1986–90; Founder-Dir Inter-Univ. Centre for Astronomy and Astrophysics (IUCAA), Pune 1988–2003, Homi Bhabha Prof. 1998–2003, Prof. Emer. 2003–; Pres. Cosmology Comm. of Int. Astronomical Union 1994–97; Fellow, Indian Nat. Science Acad., Indian Acad. of Sciences, Nat. Acad. of Sciences (India); Assoc., Royal Astronomical Soc., London, Acad. of Sciences for the Developing World; Hon. Prof., Jawaharlal Nehru Centre for Advanced Scientific Research 1990–99; Dr hc from several Indian univs and from Univ. of Natal, South Africa; Tyson Medal 1960, Smith's Prize 1962, Padma Bhushan 1965, S. S. Bhatnagar Award 1978, Rashtrabhushan Award of FIE Foundation 1981, Rathindra Award 1985, INSA Vainu Bappu Award 1988, INSA Indira Gandhi Award for Science Popularization 1990, UNESCO Kalinga Award for Science Popularization 1996, Padma Vibhushan 2004, Janssen Medal, French Astronomical Soc., Maharashtra Bhushan 2011. *Radio:* series for children in Marathi (All India Radio) early 1980's. *Television:* Brahmand (The Universe) (series on nat. channel in Hindi) 1990's. *Publications include:* articles on cosmology, general relativity and gravitation, quantum theory, astrophysics etc. in the Proceedings of the Royal Soc., London, The Monthly Notices of the Royal Astronomical Soc., London, The Astrophysical Journal, Nature, Observatory and scientific articles in various magazines; Action at a Distance in Physics and Cosmology (with Sir F. Hoyle) 1974, The Structure of the Universe 1977, General Relativity and Cosmology 1978, The Physics Astronomy Frontier (with Sir F. Hoyle) 1980, Violent Phenomena in the Universe 1982, The Lighter Side of Gravity 1982, Introduction to Cosmology 1983, From Black Clouds to Black Holes 1985, Gravity Gauge Theories and Quantum Cosmology (with T. Padmanabhan) 1986, The Primeval Universe 1988, Highlights in Gravitation and Cosmology 1989, Philosophy of Science: Perspectives from Natural and Social Sciences 1992, Seven Wonders of the Cosmos 1999, Quasars and Active Galactic Nuclei: An Introduction 1999, The Scientific Edge 2003, A Different Approach to Cosmology 2000, Current Issues in Cosmology 2006, Facts and Speculations in Cosmology 2008, An Introduction to Relativity 2010. *Leisure interests* reading, going for walks, listening to music. *Address:* Inter-University Centre for Astronomy and Astrophysics, Post Bag 4, Ganeshkhind, Pune University Campus, Pune 411 007, India (office). *Telephone:* (20) 25604100 (office). *Fax:* (20) 25604698 (office). *E-mail:* jayant@iucaa.ernet.in (office). *Website:* www.iucaa.ernet.in (office).

NARRO ROBLES, José, MD; Mexican physician, government official and university administrator; *Rector, Universidad Nacional Autónoma de México;* b. 5 Dec. 1948, Saltillo, Coahuila; ed Universidad Nacional Autónoma de México, Univ. of Birmingham, UK; fmr Gen. Dir of Health Services of Mexico City; fmr Sec.-Gen. Mexican Inst. of Social Security; fmr Under-Sec. of Migratory Services and Population, Ministry of the Interior (Secretaría de Gobernación), later Under-Sec. of Health, Fed. Secr. of Health; Dir Faculty of Medicine, Universidad Nacional Autónoma de México 2003–07, Rector Universidad Nacional Autónoma de México 2007–; Adviser to WHO; mem. Academia Nacional de Medicina (Nat. Acad. of Medicine). *Address:* Office of the Rector, Universidad Nacional Autónoma de México, Ciudad Universitaria, Del. Coyoacán, 04510 México DF, Mexico (office). *Telephone:* (55) 5622-0958 (office). *Fax:* (55) 5616-0245 (office). *Website:* www.dgi.unam.mx/rector (office).

NARS, Kari, DrSc; Finnish banker; m.; two c.; ed Univ. of Helsinki, Helsinki Swedish School of Econs; economist, Bank of Finland 1964–66, Sec. of Bank 1967, Head Foreign Exchange Policy Dept 1972–75, Dir (Int.) 1977–83; Exec. Man. Dir Bank of Helsinki 1984–85; Economist, IMF, Washington, DC 1967–71; Dir Council of Econ. Orgs 1975–76; Dir of Finance, Ministry of Finance 1986–91, 1994; Exec. Dir EBRD, London 1991–94; Chair Admin. Cttee, Social Devt Fund of Council of Europe 1993, fmrly Pres. Governing Bd, Council of Europe Devt Bank; Alt. Gov. for Finland, IMF 1981–82; mem. Bd Nordic Investment Bank 1989–91; Co-Chair. Govt Borrowers' Forum 1988–91. *Publications include:* Corporate Foreign Exchange Strategies 1980, Foreign Financing and Foreign Exchange Strategy (co-author) 1981, Financial Sector Study on Mozambique – A World Bank Study (co-author) 1992, Cross Currency Swaps (contrib.) 1992; numerous articles and speeches. *Address:* c/o Ministry of Finance, Snellmaninkatu 1A, 00170 Helsinki, Finland.

NARUHITO, Crown Prince, MA; Japanese; b. 23 Feb. 1960, Tokyo; s. of Emperor Akihito (q.v.) and Empress Michiko; m. Masako Owada (now Crown Princess Masako) 1993; one d.; ed Gakushuin Univ., Merton Coll., Oxford, UK; invested as Crown Prince following the death of his grandfather, Emperor Shōwa in 1989, 23 Feb. 1991; mem. IOC 1998–; Patron Global Water Partnership, Japanese Olympic Games Cttee –1998; Hon. Vice-Pres. Japanese Red Cross Soc. 1994; Hon. Pres. Third World Water Forum 2003, Expo 2005, UN Sec.-Gen.'s Advisory Bd on Water and Sanitation; Hon. mem. World Comm. on Water for the 21st Century; Grand Cross, Order of Christ (Portugal) 1993, Grand Decoration of Honour in Gold with Sash, Decoration of Honour for Services to the Repub. of Austria 1999, Collar, Order of al-Khalifa (Bahrain), Grand Cordon, Order of Leopold (Belgium), Kt, Order of the Elephant (Denmark) 2004, Kt Grand Cross, Order of Merit of the Italian Repub., Grand Cross, Order of the Crown (Netherlands), Kt Grand Cross, Order of St Olav (Norway), Necklace of Merit (Qatar), Grand Cross, Order of Charles III (Spain) 2008, Kt, Royal Order of the Seraphim (Sweden), Grand Collar, Royal Order of Pouono (Tonga); hon. degree from Univ. of Oxford. *Publications:* Temuzu to tomoni: Eikoku no ninenkan 1993, The Thames and I: A Memoir of Two Years at Oxford (with Hugh Cortazzi) 2006; several papers. *Leisure interests:* music, playing viola and violin, jogging, hiking, mountaineering, tennis. *Address:* The Imperial Palace, 1-1 Chiyoda, Chiyoda-ku, Tokyo 100, Japan. *Telephone:* (3) 32131111.

NARVEKAR, Prabhakar R., BCom, MCom; American (b. Indian) international civil servant; *Vice-Chairman, Centennial Group of Consultants;* b. 5 Jan. 1932, Mumbai; s. of Ramkrishna Manjunath Narvekar and Indira Narvekar; m. (wife deceased); one s. one d.; ed Bombay, Columbia and Oxford Univs; Research Asst IMF 1953; subsequently held various positions in Asian and European Depts of

IMF; Dir Asian Dept, IMF 1986–91, Special Adviser to Man. Dir 1991–94, Deputy Man. Dir 1994–97; Special Adviser to Pres. of Indonesia 1998; Sr Adviser to the Pres. Nikko Securities, Japan 1997–2004; Vice-Chair. and Founding Dir Centennial Group of Consultants. *Leisure interest:* reading. *Address:* Centennial Group, 2600 Virginia Avenue, Washington, DC 20037 (office). *Telephone:* (202) 393-6663 (office). *Fax:* (202) 393-6556 (office). *E-mail:* narvekarpr@yahoo.com (home). *Website:* www.centennial-group.com (office).

NARYSHKIN, Sergei Yevgenyevich; Russian engineer and government official; *Chairman, Gosudarstvennaya Duma (State Duma);* b. 27 Oct. 1954, Leningrad (now St Petersburg); ed Leningrad Inst. of Mechanics, Petersburg Int. Man. Inst.; apptd Deputy Vice-Rector of Leningrad Polytechnical Inst. 1982; served in the Soviet Embassy in Brussels 1980s; worked in Cttee for Economy and Finance, Office of the Mayor of St Petersburg 1992–95; Head of Foreign Investments Dept, Promstroybank 1995–97; with Leningrad Regional Govt, positions including Head Investments Dept, Head of Int. Affairs Cttee 1997–98; Chair. Cttee for External Economic and Int. Relations, Leningrad Regional Govt 1998–2004; Deputy Head of Govt Staff, Russian Fed. 2004, Chief of Staff 2004–07, Deputy Prime Minister responsible for external econ. activity 2007–08; Head of Presidential Admin 2008–11; Chair. Historical Truth Comm. 2009–12; Chair. Gosudarstvennaya Duma (State Duma) 2011–; Chair. Channel One 2004–; apptd Deputy Chair. Rosneft 2004; fmr mem. Bd of Dirs Sovkomflot. *Address:* Office of the Chairman, Gosudarstvennaya Duma, 103265 Moscow, Okhotnyi ryad 1, Russia (office). *Telephone:* (495) 692-62-66 (office). *Fax:* (495) 697-42-58 (office). *E-mail:* stateduma@duma.gov.ru (office). *Website:* www.duma.gov.ru (office).

NASARI, Muhammad Ashraf; Afghan politician; *Governor of Zabul Province;* b. Paktia Prov.; fmr mem. Ittihad-e Islami; fmr Gov. Badghis Prov.; Gov. Zabul Prov. 2009–. *Address:* Office of the Governor, Qalat, Zabul Province, Afghanistan (office).

NASCIMENTO, Lopo Fortunato Ferreira do; Angolan politician; *Chairman, National Centre for Social and Development Studies;* b. 10 July 1940, Luanda; s. of Vaz I. do Nascimento and Arminda F. do Nascimento; m. Maria do Carmo Assis 1969; two s. two d.; ed Commercial Inst., Luanda; mem. Presidential Collegiate in transitional govt before independence from Portugal Jan.–Nov. 1975; Prime Minister of Angola 1975–78; Minister of Internal Trade 1977–78, of Foreign Trade 1979–82, of Planning 1980–86; Deputy Exec. Sec. UN ECA, Addis Ababa 1979; Head Fifth Mil. Region 1986–90; Gov. Huila Prov. 1986–90; Presidential Adviser for Special Political Affairs 1990; Head Govt Del. at negotiations on a peace agreement for Angola 1991; Minister of Territorial Admin. 1991; Sec.-Gen. Movimento Popular de Libertação de Angola –1993; Deputy Speaker of Parl.; currently MP and Chair. Nat. Centre for Social and Devt Studies. *Leisure interests:* music, writing, walking. *Address:* 93 Amilcar Cabral Street, First Floor, Luanda (office); 47 Ambuíla Street, PO Box 136, Luanda, Angola (home). *Telephone:* (2) 399640 (office); (222) 339314 (office); (222) 444229 (home); 91-205732 (mobile); 92-3642051 (mobile). *Fax:* (2) 399639 (office); (222) 337551 (office); (2) 443088 (home); (2) 328451 (home). *E-mail:* loponascimento1@netcabo.ao (home); mcir@netangola .com (office).

NASCIMENTO, Milton; Brazilian singer, songwriter, composer and musician (piano, accordion, guitar, bass guitar); b. 26 Oct. 1942, Rio de Janeiro; one s.; DJ, announcer, dir, Rádio Três Pontas, early 1960s; composer 1963–; played Carnegie Hall 1994; collaborations with Art Blakey, Laudir De Oliviera, Deodato, João Gilberto, Herbie Hancock, Airto Moreira, Flora Purim, Charlie Rouse, Wayne Shorter, Roberto Silva; Chevalier des Arts et des Lettres 1984, Ordem do Rio Branco 1985; Dr hc (Universidade Federal de Ouro Preto) 2000; Festival of Brazilian Popular Music Best Performer 1965, Villa-Lobos Prize 1977, Santos Dumont Medal 1998, Sisac Gold Medal, Chile 2000, Latin Grammy Awards for Best Brazilian song (for Tristesse) 2004, (for A Festa) 2005, Gold Medal, Acad. des Arts, Sciences et Belles-Lettres (France) 2006. *Recordings include:* albums: Milton Nascimento (aka Travessia) 1967, Courage 1968, Milton Nascimento 1969, Milton 1970, Clube Da Esquina – Milton Nascimento E Lo Borges 1972, Milagre Dos Peixes 1973, Milagre Dos Peixes – Gravado Ao Vivo – Milton Nascimento E Som Imaginário 1974, Native Dancer 1974, Minas 1975, Geraes 1976, Clube Da Esquina Dois 1978, Journey To Dawn 1979, Sentinela 1980, Caçador De Mim 1981, Missa Dos Quilombos 1982, Anima 1982, Milton Nascimento Ao Vivo 1983, Encontros E Despedidas 1985, A Barca Dos Amantes 1986, Yauarete 1987, Miltons 1988, Txai 1990, O Planeta Blue Na Estrada Do Sol 1991, Angelus 1993, Amigo 1995, Nascimento (Grammy Award for Best World Music Record of the Year 1998) 1997, Tambores De Minas – Ao Vivo 1998, Crooner (Latin Grammy Award for Best Brazilian Contemporary Pop Album 2000) 1999, Gil E Milton (with Gilberto Gil) 2001, Pietá 2002, Bossas Novas (with Jobim Trio) 2008, . . .E a Gente Sonhando 2010. *Address:* c/o Tribo Produções Artísticas, Avenida Armando Lombardi 800, gr 225, Barra da Tijuca, 22640-000 Rio de Janeiro, RJ, Brazil (office). *Telephone:* (21) 3154-8200 (office); (21) 2294-7294 (office). *Fax:* (21) 3154-8220 (office). *E-mail:* miltonnascimento@triboproducoes.com.br (office); amaurylinhares@ mpbproducoes.com.br (office). *Website:* www.triboproducoes.com.br (office); www .miltonnascimento.com.br.

NASEEM, Ahmed; Maldivian diplomatist and politician; b. 1948; m.; one s. three d.; ed Wesley Coll., Sri Lanka; joined govt service 1967, served in numerous positions including Sec., Ministry of Foreign Affairs, Under-Sec. Ministry of Fisheries (later Deputy Minister); fmr Perm. Rep., UN, New York; fmr First Sec., Embassy in Washington, DC; Dir-Gen. of Investments, Foreign Investment Services Bureau 1998–2005; Minister of State for Foreign Affairs 2008–11; Minister of Foreign Affairs 2011–12; fmr mem. Bd of Dirs Regional Centre for Strategic Studies, Sri Lanka, Maldives Asscn of Tourism Industry; joined Maldivian Democratic Party 2005. *Address:* c/o Ministry of Foreign Affairs, Boduthakurufaanu Magu, Malé 20-077, Maldives.

NASEER, Umar; Maldivian business executive, politician and fmr police officer; *Minister of Home Affairs;* ed English Prep School, Malé; conscripted into Nat. Security Service, later sent to Scotland Yard, London, UK for police training, promoted to Sergeant on return, later transferred to Maldives Water Supply Unit; opened fire safety equipment dealership Alarms Pvt. Ltd; unsuccessful cand. in parl. elections for Malé constituency; started tour co. Whale Submarine to promote underwater sightseeing, later sold his share of co. to Qasim Ibrahim; Co-founder and Pres. Islamic Democratic Party 2005–10; Vice-Pres. Dhivehi Rayyithunge

Party Sept.–Dec. 2010 (expelled); currently Interim Vice-Pres., Progressive Party of Maldives; Minister of Home Affairs 2013–. *Address:* Ministry of Home Affairs, Velaanaage Building, 10th Floor, Ameer Ahmed Magu, Malé 20-096, Maldives (office). *Telephone:* 3323820 (office). *Fax:* 3324739 (office). *E-mail:* info@ homeaffairs.gov.mv (office). *Website:* www.homeaffairs.gov.mv (office).

NASH, David, OBE, RA; British sculptor; b. 14 Nov. 1945, Surrey; s. of Lt-Col W. C. E. Nash and Dora Nash (née Vickery); m. Claire Langdown 1972; two s.; ed Brighton Coll., Kingston Art School and Chelsea School of Art; has exhibited widely in Britain, Europe, USA and Japan; first exhbn Briefly Cooked Apples, York Festival 1973; works in over 100 public collections including Tate Gallery and Guggenheim Museum; Research Fellow, Dept of Visual and Performing Arts, Univ. of Northumbria 1999–2002; Hon. Fellow, Univ. of Wales (Cardiff) 2003; Dr hc (Kingston) 1999; Hon. DH (Glamorgan) 2002. *Publications:* Forms into Time 1996, The Sculpture of David Nash 1996, Twmps 2000, Black and Light 2001, The Return of Art to Nature 2003, Pyramids Rise, Spheres Turn, Cubes Stay Still, David Nash 2008, David Nash at the Yorkshire Sculpture Park 2010, David Nash: A Natural Gallery 2013. *Address:* Capel Rhiw, Blaenau Ffestiniog, Gwynedd, LL41 3NT, Wales; c/o Annely Juda Fine Art, 23 Dering Street, London, W1S 1AW, England. *Telephone:* (20) 7629-7578 (London). *Fax:* (1766) 831179 (Blaenau Ffestiniog); (20) 7491-2139 (London).

NASH, John Forbes, Jr, MS, PhD; American mathematician, economist, scientist and academic; *Senior Research Mathematician, Department of Mathematics, Princeton University;* b. 13 June 1928, Bluefield, W Va; s. of John F. Nash and Margaret Virginia Martin Nash; m. Alicia Larde 1957; one s.; ed Carnegie Mellon Univ., Princeton Univ.; Research Asst, Instructor, Princeton Univ. 1950–51; Moore Instructor, MIT 1951–53, Asst Prof. 1953–57, Assoc. Prof. 1957–59, Research Assoc. in Math. 1966–67; Sr Research Mathematician, Princeton Univ. 1959–, Visiting mem. Inst. of Advanced Study 1956–57, 1961–62, 1963–64; mem. NAS 1996, American Acad. of Arts and Sciences, American Philosophical Soc.; Fellow, Econometric Soc.; Hon. ScD (Carnegie-Mellon) 1999; Hon. PhD (Athens) 2000; Dr hc (Naples) 2003, (Charleston) 2003, (Univ. of Medicine and Dentistry, NJ) 2008, (Hong Kong Polytechnic Univ.), (City Univ. of Hong Kong); Sloan Fellow, NSF Fellow, George Westinghouse Scholar, Von Neumann Medal, Operations Research Soc. of America, shared Nobel Prize for Econs for pioneering work on game theory 1994, Business Week Award, Erasmus Univ., Rotterdam 1998, Leroy P. Steele Prize, American Mathematical Soc. 1999. *Publications:* Essays on Game Theory, The Essential John Nash; articles on econometric and math. theory. *Address:* Department of Mathematics, Fine Hall, Room 910, Princeton University, Washington Road, Princeton, NJ 08544, USA (office). *Telephone:* (609) 258-4200 (office). *Fax:* (609) 258-1367 (office). *E-mail:* xkjfnj@princeton.edu (office). *Website:* web.math.princeton.edu/jfnj (office).

NASH, Ronald Peter, CMG, LVO, BA, MCIL; British fmr diplomatist and consultant; b. 18 Sept. 1946; m.; three s.; ed Univ. of Manchester; joined FCO 1970, Personnel Operations Dept 1970, Western Orgs Dept 1970–72, full-time Russian language training 1972–73, Second, later First Sec., Chancery, Moscow 1974–76, First Sec., UK Del., Vienna 1976–79, Western European Dept, FCO 1979–81, UN Dept 1981–83, First Sec. (Information), New Delhi 1983–86, Deputy Head of E European Dept, FCO 1986–87, Deputy Head of Mission, Vienna 1988–92, Deputy High Commr, Colombo 1992–95, Coordinator, London Peace Implementation Conf. for Bosnia 1995, Head of Human Rights Policy Dept, FCO 1996–99, Amb. to Nepal 1999–2002, to Afghanistan 2002–03, High Commr to Trinidad and Tobago 2003–06 (retd); consultant to various pvt. sector, govt and int. orgs 2006–; mem. Chartered Inst. of Linguists. *Address:* c/o Foreign and Commonwealth Office, King Charles Street, London, SW1A 2AH, England.

NASH, Steve, OC, OBC, BA; Canadian professional basketball player; b. 7 Feb. 1974, Johannesburg, SA; s. of John Nash and Jean Nash; m. Alejandra Nash (née Amarilla); two d.; ed St Michael's Univ. School, Santa Clara Univ., USA; plays point guard; selected 15th overall in Nat. Basketball Asscn (NBA) draft by Phoenix Suns 1996, played with Suns 1996–98, moved to Dallas Mavericks 1998–2004, returned to Phoenix Suns 2004–12, with Los Angeles Lakers 2012–; Capt. Canadian Men's Basketball Team, Olympic Games, Sydney 2000, qualifying stages of Athens Olympics 2004; Gen. Man. Canada's sr men's basketball team 2012–; f. Steve Nash Foundation 2001, Steve Nash Sports Club, Vancouver, Meathawk (production co.); part-Owner Vancouver Whitecaps (Major League Soccer team); Order of British Columbia 2006; Dr hc (Univ. of Victoria) 2008; NBA West Conference Player of the Year 1995, 1996, NBA Most Valuable Player Award 2005, 2006, All-Star 2002, 2003, 2005, 2006, 2007, 2008, All-NBA First Team 2005, 2006, 2007, Second Team 2008, 2010, Third Team 2002, 2003, Lou Marsh Trophy 2004, Lionel Conacher Award 2002, 2005, 2006, Canada's Most Influential Sports Figure, The Globe and Mail 2006, J. Walter Kennedy Citizenship Award 2007. *Address:* c/o Los Angeles Lakers Inc., 555 North Nash Street, El Segundo, CA 90245; Steve Nash Foundation, 3921 East 86th Avenue, Anchorage, Alaska 99507, USA. *Website:* www.stevenash.org; www.nba.com/lakers.

NASHAAT, Soha, MBA; Egyptian/Syrian banking executive; *Senior Advisor, Barclays Wealth Switzerland;* b. Kuwait; m.; ed Columbia Univ., Univ. of San Francisco, USA; Product Man. Merrill Lynch, New York 1991–97, Sales Man., Merrill Lynch Int. Private Client Group, Buenos Aires 1997–2000, Head of Int. Private Client Group in Middle East 2000–06; CEO Barclays Wealth Middle East and N Africa 2006–11; Sr Advisor and mem. Bd of Dirs Barclays Wealth Switzerland 2011–; Middle East Excellence Award Inst. Award for Woman Banker of the Year 2007. *Address:* Barclays Wealth, Barclays Bank PLC, Dubai International Financial Centre, The Gate Village, Level 6, Building No. 10, PO Box 506674, Dubai, United Arab Emirates (office). *Telephone:* 43652900 (office). *Fax:* 43652999 (office). *Website:* www.barclayswealth.com (office).

NASHEED, Mohamed (Anni), BSc; Maldivian journalist, political and human rights activist and fmr head of state; b. 17 May 1967, Malé; m. Laila Ali Abdulla; two d.; ed Overseas School of Colombo, Sri Lanka, Dauntsey's School, Wilts. and John Moores Univ., Liverpool, UK; fmr journalist for Sangu magazine; arrested several times for political reasons, declared prisoner of conscience by Amnesty International 1991; arrested and sentenced several times for criticism of the govt; Dir Safari Tours Maldives 1994–96; mem. Parl. 1999–2001; apptd Dir Oriental Acad. Centre 2001; Co-founder and mem. Gen. Council, Maldivian Democratic

Party 2003, fmr Chair.; Pres. of the Maldives 2008–12 (resgnd); cand. in presidential election 2013; Hon. mem. International PEN, Hon. Fellow, Liverpool John Moores Univ.; Anna Lindh Award 2009, UN Champions of Earth Award 2010, James Lawson Award, Int. Center on Nonviolent Conflict, Tufts Univ. 2012. *Film:* The Island President (documentary) 2011. *Publications include:* Dhagadu Dhahanan: Internal Feuding and Anglo-Dhivehi Relations 1800–1900 1995, Maldives: Historical Overview of Dhivehi Policy, Hithaa Hithuge Gulhuu. *Leisure interests:* tennis, music, reading, writing. *Address:* Maldivian Democratic Party, H. Sharaashaa, 2nd Floor, Sosun Magu, Malé 20-059 (office); G. Canaray-ge, Malé, Maldives (home). *Telephone:* 3340044 (office); 3342776 (home). *Fax:* 3322960 (office). *E-mail:* secretariat@mdp.org.mv (office). *Website:* www.mdp.org.mv (office).

NASHID, Ahmed; Maldivian business executive; *Chairman, ADK Group of Companies;* opened small medical clinic with a single doctor and attached pharmacy 1987; opened ADK Pharmacy 1990; Founder-chair. ADK Group of Companies 1987–; expanded medical, clinical and pharmaceutical operations under ADK Co. Pvt. Ltd, ADK Enterprises Pvt. Ltd; est. ADK Hospital (first pvt. hospital in the Maldives); Founder-mem. Jumhooree Party (Republican Party); fmr Chair. Horizon Fisheries Pvt. Ltd. *Address:* ADK Hospital, Sosun Magu, Malé 20040, Maldives (office). *Telephone:* 3313553 (office). *Fax:* 3313554 (office). *E-mail:* info@adkenterprises.com (office). *Website:* www.adkhospital.mv (office).

NASIM, Anwar, PhD; Pakistani geneticist and academic; *Science Adviser, OIC Standing Committee on Scientific and Technological Co-operation (COMSTECH);* b. 7 Dec. 1935, Pasrur; ed Univ. of the Punjab, Univ. of Edinburgh, UK; Lecturer, Govt Coll., Multan and Lahore 1957–62; Research Officer, Atomic Energy of Canada Ltd, Chalk River 1966–73; Sr Research Officer, Nat. Research Council of Canada 1973–89; Adjunct Prof., Carleton Univ., Ottawa 1984–89, Univ. of Ottawa 1983–89; Prin. Scientist and Head, Molecular Genetics Group, Biology and Medical Research Dept, King Faisal Specialist Hosp. and Research Centre, Riyadh 1989–93; Exec. Sec. Pakistan Acad. of Sciences 1994–96; Science Adviser, OIC Standing Cttee on Scientific and Technological Co-operation (COMSTECH) 1996–; Fellow, Third World Acad. of Sciences 1987, Islamic Acad. of Sciences 1998, Pakistan Acad. of Medical Sciences 2000; Foreign Fellow, Pakistan Acad. of Sciences 1988; Gold Medal, MSc (Punjab); Civil Award Prime of Performance in Molecular Genetics 1995, Award for Outstanding Service, Overseas Pakistanis Inst. 1995, Sitara-e-Imtiaz Civil Award in Molecular Genetics 1999. *Publications:* Repairable Lesions in Microorganisms (co-author) 1984, Recombinant DNA Methodology (co-author) 1985, Molecular Biology of the Fission Yeast (co-author) 1989, Genetic Engineering and Biotechnology (co-author) 1990, Genetic Engineering – State of the Art (monograph) 1992, Biotechnology for Sustainable Development (co-author) 1995; more than 100 scientific papers published in int. journals since 1965. *Leisure interests:* reading literature, music. *Address:* COMSTECH Secretariat, 3 Constitution Avenue, G-5, Islamabad 44000, Pakistan (office); 237, Street 23, F-11/2, Islamabad (home). *Telephone:* (51) 9226813 (office); (51) 2299838 (home). *Fax:* (51) 9221115; (51) 9222026. *E-mail:* advisersc@comstech .org.pk (office); comstech@isb.comsats.net.pk (office); anwar_nasim@yahoo.com (home); comstech@isb.apollo.net.pk (office). *Website:* www.comstech.org.pk (office).

NASIR, Agha, MA; Pakistani television executive and playwright; *Executive Director, Geo TV Network;* b. 9 Feb. 1937, Meerut, UP, India; s. of Ali Ahmad Khan and Ghafari Begum; m. Safia Sultana 1957; one s. two d.; ed Karachi Univ.; Programmes Man. Pakistani TV 1967–68, Additional Gen. Man. 1967, Gen. Man. 1969–72, Dir Programmes Admin. 1972–86, Deputy Man. Dir 1986–87, Man. Dir 1987–88; Man. Dir Nat. Film Devt Corpn 1979; Dir-Gen. Pakistan Broadcasting Corpn 1989–92; Chief Exec. Shalimar Recording and Broadcasting Co. 1992–97; media consultant 1997–; Exec. Dir Geo TV Network 1998–; recipient of numerous awards for radio and TV plays; Pride of Performance Award from Pres. of Pakistan for services in the field of broadcasting 1993, Sitara-i-Imtiaz from Pres. of Pakistan in the field of literature 2011. *Radio:* has written numerous features and plays for radio and produced more than 500 programmes. *Television:* has written more than 20 plays for TV and has produced about 100. *Publications:* Saat Dramay (plays), Television Dramey (TV plays), Gumshuda Log (collection of articles), Gulshan-e-Yaad, Hum Jeetay Jee Masroof Rahey (collection and comments on poet Faiz Ahmad Faiz), This is PTV (history or Pakistan Television). *Leisure interests:* reading, walking. *Address:* Geo TV Network, 40 Blue Area, Fazal-ul-huq Road, Islamabad (office); House No. 23, Street No. 3, F-8/3, Islamabad, Pakistan (home). *Telephone:* (51) 2263685 (home); (51) 2852619 (home). *Fax:* (51) 2827396 (office); (51) 2263685 (home). *E-mail:* agha.nasir@geo.tv (office); agha.nasir09@yahoo.com (home). *Website:* www.geo.tv (office).

NASR, Farouk Mahmoud Sayf an-; Egyptian politician; b. Dec. 1922; fmr Pres. Supreme Constitutional Court; Dir Tech. Office, Ministry of Justice; worked on the preparation of laws, on Nationalist Councils; Minister of Justice 1987–2004. *Address:* c/o Ministry of Justice, Justice and Finance Building, Sharia Majlis ash-Sha'ab, Lazoughli Square, Cairo, Egypt.

NASR, Ramsey; Dutch poet, writer, actor and musical theatre director; b. 28 Jan. 1974, Rotterdam; ed Studio Herman Teirlinck, Antwerp; actor, Het Zuidelijk Toneel 1995–90; leading parts in several films and TV series; also dir of musical theatre productions, including Mozart's The Abduction from the Seraglio; numerous poetry performances at int. festivals; Dichter des Vaderlands (Poet Laureate) 2009–13; City Poet of Antwerp 2005; Dr hc (Antwerp); Mary Dresselhuys Prize for outstanding acting performance 2000, Hugues C. Pernath Prize (biennial prize for best vol. of poetry) 2004, Journalist for Peace, Humanistic Peace Council 2006, Humanistic Peace Council Journalist for Peace 2006. *Plays:* theatrical monologues (as writer and actor): De doorspeler – Geen lied (Taalunie Toneelschrijfprijs— Playwright's Prize for Best Theatre Text) 2000); other: Leven in Hel – de operette (libretto writer, actor, singer, director), Il Re Pastore, opera by Mozart (trans./ adaptation, dir), Een totale Entführung (adaptation/trans., dir of new adaptation of Mozart's The Abduction from the Seraglio). *Films include:* as actor: Frans en Duits 1995, Thuisfront 1998, De man met de hond 1998, Mariken 2000, Liefje 2001, Magonia 2001, The Enclave 2002, Hotel Bellevue 2003, Armando 2004, Mon ange 2004, Live! 2005, Het echte leven 2008, Goltzius and the Pelican Company 2011. *Television:* actor in series De Enclave – Overspel. *Publications:* poetry collections: 27 gedichten & Geen lied 2000, onhandig bloesemend (Hugues C.

Pernath Prize) 2004, onze-lieve-vrouwe-zeppelin 2006, tussen lelie en waterstofbom 2009, anthology of poetry in English: Heavenly Life (trans. David Colmer) 2010; prose: Kapitein Zeiksnor & De Twee Culturen (novella) 2001; music theatre: Twee libretto's 2002; essays and opinion articles: Van de vijand en de muzikant 2006; travel diaries: Homo safaricus 2009, In de gouden buik van Boeddha (Burma/ Myanmar) 2010; contrib. of articles to newspapers and journals. *Address:* c/o Uitgeverij De Bezige Bij, Van Miereveldstraat 1, 1071 Amsterdam, Netherlands (office). *Telephone:* (20) 305-9810 (office). *E-mail:* info@debezigebij.nl (office). *Website:* www.ramseynasr.nl.

NASR, Seyyed Hossein, MS, PhD; Iranian academic; *University Professor of Islamic Studies, George Washington University;* b. 7 April 1933, Tehran; s. of Valiallah Nasr and Ashraf Kia; m. Soussan Daneshvari 1958; one s. one d.; ed Massachusetts Inst. of Tech. and Harvard Univ.; Teaching Asst Harvard Univ. 1955–58, Visiting Prof. 1962, 1965; Assoc. Prof. of History of Science and Philosophy, Tehran Univ. 1958–63, Prof. 1963–79, Dean, Faculty of Letters 1968–72, Vice-Chancellor 1970–71; Chancellor (Pres.) Aryamehr Univ. 1972–75; First Prof. of Islamic Studies, American Univ. of Beirut 1964–65; Prof. of Islamic Studies, Temple Univ. 1979–84; Univ. Prof. of Islamic Studies, George Washington Univ. 1984–; Visiting Prof., Harvard Univ. 1962, 1965, Princeton Univ. 1975, Univ. of Utah 1979; A.D. White Prof.-at-Large, Cornell Univ. 1991–98; Founder and first Pres. Iranian Acad. of Philosophy 1974–79; mem. Inst. Int. de Philosophie, Greek Acad. of Philosophy, Royal Acad. of Jordan; Dr hc (Uppsala) 1977, (Lehigh) 1996; Gifford Lecturer, Univ. of Edinburgh 1981, The Library of Living Philosophers dedicated to his thought 2001. *Publications:* more than 50 books and 500 articles in Persian, Arabic, English and French in leading int. journals. *Leisure interests:* classical music (both Western and Eastern), tennis, hiking. *Address:* 709R Gelman Library, The George Washington University, Washington, DC 20052, USA (office). *Telephone:* (202) 994-5704 (office). *Fax:* (202) 994-4571 (office). *E-mail:* msirat@ gwu.edu (office). *Website:* www.nasrfoundation.org (office).

NASRALLAH, Sheikh Hasan; Lebanese ecclesiastic and political leader; *Secretary-General, Hezbollah;* b. 31 Aug. 1960, Beirut; m. Fatima Yassin; five c. (one deceased); at age 15 joined Amal movt, Bassouriyeh, 1975, then moved to Najaf, Iraq to study at Hawza (Islamic Seminary); forced to leave Iraq and returned to Lebanon to study with Amal leader Sheikh Abbas al-Musawi; elected Amal political del. Biqaa; resgnd from Amal and joined Hezbollah 1982, chief exec. and mem. Consultative Council, Beirut 1987–89, moved to Qom, Iran to resume studies 1989; returned briefly to Lebanon then back to Tehran to represent Hezbollah 1989; Sec.-Gen. Hezbollah 1992–. *E-mail:* hizbollahmedia@hizbollah .org. *Website:* www.moqawama.org/english; www.hizbollah.org.

NASREDDIN, Mahmoud; Lebanese international organization executive and academic; Dir-Gen. Arab Atomic Energy Agency –2009. *Address:* c/o Arab Atomic Energy Agency, PO Box 402, 7, rue Fatma El Fehria, Mutuelle Ville, El Manzeh, 1004 Tunis, Tunisia. *Telephone:* (71) 800148; (71) 800099. *E-mail:* aaea@gnet.tn; aaea@aaea.org.tn.

NASREEN, Taslima, BS, MD, MB; Bangladeshi/Swedish feminist, writer and doctor; *Research Scholar, New York University;* b. 25 Aug. 1962, Mymensingh, East Pakistan (now Bangladesh); d. of Rajab Ali and Edul Wara; m. 1st Rudra Mohammad Shahidullah 1982 (divorced 1986); m. 2nd Nayeemul Islam Khan (divorced 1991); m. 3rd Minar Mahmood 1991 (divorced 1992); ed Mymensingh Medical Coll., Dhaka Univ.; practised as a gynaecologist and anaesthesiologist 1986–93; columnist, Khoborer Kagoj 1989; books banned in Bangladesh and Indian state of West Bengal 1993–2004, first fatwa (death threat) pronounced against her 1993; forced to leave Bangladesh for Sweden 1994, later in Germany, USA, France and India; further fatwas issued against her in India 2004–08, forced to leave there 2008; currently Research Scholar, New York Univ., USA; lectures on human rights world-wide; Hon. Citizen, Esch, Luxembourg, Metz, France, Thionville, France 2011; Dr hc (Ghent Univ., Belgium) 1995, (American Univ. in Paris) 2005, (Université Catholique de Louvain, Belgium) 2010; Ananda Puroshkar, India 1992, Kurt Tukholsky Prize, Sweden 1994, Feminist of the Year, USA 1994, Human Rights Award, French Govt 1994, Edit de Nantes Award, France 1994, Monismanien Prize, Sweden 1995, Sakharov Prize, European Parl. 1995, Int. Humanist Award, Int. Humanist and Ethical Union 1996, Erwin Fischer Award 2002, UNESCO Prize 2004, Grand Prix International Condorcet-Aron 2005, Prix Simone de Beauvoir 2008, Citoyenne d'honneur, France 2008, Woodrow Wilson Fellowship, USA, Crossing Border Award 2009, Prins Global Scholars Fellowship, New York Univ., USA 2009, Medal of Honour, City of Lyon, France 2009. *Publications include:* Shikore Bipul Khudha 1986, Nirbashito bahire Ontore 1989, Amar Kichu Jay Ashe Ne 1990, Atole Ontorin 1991, Nirbachito Kolam 1991, Nosto meyer nosto goddo 1992, Oporpokkho 1992, Shodh 1992, Balikar Gollachut 1992, Nimontron 1993, Laija (novel) 1993, Phera 1993, Choto choto dukkho kotha (selected columns) 1994, Bhromor koio gia 1994, Nirbashito Narir Kobita 1996, Amar Meyebela (autobiog.) 1999, Jolopodyo 2000, Utal Hawa (autobiog.) 2002, Forashi Premik 2002, Dwihkandita (autobiog.) 2003, Ko 2003, Sei Sob Ondhokar (autobiog.) 2004, Khali Khali Lage 2004, Kicchukhan Thako 2005, Ami bhalo nei, tumi bhalo theko prio desh (autobiog.) 2006, Minu (short stories) 2007, Narir Kono Desh Nei 2007, Bhalobaso? Cchai Baso 2008, Bondini 2008, Shorom 2009, Nei, kichu nei 2010 (autobiog.). *Telephone:* (718) 419-4713 (New York). *E-mail:* taslima .nasrin@gmail.com; email@taslimanasrin.com. *Website:* taslimanasrin.com.

NASSER, Jacques A. (Jac), AO; Australian business executive; *Chairman, BHP Billiton;* b. 12 Dec. 1947, Amyoun, Lebanon; m.; ed Royal Melbourne Inst. of Tech.; with Ford of Australia 1968–73, mem. financial staff, N American Truck operations, Ford Motor Co. 1973, profit analysis, product programming Ford Motor Co., Australia 1973–75, various positions, Int. Automotive Operations, Ford Motor Co. 1975–87, Dir, Vice-Pres. Finance and Admin., Autolatina jt venture, Brazil and Argentina 1987–90, Pres., CEO Ford of Australia 1990–93, Chair. Ford of Europe 1993–96, Vice-Pres. Ford Motor Co. 1993–96, CEO 1999–2001, Chair. Ford of Europe, Pres. Ford Automotive Operations, Exec. Vice-Pres. 1996–2002; Sr Partner, One Equity Partners LLC (JPMorgan Chase & Co.) 2002–10, Advisory Partner (non-exec.) 2010–, Chair. (non-exec.), Polaroid Holding Co. 2002–05 (after acquisition of Polaroid by One Equity Partners); mem. Bd of Dirs BHP Billiton Ltd, Melbourne, Australia and BHP Billiton Plc 2006–, Chair. 2010–; Dir (non-exec.) BSkyB Ltd 2002–12, Brambles Industries 2004–08, Quintiles Transnational Corpn –2008, 21st Century Fox 2013–; mem. Int. Advisory Bd Allianz AG 2001–;

Order of the Cedar (Lebanon); Hon. Doctorate of Tech. (RMIT Univ. of Melbourne); Centenary Medal (Australia), Ellis Island Medal of Honor for outstanding contribs to American Society 2008. *Leisure interest:* opera. *Address:* BHP Billiton Ltd, BHP Billiton Centre, 180 Lonsdale Street, Melbourne, Vic. 3000, Australia (office). *Telephone:* (3) 9609-3333 (office); 1300-55-4757 (office). *Fax:* (3) 9609-3015 (office). *E-mail:* webmaster@bhpbilliton.com (office). *Website:* www.bhpbilliton.com (office).

NASSER, Nassir bin Abdulaziz al-; Qatari diplomatist and UN official; *High Representative of the Secretary-General for the Alliance of Civilizations, United Nations;* b. 15 Sept. 1953, Doha; m. Muna Rihani; one s.; joined Ministry of Foreign Affairs (MFA) 1971, Attaché, Embassy in Beirut 1972–74, mem. Qatari Del. to Org. of the Islamic Conf. 1974–75, Gen. Counsellor, Embassy in Dubai 1975–81, with MFA 1981–85, Deputy Foreign Minister 1984–85, Minister at Perm. Mission to UN, New York 1986–93, Amb. to Jordan 1993–98, Amb. and Perm. Rep. to UN, New York 1998–2011, Vice-Pres. UN Gen. Ass. 2002–03, Pres. Security Council Dec. 2006, Chair. Group of 77 2004, Pres. UN Gen. Ass. 2011–12; High Rep. of the Sec.-Gen. for the Alliance of Civilizations, UN 2013–; mem. Bd of Advisers, New York Univ. Center for Dialogues; Hon. Fellow, Foreign Policy Asscn, New York 2009; Grand Officer, Order of Merit (Italy) 2004, Medal of Grand Commdr of Order of Makarios III (Cyprus) 2007, Nat. Order of Doctor José Matias Delgado (El Salvador) 2007, Commdr, Nat. Order (Côte d'Ivoire) 2008; Dr hc (Chongqing Univ.) 2007, (Fordham Univ.); Medal of Independence (Jordan) 1998, High Honour Awards (Italy) 2005. *Address:* United Nations Alliance of Civilizations, The Chrysler Building, 405 Lexington Avenue, 5th floor, New York, NY 10174, USA (office). *Telephone:* (212) 457-1751 (office). *E-mail:* contactaoc@unops.org (office). *Website:* www.unaoc.org (office).

NASSOUR, Gen. Mahamat Ali Abdallah; Chadian army officer and politician; fmr Minister of Territorial Admin; State Minister and Minister of Mines and Energy 2006–08; Minister of Nat. Defence Feb.–March 2008; fmr Minister of Urban and Rural Water Supply; Vice-Pres. African Ministers Council on Water 2012–. *Address:* c/o Ministry of Urban and Rural Water Supply, N'Djamena, Chad (office).

NĂSTASE, Adrian, LLM, PhD; Romanian academic and politician; b. 22 June 1950, Bucharest; s. of Marin Năstase and Elena Năstase; m. Daniela Miculescu 1985; two s.; ed Bucharest Univ.; Research Fellow, Inst. of Legal Research, Bucharest 1973–90; Prof. of Public Int. Law, Bucharest Univ. 1990–, Titu Maiorescu, Dimitrie Cantemir and Nicolae Titulescu pvt. univs 1992–; Assoc. Prof. of Public Int. Law, Paris-Panthéon Sorborne I 1994–; Minister of Foreign Affairs 1990–92; Speaker Chamber of Deputies 1992–96, Deputy Speaker 1996–; Exec. Pres. Social Democracy Party of Romania 1992–97, First Vice-Pres. 1997–2000, Pres. 2001–06 (resgnd); Prime Minister of Romania 2000–04; Vice-Chair. Camera Deputaților (Chamber of Deputies) 1996–2000, Chair. 2004–06 (resgnd); apptd mem. Romanian Parl. Del. to Parl. Asscn Council of Europe 1996; Vice-Pres. Asscn of Int. Law and Int. Relations, Bucharest 1977–; Dir of Studies, Int. Inst. of Human Rights, Strasbourg 1984; Pres. Titulescu European Foundation 1990–92 (Hon. Pres. 1992–); Exec. Pres. Euro-Atlantic Centre, Bucharest 1991–92; mem. Bd of Dirs Inst. for East-West Studies, New York 1991–97; mem. Human Rights Information and Documentation System; mem. French Soc. of Int. Law 1984–, American Soc. of Int. Law 1995–; indicted by Romanian prosecutors on corruption charges Jan. 2009, sentenced by Supreme Court to four years in prison for taking bribes 2014, also sentenced to three years for blackmail to run concurrently; Order of Diplomatic Service Merit 1991, Gwanghwa Medal (Repub. of Korea) 1991, Grande Croix de Mérite, Sovereign Order of Malta 1992; Nicolae Titulescu Prize, Romanian Acad. 1994, The Political Man of 1995, Turkish Businessmen's Asscn, Global Leader for Tomorrow Prize 1993. *Publications include:* Human Rights: An End-of-the-Century Religion 1992, International Law: Achievements and Prospects (co-author) 1992, Human Rights, Civil Society, Parliamentary Diplomacy 1994, Public International Law (co-author) 1995, Nicolae Titulescu – Our Contemporary 1995, Parliamentary Humour 1996, International Economic Law II 1996, Romania and the New World Architecture 1996, Documenta universales I (with law documents) 1997, 1998, The Treaties of Romania (1990–1997) 1998, Documenta universales II: The Rights of Persons Belonging to National Minorities 1998, Battle for the Future 2000, Contemporary International Law – Essential Texts 2001; more than 240 articles and papers. *Leisure interests:* hunting, music, modern art, collecting antiques, gardening, tennis.

NĂSTASE, Ilie; Romanian fmr professional tennis player; b. 19 July 1946, Bucharest; m. 1st; one d.; m. 2nd Alexandra King 1984; m. 3rd Amalia Năstase 2004 (divorced 2010); nat. champion (13–14 age group) 1959, (15–16 age group) 1961, (17–18 age group) 1963, 1964; 58 ATP singles titles: Salisbury, USA 1970, 1974, 1976, Rome 1970, 1973, Richmond, USA 1971, Hampton, USA 1971, Nice 1971, 1972, Monte Carlo 1971, 1972, 1973, Båstad, Sweden 1971, Wembley, UK 1971, Tennis Masters Cup, Paris 1971, Baltimore 1972, Omaha 1972, 1973, Madrid 1972, 1973, 1974, 1975, Düsseldorf 1972, Toronto 1972, US Open 1972, South Orange, USA 1972, 1975, 1976, Seattle 1972, London 1972, Tennis Masters Cup, Barcelona 1972, Calgary 1973, Washington 1973, 1974, Barcelona 1973, 1975, Florence 1973, French Open 1973, Queen's Club, London 1973, Gstaad, Switzerland 1973, Cincinnati 1973, Torneo Godó-Barcelona 1973, 1974, Paris 1973, Tennis Masters Cup, Boston 1973, Bournemouth, UK 1974, Cedar Grove, USA 1974, Valencia 1975, Tennis Masters Cup, Stockholm 1975, Atlanta 1976, La Costa, USA 1976, Pepsi Grand Slam, Myrtle Beach 1976, Honolulu Challenge Cup 1976, Las Vegas Challenge Cup 1976, Mexico City 1977, Aix en Provence 1977, Miami 1978, Montego Bay Challenge Cup, Jamaica 1978; winner of doubles, French Open (with Ion Țiriac) 1970, mixed doubles, Wimbledon (with Rosemary Casals) 1970, 1972, doubles, Wimbledon (with Jimmy Connors q.v.) 1973, doubles, US Open (with Jimmy Connors) 1975; winner Tour Finals 1971, 1972, 1973, 1975; winner of ILTF Grand Prix 1972, 1973; won 108 pro titles in his career; played 130 matches for the Romanian team in the Davis Cup; elected to Nat. Council of Romania's Social Democracy Party (Partidul Social Democrat—PSD) 1995; PSD cand. in elections for Mayor of Bucharest 1996; Pres. Romanian Tennis Fed.; currently competes on Delta Tour of Champions; rank of Maj. Gen.; mem. Laureus World Sports Acad.; Chevalier, Légion d'honneur 2009; Best Romanian Sportsman of the Year 1969, 1970, 1971, 1973, Int. Tennis Hall of Fame 1991, ranked 28th by

Tennis Magazine on its list of 40 Greatest Players of the Tennis Era 2005. *Publications:* Breakpoint 1986; wrote several novels in French 1980s. *Address:* Clubul sportiv Steaua, Calea Plevnei 114, Bucharest, Romania.

NASUTION, Darmin, PhD; Indonesian fmr central banker; b. 21 Dec. 1948, Tapanuli; ed Fakultas Ekonomi Universitas Indonesia, Univ. of Paris (Sorbornne), France; held several sr ministerial posts including Asst Minister of Trade and Industry Co-ordinator, Asst Minister for Production and Distribution Co-ordinator, Asst to Co-ordinating Minister for Devt Supervision and Admin. Reform; Dir Gen. Financial Insts, Bank Indonesia 2000–05, Chair. Capital Market and Financial Inst. Supervisory Agency 2006, Dir Gen. of Taxation 2006–09, Sr Deputy Gov. Bank Indonesia 2009, Acting Gov. then Gov. 2010–13 mem. Bd of Dirs FEUI LPEM 1989–93. *Address:* c/o Bank Indonesia, Jl. MH. Thamrin 2, Jakarta 10350, Indonesia (office).

NATADZE, Nodar, (Nodar Tskhireli); Georgian politician and academic; *Chairman, People's Front of Georgia;* b. 27 May 1929, Tbilisi; s. of Revas Natadze and Tina Natadze (née Tatiana); m. Nana Gadyatska 1968; two s.; Philologist Inst. of Philosophy, Georgian Acad. of Sciences; Leader Popular Front of Georgia (now People's Front of Georgia) 1989–; Ed.-in-Chief Sakartvelo; mem. Supreme Council (Parl.) of Georgia 1989–90, 1990–91, 1992–95; mem. Tskhumi-Abkhazian Acad. of Sciences. *Leisure interests:* mountaineering, skiing, literary criticism. *Address:* People's Front of Georgia, Pushkin 5, Tbilisi, Georgia. *Telephone:* (32) 93-17-10; (32) 36-16-32.

NATAPEI, Edward Nipake; Ni-Vanuatu politician; *Minister of Foreign Affairs;* b. 17 July 1954, Futuna Island; ed Fiji Inst. of Tech. and Malapoa Coll., Vanuatu; mem. Parl. for Port Vila 1983–; Minister of Health 1987; fmr Minister of Public Works, of Civil Aviation, of Meteorology, of Posts and Telecommunications and Tourism and of Foreign Affairs; Speaker of Parl. 1996–99; Pres. (acting) of Vanuatu March 1999; Leader of Opposition 2000; Prime Minister of Vanuatu 2001–04; Deputy Prime Minister and Minister of Infrastructure and Public Utilities 2007–08; Prime Minister 2008–10; Minister of Foreign Affairs 2013–; Pres. Vanua'aku Pati (Our Land Party). *Address:* Ministry of Foreign Affairs, PMB 9051, Port Vila (office); Vanuaaku Pati (Our Land Party), POB 472, Port Vila, Vanuatu (office). *Telephone:* 22584 (party) (office). *Fax:* 22863 (party) (office).

NATARAJAN, Jayanthi, BA, BL; Indian politician and lawyer; *Minister of State for Environment and Forests;* b. 7 June 1954, Madras (now Chennai); d. of Dr C. R. Sundararajan; m. V. K. Natarajan 1974; one s.; ed Ethiraj Coll. and Madras Law Coll.; mem. Rajya Sabha (Council of States, Parl.) 1986–2001, 2008–; mem. Cttee on Privileges, Social Welfare Bd 1988; social worker All India Women's Conf.; lawyer with interest in legal aid for the underprivileged; Minister of State for Civil Aviation and Parl. Affairs 1997–98; Pres. Tamil Maanila Congress (TMC) Women's Wing 1997–2001; Minister of State for Environment and Forests 2011–; currently Spokesperson All India Congress Cttee (AICC); Fellow Inst. of Politics, Kennedy School of Govt 2001. *Leisure interests:* playing veena, reading. *Address:* Ministry of Environment and Forests, Paryavaran Bhavan, CGO Complex, Lodhi Rd, New Delhi 110 003 (office); 'Badri', 47 Warren Rd, Mylapore, Chennai 600 004, India (home). *Telephone:* (11) 24361727 (office); (44) 24992440 (home). *Fax:* (11) 24362222 (office). *E-mail:* envisect@nic.in (office); jayanthi.n@sansad.nic.in (office). *Website:* www.moef.nic.in (office).

NATH, Amar, BE, MA; Indian civil servant and government official; ed Nat. Inst. of Technology, Kurukshetra Univ., Duke Univ., USA; worked as Man. Trainee, Steel Authority of India Ltd; fmr Probationary Officer, State Bank of India; Officer, Trainee Admin. Service 1994–95; worked in Govt of Rajasthan 1995–96; Sec., Dept of Industrial Devt, Dept of Labour and Man. Dir, Pondicherry Distilleries Ltd, Govt of Pondicherry 1998–99; Sec., Dept of Planning and Programme Implementation, Dept of Econs and Statistics, Dept of Tourism, Govt of Arunachal Pradesh 1999–2003, also served as Deputy Commr/Dist Magistrate Govt of Arunachal Pradesh; Sec., Delhi Subordinate Services Selection Bd 2003–05; CEO Chandigarh Housing Bd and Dir Dept of Rural Devt 2005–08, also served as Sub-Div. Magistrate and officer in charge of various depts, Chandigarh Admin; fmr CEO Delhi Urban Shelter Improvement Bd; Vice-Chair., Delhi Agricultural Marketing Bd 2008–11; Admin. of Union Territory of Lakshadweep 2011–12. *Address:* c/o Central Secretariat, Kavaratti 682 555, India. *E-mail:* lk-admin@ hub.nic.in.

NATH, Indira, MD, FRCPath, FAMS, FNASc, FASc; Indian immunologist and academic; *Professor Emeritus, Raja Ramanna Fellow and Chairman, Research Advisory Committee, Institute of Pathology, Indian Council of Medical Research;* b. 14 Jan. 1938; m.; one d.; ed All India Inst. of Medical Sciences, New Delhi; studied leprosy and immunology at MRC Lab. and Royal Coll. of Surgeons, UK; Nuffield Postdoctoral Fellow, UK, 1971–72; mem. Faculty, Dept of Biotechnology, All India Inst. of Medical Sciences, New Delhi, 1972–87, Prof. and Head 1987–98, Indian Nat. Science Acad. Sr Scientist 1998–2003; Dean, School of Medicine, Asian Inst. of Medicine, Science and Tech. 2004–05; Dir LEPRA-Blue Peter Research Centre, Hyderabad 2006–08; Prof. Emer., Raja Ramanna Fellow and Chair. Research Advisory Cttee, Inst. of Pathology, Indian Council of Medical Research, New Delhi 2009–; Country Rep. to UN Comm. on Science and Tech. for Devt (UNCSTD) 2003–05; served on several ICSU cttees including the Cttee on Science and Social Responsibility 2003, Scoping Group on Health 2006–07; mem. Science Advisory Cttee of Govt of India 2003–08; Fellow, Indian Acad. of Sciences 1988– (mem. Council 1992–94, Vice-Pres. 2001–03), Indian Nat. Science Acad., Nat. Acad. of Sciences (India), Nat. Acad. of Medical Sciences (India), Acad. of Sciences for the Developing World (TWAS), Royal Coll. of Pathologists (UK); Padmashri 1999, Silver Banner (Italy) 2002, Chevalier, Ordre nat. du Mérite 2004; Hon. DSc (Pierre and Marie Curie Univ., Paris) 2003; S.S. Bhatnagar Award, Council for Scientific and Industrial Research 1983, Shri Om Prakash Bhasin Foundation Award 1990, Padma Shri (India) 1999, L'Oréal-UNESCO For Women in Science Award 2002, K.K. Shastri Oration 2006. *Publications:* numerous articles in scientific and medical journals on leprosy. *Address:* Institute of Pathology (ICMR), Safdarjang Hospital Campus, PO Box 4909, New Delhi 110 029 (office); 707 Sarvapriya Apartments, Sarvapriya Vihar, New Delhi 110 016, India (home). *Telephone:* (11) 26517707 (home). *Fax:* (11) 26100754 (office). *E-mail:* indiranath@gmail.com; indiran@hotmail.com. *Website:* www.icmr.nic.in (office).

NATH, Kamal, BCom; Indian politician; *Minister of Urban Development and of Parliamentary Affairs;* b. 18 Nov. 1946, Kanpur; m. Alka Nath; two s.; ed Doon

School, Dehra Dun, St Xavier's Coll., Calcutta (now Kolkata); joined Indian Nat. Congress 1968 as youth worker; first elected to Parl. for Chhindwara 1980, re-elected 1985, 1989, 1991, 1998, 1999, 2004; mem. Del. to UN Gen. Ass. 1982–83; Minister of Environment and Forests 1991–95, of Textiles 1995–96, of Commerce and Industry 2004–09, of Road Transport and Highways 2009–11, of Urban Devt and of Parl. Affairs 2011–; Sec.-Gen. Indian Nat. Congress; mem. Congress Working Cttee; Pres. Bd Govs Inst. of Man. Tech.; Chair. Madhya Pradesh Devt Council; Patron, Child Devt Council of Madhya Pradesh; Dr hc (Rani Durgavati Univ., Jabalpur) 2006. *Address:* Ministry of Urban Development, Nirman Bhavan, Maulana Azad Road, New Delhi 110 011 (office); No. 1 Tughlak Road, New Delhi 110 011, India (home). *Telephone:* (11) 23062377 (office); (11) 23792233 (home). *Fax:* (11) 23061459 (office). *E-mail:* secyurban@nic.in (office); knath@knath.com (home). *Website:* urbanindia.nic.in (office).

NATHAN, S(ellapan) R(amanathan), Dip in Social Studies with Distinction; Singaporean fmr head of state; b. (Sellapan Ramanathan), 3 July 1924; s. of V. Sellapan and Mdm Abirami; m. Urmila (Umi) Nandey; one s. one d.; ed Victoria School and Univ. of Malaya, Singapore; almoner, Medical Dept, Gen. Hosp. 1955–56; Seaman's Welfare Officer, Ministry of Labour 1956–62; Asst Dir, Labour Research Unit 1962–63, Dir 1964–66; Asst Sec., Ministry of Foreign Affairs Feb.–June 1966, Prin. Asst Sec. 1966–67, Deputy Sec. 1967–71; Dir, Security and Intelligence Div., Ministry of Defence 1971–79; First Perm. Sec., Ministry of Foreign Affairs 1979–82; Exec. Chair., The Straits Times Press 1982–88; High Commr in Malaysia 1988–90; Amb. to USA 1990–96; Amb.-at-Large, Ministry of Foreign Affairs 1996–99; Dir, Inst. of Defence and Strategic Studies, Nanyang Technological Univ. 1996–99; Pres. of Singapore 1999–2011; Pro-Chancellor, Nat. Univ. of Singapore; Chair., Hindu Endowments Bd, Mitsubishi Singapore Heavy Industries (Pte) Ltd; mem. Bd of Trustees, NTUC Research Unit, Singapore Indian Devt Asscn; Dir, Singapore Nat. Oil Co. (Pte) Ltd, New Nation Publishing Berhad, Times Publishing Berhad, Singapore Press Holdings Ltd, Marshall Cavendish Ltd, Singapore Mint (Pte) Ltd, Singapore Int. Media (Pte) Ltd; mem. Bd of Govs, Civil Service Coll.; Order of Temasek (First Class), Nat. Day Honours 2013; Friend of Labour Award 1962, Public Service Star 1964, Public Admin Medal (Silver) 1967, Meritorious Service Medal 1974, NTUC May Day Meritorious Service Award 1984. *Publications:* Why Am I Here?: Overcoming Hardships of Local Seafarers 2010, Winning Against the Odds 2011, An Unexpected Journey: The Path to the Presidency (autobiography) 2012. *Leisure interests:* walking, reading. *Address:* Katong Post Box No. 0205, Singapore 914307 (home).

NATOCHIN, Yury Viktorovich, DSc; Russian physiologist and academic; *Head of Laboratory, Sechenov Institute of Evolutionary Physiology and Biochemistry, Russian Academy of Sciences;* b. 6 Dec. 1932, Kharkov, USSR (now Ukraine); s. of Victor Natochin and Frida Kohan; m. 1957; one s. one d.; ed Novosibirsk High Medical School; Jr, then Sr Researcher, Sechenov Inst. of Evolutionary Physiology and Biochemistry, St Petersburg 1959–64, Head of Lab. 1964–; Dean, Medical Faculty, St Petersburg State Univ. 1995–2002, Prof. of Physiology 1996–; Acad.-Sec. Dept of Physiology, Russian Acad. of Sciences 1996–2002, 2011–; Ed.-in-Chief Russian Journal of Physiology 1995–2013; main research in physiology of the kidney, functional nephrology, molecular physiology; Hon. mem. Hungarian Physiology Soc. 1984; Hon. Prof., Univ. of St Petersburg 1999; Dr hc (Inst. of Experimental Medicine, St Petersburg) 2012, (Pirogov Centre, Moscow) 2012, (Medical Mil. Acad., St Petersburg) 2012; I.A. Orbeli Prize 1980, Jan Parkinje Gold Medal 1982, S. Rach Medal 1986, S. Korolev Medal 1992, Science Prize of Govt of Russia 1997, I. Pavlov Gold Medal 2001, Triumph Prize 2009. *Publications include:* Ion-Regulating Function of the Kidney 1976, Physiology of the Kidney 1982, Problems of Evolutionary Physiology of Water-Salt Balance 1984, Kidney 1997, Fluid and Electrolyte Regulation in Spaceflight 1998, Introduction in Nephrology 2007. *Leisure interests:* photography, poetry, travelling. *Address:* Sechenov Institute of Evolutionary Physiology and Biochemistry, 44 M. Thorez prospekt, 194223 St Petersburg (office); 8/2 Vernosty str., Apt 25, St Petersburg, Russia (home). *Telephone:* (812) 552-30-86 (office). *Fax:* (812) 552-30-86 (office). *E-mail:* natochin@iephb.ru (office). *Website:* www.iephb.ru (office).

NATSUKI, Shizuko; Japanese novelist; b. (Shizuko Idemitsu), 21 Dec. 1938, Tokyo; m. Yoshihide Idemitsu 1963; one s. one d.; ed Keio Univ.; screenplay for Only I Know (Japanese TV); followed by numerous novels, short stories and screenplays; Mystery Writers of Japan Prize 1973, Prix du Roman d'Aventures (France) 1989, Nishinippon Shinsbeen Cultural Award 1999, Fukuoka Pref. Cultural Award 2001. *Plays:* novels adapted for the stage: Tragedy of W 1993, Actress X 1994. *Film:* Tragedy of W 1984. *Works adapted for television include:* The Angel Vanishes 1972 and more than 200 others. *Publications include:* 39 novels including The Angel Vanishes 1970, Disappearance 1973, Murder at Mt. Fuji 1984, Dome 1986, The Third Lady 1987, The Obituary arrives at Two O'Clock 1988, Portal of the Wind 1990, Marianne 1997, Mariko 1999, The Punishment 2001, and about 240 novelettes and short stories. *Leisure interests:* golf, Go (started own Go tournament using Go stone she developed herself).

NATTIEZ, Jean-Jacques, OC, LèsL, MèsL, PhD; Canadian (b. French) musicologist and academic; *Titular Professor of Musicology, Faculty of Music, University of Montreal;* b. 30 Dec. 1945, Amiens, France; ed Amiens Conservatoire, Université d'Aix-en-Province, Université de Paris VIII-Vincennes, France; naturalized Canadian 1975; Prof., Depts of Linguistics and French Studies, Univ. of Montreal 1970–72, Prof. of Musicology, Faculty of Music 1972–; Co-Ed. first six issues of CUMR 1980–85; fmr Ed. Circuit periodical; pioneer in br. of musicology known as musical semiology (analysis of music dealing with musical meaning, sometimes inspired by structural linguistics); Co-Ed. series Musique/ Passé/Présent, Christian Bourgois publishing house, Paris 1981; Musical Dir Joliette-Lanaudière Symphony Orchestra 1984–87; currently Gen. Ed. five-volume Encyclopedia of Music; contrib. to EMC; in field of ethnomusicology, has produced several recordings of Inuit (Canada), Ainu (Japan) and Baganda (Uganda) music; mem. RSC 1988–; Ordre nat. du Québec 2001; Killam Research Fellowship 1988–90, Dent Medal, Royal Musical Asscn (England) for his complete works 1988, Prix André-Laurendeau pour les sciences humaines, Asscn canadienne française pour l'avancement des sciences 1989, Molson Prize 1990, Prix Léon-Gérin pour les sciences sociales du Gouvernement du Québec 1994, Prize for Teaching Excellence, Univ. of Montreal in 2004, Killam Prize (Humanities), Canada Council for the Arts 2004. *Recordings include:* Inuit Games and Songs

(UNESCO's Musical Sources series) (Grand prix du disque de l'Acad. Charles-Cros 1979) 1978, Jeux vocaux des Inuit (Inuit du Caribou, Netsilik et Igloolik); contributed to Chants des Aïnou 1982, LP and disc of oral music recordings made by Romanian ethnomusicologist Constantin Brailoïu in the 1950s, under the title Collection universelle de musique populaire enregistrée (Grand prix Charles-Cros 1987) 1985. *Publications:* Fondements d'une sémiologie de la musique 1975, Tétralogies 1983, Proust musicien 1984, Music and Discourse 1987, Wagner androgyne 1990; has edited texts by composer Pierre Boulez and published several major articles on the composer; Opera (novel); has published three collections of articles: De la sémiologie à la musique 1988, Le combat de Chronos et d'Orphée and La musique, la recherche et la vie; more than 150 papers. *Address:* Faculté de musique, Université de Montréal, 200 avenue Vincent-d'Indy, CP 6128, succursale Centre-ville, Montréal, PQ H3C 3J7, Canada (office). *Telephone:* (514) 343-6427 (office). *Fax:* (514) 343-5727 (office). *E-mail:* musique@umontreal.ca (office). *Website:* www.musique.umontreal.ca (office).

NATTRASS, E. M. B. (Sue), AO, FAIM, FAIAM; Australian arts administrator, director and trustee; *Consultant and Co-Director, The Yarts Consulting;* b. (Elizabeth Margaret Barrett Nattrass), 15 Sept. 1941, Horsham, Vic.; d. of John Elliott Nattrass and Elizabeth Claven Saul; ed Univ. of Melbourne and Melbourne Business School; Stage Man., Lighting Designer and Production Dir 1963–79; Gen. Man. J. C. Williamson Productions Ltd 1980–83; Dir Playbox Theatre Co. 1981–84; Theatre Operations Man., Victorian Arts Centre 1983–88, Deputy Gen. Man. 1988–89, Gen. Man. 1989–96; Artistic Dir Melbourne Int. Festival of the Arts 1997–99; Exec. Dir Producer Services Millmaine Entertainment 2000–04; CEO and Artistic Dir Adelaide Festival 2002; Owner The Yarts Consulting 2004–, currently Consultant, Co-Dir and Trustee; Pres. Australian Entertainment Industry Asscn 1994–2003; Councillor, Victorian Coll. of Arts 1989–2004, Deputy Pres. 1992–2002, Pres. 2002–04; Dir John Truscott Design Foundation 1994–, Leadership Vic. 1996–2003, Theatre Royal Hobart 2000–08, Fed. Square Pty Ltd 2000–08, Harold Mitchell Foundation 2000–09, Melbourne Football Club 2004–08; Adjunct Prof. and Chair. Academic Advisory Bd of Arts and Entertainment Management Course, Deakin Univ. 2009–12; Patron Victorian Theatres Trust 2000–, The Song Room Inc. 1999–2007; mem. Drama Advisory Panel, Vic. Ministry for the Arts 1983–85, 1987–88, mem. Bicentennial Arts and Entertainment Cttee 1987–88; mem. Ministerial Advisory Cttee, Queen Victoria Women's Centre 1993–94, Patron 1994–2001; mem. Melbourne and Olympics Parks Trust 2000–12, Brian Stacey Memorial Trust 2003–, Sydney Opera House Trust 2006–12, Australian Int. Cultural Council 2004–09; Chair. Collections Council of Australia 2004–09, City of Melbourne Cultural Devt Bd 2007–13; Bd mem. Melbourne Workers' Theatre 2010–13; George Fairfax Fellow, Deakin Univ. 2009; Premier Award, The Age 2001 Performing Arts Awards, St Michael's Medal 1996, Vic. Day Award for Community and Public Service 1999, Centenary Medal 2001, Dame Elisabeth Murdoch Cultural Leadership Award 2006, The Green Room Award for Lifetime Achievement 2007, J.C. Williamson Award for outstanding contrib. to Australian live performance industry 2008. *Leisure interests:* cooking, walking, staring at trees, the bush, people and what makes them tick, medicine, sport. *Address:* The Yarts Consulting, 19 Myross Avenue, Ascot Vale, Vic. 3032, Australia. *Telephone:* (3) 9370-7062. *E-mail:* sue@theyarts.com.au.

NATYNCZYK, Gen. (retd) Walter J., BBA, CD; Canadian army officer and government official; *President, Canadian Space Agency;* b. 1958, Winnipeg; m. Leslie Natynczyk; two s. one d.; ed Royal Roads Mil. Coll., Collège militaire royal, Canadian Forces Command and Staff Coll., All Arms Tactics Course, UK, US Army War Coll., Pa; joined Canadian Forces 1975; served in numerous regimental command positions, becoming CO Royal Canadian Dragoons; four years with Royal Canadian Dragoons on NATO duty, Germany; Squadron Commdr, Royal Mil. Coll., Kingston, Ont. 1983–86; six months UN peace-keeping duties, Cyprus 1984; one-year mission with British forces for UN as Sector SW Chief of Operations, Bosnia-Herzegovina 1994, later Chief of Land Operations, UNPRO-FOR HQ, Zagreb, Croatia, Canadian Contingent Commdr, Bosnia-Herzegovina 1998; fmr Deputy Commanding Gen., III Corps and Fort Hood, Texas, USA; deployed with III Corps to Baghdad, Iraq 2004, serving first as Deputy Dir of Strategy, Policy and Plans, later Deputy Commanding Gen. of Multi-National Corps; fmr Asst Dir to Nat. Defence HQ Secr., Ottawa; Vice-Chief of Defence Staff 2006–08, Chief of Defence Staff 2008–12 (retd); Pres. Canadian Space Agency 2013–; attained rank of Lt Gen. 2006, Gen. 2008; Order of Mil. Merit, Meritorious Service Cross 2006. *Leisure interests:* jogging and sailing. *Address:* Canadian Space Agency, 6767 Route de l'Aéroport, Saint-Hubert, PQ J3Y 8Y9, Canada (office). *Telephone:* (450) 926-4800 (office). *Website:* www.asc-csa.gc.ca (office).

NAUGHTIE, (Alexander) James, MA; British journalist; b. 9 Aug. 1951, Aberdeen, Scotland; s. of Alexander Naughtie and Isabella Naughtie; m. Eleanor Updale 1986; one s. two d.; ed Univ. of Aberdeen and Syracuse Univ., USA; journalist, The Scotsman (newspaper) 1977–84; with The Guardian 1984–88, becoming Chief Political Corresp. 1985; Laurence Sterne Fellow, The Washington Post, Washington, DC 1981; Presenter, The World at One, BBC Radio 1988–94, The Proms, BBC Radio and TV 1991–, Today, BBC Radio 4 1994–, Book Club BBC Radio 4 1998–; mem. Council, Gresham Coll. 1997–; Hon. LLD (Aberdeen), (St Andrews), Hon. DUniv (Stirling). *Publications include:* The Rivals 2001, The Accidental American: Tony Blair and the Presidency 2004, The Making of Music: A Journey with Notes 2007, The New Elizabethans 2012, The Madness of July (novel) 2014. *Leisure interests:* books, opera. *Address:* BBC News Centre, London, W12 8QT, England. *Telephone:* (20) 8624-9644. *Website:* www.bbc.co.uk/radio4/ today.

NAUMAN, Bruce, MFA; American artist; b. 6 Dec. 1941, Fort Wayne, Ind.; ed Univ. of Wisconsin, Madison and Univ. of California, Davis, studied with Italo Scango, William Wiley, Robert Arneson, Frank Owen, Stephen Kaltenbach; Instructor, San Francisco Art Inst. 1966–68, Univ. of California, Irvine 1970; has participated in numerous group exhbns in USA and Europe; work in many perm. collections, including Whitney Museum, LA County Museum of Art, Tate Modern (London); first solo exhbn 1966; Dr hc (San Francisco Art Inst.) 1989; Artist Fellowship Award, Nat. Endowment for the Arts 1968, Max Beckmann Prize (Frankfurt) 1990, Wolf Prize 1993, Aldrich Prize 1995, ranked ninth in ArtReview magazine's Power 100 list 2005. *Publications:* Pictures of Sculptures in a Room 1966, Clear Sky 1968, Burning Small Fires 1968, Bruce Naumann 1988, Bruce

Naumann Prints 1989. *Address:* c/o Leo Castelli Gallery, 59 East 79th Street, New York, NY 10021, USA.

NAUMANN, Gen. Klaus, OBE; German army officer (retd); b. 25 May 1939, Munich; m. Barbara Linke; one s. one d.; joined Bundeswehr 1958, Col staff of German Mil. Rep., NATO Mil. Cttee, Brussels 1981–84; Brigade Commdr Armoured Infantry Brigade, Ellwangen 1984–86; Brig. Dept Head of Force Planning, Gen. Staff, Ministry of Defence 1986–88; Maj.-Gen., Head of Defence Policy and Operations staff 1988–90; adviser in two-plus-four negotiations on German Unification 1990; Lt-Gen., Commdr first German corps April–Oct. 1991; Insp.-Gen. of the Bundeswehr 1991; Chair. NATO Mil. Cttee 1996–99; mem. Int. Advisory Bd Worldsecuritynetwork.com; Great Distinguished Service Cross 1993, Commdr Legion of Merit 1993, Grand Officier, Légion d'honneur 1994, Grosses Bundesverdienstkreuz mit Stern 1998, Commdr's Cross of Merit (FRG), Gold Cross of Honour of Fed. Armed Forces, Gran Cruz de la Orden del Mérito Militar con Distintivo Blanco (Spain), KBE (Mil.) (UK), Grootofficier, Kroonorde (Belgium), Commdr's Cross, Legion of Merit (USA), Grand Cross, 2nd Class, Order of Merit (Austria), Kommandor m/Stjerne av den Kongelige Norske Fortjenstorden (Norway), Defence Medal, 1st Class (Hungary), Grand Officier, Ordre de Leopold (Mil.) (Belgium), Grootofficier, Orde van Oranje-Nassau (Netherlands), Commdr's Grand Cross of the Order of the Lion of Finland. *Publication:* Die Bundeswehr in einer Welt im Umbruch; numerous articles in newspapers and journals. *Leisure interests:* politics, history, art, photography, Latin American culture. *Address:* c/o World Security Network Foundation, 945 Fifth Avenue, New York, NY 10021, USA.

NAUMANN, Michael, DPhil; German publisher and editor; b. 8 Dec. 1941, Köthen; s. of Eduard Naumann and Ursula Naumann (née Schönfeld); m. Christa Wessel 1969 (divorced); one s. one d.; ed Univ. of Munich and Queen's Coll., Oxford, UK; Asst Prof., Univ. of Bochum 1971–76; Florey Scholar, Queen's Coll. Oxford 1976–78; Ed., Foreign Corresp. Die Zeit, Hamburg 1978–82; Sr Foreign Ed. Der Spiegel, Hamburg 1982–84; Publr Rowohlt Verlag, Reinbek 1984–95; Pres. and CEO Henry Holt and Co., New York 1996–98; Minister of State for Culture 1998–2000; Chief Ed. and Publisher, Die Zeit 2001–07; SPD cand. for Hamburg mayoral elections 2008; Ed. Cicero (magazine) 2010–; Trustee, Thomson Reuters 2010–; Commdr, Légion d'honneur. *Publications include:* Der Abbau einer Verkehrten Welt 1969, Amerika liegt in Kalifornien 1983, Strukturwandel des Heroismus 1984, Die Geschichte ist offen 1990, Die schönste Form der Freiheit 2001. *Leisure interests:* books, motorcycling, sailing. *Address:* Cicero, Friedrichstraße 140, 10117 Berlin, Germany (office). *Telephone:* (30) 981941100 (office). *Fax:* (30) 981941199 (office). *E-mail:* verlag@cicero.de (office). *Website:* www.cicero.de (office).

NAUMI, Najeeb an-, PhD; Qatari lawyer and politician; b. 21 March 1954, Doha; m.; four s. one d.; ed Alexandria Univ., Egypt, Univ. of Dundee, UK; legal adviser, Qatar Gas and Petrochemical Co. 1981–88, Diwan Amiri 1988–92; Minister and Legal Adviser, Office of HH The Heir Apparent and Minister of Defence 1992–95; Minister of Justice 1995–97; advocate and legal consultant 1997–. *Publication:* International Legal Issues Arising under the United Nations Decade of International Law 1995. *Leisure interests:* boating, Internet, reading, writing. *Address:* PO Box 9952, Doha, Qatar (office). *Telephone:* (974) 675374 (office). *Fax:* (974) 675378.

NAUMOV, Vladimir Naumovich; Russian film director and screenwriter; *CEO, Soyuz-Navona Film Production Company;* b. 6 Dec. 1927, Leningrad (now St Petersburg); m. Natalia Belokhvostikova; one s. one d.; ed Dept of Directing, State Inst. of Cinematography (under I. A. Savchenko); Artistic Dir workshop unit at Mosfilm 1961–89 (with A. Alov until 1983); Chair. Bd Mosfilm Studios Co. 1989–; Prof. VGIK 1980–; currently CEO Soyuz-Navona film production co.; Head of Dept, Nesterova Univ.; Pres. Nat. Film Acad.; Sec. Nat. Union of Cinematographers; Academician, European Film Acad.; mem. Bd Mosfilm Cinema Concern; Order of Honour 1971, Order of the Red Banner of Labour 1972, Order of the Friendship of Peoples 1987, Order of Merit for the Country 1997, Golden Cross for the Resurrection of Russia 2004; Meritorious Art Worker 1965, People's Artist of the RSFSR 1974, People's Artist of USSR 1983, USSR State Prize 1984, First Degree Peacemaker Award for charity work 2007, Second Degree Merit Award for outstanding contrib. to cinema art 2007, Golden Eagle Award for outstanding contrib. to cinematography 2008. *Films include:* (in collaboration with Alov to 1983) Uneasy Youth 1955, Pavel Korchagin (based on Ostrovsky's novel How the Steel Was Tempered) 1957, Wind 1959, Peace to Him Who Enters (two prizes at 22nd Venice Film Festival) 1961, A Nasty Story (based on Dostoevsky) 1966 (banned, shown 1989), Flight (based on M. Bulgakov's play) 1971, How the Steel Was Tempered (TV series) 1974, Legend about Til (three prizes at All-Union Festival, First Prize Int. Festival Haugesunde, Norway, Int. Festival Brussels) 1976, Tehran-43 (Golden Prize at 12th Int. Film Festival, Moscow, Golden Prize All-Union Festival) 1981, The Shore (First Prize at 17th Int. Film Festival, Kiev) 1984, The Choice 1987, The Law 1989, Ten Years of Confinement 1990, The White Holiday (two prizes Int. Film Festival Rimini 1995) 1994, Nardo's Mystery (aka White Dog's Dream) (Moscow Film Festival Prize 1998) 1998, Clock without Hands (Russian 'Window to Europe' Film Festival Prize 2000, Grand Gold Pegasus Prize from the Moscow Film Festival 2001, Moscow Mayor's Prize 2001) 2000, Joconda on Asphalt 2007. *Address:* 123056 Moscow, Bolshaya Gruzinskaya 39, Apt 214, Russia. *Telephone:* (495) 147-23-10 (office); (495) 253-87-32. *Fax:* (495) 938-20-88.

NAUMOVSKI, Vasko, MA, LLM, PhD; Macedonian lawyer, academic and politician; *Assistant Professor, SS Cyril and Methodius University;* b. 1980, Skopje; ed SS Cyril and Methodius Univ., Iustininavs Primus Law School, Skopje, Rheinische-Friedrich-Wilhelms Univ., Bonn, Germany; mem. staff, Faculty for Int. Relations, Policy and European Studies, New York Univ., Skopje 2005–, Asst Prof. of Int. Law and Law within the EU 2008–; has participated in several int. scientific confs in Europe and USA; Deputy Prime Minister, responsible for European Integration 2009–11; Asst Prof., SS Cyril and Methodius Univ.; scholarships from Konrad Adenauer Foundation (Germany), from US State Dept for study in USA. *Publications:* numerous scientific papers on European integration and int. law. *Leisure interests:* skiing, hiking. *Website:* www.pf.ukim.edu.mk (office).

NAUR, Peter, Mag. Scient., DrPhil; Danish computer scientist and academic; b. 25 Oct. 1928, Frederiksberg; ed Copenhagen Univ. Astronomical Observatory; began career as astronomer; employed at Regnecentralen (Danish computing inst.) 1959–69; Lecturer, Niels Bohr Inst. and Danmarks Tekniske Højskole (Tech. Univ. of Denmark) 1959–69; Prof. of Datalogi (Computer Science), Copenhagen Univ. 1969–98; currently developing theory of human thinking called Synapse-State Theory of Mental Life; A.M. Turing Award, Association for Computing Machinery for his work on defining the ALGOL 60 programming language 2005. *Achievements include:* last name is the N in BNF notation (Backus-Naur form), attributed to him by Donald Knuth, used in description of syntax for most programming languages; contributed to creation of ALGOL 60 programming language. *Publications:* Computing: A Human Activity 1992, Report on the Algorithmic Language ALGOL 60 (ed.), Antiphilosophical Dictionary 2001, Psykologi i videnskabelig rekonstruktion 2002; large number of articles and chapters on astronomy, computer science, issues in society, classical music, psychology and educ. *Address:* c/o Universitetsparken 13, 2100 Copenhagen Ø, Denmark. *Telephone:* 35-37-11-33. *E-mail:* naturfag@unibog.dk; info@naur.com. *Website:* www.naur.com.

NAVALNYI, Aleksei Anatolievich; Russian lawyer, politician and political activist; b. 4 June 1976, Butyn, Odintsovo Dist, Moscow Oblast; s. of Anatoliy Navalnyi; m. Yuliya Navalnaya; two c.; ed Peoples' Friendship Univ. of Russia, Finance Univ. under the Govt of the Russian Fed., Yale Univ., USA; joined Russian United Democratic Party Yabloko 2000, mem. Fed. Political Council, elected to regional council of Moscow br. 2002, expelled from Yabloko "for causing political damage to the party; in particular, for nationalist activities" 2007; minor stockholder in several Russian state-related corpns; gained prominence within Russian media as a critic of state corruption from 2009; has organized large-scale demonstrations against alleged electoral fraud; writes regularly articles in several publs, including Forbes Russia; arrested, convicted and sentenced to 15 days in jail "for defying a government official" Dec. 2011; helped lead anti-Putin rally following the latter's election as Pres. March 2012, arrested along with Sergei Udaltsov following another anti-Putin rally and given 15-day jail sentence May 2012; f. Foundation for the Combating of Corruption (FBK) 2011, projects include RosPil (analysis of govt contracts), RosVybory (election monitoring); accusations of embezzlement and fraud brought against him by Russian federal authorities 2012, found guilty July 2013, sentenced to five years' imprisonment, but released on bail; announced his intention to run for Pres. of Russia April 2013; placed second in election to Mayor of Moscow Sept. 2013; mem. Bd Aeroflot 2012–13; named by Russian business newspaper Vedomosti as Person of the Year 2009, World Fellow, Yale Univ.'s World Fellows Program 2010, named by Foreign Policy magazine to the FP Top 100 Global Thinkers 2011, 2012. *Address:* Foundation for the Combating of Corruption (Fond borby s korruptsiei), 109240 Moscow, ul. Nikoloyamskaya 26, korp 1-1A, Russian Federation. *Telephone:* (499) 653-75-52. *E-mail:* navalny_en@livejournal.com (office); fbk@fbk.info. *Website:* navalny.ru; navalny.livejournal.com; rospil.info; fbk.info; rosyama.ru; navalny-en.livejournal.com.

NAVARRE, Christophe, BBA; Belgian business executive; *CEO, Moët Hennessy;* b. 1958; ed Univ. de Liège, INSEAD (France) European Marketing Programme; joined Continental Bank 1980; moved to Exxon where he held marketing and sales positions with the Esso group; joined Interbrew 1989, headed several different Italian and French subsidiaries; Pres. and CEO JAS Hennessy & Co., LVMH 1997–2001, CEO Moët Hennessy (Wines and Spirits div. of LVMH) 2001–; mem. Bd Comité Colbert; mem. Advisory Bd Heineken NV 2009–; Chevalier, Légion d'honneur; Commdr, Ordre du Mérite agricole; Officier, Ordre de la Couronne (Belgium). *Address:* LVMH Moët Hennessy Louis Vuitton, 22 avenue Montaigne, 75008 Paris, France (office). *Telephone:* 1-44-13-22-22 (office). *Fax:* 1-44-13-22-23 (office). *E-mail:* info@lvmh.com (office). *Website:* www.lvmh.com (office).

NAVARRETE LÓPEZ, Jorge Eduardo; Mexican economist, diplomatist and academic; *Head of Research on International Affairs, National Autonomous University of Mexico;* b. 29 April 1940, Mexico City; m. Martha L. López; one s.; ed Nat. Autonomous Univ. of Mexico (UNAM); Prof., Nat. School of Econs and Nat. School of Political and Social Sciences, UNAM 1964–71, Head of Research on Int. Affairs, 2004–; various positions with Foreign Trade Nat. Bank 1966–72; Ed. Comercio Exterior; with Secr. of Finance and Public Credit –1972; Amb. to Venezuela 1972–75, to Austria 1975–77, to Yugoslavia 1977–78, to UK 1986–89, to People's Repub. of China 1989–93, to Chile 1993–95, to Brazil 1997–2001, to Germany 2002–04; Rep. of Mexico at Int. Conf. for Co-operation and Devt, Paris 1976–77; Deputy Perm. Rep. to UN and Vice-Pres. Econ. and Social Council 1978–79, Perm. Rep. to UN 2001–02; Under-Sec. for Econ. Affairs, Secr. of Foreign Relations 1979–86; Under-Sec. for Policy and Devt, Secr. of Energy 1995–97; fmr consultant for Inter-American Bank and UNDP; fmr Perm. Rep. to UNIDO; fmr mem. Bd of Govs IAEA; fmr mem. South Comm. *Publications include:* The International Transference of Technology: The Mexican Case (with Gerardo Bueno and Miguel Wionczek) 1969, Mexico: The Economic Policy of the New Government 1971, The Latin American External Debt 1986. *Address:* National Autonomous University of Mexico, Ciudad Universitaria, Del. Coyoacán, 04510, Mexico (office). *Telephone:* (55) 5623-0264 (office). *Fax:* (55) 1107-6963 (office). *E-mail:* joredune@servidor.unam.mx (office). *Website:* www.unam.mx (office).

NAVARRO, Samuel Lewis, BA, MBA; Panamanian politician and business executive; b. 1957, Panama City; s. of Gabriel Lewis Galindo; m. 1st, two c.; m. 2nd Anagrethel González, two c.; ed Georgetown and American Univs, Washington, DC, USA; Founder, Partido de Solidaridad 1993, est. alliance with Partido Revolucionario Democrático 1999, left to serve as running mate to presidential cand. Martín Torrijos 2004; Vice-Pres. of Panama and Minister of Foreign Affairs 2004–09; Pres. and Dir Empaques de Colón (family business) 1985–2001, Grupo ELE 1985–2001, Northsound Corpn, Inc. 1985–2001; mem. Bd of Dirs Panama Canal Authority 1997–2001; fmr mem. Bd of Dirs Distribuidora de Productos de Papel, Inmobiliaria Costa Azul, Cervecería Nacional, Red Crown Corpn. *Address:* c/o Ministry of Foreign Affairs, Altos de Ancón, Complejo Narciso Garay, Panamá 4, Panama (office).

NAVARRO GONZÁLEZ, Alberto; Spanish diplomatist and government official; *Ambassador to Morocco;* b. 27 March 1955, Santa Cruz de Tenerife, Canary Islands; joined Diplomatic Service 1980, served in Embassy in Tegucigalpa, Honduras, Prague, Czechoslovakia and Mission of Spain to the European

Communities, later served as Deputy Dir Gen. for Co-ordination of Community Programs of Co-operation, as Dir Gen. for Community, Legal and Institutional Co-ordination and Dir Gen. Chief of Staff, Minister of Foreign Affairs, apptd Dir Dept for Humanitarian Aid (ECHO) 1997, and later Chief of Staff of Sec. Gen., High Rep. for the Common Foreign and Security Policy of the Council of EU, Javier Solana, Amb. and Head of EC in Brazil 2003–04, Sec. of State for the EU 2004–08, Amb. to Portugal 2008–10, to Morocco 2010–. *Address:* Embassy of Spain, 3 rue Aïn Khalouiya, km 5.3, route des Zaërs, Souissi, 10000 Rabat, Morocco (office). *Telephone:* (537) 633906 (office). *Fax:* (537) 630595 (office). *E-mail:* emb.rabat@maec.es (office). *Website:* www.maec.es/subwebs/Embajadas/Rabat (office).

NAVARRO NAVARRO, Miguel; Spanish sculptor and set designer; b. 29 Sept. 1945, Mislata, Valencia; s. of Vicente Navarro Lopez and Valentina-Francisca Navarro Hernandez; ed Escuela Superior de Bellas Artes de San Carlos, Valencia; began career as a painter; from 1972 devoted himself mainly to sculpture; works in public spaces include public fountains, Valencia 1984, Turis (Valencia) 1986, Minerva Paranoica (sculpture), Castellón 1989, Torre del Sonido (sculpture), Universidad Carlos III, Getafe 1990, Fraternitat (sculpture), Barcelona 1992, Boca de Luna (fountain), Brussels 1994, Casco Industrial (sculpture) Bilbao 1999, Vigía (sculpture) Las Palmas 2000, Cabeza con Luna Menguante, Mislata 2001, La Mirada (sculpture) Vitoria-Gasteiz 2002, Palera (sculpture), Malaga 2002, Palas Fundición (sculpture) Ceuti, Murcia 2003, El Parotet, Valencia 2003, Conexion, Bilbao 2006, Mantis, Murcia 2007, Valvula con alberca, Zaragoza 2008, Almassil, Mislata (Valencia) 2010; works in public collections including Guggenheim Museum, New York, Fundació Caixa de Pensions, Barcelona, Instituto Valenciano de Arte Moderno, Valencia, Museo Nacional Centro de Arte Reina Sofía, Madrid, Fondation Lambert, Brussels, Diputación Prov. de Valencia, Centre Georges Pompidou, Paris, Museu d'Art Contemporani, Barcelona, Colección Argentaria, Madrid, Colección Banco de España, Madrid, Fundación Coca Cola España, Madrid, Fundazion ICO, Madrid, Universidad Politécnica de Valencia, Museo de Arte Contemporáneo Sofía Imbert, Caracas, Mie Prefectural Art Museum, Japan; has designed sets for plays including Fernando Sabater's Vente a Sinopia and Calderon de la Barca's Absalon; Premio Nacional de Artes Plásticas 1986, Premio Alfons Roig, Valencia 1987, Premio CEOE a las Artes 1990, Premio Nacional de la Asociación de Críticos de Arte ARCO 95 1995, Premio Valencianos para el Siglo XXI 2001, Distinción de la Generalidad Valenciana al Merito Cultural 2002, Julio Gonzalez Int. Prize, IVAM. *Leisure interests:* cooking, countryside. *Address:* c/o San Martín 13, 46920 Mislata, Valencia, Spain. *Telephone:* (6) 3792624. *E-mail:* info@cifo.org.

NAVASKY, Victor Saul, AB, LLB, JD; American writer, editor and academic; *Chairman, Columbia Journalism Review;* b. 5 July 1932, New York, NY; s. of Macy Navasky and Esther Goldberg; m. Anne Landey Strongin 1966; one s. two d.; ed Swarthmore Coll., Yale Univ. Law School; Special Asst to Gov. G. Mennen Williams, Mich. 1959–60; Founding Ed. and Publr Monocle quarterly 1961–65; Ed. New York Times Magazine 1970–72, wrote monthly column (In Cold Print) for The New York Times Book Review; Ed.-in-Chief The Nation magazine 1978–94, Editorial Dir and Publr 1995–2007, Publr Emer. 2007–; George Delacorte Prof. of Magazine Journalism, Grad. School of Journalism, Columbia Univ. 1999–, Dir Delacorte Center of Magazines, Chair. Columbia Journalism Review; Visiting Scholar, Russell Sage Foundation 1975–76; Ferris Visiting Prof. of Journalism, Princeton Univ. 1976–77; Visiting Prof. of Social Change, Swarthmore Coll. 1982; Fellow, John F. Kennedy School of Govt, Harvard Univ. 1994, Freedom Forum Media Studies Center 1995; has taught at numerous colls and univs; mem. Man. Bd Swarthmore Coll. 1991–94; fmr mem. Bd Authors' Guild, Cttee to Protect Journalists, Bd of Govs New School for Social Research; fmr Vice-Pres. PEN; mem. American Acad. of Arts and Sciences; numerous hon. degrees; Guggenheim Fellow 1975–76, Carey McWilliams Award, American Political Science Assn 2001. *Play:* Starr's Last Tape (with Richard R. Lingeman) 1999. *Publications include:* Kennedy Justice, Naming Names (Nat. Book Award), The Experts Speak: The Definitive Compendium of Authoritative Misinformation, A Matter of Opinion (George Polk Book Award 2005, Ann M. Sperber Prize 2006) 2005, Mission Accomplished: The Experts Speak about Iraq (with Christopher Cerf) 2008; numerous articles and reviews published in magazines and journals of opinion. *Address:* Room 802, Columbia Graduate School of Journalism, 2950 Broadway, New York, NY 10027 (office); The Nation, 33 Irving Place, 8th Floor, New York, NY 10003 (office); 33 W 67th Street, New York, NY 10023, USA (home). *Telephone:* (212) 854-5751 (Columbia Grad. School) (office); (212) 209-5411 (The Nation) (office). *Fax:* (212) 982-9000 (The Nation) (office). *E-mail:* vic@thenation.com (office). *Website:* thenation.com (office).

NAVICKAS, Vytas, PhD; Lithuanian economist and politician; b. 14 March 1952, Lazdijai Dist; m.; two d.; ed Vilnius Univ.; Research Fellow, Inst. of Econs, Lithuanian Acad. of Sciences 1975–89; Lecturer, Vilnius Univ., Vilnius Peda-gogical Univ. and Vilnius Gediminas Tech. Univ. 1983–90, 1997–2004; Head of Div. for Econ. Reforms, Council of Ministers 1989; Minister of the Economy 1990–91, 1995–96, 2006–08, Deputy Minister 1991–95; Dir UAB Draudos Asistavimas 1996–2004; Pres. Vilnius Chamber of Commerce, Industry and Crafts 2001–05; mem. Lithuanian Peasant Nationalists' Union. *Address:* c/o Ministry of the Economy, Gedimino pr. 38/2, Vilnius 01104, Lithuania.

NAVON, Yitzhak; Israeli fmr head of state and teacher; b. 9 April 1921, Jerusalem; s. of Yosef Navon and Miriam Ben-Atar; m. Ofira Reznikov-Erez 1963 (died 1993); one s. one d.; ed Hebrew Univ. of Jerusalem; Dir Hagana Arabic Dept, Jerusalem 1946–49; Second Sec., Israel Legation in Uruguay and Argentina 1949–51; Political Sec. to Foreign Minister 1951–52; Head of Bureau of Prime Minister 1952–63; Head, Dept of Culture, Ministry of Educ. and Culture 1963–65; mem. Knesset (Parl.) 1965–78; fmr Deputy Speaker; fmr Chair. Knesset Defence and Foreign Affairs Cttee; Chair. World Zionist Council 1973–78; Pres. of Israel 1978–83; Vice-Premier and Minister of Educ. and Culture 1984–90; mem. Mapai Party 1951–65, Rafi 1965–68, Israel Labour Party 1968–; Chair. Acad. of Music and Dance, Nat. Authority of Ladino, Neot Kedumim (Biblical Gardens); voted the 108th greatest Israeli of all time in a poll by Israeli news website Ynet 2005. *Television:* Out of Spain – series of five programmes on the history of the Jews in Spain. *Publications:* musicals: Romancero Sephardi 1968, Bustan Sephardi (Spanish Garden) 1970; Six Days and Seven Gates 1979; collection of articles on Ben Gurion. *Leisure interests:* theatre, folklore, cantorial music. *Address:* 31

Hanevi'im Street, Jerusalem (office); 39 Jabotinsky Street, Jerusalem, Israel (home). *Telephone:* (2) 623-63-53 (office); (2) 563-85-66 (home). *Fax:* (2) 623-63-55 (office). *E-mail:* fpnavon@netvision.net.il (office).

NAVRACSICS, Tibor, PhD; Hungarian lawyer, political scientist, academic and politician; *Deputy Prime Minister and Minister of Public Administration and Justice;* b. 13 June 1966, Veszprém; m.; two d.; ed Eötvös Loránd Univ., Budapest; Tribunal Clerk, Municipal Court, Veszprém 1990–92; Lecturer, Dept of Social Sciences, Univ. of Veszprém 1990–92; Research Fellow, Regional Ass. of Veszprém Co. 1992–93; Lecturer, Dept of Sociology and Political Sciences, Dániel Berzsenyi Teacher's Coll., Szombathely 1992–98; Asst Prof., Dept of Political Sciences, Univ. of Econs, Budapest 1993–97, Assoc. Prof. 1997–2001; Sr Assoc. Prof., Dept of Political Sciences, Eötvös Loránd Univ. 2001–; Head of Communications Dept (Viktor Orbán's Cabinet), Prime Minister's Office 1998–99, Head of Dept for Press and Information 1999–2002; Head of Dept for Political Analyses, Parl. Group of Fidesz—Hungarian Civic Union 2002–03, Chief of Pres.'s Cabinet 2003–06; Leader of programme-creating team (referred to as Civic Governance) 2004–; mem. Parl. 2006–, Head of Parl. Group of Fidesz—Hungarian Civic Alliance 2006–10; Deputy Prime Minister and Minister of Public Admin and Justice 2010–; Acting Minister of Nat. Devt 2011; Sec. Gen. Hungarian Asscn of Political Scientists 1998–2000; Vice-Pres. Asscn of the Hungarian Inst. for Political Science 1996–; Ed. Periodical Comitatus 1992–93; mem. Editorial Bd Politikatudományi Szemle (Political Science Review) 1999–; mem. of the Presidency, Hungarian Asscn of Political Science 2001–; mem. Political Sciences Asscn; Scholarship of the Soros Foundation 1994–96, CEEPUS Scholarship, Univ. of Zagreb 1995, Leverhulme Research Fellow/Scholarship, European Inst., Univ. of Sussex, Brighton, UK 1996–97, Winner, OTKA Competition: The Democracy in Central Eastern Europe 1996–99, Jean Monnet Scholarship 1998–2001, elected Teacher of the Year by the students of Eötvös Loránd Univ. 2007. *Publications include:* Európai belpolitika (Internal Politics in the European Union) 1996, Political Analysis of the European Union 1996, Political Communication (with István Hegedűs, Mihály Szilágyi and Sipos Balázs) 2004. *Address:* Ministry of Public Administration and Justice, 1055 Budapest, Kossuth Lajos tér 2–4 (office); Ministry of Public Administration and Justice, 1357 Budapest, Pf.: 2, Hungary (office). *Telephone:* (1) 795-3033 (office). *Fax:* (1) 795-0502 (office). *E-mail:* miniszter@kim.gov.hu (office); info@kim.gov.hu (office). *Website:* www.kormany.hu/en/ministry-of-public-administration-and -justice (office).

NAVRATILOVA, Martina; American/Czech fmr professional tennis player; b. 18 Oct. 1956, Prague, Czech Repub.; d. of Miroslav Navratil and Jana Navratilova; left-handed, one-handed backhand; professional since 1975, the year she defected to USA; ranked No. 1 July 1978, 1982–85; Wimbledon singles champion 1978, 1979, 1982, 1983, 1984, 1985, 1986, 1987, 1990, finalist 1988, 1989, 1994; (doubles 1976, 1979, 1982, 1983, 1984, 1985); French champion 1982, 1984; Australian champion 1981, 1983, 1985; Avon champion 1978, 1979, 1981; US Open champion 1983, 1984, 1986, 1987; 57 Grand Slam titles (18 singles, 37 women's doubles, 2 mixed doubles); won 167 singles and 177 doubles titles (more than any other player, male or female); World No. 1 for 332 weeks at retirement (Nov. 1994); 19 Wimbledon titles (1995); set professional women's record for consecutive victories 1984; won 100th tournament of career 1985; only player to win 100 matches at Wimbledon 1991; record of 158 wins (Feb. 1992) in singles beating the record of Chris Evert Lloyd; Pres. WTA (Women's Tennis Asscn) 1979–80, 1983–84, 1994–95; World Champion 1980; played Fed. Cup for Czechoslovakia 1973, 1974, 1975, for USA 2003; 1,442 victories, 219 defeats; designer own fashion wear; made comeback (in doubles only) 2000; winner Mixed Doubles, Australian Open 2003, Wimbledon 2003 (at age 46 years and 6 months, oldest winner of a Grand Slam title); retd 2006; Dr hc (George Washington Univ.) 1996; WTA Player of the Year 1978, 1979, 1982, 1983, 1984, 1985, 1986, ITF World Champion 1979, 1982, 1983, 1984, 1985, 1986, Female Athlete of the Decade for the 1980s, Nat. Sports Review, Sportswomen of the Year 1982–84, Women's Sports Foundation, Int. Tennis Hall of Fame 2000. *Television:* I'm a Celebrity... Get Me Out of Here! (ITV) 2008. *Publications include:* Being Myself (autobiog.) 1985, The Total Zone (novel with Liz Nickles) 1994, The Breaking Point (with Liz Nickles) 1996, Killer Instinct (with Liz Nickles) 1998, Shape Yourself 2006. *Leisure interests:* golf, snowboarding, skiing, basketball. *Address:* c/o IMG, 1360 East 9th Street, Cleveland, OH 44114, USA (office). *Website:* www.martinanavratilova.com.

NAWAR, Ahmed, PhD; Egyptian arts administrator; b. 3 June 1945, el-Shin, Gharbia dist; s. of Mohamed Ismail Nawar and Fakiha Karam Mostafa Ghali; m. Wafaa Mossallem 1969; three d.; ed Cairo Univ. and St Fernando Acad., Madrid, Spain; Prof. of Graphics, Faculty of Fine Art, Helwan Univ. 1967–; Founder and Dean, Faculty of Fine Art, Menia Univ. 1983–88; Head, Nat. Centre for Fine Arts, Ministry of Culture 1988–; Head, Museums Service, Higher Council for Antiqui-ties 1994–99; Gen. Supervisor Nubia Savings Fund 1996–98; Adviser to People's Ass. 1999–; Nobel Gold Medal 1986; State Order of Arts and Sciences, First Class 1979, Order of Merit (Spain) 1992, Officier, Ordre des Arts et des Sciences. *Address:* 78 el-Shishiny Street, off Al-Mariyoutiyah Canal Street, Al-Hram, Giza (studio); 54 Dimashk Street, Madinat al-Mohandeseen, Flat 16, Giza, Egypt (home). *Telephone:* (2) 7448336. *E-mail:* a-nawar@a-nawar.com. *Website:* www.a-nawar.com.

NAWAWI AYOB, Ahmad, PhD; Malaysian botanist, academic and fmr university vice-chancellor; *Professor Emeritus, Institute of Biological Sciences, University of Malaya;* b. 11 Feb. 1937, Perak; m.; two c.; ed Queen's Univ., Belfast, Northern Ireland; Demonstrator in Botany, Mycology and Plant Pathology, Queen's Univ., Belfast 1963–65; botanist and plant pathologist, Ministry of Agric., Malaysia 1966–67; Post-doctoral Research Fellow, Wageningen Agricultural Univ., Nether-lands 1970, Queen's Univ. Belfast 1971–72; Lecturer in Botany, Univ. of Malaya 1967–74, Assoc. Prof. 1974–78, now Emer., Head Dept of Botany 1974–75, Prof. of Botany 1978, Dean Faculty of Sciences 1976–78, Acting Deputy Vice-Chancellor 1977, Deputy Vice-Chancellor for Finance and Devt 1983–86, Acting Vice-Chancellor 1986, Deputy Vice-Chancellor 1991; Pres. Malaysian Soc. for Micro-biology 1986–87; fmr Pres. Malaysian Soc. for Applied Biology; mem. Council Malaysian Agricultural Research and Devt Inst., Malaysian Nat. Science Council 1981–, Man. Cttee Nat. Scientific Research and Devt Trust Fund 1981–, Council Nat. Inst. of Public Admin.; mem. Acad. of Sciences Malaysia; Fellow, Islamic Acad. of Sciences, Malaysian Acad. of Sciences; Hon. DSc (Portsmouth), (Belfast)

1995; Johan Mangku Negara 1982, Datuk Paduka Cura Si Manja Kini 1986, Dato Paduka Cura Simanja Kini (DPCM). *Publications:* over 60 specialized publs. *Address:* Institute of Research Management and Consultancy, IPS Building, University of Malaya, 50603 Kuala Lumpur, Malaysia (office). *Telephone:* (3) 79674370 (office). *Fax:* (3) 79674178 (office). *E-mail:* nawawi@um.edu.my (office). *Website:* www.ippp.um.edu.my (office).

NAYLOR, David, OC, MD, DPhil, FRSC, FRCPC; Canadian medical researcher and fmr university administrator; b. 1954, Woodstock, Ont.; m. Ilse Treurnicht; ed Univ. of Toronto, Univ. of Oxford, UK, Univ. of Western Ontario; fmr Sr Scientist, Medical Research Council of Canada; mem. Faculty Univ. of Toronto 1981–, Dean of Medicine and Vice-Provost, Relations with Health Care Insts 1999–2005, Pres. Univ. of Toronto 2005–13; Founding CEO Inst. for Clinical Evaluative Sciences 1991–98; Chair. Nat. Advisory Cttee on SARS and Public Health 2003; fmr Gov. Canadian Insts of Health Research; fmr mem. Bd Mount Sinai Hosp., St Michael's Hosp., Univ. Health Network, Sunnybrook Health Science Centre, Toronto Rehabilitation Inst.; Fellow, Royal Coll. of Physicians and Surgeons of Canada, Canadian Acad. of Health Sciences; Foreign Assoc. Fellow, US Inst. of Medicine; Hon. DSc (Univ. of Manitoba) 2009; Hon. LLD (Western Univ.) 2011; Royal Australasian Coll. of Physicians John Dinham Cottrell Medal 1996, Royal Coll. of Physicians and Surgeons of Canada G. Malcolm Brown Award 1996, Medical Research Council of Canada Michael Smith Award 1999, Canadian Cardiovascular Soc. Research Achievement Award 2002, R.D. Defries Award, Canadian Public Health Asscn. *Publications:* more than 300 scholarly works. *Leisure interests:* music, golf. *Telephone:* (416) 987-2121 (office). *E-mail:* david.naylor@utoronto.ca (office).

NAYLOR, Sir Robert, Kt, BSc; British health services executive; *CEO, University College London Hospitals;* b. 1950, Manchester; ed Univ. of Greenwich; began career as graduate trainee, later Hosp. Admin. Nat. Hosp., Queen Square, London; CEO Birmingham Heartlands & Solihull NHS Trust 1985–2000; CEO Univ. Coll. London Hosps (UCLH) 2000–; Sr Assoc. Fellow, Univ. of Warwick Inst. of Governance and Public Man. *Leisure interests:* football (Manchester United), opera, scuba diving. *Address:* UCLH, 250 Euston Road, London, NW1 2PG, England (office). *Website:* www.uclh.nhs.uk (office).

NAYYER HUSSAIN BOKHARI, Syed, BA, LLB; Pakistani lawyer and politician; *Chairman of the Senate;* b. 23 Dec. 1952, Rawalpindi; m.; one s. two d.; ed Gordon Coll., Univ. of the Punjab, Lahore; joined Pakistan People's Party (PPP) 1968, Gen.-Sec. 1983–87, Pres. PPP Islamabad 1987–; apptd mem. of Nat. Ass. 2002, Deputy Chief Whip 2002–07; Advocate, High Court 1981, Supreme Court 2010; Admin. People's Works Program, Islamabad Dist 1989–90; mem. Bd of Man. Bait-ul-Mal 1994–96; elected to Senate, Leader of the House 2009–12, Chair. 2012–; Gen.-Sec., Islamabad Bar Asscn 1982–83, apptd Pres. 1984, 1992 and 2000. *Address:* Office of the Chairman of the Senate, Parliament House, Constitution Avenue, Islamabad, Pakistan (office). *Telephone:* (51) 9223475 (office). *Fax:* (51) 9103125 (office). *E-mail:* chairman@senate.gov.pk (office). *Website:* www.senate.gov.pk (office).

NAZARBAEV, Nursultan Abishuh, DSc; Kazakhstani politician and head of state; *President;* b. 6 July 1940, Chemolgan, Kaskelen Dist, Almatı Oblast; s. of Abish Nazarbaev and Aizhan Nazarbaeva; m. Sara Alplisovna Kunakaeva 1962; three d.; ed Higher Tech. Course at Qarağandi Metallurgical Combine, Russian Acad. of Management and Higher Party School of Cen. Cttee CPSU; mem. CPSU 1962–91; worked for Qarağandi Metallurgical Plant 1960–64, 1965–69; Sec. Temirtau City Cttee of Kazakh CP 1969–84; Sec. Party Cttee of Qarağandi Metallurgical Combine 1973–77; Second, then First Sec. Qarağandi Dist Cttee of Kazakh CP 1977–79; Sec. Cen. Cttee of Kazakh CP 1979–84; Chair. Council of Ministers of Kazakh SSR 1984–89; USSR People's Deputy 1989–91; First Sec. Cen. Cttee of Kazakh CP 1989–91, Socialist Party 1991–; Chair. Kazakh Supreme Soviet 1989–90; Exec. Pres. Kazakh SSR 1990–91; Pres. Repub. of Kazakhstan 1991–; Chair. World Kazakh Union 1992–; mem. Int. Eng Acad. 1993, Acad. of Social Sciences of the Russian Fed. 1994, Nat. Acad. of Sciences of the Repub. of Kazakhstan 1995; Hon. Citizen of Temirtau 1991, Duluth, USA 1991, Almatı 1995; Diploma of Freeman of Municipality of Bucharest 1998; Hon. Prof., Al-Farabi Kazakh State Nat. Univ., M.V. Lomonosov Moscow State Univ. 1996; Hon. mem. Belarusian Acad. of Sciences 1996, Nat. Acad. of Applied Sciences of Russia 1997; numerous decorations, including Order of the Red Banner of Labour, Kt, Order of St Andrew (Russia), Grand Collar, Order of Vytautas the Great (Lithuania), Collar of the Order of the Star of Romania, Kt Grand Cross with Grand Cordon, Order of Leopold (Belgium), Grand Cordon, Order of the Chrysanthemum (Japan), Grand Cordon, Order of the Nile (Egypt), Kt Grand Cross, Order of Merit (Hungary), Kt Grand Cross, Order of the Oak Crown (Luxembourg), Kt, Order of the Three Stars (Latvia), Mem. Order of the White Double Cross (Slovakia), Medal of Astana (Kazakhstan), Order of Akhmad Kadyrov (Chechnya), Badge of Honour 1972, Order of Prince Daniil of Moscow (First Class) 1996, Order of the Golden Eagle (Kazakhstan) 1996, The First Class of the Order of Prince Yaroslav the Wise (Ukraine) 1997, Order of Holy Apostle Andrei Pervosvannyi (Russia) 1998, Cavaliere di Gran Croce con Gran Cordone (Italy) 1998, GCMG 2000, Great Star of the Order of Merit (Austria) 2000, Order of Ismoili Samoni (Tajikistan) 2000, Kt Grand Cross of the Order of the Redeemer (Greece) 2001, Kt Grand Cross, Grand Order of King Tomislav 2001, Order of Pius (Vatican) 2001, Order of the White Eagle (Poland) 2002, Kt Grand Cross with Grand Cordon, Order of the White Rose (Finland) 2008, Grand Croix, Ordre de la Légion d'honneur 2008, Grand Cross, Order of the Lion (Finland) 2009, Order of Liberty (Ukraine) 2010, Collar of the Cross of Terra Mariana (Estonia) 2011; Dr hc (Kazakh Inst. of Man., Economy and Forecasting) 1995, (Bilkent Univ., Ankara) 1998; Capri Award (Italy) 1992, Rukhaniyat Man of the Year 1993, Gold Medal of Guild of Econ. Devt and Marketing of the City of Nuremberg (Germany) 1993, Award of Crans-Montana Int. Forum 1996, star No. Perseus RA 3h 23v Osd 40* 43 named after him 1997, Medal No. 1 of Al-Farabi Kazakh State Nat. Univ. 1998, Award for Int. Understanding, Indian Fund Unity Int. 1998, Award For Service to Turkish World 1998, Gold Medal and Diploma for Special Contrib. to Devt of CIS Aviation, Int. Aviation Comm. 1998, Peace Dove Prize, UNESCO Club of Dodecanese Islands (Greece) 1999, Man of the Century Award, Abylai Khan Int. Fund 2000, Man of the Year Nat. Award (State Policy category) 2012. *Publications:* Steel Profile of Kazakhstan, With Neither the Right nor the Left, Strategy of Resource

Saving and Market Transition, Strategy of Formation and Development of Kazakhstan as a Sovereign State, Market and Social-and-Economic Development, On the Threshold of the XXIst Century, Eurasian Union: Ideas, Practice, Prospects 1994–1997, In the Flood of History, The Epicenter of Peace, and others; numerous scientific articles and articles on econs. *Leisure interests:* tennis, water-skiing, horses, reading history books. *Address:* Office of the President, 010000 Astana, Beibitshilik 11, Kazakhstan (office). *Telephone:* (7172) 32-13-99 (office). *Fax:* (7172) 32-61-72 (office). *E-mail:* egov@nitec.kz (office). *Website:* www.akorda.kz (office).

NAZARBAEVA, Dariga Nursultanqizi, Dr rer. pol; Kazakhstani politician and media executive; b. 7 May 1963, Temirtau, Kazakh SSR, USSR; d. of Pres. Nursultan Nazarbaev; m. Rakhat Aliyev (divorced 2007); two s. one d.; ed Moscow M.V. Lomonosov State Univ., S.M. Kirov State Univ., Russian Presidential Acad. of Public Service; Vice-Pres. Khabar Broadcasting Agency 1994–95, Gen. Dir 1995–98, Pres. 1998–2001, Chair. Council of Dirs 2001–03; Founder and Chair. Mutual Help Republican Party (Asar, later Fatherland Republican Political Party, Otan' Respublikalyk Sayasi Partiyasy, following merger) 2003–06, Chair. Light of the Fatherland People's Democratic Party 2006; Chair. Eurasian Media Forum; Leader, Congress of Journalists of Kazakhstan; Chair., Supervisory Bd of Int. Inst. for Modern Politics, Kazakhstan; mem. Bd Int. TV Acad., New York; Pres. Eurasian Centre for Strategic Studies, Russia; Vice-Pres. Eurasian TV Acad., Russia; Co-Chair. Eurasian TV Forum Organizing Cttee; Assoc. mem. Int. Econ. Acad. Eurasia; Vice-Pres. Children's Charitable Fund Bobek 1992–94; mem. Nat. Comm. of Repub. of Kazakhstan for UNESCO; fmr Pres. Sports Gymnastics Fed. of Repub. of Kazakhstan; jury mem., second season of SuperStar KZ. *Publications:* Democratization of Political Systems in the Commonwealth of Independent States 1997, The Eurasian Commonwealth 2000, From the Union Towards the Commonwealth (ed. and co-author) 2001, Ten Years of the Commonwealth of Independent States: Experience, Problems, Future Prospects (co-author) 2001. *Leisure interest:* amateur opera singer. *Address:* Light of the Fatherland People's Democratic Party ('Nur Otan' Khalyktyk Demokratiyalyk Partiyasy), 050000 Almaty, Abylai khana 79, Kazakhstan (office). *Telephone:* (727) 279-78-00 (office). *Fax:* (727) 279-40-66 (office). *E-mail:* partyotan@nursat.kz (office). *Website:* nurotan.kz (office).

NAZARE, Alexandru; Romanian politician; *Minister of Transport and Infrastructure;* b. 25 June 1980; ed Nat. School of Political and Admin. Studies, Bucharest, European Coll. of Liberal Arts, Berlin; Minister Counsellor, Ministry of European Integration 2005–07; Counsellor, Del. of Democratic Liberal Party-European People's Party to the European Parl. 2007–08; mem. European Parl. 2008–09, Parl. Adviser Aug.–Oct. 2009; Sec. of State, Dept for European Affairs 2009–10; Sec. of State, Ministry of Finance April–Nov. 2010, Ministry of Transport 2010–12; Minister of Transport and Infrastructure 2012–. *Address:* Ministry of Transport and Infrastructure, 010873 Bucharest 1, Bd. Dinicu Golescu 38, Romania (office). *Telephone:* (21) 3196161 (office). *Fax:* (21) 3120772 (office). *E-mail:* relpub@mt.ro (office). *Website:* www.mt.ro (office).

NAZARENKO, Tatyana Grigorievna; Russian painter; *Professor of Art, Moscow Surikov State Fine Arts Institute;* b. 24 June 1944, Moscow; m.; two s.; ed Moscow Surikov State Fine Arts Inst.; worked in Studio of USSR Acad. of Fine Arts 1969–72; mem. USSR (now Russian) Union of Painters 1969; works in collections of approx. 42 major museums world-wide and in numerous important pvt. collections; Assoc., Russian Acad. of Fine Arts 1998, Full mem. and mem. Bd of Dirs 2001–; Prof. of Art, Moscow Surikov State Fine Arts Inst. 1999–; Acad. of Arts Silver Medal 1987, Russian State Prize 1993, Moscow Govt Prize 1999, Honored Artist of Russia 2003, Triumph Prize 2008. *Television:* Artist's Portrait – Life and Work of Tatiana Nazarenko, 'Kultura' (Russian TV), Classics in Contemporary Art, 'Kultura' (Russian TV). *Publications:* Vanishing Reality 2006. *Address:* c/o Volga Art Gallery, 125009 Moscow, Bolshoi Gnezdnikovsky per. 10, Russia. *Telephone:* (495) 629-75-18; (925) 507-45-58. *E-mail:* tatyana@nazarenko-art.ru. *Website:* www.nazarenko-art.ru; volga-gallery.com.

NAZAREWICZ, Witold (Witek), MSc, PhD, Dr habil., FInstP; American (b. Polish) physicist and academic; *James McConnell Distinguished Professor in Physics, University of Tennessee;* b. 26 Dec. 1954, Warsaw, Poland; s. of Ryszard Nazarewicz and Hanna Blonska; m. Krystyna Nazarewicz; one s. one d.; ed Warsaw Univ. of Tech., Inst. for Nuclear Research, Warsaw, Warsaw Univ.; Teaching Asst, Warsaw Univ. of Tech. 1977–81; Asst Prof., Warsaw Univ. 1981–88, Assoc. Prof. 1988–91, Prof. 1994–; Visiting Research Fellow, Lund Univ., Sweden 1982–84, Visiting Prof. 1990; Visiting Research Fellow, Niels Bohr Inst., Copenhagen, Denmark 1984–85; Visiting Prof., Jt Inst. for Heavy Ion Research, Oak Ridge, TN, USA 1985–86, 1991–95, Scientific Dir, Oak Ridge Nat. Lab. Holifield Radioactive Ion Beam Facility 1996–; Visiting Prof., Florida State Univ. 1986, 1991, Cologne Univ., Germany 1987, KTH (Royal Inst. of Tech.), Stockholm, Sweden 1988; Visiting Sr Lecturer, Univ. of Liverpool, UK 1988–89; Visiting Prof., Univ. of Lund, Sweden 1990, Kyoto Univ., Japan 1992, Univ. of Liverpool 1995; Prof. of Physics, Univ. of Tennessee, Knoxville 1995–, James McConnell Distinguished Prof. in Physics 2012–; mem. Editorial Bd, Physical Review C 1994–96, Reports on Progress in Physics 2001–06, Reviews of Modern Physics 2006–, European Physical Journal A 2006–; mem. numerous expert panels; mem. Bd of Physics and Astronomy, Nat. Research Council 1996–99, Nat. Advisory Cttee, Inst. for Nuclear Theory, Seattle 1996–98; Co-Chair., later Chair. RIA Steering Group 2000–04; mem. and Chair. RIA Users Organization Exec. Cttee 2004–05; mem. Bd Mazurian Lakes Confs on Physics, Warsaw 2006, Steering Cttee Japan US Theory Inst. for Physics with Exotic Nuclei 2006–, Jefferson Lab. Program Advisory Cttee 2007–; Chair. Bd Zdzisław Szymanski Prize, Warsaw Univ. 2002–; Scientific Expert, Scientific Advisory Bd for Finnish Centre of Excellence in Nuclear and Accelerator Based Physics, Univ. of Jyvaskyla 2006–; mem. European Physical Soc. 1992–95, Polish Physical Soc.; Fellow, American Physical Soc. 1994, Inst. of Physics 2004, AAAS 2009; Univ. of Tennessee-Battelle Corp. Fellow, ORNL 2013; Carnegie Centenary Prof. (Scotland, UK) 2008; Hon. Guest Prof., Peking Univ. 2013–(15); Hon. DUniv (Univ. of the West of Scotland) 2009; Individual Scientific Award, Polish Ministry of Educ. 1982, 1987, 1989, Individual Scientific Award, Polish Nuclear Energy Comm. 1983, Individual Scientific Award, Polish Physical Soc. 1986, Lockheed Martin Tech. Achievement Award 1999, Univ. of Tennessee Battelle Tech. Achievement Award 2000, Coll. of Arts and Sciences Sr Research/ Creative Achievement Award 2001, Univ. of Tennessee Research and Creative

Achievement Award 2002, Tom W. Bonner Prize, American Physical Soc. 2012, Distinguished Scientist Award, Oak Ridge Nat. Lab. 2012. *Publications:* author of editor of five books, nine review papers and more than 350 refereed research papers on theoretical nuclear physics, nuclear structure, and the many-body problem, listed by ISI among the most highly cited in physics. *Leisure interest:* map collecting. *Address:* Department of Physics and Astronomy, University of Tennessee, 104 South College, Knoxville, TN 37996-1200 (office); Oak Ridge National Laboratory, 8W Building 6025, 1 Bethel Valley Road, Oak Ridge, TN 37830, USA (office). *Telephone:* (865) 974-4375 (Knoxville) (office); (865) 574-4580 (Oak Ridge) (office). *Fax:* (865) 974-7843 (Knoxville) (office). *E-mail:* witek@utk .edu (office). *Website:* www.phys.utk.edu/faculty/faculty-nazarewicz.html (office).

NAZARIAN, Garen A., MA; Armenian diplomatist; *Permanent Representative, United Nations;* b. 29 Nov. 1966, Yerevan; m. Siranush Nazarian-Shahnazarova; two c.; ed Faculty of Oriental Studies, Yerevan State Univ., Faculty of Int. Relations, Moscow Diplomatic Acad.; worked in Dept on Mil.-Political Problems, Ministry of Foreign Affairs 1991–92, at Embassy of Armenia, Moscow 1992–94; Chief of Secr., Ministry of Foreign Affairs 1994–96; Perm. Rep. to UN and other Int. Orgs, Geneva 1996–2002; Adviser to Minister of Foreign Affairs 2002–05; Amb. to Iran 2005–09; Perm. Rep. to UN, New York 2009–; apptd Vice-Pres. World Conf. against Racism, Racial Discrimination, Xenophobia and Related Intolerance, Durban, South Africa 2001; apptd Chair. 8th Meeting of the State Parties to the UN Convention against Torture 2002; Chair. UN Comm. on the Status of Women 2009–11; fmr mem. Armenian-American Inter-Governmental Comm. *Leisure interests:* skiing, music. *Address:* Permanent Mission of Armenia to United Nations, 119 East 36th Street, New York, NY 10016, USA (office). *Telephone:* (212) 686-9079 (office). *Fax:* (212) 686-3934 (office). *E-mail:* armenia@un.int (office). *Website:* www.un.mfa.am (office).

NAZAROV, Talbak Nazarovich, DEconSc; Tajikistani politician and academic; b. 15 March 1938, Danghara, Kulyab District; s. of Khojaev Nazar and Ismailova Hanifa; m. Tatyana Grigorievna Teodorovich 1959; one s. one d.; ed Leningrad (now St Petersburg) Inst. of Finance and Econs; Asst, then Deputy Dean of Econs Faculty, Tajik State Univ. 1960–62, Head of Dept, Dean 1965–80, Rector 1982–88; Chair. Supreme Soviet Tajik SSR 1986–88; Minister of Public Educ. 1988–90; USSR People's Deputy 1989–92; First Deputy Chair. Tajikistan Council of Ministers, Chair. State Planning Cttee 1990–91; Minister of Foreign Affairs 1994–2006, Amb.-at-Large 2006–; mem. Presidium, Acad. of Sciences of the Repub. of Tajikistan 1980–, currently Vice-Pres.; Merited Worker of Science and many other awards and medals. *Publications:* books and articles on Tajikistan's economy and external policies. *Leisure interests:* reading fiction and political literature. *Address:* 33 Rudaki Avenue, 734025 Dushanbe, Tajikistan (office).

NAZDRATENKO, Yevgeny Ivanovich; Russian politician; b. 16 Feb. 1949, Severo-Kurilsk, Sakhalin Region; m.; two s.; ed Far East Inst. of Tech.; served with Pacific Fleet; Head of sector Bor Co.; mechanic, Vice-Pres., Pres. Primorsk Mining Co., Vostok 1980–93; Peoples' Deputy of Russian Fed. 1990–93; Head of Admin. Primorsk Territory 1993–95, Gov. 1995–2001; mem. Council of Fed. of Russia 1996–2001; Chair. State Cttee for Fisheries 2001–03; Deputy Sec. Russian Security Council 2004–; Dr hc (St Petersburg Mining Univ., Seoul Univ.); Order for Personal Courage 1994, hon. Citizen of Russia 1995. *Address:* Security Council, 103132 Moscow, Ipat'yevski per. 4/10, Russia.

NAZER, Sheikh Hisham Mohieddin, BA, MA; Saudi Arabian politician and diplomatist; b. 1932, Jeddah; ed Victoria Coll., Alexandria, Egypt, Univ. of California, Los Angeles, USA; legal adviser 1958; assisted in foundation of OPEC 1960; Deputy Minister of Petroleum 1962–68; with Ministry of Planning from 1975, Acting Minister of Planning 1986–91; Minister of Petroleum and Mineral Resources 1986–95; Pres. Cen. Org. for Planning from 1968; mem. Supreme Council for Petroleum and Minerals from 1968; fmr Chair. SAMAREC; Chair. Saudi Arabian Oil Co. (Saudi Aramco) 1988; mem. Advisory Bd Aspect Enterprise Solutions Ltd; Amb. to Egypt 2005–11; Hon. LLD (Univ. of Korea), (American Univ., Cairo) 1991. *Publication:* Power of a Third Kind 1998. *Leisure interests:* poetry, football. *Address:* Aspect Enterprise Solutions Ltd, Castlewood House, 77–91 New Oxford Street, London, WC1A 1DG, England. *Telephone:* (20) 7632-0170. *Fax:* (20) 7836-8030. *E-mail:* moreinfo@aspectenterprise.com. *Website:* www .aspectenterprise.com.

NAZIF, Ahmad Mahmoud Muhammad, BSc, MA, PhD; Egyptian computer engineer and government official; b. 8 July 1952, Alexandria; m.; two s.; ed Cairo Univ., McGill Univ., Canada; Prof. of Computer Eng, Cairo Univ. 1994; Exec. Man. IDSC 1989–95; apptd Minister for Communications and Tech. 1999; Prime Minister 2004–11 (dismissed); First Order Medal of Science and Art. *Address:* 2 Magles El Shaab Street, Kasr El Aini St., Cairo; c/o Office of the Prime Minister, Sharia Majlis ash-Sha'ab, Cairo, Egypt.

NAZIM, Col (retd) Mohamed; Maldivian fmr army officer and government official; *Minister of Defence and National Security;* b. Malé; m. Afaaf Abdul Majeed; two d.; ed Royal Mil. Acad. Sandhurst, UK, Mubarak Al Abdullah Command and Staff Coll., Kuwait, Asia-Pacific Centre for Security Studies, Coll. of Security Studies, USA, Near East South Asia Center for Strategic Studies, Nat. Defence Univ., USA; fmr Instructor, Grifushi Training Centre; CO Nat. Cadet Corps, Regional HQ Seenu Gan, Quick Reaction Force 2; Admin. Officer, Integrated HQ, Nat. Defence Force –2011; Minister of Defence and Nat. Security 2012–; fmr Pres. Dhivehi Sifainge Club; mem. Asscn of US Army; Presidential Medal, Dedicated Service Medal, Distinguished Service Medal, 3rd November Medal, Presidential Ribbon, Dedicated Service Ribbon, Long Service Ribbon, Achievement Ribbon, Ribbon of Skill. *Address:* Ministry of Defence and National Security, Ameer Ahmed Magu, Malé 20-126, Maldives (office). *Telephone:* 3322607 (office). *Fax:* 3332689 (office). *E-mail:* mnazim@defence.gov.mv (office). *Website:* www.defence.gov.mv (office).

NAZIR-ALI, Rt Rev. Michael James, BA, BLitt, MLitt, ThD, DHLitt, DD; British/Pakistani ecclesiastic and academic; *Founder and Director, OXTRAD (Oxford Centre for Training, Research, Advocacy and Dialogue);* b. 19 Aug. 1949, Karachi, Pakistan; s. of James Nazir-Ali and Patience Nazir-Ali; m. Valerie Cree 1972; two s.; ed St Paul's High School, Karachi, St Patrick's Coll., Karachi, Univ. of Karachi, Fitzwilliam Coll. Cambridge, Ridley Hall, Cambridge, St Edmund Hall, Oxford, Australian Coll. of Theology with assistance from the Centre for World

Religions, Harvard etc.; Tutorial Supervisor in Theology, Univ. of Cambridge 1974–76; Asst Curate, Holy Sepulchre, Cambridge 1974–76; Tutor then Sr Tutor, Karachi Theological Coll. 1976–81; Assoc. Priest Holy Trinity Cathedral, Karachi 1976–79; Priest-in-Charge St Andrew's Akhtar Colony, Karachi 1979–81; Provost Lahore Cathedral 1981–84; Bishop of Raiwind 1984–86; fmr Visiting Lecturer, Selly Oak Colls, Birmingham; Asst to Archbishop of Canterbury; Co-ordinator of Studies for 1988 Lambeth Conf. 1986–89; Gen. Sec. Church Mission Soc. 1989–94; Asst Bishop, Diocese of Southwark 1990–94; Canon Theologian, Leicester Cathedral 1992–94; Bishop of Rochester 1994–2009; mem. House of Lords 1999–2009; Founder and Dir OXTRAD (Oxford Centre for Training, Research, Advocacy and Dialogue) 2009–; Chair. Mission Theological Advisory Group 1992–2001, Chair. Governing Council, Trinity Coll. Bristol 1996–2009; Dir Oxford Centre for Mission Studies, Christian Aid; mem. Design Group for 1998 Lambeth Conf., Anglican Roman Catholic Int. Comm. 1991–2010, Bd of Mission Gen. Synod, Church of England 1992–94, 1996–2000, Human Fertilization and Embryology Authority 1998–2003 (Chair. of Ethics and Law Cttee); Fellow, St Edmund Hall Oxford 1998–; Fellow, Fitzwilliam Coll. Cambridge; Visiting Prof. of Theological and Religious Studies, Univ. of Greenwich 1996–; mem. Archbishop's Council 2001–06, House of Bishops' Standing Cttee 2001–06, Anglican-Roman Catholic Jt Working Group 2001–, Chair. Working Party on Women in the Episcopate, Chair. House of Bishops' Theological Group, Lecturer Royal Coll. of Defence Studies; Paul Harris Fellow, Rotary International 2005; Sr Fellow, Wycliffe Hall Oxford; Visiting Bishop, Anglican Communion, SC, USA; Hon. DLitt (Bath), (Greenwich), Hon. DD (Kent) 2004, (Nashotah House, USA) 2010; Radio Pakistan Prize for English Language and Literature 1964, Burney Award (Cambridge) 1973, 1975, Oxford Soc. Award for Grads 1973, Langham Scholarship 1974, Shaikh Yamani Gold Medal in Islamic Studies 2008. *Publications:* Islam, a Christian Perspective 1983, Frontiers in Christian–Muslim Encounter 1987, Martyrs and Magistrates: Toleration and Trial in Islam 1989, The Roots of Islamic Tolerance: Origin and Development 1990, From Everywhere to Everywhere 1991, Mission and Dialogue 1995, The Mystery of Faith 1995, Citizens and Exiles 1998, Shapes of the Church to Come 2001, Understanding My Muslim Neighbour 2002, Conviction and Conflict 2006, The Unique and Universal Christ 2008, Triple Jeopardy for the West 2012; contrib. to The Jesus Accounts on the 4 Gospels (DVD) 2009; numerous articles on Islam, Christianity, mission, inter-faith dialogue, Anglican and ecumenical affairs, public policy and int. affairs. *Leisure interests:* cricket, hockey, table tennis, reading and writing poetry. *Address:* 70 Wimpole Street, London, W1G 8AX, England (office). *Telephone:* (20) 7935-1488 (office). *E-mail:* oxtrad@ gmail.com (office). *Website:* www.michaelnazirali.com.

NAZRUL-ISLAM, Jamal, PhD; Bangladeshi professor of mathematics; *Director, Centre for Mathematics and Physical Sciences, University of Chittagong;* b. 24 Jan. 1939, Jhenidah, Jessore; ed Trinity Coll. Cambridge, UK and Calcutta Univ., India; Postdoctoral Fellow, Dept of Physics and Astronomy, Univ. of Maryland, USA 1963–65; staff mem. Inst. of Theoretical Astronomy, Univ. of Cambridge 1967–71; Visiting Assoc. in Physics, Calif. Inst. of Tech. 1971–72; Sr Research Assoc., Dept of Astronomy, Univ. of Wash. 1972–73; Lecturer in Applied Math., King's Coll., London 1973–74; Science Research Council Fellow, Univ. Coll. Cardiff 1975–78; Lecturer and Reader, Dept of Math., City Univ., London 1978–84; Prof. of Math., Founder and Dir Centre for Math. and Physical Sciences, Univ. of Chittagong; Fellow, Third World Acad. of Sciences, Cambridge Philosophical Soc., Royal Astronomical Soc., Bangladesh Acad. of Sciences, Islamic Acad. of Sciences; mem. Bd. of Trustees Gono Bishwabidyalay University; Gold Medal, Bangladesh Acad. of Sciences for Physical Sciences, Sr Group 1985. *Address:* Department of Mathematics, University of Chittagong, 4331 Chittagong, Bangladesh (office). *Telephone:* (31) 210133 (office). *Fax:* (31) 210141 (office).

NCUBE, Most Rev. Pius Alick, LTh; Zimbabwean ecclesiastic; b. (Mvundla Ncube), 1 Jan. 1947, Mtshabezi, Gwanda; s. of Amos Ncube and Ivy Mkwananzi; ed Chishawasha Major Seminary, Harare, Lateran Univ., Rome, Italy; ordained Priest, Bulawayo 1973, Parish Priest, St Patrick's 1986–90, St Mary's Cathedral 1990–1995; Vicar Gen., Bulawayo Archdiocese 1995–98, Archbishop of Bulawayo 1998–2007 (resgnd); Human Rights Award, Lawyers Cttee for Human Rights, New York 2003. *Radio:* one week per month of morning and evening prayers on nat. radio 1990–98; interviews on human rights issues. *Publications include:* Imfundiso. Yebandla. Elikhatholike (Catholic catechism). *Leisure interests:* reading, writing articles. *Address:* 73 Marigold Road, North Trenance, Bulawayo, Zimbabwe (home). *Telephone:* (9) 204951 (home); (23) 226932 (mobile) (home).

NCUBE, Welshman, MPhil, LLB; Zimbabwean politician, academic and judge; *President, Movement For Democratic Change;* b. 7 July 1961, Gweru; m. Thobekile Ncube; five c.; ed Univ. of Zimbabwe; Prof. of Law, Univ. of Zimbabwe 1992–; serves as Advocate of High Court and Supreme Court of Zimbabwe; Pres. Movement for Democratic Change (MDC) 1999–2011, Co-leader pro-Senate faction of MDC 2006–; mem. of House of Ass. of Zimbabwe for Bulawayo North East 2000–, Chair. Parl. Legal Cttee; charged with high treason over alleged plot to assassinate Pres. Robert Mugabe 2002, found not guilty; Minister of Industry and Commerce 2009–13; unsuccessful cand. in presidential election 2013; mem. Bd of Trustees, Amani Trust; mem. Advisory Bd, ZimRights; mem. Zimbabwe Lawyers for Human Rights; Dr hc (Oslo) 2005. *Publications include:* numerous books and articles on family law, women's law, human rights law and constitutional law. *Address:* Movement for Democratic Change, 11 Creswick Road, Hillside, Harare, Zimbabwe (office). *Telephone:* (4) 747071 (office). *Website:* www.mdczim.net (office).

NDAYIZEYE, Domitien; Burundian politician and fmr head of state; Sec.-Gen. opposition pro-Hutu party Front pour la démocratie au Burundi (FRODEBU); Vice-Pres. of Burundi responsible for Political and Admin. Affairs 2001–03; Pres. of Burundi 2003–05. *Address:* c/o Office of the President, Bujumbura, Burundi (office).

NDEBELE, Njabulo Simakahle, PhD; South African academic, writer and university administrator; *Chancellor, University of Johannesburg;* b. 4 July 1948, Johannesburg; m. Kathleen Mpho; one s. two d.; ed Univs of Botswana, Lesotho and Swaziland, Univ. of Cambridge, UK, Univ. of Denver, USA; Head of Dept, Nat. Univ. of Lesotho, Dean of Humanities Faculty 1987, Pro-Vice-Chancellor 1988–90; Chair. and Head of Dept of African Literature, Wits Univ. 1991; Vice-Rector, Univ. of the Western Cape 1992–93; Vice-Chancellor and Prin. Univ. of the North 1993–98, Scholar-in-Residence, Ford Foundation 1998–2000; Vice-Chancellor and

Prin. Univ. of Cape Town 2000–08; Chancellor Univ. of Johannesburg 2012–; Chair. South African Broadcasting Policy Project, Ministry of Post, Telecommunications and Broadcasting 1997, South African Univs Vice-Chancellors' Asscn –2000; mem. Exec. Bd AA4, AC4; Bd mem. and Chair. Inst. for Democracy in Africa; Dr hc (Natal Univ.) 1999, (Chicago State Univ.) 1996, (Vrije Univ. Amsterdam), (Soka Univ., Japan), (Wesleyan Univ.) 2005, (Univ. of Cambridge) 2006, (Univ. Coll. London) 2006, (Univ. of Michigan) 2008; Lincoln Univ. Pres.'s Award, Nat. Univ. of Lesotho 50th Anniversary Distinguished Service Award, NOMA Award for Publishing in Africa 1984, Sanlam Award for Outstanding Fiction, Pringle Prize for Outstanding Criticism. *Publications include:* Fools and Other Stories 1983, Bonolo and the Peach Tree 1991, Rediscovery of the Ordinary 1991, The Prophetess 1992, Sarah, Rings and I 1993, South African Literature and Culture: Rediscovery of the Ordinary 1994, Death of a Son 1996, The Cry of Winnie Mandela (novel) 2004, Telling Tales (contrib. to charity anthology) 2004, Fine Lines from the Box 2007. *Leisure interests:* bird watching, computer simulation games. *Address:* Office of the Chancellor, University of Johannesburg, PO Box 524, Auckland Park, 2006 (office); Glenara, Burg Road, Rondebosch 7700, Cape Town, South Africa (home). *Telephone:* (11) 5594555. *Website:* www.uj.ac.za (office).

NDEREBA, Catherine; Kenyan athlete; b. 21 July 1972, Nyeri; m. Anthony Maina 1996; one d.; ed Ngorano Secondary School, Nairobi; long distance and marathon runner; rep. Kenya at women's relay race in Seoul, S Korea 1995; won individual bronze and team gold medals at World Half-Marathon Championships 1999; ran world's fastest times at 5,000m (15:09), 12,000m (38:37), 15,000m (48:52) and 10 miles (53:07) 1999; marathon debut in Boston Marathon, finishing sixth 1999; runner-up, New York Marathon 1999, 2003; won both Boston and Chicago Marathons 2000, 2001; gold medal, World Championships Marathon 2003 (Championship Record time of 2 hours, 23 minutes, 55 seconds); silver medal, Olympic Games marathon, Athens 2004, Beijing 2008; set the then women's world marathon record time of 2 hours, 18 minutes, 47 seconds in Chicago Marathon Oct. 2001; ranked No. 1 by Runner's World for three consecutive years; works as telephone operator at a Kenyan prison; Runner's World magazine Road Runner of the Year 1996, 1998, Running Times Road Racer of the Year 1996, 1998, 1999, IAAF Athlete of the Year 2001, Asscn of Int. Marathon and Road Races (AIMS)/ASICS Golden Shoe World Athlete of the Year Award 2001. *Address:* c/o Lisa Buster, IAAF Authorized Athlete Representative President, Promotion in Motion International Limited, 1039 Colin Drive, Royersford, PA 19468-3137, USA (office). *Telephone:* (610) 948-5966 (office). *E-mail:* lbuster.pmi@comcast.net (office). *Website:* www.marathonchamps.com (office).

N'DIAYE, Babacar; Senegalese banker; b. 11 June 1936, Conakry, Guinea; joined African Devt Bank 1965, subsequently Group Dir of Finance, then Vice-Pres. for Finance, Pres. 1985–95, now Hon. Pres.; Chair. African Business Round Table; LLD (Clark Atlanta Univ., Ga) 1992, (Lincoln Univ., Pa) 1993. *Address:* c/o African Development Bank, 01 BP 1387, Abidjan 01, Côte d'Ivoire.

NDIAYE, Mankeur; Senegalese diplomatist and politician; *Minister of Foreign Affairs;* b. 15 March 1960, Dagana, Saint-Louis region; m.; two s. one d.; ed Teaching Middle School Gen. Dagana, École Normale St Louis, École Normale Supérieure de Dakar, Nat. School of Admin and Magistracy (ENAM) Diplomatic Section, courses at UN Conf. on Trade and Devt, UN Inst. for Training and Research and Institut des Hautes Études de Defense Nationale de Paris; teacher in charge of Goudoudou Diobé School (Dept of Matam) 1982–83; Lecturer, Coll. of Educ., Middle Neuville, St Louis 1983–86; Head of Div. of Personnel and Social Affairs, Ministry of Foreign Affairs 1991–93, Deputy Dir Gen. Admin and Equipment and Deputy Dir Dept of Credit, Dir of Cabinet of the Minister Del. to the Prime Minister of the African Econ. Integration 1993–95, mem. Bd of Dirs Solidarity Fund and Devt Intervention in Econ. Community of West African States (FOSIDEC), mem. Bd of Dirs ECOWAS Fund (Fund Econs of West Africa) became EBID (Bank for Investment and Devt of ECOWAS); Dir Cabinet of the Minister Del. to the Minister of Economy, Finance and Planning 1995; Tech. Adviser to the Minister of State, Minister of Foreign Affairs and Senegalese Abroad 1995–97; Second, then First Counsellor, Perm. Mission of Senegal to the UN, New York 1997–2003, Vice-Pres. Comm. on the Status of Women, mem. NGO Cttee of the UN and of several working groups of the UN Gen. Ass., mem. numerous official dels at int. confs or official state visits, Dir of Cabinet of the Minister of State, Minister of Foreign Affairs 2003–09, rank of Amb. 2003, Interim Dir of Cabinet Oct.–Nov. 2009, Amb. to France 2009–12; Minister of Foreign Affairs 2012–; Fellow, ENAM Diplomatic Section 1991; Chevalier, Ordre du Mérite. *Publications:* numerous articles on int. affairs and African issues. *Leisure interests:* running, playing chess and draughts. *Address:* Ministry of Foreign Affairs, place de l'Indépendance, BP 4044, Dakar, Senegal (office). *Telephone:* (33) 889-1300 (office). *Fax:* (33) 823-5496 (office). *E-mail:* maeuase@senegal.diplomatie.sn (office). *Website:* www.diplomatie.gouv.sn (office).

NDIAYE, Souleymane Ndéné, LLM; Senegalese lawyer and politician; b. 6 Aug. 1958, Kaolack; m.; four c.; Mayor of Guinguinéo 2002–; Minister of Civil Service, Labour, Employment and Professional Orgs March–Aug. 2005; Dir of Cabinet, Office of the Pres. Aug. 2005–07; mem. Nat. Ass. 2007–; Minister of State for the Environment and Protection of Nature June–July 2007, for Maritime Economy July 2007–09; Prime Minister of Senegal 2009–12. *Address:* c/o Office of the Prime Minister, Bldg Administratif, avenue Léopold Sédar Senghor, BP 4029, Dakar, Senegal.

NDIMIRA, Pascal-Firmin; Burundian politician; b. 1956; fmr univ. rector, IBRD official; fmr Minister of Agric.; Prime Minister of Burundi 1996–98; mem. Union pour le progrès national (UPRONA). *Address:* c/o Union pour le progrès national (UPRONA), BP 1810, Bujumbura, Burundi. *Telephone:* 2225028.

NDOLOU, Brig. Gen. Jacques Yvon; Republic of the Congo army officer and politician; *Minister of Sports and Sports Education;* b. 1944, Mossaka; 12 c.; fmr professional football player (capt. of Repub. of Congo football team Les Diables-Rouges 1969–72), also fmr volleyball and basketball player; Minister-Del. at the Presidency, responsible for Nat. Defence 2002–09; Minister of Sports and Sports Educ. 2009–; Pres. Fédération congolaise de basketball 1993; fmr Vice-Pres. Comité nat. olympique et sportif congolais. *Address:* Ministry of Sports, BP 2061, Brazzaville, Republic of the Congo (office). *Telephone:* 660-89-24 (office).

NDONG, Jean Eyéghé; Gabonese politician; b. 12 Feb. 1946, Libreville; m. Gisèle Biyoghé; six c.; ed Ecole des Hautes Études en Sciences Sociales, Paris, Université de Paris X Nanterre, France; Admin. Dir Nat. Social Security Fund (CNSS) 1984–90, Deputy Dir-Gen. 1990–91; Deputy Dir-Gen. Nat. Social Guarantee Fund 1991–96; mem. Nat. Ass. for Libreville constituency 1996–2001; mem. Senate 2002; Sec. of State for Finance 1996, later Minister-Del. to Minister of State, Minister of Economy, Finance, Budget and Privatization; Prime Minister and Head of Govt 2006–09; fmr mem. Gabonese Democratic Party; mem. Nat. Union party, Vice-Pres. 2010–. *Address:* Unon Nationale, Libreville, Gabon (office).

N'DONG, Léon; Gabonese diplomatist; b. 15 Feb. 1935, Libreville; s. of the late Jean-Martin Bikègne and of Marthe Kemeboune; m. Chantal Annette Bekale 1971; four s. one d.; ed School of Law and Econ. Sciences, Rennes, France; Under-Sec.-Gen. of Ministry of Foreign Affairs, later Sec.-Gen.; Teacher, Nat. School of Admin. 1969–72; Amb. to Cen. African Repub. and Sudan 1972–73, to Morocco 1973–74, to UN Office at Geneva 1974–76, to UN 1976–80, to UK 1980–86, to FRG 1986–90 (also accred to Norway, Denmark, Finland and Sweden); Amb. du Gabon, Diplomatic Adviser to Prime Minister 1990–99; High Commr, Office of Prime Minister 1997–; Commdr de l'Etoile Equatoriale, Grand Cordon of Order of the Brilliant Star (China), Commdr, Order of Devotion (Malta), Commdr Nat. Order of Dahomey, Order of Nile (Sudan), Ordre Nat. du Mérite (Gabon), Diplomatic Order of Repub. of Korea, Ordre de la Pléïade (France), Grand Officier Etoile Equatoriale, Grand Officier Ordre du Mérite, Officier Courtoisie française. *Leisure interests:* swimming, walking, music, reading, fishing, gardening. *Address:* BP 848, Libreville, Gabon. *Telephone:* (241) 263175; (241) 071952.

NDONG SIMA, Raymond; Gabonese economist and politician; b. 23 Jan. 1955, Oyem, Woleu-Ntem Prov.; began career as Research Asst, Ministry of Planning and the Economy 1983, assigned to cabinet of Minister 1986, Dir-Gen. Econs Dept 1992, responsible for structural adjustment and relations with IMF and World Bank –1994; Dir-Gen. Hévégab (state-owned rubber co.) 1994–98; Minister for Agric., Fisheries and Rural Devt 2009; mem. Assemblée Nationale (Parl.) for Kyé constituency 2011–; Prime Minister 2012–14; mem. Parti démocratique gabonais. *Address:* c/o Office of the Prime Minister, BP 546, Libreville, Gabon (office).

NDONGOU, Jean-François; Gabonese politician; *Minister of the Interior, Public Security, Immigration and Decentralization;* b. 1960; apptd Minister 1999, several portfolios including Minister for Relations with Parl. and Constitutional Insts, Deputy Minister for Foreign Affairs, Co-operation, Francophony and Regional Integration –2007, Deputy Prime Minister for Social Affairs, Welfare, Nat. Solidarity and Poverty Reduction 2007, Minister of the Interior, Local Authorities, Immigration and Security, in charge of Civil Defence and Nat. Defence 2009–10, Minister of the Interior, Public Security, Immigration and Decentralization 2010–. *Address:* Ministry of the Interior, Public Security, Immigration and Decentralization BP 2110, Libreville, Gabon (office). *Telephone:* 01-74-35-06 (office). *Fax:* 01-72-13-89 (office).

N'DOUR, Youssou; Senegalese singer, songwriter and government official; *Minister-Counsellor to the Presidency;* b. Oct. 1959, Dakar; s. of Elimane N'Dour and Ndeye Sokhna Mboup; m. 1st Mami Camara (divorced), four c.; m. 2nd Aida Coulibaly, two. d; mem. Sine Dramatic 1972, Orchestre Diamono 1975, The Star Band (house band of Dakar nightclub, the Miami Club) 1976–79; formed band Etoile de Dakar (changed name to Super Etoile 1982) 1979–; has performed with Peter Gabriel, Paul Simon, Bob Dylan, Branford Marsalis; sings in English, French, Fulani, Serer and native Wolof; Goodwill Amb. to UN, UNICEF, Int. Bureau of Work; Owner Jololi Records recording studio, radio station, Thoissane nightclub, Dakar; f. political group Fekke ma ci bolle (I am involved) Nov. 2011, announced candidacy for presidential election 2012 (subsequently barred from standing by Constitutional Council ruling); Minister of Tourism and Culture 2012–13, Minister-Counsellor to the Presidency 2013–; Hon. DMus (Yale) 2011; Best African Artist 1996, African Artist of the Century 1999, MOBO Award for Best African Act 2005. *Recordings include:* albums: A Abijan 1980, Xalis 1980, Tabaski 1981, Thiapathioly 1983, Absa Gueye 1983, Immigrès 1984, Nelson Mandela 1985, Inedits (1984–1985) 1988, The Lion 1989, African Editions Vols 5–14 1990, Africa Deebeub 1990, Jamm La Prix 1990, Kocc Barma 1990, Set 1990, Hey You: The Essential Collection 1988–90, Eyes Open 1992, The Best of Youssou N'Dour 1994, The Guide 1994, Gainde–Voices From The Heart Of Africa (with Yande Codou Sene) 1996, Lii 1996, Immigrès/Bitim Rew 1997, St Louis 1997, Best of the 80s 1998, Special Fin D'annee Plus Djamil 1999, Rewmi 1999, Joko: From Village to Town 2000, Le Grand Bal, Bercy 2000, Le Grand Bal 1 & 2 2001, Batay 2001, Birth of a Star 2001, Nothing's In Vain (Coono Du Réér) 2002, Et Ses Amis 2002, Sant Allah (Homage to God) 2003, Egypt (BBC Radio 3 World Music Award for Album of the Year 2005) 2004, Hey You! The Essential Collection 2005, Rokku Mi Rokka 2007, I Bring What I Love 2010, Etoile de Dakar/Once Upon a Time in Senegal 2010, Dakar-Kingston 2010. *Film roles include:* Picc Mi 1992, Amazing Grace 2006. *Leisure interest:* football. *Address:* c/o Office of the President, ave Léopold Sédar Senghor, BP 168, Dakar, Dakar (office); Youssou N'Dour Head Office, 8 Route des Almadies Parcelle, BP 1310, Dakar, Senegal. *Telephone:* 33-822-4303 (office); 33-865-1039. *Fax:* 33-822-1638 (office); 33-865-1068. *E-mail:* yncontact@yahoo.fr. *Website:* www.youssou.com.

N'DOURO, Issifou Kogui, Benin government official; b. Bembereke; ed Université Louis Pasteur, Strasbourg, France; consultant to UNSO Tree Planting Project, FAO 1979; fmr Finance Dir Organisation Internationale de la Francophonie; fmr Dir Office of Minister of Rural Devt; Minister of Nat. Defence 2006–12. *Address:* c/o Ministry of National Defence, BP 2493, Cotonou, Benin (office).

NDULU, Benno J., PhD; Tanzanian economist and central banker; *Governor and Chairman, Bank of Tanzania;* ed Northwestern Univ., USA; began career as econs teacher; Prof., Univ. of Dar es Salaam early 1980s; Research Dir, later Exec. Dir African Econ. Research Consortium, Nairobi; African Country Dir, World Bank, Dar es Salaam; Deputy Gov., Bank of Tanzania (Benki Kuu Ya Tanzania) –2008, Gov. and Chair. 2008–; fmr Chair. Tanzania Revenue Authority; Dr hc (Int. Inst. of Social Studies, The Hague). *Publications include:* Agenda for Africa's Economic Renewal (co-author) 1996, New Directions in Development Economics 1996, Regional Integration and Trade Liberalization in Africa (co-author) 1999, Challenges of African Growth (co-author) 2007; numerous articles in The Journal of Development Studies. *Address:* Bank of Tanzania, 10 Mirambo Street, PO Box

2939, Dar es Salaam, Tanzania (office). *Telephone:* (22) 2233021 (office). *Fax:* (22) 2234075 (office). *E-mail:* info@hq.bot-tz.org (office). *Website:* www.bot-tz.org (office).

NDUNGANE, Most Rev. Njongonkulu Winston Hugh, MTh, DD, AFTS; South African ecclesiastic; *Anglican Archbishop of Cape Town;* b. 2 April 1941, Kokstad; s. of Foster Ndungane and Tingaza Ndungane; m. 1st Nosipo Ngcelwane 1972 (died 1986); 2nd Nomahlubi Vokwana 1987; one step-s. one step-d.; ed Lovedale High School, Univ. of Cape Town, Fed. Theological Seminary and King's Coll. London, UK; Rector St Nicholas Church, Matroosfontein, Cape Town 1980–81; Prov. Liaison Officer, Johannesburg 1982–84; Prin., St Bede's Theological Coll. Umtata 1985–86; Exec. Officer, Church of the Prov. of Southern Africa (Anglican) 1987–91; Bishop of Kimberley and Kuruman 1991–96; Archbishop of Cape Town 1996–; mem. Bd SABC, Johannesburg 1992–96; Chair. Hearings into Poverty in S Africa; Patron Jubilee 2000 1998–; Hon. DD (Rhodes) 1997, (Protestant Episcopal Theological Seminary, Virginia) 2000; Hon. DHumLitt (Worcester State Coll., Mass) 2000; Hon. DScS (Natal) 2001. *Publications:* The Commuter Population for Claremont, Cape 1973, Human Rights and the Christian Doctrine of Man 1979, A World with a Human Face: A Voice from Africa 2003. *Leisure interests:* music, walking. *Address:* Bishopscourt, 20 Bishopscourt Drive, Claremont 7708, South Africa. *Telephone:* (21) 761-2531. *Fax:* (21) 761-4193. *E-mail:* archbish@bishopscourt-cpsa.org.za (home).

NDUWIMANA, Martin, MD; Burundian politician and physician; b. Mugamba, Prov. of Bururi; currently Prof. of Paediatrics, Univ. of Burundi; fmr Dir Nat. Centre for Public Health; fmr MP for Bururi Prov.; First Vice-Pres. of Burundi in charge of Political and Admin. Affairs 2005–07 (resgnd); mem. Union pour le progresse nationale (Uprona). *Address:* University of Burundi, Faculty of Medicine, BP 1020, Bujumbura, Burundi (office). *Telephone:* (257) 232074 (office). *Fax:* (257) 232267 (office). *E-mail:* m.nduwim@medecine.ub.edu.bi (office). *Website:* www.ub.edu.bi (office).

NEAL, Sir Eric James, Kt, AC, CVO, CEng, CPEng, FAIM; Australian state governor, business executive and chartered engineer; *Chair, State Government's Veterans Advisory Council;* b. 3 June 1924, London, UK; s. of James Neal and May Neal (née Johnson); m. Thelma Joan Bowden 1950; two s.; ed South Australian School of Mines; Dir Boral Ltd 1972–92, Chief Exec. 1973–82, Man. Dir 1982–87; Dir Oil Co. of Australia NL 1982–87, Chair. 1984–87; Dir Westpac Banking Corpn 1985–92, Chair. 1989–92; Dir Atlas Copco Australia Ltd 1987–96, Chair. 1990–96; Dir Metal Manufactures Ltd 1987–96, Chair. 1990–96; Dir Wormald Int. Ltd 1978–85, John Fairfax Ltd 1987–88, Cola-Cola Amatil Ltd 1987–96, BHP 1988–94; Gov. S Australia 1996–2001; Chancellor The Flinders Univ. of S Australia 2002–10; Chair. State Govt's Veterans Advisory Council 2009–; Nat. Pres. Australian Inst. of Co. Dirs 1990–93, currently Fellow; mem. Gen. Motors Australia Advisory Council 1987–94; Chief Commr Council of City of Sydney 1987–88; Life Fellow, Australian Inst. of Building; Int. Trustee, The Duke of Edinburgh's Award Int. Foundation 1987–97; Chair. of Trustees, Sir David Martin Foundation 1991–94; Patron Soccer Club Blacks, Adelaide Univ. 2007–, Freemasons Foundation Centre for Men's Health –2012; KStJ; Hon. DEng (Sydney) 1989, Hon. DUniv (S Australia) 1996, (Flinders) 2001; numerous awards and medals. *Leisure interests:* reading, walking, motor boating, sailing, naval and eng history, opera. *Address:* 82/52 Brougham Place, North Adelaide 5006, Australia (home). *Telephone:* (8) 8361-7014 (home). *Fax:* (8) 8267-1715 (home). *E-mail:* nj@internode.on.net.

NÉAOUTIYNE, Paul; New Caledonian politician; b. 1952, St Michel Village; ed Univ. of Lyon; teacher of econs at secondary coll. in Nouméa until 1980; jailed for participation in pro-independence demonstration 1980; reinstated as teacher 1983; Aide to Jean-Marie Tjibaou (Pres. Northern Regional Council) 1985; Leader, Party of Kanak Liberation (Palika); Mayor of Poindimie; mem. Northern Prov. Govt; Leader Parti de Libération Kanak (PALIKA) (merged with Kanak Socialist Nat. Liberation Front 1984).

NEARY, J. Peter, DPhil, FBA, MRIA; Irish economist and academic; *Professor of Economics, University of Oxford;* b. 11 Feb. 1950, Drogheda, Co. Louth; s. of Peter Neary and Anne Loughran; m. 1st Frances Ruane 1972 (divorced); two s.; m. 2nd Mairéad Hanrahan 1997; two d.; ed Clongowes Wood Coll., Co. Kildare, Univ. Coll. Dublin, Univ. of Oxford; Jr Lecturer, Trinity Coll. Dublin 1972–74, Lecturer 1978–80; Heyworth Research Fellow, Nuffield Coll. Oxford 1976–78; Prof. of Political Economy, Univ. Coll. Dublin 1980–2006; Prof. of Econs, Univ. of Oxford 2006–, Professorial Fellow, Merton Coll. 2006–11; Visiting Prof., Princeton Univ. 1980, Univ. of California, Berkeley 1982, Queen's Univ., Ont. 1986–88, Univ. of Ulster at Jordanstown 1992–93; Research Assoc. Centre for Econ. Performance, LSE 1993–2003; Dir de Recherche, Ecole Polytechnique, Paris 1999–2000; mem. Council Royal Econ. Soc. 1984–89, European Econ. Asscn 1985–92, Econometric Soc. 1994–99; Co-Ed. Journal of International Economics 1980–83; Assoc. Ed. Economic Journal 1981–85, Econometrica 1984–87, Review of Economic Studies 1984–93, Economica 1996–2000; Ed. European Economic Review 1986–90; Pres. Irish Econ. Asscn 1990–92, Int. Trade and Finance Soc. 1999–2000, European Econ. Asscn 2002, Econs Section, BAAS 2005; mem. Academia Europaea 1989–; Fellow, Centre for Econ. Policy Research, London 1983–, Econometric Soc. 1987–, European Econ. Asscn 2004–, British Acad. 2008–; Royal Irish Acad. Gold Medal in the Social Sciences 2006, Advanced Grant, European Research Council 2012–17. *Publications:* Measuring the Restrictiveness of International Trade Policy (with J. E. Anderson) 2005; three edited books and more than 100 publs on econs, especially int. econs. *Leisure interests:* family, travel, reading, music. *Address:* Department of Economics, University of Oxford, Manor Road Building, Manor Road, Oxford, OX1 3UQ, England (office). *Telephone:* (1865) 271085 (office). *Fax:* (1865) 271094 (office). *E-mail:* peter.neary@economics.ox.ac.uk (office). *Website:* users.ox.ac.uk/~econ0211 (office).

NEARY, Martin Gerard James, LVO, MA, DMus, FRCO; British conductor and organist; b. 28 March 1940, London, England; s. of the late Leonard W. Neary and of Jeanne M. Thébault; m. Penelope J. Warren 1967; one s. two d.; ed City of London School and Gonville & Caius Coll., Cambridge; Asst Organist, St Margaret's Westminster 1963–65, Organist and Master of Music 1965–71; Prof. of Organ, Trinity Coll. London 1963–72; Organist and Master of Music, Winchester Cathedral 1972–87; Founder and Conductor Martin Neary Singers 1972–;

Conductor Waynflete Singers 1972–87; Organist and Master of Choristers, Westminster Abbey 1988–98; has led Westminster Abbey Choir on tours to France, Germany, Switzerland, Hungary, USA, Russia, Ukraine; Guest Conductor Australian Youth Choir 1999–; Founder and Conductor Millennium Consort Singers 2007, including appearances at Disney Hall, Los Angeles; Pres. Cathedral Organists Asscn 1985–88, Organists' Charitable Trust 1988–, Royal Coll. of Organists 1988–90, 1996–98; Chair. Church Services Cttee, Musicians Benevolent Fund 1993–98, Herbert Howells Soc. 1993–; Artistic Dir Paulist Boy Choristers of California 1999–2003; many organ recitals and broadcasts in UK (including First Night of the Proms 2004), Europe, USA, Canada, the Far East and Australia; many choral premières; guest conductor English Chamber Orchestra, London Symphony Orchestra, Netherlands Chamber Choir, Netherlands Radio Choir, Nat. Lutheran Choir, University Voices Canada; numerous recordings; Hon. RAM; Hon. FTCL; Hon. Fellow, Royal School of Church Music. *Compositions include:* Responses, carol arrangements, All Saints Mass, Mass of the Redeemer, O Worship the Lord, Joy and Woe, Christmas Recordings. *Recordings:* numerous. *Publications:* edns of early organ music, contribs to organ journals. *Leisure interest:* watching cricket. *Address:* 44 Radipole Road, Fulham, London, SW6 5DL, England. *Telephone:* (20) 7736-5268. *E-mail:* martin@mneary.co.uk.

NEČAS, Petr, DrScNat; Czech politician; b. 19 Nov. 1964, Uherské Hradiště; m. Radka Nečasová (divorced); two s. two d.; ed Gymnasium in Uherské Hradiště, Masaryk Univ., Brno; mil. service, helicopter regt in Prostejov 1988–89; technologist and research engineer, Tesla Rožnov 1988–92; mem. Civic Democratic Party (Občanská demokratická strana—ODS) 1991–, Jt Vice-Chair. 1999–2004, First Deputy Chair. 2004–10, Leader 2010–13; mem. Parl. for Zlín 1992–; mem. Parl. Cttee for Foreign Affairs 1992–96; Deputy Minister of Defence 1995–96; Chair. Parl. Cttee for Defence and Security 1996–2002; Vice-Chair. Parl. Cttee for European Affairs 2002–06; Deputy Prime Minister and Minister for Labour and Social Affairs 2006–09; Prime Minister 2010–13 (resgnd); Minister of Defence 2012–13; charged with bribery Feb. 2014. *Leisure interest:* history. *Address:* Civic Democratic Party (Občanská demokratická strana), Polygon House, Doudlebská 1699/5, 140 00 Prague 4 (office); Na Příkopě 814/36, 755 01 Vsetín, Czech Republic (home). *Telephone:* (2) 34707111 (office); (57) 1413596 (office); 602-622416 (mobile). *Fax:* (2) 34707103 (office). *E-mail:* petr.necas@odsvs.cz (office). *Website:* www.ods.cz (office); www.petr-necas.cz.

NECHAEV, Andrey Alekseevich, PhD; Russian politician, economist, academic, banker and journalist; *President, Russian Financial Corporation;* b. 2 Feb. 1953, Moscow; s. of Aleksey Nechaev and Marseliesa Nechaev; m. 1st Elena Belyanova 1975; one d.; m. 2nd Margarita Kitova 1986; m. 3rd Svetlana Sergienko 1997; ed Moscow State Univ.; Researcher, USSR Acad. of Sciences 1979–90, Deputy Dir Inst. of Econ. Policy, Acad. of Nat. Economy 1990–91; First Deputy Minister of Economy and Finance of Russia 1991–92; Minister of Economy 1992–93; mem. Security Council of Russia 1992–93; Pres. Russian Financial Corpn 1993–, Moscow Finance Club 1994–; mem. Political Consultative Council under Pres. of Russia 1996–2000, Scientific Council under Security Council of Russia 1997–2002; mem. Expert Council. Financial Control Chamber of Russia, Nat. Econ. Council; Prof., Russian Acad. of Econs; Pres. Int. Youth Exchanges Foundation (Coordinator Russian-German youth exchanges); mem. Russian Union of Journalists, Political Council 'Right Deal' (political party), Council of Moscow Banks Union; mem. Acad. of Nat. Sciences, Int. Acad. of Informatization, Acad. of Security and Defence, Advisory Bd RBC-TV; Order of State Statistical Comm. 2002, Order of Ministry of Internal Affairs 2003, Leader of Russian Economy 2003, 2005, Public Order Glory of Russia 2003; State Medal 1997, 2003, Public Recognition Prize 2001, Honour Staff of Ministry of Economy and Trade 2003, Best Pen of Russia Prize, Honour Bookkeeper and Accounter. *Radio:* author and presenter of 'Financial Club' and 'Credit of Trust' radio programmes, econ. analyst on Russian radio. *Television:* author and presenter of 'Money Matter' programme; econs expert on main Russian channels. *Publications:* 250 books and publs on econs and econ. policy. *Leisure interests:* journalism, publicity, politics, history, theatre, travelling, tennis, gardening. *Address:* Russian Financial Corporation, Georgievsky pereulok 1, 125009 Moscow, Russia (office). *Telephone:* (495) 692-74-82 (office). *Fax:* (495) 692-35-62 (office). *E-mail:* nechaev@rusfincorp.ru (home); rfc@rusfincorp.ru (office). *Website:* (office).

NEDERLANDER, James Morton; American impresario; *Chairman, Nederlander Producing Company Of America, Inc.;* b. 31 March 1922, Detroit, Mich.; s. of David T. Nederlander and Sarah L. Applebaum; m. Charlene Saunders 1969; one s. two d.; ed Pontiac Sr High School and Detroit Inst. of Tech.; fmr usher, box-office asst and press agent for father's Schubert-Lafayette Theatre; served in USAF during World War II; Man. Lyceum Theatre, Minneapolis for eight years; returned to Detroit to assist in devt of Nederlander theatre chain in Detroit and Chicago in 1950s; chain expanded to Broadway with purchase of Palace Theatre 1965; now Chair. Bd Nederlander Org. (now Nederlander Producing Co. Of America, Inc.) 1966–, owners and operators of largest chain of theatres in world including 11 Broadway theatres and Adelphi and Aldwych theatres, London and producers and backers of major Broadway musicals such as Annie, La Cage aux Folles and Will Roger Follies; est. Nederlander TV and Film Production (creating films, miniseries, etc. for TV) in 1980s. *Address:* Nederlander Producing Company Of America, Inc., 1450 Broadway, Floor 6, New York, NY 10018, USA. *Telephone:* (212) 840-5577. *Website:* www.nederlander.org.

NEDVĚD, Pavel; Czech fmr professional footballer; b. 30 Aug. 1972, Cheb, Czechoslovakia (now Czech Repub.); s. of Vaclav Nedvěd and Ana Nedvěd; left winger/attacking midfielder; youth player for TJ Skalná 1977–85, RH Cheb 1985–86, Škoda Plzeň 1986–90, VTJ Tábor 1990–91, Dukla Prague 1991–92; sr player for Dukla Prague (19 league appearances, three goals) 1991–92, Sparta Prague (98 league appearances, 23 goals) 1992–96 (won Czechoslovak League 1992/93, Czech Gambrinus Liga 1993/94, 1994/95, Czech Repub. Football Cup 1996), Lazio, Italy (138 appearances, 33 goals) 1996–2001 (won Coppa Italia 1997/98, 1999/2000, Supercoppa Italiana 1998, 2000, UEFA Cup Winners' Cup 1998/99, UEFA Super Cup 1999, Serie A 1999/2000), Juventus, Italy (244 appearances, 51 goals) 2001–09 (won Serie A 2001/02, 2002/03, 2004/05, 2005/06, Supercoppa Italiana 2002, 2003, Serie B 2006/07); 83 caps and 17 goals for Czech Repub. 1994–2006 (silver medal, UEFA Euro 1996, bronze medal, UEFA Euro 2004); retd 2009; mem. Bd of Dirs Juventus Football Club SpA; Czech Player of the Year 1998,

2000, 2001, 2003, 2004, 2008, Czech Athlete of the Year 2003, World Soccer Magazine Player of the Year 2003, Serie A Footballer of the Year 2003, Serie A Foreign Footballer of the Year 2003, Ballon d'Or (European Footballer of the Year) 2003, Champions League Best Midfielder 2003, Sportske Novosti Award 2003, Czech Player of the Decade 2003, UEFA Team of the Year 2003, 2004, 2005, Golden Foot 2004, named to FIFA 100. *Address:* Juventus Football Club SpA, C.so Galileo Ferraris 32, 10128 Turin, Italy. *E-mail:* info@pavelnedved.cz. *Website:* www.pavelnedved.cz.

NEEDLEMAN, Jacob, PhD; American philosopher and academic; *Professor of Philosophy, San Francisco State University;* b. 6 Oct. 1934, Philadelphia, Pa; s. of Benjamin Needleman and Ida Needleman; m. 1st Carla Satzman 1959 (divorced 1989); one s. one d.; m. 2nd Gail Anderson 1990; ed Research Assoc., Rockefeller Inst., New York 1960–61, Harvard Coll., Yale Univ.; Assoc. Prof. of Philosophy, San Francisco State Univ. 1962–66, Prof. 1967–; Dir Center for the Study of New Religions, Grad. Theological Union, Berkeley, Calif. 1977–83; Vice-Pres. Audio Literature Co. 1987–; Rockefeller Humanities Fellow, Fulbright Scholar. *Publications:* The New Religions 1970, A Sense of the Cosmos 1975, Lost Christianity 1980, The Heart of Philosophy 1982, The Way of the Physician 1985, Sorcerers 1986, Money and the Meaning of Life 1991, A Little Book on Love 1996, Time and the Soul 1998, The American Soul 2002, The Wisdom of Love 2005, Why Can't We Be Good 2007, What Is God? 2009, An Unknown World: Notes on the Meaning of the Earth 2012. *Address:* San Francisco State University, Department of Philosophy, 1600 Holloway Avenue, San Francisco, CA 94132, USA (office). *Telephone:* (415) 338-1596 (office). *E-mail:* jacob.needleman@gmail.com (home). *Website:* www.jacobneedleman.com.

NEEMAN, Yaakov, LLB, LLM, JSD; Israeli politician and lawyer; *Founding Partner, Herzog, Fox & Neeman;* b. 1939, Tel-Aviv; m.; six c.; ed Hebrew Univ. of Jerusalem, New York Univ. Law School; mem. Israeli Bar Asscn 1966–; Founding and Sr Pnr, Herzog Fox & Neeman (law firm) 1972– (with two-year interruption); Visiting Prof. of Law, UCLA, USA 1976, Tel-Aviv Univ. 1977–79, New York Univ. 1989–90, Hebrew Univ. of Jerusalem 1990, 1994; Dir-Gen. Ministry of Finance 1979–81; Chair. Cttee of Inquiry into Inter-Relation between Tax Laws and Foreign Currency Restrictions 1977–78, Public Cttee on Allocation of Distributions by Ministry of Interior 1991–92, Nat. Cttee for the Identification of Fallen Soldiers in Times of Emergency 1991, Cttee for the Conversion Law 1997–98, Public Cttee on Privatisation Issues of El Al, Public Cttee on Educational Centres 2000, Public Cttee apptd by the Cabinet for the Drafting of the Constitution 2002–03, Exec. Cttee, Bar Ilan Univ. 2000–; mem. Cen. Cttee of World Bank 1979–81, Cttee for Atomic Energy 1979–81, Investigation Cttee on Temple Mount Affair 1991, Public Cttee apptd by the Speaker of Parl. to determine salaries and other payments to cabinet members, Knesset mems, judges and other govt officials 2000–02; mem. Bd of Govs Bank of Israel 1992–96, 2003–; mem. Bd of Dirs El Al Ltd 1979–81, Israel Aircraft Industries Ltd 1979–81; Minister of Justice 1996, of Finance 1997. *Publications:* seven books and over 30 articles on taxation, corpn and securities law. *Address:* Herzog, Fox & Neeman, Asia House, 4 Weizmann Street, 64239 Tel-Aviv, Israel (office). *Telephone:* 3-6922032 (office). *Fax:* 3-6966464 (office). *E-mail:* neeman@hfn.co.il (office). *Website:* www.hfn.co.il (office).

NEESON, Liam, OBE; British actor; b. 7 June 1952, Ballymena, Co. Antrim, Northern Ireland; m. Natasha Richardson 1994 (died 2009); two s.; ed St Mary's Teachers' Coll., London, Queen's Univ., Belfast; worked as forklift operator, then as architect's asst; acting debut with Lyric Players' Theatre, Belfast, in The Risen 1976. *Theatre includes:* Of Mice and Men (Abbey Theatre Co., Dublin), The Informer (Dublin Theatre Festival), Translations (Nat. Theatre, London), The Plough and the Stars (Royal Exchange, Manchester), The Judas Kiss. *Films include:* Excalibur 1981, Krull 1983, The Bounty 1984, The Innocent 1985, Lamb 1986, The Mission 1986, Duet for One 1986, A Prayer for the Dying 1987, Suspect 1987, Satisfaction 1988, High Spirits 1988, The Dead Pool 1988, The Good Mother 1988, Next of Kin 1989, Darkman 1990, The Big Man 1990, Under Suspicion 1991, Husbands and Wives 1992, Leap of Faith 1993, Ethan Frome 1993, Ruby Cairo 1993, Schindler's List 1993, Nell 1994, Rob Roy 1995, Before and After 1996, Michael Collins (Best Actor Evening Standard Award 1997) 1996, Les Misérables 1998, The Haunting 1999, Star Wars: Episode 1 – The Phantom Menace 1999, Gun Shy 2000, Reflections of Evil (voice, uncredited) 2002, K-19: The Widowmaker 2002, Gangs of New York 2002, Love Actually 2003, Kinsey (Best Actor, Los Angeles Film Critics' Asscn) 2004, Kingdom of Heaven 2005, Batman Begins 2005, The Proposition 2005, Breakfast on Pluto 2005, The Chronicles of Narnia: The Lion, the Witch and the Wardrobe (voice) 2005, Seraphim Falls 2006, Taken 2008, The Other Man 2008, The Chronicles of Narnia: Prince Caspian (voice) 2008, Gake no ue no Ponyo (aka Ponyo on the Cliff) (voice: English version) 2008, Fallout 3 (video game) 2008, Five Minutes of Heaven 2009, Chloe 2010, Clash of the Titans 2010, The Chronicles of Narnia: The Voyage of the Dawn Treader (voice) 2010, The Next Three Days 2010, The Grey 2012, Wrath of the Titans 2012, Battleship 2012, Taken 2 2012, The Gentleman Prizefighter 2012, Jeff Wayne's Musical Version of the War of the Worlds Alive on Stage! The New Generation 2013, Khumba (voice) 2013, Third Person 2013, Anchorman 2: The Legend Continues (uncredited) 2013, The Nut Job (voice) 2014, A Walk Among the Tombstones 2014, The Lego Movie (voice) 2014, Non-Stop 2014, A Million Ways to Die in the West 2014. *Television includes:* An Audience with Mel Brooks 1983, A Woman of Substance 1983, Ellis Island (mini-series) 1984, Arthur the King 1985, If Tomorrow Comes (mini-series) 1986, Hold the Dream 1986, Sweet As You Are 1987, Sworn to Silence 1987, The American Film Institute Salute to Steven Spielberg 1995, Out of Ireland (voice) 1995, Riverdance: The New Show (video) 1996, Kiss Me Goodnight, The Great War and the Shaping of the 20th Century (mini-series) (voice) 1996, Comic Relief VIII 1998, Empires: The Greeks – Crucible of Civilization (narrator) 2000, The Endurance: Shackleton's Legendary Antarctic Expedition (voice) 2000, Inside the Space Station (voice) 2000, The Man Who Came to Dinner 2000, The Greeks (mini-series) (voice) 2001, Revenge of the Whale 2001, Nobel Peace Prize Concert (host) 2001, Uncovering the Real Gangs of New York 2002, The Maze (voice) 2002, Inside the Playboy Mansion (uncredited) 2002, Martin Luther (voice) 2002, Evolution (mini-series) (narrator) 2002, Liberty's Kids: Est. 1776 (series) (voice) 2002, Happy Birthday Oscar Wilde 2004, Patrick (voice) 2004, The Simpsons (voice) 2005, The Big C 2010. *Address:* c/o Ed Limato, ICM, 8942 Wilshire Boulevard, Beverly Hills, CA 90211-1934, USA (office). *Telephone:* (310) 550-4000 (office). *Website:* www.icmtalent.com (office).

NEEWOOR, Anund Priyay, BA (Hons); Mauritian diplomatist and international organization official; *Secretary for Foreign Affairs;* b. 26 June 1940; m. Chandranee Neewoor 1971; two s. one d.; ed Delhi Univ., Makerere Univ., Uganda; teacher, Prin. Northern Coll. (secondary school), Mauritius 1964–67; joined Ministry of External Affairs, Tourism and Emigration (in charge of UN affairs and West Asia affairs) 1970; Admin. Asst, Civil Service 1972; Second Sec., High Comm., London 1973–75; First Sec., High Comm., New Delhi 1975–81; Minister-Counsellor, Embassy, Washington, DC 1982; Amb. to Pakistan 1983, to USA 1993–96; High. Commr to India 1983–93; Amb. in Ministry of External Affairs in charge of Multilateral Econ. Affairs 1996; Sec. for Foreign Affairs 1996–99, Amb. and Perm. Rep. to UN, New York 1999–2001, Sec. for Foreign Affairs 2005–; Commdr, Order of the Star and Key of the Indian Ocean (CSK) 2003, Grand Officer (GOSK) 2008. *Leisure interests:* reading, sports. *Address:* Ministry of Foreign Affairs, Regional Integration and International Trade, 9th, 10th, 11th & 14th Floors, Newton Tower, Sir William Newton Street, Port Louis (office); 17 Avenue des Dodos, Sodnac, Quatre Bornes, Mauritius (home). *Telephone:* (230) 4052517 (office). *Fax:* (230) 2088087 (office). *E-mail:* aneewoor@mail.gov.mu (office); apneewoor@hotmail.com (office). *Website:* foreign.gov.mu (office).

NEFEDOV, Oleg Matveyevich, DSc; Russian chemist; *Head of Laboratory, N. D. Zelinksky Institute of Organic Chemistry, Russian Academy of Sciences;* b. 25 Nov. 1931, Dmitrov, Moscow region; s. of Matvey Kondrat'evich Nefedov and Mariya Adolfovna Teodorovich; m. Galina Gimelfarb 1954; one s. one d.; ed D. I. Mendeleev Inst. of Chem. and Tech.; worked as jr then sr researcher; Head, Lab. N. D. Zelinsky Inst. of Organic Chem., USSR (now Russian) Acad. of Sciences 1968–; Corresp. mem. USSR (now Russian) Acad. of Sciences (RAS) 1979–87, mem. 1987–, Academic Sec. Div. of Gen. and Applied Chem. 1988–91, Vice-Pres. RAS 1988–2001, Rector Higher Chemical Coll. 1990–, Counsellor, RAS 2001–; Ed.-in-Chief Mendeleev Communications 1990–, Russian Chemical Bulletin 1991–, Russian Chemical Reviews 1995–; Chair. Nat. Cttee of Russian Chemists 1996–; mem. IUPAC Bureau and Exec. Cttee 1999–; Pres. Mendeleev Congresses on Gen. and Applied Chem., Tashkent 1989, Minsk 1993, St Petersburg 1998, Kazan 2003; USSR People's Deputy 1989–91; USSR State Prize 1983, 1990, ND Zelinsky Prize 1987, Prize of USSR and Hungarian Acads 1988, N. Semyonov Prize 1991, A. Karpinsky Prize 1993, D. I. Mendeleev Gold Medal 1998, Russian Fed. State Prize in Science and Tech. 2002. *Publications:* The Structure of Cyclopropane Derivatives 1986, Chemistry of Carbenes and Small-sized Cyclic Compounds (ed.) 1989, Carbenes Chemistry 1990; more than 700 articles and 201 patents. *Leisure interests:* sport, gathering mushrooms. *Address:* N. D. Zelinsky Institute of Organic Chemistry, GSP-1, Leninsky prospekt 47, Moscow, Russia (office). *Telephone:* (495) 938-18-73 (office). *Fax:* (495) 135-63-90 (office). *E-mail:* nefedov@ras.ru (office).

NEGERI SEMBILAN, Yang di-Pertuan Besar; Tuanku Muhriz ibni al-Marhum Tunku Munawir, LLB; Malaysian; b. 14 Jan. 1948; s. of the late Tuanku Munawir ibni al-Mmarhum Tuanku Abdul Rahman and of Tunku Ampuan Durah binti al-Marhum Tunku Besar Burhanuddin; m. Tuanku Aishah Rohani Tengku Besar Mahmud; three s.; ed Tuanku Muhammad and Tunku Besar Schools, Tampin, King George V School, Seremban, Negeri Sembilan, Aldenham School and Univ. Coll. of Wales at Aberystwyth (now the Univ. of Wales, Aberystwyth), UK; named Tunku Besar (Heir Presumptive) 1960, bypassed by the Council of Undangs to become Yang di-Pertuan Besar on the death of his father in 1967 for his uncle, Tuanku Jaafar ibni Abdul Rahman; proclaimed 11th Yang di-Pertuan Besar of Negeri Sembilan 29 Dec. 2008; began career in int. bank in Malaysia, became a dir and shareholder of a co. licensed as brokers in interbank foreign exchange and in currency deposits market 1973–86; chair. and shareholder of a Malaysian jt venture with a worldwide advertising agency 1981–92; chair. and dir of a jt venture co. involved in the manufacturing of building products 1995–98; dir and shareholder of an electrical eng and construction co. 1995–; mem. Bd of Dirs Bangkok Bank 2006–.

NEGISHI, Akio, BSc; Japanese business executive; *Director, President and Representative Executive Officer, Meiji Yasuda Life Insurance Company;* b. 1958; ed Waseda Univ.; joined Meiji Yasuda Life Insurance Co. 1981, Gen. Man. Shiga Regional Office 2003–04, Gen. Man. Shiga Regional Office, Meiji Yasuda Life Insurance Co. 2004–05, Gen. Man. Corp. Planning and Research Dept 2005–07, Gen. Man. Marketing Planning and Research Dept 2007–09, Exec. Officer and Gen. Man. Marketing Planning and Research Dept 2009–11, Exec. Officer 2011–12, Man. Exec. Officer 2012–13, Dir, Pres. and Rep. Exec. Officer 2013–. *Address:* Meiji Yasuda Life Insurance Company, 1-1, Marunouchi 2-chome, Chiyoda-ku, Tokyo 100-0005, Japan (office). *Telephone:* (3) 3283-8293 (office). *Fax:* (3) 3215-8123 (office). *E-mail:* info@meijiyasuda.co.jp (office). *Website:* www.meijiyasuda.co.jp (office).

NEGISHI, Ei-ichi, BS, PhD; Japanese chemist and academic; *Herbert C. Brown Distinguished Professor of Chemistry, Purdue University;* b. 14 July 1935, Changchun (fmr capital of Japanese-controlled Manchukuo, now capital of Jilin, China); ed Univ. of Tokyo, Univ. of Pennsylvania; research chemist, Teijin Ltd 1958–60, 1963–66; Postdoctoral Assoc., Purdue Univ., West Lafayette, Ind. 1966–68, Asst to Nobel laureate Herbert C. Brown 1968–72, Prof. of Chem. 1979–99, Herbert C. Brown Distinguished Prof. of Chem. and Teijin Ltd Dir of the Negishi-Brown Inst. 1999–; Asst Prof., Syracuse Univ. 1972–76, Assoc. Prof. 1976–79; Visiting Prof., Univ. of California, Santa Cruz 1980, Univ. of Tokyo 1987, Nat. Univ. of Singapore 2000; First Burroughs-Welcome Visiting Prof., Duke Univ., Durham, NC 1994; mem. ACS 1979–, AAAS 1975–80, 1992–94, Japan Chemical Soc. 1985–; Chair. NIH Medicinal Chem. Study Section 1986–90 (Ad hoc mem. 1980, 1985, 1994), ACS Purdue Section 1986; Co-Chair. Pre-OMCOS-8 Symposium 1995, OMCOS-8 1995; mem. IUPAC-OMCOS Int. Scientific Cttee 1993–; Guest Ed. Tetrahedron Symposium-in-print 1995; Co-Guest Ed. Journal of Organometallic Chemistry Special Issue 1998, Special Issue, 2002; mem. Editorial Advisory Bd Organometallics 1999–2001; consultant, Hoffmann-LaRoche & Co., Basel, Switzerland 1983–2002, Kaneka, Takasago, Japan 1991–2003; consultant to Pres. of Hokkaido Univ., Japan 2002; Fullbright-Smith-Mund Scholarship 1960–63, Harrison Fellowship 1962–63, Visiting Lectureship, sponsored by Western Swiss Univs (seven invited lectures) 1983, Syntex Distinguished Lecturer, Univ. of Colorado, Boulder 1985, John E. Mahler Lecturer, Univ. of Texas, Austin 1986, John S. Guggenheim Memorial Foundation Fellowship 1987,

Nat. Science Council Lectureship, Taiwan 1987, NSF Special Creativity Extension Award 1988–90, Robert A. Welch Foundation Lectureship 1989, NATO Invited Lecturer, Ankara Univ., Turkey 1991, Alan R. Day Award (POCC) 1996, J.C. Karcher Lecturer, Univ. of Oklahoma 1996, The Chemical Soc. of Japan Award 1996, K. Nakamoto Distinguished Lectureship, Marquette Univ. 1997, Sr Researcher Award, Alexander von Humbolt Foundation 1998–2001, ACS Organometallic Chem. Award 1998, Herbert N. McCoy Award 1998, RSC Sir Edward Frankland Prize Lectureship 2001, inclusion of the Negishi Cross-Coupling in Merck Index, 13th edn 2001, Weissberger-Williams Lectureship, Eastman Kodak, Rochester, NY 2002, Sigma Xi Award, Purdue Univ. 2003, Professional/Scholarly Publishing Div. Award (Chem.), Asscn of American Publrs 2003, Merck Frosst Award Lectureship, Univ. of Waterloo 2004, Roche Distinguished Lectureship, Colorado State Univ., Fort Collins 2005, Merck-Frosst Award Lecturer, Univ. of Montreal 2006, Merck-Frosst Award Lecturer, Univ. of California, Irvine 2006, Yamada-Koga Prize (Japan) 2007, Gold Medal of Charles Univ., Prague, Czech Repub. 2007, ACS Award for Creative Work in Synthetic Organic Chem. 2010, Nobel Prize in Chem. (jtly with Richard Heck and Akira Suzuki) "for palladium-catalyzed cross couplings in organic synthesis" 2010. *Publications:* Handbook of Organopaladium Chemistry for Organic Synthesis, two vols (ed.) 2002; more than 400 papers in professional journals; several patents. *Address:* Room WTHR 465B, H.C. Brown Laboratories of Chemistry, Purdue University, 560 Oval Drive, West Lafayette, IN 47907-2084, USA (office). *Telephone:* (765) 494-5301 (office); (765)463-4439 (home). *Fax:* (765) 496-3380 (office); (765) 494-0239 (office). *E-mail:* negishi@purdue.edu (office). *Website:* www .chem.purdue.edu/negishi (office).

NEGISHI, Takashi, PhD; Japanese economist and academic; *Emeritus Professor, Tokyo University;* b. 2 April 1933, Tokyo; s. of Setsuko Negishi and Suteta Negishi; m. Aiko Mori 1964; one d.; ed Univ. of Tokyo; Research Asst, then Research Assoc., Stanford Univ., Calif. 1958–60; Research Asst, Univ. of Tokyo 1963–65, Assoc. Prof. 1965–76, Prof. 1976–94, Prof. Emer. 1994–, also Dean, Faculty of Econs 1990–92; Prof., Aoyama Gakuin Univ. 1994–2002, Toyo Eiwa Univ. 2002–06; Fellow Econometric Soc. 1966–, Vice-Pres. 1992–93, Pres. 1994; Pres. Japan Asscn of Econs and Econometrics 1985; Pres. The Soc. for the History of Econ. Thought, Japan 1997–99; mem. Exec. Cttee Int. Econ. Asscn 1989–92, Science Council of Japan 1985–88, Japan Acad. 1998–; Foreign Hon. mem. American Econ. Asscn 1989; Distinguished Fellow, History of Econs Soc. 2005; Japan Acad. Prize 1993. *Television:* Introduction to History of Economic Thought, Univ. of the Air, Japan 2001. *Publications:* General Equilibrium Theory and International Trade 1972, Microeconomic Foundations of Keynesian Macro Economics 1979, Economic Theories of a Non-Walrasian Tradition 1985, History of Economic Theory 1989, The Collected Essays of Takashi Negishi 1994, 2000. *Address:* 1-3-1-2003, Motoazabu, Minato-ku, Tokyo 106-0046, Japan. *Telephone:* (3) 3440-0630. *E-mail:* tnegishi@bk9.so-net.ne.jp.

NEGMATULLAEV, Sabit, DTechSc; Tajikistani physicist; b. 16 Sept. 1937, Ura-Tube; ed Tajik Polytech. Inst.; mem. CPSU 1966–91; jr researcher, Tajik Inst. of Seismic Resistance, Construction and Seismology of Seismology, Tajik Acad. of Sciences, Scientific Sec. 1964–65, Vice-Dir 1965–69, Dir 1969, now Hon. Dir; mem. Tajik Acad. of Sciences 1987–, Pres. 1988–95; Chair. Scientific-Publishing Council of Acad. of Sciences; mem. Cen. Cttee CPSU 1990–91. *Address:* c/o Academy of Sciences of Tajikistan, Rudaki Prospect 33, 734025 Dushanbe, Tajikistan. *Telephone:* (3772) 27-91-61. *E-mail:* pmp_international@yahoo.com.

NEGOIȚĂ, Liviu Gheorghe, LLB; Romanian lawyer and politician; b. 22 March 1962, Brăila; ed Univ. of Bucharest; mem. Democratic Liberal Party (DLP) 1997–; mem. Camera Deputaților (Chamber of Deputies) 1996–2000, 2000–04, Leader DLP Parl. Group 2003–, mem. several parl. cttees; Mayor of Bucharest Sector 3 2004–; Prime Minister Desig. 2009 (stepped down before taking office Dec. 2009). *Address:* c/o Partidul Democrat Liberal, 011825 Bucharest, Al. Modrogan 1, Romania (office). *E-mail:* liviunegoita@liviunegoita.ro (office). *Website:* www .liviunegoita.ro (office).

NEGRI, Barjas; Brazilian politician; *Mayor of Piracicaba;* b. 8 Dec. 1950, Santo Amaro, São Paulo; s. of Affonso Negri Neto and Hirce Rodrigues Negri; m. Sandra Regina Bonsi; one s. two d.; ed Methodist Univ. of Piracicaba; Prof. of Econs, Univ. of Piracicaba 1974–95; Researcher and Lecturer, UNIVCAMP Univ. 1986–; Sec. of Educ., São Paulo State Parl. 1979–82, Sec. of Planning 1993–94; Sec. Dept of Educ., Fed. Govt 1995–96; Sec. Dept of Health 1997–2001, Minister for Health 2002; Mayor of Piracicaba 2005–. *Address:* Prédio da Prefeitura Municipal, Rua Amadeu Amaral, 255, 13380 Piracicaba São Paulo, Brazil (office). *Website:* www .piracicaba.sp.gov.br (office).

NEGRITOIU, Misu, MS, PhD; Romanian politician, economist and banker; *Chairman, ING Bank Romania;* b. 25 May 1950, Dăbuleni, Dolj Co.; s. of Marin Negritoiu and Floarea Negritoiu; m. Paulina Urzica 1977; one s. one d.; ed Bucharest Acad. of Econ. Studies, Law School, Bucharest Univ., HDS Hertfordshire Univ.; foreign trade economist and then foreign trade co. dir 1973–90; Minister-Counsellor, Embassy, Washington; Pres. Romanian Devt Agency 1990–92; Deputy Prime Minister, Chair. Council for Strategy and Econ. Reform Co-ordination 1993; Chief Econ. Adviser to Pres. of Romania 1994–96; mem. Parl. 1996–97; Exec. Dir Wholesale Banking, ING Bank Romania 1997–2006, Gen. Man. 2006–10, CEO ING Bank Romania 2010–12, Chair. 2012–; Chair. Advisory Bd Maastricht School of Man. 2012–; Prof., Acad. of Econ. Studies, School of Political Studies and Public Admin., Bucharest; Chair. Grad. School of Man., MBA Canadian Programme; Pres. Forum for European Integration; mem. Romanian Econ. Soc. (SOREC), Romanian Soc. for Club of Rome, Romanian Asscn for Energy Policy (APER), American Asscn for Arbitration, Centre for European Policy Studies, Econ. Policy Forum, Faculty for Int. Econs and Business, Business Advisory Council – South-East European Co-operation Initiative/Stability Pact; Banker of the Year, Bucharest Business Week magazine 2004, Banker of the Year, Piata Financiara magazine 2006, Best Banker, Bucharest Business Week magazine 2008. *Publications:* Jumping Ahead – Economic Development and FDI 1996, International Finance (textbook) 1994, Management in International Trade 1997; numerous studies and articles on int. and domestic econ. issues, presentations to int. and domestic confs and seminars. *Leisure interest:* golf. *Address:* ING Building, 48 Iancu de Hunedoara Avenue, 011745 Bucharest 1 (office); 16 Dionisie Fotino Street, Apt 3, Bucharest 1, Romania (home). *Telephone:* (21) 2091103

(office). *Fax:* (21) 2229385 (office). *E-mail:* misu.negritoiu@ing.ro (office). *Website:* www.ing.ro (office).

NEGROPONTE, John Dimitri, BA; American diplomatist and academic; *Vice-Chairman, McLarty Associates;* b. 21 July 1939, London, England; s. of Dimitri J. Negroponte and Catherine C. Negroponte; m. Diana Mary Villiers 1976; two s. three d.; ed Phillips Exeter Acad., NH, Yale Univ., New Haven, Conn.; entered Foreign Service 1960, Amb. to Honduras 1981–85; Asst Sec. of State for Oceans and Int. Environmental Scientific Affairs 1985–87; Deputy Asst to Pres. for Nat. Security Affairs 1987–89; Amb. to Mexico 1989–93, to the Philippines 1993–96; Special Co-ordinator for post-1999 US Presence in Panama 1996–97; Exec. Vice-Pres. Global Markets McGraw-Hill 1997–2001; Perm. Rep. to UN 2001–04; Amb. to Iraq 2004–05; Dir of Nat. Intelligence 2005–07; Deputy Sec. of State 2007–09; Brady-Johnson Distinguished Fellow in Grand Strategy and Sr Lecturer in Global Affairs, Jackson Inst., Yale Univ. 2009–; Vice-Chair. McLarty Associates (strategic advisory firm), Washington, DC 2009–; Chair. Council of the Americas/Americas Soc., New York 2009–, Intelligence and Nat. Security Alliance (INSA) 2013–; Co-Chair. US-Philippines Soc. 2012–; Bd Advisor, Libra Group, London and New York; mem. Council on Foreign Relations, American Acad. of Diplomacy, Sec. of State's Foreign Affairs Policy Bd; Sec. of State's Distinguished Service Award 2005, 2009, Pres.'s Nat. Security Medal 2009. *Leisure interests:* swimming, skiing, reading, history. *Address:* McLarty Associates, 900 17th Street, NW, Washington, DC 20006, USA (office). *Telephone:* (202) 419-1400 (office). *Fax:* (202) 419-1421 (office). *E-mail:* jnegroponte@maglobal.com (office). *Website:* www.yale.edu/jackson (office); www.maglobal.com (office).

NEGRUȚA, Veaceslav; Moldovan economist and politician; *Minister of Finance;* b. 4 March 1972, Delacău, Grigoriopol; m.; two c.; ed Acad. of Econ. Studies of Moldova; Head of Macroeconomic and Financial Analyses Unit, Ministry of Finance 1994–97; Macroeconomist, Centre for Strategic Research and Reforms, World Bank /UNDP 1997–99; Sr State Adviser to Prime Minister Ion Sturza 1999; Dir Dept of Monetary Policy and Research, Nat. Bank of Moldova 2000–01; Sr Economist, KPMG Barents Group LLC/Bearing Point, USAID Moldovan Fiscal Reform Project 2001–05; Deputy Exec. Dir Moldova CASE (Centre of Social-Economic Analyses) Foundation 2003–07; worked as financial consultant 2005–09; Minister of Finance 2009–; mem. Liberal Democratic Party of Moldova. *Address:* Ministry of Finance, 2005 Chișinău, str. Cosmonauților 7, Moldova (office). *Telephone:* (22) 22-66-29 (office). *Fax:* (22) 24-00-55 (office). *E-mail:* cancelaria@minfin.moldova.md (office). *Website:* www.minfin.md (office).

NEHER, Erwin; German research scientist and academic; *Research Director, Max-Planck-Institut für biophysikalische Chemie, Göttingen;* b. 20 March 1944, Landsberg; s. of Franz Xaver Neher and Elisabeth Neher; m. Dr Eva-Maria Neher 1978; three s. two d.; ed Tech. Univ. Munich, Univ. of Wisconsin-Madison, USA; Research Assoc., Max-Planck-Institut für Psychiatrie, Munich 1970–72, Max-Planck-Institut für biophysikalische Chemie, Göttingen 1972–75, 1976–83, Research Dir 1983–; Research Assoc., Yale Univ., New Haven, Conn., USA 1975–76; Fairchild Scholar, California Inst. of Tech. 1988–89; shared Nobel Prize for Medicine 1991; several nat. and int. scientific awards; Bundesverdienstkreuz mit Stern und Schulterband 1998. *Publications:* Elektronische Messtechnik in der Physiologie 1974, Single Channel Recording (ed.) 1983. *Address:* Max-Planck-Institut für biophysikelische Chemie, Am Fassberg 11, 37077 Göttingen, Germany (office). *Telephone:* (551) 2011630 (office). *Fax:* (551) 2011688 (office). *E-mail:* eneher@gwdg.de (office). *Website:* www.mpibpc.gwdg.de (office).

NEHWAL, Saina; Indian professional badminton player; b. 17 March 1990, Hisar, Haryana; d. of Dr Harvir Singh Nehwal and Usha Rani; ed St Ann's Coll., Mehdipatnam; took part in Jr Asian Championship, Hwacheon, Repub. of Korea aged 14; turned professional 2003; winner, Czech Jr Open 2003, Asian Satellite Tournament 2005, 2006, Philippines Open 2006, Indian Nat. Championships 2007, 2008, Indian Int. Challenge 2007, Yonex Chinese Taipai Open 2008, World Jr Badminton Championships (first Indian), Pune 2008, 2010, Indonesian Open Super Series (first Indian) 2009, 2010, Nat. Games of India (gold medal) 2007, Commonwealth Youth Games (gold medal) 2008, Indian Open Grand Prix 2009, 2010, Badminton Asia Championships (bronze medal) 2010, Singapore Open Super Series 2010, Commonwealth Games (gold medal) 2010, Hong Kong Super Series 2010, Swiss Open Grand Prix Gold trophy 2011, 2012, Indonesia Open Super Series Premier (silver medal) 2011, 2012, Malaysia Open Grand Prix Gold (silver medal) 2011; represented India (quarterfinalist) at Beijing Olympics 2008, London Olympics (bronze medal) 2012, Denmark Open 2012; Most Promising Player, Badminton World Fed. 2008, Sports Illustrated India Sportsperson of the Year 2009, MSN Sportsperson of the Year 2009, Rajiv Gandhi Khel Ratna Award 2010. *Address:* Globosport India Pvt. Ltd, 1st Floor, 2nd Cross, Amarjyoti Layout, off Intermediate Ring Road, Domlur, Bangalore 560 071, India. *Telephone:* (80) 41154214. *Fax:* (80) 41154043130. *E-mail:* info@globosportworld.com.

NEI, Masatoshi, BS, MS, PhD; American (b. Japanese) biologist and academic; *Evan Pugh Professor of Biology and Director, Institute of Molecular Evolutionary Genetics, Pennsylvania State University;* b. 2 Jan. 1931, Miyazaki; m. Nobuko Nei; one s. one d.; ed Miyazaki and Kyoto Univs, Univ. of California, Davis and North Carolina State Univ., USA; Asst Prof., Kyoto Univ. 1958–62; Geneticist, Nat. Inst. of Radiological Sciences, Chiba 1962–65, Head, Population Genetics Lab. 1965–69; Assoc. Prof. of Biology, Brown Univ., Providence, RI 1969–71, Prof. of Biology 1971–72; Prof. of Population Genetics, Center for Demographic and Population Genetics, Univ. of Texas, Houston 1972–90, Acting Dir 1978–80; Distinguished Prof. of Biology, Pennsylvania State Univ. 1990–94, Dir Inst. of Molecular Evolutionary Genetics 1990–, Evan Pugh Prof. of Biology 1994–; Visiting Prof. of Biology, Tokyo Inst. of Tech. 2001; Ed. Molecular Biology and Evolution 1983–93; mem. Editorial Bd, Proceedings of the National Academy of Sciences (USA) 2003–; mem. Bd of Overseers, Harvard Univ. 1988–94; mem. Advisory Bd Gene: Evolutionary Genomics 2004–; mem. NAS 2003– (mem. Nat. Research Council Cttee 1994–96), American Genetic Asscn (Pres. 1999), Soc. for Molecular Biology and Evolution (Pres. 1994); Hon. mem. Genetics Soc. of Japan 1989, Japan Soc. of Human Genetics 1996, Japan Soc. for Histocompatibility and Immunogenetics 2000, Japan Soc. of Animal Genetics and Breeding 2001; Dr hc (Miyazaki Univ.) 2002; Japan Soc. of Human Genetics Award 1977, Kihara Prize, Genetics Soc. of Japan 1990, P.R. Krishnaiah Memorial Lecture, Pennsylvania State Univ. 1999, Masatoshi Nei Annual Lecture, est. for the Soc. for Molecular Biology and

Evolution 2000, Certificate of Award 'Highly Cited Researchers', Inst. for Scientific Information 2000, Wilhelmine E. Key Invitational Lecture, Annual Meeting of American Genetic Asscn 2001, Int. Prize for Biology, Japan Soc. for the Promotion of Sciences 2002, Barbara Bowman Award, Texas Geneticist Soc. 2003, Thomas Hunt Morgan Medal, Genetics Soc. of America 2006, Masatoshi Nei Legacy Symposium held at the Molecular Biology and Evolution Soc. meeting, Tempe, Ariz. 2006, Kyoto Prize, Inamori Foundation (co-recipient) 2013. *Publications:* more than 260 articles in scientific journals. *Address:* Institute of Molecular Evolutionary Genetics, Pennsylvania State University, Department of Biology, 328 Mueller Laboratory, University Park, PA 16801, USA (office). *Telephone:* (814) 863-7334 (office). *Fax:* (814) 863-7336 (office). *E-mail:* nxm2@psu.edu (office). *Website:* bio.psu.edu/directory/nxm2 (office); www.personal.psu.edu/nxm2 (office).

NEID, Silvia; German football coach and fmr professional football player; *Head Coach, Germany Women's National Football Team;* b. 2 May 1964, Walldürn, Baden-Württemberg; midfielder; as a youth played with SV Schlierstadt 1975–80; sr career: played with Klinge Seckach 1980–83, SSG Bergisch Gladbach 1983–85 (Fußball-Bundesliga (women) 1984, Frauen DFB Pokal 1984), TSV Siegen 1985–86 (Fußball-Bundesliga (women) 1987, 1990, 1991, 1992, 1994, 1996, Frauen DFB Pokal 1986, 1987, 1988, 1989, 1993); mem. Germany Women's Nat. Football Team 1982–96 (won UEFA Women's Championship 1989, 1991, 1995, runners-up, FIFA Women's World Cup 1995), managed Under-19 Germany Women's Nat. Football Team, winning World Championship 2004, runners-up, Women's Championship, Asst Coach Germany Women's Nat. Football Team 1996–2005, Head Coach 2005–, as coach has won the World Cup 2007, bronze medal, Summer Olympics, Beijing 2008, European Championship 2009; Bundesverdienstkreuz am Bande 2007, Verdienstorden des Landes Nordrhein-Westfalen 2011, Verdienstorden des Landes Baden-Württemberg 2013; FIFA World Coach of the Year 2010, 2013. *Address:* Deutscher Fußball-Bund, Hermann-Neuberger-Haus, Otto-Fleck-Schneise 6, 60528 Frankfurt am Main, Germany (office). *Telephone:* (69) 67880 (office). *Fax:* (69) 6788266 (office). *E-mail:* info@dfb.de (office). *Website:* www.dfb.de (office).

NEIL, Andrew Ferguson, MA, FRSA; British publisher, broadcaster, editor and business executive; *Publisher, Spectator Magazine Group;* b. 21 May 1949, Paisley, Renfrewshire, Scotland; s. of James Neil and Mary Ferguson; ed Paisley Grammar School, Univ. of Glasgow; with Conservative Party Research Dept 1971–73; with The Economist 1973–83, Ulster Political then Industrial Corresp. 1973–79, American Corresp. 1979–82, UK Ed. 1982–83; Ed. The Sunday Times 1983–94; Exec. Ed. Fox TV News, USA 1994; Exec. Chair. Sky TV 1988–90; Publr The Scotsman, Scotland on Sunday, Edinburgh Evening News 1996–2006; Publr, The Business 1999–2007; regular anchorman and TV commentator UK and USA; anchorman, The Daily Politics (BBC 2) 2003–, This Week (BBC 1) 2003–, Straight Talk with Andrew Neil (BBC News Channel) 2004–09, Sunday Politics (BBC 1) 2012–; Contrib. Ed. Vanity Fair, New York 1994–2007; Chief Exec., then Chair. The Spectator and Apollo magazines 2004–13, Publr 2013–; Chair. World Media Rights (WMR) 2005–, ITP Magazines (Dubai) 2005–, Peters Fraser & Dunlop (talent agency) 2008–10; Lord Rector Univ. of St Andrews 1999–2002; Hon. DLit (Napier Univ.) 1998, Hon. DUniv (Paisley) 2001, Hon. LLD (St Andrews) 2002. *Publications include:* The Cable Revolution 1982, Britain's Free Press: Does It Have One? 1989, Full Disclosure 1996, British Excellence 1999, 2000, 2001. *Leisure interests:* dining out in New York, London, Dubai and Côte d'Azur, cycling when not chairing companies. *Address:* Glenburn Enterprises, 8 Cadogan Square, London, SW1X 0JU (office); c/o 22 Old Queen Street, London, SW1H 9HP, England (office). *Telephone:* (845) 299-7225 (office); (20) 7961-0000 (office). *E-mail:* afneil@icloud.com.

NEILAND, Brendan Robert, MA; British artist and professor of painting; b. 23 Oct. 1941, Lichfield, Staffs., England; s. of Arthur Neiland and Joan Whiley; m. Hilary Salter 1970; two d.; ed St Philip's Grammar School, Birmingham, St Augustine's Seminary, Ireland, Birmingham School of Art and Royal Coll. of Art, London; painter and printmaker; best known for his paintings of reflections in modern city buildings; gallery artist, Angela Flowers Gallery 1970–78, Fischer Fine Art 1978–92, Redfern Gallery 1992–; solo and group shows throughout Europe, Middle East, USA and Australia; Lecturer in Fine Art, Univ. of Brighton 1983–96, Prof. of Painting 1996–98; Keeper (Dir), Royal Acad. Schools 1998–2004 (resgnd), expelled from membership of RA 2004; Visiting Prof. of Fine Art, Loughborough Univ. 1999; Daler Rowney Award, Royal Acad. Summer Exhbn 1989. *Publication:* Upon Reflection 1997. *Leisure interests:* cricket, golf, fine wines. *Address:* c/o Redfern Gallery, 20 Cork Street, London, W1S 3HL; 2 Granard Road, London, SW12 8UL, England (home); Crepe, La Grévé sur Mignon, 17170 Courcon, France. *Telephone:* (20) 7734-1732 (Redfern Gallery); (20) 8673-4597 (home); (5) 46-01-62-97 (Courcon). *E-mail:* neilands@talktalk.net. *Website:* www.brendanneiland.com.

NEILD, Robert Ralph; British economist, academic and writer; *Professor Emeritus of Economics, University of Cambridge;* b. 10 Sept. 1924, Peterborough, Cambs., England; s. of Ralph Neild and Josephine Neild; m. 1st Nora Clemens Sayre (divorced 1961); m. 2nd Elizabeth W. Griffiths 1962 (divorced 1986); one s. four d.; m. 3rd Virginia Meagher 2004; ed Charterhouse and Trinity Coll. Cambridge; RAF 1943–44, Operational Research, RAF, 1944–45; Secr., UN Econ. Comm. for Europe, Geneva 1947–51; Econ. Section, Cabinet Office (later Treasury) 1951–56; Lecturer in Econs, Fellow and Steward of Trinity Coll. Cambridge 1956–58; Nat. Inst. of Econ. and Social Research 1958–64; Econ. Adviser to Treasury 1964–67; mem. Fulton Cttee on the Civil Service 1966–68; Dir Stockholm Int. Peace Research Inst. 1967–71, mem. Governing Bd 1972–82; Prof. of Econs, Univ. of Cambridge 1971–84, Prof. Emer. 1984–; mem. Governing Body Queen Elizabeth Coll., Oxford 1978–87; Fellow, Trinity Coll. 1971–. *Publications:* Pricing and Employment in the Trade Cycle 1964, The Measurement and Reform of Budgetary Policy (with T. S. Ward) 1978, How to Make up Your Mind about the Bomb 1981, An Essay on Strategy 1990, The Foundations of Defensive Defence (ed. with A. Boserup) 1990, The English, the French and the Oyster 1995, Public Corruption: The Dark Side of Social Evolution 2002, Riches and Responsibility: The Financial History of Trinity College, Cambridge 2008. *Leisure interests:* painting, oysters. *Address:* Trinity College, Cambridge, CB2 1TQ, England (office). *Telephone:* (1223) 338400 (office); (1223) 338444 (home). *E-mail:* RRN20@cam.ac.uk (office).

NEILL, Rt Hon. Sir Brian (Thomas), Kt, PC, MA; British judge and arbitrator; b. 2 Aug. 1923; s. of Sir Thomas Neill and Lady (Annie Strachan) Neill (née Bishop); m. Sally Margaret Backus 1956; three s.; ed Highgate School, Corpus Christi Coll., Oxford, Notre Dame Law School, London; served with Rifle Brigade 1942–46; called to Bar, Inner Temple 1949, Bencher 1976; in practice at jr Bar specialising in media law and in drafting banking and other documents for financial institutions 1949–68; QC 1968; a Recorder of the Crown Court 1972–78; a Judge of the High Court, Queen's Bench Div. 1978–84; a Lord Justice of Appeal 1985–96 (retd), sitting occasionally as retd Lord Justice in Court of Appeal and Judicial Cttee of Privy Council 1997–98; Justice, Court of Appeal, Gibraltar 1997–; Pres. (part-time) 1998–2003; Pres. Soc. for Computers and Law 1983–93, Vice-Pres. 1993–; first Chair. Information Tech. and the Courts Cttee (ITAC) 1985–95; mem. Departmental Cttee to examine operation of Section 2 of Official Secrets Act 1971; Chair. Advisory Cttee on Rhodesia Travel Restrictions 1973–78; mem. Court of Assistants 1972– (Master 1980–81), Lord Chancellor's Dept's Civil Justice IT Strategy Devt Group, City Disputes Panel, London Court of Int. Arbitration; mem. Worshipful Co. of Turners; Certified Mediator in Alternative Dispute Resolution 2000; Chair. of Trustees, Lord Slynn of Hadley European Law Foundation; Liveryman, Worshipful Co. of Information Technologists; Hon. Fellow, Corpus Christi Coll., Oxford 1986–. *Publication:* Defamation (with Colin Duncan) 1978. *Address:* 20 Essex Street, London, WC2R 3AL, England (office); ADR Chambers UK & Europe, Equity House, Blackbrook Park Avenue, Taunton, TA1 2PX, Somerset. *Telephone:* (20) 7842-1200 (office). *Fax:* (20) 7842-1270 (office). *E-mail:* clerks@20essexst.com (office); mail@adrchambers.co.uk. *Website:* www.adrchambers.co.uk.

NEILL, Sam, DCNZM, OBE; New Zealand actor; b. (Nigel Neill), 14 Sept. 1947, Omagh, Co. Tyrone, Northern Ireland, UK; m. Noriko Watanabe; one d.; one s. by Lisa Harrow; ed Univ. of Canterbury; toured for one year with Players Drama Quintet; appeared with Amamus Theatre in roles including Macbeth and Pentheus in The Bacchae; joined NZ Nat. Film Unit playing leading part in three films 1974–78; moved to Australia 1978, to England 1980; owns a small family wine-producing business called Two Paddocks at Gibbston, Central Otago in the South Island of NZ. *Films include:* Ashes 1975, Landfall 1975, Sleeping Dogs 1977, The Journalist 1979, Just Out of Reach 1979, My Brilliant Career 1979, The Final Conflict (Omen III) 1981, Possession 1981, Attack Force Z 1982, From a Far Country, Enigma 1983, Le Sang des Autres 1984, Robbery Under Arms 1985, Plenty 1985, For Love Alone 1986, Peter Kenna's The Good Wife 1987, A Cry in the Dark 1988, Dead Calm 1989, La révolution française 1989, The Hunt for Red October 1990, Shadow of China 1990, Death in Brunswick 1990, Until the End of the World 1991, Memoirs of an Invisible Man 1992, Hostage 1992, The Piano 1993, Jurassic Park 1993, Sirens 1993, Country Life 1994, The Jungle Book 1994, In the Mouth of Madness 1994, Restoration 1995, Children of the Revolution 1996, Victory 1996, Snow White: A Tale of Terror 1997, Event Horizon 1997, The Horse Whisperer 1998, The Revengers' Comedies 1998, Molokai: The Story of Father Damien 1999, Bicentennial Man 1999, My Mother Frank 2000, The Dish 2000, The Magic Pudding (voice) 2000, Jurassic Park III 2001, The Zookeeper 2001, Dirty Deeds 2002, Leunig: How Democracy Actually Works (short) (voice) 2002, Perfect Strangers 2003, Yes 2004, Wimbledon 2004, Little Fish 2005, Irresistible 2006, Angel 2007, My Talks with Dean Spanley 2008, Skin 2008, In Her Skin 2009, Under The Mountain 2009, Daybreakers 2009, Legend of the Guardians: The Owls of Ga'Hoole (voice) 2010, The Dragon Pearl 2011, The Hunter 2011, The Vow 2012, Escape Plan 2013, Mariah Mundi and the Midas Box 2013, A Long Way Down 2014. *Television includes:* Lucinda Brayford (series) 1980, Young Ramsay (series) 1980, The Sullivans (series) 1980, Ivanhoe (film) 1982, Reilly: Ace of Spies (mini-series) 1983, The Country Girls (film) 1984, Kane and Abel (mini-series) 1985, Strong Medicine (film) 1986, Amerika (mini-series) 1987, Leap of Faith (film) 1988, Fever (film) 1991, One Against the Wind (film) 1991, Family Pictures (film) 1993, The Rainbow Warrior (film) 1993, The Simpsons (series) 1994, In Cold Blood (film) 1996, Merlin (mini-series) 1998, The Games (series) 1998, Sally Hemings: An American Scandal (film) 2000, Submerged (film) 2001, Framed (film) 2002, Dr Zhivago (film) 2002, Stiff (film) 2004, Jessica (film) 2004, To the Ends of the Earth (mini-series) 2005, Mary Bryant (mini-series) 2005, To the Ends of the Earth (mini-series) 2005, Sci Fi Inside: 'The Triangle' (film) 2005, The Triangle (mini-series) 2005, Merlin's Apprentice (mini-series) 2006, Two Twisted (series) 2006, The Tudors (series) 2007, Crusoe (series) 2008–10, Iron Road (mini-series) 2009, Happy Town 2010, Rake (series) 2010, Ice (mini-series) 2011 Alcatraz (series) 2012, Peaky Blinders (series) 2013, Harry (series) 2013, The Ordained (film) 2013. *Address:* c/o ICM, 10250 Constellation Boulevard, Los Angeles, CA 90067, USA (office). *Telephone:* (310) 550-4000 (office). *Fax:* (310) 550-4100 (office). *Website:* www.icmtalent.com (office); www.twopaddocks.com.

NEILL OF BLADEN, Baron (Life Peer), cr. 1997, of Briantspuddle in the County of Dorset; **Francis Patrick Neill,** QC; British lawyer; b. 8 Aug. 1926; s. of the late Sir Thomas Neill and of Annie Strachan Neill (née Bishop); m. Caroline Susan Debenham 1954; three s. two d. (and one s. deceased); ed Highgate School and Magdalen Coll. Oxford; served with Rifle Brigade 1944–47; GSO III (Training), British Troops Egypt 1947; called to the Bar, Gray's Inn 1951; Recorder of the Crown Court 1975–78; Judge of the Court of Appeal of Jersey and Guernsey 1977–94; Fellow of All Souls Coll., Oxford 1950–77, Sub-Warden 1972–74, Warden 1977–95; Vice-Chancellor Oxford Univ. 1985–89; Chair., Justice–All Souls Cttee for Review of Admin. Law 1978–87, Press Council 1978–83, Council for Securities Industry 1978–85; mem. DTI Cttee of Inquiry into Regulatory Arrangements at Lloyds 1986–87; Bencher, Gray's Inn 1971, Vice-Treas. 1989, Treas. 1990; mem. Bar Council 1967–71, Vice-Chair. 1973–74, Chair. 1974–75; Chair. Senate of the Inns of Court and the Bar 1974–75; Chair. Cttee on Standards in Public Life 1997–2001; Dir Times Newspapers Holdings Ltd 1988–97; mem. (Crossbench), House of Lords 1997–; mem. Hon. Soc. of Gray's Inn, Gen. Council of the Bar, American Law Inst., British Inst. of Int. and Comparative Law, Int. Law Asscn; Hon. Fellow, Magdalen Coll. Oxford 1988; Hon. Prof. of Legal Ethics, Univ. of Birmingham 1983–84; Hon. DCL (Oxford) 1987; Hon. LLD (Hull) 1978, (Buckingham) 1994. *Publication:* Administrative Justice: Some Necessary Reforms 1988. *Leisure interests:* music, forestry. *Address:* House of Lords, Westminster, London, SW1A 0PW (office); Serle Court, 6 New Square, Lincoln's Inn, London, WC2A 3QS (office); 1 Hare Court, Temple, London, EC4Y 7BE, England. *Telephone:* (20) 7242-6105 (office). *Fax:* (20) 7405-4004 (office). *E-mail:* pneill@serlecourt.co.uk (office).

Website: www.parliament.uk/biographies/lords/lord-neill-of-bladen/1921 (office); www.serlecourt.co.uk (office).

NEILSON, Kerr; Australian investment fund manager; *Managing Director, Platinum Asset Management Limited;* b. South Africa; m. Judith Neilson; two c.; early career as stockbroker in London; with Banker's Trust, SA, moved to Australia to work for Banker's Trust Asset Man. Div. 1984; Founder and Man. Dir Platinum International Fund 1994–. *Address:* Platinum Asset Management Ltd, Level 8, 7 Macquarie Place, Sydney, NSW 2000, Australia. *Telephone:* (2) 9254-5590. *Website:* www.platinum.com.au.

NEIZVESTNY, Ernst Iosifovich; Russian artist and sculptor; b. 9 April 1925, Sverdlovsk; ed V. I. Surikov State Inst. of Arts (M. G. Maniser's studio); Soviet Army 1942–45; sculptor at studios of USSR Agricultural Exhbn (later Econ. Achievements of USSR Exhbn) 1953–54; mem. Artists' Union of USSR 1955–57; granted permission to emigrate to Geneva 1976; moved to New York 1977; Soviet citizenship restored 1990; mem. Royal Acad. of Fine Arts, Sweden, New York Acad. of Sciences 1986, European Acad. of Arts, Sciences and Humanities, Paris, Swedish Acad. of Sciences, Latvian Acad. of Sciences 1997, Int. Soc. for Human Rights; Guest Prof., Columbia Univ., New York Univ., Harvard Univ., Yale Univ., Univ. of Calif., Berkeley; fmr American Asscn for the Advancement of Slavic Studies and Humanist in Residence, Univ. of Ore.; Order of Red Star for heroism on the Second Ukrainian front 1945, Russian State Award for Merit 1995, Order of Honour 2000; Dr hc (Moscow State Univ. for Humanic Studies) 1996; Russian Govt Award for Achievement in the Arts 1996, Lifetime Achievement Award, Nat. Children's Leukemia Foundation 1997, Russian Medal of Honor for Artistic Achievements 2000. *Television:* Monumental Statues 1998, Cold War Postscript, CNN 1999. *Main works:* Kremlin Builder, First Wings, The Youth, Mother, series: War – is. . .; Robots and Semi-robots, Great Mistakes, Nikita Krushchev Memorial, Lotus Blossom, Aswan Dam, Egypt 1968, Monument to the Golden Child, Odessa, Ukraine 1995, Monument to Victims of Stalinism, Magadan, Russia 1990–96, Bust of Boris Yeltsin 1996, Monument to the Kalmykia Deportation 1996, The Great Centaur, Palace of Nations, Geneva 1997; illustrations to works of Dante, Beckett and Dostoyevsky. *Publications:* Space, Time and Synthesis in Art 1990, Artist's Fate 1992. *Leisure interests:* building sculpture garden on Shelter Island, New York. *Address:* Ernst Neizvestny Studio, 81 Grand Street, New York, NY 10013, USA (office). *Telephone:* (212) 226-2677 (office). *E-mail:* enstudio@yahoo.com (office). *Website:* www.enstudio.com (office).

NEJAD-HOSSEINIAN, Seyed Mohammad Hadi, MS, PhD; Iranian diplomatist and politician; *Secretary-General, Asian Parliamentary Assembly;* b. 2 Jan. 1947, Karbala; s. of Hossein Nejad Hosseinian and Razie Haj Tarkhani; m. Fatemeh Tadbir; two s. two d.; ed Tehran Univ., George Washington Univ., Washington, DC; Adviser to Deputy Prime Minister 1979–81; Deputy Minister, Plan and Budget Org. 1981; Minister for Roads and Transportation 1981–85; Deputy Minister of Oil 1985–89, 1994–97, 2002–07; Minister for Heavy Industry 1989–94; Amb. and Perm. Rep. to UN, New York 1997–2002; Sec.-Gen. Asian Parl. Ass. 2007–. *Publications:* International Business, Environments and Operations (2 vols, trans. from English), Dolate Dolatgera: Challenges and Road Map for the Next Government, Competition among Dolat abad and Mardom shar. *Address:* Asian Parliamentary Assembly, No. 4 Milad Alley, Takhti Street, Aref Nasab Street, Vali Asr Avenue, Tehran, Iran (office). *Telephone:* (21) 22694405–6 (office). *Fax:* (21) 22236540 (office). *E-mail:* secretariat@asianparliament.org (office). *Website:* www.asianparliament.org (office).

NEKIPELOV, Alexander Dmitriyevich, DrEcon; Russian economist, academic and business executive; *Director, Moscow School of Economics, Lomonosov Moscow State University;* b. 16 Nov. 1951, Moscow; m.; one d.; ed Moscow State Univ.; jr researcher, sr researcher, Head of Sector, Deputy Dir, Inst. of Int. Econ. and Political Studies, Russian Acad. of Sciences 1973–98, Dir 1998–; Dir Moscow School of Econs, Lomonosov Moscow State Univ. 2004–; mem. Russian Acad. of Sciences 1997–, Vice-Pres. 2001–; Ind. Dir, Rosneft 2006–, currently Chair.; mem. Bd of Dirs OJSC Zarubezhneft, OJSC AK Transneft; Co-Chair. Bd of Trustees Nat. Investment Council; Medal of Order for Service to Motherland, and other state awards. *Publications:* three scientific works and more than 200 academic papers published in Russia and abroad, including monograph Essays on Economics of Postcommunism 1996. *Leisure interest:* chess. *Address:* Moscow School of Economics, 119992 Moscow, 1, Building 61, Leninskie Gory, M.V. Lomonosov MSU, Russia (office). *Telephone:* (495) 510-52-67 (office). *E-mail:* mail@mse-msu .ru (office). *Website:* www.mse-msu.ru (office).

NEKROŠIUS, Eimuntas; Lithuanian theatre director and actor; *Director, Meno Fortas Theatre Studio;* b. 21 Nov. 1952, Pažobris; s. of Petras Nekrošius and Elena Nekrošienė; m. Nadezhda Gultyaeva 1976; two s.; ed State Inst. of Theatre Art in Moscow; Dir Kaunas Drama Theatre 1978–79; Dir State Youth Theatre, Lithuanian SSR (now Lithuania), Vilnius 1978–79, 1980–91, Dir LIFE Int. Theatre Festival 1991–97; Founder and Dir Meno Fortas Theatre Studio 1998–; Order of Grand Duke Gediminas; USSR State Prize 1987, Award of European Theatre Union 1991, Baltic Ass. Award 1994, Special Prize for Best Dir of the Year, Lithuanian Theatre Union 1994, Nat. Culture and Art Award, Konstantin Stanislavski Award 2001, Prize for the Best Professional Theatre Artists of the Season, Ministry of Culture 2003, 'Golden Mask' (Moscow) Prize 2004, Herder Prize 2005, Award of Italian Critics Asscn for the best foreign performance shown in Italy 2007, Hon. Award, Int. Istanbul Theatre Festival 2008. *Productions include:* A Taste of Honey 1976, Duokishkis Ballad 1978, Ivanov 1978, The Square 1980, Pirosmani, Pirosmani 1981, Love and Death in Verona (Rock opera) 1982 (renewed 1996), The Day Lasts More Than a Hundred Years 1983, Uncle Vanya 1986, The Nose 1991, Mozart and Salieri, Don Juan, Plague 1994, Three Sisters 1995, Hamlet (Lithuanian Nat. Prize, Konrad Swinarski Award, miesięcznik 'Teatr' monthly journal) 1997, Macbeth 1999, Othello 2001, Ivanov 2002, Veridi's Macbeth 2002, The Seasons 2003, The Children of Rosenthal (Bolshoi Theatre, Moscow) 2005, Faust 2006, Idiot (UBU Prize 2008) 2007, Valkyrie (opera, Lithuanian Nat. Opera and Ballet Theatre) 2007, Anna Karenina (Teatro Storchi, Modena, Italy) 2008. *Film roles include:* Girenas in Flight Through Atlantics 1983, Father in Lessons of Hatred 1984, Minister in Team 1985. *Address:* Bernardinų 8/8, 01124 Vilnius, Lithuania. *Telephone:* (5) 22312110. *E-mail:* mail@menofortas.lt. *Website:* www.menofortas.lt.

NEKVASIL, Lt-Gen. Jiří; Czech army officer and diplomatist; *Ambassador to Mongolia;* b. 24 April 1948, Benešov; m. 1st Jaroslava Papeová; m. 2nd Danuše Kadlečková; two s. three d.; m. 3rd Nanuli Kobaladze; two s. three d.; ed Tech. Inst. Liptovský Mikuláš, Mil. Acad., Kalinin, Acad. of Gen. Staff of Mil. Forces, Moscow, NATO Defence Coll., Rome; 2nd in Command Czech AF and Anti-Air Defence System 1990–92; Commdr of Gen. Staff 1993–98; Adviser to Ministry of Defence 1998–99; Amb. to Georgia 2000–04, to Mongolia 2004–07, to Afghanistan 2007–10; Order of Red Star (Czechoslovakia) 1985, Commdr, Legion of Merit 1996, Legion d'honneur 1996, Bundeswehr Gold Cross (Germany) 1998, Gold Cross (Austria) 1998. *Leisure interests:* mushrooming, tennis, gardening, photography. *Address:* c/o Ministry of Foreign Affairs, Loretánské nám. 101/5, 118 00 Prague 1, Czech Republic (office).

NELIDOV, Andrey Vitalievich, DEcon, PhD; Russian engineer and politician; b. 12 June 1957, Leningrad (now St Petersburg); ed Leningrad Inst. of Water Transportation; Soviet Army service 1978–80; Equipment Engineer, Deputy Chief of Procurement Dept, Leningrad Experimental Research Plant, Leningrad Inst. of Water Transportation 1980–85; Sr Engineer, Housing Services Enterprises, Petrograd Dist Housing Admin 1985–88; car mechanic, Leningrad 1988–89; Marketing Dir and Dir Gen., Nord-Kemp Co. (scientific mfr), later Deputy Dir Gen. for Forestry, Nord-Kemp Jt Stock Co. 1989–96, Chair. Bd of Dirs Aug.–Oct. 1999; Chair. Timber Processing Complex Cttee, St Petersburg 1996–99; Chair. Lesnaya Birzha (timber yard), St Petersburg 1999–2000; Dir Gen. White Sea Onego Shipping Co. Inc., Petrozavodsk 2000–02; mem. St Petersburg Region Legis. Ass. 2002–04, Vice-Chair. 2004–06; Repub. of Karelia Rep. to Russian Fed. Ass., Moscow and mem. Council 2006–10; Pres. Repub. of Karelia 2010–12 (resgnd); Order of Honour 2007, Council of Russian Fed. 15 Year Medal 2008, 300 Years of Russian Navy Jubilee Medal 1996, Letter of Award of Federal Ass. of the Russian Fed. 2010. *Address:* c/o Office of the President, 185028 Petrozavodsk, Lenin Street 19, Karelia, Russia.

NELISSEN, Roelof J., MA; Dutch politician and banker; b. 4 April 1931, Hoofdplaat, Zeeland Prov.; m. A. M. van der Kelen; three s. one d.; ed grammar school at Dongen and Faculty of Law, Catholic Univ. of Nijmegen; various posts in employers' asscns, Amsterdam and The Hague 1956–69; mem. Second Chamber, States-Gen. (Parl.) 1963–70; Minister of Econ. Affairs 1970–71; First Deputy Prime Minister, Minister of Finance 1971–73; mem. Bd of Man. Dirs Amsterdam-Rotterdam Bank NV 1974–, Vice-Chair. 1979–82, Chair. 1983–92; Chair. Bd of Man. Dirs ABN-AMRO Holding NV 1990–92; Commdr, Order of Orange-Nassau 1973. *Address:* PO Box 552, 1250 AN Laren, Netherlands.

NELLIGAN, Kate; Canadian actress; b. 16 March 1950, London, Ont.; d. of Patrick Joseph Nelligan and Alice Nelligan (née Dier); one s.; ed St Martin's Catholic School, London, Ont., York Univ., Toronto and Cen. School of Speech and Drama, London, UK; professional stage debut as Corrie in Barefoot in the Park, Little Theatre, Bristol 1972; other parts there and at Theatre Royal for Bristol Old Vic 1972–73 include: Hypatia in Misalliance, Stella Kowalski in A Streetcar Named Desire, Pegeen Mike in The Playboy of the Western World, Grace Harkaway in London Assurance, title role in Lulu, Sybil Chase in Private Lives; London debut as Jenny in Knuckle, Comedy Theatre 1974; joined Nat. Theatre Co. at Old Vic 1975 to play Ellie Dunn in Heartbreak House, also in Plenty and Moon for the Misbegotten 1984; As You Like It for RSC, Stratford; Serious Money, Broadway 1988, Spoils of War 1988, Eleni; Evening Standard Best Actress Award 1978. *Films include:* The Count of Monte Cristo, The Romantic Englishwoman 1975, Dracula 1979, Mr. Patman 1980, Agent 1980, Eye of the Needle 1981, Without a Trace 1983, Eleni 1985, Il Giorno prima 1987, White Room 1990, The Prince of Tides 1991, Frankie and Johnny 1991, Shadows and Fog 1992, Fatal Instinct 1993, Wolf 1994, Margaret's Museum 1995, How to Make An American Quilt 1995, Up Close and Personal 1996, U.S. Marshals 1998, Stolen Moments (voice), Boy Meets Girl 1998, The Cider House Rules 1999, Blessed Stranger 2000, Premonition 2007. *Television includes:* The Onedin Line (series) 1971, The Arcata Promise 1974, Count of Monte Cristo 1975, The Lady of the Camellias 1976, Bethune 1977, Measure for Measure 1979, Licking Hitler, Thérèse Raquin (mini-series) 1980, Forgive Our Foolish Ways 1980, Victims 1982, Kojak: The Price of Justice 1987, Love and Hate: The Story of Colin and Joanne Thatcher 1989, Golden Fiddles (mini-series) 1990, Three Hotels 1991, Old Times 1991, Terror Stalks the Class Reunion 1992, The Diamond Fleece 1992, Liar, Liar 1992; Shattered Trust: The Shari Karney Story 1993, Spoils of War 1994, Million Dollar Babes 1994, A Mother's Prayer 1995, Captive Heart: The James Mink Story 1996, Calm at Sunset 1996, Love is Strange 1999, Swing Vote 1999, Blessed Stranger: After Flight 111 2000, Walter and Henry 2001, A Wrinkle in Time (mini-series) 2003, Human Cargo (mini-series) 2004, In From the Night 2005. *Leisure interests:* reading, cooking. *Address:* c/o Innovative Artists, 235 Park Avenue South, Suite 7, New York, NY 10003, USA. *Telephone:* (212) 253-6900.

NELSON, Bill, JD; American politician; *Senator from Florida;* b. 29 Sept. 1942, Miami, Fla; s. of C. W. Nelson and Nannie Nelson; m. Grace H. Cavert 1972; one s. one d.; ed Yale Univ., Univ. of Virginia; with US Army Reserves 1965–75, Army 1968–71, rank of Capt.; admitted to the Bar, Fla; pvt. law practice Melbourne, Fla 1970–79; mem. House of Reps, Fla 1972–78, US Congress 1979–91, Chair. Space Sub-cttee of the Science, Space and Tech. Cttee (flew with crew on 24th flight of NASA Space Shuttle); State Treas., Insurance Commr and Fire Marshall, Fla 1995–2000; Senator from Florida 2000–, mem. Commerce, Budget and Finance Cttee, Intelligence Cttee, Aging Cttee. *Address:* 716 Hart Senate Building, Washington, DC 20510, USA (office). *Telephone:* (202) 224-5274 (office). *Fax:* (202) 228-2183 (office). *Website:* billnelson.senate.gov (office).

NELSON, Brendan; Australian diplomatist, physician and politician; *Director, Australian War Memorial;* b. 19 Aug. 1958, Melbourne; m. Gillian Nelson; three c.; ed Flinders Univ.; Gen. Practitioner, Hobart, Tasmania 1985–95; Dir Hobart and Launceston After Hours Medical Services 1987–91; Tasmanian State Pres. Australian Medical Asscn 1990–92, Fed. Vice-Pres. 1991–93, Fed. Pres. 1993–95; MP for Bradfield (Liberal) 1996–, Chair. House of Reps Standing Cttee on Employment, Educ. and Workplace Relations 1998; Chair. Sydney Airport Community Forum –2000; Parl. Sec. to Minister for Defence 2000–01; Minister for Educ., Science and Training 2001–06, for Defence 2006–07; Fed. Parl. Leader, Liberal Party of Australia 2007–08; Amb. to Belgium, Luxembourg and the EU 2010–12; Dir Australian War Memorial 2012–; Hon. Fellow, Royal Australasian

RACP; AMA Gold Medal for Distinguished Service to Medicine and Humanity 1995, Sydney Univ. John Lowenthal Medal. *Leisure interests:* music, motorcycles, tennis. *Address:* Australian War Memorial, GPO Box 345, Canberra ACT 2601, Australia (office). *E-mail:* brendan.nelson@awm.gov.au (office). *Website:* www .awm.gov.au (office).

NELSON, David Daniel, BA, MA; American diplomatist and business executive; *Senior Manager, Global Government Affairs and Policy, General Electric Company;* b. Minn.; m. Gloria Nelson; one s.; ed Univs of Wisconsin; has served in various Foreign Service positions including Jr Political Officer, Embassy in Montevideo 1982–84, Exec. Asst to Under-Sec. for Econ., Energy and Agricultural Affairs, Dir Office of Terrorism Finance and Econ. Sanctions, Dir Iraq Reconstruction Task Force, Dir Office of Monetary Affairs 1997–2000, Minister Counselor for Econs, Embassy in Berlin 2001–03, Sr Co-ordinator, Sea Island G-8 Summit 2003–04, Dir Office of Terrorism Finance and Sanctions 2004–07, Exec. Asst to Under-Sec. for Econs 2007–08, Prin. Deputy Asst Sec. of State, Econ., Energy and Business Affairs 2008, Acting Asst Sec. 2009, Amb. to Uruguay 2010–11, served with Nat. Security Council, postings include Embassies in Berlin, Madrid, Bonn, Quito, Montevideo, Merida; Sr Man. Global Govt Affairs and Policy, General Electric Co. 2011–. *Address:* General Electric Company, 1299 Pennsylvania Avenue NW, Suite 1100, Washington, DC 20004-2407, USA (office). *Website:* www.ge.com (office).

NELSON, E. Benjamin (Ben), MA, JD; American lawyer, organization executive and fmr politician; *CEO, National Association of Insurance Commissioners;* b. 17 May 1941, McCook, Neb.; s. of Benjamin E. Nelson and Birdella Nelson; m. Diane Nelson (née Gleason); two s. two d. from previous m.; one step-s. one step-d.; ed Univ. of Nebraska; Instructor Dept of Philosophy, Univ. of Neb. 1963–65; Dir of Compliance Neb. Dept of Insurance 1965–72, Dir 1975–76; admitted to Neb. Bar 1970; Gen. Counsel, Cen. Nat. Insurance Group of Omaha 1972–74, Exec. Vice-Pres. 1977, Pres. 1978–79, Pres. and CEO 1980–81; Exec. Vice-Pres. Nat. Assen of Insurance Commrs 1982–85, CEO 2013–; Attorney of Counsel, Kennedy, Holland DeLacy and Svoboda, Omaha 1985–90; Gov. of Nebraska 1990–98; Senator from Nebraska 2001–13 (retd), mem. Agric., Nutrition and Forestry, Armed Services Cttee, Appropriations Cttee, Rules and Admin Cttee; mem. of Counsel Lumson, Dugan and Murray 1999; Chair. Nat. Educ. Goals Panel 1992–94, Govs Ethanol Coalition (also f.) 1991, 1994, Midwestern Govs Conf. 1994; fmr Chair. Interstate Oil and Gas Compact Comm., Western Govs Assen and Co-Lead Gov. on Int. Trade; Pres. Council of State Govts 1994; Chair. Nat. Resources Cttee and Co-Lead Gov. on Federalism, Nat. Govs Assen; Co-Chair. Nat. Summit on Federalism 1995; fmr Vice-Chair. Democratic Govs Assen; Democrat; Hon. LLD (Creighton Univ.) 1992, (Peru State Coll.) 1993; Hon. DHumLitt (Coll. of St Mary) 1995; numerous awards. *Leisure interests:* spending time with my family, hunting and fishing, reading and collecting clocks. *Address:* National Association of Insurance Commissioners, 444 North Capitol Street, NW, Suite 701, Washington, DC 20001, USA (office). *Telephone:* (202) 471-3990 (office). *Fax:* (816) 460-7493 (office). *Website:* www.naic .org (office).

NELSON, John Frederick, FCA (ACA); British chartered accountant and banking executive; *Chairman, Lloyd's;* b. 26 July 1947; s. of George Frederick Nelson and Betty Violet Roddick; m. Caroline Vivien Hannam 1976; two s. one d.; qualified as a chartered accountant 1970; with Kleinwort Benson 1971–86, worked in UK and USA, Vice-Pres. 1973–75, mem. Bd of Dirs 1980–86; joined Lazard Brothers 1986, Man. Dir 1986–98, ran Corp. Finance Div. 1986–99, Vice-Chair. 1990–99, also Chair. Lazard SpA, Italy and Man. Dir Lazard Freres, New York; Chair. Credit Suisse First Boston Europe 1999–2002; Deputy Chair. Kingfisher plc 2002–11; Chair. Lloyd's 2011–; Dir (non-exec.) Woolwich plc 1998–2000, BT Group 2002–08, Hammerson plc 2004–13 (Chair. (non-exec.) 2005–13), JP Morgan Cazenove and Cazenove Group 2008–10; Chair. London Investment Banking Assen 2001–02; Sr Adviser, Charterhouse Capital Partners LLP 2010–; Dir ENO 2002–10; Trustee, Nat. Gallery 2010–. *Leisure interests:* sailing, opera. *Address:* Lloyd's, One Lime Street, London, EC3M 7HA, England (office). *Telephone:* (20) 7327-6556 (office). *Fax:* (20) 7327-5926 (office). *E-mail:* john.nelson@lloyds.com (office). *Website:* www.lloyds.com (office).

NELSON, M. Bruce, BBA; American business executive; b. 1945; m. La Vaun Nelson; one s. one d.; ed Idaho State Univ.; man. positions with Boise Cascade, BT Office Products USA; Pres. and CEO Viking Inc. –1998; Pres. and CEO Viking Office Products (following merger of Viking and Office Depot 1998) 1998–2000, Pres. Office Depot International Inc. 1998–2000, CEO Office Depot Inc. 2000–04 (resgnd); mem. Advisory Council Idaho State Univ., Exec.-in-Residence 2001; Distinguished Alumnus Award, Idaho State Univ. 2001; Entrepreneur Business Leader of the Year, Florida Atlantic Univ. 2001. *Address:* c/o Office Depot Inc., 2200 Old Germantown Road, Delray Beach, FL 33445, USA.

NELSON, Marilyn Carlson; American business executive; *Chairman, Carlson Companies;* b. 1939, Minneapolis, Minn.; m. Glen Nelson; ed Smith Coll., Mass, Sorbonne Univ., Paris, France and Inst. des Hautes Etudes Economiques Politiques, Geneva, Switzerland; began career as Securities Analyst with PaineWebber; Dir of Community Relations, Carlson Co. Inc. 1968–88, Sr Vice-Pres. 1989–91, COO 1997–2003, Chair. and CEO 1998–2008, Chair. 2008–; Co-founder and mem. Minn. Women's Econ. Roundtable 1974–; mem. Bd of Dirs First Bank System 1978–97, Nat. Tourism Org. 1996–98, Exxon Mobil Corpn 1991–, US West Inc., Singapore Tourism Bureau 1999–, Travel Industry Assen of America 2000–09, Juran Center for Leadership in Quality 1999–2005, Univ. of Minnesota Foundation 1999–; Chair. Nat. Women's Business Council 2002–05, Pres.'s Cttee on Trade and Industry 2002, Scandinavia Today celebration in USA; Co-Chair. Annual Meeting, Davos, Switzerland 2004, US Travel Advisory Bd; mem. Bd of Dirs Mayo Clinic 2001–, Chair. 2010–; mem. Minn. Orchestral Assen 1972–, Business Roundtable, Int. Business Council, World Travel and Tourism Council, World Econ. Forum 2000–; Bd mem. Cttee Encouraging Corp. Philanthropy 2004–, Overseers Curtis L. Carlson School of Man. 1999–; Del., White House Conf. on Tourism 1996, Kennedy Center for Performing Arts 2009–; Distinguished Visiting Prof., Johnson & Wales Univ.; Leader Gov.'s Task Force to bring 1992 Super Bowl to Minnesota; fmr Pres. United Way of Minneapolis; fmr Chair. New Sweden '88; fmr Bd mem. United Way of America 1984–90; Chevalier, Légion d'honneur, Royal Order of the North Star (First Class) (Sweden), Order of the White Rose (Finland), Commdr, Royal Norwegian Order of Merit; Hon. DBA (Johnson & Wales Univ.);

Hon. DHumLitt (Coll. of St Catherine), (Gustavus Adolphus Coll.); Hon. DJur (Univ. of Minnestoa); Outstanding Business Leader 1996, ranked by Travel Agent magazine as The Most Powerful Woman in Travel 1997–2004, Woodrow Wilson Award for Corp. Citizenship, Woodrow Wilson Int. Center 2000, Penn State Hotel and Restaurant Soc. Hospitality Exec. of the Year 2000, FIRST magazine Responsible Capitalism Award, London, UK 2001, Businesswoman of the World, Business Women's Network 2001, American Hotel & Lodging Assen Cutting Edge Award 2001, Int. Hotel Investment Forum Lifetime Achievement Award, Berlin, Germany 2002, Great Swedish Heritage Award, Swedish Council of America 2002, inducted into Travel Industry Assen of America's Hall of Fame 2003, inducted into Sales and Marketing Execs Int. Hall of Fame 2003, Swedish-American of the Year, King Carl XVI Gustaf and Queen Silvia of Sweden 2003, ranked by Fortune magazine amongst 50 Most Powerful Women in Business in the US 2002–04, ranked by Forbes magazine amongst 100 Most Powerful Women 2004–07, ranked by Business Week as one of Top 25 Executives in Business, Athena Award 2004, Businesswoman of the Year, US Commerce Dept's Small Business Admin 2005, 18th Annual Lucia Trade Award, Swedish-American Chamber of Commerce 2005, UN.GIFT/End Human Trafficking Now! Business Leader Award 2010. *Address:* Carlson Companies, 701 Carlson Parkway, Minnetonka, MN 55305-8212, USA (office). *Telephone:* (763) 212-1272 (office). *Fax:* (763) 212-2219 (office). *E-mail:* mnelson@carlson.com (office). *Website:* www.carlson.com (office).

NELSON, Ralph Alfred, MD, PhD, FACP; American physician and academic; *Director of Medical Research, Carle Foundation Hospital;* b. 19 June 1927, Minneapolis; s. of Alfred Walter Nelson and Lydia Nelson (née Johnson); m. Rosemarie Pokela 1954; three s. two d.; ed Univ. of Minnesota; Pathology Residency, Univ. of Minnesota 1954–55; Fellowship in Physiology, Mayo Grad. School, Mayo Clinic, Rochester 1957–60, Resident Internal Medicine 1976–78; Asst Prof. of Nutrition, Cornell Univ. 1961–62; Assoc. Prof. of Physiology, Assoc. Prof. of Nutrition, Mayo Medical School, Rochester 1967–78; Prof. of Nutrition, Dept of Medicine, Univ. of Ill. 1979–2002, Prof. Emer. 2002–, Prof. of Medicine, Food Science, Prof. of Physiology, Univ. of Ill. 1979–84, Exec. Head, Dept of Internal Medicine, Univ. of Ill. Coll. of Medicine at teaching sites of Urbana-Champaign, Chicago, Ill., Rockford, Ill. and Peoria, Ill. 1986–2002, Head, Dept of Medicine 1989–2002; Consultant for Nutritional Support Service, Danville Veterans Admin. Hosp.; Dir of Medical Research, Carle Foundation Hosp., Urbana 1979–; mem. American Physiological Soc., American Inst. of Nutrition, American Soc. of Clinical Nutrition, American Soc. of Gastroenterology; Mayo Clinic Alumni Award for Outstanding Research 1959, Fulbright Scholar 1988, Lifetime Achievement Award, Carle Foundation Hosp. 2004. *Publications:* Mayo Clinic Renal Diet Cook Book 1974, numerous learned papers, including over 140 on the metabolism of bears and clinical nutrition. *Leisure interests:* walking, bicycling, canoeing, mountain hiking. *Address:* Carle Foundation Hospital, Department of Medical Research, 611 West Park Street, Urbana, IL 61801 (office); 2 Illinois Circle, Urbana, IL 61801, USA (home). *Telephone:* (217) 383-3036 (office); (217) 344-4676 (home). *Fax:* (217) 383-3993 (office). *E-mail:* ralph.nelson@carle.com (office). *Website:* www.med.uiuc.edu/departments/internalMed (office).

NELSON, Ronald L., BA, MBA; American car rental industry executive; *Chairman and CEO, Avis Budget Group, Inc.;* ed Univ. of California, Berkeley, Univ. of California, Los Angeles; Exec. Vice-Pres., Chief Financial Officer and mem. Bd of Dirs, Paramount Communications, Inc. (fmrly Gulf & Western Industries, Inc.) 1987–94; Co-COO DreamWorks SKG 1994–2003; Pres., Chief Financial Officer and mem. Bd of Dirs, Cendant Corpn (now Avis Budget Group, Inc.) 2003–06, Chair. and CEO 2006–. *Address:* Avis Budget Group Inc., 6 Sylvan Way, Parsippany, NJ 07054, USA (office). *Telephone:* (973) 496-3500 (office). *Fax:* (888) 304-2315 (office). *Website:* www.avisbudgetgroup.com (office).

NELSON, Willie Hugh; American country and western singer, musician and songwriter; b. 30 April 1933, Abbott, Tex.; m. Annie Marie Nelson; three s. four d.; ed Baylor Univ.; fmr salesman, announcer, host and DJ, country music shows in Tex.; bass player, Ray Price's band; formed own band; appearances at Grand Ole Opry, Nashville and throughout USA 1964–; tours to NZ, Australia, USA, Canada, Europe, Japan; annual Fourth of July picnics throughout USA 1972–; performed with Frank Sinatra, Neil Young, Dolly Parton, Linda Ronstadt, ZZ Top, Waylon Jennings, Ray Charles, Santana, Joni Mitchell, Kris Kristofferson, Bob Dylan, Patsy Cline; six Grammy (NARAS) Awards, eight CMA Awards, Nashville Songwriters' Assen Hall of Fame 1973, Nat. Acad. of Popular Music Lifetime Achievement Award 1983, three ACM Awards, Tex Ritter Songwriting Award (with Kris Kristofferson) 1984. *Film appearances:* Electric Horseman 1980, Honeysuckle Rose 1980. *Compositions include:* Crazy (performed by Patsy Cline), Hello Walls (performed by Faron Young). *Recordings include:* albums: The Sound In Your Mind 1976, The Troublemaker 1976, Willie Nelson And His Friends 1976, To Lefty From Willie 1977, Willie Before His Time 1978, Wanted/The Outlaw 1978, The Willie Way 1978, Stardust 1978, One For The Road 1979, Willie And Family Live 1979, Pretty Paper 1979, Willie Sings Kristofferson 1979, San Antonio Rose 1980, Honeysuckle Rose 1980, Family Bible 1980, Tougher Than Leather 1983, City Of New Orleans 1984, Me And Paul 1985, Highwayman 1985, The Promised Land 1986, Partners 1986, Island In The Sea 1987, Seashores Of Old Mexico 1987, What A Wonderful World 1988, A Horse Called Music 1989, Highwayman II 1990, Born For Trouble 1990, Clean Shirt Waylon And Willie 1991, Across The Borderline 1993, Six Hours At Pedernales 1994, Healing Hands Of Time 1994, Just One Love 1995, Spirit 1996, How Great Thou Art 1996, Christmas With Willie Nelson 1997, Hill Country Christmas 1997, Teatro 1998, Nashville Was The Roughest 1998, Night And Day 1999, Forever Gold 2000, Me And The Drummer 2000, Milk Cow Blues 2000, Rainbow Connection 2001, Joy 2001, The Great Divide 2002, All The Songs I've Loved Before 2002, Crazy: The Demo Sessions 2003, Picture In A Frame (with Kimmie Rhodes) 2003, It Always Will Be 2004, Countryman 2005, Songbird 2006, Last Of The Breed (with Merle Haggard and Ray Price) 2007, Moment Of Forever 2008, Two Men With The Blues (with Wynton Marsalis) 2008, Willie And The Wheel (with Asleep at the Wheel) 2009, American Classic 2009, Country Music 2010. *Address:* c/o Mark Rothbaum and Associates Inc., PO Box 2689, Danbury, CT 06813-2689, USA (office). *Website:* www .willienelson.com.

NEMBANG, Subas Chandra, BA, BL; Nepalese barrister and politician; *Chairman, Constituent Assembly;* b. 11 March 1953; m.; fmr Minister of Law,

Justice and Parl. Affairs; fmr mem. Standing Cttee; Leader of Communist Party of Nepal (Unified Marxist-Leninist—UML), mem. Cen. Cttee; Sr Most Advocate, Supreme Court of Nepal; Speaker of the Interim Parl. ('Legislature-Parl.') –2008, Chair. Security Special Cttee, House of Reps Proclamation Implementation Special Cttee, Business Man. Advisory Cttee, Chair. Constituent Ass. (Speaker) 2008–12, 2014–. *Address:* Constituent Assembly Secretariat, Singh Durbar, Kathmandu, Nepal (office). *Telephone:* (1) 4227480 (office). *Fax:* (1) 4222923 (office). *E-mail:* info@can.gov.np (office); nepal.ipu@can.gov.np (office). *Website:* www.can.gov.np (office).

NĚMCOVÁ, Miroslava; Czech politician; *Leader, Civic Democratic Party;* b. 17 Nov. 1952, Nové Město na Moravě; m.; one s.; officer, Czech Statistical Office 1972–92; bookshop owner in Žďár nad Sázavou 1992–2007; mem. Civic Democratic Party (Občanská demokratická strana—ODS), fmr Deputy Chair., Leader 2013–; Alderman in Žďár nad Sázavou 1994–97; fmr mem. Žďár City Council; cand. for office of Deputy, became leader of ODS in Southern Region; mem. Chamber of Deputies for Highlands (Vysočina) 1998–, later for Capital Prague, Chair. (Speaker) 2010–13. *Address:* Civic Democratic Party (Občanská demokratická strana), Polygon House, Doudlebská 1699/5, 140 00 Prague 4 (office); Poslanecká sněmovna (Chamber of Deputies), Sněmovní 4, 118 26 Prague 1 (office); Constituency Office, Doudlebska 1699/5, 140 00 Prague 4, Czech Republic. *Telephone:* (2) 34707111 (office). *Fax:* (2) 34707103 (office). *E-mail:* miroslava.nemcova@ods.cz (office); nemcovam@psp.cz (office). *Website:* www.ods.cz (office); www.psp.cz (office); www.miroslavanemcova.cz.

NĚMEC, Jaroslav, DrTech, DrSc; Czech engineer and metallurgist (retd); *Consultant, Czech Academy of Sciences;* b. 15 March 1921, Horažďovice, Klatovy Dist; s. of Karel Němec and Bohuslava Němcová; m. Zdenka Němcová 1944 (died 1996); ed Eng Faculty, Tech. Univ. of Prague (ČVUT); design engineer 1942–45; Dir of Research and Devt, ČKD Sokolovo 1945–53; Prof., Coll. of Transport (VŠD), Dean 1953–55, Deputy Rector 1955–59; Prof., Head of Materials Dept, Faculty of Nuclear and Physical Eng, ČVUT 1969–86, Deputy Dean 1967–74, Deputy Rector 1973–79; Corresp. mem. Czechoslovak (now Czech) Acad. of Sciences (ČSAV) 1972–75, mem. Presidium 1979–87, Dir Acad. Inst. of Theoretical and Applied Mechanics, Prague 1979–87, Consultant 1991–; mem. Czechoslovak Atomic Comm.; Expert Adviser, Skoda Works, ČKD and others; mem. various foreign scientific and eng socs; Hon. mem. Int. Conf. on Fracture, Nat. Tech. Museum; Dr hc (Pardubice Univ.) 1999; All States Prize of Sciences 1965, 1974, Kaplan Medal 1968, Felber Medal 1971, Křížík Medal 1976, Order of Labour 1981, Nat. Prize 1985, Komensky Medal 1986, Medal of Sciences and Humanities, Acad. of Sciences 1986 and many others. *Publications:* over 400 original papers on mechanics, material eng and strength; 24 books including: Strength of Pressure Vessels under Different Operational Conditions, Toughness and Strength of Steel Parts, Failure of Strength of Plastics (with Acad. Serensen, Moscow), Shape and Strength of Metal Bodies (with Prof. Puchner), New Methods of Calculations of Rigidity and Strength of Machines (with Prof. Valenta), Fracture Dynamics, Dynamics and Reliability of Locomotive Parts, The Problem of Nuclear Equipment, with Special Reference to Reliability and Safety, Endurance of Mechanical Structures (with Dr Drexler), Strength and Lifetime of Gas Pipes (co-author); subject of book 'Five Minutes to Crash. . . Call Prof. Němec' 1998. *Leisure interest:* painting. *Address:* ITAM, Czech Academy of Sciences, Prosecká 809/76, 190 00, Prague 9 (office); Letohradská 60, 7 Prague 17000, Czech Republic (home). *Telephone:* (2) 86882121 (office); (2) 33376423 (home). *Fax:* (2) 86884634 (office). *E-mail:* itam@itam.cas.cz (office). *Website:* www.itam.cas.cz (office).

NÉMETH, János, PhD Habil.; Hungarian academic and lawyer; *Senior Partner, Békés-Németh-Vékás & Company, and Chairman, Editorial Board, European Law;* b. 31 July 1933, Újpest; s. of János Németh and Erzsébet Németh (née Nemes); m. Izabella Vass 1959, two d.; ed Eötvös Loránd Univ. of Budapest; jr legal official in law firm 1957, teacher at Dept of Civil Procedural Law at Eötvös Loránd Univ. 1957–2003, Vice-Chancellor 1993–97, Head of Dept and Prof. 1994–2003, Prof. Emer. 2004–; Ed. Hungarian Law (journal) 1991–; Chief Ed. Pres. Comm. for Hungarian Lawyers Asscn 1991–; Chair. Editorial Bd European Law (review) 2001–, JogOk (Lawyer's Training) 2005–06; mem. of Nat. Legal Comm. of Hungarian Acad. of Sciences, Nat. Legal Cttee of Experts for Doctorates at Hungarian Acad. of Sciences 2005–08; Sr Partner Békés-Németh-Vékás and Co. law firm 1986–; Chair. of Nat. Electoral Cttee 1990–97; judge, Constitutional Court of Hungary 1997–98, Pres. 1998–2003; Arbitrator, Arbitration Court attached to Hungarian Chamber of Commerce and Industry; Cross of Honours with Spurs of Hungarian Repub. 1995, Order of the Rising Sun (Japan) 2002, Grand Cross of Honours of Hungarian Repub. 2003, Grand Gold Honours on Sash for Service to Repub. of Austria 2004. *Publications:* more than 100 legal publs. *Leisure interest:* hunting. *Address:* ELTE Polgári Eljárásjogi Tanszék, 1053 Budapest, Egyetem tér 1–3 (office); Brassó köz 8, 1112 Budapest, Hungary (home). *Telephone:* (1) 411-6522 (office). *Fax:* (1) 411-6522 (office). *E-mail:* nemethj@ajk .elte.hu (office).

NÉMETH, Miklós; Hungarian politician; b. 24 Jan. 1948, Monok; s. of András Németh and Margit Németh (née Stajz); m. Erzsébet Szilágyi 1971; two s.; ed Karl Marx Univ. of Budapest; Lecturer in Political Economy, Karl Marx Univ. 1971–77; Deputy Section Head, Nat. Planning Office 1977–81; worked on staff, later as deputy leader, of HSWP Cen. Cttee Dept of Political Economy, Dept Leader 1987–88; mem. of Cen. Cttee, Secr. 1987–88; mem. Political Cttee 1987–88; mem. Parl. 1988–90; Prime Minister of Hungary 1988–90; apptd to four-mem. Presidium of HSWP 1989; mem. Presidium, HSP Oct.–Dec. 1989 (resgnd); Vice-Pres. (Personnel and Admin) EBRD, London, UK 1991–2000. *Leisure interests:* sailing, tennis, classical music. *Address:* c/o Keszi u. 7, 1029 Budapest II, Hungary.

NÉMETH, Zsolt; Hungarian politician; *Deputy Foreign Minister;* b. 14 Oct. 1963, Budapest; m.; three c.; ed Radnóti Miklós Grammar School, Budapest, Karl Marx Univ. of Economics (MKKE), St Anthony's Coll., Oxford, UK; trainee, Inst. for Hungarian Studies 1987–90; resident educator, Széchenyi István Coll., MKKE 1987–90; Founding mem. Alliance of Free Democrats (FIDESZ), Party Spokesman 1988–89, mem. Nat. Cttee 1989–93, Vice-Pres. 1993–2003, Deputy Faction Leader 2003–; Pres. Széchenyi Coll. Asscn 1992–95; Chief Trustee, then Hon. Chief Trustee, Transylvanian (Calvinist) Church 1995–; mem. Kts of St John 1999–; mem. Nat. Ass. 1990–; mem. Council of Europe Parl. Ass. 1994–98; State Sec., Ministry of Foreign Affairs 1998–2002, Deputy Foreign Minister 2010–; Deputy

Leader, Hungarian Delegation to Council of Europe 2002–; Chair. Foreign Affairs Cttee, Nat. Ass. 2002–06, Foreign Affairs and Hungarian Minorities Abroad Cttee 2006–. *Address:* Ministry of Foreign Affairs, 1027 Budapest, Bem rkp. 47, Hungary (office). *Telephone:* (1) 456-1240 (office); (1) 456-1420 (office). *Fax:* (1) 201-9970 (office). *E-mail:* at@kum.hu (office). *Website:* www.kulugyminiszterium.hu (office).

NEMITSAS, Takis; Cypriot fmr politician, industrialist and business administrator; *President, Takis & Louki Nemitsas Foundation;* b. 2 June 1930, Limassol; s. of Xanthos Nemitsas and Vassiliki Nemitsa; m. 1st Daisy Petrou 1958 (died 1983); three d.; m. 2nd Louki Loucaides 1986; ed English and Commercial courses in Cyprus, courses abroad in business admin and marketing; mem. House of Reps 1976–81; fmr Pres. Parl. Cttee on Commerce and Industry; Minister of Commerce, Industry and Tourism 1988–93; Exec. Chair. and Man. Dir Nemitsas Group 1993–95, Chair. Bd of Dirs 1995–, Pres. Takis & Louki Nemitsas Foundation; fmr mem. Bd Bank of Cyprus, Cyprus Employers' and Industrialists' Fed., Chamber of Commerce and Industry, Cyprus Tourism Org.; Grand Cross of Leopold II (Belgium), Grand Officer Kt of the Order of Merit (Italy). *Publications:* Environmental policy and the EU, Recycling of Scrap Metal in Cyprus. *Leisure interest:* swimming. *Address:* 159 Leontiou A' Str., Maryvonne Building, Office 104, PO Box 50124, 3601 Limassol (office); Thera Complex, 2 Megalou Alexandrou Str., Pyrgos, 4534 Limassol, Cyprus (home). *Telephone:* (25) 569222 (office); (25) 636844 (home). *Fax:* (25) 569275 (office); (25) 636050 (home). *E-mail:* foundation@nemitsas.org (office). *Website:* www.nemitsasfoundation.org (office).

NEMTSOV, Boris Yefimovich, CTechSc; Russian politician; *Co-Chairman, Republican Party of Russia—Party of People's Freedom (RPR—PARNAS);* b. 9 Oct. 1959, Sochi; s. of Efim Davidovich Nemtsov and Dina Yakovlevna Nemtsova (née Eidman); m.; one s. three d.; ed Gorkii (now Nizhnyi Novgorod) State Univ.; Researcher, then Sr Researcher, Research Inst. of Radiophysics 1981–91; elected to Supreme Soviet of the Russian Fed. 1990; Rep. of Pres. of Russia in Nizhnyi Novgorod Oblast 1991; Gov. of Nizhny Novgorod Oblast 1991–97; People's Deputy of Russia 1990–93; mem. Fed. Council 1993–97; First Deputy Chair. Russian Govt 1997–98 (resgnd); Minister of Fuel and Power Eng March–Nov. 1997; f. Young Russia Movt; joined pre-election coalition Pravoye delo (The Right Thing) 1999; mem. State Duma (Parl.) 1999–2003, Deputy Chair. Feb.–June 2000; mem. Union of Rightist Forces 1998–2008, Leader 1999–2005; Co-founder and mem. Cttee Free Choice 2008 for democratic elections 2004; Chair. Neftyanoi 2004–05 (resgnd); apptd adviser to Pres. of Ukraine 2005; mem. Solidarnost 2008–, PARNAS 2010–12, Republican Party of Russia—Party of People's Freedom (RPR—PARNAS) 2012– (Co-Chair. 2012–); arrested by police during an unauthorized protest against Pres. Putin 2007, released later that day; unsuccessful cand. for Mayor of Sochi 2009; among the 34 original signatories of the online anti-Putin manifesto 'Putin must go' published in March 2010; again arrested with other opposition leaders during a rally against govt restrictions on public protests Dec. 2010, sentenced to 15 days in jail Jan. 2011, declared a prisoner of conscience by Amnesty International, once again arrested, with other demonstrators, during protests in Moscow Dec. 2011; regular participant in various Russian TV programmes; Order of Prince Yaroslav the Wise (Ukraine) 2007. *Publications:* The Provincial 1997, The Provincial in Moscow 1999; with Vladimir Milov, has published several reports criticising Putin's regime and proposing alternative ways of development for the country 2008–11. *Leisure interests:* tennis, windsurfing, fishing. *Address:* Republican Party of Russia—Party of People's Freedom (Respublikanskaya partiya Rossii—Partiya narodnoy svobody), 119017, Moscow, per. Klimentovskii 9/1, Russia (office). *Telephone:* (495) 959-48-04 (office). *E-mail:* secretsolfed@gmail.com (office). *Website:* svobodanaroda.org (office); rusolidarnost.ru/ leaders/boris-nemtsov; www.nemtsov.ru; b-nemtsov.livejournal.com.

NEMYRYA, Hryhoriy, BA, PhD; Ukrainian academic and politician; b. 5 April 1960, Donetsk; m.; one s.; ed Donetsk State Univ., Kyiv Shevchenko Univ.; began career as Lecturer, Dept of History, Donetsk State Univ., becoming Head Centre for Political Research 1992–96; Nat. Forum Foundation Fellow, Centre for Strategic and Int. Studies, Washington, DC, USA 1994; Dean, Mohyla Acad., Kiev 1996–98; fmr Deputy Head European Integration Faculty, Nat. Acad. of Public Admin; fmr Head Centre for European and Int. Studies, Shevchenko Univ.; Chair. George Soros Int. Renaissance Foundation, Kyiv 2002; fmr Ed. Noval Bezpeka (New Security); mem. Tymoshenko Bloc, Adviser to Yuliya Tymoshenko 2005–; mem. Verkhovna Rada (Supreme Council, Parl.) 2006–; Deputy Prime Minister for European and Int. Integration 2007–10; mem. Socialist Group, Council of Europe 2006–. *Address:* Verkhovna Rada, Grushevsky 5, 01008 Kyiv, Ukraine (office). *Telephone:* (44) 253-32-17 (office). *Fax:* (44) 253-32-17 (office). *E-mail:* Nemyria.Hrihorii@rada.gov.ua (office). *Website:* www.kmu.gov.ua/control (office).

NEOH, Anthony Francis, LLB, QC, JP; Chinese lawyer; b. 9 Nov. 1946, Hong Kong; ed Univ. of London, UK; teacher 1964–66; Hong Kong Civil Service 1966–79; pvt. practice, Hong Kong Bar 1979–95, Calif. Bar 1984–95; Hong Kong public service in educ., health etc. 1985–; Chair. Securities and Futures Comm., Hong Kong 1995–98; mem. Hong Kong SAR Basic Law Cttee 1997–2008; People's Repub. of China public service in teaching, Govt advisory work etc., including Chief Adviser to China Securities Regulatory Comm. 1998–2004; Visiting Scholar, Harvard Univ., USA 1990–91; Chair. IOSCO Tech. Cttee 1996–98; Nomura Visiting Prof. of Int. Financial Systems, Harvard Law School, USA 2004; Vice-Chair. Exec. Cttee, School of Law, Chinese Univ. of Hong Kong 2005–. *Leisure interests:* reading, music. *Address:* 12th Floor, The Landmark, 15 Queen's Road Central, Hong Kong Special Administrative Region, People's Republic of China. *Telephone:* 28409201. *Fax:* 28101872.

NEPAL, Madhav Kumar; Nepalese politician; b. 6 March 1953, Rautahat Dist; s. of Mangal Kumar Upadhyaya and Durgadevi Upadhyaya; ed Thakur Ram Campus, Birgunj, Tribhuvan Univ.; dropped surname Upadhyaya since it indicates caste; joined Communist movt 1969; became mem. Dist Cttee Nepal Revolutionary Org. (Marxist-Leninist) 1971; elected mem. Bureau All Nepal Communist Revolutionary Co-ordination Cttee (Marxist-Leninist) 1975, latter f. Communist Party of Nepal (Marxist-Leninist) 1978, elected mem. Politburo 1978–, mem. Communist Party of Nepal (Unified Marxist Leninist—UML), Gen. Sec. 1993–2008, Head of Foreign Dept 2008–09, mem. Standing Cttee; Deputy Prime Minister during CPN (UML) minority govt as well as Leader of Opposition in Nat. Ass. 1995; arrested during crackdown on anti-govt protest 2001; Prime Minister of

Nepal 2009–10 (resgnd); known in Nepal as Ma-Ku-Ne. *Address:* c/o Prime Minister's Office, Singha Durbar, PO Box 43312, Kathmandu, Nepal. *E-mail:* bishnurijal@gmail.com; info@opmcm.gov.np. *Website:* www.madhavnepal.com.

NERI, Romulo L., MBA; Philippine government official and business executive; b. 1 Feb. 1950; ed Ateneo de Manila, Coll. of Business Admin, Univ. of the Philippines, Grad. School of Man., Univ. of California, Los Angeles, USA; fmr Eugenio Lopez Assoc. Prof. for Corp. Financial Man., Asian Inst. of Man.; fmr Corp. Planning and Finance Officer, Canlubang Sugar Estate, Canlubang Pulp and Manufacturing Corpn, C-J Yulo and Sons Inc., Philippine Nat. Oil Co., Luzon Stevedoring Corpn, Mobil Oil Philippines Inc.; Dir-Gen. Nat. Econ. and Devt Authority –2005, 2007–08; Dir-Gen. House of Reps Congressional and Budget Office –2005; Sec. of the Budget and Man. 2005–07; Pres. Social Security System 2008–; Chair. Comm. on Higher Educ. 2007–08. *Address:* c/o National Economic and Development Authority, NEDA-sa-Pasig Building, 12 St Josemaria Escriva Street, Pasig City, 1605 Metro Manila, Philippines.

NERLOVE, Marc L., MA, PhD; American academic; *Professor of Agricultural and Resource Economics, University of Maryland;* b. 12 Oct. 1933, Chicago, Ill.; s. of Samuel Henry Nerlove and Evelyn Nerlove (née Andelman); two d.; ed Univ. of Chicago and Johns Hopkins Univ.; Analytical Statistician, US Dept of Agric., Washington, DC 1956–57; Assoc. Prof., Univ. of Minnesota, Minneapolis 1959–60; Prof., Stanford Univ. 1960–65, Yale Univ. 1965–69; Prof. of Econs, Univ. of Chicago 1969–74; F.W. Taussig Research Prof., Harvard Univ. 1967–68; Visiting Prof., Northwestern Univ., 1973–74, Cook Prof. 1974–82; Prof. of Econs, Univ. of Pennsylvania 1982–86, Univ. Prof. 1986–93; Prof. of Agric. and Resource Econs, Univ. of Maryland, College Park 1993–; mem. NAS 1979; Fellow and Past Pres. Econometric Soc.; Fellow, American Statistical Asscn 1964; Distinguished Fellow, American Agricultural Econ. Asscn 1993; John Bates Clark Medal 1969, P.C. Mahalinobis Medal 1975. *Publications:* Dynamics of Supply 1958, Distributed Lags and Demand Analysis 1958, Estimation and Identification of Cobb-Douglas Production Functions 1965, Analysis of Economic Time Series: A Synthesis 1979, Household and Economy: Welfare Economics of Endogenous Fertility 1987; numerous articles. *Address:* Department of Agricultural and Research Economics, 2105 Symons Hall, University of Maryland, College Park, MD 20742, USA (office). *Telephone:* (301) 405-1388 (office). *E-mail:* mnerlove@arec.umd.edu (office). *Website:* www.arec.umd.edu (office).

NERO, Franco; Italian actor; b. (Francesco Sparanero), 23 Nov. 1941, Parma; m. Vanessa Redgrave (q.v.) 2006; two s. *Films include:* Wild, Wild Planet 1965, The Bible: In the Beginning 1966, Django 1966, Camelot 1967, The Mercenary 1968, The Day of the Owl 1968, Mafia 1968, Un detective 1969, Battle of the Neretva 1969, A Quiet Place in the Country 1969, Vendetta, Companeros 1970, Tristana 1970, The Virgin and the Gypsy 1970, Confessions of a Police Commissioner to the District Attorney 1971, Vacation 1971, Pope Joan 1972, Deaf Smith & Johnny Ears 1973, Victory March 1976, Last Days of Mussolini 1975, Force Ten from Navarone 1978, The Man With Bogart's Face 1980, Il giorno del Cobra 1980, Mimi 1983, Enter the Ninja 1981, The Salamander 1981, Querelle 1982, Kamikaze '89 1982, Red Bells Part I: Mexico on Fire 1982, Red Bells Part II: I Saw the Birth of a New World 1983, The Repenter 1985, The Girl 1987, Sweet Country 1987, Die Hard 2 1990, Breath of Life 1990, Jonathan degli orsi 1994, The Innocent Sleep 1996, The Versace Murder 1998, Talk of Angels 1998, White Smoke 2002, Ultimo stadio 2002, Die 8. Todsünde: Das Toskana-Karussell 2002, L'ultimo pistolero (short) 2002, Cattive inclinazioni 2003, Post coitum 2004, Guardiani delle nuvole 2004, Forever Blues 2005, Hans 2006, Amore e libertà – Masaniello 2006, Two Families 2007, Mineurs 2007, Márió a varázsló 2008, Bastardi 2008, La rabbia 2008, Bathory: Countess of Blood 2008, Una storia di lupi (short) 2008, Ti stramo: Ho voglia di un'ultima notte da manuale prima di tre baci sopra il cielo 2008, Elena (short) 2008, Killing Is My Business, Honey 2009, Lullaby (short) 2009, Palestrina – princeps musicae (documentary) 2009, Angelus Hiroshimae 2010, Letters to Juliet 2010, Prigioniero di un segreto 2010, Rasputin (narrator) 2010, Cars 2 (voice) 2011, New Order 2012, Canepazzo 2012, A Memória que me Contam 2012, The Woods 2012, Django Unchained 2012, The Last Alchemist (short) 2012, Cadences obstinées 2013, Dante's Hell Animated (short) (Italian version, voice) 2013, Father 2013, Dark Sea 2014, Dante's Hell Documente (Italian version, voice) 2014. *Television includes:* The Legend of Valentino (film) 1975, 21 Hours at Munich (film) 1976, The Pirate (film) 1978, Wagner (series) 1983, The Last Days of Pompeii 1984, Garibaldi: The General (mini-series) 1987, Young Catherine (film) 1991, Das Babylon Komplott (film) 1993, The Dragon Ring (film) 1994, Love, Lies, Passions (mini-series) 2003, The Uncrowned Heart (film) 2003, Summer Solstice (film) 2005, The Holy Family (film) 2006, Der Fürst und das Mädchen (series) 2007, Il sangue e la rosa (series) 2008, A Night at the Grand Hotel (film) 2008, Mein Herz in Chile (film) 2008, Four Seasons (mini-series) 2008, Augustine: The Decline of the Roman Empire (film) 2010, Law & Order: Special Victims Unit (series) 2011. *Address:* c/o Anne Alvares Correa, 34 rue Jouffroy d'Abbans, 75017 Paris, France (office). *Telephone:* 1-42-67-80-85 (office). *Fax:* 1-44-09-00-27 (office). *E-mail:* arac2@ wanadoo.fr (office). *Website:* www.agence-annealvarescorrea.com/artiste.cfm/ 297008-franco_nero.html (office).

NERURKAR, Hemant M., BTech; Indian steel industry executive; *Managing Director, Tata Steel Ltd;* ed Coll. of Eng, Pune Univ., several man. courses in India and overseas, including CEDEP in France; joined Tata Steel 1982, held various positions, including Chief Metallurgist, Sr Deputy Man. (LD-2 Projects), Deputy Gen. Man. (Steel and Primary Mills), Gen. Man. (Marketing), Sr Gen. Man. (Supply Chain) and COO (Steel), Vice-Pres. (Flat Products) 2002–07, COO (Steel) 2007–09, Exec. Dir, India and SE Asia, Tata Steel Ltd April 2009–, Man. Dir Oct. 2009–; Chair. TM International Logistics Ltd, Kolkata, Tata Metaliks Ltd, Kolkata, Centennial Steel Co. Ltd, Mumbai, JAMIPOL Ltd, Jamshedpur; Vice-Chair. Tata Steel (Thailand) Public Co. Ltd, Bangkok; fmr Chair. Hooghly Met Coke & Power Co. Ltd, Gopalpur Special Econ. Zone Ltd; mem. Bd of Dirs NatSteel Asia Pte Ltd, NatSteel Holdings Pte Ltd, Singapore, Tata BlueScope Steel Ltd, Pune; fmr Dir Tata Ryerson Ltd, Dhamra Port Co. Ltd, Jajpur Cluster Development Ltd; Pres. Jamshedpur Kennel Club; Vice-Pres. (Ferrous Div.), Indian Inst. of Metals; Vice-Chair. Man. Cttee Indian Cancer Soc., Jamshedpur Br.; mem. CII Nat. Cttee on Steel, Internal Security Task Force of CII Eastern Region (also Chair.), Inst. for Steel Devt and Growth (INSDAG), Man. Cttee Tata Steel Rural Devt Soc.; Special Invitee, All India Man. Asscn; mem. Bd of Govs Xavier Inst. of

Man., Bhubaneshwar; mem. All India Man. Asscn Governing Council, Gen. Body of the Sports Authority of India 2010–, amongst others; NMD Award 1987, Visvesvaraya Award 1988, SAIL Gold Medal 1989, Steel 80s Award 1990, SMS Demag Excellence Award 2002, Tata Gold Medal 2004. *Address:* Tata Steel Ltd, Bombay House, 24 Homi Mody Street, Mumbai 400 001 (office); Tata Steel Ltd, Commercial Headquarters, Tata Centre, 43 Jawaharlal Nehru Road, Kolkata 700 071, India (office). *Telephone:* (22) 66658282 (Mumbai) (office); (33) 22881962 (Kolkata) (office); (33) 22248511 (Kolkata) (office); (33) 22881558 (Kolkata) (office). *E-mail:* info@tatasteel.com (office). *Website:* www.tatasteel.com (office).

NESBØ, Jo, MBA; Norwegian singer, songwriter and crime novelist; b. 29 March 1960, Oslo; fmr freelance journalist; fmr mem. De Tusen Hjem, Di Derre; numerous concerts; currently crime writer, creator of Harry Hold series of detective novels. *Recordings:* albums: with Di Derre: Den Derre 1992, Jenter and Sånn 1994. *Publications:* Harry Hole novels: Flaggermusmannen (The Bat) (Riverton Prize for Best Norwegian Crime Novel of the Year 1997, Glass Key Award for Best Nordic Crime Novel of the Year 1998) 1997, Kakerlakkene (The Cockroaches) 1998, Rødstrupe (The Redbreast) (Norwegian Booksellers' Prize for Best Novel of the Year 2000, Norwegian Book Clubs' Award for Best Norwegian Crime Novel Ever Written 2004) 2000, Sorgenfri (Nemesis) (Mads Wiel Nygaards Bursary 2002) 2002, Marekors (The Devil's Star) (Finnish Acad. of Crime Writers Special Commendation for Excellence in Foreign Crime Writing 2007) 2003, Frelseren (The Redeemer) 2005, Snømannen (The Snowman) (Norwegian Booksellers' Prize for Best Novel of the Year 2007, Norwegian Book Club Prize for Best Novel of the Year 2008) 2007, Panserhjeerte (The Leopard) 2009, Gjenferd (Phantom) 2011; Doktor Proktor novels: Doktor Proktors prompepulver (trans. as Doctor Proctor's Fart Powder) 2007, Doktor Proktors Tidsbadekar (trans. as Doktor Proktor's Time Bathtub) 2008, Doctor Proctor and the Armageddon: Maybe 2010; other stand-alone novels: Stemmer fra Balkan (trans. as Figures in the Balkans) 1999, Det hvite hotellet (trans. as The White Hotel) 2007, Hodejegerne (trans. as Headhunters) 2008; short stories: Karusellmusikk 2001. *Address:* c/o Solomonsson Agency, Svartensgatan 4, 116 20 Stockholm, Sweden (office). *Telephone:* (8) 22-32-11 (office). *E-mail:* info@salomonssonagency.com (office). *Website:* www.salomonssonagency.com (office); www.jonesbo.com.

NESTERENKO, Evgeni, DipEng; Russian/Austrian singer (bass) and teacher; b. 8 Jan. 1938, Moscow, USSR; s. of Evgeni Nesterenko and Velta Baumann; m. Ekaterina Alexeyeva 1963; one s.; ed Leningrad Eng Inst. and Leningrad Conservatory with V. Lukanin; debut as General Ermolov in War and Peace, Maly Theatre, Leningrad 1963; soloist with Leningrad Maly Opera and Ballet Theatre 1963–67; soloist with Kirov Opera 1967–71; teacher of solo singing, Leningrad Conservatory 1967–72, Moscow Conservatory 1975–93, Konservatorium Wien 1993–2003; soloist with the Bolshoi 1971–2003; mem. staff, Moscow Musical Pedagogical Inst. 1972–74; Chair. of Singing at Moscow Conservatoire 1975–93, Prof. 1981–93; USSR People's Deputy 1989–91; seasons at Budapest 1970, Vienna Staatsoper 1975, Metropolitan Opera 1975, Teatro Colón, Buenos Aires 1975, La Scala, Milan 1977, Covent Garden 1978, Verona Festival 1978, Munich 1978, Estonia 1980, Japan 1983, Barcelona 1984, Bregenz Festival 1986, Savonlinna Festival 1987, Hamburg 1986, Orange Festival 1990, Antwerp 1993, Hong Kong 2002, São Paulo 2006; mem. Int. Acad. of Creative Endeavours, Moscow 1991; People's Artist of the USSR 1976, Viotti d'Oro Prize, City of Vercelli (Italy) 1981, Lenin Prize 1982, Melodia Golden Disc, USSR 1984, Giovanni Zenatello Prize, Verona (Italy) 1986, Hero of Labour 1988, Chaliapin Prize 1992, Wilhelm Furtwängler Prize (Germany) 1992, Austrian Kammersänger 1992, Casta Diva Prize 2001, Golden Pegasus Theatre Prize (Poland) 2004, Centaur with Gold Flower 2009. *Roles include:* Boris Godunov, Ivan Khovansky and Dosifey (Khovanshchina), Igor and Khan Konchak (Prince Igor), Mephistopheles (Faust), Grigori (Quiet Flows the Don), General Ermolov and Kutuzov (War and Peace), Filippo II (Don Carlo), Attila, Zaccaria (Nabucco), Don Pasquale, Sarastro (Magic Flute), Bluebeard, Gremin (Eugene Onegin), Ivan Susanin, Old Convict (Lady Macbeth), Don Basilio, Enrico VIII, Moses, Water-Sprite (Rusalka), Don Bartolo. *Recordings:* Glinka's Ruslan and Lyudmila and Ivan Susanin, Tchaikovsky's Mazeppa, Iolanta and Eugene Onegin, Rachmaninov's Francesca da Rimini and Aleko, Songs by Shostakovich and Mussorgsky, Suite on Poems of Michelangelo and 14th Symphony by Shostakovich, Verdi Requiem, Nabucco, Attila and Trovatore, Gounod's Faust, Dvořák's Rusalka, Donizetti's Don Pasquale and L'Elisir d'amore, Bela Bartók's Bluebeard's Castle; videos: Verdi's Attila, Rachmaninov's Aleko, Mussorgsky's Boris Godunov and Khovanshchina, Glinka's A Life for the Tsar. *Publications:* Evgeni Nesterenko, Thoughts on My Profession 1985, Evgeni Nesterenko, Memoirs of a Russian Bass 2011. *Leisure interests:* tea collecting and testing.

NESTERIKHIN, Yuri Yefremovich; Russian nuclear physicist; *Head, Synchrotron and Applied Electronics Divisions, Kurchatov Institute;* b. 10 Oct. 1930, Ivanovo; s. of Yefrem Nesterikhin and Maria Morozova; m. 1954; one s. one d.; ed Moscow Lomonosov State Univ.; mem. CPSU 1960–91; Jr Researcher, Inst. of Atomic Energy 1954–61; Sector Head and Head of Lab., Inst. of Nuclear Physics (Siberian Br.) 1961–65; Prof. 1970; Corresp. mem., USSR (now Russian) Acad. of Sciences 1970, Full mem. 1981–; Dir, Inst. of Automation and Electrometrics, Siberian Br. of Acad. of Sciences 1967–87; Head of Synchrotron and Applied Electronics Divs, Kurchatov Inst., Moscow 1987–; Dir Multimedia Centre, Acad. of Nat. Economy 1992–; mem. Bd Ranet (jt stock co.) 1992–95; Chair. Moscow Physics and Tech. Inst. 2001–; Deputy Chair. Scientific Council for Cybernetics; most important works on plasma physics and thermonuclear synthesis; USSR Council of Ministers Prize. *Publications:* Methods of Speed Measurements in Geodynamics and Plasma Physics 1967; several other works on nuclear physics and automation of research. *Leisure interest:* sauna. *Address:* Kurchatov Institute, Kurchatova ploshchad 46, R-123182 Moscow (office); Leninski Prosp. 13, Apt. 93, 117071 Moscow, Russia. *Telephone:* (495) 196-97-79 (office); (495) 237-43-47 (home). *Fax:* (495) 420-22-66.

NESTEROVA, Natalia Igorevna; Russian painter; b. 23 April 1944, Moscow; one s.; ed Moscow Surikov State Fine Arts Inst.; mem. USSR (now Russian) Union of Painters; Stage Designer, Bolshoi Theatre 1958; participated in over 170 exhbns including solo exhbns Russia, Europe, N America 1988– (Moscow 1997); Prof., Russian Acad. of Theatre Art 1992–; works in collections of Tretyakov Gallery, Moscow, Ludwig Collection, Germany, Guggenheim Museum, New York; State

Prize of Russia 1998. *Address:* c/o Moscow Artists Union, 101000 Moscow, Starosadsky per. 5, Russia.

NETANYAHU, Benjamin, MSc; Israeli politician and diplomatist; *Prime Minister;* b. 21 Oct. 1949, Tel-Aviv; m. 1st Miriam Weizmann; m. 2nd Fleur Cates (divorced 1984); m. 3rd Sara Ben-Artzi; three c.; ed Massachusetts Inst. of Tech., USA; Man. Consultant, Boston Consulting Group 1976–78; Exec. Dir Jonathan Inst., Jerusalem 1978–80; Sr Man. Rim Industries, Jerusalem 1980–82; Deputy Chief of Mission, Israeli Embassy in Washington, DC 1982–84; Perm. Rep. to UN, New York 1984–88; mem. Knesset 1988–; Deputy Minister of Foreign Affairs 1988–91; Deputy Minister, Prime Minister's Office 1991–92; Prime Minister of Israel and Minister of Housing and Construction 1996–99; Minister of Foreign Affairs 2002–03, 2012–13, of Finance 2003–05; Prime Minister of Israel 2009–, also Minister of Econ. Strategy, of Pensioner Affairs and of Health 2009–13, Minister of Public Diplomacy and Diaspora Affairs 2013–; Leader of Likud 1993–99, 2005–; ranked by Forbes magazine amongst The World's Most Powerful People (46th) 2009, (24th) 2010, (25th) 2011, (23rd) 2012, (26th) 2013. *Publications include:* Yoni's Letters (ed.) 1978, Terror: Challenge and Reaction (ed.) 1980, Terrorism: How the West Can Win (ed.) 1986, International Terrorism: Challenge and Response (ed.) 1991, A Place Among the Nations: Israel and the World 1993, Fighting Terrorism: How Democracies Can Defeat Domestic and International Terrorism 1995, A Durable Peace 2000. *Address:* Office of the Prime Minister, PO Box 187, 3 Kaplan Street, Kiryat Ben-Gurion, Jerusalem 91950 (office); Likud (Consolidation), 38 Rehov King George, Tel-Aviv 61231, Israel (office). *Telephone:* 2-6705555 (office); 3-5630666 (Likud) (office). *Fax:* 2-5664838 (office); 3-5282901 (Likud) (office). *E-mail:* pm_eng@pmo.gov.il (office); likud@likud.org.il (office). *Website:* www.pmo.gov.il (office); www.likud.org.il (office).

NETREBKO, Anna; Austrian (b. Russian) singer (soprano); b. 18 Sept. 1971, Krasnodar, Russia; m. Erwin Schrott; one s.; ed Rimsky-Korsakov Conservatory; debut at Mariinsky Opera Theatre, St Petersburg 1994, as Susanna; roles include Glinka's Ludmila with Kirov Opera, Gilda in Rigoletto and Kundry in Parsifal at St Petersburg; first appearance at Salzburg Festival 1998; tours with Kirov Opera as Pamina and Bizet's Micaela; sang Gilda at Washington 1999 and New York, Mimi at San Francisco 1999–2000 and New York; concerts with Rotterdam Philharmonic Orchestra include London Proms and Teresa in Benvenuto Cellini, Royal Festival Hall 1999; sang Natasha in War and Peace at St Petersburg and London 2000; other roles include Zerlina and Louisa in Prokofiev's Betrothal in a Monastery at San Francisco, Rosina, Pamina and Xenia in Boris Godunov, Mozart's Servilia at Covent Garden 2002, Donna Anna in Don Giovanni at Salzburg 2003 and Covent Garden 2007, Violetta in La Traviata at Salzburg 2005, Norina in Don Pasquale in New York 2005, and Elvira in I Puritani 2006; season 2011–12 included Don Pasquale at the Met, first production of La Bohème at the Salzburg Festival; season 2012–13 included Adina in Donizetti's L'Elisir d'amore at the Metropolitan Opera, La Bohème at La Scala, a European concert tour in title role of Tchaikovsky's Iolanta, Don Giovanni in Baden-Baden and role debut in title role of Verdi's Giovanna d'Arco in Salzburg, role debut as Tatiana in Tchaikovsky's Eugene Onegin at Vienna State Opera; season 2013–14 includes Tatiana at the Metropolitan Opera New York, role debuts as Leonora in Il trovatore at the Berlin Staatsoper, in title role of Puccini's Manon Lescaut, Lady Macbeth in Bavarian State Opera's Macbeth, Marguerite in Gounod's Faust at Covent Garden, Vienna's Staatsoper and Festspielhaus, Baden-Baden; People's Artist of Russia 2008; First Prize, All-Russian Glinka Vocal Competition, Moscow 1993, Third Prize, Rimsky-Korsakov Int. Competition for Young Opera Singers, St Petersburg 1996, Costa Diva Prize 1998, Golden Sophit Prize, St Petersburg 1999, Classical BRIT Award for Singer of the Year 2007, named as one of 100 People Who Shape Our World, TIME magazine 2007, Musician of the Year, Musical America Awards 2008. *Recordings include:* Glinka's Ruslan and Ludmila, Mozart Album 2006, Souvenirs 2008, In the Still of Night 2010, Rossini's Stabat Mater (Gramophone Editor's Choice Award 2011), Anna Netrebko – Live at the Metropolitan Opera 2011, Anna Netrebko – Verdi. *Address:* c/o Judith Neuhoff, Centre Stage Artist Management, Stralauer Allee 1, 10245 Berlin, Germany (office). *E-mail:* judith.neuhoff@centrestagemanagement.com (office). *Website:* www.annanetrebko.com.

NEUBERGER, Baroness (Life Peer), cr. 2004, of Primrose Hill in the London Borough of Camden; **Rabbi Julia Babette Sarah Neuberger,** DBE, MA; British rabbi, author, broadcaster and politician; *Senior Rabbi, West London Synagogue;* b. 27 Feb. 1950, London, England; d. of the late Walter Schwab and Alice Schwab; m. Anthony John Neuberger 1973; one s. one d.; ed South Hampstead High School, Newnham Coll. Cambridge and Leo Baeck Coll. London; Rabbi, South London Liberal Synagogue 1977–89, currently Sr Rabbi, West London Synagogue; Lecturer and Assoc. Fellow, Leo Baeck Coll. 1979–97; Assoc. Newnham Coll. Cambridge 1983–96; Sec. and Chief Exec. The King's Fund 1997–2004; Chancellor Univ. of Ulster 1994–2000; Chair. Rabbinic Conf. Union of Liberal and Progressive Synagogues 1983–85; Camden and Islington Community Health Services Nat. Health Service (NHS) Trust 1993–97; mem. Policy Planning Group, Inst. of Jewish Affairs 1986–90, NHS Complaints Review 1993–94, Gen. Medical Council 1993–2001, Council, Univ. Coll. London 1993–97, MRC 1995–2000, Council, Save the Children Fund 1995–96; Visiting Fellow, King's Fund Inst. 1989–91; Chair. Patients Asscn 1988–91, Royal Coll. of Nursing Comm. on Health Service; mem. Nat. Cttee Social Democratic Party 1982–88, Funding Review of BBC 1999, Cttee on Standards in Public Life 2001–04; Civil Service Commr 2001–02; mem. Bd of Visitors, Memorial Church, Harvard Univ. 1994–2000, Bloomberg Prof. of Philanthropy and Public Policy, Divinity School 2006; Prime Minister's Champion for Volunteering 2007–09; Chair. Liberal Judaism –2011, One Housing Group, Advisory Panel Judicial Diversity –2010; other public and charitable appointments; Harkness Fellow, Commonwealth Fund of New York; Visiting Fellow, Harvard Medical School 1991–92; Chair. Responsible Gambling Strategy Bd –2011, Responsible Gambling Fund –2011, Trustee, Runnymede Trust 1990–97; fmr Trustee, Imperial War Museum, British Council, Booker Prize Foundation, Jewish Care; Chair. W & L Schwab Charitable Trust; mem. House of Lords (Liberal Democrat) 2004–11, (Crossbench) 2011–; Hon. FRCP 2004; Hon. Fellow, Royal Coll. of Gen. Practitioners, Royal Coll. of Psychiatrists, City and Guilds Inst.; Hon. Fellow, Mansfield Coll. Oxford; Dr hc (Open Univ., City Univ. London, Humberside, Ulster, Stirling, Oxford Brookes, Teesside, Queen's Belfast, Aberdeen). *Radio:* Pause for Thought (BBC Radio 2). *Television:* Presenter, Choices (BBC) 1986, 1987. *Publications:* The Story of Judaism 1986,

Days of Decision (ed., four vols) 1987, Caring for Dying Patients of Different Faiths 1987, Whatever's Happening to Women? 1991, A Necessary End (co-ed. with John White) 1991, Ethics and Healthcare: The Role of Research Ethics Committees in the UK 1992, The Things That Matter 1993, On Being Jewish 1995, Dying Well: A Health Professional's Guide to Enabling a Better Death 1999, Hidden Assets: Values and Decision-Making in the NHS Today (co-ed. with Bill New) 2002, The Moral State We're In 2005, Not Dead Yet: A Manifesto for Old Age 2008, Is That All There Is? Thoughts on Leaving a Legacy 2011; contribs to various books on cultural, religious and ethical factors in nursing; contribs journals and newspapers, including Nursing Times, Jewish Chronicle, Times, Irish Times, The Independent, Guardian, Telegraph, Sunday Express, Mail on Sunday, Evening Standard. *Leisure interests:* riding, sailing, Irish life, opera, setting up the old girls' network, children, theatre, family. *Address:* House of Lords, Westminster, London, SW1 0PW, England (office). *Telephone:* (20) 7219-2716 (office); (20) 7535-0255 (office). *E-mail:* paolachurchill@googlemail.com (office); paola.churchill@wls.org .uk (office).

NEUGER, Tim; German art dealer and gallery curator; *Co-Director, Neugerriemschneider Kunstgalerie;* Co-founder and Co-dir, with Burkhard Riemschneider, Neugerriemschneider Kunstgalerie, Berlin, represents artists including Franz Ackermann, Keith Edmier, Olafur Eliasson, Isa Genzken, Sharon Lockhart, the late Michel Majerus, Antje Majewski, Jorge Pardo, Elizabeth Peyton, Tobias Rehberger, Simon Starling, Thaddeus Strode, Wolfgang Tillmans, Rirkrit Tiravanija, Pae White and Jorge Pardo; mem. Art Basel Cttee. *Address:* Neugerriemschneider Kunstgalerie, Linienstraße 155, 10115 Berlin, Germany (office). *Telephone:* (30) 288772-77 (office). *E-mail:* mail@neugerriemschneider .com (office). *Website:* www.neugerriemschneider.com (office).

NEUHAUSER, Duncan von Briesen, PhD, MBA, MHA; American professor of epidemiology and biostatistics; *The Charles Elton Blanchard MD Professor of Health Management Emeritus, Medical School, Case Western Reserve University;* b. 20 June 1939, Philadelphia, Pa; s. of Edward B. D. Neuhauser and Gernda von Briesen Neuhauser; m. Elinor Toaz Neuhauser 1965; one s. one d.; ed Harvard Univ. and Univs of Michigan and Chicago; Research Assoc. (Instructor), Center for Health Admin. Studies, Univ. of Chicago 1965–70; Asst Prof., then Assoc. Prof., Harvard School of Public Health 1970–79; Assoc. Chair., Program for Health Systems Man., Harvard Business School 1972–79; Consultant in Medicine, Massachusetts Gen. Hosp. 1975–80; Prof. of Epidemiology and Biostatistics, Case Western Reserve Univ. 1979–, Prof. of Organizational Behavior 1979–, Prof. of Medicine 1981–, Keck Foundation Sr Research Scholar 1982–, Prof. of Family Medicine 1990–, Charles Elton Blanchard MD Prof. of Health Man. 1995–2011, Emer. 2011–; Adjunct Prof. of Nursing, Vanderbilt Univ. 1998–; mem. bioscientific medical staff, Cleveland Metropolitan Gen. Hosp. 1981–2012; Adjunct mem., Medical Staff, Cleveland Clinic Foundation 1984–99; Co-Dir Health Systems Man. Centre, Case Western Reserve Univ. 1985–2012; Ed. Medical Care 1983–97, Health Matrix 1982–90, Non-Profit Management and Leadership 2012–14; mem. Inst. of Medicine (NAS) 1983–; Visiting Prof. of Health Man., Karolinska Inst., Stockholm, Sweden 2002–; Festschrift Issue of Medical Care, Aug. 1998, The Duncan Neuhauser PhD Endowed Chair in Community Health Improvement created at Case Western Reserve Univ. 2003. *Achievements include:* est. annual Duncan Neuhauser Curricular Innovation Award, Acad. of Health Care Improvement 2009; conference room at Medical Management Centre, Karolinska Inst., dedicated in his name 2011. *Publications:* (co-author) Health Services in the US 1976, The Efficient Organization 1977, The Physician and Cost Control 1979, Clinical Decision Analysis 1980, Competition, Co-operation or Regulation 1981, The New Epidemiology 1982, Coming of Age 1984, 1995, Clinical CQI 1995, Health Services Management 1997 (nine edns); numerous scientific papers in professional journals. *Leisure interests:* sailing, curling. *Address:* Department of Epidemiology and Biostatistics, Medical School, Case Western Reserve University, 10900 Euclid Avenue, Cleveland, OH 44106-4945 (office); 14 S.C. Lane, PO Box 932, Blue Hill, ME 04614, USA (home). *Telephone:* (216) 368-3726 (office); (207) 374-5325 (Blue Hill) (home). *Fax:* (216) 368-3970 (office). *E-mail:* dvn@case.edu (office).

NEUHOFF, Eric; French writer and journalist; b. 1956, *Publications:* Des gens impossibles 1986, Lettre ouverte à François Truffaut 1987, Les Hanches de Laetitia 1989, Actualités françaises 1992, Comme hier 1993, Pas trop près de l'écran 1993, Michel Déon 1994, Barbe à Papa 1996, La Petite française (Prix Interallié) 1997, Champagne! 1998, La Séance du mercredi à 14 heures 1998, Précautions d'usage 2001, Un Bien fou (Grand Prix du Roman) 2001, Rendez-vous à Samarra 2005, Folie dans la famille 2005, Histoire de Franck 2005. *Address:* c/o Albin Michel, 22 rue Huyghers, 75680 Paris Cedex 14, France.

NEUKIRCHEN, Karl-Josef (Kajo), Dr rer. pol; German business executive; *Partner, Kajo Neukirchen GmbH;* b. 17 March 1942, Bonn; Chair. Man. Bd Klöckner-Humboldt-Deutz AG, Cologne –1988, Hösch AG, Dortmund 1991–92; Chair. Supervisory Bd Klöckner-Werke AG Duisburg 1992–95, Dynamit Nobel AG 1994–, FAG Kugelfischer Georg Schäfer AG, Vossloh AG, Sixt AG; CEO Metallgesellschaft AG 1993–2004; ind. consultant to EnBW AG and mem. Supervisory Bd of subsidiary Stadtwerke Düsseldorf AG; Partner, Kajo Neukirchen GmbH; CEO Ingrid-to-Solms Foundation; mem. Exec. Bd German Lung Foundation. *Address:* Kajo Neukirchen Management und Beteiligungs GmbH, Bockenheimer Landstraße 24, 60323 Frankfurt am Main, Germany. *Telephone:* (69) 7137478-0. *Fax:* (69) 713747829. *E-mail:* info@kaneco.de. *Website:* kaneco.de.

NEUMEIER, John, BA; American/German choreographer and ballet director; *Chief Choreographer, Ballet Director and Ballettintendant, The Hamburg Ballet;* b. 1942, Milwaukee, Wis.; s. of Albert Neumeier and Lucille Neumeier; ed Marquette Univ., Milwaukee; dance training in Milwaukee, Chicago, Royal Ballet School, London and in Copenhagen with Vera Volkova; soloist, The Stuttgart Ballet 1963; Ballet Dir Frankfurt 1969; Ballet Dir and Chief Choreographer, Hamburg Ballet 1973–, Balletintendant 1996–; Prof., City of Hamburg 1987; f. John Neumeier ballet centre, Hamburg 1989; f. a ballet training school in Hamburg 1978; appears as soloist, notably in The Chairs with Marcia Haydée, a ballet cr. for them by M. Béjart; dances lead role of St Matthew Passion 1981–; Hon. mem. Semper Oper (Germany) 2002; Hon. Citizen of Hamburg 2007; Bundesverdienstkreuz, Chevalier, Légion d'honneur, Ordre des Arts et des Lettres, Medal of the Kt's Cross of the Dannebrog in Gold 2000; Hon. DFA (Marquette); Golden Camera Award for TV series of his Ballet Workshops 1978,

Dance Magazine Award 1983, Deutscher Tanzpreis 1988, Diaghilev Prize 1988, Benois de la Danse 1992, Medal of Honour (City of Tokyo) 1994, Carina-Ari Gold Medal (Sweden) 1994, Nijinsky Medal (Polish Ministry of Culture) 1996, Min-On Int. Award for Arts (Tokyo) 1997, European Prince Henrik of Denmark Award 2000, Danza Magazine Award for production of Messiah 2001, Bayerischers Theaterpreis for production of Nijinsky 2001, Gold Mask (Russia) 2002, Wilhelm Hausen Prize (Denmark) 2002, Medal for Art and Science, Hamburg 2003, Kt of the Region of Knox, Pres. of France, Jacques Chirac 2003, Porselli Prize (Italy) 2004, Hans Christian Andersen Ambassador 2004–05, Saeculum Prize for his life's work, Dresden 2005, Steffen Kempe Prize 2005, Golden Mask for Moscow's Best Contemporary Dance Production 2005, Portugaleser in Silver, Hamburg 2006, Nijinsky Award for Lifetime Achievement 2006, Citizen of the Year Hamburg 2006, German Critic Prize for Life Achievement 2007, Herbert von Karajan Music Prize 2007, German Anniversary Dance Prize 2008. *Works choreographed include:* Romeo and Juliet, The Nutcracker 1971, Daphnis and Chloë 1972, Third Symphony of Gustav Mahler 1975, Illusions-Like Swan Lake 1976, A Midsummer Night's Dream 1977, Sleeping Beauty, Lady of the Camellias 1978, St Matthew Passion 1981, Giselle 1983, Sixth Symphony of G. Mahler 1984, Peer Gynt 1989, Fifth Symphony of G. Mahler 1989, Requiem 1991, A Cinderella Story 1992, Odyssee 1995, Vivaldi Or What You Will 1996, Sylvia 1997, Images from Bartók 1998, Messias 1999, Nijinsky 2000, Giselle 2000, Sounds of Empty Pages, Winterreise 2001, The Seagull 2002, Death in Venice 2003, Preludes CV 2003, The Little Mermaid, a homage to Hans Christian Andersen for his 200th birthday celebrations 2005, Songs of the Night 2005, Parzival Episodes and Echo 2006, Christmas Oratorio 2007, Verklungene Feste 2008, Le Pavillon d'Armide 2009, Orpheus 2009, Purgatorio 2011, Liliom 2011. *Films:* The Legend of Joseph, Lady of the Camellias, Illusions – Like 'Swan Lake' (DVD), The Little Mermaid (DVD), St Matthew Passion (DVD). *Television includes:* series of ballet workshops (also on DVD), Wendungen (String Quintet in C Major by Franz Schubert), The Chairs (WDR), Third Symphony of Gustav Mahler (ZDF), Othello (ZDF), Scenes of Childhood (NDR3), Death in Venice (ARTE), St Matthew Passion (SWR). *Publications:* John Neumeier Unterwegs 1972, John Neumeier und das Hamburg Ballett 1977, Matthäus-Passion 1983, John Neumeier Traumwege 1980, 10 Jahre – John Neumeier und das Hamburg Ballett 1983, 20 Jahre – John Neumeier und das Hamburg Ballett 1993, My Favourite Pictures for John 1998, John Neumeier 2004, In Bewegung 2007, John Neumeier: Pictures from a Life (text by Horst Koegler) 2010. *Address:* Hamburg Ballet, Ballettzentrum Hamburg, Caspar-Voght-Str. 54, 20535 Hamburg, Germany (office). *Telephone:* (40) 211188-11 (office). *Fax:* (40) 211188-18 (office). *E-mail:* presse@hamburgballett.de (office). *Website:* www.hamburgballett.de (office).

NEUVILLE, Colette Jeannine Michelle Claude, LenD; French lawyer, organization executive and economist; *President, Association de défense des actionnaires minoritaires (Adam);* b. 21 Jan. 1937, Coutances (Manche); d. of Pierre Wacongne and Suzanne Wacongne (née Piquot); m. Christian Neuville 1961; one s. four d.; ed Lycée de jeunes filles et Ecole Saint-Julien, Le Mans, Faculté de droits, Caen, Faculté de droit et de sciences économiques, Paris; economist with Kléber Colombes group 1959–60; with NATO 1960–63; with Nat. Office of Irrigation, Rabat, Morocco 1963–68; with Financial Agency, Loire Bretagne 1968–69; Founder-Pres. Asscn de défense des actionnaires minoritaires (Adam) 1991–; mem. Supervisory Council Paribas 1995–2000; Dir (non-exec.) Eurotunnel plc 2005–, mem. Jt Bd 2005–, Dir Eurotunnel SA 2007–. *Leisure interests:* music, walking in the mountains. *Address:* Adam, 4 rue Montescot, BP 208, 28004 Chartres Cedex, France.

NEUVO, Yrjö A., PhD, FIEEE; Finnish electronics engineer and academic; *Technology Advisor, Nokia Corporation;* b. 21 July 1943, Turku; s. of Olavi Neuvo and Aune Neuvo (née Vaisala); m. Tuula Halsas 1968; two s. one d.; ed Cornell Univ., NY, USA and Helsinki Univ. of Tech.; Acting Prof., Helsinki Univ. of Tech. 1975–76; Prof. of Electronics, Tampere Univ. of Tech. 1976–92; Sr Vice-Pres., Tech. and Chief Tech. Officer Nokia Corpn 1993–; Sr Research Fellow Acad. of Finland 1979–80, Research Prof. 1984–; Visiting Prof., Univ. of California 1981–82; Commdr Order of Lion of Finland 1992; Hon. MD (Tampere Univ. of Tech.) 1992; IEEE Bicentennial Award 1986, Asscn in Finland Hon. Prize 1988, Nokia Prize 1989. *Publications:* more than 300 scientific publs on computer eng and new technologies. *Address:* Nokia Corporation, Keilalahdentie 4, 00045 Espoo, Finland (office). *Telephone:* (0) 18071 (office). *Fax:* (0) 716015 (office). *Website:* www.nokia.com (office).

NEVANLINNA, (Eero) Olavi, DipEng, DTech; Finnish academic; *Professor of Mathematics, Institute of Mathematics, Helsinki University of Technology;* b. 17 April 1948, Helsinki; m. Marja Lähdesmäki 1968; three s. one d.; ed Helsinki Univ. of Technology; Asst Prof. of Math., Helsinki Univ. of Tech. 1971–74, Prof. 1980–, Vice-Rector 2003–05; Sr Researcher Acad. of Finland 1975–77; Assoc. Prof. of Applied Math., Oulu Univ. 1978–79; Research Prof., Acad. of Finland 1986–92; Visiting Prof. at several US univs and ETH, Zurich; Chair. Rolf Nevanlinna Inst. 1989–90; Chair. Supervisory Bd Suomi Mutual Life Assurance Co. 1996–98; Pres. Int. Council for Industrial and Applied Math. 1999–2003, Past Pres. 2003–05; mem. Bd Pohjola Insurance Co. Ltd 1997–99; mem. Editorial Bd BIT, Finnish Acad. of Tech. Sciences 1984, Finnish Acad. of Sciences and Letters 1986, Nat. Cttee in Math. 1984–. *Publications:* Convergence of Iterations for Linear Equations 1993, Meromorphic Functions and Linear Algebra 2003. *Address:* Institute of Mathematics, Helsinki University of Technology, PO Box 1100, 02015 HUT, Helsinki, Finland (office). *Telephone:* (9) 4513034 (office). *Fax:* (9) 4513016 (office). *Website:* www.tkk.fi (office).

NEVES, José Maria Pereira, BA; Cape Verde politician; *Prime Minister;* b. 28 March 1960, Santa Catarina; three s.; ed São Paulo School of Business and Admin; consultant in organizational devt and human resources man., Cape Verde 1987–96; Dir Nat. Public Admin Training Centre 1988–89; Co-ordinator Admin Reform and Modernization Projects 1987–88; mem. Parl. 1996–; Mayor of Santa Catarina 2000–01; Chair. Partido Africano da Independência de Cabo Verde 2000–; Prime Minister of Cape Verde 2001–; Asst Prof. of Man., Higher Educ. Inst.; Marechal Floriana Peixoto Merit Award, Brazil 2005, Patrons of Century Ruby Cross 2006. *Leisure interests:* reading, walking, music. *Address:* Office of the Prime Minister, Palácio do Governo, Várzea, CP 16, Praia, Santiago, Cape Verde (office).

Telephone: 2610411 (office). *Fax:* 2613099 (office). *E-mail:* gab.imprensa@gpm.gov.cv (office). *Website:* www.primeirominstro.cv (office).

NEVES DA CUNHA, Aécio; Brazilian politician; b. 10 March 1960, Belo Horizonte; s. of Aécio Ferreira da Cunha and Inês Maria Neves; grandson of fmr Brazilian Pres. Tancredo Neves; divorced; one d.; ed Pontifícia Universidade Católica de Minas Gerais; Sec. to Tancredo Neves 1980–85; Fed. Deputy for Minas Gerais 1986–2002; co-f. Partido da Social Democracia Brasileira 1988, Leader in Chamber of Deputies 1997–2001, Pres. Chamber of Deputies 2001–02; Gov. Minas Gerais 2002–10; mem. Senado Federal for Minas Gerais 2011–. *Address:* Senado Federal, National Congress Building, Praça dos Três Poderes, 70165-900 Brasília, Brazil. *Telephone:* (61) 3303-4141. *Website:* www.senado.gov.br.

NEVO, Ruth, PhD; Israeli painter and fmr professor of English literature; b. 8 July 1924, Johannesburg, SA; d. of Benjamin Weinbren and Henrietta Weinbren (née Goldsmith); m. Natan Nevo 1952; three s.; ed Univ. of the Witwatersrand, Hebrew Univ.; tutor, Dept of English, Hebrew Univ. 1952, Prof. 1973, Renee Lang Prof. of Humanities 1982–90, Prof. Emer. 1990–; full-time painter 1987–; nine solo exhbns 1987–2005; mem. Israel Acad. 1985–, Israel Asscn of Painters and Sculptors 1989–, Int. Asscn of English Profs, Int. Shakespeare Asscn. *Publications:* The Dial of Virtue 1963, Tragic Form in Shakespeare 1972, Comic Transformations in Shakespeare 1980, Shakespeare's Other Language 1987; trans. Selected Poems by Bialik 1981, Travels by Amichai 1986, The Challenge of Poetry 2008. *Address:* c/o Department of English, Hebrew University, Mount Scopus, Jerusalem, Israel. *E-mail:* ruth.nevo@mail.huji.ac.il.

NEWALL, James Edward Malcolm (Ted), OC, BComm; Canadian business executive; *Chairman, NOVA Chemicals Corporation;* b. 20 Aug. 1935, Holden, Alberta; m. Margaret Elizabeth Lick; ed Prince Albert Coll. Inst., Univ. of Saskatchewan; joined Du Pont Canada Inc. 1957, various posts in marketing and gen. man. in fibres business, leading to Dir Fibres Group 1972, Vice-Pres., Corp. Devt 1974, Marketing 1975, Exec. Vice-Pres. 1975, Dir 1976, Pres. and CEO 1978–89, Chair. 1979, Chair. and CEO du Pont Canada –1994 and responsible for E.I. du Pont's int. businesses outside Canada and USA 1989–91, Sr Vice-Pres. E.I. du Pont de Nemours Agricultural Products 1989–91; Vice-Chair., CEO and Dir NOVA Chemicals Corpn 1991–98, Chair. 1998–; Chair. Canadian Pacific Railway Ltd, Maritime Transport Services 1994–; Newall & Assocs 1998–; Chair. Business Council on Nat. Issues; Dir Alcan Inc., BCE Inc., The Molson Cos Ltd, Pratt & Whitney Canada Inc., The Royal Bank of Canada; Chair. Business Council on Nat. Issues; fmr Chair. and Dir Conf. Bd of Canada; mem. Advisory Group to Prime Minister on exec. compensation in the public service. *Address:* NOVA Chemicals Corporation, 645 Seventh Avenue, SW, POB 2518, Calgary, Alberta T2P 5C6; Canadian Pacific Railway, Gulf Canada Square, 401-9th Avenue, SW, Calgary, Alberta T2P 4Z4; Newall & Associates, 2015 Bankers Hall, 855 2nd Street, SW, Calgary, Alberta, T2P 4J7, Canada (office).

NEWBERY, David Michael Garrood, CBE, PhD, ScD, FBA; British economist and academic; *Professor Emeritus of Economics, University of Cambridge;* b. 1 June 1943, Bucks.; m. Terri E. Apter 1975; two d.; ed Portsmouth Grammar School, Trinity Coll. Cambridge; Economist, Treasury of Tanzanian Govt 1965–66; Asst Lecturer, Faculty of Econs and Politics, Univ. of Cambridge 1966–71, Lecturer 1971–86, Reader in Econs 1986–88, Prof. of Applied Econs (Prof. of Econs from 2004) 1988–2008, Prof. Emer. of Econs 2008–; Dir Dept of Applied Econs 1988–2003, Fellow, Churchill Coll. 1966–; Div. Chief, World Bank 1981–83; Fellow, Econometric Soc. 1989; Vice-Pres. European Econ. Asscn 1994–95, Pres. 1996; Vice-Chair. Cambridge Econ. Policy Assocs; Dir Cambridge Electricity Policy Research Group; occasional consultant to the World Bank; mem. Monopolies and Mergers Comm. (later Competition Comm.) 1996–2002; fmr Chair. Dutch electricity market surveillance cttee; mem. Academic Panel for Environment, Food and Rural Affairs (Defra); Fellow, Econometric Soc. 1989; hon. degree (Antwerp) 2004; Frisch Medal, Econometric Soc. 1990, Harry Johnson Prize (jtly), Canadian Econ. Asscn 1993, Int. Asscn for Energy Econs 2002 Outstanding Contribs to the Profession Award 2003. *Publications:* Project Appraisal in Practice (co-author) 1976, The Theory of Commodity Price Stabilization: A Study in the Economics of Risk (with J. E. Stiglitz) 1981, The Theory of Taxation for Developing Countries (with N. H. Stern) 1987, Hungary: An Economy in Transition (with I. Székely) 1993, Tax and Benefit Reform in Central and Eastern Europe 1995, A European Market for Electricity? (co-author) 1999, Privatization, Restructuring and Regulation of Network Utilities 2000; numerous articles. *Address:* Faculty of Economics, Sidgwick Avenue, Cambridge, CB3 9DE (office); 9 Huntingdon Road, Cambridge, CB3 0HH, England (home). *Telephone:* (1223) 335248 (office). *Fax:* (1223) 335299 (office). *E-mail:* dmgn@cam.ac.uk (office); david.newbery@econ.cam.ac.uk (office). *Website:* www.econ.cam.ac.uk/faculty/newbery (office).

NEWBIGGING, Sir David Kennedy, Kt, OBE; British business executive; *Chairman, Academic Partnerships International Limited;* b. 19 Jan. 1934, Tientsin, China; s. of the late D. L. Newbigging, CBE, MC, Bar and of L. M. Newbigging; m. Carolyn S. Band 1968; one s. two d.; ed Oundle School; joined Jardine, Matheson & Co. Ltd 1954, Dir 1967, Man. Dir 1970, Chair. and Sr Man. Dir 1975–83; Chair. Hong Kong & Kowloon Wharf & Godown Co. Ltd 1970–80; Chair. and Man. Dir Hong Kong Land Co. Ltd 1975–83; Dir Hong Kong & Shanghai Banking Corpn 1975–83; Dir Hong Kong Electric Holdings Ltd 1975–83, Chair. 1982–83; Dir Hong Kong Telephone Co. Ltd 1975–83; Chair. Jardine, Fleming & Co. Ltd 1975–83; Dir Rennies Consolidated Holdings Ltd 1975–83, Chair. and Man. Dir 1975–83; Dir Safmarine and Rennies Holdings Ltd 1984–85, Provincial Insurance PLC 1984–86 (Deputy Chair. Provincial Group PLC 1985–91); Deputy Chair. Ivory & Sime PLC 1990–95, Chair. 1992–95 (Dir 1987–95); Dir NM UK (Chair. 1990–93), Rentokil Group PLC 1986–94 (Chair. 1987–94), PACCAR (UK) Ltd 1986–97, Mason Best International Ltd 1986–90 (Chair. 1987–90), International Financial Markets Trading Ltd 1986–93, United Meridian Corpn 1987–97, Thai Holdings Ltd 1989–91, Merrill Lynch and Co. Inc., USA 1997–2007, Ocean Energy Inc., USA 1998–, PACCAR Inc., USA 1999–; Deputy Chair. Benchmark Group PLC 1996–2004; Chair. Redfearn PLC March–Dec. 1988, Faupel PLC 1994–2005 (Dir 1989–2005), London Capital Holdings PLC March–Dec. 1994, Talbot Holdings Ltd 2003–07; Dir Wah Kwong Shipping Holdings Ltd 1992–99, Lloyd's Market Bd 1993–95, Friends' Provident Life Office 1993–2001 (Deputy Chair. 1996–98, Chair. 1998–2001, Chair. Friends Provident PLC 2001–05); Chair. Equitas Holdings Ltd 1995–98, Maritime Transport Services Ltd 1993–95; Trustee, Cancer Research UK

2001–10 (Deputy Chair. Council of Trustees 2002–04, Chair. 2004–10), King Mahendra UK Trust for Nature Conservation 1988–; Chair. of Trustees, Wilts Community Foundation 1991–97; Chair. of Council, Mission to Seafarers (fmrly Mission to Seaman) 1993–; mem. Legis. Council of Hong Kong 1978–82, mem. Exec. Council 1980–84; mem. Int. Council, Morgan Guaranty Trust Co. of New York 1977–85, Supervisory Bd DAF Trucks NV 1997–99; mem. British Coal Corpn (fmrly Nat. Coal Bd) 1984–87, CIN Man. 1985–87; DL of Wilts. 1994–, High Sheriff of Wilts. 2003–04; Liveryman, Worshipful Co. of Grocers. *Leisure interests:* most outdoor sports, Chinese art. *Address:* 119 Old Church Street, London, SW3 6EA, England. *Telephone:* (20) 7352-1558. *E-mail:* david@newbigging.co.

NEWBY, Sir Howard Joseph, KCB, CBE, BA, PhD, AcSS, FRSA; British sociologist, academic and university vice-chancellor; *Vice-Chancellor, University of Liverpool;* b. 10 Dec. 1947, Derby, England; s. of Alfred J. Newby and Constance A. Potts; Lecturer in Sociology, Univ. of Essex 1972–75, Sr Lecturer 1975–79; Prof. of Sociology, Univ. of Wisconsin, USA 1979–83, Univ. of Essex 1983–88; Chair. Econ. & Social Research Council 1988–94, Chief Exec. 1994; Vice-Chancellor, Univ. of Southampton 1994–2001; mem. Rural Devt Comm. 1991–99, S & W Regional Health Authority 1994–96, European Sciences and Technology Assen 1997–; Chair. Centre for Exploitation of Science and Tech. 1995, Cttee of Vice-Chancellors and Prins 1999–2001; Pres. BAAS 2001–02; Chief Exec. Higher Educ. Funding Council for England 2001–06; Vice-Chancellor, Univ. of the West of England 2006–07, Univ. of Liverpool 2008–; visiting appointments include Univs of New South Wales 1976, Sydney, Australia 1976, Wisconsin, USA 1977–78, Newcastle 1983–84; ten hon. degrees. *Publications include:* Community Studies (co-author) 1971, The Deferential Worker 1977, Property, Paternalism and Power (co-author) 1978, Green and Pleasant Land? 1979, The Problem of Sociology (co-author) 1983, Country Life 1987, The Countryside in Question 1988, Social Class in Modern Britain 1988 (co-author), The National Trust: The Next 100 Years 1995. *Leisure interests:* family life, gardening, Derby County, railway enthusiasms. *Address:* Office of the Vice-Chancellor, University of Liverpool, Liverpool, L69 3BX, England (office). *Telephone:* (151) 794-2000 (office). *E-mail:* howard.newby@liverpool.ac.uk (office). *Website:* www.liv.ac.uk (office).

NEWCOMBE, John David, AO, OBE; Australian fmr professional tennis player; b. 23 May 1944, Sydney, NSW; s. of George Ernest Newcombe and Lillian Newcombe; m. Angelika Pfannenberg (fmr German pro tennis player) 1966; one s. two d.; ed Sydney Church of England Grammar School; winner Wimbledon Singles Championship 1967 (last amateur), 1970, 1971, US Singles Championship 1967, 1973, Australian Singles Championship 1973, 1975, World Championship Tennis Crown 1974, Wimbledon Doubles Championship 1965–66, 1968–70, 1974; won 73 pro titles; played with Australian Davis Cup Team 1963–67, 1973–76, Capt. (non-playing) 1994–2000; set up a tennis camp, the John Newcombe Tennis Ranch, in Tex. 1968; Pres. Assen of Tennis Professionals (Int.) 1976–78, Nat. Australia Day Council 1981–91; Chair. Player Devt Bd, Tennis Australia 1985–94; Hon. Life mem. Australian Wheelchair Tennis Assen; Dr hc (Bond, Queensland) 1999; inducted into Int. Tennis Hall of Fame 1986. *Television:* has appeared as a commentator for various networks on numerous tennis tournaments in Australia, USA and UK. *Publications:* The Family Tennis Book 1975, The Young Tennis Player 1981, Bedside Tennis 1983, Newk 2002, No-one's Indestructible 2003, The Power Within 2012. *Leisure interests:* skiing, water-skiing, golf, fishing. *Address:* c/o Tennis Australia, Batman Avenue, Melbourne, Vic. 3000, Australia.

NEWELL, Frances Mary, FRSA, FCSD; British design consultant; *Founder, The Sorrell Foundation;* b. 19 Jan. 1947, Surrey, England; d. of the late Alexander C. Newell and of Julie S. Newell; m. John William Sorrell 1974; two s. one d.; Founder and Chair. Newell & Sorrell (identity & design consultants, merged with Interbrand 1997) 1976–97; apptd Group Creative Dir Interbrand Newell and Sorrell 1997; Chair. City & Guilds Nat. Advisory Cttee on Art, Craft and Design 1994–96, mem. Colour Group 1996–, City & Guilds Sr Awards Cttee 1996–; Founder The Sorrell Foundation 1999; Bd Dir Royal Acad. Enterprises 1996–99; mem. Exec. Cttee Mencap Blue Sky Appeal 1996–98, Advisory Bd of Nat. Museum of Photography, Film and TV; 11 DBA Design Effectiveness Awards, 5 Silver D&ADs, 5 Clios, 1 Grand Award for British Airways Corp. Identity and 5 Gold Awards in New York Festivals, 2 Art Directors' Club of Europe Awards. *Publications:* joinedupdesignforschools (with John Sorrell) 2005. *Leisure interests:* art, travel, gardening. *Address:* The Sorrell Foundation, Somerset House, The Strand, London, WC2R 1LA, England (office). *Website:* www.thesorrellfoundation.com (office).

NEWELL, Mike; British film director; b. 1942, St Albans, Herts., England; s. of Terence William Newell and Mollie Louise Newell; m. Bernice Stegers 1979; one s. one d.; ed Univ. of Cambridge; trainee dir, Granada TV 1963; Dir European premiere of Tennessee Williams' The Kingdom of the Earth, Bristol Old Vic. *Films as director:* The Man in the Iron Mask 1976, The Awakening 1979, Bad Blood 1980, Dance with a Stranger (Prix de la Jeunesse, Cannes) 1984, The Good Father 1985, Amazing Grace and Chuck 1986, Soursweet 1987, Common Ground 1990, Enchanted April 1991, Into the West 1992, Four Weddings and a Funeral (BAFTA Award for Best Film and Best Achievement in Direction 1995, Cesar Award for Foreign Film) 1994, An Awfully Big Adventure 1994, Donnie Brasco 1997, Pushing Tin 1998, Mona Lisa Smile 2003, Harry Potter and the Goblet of Fire 2005, Love in the Time of Cholera 2007, Prince of Persia 2010. *Films as executive producer:* Photographing Fairies 1997, 200 Cigarettes 1999, Best Laid Plans 1999, High Fidelity 2000, Traffic 2000, I Capture the Castle 2003. *Television films:* Ready When You Are, Mr McGill, Tales out of School, Birth of a Nation (Prix Futura, Berlin), The Melancholy Hussar, Lost Your Tongue, Baa Baa Black Sheep, Common Ground (for CBS), Blood Feud (for Fox) 1983. *Television work includes:* Mr and Mrs Bureaucrat, Destiny, The Gift of Friendship, Brassneck (play), Just Your Luck (play). *Leisure interests:* reading (anything but fiction), walking. *Address:* c/o ICM, 3rd Floor, Marlborough House, 10 Earlham Street, London, WC2H 9LN, England (office). *Telephone:* (20) 7836-8564 (office). *Website:* www.icmtalent.com (office).

NEWHOUSE, Samuel I., Jr; American publishing executive; *Chairman and CEO, Advance Publications, Inc.;* b. 8 Nov. 1927; s. of the late Samuel Irving Newhouse and Mitzi Newhouse (née Epstein); m. 1st Jane Franke (divorced); three c.; m. 2nd Victoria Newhouse; took over father's Staten Island Advance co. 1922 and built newspaper and magazine chain; Publr Vogue magazine 1964; Chair.

Condé Nast Publs Inc., New York 1975–, also Chair. and CEO Advance Publs Inc., New York 1979–; fmr mem. Bd Museum of Modern Art; Henry Johnson Fisher Award, Magazine Publishers' Assen 1985. *Address:* Advance Publications, Inc., 950 Fingerboard Road, Staten Island, NY 10305, USA (office). *Telephone:* (212) 286-2860 (office). *Fax:* (212) 981-1456 (office). *Website:* www.advance.net (office).

NEWLAND, Martin, BA, MA (Theol); British newspaper editor; *Editorial Director, The National;* b. 1961, Nigeria; m.; four c.; ed Univ. of London; reporter The Catholic Herald 1986–89; night reporter The Daily Telegraph 1989, News Ed. mid-1990s, Ed. 2003–05; Deputy Ed. The National Post, Canada 1998–2003; Founder and Ed.-in-Chief, The National newspaper, UAE 2008–09, Editorial Dir 2009–. *Leisure interest:* working out in the gym. *Address:* Abu Dhabi Media Co., 4th Street, Sector 18, Zone 1, Abu Dhabi, United Arab Emirates. *Telephone:* (2) 4144000. *Website:* thenational.ae.

NEWMAN, Frank Neil, BA; American banker; b. 20 April 1942, Quincy, Mass; m. Lizabeth Newman; one s.; ed Harvard Univ.; Man. Peat Marwick Livingston & Co. 1966–69; Vice-Pres. Citicorp 1969–73; Exec. Vice-Pres., Chief Financial Officer Wells Fargo Bank 1973–86; Vice-Chair., Chief Financial Officer Bank America Corp. 1986–93; Under-Sec. of the Treasury for Domestic Finance 1993–94, Deputy Sec. of the Treasury 1994–95; Sr Vice-Chair. Bankers Trust Co. 1995–96, Chair., Pres. and CEO 1996–99, resgnd as Chair., now Chair. Emer.; CEO Shenzhen Development Bank Co. Ltd (renamed Ping An Bank Co. Ltd following merger with Ping An Bank Co. Ltd 2012) from 2005; fmr Vice-Chair. The Broad Center for Man. of School Systems, Los Angeles; mem. Bd Deutsche Bank 1999, Dow Jones & Co., Korea First Bank, GUS; Alexander Hamilton Award (US Treasury Dept). *Address:* c/o The Broad Center for the Management of School Systems, 10900 Wilshire Boulevard, Los Angeles, CA 90024, USA. *E-mail:* info@broadcenter.org.

NEWMAN, Jocelyn Margaret, LLB; Australian public official and fmr politician; b. 8 July 1937; m. Kevin Newman; ed Melbourne Univ.; Senator (Liberal Party) for Tasmania 1986–2002; Shadow Minister for Defence, Science and Personnel 1988–92, Veterans' Affairs 1990–92; Shadow Minister Assisting Leader on Status of Women 1989–93; Shadow Minister for the Aged and Veterans' Affairs 1992–93; Shadow Minister for Family Health, Shadow Minister Assisting Leader on Family Matters, Chair. Health, Welfare and Veterans' Affairs Group 1993–94; Shadow Minister for Defence 1994–96; Minister for Social Security and Minister Assisting Prime Minister on Status of Women 1996–98, for Family and Community Services and Minister Assisting Prime Minister on Status of Women 1998–2001; mem. Bd Australian Strategic Policy Inst. 2001–; mem. Australian War Memorial Council 2002–. *Address:* Australian Strategic Policy Institute, Level 2, Arts House, 40 Macquarie Street, Barton, ACT 2600 (office); PO Box 146, Red Hill, ACT 2063, Australia. *Website:* www.aspi.otr.au (office).

NEWMAN, Sir Kenneth Leslie, Kt, GBE, QPM, LLB, FIBM, CIMgt; British police officer (retd) and academic; b. 15 Aug. 1926, Sussex, England; s. of John William Newman and Florence Newman; m. Eileen Lilian Newman 1949; one s. one d.; ed Univ. of London; with RAF 1942–46; mem. Palestine Police 1946–48; with Metropolitan Police, London 1948–73, Commdr, New Scotland Yard 1972; with Royal Ulster Constabulary 1973–79, Sr Deputy Chief Constable 1973, Chief Constable 1976–79; Commdt, Police Staff Coll. 1980–82; Insp. of Constabulary 1980–82; Commr Metropolitan Police 1982–87 (retd); Prof. of Law, Univ. of Bristol 1987–88; Registrar, Imperial Soc. of Kts Bachelor 1991–98; Dir Control Risks 1987–92; Chair. Disciplinary Cttee, Security Systems Inspectorate, British Security Industry Assen 1987–95, Assen for Prevention of Theft in Shops 1987–91; Pres. Assen of Police and Public Security Suppliers 1993–2000; Vice-Pres. Defence Mfrs Assen 1987–2000; Trustee, Community Action Trust 1987–99, World Humanity Action Trust 1993–98; Patron, The Police Foundation; numerous foreign decorations; Queen's Police Medal 1982, COTY Award, British Assen of Communicators in Business 1984. *Leisure interests:* bridge, walking. *Address:* c/o The Police Foundation, First Floor, Park Place, 12 Lawn Lane, London, SW8 1UD, England.

NEWMAN, Kevin, BA; Canadian broadcast journalist; b. Toronto, Ont.; m. Cathy Newman; one s. one d.; ed Univ. of Western Ontario; corresp., Global News, Global TV Network, Toronto, Parl. Bureau, Ottawa 1983–87; later with CTV Nat. News, CBC The National, CBC Midday; joined ABC (American Broadcasting Corpn) News, New York 1994, positions including Substitute Anchor and Corresp., World News Tonight with Peter Jennings, Sr Corresp., Nightline, Co-host, Good Morning America; Anchor and Exec. Ed., Global National with Kevin Newman, Global TV Network, BC 2001–10; Co-anchor, CTV 2011–; fmr Instructor in Broadcast Journalism, Ryerson Univ. School of Journalism; Rogers Communication Lecturer, Univ. of Western Ontario 1999; Emmy Award for Outstanding News and Documentary Program Achievement 2000, Emmy Award for Outstanding Coverage of a Breaking News Story 2000, George Foster Peabody Award for ABC 2000 Millennium Coverage 2000, Women's Sport Foundation Award for Outstanding Network TV Journalism 2000, Leo Award for Best Anchor 2002, 2003, Canadian Radio and TV News Dirs Assen Best Breaking News Coverage Award 2001, Best Continuing Coverage Award 2001. *Address:* CTV Television Network, PO Box 9, Station O, Toronto, ON M4A 2M9, Canada. *Telephone:* (416) 384-5000. *Website:* www.ctvnews.ca.

NEWMAN, Maurice Lionel, AM; Australian banker and business executive; *Chairman, Australian Stock Exchange;* b. 20 March 1938, Ilford, England; s. of J. Newman; m. 1st 1963 (divorced); two s.; m. 2nd Jeanette Newman 1994; ed Univ. of Sydney; Partner, Bain and Co. 1966–73, Man. Dir Bain and Co. Group 1983–85; Exec. Chair. Deutsche Bank Australia Group (fmrly Deutsche Morgan Grenfell Group) 1985–; Chair. Australian Stock Exchange Ltd 1994–, Australian-Taiwan Business Council 1995–, E Asian and Oceanic Stock Exchanges Fed. 1995–96, Axiom Funds Man. Ltd 1997–, Benchmark Securities Man. Ltd 1997–, Commercial Investment Trust 1998–, Financial Sector, Advisory Council 1998–; Dir Financial Futures Market 1990–, Securities Industry Research Centre Australia; mem. Australian Inst. of Co. Dirs; Trustee Stock Exchange Superannuation and Accumulation Fund 1990–; mem. Bd of Dirs Australian Broadcasting Corpn— 2004. *Leisure interests:* cycling, horse riding, tennis. *Address:* Australian Stock Exchange Ltd, Level 9, 20 Bridge Street, Sydney, NSW 2001 (office); 35 Burran Avenue, Mosman, NSW 2088, Australia (home). *Telephone:* (2) 9321-4000 (office). *Fax:* (2) 9235-0056 (office). *Website:* www.asx.com.au.

NEWMAN, Nanette; British actress and writer; b. Northampton, England; d. of Sidney Newman and Ruby Newman; m. Bryan Forbes 1955 (died 2013); two d.; ed Sternhold Coll., London, Italia Conti Stage School, Royal Acad. of Dramatic Art. *Film appearances include:* The L-Shaped Room 1962, The Wrong Arm of the Law 1962, Seance on a Wet Afternoon 1963, The Wrong Box 1965, The Whisperers 1966, The Madwoman of Chaillot 1968, The Raging Moon (Variety Club Best Actress Award) 1971, The Stepford Wives 1974, International Velvet 1978. *Television appearances include:* The Fun Food Factory, London Scene, Stay with Me Till Morning, Jessie, Let There Be Love, Late Expectations, The Endless Game 1988, Ideal Home Cooks, Newman Meets (series), Celebrations (series). *Publications:* God Bless Love 1972, Lots of Love 1973, Fun Food Factory 1976, All Our Love 1978, The Root Children 1978, Amy Rainbow 1980, That Dog 1980, Reflections 1981, Dog Lovers Coffee Table Book 1982, Cat Lovers Coffee Table Book 1983, My Granny Was a Frightful Bore 1983, 2004, Christmas Cookbook 1984, Cat and Mouse Love Story 1984, The Best of Love 1985, Pigalev 1985, Archie 1986, The Summer Cookbook 1986, Small Beginnings 1987, Bad Baby 1988, Entertaining with Nanette Newman 1988, Charlie the Noisy Caterpillar 1989, Sharing 1989, ABC 1990, 123 1991, Cooking for Friends 1991, Spider, The Horrible Cat 1992, There's a Bear in the Bath 1993, There's a Bear in the Classroom 1996, Take 3 Cooks 1996, Up to the Skies and Down Again 1999, To You with Love 1999, Bad Baby Good Baby 2002, Small Talk 2004, Ben's Book 2005, Eating In 2005. *Leisure interests:* needlepoint, china painting. *Address:* c/o Chatto & Linnit Ltd, 123A King's Road, London, SW3 4PL, England (office). *Telephone:* (20) 7352-7722 (office).

NEWMAN, Peter Charles, CC, CD; Canadian author and journalist; b. 10 May 1929, Vienna, Austria; s. of Oscar Newman and Wanda Newman; m. 1st Christina McCall (divorced); m. 2nd Camilla J. Turner 1978; two d.; m. 3rd Alvy Björkland 1992; ed Upper Canada Coll., Univ. of Toronto and McGill Univ.; Asst Ed. The Financial Post 1951–55; Ottawa Ed., Maclean's 1955–64; Ottawa Ed., Toronto Daily Star 1964–69; Ed.-in-Chief 1969–71; Ed.-in-Chief, Maclean's (now Rogers Publishing) 1971–82; Sr Contributing Ed. 1982–; Dir Maclean Hunter Ltd 1972–83, Key Radio Ltd 1983–; Prof. of Creative Writing, Univ. of Victoria 1985–90, Univ. of British Columbia; Visiting Prof., Ryerson Univ. 2009; Kt Commdr, Order of St Lazarus; Hon. LLD (Brock) 1974, (Wilfrid Laurier) 1983, (Royal Mil. Coll.) 1986, (Queens) 1986; Hon. DLitt (York) 1975, (British Columbia) 1998. *Publications include:* Flame of Power 1959, Renegade in Power 1963, The Distemper of Our Times 1968, Home Country 1973, The Canadian Establishment: Vol. I 1975, Bronfman Dynasty 1978, The Acquisitors – The Canadian Establishment: Vol. II 1981, The Establishment Man 1982, True North – Not Strong and Free 1983, Debrett's Illustrated Guide to the Canadian Establishment 1983, Company of Adventurers 1985, Caesars of the Wilderness 1987, Sometimes A Great Nation 1988, Empire of Bay 1989, Merchant Princes 1991, The Canadian Revolution 1995, Defining Moments 1996, Titans: How the New Canadian Establishment Seized Power 1998, Sometimes a Great Nation – Will Canada Belong to the 21st Century? 1998, Here Be Dragons: Telling Tales of People, Passion and Power 2004, The Secret Mulroney Tapes: Unguarded Confessions of a Prime Minister 2005, Izzy: The Passionate Life and Turbulent Times of Izzy Asper, Canada's Media Mogul 2008, Heroes: Canadian Champions, Dark Horses, and Icons 2010, Mavericks: Canadian Rebels, Renegades, and Anti-Heroes 2010, When the Gods Changed: The Death of Liberal Canada 2011. *Leisure interest:* sailing. *Address:* c/o Random House of Canada Ltd, One Toronto Street, Unit 300, Toronto, ON M5C 2V6, Canada.

NEWMAN, Thomas Montgomery, MMus; American composer; b. 29 Oct. 1955, Los Angeles, Calif.; s. of Alfred Newman; m. Ann Marie Zirbes; three c.; ed Univ. of Southern California, Yale Univ.; mem. Broadcast Music, Inc. *Compositions for film:* Summer's End 1984, Reckless 1984, Revenge of the Nerds 1984, Grandview, USA 1984, Desperately Seeking Susan 1985, Girls Just Want to Have Fun 1985, The Man with One Red Shoe 1985, Real Genius 1985, Gung Ho 1986, Jumpin' Jack Flash 1986, Light of Day 1987, The Lost Boys 1987, Less Than Zero 1987, The Great Outdoors 1988, The Prince of Pennsylvania 1988, Cookie 1989, Men Don't Leave 1990, Welcome Home, Roxy Carmichael 1990, Career Opportunities 1991, Naked Tango 1991, The Rapture 1991, Deceived 1991, The Linguini Incident 1991, Fried Green Tomatoes 1991, The Player 1992, Whispers in the Dark 1992, Scent of a Woman 1992, Flesh and Bone 1993, Josh and S.A.M. 1993, Threesome 1994, The Favor 1994, Corrina, Corrina 1994, The Shawshank Redemption 1994, The War 1994, Little Women 1994, Unstrung Heroes 1995, How to Make an American Quilt 1995, Up Close & Personal 1996, Phenomenon 1996, American Buffalo 1996, The People vs Larry Flynt 1996, Mad City 1997, Red Corner 1997, Oscar and Lucinda 1997, The Horse Whisperer 1998, Meet Joe Black 1998, American Beauty (Grammy Award, BAFTA 2000) 1999, The Green Mile 1999, Erin Brockovich 2000, My Khmer Heart 2000, Pay It Forward 2000, In the Bedroom 2001, The Execution of Wanda Jean 2002, The Salton Sea 2002, Road to Perdition 2002, White Oleander 2002, Finding Nemo 2003, Lemony Snicket's A Series of Unfortunate Events 2004, Cinderella Man 2005, Jarhead 2005, Little Children 2006, The Good German 2006, Nothing is Private 2007, Wall-E 2008, Revolutionary Road 2009, Brothers 2009, The Debt 2010, Skyfall (BAFTA 2013, Grammy Award for Best Score Soundtrack for Visual Media 2014) 2012, Side Effects 2013, Saving Mr. Banks 2013. *Compositions for television:* The Paper Chase (series) 1978, The Seduction of Gina (film) 1984, Amazing Stories (episode 'Santa 85') 1985, Heat Wave (film) 1990, Against the Law (series) 1990, Those Secrets (film) 1992, Citizen Cohn (film) 1992, Arli$$ (series) 1996, Boston Public (series theme) 2000, Six Feet Under (series theme) 2001, Angels in America (mini-series) 2003, Katedralen 1.z 2004, The Newsroom (series) 2012, Lauren (series) 2013. *Address:* c/o Gorfaine/Schwartz Agency Inc., 4111 West Alameda Avenue, Suite 509, Burbank, CA 91505, USA (office). *Telephone:* (818) 260-8500 (office). *Website:* www .gsamusic.com (office).

NEWSOME, William T., III, BS, PhD; American neuroscientist and academic; *Professor, Department of Neurobiology, Stanford University;* ed Stetson Univ., California Inst. of Tech.; Postdoctoral Researcher, Nat. Eye Inst.; fmr mem. Faculty, State Univ. of New York, Stony Brook; Prof., Dept of Neurobiology, Stanford Univ. School of Medicine 1988–; Investigator, Howard Hughes Medical Inst., Chevy Chase, Md; mem. NAS; Rank Prize in Optoelectronics, Spencer Award, Columbia Univ. Coll. of Physicians and Surgeons, Distinguished Scientific Contrib. Award, American Psychological Asscn 2002, Dan David Prize (Brain

Sciences), Dan David Foundation and Tel-Aviv Univ. 2004. *Publications:* numerous scientific papers in professional journals on the neural mechanisms underlying visual perception, visually based decision-making, and related issues in cognitive neuroscience. *Address:* Department of Neurobiology, Fairchild Building, Room D209, Stanford University School of Medicine, Stanford, CA 94305-2130, USA (office). *Telephone:* (650) 725-5814 (office). *Fax:* (650) 725-3958 (office). *E-mail:* bill@monkeybiz.stanford.edu (office). *Website:* monkeybiz.stanford.edu (office).

NEWSOM, Gavin, BA; American politician; *Lieutenant-Governor of California;* b. 10 Oct. 1967, San Francisco; s. William Newsom and Tessa Newsom; ed Santa Clara Univ., Calif.; opened first business, PlumpJack Wine Shop 1992; gen. pnr in several business ventures including Squaw Valley Inn, PlumpJack Man. Group; Pres. Parking and Traffic Comm., San Francisco 1996, mem. Bd of Supervisors 1996–2003; mem. Democratic Party; Mayor of San Francisco 2004–11; Lt Gov. of California 2011–. *Address:* Office of the Lieutenant-Governor, State Capitol, Rm 1114, Sacramento, CA 95814, USA (office). *Telephone:* (916) 445-8994 (office). *Fax:* (916) 323-4998 (office). *E-mail:* lt.governor@ltgov.ca.gov (office). *Website:* www.ltg .ca.gov (office).

NEWSON, Marc Andrew, CBE, RDI; Australian designer; b. 20 Oct. 1963, Sydney, NSW; m. Charlotte Stockdale 2008; two c.; ed Sydney Coll. of the Arts; staged first exhbn at Rosyln Oxley Galery, Sydney 1986; designed first of pod series of watches 1986; designer, Idée Co., Tokyo, Japan 1987–91; set up studio in Paris, France 1991; began to work for Flos for Lighting, Cappellini and Moroso 1991; est. Ikepod Watch Co. (jt venture) 1991; designed Shiseido Men's Toiletries Range, Paris 1992; Visiting Prof. European Inst. of Design, Milan, Italy 1992, Vitra Design Museum Summer Workshop, Germany 1992; designed Gluon Chair and TV Chair for Moroso 1993, Helice Lamp for Flos 1993, Gello Table for 3 Suisses 1994; co-f. Ikepod, Switzerland (with Oliver Ike) 1994; set up Marc Newson Ltd, London 1997; designed Walter Van Beirendonck's Streetwear Label W&LT 1997, Dishdoctor and Rock Doorstep for Magis 1997, Cookware for Tefal, clothes for clothing co. G-Star Raw, Lo Table for B&B Italia 1998, Glassware for Iittala, Finland 1998, MNO1 Aluminium Bicycle for Biomega, Denmark 1999, O21C Concept Car for Ford Motor Co. (Concept Car Design Award, Tokyo Motor Show 1999) 1999, Canteen, New York 1999, Hair Care Products for Vidal Sassoon, New York 2000, Lever House Restaurant and Bar, New York 2002, interiors of Hotel Puerta America, Madrid 2005, Qantas first class lounges in Melbourne and Sydney, Qantas 'Skybed' business class seat and Airbus 380 Economy Class Seat (Australian Int. Design Award of the Year 2009), Cabin design for the 'Sky Jet' 2007, airline/rocketship (by EADS Astrium) planning to take passengers into space from 2012, Riva Aquariva speedboat 2010, Kelvin 40 concept plane as a personal project; design work for Nike, Idée-Sputnik 2000; est. Partnership with Syn to develop products for Japanese market 2000; Artistic Dir Sydney New Year's Eve fire works display 2011; works in several major museum collections, including MoMA, New York, Design Museum, London, Victoria and Albert Museum, London, Centre Georges Pompidou, Paris, Vitra Design Museum; Adjunct Prof., Sydney Coll. of the Arts, Hong Kong Polytechnic Univ.; Royal Designer for Industry (UK) 2006; Hon. Dr of Visual Arts (Sydney) 2010; Australian Crafts Council Award 1984, Visual Arts Bd Grant, Australia Council 1988, Prix du créateur de l'année, Salon du Meuble, Paris 1993, Top 50 Designers Award, I.D. Magazines 1998, Sydney Design Convention Award 1999, Red Dot Design Award (Germany) 1999, 2006, George Nelson Design Award (USA) 1999, Compasso D'Oro Award, X1X Premio (Italy) 2000, Design Innovationen 2000, Design Zentrum Nordrhein Westfalen, Germany, 2000, Chicago Athenaeum Good Design Award 2001, 2003 (twice), 2005, 2006, 2009, 2010, Australian Design Award 2003, 2009 (twice), Elle Decoration Design Awards, UK 2003, ADI Compasso d'Oro Award 2004, Good Design Award (G Mark) (Japan) 2004, L'Observateur du Design Award, Paris 2005, Time Out Awards NY Reader's Choice, Best New Restaurant Design 2005, Classic Design Awards, Homes & Gardens with V&A Museum 2005, Product Innovation Award, Bathroom & Kitchen Magazine 2005, Design & Decoration Awards, best bathroom product (UK) 2005, SIFA Awards, Berlin 2005, included in TIME magazine's 100 Most Influential People in the World 2005, Designer of the Year Award, Design Miami/ Basel 2006, Australian Travel Innovator Award 2007, Australian Int. Design Awards 2008, Skytrax World Airline Award 2008, London Design Medal, London Design Festival 2008, Man of the Year Award, for Design, GQ Germany 2008, Wallpaper Design Award, Smeg Ovens & Hobs 2009, Condé Nast Traveller Innovation & Design Award 2009, Lifetime Achievement Award, The Design Awards (UK) 2010. *Designs include:* Lockheed Lounge 1984, Orgone Lounge, Charlotte Chair, Sugar Guppy Lamp 1987, Black Hole Table and Felt Chair 1988, Wood Chair for House of Fiction Exhbn, Sydney 1988, Embryo Chair for Powerhouse Museum, Sydney 1988, Andoni Shop Interior, Sydney 1988, Pod Bar Interior, Tokyo 1989, Orgone Fibreglass Chair and Lounge, Sydney 1989, Carbon Fibre Mystery Clock 1990, Event Horizon Table 1991, Interiors of Hysterie and Skoda Boutiques, Germany 1992, Seaslug Watch 1994, Interior of Coast Restaurant, London 1995, Hemipode Watch 1996, Interior of Syn Recording Studio, Tokyo 1996, Interior of Komed Restaurant, Cologne 1996, Falcon 900B Business Jet, London 1999, Llama Apartments Project, Brisbane 2000, Interior of Lever Bar, New York 2000, Miniature Lockheed Lounge 2000, Magnum Presentation Set for Dom Perignon 2006 and Black Box 2010, new range for Smeg (appliances) 2009–10. *Museum collections:* Art Gallery of S Australia, Adelaide, Carnegie Museum, Pittsburgh, Design Museum, London, Musée des Arts Decoratifs, Paris, Powerhouse Museum, Sydney, San Francisco Museum of Modern Art, Vitra Design Museum, Weil am Rhein (Germany). *Publication:* Marc Newson 1999. *Address:* Marc Newson Ltd, 7 Howick Place, London, SW1P 1BB, England (office). *Telephone:* (20) 7932-0990 (office). *Fax:* (20) 7630-6017 (office). *E-mail:* pod@marc-newson.com (office). *Website:* www.marc-newson.com (office).

NEWTON, Christopher, CM, BA, MA; Canadian (b. British) actor, director and author; *Artistic Director Emeritus, The Shaw Festival;* b. 11 June 1936, Deal, Kent, England; s. of Albert E. Newton and Gwladys M. Emes; ed Sir Roger Manwood's School, Sandwich, Kent and Univ. of Leeds, UK, Illinois and Purdue Univs, USA; actor, Stratford Festival, New York; Founding Artistic Dir, Theatre Calgary, Calgary, Alberta 1968–71; Artistic Dir, Vancouver Playhouse and Founder (with the late Powys Thomas), The Playhouse Acting School 1973–79; Artistic Dir, The Shaw Festival, Niagara-on-the-Lake 1979–2002, Artistic Dir Emer. 2002–; Hon. Fellow, Ryerson Univ., Royal Conservatory of Music; Hon. LLD (Brock Univ.,

Guelph, Toronto); Hon. DLitt (Wilfrid Laurier Univ.); Hon. DHL (State Univ. of NY at Buffalo); Gov.-Gen.'s Award, Molson Prize, Gascon-Thomas Award, Chalmers Award. *Plays directed include:* (for the Shaw Festival) Heartbreak House, Cavalcade, Man and Superman, Pygmalion, The Importance of Being Earnest, Easy Virtue, The Doctor's Dilemma, Lady Windermere's Fan, Caesar and Cleopatra, The Return of the Prodigal; (for Melbourne Theatre Co.) Misalliance; (for Vancouver Playhouse) She Stoops to Conquer, Hamlet, Julius Caesar, The Taming of the Shrew; (for Theatre Calgary) An Inspector Calls; (for YPT) Great Expectations; (for Stratford Festival) Much Ado About Nothing. *Operas directed include:* (for Canadian Opera Co.) Madama Butterfly, Patria I, The Turn of the Screw, Albert Herring; (for Nat. Arts Centre and Vancouver Opera) The Barber of Seville; (for Opera Hamilton) I due Foscari. *Publications:* plays: You Two Stay Here the Rest Come with Me, Slow Train to St Ives, Trip, The Sound of Distant Thunder, The Lost Letter (adaptation). *Leisure interest:* landscape architecture. *Address:* Shaw Festival, Box 774, Niagara-on-the-Lake, ON L0S 1J0 (office); 22 Prideaux Street, PO Box 609, Niagara-on-the-Lake, ON L0S 1J0, Canada (home). *Telephone:* (905) 468-2153 (office); (905) 468-4169 (home). *E-mail:* c_newton@ sympatico.ca (home). *Website:* www.shawfest.com (office).

NEWTON, John Oswald, MA, PhD, DSc, FAA; Australian/British nuclear physicist and academic; *Professor Emeritus and Visiting Fellow, Department of Nuclear Physics, Australian National University;* b. 12 Feb. 1924, Birmingham; s. of O. J. Newton and R. K. Newton; m. 2nd Silva Dusan Sablich 1964; two s. one d.; ed Bishop Vesey's Grammar School, Sutton Coldfield, St Catharine's Coll. Cambridge, Cavendish Lab., Cambridge; Jr Scientific Officer, Telecommunications Research Establishment, Great Malvern 1943–46; Harwell Fellow 1951–54; Prin. Scientific Officer, AERE Harwell 1954–59; Sr Lecturer, Univ. of Manchester 1959–67, Reader 1967–70; Prof. of Nuclear Physics, ANU 1970–89, Head of Dept of Nuclear Physics, Inst. of Advanced Studies 1970–88, Prof. Emer. and Visiting Fellow in Dept of Nuclear Physics 1990–; Visiting Physicist, Lawrence Berkeley Lab. (several times since 1956); Visiting Prof., Univ. of Manchester 1985–86; Centenary Medal 2003. *Publications:* more than 100 publns in nuclear physics and several book chapters. *Leisure interests:* painting, chess, music, walking, tennis. *Address:* Department of Nuclear Physics, IAS, Australian National University, Canberra, ACT 0200 (office); 8 Mackenzie Street, Hackett, ACT 2602, Australia (home). *Telephone:* (2) 6125-2074 (office). *Fax:* (2) 6125-0748 (office). *E-mail:* jon@ nuc.anu.edu.au (office). *Website:* wwwrsphysse.anu.edu.au/nuclear (office).

NEWTON, Thandiwe (Thandie) Melanie; British actress; b. 6 Nov. 1972, London, England; d. of Nick Newton and Nyasha Newton; m. Oliver Parker 1998; two d.; ed Downing Coll. Cambridge. *Films:* Flirting 1991, The Young Americans 1993, Bloody Weekend 1994, Interview with the Vampire: The Vampire Chronicles 1994, Loaded 1994, Jefferson in Paris 1995, The Journey of August King 1995, The Leading Man 1996, Gridlock'd 1997, Besieged 1998, Beloved 1998, Mission: Impossible II 2000, It Was an Accident 2000, The Truth About Charlie 2002, Shade 2003, The Chronicles of Riddick 2004, Crash (BAFTA Award for Best Actress in a Supporting Role 2006) 2005, The Interrogation of Leo and Lisa (short) 2006, The Pursuit of Happyness 2006, Norbit 2007, Run Fat Boy Run 2007, RocknRolla 2008, W. 2008, How to Lose Friends & Alienate People 2008, 2012 2009, Huge 2010, Vanishing on 7th Street 2010, For Colored Girls 2010, Retreat 2011, Good Deeds 2012, Half of a Yellow Sun 2013. *Television:* Pirate Prince (film) 1991, In Your Dreams (film) 1996, ER (series) 2003–09, American Dad! (series) 2006, Rogue (series) 2013–14. *Address:* c/o WME Entertainment, 9601 Wilshire Boulevard, Beverley Hills, CA 90210-5213, USA. *Telephone:* (310) 285-9000. *Fax:* (310) 285-9010. *Website:* www.wma.com.

NEWTON, Sir Wilfrid (see NEWTON, Sir (Charles) Wilfrid).

NEWTON-JOHN, Olivia, AO, OBE; British singer and actress; b. 26 Sept. 1948, Cambridge, England; d. of Brin Newton-John and Irene Born; m. Matt Lattanzi 1984; one d.; Co-owner Koala Blue 1982–; UNEP Goodwill Amb. 1989–; Grammy Awards, American Music Awards, Humanitarian Award, US Red Cross 1999, People's Choice Awards, Medal of the Order of Australia 2010 and numerous other awards. *Albums include:* If Not For You 1971, Let Me Be There 1974, Music Makes My Day 1974, Long Live Love 1974, If You Love Me Let Me Know (No. 1, USA) 1974, Have You Ever Never Been Mellow 1975, Clearly Love 1975, Come On Over 1976, Don't Stop Believin' 1976, Making A Good Thing Better 1977, Greatest Hits 1978, Grease (film soundtrack) 1978, Totally Hot 1979, Xanadu (film soundtrack) 1980, Physical 1981, 20 Greatest Hits 1982, Olivia's Greatest Hits Vol. 2 1983, Two Of A Kind 1984, Soul Kiss 1986, The Rumour 1988, Warm And Tender 1990, Back To Basics: The Essential Collection 1971–92 1992, Gaia – One Woman's Journey 1995, More Than Physical 1995, Greatest Hits 1996, Olivia 1998, Back With A Heart 1998, Highlights From The Main Event 1999, Greatest Hits: First Impressions 1999, Country Girl 1999, Best Of Olivia Newton John 1999, Love Songs: A Collection: One Woman's Live Journey 2000, Grace and Gratitude 2007, Christmas Collection 2010, Magic 2011, This Christmas 2012. *Films include:* Grease 1978, Xanadu 1980, Two of a Kind 1983, It's My Party 1995, Sordid Wives 1999, 1 a Minute (documentary) 2009, A Few Best Men 2012. *Television includes:* It's Cliff Richard (BBC series). *Publication:* LivWise: Easy Recipes for a Healthy, Happy Life 2011. *Leisure interests:* horse riding, songwriting, cycling, astrology, conservation, animals. *Address:* c/o Fitzgerald Hartley Co., 34 North Palm Avenue, Suite 100, Ventura, CA 93001, USA (office). *Website:* www.olivianewton-john.com.

NEYNSKY, Nadezhda; Bulgarian politician; b. (Nadezhda Mihaylova), 9 Aug. 1962, Sofia; ed Spanish Language High School, Sofia, St Kliment Ohridski Univ. of Sofia, John F. Kennedy School of Govt, Harvard Univ., USA; freelance journalist 1986–88; trans. of Spanish poetry and English literature 1988–90; Head of Foreign Relations, Dept of the Radical Democratic Party 1990–91; gained US Congress Foreign Policy and Public Relations Certificate through working in office of Rep. David Drier (Republican) 1991; Spokesperson and Chief of the Press Centre, Union for Democratic Forces during election campaign 1991; Spokesperson of centre-right cabinet and Chief of the Govt Press Centre 1991–93; took public relations course, BBC, London, UK 1993; Deputy Chair. Union of Democratic Forces 1994–97, Chair. 2002–05; Chair. Right Alternative Union 2006–; Vice-Pres. European People's Party (EPP), Co-Chair. EPP's Foreign Relations Cttee 1999–2006, Vice-Pres. SME Central, SME Union of the EPP 2007–; mem. Parl. (37th Nat. Ass.), mem. Foreign Policy Cttee, mem. Bulgarian Del. to the Council of Europe, Chair. Cttee for Parl. and Public Relations 1994–97, 38th Nat. Ass. 1997,

39th Nat. Ass., mem. Foreign Policy, Defence and Security Cttee 2001–05, Chair. Parl. Group of the United Democratic Forces 2002–05, 40th Nat. Ass., mem. Foreign Affairs Cttee, European Affairs Cttee 2005–09, Deputy Speaker, Nat. Ass. 2008–09; Minister of Foreign Affairs 1997–2001; mem. European Parl. (Group of the European People's Party (Christian Democrats) 2009–, mem. Cttee on Budgets, Del. to EU-Russia Parl. Co-operation Cttee, Del. for Relations with the NATO Parl. Ass., Substitute mem. Cttee on Foreign Affairs, Sub-cttee on Security and Defence, Del. for Relations with the Maghreb countries and the Arab Maghreb Union; Chair. Inst. for Democracy and Stability in South-East Europe 2004–; mem. Int. Advisory Cttee to the Democracy Coalition Project, in partnership with Bertelsmann Foundation, Freedom House and Ghana Centre for Democratic Devt 2006–, Advisory Group for Southern Leaders' Round Tables to the Special Unit for South–South Cooperation 2006–; Chair. Small and Medium Enterprises in Bulgaria 2007–; Order of the Kingdom of Denmark (First Class), Medal awarded by Repub. of Malta, Chevalier, Légion d'honneur, Cross of the Order for Public Service (Spain); Special Golden Distinction of US Acad. of Achievements, Badge of Honour, Venice, B'nai B'rith Medal of Tolerance. *Address:* European Parliament, Bâtiment Altiero Spinelli, 03F142, 60 rue Wiertz, 1047 Brussels, Belgium (office). *Telephone:* (2) 284-52-42 (office). *Fax:* (2) 284-92-42 (office). *E-mail:* nadezhda .neynsky@europarl.europa.eu (office). *Website:* www.europarl.europa.eu (office). www.nadezhdaneynsky.eu.

NEZVAL, Jiří; Czech automobile executive; b. 5 April 1941, Brno; s. of František Nezval and Květa Nezvalová; m. Silva Moltašová 1963; two d.; ed Railway Coll. Žilina and Polytechnic Inst. Brno; designer and design office man. in automation of rail transport, Prague; involved in Czechoslovak Scientific and Tech. Soc., Peace Movt; Fed. Minister of Transport 1990–92; mem. Civic Movt Party 1991–93, Free Democrats Party 1993– (merged with Liberal Nat. Social Party 1995); Dir Denzel Praha Co. 1992–; Chair. Union of Motor Car Importers 1995–; Exclusive Mitsubishi dealership in Czech Repub. 1997–. *Leisure interests:* computer art, man. systems, reading books, sports (skiing, cycling, volleyball). *Address:* Denzel Praha s.r.o., Revoluční 2, Prague 1, Czech Republic. *Telephone:* (2) 24810836 (office). *Fax:* (2) 22315926 (office).

NFUBEA, Ricardo Mangue Obama; Equatorial Guinean lawyer and politician; mem. Democratic Party of Equatorial Guinea (PDGE); fmr State Minister for Labour and Social Security; Minister of State in charge of the Civil Service and Admin. Co-ordination 2003; Deputy Prime Minister 2004–06, Prime Minister 2006–08 (resgnd). *Address:* c/o Office of the Prime Minister, Malabo, Equatorial Guinea.

NG, Andrew Y., MSc, PhD; American computer scientist; *Director, Stanford University Artificial Intelligence Laboratory;* b. 1976, UK; ed Carnegie Mellon Univ., Massachusetts Inst. of Tech., Univ. of California, Berkeley; Assoc. Prof., Dept of Computer Science and Dept of Electrical Eng, Stanford Univ. 2002–, Dir Stanford Artificial Intelligence Lab., led devt of Stanford main MOOC (Massive Open Online Courses) platform 2011; f. Google Brain project, Google, Inc. 2011; Co-founder Coursera (online educ. platform) 2012; Int. Jt Conf. on Artificial Intelligence Computers and Thought Award 2009. *Address:* Computer Science Department, Stanford University, Room 156, Gates Building, Stanford, CA 94305-9010, USA (office). *Telephone:* (650) 725-2593 (office). *Fax:* (650) 725-1449 (office). *E-mail:* ang@cs.stanford.edu (office). *Website:* cs.stanford.edu/people/ang (office).

NG, Eng Hen, MBBS, MCh, FRCSE; Singaporean physician and politician; *Minister of Defence;* b. 10 Dec. 1958, Singapore; m. Ivy Lim Swee Lian; two s. two d.; ed Nat. Junior Coll., Nat. Univ. of Singapore, M.D. Anderson Cancer Center, Houston, USA; Consultant Surgeon, Singapore Gen. Hosp. 1992–97; pvt. practice, Mount Elizabeth Hosp. 1997–2001; MP for Bishan-Toa Payoh Group Representation Constituency 2001–; Minister of State for Educ. and Manpower 2002–04, Minister of Manpower and Second Minister for Educ. 2004–07, Minister of Manpower 2005–07, Second Minister for Defence 2005–11, Minister of Educ. 2008–11, of Defence 2011–; mem. People's Action Party; Founder-mem. Breast Cancer Foundation, Singapore 1998; Fellow, Singapore Acad. of Medicine 1990, American Soc. of Surgical Oncology 1992, American Soc. of Clinical Oncology 1999. *Address:* Ministry of Defence, Gombak Drive, off Upper Bukit Timah Road, Mindef Bldg, Singapore 669645, Singapore (office). *Telephone:* 67608844 (office). *Fax:* 67646119 (office). *Website:* www.mindef.gov.sg (office).

NGANFUAN, Augustine Kpehe; Liberian economist and politician; *Minister of Foreign Affairs;* ed Univ. of Liberia, Simon Graduate School of Business, Univ. of Rochester, USA; Pres. Univ. of Liberia Student Union 1998–99; fmrly with Central Bank of Liberia; Prof. of Auditing and Accounting, Univ. of Liberia; Dir-Gen., Bureau of Budget, Ministry of Finance –2008, Minister of Finance 2008–12, of Foreign Affairs 2012–. *Address:* Ministry of Foreign Affairs, Mamba Point, POB 10-9002, 1000 Monrovia 10, Liberia (office). *Telephone:* 226763 (office). *Website:* www.mofa.gov.lr (office).

NGAUJAH, Sahr; American theatre director, actor and musician; b. 1978; m. Ayesha Ngaujah; ed Dasarts Theatre School, Amsterdam; early career in dance, music and acting with Freddie Hendricks Youth Ensemble of Atlanta, later also Asst Dir; fmr Theatre Dir and Developer, Lef Club, ACT Festival, Rotterdam; collaborator, Made n da Shade theatre co., Amsterdam; Art Dir, Bajah+The Dry Eye Crew (Sierra Leone hip-hop act). *Films include:* How I Spent My Summer Vacation 1997, A Lesson Before Dying (TV film) 1999, Big Ain't Bad 2002, The Signal 2007, Stomp the Yard 2007. *Plays:* The Eternal Curse on the Reader of These Pages (touring Rotterdam, Amsterdam and London), Conversations of Ice, title role in Fela! The Musical (Broadway) (Audelco Award 2008, Obie Award 2008) 2008–09, (Nat. Theatre, London) 2010–11. *Address:* c/o American Theatre Wing, 570 Seventh Avenue, Suite 501, New York, NY 10018, USA (office).

NGCOBO, S. Sandile, BProc, LLB, LLM; South African judge and academic; *Chief Justice of South Africa;* b. 1 March 1953, Durban; m. Zandile Ngcobo; two s. one d.; ed Univ. of Zululand, Univ. of Natal, Durban, Int. Law Inst. at Georgetown Law Center, Washington, DC and Harvard Law School, USA; in detention 1976–77; worked in Maphumulo magistrate's office 1977–78; articled clerk, then assoc. attorney, KK Mthiyane & Co. law firm, Durban 1978–82; attorney at law, Legal Resources Centre, Durban 1982–86; law clerk and research assoc. of the late Hon. A Leon Higginbotham Jr, fmr Chief Judge of US Court of Appeals for the Third Circuit, USA 1986–87; Visiting Foreign Attorney, Pepper, Hamilton &

Scheetz, Phila, Pa Aug.–Nov. 1987, Assoc. Attorney 1989–92; Acting Dir Legal Aid Services Clinic, Univ. of Natal, Durban 1988–92, also taught course on race legislation; practised as advocate in Durban 1988–89, 1992–94; lectured part-time in constitutional litigation 1994; Acting Judge of Supreme Court, Cape of Good Hope Prov. Div. April–Aug. 1996, Judge Sept. 1996–97; Acting Judge of Labour Appeal Court Jan.–Dec. 1997, apptd Judge of Court Nov. 1997; apptd Acting Judge Pres. of Labour Court and Labour Appeal Courts 1999; Judge in Constitutional Court of S Africa 1999–, Chief Justice of S Africa 2009–; Visiting Prof. of Law, Harvard Law School and Columbia Law School, USA; mem. Industrial Court of KwaZulu 1993; Co-ordinator Equal Opportunities Project, Centre for Socio-Legal Studies, Univ. of Natal, Durban 1993; a Presiding Officer of Ind. Election Comm.'s Electoral Tribunal 1994; apptd to serve on Amnesty Cttee of Truth and Reconciliation Comm. 1998; fmr mem. and Chair. Rules Bd for Courts of Law; Trustee Dehler Foundation; fmr Trustee Centre for Socio-Legal Studies; Hon. Prof. of Law, Univ. of Cape Town 1999; scholarship from Barclays Bank 1973–76, Fulbright Scholarship 1985, Human Rights Fellowship, Harvard Law School 1986. *Publications:* numerous papers on topics such as justice, the Truth and Reconciliation Comm., housing segregation and gender equality. *Address:* Constitutional Court, Private Bag X 1, 1 Hospital Street, Constitution Hill, Braamfontein 2017, South Africa (office). *Telephone:* (11) 359-7539 (office). *Fax:* (11) 339-7449 (office); 86-6490944 (mobile). *E-mail:* info@constitutionalcourt.org.za (office). *Website:* www.constitutionalcourt.org.za (office).

NGEMA, Mbongeni; South African writer, producer and composer; b. 1955, Hlabisa; m. Leleti Khumalo (divorced); mem. Gibson Kente's acting co., f. Cttee Artists; est. South African struggle theatre in London and New York stages 1981. *Plays include:* Woza Albert! (with Percy Mtwa and Barney Simon) 1981, Asinamali 1986, Sarafina! 1987, Township Fever 1989, Sarafina 2! 1996, The Zulu 2000, The House of Shaka 2006. *Recordings include:* Sarafina! 1990, Time to Unite 1990, Woza My Fohlaza 1998, AmaNdiya 2002, Best of Mbongeni Ngema 2002, Nikeziwe 2005, Lion of the East 2009. *Publications include:* Voices of Sarafina! Songs of Hope and Freedom 1988; contrib. to Woza Afrika!: A Collection of South African Plays 1986, Where is the Way: Song and Struggle in South Africa 1990.

NGENZEBUHORO, Frederic; Burundian politician; mem. Union pour le progrès nat. (Uprona, main Tutsi party); Minister of Information, then of Communication, then of Sports and Culture, then of Transport 1987–93; Deputy Pres. Nat. Ass. 1998–2004; Vice-Pres. of Burundi 2004–05. *Address:* c/o Union pour le progrès national, BP 1810, Bujumbura, Burundi (office).

NGHIMTINA, Erikki; Namibian politician; *Minister of Works and Transport;* fmr Man. Dir Prin. Bank for Devt and Agricultural Credit; Minister of Defence 1997–2005, of Works and Transport 2010–. *Address:* Ministry of Works and Transport, PMB 13341, Windhoek, Namibia (office). *Telephone:* (61) 2088111 (office). *Fax:* (61) 228560 (office).

NGO, Bao Chau, PhD (Habil.); Vietnamese/French mathematician and academic; *Francis and Rose Yuen Distinguished Service Professor, University of Chicago;* b. 28 June 1972, Hanoi; s. of Prof. Ngo Huy Can and Tran Luu Van Hien; m.; three c.; ed École Normale Supérieure, Université Paris-Sud, Université Paris-Nord; mem. CNRS, Paris 13 Univ. 1998–2005; Prof., Université Paris-Sud 11 2005– (currently on leave); works at Inst. for Advanced Study, Princeton, NJ, USA 2007–, Hanoi Inst. of Math. 2007–; Francis and Rose Yuen Distinguished Service Prof., Univ. of Chicago, USA 2010–; Scientific Dir Vietnam Inst. for Advanced Study 2011–; mem. Editorial Bd, Grundlehren der mathematischen Wissenschaften, Inventiones Mathematicae, Compositio Mathematica, Acta Mathematica Vietnamica, Vietnam Journal of Mathematics; Fellow, American Math. Soc. 2012; Chevalier, Légion d'honneur 2010; Dr hc (Vietnamese Nat. Univ.); Clay Research Award 2004, invited address at Int. Congress of Mathematicians, Madrid 2006, Prix Sophie Germain, Acad. des sciences 2007, Oberwolfach Prize 2007, invited plenary address at Int. Congress of Mathematicians, Hyderabad 2010, Fields Medal (co-recipient) 2010. *Publications:* numerous papers in professional journals on algebraic geometry, group theory and automorphic representations. *Address:* Department of Mathematics, Eckhart 303, 5734 University Avenue, Chicago, IL 60637-1514, USA (office). *Fax:* (773) 702-9787 (office). *E-mail:* ngo@math.uchicago .edu (office). *Website:* www.math.uchicago.edu (office).

NGOKWEY, Ndolamb, BA, MA, PhD; Democratic Republic of the Congo academic and UN official; *Deputy Special Representative of the Secretary-General, Resident Coordinator and Humanitarian Coordinator, United Nations Operation in Côte d'Ivoire (UNOCI);* b. 1952; m.; four c.; ed Univ. of Zaïre, Univ. of California, USA; Prof. of Anthropology and Public Health, Univ. of Lubumbashi 1984–86; joined UN 1986, has held several positions including UNICEF Asst Rep., Cape Verde 1986–89, UNICEF Programme Officer, Benin 1989–92, UNICEF Sr Programme Officer, Senegal 1992–95, UNICEF Area Rep. in Guinea 1995–98, in Barbados 1998–2000, Deputy Regional Dir UNICEF W and Cen. Africa Regional Office, Abidjan 2000–02, Dir Office of Sec. to UNICEF Exec. Bd 2002–06, UN Resident Co-ordinator and Devt Programme Resident Rep. in Mozambique 2006–10, Deputy Special Rep. of Sec.-Gen., UN Resident Co-ordinator and Humanitarian Co-ordinator, UN Operation in Côte d'Ivoire (UNOCI) 2010–. *Address:* United Nations Operation in Côte d'Ivoire (ONUCI), Hôtel Sebroko, Blvd de la Paix 08, BP 588, Abidjan 08, Côte d'Ivoire (office); Office of the Secretary-General, United Nations, New York, NY 10017, USA (office). *E-mail:* questions_onuci@un.org (office). *Website:* www.un.org/en/peacekeeping/missions/ unoci (office).

NGOMA, Angélique; Gabonese politician; b. 19 March 1964, Libreville; ed Institut Nat. des Sciences de Gestion, Libreville, Ecole Normale Nat. d'Apprentissage, Paris, France; Dir Coll. d'Enseignement technique commercial, Owendo 1991–93; Dir Ecole Nat. de Commerce, Port-Gentil 1993–94; mem. Parti démocratique gabonais (PDG), Leader, Union des femmes du PDG; mem. Assemblée Nationale (Parl.) for Nyanga constituency 1996–; Sr Commr, Ministry of Educ., Youth and Sport 1995–97, Sec. of State, Ministry of Social Affairs 1997–2000, Ministry of Health 1999, Minister of Family, Children's Welfare and Women's Advancement 1999–2007, of Health and Public Hygiene, also responsible for Family and Women's Advancement 2007–08, Minister of Social Affairs and the Fight against AIDS 2008–09, also Minister of Protection of Widows and Orphans –Oct. 2009, Minister of Nat. Defence 2009–11, of Labour, Employment and Social

Provision and Govt Spokesperson 2011–13. *Address:* c/o Office of the Prime Minister, BP 546, Libreville, Gabon.

NGOUBEYOU, François Xavier; Cameroonian politician; b. 1937; mem. Rassemblement Démocratique du Peuple Camerounais (RDPC); fmr Perm. Rep. to UN, Geneva; Minister of State in charge of External Relations 2001–04. *Address:* c/o Ministry of External Relations, Yaoundé, Cameroon (office).

NGOUPANDE, Jean-Paul; Central African Republic politician and fmr diplomatist; b. 6 Dec. 1948, Dekoa; m.; three s. three d.; Dean Faculty of Letters, Université de Bangui 1982–85; Minister of Educ. 1985–87; fmr Amb. to France and to Côte d'Ivoire; Prime Minister of Cen. African Repub. 1996–97; mem. Parl. 1998–; Leader Parti pour l'union nationale; Minister of Foreign and Francophone Affairs and Regional Integration 2006; Commdr, Meritorious Order of Cen. African Rep., Commdr, Ordre des Palmes académiques, Grand Officier, Ordre Nat. de Côte d'Ivoire. *Publications include:* Racines historiques et culturelles de la crise africaine 1994, Chronique de la crise centrafricaine 1997. *Leisure interests:* reading, music. *Address:* National Assembly of Central African Republic, Bangui (office); PO Box 179, Bangui, Central African Republic (home). *Telephone:* 61-82-96. *Fax:* 61-78-66 (home).

NGOWENUBUSA, Dieudonné; Burundian politician; b. 8 Sept. 1964, Ngagara; Minister of Finance 2005–06, of Devt Planning and Nat. Reconstruction 2007; Dir-Gen. Hôpital populaire de Mirango II; mem. Conseil nat. pour la défense de la democratie-Forces pour la défense de la democratie (CNDD-FDD). *Address:* c/o Ministry of Finance, BP 1830, Bujumbura, Burundi.

NGUBANE, Ben, MB, ChB; South African politician and doctor; *Minister of Arts, Culture, Science and Technology;* b. 22 Oct. 1941, Camperdown; m. Sheila Buthelezi; four c.; ed St Francis Coll., Marrianhill, Durban Medical School, Univ. of Witwatersrand, Natal Medical School; fmr Latin teacher; mem. Inkatha Freedom Party Cen. Cttee Exec. 1977–; mem. KwaZulu Legis. Ass. 1978–; led KwaZulu Govt del. to Constitutional negotiations; Minister of Health, KwaZulu Govt 1991–94, Premier 1997–99; Minister of Arts, Culture, Science and Tech. 1994–96, 1999–; mem. S African Red Cross Soc. 1977–, Regional Counsellor 1978–; mem. Council Univ. of Zululand; mem. Nat. Boxing Bd of Control 1991–. *Leisure interests:* tennis, reading, photography. *Address:* Ministry of Arts, Culture, Science and Technology, Oranje Nassau Building, 188 Schoeman Street, Pretoria 0002 (office); Empangeni, KwaZulu-Natal, South Africa (home). *Telephone:* (12) 3378378 (office); (12) 3242687. *E-mail:* frans@dacsts.pwv.gov.za (office). *Website:* www.dacst.gov.za (office); www.gov.za (home).

N'GUESSAN, Pascal Affi; Côte d'Ivoirian politician; b. 1953, Bouadikro; ed Lycée Moderne de Dimbokro, Lycée Technique d'Abidjan; Dir of Studies and Work Placements, École Nat. Supérieure des Postes et Télécommunications 1989–1993; Vice-Pres. Union des villes et commune de Côte d'Ivoire (UVICOCI) 1990–95; mem. nat. directorate, Front populaire ivoirien—FPI (Ivorian Popular Front) 1990–, Pres. 2001–11; Special Adviser to the Regional Dir, Ci-Télécom, Bouaké 1993–97; Head Dept of Resources and Standards, Côte d'Ivoire Télécom 1997–2000; Campaign Man. for Laurent Gbagbo in presidential elections 2000; Minister of Industry and Tourism 2000; Prime Minister of Côte d'Ivoire 2000–03; Minister for Planning and Devt 2000–03; arrested following capture of Laurent Gbagbo April 2011; Officier du mérite sportif 1995.

NGUYEN, Duc Doan; Vietnamese business executive; *Chairman, Hoang Anh Gia Lai Joint Stock Company;* b. 1962, Nhon My, An Nhon dist, Binh Dinh Prov.; began career as forest products developer, f. Hoang Anh 1993, renamed Hoang Anh Gia Lai Jt Stock Co. 2006, currently Chair. Hoang Anh Gia Lai Group, also Chair. Hoang Anh Gia Lai Football Club; also owns rubber plantations and tourist resorts. *Leisure interest:* football. *Address:* HAGL Joint Stock Company, 15 Truong Chinh Street, Phu Dong Ward, Pleiku City, Gia Lai Province, Viet Nam (office). *Telephone:* (592) 225888 (office); (592) 3820288 (office). *Fax:* (592) 222335 (office); (592) 2211726 (office). *E-mail:* contact@hagl.com.vn (office); hoa.pleiku@dng.vnn .vn (office). *Website:* www.hagl.com.vn (office).

NGUYEN, Dy Nien; Vietnamese politician; b. 9 Dec. 1935, Hoang Anh, Hoang Hoa, Thanh Hoa Prov.; m.; three d.; ed Banaras Hindu Univ., India; mem. Nat. Liberation Movt 1951; joined Ministry of Foreign Affairs 1954, postings to Consulate Gen. in New Delhi 1956–59, 1964–69, work in Asia and at Ministry of Foreign Affairs 1970–72, Chargé d'affaires a.i. in Canberra 1973–75, Asst Dir Ministry of Foreign Affairs 1976–79, Deputy Dir, then as Acting Dir of Asia 4 1980–81, Chief's Office, Dept of State 1982–83, Asst Minister of Foreign Affairs 1984–86, Deputy Minister of Foreign Affairs 1987–2000, Minister of Foreign Affairs 2000–06; Deputy, Nat. Ass. 2002–06; mem. Cen. Cttee, CP of Viet Nam 1991–; Pres. Viet Nam Nat. Comm. for UNESCO 1987, Nat. Cttee for Overseas Vietnamese 1995; mem. Council of Defence 2002–07 (retd); Medal of the American Struggle against the First Div., Labour Medal First Class; Coat 40-year Party. *Address:* c/o Ministry of Foreign Affairs, 1 Ton That Dam, Ba Dinh District, Hanoi, Viet Nam (office).

NGUYEN, Minh Triet, BS; Vietnamese politician and fmr head of state; b. 8 Oct. 1942, Ben Cat dist, Binh Duong Prov.; m. Tran Thi Kim Chi; ed Nguyen Ai Quoc Party School, Saigon Univ.; taught Math. in Saigon; active in Sai Gon Students' Movt 1960–63; mem. Cadre of Cen. Cttee of the People's Revolutionary Youth Union and Youth Mobilization of Party Cen. Cttee's Dept for S Vietnam, also Sec. Agency's Youth Union 1963–73, Deputy Dir Office of Youth Union and Deputy Chief Youth Union Cen. Cttee's Bd for Voluntary Young People 1974–79; apptd additional mem. Party Cttee of Song Be Prov., Perm. Deputy Sec. 1989–91; mem. Party Cen. Cttee 1991–; Deputy, Nat. Ass. 1991–2006; mem. Politburo 1997–; Dir Cen. Party Cttee's Comm. for Mass Mobilization 1997–2000; Sec. Ho Chi Minh City Party Cttee 1997–2000, Gen. Sec. 2000–06; Pres. of Viet Nam 2006–11. *Address:* c/o Dang Cong San Viet Nam (Communist Party of Viet Nam), 1 Hoang Van Thu, Hanoi, Viet Nam. *E-mail:* cpv@hn.vnn.vn. *Website:* www.cpv.org.vn.

NGUYEN, Phu Trong; Vietnamese politician; *General Secretary, Communist Party of Viet Nam;* b. 14 April 1944, Dong Hoi Commune, Dong Anh Dist, Hanoi; ed Vietnam Nat. Univ., Hanoi, USSR Acad. of Social Sciences, Ho Chi Minh Nat. Political Admin. Inst.; mem. Dang Cong San Viet Nam (CP of Viet Nam, fmrly Viet Nam Workers' Party) 1968–, mem. Cen. Cttee 1994–, mem. Political Bureau 1997–, Gen. Sec. 2011–; Sec. Hanoi CP Cttee 2000–06; Ed.-in-Chief Tap chi Cong

San (Communist Review) 1991–96; Deputy, Quoc Hoi (Nat. Ass.) 2002–, Chair. 2006–11. *Address:* Dang Cong San Viet Nam (Communist Party of Viet Nam), 1A Hung Vuong, Hanoi, Viet Nam (office). *E-mail:* dangcongsan@cpv.org.vn (office). *Website:* www.cpv.org.vn (office); nguyenphutrong.net.

NGUYEN, Quoc Cuong, BA, MA; Vietnamese government official and diplomatist; *Ambassador to USA;* m.; one s. one d.; ed Univ. of Foreign Affairs, Fletcher School of Law and Diplomacy, Tufts Univ., Maxwell School of Public Admin, Syracuse Univ., Vietnam Exec. Leadership Program, Kennedy School of Govt, Harvard Univ., USA; joined Ministry of Foreign Affairs 1981, worked as an officer at China Dept and as a researcher at Inst. of Int. Relations, Second Sec., Embassy in Beijing 1990–93, Minister Counsellor and Deputy Chief of Mission, Embassy in Ottawa 2002–05, Deputy Dir-Gen. Dept of Multilateral Econ. Co-operation 2005–07, Head of Political and Security Section of APEC Viet Nam 2006, Secr., Dir-Gen. and Exec. Asst to Deputy Prime Minister cum Minister of Foreign Affairs 2007–08; Asst Minister of Foreign Affairs 2008, Deputy Minister of Foreign Affairs in charge of relations of Viet Nam with European countries, and Press and Information Affairs, also Chief Negotiator with the Vatican 2008–11; Amb. to USA 2011–. *Address:* Embassy of Viet Nam, 1233 20th Street NW, Suite 400, Washington, DC 20036, USA (office). *Telephone:* (202) 861-0737 (office). *Fax:* (202) 861-0917 (office). *E-mail:* info@vietnamembassy.us (office). *Website:* www.vietnamembassy-usa.org (office).

NGUYEN, Sinh Hung, PhD; Vietnamese economist and politician; *Chairman, National Assembly;* b. 18 Jan. 1946, Nam Dan, Nghe An; previous posts include accountant in Finance Ministry, econ. researcher in Bulgaria, Deputy Dir then Dir Treasury, Vice-Minister of Finance, Minister of Finance –2006; Standing Deputy Prime Minister 2006–11; Chair. Nat. Ass. (Quoc Hoi) 2011–; mem. Cen. Standing Cttee Dang Cong San Viet Nam (CP of Viet Nam), also mem. Political Bureau (Politburo). *Address:* Office of the Chairman, National Assembly of Viet Nam, 35 Ngo Quyen Street, Hoan Kiem, Hanoi, Viet Nam (office). *E-mail:* webmaster@qh .gov.vn (office). *Website:* www.na.gov.vn (office).

NGUYEN, Tan Dung, LLB; Vietnamese politician and fmr central banker; *Prime Minister;* b. 17 Nov. 1949, Ca Mau City, Ca Mau Prov.; m.; one s. one d.; served in Viet Nam People's Army 1961–81; mem. CP of Viet Nam 1968–, mem. Police Party Cttee 1995–96, mem. Politburo 1997–; Deputy, 10th, 11th, 12th and 13th Nat. Ass.; Deputy Minister of Public Security 1995–96; First Deputy Prime Minister of Viet Nam 1997–2006; Gov. State Bank of Viet Nam and Sec. State Bank of Viet Nam's Party Cttee 1998–99; Prime Minister 2006–; currently also Vice-Pres. Nat. Defence and Security Council. *Address:* Office of the Prime Minister, Hanoi, Viet Nam (office). *Website:* www.chinhphu.vn (office).

NGUYEN, Thi Doan, PhD; Vietnamese economist, academic and politician; *Vice-President;* b. 11 Jan. 1951, Ha Nam Prov.; ed Univ. of Commerce, Hanoi, Sofia Econ. Univ., Bulgaria; admitted to CP of Viet Nam 1981; mem. Nat. Ass. representing Ha Nam Prov.; mem. 10th Cen. Cttee, CP of Viet Nam 2006; fmr Deputy Sec., Party Cttee of Block-I Cen. Agencies; mem. Party Cen. Cttee's Comm. for Inspection 1998, Deputy Perm. Head –2007; Vice-Pres. of Viet Nam 2007–. *Address:* Dang Cong San Viet Nam (Communist Party of Viet Nam), 381 Doi Can Street, Ba Dinh District, Hanoi, Viet Nam (office). *Telephone:* (80) 48161 (office). *Fax:* (80) 44175 (office). *E-mail:* dangcongsan@cpv.org.vn (office). *Website:* www .cpv.org.vn (office).

NGUYEN, Van Binh; Vietnamese economist and central banker; *Governor, State Bank of Viet Nam;* b. 4 March 1961; ed Cen. Inst. for Math. Econs, USSR Acad. of Sciences; joined Foreign Econ. Relations Dept, State Bank of Viet Nam 1986, becoming Deputy Head of Int. Financial Insts Dept, Deputy Head of Int. Project Man. and Int. Co-operation Dept 1996, Chief Insp., Deputy Gov. 2008–11, Gov. 2011–; Vice-Pres. and Acting Chair. Int. Investment Bank, Moscow 2001–05; mem. Exec. Cttee CP of Viet Nam. *Address:* Office of the Governor, State Bank of Viet Nam, 49 Ly Thai To, Hanoi, Viet Nam (office). *Telephone:* (4) 39343327 (office). *Fax:* (4) 39349569 (office). *E-mail:* webmaster@sbv.gov.vn (office). *Website:* www .sbv.gov.vn (office).

NGUYEN, Van Giau, DEcon; Vietnamese fmr central banker and politician; b. 8 Dec. 1957, An Giang Prov.; Dir An Giang Br. of Viet Nam Bank for Agriculture and Rural Development (Agribank) 1988–90, Deputy Gen. Dir Agribank 1991–96, Gen. Dir 1996–97; Deputy Gov. State Bank of Viet Nam 1998–2003, Gov. 2007–11; mem. Party Cen. Cttee, Deputy Party Sec., Ninh Thuan Prov. 2003–05, Party Sec. 2005–07. *Address:* c/o State Bank of Viet Nam, 49 Ly Thai To Street, Hoankiem District, Hanoi, Viet Nam (office).

NGUYEN, Van Tho; Vietnamese diplomatist; *Ambassador to People's Republic of China;* fmr Pres. Dept for External Relations, Ministry of Foreign Affairs, Deputy Minister of Foreign Affairs –2008, Amb. to People's Repub. of China 2008–; Chair. ASEAN Cttee, Beijing 2010. *Address:* Embassy of Viet Nam, 32 Guang Hua Lu, Jian Guo Men Wai, Beijing 100600, People's Republic of China (office). *Telephone:* (10) 65321155 (office). *Fax:* (10) 65325720 (office). *E-mail:* suquanbk@yahoo.com (office). *Website:* www.vnemba.org.cn (office).

NGWENYA, Sindiso, BSc, MSc; Zimbabwean international organization official; *Secretary General, Common Market for Eastern and Southern Africa (COMESA);* b. 16 April 1951; m.; three c.; ed Middlesex Polytechnic, Univ. of Birmingham, UK; Corp. Planning Officer, Ethiopia Airlines 1979–80; Planning Officer, Nat. Railways of Zimbabwe 1980–83; Sr Transport Expert, Common Market for Eastern and Southern Africa (COMESA) 1994–98, Asst Sec. Gen., in charge of Programming 1998–2008, Sec. Gen. 2008–; mem. Interim Cttee Food, Agric. and Natural Resources Policy Analysis Network 2007. *Address:* COMESA Secretariat, PO Box 30051, Ben Bella Road, 101101 Lusaka, Zambia (office). *Telephone:* (211) 229725 (office). *Fax:* (211) 225107 (office). *E-mail:* webmaster@comesa.int (office). *Website:* www.comesa.int (office).

NHASSÉ, Alamara; Guinea-Bissau politician; b. 1957; Pres. Partido para a Renovação Social (PRS); Minister of Internal Admin. 2001; Prime Minister of Guinea-Bissau 2001–02. *Address:* c/o Office of the Prime Minister, Avda Unidade Africana, CP 137 Bissau, Guinea-Bissau.

NHIEK, Bun Chhay; Cambodian politician; *Deputy Prime Minister;* b. 7 Feb. 1956; Second Vice-Pres. of the Senate 1999–2004; Acting Head of State July 2004;

Deputy Prime Minister 2004–; Minister of Defence 2004–06; Sec.-Gen. United Nat. Front for an Ind., Neutral, Peaceful and Co-operative Cambodia Party (Funcinpec) 2006–. *Address:* Funcinpec, 11 boulevard Monivong (93), Sangkat Sras Chak, Khan Daun Penh, BP 1444, Phnom-Penh, Cambodia (office). *Telephone:* (23) 428864 (office). *Fax:* (23) 218547 (office). *E-mail:* funcinpec@funcinpec.org (office). *Website:* www.funcinpec.org (office).

NI, Runfeng; Chinese business executive; b. 1944, Rongcheng, Shandong Prov.; ed Dalian Eng Coll.; Dir, later Gen. Man., later Chair. Changhong Machinery Factory, Sichuan Prov. 1985, Gen. Man. Changhong Electronics Corpn 1995–2000, Chair. 1996–2004; mem. CCP; Del., 14th CCP Nat. Congress 1992–97; Deputy, 8th NPC 1993–98; Alt. mem. 15th CCP Cen. Cttee 1997–2002; named Prof.-grade Sr Engineer, named Most Outstanding Man. by All-China Fed. of Trade Unions 1990, Nat. Wuyi Labour Medal 1990, Awarded Special Governmental Subsidy 1991, named amongst Ten Most Outstanding Persons of Sichuan 1993, named amongst Fifth Nat. Most Outstanding Entrepreneurs 1994, Nat. Model Worker, State Council 1995, chosen as one of 1995 Ten Men of the Moment in Chinese Business Circles 1996, Nikkei Asian Prize 1998, named amongst Ten Most Outstanding Operators of Industrial Enterprises of People's Repub. of China 1998, honoured as Man. Guru by Int. Statistics Conf. 1998, named amongst Ten Most Outstanding Entrepreneurs 1998, Most Outstanding Entrepreneurs of Sichuan Prov. 1998, Award for Achievement of Asian Entrepreneurs 1998. *Address:* c/o Changhong Electronics Corporation, Chengdu, Sichuan Province, People's Republic of China.

NÍ DHOMHNAILL, Nuala, BA; Irish poet and academic; b. 16 Feb. 1952, St Helens, Lancs., England; d. of Séamus Ó Domhnaill and Eibhlín Ní Fhiannachta; m. Dogan Leflef 1973; one s. three d.; ed Laurel Hill Convent, Limerick and Univ. Coll., Cork; travel overseas 1973–80; Writer-in-Residence, Univ. Coll., Cork 1992–93; Visiting Prof., New York Univ. 1998, Villanova Univ. 2001; Ireland Prof. of Poetry 2002–04; mem. Aosdána, Irish Writers' Union, Poetry Ireland; Oireachtas Poetry Awards, 1982, 1989, 1990, 1998; Irish Arts Council Awards, 1985, 1988; Irish American O'Shaughnessy Award 1988, Ireland Fund Literary Prize 1991. *Publications include:* An Dealg Droighinn 1981, Fear Suaithinseach 1984, Raven Introductions (with others) 1984, Selected Poems/Rogha Danta 1986, Pharoah's Daughter 1990, Feis 1991, The Astrakhan Cloak 1992, Jumping off Shadows: Selected Contemporary Irish Poets (co-ed) 1995, Cead Aighnis 1998, In the Heart of Europe: Poems for Bosnia 1998, The Water Horse 1999, The Fifty Minute Mermaid: Poems in Irish 2007; contribs to many anthologies and magazines. *Leisure interests:* swimming, mountain walks, reading. *Website:* www.nualanidhomhnaill.com.

NIANG, Madické, LLM; Senegalese lawyer and politician; b. 1953; ed Univ. of Abidjan, Côte d'Ivoire; legal practice, chambers of Bassine Niang 1982–85; Adviser to Pres. Abdoulaye Wade 2000; Minister of Housing 2002–03, of Energy and Mines 2003–07, of Mines, Industry and Energy Feb.–Mar 2007, of Mines and Industry 2007–08, Minister of Justice and Keeper of the Seals 2008–09, Minister of Foreign Affairs 2009–12; mem. Bd Caisse des Règlements Pécuniaires des Avocats (legal deposit fund) 1991–, Sec. 1995–; mem. Bd Ordre des Avocats du Sénégal 1992–; mem. World Jurist Asscn. *Publications:* Pour qui triomphe la vérité: l'assassinat de Maître Babacar Seye 2002, Sénégal, affaire maître Sèye: les pièges de l'acharnement 2006. *Address:* c/o Ministry of Foreign Affairs, pl. de l'Indépendance, BP 4044, Dakar, Senegal (office).

NIANG, Souleymane, PhD; Senegalese mathematician, academic and university administrator; *President, Académie des Sciences et Techniques du Sénégal;* b. Dec. 1929, Matam; ed Univ. of Toulouse; teacher, Lycée Fermat, Toulouse, William Ponty Teachers' School, Dakar 1956–60; Lecturer, Faculty of Sciences, Univ. of Dakar 1960, Sr Lecturer 1964, Prof. 1969–; Dir Research Inst. on the Teaching of Math., Physics and Tech. 1970; Rector and Pres. Univ. Cheikh Anta Diop 1986, currently Prof., Dept of Math.; Pres. Acad. des Sciences et Techniques du Sénégal; fmr Pres. Scientific Section, UNESCO Nat. Comm., Nat. Cttee of Int. Comm. for Teaching Math.; Pres. Math. and Physics Section, Africa and Mauritius Advisory Cttee on Higher Educ.; mem. Office of African Comm. for Teaching Math., Scientific Council, OAU; Officer, Ordre nat. du Lion, Ordre nat. du Mérite; Chevalier, Ordre des Palmes académiques sénégalaises; Commdr, Ordre des Palmes académiques; Zoa D. Shilling Award, Western Mich. Univ. 2002. *Address:* Académie des Sciences et Techniques du Sénégal, 61, Avenue Djily Mbaye, BP 4344, RP Dakar (office); Université Cheikh Anta Diop, BP 5005, Dakar-Fann, Senegal. *Telephone:* 849-10-99 (office). *Fax:* 849-10-96 (office). *E-mail:* Academ.sc@ sentoo.sn (office). *Website:* www.ucad.sn (office).

NIASSE, Cheikh Moustapha; Senegalese politician, UN official and company director; b. 4 Nov. 1939, Keur Madiabel; ed Lycée Faidherbe, St Louis, Univs of Dakar and Paris, Nat. School of Admin, Dakar; Dir for Information and Press Affairs, Ministry of Information 1968–69; Dir de Cabinet at Presidency 1970–78; Minister of Town Planning, Housing and Environment March–Sept. 1978, of Foreign Affairs 1978–84; Minister of Foreign Affairs of the Confed. of Senegambia 1982–84; fmr Minister of State, Minister of Foreign Affairs and Senegalese Abroad; presidential cand. 2000, 2007, 2012; Prime Minister of Senegal 2000–01; UN Special Envoy to Peace Process of the Democratic Repub. of the Congo 2002; Political Sec. Union Progressiste Sénégalaise until 1984; Founder and Sec.-Gen. Alliance des forces de progrès 1999–; mem. bd of dirs several pvt.-sector cos worldwide. *Address:* Alliance des forces de progrès, rue 1, angle rue A, point E, BP 5825, Dakar, Senegal (office). *E-mail:* admin@afp-senegal.org (office); afp.net@yahoo.fr (office). *Website:* www.afp-senegal.org (office).

NIBBERING, Nicolaas Martinus Maria, PhD; Dutch scientist and academic; *Professor Emeritus of Chemical Mass Spectrometry, University of Amsterdam;* b. 29 May 1938, Zaandam; s. of Dirk Nibbering and Hendrika Clijnk; m. Christina A. de Waart 1964; three s. one d.; ed Gymnasium B Zaanlands Lyceum Zaandam and Univ. of Amsterdam; mem. Faculty, Univ. of Amsterdam 1967–75, Assoc. Prof. 1975–80, Prof. of Organic Mass Spectrometry 1980–88, Prof. of Chemical Mass Spectrometry 1988–2000, Prof. Emer. 2000–, Scientific Dir Inst. of Mass Spectrometry 1988–2000; Visiting Faculty mem. Cornell Univ. 1974; Guest Prof., Univ. of Colorado 1980, Univ. of Rome 'La Sapienza' 2002; Chair. 12th Int. Mass Spectrometry Conf., Amsterdam 1991; Chair. European Soc. for Mass Spectrometry 1993–97, Pres. 1997–2000; Treas. Int. Mass Spectrometry Soc. 1997–2000, Pres. 2000–03; Co-Ed. Scientific Journal of Mass Spectrometry Reviews

1991–2000; Ed. Scientific Journal of Mass Spectrometry 1995–2000; mem. Royal Netherlands Acad., New York Acad. of Sciences; Hon. mem. Netherlands Soc. for Mass Spectrometry 1999; Hon. Life mem. British Mass Spectrometry Soc. 1999, Indian Soc. for Mass Spectrometry 2000, Mass Spectrometry Soc. of Japan 2003; Unilever Chem. Prize 1964, Shell Research Chem. Prize 1968, J.J. Thomson Award 1991, Joannes Marcus Marci Award 1992. *Publications include:* Encyclopedia of Mass Spectrometry Vol. 4 (ed.) 2004; articles in books and journals. *Leisure interests:* motorbike races, classical music, opera, musicals, travelling, history. *Address:* LaserLab Amsterdam and Physics Department, Vrije Universiteit, De Boelelaan 1081, 1081 HV Amsterdam (office); Janshof 39, 1391 XK Abcoude, The Netherlands (home). *Telephone:* (20) 5987646 (office); (294) 283211 (home). *Fax:* (20) 5987643 (office); (294) 283211 (home). *E-mail:* nibberin@chem.vu .nl (office); n.m.m.nibbering@vu.nl (office).

NIBLETT, Robin, BA, MPhil, DPhil; British political scientist and academic; *Director, Chatham House;* b. 1962; ed Univ. of Oxford; Research Assoc., Political-Mil. Studies Program, Center for Strategic and Int. Studies (CSIS) 1988–92, European Rep. 1992–97, Dir Strategic Planning 1997–2001, Exec. Vice-Pres. 2001–07, Dir Europe Program 2004–07; Politics Lecturer, Univ. of Oxford 1995–98; Dir Chatham House 2007–. *Publications include:* Rethinking European Order (co-ed.) 2001, Ready to Lead? Rethinking America's Role in a Changed World, Chatham House 2009, America and a Changed World: A Question of Leadership (ed.) 2010, The Chatham House-YouGov Survey 2011: British Attitudes Towards the UK's International Priorities 2011, Hard Choices Ahead: The Chatham House-YouGov Survey 2012; contribs to International Affairs, The Washington Quarterly, The World Today, Strategic Europe: A Carnegie Europe Series, Royal Elcano Institute. *Address:* Office of the Director, Chatham House, 10 St James's Square, London, SW1Y 4LE, England (office). *Telephone:* (20) 7314-2798 (office). *Fax:* (20) 7957-5710 (office). *E-mail:* kburnet@chathamhouse.org.uk (office). *Website:* www.chathamhouse.org.uk (office).

NIBLOCK, Robert A., BA; American accountant and business executive; *Chairman, President and CEO, Lowe's Companies, Inc.;* b. 1963, Fla; m. Melanie Niblock; two c.; ed Univ. of North Carolina-Charlotte; certified public accountant; began career with Ernst & Young 1984–93; joined Lowe's Companies Inc. as Dir of Taxation 1993, Vice-Pres. and Treas. 1997–99, Sr Vice-Pres. 1999–2000, Sr Vice-Pres. and Chief Financial Officer 2000–01, Exec. Vice-Pres. and Chief Financial Officer 2001–03, Pres. 2003–06, mem. Bd of Dirs 2004–, Chair. and CEO 2005–11, Chair., Pres. and CEO 2011–; mem. Bd of Dirs Retail Industry Leaders Asscn 2003– (Vice-Chair. 2006–07, Chair. 2008–09), ConocoPhillips 2010– (mem. Audit and Finance Cttee). *Address:* Lowe's Companies, Inc., 1000 Lowe's Boulevard, Mooresville, NC 28117, USA (office). *Telephone:* (704) 758-1000 (office). *Fax:* (336) 658-4766 (office). *E-mail:* info@lowes.com (office). *Website:* www.lowes.com (office).

NICA, Dan, PhD; Romanian telecommunications engineer and politician; *Minister of Communications and the Information Society;* b. 2 July 1960, Panciu, Vrancea Co.; m.; one c.; ed Faculty of Electronics and Telecommunications, Iasi, specializations in man. and communications in France, Sweden, Austria and Canada; various positions at Galati Co. Telecommunications Directorate 1985–96, Dir Galati Co. Telecommunications Directorate 1991–96; Assoc. Prof., Univ. 'Lower Danube' for Telecommunications and Data Transmission 1993–96; mem. Partidul Social Democrat (PSD—Social Democratic Party) Cen. Exec. Bureau 1999–2004, Pres. Galati Municipal PSD Org. 1997–2003, First Vice-Pres. PSD Galati Co. Org. 1999–2003, Pres. 2003–, mem. PSD Co-ordinating Bureau 2004–05, Vice-Pres. PSD and Pres. Dept of Transportation and Communications 21 April 2005, Vice-Pres. PSD and Co-ordinator Dept of Transport and Communications 2006–; mem. Chamber of Deputies (PSD) for Galati Electoral Ward 1996–, mem. Parl. Comm. for Industries and Services, mem. Parl. Groups of Friendship with Egypt, Syria and Sweden, mem. Parl. Comm. for Public Admin, Territory Man. and Ecological Balance 2000–04, Vice-Pres. Comm. for Communication and Information Tech. 2004–08; Minister of Communication and Information Tech. 2000–04; Deputy Prime Minister and Minister of the Interior and Admin. Reform 2008–09; Pres. Romania-Bavaria Governmental Comm. 2001–04; Minister of Communications and the Information Soc. 2012–; mem. UN Information and Communication Technologies Task Force 2002–04, Nat. Council for Science and Tech. Policy; Kt, Steaua României Nat. Order (Order of the Star of Romania) 2002; Prize for Excellence for the promotion of Romanian IT industry abroad, CHIP Review 2002, Prize for Excellence for the promotion and development of e-governance and transparency, ARIES 2003, 'Ion Irimescu – 100' Homage Medal, Ministry of Culture and Denominations 2004, Personalitatea anului (Personality of the Year) Prize, eFinance Review 2004. *Publications include:* Government, Citizen, IT Society 2001, Le Gouvernement électronique (Concepts Appliqués en Roumanie) (Tudor Tanasescu Prize, Romanian Acad. 2007) 2005. *Address:* Ministry of Communications and the Information Society, 050706 Bucharest 5, Bd. Libertăţii 14 (office); Partidul Social Democrat, 011346 Bucharest 1, Şos. Kiseleff 10, Romania (office). *Telephone:* (21) 4001190 (Ministry of Communications and the Information Society) (office); (21) 4135155 (Partidul Social Democrat). *Fax:* (21) 3114131 (Ministry of Communications and the Information Society) (office). *E-mail:* office@mcsi.ro (office); psd@psd.ro (office). *Website:* www.mcsi.ro (office); www.psd.ro (office).

NICHOLAS, Sir David, Kt, CBE; British television executive and editor; b. 25 Jan. 1930, Tregaron; m. Juliet Davies 1952; one s. one d.; ed Neath Grammar School, Univ. Coll. of Wales, Aberystwyth; Nat. Service 1951–53; journalist with Yorkshire Post, Daily Telegraph, Observer; joined ITN (Ind. TV News) 1960, Deputy Ed., Ed. 1963–77, Ed. and CEO 1977–89, Chair. 1989–91; Dir (non-exec.) Channel 4 TV 1992–97; Chair. Sports News TV 1996–2003; Visiting Ed. 10 US Schools of Journalism 1992–99; Hon. LLD (Univ. Coll. of Wales, Aberystwyth); Hon. DHumLitt (Univ. of Southern Illinois). *Leisure interests:* walking, sailing, golf. *Address:* Lodge Stables, 2F Kidbrooke Park Road, London, SE3 0LW, England (home). *Telephone:* (20) 8319-2823 (home). *E-mail:* dnicholas1@btinternet.com (home).

NICHOLAS, Nicholas John, Jr, AB, MBA; American communications industry executive; b. 3 Sept. 1939, Portsmouth, NH; s. of Nicholas John Nicholas; brother of Peter M. Nicholas (q.v.); m. Llewellyn Jones 1972; two s. three d.; ed Phillips Acad., Andover, Mass, Princeton Univ and Harvard Business School; Dir of Financial Analysis, Time Inc., New York 1964–69, Asst to Pres. 1970, Asst Treas.

1971–73, Vice-Pres. 1975–86, Pres. and COO 1986–90, Co-CEO Time Warner Inc. 1990–92; Pres. Manhattan Cable TV 1973–76; Pres. Home Box Office, New York 1976–80, Chair. 1979–82; mem. Bd of Dirs Xerox Corpn 1987–, Bankers Trust 1989–, Boston Scientific Corpn 1994–, Priceline 1998–2003, Time Warner Cable Inc.; Advisor, Accelergy 2006; fmr Dir Turner Broadcasting; mem. Council on Foreign Relations; fmr mem. Pres.'s Advisory Cttee for Trade Policy and Negotiations, Pres.'s Comm. on Environmental Quality; mem. Advisory Bd, Upromise, Inc., Grad. School of Journalism, Columbia Univ; mem. Council on Foreign Relations; Trustee, Environmental Defense Fund. *Address:* c/o Board of Directors, Boston Scientific, Corporate Headquarters, One Boston Scientific Place, Natick, MA 01760-1537, USA. *E-mail:* info@bostonscientific.com.

NICHOLAS, Peter M., MSc; American medical device industry executive; *Chairman, Boston Scientific Corporation;* s. of Nicholas John Nicholas; brother of Nicholas John Nicholas, Jr; m.; three c.; ed Duke Univ., Univ. of Pennsylvania Wharton School; Founder, Chair. and CEO Boston Scientific 1979–99, Chair. 1999–; fmr Chair. Bd of Trustees, Duke Univ.; Fellow, American Acad. of Arts and Sciences (Vice-Chair. Academy Trust); mem. American Acad. of Achievement; Founder Nicholas School of the Environment, Duke Univ.; Phoenix Lifetime Achievement Award, Ellis Island Medal of Honor. *Address:* Boston Scientific Corporation, 1 Boston Scientific Place, Natick, MA 01760-1537, USA (office). *Telephone:* (508) 650-8000 (office). *Fax:* (508) 647-2393 (office). *Website:* www .bostonscientific.com (office).

NICHOLLS OF BIRKENHEAD, Baron (Life Peer), cr. 1994, of Stoke D'Abernon in the County of Surrey; **Donald James Nicholls,** PC, MA, LLB; British judge; b. 25 Jan. 1933, Bebington, Cheshire; s. of the late William Greenhow Nicholls and of Eleanor J. Nicholls; m. Jennifer Mary Thomas 1960; two s. one d.; ed Birkenhead School, Univ. of Liverpool and Trinity Hall, Cambridge; Nat. service 1951–53 (2nd Lt, Royal Army Pay Corps); called to Bar, Middle Temple 1958; in practice at Chancery Bar, London 1958–83; QC 1974; Judge, High Court of Justice, Chancery Div. 1983–86; Lord Justice of Appeal 1986–91; Vice-Chancellor, Supreme Court 1991–94; a Lord of Appeal in Ordinary 1994–2007, Second Sr Lord of Appeal 2002–07; Chair. Lord Chancellor's Advisory Cttee on Legal Educ. and Conduct 1996–97, Jt Cttee on Parl. Privilege 1997–99; a non-perm. Judge, Hong Kong Court of Final Appeal 1998–2004; Hon. Fellow, Trinity Hall, Cambridge 1986; Treas. Middle Temple 1997; Hon. LLD (Liverpool) 1987. *Leisure interests:* history, music, walking. *Address:* House of Lords, Westminster, London, SW1A 0PW, England (office).

NICHOLS, Mike; American director and producer; b. (Michael Igor Peschowsky) 6 Nov. 1931, Berlin, Germany; s. of Paul Nikolaievich Peschowsky and Brigitte Landauer; m. 1st Patricia Scot 1957 (divorced); m. 2nd Margot Callas 1974 (divorced); one d.; m. 3rd Annabel Nichols (divorced); m. 4th Diane Sawyer 1988; ed pvt. schools and Univ. of Chicago; started Playwrights Theatre Club, Chicago which became the Compass Players and later Second City; formed improvised nightclub double-act with Elaine May, touring for two years and recording TV programmes and record albums; appeared in An Evening with Mike Nichols and Elaine May, New York 1961–62; acted in Shaw's St Joan and directed The Importance of Being Earnest, Vancouver; Antoinette Perry (Tony) Awards for Direction: Barefoot in the Park, Luv, The Odd Couple, Plaza Suite, The Real Thing, Death of a Salesman 2012; Acad. Award for The Graduate; Emmy Award for TV programme Julie and Carol at Carnegie Hall; Nat Asscn Theatre Owners' Achievement Award for Direction for Who's Afraid of Virginia Woolf?. *Plays:* Streamers 1976, Comedians 1976, The Gin Game 1978, Lunch Hour 1980, The Real Thing 1984, Hurlyburly 1984, Waiting for Godot 1988, Death and the Maiden 1992, Blue Murder 1995, The Seagull 2001, Spamalot (Tony Awards for Best Musical, Best Dir) 2005; Producer: Annie (New York) 1977. *Shows:* Barefoot in the Park, New York 1963, The Knack 1964, Luv 1964, The Odd Couple 1965, The Apple Tree 1966, The Little Foxes 1967, Plaza Suite 1968. *Films:* Who's Afraid of Virginia Woolf? 1966, The Graduate 1967, Catch-22 1969, Carnal Knowledge 1971, Day of the Dolphin 1973, The Fortune 1975, Gilda Live 1980, Silkwood 1983, Heartburn 1985, Biloxi Blues 1987, Working Girl 1988, Postcards From the Edge 1990, Regarding Henry (also producer) 1991, Wolf 1994 (co-producer), Mike Nichols 1995, The Birdcage (co-producer), Primary Colors 1998, What Planet Are You From? (also producer) 2000, Closer (also producer) 2004, Charlie Wilson's War 2007. *Television:* Wit (dir, producer and writer) 2001, Angels in America (dir and producer) 2003. *Leisure interest:* Arabian horse breeding. *Address:* c/o Creative Artists Agency, 2000 Avenue of the Stars, Los Angeles, CA 90067, USA (office). *Telephone:* (424) 288-2000 (office). *Fax:* (424) 288-2900 (office). *Website:* www.caa .com (office).

NICHOLS, Peter Richard, FRSL; British playwright; b. 31 July 1927, Bristol, England; s. of Richard G. Nichols and Violet A. Poole; m. Thelma Reed 1960; one s. two d. (and one d. deceased); ed Bristol Grammar School, Bristol Old Vic School and Trent Park Training Coll.; actor, mostly in repertory 1950–55; schoolteacher 1958–60; mem. Arts Council Drama Panel 1973–75; Playwright-in-Residence, Guthrie Theatre, Minneapolis; Visiting Writer, Nanyang Coll., Singapore 1994; directed revivals of Joe Egg and Forget-Me-Not Lane (Greenwich), National Health (Guthrie, Minneapolis) and first productions of Born in the Gardens (Bristol), A Piece of My Mind (Southampton), Blue Murder (Bristol), Nicholodeon (Bristol); Tony Award, New York 1985, several SWET and four Evening Standard Drama Awards, Ivor Novello Award for Best Musical 1977. *Plays:* A Day in the Death of Joe Egg 1967, The National Health 1969, Forget-Me-Not Lane 1971, Chez Nous 1973, The Freeway 1974, Privates on Parade 1977, Born in the Gardens 1979, Passion Play 1980, Poppy (musical) 1982, A Piece of My Mind 1986, Blue Murder 1995, So Long Life 2000, Nicholodeon 2000, Lingua Franca 2010. *Films:* Catch Us If You Can 1965, Georgy Girl 1967, Joe Egg 1971, The National Health 1973, Privates on Parade 1983. *Radio:* Something In The Air, Jam Yesterday. *Television:* plays include Walk on the Grass 1959, Promenade 1960, Ben Spray 1961, The Reception 1961, The Big Boys 1961, Continuity Man 1963, Ben Again 1963, The Heart of the Country 1963, The Hooded Terror 1963, When the Wind Blows 1964, The Brick Umbrella 1968, Daddy Kiss It Better 1968, The Gorge 1968, Hearts and Flowers 1971, The Common 1973, Greeks Bearing Gifts (Inspector Morse series) 1991. *Publications:* Feeling You're Behind (memoirs) 1984, Nichols: Plays One and Two 1991, Diary 1969–71, Diary Selection 2000; all listed plays published separately; archive now available in Manuscripts Dept, British Library.

Leisure interests: listening to jazz, looking at cities. *Address:* c/o Alan Brodie Representation, Fairgate House, 6th Floor, 78 New Oxford Street, London, WC1A 1HB, England (office). *Telephone:* (20) 7253-6226 (office). *E-mail:* abr@alanbrodie .com (office).

NICHOLS, HE Cardinal Vincent Gerard, STL, PhL, MA; British ecclesiastic; *Archbishop of Westminster;* b. 8 Nov. 1945, Crosby, Merseyside; s. of Henry Joseph Nichols and Mary Russell; ed St Mary's Coll., Crosby, Gregorian Univ., Rome, Manchester Univ. and Loyola Univ., Chicago; Chaplain St John Rigby VI Form Coll., Wigan 1972–77; priest in inner city of Liverpool 1978–81; Dir Upholland Northern Inst., Lancs. 1981–84; Gen. Sec. Catholic Bishops' Conf. of England and Wales 1984–91; Auxiliary Bishop of Westminster 1992–2000; Archbishop of Birmingham 2000–09, of Westminster 2009–; cr. Cardinal (Cardinal-Priest of Santissimo Redentore e Sant'Alfonso in Via Merulana) 2014–; Adviser to HE Cardinal Hume and Archbishop Worlock at the Int. Synods of Bishops 1980, 1983, 1985, 1987, 1990, 1991; Del. of Bishops' Conf. to Synod of Bishops 1994, 1999. *Publications:* Promise of Future Glory – Reflections on the Mass 1997, Missioners, Priest and People Today 2007, St John Fisher, Bishop and Theologian in Reformation and Controversy 2011. *Address:* Archbishop's House, Ambrosden Avenue, London, SW1P 1QJ, England (office). *Telephone:* (20) 7798-9033 (office). *Fax:* (20) 7798-9077 (office). *E-mail:* archbishop@rcdow.org.uk (office). *Website:* www.rcdow.org.uk/archbishop (office).

NICHOLSON, Arnold Joseph, QC; Jamaican lawyer and politician; *Minister of Foreign Affairs and Foreign Trade;* b. 28 Feb. 1942, Rock River, Clarendon; s. of Arnold A. Nicholson and Bernice Nicholson; m. Yvonne Nicholson; two s.; ed Univ. Coll. of the West Indies, Middle Temple Inn of Court, London, Univ. of London, UK; early career in banking 1964–68; called to the Bar 1972, practised law in Jamaica and Grenada 1972–92; MP for W Central St Andrew 1989–97; Parl. Sec. in Ministry of Educ. and Culture 1992–95, Minister of State, Ministry of Legal Affairs Jan.–Sept. 1995, Attorney-Gen. 1995–2007; apptd to Senate 1998; Minister of Justice 2001, of Foreign Affairs and Foreign Trade 2012–. *Leisure interests:* reading, music, cricket and dancing. *Address:* Ministry of Foreign Affairs and Foreign Trade, 21 Dominica Dr., POB 624, Kingston 5, Jamaica (office). *Telephone:* 926-4220 (office). *Fax:* 929-5112 (office). *E-mail:* mfaftjam@cwjamaica.com (office). *Website:* www.mfaft.gov.jm (office).

NICHOLSON, Sir Bryan Hubert, Kt, GBE, MA, FRSA, CBIM, FCIM; British business executive; b. 6 June 1932, Rainham, Essex, England; s. of the late Reginald H. Nicholson and of Clara Nicholson; m. Mary E. Harrison 1956; one s. one d. (and one s. deceased); ed Palmers School, Grays and Oriel Coll. Oxford; man. trainee, Unilever 1955–58; Dist Man. Van den Berghs 1958–59; Sales Man. Three Hands/Jeyes Group 1960–64; joined Sperry Rand 1964, Sales Dir UK Remington Div. 1964–66, Gen. Man. Australia, Remington Div. 1966–69, Man. Dir UK and France, Remington Div. 1969–72; Dir Operations, Rank Xerox (UK) 1972–76, Dir Overseas Subsidiaries 1976, Exec. Dir 1976–84, Chair. Rank Xerox (UK) and Rank Xerox GmbH 1979–84; Chair. Manpower Services Comm. 1984–87, The Post Office 1987–92; Chair. BUPA 1992–2001, Varity Holdings Ltd (now Varity Europe Ltd) 1993–96, Cookson Group PLC 1998–2003; Sr Adviser, Penfida Partners LLP 2006–; Pres. Involvement and Participation Assen 1990–94; Chair. CBI Vocational Educ. and Training Task Force 1988–89, CNAA 1988–91, Nat. Council for Vocational Qualifications 1990–93, CBI Educ. and Training Affairs Cttee 1990–93, Industrial Soc. 1990–93, Deputy Pres. CBI 1993–94, Pres. 1994–96; Dir (non-exec.) GKN 1990–2000, Varity Corpn, USA 1993–96, LucasVarity 1996–99, Equitas Holdings Ltd 1996–2005, Newsquest PLC 1997–99, Action Centre for Europe Ltd 1997–2004, Accountancy Foundation 2000–04; mem. Nat. Econ. Devt Council 1985–92; Pres. Oriel Soc. 1988–92; Vice-Pres. Nat. Children's Home 1990–2002, Industrial Trust 1999–2010; Deputy Chair. Educ. Devt International 2003–04, Chair. 2004–05; Chancellor, Sheffield Hallam Univ. 1992–2001; Pro-Chancellor and Chair. Council The Open Univ. 1996–2004; Chair. United Oxford and Cambridge Univ. Club 1995–97, Financial Reporting Council 2001–05, Goal PLC 2001–02; mem. International Advisory Bd, Active International 2001–; mem. Public Interest Oversight Bd, International Fed. of Accountants; Trustee, International Accounting Standards Cttee Foundation 2006–12; Pres. Young Epilepsy (fmrly Nat. Centre for Young People with Epilepsy) 2005–11, Life Vice-Pres. 2011–; Fellow, Open Univ. 2006; Patron, Inst. of Financial Accountants 2012–; Hon. FCGI 1988, Hon. Fellow, Oriel Coll. Oxford 1989, Manchester Metropolitan Univ. 1990, Scottish Vocational Ed. Council 1994, Scottish Qualifications Authority 1997, Hon. Companion Inst. of Personnel and Devt 1994; Dr hc (CNAA) 1994, (Open Univ.) 1994, (Sheffield Hallam) 2001, Hon. DLitt (Glasgow Caledonian) 2000. *Leisure interests:* tennis, bridge, opera, political history. *Address:* Point Piper, Lilley Drive, Kingswood, KT20 6JA, England (home). *Telephone:* (1737) 832208 (home). *Fax:* (1737) 832208 (home). *E-mail:* bryanhnicholson@aol.com (home).

NICHOLSON, Jack; American actor and film director; b. 22 April 1937, Neptune, NJ; s. of John Nicholson and Ethel May Nicholson; m. Sandra Knight 1961 (divorced 1966); two d.; f. Proteus Films Inc. (production co.); Commdr des Arts et des Lettres; American Film Inst. Lifetime Achievement Award 1994, Cecil B. De Mille Award 1999, Kennedy Center Honor 2001. *Films:* The Cry-Baby Killer 1958, Teenage Lovers 1960, The Wild Ride 1960, Too Soon to Love 1960, The Little Shop of Horrors 1960, Studs Lonigan 1960, The Broken Land 1962, The Raven 1963, The Terror 1963, Ensign Pulver 1964, Flight to Fury 1964, Back Door to Hell 1964, Ride the Whirlwind (also writer and producer) 1965, The Shooting (also producer) 1967, Hell's Angels on Wheels 1967, The Trip (screenplay) 1967, Head (co-scriptwriter, co-producer) 1968, Psych-Out 1968, Easy Rider (Acad. Award for Best Supporting Actor) 1969, The Rebel Rousers 1970, On a Clear Day You Can See Forever 1970, Five Easy Pieces 1971, Drive, He Said (dir) 1971, A Safe Place 1971, Carnal Knowledge 1971, The King of Marvin Gardens 1972, The Last Detail 1973, Chinatown 1974, The Passenger 1974, Tommy 1974, The Fortune 1975, One Flew over the Cuckoo's Nest (Acad. Award for Best Actor 1976) 1975, The Missouri Breaks 1976, The Last Tycoon 1976, Goin' South (also dir) 1978, The Shining 1980, The Postman Always Rings Twice 1981, Reds 1981, The Border 1982, Terms of Endearment (Acad. Award for Best Supporting Actor) 1984, Prizzi's Honor 1984, Heartburn 1985, The Witches of Eastwick 1986, Broadcast News 1987, Ironweed 1987, Batman 1989, The Two Jakes (also dir) 1989, Man Trouble 1992, A Few Good Men 1992, Hoffa 1993, Wolf 1994, The Crossing Guard 1995, Mars Attacks! 1996,

The Evening Star 1996, Blood and Wine 1996, As Good As It Gets 1997, The Pledge 2001, About Schmidt (Golden Globe for Best Dramatic Actor 2003) 2002, Anger Management 2003, Something's Gotta Give 2003, The Departed 2006, The Bucket List 2007, How Do You Know 2010. *Television:* Matinee Theatre (series) 1956, Mr. Lucky (series) 1960, The Barbara Stanwyck Show (series) 1960, Tales of Wells Fargo (series) 1961, Sea Hunt (series) 1961, Bronco (series) 1961, Little Amy (film) 1962, Hawaiian Eye (series) 1962, Dr. Kildare (series) 1966, Voyage to the Bottom of the Sea (series) 1966, The Andy Griffith Show (series) 1966–67, The Guns of Will Sonnett (series) 1967, Elephant's Child (film) 1986. *Address:* c/o Bresler Kelly and Associates, 11500 West Olympic Boulevard, Suite 510, Los Angeles, CA 90064, USA (office).

NICHOLSON, Pamela M., BA; American business executive; *President and Chief Operating Officer, Enterprise Holdings;* b. St Louis, Mo.; ed Univ. of Missouri; joined Enterprise Rent-A-Car as man. trainee in St Louis 1981, Asst Br. Man. 1982, transferred to Southern California group 1982, rose through ranks to become Regional Vice-Pres. 1994, returned to St Louis to become Corp. Vice-Pres. 1994–97, Gen. Man. Enterprise's New York group 1997–99, Sr Vice-Pres., North American operations 1999–2003, Exec. Vice-Pres. and COO Enterprise Rent-A-Car 2003–08, Pres. and COO Enterprise Holdings 2008–, mem. Bd of Dirs Crawford Group (parent co.), Dir Enterprise Rent-A-Car Foundation; mem. Bd of Dirs Energizer Holdings, Inc.; mem. Bd of Dirs Humane Soc. of Missouri; mem. Bd Trustees St Louis Regional Chamber and Growth Assen; fmr mem. Bd United Way of Bergen Co., NJ, Bd INROADS, St Louis; ranked by Fortune magazine amongst the 50 Most Powerful Women in Business in the US (44th) 2007, (29th) 2008, (34th) 2009, (29th) 2010, (26th) 2011, (30th) 2012, ranked by Forbes magazine amongst The World's 100 Most Powerful Women (92nd) 2008, (89th) 2009. *Address:* Enterprise Holdings, 600 Corporate Park Drive, St Louis, MO 63105, USA (office). *Telephone:* (314) 512-1000 (office). *Fax:* (314) 512-4706 (office). *E-mail:* info@ enterprise.com (office). *Website:* www.enterpriseholdings.com (office); www .enterprise.com (office); www.erac.com (office).

NICHOLSON, The Hon. Robert Douglas, PC, QC, BA; Canadian lawyer and politician; *Minister of National Defence;* b. 1952, Niagara Falls; m. Arlene Nicholson; three c.; ed Queen's Univ., Univ. of Windsor; fmr Niagara Regional Councillor, Conservation Authority Dir, Niagara Escarpment Commr; MP for Niagara Falls 1983–93, 2004–; Parl. Sec. to the Leader of the Govt in the House of Commons 1989–90, to the Attorney-Gen. 1989–93; Minister for Science and Minister responsible for Small Business 1993; fmr Transport Critic; Chief Opposition Whip 2005; Leader of the Govt in the House of Commons and Minister for Democratic Reform 2006–07; Minister of Justice and Attorney-Gen. of Canada 2007–13, of Nat. Defence 2013–; mem. Upper Canada Law Soc. *Address:* Department of National Defence, National Defence HQ, Maj.-Gen. George R. Pearkes Building, 101 Colonel By Dr., Ottawa, ON K1A 0K2, Canada (office). *Telephone:* (613) 995-2534 (office). *Fax:* (613) 992-4739 (office). *E-mail:* dnd_mdn@ forces.gc.ca (office). *Website:* www.forces.gc.ca (office); www.robnicholson.ca.

NICHOLSON, Robin, CBE, MA (Cantab.), MSc (Lon), RIBA, FRSA; British architect; *Senior Partner, Edward Cullinan Architects;* b. 27 July 1944, Hertford, Herts.; s. of Gerald Nicholson and Margaret Hanbury; m. Fiona Mary Bird; three s.; ed Eton Coll., Magdalene Coll. Cambridge, Bartlett School, Univ. Coll. London; worked for James Stirling Chartered Architects, London 1969–76; Boza Lührs Muzard, Santiago, Chile 1973; Polytechnic of North London 1976–79; Partner, Edward Cullinan Architects 1980–90, Dir 1989–, now Sr Pnr; Vice-Pres. RIBA 1992–94; Comm. for Architecture and the Built Environment Commr 2002–10, Jt Deputy Chair. 2008–10; Dir Nat. House-Building Council 2007–; Chair. Dept for Children, Schools and Families Zero Carbon (Schools) Task Force 2008–10; Chair. Cambridgeshire Quality Panel; Chair. The Edge; Hon. Fellow, Inst. of Structural Eng; RIBA Student Design Prize 1969. *Publications:* Innovations in Healthcare Design 1995, The Cost of Bad Design 2006. *Leisure interests:* gardening, making things. *Address:* Edward Cullinan Architects, 1 Baldwin Terrace, London, N1 7RU, England (office). *Telephone:* (20) 7704-1975 (office). *Fax:* (20) 7354-2739 (office). *E-mail:* eca@ecarch.co.uk (office). *Website:* www.edwardcullinanarchitects .com (office).

NICHOLSON, Sir Robin Buchanan, Kt, BA, MA, PhD, FRS, FREng, FIM, MInstP; British metallurgist, academic and businessman; *Member of Council, University of Exeter;* b. 12 Aug. 1934, Sutton Coldfield, West Midlands, England; s. of the late Carroll Nicholson and Nancy Nicholson; m. 1st Elizabeth Mary Caffyn 1958 (died 1988); one s. two d.; m. 2nd Yvonne Appleby 1991; ed Oundle School and St Catharine's Coll., Cambridge; Demonstrator in Metallurgy, Univ. of Cambridge 1960–64, Lecturer 1964–66, Fellow of Christ's Coll. 1962–66; Prof. of Metallurgy, Univ. of Manchester 1966–72; Dir of Research Lab., Inco Europe Ltd 1972–76, Dir 1975–81, Man. Dir 1976–81; Co.-Chair. Biogen NV 1979–81; Chief Scientist, Cen. Policy Review Staff 1981–83; Chief Scientific Adviser, Cabinet Office 1983–86; Chief. Exec., Chair. Electro-Optical Div., Pilkington PLC 1986–96, Dir Pilkington PLC (fmrly Pilkington Bros PLC) 1986–96, Pilkington Optronics Ltd 1991–98; Dir Rolls-Royce 1986–2005, BP PLC 1987–2005; Chair. Centre for Exploitation of Science and Tech. 1987–90, Advisory Council on Science and Tech. 1990–93; Pres. Inst. of Materials 1997–98; mem. Council for Science and Tech. 1993–2000; mem. Council Univ. of Exeter 2005–; fmr Pro Chancellor UMIST; Fellow, Royal Acad. of Eng, Royal Soc. (mem. Council 1983–85); Hon. DSc (Cranfield, Aston) 1983, (Manchester) 1985, (Nottingham) 2000; Hon. DMet (Sheffield) 1984; Hon. DEng (Birmingham) 1986; Rosenhain Medal, Inst. of Metals 1971, Platinum Medal, Metals Soc. 1981. *Publications:* Precipitation Hardening (co-author) 1962, Electron Microscopy of Thin Crystals (co-author) 1965, Strengthening Methods in Crystals (co-ed. and contrib.) 1971. *Leisure interests:* family life, gardening, music. *Address:* Penson Farm, Diptford, Totnes, Devon, TQ9 7NN, England. *E-mail:* pensonfarm@aol.com (home).

NIČIĆ, Radovan; Serbian politician; *Speaker, 'Assembly of the Union of Municipalities of Kosovo and Metohija';* b. 1971, Caglavica; ed Univ. of Prishtina; worked at Inst. for the Protection of Cultural Monuments, City of Prishtina 1990s; mem. Nat. Ass. (Serbian Radical Party); Speaker, 'Ass. of the Union of Municipalities of Kosovo and Metohija', Mitrovica 2008–; Pres. 'Municipal Ass. of Prishtina' 2008–. *Address:* Srpska Radikalna Stranka, 11080 Belgrade, Zemun, Magistratski trg 3, Serbia (office). *Telephone:* (11) 3164621 (office). *E-mail:* info@ srs.org.yu (office). *Website:* www.srs.org.yu (office).

NICKELL, Stephen John, CBE, BA, MSc, FBA, FES; British economist and academic; *Warden, Nuffield College Oxford*; b. 25 April 1944; s. of John Edward Hilary Nickell and Phyllis Nickell; m. Susan Elizabeth Pegden; one s. one d.; ed Merchant Taylors' School, Pembroke Coll., Cambridge, London School of Econs; math. teacher, Hendon Co. School 1965–68; Lecturer, LSE 1970–77, Reader 1977–79, Prof. of Econs 1979–84, 1998–2005; Dir Inst. of Econs and Statistics, Prof. of Econs and Fellow, Nuffield Coll., Oxford 1984–98, Warden Nuffield Coll. 2006–; mem. Academic Panel, HM Treasury 1981–89, Council of Royal Econ. Soc. 1984–94 (Pres. Royal Econ. Soc. 2001–04), Econ. and Social Research Council 1990–94; external mem. Monetary Policy Cttee Bank of England 2000–06; Fellow, Econometric Soc. 1980; Hon. mem. American Econ. Asscn 1997, American Acad. of Arts and Sciences; Hon. Fellow, Nuffield Coll. Oxford 2003. *Publications:* The Investment Decisions of Firms (jtly) 1978, The Performance of the British Economy (jtly) 1988, Unemployment (jtly) 1991, The Unemployment Crisis 1994, The Performance of Companies 1995; numerous articles in learned journals. *Leisure interests:* reading, riding, cooking. *Address:* Nuffield College, New Road, Oxford, OX1 1NF, England (office). *Telephone:* (1865) 278520 (office). *Fax:* (1865) 278621 (office). *E-mail:* wardens.secretary@nuffield.ox.ac.uk (office). *Website:* www.nuffield.ox.ac.uk (office).

NICKLAUS, Jack William; American professional golfer; b. 21 Jan. 1940, Columbus, Ohio; s. of L. Charles Nicklaus and Helen Nicklaus (née Schoener); m. Barbara Bash 1960; four s. one d.; ed Ohio State Univ.; professional golfer 1961–; won US Amateur Championship 1959, 1961; US Open Championship 1962, 1967, 1972, 1980, US Masters 1963, 1965, 1966, 1972, 1975, 1986, US PGA Championship 1963, 1971, 1973, 1975, 1980, The Open Championship 1966, 1970, 1978; by 1973 had won more major championship titles (totals now: 18 as professional, two as amateur) than any other player; Australian Open Champion six times, World Series winner five times, record three times individual winner World Cup, six times on winning team; rep. USA in six Ryder Cup matches; 97 tournament victories, 76 official tour victories, 58 times second, 36 times third; joined Seniors Tour 1990; won US Sr Open; 136 tournament appearances 1996; played in 154 consecutive majors 1999; has also designed over 100 golf courses in 26 countries; Co-Chair. The First Tee's Capital Campaign, More Than A Game 2000; Capt. US team, President's Cup 2003; f. Nicklaus Design (golf course design co.); Founder and Chair. Nicklaus Children's Health Care Foundation; Hon. LLD (St Andrews) 1984; five times US PGA Player of the Year; Golfer of the Century 1988, Athlete of the Decade Award 1970s, Golf World's Golf Course Architect of the Year 1993, Presidential Medal of Freedom 2005. *Publications:* My Story 1997 and numerous books about golf. *Leisure Interests:* fishing, hunting, tennis. *Address:* Nicklaus Design, 11780 US Highway 1, Suite 500, North Palm Beach, FL 33408, USA (office). *Telephone:* (561) 227-0300 (office). *Fax:* (561) 227-0548 (office). *Website:* www.nicklaus.com (office).

NICKLES, Don; American business executive and fmr politician; *Chairman and CEO, Nickles Group LLC*; b. 6 Dec. 1948, Ponca City, Okla; s. of Robert Nickles and Coeweene Nickles; m. Linda Morrison 1968; one s. three d.; mem. Nat. Guard 1971–76; mem. Okla State Senate 1978–80, US Senator from Oklahoma (Republican) 1981–2005; Asst Majority Leader, US Senate; Founder, Chair. and CEO Nickles Group LLC (lobbyist firm), Washington, DC 2005–; Vice-Pres., Gen. Man. Nickles Machine Co. 1972–80; mem. Bd of Dirs Fortress America Acquisition Corpn 2005–, Chesapeake Energy Corpn 2005–. *Address:* Nickles Group LLC, 601 13th Street, NW, Suite 250 North, Washington, DC 20005, USA (office). *Telephone:* (202) 637-0214 (office). *E-mail:* mail@nicklesgroup.com (office). *Website:* www.nicklesgroup.com (office).

NICKS, Stephanie (Stevie); American singer and songwriter; b. 26 May 1948, Phoenix, Ariz.; m. Kim Anderson 1983 (divorced 1984); fmr mem. Fritz (with Lindsey Buckingham); mem. duo, Buckingham Nicks (with Lindsey Buckingham) 1971–74; mem. Fleetwood Mac 1975–93, 1997–; solo artist 1978–; numerous worldwide tours and concert appearances; American Music Award for Favorite Pop/Rock Group 1978, Billboard Award for Group of the Year 1977, BRIT Award for Outstanding Contribution 1998, Grammy Hall of Fame Award 2003. *Recordings include:* albums: with Lindsey Buckingham: Buckingham Nicks 1973; with Fleetwood Mac: Fleetwood Mac 1975, Rumours (Billboard Award for Album of the Year 1977, American Music Award for Favorite Pop/Rock Album 1978, Grammy Award for Album of the Year 1978) 1977, Tusk 1979, Fleetwood Mac Live 1980, Mirage 1982, Tango In The Night 1987, Behind The Mask 1990, The Dance 1997, Say You Will 2003, Pious Bird Of Good Omen 2004; solo: Bella Donna 1981, The Wild Heart 1983, Rock A Little 1985, The Other Side Of The Mirror 1989, Street Angel 1994, Maybe Love Will Change Your Mind 1994, Trouble In Shangri-La 2001, The Divine 2001, The Soundstage Sessions 2009, In Your Dreams 2011. *Address:* PO Box 112083, Carrolton, TX 75011-2083, USA (office). *E-mail:* jk@nicksfix.com. *Website:* www.nicksfix.com.

NICKSON, Baron (Life Peer), cr. 1994, of Renagour in the District of Stirling; **David Wigley Nickson,** KBE, CBE, FRSE; British business executive (retd); b. 27 Nov. 1929, Eton, Berks., England; s. of Geoffrey W. Nickson and Janet M. Nickson; m. Helen L. Cockcraft 1952; three d.; ed Eton and Royal Mil. Acad. Sandhurst; man. trainee, Wm. Collins, Publrs, Glasgow 1954, Dir 1961, Jt Man. Dir 1967, Vice-Chair. 1976, Vice-Chair. and Group Man. Dir 1979–82, Dir (non-exec.) 1982–85; Dir (non-exec.) Scottish & Newcastle Breweries PLC 1981–95, Deputy Chair. 1982, Chair. 1983–89; Chair. Atlantic Salmon Trust 1989–96 (Vice-Chair. 1985–88), Sec. of State for Scotland's Atlantic Salmon Task Force 1996, Scottish Devt Agency 1989–90, Scottish Enterprise 1990–92; Deputy Chair. Clydesdale Bank PLC 1989–91 (Chair. 1991–98), General Accident 1993–98; Dir (non-exec.) General Accident Fire & Life Assurance Corpn PLC, Edinburgh Investment Trust PLC 1983–94; Pres. CBI 1986–88; Chair. Top Salaries Review Body 1989–95; Chancellor Glasgow Caledonian Univ. 1993–2002; Vice-Lord Lt of Stirling and Falkirk 1997–2004; Hon. DL; Hon. DUniv (Stirling) 1986, (Glasgow) 1993; Hon. DBA (Napier) 1990, (Paisley) 1991. *Leisure interests:* fishing, birdwatching, shooting, the countryside. *Address:* The River House, Doune, Perthshire, FK16 6DA, Scotland. *Telephone:* (1876) 841614. *Fax:* (1876) 841062.

NICOL, Peter Franz, MBE; British professional squash player; b. 5 April 1974, Inverurie, Scotland; s. of Patrick Nicol; professional debut 1992; achieved World No. 1 ranking Feb. 1998, ranked World No. 1 Dec. 2003; major singles titles include US Open 1994, Canadian Open 1995, Mahindra International 1995, 1996, 1997,

Al-Ahram International 1997, 2000, 2001, Kuwait Open 1997, British Open 1998, 2002, Commonwealth Games 1998 (silver medal 2002), PSA Super Series Final 1999, 2000, 2001, Hong Kong Open 1999, 2000, 2002, World Open 1999, 2001, Flanders Open 2000, Irish Open 2000, 2001, PSA Masters 2000, Tournament of Champions 2001, 2003, Scottish Open 2001, Qatar Classic 2001, 2003, YMG Capital Classic 2001, Memorial US Open 2002, British Nat. Championship 2003; 67 appearances for Scotland (66 wins, 1 defeat); switched allegiance from Scotland to England 2001 (qualified for England May 2002); doubles gold for England (with Lee Beachill) Commonwealth Games 2002; winner (with England team) European Team Championships 2003; Dr hc (Robert Gordon Univ., Aberdeen). *Leisure interests:* golf, shopping. *Website:* www.pnsquash.com.

NICOLĂESCU, Gheorghe-Eugen; Romanian economist and politician; b. 2 Aug. 1955, Grădiștea, Giurgiu County; m.; two c.; ed Bucharest Acad. of Econ. Studies; began career with Ministry of Tourism, worked at several hotels including Athénée Palace, Bucharest, as Technologist 1976, Commodities Economist 1978–82, Economist 1982–85; Computer Analyst, Ministry of Industry and Resources equipment factory 1985–87, Economist, Supplies Div. 1987–90; Head of Supplies, Ratmil (mil. equipment co.) 1990–91, Supplies Economist 1991–92, Head of Budget and Econ. Analysis 1992–94, Econ. Dir 1994–97, Gen. Dir 1997–99; Asst Sec.-Gen., Ministry of Public Finance 1999–2000; mem. Chamber of Deputies for Mureș County 2000–08, for Calarasi 2008–; Minister of Health 2005–08; Asst Prof., Spiru Haret Univ. 2000–01, Bucharest Acad. of Econ. Studies 2001–02; Vice-Pres. Chamber of Financial Auditors of Romania; mem. Partidul Național Liberal 1997–. *Address:* Partidul Național Liberal, 011866 Bucharest 5, Bd. Aviatorilor 86, Romania (office). *Telephone:* (21) 2310795 (office). *Fax:* (21) 2310796 (office). *E-mail:* dre@pnl.ro (office). *Website:* www.pnl.ro (office).

NICOLAOU, Kyriacos C., BSc, PhD; Cypriot chemist and academic; *Aline W. and L. S. Skaggs Professor of Chemical Biology, Scripps Research Institute*; b. 5 July 1946; ed Bedford Coll., London and Univ. Coll., London, UK; Research Assoc., Columbia Univ., USA 1972–73; Research Assoc., Harvard Univ. 1973–76; Asst Prof. of Chem., Univ. of Pennsylvania 1976–80, Assoc. Prof. 1980–81, Prof. 1981–88, Rhodes-Thompson Prof. of Chem. 1988–89; Prof. of Chem., Univ. of California, San Diego 1989–; Chair. Dept of Chem. and Darlene Shiley Chair. in Chem., Scripps Research Inst., La Jolla, Calif. 1989–, also Aline W. and L. S. Skaggs Prof. of Chemical Biology 1996–; mem. Editorial Bd of numerous journals; mem. NAS 1996, ACS, German Chemical Soc., European Chemical Soc., German Acad. of Sciences Leopoldina 2009, American Philosophical Soc. 2011; Foreign mem. Acad. of Athens 2001; Fellow, American Acad. of Arts and Sciences 1993, AAAS 1999; Hon. mem. Pharmaceutical Soc. of Japan 1996, Israel Chemical Soc. 2009; Hon. Life Fellow, Singapore Nat. Inst. of Chem. 2011; Honorary Fellowship, Honorary Fellowship, Chemical Research Society of India, India, 2004, Indian Academy of Sciences, India, 2007; Order of the Commdr of Honour (Greece) 1998; Hon. MA (Univ. of Pennsylvania) 1980; Hon. DSc (Univ. Coll., London) 1994; Hon. PhD (Univ. of Athens) 1995, (Univ. of Thessaloniki) 1996, (Univ. of Cyprus) 1997, (Univ. of Crete) 1998, (Univ. of Alcala) 1998, (Agric. Univ. of Athens) 2000, (Univ. of Rome, La Sapienza) 2003; numerous awards, including US Sr Scientist Award, Alexander von Humboldt Foundation 1987, ACS Award for Creative Work in Synthetic Organic Chem. 1993, RSC Rhone-Poulenc Medal 1995, Max Tischler Prize, Harvard Univ. 2000, RSC Centenary Medal 2000, Ernst Schering Prize 2001, Nagoya Medal of Organic Chem., Nagoya Univ. (Japan) 2001, Greek American Scientists, Engineers, and High Tech Entrepeneurs Award 2001, Tetrahedron Prize for Creativity in Organic Chem. (Int.) 2002, ACS Nobel Laureate Signature Award for Grad. Educ. in Chem. (shared with Phil S. Baran) 2003, Aristeio Bodossaki Prize, Bodossaki Foundation (Greece) 2004, Burckhardt-Helferich Prize (Germany) 2006, ACS Arthur C. Cope Award 2005, ACS Western Regional Meeting Award of Excellence 2007, ACS (Auburn Section) G.M. Kosolapoff Award 2006, ISHC Sr Award in Heterocyclic Chem. (Int.) 2007, August Wilhelm von Hofmann-Denkmünze Award (Germany) 2008, Charles Chandler Medal, Columbia Univ. 2008, San Diego BioPharma Achievement Award 2009, Lampousa Lifetime Achievement Award, Cypriot American Asscn 2009, Science Award, Ministry of Educ. and Culture (Cyprus) 2010, Benjamin Franklin Medal in Chem., The Franklin Inst. 2011, ACS (NJ Section) Creativity in Molecular Design and Synthesis Award 2012. *Publications:* Selenium in Natural Products Synthesis (co-author) 1984, Classics in Total Synthesis (co-author) 1996, Handbook of Combinatorial Chemistry, Vols 1 and 2 (co-ed.) 2002, Classics in Total Synthesis II (co-author) 2003, Molecules That Changed The World (co-author) 2008, Classics in Total Synthesis III (co-author) 2011; more than 720 publs and 67 patents. *Address:* Department of Chemistry, Scripps Research Institute, 10550 North Torrey Pines Road, La Jolla, CA 92037, USA (office). *Telephone:* (858) 784-2400 (office). *Fax:* (858) 784-2469 (office). *E-mail:* kcn@scripps.edu (office); knicolaou@ucsd.edu (office). *Website:* www.scripps.edu/nicolaou (office).

NICOLAS, Alrich; Haitian diplomatist and politician; b. 1956; ed Freie Univ. Berlin, Germany; fmr Dean, Latin America Inst., Freie Univ. Berlin; fmr Visiting Prof., Costa Rica; fmr Chief, Strategy and Policy Unit, Haiti, UNDP; Amb. to Germany (also accred to Denmark) 1996–2005; Minister of Foreign Affairs 2008–09. *Address:* c/o Ministry of Foreign Affairs, boulevard Harry S Truman, Cité de l'Exposition, Port-au-Prince, Haiti (office).

NICOLAS, Gwenael, MA; French interior designer and product designer; *President, Curiosity Inc.*; b. 6 June 1966, Rosporden; ed Ecole supérieure d'art graphique et d'architecture d'intérieure, Royal Coll. of Art, London; Pres. Curiosity Inc.; Nintendo Game Boy Advance Design Consultant 2000; American Inst. of Architecture Citation 1998, I.D. Magazine Distinction 1999, 2000, I.F. Design Award 2003, Japan Display Design Award 2005. *Achievements:* Tag Heuer Shops, Tokyo, New York, London, Sony LCD TV 'Capujo', Sony Showroom, Tokyo 2003, Nissan Booth, Tokyo Motor Show 2004, 2005. *Publication:* Curiosity 2002. *Address:* Curiosity Inc. 2-13-16, Tomigaya, Shibuya-ku, Tokyo 151-0063, Japan (office). *Telephone:* (3) 5452-0095 (office). *Fax:* (3) 5454-9691 (office). *E-mail:* nicolas@curiosity.jp (office). *Website:* www.curiosity.jp (office).

NICOLET, Claude; French historian and academic; *Professor Emeritus, University of Paris, Sorbonne*; b. 15 Sept. 1930, Marseilles; s. of Edmond Nicolet and Suzanne Nicolet; m. 1st Michelle Brousset 1956 (divorced, deceased); one s.; m. 2nd Hélène Pierre 1963; three s.; ed Ecole Normale Supérieure and Ecole Française de Rome; served on Staff of Minister of State Pierre Mendès-France 1956; Editorial

Sec., Cahiers de la République 1956–57; mem. Ecole Française de Rome 1957–59; Lecturer, Univ. of Tunis 1959–61; Lecturer and Prof., Univ. of Caen 1961–69; Prof. of Roman History, Univ. of Paris, Sorbonne 1969–92, Emer. Prof. 1992–; Dir of Studies, Ecole Pratique des Hautes Etudes (Section IV) 1969–; mem. Inst. for Advanced Studies, Princeton 1966–67, 1972; Prof., Univ. Paris I 1971–; Dir Era 757, CNRS 1978–91; Dir, Centre Gustav Glotz 1981–92, Ecole Française de Rome 1992–95; Pres., Soc. for Latin Studies 1983, Conseil scientifique du Centre d'études et des prévisions du Ministère de l'Interiéur 1998; mem. Acad. des Inscriptions et Belles Lettres (Inst. de France); Assoc. mem. Acad. dei Lincei; Corresp. Fellow, British Acad. 1987; Officier, Légion d'honneur; Officier des Palmes académiques; Prix Galileo Galilei des Rotary italiens 1994, Grand Prix Nat. (histoire) 1996, Prix des Cultori di Roma 1997. *Publications include:* Le radicalisme 1957, Pierre Mendès France ou le métier de Cassandre 1959, Cicéron 1961, Les idées politiques à Rome sous la République 1964, L'ordre équestre à l'époque républicaine Vol. I 1966, Vol. II 1978, Les Gracques, crise agraire et révolution à Rome 1967, Le métier de citoyen dans la République romaine 1976, Rome et la conquête du monde méditerranéen 1977, L'idée républicaine en France 1982, Des ordres à Rome 1984, L'inventaire du monde: Géographie et politique aux origines de l'Empire romain 1988, Rendre à César 1988, La République en France: état des lieux 1992, Nation, Histoire, République 2000, Censeurs et Publicains 2000, La fabrique d'une nation: La France entre Rome et les Germains 2003. *Address:* Université Paris-Sorbonne (Paris IV), 1 rue Victor Cousin, 75005 Paris (office); Institut de France, 23 quai Conti, 75006 Paris; 2 rue de Paradis, 75010 Paris, France. *Telephone:* 1-47-70-02-91. *Website:* www.paris4.sorbonne.fr/en/sommaire.php3 (office).

NICOLI, Eric Luciano, CBE, BSc; British business executive; b. 5 Aug. 1950, Pulham Market, Norfolk, England; s. of Virgilio Nicoli and Ida Nicoli; m. Rosalind West 1977; one s. one d.; ed Diss Grammar School, Norfolk, King's Coll. London; worked briefly in market research, then various positions with Rowntree Marketing Dept 1972–80; Sr Marketing Controller Biscuit Div., United Biscuits 1980–81, Marketing Dir Biscuits 1981–84, and Confectionery 1982–84; UK Business Planning Dir 1984, Man. Dir UB Frozen Foods 1985, UB Brands 1986–89, apptd. to Bd of UB (Holdings) PLC 1989, CEO European Operations 1989–90, Group CEO United Biscuits (Holdings) PLC 1991–99, Acting Chair. 2001; Non-Exec. Dir EMI Group PLC 1993–99, Exec. Dir and Chair. 1999–2007, CEO Jan.–Aug. 2007; Deputy Chair. Business in the Community 1991–2003; Chair. (non-exec.) HMV Media Group PLC 2001–04, Tussauds Group Ltd 2001–, Vue Entertainment 2006–10, R&R Music 2008–; Chair. Per Cent Club 1993–, EMI Music Sound Foundation 2003–07; adviser, Nick Stewart and Assocs 2008–. *Leisure interests:* all sports (especially golf), music, food. *Address:* R&R Music Ltd, 2 Melville Street, Falkirk, FK1 1HZ, Scotland.

NICOLL, Roger, BA, MD; American neuroscientist and academic; *Professor of Cellular and Molecular Pharmacology, University of California, San Francisco;* b. 15 Jan. 1941, Camden, NJ; m.; one c.; ed Lawrence Univ., Wis., Univ. of Rochester Medical School, Nat. Insts of Health; Research Fellow, Public Health Service, Nat. Inst. of Mental Health Lab. of Neuropharmcology, Bethesda, Md 1965–66, Research Assoc. (Mil.) 1969–73; Intern in Medicine, Univ. of Chicago Hosps and Clinic 1968–69; Research Assoc. Prof., State Univ. of NY, Lab. of Neurobiology, Buffalo 1973–75; Asst Prof., Depts of Pharmacology and Physiology, Univ. of California, San Francisco 1975–76, Assoc. Prof. 1977–80, Prof. 1980–, currently Prof. of Cellular and Molecular Pharmacology, Interim Dept Chair. 1991–93; Visiting Assoc. Prof., Salk Inst. for Biological Studies 1976; mem. Editorial Bd Current Opinion in Neurobiology 1991–, Hippocampus 1993–, Molecular and Cellular Neurobiology 1996–, Physiological Reviews 1998–; mem. NAS 1994–, American Acad. of Arts and Sciences 1999–; numerous awards including Gruber Neuroscience Prize, The Peter and Patricia Gruber Foundation (co-recipient) 2006. *Publications:* numerous scientific papers in professional journals on the cellular and molecular mechanisms underlying learning and memory in the mammalian brain. *Address:* Department of Cellular and Molecular Pharmacology, University of California, San Francisco, Genentech Hall, 600 16th Street, Box 2140, San Francisco, CA 94143-2140, USA (office). *Telephone:* (415) 476-2018 (office). *E-mail:* nicoll@phy.ucsf.edu (office). *Website:* keck.ucsf.edu/neurograd/faculty/nicoll.html (office).

NICORA, HE Cardinal Attilio; Italian ecclesiastic; *President Emeritus, Administration of the Patrimony of the Apostolic See;* b. 16 March 1937, Varese; ed Pontifical Gregorian Univ., Rome, Theological Faculty, Milan; ordained priest 1964; Prof. of Canon Law, Theological Seminary of Venegano 1964–77; Auxiliary Bishop of Milan and Titular Bishop of Furnos Minor 1977–92; Bishop of Verona 1992–97, Bishop Emer. 1997–; Bishop of Roman Curia 1997–2002; Pres. Admin of the Patrimony of the Apostolic See 2002–05, 2005–11, Pres. Emer. 2011–; cr. Cardinal (Cardinal-Deacon of San Filippo Neri in Eurosia) 2003; participated in Papal Conclave 2005, 2013; oversaw revision of Concordat between Italy and the Vatican 1984. *Address:* Administration of the Patrimony of the Apostolic See, Palazzo Apostolico, 00120 Città del Vaticano, Italy (office). *Telephone:* (06) 69883247 (office). *Fax:* (06) 69885512 (office). *E-mail:* segreteria.presidenza@aosa.va (office).

NICULESCU, Alexandru A.; Romanian diplomatist; b. 1 Jan. 1941, Bucharest; s. of Alexandru Niculescu and Elisabeth Niculescu; m.; three c.; ed Polytechnical Inst. and Univ. of Law, Bucharest; Chargé d'affaires a.i., Perm. Mission to UN, Geneva 1990–91, Deputy Perm. Rep. 1991–95; Dir Div. for UN and Specialized Agencies, Ministry of Foreign Affairs, Bucharest 1995–98; Deputy Perm. Rep., UN, New York 1999–2000, Amb. and Perm. Rep. 2001–03, Chair. Second Cttee (Econ. and Int. Financial Co-operation), UN Gen. Ass. at the Millennium Session 2000–01; Nat. Order 'Serviciu Credincios' 2002. *Publications:* Diplomacy and Destiny 2005; essays and articles on world econ. relations, globalization and UN system's activities. *Leisure interests:* literature, music, economic literature (on globalization). *Address:* 13A Dumbrava Rosie Street, Apt 6, Sector 2, Bucharest, Romania. *Telephone:* (1) 2117877. *E-mail:* alniculescu@hotmail.com.

NIE, Lt-Col Haisheng; Chinese astronaut; b. Sept. 1964, Zaoyang, Hubei Prov.; m. Nie Jielin; one d.; served as fighter pilot in PLA Air Force; attained rank of Lt-Col; selected to be astronaut, Shenzhou Program 1998; support crew for Shenzhou 5, (China's first manned space mission) 2003; debut space flight on board Shenzhou 6, with astronaut Fei Junlong (q.v.), launched from Jiuquan Satellite Launch Centre, Gobi Desert (China's second space mission) 12 Oct. 2005; Commdr,

Shenzhou 10 mission 11–26 June 2013. *Address:* China National Space Administration, c/o State Commission of Science, Technology and Industry for National Defence, 2a Guang'anmennan Jie, Xuanwu Qu, Beijing 100053, People's Republic of China. *Website:* www.cnsa.gov.cn.

NIE, Lt-Gen. Li (Lili); Chinese public official; b. 1930; d. of the late Marshal Nie Rongzhen; m. Ding Henggao; joined CCP 1950; Vice-Chair. of Scientific and Tech. Cttee under Comm. of Science, Tech. and Industry for Nat. Defence 1982–85; rank of Maj.-Gen. PLA 1988; Vice-Chair. Nat. Examination Cttee for Science Award; Deputy, 6th NPC 1983–88, 7th NPC 1988–93, mem. Standing Cttee 8th NPC 1993–98 (mem. Internal and Judicial Affairs Cttee 1994–98), mem. Standing Cttee 9th NPC 1998–2003; rank of Lt-Gen. 1993–; Vice-Pres. All-China Women's Fed. 1993–98. *Address:* c/o National Examination Committee for Science Award, Sanlihe, Beijing, People's Republic of China.

NIEBEL, Dirk, MPA; German politician; b. 29 March 1963, Hamburg; m. Andrea Niebel 1990; three s.; ed Univ. of Mannheim; paratrooper, Bundeswehr (airborne infantry), Calw 1984–92; Placement Officer, Fed. Employment Office, Heidelberg 1993–98; mem. CDU 1979–81; mem. FDP 1990–, Sec.-Gen. 2005–09; mem. Bundestag (Parl.) for Heidelberg-Weinheim constituency 1998–, FDP Parl. Group Speaker on Labour Market Policy 1998–, mem. Parl. Cttee on Labour and Social Affairs; Fed. Minister of Econ. Co-operation and Devt 2009–13; Vice Pres. German-Israeli Asscn 2000–10; Deputy Chair. German-Israeli Parl. Friendship Group; mem. Bd of Trustees Friedrich Naumann Foundation for Freedom 2003–, Pres. Friedrich Ebert Memorial 2009–. *Address:* c/o Federal Ministry of Economic Co-operation and Development, Dahlmannstr. 4, 53113 Bonn, Germany (office). *Website:* www.dirk-niebel.de (office).

NIEDERAUER, Duncan L., BA, MBA; American business executive; *CEO, NYSE Euronext Inc.;* b. 7 Sept. 1959; m.; three c.; ed Colgate Univ., Emory Univ.; joined Goldman Sachs & Co. 1985, joined Equities Div. 1987, relocated to HQ of Spear, Leeds & Kellogg (subsidiary) 2000, Man. Dir and co-head, Equities Div. Execution Services, Goldman Sachs & Co. –2007; Pres. and Co-COO New York Stock Exchange (now NYSE Euronext Inc.) and Head, US Cash Markets April–Nov. 2007, CEO Nov. 2007–; mem. NYSE Euronext Man. Cttee April 2007–; mem. Colgate Univ. Alumni Corpn Bd of Dirs, also Alumni Trustee 2006–; fmr mem. Bd of Mans, Archipelago Holdings LLC; fmr mem. Bd of Dirs EzeCastle Software. *Address:* NYSE Euronext Inc., 11 Wall Street, New York, NY 10005, USA (office). *Telephone:* (212) 656-3000 (office). *Fax:* (212) 656-2126 (office). *Website:* www.nyse.com (office).

NIEDERHUBER, John Edward, MD; American surgeon, academic, researcher and institute director; *Director, National Cancer Institute;* b. 21 June 1938, Steubenville, Ohio; s. of William Henry Niederhuber and Helen (Smittle) Niederhuber; one s.; ed Bethany Coll., W Va, Ohio State Univ. School of Medicine; NIH Academic Trainee in Surgery, Univ. of Michigan 1969–70, completed training in surgery 1973, mem. Faculty 1973–87, apptd Prof. of Microbiology/Immunology and Prof. of Surgery 1980; Visiting Fellow, Div. of Immunology, Karolinska Inst., Stockholm, Sweden 1970–71; Visiting Prof., Dept of Molecular Biology and Genetics, Johns Hopkins Univ. School of Medicine, Baltimore, Md 1986–87, Prof. of Surgery, Oncology, and Molecular Biology and Genetics 1987–91; Emile Holman Prof. of Surgery, Prof. of Microbiology and Immunology, and Chair. Dept of Surgery, Stanford Univ. 1991–97; Prof. of Surgery and Oncology, Univ. of Wisconsin School of Medicine 1997–2002, Dir Univ. of Wisconsin Comprehensive Cancer Center 1997–2002; Chair. Nat. Cancer Advisory Bd (NCAB) 2002–05; COO and Deputy Dir for Translational and Clinical Sciences, Nat. Cancer Inst. (NCI) 2005–, Dir NCI 2006–, external adviser to NCI, mem. NCI Cancer Centers Review Cttee 1984–86, mem. NCI Div. of Cancer Treatment's Bd of Scientific Counselors 1986–91 (Chair. 1987–91), mem. NCAB's Sub-cttee to Evaluate the Nat. Cancer Program (Cttee to Assess Measures of Progress Against Cancer) and Chair. Molecular Medicine Panel 1993–95, Lab. Investigator supported by NCI and NIH, Leader, Lab. of Tumor and Stem Cell Biology (part of Cell and Cancer Biology Br. of NCI's Center for Cancer Research); holds clinical appointment on NIH Clinical Center Medical Staff; mem. Bd C-Change; mem. CEO Roundtable, fmr Co-Chair. Task Force to develop a plan for future oncology devt; Pres. Asscn of American Cancer Insts 2001–03; Founding mem. and Exec. Cttee mem. American Coll. of Surgeons Oncology Co-operative Group; mem. American Coll. of Surgeons Comm. on Cancer 1983–95, Chair. 1989–90, General Motors Cancer Research Foundation Kettering Prize Selection Cttee 1988–89, GMCRF Awards Assembly 1988–92, 1998–2002, Burroughs-Wellcome Foundation Translational Research Advisory Cttee 1999–2006; Chair. American Soc. of Clinical Oncology Surgical Oncology Task Force Strategic Planning Process 2001–02, ASCO Public Policy and Practice Cttee 2002, 2003; mem. 10 scientific journal editorial bds, including Journal of Clinical Oncology 1993–95; mem. Soc. of Surgical Oncology 1978 (Pres. 2001–02); mem. NAS Inst. of Medicine 2008; numerous hon. professorships; Hon. DSc (Bethany Coll.) 2007; US Public Health Service Career Devt Award, Nat. Inst. of Allergy and Infectious Diseases, Distinguished Faculty Service Award, Univ. of Michigan, Alumni Achievement Award, Ohio State Univ. Coll. of Medicine 1989, Distinguished Alumni Award in Medicine, Bethany Coll. 1995, Professional Achievement Award, Ohio State Univ. 2007, Annual Heritage Award, Soc. of Surgical Oncology 2009. *Achievements include:* recognized for pioneering work in hepatic artery infusion chemotherapy and was first to demonstrate feasibility of totally implantable vascular access devices. *Publications:* editor of four books, including Clinical Oncology; author or co-author of more than 180 publs. *Address:* National Cancer Institute, NCI Public Inquiries Office, 6116 Executive Boulevard, Room 3036A, Bethesda, MD 20892-8322, USA (office). *Telephone:* (301) 496-5615 (office). *Fax:* (301) 402-0338 (home). *E-mail:* niederj@mail.nih.gov (office). *Website:* www.cancer.gov (office).

NIELSEN, Holger Kirkholm, PhD; Danish politician; b. 23 April 1950, Ribe; ed Univ. of Aarhus, Univ. of Belgrade; mem. Folketing (Parl.) 1981, 1984, 1987–; mem. European Affairs Cttee, Econ. and Political Affairs Cttee, Foreign Policy Cttee; mem. Socialist People's Party, Chair. 1991–2005; mem. Parliamentary Bureau 2007–; Minister of Taxation 2012–13, of Foreign Affairs 2013–14. *Address:* c/o Ministry of Foreign Affairs, Asiatisk Pl. 2, 1448 Copenhagen K, Denmark (office).

NIELSEN, Jakob, PhD; American (b. Danish) software designer; *Principal, Nielsen Norman Group;* b. 5 Oct. 1957, Copenhagen; s. of Gerhard Nielsen and Helle Nielsen; m. Hannah Kain; ed Tech. Univ. of Denmark, Copenhagen; fmr researcher, Aarhus Univ., Tech. Univ. of Denmark, Bellcore, IBM; Distinguished Engineer, Sun Microsystems 1994–98; Co-founder and Prin., Nielsen Norman Group; mem. editorial bd of several professional journals, including Morgan Kaufmann Publrs, ACM Interactions, Behaviour & Information Technology, Personal and Ubiquitous Computing; mem. Bd of Trustees, San Jose Ballet; inducted into Scandinavian Interactive Media Hall of Fame 2000, inducted into Asscn for Computing Machinery (ACM) Computer-Human Interaction Acad. 2006, Lifetime Achievement Award, Special Interest Group on Computer–Human Interaction 2013. *Publications:* Usability Engineering 1994, Multimedia and Hypertext: The Internet and Beyond 1995, Designing Web Usability: The Practice of Simplicity 2000, Homepage Usability: 50 Websites Deconstructed 2001, Prioritizing Web Usability 2006, Eyetracking Web Usability 2008, Mobile Usability 2012; more than 70 US patents; author of monthly newsletter on web design. *Address:* Nielsen Norman Group, 48105 Warm Springs Boulevard, Fremont, CA 94539, USA (office). *Telephone:* (415) 682-0688 (office). *E-mail:* nielsen@nngroup .com (office). *Website:* www.nngroup.com (office).

NIELSON, Poul, MPolSci; Danish civil servant, academic and fmr politician; *Adjunct Professor, Department of History, International and Social Studies, University of Aalborg;* b. 11 April 1943, Copenhagen; m. Anne-Marie Nielson 1967; three c.; ed Univ. of Arhus; Chair. Nat. Social Democratic Students Org. 1966–67; mem. Social Democratic Foreign Affairs Cttee 1965–79 (Chair. 1974–79, 2009–); mem. Parl. 1971–73, 1977–84, 1986–99; Head of Section, Ministry of Foreign Affairs 1974–79, 1984–85; Chair. Danish European Movt 1977–79; Chair. Parl. Commerce Cttee 1979; Minister of Energy 1979–82; Asst Prof., Danish School of Public Admin. 1985–86; CEO LD-Energy Inc. 1988–94; Minister for Devt Co-operation 1994–99; EU Commr for Devt and Humanitarian Aid 1999–2004; mem. UN Sec. Gen.'s Advisory Bd on Water and Sanitation 2004–; Adjunct Prof., Dept of History, Int. and Social Studies, Univ. of Aalborg 2005–. *Publications:* Power Play and Security 1969, The Wage Earners and the Company Act 1974, Politicians and Civil Servants 1987, En hel Nielson (memoirs) 2011. *Leisure interests:* photography, gardening. *Address:* University of Aalborg, Department of History, International and Social Studies, Fibigerstræde 2, 9220 Aalborg East, Denmark (office). *Telephone:* 72-30-08-00 (Danish Social Democratic Party) (office). *E-mail:* poulnielson@gmail.com (home).

NIEMCZYCKI, Zbigniew Marian; Polish entrepreneur and business executive; *Chairman, Curtis Group;* b. 23 Jan. 1947, Nisko; m. Katarzyna Frank; one d. three s.; ed Warsaw Univ. of Tech.; Owner and Chair. Curtis Group; Founder and Chair. Polish Eagles Aviation Foundation; Pres. Bd Polish Business Roundtable; Vice-Pres. Main Council Business Centre Club; mem. Council of European Integration affiliated to Prime Minister's Office, Council to the Rector of Warsaw Univ.; Hon. Citizen, City of Mtawa 2011; Commdr's Cross, Order of St Gregory with Star (Second Class) 1992, Kt's Cross, Order of Polonia Restituta, Pope John Paul II 1998; Oscar Heart, Cardiosurgery Devt Foundation, Businessman of the Year 1992, Leader of Polish Business 1992. *Leisure interests:* piloting helicopters and planes, tennis. *Address:* Curtis Group, ul. Wołoska 18, 02-675 Warsaw, Poland (office). *Telephone:* (22) 640-27-06 (office). *Fax:* (22) 640-27-18 (office). *E-mail:* info@ curtisgroup.pl (office). *Website:* www.curtisgroup.pl (office).

NIGHTINGALE, Anthony John Liddell, CMG; British business executive; joined Jardine Matheson Group 1969, served in several exec. positions, mem. Bd of Dirs Jardine Matheson Holdings 1994–, Man. Dir 2006–12, Chair. and Man. Dir Jardine Matheson Ltd 2006–12, Chair. Jardine Cycle & Carriage, Jardine Motors, Jardine Pacific; Man. Dir Dairy Farm, Hongkong Land, Jardine Strategic, Mandarin Oriental; Commr of Astra; Chair. Business Facilitation Advisory Cttee est. by Financial Sec. in Hong Kong; Hong Kong Rep. to APEC Business Advisory Council; Vice-Pres. Real Estate Developers' Asscn of Hong Kong; mem. Greater Pearl River Delta Business Council, Employers' Fed. of Hong Kong; non-official mem. Comm. on Strategic Devt. *Address:* Jardine Matheson Ltd, 48th Floor, Jardine House, GPO Box 70, Hong Kong Special Administrative Region, People's Republic of China (office). *Telephone:* 2843-8288 (office). *E-mail:* jml@jardines.com (office). *Website:* www.jardines.com (office).

NIGHTINGALE, (William) Benedict Herbert, BA; British writer and theatre critic; b. 14 May 1939, London; s. of R. E. Nightingale and Hon. Mrs Nightingale (née Gardner); m. Anne B. Redmon 1964; two s. one d.; ed Charterhouse School, Magdalene Coll., Cambridge and Univ. of Pennsylvania, USA; gen. writer, The Guardian 1963–66; Literary Ed., New Society 1966–67; Theatre Critic, New Statesman 1968–86; Prof. of English, Theatre and Drama, Univ. of Michigan 1986–89; Chief Drama Critic, The Times 1990–2010 (retd); Sunday Theatre Critic, New York Times 1983–84. *Publications:* Charities 1972, Fifty British Plays 1982, Fifth Row Center 1986, The Future of the Theatre 1998, What's So Flinking Bunny 2010, Great Moments in the Theatre 2012, Les Misérables: From Stage to Screen (with Martyn Palmer) 2013; numerous articles on cultural and theatrical matters in British and American journals. *Leisure interests:* music, literature, watching soccer. *Address:* 40 Broomhouse Road, London, SW6 3QX, England.

NIGHY, Bill; British actor; b. 12 Dec. 1949, Caterham, Surrey, England; s. of Alfred Nighy and Catherine Whittaker; fmr partner Diana Quick; one d.; ed John Fisher Grammar, Purley; Theatre Managers Best Actor 1996, Barclays Best Actor Award 2004. *Stage appearances include:* Arcadia, Rosencrantz & Guildenstern, Entertaining Mr Sloane, Speak Now, Under New Management, Freedom of the City, Comings and Goings, Illuminations, Map of the World, The Seagull, Skylight, Blue Orange, Mean Tears, King Lear, Pravda, Betrayal, Skylight (Best Actor, Barclays Theatre Award 1996), A Kind of Alaska, Blue/Orange, The Vertical Hour 2006. *Film appearances include:* The Bitch (uncredited) 1979, The Girl in the Cafe, Underworld: Evolution, Flushed Away, The Constant Gardener, The Threepenny Opera, The Bass Player, Eye of the Needle 1981, Curse of the Pink Panther 1983, The Little Drummer Girl 1984, The Phantom of the Opera 1989, Mack the Knife 1990, Being Human 1993, True Blue 1996, Indian Summer 1996, Fairy Tale – A True Story 1997, The Canterbury Tales (series) 1998, Still Crazy (Best Comedy Performance, Evening Standard Peter Sellers Award 1998) 1998, Guest House Paradiso 1999, The Magic of Vincent 2000, Blow Dry 2001, The Lawless Heart (Best Supporting Actor, LA Critics' Circle Award 2004) 2001, Lucky Break 2001,

AKA 2002, I Capture the Castle (Best Supporting Actor, LA Critics' Circle Award 2004) 2003, Love Actually (London Film Critics' Award 2004, Best Supporting Actor, LA Critics' Circle Award 2004, BAFTA Award for Best Actor in a Supporting Role 2004) 2003, Underworld 2003, Shaun of the Dead 2004, Enduring Love 2004, The Magic Roundabout (voice) 2005, The Hitchhiker's Guide to the Galaxy 2005, The Constant Gardener 2005, Underworld Evolution 2006, Pirates of the Caribbean: Dead Man's Chest 2006, Stormbreaker 2006, Flushed Away (voice) 2006, Notes on a Scandal 2006, Hot Fuzz 2007, Pirates of the Caribbean: At World's End 2007, Slapper 2008, Valkyrie 2008, Underworld: Rise of the Lycans 2009, The Boat That Rocked 2009, G-Force 2009, Wild Target 2010, Harry Potter and the Deathly Hallows: Part 1 2010, The Best Exotic Marigold Hotel 2011, Total Recall 2012. *Radio:* Lord of the Rings 1981, No Commitments, Bleak House, Private Lives 2010, numerous others. *Television includes:* Auf Wiedersehen Pet, Insiders, Kavanagh Series III, Wycliffe, Peak Practice, Bergerac, Antonia and Jane 1991, The Cat Bought It In, South of the Border, Under the Skin, Dreams of Leaving, Soldiers Talking Cleanly, Fat, Standing in for Henry; Agony (series) 1979, Fox 1980, Easter 2016 1982, Reilly: The Ace of Spies (mini-series) 1983, The Last Place on Earth (mini-series) 1985, Hitler's S.S.: Portrait in Evil 1985, Thirteen at Dinner (film) 1985, Making News (series) 1989, Absolute Hell 1991, The Men's Room (mini-series) 1991, A Masculine Ending 1992, Eye of the Storm (mini-series) 1993, Unnatural Causes 1993, Don't Leave Me This Way 1993, The Maitlands 1993, Kiss Me Kate (series episode) 1998, Longitude 2000, The Inspector Lynley Mysteries: Well Schooled in Murder 2002, Ready When You Are Mr. McGill 2003, The Lost Prince (Best Actor, Broadcasting Press Guild Award 2003) 2003, State of Play (series) (Best Actor, Broadcasting Press Guild Award 2003) 2003, BAFTA Award for Best Actor in a Television Drama 2004) 2003, The Canterbury Tales (mini-series, The Wife of Bath's Tale) 2003, The Young Visiters (sic) (Best Actor, Broadcasting Press Guild Award 2003) 2003, Life Beyond the Box: Norman Stanley Fletcher (narrator) 2003, He Knew He Was Right (mini-series) 2004, Gideon's Daughter (Golden Globe Award for Best Actor in a mini-series or film made for TV 2007) 2005, The Girl in the Café 2005, The Armstrongs (series) 2006. *Leisure interests:* reading, rhythm and blues. *Address:* c/o Markham & Froggatt Ltd Personal Management, 4 Windmill Street, London, W1T 2HZ, England (office). *Telephone:* (20) 7636-4412 (office). *Fax:* (20) 7637-5233 (office). *Website:* www.markhamfroggatt.com (office).

NIGMATULIN, Nurlan, PhD; Kazakhstani politician, government official and business executive; *Chairman, Majlis;* b. 1962; m. Baimurzayeva Venera; three s.; ed Qarağandi Polytechnic Inst.; Deputy Akim (head of a local govt) of Astana 1999–2002; Vice-Minister of Transport and Communications 2002–04; Deputy Chief of Presidential Admin 2004–06; Akim of Qarağandi Oblast 2006–09; mem. Political Council of Light of the Fatherland People's Democratic Party (Nur Otan) ('Nur Otan' Khalyktyk Demokratiyalyk Partiyasy) 1999–2000, Chair. Astana City Br. 2000–02, First Deputy Chair. Nur Otan 2009–; Chair. (Speaker), Majlis (Parl.) 2012–; mem. Bd of Dirs CJSC Nat. Information Technologies 20002–03; Chair. Astana Int. Airport 2002–03, KazakhTelecom 2003, Air Astana 2007; Kurmet Order 2004, II Degree Barys Order 2009, Medal '10 Years of Astana City' 2008; Medal '20 Years of the Independence of the Republic of Kazakhstan' 2011. *Leisure interests:* tennis, football. *Address:* Office of the Chairman, Majlis, 010000 Astana, Parliament House (office); Light of the Fatherland People's Democratic Party (Nur Otan), 050000 Almaty, Kunaev kosh. 12/1, Kazakhstan. *Telephone:* (7172) 74-71-42 (office); (7172) 55-55-62. *Fax:* (7172) 24-26-19 (office); (727) 279-40-66. *E-mail:* smimazh@parlam.kz (office); partyotan@nursat.kz. *Website:* www.parlam.kz (office); nurotan.kz.

NIGMATULIN, Robert I., MS, PhD, DrSc; Russian mechanical engineer and academic; *Director, P.P. Shirsov Institute of Oceanology, Russian Academy of Sciences;* b. 17 June 1940; m. 1968; two c.; ed Bauman Tech. Univ., Lomonosov Univ., Moscow; Jr Researcher, Inst. of Mechanics, Lomonosov Univ., Moscow 1963–70, Sr Researcher 1970–74, Prof. and Scientific Chief of Lab. 1974–86, currently Prof.; Vice-Dir Inst. of North Devt Problems and Inst. of Thermophysics, Siberian Br. of Russian Acad. of Sciences, Tyumen 1986–90, Dir Tyumen Inst. of Mechanics of Multiphase Systems 1990–95; Prof. and Chair. Dept of Mechanics, Tyumen Univ. 1986–93; Deputy in State Duma 1999–2003, Chair. Highest Ecology Council; Pres. Ufa (Bashkortostan) Br., Russian Acad. of Sciences 1993–2006, Scientific Chief, Inst. of Mechanics, Ufa Br. 2006–; mem. Presidium Russian Acad. of Sciences 2006–; Dir P.P. Shirsov Inst. of Oceanology, Moscow 2006–; Visiting Scholar and Prof., Centre for Multiphase Research, Rensselaer Polytechnic Inst. 1993–2006; Academician, Russian Acad. of Sciences 1991–, Bashkortostan Acad. of Sciences 1991–; mem. Russian Nat. Cttee of Theoretical and Applied Mechanics 1976–, Cen. Asia Acad., Uzbekistan 1993–, Int. Eastern Petroleum Acad., Azerbaijan 1993–; Hon. mem. Acad. of Natural Sciences of Russian Fed. 1995, Acad. of Sciences of Tatarstan 2007; Order of Honour (Decree of the Pres. of Russia) 2000; Lenin Komsomol Prize 1973, USSR State Prize 1983, Gold Medal, Nat. Econ. Achievements Exhbn 1989, First Prize, Siberian Br. of Russian Acad. of Sciences 1990, Makeev Medal, Russian Fed. of Astronautica 1996, Tsiolkovski Gold Medal, Russian Fed. of Astronautica 2000. *Publications:* eight books, 200 papers and 20 preprints; 13 patents. *Address:* P.P. Shirsov Institute of Oceanology, 36, Nahimovsky prospect, 117997 Moscow, Russia (office). *Telephone:* (495) 124-59-96 (office). *Fax:* (495) 124-59-83 (office). *Website:* www.ocean.ru (office); www .nigmatulin.ru.

NIGO; Japanese fashion designer, music producer and DJ; b. (Tomoaki Nagao), 23 Dec. 1970; ed Bunka Fashion Coll., Tokyo; fashion student, magazine stylist, DJ early 1990s; DJ of Japanese hip hop group Teriyaki Boyz; began making T-shirts and selling them at parties and DJ shows; opened store Nowhere with Jun Takahashi 1993; set up A Bathing Ape fashion label 1993, label now has stores across Japan and in Hong Kong, London, New York; built Ape Sounds the studio and f. The Bapesounds music label; f. A Bathing Ape fashion label 1993 with stores across Japan and in Hong Kong and London, opened New York store 2005, Los Angeles (closed 2010); with Pharrell Williams, responsible for helping produce the Billionaire Boys Club and Ice Cream Footwear brands; Creative Dir for Uniqlo's UT brand; also has interests in music, art, cafés, hairstyling; f. Bapesta!!Wrestling (professional wrestling), Bape Gallery; Best Producer Award, Tokyo Art Dirs Club (ADC) 2002, one of 30 Best Asian Heroes, Time Asia 2004, Style Award, MTV Asia Awards 2005. *Television:* Nigoideneye (MTV Japan). *Broadcasts:* (B)ape TV, live show Bape Heads Show. *Recordings include:* Ape Sounds 2000, Return of the Ape Sounds 2005.

NIILUS, Leopoldo Juan (Leopold Johannes); Argentine lawyer and international human rights consultant; b. 19 Jan. 1930, Tallinn, Estonia; s. of the late Jaan Eduard Niilus and Meta Kiris; m. Malle Reet Veerus 1961; one d.; ed Faculty of Law, Univ. Buenos Aires, Argentina, Southern Methodist Univ., Dallas, Tex., USA; left Estonia 1944; fmrly practising lawyer, Buenos Aires; fmr Chair. Argentine Student Christian Movt; fmr mem. World Student Christian Fed.; Dir Argentine Dept, River Plate Centre of Christian Studies 1966–67; Gen. Sec. ISAL (Comm. for Church and Soc. in Latin America) 1968–69; Dir Comm. of the Churches on Int. Affairs of WCC, Geneva 1969–81; Dir Int. Ecumenical Relations, Middle East Council of Churches 1982–95; Consultant on int. affairs and human rights, Lutheran World Fed. 1988–95; ind. political consultant 1996–; participated in mediation for Sudan peace negotiations 1972, Guatemala peace negotiations, signed as witness, Oslo accords on Guatemala 1990; Order of Two Niles, 1st Grade (Sudan). *Publications:* On Penal Law (essays); numerous articles and essays in ecumenical publs on peace, disarmament, North–South relations, Middle East, Central America. *Address:* 7 chemin du Champ d'Anier, 1209 Geneva, Switzerland. *Telephone:* (22) 7983259. *Fax:* (22) 7884448. *E-mail:* niilus@bluewin.ch.

NIINILUOTO, Ilkka, BSc, MSc, PhD; Finnish philosopher, mathematician, academic and fmr university administrator; *Professor, University of Helsinki;* b. 12 March 1946, Helsinki; m. Ritva Pelkonen; three c.; ed Univ. of Helsinki, Stanford Univ., USA; Teaching Asst, Dept of Philosophy, Univ. of Helsinki 1969–71, Assoc. Prof. of Math. 1973–77, Docent of Theoretical Philosophy 1974–81, Acting Prof. of Theoretical Philosophy 1977–81, Prof. 1981–, Chair. Dept of Philosophy 1988–88, 1992, 1995–2000, Vice-Dean, Faculty of Arts 1988–89, 1991, 1995–98, Dean 1990, 1993–94, Vice-Rector 1998–2003, Rector 2003–08, Chancellor 2008–13; Research Asst, Dept of Philosophy, Acad. of Finland 1971–73; Chair. Finnish Cultural Foundation 1993–94, Helsinki Inst. of Physics 1998–2003; Pres. Philosophical Soc. of Finland 1975–, Finnish Soc. for Science Studies 1985–86, Fed. of Finnish Learned Socs 2000–, Finnish Council of Univ. Rectors 2006–07; mem. Finnish Acad. of Science 1985–, British Soc. for the Philosophy of Science; Public Information Award, Univ. of Helsinki 1986, Chydenius Award 1990. *Publications:* Is Science Progressive? 1984, Truthlikeness 1987, Critical Scientific Realism 1999; numerous journal articles. *Address:* PO Box 24, Unioninkatu 40A, 00014 Helsinki, Finland (office). *Telephone:* (9) 5884252 (office). *E-mail:* ilkka.niiniluoto@helsinki .fi (office). *Website:* www.helsinki.fi (office).

NIINISTÖ, Sauli Väinämö, LLM; Finnish politician, lawyer and head of state; *President;* b. 24 Aug. 1948, Salo; m. 1st (wife deceased); two s.; m. 2nd Jenni Haukio; own law office in Salo 1978–88; Sr Sec., Turku Court of Appeal 1976; mem. Salo City Council 1977–92, Chair. 1989–92, mem. City Bd 1977–88; mem. Nat. Coalition Party (KOK) Council 1979–81, Party Chair. 1994–2001; mem. Parl. 1987–2003, 2007–11, Chair. Constitutional Cttee of Parl. 1993–95, Speaker 2007–11; Deputy Prime Minister 1995–2001; Minister of Justice 1995–96, of Finance 1996–2003; Vice-Pres. EIB 2003–07; Pres. of Finland 2012–; Chair. European Democratic Union 1998–2002, Econ. and Financial Affairs Council and the Eurogroup 1999; apptd Gov. for Finland, World Bank 2001; mem. Bd of Govs EBRD 1996–2003, Chair. 1999–2000. *Address:* Office of the President, Mariankatu 2, 00170 Helsinki, Finland (office). *Telephone:* (9) 661133 (office). *Fax:* (9) 638247 (office). *E-mail:* presidentti@tpk.fi (office). *Website:* www.presidentti.fi (office).

NIKAI, Toshihiro; Japanese politician; b. 17 Feb. 1939; ed Faculty of Law, Chuo Univ.; Sec. to Saburo Endo 1961; mem. Wakayama Prefectural Ass. 1975; mem. House of Reps (Wakayama 3rd Dist; elected eight times) 1983–, Chair. Standing Cttee on Construction 1997, Special Cttee on Postal Privatization 2005; State Sec. of Transportation 1990, 1993; Dir Election Div., New Frontier Party 1995; Minister of Transport and Dir-Gen. Hokkaido Devt Agency 1999, 2000; Sec.-Gen. and Rep. New Conservative Party 2002; joined Liberal Democratic Party (LDP) 2003, Chair. Special Cttee on Tourism, Dir-Gen. Election Bureau 2004–05, Chair. Diet Affairs Cttee 2006, Chair. Gen. Council 2007–; Minister of Economy, Trade and Industry 2005–06, 2008–09. *Address:* Liberal-Democratic Party, 1-11-23, Nagata-cho, Chiyoda-ku, Tokyo 100-8910, Japan (office). *Telephone:* (3) 3581-6211 (office). *E-mail:* koho@ldp.jimin.or.jp (office). *Website:* www.jimin.jp (office).

NIKITIN, Nikolai F.; Russian mechanical engineer and aviation engineer; *Director-General, Russian Aviation Production Corporation MIG;* b. 1 Jan. 1950, Orudyevo, Moscow region; ed Moscow State Aviation Inst.; worked for OKB Sukhoi 1973–91; Deputy Dir-Gen. 1991–97, Dir-Gen., mem. Bd of Dirs 1997–99; First Deputy Dir-Gen. ABPK Sukhoi 1999; Dir-Gen. Russian Aviation Production Corporation MIG 1999–; gen. constructor of SU-27M, S-80, SU-35, SU-37MP; USSR State Prize for aviation complex SU-27 1991. *Address:* Russian Aviation Production Corporation MIG, 1 Botkinsky proyezd 7, Moscow 125040, Russia (office). *Telephone:* (495) 207-04-75 (office); (495) 207-07-57 (office). *Website:* www .migavia.ru (office).

NIKOIAN, Samvel; Armenian politician; b. 13 Feb. 1958, Sarnaghbyur, Ani region (now Shirak Prov.); m.; three c.; ed State Eng Univ. of Armenia, Armenian Br. of Marxism-Leninism Univ. adjunct to USSR Cen. Cttee; worked as engineer-constructor 1982–90, later as Sr Engineer, Head of Div., Deputy Head of Production Unit and Head of Production Unit in Yerevan Hydro Apparatus Plant; Deputy Chief Engineer, Yerevan Experimental Machinery Plant 1995; Head of Div. in Chamber of Commerce and Industry of Armenia 1995–98; Deputy Dir 'Haymamul' (Armenian Media) CJSC 1998–2001; involved in production of ammunition and its delivery during the years of Artsakh freedom fighting; mem. Nat. United Party acting underground in USSR; mem. Republican Party of Armenia (RPA), Chair. RPA Org. Cttee 2001–03, Sec. RPA Faction 2007–09, mem. Foreign Relations Cttee 2008–09, mem. Bd; mem. 'Yerkrapah' Volunteer Union 1997–; Deputy (RPA) in Nat. Ass. 2003–, mem. Standing Cttee on Foreign Relations, mem. ad-hoc Cttee Studying the Effectiveness of the Use of Loans, Credits, Grants and Humanitarian Aid Received from Foreign States and Int. Orgs, mem. Armenian del. of OSCE Parl. Ass., Head of Armenian del. of Inter-parl. Union 2008– Deputy-Chair. Nat. Ass. 2009–11, Chair. (Speaker) 2011–12; Medal of 'Andranik Ozanyan' of the Armenian Armed Forces 2005, Commemorative Medal from the Prime Minister 2006. *Address:* Azgayin Zhoghov (National Assembly), 0095 Yerevan, Marshal Baghramian Street 19, Armenia (office). *E-mail:* samvel.nikoyan@parliament.am (office). *Website:* www.parliament.am (office).

NIKOLAISHVILI, Col Ramaz; Georgian economist and politician; b. 17 June 1965, Tbilisi; m.; three c.; ed Polytechnic Inst. of Georgia, Ivane Javakhishvili Tbilisi State Univ.; served in various man. positions in Operations Div., Georgian Nat. Tax Inspectorate 1994–2000; Deputy Head of Special Tasks Div., Special Legion 2000–03; Deputy Head of Information and Analytical Dept of Financial Police Div., Ministry of Finance 2003–04, Head of Statistical and Information Service of Financial Police 2004–05, Head of Tbilisi Main Div. of Financial Police Investigation Dept 2005–07, Head of Tbilisi Main Div. of Revenue Service Investigation Dept 2007–08; Gov. Lanchkhuti, Ozurgeti and Chokhatauri Dists 2008; Deputy Minister of Defence 2008; Chair. Nat. Roads Dept 2008–10; Minister of Regional Devt and Infrastructure 2010–12, resgnd in order to run for parl. election; Medal of Honour 2007, Order of Honour 2009, Presidential Order of Excellence 2010; Engineer of the Year, Union Scientific and Engineering Asscn of Georgia 2010. *Address:* c/o Ministry of Regional Development and Infrastructure, 0177 Tbilisi, Al. Qazbegi 12, Georgia. *E-mail:* press@mrdi.gov.ge.

NIKOLAYEV, Army Gen. Andrei Ivanovich; Russian politician and fmr army officer; b. 21 April 1949, Moscow; m. Tatyana Yuryevna Nikolayeva; two s.; ed Moscow Gen. Troops Commdg School of RSFSR Supreme Soviet, M. Frunze Mil. Acad., Gen. Staff Acad.; commdr of platoon, co., regt; First Deputy Head Main Admin. of Gen. HQ of USSR Armed Forces; First Deputy Head of Gen. HQ of Russian Army 1992–94; C-in-C of Border troops of Russian Fed. 1994–; Head of Fed. Border Troops Service 1995–97; mem. State Duma (Parl.) 1998–2003; Chair. Cttee of Defence 2000–03; Adviser to the Pres. on Military and Naval Matters 2004; f. Union of People's Power and Labour 1998. *Leisure interests:* theatre, organ music. *Address:* c/o Office of the President, 103132 Moscow, Staraya pl. 4, Russia.

NIKOLAYEV, Mikhail Yefimovich; Russian/Yakut politician; b. 13 Nov. 1937, Ordzhonikidze Region, Yakutia; m.; three c.; ed Omsk Veterinary Inst., Higher CP School; worked as veterinarian, then Sec. Zhigan Regional Comsomol Cttee, First Sec. Yakut Comsomol Cttee, Sec., then First Sec. Verkhneviluysk Regional CP Cttee 1971–75; Deputy Chair. Council of Ministers Yakut ASSR 1975–79; Minister of Agric. 1979–85; Sec. Yakut Regional CP Cttee 1985–89; Chair. Presidium of Supreme Soviet Yakut ASSR 1989–91; Pres. Repub. of Sakha (Yakutia) 1991–2001; mem. Council of Fed. of Russia 1993, Rep. Sakha-Yakutia Rep. In Council of Fed. 2001, Deputy Chair. 2002; Order of Red Banner of Labour, Order of Friendship, Order for Prominent Services to the Fatherland and other honours. *Publications include:* My People are My Republic 1992, The Arctic: The Pain and Hope of Russia 1994, The Arctic. XXI Century 1999.

NIKOLIĆ, Tomislav; Serbian politician and head of state; *President;* b. 15 Feb. 1952, Kragujevac; s. of Radomir Nikolić and Živadinka Nikolić (née Đoković); m. Dragica Ninković; two s.; ed Univ. of Belgrade; Deputy, Fed. Ass. of Serbia and Montenegro 1991–2006, mem. Cttee on Constitutional Charter Issues, Cttee on Foreign Affairs; mem. del. to Parl. Ass. of Council of Europe; Vice-Pres. of Serbia 1998, of Serbia and Montenegro 1999; unsuccessful presidential cand. (Serbian Progressive Party) 2000, 2003, 2004, 2008; Co-founder (with Vojislav Šešelj) and Vice-Pres. Serbian Radical Party (Srpska Radikalna Stranka), Acting Leader 2003–08; Speaker, Serbian Parl. 8–13 May 2007; Leader Serbian Progressive Party (Srpska napredna stranka) 2008–12; Pres. of Serbia 31 May 2012–. *Publications:* (13 political books all in Serbo-Croatian): Neither Victory Nor Defeat, All for Kosovo and Metohija, Abducted Victory, Šešelj for President, Through the Darkness of the Media, The Letter with an Address, In the Grip of Hatred, I Spoke, The Parliamentary Walk on Torture, Neo-Communist Parliament, Since the Beginning, When the Government Falls, Milošević Falls, The Trenches in the National Assembly. *Address:* Office of the President 11000 Belgrade, Andrićev venac 1, Serbia (office). *Telephone:* (11) 3043068 (office). *Fax:* (11) 3043280 (office). *E-mail:* predstavkegradjana@predsednik.rs (office). *Website:* www.predsednik.rs (office).

NIKOLSKY, Boris Vassilyevich; Russian politician; *Moscow Representative to Council of Federation;* b. 1 May 1937, Moscow; m.; two c.; ed Moscow Inst. of Agric. Eng, Higher School Cen. Cttee CPSU; master, chief engineer in a factory; Deputy Chair. Moscow Municipal Exec. Cttee on problems of energy and fuel 1976–82; Sec. Moscow City CP Cttee 1982–84; Sec., then Second Sec. Cen. Cttee of Georgian CP 1984–; First Deputy Chair. Moscow City Planning Cttee 1989–; First Deputy Chair. Moscow City Construction Cttee 1990–91; Deputy Prime Minister Moscow Govt 1991–92, First Deputy Chair. 1992–2002; Moscow Rep. to Council of Fed. 2002–. *Address:* Moscow Government, Tverskaya str. 13, 103032 Moscow, Russia (office). *Telephone:* (495) 229-24-24 (office). *Fax:* (495) 230-20-69. *E-mail:* mayor@ mos.ru (office).

NIKONENKO, Sergey Petrovich; Russian actor, film director and scriptwriter; b. 16 April 1941, Moscow; s. of Peter Nikonenko and Nina Nikonenko; m. Yekaterina Voronina-Nikonenko; one s.; ed All-Union Inst. of Cinematography; mem. Union of Cinematographers 1968–; f. Yesenin Cultural Foundation 1994–; Order of Honour 1971; Comsomol Prize 1976, A. Dovzhenko Medal 1988, Grand Prix. Int. Film Festival in Oberhausen (Germany), People's Artist of Russia 1991. *Film appearances include:* War and Peace 1965–67, Wings 1966, They Are Ringing, Open the Door 1966, Strange People 1969, Journalist, I Have Come This Way, Crime and Punishment, White Explosion 1969, Sing a Song, Poet 1971, Inspector of Road Police 1982, Unfinished Piece for a Mechanical Piano 1976, Winter Evening in Gagry 1986, Tomorrow Was War 1987, The Red Wine of Victory 1990, Family Man 1991, Unwilling to Marry 1992, Time of the Dancer 1996, Kids of Monday 1997, Sinful Love 1997, Chinese Service 1999, Classic 1998, Istinnyye proishestviya (True Stories) 2002, Interesnyye muzhchiny (Interesting Men) 2003. *Films directed include:* Gypsy's Happiness, Birds Above the Town, Love, Wait, Lyonya, I Want Your Husband. *Television appearances include:* Kamenskaya 2000, Igry v podkidnogo (Tricky Games) 2001, Nevozmozhnye zelyonye glaza 2002, In the Service of My Country 2003. *Leisure interests:* classical literature and music, opera music, painting. *Address:* Sivcev-Vrasheu 44/14, 119002 Moscow (office); Sivtsev Vrazhek str. 44, Apt. 20, 121002 Moscow, Russia (home). *Telephone:* (495) 244-03-44 (office); (495) 241-78-72 (home).

NIKONOV, Vyacheslav Alekseyevich, DrHis; Russian politician, academic and consultant; *President, Polity Foundation;* b. 5 June 1956, Moscow; s. of Aleksey Dmitrievich Nikonov and Svetlana Vyacheslavovna Molotova; grandson of Vyacheslav Molotov; m. 1st Viktoria Makarovna Kostyuk 1976; m. 2nd Olga

Mikhailovna Rozhkova 1987; three s.; ed Moscow State Univ.; researcher, Moscow State Univ.; on staff Admin. Cen. Cttee CPSU 1989–90; on staff of Pres. Gorbachev 1990–91; Asst to Chair. USSR State Security Cttee (KGB) 1991–92; Prof. of Political Science, California Inst. of Tech., USA 1992; counsellor, Dept of Political Problems, Int. Foundation of Econ. and Social Reforms (Foundation Reforma) 1992–93; mem. State Duma (Parl.) 1994–96, Chair. Sub-cttee on Int. Security and Arms Control 1994–95; Deputy Chair. Cttee to Re-elect the Pres. 1996; Dean of History and Political Science, Moscow Int. Univ. 2001; Deputy Chair. Editorial Bd Russia in Global Affairs 2002; Pres. Polity Foundation 1993–, Unity for Russia Foundation 2003–; Head, Int. Cooperation and Public Diplomacy Cttee, Public Council of the Russian Fed. 2006–; Ed.-in-Chief Strategy for Russia Journal 2003–; mem. Bd of Dirs Council on Foreign and Defense Policy, Russian Public Policy Center; mem. Advisory Council Carnegie Endowment (Moscow Br.). *Publications:* Republicans: From Eisenhower to Nixon 1984, Iran-Contra Affair 1988, Republicans: From Nixon to Reagan 1989, The Age of Change: Russia in the 90s as Viewed by a Conservative 1999, Contemporary Russian Politics (ed.) 2003, 2005, Agenda for Russia 2004 (ed.), Russia in Contemporary Politics 2005 (ed.), Agenda for Russia 2005 (ed.), Molotov: Youth 2005, A Code to Politics 2006. *Leisure interests:* reading, gardening. *Address:* Polity Foundation, 101000 Moscow, Bolshoy Zlatoustinsky per. 8/7, Russia (office). *Telephone:* (495) 206-81-49 (office). *Fax:* (495) 206-86-61 (office). *E-mail:* info@polity.ru (office). *Website:* www.polity.ru (office).

NIKŠIĆ, Nermin (Dževad); Bosnia and Herzegovina lawyer and politician; *Prime Minister of the Federation of Bosnia and Herzegovina;* b. 27 Dec. 1960, Konjic; s. of Džemal Nikšić and Amila Nikšić; m. Nadja Nikšić; one s. one d.; ed Univ. of Mostar; employed in Dept of Urban Planning, Construction and Housing and Utilities, municipality of Konjic 1988, later Dept of Hotel Inspection, Chief Inspector 1990–92, Asst Head of Legal Affairs 1992–95, Chair. Exec. Bd, Municipality of Konjic 1995–98, apptd Deputy Mayor of Konjic 2000, resgnd after being elected to Parl.; mem. House of Reps of Fed. of Bosnia and Herzegovina 2000–07; mem. Social Democratic Party (SDP) 1993–, Pres. Konjic Municipal Br. 1994, Pres. Herzegovina-Neretva Canton Br. 2007, SDP Gen. Sec. 2007–; Prime Minister, Fed. of Bosnia and Herzegovina 2011–. *Leisure interest:* sport. *Address:* Office of the Prime Minister, 71000 Sarajevo, Alipašina 41, Bosnia and Herzegovina (office). *Telephone:* (33) 650457 (office). *Fax:* (33) 664816 (office). *E-mail:* premijer@fbihvlada.gov.ba (office). *Website:* www.fbihvlada.gov.ba (office).

NILEKANI, Nandan M., BEng, BTech; Indian business executive and government official; *Chairman, Unique Identification Authority of India;* b. 2 June 1955, Bangalore, Karnataka; s. of Mohan Rao Nilekani and Durga Nilekani; m. Rohini Nilekani; two c.; ed Indian Inst. of Tech., Bombay (now Mumbai); Co-founder and mem. Bd of Dirs Infosys Technologies Ltd 1981–, later Man. Dir, Pres. and COO, CEO, Pres. and Man. Dir 2002–07, Co-Chair. 2007–09; Chair. (with rank of cabinet minister) Unique Identification Authority of India 2009–; Co-founder India's Nat. Asscn of Software and Service Cos (NASSCOM), Bangalore Chapter of The IndUS Entrepreneurs (TiE); Chair. Govt of India's IT for the Power Sector task force, Bangalore Agenda task force; Co-Chair. Business Leaders Dialogue, Initiative for Social Innovation Through Business, Aspen Inst., Advisory Bd IIT Bombay Heritage Fund; mem. Asia Pacific Regional Advisory Bd, London Business School, Global Advisory Council, The Conf. Bd, World Econ. Forum Foundation Bd 2006–, Bd of Govs Indian Inst. of Tech. Bombay, Review Cttee Jawaharlal Nehru Nat. Urban Renewal Mission; Padma Bhushan 2006; Alumnus Award, Indian Inst. of Tech. 1999, named in global survey by Financial Times and PricewaterhouseCoopers amongst "World's most respected business leaders" 2002, 2003, Fortune Asian Businessman of the Year (co-recipient) 2003, Corporate Citizen of the Year Award, CNBC Asia Business Leader Awards 2004, Asia Business Leaders Awards 2004, Joseph Schumpeter Prize 2005, Forbes Businessman of the Year for Asia 2007, Legend in Leadership Award, Yale Univ. 2009, named by TIME magazine on Time 100 list of World's Most Influential People 2009. *Publication:* Imagining India: Ideas for the New Century (Indiaplaza Golden Quill Readers' Choice Award for Non-fiction) 2009. *Address:* Unique Identification Authority of India, Planning Commission of India, Government of India, 3rd Floor, Tower II, Jeevan Bharti Building, Connaught Circus, New Delhi 110 001 (office); 856, 13th Main, III Block, Koramangala, Bangalore 560 034, India (home). *Telephone:* (11) 23096620 (office). (80) 25536150 (home). *Fax:* (80) 25534654 (home). *E-mail:* plancom@nic.in (office); webadmin-uidai@nic.in (office). *Website:* www.planningcommission.nic.in (office).

NILES, Thomas Michael Tolliver, MA; American diplomatist; *Vice-Chairman, United States Council for International Business;* b. 22 Sept. 1939, Lexington, Ky; s. of John Jacob Niles and Rena Niles (née Lipetz); m. Carroll C. Ehringhaus 1967; one s. one d.; ed Harvard Univ. and Univ. of Kentucky; Foreign Service Officer, Dept of State 1962; posts in Moscow, Belgrade and Brussels; Amb. to Canada 1985–89, to Greece 1993–97; Perm. Rep. to the EEC, Brussels 1989; Vice-Pres. Nat. Defense Univ. 1997–98 (retd); Pres. US Council for Int. Business 1998–2005, Pres. Emer. and Vice-Chair. 2005–; mem. Bd of Dirs Jacobs Eng Group Inc., Internet Corpn for Assigned Names and Numbers (ICANN) 2003–05; Superior Honor Award, Dept of State 1982, 1985. *Address:* United States Council for International Business, 1212 Avenue of the Americas, New York, NY 10036, USA (office). *Telephone:* (212) 354-4480 (office). *Fax:* (212) 575-0327 (office). *E-mail:* info@uscib.org (office). *Website:* www.uscib.org (office).

NIMATALLAH, Yusuf A., PhD; Saudi Arabian economist; b. 1936; ed American Univ., Beirut and Univ. of Massachusetts, USA; with Banque de l'Indochine 1952–57; Teaching Asst in Econs, Univ. of Massachusetts 1963–65; Prof. of Monetary and Int. Econs, Univ. of Riyadh (King Saud Univ. 1982–) 1965 (on leave 1973); Adviser to Minister of Finance on Money and Banking, Oil Finance and Planning 1967–73; Adviser to Sultan of Oman on Oil, Finance, Money and Banking; Deputy Chair. and Pres. Cen. Bank of Oman 1975–78; Deputy Chair. UBAF Arab American Bank, New York 1976–78; Exec. Dir Fund for Saudi Arabia 1979–89; currently Head of Injaz Money Exchange Co. (Yousuf Abdul Wahab Niamatullah Co.) Jeddah. *Address:* Injaz Money Exchange Company, PO Box 7039, Behind Al Shoalah Centre 88, Moh Taweel Street, 21462 Jeddah, Saudi Arabia. *Telephone:* (2) 667-6025. *Fax:* (2) 665-8858.

NIMETZ, Matthew, LLB, MA; American diplomatist, lawyer, business executive and UN official; *Personal Envoy of the Secretary General for the Greece-FYROM talks, United Nations;* b. 17 June 1939, Brooklyn, NY; m. Gloria S. Lorch; one s. one

d.; ed Williams Coll., Balliol Coll. Oxford, UK, Harvard Univ.; called to Bar, NY 1966, DC 1968; law clerk to Justice John M. Harlan, Supreme Court 1965–67; Staff Asst to Pres. Johnson 1967–69; Assoc. with Simpson Thatcher and Bartlett LLC, New York 1969–74, Pnr 1974–77; Pnr, Paul, Weiss, Rifkind, Wharton & Garrison LLC 1981–2000; Man. Dir General Atlantic Pnrs (now General Atlantic) LLC, Greenwich, Conn. 2000–; Counsellor, Dept of State 1977–80, Acting Co-ordinator of Refugee Affairs 1979–80; Presidential Envoy to Greece–Macedonian Negotiations 1994–95, Chair. 1997, Personal Envoy of UN Sec.-Gen. for Greece-FYROM Talks 1999–; Commr Port Authority of NY and NJ 1975–77; Dir and Chair. World Resources Inst. 1982–94 Chair. UN Devt Corpn 1986–94, Carnegie Forum in USA, Greece and Turkey 1996–98, Centre for Democracy and Reconciliation in SE Europe 1997–; mem. Bd of Dirs Charles H. Revson Foundation 1990–98, NY State Nature Conservancy 1997–; Dir Inst. Public Admin. 1999–; mem. NY State Advisory Council on State Productivity 1990–92; mem. Bd of Trustees, Cen. European Univ., Budapest, Hungary 1998–, Asscn of Bar of City of NY, Council on Foreign Relations; Trustee, William Coll. 1981–96; Rhodes Scholar, Balliol Coll. Oxford, UK 1962; Hon. LLD (Williams Coll.) 1979. *Address:* c/o Office of the Secretary-General, United Nations, New York, NY 10017, USA.

NIMLEY, Thomas Yaya; Liberian politician; b. 5 Nov. 1956, Pleebo, Maryland County; Minister of Foreign Affairs 2003–06; Chair. Movt for Democracy in Liberia (MODEL). *Address:* Ministry of Foreign Affairs, Mamba Point, POB 10-9002, 1000 Monrovia 10, Liberia (office).

NIMOY, Leonard; American actor and director; b. 26 March 1931, Boston, Mass; s. of Max Nimoy and Dora Nimoy (née Spinner); m. 1st Sandi Zober 1954 (divorced); one s. one d.; m. 2nd Susan Bay 1988; ed Boston Coll. and Antioch Univ.; served in US Army 1954–56; trained at the Pasadena Playhouse, Calif. 1960–63. *Film appearances include:* Queen for a Day, Rhubarb 1951, Kid Monk Baron, Francis Goes to West Point 1952, Old Overland Trail 1953, Satan's Satellites 1958, The Balcony 1963, Deathwatch 1966, Valley of Mystery (co-producer) 1967, Catlow (co-producer) 1971, Invasion of the Bodysnatchers (co-producer) 1978, Star Trek: The Motion Picture (also co-producer) 1979, Star Trek: The Wrath of Khan (also co-producer) 1982, Star Trek III: The Search for Spock (also dir) 1984, Star Trek IV: The Voyage Home (also dir) 1986, Star Trek V: The Final Frontier 1989, Star Trek VI: The Undiscovered Country 1991, The Pagemaster (voice) 1994, Carpati: 50 Miles, 50 Years (narrator) 1996, A Life Apart: Hasidism in America (narrator) 1997, Armageddon: Target Earth 1998, Sinbad: Beyond the Veil of Mists (voice) 2000, Atlantis: The Lost Empire (voice) 2001, Star Trek (played role of Spock Prime) 2009, Land of the Lost (voice) 2009, Transformers: Dark of the Moon (voice) 2011, Zambezia (voice) 2012, Star Trek: Into Darkness (as Spock Prime) 2013. *Films directed:* Three Men and A Baby 1987, The Good Mother 1988, Body Wars 1989, Funny About Love 1990, Holy Matrimony 1994. *Television includes:* Bonanza (series) 1960, Rawhide (series) 1961, Dr. Kildare 1963, The Eleventh Hour 1963–64, The Virginian 1963–65, Star Trek 1966–69, 1973–74, 1986, 1991, Mission: Impossible (series) 1969–71, Columbo (series) 1973, Rod Serling's Night Gallery (series) 1972, (dir) 1973, The Missing Are Deadly (film) 1975, Vincent (film) (also dir) 1981, The Powers of Matthew Star (series) (also dir) 1982, Marco Polo (mini-series) 1983, T.J. Hooker (series) (also dir) 1983, Faerie Tale Theatre (series) 1986, Never Forget 1991, The Halloween Tree (film) 1993, The Simpsons (series) 1993–97, Bonanza: Under Attack 1995, The Outer Limits (series) 1995, Deadly Games (series) (dir) 1995, David (film) 1997, Duckman: Private Dick/Family Man (series) 1997, The Lost World (film) 1998, Brave New World (film) 1998, Invasion America (voice) 1998, Futurama (series) 1999–2002, Becker (series) 2001, Fringe (series) 2009–12, The Big Bang Theory (series) 2012. *Publications include:* I Am Not Spock (autobiog.) 1975, We Are All Children 1977, Come Be With Me 1979, I Am Spock 1995, The Full Body Project 2008. *Address:* c/o Gersh Agency Inc., 232 North Cannon Drive, Beverly Hills, CA 90210, USA (office).

NIMROD, Elvin, MA, DJur; Grenadian politician; *Deputy Prime Minister;* b. 1943, Carriacou; ed Brooklyn Coll., John Jay Coll. of Criminal Justice, New York, New York Law School, USA, Hugh Wooding Law School, Port-of-Spain, Trinidad and Tobago; teacher Mt. Pleasant Govt Primary School, Carriacou; called to the Bar, Grenada 1993; Minister of Labour 1999, of Foreign Affairs and Int. Trade and of Carriacou and Petit Martinique Affairs 1999–2008, and of Legal Affairs 1999–2007; Deputy Prime Minister and Minister for Legal Affairs, Labour, Local Govt and Carriacou and Petite Martinique Affairs 2013–; fmr Attorney-Gen. of Grenada; fmr Chair. New Nat. Party (NNP). *Address:* Ministry of Carriacou and Petit Martinique Affairs, Beauséjour, Carriacou, Grenada (office). *Telephone:* 443-6026 (office). *Fax:* 443-6040 (office). *E-mail:* minccoupm@spiceisle.com (office). *Website:* www.gov.gd (office).

NIN NOVOA, Rodolfo; Uruguayan politician; *Leader, Alianza Progresista;* b. 25 Jan. 1948, Montevideo; m. Patricia Damiani; three s. one d.; active in Agricultural Soc. of Cerro Largo and Fed. of Rural Uruguay during 1970s; elected Nat. Party rep. for Cerro Largo 1982; Mayor of Cerro Largo 1985–95; left Nat. Party 1994; Co-founder Encuentro Progresista party 1994, Vice-Pres. Encuentro Progresista–Frente Amplio 1995; Founder Alianza Progresista 738 political alliance 1999, currently Leader; Senator 2000–05, 2010–, Pres., Chamber of Senators 2005–10, mem. various senate cttees including Budget Cttee (Vice-Chair. 2002) 2000–04, Livestock, Agric. and Fisheries (Vice-Chair. 2002) 2000–04, Admin. Affairs (Vice-Chair. 2002) 2000–04; Vice-Pres. of Uruguay 2005–10. *Address:* Alianza Progresista 738, Col. 1831, Montevideo, Uruguay (office). *Telephone:* (2) 4016365 (office). *E-mail:* a738@alianza738.org.uy (office). *Website:* www.alianza738.org.uy (office).

NINA FERNÁNDEZ, Col Oscar Hugo; Bolivian police officer; *Chief of Police;* joined Policia Nacional de Bolivia, reaching rank of Col, Dir Gen. Força Especial de Luta Contra o Narcotráfico (anti-drugs div.) –2010, Comandante Gen., Policia Nacional de Bolivia (Chief of Police) Jan. 2010–. *Address:* Comando General de la Policia Boliviana, Av. 20 de Octubre, Esq. Lisimaco Gutierrez, Murillo, La Paz, Bolivia (office). *Telephone:* (2) 243-4256 (office). *Website:* www.policia.bo (office).

NINAGAWA, Yukio; Japanese theatre director; b. 15 Oct. 1935, Kawaguchi, Saitama Prefecture; known for his direction of Western classic plays, especially Shakespeare, in a Japanese style; debut as a director with Shinjo afururu keihakusa 1969; his co. appeared at Edin. Festival with samurai-style Macbeth

1985, Suicide of Love, Nat. Theatre, London 1989, Medea, Suicide for Love and a Noh-inspired version of The Tempest, Barbican Theatre, London 1992; also Dir Tango at the End of Winter, King Lear 1999, Ninagawa Twelfth Night 2005, Titus Andronicus 2006; f. Saitama Gold Theatre group (for actors over 55 years old) 2006; Pres. Toho Gakuen Coll. of Drama and Music; Dr hc (Edinburgh) 1992; Hon. CBE 2002; Person of Cultural Merit Award 2004, Kan Kikuti 2005, Kennedy Center Gold Medal in the Arts 2010. E-mail: ninagawa@my-pro.co.jp. Website: www.my-pro.co.jp/ninagawa.

NINEHAM, Rev. Canon Dennis Eric, MA, DD; British professor of theology and ecclesiastic (retd); b. 27 Sept. 1921, Southampton, Hants., England; s. of Stanley Martin Nineham and Bessie Edith Gain; m. Ruth Corfield Miller 1946; two s. two d. (one d. deceased); ed King Edward VI School, Southampton, The Queen's Coll., Oxford and Lincoln Theological Coll.; Chaplain, The Queen's Coll., Oxford 1944–54, Fellow 1946–54; Prof. of Biblical and Historical Theology, Univ. of London 1954–58, Prof. of Divinity 1958–64; Regius Prof. of Divinity, Univ. of Cambridge 1964–69; Fellow, Emmanuel Coll. 1964–69; Warden Keble Coll. Oxford 1969–79; Prof. of Theology, Univ. of Bristol 1980–86; Visiting Prof., Rikkyo Univ., Tokyo 1994; Fellow, King's Coll. London; Hon. Canon Emer., Bristol Cathedral; Hon. Fellow, Keble Coll. Oxford, The Queen's Coll., Oxford; Hon. DD (Yale) 1965, (Birmingham) 1972. Publications: The Study of Divinity 1960, The Gospel of St Mark 1963, The Use and Abuse of the Bible 1976, Explorations in Theology 1977, Christianity Medieval and Modern: A Study in Religious Change 1993. Leisure interests: walking and reading. Address: 9 Fitzherbert Close, Iffley, Oxford, OX4 4EN, England. Telephone: (1865) 715941.

NING, Frank Gaoning, BA, MBA; Chinese business executive; Chairman, China National Cereals, Oils and Foodstuffs Corporation (COFCO); b. 1958, Shandong Prov.; m.; one d.; ed Shandong Univ., Univ. of Pittsburgh, USA; previous positions include Gen. Man. China Resources Enterprise Ltd 1990–99, Chair. 1999–2004; fmr Chair. China Resources Land Ltd, Vice-Chair. and Pres. China Resources (Holdings) Co. Ltd, China Resources National Corpn; Chair. China Nat. Cereals, Oils and Foodstuffs Corpn (COFCO) 2005–; mem. Bd of Dirs HIT Investments Ltd, SAB Miller; mem. Asia Business Council; named by Sixth Chinese Business Leaders Annual Meeting as one of the 25 most influential business leaders 2007. Address: China National Cereals, Oils and Foodstuffs Corporation, 19F, COFCO Fortune Plaza No. 8, Chao Yang Men South Street, Chao Yang District, Beijing 100020, People's Republic of China (office). Telephone: (10) 85006637 (office). Fax: (10) 85006637 (office). E-mail: cofco-news@cofco.com (office). Website: www.cofco.com.cn (office).

NINN-HANSEN, Erik, LLD; Danish politician; b. 12 April 1922, Skørpinge, Western Zealand; s. of Christian Hansen; in pvt. law practice 1955–; mem. Folketing (Parl.) 1953–94; Minister of Defence 1968–71, of Finance 1971, of Justice 1982–89; Pres. of the Folketing Jan.–Oct. 1989; Nat. Chair. Conservative Youth 1948–50. Publications: Syv år for VKR 1974, Fra Christmas til Baunsgaard 1985, Ret Fœrd mellem jura og politik 1990, Christmas Møller, En stridsmand i dansk politik 1991, Vaerelse 28 Dansk politik 1974–94 1997. Address: Bregnegårdsvej 11, 2920 Charlottenlund, Denmark.

NIRENBERG, Louis, PhD; American mathematician and academic; b. 28 Feb. 1925, Hamilton, Ont., Canada; s. of Zuzie Nirenberg and Bina Katz; m. Susan Blank 1948 (deceased); one s. one d.; ed McGill and New York Univs; Instructor, New York Univ. 1949–51, Asst Prof. 1951–54, Assoc. Prof. 1954–57, Prof. 1957–; Dir Courant Inst. of Math. Sciences 1970–72; mem. NAS, American Acad. of Arts and Sciences, American Philosophical Soc., Accad. dei Lincei, Acad. des sciences, Istituto Lombardo, Accad. di Scienze e Lettere; Hon. mem. European Acad. of Sciences 2004; Hon. Prof., Nankai Univ., Zhejiang Univ.; Hon. DSc (McGill Univ., Univ. of Pisa, Univ. of Paris, Dauphine, McMaster Univ.); Bôcher Prize and Steele Prize of American Math. Soc., Crafoord Prize, Royal Swedish Acad. of Sciences 1982. Publications: various papers in mathematical journals. Leisure interests: classical music, reading, cinema, walking. Address: 221 West 82nd Street, New York, NY 10024, USA (home). Telephone: (212) 998-3192 (office); (212) 724-1069 (home). Fax: (212) 995-4121 (office); (212) 724-1069 (home). E-mail: nirenl@cims.nyu.edu (office).

NISBET, Robin George Murdoch, MA, FBA; British classical scholar; b. 21 May 1925, Glasgow; s. of Robert George Nisbet and Agnes Thomson Husband; m. Anne Wood 1969 (died 2004); ed Glasgow Acad., Glasgow Univ. and Balliol Coll. Oxford; Fellow and Tutor in Classics, Corpus Christi Coll. Oxford 1952–70, Prof. of Latin 1970–92; Hon. Fellow, Balliol Coll. 1989, Corpus Christi Coll. 1992; Kenyon Medal, British Acad. 1997. Publications: Commentary on Cicero, In Pisonem 1961, Horace, Odes I, II (with M. Hubbard) 1970, 1978, III (with N. Rudd) 2004, Collected Papers on Latin Literature 1995. Address: 80 Abingdon Road, Cumnor, Oxon., OX2 9QW, England (home). Telephone: (1865) 862482 (home).

NISH, David, BAcc; British business executive; Chief Executive, Standard Life plc; m. Caroline Nish; two c.; ed Paisley Grammar School, Univ. of Glasgow; fmr Pnr, Price Waterhouse; Finance Dir Scottish Power plc 1999–2005, subsequently Exec. Dir, Infrastructure Div.; mem. Bd of Dirs Standard Life plc 2006–, Group Finance Dir 2006–09, Chief Exec. 2010–; Dir (non-exec.) Thus plc 2001–02, Royal Scottish Nat. Orchestra 2002–08, Northern Foods plc 2005– (Chair. Audit Cttee); mem. Bd and Deputy Chair. Asscn of British Insurers, Chair. Long Term Savings and Life Insurance Cttee; Dir (non-exec.) UK Green Investment Bank plc; mem. UK Strategy Cttee of TheCityUK, Financial Services Advisory Bd of the Scottish Govt; mem. Govt Employers Pension Task Force 2004–05; mem. Inst. of Chartered Accountants of Scotland; Scottish Business Awards Finance Dir of the Year 2000, 2009. Leisure interests: travel, trekking, rugby, cycling. Address: Standard Life House, 30 Lothian Road, Edinburgh, EH1 2DH, Scotland (office). Telephone: (131) 245-6012 (office). Fax: (131) 245-6010 (office). E-mail: info@standardlife.com (office). Website: www.standardlife.com (office).

NISHANI, Bujar Faik, MA; Albanian politician and head of state; President; b. 29 Sept. 1966, Durrës; m. Odeta Nishani; two c.; ed Ushtarake Skënderbej Mil. Acad., Univ. of Tirana, Univ. of Texas at San Antonio, USA; Lecturer, Ushtarake Skënderbej Mil. Acad. 1988–93; with Foreign Relations Dept, Ministry of Defence 1993–94; with NATO Relations Dept, Ministry of Foreign Affairs 1994–96; mem. Cabinet of Ministry of Defence 1996–97; Freelance Chair. European-Atlantic Mil. Forum 1997–99; mem. Democratic Party of Albania (Partia Demokratike e

Shqipërisë) 2001–12, Gen. Sec., Tirana br. 2001–03, mem. Nat. Council 2004–, mem. Chairmanship 2005–, Sec. Nat. Council Comm. 2005–; mem. Municipal Council of Tirana 2003–; mem. Parl. for Constituency 34 in Tirana 2005–12 (re-elected 2009), mem. DPA Parl. Group 2005–12; Minister of the Interior 2007–09, 2011–12, of Justice 2009–11; Pres. of Albania 2012–; mem. Bd Goethe Inst. 1997. Address: Office of the President, Bulevardi Dëshmorët e Kombit, Tirana, Albania (office). Telephone: (4) 2389811 (office). E-mail: gen_sec@president.al (office). Website: www.president.al (office).

NISHANK, Ramesh Pokhriyal, MA, PhD; Indian writer and politician; Chief Minister of Uttarakhand; b. 15 Aug. 1958, Pinani, Uttar Pradesh; s. of Parmanand Pokhriyal and Vishwambhari Devi Pokhriyal; m. Kusum Kanta Pokhriyal; three d.; entered politics in 1991; elected to Karnaprayag Vidhan Sabha (state ass.), becoming state Minister for Hill Devt 1997–98; Minister for Culture and Religion 1998; Finance and Excise Minister 2000; mem. Uttarakhand Vidhan Sabha for Thalisen constituency 2007–; State Minister of Health, Family Welfare, Science and Tech., Biotechnology and Language 2007–09; Chief Minister of Uttarakhand 2009–; mem. Bharatiya Janata Party; Hon. DSc (Int. Open Univ., Sri Lanka) 2007; Hon. DLitt (Int. Open Univ., Sri Lanka) 2009; numerous honours and awards. Publications: poetry: Samarpan 1983, Navaankur 1984, Mujhe vidhata banana hai 1985, Tum bhi mere saath chalo 1986, Desh hum na jalne denge 1988, Jeevan path mein 1989, Matrabhoomi ke liye 1992, Koi mushkil nahin 2005; fiction: Roshni ki ek kiran 1986, Bus ek hi ichha 1989, Kya nahi ho sakta 1993, Khade hue prashn (Sahitya Bharti Samman Award) 2007. Address: Office of the Chief Minister, 248001 Dehradun (office); 37/1 Vijay Colony, Rabindranath Tagore Marg, Dehradun, India (home). Telephone: (135) 2665090 (office); (135) 2740104 (home). Fax: (135) 2665722 (office). E-mail: nishankramesh@gmail.com (office); cm-uk@nic.in (office). Website: www.rameshpokhriyalnishank.com (office).

NISHIDA, Atsutoshi, MA; Japanese electronics industry executive; Chairman, Toshiba Corporation; b. 29 Dec. 1943; ed Waseda Univ., Tokyo Univ.; joined Toshiba Corpn 1975, Sr Vice-Pres. Toshiba Europe 1984, Pres. Toshiba America Information Systems Inc. 1992, Gen. Man. Personal Computer Div. 1995, Vice-Pres., Deputy Group Exec. Information Equipment Group 1997, Vice-Chair. Toshiba America Inc., Pres. Toshiba America Information Systems Inc. 1997–99, Corp. Vice-Pres., Exec. Vice-Pres. Digital Media Equipment & Services Co. 1998–2000, Gen. Man. Corp. Devt Centre, Electronic Commerce Strategy Planning Div. 2000–01, Corp. Sr Vice-Pres. 2000–03, Pres. and CEO Digital Media Network Co. 2001–03, CEO Digital Products Group 2003, Pres. and CEO Personal Computer and Network Co., Dir, Corp. Exec. Vice-Pres. 2003–05, Pres. and CEO Toshiba Corpn 2005–09, Chair. 2009–. Address: Toshiba Corpn, 1-1, Shibaura 1-chome, Minato-ku, Tokyo, 105-8001, Japan (office). Telephone: (3) 3457-4511 (office). Fax: (3) 3455-1631 (office). E-mail: info@toshiba.co.jp (office). Website: www.toshiba.co.jp (office).

NISHIDA, Tsuneo; Japanese diplomatist; Permanent Representative, United Nations; m. Keiko Nishida; ed Higher Diplomatic Service Examination, Ministry of Foreign Affairs, Univ. of Tokyo, Faculty of Law; joined Ministry of Foreign Affairs 1970, First Sec., Embassy in Moscow 1981–86, Dir Eastern Europe Div., European and Oceanic Affairs Bureau 1986–87, Dir Legal Affairs Div., Treaties Bureau 1987–89, Counsellor, Embassy in Washington, DC 1989–92, Dir Press Div. 1992–93, Dir Russian Div., European and Oceanic Affairs Bureau 1993–94, Deputy Dir-Gen. European and Oceanic Affairs Bureau 1994–96, Deputy Dir-Gen. Econ. Co-operation Bureau 1996–98; Councillor, Cabinet Secr. April–July 1998, Asst Vice-Minister July 1998–99; Consul-Gen. in Los Angeles 1999–2001, Dir-Gen. Econ. Co-operation Bureau 2001–02; Deputy Vice-Minister for Foreign Policy/Dir-Gen. Foreign Policy Bureau 2002–05, Deputy Minister for Foreign Affairs 2005–07; Amb. to Canada 2007–10; Amb. and Perm. Rep. to UN, New York 2010–. Address: Permanent Mission of Japan to United Nations, 866 United Nations Plaza, 2nd Floor, New York, NY 10017, USA (office). Telephone: (212) 223-4300 (office). Fax: (212) 751-1966 (office). E-mail: p-m-j@dn.mofa.go.jp (office). Website: www.un.emb-japan.go.jp/index.htm (office).

NISHIHARA, Haruo, LLD; Japanese professor of law and academic administrator; b. 13 March 1928, Tokyo; s. of Keiichi Nishihara and Makoto Tateyama Nishihara; m.; one s.; ed Waseda Univ.; Asst. School of Law, Waseda Univ. 1953–59, Asst Prof. 1959–63, Assoc. Prof. 1963–67, Prof. from 1967, Dean School of Law 1972–76, Exec. Dir 1978–80, Vice-Pres. 1980–82, Pres. and mem. Bd of Trustees 1982–95; fmr Pres. Kokushikan Univ.; Hon. LLD (Korea Univ.) 1985, (Earlham Coll.) 1988; Hon. DUniv (Sydney) 1989; Educational Man. Prize, De La Salle Univ. 1988. Publications: Das Abge Nderte Japanische Strafgesetzbuch Vom 10. August 1953 (trans.) 1954, On the Theory of 'mittelbare Täterschaft' 1962, Traffic Accidents and the Principle of Trust 1962, Particular Aspects of Criminal Law 1974, 1983, General Aspects of Criminal Law 1977, What Governs the Criminal Law? 1979, Kyu Keiho: Meiji 13-nen (Nihon rippo shiryo zenshu) 1994, Die Idee des Lebens im japanischen Strafrechtsdenken: Vortrag und Ansprachen anlässlich der Verleihung der Ehrendoktorwürde durch die Juristische . . . 2. Juli 1996 1997, Hanzai jikko koiron 1998. Leisure interests: swimming, skiing. Address: c/o Kokushikan University, 4-28-1 Setagaya, Setagaya-ku, Tokyo 154-8515 (office); 619-18 Nohgaya-cho, Machida-shi, Tokyo, Japan. E-mail: info@kokushikan.ac.jp.

NISHIKAWA, Yoshifumi; Japanese financial executive; Special Advisor, Ichiryu Associates Inc.; b. 1939; ed Osaka Univ.; Pres. Sumitomo Bank 1997–2001, Pres. and CEO Sumitomo Mitsui Financial Group (Sumitomo Mitsui Banking Corpn) 2001–05, Hon. Advisor 2005–; Chair. Nat. Banking Asscn 2003–05; Pres. and CEO Japan Post Holdings Co. Ltd 2007–10, Dir Japan Post Network Co. Ltd, Japan Post Service Co. Ltd and Japan Post Bank Co. Ltd; Special Advisor, Ichiryu Assocs Inc. 2010–; Dir, Panasonic Corpn (fmrly Matsushita Electric Industrial Co. Ltd 2005–07, Nippon Venture Capital Co. Ltd, Daiichi Pharmaceutical Co. Ltd; Outside Dir, Internet Initiative Japan Inc. 2005–07, Daiichi Sankyo Co. Ltd 2005–. Leisure interest: supporting Hanshin Tigers baseball team. Address: Ichiryu Associates Inc., Iidabasi Masumoto Bldg, 3F, 1-21, Ageba-cho, Sinjyuku-ku, Tokyo, Japan (office). Telephone: (3) 3266-7596 (office). Fax: (3) 3266-7172 (office). E-mail: webmaster@ichiryu.org (office). Website: www.ichiryu.org (office).

NISHIMATSU, Chikara, BSME; Japanese business executive; b. 3 Nov. 1931, Osaka; m. Michiko Yamada 1959; two s. one d.; ed Pratt Inst.; joined Itochu Co.,

Ltd 1959, mem. Bd Dirs 1984–91, Gen. Man. Itochu Asian Operations 1985, Man. Dir 1986, Gen. Man. Itochu Europe and Africa Operation 1989–91; Pres. and CEO Matsubo Co. Ltd (fmrly. known as Matsuzaka Co. Ltd) 1992–98, Chair. and CEO 1998–2000, Adviser 2000–02; CEO The Mirai Creative Co. Inc. *Address:* 3-21-6, Katsuta-Dai, Yachiyo City, Chiba-ken 276-0023, Japan (home). *Telephone:* (47) 480-1436 (home). *Fax:* (47) 480-1436 (home). *E-mail:* chik-ni@ma.kcom.ne.jp (home).

NISHIMATSU, Haruka; Japanese airline industry executive; *President and CEO, Japan Airlines Corporation;* b. 5 Jan. 1948, Hamamatsu, Shizuoka Pref.; m.; one s. one d.; ed Tokyo Univ.; joined Japan Airlines 1972, assigned to Flight Crew Training Dept in charge of preparing schedules for pilot trainees; moved to Finance Dept 1974 and held several positions in finance and investor relations –1980, Traffic Div., Admin in charge of budgets for airport offices 1980–83, worked in Corp. Planning 1983–87, Admin Man., Frankfurt, Germany 1987–91, returned to Finance Dept 1991, Dir 1999–2001, Exec. Officer, Finance and Investor Relations 2003–05, Sr Vice-Pres., Finance and Investor Relations 2005–06, Sr Man. Dir, Finance and Investor Relations 2006, Pres. and CEO 2006–. *Leisure interests:* golf, reading. *Address:* Japan Airlines Corpn, 4-11, Higashi-shinagawa 2-chome, Shinagawa-ku, Tokyo 140-8605, Japan (office). *Telephone:* (3) 5769-6098 (office). *E-mail:* info@jal.com (office). *Website:* www.jal.com (office).

NISHIMI, Toru; Japanese retail industry executive; *President, The Daiei Inc.;* Corporate Sr Vice-Pres. Marubeni Corpn –2006, mem. Bd of Dirs Marubeni-Itochu Steel Inc. 2006–; Pres. The Daiei Inc. retail group 2006–. *Address:* The Daiei Inc., 4-1-1, Minatojima Nakamachi, Chuo-ku, Kobe 650-0046, Japan (office). *Telephone:* (78) 302-5001 (office). *Fax:* (3) 3433-9226 (office). *Website:* www.daiei.co.jp (office).

NISHIMURA, Hidetoshi; Japanese business executive; Sr Man. Exec. Officer Nissho Iwai Corpn –2002, Pres. 2002, Pres. and CEO 2002–03, Pres. and Co-CEO Nisho Iwai-Nichimen Holdings Corpn (est. as holding corpn of Nichimen Corpn and Nissho Iwai Corpn 2003) 2003–04 (cos merged to form Sojitz Corpn 2004); fmr Gov. Ehime Pref., also Vice-Gov. in charge of Educ. and Foreign Affairs. *Address:* c/o Sojitz Corporation, 1-23 Shiba 4-chome, Minato-ku, Tokyo 108-8408, Japan.

NISHIMURA, Hiroshi; Japanese insurance executive; *Advisor, Mitsui Mutual Life Insurance Company Limited;* joined Mitsui Mutual Life Insurance Co. Ltd 1967, Dir and Gen. Man. Gen. Accounting Div. 1996–99, Sr Dir 1998–2009, Gen. Man. Marketing Dept 1999–2000, Gen. Man. Gen. Man. Corp. Planning Dept 2000–01, Pres. and Rep. Dir 2001–09, Advisor 2009–, negotiated jt pension man. venture and marketing collaborations with Sumitomo Life 2001; Dir, Sanki Engineering Co. Ltd 2004–. *Address:* Mitsui Mutual Life Insurance Co. Ltd, 1-2-3 Ohtemachi, Chiyoda-ku, Tokyo 100-8123, Japan (office). *Telephone:* (3) 3211-6111 (office). *Fax:* (3) 3215-1580 (office). *Website:* www.mitsui-seimei.co.jp (office).

NISHIMURA, Kiyohiko G., PhD; Japanese economist, academic and fmr central banker; *Dean, Graduate School of Economics and Chairman, Faculty of Economics, University of Tokyo;* b. 30 March 1953, Tokyo; s. of Giichi Nishimura and Sumiko Otsuka; m. Yukiko Kurihata 1979; two d.; ed Univ. of Tokyo, Yale Univ., USA; Arthur Okun Research Fellow, Brookings Inst., USA 1981–82; Assoc. Prof. of Econs, Univ. of Tokyo 1983–94, Prof. 1994–2005, 2013–, Dean, Grad. School of Econs and Chair. Faculty of Econs 2013–; Assoc. Ed. Economic Studies Quarterly 1989–93; Research Assoc. US-Japan Center, New York Univ. 1989–; Dir Tokyo Centre for Econ. Research 1990–91; Visiting Scholar, MIT, USA 1991–92; Visiting Research Fellow, Inst. for Int. Econ. Studies, Sweden 1993; Visiting Prof., Louis Pasteur Univ. 1994, Arhus Univ., Denmark 1996; Special mem. Econ. Council, Japanese Govt 1994–98; mem. Regulatory Reform Cttee, Japanese Govt 1999–2001, Council Japanese Econ. Asscn 1999–2005, Statistic Council, Japanese Govt 2003–05, Financial System Council, Japanese Govt 2003–05; mem. Policy Bd Bank of Japan 2005–08, Deputy Gov. 2008–13; Co-Ed. Journal of Industry, Competition and Trade 2000–; Sr Advisor, Asian Econ. Panel 2001–; Exec. Research Fellow, Cabinet Office, Japanese Govt 2003–05; Fellow, East Asian Econ. Asscn 2005; Nikkei Prize 1993, Japan Economist's Prize 1997, Nakahara Prize, Japanese Econ. Asscn 1998, Prize of the Japan Asscn for Real Estate Sciences 2005, Telecom Social Science Award, 2006. *Publications:* Stock and Land Prices in Japan (in Japanese) 1990, The Distribution System in Japan (ed., in Japanese) 1991, Imperfect Competition, Differential Information and Microfoundations of Macroeconomics 1992, Macroeconomics of Price Revolution 1996, The Grief of a Prairie Dog (socioeconomic essays) 1998, The Distribution in Japan 2002, The Japanese Economy: Inconspicuous Structural Transformation 2004, Advancement of Information and Communication Technology and Its Impacts on the Japanese Economy 2004, Socially-Oriented Investment Trusts – Beyond Private Finance Initiative 2004, Information Technology Innovation and the Japanese Economy 2010. *Leisure interest:* photography. *Address:* 7-3-1, Hongo, Bunkyo-Ku, Tokyo 113-0033 (office). *Telephone:* (3) 5841-5500 (office). *Fax:* (3) 5841-8732 (office). *Website:* www.e.u-tokyo.ac.jp/fservice/faculty/nishimura/nishimura.e/nishimura01.e.html (office); www.e.u-tokyo.ac.jp/kenkyuka/from-the-dean-e.html (office).

NISHIMURO, Taizo, BEcons; Japanese business executive; *President, Japan Post Holdings Company Limited;* b. 19 Dec. 1935, Yamanashi; ed Faculty of Econs, Keio Univ.; joined Toshiba Corpn 1961, Dir Industrial Mfg Div., Iwate Prefectural Office 1984–86, Gen. Man. Semiconductor Marketing & Sales Div. 1986–90, Gen. Man. Overseas Operations Promotion Div. 1990–92, Vice-Pres. and Dir 1992–94, Sr Vice-Pres. and Dir 1994–95, Exec. Vice-Pres. and Dir 1995–96, Pres. and CEO 1996–2000, Chair. 2000–05, Adviser 2005–13; Chair. Tokyo Stock Exchange Inc. June–Dec. 2005, Pres. and CEO 2006–07; Pres. Japan Post Holdings Co. Ltd 2013–; Chair. Japan-US Business Council 2002; Vice-Chair. Japan Business Fed. 2003. *Address:* Japan Post Holdings Co. Ltd, 1-3-2 Kasumigaseki, Chiyoda-ku, Tokyo 100-8798, Japan (office). *Telephone:* (3) 3504-4411 (office). *Fax:* (3) 3504-5399 (office). *E-mail:* info@japanpost.jp (office). *Website:* www.japanpost.jp (office).

NISHIO, Shinji; Japanese petroleum industry executive; *Executive Consultant, JX Holdings, Inc.;* joined Nippon Oil Co. 1964, positions include Dir of Accounting, Chief Dir of First Man. Admin, Chief Dir of Second Man. Admin, Man. Dir and Vice-Pres., Exec. Vice-Pres. and Chief Financial Officer Nippon Oil Corpn –2005, Pres. 2005–12, also Rep. Dir, Chair. and Rep. Dir, JX Holdings, Inc. (following incorporation of Nippon Oil Corpn and Nippon Mining Holdings in JX Holdings, Inc. through a share transfer) 2010–12, Exec. Consultant 2012–. *Address:* JX Holdings, Inc., 2-6-3, Ote-machi, Chiyoda-ku, Tokyo 100-0004, Japan (office). *Telephone:* (3) 3502-1131 (office). *Fax:* (3) 3502-9352 (office). *E-mail:* info@hd.jx -group.co.jp (office). *Website:* www.hd.jx-group.co.jp (office).

NISHIOKA, Takashi; Japanese manufacturing executive; *Representative Director and Chairman, Mitsubishi Motors Corporation;* b. 5 March 1936; joined Mitsubishi Heavy Industries Ltd 1959, mem. Bd 1992–, Man.-Dir 1995–98, Exec. Vice-Pres. 1998–99, Pres. 1999–2003, Chair. 2003–08, Sr Adviser 2008–, also mem. Bd Mitsubishi Motors Corpn 2003–, Rep. Dir and Chair. 2006–, led negotiations with Caterpillar Inc. to est. jt venture Shin Caterpillar Mitsubishi Ltd 2003, Chair. Mitsubishi Aircraft Corpn –2010; mem. Bd of Dirs Japan Post Holdings Co. Ltd 2006–13, Chair. 2009–13; Dir, Seiryo Electric Corpn. *Address:* Mitsubishi Motors Corpn, 2-16-4 Konan, Minato-ku, Tokyo 108-8410, Japan (office). *Telephone:* (3) 6719-2111 (office). *Fax:* (3) 6719-0059 (office). *E-mail:* info@mitsubishi-motors.co .jp (office). *Website:* www.mitsubishi-motors.co.jp (office).

NISHIZAWA, Jun-ichi, BS, DEng, FIEE; Japanese electrical engineer, academic and university administrator; *Professor (Special Appointment), Sophia University;* b. 12 Sept. 1926, Sendai; s. of Kyosuke Nishizawa and Akiko (née Ishii) Nishizawa; m. Takeko Hayakawa 1956; one s. two d.; ed Tohoku Univ.; Research Asst, Electrical Communication Research Inst., Tohoku Univ. 1953–54, Asst Prof. 1954–62, Prof. 1962–90, Dir 1983–86, 1989–90, Pres. of Univ. 1990–96; Dir Semiconductor Research Inst., Sendai 1968–2004; Pres. Iwate Prefectural Univ. 1998–2005; Chair. Japan Atomic Industrial Forum 2000–06, Eng. Acad. of Japan; Pres. Tokyo Metropolitan Univ. 2005–09; Prof. (Special Appointment), Sophia Univ., Tokyo 2009–; mem. Japan Acad.; Foreign mem. Polish Acad. of Sciences, Russian Acad. of Sciences, Korea Acad. of Science and Tech., Serbian Acad. of Eng, Nat. Acad. of Eng; Life mem. IEEE; Hon. Citizen of Sendai City 1984, First Hon. Citizen of Miyagi Pref. 1990; Person of Cultural Merits (Bunka-Korosha), conferred by Japanese Govt 1983, Order of Cultural Merits from the Emperor 1989; Dr hc (Humboldt Univ., Berlin) 1989; Dirs Award of Japanese Science and Tech. Agency 1965, 1970, Invention Prize by the Emperor 1966, Matsunaga Memorial Award 1969, Okochi Memorial Tech. Prize 1971, Japan Acad. Prize 1974, Science and Tech. Merits Award 1975, Purple Ribbon Medal conferred by Japanese Govt 1975, Achievement Award from Inst. of Electronics and Communication Engineers of Japan 1975, Dir Award of Patent Agency 1980, Okochi Memorial Tech. Prize 1980, IEEE Jack A. Morton Award 1984, Honda Prize 1986, Laudise Prize of Int. Org. of Crystal Growth 1989, Power Conversion and Intelligent Motion (PCIM) Award 1989, Kenneth J. Button Prize 1993, Harushige Inoue Award 1993, The Okawa Prize 1996, IEEE Edison Medal 2000. *Publications:* Semiconductor Devices 1961, Semiconductor Materials 1968, Optoelectronics 1977; approx. 615 patents in Japan, 345 patents abroad. *Leisure interests:* classical music, reading, pottery, pictures (especially Impressionist school). *Address:* Sophia University, 7-1 Kioi-cho, Chiyoda-ku, Tokyo 102-8554, Japan (office). *Telephone:* (3) 3238-3024 (office). *Fax:* (3) 3238-3137 (office). *Website:* www.sophia .ac.jp (office).

NISHIZAWA, Ryue; Japanese architect; b. 1966, Tokyo; has worked with Kazuyo Sejima at their architects' office SANAA in Tokyo since 1995; their architecture has been described as "translucent minimalism", in which glass walls and thin, white textiles divide interior from exterior; Rolf Schock Prize in the Visual Arts, Royal Swedish Acad. of Sciences (co-recipient) 2005, Pritzker Prize (co-recipient) 2010. *Works include:* Gifu Kitagata Apartment Bldg, Motosu 1994–98, N-Museum, Nakahechi 1995–97, O-Museum, Iida 1995–99, K Bldg, Hitachi 1996–97, M-House, Tokyo 1996–97, Park Café, Koga 1996–98, Multi-Media Workshop, Oogaki 1996–97, Weekend House, Usui-gun 1997–98, New Campus Center for Illinois Inst. of Tech., Chicago 1997–98, Museum für Zeitgenössische Kunst, Sydney 1997–2001, Day Care Centre for the Elderly, Yokohama 1997–2000, S-House, Okayama 1997, Centre for the Contemporary Arts, Rome 1998–99, Stadstheater, Almere 1998, Renovation of the Antique Quarter, Salerno 1998, pvt. residence, Kamakura 1999–2001, Contemporary Art Museum, Kanazawa 1999, Wochenenhaus, Japan 2000, Christian Dior Shop, Tokyo-Minato-ku 2004, Museum of Contemporary Art, Kanazawa 2004, new bldg for The New Museum, New York 2006. *Address:* Sanaa Ltd/Kazuyo Sejima, Ryue Nishizawa & Associates, 7-A Shinagawa-Soko, 2-2-35-6B, Higashi-Shinagawa, Shinagawa-ku, Tokyo 140-0002, Japan (office). *Telephone:* (3) 34501117 (office). *Fax:* (3) 34501757 (office). *E-mail:* sanaa@sanaa.co.jp (office); office@ryuenishizawa.com (office). *Website:* www.sanaa .co.jp (office); www.ryuenishizawa.com (office).

NISHIZAWA, Toshio; Japanese business executive; ed Kyoto Univ. School of Econs; joined Tokyo Electric Power Co., Inc. (TEPCO) 1975, rose through ranks and served as Exec. Officer and Gen. Man. Corp. Planning Dept, Man. Dir TEPCO –2011, Pres. 2011–12. *Address:* c/o Tokyo Electric Power Co., Inc., 1-1-3 Uchisaiwai-cho, Chiyoda-ku, Tokyo 100-8560, Japan.

NISKALA, Markku, MPA; Finnish Red Cross official (retd); b. 5 Dec. 1945; m.; ed Tampere Univ.; worked for Student Health Foundation 1969–70; Dist Sec., Red Cross, Helsinki 1970, various positions in Red Cross Soc. of Finland 1970–78, Rep. of League of Red Cross and Red Crescent Socs, Zambia, Tanzania and Zimbabwe 1978–81, oversaw implementation of S African Programme –1985, Head of Europe Dept, Int. Fed. of Red Cross and Red Crescent Socs (IFRC) Secr., Geneva 1985–87, missions to Tanzania, Zambia, Zimbabwe and Ethiopia, IFRC 1987–88, Sec. Gen. Finnish Red Cross 1988–2003, Chair. Comm. of the Financing of Int. Cttee of Red Cross 1992–, Acting Sec. Gen. IFRC July–Nov. 2003, Sec.-Gen. Nov. 2003–08, mem. Standing Comm. 2007–08; Golden Order of Merit, Japanese Red Cross Soc. 2008, Cross of Merit, Finnish Red Cross Soc. 2008. *Address:* c/o International Federation of Red Cross and Red Crescent Societies, PO Box 372, 1211 Geneva 19, Switzerland.

NISSIM, Moshe Binyamin, LLB, MJ; Israeli politician and lawyer; *Head of Law Office, Moshe Nissim, Rinkov, Senderovitch;* b. 10 April 1935, Jerusalem; s. of Isaac Nissim (Chief Rabbi of Israel) and Victoria Nissim; m.; five c.; ed Hebrew Univ. of Jerusalem; elected to Knesset (Parl.) (youngest-ever mem.) 1959–96 (as rep. of Union of Gen. Zionists 1959, subsequently as rep. of Gahal faction of the Liberal Party, then of the Likud Bloc); has served on Defence, Foreign Affairs and Security, Constitution Law and Legislation, Labour and Housing Cttees in the Knesset; Co-Chair. Likud Group 1975–79, Chair. Exec. Cttee 1978–; Minister without Portfolio 1978–80, 1988–89; Minister of Justice 1980–86, of Finance

1986–88, of Trade and Industry 1989–92; Deputy Prime Minister 1990–92; currently Head of Law Office, Moshe Nissim, Rinkov, Senderovitch; mem. Public Comm. on the Status and Authority of Attorney Gen.; Chair. several comms; Dr hc (Ben-Gurion Univ.). *Publications include:* numerous articles in monthly and quarterly journals. *Address:* 12 Aba Hilel Street, Ayalon Tower, Ramat-Gan 5250606 (office); 4 Shalom Aleichem Street, Jerusalem 92148, Israel (home). *Telephone:* 3-6133333 (office); 2-5619414 (home). *Fax:* 3-6133334 (office); 2-5617155 (home). *E-mail:* nrs@nrs-law.com (office). *Website:* www.nrs-law.com (office).

NISSINEN, Mikko; Finnish artistic director, teacher, ballet dancer and choreographer; *Artistic Director, Boston Ballet;* b. 1962, Helsinki; ed Stanford Univ., USA; began dance training at Finnish Nat. Ballet School 1973; began performing as soloist 1977; joined Kirov Ballet School 1979; performer with Dutch Nat. Ballet and Basel Ballet; Prin. Dancer, San Francisco Ballet, USA 1986–96; guest artist at numerous int. galas; Artistic Dir, Marin Ballet, San Rafael, Calif., USA 1996–98, Alberta Ballet, Calgary, Canada 1998–2001; Artistic Dir, Boston Ballet and Boston Ballet Center for Dance Educ. 2001–; mem. Artistic Cttee, New York Choreographic Inst.; mem. Advisory Bd, Albert Schweitzer Fellowship, Armitage Gone! Dance; First Prize, Nat. Ballet Competition, Kuopio 1978, UN Asscn of Greater Boston Leadership Award 2007, Finlandia Foundation Arts and Letters Award 2008. *Dance:* as choreographer: The Nutcracker, Alberta and Boston Ballets 2003, Swan Lake, Boston Ballet 2004, Raymonde (Act III), Alberta and Boston Ballets. *Address:* Boston Ballet, 19 Clarendon Street, Boston, MA 02116-6100, USA (office). *Telephone:* (617) 695-6950 (office). *Fax:* (617) 695-6995 (office). *Website:* www.bostonballet.org (office).

NIȚA, Constantin, PhD; Romanian economist, academic and politician; *Minister of the Economy;* b. 27 Nov. 1955; ed Theoretical High School No. 1, Pașcani, Iași Co., Faculty of Econ. Studies, Iași, Faculty of Law, Iași, Faculty of Econ. Sciences, Iași; Economist, Export and Distribution Dir, Brașov Truck Plant 1978–83; Economist, ICE Brașov Car 1983–86; Head of BTT Brașov 1986–93; Dir Pîrîul Rece Resort, Brașov 1990–93; Dir Gen. Valea Prahovei Representation and Protocol Dept 1993–97; Dir SC Nimpex SRL, Brașov 1997–2000; mem. Social Democratic Party (PSD) (Partidul Social Democrat) 1994–, Vice-Pres. Brașov Municipal PDSR Org. 1994–97, Pres. Brașov PSD Co. Org. 1997–, mem. PSD Nat. Council 1997–, mem. PSD Exec. Bureau 1998–2004, mem. PSD Exec. Cttee 2005–06; mem. Chamber of Deputies 2000–, Sec. 2000–03, Vice-Pres. 2003–04, Deputy Leader, PSD Parl. Group 2004–08, Vice-Pres. Special Cttee of Chamber of Deputies and Senate for the Exercise of Parl. Control over the Foreign Intelligence Service 2004–07, mem. Cttee for Defence, Public Order and Nat. Security 2008–; Minister, Ministry of Small and Medium-Sized Enterprises, Trade and Business Environment 2008–09; Lecturer, Transylvania Univ. of Brașov 1998–2001, Assoc. Prof., Faculty of Econ. Sciences 2010–; Reader, Faculty of Econ. Sciences, George Barițiu Univ. of Brașov 2001–05, Prof. 2005–; Pres. Brașov Economists Club Asscn; Ed. Convorbiri economice review; Founding mem. ASCOT (Trade and Tourism Employees' Asscn), Brașov, Transilvania Brașov Regional Foundation, Foundation for Political, Admin. and Civic Educ. (FEPAC), Brașov, 'Pro Brașov' Asscn, Asscn for the Construction of the Nasterea Domnului Cathedral, Brașov; Kt, Nat. Order 'Faithful Service' 2004. *Publications:* Dictionary of Marketing and Business (co-author) 1999, Marketing Audit (co-author) 1999, Industrial Marketing (co-author) 1999, Romania's Tourism Market (co-author) 2000, Practical Guide for Business Correspondence Drafting Methods (co-author) 2005, Marketing Bases 2004; several book chapters, reviews and articles in professional journals. *Address:* Ministry of the Economy, 010096 Bucharest 1, Calea Victoriei 152, Romania (office). *Telephone:* (21) 2025426 (office). *Fax:* (21) 2025108 (office). *E-mail:* birou_presa@minind.ro (office). *Website:* www.minind.ro (office).

NITTVE, Lars; Swedish museum director, art historian, academic and writer; *Executive Director, M+ and Exhibition Centre, West Kowloon Cultural District Authority;* b. 17 Sept. 1953, Stockholm; m. Shideh Shaygan; one c. from previous m.; fmr Stockholm newspaper critic; fmr journalist for Artforum; Sr Curator Moderna Museet (nat. contemporary art museum) 1986–89, Dir 2001–09, also Deputy Chair. Bd Dirs; Dir Rooseum, Malmö 1990–95, Louisiana Museum of Modern Art, Humlebæk, Denmark 1995–98, Tate Modern, London 1998–2001; Exec. Dir M+ and Exhbn Centre, West Kowloon Cultural Dist Authority 2011–; Prof., Umeå Univ. 2010–; mem. Royal Swedish Acad. of Fine Art; HM The King's Medal in Gold, 12th Size in the Order of the Serafim's Ribbon 2010; Hon. PhD (Umeå Univ.). *Address:* M+ and Exhibition Centre, West Kowloon Cultural District Authority, 29/F, Tower 6, The Gateway, 9 Canton Road, Tsim Sha Tsui, Kowloon, Hong Kong Special Administrative Region, People's Republic of China (office). *Telephone:* 2200-0008 (office). *Fax:* 2895-0016 (office). *E-mail:* lars.nittve@wkcda.hk (office). *Website:* www.wkcda.hk (office).

NIU, Maosheng; Chinese government official; b. 1939, Beijing; ed Beijing Agricultural Inst.; joined CCP 1961; sent to the countryside 1963–65; Sec., later Deputy Dir Office, Bureau for Water Resources and Meteorology, Beijing 1965–73 (mem. CCP Party Cttee), Dir Water Conservancy Man. Div.; Deputy Dir Water Conservancy Bureau, Beijing 1973–82 (Deputy Sec. CCP Party Cttee); Sec. CCP Miyun Co. Cttee, Beijing 1982–85; Vice-Chair. and Gen. Man. China Water Resources Devt Corpn 1980s; First Deputy Dir, later Dir Yellow River Man. Cttee, Ministry of Water Resources 1980s; mem. CCP Beijing Municipal Cttee 1982–85; Sec.-Gen. State Flood Control and Drought Relief HQ 1985–88, Deputy Head 1993–98; Vice-Minister of Water Resources 1988–93, Minister 1993–98; Head, Leading Group, Construction Comm. for Diverting Water from the South to the North Project 1998; Vice-Gov. Hebei Prov. 1998, Acting Gov. 1998–99, Gov. 1999–2002; mem. 15th CCP Cen. Cttee 1997–2002, 16th CCP Cen. Cttee 2002–07; mem. Standing Cttee 10th CPPCC Nat. Cttee 2003–, Chair. CPPCC Sub-cttee of Ethnic and Religious Affairs 2003–. *Leisure interests:* painting, calligraphy. *Address:* Chinese Communist Party Provincial Committee, Shijiazhuang City, Hebei Province, People's Republic of China (office).

NIU, Qun; Chinese actor and government official; b. Dec. 1949, Tianjin; joined PLA 1971; actor Zhanyou Art Troupe of PLA Beijing Mil. Command 1974–93; actor China Broadcasting Art Troupe 1993–; performs comic dialogues with Feng Gong; Vice-Mayor Mengcheng Co., Anhui Prov. 2001; mem. National United Asscn of China; numerous prizes. *Publications:* In Various Ingenious Names (five cassettes of comic dialogues). *Address:* China Broadcasting Art Troupe, Beijing, People's Republic of China (office).

NIU, Ximing, MA; Chinese economist and banking executive; *Chairman and President, Bank of Communications;* ed Harbin Inst. of Tech.; worked at Qinghai Br. of The People's Bank of China 1983–86, served as an official and Deputy Div. Chief of Industrial and Commercial Credit Div.; served successively from 1986 to 2009 as Vice-Pres. then Pres. of Xining Br. of Industrial and Commercial Bank of China Ltd, Qinghai Prov., a temporary transferred official, Div. Chief of Div. 1, a Deputy Dir, a Dir and Gen. Man. of Industrial and Communication Credit Dept, Industrial and Commercial Bank of China Ltd, Pres. of Beijing Br. of Industrial and Commercial Bank of China Ltd, an Asst to Pres. of Industrial and Commercial Bank of China Ltd (and Pres. Beijing Br. concurrently), Vice-Pres. Industrial and Commercial Bank of China Ltd, an Exec. Dir and Vice-Pres. Industrial and Commercial Bank of China Ltd; Exec. Dir, Vice-Chair. and Pres. Bank of Communications 2009–13, Exec. Dir, Chair. and Pres. 2013–. *Address:* Bank of Communications, 188 Yin Cheng Zhong Lu, Shanghai 200120, People's Republic of China (office). *Telephone:* (21) 95559 (office). *E-mail:* info@bankcomm.com (office). *Website:* www.bankcomm.com (office).

NIWA, Toshiyuki, BA, MALD; Japanese diplomatist and UN official; m.; four c.; ed Waseda Univ., Fletcher School of Law and Diplomacy, USA; worked in pvt. sector; joined UNDP 1971, served in various positions including UN Resident Co-ordinator and UNDP Resident Rep. in Yemen 1980–83, Nepal 1983–88, Thailand and Dir UN Border Relief Operation (UNBRO) for displaced Cambodians along Thai–Cambodian border 1988–90, Asst Sec.-Gen. and Asst Admin. and Dir Bureau for Finance and Admin. 1990–97, Acting Assoc. Admin. 1994; Exec. Co-ordinator for Common Services at UN Secr. 1977, responsible for common services, Asst Sec.-Gen. for Cen. Support Services, Asst Sec.-Gen. 1998–2003, Exec. Dir Capital Master Plan 2003–04; Deputy Exec. Dir UNICEF 2004–07 (retd); Head of Japan Election Observation Mission during legis. elections in Nepal 2008. *Address:* c/o Ministry of Foreign Affairs, Kasumigaseki 2-2-1, Chiyoda-ku, Tokyo 100-8919, Japan.

NIWA, Uichiro; Japanese diplomatist and business executive; *Ambassador to China;* ed Nagoya Univ.; joined Itochu Corpn (gen. trading co. involved in aerospace, electronic, multimedia, chemicals, energy, finance, automobile and textiles industries) 1966, Pres. and CEO 2000–04, Chair. 2004–10; Pres. Keidanren Cttee on Agric. Policy 2000–; Amb. to People's Repub. of China 2010–. *Address:* Embassy of Japan, 7 Ri Tan Lu, Jian Guo Men Wai, Beijing 100600, People's Republic of China (office). *Telephone:* (10) 65322361 (office). *Fax:* (10) 65324625 (office). *E-mail:* info@pk.mofa.go.jp (office); info@eoj.cn (office). *Website:* (office).

NIWA, Yuya; Japanese politician; mem. House of Reps; fmr Parl. Vice-Minister for Health and Welfare; fmr Health and Welfare Minister; fmr Chair. LDP Policy Research Council; Minister for Health and Welfare 1999–2000. *Address:* c/o Ministry of Health and Welfare, 1-2-2, Kasumigaseki, Chiyoda-ku, Tokyo 100-0013, Japan. *Telephone:* (3) 3503-1771 (office). *Fax:* (3) 3501-2532 (office). *E-mail:* www-admin@mhw.ho.jp (office).

NIWANO, Rev. Nichiko; Japanese religious leader; *President, Rissho Kosei-kai;* b. 1938; s. of Nikkyo Niwano; ed Rissho Univ.; entered Rissho Kosei-kai 1968, later Head, Dissemination Dept, later Pres. Rissho Kosei-kai Seminary, Pres. Rissho Kosei-kai 1991–; Pres. Niwano Peace Foundation, World Conf. on Religion and Peace, Asian Conf. on Religion and Peace; Chair. Shinshuren; chaired a plenary session during the Millenium World Peace Summit of Religious and Spiritual Leaders 2000. *Publications:* Modern Meditations – The Inward Path; My Father, My Teacher. *Address:* Rissho Kosei-kai, 2-11-1, Wada Suginami-ku, Tokyo 166-8537, Japan (office). *Telephone:* (3) 3380-5185 (office). *Fax:* (3) 3381-9792 (office). *E-mail:* info@rk-world.org (office). *Website:* www.rk-world.org (office).

NIXON, Gordon M., BComm; Canadian banking executive; *President and CEO, Royal Bank of Canada Financial Group;* b. 1957, Montreal; m.; three c.; ed Queen's Univ., Kingston, Ont.; began investment banking career with Dominion Securities, 1979, with Fixed Income and Govt Finance Divs 1979–86, Head of Operations, Japan 1986–89, Man. Dir Investment Banking, Royal Bank of Canada (following RBC's acquisition of Dominion) 1989–95, Head of Global Investment Banking 1995–98, Head of Banking RBC Financial Group 1998–99, CEO RBC Dominion Securities 1999–2001, mem. Exec. Cttee RBC Financial Group 1999–, Pres. and CEO RBC Financial Group 2001–; Dir RBC and Chair. Group Man. Cttee; Chair. MaRS; Co-Chair. The Toronto Region Immigrant Employment Council; Dir and Past Chair. Canadian Council of Chief Execs; mem. Bd of Dirs The Int. Monetary Conf.; fmr mem. Bd of Dirs several orgs in the arts, health care and education and has chaired numerous events and fundraising campaigns, including the United Way of Greater Toronto; current Chair. Queen's Univ. Capital Campaign; Order of Canada, Order of Ontario; Hon. LLD (Queen's Univ., Dalhousie Univ.); Rotary Foundation Paul Harris Fellowship, Queen's Golden Jubilee Medal 2002, Outstanding CEO of the Year Award, Canadian Business Leader Award, included in Barron's list of the World's Best CEOs, Honouree of the Public Policy Forum, CIJA/UJA Words and Deeds Leadership Award, Learning Partnership Champion of Public Educ. Tribute, American Banker Innovator of the Year Award. *Address:* Royal Bank of Canada, 123 Front Street West, Suite 600, Toronto, M5J 2M2, Canada (office). *Telephone:* (416) 955-7802 (office). *Fax:* (416) 955-7800 (office). *E-mail:* info@rbc.com (office). *Website:* www.rbc.com (office).

NIXON, Jeremiah Wilson (Jay), BA, JD; American lawyer, politician and state governor; *Governor of Missouri;* b. 13 Feb. 1956, De Soto, Mo.; s. of Jeremiah 'Jerry' Nixon and Betty Lea Nixon (née Willson); m. Georganne Wheeler; two s.; ed Univ. of Missouri, Columbia; Pnr, Nixon, Nixon Breeze & Roberts law firm 1981–86; mem. Mo. State Senate from Dist 22 1986–93; Attorney-Gen. for State of Mo. 1993–2009; Democrat. *Address:* Office of the Governor, Room 218, Capitol Building, PO Box 720, Jefferson City, MO 65102, USA (office). *Telephone:* (573) 751-3222 (office). *Fax:* (573) 526-3291 (office). *E-mail:* media@mo.gov (office). *Website:* governor.mo.gov (office).

NIXON, John Forster, PhD, DSc, FRS; British scientist and academic; *Professor Emeritus of Chemistry, University of Sussex;* b. 27 Jan. 1937, Whitehaven,

Cumbria, England; s. of Edward Forster Nixon, MBE and Mary Nixon (née Lytton); m. 'Kim' Smith 1960; one s. one d.; ed Univs of Manchester and Cambridge; Research Assoc. in Chem., Univ. of Southern California 1960–62; ICI Fellow, Inorganic Chem. Dept, Univ. of Cambridge 1962–64; Lecturer in Inorganic Chem., Univ. of St Andrews 1964–66; Lecturer in Chem., Univ. of Sussex 1966, Reader 1976, Subject Chair. in Chem. 1981–84, Prof. of Chem. 1986–, now Research Prof., Dean School of Chem. and Molecular Sciences 1989–92; Visiting Assoc. Prof. of Chem., Univ. of Victoria, BC 1970–71; Visiting Prof., Simon Fraser Univ., Vancouver BC 1975; Chair. Downland Section, Chemical Soc. 1973–74; mem. Int. Cttee on Phosphorus Chem. 1983–, Inorganic Chem. Panel Science and Eng Research Council Cttee 1986–89, Int. Cttee Inorganic Ring Systems (IRIS) 2002–06, Main Group Element Council 2002–06; elected Titular mem. IUPAC Comm., Inorganic Nomenclature 1985; Royal Soc.-Leverhulme Sr Research Fellow 1993; Visiting Prof., Indian Inst. of Science, Bangalore 2002, 2005–06, IISER Trivandrum 2010; Visiting Fellow, ANU, Canberra 2004; RSC Corday-Morgan Medal and Prize 1973, RSC Main Group Element Prize 1985, RSC Tilden Lectureship 1991–92, RSC Ludwig Mond Lectureship and Prize 2003, Alexander von Humbold Prize Winner 2001–02, 2009–12, Geza Zemplen Medal, Budapest Inst. of Tech. 2003, Alexander Von Humboldt Awardee, Univ. of Regensburg, Germany 2009–14, numerous invited lectures to int. confs and univ. depts. *Publications:* Phosphorus: The Carbon Copy (co-author) 1998 and about 400 publs in chemical journals. *Leisure interests:* walking, theatre, music, watching cricket, playing tennis. *Address:* Chemistry Department, School of Life Sciences, Arundel Building 312, University of Sussex, Brighton, Sussex, BN1 9RQ (office); Juggs Barn, The Street, Kingston, Lewes, Sussex, BN7 3PB, England (home). *Telephone:* (1273) 678536 (office); (1273) 483993 (home). *Fax:* (1273) 876876 (office). *E-mail:* j.nixon@sussex.ac.uk (office). *Website:* www.sussex.ac.uk/profiles/1954 (office).

NIXON, Patrick Michael, CMG, OBE; British diplomatist (retd); b. 1 Aug. 1944, Reading, Berks., England; m. Elizabeth Carlton 1968; four s.; ed Downside School, Magdalene Coll., Cambridge; joined Diplomatic Service 1965, served Middle East Centre for Arab Studies, Lebanon, Cairo, Lima, Tripoli, British Information Services, New York 1980–83; Asst, later Head Near East and N Africa Dept, FCO 1983–87; Amb. to Qatar 1987–90; Counsellor, FCO 1990–93; High Commr in Zambia 1994–97; Dir FCO 1997–98; Amb. to UAE 1998–2003; Coordinator Coalition Provision Authority, Southern Iraq 2004; Gov., All Hallows School 2003–12 (Chair. 2005–12), Downside School 2005–12. *Address:* The Old Vicarage, Maiden Bradley, Warminster, Wilts., BA12 7HN, England. *Telephone:* (1985) 844242. *E-mail:* patricknixon@onetel.com.

NIYOYANKANA, Lt-Gen. Germain; Burundian politician; commdr during civil war; Armed Forces Chief of Staff, Nat. Defence Force 2004–05; Minister of Nat. Defence and War Veterans 2005–10; mem. Union pour le progresse nationale (Uprona). *Address:* c/o Ministry of National Defence, Bujumbura, Burundi (office).

NIYUNGEKO, Vincent; Burundian politician; Minister of Defence 2002–05. *Address:* c/o Ministry of Defence, Bujumbura, Burundi (office).

NIZAMI, Farhan Ahmad, CBE, BA (Hons), MA, DPhil; Indian/British professor of history; *Director, Oxford Centre for Islamic Studies;* b. 25 Dec. 1956; s. of the late Khaliq Nizami and Razia Nizami; m. Farah Deba Ahmad 1983; one s. one d.; ed Aligarh Muslim Univ., Wadham Coll., Oxford (Overseas Scholar); mem. Faculties of Modern History and Oriental Studies, Univ. of Oxford, Rothman's Fellow in Muslim History, St Cross Coll., Oxford 1983–85, Fellow 1985–97, Emer. Fellow 1997–, Founding Dir Oxford Centre for Islamic Studies 1985–, Sec., Bd of Trustees 1985–, Prince of Wales Fellow, Magdalen Coll., Oxford 1997–, Gov. Magdalen Coll. School, Oxford 2005–10; Founder-Ed. Journal of Islamic Studies 1990–; Series Ed. Makers of Islamic Civilization 2004–; Founding Ed. Journal of Islamic Studies, Oxford University Press 1990–; Series Ed. Makers of Islamic Civilization 2004–; mem. Bd of Dirs Oxford Trust for Islamic Studies 1998–; Dir Oxford Inspires 2002–03; Chair. Oxford Endeavours 2003–; mem. Council Al-Falah Programme, Univ. of California, Berkeley 1997–2004; mem. Advisory Council, Wilton Park 2000–04 (Chair. 2004–09), Court of Oxford Brookes Univ. 2000–10, Advisory Bd Dialogues Project, New York Univ. 2003–, Archbishop of Canterbury's Reference Group for Christian–Muslim Relations 2001–04; Scholar Consultant to the Christian-Muslim Forum 2005–09; mem. Academic Consultative Cttee, Cumberland Lodge 2003–; mem. Steering Cttee C-100, World Econ. Forum, Davos 2003–07, Int. Advisory Panel, World Islamic Econ. Forum, Malaysia 2004–08; Patron Oxford Amnesty Lectures 2003–; Order of the Crown of Brunei (Class IV) 1992; Univ. Medal for standing First in Order of Merit 1977, 1979, Begam Khursheed Nurul Hasan Gold Medal for Standing First in Order of Merit 1977. *Publication:* Makers of the Islamic Civilization (series ed.) 2004–. *Leisure interests:* reading, cricket. *Address:* Oxford Centre for Islamic Studies, George Street, Oxford, OX1 2AR, England (office). *Telephone:* (1865) 278731 (office). *Fax:* (1865) 248942 (office). *E-mail:* farhan.nizami@oxcis.ac.uk (office). *Website:* www.oxcis.ac.uk (office).

NIZIGAMA, Clotilde; Burundian politician; fmr Dir-Gen. Office Nat. Pharmaceutique (ONAPHA); Minister of the Economy, Finance and Co-operation and Devt 2007–12; mem. Conseil nat. pour la défense de la démocratie—Force pour la défense de la démocratie (CNDD—FDD). *Address:* c/o Ministry of Finance, BP 1830, Bujumbura, Burundi.

NJIE, Mambury, BA, MSc; Gambian economist, politician and fmr diplomatist; *Minister of Foreign Affairs, International Co-operation and Gambians Abroad;* b. 27 June 1962; ed World Bank Econ. Devt Inst., Zimbabwe, East Stroudsburg Univ., Pa, Columbia Univ., Harvard Univ., USA; Jr Economist, Special Studies Unit, Ministry of Finance and Trade 1988–89; Policy Analyst, Office of the Pres. 1989, Economist, Dept of State for Finance and Econ. Affairs 1990–92, later becoming Prin. Economist; Econ. Counsellor, Gambian Embassy in Taiwan and the Philippines 1996, Acting Head of Mission 1997, Amb. to Taiwan and the Philippines 1997–2001; Perm. Sec. in Office of the Pres. 2001–04; Man. Dir of Social Security and Housing Finance 2004; Chair. Gambia Nat. Petroleum Co. 2005–06; Sec.-Gen. and Head of Civil Service of The Gambia 2005–06; Amb. to UAE 2008–10; Minister of Econ. Planning and Industrial Devt 2010–11, of Finance and Econ. Affairs 2011–12, of Foreign Affairs, Int. Co-operation and Gambians Abroad 2012–; apptd Chair. Governing Council, West African Insurance Inst. 2011; apptd Chair. ECOWAS Bank for Investment and Devt 2011; Gov. Islamic Devt Bank, IMF, World Bank, African Devt Bank; mem. Bd of Dirs Nat. Water and Electricity Co. Ltd 2001–04, Jammeh Foundation for Peace 2002–06, Ocean Bay Hotel and Resort 2004–05, CFAO Gambia 2004–05, Gambia Agricultural Marketing Co. 2004–05, Trust Bank Ltd 2004–05, Skye Bank 2008–09 (Chair. Jan.–July 2010); Thomas Jefferson Int. Fellow, USAID 1992–93; Order of Brilliant Star with Grand Cordon (Repub. of China) 2001, Insignia of Officer of Nat. Order of the Repub. of The Gambia 2005. *Leisure interests:* sports, soccer, travelling, community work. *Address:* Ministry of Foreign Affairs, International Co-operation and Gambians Abroad, 4 Marina Parade, Banjul, Gambia (office). *Telephone:* 4223577 (office). *Fax:* 4227917 (office). *E-mail:* info@mofa.gov.gm (office). *Website:* www.mofa.gov.gm (office).

NJIE-SAIDY, Isatou, MSc; Gambian teacher and politician; *Vice-President and Minister of Women's Affairs;* b. 5 March 1952, Kuntaya, N Bank Div.; m.; four c.; ed Yundum Teacher's Training Coll., Univ. Coll. of Swansea, Univ. of Wales, UK; schoolteacher 1970–76; Sr Business Advisory and Training Officer, Indigenous Business Advisory Services 1976–83; Deputy Exec. Sec., Women's Bureau (exec. arm of Nation's Women's Council) 1983–89; Minister of Health, Social Welfare and Women's Affairs 1996, Vice-Pres. and Minister of Women's Affairs 1997–. *Address:* Office of the Vice-President, State House, Banjul, The Gambia. *Telephone:* 227605 (office). *Fax:* 224012 (office). *E-mail:* vicepresident@statehouse.gm (office).

NJOJO, Rt Rev. Patrice Byankya; Democratic Republic of the Congo ecclesiastic; *Bishop of Boga and Honorary Archbishop of the Province of the Congo;* b. 1935, Boga; m. Kamanyoho Njojo; seven c.; ed teachers' coll., schools' inspector training, Univ. of Montreal, Canada; teacher, schools inspector, priest, currently Bishop of Boga; Archbishop of the Prov. of the Congo 1992–2002; Bronze Medal 1968, Gold Medal 1972. *Leisure interests:* cattle breeding, music. *Address:* PO Box 25586, Kampala, Uganda (office); Bishop's Residence, CAC-Boga, PO Box 25586, Kampala, Uganda (home). *Telephone:* 78321454 (office); 77847365 (home). *E-mail:* eac-mags@infocom.co.ug (office); njojob2000@yahoo.com (office).

NJUE, HE Cardinal John, MA; Kenyan ecclesiastic; *Archbishop of Nairobi;* b. 1944, Kiriari Village, Mukangu Sub-Ngandori, Embu Dist; s. of Joseph Nyaga Kibariki and Monica Ngima Nyaga; ed Nguviu Intermediate School, Kyaweru, Nkubu Jr Seminary, Pontifical Urbanian Univ. and Pontifical Lateran Univ., Rome; ordained priest of Embu 1973; served in Kariakomu Parish, Meru South Dist, Meru Diocese 1973–75; apptd Prof. of Philosophy and Dean of Students at St Augustine Sr Seminary, Mabanga, Bungoma 1975, Rector 1978–82; went to USA and undertook spiritual renewal programme course for six months; appointed Father-in-Charge of Chuka Parish (first African priest to be assigned in the parish as Parish Priest after Consolata Missionaries left) 1982; Rector St Joseph's Philosophicum Seminary, Nairobi 1985–86; Bishop of Embu 1986–2002; Coadjutor Archbishop of Nyeri 2002–07; Apostolic Admin. of Vicariate of Isiolo –2006; Archbishop of Nairobi 2007–; currently Apostolic Admin. of Catholic Diocese of Muranga; cr. Cardinal (Cardinal-Priest of Preziosissimo Sangue di Nostro Signore Gesù Cristo) 2007; Chair. Seminary Episcopal Comm. for Major Seminaries in Kenya 1987–91, Kenya Episcopal Conf. 1997–2003, Kenya Episcopal Conf. Justice and Peace Comm., Devt and Social Services Dept of Kenya Catholic Secr. *Address:* Archdiocese of Nairobi, PO Box 14231, Nairobi, Kenya (office). *Telephone:* (2) 441919 (office). *Fax:* (2) 447027 (office).

NKATE, Jacob, LLB; Botswana politician and lawyer; *Minister of Education;* ed Univ. of Botswana, Univ. of Edin., UK; Attorney at Law, Magistrate Grade I, Francistown and Palapye 1986–88; Attorney at Law and pvt. practitioner 1988–95; mem. of Parl. 1994–; Asst Minister of Finance and Devt Planning 1997–99; Minister of Lands, Housing and Environment 1999–2002; Minister of Trade and Industry 2002–05, of Education 2005–; del. to numerous int. and multilateral confs including Commonwealth and Trade Conf., UK and S Korea, IPU and UNESCO Conf. in Educ. Science, UNEP Governing Council, Malmo; Chair. Parl. Law Reform; mem. Presidential Task Force on Vision 2016; Gov. and Chair. African Devt Bank. *Address:* Ministry of Education, Private Bag 005, Gaborone, Botswana (office). *Telephone:* 3655400 (office). *Fax:* 3655458 (office). *E-mail:* moe.webmaster@gov.bw (office). *Website:* www.moe.gov.bw/moe/index.html (office).

NKOANA-MASHABANE, Maite Emily; South African diplomatist and politician; *Minister of International Relations and Co-operation;* b. 30 Sept. 1963, Ga-Makanye, Limpopo; m. Amb. Norman Mashabane (died 2007); activist during apartheid era in United Democratic Front; apptd South African High Commr to India and Malaysia in 1990s; fmr mem. Limpopo Local Govt and Housing Exec. Council; mem. Nat. Exec. Cttee of African Nat. Congress (ANC) 2007–; Minister of Int. Relations and Co-operation 2009–. *Address:* Department of Foreign Affairs, Private Bag X152, Pretoria 0001 (office); Department of Foreign Affairs, East Wing, Union Building, 1 Government Avenue, Arcadia, Pretoria 0002 (office); 120 Plein Street, Parliamentary Precinct, Cape Town, South Africa (office). *Telephone:* (12) 3511000 (Pretoria) (office); (21) 4643700 (Cape Town) (office). *Fax:* (12) 3510165 (Pretoria) (office). *E-mail:* minister@foreign.gov.za (office). *Website:* www.dfa.gov.za (office).

NKOMO, John Landa; Zimbabwean politician; *Vice-President;* b. 22 Aug. 1934; s. of Lufele Nkomo; m. Georgina Nkomo 1963; five s. one d.; school teacher 1957–64; mem. Cen. Cttee Zimbabwe African People's Union (ZAPU) 1975–89, mem. Political Bureau Zimbabwe African Nat. Union-Patriotic Front (ZANU-PF) and Cen. Cttee 1989–; MP for Bulawayo Constituency 1990–; Deputy Minister of Industry 1981–82, Minister of State, Prime Minister's Office 1982–84, Minister of Labour, Manpower Planning and Social Welfare 1988; Pres. Int. Labour Conf. 1989–; Minister of Local Govt and Nat. Housing –2001, of Home Affairs 2001–02, Minister for Special Affairs in the Pres.'s Office responsible for Lands, Land Reform and Resettlement 2002–05, Vice-Pres. of Zimbabwe 2009–; Speaker, Parl. of Zimbabwe 2005–08; mem. Public Accounts Cttee 1980–81; Chair. Cttee of Estimates of Expenditure 1985–87, African Regional Labour Centre; Exec. mem. Southern Rhodesia Teachers' Asscn; Trustee Devt Trust of Zimbabwe, The Pres. Fund; Hon. Life Pres. Matebeleland Turf Club; mem. Highlanders Football Club, Bulawayo Club; Zimbabwe Gold Liberation Medal. *Leisure interest:* reading. *Address:* Office of the Vice-Presidents, Munhumutapa Bldg, Samora Machel Ave, Private Bag 7700, Causeway, Harare, Zimbabwe (office). *Telephone:* (4) 707091 (office).

NKUHLU, Wiseman Lumkile, BCom, MBA; South African accountant, academic and university administrator; *Chancellor, University of Pretoria*; b. 5 Feb. 1944, Cala, Eastern Cape; Nondima Mahlulo; four c.; ed Univs of Fort Hare and Cape Town, New York Univ., USA; qualified as Chartered Accountant (first black African) 1976; moved to Umtata to manage an audit practice and to lecture in Dept of Accounting, Univ. of Transkei, Sr Lecturer, later Prof. and Head of Dept of Accounting 1977–82, Vice-Prin. Univ. of Transkei 1983–87, Prin. and Vice-Chancellor 1987–91; served articles with Hoek Wiehahn & Cross, Pnr in charge of Umtata office (merged with Price Waterhouse, now PricewaterhouseCoopers 1988), resigned from partnership to join Ind. Devt Trust 1990, Chief Exec. for three years; Econ. Adviser to Nat. African Federated Chamber of Commerce 1989–93; served as Econ. Adviser to Pres. T. M. Mbeki and as Chief Exec. of Secr. of new Partnership for Africa's Devt 2000–05; Chancellor Univ. of Pretoria 2007–; Chair. Devt Bank of Southern Africa 1993–2000; Chair. Pan-African Capital Holdings (Pty) Ltd, MEEG Bank, Eastern Cape 1998–2009, Metropolitan Ltd 2007–09; Chair. (non-exec.) Bigen Africa (Pty) Ltd, Kagiso Trust Investments; mem. Bd of Dirs Standard Bank, South African Breweries, Old Mutual, Tongaat Hulett, BMW and JCI 1989–2000, AngloGold Ashanti (Pty) Ltd, Datatec Ltd; first Chair. Council on Higher Educ. 1998–2002; Pres. Black Management Forum 1992–95, South African Inst. of Chartered Accountants 1998–2000, Int. Org. of Employers, Geneva 2008–11; mem. Global Financial Crisis Advisory Panel (est. jtly by Int. Accounting Standards Bd and Financial Accounting Standards Bd) 2009–; Chevalier, Légion d'honneur 2005, Grand Counsellor, Order of the Baobab 2008; Dr hc (Free State), (Stellenbosch), (Cape Town), (Pretoria), (Nelson Mandela Metropolitan), (Witwatersrand), (Fort Hare); several awards, including merit awards from Nat. African Federated Chamber of Commerce, Asscn of Advancement of Black Accountants, Black Man. Forum, Pres. of Convocation Medal, Univ. of Cape Town 2004. *Publications:* various articles on socio-economic devt issues. *Address:* Office of the Chancellor, University of Pretoria, Private Bag X20, Hatfield, Pretoria 0028, South Africa (office). *Telephone:* (12) 4203111 (office). *Fax:* (12) 4204555 (office). *E-mail:* csc@up.ac.za (office). *Website:* web.up.ac.za (office).

NKURUNZIZA, Pierre, BA; Burundian politician and head of state; *President*; b. Dec. 1963, Mwumba, Ngozi Prov.; s. of the late Eustache Ngabisha; m.; three s.; ed Gitega Secondary School, Univ. of Burundi, Bujumbura; began career as sports teacher, Vugizo and Muramvya Secondary Schools 1991; fmr Asst Lecturer, Faculty of Physical Educ. and Sports, Univ. of Burundi and ISCAM Mil. Acad. of Burundi; coached Army Football Team, Muzinga, and Union Sporting (first div. football team); forced into exile following inter-ethnic clashes 1995; joined Hutu rebellion CNDD-FDD (Force for the Defence of Democracy) 1995, elected Leader of CNDD-FDD 2001; signed ceasefire accord with Govt Nov. 2003; Minister of State for Good Governance 2004–05; Pres. of Burundi 2005–; several int. awards including Accord Peace Prize, Durban 2006, Interfaith Peacebuilding Peace Prize 2007. *Address:* Office of the President, Bujumbura, Burundi. *Telephone:* 22226063. *E-mail:* ikiyago@burundi-gov.bi (office). *Website:* www.presidence.bi (office).

NNAJI, Genevieve; Nigerian actress, model and singer; b. 3 May 1979, Mbaise, Imo State; ed Methodist Girls' Coll., Yaba, Univ. of Lagos; grew up in Lagos; began career as child actress in TV soap opera Ripples aged eight; debut in Nigerian film industry with film Most Wanted 1998; became known outside Nigeria following performance in Sharon Stone 2002; signed recording contract with EKB Records (Ghana) 2004; selected as the 'Face of Lux' soap in Nigeria 2004; launched clothing line, St. Genevieve 2008 (donates proceeds to charity); apptd as official Face of MUD cosmetics in Nigeria 2010; numerous awards, including Best Actress of the Year, City People Awards 2001, Best Actress in a Leading Role, African Movie Acad. Awards 2005. *Album:* debut album One Logologo Line (mix of R&B, Hip-Hop and Urban music). *Films include:* Most Wanted 1998, Camouflage 1999, Love Boat 2001, Death Warrant 2001, Valentino 2002, Sharon Stone 2002, Runs! 2002, Power of Love 2002, Formidable Force 2002, Battle Line 2002, Above Death: In God We Trust 2003, Blood Sister 2003, Break Up 2003, Butterfly 2003, By His Grace 2003, Church Business 2003, Deadly Mistake 2003, Emergency Wedding 2003, Emotional Tears 2003, For Better for Worse 2003, Honey 2003, Jealous Lovers 2003, Keeping Faith: Is That Love? 2003, Last Weekend 2003, Late Marriage 2003, Love 2003, My Only Love 2003, Not Man Enough 2003, Passion & Pain 2003, Passions 2003, Player: Mr. Lover Man 2003, Private Sin 2003, Sharon Stone in Abuja 2003, Super Love 2003, The Chosen One 2003, Women Affair 2003, Bumper to Bumper 2004, Critical Decision 2004, Dangerous Sister 2004, Goodbye New York 2004, He Lives in Me 2004, Into Temptation 2004, My First Love 2004, Never Die for Love 2004, Promise Me Forever 2004, Stand by Me 2004, Treasure 2004, Unbreakable 2004, We Are One 2004, Darkest Night 2005, Games Women Play 2005, Rip-Off 2005, Girls Cot 2006, 30 Days 2006, Letters to a Stranger 2007, Warrior's Heart 2007, Beautiful Soul 2008, Broken Tears 2008, Critical Condition 2008, River of Tears 2008, My Idol 2008, Silent Scandal 2009, Ijé: The Journey 2010, Tango with Me 2010, Bursting Out 2010, Mirror Boy 2010. *Address:* 213 Igbosere Road, 4th Floor, Lagos, Nigeria. *Telephone:* 803-3133587 (mobile). *E-mail:* admin@genevievennajionline.com. *Website:* genevievennajionline.com; www.genevievennajifanbook.com.

NOAH, Harold Julius, MA, PhD; American (b. British) academic; *Gardner Cowles Professor Emeritus of Economics and Education, Teachers College, Columbia University*; b. 21 Jan. 1925, London, England; s. of Abraham Noah and Sophia Cohen; m. 1st Norma Mestel 1945 (divorced 1966); m. 2nd Helen Claire Chisnall 1966; two s. two d.; ed Stratford Grammar School, London School of Econs, King's Coll. London, Teachers Coll. Columbia Univ., New York; Asst Master then Head of Econs, Henry Thornton School, London 1949–60; Asst, later Assoc. and Gardner Cowles Prof. of Econs and Educ., Teachers Coll., Columbia Univ., New York 1964–87, now Prof. Emer., also Dean 1976–81; Prof. of Educ., State Univ. of New York, Buffalo 1987–91; has received numerous academic honours and awards. *Publications include:* Educational Financing and Policy Goals for Primary Schools: General Report (with Joel Sherman) 1979, The National Case Study: An Empirical Comparative Study of Twenty-one Educational Systems (with Harry Passow and others) 1976, Canada: Review of National Policies for Education 1976, International Study of Business/Industry Involvement in Education 1987, Secondary School Examinations: International Perspectives on Policies and Practice 1993, Doing Comparative Education: Three Decades of Collaboration (with Max Eckstein) 1998, Fraud in Education: The Worm in the Apple 2001. *Leisure interests:* chess, reading German, French and Russian literature. *Address:*

Teachers College, Columbia University, New York, NY 10027, USA (office). *E-mail:* hjn9@columbia.edu (office).

NOAKES, Michael; British painter; b. 28 Oct. 1933, Brighton, Sussex, England; s. of the late Basil Noakes and Mary Noakes; m. Vivien Langley 1960; two s. one d.; ed Downside, Reigate School of Art, The Royal Acad. Schools; mil. service 1954–56; has painted numerous portraits of mems of Royal Family including Queen Elizabeth II, Queen Elizabeth The Queen Mother, Prince of Wales, Prince Philip, the Duke and Duchess of York, the Princess Royal, Princess Margaret, The Duchess of Kent, Princess Alice Countess of Athlone and of other leading figures, including Earl Mountbatten, Earl of Snowdon, Lady Thatcher as Prime Minister, Pres. Clinton, Archbishop Hope when Bishop of London, Duke of Norfolk, HE Cardinal Hume, Lord Aberconway, Princess Ashraf of Iran, Lord Charteris, Lord Denning, Sir Alec Guinness, Haham Dr Solomon Gaon, Gen. Sir John Hackett, Robert Hardy, Cliff Michelmore, Robert Morley, Malcolm Muggeridge, Airey Neave, Valerie Hobson Profumo, Sir Ralph Richardson, Lord Runcie when Archbishop of Canterbury, Dame Margaret Rutherford, Dennis Wheatley, Sir Mortimer Wheeler, etc.; exhbns internationally, including Royal Acad., Royal Inst. of Oil Painters, Royal Soc. of British Artists, of Marine Artists, of Portrait Painters, Nat. Soc. etc.; represented in perm. collections, The Queen, The Prince of Wales, The British Museum, Nat. Portrait Gallery, House of Commons, Frank Sinatra, etc.; mem. Royal Inst. of Oil Painters 1964, Vice-Pres. 1968–72, Pres. 1972–78, Hon. mem. Council 1978–; mem. Royal Soc. of Portrait Painters 1967–, served Council, 1969–71, 1972–74, 1978–80, 1993–95; Gov. Fed. of British Artists 1972–83, a Dir 1981–83; Liveryman Co. of Woolmen; fmr Chair. Contemporary Portrait Soc.; designed Crown Piece (£5 coin) as a mark of 50th Birthday of Prince of Wales and the work of the Prince's Trust 1998; throughout 1999 illustrated The Daily Life of The Queen: An Artist's Diary; has broadcast frequently in UK and also in USA on art subjects; Freeman City of London; Hon. mem. numerous socs including Nat. Soc., United Soc.; Platinum Disc Award for record sleeve, Portrait of Sinatra 1977. *Publications:* A Professional Approach to Oil Painting 1968, The Daily Hope of the Queen 2000; numerous contribs to art journals and books on art. *Leisure interest:* idling. *Address:* 146 Hamilton Terrace, St John's Wood, London, NW8 9UX, England. *Telephone:* (20) 7328-6754. *Fax:* (20) 7625-1220. *E-mail:* mail@michael-noakes.co.uk. *Website:* www.michael-noakes.co.uk.

NOAKES, Baroness (Life Peer), cr. 2000, of Goudhurst in the County of Kent; **Sheila Valerie Noakes,** DBE, LLB, FCA; British chartered accountant and company director; b. (Sheila Valerie Masters), 23 June 1949, London, England; d. of Albert Frederick Masters and Iris Sheila Ratcliffe; m. Colin Barry Noakes 1985; ed Univ. of Bristol; joined Peat Marwick Mitchell & Co. 1970; seconded to HM Treasury 1979–81; Partner, KPMG (fmrly Peat Marwick Mitchell & Co., then KPMG Peat Marwick) 1983–2000; seconded to Dept of Health as Dir of Finance, Nat. Health Service Man. Exec. 1988–91; Dir Bank of England 1994–2001, Chair. Cttee of Non-Exec. Dirs 1998–2001; mem. Council, Inst. of Chartered Accountants in England and Wales 1987–2002 (Pres. 1999–2000), Inland Revenue Man. Bd 1992–99, Chancellor of Exchequer's Pvt. Finance Panel 1993–97; mem. Bd of Dirs (non-exec.) Royal Bank of Scotland Group PLC, Carpetright PLC 2001–, Severn Trent plc 2008–; Trustee, Reuters Founders Share Co. 1998–; Dir Social Market Foundation 2002–05; mem. Bd ENO 2000–08; Gov. London Business School 1998–2001, Eastbourne Coll. 2000–06, Marlborough Coll. 2000–02; Hon. LLD (Bristol) 2000; Hon. DSc (Buckingham) 2001; Hon. DBA (London Guildhall) 1999. *Leisure interests:* opera, early classical music, horse racing, skiing. *Address:* House of Lords, Westminster, London, SW1A 0PW, England (office). *Telephone:* (20) 7219-5353 (office). *Fax:* (20) 7219-5979 (office). *E-mail:* noakess@parliament.uk (office).

NOAM, Eli M., BA, MA, PhD, JD; American economist, lawyer, academic and author; *Professor of Finance and Economics, Columbia Business School and Director, Institute for Tele-Information, Columbia University*; b. 1946; m. Nadine Strossen 1980; ed Harvard Univ. and Harvard Law School; mil. service in Israel 1966–68, 1973; Visiting Asst Prof., Princeton Univ. 1975–76; Prof. of Econs and Finance, Columbia Business School, Columbia Univ. 1976–, Founder and Dir Inst. for Tele-Information 1983–87, 1991–, Faculty mem. School of Public and Int. Affairs, has also taught at Columbia Law School; Commr, New York State Public Service Comm. 1987–90; Virtual Visiting Prof., Univ. of St Gallen, Switzerland 1998–2002; mem. numerous panels including NAS Cttee on Future of Broadband Communications, Comm. on the Status of Women in Computing, NY Gov.'s Task Force on New Media and the Internet; mem. numerous bds and advisory bds, including Electronic Privacy Information Center, European Inst. on the Media, France Telecom Scientific Advisory Bd, Intek Corpn, Minority Media Telecommunications Council, Oxford Internet Inst.; mem. Editorial Bd, The Communications Review, Information Law Series, New Media, Telecommunications Policy, Telematics, Transborder Data Report, Utility Policy, Communications and Strategies, International Journal of Media Management, Info: The International Journal of Information; columnist for Financial Times online edn; Trustee, Jones Int. Univ. (online coll.); Dr hc (Munich) 2004. *Publications:* Telecommunications Regulation: Today and Tomorrow (ed.) 1982, Video Media Competition: Regulation, Economics, and Technology (ed.) 1985, Services in Transition: The Impact of Information Technologies on the Service Sector (co-ed.) 1986, Law of International Telecommunications in the United States (co-ed.) 1988, The Cost of Libel (co-ed.) 1989, Technologies without Boundaries (ed.) 1990, Television in Europe 1991, Telecommunications in Europe 1992, The Telecommunications Revolution (co-ed.) 1992, The International Market for Film and Television (co-ed.) 1992, Asymmetric Deregulation (co-ed.) 1992, Privacy in Telecommunications: Markets, Rights, and Regulations 1994, Telecommunications in the Pacific Basin (co-ed.) 1994, Private Networks and Public Objectives (co-ed.) 1996, Globalism and Localism in Telecommunications (co-ed.) 1997, Telecommunications in Western Asia 1997, Public Television in America 1998, Telecommunications in Latin America 1998, Telecommunications in Africa 1999, The New Investment Theory of Real Options and its Implication for Telecommunications Economics (co-ed.) 1999, Interconnecting the Network of Networks 2001, Internet Television (co-ed.) 2004, Competition for the Mobile Internet (co-ed.) 2004, Telecommunications Meltdown (co-author) 2005, Mobile Media: Content and Services for Wireless Communications (co-ed.) 2006, Media Ownership and Concentration in America 2007; Gen. Ed. Business, Government and Society, Columbia Univ. Press Book series; over 400 articles in econ., legal, communications and other journals. *Address:* Columbia

Institute for Tele-Information, Graduate School of Business, Uris Hall, Suite 1A, 3022 Broadway, Columbia University, New York, NY 10027 (office); Riverside Drive, Apt 51, New York, NY 10027, USA (home). *Telephone:* (212) 854-8332 (office); (212) 864-3776 (home). *Fax:* (212) 854-1471 (office); (212) 851-1846 (home). *E-mail:* noam@columbia.edu (office). *Website:* www.citi.columbia.edu (office).

NOBLE, Adrian Keith, BA; British theatre director; b. 19 July 1950; s. of the late William John Noble and Violet Ena Noble (née Wells); m. Joanne Pearce 1991; one d. one s.; ed Chichester High School for Boys, Univ. of Bristol, London Drama Centre; Resident Dir then Assoc. Dir Bristol Old Vic 1976–79; Resident Dir RSC 1980–82, Assoc. Dir 1982–90, Artistic Dir 1991–2003; Guest Dir Royal Exchange Theatre, Man. 1980–81; Visiting Prof., London Inst. 2001; Hon. Bencher, Middle Temple; Hon. DLitt (Birmingham) 1994, (Bristol) 1996, (Exeter) 1999, (Warwick) 2001. *Film directed:* A Midsummer Night's Dream 1995. *Stage productions include:* Ubu Rex 1977, A Man's a Man 1977, A View from a Bridge 1978, Titus Adronicus 1978, The Changeling 1978, Love for Love 1979, Timon of Athens 1979, Recruiting Officer 1979, The Duchess of Malfi (Best Dir, Plays and Players) 1980, Dr Faustus 1981, The Forest (Best Revival, Drama Awards) 1981, A Doll's House (Best Dir, Best Revival, Critics' Awards) 1981, King Lear 1982, Antony and Cleopatra 1982, A New Way to Pay Old Debts 1983, The Comedy of Errors 1983, Measure for Measure 1983, Henry V 1984, The Winter's Tale 1984, As You Like It 1985, Mephisto 1986, The Art of Success 1986, Macbeth 1986, Kiss Me Kate 1987, The Plantagenets 1989, The Master Builder 1989, The Fairy Queen (Aix-en-Provence), Three Sisters 1990, Henry IV Parts 1 and 2 1991, The Thebans 1991, Hamlet, The Winter's Tale 1992, Travesties, King Lear, Macbeth 1993, A Midsummer Night's Dream 1994, Romeo and Juliet 1995, The Cherry Orchard 1995, Little Eyolf 1996, Cymbeline 1997, Twelfth Night 1997, The Tempest 1998, The Lion, the Witch and the Wardrobe 1998, The Seagull, The Family Reunion 2000, The Return of Ulysses (Aix-en-Provence) (Grand Prix des Critiques) 2000, The Secret Garden 2000–01, Chitty Chitty Bang Bang 2002, Pericles 2002, Brand 2003, A Woman of No Importance 2003, The Home Place (Dublin and London) 2005; opera: Don Giovanni (Kent Opera) 1983, The Faery Queen (Aix-en-Provence Festival) (Grand Prix des Critiques) 1989, Falstaff (Gothenburg Opera) 2005, Così fan tutte (Opera de Lyon) 2006, The Marriage of Figaro (Opera de Lyon) 2007, Macbeth (Metropolitan Opera) 2007. *Address:* c/o Independent, Oxford House, 76 Oxford Street, London, W1D 1BS, England (office). *Telephone:* (20) 7636-6565 (office). *Website:* www.independenttalent.com (office).

NOBLE, Denis, CBE, PhD, FRS; British scientist and academic; *Director of Computational Physiology, University of Oxford;* b. 16 Nov. 1936, London, England; s. of George Noble and Ethel Rutherford; m. Susan Jennifer Barfield 1965; one s. (adopted) one d.; ed Emanuel School and Univ. Coll. London; Asst Lecturer, Univ. Coll. London 1961–63; Fellow, Lecturer and Tutor in Physiology, Balliol Coll. Oxford 1963–84, Praefectus, Balliol Grad. Centre 1971–89, Burdon Sanderson Prof. of Cardiovascular Physiology and Professorial Fellow, Univ. of Oxford 1984–2004, currently Dir of Computational Physiology; Visiting Prof., Univ. of Alberta 1969–70; Ed., Progress in Biophysics 1967–; Founder/Dir, Oxsoft Ltd 1984–, Physiome Sciences Inc. 1994–; Chair. Jt Dental Cttee 1984–90; Pres. Medical Section, British Assocn 1992; Gen.-Sec. Int. Union of Physiological Sciences 1993–2001, Pres. 2009–(17); Hon. Sec. Physiological Soc. 1974–80, Foreign Sec. 1986–92; Fellow, Univ. Coll., London 1986; Adjunct Prof., Xi'an Jiaotong Univ., China 2003–07; Visiting Prof., Osaka Univ., Japan 2006–11; Founder-Fellow, Acad. of Medical Sciences 1998; Founder and performer, Oxford Trobadors; Hon. FRCP; Hon. mem. Acad. de Médecine de Belgique, American Physiological Soc., Academia Europaea 1989, Japanese Physiological Soc. 1998, The Physiological Soc. 1999; Hon. DSc (Sheffield) 2004, (Warwick) 2008; Dr hc (Bordeaux) 2005; Darwin Lecturer, British Assocn 1966, Scientific Medal, Zoological Soc. 1970, Nahum Lecturer, Yale Univ. 1977, British Heart Foundation Gold Medal and Prize 1985, Lloyd Roberts Lecturer 1987, Bowden Lecturer 1988, Alderdale Wyld Lecturer 1988, Pierre Rijlant Prize, Belgian Royal Acad. 1991, Baly Medal, Royal Coll. of Physicians 1993, Pavlov Medal Russian Acad. of Science 2004, Hodgkin-Huxley-Katz Prize, Physiological Soc. 2004, Mackenzie Prize, British Cardiac Soc. 2005, Gordon Moe Lecturer, Cardiac Electrophysiology Soc. 2010. *Publications:* Initiation of the Heartbeat 1975, Electric Current Flow in Excitable Cells 1975, Electrophysiology of Single Cardiac Cells 1987, Goals, No Goals and Own Goals 1989, Sodium-Calcium Exchange 1989, Logic of Life 1993, Ionic Channels and the Effect of Taurine on the Heart 1993, Ethics of Life 1997, The Music of Life 2006, The Selected Papers of Denis Noble CBE, FRS, A Journey in Physiology towards Enlightenment 2012; scientific papers mostly in Journal of Physiology. *Leisure interests:* Occitan language and music, Indian and French cooking, classical guitar. *Address:* Department of Physiology, Anatomy and Genetics, Parks Road, Oxford, OX1 3PT (office); 49 Old Road, Oxford, OX3 7JZ, England (home). *Telephone:* (1865) 272528 (office); (1865) 762237 (home). *Fax:* (1865) 272554 (office). *E-mail:* denis.noble@dpag.ox.ac.uk (office). *Website:* www.dpag.ox.ac.uk/team/h-n/denis-noble (office); www.musicoflife.co.uk.

NOBLE, Ronald Kenneth, BA, JD; American lawyer, law enforcement executive and academic; *Secretary-General, International Criminal Police Organization (INTERPOL);* ed Univ. of New Hampshire, Stanford Univ. Law School; fmr Asst to US Attorney, then Deputy Asst to Attorney-Gen., Dept of Justice; Pres. Financial Action Task Force (26 mem. multi-nat. org. est. to fight money-laundering by G7) 1989; Chief Law Enforcement Officer, US Treasury Dept 1989–96, responsible for The Secret Service, Customs Service, Bureau of Alcohol, Tobacco and Firearms, Fed. Law Enforcement Training Center, Financial Crimes Enforcement Network, Office of Foreign Assets Control and Criminal Investigation Div. of Internal Revenue Service; Prof. of Law, New York Univ. School of Law; fmr mem. Exec. Cttee INTERPOL, Sec.-Gen. 2000–; Chevalier, Légion d'honneur 2008. *Address:* International Criminal Police Organization (INTERPOL), 200 quai Charles de Gaulle, 69006 Lyon, France (office). *Telephone:* (4) 72-44-70-00 (office). *Fax:* (4) 72-44-71-63 (office). *E-mail:* cp@interpol.int (office). *Website:* www.interpol.int (office).

NOBOA BEJARANO, Gustavo, PhD; Ecuadorian politician and academic; b. 21 Aug. 1939, Guayaquil; m. Marta Baquerizo; six c.; teacher of social sciences and politics 1962–; fmr Rector of Catholic Univ. of Guayaquil; fmr Rector of Public Univ. of Guayaquil; Gov. of Guayas Prov. 1983; mem. of peace comm. on border dispute with Peru 1996; Vice-Pres. of Ecuador 1998–2000, Pres. 2000–02; investigated for allegedly mishandling $126 million in govt bonds to bail out

state-run banks during his presidency; granted asylum by Govt of Dominican Repub. 2003; Order of St Sylvester, Commdr, State of the Vatican.

NOBOA PONTÓN, Alvaro Fernando; Ecuadorean business executive and politician; *President, Noboa Corporation;* b. 21 Nov. 1950, Guayaquil; s. of Luis Noboa Naranjo; m. Anabella Azín; three s.; ed Le Rosey School, Switzerland, State Univ. of Guayaquil; est. first business Promandato Global SA 1973; f. La Verdad (monthly magazine) 1986, Banco del Litoral 1990, Global Financing Co. and other investment cos 1992, joined these cos with Banco del Litoral to form Grupo de Empresas Ab. Alvaro Noboa P. 1994; inherited portion of Noboa Corpn following death of father 1994; Pres. Noboa Corpn (controls 105 cos in Ecuador, Europe, USA and NZ with interests in coffee, bananas, real estate and flour) 1995–, cos include Bonita Bananas (largest banana co. in Ecuador), four shipping cos, one bank, two insurance cos, La nica (edible oils), Valdez (sugar refinery), Los Álamos and 14 other banana plantations, mines, media cos and other Ecuadorean businesses; Pres. Monetary Bd 1996; presidential cand. for Partido Roldosista Ecuatoriano (PRE) 1998, for Partido Renovador Institucional Acción Nacional (PRIAN) 2002, 2006 (also Founder and Leader); f. Fundación Cruzada Nueva Humanidad (charity) 1977. *Address:* Corporacion Noboa, El Oro y La Ria, Guayaquil (office); Partido Renovador Institucional de Acción Nacional (PRIAN), Quito, Ecuador. *Website:* www.alvaronoboa.com (office); www.prian.org.ec.

NÓBREGA SUÁREZ, Tobías, DEcon; Venezuelan economist and politician; b. 30 Jan. 1961, Puerto Cabello, Carabobo; ed Univ. Central de Venezuela, Univ. Complutense de Madrid, Spain; Lecturer, Dept of Econs, Univ. Central de Venezuela 1986–97; Chief Economist, Central Hipotecaria 1988, Asociácion Bancaria de Venezuela 1995–97, Asociácion de Gobernadores de Venezuela 1993–98; ind. financial consultant 1986–, also financial adviser to Nat. Govt and several regional govts; Dir Oficina de Asesoría Económica del Parlamento Nacional (OAEF) 2000; adviser to numerous parl. cttees, including Parl. Finance Sub-cttee 2000; Minister of Finance 2002–04. *Publications:* numerous articles in econ. journals. *Address:* c/o Ministry of Finance, esq. de Carmelitas, Avda Urdaneta, Caracas, Venezuela.

NODA, Seiko; Japanese politician; b. 3 Sept. 1960, Kitakyushu, Fukuoka; m. Yosuke Tsuruho 2001; ed Futaba Acad. Secondary School, Tokyo, Jonesville High School, Michigan, USA, Sophia Univ.; mem. staff Imperial Hotel 1983–87; elected mem. Gifu Prefectural Ass. 1987; mem. LDP; mem. for Gifu No. 1 Dist, House of Rep. 1993–; Parl. Vice-Minister of Posts and Telecommunications, Minister 1998–99; Minister of State for Science and Tech. Policy and Food Safety, Consumer Affairs, Space Policy 2008–09; adviser to Sake Mfrs Asscn; Pres. Sake-Loving Female Diet Members Club. *Publications:* (in Japanese): I am Seeing 1987, Under the Pretext of Reform 1994, Things I Want to Get Across to the People – Politics Spoken with Sincerity 1996, Japan Will Win the Post-IT Era! – Proposals of Seven Leading Figures (co-author) 2001, I Want to Give Birth 2004, Who is Taking Away Our Future – Fighting the Declining Birthrate 2005, Easy-to-understand Guide to the Revised Child Prostitution/Pornography Law (co-author) 2005. *Leisure interests:* reading, watching movies, karaoke, using the computer. *Address:* Liberal-Democratic Party, 1-11-23, Nagata-cho, Chiyoda-ku, Tokyo 100-8910, Japan (office). *Telephone:* (3) 3581-6211 (office). *E-mail:* koho@ldp.jimin.or.jp (office). *Website:* www.jimin.jp (office).

NODA, Tetsuya, MA; Japanese printmaker and academic; *Professor Emeritus, Tokyo University of the Arts (formerly Tokyo National University of Fine Arts and Music);* b. 5 March 1940, Kumamoto Pref.; s. of Tesshin Noda and Sakae Noda; m. Dorit Bartur; one s. one d.; ed Tokyo Univ. of the Arts (fmrly Tokyo Nat. Univ. of Fine Arts and Music); Visiting Artist, Alberta Univ., Canada 1984, Betzalel Art Acad., Israel 1985, Canberra Art School, Australia 1990, Columbia Univ., USA 1998; Prof., Tokyo Nat. Univ. of Fine Arts and Music (renamed Tokyo Univ. of the Arts) 1990–2007, Prof. Emer. 2007–; Cultural Envoy, Japanese Govt Agency of Cultural Affairs 2010–, to Hebrew Univ., Israel 2011, London Metropolitan Univ.; mem. Int. Jury for the British Int. Print Biennale 1976, Korean Int. Print Biennale 1996, Space Int. Print Biennale, Seoul 2002, First Int. Print Biennale, Istanbul 2008, Edmonton Print Int. 2008, 2nd Bangkok Triennale Int. Print and Drawing Exhbn 2008; Hon. DLitt (London Metropolitan); prizes include Int. Grand Prize (Tokyo Int. Print Biennale) 1968, Grand Prix (Ljubljana Int. Print Biennale) 1977 and Grand Prize of Honour 1987, Grand Prize (Norwegian Int. Print Biennale) 1978, Friends of Bradford Art Galleries and Museum Prize (British Int. Print Biennale) 1986, Gen Yamaguchi Memorial Grand Prize, City of Numazu 1993; Medal of Purple Ribbon (Japanese Govt). *Publications:* Tetsuya Noda – The Works III 1992–2000 2001. *Leisure interest:* gardening. *Address:* 2-12-4 Kikkodai-cho, Kashiwa-shi, Chiba-ken 277-0031, Japan (home). *Telephone:* (471) 63-5332 (home). *Fax:* (471) 63-5332 (home). *E-mail:* tetsuyanoda@hotmail.com (home).

NODA, Yoshihiko; Japanese politician; b. 20 May 1957, Funabashi, Chiba Pref.; ed Waseda Univ., Matsushita Inst. of Govt and Man.; mem. Chiba Prefectural Ass. 1987–93; mem. House of Reps Japan New Party (now Democratic Party of Japan–DPJ) 1993–, Pres. 2011–12, Chair. Diet Affairs Cttee 2002, 2005, Public Relations Cttee 2007; Acting Sec. Gen. DPJ 2009; Sr Vice-Minister of Finance 2009, Minister of Finance 2010–11; Prime Minister 2011–12; ranked by Forbes magazine amongst The World's Most Powerful People (62nd) 2011, (60th) 2012. *Address:* Democratic Party of Japan, 1-11-1, Nagata-cho, Chiyoda-ku, Tokyo 100-0014, Japan (office). *E-mail:* Post@Nodayoshi.gr.jp (office). *Website:* www.dpj.or.jp; www.nodayoshi.gr.jp (office).

NODDLE, Jeffrey (Jeff), BA; American retail executive; s. of the late Robert Noddle and Edith Noddle; ed Univ. of Iowa; began career as Dir of Retail Operations, JM Jones Div., Supervalu Inc. 1976, held various positions including Merchandising Dir, Vice-Pres. Marketing JM Jones Div. –1982, Pres. Fargo and Miami Divs 1982–85, Corp. Vice-Pres. Merchandising, Supervalu Inc. 1985–88, Sr Vice-Pres. Marketing 1988–92, Corp. Exec. Vice-Pres. Marketing 1992–93, Corp. Exec. Vice-Pres. 1993–95, COO Distribution Food Cos 1995–2000, Pres. and COO 2000–01, Pres. and CEO 2001–02, Chair. and CEO Supervalu Inc. 2002–09, Exec. Chair. 2009–10, mem. Finance Cttee; mem. Bd of Dirs General Cable Corpn 1998–2004, Donaldson Co. Inc. 2000–; Ind. Dir Ameriprise Financial Inc. 2005–; Vice-Chair. and mem. Exec. Cttee Food Marketing Inst. (FMI); mem. Bd Ind. Grocers Alliance Inc. (IGA), Bd Sarah W. Stedman Center for Nutritional Studies, Duke Univ. Medical Center, Exec. Cttee Minneapolis Business Partnership, Bd of Overseers Univ. of Minnesota Carlson School of Man.; Chair. Greater Twin Cities United Way 2009; Executive of the Year, Minneapolis/St Paul Business Journal 2008, Herbert Hoover Award, Food Marketing Inst. 2009, named the Network of Executive Women's Outstanding Champion for 2009, inducted into Minnesota Grocers Asscn's Hall of Fame 2009. *Address:* c/o Supervalu Inc., 11840 Valley View Road, Eden Prairie, MN 55344, USA.

NOE PINO, Hugo, PhD; Honduran economist, diplomatist and politician; b. 11 Jan. 1955, Tegucigalpa; s. of Roberto Noe and Elidia Pino; m. Vivian Bustamante; two s. one d.; ed Universidad Nacional Autonoma de Honduras (UNAH), Univ. of Texas at Austin, USA; fmr teaching Asst, Dept of Econs, Univ. of Tex.; Pres. Cen. Bank of Honduras 1994–97; Dir Master's Programme in Econs for Cen. American and Caribbean Region, UNAH; Pres. Asscn of Economists of Honduras; mem. Editorial Council of various magazines published in Honduras; Spokesman of Shadow Cabinet 1993; Amb. to USA –1999; mem. Partido Liberal (PL), campaign man. for successful presidential cand. José Manuel (Mel) Zelaya Rosales 2005; Minister of Finance Jan.–July 2006. *Publications:* An Assessment of the Campesino Associative Enterprise of Isletas 1987, Honduras: Structural Adjustment and Agrarian Reform 1992. *Leisure interests:* reading, music. *Address:* Partido Liberal (PL), Col. Miramonte, Tegucigalpa, Honduras. *Telephone:* 232-0520. *Fax:* 232-0797. *Website:* www.partidoliberal.net.

NOFAL, María Beatriz, MA, PhD; Argentine economist, politician and academic; *President, National Agency for Investment Development;* b. 7 Oct. 1952, Mendoza; ed Universidad Nacional de Cuyo, Inst. of Social Studies, Netherlands, Univ. of Paris, France, Johns Hopkins Univ., Baltimore, Md, USA; Assoc. Prof., Johns Hopkins Univ. 1983–84, MIT 1985; Prof., Univ. of Bologna based in Buenos Aires 1999; Visiting Prof., Univ. of Toronto, Canada 2004; Prof., Universidad Católica Argentina 2005; Under-Sec. of Industrial Devt, Industry and Foreign Trade Secr., Ministry of Economy 1986–89; Pres. of ECO-AXIS, SA consultants 1993–99, 2002–06; Congresswoman (Unión Cívica Radical) 1999–2002; Pres. Nat. Agency for Investment Devt (ANDI) 2006–; Dir, Arthur D. Little (consultancy firm), Argentina 1999–2000; Dir (non-exec.), Nobleza Piccardo/British American Tobacco 2006; mem. Interamerican Dialogue (US-based think tank) 2001–; adviser to Argentine Council for Int. Relations (CARI); Ed. and Prin. Author Mercosur Journal 1995–99. *Publications include:* Absentee Entrepreneurship and the Dynamics of the Motor Vehicle Industry in Argentina 1989; numerous articles in newspapers, magazines and professional journals. *Address:* Ministry of Economy and Production, Hipólito Yrigoyen 250, C1086AAB, Buenos Aires, Argentina (office); Inter-American Dialogue, 1211 Connecticut Avenue NW, Suite 510, Washington, DC 20036, USA. *Telephone:* (11) 4349-5000 (Buenos Aires) (office); (202) 822-9002 (Washington, DC). *Fax:* (202) 822-9553 (Washington, DC). *E-mail:* sagpya@mecon.gov.ar (office). *Website:* www.mecon.gov.ar (office); www.thedialogue.org.

NOGAMI, Tomoyuki, PhD; Japanese educationalist, university administrator and academic; *President, Kobe University;* b. 1946; ed Hiroshima Univ.; Research Assoc., Faculty of Educ., Hiroshima Univ. 1979–80; Lecturer, Faculty of Home Econs, Hiroshima Women's Univ. 1980–83, Assoc. Prof. 1983–86; Visiting Scholar, Teachers' Coll., Columbia Univ., New York 1986–88; Assoc. Prof., Faculty of Educ., Kobe Univ. 1988–92, Prof., Faculty of Human Devt 1992–94, Dir Research Centre for Human Science 1994–96, Prin. Kindergarten/Akashi Elementary School/ Akashi Jr High School attached to Faculty of Human Devt 1996–98, Dean Faculty of Human Devt 1998–2001, Dean Grad. School of Cultural Studies and Human Science 2001, Pres. Kobe Univ. 2001–; mem. Japanese Nat. Comm. for UNESCO 2003–. *Address:* Office of the President, Kobe University, 1-1, Rokkodai-cho, Nada-ku Kobe 657-8501, Hyogo, Japan (office). *Telephone:* (78) 881-5040 (office). *E-mail:* intl-plan@office.kobe-u.ac.jp (office). *Website:* www.kobe-u.ac.jp (office).

NOGAMI, Yoshiji; Japanese diplomatist; *President, Japan Institute of International Affairs;* b. 19 June 1942; m. Geraldine Nogami; three s.; ed Tokyo Univ.; joined Ministry of Foreign Affairs 1966, held positions as Dir-Gen. Econ. Affairs Bureau, Deputy Minister, later Vice-Minister for Foreign Affairs 2001, Consul-Gen. to Hong Kong, Amb. to OECD, Paris, to UK 2004–08; Adviser to the Cabinet 2008; Sr Visiting Fellow, Chatham House (fmrly Royal Inst. of Int. Affairs) 2002; Pres. Japan Inst. of Int. Affairs 2009–. *Address:* Japan Institute of International Affairs, 3rd Floor, Toranomon Mitsui Building, 3-8-1 Kasumigaseki Chiyodaku, Tokyo 100-0013, Japan (office). *Telephone:* (3) 3503-7261 (office). *Fax:* (3) 3503-7292 (office). *Website:* www2.jiia.or.jp (office).

NOGHAIDELI, Zurab; Georgian business executive, academic and politician; b. 22 Oct. 1964, Kobuleti, Ajara; s. of Nazi Katamadze; m. Nino Tsintsabadze; one s.; ed Moscow M.V. Lomonosov State Univ., USSR (now Russian Fed.); Asst, Inst. of Geography, Acad. of Sciences of Georgia, Batumi 1988–89; Guest Researcher, Inst. of Geology, Acad. of Sciences of Estonia, Tallinn 1989–91; Sr Researcher and Head of Lab., Niko Berzenishvili Research Inst., Acad. of Sciences of Georgia, Batumi 1989–92; Exec. Sec. Georgia Greens 1992–93; mem. Parl., Chair. Cttee of Environment Protection and Natural Resources 1992–95, Chair. Cttee of Tax and Revenue 1999–2000; Co-ordinator Office of the Chair. 1995–99; Int. Sec., Citizens' Union of Georgia 1995–98; mem. Supreme Council, Adjara Autonomous Rep. 1996–98; Minister of Finance 2000–02, 2004–05; Prime Minister of Georgia 2005–07 (resgnd); mem. Bd People's Bank of Georgia 2002–03; Partner, Solidary Responsibilities Soc. Damenia, Varshalomidze, Noghaideli and Kavtaradze April–Nov. 2003; Chair. Kala Capital (investment co.) 2007–; Chair. Int. School of Econs Business Council, Tbilisi State Univ. 2008–. *Address:* Kala Capital 4A, 1st Drive, I. Chavchavadze, 0179 Tbilisi, Georgia (office). *Telephone:* (32) 91-92-22.

NOGOYBAYEV, Bolotbek, CandJur; Kyrgyzstani politician; b. 10 Nov. 1955, Telman village, Panfilov Dist; m. Mariya Boronbayevna Nogoybayeva; two s. one d.; ed Kyrgyz State Univ.; served in Soviet Army 1973–75; served in various policing roles including police officer, Inspector and Head, Criminal Investigation Dept, Dept of Transport, Pishpek (now Bishkek) office 1976–85, Head, Transport Police Div. 1987–90; Dir Internal Affairs Dept, Sverdlov region 1990–95; Deputy Head of Internal Affairs, Talas Oblast 1995–96; Head, Criminal Investigation Dept, Ministry of Internal Affairs 1996–98; Head of Internal Affairs, Osh Oblast 1998–99; Deputy Minister of Internal Affairs 1999–2001, 2002–05; Chief Inspector, Kyrgyz Security Council Feb.–Aug. 2005; Dir Kyrgyz Drug Control Agency 2005–07; Minister of Internal Affairs 2007–08. *Publications:* Narcotics:

Theory and Practice of Counteraction; numerous articles on drug control. *Address:* c/o Ministry of Internal Affairs, 720040 Bishkek, Frunze 469, Kyrgyzstan (office).

NOGUCHI, Teruhisa, PhD; Japanese business executive; b. 22 Oct. 1924, Chiba Pref.; m.; one s. three d.; ed Schools of Medicine, Kanazawa and Tokyo Univs; with Nihon Soda Co. 1949–72; with Teijin Ltd 1972–79, Dir 1973, Dir Teijin Inst. for Biomedical Research 1976; with Suntory Ltd 1979–92, Dir 1979, Exec. Man. Pharmaceutical Div. 1981, Sr Man. Dir 1987–, Chief Exec. 1991; Exec. Vice-Pres. Yamanouchi Pharmaceutical Co. Ltd 1992–; Adjunct Prof., The Rockefeller Univ. 1984–; Fellow, American Acad. of Microbiology; several prizes and awards. *Publications include:* Biochemistry of Interferons 1982, New Trends in Neuro-Science 1984. *Leisure interests:* fine arts, golf. *Address:* 2-18-11, Kugenuma Kaigan, Fujisawa City, Kanagawa Prefecture 251, Japan.

NOHRIA, Nitin, BTech, PhD; Indian chemical engineer, academic and university administrator; *Dean, Harvard Business School;* b. 1962, Mumbai; s. of Kewal Nohria; m. Monica Norhia; two d.; ed Indian Inst. of Tech., Bombay, Sloan School of Man., Massachusetts Inst. of Tech., USA; Asst Prof., Harvard Business School 1988–93, Assoc. Prof. 1993–99, Richard P. Chapman Prof. of Business Admin 1999–, Co-Chair. Leadership Initiative 2009–, Dean, Harvard Business School 2010–, Dir Div. of Research 2003–04, Sr Assoc. Dean of Faculty Devt 2006–09, Head of Organizational Behavior unit 1998–2002; Visiting Faculty mem. London Business School 1996; Distinguished Alumnus Medal, Indian Inst. of Tech. 2007. *Publications include:* co-author or co-editor of 16 books, including Networks and Organizations: Structure, Form, and Action, Building the Information Age Organization, Beyond the Hype: Rediscovering the Essence of Management, Differentiated Network: Organizing Multinational Corporations for Value Creation (George R. Terry Award, Academy of Management 1998) 1997, Portable MBA Desk Reference, Breaking the Code of Change, Arc of Ambition: Defining the Leadership Journey (co-author) 2000, Master Passions: Emotion, Narrative, and the Development of Culture, Driven: How Human Nature Shapes Our Choices (co-author) 2001, Changing Fortunes: Remaking the Industrial Corporation (co-author) 2002, What Really Works: The 4+2 Formula for Sustained Business Success (co-author) 2003, In Their Time: The Greatest Business Leaders of the 20th Century, Paths to Power: How Insiders and Outsiders Shaped American Business Leadership (co-author) 2006, Handbook of Leadership Theory and Practice (co-ed.) 2010; over 50 journal articles, book chapters, cases, working papers and notes. *Address:* Office of the Dean, Harvard Business School, Soldiers Field, Boston, MA 02163, USA. *Website:* www.hbs.edu/dean.

NØJGAARD, Morten, DPhil; Danish academic; *Romance Editor, Orbis Litterarum;* b. 28 July 1934, Holbaek; s. of Niels Nøjgaard and Annie Nøjgaard (née Bay); m. Stina Lund 1962; two s. two d.; secondary school teacher, Roedovre Statskole 1960–63; Research Scholar, Univ. of Copenhagen 1963–65; Prof. of Romance Philology, Univ. of Southern Denmark, Odense 1966–2004; Chief Ed. Orbis Litterarum 1968–99, Romance Ed. 1999–; Pres. Asscn of French Prof. 1962–63, Alliance Française, Odense 1970–; mem. Soc. of Letters (Lund, Sweden) 1978, Royal Danish Acad. of Science 1982, Royal Norwegian Acad. of Science 1991, Royal Swedish Acad. of Antiquities 1997; Ordre du Mérite 1980; Fnske Bladfond Research Award 1975. *Publications:* La Fable Antique, (Vols I–II) 1964–67, Elévation et Expansion. Les deux dimensions de Baudelaire 1973, An Introduction to Literary Analysis 1975, Romain-Gary-Emile Ajar, Homo Duplex 1986, Les Adverbes français, Vol. I 1992, Vol. II 1993, Vol. III 1995, Plaisir et vérité, Le paradoxe de l'évaluation littéraire 1993, Le Temps de la littérature. Sur Paul Ricoeur et les paradoxes du temps raconté 1999, Temps, réalisme et description – Essais de théorie littéraire 2004; numerous scientific articles. *Address:* University of Southern Denmark, Campusvej 55, 5230 Odense M (office); Åløkken 48, 5250 Odense SV, Denmark (home). *Telephone:* 65-50-10-00 (office); 65-96-18-06 (home). *Fax:* 65-93-51-41 (office). *E-mail:* mno@litcul.sdu.dk (office). *Website:* www.humaniora.sdu.dk (office).

NOJI, Kunio; Japanese business executive; *President and CEO, Komatsu Ltd;* b. 17 Nov. 1946, Fukui Pref.; m.; two d.; ed School of Eng Science, Osaka Univ.; joined Komatsu Ltd 1969, Gen. Man. Production Control Dept, Tech. Div. 1993–95, Plant Man. Chattanooga Manufacturing Operation, Komatsu Dresser Co. (currently Komatsu America Corpn) 1995–97, Gen. Man. Information Systems Div. 1997–99, Dir June 1997, Exec. 1999–2000, Exec. Officer and Pres. Production Div. and Vice-Pres. e-Komatsu Tech. Centre April–June 2000, Sr Exec. Officer, Pres. Production Div. and Vice-Pres. e-Komatsu Tech. Centre 2000–01, Man. Dir and Pres. Production Div. and e-Komatsu Tech. Centre 2001–03, Dir and Sr Exec. Officer, Pres. of Construction and Mining Equipment Marketing Div. 2003–05, Dir and Sr Exec. Officer, Supervising Construction and Mining Equipment Business and e-Komatsu Tech. Centre 2005–06, Dir and Sr Exec. Officer, Supervising Construction and Mining Equipment Business, e-Komatsu Tech. Centre and Komatsu Way April–July 2006, Dir and Sr Exec. Officer, Gen. Man. of Komatsu Way Dept, Supervising Construction and Mining Equipment Business and e-Komatsu Tech. Centre 2006–07, Dir and Sr Exec. Officer, Pres. of Production Div. and Gen. Man. Komatsu Way Dept, Supervising Construction and Mining Equipment Business and e-Komatsu Tech. Centre Jan.–June 2007, Pres. and CEO Komatsu Ltd 2007–. *Leisure interests:* golfing, mountain climbing. *Address:* Komatsu Ltd, 2-3-6, Akasaka, Minato-ku, Tokyo 107-8414, Japan (office). *Telephone:* (3) 5561-2616 (office); (3) 5561-2687 (office). *Fax:* (3) 3505-9662 (office). *E-mail:* info@komatsu.com (office). *Website:* www.komatsu.com (office).

NOJIMA, Hideo; Japanese retail executive; fmrly with Okadaya Corpn; fmr Man. Dir AEON Co. Ltd, later Sr Man. Dir, Chair. and Rep. Dir 2006–08, part-time Auditor AEON Environmental Foundation as of 2012. *Address:* AEON Environmental Foundation, 1-5-1 Nakase, Mihama-ku, Chiba-shi, Chiba 261-8515, Japan (office). *Telephone:* (43) 212-6022 (office). *Fax:* (43) 212-6815 (office). *E-mail:* ef@aeon.info (office). *Website:* www.aeon.info/ef (office).

NOKA, Flamur, MD; Albanian physician and politician; b. 3 March 1971, Kukës; m.; two c.; held positions within Democratic Party of Albania (DPA), including Organizing Sec. 2005, mem. Nat. Council of DPA; mem. (DPA) Ass. of Repub. of Albania for Kukës dist 2009–; Minister of the Interior 2012–13. *Address:* c/o Ministry of the Interior, Sheshi Skënderbej 3, Tirana, Albania. *Telephone:* 69-4133588 (mobile). *E-mail:* minister@moi.gov.al.

NOKED, Orit; Israeli politician; *Minister of Agriculture and Rural Development;* b. 25 Oct. 1952, Jerusalem; m.; three c.; ed Hebrew Univ. of Jerusalem; legal adviser of the Kibbutz Movt 1986–92, Dir Legal Dept 1996–2002; unsuccessful cand. for Knesset (Parl.) 1999, mem. Knesset 2002–, served on Finance Cttee, Cttee on the Status of Women, Cttee on the Rights of the Child, Labour, Welfare and Health Cttee, Cttee for the Appointment of Judges; Asst to Shimon Peres, Deputy Prime Minister and Minister for Devt of the Negev and Galilee Jan.–Nov. 2005, headed Team for Settlement-Related Issues in Outlying Areas; Deputy Minister of Industry, Trade, and Labour –2011; Minister of Agric. and Rural Devt 2011–; mem. Labour Party 2002–11, Independence 2011–; mem. Jewish Nat. Fund's directorate, Agricultural Asscn's Secr., Nat. Council for Environmental Quality, Bd of Israel Lands Admin, Kibbutz Shefayim. *Address:* Ministry of Agriculture and Rural Development, PO Box 50200, Agricultural Centre, Beit Dagan 50250, Israel (office). *Telephone:* (3) 9485555 (office). *Fax:* (3) 9485858 (office). *E-mail:* pniot@moag.gov.il (office). *Website:* www.moag.gov.il (office).

NOLAN, Christopher Jonathan James; British/American director, writer and producer; b. 30 July 1970, London; s. of an English father and American mother; m. Emma Thomas 1997; three c.; ed Haileybury Coll., Herts., UK, Univ. Coll., London; filmed several short films in his univ. film soc., London; short film Tarantella shown on Image Union, an ind. film and video showcase featured on PBS 1989; short film Larceny shown during Cambridge Film Festival in 1996; Visionary Award, Palm Springs Int. Film Festival 2003. *Films directed:* Doodlebug (as Chris Nolan; also writer, cinematographer, ed. and set designer) 1997, Following (also writer, producer, cinematographer and ed.) (Silver Hitchcock, Dinard British Film Festival 1999, Best Dir Award, Newport Int. Film Festival 1999, Tiger Award, Rotterdam Int. Film Festival 1999, Black & White Award, Slamdance Film Festival 1999) 1998, Memento (also screenplay) (CinéLive Award, Critics' Award and Jury Special Prize, Deauville Film Festival 2000, Prize of the Catalan Screenwriter's Critic and Writer's Asscn, Sitges-Catalonian Int. Film Festival 2000, Boston Soc. of Film Critics' Award for Best Screenplay 2001, ALFS Award for British Screenwriter of the Year, London Critics' Circle Film Awards 2001, Los Angeles Film Critics' Asscn Award for Best Screenplay 2001, SEFCA Award for Best Original Screenplay, Southeastern Film Critics' Asscn Awards 2001, Waldo Salt Screenwriting Award, Sundance Film Festival 2001, Toronto Film Critics' Asscn Award for Best Screenplay 2001, AFI Screenwriter of the Year 2002, Bram Stoker Award for Best Screenplay 2002, Critics' Choice Award for Best Screenplay, Broadcast Film Critics' Asscn Awards 2002, Chicago Film Critics' Asscn Award for Best Screenplay 2002, Chlotrudis Award for Best Dir 2002, Russell Smith Award, Dallas-Fort Worth Film Critics' Asscn Awards 2002, Edgar for Best Motion Picture, Edgar Allan Poe Awards 2002, Florida Film Critics' Circle Award for Best Screenplay 2002, Independent Spirit Awards for Best Dir and Best Screenplay 2002, Sierra Award for Best Screenplay, Las Vegas Film Critics' Soc. Awards 2002, MTV Movie Award for Best New Filmmaker 2002, Online Film Critics' Soc. Award for Best Breakthrough Filmmaker 2002, Phoenix Film Critics' Soc. Awards for Best Newcomer and Best Original Screenplay 2002) 2000, Insomnia (ALFS Award for British Dir of the Year, London Critics' Circle Film Awards 2003) 2002, Cinema16: British Short Films (video) 2003, Batman Begins (also screenplay) (Saturn Award for Best Writing, Academy of Science Fiction, Fantasy & Horror Films, USA 2006) 2005, The Prestige (also screenplay and producer) (Empire Award for Best Dir 2007) 2006, The Dark Knight (also story and producer) 2008, Inception 2010, The Dark Knight Rises 2012. *Address:* c/o Dan Aloni, WME, 9601 Wilshire Blvd, Beverly Hills, CA 90212, USA (office). *Website:* www .christophernolan.net.

NOLAN, Philip, MBA, PhD; British telecommunications executive; *Chief Executive Officer, Eircom plc;* b. Enniskillen, Northern Ireland; ed Queen's Univ., Belfast, London Business School; fmr Lecturer in Geology, Univ. of Ulster; with British Petroleum (BP) Exploration –1996, numerous roles including Man. of Acquisitions and Disposals; Dir Transco East Area, BG Group 1996–97, Man. Dir Transco 1997–, CEO 1999–2000, mem. Bd BG Group 1998–2000; CEO Lattice Group (fmrly part of the BG Group) 2000–02; CEO Eircom plc 2002–. *Address:* Eircom plc, 114 St Stephen's Green, Dublin 2, Ireland. *Website:* www.eircom.ie.

NOLL, João Gilberto, BA; Brazilian writer; b. 15 April 1946, Porto Alegre; s. of João Noll and Ecila Noll; columnist, Folha de São Paulo newspaper; Writer-in-Residence, Univ. of California, Berkeley, also teaching Brazilian literature 1996, 1997, 1998; Guggenheim Fellowship 1999–2000; residency, Centre for the Study of Brazilian Culture and Society, King's Coll. London 2004; Prêmio Jabuti (five times), Prize for Fiction, Brazilian Acad. of Letters 2004. *Play:* Quero Sim 1992. *Publications:* short stories: O cego e a dançarina; novels: A fúria do corpo, Bandoleiros, Hotel Atlântico, Harmada, A céu aberto, Canoas e marolas, Rastros do verão, O quieto animal da esquina, Lorde, Mínimas Múltiplos Comuns. *Leisure interests:* music, travelling. *Address:* Rua José do Patrocínio 557/306, 90050-003 Porto Alegre, RS, Brazil. *Telephone:* (50) 224-8766. *Fax:* (50) 224-8766. *E-mail:* jgnoll@via-rs.net. *Website:* www.joaogilbertonoll.com.br.

NOLTE, Nick; American film actor; b. 8 Feb. 1941, Omaha, Neb.; m. Rebecca Linger 1984 (divorced 1995); one s.; pnr Clytie Lane; one d.; ed Pasadena City Coll., Phoenix City Coll.; stage appearance in The Last Pad 1973; TV films 1974–75 and drama mini-series Rich Man, Poor Man 1976; f. Kingsgate Films Inc. (production co.). *Films include:* Return to Macon County 1975, The Deep 1977, Who'll Stop the Rain 1978, North Dallas Forty 1979, Heartbeat 1980, Cannery Row 1982, 48 Hours 1982, Under Fire 1983, The Ultimate Solution of Grace Quigley 1984, Teachers 1984, Down and Out in Beverly Hills 1986, Weeds 1987, Extreme Prejudice 1987, Farewell to the King 1989, New York Stories 1989, Three Fugitives, Everybody Wins, Q & A 1990, Prince of Tides 1990, Cape Fear 1991, Lorenzo's Oil 1992, Blue Chips 1994, I'll Do Anything 1994, Love Trouble 1994, Jefferson in Paris 1994, Mulholland Falls 1996, Mother Night 1996, Afterglow 1997, Affliction 1998, U-Turn, Breakfast of Champions 1998, The Thin Red Line 1998, Trixie 2000, The Golden Bowl 2000, Investigating Sex 2001, Double Down 2001, The Good Thief 2003, Hotel Rwanda 2004, Neverwas 2005, Over the Hedge (voice) 2006, Paris, je t'aime 2006, A Few Days in September 2006, Off the Black 2006, Peaceful Warrior 2006, The Spiderwick Chronicles 2007, Tropic Thunder 2008, Arcadia Lost 2009, Arthur 2011, Warrior 2011. *Address:* Kingsgate Films, Inc., 18954 West Pico, 2nd Floor, Los Angeles, CA 90035; Creative Artists Agency, Inc., 2000 Avenue of the Stars, Los Angeles, CA 90067; 6153 Bonsall Drive, Malibu, CA 90265, USA.

NOMAKUCHI, Tamotsu, MS, PhD; Japanese business executive and institute director; *President, National Institute of Advanced Industrial Science and Technology;* b. 18 Nov. 1940, Kagoshima; ed Kyoto Univ., Osaka Univ.; joined Mitsubishi Electric Corpn 1965, various positions including researcher Cen. Research Laboratory, Dir Mitsubishi Information Tech. Research and Devt Centre 1996–97, mem. Bd of Dirs 1997–, Sr Vice-Pres. and Vice-Pres. of Corp. Research and Devt 1997–2001, Exec. Vice-Pres. and Vice-Pres. of Information Systems & Network Services 2001–02, Pres. and CEO Mitsubishi Electric Corpn 2002–06, Chair. 2006–10; Pres. Nat. Inst. of Advanced Industrial Science and Tech.; Chair. Echonet Consortium; Vice-Chair. Bd of Councillors, Nippon Keidanren (Japan Business Fed.) 2008–; mem. Intellectual Property Strategy Headquarters, Japan 2009. *Address:* National Institute of Advanced Industrial Science and Technology, 1-3-1 Kasumigaseki, Chiyoda-ku, Tokyo 100-8921, Japan (office). *Telephone:* (3) 5501-0900 (office). *E-mail:* info@aist.go.jp (office). *Website:* www.aist.go.jp (office).

NOMIYAMA, Akihiko, LLB; Japanese business executive; *Special Adviser, Nippon Mining Holdings Incorporated;* b. 15 June 1934, Fukuoka Pref.; one s. one d.; ed Tokyo Univ.; joined Nippon Mining Co. 1957, assignments in budget control, corp. financing, Gen. Man. Admin. Dept, Petroleum Operation 1981–92, Man. Dir Japan Energy Corpn (formed from merger with Kyodo Oil Co.) 1992–96, apptd Pres., CEO and Dir 1996, Chair. and Rep. Dir Nippon Mining Holdings Inc. –2006, Special Adviser 2006–; Vice-Chair. Petroleum Asscn of Japan. *Leisure interests:* golf, classical music. *Address:* Nippon Mining Holdings Incorporated, 2-10-1, Toranomon, Minato-ku, Tokyo 105-0001, Japan (office). *Telephone:* (3) 5573-5123 (office). *Fax:* (3) 5573-6784 (office). *Website:* www.shinnikko-hd.co.jp (office).

NOMURA, Masayasu, PhD; American (b. Japanese) molecular biologist and academic; *Grace Bell Professor of Biological Chemistry, Department of Biological Chemistry, University of California, Irvine;* b. 27 April 1927, Hyogo-Ken, Japan; s. of Hiromichi Nomura and Yaeko Nomura; m. Junko Hamashima 1957; one s. one d.; ed Univ. of Tokyo; Research Assoc., Prof. S. Spiegelman's Lab., Univ. of Illinois and Prof. J. D. Watson's Lab., Harvard Univ. 1957–59; Prof. S. Benzer's Lab., Purdue Univ. 1959–60; Asst Prof., Inst. for Protein Research, Osaka Univ., Japan 1960–63; Assoc. Prof., Dept of Genetics, Univ. of Wisconsin 1963–66, Prof. 1966–70; Elvehjem Prof. of Life Sciences, Inst. for Enzyme Research, with jt appointments in Depts of Genetics and Biochemistry 1970–84; Grace Bell Prof. of Biological Chem., Univ. of California, Irvine 1984–; mem. American Acad. of Arts and Sciences 1969, NAS 1978; Foreign mem. Royal Danish Acad. of Sciences and Letters 1977, Royal Netherlands Acad. of Arts and Sciences 1989; Fellow, AAAS 1979, American Acad. of Microbiology 1997; Hon. DSc (Purdue) 1996; NAS Award in Molecular Biology 1971, Japanese Acad. of Sciences Award 1972, Y. D. Mattia Award, Roche Inst. 1973, Abbott-ASM Lifetime Achievement Award 2002. *Leisure interests:* hiking, reading. *Address:* University of California, Department of Biological Chemistry, 109 Plumwood House, Irvine, CA 92697-1700 (office); 74 Whitman Court, Irvine, CA 92612, USA (home). *Website:* www.biochem.uci.edu/ faculty/nomura.html (office).

NOMURA, Tetsuya; Japanese construction industry executive; *Representative Director and Chairman, Shimizu Corporation;* joined Shimizu Corpn (contractor in eng and construction projects) 1961, served in various exec. roles including Man. of Kyushu Office, Man. Dir, Sr Man. Dir and Vice-Pres., Pres. and CEO –2007, Chair. and Rep. Dir 2007–, led negotiations with NTT Data Corpn to est. jtly funded corpn NTT Data Billing Service 2002; Dir Global Industrial and Social Progress Research Inst. (GISPRI) 2003–, Japan Productivity Centre for Socio-Econ. Devt (JPC-SED) 2003–. *Address:* Shimizu Corporation, Seavans South, 1-2-3 Shibaura, Minato-ku, Tokyo 105-8007, Japan (office). *Telephone:* (3) 5441-1111 (office). *Fax:* (3) 5441-0526 (office). *E-mail:* info@shimz.co.jp (office). *Website:* www .shimz.co.jp (office).

NOMURA, Yoshihiro; Japanese legal scholar and academic; *Professor Emeritus of Civil Law, Meiji-Gakuin University;* b. 3 Jan. 1941, Nagoya City; s. of Akio Nomura and Michiko Nomura; m. 1966; three s. one d.; ed Univ. of Tokyo; Asst Researcher in Law, Univ. of Tokyo 1963; Lecturer, Tokyo Metropolitan Univ. 1966–67, Assoc. Prof. 1967–77, Prof. of Civil and Environmental Law 1977; later Prof. of Civil Law, Meiji-Gakuin Univ., now Prof. Emer. *Publications:* Automobile Accident Damages 1970, Environmental Law 1981. *Leisure interest:* nature watching. *Address:* Faculty of Law, Meiji-Gakuin University, 1-2-37 Shirokanedai, Minato-ku, Tokyo 108-8636, Japan (office). *Telephone:* (3) 5421-5209 (office). *Fax:* (35) 421-5692 (office). *Website:* www.meijigakuin.ac.jp/law (office).

NONAKA, Tomoyo, BA, MA; Japanese television journalist and business executive; *Chairman, Gaia Initiative;* b. 18 June 1954; ed Sophia Univ., Tokyo, Univ. of Missouri at Columbia, USA; worked as TV anchor on Japan Broadcasting Corpn (NHK) programme International News Weekly (Kaigai Weekly) 1979–92; main newscaster for TV Tokyo's World Business Satellite programme 1992–96; has served as mem. of numerous advisory and discussion councils, including at Ministry of Finance, Ministry of Posts and Telecommunications (now Ministry of Public Man., Home Affairs, Posts and Telecommunications) and Ministry of Educ. and Science and Tech. Agency (now Ministry of Educ., Culture, Sports, Science and Tech.); mem. Council on the Financial System, Ministry of Finance, Council on Science and Tech.; mem. Bd of Dirs, Sanyo Electric Co. Ltd 2002–07, Chair. and CEO 2005–06, Chair. 2006–07; Founder and Chair. Gaia Initiative (non-profit org.) 2007–; mem. Bd of Dirs, Asahi Breweries 2002–07; Exec. mem. Advisory Bd, Mitsui Fudosan Co. Ltd 2001–; ranked by Fortune magazine amongst the 50 Most Powerful Women in Business outside the US (fifth) 2005, (24th) 2006. *Publications include:* Ganbare, Jibun! (Do the Best for Yourself!), Iron John no Kokoro (The Shadow of Iron John) (trans.). *Address:* Gaia Initiative, 6-10-45-305 Akasaka, Minato-ku, Tokyo 107-0052, Japan (office). *Telephone:* (3) 5574-7716 (office). *Fax:* (3) 5574-7718 (office). *E-mail:* info@gaiainitiative.org (office). *Website:* www .gaiainitiative.org (office).

NONGXA, Loyiso G., BSc, BSc (Hons), MSc, DPhil (Oxon.); South African mathematician, academic and university administrator; *Vice-Chancellor and Principal, University of the Witwatersrand;* b. 22 Oct. 1953, Indwe, Eastern Cape; s. of Arthur Tamsanqa Nongxa and Tuddie Ruth Nongxa; m. Nomthunzi Jacobs; three c.; ed Healdtown Coll., Eastern Cape, Univ. of Fort Hare, Balliol Coll., Oxford (Rhodes Scholar), UK; Lecturer, Dept of Math., Univ. of Fort Hare 1978–82; Lecturer, Dept of Math. and Computer Sciences, Nat. Univ. of Lesotho 1982–85; Sr

Lecturer, Dept of Pure and Applied Math., Univ. of KwaZulu-Natal 1986–90; Prof. of Math. and Dean of Faculty of Natural Sciences, Univ. of the Western Cape, Belville 1990–2000; Vice-Prin. and Dept Vice-Chancellor – Research, Univ. of the Witwatersrand 2000–03, Vice-Chancellor and Prin. 2003– (first ever black CEO in its history); Visiting Fellow, Harvard Univ., Univ. of Illinois; Visiting Researcher, Univ. of Colorado, Univ. of Hawaii, Univ. of Connecticut, Baylor Univ., USA; Chair. TENET Bd; mem. Rhodes Scholarships Selection Cttee, South Africa Netherlands Programme for Alternative Devt, South African Univ. Vice-Chancellor's Asscn and its successor Higher Educ. South Africa; mem. South African Math. Soc., American Math. Soc.; top student in South Africa 1969 (Jr Certificate, Healdtown Coll.), 1972 (Sr Certificate, Healdtown Coll.), Univ. of Fort Hare Council Prize for best performance by an undergraduate student at the Univ. 1976, Rhodes Scholarship 1978, South Africa/Harvard Fellowship. *Achievements include:* South Africa's first African Rhodes Scholar to graduate from Univ. of Oxford with a doctoral degree in math. 1982. *Publications:* numerous papers in professional journals on Abelian group theory and universal algebra. *Leisure interest:* watching football. *Address:* University of the Witwatersrand, Private Bag 3, Wits, Johannesburg, 2050, South Africa (office). *Telephone:* (11) 7171102 (office). *Fax:* (11) 3395708 (office). *E-mail:* loyiso.nongxa@wits.ac.za (office); nkolonzin@vco .wits.ac.za (office). *Website:* www.wits.ac.za (office).

NOON, Baron (Life Peer), cr. 2011, of St John's Wood in the London Borough of Camden; **Gulam Noon,** Kt, MBE; Indian/British business executive; *Chairman, Noon Products Ltd;* b. 1936, India; f. and operated several food product cos in Southall, London, specializing in Indian cuisine; Founder and Chair. Noon Products Ltd 1989– (survived major factory fire 1994, co. taken over by Irish food conglomerate Kerry Group 2005); backer of fmr Britain in Europe group (pro-European pressure group); Founder and Chair. Noon Foundation; Trustee, Maimonides Foundation (promotes dialogue between Jews and Muslims); hon. degree from Univ. of East London 2009. *Radio:* a 'castaway' on Desert Island Discs (BBC Radio 4) 2004. *Publication:* Noon, with a View: Courage and Integrity 2009. *Address:* Noon Products Ltd, Windmill Lane, Middx, Southall, UB2 4NA (office); House of Lords, Westminster, London, SW1A 0PW, England. *Telephone:* (20) 8843-4000 (office); (20) 7219-5353. *Fax:* (20) 8571-2672 (office). *E-mail:* info@noon.co.uk (office). *Website:* www.noon.co.uk (office).

NOOR, Gen. Ata Mohammad; Afghan military commander; *Governor of Balkh Province;* b. 5 Jan. 1964, Qalander Shah Colony, Mazar e Sharif; m. 1992; six c.; ed Bakhter High School, studied political science at univ. in Tajikistan; fought Soviet occupation in Mazar-i-Sharif as Mujahed mil. officer under the command of Ustad Zabiullah 1985, following assassination of Ustad Zabiullah was selected as Deputy Commdr of Mujahed forces that belonged to Zabiullah 1987; his forces captured Balkh from forces of communist govt 1993; rank of Lt-Gen. 1993; apptd Chief of Politics and Mil. of Jamiat e Mili Islami (Islamic Soc.) and mem. High Comm. of Islamic Govt of Afghanistan 1993; apptd Commdr 7th Army Corps 1994; led troops to recapture northern provs 2001; promoted to Gen. 2002; Gov. of Balkh Prov. 2004–; Medal of Educ., Ministry of Educ., Shining Star of Educ., Educ. Presidency, title of Man of Peace, Univ. of Mazar e Sharif, honoured by Ministry of Information, Culture and Tourism and by Ministry of Women's Affairs, numerous other honours and awards. *Address:* Office of the Governor, Mazar-i-Sharif, Balkh Province, Afghanistan (office). *Telephone:* (700) 500500 (mobile) (office). *E-mail:* The_Balkh_Government@yahoo.com (office).

NOOR, Dato' Mohamad Yusof, MA, PhD; Malaysian politician and teacher; b. 5 Feb. 1941, Raja, Terangganu; m.; two c.; ed Islamic Coll., Klang, Selangor, Al Azhar Univ., Ein Shams Univ. and Univ. of Cairo; secondary school teacher 1969–70; Insp. of Secondary Schools, Terengganu State 1970; Prin., Sultan Zainal Abidin Secondary Religious School 1970; Lecturer and Head of Coll., Nat. Univ. of Malaysia 1974, Dean, Faculty of Islamic Studies 1975–79, Deputy Vice-Chancellor for Student Affairs 1980–84; mem. Senate 1984; Deputy Minister responsible for Islamic Affairs, Prime Minister's Dept 1984; mem. House of Reps 1987–; mem. Supreme Council, United Malays Nat. Org. (UMNO) 1987–; Minister, Prime Minister's Dept 1987; Chair. Religious Council for Fed. Territory; many other appointments in Islamic and religious field. *Publications:* numerous articles in fields of educ. and Islamic affairs. *Address:* c/o House of Representatives, Parliament Building, Kuala Lumpur, Malaysia.

NOOR, Muhamad; Malaysian diplomatist, government official and international organization official; ed Univ. of Malaya, Univ. of Wisconsin-Madison, USA, Advanced Man. Programme, Harvard Business School, USA; Asst Sec., Int. Affairs Div., Ministry of Plantation Industry and Commodities 1974–84; Trade Commr (Commodities), Malaysian High Comm., London 1984–87; Prin. Asst Sec., Ministry of Plantation Industry and Commodities 1987–96; Head of Planning and Policy Research and Chief Information Officer, Ministry of Human Resources 1996–2001, concurrently Dir of Electronic Labour Exchange Project; Deputy Sec.-Gen., Ministry of Women, Family and Community Devt 2001–03; Amb. and Perm. Rep. to WTO 2003–09, Chair. WTO Negotiating Group on Trade Facilitation 2004–05, Chair. WTO Dispute Settlement Body 2006, Chair. Gen. Council 2007; Exec. Dir APEC 2010–12; fmr Chair. Exec. Cttee Int. Rubber Study Group, Man. Bd Int. Tin Research Inst.; fmr Vice-Chair. Int. Cocoa Council; Excellent Public Service Award, Ministry of Plantation Industry and Commodities 1995, Kesatria Mangku Negara, HM King of Malaysia 1996, Darjah Indera Mahkota Pahang (carries the title Dato'), HRH Sultan of Pahang 2006, Johan Mangku Negara, HM King of Malaysia 2006. *Address:* c/o APEC Secretariat, 35 Heng Mui Keng Terrace, Singapore 119616, Singapore.

NOOR AL-HUSSEIN, HM Queen, BA; Jordanian public servant and inter-national humanitarian activist; b. (Lisa Najeeb Halaby), 23 Aug. 1951, USA; d. of the late Najeeb Halaby; m. King Hussein I of Jordan 1978 (died 1999); two s.: HRH Prince Hamzah (b. 29 March 1980), HRH Prince Hashim (b. 10 June 1981) two d.: HRH Princess Iman (b. 24 April 1983), HRH Princess Raiyah (b. 9 February 1986); ed attended schools in Los Angeles, Washington, DC and New York City, Concord Acad., Mass, Princeton Univ., USA; architectural and urban planning projects in Australia, Iran and Jordan 1974–78; f. in Jordan: Royal Endowment for Culture and Educ. 1979, annual Arab Children's Congress 1980, annual int. Jerash Festival for Culture and Arts 1981 (also Chair.), Noor Al-Hussein Foundation 1985 (also Chair.), King Hussein Foundation (also Chair.) 1999; Chair. UN Univ. Int. Leadership Inst. (UNU/ILI), Amman; UN Expert Adviser 2004–05; Founding

mem. Int. Comm. on Peace and Food 1992; Pres. United World Colls 1995; mem. Int. Eye Foundation, Int. Council Near East Foundation, Int. Comm. on Missing Persons, The Mentor Foundation, Hunger Project; Trustee, Refugees Inter-national, Conservation International, WWF International, Aspen Inst. 2004–; Adviser, Women Waging Peace and Seeds of Peace; Patron Royal Soc. for the Conservation of Nature, World Conservation Union 1988, Int. Campaign to Ban Landmines, Landmine Survivors Network (also Chair.) 1998, Int. Alert's Women and Peace-building Campaign, Council of Women World Leaders' Advisory Group 2004–; Hon. Pres. Jordan Red Crescent, Birdlife International 1996–2004 (Hon. Pres. Emer. 2004–); Hon. Chair. Petra Nat. Trust, SOS Children's Asscn, McGill Middle East Program in Civil Society and Peace Building; numerous hon. doctorates, numerous int. awards and decorations for the promotion educ., culture, women and children's welfare, sustainable community devt, environmental conservation, human rights, conflict resolution, cross-cultural understanding and world peace, ranked 83rd by Forbes magazine amongst 100 Most Powerful Women 2004. *Publication:* Leap of Faith: Memoirs of an Unexpected Life 2002. *Leisure interests:* skiing, water skiing, tennis, horse riding, reading, gardening, photography, biking, sailing. *Address:* Office of Her Majesty Queen Noor, Bab Al Salam Palace, Amman, Jordan. *Telephone:* (6) 551-5191. *Fax:* (6) 464-7961. *E-mail:* noor@queennoor.jo. *Website:* www.noor.gov.jo.

NOORISTANI, Muhammad Yosuf, MA, PhD; Afghan government official; *Chairman, Independent Election Commission;* b. 1948; ed Kabul Univ., Arizona State Univ., USA; fmr Asst Prof. of Anthropology, Kabul Univ.; Researcher, Arizona State Univ. 1975–78; Sr Cultural Specialist, US Information Service Afghan Program, Peshawar 1988–90; Project Coordinator, Basic Educ. for Afghan Refugees, Peshawar, Pakistan 1992–96; consultant and coordinator for several research and humanitarian aid orgs –2001; Chief of Media and Spokesman for Interim Admin, Kabul Jan.–June 2001; Minister of Irrigation and Environment during first Interim Admin 2001–02; Deputy Minister of Defence 2005–08; Gov. Herat Prov. 2009–10; currently Chair. Independent Election Comm.; Founding mem. Writers' Union of Free Afghanistan 1985–88. *Address:* Independent Election Commission of Afghanistan (IEC), IEC Compound, Jalalabad Road, Paktia Kot, POB 979, Kabul, Afghanistan (office). *Telephone:* 752035203 (mobile) (office). *E-mail:* info@iec.org.af (office). *Website:* iec.org.af (office).

NOOTEBOOM, Cornelis (Cees) Johannes Jacobus Maria; Dutch writer and poet; b. 31 July 1933, The Hague; Hon. mem. Modern Language Asscn, USA 1997; Chevalier, Légion d'honneur 1991, Commdr, Ordre des Arts et des Lettres; Hon. DLitt (Katholieke Universiteit Brussel) 1998, Dr hc (Freie Universität Berlin) 2008; Prijs van de dagbladjournalistiek 1969, Cestoda-prijs 1982, Preis zum 3 Oktober 1990, Constantijn Huygensprijs 1992, Hugo Ball Preis 1993, Aristeion Prijs 1993, Premio Grinzane Cavour 1994, Dirk Martens-prijs 1994, Goethe-prijs 2002, Oostenrijkse staatsprijs 2002, P. C. Hooftprijs 2004, Prijs der Nederlandse Letteren 2009. *Publications include:* fiction: Philip en de anderen (Anne Frank-prijs 1957) 1954, De verliefde gevangene 1958, De koning is dood 1961, De ridder is gestorven (Lucy B. en C. W. van der Hoogtprijs 1963) 1963, Rituelen (F. Bordewijkprijs 1981, Mobil Pegasus Literatuurprijs 1982) 1980, Een lied van schijn en wezen 1981, Mokusei 1982, In Nederland (Multatuliprijs 1985) 1984, De Boeddha achter de schutting. Aan de oever van de Chaophraya 1986, Ina Rilke 1991, Allerzielen 1998, Paradijs Verloren 2004, 's Nachts kommen de vossen 2009, Roads to Berlin 2012; plays: De zwanen van de Theems (ANV-Visser Neerlandia-prijs 1960) 1959, Gyges en Kandaules. Een koningsdrama 1982; poetry: De doden zoeben een huis 1956, Koude gedichten 1959, Het zwarte gedicht 1960, Ibicenzer gedicht (Poëzieprijs van de gemeente Amsterdam) 1960, Gesloten gedichten (Poëzieprijs van de gemeente Amsterdam 1965) 1964, Gemaakte gedichten 1970, Open als een schelp – dicht als een steen (Jan Campertprijs 1978) 1978, Aas 1982, Vuurtijd, Ijstijd. Gedichten 1955–1983 1984, Het gezicht van het oog 1989, Zo kon het zijn (Gedichtendagprijzen 2000) 1999, Bitterzoet, honderd gedichten van vroeger en zeventien nieuwe 2000, Met andere woorden 2004, Die schlafenden Götter 2005; non-fiction: Een middag in Bruay 1963, Een nacht in Tunesië 1965, Een ochtend in Bahia 1968, De Parijse beroerte 1968, Bitter Bolivia, Maanland Mali 1971, Een avond in Isfahan 1978, Waar je gevallen bent, blijf je 1983, De zucht naar het Westen 1985, De wereld een reiziger 1989, Berlijnse notities 1990, Vreemd water 1991, Het volgende verhaal 1991, De omweg naar Santiago (Preis für Reiseliteratur des Landes Tirol 1996) 1992, Zurbaránk 1992, De ontvoering van Europa (essay) 1993, De koning van Suriname 1993, Van de lente de dauw. Oosterse reizen 1995, De filosoof zonder ogen: Europese reizen 1997, Terugkeer naar Berlijn 1997, Nootebooms Hotel 2002, Het geluid van Aijn naam. Reizen door de Islamitische wereld 2005, Rode regen 2007, Verleden als eigenschap. Kronieken 1961/1968 2008, Berlin 1989/2009 2009, Het raadsel van het licht 2009, Scheepsjournaal 2010, Brieven aan Poseidon 2012. *Address:* c/o De Bezige Bij, PO Box 75184, 1070 AD Amsterdam; c/o Arbeiderspers, Herengracht 370-372, 1016 CH Amsterdam, The Netherlands. *Website:* www.debezigebij.nl; www .ceesnooteboom.com.

NOOYI, Indra K., BS, MBA; Indian/American business executive; *Chairman and CEO, PepsiCo Inc.;* b. 28 Oct. 1955, Chennai, India; m. Rajkishan Nooyi; two d.; ed Madras Christian Coll., Indian Inst. of Man., Calcutta, Yale School of Man.; early position as Product Man., Johnson & Johnson, Mettur Beardsell Ltd; spent six years at Boston Consulting Group; fmr Pres. and Dir of Corp. Strategy and Planning, Motorola; Sr Vice-Pres. of Strategic Planning and Strategic Markets, Asea Brown Boveri –1994; Sr Vice-Pres. PepsiCo Inc. 1994–2001, Chief Financial Officer 2000–06, Pres. 2001–06, CEO 2006–, Chair. 2007–, mem. Bd of Dirs PepsiCo, PepsiCo Foundation; Chair. USA-India Business Council 2008–; apptd to US-India CEO Forum by Pres. Obama; mem. Bd US-China Business Council, US-India Business Council, The Consumer Goods Forum, Catalyst, Lincoln Center for the Performing Arts, The Peterson Inst. for Inst. of Int. Econs, Grocery Mfrs Asscn, Tsinghua Univ.; Successor Fellow, The Yale Corpn 2002; Fellow, American Acad. of Arts and Sciences 2008; Woman Pioneer Award 2003, Padma Bhushan Award 2007, CEO of the Year, Global Supply Chain Leaders Group 2009, ranked by Fortune magazine amongst the 50 Most Powerful Women in Business in the US (fourth) 2002, (eighth) 2003, (12th) 2004, (11th) 2005, (first) 2006–10, (second) 2011–12, ranked by Forbes magazine amongst the World's 100 Most Powerful Women (29th) 2004, (28th) 2005, (fourth) 2006, (fifth) 2007, (third) 2008–09, (sixth) 2010, (fourth) 2011, (12th) 2012, (tenth) 2013, named by The Wall Street Journal as one of 50 Women to Watch in 2005. *Address:* PepsiCo Inc., 700 Anderson Hill

Road, Purchase, NY 10577, USA (office). *Telephone:* (914) 253-2000 (office). *Fax:* (914) 253-2070 (office). *Website:* www.pepsico.com (office).

NORBU, Lyonpo Wangdi, BEcons; Bhutanese politician and civil servant; b. 15 June 1954, Galing, Trashigang Dist; m. Aum Pem Zangmo; one s. one d.; ed Scotch Coll., Australia, Univ. of Western Australia; joined Ministry of Finance 1977, has held various posts including Dir Dept of Budget and Accounts, Auditor Gen. Royal Audit Authority, Finance Sec., Minister of Finance 2003–07 (resgnd), 2008–13; Gov. for Bhutan, Asian Devt Bank; mem. Nat. Ass. from Bartsham-Shongphu constituency, Trashigang; fmr Chair. Royal Monetary Authority, Chair. 2010–11; Vice-Chair. Gross Nat. Happiness Comm.; Red Scarf (Dasho) 1998, Orange Scarf (Lyonpo) 2003. *Address:* c/o Ministry of Finance, Tashichhodzong, PO Box 117, Thimphu, Bhutan. *E-mail:* wnorbu@mof.gov.bt; wangdinorbu@nab.gov.bt.

NORDAL, Salvör, BA, MPh; Icelandic academic; *Lecturer and Director, Centre for Ethics, Faculty of History and Philosophy, University of Iceland;* b. 21 Nov. 1962; two s.; ed Univ. of Iceland, Univ. of Stirling, UK, Univ. of Calgary, Canada; journalist, Morgunbladid (newspaper) 1984–85; Gen. Man. Reykjavík Arts Festival and Reykjavík Film Festival 1985–86, Iceland Ballet 1989–94; Lecturer (part-time), Dept of Ethics, Univ. of Iceland 1998–, Dir Centre for Ethics 2001–; Co-Ed. Hugur, Journal of the Icelandic Philosophy Society 2000–02; mem. Nat. Animal Research Cttee 2001–07, Univ. Hospital Ethics Cttee 2004–08, Icelandic Journalists Asscn Ethics Cttee 2005–, Nat. Bioethics Cttee 2008–; mem. Working Group on Ethics, Special Investigation Comm. of Icelandic Parl. 2009–10; mem. Constitutional Council (Stjórnlagaráð) 2010–, Chair. 2011–; Chair. Reykjavík Acad. 2000–01, Art Gallery of Univ. of Iceland. *Publications:* Blood and Data: Ethical, Legal and Social Aspects of Human Genetic Databases (co-ed.) 2004; contrib. essays and articles in professional journals. *Address:* Centre for Ethics, Faculty of History and Philosophy, University of Iceland, 101 Reykjavík, Iceland (office). *Telephone:* 5254195 (office). *E-mail:* salvorn@hi.is (office). *Website:* www.hi.is (office).

NORDBERG, Bert, BElecEng; Swedish business executive; *President and CEO, Sony Ericsson Mobile Communications AB;* b. 1956, Malmö; ed Malmö Univ., courses in Int. Man., Marketing and Finance, Institut Européen d'Admin des Affaires (INSEAD), France; engineer in Swedish Marines, Berga 1980; various positions with Data General Corpn and Digital Equipment Corpn, Sweden 1985–96; Head of Enterprise Services, Ericsson 1996–99, Exec. Vice-Pres. Ericsson Services 1999–2000, apptd Exec. Vice-Pres. Div. Global Services July 2000, Head of Business Unit Global Services 2001–02, Head of Business Unit Systems 2002–03, Sr Vice-Pres. Group Function Sales and Marketing Jan.–April 2004, Exec. Vice-Pres. Group Function Sales and Marketing, Telefonaktiebolaget LM Ericsson 2004–07, Exec. Vice-Pres. and Head of Ericsson Silicon Valley 2008–09, Head of Sales and Marketing and Exec. Vice-Pres. Ericsson Group cos Redback and Entrisphere –2008, Exec. Vice-Pres. and Chair. 2008–09, Pres. and CEO Sony Ericsson 2009–; Chair. Litos reprotryck i Malmo AB. *Address:* Sony Ericsson Mobile Communications AB, Sony Ericsson House, 202 Hammersmith Road, London, W6 7DN, England (office). *Telephone:* (20) 8762-5800 (office). *Fax:* (20) 8762-5887 (office). *E-mail:* info@sonyericsson.com (office). *Website:* www.sonyericsson.com (office).

NORDENBERG, Mark A., BA, JD; American teacher, university administrator and academic; *Chancellor and CEO, University of Pittsburgh;* b. Duluth, Minn.; m. Dr Nikki Pirillo Nordenberg; two s. one d.; ed Thiel Coll., Univ. of Wisconsin Law School; joined Law Faculty, Univ. of Pittsburgh 1977, Dean School of Law 1985–1993, Interim Provost and Sr Vice-Chancellor for Academic Affairs 1993–94, Distinguished Service Prof. of Law 1994–, Interim Chancellor 1995, Chancellor and CEO Univ. of Pittsburgh 1996–; Chair. Citizens' Advisory Cttee on Efficiency and Effectiveness of City-County Govt; fmr mem. US Advisory Cttee on Civil Rules, Pa Civil Procedural Rules Cttee; Founding mem. Technology Collaborative, Pittsburgh Life Sciences Greenhouse (Co-Chair. both bds); mem. Asscn of American Univs, Pa Asscn of Colls and Univs, Univ. of Pittsburgh Medical Center, Allegheny Conf. on Community Devt, Pittsburgh Council on Higher Educ., Mellon Financial Corpn, Pittsburgh Post-Gazette Dapper Dan Charities, Pittsburgh-Wuhan Friendship Cttee Inc.; Univ. of Pittsburgh School of Law's Excellence-in-Teaching Award (first recipient) 1984, Chancellor's Distinguished Teaching Award 1985, Vectors Pittsburgh Person of the Year in Educ. 1997, selected by Vectors Pittsburgh as Pittsburgh's Overall Person of the Year 1998, named by Pittsburgh magazine as a Pittsburgher of the Year 1999, Pittsburgh magazine's Pittsburgher of the Year Award (co-recipient) 2001, Person of Vision Award, Pittsburgh Vision Services 2003, endowed Chancellor Mark A. Nordenberg Univ. Chair (est. to honour his ten years of leadership) 2005, Chief Exec. Leadership Award, Council for Advancement and Support of Educ., District II 2006, Nellie Leadership Award, Three Rivers Youth 2006, Kesher Award, Edward and Rose Berman Hillel Jewish Univ. Center (co-recipient) 2006. *Publications:* has published books, articles and reports on civil litigation. *Address:* Office of the Chancellor, University of Pittsburgh, CL 107, Pittsburgh, PA 15260, USA (office). *Telephone:* (412) 624-4200 (office). *Fax:* (412) 624-7539 (office). *E-mail:* norden@pitt.edu (office). *Website:* www.pitt.edu (office).

NORDH, Sture, BPA; Swedish trade union official; b. 3 June 1952, Skellefteå; m. Gudrun Nordh (née Nygren); one s. one d.; ed Univ. of Umeå; National-Sec. Swedish Union of Local Govt Employees (SKTF) 1975–79, Gen.-Sec. 1979–83, Pres. 1983–96; State Sec. Ministry of Labour 1996–98; Deputy Dir-Gen. Nat. Inst. of Working Life 1999; Pres. Swedish Confed. of Professional Employees (TCO) 1999–2011. *Publication:* Future of the Welfare State (co-author with Bengt Westerberg). *Leisure interests:* skiing, literature. *Address:* Gyllenstiernsg. 10, 115 26 Stockholm, Sweden. *Telephone:* (8) 661-34-23. *Fax:* (8) 662-16-75. *E-mail:* sture.nordh@telia.com.

NORDHAGEN, Per Jonas, DPhil; Norwegian professor of history of art; *Professor Emeritus, University of Bergen;* b. 30 Oct. 1929, Bergen; s. of Rolf Nordhagen and Elisabeth M. Myhre; m. Inger K. Noss 1978; one s. four d.; ed Univ. of Oslo; Lecturer, Univ. of Oslo 1962; Assoc. Prof., Univ. of Bergen 1969; Dir Norwegian Inst. Rome 1973; Sr Lecturer, Univ. of Oslo 1977; Prof. of History of Art, Univ. of Bergen 1986–2000, Prof. Emer. 2000–; mem. Norwegian Acad. of Sciences. *Publications:* The Frescoes of John VII (705–707 AD) in S. Maria Antiqua, Rome 1968, Frescoes of the Seventh Century 1978, Collected Papers in

the History of Byzantine and Early Medieval Art 1990, The Wooden Architecture of Bergen 1994, The Technique of Early Christian and Byzantine Mosaics 1997, Roberto Longhi: Connoisseurship as a Science 1999, Architecture of Norway (AD 1000–1900) 2003, Iconoclasm: Rupture or Interlude? 2005, Ernst Kitzinger's Thesis on the 'Perennial Hellenism' of Constantinople 2007, The Birth of the Byzantine Cross-Domed Church as a Receptacle for Pictorial Decoration 2011. *Leisure interests:* skiing, hiking, books, botany. *Address:* Heien 6, 5037 Bergen, Norway. *E-mail:* pjnordhagen@gmail.com.

NORDLI, Odvar; Norwegian politician; b. 3 Nov. 1927, Stange, Hedmark; s. of Eugen Nordli and Marie Jørgensen; ed in business admin; asst, Baerum Municipal Auditor's Office 1948–49; Chief Clerk, Hedmark Co. Auditor's Office 1949–57; Dist Auditor, Vang and Löten 1957–61; mem. and Deputy Chair. Stange Municipal Council 1952; mem. Storting (Parl.) for Hedmark 1954–85, Leader Parl. Labour Party 1973–76; Chair. Municipal Cttee of Hedmark Labour Party 1960–; Deputy mem. Cen. Cttee of Labour Party 1965, Chair. Hedmark Labour Party 1968; Chair. Trade Union and Labour Party Tax Cttee 1967–68; Vice-Chair. Parl. Municipal Cttee 1965–69; Chair. Parl. Social Welfare Cttee 1969–71; Minister of Labour and Municipal Affairs 1971–72; Chair. Comm. of Defence 1974–75; Prime Minister 1976–81; Vice-Pres. Parl. 1981; Gov. of Hedmark Co. 1981–93; mem. Norwegian Nobel Cttee 1985–96; Commdr of St Olav 1994. *Publications:* Vi så kornmoglansen: om drøm og hverdag 1996, Alvorlig talt (conversation with Kåre Willoch) 2008.

NORDLING, Carl, PhD; Swedish physicist and academic; *Professor Emeritus of Atomic and Molecular Physics, University of Uppsala;* b. 6 Feb. 1931, Edmonton, Canada; s. of Jarl Nordling and Karin Thorén; m. Gunhild Söderström 1954; two s. one d.; ed Univ. of Uppsala; Asst Prof., Univ. of Uppsala 1959–61, Lecturer 1962–64, Assoc. Prof. 1965–69, Prof. of Atomic and Molecular Physics 1970–95, Prof. Emer. 1996–; Sec.-Gen. Swedish Nat. Science Research Council 1987–93; Chair. Nobel Cttee for Physics 1992–96. *Publications:* ESCA-Atomic, Molecular and Solid State Structure Studied by Means of Electron Spectroscopy (co-author) 1967, ESCA Applied to Free Molecules (co-author) 1969, Physics Handbook (co-author) 1982; 150 scientific papers on electron, X-ray and laser spectroscopy. *Address:* Department of Physics, University of Uppsala, Box 530, 751 21 Uppsala (office); Malma Ringv. 45B, 756 45 Uppsala, Sweden (home). *Telephone:* (18) 471-35-45 (office); (18) 30-22-21 (home). *Fax:* (18) 51-22-27 (office). *E-mail:* carl.nordling@fysik.uu.se (office). *Website:* www.fysik.uu.se/english (office).

NORDLUND, Roger; Åland Islands politician; *Chairman (Lantråd) of the Landskapsregering;* b. 19 Nov. 1957; mem. Lagting (Åland Parl.) 1983–87, Ålands landskapsstyrelse, sedan 2004; Chair. Åländsk Ungcenter 1979–85, Åländsk Center (Åland Centre Party) 1986–87, 1997–; Minister of Educ. and Culture 1991–95; Deputy Chair. Landskapsregering (Deputy Premier–Vicelantråd) 1995–99, Chair. (Premier–Lantråd) 1999–. *Address:* Pb 1060, 22111 Mariehamn, Åland Islands, Gulf of Bothnia, Finland (office). *Telephone:* (18) 25370 (office). *Fax:* (18) 19155 (office). *E-mail:* roger.nordlund@regeringen.ax (office). *Website:* www.regeringen.ax (office).

NORDSTRÖM, Anders, MD; Swedish physician and international organization official; m.; two c.; ed Karolinska Institut; worked with Swedish Red Cross in Cambodia and Int. Cttee of the Red Cross in Iran; worked for Swedish Int. Devt Co-operation Agency (SIDA) for 12 years, including three years as Regional Advisor, Zambia and four years as Head of Health Div., Stockholm; Interim Exec. Dir Global Fund to Fight AIDS, Tuberculosis and Malaria 2002; Asst Dir-Gen. for Gen. Man., WHO 2003–06, Acting Dir-Gen. 2006–07; Dir-Gen. Swedish Int. Devt Cooperation Agency (Sida) 2008–10. *Address:* c/o Office of the Director-General, Sida, Valhallavägen 199, 105 25 Stockholm, Sweden.

NORDSTRÖM, Lars G.; Swedish business executive; *Chairman, Vattenfall AB;* b. 1943; ed Uppsala Univ.; with Skandinaviska Enskilda Banken 1970–93, Exec. Vice-Pres. 1989–93; Exec. Vice-Pres. and mem. Group Exec. Man., Nordbanken 1993–98, CEO 1998–2000, Exec. Vice-Pres. and mem. Group Exec. Bd, MeritaNordbanken 1998–99; Exec. Vice-Pres. and mem. Group Exec. Cttee, Nordic Baltic Holding 1999–2000; Exec. Vice-Pres. and Head of Retail Banking, Nordea 2000–02, mem. Group Exec. Man. 2000–02, Pres. and Group CEO 2002–07; Group CEO and Pres. Posten Norden AB 2008–11; mem. Bd of Dirs and Chair. Vattenfall AB 2011–; mem. Bd of Dirs TeliaSonera 2004–10; fmr Chair. Finnish-Swedish Chamber of Commerce; fmr mem. Bd of Dirs Viking Line Abp, Swedish-American Chamber of Commerce; Chair. Swedish Royal Opera 2005–09; fmr mem. Royal Swedish Acad. of Eng Sciences. *Address:* Vattenfall AB, Birger Jarlsgatan 33, 162 87 Stockholm, Sweden (office). *Telephone:* (8) 739-50-00 (office). *Fax:* (8) 17-85-06 (office). *E-mail:* info@vattenfall.com (office). *Website:* www.vattenfall.com (office).

NORÉN, Lars; Swedish playwright and director; b. 9 May 1944, Stockholm; s. of Matti Norén and Britt Norén; m. 1st Titti Mörk 1979; m. 2nd Charlott Neuhauser 1993; two d.; started career as a poet; wrote first play 1968; has written 55 plays, performed world-wide; Artistic Dir Folkteatern 2009–; Aftonbladet's Literary Prize 1971, De Nio's Pris 1985, Expressens Reviewers' Prize 1993, Pilot Prize 1994, Swedish Academy Nordic Prizeand 2003. *Plays include:* Courage to Kill 1978, Munich-Athens 1981, Night is Day's Mother 1982, Comedians 1985, Hebriana 1987, Autumn and Winter 1987, And Give Us the Shadows 1988, Trick or Treat 1989, Lost and Found 1991, The Shadow Boys 1991, Leaves in Vallombrosa 1992, Blood 1994, Some Kind of Hades 1994, The Clinic 1995, Personkrets 3:1 1997, 7:3 1998, Autumn and Winter 1997, Blood 2003, War 2008. *Leisure interests:* fishing, hunting. *Address:* Folkteatern, Olof Palmes Plats, 413 04 Göteborg, Sweden (office). *Telephone:* (76) 764-19-76 (office). *E-mail:* info@folkteatern.se (office). *Website:* www.folkteatern.se (office).

NORMAN, Archie John, MA, MBA; British business executive and fmr politician; *Chairman, ITV plc;* b. 1 May 1954, London, England; s. of Archibald Percy Norman and Aleida Elizabeth Norman; m. Vanessa Peet 1982; one d.; ed Univ. of Minnesota, Emmanuel Coll. Cambridge, Harvard Business School; with Citibank N.A. 1975–77; Pnr, McKinsey & Co. Inc. 1979–86; Group Finance Dir Kingfisher PLC 1986–91; Chief Exec. Asda Group PLC 1991–96, Chair. 1996–97; Chair. (non-exec.) French PLC 1999–2001, Energis 2002–05; MP for Tunbridge Wells 1997–2005; Vice-Chair. Conservative Party 1997–98; Chief Exec. and Deputy Chair. Conservative Party 1998–99; Shadow Foreign Affairs Post 1999–2000; Shadow Spokesman on Environment, Transport and the Regions 2000–01; Dir (non-exec.) Geest 1988–91, British Rail 1992–94, Railtrack

1994–2000, Holmes Place 2003–06; Chair. ITV plc 2010–; Deputy Chair. Coles Group, Australia 2007–; Sr Adviser, Lazard 2004–; Adviser to Board of Wesfarmers 2009–; f. Aurigo Management Partners LLP (pvt. equity firm) 2006; UK Retailer of the Year 1995, Yorks. Businessman of the Year 1995, Marketing Soc. Hall of Fame 1996, Inst. of Turnaround Professionals Lifetime Achievement Award 2010. *Leisure interests:* farming, music, opera, tennis, football. *Address:* Barbara Kyriakou (PA), ITV plc, Upper Ground, London, SE1 9LT, England (office). *Telephone:* (20) 7157-3070 (office). *E-mail:* barbara@itv.com (office). *Website:* www.itvplc.com (office).

NORMAN, Barry Leslie, CBE; British author and broadcaster; b. 21 Aug. 1933, London; s. of Leslie Norman and Elizabeth Norman; m. Diana Narracott 1957 (died 2011); two d.; ed Highgate School, London; Entertainment Ed., Daily Mail, London 1969–71; weekly columnist, The Guardian 1971–80; Writer and Presenter of BBC 1 Film 1973–81, 1983–98, The Hollywood Greats 1977–79, 1984, The British Greats 1980, Omnibus 1982, Film Greats 1985, Talking Pictures 1988, Barry Norman's Film Night, BSkyB 1998–2001, Radio 4 Today 1974–76, The News Quiz 1978–79, Going Places 1977–81, Breakaway 1979–80; Barry Norman's Film Night, Sky 1998–2001; Hon. DLitt (East Anglia) 1991, (Hertfordshire) 1996; Richard Dimbleby Award, BAFTA 1981, Columnist of the Year Award 1990. *Publications include:* novels: The Matter of Mandrake 1967, The Hounds of Sparta 1968, End Product 1975, A Series of Defeats 1977, To Nick a Good Body 1978, Have a Nice Day 1981, Sticky Wicket 1984, The Birddog Tape 1992, The Mickey Mouse Affair 1995, Death on Sunset 1998; non-fiction: Tales of the Redundance Kid 1975, The Hollywood Greats 1979, The Movie Greats 1981, The Film Greats 1985, Talking Pictures 1987, The Good Night In Guide 1992, 100 Best Films of the Century 1992, And Why Not? (autobiography) 2002, Barry Norman's Book of Cricket 2009. *Leisure interest:* cricket. *Address:* c/o Curtis Brown Group Limited, Haymarket House, 28–29 Haymarket, London, SW1Y 4SP, England (office). *Telephone:* (1438) 812087 (office); (20) 7393-4400 (office). *Fax:* (20) 7393-4401 (office). *E-mail:* barry@datchworth.org (office); presenters@curtisbrown.co.uk (office). *Website:* www.curtisbrown.co.uk/barry-norman (office).

NORMAN, Donald (Don) A., BS, MS, PhD; American design consultant, author and academic; *Co-founder and Partner, Nielsen Norman Group;* b. 25 Dec. 1935, New York; s. of Noah N. Norman and Miriam F. Norman; m. Julie J. Norman; two s. one d.; ed Massachusetts Inst. of Tech., Univ. of Pennsylvania; Jr Faculty mem. Center for Cognitive Studies, Harvard Univ.; joined Dept of Psychology, Univ. of California, San Diego, fmr Chair. Dept of Psychology and Dept of Cognitive Science, currently Prof. Emer. of Cognitive Science; acted as consultant on Three Mile Island nuclear accident, realized his unique combination of eng and psychology could be combined in study of design; research moved to study of aviation safety and computers, then to everyday items; Exec. at Apple Computer (Vice-Pres. Advanced Tech. Group), Hewlett-Packard and Cardean Learning Systems, UNext; currently Breed Prof. Emer. of Design and Prof. of Electrical Eng and Computer Science, Northwestern Univ., Evanston, Illinois; Visiting Distinguished Prof. of Design, Korea Advanced Inst. of Science and Tech. (KAIST), Daejeon, S Korea; Co-founder and Partner, Nielsen Norman Group, Palo Alto, California; Founding mem. and Fellow, Cognitive Science Soc.; Charter Fellow, American Psychological Soc.; Fellow, American Acad. of Arts and Sciences, Asscn for Computational Machinery, American Psychological Asscn, Design Research Soc.; mem. Industrial Design Soc. of America, Nat. Acad. of Eng; Dr hc (Univ. of Padua), (Tech. Univ. of Delft); Franklin V. Taylor Award, American Psychological Asscn, Presidential Citation and Lifetime Achievement Award, ACM Human-Computer Interaction Group, Benjamin Franklin Medal in Computer and Cognitive Science, The Franklin Inst. 2006. *Publications include:* Human Information Processing: An Introduction to Psychology (co-author) 1975, Memory and Attention 1977, Learning and Memory 1982, Direct Manipulation Interfaces (co-author) 1985, User Centered System Design: New Perspectives on Human-Computer Interaction (co-ed) 1986, The Design of Everyday Things (originally under the title The Psychology of Everyday Things) 1988, Turn Signals Are the Facial Expressions of Automobiles 1992, Things That Make Us Smart: Defending Human Attributes in the Age of the Machine 1993, The Invisible Computer: Why Good Products Can Fail, the Personal Computer Is So Complex and Information Appliances Are the Solution 1999, Emotional Design 2003, The Design of Future Things 2007, Living with Complexity 2011. *E-mail:* norman@nngroup.com. *Website:* www.jnd.org (office).

NORMAN, Gregory (Greg) John, AO; Australian professional golfer; *Chairman and CEO, Great White Shark Enterprises, Inc.;* b. 10 Feb. 1955, Queensland; s. of M. Norman; m. Laura Andrassy 1981 (divorced 2006); one s. one d.; m. Chris Evert 2008 (divorced 2010); ed Townsville Grammar School, High School, Aspley, Queensland; turned professional 1976; won West Lake Classic, Australia 1976, Martini Int., Kuzuhz Int., Japan 1977, NSW Open, South Seas Classic, Fiji 1978, Martini Int., Hong Kong Open 1979, Australian Open, French Open, Scandinavian Open 1980, Australian Masters, Martini Int., Dunlop Masters 1981, Dunlop Masters, State Express Classic, Benson & Hedges Int. 1982, Australian Masters, Nat. Panasonic NSW Open, Hong Kong Open, Cannes Invitational, Suntory World Match Play Championship 1983, Canadian Open, Victorian Open, Australian Masters, Toshiba Australian PGA Championship 1984, Toshiba Australian PGA Championship, Nat. Panasonic Australian Open 1985, European Open, British Open, Suntory World Matchplay Championship, Panasonic-Las Vegas Invitational, Kemper Open 1986, Australian Masters, Nat. Panasonic Australian Open 1987, Palm Meadows Cup, Australia, PGA Nat. Tournament Players Championship, Australia, Panasonic NSW Open, Lancia Italian Open 1988, Australian Masters, PGA Nat. Tournament Players Championship 1989, Australian Masters, The Memorial Tournament 1990, Canadian Open 1992, British Open, Taiheyo Masters, Japan 1993, Johnnie Walker Asian Classic, The Players Championship 1994, Australian Open, Memorial Tournament, Canon Greater Hartford Open 1995, Doral-Ryder Open, S African Open 1996, World Championship, FedEx St Jude Classic 1997, Greg Norman Holden Int. 1998, Franklin Templeton Shootout 1998, Skins Game 2001; Chair. and CEO Great White Shark Enterprises, Inc.; apptd Australian Amb. for Sport by Prime Minister 1998; inducted into World Golf Hall of Fame 2001. *Publications:* My Story 1983, Shark Attack 1988, Greg Norman's Instant Lessons 1993, Greg Norman's Better Golf 1994. *Leisure interests:* family, fishing, hunting, scuba diving. *Address:* Great White Shark

Enterprise Inc., 2041 Vista Parkway, Level 2, West Palm Beach, FL 33411, USA. *Telephone:* (561) 640-7000 (office). *Website:* www.shark.com (office).

NORMAN, Jessye, MMus; American singer (soprano); b. 15 Sept. 1945, Augusta, Ga; d. of Silas Norman and Janie Norman (née King); ed Howard Univ., Washington, DC, Peabody Conservatory, Univ. of Michigan; Vocal Winner, Int. Musikwettbewerb, Bayerischer Rundfunk, Munich, FRG 1968; operatic debut, Deutsche Oper Berlin 1969; debut La Scala, Milan 1972, Royal Opera House, Covent Garden 1972; American operatic debut, Hollywood Bowl 1972; performer at Lincoln Center 1973–; tours in N and S America, Europe, Middle East, Australia; int. festivals including Aix-en-Provence, Aldeburgh, Berliner Festwochen, Edin., Flanders, Helsinki, Lucerne, Salzburg, Tanglewood, Spoleto, Hollywood Bowl, Ravinia; with leading orchestras from USA, UK, Israel, Australia; other performances include La Voix Humaine, Orchestre nat. de Lyon 2002; Founder and Pres. L'Orchidée Inc.; mem. Bd of Dirs Ms. Foundation, New York Botanical Garden, Nat. Music Foundation, City-Meals-on-Wheels (New York City); Trustee, Paine Coll., Augusta, Ga; spokesperson for Partnership for the Homeless; Fellow, American Acad. of Arts and Sciences; Commdr des Arts et des Lettres 1984; Hon. MusDoc (Howard) 1982, (Univ. of the South, Sewance) 1984, (Univ. of Michigan) 1987, (Edinburgh) 1989; Hon. DMus (Cambridge) 1989; Grand Prix du Disque (Acad. du Disque Français) 1973, 1976, 1977, 1982; Deutsche Schallplatten Preis für Euryanthe 1975; Cigale d'Or (Aix-en-Provence Festival) 1977; Grammy Award 1980, 1982, 1985, Musician of the Year (Musical America) 1982, IRCAM Record Award 1982, Alumna Award (Univ. of Michigan) 1982, Edison Award for Lifetime Achievement, Amsterdam 2006, Nat. Medal of Arts 2009. *Leisure interests:* reading, cooking, houseplant growing, fashion designing. *Address:* 244 Mount Airy Road West, Croton On Hudson, NY 10520-3311; c/o Philips Records Polygram, 825 8th Avenue, New York, NY 10019, USA.

NORMAN, Marsha, BA, MA; American playwright and writer; *Co-director of Playwrights Program, Juilliard School;* b. 21 Sept. 1947, Louisville, Ky; d. of Billie Williams and Bertha Conley; m. 1st Michael Norman 1969 (divorced 1974); m. 2nd Dann C. Byck Jr 1978 (divorced); m. 3rd Timothy Dykman 1987; one s. one d.; ed Agnes Scott Coll. and Univ. of Louisville; Rockefeller Playwright-in-Residence grantee 1979–80; American Acad. and Inst. for Arts and Letters grantee; Instructor, MFA in Theatre Program, Stony Brook Southampton, State Univ. of New York at Stony Brook; currently Co-Dir of Playwrights Program, Juilliard School; fmr Vice-Pres. Dramatists Guild of America; Co-founder The Lilly Awards; mem. Bd of Dirs Writers Guild of America East Foundation; William Inge Distinguished Lifetime Achievement in Theatre Award 2011. *Plays include:* Getting Out 1977, Third and Oak 1978, Circus Valentine 1979, Merry Christmas 1979, The Holdup 1980, 'Night, Mother (Pulitzer Prize for Drama 1983) 1982, Traveler in the Dark 1984, The Fortune Teller 1987, Sarah and Abraham 1987, The Secret Garden (musical) (Tony Award, Drama Desk Award for Outstanding Book of a Musical) 1991, D. Boone 1991–92, Loving Daniel Boone 1992, The Red Shoes 1992, Trudy Blues 1995, Love's Fire 1998, 140 1998, Last Dance 2003, The Color Purple 2005, The Master Butchers Singing Club 2010. *Television plays:* It's the Willingness 1978, In Trouble at Fifteen 1980, The Laundromat 1985, The Pool Hall 1989, Face of a Stranger 1991. *Publication:* The Fortune Teller (novel) 1987. *Address:* c/o John Buzzetti, WME Entertainment, 9601 Wilshire Boulevard, Beverly Hills, CA 90210-5213, USA (office); MFA in Theatre Program, Stony Brook Southampton, Chancellors Hall, 239 Montauk Highway, Southampton, NY 11968, USA (office). *Telephone:* (310) 285-9000 (office); (631) 632-5071 (office). *Fax:* (310) 285-9010 (office). *Website:* www.wma.com (office); www.stonybrook.edu/southampton/mfa/theatre (office); www.juilliard.edu (office); www.marshanorman.com. *E-mail:* mnorman@juilliard.edu (office); info@marshanorman.com.

NORMURODOV, Mamarizo Berdimurodovich; Uzbekistani politician; Minister of Finance 2000–04. *Address:* c/o Ministry of Finance, Mustaqillik maydoni 5, 100008 Tashkent, Uzbekistan (office). *Telephone:* (71) 133-70-73 (office). *Fax:* (71) 144-56-43 (office).

NORODOM RANARIDDH, Prince; Cambodian politician; b. 2 Jan. 1944; s. of King Norodom Sihanouk; m. 1968; two s. one d.; ed Univ. of Aix-Marseilles, France; worked with resistance leaders during early 1970s, arrested, acquitted on charges of engaging in terrorism 1971, returned to France in mid-1970s to teach at alma mater; Supreme Commander ANS 1985, C-in-C and Chief of Staff 1986; Pres. United Nat. Front for an Ind., Neutral, Peaceful and Co-operative Cambodia (FUNCINPEC); Co-Chair. Provisional Nat. Govt of Cambodia, also Minister of Nat. Defence, Interior and Nat. Security June–Sept. 1993; mem. Nat. Ass. 1993 (fmr Pres.); Co-Prime Minister and mem. Throne Council Sept.–Oct. 1993; First Prime Minister of Royal Govt of Cambodia 1993–97; Chair. Nat. Devt Council 1993–97; found guilty of conspiracy with Khmer Rouges to overthrow the Govt, sentenced to 30 years' imprisonment; in exile; returned from exile May 1998; Prof. of Public Law. *Leisure interest:* aviation.

NORODOM SIHAMONI, HM King of Cambodia; b. 14 May 1953, Phnom Penh; s. of HM King Norodom Sihanouk and HM Queen Norodom Monineath Sihanouk; ed Norodom School, Descartes High School, Phnom Penh, Prague High School, Nat. Conservatory of Prague, Acad. of Musical Art, Prague, Czechoslovakia (now Czech Repub.); studied dance, music, theatre and cinematography; Prof. of Classical Dance and Artistic Pedagogy, Marius Petipa Conservatory, Gabriel Faure Conservatory, W. A. Mozart Conservatory, Paris 1981–2004; Pres. Khmer Dance Asscn, France 1984–2004; Dir-Gen. and Artistic Dir Deva Ballet Group 1984–2004; Dir-Gen. and Artistic Dir Khmer Cinematographic Soc. 'Khemara Pictures' 1990–2004; Amb. and Perm. Rep. to UN 1992–2004; Amb. to UNESCO 1993–2004; elevated to rank of Sdech Krom Khun (Great Prince) 1994; crowned King of Cambodia Oct. 2004; Hon. Citizen of the City of Prague 2006; Grand Collier, Ordre Nat. de l'Independence, Grand Cross, Royal Order of Monisaraphon; Grand Officier, Légion d'honneur 2004, Grand Croix 2010; Grand Cross, Royal Order of Cambodia, Grand Cordon, Order of the Chrysanthemum 2010; Silver Medal of the City of Paris. *Address:* Royal Palace, Phnom Penh, Cambodia. *E-mail:* cabinet@norodomsihanouk.info. *Website:* www.norodomsihamoni.org.

NORONHA NASCIMENTO, Luís António; Portuguese judge (retd); b. 2 Dec. 1943, Porto; m. Maria Clara Nascimento; early career as Asst to Public Prosecutor for Comarcas de Paredes, Pombal e Santo Tirso; Judge for Trancoso, Marco de Canavezes, Vila Nova de Famalicão, Vila Nova de Gaia and Porto; Judge Court of

Appeal, Lisbon –1994; mem. Superior Council of Magistrates 1989–90, Vice-Pres. 2001–; Judge Supreme Court of Justice 1994–98, Vice-Pres. 1998–2006, Pres. 2006–13 (retd); mem. Portuguese Asscn of Judges 1984–88, Pres. 1992–96. *Address:* c/o Supremo Tribunal da Justiça, Praça do Comércio, 1149-012 Lisbon, Portugal.

NORRBACK, Johan Ole; Finnish diplomatist and politician; *Ambassador for Baltic Sea Issues, Ministry of Foreign Affairs;* b. 18 March 1941, Övermark; m. Vivi-Anna Lindqvist 1959; two c.; teacher 1966–67; Dist Sec. Swedish People's Party in Ostrobothnia 1967–71; Exec. Man. Prov. Union of Swedish Ostrobothnia 1971–91; Political Sec. to Minister of Communications 1976–77; mem. Parl. 1979–87, 1991–99; mem. Exec. Cttee Svenska Folkpartiet (SFP) (Swedish People's Party) 1983–89, Chair. 1990–99; Minister of Defence 1987–90, of Educ. and Science 1990–91, of Transport and Communications 1991–95, for Europe and Foreign Trade 1995–99; Amb. to Norway 1999–2003, to Greece 2003–07; Amb. for Baltic Sea Issues, Ministry for Foreign Affairs 2007–, Special Adviser to the Prime Minister on border obstacles between Nordic countries 2007–. *Address:* Ministry for Foreign Affairs, Maringatan 22H, 00161 Helsingfors, Finland (office); c/o Svenska Folkpartiet (SFP), Simonsgatan 8A, 00100 Helsinki, Finland. *Telephone:* (9) 16055438 (office). *Fax:* (9) 16055653 (office). *E-mail:* ole.norrback@formin.fi (office).

NORRINGTON, Sir Roger Arthur Carver, Kt, CBE, FRAM; British conductor; *Principal Conductor, Zurich Chamber Orchestra;* b. 16 March 1934; s. of Sir Arthur Norrington and Edith Joyce Carver; m. 1st Susan Elizabeth McLean May 1964 (divorced 1982); one s. one d.; m. 2nd Karalyn Mary Lawrence 1986; one s.; ed Dragon School, Oxford, Westminster School, Clare Coll. Cambridge, Royal Coll. of Music, London; freelance singer 1962–72; Prin. Conductor, Kent Opera 1966–84; Guest Conductor with numerous British, American and European orchestras, appearances at BBC Proms and City of London, Bath, Aldeburgh, Edin. and Harrogate festivals; regular broadcasts UK, Europe, USA; Musical Dir London Classical Players 1978–97, London Baroque Players 1975–, Schütz Choir of London 1962, Orchestra of St Luke's, New York 1990–94; Prin. Conductor Bournemouth Sinfonietta 1985–89; Chief Conductor Camerata Salzburg 1997–2006; Prin. Conductor Radio Sinfonieorchester, Stuttgart 1998–2011, Zurich Chamber Orchestra 2011–; Co.-Dir Early Opera Project 1984–90, Historic Arts 1986–90; numerous gramophone recordings; Cavaliere, Ordine al Merito della Repubblica Italiana, Ehrenkreuz Erster Klasse (Austria) 1999; Ehrenkreuz Erste Klasse (FRG) 2011; Hon. DMus (Kent) 1994, (York) 2013; ECHO Klassik Award for Symphonic Recording of the Year – 19th Century (for Elgar Enigma Variations) 2012. *Leisure interests:* reading, walking, sailing. *Address:* Zürcher Kammerorchester, Seefeldstrasse 305, 8034 Zurich, Switzerland (office). *Telephone:* (44) 388-36-00 (office). *E-mail:* info@zko.ch (office). *Website:* www.zko.ch (office).

NORRIS, David Owen, MA, FRAM, FRCO; British pianist and broadcaster; *Professor of Musical Performance, University of Southampton;* b. 16 June 1953, Northampton, England; s. of Albert Norris and Margaret Norris; two s.; ed Keble Coll. Oxford, Royal Acad. of Music, London and privately in Paris; Prof., RAM 1977–89; Dir Petworth Festival 1986–92; Artistic Dir Cardiff Festival 1992–95; Chair. Steans Inst. for Singers, Chicago 1992–98; Gresham Prof. of Music, London 1993–97; Prof., Royal Coll. of Music 2000–; Lecturer in Music and Head of Keyboard, Univ. of Southampton 2000–07, Prof. of Musical Performance 2007–; Hon. Fellow, Keble Coll. Oxford 2006; First Gilmore Artist Award 1991. *Recordings:* complete piano music of Elgar, Dyson, Quilter and the World's First Piano Concertos. *Achievements:* gave world premieres of Schubert's First Song Cycle and Elgar's Piano Concerto (also on CD). *Leisure interests:* naval and detective fiction. *Address:* c/o Ikon Arts, 114 Business Design Centre, 52 Upper Street, London, N1 0QH, England (office); 17 Manor Road, Andover, Hants., SP10 3JS, England. *Telephone:* (20) 7354-9199 (office); (1264) 355409. *Fax:* (20) 7281-9687 (office). *E-mail:* info@ikonarts.com (office); info@davidowennorris.com. *Website:* www.ikonarts.com (office); davidowennorris.com.

NORRIS, Elwood (Woody); American inventor and engineer; *CEO, Parametric Sound Corporation;* b. Barrelville, Cumberland, Md; m.; eleven c.; ed Univ. of New Mexico; joined USAF 1956, trained as Nuclear Weapons Specialist, Monzano Base, New Mexico; cameraman, American Broadcasting Corpn (ABC) TV network, Albuquerque 1958; joined Tech. Staff, Univ. of Wash. 1959, Dir Eng Experiment Station –1970; worked for Heath Technic Corpn 1970s; f. American Tech. Corpn (LRAD Corpn since 2010), San Diego 1980, Chair. 1980–2010; Founder and CEO Parametric Sound Corpn (fmr subsidiary of LRAD Corpn) 2010–; licensed pilot; Lemelson-MIT Inventor of the Year Award 2005. *Achievements include:* inventions include Transcutaneous Doppler System (precursor to sonogram) 1967, tone arm, unidirectional microphone, virtual speaker, electrostatic transducer, holographic transparent speaker, magnetic film, ear-mounted speaker/microphone device (designed for NASA astronaut helmets, now used for cell phone headsets), Flashback®, HyperSonic Sound®, AirScooter® ultralight helicopter, hydrogen-poweres automobiles, artificial hip alarm; holds 47 US patents and over 300 patents world-wide. *Leisure interest:* flying aeroplanes. *Address:* Parametric Sound Corporation, 1941 Ramrod Avenue, Suite 100, Henderson, NV 89014-0826, USA (office). *Telephone:* (888) 477-2150 (office). *Website:* www .parametricsound.com (office); www.woodynorris.com.

NORRIS, Sir Ralph James, Kt, KNZM; New Zealand banking executive; b. Auckland; ed Lynfield Coll.; began career as commercial cadet, Mobil Oil NZ 1967–69; joined Auckland Savings Bank (ASB) Ltd 1969, Man. Dir and CEO 1991–2001; mem. Bd of Dirs Air New Zealand Ltd 1998–2005, Man. Dir and CEO 2002–05; Head of Int. Financial Services, Commonwealth Bank of Australia 1999–2001, Man. Dir and CEO 2005–11; Chair. Australian Bankers' Asscn, CommFoundation Pty Ltd; fmr Chair. NZ Bankers Asscn, Business Roundtable, Hosting Cttee of Asia-Pacific Econ. Council CEO Summit; mem. Bd of Dirs Fletcher Building Ltd 2001–05, Team NZ Defence 2003, Business Council of Australia, Financial Markets Foundation for Children; fmr mem. Prime Minister's Enterprise Council, Prime Minister's Y2K Task Force, Pacific Basin Econ. Council; mem. Starship Foundation Trust, Knowledge Wave Trust, Northern Lifeguard Services Trust; Fellow, NZ Inst. of Man.; Amb., Australian Indigenous Educ. Foundation; Hon. Fellow, NZ Computer Soc.; Distinguished Companion, NZ Order of Merit 2006, Kt, NZ Order of Merit; NZ Exec. of the Year Award 1997, 2004.

Address: c/o Commonwealth Bank of Australia, Ground Floor, Tower 1, 201 Sussex Street, Sydney, NSW 2000, Australia. *E-mail:* info@commbank.com.au.

NORRIS, Steve, FRSA; British film producer; *CEO, Apollo Productions;* b. 1959, Harefield, England; fmrly with The Rank Org.; fmr exec., Columbia Pictures, Warner Brothers, Enigma, USA 1989–99; fmr Vice-Pres. Producers' Alliance for Cinema and TV, Chair. Film Cttee; British Film Commr 1998–2006; Man. Dir of Film, Framestore 2006–13; Exec. Producer, Pinewood Films Ltd; CEO Apollo Productions 2013–; has consulted for several key industry clients including nat. govts; fmr mem. Council, BAFTA, Producers Alliance for Cinema and Televisio, British Screen Advisory Council, amongst others; Chair. UK Screen (trade body for UK film, TV and commercial sector cos); Hon. mem. Production Guild of GB; several awards, including Golden Globe for The Burning Season. *Films include:* Memphis Belle 1990, Being Human 1994, War of the Buttons 1994, Le Confessional (Canadian Academy Award for Best) 1995, Diane & Me 1997, My Life So Far 1999, Freakdog 2008, Me and Orson Welles 2008, Triangle 2009, Heartless 2009, harry Brown 2009, Ghost Machine 2009, A Fantastic Fear of Everything 2012, Last Passenger 2013, Dom Hemingway 2013, Belle 2013, Powder Room 2013, Camera Trap (documentary) 2014, Robot Overlords 2014, Posh 2014. *Television includes:* The Burning Season (film) 1994. *Address:* Apollo Productions, Pinewood Studios, Pinewood Road, Iver Heath, Bucks., SL0 0HH, England. *E-mail:* julia@apolloprods.com. *Website:* www.apolloprods.com.

NORRIS, Steven, MA; British politician and business executive; *Executive Chairman, Jarvis plc;* b. 24 May 1945, Liverpool; s. of John Francis Birkett and Eileen Winifred Walsh; m. 1st Peta Veronica Cecil-Gibson 1969 (divorced); two s.; m. 2nd Emma Courtney 2000; one s.; ed Liverpool Inst. High School, Worcester Coll., Oxford; Berks. Co. Councillor 1977–85; various man. positions in industry –1983; MP for Oxford E 1983–87, for Epping Forest 1988–97; Parl. Pvt. Sec. to William Waldegrave, Minister of State, Dept of Environment 1985–87, to Nicholas Ridley, Sec. of State for Trade and Industry 1990, to Kenneth Baker, Home Sec. 1991–92; Minister for Transport in London 1992–96; Dir-Gen. Road Haulage Asscn 1997–99; Conservative cand. for Mayoralty of London 2000, 2004; Vice-Chair. Conservative Party 2000–01; mem. Bd Transport for London –2001; Sr Partner, Park Place Communications 2003–; Exec. Chair. Jarvis plc 2004–; Chair. AMT-Sybex Ltd; Sr Ind. Dir ITIS Holdings plc; Chair. East Side Young Leaders Acad., British Urological Foundation; Companion Inst. of Civil Engineers; Trustee London Action Trust; Freeman of the City of London; Liveryman of the Worshipful Co. of Coachmakers and Coach Harness Makers, Worshipful Co. of Carmen; Craftowning Freeman of Co. of Watchmen and Lightermen of City of London. *Publication:* Changing Train 1996. *Leisure interests:* football, opera, reading. *Address:* Jarvis plc, Meridian House, The Crescent, York, YO24 1AW, England (office). *Telephone:* (1904) 712712 (office). *Website:* www.jarvis-uk.com (office).

NORSHTEIN, Yuri Borisovich; Russian film director, animator and script-writer; b. 15 Sept. 1941, Andreyevka, Penza Region; s. of Berko Leipovich Norshtein and Basya Girshevna Krichevskaya; m. Francesca Alfredovna Yarbu-sova; one s. one d.; ed Soyuzmultfilmstudio courses; debut as film dir The 25th is the First Day 1968 (co-dir with Arkady Tyurin); cutout film Battle at Kerzhenets 1971 (co-dir with I. Ivanov-Vano); later with his wife (art dir Yarbusova): Fox and Hare 1973, Heron and Crane 1974, Hedgehog in Mist 1975, The Tale of Tales 1979, Great Coat 2002; Tale of Tales voted best animated film of all time 1984 in int. survey, LA Animation Olympiad; Tarkovsky Prize 1989; Grand Prix Zagreb Animation Festival 1980; USSR State Prize 1979, Triumph Prize 1995. *Address:* Butlerov str. 4, korp. 2, Apt. 88, 117485 Moscow, Russia (home). *Telephone:* (495) 335-08-21 (home).

NORTEN, Enrique, BArch, MArch; Mexican architect and teacher; *Principal, TEN Arquitectos (Taller de Enrique Norten Arquitectos, SC);* b. 27 Feb. 1954, Mexico City; ed Universidad Iberoamericana, Mexico City, Cornell Univ., USA; f. TEN (Taller de Enrique Norten) Arquitectos 1986, currently Prin., involved in projects of different types and scales, including furniture design, single-family houses, residential, cultural and institutional bldgs, as well as landscape and master planning, opened New York office 2003; Prof. of Architecture, Universidad Iberoamericana, Mexico City 1980–90; Coordinator of Grad. Urban Design Program 1983–85; has held Miller Chair, Univ. of Pennsylvania, Phila 1998–; fmr holder of O'Neal Ford Chair in Architecture, Univ. of Texas at Austin; fmr Lorch Prof. of Architecture, Univ. of Michigan; fmr Eero Saarinen Visiting Prof. of Architectural Design, Yale School of Architecture; fmr Distinguished Visiting Prof., Cornell Univ.; fmr Visiting Prof., UCLA Dept of Architecture and Urban Design, Yale School of Architecture, Sci-Arc, Rice Univ., Univ. of Houston, Columbia Univ., Pratt Inst., Parsons School of Design; fmr Elliot Noyes Visiting Design Critic, Harvard Univ.; has lectured world-wide and is a regular speaker at Urban Age Conf.; has participated on int. juries and award cttees, including the World Trade Center Site Memorial Competition in New York City and Holcim Foundation Awards for Sustainable Construction; mem. Bd Trustees, Deutsche Bank 2006–; mem. Bd Mexican Cultural Inst. of New York 2007–, Americas Soc./ Council of the Americas 2008–; Hon. mem. AIA 1999; Hon. Mention, I Bienal de Arquitectura Mexicana 1990, Grant for Creators and Intellectuals, Nat. Council for Culture and the Arts (CONACULTA) 1990, Medalla a la Excelencia Profesional Colegio de Arquitectos de México 1990, Architectural Record Awards (House 'O') 1992, Hon. Mention, II Bienal de Arquitectura Mexicana 1992, Latin American Award, Bienal de Arquitectura de Buenos Aires 1993, Consejo Internacional de Críticos de Arquitectura 1993, Progressive Architecture Award, P/A Awards 1994, Hon. Mention, III Bienal de Arquitectura Mexicana 1994, Progressive Architecture Award, P/A Awards 1995, First Prize, IV Bienal de Arquitectura Mexicana 1996, Hon. Mention, IV Bienal de Arquitectura Mexicana 1996, Hon. Mention, P/A Awards (Museum of Natural History) 1996, Ciudad de México Award, Departamento del DF 1997, Progressive Architecture Award, P/A Awards 1999, Creador Artístico 2000, Grant, CONACULTA 2000, Sistema Nacional de Creadores de Arte Gold Mention 2000, Quorum Design Award 2000, Graphic Design for the Book TEN Arquitectos 2000, Hon. Mention, VI Bienal de Arquitectura Mexicana 2000, Hon. Mention, P/A Awards (JVC Convention & Exhbn Center) 2000, DuPont Benedictus Awards for Innovation in Architectural Glass, DuPont Benedictus (House IA) 2001, AIA Gold Medal 2002, Gold Medal, Soc. of American Registered Architects 2003, 'Leonardo da Vinci' World Award of Arts, World Cultural Council 2005, Design Awards 2006, Hon. Mention, IX Bienal de Arquitectura Mexicana

(House C) 2006, 'Legacy Award', Smithsonian Latino Center, Smithsonian Inst. 2007, Hon. Mention, CAF Office Bldg Competition, Caracas, Venezuela 2008, Excellence in Architecture and Design Award, PODER – The Boston Consulting Group Business Awards 2008, Design and Construction Excellence Program, NYC DC, New York 2009, Calli de Cristal, Colegio de Arquitectos de Nuevo Léon, Mexico, XV Bienal de Arquitectura CANL 2009. *Projects include:* Nat. School of Theater at Nat. Center of the Arts, Churubusco, Mexico City, Televisa Mixed Use Bldg, Mexico City (first Mies van der Rohe Pavillion Award for Latin American Architecture, Barcelona 1998), House RR, Mexico City (Design Excellence in Housing, Boston Soc. of Architects 2004), Hotel HABITA (AR Awards for Emerging Architecture 2001, DuPont Benedictus Awards for Innovation in Architectural Glass, DuPont Benedictus 2001, Latin American Bldg of the Year, World Architecture Awards 2002, RIBA Worldwide Architecture Award 2002, Mexican, XIII Bienal de Arquitectura de Quito, Ecuador 2002, Silver Medal, VII Bienal de Arquitectura Mexicana 2002, Business Week/Architectural Record Award 2003, AIA Architecture Award, New York Chapter Design Awards 2003), Educare in Zapopan, Jalisco (Hon. Mention, VII Bienal de Arquitectura Mexicana (Educare) 2002 2002, First Prize of Int. Design, XIII Bienal de Arquitectura de Quito, Ecuador 2002, AIA Architecture Award, New York Chapter Design Awards 2003), Princeton Parking Structure (Gold Medal, AIA/New Jersey Design Awards 2002), Parque España Residential Bldg, Colonia Condesa, Mexico City (Design Excellence in Housing, Boston Soc. of Architects 2004, Guggenheim Museum, Guadalajara (Project Citation, AIA New York Chapter 2006) 2005, One York Residential Bldg, New York City 2009, Orange County Great Park (AIA Inst. Honor Award for Regional and Urban Design) 2009. *Commissions include:* Guggenheim Museum, Guadalajara, Xochimilco Master Plan and Aquarium, Mexico City (AIA Inst. Merit Award, New York Chapter Design Awards 2009), new vision for Rutgers Univ.'s Coll. Avenue Campus and Livingston Campus, New Brunswick, NJ, plan for the recovery of a 4½ mile stretch of the New Orleans Riverfront, New Orleans, La, Chopo Museum, Mexico City, Nat. Lab. of Genomics, Irapuato, Guanajuato, Mexico, Cassa Residential Bldg at 45th Street, New York City, High Line Hotel, New York City, 580 Carroll Street Residential Bldg, Brooklyn, NY, 1.3 million square feet Clinton Park, New York City. *Publications:* several monographs, including TEN Arquitectos 1998, Enrique Norten: Temas y Variaciones 2004, Working: Enrique Norten/TEN Arquitectos 2007; numerous articles in nat. and int. publs. *Address:* TEN Arquitectos, 127 W 25th Street, New York, NY 10001, USA (office); TEN Arquitectos, Cuernavaca 114/PB, Colonia Condesa, 06140 Mexico City DF, Mexico (office). *Telephone:* (212) 620-0794 (New York) (office); (55) 5211-8004 (Mexico City) (office). *Fax:* (212) 620-0798 (New York) (office); (55) 5286-1735 (Mexico City) (office). *E-mail:* ten@ten-arquitectos.com (office). *Website:* www.ten-arquitectos.com (office).

NORTH, Alastair Macarthur, OBE, PhD, DSc; British chemist and academic (retd); b. 2 April 1932, Aberdeen, Scotland; s. of Norman R. North and Anne North; m. Charlotte Muriel Begg 1957; two s. two d.; ed Univs of Aberdeen and Birmingham; Lecturer, Dept of Inorganic, Physical and Industrial Chem., Univ. of Liverpool 1959–67; apptd to Burmah Chair of Physical Chem., Univ. of Strathclyde 1967, Dean, School of Chemical and Materials Science 1972–75, Vice-Prin. of the Univ. 1976–80; Pres., Asian Inst. of Tech. 1983–96; Visiting Prof. Chiang Mai Univ. 1984–2003, Mahidol Univ., Bangkok 1989–; mem. several nat. cttees on formation of science policy; Commdr des Palmes académiques; Commdr, Order of King Leopold II (Belgium); Prasidda Prabala Gorkha Dakshin Bahu (Nepal); Hon. ScD (Politechnika Lodzka), Hon. PhD (Ramkhamhaeng Univ.), Hon. DUniv (Strathclyde), Hon. DTech (AIT), Hon. LLD (Aberdeen), Dr hc (Inst. Nat. Polytechnique de Toulouse). *Leisure interest:* gardening. *Address:* 79/78 Soi 7/1 Mooban Tararom, Ramkhamhaeng Soi 150, Sapansoong, Bangkok 10240, Thailand (home). *Telephone:* (2) 373-2818 (home). *Fax:* (2) 373-3052 (home).

NORTH, Douglass Cecil, PhD; American economist and academic; *Spencer T. Olin Professor in Arts and Sciences, Department of Economics, Washington University;* b. 5 Nov. 1920, Cambridge, Mass; s. of Henry North and Edith Saitta; m. Elisabeth Willard Case 1972; three s. by previous m.; ed Univ. of California, Berkeley; Asst Prof., Univ. of Washington 1950–56, Assoc. Prof. 1957–60, Prof. of Econs 1960–63, Prof. Emer. 1983–, Chair. Dept of Econs 1967–79; Dir Inst. of Econ. Research 1960–66, Nat. Bureau of Econ. Research 1967–87; Pitt Prof. of American History and Inst., Univ. of Cambridge, UK 1981–82; Luce Prof. of Law and Liberty, Prof. of Econs, Washington Univ., St Louis 1983–; Spencer T. Olin Prof. in Arts and Sciences 1996–; Bartlett Burnap Sr Fellow, Hoover Inst. 2000–; mem. Bradley Foundation 1986–; Fellow, Center for Advanced Study on Behavioral Sciences 1987–88; Guggenheim Fellow 1972–73; Fellow, American Acad. of Arts and Sciences; mem. American Econ. Asscn, Econ. History Asscn; Hon. Dr rer. pol (Cologne) 1988, (Zurich) 1993, (Stockholm School of Econs) 1994, (Prague School of Econs) 1995; shared Nobel Prize for Econs 1993. *Publications:* The Economic Growth of the US 1790–1860 1961, Growth and Welfare in the American Past 1971, Institutional Change and American Economic Growth (with L. Davis) 1971, The Economics of Public Issues (with R. Miller) 1971, The Rise of the Western World (with R. Thomas) 1973, Structure and Change in Economic History 1981, Institutions, Institutional Change and Economic Performance 1990, Understanding the Process of Economic Change 2004. *Address:* Department of Economics, Washington University, Campus Box 1208, St Louis, MO 63130-4899, USA (office). *Telephone:* (314) 935-5809 (office); (314) 935-5670 (office). *Fax:* (314) 935-4156 (office). *E-mail:* north@economics.wustl.edu (office). *Website:* economics.wustl.edu (office).

NORTH, Oliver L.; American radio show host and fmr marine officer; b. 7 Oct. 1943, San Antonio, Tex.; s. of Oliver Clay North and Ann North; m.; c.; ed US Naval Acad., Annapolis; served 22 years with US Marines, platoon Commdr Viet Nam; marine instructor 1969; leader marine mission, Turkey 1980; mem. Nat. Security Council staff as Deputy Dir for Political Mil. Affairs 1981–86; dismissed Nov. 1986 because of involvement with secret operation to sell arms to Iran and the diversion of proceeds from the sales to aid anti-govt 'Contra' guerrillas in Nicaragua; rank of Lt-Col 1983, retd from Marines 1988; found guilty on three counts May 1989, appeal court reversed one count 1990, three convictions set aside 1990; cleared of all charges 1991; f. Freedom Alliance 1990, now Hon. Chair.; radio show host 1995–; TV host War Stories with Oliver North; Dr hc (Liberty Univ.) 1988. *Publication:* Under Fire: An American Story 1991. *Address:* c/o Freedom Alliance,

22570 Markey Court, Suite 240, Dulles, VA 20166, USA. *Telephone:* (703) 444-7940. *Fax:* (703) 444-9893. *Website:* www.freedomalliance.org.

NORTH, Sir Peter Machin, Kt, CBE, QC, MA, DCL, FBA; British academic and lawyer; b. 30 Aug. 1936, Nottingham, Notts., England; s. of Geoffrey Machin North and Freda Brunt North (née Smith); m. Stephanie Mary Chadwick 1960; two s. one d.; ed Oakham School, Rutland, Keble Coll., Oxford; Teaching Assoc., Northwestern Univ. Law School, Chicago 1960–61; Lecturer, Univ. Coll. of Wales, Aberystwyth 1961–63, Univ. of Nottingham 1964–65; Fellow and Tutor in Law, Keble Coll. Oxford 1965–76; Chair. Faculty of Law, Univ. of Oxford 1971–75; Prin. Jesus Coll., Oxford 1984–2005; Pro-Vice-Chancellor Univ. of Oxford 1988–93, 1997–2005, Vice-Chancellor 1993–97; Ed. Oxford Journal of Legal Studies 1987–92; Law Commr for England and Wales 1976–84; mem. Lord Chancellor's Advisory Cttee on Legal Educ. 1973–75, Council of Man., British Inst. of Int. and Comparative Law 1976–, Econ. and Social Research Council Cttees 1982–87, Council, Univ. of Reading 1986–89, Finance Cttee, Oxford University Press 1993–2008 (Chair. 2005–08), Sr Salaries Review Body 2004–12, Accountancy Investigation and Discipline Bd Tribunal 2005–13; Chair. Conciliation Advisory Cttee 1985–88, Road Traffic Law Review 1985–88, Ind. Review of Parades and Marches in Northern Ireland 1996–97, Ind. Cttee for Supervision of Standards of Telephone Information Services 1999–2006, Review of Drink and Drug Driving Law 2009–10; mem. Inst. de droit int.; Visitor, Ashmolean Museum, Oxford 2004–08; Hon. Bencher, Inner Temple; Hon. Fellow, Keble Coll. Oxford, Jesus Coll. Oxford, Univ. Coll. of N Wales, Bangor, Trinity Coll., Carmarthen, Univ. of Wales, Aberystwyth; Hon. LLD (Reading) 1992, (Nottingham) 1996, (Aberdeen) 1997, (New Brunswick) 2002; Hon. DHumLitt (Arizona) 2005. *Publications:* Occupier's Liability 1971 (second edn 2014), Modern Law of Animals 1972, Chitty on Contracts (ed.) 1968–89, Private International Law of Matrimonial Causes 1977, Contract Conflicts (ed.) 1982, Cases and Materials on Private International Law (with J. H. C. Morris) 1984, Cheshire and North's Private International Law (ed.) 1970–2008, Private International Law Problems in Common Law Jurisdictions 1993, Essays in Private International Law 1993, Civil Liability for Animals 2012. *Telephone:* (1865) 557011. *E-mail:* peter.north@jesus.ox.ac.uk.

NORTH, Richard Conway, FCA, ACA; British accountant and business executive; b. 20 Jan. 1950; joined Coopers and Lybrand 1971, seconded to New York 1976–78, seconded to Midland Bank plc 1981–82, Partner 1983–91; Group Finance Dir The Burton Group PLC 1991–94, later Chair.; Group Finance Dir Bass PLC (later Six Continents plc) 1994–2003, Chief Exec., Hotels Div. 2002; apptd Chair. Britvic Soft Drinks 1997; CEO InterContinental Hotels Group PLC 2003–04; mem. Bd of Dirs Woolworths Group PLC 2006–08, Chair. 2007–08; mem. Bd of Dirs Mecom Group PLC 2007; Dir (non-exec.) Asda PLC 1997–99, Leeds United plc 1998–2002, FelCor Lodging Trust 1998, Logica plc 2002–04, Majid al Futtaim Group LLC 2006; Chair. Payments Council; mem. Senate Inst. of Chartered Accountants in England and Wales 1991–2000, Hundred Group Cttee 1996–2000, Exec. Cttee World Travel and Tourism Council 2004–. *Leisure interests:* golf, tennis, sailing, football, opera. *Address:* 8 St Simon's Avenue, Putney, London, SW15 6DU, England.

NORTHFLEET, Ellen Gracie, LLB; Brazilian judge; b. 16 Feb. 1948, Rio de Janeiro; d. of José Barros Northfleet and Helena Northfleet; m. (divorced); one d.; ed Universidade do Estado da Guanabara, Universidade Federal do Rio Grande do Sul; Public Prosecutor (1st Level) 1980–89; Prof. of Law, Universidade Federal do Rio Grande do Sul 1983–87, Universidade do Vale do Rio dos Sinos 1987–; mem. Fed. Public Ministry 1973–89; mem. Regional Electoral Tribune, Rio Grande do Sul 1989–2000, Pres. 1997–2000; Minister for Supreme Fed. Tribunal 2000–04, Vice-Pres. 2004–06, Pres. 2006–08; Pres. Nat. Justice Council 2006–08; Fulbright Scholar, American Univ., Washington DC 1991–92; mem. Fulbright Alumni Asscn of Brazil; Jurist in Residence, Library of Congress, USA 1992; Hon. mem. Fed. Judiciary of the USA 2006; Santos Dumont Medal 1977, Grand Official of the Order of Merit 2001, Grand Cross of the Order of Rio Branco 2006, numerous other decorations. *Publications:* numerous articles in professional journals. *Address:* c/o Supremo Tribunal Federal, Praça dos Três Poderes, 70175-900 Brasília, DF, Brazil.

NORTON, Edward Harrison, BA; American actor, screenwriter, film director and producer; b. 18 Aug. 1969, Columbia, Md; s. of Edward Mower Norton, Jr and the late Lydia Robinson 'Robin' Norton (née Rouse); ed Wilde Lake High School, Md, Yale Univ., Columbia School for Theatrical Arts, Md; fmr consultant Enterprise Foundation, Osaka, Japan, currently mem. Nat. Bd; mem. Signature Theatre Repertory Co. 1994–, performed in the premiere of Edward Albee's Fragments, mem. Bd 1996–; Co-founder Class 5 Films (production co.). *Plays:* Burn This (Obie Award). *Films include:* Primal Fear (Golden Globe, Best Supporting Actor) 1996, Everyone Says I Love You 1996, The People vs. Larry Flynt 1996, American History X 1998, Rounders 1998, Fight Club 1999, Keeping the Faith (also dir and producer), The Score, Death to Smoochy, Red Dragon 2002, The 25th Hour 2001, Frida 2002 (also co-wrote screenplay), The Italian Job 2003, Down in the Valley 2004, Kingdom of Heaven 2005, The Illusionist 2006, The Painted Veil 2006, Pride and Glory 2007, The Incredible Hulk 2008, Pride and Glory 2008, The Invention of Lying 2009, Leaves of Grass (also producer) 2010, Stone 2010, Moonrise Kingdom 2012, All in for the 99% (short) 2012, The Dictator 2012, The Bourne Legacy 2012. *Television includes:* host, National Geographic's Strange Days on Planet Earth; Modern Family (series) 2009. *Address:* c/o WME Entertainment, 9601 Wilshire Boulevard, Beverley Hills, Ca 90210-5213, USA. *Telephone:* (310) 285-9000. *Fax:* (310) 285-9010. *Website:* www.wma.com.

NORTON, The Honorable Gale Ann, BA, JD; American lawyer and fmr government official; *President, Norton Regulatory Strategies;* b. 11 March 1954, Wichita, Kan.; d. of Dale Bentsen Norton and Anna Jacqueline Norton (née Lansdowne); m. John Goethe Hughes 1990; ed Univ. of Denver; lawyer, Colorado 1978, Supreme Court 1981; judicial clerk, Colorado Court of Appeals 1978–79, Sr Attorney, Mountain States Legal Foundation 1979–83; Nat. Fellow, Hoover Inst., Stanford Univ. 1983–84; Asst to Deputy Sec., Dept of Agric., Washington, DC 1984–85; Assoc. Solicitor, Dept of Interior 1985–87; pvt. law practice 1987–90; Attorney-Gen., Colorado 1991–99; Sr Counsel, Brownstein, Hyatt & Farber, PC 1999–2001; Sec. of the Interior, Washington, DC 2001–06; Gen. Counsel, Royal Dutch Shell 2006–10; Pres. Norton Regulatory Strategies 2011–; Corp. Dir American Transmission Co. 2012–; Transportation Law Program Dir, Univ. of

Denver 1978–79; Lecturer, Univ. of Denver Law School 1989; mem. Bd of Dirs Federalist Soc. and Univ. of Colorado Energy Inst.; fmr Chair. Nat. Asscn of Attorneys Environmental Cttee; Co-Chair. Nat. Policy Forum Environmental Council; Chair. Environmental Comm. of Republican Nat. Lawyers Asscn; Policy Analyst, Presidential Council on Environmental Quality 1985–88; Founding mem., Conservation Leadership Council 2012–; Hon. DEng (Colorado School of Mines); Hon. PhD (Univ. of Denver); Trailblazer Award, Colo Women's Bar Asscn 1999, Conservation Patriot Award, Nat. Fish and Wildlife Foundation, Western Business Roundtable Spirit of the West Award, Ind. Inst. Award for Inspired Leadership, Boone and Crockett Club Conservation Award, American Recreation Coalition Coleman Outdoor Award. *Publications:* chapters in several books; articles in various legal journals. *Leisure interest:* skiing, travel, golf. *Address:* Norton Regulatory Strategies, PO Box 460971, Aurora, CO 80046, USA (office).

NORTON, Hugh Edward, BA; British business executive; b. 23 June 1936, London, England; s. of Lt-Gen. Edward F. Norton and I. Joyce Norton; m. 1st Janet M. Johnson 1965 (died 1993); one s.; m. 2nd F. Joy Harcup 1998; ed Winchester Coll., Trinity Coll., Oxford; joined British Petroleum Co. 1959, Exploration Dept 1960, in Abu Dhabi, Lebanon and Libya 1962–70, subsequently held appointments in Supply, Cen. Planning, Policy Planning, Regional Directorate Middle East and Int. and Govt Affairs Depts; Man. Dir BP's assoc. cos, Singapore, Malaysia, Hong Kong 1978–81, Dir of Planning 1981–83, Regional Dir for Near East, Middle East and Indian subcontinent 1981–86, Dir of Admin. 1983–86, Man. Dir and CEO BP Exploration Co. 1986–89, Chair. 1989–95, Man. Dir The British Petroleum Co. PLC 1989–95; Chair. BP Asia Pacific Pvt. Co. Ltd 1991–95; Dir (non-exec.), Inchcape PLC 1995–2004; Ind. Dir (non-exec.), Standard Chartered PLC 1995– (Sr Ind. Dir (non-exec.) 2003–06), Standard Chartered Bank Australia 1995–; Sr Ind. Dir (non-exec.), Standard Chartered Bank (Thai) Public Co. Ltd 1995–; Lasmo PLC 1997–; mem. Council Royal Inst. of Econ. Affairs 1991–, Chancellor's Court of Benefactors, Univ. of Oxford. *Leisure interests:* painting, ornithology, tennis, travel. *Address:* Standard Chartered Bank Australia, Level 1, 345 George Street, Sydney, NSW 2000, Australia. *Telephone:* (2) 9232-9333. *Fax:* (2) 9232-9345. *E-mail:* info@standardchartered.com. *Website:* www.standardchartered.com/au.

NORVIK, Harald J., MS; Norwegian business executive; b. 21 June 1946, Vadsø; ed Norwegian School of Econs and Business Admin., Bergen; Adviser, Nat. Inst. of Tech. 1971–73; Group Sec. for Industrial and Financial Affairs 1973–75; trainee course, Ministry of Foreign Affairs 1975–76; Personal Sec. to Prime Minister 1976–79; Minister of Petroleum and Energy 1979–81; Dir of Finance Aker mek. Verksted A/S 1981–85, Sr Exec. Vice-Pres. 1985–86; Pres. Astrup Hoyer A/S 1986–87; Pres. and Chair. Exec. Bd Statoil Group 1988–99; Chair. and Partner, Econ Management AS 2002–08, strategic adviser 2008–10; alternating Chair. Bd of Dirs SAS Norge ASA, Scandinavian Airlines System (SAS); Chair. Telenor ASA 2007–12; fmr Chair. Supervisory Bd Den Norske Bank; mem. Bd of Dirs DeepOcean Group Holding AS 2011–, ConocoPhillips, Petroleum Geo-Services ASA; Commdr Order of the Lion of Finland (1st Class), Grosses Bundesverdienstkreuz. *Address:* c/o Board of Directors, DeepOcean AS, Karmsundsgt. 74, Haugesund Norway, PO Box 2144, Postterminalen, 5504, Norway. *Telephone:* 52-70-04-00. *E-mail:* post@deepoceangroup.com. *Website:* www.deepoceangroup.com.

NORWICH, 2nd Viscount, cr. 1952, of Aldwick; **John Julius Cooper,** (John Julius Norwich), CVO, FRSL, FRGS; British author and broadcaster; b. 15 Sept. 1929, London, England; s. of 1st Viscount Norwich, PC, GCMG, DSO and of the late Lady Diana Cooper; m. 1st Anne Clifford 1952 (divorced 1985); one s. one d.; m. 2nd Mollie Philipps 1989; ed Upper Canada Coll. Toronto, Eton Coll., Univ. of Strasbourg, France and New Coll., Oxford; entered Foreign Office 1952; Third Sec. Belgrade 1955–57; Second Sec. Beirut 1957–60; Foreign Office and British del. to Disarmament Conf., Geneva 1961–63; Chair. British Theatre Museum 1966–71, Venice in Peril Fund 1970–99, World Monuments Fund in Britain 1994–2009; mem. Exec. Cttee Nat. Trust 1969–95; mem. Franco-British Council 1972–79; mem. Bd ENO 1977–81; Commendatore, Ordine al Merito della Repubblica Italiana; Commendatore della Solidarità Italiana; Hadrian Award, World Monuments Fund, New York 2005. *Television:* has made over 30 documentary films for TV, mainly on history and architecture. *Publications:* as John Julius Norwich: Mount Athos (with R. Sitwell) 1966, The Normans in the South 1967, Sahara 1968, The Kingdom in the Sun 1970, Great Architecture of the World (ed.) 1975, A History of Venice Vol. I 1977, Vol. II 1981, Christmas Crackers 1970–79 1980, Britain's Heritage (ed.) 1982, The Italian World (ed.) 1983, Fifty Years of Glyndebourne 1985, A Taste for Travel (anthology) 1985, The Architecture of Southern England 1985, Byzantium, the Early Centuries 1988, More Christmas Crackers 1980–89 1990, Venice: a Traveller's Companion 1990, The Oxford Illustrated Encyclopaedia of the Arts, Vol. V (ed.) 1990, Byzantium: The Apogee 1991, Byzantium: Decline and Fall 1995, The Twelve Days of Christmas 1998, Shakespeare's Kings 1999, Still More Christmas Crackers 1990–99 2000, Paradise of Cities 2003, The Middle Sea 2007, Great Cities in History (ed.) 2009, The Popes: A History 2011, A History of England in 100 Places 2011. *Leisure interests:* sightseeing, walking at night through Venice, nightclub piano. *Address:* 24 Blomfield Road, London, W9 1AD, England. *Telephone:* (20) 7286-5050; 7799-625598 (mobile). *E-mail:* jjnorwich@dial.pipex.com (home).

NOSSAL, Sir Gustav Joseph Victor, AC, CBE, MB, BS, PhD, FRS, FRCP, FRACP, FRCPA, FRCPath, FRSE, FTSE, FAA; Australian medical research scientist and academic; *Professor Emeritus, University of Melbourne;* b. 4 June 1931, Bad Ischl, Austria; s. of R.I. Nossal and I.M.C. Lowenthal; m. Lyn B. Dunnicliff 1955; two s. two d.; ed St Aloysius Coll., Sydney, Univs of Sydney and Melbourne; Jr and Sr Resident Officer, Royal Prince Alfred Hosp., Sydney 1955–56; Research Fellow, The Walter and Eliza Hall Inst. of Medical Research, Melbourne 1957–59, Deputy Dir (Immunology) 1961–65, Dir 1965–96; Asst Prof., Dept of Genetics, Stanford Univ. School of Medicine, Calif., USA 1959–61; Prof. of Medical Biology, Univ. of Melbourne 1965–96, Prof. Emer. 1996–; Chair. WHO Global Programme for Vaccines and Immunization 1992–2002; Pnr, Foursight Assocs Pty Ltd 1996–; Dir CRA Ltd 1977–97; Pres. Australian Acad. of Science 1994–98; Foreign Assoc. NAS; mem. or hon. mem. many other nat. and foreign acads and learned socs; Hon. FRACOG; Hon. LLD (Monash, Melbourne); Hon. MD (Mainz, Newcastle, Leeds, Univ. of Western Australia); Hon. DSc (Sydney, Queensland, ANU, Univ. of NSW, La Trobe, McMaster, Oxford); Robert Koch Gold Medal, Albert Einstein World Award of Science, Emil von Behring Prize, Rabbi

Shai Shacknai Prize, Burnet Medal of the Australian Acad. of Science, Australian of the Year 2000, Australia Post 6th Annual Australian Legends Award and many other awards and prizes. *Publications:* Antibodies and Immunity 1968, Antigens, Lymphoid Cells and Immune Response 1971, Medical Science and Human Goals 1975, Nature's Defences (1978 Boyer Lectures), Reshaping Life: Key Issues in Genetic Engineering 1984, Immunology: the Making of a Modern Science 1988, Diversity and Discovery 2007; 540 publs on immunology. *Leisure interests:* golf, literature. *Address:* Department of Pathology, University of Melbourne, Melbourne, Vic. 3010 (office); 46 Fellows Street, Kew, Vic. 3101, Australia (home). *Telephone:* (3) 8344-6946 (office); (3) 9853-8256 (home). *E-mail:* gnossal@bigpond .net.au (home).

NOSSOL, Most Rev. Archbishop Alfons, PhD; Polish ecclesiastic and professor of theology; *Archbishop ad personam of Opole;* b. 8 Aug. 1932, Brożec, Opole Prov.; ed Higher Ecclesiastic Seminary in Opole Silesia, Catholic Univ. of Lublin (KUL); ordained priest, Opole 1957; Lecturer, Higher Ecclesiastic Seminary, Opole Silesia 1962–; Lecturer, Catholic Univ. of Lublin 1968, Asst Prof. 1976, Head, Second Dept of Dogmatic Theology 1977, Prof. 1981, Head Ecumenical Inst. 1983; Prof., Theological Dept, Jan Gutenberg Univ., Mainz 1977; Prof., Pontifical Theology Dept, Wrocław 1978; Prof., Diocesan Theology and Pastoral Inst., Opole 1981; Bishop of Opole 1977–; Archbishop ad personam of Opole 1999–; High Chancellor and Prof., Opole Univ. Theological Dept 1994–; mem. Main Council Polish Episcopate; mem. Scientific Council of the Episcopate of Poland; Chair. Episcopate Cttee for Ecumenism; Vice-Leader Episcopate Cttee for Catholic Learning; mem. Christian Unity Pontifical Council, int. cttees for theological dialogue with the Orthodox Church and the Lutheran Church; mem. European Acad. of Science and Art, Salzburg; Dr hc (Munster) 1991, (Mainz) 1992, (Opole) 1995, (Christian Acad. of Theology, Warsaw) 1997, (Bamberg) 1998, (Olomuniec) 2000; Augsburger Friedenspreis 1997, Kulturpreis Schlesien des Landes Niedersachsen 2001. *Publications:* Theology for the Service of Faith 1968, Cognito Dei experimentalis 1974, Karol Barth Christology 1979, Truth and Love 1982, Towards a Civilization of Love 1984, Theology Closer to Life 1984, Der Mensch braucht Theologie 1986, Love the Victor of Truth 1987, Gelebte Theologie Heute 1991, By Truth to Love 1994, Love Rejoices Together with Truth 1996, Ecumenism as Imperative of Christian Conscience 2001, Brücken bauen Wege zu einem christlichen Europa von Morgen 2002. *Leisure interests:* classical literature, philosophy, the history of art. *Address:* Kuria Diecezjalna, ul. Książąt Opolskich 19, 45-005 Opole, Poland (office). *Telephone:* (77) 454-38-37 (home). *Fax:* (77) 453-79-61 (office). *E-mail:* kuria@diecezja.opole.pl. *Website:* www.diecezja.opole.pl (office).

NOTE, Kessai H.; Marshall Islands politician and fmr head of state; b. 7 Aug. 1950, Ailinglablab Atoll; m. Mary Note; five c.; Senator from Jabat, fmr Speaker of Nitijela (Parl.); mem. United Democratic Party (UDP); Pres. of the Marshall Islands 2000–08; unsuccessful cand. in 2008 presidential election. *Address:* c/o Office of the President, PO Box 2, Majuro, MH 96960, Marshall Islands.

NOTEBAERT, Richard C. (Dick), BA, MBA; American business executive; m. Peggy Notebaert; two c.; ed Univ. of Wisconsin; began career with Amitech Corpn 1969, various positions including Pres. Amitech Mobile Communications 1986–89, Pres. Indiana Bell 1989–92, Pres. Amitech Services 1992–93, Pres. and COO Amitech Corpn 1993–94, Pres. and CEO 1994, Chair. and CEO 1994–99; Pres. and CEO Tellabs 2000–02; Chair. and CEO Qwest Communications International Inc. 2002–07 (retd); mem. Bd Dirs AON Corpn, Cardinal Health Inc., Denver Center for Performing Arts, Qwest Communications International Inc., Univ. of Notre Dame; mem. Business Council, Reliability and Interoperability Council, Nat. Security Telecommunications Advisory Cttee (NSTAC), US Dept of State 2003–; fmr Vice-Chair. Civic Cttee of Commercial Club of Chicago; fmr Co-Chair. Alexis de Tocqueville Soc., United Way; mem. Bd Execs Club of Chicago; Trustee, Univ. of Notre Dame; Distinguished Alumni Award, Univ. of Wisconsin 1999. *Address:* c/o Qwest Communications International Inc., 1801 California Street, Denver, CO 80202, USA.

NOTEBOOM, Ben J.; Dutch business executive; *Chairman of the Executive Board and CEO, Randstad Holding NV;* b. 1958; following graduation held int. man. positions with a major chemical co.; joined Randstad 1993, later held series of sr man. positions and started in-house services, with Europe-wide responsibility from 2000, mem. Exec. Bd 2001–, Chair. Exec. Bd and CEO 2003–, also responsible for Randstad in the Netherlands, Group HR, Group Marketing and Communications, Business Concept Devt, Group Legal and Public Affairs; mem. Supervisory Bd Corporate Express NV (fmrly Buhrmann NV) 2005–, Coastwide Laboratories, Inc., Koninklijke Ahold NV 2009–. *Address:* Randstad Holding NV, PO Box 12600, 1100 AP Amsterdam z.o. (office); Randstad Holding NV, Diemermere 25, 1112 TC Diemen, Netherlands (office). *Telephone:* (20) 569-59-11 (office). *Fax:* (20) 569-55-20 (office). *E-mail:* info@randstad.com (office). *Website:* www.randstad.com (office).

NÖTH, Heinrich, Dr rer. nat; German scientist and academic; *Professor Emeritus of Inorganic Chemistry, University of Munich;* b. 20 June 1928, Munich; s. of Hans Nöth and Eugenie Nöth; m. 1951; two d.; ed Univ. of Munich; Scientific Asst, Univ. of Munich 1952–55, 1957–62, Research Officer 1956, Lecturer 1962–64, Assoc. Prof. 1964–65, Prof. 1965–, Prof. Emer. 1997–, Head Inst. of Inorganic Chem. 1969–97; Pres. German Chemical Soc. 1988–89, 1991–92, Hon. mem.; Pres. Bavarian Acad. of Sciences 1998–2005; Foreign mem. Russian Acad. of Sciences, Mexican Acad. of Sciences; Corresp. mem. Acad. of Sciences, Göttingen, Austrian Acad. of Sciences; mem. Academia Europaea; Hon. mem. Austrian Chemical Soc., Royal Soc. of Chem.; Verdienstkreuz First Class, Bavarian Order of Maximilian for Science and Art; Dr hc (Marburg); Hon. DSc (Leeds); Alfred Stock Medal, IMEBORON Award, Bavarian Constitutional Gold Medal. *Publications:* Nuclear Magnetic Resonance of Boron Compounds 1973, Cluster Compounds of Main Group Elements 2004 and more than 880 original research papers. *Leisure interests:* hiking, gardening, music. *Address:* Department of Inorganic Chemistry, Office D1.036, University of Munich, Butenandtstr. 5-13, 81377 Munich (office); Eichleite 25A, 82031 Grünwald, Germany (home). *Telephone:* (89) 21807454 (office); (89) 6413461 (home). *Fax:* (89) 21807455 (office). *E-mail:* H.Noeth@lrz.uni -muenchen.de (office). *Website:* www.cup.uni-muenchen.de/ac/noeth (office).

NOTT, Rt Hon. Sir John William Frederic, KCB, PC, BA; British fmr politician and business executive; b. 1 Feb. 1932; s. of Richard Nott and Phyllis Nott (née Francis); m. Miloska Sekol 1959; two s. one d.; ed Bradfield Coll. and

Trinity Coll., Cambridge; Lt with 2nd Gurkha Rifles, (regular officer) 1952–56; Pres. Cambridge Union 1959; called to the Bar, Inner Temple 1959; MP for St Ives, Cornwall 1966–83; Minister of State at Treasury 1972–74; Sec. of State for Trade 1979–81, for Defence 1981–83; Man. Dir, Lazard Brothers 1983–90, Chair. and CEO 1985–90; Chair., Hillsdown Holdings PLC 1993–99 (Dir 1991–), Maple Leaf Foods Inc., Toronto 1993–95; Deputy Chair., Royal Insurance PLC 1986–89; Chair. (non-exec.), Etam 1991–95; Dir, Apax Partners & Co. Capital 1996–. *Publications:* Here Today, Gone Tomorrow, Mr Wonderful Takes a Cruise 2004. *Leisure interests:* farming, fishing, golf. *Address:* 31 Walpole Street, London, SW3 4QS, England. *Telephone:* (20) 7730-2351. *Fax:* (20) 7730-9859.

NOTT, Rt Rev. Peter John, MA; British ecclesiastic; *Assistant Bishop, Diocese of Oxford;* b. 30 Dec. 1933, Belfast, Northern Ireland; s. of Cecil Frederick Wilder Nott and Rosina Mabel Nott; m. Elizabeth May Maingot 1961; one s. three d.; ed Bristol Grammar School, Dulwich Coll., London, Royal Mil. Acad. Sandhurst, Fitzwilliam House, Cambridge, Westcott House, Cambridge; served in regular army, commissioned RA 1951–55; Curate of Harpenden 1961–64; Chaplain and Fellow of Fitzwilliam Coll. Cambridge 1966–69, Hon. Fellow 1993; Chaplain of New Hall, Cambridge 1966–69; Rector of Beaconsfield 1969–77; Bishop of Taunton 1977–85; Bishop of Norwich 1985–99; Asst Bishop, Diocese of Oxford 1999–; Archbishop's Adviser to HMC 1980–85; Vice-Chair. Archbishops' Comm. on Rural Areas 1988–90; Pres. SW Region of Mencap 1978–84, Somerset Rural Music School 1981–85, Royal Norfolk Agricultural Asscn 1996; Dean, Priory of England, Order of St John of Jerusalem 1999–2003; Trustee, Nat. Army Museum 2001–09; KStJ 1999. *Publications:* Moving Forward in Prayer 1991, Bishop Peter's Pilgrimage: His Diary and Sketchbook 1996. *Leisure interests:* gardening, sketching, fishing. *Address:* Westcot House, Westcot, Wantage, Oxon., OX12 9QA, England (home). *Telephone:* (1235) 751233 (office).

NOTTAGE, Bernard Jonathon, MD; Bahamian physician and politician; *Minister of National Security;* b. 23 Oct. 1945; m. Portia Butterfield; two s.; ed Univ. of Aberdeen and Royal Coll. of Obstetricians and Gynaecologists, UK; fmr consultant in obstetrics and gynaecology, Princess Margaret Hosp., Nassau; mem. House of Ass. (PLP) for Garden Hills 1987–92, for Bain Town and Grants Town 2012–; apptd to Senate 2005, Leader of Opposition Business 2007; Minister of Health and Nat. Insurance 2006, Minister of Nat. Security and Leader of Govt Business in House of Ass. 2012–; Chair. Nat. Insurance Bd 1982–87; Pres. Central American and Caribbean Athletic Confed. 1982–90; fmr Pres. Scottish Univs Athletic Asscn, Bahamas Asscn of Athletic Asscns, Medical Asscn of the Bahamas, Bahamas Doctors' Union, Bahamas Family Planning Asscn; mem. Progressive Liberal Party (PLP) –1998, 2005–; Chair. Centre for Positive Change 1998–2006; CEO Coalition for Democratic Reform 2000–05; inducted into Central American and Caribbean Athletic Confed. Hall of Fame 2008. *Achievements include:* represented Bahamas in athletics (200 metres) at 1966 Commonwealth Games, 1967 Pan American Games, 1968 Mexico Summer Olympic Games and 1970 Commonwealth Games. *Address:* Ministry of National Security, East Hill Street POB N-3746, Nassau, Bahamas (office). *Telephone:* 322-7624 (office). *Fax:* 328-8212 (office).

NOTTAGE, Lynn; American playwright; b. 2 Nov. 1964, Brooklyn, NY; d. of Wallace Nottage and Jeannette Nottage; m. Tony Gerber; two c.; ed Brown Univ., Yale Univ. School of Drama; Visiting Lecturer, Yale Univ. School of Drama; Bd mem. BRIC Arts/Media/Brooklyn, Voice and Vision; NEA/TCG residency grant 1999, Manhattan Theatre Club Fellowship, New Dramatists Fellowship, New York Foundation for the Arts Fellowship 2000, 2004, Audelco Award for Best Production of the Year and Best Playwright 2004, American Theatre Critics'/ Steinberg New Play Award 2004, PEN/Laura Pels Award for Drama 2004, John Gassner Award for Best Playwright 2004, Outer Critics' Circle Award for Best Play 2004, Guggenheim Foundation Fellowship 2005, Nat. Black Theatre Festival August Wilson Playwriting Award 2005, Lucille Lortel Foundation Fellowship 2007, MacArthur Genius Award 2007, Obie Award for Playwriting 2009, Outer Critics' Circle Award 2009, Lucille Lortel Award 2009, New York Drama Critics' Circle Award 2009, Jeff Award 2009, Audelco 2009, Steinberg Distinguished Playwrights' Award, Dramatists' Guild Hull-Warriner Award, inaugural Horton Foote Prize for Outstanding New American Play, Helen Hayes Award, Lee Reynolds Award, Jewish World Watch iWitness Award. *Plays:* Poof! (Heideman Award) 1993, Crumbs from the Table of Joy 1995, Mud, River, Stone 1998, Becoming American 2002, Snapshot 2002, Las Meninas (AT&T OnStage Award) 2002, Intimate Apparel (New York Drama Critics' Circle Award for Best Play 2004, AT&T OnStage Award) 2003, A Walk Through Time (children's musical), Por'Knockers, Fabulation (Obie Award for Playwriting 2005) 2003, Give Again? 2006, Point of Revue 2006, A Stone's Throw, Ruined (Manhattan Theatre Club, New York) (Pulitzer Prize for Drama) 2009, By The Way, Meet Vera Stark 2011. *Publications:* Poof! 1993, Crumbs From the Table of Joy 1998, Mud, River, Stone 1999, Las Meninas 2004, Intimate Apparel/Fabulation 2006, Ruined 2009, By The Way, Meet Vera Stark 2013. *Address:* c/o Oliver Sultan, Creative Artists Agency, 162 Fifth Avenue, 6th Floor, New York, NY 10010, USA (office). *Telephone:* (212) 277-9000 (office). *Fax:* (212) 277-9099 (office). *E-mail:* osultan@caa.com (office); info@lynnnottage.net (home). *Website:* www.caa.com (office); www.lynnnottage .net.

NOTTEBOHM, Fernando, BA, PhD; American (b. Argentine) neuroscientist and academic; *Dorothea L. Leonhardt Professor, Head of the Laboratory of Animal Behavior and Director, Field Research Center for Ecology and Ethology, The Rockefeller University;* b. Buenos Aires, Argentina; ed Univ. of California, Berkeley; joined Faculty, The Rockefeller Univ., New York 1967, currently Dorothea L. Leonhardt Prof., Head of Lab. of Animal Behavior and Dir Field Research Center for Ecology and Ethology; mem. NAS, Soc. for Neuroscience, American Philosophical Soc.; Fellow, American Acad. of Arts and Sciences, AAAS; Kenneth Caik Research Award, St John's Coll. Cambridge (UK) 1983, Karl Spencer Lashley Award (co-recipient) 1983, Charles A. Dana Award (co-recipient) 1983, Lewis S. Rosensteil Award for Distinguished Work in the Basic Medical Sciences (co-recipient) 2004, French Fondation Ipsen Neuronal Plasticity Prize 2004, MERIT Award, Nat. Insts of Mental Health 2004, Pattison Award for Distinguished Research in the Neurosciences 2004, Benjamin Franklin Medal in Life Science, The Franklin Inst. 2006, Sven Berggren Lecture and Prize, Royal Physiographic Soc., Lund 2006. *Achievement:* most famous for providing definitive

proof that neurogenesis occurs in the vertebrate brain. *Publications:* more than 135 scientific papers in professional journals. *Address:* Laboratory of Animal Behavior, The Rockefeller University, 1230 York Avenue, New York, NY 10065, USA (office). *Telephone:* (212) 327-8000 (office). *E-mail:* nottebo@rockefeller.edu (office). *Website:* lab.rockefeller.edu/nottebohm (office).

NOUGAYRÈDE, Natalie; French journalist and editor; *Director and Editor-in-Chief, Le Monde;* b. 29 May 1966, Dijon; ed educated in UK and Canada, Institut d'Etudes Politiques, Strasbourg, Centre de formation des journalistes, Paris; as a journalist, specialized in int. issues, including Eastern Europe and the post-Soviet space; began career as corresp. in Prague, Czechoslovakia for Libération newspaper and the BBC 1991, then as corresp. in the Caucasus for Libération and RFI; reporter in Caucasus region, covering Georgia, Azerbaijan and Ukraine 1993–95; Ed. Portraits pages of Libération 1995–96; Eastern Europe Corresp. for Le Monde newspaper in Ukraine and Russia 1996–2001, Moscow Corresp. 2001–05, Diplomatic Corresp. 2005–13, Dir and Ed.-in-Chief Le Monde 2013–; Prix de la Presse diplomatique 2004, Prix Albert-Londres for her reporting on Chechnya and the hostage crisis in Beslan 2005. *Address:* Le Monde, 80 boulevard Auguste Blanqui, 75707 Paris Cedex 13, France (office). *Telephone:* 1-76-26-32-89 (office). *Fax:* 1-57-67-44-95 (office). *Website:* www.lemonde.fr (office).

NOUR, Momtaz Saed Abu el-, BCom; Egyptian politician; *Minister of Finance;* b. 16 Dec. 1948; m.; ed Ain Shaims Univ.; joined Ministry of Finance 1972, Gen. Man. Int. Org. Div. 1990–96, Head of Cen. Treasury Dept in the State Gen. Budget Sector 1996–2003, Head of Minister of Finance Office Sector 2003–08, Councillor to the Minister of Finance 2008–11, Pvt. Adviser to the Minister of Finance 2011, Deputy Minister of Finance 2011, Minister of Finance 2011–; mem. Bd of Dirs Nat. Investment Bank; fmr mem. Bd of Dirs Egyptian Postal Authority, South Cairo Electricity Distribution Co. *Address:* Ministry of Finance, Ministry of Finance Towers, Cairo (Nasr City), Egypt (office). *Telephone:* (2) 23428886 (office). *Fax:* (2) 26861561 (office). *E-mail:* finance@mof.gov.eg (office). *Website:* www.mof.gov.eg (office).

NOUVEL, Jean; French architect; b. 12 Aug. 1945, Fumel, Lot-et-Garonne; s. of Roger Nouvel and Renée Barlangue; m. Catherine Richard 1992; one d.; two s. by Odile Fillion; ed Ecole des Beaux Arts, Paris; has headed own architectural practice since 1970; amongst major completed buildings are: Arab World Inst., Paris 1987, Lyon Opera House, Cartier Foundation, Paris 1994, The Galeries Lafayette dept store, Berlin, Lucerne Culture and Congress Centre, Tours Conf. Centre, The Hotel, Lucerne, Andel office bldg, Prague, Nantes Justice Centre, Dentsu Tower, Tokyo, tech. centre, Wismar, museum of archaeology, Périgueux, Agbar office tower, Barcelona 2003, extension to Queen Sophia museum, Madrid 2005, Quai Branly Museum, Paris 2006, Guthrie Theater, Minneapolis 2006, Brembo's research and devt centre, Richemont Corpn HQ, Geneva, swimming pool of Les Bains des docks, Le Havre, Symphonic House, Copenhagen 2009, apartment bldg, 40 Mercer Street, Soho, New York, apartment bldg, Chelsea, New York, Ferrari factory in Maranello Modena, Pavilion B, Fiera di Genova; commission to design 10th Serpentine Gallery Pavillion, Theatre 'Archipel', Perpignan, One New Change, London 2010, Doha 9 skyscraper, Doha, Qatar 2012, City Hall, Montpellier 2012; current projects under study or construction include sea centre museum, Le Havre, office bldg Horizons, Boulogne Billancourtan, two apartment bldgs, Ibiza, Spain, hotel in Barcelona, Louvre Museum, Abu Dhabi, Philharmonic Hall, Paris, Tour de Verre, New York, a mixed use high-rise bldg in Sydney, two apartment bldgs in Singapore, the Grand Paris with Jean Marie Duthilleul and Michel Cantal-Dupart, Nat. Qatar Museum, design showroom RBC, Montpellier, two office bldgs in the dist of Brussels Midi train station, Foundation Imagine, Paris, police station and extension of Charleroi Danses, Charleroi; Architect Man. l'Ile Seguin; Chevalier, Ordre nat. du Mérite, des Arts et des Lettres; Officier, Légion d'honneur; hon. fellowships in AIA; Gold Medal, French Acad. of Architecture, RIBA Royal Gold Medal, Aga Khan Prize for the Arab World Inst., Nat. Grand Prize for Architecture, Francesco Borromini Int. Architecture Prize for Lucerne Culture and Congress Centre (Italy) 2001, Praemium Imperiale Career Prize, Japan Art Asscn 2001, Wolf Prize in the Arts 2005, Arnold W. Brunner Memorial Prize in Architecture 2005, Int. Highrise Award for the Agbar tower 2006, Pritzker Prize 2008. *Address:* Ateliers Jean Nouvel, 10 Cité d'Angoulême, 75011 Paris, France (office). *Telephone:* 1-49-23-83-83 (office). *Fax:* 1-43-14-81-10 (office). *E-mail:* info@jeannouvel.fr (office). *Website:* www.jeannouvel.com (office).

NOVÁK, Jiří, JUDr; Czech politician and lawyer; *Partner, Brož & Sokol & Novák Attorneys at Law;* b. 11 April 1950, Hranice, Přerov Dist; m.; one s. one d.; ed J.E. Purkyně (now Masaryk) Univ., Brno; practising lawyer 1976–89; mem. Standing Comm. of the Presidium of Czech Nat. Council for Prison System Issues 1989–92; Deputy to Czech Nat. Council Feb.–June 1990; mem. Presidium, Czech Nat. Council 1990–92; Chair. Cttee on Law and Constitution of Czech Nat. Council 1990–92; Minister of Justice, Czech Repub. 1992–96; Chair. Legis. Council of Govt of Czech Repub. Feb.–July 1992; mem. Parl. 1996–98; Chair. Parl. Cttee for Petitions 1996–98; Vice-Chair. Interdepartmental Antidrug Comm. 1996; mem. Civic Democratic Party 1991–98; advocate 1998–, currently Partner, Brož & Sokol & Novák Attorneys at Law. *Address:* Nám. T.G. Masaryka 15, 750 02 Přerov, Czech Republic (home). *Telephone:* (2) 24941946 (home). *Fax:* (2) 24941940 (office). *E-mail:* advokati@akbsn.eu (office). *Website:* www.akbsn.eu (office).

NOVAK, Michael, BT, MA; American theologian and writer; *George Frederick Jewett Scholar in Religion, Philosophy and Public Policy, American Enterprise Institute;* b. 9 Sept. 1933, Johnstown, Pa; s. of Michael J. Novak and Irene Sakmar; m. Karen R. Laub 1963; one s. two d.; ed Stonehill Coll., North Easton, Mass. and Gregorian Univ., Rome; Teaching Fellow, Harvard Univ. 1961–63; Asst Prof. of Humanities, Stanford Univ. 1965–68; Assoc. Prof. of Philosophy and Religious Studies, State Univ. of NY, Old Westbury 1969–71; Assoc. Dir Humanities, Rockefeller Foundation 1973–74; Ledden-Watson Distinguished Prof. of Religion, Syracuse Univ. 1976–78; Resident Scholar, American Enterprise Inst. 1978–, George Frederick Jewett Prof. of Religion, Philosophy, and Public Policy 1983–, Dir Social and Political Studies 1987–; Visiting Prof., Univ. of Notre Dame 1987–88; columnist, The National Review 1979–86, Forbes magazine 1989–; Founder and Publr Crisis 1982–95, Ed.-in-Chief 1993–95; mem. Bd for Int. Broadcasting 1983; Judge, Nat. Book Awards, DuPont Awards in Broadcast Journalism; Head, US Del. to UN Human Rights Comm., Geneva 1981, 1982, to CSCE, Berne 1996; Kt of Malta; several hon. degrees; Freedom Award, Coalition for a Democratic Majority 1979, George Washington Honor Medal, Freedom Foundation 1984, Angel Award 1985, Ellis Island Medal of Honor 1986, Templeton Prize 1994, Bratislava Medal 1998, Boyer Award 1999, Masaryk Medal 2000, Econs Medal, Inst. of Italian Mans and Entrepreneurs 2000. *Publications include:* Belief and Unbelief 1965, The Rise of the Unmeltable Ethnics 1972, Choosing Our King 1974, The Spirit of Democratic Capitalism 1982, Freedom with Justice: Catholic Social Thought and Liberal Institutions 1984, Taking Glasnost Seriously 1988, Free Persons and the Common Good 1989, This Hemisphere of Liberty 1990, The Catholic Ethic and the Spirit of Capitalism 1993, Business as a Calling 1996, The Experience of Nothingness 1998, Tell Me Why 1998, On Cultivating Liberty 1999, A Free Society Reader (ed.) 2000, Three in One 2001, On Two Wings 2002, The Universal Hunger for Liberty 2004, Washington's God 2006, No One Sees God 2008, All Nature is a Sacramental Fire 2011, Living the Call 2011, The Myth of Romantic Love and Other Essays 2012 and more than 500 articles in journals. *Address:* American Enterprise Institute, 1150 17th Street NW, Washington, DC 20036, USA (office). *Telephone:* (202) 862-5839 (office). *Fax:* (202) 862-5821 (office). *E-mail:* mnovak@aei.org (office). *Website:* www.aei.org (office); www.michaelnovak .net.

NOVAKOVIC, Phebe N.; American business executive; *Chairman and CEO, General Dynamics Corporation;* fmr Deputy Assoc. Dir Office of Man. and Budget, US Dept of Defense, Washington, DC, later Special Asst to Sec. and Deputy Sec. of Defense –2001; joined General Dynamics Corpn 2001, Vice-Pres., Strategic Planning 2002–05, Sr Vice-Pres., Planning and Devt 2005–10, Exec. Vice-Pres., Marine Systems 2010–12, Pres. and COO General Dynamics Corpn May–Dec. 2012, Chair. and CEO 2013–; Dir, Abbott Diabetes Care, Inc., Abbott Laboratories 2010–; ranked by Fortune magazine amongst the 50 Most Powerful Women in Business in the US (49th) 2010, (41st) 2011, (16th) 2012, ranked by Forbes magazine amongst The World's 100 Most Powerful Women (75th) 2013. *Address:* General Dynamics Corporation, 2941 Fairview Park Drive, Suite 100, Falls Church, VA 22042, USA (office). *Telephone:* (703) 876-3000 (office). *Fax:* (703) 876-3125 (office). *E-mail:* info@generaldynamics.com (office). *Website:* www .generaldynamics.com (office).

NOVELLI, Hervé; French politician; b. 6 March 1949, Paris; ed Univ. of Paris-Dauphine; began his career at Chambre Syndicale de la Sidérurgie Française (French Steel Industry Employers' Asscn); Chair. and Man. Dir family-owned prosthesis and orthesis maker based in Richelieu (Indre-et-Loire Dist) 1982–2006; Head of Minister's Office, Ministry of Industry, the Post Office and Tourism 1986–90; apptd Gen. Sec. Republican Party 1990, subsequently became mem. Exec. Bureau; elected Deputy to Nat. Ass. for Indre-et-Loire Dist 1993, re-elected for UMP party 2002, 2007; joined Audace Pour l'Emploi group made up of 50 mems Parl. with entrepreneurial backgrounds 1993; elected to Conseil Général (deliberative ass.) as Rep. of Richelieu canton 1997, Vice-Pres. Conseil Général 1998–2001; Co-founder and first Gen. Del. Démocratie Libérale party 1998; mem. European Parl. 1999–2002; Deputy Mayor of Richelieu 2001–08, Mayor 2008–; elected mem. Conseil Régional (governing body) of Centre region 2004 (resigned when appointed to Govt 2007); Pres. Les Réformateurs (asscn formed under aegis of UMP) 2002–; Co-founder Euro 92 Inst. to prepare French businesses for European Single Market 1988; Minister of State for Businesses and Foreign Trade 2007–09, for Commerce, Arts and Crafts, Small and Medium Businesses, Tourism and Services 2009–10. *Address:* c/o Ministry of the Economy, Industry and Employment, 139 rue de Bercy, 75572 Paris Cedex 12, France (office). *E-mail:* info@herve-novelli.com (office). *Website:* www.herve-novelli.com.

NOVELLO, Antonia Coello, MD, MPH, DPhil; American paediatrician and public health official; b. 23 Aug. 1944, Fajardo, Puerto Rico; m. Joseph Novello 1970; ed Univ. of Michigan, Univ. of Puerto Rico, Johns Hopkins Univ.; intern, Mott Children's Hosp., Univ. of Michigan, Ann Arbor 1970–71; Univ. of Michigan Medical Center 1971–73, postgraduate training in nephrology, Dept of Internal Medicine 1973–74; postgraduate training, Dept of Pediatrics, Georgetown Univ. 1974–75; pvt. practice in pediatrics, Springfield, Va 1976–78; entered US Public Health Service 1978; various posts at NIH, Bethesda, Md 1978–90, Deputy Dir Nat. Inst. of Child Health and Human Devt 1986–90; apptd Clinical Prof. of Pediatrics, Georgetown Univ. Hosp., Washington, DC 1986, 1989, Uniformed Services Univ. of the Health Services, Bethesda 1989; Adjunct Prof. of Pediatrics and Communicable Diseases, Univ. of Michigan, of Int. Health, Johns Hopkins School of Public Health; Surgeon-Gen., US Public Health Service (first woman and first Hispanic) 1990–93; UNICEF Special Rep. for Health and Nutrition 1993–96; Visiting Prof. of Health Policy and Man., Johns Hopkins Univ. School of Hygiene and Public Health 1996–99 (also Special Dir for Community Health Policy); New York State Commr of Health 1999–2007, Pres. Health Research, Inc.; mem. Alpha Omega Alpha, American Soc. of Nephrology, American Soc. of Pediatric Nephrology, American Pediatrics Soc., Soc. for Pediatric Research; Fellow, American Acad. of Pediatrics; numerous professional appointments, memberships and affiliations; 50 hon. doctorates; recipient of numerous awards, including Surgeon Gen.'s Exemplary Service Medallion and Medal, USPHS Distinguished Service Medal, Army Legion of Merit, Coast Guard Meritorious Medal, US Dept of the Navy Distinguished Public Service Award, American Medical Asscn Nathan B. Davis Award, Congressional Hispanic Caucus Medal, Johns Hopkins Soc. of Scholars Award and Univ. Alumni Asscn's Woodrow Wilson Award for Distinguished Govt Service, Elizabeth Blackwell Award, Univ. of Michigan Medical Center Alumni Award and Alumna Council Athena Award, Public Health Service Commissioned Officer's Asscn Health Leader of the Year Award, Ellis Island Medal of Honor, Elizabeth Ann Seton Award, Charles C. Shepard Science Award for Scientific Excellence, American Medical Women's Asscn Leadership Award, Nat. Council of La Raza Pres.'s Award, Nat. Council of Alcohol and Drug Dependency Golden Key Award, American Acad. of Pediatrics Excellence in Public Service Award, Healthy American Fitness Leaders Award, Nat. Women's Hall of Fame, Ronald McDonald Children's Charities Award of Excellence, Hispanic Hero Award, Miami Children's Hosp. Int. Hall of Fame, Women at Work Science Award, Award for Leadership, Hispanic Heritage Awards 1998, James Smithson Bicentennial Medal 2002. *Leisure interest:* collecting antique furniture. *Address:* 5438 Coral Ridge Drive, Grand Blanc, MI 48439, USA. *E-mail:* novello.antonia@gmail .com.

NOVIKOV, Arkady; Russian restaurateur; b. 1962, Moscow; m. Nadezhda Advokatova; two c.; ed Culinary Coll. No. 174, G.V. Plekhanov Econs Acad.; started career as chef, Universitetsky restaurant; deputy chef, Havana restaurant, later chef, Olympic Lights restaurant; Chef, Hard Rock Cafe, Gorky Park Green Theatre 1990; opened Sirena fish restaurant 1992, followed by White Sun of the Desert 1997; Founder and Owner Yolki-Palki chain of over 60 restaurants 1996–; est. Vogue Café in jt venture with Condé Nast; opened Gallery restaurant 2004, Cantinetta Antinori 2004, numerous other restaurants; f. Rodnik NT to open and operate chain of grocery stores in Moscow 2004; opened his first restaurant in London 2011; Founding Dir Fed. of Restaurateurs and Hoteliers; TV presenter, The Candidate 2005;*Website:* www.novikovrestaurant.co.uk/arkady-novikov.

NOVIKOV, Sergey Petrovich; Russian mathematician and academic; *Distinguished University Professor, Department of Mathematics, University of Maryland;* b. 20 March 1938, Gorky (now Nizhniy Novgorod); s. Petr Novikov and Ludmila Keldysh; m. Eleonora Tsoi 1962; one s. two d.; ed Moscow Univ., Steklov Math. Inst.; Prof., Moscow Univ. 1966–; Head, Dept, Landau Inst. for Theoretical Physics 1975–, Chair. Dept of Geometry and Topology, Moscow Univ. 1984–; Head, Dept, Steklov Math. Inst. 1983–; Distinguished Univ. Prof., Univ. of Maryland, USA 1997–; Corresp. mem. USSR (now Russian) Acad. of Sciences 1966–, mem. 1981–; Foreign mem. Accad. dei Lincei 1991; Foreign Assoc., NAS 1994, European Acad. of Sciences 2003; Hon. mem. London Math. Soc. 1987, Serbian Acad. of Art and Science 1988, Academia Europaea 1993, Pontifical Acad. of Sciences 1996; Dr hc (Athens) 1989, (Tel-Aviv) 1999; Moscow Math. Soc. Prize 1964, Lenin Prize 1967, Field's Medal, Int. Math. Union 1970, Lobachevsky Int. Prize, USSR Acad. of Sciences 1981, Wolf Foundation Prize in Math. 2005. *Publications:* Algebraic and Differential Topology 1960, General Relativity 1971–75, Theory of Solitons 1974, Topological Phenomena in Physics 1981, Riemannian Geometry and Poisson Structures 1983. *Leisure interest:* history. *Address:* University of Maryland, College Park, IPST, MD 20742, USA (office); Landau Institute for Theoretical Physics, Kosygina 2, 117334 Moscow, Russia (office). *Telephone:* (301) 405-5133 (College Park) (office); (495) 137-32-44 (Moscow); (495) 135-12-24 (Moscow) (home); (301) 779-7472 (USA) (home). *Fax:* (301) 314-9363 (USA) (office). *E-mail:* novikov@ipst.umd.edu (office). *Website:* www.ipst.umd.edu/researchandfaculty/ novikov.php (office).

NOVITSKY, Gennady; Belarusian politician and construction engineer; *Chairperson, Standing Committee, Council of the Republic, National Assembly;* b. 2 Jan. 1949, Mogilev; m.; two s.; ed Belarus State Polytechnic Inst. Acad. of Social Sciences; foreman, supervising foreman, Head of Construction Div., Mogilev Construction Trust No. 12 1971–77; worked in econ. man. and as a party exec. 1977–94, Chief Engineer of Mogilev Region Agricultural Construction Enterprise, Instructor and Head of Construction Dept at Mogilev Region CP Cttee, Head of Mogilev Agricultural Construction Enterprise Bd; Minister of Architecture and Construction 1994–97; Deputy, later Acting Prime Minister 1997–2001; Prime Minister 2001–03; Chair. Council of the Repub., Nat. Ass. of Repub. of Belarus 2003–11, Chair. Standing Cttee 2011–; Certificate of Honour, Council Ministers, Repub. of Belarus. *Leisure interests:* simple sports like jogging. *Address:* 4 Krasnoarmeyskaya str., 220016 Minsk, Belarus (office). *Telephone:* (17) 227-25-82 (office). *Fax:* (17) 227-23-18 (office). *E-mail:* novitsky@sovrep.gov.by (office). *Website:* www.sovrep.gov.by (office).

NOVOSELOV, Sir Konstantin (Kostya) Sergeevich, Kt, MSc, PhD, FRS; Russian/British physicist and academic; *Royal Society Research Fellow and Professor of Physics, University of Manchester;* b. 23 Aug. 1974, Nizhny Tagil, Russian SFSR, USSR; ed Moscow Physical-Technical Univ., High Magnetic Field Lab., Univ. of Nijmegen, the Netherlands; Researcher, Inst. for Microelectronics Tech., Chernogolovka 1997–99; Researcher, High Magnetic Field Lab., Univ. of Nijmegen 1999–2001; Researcher, Univ. of Manchester 2001–05, Leverhulme Research Fellow 2005–06, Royal Soc. Research Fellow 2007–, Prof. of Physics 2010–; Hon. FInstP 2011, Hon. FRSC 2011; Hon. DSc (Manchester) 2011; Early Career Fellowship, Leverhulme Trust 2004, Nicholas Kurti European Prize 2007, Univ. of Manchester Researcher of the Year 2008, Young Scientist Prize, Int. Union of Pure and Applied Science 2008, Technology Review-35 Young Innovator 2008, Europhysics Prize (jtly) 2008, Nobel Prize in Physics (with Andre Geim) 2010, Leverhulme Medal, Royal Soc. 2013. *Achievements include:* best known for his discovery, with Andre Geim, of two-dimensional crystals made of carbon atoms – and most notably graphene – in 2004 at Univ. of Manchester; original jt paper on graphene in Science in 2004 acknowledged by ISI citation index as "one of the most cited recent papers in the field of Physics". *Publications:* more than 90 peer-refereed research papers, including many in Nature and in Science, on condensed matter physics. *Address:* Room 2.09, Schuster Building, The School of Physics and Astronomy, University of Manchester, Manchester, M13 9PL, England (office). *Telephone:* (161) 275-4119 (office). *E-mail:* konstantin.novoselov@manchester.ac .uk (office); kostya@manchester.ac.uk (office). *Website:* www.physics.manchester .ac.uk (office); www.condmat.physics.manchester.ac.uk/people/academic/ kostyanovoselov (office).

NOVOTNÝ, Petr; Czech actor, writer and producer; b. 6 Aug. 1947, Olomouc; m. Miroslava Novotný; four c.; ed Charles Univ., Prague; mem. Laterna Magika Theatre, Prague; Owner Firma 6P and Amfora Football Club. *Awards:* Best Comedian and Best Programme (Novotný), TYTY Awards 1999, Most Popular Male Actor, TYTY Awards 2000. *Theatre productions directed:* Sugar (Some Like It Hot), Gypsies Go to Heaven, Libuse (opera) 1995, Hello Dolly! 1996, My Fair Lady, Evita 1999, Pokuseni sv. Antonina 2001. *Television includes:* Big Ear; writer and presenter of numerous programmes. *Leisure interests:* football, cooking. *Address:* Firma 6P—Petr Novotný, s.r.o, Koterovská 833, 15500 Prague 5, Czech Republic (office). *Telephone:* (2) 57960560 (office). *Fax:* (2) 57960562 (office). *E-mail:* firma6p@decent3000.cz (office). *Website:* www.firma6p.cz (office); www .petr-novotny.cz.

NOVOZHILOV, Genrikh Vasilievich; Russian mechanical engineer and aircraft designer; b. 27 Oct. 1925, Moscow; m.; one s.; ed Moscow Aviation Inst.; mem. CPSU 1951–91; constructor, constructing engineer, leading engineer, Sec. CP Cttee aviation plant 1948–57; Deputy Constructor-in-Chief, Chief Constructor, Constructor-Gen. USSR Ministry of Aviation Industry 1958–86; simultaneously First Deputy Constructor-Gen. Moscow Ilyushin Machine Constructing Plant 1964–, Constructor-Gen. 1976–2000, Adviser and Gen. Designer Illushin Design

Bureau 2000–; Deputy to USSR Supreme Soviet 1974–89, USSR People's Deputy, 1989–91; mem. Cen. CPSU Cttee 1986–91; Head of Production of IL76T, IL86 and IL96-300 aircraft; Hero of Socialist Labour (twice), Lenin Prize and other awards and decorations. *Publications:* works in the field of new samples of aviation tech., including Theory and Practice of Designing Passenger Aircraft 1976, Design, Testing and Production of Wide-Fuselage Passenger Aircraft 1980, essays on History of Constructions and Systems of Aircraft 1983. *Leisure interests:* tennis, photography. *Address:* Ilyushin Design Bureau, 125190 Moscow, Leningradsky prospekt 45G, Russia (office). *Telephone:* (495) 943-81-16 (office); (495) 212-21-32 (office). *E-mail:* ilyushin@online.ru (office).

NOWAK, Rev. Arkadiusz; Polish ecclesiastic and charity worker; b. 28 Nov. 1966, Rybnik; ed Pontifical Faculty of Theology, Warsaw, Szczecin Univ.; mem. Camillian Order (Ordo Clericorum Regularium Ministrantium Infirmis—OSCam.) 1985–; opened first AIDS hospice in Poland; Dir Centre of Re-adaptation Ministry of Health, Konstancin (brs in Piastów and Anielin) 1990–; ordained priest 1993; Co-founder Polish Humanitarian Aid Foundation Res Humanae 1993–; Adviser on Issues of AIDS and Drugs to Minister of Health 1995–2001, Plenipotentiary 2001; Order of the Smile 1995; numerous prizes include Medal of St Georges (Tygodnik Powszechny Award) 1993, Award for Acting Against Intolerance, Xenophobia and Racialism (Finland), Global Leader for Tomorrow, World Econ. Forum 2000, UN Award for Breaking the Silence on HIV/AIDS 2000. *Address:* National AIDS Centre, ul. Samsonowska 1, 02-829 Warsaw, Poland (office). *Telephone:* (22) 6418301 (office). *Fax:* (22) 6412190 (office). *E-mail:* arknowak@poczta.onet.pl (office).

NOWELL, Peter C., MD, FAAS; American pathologist and academic; *Gaylord P. and Mary Louise Harnwell Professor of Pathology and Laboratory Medicine, University of Pennsylvania School of Medicine;* ed Wesleyan Univ., Middletown, Conn., Univ. of Pennsylvania School of Medicine; Rotating Internship, Philadelphia Gen. Hosp. 1952–53, Clinical Asst, Lab. Service 1956–70, Consultant, Lab. Service, Philadelphia Gen. Hosp. and Philadelphia Veterans' Admin Hospital 1970–77; Resident in Pathology, Presbyterian Hosp., Philadelphia (Trainee of Nat. Cancer Inst.) 1953–54; Lt, Medical Corps, USNR (Pathologist for US Naval Radiological Defense Lab., San Francisco, Calif.) 1954–56; Sr Research Fellowship, US Public Health Service 1956–61; Instructor to Prof. of Pathology, Univ. of Pennsylvania School of Medicine 1956–64, Prof. of Pathology 1964–, Chair. of Pathology 1967–73, Dir Univ. of Pennsylvania Cancer Center 1973–75, Deputy Dir 1975–, Academic Co-ordinator, Dept of Pathology and Lab. Medicine 1980–87, Gaylord P. and Mary Louise Harnwell Prof. of Pathology and Lab. Medicine 1990–; Consultant in Pathology, Children's Hosp. of Philadelphia 1974–; mem. Nat. Cancer Inst. DCBD Bd of Scientific Counselors 1982–86, American Cancer Soc. Advisory Bd on Institutional Grants 1982–84, Leukemia Soc. of America Grants Review Bd 1987–90, Advisory Cttee to Dir NIH 1990–94; mem. NAS 1976, Inst. of Medicine 1991, American Soc. for Experimental Pathology (mem. Council 1967–71, Pres. 1970–71), American Asscn for Cancer Research (Dir 1970–73, 1990–93) Pathological Soc. of Philadelphia, Coll. of Physicians of Philadelphia, American Soc. for Investigative Pathology, American Asscn of Immunologists, Acad. of Clinical Lab. Physicians and Scientists; mem. Editorial Bd Cancer Research 1973–76, 1982–85, 1990–93, Journal of Immunology 1977–80, American Journal of Pathology 1980–, Cancer Genetics and Cytogenetics 1980–, Cancer Reviews 1985–, Cancer and Metastasis Reviews 1985–, Hematological Oncology 1987–89, Genes, Chromosomes and Cancer 1989–, International Review of Experimental Pathology 1990–; Fellow, American Acad. of Arts and Sciences 2009–; Hon. mem. Asscn of American Physicians 1992; Research Career Devt Award, US Public Health Service 1961–64, Research Career Award, US Public Health Service 1964–67, Parke Davis Award in Experimental Pathology 1965, Lindback Distinguished Teaching Award 1967, Distinguished Alumnus Award, Wesleyan Univ. 1968, Gerhardt Medal, Philadelphia Pathological Soc. 1974, American Cancer Soc. (Phila) Scientific Award 1976, Shubitz Prize, Univ. of Chicago 1980, La Madonnina Award, Milan 1982, Passano Foundation Award 1984, Rous-Whipple Award, American Asscn of Pathologists 1986, NIH Outstanding Investigator Grant 1986, Robert de Villiers Award, Leukemia Soc. of America 1987, Cotlove Award, Acad. of Clinical Lab. Physicians and Scientists 1987, Philip Levine Award, American Soc. of Clinical Pathologists 1989, Fred W. Stewart Award, Memorial Sloan-Kettering Cancer Center 1989, Mott Prize, General Motors Cancer Research Foundation 1989, Distinguished Graduate Award, Univ. of Pennsylvania School of Medicine 1992, 3M Life Sciences Award, Fed. of American Socs for Experimental Biology 1993, American Philosophical Soc. 1993, Leukemia Soc. of America Award (Eastern Pennsylvania Chapter) 1995, Gold-Headed Cane Award, American Soc. for Investigative Pathology 1997, Albert Lasker Award for Clinical Medical Research (jt recipient) 1998. *Publications:* numerous articles in medical journals. *Address:* University of Pennsylvania School of Medicine, Department of Pathology, M163 John Morgan/6082, Philadelphia, PA 19104, USA (office). *E-mail:* nowell@mail.med.upenn.edu (office). *Website:* www .med.upenn.edu (office).

NOWINA-KONOPKA, Piotr Maria, MSc (Econs), PhD; Polish politician, economist and diplomatist; *Ambassador to the Holy See;* b. 27 May 1949, Chorzów; s. of Mikołaj Nowina-Konopka and Anna Nowina-Konopka; m. Wanda Nowina-Konopka 1975; two d.; ed Higher School of Econs, Sopot, Univ. of Gdańsk; Asst, Gdańsk Tech. Univ. 1972–74; post-doctoral studies, Univ. of Gdansk 1975–77; Deputy Head, Centre of Revocatory Maritime Chamber, Gdynia 1977–79; Lecturer, Foreign Trade Econs Inst. of Gdańsk Univ. 1979–89; Co-founder and Sec. Catholic Intelligentsia Club in Gdańsk 1980–81; mem. Solidarity Independent Self-governing Trade Union 1980–1990, aide to Pres. Lech Wałęsa 1982–89, Press Spokesman 1988–89, Chief of Press 1989; mem. Civic Cttee attached to Lech Wałęsa (q.v.) 1988–91; Lecturer, Gdańsk Theology Inst. 1988–89; Minister of State in Chancellery of Pres. of Poland 1989–90; Sec.-Gen. Democratic Union 1990–94; Union for Freedom Sec. for Foreign Affairs 1994–98; Deputy to Sejm (Parl.) 1991–2001, Vice-Chair. Cttee for the European Treaty 1992–97, Deputy Chair. Jt Parl. Cttee Poland-European Parl. 1993–97; Sec. of State Office of the Cttee for European Integration 1998; Sec. of State in Chancellery of Prime Minister 1998–99; Vice-Rector Coll. of Europe, Bruges/Warsaw 1999–2004; adviser to Nat. Parl. of Georgia 2005–06; Dir for Relations with Nat. Parls, European Parl. 2006–09; Dir European Parl. Liaison Office with US Congress, Washington, DC 2010–2012; Amb. to the Holy See 2013–; Prof., Giedroyć Coll., Warsaw 2006–;

mem. Foreign Affairs Comm. 1991–2001; Pres. Robert Schuman Foundation 1996, now mem. Bd of Founders; Deputy Chief Negotiator for negotiations with EU 1998–99; Chevalier, Ordre nat. du Mérite, Officer, Légion d'honneur, Verdienstkreuz Erste Klasse des Verdienstordens, Officer, Polonia Restituta, Commdr, Ordre de Roi Leopold (Belgium). *Publications:* weekly columnist in Wprost, political articles in different books/periodicals. *Leisure interests:* family life, reading, social sciences, yachting, riding, skiing. *Address:* Embassy of Poland, Via dei Delfini 16, Int. 3, 00186 Rome Italy (office). *Telephone:* (06) 6990958 (office). *Fax:* (06) 6990978 (office). *E-mail:* watykan.amb.sekretariat@msz.gov.pl (office).

NOWITZKI, Dirk Werner; German professional basketball player; b. 19 June 1978, Würzburg; s. of Jörg-Werner Nowitzki and Helga Nowitzki; ed Röntgen Gymnasium, Würzburg; plays power forward for the Dallas Mavericks, Nat. Basketball Asscn (NBA), USA; played for DJK Würzburg basketball club 1994–98; drafted ninth overall by the Milwaukee Bucks in 1998 NBA Draft and immediately traded to Mavericks 1998–, led team to 11 consecutive NBA Playoffs 2000/01–10/11, including an NBA Finals appearance 2006 and franchise's first championship 2011, one of only five players in NBA history to win a championship while being the only NBA All-Star on the team; 10-time All-Star and 11-time mem. All-NBA Teams; one of only four players to have averaged more than 25 points and 10 rebounds in NBA playoffs; one of only two players to have managed four consecutive 30-point 15-rebound games in playoffs; only player in NBA history to get over 100 blocks and 150 three-pointers in a single season; led German nat. basketball team to a bronze medal in FIBA World Championship 2002, silver medal in EuroBasket 2005; f. Dirk Nowitzki Foundation (charity aiming to fight poverty in Africa); seven-time European Player of the Year: Euroscar European Basketball Player of the Year, Gazzetta dello Sport 2002–06, Mister Europa European Player of the Year, Superbasket magazine 2005, FIBA Europe Basketball Player of the Year 2005; All-NBA Third Team 2001, 2004, All-NBA Second Team 2002–03, 2008, 2010–11, All-NBA First Team 2005–07, 2009, NBA All-Star 2002–11, FIBA World Championship Most Valuable Player (MVP) 2002, Euro-Basket MVP 2005, NBA Three-Point Shootout Champion 2006, NBA MVP (first European player) 2007, NBA Finals MVP 2011. *Leisure interests:* reading, playing the saxophone. *Address:* c/o Helga Nowitzki, Am Kirschberg 18, 97218 Gerbrunn, Germany; c/o Lisa Tyner, 2909 Taylor Street, Dallas, TX 75226, USA. *Telephone:* (214) 658-7186 (Dallas). *Website:* www.41-world.com; www.dirk-nowitzki -foundation.org.

NOWOTNY, Ewald, DrIur; Austrian economist, academic, central banker and fmr politician; *Governor, Oesterreichische Nationalbank;* b. 1944, Vienna; m.; one s.; ed Vienna Univ. of Econs, Inst. for Advanced Studies, Vienna, Univ. of Vienna; Asst, Inst. of Econs and Finance, Johannes Kepler Univ., Linz 1968–73; mem., later Chair., Österreichischen Postsparkasse 1971–79; mem. Nationalrat (Parl., SPÖ) 1979–99, mem. Finance Cttee 1985–99; Visiting Prof., Harvard Univ. 1971–72, Technische Universität Darmstadt 1972; Prof., Inst. für Finanzwissenschaften, Univ. of Linz 1973–82; Prof., Vienna Univ. of Econs 1982–, Vice-Rector 2003–04; Vice-Pres. and mem. Bd of Man. European Investment Bank (EIB), Luxembourg 1999–2003; CEO BAWAG PSK Group 2006–07; mem. Gen. Council, Oesterreichische Nationalbank 2007–08, Gov. 2008–; mem. Governing Council, European Central Bank; Grosses Goldenes Ehrenzeichen für Verdienste um die Republik Österreich; Hon. DEcon (Alpen-Adria Univ., Klagenfurt) 2008. *Publications include:* Der öffentliche Sektor – Einführung in die Finanzwissenschaft; numerous contribs to econ. journals. *Address:* Office of the Governor, Oesterreichische Nationalbank, Otto-Wagner-Pl. 3, 1090 Vienna, Austria (office). *Telephone:* (1) 404-20 (office). *Fax:* (1) 404-23-99 (office). *E-mail:* oenb.info@oenb.co .at (office). *Website:* www.oenb.at (office).

NOWRA, Louis; Australian writer and scriptwriter; b. 12 Dec. 1950; m. Mandy Sayer; Dr hc (Griffiths Univ.) 1996; Literature Board Grants 1975, 1977, 1979, 1980, 1981, 1982; Prix Italia 1990, NSW Premier's Literary Prize 1992, Victoria Premier's Prize 1994, Australian Literary Soc. Gold Medal 1994, The Australia/Canada Award 1994, The Green Room Award for Best New Play 1995, Courier-Mail Book of the Year 2000, Winner, Green Room Awards, New Australian Opera (Librettist) – Midnight Son, Patrick White Literary Award 2013. *Radio:* Albert Names Edward 1975, The Song Room 1980, The Widows 1984, Summer of the Aliens 1989, Sydney 1993, Moon of the Exploding Trees 1995, The Divine Hammer 2001, Jez 2006, Far North 2008. *Publications:* The Misery of Beauty 1976, The Cheated 1978, Albert Names Edward 1975, Inner Voices 1978, Visions 1979, Inside The Island/The Precious Woman 1981, The Song Room 1982, Sunrise 1983, The Golden Age 1985, Palu 1987, Capricornia 1988, The Watchtower 1992, Summer of the Aliens 1992, Cosi 1992, Radiance 1993, The Temple 1993, Crow 1994, The Incorruptible 1995, Cosi (Australian Film Inst. Award for Best Adapted Screenplay 1996) 1996, Red Nights 1997, The Jungle 1998, Language of the Gods 1999, The Twelfth of Never 1999, Byzantine Flowers 2000, Radiance 2000, In the Gutter... Looking at the Stars (anthology, co-ed.) 2000, Abaza 2001, Warne's World 2002, Walkabout 2003, Shooting the Moon 2004, Chihuahuas, Women and Me 2005, Bad Dreaming 2007, The Boyce Trilogy Includes: The Woman with Dog's Eyes, The Marvellous Boy, The Emperor of Sydney 2007, Ice 2008. *Leisure interests:* cricket, mycology. *Address:* c/o HLA Management, PO Box 1536, Strawberry Hills, NSW 2012, Australia (office). *Telephone:* (2) 9549-3000 (office). *Fax:* (2) 9310-4113 (office). *E-mail:* hla@hlamgt.com.au (office). *Website:* www .hlamgt.com.au (office).

NOYCE, Phillip; Australian film director; b. 29 April 1950, Griffith, NSW; ed Univ. of Sydney, Australian Film and Television School. *Films include:* That's Showbiz 1973, Castor and Pollux (Rouben Mamoulien Award, Sydney Film Festival) 1974, God Knows Why But It Works 1975, Backroads (writer, dir and producer) 1977, Newsfront 1978, Heatwave 1982, Echoes of Paradise (1987), Dead Calm 1989, Blind Fury 1989, Patriot Games 1992, Sliver 1993, Clear and Present Danger 1994, The Saint 1997, The Bone Collector 1999, Rabbit Proof Fence (dir and producer) 2002, The Quiet American 2002. *Television includes:* The Dismissal (mini-series) 1983, Cowra Breakout (mini-series) 1984, The Hitchhiker (various episodes) 1983, Tru Calling (series pilot) 2003. *Address:* c/o Endeavor Talent Agency, 9701 Wiltshire Boulevard, #1000, Beverly Hills, CA 90212, USA (office); c/o The Cameron Creswell Agency Pty Ltd, 5/2 New McLean Street, Edgcliff, NSW 2027, Australia (office).

NOYER, Christian; French central banker and civil servant; *Governor, Banque de France;* b. 6 Oct. 1950, Soisy-sous-Montmorency, Val d'Oise; ed Univs of Rennes and Paris, Inst. of Political Science, Ecole Nat. d'Admin; mil. service as naval officer 1972; joined French Treasury 1976, Chief of Banking Office, then of Export Credit Office 1982–85, Deputy Dir in charge of Int. Multilateral Issues 1988–90, then of Debt Man., Monetary and Banking Issues 1990–92, Dir of Dept responsible for public holdings and public financing 1992–93, Dir of Treasury 1993–95; financial attaché, French Del. to EC, Brussels 1980–82; Econ. Adviser to Minister for Econ. Affairs and Finance, Edouard Balladur 1986–88, Chief of Staff to E. Alphandéry 1993, to Jean Arthuis (q.v.) 1995–97; Dir, Ministry for Econ. Affairs, Finance and Industry 1997–98; Alt. Gov., IMF and World Bank 1993–95; Vice-Pres., European Cen. Bank 1998–2002; Gov., Banque de France 2003–; Alt. mem. European Monetary Cttee 1988–90, mem. 1993–95, 1998; Alt. mem. G7 and G10 1993–95; mem. Working Party No. 3 OECD 1993–95; Chair. Paris Club of Creditor Countries 1993–97; mem. European Econ. and Financial Cttee 1999–2002; Chair. BIS, Basel, Switzerland 2010–; Officier, Légion d'honneur, Chevalier, Ordre nat. du Mérite, Commdr, Nat. Order of the Lion (Senegal), Grand Cross, Orden del Mérito (Spain). *Publications:* Banks: The Rules of the Game 1990; various articles. *Leisure interest:* sailing. *Address:* Banque de France, 3 rue de la Vrillière, 75001 Paris (office); 39 rue Croix des Petits Champs, 75001 Paris, France (office); Bank for International Settlements, Centralbahnplatz 2, 4002 Basel, Switzerland. *Telephone:* 1-42-92-20-05 (office); 1-42-92-20-01 (office). *Fax:* 1-42-92-20-10 (office). *E-mail:* secretariat.gouv@banque-france.fr (office). *Website:* www.banque-france.fr (office).

NOYORI, Ryōji, MEng, PhD; Japanese scientist and academic; *President, RIKEN;* b. 3 Sept. 1938, Kobe; m. Hiroko Oshima; two s.; ed Kyoto Univ.; Research Assoc. Dept of Industrial Chem., Kyoto Univ. 1963–68; Assoc. Prof., Dept of Chem., Nagoya Univ. 1968–72, Prof. 1972–2003, Dir Chemical Instrument Center 1979–91, Dean Grad. School of Science 1997–99, Dir Research Center for Materials Science 2000–03; Pres. RIKEN (scientific research inst.) 2003–; Dir ERATO Molecular Catalysis Project, Research Devt Corpn of Japan 1991–96; Science Adviser, Ministry of Educ., Science and Culture 1992–96, mem. Scientific Council 1996–2003; Prof. for Fundamental Research on Organic Chem., Kyushu Univ. 1993–96; Cttee Chair. Research for the Future Program on Advanced Processes, Japan Soc. for the Promotion of Science 1996–2002; Pres. Soc. of Synthetic Organic Chem. 1997–99; Visiting Prof. at numerous int. univs; mem. editorial bd of 30 learned journals; mem. numerous professional bodies including Chemical Soc. of Japan, Pharmaceutical Soc. of Japan, ACS, RSC (UK); numerous hon. degrees, including Hon. Dr (Univ. of Rennes 1) 2000, (Technical Univ. of Munich) 2005, (RWTH Aachen Univ., Germany) 2005; numerous awards and prizes, including Chemical Soc. of Japan Award 1985, Japan Acad. Prize 1995, Wolf Prize (jtly) 2001, Nobel Prize in Chem. (jt recipient) 2001, Lomonosov Gold Medal, Russian Acad. of Sciences 2009, and several ACS awards. *Address:* RIKEN, 2-1, Hirosawa, Wako, Saitama 351-0198 (office); Department of Chemistry, Graduate School of Science, Nagoya University, Furo-cho, Chikusa, Nagoya, Aichi, 464-8602 (office); 1105 Luxembourg House, 8-9, Yonban-cho, Chiyoda, Tokyo 102-0081, Japan (home). *Telephone:* (48) 463-9900 (RIKEN) (office); (52) 789-2956 (Nagoya University) (office). *Fax:* (48) 462-4604 (RIKEN) (office); (52) 783-4177 (Nagoya University) (office). *E-mail:* noyori@riken.jp (office); noyori@chem3.chem.nagoya-u.ac.jp (office). *Website:* www.riken.jp/engn/index.html (office); www.nagoya-u.ac.jp/en/ (office).

NOZARI, Gholamhossein, BS, MA; Iranian petroleum industry executive; b. 1954; responsible for air defence in southern Iran during Iran–Iraq War; fmr Head of Security, Nat. Iranian South Oil Co.; fmr mem. Cen. Council, Islamic Republic Party; fmr Deputy Chair. Majlis Energy Comm., fmr mem. Majlis Devt Comm.; fmr Man. Dir Nat. Iranian Cen. Oil Co., then Man. Dir Nat. Iranian Oil Co. –2007; Minister of Petroleum 2007–09. *Address:* c/o Ministry of Petroleum, Hafez Crossing, Taleghani Avenue, Tehran, Iran.

NOZIÈRES, Philippe Pierre Gaston François; French physicist; b. 12 April 1932, Paris; s. of Henri Nozières and Alice Noël; m. Catherine Michel 1982; one d. (one s. and one d. by previous m.); ed Ecole Normale Supérieure and Princeton Univ., USA; Prof. of Physics, Univ. of Paris 1961–72; Physicist, Laue-Langevin Inst. 1972–76; Prof. of Physics, Grenoble Univ. 1976–83; Prof. of Statistical Physics, Collège de France 1983–2001; mem. Acad. des Sciences (Inst. de France); Foreign Assoc. NAS; Holweck Prize 1976, Prix du CEA (Acad. des Sciences) 1979, Wolf Prize 1985, Gold Medal CNRS 1988, Feenberg Medal 2000. *Publications:* papers on theoretical and statistical physics. *Address:* ILL, BP 156, 38042 Grenoble Cedex (office); 15 route de Saint Nizier, 38180 Seyssins, France (home). *Telephone:* (4) 76-20-72-74 (office); (4) 76-21-60-28 (home). *Fax:* (4) 76-88-24-16 (office). *E-mail:* nozieres@ill.fr (office).

NOZOE, Kuniaki, BA; Japanese business executive; *President and Representative Director, Fujitsu Limited;* ed Waseda Univ.; joined Fujitsu Ltd 1971, has held several exec. positions including Corp. Sr Vice-Pres. Fujitsu Ltd –2007, Corp. Vice-Pres., Group Support, and Corp. First Sr Vice-Pres. 2007–, Corp. Sr Exec. Vice-Pres. April–June 2008, Pres. and Rep. Dir Fujitsu Ltd June 2008–; mem. Bd of Dirs Fujitsu Frontech Ltd, Asscn of Radio Industries and Businesses. *Address:* Fujitsu Headquarters, Shiodome City Center, 1-5-2 Higashi-Shimbashi, Minato-ku, Tokyo 105-7123, Japan (office). *Telephone:* (3) 6252-2220 (office). *Fax:* (3) 6252-2783 (office). *E-mail:* info@fujitsu.com (office). *Website:* www.fujitsu.com (office).

NQAKULA, Charles; South African politician; b. 13 Sept. 1942; m.; ed Cradock, Lovedale; fmr waiter, wine steward; fmr clerk, Dept of Bantu Educ.; journalist, Midland News 1966; Political Reporter, Imvo Zabantsundu 1973; with Daily Dispatch, London 1976; placed under banning order 1981, declared prohibited immigrant, forbidden to enter S Africa 1982; est. Veritas News Agency, Zwelitsha 1982; Publicity Sec. United Democratic Front (UDF) 1983; fmr underground operative African Nat. Congress (ANC), mem. Nat. Exec. Cttee 1994; granted amnesty 1991; mem. S African Communist Party (SACP), Deputy Gen. Sec. 1991, later Gen. Sec., currently Chair.; Parl. Counsellor to Pres. –2001; Deputy Minister of Home Affairs 2001–02; Minister of Safety and Security 2002–08, of Defence 2008–09; mem. Union of Black Journalists, Vice-Pres. 1976; Vice-Pres. Writers' Asscn of S Africa (later Media Workers' Asscn of S Africa) 1979. *Leisure interests:* composing choral music, writing poetry. *Address:* c/o Ministry of Defence, Armscor

Building, Block 5, Nossob Street, Erasmusrand 0181 Private Bag X161, Pretoria 0001, South Africa (office).

NSANZE, Augustin, PhD; Burundian politician, diplomatist, historian and academic; b. 1953, Kibumbu, Mbuye; m.; ed Univ. of Burundi, Univ. of Paris, France; Instructor, Lycée Clarte-Notre Dame, Bujimbura 1978–79; Lecturer, Univ. of Burundi 1979–1990, Prof. 1987–90, Advisor to Dir of Dept of Scientific Research 1989, Chief of Scientific Research Service 1990; First Advisor to Pres. on social and cultural issues 1992–98; Consultant on the history of Burundi, UNESCO 1998; Researcher, Univ. of Lieden 1999; Research Asst, Univ. of Laval, Canada 2001–03; Counsellor, Perm. Mission to UN, New York 2004–06; Amb. to Ethiopia (also accred to Djibouti) and Rep. to African Union and Econ. Comm. for Africa 2006–08; Amb. and Perm. Rep. to UN, New York 2008–09; Minister for External Relations 2009–11. *Publications:* several books and academic articles. *Address:* c/o Ministry of External Relations and International Co-operation, Bujumbura, Burundi.

NSEREKO, Daniel David Ntanda, LLB, MCJ, LLM, JSD; Ugandan judge; *Judge, Appeals Division, International Criminal Court;* m.; ed Univ. of East Africa, Dar es Salaam, Tanzania, Howard Univ. School of Law, Washington, DC, USA, The Hague Acad., Netherlands, New York Univ. School of Law, USA; pupil advocate with Kiwanuka & Co., Advocates, Kampala 1968; Advocate, High Court of Uganda 1972–, included on List of Counsel eligible for appointment to represent accused or victims before Int. Criminal Court 2007; Lecturer in Law, Makerere Univ., Kampala 1971–75, Sr Lecturer in Law 1975–78; full-time pvt. law practice, Kampala 1978–82; expert consultant, Crime Prevention and Criminal Justice Br. of UN Centre for Social Devt and Humanitarian Affairs, New York, USA 1983–84, Social Affairs Officer, UN Centre for Social Devt and Humanitarian Affairs 1983; Sr Lecturer in Law, Univ. of Botswana, Gaborone 1984–92, Head of Dept of Law 1985–93, Assoc. Prof. of Law 1992–96, Prof. of Law 1996–; Walter S. Owen Visiting Prof. of Law, Univ. of British Columbia, Canada 1993–94; Visiting Scholar, Max Planck Inst. for Foreign and Int. Criminal Law, Freiburg, Germany 1995, 2006; Judge, Trial Div., Int. Criminal Court, The Hague 2008–09, Appeals Div. 2009–; served as Amnesty International Trial Observer to Swaziland 1990, Amnesty International mission to Swaziland to investigate allegations of human rights abuses and to inspect prison conditions 1991, Amnesty International Trial Observer to Ethiopia 1996, Head of an Amnesty International del. to Lesotho to investigate allegations of human rights and humanitarian law violations and inspecting prison conditions following S African and Botswana mil. intervention 1998; mem. Exec. Cttee Uganda Red Cross Soc. 1975–80, Bd Int. Soc. for Reform of Criminal Law, Vancouver, Canada 1988–, Advisory Exec. War Crimes Research Office, American Univ., Washington, DC 2006–; mem. Editorial Council Journal of Church and State 1985–, Editorial Bd Journal Violence, Aggression and Terrorism 1986–90, Criminal Law Forum: An International Journal 1990–, University of Botswana Law Journal 2005–; mem. Int. Advisory Bd Int. Doctorate School of Excellence, Univ. of Cologne, Germany 2006–; mem. Uganda Law Soc. 1972– (mem. Law Council (Exec. Cttee) 1975–80), East African Law Soc. 2004–; Fellow, Inst. of Int. Law and Int. Relations Research, The Hague Acad. of Int. Law 1982; Medal of Int. Soc. for Reform of Criminal Law 1996. *Publications:* Police Powers and the Rights of the Individual in Uganda 1973, The International Protection of Refugees (doctoral dissertation) 1975, Antigone: A Greek Play by Sophocles (trans. into the Luganda language) 1989, English–Luganda Law Dictionary 1993, Eddembe Lyaffe (Our Rights; treatise written in the Luganda language) 1995, Criminal Law and Procedure in Uganda (in, International Encyclopaedia of Laws) 1996, Criminal Procedure in Botswana: Cases and Materials (third edn) 2002, Constitutional Law in Botswana (in, International Encyclopaedia of Laws) 2002, Legal Ethics in Botswana: Cases and Materials (with K. Solo) 2004, Criminal Law and Procedure in Botswana 2007; several book chapters and reviews and numerous articles in professional journals. *Address:* International Criminal Court, PO Box 19519, 2500 CM The Hague, The Netherlands (office). *Telephone:* (70) 515-8515 (office). *Fax:* (70) 515-8555 (office). *E-mail:* info@icc-cpi.int (office). *Website:* www.icc-cpi.int (office).

NSHUTI, Paul Manasseh, PhD; Rwandan government official and academic; Minister of Commerce, Industry, Investment, Tourism and Co-operation –2005, of Finance and Econ. Planning 2005–06. *Address:* c/o Ministry of Finance and Economic Planning, BP 158, Kigali, Rwanda (office).

NSIMBAMBI, Apollo Robin, BSc, MSc, PhD; Ugandan politician; b. 27 Nov. 1938; m. 1st Rhoda Nsimbambi (deceased); m. 2nd Esther Nsimbambi; ed Univ. of London, UK, Univ. of Chicago, USA, Univ. of Nairobi, Kenya; Dean, Faculty of Social Science, Makerere Univ. 1978–83, 1985–87, Head, Dept of Political 1987–90, Dir Makerere Inst. of Social Research 1994–96, Chancellor of Makerere Univ. 2003–07; Minister of Public Service 1996–98, of Educ. and Sports 1998–99; Prime Minister of Uganda 1999–2011; mem. Nat. Resistance Movt. *Address:* c/o Office of the Prime Minister, PO Box 341, Kampala, Uganda.

N'SINGA UDJUU ONGWABEKI UNTUBE, Joseph; Democratic Republic of the Congo politician; *President, Union chrétienne pour le renouveau et la justice;* b. (Joseph N'Singa Udjuu), 29 Oct. 1934, Nsontin, Bandundu Prov.; s. of Nshue O. N'singa and Monkaju Medji; m. Mbu Modiri Marie; four s. four d.; ed Kokoro and Kabue Seminaries, Bandundu Prov., Univ. of Lovanium (now Kinshasa); Juridical adviser of the provisional Govt, Inongo, Bandundu Prov. 1963; Provincial Minister of the Interior (Home Affairs) and Information 1963–64; elected Nat. Deputy 1964; Vice-Minister of the Interior (Home Affairs) 1965, of Justice 1965; Minister of Justice 1966–69; Minister of State for Home Affairs 1968; Minister of State at the Presidency Sept. 1970; Chair. Nat. Inst. of Social Security 1975–80; Co-founder and mem. Cen. Cttee, Mouvement Populaire de la Révolution (MPR) 1980–83 (Exec. Sec. 1981–83), First Vice-Pres. 1980–83; Chair. 1990–91; Prime Minister (first State Commissary) 1981; Pres. Judiciary Council 1987–90; mem. Sovereign Nat. Conf. and elected Counsellor of the Repub. during Nat. Conf.; mem. transition Parl.; Minister of Transportation 1994–95, of Justice 1995–96, of Reconstruction and Planning 1997; participant at nat. consultation assizes conf., Kinshasa 2000; mem. Jt Comm. Cttee in charge of Law Review 2001; Founder and Pres. own political party Union chrétienne pour le renouveau et la justice (UCRJ); Grand Cordon of the Leopard Nat. Order, Commdr of the Belgian King Leopold II Cross, Commdr of the Cen. African Repub. Order of Merit. *Leisure interests:* walking, jogging. *Address:* 68 Avenue Uvira, #5 Commune de Gombe, Kinshasa, Democratic Republic of the Congo (home). *E-mail:* nsinga5@hotmail.com.

NTIBANTUNGANYA, Sylvestre; Burundian politician; b. 8 May 1956, Nyamutobo; m. 1st Eusebie Ntibantunganya (deceased); m. 2nd Pascasie Minani; one s. two d.; ed Nat. Audiovisual Inst. Paris, Nat. Univ. of Rwanda; worked for Burundi State TV and Radio 1984–87; joined Nat. Secr. Unity for Nat. Progress (UPRONA); in exile in Rwanda 1979–83; Founding mem. Sahwanya-Frodebu Party, mem. Exec. Cttee 1991, Leader 1993–; Chief Ed. Aube de la Démocratie (Frodebu Party newspaper) until 1993; Deputy for Gitega 1993; Minister for External Relations 1993; fmr Speaker of Parl.; Pres. of Burundi 1994–96; Chair. Nat. Security Council 1996; mem. Senate 2002–. *Publications:* Une démocratie pour tous les Burundais 1999. *Address:* Senate of Burundi, Bujumbura (office); 82 Chaussée Prince Louis Rwagasore, Bujumbura, Burundi (home). *Telephone:* (257) 22219474 (home). *Fax:* (257) 22258686 (home). *E-mail:* ntibasy@yahoo.fr (home).

NTISEZERANA, Gabriel; Burundian economist, fmr central banker and politician; *President, Senate;* m.; three c.; Customers Officer, Credit Dept, Interbank Burundi s.a. in charge of business portfolio 1993–99, Man. Cen. Market Br. 1999–2000, Head of Asian Area br. Jan.–Aug. 2001; Chair. Banque nationale de développement économique (Nat. Bank for Econ. Devt) –2006; Gov. Cen. Bank 2006–07, Gov. for Burundi, IMF 2006; mem. Conseil nat. pour la défense de la démocratie-Forces pour la défense de la démocratie (CNDD-FDD—Nat. Council for the Defence of Democracy-Forces for the Defence of Democracy); Second Vice-Pres. of Burundi 2007–10; Pres. Senate 2010–. *Address:* Office of the President, Senate, Bujumbura, Burundi (office).

NTOUTOUME EMANE, Jean-François; Gabonese politician; b. 6 Oct. 1939; Minister of State, Minister of Land Registry, Town Planning and Housing and Minister for State Control, Decentralization, Territorial Admin and Regional Integration 1997–99; Prime Minister of Gabon and Head of Govt 1999–2006, also fmrly Minister of Housing and Urbanization. *Address:* c/o Office of the Prime Minister, BP 546, Libreville, Gabon (office).

NTSHANGASE, Rev. Abednego Mandla; Swazi politician, diplomatist and church leader; *Ambassador to USA;* b. 1 May 1954; m. Phindile Ntshangase; ed Rhema Bible Coll.; fmr production plant operator; fmr Industrial Relations Officer; Minister of Educ. 1998–2001, of Foreign Affairs and Trade 2001–03, of Public Service and Information 2003–10; Amb. to USA 2010–; fmr Dir Youth for Christ; fmr Leader New Life Christian Fellowship Church. *Address:* Embassy of Swaziland, 1712 New Hampshire Avenue NW, Washington, DC 20009, USA (office). *Telephone:* (202) 234-5002 (office). *Fax:* (202) 234-8254 (office). *E-mail:* swaziland@compuserve.com (office); info@swazilandembassyus.com (office).

NUAIMI, Ali ibn Ibrahim an-, MS; Saudi Arabian government official and fmr oil industry executive; *Minister of Petroleum and Mineral Resources;* b. 1935, Eastern Prov.; m. 1962; four c.; ed Int. Coll. Beirut, American Univ., Beirut and Lehigh Univ., Pennsylvania and Stanford Univ., USA; Asst Geologist, Exploration Dept, Aramco 1953, Hydrologist and Geologist 1963–67, worked in Econs and Public Relations Dept 1967–69, Vice-Pres. Aramco 1975, Sr Vice-Pres. 1978, Dir 1980, Exec. Vice-Pres., Operations 1982, Pres. 1984, CEO 1988; Minister of Petroleum and Mineral Resources 1995–; ranked by Forbes magazine amongst The World's Most Powerful People (31st) 2011, (32nd) 2012, (40th) 2013. *Leisure interests:* hunting, hiking. *Address:* Ministry of Petroleum and Mineral Resources, PO Box 247, Al Ma'ather Street, Riyadh 11191, Saudi Arabia (office). *Telephone:* (1) 478-1661 (office). *Fax:* (1) 479-3596 (office). *E-mail:* info@mopm.gov.sa (office). *Website:* www.mopm.gov.sa (office).

NUAIMI, HH Sheikh Humaid bin Rashid an-, (Ruler of Ajman); United Arab Emirates Ruler of Ajman 1981–; mem. Supreme Council of UAE 1981–; Patron, Sheikh Humaid bin Rashid Prizes for Culture and Science 1983–. *Address:* Ruler's Palace, PO Box 1, Ajman, United Arab Emirates.

NUAIMI, Rashid Abdullah an-; United Arab Emirates politician; Acting Minister of Foreign Affairs 1980–90, Minister of Foreign Affairs 1990–2006. *Address:* c/o Ministry of Foreign Affairs, PO Box 1, Abu Dhabi, United Arab Emirates (office).

NUDER, Pär, BL; Swedish politician; b. 1963; m.; two d.; mem. Österåker Municipal Exec. Cttee 1982–94; Chair. Stockholm Co. Br. Swedish Social Democratic Youth League 1986–89, mem. Nat. Exec. Cttee 1989–90; Political Adviser to Minister for Justice 1986–87, to Prime Minister's Office 1988–91, to Prime Minister 1994–96, 1996–97; Alt. mem. Riksdag 1988–94, mem. 1994–, mem. Parl. Cttee on Justice 1994–97; Political Sec. Social Democratic Parl. Party Group 1992–94, mem. Exec. Cttee, Stockholm Co. Br. of Social Democratic Party (SDP) 1992–94; Exec. mem. Prime Minister's Advisory Council for Baltic Sea Co-operation 1996–2000; Chair. Task Force on Organized Crime in the Baltic Sea Area 1996–2000; State Sec., Prime Minister's Office 1997–2002; Minister for Policy Co-ordination 2002–04, for Finance 2004–06; econ. adviser to SDP –2010; Chair. Vasallen AB 2001–02; Dir, Vin & Sprit AB 2001–02; Vice-Pres. Bd Nat. Swedish Art Museums 1995–97. *Address:* c/o Sveriges Socialdemokratiska Arbetareparti (Swedish Social Democratic Party), Sveavägen 68, 105 60 Stockholm, Sweden.

NUJOMA, Sam; Namibian fmr head of state; *Founding President of the Republic of Namibia and Founding Father of the Namibian Nation;* b. (Samuel Shafiihuma Nujoma), 12 May 1929, Etunda Village, Ongandjera Dist; s. of the late Daniel Uutoni Nujoma and of Helvi Mpingana Kondombolo; m. Kovambo Theopoldine Katjimune 1956; three s. one d.; ed Okahaol Finnish Mission School, St Barnabas School, Windhoek; with State Railways until 1957; Municipal Clerk, Windhoek 1957; clerk in wholesale store 1957–59; elected Leader of Ovamboland People's Org. (OPO) 1959; arrested Dec. 1959; went into exile 1960; Founder, with Herman Toivo ja Toivo (q.v.) and Pres. SWAPO (SW Africa People's Org.) April 1960–2007; appeared before UN Cttee on SW Africa June 1960; set up SWAPO provisional HQ in Dar es Salaam, Tanzania March 1961; arrested on return to Windhoek and formally ordered out of the country March 1966; turned to armed struggle after rejection by Int. Court of Justice of SWAPO complaint against S Africa Aug. 1966; gave evidence at UN Security Council Oct. 1971; led SWAPO negotiations at numerous int. negotiations culminating in implementation in March 1989 of UN Resolution 435 providing for independence of Namibia; returned to Namibia Sept. 1989; mem. Constituent Ass. 1989–90; Pres. of Namibia 1990–2005, also Minister

of Home Affairs 1995–96; Fellow, Inst. of Governance and Social Research – Jos, Plateau State, Nigeria 2003–; Grand Master, Order of Merit Grand Cruz (Brazil), Companion of the Order of Star of Ghana 2004; Hon. LLD (Ahmadu Bello Univ., Nigeria) 1982, (Lincoln Univ., USA) 1990, (Ohio Cen. State Univ., USA) 1993, (State Univ. of NJ, USA) 1997; Hon. DTech (Fed. Univ. of Tech., Minna) 1992, Hon. DEd (Univ. of Namibia) 1993; Hon. DSc (Abubakar Tafawa Balewa Univ., Nigeria) 2003; Dr hc (Academic Council, Russian Econ. Acad.) 1998, (People's Friendship Univ. of Russia); Lenin Peace Prize 1973, Frederic Joliot Curie Gold Medal 1980, Ho Chi Minh Peace Award 1988, Indira Gandhi Peace Prize 1990, Africa Prize for Leadership for Sustainable End to Hunger, New York 1995, Order of Friendship Award (Viet Nam) 2000; numerous honours and awards. *Publications:* To Free Namibia 1994, Where Others Wavered – My Life in SWAPO and My Participation in the Liberation Struggle of Namibia (autobiog.) 2001. *Address:* The Sam Nujoma Foundation, Private Bag 13220, Robert Mugabe Avenue, Windhoek, Namibia (office). *Telephone:* (61) 377700 (office). *Fax:* (61) 253098 (office). *E-mail:* jnauta@iway.na (office). *Website:* www.samnujomafoundation.org (office).

NUJOMA, Utoni Daniel, LLB; Namibian politician; *Minister of Justice;* b. 8 Sept. 1952, Kapako; s. of Sam Nujoma (fmr SWAPO leader and Pres. of Namibia); ed Univ. of Warwick, UK, Lund Univ., Sweden; grew up in exile in Angola; mem. SWAPO Cen. Cttee 2002–; mem. Nat. Ass. (Parl.) 2005–; Deputy Minister of Justice 2005–10; Minister of Foreign Affairs 2010–12; Minister of Justice 2012–. *Address:* Ministry of Justice, Justitia Building, Independence Avenue, PMB 13248, Windhoek, Namibia (office). *Telephone:* (61) 2805111 (office). *Fax:* (61) 221615 (office).

NUKAGA, Fukushiro; Japanese politician and fmr journalist; b. 1944; ed Waseda Univ.; fmr political and econ. reporter for Sankei Shimbun; fmr mem. Ibaraki Prefectural Ass.; mem. LDP, fmr Chair. Policy Research Council (Jiyu-Minshuto); mem. for Kitakanto Block, House of Reps; fmr Deputy Chief Cabinet Sec.; Dir-Gen. Defence Agency 1998–2000, of Econ. Planning Agency 2000–01; Minister of State for Defence 2005–06; Minister of Finance 2007–08. *Address:* Liberal Democratic Party, 1-11-23, Nagata-cho, Chiyoda-ku, Tokyo 100-8910, Japan (office). *Telephone:* (3) 3581-6211 (office). *E-mail:* koho@ldp.jimin.or.jp (office). *Website:* www.jimin.jp (office).

NUMAN, Yasin Said; Yemeni politician; *General Secretary, Yemeni Socialist Party (Al-Hizb Al-Ishtiraki Al-Yamani);* fmr Deputy Prime Minister and Minister of Fisheries; Prime Minister of Democratic Republic of Yemen 1986–90, Minister of Labour and Civil Service 1986; Gen. Sec. Yemeni Socialist Party (Al-Hizb Al-Ishtiraki Al-Yamani) 2005–. *Address:* Yemeni Socialist Party (Al-Hizb Al-Ishtiraki Al-Yamani), San'a, Yemen. *E-mail:* info@aleshteraki.net. *Website:* www.aleshteraki.net.

NUMATA, Sadaaki; Japanese diplomatist; b. 1943, Hyogo Pref.; m. Kyoko Numata; one s. one d.; ed Tokyo Univ., Univ. Coll., Oxford, UK; served in Embassy in London 1968–70; positions at Ministry of Foreign Affairs, Tokyo dealing with econ. co-operation, then N American affairs 1970–76; served in Embassy in Jakarta, Indonesia 1976–78; Politico-Mil. Officer, Embassy in Washington, DC 1978–82; Dir, First Int. Orgs (GATT) Div., Econ. Affairs Bureau, Tokyo 1982–84; Dir Japan–US Security Div., N American Affairs Bureau 1984–85, Dir First N America Div. 1985–87; Deputy Japanese Rep. to Conf. on Disarmament, Geneva 1987–88; Deputy Head of Mission, Embassy in Canberra, Australia 1989–91; Deputy Spokesman of Foreign Ministry, Tokyo 1991–94; Deputy Head of Mission, Embassy in London 1994–98; Foreign Ministry Spokesman and Dir Gen. for Press and Public Information, Tokyo 1998–2000; Amb. to Pakistan 2000–02; Amb. in Charge of Okinawan Affairs 2003–04; Amb. to Canada 2005–07; Exec. Dir Centre for Global Partnership, Japan Foundation 2007–10; Chair. English-Speaking Union of Japan 2010–. *Leisure interests:* singing folk songs, fly fishing, skiing. *Address:* English-Speaking Union of Japan, Fujikage-Building 9th Floor, Motoakasaka 1-1-5, Minato-ku, Tokyo 107-0051, Japan (office). *Telephone:* (03) 3423-0970 (office). *Fax:* (03) 3423-0971 (office). *Website:* www.esuj.gr.jp (office).

NÚÑEZ DE REYES, Gabriela, MEconSc; Honduran economist and politician; ed Univ. Nacional Autonoma de Honduras, State Univ. of New York at Albany, USA; Financial Analyst, Banco Cen. de Honduras 1985–94, eventually becoming Pres.; Tech. Sec. UDAPE (econ. policy analysis unit) 1993–95; Under-Sec. of Finance 1995–96, Minister of Finance 1998–2002, 2009–10; Honduras Rep. at IDB, IMF and World Bank 1996–98; fmr Vice-Pres. Banco Atlántida; mem. Bd of Dirs Asociación de Instituciones Bancarias de Honduras; included by CNN/TIME among 50 Latin American Leaders for the New Millennium 1999, and by World Econ. Forum among Global Leaders for Tomorrow. *Address:* c/o Ministry of Finance, 5A Avda, 3A Calle, Tegucigalpa, Honduras.

NÚÑEZ FÁBREGA, Fernando; Panamanian journalist, economist and politician; *Minister of Foreign Affairs;* b. 1946; s. of Emilio Núñez Portuondo and Olga Fábrega y Fábrega; ed Univ. of Missouri, USA; fmr Pres. Société Panamericane de Bourse, Andorra; fmr Man. Dir El Siglo (daily newspaper); fmr Exec. Vice-Pres. Vision Group (news media conglomerate in Spanish, based in London); several diplomatic postings including Consul Gen. in Tampa, Fla USA, Vice-Consul in Nassau, Bahamas and Sec. Gen., Consulate in Maracaibo, Venezuela; fmr Sec.-Gen., Ministry of Agric.; Exec. Sec., Consejo Nacional de Transparencia contra la Corrupción (anti-corruption agency) 2009–11; Gov. Coclé Prov. 2011–13; Minister of Foreign Affairs 2013–; fmr Pres. Nat. Broadcasting Asscn of Panama. *Address:* Ministry of Foreign Affairs, Edif. 26, Palacio Bolívar, Calle 3, San Felipe, Panamá 4, Panama (office). *Telephone:* 511-4100 (office). *Fax:* 511-4022 (office). *E-mail:* prensa@mire.gob.pa (office). *Website:* www.mire.gob.pa (office).

NUNN, Hon. Samuel Augustus (Sam), LLB; American lawyer and politician; *Co-Chairman and CEO, Nuclear Threat Initiative;* b. 8 Sept. 1938, Macon, Ga; s. of Samuel Augustus Nunn and Elizabeth Cannon Nunn; m. Colleen O'Brien 1965; one s. one d.; ed Georgia Inst. of Tech., Emory Univ. and Emory Univ. Law School, Atlanta; pvt. law practice 1964–72; mem. Georgia House of Reps 1968–72; US Senator from Georgia (Democrat) 1972–97, mem. Armed Services Cttee, Govt Affairs Cttee, Small Business Cttee; Sr Partner, King & Spalding, Atlanta 1997 (now retd); currently Co-Chair. and CEO Nuclear Threat Initiative, Washington; also currently Distinguished Prof., Sam Nunn School of Int., Georgia Inst. of Tech.; also currently Chair. Bd of Trustees, Center for Strategic and Int. Studies, Washington; mem. Bd of Dirs, ChevronTexaco Corpn, The Coca-Cola Co., Dell Inc.,

General Electric Co., Internet Security Systems. Inc., Scientific-Atlanta Inc., Hess Corpn 2012–; mem. Supervisory Council, Int. Luxembourg Forum on Preventing Nuclear Catastrophe, Bd of Advisors, Nat. Bureau of Asian Research; teamed up with fmr Senator Fred Thompson to promote a new film, Last Best Chance, on the dangers of excess nuclear weapons and materials 2005; Kt Commdr, Order of Merit (FRG) 2013; US Senator John Heinz Award for Greatest Public Service by an Elected or Appointed Official, Jefferson Awards 1996, Chairman's Medal, Heinz Awards (jtly) 2004, Hessian Peace Prize 2008, Georgia Trustee, Georgia Historical Soc. in conjunction with the Gov. of Georgia 2011, Inaugural recipient of Ivan Allen Jr Prize for Social Courage, Georgia Inst. of Tech. and Georgia Tech's Ivan Allen Coll. of Liberal Arts 2011. *Film:* Nuclear Tipping Point (documentary) 2010. *Leisure interests:* golf, reading. *Address:* Nuclear Threat Initiative, 1747 Pennsylvania Avenue NW, Seventh Floor, Washington, DC 20006 (office); The Sam Nunn School of International Affairs, 781 Marietta Street NW, Atlanta, GA 30318 (office); Center for Strategic and International Studies, 1616 Rhode Island Avenue NW, Washington, DC 20036, USA (office). *Telephone:* (202) 296-4810 (NTI) (office); (404) 894-3195 (Georgia Tech) (office); (202) 887-0200 (CSIS) (office). *Fax:* (202) 296-4811 (NTI) (office); (404) 894-1900 (Georgia Tech) (office); (202) 775-3199 (CSIS) (office). *E-mail:* contact@nti.org (office). *Website:* www.nti.org/about/leadership-staff/sam-nunn (office); www.inta.gatech.edu/mission/senator-sam -nunn (office); csis.org/expert/sam-nunn (office).

NUNN, Sir Trevor Robert, Kt, CBE; British theatre director; *Director Emeritus, Royal Shakespeare Company;* b. 14 Jan. 1940, Ipswich; s. of Robert Alexander Nunn and Dorothy May Nunn (née Piper); m. 1st Janet Suzman (q.v.) 1969 (divorced 1986); one s.; m. 2nd Sharon Lee Hill 1986 (divorced 1991); two d.; m. 3rd Imogen Stubbs 1994; one s. one d.; ed Northgate Grammar School, Ipswich and Downing Coll. Cambridge; Trainee Dir Belgrade Theatre, Coventry; Assoc. Dir Royal Shakespeare Co. 1964–86, Artistic Dir 1968–78, CEO 1968–86, Jt Artistic Dir 1978–86, Dir Emer. 1986–; f. Homevale Ltd and Awayvale Ltd; Artistic Dir Royal Nat. Theatre 1996–2001; Cameron Mackintosh Prof. of Contemporary Theatre, Univ. of Oxford 2010–11; toured USA, Australia with own version of Hedda Gabler 1975; mem. Arts Council of England 1994–; Hon. LittD (Warwick) 1982; Hon. MA (Newcastle-upon-Tyne) 1982; Hon. DLitt (Suffolk) 1997; Laurence Olivier Award for Outstanding Achievement 2002. *Productions:* Tango 1965, The Revenger's Tragedy (London Theatre Critics' Best Dir Award) 1965, 1969, The Taming of the Shrew, The Relapse, The Winter's Tale (London Theatre Critics' Best Dir Award) 1969, Hamlet 1970, Henry VIII 1970, Roman Season: Antony and Cleopatra (Soc. of Film and TV Arts Award 1975), Coriolanus, Julius Caesar, Titus Andronicus 1970, Macbeth 1974, 1976, Hedda Gabler (own version) 1975, Romeo and Juliet 1976, The Comedy of Errors (Ivor Novello Award for Best British Musical of 1976 (Lyrics), Soc. of West End Theatre Award for Best Musical of the Year 1977) 1976, Winter's Tale (co-dir) 1976, King Lear (co-dir) 1976, Macbeth 1976, The Alchemist 1977, As You Like It 1977, Every Good Boy Deserves Favour 1977, Three Sisters 1978, The Merry Wives of Windsor 1979, Once in a Lifetime (Plays and Players Award 1978, 1979 for Best Production (Dir), Sydney Edwards Award for Best Dir, Evening Standard Drama Awards 1978, 1979) 1979, Juno and the Paycock 1980, The Life and Adventures of Nicholas Nickleby (Laurence Olivier Award for Best Dir 1980, Tony Award for Best Direction of a Play 1982, Soc. of West End Theatres Awards, including Best Dir, Best New Play, Evening Standard Award, Best Dir, Drama Award for Best Dir, Mr. Abbott Award (Broadway) 1980 (with John Caird) (New York 1981), Cats (Tony Award for Best Direction of a Musical 1983) 1981, All's Well That Ends Well (Drama Desk Award for Outstanding Director of a Play 1983) 1981, Henry IV (Parts I & II) 1981, 1982, Peter Pan (with John Caird) 1982, Starlight Express 1984, Les Misérables (with John Caird) (Tony Award for Best Direction of a Musical 1987) 1985, Chess 1986, The Fair Maid of the West 1986, Aspects of Love 1989, Othello 1989, The Baker's Wife 1989, Timon of Athens 1991, The Blue Angel 1991, Measure for Measure 1991, Heartbreak House 1992, Arcadia 1993, Sunset Boulevard 1993, Enemy of The People 1997, Mutabilitie 1997, Not About Nightingales (Drama Desk Award for Outstanding Dir of a Play 1999) 1998, Oklahoma! 1998, Betrayal 1998, Troilus and Cressida 1999, The Merchant of Venice 1999, Summerfolk (Laurence Olivier Award for Best Dir 2000) 1999, Love's Labour's Lost 2002, We Happy Few 2004, The Woman in White 2004, Acorn Antiques: The Musical! 2005, Porgy and Bess 2006, Katya Kabanova 2007, The Seagull 2007, King Lear 2007, Gone with the Wind 2008, Inherit the Wind 2009, A Little Night Music 2009, Aspects of Love 2010, Birdsong 2010, Flare Path 2011, The Lion in Winter 2011, A Chorus of Disapproval 2012. *Films:* Hedda (dir and adaptation), Lady Jane (dir) 1985, Twelfth Night: Or What You Will (dir and adaptation) 1996. *Operas:* Idomeneo 1982, Porgy and Bess 1986, Così fan tutte 1991, Peter Grimes 1992, Katya Kabanova 1994, Sophie's Choice 2002, Porgy and Bess 2006. *Television:* Antony and Cleopatra 1975, Comedy of Errors 1976, Every Good Boy Deserves Favour 1979, Macbeth 1978, Shakespeare Workshops Word of Mouth (written and directed by T. Nunn) 1979, Three Sisters 1981, The Life and Adventures of Nicholas Nickleby (mini-series) 1982, Othello 1990, Porgy and Bess 1993, Oklahoma! 1999, The Merchant of Venice 2001, King Lear 2008. *Publication:* British Theatre Design 1989. *Address:* c/o Royal Shakespeare Company, Royal Shakespeare Theatre, Waterside, Stratford-upon-Avon, Warwicks., CV37 6BB, England.

NURBERDIYEVA, Akja Tajiyevna; Turkmenistani politician; *Chairman, Majlis;* b. 1957, Aşgabat; m.; two s.; ed Turkmen State Art Inst., Management Acad., Moscow (Russia); mem. Democratic Party of Turkmenistan; mem. Majlis (Parl.) 1994–, Vice-Chair. 2003–06, Acting Chair. 2006–07, Chair. 2007–; Chair. Nat. Centre of Trade Unions 2005–07. *Address:* Majlis, 744000 Aşgabat, Garaşsyzlyk Şaýoly 110, Turkmenistan (office). *Telephone:* (12) 35-31-25 (office). *Fax:* (12) 35-31-47 (office).

NURGALIYEV, Col-Gen. Rashid Gumarovich, PhD; Russian politician and security officer; *Deputy Secretary of the Security Council;* b. 8 Oct. 1956, Jetikar, Kazakh SSR, USSR; m.; two s.; ed Kuusinen State Univ., Petrozavodsk; ethnic Tatar; physics teacher, Nadvoitsy 1979–81; with KGB, and its successor, since 1981, Head of Anti-Terrorist Dept, Karelian Republican KGB 1991–95, Chief Inspector, Fed. Counterespionage Service (FSB) 1995–98, Head, Office for Drug Trafficking Control, Dept of Econ. Security 1999–2000, Deputy Dir, Head of Inspectors Admin 2000–02; First Deputy Minister of Internal Affairs 2002–03, Head of Criminal Militia Service 2002–03, Minister of Internal Affairs 2003–12;

Deputy Sec. Security Council 2012–; Hon. Citizen of the Repub. of Karelia; Order of Merit for the Fatherland (Third and Fourth Classes), Order of Honour, Order of Saint Blessed Prince Dimitry Donskoy Great (First Class) (Russian Orthodox Church) 2005, Order of Akhmad Kadyrov (Chechen Repub.) 2006, Medal 'In Commemoration of the 1000th Anniversary of Kazan', Medal for Distinction in Mil. Service (Second Class), Medal of Merit in the conduct of national census, Jubilee Medal '100 Years of the Trans-Siberian Railway', Medal 'In Commemoration of the 300th Anniversary of Saint Petersburg', Jubilee Medal '70 Years of the Armed Forces of the USSR', Medal for Strengthening Mil. Co-operation (Defence), Medal '200 Years of the Ministry of Defence', Medal 'For Military Merit' (MIA), Medal 'For Impeccable Service' (First Class); Yuri Andropov Award. *Address:* Security Council of Russian Federation, 103132 Moscow, Ipatyevskii per. 4/10, Russia (office). *Telephone:* (495) 206-35-96 (office). *Website:* www.scrf.gov.ru (office); state.kremlin.ru/security_council (office).

NURSE, Sir Paul Maxime, Kt, MA, PhD, FRS, PRS; British university president and scientist; *President, Royal Society;* b. 25 Jan. 1949, Norfolk, England; s. of Maxime Nurse and Cissie Nurse (née White); m. Anne Teresa Talbott 1971; two d.; ed Harrow Co. Grammar School, Univ. of Birmingham, Univ. of East Anglia; Research Fellow, Dept of Zoology, Univ. of Edin. 1974–78; Sr Research Fellow, School of Biology, Univ. of Sussex 1980–84; Head Cell Cycle Control Lab., Imperial Cancer Research Fund (ICRF), London 1984–87; Iveagh Prof. of Microbiology, Univ. of Oxford 1987–91; Dir of Research (Labs) and Head Cell Cycle Lab., ICRF 1993–96, Dir-Gen. ICRF 1996–2002, Dir-Gen. (Science) and CEO Cancer Research UK 2002–03; Pres. Rockefeller Univ., New York, USA 2003–11; Dir Francis Crick Inst. (fmrly UK Centre for Medical Research and Innovation) 2011–; mem. EMBO 1987–; Pres. Genetical Soc. 1990–93; mem. Academia Europaea 1991; Foreign Assoc. NAS 1995–; Fellow, Royal Soc. 1989–, Pres. 2010–; Hon. FRCP, Hon. FRCPath 2000, Hon. mem. American Acad. of Arts and Sciences 2006; Chevalier, Légion d'honneur 2002; Dr hc numerous univs; Fleming Lecturer, Soc. of Gen. Microbiology 1984, Florey Lecturer, Royal Soc. 1990, Marjory Stephenson Lecturer, Soc. of Gen. Microbiology 1990, Feldberg Prize for Medical Research (UK/Germany) 1991, CIBA Medal, Biochemical Soc. 1991, Louis Jeantet Prize for Medicine in Europe (Switzerland) 1992, Gairdner Foundation Int. Award (Canada) 1992, Royal Soc. Wellcome Medal 1993, Jiménez Díaz Memorial Award and Medal (Spain) 1993, Purkyne Medal, Czech Acad. 1994, Pezcoller Award for Oncology Research (Italy) 1995, Royal Soc. Medal 1995, Dr Josef Steiner Prize, Switzerland 1996, Dr H.P. Heineken Prize for Biochemistry and Biophysics (Netherlands) 1996, Alfred P. Sloan, Jr Prize and Medal, General Motors Cancer Research Foundation 1997, Berkan Judd Award (USA) 1998, Albert Lasker Award for Basic Medical Research (USA) 1998, Nobel Prize in Physiology or Medicine 2001, Copley Medal 2005. *Publications:* The Great Ideas of Biology: The Romanes Lecture for 2003 2004; numerous articles in scientific journals concerned with cell and molecular biology. *Leisure interests:* gliding, motorcycling, running, astronomy, talking. *Address:* Royal Society, 6–9 Carlton House Terrace, London, SW1Y 5AG, England (office). *Telephone:* (20) 7451-2500 (office). *E-mail:* president@royalsociety.org (office). *Website:* www.royalsociety.org (office).

NUSSBAUM, Martha Craven, MA, PhD; American academic; *Ernst Freund Distinguished Service Professor of Law and Ethics, University of Chicago;* b. 6 May 1947, New York, NY; d. of George Craven and Betty Craven; m. Alan J. Nussbaum 1969 (divorced 1987); one d.; ed New York and Harvard Univs; Jr Fellow, Soc. of Fellows, Harvard Univ. 1972–75, Asst Prof. of Philosophy and Classics 1975–80, Assoc. Prof. 1980–83; Assoc. Prof. of Philosophy and Classics, Brown Univ. 1984–85, Prof. of Philosophy, Classics and Comparative Literature 1985–87, David Benedict Prof. 1987–89, Prof. 1989–95; Visiting Prof. of Law, Univ. of Chicago 1994, Prof. of Law and Ethics 1995–96, Prof. of Philosophy 1995–, Prof. of Divinity 1995–, Ernst Freund Prof. of Law and Ethics 1996–, Assoc. mem. Classics Dept 1996–, Assoc. mem. Dept of Political Science 2003–, Founder and Co-ordinator, Center for Comparative Constitutionalism 2002–; Visiting Prof., Jawaharlal Nehru Univ., New Delhi, India 2004; Fellow, American Acad. of Arts and Sciences; mem. American Philosophical Asscn (Chair. Cttee on Status of Women 1994–97); Brandeis Creative Arts Award 1990, PEN Spielvogel-Diamondstein Award 1991, NY Univ. Distinguished Alumni Award 2000, Grawemeyer Award in Educ. 2002, Barnard Medal of Distinction 2003; many other awards. *Publications:* Aristotle's De Motu Animalium 1978, Language and Logic (ed.) 1983, The Fragility of Goodness 1986, Love's Knowledge 1990, Essays on Aristotle's De Anima (ed. with A. Rorty) 1992, The Therapy of Desire 1994, The Quality of Life (ed. with A. Sen) 1993, Passions and Perceptions (ed. with J. Brunschwig) 1993, Women, Culture and Development (ed. with J. Glover) 1995, Poetic Justice 1996, For Love of Country 1996, Cultivating Humanity 1997, Sex and Social Justice 1998, Hiding from Humanity: Disgust, Shame and the Law 2004, Liberty of Conscience 2008, From Disgust to Humanity: Sexual Orientation and Constitutional Law 2010, Not for Profit: Why Democracy Needs the Humanities 2010, Creating Capabilities: The Human Development Approach 2011, The New Religious Intolerance: Overcoming the Politics of Fear in an Anxious Age 2012. *Leisure interests:* music, running, hiking. *Address:* 520 Law Quad, Law School, University of Chicago, 1111 East 60th Street, Chicago, IL 60637, USA (office). *Telephone:* (773) 702-3470 (office). *Fax:* (773) 702-0730 (office). *E-mail:* martha_nussbaum@law.uchicago.edu (office). *Website:* www.law.uchicago.edu/faculty/nussbaum (office).

NUSSLE, James (Jim) Allen, BA, JD; American lawyer, politician and fmr government official; b. 27 June 1960, Des Moines, Ia; m. 1st Leslie Jeanne Harbison 1986 (divorced 1996); one s. one d.; m. 2nd Karen Chiccehitto 2001; ed Luther Coll., Drake Univ.; called to the Bar, Iowa 1985, States Attorney for Delaware Co., Ia 1986–90; mem. US House of Reps (Ia 2nd Dist) 1991–2006 (retd), Chair. House Budget Cttee 2001–06; ran unsuccessfully for Gov. of Ia 2006; Dir Office of Man. and Budget 2007–09; f. Nussle Group (consultancy), Alexandria, Va 2009; Republican. *Address:* Nussle Group, 828 Slaters Lane, Suite 104, Alexandria, VA 22314, USA (office). *Telephone:* (202) 540-9045 (office). *E-mail:* info@thenusslegroup.com (office). *Website:* thenusslegroup.com (office).

NÜSSLEIN-VOLHARD, Christiane, PhD, FRS; German scientist and academic; *Director, Max Planck Institute for Developmental Biology, Tübingen;* b. 20 Oct. 1942, Magdeburg; d. of Rolf Volhard and Brigitte Volhard (née Haas); ed Univ. of Tübingen; Research Assoc., Lab. of Dr Schaller, Max-Planck-Inst. für Virusforschung, Tübingen 1972–74; Postdoctoral Fellow (EMBO Fellowship),

Lab. of Prof. Dr W. Gehring, Biozentrum Basel, Switzerland 1975–76, Lab. of Prof. Dr K. Sander, Univ. of Freiburg 1977; Head of Group, European Molecular Biology Lab. (EMBL), Heidelberg 1978–80; Group Leader, Friedrich-Miescher-Laboratorium, Max-Planck-Gesellschaft, Tübingen 1981–85, Scientific mem. Max-Planck-Gesellschaft and Dir Max-Planck-Institut für Entwicklungsbiologie, Tübingen 1985–90, Dir Dept of Genetics 1990–; mem. Scientific Council of the European Research Council (ERC) 2005–12; Chancellor, Order Pour le mérit 2013–; head of the curatorium, International Hugo Wolf Acad., Stuttgart 2010–; f. Christiane Nüsslein-Volhard Stiftung 2004; mem. NAS; Grosses Verdienstkreuz mit Stern 1996, Ordre pour le Mérite 1997, Grosses Verdienstkreuz mit Stern und Schulterband 2005; Hon. ScD (Yale) 1990, (Oxford) 2005; Dr hc (Utrecht) 1991, (Princeton) 1991, (Harvard) 1993; Albert Lasker Medical Research Award, New York 1991, Prix Louis Jeantet de Médicine, Geneva 1992, Ernst Schering Prize, Berlin 1993, Nobel Prize in Medicine (jtly) 1995. *Publications:* 135 Zebra Fish: A Practical Approach 2002; numerous scientific articles. *Address:* Max-Planck-Institut für Entwicklungsbiologie, Spemannstrasse 35, 72076 Tübingen, Germany (office). *Telephone:* (7071) 601487 (office). *Fax:* (7071) 601384 (office). *E-mail:* christiane.nuesslein-volhard@tuebingen.mpg.de (office). *Website:* www.eb .tuebingen.mpg.de/departments/3-genetics/christiane-nusslein-volhard (office); www.cnv-stiftung.de.

NUTBEAM, Don, PhD, FFPH; British public health scientist, academic and university administrator; *Vice-Chancellor, University of Southampton;* m.; two c.; ed Univ. of Southampton; Head of Public Health, UK Dept of Health 2000–03; Academic Provost, Univ. of Sydney 2003–09; Vice-Chancellor Univ. of Southampton 2009–; has worked as an adviser and consultant for WHO over 20 years and as consultant and team leader in projects for the World Bank; Fellow, Faculty of Public Health. *Publications include:* two public health text books; more than 100 papers in peer-reviewed journals on public health intervention, health literacy and adolescent health behaviour. *Leisure interests:* sport, especially football, rugby, skiing, tennis and golf, vegetable gardening. *Address:* Office of the Vice-Chancellor, University of Southampton, University Road, Southampton, Hants., SO17 1BJ, England (office). *Telephone:* (23) 8059-6686 (office). *E-mail:* g.costigan@ southampton.ac.uk (office). *Website:* www.southampton.ac.uk (office).

NUTT, Jim, BFA; American artist; b. 28 Nov. 1938, Pittsfield, Mass.; s. of Frank E. Nutt and Ruth Tureman Nutt; m. Gladys Nilsson 1961; ed School of Art Inst. of Chicago, Washington Univ. and Univ. of Pennsylvania; Prof. of Art, Calif. State Univ., Sacramento 1968–75, School of Art Inst. of Chicago 1990; Cassandra Foundation Award 1969, Nat. Endowment for the Arts Award 1975, 1990. *Address:* c/o David Nolan Gallery, 527 West 29th Street, New York, NY 10001, USA.

NWANZE, Kanayo F., BSc, MSc, PhD; Nigerian agricultural scientist and international organization official; *President, International Fund for Agricultural Development;* ed Univ. of Ibadan, Kansas State Univ., USA; experience in poverty reduction through agric., rural devt and research world-wide since late 1970s; Dir-Gen. Africa Rice Centre (WARDA) for ten years; held sr positions at several research centres affiliated to Consultative Group on Int. Agricultural Research (CGIAR), Chair. Centre Dirs' Cttee, helped establish Alliance of CGIAR Centres; Vice-Pres. IFAD, Rome, Italy 2007–09, Pres. 2009–; has served on exec. bds of various insts; mem. several scientific asscns; numerous prizes and awards. *Achievements include:* instrumental in introducing and promoting New Rice for Africa (NERICA), a high-yield, drought- and pest-resistant rice variety developed specifically for the African landscape. *Publications:* numerous publs and articles in scientific journals. *Address:* International Fund for Agricultural Development, Via Paolo di Dono 44, 00142 Rome, Italy (office). *Telephone:* (06) 54591 (office). *Fax:* (06) 5043463 (office). *E-mail:* ifad@ifad.org (office). *Website:* www.ifad.org (office).

NYAKLYAEU, Uladzimer; Belarusian poet, writer, journalist, editor and politician; b. 11 July 1946, Smarhon, Grodno Region; s. of Prokofiy Neklyayev and Anastasiya Mahyer; m. 1st Ludmila Nyaklyaeu 1965; one d. one step-c.; m. 2nd Volha Nyaklyaeu 1999; ed Higher State Communications Coll., Minsk Pedagogical Inst., Moscow Literature Inst.; began working in Vladivostok, Taishet and Norilsk following graduation; returned to Belarus 1967, worked as a radio mechanic at Minsk TV custom shop –1971; literature worker, Znamya Yunosti newspaper 1972–75; Ed. Theatrical Minsk bulletin 1975–87; Chief Ed. main editorial bd of literature and drama programmes, Belarusian TV 1978–87; Chief Ed. Krynitsa magazine 1987–98; Chief Ed. Litaratura i Mastatstva weekly 1996–99; left Belarus to lived in Poland for political reasons June 1999, also lived in Finland, returned to Minsk 2003; initiator of civil campaign 'Tell the Truth!' 2010; opposition leader and presidential cand. 2010; beaten unconscious by men in black uniform in Minsk before the closure of the polls 19 Dec. 2010, spent more than a month in custody following the post-election street protest before being released and placed under house arrest 28 Jan. 2011; given a two-year suspended sentence for his role in a protest in Minsk on 19 Dec. 2010 following announcement of Pres. Lukashenka's re-election May 2011; barred by court from leaving Minsk without written permission and from travelling outside Belarus for duration of sentence, also barred from attending public gatherings and meetings, ordered to present himself at a police station once a week, and told to stay at home between 8 pm and 6 am; attended OSCE conf. on human rights in Warsaw and thereafter summoned by the police Sept. 2011; named a prisoner of conscience by Amnesty International who called for his immediate and unconditional release; exempted by Leninski Dist Court in Minsk from serving two-year imprisonment sentence July 2013; mem. Union of Writers of USSR 1978; Order of the Badge of Honour 1986; First Prize, First Int. Festival of Slavic Poetry 'Singing Letters', Tver, Russia 2009. *Publications include:* Adkryccio (Disovery) 1976, Vynachodcy viatrou (Inventors of the Winds) (Prize of Lenin Komsomol) 1979, Znak achovy (The Sign of Protection) 1983, Mestnoe vremja (Local Time) 1983, Naskroz (Throughout) 1985, Halubinaja posta (Pigeon Mail) 1987, Derevo boli (The Tree of Pain) 1989, Prosca (Proshcha) (State Award of Belaru 'Janka Kupala') 1996, Vybranaje (Selected Works) 1998, Labuch (Musician) (novel) 2003, Tak (Yes) 2004, Centar Europy (The Centre of Europe) (prose works) 2009, Kon (Con) 2010.

NYAMDORJ, Tsendiin, LLB, PhD; Mongolian lawyer and politician; *Minister of Justice and Home Affairs;* b. 1956, Aimag Uws; ed Leningrad Univ.; Div. Prosecutor and Head of Div., State Gen. Authority of Prosecutor 1981–88; First Deputy, Gen. Prosecutor's Office of Mil Affairs 1988–90; First Deputy Minister of Justice 1990–92; mem. People's Grand Hural (Parl.) 1992–, Chair. (Speaker)

2005–07; Minister of Justice and Home Affairs 2000–05, 2008–; mem. Mongolian People's Revolutionary Party. *Address:* Ministry of Justice and Home Affairs, Government Bldg 5, Khudaldaany Gudamj 6/1, Chingeltei District, Ulan Bator, Mongolia (office). *Telephone:* (11) 267014 (office). *Fax:* (11) 325225 (office). *E-mail:* admin@mojha.gov.mn (office). *Website:* www.mojha.gov.mn (office).

NYAN WIN, Maj.-Gen.; Myanma government official; *Chief Minister of Bago Region;* b. 22 Jan. 1953; m. Myint Myint Soe; ed Defence Services Acad.; fmr mem. of staff, Office of Strategic Studies; served as Commdt, Command and Gen. Staff Coll.; Deputy Chief of Defence Services Training –2004; Minister of Foreign Affairs 2004–11; won a Regional Hluttaw seat in an uncontested election, representing Zigon Township 2010; Chief Minister of Bago Region 2011–; mem. Nat. Convention Convening Comm.

NYANDA, Gen. Siphiwe, (Gebhuza), BA, MSc; South African army officer (retd); b. 22 May 1950, Soweto; s. of Henry Nyanda and Betsy Nyanda; two s. five d.; ed Orlando High School, Soweto, Univ. of S Africa, Univ. of London, UK; fmrly sports journalist; trained in fmr GDR and USSR as platoon commdr, artilleryman and in intelligence; mem. African Nat. Congress (ANC), fmrly guerrilla fighter for ANC, Commissar of Transvaal Region 1979–86, mem. Nat. Exec. Cttee 1991–96, 2007–; Deputy Chief, S African Nat. Defence Force 1997–98, Chief 1998–2005; Minister of Communications 2009–10; Parl. Counsellor to Pres. Jacob Zuma 2010–; Chief of Staff, Mkhonto we Sizwe 1992–94; Chevalier, Légion d'honneur and other decorations; Mil. Merit Medal 1995, Gold Star of South Africa 1998, American Legion of Honor, Star of South Africa. *Publications:* articles in newspapers and ANC publs. *Leisure interests:* reading, watching soccer, playing golf, aerobics, chess. *Address:* 15 Westminster Avenue, Bryanstown, South Africa (home). *Telephone:* (11) 4632778 (home). *Fax:* (11) 4632847 (home). *E-mail:* s.nyanda@ mweb.co.za (home).

NYCZ, HE Cardinal Kazimierz; Polish ecclesiastic; *Archbishop of Warsaw and Bishop of Poland, Faithful of Eastern Rites;* b. 1 Feb. 1950, Stara Wieś, Gmina Wilamowice dist, Bielsko Co., Silesian Voivodeship; ed Lyceum of Maria Skłodowska-Curie, Czechowice-Dziedzice, Major Seminary of Kraków, Faculty of Theology of Papieska Akademia Teologiczna (Pontifical Acad. of Theology), Kraków, Catholic Univ. of Lublin; ordained deacon, Diocese of Kraków 1972; ordained priest, Diocese of 1973; vicar in a parish of St Elisabeth, Jaworzno 1973–75; Vice-Rector Major Seminary of Kraków 1987–88; Auxiliary Bishop of Kraków and Titular Bishop of Villa Regis 1988–2004; apptd Chair. Cttee for Catholic Educ. 1999; served as Chair. Comm. for Educ. of Conf. of the Polish Episcopate; Bishop of Koszalin-Kołobrzeg 2004–07; Archbishop of Warsaw 2007–; Bishop of Poland, Faithful of Eastern Rites 2007–; cr. Cardinal (Cardinal-Priest of Santi Silvestro e Martino ai Monti) 2010; participated in Papal Conclave 2013. *Address:* Archdiocese of Warsaw, 00-246 Warsaw, ul. Miodow 17–19, Poland (office). *Telephone:* (22) 531-72-00 (office). *Fax:* (22) 635-43-24 (office). *E-mail:* info@ archidiecezja.warszawa.pl (office). *Website:* www.archidiecezja.warszawa.pl (office).

NYE, John Frederick, MA, PhD, FRS, FInstP; British physicist and academic; *Professor Emeritus of Physics, University of Bristol;* b. 26 Feb. 1923, Hove, Sussex, England; s. of Haydn Percival Nye and Jessie Mary Nye (née Hague); brother of Peter Hague Nye; m. Georgiana Wiebenson 1953; one s. two d.; ed Stowe School, King's Coll., Cambridge; Demonstrator, Dept of Mineralogy and Petrology, Univ. of Cambridge 1949–51; mem. of Tech. Staff, Bell Telephone Labs, NJ 1952–53; Lecturer in Physics, Univ. of Bristol 1953–65, Reader 1965–69, Prof. 1969–88, Prof. Emer. 1988–; Pres. Int. Glaciological Soc. 1966–69, Int. Comm. of Snow and Ice 1971–75; Foreign mem. Royal Swedish Acad. of Sciences 1977; glacier in Palmer Peninsula, Antarctica officially named Nye Glacier 1963, Seligman Crystal Int. Glaciological Soc. 1969, Antarctic Service Medal (USA) 1974, Charles Chree Medal and Prize, Inst. of Physics 1989. *Publications:* Physical Properties of Crystals 1957, Natural Focusing and Fine Structure of Light 1999; numerous papers in scientific journals on glaciers, physics of ice, waves and math. catastrophes. *Leisure interest:* gardening. *Address:* University of Bristol, H.H. Wills Physics Laboratory, Royal Fort, Tyndall Avenue, Bristol, BS8 ITL (office); 45 Canynge Road, Bristol, BS8 3LH, England (home). *Telephone:* (117) 928-8727 (office); (117) 973-3769 (home). *E-mail:* john.nye@bristol.ac.uk (office). *Website:* www.phy.bris.ac.uk (office).

NYE, Joseph Samuel, Jr, BA, PhD, FBA; American political scientist, academic and fmr government official; *University Distinguished Service Professor, Harvard University;* b. 19 Jan. 1937, NJ; s. of Joseph Nye and Else Ashwell; m. Molly Harding 1961; three s.; ed Princeton and Harvard Univs, Univ. of Oxford, UK; Prof. of Govt, Harvard Univ. 1969–, also Dir Centre for Int. Affairs 1989–93, Dean and Don K. Price Prof. of Public Policy, John F. Kennedy School of Govt 1995–2004, Univ. Distinguished Service Prof. 2004–; Deputy Under-Sec. Dept of State, Washington, DC 1977–79, Chair. Nat. Intelligence Council 1992–; Asst Sec. of Defense for Int. Security Affairs 1994–95; mem. Trilateral Comm.; mem. Council, Int. Inst. of Strategic Studies; mem. Council on Foreign Relations; Fellow, American Acad. of Arts and Sciences, American Acad. of Diplomacy, Aspen Inst.; Dept of State Distinguished Honor Award 1979, Intelligence Distinguished Service Award 1994, Dept of Defense Distinguished Service Medal 1995, Charles E. Merriman Award, American Political Science Asscn 2003, Woodrow Wilson Award, Princeton Univ. 2004. *Publications include:* Power and Independence (co-author) 1977, The Making of America's Soviet Policy (co-author and ed.) 1984, Hawks, Doves and Owls (co-author and ed.) 1985, Nuclear Ethics 1986, Fateful Visions (co-ed.) 1988, Bound to Lead: The Changing Nature of American Power (co-ed.) 1990, Understanding International Conflicts: An Introduction to Theory and History 1993 (fourth edn) 2002, Governance in a Globalizing World 2000, The Paradox of American Power 2002, Soft Power: The Means to Success in World Politics 2004, Power in a Global Information Age 2004, The Power Game (novel) 2004, The Powers to Lead 2008, The Future of Power 2011, Presidential Leadership and the Creation of the American Era 2013. *Leisure interests:* fly fishing, skiing, hiking, hunting, gardening. *Address:* John F. Kennedy School of Government, Harvard University, Mailbox 124, 79 John F. Kennedy Street, Cambridge, MA 02138-5801, USA (office). *Telephone:* (617) 495-1123 (office). *Fax:* (617) 496-3337 (office). *E-mail:* joseph_nye@hks.harvard.edu (office). *Website:* www.hks.harvard.edu/about/faculty-staff-directory/joseph-nye (office).

NYE, Robert, FRSL; British poet, novelist and critic; b. 15 March 1939, London, England; s. of Oswald William Nye and Frances Dorothy Weller; m. 1st Judith Pratt 1959 (divorced 1967); three s.; m. 2nd Aileen Campbell 1968; one d. one step-s. one step-d.; ed Southend High School; freelance writer 1961–; Chief Book Reviewer, The Scotsman 1965–2000; contributes critical articles and reviews to British periodicals, including The Times and The Scotsman; Poetry Critic, The Times 1971–96; Eric Gregory Award 1963, Scottish Arts Council Bursary 1969, James Kennaway Memorial Award 1970, Guardian Fiction Prize 1976, Hawthornden Prize 1977, Soc. of Authors Travelling Scholarship 1991, Authors' Foundation Award 2003, 2007, Cholmondeley Award 2007. *Publications include:* poetry: Juvenilia 1 1961, Juvenilia 2 1963, Darker Ends 1969, Agnus Dei 1973, Two Prayers 1974, Five Dreams 1974, Divisions on a Ground 1976, A Collection of Poems 1955–1988 1989, 14 Poems 1994, Henry James and Other Poems 1995, Collected Poems 1995, 1998, The Rain and the Glass: 99 Poems, New and Selected 2005, Sixteen Poems 2005, One or Two Swallows 2008, An Almost Dancer 2012; novels: Doubtfire 1967, Falstaff 1976, Merlin 1978, Faust 1980, The Voyage of the Destiny 1982, The Facts of Life and Other Fictions 1983, The Memoirs of Lord Byron 1989, The Life and Death of My Lord Gilles de Rais 1990, Mrs Shakespeare: The Complete Works 1993, The Late Mr. Shakespeare 1998, and several children's books; plays; ed.: A Choice of Sir Walter Ralegh's Verse 1972, William Barnes of Dorset: A Selection of His Poems 1973, A Choice of Swinburne's Verse 1973, The English Sermon 1750–1850 1976, The Faber Book of Sonnets 1976, PEN New Poetry I 1986, First Awakenings: The Early Poems of Laura Riding (co-ed.) 1992, A Selection of the Poems of Laura Riding 1993, Some Poems by Ernest Dowson 2006, Some Poems by Thomas Chatterton 2007, Some Poems by Clere Parsons 2008, The Liquid Rhinoceros and other uncollected poems by Martin Seymour-Smith 2009, Some Poems by James Reeves 2009. *Address:* c/o Curtis Brown Ltd, 28–29 Haymarket, London, SW1Y 4SP, England (office). *Telephone:* (20) 7393-4400 (office). *Fax:* (20) 7393-4401 (office). *E-mail:* cb@curtisbrown.co.uk (office). *Website:* www.curtisbrown.co.uk (office).

NYEMBEZI-HEITA, Nonkululeko (Nku), BSc (Hons), MSc, MBA; South African business executive; *CEO, ArcelorMittal South Africa;* b. 22 March 1960, Pietermaritzburg, KwaZulu-Natal; d. of Aubrey Vulindlela Nyembezi and Dibiya Merina; m. Sam Ndahupula Heita; one s. one d.; ed Univ. of Manchester Inst. of Science and Tech. and Open Univ., UK, California Inst. of Tech., USA; engineer, IBM, Research Triangle Park, NC, USA 1984–86, moved to S Africa, Account Sales Rep., IBM SA 1986–93, Regional Man. 1993–98, also involved in establishment of IBM in Namibia; CEO Alliance Capital SA 1998–2005, Chair. Alliance Capital Namibia; Head of Mergers and Acquisitions, Vodacom Group 2005–08; CEO ArcelorMittal SA 2008–; mem. Bd of Dirs Macsteel International, Kalagadi Manganese, Arivia.kom; Chair. Bond Exchange of SA 2004–; Anglo-American Prize Scholarship, ranked by Forbes magazine amongst The World's 100 Most Powerful Women (97th) 2011. *Leisure interests:* reading, walking, Pilates, yoga, listening to jazz and classical music. *Address:* ArcelorMittal South Africa Corporate Office, Delfos Boulevard, Vanderbijlpark, South Africa (office). *Telephone:* (16) 8899111 (office). *Fax:* (16) 8894318 (office). *E-mail:* info@arcelormittalsa.com (office). *Website:* www.arcelormittalsa.com (office).

NYEMBO SHABANI, DSc (Econ); Democratic Republic of the Congo politician, economist and academic; b. 5 Aug. 1937, Kayanza; ed Inst. Saint Boniface, Elisabethville (now Lubumbashi) and Univ. Catholique de Louvain, Belgium; Dir, Bureau of Econ. Co-operation attached to the Prime Minister's Office 1964–65; Research in Econs, Univ. Catholique de Louvain 1967–76; Prof., Faculty of Econ. Science, Nat. Univ. of Zaïre Oct. 1976; State Commr for Nat. Econ. and Industry Feb.–Aug. 1977, for Nat. Econ. 1977–78, for the State Portfolio (Investments) 1978–80, for Agric. and Rural Devt 1980–81, 1983–84, for Econ., Industry and Foreign Trade 1982–83, for Finance and Budget 1986–88, for Agric. 1988–89; Pres. Gécamines Holdings 1985. *Publications:* L'industrie du cuivre dans le monde, Le progrès économique du Copperbelt Africain, Bruxelles, La Renaissance du Livre 1975. *Address:* BP 3.824, Kinshasa 1, Democratic Republic of the Congo.

NYMAN, Michael, CBE; British composer; b. 23 March 1944, London; ed Royal Acad. of Music, King's Coll. London; composer, writer and music critic 1968–78; lecturer 1976–80; established MN Records label 2005–; Hon. DLitt. *Film and television soundtracks:* Peter Greenaway films: 5 Postcards from Capital Cities 1967, Vertical Features Remake 1976, Goole by Numbers 1976, A Walk Through H: The Reincarnation of an Ornithologist 1978, 1–100 1978, The Falls 1980, Act of God 1980, Terence Conran 1981, The Draughtsman's Contract 1982, The Coastline 1983, Making a Splash 1984, A Zed and Two Noughts 1985, Inside Rooms: 26 Bathrooms, London & Oxfordshire 1985, Drowning by Numbers 1988, Fear of Drowning 1988, Death in the Seine 1988, The Cook, The Thief, His Wife and Her Lover 1989, Hubert Bals Handshake 1989, Prospero's Books 1991; other films: Keep It Downstairs 1976, Tom Phillips 1977, Brimstone and Treacle 1982, Nelly's Version 1983, Frozen Music 1983, The Cold Room 1984, Fairly Secret Army 1984, The Kiss 1985, L'ange frénétique 1985, I'll Stake My Cremona to a Jew's Trump 1985, The Disputation 1986, Ballet méchanique 1986, Le miraculé 1987, The Man Who Mistook His Wife for a Hat 1987, Monsieur Hire 1989, Out of the Ruins 1989, Le mari de la coiffeuse 1990, Men of Steel 1990, Les enfants volants 1990, Not Mozart: Letters, Riddles and Writs 1991, The Final Score 1992, The Fall of Icarus 1992, The Piano 1993, Ryori no tetsujin 1993, Mesmer 1994, A la folie (Six Days, Six Nights) 1994, Carrington 1995, Anne no nikki (The Diary of Anne Frank) 1995, Der Unhold (The Ogre) 1996, Enemy Zero 1996, Gattaca 1997, Titch 1998, Ravenous 1999, How to Make Dhyrak: A Dramatic Work for Three Players and Camera, Truncated with Only Two Players 1999, Wonderland 1999, Nabbie no koi (Nabbie's Love) 1999, The End of the Affair 1999, The Claim 2000, Act Without Words I 2000, That Sinking Feeling 2000, La Stanza del figlio 2001, Subterrain 2001, 24 heures de la vie d'une femme 2002, The Man with a Movie Camera 2002, The Actors 2003, Nathalie. . . 2003, Charged 2003, Ident (Channel 5) 2004, Man on Wire 2007, The Eleventh Year 2009, The Trip 2010, 2 Graves 2010, Everyday 2012. *Other compositions:* orchestral: A Handsome, Smooth, Sweet, Smart, Clear Stroke: Or Else Play Not At All 1983, Taking a Line for a Second Walk 1984, L'Orgie Parisienne 1989, Six Celan Songs 1990, Where the Bee Dances 1991, Self Laudatory Hymn of Inanna and Her Omnipotence 1992, The Upside-Down Violin 1992, MGV (Musique à Grande Vitesse) 1993, On the Fiddle 1993, Concerto for

Harpsichord and Strings 1995, Concerto for Trombone 1995, Double Concerto 1996, Strong on Oaks, Strong on the Causes of Oaks 1997, Cycle of Disquietude 1998, a dance he little thinks of 2001, The Draughtsman's Contract for Orchestra 2001, Dance of the Engines 2002, Gattaca for Orchestra 2003, The Claim for Orchestra 2003, The Piano: Concert Suite 2003, Violin Concerto 2003; chamber music: First Waltz in D, Bell Set No. 1 1974, 1–100 1976, Waltz in F 1976, Think Slow, Act Fast 1981, 2 Violins 1981, Four Saxes (Real Slow Drag) 1982, I'll Stake My Cremona to a Jew's Crump 1983, Time's Up 1983, Child's Play 1985, String Quartet No. 1 1985, Taking a Line for a Second Walk 1986, String Quartet No. 2 1988, String Quartet No. 3 1990, In Re Don Giovanni 1991, Masque Arias 1991, Time Will Pronounce 1992, Songs for Tony 1993, Three Quartets 1994, H.R.T. 1995, String Quartet No. 4 1995, Free for All 2001, Five Who Figured Four Years Ago 2002, Mapping 2002, Yellow Beach 2002, 24 Hour Sax Quartet 2004, For John Peel 2004; instrumental: Shaping the Curve 1990, Six Celan Songs 1990, Flugelhorn and Piano 1991, For John Cage 1992, The Convertibility of Lute Strings 1992, Here to There 1993, Yamamoto Perpetuo 1993, On the Fiddle 1993, To Morrow 1994, Tango for Tim 1994, Elisabeth Gets Her Way 1995, Viola and Piano 1995, Titch 1997, Fourths, Mostly (for organ) 2001; dramatic works: Strange Attractors, The Princess of Milan, A Broken Set of Rules 1984, Basic Black 1984, Portraits in Reflection 1985, And Do They Do 1986, The Man Who Mistook His Wife for a Hat 1986, Miniatures/Configurations 1988, Letters, Riddles and Writs 1991, Noises, Sounds and Sweet Airs 1994, Facing Goya 2000, Man and Boy: Dada (opera) 2003, Love Counts 2004; vocal: A Neat Slice of Time 1980, The Abbess of Andouillets 1984, Out of the Ruins 1989, Polish Love Song 1990, Shaping the Curve 1991, Anne de Lucy Songs 1992, Mozart on Mortality 1992, Grounded 1995, The Waltz Song 1995, The Ballad of Kastriot Rexhepi 2001, Mosè 2001, A Child's View of Colour 2003, Acts of Beauty 2004; with Michael Nyman Band: In Re Don Giovanni 1977, The Masterwork/Award-Winning Fishknife 1979, Bird List Song 1979, Five Orchestral Pieces Opus Tree 1981, Bird Anthem 1981, M-Work 1981, Love is Certainly, at Least Alphabetically Speaking 1983, Bird Work 1984, The Fall of Icarus 1989, La Traversée de Paris 1989, The Final Score 1992, AET (After Extra Time) 1996, De Granada a la Luna 1998, Orfeu 1998, The Commissar Vanishes 1999, Man with a Movie Camera 2001, Compiling the Colours (Samhitha) 2003, Three Ways of Describing Rain (Sawan; Rang; Dhyan) 2003, Zeit und Ziel 1814–2002, Manhatta 2003; dance: Flicker 2005. *Films:* Cine Opera 2009, Nyman with a Movie Camera 2010. *Recordings include:* film soundtracks, The Piano Sings 2005. *Publications:* Libretto for Birtwistle's Dramatic Pastoral, Down by the Greenwood Side 1968–69, Experimental Music: Cage and Beyond 1974; contribs: critical articles to journals, including The Spectator. *E-mail:* myriam@michaelnyman.com (office); office@michaelnyman.com. *Website:* www.michaelnyman.com.

NYRUP RASMUSSEN, Poul; Danish politician; b. 15 June 1943, Esbjerg, Western Jutland; s. of Olof Nyrup Rasmussen and Vera Nyrup Rasmussen; m. 1st (divorced); m. 2nd (divorced); m. 3rd Lone Dybkjær; one c. (deceased); ed Esbjerg Statsskole and Univ. of Copenhagen; worked for Danish Trade Union Council in Brussels for a year; Chief Economist, Danish Trade Union Council 1981; Man. Dir Employees' Capital Pension Fund 1986–88; Deputy Chair. SDP 1987–92, Chair. 1992–2002; mem. Folketing (Parl.) 1988–2004; Prime Minister 1993–2001; MEP 2004–09, Pres. Party of European Socialists 2004–11. *Leisure interests:* music, spending time with his wife and grandchild. *Address:* c/o Office 11, G 130, European Parliament, Rue Wiertz, 1047, Brussels, Belgium. *Website:* www.nyrup.dk.

NYUSI, Filipe Jacinto, MA; Mozambican engineer and politician; b. 9 Feb. 1959, Namaua, Mueda, Cabo Delgado; s. of the late Jacinto Nhussi Chimela and Angelina Daima; ed Mil. Acad., Brno, Czechoslovakia, Univ. of Manchester, UK, Indian Inst. of Man., Ahmadbad; Exec. Dir CMF-Norte, Mozambique Ports and Railways 1992–2007, mem. Bd of Dirs 2007–; Minister of Nat. Defence 2007–14; Pres. Clube Ferroviário de Nampula (football club) 1993–2002; Fellow, Africa Leadership Initiative; mem. Frente de Libertação de Moçambique (Frelimo), mem. Cen. Cttee 2012–, selected as Frelimo cand. in presidential elections March 2014; Hon. Mention in Czechoslovakia 1990. *Leisure interests:* singing, football. *Address:* Frelimo, Rua Pereira do Lago 10, Bairro de Sommerschield, Maputo, Mozambique (office). *Telephone:* 21490181 (office). *Fax:* 21490008 (office). *E-mail:* info@frelimo.org.mz (office). *Website:* www.frelimo.org.mz (office).

NZAMBIMANA, Lt-Col Édouard; Burundian politician and army officer; b. 20 Dec. 1945; Minister of Public Works, Transport and Equipment 1974–76; participated in coup that overthrew Pres. Micombero Nov. 1976; Prime Minister 1976–78 and Minister of Planning 1976–78, of Agric., Livestock and Rural Devt 1978, of Foreign Affairs and Co-operation 1978–82; later Chair. Union Commerciale d'Assurances et de Réassurance (UCAR). *Address:* Union Commerciale d'Assurances et de Réassurance, BP 3012, Bujumbura, Burundi. *Telephone:* 223638. *Fax:* 223695. *E-mail:* info@ucar.bi.

NZAPAYÉKÉ, André; Central African Republic international banking official and government official; *Prime Minister;* b. 20 Aug. 1951, Bangassou; ed Univ. of Amsterdam, The Netherlands; Minister of Rural Devt in 1990s; f. COSSOSIM (research consultancy), Bangui; postings with several int. orgs including World Bank, UN, Luxembourg Devt Corpn; Governance and Institutional Reforms Expert, African Devt Bank, Tunis 2001–09, Chair., Staff Council 2009–10, Exec. Dir 2010–12; Vice-Pres. Banque de Développement des Etats de l'Afrique Centrale (Central African States Devt Bank) 2012–14; Prime Minister 2014–. *Address:* Office of the Prime Minister, BP 932, Bangui, Central African Republic (office). *Telephone:* 21-61-59-23 (office). *E-mail:* contact@primature-rca.org (office). *Website:* www.primature-rca.org (office).

NZOMUKUNDA, Alice; Burundian politician; b. 12 April 1966; trained as accountant; elected mem. Parl. for Bujumbura, First Vice-Pres. of Nat. Ass. 2007–08; Second Vice-Pres. of Burundi in charge of Econ. and Social Affairs 2005–06 (resgnd); Founder and Leader, Alliance Démocratique pour le Renouveau 2008–; Vice-Pres. for Southern Africa, Africa Liberal Network 2012–. *Address:* Alliance Democratique pour le Renouveau, Bwiza, 4ème Avenue, BP 3055, Bujumbura, Burundi.

O

OAKDEN, Edward Anthony, CMG; British government official and diplomatist; *Managing Director, Sectors Group, UK Trade and Investment;* b. 3 Nov. 1955; m. Ana Oakden; two d.; ed School of Oriental and African Studies, London; Repub. of Ireland Dept, FCO 1981–82, Third Sec. (Chancery), Embassy in Baghdad 1984–85, Second Sec. (Chancery), Embassy in Khartoum 1985–88, Pvt. Sec. to the Amb., Embassy in Washington, DC 1988–92, Asst Head of EC Dept (External), FCO 1992–94, Asst Head of Eastern Adriatic Unit 1994–95, Pvt. Sec. to Prime Minister 1995–97, Deputy Head of EU Union Dept (Internal), FCO 1997–98, Deputy Head of Mission, Embassy in Madrid 1998–2002, Head of Security Policy Dept, FCO 2002, Dir for Defence and Strategic Threats and Envoy for Counter-Terrorism 2002–06, Amb. to UAE 2006–10; Man. Dir, Sectors Group, UK Trade and Investment 2010–. *Address:* UK Trade and Investment, Kingsgate House, 66–74 Victoria Street, London, SW1E 6SW, England (office). *Telephone:* (20) 7215-8000 (office). *E-mail:* enquiries@ukti.gsi.gov.uk (office). *Website:* www.uktradeinvest.gov.uk (office).

OAKLEY, Ann, BA, MA, PhD; British sociologist, writer and academic; *Professor of Social Policy and Founding Director, Social Science Research Unit, Institute of Education, University of London;* b. 17 Jan. 1944, London, England; d. of the late Richard Titmuss and Kay Titmuss; m. Robin Oakley; three c.; ed Chiswick Polytechnic, Somerville Coll., Oxford, Bedford Coll., London; Research Fellow, Bedford Coll., Univ. of London 1974–79, Univ. of Oxford 1979–84; Deputy Dir Thomas Coram Research Unit, Univ. of London 1985–90; Prof. of Social Policy and Dir Social Science Research Unit, Inst. of Educ., Univ. of London 1991–2005, Founding Dir Social Science Research Unit 2005–; mem. Acad. of Social Sciences; Hon. Prof., Univ. Coll. London 1996–2005; Hon. Fellow, Somerville Coll., Oxford 2001–; Hon. DLitt (Salford) 1995; Hon. DSc (Edinburgh); Lifetime Achievement Award, British Sociological Asscn 2011. *Publications include:* novels: The Men's Room (adapted for TV 1991) 1988; as Rosamund Clay: Only Angels Forget 1990; as Ann Oakley: Matilda's Mistake 1991, The Secret Lives of Eleanor Jenkinson 1992, Scenes Orginating in the Garden of Eden 1993, A Proper Holiday 1996, Overheads 1999; two short stories; non-fiction: Sex, Gender and Society 1972, Housewife 1974, The Sociology of Housework 1974, The Rights and Wrongs of Women (co-ed.) 1976, Becoming a Mother (also published as From Here to Maternity 1981) 1979, Women Confined: Towards a Sociology of Childbirth 1980, Subject Women 1981, Miscarriage (with A. McPherson and H. Roberts) 1984, The Captured Womb: A History of the Medical Care of Pregnant Women 1984, Taking It Like a Woman 1984, What is Feminism? (co-ed.) 1986, Telling the Truth about Jerusalem: Selected Essays 1986, Helpers in Childbirth: Midwifery Today (with S. Houd) 1990, Social Support and Motherhood: The Natural History of a Research Project 1992, Essays on Women, Medicine and Health 1993, Young People, Health and Family Life (with others) 1994, The Politics of the Welfare State (co-ed.) 1994, Evaluating Social Interventions: A Report on Two Workshops (co-ed.) 1996, Man and Wife: Richard and Kay Titmuss, My Parents' Early Years 1996, Who's Afraid of Feminism? (co-ed.) 1997, The Gift Relationship: From Human Blood to Social Policy (co-ed.) 1997, Welfare Research: A Critical Review (co-ed.) 1998, Experiments in Knowing: Gender and Method in the Social Sciences 2000, Welfare and Being: Richard Titmuss's Contribution to Social Policy (co-ed.) 2001, Gender on Planet Earth 2002, The Ann Oakley Reader 2005, Fracture: Adventures of a Broken Body 2007, A Critical Woman: Barbara Wootton, Social Science and Public Policy in the Twentieth Century 2011. *Leisure interests:* cycling, grandchildren. *Address:* c/o The Sayle Literary Agency, 1 Petersfield, Cambridge, CB1 1BB, England (office); Social Science Research Unit, Institute of Education, University of London, Room 102, 18 Woburn Square, London, WC1H 0NR, England (office). *Telephone:* (1223) 303035 (office); (20) 7612-6380 (office). *E-mail:* info@sayleliteraryagency.com (office); a.oakley@ioe.ac.uk (office). *Website:* www.sayleliteraryagency.com (office); www.ioe.ac.uk/SSRU (office); www.annoakley.co.uk (home). *Fax:* (20) 7612-6400 (office).

OATES, Joyce Carol, (Rosamond Smith, Lauren Kelly), MA; American writer, poet, publisher and academic; *Roger S. Berlind '52 Professor in the Humanities, Princeton University;* b. 16 June 1938, Lockport, NY; d. of Frederic J. Oates and Caroline Bush; m. Raymond J. Smith 1961; ed Syracuse Univ. and Univ. of Wisconsin; instructor, Univ. of Detroit 1961–65, Asst Prof. of English 1965–67; Faculty mem. Dept of English, Univ. of Windsor, Ont. 1967–78; publr (with Raymond Joseph Smith) Ontario Review 1974–; Writer-in-Residence, Princeton Univ. 1978–81, Prof. 1987–, currently Roger S. Berlind '52 Prof. in the Humanities; mem. American Acad., Inst. of Arts and Letters; Guggenheim Fellow 1967–68; O. Henry Prize Story Award 1967, 1968, Rea Award for Short Story 1990, Elmer Holmes Bukst Award 1990, Ivan Sandrof Lifetime Achievement Award, Nat. Book Critics' Circle 2009. *Plays:* Three Plays: Ontological Proof of My Existence, Miracle Play, The Triumph of the Spider Monkey 1980, Twelve Plays 1991, The Perfectionist and Other Plays 1995. *Publications:* novels: With Shuddering Fall 1964, A Garden of Earthly Delights 1967, Expensive People 1968, Them 1969, Wonderland 1971, Do with Me What You Will 1973, The Assassins: A Book of Hours 1975, Childworld 1976, Son of the Morning 1978, Unholy Loves 1979, Cybele 1979, Bellefleur 1980, A Sentimental Education 1981, Angel of Light 1981, A Bloodsmoor Romance 1982, Mysteries of Winterthurn 1984, Solstice 1985, Marya: A Life 1986, You Must Remember This 1987, American Appetites 1989, Because It is Bitter and Because It is My Heart 1990, Black Water 1992, Foxfire 1993, What I Lived For 1994, Zombie 1995, First Love: A Gothic Tale 1996, We Were the Mulvaneys 1996, Man Crazy 1997, My Heart Laid Bare 1998, Come Meet Muffin 1998, The Collector of Hearts 1999, Broke Heart Blues 1999, Blonde: A Novel 2000, Middle Age: A Romance 2002, I'll Take You There 2002, Big Mouth and Ugly Girl 2002, The Tattooed Girl 2004, Rape: A Love Story 2004, I Am No One You Know 2004, The Falls 2004, Mother, Missing 2005, The Gravedigger's Daughter 2007, My Sister, My Love: The Intimate Story of Skyler Rampike 2008, Little Bird of Heaven 2009, A Fair Maiden 2010, Blonde 2011, Mudwoman 2012, Two or Three Things I Forgot to Tell You 2012, The Accursed 2013; short story collections: By the North Gate 1963, Upon the Sweeping Flood and Other Stories 1966, The Wheel of Love 1970, Cupid and Psyche 1970, Marriages and Infidelities 1972, A Posthumous Sketch 1973, The Girl 1974, Plagiarized Material 1974, The

Goddess and Other Women 1974, Where Are You Going, Where Have You Been?: Stories of Young America 1974, The Hungry Ghosts: Seven Allusive Comedies 1974, The Seduction and Other Stories 1975, The Poisoned Kiss and Other Stories from the Portuguese 1975, The Triumph of the Spider Monkey 1976, Crossing the Border 1976, Night-Side 1977, The Step-Father 1978, All the Good People I've Left Behind 1979, Queen of the Night 1979, The Lamb of Abyssalia 1979, A Middle-Class Education 1980, A Sentimental Education 1980, Last Day 1984, Wild Saturday and Other Stories 1984, Wild Nights 1985, Raven's Wing 1986, The Assignation 1988, Heat and Other Stories 1991, Where is Here? 1992, Haunted Tales of the Grotesque 1994, Faithless: Tales of Transgression 2001, The Female of the Species 2006, High Lonesome: New & Selected Stories 1966–2006 2006, Wild Nights! 2008, Museum of Doctor Moses 2008, Sourland 2010, Give Me Your Heart 2011, The Maiden and Other Nightmares 2011; poetry: Women in Love and Other Poems 1968, Anonymous Sins and Other Poems 1969, Them (Nat. Book Award 1970) 1969, Love and its Derangements 1970, Wooded Forms 1972, Angel Fire 1973, Dreaming America and Other Poems 1973, The Fabulous Beasts 1975, Seasons of Peril 1977, Women Whose Lives are Food, Men Whose Lives are Money 1978, Celestial Timepiece 1980, Nightless Nights: Nine Poems 1981, Invisible Women: New and Selected Poems 1970–1982 1982, Luxury of Sin 1984, The Time Traveller: Poems 1983–1989 1989; non-fiction: The Edge of Impossibility: Tragic Forms in Literature 1972, The Hostile Sun: The Poetry of D. H. Lawrence 1973, New Heaven, New Earth: The Visionary Experience in Literature 1974, The Stone Orchard 1980, Contraries: Essays 1981, The Profane Art: Essays and Reviews 1983, Funland 1983, On Boxing 1987, (Woman) Writer: Occasions and Opportunities 1988, George Bellows: American Artist (biog.) 1995, The Faith of a Writer: Life, Craft, Art 2004, Black Girl/White Girl 2006, The Journals of Joyce Carol Oates: 1973–1982 2007, In Rough Country: Essays and Reviews 2010; editor: Scenes from American Life: Contemporary Short Fiction 1973, The Best American Short Stories 1979 (with Shannon Ravenel) 1979, Night Walks: A Bedside Companion 1982, First Person Singular: Writers on Their Craft 1983, Story: Fictions Past and Present (with Boyd Litzinger) 1985, Reading the Fights (with Daniel Halpern) 1988, The Oxford Book of American Short Stories 1993, The Best American Mystery Stories 2006; as Rosamond Smith: The Lives of the Twins 1987, Kindred Passions 1988, Soul-Mate 1989, Nemesis 1990, Snake Eyes 1992, You Can't Catch Me 1995, Double Delight 1997, Starr Bright Will Be with You Soon 1999, The Barrens 2001, Beasts 2003; fiction in nat. magazines. *Address:* Department of Creative Writing, Princeton University, 185 Nassau Street, Princeton, NJ 08544 (office); c/o John Hawkins, 71 West 23rd Street, Suite 1600, New York, NY 10010, USA. *Website:* www.princeton.edu/~visarts/cwr.

OBADIA, Nathalie, MA; French art dealer; ed Univ. Panthéon-Assas, Institut d'études politiques de Paris (Sciences-Po); worked as a sr dir at Galerie Daniel Templon, Paris 1988–93; opened own gallery Rue de Normandie in the Marais 1993; has introduced artists including Huma Bhabha, Guy Ben-Ner, Cameron Jamie, Frank Nitsche and Chloe Piene; Galerie Obadia opened in Oct. 2008, joined by Sarkis, a French artist from Turkey with second gallery opening in Brussels; mem. bureau of the French professional cttee of art galleries, Vice-Chair. 2005–08; Officier des Arts et des Lettres 2009. *Publication:* published in partnership with Thea Westreich/Ethan Wagner a significant monograph on Martin Barré, including the English trans. of the reference text by Yve-Alain Bois. *Address:* Galerie Obadia, 18 rue du Bourg-Tibourg, 75004 Paris, France (office). *Telephone:* 1-53-01-99-76 (office). *E-mail:* nathalie.obadia@galerie-obadia.com (office). *Website:* www.galerie-obadia.com (office).

OBAID, Thoraya Ahmed, BA, MA, PhD; Saudi Arabian fmr UN official; b. 2 March 1945, Baghdad, Iraq; m. Mahmoud Saleh; two d.; ed Mills Coll., Oakland, Wayne State Univ., Detroit, Mich., USA; mem. League of Arab States working group for formulating the Arab Strategy for Social Devt 1984–85; mem. Editorial Bd Journal of Arab Women 1984–90; mem. Int. Women's Advisory Panel, Int. Planned Parenthood Fed. 1993; Chair. UN Inter-agency Task Force on Gender, Amman 1996; mem. UN Inter-agency Gender Mission to Afghanistan Nov. 1997, UN Strategic Framework Mission to Afghanistan 1997; Assoc. Social Affairs Officer (Women and Devt), Econ. and Social Comm. for W Africa (ESCWA) Social Devt and Population Div. (SDPD) 1975–81, Women and Devt Programme Man., ESCWA SDPD 1981–92, Chief of ESCWA SDPD 1992–93, Deputy Exec. Sec. ESCWA 1993–98; Dir Div. for Arab States and Europe, UN Population Fund (UNFPA) 1998–2000, Exec. Dir and Under-Sec. Gen. UNFPA 2001–10; mem. Middle East Studies Asscn, Al-Nahdha Women's Philanthropic Asscn; Order of Dionisio de Herrera (Honduras) 2005; Dr hc of Law (Mills Coll.) 2002, (Kwansei Gakuin Univ., Japan) 2004; George P. Younger Award, UN Cttee of Religious NGOs 2002, Medal and Key to the City of Managua, Nicaragua 2003, Pedro Joaquin Chamorro Award, Nicaragua 2003, Second Century Award for Excellence in Health Care, Columbia Univ. 2003, Commemorative Medal, Bulgaria 2006, Louis B. Sohn Human Rights Award 2009. *Address:* c/o UN Population Fund, 220 East 42nd Street, 19th Floor, New York, NY 10017, USA.

OBAIDI, Gen. Abd al-Qader Jasim al-; Iraqi army officer and government official; b. 1947, Ramadi; fmr Gen. in Iraqi army under Saddam Hussein, rejoined army 2003, served as Commdr of Operations Centre, then Mil. Commdr in western Iraq, then Commdr infantry commando units; Minister of Defence 2006–10. *Address:* c/o Ministry of Defence, Baghdad, Iraq.

OBAMA, Barack Hussein, Jr, BA, JD; American lawyer, politician and head of state; *President;* b. 4 Aug. 1961, Honolulu, Hawaii; s. of the late Barack Obama, Sr and Ann Dunham; m. Michelle Obama (née Robinson) 1992; two d.; ed Punahou School, Hawaii, Occidental Coll., Columbia Univ., Harvard Law School; family lived in Hawaii and Indonesia; Ed.-in-Chief Harvard Law Review (first African-American) and mem. Exec. Bd Black Law Students Asscn, Harvard Univ.; writer and financial analyst, Business Int. Corpn 1984–85; Dir Developing Communities Project, Chicago 1985–88; worked for Bill Clinton's presidential election campaign as Dir Ill. Project Vote 1992; Assoc., Davis, Miner, Barnhill & Galland, PC (law firm), Chicago 1993–96, Of Counsel 1996–2004; Sr Lecturer, Univ. of Chicago Law School 1993–2004; mem. Ill. State Senate for 13th Senate Dist, S Chicago

1997–2005, Chair. Public Health and Welfare Cttee, mem. Judiciary Cttee, Revenue Cttee; lost Democratic primary for US House of Reps to incumbent Congressman Bobby Rush 2000; Senator from Ill. (third-ever African-American mem. of Senate) 2005–08; Pres. of USA (first African-American) 2009–; fmr Chair. Chicago Lawyers Cttee for Civil Rights under the Law, Chicago Annenberg Challenge; mem. Ill. Bar Asscn, Cook Co. Bar Asscn; Democrat; Hon. LLD (Knox Coll.) 2005, (Northwestern Univ.) 2005, (Univ. of Massachusetts) 2006, (Xavier Univ.) 2006, (Southern New Hampshire Univ.) 2007, (Harvard Univ.) 2007, (Wesleyan Univ.) 2008, (Univ. of Notre Dame) 2009; Grammy Award for Best Spoken Word Album (for audio-book version of The Audacity of Hope) 2008, named by TIME magazine as its Person of the Year 2008, Nobel Peace Prize 2009, ranked by Forbes magazine amongst The World's Most Powerful People (first) 2009, (second) 2010, (first) 2011–12, (second) 2013. *Publications:* Dreams from My Father 1995, The Audacity of Hope 2006, Of Thee I Sing: A Letter to My Daughters 2010. *Address:* The White House, 1600 Pennsylvania Avenue NW, Washington, DC 20500, USA (office). *Telephone:* (202) 456-1414 (office). *Fax:* (202) 456-2461 (office). *E-mail:* president@whitehouse.gov (office). *Website:* www.whitehouse.gov (office).

OBAMA, Michelle LaVaughn Robinson, BA, JD; American lawyer; *First Lady;* b. 17 Jan. 1964, Chicago, Ill.; d. of Fraser Robinson III and Marian Shields Robinson; m. Barack Obama 1992; two d.; ed Whitney Young High School, Chicago, Princeton Univ., Harvard Law School; Assoc., Sidley Austin (law firm), Chicago 1988–91; Asst to Chicago Mayor Richard M. Daley 1991–93, also Asst Commr of Planning and Devt; Exec. Dir Public Allies, Chicago 1993–96; Assoc. Dean of Student Services, Univ. of Chicago 1996–2002; Exec. Dir for Community Affairs, Univ. of Chicago Hosps 2002–05, Vice-Pres. for Community and External Affairs 2005–09; First Lady of USA 2009–; mem. Bd of Dirs Chicago Council on Global Affairs; ranked by Forbes magazine amongst World's 100 Most Powerful Women (40th) 2009, (first) 2010, (eighth) 2011, (seventh) 2012, (fourth) 2013. *Address:* The White House, 1600 Pennsylvania Avenue NW, Washington, DC 20500, USA (office). *Telephone:* (202) 456-1414 (office). *Fax:* (202) 456-2461 (office). *Website:* www.whitehouse.gov/administration/first-lady-michelle-obama (office).

OBANDO Y BRAVO, HE Cardinal Miguel; Nicaraguan ecclesiastic; *Archbishop Emeritus of Managua;* b. 2 Feb. 1926, La Libertad (Chontales), Juigalpa; ordained priest of Salesians of St John Bosco 1958; consecrated Bishop (Titular Church of Puzia in Byzacena) and apptd Auxiliary Bishop of Matagalpa 1968–70, Archbishop of Managua 1970–2005, Archbishop Emer. 2005–; cr. Cardinal (Cardinal-Priest of San Giovanni Evangelista a Spinaceto) 1985; Chair. Nat. Reconciliation Comm. for Nicaragua 1987; Pres. Episcopal Conf. of Nicaragua 1971–74, 1979–83, Episcopal Secr. of Cen. America and Panamá 1976–80; participated in Papal Conclave 2005; presided over the Peace and Reconciliation Comm. 2007; Order of Francisco Miranda (Venezuela) 1981; Dr hc (Universidad Francisco Marroquín) 1986; Bruno Kreysky Award (Austria), Plaque for Peace and Freedom of the Nicaraguan People, San Francisco, United States of America 1980, Letter of Brotherhood of the Piarist Soc., Managua 1980, Distinction of Loyalty to the Pope, the Church and the Nicaraguan People, Central of Nicaraguan Workers 1982. *Address:* c/o Arzobispado, Apartado 3058, Managua, Nicaragua. *Telephone:* (2) 277-1754. *Fax:* (2) 276-0130. *E-mail:* cen@tmx.com.ni (office). *Website:* www.curiamanagua.org.

OBASANJO, Gen. (retd) Olusegun Mathew Okikiola Aremu; Nigerian politician, UN official, fmr army officer and fmr head of state; b. 5 March 1937, Abeokuta, Ogun State; m. 1st Oluremi Akinbwon; two s. four d.; m. 2nd Stella Abebe (died 2005); ed Abeokuta Baptist High School and Mons Officers' Cadet School, UK; joined Nigerian Army 1958, commissioned 1959; served in Congo (now Democratic Repub. of the Congo) 1960; promoted Capt. 1963, Maj. 1965, Lt-Col 1967, Col 1969, Brig. 1972, Lt-Gen. 1976, Gen. 1979; Commdr Eng Corps 1963, later Commdr 2nd Div. (Rear), Ibadan; GOC 3rd Infantry Div. 1969; Commdr 3rd Marine Commando Div. during Nigerian Civil War, accepted surrender of Biafran forces Jan. 1970; Commdr Eng Corps 1970–75; Fed. Commr for Works and Housing Jan.–July 1975; Chief of Staff, Supreme HQ 1975–76; mem. Supreme Mil. Council 1975–79; Head of Fed. Mil. Govt and C-in-C of Armed Forces 1976–79; mem. Advisory Council of State 1979; arrested March 1995, interned 1995; Pres. of Nigeria and C-in-C of Armed Forces 1999–2007; Chair. Bd of Trustees, People's Democratic Party 2007; apptd UN Special Envoy for the Democratic Repub. of the Congo 2008; UN Special Rep. of Sec.-Gen. for the Great Lakes Region Dec. 2008–12; fmr Chair. African Union; Fellow, Univ. of Ibadan 1979–81; mem. Ind. Comm. on Disarmament and Security 1980, mem. Exec. Cttee Inter-Action Council of fmr Heads of Govt; Chair. Africa Leadership Forum and Foundation; Co-Chair. Eminent Persons Group on S Africa 1985; Grand Commdr, Order of the Fed. Repub. of Nigeria 1980; Hon. DHumLitt (Howard), Hon. LLD (Maiduguri) 1980, (Ahmadu Bello Univ., Zaria) 1985, (Ibadan) 1988, Dr hc (Namibia), (Bowen); Human Rights Prize, Friedrich–Ebert Foundation, Germany 1996, Indira Gandhi Peace Prize, India. *Publications include:* My Command 1980, Africa in Perspective 'Myths and Realities' 1987, Nzeogwu 1987, Africa Embattled 1988, Constitution for National Integration and Development 1989, Not My Will 1990, Elements of Development 1992, Elements of Democracy 1993, Africa: Rise to Challenge 1993, Hope for Africa 1993, Guide to Effective Prayer 1999, This Animal Called Man 1999, Women of Virtue 1999, A New Dawn 2000), Exemplary Youth in a Difficult World 2002, I See Hope 2002, Sermons from Prison 2002. *Leisure interests:* table tennis, squash, reading, writing. *Address:* Olusegun Obasanjo Presidential Library Foundation, Presidential Blvd, Oke-Mosan Abeokuta, Ogun State, Nigeria (office). *E-mail:* ortesev@yahoo.com (office); ooplibrary@yahoo.com (office). *Website:* www.ooplproject.org (office).

OBAYASHI, Takeo, MS; Japanese construction industry executive; *Chairman, Obayashi Corporation;* s. of the late Yoshiro Obayashi; m.; ed Keio Univ., Stanford Univ., Calif., USA; trained as civil engineer; joined Obayashi Corpn 1977, apptd Dir 1983, Rep. Dir 1989–, Vice-Pres. 1997–2003, Vice-Chair. 2003–07, Chair. 2007–; Chair. Obayashi Foundation; Man.-Dir Kansei Asscn of Corp. Execs; Vice-Chair. Osaka Chamber of Commerce and Industry; mem. Bd, Kansei Econ. Fed., Bd of Councillors, Int. Inst. for Advanced Studies Foundation, Bd of Visitors, Stanford Inst. for Int. Studies, Research Governance Cttee, Stanford Japan Center, Japanese Cttee of Honour, Royal Acad. of Arts, London, Int. Council, Tate Gallery, London, UK, Advisory Group, Asian Art Fairs Ltd; Trustee and mem.

Council, Museum of Modern Art; Hon. Consul of the Repub. of Lithuania 2008–. *Address:* Obayashi Corporation, Shinagawa Intercity Tower B, 2-15-2 Konan, Minato-ku, Tokyo 108-8502, Japan (office). *Telephone:* (3) 5769-1906 (office). *Fax:* (3) 5769-1910 (office). *E-mail:* info@obayashi.co.jp (office). *Website:* www.obayashi.co.jp (office).

OBEID, Atif Muhammad, MA, PhD; Egyptian politician; m.; two c.; ed Faculty of Commerce, Cairo Univ. and Univ. of Illinois; mem. Arab League Media Policy Co-ordinating Cttee 1970; fmr Prof. of Business Admin, Faculty of Commerce, Cairo Univ. and Pres. Int. Man. Centre; Minister of Cabinet Affairs and Minister of State for Admin. Devt 1985–93, Minister of the Public Enterprise Sector 1993–99; Prime Minister of Egypt 1999–2004 (resgnd). *Address:* c/o Sharia Majlis ash-Sha'ab, Lazoughli Square, Cairo, Egypt.

OBEID, Jean, BA; Lebanese politician; b. 8 May 1939, Alma, Zghorta; m. Loubna Emile El-Boustani; two s. three d.; ed Collège de Frères-Pères Carmélites-Lycée Officiel, Tripoli, St Joseph's Univ., Beirut; journalist, Magazine and Isbouh El Arabi 1959–62, Lissan Al Hal 1960–63, Al Nahar 1963–66, Assayad 1963–66, Ed. Assayad 1966–72; began political career 1973; adviser to Pres. Elias Sarkis of Lebanon 1973; counsellor and presidential del. to Summit of Non-Aligned States, New Delhi, India 1983; participated in Inter-Lebanese Nat. Reconciliation Conf., Geneva, Switzerland; Deputy of the Chouf 1991; Deputy for Tripoli, N Lebanon 1992; Minister of State 1993; Deputy for N Lebanon 1996–2004; Minister of Nat. Educ., Sports and Youth 1996–2003, of Foreign Affairs and Emigrants 2003–04; unsuccessful cand. for Pres. of Lebanon 2007. *Address:* c/o Ministry of Foreign Affairs and Emigrants, rue Sursock, Achrafieh, Beirut, Lebanon.

OBEIDAT, Ahmad Abdul-Majeed; Jordanian politician; b. 1938, Hartha, Irbid; m.; five c.; ed Salahiyah School and Univ. of Baghdad; teacher, Minister of Educ. 1957; Customs Officer 1961; First Lt-Gen. Security Service 1962–64; Asst Dir Gen. Intelligence Service 1964–74, Dir 1974–82; Minister of the Interior 1982–84; Prime Minister of Jordan and Minister of Defence 1984–85; Partner, Law and Arbitration Centre 1985–; fmr Deputy Speaker of the Senate; Pres. Jordan Environment Soc.; Chair. Bd of Trustees Nat. Centre for Human Rights. *Address:* Law and Arbitration Centre, PO Box 926544, Amman, Jordan. *Telephone:* 672222.

OBENG, Letitia Eva, BSc, MSc, PhD, FRSA; Ghanaian scientist, research director and environmental manager; b. (Takyibea Asihene), 10 Jan. 1925, Anum; d. of Rev. E. V. Asihene and Dora Asihene; m. George A. Obeng 1953; two s. one d.; ed Achimota Coll., Ghana, Univs of Birmingham and Liverpool, UK; Lecturer, Coll. of Science and Tech., Kumasi 1952–59; Research Scientist, Nat. Research Council, Ghana 1960–62; mem. research staff, Ghana Acad. of Sciences 1963–65; built and served as first Dir, Inst. of Aquatic Biology, Council for Scientific and Industrial Research, Ghana 1965–74; Project Co-Man., Ghana Govt/UNDP Volta Lake Research Project; Sr Programme Officer and Chair. Soil and Water Task Force, UNEP, Nairobi 1974–80; Regional Dir and Rep. of UNEP to Africa 1980–85; Dir Environmental Man. Services 1986; Distinguished Int. Visitor, Radcliffe Coll., USA 1992; mem. Exec. Council, Africa Leadership Forum 1991, Bd of Stockholm Environment Inst., PANOS 1986–95; Affiliate mem. Africa Leadership Forum, Royal Soc. (UK), New York Acad. of Sciences 1995, Int. Rice Research Inst., Int. Irrigation Man. Inst., Stockholm Environment Inst.; Fellow, Ghana Acad. of Arts and Sciences (fmr Pres.); Trustee, Bd of Int. Rice Research Inst., Int. Irrigation Man. Inst., Human Ecology Foundation; Star of Ghana 2006; Silver Medal, Royal Soc. of Arts, Ghana Council for Scientific and Industrial Research (CSIR) Award 1997, Ghana Govt Award for Biological Sciences 1998, CSIR Bldg named The Letitia Obeng Block 1998; featured on nat. commemorative postage stamp. *Publications:* Man-made Lakes (ed.) 1969, Environment and the Responsibility of the Privileged, Environment and Population, The Right to Health in Tropical Agriculture; Parasites: The Sly and Sneaky Enemies Inside You 1997, Ephraim Amu – A Portrait of Cultured Patriotism, Kwame Mkrumah and the Sciences 2005, A Silent Heritage 2010; scientific articles; book chapters. *Leisure interests:* poetry, painting flowers, Akan culture and traditions. *Address:* c/o Ghana Academy of Arts and Sciences, PO Box KD 1178, Kandra, Accra, Ghana. *E-mail:* info@gaas-gh.org. *Website:* www.gaas-gh.org.

OBENG, Lt-Gen. Seth Kofi, MSc; Ghanaian army officer; *Member, Council of the Wise, Economic Community of West African States (ECOWAS);* b. 26 Jan. 1945, Lagos, Nigeria; s. of Nicholas Emmanuel Obeng and Dina Kwaley Obeng; m. Barbara Baaba Obeng; six c.; ed US Command and Staff Coll., Fort Leavenworth, Kansas, London School of Econs, UK, Nat. Defence Coll., Delhi, India (Postgraduate Diploma in Int. and Comparative Politics; commissioned into Ghanaian Army as artillery officer 1965, various sr command and staff appointments including Commdt Mil. Acad. and Training School and Ghana Armed Forces Command and Staff Coll. as well as Chief of Staff/Gen. HQ; Defence Adviser, Ghana High Comm., London 1984–88; Chief Staff Officer, Army HQ 1988–89; Man. Dir State Housing Corpn (now State Housing Co. 1989–92, 1992–93; Deputy Force Commdr Econ. Community of West African States (ECOWAS) Monitoring Group in Liberia 1994–96; Force Commdr UN Observer Mission to Angola 1998–99; Force Commdr UN Interim Force in Lebanon (UNIFIL) 1999–2001; Chief of Defence Staff 2001–05; Chair. ECOWAS Defence and Security Comm., mem. ECOWAS Council of the Wise 2006–, mem. Bd of Govs Small Arms and Light Weapons Contol Programme; Under-Sec. Gen., UN Secr. 2006–, mem. Follow Up Cttee of the Greentree Agreement of 12th June 2006; Special Adviser on Mil. Affairs to African Union Chair. 2007; appointed by ECOWAS Comm. as mem. of Mediation Team to help resolve political and constitutional crisis in Niger Nov. 2009; has participated in several ECOWAS Observer Missions in Nigeria, Sierra Leone (as Head of Mission), Guinea (Conakry), Côte d'Ivoire, Liberia (Special Envoy of the Pres. of ECOWAS Comm.) 2011; ECOMOG Medal (Liberia) 1996, MONUA Medal (Angola) 1999, UNIFIL Medal 2001; Commdr, Nat. Legion of Cedars (Lebanon) 2001, Officer Nat. Order of Côte d'Ivoire 2002, Meritorious Service Medal (USA) 2004, Order of the Star of Ghana 2006, Commdr, Nat. Order of Merit (Niger) 2012; ECOWAS Award 1996, Int. Officer Hall of Fame (USA) 2004, Ghana Mil. Acad. Jubilee Award for outstanding contrib. to Int. Peace Support Operations from Vice-Pres. of Ghana and Chair. Armed Forces Council 2010. *Leisure interests:* reading, keeping fit, football, hockey, volleyball. *Telephone:* 24-2861246 (mobile). *E-mail:* sethobeng@gmail.com (office).

OBERHELMAN, Douglas R., BA; American business executive; *Chairman and CEO, Caterpillar Inc.;* ed Millikin Univ.; joined Caterpillar 1975, held a variety of positions, including Sr Finance Rep. based in S America for Caterpillar Americas Co., Region Finance Man. and Dist Man. for the co.'s N American Commercial Div., Man. Dir and Vice-Gen. Man. for Strategic Planning at Caterpillar Japan Ltd, Tokyo, Japan, Vice-Pres. 1995, served as Caterpillar's Chief Financial Officer 1995–98, Vice-Pres. with responsibility for the Engine Products Div. 1998–2002, Group Pres. and mem. Exec. Office 2002–09, Vice-Chair. and CEO-elect 2009–10, mem. Bd of Dirs and CEO July 2010–, Chair. Nov. 2010–; mem. Bd of Dirs Eli Lilly & Co., Illinois Chapter, The Nature Conservancy, Asscn of Equipment Mfrs, Nat. Asscn of Mfrs, Manufacturing Inst., Wetlands America Trust; fmr mem. Bd of Dirs Ameren Corpn (Chair. Audit Committee and mem. Nominating and Governance Cttee and the Public Policy Cttee), South Side Bank, Millikin Univ. (Chair. Bd of Trustees), Easter Seals (Chair.). *Address:* Caterpillar Inc., 100 NE Adams Street, Peoria, IL 61629, USA (office). *Telephone:* (309) 675-1000 (office). *Fax:* (309) 675-1182 (office). *E-mail:* info@cat.com (office). *Website:* www.cat.com (office).

OBERMANN, René; German business executive; *CEO, Ziggo;* b. March 1963, Düsseldorf; m.; two d.; ed Univ. of Muenster; traineeship with BMW AG 1984–86; f. ABC Telekom (subsequently Hutchison Mobilfunk), Muenster 1986, Man. Partner 1991, Chair. Man. Bd 1994–98; Man. Dir of Sales, T-Mobile Deutschland 1998–2000, CEO T-Mobile International AG (holding co. for Deutsche Telekom AG mobile operations) 2000–02, mem. Man. Bd responsible for European operations 2001–02, responsible for mobile operations 2002–06, also responsible for mobile communications strategic business area, CEO Deutsche Telekom AG 2006–13, responsible for innovation 2012–13; CEO Ziggo 2014–; Chair. VAM – Verband der Anbieter von Mobilfunkdiensten (Asscn of Mobile Communications Service Providers) 1995–96; Presidium mem. BITKOM German industry asscn 2007–; mem. Supervisory Bd E.ON AG 2011–, Senate of the Fraunhofer Gesellschaft 2011–. *Address:* Ziggo, Atoomweg 100, 3542 AB Utrecht, The Netherlands (office). *Telephone:* (88) 7170717 (office). *Website:* www.ziggo.com (office).

OBERMEIER, Georg, DPhil; German business executive; b. 21 July 1941, Munich; m.; ed Ludwig-Maximilians-Universität, Munich; with Knorr-Bremse GmbH 1964–72; Bayernwerk AG, Munich, latterly Dir of Finance and Org. 1973–89; apptd mem. Man. Bd VIAG AG 1989–98, Chair. 1995–98; Chair. Ryhag, Vienna 1999–2001; fmr Chair. Supervisory Bd Isar-Amperwerke AG, Munich, Rheinhold & Mahla AG, Munich, SKW Trostberg AG, Trostberg; Vice-Chair. and mem. Supervisory Bd Kühne & Nagel International AG 1992–2011; Chair. Supervisory Bd Gigaset AG (fmrly Arques Industries AG) 2007–09, 2009–10; mem. or fmr mem. Supervisory Bd Bayernwerk AG, Munich, Didier-Werke AG, Wiesbaden, Gerresheimer Glas AG, Düsseldorf, Klöckner & Co. AG, Duisburg, Schindellegi, Mobil Oil AG, Hamburg, Schmalbach-Lubeca AG, Brunswick, Thomassen & Drijver Verblifa NV, Deventer, Thyssengas GmbH, Duisburg, VAW Aluminium AG, Berlin/Bonn, SKW Stahl-Metallurgie Holding GmbH 2006–; mem. Int. Advisory Bd and Jt Advisory Council, Allianz SE; mem. Supervisory Cttee Energie-Control GmbH, Spaten-Franziskaner KGaA, Munich. *Address:* c/o Allianz SE, Koeniginstrasse 28, 80802 Munich, Germany.

OBETSEBI-LAMPTEY, Jake; Ghanaian politician and advertising executive; b. 4 Feb. 1946, Accra; scriptwriter, commentator and TV and radio presenter, Ghana Broadcasting Corpn 1966–69; Account Exec. and radio and TV producer Lintas West African advertising agency 1969, Client Service Man., Ghana 1971, wrote, co-ordinated and executed Ghana Nat. Family Planning Programme motivation campaign, Gen. Man. Lintas Ghana Ltd 1974–84; devised operation manuals and presentations for WHO and SOMARC Futures Group 1984–99; Nat. Campaign Man. for New Patriotic Party, presidential elections 2000; Minister of Information and Presidential Affairs and Chief of Staff 2001, Minister of Tourism and the Modernization of the Capital City –2007; fmr Pres. Advertising Asscn of Ghana. *Publications:* Using Commercial Resources in Family Planning Programmes: The International Experience, The Handbook for AIDS Prevention in Africa. *Address:* c/o Ministry of Tourism and the Modernization of the Capital City, PO Box 4386, Accra, Ghana.

OBI, Onyeabo C., LLB, FCIArb; Nigerian international business lawyer; b. 20 Nov. 1938, Ogidi; s. of Chief Z. C. Obi; m. Evelyn Nnenna Obioha 1967; two s. three d.; ed London School of Econs, UK; called to the Bar, Gray's Inn, London 1962; in pvt. practice as barrister and solicitor of Supreme Court of Nigeria 1963–; Dir Nigerian Rubber Bd 1977–79; Senator, Fed. Repub. of Nigeria 1979–83; mem. of Council (and Vice-Chair. Cttee on Procedures for Settling Disputes), Section on Business Law, Int. Bar Asscn 1986–92; mem. Advisory Cttee on Rules of the Supreme Court of Nigeria (by appointment of Hon. Chief Justice) 1986–92; mem. Panel of Arbitrators held at Int. Center for the Settlement of Investment Disputes, World Bank, Washington, DC, USA 2009–. *Leisure interest:* short walks. *Address:* Western House (13th Floor), 8–10 Broad Street, PO Box 4040, Lagos, Nigeria (office). *Telephone:* (1) 263-0843 (office); (1) 743-2365 (office); (1) 263-4604 (office). *Fax:* (1) 263-7609 (office). *E-mail:* abobi@hyperia.com (office); niger.lex@gmail.com (office).

OBIALA, Edmund, MESc; Polish/Australian civil and structural engineer; *Operations Director, Bovis Lend Lease Ltd;* b. 9 Feb. 1946, Poland; m. Grażyna Guth; ed Poznań Univ. of Tech., Bydgoszcz Univ. of Tech.; geodesist Pomeranian Mil. Dist 1966–72; construction designer, head of designer team, Eltor, Bydgoszcz 1972–78; research worker, Ibmer Warsaw, constructed works in Bydgoszcz 1977–80; mem. staff, Civil and Civic Pty Ltd, Sydney 1982–88, Multiplex Constructions Pty Ltd 1988–2000; Operations Dir Bovis Lend Lease Ltd 2000–; Award for Excellence, Concrete Inst. of Australia 1999, Grand Award for Excellence in Arboriculture, Nat. Arborist Asscn 1999, British Construction Award for Olympic Stadium in Sydney 2000, Structural Special Award 2000, Green Apple Award 2004. *Works:* constructions designed include Nat. Bank of Australia, Sydney 1982–85, sports stadium Parramatta and football stadium, Sydney 1985–88, Chiefley Tower, Coles Myer Centre and re-building of Chelsea football team stadium, London 1988–2000. *Achievements:* project director on major constructions including Olympic Stadium, Sydney 1994–99, Wembley Stadium 1999–2001, Chelsea Stadium 1999–2001, Munich City Tower 2001–02, Everton Stadium, Liverpool 2002–03, Chapelfield Shopping Centre, Norwich 2003–. *Leisure interests:* cinema, literature, tennis, volleyball. *Address:* Bovis Lend Lease Ltd, Bovis House, Northolt Road, Harrow, Middx, HA2 OEE (office); 42 Wherry Road, Norwich, NR1 1WS, England (home). *Telephone:* (20) 8271-8000 (office); (1603) 285050 (office); (1603) 766584 (home). *E-mail:* edmund.obiala@eu.bovislendlease.com (office); eobiala@onetel.com (home); gguth@onetel.net (home).

OBRAZTSOVA, Elena Vasilyevna; Russian singer (mezzo-soprano); *Director, Elena Obraztsova Cultural Centre, St Petersburg;* b. 7 July 1939, Leningrad (now St Petersburg); d. of Vasily Alekseevich Obraztsov and Nataliya Ivanovna Obraztsova (née Bychkova); m. 1st Vyacheslav Makarov (divorced 1983); one d.; m. 2nd Algis Žiuraitis 1983 (died 1998); ed Leningrad Conservatoire (under tuition of Prof. Grigoriyeva); Prof., Moscow Conservatoire 1973–94; mem. and Prin. Soloist Bolshoi Theatre, Moscow 1964–; Dir St Petersburg Elena Obraztsova Cultural Centre 1999–, Mikhailovsky Opera, St Petersburg 2007–; has appeared at most leading opera houses of Europe and America, including Vienna State Opera 1975, Metropolitan Opera New York 1976, La Scala Milan 1976, Salzburg 1978, Covent Garden, London 1981 and has toured extensively in Russia and throughout world; gives masterclasses in Europe and Japan; judge of int. vocal competitions; est. Int. Elena Obraztsova Competition for young opera singers, St Petersburg 1999, Elena Obraztsova Int. Competition for young vocalists, St Petersburg 2006 and for chamber music singers, Moscow 2000; Academician Acad. of Russian Art 1999–; Hon. mem. Pushkin Acad. 1995–, Russian Acad. of Art Critics and Musical Performance 1999–; Order for Services to the Fatherland 1999 and other decorations; gold medals at competitions Helsinki 1962, Moscow 1962, 1970, Barcelona 1970, Medal of Granados 1971, Gold Pen of Critics, Wiesbaden 1972, Award of Merit, San Francisco 1977, Gold Verdi, Italy 1978, Bartók Memorial Medal, Hungary 1982, State Prize of Russia 1974, Lenin Prize 1976, People's Artist of USSR 1976, Gold Star-Hero of Labour 1990. *Roles include:* Marina Mniszek in Boris Godunov (debut, Bolshoi 1963), Countess in Queen of Spades, Konchakovna in Prince Igor, Marfa in Khovanshchina, Lyubasha in The Tsar's Bride, Helene Bezukhova in War and Peace, Frosia in Semionkotko, Princess de Bouillon in Adriana Lecouvreur, Jocasta in Oedipus Rex, Oberon in A Midsummer Night's Dream, Eudosya in La Fiamma, Giovanna Seymour in Anna Bolena, Herodiade, Amneris in Aida, Azucena in Il Trovatore, Eboli in Don Carlos, Santuzza in Cavelleria Rusticana, Ulrica in Un Ballo in Maschera, Adalgiza in Norma, Orfeo in Orfeo ed Euridice, Neris in Medea, Leonora in La Favorita, Aunt Princess in Suor Angelica, Frederica in Luisa Miller, Carmen, Charlotte in Werther, Delilah in Samson and Delilah, Judith in Duke Bluebeard's Castle, Granny in The Gambler, the Countess in The Queen of Spades and others; recital repertoire includes works by more than 100 composers; staged Werther at Bolshoi Theatre 1986. *Play:* Amalia in Antonia von Elba 1999. *Film:* Cavalleria Rusticana 1981. *Television includes:* My Carmen 1977, And My Image Will Rise Before You 1979, The Merry Widow 1984, Higher Than The Love 1991, Elena The Great 1995, People, Years, Life 2007. *Recordings:* over 50 recordings for Melodia, Polydor, DG, EMI, CBS, Philips etc., including operas, oratorios, cantatas, solo discs of arias and chamber music. *Publication:* Bolshoi (poetry) 2001. *Leisure interests:* dogs, horses, fishing, mushrooms. *Address:* Bolshoi Theatre, Teatralnaya pl. 1, 125009 Moscow (office). *Telephone:* (495) 692-31-08 (office); (495) 692-06-58 (office); (495) 692-66-90 (office). *Fax:* (495) 692-66-90 (office). *E-mail:* admin@elenaobraztsova.ru (office). *Website:* www.elenaobraztsova.ru (office); www.obraztsova.org.

O'BRIEN, Conan Christopher, AB; American comedian, television writer and talk show host; b. 18 April 1963, Brookline, Mass; s. of Thomas Francis O'Brien and Ruth O'Brien (née Reardon); m. Elizabeth Ann (Liza) Powel 2002; one s. one d.; ed Brookline High School, Harvard Univ.; was Man. Ed. of school newspaper; wrote for Harvard Lampoon humour magazine, later Pres. Harvard Lampoon; moved to Los Angeles following graduation to join writing staff of HBO's Not Necessarily the News 1985–87; performed regularly with improvisational groups, including The Groundlings; was hired as writer for Saturday Night Live (SNL) 1988–92, put on improvisational comedy revue in Chicago, with fellow SNL writers Bob Odenkirk and Robert Smigel, called Happy Happy Good Show, occasionally appeared as an extra in sketches, returned to host the show 2001; co-wrote TV pilot Lookwell, NBC 1991; writer and producer for The Simpsons 1991–93 (credited as writer or co-writer of four episodes); host, Late Night with Conan O'Brien 1993–2009, The Tonight Show with Conan O'Brien 2009–10, Conan 2010–; ordained as a minister by the Universal Life Church Monastery 2011. *Films include:* Space Ghost: Coast to Coast (as himself) 1994, Mr. Show with Bob and David 1995, The Single Guy (TV) 1996, Good Money 1996, Arli$$ 1996, Spin City (TV) 1998, Futurama 1999, Storytelling 2001, Vanilla Sky 2001, Sugar & Spice (cameo in end credits) 2001, Andy Richter Controls the Universe (TV) 2003, End of the Century 2003, Bewitched (as himself) 2005, Robot Chicken 2005, The Denial Twist (the White Stripes music video) 2005, O'Grady (TV) 2006, The Office (cameo) 2006, Queer Duck (as himself) 2006, 30 Rock (as himself) 2007, 2009, Robot Chicken: Star Wars (TV; voice) 2007, Robot Chicken: Star Wars Episode II (TV; voice) 2008, The Backyardigans 2009. *TV writer/producer:* Not Necessarily the News (writer 5 episodes) 1983–85, The Rich Hall Show (writer) 1987, The Wilton North Report (series writer and producer) 1987, Saturday Night Live (aka NBC's Saturday Night, aka SNL 25; writer 73 episodes) 1987–91, Lookwell (writer and producer) 1991, Best of Saturday Night Live: Special Edition (writer) 1992, The Simpsons (writer 4 episodes; producer 52 episodes) 1991–93, Saturday Night Live: The Best of Phil Hartman (writer) 1998, Late Night with Conan O'Brien: 5th Anniversary Special (writer) 1998, Saturday Night Live: 25th Anniversary (writer; uncredited) 1999, 50 Years of NBC Late Night (writer) 2001, The Greg Giraldo Show (exec. producer) 2002, Beat Cops (exec. producer) 2003, Late Night with Conan O'Brien: 10th Anniversary Special (writer) 2003, Foster Hall (exec. producer) 2004, Saturday Night Live: The Best of Jon Lovitz (writer; uncredited) 2005, Marsha Potter Gets a Life (exec. producer) 2005, Haskett's Chance (exec. producer) 2006, The 58th Annual Primetime Emmy Awards (writer) 2006, Andy Barker, P.I. (creator and exec. producer 6 episodes) 2007, Wildlife (exec. producer) 2007, Late Night with Conan O'Brien (writer 1,494 episodes; producer 7 episodes) 1993–2008, Man of Your Dreams (exec. producer) 2008, The Tonight Show with Conan O'Brien (writer 51 episodes; also consulting producer) 2009, Outnumbered (series; exec. producer) 2009, Operating Instructions (exec. producer) 2009. *Address:* c/o WME Entertainment, 9601 Wilshire Boulevard, Beverley Hills, CA 90210-5213, USA (office). *Telephone:* (310) 285-9000 (office). *Fax:* (310) 285-9010 (office). *Website:* www.wma.com (office).

O'BRIEN, David P., OC, BA, BCL; Canadian business executive; *Chairman, Royal Bank of Canada;* b. 9 Sept. 1941, Montreal; s. of John Lewis and Ethel

O'Brien (née Cox); m. Gail Baxter Cornell 1968; two s. one d.; ed Loyola Coll., McGill Univ.; Assoc. Ogilvy Renault 1967, later Pnr; joined Petro-Canada 1978, positions including Exec. Vice-Pres. 1985–89; Pres. and CEO Noverco Inc. 1989; with PanCanadian Petroleum 1990–95, Chair., Pres. and CEO –1995; Pres. and COO Canadian Pacific Ltd 1995–96, Chair., Pres. and CEO 1996–2001; Chair. and CEO PanCanadian Energy Corpn 2001–02, Chair. EnCana Corpn (following merger of PanCanadian Energy Corpn and Alberta Energy Co.) 2002–; mem. Bd of Dirs, Royal Bank of Canada 1996–, Chair. 2004–; mem. Bd Dirs Fairmont Hotel and Resorts, Inco Ltd, TransCanada Pipelines Ltd, Molson Inc., C. D. Howe Inst.; Hon. DCL (Bishops Univ.) 1998, Hon. BA (Mount Royal Coll.) 2000. *Address:* Royal Bank of Canada, 200 Bay Street, Toronto, ON M5J 2J5, Canada (office). *Telephone:* (416) 974-5151 (office). *Fax:* (416) 955-7800 (office). *E-mail:* info@rbc.com (office). *Website:* www.rbc.com (office).

O'BRIEN, Derek, BA; Indian television presenter and author; b. 1961, Kolkata; s. of Neil O'Brien and Joyce O'Brien; m. 1st Rila Banerjee 1991 (divorced); m. 2nd Tonuca O'Brien; one d.; ed St Xavier's Collegiate School, Kolkata, St Columba's School, Delhi, Scottish Church Coll., Kolkata; early career as journalist for Sportsworld; worked for Ogilvy and Mather advertising firm; f. Derek O'Brien & Assocs Pvt. Ltd 1991 (direct marketer and developer of quiz shows); Host, Brand Equity Quiz 1991–, Cadbury Bournvita Quiz Contest 1992–, Mind Grind (Pakistan) 2008–; conducts inter-school quiz contests in India, UAE, Oman, Kuwait, Qatar, Saudi Arabia, Bahrain, Bangladesh, Pakistan and Nepal; joined All India Trinamool Congress (political party) 2005, fmr Spokesperson; Chair. Passenger Services Cttee, Indian Railways 2009–; Hero Honda Indian TV Acad. Award (Best Anchor of a Game/Quiz Show) 2003. *Publications include:* Penguin India Reference Yearbook (ed.), Bournvita Book of Knowledge (ed.), C B Book Of Knowledge (Vols 1–3), Discover with Derek (Vols 1–3) GK with Derek—Box Set (Vols 1–6) 2004, Ultimate Quiz Challenge 2005, Essential Knowledge Quiz Book 2006, Penguin CNBC Business YRBK-07 2007, The Ultimate India Quiz Book 2007, Derek's Picks 2008, Penguin CNBC TV18 Business Yearbook 2010. *Leisure interests:* horses, cricket. *Address:* Derek O'Brien & Associates Pvt. Ltd, 23E Ahiripukur 1st Lane, Kolkata 700 019, West Bengal (office); 7/2Y Jamir Lane, Ballygunge, Kolkata 700 019, West Bengal, India (home). *Telephone:* (33) 22804093 (office); (33) 22804094 (office); (33) 4404126 (home). *Fax:* (33) 22804092 (office); (33) 4405844 (home). *E-mail:* shows@derek.co.in (office). *Website:* www.derek.co.in (office).

O'BRIEN, Edna; Irish writer; b. Tuamgraney, Co. Clare; d. of Michael O'Brien and Lena Cleary; m. Ernest Géblev 1954 (divorced 1964); two s.; ed convents, Pharmaceutical Coll. of Ireland; Hon. DLitt (Queen's) 1999; Yorkshire Post Novel Award 1971, Kingsley Amis Award, Writers' Guild of GB Award 1993, European Prize for Literature 1995, American Nat. Arts Gold Medal, Bob Hughes Lifetime Achievement Award, Irish Book Awards 2009. *Play:* Haunted 2010. *Publications include:* The Country Girls 1960 (film 1983), The Lonely Girl 1962, Girls in Their Married Bliss 1963, August is a Wicked Month 1964, Casualties of Peace 1966, The Love Object 1968, A Pagan Place 1970 (play 1971), Night 1972, A Scandalous Woman (short stories) 1974, Mother Ireland 1976, Johnny I Hardly Knew You (novel) 1977, Arabian Days 1977, Mrs. Reinhardt and other stories 1978, Virginia (play) 1979, Mrs. Reinhardt (adapted for TV) 1981, The Dazzle (children's book), Returning: A Collection of New Tales 1982, A Christmas Treat 1982, A Fanatic Heart (Selected Stories) 1985, Madame Bovary (play) 1987, Vanishing Ireland 1987, Tales for the Telling (children's book) 1987, The High Road (novel) 1988, On the Bone (poetry) 1989, Scandalous Woman and Other Stories 1990, Lantern Slides (stories) 1990, Time and Tide (novel) 1992, House of Splendid Isolation (novel) 1994, Down by the River (novel) 1997, Maud Gonne (screenplay) 1996, James Joyce 1999, Wild Decembers 1999, In the Forest (novel) 2002, Iphigenia (play) 2003, Triptych (play) 2004, The Light of Evening (novel) 2006, Byron in Love (biography) 2009, Saints and Sinners (novel) 2012, Country Girl (memoir) 2012. *Leisure interests:* reading, walking, meditating. *Address:* c/o Faber and Faber Ltd, Bloomsbury House, 74–77 Great Russell Street, London, WC1B 3DA, England. *Website:* www.faber.co.uk/catalog/author/edna-obrien.

O'BRIEN, HE Cardinal Edwin Frederick, BA, MDiv, MA, DST; American ecclesiastic; *Grand Master, Equestrian Order of the Holy Sepulchre of Jerusalem;* b. 8 April 1939, Bronx, NY; s. of Edwin Frederick O'Brien, Sr and Mary Winifred O'Brien; ed Our Lady of Solace School, St Mary's High School, Katonah 1953–57, St Joseph's Seminary, Yonkers, Pontifical North American Coll., Rome, Angelicum Univ.; ordained priest, Archdiocese of New York 1965; served as civilian chaplain at US Mil. Acad., West Point –1970; army chaplain with rank of Capt. 1970, chaplain at Fort Bragg, NC with 82nd Div. 1970–71, in Vietnam with 173rd Airborne Brigade and 1st Cavalry Brigade 1971–72; post chaplain at Fort Gordon, Ga 1972–73; Vice-Chancellor Archdiocese of New York and Assoc. Pastor, St Patrick's Cathedral 1976–81; co-ordinated Pope John Paul II's visit to New York 1979; Archdiocesan Dir of Communications 1981–83; Pvt. Sec. to Cardinal Cooke and then to Cardinal John Joseph O'Connor 1983–85; rank of Hon. Prelate of His Holiness 1986; Rector, St Joseph's Seminary, Yonkers 1985–89, 1994–97, Pontifical North American Coll., Rome 1990–94; apptd Auxiliary Bishop of New York and Titular Bishop of Thizica 1996, Coadjutor Archbishop of USA, Mil. and Titular Archbishop of Thizica 1997–98; Archbishop of USA Mil. 1997–2007; Archbishop of Baltimore 2007–11, Apostolic Admin. of Baltimore 2011–12; Pro-Grand Master of the Equestrian Order of the Holy Sepulchre of Jerusalem 2011–12, Grand Master 2012–; cr. Cardinal (Cardinal-Deacon of San Sebastiano al Palatino) 2012; participated in Papal Conclave 2013. *Address:* Equestrian Order of the Holy Sepulchre of Jerusalem, Borgo Spirito Santo 73, 00193 Rome, Italy (office). *Telephone:* (06) 69892943 (office); (06) 69892901 (office). *Fax:* (06) 69892930 (office). *E-mail:* gm@oessh.va (office). *Website:* www.vatican.va/roman_curia/institutions_connected/oessh/ (office).

O'BRIEN, Grant; Australian business executive; *Managing Director and CEO, Woolworths Ltd;* m. Mary O'Brien; three c.; with Woolworths since 1980s starting as an Accountant in Purity (Supermarkets) in Tasmania (div. of Woolworths Ltd), held positions as COO Australian Food and Petrol, Dir New Business Devt 2008–10, Gen. Man. Woolworths Liquor, Nat. Operations Man. Freestanding Liquor, Sr Business Man. Marketing Supermarkets, and Marketing and Merchandise Man. for Purity –2010, COO for Australia Food and Petrol, with responsibility for Supermarket Operations, Online and Petrol 2010–11, mem. Bd

of Dirs, Deputy CEO and CEO-designate April–Oct. 2011, Man. Dir and CEO Oct. 2011–; Dir, Global Consumer Goods Forum, Avner Nahmani Pancreatic Cancer Research Fund; mem. Business Council of Australia. *Address:* Woolworths Ltd, PO Box 8000, Baulkham Hills, NSW 2153 (office); Woolworths Ltd, 1 Woolworths Way, Bella Vista, NSW 2153, Australia (office). *Telephone:* (2) 8885-0000 (office). *E-mail:* info@woolworthslimited.com.au (office). *Website:* www.woolworthslimited.com.au (office).

O'BRIEN, Gregory Michael St Lawrence, BA, MA, PhD; American academic and university chancellor; b. 7 Oct. 1944, New York, NY; s. of Henry Joseph O'Brien and Mary Agnes O'Brien (née McGoldrick); m. Mary K. McLaughlin 1968; two d.; ed Lehigh Univ., Pa and Boston Univ.; Dean and Prof., School of Social Welfare, Univ. of Wisconsin-Milwaukee 1974–78; Provost and Prof. of Psychology, Univ. of Michigan-Flint 1978–80; Prof. of Psychology, Univ. of South Florida 1980–83, Prof. of Social Work 1980–83, Prof. of Man. 1986–87, Vice-Pres. for Academic Affairs 1980–83; Provost 1983–87; Chancellor, Univ. of New Orleans 1987–2003; Chair. Metro Council Govts Metrovision 1992–94; Vice-Chair. State of Louisiana Film and Video Comm. 1993–94 (mem. 1993–2003); Supt New Orleans Public Schools 1999–2000; Pres. Argosy Univ. Systems 2004–07; mem. Bd of Dirs WLAE-TV (PBS), Bank One New Orleans Region, Entergy New Orleans, Nat. Coalition for Advanced Manufacturing, Nat. Asscn of State Univs and Land-Grant Colls; mem. Kellogg Comm. on Future of Land Grant Colls and State Univs 1996–98, State of Louisiana Econ. Devt Council 1997; Advisory mem. Business Council New Orleans and the River Region; mem. Bd of Dirs The Chamber/New Orleans and the River Region 1988–2003; mem. NCAA (Chair. and Pres. Comm. 1992–93), Nat. Asscn of Social Workers, Nat. Conf. on Social Welfare, Society General Systems Research, American Psychological Asscn, American Public Health Asscn, Metrovision Partnership Foundation 1992–93, Council on Social Work Educ. (presidential task force on structure of the asscn), Industrial Relations Research Asscn; Fellow, American Coll. of Mental Health Admins (Founding Fellow, Pres. 1984–86); Nat. Inst. of Mental Health Fellow 1968–69, Gambit Weekly's New Orleanian of the Year 1999. *Publications:* contrib. of chapters to books and articles to professional journals. *Address:* c/o Office of the Chancellor, University of New Orleans, Lakefront, New Orleans, LA 70148-2468; Lark Street, New Orleans, LA 70122, USA.

O'BRIEN, HE Cardinal Keith Michael Patrick, KM, GCHS, BSc; British ecclesiastic; *Archbishop Emeritus of St Andrews and Edinburgh;* b. 17 March 1938, Ballycastle, Co. Antrim, Northern Ireland; s. of Mark Joseph O'Brien and Alice Mary Moriarty; ed St Patrick's High School, Dumbarton, Holy Cross Acad., Edin., Univ. of Edin., St Andrew's Coll., Drygrange and Moray House Coll. of Educ.; ordained to priesthood 1965, Asst Priest, Holy Cross, Edin. 1965–66, St Bride, Cowdenbeath 1966–71; Chaplain and teacher, St Columba's High School, Dunfermline 1966–71; Asst Priest, St Patrick's, Kilsyth 1972–75, St Mary's, Bathgate 1975–78; Spiritual Dir St Andrew's Coll., Drygrange 1978–80; Rector St Mary's Coll., Blairs 1980–85; RC Archbishop of St Andrews and Edin. 1985–2013 (resgnd), Archbishop Emer. 2013–; Apostolic Admin. Diocese of Argyll and the Isles 1996–99; cr. Cardinal (Cardinal-Priest of Santi Gioacchino ed Anna al Tuscolano) 2003; participated in Papal Conclave 2005; Grand Cross, Conventual Chaplain of Sovereign Mil. Order of Malta 1985, Grand Prior of Scottish Lieutenancy of Equestrian Order of Holy Sepulchre of Jerusalem 2001, Kt Grand Cross 2003, Bailiff Grand Cross of Honour and Devotion, Sovereign Mil. Order of Malta 2005; Hon. LLD (Univ. of St Francis Xavier, Antigonish, Nova Scotia) 2004; Hon. DD (St Andrews) 2004, (Edinburgh) 2004. *Address:* Archdiocesan Offices, 100 Strathearn Road, Edinburgh, EH9 1BB, Scotland (office). *E-mail:* kpobrien247@gmail.com (home).

O'BRIEN, Patricia, BA, MA, BL, LLB; Irish lawyer and diplomatist; *Permanent Representative, United Nations, Geneva;* b. 8 Feb. 1957; m.; three c.; ed Trinity Coll., Dublin, Kings Inns, Dublin, Univ. of Ottawa, Canada; lawyer, Irish Bar 1979–88; called to Bar of England and Wales 1986; fmr lawyer, Bar of BC, Canada; Lecturer, Dept of Law, Univ. of British Columbia 1989–92; fmr Sr Legal Adviser to Irish Attorney-Gen.; fmr Legal Counsellor, Irish Perm. Representation to EU, Brussels; Legal Adviser, Dept of Foreign Affairs, Dublin 2003–08; Under-Sec.-Gen. for Legal Affairs and Legal Counsel, UN 2008–13; Amb. and Perm. Rep. to UN, Geneva 2013–; Fellow, Soc. for Advanced Legal Studies, Inst. of Advanced Legal Studies, London. *Address:* Permanent Mission of Ireland to the United Nations, Rue de Moillebeau 58, 1209 Geneva, Switzerland (office). *Telephone:* (22) 919-19-50. *Fax:* (22) 919-19-51. *E-mail:* genevapmun@dfa.ie. *Website:* www.dfa.ie.

O'BRIEN, Patrick Karl, BSc (Econ), MA, DPhil, FRSA, FRHistS, FBA; British historian and academic; *Professor of Global Economic History, London School of Economics;* b. 12 Aug. 1932, London, England; s. of William O'Brien and Elizabeth O'Brien Stockhausen; m. Cassy Cobham 1959; one s. two d.; ed London School of Econs, Nuffield Coll. Oxford; Lecturer, SOAS, Univ. of London 1963–70; Reader in Econs and Econ. History, Univ. of London 1967–70; Univ. Lecturer in Econ. History and Faculty Fellow, St Antony's Coll. Oxford 1970–84, Univ. Reader in Econ. History and Professorial Fellow 1984–90; Prof. of Econ. History, Univ. of London 1990–98; Sr Research Fellow and Convener of Programme in Global History, Inst. of Historical Research, Univ. of London 1998– (now Dir); Prof. of Global Econ. History, LSE 2009–, Convenor of European Research Council-funded Research Programme 'Regimes for the Production and Diffusion of Useful and Reliable Knowledge in the East and the West from the Accession of the Ming in 1368 to The Opium War 1839'; Fellow, Academia Europaea; Dr hc (Carlos III Univ., Madrid) 1999, (Uppsala) 2000. *Publications:* The Revolution in Egypt's Economic System 1966, The New Economic History of Railways 1977, Two Paths to the 20th Century: Economic Growth in Britain and France 1978, The Economic Effects of the Civil War 1988. *Leisure interests:* theatre, Western art, foreign travel. *Address:* Department of Economic History, Room E488, London School of Economics, Houghton Street, Aldwych, London, WC2A 2AE (office); 66 St Bernard's Road, Oxford, OX2 6EJ, England (home). *Telephone:* (20) 7955-6586 (office); (1865) 512004 (home). *Fax:* (20) 7955-7730 (office). *E-mail:* p.o'brien@lse.ac .uk (office). *Website:* www.lse.ac.uk (office).

O'BRIEN QUINN, James Aiden, BA, LLB, QC; Irish lawyer; b. 3 Jan. 1932, Tipperary; s. of the late William Patrick Quinn and Helen Mary Quinn (née Walshe); m. Christel Mary Tyner 1960; two s. one d.; ed Presentation Coll., Bray, Univ. Coll., Dublin and King's Inns, Dublin; studied banking, Nat. City Bank,

Dublin 1949–53; Crown Counsel and Acting Sr Crown Counsel, Nyasaland (Malawi) 1960–64; Asst Attorney-Gen. and Acting Attorney-Gen., West Cameroon 1964–66, Attorney-Gen. 1966–68; Avocat-Général près la Cour Fédérale de Justice, Cameroon 1966–68; Conseiller à la Cour Fédérale de Justice, Yaoundé, Cameroon 1968–72; Président du Tribunal Administratif du Cameroun Occidental 1968–72; Conseiller Technique (Harmonisation des Lois), Yaoundé, Cameroon 1968–72; Attorney-Gen. of Seychelles and British Indian Ocean Territory 1972–76; Chief Justice of Seychelles 1976–77; acted as Deputy Gov. of Seychelles for a period during 1974; mem. Seychelles dels on self-govt and independence constitutions 1975, 1976; Chief Justice of Gilbert Islands (later Kiribati), Pacific Ocean 1977–81; Judge of High Court of Solomon Islands 1977–81; Special Prosecutor, Falkland Islands 1980; Chief Justice of Botswana 1981–87; Chair. of Judicial Service Comm., Botswana 1981; Adjudicator, Immigrations Appeals 1990–96; Vice-Pres. Immigration Appeal Tribunal 1996–; BESO Adviser, Dominica 1992; Third Place, Inst. of Bankers in Ireland 1950; QC, Seychelles 1973; Kiribati Independence Medal 1979; Chevalier, Ordre Nat. de la Valeur (Cameroon) 1967. *Publications:* West Cameroon Law Reports (ed.) 1961–68, Gilbert Islands Law Reports (ed.), Kiribati Law Reports (ed.) 1977–79, Magistrates' Courts' Handbook, West Cameroon 1968, Magistrates' Courts' Handbook, Kiribati 1979. *Leisure interests:* swimming, reading, languages, travel. *Address:* Field House, 15–25 Bream's Buildings, London, EC4A 1DZ (office); 9 Lorane Court, Langley Road, Watford, Herts., WD1 3LZ, England. *Telephone:* (1923) 232861.

OBRIST, Hans Ulrich; Swiss gallery curator; *Co-Director, Exhibitions and Programmes and Director of International Projects, Serpentine Galleries, London;* b. 1968, Zurich; Founder and Curator, Robert Walser migratory museum, Vienna, Austria 1993–2000; Curator, Musée d'Art Moderne de la Ville de Paris, France 2000–06; Lecturer, Arts Faculty, Univ. IUAV, Venice, Italy 2001–; Co-Dir Exhbns and Programmes and Dir of Int. Projects, Serpentine Gallery, London 2006–. *Publications include:* A Brief History of Curating 2008, Everything You Always Wanted to Know About Curating but Were Afraid to Ask 2011, Ai Weiwei Speaks 2011, Do It: The Compendium 2013, Think Like Clouds 2014, along with new vols of the Conversation Series. *Address:* Serpentine Galleries, Kensington Gardens, London, W2 3XA, England (office). *Telephone:* (20) 7298-1543 (office); (20) 7298-1508 (PA) (office). *Fax:* (20) 7402-4103 (office). *E-mail:* information@serpentinegallery.org (office). *Website:* www.serpentinegallery.org (office).

OBSITNIK, Vincent, BS, MBA; American business executive and diplomatist (retd); *President and CEO, East West Ventures LLC;* b. 24 Jan. 1938, Moravany, Slovakia; m. Annemarie Harden; four s.; ed Linden High School, NJ, US Naval Acad., American Univ., Washington, DC, IBM Advanced Man. School, Sands Point, Long Island, NY, IBM Int. Man. School, La Hulpe, Belgium, Unisys Exec. Program, Wharton School, Univ. of Pennsylvania, Phila; moved to USA with parents prior to occupation of Czechoslovakia by Nazi Germany 1938; served as officer in USN in destroyers and submarines 1959–64; fmr Pres. Systems Devt Div., Unisys Corpn; fmr Vice-Pres., International, Litton Corpn; spent 27 years at IBM Corpn, responsible for Marketing, Sales, Mfg, Eng and Program Man., spent eight years with IBM World Trade Corpn with mfg responsibilities in Europe, Latin America and Asia; Founder and Pres. International Investments, Inc.; Pres. and CEO East West Ventures LLC; apptd by Pres. George W. Bush to US Comm. for Preservation of America's Heritage Abroad 2001–06, to US Presidential Del. for Austrian State Treaty Anniversary 2005, to US Presidential Del. to Commemoration of 65th Anniversary of Tragedy in Babyn Yar in Ukraine 2006; Amb. to Slovakia 2007–09. *Leisure interests:* running marathons, playing tennis and squash. *Address:* 6849 Grenadier Blvd, #904, Naples, FL 34108 USA (home).

OBUKHOV, Alexey Aleksandrovich, PhD; Russian diplomatist (retd); b. 12 Nov. 1937, Moscow; s. of Alexander Ivanovich Obukhov and Klaudia Ivanovna Obukhov; m. Olga Obukhov; two s.; ed Moscow Inst. of Int. Relations and Univ. of Chicago; joined Ministry of Foreign Affairs 1965; served in Embassy in Thailand; took part in Soviet-American Strategic Arms Limitation Talks on Threshold Test Ban Treaty (TTBT), Moscow 1974; Deputy Dir US Dept, Ministry of Foreign Affairs 1980–86; mem. Soviet negotiating team in arms control talks, responsible for negotiations on long-range strategic weapons, subsequently for negotiations on medium-range nuclear weapons, Geneva 1985; Deputy Head Soviet Del., Nuclear and Space Talks, Geneva 1987, Head 1988; Head, Dept of USA and Canada, Ministry of Foreign Affairs 1989–90; Deputy Minister of Foreign Affairs 1990–91; Amb. to Denmark 1992–96; Amb.-at-Large 1996–2002; Head of Del. to Russian-Lithuanian talks on border issues 1996–2012; Head of Del. to Joint Russian-Lithuanian Comm. on Demarcation 2005–12; Chair. Cttee of Sr Officers (CSO) of the Barents Euro/Arctic Council 2000–01, CSO of the Council of Baltic Sea States 2001–02; Order of the Red Banner 1988; Harold Weill Medal for Outstanding Contrib. to Peace and Understanding through the Rule of Law, New York Univ. 1988, Medal of Merit, Russian Acad. of Arts 2006. *Publications:* Russia and Denmark: Painters of the Royal Courts from Catherine the Great to Margrethe II and numerous texts on diplomatic affairs. *Leisure interests:* art, photography. *Address:* 117049 Moscow, 40/7/71 Bolshaya Yakimanka str. (home); c/o Ministry of Foreign Affairs, 119200 Moscow, Smolenskaya-Sennaya pl. 32/34, Russian Federation (office). *Telephone:* (495) 238-00-48 (home); (495) 244-16-06 (office). *Fax:* (495) 238-00-48 (home); (495) 230-21-30 (office). *E-mail:* moscowsuper@mtu-net.ru (home). *Website:* www.mid.ru (office).

OCAMPO, José Antonio, PhD; Colombian academic and UN official; *Professor of Professional Practice, Columbia University;* b. 20 Dec. 1952; m. Ana Lucía Lalinde; three c.; ed Univ. of Notre Dame, Yale Univ., USA; researcher, Centre for Devt Studies, Universidad de los Andes 1976–80, Dir 1980–82; at Foundation for Higher Educ. and Devt 1983–93, Deputy Dir 1983–84, Exec. Dir 1984–88, Sr Researcher and mem. Bd of Dirs; Minister of Agric. 1993–94, of Planning 1994–96, of Finance and Public Credit 1996–97; Exec. Sec. UN Econ. Comm. for Latin America and the Caribbean 1998–2003; UN Under-Sec.-Gen. for Econ. and Social Affairs 2003–07; Co-Dir UNDP/OAS Project 'Agenda for a Citizens' Democracy in Latin America' 2008–10; mem., Comm. of Experts, UN Gen. Ass. on Reforms of the Int. Monetary and Financial System 2009; Prof. of Professional Practice and mem. Cttee on Global Thought, Columbia Univ., New York 2007–; Nat. Dir Employment Mission 1985–86; Adviser, Colombian Foreign Trade Bd 1990–91, Colombian Nat. Council of Entrepreneurial Asscn; mem. Tech. Comm. on Coffee Affairs, Public Expenditure Comm., Advisory Comm. for Fiscal Reform, Mission on Intergovernmental

Finance; consultant to IBRD, IDB and UN; mem. Colombian Acad. of Econ. Science 1987; Visiting Fellow, Univ. of Oxford, Yale Univ.; Grand Cross, Order of Boyacá, 1997, Order of Merit of Chile 2003; Alejandro Angel Escobar Colombian Nat. Science Prize 1988, Leontief Prize for Advancing the Frontiers of Economic Thought 2008. *Publications:* author or ed. of over 40 books. *Address:* School of International and Public Affairs, Columbia University, 116th and Broadway, New York, NY 10027, USA (office). *Telephone:* (212) 854-6339 (office). *E-mail:* jose.ocampo@sipa.columbia.edu (office). *Website:* sipa.columbia.edu (office).

OCANTE DA SILVA, Aristides; Guinea-Bissau politician; *Minister of State, Minister of the Civil Service, State Reform, Labour and Social Security;* fmr Minister of Energy, of Natural Resources and Environment 2005, of Nat. Educ., Culture and Science –2009, Minister of Nat. Defence 2009–11, of the Civil Service, Employment and Modernization of the State 2011–12, Minister of State, Minister of the Civil Service, State Reform, Labour and Social Security 2013–; mem. Partido Africano da Independência da Guiné e Cabo Verde. *Address:* Ministry of the Civil Service, State Reform, Labour and Social Security, Bissau, Guinea-Bissau.

O'CATHAIN, Baroness, cr. 1991 (Life Peer), of The Barbican in the City of London; **Detta O'Cathain,** OBE, BA, FCIM; British economist, business executive and parliamentarian; b. 3 Feb. 1938, Cork, Ireland; d. of Caoimhghin O'Cathain and Margaret Prior; m. William Ernest John Bishop 1968 (died 2001); ed Loreto School, Rathfarnham, Co. Dublin, Laurel Hill, Limerick, Univ. Coll. Dublin; Asst Economist, Aer Lingus 1961–66; Group Economist, Tarmac Ltd 1966–69; Econ. Adviser, Rootes Motors Ltd 1969–72; Sr Economist, Carrington Viyella 1972; Market Planning Dir, British Leyland 1973–76; Corp. Planning Exec., Unigate PLC 1976–81; Head of Strategic Planning, Milk Marketing Bd 1981–83, Dir and Gen. Man. 1983, Man. Dir Milk Marketing 1984–88; Man. Dir Barbican Centre, London 1990–95; Dir (non-exec.) Midland Bank PLC 1984–93, Tesco PLC 1985–2000, Sears PLC 1987–94, British Airways 1993–2004, BET PLC 1994–96, BNP Paribas (UK) PLC 1995–2005, Thistle Hotels 1996–2003; Pres. Chartered Inst. of Marketing 1998–2001, Southeast Water PLC 1998, Allders PLC 2000–03, William Baird PLC 2000–02; Commdr, Royal Norwegian Order 1992, Commdr, Order of Lion of Finland 1992, Order of Azerbaijan 2010. *Leisure interests:* music, reading, swimming, gardening. *Address:* House of Lords, Westminster, London, SW1A 0PW, England (office). *Telephone:* (20) 7219-0662 (office). *Fax:* (20) 7219-0785. *E-mail:* ocathaind@parliament.uk (office).

OCCHETTO, Achille; Italian politician; b. 3 March 1936, Turin; joined Italian Communist Party (PCI) and Young Communists' Fed. 1953, apptd Nat. Sec. Young Communists 1962, Sec. PCI Palermo 1969, subsequently Regional Sec. for Sicily; moved to Rome, held succession of party posts 1976; mem. Chamber of Deputies 1976–2001; Deputy Leader PCI (name changed to Partito Democratico della Sinistra 1991) 1987–88, Gen.-Sec. 1988–94, mem. –1998; Senator 2001–06, Alternate Chair. Cttee on Rules of Procedure and Immunities, Cttee on Migration, Refugees and Population; mem. European Parl. 2004 (resgnd), 2006–07; mem. Democrats of the Left 1994–2007, Democratic Left 2007–09, Left Ecology Freedom party (Sinistra Ecologia Libertà) 2009–. *Address:* c/o Sinistra Ecologia Libertà, via Arenula 29, 00186 Rome, Italy. *Telephone:* (06) 44700403. *Fax:* (06) 4455832. *E-mail:* selnazionale@sxmail.it; achille@achilleocchetto.it. *Website:* www.sinistraecologialiberta.it.

OCHIRBAT, Punsalmaagin, DSc; Mongolian politician; *President, Ochirbat Fund;* b. 23 Jan. 1942, Tudevtei Dist, Zavkhan Prov.; s. of Gonsiin Gendenjav and Tsogtiin Punsalmaa; m. Sharaviin Tsevelmaa 1965; two d.; ed Mining Inst. of USSR; apptd official at Ministry of Industry 1966, Chief Engineer, Sharyn Gol coal mine 1967, Deputy Minister, Ministry of Fuel and Power Industry and Geology 1972–76, Minister 1976; Chair. State Cttee External Econ. Relations 1985–87, Minister 1987; elected mem. Mongolian People's Revolutionary Party (MPRP) Cen. Cttee 17th, 18th and 19th Party Congresses and at 1990 Extraordinary Congress; resgnd from MPRP 1991; elected Deputy to Great People's Hural 9th, 10th and 11th elections, Chair. 1990; Pres. of Mongolia 1990–97, C-in-C of the Armed Forces 1993–97; Pres. Ochirbat Fund 1997–; Altan Gadas 1972, Mu Gung Hwa (Repub. of Korea) 1991, Liberty Award (USA) 1995. *Publications:* Black Gold, Art of Management, Organisation and Management of Fuel and Energy Complex, Heavenly Hour, Without the Right to Mistakes, Ecolog-Steady Development. *Address:* Olympic Street 14, Sky Plaza, 3rd Floor of Office Building 1, Ulan Bator 210648, Mongolia (office). *Telephone:* (11) 327215 (office). *Fax:* (11) 327233 (office). *E-mail:* pobmongolia@magicnet.mn (office). *Website:* www.ochirbatfoundation.mn (office).

OCHMAN, Wiesław; Polish tenor, producer and painter; b. 6 Feb. 1937, Warsaw; s. of Jan Ochman and Bronisława Ochman; m. Krystyna Ochman 1963; one s. one d.; ed Acad. of Mining and Metallurgy, Kraków 1960, studied with Prof. Gustaw Serafin, Kraków and with Prof. Maria Szłapak, Jerzy Gaczek and Sergiusz Nadgryzowski; debut in Silesian Opera, Bytom 1960; soloist, Silesian Opera, Bytom 1960–63, Opera in Kraków 1963–64, Great Theatre, Warsaw 1964–75, Deutsche Staatsoper 1967, Hamburgische Staatsoper 1967–, Metropolitan Opera, New York 1975–, La Scala, Milan 1981; festivals at Glyndebourne, Salzburg, Orange; guest performances in operas in Paris, Munich, Frankfurt am Main, San Francisco, Miami, Chicago, Geneva, Budapest, Washington, Staatsoper in Vienna, Grand Theatre in Moscow, Staatsoper and Deutsche Oper in W Berlin, Teatro Colón in Buenos Aires, Gran Teatre del Liceu in Barcelona, Accademia Santa Cecila in Rome, Carnegie Hall in New York, Teatro de la Maestranza in Seville; participation in TV films including Eugene Onegin, Tcharevitch, Salome, Don Giovanni; numerous recordings; mem. Pres. Council for Culture 1992–95; Goodwill Amb. for UNICEF 1996; Commdr's Cross with Star, Order of Polonia Restituta 2001; Minister of Culture and Art Prize 1973, The City of Warsaw Prize 1976, Pres. of Radio and TV Cttee Prize (1st Class) 1979, Prime Minister Prize (1st Class) 1979, Minister of Foreign Affairs Diploma 1977, 1986, Medal Maecenas of Art 1976, The City of Kraków Gold Award, Medal of Merit for Nat. Culture 1986. *Operatic roles include:* Faust, Don Carlos, Cavaradossi in Tosca, Don José in Carmen, Dimitri in Boris Godunov, Edgardo in Lucia di Lammermoor, Arrigo in I vespri siciliani, Alfredo in La Traviata, Don Carlos in Don Carlos, Stefan in The Hunted Manor, Turiddu in Cavalleria Rusticana, Lensky in Eugene Onegin, Herman in Pique Dame, Tamino in Der Zauberflöte, Idomeneo in Idomeneo, Titus in La clemenza di Tito, Eric in Der Fliegende Holländer, Florestan in Fidelio, Shepherd in King Roger, Les pêcheurs de perles, Herod in Salome, Prince Golitsyn in Khovanshchina, Jontek in Halka, Laca in Jenůfa, Prince in Rigoletto, Don Ottavio in Don Giovanni. *Operas directed:* Mozart's Don Giovanni, Verdi's La Traviata 2000, Lehar's Tcharevitch 2001, Tchaikovsky's Eugene Onegin 2002. *Recordings:* Jenůfa 1995, 2002, Halka 1995, Bruckner Masses 1996, Armida 1996, Stabat Mater/Legends 1997, Rusalka 1998, King Roger 1999, Great Operas of Richard Strauss 2001, Orchestral & Choral Works 2002, Te Deum/Lachrimosa 2003, Prokofiev: 50th Anniversary Edition – Limited Edition 2003, Cantatas 2004. *Leisure interests:* painting, collecting objects of art. *Address:* ul. Miączyńska 46B, 02-637 Warsaw, Poland. *Telephone:* 603-640-845.

OCHOA, Lorena; Mexican professional golfer; b. (Lorena Ochoa Reyes), 15 Nov. 1981, Guadalajara; m. Andrés Conesa Labastida 2009; ed Univ. of Arizona; won first nat. event aged seven; 27 wins 2003–10, including Ricoh Women's British Open 2007, Kraft Nabisco Championship 2008; ranked No. 1 female golfer 2007–10; retired 2010; Nat. Sports Award (youngest ever winner) 2001, Futures Tour Player of the Year 2002, AP Female Athlete of the Year 2006, 2007, Ladies Professional Golf Asscn (LPGA) Rolex Player of the Year 2006–09, LPGA Tour Money Winner 2006–08, LPGA Vare Trophy 2006–09, Golf Writers Asscn of America Female Player of the Year 2006–09, Heather Farr Player Award 2007, Best Int. Athlete ESPY Award 2008, 2009. *Address:* Alejandro Ochoa, Morelos No. 2179, Col. Arcos Vallarta, CP 44130, Guadalajara Jalisco, Mexico (office). *Telephone:* (33) 1202-0877 (office). *Fax:* (33) 1202-0877 (office). *E-mail:* aochoa@ grupoochoa.com (office). *Website:* www.grupoochoa.com.mx (office); www .lorenaochoa.com.

OCHOJSKA-OKOŃSKA, Janina; Polish charity administrator; *Chairman, Polska Akcja Humanitarna;* b. 12 March 1955, Gdańsk; m. Michał Okoński; ed Nicolaus Copernicus Univ., Toruń; Asst. Astrophysics Lab. of Astronomy Centre of Polish Acad. of Sciences (PAN), Toruń 1980–92; co-f. EquiLibre Foundation 1989, Co-founder and Dir Warsaw br. 1992–94; Co-founder and Chair. Polska Akcja Humanitarna (Polish Humanitarian Org.) 1994–; Order of the Smile awarded by Polish children 1995; EU Woman of Europe 1994, Feliks Civic Prize, Gazeta Wyborcza 1994, St George Medal, Tygodnik Powszechny magazine 1994, Pax Christi Int. Peace Award 1995, Woman of the Year, Poland 1995, Atsushi Nakata Memorial, Japan 1996, Romers' Foundation Award, Canada 1997, European German Culture Award 1999, Life Guide Award, Lublin Archdiocese's Youth Council 2000, Jt Winner, Twój Styl Magazine poll for the 50 Most Influential Woman in Poland 2000, 2001, Gold Medal of Voluntary Fire Brigades of Poland, Winner, first Jan Karski Freedom Award for Valour and Compassion, American Center of Polish Culture, Washington, DC 2002. *Leisure interests:* music, books, cooking. *Address:* Polska Akcja Humanitarna, 00-031 Warsaw, ul. Szpitalna 5 lok. 3, Poland (office). *Telephone:* (22) 8288882 (office). *Fax:* (22) 8319938 (office). *E-mail:* pah@pah.org.pl (office). *Website:* www.pah.org.pl (office).

OCKRENT, Christine; Belgian journalist and broadcaster; b. 24 April 1944, Brussels; d. of Roger Ockrent and Greta Bastenie; m. Bernard Kouchner (q.v.); one s.; ed Collège Sévigné, Paris, Univ. of Cambridge, UK, Institut d'Etudes Politiques de Paris; journalist, Information Office, EEC 1965–66; Researcher, NBC News, USA 1967–68; producer and journalist, CBS News, USA 1968–77; journalist and producer, FR3, France 1976–80; Ed. and Anchor, news programme on Antenne 2 1980–85; Chief Ed. RTL 1985–86; Deputy Dir-Gen. TF1 1986–87; Ed., anchor and producer, news programmes on Antenne 2 1988–92, on France 3 1992–95; Chief Ed. L'Express 1995–96; Deputy Dir BFM 1996–2000; Ed.-in-Chief Dimanche Soir programme France 3 1996–98; Ed.-in-Chief and Presenter, France Europe Express 1997; currently columnist, International Herald Tribune, El Pais, The Guardian and several other European newspapers; Pres. BFMbiz.com; mem. Bd of Dirs International Crisis Group, French Council on Foreign Relations, European Council on Foreign Relations, Centre for European Reform, Human Rights Watch France, Reporters sans Frontières, Women's Forum for the Economy and Society; Chevalier, Légion d'honneur 2000. *Publications include:* Dans le secret des princes 1986, Duel 1988, Les uns et les autres 1993, Portraits d'ici et d'ailleurs 1994, La mémoire du cœur 1997, Les grands patrons (co-author) 1998, L'Europe racontée à mon fils, de Jules César à l'euro 1999, La double vie d'Hillary Clinton 2000, Françoise 2003. *Leisure interests:* riding, skiing, tennis. *Address:* The Guardian, Kings Place, 90 York Way, London, N1 9GU, England. *E-mail:* christine.ockrent@ guardian.co.uk. *Website:* www.guardian.com/profile/christine-ockrent.

O'CONNELL, Robert J., MA; American insurance executive; b. 1943; ed Univ. of Pennsylvania; with American Int. Group Inc. (AIG) 1989–98; joined MassMutual Life Insurance 1998, Pres. and CEO 1999–2000, Chair., Pres. and CEO 2000–05; mem. Bd of Dirs, Oppenheimer Acquisition Corpn, DLB Acquisition Corpn, American Council of Life Insurance, Life Office Man. Asscn, US Chamber of Commerce, CM Life Insurance Co. 1999, Yankee Holding Corpn (fmrly Yankee Candle Co. Inc.) 2004–05. *Address:* c/o Massachusetts Mutual Life Insurance Co., 1295 State Street, Springfield, MA 0111-0001, USA. *E-mail:* info@massmutual .com.

O'CONNOR, Gordon, PC, OMM, CD, BSc, BA; Canadian politician and fmr military officer; b. 18 May 1939, Toronto, Ont.; m.; two c.; ed Concordia and York Univs; fmr mil. officer, Second Lt Armour Br., later Brig. Gen.; fmr Sr Assoc., Hill and Knowlton Canada; MP for Carleton-Mississippi Mills 2004–, mem. Standing Cttee on Nat. Defence and Veterans Affairs, Sub-cttee on Veterans Affairs; fmr Official Opposition Critic for Nat. Defence; Minister of Nat. Defence 2006–07, of Nat. Revenue 2007–08; Minister of State and Chief Govt Whip 2008–11; Order of Mil. Merit (Canada). *Address:* Room 1100, La Promenade, 151 Sparks Street, Ottawa, ON K1A 0A6, Canada (office). *Telephone:* (613) 992-1119 (office). *Fax:* (613) 992-1043 (office). *E-mail:* gordon.oconnor@parl.gc.ca (office). *Website:* www .gordonoconnor.ca.

O'CONNOR, Sandra Day, BA, LLB; American lawyer and judge (retd); b. 26 March 1930, El Paso, Tex.; d. of Harry A. Day and Ada Mae Day (née Wilkey); m. John Jay O'Connor III 1952 (died 2009); three s.; ed Stanford Univ.; pvt. law practice, Phoenix, Ariz. 1959–65; served in Ariz. Senate 1969–75, Majority Leader 1972–75; Superior Court Judge, Ariz. 1975–79, Judge of Appeals 1979–81; Assoc. Justice, US Supreme Court 1981–2006 (retd); mem. Nat. Bd, Smithsonian Assocs 1981–, Exec. Bd, Cen. European and Eurasian Law Initiative (ABA) 1990–; Chancellor Coll. of William and Mary 2005–11; mem. Bd of Trustees, Rockefeller Foundation 2006–; mem. Iraq Study Group, US Inst. of Peace 2006; Harry

Rathbun Visiting Fellow, Office for Religious Life, Stanford Univ. 2008; f. iCivics.org 2009; mem. ABA, State Bar of Ariz., State Bar of Calif., Maricopa Co. Bar Asscn, Ariz. Judges' Asscn, Nat. Asscn of Women Judges, Ariz. Women Lawyers' Asscn; Fellow, American Acad. of Arts and Sciences 2007; 15th Hendrick Fellow by the US Coast Guard Acad. 2009; 25 hon. degrees, including Dr hc (Yale Univ.) 2006; numerous awards, including Elizabeth Blackwell Award, Hobart and William Smith Coll. 1985, Service to Democracy Award, American Ass. 1982, Fordham-Stein Prize, Fordham Univ. 1992, Award of Merit, Stanford Law School 1990, Nat. Women's Hall of Fame, Seneca Falls, NY 1995, ABA Medal 1997, ranked by Forbes magazine amongst 100 Most Powerful Women (sixth) 2004, (36th) 2005, Sylvanus Thayer Award, US Mil. Acad. 2005, Harry F. Byrd Jr. '35 Public Service Award, Virginia Mil. Inst. 2008, Franklin Award, Nat. Conf. on Citizenship 2008, Presidential Medal of Freedom 2009, Brigham-Kanner Property Rights Prize 2011. *Publications:* Lazy B: Growing Up on a Cattle Ranch in the American Southwest 2002, The Majesty of Law: Reflections of a Supreme Court Judge 2003, Chico (children's book) 2005, Finding Susie (children's book) 2009, Out of Order: Stories from the History of the Supreme Court 2013. *Website:* www .icivics.org.

O'CONNOR, Sean; South African business executive; *CEO, INTL FCStone Inc.;* ed Univ. of Stellenbosch, Univ. of Cape Town; qualified as Chartered Accountant in SA; began career with Standard Bank as investment banking exec., spent 14 years as mem. man. team that est. bank's int. operations, CEO Standard New York Securities 1994–2002, Exec. Dir Standard Bank London Ltd (subsidiary of Standard Bank of South Africa) 1999–2002; mem. Bd of Dirs and CEO International Assets Holding Corpn (INTL) 2002– (merged with FCStone Sept. 2009). *Address:* INTL FCStone Inc., 708 Third Avenue, 15th Floor, New York, NY 10017, USA (office). *Telephone:* (212) 485-3500 (office). *Fax:* (212) 485-3505 (office). *E-mail:* info@intlfcstone.com (office). *Website:* www.intlfcstone.com (office).

O'CONNOR, Sinéad; Irish singer, songwriter and musician (guitar, piano, keyboards, percussion, low whistle); b. (Sinéad Marie Bernadette O'Connor), 8 Dec. 1966, Glenageary, Co. Dublin; d. of John O'Connor and the late Marie O'Connor; m. 1st John Reynolds (divorced); one d. (by John Waters); m. 2nd Nicholas Sommerland 2002; one c. with Frank Bonadio 2007; m. 3rd Steve Cooney 2010 (divorced 2011); m. 4th Barry Herridge 9 Dec. 2011 (divorced 26 Dec. 2011); ed Dublin Coll. of Music; mem. Ton Ton Macoute 1985–87; rose to fame with debut album The Lion and the Cobra late 1980s; worldwide success with cover version of song Nothing Compares 2 U 1990; refused to accept Grammy Award for Best Alternative Album 1991; now Tridentine priest Mother Bernadette Mary; MTV Award for Best Video, MTV Award for Best Single (both for Nothing Compares 2 U) 1990, MTV Award for Best Female Singer 1990, Rolling Stone Artist of the Year Award 1991, BRIT Award for Best Int. Solo Artist 1991. *Recordings include:* albums: The Lion and the Cobra 1987, I Do Not Want What I Have Not Got (Grammy Award for Best Alternative Album 1991) 1990, Am I Not Your Girl? 1992, Universal Mother 1994, Gospeloak 1997, Sean-Nós Nua 2002, Throw Down Your Arms 2005, Theology 2007, How About I Be Me (And You Be You)? 2012. *Video films:* Value of Ignorance 1989, The Year of the Horse 1991. *Television:* Hush-a-Bye-Baby. *Website:* www.sineadoconnor.com.

O'CONNOR-CONNOLLY, Julianna, JP; Cayman Islands lawyer and politician; b. Cayman Brac; ed Univ. of Liverpool, UK; mem. Legis. Ass. for Cayman Brac and Little Cayman 1996–, Speaker 2001–03; Minister of Community Affairs, Sports, Women, Youth and Culture 1997, Minister for Planning, Communications, Dist Admin and Information Tech. 2003–05, Minister of Finance, Dist Admin, Works, Lands and Agric. 2009–; Deputy Premier of Cayman Islands 2009–12, Premier (first woman) 2012–13; Founding mem. United Democratic Party 2001. *Address:* c/o Government Administration Bldg, Elgin Avenue, George Town, Grand Cayman, Cayman Islands (office).

ODA, Beverley J., PC, BA; Canadian politician and broadcasting executive; *Minister of International Co-operation;* b. 27 July 1944, Thunder Bay, Ont.; ed Univ. of Toronto; joined TVO 1973; various positions in broadcasting industry; Commr CRTC 1987–93; Sr Vice-Pres., Industry Affairs, CTV Inc. 1999; fmr Chair. Lakeridge Health Hosp. Network, Co-Chair. Task Force on Diversity on Canadian TV; MP for Durham 2004–; Minister of Canadian Heritage and Status of Women 2006–07, of Int. Co-operation 2007–; Queen's Golden Jubilee Medal 2002, Canadian Broadcasters Hall of Fame 2003. *Address:* House of Commons, Ottawa, ON K1A 0A6, Canada (office). *Telephone:* (613) 992-2792 (office). *Fax:* (613) 992-2794 (office). *E-mail:* Oda.B@parl.gc.ca (office). *Website:* www.parl.gc.ca (office); www.bevoda.ca (home).

ODA, Shigeru, LLM, JSD, LLD; Japanese international judge, lawyer and academic; *Professor Emeritus, Tôhoku University;* b. 22 Oct. 1924; s. of Toshio and Mioko Oda; m. Noriko Sugimura 1950; one s. one d.; ed Univ. of Tokyo, Yale Univ.; Research Fellow, Univ. of Tokyo 1947–49; Asst Prof. Tôhoku Univ. 1950–53, Assoc. Prof. 1953–59, Prof. 1959–76, Prof. Emer. 1985–; Tech. Adviser, Atomic Energy Comm. 1961–64; Special Asst to Minister for Foreign Affairs 1973–76; mem. Science Council of Ministry of Educ. 1969–76, of Council for Ocean Devt in Prime Minister's Office 1971–76, Advisory Cttee for Co-operation with UN Univ. 1971–76; Judge, Int. Court of Justice 1976–85, 1985–94, 1994–2003, (Vice-Pres. 1991–94); del. to UN Confs on Law of the Sea 1958, 1960, 1973–75; Rep. at 6th Gen. Conf. of Inter-Governmental Oceanographic Comm., UNESCO 1969; consultative positions with bodies concerned with marine questions; Counsel for FRG before Int. Court of Justice 1968; Ed.-in-Chief, Japanese Annual of International Law 1973–77; Assoc. Inst. de Droit Int. 1969 (mem. 1979, Hon. mem. 2003); mem. Curatorium, Hague Acad. of Int. Law 1989–2004, fmr mem. Bd Dirs, Int. Devt Law Inst., Rome, Int. Council of Arbitration for Sport, Lausanne 1994–2006; mem. Japan Acad. 1994–; Hon. mem. American Soc. of Int. Law 1975, Inst. of Int. Law 2001; Hon. Citizen of the City of Sendai 2004; Grand Order of the Sacred Treasure (by the Emperor of Japan), Person of Cultural Merit, Govt of Japan 2007; Hon. DJur (Bhopal) 1980, (New York Law School) 1981. *Publications:* in Japanese: International Law of the Sea 1956–85 (eight vols), International Law and Maritime Resources 1971–75, Judicial Decisions relating to International Law before Japanese Courts 1978; in English: International Control of Sea Resources 1962, International Law of Sea Resources 1969, The International Law of Ocean Development (four vols) 1972–79, The Law of the Sea in Our Times (two vols) 1977, The Practice of Japan in International Law 1961–70 1982, The International Court of Justice 1987, 1993, Fifty Years of the Law of the Sea 2002, Sixty Years as Scholar and Judge of International Law 2009; various articles. *Address:* c/o Japan Academy, Ueno Koen 7-32, Taito-ku, Tokyo, 110-0007 (office); Akashicho 8-2-704, Chuo-ku, Tokyo 104-0044, Japan (home). *Telephone:* (3) 3822-2101 (office); (3) 5550-6666 (home). *Fax:* (3) 3822-2105 (office); (3) 5550-6694 (home). *E-mail:* oda .icj@bma.biglobe.ne.jp (home).

ODAGIRI, Joe, (Odajo); Japanese actor and singer; b. (Jô Odagiri), 16 Feb. 1976, Tsuyama City, Okayama; m. Yuu Kashii 2008; one s.; ed Fresno State Univ., USA. *Films include:* Kamen Rider Kuuga 2000, Platonic Sex 2001, Terrors 2001, Satorare 2002, Mokka no Kobito 2002, Azumi (Japan Acad. Award for Best New Actor) 2003, Bright Future (Japanese Professional Movie Award) 2003, Kaikyo wo wataru violin 2004, Pacchigil 2004, Blood and Bones (Blue Ribbon Best Supporting Actor Award 2004, Japan Acad. Award for Best Supporting Actor 2004, Kinema Junpo Best Supporting Actor Award 2004, Mainichi Film Concours Award for Best Supporting Actor 2004, Nikkan Sports Film Ishihara Yujiro New Actor Award 2004) 2004, Black Kiss 2004, In the Pool 2005, HAZARD 2005, House of Himiko (Yokohama Film Festival Best Actor Award 2005, Kinema Junpo Best Actor Award 2005) 2005, Shinobi: Heart Under Blade 2005, Scrap Heaven 2005, Princess Raccoon 2005, Big River 2006, The Uchôten Hotel 2006, Jikou Keisatsu 2006, Retribution 2006, Mushishi 2006, The Pavilion Salamandre 2006, Sway 2006, Tokyo Tower: Mom and Me and Sometimes Dad 2007, Sad Vacation 2007, Adrift in Tokyo 2007, Plastic City 2008, Dream 2008, The Warrior and the Wolf 2009, Air Doll 2009, I Wish 2011, My Way 2011, Real 2013, Mr. Go 2013, The Human Trust 2013, Present for You 2013; as writer and dir: Looking for Cherry Blossoms 2009. *Television includes:* Kamen Raidâ Kûga (series) 2000, Sitto no nioi (mini-series) 2001, Hatsu taiken (series) 2002, Satoukibi batake no uta (film) 2003, Prayer Beads (series) 2004, Shinsengumi!! Hijikata Toshizô saigo no ichi-nichi (film) 2004, Kaikyou o wataru baiorin (film) 2004, Fukigen na jiin (series) 2005, Kaette kita jikô keisatsu (series) 2007, Boku no imôto (series) 2009, Atami no Sôsakan (series) 2010, Hei no naka no chûgakkô (film) 2010, Kazoku no uta (series) 2012, Toshi densetsu no onna (series) 2012, Yae no sakura (series) 2013, Airport 2013 (film) 2013, River's Edge: The Ohkawabata Detective Agency (mini-series) 2014. *Recordings:* albums: White 2006, Black 2006. *Address:* c/o Dongyu, JPL 6F, Shibuya 2-10-15, Shibuya-ku, Tokyo, 150-0002, Japan (office). *Telephone:* (81) 3-3400-2131 (office). *Fax:* (81) 3-3400-2132 (office). *E-mail:* contact@dongyu.co.jp (office). *Website:* www.dongyu.co.jp/English/profile/odagiri.html (office); www .odagiri-joe.com (home).

ODDSSON, David; Icelandic politician and fmr central banker; b. 17 Jan. 1948, Reykjavik; s. of Oddur Ólafsson and Ingibjörg Kristín Lúðvíksdóttir; m. 1st Astríður Thorarensen 1951; one s.; m. 2nd Þorsteinn Daviðsson 1971; ed Reykjavik Coll., Univ. of Iceland; Chief Clerk Reykjavik Theatre 1970–72; parl. reporter for Morgunbladid newspaper 1973–74; worked for Almenna bokafelagid publishing co. 1975–76; Office Man., Reykjavik Health Insurance Fund 1976–78, Man. Dir 1978–82; mem. Reykjavik City Council 1974–99; Mayor of Reykjavik 1982–91; Vice-Chair. Independence Party 1989–91, Chair. 1991–; mem. Parl. 1991–; Prime Minister of Iceland 1991–2004; Minister of the Statistical Bureau of Iceland; Minister of Foreign Affairs 2004–05; Gov. Cen. Bank of Iceland 2005–09; Chair. of Exec. Cttee Reykjavik Arts Festival 1976–78; Hon. LLD (Univ. of Manitoba) 2000. *Publications:* plays: For My Country's Benefit (Nat. Theatre 1974–75), Icelandic Confabulations (Reykjavik Theatre 1975–76); TV dramas: Robert Eliasson Returns From Abroad 1977, Stains on the White Collar 1981; short stories: A Couple of Days Without Gudny 1997, Stolen from the Author of the Alphabet 2002; essay The Independence Movement 1981; trans. A Small Nation Under the Yoke of a Foreign Power by Anders Küng-Estonia 1973. *Leisure interests:* bridge, salmon fishing, forestry. *Address:* c/o Central Bank of Iceland, Kalkofnsvegi 1, 150 Reykjavik, Iceland (office).

O'DEA, Willie, LLM, CA; Irish politician; b. Nov. 1952, Limerick; m. Geraldine Kennedy; ed Patrician Brothers Coll., Ballyfin, Co. Laois, Univ. Coll. Dublin (UCD), Kings Inns, Inst. of Certified Accountants; fmr barrister and accountant; fmr Lecturer, UCD and Univ. of Limerick; TD 1982–, Minister of State at Dept of Justice 1992–93, at Depts of Justice and Health 1993–94, at Dept of Educ. 1997–2002, at Dept of Justice, Equality and Law Reform with special responsibility for Equality Issues 2002–04, Minister for Defence 2004–10; regular columnist, Sunday Independent and other nat. newspapers. *Address:* c/o Department of Defence, Parkgate, Infirmary Road, Dublin 7, Ireland (office). *Website:* www .willieodea.ie.

ØDEGÅRD, Knut, LittD; Norwegian poet, writer, critic and diplomatist; *Consul General, Republic of Macedonia;* b. 6 Nov. 1945, Molde; m. Thorgerdur Ingólfsdóttir 1981; two d.; ed Univ. of Oslo; poetry critic, Aftenposten newspaper 1968–2009, Vårt Land 2009–; Publr Noregs Boklag 1975–77; Cinema and Cultural Dir, Kristiansund Municipality 1977–78; Cultural Dir, Sør-Trøndelag Co. 1978–84; Man. Dir Scandinavian Centre, Nordens Hus, Reykjavík 1984–89; Founder and Pres. Bjornson Festivalen, Norwegian Festival of Int. Literature 1992–2002; Consul, Repub. of Slovakia 1995–97; Consul Gen., Repub. of Macedonia 1997–; Pres. Bjornstjerne Bjornson Acad., Norwegian Acad. of Literature and Freedom of Expression 2003–; mem. Icelandic Soc. of Authors, Literary Acad. of Romania, Norwegian Soc. of Authors, European Acad. of Poetry (Sec. Gen. 2009–); Norwegian State Scholar for Life 1989–; knighted by Pres. of Iceland 1987, Grand Kt Commdr, Order of the Icelandic Falcon 1993, Int. Order of Merit 1993, Kt, Norwegian Order of Literature 1995, knighted by King of Norway 1998, Kt, Equestrial Order of Holy Sepulchre of Jerusalem (Vatican) 2009; Jan Smrek Int. Poetry Award, Slovakia 2008, Bastian Prize 1984, Anders Jahre Cultural Prize 2001, Dobloug Prize, Swedish Acad. 2010. *Publications include:* poetry: Bee-buzz, Salmon Leap 1968, Cinema Operator 1991, Ventriloquy 1994, Selected Poems 1995, Missa 1998, The Stephensen House 2003, Look-out 2005, It Flowered So Insane 2009; books of prose and essays, a play, two non-fiction books about Iceland 1992, 1998 and a book about St Olaf 2011; works trans. into 29 languages. *Address:* Postboks 326, 6401 Molde, Norway. *Telephone:* 71-21-59-91 (office); 91-83-86-67 (office). *E-mail:* knutode@mimer.no (office).

ODEH, Ayman, LLM; Jordanian lawyer and politician; *Minister of State for Prime Ministry Affairs and Legislation;* b. 1961; ed Univ. of Jordan, Miami Univ., USA; practising lawyer 1985–; mem. various legal cttees including Jordan First Comm. Anti-Corruption Cttee, We Are All Jordan Cttee; Minister of Justice

2007–10; Minister of State for Prime Ministry Affairs and Legislation 2011–. *Address:* The Prime Ministry of Jordan, POB 80, Amman 11180, Jordan (office).

ODEIN AJUMOGOBIA, Henry, LLB; Nigerian lawyer and politician; *Minister of Foreign Affairs;* Founding Pnr, Ajumogobia & Okeke (legal practice), Lagos 2003–; fmr Attorney-Gen. and Commr of Justice, Rivers State; Fed. Minister of State for Petroleum 2007; Fed. Minister of Foreign Affairs 2010–; Sr Advocate of Nigeria 2003. *Address:* Ministry of Foreign Affairs, Maputo St, Zone 3, Wuse District, PMB 130, Abuja, Nigeria (office). *Telephone:* (9) 5230570 (office). *E-mail:* omaduekwe@nigeria.gov.ng (office). *Website:* www.mfa.gov.ng (office).

ODENBERG, Mikael; Swedish politician; b. 1953, Stockholm; m. Catherine Odenberg; two s. two d.; ed Östra Real Upper Secondary School, Stockholm, Stockholm Univ., Stockholm School of Econs, Reserve Officer Training, Nat. Defence Coll.; Maj. (reserve) in Swedish Marines; Local Govt Ombudsman, Swedish Young Conservatives and Moderate Party, Nacka 1972–73; Sec. Moderate Youth (MUF) 1978; Deputy Sec. to Stockholm City Commr (real estate, town-planning and highways depts) and Sec. to Moderate City Council Group 1979–85; self-employed 1985–2004; mem. Riksdag (Parl.) 1987, 1990, 1991–2006, mem. Cttee on Housing 1991–94, Cttee on Industry and Trade 1994–98, Cttee on Labour Market and Cttee on EU Affairs 1998–2002, Deputy Chair. Cttee on Industry and Trade 2002–03, mem. War Del. 2003–, Leader Moderate Party Parl. Group 2003–06, Deputy Chair. Cttee on Finance 2003–06, mem. Advisory Council on Foreign Affairs 2003–06, mem. Riksdag Bd 2003–06, mem. Parl. Review Comm. 2003–06; Minister for Defence 2006–07; Leader Moderate Party's group on healthcare matters, Stockholm Co. Council 1988–91.

ODENT, Michel, MD; French obstetrician and writer; *Director, Primal Health Research Centre, London;* b. 7 July 1930, Bresles, Oise; m. Nicole Odent; two s. (one deceased) one d.; ed Univ. of Paris; developed and led surgical unit and maternity unit at the Pithiviers state hosp. 1962–85; commissioned by WHO to report on planned home birth in industrialized countries 1986–90; moved to London, UK 1990; Founder and Dir Primal Health Research Centre, London, for study of long-term consequences of early experiences; introduced concepts of home-like birthing rooms and birthing pools in maternity hosps 1970s; Contributing Ed. Midwifery Today, USA. *Achievements:* author of the first article in the medical literature about the use of birthing pools (Lancet 1983), of the first article about the initiation of lactation during the hour following birth, and of the first article applying the 'Gate Control Theory of Pain' to obstetrics. *Publications:* 12 books, published in 22 languages, including Birth Reborn 1984, Primal Health 1986, The Scientification of Love 2001, The Farmer and the Obstetrician 2002, The Caesarean 2004, The Functions of the Orgasms 2009, Childbirth in the Age of Plastics 2011; more than 90 medical articles. *Address:* 72 Savernake Road, London, NW3 2JR, England (office). *Telephone:* (20) 7485-0095 (office); (20) 7475-0095 (home). *Fax:* (20) 7267-5123 (office). *E-mail:* modent@aol.com (home). *Website:* www.wombecology.com (home); www.primalhealthresearch.com (home).

ODGERS, Sir Graeme David William, Kt, MA, MBA; British business executive; b. 10 March 1934, Johannesburg, SA; s. of the late William Arthur Odgers and of Elizabeth Minty (née Rennie); m. Diana Patricia Berge 1957 (died 2012); one s. three d. (one deceased); ed St John's Coll., Johannesburg, Gonville and Caius Coll., Cambridge, Harvard Business School, USA; Investment Officer, IFC, Washington, DC 1959–62; Man. Consultant, Urwick Orr & Partners Ltd 1962–64; Investment Exec., Hambros Bank Ltd 1964–65; Dir, Keith Shipton Ltd 1965–72, C.T. Bowring (Insurance) Holdings Ltd 1972–74; Chair. Odgers & Co. Ltd (Exec. Recruitment Consultants) 1970–74; Dir, Industrial Devt Unit, Dept of Industry 1974–77; Assoc. Dir (Finance), General Electric Co. 1977–78; Group Finance Dir, Tarmac PLC 1979–86, Group Man. Dir 1983–86, Dir (non-exec.) 1986–87; Dir (non-exec.), Dalgety PLC 1987–93; part-time Bd mem., British Telecommunications PLC 1983–86, Govt Dir 1984–86, Deputy Chair. and Chief Finance Officer 1986–87, Group Man. Dir 1987–89; Chief Exec., Alfred McAlpine 1990–93; Chair., Monopolies and Mergers Comm. 1993–97; Dir (non-exec.), Southern Electric PLC 1998–; Dir, Scottish and Southern Energy PLC 1999–; Chair., Locate in Kent Ltd 1998–2005, Kent Econ. Bd 2001–09; DL, Co. of Kent 2002–09; Chair., later Pres. New Marlowe Theatre Devt Trust 2007–11; Hon. Fellow, Christ Church Univ. 2010; Hon. LLD (Greenwich) 2004, (Kent) 2005; Invicta Award, Co. of Kent 2009. *Leisure interest:* golf. *Address:* 5 The Coach House, Springwood Park, Tonbridge, Kent, TN11 9LZ, England. *Telephone:* (1732) 773611. *E-mail:* graeme@theodgers.plus.com.

ODIER, Patrick, BA (Econ), MBA; Swiss banking executive; *Chairman, Swiss Bankers Association;* b. 1955; ed Univ. of Geneva, Univ. of Chicago, USA; joined Lombard Odier & Cie (pvt. bankers) 1982, completed training in Zurich, New York and Montreal, Man. Partner 1986–2008, Sr Partner, Lombard Odier Darier Hentsch & Cie 2008–; Chair. Swiss Bankers Asscn 2009–; Vice-Chair. economie-suisse (Swiss fed. of trade and industry); mem. Bd several Swiss and int. academic insts and non-profit orgs. *Address:* Swiss Bankers Association, Aeschenplatz 7, PO Box 4182, 4002 Basel, Switzerland (office). *Telephone:* (61) 2959393 (office). *Fax:* (61) 2725382 (office). *E-mail:* office@sba.ch (office). *Website:* www.swissbanking .org (office).

ODIERNO, Gen. Raymond (Ray) T., BSc, MS, MA; American army officer; *Chief of Staff, US Army;* b. 8 Sept. 1954, Rockaway, NJ; s. of Ray Odierno and Helen Odierno; m. Linda Burkarth; two s. one d.; ed US Mil. Acad., West Point, North Carolina State Univ., Naval War Coll.; began army career with US Army Europe and US Seventh Army, Germany, becoming Platoon Leader and Survey Officer, 1st Bn, US 41st Field Artillery Brigade, 56th Field Artillery Brigade, and ADC to Commdg Gen.; Exec. Officer, 2nd Bn, 3rd Field Artillery and later Div. Artillery, 3rd Armored Div., Operation Desert Storm 1990–91; fmr Chief of Staff, US States V Corps, US Army Europe; Commdr, US 4th Infantry Div. (4th ID) 2001–04; Asst to Chair. of Jt Chiefs of Staff and Sr Mil. Adviser to Sec. of State, Washington, DC 2004–06; Commdg Gen., US III Corps, Iraq, also Commdg Gen. Multi-Nat. Force—Iraq, Baghdad 2008–10, Commdg Gen., US Forces—Iraq, Operation Iraqi Freedom Jan.-Oct. 2010; Commdr, US Jt Forces Command, Norfolk, Va 2010–11; Chief of Staff of US Army 2011–; decorations include four Defense Distinguished Service Medals, two Army Distinguished Service Medals, Defense Superior Service Medal, six Legions of Merit, Bronze Star Medal, Defense Meritorious Service Medal, four Meritorious Service Medals, Army Commendation

Medal, Army Achievement Medal, Combat Action Badge; Orders of Mil. Merit from Brazil, Colombia, Romania and Italy; Officier, Légion d'honneur; numerous medals, including Army Distinguished Service Medal, Defense Superior Service Medal, Legion of Merit, Bronze Star, State Department Sec.'s Distinguished Service Award. *Address:* Chief of Public Affairs, Department of the Army, 1500 Army Pentagon, Washington, DC 20310-1500, USA (office). *Website:* www.army .mil/leaders/csa (office).

ODINGA, Raila Amollo, MSc; Kenyan politician; *Prime Minister;* b. 7 Jan. 1945, Nyanza; s. of Jaramogi Odinga and Mary Emma Odinga; m. Ida Anyango Oyoo; four c.; ed Herder Inst., Leipzig, Otto von Guericke Tech. Univ., Magdeburg, Germany; Asst Lecturer, Dept of Mechanical Eng, Univ. of Nairobi 1971–72; f. Spectre Ltd (later East African Spectre Ltd) eng co. 1971; Group Standards Man. Kenya Bureau of Standards 1974–78, Deputy Dir 1978–82; detained without trial following coup attempt by Kenya Air Force personnel 1982–88, re-arrested and detained 1988, 1990, spent four months in political asylum in Norway 1991; Co-founder Forum for the Restoration of Democracy 1991; elected MP for Langata 1992, joined Nat. Devt Party 1996; finished cand. in presidential elections 1997, 2007, 2013; Minister for Energy 2001–02; joined Liberal Democratic Party 2002; Minister for Roads and Public Works 2002–05; Co-founder Orange Democratic Movt 2005, Leader 2007–; Prime Minister 2008–. *Address:* Orange Democratic Movement – Kenya, Orange House, Vanga Road, PO Box 2478, 00202 Nairobi, Kenya (office). *E-mail:* odmk2007@yahoo.com (office); contact@raila07.com (office). *Website:* odmk.org (office); www.raila2007.com (office).

ODIO BENITO, Elizabeth; Costa Rican politician, lawyer, judge and international arbitrator; b. 15 Sept. 1939, Puntarenas; d. of Emiliano Odio Madrigal and Esperanza Benito Ibañez; ed Colegio Superior de Señoritas, Univ. of Costa Rica, Univ. of Buenos Aires; Minister of Justice and Attorney-Gen. 1978–82; Minister of Justice 1990–94; Second Vice-Pres. of Costa Rica and Minister of Environment and Energy 1998–2002; Perm. Rep. to UN, Geneva 1993; mem. Sub-comm. for the Prevention of Discrimination and Minorities Protection, Human Rights Comm., UN 1980–83, Special Rapporteur, Sub-comm. on Discrimination and Intolerance Based on Religion or Creed 1983–86; Vice-Pres. Criminal Tribunal for the Fmr Yugoslavia 1993–95, Judge, Int. Tribunal for the Fmr Yugoslavia (ICTY) 1993–98; mem. Admin. Tribunal, IDB 1997–98; mem. and Vice-Pres. Bd of Dirs Univ. para la Paz, UNESCO 1999–, Pres. Working Group on Optional Protocol for the Int. Convention against Torture 1998; mem. Costa Rican Nat. Group to the Perm. Court of Arbitration 2000–03; Judge, Trial Div., Int. Criminal Court, The Hague 2003–12 (served term as Second Vice-Pres. 2003–06); Prof., Univ. of Costa Rica 1986–94, Vice-Pres. of Academic Affairs 1988–90, Prof. Emer. 1994–; Prof. Inter-American Inst. of Human Rights, Costa Rica 1992–; Visiting Prof., Univs of Strasbourg, France 1986, Utrecht, Netherlands 1995, Zaragoza, Spain 1996, Leiden, The Netherlands 1998, Barcelona, Spain 1998; mem. Costa Rican Law Asscn, Steering Cttee Asser Inst., The Hague, Bd Dirs Inter-American Inst. of Human Rights, Int. Comm. of Jurists; Dr hc (St Edward's Univ.) 2004. *Address:* International Criminal Court, PO Box 19519, 2500 CM The Hague, The Netherlands (office); PO Box 2292/1000, San José, Costa Rica. *Telephone:* (70) 515-8515 (office); 2809654 (home). *Fax:* (70) 515-8555 (office); 2536984 (home). *E-mail:* pio@icc-cpi.int (office); eodio@racsa.co.cr (home). *Website:* www.icc-cpi.int (office).

ODLAND, Steve, BBA, MM; American business executive; *Chairman and CEO, Office Depot Inc.;* ed Univ. of Notre Dame, Northwestern Univ.; with Quaker Oats Co. 1981–96; Sr Vice-Pres., Gen. Man. Snacks Div., Sara Lee 1996–98, Pres. Foodservice Div. 1997–98; Exec. Ahold USA 1998–2000; Chair., CEO, Pres. and Dir AutoZone Inc. 2001–05; Chair. and CEO Office Depot Inc. 2005–; mem. Bd of Dirs General Mills Inc. *Address:* Office Depot Inc., 2200 Old Germantown Road, Delray Beach, FL 33445, USA (office). *Telephone:* (561) 438-4800 (office). *Fax:* (561) 438-4001 (office). *Website:* www.officedepot.com (office).

ODLING-SMEE, John Charles, CMG, MA; British economist (retd); b. 13 April 1943, Leeds, Yorks., England; s. of the late Rev. Charles William Odling-Smee and Katherine Hamilton Odling-Smee (née Aitchison); m. Carmela Veneroso 1996; ed Durham School, St John's Coll., Cambridge; Jr Research Officer, Dept of Applied Econs, Cambridge 1964–65; Asst Research Officer, Inst. of Econs and Statistics, Oxford 1968–71, 1972–73; Econ. Research Officer, Govt of Ghana 1971–72; Sr Research Officer, Centre for Urban Econs LSE 1973–75; Econ. Adviser, Cen. Policy Review Staff, Cabinet Office 1975–77; Sr Econ. Adviser, HM Treasury 1977–80; Sr Economist, IMF 1981–82; Under-Sec., HM Treasury 1982–89; Deputy Chief Econ. Adviser, HM Treasury 1989–90; Sr Adviser, IMF 1990–91, Dir IMF European II Dept 1992–2003 (dept dissolved), retd 2004. *Publications:* Housing Rent Costs and Subsidies 1978, British Economic Growth 1856–1973 1982; various articles in books and learned journals. *Address:* 3506 Garfield Street NW, Washington, DC 20007, USA. *E-mail:* jodlingsmee@juno.com.

ODOKI, Hon. Benjamin Joses, LLB; Ugandan lawyer; *Chief Justice of Uganda;* b. 23 March 1943, Busia; m. Veronica Odoki; three s. one d.; ed Kings Coll. Budo, Kampala, Univ. of Dar-es-Salaam; State Attorney 1969–72; Advocate, High Court of Uganda 1970; Dir Law Devt Centre 1974–78; Judge, High Court of Uganda 1978–81, Dir Public Prosecution 1981–84; Judge, Supreme Court 1986–2001; Chair. Uganda Constitutional Comm. 1989–93; Chair. Judicial Service Comm. 1996–2000; Chief Justice of Uganda 2001–; Gen. Ed. Uganda Law Focus 1974–78, Ed.-in-Chief Uganda Law Reports 1974–78; mem. Editorial Advisory Bd Commonwealth Law Bulletin 2005–; Independence Medal 1974, Order of Merit, Uganda Law Soc. 1998, Distinguished Jurist Award (Nigeria) 2002. *Publications include:* A Guide to Criminal Procedure in Uganda 1990, An Introduction to Juridical Conduct and Practice 1992, A Guide to the Legal Profession in Uganda 1992, Criminal Investigation and Prosecutions 1999. *Leisure interests:* music, fine art, drama. *Address:* Chambers of the Chief Justice, Courts of Judicature, POB 7085, Kampala (office); Plot 4 Philip Road, Kololo, Kampala, Uganda (home). *Telephone:* (41) 231727 (office); (41) 343576 (home). *Fax:* (41) 343971 (office). *E-mail:* bodoki2000@yahoo.com (home). *Website:* www.judicature.go.ug (office).

O'DONNELL, Baron (Life Peer), cr. 2012, of Clapham in the London Borough of Wandsworth; **Rt Hon. Augustine Thomas (Gus) O'Donnell,** Kt, GCB, KCB, CB, BA, MPhil; British economist and civil servant; *Chairman, Frontier Economics;* b. 1 Oct. 1952, South London, England; s. of James O'Donnell and Helen O'Donnell (née McLean); m. Melanie Timmis 1979; one d.; ed Salesian Coll.,

Battersea, Univ. of Warwick and Nuffield Coll., Oxford; Lecturer, Dept of Political Economy, Univ. of Glasgow 1975–79; economist, HM Treasury 1979–85; First Sec. (Econ.) Embassy in Washington, DC 1985–88; Sr Econ. Adviser, HM Treasury 1988–89, Press Sec. to Chancellor of the Exchequer 1989–90; Press Sec. to Prime Minister John Major 1990–94; Under-Sec. (monetary group) HM Treasury 1994–95, Deputy Dir Macroeconomic Policy and Prospects Directorate 1995–96, Minister (Econs), Embassy in Washington, DC; Exec. Dir IMF, World Bank 1997–98, Man. Dir Macroeconomic Policy and Prospects Directorate 1998–2002; Head of Govt Econ. Service, HM Treasury 1998–2002, Perm. Sec. (with responsibility for Euro entry tests) 2002–05; Sec. to Cabinet, Head of Home Civil Service and Perm. Sec. of the Cabinet Office 2005–11; mem. (Crossbench), House of Lords 2012–; Visiting Fellow, Nuffield Coll., Oxford; Visiting Prof. LSE, Univ. Coll. London; Chair. Frontier Economics 2013–; Adviser TD Bank; Dir (non-exec.) Brookfield Asset Management; Trustee, The Tablet newspaper. *Publications:* The O'Donnell Review of the Revenue Departments, Reforming Britain's Economic and Financial Policy (ed.), Microeconomic Reform in Britain (ed.); various articles in econ. journals and contrib. to Scotland's Future (ed. A. Goudie). *Leisure interests:* football, cricket, tennis, golf. *Address:* House of Lords, Westminster, London, SW1A 0PW, England (office). *Telephone:* (20) 7031-7000 (office). *Fax:* (20) 7031-7001 (office). *E-mail:* gus.odonnell@frontier-economics.com. *Website:* www .parliament.uk/biographies/lords/augustine-o%27donnell/18039 (office).

O'DONNELL, Christopher (Chris) Eugene; American actor; b. 26 June 1970, Winnetka, Ill.; m. Caroline Fentress 1997; five c.; f. George Street Pictures (production co.). *Films:* Men Don't Leave 1990, Fried Green Tomatoes at the Whistle Stop Cafe 1991, School Ties 1992, Scent of a Woman 1992, The Three Musketeers 1993, Blue Sky 1994, Circle of Friends 1995, Mad Love 1995, Batman Forever 1995, The Chamber 1996, In Love and War 1996, Batman and Robin 1997, Cookie's Fortune 1999, The Bachelor (producer and actor) 1999, Vertical Limit 2000, 29 Palms 2002, Kinsey 2004, The Sisters 2005, Kit Kittredge: An American Girl 2008, Max Payne 2008, A Little Help 2010, Cats & Dogs: The Revenge of Kitty Galore 2010, The Tournament Challenge Challenged (short) 2012. *Television:* Jack and Mike (series) 1986, The Practice (series) 2003, The Amazing Westerbergs (film) 2004, Two and a Half Men (series) 2004, Head Cases (series) 2005, Grey's Anatomy (series) 2006, The Company (mini-series) 2007, NCIS (series) 2009, NCIS: Los Angeles (series) 2009–14, WWII in HD: The Air War (film documentary) 2010, Hawaii Five-0 (series) 2012. *Address:* c/o Josh Lieberman, Creative Artists Agency, 2000 Avenue of the Stars, Los Angeles, CA 90067, USA (office); George Street Pictures, 4000 Warner Blvd, Building 81, Room 203, Burbank, CA 91522. *Telephone:* (424) 288-2000 (office); (818) 954-4361. *Fax:* (424) 288-2900 (office). *Website:* www.caa.com (office).

O'DONNELL, Daniel, MBE; Irish singer; b. 12 Dec. 1961, Kincasslagh, Co. Donegal; m. Majella McLennan 2002; backing vocalist for sister Margo O'Donnell early 1980s; tours of UK and Ireland 1985–, Australia and NZ 1993–, USA 2003–; numerous live appearances. *Radio:* numerous interviews in Ireland, UK, USA and Australia. *Television:* series, Ireland, Pledges (PBS TV, USA). *Recordings include:* albums: Two Sides Of Daniel O'Donnell 1985, I Need You 1986, Don't Forget To Remember 1987, The Boy From Donegal 1987, Love Songs 1988, From The Heart 1988, Thoughts Of Home 1989, Favourites 1990, The Last Waltz 1990, The Very Best Of… 1991, Follow Your Dream 1992, Christmas With Daniel 1994, Especially For You 1994, The Classic Collection 1995, Irish Collection 1996, Timeless (with Mary Duff) 1996, Songs Of Inspiration 1996, Country Collection 1997, This Is Daniel O'Donnell 1997, I Believe 1997, Love Hope & Faith 1998, Greatest Hits 1999, Faith And Inspiration 2000, Live Laugh Love 2001, Heartbreakers 2002, Songs Of Love 2002, Irish Album 2002, Yesterday's Memories 2002, Dreaming 2002, The Daniel O'Donnell Show 2003, Welcome To North America 2003, Date With (live) 2003, Daniel In Blue Jeans 2003, Daniel O'Donnell And Friends (live) 2003, At The End Of The Day 2003, The Jukebox Years 2004, Welcome To My World 2004, Until The Next Time 2006, Together Again (with Mary Duff) 2008, Country Boy 2008, Peace In The Valley 2009, O Holy Night 2010. *Videos include:* Daniel O'Donnell Live In Concert 1988, Thoughts Of Home 1989, TV Show Favourites 1990, An Evening With Daniel O'Donnell 1990, Follow Your Dream 1992, Daniel And Friends Live 1993, Just For You 1994, The Classic Concert 1995, Christmas With Daniel 1996, The Gospel Show, Live At The Point 1997, Give A Little Love 1998, Peaceful Waters 1999, Faith And Inspiration 2000, Live Laugh Love 2001, The Daniel O'Donnell Show 2001, Shades Of Green 2002, Songs Of Faith 2003. *Publications:* My Story (autobiog.) 2000, Daniel O'Donnell: My Pictures and Places 2004. *Address:* c/o Brockwell Ltd, Unit 6, 90B Lagan Road, Dublin Industrial Estate, Glasnevin, Dublin 11, Ireland (office). *Telephone:* (1) 830 1707 (office). *Fax:* (1) 830 1981 (office). *E-mail:* srmanagement@eircom.net (office). *Website:* www.danielodonnell.org.

O'DONNELL, Edward B., BA, MA; American economist, diplomatist and business executive; *Director of International Business Development. American Business Development Group International;* b. Memphis, Tenn.; m.; three c.; ed Southern Methodist Univ., American Univ. and Univ. of Heidelberg, Germany; served with US Army 1968–72; joined Foreign Service 1975, positions included West German and East German Desk Officer, Econ. Counsellor, Embassy in Vienna, Commercial Officer, US Mission in Berlin, Chargé d'affaires a.i. and Deputy Chief, Embassy in Panama, Econ. and Commercial Officer, Embassies in Bogotá and Asunción, Prin. Officer and Consul-Gen., Frankfurt, Germany; served as Exec. Asst to three Under-Secs and as Special Asst to two Dirs of Policy Planning Staff, US State Dept; fmr Dir Dept of State Liaison Office to US House of Reps; Special Envoy for Holocaust Issues, US State Dept 2003–06; currently Special Negotiator, US Mission to OAS; Dir Int. Business Devt, American Business Development Group International, Columbia, SC 2007–; returned to Dept of State for 90 days to assist with transition of Sec. Hillary Clinton's new leadership team 2009. *Address:* American Business Development Group International, 1201 Gervais Street, Columbia, SC 29201, USA (office). *Telephone:* (803) 929-1414 (office). *Website:* www.abdg.com.

O'DONNELL, Norah, BA, MA; American journalist and television presenter; *Co-Host, CBS This Morning;* b. 23 Jan. 1974, Washington, DC; m. Geoff Tracy 2001; one s. two d.; ed Douglas MacArthur High School, San Antonio, Tex., Georgetown Univ.; grew up in San Antonio, Tex., Landstuhl, Germany, Seoul, South Korea and Washington, DC; worked as staff reporter, Roll Call; worked as a contrib. and analyst for MSNBC, joined NBC News 1999, Chief Washington Corresp. for MSNBC and contributing corresp. for NBC News' Today and Weekend Today programmes, White House Corresp. for NBC 2003–05, was also regular contrib. to all of NBC News platforms and served as substitute anchor on 9:00 AM hour of Today –2011; joined CBS News as Chief White House Corresp. 2011, also serves as primary substitute anchor for Face The Nation and reports for all CBS News broadcasts and platforms, Co-host, with Charlie Rose and Gayle King, CBS This Morning 2012–; Sigma Delta Chi Award for Breaking News Coverage 2001, Emmy Award as part of NBC News' election night coverage 2008, named by Washingtonian Magazine as one of Washington's 100 Most Powerful Women, named to Irish American Magazine's 2000 Top 100 Irish Americans list. *Address:* CBS News, 555 West 57th Street, New York, NY 10019, USA (office). *Telephone:* (212) 975-4114 (office). *Website:* www.cbsnews.com/cbsthismorning (office).

O'DONOGHUE, John, BCL, LLB; Irish politician; b. 28 May 1956, Cahirciveen, Co. Kerry; m. Kate Ann Murphy; two s. one d.; ed Christian Brothers' Secondary School, Cahirciveen, Univ. Coll., Cork, Inc. Law Soc. of Ireland; fmrly solicitor; mem. Dáil Éireann (lower house of parl.) Feb. 1987–; Minister of State, Dept of Finance 1991–92; fmr Fianna Fáil Spokesperson on Justice; Minister of Justice, Equality and Law Reform June 1997–2002, for Arts, Sport and Tourism 2002–07; Chair., Dáil Éireann 2007–09; mem. Kerry Co. Council (Chair. 1990–91), mem. Kerry Co. Library Cttee, Kerry Fisheries and Coastal Man. Cttee, Southern Health Bd Psychiatric Services Cttee, Caherciveen Social Services Cttee, British–Irish Parl. Body. *Leisure interests:* English literature, history, Gaelic games, horse racing. *Address:* 14 Main Street, Cahirciveen, Co. Kerry (office); Garranearagh, Cahirciveen, Co. Kerry, Ireland (home). *Telephone:* (66) 9473221 (office); (66) 72413 (home). *Fax:* (66) 9473222 (office); (66) 72667 (home). *Website:* www .johnodonoghue.ie.

ODROWĄŻ-PIENIĄŻEK, Janusz, MA; Polish writer, literary historian and museum director; *Senior Director, Adam Mickiewicz Museum of Literature;* b. 2 July 1931, Opatowice; s. of Ludwik Odrowąż-Pieniążek and Helena Korybut-Daszkiewicz; m. Izabella Romanowska; one s.; ed Warsaw Univ., Lublin Catholic Univ.; scientific worker, Inst. of Literary Research, Polish Acad. of Science, Warsaw 1956–72; Dir Adam Mickiewicz Museum of Literature, Warsaw 1972–2009, Sr Dir 2010–; Ed.-in-Chief Muzealnictwo (journal) 1981–2010; mem. Asscn of Friends of Books 1958–, Adam Mickiewicz Literature Asscn 1992–, Soc. of Authors ZAiKS 1962–, Pen Club 1969–, Accad. di Storia e Letteratura Polacca e Slava 'Adamo Mickiewicz', Bologna 1976–, Deutsche Schillergesellschaft (Marbach am Neckar) 1995–, mem. Polish Nat. Cttee, ICOM 1972–, Vice-Chair. 2002–08; Pres. Int. Cttee Museum of Literature ICOM 1995–2001; mem. Man. Bd SEC 1975–; Vice-Chair. Polish Writers' Asscn 1996–99, Chair. 1999–2002; Golden Cross of Merit 1974, Kt's Cross, Order of Polonia Restituta 1988, Commdr's Cross 1999, Commdr's Cross with Star 2012; Diploma of Merit, Acad. Internationale des Sciences de l'Homme du Canada 1982, Warsaw Award 1983, Editor's Award, Polish Pen Club 1998, Minister of Culture Award 2003, Zygmunt Gloger Award 2004, Gloria Artis Silver Medal 2005, Gold Medal 2009, Reymont Award 2010. *Publications:* short stories: Opowiadania paryskie 1963, Ucieczka z ciepłych krajów 1968, Wielki romans w Bucharze 1984, Bulwar Wilshire 2004; poetical prose: Teoria fal 1964, Głos z szuflady 2002; novels: Małżeństwo z Lyndą Winters 1971, Mit Marii Chapdelaine 1985, Bulwar Wilshire albo lądowanie w Kizył Kija 2004; essays: Polonika zbierane po świecie 1992, Mickiewicziana zbierane po świecie 1998; Paul Cazin, diariste, epistolier, traducteur (co-author) 1997; numerous works on literary history in scientific journals. *Leisure interest:* travelling. *Address:* Adam Mickiewicz Museum of Literature, Rynek Starego Miasta 20, 00-272 Warsaw (office); Uniwersytecka 1 Apt. 2, 02-036 Warsaw, Poland (home). *Telephone:* (22) 8314061 (office); (22) 8225913 (home). *Fax:* (22) 8317692 (office); (22) 8225913 (home). *E-mail:* sekretariat@muzeumliteratury.pl (office).

ODUBER, Nelson Orlando; Dutch politician; b. 7 Feb. 1947; m. Glenda Oduber; three s.; ed St Antonius Coll., Santa Cruz, Admin. Acad. of Brabant, Tilburg, Univ. of Utrecht; Teacher, Governmental Org. and mem. Exams Preparatory Cttee 1973–75; mem. Cttee of the Kingdom to prepare the independence of Suriname 1973–75; Deputy in charge of Dept for Legis. and Constitutional Affairs 1975–85; Vice-Pres. Consultative Cttee for Independence of Aruba 1978–85; mem. Kingdom Cttee for political restructuring of Antilles 1978–80; Leader Movimento Electoral di Pueblo (MEP) (People's Electoral Movt); Prime Minister of Aruba 1989–94, 2001–09, also Minister of Gen. Affairs 1989–94, 2001–09; Ordén Francisco de Miranda (Venezuela) 1989, Order of the Liberatador First Class (Venezuela) 1991, Kt, Order of Orange Nassau 1995; Man of the Year (Diario) 1980, Gold Award for contributing to educ. of Aruba 1983, Politician of the Year by readers of Extra 1990, Man of the Year (MEP) 1993, Man of the Year 2001. *Leisure interests:* swimming, gardening, keeping fit. *Address:* Nayostraat 5, Oranjestad (home); MEP, Nayostraat 5, Oranjestad, Aruba. *Telephone:* (297) 5824206 (home).

ODUNTON, Nii Allotey, MS; Ghanaian mining engineer, administrative officer and international organization official; *Secretary-General, International Seabed Authority;* b. 14 June 1951; m. Nijama Odunton; four c.; ed Achimota Secondary School, Accra, Henry Krumb School of Mines, Columbia Univ., USA; Mine Planning Officer, Bethlehem Steel Corpn, Morgantown, Pa 1974–75; Econ. Affairs Officer, Dept of Int. Econ. Social Affairs, UN Secr., New York 1980–83, held several other UN positions 1984–88 including Chief of Mineral Resources Section and Ocean Econs and Tech. Br., First Officer in Charge, UN Office for Law of the Sea, Kingston, Jamaica 1988–; Adviser to Minerals Comm. of Govt of Ghana 1984–87; Interim Dir-Gen. and Programme Co-ordinator, Int. Seabed Authority 1996–2008, Head of Office of Resources and Environmental Monitoring 2008, Deputy to Sec.-Gen. 2008, Sec.-Gen. 2009–; mem. American Inst. of Mining, Metallurgical and Petroleum Engineers, Ghana Inst. of Engineers; African Scholarship Programme of American Univs Award 1969, 1969–72, Henry Krumb Research Fellow 1972, Henry Krumb Fellow 1974–75. *Address:* International Seabed Authority, 14–20 Port Royal Street, Kingston, Jamaica (office). *Telephone:* 922-9105 (office). *Fax:* 922-0195 (office). *Website:* www.isa.org.jm (office).

ŌE, Kenzaburō, BA; Japanese writer; b. 31 Jan. 1935, Ehime, Shikoku; m. Yukari Itami 1960; two s. one d.; ed Tokyo Univ.; first stories published 1957; first full-length novel Pluck the Flowers, Gun the Kids 1958; represented young Japanese writers at Peking (now Beijing) 1960; travelled to Russia and Western

Europe writing a series of essays on Youth in the West 1961; Commdr, Légion d'honneur 2002; Hon. DLit (Harvard) 2000; Shinchosha Literary Prize 1964, Tanizaka Prize 1967, Europelia Arts Festival Literary Prize 1989, Nobel Prize for Literature 1994. *Publications include:* fiction: Shisha no ogori (trans. as The Catch) (Japanese Soc. for the Promotion of Literature Akutagawa Prize) 1958, Memushiri kouchi (trans. as Nip the Buds, Shoot the Kids) 1958, Miru mae ni tobe 1958, Our Age (in trans.) 1959, Screams (in trans.) 1962, The Perverts (in trans.) 1963, Nichijo seikatsu no boken 1963, Kojinteki na taiken (trans. as A Personal Matter) 1964, Adventures in Daily Life (in trans.) 1964, Man'en gannen no futtoburu (trans. as The Silent Cry) 1967, Football in The First Year of Mannen (in trans.) 1967, Pinchi ranna chosho (trans. as The Pinch Runner Memorandum) 1976, Warera no kyoki o iki nobiru michi o 1969, Shosetsu no hoho 1978, Natsukashii toshi e no tegami 1986, M/T to mori no fushigi no monogatari 1986, A Healing Family (in trans.) 1996, A Quiet Life (in trans.) 1998, Rouse Up, O Young Men of the New Age (in trans.) 2002, Somersault (in trans.) 2003, Telling Tales (contrib. to charity anthology) 2004, Torikaeko (trans. as The Changeling) 2000, Jibun no Ki'no Sitade (trans. as Under My Tree) 2000, Sakokushiteha Naranai 2001, Iigataki Nagekimote 2001, Ureigao no Douij 2002, Bouryoku ni Sakaratte kaku (trans. as Writing against Violence) 2003, Atarasii hito' no houe 2003, Nihyakunen no kodomo 2003, Sayounara, Watashi no Hon yo! 2005, Routashi Anaberu rī souke dachitu mimakaritu (trans. as The Beautiful Annabel Lee was Chilled and Killed) 2007, Sui Si 2009; non-fiction: Hiroshima noto (trans. as Hiroshima Notes) 1963, Okinawa noto 1970, Chiryo noto 1990, Japan, the Ambiguous and Myself (the Nobel Prize speech and other lectures) 1995. *Address:* 585 Seijo-machi, Setagaya-ku, Tokyo, Japan. *Telephone:* 482-7192.

OELZE, Christiane; German singer (soprano); b. 9 Oct. 1963, Cologne; m. Bodo Primus; one d.; ed studied with Klesie Kelly-Moog and Erna Westenberger; began singing in opera 1990; recital tours USA, S America, Japan; has worked with numerous major int. conductors and has appeared on all important European concert stages and at int. festivals, including Salzburg Festival; roles include Despina (Ottawa), Pamina (Leipzig, Lyon, Hamburg, Munich), Konstanze (Salzburg, Zurich), Anne Trulove (Glyndebourne), Regina (in Mathis der Maler, Covent Garden), Zdenka (Covent Garden), Zerlina (Covent Garden), Ännchen (in Der Freischütz, Covent Garden), Mélisande (Glyndebourne), Servilia (in La Clemenza di Tito, Covent Garden), Susanna (Salzburg), Ilia (in Idomeneo, Glyndebourne), Igluno (Palestina, Covent Garden), Sophie (in Rosenkavalier, Hamburg); taught at Robert-Schumann-Hochschule, Dusseldorf, Germany 2003–08; winner, several lieder competitions, including Hugo-Wolf-Wettbewerb 1987, Hochschule Wettbewerb für Lied-Duo 1988. *Recordings include:* several solo recitals, concert arias, Mass in C minor (Mozart), Christmas Oratorio, St John and St Matthew Passions, Webern songs and cantatas, Le nozze di Figaro and many others. *Television:* Pelléas et Mélisande, Glyndebourne 1999. *Address:* c/o Künstleragentur, Augstein & Hahn, Sendlinger Str. 56, 80331 Munich, Germany (office). *E-mail:* hahn@augstein.info (office). *Website:* www.christianeoelze.com.

OESTREICHER, Rev. Canon Paul, MA; British/New Zealand/German clergyman and journalist; b. 29 Sept. 1931, Meiningen, Germany; s. of Paul Oestreicher, MD and Emma Oestreicher (née Schnaus); m. 1st Lore Feind 1958 (died 2000); two s. (one deceased) two d.; m. 2nd Dr Barbara Einhorn 2002; ed Otago and Victoria Univs, NZ, Bonn Univ., FRG, Lincoln Theological Coll., UK; emigrated to NZ with parents 1939; Ed. Critic student newspaper, Otago Univ. 1952–53; Humboldt Research Fellow, Bonn Univ. 1955, Berlin 1992; studied industrial mission (Opel, Gen. Motors), Rüsselsheim 1958–59; ordained in Church of England 1959; freelance journalist and broadcaster in FRG and UK 1959–; Curate in Dalston, London 1959–61; Programme Producer, Religious Dept, BBC Radio 1961–64; Assoc. Sec., Dept of Int. Affairs, British Council of Churches, with special responsibility for East–West relations 1964–69, Hon. Sec. East–West Relations Cttee 1969–81, Asst Gen. Sec. and Div. Sec. for Int. Affairs 1981–86; Vicar, Church of the Ascension, Blackheath, London 1968–81; Dir of Lay Training, Diocese of Southwark 1969–72; mem. Gen. Synod of Church of England 1970–86, 1996–97, Int. Affairs Cttee 1965–2001; mem. Exec. Council Amnesty International (UK Section) 1969–80, Chair. 1974–79; Founder and Trustee, Christian Inst. (of Southern Africa) Fund 1974–94, Chair. Trustees 1983–94; Hon. Chaplain to Bishop of Southwark 1975–80; Hon. Canon of Southwark Cathedral 1978–83, Canon Emer. 1983–86; Public Preacher, Diocese of Southwark 1981–86; Dir Int. Ministry of Coventry Cathedral 1986–97, Canon Residentiary 1986–97, Canon Emer. 1998–; int. consultant 1997–2000; Chair. Christians Aware 1999–2000; mem. Council Keston Coll. 1975–83; mem. Nat. Council Campaign for Nuclear Disarmament 1980–82, Vice-Chair. 1983–85, Vice-Pres. 1985–; mem. Religious Soc. of Friends (Quakers) 1982; Quaker Chaplain, Univ. of Sussex 1994–; Hon. Citizen of Meiningen 1995; Bundesverdienstkreuz (Cross of Merit First Class), Germany 1995, Verdienstorden of Free State of Saxony 2004; Hon. DLitt (Coventry); Hon. LLD (Sussex); Wartburg Prize for Promotion of European Unity 1997, City of Coventry Distinguished Citizen Award 2002. *Publications:* Ed.: Gollwitzer: The Demands of Freedom (English edn) 1965, The Christian Marxist Dialogue 1969, (with J. Klugmann) What Kind of Revolution 1969, The Church and the Bomb (co-author) 1983, The Double Cross 1986; trans. Schulz: Conversion to the World 1967; contrib. to British Council of Churches working party reports on Eastern Europe and Southern Africa. *Address:* 97 Furze Croft, Furze Hill, Brighton, BN3 1PE, England. *Telephone:* (1273) 728033. *E-mail:* paulo@reconcile .org.uk.

OETTINGER, Günther H.; German lawyer, politician and international organization official; *Commissioner for Energy, European Commission;* b. 15 Oct. 1953, Stuttgart; m. Inken Oettinger; one s.; ed Tübingen Univ.; mem. town council, Ditzingen 1980–94; practised as lawyer 1984–2005; mem. CDU, Chair. Baden-Württemberg Junge Union (CDU youth div.) 1983–89, Chair. Baden-Württemberg CDU 2005–09, Chair. CDU Fed. Cttee for Media Politics; mem. Landtag (regional ass.), Baden-Württemberg 1984–09, Minister-Pres. of Baden-Württemberg 2005–09; Commr for Energy, EC 2010–. *Address:* European Commission, rue de la Loi 200, 1049 Brussels, Belgium (office). *Telephone:* (2) 299-11-11 (office). *Fax:* (2) 295-01-38 (office). *Website:* ec.europa.eu (office); www.guenther-oettinger.de (office).

O'FARRELL, Anthony (Tony) Gilbert, PhD, MRIA, FIMA; Irish mathematician and academic; *Professor Emeritus of Mathematics, National University of*

Ireland, Maynooth; b. 28 May 1947, Dublin; s. of Patrick O'Farrell and Sheila O'Farrell (née Curtis); m. Lise Pothin 1972; three s. one d.; ed Univ. Coll. Dublin, Brown Univ., USA; Meteorological Officer, Irish Meteorological Service 1967–68; Fellow and Teaching Asst, Brown Univ., USA 1970–73; Asst Prof., UCLA 1973–75; Prof. of Math., Maynooth Coll. (now Nat. Univ. of Ireland, Maynooth) 1975–2013, Prof. Emer. 2013–, also Head of Dept, Head of Computer Science 1992–95; Research Assoc., Dublin Inst. for Advanced Studies 1979–; mem. Irish Math. Soc. (Pres. 1982–84, Sec. 1984–85, 1987–89), London Math. Soc., Soc. Mathématique de France –2012, American Math. Soc., Math. Asscn of America, Irish Meteorological Soc.; Fellow, Inst. of Math. and its Applications –2012; Nat. Univ. Travelling Studentship 1969. Publications: numerous research papers. Leisure interests: literature, walking, music. Address: Department of Mathematics and Statistics, National University of Ireland, Maynooth, Co. Kildare, Ireland (office). Telephone: (1) 7083914 (office). Fax: (1) 7083913 (office). E-mail: admin@maths.nuim.ie (office). Website: www.maths.nuim.ie/aofarrell (office).

OFER, Idan, BA, MBA; Israeli business executive; Chairman, Israel Corporation Limited; ed Haifa Univ., London School of Business, UK; spent 15 years in Hong Kong, Singapore and USA in shipping and offshore oil storage industries, est. and managed Tanker Pacific Man.; Co-founder and Adviser, Synergy Ventures; Chair. Tower Semiconductor Ltd –1999; Chair. Israel Corpn Ltd ('Israel Corp.') 1999–; Chair. ZIM Integrated Shipping Services Ltd, Project Better Place 2007–; mem. Bd of Dirs Israel Chemicals, Zim Israel Navigation Co. Ltd, Dead Sea Works, and other subsidiaries and related cos of Israel Corp. and Ofer Group; also engaged in several venture capital and energy projects, including Chair. Energy Horizons and Ofer Power Stations and as a Dir of Yozma Venture Capital and Ofer Hi-Tech; Fellow, London School of Business 1999. Address: Israel Corp., Millennium Tower, 23 Aranha Street, PO Box 20456, Tel-Aviv 61204, Israel (office). Telephone: (3) 684-4500 (office). Fax: (3) 684-4570 (office). E-mail: info@israelcorp.com (office). Website: www.israelcorp.com (office).

OFFORD, Robin Ewart, MA, PhD; British medical scientist, biochemist and academic; Executive Director, Mintaka Foundation for Medical Research; b. 28 June 1940, Stondon, Beds., England; s. of Frank Offord and Eileen Offord; m. Valerie Wheatley 1963; one s. two d.; ed Dame Alice Owen's School, London, Peterhouse, Univ. of Cambridge; scientific staff (part-time), UKAEA 1959–62; grad. student, MRC Lab. for Molecular Biology 1962–65, on scientific staff 1965–66; scientific staff, Lab. of Molecular Biophysics, Oxford 1966–72; Fellow, Univ. Coll., Oxford 1968–73, Univ. Lecturer in Molecular Biophysics, Univ. of Oxford 1972–80, Tutor in Biochemistry and Official Fellow, Christ Church Coll., Oxford 1973–80; Prof., Dir Dept of Medical Biochemistry, Univ. of Geneva 1980–2005, Pres. Pre-Clinical Medicine 1994–2000; Dir Geneva Bioinformatics SA 1999–2000; Pres. and Exec. Vice-Chair. GeneProt Inc. 2000–01; Chair. Scentific and Econ. Advisory Bd Eclosion SA 2003–; Co-founder and Exec. Dir Mintaka Foundation for Medical Research 2005–; Chair. Bd of Trustees, Torrey Pines Inst. for Molecular Studies 2009–; mem. Council, American Petide Soc. 1999–, Sec. 2003–11, Pres. 2013–; Agefi Man. of the Year Award (Switzerland) 2002, Makineni Award, American Peptide Soc. 2005, Tribune de Genève Personality of the Year-Society 2008. Publications: author, co-author or ed. six scientific books; author or co-author of approx. 190 articles in scientific journals. Leisure interests: scuba diving (PADI Master Instructor), windsurfing, cross-country skiing, comparative linguistics. Address: Mintaka Foundation, 31 route Pré-Marais, 1233 Bernex, Switzerland (office). Telephone: (79) 293-5781 (office). E-mail: robin.offord@unige .ch (office). Website: www.mintakafoundation.org (office).

OGATA, Sadako, PhD; Japanese international organization official; b. 1927; one s. one d.; ed Univ. of Sacred Heart, Tokyo, Georgetown Univ., Univ. of California, Berkeley, USA; Minister, Japan's Mission to UN 1978–79; UN special emissary investigating problems of Cambodian refugees on Thai-Cambodian border; fmr Head of Japan on UN Comm. for Human Rights 1982–85; fmr Chair. Exec. Bd UNICEF; fmr Dir Inst. of Int. Relations, Sophia Univ. Tokyo; Dean, Faculty of Foreign Studies, Sophia Univ. –1990; UN High Commr for Refugees 1991–2000; Co-Chair. Comm. for Human Security 2001–03; Prime Minister's Special Rep. for Afghanistan 2002–04; mem. UN High Level Panel on Threat, Challenges and Change 2003–04, Chair. Advisory Bd on Human Security 2003–; Pres. Japan Int. Co-operation Agency 2003–12; Ford Foundation Scholar-in-Residence 2002; Dr hc (Harvard) 1994; Hon. DCL (Oxford) 1998; Grand Officer, Order of Orange-Nassau 2008; Hon. DCMG 2011; UNESCO Houphouët-Boigny Peace Prize 1996, Ramon Magsaysay Award for Int. Understanding 1997, Seoul Peace Prize 2000, Delta Prize for Global Understanding 2002, J. William Fulbright Prize for Int. Understanding 2002, Eleanor Roosevelt Val-Kill Medal 2002, Indira Gandhi Prize 2002, Great Negotiator Award, Harvard 2005, Woodrow Wilson Award for Public Service 2007. Publications: The Turbulent Decade: Confronting the Refugee Crises of the 1990s 2005, Defiance in Manchuria: The Making of Japanese Foreign Policy, 1931–1932. Address: Shinjuku Maynds Tower, 1-1 Yoyogi, 2-chome, Shibuya-ku, Tokyo 151-8558, Japan.

OGAWA, Seiji, BS, PhD; Japanese neuroscientist; Director, Ogawa Laboratories for Brain Function Research; b. 19 Jan. 1934; ed Univ. of Tokyo, Stanford Univ., USA; pioneer in devt of nuclear magnetic resonance (NMR) and functional magnetic resonance imaging (fMRI) of brain; Research Assoc., Radiation Research Labs, Mellon Inst., Pittsburgh, USA 1962–64; Postdoctoral Fellow, Stanford Univ. 1967–68; mem. Tech. Staff, Biophysics Research (later Biological Computation Research) Dept, Bell Labs, AT&T, Murray Hill, NJ 1968–80, Distinguished mem. of Tech. Staff and Prin. Investigator, Biophysics Research 1984–96; Distinguished mem. of Tech. Staff and Prin. Investigator, Bell Labs, Lucent Technologies 1996–2001; Visiting Prof., Dept of Biophysics and Physiology, Albert Einstein Coll. of Medicine, Yeshiva Univ., Bronx, NY 2001; Dir Ogawa Labs for Brain Function Research, Hamano Life Science Research Foundation, Tokyo 2001–; Fellow, Int. Soc. for Magnetic Resonance in Medicine 1997; mem. Inst. of Medicine, NAS 2000, Soc. for Neuroscience; Hon. mem. Japanese Soc. of Magnetic Resonance in Medicine 2004, Japanese Soc. of Nuclear Magnetic Resonance 2004; Eastman Kodak Award in Chem. 1967, Gold Medal Award, Soc. of Magnetic Resonance in Medicine 1995, Biological Physics Prize, American Physical Soc. 1996, Nakayama Prize, Nakayama Foundation for Human Science 1998, Asahi Prize, Asahi-Shinbun Cultural Foundation 1999, Japan Int. Prize, Japan Foundation for Science and Tech. 2003, Gairnder Int. Award, Gairdner Foundation, Canada 2003.

Publications: numerous articles in scientific journals. Address: Ogawa Laboratories for Brain Function Research, Hamano Life Science Research Foundation, 12 Daikyo-cho, Shinjuku-ku, Tokyo 160-0015, Japan (office). Telephone: (3) 5919-3991 (office). Fax: (3) 5919-3993 (office). E-mail: info@hlsrf.or.jp (office). Website: www .hlsrf.or.fp (office).

OGAWA, Tadashi, LLB; Japanese tobacco industry executive; Chairman, Bank of Yokohama Ltd; b. 26 Feb. 1940, Tokyo; ed Faculty of Law, Univ. of Tokyo; began career with Ministry of Finance, later Dir-Gen. of Tax Bureau, Commr of Nat. Tax Agency, Admin. Vice-Minister of Finance 1996–97; Visiting Prof., Research Centre for Advanced Science and Tech., Univ. of Tokyo 1997–2001; Rep. Dir and Chair. Japan Tobacco Inc. 2001–04; Pres. Bank of Yokohama 2005–11, Dir and Chair. 2011–; Chair. Regional Banks Asscn of Japan 2007–; mem. Bd of Dirs AEON Co. Ltd. Publications: Detailed Explanation of the Tobacco Consumption Tax (co-author). Address: Bank of Yokohama Ltd, 1-1 Minatomirai 3-chome, Nishi-ku, Yokohama 220-8611, Japan (office). E-mail: info@boy.co.jp (office). Website: www .boy.co.jp (office).

OGI, Adolf; Swiss politician, international consultant, fmr head of state and fmr UN official; b. 18 July 1942, Kandersteg; s. of Adolf Ogi and Anna Ogi; m.; two c.; ed Ecole Supérieure de Commerce, La Neuveville, Swiss Mercantile School, London; Man. Soc. for the Devt and Improvement of Meiringen and the Hasli Valley 1963–64; joined Swiss Ski Asscn 1964, Tech. Dir 1969–74, Dir 1975–81; Maj. in Army 1981–83, Staff Liaison Officer 1984–87; mem. Swiss People's Party 1978–, Chair. 1984–87; mem. Parl. 1979–; mem. Fed. Council 1987, Vice-Pres. 1999; Head Fed. Dept of Transport, Communications and Energy 1988–95; Pres. of Switzerland Jan.–Dec. 1993, Jan.–Dec. 2000; Special Adviser to UN Sec.-Gen. on Sport for Devt and Peace 2001–07; Head Fed. Mil. Dept 1995–97, Fed. Dept of Defence, Civil Protection and Sports 1998–2002; Chair. Candidature Cttee for Winter Olympic Games Sion 2006 1998–99; Vice-Chair. Int. and European Cttee, Int. Ski Fed. 1971–83; Dir-Gen. and mem. of Bd Intersport Schweiz Holding AG 1981–; mem. Int. Olympic Truce Cttee; mem. Bd of Dirs NGO Right to Play International; Hon. Pres. Swiss Olympic Asscn; Hon. mem. Swiss Ski Asscn; Citizen of Honour, Kandersteg 1992, Fraubrunnen 1999, Sion 2000, Crans Montana, Gondo; Dr hc (Univ. of Berne, Int. Univ. in Geneva, Geneva School of Diplomacy and Int. Relations, American Coll. of Greece); European Solar Prize, Human Rights Prize (Switzerland). Address: Bureau Ogi, Schürmattstrasse 6, 3073, Gümligen, Switzerland (office). Telephone: (31) 952-54-77. E-mail: info@adolfogi.ch (office).

OGI, Chikage; Japanese politician; b. (Hiroko Hayashi), 10 May 1933, Hyogo; m. Nakamura Ganjiro; ed Kobe High School; fmr actress of all-female Takarazuka Revue theatre group, also fmr singer and broadcaster; mem. House of Councillors 1977–89, 1993–07, Speaker 2004–07; apptd Minister of State, Dir-Gen. Nat. Land Agency 2000; Minister of Construction 2000, of Land, Infrastructure and Transport 2001–03; mem. LDP –1994, Head of Hoshuto (New Conservative Party) 2000–01, returned to LDP 2003. Address: c/o House of Councillors, Nagatacho 1-7-1, Chiyoda-ku, Tokyo, Japan.

OGILVIE, Dame Bridget Margaret, AC, DBE, ScD, FRS, FIBiol, FRCPath, FMedSci; Australian scientist and academic; Visiting Professor, University College London; b. 24 March 1938, Glen Innes, NSW; d. of the late John Mylne Ogilvie and Margaret Beryl McRae; ed New England Girls School, Armidale, NSW, Univ. of New England, NSW, Univ. of Cambridge; Fellow, Wellcome Animal Health Trust 1963–66; mem. scientific staff MRC 1966–81; mem. staff of The Wellcome Trust (various capacities) 1979–, Dir 1991–98; Visiting Prof., Univ. Coll. London 1997–; Chair. Governing Body, Inst. for Animal Health 1997–2003, Cttee on the Public Understanding of Science 1998–2002, British Library Advisory Cttee for Science and Business 1999–2002, Asscn of Medical Research Charities 2002–, Medicines for Malaria Venture 1999–2006, Lister Inst. Governing Body 2002–; High Steward Univ. of Cambridge 2002–; Dir (non-exec.) Lloyds Bank 1995–96, Lloyds TSB Group PLC 1996–2000, Zeneca Group PLC 1997, AstraZeneca 1999–2006; mem. UK Council for Science and Tech. 1993–2000, Advisory Council for Chem., Univ. of Oxford 1997–2001, Australian Health and Medical Research Strategic Review 1998, Australian Acad. of Science 2008–; Trustee Nat. Museum of Science and Industry 1992–2002, Royal Coll. of Veterinary Surgeons Trust Fund 1998–2001, Nat. Endowment for Science and Tech. and the Arts 1998–2002, Cancer Research Campaign 2000–02, Research UK 2002–; Ian McMaster Fellow 1971–72; Vice-Chair. Sense About Science; Hon. mem. British and American Socs of Parasitology, British Veterinary Asscn; Hon. MRCP; Hon. FRCP; Hon. Assoc. Royal Coll. of Veterinary Surgeons; Hon. Fellow, Univ. Coll. London, Girton Coll., Cambridge, St Edmunds Coll., Cambridge, Royal Australasian Coll. of Physicians, Inst. of Biology, Royal Soc. of Medicine; Foundation Hon. Fellow, Royal Veterinary Coll.; Hon. MD (Newcastle); Hon. DSc (Nottingham, Salford, Westminster, Bristol, Glasgow, ANU, Buckingham, Dublin, Nottingham Trent, Oxford Brookes, Greenwich, Auckland, Durham, Kent, Exeter, London, Leicester, Manchester, St Andrews, Wollongong); Hon. LLD Trinity Coll., Dundee; Dr hc (Edin.); Univ. Medal (Univ. of New England); Inaugural Distinguished Alumni Award (Univ. of New England); Lloyd of Kilgerran Prize 1994, Wooldridge Memorial Medal 1998, Australian Soc. of Medical Research Medal 2000, Kilby Award 2003, Duncan Davies Memorial Medal 2004, Ralph Doherty Memorial Medal, Queensland Inst. of Medical Research 2006. Publications: various scientific papers, reviews, book chapters on the immune response to parasitic infections of man and animals 1964–84. Leisure interests: the company of friends, looking at landscape, swimming, walking, music, gardening. Address: c/o Medical Administration, University College London, Gower Street, London, WC1E 6BT, England. Telephone: (20) 7679-6939. Fax: (20) 7383-2462. E-mail: rachel.chapman@ucl.ac.uk.

OGILVIE THOMPSON, Julian, MA; South African business executive (retd); b. 27 Jan. 1934, Cape Town; s. of the late Hon. Newton Ogilvie Thompson and Eve Ogilvie Thompson; m. the Hon. Tessa M. Brand 1956; two s. two d.; ed Diocesan Coll., Rondebosch and Worcester Coll., Oxford; Dir (non-exec.) De Beers Consolidated Mines Ltd 1966–, Chair. 1985–97, Deputy Chair. 1998–2001; Chair. Mineral and Resources Corpn 1982–99; Deputy Chair. Anglo-American Corpn of South Africa Ltd 1983–90, Chair. 1990–2002, Chair. Anglo-American PLC 1999–2002; Dir Anglogold Ltd 1998–2004; Rhodes Trustee 2002–; Trustee Mandela-Rhodes Foundation 2003–; Commdr, Order of Leopold (Belgium), Grand Official, Order of Bernardo O'Higgins (Chile), Presidential Order of Honour (Botswana); Hon. LLD (Rhodes Univ.); Rhodes Scholar 1953. Leisure interests: golf, fishing, shooting.

Address: PO Box 61631, Marshalltown 2107 (office); Froome, Froome Street, Athol Ext. 3, Sandton, Gauteng, South Africa (home). *Telephone:* (11) 274-2040 (office); 884-3925 (home). *Fax:* (11) 643-2720 (office). *E-mail:* odonnellt@coson.co.za (office).

OGILVY, HRH Princess Alexandra, the Hon. Lady, KG, GCVO; b. 25 Dec. 1936; d. of the late Duke of Kent (fourth s. of King George V) and Princess Marina (d. of the late Prince Nicholas of Greece); m. Sir Angus James Bruce Ogilvy (second s. of the late 12th Earl of Airlie, KT, GCVO, MC) 1963 (died 2004); one s. one d.; ed Heathfield School, Ascot; Chancellor, Univ. of Lancaster 1964–2004; Col-in-Chief, the King's Own Royal Border Regt –2006, The Queen's Own Rifles of Canada –2010, Canadian Scottish Regt (Princess Mary's); Col-in-Chief, The Light Infantry –2007; Deputy Col-in-Chief, Queen's Royal Lancers 1993–; Royal Col, Third Battalion, The Rifles; Patron and Air Chief Commdt, Princess Mary's Royal Air Force Nursing Service; Patron, Queen Alexandra's Royal Naval Nursing Service; Pres. or Patron of many charitable and social welfare orgs; rep. HM Queen Elizabeth II at independence celebrations of Nigeria 1960 and St Lucia 1979, 150th anniversary celebrations, Singapore 1969; Hon. Royal Col The Royal Yeomanry (Territorial Army Voluntary Reserves); Hon. Liverywoman, Worshipful Co. of Clothworkers; Royal Hon. Freeman, Worshipful Co. of Barbers; Hon. Freeman, City of Lancaster, City of London; Hon. Fellow, Royal Coll. of Physicians and Surgeons of Glasgow, Royal Coll. of Anaesthetists, Royal Coll. of Obstetricians and Gynaecologists, Royal Coll. of Physicians; decorations from Mexico, Peru, Chile, Brazil, Japan, Finland, Luxembourg, Netherlands, Canada; hon. degrees (Queensland, Hong Kong, Mauritius, Liverpool); Hon. DMus (Lancaster) 2005. *Address:* Buckingham Palace, London, SW1A 1AA, England. *Telephone:* (20) 7024-4270 (office). *Fax:* (20) 7839-3371 (office).

OGIO, Michael; Papua New Guinea politician; *Governor-General;* b. 7 July 1942; fmr Minister of Forestry; fmr Deputy Prime Minister; Minister for Higher Educ., Research, Science and Tech. –2011; Gov.-Gen. 2011–; mem. People's Democratic Movement. *Address:* Office of the Governor-General, Waigani, NCD, Papua New Guinea (office).

O'GRADY, Frances, BA; British trade union executive; *General Secretary, Trades Union Congress;* b. 9 Nov. 1959, Oxford; two c.; ed Milham Ford School, Univ. of Manchester, Middlesex Polytechnic, London; has spent career as trade unionist and campaigner; employed in a range of jobs from shop work to the voluntary sector; worked for Transport and General Workers Union on campaigns to prevent abolition of the Agricultural Wages Bd and for introduction of nat. minimum wage, equal pay for women, and on a range of industrial wage claims; Campaigns Officer, Trades Union Congress (TUC) 1994–97, Head of New Unionism campaign 1997–99, launched the TUC's Organising Acad., Head of TUC's org. dept 1999–2003, Deputy Gen. Sec. TUC 2003–12, Gen. Sec. (first woman) 2013–; fmr mem. Resolution Foundation's Comm. on Living Standards, Low Pay Comm., High Pay Comm. *Address:* Trades Union Congress, Congress House, Great Russell Street, London, WC1B 3LS, England (office). *Telephone:* (20) 7467-1215 (office). *E-mail:* info@tuc.org.uk (office). *Website:* www.tuc.org.uk (office).

OGRIS, Werner, DIur; Austrian academic; *Professor Emeritus of Law, University of Vienna;* b. 9 July 1935, Vienna; s. of Alfred Ogris and Maria Erber; m. Eva Scolik 1963; two s.; ed Univ. of Vienna; Asst, Inst. für Deutsches Recht, Vienna 1958–61; Prof., Freie Univ. Berlin 1962, Univ. of Vienna 1966, now Prof. Emer.; Prof., Bratislava School of Law 2004, Dean 2005–07; mem. Austrian Acad. of Sciences; Corresp. mem. Saxon Acad.; Foreign mem. Royal Netherlands Acad.; Großes Silbernes Ehrenzeichen für Verdienste um die Republik Österreich 2003, Ehrenkreuz für Wissenschaft und Kunst, Klasse 2010; Hon. DrIur (Prague, Bratislava, Pécs); Theodor-Körner-Stiftung Prize 1961, Brothers Grimm Prize, Univ. of Marburg 1997. *Publications:* Der mittelalterliche Leibrentenvertrag 1961, Der Entwicklungsgang der österreichischen Privatrechtswissenschaft im 19. Jahrhundert 1968, Die Rechtsentwicklung in Österreich 1848–1918 1975, Personenstandsrecht 1977, Recht und Macht bei Maria Theresia 1980, Goethe—amtlich und politisch 1982, Jacob Grimm. Ein politisches Gelehrtenleben 1986, Friedrich der Grosse und das Recht 1987, Joseph von Sonnenfels als Rechtsreformer 1988, Zur Entwicklung des Versicherungsaufsichtsrechts und des Versicherungsvertragsrechts in Österreich von 1850 bis 1918 1988, Deutsche und österreichische Rechtsgeschichte in Japan 1991, Tatort Rechtsgeschichte 1994, Vom Galgenberg zum Ringtheaterbrand 1997, Tatort Rechtsgeschichte 2 1998, Mozart im Familien- und Erbrecht seiner Zeit 1999, Die Universitätsreform des Ministers Leo Graf Thun-Hohenstein 1999, Joseph von Sonnenfels (Grundsätze) 2003, Elemente europäischer Rechtskultur 2003, Die Zensur in der Ära Metternich 2006, Ubi sponsa ibi sponsalia 2006, Einige Aspekte der Beziehungen Böhmens zum Reichshofrat (with Eva Ortlieb) 2006. *Address:* Österreichische Akademie der Wissenschaften, Dr Ignaz Seipel-Platz 2, 1010 Vienna (office); Mariahilferstrasse 71/21, 1060 Vienna, Austria (home). *Telephone:* (1) 4277 34530 (office); (1) 586-41-57 (home). *E-mail:* werner.ogris@oeaw.ac.at (office); www.oeaw.ac.at/krgoe (office).

OH, Byung-wook; South Korean business executive; *President and CEO, Hyundai Samho Heavy Industries;* joined Hyundai Heavy Industries 1974, COO, Offshore & Eng and Industrial Plant & Eng Divs and Sr Exec. Vice-Pres., Hyundai Heavy Industries Co. Ltd 2006–09, Pres. 2009–10, Pres. and CEO Hyundai Samho Heavy Industries Co. Ltd 2010–; Chair. The Korea Shipbuilders' Asscn (KOSHIPA) 2009. *Address:* Hyundai Samho Heavy Industries Co. Ltd, 1700 Yongdang-Ri, Samho-Eup, Jeollanam-Do, Yeongam 526-701, South Korea (office). *Telephone:* (61) 460-2641 (office). *Fax:* (61) 460-3707 (office). *E-mail:* asteam@hshi .co.kr (office). *Website:* www.hshi.co.kr (office).

OH, Yeon-cheon, BA, MPA, PhD; South Korean economist, academic and university administrator; *President, Seoul National University;* ed Seoul Nat. Univ., New York Univ., USA; passed the 17th Sr Civil Service Examination for Admin. Service 1975; Chief Researcher, Korea Econ. Research Inst. 1982–83; Asst Prof., Assoc. Prof. and Prof., Grad. School of Public Admin, Seoul Nat. Univ. (SNU) 1983–2010, Dean, Grad. School of Public Admin 2000–04, Pres. SNU 2010–; Visiting Prof., Univ. of Berlin, Germany 1991–92; Pres. Korea Taxation Asscn 1997; Cttee mem., Planning and Budget Bd 1998–99; consultant to World Bank on privatization 1999; Chair. Korea Congressional Devt Foundation, Nat. Ass. 2000–06, Public Enterprise Evaluation Task Force, Ministry of Planning and

Finance 2001–03, Information and Communication Policy Review Cttee 2003–07, Korea Evaluation Inst. of Industrial Tech., Ministry of Commerce 2005–09, Cttee of Industry Devt Advisory Cttee, Ministry of Knowledge and Econs 2007–09, Korea Biotech R&D Group 2008–10, Korea Childhood Leukemia Foundation 2009–; Pres. Korea Academic Asscn of Public Choice 2007; Order of Service Merit (Red Stripes) 2005. *Publications:* Fiscal Policy and Economic Well-being (co-ed.) 1989, A Theory of Korean Local Public Finance 1989, A Theory of Korean Taxation 1992, Prospect for Fiscal Policy and Directions for Property Tax 1996, Strong Market and Responsible Government 2009; numerous papers in professional journals. *Address:* Office of the President, Seoul National University, Building 60, 1 Gwanak-ro, Gwanak-gu, Seoul 151-742, South Korea (office). *Telephone:* (2) 880-7137 (office). *Fax:* (2) 889-7515 (office). *E-mail:* snuop@snu.ac.kr (office). *Website:* www.useoul.edu (office).

O'HALI, Abdulaziz A., PhD; Saudi Arabian business executive; b. 1935; one s. three d.; ed Univ. of Puget Sound, Tacoma, Wash. and Claremont Grad. School, Calif.; entered govt service 1957, held various posts, including Mil. Advisory Dir, Prime Minister's Office, Acting Dir of Planning and Budgeting, Dir Cultural and Educ. Directorate, Ministry of Defense and Aviation; retd with rank of Col 1979; founding shareholder United Saudi Commercial Bank, Nat. Industrialization Co. 1983; Chair. Saudi Investment Bank; Man. Dir Gulf Center Man. Consultants; mem. Jt Econ. and Tech. Comm. of Saudi Arabia and USA, of Saudi Arabia and Germany. *Address:* Saudi Investment Bank, PO Box 3533, Riyadh 11481 (office); Gulf Center Management Consultants, PO Box 397, Riyadh 11411, Saudi Arabia (office). *Telephone:* 476-0287 (office). *Fax:* 478-1557 (office).

OHANIAN, Col-Gen. Seyran, PhD; Armenian government official and fmr army officer; *Minister of Defence;* b. 1 July 1962, Shushi (Şuşa), Nagornyi Karabakh Autonomous Oblast, Azerbaijan SSR, USSR; m.; three s. one d.; ed high school, Mrgashen Village, Nairi region, Baku Higher Jt Command Coll., Azerbaijan SSR; began mil. service serving as Platoon Commdr with USSR motorized rifle platoon, GDR 1987–88, Co. Commdr 1987–88; Co. Commdr, 366th motorized rifle regt, Stepanakert 1988–89, Battalion Deputy Commdr 1989–90, Battalion Commdr 1990–92; Chief of Staff of Self-Defence Forces, 'Repub. of Nagornyi Karabakh' 1992–94, First Deputy Commdr of Defence Army 1994–98; Commdr 5th Army Corps of Armenia 1998–99; rank of Maj.-Gen. 1995, Lt-Gen. 2000, Col-Gen. 2007; Minister of Defence, 'Repub. of Nagornyi Karabakh' 1999–2000, Minister of Defence and Commdr of Defence Army 2000–07; Chief of Staff, Armenian Armed Forces 2007–08; Minister of Defence 2008–; 70th Anniversary of USSR Armed Forces, For Perfect Service, For Excellency, Soviet Union Marshal Zhukov (all from USSR); Hero of Artsakh, Golden Eagle, Combat Cross, 1st Degree, For the Liberation of Shushi (Nagornyi Karabakh); Combat Cross, 1st Degree, Tigranes the Great, For Service to the Motherland, For Perfect Service, 1st and 2nd Degrees, Drastamat Kanayan, Marshal Baghramyan, For the Strengthening of Co-operation, Maternal Gratitude, Coat of Arms. *Address:* Ministry of Defence, 0044 Yerevan, Bagrevand Str. 5, Armenia (office). *Telephone:* (10) 29-46-99 (office). *Fax:* (10) 29-45-31 (office). *E-mail:* modpress@mil.am (office). *Website:* www.mil.am (office).

O'HANLON, Rory, MB, BCh, BAO, DCH; Irish politician and physician; b. 7 Feb. 1934, Dublin; s. of Michael O'Hanlon and Anna Mary O'Hanlon; m. Teresa Ward 1962; four s. two d.; ed Blackrock Coll. Dublin and Univ. Coll. Dublin; mem. Dáil 1977–; mem. Monaghan Co. Council 1979–87; Minister of State, Dept of Health and Social Welfare Oct.–Dec. 1982; Minister of Health 1987–91, for the Environment 1991–92; Chair. Fianna Fáil Parl. Party 1994–2002; Deputy Speaker of Dáil 1997–2002, Ceann Comhairle (Speaker) 2002–07; Fellow, Royal Acad. of Medicine; mem. British-Irish Parl. Group 1992–2002, Jt Cttee on Foreign Affairs 1993–97. *Leisure interests:* swimming, reading, walking, computers.

O'HARA, Michael John, MA, PhD, FRS, FRSE; British scientist (retd); b. 22 Feb. 1933, Sydney, Australia; s. of the late Michael Patrick O'Hara and Dorothy Winifred Avis; m. 1st Janet Prudence Tibbits 1962 (divorced 1977); one s. two d.; m. 2nd Susan Howells 1977; two s. one d.; ed Dulwich Coll. Prep., London, Cranleigh School, Surrey and Peterhouse, Cambridge; Univ. of Edin., Grant Inst. of Geology 1958–78, Reader 1967, Prof. 1971–78; Research Fellow, Carnegie Inst. of Washington Geophysical Lab. 1962–63; Prof., Univ. Coll. Aberystwyth, Dept of Geology 1978–88, Head of Dept 1978–87, Prof., Inst. of Earth Sciences 1988–93; Distinguished Research Prof., Earth Sciences Dept, Univ. of Cardiff 1994–2003; Sherman-Fairchild Distinguished Visiting Scholar, Calif. Inst. of Tech. 1984–85; Visiting Prof., Dept of Earth Sciences, Harvard Univ. 1986; Prof. and Head of Dept, Sultan Qaboos Univ., Oman 1988–90; Visiting Prof., North West Univ., Xi'an, People's Repub. of China 2004; Concurrent Prof., Nanjing Univ., People's Repub. of China 2004; mem. Natural Environment Research Council 1986–88; mem. Univ. Grants Cttee 1987–89, Chair. Univ. Grants Cttee, Earth Sciences Review; Geochemistry Fellow, jt geochemical socs of America and Europe 1997; Fellow, American Geophysical Union 2004; Hon. Prof., Aberystwyth Univ. 2004, China Univ. of Geosciences, Beijing 2004, Univ. of Durham 2005; Hon. mem. Geological Soc. France; Geological Soc. of London Murchison Medal 1983, American Geophysical Union Bowen Award 1984. *Publications:* over 100 articles in scientific journals 1961–2004. *Leisure interests:* mountaineering, hill walking.

O'HARE, Joseph Aloysius, MA, PhL, STL, PhD; American priest, editor and fmr university president; *Associate Editor, America Magazine;* b. 12 Feb. 1931, New York; ed Berchmans Coll., Cebu City, Philippines, Woodstock Coll., Md and Fordham Univ., New York; Instructor in Humanities, Ateneo de Manila Univ. 1955–58, Assoc. Prof. in Philosophy 1967–72; Assoc. Ed. America Magazine, New York 1972–75, 2003–, Ed.-in-Chief 1975–84; Pres. Fordham Univ. 1984–2003 (retd); Chair. NY City Campaign Financial Bd; numerous hon. degrees. *Leisure interests:* contemporary fiction, Irish folk music. *Address:* America Magazine, 106 West 56th Street, New York, NY 10019-3803, USA (office). *Telephone:* (212) 581-4640 (office). *Fax:* (212) 399-3596 (office). *Website:* www.americamagazine.org (office).

O'HARE, Kevin; British ballet director and fmr professional ballet dancer; *Director, The Royal Ballet;* b. Kingston upon Hull, England; born to Irish parents; ed Vera Skelton School of Dance, Louise Browne Yorkshire Ballet Scholarship Centre, Royal Ballet School, London, Royal Danish Ballet (exchange programme); as a child, appeared with his brother in the film Bugsy Malone with Jodie Foster;

joined Sadler's Wells Ballet 1984, Prin. 1990, remained with the co. (now called Birmingham Royal Ballet) until his retirement from dancing 2000; worked with Frederick Ashton, Kenneth MacMillan, David Bintley and Sir Peter Wright; studied co. man. and worked at RSC, returned to Birmingham Royal Ballet as Co. Man. 2001–04; Co. Man., The Royal Ballet 2004–09, Admin. Dir 2009–12, Artistic Dir 2012–. *Address:* The Royal Ballet, Covent Garden, London, WC2E 9DD, England (office). *Telephone:* (20) 7240-1200 (office). *E-mail:* info@roh.org.uk (office). *Website:* www.roh.org.uk (office).

OHASHI, Nobuo; Japanese business executive; *Chairman and Executive Director, Mitsui & Company Ltd;* Sr Man.-Dir Kawasaki Steel Corpn 1990; Pres. Techno-Research Corpn (subsidiary of Kawasaki Steel Corpn) 1991; mem. Bd Dirs (Dir, Gen. Man. Seoul Br.) 1994–97, Rep. Dir, Exec. Man. Dir, COO Foods Unit 1997–99, Rep. Dir, Sr Exec. Man. Dir, Gen. Man. Corp. Planning Div. 1999–2000, Rep. Dir, Exec. Vice-Pres. 2000–02, Rep. Dir, Exec. Vice-Pres., Group Pres. Consumer Products and Services Group 2002, Rep. Dir, Chair. and Exec. Dir 2002–04, Chair. and Dir 2004–; Chair. Japan-India Business Co-operation Cttee; mem. Exec. Cttee Japan-US Business Council 2004; mem. Bd of Dirs The Angel Foundation 2002. *Address:* Mitsui & Company Ltd, 2-1 Ohtemachi 1-chome, Chiyoda-ku, Tokyo 100-0004, Japan (office). *Telephone:* (3) 3285-1111 (office). *Fax:* (3) 3285-9819 (office). *E-mail:* info@mitsui.co.jp (office). *Website:* www.mitsui.co.jp (office).

OHATA, Akihiro; Japanese engineer and politician; b. 5 Oct. 1947; m.; two c.; ed Musashi Inst. of Tech.; began career as engineer in power plant design team, Hitachi Ltd 1971; elected to Ibaraki Prefectural Ass. 1986; mem. House of Reps (lower house of parl.) for Ibaraki No. 5 Constituency 1990–, Chair. Fundamental Nat. Policies Cttee; Minister of Economy, Trade and Industry 2010–11, of Land, Infrastructure, Transport and Tourism 2011; Founding mem. Democratic Party of Japan. *Leisure interests:* kendo (second-degree black belt), cinema, mountain trekking, swimming. *Address:* c/o Democratic Party of Japan (DPJ) 1-11-1, Nagata-cho, Chiyoda-ku, Tokyo 100-8901, Japan (office). *Website:* www.oohata.com.

OHENE, Elizabeth Akua, BA; Ghanaian journalist and politician; b. 24 Jan. 1945, Ho; ed Mawuli High School, Univ. of Ghana, Indiana Univ., USA; work experience with newspapers in USA; reporter, staff writer, columnist, leader writer, then Ed. The Daily Graphic and Mirror 1967–82; f. Talking Drum Publications 1986, Publr and Ed.; joined BBC, London, UK 1986, worked successively as Producer of Radio Programmes, Presenter, Sr Producer World Service and BBC Domestic Radio, researcher and columnist, Focus on Africa Magazine, Deputy Ed. African Service for English Daily Programmes, Ed. Focus on Africa Programme, Dir Operational Budget, Corresp. 1993–94; conducted training programmes for BBC in SA, Nigeria, Liberia, Senegal, Sierra Leone, Kenya, Ethiopia and Somalia; Minister of State for Media Relations 2001–02; Govt Spokesperson 2002–03; Minister of State in charge of Tertiary Educ. 2003–08; mem. Int. Women Media Foundation, Bd Int. Comm. of Investigative Journalists, CNN Africa Journalist of the Year Competition 1997–; Order of the Volta; Hon. DLitt (Univ. of Mines and Tech.). *Address:* c/o Ministry of Education, Youth and Sports, POB M45, Accra, Ghana.

OHIN, Elliot, MBA; Togolese business executive and government official; *Minister of State, Minister of Foreign Affairs and Co-operation;* b. 3 Oct. 1951, Lomé; m.; three c.; ed Sullivan Univ., USA and Ecole Superieure des Ingenieurs Commerciaux en Informatique, France; Commercial Engineer, Athena Informatique, Paris, France 1986–92; Dir PNC Bank, Louisville, Kentucky, USA 2001–07; Dir Marathon Petroleum Corpn, Louisville 2007–10; Minister of State, Minister of Foreign Affairs and Co-operation 2010–; mem. Union of Forces for Change. *Address:* Ministry of Foreign Affairs and Co-operation, place du Monument aux Morts, Avenue Georges Pompidou, BP 900, Lomé, Togo (office). *Telephone:* 22-21-29-10 (office). *Fax:* 22-21-39-74 (office). *E-mail:* maeirtgce@yahoo.fr (office). *Website:* www.diplomatie.gouv.tg (office).

OHLSSON, Garrick; American pianist; b. 3 April 1948, White Plains, NY; ed Westchester Conservatory, Juilliard School with Sascha Gorodnitsky, studied with Olga Barabini, Rosina Lhevinne and Claudio Arrau; appears regularly with major orchestras, including New York Philharmonic, Chicago Symphony, Boston Symphony, Philadelphia Orchestra, Los Angeles Philharmonic and with orchestras and in recital series throughout the world; complete cycle of Beethoven piano sonatas at the Verbier, Tanglewood and Ravinia festivals; prizewinner at Busoni Piano Competition, Italy 1966, Chopin Int. Piano Competition, Warsaw 1970, Montreal Int. Piano Competition 1970, Avery Fisher Prize 1994, Grammy Award for Best Instrumental Soloist Performance 2008. *Recordings include:* Complete Solo Works of Chopin and numerous other recordings. *Address:* Opus 3 Artists, 470 Park Avenue South, 9th Floor North, New York, NY 10016, USA (office). *Telephone:* (212) 584-7500 (office). *Fax:* (646) 300-8200 (office). *E-mail:* info@opus3artists.com (office). *Website:* www.opus3artists.com (office).

OHLSSON, Mikael, MSc; Swedish retail executive; *President and CEO, Inter IKEA Systems B.V.;* b. 1957; m.; two s. one d.; ed Linköping Tekniske Högskola; joined IKEA in 1979, worked in carpet dept, Linköping Br., becoming Store Man., IKEA Sundsvall Br. 1981–84, Training and Devt Man. IKEA Sweden 1984–86, Marketing Man. IKEA Sweden 1986–88, Country Man. IKEA Belgium 1988–91, Country Man. IKEA Canada 1991–95, mem. IKEA Exec. Man. Group 1995–, Man. Dir IKEA Sweden 1995–2000, Regional Man. IKEA (various regions) 2000–09, Regional Man. for Retail, S Europe and N America –2009, Pres. and CEO, Inter IKEA Systems B.V. 2009–. *Address:* Inter IKEA Systems B.V., Olof Palmestraat 1, 2616 Delft, Netherlands (office). *Telephone:* (15) 215-0750 (office). *Fax:* (15) 219-0533 (office). *Website:* www.ikea-group.ikea.com (office).

OHLSSON, Per Evald Torbjörn; Swedish journalist and author; *Senior Columnist, Sydsvenska Dagbladet;* b. 3 March 1958, Malmö; s. of Ulla Ohlsson and Torsten Ohlsson; m. Maria Rydqvist-Ohlsson 1989; one s.; ed Lund Univ.; Ed. Lundagard 1980–81; editorial writer, Expressen, Stockholm 1981–85; New York Corresp., Sydsvenska Dagbladet 1985–88, Ed.-in-Chief 1990–2005, Sr Columnist 2005–; Soderberg Foundation Prize for Journalism 1998. *Publications:* Over There: Banden Över Atlanten 1992, Gudarnas Ö 1993, 100 År av Tillväxt 1994, Konservkungen: Herbert Felix – ett flyktingöde i 1900-talets Europa 2006, Den enda supermakten – hur förhåller vi oss till den? 2006. *Leisure interests:* music,

literature, sports. *Address:* Sydsvenska Dagbladet, 205 05 Malmö, Sweden (office). *Telephone:* 40-28-12-00 (office). *Fax:* 40-28-13-86 (office). *E-mail:* per.t.ohlsson@sydsvenskan.se (office).

OHMORI, Kazuo; Japanese business executive; *Chairman, Sumitomo Corporation;* joined Sumitomo Corpn 1971, Gen. Man., Transportation Project and System Dept, thereafter Gen. Man., Ship and Marine Project Dept, Corp. Officer, Gen. Man., Ship, Aerospace and Transportation Systems Div. 1996–2003, Exec. Officer and Gen. Man., Ship, Aerospace and Transportation Systems Div. 2003–05, Man. Exec. Officer and Asst Gen. Man., Transportation and Construction Systems Business Unit, Gen. Man., Ship, Aerospace and Transportation Systems Div. 2005–06, Man. Exec. and Gen. Man., Transportation and Construction Systems Business Unit, Rep. Dir, Man. Exec. and Gen. Man. 2006–07, Rep. Dir, Sr Man. Exec. and Gen. Man. 2007–09, Rep. Dir, Exec. Vice-Pres. and Gen. Man. 2009–12, Rep. Dir and Asst to Pres.'s Office April–June 2012, Special Adviser June 2012–13, Chair. Sumitomo Corpn 2013–. *Address:* Sumitomo Corporation, 8-11 Harumi 1-chome, Chuo-ku, Tokyo 104-8610, Japan (office). *Telephone:* (3) 5166-5000 (office). *Fax:* (3) 5166-6292 (office). *E-mail:* info@sumitomocorp.co.jp (office). *Website:* www.sumitomocorp.co.jp (office).

OHNISHI, Minoru; Japanese business executive; b. 28 Oct. 1925, Hyogo Pref.; s. of Sokichi Ohnishi and Mitsu Ohnishi; m. Yaeko Yui 1951; two s.; ed School of Econs, Tokyo Univ.; joined Fuji Photo Film Co. Ltd 1948, Man. Tokyo Sales Dept of Consumer Products Div. 1957–61, Sales Dept of Industrial Products Div. 1961–62, Fukuoka Br. Office 1962–64, Exec. Vice-Pres. Fuji Photo Film USA Inc. 1964–68, Man. Export Sales Div. Fuji Photo Film Co. Ltd 1968–76, Dir 1972–, Man. Dir 1976–79, Sr Man. Dir 1979–80, Pres. 1980–96, Chair. and CEO 1996–2002, Chair. 2003–12; Pres. Photo-Sensitized Materials Mfrs Asscn of Japan 1980–96; mem. Photography Soc. of Japan (Chair. 1997–). *Leisure interests:* golf, reading. *Address:* c/o Fujifilm Holdings Corporation, 7-3, Akasaka 9-chome, Minato-ku, Tokyo 107-0052, Japan. *E-mail:* info@fujifilm.com.

OHNO, Hideo, PhD; Japanese physicist and academic; *Professor, Laboratory for Nanoelectronics and Spintronics, Research Institute of Electrical Communication, and Director, Centre for Spintronics Integrated Systems, Tohoku University;* ed Univ. of Tokyo; began career as Lecturer, then Assoc. Prof., Dept of Electrical Eng, Hokkaido Univ.; currently Prof. of Lab. for Nanoelectronics and Spintronics, Research Inst. of Electrical Communication and Dir Centre for Spintronics Integrated Systems, Tohoku Univ.; Visiting Scientist, IBM T.J. Watson Research Center 1988–90; currently leading an IT-Program of Research Revolution 2002, Development of Universal Low-Power Spin Memory project, Ministry of Educ., Culture, Sports, Science and Tech.; Leader of Exploratory Research for Advanced Tech. (ERATO) Project 'Semiconductor Spintronics', Japan Science and Tech. Corpn; Japan IBM Science Award 1998, IUPAP Magnetism Prize 2003. *Publications:* more than 300 papers in professional journals on spintronics, physics and the application of semiconductor quantum structures, and semiconductor crystal growth. *Address:* Centre for Spintronics Integrated Systems, Tohoku University, 2-1-1 Katahira, Aoba-ku, Sendai 980-8577, Japan (office). *Telephone:* (22) 217-5553 (office); (22) 217-5555 (Lab.) (office). *Fax:* (22) 217-5553 (office). *E-mail:* ohno@riec.tohoku.ac.jp (office). *Website:* www.riec.tohoku.ac.jp/lab/ohno/index-e.html (office); www.ohno.riec.tohoku.ac.jp (office).

OHNO, Naotake; Japanese business executive; *President and Chief Operating Officer, Daiwa House Industry Company Ltd;* b. 1948; joined Daiwa House Industry 1971, Dir 2000–, Exec. Vice-Pres. 2007–11, Pres. and COO Daiwa House Industry Co. Ltd 2011–. *Address:* Daiwa House Industry Co. Ltd, 3-3-5 Umeda, Kita-ku, Osaka 530-8241, Japan (office). *Telephone:* (6) 6346-2111 (office). *Fax:* (6) 6342-1419 (office). *E-mail:* info@daiwahouse.com (office). *Website:* www.daiwahouse.com (office); www.daiwahouse.co.jp (office).

OHNO, Shigeru; Japanese energy industry executive; Dir Japan Nuclear Fuel Ltd 1997; fmr Chair. Kyushu Electric Power Co. Inc.; Chair. Fukuoka Venture Market Asscn; fmr Chair. Kyushu Industrial Tech. Centre; mem. Kyushu Economy Int.; Auditor, Nisseki Plasto Co. Ltd 2002; Hon. mem. Bd of Dirs Asian-Pacific Children's Convention (APCC), Fukuoka 2003–. *Address:* c/o Kyushu Electric Power Company Inc., 1-82 Watanabe-dori, 2-chome, Chuo-ku, Fukuoka 810-8720, Japan.

OHNO, Yoshinori; Japanese politician; b. 16 Oct. 1935; ed Univ. of Tokyo, Univ. of Pennsylvania, USA (Fulbright Exchange Student); joined Ministry of Finance 1958, First Sec., Perm. Del. of Japan, Geneva, Switzerland 1971–75, Dir Int. Orgs Section, Int. Finance Bureau 1976; mem. House of Reps 1986–2012, Chair. Standing Cttee on Transport 1997, Standing Cttee on Rules and Admin 2002, Research Comm. on the Annuities System 2003; Parl. Vice-Minister of Posts and Telecommunications 1990; Dir Nat. Defence Div., LDP 1994; Sr State Sec. for Finance 1999–2000, for Science and Tech. 2000–01; Sr Vice-Minister of Educ., Culture, Sports, Science and Tech. 2001–04; Minister of State for Defence 2004–05; Chair. Research Comm. on the Finance and Banking Systems, LDP, Deputy Chair. Research Comm. on the Tax System; Order of Merit of Duarte, Sanchez and Mella, Légion d'honneur 2011, Asahidai Jusho 2013. *Address:* Room #432, 1st Members' Office Building, 2-2-1, Nagata-cho, Chiyoda-ku, Tokyo 100-8981, Japan (office). *Telephone:* (3) 3508-7132 (office). *Fax:* (3) 3502-5870 (office).

OHSAN BELLEPEAU, (Agnès) Monique, GOSK; Mauritian politician, journalist and news broadcaster; *Vice-President;* b. 3 May 1942, grand-d. of Bartholomée Ohsan, a founding mem. of Mauritian Labour Party; m. Yves Joseph Bellepeau (died 2010); two c.; fmr news announcer, Mauritius Broadcasting Corpn; Parl. Pvt. Sec. 1997–2000; fmr mem. Parti Travailliste (Labour Party), Pres. 2007–10; Vice-Pres. of Mauritius (first woman) 2010–, Acting Pres. March–July 2012; Grand Officer, Star and Key of the Indian Ocean 2009. *Address:* Office of the Vice-President, 30 Farquhar Avenue, Quatre Bornes, Port Louis, Mauritius (office). *Telephone:* 427-1279 (office); 427-6110 (office). *Fax:* 464-1487 (office). *E-mail:* ovp@mail.gov.mu (office). *Website:* ovp.gov.mu (office).

OHSUMI, Yoshinori, BSc, PhD; Japanese cell biologist and academic; *Professor, Frontier Research Centre, Tokyo Institute of Technology;* b. 9 Feb. 1945, Fukuoka; ed Tokyo Univ.; Postdoctoral Fellow, The Rockefeller Univ., USA 1974–77; Research Assoc., Tokyo Univ. 1977–86, Lecturer 1986–88, Assoc. Prof. 1988–96, began work on identifying the genes connected with autophagy 1988; Prof., Nat.

Inst. for Basic Biology, Okazaki, Aichi Pref. 1996–2009, Prof. Emer. 2009–; Prof., Grad. Univ. for Advanced Studies, Hayama 2004–09, Prof. Emer. 2009–; Prof., Frontier Research Centre, Tokyo Inst. of Tech. 2009–; Fujihara Award 2005, Japan Acad. Prize 2006, Asahi Prize 2008, Kyoto Prize for Basic Science, Inamori Foundation (co-recipient) 2012. *Publications:* numerous papers in professional journals. *Address:* Frontier Research Centre, Tokyo Institute of Technology, S2-2, 4259 Nagatsuta-cho, Midori-ku, Yokohama 226-8503, Japan (office). *Telephone:* (45) 924-5113 (office); (45) 924-5879 (office). *Fax:* (45) 924-5121 (office). *E-mail:* kenkik.suzu@jim.titech.ac.jp (office). *Website:* www.fcrc.titech.ac.jp/english (office); www.ohsumilab.aro.iri.titech.ac.jp (office).

OHTA, Tomoko Harada, PhD; Japanese geneticist and academic; *Professor Emerita, National Institute of Genetics;* b. (Tomoko Harada), 7 Sept. 1933, Aichi-Ken; d. of Mamoru Harada and Hatsu Harada; m. Yasuo Ohta 1960 (divorced 1972); one d.; ed Tokyo Univ., North Carolina State Univ., USA; researcher, Kihara Inst. for Biological Research 1958–62; Postdoctoral Fellow, Nat. Inst. of Genetics 1967–69, Researcher 1969–76, Assoc. Prof. 1976–84, Prof. 1984–97, Prof. Emer. 1997–, Head of Dept of Population Genetics 1988–97; Vice-Pres. Soc. for the Study of Evolution 1994; Fellow, AAAS 2000; Foreign mem. NAS 2002; Foreign Hon. mem. American Acad. of Arts and Sciences 1984; Saruhashi Prize 1981, Japan Acad. Prize 1985, Weldon Memorial Prize, Oxford Univ. 1986, Person of Cultural Merit 2002. *Publications:* Evolution and Variation of Multigene Families, Lecture Notes in Biomathematics Vol. 37 1980. *Leisure interest:* reading. *Address:* 20-20 Hatsunedai, Mishima-shi, Mishima-ken 411-0018 (home); National Institute of Genetics, Mishima 411-8540, Japan (office). *E-mail:* tohta@nig.ac.jp (office). *Website:* www.nig.ac.jp (office).

OHTANI, Monshu Koshin, MA; Japanese ecclesiastic; *Monshu (Ecclesiastic Patriarch);* b. 12 Aug. 1945, Kyoto; s. of Kosho Ohtani and Yoshiko Ohtani; m. Noriko Tanaka 1974; two s. two d.; ed Tokyo Univ. and Ryukoku Univ.; ordained Priest of Jodo Shinshu Hongwanji-ha Aug. 1960, Monshu (Ecclesiastic Patriarch) Apparent 1970–1977, Monshu 1977–; Pres. All-Japanese Buddhist Fed. 1978–80, 1988–90, 2002–04. *Publications:* The Buddha's Wish for the World 2009, The Buddha's Call to Awaken 2012. *Leisure interests:* classical music, skiing. *Address:* Horikawa-dori, Hanayacho-sagaru, Shimogyo-ku, Kyoto 600-8501, Japan. *Telephone:* (75) 371-5181 (office). *Fax:* (75) 351-1211 (office). *Website:* www.hongwanji .or.jp (office).

OHTSUBO, Fumio, MA; Japanese business executive; *Executive Advisor, Panasonic Corporation;* ed Kansai Univ., Osaka; joined Matsushita Electric Industrial Co. in 1971, mem. Bd of Dirs 1998–2013, Vice-Pres. Audio and Video Sector (now Panasonic AVC Networks Co.) 1998–2000, Man. Dir 2000–03, Pres. Panasonic AVC Networks Co., Business Group Exec. AVC Network Business Group, and in Charge of Storage Device Business Jan.–June 2003, Sr Man. Dir Matsushita Electric Industrial Co. Ltd –2006, Pres. and Rep. Dir Matsushita Electric Industrial Co. Ltd 2006–12 (renamed Panasonic Corpn Oct. 2008), Chair. 2012–13, Exec. Advisor, also responsible for Storage Device Business 2013–; Chair. Exec. Bd Japan Electronics and Information Tech. Industries Asscn. *Address:* Panasonic Corpn, Corporate Headquarters, 1006 Oaza Kadoma, Kadoma-shi, Osaka 571-8501, Japan (office). *Telephone:* (6) 6908-1121 (office). *Fax:* (6) 6908-2351 (office). *E-mail:* info@panasonic.net (office). *Website:* panasonic.net (office).

OHURUOGU, Christine Ijeoma, MBE; British athlete; b. 17 May 1984, Newham, East London; ed Univ. Coll., London; sprinter; specializes in 400m, Commonwealth, World and Olympic Champion; bronze medal, 400m, European Jr Championships 2003; AAA Champion in 400m 2004; semi-finalist in 400m, Olympic Games, Athens 2004, also took part in 4×400m relay team that finished 4th; silver medal, 400m and 4×400m relay, European Under 23 Championships 2005; semi-finalist in 400m, World Championships, Helsinki 2005, bronze medal, 4×400m relay; gold medal, 400m, Commonwealth Games, Melbourne 2006; banned from athletics for one year for missing three out-of-competition drugs tests 2006, also banned by British Olympic Asscn from competing at future Olympic Games for GB, appealed to Court of Arbitration for Sport, original decision upheld, appealed against her Olympic ban which was overturned Nov. 2007; gold medal, 400m, bronze medal, 4×400m relay, World Championships, Osaka 2007, World Championships, Moscow 2013; gold medal, Olympic Games, Beijing 2008, silver medal, 400m, Olympic Games, London 2012; gold medal, 4×400m, World Indoor Championships, Istanbul 2012; gold medal, 4×400m, European Indoor Championships, Gothenburg 2013; first British female to win two World Championship titles, first British female to win three global titles, first British athlete to win three global titles in the same event; mem. Newham and Essex Beagles Athletics Club; coached by Lloyd Cowan. *E-mail:* info@chrissyo.com. *Website:* www.chrissyo .com.

OIKE, Kazuo, BSc, DSc; Japanese geophysicist and university administrator; b. 1940, Tokyo; ed Kyoto Univ.; Research Assoc., Disaster Prevention Research Inst., Kyoto Univ. 1963–73, Assoc. Prof. 1973–88, Prof. of Seismology, Grad. School of Science 1988–2003, Dean Grad. School of Science 1997–99, Dir Fmr Research Centre for Sports Science 2001–03, Vice-Pres. Kyoto Univ. 2001–03, Pres. 2003–08; f. observation network of microearthquakes in Inner Zone of south-western Japan to study stress field. *Publications:* numerous scientific papers in professional journals. *Address:* Kyoto University, Yoshida-Honmachi, Sakyo-ku, Kyoto 606-8501, Japan (office). *Telephone:* (75) 753-7531 (office). *Fax:* (774) 334598 (home). *E-mail:* koryu52@mail.adm.kyoto-u.ac.jp (office); konamazu@infoseek.to (office). *Website:* www.kyoto-u.ac.jp (office); homepage2.nifty.com/cat-fish.

OISHI, Katsuro; Japanese insurance industry executive; Dir and Gen. Man. Investment Planning Dept, Taiyo Mutual Life Insurance Co. 1999–2004, Rep. Dir and Pres. Taiyo Life Insurance Co. 2004–09, Rep. Dir and Chair. 2009–13, Advisor 2013–, Dir T&D Holdings Inc. (holding co. for Taiyo Life Insurance Co., Daido Life Insurance Co. and T&D Financial Life Insurance Co.) 2004–13. *Address:* Taiyo Life Insurance Co., 11-2 Nihonbashi 2-chome, Chuo-ku, Tokyo 103-0027, Japan. *E-mail:* info@td-holdings.co.jp.

OJEDA PAULLADA, Pedro; Mexican lawyer; b. 19 Jan. 1934, México, DF; s. of Manuel Ojeda Lacroix and Adela Paullada de Ojeda; m. Olga Cárdenas de Ojeda 1959; two s. three d.; ed Univ. Nacional Autónoma de México (UNAM); Head of Personnel and lawyer, Técnica y Fundación, SA de CV 1955, Sub-Man. 1955–57; Gen. Man. Industria Química de Plásticos SA 1957–58; Deputy Dir-Gen. Juntas Federales de Mejoras Materiales 1959–65; Dir-Gen. of Legal Affairs, SCT 1966–70; Sec.-Gen. Presidential Secr. 1970–71; Attorney-Gen. 1971–76; Sec. of Labour and Social Welfare 1976–81; Minister of Fisheries 1982–88; Gen. Co-ordinator Nat. Food Comm. 1988–91; Pres. Fed. Court of Conciliation and Arbitrage 1995–; Prof. of Law and Economics, UNAM, Prof. of Social Security; rep. Mexico on many int. and regional comms etc., including Pres. Perm. Conf. of Political Parties of Latin America (COPPAL) 1981–82, Chair. World Conf. of Int. Women's Year 1975, 64th Int. Conf. of ILO 1978, World Conf. on Fishing Devt (FAO) 1984; Fed. Congressman 1991–94; Pres. Energy Comm. of the Mexican Congress 1991–94, Nat. Fed. of Lawyers in the Service of Mexico (FENASEM) 1992–, Tech. Comm. of Foreign Relations of Fundación Mexicana Luis Donaldo Colosio, AC 1992–94, Mexican Coll. of Lawyers 1994–, Mexican Acad. of Law and Econs 1995–; Mexican Soc. of Geography and Statistics, 1994–97; mem. Institutional Revolutionary Party (PRI) 1951–, Pres. Nat. Exec. Cttee 1981–82; mem. Nat. Acad. of History and Geography, American Law and Econs Asscn 1991–; Order of Merit (Italy), Gran Cruz al Mérito (Italy), Orden de Isabel la Católica (Spain) and other decorations. *Leisure interests:* art, dominoes, reading, tennis. *Address:* Avenida del IMAN 660, 3° piso, Col Pedregal del Maurel, CP 04720, Del. Coyoacan, México, DF, Mexico. *Telephone:* (5) 568-1878; (5) 606-8881. *Fax:* (5) 606-9070.

OJEDA Y EISELEY, Jaime de, LLB; Spanish diplomatist; *Ambassador-in-Residence, Shenandoah University;* b. 5 Aug. 1933; ed Univ. of Madrid, Int. Acad. of The Hague, Naval War Coll. of Madrid and Sr Centre for Nat. Defence Studies (CESEDEN), Madrid; Prof. of Political Law, Complutense Univ. of Madrid 1958; joined diplomatic service 1958; served Washington, DC 1962–69; Minister-Counsellor, Beijing 1973–76; Consul-Gen. of Spain in Hong Kong and Macao 1976–79; Fellow, Center for Int. Relations, Harvard Univ. 1979–80; Deputy Perm. Rep. to North Atlantic Council 1982–83, Perm. Rep. to NATO 1983–90; Amb. to USA 1990–97; Pres. Sr Council on Foreign Affairs 1997–98; Amb.-in-Residence Shenandoah Univ. 1998–; Great Cross, Mil. Merit, Great Cross, Civil Merit, Kt Order of Carlos III. *Publications:* El 98 en el Congreso y en la Prensa de los Estados Unidos 1999; trans. Alice in Wonderland (Lewis Carroll) 1971, Through the Looking Glass (Lewis Carroll) 1974, Spain and America: The Past and the Future 1994. *Leisure interests:* music, botany, sailing. *Address:* 1460 University Drive, Winchester, VA 22643 (office); 3770 Leed's Manor Road, Markham, VA 22643, USA (home). *Telephone:* (540) 665-4696 (office); (540) 364-2275 (home). *Fax:* (540) 665-4698 (office); (540) 364-9281 (home). *E-mail:* wsherdow@su.edu (office).

OJO, Bayo, LLM; Nigerian lawyer and politician; ed Univ. of Lagos, Royal Inst. of Public Admin, London, LSE, London; began career as civil servant, fmr Kwara State; called to Nigerian Bar 1978; fmr State Counsel, Ministry of Justice, Kwara State; Head of Chambers, Oniyangi & Co. 1983–86; Prin. Pnr, Bayo Ojo & Co. (law firm) 1986–; Minister of Justice and Attorney-Gen. 2005–07; Solicitor of Supreme Court of England and Wales; Fellow, Chartered Inst. of Arbitrators, UK; Chair. Nigeria Legal Aid Council; fmr Pres. Nigeria Bar Asscn, also mem. Nat. Exec. Cttee; Sr Advocate of Nigeria (SAN). *Address:* c/o Ministry of Justice, New Federal Secretariat Complex, Shehu Shagari Way, Central Area District, Abuja, Nigeria (office).

OKA, Motoyuki; Japanese business executive; *Senior Adviser, Sumitomo Corporation;* b. 15 Sept. 1943; joined Sumitomo Corpn (gen. trading co.) 1966, served as Gen. Man. Tubular Products Import and Export Dept No. 1 and Gen. Man., Sumitomo Corpn of America, Houston Office, Dir and Gen. Man. Iron and Steel Div. No. 3 and Gen. Man. Planning and Co-ordination Div. 1994–98, Man. Dir and Gen. Man. Planning and Co-ordination Div., Responsible for Personnel Div., C&C System Div. 1998–2001, Sr Man. Dir Responsible for Legal Div., Personnel and Gen. Affairs Div., Planning and Co-ordination Div. April–June 2001, Pres. and CEO Sumitomo Corpn 2001–07, Chair. 2007–12, Sr Adviser 2012–; Outside Dir, Japan Tobacco Inc. 2012–; Dir, NEC Corpn 2013–; Chair. Int. Market Cttee, Japan Foreign Trade Council 2001–. *Address:* Sumitomo Corpn, 8-11 Harumi 1-chome, Chuo-ku, Tokyo 104-8610, Japan (office). *Telephone:* (3) 5166-5000 (office). *Fax:* (3) 5166-6292 (office). *E-mail:* info@sumitomocorp.co.jp (office). *Website:* www.sumitomocorp.co.jp (office).

OKA, Takeshi, PhD, FRS, FRSC; Canadian/American (b. Japanese) scientist and academic; *Robert A. Millikan Distinguished Service Professor Emeritus of Chemistry, Astronomy and Astrophysics, Enrico Fermi Institute, University of Chicago;* b. 10 June 1932, Tokyo, Japan; s. of Shumpei Oka and Chiyoko Oka; m. Keiko Nukui 1960; two s. two d.; ed Univ. of Tokyo; Fellow, Japan Soc. for the Promotion of Science 1960–63; Postdoctoral Fellow, Nat. Research Council of Canada 1963–65; Research Physicist, Herzberg Inst. of Astrophysics 1965–81; Prof. of Chem. and Astronomy and Astrophysics, Enrico Fermi Inst., Univ. of Chicago, USA 1981–, Robert A. Millikan Distinguished Service Prof. 1989–2003, Prof. Emer. 2003–; Fellow, American Acad. of Arts and Sciences, American Physical Soc.; Hon. DSc (Waterloo) 2001, (Univ. Coll. London) 2004; Steacie Prize 1972, Plyler Prize 1982; Meggers Award 1997, Lippincott Award 1998, Wilson Award 2002, Davy Medal 2004. *Leisure interest:* history of science. *Address:* Department of Chemistry, Astronomy and Astrophysics, University of Chicago, 5735 S Ellis Avenue, Chicago, IL 60637, USA (office). *Telephone:* (773) 702-7070 (office). *Fax:* (773) 702-0805 (office). *E-mail:* t-oka@uchicago.edu (office). *Website:* www.fermi.uchicago.edu (office).

OKABE, Hiromu, BSc; Japanese business executive and economist; ed Faculty of Econs, Nagoya Univ., Aichi; joined Denso Corpn 1960, held various positions in Accounting Dept and Corp. Planning Dept, Head of Planning Centre No. 2 (Electrical Products), Head of Corp. Planning 1989–95, apptd Dir 1989, Man.-Dir in charge of Engine Electrical Systems Product Div. 1995–96, Pres. and CEO 1996–2003, Vice-Chair. 2003–04, Chair. 2004–09; Dir, Nagoya Railroad Co. Ltd 2007–; Japanese Prime Minister's Award for a Treatise on Econs 1971. *Leisure interests:* reading, writing, playing the traditional board game Go. *Address:* Nagoya Railroad Co. Ltd, 1-2-4 Meieki, Nagoya, Aichi 450-8501, Japan (office). *Telephone:* (52) 588-0813 (office). *Fax:* (52) 588-0815 (office). *Website:* www .meitetsu.co.jp (office).

OKABE, Keiichiro; Japanese oil industry executive; b. 1946; fmr Pres. AOC Holdings; Pres. and CEO Cosmo Oil Co. Ltd –2004, Rep. Dir and Chair. 2004–12; Chair. Japan Oil Asscn 2000, Petroleum Asscn of Japan 2002–; Pres. Qatar Petroleum Devt Co.; mem. Business Leaders' Inter-Forum for Environment 2002;

mem. Bd Auditors Tokyo Broadcasting System Inc. (TBS) 2003–; mem. Bd of Dirs Japan Co-operative Centre for the Middle East. *Address:* c/o Cosmo Oil Co. Ltd, 1-1-1, Shibaura, Minato-ku, Tokyo 105-8528, Japan. *E-mail:* info@cosmo-oil.co.jp.

OKABE, Masahiko; Japanese business executive; *Chairman, Nippon Express Company Ltd;* joined Nippon Express Co. Ltd 1961, various positions within Corp. Admin and Human Resources Depts, Gen.-Man. Chugoku Regional Br. Office 1995–97, Man.-Dir Nippon Express Co. Ltd 1997–99, Pres. 1999–2001, Pres. and CEO 2001–05, Chair. 2005–; Co-Chair. Cttee on Transportation, Nippon Keidanren 2003–. *Address:* Nippon Express Company Ltd, 1-9-3 Higashi-Shimbashi, Minato-ku, Tokyo 105-8322, Japan (office). *Telephone:* (3) 6251-1111 (office). *Website:* www.nittsu.co.jp (office).

OKADA, Akashige; Japanese banking executive; Pres. Sakura Bank –2001; Chair. Sumitomo Mitsui Banking Corpn 2001–05; Chair. and Rep. Dir Sumitomo Mitsui Financial Group Inc. 2004–05; Dir Sony Corpn 2002– (also Chair. Compensation Cttee 2004–), Mitsui & Co. Ltd, Kao Corpn 2002–; mem. Japan Cttee, Pacific Basin Econ. Council; Auditor Toray Science Foundation. *Address:* c/o Sumitomo Mitsui Financial Group Inc., 1-2 Yurakucho 1-chome, Chiyoda-ku, Tokyo 100-0006, Japan (office).

OKADA, Katsuya; Japanese lawyer and politician; b. 14 July 1953; ed Univ. of Tokyo and Harvard Univ., USA; entered Ministry of Int. Trade and Industry; joined Takeshita faction of LDP; joined Shinsheito 1993; later mem. Shinshinto and Taiyo Party, then Minseito, finally Democratic Party of Japan, DPJ, following merger with Minseito 1998–, Pres. 2004–05 (resgnd), Vice-Pres. 2006–10, Sec.-Gen. 2010–; mem. House of Reps for Mie Pref.; Minister for Foreign Affairs 2009–10, Deputy Prime Minister and Minister for Total Reform of Social Security and Tax Jan.–Dec. 2012. *Address:* Democratic Party of Japan, 1-11-1, Nagata-cho, Chiyoda-ku, Tokyo 100-0014, Japan (office). *Telephone:* (3) 3595-9988 (office). *Fax:* (3) 3595-9961 (office). *E-mail:* dpjenews@dpj.or.jp (office). *Website:* www.dpj.or.jp (office).

OKADA, Motoya, MBA; Japanese retail executive; *President and Representative Executive Officer, AEON Company Limited;* ed Babson Coll., USA; mem. Bd Dirs Jusco Co. Ltd (retail co.) 1990–92, Man. Dir 1992–95, Sr Man. Dir 1995–97, Pres. and CEO 1997–2009 (renamed AEON Co. Ltd 2001), Pres. and Rep. Exec. Officer 2009–, Pres. Talbots Japan Co. Ltd (subsidiary of AEON) 1990–97, mem. Bd Dirs AEON Co. (Malaysia) Berhad, The Talbots, Inc. 1993–; Chair. Mycal; mem. Bd of Dirs CIES – The Food Business Forum 2000–. *Address:* AEON Co. Ltd, 1-5-1 Nakase, Mihama-ku, Chiba-shi, Chiba 261-8515, Japan (office). *Telephone:* (4) 3212-6042 (office). *Fax:* (4) 3212-6849 (office). *E-mail:* info@aeon.info (office). *Website:* www.aeon.info (office).

OKAFUJI, Masahiro; Japanese business executive; *President, CEO and Representative Director, ITOCHU Corporation;* b. 1949, Osaka Pref.; ed Tokyo and Osaka Univs; joined ITOCHU 1974, positions include Vice-Pres., Pres. of Fibre Co., Dir of Brand Marketing Business, Exec. Officer 2002, Man. Exec. Officer, Sr Man. Dir, Pres. of Textiles and Man. Dir ITOCHU Corpn 2004–06, Sr Man. Dir 2006–10, Pres., CEO and Rep. Dir 2010–. *Address:* ITOCHU Corporation, 5-1 Kita-Aoyama 2-chome, Minato-ku, Tokyo 107-8077, Japan (office). *Telephone:* (3) 3497-2121 (office). *Fax:* (3) 3497-4141 (office). *E-mail:* info@itochu.co.jp (office). *Website:* www .itochu.co.jp (office).

OKALIK, Paul, BA, LLB; Canadian politician; b. 1964, Pangnirtung, NWT; s. of Auyaluk; m.; 2 c.; ed Carleton Univ., Univ. of Ottawa; first Inuit law grad.; called to the Bar 1999; mem. Nunavut Legis. Ass. 1999–; first Premier of Nunavut, Minister of Exec. and Intergovernmental Affairs and Minister of Justice 1999–2008. *Leisure interests:* hunting, fishing, golf. *Address:* Nunavut Legislative Assembly, PO Box 1200, Iqaluit, NU X0A 0H0, Canada (office). *Telephone:* (867) 975-5017 (office). *Fax:* (867) 975-5112 (office). *Website:* www.assembly.nu.ca (office).

OKAMOTO, Kunie; Japanese insurance company executive; *Chairman, Nippon Life Insurance Company;* ed Univ. of Tokyo; joined Nippon Life Insurance Co. 1969, Dir 1999, Man. Dir 1999–2002, Sr Man. Dir 2002–05, Pres. 2005–11, Chair. 2011–; Corp. Auditor, Sapporo Holdings Ltd, UFJ Holdings, Inc. June–Sept. 2005, Mitsubishi Financial UFJ Group 2005–, Tokyu Corpn 2005–; Dir Kintetsu Corpn 2010–; External Corp. Auditor, Daicel Chemical Industries Ltd; Vice-Chair. Life Insurance Asscn of Japan. *Address:* Nippon Life Insurance Co., 3-5-12 Imabashi, Chuo-ku, Osaka 541-8501, Japan (office). *Telephone:* (6) 6209-5525 (office). *Fax:* (3) 5510-7340 (office). *E-mail:* info@nissay.co.jp (office). *Website:* www.nissay.co.jp (office).

OKAMOTO, Tao; Japanese fashion model and actress; b. 22 May 1987, Tokyo; signed with Elite model agency 2006, catwalk debut at spring Emanuel Ungaro and Martin Grant shows, Paris 2006; has modelled for Vogue, Dolce & Gabbana, Julien Macdonald, Yves Saint Laurent, Ralph Lauren. *Film:* The Wolverine 2013. *Address:* The Society Management, 156 5th Avenue, 8th Floor, New York, NY 10010, USA (office). *Website:* taookamoto.com (office).

OKAMOTO, Tsuyoshi; Japanese business executive; *Representative Director and President, Tokyo Gas;* b. 23 Sept. 1947; joined Tokyo Gas 1970, Dir, Sr Exec. Officer, Chief Exec. of Corp. Communication Div. and in charge of Compliance Dept, Internal Audit Dept 2006–07, Rep. Dir, Exec. Vice-Pres., and in charge of Personnel Dept, Secretary Dept, Gen. Admin Dept, Compliance Dept and Internal Audit Dept 2007–09, Rep. Dir, Exec. Vice-Pres., and in charge of Personnel Dept, Secretary Dept, Gen. Admin Dept and Compliance Dept 2009–10, Rep. Dir and Pres. Tokyo Gas 2010–. *Address:* Tokyo Gas, 1-5-20 Kaigan, Minato-ku, Tokyo 105-8527, Japan (office). *Telephone:* (3) 3344-9100 (office). *E-mail:* tgir@tokyo-gas.co.jp (office). *Website:* www.tokyo-gas.co.jp (office).

OKAMURA, Tadashi, LLB; Japanese electronics industry executive; *Chairman, Toshiba Corporation;* ed Univ. of Tokyo; joined Toshiba Corpn 1962, Gen.-Man. Marketing Planning Div. 1989–93, Group Exec. Information Processing and Control Systems Group 1993–94, Dir 1994–, Vice-Pres. 1994–96, Sr Vice-Pres. 1996–2000, Pres. and CEO Toshiba Corpn 2000–05, Chair. 2005–. *Address:* Toshiba Corporation, 1-1 Shibaura 1-chome, Minato-ku, Tokyo 105-8001, Japan (office). *Telephone:* (3) 3457-4511 (office). *Fax:* (3) 3455-1631 (office). *Website:* www .toshiba.com (office).

O'KANE, Dene Philip; New Zealand professional snooker player; b. 24 Feb. 1963, Christchurch; s. of Robert John O'Kane and Lesley Joan Marshall; ed Northcote Coll.; NZ Under-21 Champion 1977; youngest-ever NZ Champion 1980; turned professional 1984; tournament record includes Embassy World Championship Quarter Final 1987, World Cup Runner Up (Rest of World Team) 1989, Hong Kong Open runner up 1989; highest ranking: 18; retd 2001; NZ Seniors Champion 2004, IBSF World Masters Championship 2004, 2005, 2008, Bob Hawke AC Australian Open Snooker Championship 2005, Oceania Championship 2005, 2006, 2007; Chair. NZ Confed. of Billiard Sports; Overseas (non-British) Player of the Year 1987. *Leisure interests:* golf, skin-diving, Formula One motor-racing, wine, clothes. *Address:* c/o Speakers New Zealand, PO Box 51 266, Auckland 1730, New Zealand.

O'KANE, Margaret (Maggie) Mary, BA (Hons); Irish journalist; *Multimedia Editor, Investigations, The Guardian;* b. 8 June 1962, Ardglas, Co. Down, Northern Ireland; d. of Peter O'Kane and Maura McNeil; m. John Mullin 1995; one s. two d.; ed Loreto Convent (Balbriggan, Co. Dublin), Univ. Coll., Dublin, Coll. de Journalistes en Europe, Paris and Coll. of Commerce, Dublin; reporter on Irish TV 1982–84, for Sunday Tribune newspaper 1984–87; reporter, TV Producer and Presenter 1987–89; Foreign Corresp. and Feature Writer, The Guardian 1989–2003; has reported from world trouble spots: Eastern Europe 1989–91, Baghdad 1991, Kurdistan 1991–92, Yugoslavia 1992–94, Bosnia, Haiti, Cuba 1994–96, Afghanistan, Cambodia, Kosovo, Yugoslavia 2000 etc.; Editorial Dir Guardian Films 2003, now Multimedia Ed., Investigations; Dr hc (Bradford); Journalist of the Year 1992, Foreign Corresp. of the Year 1992, Reporter of the Year (commended) (jt award) 1994, Amnesty International Foreign Corresp. of the Year 1993, James Cameron Award for Journalism 1996, European Journalist of the Year 2002, 2003. *Films:* (documentaries) Milosevic: Puppet Master of the Balkans (Channel 4) (Royal TV Soc. (RTS) Documentary of the Year 1993), Bloody Bosnia (RTS Documentary of the Year 1994), Looking for Karadzic (Guardian Films) (European Journalist of the Year 2002, RTS Best Documentary 2004, International Emmy 2008), Baghdad: A Doctor's Story (Best News Award 2009, Zimbabwe Emmy Award 2008) 2008. *Publications:* A Woman's World: Beyond the Headlines 1996, Mozambique. *Leisure interests:* outdoor and swimming, cooking, bikram yoga training in Co. Mayo, gardening. *Address:* The Guardian, Kings Place, 90 York Way, London, N1 9GU, England (office). *Telephone:* (20) 3353-2000 (office). *E-mail:* maggie.okane@guardian.co.uk (office). *Website:* www.guardian.co .uk/guardianfilms (office).

OKANLA, Moussa, PhD; Benin politician and academic; b. 2 Sept. 1950; m.; ed Univ. of Michigan, USA; Prof. of Law, Univ. of Benin; Benin Rep., African and Afroamerican Inst., New York 1987–94; Specialist in Democracy and Governance for USAID regional office, Abidjan, Côte d'Ivoire 1994–98; Governance Adviser, UNDP, Cotonou 1999–2000; Deputy Dir, later Dir, Benin School of Public Admin 2001–03; Program Officer, PGDP (Danish-funded governance programme) 2004–07; Minister of Foreign Affairs, African Integration, Francophony and Beninese Diaspora 2007–08; Chair. Group of Least Developed Countries, UNDP; currently Lecturer in Political Science, Univ. of Abomey-Calavi; Commdr, Ordre Nat. du Bénin. *Address:* University of Abomey-Calavi, BP 526, Abomey-Calavi, Cotonou, Benin (office). *Telephone:* 36-00-74 (office). *Website:* www.uac.bj (office).

OKAWA, Ryuho; Japanese religious leader; *Leader, Kofuku-no-Kagaku;* b. 7 July 1956, Tokushima Pref.; ed Univ. of Tokyo, Graduate Center, City Univ. of New York, USA; attained enlightenment 23 March 1981, realized his identity as El Cantare, saviour of humanity; f. Kofuku-no-Kagaku (Inst. for Research in Human Happiness) 1986; holds numerous open lecture sessions with large audiences that are broadcast by satellite throughout Japan. *Publications include:* more than 400 books including The Starting Point of Happiness – A Practical and Intuitive Guide to Discovering Love, Wisdom, and Faith 2001, Love, Nurture, and Forgive – A Handbook on Adding New Richness in Your Life 2002, An Unshakeable Mind – How to Cope with Life's Difficulties and Turn Them into Food for Your Soul 2002, A Revolution of Happiness – The Power of Thought to Change the Future, The 'Inability to Attain Happiness' Syndrome – Say Good-bye to a Life of Gloom, Work and Love – Become a True Leader in the Business World, Invincible Thinking – Become a Master of Your Own Destiny 2003, The Science of Happiness 2009. *Address:* Kofuku-no-Kagaku, 1-6-7 Togoshi, Shinagawa-ku, Tokyo, 142-0041, Japan (office). *Telephone:* (3) 6384-5770 (office). *Fax:* (3) 6384-5776 (office). *E-mail:* tokyo@happy-science.org (office). *Website:* www.happy-science.org; www.kofuku -no-kagaku.or.jp (office).

OKAYAMA, Norio; Japanese electronics industry executive; fmrly with Juki Corpn; apptd Pres. Sumitomo Electric Industries Ltd 1999, Chair. –2008; mem. Bd of Dirs Dunlop Co. 2000–, Optoelectronic Industry and Tech. Devt Asscn (OITDA); Acting Pres. Int. Cablemakers Fed. 2006. *Address:* c/o Sumitomo Electric Industries Ltd, 5-33 Kitahama 4-chome, Chuo-ku, Osaka 541-0041, Japan. *E-mail:* info@global-sei.com.

OKAZAKI, Tomiko; Japanese politician; b. 16 Feb. 1944, Fukushima; ed Fukushima Prefectural Women's High School; TV presenter, Tohoku Broadcasting Co. 1968–90; mem. House of Reps (Social Democratic Party) for Miyagi 1st dist 1990–96, House of Councillors (Democratic Party of Japan—DPJ) for Miyagi dist 1997–; Minister of State for Consumer Affairs and Food Safety and for Social Affairs and Gender Equality 2010–11; Chair. Nat. Public Safety Comm. 2010–11; Vice-Pres. DPJ 1996. *Address:* Office 415, Members' Office Building, House of Councillors, Nagatachō, Chiyoda-ku, Tokyo, Japan (office). *Telephone:* (3) 6550-0415 (office). *Fax:* (3) 6551-0415 (office). *Website:* okazaki-tomiko.jp (office).

OKAZAKI, Tsuneko, MSc, DSc; Japanese molecular biologist, cellular biologist, academic and business executive; b. (Tsuneko Hara), 7 Aug. 1933, Nagoya; d. of Takima Hara and Hama Hara; m. Reiji Okazaki; ed Nagoya Univ., studies in USA; Fellowship with J. L. Strominger at Washington Univ., St Louis, Mo., USA 1960–61; Fellowship with A. Kornberg at Stanford Univ., USA 1961–63; Dept of Molecular Biology, Faculty of Science, Nagoya Univ. 1963–97, Prof. 1997–2002, Visiting Prof. 2002-08, currently Prof. Emer.; Prof. and Visiting Prof., Div. of Artificial Chromosome Project, Inst. for Comprehensive Medical Science, Fujita Health Univ., Toyoake, Aichi 1997–2008; Dir JSPS Stockholm Office, Sweden; CEO Chromo Research Inc., Nagoya 2008–13; Order of the Sacred Treasure 2008; L'Oréal-UNESCO For Women in Science Award 2000, Purple Ribbon Prize 2000. *Achievements include:* co-discoverer of Okazaki Fragments of DNA; discoverer of

Primer RNA for DNA synthesis; elucidation of detail mechanisms of discontinuous way of DNA synthesis; construction of human artificial chromosome. *Publications include:* numerous articles in scientific journals on mechanisms of DNA replication and the human artificial chromosome. *Address:* c/o Chromo Research Inc., 1212 Shihongi, Midori-ku, Nagoya 458-0039, Japan.

OKAZAKI, Yoichiro; Japanese engineering executive; *Chairman, President and CEO, Mitsubishi Motors Corporation;* b. 1943; joined Mitsubishi Heavy Industries Ltd 1965, Deputy Gen. Man., Sagamihara Machinery Works 1995–97, Chief Engineer, Gen. Machinery & Components HQ 1997, Pres. Mitsubishi Caterpillar Forklift America Inc. 1997–2001, Dir and Chief Co-ordinator, Gen. Machinery & Components HQ 1999–2000, Gen. Machinery & Special Vehicle HQ 2000–01, Dir, Gen. Man. then Man.-Dir 2001–04; Chair., Pres. and CEO Mitsubishi Motors Corpn 2004–; Dir Shin Caterpillar Mitsubishi Ltd 2001, Mitsubishi Heavy Industries Ltd 2004–; mem. Hon. Cttee FISITSA. *Address:* Mitsubishi Motors Corporation, 2-16-4 Konan, Minato-ku, Tokyo 108-8410, Japan (office). *Telephone:* (3) 6719-2111 (office). *Fax:* (3) 6719-0014 (office). *Website:* www.mistubishi-motors .co.jp (office).

OKDAH, Farouk Abd el-Baky el-, BS, MS, MBA, PhD; Egyptian economist and central banker; b. Aug. 1946; m.; two c.; ed Ain Shams Univ., Cairo Univ., The Wharton School, Univ. of Pennsylvania, USA; Instructor in Accounting and Finance, The Wharton School, Univ. of Pennsylvania 1978–82; Asst Vice-Pres., Middle East Div., later Vice-Pres. and Africa District Man., Irving Trust Co., New York 1984–88; Vice-Pres., Regional Man. and Adviser, Bank of New York 1989–2002; Man. Dir, Int. Co. for Leasing 'Incolease' 1997–2002; Chair. and CEO Nat. Bank of Egypt Jan.–Dec. 2003; Gov. Cen. Bank of Egypt Dec. 2003–13; Gov. African Devt Bank, Arab Monetary Fund; Alt. Gov. IMF; Chair. Nat. Bank of Egypt, London, Union de Banques Arabes et Françaises; mem. Bd of Dirs Egyptian Air Holding Co. 1998–; Dir British Arab Commercial Bank Ltd 2003–10; mem. Bd of Dirs Egyptian Banking Fed., Arab Bankers Asscn–N America (also Treas.) 1987–89. *Address:* c/o Office of the Governor, Central Bank of Egypt, 31 Sharia Qasr el-Nil, Cairo, Egypt. *E-mail:* info@cbe.org.eg.

OKE, Timothy Richard, OC, FRSC, PhD; Canadian/British geographer and academic; *Professor Emeritus of Geography, University of British Columbia;* b. 22 Nov. 1941, Kingsbridge, Devon, England; s. of the late Leslie Oke and Kathleen Oke; m. Margaret 1967; one s. one d.; ed Lord Wandsworth Coll., Univ. of Bristol and McMaster Univ.; Asst Prof., McGill Univ. 1967–70; Asst Prof., Univ. of British Col 1970–71, Assoc. Prof. 1971–78, Prof. of Geography 1978–, now Prof. Emer., also Head, Dept of Geography 1991–96; Ed.-in-Chief, Atmosphere-Ocean 1977–80; Hooker Distinguished Visiting Prof., McMaster Univ. 1987; Visiting Fellow, Keble Coll. Oxford 1990–91; Research Scholar (Rockefeller Foundation) Bellagio, Italy 1991; consultant to WMO and other orgs; Founder and Pres. Int. Asscn for Urban Climate 2000–03; Fellow, Royal Canadian Geographical Soc., Canadian Meteorological and Oceanographic Soc. 2003, American Meteorological Soc. 2004; Dr hc (Łódź) 2005; Pres.'s Prize, Canadian Meteorological Soc. 1972, Killam Prize 1988, Award for Scholarly Distinction, Canadian Asscn of Geographers 1986, Guggenheim Fellow 1990, American Meteorological Soc. Outstanding Achievement in Biometeorology Award 2002, Patterson Medal, Meteorological Service of Canada, Environment Canada 2002, Luke Howard Award, Int. Asscn for Urban Climate 2004, Massey Medal, Royal Canadian Geog Soc. 2005, Helmut E. Landsberg Award, American Meteorological Soc. 2006, Founder's Medal, Int. Asscn for Urban Climate 2012. *Publications:* Boundary Layer Climates 1978, Vancouver and its Region 1992, The Surface Climates of Canada 1997; more than 200 articles on the climate of cities. *Leisure interests:* golf, music, walking, art. *Address:* Department of Geography, University of British Columbia, 1984 West Mall, Vancouver, BC, V6T 1Z2, Canada (office). *Telephone:* (604) 822-2900 (office). *Fax:* (604) 822-6150 (office). *Website:* www.geog.ubc.ca/~toke (office).

O'KEEFE, Sean Charles; American space research administration official and fmr university administrator; *Chairman and CEO, EADS North America;* b. 27 Jan. 1956, New Orleans, La; m. Laura McCarthy O'Keefe; three c.; fmr staff dir and professional staff mem. Defense Sub-cttee of Senate Appropriations Cttee; Comptroller, Dept of Defense 1989, Sec. of the Navy 1992–93; Prof. of Business Admin., Sr Vice-Pres. for Research, Dean of Grad. School, Pennsylvania State Univ. 1993–96; Louis A. Bantle Prof. of Business and Govt Policy, Maxwell Grad. School of Citizenship and Public Affairs, Syracuse Univ., NY 1996–2001, Dir Nat. Security Studies, Syracuse Univ. and Johns Hopkins Univ. 1996–2001; Deputy Dir Office of Man. and Budget March–Dec. 2001; Admin. NASA Dec. 2001–05 (resgnd); Chancellor Louisiana State Univ. 2005–08; CEO EADS North America (subsidiary of European Aeronautic Defence and Space Co. NV) 2009–, Chair. 2012–; Vice-Chair. Exec. Cttee, Nat. Defense Industrial Asscn –2011, Chair. 2011–; mem. Bd of Advisors, Naval Postgraduate School; Fellow, Nat. Acad. of Public Admin, Int. Acad. of Astronautics; survived a plane crash nr Aleknagik, Alaska 2010; Hon. Engineer of the Year Award, Engineer's Council 2005; Distinguished Public Service Award 1993, Chancellor's Award for Public Service, Syracuse Univ. 1999, Public Service Award, Dept of the Navy 2000, Navigator Award, Potomac Inst. for Policy Studies 2005, inducted into Louisiana Political Hall of Fame 2007, Asteroid 78905 Seanokeefe named in his honour. *Publications:* The Defense Industry in the Post-Cold War Era: Corporate Strategies and Public Policy Perspectives (co-author) 1998, Keeping the Edge: Managing Defense for the Future (contrib.) 2000; several journal articles. *Address:* EADS North America, 2550 Wasser Terrace, Suite 9000, Herndon, VA 20171, USA (office). *Telephone:* (703) 466-5600 (office). *E-mail:* info@eadsnorthamerica.com (office). *Website:* www.eadsnorthamerica.com (office).

O'KEEFFE, Michael, BSc, PhD, DSc; American (b. British) chemist and academic; *Regents' Professor Emeritus and Research Professor Emeritus of Chemistry, Arizona State University;* b. 3 April 1934, Bury St Edmunds, Suffolk; ed Univ. of Bristol, UK; Research Scientist, Mullard Research Labs and Philips Research Labs, UK 1958–60; Postdoctoral Assoc., Indiana Univ., USA 1960–63; Asst Prof., Arizona State Univ. 1963–66, Assoc. Prof. 1966–70, Prof. 1970–94, Regents' Prof. and Research Prof. of Chem. 1994, now Prof. Emer. *Publications:* three books, including Crystal Structures: Patterns & Symmetry (with Bruce Hyde); more than 280 papers in professional journals. *Address:* PSC-208, Physical Sciences Building, Department of Chemistry and Biochemistry, Arizona State University, Tempe, AZ 85287-1604, USA (office). *Telephone:* (480) 965-3670

(office). *Fax:* (480) 965-2747 (office). *E-mail:* mokeeffe@asu.edu (office). *Website:* chemistry.asu.edu/faculty/M_Okeeffe.asp (office); www.public.asu.edu/~rosebudx/ okeeffe.htm (office).

OKEKE, Francisca Nneka, PhD, FAS; Nigerian physicist, space scientist and academic; *Professor of Physics, University of Nigeria, Nsukka;* Visiting Research Fellow, Univ. of Natal, South Africa 1998; Prof. of Physics, Univ. of Nigeria, Nsukka 2000–, Head of Dept of Physics and Astronomy (first woman) 2003–06, Dean, Faculty of Physical Sciences 2008–10 (first woman); research visits to Harvard Smithsonian Centre, USA 2004, Morgan State Univ., USA 2003, etc.; Fellowship Int. Award (as Fellow, Japan Soc. for Promotion of Science), Univ. of Tokyo 1999–2000, Visiting Assoc., CPTEC Brazil, Laureate for Africa and Arab States, L'Oréal-UNESCO Awards for Women in Science 2013. *Publications:* several physics textbooks and numerous papers in professional journals. *Address:* Department of Physics and Astronomy, Faculty of Physical Sciences, University of Nigeria, Nsukka, Nigeria (office). *Telephone:* 803-5079686 (mobile) (office). *E-mail:* francisca.okeke@unn.edu.ng (office); franciscaokeke@yahoo.com. *Website:* www .unn.edu.ng/profile/prof-francisca-nneka-okeke (office).

O'KENNEDY, Michael, MA; Irish politician; b. 21 Feb. 1936, Nenagh, Co. Tipperary; s. of Éamonn O'Kennedy and Helena (Slattery) O'Kennedy; m. Breda Heavey 1965; one s. two d.; ed St Flannan's Coll., Ennis, Univ. Coll. Dublin, King's Inns, Dublin; practised as barrister 1961–70, as Sr Counsel 1973–77, 1982–; mem. Senate 1965–69, 1993–, Front Bench Spokesman on Educ. and Justice, Senate Statutory Instruments Cttee on the Constitution until 1967; mem. Dáil for N Tipperary 1969–80, 1982–93, 1997–2002; presidential cand. 1997; Parl. Sec. to Minister of Educ. 1970–72, Minister without Portfolio 1972–73, Minister for Transport and Power 1973; Opposition Spokesman on Foreign Affairs 1973–77; Minister for Foreign Affairs 1977–79, of Finance 1979–80; mem. Comm. of European Communities 1980–82; Commr for Personnel, Consumer Affairs, Environment 1981–82; Opposition Spokesman for Finance 1982–87, Minister of Agric. 1987–92; mem. All-Parties Cttee on Irish Relations, Chair. 1973–80; mem. Informal Cttee on Reform of Dáil Procedure until 1972, Dáil and Senate Joint Cttee on Secondary Legislation of EEC 1973–80, Anglo-Irish Parl. Body 1993– (Co-Chair. 1997–); mem. Inter-Parl. Union, mem. Exec. of Irish Council of European Movt; Pres. EEC Council of Ministers July–Dec. 1979; Pres. EC Council of Agric. Ministers Jan.–June 1990; Pres. Re-negotiation EEC/ACP at 2nd Lomé Convention 1979; Nat. Trustee Fianna Fáil. *Leisure interests:* reading, philosophy, history, politics, drama, music, sports. *Address:* Gortlandroe, Nenagh, Co. Tipperary, Ireland. *Telephone:* (67) 31366 (home).

OKETA, Gazmend; Albanian engineer and politician; b. 14 Dec. 1968, Durrës; s. of Nuri Oketa; m.; two c.; ed General High School 'Gjergj Kastrioti', Durrës, Faculty of Civil Eng, Tirana Polytechnic Univ., Siegen Univ., Germany; Prof., Faculty of Civil Eng, Tirana 1994–95; Specialist of World Bank project on water supply rehabilitation, Durrës 1995–97; designing engineer and pvt. admin. in pvt. construction enterprises 1997–2003; adviser to Voith Siemens (Austria), project on Bistrica hydroelectric power station rehabilitation 2003–04; mem. Democratic Party of Albania (Partia Demokratike e Shqipërisë), Deputy Head of DPA, Durrës Br. 2004, Head of DPA and Spokesman Nov. 2005; mem. Durrës Municipal Council 2003–05; mem. Parl. for Durrës City, Zone No. 29 2005–, mem. Parl. Comm. for Legal Issues, Public Admin and Human Rights; Successive Pres. Cen. European Initiative Parl. Dimension Jan. 2006; Deputy Prime Minister 2007–08; Minister of Defence 2008–09. *Address:* c/o Partia Demokratike e Shqipërisë, Rruga Punëtorët e Rilindjes 1, Tirana, Albania (office). *Telephone:* (4) 2228091 (office). *Fax:* (4) 2223525 (office). *E-mail:* profsberisha@albaniaonline.net (office). *Website:* www .partiademokratike.al (office).

OKHOTNIKOV, Nikolai Petrovich; Russian singer (bass); b. 5 July 1937, Glubokoye, Kazakh Repub.; s. of P.Y. Okhotnikov and K.A. Okhotnikov; m. Larkina Tamara 1973; two s.; ed Leningrad Conservatoire with I.I. Pleshakov; mem. CPSU 1974–90; soloist with Leningrad Concert Union; with Maly Theatre, Leningrad 1967–71, with Kirov (now Mariinsky) Opera 1971–; teacher of singing at Leningrad (later St Petersburg) Conservatoire 1976–; Grand Prix, Barcelona 1972, People's Artist of USSR 1983, USSR State Prize 1985. *Major roles include:* Kochubey in Mazeppa, René in Iolanta, the Miller in Rusalka, Susanin in Glinka's Ivan Susanin, Dosifey in Mussorgsky's Khovanshchina, Kutuzov in Prokofiev's War and Peace, Philip II in Don Carlos, Heinrich in Lohengrin, Gremin in Eugene Onegin, Boris Godunov and Pimen in Boris Godunov, Don Basilio in The Barber of Seville. *Leisure interests:* fishing, photography. *Address:* Canal Griboedova 109, Apt 13, 190068 St Petersburg, Russia (home).

OKIHARA, Takamune; Japanese banking executive; *Chairman, Mitsubishi UFJ Financial Group, Inc.;* Exec. Officer, Sanwa 2001–02; Exec. Officer, UFJ Bank Ltd 2002–03, Sr Exec. Officer 2003–04, Pres. and CEO 2004–05, Man. Officer and Group Head of Integrated Corp. Banking Business Group, Mitsubishi UFJ Financial Group, Inc. 2005–06, Deputy Pres. and Chief Exec., Commercial Banking Business Unit, Bank of Tokyo-Mitsubishi UFJ Ltd 2006–08, Deputy Chair. Bank of Tokyo-Mitsubishi UFJ Ltd 2008–10, Chair. Mitsubishi UFJ Financial Group, Inc. 2010–; Dir UFJ Central Leasing Co. Ltd 2005–, Bank of Tokyo-Mitsubishi UFJ Ltd 2006–, UFJ Holdings Inc. *Address:* Mitsubishi UFJ Financial Group, Inc., 7-1, Marunouchi 2-chome, Chiyoda-ku, Tokyo 100-8330, Japan (office). *Telephone:* (3) 3240-8111 (office). *Fax:* (3) 3240-8203 (office). *E-mail:* info@mufg.jp (office). *Website:* www.mufg.jp (office).

OKOGIE, HE Cardinal Anthony Olubunmi, STL, DD; Nigerian ecclesiastic; *Archbishop Emeritus of Lagos;* b. 16 June 1936, Lagos; s. of Prince Michael Okogie and Lucy Okogie; ed St Gregory's Coll., Lagos, St Theresa Minor Seminary, Ibadan, St Peter and St Paul's Seminary, Ibadan, Urban Univ., Rome; ordained priest 1966; Acting Parish Priest, St Patrick's Church, Idumagbo, Lagos; Asst Priest, Holy Cross Cathedral, Lagos; Religious Instructor, King's Coll., Lagos; Dir of Vocations, Archdiocese of Lagos; Man. Holy Cross Group of Schools, Lagos; Master of Ceremonies, Holy Cross Cathedral; broadcaster of religious programmes, NBC-TV; Auxiliary Bishop of Oyo Diocese 1971–72; Auxiliary Bishop to the Apostolic Admin., Archdiocese of Lagos 1972–73; Archbishop of Lagos 1973–2012, Archbishop Emer. 2012–; cr. Cardinal (Cardinal-Priest of Beata Vergine Maria del Monte Carmelo a Mostacciano) 2003; participated in Papal Conclave 2005, 2013; Vice-Pres. Catholic Bishops' Conf. of Nigeria 1985–88, Pres.

1988–94; Nat. Pres. Christian Asscn of Nigeria 1988–96; mem. Prerogative of Mercy, Religious Advisory Council; Commdr, Order of the Niger 1999. *Leisure interests:* reading, watching films, table tennis. *Address:* Archdiocese of Lagos, 19 Catholic Mission Street, PO Box 8, Lagos, Nigeria (office). *Telephone:* (1) 2635729 (office). *Fax:* (1) 2633841 (office). *E-mail:* arclagos@yahoo.com.

OKONJO-IWEALA, Ngozi, AB, PhD; Nigerian economist, politician and international organization official; *Minister of Finance;* b. 13 June 1954; m. Ikemba Iweala; four c.; ed Harvard Univ., Massachusetts Inst. of Tech., USA; joined World Bank 1982, various positions including Economist, Country Dir in E Asia Region responsible for Malaysia, Cambodia, Laos and Mongolia 1997–99, Dir of Operations Middle East Region 2001–02, Vice-Pres. and Corp. Sec., World Bank Group 2002–03, Man. Dir 2007–11; Adviser on Econ. Issues to Pres. of Nigeria 2000; Minister of Finance and Economy (first woman) 2003–06, 2011–, of Foreign Affairs (first woman) June–Aug. 2006 (resgnd); Distinguished Visiting Fellow, Global Economy and Devt Program, Brookings Inst., Washington, DC 2007; Founder NOI-Gallup polls; Co-founder African Inst. for Applied Econs, Enugu (apptd Chair.), Makeda Fund; mem. bd several NGOs and think-tanks, including DATA, World Resources Inst., Clinton Global Initiative, Nelson Mandela Inst. and African Insts of Science and Tech., Mo Ibrahim Foundation Governance Prize Cttee, Friends of the Global Fund Africa; adviser to World Bank on the Stolen Assets Recovery (STAR) initiative; fmr mem. Malan Cttee on Bank-Fund collaboration; Hon. LLD (Brown Univ.) 2006, (Colby Coll.) 2007, Hon. DHumLitt (Northern Caribbean Univ., Jamaica), Dr hc (Trinity Coll., Dublin); Euromarket Forum Award for Vision and Courage 2003, Time Magazine European Hero 2004, This Day Nigeria Minister of the Year 2004, 2005, Euromoney Magazine Global Finance Minister of the Year 2005, Financial Times/The Banker African Finance Minister of the Year 2005, ranked by Forbes magazine amongst The World's 100 Most Powerful Women (62nd) 2006, (87th) 2011, (81st) 2012, (83rd) 2013. *Publications include:* The Debt Trap in Nigeria: Towards a Sustainable Debt Strategy (co-ed.), several papers in devt journals. *Address:* Ministry of Finance, Ahmadu Bello Way, Central Area, PMB 14, Garki, Abuja, Nigeria (office). *Telephone:* (9) 2346290 (office). *E-mail:* susman@nigeria.gov.ng (office). *Website:* www.fmf.gov.ng (office).

OKOUNKOV, Andrei Yurovich, PhD; Russian mathematician and academic; *Professor, Princeton University;* b. 1969, Moscow; two d.; ed Moscow State Univ.; fmr Research Fellow, Dobrushin Math. Lab., Inst. for Problems of Information Transmission, Russian Acad. of Sciences; has taught at Inst. for Advanced Study in Princeton and Univ. of Chicago; Asst Prof., Univ. of Calif., Berkeley –2002; Prof., Princeton Univ. 2002–; Sloan Research Fellowship 2000, Packard Fellowship 2001; European Math. Society Prize 2004, Fields Medal (co-recipient) 2006. *Publications:* numerous papers in professional journals on probability, representation theory, algebraic geometry and math. physics. *Leisure interests:* cooking, playing football and ping-pong, reading. *Address:* Princeton University, Department of Mathematics, Fine 701, Fine Hall, Washington Road, Princeton, NJ 08544, USA (office). *Telephone:* (609) 258-4200 (office). *Fax:* (609) 258-1367 (office). *E-mail:* okounkov@math.princeton.edu (office). *Website:* www.math.princeton .edu/~okounkov (office).

OKOUR, Abdul Rahim, BA; Jordanian politician; b. 1939; ed Univ. of Damascus; worked as secondary school teacher for two years; fmr Lecturer, Howwara Coll., Yarmouk Univ.; served 22 years in various civil service positions; mem. House of Reps, Majlis al-Umma for eight years; fmr mem. Consultative Council, Irbid Governorate; fmr mem. Islamic Action Front (IAF); Minister of State for Parl. Affairs 2007–, of Awqaf (Religious Endowments) and Islamic Affairs 2011. *Address:* c/o Ministry of Awqaf (Religious Endowments) and Islamic Affairs, POB 659, Amman 11118, Jordan.

OKPAKO, David Tinakpoevwan, PhD, CBiol, FIBiol, FNIBiol, FAAS, FAS, FRPharmS; Nigerian pharmacologist and pharmacist; b. 22 Nov. 1936, Owahwa, Delta; s. of Okun Okoro-Okpako Tsere and Obien Rebayi-Tsere; m. Kathleen Gweneth Jones-Williams 1967; one s. one d.; ed Urhobo Coll. Effurun, Nigerian Coll. of Arts, Science & Tech. Ibadan, Univ. of Bradford and Univ. Coll., London; Visiting Fellow, Corpus Christi Coll., Cambridge 1973–74, 1983–84; Prof. and Head, Dept of Pharmacology and Therapeutics, Univ. of Ibadan 1978–81, 1986–87, Dean, Faculty of Pharmacy 1987–91; Pres. W African Soc. for Pharmacology 1987–90; Foundation Pres. Nigeria Inst. of Biology 1990–92; Chair. Council, Nigerian Field Soc. 1991–2000; Visiting Prof., Univ. of the Western Cape, SA 1995–96; Visiting Fellow, Humanities Research Centre, ANU, Canberra 1996, Fitzwilliam Coll., Cambridge 1997; Visiting Scientist, Research Inst. Hosp. for Sick Children, Univ. of Toronto; now working as consultant pharmacist and pharmacologist. *Publications:* Principles of Pharmacology – A Tropical Approach 1991, 2001, Pharmacological Methods in Phytotherapy Research, Vol. 1. Selection, Preparation and Pharmacological Evaluation of Plant Material (with E. M. Williamson and F. J. Evans) 1996; articles in professional journals; several book chapters. *Leisure interests:* golf, tennis, reading, fishing. *Address:* PO Box 20334, University of Ibadan Post Office, Oyo Road, Ibadan (office); 22 Sankore Avenue, University of Ibadan, Ibadan, Nigeria (office). *Telephone:* (234) 28107602 (home). *E-mail:* dpc@skannet.com.ng (office).

OKREPILOV, Vladimir V., Dr.sc.oec; Russian economist; *General Director, TEST-St Petersburg;* b. 23 Feb. 1944, Leningrad; m.; two s.; ed Leningrad State Inst. of Mechanics; engineer, sr engineer-constructor, Leningrad factory of radiotechnology equipment 1965–70; Komsomol and CP service 1970–79; Chief Engineer, Research-Production Co. Mendeleyev VNIIM 1979–86; Dir Leningrad Centre of Standardization and Metrology of USSR State Cttee of Standards 1986–90; Gen. Dir TEST-St Petersburg 1986–; Prof., Head of Chair, St Petersburg Univ. of Econs and Finance; Pres. St Petersburg Br. of Acad. of Quality Problems; mem. Presidium Russian Acad. of Sciences 2003–, Acad. of Electrotechnological Sciences, St Petersburg Acad. of Eng, Int. Acad. of Ecological Sciences, Security of Man and Nature; Corresp. mem. Russian Acad. of Sciences 2000–; Merited Worker of Science and Tech. of Russian Fed., Order of Friendship of Peoples 1988, Order for Merits to the Fatherland, Fourth Grade 1997; hon. prize for merits in standardization 1984, State Prize of Russian Fed. 1997, Prize of Pres. of Russian Fed. for Educ. 2002. *Publications include:* more than 300 scientific publs. *Address:* Kurlyandskaya str. 1, St Petersburg 190103, Russia (office). *Telephone:* (812) 251-

39-50 (office). *Fax:* (812) 251-41-08 (office). *E-mail:* letter@rustest.spb.ru (office). *Website:* www.rustest.spb.ru (office).

OKRI, Ben, OBE, FRSL, FRSA; Nigerian/British novelist, poet, essayist and short-story writer; b. 15 March 1959, Minna; s. of Silver Okri and Grace Okri; ed John Donne's School, Peckham, London, Children's Home School, Sapele, Nigeria, Christ High School, Ibadan, Urhobo Coll., Warri and Univ. of Essex, UK; staff writer and librarian, Afriscope magazine 1978; Poetry Ed. West Africa magazine 1983–86; broadcaster with BBC 1983–85; Fellow Commoner in Creative Arts, Trinity Coll. Cambridge 1991–93; Visiting Prof. School of English, Univ. of Leicester 2012–; mem. Int. PEN, a Vice-Pres. English Centre of Int. PEN 1997–; mem. Bd Royal Nat. Theatre of GB 1999–2006; mem. Soc. of Authors, RSL (mem. of Council 1999–2004); Hon. DLitt (Westminster) 1997, (Essex) 2002, (Exeter) 2004, (SOAS, London) 2010; Dr hc (Universiteit voor het Algemeen Belang, Belgium) 2009; Hon. Dr of Arts (Bedfordshire) 2010; Commonwealth Prize for Africa 1987, Paris Review Aga Khan Prize for Fiction 1987, Premio Letterario Internazionale, Chianti Ruffino-Antico Fattore 1992, Premio Grinzane Cavour 1994, The Crystal Award (World Econ. Forum, Switzerland) 1995, Premio Palmi 2000, Grinzane for Africa Mainstream Prize 2008, Int. Literary Award of Novi Sad, Serbia 2008. *Plays:* In Exilus (The Studio, Royal Nat. Theatre of GB) 2001, The Heart's Tent is Broken (Tristam Bates Theatre) 2011. *Television:* Great Railway Journey: London to Arcadia 1996. *Publications:* Flowers and Shadows 1980, The Landscapes Within 1982, Incidents at the Shrine 1986, Stars of the New Curfew 1988, The Famished Road (Booker Prize) 1991, An African Elegy (vol. of poems) 1992, Songs of Enchantment 1993, Astonishing the Gods 1995, Birds of Heaven (essays) 1996, Dangerous Love (novel) 1996, A Way of Being Free (non-fiction) 1997, Infinite Riches (novel) 1998, Mental Fight (epic poem) 1999, In Arcadia (novel) 2002, Starbook (novel) 2007, Tales of Freedom 2009, A Time for New Dreams (poetic essays) 2011, Wild (vol. of poems) 2012. *Leisure interests:* chess, music, travel, theatre, cinema, art, walking, good conversation, silence. *Address:* The Marsh Agency, 50 Albemarle Street, London, W1S 4BD, England (office). *Website:* www .marsh-agency.co.uk (office).

OKRUASHVILI, Irakli; Georgian lawyer and politician; b. 6 Nov. 1973, Tskhinvali, South Ossetian Autonomous Oblast, Georgian SSR, USSR; s. of Koba Okruashvili and Eter Giguashvili; m. Irina Gordeladze; one d.; ed Tbilisi State Univ.; leading specialist, Elections Cen. Comm. 1995; consultant, TACIS project, State Service Div. 1996; lawyer, Korzadze, Svanidze & Okruashvili, Okruashvili & Partners 1996–2000; Lecturer in Int. Trade Law, Tbilisi State Univ. 1997–2001; Deputy Minister of Justice 2000–01; mem. Tbilisi Sakrebulo (City Ass.) 2002–, Head of Revision Comm. Nov. 2002; Pres.'s plenipotentiary in Shida Kartli Mkhare (region) Nov. 2003; Gen. Prosecutor Jan.–June 2004; Minister of Internal Affairs June–Dec. 2004, of Defence Dec. 2004–06, of Econ. Devt Nov. 2006; f. Movt for a United Georgia 2007, resgnd his position and joined with several politicians in Georgia to establish the Georgian Party Oct. 2010; mem. Georgian Young Lawyers' Asscn, World Lawyers' Asscn, Lawyers' Int. Asscn; sentenced in absentia to 11 years' imprisonment on corruption charges March 2008; granted asylum in France April 2008; returned to Georgia and arrested upon arrival at Tbilisi airport Nov. 2012, cleared of bribe-taking and extortion charges and released from court on bail Jan. 2013, awaiting trial on charges of negligence in Tbilisi City Court. *Leisure interest:* hunting.

OKU, Masayuki; Japanese banking executive; *Chairman and Representative Director, Sumitomo Mitsui Financial Group, Inc.;* joined Sumitomo Bank Corpn 1968, Dir 1994–, later Deputy Pres. and Head of Corp. Banking Unit and Head of Int. Banking Unit, Sumitomo Mitsui Banking Corpn (unit of Sumitomo Mitsui Financial Group Inc.), Man. Dir 1998–99, Man. Exec. Officer 1999–2001, Sr Man. Dir and Sr Exec. Officer 2001–02, Sr Man. Dir Sumitomo Mitsui Financial Group, Inc. 2002–05, Chair. 2005–, Pres. Sumitomo Mitsui Banking Corpn 2005–, Pres. and Rep. Dir Sumitomo Mitsui Banking Corpn (SMBC) Friend Securities Co. Ltd; Chair. Japanese Bankers Asscn; Exec. Dir Nikko Cordial Securities Inc.; Standing Auditor, Nankai Electric Railway Co. Ltd 2008–; Dir, Panasonic Corpn 2008–, Mitsui Oil Exploration Co. *Address:* Sumitomo Mitsui Financial Group, Inc., 1-2, Yurakucho 1-chome, Chiyoda-ku, Tokyo 100-0006, Japan (office). *Telephone:* (3) 5512-3411 (office). *Fax:* (3) 5512-4429 (office). *E-mail:* info@smfg.co.gp (office). *Website:* www.smfg.co.jp (office).

OKUDA, Hiroshi; Japanese automotive industry executive; *Senior Adviser, Toyota Motor Corporation;* b. 29 Dec. 1932; ed Hitotsubashi Univ.; fmr Exec. Dir Toyota Motor Corpn, Pres. 1995, Chair. –2006, now Sr Adviser; Chair. Nippon Keidanren (business fed.) –2006, Japan Business Fed. –2006. *Leisure interests:* reading, watching films. *Address:* Toyota Motor Corporation, 1 Toyota-cho, Toyota, Aichi 471-8571, Japan (office). *Telephone:* (565) 28-2121 (office). *Fax:* (565) 23-5800 (office). *Website:* www.global.toyota.com (office).

OKUDA, Takashi; Japanese business executive; joined Sharp Corpn 1978, Gen. Man. Global Procurement Dept, Global Procurement Operations Group 1996–97, Gen. Man. Global Procurement, Sharp Electronics (Malaysia) Sdn Bhd (SEM) and Gen. Man. Singapore Br. 1997–2000, Gen. Man. Procurement and Quality of Audio-Visual Systems Group 2000–01, Gen. Man. Visual Systems Div., Audio-Visual Systems Group 2001–02, Deputy Gen. Man. Audio-Visual Systems Group and Gen. Man. Visual Systems Div. 2002–05, Gen. Man. Audio-Visual Systems Group from 2005, later Gen. Man. Int. Production Planning Group, Exec. Officer and Gen. Man. Strategic Business Promotion of Growing Markets, Exec. Man. Officer, Gen. Man. Global Business, Admin and Manufacturing Promotion and Gen. Man. Global Business Group –2012, Rep. Dir, Pres. and CEO Sharp Corpn 2012–13; Dir, Permasteelisa SpA 2011–. *Address:* c/o Sharp Corpn, 22-22 Nagaike-cho, Abeno-ku, Osaka 545-8522, Japan. *E-mail:* info@sharp.co.jp.

OKUI, Isao; Japanese business executive; Chair. and Rep. Dir Sekisui House Ltd –2004; Chair. Kansai Employers' Asscn; Vice-Chair. Nippon Keidanren 2002, Japan Fed. of Employers' Asscns (Nikkeiren) 2002; mem. Advisory Cttee, Ritsumeikan Asia-Pacific Univ. (APU); mem. Cttee, The 3rd World Water Forum. *Address:* c/o Sekisui House Ltd, 1-1-88 Oyodonaka, Kita-ku, Osaka 531-0076, Japan. *E-mail:* info@sekisuihouse.co.jp.

OKULOV, Valery Mikhailovich; Russian business executive and pilot; *Chairman of the Managing Board and General Director, Aeroflot;* b. 22 April 1952, Kirov; m. Yelena Yeltsin (d. of fmr Pres. Boris Yeltsin); one s. two d.; ed Acad. of Civil

Aviation; navigator, instructor, Sverdlovsk aviation team 1976–85; leading navigator, First Deputy Gen. Dir Aviation Co. Aeroflot (now Aeroflot Russian Airlines JSC) 1996–97, Gen. Dir 1997–, also Chair. of Man. Bd. *Leisure interest:* boating. *Address:* Aeroflot, Leningradsky prosp. 37, korp. 9, 125167 Moscow, Russia (office). *Telephone:* (495) 155-6648 (office). *Fax:* (495) 752-9016 (office). *Website:* www.aeroflot.ru (office).

OKUN, Lev Borisovich; Russian theoretical physicist; *Head of Laboratory, A.I. Alikhanov Institute of Theoretical and Experimental Physics;* b. 7 July 1929, Sukhinichi, Kaluga Dist; s. of B. G. Okun and B. R. Ginzburg; m. Erica Gulyaeva 1954; one s. two d.; ed Moscow Physics and Eng Inst.; mem. of staff, A.I. Alikhanov Inst. of Experimental and Theoretical Physics, now Head of Lab. 1954–; Prof., Moscow Inst. of Physics and Tech. 1967–; main work has been on the theory of elementary particles; Corresp. mem. USSR (now Russian) Acad. of Sciences 1966–90, mem. 1990–, mem. Bureau Nuclear Physics Div., mem. Bureau Div. of Physical Sciences 2002–; mem. Science Policy Cttee CERN, Geneva, Switzerland 1981–86, Super Conducting Super Collider Lab., Dallas, Tex., USA 1989–93; mem. Extended Scientific Council of Deutsches Elektronen-Synchrotron (DESY) 1992–98, Bd Int. Science Foundation 1993–97, Council of Scientists of Int. Asscn for the Promotion of Co-operation with Scientists from the Ind. States of the Fmr Soviet Union (INTAS), Brussels 1993–97; mem. Academia Europaea 1991; Regents Prof., Univ. of California, Berkeley 1990; Visiting Prof., CERN 1992; Schrödinger Professorship, Univ. of Vienna, Austria 1994; invited lecturer at numerous major int. confs on high energy physics; Hon. Life mem. New York Acad. of Sciences 1993; Matteucci Prize (Italy) 1988, Lee Page Prize, Yale Univ. 1989, Loeb Lecturer, Harvard Univ. 1989, Karpinsky Prize, F.V.S. Foundation (FRG) 1990, Buhl Lecturer, Carnegie Mellon Univ. 1991, Humboldt Research Award 1993, Fermi Lecturer, Scuola Normale Superiore, Pisa 1993, AUI Distinguished Lecturer, Brookhaven Nat. Lab., USA 1995, Bruno Pontecorvo Prize, Jt Inst. for Nuclear Research, Dubna 1996, Open Soc. Inst. Prize 1997, Henry Primakoff Lecturer, Univ. of Pennsylvania 2001, L.D. Landau Gold Medal, Russian Acad. of Sciences 2003. *Achievements:* formulation of the theoretical model of strongly interacting particles based on three fundamental fermions 1957, coining of the term hadron 1961, notion of vacuum domains and unstable vacuum 1974. *Publications include:* The Weak Interaction of Elementary Particles 1963, Leptons and Quarks 1981, Particle Physics: The Quest for the Substance of Substance 1984, A Primer in Particle Physics 1987, The Relations of Particles 1991; more than 200 research and review articles in leading physics journals. *Address:* A.I. Alikhanov Institute of Theoretical and Experimental Physics, B. Cheremushkinskaya 25, 117218 Moscow, Russia (office). *Telephone:* (499) 123-31-92 (office); (499) 124-19-41 (home). *Fax:* (499) 127-08-33 (office). *E-mail:* okun@itep.ru (office). *Website:* www.itep.ru (office).

OKURUT, Mary Karooro, MA; Ugandan lecturer, novelist and politician; *Minister of Gender, Labour and Social Development;* b. Bushenyi Dist; d. of Erinesti Karooro; m. Stanislaus Okurut; ed Makerere Univ.; fmr Lecturer, Dept of Literature, Makerere Univ.; fmr Commr Educ. Service Comm.; fmr Press Sec. to Pres. Museveni; mem. Parl. (Nat. Resistance Movt) for Bushenyi Dist; Minister of Information and Nat. Guidance 2011–13, of Gender, Labour and Social Devt 2013–; Founder, Uganda Women Writers Asscn; Woman Writer of the Millennium 1999. *Publications include:* The Invisible Weevil 1998, The Official Wife (Nat. Book Trust of Uganda 2004) 2003. *Address:* Ministry of Gender, Labour and Social Development, Plot 2, Lumumba Avenue, Simbamanyo House, POB 7136, Kampala, Uganda (office). *Telephone:* (41) 347854 (office). *Fax:* (41) 256374 (office). *E-mail:* ps@mglsd.go.ug (office). *Website:* www.mglsd.go.ug (office).

OKWO-BELE, Jean-Marie, MD, MPH; Democratic Republic of the Congo physician, epidemiologist, public health official and international organization official; *Director, Department of Immunization, Vaccines and Biologicals, World Health Organization;* b. 23 Feb. 1957, Bandundu, Belgian Congo (now Democratic Repub. of the Congo—DRC); ed Univ. of Zaïre Kinshasa Campus (now Univ. of Kinshasa), Johns Hopkins School of Hygiene and Public Health (now the Johns Hopkins Bloomberg School of Public Health), USA; Expanded Programme on Immunization (EPI) Man. at prov. and nat. levels, within EPI-Combatting Child Communicable Diseases Div., Dept of Health, DRC 1982–89; Medical Officer with WHO/African Region 1989–2002; Regional Adviser, Vaccine-Preventable Disease Unit, WHO African Regional Office 1993–2002; Chief of Immunization Activities, UNICEF HQ, New York, USA 2002–04; Dir Dept of Immunization, Vaccines and Biologicals, WHO, Geneva, Switzerland 2004–; directed Polio Eradication Initiative in Africa 1993–2002; ensured oversight and co-ordination of devt of WHO/ UNICEF Global Immunization Vision and Strategy for 2006–2015 (adopted by World Health Ass. 2005). *Address:* World Health Organization, Avenue Appia 20, 1211 Geneva 27, Switzerland (office). *Telephone:* (22) 791-21-11 (office). *Fax:* (22) 791-31-11 (office). *E-mail:* info@who.int (office). *Website:* www.who.int (office).

OLAFSSON, Thröstur; Icelandic government official and business consultant; *Chairman, Reykjavik Forestry Society;* b. 4 Oct. 1939, Husavík; m. 1st Monika Büttner 1966 (divorced); m. 2nd Thorunn Klemenzdóttir 1975; three s. one d. (and one s. deceased); ed Akureyri Gymnasium, Free Univ. of Berlin, Ruhr Univ., Bochum, Germany; economist, Nat. Bank of Iceland 1968–69, Civil Servants' Org. 1969–71; specialist adviser to Minister of Industry 1971–73; Man. Dir Mál og Menning (publishing co.) 1973–80; Asst to Minister of Finance 1980–83; Man. Dir Gen. Workers and Transport Union 1983–88; Exec. Dir Mikligardur Ltd 1989–90; Political Asst to Minister of Foreign Affairs 1991–95; Chair. Cen. Bank of Iceland 1994–98; Sec.-Gen. Social Democratic Party's Parl. Group 1995–97; consultant 1997–98; Chair. Icemarkt Ltd 1989–99, Icelandic Int. Devt Agency 1991–95, Social Housing Co. Felagsbustadir Ltd, Minjaverand (Icelandic Heritage Inst.), Reykjavik Forestry Soc. 2007–; Gen. Man. Iceland Symphony Orchestra 1998–2009; mem. Bd Edda Ltd (publishing co.); mem. Admin. Council of Europe Devt Bank 1995–2004. *Publications:* numerous articles on Icelandic econs and politics. *Leisure interests:* music, literature, skiing, forestry. *Address:* Brædraborgarstígur 21B, 101 Reykjavik, Iceland (home); Háskólabió v. Hagetorg 107, Reykjavik (office). *Telephone:* 5452500 (office); 5519698 (home). *Fax:* 5624475 (office). *E-mail:* throl@sinfonia.is (office).

OLAH, George Andrew, PhD; American chemist and academic; *Distinguished Professor of Chemistry and Engineering and Director, Donald P. and Katherine B. Loker Hydrocarbon Research Institute and Department of Chemistry, University of*

Southern California; b. 22 May 1927, Budapest, Hungary; s. of Julius Olah and Magda Krasznai; m. Judith Lengyel 1949; two s.; ed Tech. Univ. Budapest; mem. Faculty, Tech. Univ. Budapest 1949–54; Assoc. Dir Centre for Chemical Research, Hungarian Acad. of Sciences 1954–56; research scientist, Dow Chemical Canada Ltd 1957–64, Dow Chemical Co. Framingham, Mass 1964–65; Prof. of Chem., Case Western Reserve Univ. 1965–69, C.F. Mabery Research Prof. 1969–77; Distinguished Prof. of Chem. and Eng and Dir Donald P. and Katherine B. Loker Hydrocarbon Research Inst. and Dept of Chem., Univ. of Southern California 1977–; consultant to industry; numerous visiting professorships; mem. NAS, Accad. dei Lincei, Hungarian Acad. of Sciences, European Acad. of Arts, Sciences and Humanities, Nat. Acad. of Eng; Foreign Fellow, Royal Soc. (UK), Canadian Royal Soc.; Hon. mem. RSC, German Chemical Soc. etc.; Grand Cordon, Order of the Rising Sun (Japan) 2003, Hungarian Order of Merit 2006; Dr hc (Durham) 1988, (Budapest) 1989, (Munich) 1990, (Crete) 1994, (Southern Calif., Case Western, Szeged, Veszprem) 1995, (Montpellier) 1996, (NY State Univ.) 1998, (Pecs, Debrecen, Hungary) 2003, (Ohio State Univ.) 2009, (Obuda) 2011; Alexander von Humboldt Sr US Scientist Award 1979, Pioneer of Chem. Award, American Inst. of Chemists 1993, Nobel Prize in Chem. 1994, Priestley Medal (ACS) 2005, Szechenyi Grand Prize (Hungary) 2011. *Publications include:* Friedel-Crafts Reactions (Vols I–IV) 1963–64, Carbonium Ions (Vols I–V) 1969–76 (co-author), Carbocations and Electrophilic Reactions 1973, Superacids (co-author) 1984, Hypercarbon Chemistry (co-author) 1987 (second edn 2010), Nitration (co-author) 1989, Cage Hydrocarbons 1990, Electron Deficient Boron and Carbon Clusters (co-author) 1991, Synthetic Fluorine Chemistry (co-author) 1992, Hydrocarbon Chemistry 1995, Onium Ions (co-author) 1998, A Life of Magic Chemistry 2001, Across Conventional Lines (selected papers with commentary, co-author) 2003, Beyond Oil and Gas: The Methanol Economy (co-author) 2006 (Chinese, Swedish and Hungarians edns 2007) (second revised and enlarged English edn) 2009, Superelectrophiles and Their Chemistry (co-author) 2008, Superacid Chemistry (co-author) 2009, George Olah, La ricerca di una vita 2010; several book chapters, 1,400 scientific papers and 140 patents. *Leisure interests:* reading, swimming. *Address:* Loker Hydrocarbon Research Inst., University of Southern California, Los Angeles, CA 90089, USA (office). *Telephone:* (213) 740-5976 (office). *Fax:* (213) 740-5087 (office). *E-mail:* olah@usc.edu (office). *Website:* chem.usc.edu/faculty/Olah.html (office).

OLARREAGA, Manuel; Uruguayan academic; *Professor of International Marketing, Catholic University of Uruguay;* b. 1 June 1937, Salto; s. of Manuel Olarreaga and Hilda Leguisamo; m. Marina Rico 1966; three s.; ed Univ. of Paris; Minister-Counsellor, Uruguay's Perm. Del. to GATT 1982–87; First Exec. Sec. Latin American and Caribbean Program of Commercial Information to Support Foreign Trade 1988–91; Co-ordinator, Admin. Secr., Mercado Común del Sur, (Mercosur) 1991–96, Head Regulations Div. 1997–2003, Ed. Official Bulletin of Mercosur 1997–2003; Prof. of Int. Marketing, Catholic Univ. of Uruguay 1993–; Chair. Cttee of Countries Participating in Protocol Relating to Trade between Developing Countries, GATT; Deputy Chair. 18th, 19th and 20th Consultative Groups, UNCTAD-GATT Int. Trade Centre. *Publications:* several publs on int. trade. *Leisure interests:* reading, collecting antique keys. *Address:* avenue 8 de octubre 2738, CP 11600, Montevideo (office); Tomás Diago 769, Ap. 601, CP 11300, Montevideo, Uruguay (home). *Telephone:* (2) 487-27-17 (office); (2) 710-24-33 (home). *Fax:* (2) 487-32-27 (office). *E-mail:* molarrea@ucu.edu.uy (office); olarreaga@hotmail.com (home). *Website:* www.ucu.edu.uy (office).

ÓLASON, Vésteinn, PhD; Icelandic academic and university administrator; *Professor Emeritus, University of Iceland;* b. 14 Feb. 1939, Höfn; s. of Oli K. Gudbrandsson and Adalbjörg Gudmundsdóttir; m. Unnur Alexandra Jónsdóttir 1960; one s. one d.; ed Menntaskólinn Laugarvatni, Univ. of Iceland Háskóli Íslands, Univ. of Iceland; Lecturer in Icelandic Language and Literature, Univ. of Copenhagen 1968–72; Lecturer in Comparative Literature, Univ. of Iceland 1972–80, docent in Icelandic Literature 1980–85, Prof. of Icelandic Literature 1991–2009, Dean, Faculty of Arts 1993–95, Prorektor 1993–94, currently Prof. Emer.; Prof. of Icelandic, Univ. of Oslo 1985–91; mem. Icelandic Soc. of Sciences and Letters 1983–, Norwegian Acad. of Sciences and Letters 1994–, Icelandic Research Council 1994–, Royal Gustaf Adolf Acad. of Letters 1999–, Royal Norwegian Soc. of Sciences and Letters 2000–; Dir Árni Magnússon Inst. 1999–2009; Hon. mem. Soc. of Antiquaries of London 2005; Iceland Literary Prize for Non-Fiction 1993, Gad Rausing Prize, Royal Swedish Acad. of Letters, History and Antiquities 2010. *Publications include:* Sagnadansar: Edition and Study 1979, The Traditional Ballads of Iceland 1982, Islensk Bókmenntasaga I–II (History of Icelandic Literature 870–1720) 1992–93, Dialogues with the Viking Age: Narration and Representation in the Sagas of the Icelanders 1998; more than 100 articles in professional publs. *Address:* Nylendugata 43, 101 Reykjavik, Iceland. *Telephone:* 5521792. *E-mail:* vesteinn@hi.is.

OLAYAN, Khaled S., BS, MBA; Saudi Arabian business executive; *Chairman, Olayan Group;* b. 4 July 1945, Unayzah; s. of Suliman Saleh Olayan; m.; three c.; ed in Saudi Arabia and Lebanon, Menlo Coll., Calif. and American Univ., Washington, DC, USA; following return to Saudi Arabia, worked with Ministry of Finance and Nat. Economy; joined The Olayan Group 1974, Chair. Olayan Group 2002–, Olayan Saudi Holding Co. (OSHCO) and its parent, Olayan Financing Co., serves on bds of numerous Olayan joint ventures; has also been on bds of several outside cos; mem. Bd of Dirs and Man. Dir Saudi Cement Co.; apptd to Eastern Prov. Council 1997; mem. Bd of Dirs Saudi British Bank (SABB) 2002–, Chair. 2009–. *Leisure interests:* reading (especially the works of Naguib Mahfouz, Ahmed Shawky, Ilya Abumadi and Taha Hussein, as well as historical stories, biographies and poetry, especially the works of Khaled Al-Faisal), sports, travelling, meeting people. *Address:* Olayan Financing Co., PO Box 8772, Riyadh 11492, Saudi Arabia (office). *Telephone:* (1) 474-9000 (office). *Fax:* (1) 474-9108 (office). *E-mail:* info@ olayan.com (office). *Website:* www.olayan.com (office).

OLAYAN, Lubna Suliman, BSc, MBA; Saudi Arabian business executive; *CEO and Deputy Chairperson, Olayan Financing Group;* b. 4 Aug. 1955; d. of the late Suliman Saleh Olayan and Maryam bint Jassim Al Abdulwahab; sister of Khaled S. Olayan; m. John Xefos; three d.; ed Cornell and Indiana Univs, USA; CEO and Deputy Chair. Olayan Financing Co. 1986–, mem. Bd of Dirs Olayan Investments Co. Establishment; Co-Chair. Arab World Competitiveness Forum, Geneva, Switzerland 2002; Dir (non-exec.) WPP 2005–; mem. Bd Chelsfield Plc (UK)

1996–2004, Saudi Hollandi Bank 2004–; mem. Int. Council of Institut Européen d'Admin des Affaires (INSEAD) 1997– (mem. Bd of Dirs INSEAD 2006–), Arab Business Council of World Econ. Forum, Int. Business Council of World Econ. Forum 2005–, Advisory Bd Effat Coll., Jeddah 2006–; mem. Int. Advisory Bds Council on Foreign Relations 2005–, Rolls Royce 2006–, Citigroup 2007–; mem. Bd Al Fanar 2006–, Down Syndrome Charitable Asscn, Riyadh 2005–; mem. Bd of Trustees, Arab Thought Foundation, Beirut 2002–, King Abdullah Univ. for Science and Tech. (KAUST) 2005–, Cornell Univ. 2007–; spokesperson for women's rights in the Middle East, first woman to speak at a 'mixed' conf. in Saudi Arabia, Jeddah Econ. Conf. 2004; Co-Chair. World Econ. Forum, Davos, Switzerland 2005; ranked by Fortune magazine amongst the 50 Most Powerful Women in Business outside the US (40th) 2003, (37th) 2004, (35th) 2005, (33rd) 2006, (29th) 2007–10, (28th) 2011–12, Middle East Award for Distinguished Businesswoman (UAE) 2003, named Female Exec. of the Year, Arabian Business Achievement Awards 2004, Arab Bankers Asscn of North America Achievement Award 2004, Distinguished Arabic Woman Award in the Businesswomen Sector in the Arab World, Sec.-Gen. Arab League, Cairo 2004, listed by Time magazine as one of the top 100 Most Influential People 2005, ranked by Forbes magazine amongst The World's 100 Most Powerful Women (97th) 2005–06, (63rd) 2011, (92nd) 2013, ranked by Arabian Business amongst its Power 100: The World's Most Influential Arabs (44th) 2008, (32nd) 2009, and amongst its Power 500: The World's Most Influential Arabs (35th) 2012, (50th) 2013. *Address:* Olayan Financing Group, PO Box 8772, Riyadh, Saudi Arabia (office). *Telephone:* (1) 477-9000 (office). *Fax:* (1) 478-9207 (office). *Website:* www.olayan.com (office).

OLAZÁBAL, José María; Spanish professional golfer; b. 5 Feb. 1966, Hondarribia (Fuenterrabía), Gipuzkoa, Basque Country; s. of Gaspar Olazábal and Julia Olazábal; won Italian Open, Spanish Open and British Boys' Amateur Championships 1983, Belgian Int. Youth Championship 1984, Spanish Open Amateur Championship 1984, British Youths' Amateur Championship 1985; turned professional 1985; winner Ebel European Masters Swiss Open 1986, Sanyo Open 1986, Volvo Belgian Open 1988, German Masters 1988, Tenerife Open 1989, KLM Dutch Open 1989, Benson & Hedges International Open 1990, 2000, Carroll's Irish Open 1990, Lancome Trophy 1990, NEC World Series of Golf 1990, 1994, Open Catalonia 1991, Epson Grand Prix of Europe 1991, The International (USA) 1991, Turespana Open de Tenerife 1992, Open Mediterrania 1992, Turespana Open Mediterrania 1994, US Masters 1994, 1999, Volvo PGA Championship 1994, Turespana Masters Open de Canarias 1997, Dubai Desert Classic 1998, Open de France 2001, Omega Hong Kong Open 2001, Buick Invitational 2002, Mallorca Classic 2005; mem. European Ryder Cup Team 1987, 1989, 1991, 1993, 1997, 1999, Capt. of winning European Ryder Cup Team, Medinah Country Club, Ill., USA 2012; golf-course designer (15 designed). *Leisure interests:* cinema, music, hunting, wildlife, ecology. *Address:* c/o PGA, 100 Avenue of Champions, Palm Beach Gardens, FL 33418, USA.

OLBRYCHSKI, Daniel; Polish actor; b. 27 Feb. 1945, Łowicz; m. 1st Monika Dzienisiewicz-Olbrychska 1967 (divorced 1977); one s.; m. 2nd Zuzanna Lapicka 1978 (divorced 1988); one d.; m. 3rd Krystyna Demska 2003; one s. with Barbara Sukowa; ed State Higher School of Drama, Warsaw; actor, Nat. Theatre 1969–77; best known for leading roles in several Andrzej Wajda films; mem. Polish Film Union; Officier des Arts et des Lettres 1986; State Prize (Second Class) 1974; numerous awards at Polish and foreign film festivals, including Stanislavsky Award at 29th Moscow Int. Film Festival 2007. *Roles include:* Koral in Wounded in the Forest 1964, Rafał Olbromski in Ashes 1965, boxer in Boxer 1966, Marek in Jowita 1967, Daniel in All for Sale 1968, Azja in Michael Wołodyjowski 1969, Angel of Death in Agnus Dei 1970, Tadeusz in Landscape After Battle 1970, Bolesław in The Birch Wood (Best Actor, 7th Moscow Int. Film Festival) 1971, Wit in Family Life 1971, Pan Młody in The Wedding 1972, Mateusz in Pilatus und Andere 1972, Kmicic in The Deluge 1974, Karol Borowiecki in The Promised Land 1975, Przybyszewski in Dagny 1976, Wiktor in The Maids of Wilko 1978, Jan in Little Tin Drum 1978, Saint-Genis in The Trout 1982, Pisarz in Flash-Back 1983, Love in Germany 1983, I'm Against 1985, Leon in Rosa Luxemburg 1986, Scope in Ga-ga 1986, Michał Kątny in Siekierezada 1986, Pitt in Tiger's Fight 1987, The Unbearable Lightness of Being 1988, Borys in Pestka 1995, Old Tuchajbej in With Fire and Sword 1998, Gerwazy in Last Foray in Lithuania 1999, Seweryn in It's Me, the Thief 2000, Szymon Gajowiec in The Spring to Come 2001, Prince of Elfs in The Hexer 2001, Konrad Sachs in Gebürtig (2002) 2002, Dyndalski in The Revenge 2002, Piastun in Stara basn. Kiedy slonce bylo bogiem 2003, Nitschewo 2003, Break Point 2004, Anthony Zimmer 2005, The Turkish Gambit 2005, Dwie strony medalu 2007, Taras Bulba 2008, A Man and His Dog 2009, Czas honoru as Doctor 2009–11, Salt as Vasily Orlov 2010, Józef Piłsudski in Battle of Warsaw 1920 2011, Hans Kloss: Stawka większa niż śmierć 2012. *Stage appearances:* Hamlet 1970, Rhett in Gone With the Wind, Rodric in Cyd 1985, Cześnik in Revenge 1998. *Television:* Raskolnikow in Crime and Punishment 1980, Chello 1985, Kean 1993, Milady (TV) 2004. *Leisure interests:* tennis, horses, family life.

OLDENBURG, Claes Thure, BA; American (b. Swedish) artist; b. 28 Jan. 1929, Stockholm, Sweden; s. of Gösta Oldenburg and Sigrid E. Oldenburg (née Lindforss); brother of Richard Oldenburg (q.v.); m. Patricia Joan Muschinski 1960 (divorced 1970); m. Coosje van Bruggen 1977 (died 2009); ed Yale Coll. and Art Inst. of Chicago; arrived in USA 1929 (naturalized 1953); moved to New York City 1956; took up fabrication on large scale 1969; has worked in partnership with Coosje van Bruggen 1976–; mem. American Acad. of Arts and Letters, American Acad. of Arts and Sciences; Dr hc (Oberlin Coll.) 1970, (Art Inst. of Chicago) 1979, (Bard Coll.) 1995, (RCA) 1996, (Nova Scotia Coll. of Art and Design—NSCAD Univ.) 2005, (Coll. for Creative Studies, Detroit) 2005, (Pennsylvania Acad. of Fine Arts) 2011; Skowhegan Medal for Sculpture 1972, Brandeis Univ. Sculpture Award 1976, Art Inst. of Chicago Sculpture Award 1976, Medal American Inst. of Architects 1977, Wilhelm Lehmbruck Sculpture Award 1981, Wolf Foundation Prize for the Arts 1989, Brandeis Univ. Creative Arts Award for Lifetime Artistic Achievement 1993, Lifetime Achievement Award, Int. Sculpture Center, New York 1994, Distinction in Sculpture, New York 1994, Rolf Schock Foundation Stockholm 1995, Nathaniel S. Saltonstall Award, Boston 1996, National Medal of Arts, Washington, DC 2000, Partners in Educ. Award, Solomon R. Guggenheim Museum 2002, Medal Award, School of the Museum of Fine Arts, Boston 2004. *Public sculptures with Coosje van Bruggen include:* Trowel I, Rijksmuseum Kröller-Müller, Otterlo, The Netherlands 1971–76, Crusoe Umbrella, Nollen Plaza, Civic

Center of Greater Des Moines, Ia 1979, Balancing Tools, Vitra International AG, Weil am Rhin, Germany 1984, Spoonbridge and Cherry, Minneapolis Sculpture Garden, Walker Art Center, Minn., Bicyclette Ensevelie Parc de la Villette, Paris 1990, Bottle of Notes, Central Gardens, Middlesbrough, UK 1993, Shuttlecocks, Nelson-Atkins Museum of Art, Kansas City, Mo. 1994, Saw Sawing, Tokyo Int. Exhbn Centre 1996, Soft Shuttlecocks, Guggenheim Foundation 1996, Ago, Filo e Nodo, Piazzale Cadorna, Milan 2000, Flying Pins, Eindhoven, Netherlands 2000, Dropped Clone, Neumarkt Galerie, Cologne, Germany 2001, Cupid's Span, San Francisco 2002, Big Sweep, Denver, Colo 2006. *Publications include:* Store Days 1967, Notes in Hand 1971, Raw Notes 1973, Multiples in Retrospect 1991; with Coosje van Bruggen: Claes Oldenburg: Sketches and Blottings Toward the European Desk Top 1990, Large Scale Projects 1994, Claes Oldenburg Coosje van Bruggen 1999, Down Liquidambar Lane: Sculpture in the Park 2001, Images á la Carte 2004. *Address:* 556 Broome Street, New York, NY 10013-1517, USA (office). *Telephone:* (212) 966-2290 (office). *Fax:* (212) 226-4315 (office). *E-mail:* office@oldenburgvanbruggen.com (office). *Website:* www.oldenburgvanbruggen .com (office).

OLDENBURG, Richard Erik, AB; American museum director; b. 21 Sept. 1933, Stockholm, Sweden; s. of Gösta Oldenburg and Sigrid E Lindfors; brother of Claes Oldenburg (q.v.); m. 1st Harriet L. Turnure 1960 (died 1998); m. 2nd Mary Ellen Meehan 2003; ed Harvard Coll.; Man. Ed., Macmillan Co. 1964–69; Dir of Publs, Museum of Modern Art, New York 1969–71, Acting Dir Jan.–June 1972, Dir 1972–94, Dir Emer. and Hon. Trustee 1995–; Chair. Sotheby's N and S America 1995–2000, Hon. Chair. 2000–06, Consultant 2006–. *Leisure interest:* reading. *Address:* Sotheby's Inc., 1134 York Avenue, New York, NY 10021 (office); 447 East 57th Street, New York, NY 10022, USA (home).

OLDFIELD, Bruce, OBE; British fashion designer; *Managing Director, Bruce Oldfield Limited;* b. 14 July 1950, brought up in Dr Barnardo's charity home, Ripon; ed Ripon Grammar School, Sheffield City Polytechnic, Ravensbourne Coll. of Art and St Martin's Coll. of Art; designed for Henri Bendel, New York and other stores 1973–74; freelance comms include film wardrobe for Charlotte Rampling 1974–75; first collection 1975; est. couture div. 1978; opened London boutique and redeveloped ready-to-wear collection with couture collection 1984–, opened Bruce Oldfield Wedding boutique at 34 Beauchamp Place, Knightsbridge 2009; British Rep., Australian Bicentennial Wool Collection Fashion Show, Sydney Opera House 1988; lectures: Fashion Inst., New York 1977, Los Angeles Co. Museum 1983, Int. Design Conf., Aspen, Colo (speaker and show) 1986; Vice-Pres. Barnardo's 1998–; mem. panel, Whitbread Literary Awards 1987; organized Bruce Oldfield for Barnardo's gala evenings attended by HRH The Princess of Wales 1985, 1988; Northern Personality of the Year Variety Club 1985; Gov. London Inst. 1999–2002; Trustee, Royal Acad. of Arts 2000–02; Hon. Fellow, Sheffield Hallam Univ. 1987, RCA 1990, Hatfield Coll. Durham 1991; Hon. DCL (Univ. of Northumbria at Newcastle) 2001; Hon. DUniv (Univ. of Cen. England) 2005; Hon. DL (Hull) 2009. *Television:* A Journey into Fashion (Tyne Tees TV documentary) 1990. *Publications:* Bruce Oldfield's Season (contrib.) 1987, Bruce Oldfield: Rootless (autobiog.) 2004. *Leisure interests:* music, reading, gardening, working, cooking, playing piano. *Address:* 27 Beauchamp Place, London, SW3 1NJ, England. *Telephone:* (20) 7584-1363. *Fax:* (20) 7761-0351. *E-mail:* hq@ bruceoldfield.com (office). *Website:* www.bruceoldfield.com.

OLDMAN, Gary; British actor; b. 21 March 1958, New Cross, S London; m. 1st Lesley Manville; one s.; m. 2nd Uma Thurman (q.v.) 1991 (divorced 1992); m. 3rd Donya Fiorentino (separated 2001); two c.; m. 4th Alexandra Edenborough 2008; ed Rose Bruford Drama Coll.; studied with Greenwich Young People's Theatre; acted with Theatre Royal, York and then with touring co.; appeared at Glasgow Citizens Theatre in Massacre at Paris, Chinchilla, Desperado Corner, A Waste of Time; London stage appearances: Minnesota Moon, Summit Conference, Real Dreams, The Desert Air (RSC), War Play I, II, III (RSC), Serious Money (Royal Court), Women Beware Women (Royal Court), The Pope's Wedding; appeared in The Country Wife, Royal Exchange Theatre, Manchester; Co-founder SE8 Group (production co.) 1995. *Films include:* Sid and Nancy 1986, Prick Up Your Ears 1987, Track 29 1988, Criminal Law 1988, We Think the World of You 1988, Chattahoochee 1989, State of Grace 1990, Rosencrantz and Guildenstern are Dead 1990, JFK 1991, Dracula 1992, True Romance 1993, Romeo is Bleeding 1993, Léon 1994, Immortal Beloved 1994, Murder in the First 1995, The Scarlet Letter 1995, Basquiat 1996, Nil by Mouth (producer, BAFTA Award) 1997, The Fifth Element 1997, Air Force One 1997, Lost in Space 1998, Anasazie Moon 1999, Plunkett & Macleane (exec. producer) 1999, The Contender (also exec. producer) 2000, Nobody's Baby 2001, Hannibal 2001, Interstate 60 2002, The Hire: Beat the Devil 2002, Tiptoes 2003, Sin 2003, Harry Potter and the Prisoner of Azkaban 2004, Who's Kyle? 2004, Dead Fish 2004, Batman Begins 2005, Harry Potter and the Goblet of Fire 2005, BackWoods 2006, The Legend of Spyro: A New Beginning (video game, voice) 2006, Harry Potter and the Order of the Phoenix 2007, The Legend of Spyro: The Eternal Night (video game, voice) 2007, The Legend of Spyro: Dawn of the Dragon (video game, voice) 2008, The Dark Knight 2008, Call of Duty: World at War (video game, voice) 2008, The Unborn 2009, Rain Fall 2009, A Christmas Carol 2009, Planet 51 (voice) 2009, The Book of Eli 2010, Tinker, Tailor, Soldier, Spy 2011, The Dark Knight Rises 2012, Lawless 2012. *Television includes:* Remembrance, Meantime (Channel 4); Honest, Decent and True (BBC); Rat in the Skull (Central), The Firm, Heading Home, Fallen Angels. *Address:* c/o Douglas Urbanski, Douglas Management Inc., PO Box 691763, West Hollywood, CA 90069, USA (office); SE8 Group, 12 Great James Street, Camden, London, WC1N 3DR, England (office). *Telephone:* (310) 285-6090 (office). *Fax:* (310) 285-6097 (office). *Website:* www.douglasmanagementgroup.com (office).

OLDSTONE, Michael Beauregard Alan, MD, PhD; American neuropharmacologist and academic; *Head, Viral-Immunobiology Laboratory, Scripps Research Institute;* b. New York; m. Elizabeth Hoster Oldstone; ed Univ. of Maryland School of Medicine and Johns Hopkins McCullom Pratt Inst. of Biochemistry; Postdoctoral Fellow, Dept of Experimental Pathology, Scripps Research Inst. 1966, Assoc. mem. Dept of Immunopathology 1972–78, mem. Dept of Immunology 1978–89, Head, Div. of Virology and mem. Dept of Neuropharmacology 1989, currently Head, Viral-Immunobiology Lab.; mem. Nat. Advisory Cttee, PEW Scholars Program in the Biomedical Sciences, WHO Cttee for the Eradication of Poliomyelitis and Measles Virus; Ed. Virology; mem. Editorial Bd Current Topics in Microbiology and Immunology, Journal of Experimental Medicine, Immunity; mem. Inst. of Medicine of NAS, American Asscn of Physicians, American Soc. for Clinical Investigation, Scandinavian Soc. of Immunology; Fellow, American Acad. of Microbiology; Burroughs Wellcome Professorship Award, Cotzias Award 1986, Abraham Flexner Award 1988, Rous-Whipple Award 1993, Biomedical Science Award, Karolinska Inst. (Sweden) 1994, J. Allyn Taylor Int. Prize in Medicine 1997, R. E. Dyer Lectureship and Directors Award, NIH 2000. *Publications:* HIV and Dementia 1995, Transgenic Models of Human Viral and Immunology Disease 1995, Arenaviruses I: The Epidemiology, Molecular and Cell Biology of Arenaviruses 2002, Arenaviruses II: The Molecular Pathogenesis of Arenavirus Infections 2002; numerous articles in scientific journals. *Address:* The Scripps Research Institute, Department of Immunology & Microbial Science (IMM-6), 10550 North Torrey Pines Road, La Jolla, CA 92037, USA (office). *Telephone:* (858) 784-8054 (office). *Fax:* (858) 784-9981 (office). *E-mail:* mbaobo@scripps.edu (office). *Website:* www.scripps.edu (office).

OLE-MOIYOI, Onesmo K.; Kenyan molecular biologist and immunologist; *Chairman, Council, Kenyatta University;* b. Tanzania; ed Harvard Coll. (Aga Khan Scholar) and Harvard Medical School, USA; looked after Maasai village cattle herd of 800 cows as a boy; Head of Biochemistry and Molecular Biology Lab. and Leader in Programme on Pathophysiology and Genetics, Int. Lab. for Research on Animal Diseases, Int. Livestock Research Inst., Nairobi 1987–2001; est. Inst. of Molecular and Cell Biology, Nairobi; Dir of Research and Partnerships, Int. Centre of Insect Physiology and Ecology (now African Insect Science for Food and Health—ICIPE), Nairobi 2001–07; fmr Asst Prof. and Capps' Scholar, Harvard Medical School; fmr Visiting Prof., Harvard School of Public Health; mem. Science Council for the Consultative Group of Int. Agricultural Research, Steering Cttees of HUGO (Human Genome Org.), among other appointments; Chair. Kenyatta Univ. Council in Kenya 2007–; Elder of the Order of the Burning Spear; Dr hc (Soka Univ., Japan); Kilby Int. Award 2003. *Address:* Kenyatta University, PO Box 43844-00100, Nairobi 30772, Kenya (office). *Telephone:* (20) 810901 (office). *Fax:* (20) 811575 (office). *E-mail:* info@ku.ac.ke (office). *Website:* www.ku.ac.ke (office).

O'LEARY, Hazel, BA, JD; American lawyer, academic administrator and fmr government official; *President, Fisk University;* b. 17 May 1937, Newport News, Va; d. of Russell Reid and Hazel Palleman; m. John F. O'Leary 1980 (deceased); one s.; ed High School of Fine and Performing Arts, Newark, NJ, Fisk Univ., Rutgers Univ. Law School; fmr prosecutor, then an Asst Attorney-Gen., NJ; fmr mem. staff US Dept of Energy and Fed. Energy Admin.; Vice-Pres. and Gen. Counsel, O'Leary Assocs (consultants on energy econs and planning) 1981–89, 1997–2000; joined Northern States Power Co., Minn. 1989, subsequently Exec. Vice-Pres.; US Sec. of Energy 1993–97; COO Blaylock & Pnrs (investment banking firm), New York 2001–02; Pres. Fisk Univ., Nashville 2004–. *Address:* Office of the President, Fisk University, 1000 Seventeenth Avenue North, Nashville, TN 37208-3051 (office); 4215 Harding Pike, Apt 301, Nashville, TN 37205-2029, USA. *Telephone:* (615) 329-8500 (office). *Website:* www.fisk.edu (office).

O'LEARY, Michael Kevin; Irish airline industry executive; *CEO, Ryanair Holdings PLC;* b. 20 March 1961, Kanturk, Co. Cork; s. of Ted O'Leary and Ger O'Leary; m. Anita Farrall 2003; four c.; ed Clongowes Wood Coll., Co. Kildare, Trinity Coll. Dublin; trainee with Stokes Kennedy Crowley (later KPMG) 1984–86; Dublin property developer and financial adviser to Tony Ryan; Dir Ryanair Holdings PLC 1988–91, Deputy CEO 1991–93, COO 1993–94, CEO 1994–; breeds Aberdeen Angus cattle and horses at his Gigginstown House Stud, Co. Westmeath, his horse War of Attrition won the Cheltenham Gold Cup 2006; European Businessman of the Year, Fortune Magazine 2001. *Leisure interests:* horse riding, farming, watching rugby, Manchester City Football Club. *Address:* Ryanair Ltd, Corporate Head Office, Airside Business Park, Swords, Co. Dublin, Ireland (office). *Telephone:* (1) 8121212 (office). *Fax:* (1) 8121213 (office). *E-mail:* info@ryanair.com (office). *Website:* www.ryanair.com (office).

OLECHNOWICZ, Paweł, BEcons, PhD; Polish business executive; *Chairman, President and CEO, Grupa LOTOS SA;* b. 2 Jan. 1952, Puszcza Obalska; s. of Leon Olechnowicz and Janina Olechnowicz (née Rodziewicz); m. Krystyna Olechnowicz 1975; one s.; ed Acad. of Mining and Metallurgy, Krakow, INSEAD, Fontainebleau, France, Tech. Univ., Gdansk; Technologist, Zamech Mechanical Works, Elblag 1976–77, Foreman, Metallurgical Dept, 1977–80, Man. 1980–90, Gen. Man. Elzam and Zamech 1990, CEO ABB Zamech Ltd 1990–96, Dir Power Generation Div. 1993–96, Vice-Pres. Cen. and E Europe Power Generation Div. 1996–98; Vice-Pres. and Deputy CEO, ZML Kęty SA 1999–2000; Dir Paweł Olechnowicz Consulting 2001; Chair., Pres. and CEO Grupa Lotos SA (fmrly Rafineria Gdanska), Gdansk 2002–; mem. Polish Tech. Cttee, Det Norske Veritas Classification AS, Norway 1993–; Chair. Supervisory Bd Rekoenergo, Warsaw 1991; mem. Polish Council for Econ. Devt, Warsaw 1993; Dir Business Forum, Polish Higher Educ.; mem. Polish Centre Club, Int. Inst. of Man. Devt; Orderu Odrodzenia Polski 2011. *Leisure interests:* chess, sports, playing guitar and piano. *Address:* Grupa Lotos SA, ul. Elbląska 135, 80–718 Gdansk, Poland (office). *Telephone:* (58) 3087111 (office). *Fax:* (58) 3018838 (office). *E-mail:* lotos@grupalotos.pl (office). *Website:* www.lotos.pl (office).

OLECHOWSKI, Andrzej, MA, PhD; Polish politician, economist and writer; *European Deputy Chairman, Trilateral Commission;* b. 9 Sept. 1947, Kraków; m. Irena Olechowska 1951; two s.; ed Cen. School of Planning and Statistics, Warsaw; Assoc. Econ. Affairs Officer, UNCTAD Multilateral Trade Negotiations Project, Geneva 1973–78; Head, Dept of Analysis and Projections, Foreign Trade Research Inst. Warsaw 1978–82; Econ. Affairs Officer, UNCTAD, Geneva 1982–84; Economist, IBRD, Washington, DC 1985–87; Adviser to Gov. Nat. Bank of Poland 1987; Dir World Bank Co-operation Bureau, Nat. Bank of Poland 1988; Dir Ministry of Foreign Econ. Relations 1988–89; Deputy Gov. Nat. Bank of Poland 1989–91; Sec. of State, Ministry of Foreign Econ. Relations and Chief Negotiator of Asscn Treaty with EU and Cen. European Free Trade Agreement 1991–92; Minister of Finance Feb.–May 1992; Sr Adviser, EBRD 1992–93; Econ. Adviser to Pres. of Repub. 1992–93, 1995; Minister of Foreign Affairs 1993–95; Chair. Bank Handlowy 1991–96, 1998–2000; presidential cand. 2000; Chair. Program Council, Civic Platform (Platforma Obywatelska—PO, a centrist political movt) 2001–04; currently European Deputy Chair. Trilateral Comm.; mem. Bd of Dirs Bank Handlowy, Euronet, MCI; mem. Advisory Bd Baltic Devt Forum, ACE, Citigroup

Europe, Macquarie European Infrastructure Funds. *Publications include:* Wygrac przyszlosc; publs on int. trade and foreign policy. *Address:* ul. Traugutta 7/9, 00-067 Warsaw, Poland (office). *Telephone:* (22) 629-80-70 (office). *Fax:* (22) 692-50-09 (office). *E-mail:* a.olechowski@olechowski.pl (office). *Website:* www.olechowski.pl (office).

OLEKAS, Juozas; Lithuanian physician and politician; *Minister of National Defence;* b. 30 Oct. 1955, Krasnojarsk Kraj, Siberia; m. Aurelija Olekas; one s. two d.; ed Kaunas Medical Inst., Vilnius Univ.; worked at hosp. in Vilnius 1980–90; physician and sr researcher, Vilnius Univ. Microsurgery Centre 1982–89; participated in Sàjûdis activity, elected mem. Sàjûdis Seimas 1988, People's Deputy of USSR 1989; mem. Lithuanian Del., Supreme Council of USSR 1989–91; Minister of Health 1990–92 (resgnd), 2003–04; surgeon, Vilnius Ambulance Univ. Hosp. 1993–94; Chief Physician, Vilnius Univ. Hosp. 1994; staff mem. Stomatology Clinic, Medical Faculty, Vilnius Univ. Hosp. 1994–99; mem. Social Democratic Party 1989–, mem. Seimas 1996–; Minister of Nat. Defence 2006–08, 2013–; mem. Org. Comm., European Regional Bureau of WHO 1992–93; Chair. Lithuanian Trade Union Centre 1997; Medal of Independence 2000; Nat. Award of Lithuania 1998. *Publications include:* over 100 scientific articles. *Leisure interests:* gardening, sport, dancing, theatre. *Address:* Ministry of National Defence, Totorių 25/3, Vilnius 01121, Lithuania (office). *Telephone:* (5) 273-5673 (office). *Fax:* (5) 264-8517 (office). *E-mail:* pilieciuaptarnavimas@kam.lt (office). *Website:* www.kam.lt (office).

OLEKSY, Józef, DEcon; Polish politician and economist; b. 22 June 1946, Nowy Sącz; s. of Józef Oleksy and Michalina Oleksy; m. Maria Oleksy 1983; one s. one d.; ed Warsaw School of Econs, European Faculty of Comparative Law, Strasbourg; researcher, Faculty of Foreign Trade, Vice-Dir Int. Law Dept, Warsaw School of Econs (SGH) 1969–; Founder-Pres. Movt of Young Scientists in Poland 1969–72; mem. Democratic Left Alliance (Sojusz Lewicy Demokratycznej) –2007, Chair. 2004–05; Minister, mem. of Council of Ministers 1989; mem. Polish Group of IPU; Deputy to Sejm (Parl.) 1989–2005, Marshal (Speaker) of Sejm 1993–95, 2004–05 (resgnd), Chair. European Cttee 2001–04; Prime Minister of Poland 1995–96; fmr Deputy Prime Minister and Minister for Internal Affairs; mem. Polish United Workers' Party (PZPR) 1968–90, First Sec. Voivodship Cttee 1987–89; mem. Parl. Asscn of OSCE 1989–93; mem. Governing Bd of the Council for Social Democracy of the Repub. of Poland (SDRP) from 1990, Vice-Chair. 1992–96, Chair. 1996–97; Pres. Polish Council of Young Scientists 1969–76; participant, Historical Compromise in Poland Round Table 1989; mem. Cttee on Foreign Affairs and Cttee on European Integration; Rep. EU-Poland Jt Parl. Cttee 1997, Co-Chair. 2001–04. *Publications:* numerous articles on econ. and int. affairs. *Leisure interests:* walking, hunting, history, futurology, parapsychology, cosmology. *Address:* c/o Sejm RP, ul. Wiejska 4/6/8, 00-902 Warsaw, Poland. *Website:* jozef-oleksy.blog.onet .pl.

OLESEN, Poul; Danish physicist and academic; *Professor of Theoretical Physics, The Niels Bohr International Academy, University of Copenhagen;* b. 28 April 1939, Alborg; s. of Viktor Olesen and Herdis Olesen; m. Birgitte Sode-Mogensen 1984; ed Univ. of Copenhagen; Research Assoc., Univ. of Rochester, NY, USA 1967–69; Research Assoc., CERN, Geneva, Geneva 1969–71, Visiting Fellow 1985; Assoc. Prof. of Theoretical Physics, The Niels Bohr Inst., Copenhagen 1971–97, Prof. 1997–2009, Prof., The Niels Bohr Int. Acad. 2009–, Chair. Research Cttee 1993–95, 2005–08, mem. Governing Body 1996–99; mem. Faculty of Science Council, Univ. of Copenhagen 1989–2005, Exec. Cttee 1990–93, Research Cttee 1998–2003; mem. Royal Danish Acad.; Hermer Prize. *Publications:* articles in int. journals on particle physics. *Leisure interests:* mountain biking. *Address:* The Niels Bohr International Academy, Blegdamsvej 17, 2100 Copenhagen, Ø (office); Malmmosevej 1, 2840 Holte, Denmark (home). *Telephone:* 31-42-16-16 (office). *Fax:* 35-32-50-16 (office). *E-mail:* polesen@nbi.dk (office). *Website:* www.nbia.dk (office).

OLHAYE, Roblé; Djibouti diplomatist; *Permanent Representative, United Nations;* b. 24 April 1944; m.; five c.; ed Commercial School of Addis Ababa; worked in area of financial and admin. man. in various orgs in Ethiopia engaged in communication, printing, export trade, insurance and mfg 1964–73; apptd Regional Accountant, TAW International Leasing Corpn, Nairobi 1973, Financial Dir 1975; Ind. Consultant 1980–82; Hon. Consul to Kenya 1980–85; f. (as jt venture with Middle East Bank of Dubai) Banque de Djibouti et du Moyen Orient, SA 1982; Perm. Rep. to UNEP and UN Centre for Human Settlements (Habitat), Nairobi 1986–88; Amb. to USA 1988– (also accred to Canada 1989–), Amb. and Perm. Rep. to UN, New York 1988–; apptd Pres. of Council 1994, Chair. of Sanctions Cttee 1994, mem. Security Council Mission to Mozambique 1994, Dean of African Diplomatic Corps 1999–, Chair. Second Cttee (Econ. and Social) 1999–; Fellow, Asscn of Int. Accountants (UK); mem. British Inst. of Man. *Address:* Permanent Mission of Djibouti to United Nations, 866 United Nations Plaza, Suite 4011, New York, NY 10017 (office); Embassy of Djibouti, 1156 15th Street NW, Suite 515, Washington, DC 20005 (office). *Telephone:* (212) 753-3163 (New York) (office); (202) 331-0270 (DC) (office). *Fax:* (212) 223-1276 (New York) (office); (202) 331-0302 (DC) (office). *E-mail:* djibouti@nyct.net (office). *Website:* www.un.int/wcm/content/site/djibouti/pid/3758 (office).

OLI, K. P. Sharma; Nepalese politician; b. 22 Feb. 1952; m.; mem. CP of Nepal 1970–, mem. Area Cttee 1970, Dist Cttee 1971, Head, Jhapa Movt Organizing Cttee 1972; imprisoned 1973–87; mem. CP Cen. Cttee 1987, head of Lumbini zone –1990; mem. Standing Cttee and Head of Foreign Dept 1992–; Founder and Pres. Nat. Democratic Youth Fed. 1990; Head, Dept of Publicity and Propaganda 1993; Head, Parl. Affairs 1995–, Deputy Leader 1999–2002, Head, Party School 2004–; mem. House of Reps for Jhapa Dist 1991–2002, 2006–; Minister for Home Affairs, 1994–95; Deputy Prime Minister and Minister for Foreign Affairs 2006–07; led comm. investigating Dasdhunga jeep accident 1993; mem. Presidium of Afro-Asian Peoples' Solidarity Org. (AAPSO) in Nepal 1994–2000, Pres. 2000–. *Address:* Parliament of Nepal, Singha Durbar, Kathmandu, Nepal (office). *Telephone:* 4227480 (office). *Fax:* 4222923 (office). *E-mail:* nparl@ntc.net.np (office). *Website:* www.parliament.gov.np (office).

OLIPHANT, Patrick (Pat), DHumLitt; American political cartoonist, artist and sculptor; b. 24 July 1935, Adelaide, Australia; copyboy, press artist, Adelaide Advertiser 1953–55, cartoonist 1955–64; cartoonist, Denver Post 1964–75,

Washington Star 1975–81; ind. cartoonist syndicated through Universal Press Syndicate 1980–; Hon. LHD (Dartmouth Coll.) 1981; Pulitzer Prize 1967, Reuben Award 1968, 1972, Nat. Cartoonist of Year Award 1971, 1973, 1974, 1984, 1989, 1990, 1991, Washington Journalism Review 'Best in the Business' Award 1985, Thomas Nast Prize (Germany), Premio Satira Politica of Italy. *Publications:* The Oliphant Book 1969, Four More Years 1973, An Informal Gathering 1978, Oliphant, A Cartoon Collection 1980, The Jellybean Society 1981, Ban This Book 1982, But Seriously Folks 1983, The Year of Living Perilously 1984, Make My Day! 1985, Between Rock and a Hard Place 1986, Up to Here in Alligators 1987, Nothing Basically Wrong 1988, What Those People Need is a Puppy 1989, Oliphant's Presidents: Twenty-Five Years of Caricature 1990, Fashions for the New World Order 1991, Just Say No 1992, Waiting for the Other Shoe to Drop 1994, Off to the Revolution 1995, Maintain the Status Quo 1996, So That's Where They Came From 1997, Are We There Yet? 1999, Now We'll Have to Spray for Politicians! 2000, When We Can't See the Forest for the Bushes 2001, Leadership: Cartoon and Sculptures from the Bush Years 2008. *Address:* Universal Press Syndicate, 4520 Main Street, Suite 700, Kansas City, MO 64112; c/o Susan Conway Gallery, 1214 Thirtieth Street NW, Washington DC 20007, USA. *Telephone:* (505) 670-6266 (office). *E-mail:* sconwaygly@aol.com (office). *Website:* www.ucomics.com/patoliphant.

OLIVEIRA, Manoel de; Portuguese film director and screenwriter; b. 11 Dec. 1908, Oporto; s. of Francisco José de Oliveira; m. Maria Isabel Brandão Carvalhais de Oliveira; two c.; Order of St James of the Sword (Portugal); Dr hc (Univ. of the Algarve) 2008; Golden Lion 1985, 2004, Golden Palm 2008. *Films include:* Douro, Faina Fluvial 1931, Aniki-Bóbó 1942, O Pinto e a Cidade 1956, O Pão 1959, O Acto da Primavera 1963, A Caça 1964, O Passado e Presente 1972, Benilde ou A Virgem Mãe 1975, Amor de Perdição 1979, Francisca 1981, Visita ou Memórias e Confissões 1982, Nice: À propos de Jean Vigo 1983, Lisboa Cultural 1983, Le Soulier de satin 1985, Mon cas 1986, Os Canibais (Critics Special Award) 1988, Non', ou A Vã Glória de Mandar 1990, A Divina Comédia 1991, O Dia do Desespero (Golden Leopard Award) 1992, Vale Abraão (Critics Award, Best Artistic Contribution Award) 1993, A Caixa 1994, O Convento 1995, Party 1996, Viagem ao Princípio do Mundo 1997, Inquietude 1998, La Lettre 1999, Palavra e Utopia 2000, Je rentre à la maison 2001, Porto da Minha Infância 2001, O Princípio da Incerteza 2002, Um Filme Falado 2003, O Quinto Império: Ontem Como Hoje 2004, O Espelho Mágico 2005, Belle Toujours 2006, Os Invisíveis 2006, Cristóvão Colombo – O Enigma 2007, Eccentricities of a Blonde-haired Girl 2009, O Estranho Caso de Angélica 2010, Gebo et l'Ombre 2012. *Address:* c/o Madragoa Filmes, Rua da Palmeira, 6, 1200-313 Lisbon, Portugal.

OLIVER, Jamie, MBE; British chef, restaurateur, television personality and cookery writer; b. (James Trevor Oliver), 27 May 1975; m. Jools Oliver 2000; one s. three c.; ed Westminster Catering Coll.; began cooking at parents' pub/restaurant The Cricketers, Cambridge; fmr Head Pastry Chef, The Neal Street Restaurant; fmr Chef, The River Café; numerous TV series; advertising contract with Sainsbury's Co.; cookery show tour The Happy Days Tour, UK, NZ and Australia 2001; designed range of cooking and tableware for Royal Worcester; Consultant Chef, Monte's Restaurant, London; est. restaurant Fifteen, London 2003; est. Jamie's Italian chain of restaurants 2008; opened Barbecoa 2011; sometimes known as the Naked Chef; British Book Awards Outstanding Achievement Award 2006. *Television includes:* Presenter, The Naked Chef (Optomen TV) 1998–99, Pukka Tukka (Channel 4) 2000, Oliver's Twist 2002, Jamie's Kitchen 2002, Jamie's School Dinners (Channel 4, UK and internationally) 2005, Jamie's Great Italian Escape (Channel 4) 2005, Jamie's Kitchen Australia 2006, Jamie's Chef 2007, Jamie at Home 2007, Jamie's Fowl Dinners 2008, Jamie's Ministry of Food 2008, What's Cooking? with Jamie Oliver (video game) 2008, Jamie Saves Our Bacon (Channel 4) 2009, Jamie's American Roadtrip (Channel 4) 2009, Jamie's Family Christmas (Channel 4) 2009, Jamie Oliver's Food Revolution (ABC; aired in UK on Channel 4 as Jamie's American Food Revolution) (Emmy Award for Outstanding Reality Programme 2010) 2010–, Jamie Does… (Channel 4) 2010, Jamie's 30 Minute Meals (Channel 4) 2010–11, Jamie's Dream School 2011; other: twice guest-hosted Channel 4's The Friday Night Project, two appearances in 'Star in a Reasonably-Priced Car' segment of BBC 2's Top Gear, second British celebrity chef to appear as a challenger on Iron Chef America, starred as a judge in series Oprah's Big Give (ABC) 2008. *Publications include:* The Naked Chef (three cookery books), Jamie's Kitchen 2002, Jamie's Dinners 2004, Jamie's Italy 2005, Cook with Jamie 2006, Jamie at Home 2007, Jamie's Ministry of Food 2008, Jamie's America 2009, Jamie Does… 2010, Jamie's 30-Minute Meals: A Revolutionary Approach to Cooking Good Food Fast 2010. *Address:* 19–21 Nile Street, London, N1 7LL, England (office). *Telephone:* (20) 7566-1770 (office). *Fax:* (20) 7251-2749 (office). *Website:* www.jamieoliver.com (office).

OLIVER, Joseph (Joe), PC, BA, BCL, MBA; Canadian lawyer, politician and fmr investment banker; *Minister of Finance;* b. 20 May 1940, Montreal; m. Golda Goldman; two s.; ed McGill Univ., Rotman School of Man., Harvard Graduate School of Business; called to Quebec Bar; early career as investment banker with Merrill Lynch; sr positions with other investment dealers; fmr Exec. Dir Ontario Securities Comm.; Pres. and CEO Investment Dealers Asscn of Canada 1995–2007; mem. House of Commons for Eglinton-Lawrence (Ont.) 2011–; Minister of Natural Resources 2011–14, of Finance 2014–; fmr Chair. Advisory Cttee, Int. Council of Securities Asscn; fmr Chair. Consultative Cttee, Int. Asscn of Securities Comms; mem. Canadian Inst. of Chartered Business Valuators; fmr Dir Canadian Securities Inst. Research Foundation; mem. Conservative Party. *Address:* Department of Finance Canada, East Tower, 19th Floor, 140 O'Connor Street, Ottawa, ON K1A 0G5, Canada (office). *Telephone:* (613) 992-1573 (office). *Fax:* (613) 943-0938 (office). *E-mail:* finpub@fin.gc.ca (office). *Website:* www.fin.gc.ca (office); www.joeoliver.ca.

OLLIER, Patrick; French politician; *Mayor of Rueil-Malmaison;* b. 17 Dec. 1944, Périgueux, Dordogne; m. (divorced) one s.; pnr Michèle Alliot-Marie (q.v.); Founding mem. Union des jeunes pour le progrès 1965; participated in presidential campaign of Jacques Chaban-Delmas 1974; attached to Mayor of Rueil-Malmaison (Hauts-de-Seine) 1983–89; Deputy (RPR) for Hautes-Alpes 1988–2002, Vice-Pres. Nat. Ass. 1998–2002, Deputy (Union pour un Mouvement Populaire) for Hauts-de-Seine 2002–10, Pres. Nat. Ass. March–June 2007; Mayor of La Salle les Alpes (Hautes-Alpes) 1989–2001; mem. Conseil général, Hautes-Alpes 1992–2001; Pres.

Cttee on Econ. Affairs, the Environment, and Territory, Head of French-Libyan Friendship Group; Mayor of Rueil-Malmaison, Hauts-de-Seine 2004–; Minister in the Office of the Prime Minister, in charge of Relations with Parl. 2010–12; Hon. mem. Rotary-Club of Rueil-Malmaison. *Address:* Mairie de Rueil-Malmaison, 13 boulevard Foch, 92501 Rueil-Malmaison Cedex (office); 12 rue Hervet, 92500 Rueil-Malmaison, France (home). *Telephone:* 1-47-32-65-65 (office). *E-mail:* infos@patrick-ollier.com (office); contact@patrickollier2012.fr (office). *Website:* www.mairie-rueilmalmaison.fr (office); www.patrick-ollier.com (office); patrickollier2012.fr (office).

OLLILA, Esko Juhani, LLM; Finnish bank executive; b. 14 July 1940, Rovaniemi; s. of Heikki Armas Ollila and Lempi Maria Ollila (née Häggman); m. Riitta Leena, née Huhtala 1963; two s.; Man. Dir Rovaniemi Savings Bank 1971–75; Man. Dir and Chair. Bd Regional Devt Fund of Finland 1975–79; mem. Bd Skopbank 1979–83; Minister of Trade and Industry 1982–83; Minister of Finance 1986–87; mem. Bd Bank of Finland 1983–2000; Chair. Finnish Nat. Fund for Research and Devt (SITRA) 1991–95, mem. 1995–; mem. Supervisory Bd Finnish Guarantee Bd 1995–; Chair. Advisory Bd Baltic Investment Fund 1995–; mem. Wise Men Assembly (group promoting co-operation between Finland and Estonia).

OLLILA, Jorma Jaakko, MPolSci, MSc (Econs), MSc (Eng); Finnish business executive; *Non-Executive Chairman, Royal Dutch Shell plc;* b. 15 Aug. 1950, Seinäjoki; m. Liisa Annikki (née Metsola); two s. one d.; ed Univ. of Helsinki, London School of Econs, UK and Helsinki Univ. of Tech.; rank of Sr Lt; Account Man., Corporate Bank, Citibank N.A., London UK 1978–80; Account Officer, Citibank Oy 1980–82, mem. Bd of Man. 1983–85; Vice-Pres. Int. Operations, Nokia 1985–86, mem. Group Exec. Bd 1986–, Sr Vice-Pres. Finance 1986–89, Deputy mem. Bd of Dirs 1989–90, Pres. Nokia Mobile Phones 1990–92, Pres. and CEO Nokia 1992–99, Chair. Group Exec. Bd 1992–2006, mem. Bd Nokia Corpn 1995–2006, Chair. and CEO 1999–2006, Chair. 2006–12; Chair. (non-exec.) Royal Dutch Shell plc 2006–, Chair. Nomination and Succession Cttee; Chair. Bd MTV Oy 1993–97; mem. Bd of Dirs Oy Dipoli Ab 1990–94, ICI PLC 1992–2000, Otava Books and Magazines Group Ltd 1996–, UPM-Kymmene 1997–; Dir (non-exec.) Ford Motor Co. 2000–; mem. Supervisory Bd, Oy Rastor AB 1992–93, Tietotehdas Oy 1992–95, Industrial Mutual Insurance Co., Pohjola Insurance Co. Ltd 1992–97, NKF Holding NV 1992–99, Pension-Varma Mutual Insurance Co. 1993–98, Sampo Insurance Co. Ltd 1993–2000, Merita Bank Ltd (fmr Union Bank of Finland Ltd) 1994–2000; Chair. Nat. Union of Finnish Students 1973–74; mem. Planning Bd for Defence Economy 1992–96; mem. Bd and Exec. Cttee Confed. of Finnish Industries and Employers 1992–2002, Deputy Chair. Bd 1995–2002; Chair. Supervisory Bd Finnish Foreign Trade Asscn 1993–98; Chair. Bd Dirs and Supervisory Bd Finnish Business and Policy Forum 2004–, Research Inst. of the Finnish Economy 2004–; Vice-Chair. Bd, Finnish Section, Int. Chamber of Commerce 1993–97, Advisory Cttee Helsinki Univ. of Tech. 1993–95 (Chair. 1996–); mem. Bd Econ. Information Bureau 1993–97; mem. Exec. Bd Asscn for the Finnish Cultural Foundation 1993–99; mem. Council, Centre for Finnish Business and Policy Studies 1993–2001, Helsinki School of Econs and Business Admin 1993–98; mem. Supervisory Bd Foundation for Pediatric Research 1993–98, WWF Finland 1995–97; mem. Science and Tech. Policy Council of Finland 1993–2002; mem. Council of Supervisors, Research Institute of the Finnish Economy 1993–2000; mem. Dean's Council, John F. Kennedy School of Govt, Harvard Univ. 1995–; Overseas Advisory Trustee The American-Scandinavian Foundation 1994–; mem. Int. Bd United World Coll. 1995–; mem. European Round Table of Industrialists 1997–, GBDe Business Steering Cttee 1999–; Hon. Citizen of Beijing 2002; Hon. Fellow, LSE 2003; Hon. mem. IEEE 2003; Kt, First Class, Order of White Rose of Finland 1991, Commdr, 1st Class 1996; Commdr, Order of Orange-Nassau 1995, Order of White Star (Estonia) 1995, Officer's Cross, Order of Merit (Hungary) 1996; Commdr's Cross, Order of Merit of FRG 1997, Commdr's Cross, Order of Merit of the Repub. of Poland 1999, Commdr Grand Cross, Order of the Lion of Finland 2005, Hon. CBE 2008; Hon. PhD (Helsinki) 1995; Hon. DSc (Helsinki Univ. of Tech.) 1998. *Address:* Nokia Corporation, Keilalahdentie 4, Espoo 00045, Finland (office); Royal Dutch Shell plc, Carel van Bylandtlaan 30, 2596 HR The Hague, Netherlands (office). *Telephone:* 7180-08000 (Espoo) (office); (70) 3779111 (The Hague) (office). *Fax:* 7180-38226 (Espoo) (office); (70) 3773115 (The Hague) (office). *Website:* www.nokia.com (office); www.shell.com (office).

OLMERT, Ehud, BA, LLB; Israeli politician and lawyer; b. 1945, Binyamina; m.; four c.; ed Hebrew Univ. of Jerusalem; served in Israeli Defense Force (IDF) as combat infantry unit officer; mil. corresp. for IDF journal Bamachane; mem. Likud Party; mem. Knesset 1973–98, 2003–, mem. Foreign Affairs and Security Cttee 1981–88; Minister without Portfolio responsible for Minority Affairs 1988–90; Minister of Health 1990–92; Mayor of Jerusalem 1993–2003; Vice-Prime Minister and Minister of Industry, Trade, Labor and Communications 2003–05, Vice-Premier and Minister of Finance 2005–06; left Likud party to join newly formed Kadima party Dec. 2005; Acting Chair. of Kadima Jan.–April 2006, Chair. April 2006–08; Acting Prime Minister Jan.–April 2006, Prime Minister and Minister for Social Affairs April 2006–08 (resgnd), Minister of Finance April–July 2007. *Address:* Kadima, Petach Tikva, Tel-Aviv, Israel (office). *Telephone:* 3-9788000 (office). *Fax:* 3-9788020 (office). *Website:* www.kadima.org.il (office).

OLMI, Ermanno; Italian film director; b. 24 July 1931, Bergamo, Lombardy; m. Loredana Detto; fmr clerk, Edison-Volta electric plant; later dir and producer sponsored documentary films; made first feature film 1959, f. production co. 22 December SpA 1961 and helped found Hypothesis Cinema; an exponent of Italian neorealism. *Films include:* El Frayle (short) 1953, Piccoli calabresi a Suna sul Lago Maggiore (documentary short) 1954, La pattuglia del Passo S. Giacomo (documentary short) 1954, Dialogo di un venditore di almanacchi e di un passeggiere (short) 1954, Cantiere d'inverno (short) 1955, La diga del ghiacciaio (documentary short) 1955, L'energia elettrica nell'agricoltura (documentary short) 1955, La mia valle (documentary short) 1955, L'onda (documentary short) 1955, Il pensionato (documentary short) 1955, Il racconto della Stura (documentary short) 1955, Società Ovesticino – Dinamo (documentary short) 1955, Buongiorno natura (short) 1955, Manon: Finestra 2 (short) 1956, Michelino 1A B (documentary short) 1956, Campi sperimentali (documentary short) 1957, Fibre in civiltà (short) 1957, Colonie Sicedison (documentary short) 1958, Il frumento (documentary short) 1958, Giochi di colonia (documentary short) 1958, Tre fili fino a Milano (documentary short) 1958, Venezia città moderna (documentary short) 1958, Grigio (documentary short) 1958, Il tempo si è fermato 1959, Cavo ad olio fluido a 220.000 volt (documentary short) 1959, Fertilizzanti prodotti dalla società del Gruppo Edison (documentary short) 1959, Natura e chimica (documentary short) 1959, Il grande paese d'acciaio (documentary short) 1960, Po: forza 50.000 (documentary short) 1960, Il Posto 1961, Fertilizzanti complessi (documentary short) 1961, Le grand barrage (documentary short) 1961, Un metro lungo cinque (documentary short) 1961, Pomodoro (documentary short) 1961, Sacco in plypac (documentary short) 1961, The Engagement 1963, A Man Named John 1965, Racconti di giovani amori 1967, One Fine Day 1969, I recuperanti 1970, In the Summertime 1971, La circostanza 1974, The Tree of Wooden Clogs (L'Albero degli zoccoli) (Palme d'Or, Cannes Film Festival) 1978, Walking, Walking 1983, Artigiani veneti (documentary short) 1986, Long Live the Lady! 1987, Imago urbis (documentary) 1987, The Legend of the Holy Drinker (La leggenda del santo bevitore) (Golden Lion, Venice Film Festival, David di Donatello Award) 1988, 12 registi per 12 città (documentary) (segment 'Milano') 1989, Lungo il fiume (documentary) 1992, Il segreto del bosco vecchio 1993, Genesis: The Creation and the Flood 1994, Mille anni (documentary short) 1995, The Profession of Arms (David di Donatello Award) 2001, Singing Behind Screens 2003, Tickets 2005, Atto unico di Jannis Kounellis (short) 2007, Centochiodi 2007, Terra madre (documentary) 2009, Il premio (short) 2009, Rupi del vino (documentary) 2009, The Cardboard Village 2011, Venice 70: Future Reloaded (documentary) (segment 'La moviola') 2013. *Television includes:* 700 anni fa (film documentary) 1963, Dopo secoli (film documentary) 1964, Ritorno al paese (film documentary short) 1967, Beata gioventù (film documentary) 1967, Nino il fioraio (film documentary short) 1967, The Crush (film) 1967, …Dal diario scolastico di Cesare Cornoldi (film documentary short) 1967, La borsa (film documentary) 1968, La fatica di leggere (film documentary short) 1970, In nome del popolo italiano (film documentary) 1971, Le radici della libertà (film) 1972, Nascita di una formazione partigiana (film) 1973, Alcide De Gasperi (series) 1974, Apocalypsis cum figuris (film documentary) 1979, Capitali culturali d'Europa (series documentary) – Milano '83 1983, Personaggi fortemente sospettabili (film documentary short) 1983, Il denaro non esiste (film documentary) 1999.

OLOFSSON, Lars, BBA; Swedish business executive; b. 19 Dec. 1951, Kristianstad; ed Univ. of Lund; began career with Nestlé SA, Vevey, Switzerland as Product Man. for Findus frozen products 1976, worked at Nestlé France and held various commercial and marketing positions 1981–92, apptd Gen. Man. France Glaces Findus 1992, then became Pres. Pripps-Procordia Sweden, then led the Dairy and Dietetic Products Div. of Sopad Nestlé, apptd Gen. Man. Nestlé Nordic Markets 1995, apptd CEO Nestlé France 1997, Exec. Vice-Pres. Nestlé Group, responsible for Zone Europe 2001–08, Exec. Vice-Pres. in charge of Strategic Business Units, Marketing and Sales, Nestlé 2005–08; mem. Bd of Dirs and CEO Carrefour Group 2009–12, Chair. 2011–12, Chair. Carrefour Foundation; Co-Chair. Consumer Goods Forum 2010–; Chevalier du Mérite agricole; Chevalier, Légion d'honneur 2003, Officier 2011. *Address:* c/o Groupe Carrefour, 26 Quai Michelet, TSA 20016, 92695 Levallois-Perret Cedex, France. *E-mail:* info@ carrefour.com.

OLOVSSON, Ivar (Olov Göte), DrSc; Swedish chemist and academic; *Professor Emeritus of Inorganic Chemistry, University of Uppsala;* b. 15 Oct. 1928, Rödön; s. of Erik Olovsson and Anna Andersson; m. Kristina Jonsson 1950; three s. one d.; ed Univ. of Uppsala; Teaching Asst, Univ. of Uppsala 1953–57, Asst Prof. 1961–64, Assoc. Prof. 1965–69, Prof. of Inorganic Chem. 1969–93, Prof. Emer. 1993–; Research Assoc., Univ. of California, Berkeley 1957–59, 1964–65, Visiting Miller Prof. 2002; Guest Prof., Lab. de Cristallographie, Grenoble 1977–78, Univ. of Konstanz 1982–83, 1999; mem. Royal Soc. of Sciences 1970 (Pres. 1996–97), Royal Swedish Acad. of Sciences 1974; Kt of Northern Star 1975; Chevalier des Palmes académiques 1981; Gold Medal, Royal Acad. of Sciences of Sweden 1961, Gold Medal, Swedish Chem. Soc. 1965, María Sklodowska-Curie Medal, Polish Chem. Soc. 2003. *Publications include:* about 90 scientific papers, mainly in field of structural chem. *Leisure interests:* outdoor life, mountaineering, skiing, music. *Address:* Ångström Laboratory, Department of Chemistry, PO Box 538, 751 21 Uppsala (office); Murklevägen 27, 756 46 Uppsala, Sweden (home). *Telephone:* (18) 30-22-76 (home). *E-mail:* ivar.olovsson@kemi.uu.se (office). *Website:* www.kemi.uu .se (office).

OLSEN, Matthew G., BA, JD; American lawyer and government official; *Director, National Counterterrorism Center;* ed Univ. of Virginia, Harvard Law School; Fed. Prosecutor, US Attorney's Office for Dist of Columbia 1994–2006, Chief of Nat. Security Section 2005–06; Special Counsel to Dir of FBI 2004–05; Deputy Asst Attorney Gen., Nat. Security Div. 2006–09; Assoc. Deputy Attorney Gen., Dept of Justice, also Special Counselor to Attorney Gen. and Exec. Dir Guantanamo Review Task Force 2009–11, served as Acting Asst Attorney Gen. for Nat. Security during presidential transition of Barack Obama; Gen. Counsel, Nat. Security Agency (NSA) –2011; Dir Nat. Counterterrorism Center 2011–. *Address:* US National Counterterrorism Center, c/o Director of National Intelligence, Washington, DC 20511, USA (office). *Telephone:* (703) 733-8600 (office). *Website:* www.nctc.gov (office).

OLSEN, Olaf, PhD; Danish archaeologist, historian and fmr museum director; b. 7 June 1928, Copenhagen; s. of Prof. Albert Olsen and Agnete Olsen (née Bing); m. 1st Jean Catherine Dennistoun Sword; one s; m. 2nd Rikke Agnete Clausen 1971; ed Univ. of Copenhagen; Asst, Medieval Dept, Nat. Museum 1950–58, Asst Keeper 1958–71, State Antiquary and Dir Nat. Museum 1981–95; Prof. of Medieval Archaeology, Århus Univ. 1971–81; Dir Hielmstierne-Rosencrone Foundation 1979–; Vice-Pres. Det kgl. nordiske Oldskriftselskab 1981–95, Royal Danish Acad. of Sciences and Letters 1983–89; Founding mem. Academia Europaea 1988; dir numerous archaeological excavations, mainly of Viking ships and fortresses and medieval churches and monasteries; Hon. Fellow, Soc. of Antiquaries; Dr hc (St Petersburg Univ.) 1994; GEC Gad Foundation Prize 1966, 1992, Hartmann Prize 1995, Westerby Prize 2002, Ingenio et arti Medal. *Publications:* numerous books and papers on history and medieval archaeology. *Address:* Strevelshovedvej 2, Alrø, 8300 Odder, Denmark (home). *Telephone:* 86-55-21-28 (home). *E-mail:* olaf .olsen@rikkeslyst.dk (home).

OLSEN, Øystein, Cand. oecon; Norwegian economist and central banker; *Governor, Norges Bank;* b. 1952; ed Univ. of Oslo; with Research Dept, Statistics

Norway 1977–90, 1991–94, Head of Research Dept 1996–99, Dir-Gen. Statistics Norway 2005–10; Researcher, Lawrence Berkeley Lab., Univ. of California, Berkeley, USA 1985–86; with ECON Centre for Economic Analysis, Oslo 1990–91; Prof., Norwegian School of Man. 1993–99; Deputy Dir-Gen., Econ. Policy Dept, Ministry of Finance 1994–96, Dir-Gen. 1999–2005; Gov. Norges Bank (central bank) 2011–. *Address:* Office of the Governor, Norges Bank, Bankplassen 2, POB 1179 Sentrum, 0107 Oslo, Norway (office). *Telephone:* 22-31-60-00 (office). *Fax:* 22-41-31-05 (office). *E-mail:* central.bank@norges-bank.no (office). *Website:* www .norges-bank.no (office).

OLSON, Hon. Lyndon Lowell, Jr; American insurance executive, politician and diplomatist; *Chairman, Hill+Knowlton Strategies for the United States;* b. 7 March 1947, Waco, Tex.; m. Kay Woodward Olson 1982; ed Baylor Univ., Baylor Law School, Tex.; mem. Texas State House of Reps 1973–78; Chair. Cttee on Higher Educ., House Standing Cttee on Local Govt; Chair. Texas State Bd of Insurance 1979–81, 1983–87; fmr CEO Nat. Group of Insurance Cos 1987; helped negotiate US–Israeli Free Trade Agreement; led Trade Del. on Financial Services to Russia and China 1985; Pres. and CEO Travelers Insurance Holdings and Associated Madison Cos (predecessors of Citigroup) 1990–98, sr adviser to the Chair. of Citigroup Inc. 2002–08; currently Chair. Hill+Knowlton Strategies for the US; Amb. to Sweden 1997–2001; Pres. Nat. Asscn of Insurance Commrs 1982; Pres. and CEO Travellers Insurance Holdings Inc. 1990–98, Assoc. Madison Cos Inc.; Commr and Vice-Chair. US Advisory Comm. on Public Diplomacy; Vice-Chair. Lyndon B. Johnson Foundation; mem. Bernard and Audre Rapoport Foundation; Chair. and Trustee, Texas Scottish Rite Hosp. for Children, Dallas; fmr Chair. Swedish American Chamber of Commerce, New York; mem. Bd of Trustees, Baylor Coll. of Medicine, Austin Presbyterian Theological Seminary 2009–; fmr Trustee, American Scandinavian Foundation, New York; mem. Council on Foreign Relations, Council of American Ambs; Elder Cen. Pres. Church, Tex.; Democrat; Order of the Polar Star (Sweden) 2007; Dr hc (Umeå Univ.); Gates of Jerusalem Award (Israel), Baylor Young Outstanding Alumni Award 1999, Distinguished Public Official (Texas Medical Asscn), Ellis Island Medal of Honor in 2001, Swedish-American of the Year Award, King Carl XVI Gustaf 2002, The Swedish-American of 2002, Vasa Order of America 2002, Price Daniel Distinguished Public Service Award, Baylor Univ. 2002, Anson Jones Award, Fort Worth Scottish Rite Foundation 2007. *Address:* Hill+Knowlton Strategies, 825 3rd Avenue, New York, NY 10022, USA (office). *Telephone:* (212) 885-0300 (office). *E-mail:* lyndon.olson@ hkstrategies.com (office). *Website:* www.hkstrategies.com (office).

OLSON, Maynard V., BS, PhD; American chemist, geneticist and academic; *Professor of Genome Sciences and of Medicine and Adjunct Professor of Computer Science and Engineering, University of Washington;* ed California Inst. of Tech., Stanford Univ.; chemist at Dartmouth Coll. 1970–74; Visiting Scholar and Research Assoc., Dept of Genetics, Univ. of Washington 1974–79, rejoined Dept of Molecular Biotechnology 1992–, currently Prof. of Genome Sciences and of Medicine and Adjunct Prof. of Computer Science and Eng; joined Faculty, Washington Univ., St Louis 1979; fmr Investigator, Howard Hughes Medical Inst.; mem. NAS 1994; Genetics Soc. of America Medal 1992, Gairdner Foundation Int. Award 2002, Gruber Genetics Prize, The Peter and Patricia Gruber Foundation 2007. *Achievements include:* one of main architects of Human Genome Project; created a method to break the yeast genome into manageable pieces for analysis; his pioneering work paved way for analysis of entire human genome. *Publications:* numerous scientific papers in professional journals. *Address:* Fluke Hall 316, University of Washington, Box 352145, Seattle, WA 98195, USA (office). *Telephone:* (206) 685-7346 (office). *Fax:* (206) 543-0754 (office). *E-mail:* mvo@u .washington.edu (office). *Website:* www.genome.washington.edu/UWGC (office).

OLSON, Peter, AB, MBA, JD; American publishing executive; b. 1 May 1950, Chicago, Ill.; m. 1st (divorced); three c.; m. 2nd Candice Carpenter 2001; ed Harvard Univ., Harvard Business School, Harvard Law School; Assoc. Attorney, Baker & Botts (law firm), Washington, DC 1976–77; Assoc. Attorney, Hamada & Matsumoto (law firm), Tokyo, Japan 1977–79; Officer, Int. Div. Dresdner Bank, Frankfurt am Main, Germany 1979–81, Deputy Man. Corp. Business Dept, Tokyo Br. 1981–84, Man. Credit Dept, Tokyo Br. 1984–87, Vice-Pres. Planning Dept, Treasury Div., Frankfurt 1987–88; Man. Bertelsmann AG Corp. Office, Gütersloh, Germany 1988–89; Sr Vice-Pres. Doubleday Book & Music Clubs, Inc., Garden City, NY, USA 1989–90, Pres. Bertelsmann, Inc., New York, USA 1990–92; Exec. Vice-Pres. and Chief Financial Officer Bantam Doubleday Dell Publishing Group, New York 1992–94; Chair. and CEO Bertelsmann Book Group North America, New York 1994–98 (mem. Bertelsmann Book AG Exec. Bd); Chair. and CEO Random House, Inc., New York 1998–2008 (mem. Bertelsmann Book AG Exec. Bd), mem. Bd Bertelsmann AG 2001–; Detur Prize; Phi Beta Kappa. *Leisure interest:* reading. *Address:* c/o Random House, Inc., 1745 Broadway, New York, NY 10019, USA (office).

OLSSON, Christian; Swedish athlete; b. 25 Jan. 1980, Gothenburg; competes in triple jump; Programme Seller, Gothenburg Stadium 1995; coached by Viljo Nousiainen 1995–99, Yannick Tregaro 1999–; professional debut 1999; equalled world record at World Indoor Championships 2004; winner Gold Medal for triple jump, Grand Prix, Athens 2002, World Athletics Final, St Denis 2002, Monaco 2003, World Championships, St Denis 2003, World Indoor Championships, Birmingham 2003, Budapest 2004, Super Grand Prix, Gateshead 2003, 2004, Stockholm 2003, 2004, Olympic Games, Athens 2004, Golden League, Monaco 2002, Bergen 2004, Rome 2004, Zurich 2004, St Denis 2004; winner Silver Medal for triple jump, Grand Prix, Stockholm 2001, 2002, Golden League, Oslo 2002, St Denis 2002, Brussels 2002, World Championships, Edmonton 2003; winner Bronze Medal for triple jump, Golden League, Zurich 2002; mem. Örgryte IS Club; Best Sports Achievement of the Year, Swedish Sports Awards 2001, European Athletic Asscn Athlete of the Year 2003. *Leisure interests:* cars, reading, computer games, music. *Address:* c/o Svenska Friidrottsförbundet, Box 11, 171 18 Solna, Sweden (office).

OLSSON, Hans-Olov, MBA; Swedish automobile industry executive; *Vice-Chairman, Volvo Car Corporation;* b. 1941, Snäcke, Animskogs parish; m. Monica Olsson; two d.; ed Univ. of Gothenburg, Harvard Univ., Vevey, Switzerland; joined Volvo Corpn 1966, systems engineer responsible for production control, logistics and procurement 1966–69, Man. of Material and Production Control 1969–72, Production Man. of Final Ass. Plant, Volvo Truck Corpn, Gothenburg 1972–74,

Project Man., Chesapeake Plant, Volvo Car Corpn, VA 1974–77, Gen. Plant Man., Component Supply, Volvo Daisland Plant 1977–80, Dir of Area Overseas, Global Sales and Marketing Div. 1984–87, Vice-Pres. of Div. 1987–89, est. Volvo Business Univ. 1989, Pres. of Volvo Japan, Tokyo 1990–96, Pres. of Volvo Cars Market Area Europe, Brussels, Belgium 1996–98, Pres. and CEO Volvo Cars N America, Rockleigh, NJ 1998–2000, Pres. and CEO Volvo Car Corpn 2000–05; Sr Vice-Pres. and Chief Marketing Officer, Ford Motor Co. 2005–06; Vice-Chair., Volvo Car Corpn 2010–; mem. Bd Svenskt Näringsliv (Confed. of Swedish Enterprises); Dir, Lindab AB –2010, Lindab International AB 2001–10, Höganäs AB 2006–, Elanders AB 2007–. *Leisure interests:* jogging, golf, gardening, skiing. *Address:* Volvo Car Corporation, PVH50, 50200, 405 31 Göteborg, Sweden (office). *Website:* www .volvocars.com (office).

OLSSON, Karl Erik; Swedish politician and farmer; *Chairman, Swedish Association for Senior Citizens;* b. 23 Feb. 1938, Häglinge, Kristianstad; m. Sonja Olsson; three c.; ed Colls of Agric.; farmer, Nygård Farm 1963–; Chair. Nat. Centre Party Youth League 1971–74; mem. Centre Party Nat. Bd 1981–92, Asst Vice-Chair. 1986–87, Vice-Chair. 1987–92; mem. Parl. 1976–79, 1985–95; mem. Bd Nuclear Power Inspectorate 1977–91, Foundation for the Promotion of Literature 1980–91, Swedish Univ. of Agric. Sciences 1986–91; Chair. Standing Cttee on Agric. 1985–91; Minister of Agric. 1991–94; mem. European Parl. 1995–2004, mem. European Liberal, Democrat and Reform Party Group (ELDR), Bureau European Parl., Cttee on Agric. and Rural Devt, Cttee on Fisheries, Substitute Cttee on Environment, Public Health and Consumer Policy, mem. Del. to EU–Czech Repub. Jt Parl. Cttee, Substitute Del. to EU–Bulgaria Jt Parl. Cttee; Chair. Häglinge Church Council 1983–2009, Kristianstad Council of Agric. 1997–2009, Swedish Mutual Guarantee Asscn 2004–09, Swedish Asscn for Sr Citizens 2008–; mem. ELDR Group Bureau, Exec. Bd Global Crop Diversity Trust, FAO, Rome, Advisory Council to the Nat. Bd of Health and Welfare; mem. Royal Swedish Acad. for Agric. and Forestry 1999–2011; Hon. AgrD; Gold Medal, Chamber of Agric. *Publications:* Bonde i lokalsamhället 1973, Tankar 1978, Naturresurserna och framtiden 1984, Sverige behöver en Livskraftig Landsbygd 1985, Europeiskt jordbruk i battre takt med naturen 1998, Jordbruk, Handel och Utreckling 2006. *Address:* Nygård 2116, 280 10 Sösdala, Sweden (home); SPF, Box 22574, 104 22 Stockholm, Sweden. *Telephone:* (451) 63091 (home); 708-738259 (mobile). *Fax:* (451) 63275 (home). *E-mail:* karl.erik.olsson@hotmail.com (home); karl.erik .olsson@spfpension.se. *Website:* www.haglingenygard.se (home); www.spfpension .se.

OLSZEWSKI, Jan Ferdynand; Polish politician and lawyer; *Leader, Movement for the Reconstruction of Poland;* b. 20 Aug. 1930, Warsaw; m.; ed Warsaw Univ.; mem. underground Boy Scouts in WWII; Research Asst, Legal Sciences Dept, Polish Acad. of Sciences 1954–56; journalist Po prostu 1956–57; banned from working as a journalist 1957; mem. Crooked Circle Club 1956–62; Trial Lawyer 1962–68; suspended from the Bar by Justice Minister for defending students involved in anti-Communist demonstrations 1968; returned to work as attorney 1970; Defence Counsel for anti-Communist Ruch Org. 1972; Co-founder, Leader Polish Independence Alliance 1975–80; Co-founder Workers' Defence Cttee (KOR) 1976–77; drafted (jtly) Statute of the Free Trade Union of Coast Workers 1980; Adviser Solidarity Nat. Comm. 1980–; Legal Adviser Secretariat of Polish Episcopate; Plenipotentiary to family of Father Jerzy Popiełuszko during trial of his murderers; Rep. Solidarity opposition in sub-comm. on legal and judicial reform 1989; mem. Pres. Lech Wałęsa's Advisory Cttee Jan.–Nov. 1991; Deputy to Sejm (Parl.) 1991–93, 1997–; Prime Minister 1991–92; Co-founder and Pres. Movt for the Repub. 1992–94; Co-founder and Leader Movt for the Reconstruction of Poland (Ruchu Odbudowy Polski—ROP) 1995–; Leader Homeland Patriotic Movt 1997; Founder-mem. Civic Inst. and Atlantic Club. *Address:* Ruchu Odbudowy Polski, ul. Piękna 22 Lok. 7, 00-549 Warsaw, Poland (office). *Telephone:* (22) 6253282 (office). *Fax:* (22) 6253501 (office). *E-mail:* jan.olszewski@sejm.gov.pl (office). *Website:* www.rop.sky.pl (office).

OLTEANU, Bogdan, MBA; Romanian banker and politician; *Vice-Governor, National Bank of Romania;* b. 29 Oct. 1971, Bucharest; m. Cristina Oteanu; two c.; ed Univ. of Bucharest, Romanian Banking Inst. and City Univ., Seattle, USA; mem. Nat. Liberal Party (Partidul Naţional Liberal—PNL) 1991–2009, Pres. Youth Section 1998–2000, Alt. mem. Standing Bureau 2001–02, Chair. Court of Honour and Arbitration 2002; Sec.-Gen. Org. of Liberal Students 1993–96; Adviser to State Minister, Ministry of Industry and Commerce 1997; lawyer, Bogdan Olteanu Law Firm 1998–; Govt Minister responsible for relations with Parl. 2004–06; mem. Camera Deputaţilor (Chamber of Deputies) 2004–09, Chair. 2006–08, Vice-Chair. 2008–09, mem. Culture, Arts, Mass Information Means Cttee (Chair. 2004–05) 2004–06, Investigation of Abuses, Corrupt Practices and Petitions Cttee 2006–07, Defence, Public Order and Nat. Security Cttee 2007–; Vice-Gov. Nat. Bank of Romania 2009–. *Address:* National Bank of Romania (Banca Naţională a României), 030031 Bucharest 3, Str. Lipscani 25, Romania (office). *Telephone:* (21) 3130410 (office). *Fax:* (21) 3123831 (office). *E-mail:* info@ bnro.ro (office). *Website:* www.bnro.ro (office).

OLUTOYIN AGANGA, Olusegun; Nigerian economist and politician; b. 1955, Lagos State; ed Univ. of Oxford, UK; Man. Dir Goldman Sachs, London, UK –2010; Minister of Finance 2010–11; co-f. Nigerian Leadership Initiative 2006. *Address:* c/o Ministry of Finance, Ahmadu Bello Way, Central Area, PMB 14, Garki, Abuja, Nigeria.

OLVER, Sir Richard (Dick) Lake, Kt, BSc, FREng, FICE; British engineer and business executive; *Non-Executive Chairman, BAE Systems plc;* b. 1947; m.; two d.; joined British Petroleum (BP) 1973, apptd Vice-Pres. BP Pipelines Inc., BP North America 1979, Div. Man. of Corp. Planning 1985, Gen. Man. Gas, BP Exploration Europe 1988, Chief of Staff to Chair., Head of Corp. Strategy 1990, CEO BP Exploration USA 1992, Deputy CEO BP Exploration 1995, CEO BP Exploration and Production Div. 1998–2002, apptd Deputy Group CEO BP plc 2003–04; Chair. (non-exec.) BAE Systems plc 2004–; Dir (non-exec.) Reuters, then Thomson Reuters PLC 1997–2007; Sr Adviser, Clayton, Dubilier & Rice, HSBC; mem. Prime Minister's Business Advisory Group and India/UK CEO Forum, GLF Global Leadership Foundation, Trilateral Comm.; UK Business Amb.; Fellow, Royal Acad. of Eng 2005, mem. Council 2006–09; Hon. DSc (City Univ.) 2004, (Cranfield Univ.) 2006. *Leisure interests:* grandchildren, education, sailing, ballet, fine arts. *Address:* BAE Systems plc, 6 Carlton Gardens, London, SW1Y 5AD,

England (office). *Telephone:* (1252) 373232 (office). *Fax:* (1252) 383000 (office). *E-mail:* info@baesystems.com (office). *Website:* www.baesystems.com (office).

OMAAR, Mohamed Abdullahi; Somali politician; *Minister of Foreign Affairs, 'Somaliland';* b. 1 July 1953; s. of Abdullahi Omaar; Minister for Higher Educ. and Heritage, 'Somaliland' –2010, Minister of Foreign Affairs 2010–; mem. Kulmiye Party. *Address:* Ministry of Foreign Affairs, Hargeisa, Somalia (office). *Telephone:* 252-225-3871 (office). *Fax:* 252-225-3871 (office). *Website:* www.somalilandgov.com (office).

O'MAHONY, W. I. (Liam), BE, BL, MBA, FIEI; Irish business executive; *Chairman, Smurfit Kappa Group plc;* b. 1947; began career as civil engineer in Repub. of Ireland and UK; joined CRH plc 1971, worked in Middle East, Africa and USA for CRH Cos, sr man. positions include COO of US Operations, Man.-Dir Repub. of Ireland and UK Group Cos 1991–94, mem. Bd of Dirs 1992–2011, Chief Exec. Oldcastle Inc., USA 1994–2000, Dir 2000–, Group Chief Exec. 2000–08; mem. Bd of Dirs Smurfit Kappa Group plc 2007–, Chair. 2008–; mem. The Irish Man. Inst. Council, Harvard Business School European Advisory Bd, USA. *Address:* Smurfit Kappa Group, Beech Hill, Clonskeagh, Dublin 4, Ireland (office). *Telephone:* (1) 202-7000 (office). *E-mail:* info@smurfitkappa.com (office). *Website:* www.smurfitkappa.com (office).

O'MALLEY, Bert W., MD; American biologist and academic; *Tom Thompson Distinguished Service Professor and Chairman, Department of Molecular and Cellular Biology, Baylor College of Medicine;* b. Pittsburgh, Pa; ed Univ. of Pittsburgh School of Medicine; Resident, Duke Univ. 1963–65; Clinical Assoc., NIH, Bethesda, Md 1965–67, Head of Molecular Biology Section 1967–69; Luscious Birch Prof. and Dir Reproductive Biology Center, Vanderbilt Univ. 1969–73; Tom Thompson Distinguished Service Prof. of Molecular and Cellular Biology, Baylor Coll. of Medicine 1973–, also Chair. Dept of Molecular and Cellular Biology; mem. NAS, Inst. of Medicine, Endocrine Soc. (Pres. 1985); Fellow AAAS, American Acad. of Arts and Sciences, American Acad. of Microbiology; several hon. doctorates, including (Karolinska Inst., New York Univ., Nat. Univ. of Ireland, Univ. of Maryland, Univ. of Pittsburgh, Univ. of Athens, Greece); Ernst Oppenheimer Award, British Endocrine Soc. Award, Carl G. Hartman Award 2007, Nat. Medal of Science 2008, Ernst Schering Prize 2011. *Publications:* more than 600 publs; holder of 19 patents. *Address:* Baylor College of Medicine, Interdepartmental Program in Cell and Molecular Biology, One Baylor Plaza, Room N204Q, Houston, TX 77030, USA (office). *Telephone:* (713) 798-6205 (office). *Fax:* (713) 798-5599 (office). *E-mail:* berto@bcm.edu (office). *Website:* www.bcm.edu (office).

O'MALLEY, Desmond Joseph, BCL; Irish politician, solicitor and banker; b. 2 Feb. 1939, Limerick; s. of Desmond J. O'Malley and Una O'Malley; m. Patricia McAleer 1965; two s. four d.; ed Crescent Coll., Limerick, Nat. Univ. of Ireland; practised as solicitor 1962; mem. Dáil (House of Reps) for Limerick East 1968–2002; mem. Limerick Corpn 1974–77; Parl. Sec. to Taoiseach (Prime Minister) and to Minister for Defence 1969–70; Minister for Justice 1970–73; Opposition Spokesman on Health 1973–75, on Industry and Commerce 1975–77; Minister for Industry and Commerce 1977–81, 1989–92, for Energy 1977–79; Opposition Spokesman on Industry and Commerce 1981–82; Minister for Trade, Commerce and Tourism 1982; Opposition Spokesman on Energy 1983–84; fmrly Fianna Fáil (expelled 1984); Co-founder and Leader of Progressive Democrats Party 1985–93; Chair. Foreign Affairs Cttee, Irish Parl. 1997–2002; Alt. Dir for Denmark, Ireland, Lithuania and Macedonia, EBRD 2003–10; Hon. LLD (Univ. of Limerick) 2003. *Leisure interests:* golf, horse racing.

O'MALLEY, Martin Joseph, JD; American lawyer, politician and state governor; *Governor of Maryland;* b. 18 Jan. 1963, Washington, DC; m. Catherine Curran (Katie) O'Malley 1990; two s. two d.; ed Gonzaga Coll. High School, Catholic Univ. of America, Univ. of Maryland School of Law; worked for Gary Hart for President campaign; named by US Congresswoman Barbara Mikulski as her state field dir for her primary and gen. election campaigns for US Senate 1986, served as Legis. Fellow in Senator Mikulski's office 1987–88; Asst State's Attorney for City of Baltimore 1988–90; cand. for Maryland State Senate in 43rd Dist 1990; mem. Baltimore City Council for 3rd Dist 1991–99, served as Chair. Legis. Investigations Cttee, Taxation and Finance Cttee; Mayor of Baltimore 1999–2006; Gov. of Maryland 2007–; Democrat; named by Esquire Magazine as The Best Young Mayor in the Country 2002, named by TIME magazine as one of America's Top 5 Big City Mayors 2005. *Address:* Office of the Governor, 100 State Circle, Annapolis, MD 21401-1925, USA (office). *Telephone:* (410) 974-3901 (office). *Fax:* (410) 974-3275 (office). *E-mail:* info@martinomalley.com. *Website:* www.gov.state .md.us (office); www.martinomalley.com.

O'MALLEY, HE Cardinal Sean Patrick, OFM Cap.; American ecclesiastic; *Archbishop of Boston;* b. 29 June 1944, Lakewood, Ohio; ordained priest of Order of Friars Minor Capuchin 1970; Coadjutor Bishop of St Thomas, US VI 1984–85, Bishop of St Thomas 1985–92; Bishop of Fall River, Mass 1992–2002; Bishop of Palm Beach, Fla 2002–03; Archbishop of Boston 2003–; cr. Cardinal (Cardinal-Priest of Santa Maria della Vittoria) 2006; participated in Papal Conclave 2013. *Address:* Cardinal's Residence, 2121 Commonwealth Avenue, Boston, MA 02135-3192, USA (office). *Telephone:* (617) 782-2544 (office). *Fax:* (617) 782-8358 (office). *Website:* www.rcab.org (office).

O'MALLEY, Thomas D., BA; American business executive; *Chairman, PBF Energy Company LLC;* b. 1942, New York, NY; m. Mary Alice Lucey; four c.; ed Manhattan Coll.; mailroom employee, Philipp Brothers 1963–66, commodities trader, Europe, Salomon Inc. 1966–75, various exec. roles at Salomon Inc. and its predecessor cos, Philbro/Salomon and Philipp Brothers, including Vice-Chair., Chief Exec. of oil-trading div., Chair. Phibro Energy, mem. parent co.'s Bd of Dirs and Exec. Cttee 1975–86; Chair. and CEO Argus Resources 1986–88, Chair. Comfed Bancorp (a holding of Argus) 1988–89; Pres. Tosco Corpn 1989–90, 1993–97, Chair. and CEO 1990–2001, Vice-Chair. Phillips Petroleum Co. (following acquisition of Tosco Corpn) 2001–02; Chair. Premcor Inc. 2002–05, Sr Exec. employee Jan.–Sept. 2005, CEO 2002–04, Pres. 2002–03; Pres. and CEO Argus Services Corpn 2005–06; CEO Petroplus Holdings 2006–08, Chair. 2008–11; fmr CEO PBF Energy Co. LLC, currently Chair. *Address:* 1 Sylvan Way, Parsippany, NJ 07054-3887, USA (office). *Telephone:* (973) 455-7500 (office). *E-mail:* info@ pbfenergy.com (office). *Website:* www.pbfenergy.com (office).

OMAMO, Rachelle Awuor, LLB; Kenyan lawyer, diplomatist and politician; *Secretary for Defence;* b. 1963, Nairobi; d. of William Odongo Omamo (fmr Minister of Agric.); ed Univ. of Kent at Canterbury, UK; 27 years' experience as advocate, High Court of Kenya, becoming Sr Counsel; fmr Amb. to Portugal, Vatican City and Serbia, fmr Perm. Rep. of Kenya to UNESCO, Amb. to France –2013; Sec. (Minister) for Defence 2013–; Dir Mo-Consult Ltd (consultancy firm); fmr mem. bds and governing councils of several non-profit orgs; legal counsel for numerous govt task forces and comms including Task Forces on Establishment of the Truth and Reconciliation Comm. for Kenya and on Review of Landlord and Tenant Legislation; Assisting Counsel to Ndungu Comm. on Illegal/Irregular Allocation of Public Land; fmr Chair. Law Soc. of Kenya (first woman); fmr Vice-Pres. E African Law Soc. *Address:* Ministry of State for Defence, Ulinzi House, Lenana Road, POB 40668-00100, Nairobi, Kenya (office). *Telephone:* 2721100 (office). *E-mail:* info@mod.go.ke (office). *Website:* www.mod.go.ke (office).

OMAND, Sir David Bruce, Kt, GCB, KCB, BA; British civil servant (retd); b. 15 April 1947, Glasgow, Scotland; s. of the late J. Bruce Omand and Esther Omand; m. Elizabeth Wales 1971; one s. one d.; ed Glasgow Acad., Corpus Christi Coll., Cambridge; Asst Prin., Ministry of Defence 1970, Pvt. Sec. to Chief Exec. (Procurement Exec.) 1973, Asst Pvt. Sec. to Sec. of State 1973–75, 1979–80, Prin. 1975, Asst Sec. 1981, Pvt. Sec. to Sec. of State 1981–82; Asst Under-Sec. of State (Man. Strategy) 1988–91, Deputy Under-Sec. of State (Policy) Ministry of Defence 1993–96, Dir Govt Communications HQ 1996–97; Perm. Under-Sec. of State, Home Office 1998–2001; Defence Counsellor FCO UK Del. to NATO, Brussels 1985–88; Chair. Centre for Man. and Policy Studies, Cabinet Office 2001–02, Perm. Sec. Cabinet Office, also Security and Intelligence Co-ordinator 2002–05 (retd); Visiting Prof., King's Coll. London 2005–; Deputy Chair. Windsor Leadership Trust; mem. Bd Natural History Museum 2006–; British Soc. for History and Math. Prize 2003. *Publication:* Securing the State 2010. *Leisure interests:* opera, walking. *Address:* c/o Windsor Leadership Trust, Gainsborough House, 59–60 Thames Street, Windsor, Berks., SL4 1TX, England.

OMAR, Tan Sri Dato' Seri Abu Hassan Bin Haj, MA, KMN, PPT, SMP, DSDK, JMN, DPTS; Malaysian politician and business executive; *Chairman, BASIS Holdings Sdn Bhd;* b. 15 Sept. 1940, Bukit Belimbing, Kuala Selangor; m. Datin Wan Noor bint Haj Daud; five c.; ed Klang High School, Malay Coll. Kuala Kangsar, Univ. of Hull, UK; fmr Deputy State Sec. State of Selangor and Deputy Sec.-Gen. Ministry of Land and Fed. Devt; mem. Parl. 1978–; Parl. Sec. Ministry of Commerce and Industry 1978–80; Deputy Minister of Defence 1980–81, of Transport 1981–84; Minister of Welfare Services 1984–86, of Fed. Territory 1986–87, of Foreign Affairs 1987–91, of Domestic Trade and Consumer Affairs 1991–97; Menteri Besar (Chief Minister) of Selangor 1997–2000; mem. (for Permatang) Selangor State Ass. 1997–2004; currently Chair. OILFAB Sdn Bhd, BASIS Holdings Sdn Bhd; Ind. Dir (non-exec.), LBS Bina Group Bhd 2004–13; mem. Selangor Royal Council (Dewan DiRaja Selangor); Pro-Chancellor Universiti Industri Selangor (UNISEL); mem. UMNO Supreme Council from 1978; Hon. DSc (Hull) 1985; recipient of several awards. *Leisure interests:* gardening, photography. *Address:* Wisma BASIS, Metro Centre, No. 11–15, Jalan 8/146, Bandar Tasik Selatan Sungai Besi, 57000 Kuala Lumpur, Malaysia. *Telephone:* (3) 9051-6999. *Fax:* (3) 9051-6888. *E-mail:* info@basis.com.my. *Website:* www.basis.com.my.

OMAR, Chamassi Said; Comoran politician; fmr naval officer; Prime Minister of Comoros 1998–99 (dismissed by Pres. Abdallah Ibrahim). *Address:* BP XXX, Moroni, Comoros.

OMAR, Mullah Mohammad; Afghan fmr guerrilla leader and politician; b. 1959, Uruzgan Prov.; m. Guljana Omar 1995; two other wives; five c. (one s. died 2001); studied in several Islamic schools; joined jihad (Islamic holy war) against Soviet occupation in 1980s, became a deputy chief commdr Mujahidin guerrilla movt fighting Soviet occupation forces; helped form, recruit for and consolidate the Taliban regime (with Osama bin Laden) 1994; declared Afghanistan a 'complete' Islamic State (Islamic Emirate of Afghanistan); Leader Taliban-apptd Interim Council of Ministers 1996–2001, given title Emir al-Mo'menein (Commdr of the Faithful); went into hiding during US-led mil. action against Taliban and al-Qa'ida targets in Afghanistan, following suspected al-Qa'ida terrorist attacks in USA Sept. 2001.

OMAR, Tan Sri Dato' Napsiah binti, MSc; Malaysian politician and regional organization official; b. 21 April 1943; m. (husband deceased); ed Australian Nat. Univ., Cornell Univ., USA; Admin. Officer, Fed. Land Devt Authority, Kuala Lumpur 1967–69; started Women's and Family Devt Programme 1967; Lecturer, Agricultural Coll. Malaya Serdang 1972; Co-ordinator, Food Tech., Home and Food Tech. Div. Agricultural Univ. 1972–73, Deputy Head, Dept of Home Tech. 1973–76, Head, Dept of Human Devt Studies 1978–80, Warden, Fourth Residential Coll. 1974–82; Assoc. Prof. Dept of Human Devt Studies 1981; Deputy Minister of Housing and Local Govt 1981–87; Minister of Public Enterprises 1988–90; mem. Barisan Nasional—UMNO party, mem. Exec. Cttee UMNO Women Malaysia and Chair. of Unity Bureau, UMNO Malaysia 1987–90; Chair. Econ. Bureau, UMNO 1986–88; Senator; Treas. Asian Forum of Parliamentarians on Population and Devt (AFPPD); Chair. Bd of Dirs and mem. Exec. Cttee, Nat. Population and Family Devt Bd (LPPKN). *Address:* Pengerusi LPPKN, Tingkat 21, Bangunan LPPKN, No. 12B, Jalan Raja Laut, 50350 Kuala Lumpur, Malaysia. *Telephone:* (3) 26937555. *Fax:* (3) 26937250. *E-mail:* napsiah@lppkn.gov.my. *Website:* www.lppkn.gov.my.

O'MEARA, Mark Francis; American professional golfer; b. 13 Jan. 1957, Goldsboro, NC; m. Alicia O'Meara; one s. one d.; ed Long Beach State Univ.; professional golfer 1980–; won US Amateur Championship 1979, Greater Milwaukee Open 1984, Bing Crosby Pro-Am 1985, Hawaiian Open 1985, Fuji Sankei Classic 1985, Isuzu Kapalua International (unofficial PGA Tour event) 1985, Australian Masters 1986, Lawrence Batley International 1987, AT&T Pebble Beach Nat. Pro-Am 1989, 1990, 1992, 1997, RMCC Invitational (with Curtis Strange) 1989, H-E-B Tex. Open 1990, Walt Disney World/Oldsmobile Classic 1991, Tokai Classic 1992, Argentine Open 1994, Fred Meyer Challenge (with John Cook) 1994, 2000, Honda Classic 1995, Bell Canada Open 1995, Mercedes Championships 1996, Greater Greensboro Open 1996, Buick Invitational 1997, US Masters 1998, The Open Championship 1998, Cisco World Match Play Championship (European unofficial event) 1998, Skins Game (US unofficial

event) 1998, 2002, World Cup of Golf (with Tiger Woods) 1999, Dubai Desert Classic 2004, Champions Challenge (with Mike Reid) 2007, Liberty Mutual Insurance Legends of Golf (with Nick Price) 2010, Constellation Energy Senior Players Championship 2010; best finish 2002, second in Buick Invitational and second in Buick Open; mem. Ryder Cup team 1985, 1989 (tie), 1991 (winners), 1997, 1999 (winners), Alfred Dunhill Cup team 1985, 1986, 1987, 1996 (winners), 1997, 1998, 1999, Presidents Cup team 1996 (winners), 1998, World Cup team 1999 (winners); Hon. mem. Royal Birkdale Golf Club 2013; All-American Rookie of Year, Long Beach State Univ. 1981, PGA Tour Player of the Year 1998. *Leisure interests:* golf course consulting, hunting, fishing. *Address:* Mark O'Meara Design, 12386 North Deer Mountain Blvd, Deer Mountain, UT 84036, USA. *Telephone:* (877) 663-1998. *Fax:* (435) 333-1999. *E-mail:* info@markomearadesign.com. *Website:* www.markomearadesign.com; www.pgatour.com/players/player.01887.html.

OMI, Koji; Japanese politician; b. 14 Dec. 1932, Gunma Pref.; ed Faculty of Commercial Science, Hitotsubashi Univ.; joined Ministry of Int. Trade and Industry (MITI) 1956, Consul, Consulate Gen., New York 1970–74, Dir S Asia and Eastern Europe Div., Trade Policy Bureau 1974, Dir Small Enterprise Policy Div., Small and Medium Enterprise Agency (SMEA) 1978, Dir Admin. Div., Science and Tech. Agency 1979–81, Dir-Gen. Guidance Dept, SMEA 1981–82 (retd from MITI); elected mem. House of Reps 1983, Parl. Vice-Minister for Finance 1990; Dir-Gen. Research and Investigation Bureau, LDP 1991–92, Dir-Gen. Commerce and Industry Policy Bureau 1992–93, Dir-Gen. Science and Tech. Policy Bureau 1993–94, LDP Deputy Sec.-Gen. 1994–95; Chair. House Standing Cttee on Finance 1995, Sec.-Gen. Research Council for Promotion of Science and Tech.-oriented Nation, LDP 1996, Dir Special Cttee on Taxation System Problems and Relatives Matters 1996, mem. Standing Cttee on Budget 1996, Deputy Chair. Policy Research Council, LDP 1996–97, Dir-Gen. Election Bureau, LDP 1998–99, Dir Interest Group Policy Div., LDP 1999–2000, Acting Chair. Party Org. HQ, LDP 1999–2000, Acting Sec.-Gen., LDP 2000–01, Chair. LDP Research Comm. to Promote Research and Establish a Nation of Innovative Science and Tech. 2002, Deputy Chair. LDP Gen. Council 2004, Chair. LDP Research Comm. on Oil, Resources and Energy 2005; Minister of State for Econ. Planning 1997–98, Minister of State for Okinawa and Northern Territories Affairs and Minister of State for Science and Tech. Policy 2001, Minister of Finance 2006–07. *Address:* Liberal-Democratic Party (Jiyu-Minshuto), 1-11-23, Nagata-cho, Chiyoda-ku, Tokyo 100-8910, Japan (office). *Telephone:* (3) 3581-6211 (office). *E-mail:* koho@ldp.jimin.or.jp (office). *Website:* www.jimin.jp (office).

OMI, Shigeru, MD, PhD; Japanese molecular biologist, academic and fmr international organization executive; *Professor of Public Health, Jichi Medical University;* b. 11 June 1949, Tokyo; m.; one s. one d.; ed American Field Service scholarship to Potsdam Central High School, New York, Keio Univ., Jichi Medical School; Medical Officer, Div. of Medical Affairs, Bureau of Public Health, Tokyo Metropolitan Govt (assigned as sole doctor on remote Pacific islands) 1978–87; Researcher, Div. of Immunology, Jichi Medical School 1987–89; Deputy Dir Office of Medical Guidance and Inspection, Bureau of Health Insurance, Ministry of Health and Welfare 1989–90; Medical Officer and Regional Adviser, Expanded Programme on Immunization, WHO Regional Office for the Western Pacific 1990–95, Dir Div. of Communicable Disease Prevention and Control 1995–98, Dir WHO Regional Office for Western Pacific 1999–2009, Dir Emer. 2009–; currently Prof. of Public Health, Jichi Medical School; Exec. Ed. Polio Eradication in the Western Pacific Region 2002; Hon. Fellow, Hong Kong Coll. of Community Medicine 2002, Hon. mem. Keio Univ. 2004; Dr hc (Mongolian Nat. Medical Univ.) 2002; 37th Kojima Award 2001. *Publication:* SARS: How a Global Epidemic Was Stopped (ed.) 2006. *Address:* Jichi Medical University, Jichi Medical University Hospital, 3311-1 Yakushiji, Shimotsuke-shi, Tochigi-ken, 329-0498, Japan (office). *Telephone:* (2) 8544-2111 (office). *E-mail:* omis@jichi.ac.jp (office). *Website:* www.jichi.ac.jp/dph/e (office).

OMIDYAR, Pierre M., BS; French/American internet executive; *Chairman, eBay Incorporated;* b. Paris; m.; ed Tufts Univ., Mass; family moved to Washington, DC, when he was a child; joined Claris (Apple Computer subsidiary) and wrote MacDraw application 1988–91; co-f. Ink Development (later renamed eShop and acquired by Microsoft) 1991; software engineer, General Magic 1991–96; Founder and Chair. eBay 1995–; Founder Omidyar Network (charity), now Chair. and CEO; est. (with Tufts Univ.) Univ. Coll. of Citizenship and Public Service; mem. Bd of Trustees Tufts Univ., Santa Fe Inst.; Co-founder Peer News Inc. (operating as Ginx) 2008; Fellow, American Acad. of Arts and Sciences 2009–. *Address:* Omidyar Network, 1991 Broadway, Suite 200, Redwood City, CA 94063; eBay Inc., 2145 Hamilton Avenue, San Jose, CA 95125, USA (office). *Telephone:* (408) 376–7400 (office). *Fax:* (408) 376–7401 (office). *Website:* www.ebay.com (office); www.omidyar.net.

OMIYA, Hideaki; Japanese business executive; *Chairman, Mitsubishi Heavy Industries;* joined Mitsubishi Heavy Industries in 1969, served in several exec. positions including Deputy Head of Industrial Machinery Div. and Head of Air Conditioning and Refrigeration Systems Div., mem. Bd of Dirs and Sr Exec. Vice-Pres. 2007–08, Pres. and CEO Mitsubishi Heavy Industries 2008–13, Chair. 2013–. *Address:* Mitsubishi Heavy Industries, 16-5, Konan 2-chome, Minato-ku, Tokyo 108-8215, Japan (office). *Telephone:* (3) 6716-3111 (office). *Fax:* (3) 6716-5800 (office). *E-mail:* info@mhi.co.jp (office). *Website:* www.mhi.co.jp (office).

OMIYI, Basil Efoise; Nigerian oil industry executive; joined Shell Petroleum Devt Co. of Nigeria Ltd (SPDC) as petroleum engineer 1970, worked in Nigeria, UK and the Netherlands, apptd to Bd of SPDC as Gen. Man. Relations and Environment 1996–99, External Affairs Dir 1999–2002, Production Dir 2002–04, Man. Dir Shell Petroleum Devt Co. of Nigeria Ltd (first Nigerian) 2004–09. *Address:* c/o Shell Petroleum Development Company of Nigeria Ltd, Freeman House, 21/22 Marina, PMB 2418, Lagos, Nigeria.

OMOROGBE, Oluyinka Osayame, LLB, LLM, BL, MCIArB; Nigerian academic, legal practitioner and energy consultant; *Corporation Secretary and Legal Adviser, Nigerian National Petroleum Corporation;* b. (Oluyinka Osayame Ighodaro), 21 Sept. 1957, Ibadan; d. of Samuel O Ighodaro and Irene E. B. Ighodaro; m. Allan Omorogbe 1984; one s. two d.; ed Univ. of Ife, London School of Econs, UK; Nat. Youth Service 1979–80; pvt. legal practitioner 1980–81; Lecturer,

Dept of Jurisprudence and Int. Law, Univ. of Benin 1983–90, Head of Dept 1988–89; Sr Lecturer, Univ. of Lagos 1990–; Dir Centre for Petroleum, Environment and Devt Studies, Lagos 1996–; e-publr and consultant 2001–; Prof., Dept of Public and Int. Law, Ibadan Univ. 2002–09, Dean 2005–09; Corpn Sec. and Legal Adviser, Nigerian Nat. Petroleum Corpn 2009–; mem. Exec. Cttee Petroleum Energy and Mining Law Asscn of Nigeria 1986; mem. Acad. Advisory Group, Section on Energy and Natural Resources Law, Int. Bar Asscn, African Soc. of Int. and Comparative Law; mem. Oil and Gas Sector Reform Implementation Cttee (OGIC) 1999; Treas. Nigerian Soc. of Int. Law 1994–97, Gen. Sec. 1997. *Publications:* The Oil and Gas Industry: Exploration and Production Contracts 1997, Oil and Gas Law in Nigeria 2000; numerous articles on petroleum and energy law and int. econ. law in int. journals and books. *Leisure interests:* cooking, baking, handicrafts. *Address:* Nigerian National Petroleum Corporation, NNPC Towers, Central Business District, Herbert Macaulay Way, PMB 190, Garki, Abuja, Nigeria (office). *Website:* www.nnpcgroup.com (office).

OMRAN, Mohammed Hassan, BEng; United Arab Emirates telecommunications industry executive; *Chairman, Emirates Telecommunications Corporation (Etisalat);* ed Cairo Univ., Egypt; joined Emirates Telecommunications Corpn PJSC (Etisalat) 1977, Area Man., Ras al-Khaimah 1982–84, Deputy Gen. Man. Etisalat 1984–99, Sr Exec. Vice-Pres. 1999–2004, CEO 2004–05, Chair. 2005–; Chair. Canar Telecommunications Co., Thuraya Telecommunications Co. 2007–; Lifetime Achievement Award, Abu Dhabi Econ. Forum 2008, Outstanding Achievement Award, CEO Magazine 2008, Chair. of the Year, Int. Business Awards 2010, Chair. of the Year, World Communications Awards 2010, Lifetime Achievement Award, Middle East Business Leaders Awards 2010, ranked by Arabian Business amongst the Power 500: The Worlds's Most Influential Arabs (131st) 2011, (67th) 2012. *Address:* Emirates Telecommunications Corporation, Etisalat Building, intersection of Zayed The 1st Street and Sheikh Rashid Bin Saeed Al Maktoum Street, PO Box 3838, Abu Dhabi, United Arab Emirates (office). *Telephone:* (2) 6283333 (office). *Fax:* (2) 6317000 (office). *E-mail:* info@etisalat.ae (office). *Website:* www.etisalat.ae (office).

OMRANA, Abderrahim, PhD; Moroccan economist and banker; b. 1947, Quezane; m.; three c.; with Govt Gen. Inspection Dept 1970; Head of Mission, Treasury Dept, Ministry of Finance 1973; Asst Lecturer, Univ. of Rabat 1974, Sr Lecturer 1975–78; Exec. Attaché, Banque Nationale pour le Développement Economique 1975–78; Lecturer, Univ. of Dakar, Senegal 1978–79; Deputy Dir Gen. African Centre for Monetary Studies and Fed. of African Cen. Banks 1978–87; Dir Gen. ICOMA and NASCOTEX 1989–95; Bank Sec., Islamic Devt Bank 1996–2001, 2003–, Dir Gen. Fund for Municipal Equipments 2001–03, later Adviser to Bank Pres. *Publications:* three books on finance, accountancy and modern econs and more than 100 articles on econs and finance. *Address:* c/o Islamic Development Bank, PO Box 5925, Jeddah 21432, Saudi Arabia (office).

OMURA, Satoshi, MS, PhD; Japanese biochemist and academic; *Distinguished Emeritus Professor and Special Coordinator, Research Project for Drug Discovery from Natural Products, Kitasato Institute;* b. 12 July 1935; ed Yamanashi Univ., Tokyo Univ. of Science, Univ. of Tokyo; Research Assoc., Yamanashi Univ. 1963–65; Researcher, Kitasato Inst. 1965–71, Prof. and Exec. Vice-Pres. 1984–90, Prof. and Pres. 1990–2008, Pres. Emer. 2008–12, Distinguished Emer. Prof. 2013–, also Special Coordinator, Research Project for Drug Discovery from Natural Products, Assoc. Prof., School of Pharmaceutical Sciences, Kitasato Univ. 1968–75, Prof. 1975–84, Prof., Kitasato Inst. for Life Sciences 2001–02, also Prof., Grad. School of Infection Control Sciences 2002–07; Max Tishler Prof. of Chemistry, Wesleyan Univ., USA 2005–; Pres. Joshibi Univ. of Art and Design 2007–; mem. Editorial Bd Journal of Antibiotics 1973–, Ed.-in-Chief 2004–13; mem. Japan Acad. 2001, American Chemical Soc., Japanese Biochemical Soc., Acad. des sciences 2002, Soc. for Industrial Microbiology and Biotechnology, USA; Hon. mem. American Soc. of Biochemistry and Molecular Biology, Chemical Soc. of Japan, Pharmaceutical Soc. of Japan, Japanese Soc. of Chemotherapy, Japan Soc. for Bioscience, Biotechnology and Agrochemistry; Chevalier, Ordre Nat. du Mérite (France) 1992, Chevalier, Légion d'honneur (France) 2007, Order of the Sacred Treasure, Gold and Silver Star (Nat. Medal of Japan) 2011; numerous awards including Japan Acad. Prize 1990, Robert Koch Gold Medal (Germany) 1997, Nakanishi Prize 2000, Tetrahedron Prize 2010, Arima Award 2011, Person of Cultural Merit (Japan) 2012, Norman R. Farnsworth ASP Research Achievement Award (American Soc. of Pharmacognosy) 2013, Canada Gairdner Global Health Award 2014. *Publications:* MacRolide Antibiotics: Chemistry, Biology and Practice (ed.) 1984, The Search for Bioactive Compounds from Microorganisms (ed.) 1992; co-author of over 40 books; more than 1,000 research papers. *Leisure interests:* golf, cross-country skiing, Japanese art. *Address:* Kitasato Institute for Life Sciences, Kitasato University, 9-1, Shirokane 5-chome, Minato-ku, Tokyo 108-8642, Japan (office). *Telephone:* (3) 5791-6101 (office). *Fax:* (3) 444-8360 (office). *E-mail:* omura-s@kitasato.or.jp (office). *Website:* www.kitasato.or.jp (office); www.satoshi-omura.info.

OMURA, Yukiko, BA (Econs), MA; Japanese banker, international business consultant and international organization official; b. Paris, France; ed Int. School of Geneva, Queen Mary, Univ. of London, UK, Boston Univ., USA; began career as project economist with IDB; spent ten years with J.P. Morgan, Tokyo, New York and London; fmrly Head of Emerging Markets, Asia, Lehman Brothers, Head of Credit Business, Asia; fmrly Head of Global Fixed Income and Derivatives UBS Japan; fmrly Head of Global Markets and Global Debt, Dresdner Bank, Japan; Founder, CEO and Exec. Dir HIV/AIDS Prevention Fund, London 2002–04; Exec. Vice-Pres. Multilateral Investment Guarantee Agency (MIGA), World Bank Group 2004–09; Vice-Pres. IFAD 2010–12; mem. Bd of Dirs GuarantCo Ltd, Private Infrastructure Development Group 2013–; mem. Advisory Bd CG/LA Infrastructure, LLC, Washington, DC 2008–, Columbus Frontiers Investment Management NV 2012–, Amatheon Holding NV 2013–. *Address:* CG/LA Infrastructure LLC, 1827 Jefferson Place NW, Washington, DC 20036, USA (office). *Telephone:* (202) 776-0990 (office). *Fax:* (202) 776-0994 (office). *E-mail:* info@cg-la.com (office). *Website:* www.cg-la.com (office).

OMURALIYEV, Maj.-Gen. Taalaybek; Kyrgyzstani army officer and politician; Deputy Chief, Maintenance Dept, Ministry of Defence, fmr Chief of Gen. Staff of Armed Forces; First Deputy Minister of Defence –2011, Minister of Defence 2011–14. *Address:* c/o Ministry of Defence, 720001 Bishkek, Logvinenko 26, Kyrgyzstan (office).

ONA ONDO, Daniel; Gabonese economist and politician; *Prime Minister and Head of Government;* b. 10 July 1945, Oyem; m.; seven c.; ed Univ. de Picardie, Univ. Paris 1 (Panthéon-Sorbonne 2), France; Assoc. Prof., Faculty of Law and Social Sciences, Omar Bongo Univ., Libreville; fmr Technical Adviser to Minister of Planning and Devt; apptd Adviser to Pres. Omar Bongo 1990; mem. Nat. Ass. (Parl.) for Woleu Dist No 4 1996–, First Vice-Pres., Nat. Ass. 2007–14; Minister-Del. under Minister of Health and Population 1997; Minister of Culture, Arts, Popular Educ., Youth and Sports 1999–2002, of Nat. Educ. 2002, of Posts and Telecommunications 2005; Prime Minister and Head of Govt 2014–; mem. Parti démocratique gabonais. *Address:* Office of the Prime Minister, BP 546, Libreville, Gabon (office). *Telephone:* 01-74-70-90 (office). *Fax:* 01-77-20-04 (office).

ONAIYEKAN, HE Cardinal John Olorunfemi, Lic. Sacr. Scrip., PhD; Nigerian ecclesiastic; *Archbishop of Abuja;* b. 29 Jan. 1944, Kabba, Kogi State; s. of Bartholomew Onaiyekan and Joann Onaiyekan; ed Mount St Michael's Secondary School, Aliade, Benue State, Ss. Peter & Paul Major Seminary, Bodija, Ibadan, completed his religious studies in Rome; ordained priest, Archdiocese of Lokoja 1969; taught at St Kizito's Coll., Isanlu 1969–71; Rector St Clement Jr Seminary, Lokoja 1971–77; Vice-Rector Ss. Peter & Paul 1977–82; Titular Bishop of Thunusuda 1982; Auxiliary Bishop of Ilorin 1982–84, Bishop of Ilorin 1984–90; Coadjutor Bishop of Abuja 1990–92, Bishop of Abuja 1992–94, Archbishop of Abuja 1994–; cr. Cardinal (Cardinal-Priest of San Saturnino) 2012; mem. Int. Theological Comm. 1980–85, Int. Catholic/Methodist Dialogue Comm. 1980–85; Vice-Pres. Catholic Bishops Conf. of Nigeria 1994–2000, Pres. 2000–07; Pres. Christian Asscn of Nigeria 2007–10; apptd a Synod Father for the Ordinary Gen. Ass. of Synod of Bishops on New Evangelization 2012; mem. Congregation for Doctrine of the Faith 2013–, Presidential Cttee of the Pontifical Council for the Family 2013–; named Pax Christi Int. Peace Laureate 2012. *Publications:* The Priesthood in Pre-monarchial Ancient Israel and among the Owe-Yoruba of Kabba: A Comparative Study (dissertation) 1976, The Shariah in Nigeria: A Christian Ciew, in Bulletin on Islam & Christian-Muslim Relations in Africa 1987. *Address:* Archbishop's House, Area 3, Section 2, PO Box 286, Garki, Federal Capital Territory, Abuja, Nigeria (office). *Telephone:* (803) 451-1635 (office).

ONANGA-ANYANGA, Parfait; Gabonese diplomatist and UN official; *Special Representative of the Secretary-General for Burundi and Head, United Nations Office in Burundi (BNUB);* b. 1960; m.; three c.; ed Univ. of Paris I Panthéon-Sorbonne, Univ. Omar Bongo, Libreville; served as First Counselor for Disarmament and Political Affairs, Perm. Mission to UN, New York; has held several exec. positions in the UN including Acting Sec., UN Standing Advisory Cttee for Security Questions in Cen. Africa, Prep. Comm. of Comprehensive Nuclear Test-Ban Treaty Org., Vienna and New York 1988–2004, Chef de Cabinet to Pres., 59th session of UN Gen. Ass. 2004, Special Adviser to Pres., 60th and 61st sessions of UN Gen. Ass. 2005–07, Dir UN Deputy Sec.-Gen.'s Office 2007–12, Special Rep. of the Sec.-Gen. for Burundi and Head of UN Office in Burundi (BNUB) 2012–. *Address:* United Nations Office in Burundi (BNUB), Chaussée d'Uvira, 6899 Bujumbura, Burundi (office). *E-mail:* karema@un.org (office). *Website:* bnub.unmissions.org (office).

ONDAATJE, Michael, OC, BA, MA; Canadian (b. Sri Lankan) writer, poet and filmmaker; b. 12 Sept. 1943, Colombo, Sri Lanka; s. of Philip Mervyn Ondaatje and Enid Doris Gratiaen; m. Linda Spalding; two s.; ed Dulwich Coll. London, Bishop's Univ., Queen's Univ. and Univ. of Toronto; has taught at Univ. of Western Ontario, York Univ., Univ. of Hawaii at Manoa, Brown Univ., Univ. of Toronto; Founding Trustee, Griffin Trust for Excellence in Poetry; Foreign Hon. mem. American Acad. of Arts and Letters. *Films include:* Sons of Captain Poetry 1970, Carry on Crime and Punishment 1970, The Clinton Special: A Film About The Farm Show 1974. *Publications include:* poetry: The Dainty Monsters 1967, The Man with Seven Toes 1968, The Collected Works of Billy the Kid (Gov.-Gen.'s Award) 1970, There's a Trick with a Knife I'm Learning to Do (Gov.-Gen.'s Award) 1979, Secular Love 1984, The Cinnamon Peeler 1991, Handwriting 1998; fiction: In the Skin of a Lion (City of Toronto Book Award) 1988, The English Patient (shared the Booker Prize for Fiction, Gov.-Gen.'s Award) 1992, Running in the Family 1993, The Collected Works of Billy the Kid 1996, Coming through Slaughter 1996, Anil's Ghost (Prix Médicis, Giller Prize, Gov.-Gen.'s Award, Kiriyama Pacific Rim Book Prize) 2000, The Conversations 2004, The Story 2005, Divisadero (Gov.-Gen.'s Literary Award) 2007, Divisadero 2008, The Cat's Table 2011. *Address:* c/o Trident Media Group LLC, 41 Madison Avenue, 36th Floor, New York, NY 10010, USA; 2275 Bayview Avenue, Toronto, ON N4N 3M6, Canada.

ONDAATJE, Sir (Philip) Christopher, Kt, CBE, OC, FRGS, FRSL; Canadian/British banker and author; *Chairman, The Ondaatje Foundation;* b. 22 Feb. 1933, Kandy, Ceylon (now Sri Lanka); s. of Philip Mervyn Ondaatje and Enid Doris Gratiaen; m. Valda Bulins 1959; one s. two d.; ed Blundell's School, Tiverton, Devon; Nat. and Grindlays Bank, London 1951–55; Burns Bros & Denton, Toronto 1955–56; Montrealer Magazine and Canada Month Magazine 1956–57; Maclean-Hunter Publishing Co. Ltd, Montreal 1957–62; Financial Post, Toronto 1963–65; Pitfield Mackay, Ross & Co. Ltd, Toronto 1965–69; Founder Pagurian Corpn Ltd 1967–89, Loewen, Ondaatje, McCutcheon & Co. Ltd 1970–88; Chair. The Ondaatje Foundation 1975–; major donor to Ondaatje Wing, Nat. Portrait Gallery, London 2000 and to the Ondaatje Theatre, Royal Geographical Soc.; mem. Advisory Bd Royal Soc. of Portrait Painters; Life mem. Somerset Co. Cricket Club; Trustee Portrait Fund, Nat. Portrait Gallery 2002–10; mem. Canadian Olympic Bobsled Team 1964; Hon. Vice-Pres. Royal Geographical Soc.; Hon. LLD (Dalhousie) 1994, Hon. DLit (Buckingham) 2003, (Exeter) 2003, (Macquarie) 2011. *Publications:* Olympic Victory 1964, The Prime Ministers of Canada (1867–1985) 1985, Leopard in the Afternoon 1989, The Man-Eater of Punanai 1992, Sindh Revisited 1996, Journey to the Source of the Nile 1998, Hemingway in Africa 2003, Woolf in Ceylon 2005, The Power of Paper 2006, The Glenthorne Cat 2008, The Last Colonial 2011. *Leisure interests:* golf, tennis, adventure, writing, photography. *Address:* Glenthorne, Countisbury, nr Lynton, N Devon, EX35 6NQ, England. *Website:* www.ondaatje.com

ONDEKANE, Jean-Pierre; Democratic Republic of the Congo politician; fmr leader rebel forces; Minister of Defence, Demobilization and War Veterans' Affairs

2003–05. *Address:* c/o Ministry of Defence, Demobilization and War Veterans' Affairs, BP 4111, Kinshasa-Gombe, Democratic Republic of the Congo (office).

ONDOA, Christine Joyce Dradidi, MD; Ugandan paediatrician and politician; *Adviser to the President on Health;* b. 21 Oct. 1968, Adjumani Dist; one s.; ed Makerere Univ.; paediatrician, Arua Hosp. 2000–09; Medical Supt and Sr Consultant, Jinja Hosp. 2009–10; Exec. Dir Mbarara Hosp. 2010–11; Minister of Health 2011–13; Adviser to the Pres. on Health 2013–. *Address:* Office of the President, Parliament Building, POB 7168, Kampala, Uganda (office). *Telephone:* (41) 4258441 (office). *Fax:* (41) 4256143 (office). *E-mail:* aak@statehouse.go.ug (office). *Website:* www.statehouse.go.ug (office).

ONDONGO, Gilbert; Republic of the Congo politician; *Minister of Finance, the Budget and the Public Portfolio;* b. 1960, Owando; Adviser to Pres. on the Economy, Finance and Budget 1997–2002, Sec. of State under Minister of the Economy, Finance and Budget 2002–05, Minister of Labour, Employment and Social Security 2005–09, of Finance, the Budget and the Public Portfolio 2009–; mem. Assemblée nationale (Parti Congolais du Travail) for Owando constituency 2012–; mem. PCT, mem. Political Bureau 2011–. *Address:* Ministry of Finance, the Budget and the Public Portfolio, avenue de l'Indépendance, croisement avenue Foch, BP 2083, Brazzaville, Republic of the Congo (office). *Telephone:* 281-45-24 (office). *Fax:* 281-43-69 (office). *E-mail:* mefb-cg@mefb-cg.net (office). *Website:* www.mefb-cg.org (office).

ONDZOUNGA, Rufin Pacôme; Gabonese politician; Minister of Housing and Town Planning 2009–11, also of the Environment and Sustainable Devt July–Dec. 2010, of Nat. Defence 2011–14. *Address:* c/o Ministry of National Defence, BP 13493, Libreville, Gabon (office).

O'NEAL, E. Stanley, BS, MBA; American business executive; b. 7 Oct. 1951, Roanoke, Ala; m. Nancy A. Garvey; two c.; ed Kettering Univ., Harvard Univ.; joined Treasury Dept, General Motors 1978; Dir of Investment Banking, Merrill Lynch 1986–91, Man. Dir of High Yield Finance and Restructuring 1991–95, Head of Capital Markets Group 1995–98, Exec. Vice-Pres. and Co-head of Corp. and Institutional Client Group 1997–99, Pres. US Pvt. Client Group 1999–2001, COO, mem. Bd of Dirs and Exec. Man. Cttee, Merrill Lynch 2001–07, CEO 2002–07, Chair. 2003–07 (retd); Co-head CICG 1997–, Chief Financial Officer 1998–2000, Pres. 2000–; Vice-Chair. Securities Industry Asscn; mem. Advisory Cttee New York Stock Exchange; mem. Bd of Dirs, Nasdaq Stock Market, General Motors Corpn 2001–06; mem. Bd Nat. Urban League, McDonald House of New York, Catalyst, Buckley School; mem. Advisory Council, Bronx Preparatory Charter School; named among Most Influential Black Americans, Ebony magazine 2006. *Address:* c/o Merrill Lynch & Company, Inc., 4 World Financial Center, New York, NY 10080, USA.

O'NEAL, Hon. Ralph T., OBE; British Virgin Islands business executive and politician; *Premier and Minister of Finance;* b. 1933; m. Edris O'Neal; Leader Virgin Islands Party; fmr civil servant and mem. of govt in various capacities; Deputy Chief Minister –1995; Chief Minister and Minister of Finance 1995–2003, 2007–; fmr Dir British Virgin Islands Red Cross; Founding mem. Rotary Club, Tortola. *Leisure interest:* watching cricket. *Address:* Office of the Premier, 33 Admin Drive, Wickham's Cay 1, Tortola VG1110, British Virgin Islands (office). *Telephone:* 468-3701 (office). *Fax:* 468-6413 (office). *E-mail:* premieroffice@gov.vg (office).

O'NEAL, Rodney, MEng; American business executive; *President and CEO, Delphi Corporation;* b. 1953; ed Kettering Univ., Stanford Univ.; joined General Motors (GM) 1971, Inland Div. 1976–91, Dir of Industrial Eng, Chevrolet-Pontiac-GM of Canada Group 1991–92, Gen. Dir of Mfg, Delphi Corpn (GM subsidiary spun off from parent 1999) 1992–94, Gen. Dir of Warehousing & Distribution, GM Service Parts Operations 1994–97, Vice-Pres. GM 1997, also Gen. Man. Delphi Interior Systems 1997–98, Vice-Pres. Delphi 1998–2000, also Pres. Delphi Interior Systems 1998–2000, Exec. Vice-Pres. Safety, Thermal & Electrical Architecture Sector 2000–03, Pres. Dynamics, Propulsion, and Thermal Sector 2003–05, mem. Bd of Dirs, Pres. and COO Delphi Corpn 2005–07, Pres. and CEO 2007–; mem. or fmr mem. Bd of Dirs Goodyear Tire & Rubber Co., Sprint/Nextel; fmr mem. Bd of Dirs Inroads Inc., Michigan Mfrs Asscn, Woodward Governor Co.; mem. Advisory Bd Focus: HOPE (charity); mem. Exec. Leadership Council. *Address:* Delphi Corpn, 5725 Delphi Drive, Troy, MI 48098-2815, USA (office). *Telephone:* (248) 813-2000 (office). *Fax:* (248) 813-2673 (office). *E-mail:* info@delphi.com (office). *Website:* www.delphi.com (office).

O'NEAL, Ryan; American actor; b. (Charles Patrick Ryan O'Neal), 20 April 1941, Los Angeles, Calif.; s. of Charles O'Neal and Patricia O'Neal (née Callaghan); m. 1st Joanna Moore 1963 (divorced 1967), one s. one d. Tatum O'Neal (q.v.); m. 2nd Leigh Taylor-Young 1967, one s.; one s. by the late Farrah Fawcett; ed US Army High School, Munich, Germany, UCLA Theatre Arts. *Films include:* The Big Bounce 1969, Love Story 1970 (David di Donatello Award 1972) 1970, The Wild Rovers 1971, What's Up, Doc? 1972, The Thief Who Came to Dinner 1973, Paper Moon 1973, Oliver's Story 1978, The Main Event 1979, So Fine 1981, Partners 1982, Irreconcilable Differences 1983, Fever Pitch 1985, Tough Guys Don't Dance 1986, Chances Are 1989, Faithful 1996, Hacks 1997, Burn Hollywood Burn 1997, Zero Effect 1998, Coming Soon 1999, The List 2000, People I Know 2002, Gentleman B. 2003, Malibu's Most Wanted 2003, Waste Land (short) 2007, Slumber Party Slaughter 2012, Knight of Cups 2014. *Television includes:* Dobie Gillis, Two Faces West, Perry Mason, The Virginian, This is the Life, The Untouchables, My Three Sons, Bachelor Father, Empire, Peyton Place, Epoch 2000, Miss Match (series) 2003, Desperate Housewives (series) 2005, Bones 2006–13, 90210 (series) 2010, Ryan & Tatum: The O'Neals (series) 2011. *Leisure interest:* boxing. *Address:* 21368 Pacific Coast Highway, Malibu, CA 90265, USA. *Telephone:* (310) 277-7351 (office). *Fax:* (310) 456-8310 (home).

O'NEAL, Shaquille Rashaun, BA, MBA; American professional basketball player (retd) and television presenter; b. 6 March 1972, Newark, NJ; s. of Philip A. Harrison and Lucille O'Neal; m. Shaunie Nelson 2002; four c.; two c. from previous relationships; ed Louisiana State Univ., Univ. of Phoenix; drafted in first round (first overall) by Orlando Magic 1992, played 1992–96; signed as free agent LA Lakers 1996, played 1996–2004; traded to Miami Heat 2004–08, with Phoenix Suns 2008–09, Cleveland Cavaliers 2009–10, Boston Celtics 2010–11 (retd); mem. four Nat. Basketball Asscn (NBA) championship teams (with Lakers 2000, 2001, 2002, with Heat 2006); Most Valuable Player in NBA Finals 2000, 2001, 2002; NBA Most Valuable Player 2000; 15-time NBA All-Star team 1993–98, 2000–07, 2009; NBA Rookie of the Year 1993; NBA scoring champion 1995, 2000; mem. gold-medal winning World Championship team 1994, US Olympic team, Atlanta 1996; commentator, Inside The NBA on Turner Network Television 2011–; Hon. US Deputy Marshal 2006; named one of 50 Greatest Players in NBA History 1996. *Films:* Blue Chips 1994, Kazaam 1996, Steel 1997, Freddy Got Fingered 2001, The Wash 2001, The Kid & I 2005, Scary Movie 4 2006, The House Bunny 2008. *Music:* has released five rap albums; owns record label Twism. *Publications:* Shaq Talks Back: The Uncensored Word on My Life and Winning in the NBA 2001. *Address:* c/o Inside the NBA, Turner Network Television, 1050 Techwood Drive, Atlanta, GA 30318, USA.

O'NEAL, Tatum; American actress; b. 5 Nov. 1963, Los Angeles, Calif.; d. of Ryan O'Neal and Joanna Moore; m. John McEnroe 1986 (divorced 1994); two s. one d. *Films include:* Paper Moon (Acad. Award for Best Supporting Actress) 1973, The Bad News Bears 1976, Nickelodeon 1976, International Velvet 1978, Little Darlings 1980, Circle of Two 1980, Prisoners 1981, Certain Fury 1985, Little Noises 1991, Basquiat 1996, The Scoundrel's Wife 2002, The Technical Writer 2003, My Brother 2006, Saving Grace B. Jones 2009, The Runaways 2010, Last Will 2010, This Is 40 2012, Mr. Sophistication 2013, Sweet Lorraine 2014, Squirrels to the Nuts 2015. *Television includes:* 15 and Getting Straight (film) 1989, Woman on Trial: The Lawrencia Bembenek Story (film) 1993, Sex and the City (series) 2003, 8 Simple Rules (series) 2004, Law & Order: Criminal Intent (series) 2004, Rescue Me (series) 2004–11, Wicked Wicked Games (series) 2006–07, Fab Five: The Texas Cheerleader Scandal (film) 2008. *Achievements include:* youngest person to ever win a competitive Acad. Award (1973). *Publication:* A Paper Life 2004. *Address:* c/o Innovative Artists, 1999 Avenue of the Stars, Suite 2850, Century City, CA 90067, USA (office).

O'NEIL, William Andrew, CMG, CM, BASc, FRSA, FREng, PEng; Canadian international public servant and engineer; b. 6 June 1927, Ottawa, Ont.; s. of Thomas Wilson O'Neil and Margaret O'Neil (née Swan); m. Dorothy Muir 1950; one s. two d.; ed Univ. of Toronto; engineer, Fed. Dept of Transport, Ottawa 1949–53, Resident Engineer, Special Projects Br. 1954; Div. Engineer, St Lawrence Seaway Authority 1955–59, Regional Dir 1960–63, Dir of Construction 1964–70; Deputy Admin., Marine Services, Canadian Marine Transportation Admin. 1970–79; Commr, Canadian Coast Guard and Deputy Admin., Marine Admin. 1975–89; Pres. St Lawrence Seaway Authority 1980–89; Chair. Council Int. Maritime Org. 1980–89, Sec.-Gen. 1990–2003; mem. Bd of Govs World Maritime Univ. 1983–; Chair. Governing Bd, Int. Maritime Law Inst., Malta 1991–2004; Canadian del. to Perm. Int. Asscn of Navigation Congresses 1984–90; Chair. Canadian Cttee Lloyd's Register of Shipping 1987–88; Chancellor World Maritime Univ. 1991–2004; Dir Canarctic Shipping Co.; Pres. Seaway Authority, Int. Bridge Corpn, Inst. of Chartered Shipbrokers 2004–, Videotel 2004–; mem. Bd Thousand Islands Bridge Authority 1980–90; mem. Asscn of Professional Engineers of Ont., American Soc. of Civil Engineers; Foreign mem. Royal Acad. of Eng (UK); Hon. Cdre, Canadian Coast Guard; Hon. mem. Canadian Maritime Law Asscn, Hon. Co. of Master Mariners (UK), Int. Maritime Pilots Asscn, Int. Fed. of Shipmasters' Asscns, NUMAST (Nat. Union of Marine Aviation and Shipping Transport Officers) (UK), Soc. of Naval Architects and Marine Engineers (USA), Singapore, Int. Asscn of Lighthouse Authorities, Co. of Master Mariners (India) 1998; Hon. Fellow, The Nautical Inst. (UK) 1996, Royal Inst. of Naval Architects 1998, Royal Inst. of Navigation; Hon. Titular mem. Comité Maritime Int.; Commdr, Ordre Nat. des Cèdres (Lebanon) 1995, Grand Cross, Orden Vasco Núñez de Balboa (Panama) 1998; Hon. Diploma, Canadian Coast Guard Coll.; Hon. LLD (Malta) 1993, (Memorial Univ. of Newfoundland) 1996; Hon. DSc (Nottingham Trent) 1994 (World Maritime Univ.) 2004; Eng Medal, Asscn of Professional Engineers of Ont. 1972, Distinguished Public Service Award, US Govt, Admirals' Medal 1994, Seatrade Personality of the Year Award 1995, NUMAST Award (UK) 1995, Professional Engineers Ont. Gold Medal 1995, mem. Eng Alumni Hall of Distinction, Univ. of Toronto 1996, Silver Bell Award, Seamen's Church Inst. New York 1997, Vice-Adm. Jerry Land Medal, Soc. of Naval Architects and Marine Engineers, USA 1999, Cdre Award, Conn. Maritime Asscn 1998, Dioscun Prize, Lega Navale Italiana (Italy) 1998, Halert C. Shepheard Award (USA) 2000, Medal for Distinguished Services to the Directorate Gen. for Maritime Affairs, Colombia 2001, CITIS Lifetime Achievement Award UK 2002, Freeman of the Worshipful Company of Shipwrights (hc) UK 2002, Golden Jubilee Medal, Canada 2002, '15 November 1817 Medal', Uruguay 2002. *Leisure interests:* reading, swimming, golf. *Address:* 2 Dean Wood Close, Woodcote, RG8 0PW, England. *Telephone:* (1491) 682897. *Fax:* (1491) 682625. *E-mail:* bill.oneil@imo.org.

O'NEILL, Brendan, MA, PhD, FCMA; British business executive; b. 6 Dec. 1948; s. of John Christopher O'Neill and Doris Monk; m. Margaret Maude O'Neill 1979; one s. two d.; ed Churchill Coll., Cambridge, Univ. of East Anglia; with Ford Motor Co. 1973–75, British Leyland 1975–81, BICC PLC 1981–83; Group Financial Controller Midland Bank 1983–87; Dir of Financial Control Guinness PLC 1987, Finance Dir 1988–90, Man. Dir Int. Regulation, United Distillers 1990–92, Guinness Brewing Worldwide 1993–97, CEO Guinness Diageo PLC 1997–98; COO ICI PLC 1998–99, CEO 1999–2003, Dir 1998–2003; Dir EMAP PLC 1995–, Diageo 1997–98, Endurance Specialty Holdings Ltd 2005–, Tyco International Ltd 2003–, Rank Group PLC; Life Gov., Imperial Cancer Research Fund 1994–2002; Trustee, Cancer Research UK 2002–; Fellow, Chartered Inst. of Man. Accountants. *Leisure interests:* music, reading. *Address:* c/o Board of Directors, Tyco International Ltd, 90 Pitts Bay Road, 2nd Floor, Pembroke HM 08, Bermuda.

O'NEILL, Michael E., BA, MBA; American banker; *Chairman, Citigroup Inc.;* b. 31 Oct. 1946, Santa Monica, Calif.; m. Trish O'Neill; two s.; ed Princeton Univ., Colgate W. Darden Grad. School of Business Admin, Univ. of Virginia; Lt with Marine Corps 1969–71; worked with Continental Bank 1974–84, in Belgium, Hong Kong and London (as Country Man.); ind. consultant 1985–88; returned to Continental Bank as Chief Financial Officer heading merger negotiations with BankAmerica; responsible for pvt. equity business BankAmerica Corpn following 1994 merger, Vice-Chair., Chief Financial Officer 1995, then Pres. Prin. Investing and Wealth Man. and mem. Policy Cttee Transition (fmr Chair.); Group Chief

Exec. and Dir Barclays PLC and Barclays Bank PLC Feb.– April 1999; mem. Bd of Dirs Bank of Hawaii Corpn 2000–04, Chair. and CEO 2000–04; mem. Bd of Dirs Citibank N.A. 2009–, Citigroup Inc. 2009–, Chair. Citi Holdings Oversight Cttee 2009–, Citibank N.A. 2011–, Citigroup Inc. 2012–; Trustee, Hawaii Pacific Univ., Honolulu Acad. of Arts; mem. Econ. Advisory Council, Fed. Reserve Bank of San Francisco. *Address:* Citigroup Inc., 399 Park Avenue, New York, NY 10043, USA (office). *Telephone:* (212) 559-1000 (office). *Fax:* (212) 793-3946 (office). *Website:* www.citigroup.com (office).

O'NEILL, Paul H., MPA; American business executive and fmr government official; *Principal, Value Capture;* b. 4 Dec. 1935, St Louis, Mo.; s. of John Paul O'Neill and Gayland Elsie Irvin; m. Nancy Jo Wolfe 1955; one s. three d.; ed Fresno State Coll., Indiana Univ., Claremont Grad. School and George Washington Univ.; computer systems analyst, US Veterans Admin.; later engineer, Morris-Knudsen, Anchorage, Alaska; mem. staff, Office of Man. and Budget 1967–77, Deputy Dir 1974–77; Vice-Pres. Planning, International Paper Co. 1977, Sr Vice-Pres. Planning and Finance 1981, Sr Vice-Pres. paperboard and packaging Div. 1983, Pres. 1985–87; Chair. and CEO Aluminum Co. of America (Alcoa) 1987–99, Chair. 1999–2000; Sec. of Treasury 2001–02; Co-founder and CEO Pittsburgh Regional Healthcare Initiative 2002–05, mem. Bd of Dirs 2002–; Founder and Prin., Value Capture (hosp. consulting firm) 2005–; fmr Dir Manpower Demonstration Research Group, Alcoa, Lucent Technologies, Eastman Kodak Co., RAND Corpn (fmr Chair.), American Enterprise Inst.; Dr hc (Clarkson Univ.) 1993. *Address:* c/o Board of Directors, Pittsburgh Regional Healthcare Initiative, 650 Smithfield Street, Centre City Tower, Suite 2400, Pittsburgh, PA 15222, USA.

O'NEILL, Peter Charles Paire, CMG; Papua New Guinea politician and fmr accountant; *Prime Minister;* b. 13 Feb. 1965, Pangia Dist; s. of the late Brian O'Neill; ed Ialibu High School, Goroka High School, Univ. of Papua New Guinea; Certified Practising Accountant 1989; Pres. Papua New Guinea Inst. of Certified Practising Accountants 1990; Pnr, Pratley and O'Neill Accounting Firm 1991–92; Exec. Chair. Pangia Enterprises Ltd 1993–97, Papua New Guinea Banking Corpn (PNGBC) 1997–99, Motor Vehicle Insurance Ltd 1997–99, Pacific MMI Insurance Ltd 1997–99, Finance Pacific Ltd 1997–99, Port Moresby Private Hosp. Ltd 1997–99, Remington Technologies Ltd 1999; MP for Ialibu-Pangia 2002–; Minister for Labour and Industrial Relations 2002–03, for Public Service and Leader of Govt Business 2003–04; Leader, People's Nat. Congress Party 2004–; Minister for Public Service 2007–10, for Finance and Treasury 2010–11, Works Minister 2011; Prime Minister 2011–; Minister of Finance Feb.–Aug. 2012. *Address:* Office of the Prime Minister, PO Box 639, Waigani, NCD, Papua New Guinea (office). *Telephone:* 3277316 (office). *Fax:* 3277328 (office). *E-mail:* chiefsectogov@pmnec .gov.pg (office). *Website:* www.pm.gov.pg (office).

O'NEILL, Robert John, AO, MA, BE, DPhil, FASSA; Australian historian, academic and fmr army officer; *Professor Emeritus, Australian National University;* b. 5 Nov. 1936, Melbourne, Vic.; s. of Joseph Henry O'Neill and Janet Gibbon O'Neill; m. Sally Margaret Burnard 1965; two d.; ed Scotch Coll. Melbourne, Royal Mil. Coll. of Australia, Melbourne Univ., Brasenose Coll. Oxford; served in Australian Army 1955–68, Fifth Bn, Royal Australian Regt, Viet Nam (despatches) 1966–67, Maj. 1967–68 (resgnd); Rhodes Scholar, Vic. 1961; Official Australian Historian for the Korean War 1969–82; Sr Fellow in Int. Relations, ANU 1969–77, Professorial Fellow 1977–82, Head of Strategic and Defence Studies Centre 1971–82, Prof. Emer. 2013–; Dir IISS, London 1982–87, Chair. Council 1996–2001; Chichele Prof. of the History of War, Univ. of Oxford 1987–2001, Dir Grad. Studies, Modern History Faculty 1990–92, Fellow, All Souls Coll. 1987–2001; Trustee, Imperial War Museum 1990–2001, Deputy Chair. 1996–98, Chair. 1998–2001; Gov. Ditchley Foundation 1989–2001, Int. Peace Acad. 1990–2001; Chair. Centre for Defence Studies, Centre for Australian Studies, Univ. of London 1990–95; Chair. Council of Australian Strategic Policy Inst. 2001–05; Deputy Chair. Grad. School of Govt, Univ. of Sydney 2001–05, Planning Dir, US Studies Centre 2006–07; Dir The Shell Transport and Trading Co. 1992–2002 and three mutual funds of Capital Group, Los Angeles 1988–2013, The Lowy Inst. 2001–12; mem. Advisory Bd Investment Co. of America 1988–2010; mem. Commonwealth War Graves Comm. 1990–2001, The Rhodes Trust 1995–2001; Fellow, Australian Inst. of Int. Affairs 2008; Hon. Fellow, Brasenose Coll. Oxford; Hon. Col 5th (V) Bn, The Royal Greenjackets 1993–99; mentioned in despatches, Viet Nam 1967; Hon. DLitt (ANU) 2001; Nat. Volunteer's Award 2012. *Publications include:* The German Army and the Nazi Party 1933–39 1966, Vietnam Task 1968, General Giap: Politician and Strategist 1969, The Strategic Nuclear Balance (ed.) 1975, The Defence of Australia: Fundamental New Aspects (ed.) 1977, Insecurity: The Spread of Weapons in the Indian and Pacific Oceans (ed.) 1978, Australian Dictionary of Biography Vols 7–12, 1891–1939, 1979–91 (co-ed.), New Directions in Strategic Thinking (co-ed.) 1981, Australia in the Korean War 1950–53: Vol. I Strategy and Diplomacy 1981, Vol. II Combat Operations 1985, Australian Defence Policy for the 1980s (co-ed.) 1982, Security in East Asia (ed.) 1984, The Conduct of East–West Relations in the 1980s (ed.) 1985, New Technology and Western Security Policy (ed.) 1985, Doctrine, the Alliance and Arms Control (ed.) 1986, East Asia, the West and International Security (ed.) 1987, Security in the Mediterranean (ed.) 1989, The West and the Third World (co-ed.) 1990, Securing Peace in Europe 1945–62 (co-ed.) 1992, War, Strategy and International Politics (co-ed.) 1992, Alternative Nuclear Futures 1999; articles in numerous journals. *Leisure interests:* local history, walking.

O'NEILL, Terence (Terry) Patrick; British photographer; b. 30 July 1938, London; s. of Leonard Victor O'Neill and Josephine Mary O'Neill; m. 1st Vera Day; one s. one d.; m. 2nd Faye Dunaway (q.v.) 1981; one s.; ed Gunnersbury Grammar School; fmr modern jazz drummer in leading London jazz clubs; army service as physical training instructor; subsequently took up photography, took first photographs of Beatles and Rolling Stones early 1960s; went to Hollywood 1962; has photographed leading actors and actresses, rock and classical musicians, political and sports personalities, mems. of British and other royal families; work published in The Sunday Times, Time, Life, Newsweek, Tatler, Elle, Paris Match, Stern etc. and other newspapers and magazines, in 52 countries and used on about 500 front covers worldwide a year. *Publication:* Legend S. *Leisure interests:* music, food, wine, art in all forms, literature.

O'NEILL, Thomas C., BComm, FCA; Canadian chartered accountant and business executive; *Chairman, BCE Inc. and Bell Canada;* ed Queen's Univ.;

chartered accountant 1970; client service partner for numerous multinationals, specializing in dual Canadian and US listed cos 1975–85; fmr Chair. and CEO Price Waterhouse Canada, then CEO PricewaterhouseCoopers LLP, Canada 1998–2000, COO PricewaterhouseCoopers LLP, Global 2000–02, CEO PricewaterhouseCoopers Consulting Jan.–May 2002, Chair. May–Oct. 2002; mem. Bd of Dirs BCE (Bell Canada Enterprises) Inc. 2003–, Chair. 2009–, Chair. Audit Cttee, also Chair. Bell Canada; mem. Bd of Dirs Adecco SA, Bank of Nova Scotia, Loblaw Cos Ltd, Nexen Inc.; fmr Vice-Chair. Bd Govs Queen's Univ. and past mem. Advisory Council of Queen's Univ. School of Business; mem. Bd St Michael's Hosp.; Fellow, Inst. of Corp. Dirs 2008; Hon. LLD (Queen's Univ.). *Address:* BCE Inc., 1 Carrefour Alexander Graham Bell, Building A, 4th Floor, Verdun, PQ H3E 3B3, Canada (office). *Telephone:* (514) 870-8777 (office). *Fax:* (514) 786-3970 (office). *E-mail:* bcecomms@bce.ca (office). *Website:* www.bce.ca (office).

O'NEILL OF BENGARVE, Baroness (Life Peer), cr. 1999, of The Braid in the County of Antrim; **Onora Sylvia O'Neill,** CH, CBE, BA, PhD, FBA, FMedSci; British philosopher and academic; *Chairman, Equality and Human Rights Commission;* b. 23 Aug. 1941, Aughafatten, Northern Ireland; d. of the late Sir Con O'Neill and Lady Garvey (née Rosemary Pritchard); m. Edward Nell 1963 (divorced 1976); two s.; ed St Paul's Girls' School, London, Somerville Coll., Oxford, Harvard Univ., USA; Asst Prof., Barnard Coll., Columbia Univ. 1970–76, Assoc. Prof. 1976–77; Lecturer, Univ. of Essex 1977–78, Sr Lecturer 1978–82, Reader 1982–87, Prof. 1987–92; Prin. Newnham Coll., Cambridge 1992–2006; Chair. Nuffield Foundation 1998–2010, Equality and Human Rights Comm. 2012–; Chair. Royal Irish Acad.'s Strategic Review Cttee May–Oct. 2012, Advisory Bd, Inst. of Philosophy, Insts of Advanced Study, Univ. of London; Pres. British Acad. 2005–09; mem. Council, Royal Inst. of Philosophy, Foundation for Science and Tech., British-Irish Asscn; Trustee, American Univ. of Sharjah, Sense about Science; Foreign mem. American Philosophical Soc. 2003, Leopoldina 2004, Norwegian Acad. of Sciences 2006; Fellow, Wissenschaftskolleg, Berlin 1989–90; Foreign Hon. mem. American Acad. of Arts and Sciences 1993, Austrian Acad. of Sciences 2002; Hon. Bencher of Gray's Inn 2002; Hon. MRIA 2003; Hon. FRS; Dr hc (East Anglia) 1995, (Essex) 1996, (Nottingham) 1999, (Aberdeen) 2001, (Dublin) 2002, (Oxford) 2003, (Ulster) 2003, London (2003), (Bath) 2004, (Stirling) 2005, (Queen's Univ. Belfast) 2005, (Edinburgh) 2006, (Cambridge) 2007, (Newcastle) 2008, (Lancaster) 2008, (York) 2009, (Harvard) 2010, (Glasgow) 2010, (Univ. Coll. London) 2010, (Nat. Univ. of Ireland) 2011. *Radio:* The Reith Lectures 2002. *Publications:* Faces of Hunger: An Essay on Poverty, Development and Justice 1986, Constructions of Reason: Explorations of Kant's Practical Philosophy 1989, Towards Justice and Virtue: A Constructive Account of Practical Reasoning 1996, Bounds of Justice 2000, Autonomy and Trust in Bioethics 2002, A Question of Trust 2002, Rethinking Informed Consent in Bioethcs (with Neil Manson); numerous articles in learned journals. *Leisure interests:* walking, talking. *Address:* House of Lords, Westminster, London, SW1A 0PW, England (office). *Telephone:* (20) 3117-0220 (office). *E-mail:* oon20@cam.ac.uk (home); sue.thomson@ equalityhumanrights.com (office). *Website:* www.parliament.uk/biographies/lords/ baroness-o'neill-of-bengarve/2441 (office).

ONG, Beng Seng; Singaporean hotel industry executive; *Owner and Managing Director, Hotel Properties Ltd;* m. Christina Ong; Owner and Man. Dir, Hotel Properties Ltd with 18 hotels in nine countries in Asia, Australia and Europe; acquired NatSteel through 98 Holdings consortium 2003. *Address:* Hotel Properties Ltd, 50 Cuscaden Road, #08-01, HPL House, 249724 Singapore (office). *Telephone:* 6734-5250 (office). *Fax:* 6732-0347 (office). *Website:* www.hplhotels.com (office).

ONG, John Doyle, LLB, MA; American business executive and fmr diplomatist; *Senior Visiting Policy Fellow, RTI International;* b. 29 Sept. 1933, Uhrichsville, Ohio; s. of Louis Brosee and Mary Ellen Ong (née Liggett); m. Mary Lee Schupp 1957; two s. one d.; ed Ohio State Univ., Harvard Univ.; admitted to Ohio Bar 1958; Asst Counsel, B.F. Goodrich Co., Akron 1961–66, Asst to Pres. Int. B.F. Goodrich Co., Akron 1966–69, Vice-Pres. 1969–70, Pres. 1970–72, Group Vice-Pres. 1972–73, Exec. Vice-Pres. 1973–74, Vice-Chair. 1974–75, Pres. 1975–84, Dir 1975–77, COO 1978–79, Chair., Pres. and CEO 1979–84, Chair. 1984–97, CEO 1984–96, Chair. Emer. 1997–; Amb. to Norway 2002–05; Sr Visiting Policy Fellow, RTI International 2006–; fmr mem. Bd of Dirs Cooper Industries, The Kroger Co., Ameritech Corpn, Nat. Alliance for Business; Chair. Ohio Business Roundtable 1994–97; Pres. Bd of Trustees, Western Reserve Acad., Hudson, Ohio 1977–95; Trustee, John S. and James L. Knight Foundation 1995–, Univ. of Chicago 1991–, Ohio Historical Soc. 1998–; Dr hc (Ohio State Univ., Kent State Univ., Univ. of Akron, South Dakota State Univ.); Humanities Award of Distinction, Ohio State Univ., Alumni Medal, Ohio State Univ. *Leisure interests:* fishing, hunting. *Address:* RTI International, 701 13th Street, NW, Suite 750, Washington, DC 20005-3967 (office); 230 Aurora Street, Hudson, OH 44236, USA (home). *Telephone:* (202) 728-2080 (office). *Fax:* (202) 728-2095 (office). *E-mail:* johndong@aol.com; listen@rti.org (office). *Website:* www.rti.org (office).

ONG, Keng Sen; Singaporean theatre director; *Artistic Director, TheatreWorks (Singapore) Limited;* ed Nat. Univ. of Singapore, Tisch Schools of the Arts, New York Univ.; trained as lawyer; Artistic Dir TheatreWorks, Singapore 1988–; f. Arts Networks Asia 1999; Co-Artistic Dir 'In Transit' Arts Festival (annual three-week festival) Berlin 2002–03; mem. Int. Council of The Asia Soc. of New York; Artist-in-Residence, New York Univ. Asian Pacific and American Studies Programme/Inst. 2002, Vienna Schauspielhaus 2003, Leverhulme Artist-in-Residence, Inst. for Advanced Studies in the Humanities, Univ. of Edinburgh 2008; Singapore Young Artist Award 1992, Singapore Cultural Medallion Award 2003, Distinguished Artist Award, Int. Soc. of Performing Arts 2003, Excellence for Singapore Award, Singapore Totalisator Bd 2003. *Productions include:* A Language of Their Own, New York Shakespeare Festival 1995, Lear, Tokyo 1997, The Silver River, Spoleto Festival, Charleston 2000, The Continuum: Beyond the Killing Fields, Int. Festival of Arts and Ideas, Yale Univ. and Singapore 2001, The Myths of Memory, Vienna 2003. *Address:* TheatreWorks (Singapore) Ltd, 72-13 Mohamed Sultan Road, Singapore 239007 (office). *Telephone:* 67377213 (office). *Fax:* 67377013 (office). *E-mail:* tworks@singnet.com.sg (office). *Website:* www.theatreworks.org.sg (office).

ONG, Keng Yong, LLB, MA; Singaporean international organization official and diplomatist; *Non-Resident Ambassador to Iran;* b. 6 Jan. 1954; m. Irene Tan Lee

Chen; ed Univ. of Singapore, Georgetown Univ., Washington, DC, USA; Chargé d'affaires, Embassy in Riyadh 1984–88; Counsellor, High Comm. in Kuala Lumpur 1989–91; Minister Counsellor and Deputy Chief of Mission, Embassy in Washington, DC 1991–94; Press Sec. to Minister of Foreign Affairs and Ministry Spokesperson 1994–95; High Commr to India and Amb. to Nepal 1996–98; Press Sec. to Prime Minister 1998–2002; Deputy Sec. Ministry of Information, Communication and the Arts 1998; Chief Exec. Dir The People's Asscn 1999–2002; Sec.-Gen. ASEAN 2003–08; Amb. at Large, Ministry of Foreign Affairs 2008–; Dir Inst. of Policy Studies, Lee Kuan Yew School of Public Policy, Nat. Univ. of Singapore 2008–; Amb. (non-resident) to Iran 2009–; Public Admin Silver Medal, Long Service Medal Meritorious Service Medal, Medal of Friendship (Laos), Medal of Sahametrei (Cambodia). *Address:* Ministry of Foreign Affairs, MFA Building, Tanglin, off Napier Road, Singapore 248163 (office). *Telephone:* 63798000 (office). *Fax:* 64747885 (office). *E-mail:* ongkengyong@gmail.com (home). *Website:* www.mfa.gov.sg (office).

ONG, Romualdo Añover, BSc; Philippine fmr diplomatist; b. 25 April 1939, Manila; s. of the late Juan Salido Ong and of Adelaida Añover; m. 1st Cecilia Hidalgo 1964 (deceased); m. 2nd Farita Aguilucho 1994; two s. two d.; ed Ateneo de Manila and Univ. of the Philippines; joined Ministry of Foreign Affairs 1968; served Bonn 1972–75, Geneva 1975–79, Minister Counsellor, Beijing 1979–82; Special Asst to Deputy Minister for Foreign Affairs 1983; Asst Minister for ASEAN Affairs 1984–85; Sr Econ. Consultant, Tech. Secr. for Int. Econ. Relations/Bd. of Overseas Econ. Promotion 1985; Amb. to Australia (also accred to Vanuatu) 1986–89; Asst Sec. for Asian and Pacific Affairs, Dept of Foreign Affairs, Manila 1990–93; Amb. to Russia 1993–94, to People's Repub. of China 1994–2000; Dir Foreign Service Inst. 2000; mem. Bd of Dirs First Metro Investment Corpn 2005–, PBC Capital Investment Corpn, First Metro Securities Brokerage Corpn. *Leisure interests:* reading, car driving, basketball, hiking, movies, listening to music. *Address:* c/o Board of Directors, First Metro Investment Corporation, 20th Floor, GT Tower International, Ayala Ave, corner HV Dela Costa, Makati City, Philippines.

ONGERI, Samson Kegeo, MB, DCH, MRCP; Kenyan physician and politician; b. 23 Feb. 1938; ed Univ. of Bombay, India, Univ. of London, UK; Lecturer, Univ. of Nairobi 1972–89, becoming Prof., Dept of Paediatrics and Child Health; Council Chair., OUN 1993–97; mem. Nat. Ass. (Parl.) for Nyaribari Masaba constituency 1997–; fmrly with Ministries of Health and Local Govt; Minister for Tech. Training and Applied Tech. 1988–92, for Educ. 2008–12, of Foreign Affairs 2012–13; mem. Nat. Dialogue Reconciliation team led by Kofi Annan (following post-election violence) 2008; Pres. Multilateral Fund of the Ozone Layer; Perm. Rep. of Kenya to UNEP 1992–97, becoming Vice-Chair. UNEP Governing Council; Chair. Kenya Athletic Asscn 1976–84, Ongeri Foundation (promoting health, educ., environment and devt issues); fmr Chair. Kenya Inst. of Educ., Kenya Nat. Trading Co.; mem. Kenya African Nat. Union; Elder of the Order of the Golden Heart of Kenya (EGH), Elder of the Burning Spear (EBS), Ordre Nationale Burkinabe 2012; IAAF Veteran's Pin. *Address:* c/o Ministry of Foreign Affairs, Old Treasury Building, Harambee Avenue, PO Box 30551, 00100 Nairobi, Kenya.

ONGPIN, Roberto V., CPA, MBA; Philippine business executive and fmr government official; *Chairman, Alphaland Corporation;* m.; four c.; ed Ateneo de Manila Univ., Harvard Business School, USA; with SyCip Gorres Velayo & Co. 1964–79, becoming Man. Pnr; Minister of Trade and Industry 1979–86; f. AIA Capital (financial advisory firm) 1987; CEO ISM Communications Corpn 2001–13; Chair. Alphaland Corpn 2009–; Founder and Chair. PhilWeb Corpn 2000–; Chair. Macondray Plastics Inc 2009–; Vice-Chair. SCMP Group Ltd, South China Morning Post; mem. Bd of Dirs Shangri-La Asia Ltd 2003–, Philex 2007–, Petron Corpn 2008–, San Miguel Corpn 2009–, Philippine Bank of Communications Inc 2011–, PAL Holdings, Inc. 2012–. *Address:* Alphaland Corporation, The Penthouse, Alphaland Southgate Tower 2258, Chino Roces Avenue, corner Edsa Makati, Metro Manila, Philippines (office). *Telephone:* (2) 3372031 (office). *Website:* www.alphaland.com.ph (office).

O'NIONS, Sir (Robert) Keith, Kt, MA, PhD, FRS; British geochemist, academic and university administrator; *President and Rector, Imperial College London;* b. 26 Sept. 1944, Birmingham, England; s. of William Henry O'Nions and Eva Stagg; m. Rita Bill 1967; three d.; ed Univ. of Nottingham, Univ. of Alberta; Postdoctoral Fellow, Univ. of Alberta, Canada 1969–70; Unger Vetlesen Postdoctoral Fellow, Univ. of Oslo, Norway 1970–71; Demonstrator in Petrology, Univ. of Oxford 1971–72, Lecturer in Geochemistry 1972–75; Assoc. Prof. and Prof. of Geology, Columbia Univ., New York, USA 1975–79; Royal Soc. Research Prof., Univ. of Cambridge 1979–95; Fellow, Clare Hall Cambridge 1980–95; Prof. of Physics and Chem. of Minerals, Univ. of Oxford 1995–2003; Chief Scientific Adviser, Ministry of Defence 2000–04; Dir Gen. Research Councils 2004–08; Head, Inst. for Security Science and Tech., Imperial Coll. London 2008–10, Rector, Imperial Coll. London 2010–12, Pres. and Rector 2012–; mem. UK Govt's Council of Science and Tech. 1998–2000; Trustee, then Chair. Natural History Museum 1996–2005; Fellow, St Hugh's Coll. Oxford 1995–2003; mem. Norwegian Acad. of Sciences 1980; Fellow, American Geophysical Union 1979, Indian Nat. Science Acad. 2001; hon. doctorates from 11 univs; J.B. Macelwane Award 1979, Bigsby Medal 1983, Holmes Medal 1995, Lyell Medal 1995, Urey Medal 2001. *Publications:* numerous publs in scientific journals on geochemistry. *Address:* Office of the President and Rector, Room 4.16, Faculty Building, Imperial College London, South Kensington Campus, London, SW7 2AZ, England (office). *Telephone:* (20) 7594-5001 (office). *E-mail:* k.onions@imperial.ac.uk (office); rector@imperial.ac.uk (office). *Website:* www3.imperial.ac.uk/rector (office).

ONKELINX, Laurette, BL; Belgian politician; *Deputy Prime Minister and Minister of Social Affairs and Health;* b. 2 Oct. 1958, Ougrée; Lecturer in Admin. Sciences 1982–85; barrister, Liège 1981–; Parti Socialiste (PS) Deputy for Liège 1988; Chair. Interfederal Comm. of Socialist Women; Vice-Chair. Socialist Group, House of Reps; mem. PS Party Office 1988; Chair. Justice Cttee, House of Reps; Vice-Pres. House of Reps; Minister for Social Integration, Health and Environment 1992–93; Minister-Pres. in Govt of Communauté française in charge of Civil Service, Childhood and Promotion of Health 1993–95, Minister-Pres. in charge of Educ., Audio-visual, Youth Help and Promotion of Health 1995–99; apptd. Deputy Prime Minister and Minister for Employment (later Employment and Equal Opportunities) 1999, then also Minister of Mobility and Transport 2003; Deputy

Prime Minister and Minister for Justice 2003–07; Minister of Social Affairs and Public Health 2007 (resgnd), reappointed Dec. 2007, resgnd March 2008, Deputy Prime Minister and Minister of Social Affairs and Health March–Dec. 2008 (resgnd), reappointed Dec. 2008–11, Dec. 2011–. *Publications:* Continuons le débat, Théâtre du jeune public. *Address:* Federal Public Service of Health, Eurostation II, 40 place Victor Horta, BP 10, 106 Brussels (office); c/o Parti Socialiste (PS), Maison du PS, 13 blvd de l'Empereur, 1000 Brussels (office). *Telephone:* (2) 524-94-94 (office). *Fax:* (2) 524-95-27 (home). *E-mail:* info@laurette-onkelinx.be (office); info@health.fgov.be (office). *Website:* www.laurette-onkelinx.be (home); www.health.fgov.be (office).

ONODERA, Itsunori, MPolSci; Japanese academic and politician; *Minister of Defence;* b. 5 May 1960, Kesennuma, Miyagi Pref.; m.; two s.; ed Tokyo Univ. of Marine Science and Tech., Matsushita Inst. of Govt and Man., Univ. of Tokyo; began career with Miyagi Prefectural Govt 1983; Special Lecturer, later Asst Prof. and Guest Prof., Tohoku Fukushi Univ. 1994–98, Assoc. Prof. 2002; mem. House of Reps (lower house of Parl.) for Miyagi No. 6 constituency (LDP) 1997–2000 (resgnd), 2003–, Dir Special Cttee on Prevention of Int. Terrorism and Japan's Co-operation and Support, mem. Cttee on Foreign Affairs; Parl. Sec. for Foreign Affairs 2004–05, Sr Vice-Minister for Foreign Affairs 2007; Minister of Defence 2012–; Visiting Research Fellow, School of Advanced Int. Studies, Johns Hopkins Univ., USA Sept. 2000; mem. LDP, Deputy Dir Fisheries Div., Policy Research Council 1999, Foreign Affairs Div., Deputy Chair. Diet Affairs Cttee 2006. *Address:* Ministry of Defence, 5-1, Ichigaya, Honmura-cho, Shinjuku-ku, Tokyo 162-8801, Japan (office). *Telephone:* (3) 3268-3111 (office). *Fax:* (3) 3268-3111 (office). *E-mail:* infomod@mod.go.jp (office). *Website:* www.mod.go.jp (office); www.itsunori.com.

ONODERA, Tadashi, BEng; Japanese business executive; *Chairman, KDDI Corporation;* b. 3 Feb. 1948; ed Tohuko Univ.; began career as electronic engineer Microwave Div., Nippon Telegraph and Telephone Public Corpn 1970; joined DDI Corpn 1984, Dir and Gen. Man. Microwave Eng Dept, Network Communications Group and Mobile Communications Group 1989–95, Man. Dir and Sr Gen. Man. Eng Group 1995–97, Exec. Vice-Pres. and Sr Gen. Man. Eng Group 1997–98, Exec. Vice-Pres., Chief Engineer and Sr Gen. Man. Mobile Communications Group 1998–2000, Exec. Vice-Pres. and Deputy Operating Officer Mobile Communications Sector 2000–01, Pres. KDDI Corpn (following merger of DDI Corpn, KDD Corpn and IDO Corpn 2000) 2001–05, Pres. and Chair. 2005–10, Chair. 2010–; Dir, Kyocera Corpn 2013–. *Address:* KDDI Corpn, Garden Air Tower, 3-10-10, Iidabashi, Chiyoda-ku, Tokyo 102-8460, Japan (office). *Telephone:* (3) 6678-0692 (office). *Fax:* (3) 6678-0305 (office). *E-mail:* info@kddi.com (office). *Website:* www.kddi.com (office).

ONORIO, Teima, MA; I-Kiribati politician; *Vice-President;* d. of Rota Onorio; MP for Arorae constituency 1998–2002; Vice-Pres. of Kiribati 2003–, also Minister of Commerce, Industry and Co-operatives 2007–08, for Educ., Youth and Sport Devt 2008, for Internal and Social Affairs 2012–. *Address:* c/o Office of the President, PO Box 68, Bikenibeu, Tarawa, Kiribati.

ONWUMECHILI, Ozo Ochendo Cyril Agodi, PhD, DSc; Nigerian physicist, academic and administrator; b. 20 Jan. 1932, Inyi; s. of Nwaime Onwumechili and Akuviro Onwumechili (née Orji); m. Cecilia Bedeaka (née Anyadibe) 1958; two s. one d.; ed King's Coll., Lagos, Univ. Coll., Ibadan and Univ. of London, UK; Dir of chain of observatories 1960–66; Dean, Faculty of Science, Univ. of Ibadan 1965–66; Prof. and Head of Dept, Univ. of Nigeria 1966–73, 1976–78, Dean, Faculty of Science 1970–71, Dean, Faculty of Physical Sciences 1973–76, 1978; Visiting Prof. of Geophysics, Univ. of Alaska 1971–72; Consultant, Inst. for Space Research, Nat. Research Council of Brazil 1972; Vice-Chancellor, Univ. of Ife, Ile-Ife 1979–82; Deputy Pres. Anambra State Univ. of Tech., Enugu 1983–84, Pres. 1984–85, Vice-Chancellor 1985–86; Consultant UN Econ. Comm. for Africa 1987, Commonwealth Science Council 1988; Vice-Chair. Div. II Int. Asscn of Geomagnetism and Aeronomy 1987–91, Chair. Interdivisional Comm. 1991–95; mem. Int. Scientific Programmes Cttee, Int. Symposia on Equatorial Aeronomy 1972–, UN Advisory Cttee on Science and Tech. for Devt 1981–83; Chair. Man. Cttee UNESCO African Network of Scientific and Technological Insts (ANSTI) 1985–90; Vice-Pres. Asscn of African Univs 1984–89, Consultant 1990–2002, Chair. Scientific Cttee 1993–; mem. American Geophysical Union, Soc. for Terrestrial Magnetism and Electricity of Japan; Fellow, UK and Nigerian Inst. of Physics 1969; Foundation Ed.-in-Chief Nigerian Journal of Science 1964–67; Visiting Prof. of Physics, Univ. of Wales at Cardiff 1987–88; Foundation Fellow and Former Pres. Nigerian Acad. of Science; UK Chartered Physicist 1986; Fellow, African Acad. of Sciences 1987, Third World Acad. of Sciences 1989; Foundation Fellow, Science Asscn of Nigeria 1974; Hon. DSc (Ife) 1977, (Enugu State Univ.) 1992, (Univ. of Nigeria) 2001. *Publications:* Geomagnetic Variations in the Equatorial Zone 1967, University Administration in Nigeria: The Anambra State University of Technology Approach I 1991, Cost Effectiveness and Efficiency in African Universities 1993, The Equatorial Electrojet 1997, Igho Enwe Eze?: The 2000 Ahiajoku Lecture; numerous scientific articles. *Leisure interests:* swimming, table tennis, lawn tennis. *Address:* PO Box 9059, Uwani, Enugu, Nigeria; 69 Lansdowne Drive, Hackney, London, E8 3EP, England. *Telephone:* (20) 7249-3260 (London); (42) 254987 (Enugu).

ONYSZKIEWICZ, Janusz, DMath; Polish mathematician and government official; *Chairman, International Board of Directors, International Centre for Democratic Transition;* b. 18 Dec. 1937, Lvov; s. of Stanislaw Onyszkiewicz and Franciszka Onyszkiewicz; m. 1st Witoslawa Boretti (died 1967); m. 2nd Alison Chadwick (died 1978); m. 3rd Joanna Jaraczewska 1983; two s. three d.; ed Univ. of Warsaw; Asst, Math. Engines Inst., Polish Acad. of Sciences, Warsaw 1958–61; Asst, later Sr Asst, Faculty of Math., Informatics and Mechanics, Math. Inst., Univ. of Warsaw 1963–67, Lecturer 1967–75, now Sr Lecturer; Lecturer, Univ. of Leeds, UK 1976–79; mem. Polish Teachers' Union (ZNP) 1969–80, Ind. Self-governing Trade Union of Science, Tech. and Educ. Workers 1980, Deputy Chair. Br. at Warsaw Univ. Sept.–Oct. 1980; adviser to Interfactory Founding Cttee of Solidarity Ind. Self-governing Trade Union – Mazovia Region, subsequently mem. Presidium of Nat. Comm. of Solidarity Trade Union, Bd and Press Spokesman of Mazovia Region of Solidarity Trade Union; Press Spokesman Nat. Understanding Comm. and First Nat. Congress of Solidarity Trade Union 1980–81; interned 1981–82; arrested April 1983, released under amnesty July 1983; sentenced to six weeks' confinement May 1988; Press Spokesman Nat. Exec. Comm., Solidarity

Trade Union; mem. Civic Cttee attached to Lech Wałęsa (q.v.) 1988–91; participant Round Table debates, mem. team for mass media and opposition press spokesman Feb.–April 1989; Deputy to Sejm (Parl.) 1989–2001; Vice-Minister of Nat. Defence 1990–92, Minister 1992–93, 1997–2000, Chair. Defence Cttee, Council of Ministers 1997–99; mem. European Parl. 2004–09, Vice-Pres. Foreign Affairs Cttee 2007–09; currently Chair. Int. Bd of Dirs Int. Centre for Democratic Transition, Budapest; mem. Democratic Union Parl. 1991–94, Freedom Union Parl. 1994; Vice-Pres. Polish Asia-Pacific Council 1996; mem. Nat. Council Freedom Union 1996; mem. Euro-Atlantic Asscn 1994– (Pres. 1994–98); currently Sr Fellow, Centre for Int. Relations; Pres. Polish Mountaineering Fed. 2001–; Great Cross of Gedymin (Lithuania), Great Cross of King Leopold II (Belgium); Hon. DSc (Leeds) 1991; Gold Medal (For Outstanding Sporting Achievements), Manfred Wörner Medal. *Achievements include:* mountaineer and speleologist, participant in mountaineering expeditions in Himalayas, Hindu Kush, Karakoram, Pamir. *Publications:* 15 works on foundations of math., including Complete Abstract Logics 1979; Zdobycie Gasherbrumów (co-author) 1977. *Leisure interests:* climbing, caving, tourism, classical music. *Address:* International Centre for Democratic Transition, 1022 Budapest, Árvácska u. 12, Hungary (office). *Telephone:* (1) 438-0820 (office). *Fax:* (1) 438-0821 (office). *Website:* www.icdt.hu (office).

OOKA, Makoto, Japanese poet, writer and academic; b. 16 Feb. 1931, Mishima City; s. of Hiroshi Ooka and Ayako Ooka; m. Kaneko Aizawa 1957; one s. one d.; ed Tokyo Nat. Univ.; journalist with Yomiuri (newspaper), foreign news section 1953–63; Asst Prof., Meiji Univ., Tokyo 1965–70, Prof. 1970–87; Pres. Japan Poets' Asscn 1979–81; Prof., Nat. Univ. for Fine Arts and Music 1988–93; Soshitsu Sen XV Distinguished Lecturer in Japanese Culture and Visiting Fellow, Donald Keene Center of Japanese Culture, Columbia Univ., New York 2000; Pres. Japan PEN Club 1989–93; mem. Int. Advisory Bd of Poetry International, Rotterdam; mem. Japan Art Acad. 1995–; Officier des Arts et des Lettres, Order of Cultural Merit 2003; Yomiuri Prize for Literature, Kikuchi Kan Prize, Hanatsubaki Prize for Poetry, Golden Wreath Prize, Struga Poetry Evenings Macedonia 1996, Asahi Prize 1996, Japanese Art Acad. Imperial Award 1996, Person of Cultural Merit 1997, Japan Foundation Prize 2002. *Publications include:* poetry: Memories and the Present 1956, For a Girl in Springtime 1978, City of Water 1981, Odes to the Waters of My Hometown 1989, The Afternoon in the Earthly Paradise 1992, The Last Will of Fire 1995; Criticism: The Banquet and the Solitary Mind, Aesthetics of Japanese Poetry 1978; English translations: Japanese Poetry; Past and Present, A Poet's Anthology 1979–, an anthological series for the newspaper Asahi, A String around Autumn 1982, A Play of Mirrors: Eight Major Poets of Modern Japan (co-ed) 1987, Elegy and Benediction 1991, The Colours of Poetry – Essays on Classic Japanese Verse 1991, What the Kite Thinks, a linked poem with three American poets 1994, The Range of Japanese Poetry 1994, Beneath the Sleepless Tossing of the Planets 1995, The Poetry and Poetics of Ancient Japan 1997, Love Songs from the Man'yoshu: Selections from a Japanese Classic 2000; French translations: Poèmes de tous les jours 1993, Propos sur le vent et autres poèmes 1995, Poésie et Poétique du Japon Ancien 1995, Dans l'Océan du Silence 1998, Citadelle de Lumière 2002. *Address:* 2-18-1-2606, Iidabashi, Chiyoda-ku, Tokyo 102-0072, Japan.

OPERTTI BADDAN, Didier, PhD; Uruguayan lawyer, politician and international organization official; b. 1937, Montevideo; m.; four c.; ed Univ. of Uruguay; fmr Asst Prof. of Int. Pvt. Law, Univ. of Uruguay, Prof. of Int. Relations 1986; Dir Office of Codification and Devt of Int. Law, Gen. Secr., OAS 1979–81, Perm. Rep. to OAS 1988–93, Pres. OAS Perm. Council's Comm. of Juridical and Political Matters 1989, Pres. OAS Perm. Council 1990; Dir Diplomatic Law Advisory Council, Ministry of Foreign Affairs 1985–88; Prof. of Int. Pvt. Law, Int. Law Acad., The Hague; Prof. of Int. Pvt. Law, Catholic Univ. of Uruguay 1994; Minister of the Interior 1995–98, of Foreign Affairs 1998, 2000–05; Sec.-Gen., Latin-American Integration Asscn (Asociación Latinoamericana de Integración— ALADI) 2005–08; Pres. 53rd Session of UN Gen. Ass. 1998–2000; Special Counsellor for MERCOSUR issues to IDB and Inst. for Integration of Latin America and the Caribbean 1993–94; mem. UN Law Comm.; fmr mem. Uruguayan Nat. Group of Perm. Court of Arbitration; Founder and Bd mem. Int. Law Asscn of Uruguay; mem. and Dir Uruguayan Comparative Law Inst.; mem. Lawyers Asscn of Uruguay, Portuguese-Spanish American Int. Law Inst., Int. Law Asscn of Argentina, Int. and Comparative Law Acad. of Brazil. *Address:* c/o Asociación Latinoamericana de Integración, Cebollati 1461, Casilla 577, CP 11200, Montevideo, Uruguay. *Telephone:* (2) 410-1121.

OPIE, Julian Gilbert, BA; British artist; b. 12 Dec. 1958, London, England; s. of Roger G. Opie and Norma Opie; m. Aniela Opie; one s. three d.; ed Magdalen Coll. School, Oxford, Chelsea School of Art, London and Goldsmiths' School of Art, London; exhibited Young Blood, Riverside Studios, London 1983, Sculpture 1983, Rotterdam 1983, The Sculpture Show, Hayward Gallery, London 1983, Making Sculpture, Tate Gallery, London 1983, Perspective, Basel Art Fair, Basel 1984, Home and Abroad, Serpentine Gallery, London 1984, Myth and Symbol, Tokyo Museum of Modern Art 1984, The British Show touring Australia 1984, Paris Biennale, Paris 1985, Anniotanta, Ravenna 1985, British Sculpture Louisiana Museum, Denmark 1986, De Sculptura, Vienna 1986, Correspondence Europe, Stedelijk Museum, Amsterdam 1986, Prospect 86, Frankfurt 1986, Hayward Gallery 1993 and elsewhere. *Publications include:* Julian Opie, Kunstverein Cologne: Catalogue of Works 1984, Julian Opie Drawings, ICA, London, Julian Opie New Works, Lisson Gallery. *Address:* c/o Lisson Gallery, 52–54 Bell Street, London, NW1 5DA, England (office). *E-mail:* info@julianopie.com. *Website:* www .julianopie.com.

OPIE, Lionel Henry, MD, PhD, MRCP, FACC, FRSSA; South African cardiologist and academic; *Professor Emeritus of Medicine, Hatter Institute for Cardiology Research, Cape Heart Group, University of Cape Town;* b. 6 May 1933, Hanover, SA; s. of Prof. William Henry Opie and Marie Opie (née Le Roux); m. Carol June Sancroft Baker 1969; two d.; ed Diocesan Coll., Rondebosch, Cape Town, Univ. of Cape Town, Univ. of Oxford, UK; Intern, Groote Schuur Hosp. 1956; Sr House Officer, Dept of Neurology, Radcliffe Infirmary, Oxford 1957–59; House Physician (Endocrinology), Hammersmith Hosp., London 1959; Asst in Medicine, Peter Bent Brigham Hosp., Boston, Mass, USA, Samuel A. Levine Fellow in Cardiology, Harvard Medical School 1960–61; Asst Resident in Medicine, Toronto Gen. Hosp., Canada 1961–62; Consultant Physician, Karl Bremer Hosp. and Univ. of

Stellenbosch, SA; Out-Patient Asst Physician, Radcliffe Infirmary, Wellcome Research Fellow, Dept of Biochemistry, Univ. of Oxford 1964–66; part-time Registrar, Hammersmith Hosp., London 1966–67; Research Fellow, Dept of Biochemistry, Imperial Coll., London 1966–68; Sr Registrar in Medicine (Cardiology), Hammersmith Hosp. 1967–69, Consultant in Medicine 1969; Sr Specialist Physician, Groote Schuur Hosp. 1971; Assoc. Prof. of Medicine, Univ. of Cape Town 1975, Dir MRC Research Unit for Ischaemic Heart Disease (now Hatter Inst., Cape Heart Centre) 1976, Personal Chair in Medicine, Prof. of Medicine 1980, now Prof. Emer., Dir Hypertension Clinic 1979; Visiting Prof., Div. of Cardiovascular Medicine, Stanford Univ. School of Medicine, Calif., USA 1991–94; British Heart Foundation Sr Fellow and Visiting Prof. St Thomas' Hosp., London 1992; Pres. Southern Africa Cardiac Soc. 1980–82; Chair. Council on Cardiac Metabolism, Int. Soc. and Fed. of Cardiology 1980; Pres. Southern Africa Hypertension Soc. 1986; Chair. Cttee Cardiovascular Drugs, Int. Soc. and Fed. Cardiology 1990; mem. British Cardiac Soc., Physiological Soc. (UK), SA Socs of Cardiology, Pharmacology, Biochemistry and Hypertension, Int. Hypertension Soc. *Publications:* over 300. *Address:* Hatter Institute for Cardiology Research, Cape Heart Centre, Faculty of Health Sciences, University of Cape Town, 7925 Observatory (office); 66A Dean Street, Newlands 7700, South Africa (home). *Telephone:* 471250 (office); 6853855 (home). *Website:* web.uct.ac.za/depts/chc/hatter/intro.htm (office).

OPPENHEIMER, Nicholas Frank, MA; South African business executive; *Chairman, De Beers;* b. 8 June 1945, Johannesburg; s. of Harry F. Oppenheimer and Bridget Oppenheimer (née McCall); m. Orcillia M. L. Lasch 1968; one s.; ed Harrow School, UK and Christ Church, Oxford, UK; Chair. De Beers Consolidated Mines Ltd 1998–, The Diamond Trading Co. Ltd; Exec. Chair. De Beers Centenary AG; Dir De Beers Industrial Corpn Ltd, E. Oppenheimer & Son (Pty) Ltd; Dir (nonexec.) Anglo-American Corpn of South Africa Ltd; f., Greene and Partners Investments (venture capital firm) 1999; Hon. DTech (Technikon Witwatersrand) 2003. *Leisure interests:* squash, golf, cricket, flying. *Address:* PO Box 61631, Marshalltown 2107, South Africa. *E-mail:* www.debeersgroup.com (office).

OPPENLÄNDER, Karl Heinrich, DEcon; German economist; b. 17 Jan. 1932, Dörzbach; m. Cäcilie Oppenländer 1958; one s. one d.; ed Univ. of Munich; entered IFO Inst. for Econ. Research 1958, Head of Dept 1966, mem. Exec. Cttee 1972, Pres. (Prof.) 1976–99; Lecturer, Univ. of Tübingen 1975, Univ. of Munich 1976–, Univ. of Augsburg 1980–83. *Publications:* Die moderne Wachstumstheorie 1963, Der investitionsinduzierte technische Fortschritt 1976.

OPREA, Gabriel, DIur; Romanian politician and fmr army officer; *Deputy Prime Minister and Acting Minister of Internal Affairs;* b. 1 Jan. 1961, Fundulea, Călăraşi Co.; m.; two c.; ed Active Officers' Mil. School, Sibiu, Faculty of Law, Univ. of Bucharest, Nat. Coll. of Defence; officer, Ministry of Defence 1983–90; Vice-Pres. Nat. Coll. of Defence 2000, Deputy Dir 2000–01, Prof. 2001; Sec. of State and Pres. Nat. Admin of State Reserves 2001–02; thesis adviser, Alexandru Ioan Cuza Police Acad. 2002; Prefect, Bucharest 2002–03; Del. Minister of Public Admin 2003–04; mem. Chamber of Deputies for Ilfov Co. 2004–; mem. Democrat Party (PSD) 2003–09, Pres. PSD Ilfov 2004–09, PSD Defence Dept 2008–09; Minister of Interior and Admin. Reform Dec. 2008–Jan. 2009 (resgnd), Nov.–Dec. 2009, Minister of Nat. Defence 2009–12; Prof., Nat. Intelligence Acad. 2008–; Deputy Prime Minister 2012–; Acting Minister of Internal Affairs 2014–; Exec. Pres. UNPR (Nat. Union for the Progress of Romania) 2010–; rank of four-star Gen. in the reserves 2009; Kt, Nat. Order of the Star of Romania 2000, Nat. Order of Faithful Service 2001. *Address:* Ministry of Internal Affairs, 010086 Bucharest 1, Piaţa Revoluţiei 1A, Romania (office). *Telephone:* (21) 2648526 (office). *Fax:* (21) 2648677 (office). *E-mail:* petitii@mai.gov.ro (office). *Website:* www.mai.gov.ro (office).

OPRESCU, Sorin Mircea; Romanian physician and politician; *Mayor of Bucharest;* b. 7 Nov. 1951, Bucharest; m. (divorced); one c.; ed Faculty of Medicine, Univ. of Bucharest; surgical intern 1975–78; physician, M. Kogălniceanu Int. Airport, Constanţa 1978–79; Trainee Univ. Asst, Surgery Clinic of Brancovenian Clinic Hosp. 1978, Univ. Asst 1982; surgeon, Bucharest Univ. Hosp. 1985–90, Primary Surgeon, Clinic for Higher Digestive Surgery 1990–94, Dir Bucharest Univ. Hosp. 1994–; Lecturer, Carol Davila Univ. of Medicine and Pharmacy 1996–2000, Univ. Prof. and Chair of Surgery 2000–; Adviser to Minister of Health 1993–94; Adviser to Gen. Council of Bucharest 1996–2000; Deputy Mayor of Bucharest 2000; mem. Senate 2000–08; mem. Social Democrat Party 1990–2008, Pres. Bucharest br. 2006–08; Mayor of Bucharest (Ind.) 2008–. *Address:* Office of the Mayor, Bucharest Municipal Council, 060042 Bucharest 6, Splaiul Independenţei 291–293, Romania (office). *Telephone:* (21) 3055500 (office). *Fax:* (21) 3120030 (office). *E-mail:* sorin.oprescu@bucuresti-primaria.ro (office). *Website:* www.pmb.ro (office); sorinoprescu.wordpress.com.

OQILOV, Oqil Ghaybulloyevich; Tajikistani politician and engineer; b. 2 Feb. 1944, Leninobod (now Khujand); m.; three c.; ed Moscow Inst. of Construction and Eng; various posts in construction orgs, Leninobod (now Sugdh) Viloyat 1960–76; worked for CP 1976–93; Minister of Construction of Tajikistan 1993–94; Deputy Prime Minister 1994–96; First Deputy Chair. Leninobod Viloyat 1996–99; Prime Minister 1999–2013, also Minister of Construction; mem. People's Democratic Party of Tajikistan. *Address:* c/o Secretariat of the Prime Minister, 734023 Dushanbe, Xiyoboni Rudaki 80, Tajikistan.

ORABI, Muhammad al-, MBA; Egyptian diplomatist; *Minister of Foreign Affairs;* b. 26 Jan. 1951, Heliopolis, Cairo; m.; one d.; ed Cairo Univ.; Attaché, Ministry of Foreign Affairs (MFA) 1976–78, Second Sec., Embassy in Kuwait 1978–82, in Cabinet of State Minister for Foreign Affairs and Pvt. Sec. to Minister 1982–84, First Sec., Embassy in London 1984–88, Official MFA Spokesperson 1988–89, Counsellor, Embassy in Washington, DC 1989–94, Minister Plenipotentiary and Deputy Head of Mission, Embassy in Tel-Aviv 1994–98, Dir Office of Minister of Foreign Affairs 1998–2001, Amb. to Germany 2001–08, Asst Minister of Foreign Affairs for Econ. Affairs and Int. Co-operation 2008–11, Minister of Foreign Affairs 2011–; Grosses Bundesverdienstkreuz (Germany). *Address:* Ministry of Foreign Affairs, Corniche el-Nil, Cairo (Maspiro), Egypt (office). *Telephone:* (2) 25749820 (office). *Fax:* (2) 25748822 (office). *E-mail:* info@mfa.gov .eg (office). *Website:* www.mfa.gov.eg (office).

ORAM, Jacob David Philip; New Zealand professional cricketer; b. 28 July 1978, Palmerston North, Manawatu; m. Mara Tait-Jamieson 2008; one s.; all-rounder; left-handed batsman; right-arm fast-medium pace bowler; plays for Central Districts Stags 1997–, New Zealand 2001–, Chennai Super Kings 2008–09, Rajasthan Royals 2011–, Uva Next 2012–, Chittagong Kings 2013–; First-class debut: 1997/98; Test debut: NZ v India, Wellington 12–14 Dec. 2002; One-Day Int. (ODI) debut: NZ v Zimbabwe, Wellington 4 Jan. 2001; T20I debut: S Africa v NZ, Johannesburg 21 Oct. 2005; has played in 33 Test matches, scored 1,780 runs (five centuries, six half-centuries, average 36.32), taken 60 wickets (average 33.05), best bowling (innings) 4/41, (match) 6/63; ODIs: 160 matches, scored 2,434 runs, one century, 13 half-centuries, highest score 101 not out, average 24.09, took 173 wickets, average 29.17, best bowling 5/26; T20Is: 36 matches, scored 474 runs, highest score 66 not out, took 19 wickets, best bowling 3/33; took a hat trick against Sri Lanka in a Twenty20 Int. in Colombo 2 Sept. 2009; announced retirement from Test cricket 13 Oct. 2009; name inscribed on Lords Honours Board for his Test century against England 2008. *Address:* c/o Central Districts Cricket, Chapman Pavilion, McLean Park, Latham Street, PO Box 309, Napier, New Zealand. *Telephone:* (6) 835-7617. *Fax:* (6) 835-0543. *E-mail:* info@cdcricket.co.nz. *Website:* www.cdcricket.co.nz.

ORAYEVSKY, Victor Nikolayevich, DPhysMathSc; Russian physicist; b. 9 March 1935, Poltava, Ukraine; ed Kharkov State Univ.; Jr Researcher, Inst. of Nuclear Physics, USSR Acad. of Sciences (Siberian br.) 1958–65, Head of Div. Inst. of Earth Magnetism, Ionosphere and Radiowaves Propagation (IZMIRAN) 1979–89, Dir 1989–, Head of int. Sputnik projects; Sr Researcher, Inst. of Physics, Ukrainian Acad. of Sciences 1965–70, Head of Div., Inst. of Nuclear Studies 1970–74; Head of Scientific Production Div., Energia Co. 1974–79, Head of Lab., Head of Dept 1979–89; mem. Int. Acad. of Astronautics, New York Acad. of Sciences, Russian Acad. of Sciences, Int. Acad. of Informatics; State Prize of Ukrainian SSR, USSR State Prize 1987, Merited Worker of Science, Russian Fed. 1996. *Address:* IZMIRAN, 142092 Troitsk, Moscow, Russia (office). *Telephone:* (495) 334-01-20 (office).

ORAZBAY, Askhat T.; Kazakhstani international organization official; Sec.-Gen. Econ. Co-operation Org. 2004–06. *Address:* c/o Economic Co-operation Organization, 1 Golbou Alley, Kamranieh Street, POB 14155-6176, Tehran, Iran (office).

ORAZMUKHAMEDOV, Nury Orazovich; Turkmenistani politician and diplomatist; b. 1949, Mary; ed Turkmenistan Polytech. Inst.; master, engineer, Chief Engineer, Turkmencentrstroi 1971–; Head of Ashkhabad construction units; Deputy Chair. State Construction Cttee 1990–91; Minister of Construction 1991–94, of Construction and Architecture 1994–95; Head of Admin. Khikim Ashkhabad Feb. 1995; Amb. to Russian Fed. 1996–2000, to Moldova 2000. *Address:* Ministry of Foreign Affairs, 744000 Asgabat, Archabil av. 108, Turkmenistan (office). *Telephone:* (12) 445622 (office). *Fax:* (12) 218675 (office). *E-mail:* mfatm@online.tm (office). *Website:* www.mfa.gov.tm (office).

ORBAN, Leonard; Romanian engineer and politician; b. 28 June 1961, Braşov, m.; one c.; ed Faculty of Mechanical Eng, Univ. of Braşov, Faculty of Man., Acad. of Econ. Studies, Bucharest; engineer, Inst. of Research for Machine Mfg Tech., Bucharest, Enterprise for Special Industrial Constructions, Bucharest, Tractor Mfg Co. Miercurea Ciuc 1986–93; Parl. Counsellor on European and Int. affairs, Chamber of Deputies, Romanian Parl. 1993–2001; Deputy Chief Negotiator for accession to EU 2001–04, Chief Negotiator 2004–05; State Sec., Ministry of European Integration 2005–06; Head of Romanian del. for negotiating accession to European Econ. Area 2006–; nominated as Romania's cand. for EC Oct. 2006, European Commr for Multilingualism 2007–10; Co-ordinator, Elaboration of Romanian Post Accession Strategy for 2007–2013; mem. several governmental cttees related to Romania's EU accession negotiations, including European Integration Exec. Cttee, State Aid Cttee, Cttee for the Man. of EU Funds, Romanian Steel Sector Restructuring; mem. Romanian Social and Econ. Council; Kt of 'Steaua Romaniei' Nat. Order (Star of Romania) 2002. *Publications:* articles and analyses in nat. and foreign newspapers and magazines on European integration and European affairs 2001–. *Leisure interests:* foreign policy, classical music, reading, cinema. *Address:* c/o Office of the Commissioner for Multilingualism, European Commission, 1049 Brussels, Belgium.

ORBÁN, Viktor, LLD, PhD; Hungarian politician and lawyer; *Prime Minister;* b. 31 May 1963, Székesfehérvár; s. of Győző Orbán; m. Anikó Lévai; two s. three d.; ed Eötvös Loránd Univ., Budapest and Pembroke Coll., Oxford, UK; worked as sociologist for Man. Training Inst., Ministry of Agric. and Food 1987–88; researcher, Middle Europe Research Group 1989–91; co-f. Hungarian opposition group Fed. of Young Democrats (Fidesz) 1988, Spokesman 1989, Pres. Fidesz—Hungarian Civic Alliance 1993–2000, 2003–; represented Fidesz political Sub-cttee of Opposition Round Table Discussion 1989; mem. Parl., Leader Fidesz Parl. Group 1990–94; Prime Minister 1998–2002, 2010–; Chair. Parl. Cttee on European Integration Affairs 1994–98; Pres. New Atlantic Initiative Hungarian Cttee 1996–98; Vice-Pres. Liberal International 1992–2000 (mem. Bureau 1993–2002), Christian Democrat and People's Parties International 2001–, European People's Party 2002–; Hon. Senator, European Acad. of Sciences and Arts 2000; Grande Croix, Ordre nat. du Mérite 2001, Papal Grand Cross of the Order of St Gregory the Great 2004; Freedom Prize, American Enterprises Inst. and the New Atlantic Initiative 2001, Vesek and Maria Polák Prize 2001, Franz Josef Strauss Prize 2001, Capo Circeo Prize 2001, Förderpreis Soziale Marktwirtschaft, German Club of Econs 2002, Mérite Européen Prize, European Peoples's Party 2004. *Film:* played bit part of a footballer in Hungarian family film 'Szegény Dzsoni és Árnika' 1983. *Publications:* National Policy 1988–1998, Egy az ország 2007 (translated into Polish as Ojczyzna jest jedna 2009), Rengés-Hullámok 2010. *Leisure interests:* playing football (signed player and financier of Felcsút Football Club), music (favourite band is Creedence Clearwater Revival). *Address:* Office of the Prime Minister, 1055 Budapest, Kossuth Lajos tér 4 (office); Office of the Prime Minister, 1357 Budapest, Pf. 6, Hungary (office); Fidesz—Hungarian Civic Alliance, 1089 Budapest, Visi Imre u. 6, Hungary (office). *Telephone:* (1) 795-6978 (office); (1) 555-2000 (Fidesz) (office). *Fax:* (1) 795-0381 (office); (1) 269-5343 (Fidesz) (office). *E-mail:* miniszterelnok@me.gov.hu (office); titkarsag@me.gov.hu (office); fidesz@fidesz.hu (office). *Website:* www.kormany.hu/en/prime-minister-s-office (office); www.fidesz.hu (office); www.orbanviktor.hu.

ORDE, Sir Hugh Stephen Roden, Kt, OBE, QPM, BA; British police officer; *President, Association of Chief Police Officers;* b. 27 Aug. 1958, London, England; s.

of Thomas Orde and Stella Orde; ed Univ. of Kent; joined London Metropolitan Police 1977, apptd Sergeant, Brixton 1982, Police Staff Coll. 1983, Insp., Greenwich 1984–90, Chief Insp., Deputy Asst Commdr SW London 1990, Chief Insp., Hounslow 1991–93, Supt Territorial Support 1993–95, Commdr (Community Safety and Partnership) 1997–98, Commdr (Crime), S London 1998–99, Deputy Asst Commr attached to Commr's Pvt. Office, New Scotland Yard 1999–2002; Chief Constable, Police Service of NI 2002–09; Pres. Asscn of Chief Police Officers 2009–; Visiting Prof., Univ. of Ulster; Hon. LLD (Kent) 2008, (Ulster) 2010. *Leisure interests:* marathon running, wine, gardening. *Address:* Association of Chief Police Officers, 1st Floor, 10 Victoria Street, London, SW1H 0NN, England (office). *Telephone:* (20) 7084-8950 (office). *E-mail:* info@acpo.pnn.police.uk (office). *Website:* www.acpo.police.uk (office).

ORDJONIKIDZE, Iosif Nikolaevich; Georgian engineer and politician; b. 9 Feb. 1948, Borjomi; m.; two c.; ed Georgian Polytechnic Inst.; engineer, Tbilisi Aviation plant 1971–73, Sec. Komsomol Cttee 1973–76; First Sec. Regional Komsomol Cttee of Georgia 1976–83; Sec. USSR Cen. Komsomol Cttee 1983–90; Chair. Union of Innovation Enterprises 1990–91; Deputy Premier for Int. and External Econ. Relations, Govt of Moscow 1991–2001, Deputy Mayor 2001–; Order of the Red Banner of Labour, Order of Friendship of Nations, Badge of Honour. *Address:* Moscow Government, Tverskaya str. 13, 103032 Moscow, Russia (office). *Telephone:* (495) 229-63-90 (office); (495) 230-28-56 (office).

OREFFICE, Paul F(austo), BS; American business executive; *Chairman, National Parkinson Foundation Inc.;* b. 29 Nov. 1927, Venice, Italy; s. of Max Oreffice and Elena Oreffice (née Friedenberg); m. Franca Giuseppina Ruffini 1956; one s. one d.; ed Purdue Univ.; joined Dow Chemical International, Midland, Mich. 1953, Mediterranean Area Sales Man., Milan, Italy 1955–56, Man. Dow Quimica do Brazil, São Paulo 1956–63, Gen. Man. Dow International, Spain 1963–65, Gen. Man. Dow Chemical Latin America 1965–67, Pres. Dow Chemical Inter-American Ltd 1967–69, Financial Vice-Pres. The Dow Chemical Co. 1969–75, Dir Dow Chemical Co. 1971–, Pres. Dow Chemical USA 1975–78, Chair. Exec. Cttee Dow Chemical Co. 1978–87, Pres. and CEO 1978–86, Chair., Pres. and CEO 1986–87, Chair. Bd 1987–92; Dir Cigna Corpn, Northern Telecom Ltd 1983, The Coca-Cola Company 1985, Morgan Stanley Group Inc. 1987; Chair. American Enterprise Inst., Bd of Overseers Inst. for Civil Justice; mem. Bd of Govs Nat. Parkinson Foundation, now Chair.; mem. The Business Council; Encomienda del Mérito Civil (Spain) 1966; Hon. DEng (Purdue) 1976; Hon. Dr of Industrial Man. (Lawrence Inst. of Tech.); Hon. DSc (Saginaw Valley State Coll.); Hon. DBA (Tri-State Univ.). *Leisure interests:* tennis, bridge, golf, various other sports. *Address:* c/o National Parkinson Foundation Inc., 1501 NW 9th Avenue, Bob Hope Road, Miami, FL 33136-1494, USA (office). *Website:* www.parkinson.org (office).

O'REILLY, Sir Anthony (John Francis), Kt, BCL; Irish business executive; *CEO, Independent News and Media PLC;* b. 7 May 1936, Dublin; s. of John Patrick O'Reilly and Aileen O'Reilly (née O'Connor); m. 1st Susan Cameron 1962 (divorced); three s. three d.; m. 2nd Chryss Goulandris 1991; ed Belvedere Coll., Dublin, Univ. Coll., Dublin; qualified as solicitor 1958; Demonstrator and Lecturer, Univ. Coll., Cork 1960–62; Personal Asst to Chair., Suttons Ltd, Cork 1960–62; Dir Robert McCowen & Sons Ltd, Tralee 1961–62; Gen. Man. Bord Bainne (Irish Dairy Bd) 1962–66; Man. Dir and CEO, Cómhlucht Siúicre Eireann Teo. (Irish Sugar Co.) 1966–69; Jt Man. Dir Heinz-Erin Ltd 1967–70, Man. Dir H. J. Heinz Co. Ltd, UK 1969–71, Sr Vice-Pres. N America and Pacific, H. J. Heinz Co. 1971–72, Exec. Vice-Pres. and COO 1972–73, Pres. and COO 1973–79, Chair. 1978–2000, Pres. 1979–90, CEO 1979–98; Chair. Ind. Newspapers PLC 1980–, Chair. and CEO Independent News and Media PLC 2000–04, CEO 2004–; Chair. Waterford Wedgwood PLC 1993–2009 (resgnd); Chair. European Advisory Bd Bankers Trust 1992–, Fitzwilton PLC, Atlantic Resources, Dublin, Eircom PLC 2001–; numerous other commercial appointments; Fellow, BIM, RSA; Dr hc (Bradford) 1991; Hon. LLD (Leicester) 1992. *Publications:* Prospect 1962, Developing Creative Management 1970, The Conservative Consumer 1971, Food for Thought 1972. *Leisure interests:* tennis, rugby. *Address:* Independent News and Media, Independent House, 2023 Bianconi Avenue, Citywest Business Park, Citywest Business Campus, Naas Road, Dublin 2 (office); Castlemartin, Kilcullen, Co. Kildare, Ireland (home). *Telephone:* (1) 4663200 (office). *Fax:* (1) 4663222 (office). *Website:* www.independentnewsmedia.com (office).

O'REILLY, David J., BEng; American/Irish petroleum company executive (retd); b. Jan. 1947, Dublin, Ireland; ed Univ. Coll., Dublin; joined Chevron Research Co. 1968, Sr Vice-Pres. and COO Chevron Chemical Co. 1989–91, Vice-Pres. Chevron 1991–98, Pres. Chevron Products Co. 1994–98, mem. Bd Dirs Chevron Corpn 1998–2010, Vice-Chair. Chevron Corpn 1998–99, Chair. and CEO 2000–10 (retd); fmr mem. American Petroleum Inst., Peterson Inst. for Int. Econs, The Business Council, The Business Roundtable, JPMorgan Int. Council, World Econ. Forum's Int. Business Council, Nat. Petroleum Council, American Soc. of Corp. Execs, Bd of Trustees Eisenhower Fellowships, King Fahd Univ. of Petroleum, Minerals Int. Advisory Bd. *Address:* 2158 Las Trampas Road, Alamo, CA 94507-1882, USA.

OREKHOV, Ruslan Gennadyevich; Russian politician; b. 14 Oct. 1963, Kalinin (now Tver); m.; two c.; ed Kazakh State Univ.; engineer-researcher Kazakh State Univ. 1985–87; Head of Div., Alma-Ata Dist Exec. Cttee 1987–88; instructor Moscow Dist Exec. Cttee 1989–90; expert USSR Union of Lawyers 1990; leading expert Cttee on Law Supreme Soviet of Russian Fed. 1990–91; Head Div. of Service of State Counsellors Russian Fed. 1991–93; Head State Dept of Law; Russian Presidency 1993–94; Co-Chair. Expert Council on Law, Russian Presidency 1994–96; Deputy Head of Admin. Russian Presidency, Head Dept of State Law 1996–2000, Pres. World Bank Group for Russia 2001. *Address:* The World Bank, Sadovo-Kudrinskaya str. 3, 123242 Moscow, Russia (office). *Telephone:* (495) 745-70-00 (office). *Fax:* (495) 253-06-12.

ORELLANA, José Roberto, MS; Salvadorean economist and banker; b. 20 Jan. 1944, San Salvador; s. of Roberto Orellana and Aida Milla; m. Julia Raquel Aguilar 1977; four c.; ed Trinity Coll., Conn., USA, Stanford Univ.; Vice-Pres., Gen. Man. Banco Cuscatlán 1971–81; Dir Fundación Salvadoreña para el Desarrollo Económico y Social (FUSADES) 1984–89; fmr Pres. Banco Cen. de Reserva de El Salvador; Alt. Gov. Interamerican Devt Bank 1989–95, IMF, World Bank, Banco Centroamericano de Integración Económica. *Address:* c/o Banco Central de

Reserva de El Salvador, Alameda Juan Pablo II y 17 Avenida Norte, San Salvador, El Salvador.

ORELLANA MERCADO, Angel Edmundo, DJur; Honduran diplomatist and legal executive; b. 20 Oct. 1948, Honduras; m.; ed Universidad Autónoma de Honduras, Univ. of Bologna, Italy; Asst to Legal Counsel of Nat. Housing Inst. 1968; Legal Counsel of Tech. Secr. of Council for Econ. Planning 1976–79; Dir Honduran Pre-Investment Fund 1980–84; Dir-Gen. Admin. Reform of the State Secr. for Planning, Co-ordination and Budget 1985–88; Pty Magistrate of Court of Appeals, Admin. Jurisdiction 1989–94; Attorney-Gen. 1994–99; Perm. Rep. to UN, New York 1999–2001; mem. Faculty of Law and Social Sciences, Universidad Nacional Autónoma de Honduras 1976–; Hon. Consul in Genoa, Italy 1974–75; mem. Admin. Law Comm., Honduran Bar Asscn 1980–91; Vice-Chair. for Co-ordination, Comm. on Judicial Reform 1988–93; Co-ordinator Cttee on Admin. Oversight of the Judiciary 1988–93; Minister of the Interior 2007–08, for Foreign Affairs 2008–09, of Nat. Defence 2009. *Publications include:* numerous articles and books; participated in promulgation of several bills. *Address:* c/o Ministry of National Defence, 5A Avenida, 4A Calle, Tegucigalpa, Honduras (office).

OREN, Michael B., BA, MA, PhD; Israeli (b. American) historian, academic, author and diplomatist; b. (Michael Bornstein), 1955, upstate NY, USA; m. Sally Oren 1982; two s. one d.; ed Columbia Univ., New York, Princeton Univ., NJ; grew up in NJ; youth activist in Zionist youth groups including USY; made first trip to Israel with youth movt Habonim Dror, working on Kibbutz Gan Shmuel 1970; adviser to Israeli del. to UN headed by Yehuda Blum 1978–79; emigrated to Israel and joined Israel Defense Forces (IDF) 1979, served as paratrooper in Lebanon War 1982; Israeli Liaison Officer to US Sixth Fleet during Gulf War 1991; Army Spokesman in IDF Reserves during Israel–Lebanon conflict 2006, Gaza operation Jan. 2009; Media Relations Officer during Israel–Gaza conflict 2008–09; Israeli Emissary to Jewish refuseniks in USSR, Israeli Govt's Dir of Inter-Religious Affairs; Visiting Prof., Harvard and Yale Univs 2006, Georgetown Univ.'s School of Foreign Service (as part of the Faculty associated with the Program for Jewish Civilization) 2008–09; continued teaching at Yale Univ. 2007; apptd by Pres. George W. Bush to serve on Hon. Del. to accompany him to Jerusalem for 60th anniversary of State of Israel May 2008; Amb. to USA 2009–13 (forfeited US citizenship to accept post); fmr Lady Davis Fellow, Hebrew Univ.; fmr Moshe Dayan Fellow, Tel-Aviv Univ.; fmr Distinguished Fellow, Shalem Center, Jerusalem; fmr Contributing Ed., The New Republic, Shalem Center's quarterly journal, Azure; fellowships from US Deps of State and Defense, and from UK and Canadian Govts. *Achievements include:* gold medal-winning athlete in Maccabiah Games. *Publications:* Six Days of War: June 1967 and the Making of the Modern Middle East (Los Angeles Times History Book of the Year Award, Nat. Council of the Humanities Award, Nat. Jewish Book Award) 2002, Reunion (novel) 2003, Power, Faith, and Fantasy: The United States in the Middle East, 1776 to 2006 2007, New Essays on Zionism (co-ed.) 2007; articles and essays on Middle Eastern history and current political issues. *Address:* c/o Embassy of Israel, 3514 International Drive NW, Washington, DC 20008, USA (office).

ORESHARSKI, Plamen, PhD; Bulgarian politician; *Prime Minister*; b. 21 Feb. 1960, Dupnitsa; m.; one s.; ed Univ. of Nat. and World Economy; Vice-Dean Finance Dept, Univ. of Nat. and World Economy 1992–93, Vice-Chancellor and Prof., Teaching on Finance Man., Investments, Investment Analysis 2003–05; Dir State Treasury and Debt Directorate, Ministry of Finance 1993–97, Deputy Minister 1997–2001, Minister of Finance 2005–09; mem. Union of Democratic Forces (UDF), Deputy Chair. and mem. UDF Nat. Exec. Bd –2003 (resgnd), UDF nominee for Mayor of Sofia at 2003 elections, candidature withdrawn; mem. Nat. Ass. 2009–13; Prime Minister 2013–; Pres. Man. Bd Sofiabank 1996–96; mem. Man. Bd Bulgarian Stock Exchange 1995–99, State Saving Bank 1996–97, Bulbank 1997–2000, Bulgarian Consolidation Co. 1997–2000; Emerging Markets magazine Finance Minister of the Year Award 2007, Person of the Year, Int. Tribunal for Crimes against Disabled People 2007, Knight of Book, Bulgarian Book Asscn 2007, nominated by the World Bank as one of the 10 top global reformers. *Publications:* Investment Analysis, Finance; more than 100 articles, reviews and comments. *Address:* Council of Ministers, 1594 Sofia, bul. Dondukov 1, Bulgaria (office). *Telephone:* (2) 940-29-99 (office). *Fax:* (2) 980-21-01 (office). *E-mail:* gis@government.bg (office). *Website:* www.government.bg (office).

ORGAN, (Harold) Bryan; British artist; b. 31 Aug. 1935, Leicester, England; s. of the late Harold Victor Organ and Helen Dorothy Organ; m. 2nd Sandra Mary Mills 1982; ed Loughborough Coll. of Art, Royal Acad. Schools, London; Lecturer in Drawing and Painting, Loughborough 1959–65; represented: Kunsthalle, Darmstadt 1968, Mostra Mercatao d'Arte Contemporanea, Florence 1969, 3rd Int. Exhbns of Drawing Germany 1970, São Paulo Museum of Art, Brazil; works in pvt. and public collections in England, France, Germany, Italy, Switzerland, USA, Canada, Brazil; Hon. MA (Loughborough) 1974; Hon. DLitt (Leicester) 1985. *Portraits include:* Sir Michael Tippett 1966, David Hicks 1968, Mary Quant 1969, Princess Margaret 1970, Sir Roy Strong 1971, Elton John 1973, Lester Piggott 1974, Jimmy Lindley 1974, Geoff Lewis 1974, Willie Carson 1974, Tony Murray 1974, Joe Mercer 1974, Harold Macmillan, 1st Earl of Stockton 1980, HRH The Prince of Wales 1980, Diana, Princess of Wales 1981, Alfred Thompson (Tom) Denning, Baron Denning 1982, James Callaghan, Baron Callaghan of Cardiff 1982, HRH The Duke of Edinburgh 1983, François Mitterand 1985, Richard Attenborough (later Lord Attenborough) 1985, 2003, Lord Jenkins 2002, Martin Johnson 2004, Alan Sugar, Baron Sugar 2010. *Leisure interest:* cricket. *Address:* c/o Redfern Gallery, 20 Cork Street, London, W1X 2HL; The Stables, Marston Trussell, nr Market Harborough, Leics., LE16 9TX, England. *Telephone:* (20) 7734-1732 (London). *E-mail:* art@redfern-gallery.com. *Website:* www.redfern-gallery.com/bryan-organ_1044.

O'RIORDAN, Timothy, OBE, MA, PhD, FRSA, FBA, DL; British environmental scientist and academic; *Professor Emeritus of Environmental Sciences, University of East Anglia;* b. 21 Feb. 1942, Edinburgh, Scotland; s. of the late Kevin O'Riordan and Norah O'Riordan; m. Ann Philip 1968 (died 1992); two d.; ed Univs of Edinburgh and Cambridge, Cornell Univ., USA; Asst Prof., Dept of Geography, Simon Fraser Univ. Vancouver, BC 1967–74; Visiting Lecturer, Univ. of Canterbury, NZ 1970; Visiting Assoc. Prof., Clark Univ., Worcester, Mass, USA 1972; Reader, Univ. of East Anglia 1974, Prof. of Environmental Sciences 1980–2005, Prof. Emer. 2005–; Chair. Environment Cttee Broads Authority 1989–99, Envir-

onment Science and Soc. Programme, European Science Foundation 1989–; Adviser, Environmental Research Directorate 1996–97; mem. Environmental Advisory Council, Dow Chemical 1992–97, Eastern Group PLC 1995–98; mem. UK Sustainable Devt Comm. 2000–07; Trustee, Soil Asscn 2005–; DL of Norfolk 1998; Sheriff, City of Norwich 2009–10; Gill Memorial Prize, Royal Geographical Soc. *Publications:* Environmentalism 1976, Countryside Conflicts 1986, Sizewell B: An Anatomy of the Inquiry 1987, The Greening of the Machinery of Government 1990; ed. Interpreting the Precautionary Principle 1994, The Politics of Climate Change in Europe 1996, Ecotaxation 1996, The Transition to Sustainability in Europe 1998, Environmental Science for Environmental Management 2000, Globalism, Localism and Identity 2001, Reinterpreting the Precautionary Principle 2001, Biodiversity, Sustainability and Human Communities 2002. *Leisure interests:* classical double bass playing, jogging, cycling, swimming, intuition. *Address:* Wheatlands, Hethersett Lane, Colney, Norwich, Norfolk, NR4 7TT, England. *Telephone:* (1603) 810534. *Fax:* (1603) 593739. *E-mail:* t.oriordan@uea.ac.uk (office). *Website:* www.uea.ac.uk/env (office).

ORITA, Masaki, LLB; Japanese academic and fmr diplomatist; *Professor, Faculty of Law, Chuo University;* b. 29 July 1942, Tokyo; s. of Saburo Orita and Saeko Orita; m. Masako Orita; one s.; ed Univ. of Tokyo, St Catherine's Coll., Oxford, UK; diplomatic postings to UK 1967–69, USSR 1975–77, OECD, Paris 1977–79, Washington, DC 1984–87; Exec. Asst to Prime Minister 1989–1992; Consul-Gen., Hong Kong 1992–94, Dir Gen. Treaties Bureau and N American Affairs Bureau, Ministry of Foreign Affairs 1994–97, Amb. to Denmark (also accred to Lithuania) 1997–2001, Insp. Gen., Ministry of Foreign Affairs 2001, Amb. to UK 2001–04, Special Envoy (Europe) for UN Reform, Ministry of Foreign Affairs 2005; currently Prof., Faculty of Law, Chuo Univ.; Chair. Inst. of Int. Affairs; Hon. Fellow, St Catherine's Coll., Oxford; Commdr, Order of Orange (Netherlands) 1991; Grand Cross, Order of the Dannebrog (Denmark) 1998. *Address:* Faculty of Law, Chuo University, 742-1 Higashinakano Hachioji-shi, Tokyo 192-0393 (office); c/o Board of Directors, Japan Center for Conflict Prevention, 3rd Floor Fujita Building, 1-35-20 Sekiguchi, Bunkyo-ku, Tokyo 112-0014, Japan.

ORLOV, Aleksey Maratovich; Russian politician; b. 9 Oct. 1961; ed Moscow State Inst. of Int. Relations; Perm. Rep. of Repub. of Kalmykiya, S Russia, to Pres. of Russian Fed. 1995, First Deputy Prime Minister, Repub. of Kalmykiya –2010; Pres. Repub. of Kalmykiya 2010–14; Hon. Pres. World Chess Fed. *Address:* c/o Dom Pravitelstva, pl. Lenina, 358000 Elista, Republic of Kalmykiya, Russia.

ORLOV, Alexandre; Russian diplomatist; *Ambassador to France;* b. 17 March 1948; m.; two s. one d.; ed Moscow State Inst. of Int. Relations; entered Ministry of Foreign Affairs of USSR 1971, various posts, including Minister Counsellor, Embassy in Paris 1993–98, Dir First Dept European Affairs, Ministry of Foreign Affairs 1998–2001, Perm. Rep. to Council of Europe, Strasbourg 2001–07, Dir Dept of Relationships to Federated Entities, Parl. and non-governmental orgs, Ministry of Foreign Affairs 2007–08, Amb. to France (also accred to Monaco) 2008–. *Address:* Embassy of Russia, 40–50 boulevard Lannes, 75116 Paris, France (office). *Telephone:* 1-45-04-05-50 (office). *Fax:* 1-45-04-17-65 (office). *E-mail:* ambrus@wanadoo.fr (office). *Website:* www.france.mid.ru (office).

ORLOV, Viktor Petrovich, CandGeolSc, DEconSc; Russian politician and geologist; b. 23 March 1940, Chernogorsk, Krasnoyarsk Region; s. of Petr Orlov and Eva Orlova; m.; three d.; ed Tomsk State Univ., Acad. of Nat. Econ. at USSR Council of Ministers; geologist, Chief Geologist, Team Leader, W Siberian Geological Survey 1968–75; Chief Engineer Geological Exploration, Iran 1975–78; Chief Geologist, Deputy Head Geological Div., Amalgamation Tsentrgeologiya 1979–81, Dir Gen. 1986–90; Deputy Head Geology and Production Depts, Ministry of Geology Russian Fed. 1981–84, 1986–; Deputy Minister of Geology USSR 1990–91; First Deputy Chair. State Cttee on Geology Russian Fed. 1991–92; Chair. Cttee on Geology and Use of Mineral Resources Russian Fed. 1992–96; Minister of Natural Resources Russian Fed. 1996–98, 1998–99; Pres. Russian Geological Soc. 2000–01; mem. Council of Fed., Fed. Ass. of the Russian Fed., Rep., Admin, Koryak Autonomous Area 2001–; Laureate, RF State Prize in Science and Eng 2001; Honoured Geologist of Russia 1990, Order for Services to the Native Land, IVth degree, 2001. *Publications:* Geological Forecasting 1991, Iron-Ore Base of Russia 1998, Mineral Resources and Geological Service of Russia during the Economic Reforms 1999, Reforms in Geology 2000; more than 200 scientific articles. *Leisure interests:* fishing, hunting. *Address:* Russian Geological Society, Zvenigorodskoye Shosse 9, 123022 Moscow (office); Council of Federation, Bolshaya Dmitrovka str. 26, Moscow (office); Palana, Portova str. 22, 684620 Kamchatka region, Karyak autonomous district, Russia (office). *Telephone:* (495) 292-75-43 (Geological Soc.) (office); (495) 926-69-53 (Council of Fed.) (office); (8415-43) 3-13-80 (Palana) (office); (495) 259-79-53. *Fax:* (495) 292-75-43. *E-mail:* VPOrlov@council.gov.ru (office).

ORMAN, Susan Lynn (Suze), BA; American financial adviser, television host, author, producer and magazine columnist; b. 5 June 1951, Chicago, Ill.; d. of Morry Orman and Ann Orman; partner Kathy Travis; ed Univ. of Illinois at Urbana-Champaign; Account Exec., Merrill Lynch 1980–83; Vice-Pres. of Investments, Prudential Bache Securities 1983–87; opened own financial planning firm, Suze Orman Financial Group, Emeryville, Calif. 1987, mem. Bd of Dirs 1987–97; contributing ed. to "O" The Oprah Magazine, Costco Connection Magazine; contrib., The Philadelphia Inquirer, Lowes MoneyWorks, Your Business at Home Magazine; host, weekly The Suze Orman Show (CNBC) 2001–; host, QVC Network 'Financial Freedom' Hour 1999–2009; regular guest on The View, Larry King Live, and The Oprah Winfrey Show; motivational speaker; Hon. DHumLitt (Univ. of Illinois) 2009; numerous awards including named one of Smart Money magazine's top 30 Power Brokers 1999, profiled in Worth Magazine's 100th issue as amongst those "who have revolutionized the way America thinks about money" 2001, The Suze Orman First Book Award est. by Books for a Better Life to honour first-time authors of self-improvement books 2002, Crossing Borders Award, Feminist Press 2003, American Women in Radio and Television (AWRT) Gracie Allen Award for The Suze Orman Show (National/Network/Syndication Talk Show category) 2003, Day Time Emmy Award in category of Outstanding Service Show Host for her PBS Special, AWRT Gracie Allen Award for The Suze Orman Show (Individual Achievement: Program Host category) 2005, 2006, Day Time Emmy Award for her PBS Special, The Money Show for the Young Fabulous & Broke (Outstanding Service Show Host category) 2006, AWRT Gracie Allen Award for The Suze Orman

Show (Outstanding Talk Show category) 2007, 2008, 2009, Amelia Earhart Award 2008, named by TIME magazine as one of the TIME 100, The World's Most Influential People 2008, 2009, CableFAX Program Award for Best Show or Series in the Talk Show/Commentary for The Suze Orman Show 2008, Vito Russo Media Award, Gay & Lesbian Alliance Against Defamation 2009, ranked by Forbes magazine amongst The World's 100 Most Powerful Women (61st) 2010, Touchstone Award from Women in Cable Telecommunications 2010. *Television:* co-produced and hosted six PBS Specials (based on her New York Times bestselling books). *Publications: You've Earned It, Don't Lose It* 1995, *The 9 Steps to Financial Freedom* 1997, Suze Orman's Financial Guidebook 1998, The Courage to Be Rich (Books for a Better Life Motivational Book Award 1999) 1999, Ask Suze Library System (nine-vol. set) 2000, The Road to Wealth 2001, The Laws of Money, the Lessons of Life 2003, The Money Book for the Young, Fabulous and Broke 2005, Women & Money: Owning the Power to Control Your Destiny 2007 (Spanish edn) 2007, Suze Orman's 2009 Action Plan 2009, Suze Orman's 2010 Action Plan: New Rules for New Times 2010; US Patent for her Ultimate Protection Portfolio design 2006; several non-book products, primarily CD-ROM-based services that offer educ. and various financial services, usually in conjunction with her books and writings, including Suze Orman's FICO Kit 2002, Suze Orman's Protection Portfolio 2002, Suze Orman's Will & Trust Kit 2005, Suze Orman's Insurance Kit 2007, Suze Orman's Identity Theft Kit 2008, Suze Orman's Save Yourself Retirement Program 2009, The Money Class, Learn To Create Your New American Dream 2011. *Address:* The Suze Orman Show, CNBC, 900 Sylvan Avenue, Englewood Cliffs, NJ 07632, USA (office). *Telephone:* (201) 735-2622 (office). *Fax:* (201) 735-3200 (office). *E-mail:* info@suzeorman.com (office); www.cnbc.com/id/15838016 (office); www.suzeorman.com.

ORMOND, Julia; British actress; b. 4 Jan. 1965, Epsom, Surrey, England; m. Rory Edwards (divorced); ed Guildford High School, Cranleigh School, Farnham Art School and Webber Douglas Acad.; worked in repertory, Crucible Theatre, Sheffield, Everyman Theatre, Cheltenham and on tour with Royal Exchange Theatre, Manchester; appeared in Faith, Hope and Charity (Lyric, Hammersmith), Treats (Hampstead Theatre); West End debut in Anouilh's The Rehearsal (Almeida), My Zinc Bed (Royal Court) 2000; Founding Chair. and Co-Chair, FilmAid International, mem. UK Bd of Trustees; Crystal Award, World Econ. Forum 2003. *Films include:* The Baby of Mâcon 1993, Nostradamus 1994, Captives 1994, Legends of the Fall 1994, First Knight 1995, Sabrina 1995, Calling the Ghosts (producer) 1996, Smilla's Sense of Snow 1997, The Barber of Siberia 1998, The Prime Gig 2000, Resistance 2003, Inland Empire 2006, I Know Who Killed Me 2007, Surveillance 2008, The Argentine 2008, Kit Kittredge: An American Girl 2008, La Conjura de El Escorial 2008, The Curious Case of Benjamin Button 2008, My Week with Marilyn 2011. *Television includes:* Traffik (Channel 4 mini-series) 1989, Capital City (series) 1989, Ruth Rendell Mysteries: The Best Man to Die 1990, Young Catherine 1991, Stalin 1992, Animal Farm (voice) 1999, Varian's War 2001, Iron Jawed Angels 2004. *Address:* c/o Marmont Management, Langham House, 302/8 Regent Street, London, W1R 5AL, England (office); c/o FilmAid International UK, Flat 2, 9 Colville Terrace, London, W11 2BE, England. *Telephone:* (20) 7727-1030. *Website:* www.filmaidinternational.org.

ORMOND, Richard Louis, CBE, MA; British museum director and art historian; b. 16 Jan. 1939, Bath, Avon, England; s. of Conrad E. Ormond and Dorothea Gibbons; m. Leonée Ormond 1963; two s.; ed Marlborough Coll., Brown Univ., USA and Christ Church, Oxford; Asst Keeper, Nat. Portrait Gallery 1965–75, Deputy Dir 1975–83; Head of Picture Dept Nat. Maritime Museum 1983–86; Dir Nat. Maritime Museum 1986–2000; Dir J. S. Sargent Catalogue Raisonné project. *Publications:* J. S. Sargent 1970, Catalogue of Early Victorian Portraits in the National Portrait Gallery 1973, Lord Leighton 1975, Sir Edwin Landseer 1982, The Great Age of Sail 1986, F.X. Winterhalter and the Courts of Europe 1987, Frederic, Lord Leighton (co-author) 1996, Sargent Abroad (co-author) 1997, John Singer Sargent: The Early Portraits (co-author) 1998, John Singer Sargent (co-author) 1998, Sargent (co-author) 1998, Sargent e l'Italia (co-author) 2001, John Singer Sargent: Portraits of the 1890s (co-author) 2002, John Singer Sargent: The Later Portraits (co-author) 2004, John Singer Sargent: Figures and Landscapes (co-author) 2006, John Singer Sargent: Venetian Figures and Landscapes (co-author) 2009, Edwin Landseer: The Private Drawings 2009. *Leisure interests:* opera, theatre, cycling. *Address:* Crusader House, Pall Mall, London, SW1Y 5LU (office); 8 Holly Terrace, London, N6 6LX, England (home). *Telephone:* (20) 7839-3125. *E-mail:* rormond@ceoexpress.com (office).

ORMOS, Mária, DSc; Hungarian historian and academic; b. 1 Oct. 1930, Debrecen; d. of János Ormos and Elza Förster; one s. one d.; ed Kossuth Lajos Univ., Debrecen; Asst Lecturer, Historic Science Inst. 1963; Univ. Prof., Eötvös Loránd Univ., Budapest 1982; Prof. of History then Prof. Emer., Janus Pannonius Univ. (now Univ. of Pécs), Rector 1984–92, f. Foundation of the Univ. of Pécs 1992; mem. Nat. Cttee of Historians; Pres. Italian-Hungarian Mixed Cttee of Historians; Vice-Pres. Asscn d'histoire des relations internationales; mem. Hungarian Acad. of Sciences 1993 (mem. of Presidium), European Acad. of Arts, Sciences and Humanities; Széchenyi Prize 1995, Szentgyörgyi Prize 1995, Leo Sziliard Prize 2000, Deák Ferenc Prize 2000, Pulitzer Prize 2000, Hazám-díj 2003, Grastyán-díj 2004, Húszéves a Köztársaság Díj 2009. *Publications:* Franciaország és a keleti biztonság 1931–36 (France and the Eastern Security) 1969, Europai Fasizmusok 1919–1939 (co-author) 1976, Merénylet Marseille-Ben (Assassination in Marseille) 1984, Mussolini: Politikai eletrajz (Mussolini: A Political Portrait) 1987, Nacizmus, Fasizmus (Nazism and Fascism) 1987, Never as Long as I Shall Live 1989, Civitas fidelissima 1921 1990, From Padua to the Trianon 1918–1920 1991, Hitler 1993, Documents diplomatiques français sur l'histoire du Bassin des Carpates 1918–1932: août 1919–juin 1920 (co-author) 1995, Magyarország a világháborúk korában 1914–45 (Hungary in the Age of the World Wars 1914–45) 1997, Európa a nemzetközi Küzdőtéren. Felemelkedés és hanyatlás 1814–1945 (Europe in the International Arena. Rise and Decline) (co-author) 1998, Hitler-Stálin (Hitler-Stalin) (co-author) 1999), Documents diplomatiques français sur l'histoire du Bassin des Carpates: 1918–1932 (co-author) 1999, Kozma Miklós, Egy magyar Médiavezér (Nikolaus Kozma, Life of Hungarian Media Leader) 2000, Hungary Governments and Politics 1848–2000 (co-ed.) 2001, Gazdasagi Vilagvalsag Magyar Visszhangja: 1929–1936 2004, Hungary in the Age of the Two World Wars: 1914–1945 2008. *Leisure interests:* music, books, theatre. *Address:* Department of

History, University of Pécs, 7633 Pécs, Szántó Kovács János u. 1/B, Hungary (office).

ORNSTEIN, Donald Samuel, PhD; American mathematician and academic; *Professor of Mathematics, Stanford University;* b. 30 July 1934; s. of Harry Ornstein and Rose Ornstein (née Wisner); m. Shari Richman 1964; two s. one d.; ed Swarthmore Coll. and Univ. of Chicago; mem. Inst. for Advanced Study, Princeton 1956–58; Instructor, Univ. of Wis. 1958–60; Asst Prof., Stanford Univ. 1960–63, Sloan Fellow and Assoc. Prof. 1963–65, Assoc. Prof. 1965–66, Prof. of Math. 1966–; Visiting Prof., Cornell Univ. and New York Univ. (Courant Inst.) 1967–68, Hebrew Univ., Jerusalem 1975–76, Math. Sciences Research Inst., Berkeley 1983–84;; mem. NAS 1981, American Acad. of Arts and Sciences 1991; Bocher Prize 1974. *Publications:* Ergodic Theory Randomness and Dynamical Systems 1974; mathematical papers in many journals since 1959. *Address:* Department of Mathematics, Stanford University, 450 Serra Mall, Building 380, Stanford, CA 94305-2125 (office); 857 Tolman Drive, Stanford, CA 94305, USA (home). *Fax:* (415) 725-4066 (office). *E-mail:* ornstein@math.stanford.edu (office). *Website:* math.stanford.edu (office).

OROZCO, Esther, PhD; Mexican biologist and academic; *Investigator and Professor of Experimental Pathology, Centre for Research and Advanced Studies, National Polytechnic Institute (Cinvestav-IPN);* b. 25 April 1945, Est. Pascual Orozco, Chihuahua; m. Tomás Sánchez; one s. one d.; ed Universidad Autónoma de Chihuahua, Centre for Research and Advanced Studies, Nat. Polytechnic Inst. (Cinvestav-IPN); conducted postdoctoral research for short periods at MRC, London and Netherlands Cancer Inst., Amsterdam; fmr Visiting Prof., Harvard School of Public Health; Assoc. Prof., Dept of Genetics and Molecular Biology, Centre for Research and Advanced Studies, Nat. Polytechnic Inst. (Cinvestav-IPN), now Investigator and Prof. of Experimental Pathology, est. Multidisciplinary Program of Molecular Biomedicine; Howard Hughes Medical Inst. Int. Research Scholar 1991–96, currently Howard Hughes Medical Inst. Foreign Prof.; mem. Mexican Acad. of Sciences, Instituto de las Mujeres, Nat. Researcher System (Level E); unsuccessful cand. (Revolutionary Democratic Party–PRD) for Gov. of Chihuahua (first woman) 1998; Dir Gen. Inst. of Science and Tech., Mexico City; Premio Nacional Miguel Otero, Secr. of Health 1985, Pasteur Medal, Institut Pasteur and UNESCO 1997, L'Oreal/UNESCO Award for Women in Science (Latin American) for discovery of mechanisms and control of infections by amoebae in the tropics 2006, Medal for Scientific Merit, Asamblea Legislativa, Mexico City 2006. *Publications:* numerous scientific papers in professional journals. *Leisure interests:* writing, reading, theatre. *Address:* Centro de Investigación y de Estudios Avanzados del IPN, Av. Instituto Politécnico Nacional, 2508 Col. San Pedro, Apartado Postal 14-740, 07000 Mexico City, DF, Mexico (office). *Telephone:* (52) 5061-3800 (ext 5650) (office). *Fax:* (52) 5061-7108 (office). *E-mail:* esther@cinvestav.mx (office). *Website:* www.cinvestav.mx (office); www.icyt.df.gob.mx; www.estherorozco.net.

OROZCO, Gabriel; Mexican artist; b. 27 April 1962, Jalapa, Veracruz; s. of Mario Orozco Rivera and Cristina Fèlix Romandía; m. Maria Gutierrez 1994; one s.; ed Escuela Nacional de Arte Plasticas, Mexico City, Circulo de Bellas Artes, Madrid, Spain; gained reputation with his exploration of drawing, photography, sculpture and installation early 1990s; works include Sleeping Dog 1990, Recaptured Nature 1991, Crazy Tourist 1991, My Hands are my Heart 1991, Yielding Stone 1992, Empty Shoe Box 1993, Home Run 1993, La DS 1993, Yogurt Caps 1994, Working Tables 1996, Black Kites 1997, Lintels 2001, Samurai Tree Paintings 2004, Corplegados 2011; terracotta ceramics featured at Documenta XI 2002; lives and works in New York, Paris and Mexico City; Seccio Espacios Alternativos Prize, Salon Nacional de Artes Plasticas, Mexico City 1987, DAAD Artist-in-Residence grant, Berlin 1995, German Blue Orange Prize 2006. *Leisure interests:* football (soccer), throwing boomerangs. *Address:* c/o Marian Goodman Gallery, 24 West 57th Street, New York, NY 10019, USA. *Telephone:* (212) 977-7160. *Fax:* (212) 581-5187. *E-mail:* info@mariangoodman.com. *Website:* www.mariangoodman.com/artists/gabriel-orozco.

ORR, Christopher John, MBE, MA, RCA, RA; British artist; *Professor Emeritus of Printmaking, Royal College of Art;* b. 8 April 1943, London, England; s. of Ronald Orr and Violet Townley; m. Catherine Terris 1985; one s. one d.; ed Ravensbourne Coll. of Art, Hornsey Coll. of Art, Royal Coll. of Art; worked as artist and teacher, latterly as a tutor and Visiting Lecturer, RCA 1976–, Prof. and Course Dir of Printmaking 1998–2008, Prof. Emer. 2008–; solo touring exhbns The Complete Chris Orr 1976, Many Mansions 1990; numerous exhbns world-wide; Fellow, Royal Soc. of Painters and Printmakers; elected Royal Academician 1995. *Publications:* Many Mansions 1990, The Small Titanic 1994, Happy Days 1999, Semi-antics 2001, The Disguise Factory 2003, City of Holy Dreams 2006, The Multitude Diaries 2008. *Telephone:* (20) 7738-1203. *E-mail:* info@chrisorr-ra.com. *Website:* www.chrisorr-ra.com.

ORREGO VICUÑA, Francisco, PhD; Chilean arbitrator, judge and academic; *Professor of International Law, Heildelberg University Centre at Santiago;* b. 12 April 1942, Santiago; m. Soledad Bauza; three c.; ed schools in Chile, Argentina, Spain and Egypt, Univ. of Chile and London School of Econs; fmr Dir Inst. of Int. Studies Univ. of Chile; fmr Visiting Prof., Stanford Univ., Univ. of Paris II Law School, Univ. of Miami Law School; participated in projects for Acad. of Int. Law, The Hague, UNITAR and various studies and projects undertaken by univs in Europe, USA, Asia and Latin America; fmr legal adviser to OAS; fmr del. to Law of Sea Conf.; fmr int. corresp., El Mercurio (daily newspaper); Amb. to UK 1983–85; Prof. of Int. Law, Inst. of Int. Studies, Univ. of Chile 1985–2010; Prof. of Int. Law, Heildelberg Univ. Centre at Santiago 2010–; Pres. Chilean Council on Foreign Relations 1989–2000, Chilean Acad. of Social Sciences 1995–2000; mem. Chilean-US Comm. for Settlement of Disputes; Conciliator and Arbitrator of ICSID 1995–; Judge Admin. Tribunal of IBRD 1991–2010, Pres. 2001–04; Commr UN Compensation Comm. 1998–2000; Arbitrator, Int. Chamber of Commerce, London Court of Int. Arbitration, Perm. Court of Arbitration; arbitrator, 20 Essex Street Chambers (Barristers), London, Singapore; Judge ad-hoc, Int. Tribunal for the Law of the Sea, Hamburg; Judge ad-hoc, Int. Court of Justice, The Hague; Judge, Admin. Tribunal of IMF 2012–; mem. Inst. of Int. Law (fmr Pres.); Great Cross of the Order Piana (Holy See); Nat. Award for the Humanities and Social Sciences 2001, Medal of Merit, Univ. of Heidelberg. *Publications:* Antarctic Resources Policy 1983, Antarctic Mineral Exploitation 1988, The Exclusive Economic Zone 1989, The

Changing International Law of High Seas Fisheries 1999, International Dispute Settlement in a Global Society 2004, and other books and articles. *Address:* Francisco Orrego Vicuña y Cia., Avenida El Golf No. 40, Sixth Floor, Santiago 755-0107, Chile (office). *Telephone:* (2) 4416300 (office). *Fax:* (2) 4416399 (office). *E-mail:* forregovicuna@20essexst.com (office).

ORRELL-JONES, Keith, MA, CInstM; British business executive; b. 15 July 1937; s. of Francis George Orrell-Jones and Elsie Orrell-Jones; m. Hilary Kathleen Orrell-Jones (née Pegram) 1961; four s.; ed The High School, Newcastle-under-Lyme, St John's Coll., Cambridge; Chief Exec. ARC Ltd 1986–89; Dir Consolidated Gold Fields PLC 1989; Dir Blue Circle Industries PLC 1990, Chief Exec. 1992–99; Chair. FKI PLC 1999–2004; Dir (non-exec.) Smiths Group PLC 1990, Chair. 1998–2004 (retd). *Leisure interests:* music (particularly opera), field sports, art, walking.

ORSENNA, Érik (see ARNOULT, Érik).

ORSI, Giuseppe, CBE, PhD, FRAeS; Italian business executive; *Chairman and CEO, Finmeccanica SpA;* m. Rita Orsi; two s.; ed Milan Polytechnic Univ., Wharton School, Univ. of Pennsylvania, USA; served as an officer in Italian Air Force, a qualified civil pilot; joined SIAI Marchetti 1973, later Product Support Dir; joined Agusta Corpn as staff to Marketing & Strategy Dir 1984–87, Sales Dir Agusta's Aircraft Div. 1987–89, Pres. and CEO Agusta Aerospace Corpn (North American subsidiary headquartered in Philadelphia) 1989–94, Chair. EHI Inc. (jt Agusta and Westland co. incorporated in USA) 1989–94, Sr Vice-Pres. of Govt Sales and Programs Agusta 1994–97, relocated to Italy with responsibility for worldwide military sales, Deputy Gen. Man. Agusta, responsible for Marketing and Sales 1997–99, Co-Gen. Man. Agusta 1999–2001, mem. Man. Cttee of JV, Agusta and Westland merged 2001, Man. Dir Marketing and Sales org. of AgustaWestland world-wide 2001–02, Man. Dir Agusta SpA 2002–11, CEO AgustaWestland NV 2004–11; CEO Finmeccanica SpA May 2011–, Chair. Dec. 2011–; Freeman of the City of London 2010. *Address:* Finmeccanica SpA, Piazza Monte Grappa 4, Rome 00195, Italy (office). *Telephone:* (06) 324731 (office). *Fax:* (06) 3208621 (office). *E-mail:* info@finmeccanica.it (office). *Website:* www.finmeccanica.it (office).

ORSZAG, Peter Richard, AB, MS, PhD; American economist, business executive and fmr government official; *Vice-Chairman of Global Banking, Citigroup Inc.;* b. 16 Dec. 1968, Boston; two c.; ed Princeton Univ., London School of Econs, UK; Research Officer, Centre for Econ. Performance, London School of Econs 1992–93, mem. Professional Research Staff 1994–95; Econ. Adviser, Macroeconomic and Fiscal Unit, Ministry of Finance, Russian Fed., Moscow 1993; Staff Economist, Council of Econ. Advisers, Washington, DC 1993–94, Sr Adviser 1996; Sr Econ. Advisor, Nat. Econ. Council 1997, Special Asst to Pres. Clinton for Econ. Policy 1998; consultant, McKinsey & Co. 1998; Pres. Sebago Assocs Inc. 1998–2007, Sr Dir 2002–07; Dir Congressional Budget Office, Washington, DC 2007–08; Dir Office of Man. and Budget 2009–10 (resgnd); Distinguished Visiting Fellow, Council on Foreign Relations 2010; Vice-Chair. Global Banking, Citigroup Inc. 2010–; Dir Competition Policy Assocs Inc. 2003–07; Sr Fellow in Economic Studies, Brookings Inst. 2001–07, Joseph A. Pechman Fellow in Tax and Fiscal Policy 2001–07, Co-Dir Tax Policy Center 2003–07, Dir The Hamilton Project 2005–07, Deputy Dir of Econ. Studies 2006–07; Dir Retirement Security Project, Pew Charitable Trust 2004–07; Lecturer, Univ. of California, Berkeley 1999–2000; Research Prof., Georgetown Univ. 2005–07; mem. Inst. of Medicine. *Publications:* American Economic Policy in the 1990s (co-ed.) 2002, Protecting the American Homeland: A Preliminary Analysis (co-author) 2002, Protecting the American Homeland: One Year On (co-author) 2003, Saving Social Security: A Balanced Approach (co-author) 2005, Aging Gracefully: Ideas to Improve Retirement Security in America (co-author) 2006, Protecting the Homeland 2006/7 (co-author) 2006; numerous articles. *Address:* Citigroup Inc., 399 Park Avenue, New York, NY 10043, USA (office). *Telephone:* (212) 559-1000 (office). *Website:* www.citigroup.com (office).

ORSZULIK, Most Rev. Alojzy; Polish ecclesiastic; b. 21 June 1928, Baranowice Śląskie; ed Catholic Univ. of Lublin; ordained priest, Soc. of the Catholic Apostolate 1957; Lecturer, Higher Ecclesiastic Seminar, Ołtarzew 1962–89; mem. staff, Secr. of Episcopate of Poland 1962–68, Head, Press Bureau 1968–93, Deputy Sec. 1989–94, Chair. Comm. for Social Communications 1984–94; Adviser, Pontifical Council for Social Communications 1974–2000; Sec. Jt Comm. of Gov. and Episcopate of Poland 1980; mem. Working Group for Legis. Affairs 1981–83, 1987–89; Legis. Council of Episcopate of Poland 1993–; rep. of Catholic Church during Round Table Talks 1989; Auxiliary Bishop of Siedlce, Titular Bishop of Vissalsa and Curate-Gen. 1989–92; Bishop of Łowicz 1992–2004; del. of the Holy See for negotiations with Polish Govt about the concordat 1990–93. *Publications:* numerous articles on canon law. *Address:* c/o Bishops Curie, Stary Rynek 20, 99-400 Łowicz, Poland (office). *Telephone:* (46) 837-66-15 (office). *Fax:* (46) 837-43-49 (office). *Website:* www.diecezja.lowicz.pl (office).

ORTEGA GAONA, Amancio; Spanish retail executive; *Chairman, Industria de Diseño Textil, SA;* b. March 1936, León; fmr shop assistant; f. Confecciones Goa (mfrs of bathrobes) 1963, f. Zara (chain of fashion stores, 1,500 outlets world-wide) 1975, now majority shareholder and Chair. Inditex group (Industrias de Diseño Textil SA), including Zara, Massimo Dutti and Pull and Bear and other brands. *Address:* Industria de Diseño Textil, SA, Avenida de la Diputación, 15142 Arteixo, A Coruña, Spain (office). *Telephone:* (98) 1185400 (office). *Fax:* (98) 1185544 (office). *Website:* www.inditex.com (office).

ORTEGA MARTÍNEZ, Jesús; Mexican politician; b. 5 Nov. 1952, Aguascalientes; ed Instituto Politécnico Nacional; fmr mem. Partido Socialista de los Trabajadores; fmr mem. Partido Mexicano Socialista; mem. Chamber of Deputies 1979–82, 1988–91; mem. Senate (upper house) 2000; Founding mem. Partido de la Revolución Democrática, Sec. Gen. 1996–99, Pres. 2008–11. *Address:* Partido de la Revolución Democrática, Avda Benjamín Franklin 84, Col. Escandón, 11800 México DF, Mexico (office). *Telephone:* (55) 1085-8000 (office). *Fax:* (55) 1085-8144 (office). *E-mail:* comunicacion@prd.org.mx (office); jesus.ortega@prd.org.mx (office). *Website:* www.prd.org.mx (office).

ORTEGA SAAVEDRA, José Daniel; Nicaraguan politician, fmr resistance leader and head of state; *President;* b. 11 Nov. 1945, La Libertad, Chontales; s. of

Daniel Ortega and Lidia Saavedra; m. Rosario Murillo; seven c.; ed Univ. Centroamericano, Managua; joined Frente Sandinista 1963; active in various underground resistance movt against regime of Anastasio Somoza from 1959, was imprisoned several times and tortured for revolutionary activities; ed. El Estudiante, official publ of Frente Estudiantil Revolucionaria and directed org. of Comités Cívicos Populares in Managua 1965; mem. Nat. Directorate of FSLN (Sandinista Liberation Front) 1966–67; imprisoned 1967–74; resumed position with FSLN and with José Benito Escobar, became involved in further revolutionary activities; fought on front in two-year mil. offensive which overthrew Somoza regime 1979; mem. Junta of Nat. Reconstruction Govt 1979, Co-ordinator of Junta 1981–85, Pres. of Nicaragua 1985–90, 2006–; presidential cand. 2001; Gen. Sec. FSLN. *Address:* Office of the President, Casa Presidencial, Managua, Nicaragua (office). *E-mail:* daniel@presidencia.gob.ni (office). *Website:* www.presidencia.gob.ni (office).

ORTEGA Y ALAMINO, HE Cardinal Jaime Lucas; Cuban ecclesiastic; *Archbishop of San Cristóbal de la Habana;* b. 18 Oct. 1936, Jagüey Grande, Matanzas; ed Arturo Echemendía School, Matanzas, Advanced Inst. for Secondary Studies of Matanzas, Diocesan Seminary of San Alberto Magno, Seminary of Foreign Mission in Quebec, Canada; ordained priest 1964; Coadjutor Vicar of Cárdenas 1964, detained in work camp 1966, released 1967; Parish Priest of Jagüey Grande 1967 and also of Cathedral of Matanzas, also responsible for Parish of Pueblo Nuevo in city and another two churches outside it; Pres. Diocesan Comm. for Catechesis; taught moral theology part-time at Sts Charles and Ambrose Interdiocesan Seminary, Havana; Bishop of Pinar del Rio 1979; Archbishop of San Cristóbal de la Habana 1981–; Pres. Cuban Conf. of Catholic Bishops 1988–98, 2001–, took part in fourth Gen. Conf. Latin-American Bishops, Santo Domingo; Founder Caritas Cuba 1991; Vice-Pres. Latin American Episcopal Council 1995–99; cr. Cardinal (Cardinal-Priest of Santi Aquila e Priscilla) 1994; participated in Papal Conclave 2005, 2013; attended Special Ass. for America of World Synod of Bishops, Vatican City 1997; Special Papal Envoy to Nat. Eucharistic Congress of El Salvador, San Salvador 2000; Dr hc (St John's Univ., New York); hon. degrees from Barry and St Thomas Univs, Fla, Univ. of San Francisco, Calif., Providence Coll., RI, Boston Coll., Mass 2001. *Address:* Apartado 594, Calle Habana 152, Havana 10100, Cuba (office). *Telephone:* (7) 624000 (office). *Fax:* (7) 338109 (office).

ORTEZ COLINDRES, Enrique, LLD; Honduran lawyer, diplomatist and politician; b. 29 Oct. 1931, Tegucigalpa; s. of Enrique Ortez Pinel; m. 1st Hilda Sequeira 1959; two s. one d.; m. 2nd Patricia d'Arcy Lardizabal 1995; one d.; diplomatic postings include Sec., Embassy in Paris 1955, Rep. to Org. of Cen. American States, Perm. Rep. to UN, New York in 1970s; Dir, later Pres. Banco Centroamericano de Integracion Economico; mem. Partido Liberal; Minister of Foreign Affairs June–July 2009; Minister of the Interior and Justice 2009. *Publications:* La Republica Federal de Centro America a la luz del derecho internacional publico 1963, Integracion politica de Centroamerica 1975. *Address:* c/o Ministry of the Interior and Justice, Residencia la Hacienda, Calle la Estancia, Tegucigalpa, Honduras (office).

ORTIZ, Cristina; Brazilian pianist; b. 17 April 1950, Bahia; d. of Silverio M. Ortiz and Moema F. Ortiz; m. Jasper W. Parrott 1974; two d.; ed Conservatório Brasileiro de Música, Rio de Janeiro, Acad. Int. de Piano (with Magda Tagliaferro), Paris and Curtis Inst. of Music, Philadelphia (with Rudolf Serkin); New York recital debut 1971; London debut with LSO and André Previn 1973; has appeared in concerts with the Vienna Philharmonic, Berlin Philharmonic, the Concertgebouw, Chicago Symphony, New York Philharmonic, Israel Philharmonic, Los Angeles Philharmonic, leading British orchestras and has undertaken many tours of North and South America, the Far East, New Zealand and Japan; appeared with NHK Symphony, the Bergen Philharmonic and Philharmonia under Janowski 1997; played with conductors including Previn, Mehta, Kondrashin, Ashkenazy, Leinsdorf, Chailly, Masur, Salonen, Colin Davis, Janssons, Fedoseyev, Zinman, Rattle, Järvi and Fürst; first prize, Van Cliburn Int. Competition, Texas 1969. *Leisure interests:* tennis, swimming, reading, hiking, holidaying, horse riding. *E-mail:* mscristinaortiz@gmail.com (office). *Website:* www.cristina.ortiz.name.

ORTIZ BOSCH, Milagros María; Dominican Republic politician; b. 23 Aug. 1936, Santo Domingo; one s.; niece of fmr Pres. Juan Bosch Gaviño; ed Univ. of Santo Domingo; Adviser, Chamber of Deputies 1982–90; mem. Senate 1990–2000; Vice-Pres. of the Dominican Republic 2000–04; Sec. of State for Educ. 2000–04; mem. Partido Revolucionario Dominicano, fmr Vice-Pres. *Address:* c/o Partido Revolucionario Dominicano, Avda Dr Comandante Enrique Jiménez Moya 14, Bella Vista, Santo Domingo, DN, Dominican Republic. *Telephone:* 687-2193. *E-mail:* prensa_tribunalp.r.d@hotmail.com. *Website:* www.prd.partidos.com.

ORTIZ DE LA CADENA, Fausto, MBA; Ecuadorean economist and government official; ed Universidad Católica de Guayaquil; served as State Treasurer 2005, Sub-Sec. of Public Credit 2005; Deputy Minister of Economy 2005–07, Minister of the Economy and Finance 2007–08 (resgnd); mem. Alianza País. *Address:* Alianza País, Of. 501, Edif. Torres Whimper, Diego de Almagro 32-27 y Whimper, Quito, Ecuador (office). *Telephone:* (2) 600-0630 (office). *Fax:* (2) 600-1029 (office). *E-mail:* info@rafaelcorrea.com (office). *Website:* www.rafaelcorrea.com (office).

ORTIZ DE ROZAS, Carlos; Argentine diplomatist, lawyer and academic; *Professor of International Relations, University of Belgrano;* b. 26 April 1926, Buenos Aires; s. of the late Alfredo Ortiz de Rozas and Susana del Valle; m. Carmen Sarobe 1952; ed Univ. de Buenos Aires School of Diplomacy; entered foreign service 1948; Chargé d'affaires a.i., Sofia 1952–54; Sec. Greece 1954–56; mem. Cabinet, Argentine Ministry of Foreign Affairs 1958–59; Counsellor, Argentine Mission at UN 1959–61; subsequently Dir-Gen. Policy Dept, Ministry of Foreign Affairs and later Minister at embassies in UAR and UK; Amb. to Austria 1967–70; Chief Rep. to Conf. of Cttee on Disarmament, Geneva 1969 (Chair. of Cttee 1979); Perm. Rep. to UN 1970–77; Amb. to UK 1980–82, to France 1984–89, to USA 1991–93; Under-Sec. of State for Foreign Relations 1990; Head of Argentine Special Mission to Holy See 1982; Pres. UN Security Council 1971, 1972; mem. Advisory Bd to Sec.-Gen. on Disarmament 1978–92; Prof. of Int. Relations, Univ. of Belgrano, Buenos Aires 1995–; Dir and Pres. Del. of Conf. on Law of the Sea 1973; Chair. First (Political and Security) Cttee of the 29th General Ass. 1974; has held several teaching posts including Prof. of Public Law and Int.

Relations, Univ. del Salvador, Buenos Aires (now mem. Bd Dirs); Pres. Bunge and Born Foundation 1994–99, Alliance Française de Buenos Aires 1999–2001; mem. Exec. Bd Argentine Council for Int. Relations 1994–; mem. Nat. Acad. of Social and Political Sciences, Buenos Aires 2005; decorations from Chile, Brazil, Greece, Thailand, Repub. of Korea, UAR, Nicaragua, Peru, Japan, Italy, Spain, The Holy See and France; Personality of the Year in Int. Relations, Rotary Club, Buenos Aires 1995. *Publications:* Paths to Peace: The UN Security Council and its Presidency 1981, La reunion de Palm Beach: J.F. Kennedy – A. Frondizi 1994, Contribuciones Argentinas a las Naciones Unidas 1995. *Address:* Avenida Gelly y Obes 2263, 1425 Buenos Aires, Argentina. *Telephone:* (11) 4803-3630. *Fax:* (11) 4804-6791. *E-mail:* corzas@yahoo.com.

ORTIZ DE ZEVALLOS MADUEÑO, Felipe, BA, MA; Peruvian economist, academic, business executive and diplomatist; *Chairman, Grupo APOYO;* b. Aug. 1947, Lima; ed Universidad Nacional de Ingeniería, Lima, Univ. of Rochester, NY and Owner-Pres. Man. Program, Harvard Business School, USA; worked as consulting engineer in Peru 1970–77; f. APOYO (consultancy and publishing firm) 1977, currently Chair. Grupo APOYO; ind. mem. of Bd of several businesses, educational and cultural insts, including Buenaventura Mining Co., Credicorp; Chair. Eisenhower Fellowship's Nominating Cttee Peru, mem. Eisenhower Fellowship's Advisory Int. Council; Founder-Dir Inst. of Econ. Devt, ESAN (Grad. School of Business Admin), Lima 1979–82; Chair. Nat. Devt Corpn (CONADE) and Inversiones Cofide (holding cos of all state-owned enterprises) 1982; Pres. Annual Conf. of Execs 1985; Visiting Scholar, Inst. of Latin American Studies, Univ. of Texas, Austin, USA 1983, 1984; Prof., Econs Dept, Universidad del Pacífico 1978–, Pres. Universidad del Pacífico –2006; Amb. to USA 2006–09; guest columnist in magazines; Instituto Peruano de Administracion de Empresas Award 1990, Eisenhower Exchange Fellowship 1996, Jerusalem Award of Journalism 1998, Manuel J. Bustamante de la Fuente Prize 2008. *Publications:* The Peruvian Puzzle 1989, Respuestas para los 90s (Answers to the 90s) (with Pedro Pablo Kuczynski) 1990, In the Shadow of the Debt (co-author) 1992, A Mitad de Camino (Half Way Through) 1992, El Reto 2001: Competir y Crear Empleo (The 2001 Challenge: Compete and Create Employment) (with Pedro Pablo Kuczynski) 2001; numerous articles in nat. and int. journals. *Leisure interests:* reading, swimming, collecting art. *Address:* Grupo APOYO, Camino Real 390, Torre Central Piso 11, San Isidro, Lima 27, Peru (office). *Telephone:* (1) 513-3030 (office). *Fax:* (1) 513-3035 (office). *E-mail:* info@apoyo.com (office). *Website:* www.apoyo.com (office).

ORTIZ MARTÍNEZ, Guillermo, BA, PhD; Mexican economist, academic, fmr central banker and fmr government official; *Chairman, Grupo Financiero Banorte-Ixe;* b. 21 July 1948, Mexico City; s. of Gen. Leopoldo Ortiz Sevilla and Graciela Martínez Ostos; m. Margie Simon de Ortiz; three d.; ed Universidad Nacional Autónoma de México, Stanford Univ., USA; economist, Ministry of the Presidency of Mexico 1971–72; Deputy Man., later Man. Econ. Research Dept, Banco de México 1977–84, Gov. Banco de México 1998–2009; Exec. Dir IMF 1984–88, mem. Cttee to Study Sustainable Long-term Financing of the IMF 2006–07, Cttee on IMF Governance Reform 2008–09, Chair. External Panel for the Review of the Fund's Risk Management Framework 2010–11; Undersecretary of Finance and Public Credit, Fed. Govt 1988–94; Sec. of Telecommunications and Transportation –1994, of Finance and Public Credit 1994–97; mem. Bd of Dirs BIS, Basel, Switzerland 2006–, Chair. March–Dec. 2009, also chaired Cen. Bank Governance Forum; Founder and Pres. Guillermo Ortiz & Asociados (econ. advisory and consulting firm) 2009–11; Chair. Grupo Financiero Banorte-Ixe 2011–; mem. Bd of Dirs Mexichem, Asur, Vitro, Chedraui, Weatherford International, Geneva; Dir in several corp. and non-profit bds; mem. Group of Thirty; Dir, several int. orgs, including Per Jacobsson Foundation, Int. Econ. Forum of the Americas/Conf. of Montreal, Globalization and Monetary Policy Inst., Fed. Reserve Bank of Dallas; mem. Council of Global Financial Regulation; has taught at universities in Mexico and USA; decorations from Govts of France, Spain, Germany, Japan and Brazil; Rodrigo Gómez Prize, Man of the Year, Top Central Banker, Good Neighbor Award, Best Central Bank Governor for Latin America, Central Banker of the Year. *Publications:* two books and numerous papers on topics in economics and finance in specialized journals and magazines in Mexico and abroad. *Address:* Prolongación Paseo de la Reforma 1230, Col. Cruz Manca, Santa Fe, Cuajimalpa, 05349 Mexico City, DF, Mexico (office). *Telephone:* (55) 5268-1612 (office). *Fax:* (55) 1103-6480 (office). *E-mail:* rmaria.gonzalez.r@banorte.com (office); lorena.rivera .r@banorte.com (office). *Website:* www.banorte.com (office).

OSAFO-MAAFO, Yaw, BSc; Ghanaian engineer, banker, economist and politician; *CEO, Economic and Management Consultancy;* b. (Samuel Yaw Osafo-Maafo), 24 Dec. 1942, Akim Awisa; s. of Nana Kwabena Maafo and Mary Boateng; m. Anna Osafo-Maafo; four c.; ed Kwame Nkrumah Univ. of Science and Tech., Metal Eng Inst., USA, Les Aspin Centre for Govt, Marqutee Univ., USA; Process and Quality Control Engineer, VALCO-Tema 1967–69; Sr Investment Promotions Officer, Capital Investment Bd 1969–76; Dir Ghana Investment Centre, Frankfurt, Germany 1972–76; Sr Investment Promotions Officer, Capital Investment Bd (now Ghana Investment Promotion Centre) 1969–76; Chief Operations Man., Bank for Housing and Construction 1976–79, Man. Dir 1979–89; Man. Dir Nat. Investment Bank 1990–92; Sr Consultant, Consultancy Management Enterprise 1992–94, Dir of Training 1993–96; mem. Parl. for Akim Oda Constituency 1997–2009; Minister of Finance and Econ. Planning 2001–04, of Educ. and Sports 2005–06; CEO Econ. and Man. Consultancy 2006–; mem. Consultative Ass. which drafted 1992 constitution for Repub. of Ghana; fmr mem. first World Bank financial sector mission to Uganda; Chair. W African Monetary Zone Convergence Council; Founding Deputy Chair. Ghana Stock Exchange; dir numerous corp. bodies including Nat. Trust Holding Co., Nestlé Ghana Ltd, Redco Ltd, PSCP (Gh) Ltd, Plant Pool Ltd, Consultant Management Enterprise, Donewell Insurance Co., Divestiture Implementation Cttee, Nat. Devt Planning Comm.; Dir Asante Kotoko Football Club; mem. Ghana Inst. of Engineers; Fellow, Ghana Inst. of Engineers; mem. Methodist Conf.; mem. New Patriotic Party (NPP), mem. NPP Manifesto Cttee; Hon. Fellow, Ghana Inst. of Architects; Order of the Volta Companion. *Leisure interests:* reading, football. *Address:* 27th Asafoatse Afua Street, West Airport Residential Area, Accra (home); PO Box OS 605, Osu-Accra, Ghana (office). *Telephone:* (30) 2782992 (office); 26-4632380 (mobile) (office); 24-4330000 (mobile) (office). *E-mail:* yaw@osafomaafo.net (office).

OSBALDESTON, Hon. Gordon Francis, PC, CC, BComm, MBA, LLD; Canadian academic and fmr government official; b. 29 April 1930, Hamilton, Ont.; s. of John E. Osbaldeston and Margaret Osbaldeston (née Hanley); m. Geraldine M. Keller 1953; three s. one d.; ed St Jerome's Coll., Univs of Toronto and Western Ontario; Sec. Treasury Bd 1973–76; Deputy Minister, Dept of Industry, Trade and Commerce 1976–78; Sec. Ministry of State for Econ. Devt 1978–82; Under-Sec. of State for External Affairs 1982; Clerk of Privy Council and Sec. to Cabinet 1982–86; Sr Fellow, School of Business Admin., Univ. of Western Ontario 1986–95, Prof. Emer., Ivey School of Business 1995–; Dir Great West Lifeco Inc., London Life Insurance Co.; Commemorative Medal for the 125th Anniversary of Canadian Confed. 1992, Queen's Golden Jubilee Medal 2002; Hon. DrIur (Western Ontario), (Carleton), (Dalhousie); Vanier Medal, Inst. of Public Admin. of Canada 1990. *Publications include:* Keeping Deputy Ministers Accountable 1989, Organizing to Govern 1992. *Leisure interests:* golf, stamp collecting. *Address:* 1353 Corley Drive, London, ON N6G 4L4, Canada. *Telephone:* (519) 438-9772. *Fax:* (519) 433-7605. *E-mail:* gordon5304@aol.com.

OSBORN, Frederic (Derek) Adrian, CB, BA, BPhil; British government official; b. 14 Jan. 1941, Dorset; s. of the late Rev. George Osborn and Betty Osborn; m. Caroline Niebuhr Tod 1971; one s. one d.; ed Leys School, Cambridge and Balliol Coll., Oxford; with Ministry of Housing and Local Govt 1965–70, Dept of Transport 1975–77, Dept of Environment 1977–95, Dir-Gen. (Deputy Sec.) 1990–95; Chair. European Environment Agency 1995–99; Chair. UNED, UK (name changed to Stakeholder Forum for Our Common Future 2002, renamed Stakeholder Forum for a Sustainable Future 2004) 1996–, Earth Centre 1996– (mem. Bd 1996–), Joseph Rowntree Foundation Steering Group on Reconciling Environmental and Social Objectives 1998–, UK Round Table on Sustainable Devt 1999–; mem. Bd England and Wales Environment Agency 1996–98, Severn Trent PLC 1998–; Special Adviser House of Commons Environmental Audit Cttee 1998–99; Chair. Jupiter Global Green Investment Trust 2001–; mem. Royal Soc. for Protection of Birds 1996–; mem. Bd of Trustees Green Alliance; Visiting Fellow Green Coll., Oxford 1996–97; Visiting Prof., School of Public Policy, Univ. Coll., London 1998–. *Publications:* Earth Summit II 1998, contribs. to Journal of Environmental Law etc. *Leisure interests:* music, reading. *Address:* Stakeholder Forum for a Sustainable Future, 33 Bloomsbury Place, London WC1A 2QL, England (office). *Telephone:* (20) 7580-6912 (office). *Website:* www.stakeholderforum.org (office).

OSBORN, Mary, PhD; British biologist and academic; *Professor, Max Planck Institute for Biophysical Chemistry;* lab. work in USA; Prof., Max Planck Inst. for Biophysical Chem. (Karl Friedrich Bonhoeffer Inst.), Göttingen 1978–, also Hon. Prof. in the Medical Faculty, Georgia Augusta Univ.; Pres. Exec. Cttee Int. Union of Biochemistry and Molecular Biology 2003–06; Chair. European Tech. Assessment Network expert working group on gender balance in research policy 1998; mem. Editorial Advisory Bd Encyclopedia of Human Biology; mem. Helmholtz Soc. Senate, European Strategy Forum on Research Infrastructures Group A, Descartes Prize Grand Jury of the EC; fmr Trustee, Swedish Foundation on the Environment; Dr hc (Pomerian Medical Acad., Szczecin, Poland); L'Oréal-UNESCO For Women in Science Award 2002, Meyenburg Prize. *Publications:* numerous articles in scientific journals. *Address:* Max-Planck-Institut für biophysikalische Chemie, Am Faßberg 11, 37077 Göttingen, Germany (office). *Telephone:* (551) 201-1477 (office). *Fax:* (551) 201-1578 (office). *E-mail:* mosborn@ gwdg.de (office). *Website:* www.mpibpc.gwdg.de (office).

OSBORNE, Rt Hon. George Gideon Oliver; British politician; *Chancellor of the Exchequer;* b. 23 May 1971, London, England; s. of Sir Peter Osborne, 17th Baronet; m. The Hon. Frances Victoria Howell 1998; one s. one d.; ed St Paul's School, London, Magdalen Coll., Oxford; fmr Jt Ed. Isis (Univ. of Oxford magazine); Dean Rusk Scholar (for a semester), Davidson Coll., N Carolina, USA; first job providing data entry services to Nat. Health Service; worked briefly for Selfridges and as freelance journalist; joined Conservative Research Dept in 1994, later Head of Political Section; Special Adviser, Minister of Agric., Fisheries and Food 1995–97; worked in Political Office, No. 10 Downing Street, Political Sec. to Leader of the Opposition and Sec. to Shadow Cabinet 1997–2001; MP (Conservative) for Tatton, Cheshire 2001–, Shadow Chief Sec. to the Treasury 2004, fmr Opposition Whip, fmr Shadow Work and Pensions Minister and Shadow Econ. Sec., Chair. David Cameron's leadership election campaign 2005, fmr mem. Public Accounts Cttee, Transport Select Cttee, Shadow Chancellor of the Exchequer 2005–10; Chancellor of the Exchequer 2010–; Vice-Pres. East Cheshire Hospice; Trustee, Arts and Business; Conservative; Hon. Pres. The British Youth Council; Macmillan Cancer Relief Champion 2005. *Address:* Chancellor of the Exchequer, HM Treasury, 1 Horse Guards Road, London, SW1A 2HQ, England (office). *Telephone:* (20) 7270-4558 (office). *Fax:* (20) 7270-4861 (office). *E-mail:* george.osborne.mp@parliament.uk; contact@georgeosborne.co.uk (office). *Website:* www.gov.uk/government/organisations/hm-treasury (office); www.georgeosborne .co.uk.

OSBOURNE, John (Ozzy); British musician and singer; b. 3 Dec. 1948, Aston, Warwicks., England; m. 1st Thelma; two d.; m. 2nd Sharon Arden 1982; two d. one s.; mem. and lead singer, Black Sabbath (fmrly Polka Tulk, then Earth) 1967–77 (reunion tour 1998–99); solo artist with backing group Blizzard of Ozz 1979–; cr. annual touring festival Ozzfest 1996–; numerous live performances and festival appearances; Grammy Awards for Best Metal Performance (for I Don't Want to Change the World) 1994, (for Iron Man) 2000, (for God is Dead?) 2014, Nordoff-Robbins O2 Silver Clef Award (with Sharon Osbourne) 2006. *Television series:* The Osbournes (MTV) 2001–05. *Recordings include:* albums: with Black Sabbath: Black Sabbath 1969, Paranoid 1970, Master Of Reality 1971, Black Sabbath Vol. 4 1972, Sabbath Bloody Sabbath 1973, Sabotage 1975, Technical Ecstasy 1976, Never Say Die! 1978, Reunion 1998, 13 2013; solo: Blizzard Of Ozz 1980, Diary Of A Madman 1981, Speak Of The Devil 1982, Bark At The Moon 1983, The Ultimate Sin 1986, Tribute 1987, No Rest For The Wicked 1988, Just Say Ozzy 1990, No More Tears 1991, Live & Loud 1993, Ozzmosis 1995, The Ozzman Cometh 1997, OzzFest Vol. 1 1997, Down To Earth 2001, Live At Budokan 2002, X-Posed 2002, Under Cover 2005, Black Rain 2007, Scream 2010. *Publication:* I Am Ozzy (autobiog.) 2009. *Address:* c/o Sharon Osbourne Management, 9292 Civic Centre Drive, Beverly Hills, CA 90210, USA (office). *Website:* www.ozzy.com.

OSEI, Isaac, BSc, MA; Ghanaian economist, diplomatist, politician and business executive; b. 29 March 1951; s. of Nana Osei Nkwantabisa I and Rosina Eunice

Osei (née Inkumsah); m. Marian Osei; two s. two d.; ed Achimota School, Univ. of Ghana, Legon, Econ. Inst., Univ. of Colorado, USA, Williams Coll., Mass, USA; Asst Econ. Planning Officer, Ministry of Finance and Econ. Planning 1970s; Founder and Man. Consultant, Ghanexim Econ. Consultants Ltd; fmr consultant to numerous official orgs. including Govt of Ghana, USAID, World Bank, UNCTAD, Japan Int. Co-operation Agency, Dept for Int. Devt; Man. Dir Intravenous Infusions Limited, Koforidua; fmr Chief, Commercial Operations Dept, Ghana Tourist Devt Co. Ltd; High Commr to UK 2001–06; Chair. Bd of Govs Commonwealth Secr. 2003–05; Chief Exec. Ghana Cocoa Bd (COCOBOD) 2006–08; mem. Parl. for Subin constituency (New Patriotic Party) 2009–; Officer, Order of the Volta. *Leisure interest:* football (from a distance). *Address:* Parliament House, Accra (office); PO Box OS 1402, Accra, Ghana (office). *Telephone:* (21) 777625 (office). *E-mail:* ikeosei@email.com (office); isaacosei@consultant.com (office).

OSEI-ADJEI, Akwasi, MSc; Ghanaian politician; b. 29 Dec. 1949, Onwe, Ashanti Region; m.; five c.; ed De Montfort Univ., UK; trained and qualified as an accountant, worked at Ozze Ghana Ltd; mem. Parl. for Ejisu/Juabeng constituency –2007; fmr Deputy Minister of Foreign Affairs, Regional Integration and New Partnership for Africa's Devt (NEPAD), Minister of Foreign Affairs, Regional Integration and NEPAD 2007–09; mem. New Patriotic Party. *Address:* c/o New Patriotic Party, C912/2 Duade St, Kokomlemle, POB 3456, Accra, Ghana (office). *Telephone:* (21) 227951 (office). *Fax:* (21) 224418 (office). *E-mail:* npp@africanonline.com.gh (office).

O'SHEA, Sir Timothy Michael Martin, Kt, BSc, PhD, FRSE; British university principal and professor of computer science; *Principal and Vice-Chancellor, University of Edinburgh;* b. 28 March 1949, Hamburg, Germany; s. of John Edward O'Shea and Elisabeth Hedwig Oberhof; m. Eileen Scanlon 1982; two s. two d.; ed Royal Liberty School Havering, Univs of Sussex and Leeds; postgraduate research, Univ. of Texas at Austin, USA and Univ. of Edinburgh; Founder, Computer Assisted Learning Research Group, Open Univ. 1978; Lecturer, Inst. of Educational Tech. 1980–82, Sr Lecturer 1983–87, Prof. of Information Tech. and Educ. 1987–97, Pro-Vice-Chancellor for Quality Assurance and Research 1994–97, Visiting Research Prof. 1997; Master of Birkbeck Coll. and Prof. of Information and Communication Technologies 1998–2002; Gov. Literary Inst. 1998–2000, SOAS 1998–2002, St George's Medical School, Univ. of London 2000–02; Curator, School of Advanced Study, Univ. of London 1999–2002; Provost, Gresham Coll. 2000–02; Pro-Vice-Chancellor Univ. of London 2001–02; Prin. and Vice-Chancellor, Univ. of Edinburgh 2002–; Visiting Scientist, Xerox PARC and Visiting Scholar, Univ. of California, Berkeley 1986–87; Chair. NATO programme on Advanced Educational Tech. 1988–90; Chair. London Metropolitan Network Ltd 1999–2002; Chair. HERO Ltd 2000; Dir, Edexcel Foundation 1998–2001 (mem. Exec. Cttee 1998–2001), Univs and Colls Staff Devt Agency 1999–2000; Chair. Information Systems Sector Group, Cttee of Vice-Chancellors and Principals 1999; mem. Higher Educ. Funding Council for England Cttee on Equal Opportunities, Access and Lifelong Learning 1998, Jt Information Systems Cttee 2000–13 (Chair.); mem. Bd Universities UK 2001–; Pres. Pyschology Section, BAAS 1991–92; Chair. Artificial Intelligence Soc. 1979–82; mem. Council, Royal Coll. of Music 2001; Trustee, Eduserv 1999–2000; Fellow, Birkbeck, Univ. of London, Univ. of the Highlands and Islands, Millennium Inst., European Co-ordinating Cttee on Artificial Intelligence, Acad. of Social Sciences; Hon. DUniv (Heriot-Watt), (Strathclyde); Hon. LLD (McGill); Dr hc (St Petersburg Univ. of Humanities and Social Sciences); Univ. of London Union Laurel for his services to part-time students, outstanding contrib. awards from Govt of Japan and of People's Repub. of China for promoting academic co-operation between Scotland and those countries. *Television:* The Learning Machine (series presenter and author) 1985. *Publications include:* Self-Improving Teaching Systems 1979, Learning and Teaching with Computers (co-author) 1983, Artificial Intelligence: Tools, Techniques and Applications (co-author) 1984, Advances in Artificial Intelligence (ed.) 1985, Intelligent Knowledge-based Systems: An Introduction (co-ed.) 1987, Educational Computing (co-ed.) 1987, New Directions in Educational Tech. (co-ed.) 1992. *Leisure interests:* hill walking, especially on the Pentlands and the north Kilkenny countryside, avid reader of history books, active mem. Oyster Club of Edinburgh and Caledonian Club of London. *Address:* Office of the Principal, University of Edinburgh, Old College, South Bridge, Edinburgh, EH8 9YL, Scotland (office). *Telephone:* (131) 650-2150 (office). *Fax:* (131) 650-6519 (office). *E-mail:* principal@ed.ac.uk (office). *Website:* www.ed.ac.uk/about/people/officials/principal (office).

OSHEROFF, Douglas Dean, PhD; American physicist and researcher; b. 1 Aug. 1945, Aberdeen, Wash.; s. of William Osheroff and Bessie Anne Osheroff (née Ondov); m. Phyllis S. K. Liu 1970; ed California Inst. of Tech., Cornell Univ.; mem. tech. staff, Bell Labs, Murray Hill, NY 1972–82, Head Solid State and Low Temperature Physics Research Dept 1982–87; Prof., Stanford Univ., Calif. 1987–, J.G. Jackson and C.J. Wood Prof. of Physics 1992–, Chair. Physics 1993–96; co-discoverer of superfluidity in liquid³He 1971, nuclear antiferromagnetic resonance in solid³He 1980; Fellow, American Physical Soc., American Acad. of Arts and Sciences, NAA; Simon Memorial Prize, British Inst. of Physics (co-recipient) 1976, Oliver E. Buckley Solid State Physics Prize 1981, John D. and Catherine T. MacArthur Prize Fellow 1981, shared Nobel Prize for Physics 1996. *Address:* Department of Physics, Stanford University, Stanford, CA 94305-4060, USA.

OSHII, Mamoru; Japanese film director; b. 8 Aug. 1951, Tokyo; ed Fine Arts School, Dept of Educ., Tokyo Liberal Arts Univ. (Tokyo Gakugei Daigaku); involved in anti-ANPO (US–Japan Security Treaty) student movt 1970s; began directing short films 1976; joined Tatsunoko Productions 1977; made film On the Roof using permeable light filming process; worked for Studio Pierrot under supervision of Nagayuki Toriumi 1980–84; joined Headgear as writer and dir 1980s; cr. Patlabor franchise with Masami Yuuki, Kenji Kawaï and Akemi Tadaka. *Films directed include:* Darossu 1983, Urusei Yatsura 1: Only You 1983, Urusei Yatsura 2: Beautiful Dreamer 1984, Angel's Egg 1985, The Red Spectacles 1987, Twilight Q Episode 2: Meikyu Bukken File 538 1987, Mobile Police Patlabor 1988, Patlabor: The Movie 1989, Stray Dogs: Kerberos Panzer Cops 1991, Talking Head 1992, Patlabor 2: The Movie 1993, Ghost in the Shell 1995, Avalon 2001, Ghost in the Shell 2: Innocence 2004, Open Your Mind (short) 2005, Tachiguishi retsuden 2006, The Women of Fast Food (segments The Assault Girl, The Golden Fish Girl) (also exec. producer) 2007, Ghost in the Shell 2.0 2008, The Sky Crawlers 2008, Kill

(also exec. producer) 2008, Assault Girls 2009, Halo Legends (video) (creative dir segment The Duel) 2010, 28½ mousou no kyojin 2010, 009: The Reopening (short) 2010, The Last Druid: Garm Wars 2014. *Screenplays include:* Urusei Yatsura 1: Only You 1983, Urusei Yatsura 2: Beautiful Dreamer 1984, When All's Said and Done 1984, Angel's Egg 1985, The Red Spectacles 1987, In the Aftermath 1988, Legend of a Wolf-Dog 1988, StrayDog: Kerberos Panzer Cops 1991, Talking Head 1992, Seraphim 1995, Jin Roth: The Wolf Brigade 1998, Ghost in the Shell 2: Innocence 2004, Tachiguishi retsuden 2006, The Women of Fast Food 2007, Kill 2008, Musashi: The Dream of the Last Samurai (also producer) 2009, Assault Girls 2009. *Television series:* The Wonderful Adventures of Nils 1980, Urusei Yatsura (Those Obnoxious Aliens) 1981–84, Mrs Pepperpot 1983, Blood: The Last Vampire (supervising producer) 2000, Mini-Pato 2002, Blood+ (series) (producer and co-planner) 2005, Ani*Kuri15 (series) (also writer) 2007. *Website:* www.oshiimamoru.com.

OSHIMA, Kenzo; Japanese diplomatist; *Senior Vice-President, Japan International Co-operation Agency;* b. 1943; m.; two c.; ed Tokyo Univ.; served in diplomatic posts in Australia, France, India, USA and at Perm. Mission to UN; Dir-Gen. Econ. Co-operation Bureau, Ministry of Foreign Affairs; Sec.-Gen. Secr. for Int. Peace Co-operation HQ, Office of the Prime Minister –2000; UN Under-Sec.-Gen. for Humanitarian Affairs and Emergency Relief Co-ordinator 2001–03; Amb. to Australia 2003; Perm. Rep. to UN 2004–07; Sr Vice-Pres. Japan Int. Co-operation Agency 2007–. *Address:* Japan International Co-operation Agency, 6th–13th floors, Shinjuku Maynds Tower 2-1-1 Yoyogi, Shibuya-ku, Tokyo 151-8558, Japan (office). *Telephone:* (3) 5352-5311 (office). *E-mail:* oshima.kenzo@jica.go.jp (office). *Website:* www.jica.go.jp (office).

OSHIOMHOLE, Adams Aliyu; Nigerian trade union official and regional governor; *Governor, Edo State;* b. 4 April 1953; m. Clara Oshiomhole (deceased); five c.; ed Ruskin Coll., Oxford, UK and Nat. Inst. for Policy and Strategic Studies, Kuru; began career as shop steward at textile factory; Pres. Nigeria Labour Congress 1999; Chair. Governing Bd Nigerian Social Insurance Trust Fund Scheme; Gov. Edo State 2008–; mem Action Congress of Nigeria. *Address:* Office of the Governor, Benin City, Edo State, Nigeria (office). *E-mail:* governor@edostate.gov.ng (office). *Website:* www.edostate.gov.ng (office).

OSHO, Pierre, MA; Benin politician; b. 5 May 1945, Porto Novo; m.; six c.; ed Acad. of Grenoble, Univ. of Dakar, Univ. of Aix-en-Provence, France; Prof. of History and Geography, Coll. Père Aupiais, Cotonou 1968–70, Coll. d'Enseignement Moyen Général de Gbégamey, Cotonou 1970–73; Dir of Information and Propaganda (MISON) 1976–78; mem. Cen. Cttee, Party of Popular Revolution 1979–90; Chief of Dist of Klouékanmey, Prov. of Mono 1978–84; Peoples' Commr, Nat. Ass. 1980–90; Pres. Comm. on Govt and Ass. Relations 1980–84; Dir Nat. Centre of Revolutionary Educ. 1982–84; Sec.-Gen. Perm. Cttee of Nat. Ass. 1984–89; Pres. Comm. on Constitutional Affairs 1989–90; Dir Cabinet of Pres. of Benin 1989–91; with Dept of Research of Human and Social Sciences 1991–96; Minister of Foreign Affairs and Co-operation 1996–98; Minister to Pres. of Benin 1998–2001; Minister of Nat. Defence 2001–06 (resgnd); del. to int. and multilateral confs. *Address:* c/o Ministry of National Defence, BP 2493 Cotonou, Benin.

OSIPOV, Victor Ivanovich; Russian engineer, geologist and hydrogeologist; *Director, Sergeev Institute of Environmental Geoscience, Russian Academy of Sciences;* b. 15 April 1937, Bashkortostan; ed Moscow State Univ.; Dir scientific station 1959–61; Lecturer, Prof., Moscow State Univ. 1964–90; Deputy Dir Inst. of Lithosphere 1990; Dir Centre of Eng Geology and Geoecology (now Sergeev Inst. of Environmental Geoscience), Russian Acad. of Sciences; Corresp. mem., USSR (now Russian) Acad. of Sciences 1987, mem. 1991–; main research in eng geology, environmental protection; State Prize 1988. *Publications:* more than 500 articles in scientific journals. *Leisure interests:* travelling, sports (skiing), gardening, fishing. *Address:* Sergeev Institute of Environmental Geoscience, PO Box 145, Ulansky per. 13, Building 2, 101000 Moscow, Russia (office). *Telephone:* (495) 623-31-11 (office). *Fax:* (495) 623-18-86 (office). *E-mail:* direct@geoenv.ru (office). *Website:* www.geoenv.ru (office).

OSIPOV, Yuri Sergeyevich, DPhys-MathSc; Russian mathematician and technician; *President, Russian Academy of Sciences;* b. 7 July 1936, Tobolsk; m.; one d.; ed Urals State Univ.; Corresp. mem. USSR (now Russian) Acad. of Sciences 1984, mem. 1987, Pres. 1991–; staff mem., Inst. of Mechanics and Math., Urals Scientific Cen. Acad. of Sciences 1959, Dir 1990–93; Prof., Urals Univ. 1961–70; fmr Head of Chair of Moscow State Univ.; Dir Steklov Math. Inst. 1993–; mem. American Math. Soc., American Acad. of Arts and Sciences, Mongolian Acad. of Sciences, Armenian Acad. of Sciences, Santiago Univ., Chile; Dr hc (Bar-Ilan Univ., Israel), (Santiago Univ., Chile); Lenin Prize 1976, USSR State Prize. *Publications:* more than 150 works on the theory of math., differential equations and their application. *Address:* Russian Academy of Sciences, Leninsky prospekt 14, 119991 GSP-1, Moscow; Steklov Mathematical Institute, 42 Vavilov Street, 117966 Moscow, Russia. *Telephone:* (495) 954-35-06 (Acad.); (495) 135-22-91 (Inst.). *Website:* www.ras.ru.

OSKANIAN, Vardan, BS, MSc, MA; Armenian diplomatist; *Founder and Director, Civilitas Foundation;* b. 7 Feb. 1955, Syria; m. Dr Nani Oskanian; two s.; ed Yerevan Polytechnic Inst., Tufts Univ., Mass, Harvard Univ., Fletcher School of Law and Diplomacy, USA; Founder and Ed. Armenian Int. Magazine 1990; on staff, Armenian Ministry of Foreign Affairs 1992–; Deputy Head, Middle East Dept, Head, Dept of N America 1992–94; prin. negotiator in Misk process on Nagorno-Karabakh conflict 1994–97; Visiting Asst Prof. of Int. Relations, American Univ. of Armenia 1994–96; Deputy Foreign Minister 1994–96, First Deputy Foreign Minister 1996–98, Minister of Foreign Affairs 1998–2008; f. Civilitas Foundation 2008. *Publication:* Speaking to be Heard: A Decade of Speeches 2009. *Address:* Civilitas Foundation, 0010 Yerevan, One Northern Avenue, Suite 30, Armenia (office). *Telephone:* (10) 50-01-19 (office). *Fax:* (10) 50-01-12 (office). *E-mail:* info@civilitasfoundation.org (office). *Website:* www.civilitasfoundation.org (office).

OSKARSON, Peter, (Dhyan Manyu); Swedish theatre director and actor; b. 13 June 1951, Stockholm; s. of Per-Otto Oskarson and Margareta Du Rietz; m. 1st Kajsa Reingardt 1979; m. 2nd Gunilla Kindstrand 1988 (divorced 2002); one s. four d.; m. 3rd Sofie Livebrant; one d.; ed Swedish Actors' School, Acad. of Dramatic Arts, Stockholm; Artistic Dir Skånska Teatern Landskrona 1973–82,

Folkteatern Gävleborg 1982–90; Head, Helsingegården, inst. for theatre and popular arts, N Scandinavia 1990–2004; Artistic Dir Orion Theatre 1993–2000; Gen. Man. Folkteatern Gävleborg 1997–2006; Artistic Adviser, Peking Opera, Anhui, Hefei, China 1996–2000; Artistic Dir World Theatre Project 1999–; Artistic Dir Holy Fools of Katarina Church 2009–; Artistic Leader, The Scania Anatomical 2012–; theatre plays produced also at Royal Opera House and at Royal Dramatic Theatre, Stockholm, Drottningholm Theatre, Staatsoper, Stuttgart, Intiman, Seattle, USA, Oper der Stadt, Bonn, Festwochen, Vienna, Schwetzingen Festspiele, Swedish TV, Nationaltheater Mannheim, Royal Opera House, Copenhagen etc.; mem. Swedish Theatre Acad. 1993–, Swedish World Culture Forum 1998–2001, Framtidens Kultur 2003–06; Alf Sjöberg Prize, Swedish Acad. Theatre Prize, Svenska Dagbladet Thalia Prize, Expressen Theatre Prize, Gävle and Gävleborg Culture Prize, Malmö Thalia Prize, Gefledagblad Culture Prize, Olof Hogberg Prize, Sture Linnér Prize, Poul Reumert Prize for Best Opera. *E-mail:* posk@me.com. *Website:* www.oskarson.se.

OSLON, Alexander A., Cand.Tech. sciences; Russian engineer; *President, All-Russian Foundation for Public Opinion;* b. 19 March 1952, Zlatoust, Chelyabinsk region; m.; one d.; ed Tula State Polytech. Inst.; worked as engineer, then chief constructor GSKTB 1974–87; researcher All-Union Centre of Public Opinion Studies 1988–90, Deputy Dir 1990–92; Pres. All-Russian Foundation for Public Opinion 1992–. *Publications include:* numerous articles in the press on results of public pools of population and methodical problems of sociological studies. *Address:* All-Russian Foundation for Public Opinion, Obrucheva str. 26, bldg 2, Moscow, Russia (office). *Telephone:* (495) 745-87-65 (office). *Website:* www.fom.ru (office).

OSMAN, Ahmed, LLM; Moroccan politician and diplomatist; b. 3 Jan. 1930, Oujda; m. HRH Princess Lalla Nezha (sister of King Hassan II) 1965; one s.; ed Royal High School, Rabat, Univ. of Rabat and Univ. of Bordeaux, France; Head of the Legal Section, Royal Cabinet 1956; joined Ministry of Foreign Affairs 1957; Sec.-Gen. Ministry of Nat. Defence 1959–61; Amb. to FRG 1961–62; UnderSec.-of-State for Industry and Mines 1963–64; Pres. and Gen. Man. Moroccan Navigation Co. 1964–67; Amb. to USA, Canada and Mexico 1967–70; Minister of Admin. Affairs 1970–71; Dir of Royal Cabinet 1971–72; Prime Minister 1972–79; Parl. Rep. for Oujda 1977–; Leader Rassemblement nat. des indépendants 1978–2007; mem. Nat. Defence Council 1979–; Minister of State 1983; Pres. Chamber of Reps. 1984–92; participated in UN sessions 1957, 1958, 1960, 1961, 1968, Conf. on Maritime law 1958, Conf. of the League of Arab States 1961. *Leisure interests:* bridge, sports, reading, swimming. *Address:* Rassemblement national des indépendants, 6 rue Laos, avenue Hassan II, Rabat, Morocco.

OSMAN, Salih Mahmoud; Sudanese lawyer and human rights activist; b. Darfur; m.; for 20 years has defended people who were allegedly arbitrarily detained and tortured by Sudanese govt; Lawyer, Sudanese Org. Against Torture 2003–, also works with Amal Center for Rehabilitation of Torture Victims, Nyala; imprisoned Feb.–Sept. 2004; mem. Parl., Nat. Democratic Alliance 2006–; mem. Bd of Dirs Darfur Peace and Devt Org.; Human Rights Defender Award, Human Rights Watch 2005, International Human Rights Award 2006, Sakharov Prize 2007.

OSMANI, S. R.; Bangladeshi business executive; Dir of Finance Bangladesh Oil, Gas and Mineral Corpn (PETROBANGLA), Acting Chair., then Chair. 2003–06. *Address:* c/o Petrobangla, Petrocenter Bhaban, 3 Kawran Bazar C/A, PO Box 849, Dhaka 1215, Bangladesh.

OSMIĆ, Zekerijah (Mevludin); Bosnia and Herzegovina economist and politician; *Minister of Defence;* b. 2 Aug. 1956, Brčko; m.; three c.; ed Brčko Univ.; began career as math. and physics teacher, Brčko elementary school 1976–80; Professional Sec., Youth and Cooperatives Centre, Brčko 1981–83, Dir 1983–88; engaged in private enterprise 1988–92; Head of Logistics Centre, Govt of Brčko-Rahić 1992–96, Sec. for Economy and Deputy Mayor for Economy and Finance 1996–98; mem. Nat. Ass. of Republika Srpska (Serbian Democratic Party) 1998–2006; Adviser on Economy and Finance to Mayor of Brčko Dist 2006–08; Head, Public Records Div., Govt of Brčko Dist 2008–12; Minister of Defence 2012–. *Address:* Ministry of Defence, 71000 Sarajevo, Hamdije Kreševljakovića 98, Bosnia and Herzegovina (office). *Telephone:* (33) 285500 (office). *Fax:* (33) 206094 (office). *E-mail:* zekerijah.osmic@mod.gov.ba (office). *Website:* www.mod.gov.ba (office).

OSMOND, Charles Barry, PhD, FRS, FAA; Australian biologist and academic; *Professor of Plant Science, Institute of Conservation Biology and Environmental Management, University of Wollongong;* b. 20 Sept. 1939, Cooranbong, NSW; s. of Edward Charles Osmond and Joyce Daphne Osmond (née Krauss); m. 1st Suzanne Ward 1962 (divorced 1983); one s. one d.; m. 2nd Cornelia Gauhl 1983; ed Morisset Central and Wyong High Schools and Univs of New England and Adelaide; Postdoctoral Fellow, UCLA 1965–66, Univ. of Cambridge 1966–67; Research Fellow, Dept of Environmental Biology, Research School of Biological Sciences, ANU 1967, subsequently Fellow, Sr Research Fellow, Prof. of Biology 1978–87, Dir 1991–98, Dir Research School of Biol. Sciences 1991–98, Prof., Photo Bioenergetics Group 1998–2001, currently Hon. Visiting Fellow, Div. of Plant Sciences; Prof. of Plant Science, Inst. of Conservation Biology and Environmental Man., Univ. of Wollongong 2011–; Exec. Dir Biological Science Center, Desert Research Inst., Univ. of Nevada 1982–86; Arts and Sciences Distinguished Prof., Dept of Botany, Duke Univ. 1987–91; Pres. and CEO Biosphere 2 Center, Columbia Univ. 2001–03; Sr Fulbright Fellowship, Univ. of Calif., Santa Cruz 1973–74; Guest Prof., Technical Univ., Munich 1974; Overseas Fellow, Churchill Coll., Cambridge 1980; mem. Australian Nat. Comm. for UNESCO 1980–82; mem. Council, Australian Acad. of Sciences 1982–85, Deutsche Akad. der Naturforscher, Leopoldina (German Nat. Acad. of Sciences) 2001; Research Prize, Alexander von Humboldt Foundation, Univs of Darmstadt and Göttingen 1997–2000. *Publications:* numerous publs on plant physiology. *Address:* PO Box 3252, Weston Creek, ACT 2611, Australia (home). *Telephone:* (2) 6287-1487 (home). *E-mail:* osmond@grapevine .net.au (office).

OSMOND, Donald (Donny) Clark; American singer; b. 9 Dec. 1957, Ogden, UT; m. Debra Glenn 1978; five c.; ed Brigham Young Univ.; singer with The Osmonds 1963–80; solo artist 1971–78, 1988–; also duo with sister Marie; head of own TV production co., Night Star 1980s, also satellite TV entrepreneur; Georgie Award for Best Vocal Team (with Marie Osmond) 1978. *Television includes:* Donny and Marie (show) 1976–79, Osmond Family (show) 1980, Dancing With The Stars (winner) 2009. *Films include:* Goin' Coconuts 1978, College Road Trip 2008. *Theatre includes:* Joseph and his Amazing Technicolour Dreamcoat, Toronto, Canada 1992–93, Beauty and the Beast, New York 2006. *Recordings include:* albums: with The Osmonds: Homemade 1971, Osmonds 1971, Crazy Horses 1972, Phase-III 1972, The Osmonds Live 1972, The Plan 1973, Love Me For A Reason 1974, Around The World: Live In Concert 1975, The Proud One 1975, Brainstorm 1976, The Osmond Christmas Album 1976, Osmond Family Christmas 1991; solo: The Donny Osmond Album 1971, To You With Love, Donny 1971, Portrait of Donny 1972, Too Young 1972, My Best To You 1972, A Time For Us 1973, Alone Together 1973, Donny Osmond Superstar 1973, Donny 1974, I'm Leaving It All Up To You (with Marie Osmond) 1974, Love Me For A Reason 1974, Make The World Go Away (with Marie Osmond) 1975, Donny and Marie – Featuring Songs From Their Television Show (with Marie Osmond) 1976, Donny and Marie: New Season (with Marie Osmond) 1976, Deep Purple (with Marie Osmond) 1976, Disco Train 1976, Donald Clark Osmond 1977, Goin' Coconuts (with Marie Osmond) 1978, Winning Combination 1978, Donny Osmond 1989, Eyes Don't Lie 1990, Christmas At Home 1998, This Is The Moment 2001, Somewhere In Time 2002, What I Meant To Say 2004, Love Songs of the '70s 2007, From Donny with Love 2008, Duets (with Marie Osmond) 2009, Donny & Marie (with Marie Osmond) 2011. *Publication:* Life is Just What You Make of It (autobiography) 2005. *Address:* c/o William Morris Endeavor, 9601, Wilshire Blvd, Beverly Hills, CA 90210 (office); 51 W Center Street, Suite 424, Orem, UT 84057, USA (office). *Telephone:* (310) 285-9000 (office). *Fax:* (310) 285-9010 (office). *Website:* www.wma.com (office); www.donny.com (office).

OSMONOV, Kurmanbek Ergeshovich; Kyrgyzstani politician and lawyer; b. 1 March 1953, Kara-Kulja; m.; two s. two d.; ed Kyrgyz State Univ.; Deputy Minister for Justice, subsequently First Deputy Minister 1991–94; Judge Constitutional Court 1994–2000; mem. Jogorku Kenesh (parl.) 2000–02; First Deputy Prime Minister of Kyrgyzstan and Minister of Justice 2002–04; Chair. of the Supreme Court 2004–08; Honoured Lawyer of Kyrgyz Repub.; Dank Medal (highest nat. award). *Publications:* several books on development and court reform in Kyrgyzstan. *Leisure Interests:* music, chess, cars. *Address:* 26 Keldibek Karboz Uulu Street, Orto-sai, Bishkek, Kyrgyzstan (home). *Telephone:* (312) 55-01-37 (home).

OSORI, Ayisha, LLB, LLM, MC/MPA; Nigerian lawyer, consultant and organization official; *CEO, The Nigerian Women's Trust Fund;* ed Univ. of Lagos, Harvard Law School, Sloan School of Man. at Massachusetts Inst. of Tech., Kennedy School of Govt at Harvard Univ., USA; called to Nigerian Bar 1998, NY State Bar 2000; Assoc., Arthur Andersen, Lagos 1998–2000; Vice-Pres., Corp. Services, Ocean & Oil Holdings Nigeria Ltd 2002–06; Regulatory Affairs Man., British American Tobacco (BAT) Nigeria 2006–09, Area Regulation and Compliance Counsel, West Africa Area 2006–12; CEO The Nigerian Women's Trust Fund 2012–; hosted and co-produced a local radio programme Women Talk Politics 2010–11; wrote a weekly column, Pedestrian Lawyer, in Thisday's The Lawyer for more than three years; writes a weekly column for Leadership newspaper Nigerian Citizen; lead consultant and nat. co-ordinator for the World Bank DFID Gender Dialogue Sessions; Dir, Advocates for Change & Social Justice Initiative. *Publication:* Social Studies For Primary Schools (co-author) (series) 2007. *Address:* The Nigerian Women's Trust Fund, c/o 14 Oguda Close, off Lake Chad Crescent, off IBB Boulevard, Maitama, Abuja, FCT, Nigeria (office). *Telephone:* 7029-147571 (mobile) (office). *E-mail:* mabazie-humphrey@nigerianwomentrustfund.org (office). *Website:* www.nigerianwomentrustfund.org (office).

OSORIO CHONG, Miguel Ángel, LLB; Mexican lawyer and politician; *Secretary of the Interior;* b. 5 Aug. 1964, Pachuca, Hidalgo State; s. of Eduardo Osorio Hernández and María Luisa Chong Chávez; m. Laura Vargas; one s. one d.; ed Univ. Autónoma del Estado de Hidalgo; held several positions with Pachuca municipal govt including Chief Clerk, Pachuca City Hall, Sec. of Govt, Sec. of Social Devt, Regional Devt Sec.; mem. Cámara Federal de Diputados (Parl.) for Pachuca constituency 2003–05, Deputy Coordinator of Parl. Partido Revolucionario Institucional—PRI Group; Gov., Hidalgo State 2005–11; Coordinator of Political Dialogue and Agreement, Office of Pres.-elect Enrique Peña Nieto 2012; Sec. (Minister) of the Interior 2012–. *Address:* Secretariat of State for the Interior, Abraham González 48, Col. Juárez, Del. Cuauhtémoc, 66000 México DF, Mexico (office). *Telephone:* (55) 5728-7400 (office). *Fax:* (55) 5728-7300 (office). *E-mail:* contacto@segob.gob.mx (office). *Website:* www.gobernacion.gob.mx (office).

OSOTIMEHIN, Babatunde, BM, MBBS, MD; Nigerian physician, UN official and fmr politician; *Executive Director, United Nations Population Fund;* b. 1949, Ogun State; m.; five c.; ed Univ. of Ibadan, Univ. of Birmingham, UK; Prof. of Clinical Pathology, Coll. of Medicine, Univ. of Ibadan 1980, later Head, Dept of Clinical Pathology, Provost, Coll. of Medicine 1990–94; fmr Project Man., Nigerian Nat. HIV/AIDS Programme Devt Project; Dir-Gen., Nigerian Nat. Agency for Control of AIDS 2007–08; Minister of Health 2008–10; Exec. Dir UN Population Fund (UNFPA) 2011–; Chair. Nat. Action Cttee on AIDS, Nigeria 2002–07, Cttee of Presidential Advisers of AIDS Watch Africa; Fellow, Graduate School of Medicine, Cornell Univ., New York 1979–80; Visiting Fellow, Harvard Centre for Population and Devt Studies, USA 1996–97; Fellow, Nigerian Acad. of Sciences 2006–; Distinguished Visitor, John D. and Catherine T. MacArthur Foundation, Chicago 1996; fmr Co-ordinator, Social Sciences and Reproductive Health Research Network, Ibadan; fmr Ed. African Journal of Medicine and Medical Sciences; mem. Royal Coll. of Physicians, Population Asscn of America, Int. Advisory Group, Population and Reproductive Health, John D. & Catherine T. MacArthur Foundation, Chicago, Nigerian Soc. of Endocrinology and Metabolism, Nigerian Medical Asscn, Nigerian Inst. of Man., Policy and Strategy Cttee, Global Fund for AIDS, Tuberculosis and Malaria, Global Steering Cttee on Universal Access; Officer of the Order of the Niger 2005. *Address:* United Nations Population Fund, 605 Third Avenue, New York, NY 10158, USA (office). *Telephone:* (212) 297-5000 (office). *Fax:* (212) 370-0201 (office). *E-mail:* hq@unfpa.org (office). *Website:* www .unfpa.org (office).

OSPEL, Marcel; Swiss banker; b. 8 Feb. 1950; ed Higher School of Econs and Man., Basel; joined Dept of Planning and Marketing Swiss Bank Corpn (SBC) 1977, with SBC Capital Markets, London, New York 1980, Dir 1987, mem. Enlargement Group 1990, CEO Capital Markets and Treasury 1992, SBC

Warburg 1995, Group Pres. 1996; Pres. and Group CEO Swiss Bank Corpn (SBC) 1996–98; Group CEO UBS AG 1999–2001, Chair. 2001–08 (resgnd); Dr hc (Univ. of Rochester) 2005. *Address:* c/o UBS AG, Bahnhofstrasse 45, 8098 Zürich, Switzerland (office).

OSPINA BERNAL, Camilo; Colombian academic, government official and lawyer; b. 1962, Bogotá; ed Colegio Mayor de Nuestra Señora del Rosario; Vice-Dean Faculty of Law, Colegio Mayor de Nuestra Señora del Rosario 1990–91; Legal Adviser Ministry of Finance and Public Credit 1991–92, Sec.-Gen. Budget Directorate 1992–94; Consultant UNDP 1994–95; Legal Adviser to Pres. 2002–05; Minister of Nat. Defence 2005–06; Perm Rep of Colombia to OAS 2006–12; Founding Pnr and mem. Soc. of Constitutional Rights, Sec. 1997–99. *Address:* c/o Ministry of National Defence, Centro Administrativo Nacional (CAN), 2°, Avda El Dorado, Santafé de Bogotá, Colombia (office).

OST, Friedhelm, Dipl. rer. pol.; German politician and business executive; *Chairman, PKS Kommunikations- und Strategieberatung GmbH;* b. 15 June 1942, Castrop-Rauxel; s. of Franz Ost and Barbara Ost; m. Erika Herrmann 1968; three s. two d.; ed Univs of Freiburg and Cologne; research asst of a major bank 1966–69; Speaker, Bundesverband Deutscher Banken 1969–72; Econ. Ed., moderator and commentator, Zweites Deutsches Fernsehen (ZDF) 1973–85; State Sec. and Head, Govt Press and Information Dept 1985–89; Econ. and Political Adviser to German Fed. Chancellor and freelance journalist and public relations consultant 1989–90; Gen. Man. Wirtschaftsvereinigung Bergbau –1990; mem. CDU 1980–; mem. Bundestag 1990–2002, Chair. Econ. Cttee 1991–98; Adviser, Frankfurter Rothschild GmbH 1997–; fmr Gen. Rep. Deutsche Vermögensberatungs AG; currently Chair. PKS Kommunikations- und Strategieberatung GmbH; mem. Bd of Govs Univ. of Haifa, Israel; mem. Russian Acad. of Sciences; Fed. Cross of Merit, Grand Cross, Order of Merit of the Italian Repub. 1986, Grand Cross of the Falcon 198, Grand Cross of the Portuguese Order of Merit 1989. *Leisure interests:* football, tennis. *Address:* PKS Kommunikations- und Strategieberatung GmbH, Reinhardtstr. 34, 10117 Berlin 32, Germany (office). *Telephone:* (30) 25797223 (office); (2224) 78291. *Fax:* (30) 25797225 (office); (2224) 75633. *E-mail:* friedhelm.ost@t-online.de. *Website:* www.pks-gmbh.net (office).

OSTEN, Suzanne Carlota; Swedish playwright and theatre and film director; b. 20 June 1944, Stockholm; d. of Carl Otto Osten and Gud Osten; m.; one d.; ed Lund Univ.; started directing while a student 1963; ran Fickteatern fringe theatre group performing in schools, prisons, public areas, etc. 1967–71; joined City Theatre, Stockholm 1971; f. and Artistic Dir, Unga Klara Stadsteatern ind. repertory co. 1975–; has written and directed over 30 plays, numerous radio and TV productions; began directing films 1980; Prof. of Directing, Dramatic Inst., Stockholm 1995–; Nat. Theatre Critics Prize 1982, Paris-Creteil Prize 1993, Expressens Theatre Prize 2002, Assitej Int. Prize 2002, Berns Prize, Swedish PEN 2002, numerous other awards and prizes. *Plays:* as writer and dir: Medea's Children 1975, The Haga-Princesses 1976, The Hunt for Snores 1976, Lazarillo 1977, Prince Carefree 1977, The Children from Mount Frostmo 1978, The Pork Horses 1981, The Frontier 2000; as dir: The Vampire 1975, The Sweaty Tiger 1978, Unga Klara tells Life 1982, The Smile of Hades 1982, A Clean Girl 1983, Hitler's Childhood 1 1984, Hitler's Childhood 2 1984, The Danton Affair 1986, Everybody – But Me 1987, The Toad Aquarium 1988, In the Summer House 1988, R 1990, The Piggle 1991, The Dolphin 1992, Preparation for Suicide 1994, Mirad 1994, Money 1994, Lilacs 1914 1996, Irina's New Life 1996, The Girl, the Mother and the Trash 1998, Difficult People 1999, Time of Darkness 2002, The Main Thing 2002. *Films include:* Ei inspelat, Mamma 1982, Bröderna Mozart (Guldbagge Award for Direction 1986) 1986, Livsfarlig film 1988, Skyddsängeln 1990, Tala det är så mörkt 1992, Bara du och jag 1994, Bengbulan 1996, Besvärliga Människor 2001. *Address:* Unga Klara, Stockholms Stadsteater, Box 16412, 103 27 Stockholm, Sweden (office). *Telephone:* (8) 506-20-100 (office). *E-mail:* maja.svae@stadsteatern.stockholm.se (office). *Website:* www.stadsteatern.stockholm.se (office).

OSTERWALDER, Konrad, PhD; Swiss physicist and university administrator; *Professor Emeritus, Department of Mathematics, Eidgenössische Technische Hochschule (ETH), Zürich;* b. 3 June 1942, Frauenfeld, Thurgau; m.; three c.; ed Eidgenössische Technische Hochschule (ETH) Zürich, Univ. of Zürich, Harvard Grad. School for Higher Educ., USA; Asst Prof. of Math. Physics, Harvard Univ. 1973–76, Assoc. Prof. 1976–78; Prof. of Math. Physics, ETH Zürich 1977–2007, Head Dept of Math. 1986–90, Head, Planning Cttee 1990–95, Rector 1995–2007, Prof. Emer., Dept of Math. 2007–; Guest Prof., Univ. of Austin, Tex., Univ. of Cambridge, UK, IHES, Bures-sur-Yvette, France, Max-Planck-Institut für Physik und Astrophysik, Munich, Università La Sapienza, Rome, Università di Napoli, Tokyo Univ., Weitzmann Inst., Rehovot, Israel; Rector UNU, Tokyo 2007–13; Founder-Pres. UNITECH Int.; Chair. Univ. Council, Tech. Univ., Darmstadt, Germany; mem. Admin. Cttee, Ecole Polytechnique de France, Educ. Cttee, Ecole des Mines, Paris, Conseil d'Orientation Statégique, ParisTech, Consiglio dell'Università della Svizzera, Italy, Academic Council, Int. Council on Systems Eng; mem. Swiss Acad. of Tech. Sciences 2000; Fellow, Alfred P. Sloan Foundation 1974–78, American Mathematical Soc. 2012–; Hon. mem. Riga Tech. Univ. 2002; Dr hc (Tech. Univ., Helsinki) 2003; J. Bauer Prize 1959, 1960, ETH Medaille, Kern Prize 1970, Matteo Ricci Award 2009, Leonardo da Vinci Medal 2010. *Address:* Department of Mathematics, Eidgenössische Technische Hochschule Zurich, HG building, Rämistrasse 101, 8092 Zurich, Switzerland (office). *Telephone:* 446321111 (office). *Fax:* 446321010 (office). *E-mail:* konrad.osterwalder@sl.ethz.ch (office). *Website:* www.bi.id.ethz.ch/personensuche/detail.do?pid=130CC(=EN (office).

ÖSTLING, Leif, MEng, BEcons; Swedish business executive; *Member Board of Management with responsibility for Commercial Vehicles, Volkswagen AG;* b. 25 Sept. 1945, Luleå; ed Chalmers Univ. of Tech., Univ. of Göteborg; joined Scania 1972, Head of Strategic Planning 1977–81, Marketing Man., Scania Nederland BV 1981–83, Pres. Scania Nederland 1983–88, Man. Scania Div. (part of Saab-Scania) 1988, Pres. and CEO Scania AB 1994–2012; mem. Bd of Man. Volkswagen AG with responsibility for Commercial Vehicles 2012–; Chair. ISS A/S 2005; Dir SKF AB 2005, Vice-Chair. 2006–08, Chair. 2008; mem. Bd Confed. of Swedish Enterprise, Asscn of Swedish Eng Industries; Dr hc (Royal Inst. of Technology) 2003, (Luleå Univ. of Technology) 2003. *Address:* Volkswagen AG, Berliner Ring 2, 38440 Wolfsburg, Germany (office). *E-mail:* vw@volkswagen.de (office). *Website:* www.volkswagenag.com (office).

ÖSTMAN, Arnold; Swedish conductor; b. 1939, Malmö; m. Kristina Modig; ed Univs of Paris and Stockholm; fmr Lecturer, State Acad. of Music and Drama, Stockholm; Artistic Dir Vadstena Acad. 1969, f. Norrlands Operan 1974, Gen. Admin. and Artistic Dir Drottningholm Court Theatre 1979–92; has conducted at opera houses including Covent Garden, Parma, Paris Bastille, Paris Garnier, Trieste, Cologne, Bonn, Toulouse, Nice, Vienna Staatsoper, Vienna Volksoper, Wexford, Washington, Lausanne, Gothenburg Opera, Graz Opera; symphonic conductor with orchestras including German radio orchestras of Hamburg, Cologne, Stuttgart and Baden-Baden, Stuttgart Philharmonic, Orchestre nat. de France, de Lille, orchestra of La Fenice, Venice, Adelaide Symphony Orchestra, Orchestra Sinfonia Siciliana, Scottish Chamber Orchestra, Acad. of Ancient Music, London, Royal Concertgebouw Orchestra, Amsterdam, Oslo Philharmonic Orchestra, Minneapolis Symphony Orchestra, Sydney Symphony Orchestra, Melbourne Symphony Orchestra, Rotterdam Philharmonic, Gothenburg Symphony Orchestra, Swedish Radio Orchestra; works regularly with Netherlands Radio Chamber Orchestra (symphonic and operatic); mem. Royal Swedish Acad. of Music; Chevalier, Légion d'honneur; Hon. PhD. *Recordings include:* Così fan tutte, Le Nozze di Figaro, Don Giovanni, Die Zauberflöte (Diapason d'Or and Deutsche Schallplattenpreis), Gluck's Alceste for Naxos; co-producer two TV films: Christina the Winter Queen, Gustav III (both winners of Prix d'Italia). *Address:* c/o Haydn Rawstron Ltd, 29a High Street, First Floor, West Wickham, Kent, BR4 0LP, England (office). *Telephone:* (20) 8777-6070 (office). *Fax:* (20) 8777-4073 (office). *Website:* www.haydnrawston.com (office).

OSTOJIĆ, Ranko; Croatian lawyer and politician; *Deputy Prime Minister and Minister of Internal Affairs;* b. 3 Oct. 1962, Split; ed Univ. of Split; held various positions in Split-based cos; mem. Social Democratic Party of Croatia (SDP) 1990–2000, 2004–; served as Asst to the Minister of the Interior 2001–04, held post of Director of Police; mem. 6th Sabor (Parl.) 2007–11, Chair. Parl. Cttee for Internal Affairs and Nat. Security; unsuccessful cand. for Mayor of Split 2009; Minister of Internal Affairs 2011–; Deputy Prime Minister 2013–. *Address:* Ministry of Internal Affairs, 10000 Zagreb, ul. grada Vukovara 33, Croatia (office). *Telephone:* (1) 6122129 (office); (1) 6122405 (office); (1) 6122111 (switchboard) (office). *Fax:* (1) 6122452 (office). *E-mail:* ministar@mup.hr (office). *Website:* www.mup.hr (office).

OSTRIKER, Jeremiah (Paul), PhD, FAAS; American astronomer, astrophysicist and academic; *Treasurer, National Academy of Sciences;* b. 13 April 1937, New York, NY; s. of Martin Ostriker and Jeanne Sumpf; m. Alicia S. Suskin 1958; one s. two d.; ed Harvard Univ. and Univ. of Chicago; Postdoctoral Fellow, Univ. of Cambridge, UK 1964–65; Research Assoc. and Lecturer, Princeton Univ. 1965–66, Asst Prof. 1966–68, Assoc. Prof. 1968–71, Prof. 1971–; Chair. Dept of Astrophysical Sciences and Dir Observatory 1979–95, Charles A. Young Prof. of Astronomy 1982–2002, Provost, Princeton Univ. 1995–2001, Dir, Princeton Inst. for Computational Science and Eng 2005–, Charles A. Young Prof. Emer. 2012–; Plumian Prof. of Astronomy and Experimental Physics, Inst. of Astronomy, Univ. of Cambridge 2001–04; Prof. of Astronomy, Columbia Univ. 2012–(17); mem. Editorial Bd and Trustee Princeton Univ. Press 1982–84, 1986; mem. NAS 1974–, mem. Council 1992–95, mem. Bd of Govs 1993–95, Treas. 2008–(16); mem. American Acad. of Arts and Sciences 1975–, American Astronomical Soc., Int. Astronomical Union, American Philosophical Soc. 1994–; Assoc. mem. Royal Astronomical Soc. 1994–; Foreign mem. Royal Netherlands Acad. of Arts and Sciences, Royal Soc. (London); NSF Fellow 1960–65; Alfred P. Sloan Fellowship 1970–72; Sherman Fairchild Fellowship of CalTech 1977; Trustee, American Museum of Nat. History 1997–2004; Hon. FRAS 1994; Hon. DSc (Chicago) 1992; Helen B. Warner Prize (American Astronomical Soc.) 1972, Henry Norris Russell Prize 1980; Vainu Bappu Memorial Award (Indian Nat. Science Acad.) 1993, Karl Schwarzschild Medal, Astronomische Gesellschaft (Germany) 1999, US Nat. Medal of Science 2000, American Acad. of Achievement Golden Plate Award 2001, Royal Astronomical Soc. Gold Medal 2004, Catherine Wolfe Bruce Gold Medal 2011, James Craig Watson Medal 2012. *Leisure interest:* squash. *Address:* Department of Astrophysical Sciences, Peyton Hall, Ivy Lane, Princeton University, Princeton, NJ 08544-1001 (office); 33 Philip Drive, Princeton, NJ 08540, USA (home). *Telephone:* (609) 258-4267 (office); (609) 924-5737 (home). *Fax:* (609) 258-1020 (office). *E-mail:* jpo@astro.princeton.edu (office); ostriker@astro.princeton.edu (office). *Website:* www.princeton.edu/astro/people/faculty/ostriker (office).

OSTROUMOVA, Olga Mikhailovna; Russian actress; b. 21 Sept. 1947, Buguruslan; ed Moscow Inst. of Theatre Arts; actress, Moscow Theatre of Young Spectators until 1973, Moscow Theatre on Malaya Bronnaya 1973–83, Moscow Mossoviet Theatre 1983–; Silver Nymph Prize, Sorrento and Naples 1973, USSR Official State Prize 1979, RSFSR Merited Actress 1982, Golden Dovzhenko Medal 1982, Peoples' Actress of Russian Fed. 1993. *Films include:* Garage, Stop Kidding, Fate, Snake's Spring, We'll Live up to Monday 1969, Dawns Here Are Quiet 1972, Destiny 1977, Garazh 1979, Earthly Love, Vassily and Vassilisa 1981, There Was No Sorrow 1982, Ya sdelal vsyo, chto mog 1986, The Time of Sons 1986, The Spy 1987, Tower 1987, The Charming Traveller 1990, Very Faithful Wife 1992, Zmeiny istochnik 1997, Ne valyai duraka 1997, Novogodnie priklyucheniya 2002, Photo 2003, Syn 2004, Admiral 2008. *Television includes:* Whilom at California 1978, Engineer Barkasov's Crazy Day 1983, My Sister Lucy 1985, Days and Years of Nikolai Batygin (mini-series) 1987, Zhenshchiny, kotorym povezlo (mini-series) 1989, Po tu storonu volkov (mini-series) 2002, Zachem tebe alibi? (mini-series) 2003, Bednaya Nastya (mini-series) 2003, Zhenshchiny v igre bez pravil (mini-series) 2004, Karusel (series) 2005, Ne rodis krasivoy (series) 2005, Morpekhi (series) 2011. *Music:* (CDs) Tribute to Vladimir Visotsky 2000, A Song about Earth, A Novel about Girls 2002. *Theatre includes:* White Guard, Madame Bovary, At the Threshold of the Tsardom, Cherry Orchard 2001, A Husband, a Wife and a Lover, The Eternal Husband (Dostoevsky) 2003. *Leisure interest:* travelling. *Address:* 121002 Moscow, Arboit str. 17, 4, Apt 9 (home); Moscow Mossoviet Theatre, 103050 Moscow, B. Sadovaya str. 16, Russia (office). *Telephone:* (495) 202-01-88 (home); (495) 299-33-77 (office).

OSTROVSKY, Mikhail Arkadievich, DBiolSc; Russian physiologist, biophysicist and academic; b. 22 Feb. 1935, Leningrad (now St Petersburg); m. Raisa Brook; two c.; ed Moscow State Univ.; jr then sr researcher, Inst. of Higher Nervous Activity and Neurophysiology 1959–70, Head of Sensory Reception Lab., Inst. of Biochemical Physics USSR (now Russian) Acad. of Sciences 1970–; Prof., Moscow

State Univ. 1977–; Visiting Prof., Univ. of Maryland, College Park, USA 1994–; Corresp. mem. USSR (now Russian) Acad. of Sciences 1990, mem. 1994; Ed. Russian Sensory Systems 1987–; Chair. Expert Comm. on Physiology and Medicine of Russian Foundation for Basic Research 1992–; mem. Int. Brain Research Organization 1980, Russian Pavlov Physiological Soc. 1976, Int. Eye Research Asscn 1989; mem. Bd and Chair. Cttee for Relations with E European Neuroscience Asscns. *Publications:* more than 100 articles and papers on photoreception, visual pigments, phototransduction, eye screening pigments, light damage to eye structures; patents for devices and methods in biochemistry, medicine and optics; invented UV blue light-absorbing intraocular lenses. *Address:* ul. Kosygina 4, 119991 Moscow, Russia. *Telephone:* (495) 135-70-73 (office); (495) 939-73-57 (lab.); (495) 434-15-35 (home). *Fax:* (495) 137-41-01. *E-mail:* ostrovsky@ sky.chph.ras.ru (office); ostrovsky@eye.phys.msu.su (home).

OSTROWSKI, Hartmut; German business executive; b. 25 Feb. 1958, Bielefeld; m.; one s. one d.; ed Univ. of Bielefeld; Asst to Bd of Dirs, Bertelsmann Distribution GmbH, Gütersloh, Germany 1982–83, Dept Head 1983–86, Exec. Dept Head 1986–88, Head of Business Unit, 1990–92, Man. Dir 1992–95, Chair. 1995–96, mem. Exec. Bd Bertelsmann Industrie AG (now Bertelsmann Arvato AG) 1996–2002, Chair. 2002–07, Deputy mem. Exec. Bd Bertelsmann AG, Gütersloh 2001–02, mem. 2002–11, Chair. and CEO 2008–11, mem. Supervisory Bd; Man. Dir Security Pacific Eurofinance, Inc., Munich 1988–90. *Address:* c/o Bertelsmann AG, Carl-Bertelsmann-Strasse 270, 33311 Gütersloh, Germany. *Telephone:* 5241800 (office).

OSTRY, Sylvia, CC, PhD, FRSC, OC; Canadian economist and academic; *Distinguished Research Fellow in International Studies, University of Toronto;* b. (Sylvia Knelman), Winnipeg, Man.; d. of Morris J. Knelman and B. Knelman (née Stoller); m. Bernard Ostry; two s.; ed McGill Univ., Montreal, Univ. of Cambridge, UK; Chief Statistician, Statistics Canada 1972–75; Deputy Minister of Consumer and Corp. Affairs and Deputy Registrar Gen. 1975–78; Chair. Econ. Council of Canada 1978–79; Head, Econ. and Statistics Dept, OECD 1979–83; Deputy Minister (Int. Trade) and Co-ordinator for Int. Econ. Relations, Dept of External Affairs 1984–85; Amb., Multilateral Trade Negotiations and Personal Rep. of the Prime Minister, Econ. Summit, Dept of External Affairs 1985–88; Per Jacobsson Foundation Lecture, Washington 1987; Sr Research Fellow, Univ. of Toronto 1989–90; Volvo Distinguished Visiting Fellow, Council on Foreign Relations, New York 1989; Chair. Centre for Int. Studies, Univ. of Toronto 1990–97, Distinguished Research Fellow 1997–; Chancellor, Univ. of Waterloo 1991–97; Western Co-Chair. Blue Ribbon Comm. for Hungary's Econ. Devt 1990–94; Chair. Council Canadian Inst. for Int. Affairs 1990–94; mem. Int. American Dialogue, Advisory Bd Inst. of Int. Econs, Washington, DC, Academic Advisory Council of Deputy Minister for Int. Trade; Founding mem. Pacific Council on Int. Policy; mem. Emer. Group of Thirty Consultative Group on Int. Econ. and Monetary Affairs, Inc. (G-30), Washington, DC; mem. several learned socs and professional orgs; Fellow, American Statistical Asscn; 19 hon. doctorates 1971–2003; The Per Jacobsson Foundation Lecture, Washington, DC 1987, Outstanding Achievement Award, Govt of Canada 1987, Public Policy Forum honouree, Testimonial Dinner 1991, Hon. Assoc. Award, Conf. Bd of Canada 1992, Sylvia Ostry Foundation annual lecture series launched 1992, Career Achievement Award, Canadian Policy Research 2000. *Publications include:* International Economic Policy Co-ordination (with Michael Artis) 1986, Governments and Corporations in a Shrinking World: The Search for Stability 1990, The Threat of Managed Trade to Transforming Economies 1993, Rethinking Federalism: Citizens, Markets and Governments in a Changing World (co-author) 1995, The Halifax G7 Summit: Issues on the Table (co-ed. with Gilbert Winham) 1995, Who's On First? The Post Coldwar Trading System 1997, The Future of the World Trading System 1999, Business, Trade and the Environment 2000, The Changing Scenario in International Governance 2000, The World Trading System: In Dire Need of Reform 2003, Global Integration: Currents and Counter Currents (in The World Trade Organization: Legal, Economic and Political Analysis) 2005, The WTO and Global Governance 2008, Economic Integration in the Americas 2008, The World Trade Organization: System Under Stress 2008; articles on labour econs, demography, productivity, competition policy. *Leisure interests:* films, theatre, contemporary reading. *Address:* Munk Centre for International Studies, University of Toronto, Room 361S, 1 Devonshire Place, Toronto, ON M5S 3K7, Canada (office). *Telephone:* (416) 946-8927 (office); (416) 946-8839 (office). *Fax:* (416) 946-8915 (office). *E-mail:* sylvia.ostry@utoronto.ca (office). *Website:* www .utoronto.ca/cis/ostry (office).

O'SULLEVAN, Sir Peter John, Kt, CBE; British racing correspondent and fmr commentator; b. 3 March 1918; s. of the late Col John Joseph O'Sullevan and Vera O'Sullevan; m. Patricia Duckworth 1951 (died 2010); ed Hawtreys, Charterhouse and Collège Alpin, Switzerland; attached to Chelsea Rescue Services 1939–45; then editorial work and manuscripts reading with Bodley Head Publr; Racing Corresp., Press Asscn 1945–50, Daily Express 1950–86, Today 1986–87; race-broadcaster 1946–98 (from Australia, S Africa, Italy, France, USA etc.); first regular TV (BBC) horse-racing commentator to work without a race-reader; commentator on first televised Grand National 1960, world's first televised electronic horse race from Atlas computer at London Univ. (transmitted by BBC) 1967, first horse race transmitted live via satellite from New York 1980; Dir Int. Racing Bureau 1979–93, Racing Post Ltd 1985–95; mem. Jockey Club 1986–; Chair. Osborne Studio Gallery 1999–; est. Sir Peter O'Sullevan Charitable Trust; Patron Brooke Hospital for Animals; numerous awards for services to horse-racing include Derby Award for Racing Journalist of the Year (with the late Clive Graham) 1971, Racehorse Owner of the Year Award, Horserace Writers' Asscn 1974, Sport on TV Award, Daily Telegraph 1994, Services to Racing Award, Daily Star 1995, Lester's Award, Jockeys' Asscn 1996, Special Award, TV and Radio Industries Club 1998. *Publication:* Calling the Horses: A Racing Autobiography 1989. *Leisure interests:* travel, reading, art, food and wine. *Website:* www .thevoiceofracing.com.

O'SULLIVAN, David, BA; Irish international civil servant; *Chief Operating Officer, European External Action Service;* b. 1 March 1953, Dublin; s. of Gerald O'Sullivan and Philomena Boland; m. Agnes O'Hare; one s. one d.; ed Trinity Coll. Dublin, Collège d'Europe, Bruges; Dept of Foreign Affairs, Dublin 1976–79; mem. staff External Relations, EC 1979–81, First Sec. (Econ. and Commercial), Del. of

EC in Japan 1981–85; mem. Cabinet of Commr P. Sutherland 1985–89; Head of Unit (Educ. and Youth, Training) 1989–92; mem. Cabinet of Commr P. Flynn 1993–96, Deputy Head 1994–96; Dir Social Affairs, European Social Fund 1996–98, Social Affairs, Man. of Resources 1998–99; Dir-Gen. DGXXII (Educ., Training and Youth) 1999; Head of Cabinet of Pres. of Comm. 1999–2000; Sec.-Gen. European Comm. 2000–05, Dir-Gen. for Trade 2005–10, for External Relations Oct.–Dec. 2010, COO European External Action Service 2010–; Dr hc (Dublin Inst. of Tech.) 2005; European of the Year, Irish Council of the European Movt 1999. *Leisure interests:* tennis, fitness, cinema, music, scuba-diving, yoga. *Address:* European External Action Service, 1046 Brussels (office); 87 rue Langeveld, 1180 Brussels, Belgium (home). *Telephone:* (2) 584-95-39 (office). *Fax:* (2) 584-72-22 (office). *E-mail:* david.o'sullivan@eeas.europa.eu (office). *Website:* www.eeas.europa.eu (office).

O'SULLIVAN, John, CBE, BA; British editor and journalist; *Fellow, National Review Institute;* b. 25 April 1942, Liverpool; s. of Alfred M. O'Sullivan and Margaret O'Sullivan (née Corner); m. Melissa Matthews O'Sullivan; ed Queen Mary Coll., Bedford Coll., Univ. of London; jr tutor, Swinton Conservative Coll. 1965–67, Sr Tutor 1967–69; Conservative parl. cand. 1970; Ed. Swinton Journal 1967–69; London Corresp. Irish Radio and TV 1970–72; editorial writer and parl. sketchwriter, Daily Telegraph 1972–79; Ed. Policy Review 1979–83; Asst Ed. Daily Telegraph 1983–84; columnist, The Times 1984–86, Assoc. Ed. 1986–87; Editorial Page Ed. New York Post 1984–86; Ed.-in-Chief Nat. Review 1988–97, Ed.-at-Large 1998–, Fellow, National Review Inst.; columnist, Sunday Telegraph 1988–, Independent on Sunday 1990–91; Editorial Consultant, Hollinger 1998–2001; Ed.-in-Chief, United Press International 2001–04; Ed., The National Interest 2004–06; Exec. Ed. Radio Free Europe/Radio Liberty 2008–11; Dir of Studies, Heritage Foundation 1979–83; Special Adviser to Prime Minister Margaret Thatcher 1987–88; Founder and Co-Chair. The New Atlantic Initiative, American Enterprise Inst. 1996–; mem. Exec. Advisory Bd Margaret Thatcher Foundation, Advisory Council Social Affairs Unit, Hon. Bd Civic Inst., Prague; Fellow, Inst. of Politics, Harvard Univ. 1983; Sr Fellow, Hudson Inst. 2006–09, Nixon Center 2003–05; Hon. LLB (Lewis and Clark Coll.). *Publication:* The President, the Pope, and the Prime Minister: Three Who Changed the World. *Leisure interests:* reading, cinema, theatre, dining out, walking around cities. *Address:* National Review Institute, 233 Pennsylvania Avenue, SE, 3rd Floor, Washington, DC 20003, USA (office). *Telephone:* (202) 543-9226 (office). *E-mail:* info@nrinstitute.org (office). *Website:* www.nrinstitute.org (office).

O'SULLIVAN, Kevin, BSc; Irish journalist; *Editor, The Irish Times;* b. 1960, Tramore, Co. Waterford; m. Ger O'Sullivan; two s. one d.; ed Univ. Coll. Dublin, Nat. Inst. of Higher Educ., Dublin (now Dublin City Univ.); began career as freelance journalist and Founder, Copywrite News Agency 1983–84; reporter, Tuam Herald, Co. Galway 1984–86; Sr Journalist, Connacht Tribune Newspaper Group 1986–96; joined The Irish Times 1997, becoming Environmental and Food Science Corresp. 1997–99, Deputy/Asst News Ed. 2000–01, Special Projects Ed./ Asst Ed. 2000–04, Acting Northern Ed. (based in Belfast) May–June 2001, Acting Foreign Ed. Spring 2003, Founding Ed. of Healthplus supplement 2004–05, Night Ed. 2005–06, News Ed. 2006–11, Ed. 2011–. *Address:* The Irish Times, Irish Times Building, 24–28 Tara Street, Dublin 2, Ireland (office). *Telephone:* (1) 6758000 (office). *Fax:* (1) 6758035 (office). *E-mail:* newsdesk@irishtimes.com (office). *Website:* www.irishtimes.com (office).

O'SULLIVAN, Patrick; British chartered accountant and business executive; *Non-Executive Chairman, Old Mutual plc;* experience includes positions at Bank of America, Goldman Sachs, Financial Guaranty Insurance Co. (subsidiary of GE Capital), Barclays/BZW; Chief Exec. Eagle Star Insurance Co. 1998–2002; Group Finance Dir, Zurich Financial Services 2002–07, Vice-Chair. 2007–09; Chair. (non-exec.) Old Mutual plc 2010–, also Chair. Nomination Cttee; Dir (non-exec.) COFRA Group (Switzerland), Man Group plc, Bank of Ireland. *Address:* Old Mutual plc, 5th Floor, Old Mutual Place, 2 Lambeth Hill, London, EC4V 4GG, England (office). *Telephone:* (20) 7002-7204 (office). *Fax:* (20) 7002-7299 (office). *E-mail:* matthew .gregorowski@omg.co.uk (office). *Website:* www.oldmutual.com (office).

O'SULLIVAN, Paul, BA (Hons); Australian diplomatist; *High Commissioner to New Zealand;* b. 1948, Sydney, NSW; m. Merrilyn O'Sullivan; three s.; ed Marcellin Coll., Randwick, Univ. of Sydney; joined Dept of Foreign Affairs 1971, served in Embassies in Rome, Washington, DC and Cairo, Amb. and Perm. Rep. to UN for Disarmament Issues, Geneva 1991–94, held range of sr positions in Dept of Foreign Affairs and Trade, including First Asst Sec., Americas and Europe Div. 1994–95, First Asst Sec., Int. Orgs and Legal Div. 1995–96, Deputy Chief of Mission, Washington, DC 1996–98, Amb. to Germany 1999–2003, Deputy Sec., Dept of Foreign Affairs and Trade 2003–04; Sr Adviser (Int.), Office of Prime Minister John Howard 2004–05; Dir-Gen. Australian Security and Intelligence Org. 2005–09; High Commr to NZ 2009–. *Address:* Australian High Commission, 72–76 Hobson Street, Thorndon, PO Box 4036, Wellington, New Zealand (office). *Telephone:* (4) 473-6411 (office). *Fax:* (4) 498-7135 (office). *E-mail:* nzinbox@dfat .gov.au (office). *Website:* www.australia.org.nz (office).

O'SULLIVAN, Ronald (Ronnie) Antonio; British professional snooker player and business executive; b. 5 Dec. 1975, Wordsley, West Midlands, England; one s. one d. with Jo Langley and one d. from a previous relationship; ed Wanstead High School; grew up in Chigwell, Essex; first century break (117) aged ten, maximum (147) break aged 15; amateur titles: British Under-16 Championship 1988, IBSF World Under-21 Championship 1991, Junior Pot Black 1991; turned professional 1992; won his first 38 ranking matches as a professional (record); winner of 25 ranking titles: UK Championship 1993, 1997, 2001, 2007, British Open 1994, Asian Classic 1996, German Open 1996, German Masters 2012, Scottish Open 1998, 2000, China Open 1999, 2000, World Snooker Championship 2001, 2004, 2008, 2012, 2013, European Open 2003, Irish Masters 2003, 2005, Welsh Open 2004, 2005, Grand Prix 2004, Northern Ireland Trophy 2008, Shanghai Masters 2009; minor-ranking event titles: Players Tour Championship 2011, Kay Suzanne Memorial Trophy 2011; non-ranking event titles: Nescafé Extra Challenge 1993, Benson and Hedges Championship 1993, The Masters 1995, 2005, 2007, 2009, Charity Challenge 1996, European League 1997, Riley Superstar International 1997, Scottish Masters 1998, 2000, 2002, Champions Cup 2000, Irish Masters 2001, 2007, Premier League Snooker 1997, 2001, 2002, 2005, 2006, 2007, 2008, 2009, 2011, 2012; winner, Nations Cup (with Team England) 2000; youngest winner of a ranking title 1993 (aged 17); fmr World No. 1; has made a record 11 maximum (147) breaks, including the fastest (5:20 in first round of World Championship 1997), only player to score six century breaks in a World Championship final and achieved a total of 131 centuries at the Crucible, beating Stephen Hendry's record of 127 May 2013; known for his rapid playing style and nicknamed 'The Rocket'; Founder and Owner Viva la Diva lingerie shop, London 2003; launched Ronnie O'Sullivan International Ltd 2010; named World Snooker Player of the Year 2012, voted Snooker Writers Player of the Year 2012, inducted into the Hall of Fame 2012. *Television:* appeared on Top Gear (BBC) as the 'Star in a Reasonably Priced Car', finishing with a time of 1:47.3 around test track in a Suzuki Liana 2004. *Publication:* The Autobiography of Ronnie O'Sullivan 2003. *Leisure interests:* Arsenal Football Club, motor racing. *Website:* www.ronnieosullivan.tv.

O'SULLIVAN, Sonia, BA; Irish/Australian athlete; b. 28 Nov. 1969, Cobh, Co. Cork; d. of John O'Sullivan and Mary O'Sullivan; m. Nick Bideau; two d.; ed Villanova Univ., USA; gold medal, 1,500m, silver medal, 3,000m, World Student Games 1991; holds seven nat. (Irish) records; set new world record (her first) in 2,000m TSB Challenge, Edinburgh 1994, new European record in 3,000m, TSB Games London 1994, gold medal in 3,000m, European Athletic Championships, Helsinki 1994; winner, Grand Prix 3,000m, second overall 1993; silver medal, 1,500m, World Championships, Stuttgart 1993; gold medal, 5,000m, World Championships, Gothenburg 1995; gold medal, World Cross Country Championships 4km, 8km 1998; gold medal, European Championships 5,000m, 10,000m 1998; silver medal, 5,000m Olympic Games, Sydney 2000; silver medal, 5,000m, 10,000m European Championships, Munich 2002; winner BUPA Great South Run, Portsmouth 2002 (new world 10–mile record); winner Great BUPA Ireland Run, Dublin 2003; silver medal (with Ireland team), European Cross Country Championships 2003; ran London Marathon for the first time 2005, finished 8th; chosen for the Australian team for the 5000m in Commonwealth Games, Melbourne 2006, unable to compete due to a hamstring injury; Flag bearer for Irish team, Sydney Olympic Games 2000, Ireland Chef de Mission, London Olympic Games 2012; Female Athlete of the Year 1995, Texaco Sports Star of the Year (Athletics) 2002. *Publications:* Running to Stand Still 2001, Sonia: My Story 2008. *Leisure interests:* cycling, swimming, reading, movies, food and cooking. *Telephone:* (4) 1255-0628. *E-mail:* nic@melbournetrackclub.com.

OSZKÓ, Péter, PhD; Hungarian lawyer, management consultant and government official; b. 22 March 1973; ed Eötvös Loránd Univ.; Marketing Dir and Chair. Bd of Trustees, ELTE Student Foundation 1995–97; Man. Dir HÖÖK Kht 1997–99, Vice-Pres. Asscn of Student Councils 1997–99; Man. Dir Agora Universitatis Kht 1997–99; adviser to KPMG Hungary 1996–2000, Tax Man. 2000, Man. KPMG, London 2000–01; Sr Attorney and Head of Tax Group, Freshfields Bruckhaus Deringer Budapest 2001–04; Tax Partner, Deloitte Hungary Inc. 2004–06, Head of Tax Dept 2006–07, Chair. and CEO 2007–09; Minister of Finance 2009–10; Teaching at Faculty of Financial Law, ELTE ÁJTK 1998–; Ed. Hungarian 'Collega' Journal (page of financial law) 1997–2000; mem. Bd of Trustees Pro Facultati Iuridica Foundation 1997–; mem. Bd American Chamber of Commerce 2007–, Jt Venture Asscn 2008–; Head of Tax Working Party, Reform Alliance 2008–09. *Publication:* Verlag Dashöfer's financial issues (co-author) 1998–2000; numerous articles on taxation and other financial matters. *Address:* c/o Ministry of Finance, 1051 Budapest, József Nádor tér 2–4, Hungary (office).

OTA, Akihiro, MEng; Japanese journalist and politician; *Minister of Land, Infrastructure, Transport and Tourism;* b. 6 Oct. 1945, Shinshiro, Aichi Pref.; ed Kyoto Univ.; began career as journalist with Komei Shimbun (newspaper of New Komeito political party), becoming parl. reporter and leader writer; mem. House of Reps (lower house of Parl.) for Tokyo No. 12 constituency 1993–2009, 2012–; Minister of Land, Infrastructure, Transport and Tourism 2012–; fmr mem. New Frontier Party (Shinshinto), Deputy Sec.-Gen. 1994 (party dissolved 1997); mem. New Komeito, Pres. 2006–09. *Address:* Ministry of Land, Infrastructure, Transport and Tourism, 2-1-3, Kasumigaseki, Chiyoda-ku, Tokyo 100-8918, Japan (office). *Telephone:* (3) 5253-8111 (office). *Fax:* (3) 3580-7982 (office). *E-mail:* webmaster@mlit.go.jp (office). *Website:* www.mlit.go.jp (office).

OTA, Hiroko; Japanese economist, academic and government official; b. 2 Feb. 1954; ed Faculty of Social Sciences, Hitotsubashi Univ.; with Mikimoto Corpn 1976–81; Research Fellow, Japan Inst. of Life Insurance 1981–93; Guest Lectuer, Econs Dept, Osaka Univ. 1993–96; Assoc. Prof., Grad. School of Political Science, Saitama Univ. 1996–97; Assoc. Prof. Nat. Grad. Inst. for Policy Studies 1997–2001, Prof. of Econs 2001–, Vice-Pres. 2008–11; Dir of Policy Analysis, Cabinet Office 2002–03, Deputy Dir Gen. for Econ. Research 2003–04, Dir Gen. for Econ. Research 2004–05; Minister of State for Econ. and Fiscal Policy 2006–08 (resgnd). *Address:* National Graduate Institute for Policy Studies, 7-22-1 Roppongi, Minato-ku, Tokyo 106-8677, Japan (office). *Website:* www.grips.ac.jp (office).

OTA, Hiroshi; Japanese business executive; *President and CEO, Suzuken Company Ltd;* fmr Deputy Sr Gen. Man. Sales HQ, Sr Gen. Pharmaceutical Marketing Dept and Sr Exec. Officer Suzuken Co. Ltd, later Man. Dir Suzuken Co. Ltd, mem. Bd of Dirs, Pres. and CEO 2007–. *Address:* Suzuken Co. Ltd, 8 Higashi Kataha-machi, Higashi-ku, Nagoya, Aichi 461-8701, Japan (office). *Telephone:* (52) 961-2331 (office). *E-mail:* info@suzuken.co.jp (office). *Website:* www.suzuken.co.jp (office).

OTAFIIRE, Kahinda, BA; Ugandan politician and army officer; *Minister of Justice and Constitutional Affairs;* b. 29 Dec. 1950, Mitooma Dist; m.; ed Makerere Univ.; Youth Officer 1975–76; Foreign Service Officer, Ministry of Foreign Affairs 1976–80; Chief Political Commissar, Nat. Resistance Army 1981–84, Nat. Political Commissar 1984–86; Commr Internal Affairs Interim Admin 1985–86, Minister of State for Internal Affairs 1986–88, Presidential Asst (Security) 1988–92, Dir Gen. External Security Org. 1992–94, Constituent Ass. Delegate 1994–95, Minister of State for Security 1994–95, for Local Govt 1996–98, Deputy Minister for Local Govt 1996–2001, Political Head, Congo Mil. Expedition 1998–2001, Minister of State for Regional Cooperation 2001–03, Minister of Water, Land and Environment 2003–06, of Local Govt 2006–09, of Trade and Industry 2009–11, of Justice and Constitutional Affairs and Attorney-Gen. 2011–; mem. Parl. (Nat. Resistance Movt) for Ruhinda Co. 1996–; Major Gen. Uganda People's Defence Force. *Address:*

Parliament of Uganda, PO Box 7171, Parliamentary Avenue, Kampala, Uganda (office). *Telephone:* (48) 543199 (office). *E-mail:* kotafiire@parliament.go.ug (office). *Website:* www.parliament.go.ug (office).

OTAKA, Tadaaki; Japanese conductor; *Permanent Conductor, NHK Symphony, Tokyo;* b. 8 Nov. 1947, Kamakura; s. of Hisatada Otaka and Misaoko Otaka; m. Yukiko Otaka 1978; ed Toho Gakuen Music School, Toho Gakuen Music Acad., Vienna Acad., Austria; began studying violin 1951; apptd Chief Conductor Tokyo Philharmonic Orchestra 1971–, Conductor Laureate 1991–; Chief Conductor Sapporo Symphony 1981–86, Prin. Conductor 1998–; Prin. Conductor BBC Welsh Symphony Orchestra (now BBC Nat. Orchestra of Wales) 1987–95, Conductor Laureate 1996–; Chief Conductor Yomiuri Nippon Symphony Orchestra 1992–98; Music Adviser and Prin. Conductor Kioi Sinfonietta (Tokyo) 1995–; Dir Britten Pears Orchestra 1998–2001; Perm. Conductor NHK Symphony, Tokyo 2010–; Prin. Guest Conductor Melbourne Symphony 2010–12; Artistic Dir New Nat. Theatre, Tokyo 2010–; has conducted BBC Proms, and orchestras including City of Birmingham Symphony, Royal Liverpool Philharmonic, Royal Scottish Nat., Bournemouth Symphony, BBC Symphony, London Symphony, London Philharmonic, Rotterdam Philharmonic, Bamberg Symphony, Strasbourg Philharmonic, Bergen Philharmonic and Singapore Symphony; Hon. Fellow, Welsh Coll. of Music and Drama 1993; Hon. CBE 1997; Dr hc (Univ. of Wales) 1993; Second Prize Min-On Conductors' Competition 1969, Suntory Music Award 1992, Elgar Medal 2000. *Music:* many recordings with BBC Nat. Orchestra of Wales including works by Takemitsu and Franck, and Britten's Peter Grimes with Yomiuri Nippon. *Leisure interests:* fishing, tennis, cooking. *Address:* NHK Symphony Orchestra 2-16-49 Takanawa, Minato-ku, Tokyo, 108-0074, Japan (office). *Telephone:* (3) 5793-8111 (office). *Fax:* (3) 3443-0278 (office). *Website:* www.nhkso.or.jp/en (office).

OTARI, Muhammad Naji al-; Syrian politician; b. 1944, Aleppo; ed studied architecture, diploma in town planning from the Netherlands; Head of Aleppo City Council 1983–87; fmr Gov. of Hums; mem. Ba'ath Party Cen. Cttee 2000–, mem. Regional Command 2000–; Deputy Prime Minister for Services Affairs 2000–03; Speaker of the People's Ass. (Parl.) March–Sept. 2003; Prime Minister of Syria 2003–11 (resgnd with rest of cabinet at Pres.'s request following popular protests), asked to stay on as caretaker Prime Minister 29 March 2011–; Pres. Aleppo's eng syndicate 1989–93. *Address:* Office of the Prime Minister, rue Chahbandar, Damascus, Syria (office). *Telephone:* (11) 2226000 (office). *Fax:* (11) 2237842 (office).

OTÁROLA PEÑARANDA, Luis Alberto; Peruvian lawyer, academic and politician; b. 1967; ed Univ. San Martín de Porres, Lima, American Inst. of Human Rights, San José, Costa Rica; Adviser to Ministry of Defence 2002–03, Deputy Minister of Econ. Affairs and Admin of Ministry of Defence 2003–04, Deputy Minister of Internal Order, Ministry of Interior, Aug.–Dec. 2011, Minister of Defence 2011–12; fmr Lecturer in Law, Univ. of Lima and Peruvian Naval War Coll.; fmr visiting lecturer at several int. univs; Ad-hoc Public Prosecutor for cases arising from Judgments of Inter-American Court of Human Rights. *Address:* c/o Ministry of Defence, Edif. Quiñones, Avda de la Peruanidad s/n, Jesús María, Lima 1, Peru. *Website:* www.albertootarola.com.

OTCHAKOVSKY-LAURENS, Paul, LenD; French publisher; *President Director-General, Editions P.O.L.;* b. 10 Oct. 1944, Valreas, Vaucluse; s. of Zelman Otchakovsky and Odette Labaume; adopted s. of Berthe Laurens; m. Monique Pierret 1970; one s. one d.; ed Coll. and Lycée de Sablé sur Sarthe, Coll. Montalembert de Courbevoie, Coll. St Croix de Neuilly and Faculté de Droit, Paris; Reader, Editions Christian Bourgois 1969–70; Dir of Collection, Editions Flammarion 1970–77; Dir of Collections, then Dir of Dept Editions Hachette 1977–82; Pres. Dir-Gen. Editions P.O.L. 1983–; Commdr, Ordre des Arts et des Lettres, Chevalier, Légion d'honneur. *Films:* Sablé-sur-Sarthe, Sarthe 2007. *Address:* Editions P.O.L., 33 rue Saint-André-des-Arts, 75006 Paris, France (office). *Telephone:* 1-43-54-21-20 (office). *E-mail:* otchakov@pol-editeur.fr (office). *Website:* www.pol-editeur.com (office).

OTELLINI, Paul S., BA, MBA; American business executive; b. 2 Oct. 1950, San Francisco, Calif.; m.; two c.; ed Univ. of San Francisco, Univ. of California, Berkeley; joined Intel Corpn 1974, Man. business with IBM Corpn 1980–85, Gen. Man. Peripheral Components Operations 1985–87, Folsom Microcomputer Div. 1987–89, Vice-Pres. Operating Group 1988, Asst to Pres. 1989, Gen. Man. Microprocessor Products Group 1990, Corp. Officer 1991, Exec. Vice-Pres. Sales and Marketing 1992–98, Sr Vice-Pres. 1993–96, Exec. Vice-Pres. 1996–2002, Exec. Vice-Pres. and Gen. Man. Architecture Group 1998–2002, Pres. and COO Intel Corpn 2002–05, mem. Bd of Dirs 2002–, Pres. and CEO 2005–13; mem. Bd of Dirs Google Inc.; mem. President's Council on Jobs and Competitiveness. *Address:* c/o Intel Corporation, 2200 Mission College Boulevard, Santa Clara, CA 95052-8119, USA. *E-mail:* info@intel.com.

OTHMAN BIN WOK; Singaporean company director, fmr journalist, politician and fmr diplomatist; b. 8 Oct. 1924; m. Asnah Bte Suhaimi (now called Lina Binte Abdullah) 1975; one s. two d.; ed Telok Saga Malay School, Raffles Inst. and London School of Journalism; worked on Utusan Melayu as reporter, News Ed. then Deputy Ed. 1946–63; mem. People's Action Party 1954–; MP for Pasir Panjang Constituency 1963–81; Minister for Social Affairs 1963–77; Amb. to Indonesia (also accred to Papua New Guinea) 1977–80; Dir Overseas Investment Pte Ltd 1981–, Overseas Trustees Ltd 1982–, Overseas Investment Nominees Pte Ltd 1982–, Biohealth Int. (S) Pte Ltd 1983–99, Autologous Blood Bank (S) Pte Ltd 1987–99, Sembawang Eng Pte Ltd 1989–97, Utusan Melayu (S) Pte Ltd 1988–2001, Gainall Pte Ltd 1992–, Property Services Int. 1993–99, Hale Medical Clinic (Concourse) Pte Ltd 1995–, Bright Steel Pte Ltd 1996–, Genesis School for Special Educ. 1998–; The Hale Medical Group 2001–, Dimas (S) Pte Ltd 2001–, Ms Twilight Pte Ltd 2001–02, Chair. Lion Asiapac Ltd 1996–, Mainstream Techs Pte Ltd 2000–, Mindsets Pte Ltd 2000–, d'Oz International Pte Ltd; Perm. mem. Presidential Council for Minority Rights 1981–; mem. Singapore Tourist Promotion Bd 1981–94, Sentosa Devt Corpn 1981–97 Singapore Professional Executives Co-operative Ltd 2000–, Ang Mo Kio Community Hosp. 2002; Hon. Consul, Principality of Monaco 1996–99; Jasa Utama Star for Outstanding Services (Indonesia) 1980, Order of Nila Utama for Distinguished Service 1983. *Leisure interests:* reading, music, keep-fit exercise, golf. *Address:* Overseas Investment Pte Ltd, 300 Beach Road, #02-01, The Concourse, Singapore 199555 (office); Wisma

Bahagia, 35 Carmen Street, Singapore 459756, Singapore (home). *Telephone:* (65) 63929881 (home). *Fax:* (65) 63929901 (office). *E-mail:* OthmanWok@hotmail.sg (office).

OTHMANI, Saâdeddine el-, MD; Moroccan psychiatrist and politician; b. 16 Jan. 1956, Inezgane; ed Hassan II Univ., Casablanca; gen. medical practitioner 1987–94; psychiatrist, Berrechid City Hosp. 1994–97; mem. Majlis al-Nuab (Parl.) for Mohammedia 1997–2007, Vice-Pres. Foreign Affairs Cttee 2001–02; Minister of Foreign Affairs and Co-operation 2012–13; mem. Conseil Maghrébin de la Choura (Union du Maghreb Arabe) 2002–; mem. Parti de la justice et du développement (Sec.-Gen. 2004–08). *Publications include:* several books on psychiatry and Islamic law. *Address:* c/o Ministry of Foreign Affairs and Co-operation, ave Franklin Roosevelt, Rabat, Morocco (office).

OTI, Paterson; Solomon Islands politician; mem. Parl. for Temotu and Nende 1997–; Deputy Speaker Nat. Parl. Feb.–Dec. 2005; Minister for Foreign Affairs 1997–2000, 2006–07; Minister of Communications, Aviation and Meteorology 2004–05; Deputy Prime Minister Nov.–Dec. 2007; mem. Solomon Islands Alliance for Change. *Address:* National Parliament, P.O. Box G19, Honiara, Solomon Islands (office). *Telephone:* 28520 (office). *Fax:* 24272 (office). *Website:* www .parliament.gov.sb (office).

OTMAN ASSED, Mohamed; Libyan politician; b. Oct. 1922, Fezzan; s. of Ahmed al-Badawi Assed and Fatima Nuweir; m. Lola Seif 1959; nine s.; ed Libyan religious and Arabic schools; teacher 1942–43; in Liberation Movt; Head of Fezzan Del. in Legis. Ass. 1950–51; Rep. for Fezzan, UN Council for Libya 1951; Deputy 1952–64; Minister of Health, Fed. Govt 1951–58, of Econ. Affairs Feb.–Oct. 1960; Prime Minister 1960–63; pvt. business 1964–; emigrated to Morocco 1969; Order of Independence 1954; Order of Independence (Tunisia) 1957; Order of the Throne (Morocco) 1962; Muhammad Ali al-Sanoussi Medal 1964. *Address:* Villa Rissani, Route Oued Akrach, Souissi, Rabat, Morocco. *Telephone:* 75-16-25; 75-11-83.

OTOMO, Katsuhiro; Japanese animator and manga artist; b. 14 April 1954, Tome-gun, Miyagi Pref.; m. Yoko Otomo; ed Sanuma High School; following high school, moved to Tokyo to work in manga industry, wrote short strips for Action comics, including Prosper Merimee's short novel Mateo Falcone (retitled A Gun Report) 1973; began Fireball series (unfinished) introducing themes that later became his trademark 1979; serialization of Domu (A Child's Dream) graphic novel was his first major success, selling over half a million copies 1980–82, won Science Fiction Grand Prix 1983 (first ever manga recipient); began work on his masterpiece Akira which took 10 years and over 2,000 pages to complete, animated film version released in 1988 (greatest box office success in Japan that year). *Films include:* genre filmography: Koko Erotopia: Akai seifuku (scriptwriter) 1979, Shuffle (comic strip Run) 1981, Jiyu o warera (dir) 1982, Crusher Joe (special character designer) 1983, Harmagedon: Genam taisen (Armageddon: The Great Battle with Genma) (animator, character designer) 1983, Meikyu monogatari (Labyrinth Tales) (segment scriptwriter, dir and character designer) 1987, Roboto kanibauru (segment dir) 1987, Akira (scriptwriter, dir) 1988, Akira Production Report (performed as himself) 1988, Fushigi monogatari: Hachi neko wa yoku asagata kaette kuru (scriptwriter) 1988, Rojin Z (Oldman Z) (scriptwriter) 1991, Warudo apaatoment hora (World Apartment Horror) (dir) 1991, Memories (exec. producer, scriptwriter, dir, art dir) 1995, Perfect Blue (supervisor) 1997, Spriggan (gen. supervisor) 1998, Metoroporisu (Metropolis) (scriptwriter, storyboard artist) 2001, Animax Special: The Making of Metropolis (performed as himself) 2002, Steamboy (dir) 2004, Mushishi (scriptwriter and dir) 2006, Combustible (dir and scriptwriter) 2012; non-genre filmography: Give Us Guns (dir) 1981, So What (scriptwriter) 1988. *Address:* c/o Toho Co. Ltd, 1-2-2 Yurako-cho, Chiyoda-ku, Tokyo 100-8415, Japan (office).

O'TOOLE, Shane, BArch; Irish architectural historian and critic; b. 5 July 1955, Dublin; s. of James Patrick O'Toole and Caroline Louise O'Toole (née Hannan); m. Maeve O'Neill 1984 (separated 2011); one s. one d.; ed Franciscan Coll., Gormanston, Co. Meath, Univ. Coll., Dublin (UCD); Lynch O'Toole Walsh Architects, Dublin 1979–86; Project Man. Energy Research Group, UCD 1986–92; Co-Founder and Dir urban design consortium Group 91 Architects 1990–99; Shane O'Toole Architect 1991–97, 2008–; Co. Architect Target Bldg Products Ltd 1994–2008; architecture critic, The Sunday Times 1999–2009; Pres. Architectural Asscn of Ireland 1982–83; Vice-Pres. Royal Inst. of the Architects of Ireland 1988, 1997; Founder and Sec., DoCoMoMo Ireland 1990–2012; Dir Irish Architectural Archive 2002–; Fellow, Salzburg Global Seminar 2005; inaugural Curator and Dir Irish Architecture Foundation 2005–06; mem. CICA (Int. Cttee of Architectural Critics) 2008–; Adviser to Mies van der Rohe Award for European Architecture 1992–, to Nation Building (TV series on architecture in Ireland 1922–2000) 2000, to Veronica Rudge Green Prize in Urban Design (Harvard Prize in Urbanism), Harvard Univ. Grad. School of Design 2000–04, to New Trends of Architecture in Europe and Asia-Pacific Exhbn 2002–07, to Royal Irish Acad. Irish Architecture 1600–2000 research project 2008–13, to European Prize for Urban Public Space 2012–; Judge, European Prize for Contemporary Architecture 2003, World Architecture Festival 2008–11; Hon. mem. Architectural Asscn of Ireland 1995; Silver Medal Sofia Biennale 1987, Grand Prix Kraków Biennale 1989, Irish Bldg of the Year Award 1996, Architectural Asscn of Ireland Downes Medal 1996, European Architectural Award (RIBA) 1997, Int. Union of Architects Sir Patrick Abercrombie Prize for town planning and territorial devt 2002, Gold Medal Commendation, Royal Inst. of the Architects of Ireland 2003, Int. Bldg Press Architectural Critic/Architecture Writer of the Year 2008, 2009, 2010 and other prizes and awards. *Achievements:* Co-Dir Architectural Framework Plan for Regeneration of Temple Bar, Dublin 1992–2000; Co-Designer The Ark, Europe's first cultural centre for children 1992–95; represented in architecture exhbns including 40 Under 40: Emerging British Architects, UK and USA 1988–89, The New Breed, Sydney 1988, Making a Modern Street, Zurich 1991, 20 Young Architects of the World, London 1993, Presenting Architecture, Dublin 2005, Collection Building, Dublin 2006, Group 91: 15 Years On, Belfast 2006, Notebooks and Narratives: The Secret Laboratory, Belfast, Cork and Dublin 2011, Group 91, Dublin 2011; cr. exhbns, The Pillar Project, Dublin 1988, Tales from Two Cities: Emerging Architects in Dublin and Edinburgh (Edin., Dublin, Berlin, London) 1994, Master of All the Muses: Michael Scott 1905–2005 (Cork, Dublin) 2005, Irish Commr, Venice Biennale 2004, 2006, North by Northwest: Liam McCormick 1916–1996 (Dublin, Belfast, Letterkenny, Greencastle) 2008, (Derry) 2009, New

Irish Architecture: Rebuilding the Republic, Leuven 2011, Ireland at the Venice Architecture Biennale 2000–2010, Shankill Castle 2011, Restless Pencil: Noel Moffett 1912–94, Dublin 2012. *Radio:* contrib. to RTE Arts Tonight documentary on Sam Stephenson Architect (PPI Award) 2011. *Publications:* Kevin Roche Architect 1983, Aldo Rossi: Selected Writings and Projects 1983, Collaboration: The Pillar Project 1988, The Architect and the Drawing 1989, Making a Modern Street 1991, Tales from Two Cities 1994, Transformation of an Institution 2004, SubUrban to SuperRural 2006, North by Northwest (co-author) 2008. *Leisure interests:* family, football, films, food, good buildings, a glass of wine. *Address:* Shankill Castle, Paulstown, Co. Kilkenny, Ireland (home). *Telephone:* 85-7686590 (mobile) (office). *E-mail:* shane_otoole@hotmail.com (home).

OTORBAYEV, Djoomart Kaipovich; Kyrgyzstani economist, academic and politician; *Prime Minister;* b. 18 Aug. 1955, Frunze (now Bishkek); ed Leningrad (now St Petersburg) State Univ., Russian SFSR; Lecturer, Sr Lecturer, Prof., Kyrgyz State Univ. 1985–96; Visiting Prof., Eindhoven Univ., The Netherlands 1992–96; Prof., Kyrgyz-Russian Slavonic Univ. 1996–2005; Chief Rep. of Philips Electronics Corpn in Cen. Asia 1996–99, Vice-Pres. of Representation 1999–2002; Special Rep. of Pres. of Kyrgyzstan for attracting investment 2001–04, and for econ. assistance to Afghanistan 2001–05; Deputy Prime Minister, responsible for the Economy 2002–05; f. Investment Round Table 2001; Sr Adviser for Caucasus and Cen. Asia, EBRD, London, UK 2006–12; First Deputy Prime Minister 2012–14, Prime Minister 2014–; mem. Fatherland Socialist Political Party (Ata Meken) (Ata Meken Sotsialisttik Partiyasy). *Address:* Office of the Government, 720003 Bishkek, Dom Pravitelstva, Kyrgyzstan (office). *Telephone:* (312) 66-49-23 (office). *E-mail:* ps@mail.gov.kg (office). *Website:* www.gov.kg (office).

OTSUKA, Mutsutake; Japanese transport industry executive; *Advisor, East Japan Railway Company;* b. 5 Jan. 1932, Beijing, China; ed Tokyo Univ.; began career with Japanese Nat. Railways 1965, various positions 1965–87; Man. Dir East Japan Railway Co. 1987–97, Vice-Pres. 1997–2000, Pres. and CEO JR East (formed during privatization of railways) 2000–06, Chair. East Japan Railway Co. 2006–12, Advisor 2012–; Corp. Auditor, Electric Power Development Co. Ltd. *Leisure interests:* music, golf. *Address:* East Japan Railway Co., 2-2 Yoyogi 2-chome, Shibuya-ku, Tokyo 151-8578, Japan (office). *Telephone:* (3) 5334-1310 (office). *Fax:* (3) 5334-1297 (office). *E-mail:* info@jreast.co.jp (office). *Website:* www .jreast.co.jp (office).

OTT, Hans Rudolf, PhD; Swiss physicist and academic; *Professor Emeritus, Eidgenössische Technische Hochschule, Zurich;* b. 4 July 1940, Berne; m. Marie-Louise Ott (née Gruaz); one s.; ed Eidgenössische Technische Hochschule (ETH), Zurich; Asst, ETH, Zurich 1971, Admin. Dir, Dept of Physics 1976–88, Prof. of Physics 1986–2008, Prof. Emer. 2008–, Deputy Chair., Dept of Physics 1999–2001, Chair. 2001–05, also Head, Inst. for Solid State Physics 1990–93, 1998–99; Head of Research, Paul Scherrer Inst. (PSI), Villigen 1988–91, also Dir and Chair. of Research Cttee 1991–2008; Vice-Chair., Comm. C5, IUPAP 1996–2002; Pres. Physikalische Gesellschaft, Zurich 1994–97; Sec. of Comm., Int. Inst. of Refrigeration 1976–86; mem. Council European Physical Soc. 1993–96 (mem. Cttee for Low Temperature Physics, IUPAP 1987–92, Chair. Condensed Matter Div. 1998–2005); mem. Exec. Bd Int. Council for Science (ICSU) (Treas.) 2008–; Co-Ed. Physica C 1988–2004; Assoc. Ed. Reviews of Modern Physics 1994–99; Ed.-in-Chief European Physical Journal B 2004–; mem. Research Council, Swiss Nat. Science Foundation 1997–; Chair. Platform Math., Astronomy and Physics, Swiss Acad. of Natural Sciences 2007–12; Pres. Albert Einstein Soc., Bern 2008–; Foreign mem. Finnish Acad. of Sciences 2005–; Fellow, American Physical Soc. 1989–, World Innovation Foundation 2004–; Hon. mem. Physical Soc., Zurich 2003, Swiss Physical Soc. 2005; European Physical Soc. Hewlett-Packard Europhysics Prize 1989, American Physical Soc. Int. Prize for New Materials 1990. *Publications:* several books and more than 500 articles in scientific journals. *Address:* Laboratorium für Festkörperphysik, ETH Hönggerberg Office, HPF F 4, 8093 Zurich, Switzerland (office). *Telephone:* (1) 633-2311 (office). *E-mail:* ott@phys.ethz .ch (office). *Website:* www.dscm.ethz.ch/people/otth (office).

OTTER, Clement Leroy (Butch), BA; American business executive and state official; *Governor of Idaho;* b. 3 May 1942, Caldwell, Ida; m. 1st Gay Simplot 1964 (divorced 1992); four c.; m. 2nd Lori Easley 2006; ed St Teresa's Acad. (now Bishop Kelly High School), Boise, Saint Martin's Univ., Boise Jr Coll. (now Boise State Univ.), Coll. of Idaho (now Albertson Coll. of Idaho); served in Ida. Army Nat. Guard's 116th Armored Cavalry 1968–73, received specialized training at Fort Knox, Ky; mem. Bd of Dirs J.R. Simplot Co., later Dir Food Products Div., later Pres. Simplot Livestock, Pres. Simplot Int. –1993; mem. Ida. State House of Reps from Canyon Co. 1973–76, served as Deputy Majority Whip; cand. for Gov. of Ida. 1978; remained active in Ida. Republican Party, including its Cen. Cttee, served as Chair. Canyon Co. Republican Party; Lt-Gov. of Ida. 1987–2001; mem. US House of Reps for Ida. First Congressional Dist 2001–06; Gov. of Idaho 2007–; mem. Nat. Rifle Asscn, Maple Grove State Grange, Ida. Cowboys Asscn, American Legion, Ida. 4-H Million Dollar Club; Grand Slam mem. Ducks Unlimited; Lifetime mem. Safari Club International; Republican; Dr hc (Mindanao State Univ., Philippines, Albertson Coll. of Idaho). *Address:* Office of the Governor, State Capitol, PO Box 83720, Boise, ID 83720, USA (office). *Telephone:* (208) 334-2100 (office). *Fax:* (208) 334-3454 (office). *Website:* gov.idaho.gov (office).

OTTO, Frei, PhD; German architect and engineer; b. 1925, Siegmar, Saxony; ed Tech. Univ., Berlin, Univ. of Va, USA; served as pilot with Luftwaffe 1943–45; taken prisoner and served as architect, builder and repairman for POW camp, France 1945–47; freelance architect, inventor, author and designer 1952–; led revival of tent as feature of modern architecture 1950s; f. Centre of Devt for Lightweight Structures, Berlin 1957; Founding Dir Inst. for Lightweight Structures, Univ. of Stuttgart 1964–90; f. Wide-Spanned Lightweight Structures Special Research Unit, Deutschen Forschungsgemeinschaft 1969; fmr Prof., Tech. Univ., Berlin; fmr Visiting Prof. at Yale, Wash., Harvard Univs, Univ. of Calif., Berkeley, MIT; Hon. mem. AIA 1968, RIBA 1981; Hon. Citizen of the City of Leonberg 2000; Dr hc Tech. Univ., Munich; Berlin Prize for Architecture 1967, Thomas Jefferson Medal in Architecture, Univ. of Va 1974, Aga Khan Award for Architecture 1980, 1998, Honda Prize for Architecture and Nature (Japan) 1990, Grand Prize, German Architects and Engineers Asscn 1996, Wolf Prize in Architecture 1997, Lifetime Achievement Special Prize, VII Int. Biennial for Architecture, Buenos Aires 2000, RIBA Royal Gold Medal 2005. *Architectural* *works include:* Music Pavilion, Fed. Garden Exhbn, Kassel 1955, Entrance Arch, Fed. Garden Exhbn, Cologne 1957, Snow and Rocks Pavilion, Swiss Nat. Exhbn, Lausanne 1964, W German Pavilion, Montreal Exposition, Canada 1967, Intercontinental Hotel and Conf. Centre, Mecca, Saudi Arabia 1968–72, Sport Structures Roofs, Olympic Park, Munich 1972, Multihall Complex, Mannheim 1975, Bird House, Hellabrunn Zoo 1980, Cultural Centre, Tuwaiq Palace, Riad, Saudi Arabia 1985, Ecological Houses in Berlin 1990, Stuttgart Train Station Project 2000, Japanese Pavilion for Hannover Exposition 2000. *Publications:* Natürliche Konstruktionen 1981, Gestaltwerdung. Zur Formentstehung in Nature, Technik und Baukunst 1988, Das hängende Dach 1990; various articles on tensile and pneumatic structures. *Address:* c/o Institute for Lightweight Structures, University of Stuttgart, Pfaffenwaldring 7, 70569 Stuttgart, Germany (office). *Website:* www.uni-stuttgart.de/ilek (office).

OTTO, Michael, Dr rer. pol; German business executive; *Chairman of the Supervisory Board, Otto Group;* b. 12 April 1943; joined Otto Group 1971, mem. Exec. Bd Merchandise 1971–81, Chair. Exec. Bd and CEO 1981–2007, Chair. Supervisory Bd 2007–; mem. Bd of Dirs Axel Springer Verlag AG, Berlin; Chair. Council WWF Deutschland; Chair. Bd of Trustees Soc. for Politics and Industry, Werner Otto Foundation for Medical Research; Founder and Chair. Bd of Trustees Michael Otto Foundation for Environmental Protection, Foundation for Sustainable Agriculture and Forestry (FSAF); Hon. Senator, Univs of Hamburg and Greifswald 2000; Bundesverdienstkreuz mit Stern 2006; Manager of the Year 1986, 2001, Hamburg Senate Alfred Töpfer Medal 1996, German Environment Award 1997, Corp. Ethics Award 2000, German Business Ethics Network Business Ethics Award, Sustainability Leadership Award 2002, Jewish Museum Berlin Prize for Understanding and Tolerance 2004, BAUM Sustainability Special Award 2005, Vernon A. Walters Award, Atlantik-Brücke 2005, German Incorporaters Prize (for life's work) 2006, Int. Lifetime award 2006. *Address:* Otto GmbH & Co. KG, Wandsbeker Strasse 3–7, 22179 Hamburg, Germany (office). *Telephone:* (40) 64610 (office). *Fax:* (40) 64618571 (office). *E-mail:* info@ottogroup .com (office). *Website:* www.ottogroup.com (office).

OTUDEKO, Oba, BA, FCA, FCIB, FCIS; Nigerian business executive and fmr banker; *Chairman, Honeywell Group;* b. 18 Aug. 1943; m.; ed Leeds Coll. of Commerce, UK; f. Honeywell Group (fmrly Honeywell Enterprises) in early 1980s, currently Chair.; currently also Chair. Airtel Nigeria, Fan Milk of Nigeria Plc; Pres. and Chair. of Council, Nigerian Stock Exchange 2006–09; fmr Chair. Nat. Maritime Authority, FBN Bank (UK) Ltd, Nigeria–South Africa Chamber of Commerce, Vee-Networks; f. Oba Otudeko Foundation 2003; mem. Bd of Dirs Cen. Bank of Nigeria, Guinness Nigeria Plc, Ecobank Transnational Inc.; mem. Constituent Ass. responsible for drafting new constitution 1988–89; mem. of Council, Manufacturers Asscn of Nigeria, Africa Regional Advisory Bd, London Business School, UK (also mem. Office of Distinguished Friends); Fellow, Inst. of Chartered and Corporate Accountants, UK, Inst. Chartered Secs and Admins of Nigeria; Paul Harris Fellow, Rotary International; Chancellor, Olabisi Onabanjo Univ. (fmrly Ogun State Univ.) 2001–10; Hon. Citizen of Dallas, Texas, USA, Hon. Citizen of Meziara, Lebanon; mem. Order of the Fed. Repub. 2000, Officer, Order of the Fed. Repub. 2003, Commdr, Order of the Fed. Repub. 2011; Hon. DSc (Olabisi Onabanjo Univ.). *Address:* Honeywell Group, 6B Mekunwen Road, Off Oyinkan Abayomi Drive, Ikoyi, Lagos, Nigeria (office). *Telephone:* (1) 2900525 (office). *E-mail:* info@honeywellgroup.com (office). *Website:* www.honeywellgroup.com (office).

OTUNBAYEVA, Roza Isakovna, CPhilSc; Kyrgyzstani diplomatist, politician and fmr head of state; b. 23 Aug. 1950, Frunze (now Bishkek); m.; one s. one d.; ed Moscow State Univ.; sr teacher, Head of Chair, Kyrgyz Univ. 1975–81; Second Sec., Regional CP Cttee in Frunze (now Bishkek), Sec., City CP Cttee 1979–86; Vice-Chair. Council of Ministers, Minister of Foreign Affairs of Kyrgyz SSR 1986–89; Exec. Sec., USSR Comm. on UNESCO 1989–90, Chair. 1990–91; Amb. of USSR to Malaysia 1991–92; Vice-Prime Minister and Minister of Foreign Affairs of Repub. of Kyrgyzstan Feb.–May 1992; Amb. of Kyrgyzstan to USA 1992–94 (also accred to Canada); Minister of Foreign Affairs 1994–97; Amb. to UK 1997–2002; apptd Deputy Special Rep. of UN Sec.-Gen. for Georgia (to regulate conflict between Georgia and Abkhazia) 2002; Chair. Ata-Jurt party 2004–06, amongst leaders of 'Tulip Revolution' that led to overthrow of Pres. Akayev 2005, Acting Minister of Foreign Affairs 2005; Chair. Interim Govt of Nat. Trust (following overthrow of Pres. Kurmanbek Bakiyev) April–May 2010, Acting Pres. of Kyrgyzstan May–July 2010, Pres. July 2010–Dec. 2011, also Prime Minister May–Dec. 2010; Co-Chair. Banner (Asaba) Party of Nat. Revival 2006–07; mem. Social Democratic Party of Kyrgyzstan 2008–10; mem. Advisory Bd (Moscow Br.), Carnegie Endowment for Int. Peace; f. Roza Otunbayeva's Initiative Int. Social Fund 2012. *Address:* Roza Otunbayeva's Initiative International Social Fund, 720000 Bishkek, Kyrgyzstan. *Telephone:* (312) 66-03-82. *E-mail:* office@roza.kg. *Website:* www.roza.kg.

OU, Francisco H. L., BA; Taiwanese diplomatist and politician; b. 5 Jan. 1940; ed Nat. Cheng-chi Univ.; Officer, Dept of Cen. and S American Affairs, Ministry of Foreign Affairs 1964–67; Third Sec., Embassy in Peru 1967–71, Second Sec. 1971; Section Chief, Dept of Cen. and S American Affairs, Ministry of Foreign Affairs 1971–73, Deputy Dir-Gen. 1973–75, Dir-Gen. 1981–84; Dir Far E Commercial Office, Santiago, Chile 1975–81; Amb. to Nicaragua 1984–85, to Guatemala 1990–96, 2003–08; Dir Commercial Office, Argentina 1986–90; Vice Minister of Foreign Affairs 1996–2000, Minister 2008–09; Rep. Taipei Econ. and Cultural Office, Spain 2000–03. *Address:* c/o Ministry of Foreign Affairs, 2 Kaitakeland Boulevard, Taipei 10048, Taiwan (office). *E-mail:* eyes@mofa.gov.tw (office). *Website:* www.mofa.gov.tw (office).

OU, Jinping, BS, MS, PhD; Chinese engineer and university administrator; b. 15 April 1959; ed Xiangtan Univ., Wuhan Univ. of Tech., Harbin Inst. of Tech.; Asst Prof. of Civil Eng, Harbin Inst. of Tech. 1985–87, Assoc. Prof. 1987–90, Prof. 1990–, Dean, School of Civil Eng 1997–2000; Prof., Dept of Civil Eng, Dalian Univ. of Tech. 1988–, also Univ. Pres. 2006–12; Deputy, 11th NPC 2008; mem. Chinese Acad. of Eng 2003–; winner of first Feng Kang Prize for Scientific Computing. *Address:* Dalian University of Technology, Dalian 116024, Liaoning Province, People's Republic of China (office). *Telephone:* (411) 84708114 (office). *Fax:* (411) 84708116 (office). *E-mail:* oujinping@dlut.edu.cn (office). *Website:* www.dlut.edu .cn (office).

OUALALOU, Fathallah, DèsSc; Moroccan economist and politician; *Mayor of Rabat;* b. 1942, Rabat; m.; four c.; ed Lycée Moulay Youssef, Univ. of Rabat, Univ. of Paris; began career as Research Asst, Centre Universitaire de Recherche Scientifique, also Pres. Union Nationale des Etudiants; Lecturer, Law Dept, Univs of Rabat, Casablanca and Ecole Nat. d'Admin 1968; mem. Groupe de Rabat; Co-founder Socialist Union of Popular Forces (Union socialiste des forces populaires) 1972, mem. Political Bureau 1989–, Leader Parl. Group 1984–98; Minister of Economy, Finance, Privatization and Tourism 1998–2002, of Finance and Privatization 2002–07; Mayor of Rabat 2009–; mem. Nat. Bureau, Syndicat Nat. de l'Enseignement Supérieur; Co-founder Asscn des économistes marocains 1972, Pres. 1982–; Pres. Union des économistes Arabes; mem. Chambre des Représentants. *Publications:* numerous articles on econ. theory and Maghreb economies. *Address:* Union socialiste des forces populaires, 9 avenue al-Araâr, Hay Riad, Rabat, Morocco (office). *Telephone:* (537) 565511 (office). *Fax:* (537) 565511 (office). *E-mail:* usfp@usfp.ma (office). *Website:* www.usfp.ma (office).

OUATTARA, Alassane Dramane, DSc; Côte d'Ivoirian politician, financial official and head of state; *President and Minister of Defence;* b. 1 Jan. 1942, Dimbokro; s. of Dramane Ouattara and Nabintou Cissé; m.; four c.; ed Drexel Inst. of Tech., Phila and Univ. of Pennsylvania, USA; Economist, IMF 1968–73; sr staff mem. in charge of missions Banque Centrale des Etats de l'Afrique de l'Ouest (BCEAO) 1973–75, Special Adviser to the Gov. and Dir of Research 1975–82, Vice-Gov. 1983–84, Gov. 1988–90; Dir African Dept, IMF 1984–88, Counsellor to Man. Dir 1987–88; Prime Minister of Côte d'Ivoire and Minister of Economy and Finance 1990–93; Deputy Man. Dir IMF 1994–99; Pres. UNCTAD 1979–80; mem. Bd of Dirs Global Econ. Action Inst.; Expert Adviser Comm. on Transnat.Corpns; Hon. Gov. BCEAO; Pres. Rassemblement des républicains (RDR) 1999–; in exile in Gabon; being also a citizen of Burkina Faso he was barred from standing in 2000 presidential elections of Côte d'Ivoire; granted Côte d'Ivorian citizenship 2002; declared winner of presidential election by election comm. and formally recognized by UN Security Council as winner Dec. 2010, Pres. of Côte d'Ivoire 2011– (sworn in 6 May), also Minister of Defence 2012–; Commdr Ordre du Lion du Sénégal, Ordre du Mono du Togo, Ordre Nat. du Niger, Grand Officier Ordre Nat. de Côte d'Ivoire. *Address:* Office of the President, 01 BP 1354, Abidjan, Côte d'Ivoire (office). *Telephone:* 20-22-02-22 (office). *Fax:* 20-21-14-25 (office). *Website:* www .cotedivoirepr.ci (home).

OUDÉA, Frédéric; French business executive and fmr civil servant; *Chairman and CEO, Société Générale;* b. 1963; ed Ecole Polytechnique, Ecole Nationale d'Admin; held several posts in French sr civil service, including in Audit Dept of Ministry of Finance, Ministry of Economy and Finance, Budget Ministry and in Cabinet of Ministry of Treasury and Communication 1987–95; Deputy Head, then Head of Corp. Banking arm, Société Générale, London, UK 1995–97, Head of Global Supervisory and Devt of Equities 1998–2001, Deputy Chief Financial Officer, Société Générale Group 2002–03, Chief Financial Officer 2003–March 2008, Deputy CEO March–May 2008, CEO May 2008–, Chair. 2009–, mem. Nomination Cttee; Chair. Fédération Bancaire Française 2011–12. *Address:* Société Générale, 29 boulevard Haussmann, 75009 Paris, France (office). *Telephone:* 1-42-14-20-00 (office). *E-mail:* info@socgen.com (office). *Website:* www .societegenerale.com (office).

OUDEMAN, Marjan J., LLM; Dutch lawyer, business executive and university administrator; *President of the Executive Board, Utrecht University;* b. 7 July 1958, Beverwijk; ed Univ. of Groningen; began career as company lawyer at Koninklijke Hoogovens 1982, moved to Finance Dept and rose to become Dir of canning factory (first female dir at steel co.), following merger with British Steel to become Corus, responsible for European Steel, later mem. Exec. Cttee of European part of Tata Steel Group (fmrly Corus) and Exec. Dir Strip Div. –2010; mem. Exec. Cttee AkzoNobel 2010–13, responsible for Organizational Devt and Human Resources; Pres. Exec. Bd Utrecht Univ. 2013–; Commr, Dutch Railways 2005–13; Chair. Supervisory Bd HKS Scrap Metals BV; Gov. of Training Managers, Ashorne Hill Management Coll.; mem. Exec. Bd VNO NCW; mem. Bd Foundation Sail Amsterdam, Foundation Cttee for Concertgebouw; mem. Steering Cttee of Artis, Bd of Nat. Fund 4 and 5 May, Recommendation Cttee of Young Entrepreneurs, Ronald McDonald Kinderfonds, October Knowledge Month; fmr mem. Innovatie-platform; ranked first by FEM Business magazine on list of most powerful businesswomen in the Netherlands Nov. 2005, chosen by Aside magazine as one of ten most influential women in the Netherlands and as most important woman in business category 2009. *Address:* Utrecht University, Heidelberglaan 8, PO Box 80125, 3508 Utrecht TC, Netherlands (office). *Telephone:* (30) 2535150 (office). *Fax:* (30) 2537745 (office). *E-mail:* m.j.oudeman@uu.nl (office); c.krapels@uu.nl (office). *Website:* www.uu.nl (office).

OUEDRAOGO, Ablassé, DEcon; Burkinabè international organization official; *Regional Adviser for Africa, African Development Bank;* b. 30 June 1953, Burkina Faso; ed Univ. of Nice, France; Deputy Resident Rep. of UNDP, Kinshasa 1991–93; Head of Regional Office for E Africa of UN Sudano-Sahélienne Office (also accred to OAU, ECA, UNEP) 1993–94; Minister of Foreign Affairs 1994–99; Special Adviser to Pres. of Burkina Faso 1999; Jt Deputy Dir-Gen. WTO 1999–2000; Regional Adviser for Africa, African Devt Bank 2006–; Officer of Nat. Order of Burkina Faso 1997; Officer of Equatorial Order of Gabon 2000. *Publications:* Réflexions sur la crise industrielle en France 1979, Les firmes multinationales et l'industrialisation des pays en voie de développement 1981. *Address:* African Development Bank, Rue Joseph Anoma 1, BP 1387, Abidjan 01, Cote d'Ivoire.

OUÉDRAOGO, Gérard Kango; Burkinabè politician; *Honorary President, Alliance pour la Démocratie et la Fédération-Rassemblement Démocratique Africain;* b. 19 Sept. 1925, Ouahigouya; s. of Jean Ouédraogo and Christine Ouédraogo; m. 1947; Rep. to French West African Fed. 1952; Deputy to French Nat. Ass. 1956–59; Co-founder Mouvement Démocratique Voltaïque; mem. Parl. 1957–65; Minister of Finance 1958–59; Amb. to UK 1961–66; Adviser, Ministry of Foreign Affairs; Pres. Union Démocratique Voltaïque 1970–74, now Commr; Prime Minister 1971–74; Pres. Nat. Ass. 1978–80; Jr Pres. ACP/EEC Lomé Convention 1970–80; fmr Leader Rassemblement Démocratique Africain (RDA); Deputy and Pres. Parl. Group RDA, Assemblée des Députés du Peuple; Hon. Pres. Alliance pour la Démocratie et la Fédération-Rassemblement Démocratique Africain 1998–; Grand Officier, Ordre Nat. Burkina Faso, du Mérite Français, Grand Officier, Légion d'honneur; several other decorations. *Address:* ADF-RDA, 01 BP

1991, Ouagadougou 01, Burkina Faso. *Telephone:* 50-43-03-69. *E-mail:* contact@adf-rda.com. *Website:* adf-rda.org.

OUEDRAOGO, Idrissa; Burkinabè film director and screenwriter; b. 21 Jan. 1954; ed film school in Burkina Faso; Grand Jury Prize, Cannes Film Festival 1990. *Films include:* Poko 1981, Les Écuelles 1983, Les Funérailles du Larle Naba 1984, Ouagadougou, ouaga deux roues 1985, Issa le tisserand 1985, Yam Daabo (The Choice) 1986, Yaaba 1989, Tilaï (Etalon de Yenenga/Grand Prix, Pan-African Film Festival) 1990, Obi 1991, Karim and Sala 1991, Samba Traore 1993, Afrique, mon Afrique... 1995, Lumiè et Compagnie 1995, Kini and Adams 1997, Les Parias du cinéma 1997, Scenarios from the Sahel 2001, 11'09"01 – September 11 (segment) 2002, La Colère des dieux (Anger of the Gods) 2003, Kato Kato 2006. *Address:* FEPACI, 01 BP 2524, Ouagadougou, Burkina Faso.

OUEDRAOGO, Kadré Désiré; Burkinabè politician, economist and banker; *President, Economic Community of West African States (ECOWAS) Commission;* m. Solange Ouedraogo; ed Haute Ecole, Paris, Université Paris I (Sorbonne), France; fmr Deputy Exec. Sec. Econ. Community of West African States (ECOWAS) in charge of Econ. Affairs; fmr Gov. of Cen. Bank of West African States; Prime Minister of Burkina Faso 1996–2000; Amb. to the EU (also accred to Belgium, Luxembourg, Netherlands and UK), Brussels 2001–12; Pres. Econ. Community of West African States (ECOWAS) Comm., Abuja, Nigeria 2012–; Grand Officier, Ordre Nat. du Burkina Faso 1996. *Address:* ECOWAS Executive Secretariat, 60 Yakubu Gowon Crescent, PMB 401, Asokoro, Abuja, Nigeria (office); 01 BP 3474, Ouagadougou 01, Burkina Faso (home). *Telephone:* (9) 3147647 (office). *Fax:* (9) 3147646 (office). *E-mail:* info@ecowas.int (office); ibratoure@hotmail.com. *Website:* www.ecowas.int (office).

OUÉDRAOGO, Youssouf, PhD; Burkinabè academic, politician and diplomatist; *Special Adviser to the President, African Development Bank;* b. 25 Dec. 1952, Tikaré, Bam Prov.; m.; two c.; ed Univ. of Dijon and Univ. of Clermont-Ferrand, France; Head of Business Admin Course, Univ. of Dijon, France 1979–82; Prof. of Admin, Univ. of Ouagadougou 1983–84; Minister of Planning and Population Devt 1984–87, of Planning and Co-operation 1987–89; Pres. Social and Econ. Council 1989–92; elected Deputy, Nat. Ass. (Parl.) 1992, Prime Minister 1992–94; Amb. to Belgium, the Netherlands, Luxembourg, the UK and EU 1994–99; Minister of State, Ministry of Foreign Affairs 1999–2002; State Minister and Minister of Foreign Affairs and Regional Co-operation 2002–07; Special Adviser to Pres. African Devt Bank 2007–; mem. Congress for Democracy and Progress; Silver Medal of the Torch of the Revolution 1986, Grand Officier of the Nat. Order 1994, Grand Cordon, Order of the Shining Star, Taiwan 2002, Grand Officier, Order of the Crown, Belgium 2005. *Address:* Office of the President, African Development Bank, rue Joseph Anoma, 01 BP 1387, Abidjan 01, Côte d'Ivoire (office). *Telephone:* 20-20-44-44 (office). *Fax:* 20-20-49-59 (office). *E-mail:* afdb@afdb.org (office). *Website:* www.afdb.org (office).

OUELLET, Hon. André, PC, BA, LLL; Canadian lawyer and fmr politician; b. 6 April 1939, St-Pascal, Québec; s. of Dr Albert Ouellet and Rita Turgeon; m. Edith Pagé 1965; two s. two d.; ed Pensionnat St-Louis de Gonzague, Québec Seminary, Ottawa and Sherbrooke Univs; MP for Papineau 1967–93; Parl. Sec. to Minister for External Affairs 1970, to Minister for Nat. Health and Welfare 1971; Postmaster Gen. 1972–74; Minister for Consumer and Corp. Affairs 1974–76, 1980–84, for Urban Affairs 1976–79, for Public Works 1978–79, for Canada Post Corpn 1980–83, for Labour 1983, for Regional Econ. Devt 1983–84; Pres. Privy Council 1984; Govt Leader of Commons 1984; Opposition Transport Critic 1984; Opposition External Affairs Critic 1987; Opposition Critic for Fed. Provincial Relations 1990; Minister for Foreign Affairs 1993–96; Chair. Canada Post Corpn 1996–99, Pres. and CEO 1999–2004. *Leisure interests:* tennis, swimming, squash, skiing, reading and collecting works of art.

OUELLET, HE Cardinal Marc, PSS; Canadian ecclesiastic; *Prefect of the Congregation for Bishops;* b. 8 June 1944, Lamotte; ed Collège de Berthier, Ecole Normale of Amos, Univ. of Laval, Major Seminary of Montreal, Pontifical Univ. San Tommaso d'Aquino, Pontifical Gregorian Univ., Rome, Italy; ordained priest of Soc. of Priests of St Sulpice 1968; entered Soc. of Priests of St Sulpice 1972, held several teaching positions in Colombia, Montreal and Edmonton; Prof., John Paul II Inst. for Studies on Marriage and the Family 1997–2001; apptd Sec. Pontifical Council for Promoting Christian Unity 2001; Titular Archbishop of Acropolis 2001–; Archbishop of Quebec City 2002–10; cr. Cardinal (Cardinal-Priest of Santa Maria in Traspontina) 2003; participated in Papal Conclave 2005, 2013; Prefect of the Congregation for Bishops 2010–13, 2013–; Pres. Pontifical Comm. for Latin America 2010–; Consultor, Congregation for the Doctrine of Faith, Congregation for Divine Worship; Sec. Comm. for Religious Relations with Jews; mem. Perm. Interdicasteral Comm. for the Eastern Churches in Europe, Pontifical Acad. of Theology; mem. Editorial Bd Rivista Internazionale Communio (N American edn); mem. XIth Gen. Ordinary Ass. of Synod of Bishops, Vatican City 2005. *Address:* Congregation for Bishops, Palazzo della Congregazioni, Piazza Pio XII 10, 00193 Rome, Italy (office). *Telephone:* (06) 69884217 (office). *Fax:* (06) 69885303 (office). *Website:* www.vatican.va/roman_curia/congregations/cbishops (office).

OULD ABDEL AZIZ, Gen. Mohamed; Mauritanian army officer and head of state; *President;* b. 20 Dec. 1956, Akjoujt; ed Royal Military Acad., Meknès, Morocco; joined army in 1977, attained rank of Second-Lt 1980, Capt. 1988, Maj. 1994, Lt-Col 1988, Col 2004, Gen. 2007; Commdr Presidential Guard (Bataillon de la Sécurité présidentielle) 1987–91; Chief of Staff to Pres. Sidi Ould Cheikh Abdallahi 2007–08; Pres. High Council of State (following coup d'etat of 6 Aug. 2008) 2008–09; Leader, Union for the Republic 2009 (resgnd); Pres. of Mauritania 2009–; Chair. African Union Ass. 2014–. *Address:* Office of the President, BP 184, Nouakchott, Mauritania (office). *Telephone:* 525-26-36 (office). *Fax:* 525-26-36 (office).

OULD AHMED WAGHF, Yahya; Mauritanian economist and politician; fmr Prof. of Econs, Univ. of Nouakchott; fmr Minister Sec.-Gen. of the Presidency; Chair. Nat. Pact for Devt and Democracy (PNDD-ADIL); Prime Minister 2008 (ousted in coup). *Address:* c/o Office of the Prime Minister, BP 237, Nouakchott, Mauritania.

OULD HAMADI, Hamadi Ould Baba; Mauritanian engineer and government official; b. 31 Dec. 1948, Moudjéria; one c.; ed Ecole Nat. d'Admin.; Deputy Head,

---

Hydraulic Div., Nouadhibou, Ministry of Equipment 1967–78; Sec.-Gen FIAP 1983–90; Consultant 1992–2007; Minister of Nat. Defence 2009, of Foreign Affairs and Co-operation 2011–13. *Address:* c/o Ministry of Foreign Affairs and Co-operation, BP 230, Nouakchott, Mauritania (office).

OULD SIDI MOHAMED, Zahabi, DEA; Malian politician, UN official and fmr resistance fighter; b. 1 Oct. 1957, Goundam; ed École nationale d'Admin, Bamako, Univ. of Paris-IV (Sorbonne), France; Deputy Dir, aid programme in N Mali, Aide de l'Eglise Norvégienne (non-govt org.) 1985–90; with Front islamique arabe de l'Azawad (armed rebel group) 1990s, prin. negotiator at peace talks with govt 1992; several postings with UN in Congo, Haiti, Somalia, Côte d'Ivoire and S Sudan 1996–2013; Minister of Foreign Affairs and Int. Co-operation 2013–14. *Address:* c/o Ministry of Foreign Affairs and International Co-operation, Koulouba, Bamako, Mali (office).

OULD TAH, Sidi, PhD; Mauritanian economist and politician; *Minister of Economic Affairs and Development;* fmrly with Islamic Devt Bank; fmr econ. adviser to Prime Minister; Minister of Economy and Finance 2008, of Econ. Affairs and Devt 2009–. *Address:* Ministry of Economic Affairs and Development, 303 Ilot C, BP 5150, Nouakchott, Mauritania (office). *Telephone:* 525-16-12 (office). *Fax:* 525-51-10 (office). *E-mail:* nfomaed@mauritania.mr (office). *Website:* www.maed .gov.mr (office).

OUMAROU, Mamane; Niger politician and diplomatist; b. 1945; m.; *Prime Minister of Niger Jan.–Nov. 1983, 1988–90; mem. Mouvement Nat. de la Soc. de développement (MNSD); fmr Amb. to Saudi Arabia; apptd Mediator of the Repub. 2008. *Address:* c/o Mouvement national pour la société de développement—Nassara (MNSD—Nassara), rue Issa Beri 30, cnr blvd de Zarmaganda, porte 72, BP 881, Niamey, Niger (office).

OUMAROU, Seyni; Niger politician; b. 9 Aug. 1950, Tillabéri; m.; six c.; Dir-Gen. Nigerien Paper Transformation Enterprise (ENITRAP) 1987–98; mem. Mouvement national pour la société de développement (MNSD), Pres. Tillabéry regional council 2007–08, Pres. MNSD 2008–; apptd Special Adviser to Prime Minister 1995; Minister of Trade and Industry 1999–2004; Minister of State for Equipment 2004–07; Prime Minister 2007–09. *Address:* Mouvement national pour la société de développement, rue Issa Beri 30, cnr blvd de Zarmaganda, porte 72, BP 881, Niamey, Niger (office). *E-mail:* presi@mnsd-nassara.org (office). *Website:* www .mnsd.ne (office).

OUSELEY, Baron (Life Peer) cr. 2001 Herman (George), Kt; British civil servant and race relations adviser; various public service posts 1963–86; Race Relations Adviser Lambeth Borough Council 1979–81, GLC 1981–84; Dir of Educ. ILEA 1986–88, Chief Exec. 1988–90; Chief Exec. London Borough of Lambeth 1990–93; Chair. Comm. for Racial Equality 1993–2000; Man. Dir Different Realities Partnership Ltd 2000–; Dir Focus Consultancy Ltd 2000–; mem. Council Policy Studies Inst. 1988–, Inst. of Race Relations 1990–, Inst. of Educ., Univ. of London 1995–; mem. Advisory Council Prince's Youth Business Trust 1993–; Chair. Uniting Britain Charitable Trust 1997–, Presentation Educ. and Employment Charitable Trust 1997–; Patron Presentation Housing Asscn 1990–; Dr hc (Edin.) 1999. *Publications:* The System 1981, pamphlets and articles on local govt, public services, employment, training and race equality issues. *Address:* House of Lords, London, SW1A 0PW, England (office).

OUSMANE, Kane; Mauritanian mining engineer and politician; ed Polytechnique, Paris, France; fmr Vice-Pres. for Corp. Man., African Devt Bank; Gov. Banque centrale de Mauritanie –2008; Man. Dir Societe Nationale Industrielle et Minière 2008–09; Minister of Finance 2009–10. *Address:* c/o Ministry of Finance, BP 181, Nouakchott, Mauritania (office).

OUSSEINI, Brig.-Gen. Amadou; Niger army officer and politician; *Minister of National Defence;* b. 1 Jan. 1953, Gouré; m.; six c.; ed Ecole Mil. Préparatoire Technique, Bingerville, Côte d'Ivoire, Acad. Mil. d'Antsirabé, Madagascar, Ecole d'application de l'infanterie, Montpellier, France, École d'état-major, Compiègne, Coll. Inter-Armées de Défense, Paris; joined army 1974, command roles include fmr Deputy Officer, 2nd Agadez Compagnie saharienne motorisée (CSM), Deputy Commdr, 4th CSM, 3rd Zinder CSM, Commdr 3rd Zinder CSM, 6th Dirkou CSM, Préfet (Police Commr) of Dosso, of Diffa, Head of Garde Républicaine, Commdr, Presidential Guard, Land Army Adviser, Ministry of Nat. Defence, Sec.-Gen. Ministry of Nat. Defence, Defence Attaché, Embassy in Nigeria, Deputy Chief of Gen. Staff of Land Army, Chief of Gen. Staff of Land Army –2010, Minister of Nat. Defence 2010–; rank of 2nd Lt 1977, Lt 1979, Capt. 1984, Commdr 1990, Lt-Col 1995, Col 2000, Brig.-Gen. 2006; Grand Officier, Ordre Nat. du Niger. *Address:* Ministry of National Defence, BP 626, Niamey, Niger (office). *Telephone:* 20-72-20-76 (office). *Fax:* 20-72-40-78 (office).

OUTLULE, Samuel Otsile, BPA; Botswana diplomatist; *Permanent Secretary, Ministry of Youth, Sport and Culture;* b. 8 July 1957; m.; three c.; ed Gaborone Campus, Univ. of Botswana and Swaziland, Inst. of Devt Man., Gaborone, Ranche House Coll., Harare, German Foundation for Int. Devt, Berlin; Foreign Affairs Officer, Ministry of Foreign Affairs 1982–85; served at High Comm. in Harare 1985–89, Counsellor, High Comm. in London 1993–95; First Sec. to Perm. Mission to UN, New York 1989, Political Counsellor and Alternate Rep. to Security Council 1995; Deputy Dir for Africa and Middle E, Ministry of Foreign Affairs 1997–99, Dir of Int. Relations 1999–2000; Clerk to Cabinet and Sr Pvt. Sec. to Pres. Mogae 2000–05; Perm. Rep. to UN, New York 2005–08; Foreign Sec., Ministry of Foreign Affairs 2008–09; Perm. Sec., Ministry of Youth, Sport and Culture 2009–. *Address:* Ministry of Youth, Sport and Culture, Plot 50626, Samora Machel Drive, next to Cresta Lodge, PMB 00514, Gaborone, Botswana (office). *Telephone:* 3682600 (office). *Fax:* 3913473 (office). *E-mail:* mysc_pro@gov.bw (office). *Website:* www .mysc.gov.bw (office).

OUTRAM, Dorinda, MA, PhD; British historian and academic; *Professor and Gladys I. and Franklin W. Clark Chair in History, University of Rochester;* b. 11 Dec. 1949, Leicester, England; d. of Albert Ernest Outram and Rosemary Elenor Collins; m. 1976 (divorced 1980); one s.; ed Univ. of Cambridge; Research Fellowship British Acad. 1974, Univ. of Reading 1975; Lectureship and Research Fellowships, Univ. of London 1977–81; Asst Prof. Univ. of Montreal 1981–82; Research Fellowship, Girton Coll., Cambridge 1982–84; Lecturer in Modern History, Univ. Coll., Cork 1984–98; Clark Chair and Prof. of History, Univ. of

Rochester, NY 1998–; Visiting Prof. Griffith Univ., Australia 1990; Landon Clay Visiting Assoc. Prof., Harvard Univ. 1991–92; Editorial Dir, Comité int. pour l'édition de la correspondance de Georges Cuvier 1983–; mem. Editorial panel, Dictionary of Irish Biography 1984–; Ed. Bulletin of the Irish Asscn for Research in Women's History 1987–88; Trustee, British Soc. for History of Science; Hon. Sec. Irish Nat. Cttee for Research in Women's History 1988–; Vellacott Historical Essay Prize, Cambridge 1971, Royal Soc. of London Research Award 1982, CNRS Research Award, Paris 1982. *Publications:* Science, Vocation and Authority in Post-Revolutionary France, Georges Cuvier 1984, Uneasy Careers and Intimate Lives: Women in Science 1987, The Body and the French Revolution 1989, The Enlightenment 1994, Panorama of the Enlightenment 2007; numerous articles. *Leisure interests:* walking, talking, learning languages, visiting France, Italy and Germany. *Address:* 369A Rush Rhees Library, University of Rochester, Rochester, NY 14627-0070, USA. *Telephone:* (585) 275-4097 (office). *Fax:* (585) 756-4425 (office). *E-mail:* otrm@mail.rochester.edu (office). *Website:* www.rochester.edu/College/HIS/index.php (office).

OUYAHIA, Ahmed; Algerian politician and diplomatist; *Secretary-General, Rassemblement national démocratique;* b. 2 July 1952, Bouadnane; m.; two c.; Sec., Ministry of Foreign Affairs 1975–81; Counsellor, Embassy in Abidjan 1981–84; Counsellor, Perm. Mission to UN, New York 1984–89, Deputy Rep. to Security Council 1988–89; Counsellor, Office of the Minister of Foreign Affairs 1989–90, Dir Gen. Dept of African Affairs, Ministry of Foreign Affairs 1990–91; Amb. to Mali 1992–93; Sec. of State for Cooperation and N African Affairs 1993–94; Dir of Cabinet to the Presidency 1994–95; Prime Minister of Algeria 1995–98, 2003–06 (resgnd), 2008–12; Deputy, Nat. Ass. 1997–; Minister of Justice 2000–02; Minister of State, Personal Rep. of the Pres. of the Repub. 2002–03; Sec.-Gen. Rassemblement nat. démocratique (RND) 1999–. *Address:* Rassemblement national démocratique (RND), Cité des Asphodèles, BP 10, Ben Aknoun, Algiers, Algeria (office). *Telephone:* (21) 91-64-10 (office). *Fax:* (21) 91-47-40 (office). *E-mail:* rnd@rnd-dz.org (office). *Website:* www.rnd-dz.org (office).

OUYANG, Ziyuan, MSc; Chinese scientist; *President, Chinese Society of Mineralogy, Petrology and Geochemistry;* b. Oct. 1935, Jian City, Jiangxi Prov.; ed Beijing Coll. of Geology, Inst. of Geology, Beijing, Univ. of Science and Tech., Beijing, Inst. of Atomic Energy; Asst Prof., Inst. of Geology Chinese Acad. of Sciences 1960–66, Assoc. Prof., Inst. of Geochemistry 1966–78, Prof., Vice-Dir then Dir 1978–94, Prof. 1994–, Dir Bureau of Resources and Environmental Sciences 1991–93; Vice-Pres. People's Congress of Guizhou Prov. 1993–; Chair. Asscn for Science and Tech. Guizhou Prov. 1993–; Pres. Chinese Soc. of Mineralogy, Petrology and Geochemistry 1994–; Guest Prof., Beijing, Nanjing and other univs 1993–; Standing Vice-Pres. Chinese Soc. of Mineralogy, Petrology and Geochemistry 1976–94; Vice-Pres. Chinese Soc. of Space Sciences; Chair. Cttee of Space Chem. and Space Geology, Assoc. Ed.-in-Chief Journal of Space Science, Chinese Journal of Geochemistry 1980–; Ed.-in-Chief Journal of Environmental Science, Journal of Geology-Geochemistry, Bulletin of Mineralogy, Petrology and Geochemistry 1985–; Vice-Pres. Chinese Soc. of Geology 1992–96; Academician, Chinese Acad. of Sciences 1991–; First-Class Award of Natural Science Prize, Chinese Acad. of Sciences Nat. Science Conf. Prize, Nat. Outstanding Science Worker 2010. *Publications:* Progress of Selenology Research, Space Chemistry, Progress of Geology and Geochemistry during the 1980s, Progress of Mineralogy, Petrology and Geochemistry Research in China, Riddle of Dinosaur Depopulation, Formation and Evolution of the Planets and the Earth. *Leisure interests:* music, literature, tourism, photography. *Address:* Chinese Society for Mineralogy, Petrology and Geochemistry, 73 Guanshui Road, Guiyang 550002, Guizhou Province (office); Institute of Geochemistry, China Academy of Sciences, Guiyang City, Guizhou Province, People's Republic of China. *Telephone:* (851) 5895328 (office); (851) 5891338 (office). *Fax:* (851) 5891923 (office); (851) 5891379 (home). *E-mail:* ouyangziyuan@ms.gyig.ac.cn (home); kydhtb@263.net (home). *Website:* (office).

OVALDÉ, Véronique; French novelist; b. 1972, *Publications:* novels: Le Sommeil des poissons 2000, Toutes choses scintillant 2002, Les hommes en général me plaisent beaucoup 2003, Déloger l'animal 2005, La Très Petite Zébuline (with Joëlle Jolivet) 2006, Et mon cœur transparent (Prix France Culture/Télérama 2008) 2008, Ce que je sais de Vera Candida (Prix Renaudot des Lycéens 2009, Prix France Télévisions 2009, Grand Prix des lectrices de Elle 2010) 2009, La Salle de bains du Titanic 2009, Des vies d'oiseaux 2011; novels have been translated into numerous languages, including Italian, Spanish, German, Romanian, Portuguese, English, Korean, Chinese and French. *Address:* c/o Éditions de l'Olivier, 16 boulevard du Montparnasse, 75014 Paris, France. *Telephone:* 1-41-48-84-76. *Website:* www.editionsdelolivier.fr.

OVCHINNIKOV, Vladimir Pavlovich; Russian pianist; b. 1 Jan. 1958, Beleby, Urals; ed studied with Anna Artobolevskaya and at Moscow Conservatoire with Alexey Nasedkin; London debut, Barbican Hall 1987; has since given recitals in UK, Europe, USA, Canada and Japan and appeared with BBC Symphony, Royal Liverpool Philharmonic, Netherlands Philharmonic, Moscow Philharmonic and other major orchestras; Lecturer in Keyboard Studies, Royal Northern Coll. of Music 1994–; silver medal (jtly with Peter Donohoe) Moscow Tchaikovsky Competition 1982, first prize Leeds Int. Piano Competition 1987.

OVCHINNIKOV, Col-Gen. Vyacheslav Victorovich; Russian army officer; b. 25 Oct. 1946, Tambov Region; m.; two s.; ed Leningrad Artillery Higher School, Kalinin Mil. Artillery Acad.; various posts in internal troops; service in Dept of Internal Affairs; fmr Deputy Head of Gen. Staff, Ministry of Internal Affairs, Head Dept of Punishments 1989–99, Deputy Minister of Internal Affairs 1999; Commdt of Stepanakert during Karabakh Conflict 1992, of N Osetia during Osetia-Ingush Conflict, of Grozny during mil. operations in Chechnya; First Deputy C-in-C Internal Troops, Ministry of Internal Affairs 1999, C-in-C 1999–2000, Adviser to Dir-Gen. Rosoboronexport Co. 2001; Order for Personal Courage, Order for Service to Motherland and numerous other medals. *Address:* Rosoboronexport, Gogolevski Blvd 21, 119865 Moscow, Russia (office). *Telephone:* (495) 239-52-66 (office).

OVELAR, Blanca, MEd, PhD; Paraguayan politician; b. (Blanca Margarita Ovelar de Duarte), 2 Sept. 1957, Concepcion; d. of Vicente Ovelar Lamas and Edemilda Valiente; m. Ramón Duarte Rodas; three s.; Minister of Educ. –2007; selected as cand. for 2008 presidential election by Asociación Nacional Repub-

licana—Partido Colorado (Nat. Republican Asscn—Colorado Party); Best Graduate Teacher of Primary Ed., Gold Medal of the Presidency of the Repub. *Publications:* Introduction to Basic Skills 1994, articles on education in values 1996–2000, articles on national reality 2009, Policy Papers 2009–10. *Address:* Teniente 2do Jorge Martinez N° 1140, c/ Dr. Sosa Barrio Madame Lynch, c.p: 1732, Asunción, Paraguay.

OVENDEN, Graham Stuart, MA, ARCA, ARCM; British art historian, artist and poet; b. 11 Feb. 1943, Alresford, Hants.; s. of the late Henry Ovenden and Gwendoline D. Hill; m. Ann D. Gilmore 1969; one s. one d.; ed Alresford Dames School, Itchen Grammar School, Southampton, Southampton Coll. of Art, Royal Coll. of Music and Royal Coll. of Art; corresp. and critic, Architecture Design Magazine; Founder mem. South West Acad. of Fine and Applied Art. *Publications:* Illustrators of Alice 1971, Victorian Children 1972, Clementina, Lady Harwarden 1973, Pre-Raphaelite Photography 1972, Victorian Erotic Photography 1973, Aspects of Lolita 1975, A Victorian Album (with Lord David Cecil) 1976, Satirical Poems and Others 1983, The Marble Mirror (poems) 1984, Lewis Carroll Photographer 1984; Graham Ovenden… A Monograph with Essays by Laurie Lee, etc. 1987, Sold With All Faults (poems) 1991; photographs: Alphonse Mucha 1973, Hill & Adamson 1973, Graham Ovenden – Childhood Streets (Photographs 1956–64) 1998; contribs on art to numerous journals. *Leisure interests:* music (very seriously indeed), architecture, social science. *Address:* Barleysplatt Chapel, Panters Bridge, Mount, nr Bodmin, Cornwall, PL30 3DP, England (home).

OVERY, Richard James, PhD, FRHistS, FBA, FRSA; British historian and academic; *Professor of History, University of Exeter;* b. 23 Dec. 1947, London, England; s. of James Herbert Overy and Margaret Grace Overy (née Sutherland); m. 1st Tessa Coles 1969 (divorced 1976); m. 2nd Jane Giddens 1979 (divorced 1992); m. 3rd Kim Turner 1992 (divorced 2004); one s. four d.; ed Sexey's Blackford Grammar School, Somerset, Gonville and Caius Coll., Cambridge; Research Fellow, Churchill Coll., Cambridge 1972–73; Fellow and Coll. Lecturer, Queen's Coll., Cambridge 1973–79; Asst Univ. Lecturer, Univ. of Cambridge 1976–79; Lecturer in History, King's Coll., London 1980–88, Reader in History 1988–92, Prof. of Modern History 1992–2004, Fellow 2003–; Prof. of History, Univ. of Exeter 2004–; mem. European Acad. for Sciences and Arts; T.S. Ashton Prize 1983, Cass Prize for Business History 1987, Samuel Eliot Morison Prize for lifetime contrib. to mil. history, Soc. for Mil. History 2001, Wolfson Prize for History 2004, James Doolittle Award for a lifetime contrib. to aviation history 2010. *Publications:* William Morris, Viscount Nuffield 1976, The Air War 1939–1945 1980, The Nazi Economic Recovery 1982, Goering: The Iron Man 1984, The Origins of the Second World War 1987, The Road to War 1989, War and Economy in the Third Reich 1994, The Interwar Crisis 1919–1939 1994, Why the Allies Won 1995, The Penguin Atlas of the Third Reich 1996, The Times Atlas of the Twentieth Century 1996, Bomber Command 1939–1945 1997, Russia's War 1998, The Times History of the World (Gen. Ed.) 1999, The Battle 2000, Interrogations: The Nazi Elite in Allied Lands 1945 2001, The Dictators: Hitler's Germany and Stalin's Russia (Second Prize, Wolfson Prize for History 2004, Hessell-Tiltman Prize for History (jtly) 2005) 2004, What Britain Has Done: September 1939–May 1945 A Selection of Outstanding Facts and Figures 2007, The Morbid Age 2009, 1939: Countdown to War 2009, The Battle of Britain Experience 2010, Goering: Hitler's Iron Knight 2011; contrib. to scholarly books and professional journals. *Leisure interests:* opera, art, football. *Address:* College of Humanities, Amory Building, Rennes Drive, Exeter, Devon, EX4 4RJ, England (office). *Fax:* (1392) 263291 (office). *E-mail:* r.overy@exeter.ac.uk (office). *Website:* humanities.exeter.ac.uk/history/staff/overy (office).

OVETT, Stephen Michael James (Steve), OBE; British fmr athlete; b. 9 Oct. 1955, Brighton, Sussex, England; m. Rachel Waller 1981 (divorced 2006); two s. two d.; partner Carolyn Schuwalow; ed Varndean School, Brighton Coll. of Art; middle distance runner; European Jr Champion at 800m 1973; European Champion at 1500m, Prague 1978 and silver medallist at 800m Rome 1974, Prague 1978; competed at Olympic Games, Montreal 1976, finished 5th in 800m, reached semifinal of 1,500m; Moscow 1980, won gold medal at 800m and bronze medal at 1,500m; gold medal, Int. Asscn of Athletics Feds (IAAF) World Cup, Düsseldorf 1977, Rome 1980; gold medal, 5,000m, Commonwealth Games, Edinburgh 1986; set four world records; holder of record for greatest number of mile/1,500m victories (45 to 1980); also winner of major titles at 5,000m; holds UK record for the two miles, set in 1978; known for his rivalry with Sebastian Coe; Track and field TV commentator for ITV, later for IAAF, for CBC since 1992; part of BBC's on-location commentary team for Commonwealth Games, Melbourne 2006; lives in Australia; BBC Sports Personality of the Year 1978, bronze statue of him erected in Preston Park, Brighton 1987. *Publication:* Ovett: An Autobiography. *Leisure interest:* art.

OVIA, Jim, BSc, MBA; Nigerian business executive; b. 4 Nov. 1951, Agbor; m.; ed Southern Univ., USA, Northeast Louisiana Univ. (now Univ. of Louisiana at Monroe), USA, Harvard Business School, USA; Bank Clerk, Barclays Bank (now Union Bank) 1973; part-time Computer Operator, Baton Rouge and Trust Co., Louisiana 1977; Financial Analyst, International Merchant Bank 1980, Sr Man. 1987; Head, Corporate Finance Dept, Merchant Bank of Africa 1987–1990; Co-founder Zenith Bank plc 1990, Group Man. Dir and CEO 1990–2010; Pres. Nigeria Internet Group 2001–03; Founder Visafone Communications Ltd 2007–, also mem. Bd of Dirs; Chair. Quantum Luxury Properties Ltd, Nigerian Software Devt Initiative, Nat. Information Technology Advisory Council, Cttee on Nigeria Polio-Immunisation Action Group; Proprietor, Univ. of Information and Communication Tech., Agbor, Delta State; Founder-Chair. Youth Empowerment and ICT Foundation, Mankind United to Support Total Education; mem. Bd of Dirs Africa Finance Corpn, Transnational Corpn of Nigeria plc, American International School, Lagos 2001–03; mem. Governing Council, Nigerian Investment Promotion Comm. 1999–2007, Governing Council, Lagos State Univ., Hon. International Investor Council, Digital Bridge Inst.; mem. Bd of Trustees, Redeemer's Univ. for Nations; Order of the Fed. Repub. 2000; Hon. DSc (Lagos State Univ.) 2005; Zik Award 1999, Business Day's Award for top 10 bankers in Nigeria. *Address:* c/o Board of Directors, Visafone Communications Ltd., 4th Floor, Zenon House, 2, Ajose Adeogun Street, Victoria Island, Lagos, Nigeria.

OVITZ, Michael, BA; American entertainment industry executive; *Owner, Broad Beach Ventures LLC;* b. Dec. 1946, Chicago, Ill.; m. Judy Reich 1969; three c.; ed

Birmingham High School and UCLA; tour guide at Universal Studios while at coll.; joined William Morris Agency, Beverly Hills 1968; with three others formed Creative Artists Agency (CAA) 1975, Pres. 1975–95; Pres. Walt Disney Co. 1995–97; private investor 1997–98; Head Livent Inc. Toronto 1998–99; Founder, CEO Artists Man. Group 1998–2002; Founder and Prin., CKE Assocs 1999–2002; now invests in startup technology and media cos, real estate and other ventures; Owner Broad Beach Ventures (portfolio of more than 30 cos) 2010–; mem. Bd of Dirs Museum of Modern Art, Bd of Advisors of Andreessen Horowitz; fmr mem. Bd of Dirs D.A.R.E. America, J. Crew Group Inc., Gulfstream Aviation, Opsware; Chair. Exec. Bd UCLA Hosp. and Medical Center; Trustee, Museum of Modern Art, New York; mem. Bd of Advisors UCLA School of Theater, Film and Television, Exec. Advisory Bd Pediatric AIDS Foundation, Nat. Bd of Advisors for the Children's Scholarship Fund; mem. Council on Foreign Relations; considered amongst the world's top 200 art collectors, contemporary pieces include works by Pablo Picasso, Jasper Johns, Willem de Kooning, Barnett Newman, Mark Rothko and many others; Top 100 People of the Advertising Century, Ad Age. *Address:* c/o Board of Advisors, UCLA School of Theater, Film and Television, 102 East Melnitz Hall, Box 951622, Los Angeles, CA 90095-1622, USA. *E-mail:* info@michaelovitz .com. *Website:* www.michaelovitz.com.

OWADA, Hisashi, BA, LLB; Japanese judge, academic and fmr diplomatist; b. 18 Sept. 1932, Shibata, Niigata Pref.; s. of Takeo Owada and Shizuka Tamura; m. Yumiko Egashira 1962; three d. (one d. Masako Owada; m. Crown Prince Naruhito of Japan); ed Univ. of Tokyo, Univ. of Cambridge, UK; entered Foreign Service 1955, served in various posts in Ministry of Foreign Affairs, Tokyo and embassies in USSR and USA, Pvt. Sec. to Minister for Foreign Affairs 1971–72, Pvt. Sec. to Prime Minister Takeo Fukuda 1976–78, Minister-Plenipotentiary, USSR 1981–84, Dir-Gen. Treaties Bureau and Office for Law of the Sea 1984–87, Deputy Vice-Minister, Ministry of Foreign Affairs 1987–88, Amb. to OECD 1988–89, Deputy Minister, Ministry of Foreign Affairs 1989–91, Vice-Minister for Foreign Affairs 1991–93, Adviser to Minister for Foreign Affairs 1993–94, 1999–2003; Amb. and Perm. Rep. to UN 1994–98 (twice served as Pres. Security Council); Sr Adviser to Pres. World Bank 1999–2003; Adjunct Prof., Univ. of Tokyo 1963–88; Visiting Prof., Harvard Univ. 1979–81, 1987, 1989, 1999–2002, New York Univ. Law School 1994–; Prof., Waseda Univ. 1999–2003; Pres. Japan Inst. of Int. Affairs 1999–2003; Judge, Int. Court of Justice 2003–, Pres. 2009–12; Associé de l'Institut de Droit Int.; mem. Bd of Dirs Nuclear Threat Initiative, United Nations Foundation; Al-Istiqlal Order, First Class (Jordan) 1990, Officier, Légion d'honneur 1992, Grand Cross of the Order of Merit (Germany) 1994; Hon. LLD (Keiwa Univ., Banaras Hindu Univ., Waseda Univ.). *Publications include:* US–Japan Economic Inter-action in an Independent World 1981, Japanese Perspectives on Asian Security 1982, Practice of Japan in International Law 1984, From Involvement to Engagement: A New Course for Japanese Foreign Policy 1994, Diplomacy 1997, A Treatise on International Relations 2003. *Leisure interests:* music, skiing, mountain walking. *Address:* c/o International Court of Justice, Carnegieplein 2 (Peace Palace), 2517 KJ, The Hague, Netherlands.

OWEN, Clive; British actor; b. 3 Oct. 1964, Keresley, Warwicks.; m. Sarah-Jane Fenton; two d.; ed Royal Acad. of Dramatic Arts. *Film appearances include:* Vroom 1988, Close My Eyes 1991, Century 1993, The Turnaround 1994, The Rich Man's Wife 1996, Bent 1997, Croupier 1998, Greenfingers 2000, The Hire: Ambush 2001, The Hire: Chosen 2001, The Hire: The Follow 2001, The Hire: Star 2001, The Hire: Powder Keg 2001, Gosford Park 2001, A Day in the Death of Joe Egg 2001, Beyond Borders 2002, The Bourne Identity 2002, The Hire: Hostage 2002, The Hire: Beat the Devil 2002, The Hire: Ticker 2002, I'll Sleep When I'm Dead 2003, Beyond Borders 2003, King Arthur 2004, Closer (Best Supporting Actor, Golden Globe Awards 2005, Best Actor in a Supporting Role, BAFTA Awards 2005) 2004, Sin City 2005, Derailed 2005, Inside Man 2006, Children of Men 2006, Shoot 'Em Up 2007, Elizabeth: The Golden Age 2007, The International 2009, Duplicity 2009, The Boys are Back 2009, Intruders 2011. *Television appearances include:* Precious Bane 1989, Capital City (series) 1989, Lorna Doone 1990, Chancer (series) 1990, The Magician 1993, Class of '61 1993, Nobody's Children 1994, An Evening with Gary Lineker 1994, Doomsday Gun 1994, The Return of the Native 1994, Bad Boy Blues 1995, Sharman (series) 1996, The Echo 1998, Split Second 1999, Second Sight 1999, Second Sight: Parasomnia 2000, Second Sight: Kingdom of the Blind 2000, Second Sight II: Hide and Seek 2000. *Stage appearances include:* Design for Living 1994, Closer 1997. *Address:* c/o Creative Artists Agency, 9830 Wilshire Blvd, Beverly Hills, CA 90212-1825, USA. *Telephone:* (310) 288-4545. *Fax:* (310) 288-4800. *Website:* www.caa.com.

OWEN, Baron (Life Peer), cr. 1992, of the City of Plymouth; **David Anthony Llewellyn Owen,** CH, PC, MA, MB, BChir, FRCP; British politician and business executive; b. 2 July 1938, Plymouth, Devon, England; s. of Dr John William Morris Owen and Mary Llewellyn; m. Deborah Schabert 1968; two s. one d.; ed Bradfield Coll., Sidney Sussex Coll., Cambridge, St Thomas' Hosp.; house appointments, St Thomas' Hosp. 1962–64, Neurological and Psychiatric Registrar 1964–66, Research Fellow, Medical Unit 1966–68; MP for Sutton Div. of Plymouth 1966–74, for Devonport Div. of Plymouth 1974–92; Parl. Pvt. Sec. to Minister of Defence, Admin. 1967; Parl. Under-Sec. of State for Defence, RN 1968–70; Opposition Defence Spokesman 1970–72, resgnd over party policy on EEC 1972; Parl. Under-Sec. of State, Dept of Health and Social Security (DHSS) March–July 1974; Minister of State, DHSS 1974–76, FCO 1976–77; Sec. of State for Foreign and Commonwealth Affairs 1977–79; Opposition Spokesman for Energy 1979–80; co-f. Social Democratic Party (SDP) 1981; Chair. Parl. Cttee 1981–82; Deputy Leader SDP 1982–83, Leader 1983–87, 1988–92; now Ind. Social Democrat; mem. (Crossbench) House of Lords 1992–; mem. Palme Comm. on Disarmament and Security Issues 1980–89, Ind. Comm. on Int. Humanitarian Issues 1983–88; EC Co-Chair. Int. Conf. on fmr Yugoslavia 1992–95, Carnegie Comm. on Preventing Deadly Conflict 1994–2000; Chair. Global Natural Energy 1996–2006, New Europe 1999–2005, Europe Steel 2000–, Yukos Int. 2002–05; mem. Bd of Dirs, Abbott Laboratories Inc. 1996–2011; Dir (non-exec.) Coats Viyella 1994–2001, Intelligent Energy 2003–05, Hyperdynamics Corpn 2009–; Dir Center for Int. Health and Co-operation; Chancellor Univ. of Liverpool 1996–2009; Pres. River Thames Soc.; Freeman, City of Plymouth 2000. *Publications:* Ed.: A Unified Health Service 1968; contrib.: Social Services for All 1968; author: The Politics of Defence 1972, In Sickness and in Health – The Politics of Medicine 1976, Human Rights 1978, Face the Future 1981, A Future that Will Work 1984, A United Kingdom 1986, Personally Speaking to Kenneth Harris 1987, Our NHS 1988, Time to Declare (autobiog.) 1991, Seven Ages (poetry) 1992, Balkan Odyssey 1995, The Hubris Syndrome: Bush, Blair and the Intoxication of Power 2007 (revised edn 2012), In Sickness and in Power 2008 (revised edn 2011), Time to Declare: Second Innings (updated and abridged autobiog.) 2009, Nuclear Papers 2009, Europe Restructured: The European Crisis and Its Aftermath 2012, Bosnia-Herzegovina: The Vance-Owen Peace Plan 2013; articles in The Lancet, Neurology, Clinical Science and Brain. *Leisure interest:* sailing. *Address:* House of Lords, Westminster, London, SW1A 0PW (office); 78 Narrow Street, Limehouse, London, E14 8BP, England (home). *Telephone:* (1442) 872617 (office); (20) 7987-5441 (home). *Fax:* (1442) 876108 (home). *E-mail:* davidowen@lorddavidowen.co.uk (office). *Website:* www.parliament.uk/biographies/lords/lord-owen/992 (office); www.lorddavidowen .co.uk.

OWEN, Sir Geoffrey David, Kt, MA; British newspaper editor and academic; b. 16 April 1934; s. of L. G. Owen; m. 1st Dorothy J. Owen 1961 (died 1991); two s. one d.; m. 2nd Miriam Marianna Gross 1993; ed Rugby School and Balliol Coll., Oxford; joined Financial Times as feature writer and Industrial Corresp. 1958, US Corresp. 1961, Industrial Corresp. 1967; Exec. Industrial Reorganization Corpn 1967–69; Dir of Admin, Overseas Div. of British Leyland Int. 1969, Dir of Personnel and Admin 1972; Deputy Ed. Financial Times 1974–80, Ed. 1981–90; Dir Business Policy Programme, Centre for Econ. Performance, LSE 1991–98, Sr Fellow, Inter-disciplinary Inst. of Man. 1998–; mem. Council Foundation for Mfg and Industries 1993–; Chair. Wincott Foundation 1998–; Dir Laird Group 2000–. *Publications include:* Industry in the USA 1966, From Empire to Europe 1999, Corporate Governance in the US and Europe: Where are We Now? (co-author) 2006, The Rise and Fall of Great Companies 2010. *Address:* London School of Economics and Political Science, Houghton Street, London, WC2A 2AE, England. *Telephone:* (20) 7955-7177; (20) 7405-7686. *Fax:* (20) 7242-0392. *E-mail:* g.owen@ lse.ac.uk. *Website:* www.lse.ac.uk (office).

OWEN, Michael James; British fmr professional football player and commen-tator; b. 14 Dec. 1979, Chester, Cheshire, England; s. of Terence Owen and Jeanette Owen; m. Louise Bonsall 2005; one s. three d.; ed Hawarden High School, Flintshire, Wales, Idsall High School, Shifnal, Shropshire; striker; youth player, Liverpool Football Club 1991–96, sr player 1996–2004 (306 games, 179 goals), scored during debut against Wimbledon May 1997 (youngest ever Liverpool player to score), 21 goals in European competition (club record), won FA Cup 2001, Football League Cup 2001, 2003, FA Community Shield 2001, UEFA Cup 2001, European Super Cup 2001, FA Youth Cup 1996; player for Real Madrid, Spain 2004–05 (43 games, 19 goals), Newcastle United 2005–09 (Capt. 2008–09) (74 games, 30 goals), Manchester United 2009–12 (49 games, 17 goals), won League Cup 2009–10, FA Community Shield 2010, Premier League 2010–11, Stoke City 2012–13 (eight games, one goal); player for England U-20 team 1997 (four caps, three goals), England U-21 team 1997 (one cap, one goal), England team 1998–2008 (89 caps and 40 goals, scored hat-trick in 5–1 victory over Germany in World Cup qualifier 2001, won FA Summer Tournament 2004), England B team 2006–07 (two caps, no goals); lead co-commentator, BT Sport's football coverage 2013–; Professional Footballers' Assc'n Young Player of the Year 1998, Premier League jt top scorer: 1998, 1999, BBC Sports Personality of the Year 1998, Ballon d'Or (European Footballer of the Year) 2001, Domestic Team of the Decade – Premier League 10 Seasons Awards (1992/93–2001/02), named to FIFA 100. *Film appearance:* Goal II: Living the Dream 2006. *Publication:* Michael Owen: Off the Record 2004. *Leisure interests:* golf, table-tennis, snooker. *Address:* c/o Daniel Ullmann, Eurosport Management Ltd, 6 & 7 Feast Field, Horsforth, Leeds, Yorks., LS18 4TJ, England (office). *Telephone:* (845) 0545566 (office); (7796) 178690 (mobile) (office). *E-mail:* daniel@eurosportmanagement.com (office); enquiries@ michaelowen.com. *Website:* www.eurosportmanagement.com (office); www .michaelowen.com.

OWEN, Ray David, PhD, ScD; American biologist and academic; *Professor Emeritus, Division of Biology, California Institute of Technology;* b. 30 Oct. 1915, Genesee, Wis.; s. of Dave Owen and Ida Hoeft Owen; m. June Johanna Weissenberg 1939; one s.; ed Carroll Coll., Univ. of Wisconsin; Research Fellow, Univ. of Wisconsin 1941–43, Asst Prof. of Genetics and Zoology 1943–47; Gosney Fellow, Calif. Inst. of Tech. 1946–47, Assoc. Prof. 1947–53, Prof. 1953–83, Chair. Div. of Biology 1961–68, Vice-Pres. for Student Affairs and Dean of Students 1975–80, Prof. Emer. 1983–; Research Participant, Oak Ridge Nat. Lab. 1957–58; mem. Genetics Soc. of America (Treas. 1957–60, Vice-Pres. 1961, Pres. 1962), NAS, American Acad. of Arts and Sciences, American Philosophical Soc., Soc. for the Study of Evolution, American Assc'n of Immunologists; Mendel Award, Czechoslo-vak Acad. of Sciences 1965, Morgan Award, Genetics Soc. of America 1995, Excellence in Mentoring Award, American Assc'n of Immunologists 1999, Medawar Award, Transplantation Soc. 2000. *Publications:* General Genetics (with Srb and Edgar) 1952, 1965; numerous research papers. *Website:* www.bbe .caltech.edu (office).

OWEN, Robert John Richard, MA; British financial industry official; *Chair-man, International Securities Consultancy Ltd;* b. 11 Feb. 1940, London; s. of Thomas R. Owen and Margaret Fletcher; m. Beatrice M. Voelker 1962 (divorced); two s. one d.; ed Repton School and Oriel Coll., Oxford; Foreign Office 1961–68, served in British Embassy, Washington, DC 1964–68; HM Treasury 1968–70; Morgan Grenfell & Co. Ltd 1970–79, Dir 1973; Dir Merchant Banking Div. Lloyds Bank Int., Ltd 1979–82, Dir Far East Div. 1982–84; Dir of Investment Banking, Lloyds Bank PLC and Chair. Lloyds Merchant Bank, Ltd 1984–88; Adviser to Hong Kong Govt on implementation of Securities Review Cttee Report 1988–89; Chair. Securities and Futures Comm. of Hong Kong 1989–92; Dir European Capital Co. Ltd 1992–; Regulatory Bd and Council of Lloyd's of London 1993–95; Deputy Chair. Nomura Int. Ltd, Hong Kong 1993– (now Sr Adviser), Capital Ltd, Crosby Ltd; mem. Bd of Dirs Singapore Stock Exchange, IB Daiwa Corpn, Yaohan Int. Holdings 1993–, Int. Securities Consultancy Ltd 1995– (now Chair.), Regent Pacific Group Ltd 1998–, ECK and Partners Ltd 1999–, TechPacific Ltd 1999–; Gov. Repton School; mem. Regulatory Council, Dubai Int. Financial Centre 2002–. *Leisure interests:* mountain walking, collecting oriental paintings and carvings. *Address:* International Securities Consultancy Ltd, 9A, Carfield Commercial Building, 75-77 Wyndham Street, Central, Hong Kong Special Administrative

Region, People's Republic of China (office). *Telephone:* 28773417 (office). *Fax:* 28770914 (office). *Website:* www.isc-global.com (office); www.crosby.com.

OWEN-JONES, Sir Lindsay, KBE, BA; British business executive; *Chairman, L'Oréal;* b. 17 March 1946, Wallasey; s. of Hugh A. Owen-Jones and Esmee Owen-Jones (née Lindsay); m. 1st; one d.; m. 2nd Cristina Furno 1994; ed Univ. of Oxford and European Inst. of Business Admin (INSEAD); Product Man. L'Oréal 1969, Head, Public Products Div., Belgium 1971–74, Man. SCAD (L'Oréal subsidiary), Paris 1974–76, Marketing Man. Public Products Div., Paris 1976–78, Gen. Man. SAIPO (L'Oréal subsidiary, Italy) 1978–81, Chair. 1991–, Pres. COSMAIR Inc. (exclusive L'Oréal agent) USA 1981–83, Vice-Pres. L'Oréal Man. Cttee 1984, mem. Bd of Dirs 1984, Pres. and COO 1984–88, Chair. and CEO 1988–2006, Chair. 2006–; mem. Bd of Dirs Banque Nat. de Paris 1989–, Lafarge 1993–2001, Air Liquide 1994–; Officier, Légion d'honneur; Hon. DSc (Cranfield School of Man.); named by Futuro magazine as Best European Manager 2002, Challenges magazine Best Manager of the Last 20 Years 2002, Le Nouvel Economiste magazine Manager of the Year 2002. *Leisure interest:* sailing. *Address:* L'Oréal, 41 rue Martre, 92117 Clichy Cedex, France (office). *Telephone:* 1-47-56-70-00 (office). *Fax:* 1-47-56-80-02 (office). *E-mail:* info@loreal.com (office). *Website:* www.loreal.com (office).

OWENS, James W., PhD; American economist and business executive; b. Elizabeth City, NC; ed North Carolina State Univ.; Corp. Economist, Caterpillar Inc. 1972–75, Chief Economist, Caterpillar Overseas SA, Geneva 1975–80, Man. Accounting and Product Source Planning Dept, Peoria, Ill. 1980–87, Man. Dir, P. T. Natra Raya, Indonesia 1987–90, Corp. Vice-Pres. 1990, also Pres. Solar Turbines Inc., San Diego 1990, Vice-Pres. and Chief Financial Officer, Caterpillar Corp. Services Div., Peoria 1993–95, Group Pres. Caterpillar Inc. 1995–2004, Chair. and CEO 2004–10 (retd); Dir Inst. for Int. Econs, Washington, DC, FM Global Insurance Co., IBM, Johnston, RI, Black & Veatch Holding Co., Overland Park, Kan.; Trustee, Manufacturers Alliance/MAPI, Arlington, Va; mem. Council on Foreign Relations, New York, The Business Roundtable, Washington, DC, Global Advisory Council to The Conf. Bd, New York, Community Advisory Bd, St Francis Medical Center, Peoria. *Address:* c/o Caterpillar Inc., 100 NE Adams Street, Peoria, IL 61629, USA. *Telephone:* (309) 675-1000. *E-mail:* info@cat.com. *Website:* www.cat.com.

OWENS, William (Bill) F., BA, MPA; American business executive and fmr state official; *Chairman of the Supervisory Board, Credit Bank of Moscow;* b. 22 Oct. 1950, Fort Worth, Tex.; m. Frances Owens; two s. one d.; ed Austin State Univ., LBJ School of Public Affairs, Univ. of Texas; fmrly with Touche Ross & Co., Gates Corpn; served as Exec. Dir Colorado Petroleum Asscn and Exec. Vice-Pres. Rocky Mountain Oil and Gas Asscn; mem. Colorado House of Reps 1983–89, Colorado Senate 1989–95, Colorado State Treas. 1994–99, Gov. of Colorado 1999–2007; fmr Vice-Chair. RBS Greenwich Capital Markets, Inc.; Partner, JCB Group 2007–; Man. Dir Renew Strategies, LLC, Front Range Resources; Chair. Supervisory Bd, Credit Bank Of Moscow OAO 2013–; mem. Bd of Dirs Key Energy Services Inc. 2007–, Federal Signal Corpn 2011–, Bill Barrett Corpn 2010–, Cloud Peak Energy, Inc. 2010–; mem. Bd of Dirs FESCO Transport Group 2007–12. *Publications:* contrib. to professional journals. *Address:* Credit Bank Of Moscow, 107045 Moscow, 2 Str. 1, Per. Lukov, Russia (office). *Website:* mkb.ru (office).

OWONO EDU, Marcelino; Equatorial Guinean politician; *Minister of Finance and the Budget;* Minister of Finance and the Budget 2003–08, 2012–, of Mines, Industry and Energy 2008–12; Alternate Gov. for Equatorial Guinea of the ADB Group. *Address:* Ministry of Finance and the Budget, Malabo, Equatorial Guinea (office). *Website:* www.ceiba-guinea-ecuatorial.org/guineees/indexbienv1.htm.

OWUSU-AGYEMANG, Hackman, MSc; Ghanaian politician and economist; b. 22 Nov. 1941, Effiduase-Koforidua; ed St Augustine's Coll., Cape Coast, Kwame Nkrumah Univ. of Science and Tech., Kumasi, Inst. of Social Studies, The Hague, Netherlands, Wye Coll., Univ. of London, UK; economist, Ministry of Agric. 1965–68, Sr Agricultural Economist 1968–70; economist, Econ. Analysis Div., FAO, Rome, Field Programme Officer, FAO-Regional Co-operation and Liaison Officer for Africa 1970–84; FAO Rep. in Zambia, Trinidad and Tobago 1979–84; Chief FAO Regional Bureau for Africa, Italy 1984; mem. New Patriotic Party (NPP) 1982–; mem. Parl. for New Juaben 1996–; Shadow Minister of Foreign Affairs 2000–01, Minister 2001–03; Minister of the Interior 2003–05, for Water Resources, Works and Housing 2005–07. *Address:* c/o New Patriotic Party (NPP), C912/2 Duade Street, Kokomlemle, POB 3456, Accra-North, Ghana. *Telephone:* (21) 227951. *Fax:* (21) 224418. *E-mail:* npp@africanonline.com.gh. *Website:* www.nppghana.org.

OXBURGH, Baron (Life Peer), cr. 1999, of Liverpool in the County of Merseyside; Ernest Ronald Oxburgh, Kt, KBE, PhD, FRS; British geologist/geophysicist; b. 2 Nov. 1934, Liverpool; s. of Ernest Oxburgh and Violet Bugden; m. Ursula Mary Brown 1934; one s. two d.; ed Liverpool Inst., Univ. of Oxford and Princeton Univ., USA; Departmental Demonstrator, Univ. of Oxford 1960–61, Lecturer in Geology 1962–78, Fellow St Edmund Hall 1964–78, Emer. Fellow 1978, Hon. Fellow 1986; Prof. of Mineralogy and Petrology, Univ. of Cambridge 1978–91, Head of Dept of Earth Sciences 1980–88; Chief Scientific Adviser, Ministry of Defence 1988–93; Rector Imperial Coll. of Science, Tech. and Medicine 1993–2001; Fellow, Trinity Hall, Cambridge 1978–82, Hon. Fellow 1983; Pres. Queens' Coll., Cambridge 1982–89, Hon. Fellow 1989; Chair. D1 Oils PLC 2007–09, Falck Renewables 2008–10; mem. Bd of Dirs Shell Transport and Trading Co. 1996–2005 (Chair. 2004–05), Nirex 1996–97; Sherman Fairchild Distinguished Scholar, Calif. Inst. of Tech. 1985–86; Pres. European Union of Geosciences 1987; mem. Nat. Cttee of Inquiry into Higher Educ. (Dearing Cttee) 1996–97; Trustee, Natural History Museum 1993–2002, Chair. of Trustees 1999–2002; Chair. House of Lords Select Cttee on Science and Tech. 2001–04; Chair. SETNET 2001–05; Foreign mem. Venezuelan Acad. of Sciences 1992, Deutsche Acad. der Naturforscher Leopoldina 1994; Hon. mem. Geologists Asscn, Hon. Fellow, St Edmund Univ. Coll., Oxford 1983, Hon. FREng 2002; Hon. Citizen of Singapore 2012; Officier, Ordre des Palmes Academiques 1995; Hon. DSc (Paris) 1986, (Leicester) 1990, (Loughborough) 1991, (Edin.) 1994, (Birmingham, Liverpool) 1996, (Southampton) 2003, (John Moores Univ.) 2006, (Newcastle) 2007, (Leeds) 2009, (Wyoming) 2011; Bigsby Medal, Geological Soc. of London 1979, Public Service Medal of Singapore 2009, Sir George Public Service Medal Singapore 2009, Sir Geo Thompson Gold

Medal, Inst. of Measurement and Control 2010. *Publications:* The Geology of the Eastern Alps (ed. and contrib.) 1968, Structural, Metamorphic and Geochronological Studies in the Eastern Alps 1971 and contribs to Nature, Journal of Geophysical Research, Tectonophysics, Journal of the Geological Soc. of London and other learned journals. *Leisure interests:* reading, various sports. *Address:* House of Lords, Westminster, London, SW1A 0PW, England (office). *Telephone:* (20) 7219-4341 (office). *E-mail:* oxburghe@parliament.uk (office).

ØYE, Harald Arnljot, DTech; Norwegian chemist and academic; *Professor Emeritus, Norwegian University of Science and Technology;* b. 1 Feb. 1935, Oslo; s. of Leiv C. Øye and Ingrid H. Øye; m. Tove Stiegler 1963; two s. one d.; ed Norwegian Inst. of Tech.; Postdoctoral Fellow, Argonne Nat. Lab., Illinois, USA 1963–64; Assoc. Prof., Inst. of Inorganic Chem., Norwegian Inst. of Tech. 1965–72, Prof. and Head of Inst., Norwegian Univ. of Science and Tech. (fmrly Norwegian Inst. of Tech.) 1973–90, 1992–98, Prof., Chem. Dept, later Dept of Materials Tech. 1999–2006, Prof. Emer. 2006–; Pres. Norwegian Acad. of Tech. Sciences 1985–92, Hon. Fellow 1993–; guest scientist at various insts in Germany, Italy, USA, France, New Zealand, Switzerland, UK; Brotherton Distinguished Prof., Univ. of Leeds 1985; Hon. Prof., North-Eastern Univ., Shenyang, People's Repub. of China; Kt First Class, Royal Norwegian Order of St Olav; Prize for Outstanding Research, Research Council of Norway 1997, Guldberg-Waage Medal, Norwegian Chemical Soc. 1998, Max Bredig Award, Electrochemical Soc., USA 1998, Royal Norwegian Soc. of Sciences and Letters Gunnerus Gold Medal 2004. *Publications include:* Cathodes in Aluminium Electrolysis (with M. Sørlie) 1991; more than 350 publs on electrowinning of aluminium and magnesium, characterization of silicon, carbon technology, transport properties, molten salt chem., spectroscopy and thermodynamics of high temperature systems. *Leisure interests:* reading, outdoor activities. *Address:* Department of Materials Technology, Norwegian University of Science and Technology, 7491 Trondheim (office); Steinhaugen 5, 7049 Trondheim, Norway (home). *Telephone:* 73-59-40-16 (office); 73-93-75-58 (home). *Fax:* 73-59-39-92 (office). *E-mail:* oye@material.ntnu.no (office). *Website:* www.ntnu.edu/employees/haoye (office).

OYÉ-MBA, Casimir, LLD; Gabonese banker and politician; b. 20 April 1942, Nzamal'igue Village, Libreville; s. of Ange Mba and Marie-Jeanne Nse; m. Marie-Françoise Razafimbelo 1963; three s. three d.; ed Univs of Rennes and Paris, France; trainee, Banque Centrale, Libreville 1967–69, Asst Dir 1969–70, Dir 1970–73; Nat. Dir Banque pour le Gabon 1973–76; Asst Dir-Gen. Banque Centrale 1977–78; Gov. Banque des Etats de l'Afrique Centrale 1978–90; Prime Minister of Gabon 1990–94; Minister of Foreign Affairs and Co-operation 1994–99; fmr Minister of State for Planning and Devt; Sr Minister of Mining, Oil, Energy and Water 2007–09; Alt. Gov. IMF for Gabon 1969–76; apptd Pres. Asscn des Banques Centrales Africaines 1987; elected mem. Parl. for Komo-Mondah dist 1990, re-elected 1996, 2001, 2006; mem. political bureau, Gabonese Democratic Party 1991; Campaign Man. for Pres. Omar Bongo 1993; Gabon mem. Bd of Govs of World Bank 1999–; mem. Ntoum City Council; unsuccessful presidential cand. 2009; Commdr, Légion d'honneur; Gabon, Cameroon, Congo, Equatorial Guinea and Cen. African Repub. decorations. *Leisure interests:* football, tennis, cinema, reading, traveling. *Address:* c/o Ministry of Mining, Libreville, Gabon. *E-mail:* casimir.oyemba@yahoo.fr (home). *Website:* www.oyemba.org (office).

OYELOWO, David Oyetokunbo; British actor, writer and director; *Co-Director, Inservice Productions;* b. 1 April 1976, Oxford; m. Jessica Oyelowo; three s.; ed Model Coll., Lagos, Nigeria, Highbury Grove Boys, Islington Sixth Form Centre, London Acad. of Music and Dramatic Art; left drama school early to do work on BBC TV series Maisie Raine 1998; joined the RSC 1999, played Henry VI 2000, first black actor to play an English King at the RSC, mem. Bd Dirs RSC 2005–; Amb. for the Prince's Trust 2003–; Co-Dir Inservice Productions; London Acad. of Music and Dramatic Art (LAMDA) Scholarship of Excellence, Ian Charleson Award for Best Newcomer 2001, Gold Award for Achievement beyond Further Educ., GAB (Gathering of Africa's Best) Award for Excellence. *Plays:* The Suppliants (Gate Theatre, London) 1998; Oroonoko, Volpone, Antony and Cleopatra (RSC) 1999; Henry VI Parts 1, 2, 3 (RSC) 2001, Richard III, The Godbrothers (Bush Theatre London), Prometheus Bound (Sound Theatre, London, Classic Stage Co., New York); Dir: The Man of Mode (Pavilion Theatre), The White Devil (Pavilion Theatre). *Films:* Dog Eat Dog 2000, A Sound of Thunder 2004, Spice of Life 2005, Derailed 2005, The Best Man 2006, The Last King of Scotland 2006, As You Like It 2006, Chess 2008, Red Tails 2012, Lincoln 2012, Jack Reacher 2012. *Television:* Maisie Raine 1998, Brothers and Sisters 1998, Spooks 2002, 2003, 2004, Tomorrow La Scala (film) 2002, As Time Goes By 2005, Shoot the Messenger 2006, The No. 1 Ladies' Detective Agency 2008, Small Island 2009, Blood and Oil 2010; writer: Graham & Alice (BBC). *Radio:* The Faerie Queen (BBC), Man Talk, Woman Talk (BBC), Oroonoko (BBC), The Word (BBC). *Publications:* Actors on Shakespeare: Henry VI 2003. *Leisure interests:* drawing, film, tennis, football, travel, writing. *Address:* Hamilton Hodell Management, 66–68 Margaret Street, London, W1W 8SR, England (office). *Telephone:* (20) 7636-1221 (office). *Fax:* (20) 7636-1226 (office).

ÖYMEN, Onur Basaran, PhD; Turkish diplomatist and politician; *Deputy Leader, Cumhuriyet Halk Partisi (CHP) (Republican People's Party);* b. 1940, Istanbul; s. of Münir Raşit Öymen and Nebahat Öymen; m. Nedret Gürsel 1971; one s. one d.; ed Galatasay Lisesi, Istanbul, Univ. of Ankara; joined Ministry of Foreign Affairs 1964; mil. service 1964–66; Second Sec. NATO Dept, Ministry of Foreign Affairs 1966–68, First Sec. Perm. Del. to Council of Europe, Strasbourg 1968–72, Chief of Section, Policy Planning Dept, Ministry of Foreign Affairs 1972–74, Counsellor Turkish Embassy, Nicosia 1974–78; Special Adviser to Minister of Foreign Affairs 1978–80; Counsellor, Turkish Embassy, Prague 1980–82, Madrid 1982–84; Head Policy Planning Dept, Ministry of Foreign Affairs 1984–88; Amb. to Denmark 1988–90, to Germany 1990–95; Under-Sec. Ministry of Foreign Affairs 1995–97; Perm. Rep. to NATO 1997–2002; currently Deputy Leader, Cumhuriyet Halk Partisi (CHP) (Republican People's Party); Bureaucrat of the Year, Nokta Review 1995, Diplomat of the Year, Asscn of Turkish Industrialists and Business 1995, 1996, 1997; Abdi Ipekçi Special Peace Award, Milliyet newspaper 1997. *Publications:* Türkiye 'nin Gücü (Turkish Strength) 1998, trans. into Turkish of Science and Common Sense by Oppenheimer. *Address:* Cumhuriyet Halk Partisi (CHP) (Republican People's Party), Çevre Sok. 38,

Ankara, Turkey (office). *Telephone:* (312) 4685969 (office). *Fax:* (312) 4685969 (office). *E-mail:* chpbim@chp.org.tr (office). *Website:* www.chp.org.tr (office).

OYUN, Sanjaasurengin, DPhil; Mongolian geologist and politician; b. 1964, Ulan Bator; m.; three c.; ed Univ. of Cambridge, UK, Charles Univ., Prague, Czech Repub.; worked as exploration geologist on surveys in Mongolia and for Rio Tinto-Zinc; mem. Mongolian Great Khural (Parl.) 1998–; Founder and Chair. Civil Will Party (Irgenii Zorig Nam) 2000–; Minister of Foreign Affairs 2007–08; Founder and Head of Zorig Foundation. *Address:* Government House, Ulan Bator 12, Mongolia (home). *Telephone:* (11) 323645 (office). *Fax:* (11) 327016 (office). *E-mail:* oyun@mail.parliament.mn (office). *Website:* www.zorigfoundation.org.mn (office).

OZ, Amos, BA; Israeli writer and academic; *Professor of Hebrew Literature, Ben Gurion University;* b. 4 May 1939, Jerusalem; m. Nily Zuckermann 1960; one s. two d.; ed Hebrew Univ. Jerusalem; Kibbutz Hulda 1957–86; teacher of literature and philosophy, Hulda High School and Givat Brenner Regional High School 1963–86; Visiting Fellow, St Cross Coll. Oxford 1969–70; Writer-in-Residence, Hebrew Univ. Jerusalem 1975; Visiting Prof., Univ. of Calif., Berkeley; Writer-in-Residence and Prof. of Literature, Colorado Coll., Colorado Springs 1984–85; Prof. of Hebrew Literature, Ben Gurion Univ. 1987–, Agnon Chair in Modern Hebrew 1990; Visiting Prof. of Literature, Writer-in-Residence, Boston Univ. 1987; Writer-in-Residence, Hebrew Univ. 1990; Writer-in-Residence and Prof. of Literature, Princeton Univ. 1997, Weidenfeld Visiting Prof. of European Comparative Literature, St Anne's Coll., Oxford 1998; Visiting Writer, Stanford Univ. 2007; Officier, Ordre des Arts et des Lettres; Chevalier, Légion d'honneur 1997; Dr hc (Hebrew Union Coll., Cincinnati, OH and Jerusalem) 1988, (Western New England Coll.) 1988, (Tel-Aviv) 1992; Holon Prize 1965, Brenner Prize 1976, Zeev Award for Children's Books 1978, Bernstein Prize 1983, Bialik Prize 1986, Wingate Prize, London 1988, Prix Fémina, Paris 1989 (for novel Black Box), German Publrs' Int. Peace Prize 1992, Luchs Prize for Children's Books (Germany) 1993, Hamore Prize 1993, Israeli Prize for Literature 1998, Freedom of Speech Prize, Writers' Union of Norway 2002, Int. Medal of Tolerance, Polish Ecumenical Council 2002, Goethe Cultural Prize, Frankfurt, Germany 2005, Premio Príncipe de Asturias (for literature) 2007, Dan David Prize 2008, Heinrich Heine Prize 2008, Primo Levi Prize (Italy) 2008, Stefan Heym Prize 2008. *Publications:* novels: Elsewhere, Perhaps 1966, My Michael 1968, Touch the Water, Touch the Wind 1973, A Perfect Peace 1982, Black Box 1987, To Know a Woman 1989, The Third Condition (Fima) 1991, The Same Sea 1991, Don't Call It Night 1994, Panther in the Basement 1995, The Same Sea 1999, The Silence of Heaven 2000, Suddenly in the Depths of the Forest 2005, Rhyming Life and Death 2007, Between Friends 2012; novellas and short stories: Where the Jackals Howl 1965, Unto Death 1971, Different People (selected anthology) 1974, The Hill of Evil Counsel 1976, Soumchi (children's story) 1978, Telling Tales (contrib. to charity anthology) 2004, Scenes From Village Life 2009; essays: Under this Blazing Light 1979, In the Land of Israel 1983, The Slopes of Lebanon 1987, Report of the Situation (in German) 1992, Israel, Palestine and Peace 1994, A Story Begins 1996, All Our Hopes 1998, But These Are Two Different Wars 2002, How to Cure a Fanatic 2006, Suddenly in the Depths of the Forest 2010, Jews and Words 2012; other: A Tale of Love and Darkness (memoir) (The Jewish Quarterly Wingate Literary Prize for non-fiction 2005) 2002. *Address:* Ben Gurion University of the Negev, PO Box 653, Beersheva 84105, Israel. *Telephone:* (8) 6461111. *Fax:* (8) 6237682. *E-mail:* acsec@bgumail .bgu.ac.il (office). *Website:* www.amos-oz.com (office).

OZAWA, Ichiro, BA; Japanese politician; b. 24 May 1942, Mizusawa, Iwate Pref.; s. of Saeki Ozawa and Michi Ozawa; m. Kazuko Fukuda 1973; three s.; ed Keio Univ.; mem. House of Reps representing Iwate Prefecture 1967–; Minister of Home Affairs 1985–87; fmr Deputy Chief Cabinet Sec.; fmr Dir-Gen. Liberal-Democratic Party (LDP) Election Bureau; Sec.-Gen. LDP 1989–91; Chair. Cttee on Rules and Admin.; left LDP 1993; Co-Founder and Sec.-Gen. Shinseito (Japan Renewal Party) 1993–94; Sec.-Gen. Shinshinto (New Frontier Party) 1994–95, Pres. 1995–97; Founder and Pres. Jiyuto (Liberal Party) 1998–2003 (resgnd), Acting Pres. Democratic Party of Japan (DPJ) (after merger with Liberal Party) 2003–04, Vice-Pres. 2004–05, Pres. 2006–09. *Publication:* Blueprint for a New Japan 1993. *Leisure interests:* fishing, Go. *Address:* Democratic Party of Japan (DPJ), 1-11-1, Nagata-cho, Chiyoda-ku, Tokyo, 100-0014 (office); 2-38 Fukuro-machi, Mizusawa-shi, Iwate-ken 023-0814, Japan (home). *Telephone:* (3) 3595-9960 (office). *Fax:* (3) 3595-7318 (office). *E-mail:* dpjnews@dpj.or.jp (office). *Website:* www.dpj.or.jp (office).

OZAWA, Sakihito, LLB; Japanese politician; b. 31 May 1954, Yamanashi Pref.; ed Tokyo Univ., Grad. School of Political Science, Saitama Univ.; began career in foreign currency exchange dept, Bank of Tokyo Ltd 1981; mem. House of Reps for Yamanashi 1st Dist constituency 1993–, Chief Dir Parl. Cttee on Financial Affairs 2006; fmr mem. Japan New Party; mem. Democratic Party of Japan 1996–, various party roles including Deputy Chair. Diet Affairs Cttee 1996, Deputy Chair. Policy Research Council 1998, Deputy Sec.-Gen. 1998, 2006, Chief of Office of Party Pres. 2001, Deputy Chief, Global Warming Prevention HQ 2008; Next (Shadow) Minister of Information and Communication 1999, Shadow Minister of the Economy, Trade and Industry 2002; Minister of the Environment 2009–10. *Address:* c/o Ministry of the Environment, 1-2-2, Kasumigaseki, Chiyoda-ku, Tokyo 100-8975, Japan (office).

OZAWA, Seiji; Japanese conductor; *Artistic Director, Tokyo Opera Nomori;* b. 1 Sept. 1935, Shenyang, China; m. 1st Kyoko Edo; m. 2nd Vera Ilyan; one s. one d.; ed Toho School of Music, Tokyo with Prof. Hideo Saito, Tanglewood, USA and in West Berlin under Herbert von Karajan; Asst Conductor (under Leonard Bernstein), New York Philharmonic 1961–62 (including tour of Japan 1961); Guest Conductor, San Francisco Symphony, Detroit Symphony, Montréal, Minneapolis, Toronto and London Symphony Orchestras 1961–65; Music Dir, Ravinia Festival, Chicago 1964–68; Music Dir, Toronto Symphony Orchestra 1965–69, San Francisco Symphony Orchestra 1970–76, Boston Symphony Orchestra 1973–2002, Vienna State Opera 2002–10; co-founder, Saito Kinen Orchestra 1987, Saito Kinen Festival Matsumoto 1992; co-founder and Artistic Dir, Tokyo Opera Nomori 2005–; toured Europe conducting many of the major orchestras 1966–67; Salzburg Festival 1969; toured USA, France, FRG, China 1979, Austria, UK 1981, Japan 1981, 1986, toured England, Netherlands, France, Germany, Austria and Belgium 1988; opened music acad., Geneva 2005–; makes frequent guest appearances with leading orchestras of America, Europe and Japan; has

conducted opera at Salzburg, Covent Garden, La Scala, Vienna Staatsoper and Paris Opera; conducted world premiere, Messiaen's St Francis of Assisi, Paris 1983; Hon. mem., Vienna Staatsoper 2007; Hon. DMus (Univ. of Mass., New England Conservatory, Wheaton Coll., Norton, Mass.); First Prize, Int. Competition of Orchestra Conductors, France 1959, Koussevitsky Prize for outstanding student conductor 1960, Laureate, Fondation du Japon 1988, Japan Art Asscn Praemium Imperiale 2011. *Leisure interests:* golf, tennis, skiing. *Address:* c/o Ronald A. Wilford, Columbia Artists Management Inc., Conductors Division, 165 W 57th Street, New York, NY, USA (office); c/o Harold Holt Ltd, 31 Sinclair Road, London, W14 0NS, England (office); Tokyo Opera Nomori Committee Office, Jimbo-cho Mitsui Building 17F, Kanda Jimbo-cho 1-105, Chiyoda-ku, Tokyo 101-0051, Japan. *Website:* www.tokyo-opera-nomori.com.

ÖZAYDINLI, F. Bülend; Turkish business executive; *Executive Chairman, Migros Ticaret AS;* b. 1949, Eskişehir; ed Izmir Maarif Coll., American Univ. of Beirut, Lebanon; Asst Man. Oyak 1972–76; Regional Man. Motorlu Araçlar Tic. AS 1976–79; Asst Gen. Man. Oyak 1979–87; Investments Co-ordinator, Migros Türk TAS 1987–88; Asst Gen. Man. Maret AS 1988–90; Gen. Man. Migros Türk TAS 1990–2001; Deputy CEO Koç Holding AS 2001, CEO 2002–07, also mem. Bd of Dirs; Chair. Migros Turk TAS (now Migros Ticaret AS) 2008–; Pres. Fiat Group 2001. *Address:* Migros Ticaret AS, Ataturk Mahallesi Turgut Ozal Bulvari No:7, Atasehir, Istanbul 34758, Turkey (office). *Telephone:* (216) 5793000 (office). *Website:* www.migros.com.tr (office).

OZBEK, (Ibrahim Mehmet) Rifat, BA; Turkish/British couturier; b. 8 Nov. 1953, Istanbul; s. of Melike Osbek and Abdulazim Mehmet Ismet; ed St Martin's School of Art, London; worked with Walter Albini for Trell; designer Monsoon Co.; launched O for Ozbek (now Future Ozbek) 1987; presented first collection 1984; began presenting collections for Pollini 2004–; British Fashion Council Designer of the Year 1988, 1992. *Address:* c/o Pollini SpA, via Erbosa, 2–B, 47030 Gatteo, Italy; 18 Haunch of Venison Yard, London, W1Y 1AF, England. *Telephone:* (20) 7408-0625. *Fax:* (20) 7629-1586.

ÖZDAŞ, Mehmet Nimet, DipEng, PhD; Turkish professor of engineering and administrator; b. 26 March 1921, Istanbul; m.; two c.; ed Istanbul Tech. Univ., Imperial Coll., London, UK; Visiting Prof., Case Western Reserve Univ., Ohio, USA 1953–59; Research Fellow, MIT 1955–56; Prof., Istanbul Tech. Univ. 1961; Founding Dir Computer Centre 1961; Founding Sec.-Gen. Turkish Scientific Council (TUBITAK) 1964–66, mem. Science Bd 1968–72; Founding Dir Marmara Scientific and Industrial Research; Pres. NATO Science Cttee 1973–79; mem. Bd Von Karman Inst. and Steering Cttee AGARD 1973; Minister of State for Science and Tech. 1980–83; Prof., Dept of Mechanical and Control Eng, Istanbul Tech. Univ. 1983–; Pres. Turkish Org. for Automatic Control; Founding Fellow, Islamic Acad. of Sciences 1986. *Publications:* several books and articles in various languages. *Address:* Department of Mechanical and Control Engineering, Istanbul Technical University, Ayazaga, Istanbul 80626, Turkey (office). *Telephone:* (212) 2853000 (office). *Fax:* (212) 2852916 (office). *E-mail:* mknbolum@itu.edu.tr (office). *Website:* www.mkn.itu.edu.tr (office).

OZICK, Cynthia, MA; American writer and poet; b. 17 April 1928, New York, NY; d. of William Ozick and Celia Regelson; m. Bernard Hallote 1952; one d.; ed New York Univ. and Ohio State Univ.; mem. PEN, Authors' League, American Acad. of Arts and Sciences, American Acad. of Arts and Letters; Founder-mem. Acad. Universelle des Cultures; Guggenheim Fellow 1982; Dr hc (Yeshiva) 1984, (Hebrew Union Coll.) 1984, (Williams Coll.) 1986, (Hunter Coll.) 1987, (Jewish Theological Seminary) 1988, (Adelphi) 1988, (State Univ. of NY) 1989, (Brandeis) 1990, (Bard Coll.) 1991, (Spertus Coll.) 1991, (Seton Hall Univ.) 1999, (Rutgers Univ.) 1999, (Asheville) 2000, (New York) 2001, (Bar-Ilan) 2002, (Baltimore Hebrew Univ.) 2004, (Georgetown) 2007; Mildred and Harold Strauss Living Award, American Acad. of Arts and Letters 1983; Rea Award for short story 1986, PEN/Spiegel-Diamonstein Award for the Art of the Essay 1997, Harold Washington Literary Award, City of Chicago 1997, John Cheever Award 1999, Lotos Club Medal of Merit 2000, Lannan Foundation Award 2000, Nat. Critics' Circle Award for Criticism 2001, Koret Foundation Award for Literary Studies 2001, Mary McCarthy Award, Bard Coll. 2007, Nat. Humanities Medal 2007, PEN/Malamud Prize 2008, PEN/Nabokov Prize 2008. *Publications:* Trust 1966, The Pagan Rabbi and Other Stories 1971, Bloodshed and Three Novellas 1976, Levitation: Five Fictions 1982, Art & Ardor: Essays 1983, The Cannibal Galaxy 1983, The Messiah of Stockholm 1987, Metaphor & Memory: Essays 1989, The Shawl 1989, Epodes: First Poems 1992, What Henry James Knew, and Other Essays on Writers 1993, Blue Light (play) 1994, Portrait of the Artist as a Bad Character and Other Essays on Writing 1995, The Shawl (novel) 1996, Fame & Folly: Essays 1996, The Puttermesser Papers (novel) 1997, The Best American Essays (ed.) 1998, Quarrel & Quandary (essays) 2000, Heir to the Glimmering World (novel published as The Bear Boy in UK) 2004, Collected Stories 2006, A Din in the Head: Essays 2006, Dictation: A Quartet 2008, Foreign Bodies 2010; contrib. of fiction to numerous periodicals and anthologies, including New Criterion, New Yorker, Harper's, Partisan Review, Yale Review, New York Times Magazine, Best American Short Stories, O. Henry Prize Stories, Best American Essays, The Oxford Book of Jewish Short Stories, The Norton Anthology of Jewish American Literature.

OZIM, Igor; Slovenian/German violinist and academic; *Professor of Violin, Universität Mozarteum, Salzburg;* b. 9 May 1931, Ljubljana, fmr Yugoslavia (now Slovenia); s. of Rudolf Ozim and Marija Kodric; m. Wonji Kim-Ozim; ed Akad. za glasbo Ljubljana, Royal Coll. of Music, London, UK, studied with Prof. Max Rostal; Prof. of Violin, Akad. za glasbo Ljubljana 1960–63, Staatliche Hochschule für Musik, Cologne 1963–96, Berne Conservatoire 1985–96, Hochschule für Musik, Vienna 1996–, currently Universität Mozarteum, Salzburg; mem. trio with Walter Grimmer and Ilse Dorati-von Alpenheim which performed and recorded all of Mozart's and Schubert's works –1995; concerts throughout Europe; Pres. Cen. Cttee European String Teachers' Asscn; Dr hc; First Prize, Int. Carl-Flesch Competition, London 1951, Munich 1953. *Leisure interests:* photography, table tennis. *Address:* Department of Strings, Universität Mozarteum, Mirabellplatz 1, 5020 Salzburg, Austria (office). *Telephone:* (662) 61-98-0 (office). *E-mail:* igor .ozim@moz.ac.at (office). *Website:* www.moz.ac.at (office).

ÖZKÖK, Gen. Hilmi; Turkish army officer; b. 1940, Turgutlu, Manisa; m. Özenç Özkök; two c.; ed Işıklar Mil. High School, Turkish Mil. Acad., Field Artillery School, Army War Coll., NATO Defence Coll.; Artillery 3rd Lt 1959; Platoon Leader and Anti-Aircraft Battery Commdr 1972; Chief of Operations and Training Br., 15th Training Brigade; Staff Officer, Plan and Policy Dept of Shape, HQ; Chief of Defence Research Section, Plan and Policy Dept of Shape, HQ; Dir Exec. Office of Sec.-Gen. of Nat. Security Council; Commdr Cadet Regiment, Turkish Mil. Acad.; rank of Brig.-Gen. 1984; Chief of Planning and Operations Dept, Turkish Gen. Staff (TGS) 1984–86; Commdr 70th Infantry Brigade 1986–88; rank of Maj.-Gen. 1988; Commdr 28th Infantry Div. 1988–90; Chief of Personnel, Dept of TGS 1990–92; rank of Lt-Gen. 1992; Chief of Turkish Mil. Del. to NATO, Brussels 1992–95; Commdr 7th Corps 1995–96; rank of Gen. 1996; Command of Allied Land Forces South-Eastern Europe 1996–98; Deputy Chief of TGS 1998–99; 1st Army Commdr 1999–2000; Commdr of Turkish Army 2000–02; Chief of the Gen. Staff 2002–06; fmr mem. NATO Mil. Cttee; Turkish Armed Forces Medal of Honour, Turkish Armed Forces Medal of Distinguished Service, Medal of Distinguished Service and Self-Sacrifice, Chevalier, Ordre nat. du Mérite, Legion of Merit (USA), Medal of Nishan-i-Imtiaz (Pakistan), Great Cross for Military Merit (Spain), Tong-II Medal (Repub. of Korea), Eagle Golden Medal (Albania). *Address:* c/o Ministry of National Defence, Milli Savunma Bakanlığı, 06100 Ankara, Turkey (office).

ÖZPETEK, Ferzan; Turkish/Italian film director and screenwriter; b. 3 Feb. 1959, Istanbul; Hon. Citizen of the City of Lecce 2010; Medal of Merit (Italy) 2008. *Films directed:* Hamam (Hamam: The Turkish Bath, UK) (also screenplay) (Golden Orange for Best Film and Best Direction, Antalya Int. Film Festival, Italian Nat. Syndicate of Film Journalists Silver Ribbon Award for Best Producer) 1997, Harem Suaré (also screenplay) 1999, His Secret Life 2001, Le fate ignoranti (The Ignorant Fairies) (also screenplay) (Austin Gay & Lesbian Int. Film Festival Award for Best Feature, New York Lesbian and Gay Film Festival Award for Best Feature) 2001, La finestra di fronte (The Window Opposite) (also screenplay) (David di Donatello Award 2003, also won awards for Best Film, Best Direction, Best Leading Actor and Actress) 2003, Cuore sacro (also screenplay) 2005, Saturn in Opposition (also writer) 2007, A Perfect Day (also screenplay) 2008, L'Aquila 2009 – Cinque registi tra le macerie (video documentary short) (segment 'Nonostante tutto è Pasqua') 2009, Loose Cannons (also writer) 2010, Magnifica presenza (A Magnificent Haunting) (also written by) 2012, Allacciate le cinture (also screenplay/story) 2014; other films include: Scusate il ritardo (first asst dir) 1983, Son contento (first asst dir) 1983, Il tenente dei carabinieri (asst dir) 1986, Noi uomini duri (asst dir) 1987, Il volpone (The Big Fox) (asst dir) 1988, Mortacci (first assistant director) 1989, Ultrà (assistant director) 1991, La scorta (The Escort) (asst dir) 1993, Anche i commercialisti hanno un'anima (asst dir) 1994, Il branco (The Pack) (asst dir) 1994, Vite strozzate (assistant director) 1996. *Television includes:* Qualcosa di biondo (film) (second asst dir) 1984, Il maestro del terrore (The Prince of Terror) (film) (asst dir) 1988, The Man Who Didn't Want to Die (film) (asst dir) 1988, School of Fear (film) (asst dir) 1989. *Website:* www.ferzanozpetek.com.

ÖZSOYLU, Şinasi, (Nasih), MD; Turkish physician; *Professor of Paediatrics and Haematology, Fatıh University, Ankara;* b. 29 July 1927, Erzurum; s. of Ahmet Fazil Ozsoylu and Azime Ozsoylu; m. Selma Ozsoylu; two s. one d.; ed Istanbul Univ.; paediatrician, Washington Univ. Medical School, St Louis, USA 1960; haematologist, Harvard Univ. Medical School, Boston, Mass 1963; Assoc. Prof. of Paediatrics, Hacettepe Univ., Ankara 1964–69, Prof. 1969–94, Head of Haematology 1970–94, of Paediatrics 1976–77; Prof. of Paediatrics and Haematology, Fatih Univ., Ankara 1996–; Visiting Prof., Md Univ. Medical School, Baltimore 1972; mem. Turkish Medical Soc. 1953–, Turkish Paediatrics Soc. 1958–, Turkish Haematology Soc. 1974–, Int. Paediatrics Soc. 1974–; Pres. European Soc. of Haematology and Immunology 1991–93; Fellow Islamic Acad. of Sciences 1989–; Ed. Turkish Journal of Medical Sciences 1989–94, Hon. Ed. 1994–; Ed. Yeni Tip Dergisi 1994–; invited to speak at numerous specialist congresses; Hon. mem. American Pediatric Soc. 1992–; Hon. Fellow, American Acad. of Pediatrics 1995–; numerous awards and prizes including Exceptional Scientific Achievement Award, Hacettepe Univ. 1991. *Publications:* several hundred papers on paediatrics, haematology, liver disorders, etc. *Leisure interests:* gardening, music. *Address:* Kenedi Cad. No. 148/14, GOP 06700, Ankara, Turkey (home); Fatıh University, Medical School Hospital, Alpaslan Turkes Cad. No. 57, Emek. 06510, Ankara (office). *Telephone:* (312) 2126262 (office); (312) 2121804 (office); (312) 4280975 (home). *Fax:* (312) 2213276 (office). *E-mail:* sinasi.ozsoylu@hotmail.com (office).

OZZIE, Raymond (Ray) E., BS; American software industry executive; b. 20 Nov. 1955, Chicago, Ill.; m. Dawna Bousquet 1982; one s. one d.; ed Main Township High School South, Park Ridge, Ill., Univ. of Ill.; Programmer, Protection Mutual Insurance Co. 1972–73; Technician, Dept of Nuclear Eng, Univ. of Ill. 1974, System Programmer, PLATO project, 1974–79; Co-founder Urbana Software Enterprises 1998–79; with Data Gen. Corpn 1979–81; Co-founder Microcosm Corpn 1981; with Software Arts 1981–82; with Lotus Devt 1982–84, led team that developed Lotus Symphony; Founder and Pres. Iris Assocs (back by Lotus), developed Lotus Notes 1984–97; Founder, Chair. and CEO Groove Networks Inc. (provider of collaboration software for the virtual office), Beverly, Mass 1997–2005, Chief Tech. Officer, Microsoft Corpn, Redmond, Wash. (after acquisition of Groove Networks by Microsoft) 2005–06, Chief Software Architect 2006–10 (resgnd; Founder and CEO Talko 2012–; mem. Nat. Acad. of Eng, Nat. Research Council; mem. and Gov. for IT and Telecommunications, World Econ. Forum; mem. Int. Council, John F. Kennedy School of Govt, Harvard Univ.; Person of the Year, PC Magazine 1995, W. Wallace McDowell Award, IEEE Computer Society 2000; named one of seven Windows Pioneers by Microsoft; inducted into Computer Museum Industry Hall of Fame and InfoWorld Hall of Fame. *Website:* ozzie.net; www.talko.com.

P

PÄÄBO, Svante, PhD; Swedish biologist and academic; *Director, Department of Genetics, Max Planck Institute for Evolutionary Anthropology*; b. 1955, Stockholm; ed Uppsala Univ.; worked in School of Interpreters, Swedish Defense Forces 1975–76; Researcher, Dept of Biochemistry, Univ. of California, Berkeley, USA 1987–90; Docent in Medical Genetics, Univ. of Uppsala 1990, Guest Prof. of Comparative Genomics 2003–; Prof. of Gen. Biology, Univ. of Munich 1990–98; Founding Dir Dept of Genetics, Max Planck Inst. for Evolutionary Anthropology, Leipzig, Germany 1997–; Chair. Scientific Advisory Bd Uppsala Centre for Comparative Genomics 2005–; mem. Editorial Bd PLoS Biology 2003–; mem. Academia Europaea, Swedish Royal Acad. of Sciences, Deutsche Akademie der Naturforscher Leopoldina, Halle, Saxonian Acad. of Sciences, Leipzig; Foreign mem. Finnish Soc. of Sciences and Letters, NAS, American Acad. of Arts and Sciences, USA 2011–, Royal Acad. of Eng, Stockholm 2013–; Corresponding mem. Croatian Acad. of Sciences and Arts, Croatia 2012–; Hon. Prof. of Genetics and Evolutionary Biology, Univ. of Leipzig 1999–, Grad. Univ. of the Chinese Acad. of Sciences, Beijing 2008, Hon. mem. Croatian Anthropological Soc., Croatia 2010; Order of Terra Mariana, 3rd Class (Estonia) 2008, H.M. The King's Medal 2012; Dr hc (Zurich, Helsinki, Royal Inst. of Tech., Stockholm, Karolinska Inst., Stockholm); Leibniz Prize German Science Foundation 1992, Max Delbrück Medal, Berlin, Germany 1998, Carus Medal and Prize, Halle and Schweinfurt, Germany 1999, Rudbeck Prize, Uppsala, Sweden 2000, Leipzig Science Prize 2003, Ernst Schering Prize, Berlin 2003, Louis-Jeantet Prize for Medicine 2005, Virchow Medal 2005, Gorjanovic-Kramberger Medal 2008, Kistler Prize 2009, Newcomb-Cleveland Prize, American Acad. of Arts and Sciences 2011, Biochemical Analysis Prize 2011, Gruber Genetics Prize 2013. *Achievements include:* pioneer in study of ancient DNA. *Publications include:* numerous book chapters and articles and papers in scientific journals. *Address:* Max Planck Institute for Evolutionary Anthropology, Department of Genetics, Deutscher Platz 6, Level 3, Room U3.92, 04103 Leipzig, Germany (office). *Telephone:* (341) 3550501 (office). *Fax:* (341) 3550555 (office). *E-mail:* paabo@eva.mpg.de (office). *Website:* wwwstaff.eva.mpg.de/~paabo/ (office).

PAAR, Vladimir, DSc; Croatian physicist; *Professor of Physics, Zagreb University;* b. 11 May 1942, Zagreb; s. of Vladimir Paar and Elvira Paar; m. Nada Paar-Pandur 1968; three s. one d.; ed Zagreb Univ.; Research Assoc., Zagreb Univ. 1973–76, Prof. 1981–; Visiting Prof. in Copenhagen, Julich, Paris, Moscow, Munich, Amsterdam, Livermore (Calif.) and Rio de Janeiro; participation in numerous int. confs; mem. Croatian Acad. of Arts and Sciences, Croatian Physical Soc., European Physical Soc. *Television:* Deterministic Chaos, Energy Crisis, Physics in Educ. *Publications:* author and ed. of several books and more than 300 papers on atomic nucleus structure, symmetry, supersymmetry and deterministic chaos, energetics and scientific econ. devt. *Leisure interests:* soccer, tennis, presenting science in the media. *Address:* Theoretical Physics Department, Faculty of Science, University of Zagreb, Bijenicka 32, 10000 Zagreb (office); Croatian Academy of Sciences and Arts, Zrinski trg 11, 10000 Zagreb, Croatia. *Telephone:* (1) 4605555 (office). *Fax:* (1) 4680336 (office). *E-mail:* paar@hazu.hr (office); vpaar@phy.hr (office). *Website:* www.hazu.hr/~paar (office).

PAASIO, Pertti Kullervo, MSc; Finnish politician and organization official; *Chairman, Finland Society;* b. 2 April 1939, Helsinki; s. of Rafael Paasio and Mary Wahlman; m. Kirsti Johansson 1967; two s. two d.; ed Turku Univ.; regional organizer, Nuoret Kotkat (Young Falcons) 1963–66; mem. Turku City Council 1965–91; Sec. for Tourism, City of Turku 1967–73; Political Sec. Ministry of Finance 1972; Head of Turku Labour Exchange 1973–87; Vice-Pres. Int. Falcon Movt 1975–81; Chair. Young Falcons Fed. 1978–81; Political Sec. to Prime Minister 1975; mem. Parl. 1975–79, 1982–96; mem. Exec. Cttee Social Democratic Party of Finland 1978–91; mem. Presidential Electoral Coll. 1978, 1982, 1988; Leader, Social Democratic Parl. Group 1984–87; Chair. Social Democratic Party 1987–91; Deputy Prime Minister, Minister for Foreign Affairs 1989–91; Chair. Parl. Cttee for Foreign Affairs 1991–96; mem. European Parl. 1996–99 Quaestor 1997–; currently Chair. Finland Soc. *Leisure interests:* photography, caravanning. *Address:* Finland Society, Mariankatu 8, 00170 Helsinki (office); Eerikinkatu 30, 20100 Turku, Finland. *Telephone:* (9) 6841210 (office). *Fax:* (9) 68412140 (office). *Website:* www.suomi-seura.fi (office).

PABLO ROSSO, Pedro, MD; Chilean paediatrician, academic and university administrator; *Rector, Pontificia Universidad Católica de Chile;* b. 27 Aug. 1941, Spotorno, Italy; s. of José Pablo Rosso and Laura Pablo Rosso; m. Mary Rose Streeter, two s. one d.; ed Scuola Italiana de Valparaíso, Scuola Italiana de Santiago, Pontificia Universidad Católica de Chile; Paediatrician, Roberto del Río Hosp., Santiago 1966–69; Paediatrician, Weill Cornell Medical Coll., Cornell Univ., NY 1970–74; Asst Prof. and Researcher, Coll. of Physicians and Surgeons, Columbia Univ., New York 1972–75, Assoc. Prof. of Paediatrics 1978, Dir Growth and Devt Div. 1982–84; Prof., Faculty of Medicine, Pontificia Universidad Católica de Chile 1984–, f. Director de Investigaciones Médicas 1990, Dean, Faculty of Medicine 1991, Rector, Pontificia Universidad Católica 2000–; fmr Visiting Prof., Universidad de Puerto Rico, Universidad de San Marcos, Lima; Pres., Asscn de Chilean Medical Faculties 1996–2000; Vice-Pres. Federación Internacional de Escuelas de Medicina de Universidades Católicas 1994–96; mem. Academia Chilena de Medicina 1999–; Cavalier, Order of Merit of Repub. of Italy 2008; US March of Dimes/Birth Defect Foundation Agnes Higgins Prize. *Publications:* more than 120 publs. *Address:* Office of the Rector, Pontificia Universidad Católica de Chile, 8320000 Santiago, Chile (office). *Telephone:* (2) 354-2000 (office). *Website:* www.puc.cl (office).

PABRIKS, Artis, PhD; Latvian politician, political scientist and academic; b. 22 March 1966, Jūrmala; ed Univ. of Latvia, Univ. of Arhus, Denmark; Research Asst, Acad. of Sciences 1988–90; External Lecturer, Univ. of Arhus, Denmark 1994; Lecturer, Univ. of Latvia 1995–99; First Rector, Vidzeme Univ. Coll. 1996–97, Asst Prof. 1996–2001, Assoc. Prof. 2001–; Policy Analyst, Latvian Centre for Human Rights and Ethnic Studies 2001–03, Political Educ. Foundation 2003–04; mem. Saeima (Parl.) 2004–, Chair. Foreign Affairs Comm.; Parl. Sec., Ministry of Foreign Affairs 2004, Minister of Foreign Affairs 2004–07; Deputy Prime Minister and Minister of Defence 2010–11, Minister of Defence 2011–14;

Deputy mem. for Latvia, European Comm. against Racism and Intolerance, Council of Europe 2002–; mem. Editorial Bd, Baltic Review magazine 2002–; mem. Soc. for a Different Politics (SCP); Visiting Prof., Bosphorus (Boğaziçi) Univ., Istanbul 2009–10; Prof., Rīga Int. School of Econs and Business Admin 2011–; Great Commdr, Order of Duke Gediminas. *Leisure interest:* karate (black belt). *Address:* c/o Ministry of Defence, K. Valdemāra iela 10–12, Rīga 1473, Latvia (office).

PACARI VEGA, Nina, BA, JD; Ecuadorean lawyer and politician; b. (María Estela Vega), 9 Oct. 1960, Imbabura-Cotopaxi; ed Universidad Cen. del Ecuador; Legal Advisor, Confed. of Indigenous Nationalities of Ecuador (CONAIE) 1989; elected mem. Nat. Ass. 1998–2003, Vice-Pres. (first native Quécha-Indian in position) 1999–2000, Acting Pres. 2000–03; Minister of Foreign Affairs 2003 (resgnd); mem. UN Perm. Forum on Indigenous Issues 2005–07; Judge, Constitutional Court of Ecuador 2007; mem. Faculty, Univ. of Ambato; mem. Inter-American Dialogue; Best Congresswoman of the Year, TC Television 1998. *Address:* c/o Movimiento de Unidad Pluriacional Pachakútik Nuevo País (Pachakútik), Calle Lugo 13-04 y Avda Ladrón de Guevara, La Floresta, Quito, Ecuador (office).

PACE, Gen. (retd) Peter, MBA; American management consultant and military officer (retd); *President and CEO, SM&A Strategic Advisors Inc.;* b. 5 Nov. 1945, Brooklyn, NY; m.; one s. one d.; ed US Naval Acad., George Washington Univ., Harvard Univ., Nat. War Coll.; Rifle Platoon Leader, then Asst Operations Officer, 1st Marine Div. in Viet Nam 1968–69; various positions 1969–71, including Head, Infantry Writer Unit, Marine Corps Inst., White House Social Aide; CO Marine Corps Recruiting Station, Buffalo, NY 1980–83, 2nd Battalion, 1st Marines 1983–85; assigned to Combined/Jt Staff, Seoul 1986, served as Chief, Ground Forces Br., then Exec. Officer to the Asst Chief of Staff; Chief of Staff, 2nd Marine Div., Camp Lejeune 1991–92, Asst Div. Commdr 1992; Pres. Marine Corps Univ., Commanding Gen. Marine Corps Schools, Marine Corps Combat Devt Command, Quantico, Va 1992; Deputy Commdr Marine Forces, Somalia 1992–93, Deputy Commdr Jt Task Force 1993–94; Deputy Commdr/Chief of Staff, US Forces, Japan 1994–96; Dir for Operations, Jt Staff, Washington, DC 1996–97; Commdr US Marine Corps Forces, Atlantic/Europe/South 1997–2000; C-in-C US Southern Command 2000–01; Vice-Chair. Jt Chiefs of Staff 2001–05, Chair. 2005–07; Pres. and CEO SM&A Strategic Advisors Inc. (man. consultancy) 2008–, also mem. Bd of Dirs; mem. Bd of Dirs Marine Corps Law Enforcement Foundation; promoted to Capt. 1971, Maj. 1977, Lt-Col 1982, Col 1988, Brig.-Gen. 1992, Maj.-Gen. 1994, Lt-Gen. 1996, Gen. 2000; Legion of Merit, Combat Action Ribbon; Defense Distinguished Service Medal, Defense Superior Service Medal, Bronze Star Medal with Combat V, Defense Meritorious Service Medal, Meritorious Service Medal with Gold Star, Navy Commendation Medal with Combat V, Navy Achievement Medal with Gold Star. *Address:* SM&A Strategic Advisors Inc., 4695 Macarthur Court, 8th Floor, Newport Beach, CA 92660, USA (office). *Telephone:* (949) 975-1550 (office). *Fax:* (949) 975-1624 (office). *Website:* www.smawins.com (office).

PAČES, Vaclav, DrSc; Czech biochemist and academic; *Chairman, Academy of Sciences of the Czech Republic;* b. 2 Feb. 1941, Prague; m. Magdalena Tomková Pačes 1966; two s.; ed Charles Univ., Czechoslovak Acad. of Sciences; joined Inst. of Molecular Genetics 1977, Head of Lab. 1986, Docent 1992–95, Full Prof. 1995, Dir 1999–2005; Chair. Czech Acad. of Sciences 2005–; at Yale Univ. 1990–91, has also conducted research at Univs of Chicago, Seville, Bristol and Japan; mem. Czech Soc. of Arts and Sciences (SVU), Fellow 2004–; mem. European Acad. of Sciences and Arts, European Molecular Biology Org. (EMBO); recipient of several prizes including State Prize for Science 1989, Prize for Popularization of Science 1992. *Publications:* Molecular Biology of the Gene 1982, Molecular Genetics 1983, Antibiotics: Mechanism of Action and Resistance (co-author) 1987, Highlights of Modern Biochemistry 1989; more than 100 original papers. *Address:* The Academy of Sciences of the Czech Republic, Narodni 3, 11720 Prague 1, Czech Republic (office). *Telephone:* (224) 229610 (office). *Fax:* (224) 240512 (office). *E-mail:* paces@kav.cas.cz (office). *Website:* www.cas.cz (office).

PACHACHI, Adnan, PhD; Iraqi politician and diplomatist (retd); b. (Adnan Muzahim al-Pachachi), 14 May 1923, Baghdad; m. Selwa Pachachi 1946; three d.; ed Victoria Coll., Alexandria, Egypt, American Univ., Beirut, Lebanon, Georgetown Univ, Washington, DC, USA; Perm. Rep. to UN 1959–65, 1967–69; Minister of Foreign Affairs 1965–67; left Iraq to settle in UAE 1971, Minister of State in Govt of Abu Dhabi 1971–93, Personal Rep. of the Pres. of Pres. 1974–90, returned to Iraq 2003; Founder and Pres. Ind. Democratic Movt 2003–06; led Iraqi del. to UN Security Council July 2003; mem. Iraq Governing Council 2003–04, Pres. Jan. 2004; mem. Parl. 2006–10; decorations from Italy and Morocco. *Publications:* Muzahim Pachachi – Political Career (in Arabic) 1990, Voice of Iraq in the UN 1959–1969 – Personal Record 1991. *Leisure interests:* music, swimming, theatre, visiting art galleries and exhibitions. *E-mail:* adnan@pachachi.org (office).

PACHAURI, Rajendra Kumar, MS, DEcon, DEng; Indian economist, academic, research director and international organization official; *Chairman, Intergovernmental Panel on Climate Change;* b. 20 Aug. 1940, Nainital; s. of A. R. Pachauri; m. Saroj Pachauri; three d.; ed North Carolina State Univ., USA; Asst Prof., North Carolina State Univ. 1974–75, Visiting Faculty mem., Dept of Econs and Business 1976–77; mem. Sr Faculty, Admin. Staff Coll. of India 1975–79, Dir Consulting and Applied Research Div. 1979–81; Dir The Energy Research Inst. (TERI), New Delhi 1982–2001, Dir-Gen. 2001–; Visiting Prof., Resource Econs, Univ. of West Virginia 1981–82; Sr Visiting Fellow, Resource Systems Inst., East-West Center, USA 1982; Visiting Fellow, Energy Dept, IBRD 1990; Pres. Int. Asscn for Energy Econs 1988, Chair. 1989–90; Pres. Asian Energy Inst. 1992–; Adviser on Energy and Sustainable Man. of Natural Resources to the Admin., UNDP 1994–99; Adviser, Int. Advisory Bd, Toyota Motor Corpn, Japan 2006–09; Vice-Chair. Intergovernmental Panel on Climate Change (IPCC) 1997, Chair. 2002–; Dir-Gen. Energy and Resources Inst., New Delhi; Chancellor TERI Univ.; Dir Yale Climate and Energy Inst.; mem. Bd of Dirs Int. Solar Energy Soc. 1991–97, Inst. for Global Environmental Strategies 1999–, Indian Oil Corpn Ltd 1999–2003, Nat. Thermal Power Corpn Ltd 2002–05, GAIL (India) Ltd 2003–04, Oil and Natural Gas Corpn

Ltd 2006–09; McCluskey Fellow, Yale Univ., USA Sept.–Dec. 2000; mem. Advisory Bd, Clinton Climate Initiative, USA 2010–; mem. High Panel on Peace and Dialogue among Cultures, UNESCO, France 2009–; mem. Bd of Govs, Shriram Scientific and Industrial Research Foundation 1987–90; mem. Exec. Cttee, India Int. Centre, New Delhi, mem. Bd of Trustees 1985–; Vice-Pres. Bangalore Int. Centre; mem. Governing Council, India Habitat Centre, New Delhi 1987–, Pres. 2004–06; mem. Court of Govs, Admin. Staff Coll. of India 1979–81; mem. Advisory Bd on Energy, reporting directly to Prime Minister 1983–88, World Energy Council 1990–93, Nat. Environmental Council, under Prime Minister 1993–99, Oil Industry Restructuring Group, 'R' Group, Ministry of Petroleum and Natural Gas 1994, Econ. Advisory Council to Prime Minister 2001–04, Prime Minister's Advisory Council on Climate Change 2007–; Hon. Prof., HEC Paris 2009; Officier de la Legion d'honneur 2006, Commdr of the Order of the White Rose (Finland) 2010, Order of the Rising Sun, Gold and Silver Star (Japan) 2010; Dr hc (Ritsumeikan Univ.) 2007, (Univ. of Liege) 2008, (Univ. of Athens) 2009, Hon. DHumLitt (Yale Univ.) 2008, (Brandeis Univ.) 2009, Hon. DSc (Kumaun Univ.) 2008, (Rani Durgavati Vishwavidyalaya, Jabalpur) 2008, (Univ. of New South Wales) 2008, (Univ. of Warwick) 2009, (Univ. of Kalyani) 2009, (Illinois Univ.) 2009, (Gustavus Adolphus Coll., Minnesota) 2009, Hon. ScD (Univ. of East Anglia) 2008; Millennium Pioneer Award 2000, Padma Bhushan 2001, Intergovernmental Panel on Climate Change awarded Nobel Peace Prize (shared with Al Gore) 2007, NDTV Global Indian Award 2007, Padma Vibhushan 2008, IIFA Global Leadership Award 2008, GQ Global Indian of the Year Award 2009. *Publications include:* The Dynamics of Electrical Energy Supply and Demand 1975, Energy and Economic Development in India 1977, International Energy Studies 1980, Energy Policy for India: An Interdisciplinary Analysis 1980, National Energy Data Systems (co-author) 1984, The Political Economy of Global Energy 1985, Global Energy Interactions 1986, Global Warming and Climate Change: Perspectives from Developing Countries (co-ed.) 1990, Role of Innovative Technologies and Approaches for India (co-ed.) 1991, Global Warming: Mitigation Strategies and Perspectives from Asia and Brazil (co-ed.) 1991, Energy-Environment-Development (co-ed.) 1991, Global Warming: Collaborative Study on Strategies to Limit CO2 emissions in Asia and Brazil (co-ed.) 1992, Contemporary India 1992, Climate Change in Asia and Brazil: The Role of Technology Transfer (co-ed. with Preety Bhandari) 1994, Population, Environment and Development (ed. with Lubina F. Qureshy) 1997; Energy in the Indian Sub-Continent (co-ed. with Gurneeta Vasudeva) 2000, Directions, Innovations, and Strategies for Harnessing Action for Sustainable Development 2001, Business Unusual: Championing Corporate Social Responsibility (ed) 2004, Petroleum Pricing in India: Balancing Efficiency and Equity (co-author) 2005, The Promises and Challenges of Biofuels for the Poor in Developing Countries 2006, CITIES: Steering Towards Sustainability 2009; scientific papers and newspaper articles. *Leisure interests:* cricket, flying, golf. *Address:* Intergovernmental Panel on Climate Change, World Meteorological Organization, 7 bis, Avenue de la Paix, CP 2300, 1211 Geneva 2, Switzerland (office); 160 Golf Links, New Delhi 110 003, India (home). *Telephone:* 227308208 (office); (11) 4634663 (home). *Fax:* 227308025 (office). *E-mail:* IPCC -Sec@wmo.int (office). *Website:* www.ipcc.ch (office); www.teriin.org (office).

PACHE, Bernard; French business executive and engineer; b. 13 Oct. 1934, Sallanches; s. of Joseph Pache and Sabine Pache (née Minjoz); m. Yvette Vitaly 1959; three s. (two deceased); ed Ecole Polytechnique de Paris and Ecole des Mines de Paris; mining engineer 1957–; Asst to Dir of Mines 1963–65; Tech. Adviser to Minister of Industry 1965–67; Chief Mining Engineer 1967; joined Compagnie Pechiney 1967, Asst to Dir, Uranium and Nuclear Activity Dept, then Dir of Mines Div., Nuclear Branch of Pechiney Ugine Kuhlmann 1969–73; Gen.-Man. Soc. des Electrodes et Refractaires Savoie 1972–73; Chair. Cie Générale d'Electrolyse du Palais 1972–76; Gen.-Man. Soc. Cefilac 1973–74; Dir and Gen. Man. Soc. Française d'Electrométallurgie 1974–79; Dir of Industrial Policy, Pechiney Ugine Kuhlmann Group 1979–83, Deputy Dir of Pechiney 1983–84, Chair. and CEO 1985–86, Hon. Pres. 1986–; Dir-Gen. Charbonnages de France 1986, Chair. and CEO 1987–92, Hon. Pres. 1992–; Pres., Dir-Gen. Cie des Machines Bull 1992–93, Hon. Pres. 1993–; Pres. Directoire de l'Entreprise minière et chimique 1994–99, Hon. Pres. 1999–; Chair. la Fondation Georges Besse 1994–99; Chair. NOVATEC 1999–2003; Ind. Dir on Bd of European cos; Officier, Légion d'honneur, Ordre nat. du Mérite. *Address:* 7 Résidence de l'Observatoire, 8 rue Bel Air, 92190 Meudon, France (home). *Telephone:* 1-46-26-32-90 (home). *E-mail:* yvebernpache@free.fr (home).

PACHECO, Abel; Costa Rican psychiatrist, writer and fmr head of state; b. (Abel Pacheco de la Espriella), 22 Dec. 1933, San José; ed Nat. Autonomous Univ. of Mexico, Louisiana State Univ., USA; fmr TV commentator and producer of documentaries; Pres. Partido Unidad Social Cristiana (PUSC); Pres. of Costa Rica 2002–06. *Publications:* series of novels, six books on Costa Rica and several popular songs. *Address:* c/o Partido Unidad Social Cristiana (PUSC), Del Restaurante Kentucky Fried Chicken 75 metros al sur, frente a la Embajada de España, Paseo Colón, Apdo 10.095, 1000 San José, Costa Rica (office).

PACHECO, Máximo, MBA; Chilean economist and business executive; *President, Europe, Middle East, Africa and Russia, International Paper Company;* b. 12 Feb. 1953, Santiago; s. of Máximo Pacheco and Adriana Matte; m. Soledad Flanagan 1976; four d.; ed Univ. of Chile; Man. Banco Osorno; Man. Planning, Banco Talca; Gen. Man. Leasing Andino 1983–90; mem. Bd of Dirs Cabildo SA 1982–90, Jucosa 1987–90; Pres. Chilean Leasing Asscn 1984–90; Faculty mem. Univ. de Chile; COO Codelco-Chile; Exec. Vice-Pres. for Chile and Latin America, Carter Holt Harvey 1994–2000, Exec. Pres. International Paper-Latinamerica 2000–04, named Exec. Pres. International Paper-Brazil 2004, named Sr Vice-Pres. International Paper Co. 2004, currently serves as Sr Vice-Pres. and Pres. IP Europe, Middle East, Africa & Russia. *Address:* International Paper EMEA, Chaussée de la Hulpe 166, 1170 Brussels, Belgium (office). *Telephone:* (2) 774-1201 (office). *Fax:* (2) 774-1298 (office). *E-mail:* maximo.pacheco@ipaper.com (office). *Website:* www.internationalpaper.com (office).

PACHECO GUTIERREZ, Adm. Armando; Bolivian naval officer; *Chief of Staff;* attained rank of Adm. 2009, Gen. Commdr of Naval Forces –2010, Chief of Staff of the Armed Forces Jan. 2010–. *Address:* Ministry of National Defence, Plaza Avaroa, esq. Pedro Salazar y 20 de Octubre 2502, La Paz, Bolivia (office).

Telephone: (2) 232-0225 (office). *Fax:* (2) 243-3153 (office). *E-mail:* correomaster@ mindef.gov.bo (office). *Website:* www.mindef.gov.bo (office).

PACHTA-REYHOFEN, Georg, Dipl-Ing, Dr techn; German engineer and business executive; *CEO, MAN Group;* b. 28 June 1955; ed Vienna Univ. of Tech.; worked as a univ. asst at Inst. for Internal Combustion Engines and Automotive Eng, Vienna Univ. of Tech. 1981–86; joined MAN Group at ÖAF Gräf und Stift AG, Vienna (now MAN Sonderfahrzeuge AG) 1986, held various positions –1995, Tech. Dir, MAN A.S., Ankara (now MAN Türkiye) 1996–99, mem. Exec. Bd 1998–99, Head of Engine Devt, MAN Nutzfahrzeuge AG, Nuremberg 1999–2001, mem. Exec. Bd MAN Nutzfahrzeuge Group 2001–, Exec. Bd MAN SE 2006–, Chair. Exec. Bd MAN Diesel SE –2009, CEO MAN SE and MAN Nutzfahrzeuge AG 2010–. *Address:* MAN Group, Ungererstrasse 69, 80805 Munich, Germany (office). *E-mail:* info@man.eu (office). *Website:* www.man.eu (office).

PACINO, Al (Alfredo James); American actor; b. 25 April 1940, New York, NY; s. of Salvatore Pacino and Rosa Pacino; ed High School for the Performing Arts, New York, The Actors Studio; worked as messenger and cinema usher; Co-artistic Dir The Actors Studio, Inc., New York 1982–83; mem. Artistic Directorate Globe Theatre 1997–; Broadway début in Does a Tiger Wear a Necktie? 1969; appeared with Lincoln Center Repertory Co. as Kilroy in Camino Real 1970; other New York appearances include The Connection, Hello Out There, Tiger at the Gates and The Basic Training of Pavlo Hummel 1977, American Buffalo 1981 (UK 1984), Julius Caesar 1988, Salome 1992; appearances at Charles Playhouse, Boston, include: Richard III 1973 (repeated on Broadway 1979), Arturo Ui 1975, Rats (director) 1970; f. Chal Productions (production co.); Nat. Soc. of Film Critics Award (for The Godfather), British Film Award (for The Godfather Part II) Tony Award 1996, American Film Inst. Lifetime Achievement Award 2007. *Films include:* Me, Natalie 1969, Panic in Needle Park 1971, The Godfather 1972, Scarecrow 1973, Serpico 1974, The Godfather Part II 1974, Dog Day Afternoon 1975, Bobby Deerfield 1977, And Justice For All 1979, Cruising 1980, Author! Author! 1982, Scarface 1983, Revolution 1985, Sea of Love 1990, Dick Tracy 1991, The Godfather Part III 1990, Frankie and Johnny 1991, Glengarry Glen Ross 1992, Scent of a Woman (Acad. Award for Best Actor 1993) 1992, Carlito's Way 1994, City Hall 1995, Heat 1995, Donny Brasco 1996, Looking for Richard 1996 (also producer, Dir), Devil's Advocate 1997, The Insider 1999, Chinese Coffee 1999, Man of the People 1999, Any Given Sunday 1999, People I Know 2002, Insomnia 2002, Simone 2002, The Recruit 2003, The Merchant of Venice 2004, Two for the Money 2005, 88 Minutes 2007, Ocean's Thirteen 2007, Righteous Kill 2008, The Son of No One 2011, Stand Up Guys 2012. *Television includes:* Angels in America (Golden Globe for Best Actor in a Mini-Series or TV Movie 2004, Screen Actors Guild Award for Best Actor in a Miniseries 2004, Emmy Award for Outstanding Lead Actor in a Miniseries 2004) 2003, You Don't Know Jack (film) (Emmy Award for Outstanding Lead Actor 2010, Golden Globe Award for Best Performance by an Actor in a Mini-Series or Movie Made for TV 2011) 2010, Phil Spector (film) 2013. *Address:* c/o Rick Nicita, Creative Artists Agency, 2000 Avenue of the Stars, Los Angeles, CA 90067, USA (office); Chal Productions, 301 West 57th Street, Suite 49A, New York, NY 10017, USA (office). *Telephone:* (424) 288-2000 (office); (212) 247-0227. *Fax:* (424) 288-2900 (office). *Website:* www.caa.com (office).

PACKER, James Douglas; Australian media company executive; *Executive Chairman, Consolidated Media Holdings Ltd;* b. 8 Sept. 1967; s. of the late Kerry Francis Packer and Roslyn Packer; m. 1st Jodie Meaves 1999; m. 2nd Erica Baxter 2007; ed Cranbrook School, Sydney; worked as a 'jackeroo' on a family-owned cattle station, Newcastle Walters; joined family business as magazine sales rep.; Dir Publishing & Broadcasting Ltd (PBL) 1991–, Man. Dir 1996–98, Exec. Chair. 1998–, inherited co. after father's death and split into two public cos., Consolidated Media Holdings Ltd and Crown Ltd, Dir Australian Consolidated Press Group Ltd 1991–, Gen. Man. 1993–, currently Jt CEO Consolidated Press Holdings Ltd, Chair. Crown Ltd; Chair. Burswood Ltd; Dir Nine Network Australia Ltd 1992–, Huntsman Corpn (Utah) 1994–, Optus Vision Pty Ltd 1995–, Valassas Inserts, USA, Ecorp Ltd 1999–, Challenger Int. 1999–, Crown Ltd 1999–, Hoytes Cinemas Ltd 1999–, Qantas Ltd –2007, Foxtel. *Address:* Consolidated Media Holdings Ltd, 2nd Floor, 54 Park Street, Sydney, NSW 1028, Australia (office). *Telephone:* (2) 9282-8000 (office). *Fax:* (2) 9282-8828 (office). *Website:* www.pbl.com.au (office).

PACKER, Sir Richard John, KCB, MSc; British former government official and business executive; b. 18 Aug. 1944, Bexley, England; s. of the late George Packer and Dorothy Packer; m. 1st Alison Sellwood; two s. one d.; m. 2nd Lucy Neville-Rolfe; four s.; ed City of London School and Univ. of Manchester; joined Ministry of Agric., Fisheries and Food (MAFF) 1967; on secondment, First Sec., Office of Perm. Representation to EEC 1973–76; Prin. Pvt. Sec. to Minister, MAFF 1977–78, Asst Sec. 1979–85, Under-Sec. 1985–89, Deputy Sec. 1989–93, Perm. Sec. 1993–2000; Dir (non-exec.) Express Foods (later Arla Foods) PLC 2002–07. *Publication:* The Politics of BSE 2006. *Leisure interests:* philosophy, history, arts, sport. *Address:* 113 St George's Road, London, SE1 6HY, England (home).

PACKER, William John; English artist, art critic and teacher; b. 19 Aug. 1940, Birmingham, England; s. of Rex Packer and Molly Wornham; m. Clare Winn 1965; three d.; ed Windsor Grammar School, Wimbledon School of Art; Nat. Diploma in Design (Painting); secondary school teacher 1964–67; part-time art school lecturer 1967–77; art critic, Art & Artists 1969–74, Financial Times 1974–2004; first exhibited Royal Acad. 1963; mem. Fine Art Bd of Council for Nat. Academic Awards and Specialist Adviser 1976–83, Specialist Adviser 1983–87; mem. Advisory Cttee to Govt Art Collection 1977–84, Crafts Council 1980–87; sole selector first British Art Show (Arts Council) 1979–80; external examiner at various art schools 1980–2000; mem. New English Art Club 2006; Trustee, Heatherley's School of Art 2008–14; Hon. Fellow, RCA; Hon. RBA; Hon. RBS; Hon. PS; Inaugural Henry Moore Memorial Lecturer, Florence 1986. *Publications:* Art of Vogue Covers 1980, Fashion Drawing in Vogue 1983, Henry Moore 1985, John Houston 2003, Sarah Raphael 2013. *Leisure interests:* France, books, singing. *Address:* 60 Trinity Gardens, London, SW9 8DR, England. *Telephone:* (20) 7733-4012. *E-mail:* williampacker@hotmail.com; williampacker19@gmail.com.

PACOLLI, Behgjet Isa; Kosovo/Swiss business executive and politician; *First Deputy Prime Minister;* b. 30 Aug. 1951, Marevc, Kosovo, Serbia, SFR Yugoslavia; s. of Isa Pacolli and Nazmije Pacolli; m. 1st Anna Oxa 1999 (divorced 2002); m. 2nd Maria (Masha) Pacolli; one s. four d.; ed Institut für Außenhandel, Univ. of

Hamburg, Germany, Institut Mösinger, Zurich, Switzerland; emigrated to Hamburg, Germany 1970s; mil. service in Fmr Yugoslavia; fmr Man. Interplastica (eng co.), Switzerland; f. Mabetex Project Management (construction co.) 1990, now Pres. and CEO Mabetex Group, Lugano, Switzerland; Founder and Leader, New Kosovo Alliance (AKR) 2006–; mem. (AKR) Ass. of Kosovo 2007–; Pres. of Kosovo 22 Feb.–30 March 2011 (resgnd after his election was declared to have occurred by unconstitutional means); First Deputy Prime Minister of Kosovo 15 April 2011–; Int. Councillor, Center for Strategic and Int. Studies, Washington, DC (think tank); Chief Exec. Lajm (The News); Hon. Citizen of Lezha, of Astana, Kazakhstan, of Baton Rouge, La, USA, Hon. Diplomat of Liberia; Highest honours of Russian Fed., of Peru, Cavaliere della Pace (Cavalier of Peace), Int. Union for Peace 2010; Hon. titles from Technology Univ., Rochester; Dr hc (European Univ. of Tirana); Certificate of Thanks from American Univ. in Kosovo, Honours of TMK, Recognition from Nelson Mandela Foundation, Recognition from Pres. Clinton, Gusi Peace Prize (Philippines), Chancellor's Gold Medal, Gov. of Louisiana, Key of New Orleans, copy of the key of City of Tirana on the occasion of state visit to Albania 2011. *Address:* Office of the Prime Minister, 10000 Prishtina, Rruga Nënë Terezë (office); New Kosovo Alliance (Aleanca Kosova e Re), 10000 Prishtina, Rruga UÇK 55, Kosovo (office); Mabetex Group Headquarters, Via Cattori 7, 6902 Lugano, Switzerland. *Telephone:* (38) 20114635 (office); (38) 247988 (AKR) (office); (91) 9850101. *Fax:* (38) 13814671 (office); (91) 9930636. *E-mail:* info_pmo@ks-gov .net (office); avdii@hotmail.com (office); info@mabetex.com. *Website:* www .kryeministri-ks.net (office); www.akr-ks.eu (office); www.behgjetpacolli.com; www.mabetex.com.

PACQUEMENT, Alfred; French museum administrator; *Director, Musée National d'Art Moderne, Centre Pompidou;* b. 1948; Curator, Centre Nat. d'Art Contemporain 1971–72, with Ministry of Cultural Affairs 1973, Exhbns Dir, Musée Nat. d'Art Moderne (MNAM) 1974–81, Curator 1982–87, Attached to Ministry of Culture 1987–89, Dir, Galerie Nat. du Jeu de Paume 1990–93, Dir for 'Arts plastiques', Ministry of Culture 1993–96, Dir, École Nationale Supérieure des Beaux-Arts 1996–2000, Dir MNAM, Centre Pompidou 2000–; Pres. Int. Cttee for Museums and Collections of Art (CIMAM). *Address:* Musée National d'Art Moderne, Centre Pompidou, 75191 Paris, Cedex 04, France (office). *Telephone:* (1) 44784640 (office). *Fax:* (1) 44781677 (office). *Website:* www.centrepompidou.fr (office).

PACQUIAO, Emmanuel Dapidran (Manny); Philippine professional boxer and politician; b. 17 Dec. 1978, Kibawe, Bukidnon, Mindanao; m. Jinkee Pacquiao; four c.; began professional boxing career aged 16 (light flyweight); currently fights in welterweight div.; World Boxing Council (WBC) flyweight world champion 1998–99; Int. Boxing Fed. (IBF) super bantamweight world champion 2001–03; Ring Magazine featherweight world champion 2003–05, super featherweight champion March–July 2008; WBC super featherweight world champion March–July 2008; WBC lightweight world champion 2008–09; World Boxing Org. (WBO) welterweight world champion 2009–12, 2014–; Int. Boxing Org. (IBO) light welterweight champion 2009–; Ring Magazine light welterweight champion 2009–10; 63 total fights, 56 wins (38 by knockout), 5 losses and 2 draws; rated by Ring Magazine as the No. 1 pound-for-pound boxer in the world; first boxer to win seven world titles in seven different weight divs; mem. House of Reps for Sarangani constituency 2010–; mil. reservist with rank of Master Sergeant; Champion for Life (Kampeon Habambuhay) 2006, Order of Lakandula 2006, Officer (Pinuno), Philippine Legion of Honor 2008, Grand Cross (Datu) Order of Sikatuna 2009; Presidential Medal of Merit 2003, Ring Magazine Fighter of the Year 2006, 2008, Boxing Writers Asscn of America Fighter of the Year 2006, 2008, WBC Emer. Champion, The Ring Magazine #1 Pound For Pound, 5-Time PSA Sportsman of the Year, World Boxing Hall of Fame 2007, Univ. Athletic Asscn of the Philippines Hon. Award for Sports Excellence 2008, BoxingScene.com Fighter of the Year 2008, Sports Illustrated Boxer of the Year 2008, SecondsOut.com Fighter of the Year 2008, TheSweetScience.com Boxer of the Year 2008, WBC Boxer of the Year 2008, Yahoo Sports Fighter of the Year 2008, ESPN Star's Champion of Champions 2008, ESPY Awards Best Fighter 2009, TIME 100 Most Influential People (Heroes & Icons Category) 2009, Forbes Magazine Celebrity 100 (ranked 57th) 2009, Sports Illustrated Fighter of the Year 2009, included among Most Exciting Athletes of All Time (ranked 85th), Bleacher Report 2010, Fighter of the Year, World Boxing Org. 2010, named among World's Highest-Paid Athletes (ranked 14th), Forbes Magazine 2013. *Telephone:* (949) 412-0197. *E-mail:* mpboxing@ymail.com. *Website:* www.mannypacquiao.ph.

PADAR, Ivari, BA; Estonian politician; b. 12 March 1965, Navi village, Võru county; m.; one s. one d.; ed Tartu Univ.; began career as transport worker, Võru Dairy Factory 1984–88; carpenter, Võru Dept of Repairs and Construction 1988–90; teacher, Võru School 1990–92; Deputy Mayor of Võru 1993–94; Chair. Võru Farmers' Union 1994–95; Asst to Chancellor of the Exchequer 1995–97; Dir-Gen. AS HT Hulgi (customs warehouse) 1997–99; Minister of Agric. 1999–2002, of Finance 2007–09; Chair. Võru City Council 2002–03; Advisor AS Tallink Duty Free 2002–03; mem. Riigikogu (Parl.) 2002–09; mem. Estonian Social Democratic Party (Sotsiaaldemokraatlik Erakond) 1999–, Chair. 2003–10; mem. European Parl. (Group of the Progressive Alliance of Socialists and Democrats) 2009–; mem. Farmers Union of Võru Co.; Hon. Pres. Estonian Asscn of Equestrian Sports; Hon. mem. Estonian Grilling Union, Eesti Lihakasvatajate Selts, Eesti Nortalunike Ühing, Eesti Sporthobuste Kasvatajate Selts; Order of the Nat. Coat of Arms (Third Class) 2011; Friend of the Press, Estonian Newspaper Asscn 2008. *Address:* European Parliament, 60 rue Wiertz, 1047 Brussels, Belgium (office). *Telephone:* (2) 284-55-46 (office). *E-mail:* ivari.padar@europarl.europa.eu (office). *Website:* www.padar.ee.

PADGAONKAR, Dileep, PhD; Indian journalist; *Consulting Editor and Columnist, Times of India;* b. 1 May 1944, Pune; s. of Vasant Padgaonkar and Shakuntala Padgaonkar (née Kattakar); m. Latika Tawadey 1968; two s.; ed Fergusson Coll. Pune, Institut des Hautes Etudes Cinématographiques, Sorbonne, France; Paris Corresp., The Times of India 1968–73, Asst Ed. Bombay and Delhi 1973–78, Assoc. Ed. and Exec. Ed. The Times of India Group 1986–88, Ed. 1988–94, Dir (Corp.) and Exec. Man. Ed. 1998–2002, Consulting Ed. and Columnist 2002–; f. Asia Pacific Communication Assocs 1994; Information Chief for Asia and Pacific, UNESCO 1978–81; Deputy Dir Office of Public Information, Paris 1981–85, Acting Dir 1985–86, Acting Dir Communication Sector 1986; Presenter Question Time India,

BBC World; Chevalier, Legion d'honneur 2001. *Television:* presenter, BBC World's Question Time India panel discussion programme. *Publications include:* When Bombay Burned (ed.) 1993, Under Her Spell: Roberto Rossellini in India 2008. *Leisure interests:* reading, classical music, contemporary art, cooking. *Address:* The Times of India, Times House, 7 Bahadur Shah Zafar Marg, New Delhi 110 002 (office); C-313, Defence Colony, New Delhi 110 024, India (home). *Telephone:* (11) 3312277 (office); (11) 4697949 (home). *Fax:* (11) 3323346 (office). *Website:* www .timesofindia.com (office).

PADILLA, James J., MEconSc; American automobile industry executive (retd); b. 1947, Detroit; ed Univ. of Detroit; joined Ford Motor Co. as Quality Control Engineer 1966; held various man. positions in product eng and manufacturing including manufacturing operations man. for Ford Escort and Mercury Tracer, Ford Contour and Mercury Mystique, Ford Taurus and Mercury Sable car lines 1976–92, Dir of Eng and Manufacturing, Jaguar Cars 1992–94, Dir of performance luxury vehicle lines 1994–96, Pres. S American Operations 1996–98, Group Vice Pres. for Global Manufacturing 1999, for Quality 2001, Group Vice Pres. N America 2001–02, Pres. N American Operations 2002, then Exec. Vice Pres. and Pres. the Americas, COO and Chair. Automotive Operations 2004, Pres. and COO Ford Motor Co. 2004–06 (retd); mem. US Dept of Commerce Manufacturing Council; Fellow, Nat. Acad. of Eng; Ohtli Award (Mexico) 2004. *Address:* c/o Ford Motor Company, 1 American Road, Dearborn, MI 48126–2798, USA (office).

PADILLA ARANCIBIA, Gen. David; Bolivian army officer and fmr head of state; career officer with regional commands; Pres. of Bolivia and C-in-C of the Armed Forces 1978–79.

PADILLA DE LEÓN, Gen. Freddy; Colombian army officer and government official; b. 10 Oct. 1948, Montería, Córdoba; m. Miriam Hodges de Padilla; ed Escuela Militar de Cadetes Gen. José María Córdova, Pontificia Univ. Javeriana, Univ. de Chile; Prof. of Mil. Geography and Geopolitics, Academia de Guerra del Ejército de Chile 1999; joined Colombian army 1966, attained rank of Brig.-Gen. 1997, Maj.-Gen. 2001, Gen. 2004, Gen. (Four Stars) 2009; Jt Gen. Chief of Staff 2003–06, Commdr Gen. of Mil. Forces 2006–10, also Minister of Nat. Defence 2009–10; Gran Oficial de la Región de Honor 2008; numerous awards including Orden de Boyacá, Orden de la Democracia, Servicios Distinguidos en Orden Público. *Address:* c/o Ministry of National Defence, Carrera 54, No 26–25, Centro Administrativo Nacional (CAN), 2°, Bogotá, DC, Colombia.

PADMANABAN, Anandam, MA; Indian civil servant and writer; b. 14 Dec. 1928, Pinji, Ranipet, Tamil Nadu; m. Seetha Padmanaban 1961; two s. one d.; fmrly with Indian Admin. Service; Chief Sec. Govt of Tamil Nadu 1986–87, adviser to Gov. 1988–89; mem. Union Public Service Comm. 1989–93; Gov. of Mizoram 1998–2000; Indian Ed. Poet Int.; Pres. Authors' Guild of India; Vice-Pres. World Acad. of Arts and Culture, USA; Pres. World Poetry Soc. Intercontinental; Adviser and Patron Dr Ambedkar Acad., Chennai; Gov. Indian Council for Cultural Affairs; For the Sake of Honour Award by Rotarians 1988, Eminent Poet Award, Int. Acad., India, Nat. Integration Award 1994, Michael Madhusudan Award; Soka University Award of Highest Honour, Tokyo, Melbourne Poetry Australia Gold Medallion, Dr. Ambedkar Award, Dalit Sahitya Acad., New Delhi, Underprivileged Forum Award, New Delhi. *Publications include:* Rain Drops (poetry) 1986, Saint Nandanar 1986, Light a Candle 1987, Buddha 1987, Saint Chokhamela 1988, Untouchable's Journey 1991, My Dream 1992, Story of Eight Saint Reformers 1993, Cosmic Accident 1995, Dalits at the Cross-Roads: Their Struggle Past and Present (biographical sketches) 1996, My Days and Times 2001, Daisaku Ikeda 2002, Everest 2002, Indian Panorama 2003, Poet and Peace 2007. *Leisure interests:* freelance writing, social work. *Address:* c/o Ananda Illam 14, 9th Cross Street, Shastri Nagar, Chennai 600 020, India. *Telephone:* 24910865.

PADOAN, Pier Carlo; Italian economist, international organization executive, academic and government official; *Minister of Economy and Finance;* ed Univ. of Rome; has held various academic positions in Italian and foreign univs including at Univ. of Rome, College of Europe (Bruges), Université Libre de Bruxelles, Univ. of Urbino, Universidad de La Plata and Univ. of Tokyo; Italian Exec. Dir at IMF, Washington, DC, with competence also for Greece, Portugal, San Marino, Albania and Timor Leste, served as mem. Bd and chaired several Bd Cttees, was also in charge of European Coordination; Econ. Adviser to Prime Ministers Massimo D'Alema and Giuliano Amato, in charge of int. econ. policies 1998–2001; Pres. of Econs, Univ. La Sapienza, Rome and Dir Fondazione Italianieuropei (policy think-tank) 2001–07; Deputy Sec.-Gen. OECD 2007–13, in charge of relations with other int. orgs, also Chief Economist 2009; Minister of Economy and Finance 2014–. *Address:* Ministry of the Economy and Finance, Via XX Settembre 97, 00187 Rome, Italy (office). *Telephone:* (06) 476111 (office). *Fax:* (06) 5910993 (office). *E-mail:* portavoce@tesoro.it (office). *Website:* www.mef.gov.it (office).

PADVA, Genrikh Pavlovich; Russian lawyer; *Managing Partner, Padva & Partners;* b. 20 Feb. 1931, Moscow; s. of Pavel Padva and Eva Rappoport; ed Moscow Inst. of Law; Kalinin Pedagogical Inst.; mem. Kalinin Bar 1953, Presidium 1965–71, of Moscow Bar 1971–, of the Presidium 1986, Dir Research Inst. of Bar; one of founders of the USSR (now Russian) Union of Barristers, Deputy-Chair. of the Exec. Board 1990; Vice-Pres. of the Int. Asscn of Lawyers 1990, acted as a barrister on major political and economic trials in 1970s, was a lawyer for many dissidents, rendered legal advice to the families of Andrei Sakharov, singer Vladimir Vysotsky, Pavel Borodin; represented Mikhail Khodorkovsky in criminal proceedings; investigated some major econ. and criminal cases in late 1980s–1990s, a founder and Dir-Gen. of Russian-American Int. Lawyers Co.; Man. Partner Padva & Partners, Attorneys at Law; Honoured Barrister of Russian Fed., F.N. Plevako Gold Medal. *Publications:* articles in specialized journals and newspapers on legal problems. *Address:* Padva & Partners, Bolshoi Golovin 6, Moscow 107045, Russia (office). *Telephone:* (495) 737-43-03 (office). *Fax:* (495) 737-43-08 (office). *E-mail:* padva@col.ru (office). *Website:* www.padva_.ru (office).

PAE, Chong-yeul; South Korean electronics industry executive; began career as jr economist, Research Dept, Bank of Korea 1969–76; Asst Adviser on Econ. Policy, Office of Pres. of Repub. of Korea 1973–75; Man. Planning Dept, Samsung Corpn 1976–83, Pres. Samsung Pacific Int. Inc., LA, USA 1983, Pres. Samsung America Inc., NY 1983–87, Sr Exec. Man.-Dir Sales and Marketing, Semiconductor Div., Samsung Electronics Co. Ltd 1988–90, Vice-Pres., Office of Chair., Samsung Group 1991–93, Pres. and CEO Samsung Corpn Ltd 2001; Exec. Vice-Pres. Joongang Daily News 1994–98; Pres. and CEO Cheil Communications Inc. 1998–2001. *Address:* c/o Samsung Corporation, Samsung Plaza, 263 Seohyeon-dong, Bundang-gu, Songnam, Kyonggi 463-721, Republic of Korea.

PAEK, Ryong-chon; North Korean government official and central banker; *Governor, Central Bank of the DPRK;* b. 1962; s. of the late Paek Nam-sun (fmr Minister of Foreign Affairs); fmr Dept Dir, Cabinet Secr.; mem. N Korean del. to working-level talks on inter-Korean econ. co-operation, Seoul 2002, and inter-Korean Jt Summit, Gwangju 2006; Gov. Central Bank of DPRK 2011–; Alt. mem. Korean Workers' Party Cen. Cttee. *Address:* Office of the Governor, Central Bank of the DPRK, Munsudong, Seungri Street 58-1, Central District, Pyongyang, Democratic People's Republic of Korea (office). *Telephone:* (2) 3338196 (office). *Fax:* (2) 3814624 (office). *E-mail:* kcb_idkb@co.chesin.com (office).

PAENIU, Rt Hon Bikenibeu, BAgr, MSc; Tuvaluan politician and economist; b. 10 May 1956, Bikenibeu, Tarawa; m. Foketi Paeniu; two s. two d.; ed King George V School, Tarawa, Univ. of S Pacific, Suva and Univ. of Hawaii; worked in Agric. Div. Tuvalu; later Asst Economist, South Pacific Comm. Nouméa; returned to Tuvalu 1988; MP 1989–2006; Prime Minister of Tuvalu 1989–93, 1996–99; Minister for Finance and Econ. Planning and Industries –2006. *Address:* c/o Ministry of Finance, Economic Planning and Industries PMB, Vaiaku, Funafuti (office); Nukulaezae, Tuvalu (home).

PAES, Leander Adrian; Indian professional tennis player; b. 17 June 1973, Goa; s. of Vece Paes and Jennifer Paes; m. Rhea Pillai; one d.; ed Madras Christian Coll. Higher Secondary School, St Xavier's Coll., Kolkata; winner, Davis Cup (singles) 1993, 1994, 1995, 1997, 2007, (doubles) 1995, 1997, 1998, 2005, 2007, Atlanta Olympics (bronze medal) (men's singles) 1996, ATP Championships (men's singles), Newport 1998, Wimbledon and French Open Championships (men's doubles) 1999, Wimbledon (mixed doubles) 1999, French Open (men's doubles) 2001, Asian Games (gold medal), Busan 2002, Australian Open, Wimbledon (mixed doubles) 2003, US Open (men's doubles) 2006, Asian Games (two gold medals) (men's doubles, mixed doubles), Doha 2006, US Open (mixed doubles) 2008, French Open, US Open (men's doubles) 2009, 2013, US Open (mixed doubles runner-up) 2009, Australian Open (mixed doubles) 2010, Commonwealth Games (bronze medal) (men's doubles), New Delhi 2010; Dir Leander Sport Pvt. Ltd; Rajiv Gandhi Khel Ratna 1996–97, Arjuna Award 1998, Padma Shri 2001, Padma Bhushan 2014. *Address:* Leander Sport Private Limited, 4121/B, 19th A Main, 6th Cross, HAL II Stage Extension, Bangalore 560 038, India (office). *E-mail:* ara@leandersport.com (office). *Website:* www.leandersport.com (office).

PAET, Urmas, BA; Estonian journalist and politician; *Minister of Foreign Affairs;* b. 20 April 1974, Tallinn; m. Tiina Paet; two d.; ed Univ. of Tartu, Univ. of Oslo, Norway; ed., Chief Editorial Office for Int. News, Estonian Radio 1991–92, ed., News Editorial Office 1993–94; reporter, News Editorial Office, AS Postimees 1994–98, Sr Ed. and Political Journalist 1998–99; mem. and Adviser, Estonian Reform Party 1999–; Dist Elder, Nõmme (Dist of Tallinn) 1999–2003; Minister of Culture 2003–05, of Foreign Affairs 2005–. *Leisure interests:* cycling, skiing, theatre, cinema, literature. *Address:* Ministry of Foreign Affairs, Islandi Väljak 1, Tallinn 15049, Estonia (office). *Telephone:* 637-7092 (office). *Fax:* 637-7099 (office). *E-mail:* vminfo@vm.ee (office). *Website:* www.vm.ee (office).

PAGAN, Adrian Rodney, BEcons, PhD, FASSA, FES; Australian economist and academic; *Professor of Economics, University of Technology, Sydney;* b. 12 Jan. 1947, Mungindi, Qld; m.; two c.; ed Queensland Univ., Australian Nat. Univ.; Visiting Research Fellow, Princeton Univ., USA 1973; Lecturer, then Sr Lecturer, ANU, 1974–80, Sr Research Fellow 1980–83, Sr Fellow 1983–88, Adjunct Prof. 1989–90, Prof. of Econs, Research School of Social Sciences 1992–2006; Prof. of Econs, Univ. of Rochester, USA 1986–90, 1992–95, Wilson Prof. of Econs 1990–92; Prof. of Econs, Queensland Univ. of Tech. 2005–09; Prof. of Econs, Australian School of Business, Univ. of New South Wales –2009; Prof. of Econs, Univ. of Tech., Sydney 2009–; Visiting Prof., Inst. of Advanced Studies, Vienna, Austria 1982, Yale Univ., USA 1985, Johns Hopkins Univ., USA 1996, 2000–, UCLA, USA 1997; mem. Bd Reserve Bank of Australia 1995–2000; Professorial Assoc., Univ. of Melbourne 1996–99; Professorial Fellow, Nuffield Coll. and Visiting Prof. of Econs, Univ. of Oxford, UK 2000–02; numerous assoc. editorships and editorial bd memberships; Fellow, Centre of Operations Research and Econometrics 1977–78, Econometric Soc. 1985, Journal of Econometrics 1990; University of Queensland Scholarship, Esso Prize in Accounting, Brinds Prize in Econs, Univ. Medal (Queensland), Medallist Fellow and Socio-Econ. Systems Medal, Modelling and Simulation Soc. of Australia 1997, Distinguished Fellow Award, Econ. Soc. of Australia 1999, Centenary Medal 2003. *Publications include:* The Theory of Economic Policy (with A. J. Preston) 1982, The Effects of Inflation (co-ed. with P. K. Trivedi) 1983, Non-Parametric Econometrics (with A. Ullah) 1999; numerous journal articles on macro-econ. modelling and its uses in policy analysis and for the explanation of business cycles. *Address:* School of Finance and Economics, University of Technology, Sydney, 123 Broadway, Sydney, NSW 2007, Australia (office). *Telephone:* (2) 9514-7721 (office). *Fax:* (2) 9514-7722 (office). *E-mail:* adrian .pagan@uts.edu.au (office). *Website:* www.uts.edu.au (office).

PAGANI, Rémy; Swiss writer and politician; b. 21 April 1954, Geneva; m.; two c.; active in local politics 1974–87; Union Sec., Syndicat interprofessionnel de travailleuses et travailleurs (SIT) 1987–97; Perm. Sec., Syndicat des Services Publics (trade union) 1997–2007; Deputy, Geneva City Council 1997–2005; mem. Exec. Council, City of Geneva 2007–, Head of Building and Town Planning Dept, Mayor of Geneva 2009–10; mem. A gauche toute! coalition. *Publications:* Les beaux jours reviendront, Entre chien et loup, Confession d'un commissaire de police, Étrange balade. *Address:* c/o Office of the Mayor, Rue de l'Hôtel-de-Ville 4, Geneva, Switzerland (office). *Website:* remy-pagani.isuisse.com.

PAGBALHA, Geleg Namgyai; Chinese administrator; *Vice-Chairman of National Committee, 12th Chinese People's Political Consultative Congress;* b. 1940, Litang Co., Sichuan Prov.; was confirmed by the Qangdin Lamasery as 11th incarnation of a living Buddha 1942; Vice-Chair. Qamdo Prefectural People's Liberation Cttee, Tibet Autonomous Region 1950; Vice-Chair. Tibet Autonomous Regional Preparatory Cttee 1956, Vice-Chair. Religious Affairs Cttee, Chair. Ethnic Affairs Cttee; sent to do manual labour 1966–76; Vice-Chair. People's Govt of Tibet Autonomous Region 1979–83; Acting Chair., Tibet Autonomous Region People's Congress 1983–86; Vice-Chair. Tibetan Autonomous Region Cttee of

CPPCC and Vice Chair. Standing Cttee of Tibetan Autonomous Regional People's Congress 1983–88; Vice-Chair. 3rd CPPCC Nat. Cttee 1959–64, 4th CPPCC Nat. Cttee 1964–78, mem. Presidium 4th NPC 1975–78, Vice-Chair. 5th CPPCC Nat. Cttee 1978–83, mem. Presidium 5th NPC 1978–83, Exec. Chair. 6th CPPCC 1983–88, Vice-Chair. 7th CPPCC Nat. Cttee 1988–92, 10th CPPCC Nat. Cttee 2003–08, 11th CPPCC Nat. Cttee 2008–13, 12th CPPCC Nat. Cttee 2013–; Deputy, 2nd NPC 1959, 3rd NPC 1964, 4th NPC 1975, 5th NPC 1978, Vice-Chair. Standing Cttee 8th NPC 1993–98, 9th NPC 1998–2003; Chair. CPPCC, Tibetan Autonomous Region 1993–; Vice-Pres. Buddhist Asscn of China 1993–2002, Hon. Pres. 2002–; Pres. China Tibet Devt Foundation. *Address:* Standing Committee of National People's Congress, Beijing, People's Republic of China (office).

PAGE, Ashley, OBE; British classical dancer, choreographer and artistic director; b. 9 Aug. 1956, Rochester, Kent; s. of John H. Laverty and Sheila R. Medhurst; m. Nicola J. Roberts; one s. one d.; ed St Andrew's, Royal Ballet, Lower and Upper Schools; joined Royal Ballet Co. 1975, soloist 1980, Prin. 1984, House Choreographer; leading roles in classical and modern repertoire; cr. numerous roles for MacMillan, Ashton and other leading choreographers; Choreographer Royal Opera House 1984; with numerous cos in London, Europe; Artistic Dir Scottish Ballet 2002–(12); Frederick Ashton Choreographer Award 1982, Frederick Ashton Memorial Comm. Award 1990, Time Out Dance Award 1994, Olivier Award for Best New Dance Production 1995. *Productions include:* 19 works for the Royal Ballet, 2 for the Dutch Nat. Ballet, 3 for the Rambert Dance Co. and several for Dance Umbrella, West Australian Ballet and other cos . *Films:* (all dance) Savage Water (Channel 4) 1989, Soldat (BBC) 1990; (art films) Pull-Dance for the Camera 1998. *Leisure interests:* fine arts, driving, film, music, reading, theatre, travel, photography, family, friends. *Address:* Scottish Ballet, 261 West Princes Street, Glasgow, G4 9EE, England. *Telephone:* (141) 331-6263 (office). *Fax:* (141) 331-2629 (office). *E-mail:* ashley.page@scottishballet.co.uk (home).

PAGE, Bruce; British journalist; b. 1 Dec. 1936, London; s. of Roger Page and Amy B. Page; m. 1st Anne Gillison 1964 (divorced 1969); m. 2nd Anne L. Darnborough 1969; one s. one d.; ed Melbourne High School and Melbourne Univ., Australia; trained as journalist, Melbourne Herald 1956–60; Evening Standard, London 1960–62; Daily Herald, London 1962–64; various exec. posts, Sunday Times, London 1964–76; Assoc. Ed. Daily Express 1977; Ed. New Statesman 1978–82; Dir Direct Image Systems and Communications 1992–95; currently freelance journalist and author, openDemocracy; British Newspaper Hall of Fame 2005. *Publications include:* co-author: Philby, the Spy who Betrayed a Generation, An American Melodrama, Do You Sincerely Want to be Rich?, Destination Disaster, Ulster (contrib.), The Yom Kippur War, The British Press; author: The Murdoch Archipelago 2003. *Leisure interests:* reading, sailing, computers. *Address:* openDemocracy, The Print House, 18 Ashwin Street, London, E8 3DL, England (office). Beach House, Shingle Streeet, Shottisham, Suffolk, IP12 3BE, England (home). *Telephone:* (20) 7193-0676; (1394) 411427 (home). *E-mail:* info@opendemocracy.net; bruce@pages2.ads24.co.uk (office).

PAGE, Geneviève, (pseudonym of Geneviève Bonjean); French actress; b. 13 Dec. 1927, Paris; d. of Jacques Bonjean and Germaine Lipmann; m. Jean-Claude Bujard 1959; one s. one d.; ed Lycée Racine, Paris, Univ. of Paris (Sorbonne), Conservatoire nat. d'art dramatique, École du Louvre; prin. actress in the Comédie Française, the Jean-Louis Barrault company and TNP Jean Vilar; has appeared in many famous classical and tragic stage roles, including Les larmes amères de Petra von Kant (Critics' Prize for Best Actress 1980), La nuit des rois, L'aigle à deux têtes, Angelo, tyran de Padoue 1984, Perséphone 1988, Mère Courage 1988, Le balcon 1991, Paroles de poètes 1992, La peste 1992, La femme sur le lit 1994 (Colombe Prix, Plaisir du Théâtre Best Actress), Les grandes forêts 1997, 2009, Delicate Balance 1998, Le martyre de Saint Sébastien 2005; Chevalier du Mérite sportif, du Cèdre du Liban, Officier des Arts et des Lettres 2006, Officier de la Légion d'honneur 2013. *Films include:* Ce siècle a cinquante ans, Pas de pitié pour les femmes, Fanfan la tulipe, Lettre ouverte, Plaisirs de Paris, Nuits andalouses, L'étrange désir de M. Bard, Cherchez la femme, L'homme sans passé, Foreign Intrigue, The Silken Affair, Michael Strogoff, Un amour de poche, Song Without End, Le bal des adieux, El Cid, Les égarements, La joie et l'heure, L'honorable correspondence, Youngblood Hawke, Le majordome, Les corsaires, Trois chambres à Manhattan, Grand Prix, Belle de jour, Mayerling, A Talent for Loving, The Private Life of Sherlock Holmes, Les Gémeaux, Décembre, Buffet froid, Beyond Therapy 1987, Les bois noirs 1991, Lovers 1999, Last Night 1999, Eye of the Beholder 2000, Eye 2000, Rien que du bonheur 2002, Britannicus (as Agrippine) 2011. *Television includes:* La nuit des rois 1962 (Best Actress TV), Quatre Siècles de Théâtre français 2002), La chambre 1964, La chasse aux hommes 1976, Athalie 1980, Les gens ne sont pas forcément ignobles 1990, Mémoire en fuite 2001. *Music includes:* Jeanne au Boucher-Persephone, Le Martyre de St-Sebastien, Oedipus Rex, Histoire du Soldat. *Publications include:* Pour l'amour du Grec, Les Femmes et l'Amour. *Leisure interests:* ancient artefacts, skiing, tennis, riding, skin diving. *Address:* 52 rue de Vaugirard, 75006 Paris, France.

PAGE, Lawrence (Larry) Edward, BS, MS; American computer scientist, internet industry executive and entrepreneur; *CEO, Google Inc.;* b. 26 March 1973, Lansing, Mich.; s. of Dr Carl Victor Page and Gloria Page; m. Lucinda Southworth 2007; ed East Lansing High School, Univ. of Michigan, Stanford Univ.; co-f. (with Sergey Brin) Google Inc. 1998, Co-Pres. and CEO 1998–2001, Pres., Products 2001–11, CEO 2011–; mem. Nat. Advisory Cttee, Univ. of Michigan Coll. of Eng; mem. Nat. Acad. of Eng 2004; mem. Bd of Trustees, X PRIZE; Fellow, Marconi Foundation at Columbia Univ. 2004; Hon. MBA (IE Business School) 2003, Dr hc (Univ. of Michigan) 2009; named a World Econ. Forum Global Leader for Tomorrow 2002, Marconi Prize (with Sergey Brin) 2004, Economist Innovation Award (with Sergey Brin) 2005, named one of the World's Most Influential People by Time Magazine 2005, ranked No. 1 (with Sergey Brin) by PC World Magazine amongst the 50 Most Important People on the Web 2007, ranked (with Sergey Brin) by Forbes magazine amongst The World's Most Powerful People (jt fifth) 2009, (jt 22nd) 2010, (jt 30th) 2011, (jt 20th) 2012, (jt 17th) 2013. *Film:* Broken Arrows (exec. producer) 2009. *Address:* Google Inc., 1600 Amphitheatre Parkway, Mountain View, CA 94043, USA (office). *Telephone:* (650) 253-0000 (office). *Fax:* (650) 253-0001 (office). *Website:* www.google.com (office).

PAGE, Lyman Alexander, Jr, BS, PhD; American physicist, cosmologist and academic; *Henry DeWolf Smyth Professor of Physics and Chairman, Department of*

Physics, Princeton University; b. 24 Sept. 1957, San Francisco, Calif.; m. Lisa Olson; three s.; ed Bowdoin Coll., Massachusetts Inst. of Tech.; took a job operating a cosmic ray station in McMurdo Sound, Antarctica 1978, spent two months at South Pole helping to make solar observations; worked as painter, rigger and boat carpenter while sailing a 37-foot ketch along the east coast of the USA and around Caribbean 1980–82; currently Henry DeWolf Smyth Prof. of Physics, Princeton Univ., Chair. Dept of Physics; mem. NAS 2006; Fellow, American Acad. of Arts and Sciences 2004; NASA Grad. Student Researchers Program Fellowship 1987–89, Princeton Eng Council Teaching Award 1992, 1994, NSF NYI Award 1993, Research Corpn Cottrell Scholar 1994, David & Lucile Packard Fellowship 1994, Primakoff Lectureship 2003, Marc Aaronson Lectureship and Prize 2003, Philips Lectureship 2006, Shaw Prize in Astronomy (co-recipient) 2010. *Achievements include:* one of the original co-investigators for the Wilkinson Microwave Anisotropy Probe that measured the cosmic background radiation. *Publications:* numerous papers in professional journals. *Address:* Department of Physics, Princeton Univesity, 217 Jadwin Hall, Princeton, NJ 08544, USA (office). *Telephone:* (609) 258-5578 (office). *Fax:* (609) 258-6853 (office). *E-mail:* page@princeton.edu (office). *Website:* www.princeton.edu/physics (office); phy-page-imac.princeton.edu/~page (office).

PAGLIA, Camille, BA, MPhil, PhD; American academic and writer; *University Professor of Humanities and Media Studies, University of the Arts;* b. 2 April 1947, Endicott, NY; d. of Pasquale Paglia and Lydia Paglia; ed State Univ. of New York at Binghamton, Yale Univ.; Faculty mem., Bennington Coll. 1972–80; Visiting Lecturer, Wesleyan Univ. 1980, Yale Univ. 1980–84; Asst Prof., Philadelphia Coll. of Performing Arts (now Univ. of the Arts) 1984–87, Assoc. Prof. 1987–91, Prof. of Humanities 1991–2000; Univ. Prof. of Humanities and Media Studies 2000–; columnist, Salon.com 1995–2001, 2007–; Contributing Ed. Interview magazine 2001–. *Publications include:* Sexual Personae: Art and Decadence from Nefertiti to Emily Dickinson 1990, Sex, Art and American Culture: Essays 1992, Vamps and Tramps: New Essays 1994, Alfred Hitchcock's The Birds 1998, Break, Blow, Burn: Camille Paglia Reads Forty-Three of the World's Best Poems 2005, Glittering Images: A Journey Through Art from Egypt to Star Wars 2012. *Address:* University of the Arts, 320 South Broad Street, Philadelphia, PA 19102, USA (office). *Telephone:* (212) 421-1700 (agent) (office); (215) 717-6265 (office). *Fax:* (212) 980-3671 (agent). *Website:* www.uarts.edu (office).

PĄGOWSKI, Andrzej; Polish graphic designer; b. 19 April 1953, Warsaw; ed Faculty of Poster Design, Acad. of Fine Arts, Poznań; est. own graphic studio 1990–; illustrator of books, covers of compact discs; designer of posters, TV and film billboards, TV programme credits, satirical drawings; has designed over 1,000 posters since 1977, including Husband and Wife and series highlighting dangers of alcohol, tobacco and drug abuse; began co-operation with various magazines as their artistic dir 1986; Art Dir Polish edn of Playboy from 1992 for several years; works in numerous pvt. and public collections, including Metropolitan Museum, New York; Owner and Creative Dir KreacjaPro Co. 1989–; numerous awards include Silver Medal, Biennale Polish Poster 1983, 1993, First Prize, Int. Competition for the Best Film and TV Poster, Los Angeles 1980–1993, Silver Hugon, Golden and Silver Badge (twice), Int. Competition Film Poster, Chicago 1982–87, Annual Award of Hollywood Reporters for film posters 1986, Clio Poland Award 1993. *Address:* Andrzej Pągowski Studio P, ul. Balaton 8, 01-981 Warsaw (office); KreacjaPro, ul. Lektykarska 4c/3, 01-687 Warsaw, Poland. *Telephone:* (22) 8649293 (Studio) (office); (22) 8339303 (KreacjaPro) (office). *Fax:* (22) 8649290 (Studio) (office); (22) 8328655 (KreacjaPro) (office). *E-mail:* ap@kreacjapro.pl (office); biuro@kreacjapro.pl (office). *Website:* www.kreacjapro.pl (office); www.pagowski.pl.

PAHAD, Aziz Goolam Hoosein, MA; South African politician; b. 25 Dec. 1940, Schweizer-Reneke, Western Transvaal; s. of Goolam Hoosein Ismail Pahad and Amina Pahad; m. Sandra Pahad 1994; two s. one d.; ed Cen. Indian High School, Johannesburg, Univ. of Witwatersrand, Univ. Coll., London, and Univ. of Sussex, UK; in exile 1964–90; worked in London office of African Nat. Congress (ANC) from 1968, later mem. ANC Revolutionary Council until its dissolution in 1983; rep. of ANC Revolutionary Council in Angola and Zambia; mem. ANC Nat. Exec. Cttee 1985–; Deputy Head, ANC Dept of Int. Affairs 1991; mem. Nat. Peace Exec. Cttee 1991–92; mem. Sub-Council on Foreign Affairs of Transitional Exec. Council 1993–94; MP 1994–2008; Deputy Minister of Foreign Affairs 1994–2008. *Leisure interests:* listening to music, watching sport, reading. *Address:* c/o Ministry of International Relations and Co-operation, Union Bldgs, East Wing, 1 Government Ave, Arcadia, Pretoria 0002, South Africa.

PAHADIA, Jagannath, MA, LLB; Indian government official; *Governor of Haryana;* b. 15 Jan. 1932, Bhusawar, Bharatpur Dist; m. Smt. Shanti Devi Pahadia; two s. five d.; ed M.S.J. Coll., Bharatpur, Maharaja Coll., Jaipur and Law Coll., Rajasthan Univ.; mem. Lok Sabha (Parl.) for Bayana constituency (Indian Nat. Congress) 1957–77, 1980–84; mem. Rajya Sabha (upper house of parl.) 1965, mem. Congress Party Parl. Exec. Cttee and Sec. Parl. Congress Party 1967–68; Union (Nat.) Minister of Finance 1967–69, Deputy Minister of Food and Agric. 1970–71, of Supply 1971, of Communications 1973–76, of Labour 1976–77, Union Minister of State for Finance 1980; Chief Minister of Rajasthan 1980–81; Gov. of Bihar 1989–90, of Haryana 2009–; mem. Indian Nat. Congress party. *Address:* Office of the Governor, Raj Bhavan, Chandigarh, Haryana, India (office). *Telephone:* (172) 2740654 (office). *Fax:* (172) 2740557 (office). *E-mail:* governor@hry.nic.in (office).

PAHANG, HRH The Sultan of; Haji Ahmad Shah al-Musta'in Billah ibni al-Marhum Sultan Abu Bakar Ri'ayatuddin al-Mu'adzam Shah, DKP; Malaysian; b. 24 Oct. 1930, Istana Mangga Tunggal, Pekan; m. Tengku Hajjah Afzan binti Tengku Muhammad 1954; ed Malay Coll., Kuala Kangsar, Worcester Coll., Oxford and Univ. Coll., Exeter, UK; named Tengku Mahkota (Crown Prince) 1944; Capt. 4th Bn, Royal Malay Regt 1954; Commdr 12th Infantry Battalion of Territorial Army 1963–65, Lt-Col; mem. State Council 1955; Regent 1956, 1959, 1965; succeeded as Sultan 1974; Timbalan Yang di Pertuan Agong (Deputy Supreme Head of State of Malaysia) 1975–79, Yang di Pertuan Agong (Supreme Head of State) 1979–84, 1985; Constitutional Head of Int. Islamic Univ. 1988; Hon. DLitt (Malaya) 1988; Hon. LLD (Northrop, USA) 1993. *Address:* Istana Abu Bakar, Pekan, Pahang, Malaysia.

PAHLAVI, Farah Diba, fmr Empress of Iran; b. 14 Oct. 1938; d. of Sohrab and Farida Diba; m. HIM Shah Mohammed Reza Pahlavi 1959 (died 1980); two s. two d.; ed Jeanne d'Arc School and Razi School, Tehran and Ecole Spéciale d'Architecture, Paris; Foreign Assoc. mem. Fine Arts Acad., France 1974; fmr Patron, Farah Pahlavi Asscn (admin. of Social Educ. Asscn), Iran Cultural Foundation and 34 other educational, health and cultural orgs; left Iran 1979, living in Egypt 1980–. *E-mail:* fpahlavi@hotmail.com. *Website:* www.farahpahlavi.org.

PAHOR, Borut, BA; Slovenian politician and head of state; *President;* b. 2 Nov. 1963, Postojna; m. Tanja Pečar; one s.; ed Nova Gorica Grammar School, Faculty of Sociology, Political Sciences and Journalism, Univ. of Ljubljana; mem. League of Communists –1990; mem. United List of Social Democrats (renamed Social Democrats 2005) 1990–2012, Deputy Leader 1993–97, Leader 1997–2012; Deputy to Nat. Ass. 1992–2004, mem. Comms for EU Affairs and the Supervision of Intelligence and Security Services 1992–96, Cttee on Defence 1992–96, Vice-Pres. Cttee on International Relations 1996–97, Chair. Slovenian Del. to the Parl. Ass. of the Council of Europe 1996–97, mem. Constitutional Comm 1996–97, Exec. Cttee of Inter-Parl. Union 1996–97, Pres. Nat. Ass. 2000–04; mem. European Parl. (Socialist Group) 2004–08, Vice-Chair. of Del. to EU-Croatia Jt Parl. Cttee, mem. Cttee Budgetary Control, on Constitutional Affairs; Prime Minister 2008–Sept. 2011, *pro tempore* Prime Minister Sept. 2011–Feb. 2012; Ind. 2012–; Pres. of Slovenia 22 Dec. 2012–. *Leisure interest:* sport. *Address:* Office of the President, 1000 Ljubljana, Erjavčeva 17, Slovenia (office). *Telephone:* (1) 4781222 (office); (1) 4781357 (office). *E-mail:* gp.uprs@up-rs.si (office). *Website:* www.up-rs.si (office).

PAHR, Willibald P., DrIur; Austrian diplomatist and politician; *Chairman of the Advisory Board, International Centre for Migration Policy Development;* b. 5 June 1930, Vienna; m. Ingeborg Varga 1960; one s. one d.; ed Univ. of Vienna and Coll. of Europe, Bruges, Belgium; Asst in Inst. of Int. Law and Int. Relations, Univ. of Vienna 1952–55; served in Fed. Chancellery 1955–76, Head of Section 1968, Head of Dept 1973, Dir-Gen. 1975–76; Fed. Minister for Foreign Affairs 1976–83; Amb. to FRG 1983–85; Sec.-Gen. World Tourism Org. 1986–88; Special Commr for Refugees and Migration, Austrian Ministry of the Interior 1990–95; fmr Chair. Int. Centre for Migration Policy Devt (ICMPD), now Chair. Advisory Bd. *Publications:* Der österreichische Status der dauernden Neutralität 1967, several articles in Revue des Droits de l'Homme, numerous articles on current int. problems in various periodicals; co-ed. Grundrechte, die Rechtsprechung in Europa (journal). *Address:* ICMPD, Möllwaldplatz 4, 1040 Vienna, Austria. *E-mail:* Willibald.Pahr@icmpd.org.

PAIGE, Elaine, OBE; British singer and actress; b. (Elaine Bickerstaff), 5 March 1948, Barnet, England; d. of Eric Bickerstaff and Irene Bickerstaff; ed Aida Foster Stage school; Variety Club Award for Showbusiness Personality of the Year and Recording Artist of the Year 1986, BASCA Award 1993, Lifetime Achievement Award, Nat. Operatic and Dramatic Asscn 1999,. *Theatre:* West End, London appearances in Hair 1968, Jesus Christ Superstar 1973, Grease (played Sandy) 1973, Billy (played Rita) 1974, Evita (created role of Eva Perón) (Soc. of West End Theatre Award for Best Actress in a Musical 1978) 1978, Cats (created role of Grizabella) 1981, Abbacadabra (played Carabosse) 1983, Chess (played Florence) 1986, Anything Goes (played Reno Sweeney) 1989, Piaf 1993–94, Sunset Boulevard (played Norma Desmond) 1995–96, The Misanthrope (played Célimène) 1998, The King and I (played Anna) 2000, The Drowsy Chaperone (Novello Theatre, London) 2007. *Recordings include:* albums: Sitting Pretty 1978, Elaine Paige 1981, Stages 1983, Cinema 1984, Love Hurts 1985, Christmas 1986, Memories: The Best Of Elaine Paige 1987, The Queen Album 1988, Elaine Paige: The Collection 1990, Love Can Do That 1991, An Evening With Elaine Paige 1991, Elaine Paige And Barbara Dickson 'Together' 1992, Romance And The Stage 1993, Piaf 1994, Encore 1995, Performance 1996, From A Distance 1997, On Reflection 1998, Centre Stage: The Best of Elaine Paige 2004, Essential Musicals 2006, Elaine Paige and Friends 2010; contributions to soundtrack recordings, including Nine, Anything Goes, Chess, Cats, Evita, Billy, The King And I; appears on: Tim Rice Collection: Stage and Screen Classics 1996, Christmas with the Stars Vol. 2 1999. *Leisure interests:* antiques, gardening, skiing, tennis. *Address:* c/o Nick Fiveash, The Works PR, 11 Marshalsea Road, London, SE1 1EN, England (office). *Telephone:* (20) 7940-4686 (office). *E-mail:* nick@theworkspr.com (office). *Website:* www.theworkspr.com (office); www.elainepaige.com.

PAIGE, Roderick (Rod), PhD; American educational administrator and fmr government official; *Public Policy Scholar, Woodrow Wilson International Center for Education;* b. Monticello, Miss.; ed Jackson State Univ., Indiana Univ.; mem. Bd of Educ., Houston Ind. School Dist 1989, Pres. 1992; Supt of Schools 1994; Dean Coll. of Educ. Texas Southern Univ.; US Sec. of Educ. 2001–05; Public Policy Scholar, Woodrow Wilson Int. Center for Scholars 2005–; mem. Bd of Trustees Thomas B. Fordham Foundation 2005–; mem. Houston Job Training Partnership Council; Community Advisory Bd of Texas Commerce Bank, NAACP; consultant, Greater New Orleans Educ. Foundation; Sec.-Treas. Council of the Great City Schools; Richard R. Green Award 1998, Outstanding Urban Educator Award 1999, McGraw Prize in Educ. 2000, Supt of the Year Award 2000, 2001. *Publication:* The Black-White Achievement Gap (with Elaine Witty) 2010. *Address:* Woodrow Wilson International Center for Scholars, Ronald Reagan Building and International Trade Center, One Woodrow Wilson Plaza, 1300 Pennsylvania Avenue, NW, Washington, DC 20004-3027, USA (office). *Telephone:* (202) 691-4000 (office). *Website:* wwics.si.edu (office).

PAIHAMA, Gen. Kundi; Angolan politician and army general; *Minister of Former Combatants and War Veterans;* b. 1958; with Angolan armed forces, also seconded to the Portuguese army; fmr Councillor of Benguela; fmr Minister of the Interior; Gov. of Huíla Prov. 1992–99, also of the City of Luanda; Minister of State Security 1998; elected to Congress (MPLA) 1998; Minister of Nat. Defence 1999–2010, Former Combatants and War Veterans 2010–. *Address:* Ministry of Former Combatants and War Veterans Av. Comandante Gika 2, CP 3828, Luanda, Angola (office). *Telephone:* 222321648 (office). *Fax:* 222320876 (office). *E-mail:* geral@macvg.gov.ao (office). *Website:* www.macvg.gov.ao (office).

PAIK, Kun-woo; South Korean pianist; b. 10 March 1946; ed Juilliard School, New York and in London and Italy; interpreter of piano works of Ravel, Liszt, Scriabin and Prokofiev; has played with orchestras throughout N America and

Europe, notably Indianapolis Symphony, Rotterdam Philharmonic, Royal Philharmonic, London Symphony, BBC Symphony (soloist, Last Night of the Proms 1987), Orchestre Nat. de France, Polish Radio Nat. Symphony; lives in Paris; recitals at all maj. European music festivals; three Diapason d'Or awards. *E-mail:* kw@kunwoopaik.com (office). *Website:* www.kunwoopaik.com.

PAIN, Emil Abramovich, PhD; Russian sociologist; *Director-General, Center of Ethnopolitical and Regional Studies (CEPRS);* b. 6 Dec. 1948, Kiev; m.; one s.; ed Voronezh State Univ., Moscow State Univ.; researcher on problems of regional sociology and ethnology, problems of nat. conflicts, Voronezh State Univ. and Inst. of Ethnography USSR (now Russian) Acad. of Sciences 1974–91; during perestroika was expert of Deputies' Comm. on Deported Peoples and Problems of Crimea Tartars 1989–91; Chief Adviser Int. Asscn of Foreign Policy 1991–92; Dir-Gen. Cen. Ethnopolitical and Regional Studies (CEPRS) 1993–; mem. Pres.'s Council 1993–97; mem. Expert-Analytical Dept of Pres. of Russia 1994–98; Adviser to Pres. 1996–99; Prof. Inst. of Int. Relations 1992–99, Moscow Univ. 1999–, Inst. of Sociology, Russian Acad. of Sciences; fmr Galina Starovoitova Fellow, Kennan Inst. for Advanced Russian Studies. *Publications:* Russia between the Nation and Empire 2004; numerous articles on relations between nations, prevention of social conflicts, sociology and ethnology. *Address:* CEPRS, Krzhizhanovskogo str. 24/35 Korp. 5, Suite 522, 117259 Moscow, Russia. *Telephone:* (495) 128-56-51 (office); (495) 431-56-07 (home). *Fax:* (495) 128-56-51 (office); (495) 431-56-07 (home).

PAISLEY, Baron Bannside (Life Peer), cr. 2010, of North Antrim in the County of Antrim; **Ian Richard Kyle Paisley,** DD, FRGS; British politician; b. 6 April 1926; s. of Rev. J. Kyle Paisley and Isabella Paisley; m. Eileen E Cassells 1956; two s. (twins) three d.; ed Ballymena Model School, Ballymena Tech. High School and S Wales Bible Coll. and Reformed Presbyterian Theological Coll., Belfast; ordained 1946; Minister, Martyrs Memorial Free Presbyterian Church 1946–; Moderator, Free Presbyterian Church of Ulster 1951–2008; f. The Protestant Telegraph 1966; MP (Democratic Unionist) 1974–2010 (Protestant Unionist 1970–74) resgnd seat Dec. 1985 in protest against Anglo-Irish Agreement; re-elected Jan. 1986; MP (Protestant Unionist) for Bannside, Co. Antrim, Parl. of Northern Ireland (Stormont) 1970–72, Leader of the Opposition 1972, Chair. Public Accounts Cttee 1972; mem. NI Ass. 1973–74, elected to Second NI Ass. 1982; MEP 1979–2004; MP for Antrim N, NI Ass. 1998–2000; First Minister of NI Ass. 2007–08; mem. Constitutional Convention 1975–76; Leader (co-founder) of Democratic Unionist Party 1972–2008; Chair. Agric. Cttee and Cttee of Privileges 1983; Pres. Whitefield Coll. of the Bible, Laurencetown, Co. Down 1979–; Co-Chair. World Congress of Fundamentalists 1978; mem. Political Cttee European Parl., NI Ass. 1998–2004; mem. Int. Cultural Soc. of Korea 1977. *Publications include:* History of the 1859 Revival 1959, Christian Foundations 1960, Ravenhill Pulpit Vol. I 1966, Vol. II 1967, Exposition of the Epistle to the Romans 1968, Billy Graham and the Church of Rome 1970, The Massacre of Saint Bartholomew 1972, Paisley, the Man and his Message 1976, America's Debt to Ulster 1976, Ulster – The Facts 1981 (jtly), No Pope Here 1982, Dr. Kidd 1982, Those Flaming Tennents 1983, Crown Rights of Jesus Christ 1985, Be Sure: 7 Rules for Public Speaking 1986, Paisley's Pocket Preacher 1986, Jonathan Edwards, The Theologian of Revival 1987, Union with Rome 1989, The Soul of the Question 1990, The Revised English Bible: An Exposure 1990, What a Friend We Have in Jesus 1994, Understanding Events in Northern Ireland: An Introduction for Americans 1995, My Plea for the Old Sword 1997, The Rent Veils at Calvary 1997, A Text a Day Keeps the Devil Away 1997.

PAJAZITI, Zenun; Kosovo politician; b. 12 Sept. 1966, Gjilan; m.; two s. one d.; ed Tech. Faculty, Univ. of Prishtina, Prishtina School of Politics, completed Int. Visitor Leadership Programme course on Accountability and Ethics in Govt and Business, sponsored by US Dept of State/US Office, Prishtina; served with Emergency Cttee of Kosovo in Prishtina with responsibility for displaced persons; worked as Programme Devt Co-ordinator with Int. Medical Corps 1999–2000; mem. Advisory Bd for Kosovo Action Together 2000–, Exec. Dir 2005–08; Jt Head, Dept of Sports within Jt Interim Admin. Structure (highest level advisory body to UN Interim Admin Mission in Kosovo—UNMIK) March–Nov. 2000, Head Nov. 2000–04; entered Govt of Kosovo 2004, served in Office of the Prime Minister as Head of Govt Liaison Office with UNMIK and Special Rep. of Sec.-Gen. and Co-ordinator for Standards; consultant, Public Administration International 2005–07, engaged in Support for European Integration and Standards Process (UK Dept for Int. Devt-funded project); Minister of Internal Affairs 2008–10; mem. Partia Demokratike e Kosovës (Democratic Party of Kosovo); Pres. Bd of Volleyball Fed. of Kosovo; Vice-Pres. Olympic Cttee of Kosovo; has participated in int. seminars in Albania, Italy, Turkey and other countries. *Address:* c/o Ministry of Internal Affairs, 10000 Prishtina, Bulevardi Nënë Terezë p.n. Objekti i Qeverisë, kati IX, Kosovo (office).

PAK, Gil-yon; North Korean diplomatist; b. 1943; m.; three c.; ed Univ. of Int. Relations; joined Ministry of Foreign Affairs 1964, served as Officer, Consul in Singapore and Myanmar, Section Chief, Deputy Dir, Dir of Ministry 1978–1983, Vice-Minister 1983–84, 1996–; Perm. Rep. to UN, New York 1984–96, 2001–08; Order of Kim Il Sung 1992. *Address:* c/o Ministry of Foreign Affairs, Pyongyang, Democratic People's Republic of Korea (office).

PAK, Pong-ju; North Korean government official; *Premier;* b. 23 Oct. 1939; Vice-Dir Party Light Industry Dept 1992–98, 2010–12, Dir 2012; Dir Chemical Industry 1998–2003; Premier of Democratic People's Repub. of Korea 2003–07, 2013–. *Address:* Office of the Premier, Pyongyang, Democratic People's Republic of Korea (office).

PAK, Se Ri; South Korean golfer; b. 28 Sept. 1977, Daejeon, Repub. of Korea; won 30 tournaments in Repub. of Korea as amateur; turned professional 1996; moved to USA 1997; became youngest player to capture four major tournments; 22 other Ladies Professional Golf Asscn (LPGA) victories; finished second in LPGA prize money 1998, 2001–2003; first woman in 58 years to make cut in men's golf tournament, SBS Super Tournament on Korean tour (finished tenth overall); Rolex Rookie of the Year 1998, Golf Writers Asscn of America Player of the Year 1998, Repub. of Korea Order of Merit 1998, Vare Trophy 2003, LPGA Heather Farr Award 2006, inducted into World Golf Hall of Fame 2007. *Leisure interests:* playing video games, watching television, shopping. *Address:* c/o IMG Golf Client Management, 1360 East 9th Street, Suite 100, Cleveland, OH 44114-1730, USA.

PAK, Su-gil; North Korean politician; *Vice-Premier and Minister of Finance;* mem. Korean Workers' Party, fmr Chair. North Hamgyong Prov. People's Cttee; Vice-Premier and Minister of Finance 2009–. *Address:* Ministry of Finance, Pyongyang, Democratic People's Republic of Korea (office).

PAK, Ui-chun; North Korean diplomatist and government official; b. 1932; began diplomatic career with posting at Embassy in Cameroon 1972; fmr Amb. to Algeria, Syria and Lebanon; Amb. to Russian Fed. 1998–2006; Minister of Foreign Affairs 2007–14. *Address:* c/o Ministry of Foreign Affairs, Pyongyang, Democratic People's Republic of Korea (office).

PAKENHAM, Hon. Sir Michael, Kt, KBE, CMG, MA; British consultant and fmr diplomatist; *Senior Adviser, Access Industries;* b. 3 Nov. 1943, Oxford; s. of the late Earl of Longford and Elizabeth Pakenham, Countess of Longford; brother of Antonia Fraser (q.v.); m. Mimi Doak; two d.; ed Ampleforth Coll., N Yorks., Trinity Coll. Cambridge, Rice Univ., Tex., USA; joined FCO 1965, served in Warsaw, New Delhi, Paris, Washington, DC; seconded to Cabinet Office 1971–74; Counsellor British Representation to EU 1987–91; Amb. to Luxembourg 1991–94; Deputy Sec. to Cabinet, Chair. Jt Intelligence Cttee and Intelligence Co-ordinator 1997–2000; Amb. to Poland 2000–03; Sr Adviser Access Industries 2004–, Signet Asset Management 2004–06, Droege & Co. (Dusseldorf) 2006–08; European Security Project Consultant Thales International 2004–06; Deputy Chair. King's Coll. London Council 2005–; Dir (non-exec.) Westminster Group 2008–. *Leisure interests:* golf, tennis, museums, military history. *Address:* Cope House, 15B Kensington Palace Gardens, London, W8 4QG, England (office). *Telephone:* (20) 7908-9966 (office). *E-mail:* mpakenham@accind.co.uk (office). *Website:* www .accessindustries.com (office).

PAKSAS, Rolandas; Lithuanian politician, engineer and fmr head of state; *Chairman, Order and Justice Party;* b. 10 June 1956, Telšiai; s. of Feliksas Paksas and Elena Paksienė; m. Laima Paksienė; one s. one d.; ed Žemaitės Secondary School, Telšiai, Vilnius Inst. of Civil Eng, Leningrad Inst. of Civil Aviation; flight instructor –1984; Chair. Vilnius Darius ir Girenas Aero Club, Aviation Dept, Voluntary Nat. Defence Service 1985–92; Pres. Construction Co. Restako 1992–97; elected to Vilnius City Council, Mayor of Vilnius 1997–99, 2000, elected to Vilnius City Council 2007–09; Prime Minister of Lithuania 1999–2000 (resgnd), 2000–01; Adviser Pres. of Lithuania and Plenipotentiary of Pres. for Special Assignments 1999–2000; elected Chair. newly founded Liberal Democratic Party 2002– (later renamed Order and Justice Party); Pres. of Lithuania 2003–04, charged with violating the constitution and his oath of office March 2004, impeached April 2004; fmr Chair. Lithuanian Liberal Union; mem. European Parl. 2009–, Vice-Chair. Europe of Freedom and Democracy political group. *Leisure interest:* aviation. *Address:* Order and Justice Party, Gedimino Ave. 10/1, Vilnius 01103 (office). *Telephone:* (5) 269-1618 (home). *Fax:* (5) 269-1618 (office). *E-mail:* tt@tvarka.lt (office). *Website:* www.tvarka.lt (office).

PÁL, László; Hungarian electrical engineer and politician; b. 5 Sept. 1942, Budapest; m.; two c.; ed Inst. of Energetics, Moscow, Political Acad., Budapest; Research Inst. for Electrical Eng 1966–69; mem. Nat. Cttee for Technological Devt 1969–89; State Sec. Ministry of Industry 1989–90; mem. Parl. 1990–97; Minister for Industry and Trade 1994–95; Dir and Head of Power Machinery Production, Ganz Holding Rt. –2002; fmr Chair. MOL Rt. (Hungarian Oil and Gas Co.); CEO Magyar Villamos Müvek Reszvenytarsag (MVM—nat. electricity co.) 2002–11; mem. several MTESZ (Fed. of Tech. and Scientific Socs) and GTTSZ (Fed. of Econ. and Scientific Socs) asscns; mem. Energetic Cttee of Hungarian Acad. of Sciences, AGORA Asscn, Bd AISEC Hungary; Pro Inventore Prize, Borbála Prize, Lóránd Eötvös Award 1986, János Neumann Award 1988. *Address:* c/o Magyar Villamos Muvek Zrt., Szentendrei út 207–209, 1031 Budapest, Hungary. *E-mail:* info@mvm .hu.

PÁL, Lénárd; Hungarian physicist; *Research Professor Emeritus, Centre for Energy Research, Hungarian Academy of Sciences;* b. 7 Nov. 1925, Gyoma; s. of Imre Pál and Erzsébet Varga; m. Angela Danóci 1963; one d.; ed Budapest and Moscow Univs; Dept Head, Cen. Research Inst. for Physics, Budapest 1953–56, Deputy Dir 1956–69, Dir 1970–74, Dir-Gen. 1974–78; Prof. of Nuclear Physics, Eötvös Lóránd Univ., Budapest 1961–77, 1989–98; Pres. State Office for Tech. Devt 1978–80, 1984–85, Nat. Atomic Energy Comm. 1978–80, 1984–85; mem. Science Policy Cttee, Council of Ministers 1978–85; Sec. Cen. Cttee Hungarian Socialist Workers' Party 1985–88; currently Research Prof. Emer., Centre for Energy Research, Hungarian Acad. of Sciences; fmr Vice-Pres. IUPAP; Corresp. mem. Hungarian Acad. of Sciences 1961–73, mem. 1973, Gen. Sec. 1980–84, Pres. Intercosmos Council 1980–84; Foreign mem. Acad. of Sciences of the USSR 1976, of GDR 1982, of Czechoslovakia 1983, Russian Acad. of Sciences 1996; mem. Leibniz Soc. eV 1994; Gold Medal, Order of Labour 1956, 1968, Red Banner Order of Labour (USSR) 1975, Red Banner of Work 1985; Kossuth Prize 1962, Memorial Medal 25th Anniversary of the Liberation 1970, Kurtchatov Memory Medal (USSR) 1970, Gold Medal of the Hungarian Acad. of Sciences 1975, Eötvös Lóránd Physical Soc. Medal 1976, Wigner's Award 2001. *Publications:* Science and Technical Development 1987, Science and Technology Policies in Finland and Hungary 1985, Foundation of Probability Calculus and Statistics 1995, Neutron Fluctuations, a Treatise on the Physics of Branching Processes; approx. 275 articles in Hungarian and foreign scientific journals. *Leisure interests:* hunting, angling.

PALA, Ano; Papua New Guinea politician; Parl. Clerk –2007; mem. Nat. Parl. for Rigo constituency 2007–; Parl. Sec. to Puka Temu (Deputy Prime Minister) –2010; Attorney-Gen. and Minister of Justice 2010, Minister for Foreign Affairs, Trade and Immigration 2011–12; mem. Nat. Alliance Party. *Address:* c/o Department of Foreign Affairs, Trade and Immigration, POB 422, Waigani 131, Port Moresby, NCD, Papua New Guinea.

PALACIO, Alfredo, MD; Ecuadorean politician, cardiologist and fmr head of state; b. 22 Jan. 1939, Guayaquil; m. Maria Beatriz Paret; four s.; ed Colegio San José La Salle, Universidad de Guayaquil; residency at Case Western Reserve Univ., USA, worked at various hosps in USA 1969–74, including Mount Sinai Hosp., Cleveland, OH 1969–71, Veterans Admin. Hosp., Missouri 1971–72, Barnes Hosp., Washington Univ. 1972–74; Dir Nat. Inst. of Cardiology 1980–; Prin. Prof. of Cardiology, Faculty of Medicine, Univ. of Guayaquil 1989–2003, Prof. of Public Health 2001–2003; Minister of Public Health 1994–96; Vice-Pres. of Ecuador

2003–05, Pres. 2005–07; fmr Regional Dir Ecuador Inst. of Social Security (IESS); Fellow, American Coll. of Cardiology, American Coll. of Chest Physicians, American Coll. of Physicians; mem. American Acad. of Sciences, Ecuador Acad. of Medicine, and numerous other medical socs; Dr hc (Johns Hopkins Univ.) 2007; Commdr, Al Mérito Atahualpha, Ministry of Nat. Defence 1995, Recognition of Merit, Ecuador Nat. Civil Defence 1996, Recognition of Merit, Gran Cruz, Pres. of Ecuador 1996; American Medical Asscn Award 1976, Eugenio Espejo Award, Quito Municipality 1982, Scientific Merit Award, Guayaquil Municipality 1982, 1987. *Publications include:* Atlas de Ecocardiografia Bidimensional 1981, Atlas of 2D Echocardiography 1983, Cardiopatía Isquémica (ed.) 1985, Estudio Guayaquil 1991, Hacia un Humanisco Científico 1997. *Address:* c/o Office of the President, Palacio Nacional, García Moreno 1043, Quito, Ecuador (office).

PALACIO DEL VALLE LERSUNDI, Ana; Spanish lawyer, politician and international organization official; *Elective Member, Consejo de Estado;* b. 22 Aug. 1948, Madrid; ed Complutense Univ., Madrid; early career as lawyer in pvt. practice, held numerous sr positions in Madrid Bar; MEP (PPE, PP) 1994–2002; Chair. Cttee on Legal Affairs and the Internal Market, European Parl. 1994–2002, Justice and Home Affairs Cttee 1994–2002, Conf. of Cttee Chairs 1994–2002; Minister of Foreign Affairs 2002–04; mem. Parl. 2002–06, Chair. Jt Parl. Cttee for European Affairs 2004–06; Sr Vice-Pres. and General Counsel, World Bank Group, Washington, DC 2006–08, also Sec.-Gen. Int. Centre for the Settlement of Investment Disputes; mem. Int. Advisory Bd, Council on Foreign Relations, New York; Elective mem., Consejo de Estado, Madrid 2012–; First Vice-Pres., later Pres.-elect, Council of Bars and Law Societies of the European Union, Brussels; Pres. Acad. of European Law; Trustee, Carnegie Corpn, New York; mem. Bd Council on Foreign Relations, Fundación para el Análisis y los Estudios Sociales, Fundacion for las Relaciones Internacionales y el Diálogo Exterior, CSIS Initiative for Renewed Transatlantic Partnership, Transatlantic Policy Network; mem. Bd of Govs Law Soc. of Madrid; Hon. mem. Bar of England and Wales (including the Inner Temple); Ramer Award for Diplomatic Excellence, American Jewish Cttee 2004. *Address:* Consejo de Estado, C/ Mayor 79, 28013, Madrid, (office); Palacio & Partners SC, Plaza de las Salesas, 3, 28004 Madrid, Spain. *Telephone:* (91) 5166240 (office). *Fax:* (91) 5166244 (office). *Website:* www.consejo-estado.es (office).

PALAITIS, Raimundas, BSc; Lithuanian politician; b. 23 Oct. 1957, Palanga; m. 1st (died 2004); two s. one d.; m. 2nd Vilija Venckutė-Palaitienė 2006; ed Palanga Secondary School (now Palanga Old Gymnasium), Vilnius Univ.; programmer, Palanga br. of Kaunas Inst. of Cardiology 1980–89; launched own business 1989; also employed at the Palanga Communications Unit and Municipality 1989; Founder and Dir JSC Klaipėdos vertybiniai popieriai 1997–2000; mem. Lithuanian Liberal Union 1994–2003, Liberal and Cen. Union 2003–; mem. Palanga City Municipality Bd 1995–2000, Mayor of Palanga April–Nov. 2000; mem. Seimas (Parl.) 2000–08; Minister of the Interior 2008–12 (resgnd). *Leisure interests:* music, sport. *Address:* Gedimino pr. 53, Vilnius, Lithuania. *Website:* www.palaitis.lt.

PALAU, Luis; American evangelist and writer; b. 27 Nov. 1934, Buenos Aires, Argentina; s. of Luis Palau Sr; m. Patricia Marilyn Scofield 1961; four s.; ed St Alban's Coll., Buenos Aires, Multnomah School of the Bible, Portland, Ore., USA; mem. staff Bank of London, Buenos Aires and Cordoba 1952–59; moved to USA 1960; worked as interpreter for Billy Graham 1962; began Spanish radio broadcasts as missionary in Colombia 1967; began evangelistic ministry as part of Overseas Crusades 1968; made crusade broadcasts to all Latin America 1975; named Pres. Overseas Crusades 1976; f. Luis Palau Evangelistic Assn 1978; first major crusade in USA, San Diego 1981; Dr hc (Talbot Theological Seminary) 1977, (Wheaton Coll.) 1985. *Publications:* Heart After God 1978, My Response 1985, Time To Stop Pretending 1985, So You Want To Grow 1986, Calling America and the Nations to Christ 1994; 26 books and booklets in Spanish; works have been transl. into 30 languages. *Leisure interest:* family. *Address:* Luis Palua Evangelistic Association, POB 50, Beaverton, OR 97207, USA (office). *Telephone:* (503) 614-1500 (office). *Fax:* (503) 614-1599 (office). *E-mail:* info@palau.org (office). *Website:* www.palau.org (office).

PALECKIS, Justas Vincas; Lithuanian diplomatist and politician; b. 1 Jan. 1942, Samara (Kuibyshev), Russia; s. of Justas Paleckis and Genovaite Paleckiene; m. Laima Paleckienė; two s. one d.; ed Univ. of Vilnius, Diplomatic Univ. of the Ministry of Foreign Affairs, USSR; contrib. Komjaunimo Tiesa (daily), Head of Dept 1960, 1963–66; Third Sec. USSR Embassy to Switzerland; Second, First Sec., Counsellor, USSR Embassy to GDR 1969–83; Deputy Dir, Dir of sector Lithuanian CP Cen. Cttee 1983–89; Sec., Ind. Lithuanian CP Cen. Cttee 1989–90; Deputy Chair. Foreign Affairs Cttee, Lithuanian Repub. Supreme Council (Parl.) 1990–92; Lecturer, Inst. of Journalism, Vilnius State Univ. 1990–93; Lecturer, Inst. of Int. Relations and Political Science, Vilnius State Univ. 1993–95; adviser on Foreign Affairs to Lithuanian Pres. 1993–96; rank of Amb. 1993–; Amb. to UK 1996–2001 (also accred to Portugal and Ireland 1997–2001); Deputy Minister of Foreign Affairs 2002–04; mem. European Parl. (Socialist Group) 2004–, Vice-Chair. Subcttee on Security and Defence, mem. Cttee on Foreign Affairs, Substitute mem. Cttee on the Environment, Public Health and Food Safety, Temporary Cttee on Climate Change, Del. to EU-Russia Parl. Cooperation Cttee, Del. to EU-Fmr Yugoslav Repub. of Macedonia Jt Parl. Cttee, Del. to EU-Bulgaria Jt Parl. Cttee; Kt, Royal Swedish Order of the Northern Star 1994, Lithuanian Independence Medal 2000, Commdr, Order of Merit (Lithuania) 2003. *Publications:* Swiss Pyramids 1974, At the Foot of Swiss Pyramids 1985, Life in a Triangle. Vilnius-Brussels-Strasbourg 2007. *Leisure interests:* reading, theatre, gardening, tennis, swimming. *Address:* European Parliament, Bâtiment Altiero Spinelli, ASP 13G158, 60 rue Wiertz, 1047 Brussels, Belgium (office); Europos Parlamento nario Justo Paleckio bíuras, Pylimo g. 12-10, 01118 Vilnius; K. Donelaicio 20-5, 2000 Vilnius, Lithuania (home). *Telephone:* (2) 284-79-21 (office); (5) 2635445 (home). *Fax:* (2) 284-99-21 (office). *E-mail:* justasvincas.paleckis@europarl.europa.eu (office); biuras@paleckis.lt (office). *Website:* www.europarl.europa.eu (office); www.paleckis.lt (office).

PALECZNY, Piotr; Polish pianist and academic; *Artistic Director, International Chopin Festival;* b. 10 May 1946, Rybnik; m.; one s.; ed State Higher School of Music, Warsaw (studied under Prof. Jan Ekier); f. master courses in music, Bordeaux, Amsterdam, Paris, Buenos Aires, Tokyo, Lugano, Warsaw; soloist with orchestras including Warsaw Nat. Philharmonic Orchestra, Polish Radio Nat.

Symphony Orchestra, Chicago Symphony, American Symphony, Royal Philharmonic, Concertgebouw, BBC London Orchestra, Yomiuri Nippon, Tonhalle Zürich, RAI Roma, Santa Cecilia, Mexico Nat., Buenos Aires Nat., Gewandhaus, Nat. Orchestra Madrid; has performed in major concert halls, including Carnegie Hall, Avery Fisher Hall and Alice Tully Hall, New York, Orchestra Hall, Chicago, Suntory Hall, Tokyo, Teatro Colon, Buenos Aires, Gewandhaus, Leipzig, Concertgebouw, Amsterdam, Royal Festival Hall, London; Artistic Dir, Int. Chopin Festival, Duszniki Zdrój 1993–; Prof. of Piano Performance, Frederick Chopin Acad. of Music, Warsaw; judge, int. music competitions in Warsaw, Paris, Santander, Tokyo, Hamamatsu, Prague, Taipei, Cleveland, London; judge Sendai Int. Music Competition, Japan 2010, Prix Amadèo de Piano 2011; Kt's Cross, Order of Polonia Restituta, Gold Cross of Merit; granted title of Prof. by Pres. of Poland 1998; winner, competitions in Sofia 1968, Munich 1969, Warsaw 1970, Pleven 1971, Bordeaux 1972, Grand Prix VIII Chopin Competition 1970. *Recordings include:* K. Szymanowski Concert Symphony No. 4, complete Ballads, Sonatas, and Concertos by Chopin, The Best of Fryderyk Chopin ('Fryderyk 1999' Award, Polish Phonographic Acad.), works by Paderewski, Szymanowski, Lutosławski. *Address:* International Chopin Festival, 57-340 Duszniki-Zdrój, Rynek 10, Poland (office). *Telephone:* (74) 8669280 (office). *E-mail:* chopin@festival.pl (office). *Website:* www.chopin.festival.pl (office).

PALESE, Peter, MSc, PhD; American microbiologist and academic; *Professor and Chairman, Department of Microbiology, Mount Sinai School of Medicine;* ed Univ. of Vienna, Austria; Postdoctoral Fellow, Roche Inst. of Molecular Biology 1970–71; apptd Asst Prof., Dept of Microbiology, Mount Sinai School of Medicine, New York 1971, currently Prof., Chair. Dept of Microbiology 1987–; Visiting Assoc. Prof., Dept of Microbiology and Immunology, UCLA School of Medicine 1976; Pres. Harvey Soc. 2003–04, American Soc. of Virology 2005–06; mem. NAS 2000, German Acad. of Sciences Leopoldina 2006; Corresp. mem. Austrian Acad. of Sciences 2002; Robert Koch Prize, Berlin 2006, Charles C. Shepard Science Award 2006, 2008, Wilhelm Exner Medal, Austrian Asscn for SME (Oesterreichischer Gewerbeverein—OGV) (jtly) 2007, European Virology Award 2010. *Achievements include:* built "the first genetic maps for influenza A, B and C viruses, identified the function of several viral genes, ...defined the mechanism of neuraminidase inhibitors (which are now FDA-approved antivirals)" and "pioneered the field of reverse genetics for negative-strand RNA viruses". *Publications:* numerous papers in professional journals on host-virus interactions, vaccines and antivirals, and virulence factors of RNA viruses. *Address:* Mount Sinai School of Medicine, 1 Gustave L. Levy Place, Box 1124, New York, NY 10029-6500 (office); Mount Sinai School of Medicine, Annenberg Building, Floor 16, Room 16-20, 1468 Madison Avenue, New York, NY 10029, USA (office). *Telephone:* (212) 241-7318 (office). *Fax:* (212) 722-3634 (office). *E-mail:* peter.palese@mssm.edu (office). *Website:* www.mssm.edu/research/labs/palese-laboratory (office).

PALIHOVICI, Liliana, BA, MA, MA; Moldovan politician; *Deputy Chairman (Deputy Speaker) of Parliament;* b. 26 Nov. 1971, Horodişte, Călărasi dist; m.; two c.; ed Moldovan State Univ., Centre for Grad. Studies, Acad. of Public Admin; Prof. of History, School Mircea Eliade 1993–95; specialist in youth issues, Youth Div., Dept of Youth, Ministry of Educ. 1995–2001, Head of Directorate, Youth and Sport Dept 2001–03; consultant, UNICEF project co-ordinating socio-econ. empowerment of youth 2004–07; World Bank Consultant, Co-ordinator of Youth Voices Group 2007–08; Grants Co-ordinator, Acad. of Educational Devt 2008; mem. Parl. 2009–, Chair. Social Protection, Health and Family Cttee, Deputy Chair. (Deputy Speaker) Parl. 2010–, Acting Chair. (Speaker) April–May 2013; mem. Initiative Group, Liberal Democratic Party 2007–09; mem. Alliance for European Integration 2009–. *Address:* Parlamentul Republicii Moldova, 2023 Chişinău, bd Ştefan cel Mare 105, Moldova (office). *Telephone:* (22) 23-33-52 (office). *Fax:* (22) 23-30-12 (office). *E-mail:* liliana.palihovici@parlament.md (office). *Website:* www.parlament.md (office).

PALIKOT, Janusz Marian, MA; Polish politician and business executive; *Leader, Your Movement;* b. 26 Oct. 1964, Biłgoraj; m. 1st Maria Nowińska (divorced); two s.; m. 2nd Monika Kubat; one s. one d.; ed John Paul II Catholic Univ. of Lublin, Warsaw Univ.; entrepreneur and fmr Co-owner Polmos Lublin SA (vodka business) and Ambra SA; mem. Civic Platform 2005–10; mem. Sejm (Parl.) for 6 – Lublin 2005–; Founder and Leader Movement of Support (later renamed Palikot's Movement) 2010–13; Your Movement (Twój Ruch) 2013–. *Publications:* Myśli o nowoczesnym biznesie with Krzysztof Obłój 2003, Płoną koty w Biłgoraju (autobiog.) 2007, Poletko Pana P. 2008, Pop-polityka 2009, Ja Palikot (interview by Cezary Michalski) 2010, Kulisy Platformy (interview by Anna Wojciechowska) 2011. *Address:* Your Movement (Twój Ruch), 00-029 Warsaw, ul. Nowy Świat 39, Poland (office). *Telephone:* 731-537500 (mobile). *E-mail:* biuro@twojruch.eu (office). *Website:* www.twojruch.eu (office); palikot.blog.onet.pl.

PALIN, Michael Edward, CBE, BA, FRGS; British actor, writer and traveller; b. 5 May 1943, Sheffield, Yorks., England; s. of the late Edward Palin and Mary Palin; m. Helen M. Gibbins 1966; two s. one d.; ed Birkdale School, Sheffield, Shrewsbury School, Brasenose Coll. Oxford; Pres. Transport 2000, Royal Geographical Soc. 2009–11; Vice-Pres. Michael Palin Centre for Stammering Children; Dr hc (Sheffield) 1992, (Queen's Univ., Belfast) 2000; Michael Balcon Award for outstanding contrib. to cinema (with Monty Python), BAFTA 1987, Travel Writer of the Year, British Book Awards 1993, Lifetime Achievement Award, British Comedy Awards 2002, BCA Illustrated Book of the Year Award 2002, BAFTA Special Award for Outstanding Contrib. to TV 2005, British Book Award for Outstanding Achievement 2009, BAFTA Fellowship Award 2013. *Musical theatre:* Monty Python's Spamalot 2006. *Films:* actor and co-author: And Now for Something Completely Different 1970, Monty Python and the Holy Grail 1974, Monty Python's Life of Brian 1979, Time Bandits 1980, Monty Python's The Meaning of Life 1982; actor, writer and co-producer: The Missionary 1982; actor, co-scriptwriter: American Friends 1991; actor: Jabberwocky 1976, A Private Function 1984, Brazil 1985, A Fish Called Wanda (Best Supporting Film Actor, BAFTA Award 1988) 1988, American Friends (also writer) 1991, The Wind in the Willows 1996, Fierce Creatures 1997, Not the Messiah (He's a Very Naughty Boy) 2010. *Television:* actor and writer: Monty Python's Flying Circus, BBC TV 1969–74, Ripping Yarns, BBC TV 1976–79; actor: Three Men in a Boat, BBC 1975, GBH (Channel 4 TV) 1991; writer: East of Ipswich, BBC TV 1987, Number 27, BBC TV, The Weekend (play for stage) 1994; TV series: contrib. to Great Railway

Journeys of the World, BBC TV 1980, 1993; presenter Around the World in 80 Days 1989, Pole to Pole 1992, Palin's Column 1994, Full Circle 1997, Michael Palin's Hemingway Adventure 1999, Sahara 2002, Himalaya with Michael Palin 2004, Michael Palin's New Europe 2007, Around the World in 20 Years 2008, Brazil with Michael Palin 2012; art documentaries (presenter): Palin on Redpath 1997, The Bright Side of Life 2000, The Ladies Who Loved Matisse 2003, Michael Palin and the Mystery of Hammershoi 2005. *Publications include:* Monty Python's Big Red Book 1970, Monty Python's Brand New Book 1973, Bert Fegg's Nasty Book for Boys and Girls (fiction) (with Terry Jones, illustrated by Martin Honeysett, Frank Bellamy *et al.*) 1974, Montypythonscrapbook 1979, Dr Fegg's Encyclopaedia of All World Knowledge 1984, Limericks 1985, Around the World in 80 Days 1989, Pole to Pole 1992, The Weekend (play) 1994, Hemingway's Chair (fiction) 1995, Full Circle 1997, Michael Palin's Hemingway Adventure 1999, Sahara 2002, The Pythons Autobiography (co-author) 2003, Himalaya (British Book Award for TV & Film Book of the Year 2005) 2004, Diaries 1969–1979: The Python Years 2006, New Europe 2007, Diaries 1980–88: Halfway to Hollywood – The Film Years 2009, The Truth (fiction) 2012, Brazil 2012; for children: Small Harry and the Toothache Pills 1981, Limericks or The Limerick Book 1985, Cyril and the House of Commons 1986, Cyril and the Dinner Party 1986, The Mirrorstone (with Alan Lee and Richard Seymour) 1986. *Leisure interests:* reading, running, railways. *Address:* c/o Mayday Management, 34 Tavistock Street, London, WC2E 7PB, England (office). *Telephone:* (20) 7497-1100 (office). *Fax:* (20) 7497-1133 (office). *Website:* www.palinstravels.co.uk.

PALIN, Sarah Louise, BS; American television host and fmr politician; b. 11 Feb. 1964, Sandpoint, Ida.; d. of Charles 'Chuck' Heath and Sarah 'Sally' Heath (née Sheeran); m. Todd Palin; two s. three d.; ed Wasilla High School, Hawaii Pacific Univ., North Idaho Coll., Univ. of Idaho, Matanuska-Susitna Coll.; family moved to Alaska while an infant; worked as sportscaster for KTUU-TV and KTVA-TV in Anchorage and as sports reporter for Mat-Su Valley Frontiersman; mem. Wasilla, Alaska City Council 1992–96; Mayor and Man. of Wasilla 1996–2002; unsuccessful cand. for Lt-Gov. of Alaska 2002; Chair. Alaska Oil and Gas Conservation Comm. 2003–04 (resgnd); fmr Pres. Alaska Conf. of Mayors; also served on Interstate Oil and Gas Compact Comm.; Gov. of Alaska (youngest gov. in state's history and first woman to hold the office) 2006–09 (resgnd); Republican nominee for Vice-Pres. of US 2008; political commentator, Fox News Channel 2010–Jan. 2013, June 2013–; mem. Bd Valley Hosp., Iditarod Parent-Teacher Asscn; fmr mem. American Man. Asscn, Alaska Outdoor Council, Alaska Miners Asscn, Alaska Resource Devt Council, Youth Court Steering Cttee, Salvation Army Bd; Lifetime mem. Nat. Rifle Asscn; fmr coach, Valley Youth Sports, ice hockey team man.; Hon. mem. Rotary; State Chamber 'Top 40 Under 40' Award, American Public Works Asscn Alaska Chapter Person of the Year, Distinguished Alumni Achievement Award, Alumni Asscn of North Idaho Coll. 2008, selected by TIME magazine as one of the 100 World's Most Influential People 2010, ranked by Forbes magazine amongst The World's 100 Most Powerful Women (16th) 2010, (34th) 2011. *Television:* host, Sarah Palin's Alaska 2010. *Publications include:* Going Rogue: An American Life (memoir) 2009, America by Heart 2010. *Leisure interests:* hunting, fishing, snow machining, running. *Address:* SarahPAC, PO Box 7711, Arlington, VA 22207, USA. *Website:* www.sarahpac.com.

PALIS, Jacob, PhD; Brazilian mathematician and academic; *Director Emeritus, Instituto de Matemática Pura e Aplicada (IMPA);* b. 15 March 1940, Uberaba; s. of Jacob Palis and Sames Palis; m.; three c.; ed Fed. Univ. of Rio de Janeiro, Univ. of California, Berkeley, USA; Prof., Instituto de Matemática Pura e Aplicada (IMPA), Rio de Janeiro 1971–, Dir 1993–2003, Dir Emer. 2003–; Visiting Prof. Univ. of Warwick, Inst. des Hautes Etudes Scientifiques, France, Univ. of Dijon, Ecole Polytechnique, Paris, City Univ. of New York, Steklov Inst., Moscow, ETH-Zurich, Univs of Nagoya, Tokyo, Kyoto, Toulouse, Rome, Paris-Orsay, Nice, Collège de France 1969–94; Chair. Int. Center for Theoretical Council (ICTP), Trieste, Italy 2003–05, mem. Scientific Cttee 1993–2005; mem. Exec. Bd Int. Math. Union 1982–91, Sec. 1991–99, Pres. 1999–2002; mem. Exec. Bd Int. Council for Science 1993–96, Vice-Pres. 1996–99; mem. Scientific Advisory Cttee, ETH, Zürich 1990–2006, Scientific and Strategic Council, Collège de France 2003–08; Founding Mem. Latin American and Caribean Math. Union 1995; Guggenheim Fellow 1993; mem. Brazilian Acad. of Sciences 1970 (Vice-Pres. 2004–07), Third World Acad. of Sciences (now Acad. of Sciences for the Developing World) 1991 (Sec.-Gen. 2004–06), Indian Acad. of Sciences 1995, Chilean Acad. of Sciences 1997, Mexican Acad. of Sciences 2001, US Nat. Acad. of Sciences 2002, French Acad. of Sciences 2002, European Acad. of Sciences 2004, Norwegian Acad. of Sciences 2005, Russian Acad. of Sciences 2006; Hon. mem. Peruvian Math. Soc.; Chevalier de la Légion d'honneur 2005; Dr hc (State Univ. of Rio de Janeiro) 1993, (Univ. of Chile) 1996, (Univ. of Warwick) 2000, (Univ. of Santiago de Chile) 2000, (Universidad de la Habana) 2001, (Universidad de Ingenieria, Peru) 2003; Prize Moinho Santista 1976, Math. Prize, Third World Acad. of Sciences 1988, Grand-Croix National Order of Scientific Merit, Brazil, 1994, Nat. Prize for Science and Tech., Brazil 1990, Inter-American Prize for Science, OAS 1995, Prize Mexico for Science and Technology 2001, Trieste Science Prize in Math. (co-winner with C.S. Seshadri) 2006; honoured for contribution to science by Brazil UNESCO in its 60th annniversary 2006. *Publications:* Geometric Theory of Dynamical Systems (with W. de Melo) 1982, Hyperbolicity and Sensitive-Chaotic Dynamics and Homoclinic Bifurcations, Fractal Dimensions and Infinitely Many Attractors (with F. Takens) 1994; numerous scientific papers. *Address:* Instituto Matemática Pura e Aplicada, Estrada Dona Castorina 110, Jardim Botânico, 22460-320 Rio de Janeiro, RJ, Brazil (office). *Telephone:* (21) 2529-5270 (office). *Fax:* (21) 512-4112 (office). *E-mail:* jpalis@impa.br (office). *Website:* w3.impa.br/~jpalis (office).

PALLANT, John, BA; British advertising executive; *European Creative Director, Saatchi & Saatchi;* b. 10 Aug. 1955; s. of Dennis Pallant and Doreen Pallant (née Hirst); ed St John's Coll., Southsea, Univ. of Reading; copywriter, Griffin & George Ltd 1977, Acroyd Westwood Assocs 1977, Collett Dickenson Pearce 1980, Gold Greenless Trott 1982, Boase Massimi Politt 1978, copywriter and creative group head 1983; copywriter, Saatchi & Saatchi 1988, Group Head 1991, Deputy Creative Dir and Exec. Bd Dir 1995, Creative Dir 1996–97, Jt Exec. Creative Dir 1997–98, Deputy Exec. Creative Dir 1999–; European Creative Dir 2003–; numerous awards. *Address:* Saatchi & Saatchi, 80 Charlotte Street, London, W1A 1AQ, England (office). *Telephone:* (20) 7636-5060 (office). *Fax:* (20) 7637-8489 (office). *Website:* www.saatchi.com (office).

PALLASMAA, Juhani Uolevi; Finnish architect and academic; *Principal, Juhani Pallasmaa Architects;* b. 14 Sept. 1936, Hämeenlinna; s. of Harry Alexander Pallasmaa and Aili Pallasmaa (née Kannisto); m. 1st 1957; two d.; m. 2nd Hannele Jäämeri 1980; one s. one d.; ed Helsinki Univ. of Tech.; Dir Exhbn Dept, Museum of Finnish Architecture, Helsinki 1968–72, 1974–83, Dir of Museum 1978–83; Rector Coll. of Crafts and Design, Helsinki 1970–72; Assoc. Prof., Haile Selassie Univ., Addis Ababa, Ethiopia 1972–74; Prin., Juhani Pallasmaa Architects, Helsinki 1983–; State Artist Prof., Helsinki 1983–88; Prof., Faculty of Architecture, Univ. of Tech., Helsinki 1991–97; Eero Saarinen Visiting Prof., Yale Univ., New Haven, Conn., USA 1993; Raymond E. Maritz Visiting Prof. of Architecture, Washington Univ., St Louis, Mo., USA 1999–2004; Thomas Jefferson Visiting Prof., Univ. of Virginia, USA 2002; Visiting Prof., Univ. of Florida, USA 2009; Plym Distinguished Prof., Univ. of Illinois, USA 2010; Walton Critic, Catholic Univ. of America, Washington, DC, USA 2011; participant in numerous exhbns of architecture and visual arts, designer numerous nat. and int. exhbns of architecture and visual arts, on town planning, architecture, design and visual arts; Dr hc (Helsinki Univ. of Industrial Arts) 1993, (Helsinki Univ. of Tech.) 1998, (Estonian Art Acad.) 2004; Kt, Order of White Rose 1988, Commdr, Order of the White Rose 1997; Finnish State Award for Architecture 1992, Helsinki City Culture Award 1993, Russian Fed. Architecture Award 1996, Fritz Schumacher Prize for Architecture, Germany 1997, Int. Union of Architects Jean Tschumi Prize for Architectural Criticism 1999, Finland Award 2000, Arnold W. Brunner Prize for Architecture, American Acad. of Arts and Letters 2009, Award for Merit, A. Kordelin Foundation 2010. *Publications include:* Language of Wood 1987, Animal Architecture 1995, The Melnikov House 1996, The Eyes of the Skin: Architecture and the Senses 1996, 2005, Alvar Aalto, Villa Mairea 1938–39 1998, Architecture of Image: Existential Space in Cinema 2001, Sensuous Minimalism 2002, Encounters: Architectural Essays 2005, The Thinking Hand: Existential and Embodied Wisdom in Architecture 2009, Conversaciones con Alvar Aalto 2010, Una arquitectura de la humildad 2010, The Embodied Image: Imagination and Imagery in Architecture 2011. *Leisure interests:* philosophy and psychology of artistic phenomena. *Address:* Tehtaankatu 13 B 29, 00140 Helsinki (office); Huvilakatu 14 A 8, 00150 Helsinki, Finland (home). *Telephone:* (9) 669740 (office); (9) 666625 (home). *Fax:* (9) 669741 (office). *E-mail:* jpallasmaa@gmail.com (office). *Website:* www.pallasmaa.fi (office).

PALMER, Andrew Clennel, PhD, FRS, FREng, FICE; British civil engineer and academic; b. 26 May 1938, Colchester; s. of Gerald Basil Coote Palmer and Muriel Gertrude Palmer (née Howes); m. Jane Rhiannon Evans 1963; one d.; ed Cambridge Univ., Brown Univ., USA; Lecturer, Univ. of Liverpool 1965–67, Univ. of Cambridge 1968–75; Chief Pipeline Engineer, R. J. Brown & Assocs 1975–79, Vice-Pres. Eng 1982–85; Man. Dir and Tech. Dir Andrew Palmer and Associates Ltd (consultancy) 1985–96; f. Bold Island Engineering Ltd (consultancy); Prof. of Civil Eng, Univ. Manchester Inst. of Science and Technology 1979–82; Research Prof. of Petroleum Eng, Univ. of Cambridge 1996–2005, Fellow, Churchill Coll., Cambridge 1996–; Keppel Chair. Prof., Nat. Univ. of Singapore 2006–; Dr hc (Clarkson Univ.) 2007. *Publications include:* Structural Mechanics 1976, Subsea Pipeline Engineering (with R. A. King) 2004; papers in learned journals. *Leisure interests:* travel, languages, glassblowing. *Address:* #12-06 Block C, 111 Clementi Road, Singapore 129792; Department of Civil and Environmental Engineering, National University of Singapore, 1 Engineering Drive 2, E1A 07-03, Singapore 117576, Singapore (office). *Telephone:* 65164601 (office). *E-mail:* ceepalme@nus.edu.sg (office). *Website:* andrewcpalmer.com; www.nus.edu.sg (office).

PALMER, Arnold Daniel; American professional golfer and business executive; b. 10 Sept. 1929, Latrobe, Pa; s. of Milfred J. Palmer and Doris Palmer; m. 1st Winifred Walzer 1954 (died 1999); two d.; m. 2nd Kathleen Gawthrop 2005; ed Wake Forest Univ.; served in US Coast Guard 1950–53; US Amateur Golf Champion 1954; professional golfer 1954–; winner of 92 professional titles, including British Open 1961, 1962, US Open 1960, US Masters 1958, 1960, 1962, 1964, Canadian PGA 1980, US Seniors Championship 1981; mem. US Ryder Cup team 1961, 1963, 1965, 1967, 1971, 1973, Capt. 1963, 1975; joined Seniors (Champions) Tour 1980, finished first ten times; Pres. Arnold Palmer Enterprises, one automobile agency, Latrobe Country Club, Bay Hill Club; Chair. Latrobe Area Hosp. Charitable Foundation; Hon. Nat. Chair. Nat. Foundation March of Dimes 1971–90; consultant, Golf Channel; mem. of numerous golf clubs including Royal and Ancient and Hon. Life mem. Carnoustie, Royal Birkdale, Royal Troon; designer of numerous golf courses; Hon. LLD (Wake Forest, Nat. Coll. of Educ.); Hon. DH (Thiel Coll.); Hon. DHL (Fla Southern Coll., St Vincent Coll., Allegheny Coll.); Hon. DPS (Washington and Jefferson Coll.); Athlete of Decade, Associated Press 1970; Sportsman of the Year, Sports Illustrated 1960; Hickok Belt, Professional Athlete of Year 1960. *Publications:* My Game and Yours 1965, Situation Golf 1970, Go for Broke 1973, Arnold Palmer's Best 54 Golf Holes 1977, Arnold Palmer's Complete Book of Putting 1986, Play Great Golf 1987, Arnold Palmer: A Personal Journey (with Thomas Hauser) 1994, A Golfer's Life (with James Dodson) 1999, Playing by the Rules 2002, Memories, Stories and Memorabilia 2004. *Leisure interests:* bridge, occasional hunting, fishing, aviation, business, clubmaking. *Address:* PO Box 52, Youngstown, PA 15696, USA. *Telephone:* (724) 537-7751 (office); (724) 537-7751 (home). *Fax:* (724) 537-9355 (office). *Website:* www.arnoldpalmer.com.

PALMER, Frank Robert, MA, DLitt, FBA; British academic; *Professor Emeritus of Linguistic Science, University of Reading;* b. 9 April 1922, Westerleigh, Glos., England; s. of George Samuel Palmer and Gertrude Lilian Palmer (née Newman); m. Jean Elisabeth Moore 1948; three s. two d.; ed Bristol Grammar School, New Coll., Oxford, Merton Coll., Oxford; Lecturer in Linguistics, SOAS, Univ. of London 1950–60; Prof. of Linguistics, Univ. Coll. of North Wales, Bangor 1960–65; Prof. of Linguistic Science, Univ. of Reading 1965–87, Dean, Faculty of Letters and Social Sciences 1969–72, Prof. Emer. 1987–; Vice-Pres., Philological Soc.; Chair. Linguistics Asscn (GB) 1965–68, Ed. Journal of Linguistics 1969–79, Linguistic Soc. of America Prof., Buffalo, USA 1971; Distinguished Visiting Prof., Univ. of Delaware, Newark, USA 1982; mem. Academia Europaea 1992; Hon. DLitt 1997. *Publications include:* The Morphology of the Tigre Noun 1962, A Linguistic Study of the English Verb 1965, Selected Papers of J. R. Firth (1951–58) (ed.) 1968, Prosodic Analysis (ed.) 1970, Grammar 1971, 1984, The English Verb 1974, 1987, Semantics 1976, 1981, Modality and the English Modals 1979, 1990, Mood and

Modality 1986, 2001, Studies in the History of Western Linguistics in Honour of R. H. Robins (co-ed.) 1986, Grammatical Roles and Relations 1994, Grammar and Meaning: Essays in Honour of Sir John Lyons (ed.) 1995, Modality in Contemporary English (co-ed.) 2003, English Modality in Perspective (co-ed.) 2004. *Leisure interests:* gardening, crosswords. *Address:* 'Whitethorns', Roundabout Lane, Winnersh, Wokingham, Berks., RG41 5AD, England (home). *Telephone:* (118) 978-6214 (home). *E-mail:* llspalmf@reading.ac.uk.

PALMER, Sir Geoff (Godfrey) Henry Oliver, Kt, OBE, PhD, DSc, FRSA, FRSM; British (b. Jamaican) academic; *Professor Emeritus of Brewing, Heriot-Watt University;* b. 1940, St Elizabeth, Jamaica; m.; three c.; ed Kingston Senior School, Univ. of Leicester, Heriot-Watt Univ.; researcher and later Sr Scientist, Brewing Research Foundation, British Brewing Soc., Surrey 1968–77; Lecturer, Heriot-Watt Univ. 1977–, Prof. of Brewing 1989–, now Emer.; Visiting Prof., Kyoto Univ., Japan; mem. Exec. and Hon. Pres. Edinburgh and Lothian Racial Equality Council; American Soc. of Brewing Chemists Award 1998, Good Citizen of Edinburgh Award 2002. *Publications:* The Enlightenment Abolished, Mr White and the Ravens; over 150 scientific papers. *Leisure interests:* reading, pop music, travel. *Address:* 23 Waulkmill Drive, Penicuik, EH26 8LA, Scotland. *E-mail:* geoff.palmer4@btinternet.com.

PALMER, Rt Hon. Sir Geoffrey Winston Russell, KCMG, QC, PC, AC, BA, LLB, JD; New Zealand lawyer, academic and fmr politician; b. 21 April 1942, Nelson; s. of Leonard R. Palmer and Jessie P. Palmer; m. Margaret E. Hinchcliff 1963; one s. one d.; ed Nelson Coll., Victoria Univ. of Wellington and Univ. of Chicago; solicitor, Wellington 1964–66; Lecturer in Political Science, Victoria Univ. 1968–69; Prof. of Law, Univ. of Iowa and Univ. of Virginia, USA 1969–73; Prof. of English and New Zealand Law, Victoria Univ. 1974–79, Prof. of Law 1991–95; Prin. Asst to Australian Nat. Comm. of Inquiry on Rehabilitation and Compensation 1973; Visiting Fellow, Wolfson Coll., Oxford 1978; MP for Christchurch Cen. 1979–90; Deputy Leader, New Zealand Labour Party 1983–89; Deputy Prime Minister, Minister of Justice and Attorney-Gen. 1984–89; Minister for the Environment 1987–90; Prime Minister of New Zealand 1989–90; Minister in Charge of New Zealand Security Intelligence; Prof. of Law, Victoria Univ. 1991–95; Prof. of Law, Univ. of Iowa 1991–95, Ida Beam Distinguished Visiting Prof. of Law 1991; Partner, Chen, Palmer & Partners, Wellington 1994–2005; Pres. New Zealand Law Comm. 2005–10; currently Barrister, Harbour Chambers; also currently Distinguished Fellow, Faculty of Law, Victoria Univ. of Wellington; Dr hc (Victoria Univ. of Wellington, Washington Univ. St Louis, Hofstra Univ.); UNEP Global 500 Laureate 1991. *Publications include:* Unbridled Power?: An Interpretation of New Zealand's Constitution and Government 1979, Compensation for Incapacity: A Study of Law and Social Change in Australia and New Zealand 1979, Environmental Politics: A Greenprint for New Zealand 1990, New Zealand's Constitution in Crisis 1992, Public Law in New Zealand (with Mai Chen) 1993, Environment: The International Challenge 1995, Bridled Power 1997. *Leisure interests:* cricket, golf, playing the trumpet, fishing. *Address:* Harbour Chambers, Level 10, Equinox House, 111 The Terrace, PO Box 10-242, Wellington (office); 63 Roxburgh Street, Mount Victoria, Wellington, New Zealand (home). *Telephone:* (4) 4992684 (office); (4) 8015185 (home). *Fax:* (4) 4992705 (office). *E-mail:* geoffrey.palmer@xtra.co.nz (office); cheryl@legalchambers.co.nz (office). *Website:* www.harbourchambers.co.nz (office).

PALMER OF CHILDS HILL, Baron (Life Peer), cr. 2011, of Childs Hill in the London Borough of Barnet; **Monroe Edward Palmer,** OBE, BA, FCA; British politician and chartered accountant; *Vice-President, Liberal Democrat Friends of Israel;* b. (Monroe Polikoff), 30 Nov. 1938, London, England; s. of the late Will Polikoff and Sybil Polikoff; m. Susette Palmer; three c.; ed Orange Hill Grammar School; Councillor for Childs Hill, London Borough of Barnet 1986–94, 1998–2014, Chair. Audit Cttee 2010–14; Jt Treas. Liberal Parl. Party and Liberal Party 1977–83, Treas., London Region, Liberal Democrats 2008–10; contested (Liberal) Hendon South in Gen. Election 1979, 1983, 1987, (Liberal Democrat) Hastings and Rye 1992, 1997; mem. (Liberal Democrat), House of Lords 2011–, Liberal Democrat Lead Spokesman on Defence; mem. Barnet's Area Environment Cttee, Chair. Barnet's Audit Cttee; Special Advisor to Nick Clegg on Middle East Affairs; fmr Chair. Barnet Citizens' Advice Bureau; fmr Dir, Barnet Homes; fmr Treas. Disablement Asscn of Barnet; Nat. Chair. Liberal Democrat Friends of Israel 1987–2010, Vice-Pres. 2010–. *Leisure interests:* horse riding, fishing, reading, politics. *Address:* House of Lords, Westminster, London, SW1A 0PW, England (office). *Telephone:* (20) 7219-2561 (office); (20) 8455-5140 (home). *Fax:* (20) 8209-3496 (home). *E-mail:* palmerm@parliament.uk (office). *Website:* www.parliament.uk/biographies/lords/lord-palmer-of-childs-hill/4214 (office).

PALMISANO, Samuel J.; American business executive; *Chairman, International Business Machines Corporation (IBM);* ed The Johns Hopkins Univ., Baltimore, Md; joined Int. Business Machines Corpn (IBM), Baltimore, Md 1973, subsequently Sr Man. Dir of Operations, IBM Japan, Pres., CEO ISSC (IBM subsidiary) 1993, mem. Worldwide Man. Council IBM 1994, in charge of IBM's strategic outsourcing business 1995, Sr Vice-Pres. and Group Exec. Enterprise Systems Group, IBM Global Services, Personal Systems Group, mem. Corp. Exec. Cttee 1998, Pres. and COO 2000–02, Pres. and CEO IBM Corpn 2002–11, Chair. 2003–; mem. Bd of Dirs Gannett Co. Inc.; Co-Chair. Council of Competitiveness' Nat. Innovation Initiative; mem. American Acad. of Arts and Sciences; Hon. Fellow, London Business School 2006; Hon. DHumLitt (Rensselaer Polytechnic Inst.) 2005; Distinguished Business Leadership Award, Atlantic Council 2009, inaugural Deming Cup, W. Edwards Deming Center for Quality, Productivity and Competitiveness at Columbia Business School 2010. *Address:* International Business Machines Corporation, 1 New Orchard Road, Armonk, NY 10504-1722, USA (office). *Telephone:* (914) 499-1900 (office). *Fax:* (914) 765-7382 (office). *E-mail:* info@ibm.com (office). *Website:* www.ibm.com (office).

PALOCCI, António Filho; Brazilian physician and politician; b. 4 Oct. 1960; s. of António Palocci and Antonia de Castro Palocci; m. Margareth Rose Silva Palocci; one s. two d.; ed Univ. of São Paulo; physician specializing in preventive medicine; mem. Partido dos Trabalhadores 1980–, Municipal Party Exec. 1988–89, Regional Party Directorate 1990–91 (Pres. 1997–99), Nat. Party Directorate 1996–97, Deputy Leader 2000; Pres. Rocha Lima Centre, Univ. of São Paulo 1981; Regional Dir DCE Alexandre Vanucci Leme, Univ. of São Paulo 1982; Pres. Ass. Resident Physicians of Ribeirão Pret 1984–85; Regional Dir SIMESP 1985; Pres. Regional

CUT Ribeirão Preto 1985; Regional Dir Sanitary Monitoring Service São Paulo 1986–88; Mayor of Ribeirão Preto 1993–96, 2001–02; Fed. Deputy 1999–2000, 2007–; Co-ordinator Govt transition team Oct.–Dec. 2002; Minister of Finance 2003–06; Pres. Conselho Monetário Nacional 2003–06; Cabinet Chief (Chief of Staff) Jan.–June 2011 (resgnd); UNICEF Child and Peace Prize 1995, Juscelino Kubitschek Prize, Serviço Brasileiro de Apoio às Micro e Pequenas Empresas–SEBRAE 1996. *Publications include:* Saúde do trabalhador (Health of the Worker) 1994, A reforma do Estado e os municípios: a experiência de Ribeirão Preto (State and City Reform: The Experience of Ribeirão Preto) 1996, Sobre Formigas e Cigarras (autobiography) 2007. *Address:* c/o Office of the Civilian Cabinet, Palácio do Planalto, 4° andar, Praça dos Três Poderes, 70150-900, Brasília, DF, Brazil.

PALOMÉROS, Gen. Jean-Paul; French air force officer and international organization official; *Supreme Allied Commander, Transformation, NATO;* b. 1953; m. to Agnes Paloméros; five c.; ed Royal Air Force Staff Coll., UK; Commdr SPA 124 Jeanne d'arc squadron on Mirage F1, USA, 30th Fighter Squadron in Reims 1990, Cazaux Air Base 1996–98, Head 2/12 Picardy squadron, Epervier operation, Chad 1987, Deputy Commdr Air Force, Vicenza, Italy 1993, Head, Studies and Strategic Plans Dept, Air Force staff 1998, Chair. Capability Devt Cttee, Jt Staff 2002, Deputy Chief of Staff, Air Force 2005–09, Chief of Staff, Air Force 2009–12, Supreme Allied Commdr Transformation, NATO 2012–; apptd Gen.-Sec. Coherence Officers Jt Staff Coll. 2001; attained rank of Brig.-Gen. 2000, Maj.-Gen. 2005; Grand Officier, Légion d'honneur 2009, Officier, Ordre national du Mérite, Grand Cross, Order of the Redeemer (Greece), Santos-Dumont Medal of Merit (Brazil); Aeronautical Medal, Overseas Medal, Meritorious Service Medal (Singapore), Guatemalan Armed Forces Cross (with two crossed sabres); Curtis Prize. *Leisure interests:* jogging, swimming, opera, poetry. *Address:* Allied Command Transformation, 7857 Blandy Road, Suite 100, Norfolk, VA 23551-2490, USA (office). *Telephone:* (757) 747-3400 (office). *Fax:* (757) 747-3234 (office). *Website:* www.act.nato.int (office).

PALOUŠ, Radim, PhD; Czech university rector (retd); b. 6 Nov. 1924, Prague; s. of Jan A. Palouš and Marie Paloušová; m. Anna Štausová 1949; two s.; ed Charles Univ. of Prague, Pedagogical Univ.; mem. student anti-Nazi resistance movt; Lecturer in Analytical Chem., Faculty of Natural Sciences 1957–59, Inst. of Univ. Studies, Tech. Univ. of Prague; after 1959 suffered intermittent persecution from Communist regime; Chair. Educ. Techniques Dept, Faculty of Pedagogics, Prague 1968–69; Charter 77 spokesman; Rector, Charles Univ. 1990–94; Vice-Chair. Czechoslovak Asscn of the Roman Club 1991–; Dr hc (Pittsburgh) 1990, (Omaha) 1990, (Int. Acad. for Philosophy) 1991, (Cracow) 1991, (Moravian Coll., USA) 1991, (York) 1992, Seoul 1993, (Edin.) 1993, (Pardubice) 2008; Czechoslovak Acad. of Sciences Prize 1990, mem. Pontificum Concilium de Kultura (awarded by Pope John Paul II) 1990–2003, Comenius Scheidegger Prize, Netherlands 1992, T.G. Masaryk Order 1997. *Publications include:* Die Schule den Alten 1979, The Time of Education 1983, The Czech Experience 1994, Das Weltzeitalter 1993, Totalism and Holism 1995, Letters to Godchildren of the Present Age 2001, Ars docenti (The Art of Teaching) 2004, Globalization 2005, Adventure of My Life 2006, Heretic School 2008. *Address:* Charles University, Ovocný trh 3-5, 116 36 Prague 1, Czech Republic (office). *E-mail:* rpalous@ruk.cuni.cz (office).

PÁLSSON, Thorsteinn; Icelandic politician and diplomatist; *Co-Editor, Fréttablaðið;* b. 29 Oct. 1947; m. Ingibjörg Rafnar; three c.; ed Commercial Coll., Reykjavik and Univ. of Iceland; Chair. Vaka (student's union) 1969–70; Ed. Vísir 1975; Dir Confed. of Icelandic Employers 1979–83; mem. Parl. 1983–99; Chair. Independence Party 1983–91; Minister of Finance 1985–87, Prime Minister of Iceland 1987–88, Minister of Fisheries 1991–99, of Justice 1991–99, also of Ecclesiastical Affairs –1999; Amb. to UK 1999–2002, to Denmark 2003–05; co-Ed. Fréttablaðið (daily newspaper) 2006–. *Address:* Fréttablaðið (The Newspaper), Útgáfufélagið Frétt ehf, Suðurgata 10, 101 Reykjavík, Iceland (office). *Telephone:* 5157500 (office). *E-mail:* ristjorn@frettabladid.is (office). *Website:* www.frettabladid.is (office).

PALTRIDGE, Garth William, BSc, PhD, DSc, FAA; Australian atmospheric physicist; b. 24 April 1940, Brisbane, Queensland; s. of T. B. Paltridge and A. T. Savage; m. Kay L. Petty 1965; one s. one d.; ed Brisbane Boys' Coll., Univs of Queensland and Melbourne; Postdoctoral Fellow, New Mexico Inst. of Mining and Tech. 1965; Sr Scientific Officer, Radio and Space Research Station, Ditton Park, Bucks., UK 1966–67; Research Scientist, CSIRO Div. of Meteorological Physics 1967–1981, Chief Research Scientist 1981–89; Exec. Dir PIECE, Australian Inst. of Petroleum 1980; Sr Visiting Scientist, Nat. Climate Program Office 1989–90; Prof. and Dir Inst. of Antarctic and Southern Oceans Studies (IASOS) and CEO Antarctic Co-operative Research Centre, Univ. of Tasmania 1991–2002, Prof. Emer. and Hon. Research Fellow 2002–; Visiting Fellow, ANU; WMO Research Prize. *Publications:* Radiative Processes in Meteorology and Climatology (co-author) 1976, The Climate Caper: Facts and Fallacies of Global Warming 2009; 100 research papers on environmental topics. *Leisure interests:* golf, history, furniture and cabinet making. *Address:* c/o Institute of Antarctic and Southern Ocean Studies, University of Tasmania, Private Bag 77, Hobart, Tasmania 7001 (office); 9 Waymouth Avenue, Sandy Bay, Tasmania 7005, Australia (home). *E-mail:* secretary@iasos.utas.edu.au (office).

PALTROW, Gwyneth; American actress; b. 27 Sept. 1972, Los Angeles, Calif.; d. of the late Bruce Paltrow and of Blythe Danner; m. Chris Martin 2003 (separated 2014); one s. one d.; ed Spence School, New York and Univ. of California, Santa Barbara. *Films include:* Shout 1991, Hook 1991, Malice 1993, Flesh and Bone 1993, Mrs. Parker and the Vicious Circle 1994, Higher Learning (uncredited) 1995, Jefferson in Paris 1995, Se7en 1995, Moonlight and Valentino 1995, Hard Eight 1996, The Pallbearer, Seven 1995, Emma 1996, Sydney 1996, Great Expectations 1998, Sliding Doors 1998, Hush 1998, A Perfect Murder 1998, Shakespeare in Love (Academy Award for Best Actress) 1998, The Talented Mr. Ripley 1999, Duets 2000, Bounce 2000, The Intern 2000, The Anniversary Party 2001, The Royal Tenenbaums 2001, Shallow Hal 2001, Austin Powers in Goldmember (cameo) 2002, Possession 2002, View from the Top 2003, Sylvia 2003, Sky Captain and the World of Tomorrow 2004, Proof 2005, Infamous 2006, Love and Other Disasters 2006, Running with Scissors 2006, The Good Night 2007, Iron Man 2008, Two Lovers 2008, Pashmy Dream (short) 2008, Iron Man 2 2010, Country Strong 2010, Contagion 2011, Avengers Assemble 2012, Thanks for Sharing 2012, Iron Man 3 2013, Mortdecai 2014. *Television includes:* High (film) 1989, Cruel Doubt (film)

1992, Deadly Relations (film) 1993, Spain... On the Road Again 2008, The Marriage Ref 2010, The New Normal (series pilot, uncredited) 2012, Glee (series) 2010–14. *Play:* Proof (Donmar Warehouse, London) 2002. *Address:* c/o Rick Kurtzman, Creative Artists Agency, 2000 Avenue of the Stars, Los Angeles, CA 90067, USA (office). *Telephone:* (424) 288-2000 (office). *Fax:* (424) 288-2900 (office). *Website:* www.caa.com (office).

PALTSEV, Mikhail Alexandrovich, DrMed; Russian pathologist; *Rector and Head of Pathology Department, Moscow Sechenov Academy of Medicine;* b. 9 Nov. 1949, Russia; m.; one d.; ed 1st Moscow Sechenov Inst. of Medicine; Prof., Moscow Sechenov Acad. of Medicine; active as pathology anatomist and organizer of medical sciences; mem. Presidium Russian Acad. of Sciences; Pres. Asscn of Medical and Pharmaceutical Educ.; Ed.-in-Chief Molecular Medicine, Pathology Archives; mem. Int. Acad. of Pathology, Exec. Cttee European Soc. of Pathology; Rector and Head of Pathology Dept, Moscow Sechenov Acad. of Medicine; Order of Friendship Between Peoples, USSR State Prize 1991, Order for Service to the Fatherland, Rank IV 1999; Russian Govt's Prize 2000, 2006. *Publications:* Pathological Anatomy (with N. Anichkov) 2001, 2005, Pathology (textbook, co-author) 2002, Intercellular Interactions (co-author) 2003. *Address:* Moscow Sechenov Academy of Medicine, Trubetskaya str. 8–2, 119991 Moscow, Russia (office). *Telephone:* (495) 248-05-53 (office). *Fax:* (495) 248-02-14 (office). *E-mail:* mma-sechenov@mtu-net.ru. *Website:* www.mma.ru (office).

PALUMBO, Baron (Life Peer), cr. 1991, of Walbrook in the City of London; **Peter Garth Palumbo,** MA; British property developer; b. 20 July 1935, London; s. of Rudolph Palumbo and Elsie Palumbo; m. 1st Denia Wigram 1959 (died 1986), one s. two d.; m. 2nd Hayat Morowa 1986, one s. two d.; ed Eton Coll. and Worcester Coll., Oxford; Gov. LSE 1976–94; Hon. mem. Emmanuel Coll., Cambridge 1994–; Trustee, Mies van der Rohe Archive 1977–, The Tate Gallery 1978–85, White-chapel Art Gallery Foundation 1981–87; Trustee and Hon. Treas. Writers and Scholars Educational Trust 1984–99; Chair. The Tate Gallery Foundation 1986–87, Painshill Park Trust Appeal 1986–96; Chair. The Arts Council of GB 1989–94; Chair. Pritzker Architecture Prize Jury 2004–; Chancellor Univ. of Portsmouth 1992–2007; mem. bd and Dir Andy Warhol Foundation for the Arts 1994–97; Trustee Natural History Museum 1994–2007, Design Museum 1995–2005; mem. Council, Royal Albert Hall 1995–99; Gov. RSC 1995–2000, Whitgift School 2002–; Hon. FRIBA 1986; Hon. Fellow Inst. of Structural Eng 1994; mem. Livery, Salters' Co. 1965; Dr hc (Portsmouth) 1993; Nat. Order of Southern Cross, Brazil; Cranbrook Patronage of the Arts Award, Detroit, USA 2002. *Leisure interests:* music, travel, gardening, reading.

PAMFILOVA, Ella Aleksandrovna; Russian politician; b. 12 Sept. 1953, Tashkent Region, Uzbekistan; d. of Aleksandr Lekomtsev and Polina Lekomtseva; m. 1st Nikita Leonidovich Pamfilov 1976 (divorced 1993); one d.; m. 2nd; ed Moscow Inst. of Power Eng; foreman at cen. factory Mosenergo, Chair. of trade union at factory 1981–89; USSR People's Deputy 1989–91; Sec. Comm. of Supreme Soviet on Privileges Jan.–Nov. 1991; Russian Fed. Minister for Social Security 1991–94; mem. State Duma (Parl.) 1993–99, mem. Cttee on Security 1995–98; Chair. Council on Social Policy under Presidential Admin. 1994; Founder and Head Movt for Healthy Russia (later Movt for Civic Dignity) 1996; Chair. Presidential Comm. on Human Rights 2002–08; Chair. Civil Society Insts and Human Rights Council 2004–10; Pres. Acad. Revival; Order of Honour 2010. *Leisure interest:* gardening. *Address:* c/o Civil Society Institutions and Human Rights Council, 103132 Moscow, 4, Staraya Square, Russia (office). *Telephone:* (495) 606-49-14 (office). *E-mail:* sovetpamfilova@yandex.ru (office).

PAMPURO, José Juan Bautista, MD; Argentine politician and physician; *Provisional President of the Senate;* b. 28 Dec. 1949, Buenos Aires; m.; three d.; ed Univ. of Buenos Aires; Sec. of Health, Lanús Municipality 1983–87; elected Nat. Deputy for Justice, Buenos Aires Prov. 1987–91; Minister of Health and Social Action, Buenos Aires Prov. 1991–92; in pvt. medical practice 1992–95; Gov. of Buenos Aires 1995–99; re-elected Nat. Deputy 1999–2002; Gen. Coordinator for Pres. Eduardo Duhalde 2002; Sec.-Gen. of the Nat. Presidency 2002–04; Minister of Defence 2004–05; Provisional Pres. of the Senate 2006–. *Address:* Senate, 1328 Buenos Aires, Argentina (office). *E-mail:* jose.pampuro@senado.gov.ar (office). *Website:* www.senado.gov.ar (office).

PAMUK, Orhan; Turkish novelist and academic; *Robert Yik-Fong Tam Professor of the Humanities, Columbia University;* b. 7 June 1952, Istanbul; m. Aylin Turegen 1982 (divorced 2001); one d.; ed Robert Coll., Istanbul Technical Univ., Inst. of Journalism at Istanbul Univ.; currently Robert Yik-Fong Tam Prof. of the Humanities, Columbia Univ., USA; jury mem. Cannes Film Festival 2007; mem. American Acad. of Arts and Sciences 2008–, Chinese Acad. for Social Sciences 2008–; Hon. mem. American Acad. of Arts and Letters 2005; Officier, Ordre national de la Légion d'honneur 2012; Dr hc (American Univ. of Beirut) 2003, (Georgetown Univ.) 2007, Bogaziçi Univ.) 2007, (Tilburg Univ.) 2007, (Free Univ. of Berlin) 2007, (Univ. of Bucharest) 2008, (Madrid Univ.) 2008, (Univ. of Rouen) 2009, (Univ. of Tirana) 2010, (Yale Univ.) 2010, (Sofia Univ.) 2011; First Prize, Milliyet Press Novel Contest 1979, Orhan Kemal Novel Prize 1983, Prix de la Découverte Européenne 1991, Ricardo-Huch Prize 2005, Nobel Prize in Literature 2006, Distinguished Humanist Award, Washington Univ. 2006, Puterbaugh Award 2006, Ovid Award 2008, Norman Mailer Lifetime Achievement Award 2010, Sonning Prize (Denmark) 2012. *Publications include:* Cevdet Bey ve Ogullari (Cevdet Bey and His Sons) 1983, Sessiz Ev (The Quiet House) (Madarali Novel Prize, Turkey 1984) 1983, Beyaz Kale (trans. as The White Castle) (Independent Foreign Fiction Prize 1990) 1985, Kara Kitap (trans. as The Black Book) (Prix France Culture 1995) 1990, Gizli Yuz (screenplay of Kara Kitap) 1992, Yeni Hayat (trans. as The New Life) 1995, My Name is Red (Prix du Meilleur Livre Etranger, France 2002, Premio Grinzane Cavour, Italy 2002, Int. IMPAC Dublin Literary Award 2003) 2000, Istanbul 2003, Snow (Prix Médicis Etranger, France 2005) 2004, Istanbul: Memories of a City 2006, Istanbul: City of a Hundred Names 2007, Other Colours (essays) 2007, Masumiyet Müzesi (trans. as The Museum of Innocence) 2008, Manzaradan Parçalar 'Hayat, Sokaklar, Edebiyat' 2010, The Naive and the Sentimental Novelist 2011, The Innocence of Objects 2012; contrib. to various newspapers and magazines. *Address:* School of the Arts, Columbia University, 305 Dodge Hall, 2960 Broadway, New York, NY 10027, USA (office). *Website:* arts.columbia.edu (office); www.orhanpamuk.net.

PAN, Hong; Chinese film actress; b. 4 Nov. 1954, Shanghai; m. Mi Jingshan (divorced 1990); ed Shanghai Drama Acad. 1973–76; actress, Shanghai Film Studio, Shanghai 1977–80, Omei Film Studio, Chengdu 1980–; mem. 5th Nat. Cttee, Fed. of Literary and Art Circles 1988–; Vice-Chair. China Film Asscn, China Film Performance Academic Soc.; mem. CPPCC Nat. Cttee; mem. Jury 5th Shanghai Int. Film Festival 2001. *Films include:* Troubled Laughter 1979, Sunray Through Clouds 1980, At Middle Age (3rd Golden Rooster Best Actress Award 1983) 1982, The Last Empress 1985, The Trouble-shooters 1988, Well (8th Golden Rooster Best Actress) 1988, The Last Aristocrats 1989, The Single Woman 1991, Woman-TAXI-Woman 1991, Shanghai Fever (14th Golden Rooster Best Actress, Hundred Flowers Award Best Actress) 1994, Up For the Raising Sun 1997, Destination – 9th Heaven 1997. *Television includes:* Secret Murder, Amazing Cases 2003, Beijing My Love 2005, Qing Tian Ya Men 2006, Embroiderer Lan Xin 2007, Ancestral Temple 2008. *Address:* Omei Film Studio, Tonghui Menwai, Chengdu City, Sichuan Province, People's Republic of China (office). *Telephone:* (28) 22991 (office).

PAN, Rongwen, MD; Chinese physician; b. 1 July 1931, Jiangsu Prov.; d. of Pan Yu Qi and Pan Cao Shi; m. Lu Shi Cai 1960; one s. one d.; Alt. mem. 12th CCP Cen. Cttee 1982–87; Physician-in-Charge, Changzheng Hosp. 1982, Vice-Pres. 1983–, Prof. 1986–. *Address:* Changzheng Hospital, 428 Feng Yang Road, Shanghai 200003, People's Republic of China (office). *Telephone:* (21) 3275997 (office).

PAN, Wenent P., BS, PhD; Taiwanese oil industry executive; ed Nat. Taiwan Normal Univ., Univ. of Wyoming, USA; fmrly with ACE Chemical Co. and Fluid Properties Research Inst.; joined CPC Corpn, Taiwan (fmrly Chinese Petroleum Corpn), held various roles including Man. of Process Research, Dir of Corp. Planning, Vice-Pres. then Pres. 1996–2004, Chair. 2006–09, also Vice-Chair. Kuo Kuang Power Co. (subsidiary co.) 1997–2004, Chair. 2004–09; Chair. ROC-Australia Business Council, Sino-Indonesia Cultural and Econ. Asscn, Indonesia Cttee of Chinese Int. Econ. Cooperation Asscn; fmr Pres. Chinese Asscn for Energy Econs. *Address:* c/o CPC Corpn, No. 3, Songren Road, Sinyi District, Taipei City 110, Taiwan. *E-mail:* ir@cpc.com.tw.

PAN, Xia; Chinese film director; b. Aug. 1937, Yidu, Shandong Prov.; ed Tongji Univ. Shanghai; Ed. and Dir Literature and Arts Dept, Chinese People's Cen. Radio Station 1959–75; Dir TV Drama Troupe, Cen. Broadcasting Art Co. 1975–83; Dir China TV Drama Centre 1984–; mem. Standing Cttee 8th CPPCC Nat. Cttee 1993–98, Standing Cttee 9th CPPCC Nat. Cttee 1998–2003; Best TV Drama Award 1980, Flying Apsaras Award 1982, several Gold Eagle Awards; awarded the titles of Nat. Jinguo Pacesetter for Meritorious Service 1991 and Nat. Sanba Standard-Bearer 1992. *Television:* The Sacred Mission, Multi-Prism, Walking into the Storm, Xiang Jingyu, The Pioneers' Footsteps, Madame Sun Yatsen and Her Sisters. *Publications:* more than 20 research papers. *Address:* China Television Drama Centre, Beijing, People's Republic of China (office).

PANAFIEU, HE Cardinal Bernard Louis Auguste Paul; French ecclesiastic; *Metropolitan Archbishop of Marseille;* b. 26 Jan. 1931, Châtellerault; s. of Andre Panafieu and Madeleine Doussière; ed Grand Seminary of Albi, Seminary of Issy-les-Moulineaux; ordained priest 1956; Vicar of Saint-Sauveur-de-Mazamet and Chaplain of lyceum La Perouse, Aibi 1962; chaplain of univ. parish and responsible for chaplaincy of public educ.; Student Chaplain, Toulouse 1967–70; curé-doyen of Brassac 1971–74; Sec.-Gen. Presbyteral Council 1973–74; Titular Bishop of Tibili and Auxiliary Bishop of Annecy 1974; Archbishop of Aix 1978; Coadjutor Archbishop of Marseille 1994–95, Archbishop of Marseille 1995–2002, Metropol-itan Archbishop of Marseille 2002–; cr. Cardinal (Cardinal Priest of St Gregory Barbarigo) alle Tre Fontane) 2003. *Address:* Archdiocese of Marseille, 14 place du Colonel-Edon, 13284 Marseille, France (office). *Telephone:* (4) 91-52-38-23 (office). *Fax:* (4) 91-52-45-19 (office). *Website:* catholique-marseille.cef.fr (office).

PANAGIOTOPOULOS, Panos; Greek journalist, lawyer and politician; *Minis-ter of Culture and Sports;* b. 1957, Athens; m. Maouzi Tsaldari; one s.; ed Technical Univ. of Athens, Athens Law School, Univ. of Vincennes, Paris, French Inst. of Athens; mil. service in Greek Air Force; active in ONNED and DAP-NDFK (student org. of Nea Demokratia), mem. leadership of ONNED and Ed. Demokratike Protoporia newspaper; mem. Steering Cttee (Youth Dept) of Nea Demokratia, participated in Govt Comm. programme responsible for Youth and Drugs 1984–85; mem. Political Council of New Democracy; mem. (New Democ-racy) of the Vouli (Parl.) for Athens B 2000–; Minister for Employment and Social Protection in first govt of Kostas Karamanlis March 2004; served as Govt Gen. Rapporteur for the Revision of the Constitution; Parl. Spokesman for New Democracy 2007–09, Spokesman for New Democracy 2009–11, responsible for Foreign Policy 2011–12; Minister of Nat. Defence following formation of coalition govt with Panhellenic Socialist Movt (PASOK) and Democratic Left (Dimokratiki Aristera) June 2012–13; Minister of Culture and Sports 2013–; Chair. Special Parl. Cttee on the ratification of the Treaty of Lisbon; had successful TV and print journalism career; legal career as prosecuting lawyer with own law office in Athens, specializing in criminal and corp. affairs; news reporter on Greek television; mem. Journalists Union of Athens Daily Newspapers, Athens Bar Asscn; fmr Dir, News SKY 100, 4 FM, STAR TV News; fmr Dir of Information and Broadcasting, ET1 and ANT1 TV; Founding mem. Athens radio station; political ed. and columnist at several newspapers; numerous awards, including Greek Television Award 1992, Botsis Foundation Award, Prize of the Greek Christian Literature Soc., Honour of the Panhellenic Asscn of Reserve Forces. *Address:* Ministry of Culture and Sports, Andreas Papandreou 37, 151 80 Maroussi, Greece (office). *Telephone:* (210) 3442505 (office). *E-mail:* webmaster@ypepth.gr (office). *Website:* www.culture.gr/culture/eindex.jsp (office); www.yppo.gr/0/eindex.jsp (office); www.panospanagiotopoulos.gr.

PANARITI, Edmond, DipVetMed, PhD; Albanian veterinary surgeon, academic and politician; b. 1 June 1960, Tirana; m.; two c.; ed Univ. of Agriculture, Tirana; Researcher, Dept of Radio-biology, Inst. of Veterinary Research, Tirana 1984–89, Head of Dept of Environmental Toxicology 1992–95, Deputy Dir Inst. of Veterinary Research 1998–2006; Postgraduate Researcher on Environmental Toxicology, ETH, Zurich, Switzerland 1989–92; Lecturer and Researcher, Univ. of Kentucky, USA 1995–96, Univ. of Mississippi 2000–01; Head of Food Safety Section, Inst. of Public Health 1996–98; Lecturer and Researcher on Analytical Toxicology, Veterinary Univ. of Hanover, Germany 2004–05; Officer and Project Coordinator,

WHO 2009–11; mem. Tirana Municipal Council 2011, Deputy Mayor of Tirana 2011–12; Minister of Foreign Affairs 2012–13; Minister, Ministry of Agric., Rural Devt and Water Admin 2013–; mem. Socialist Movement for Integration 2004–, Sec. for Agric. and Environment 2006–08, Chair. Nat. Steering Cttee 2008–; Chair. Cttee of European Ministers, Council of Europe –2012. *Publications:* two textbooks and numerous articles. *Address:* Ministry of Agriculture, Rural Development and Water Administration, Blvd Deshmoret e Kombit 2, Tirana, Albania (office). *Telephone:* (4) 2232796 (office). *Fax:* (4) 2227924 (office). *E-mail:* edmond.panariti@bujqesia.gov.al (office). *Website:* www.bujqesia.gov.al (office).

PANDA, Ramakanta, MCh; Indian cardiothoracic and vascular surgeon; *Consultant Cardiovascular Thoracic Surgeon, Vice-Chairman and Managing Director, Asian Heart Institute;* b. (Ramakant Madanmohan Panda), Sundargarh, Orissa; s. of Sarla Panda; m. Sanghamitra Panda; ed SCB Medical Coll., Orissa, All India Inst. of Medical Sciences; fmr Sr Registrar, Harefield Hosp. UK; Fellowship in Cardiovascular and Thoracic Surgery, Cleveland Clinic, Ohio, USA, fmr Assoc. Staff Surgeon; f. Asian Heart Inst. 2003, currently Consultant Cardiovascular Thoracic Surgeon, Vice-Chair. and Man. Dir; fmr Consultant Cardiothoracic Surgeon, Jaslok Hosp., Breach Candy Hosp., Lilavati and Nanavati Hosp.; f. Sarla Madan Charitable Trust, Asian Heart Inst., Mumbai; Rashtriya Samman, Central Bd of Taxes, Bank of Baroda Sun Lifetime Achievement Award 2009, Lifetime Achievement Award, World Congress on Clinical, Preventive & Geriatric Cardiology 2009, Padma Bhushan 2010, Think Odisha Legend Leadership Award 2011. *Achievements include:* under his leadership, his surgical team has performed more than 16,000 bypass surgeries, has also performed more than 900 repeat (redo) bypass surgeries as well as more than 2,000 surgeries on patients considered high risk by surgical definition. *Publications:* several scientific publications in nat. and int. journals. *Address:* Asian Heart Institute, Bandra Kurla Complex, Bandra (E), Mumbai 400 051, India (office). *Telephone:* (22) 66986601 (office). *Fax:* (22) 66986639 (office). *E-mail:* rp@ahirc.com (office). *Website:* www.asianheartinstitute.org (office).

PANDAY, Basdeo, BLL, BSc (Econs); Trinidad and Tobago politician; b. 25 May 1933, Prince's Town; m. 1st Norma Mohammed (died 1981); one d.; m. 2nd Oma Ramkisson; three d.; ed Lincoln's Inn, Univ. of London, UK; entered politics as mem. of Workers' and Farmers' Party 1966; trade union legal adviser; Pres.-Gen. All Trinidad Sugar and Gen. Workers' Trade Union 1973, Sugar Industry Staff Asscn 1975; founder mem. United Labour Front (ULF); Leader of the Opposition 1976–86, 1989–95, 2001–10; Minister of Foreign Affairs 1986–91; mem. Nat. Alliance for Reconciliation (NAR), expelled 1988; Founder United Nat. Congress (UNC), Leader 1989–2005, 2006–10; Prime Minister of Trinidad and Tobago 1995–2001; Pravasi Bharatiya Samman (India) 1986. *Address:* United National Congress, Rienzi Complex, 78–81 Southern Main Road, Couva; La Fantasie Gardens, St Ann's, Port of Spain, Trinidad and Tobago (home).

PANDE, Arvind, MA; Indian business executive; b. 7 Sept. 1942; ed Allahabad Univ., Univ. of Cambridge, UK; Adviser to Exec. Dir for India, Bangladesh and Sri Lanka, IBRD 1971–74; Dept of Econ. Affairs, Ministry of Finance 1974–78; Special Sec., Govt of Madhya Pradesh 1978–81; Jt Sec. to Prime Minister of India 1981–86; Dir (Corp. Planning) Steel Authority of India Ltd (SAIL) 1986–90, (Personnel and Corp. Planning) 1990–93, Vice-Chair. 1993–97, Chair. (CEO) 1997–2002; Chair. Indian Iron and Steel Co. Ltd; fmrly Dir HDFC Bank Ltd (ADR), Exec. Dir 2003–; Pres. Nat. HRD Network; Council mem. Indian Inst. of Metals, Confed. of Indian Industry; mem. Bd of Govs Int. Man. Inst.; Dir Int. Iron and Steel Inst., Belgium; mem. Bureau of Indian Standards; Chair. IVRCL Infrastructures and Projects Ltd 2003–06; Chair. (non-exec.) Burnpur Cement Ltd 2006–09; mem. Bd of Dirs Era Infra Eng Ltd 2005–, Ind. Dir VISA Steel Ltd, Coal India Ltd. *Address:* c/o Board of Directors, Coal India Ltd, 10 Netaji Subhas Road, Kolkata 700 001 (office); B-249, Asian Games Village, New Delhi 110 049, India (home). *Telephone:* (11) 6493167 (home).

PANDE, Kabinga; Zambian politician; fmr Head Public Relations, Zambian Cen. Bank; fmr Pres. Africa Travel Asscn; Minister of Science, Tech. and Vocational Training 2005, of Tourism, Environment and Natural Resources 2005–07, of Foreign Affairs 2007–11; Deputy Chair. Movt for Multi-party Democracy. *Address:* c/o Ministry of Foreign Affairs, POB RW50069, Lusaka, Zambia (office).

PANDE, Mrinal; Indian journalist, editor and broadcasting executive; *Chairman of Prasar Bharati;* b. 1946, Tikamgarh, Madhya Pradesh; d. of the late Gaura Pant Shivani; m.; two d.; ed Allahabad Univ.; taught at Univs of Allahabad, Delhi and Bhopal; Ed. Vama (women's magazine) 1984–87; Editor-Anchor (Hindi news), Star News and Doordarshan; Chief Ed. Hindustan (Hindi daily) 2000–09; Chair. Prasar Bharati (public service broadcaster) 2010–; fmr Sec. Gen. Eds Guild of India; Founder-Pres. Indian Women's Press Corps; Padmashree 2006. *Television:* Baaton Baaton Mein (host). *Publications include:* The Subject is Woman 1991, Daughter's Daughter 1993, That Which Ram Hath Ordained 1993, Devi, Tales of the Goddess in Our Time 2000, My Own Witness 2001. *Address:* Prasar Bharati, 2nd Floor, PTI Building, Sansad Marg, New Delhi 110 001, India (office). *Telephone:* (11) 23753687 (office). *Fax:* (11) 23737589 (office). *Website:* prasarbharati.gov.in.

PANDE, Prithivi Bahadur; Nepalese banker; *Chairman and Chief Executive Director, Nepal Investment Bank Limited;* m. Pratima Pande; one s.; worked at Central Bank of Nepal –1990; Gen. Man. Rastra Banijya Bank 1990, then Exec. Dir Himalayan Bank (first pvt. sector commercial bank in Nepal) 1991–2001; led consortium of investors to buy Credit Agricole shares in Nepal Indosuez Bank Ltd, renamed Nepal Investment Bank Ltd 2002, Chair. and Chief Exec. Dir 2002–; Chair. Himalayan Infrastructure Fund (pvt. equity fund). *Address:* Nepal Investment Bank Ltd, Durbar Marg, PO Box 3412, Kathmandu, Nepal (office). *Telephone:* (1) 4228229 (office). *Fax:* (1) 4226349 (office); (1) 4228927 (office). *E-mail:* info@nibl.com.np (office). *Website:* www.nibl.com.np (office).

PANDEY, Ramesh Nath; Nepalese politician; b. Feb. 1944; fmr Minister of Population and Devt, Information, Communication and Gen. Admin; fmr Minister for Industry and Communication; fmr Minister of State for Tourism, Labour and Social Welfare; fmr Govt Spokesman; mem. Parl.; Minister of Foreign Affairs 2005–06; arrested 2006 after King Gyanendra ceded control of govt; currently political analyst. *Address:* c/o Ministry of Foreign Affairs, Shital Niwas, Maharajganj, Kathmandu, Nepal (office).

PANDEY, Surendra; Nepalese sociologist and politician; elected mem. Upper House, Nat. Ass.; mem. Communist Party of Nepal (Unified Marxist-Leninist), mem. Politburo; Minister of Finance 2009–11, also Gov. for Nepal in Asian Devt Bank. *Address:* c/o Ministry of Finance Singha Durbar, Kathmandu, Nepal.

PANDIT, Vikram S., BS, MS, MBA, PhD; American (b. Indian) banking executive; b. 14 Jan. 1957, Nagpur, Maharashtra, India; s. of Shankar Pandit and the late Shailaja Pandit; m. Swati Pandit; one s. one d.; ed Dadar Parsee Youths Ass. High School, Mumbai, Gannon Univ., Columbia Univ., New York; moved to USA to study aged 16; Prof., Indiana Univ., Bloomington 1986–90; worked for 20 years with Morgan Stanley & Co., becoming Man. Dir 1990–94, Head of Equity Derivatives 1994–2000, also Man. Dir 1997–2000, Co-pres. and COO Institutional Securities Div. 2000–03, Pres. and COO Institutional Securities & Investment Banking Group 2003–05; Founder and Chair. Old Lane LP (hedge fund) 2005–07; Chair. and CEO Citigroup Alternative Investments 2007, Chair. and CEO Institutional Clients Group 2007, mem. Bd of Dirs and CEO Citigroup Inc. 2007–12 (resgnd); mem. Bd of Dirs Columbia Univ., Columbia Business School, Indian School of Business, Trinity School, NASDAQ 2000–03; fmr mem. Bd of Dirs New York City Investment Fund, American India Foundation; Padma Bhushan 2008, named Banker of the Year by Euromoney magazine 2010. *Address:* c/o Citigroup Inc., 399 Park Avenue, New York, NY 10043, USA.

PANDITHAGE, A(beyakumar) Mohan; Sri Lankan business executive; *Chairman and CEO, Hayleys PLC;* s. of the late P. D. Alexander; began career with Hayleys as a man. trainee 1969, apptd a Dir of Hayleys Advantis 1981, Man. Dir 1988, Group Exec. Dir 1996, elected mem. Bd of Dirs 1998, Deputy Chair. Hayleys PLC and CEO Hayleys Advantis Ltd 2007–09, Chair. and CEO Hayleys PLC 2009–; mem. American Bureau of Shipping, SRILPO (Trade Facilitation) Cttee, mem. of several Chambers of Commerce; mem. Bd of Dirs Sri Lanka Port Man. Consultancy Services Ltd; mem. Presidential Cttee on Maritime Matters; fmr Chair. and Vice-Chair. Ceylon Asscn of Ships' Agents; fmr mem. Bd of Dirs Sri Lanka Ports Authority, Jaya Container Terminals Ltd; Hon. Consul of Mexico to Sri Lanka 2011; Best Shipping Personality, Inst. of Chartered Shipbrokers, Sri Lanka 2004. *Address:* Hayleys Group, 400 Deans Road, Colombo 10, Sri Lanka (office). *Telephone:* (11) 2696331 (office). *Fax:* (11) 2699299 (office). *E-mail:* info@cau.hayleys.com (office). *Website:* www.hayleys.com (office).

PANDOLFI, Filippo Maria, PhD; Italian politician (retd); b. 1 Nov. 1927, Bergamo; ed Università Cattolica del Sacro Cuore, Milan; fmr co. dir; mem. Chamber of Deputies for Brescia-Bergamo 1968–89; mem. Comm. on Finance and the Treasury; fmr Under-Sec. of State in Ministry of the Budget; Minister of Finance 1976–78, of the Treasury 1978–80, of Trade and Industry 1980–81, 1982–83, of Agric. and Forestry 1983–88; EEC Commr for Science, Research, Telecommunications and Information Tech. 1989–93; mem. Group of 10, Luigi Sturzo Inst. from 2000; Christian Democrat; Cavaliere di Gran Croce dell'Ordine al Merito della Repubblica Italiana 2003. *Leisure interests:* ancient Christian literature, opera and classical music, climbing.

PANETTA, Leon E., BA, JD; American lawyer, academic, fmr government official and fmr politician; b. 28 June 1938, Monterey, Calif.; s. of Carmelo Panetta and Carmelina Panetta; m. Sylvia Varni 1962; three s.; ed Santa Clara Univ.; served US Army 1964–66; Legis. Asst to Senator Thomas Kuchel, Washington, DC 1966–69; Dir Office of Civil Rights 1969–70; Exec. Asst to Mayor of New York 1970–71; Pnr, Panetta, Thompson and Panetta (law firm), Monterey, Calif. 1971–76; mem. US House of Reps 1977–93, Washington, DC, mem. House Agric. Cttee 1977–93, Budget Cttee 1979–85 (Chair. 1989–92), Vice-Chair. New Mem. Caucus 1977, Caucus of Vietnam Era Veterans in Congress, mem. Pres.'s Comm. on Foreign Language and Int. Studies; Head of Office of Man. and Budget 1993–94; Chief of Staff to Pres. Bill Clinton 1994–97; Founder and Co-Dir Panetta Inst. for Public Policy, California State Univ., Monterey Bay 1998–2009, also Distinguished Scholar to the Chancellor, Calif. State Univ. System, Presidential Prof., Santa Clara Univ.; Dir CIA 2009–11; Sec. of Defense 2011–13; Chair. Pew Oceans Comm., Co-Chair. Jt Ocean Cttee Initiative; Co-Chair. Calif. Council on Base Support and Retention, Calif. Forward Leadership Council; mem. Iraq Study Group, US Inst. of Peace 2006; mem. Ind. Task Force on Immigration and America's Future; fmr mem. Bd of Dirs Blue Shield, Zenith, Nat. Marine Sanctuary Foundation, Bread for the World, Close Up, BP America's Public Policy Inst. of Calif.; mem. Bd of Visitors Santa Clara Univ. School of Law; fmr mem. Advisory Bd Fleishman–Hillard Int.; Trustee, Monterey Bay Aquarium; Democrat; numerous awards including John H. Chafee Coastal Stewardship Award, Julius A. Stratton Award for Coastal Leadership and Distinguished Public Service Medal, Center for the Study of the Presidency, Army Commendation Medal, NEA Lincoln Award, A. Philip Randolph Award, Smithsonian Inst. Nat. Portrait Gallery Paul Peck Presidential Award, Nat. Marine Sanctuary Foundation Lifetime Achievement Award, Natural Resources Defense Council Forces for Nature, Nat. Hospice Foundation Silver Anniversary Honouree. *Publication:* Bring Us Together 1971. *Address:* Panetta Institute for Public Policy, 100 Campus Centre, Building 86E, California State University, Monterey Bay, Seaside, CA 93955, USA (office). *Telephone:* (831) 582-4200 (office). *Fax:* (831) 582-4082 (office). *E-mail:* info@PanettaInstitute.org (office). *Website:* www.panettainstitute.org (office).

PANFILOV, Gleb Anatolyevich; Russian film director; b. 21 Dec. 1934, Magnitogorsk; m. Inna Mikhailovna Churikova; one s.; grad. Sverdlovsk Polytechnic Inst. as chemical engineer and Mosfilm Studios (course in directing); work as Dir in Sverdlovsk, Leningrad (now St Petersburg), Moscow 1976–; RSFSR People's Artist 1984, RSFSR State Prize 1985. *Films include:* No Ford in the Fire (scenario: Yevgeny Gabrilovich) 1968 (Grand Prix Locarno 1969), Début 1970, both starring Inna Churikova, I Wish to Speak 1975, Valentina 1981, Vassa Zheleznova 1983, The Theme 1986, The Mother 1989, Hamlet 1989, The Romanovs: An Imperial Family 2000; stage productions include Hamlet 1986, Sorry (A. Galin) 1992, The Romanovs: An Imperial Family 2000. *Address:* Universitetski Prosp. 6, Korp. 4, Apt 68, 117333 Moscow, Russia. *Telephone:* (495) 137-89-67.

PANGALOS, Theodoros, PhD; Greek politician, economist and lawyer; b. 17 Aug. 1938, Elefsis; m.; three s. two d.; ed Univ. of Athens, Univ. of Paris IV (Paris-Sorbonne), France; Co-founder Grigoris Lambrakis Youth Movt; stood as EDA cand. in 1964 election; active in dissident movt during mil. dictatorship; deprived of Greek citizenship by junta 1968; lecturer and researcher specializing in econ. devt, programming and town and country planning, Sorbonne, Paris and Head of Econ. Devt Inst. 1969–78; practises as lawyer in Athens; legal adviser to trade unions; active in movt to protect environment; Socialist mem. Parl. for Attica 1981–2012; Deputy Minister of Commerce 1982–84, of Foreign Affairs 1984–89, 1993–94; Minister of Transport and Communications 1994, of Foreign Affairs 1996–99, of Culture April–Nov. 2000; Deputy Chair. of Govt (Deputy Prime Minister), responsible for Co-ordination of Foreign Policy and Defence Cttee and the Econ. and Social Policy Cttee 2009–12; Rep. of Greek Del. to WEU Ass. and Council of Europe 2001–09; mem. Political Council and Head of Int. Affairs and Defence section, Panhellenic Socialist Movt (PASOK); 17 awards or honours from various countries. *Publications:* several works on econs, sociology and philosophy. *Address:* c/o Office of the Prime Minister, Maximos Mansion, Herodou Atticou 19, 106 74 Athens; 16–18 Pireos Street, 104 31 Athens, Greece (home). *Telephone:* (1) 5231142 (home). *Fax:* (1) 5231178 (home). *E-mail:* pangalos@otenet.gr (home). *Website:* www.pangalos.gr.

PANGESTU, Prajogo, (Pang Djun Phen); Indonesian business executive; *President Commissioner, PT Barito Pacific Tbk;* b. 1951; m. Herlina Tjandinegara; three c.; Dir Djajanti Timber Group, Kalimantan 1969–76, Pres. Dir 1977–93; mem. Bd of Commrs PT Astra International 1993–98; Pres. Dir PT Chandra Asri 1990–99; f. Barito Pacific Group, Pres. Commr PT Barito Pacific Tbk 1993–; Pres. Commr PT Tri Polyta Indonesia Tbk; Propr Transpacific Group; other business interests include PT Mangole Timber Producers, PT Chandra Asri Petrochemical Centre (CAPC) (jt venture). *Address:* PT Barito Pacific Tbk, Wisma Barito Pacific, Tower B, Lt.8 Jl. Letjen S. Parman Kav. 62-63, Jakarta 11410, Indonesia (office). *Telephone:* (21) 5306711 (office). *Fax:* (21) 5306680 (office). *E-mail:* corpsec@barito .co.id (office). *Website:* www.barito.co.id (office).

PANIČ, Milan; Serbian business executive and fmr politician; *Owner, MP Global Enterprises;* b. 20 Dec. 1929, Belgrade; one s. two d.; ed Univ. of Belgrade, Univ. of South Carolina, USA, and Heidelberg Univ., Germany; emigrated to USA 1956; Founder and Chair. ICN Pharmaceuticals Inc. 1960–2002; returned to Yugoslavia 1991; Prime Minister of Yugoslavia July–Dec. 1992; cand. for Presidency of Serbia 1992; Founder and Owner of MP Global Enterprises 2003–; Dir Galenica Co., Belgrade and Moscow; mem. Bd Fund for Interdisciplinary Scientific Research (ISRF); Corresp. mem. California Inst. of Tech.; mem. American Nuclear Soc., Swiss Chemical Soc., Int. Soc. of Haemotherapy; mem. Bd Freedoms Foundation of Valley Forge; Wall Street Journal European of the Year. *Leisure interests:* tennis, cycling (fmr Yugoslav Champion). *Address:* MP Global Enterprises, 650 Town Center Drive, No. 660, Costa Mesa, CA 92626 (office); 1050 Arden Road, Pasadena, CA 91106, USA (home). *Telephone:* (714) 384-4000 (office). *Fax:* (714) 384-4010 (office). *Website:* www.milanpanic.com (office).

PANIGORO, Arifin, BEng; Indonesian business executive and politician; *Adviser, Medco Group;* b. 14 March 1945, Bandung; m.; two c.; ed Institut Teknologi Bandung, Inst. of Business Admin, France; Founder Meta Epsi Drilling Co. (Medco), currently Adviser, Medco Group, majority shareholder, Bank Saudara (part of Medco Group); fmr mem. House of Reps (parl.); fmr Chair. Partai Demokrasi Indonesia Perjuangan; mem. Indonesia Petroleum Asscn, Indonesian Engineer Asscn; Dr hc (Bandung Inst. of Tech.) 2010. *Address:* Medco Group, Medco Building III, 3rd Floor, Jl. Ampera Ray,a 18-20 Cilandak, Pasar Minggu South, Jakarta 12560, Indonesia (office). *Telephone:* (21) 7821671 (office). *Fax:* (21) 7821771 (office). *Website:* www.medcogroup.com (office).

PANITCHPAKDI, Supachai, MA, PhD; Thai banker, UN official and fmr government official; b. 30 May 1946, Bangkok; m. Sasai; one s. one d.; ed St Gabriel's Coll., Netherlands School of Econs (now Erasmus Univ.), Rotterdam; worked in Research Dept, Int. Finance Div., and Financial Insts Supervision Dept, Bank of Thailand 1974–86; elected mem. Thai Parl. 1986, Deputy Minister of Finance 1986–88; Dir and Adviser, then Pres. Thai Military Bank 1988–92; apptd Senator 1992, then Deputy Prime Minister of Thailand 1992–95, Deputy Prime Minister and Minister of Commerce 1997–99; Dir-Gen. WTO 2002–05; Sec.-Gen. UNCTAD 2005–Aug. 2013; Visiting Prof., Int. Inst. for Man. Devt, Lausanne 2001; Knight Grand Cordon (Special Class) of the Most Exalted Order of the White Elephant. *Publications include:* Globalization and Trade in the New Millennium 2001, China and WTO: Changing China Changing WTO (with Mark Clifford) 2002. *Address:* c/o United Nations Conference on Trade and Development (UNCTAD), Palais des Nations 8-14, Avenue de la Paix, 1211 Geneva 10, Switzerland.

PANJIKIDZE, Maia, PhD; Georgian philologist, academic, diplomatist and politician; *Minister of Foreign Affairs;* b. 16 Oct. 1960; m.; two s.; ed Tbilisi Javakhishvili State Univ., Friedrich Schiller Univ., Jena, GDR; Lecturer and Prof. of Philology, later Prof., Guram Tavartkiladze Univ. 2010–11; joined Foreign Service and was promoted to various high-level positions in Ministry of Foreign Affairs, including First Sec. 1994, Deputy Minister 2004, Amb. to Germany 2004–07, to The Netherlands 2007–10; mem. Georgian Dream political coalition, Spokesperson and Head of Cen. Office of coalition Feb.–Oct. 2012; Minister of Foreign Affairs 2012–; Founder and fmr Chair. Union of German Language Teachers of Georgia. *Publications:* several works on German language and literature. *Address:* Ministry of Foreign Affairs, 0108 Tbilisi, Sh. Chitadze str. 4, Georgia (office). *Telephone:* (32) 294-50-00 (office). *Fax:* (32) 294-50-01 (office). *E-mail:* inform@mfa.gov.ge (office). *Website:* www.mfa.gov.ge (office).

PANKE, Helmut, PhD; German business executive; b. 31 Aug. 1946, Storkow, Fürstenwalde; ed Univ. of Munich; Researcher, Swiss Inst. for Nuclear Research, simultaneous teaching role at Univ. of Munich 1976–78; worked as consultant, McKinsey & Co. in Düsseldorf and Munich 1978–82; joined Bayerische Motoren Werke (BMW) AG as Head of Planning and Controlling, Research and Devt 1982, then served in several man. positions in corp. planning, organization and corp. strategy, Head of Corp. Strategy and Co-ordination 1990–93, Chair. and CEO BMW (US) Holding Corpn 1993–96, mem. Bd of Man. (Personnel and Information Tech.) 1996–99, mem. Bd of Man. (Finance) 1999–2002, Chair. Bd of Man. BMW AG 2002–06; mem. Supervisory Bd Bayer AG 2006–; mem. Bd of Dirs Microsoft Corpn 2003–, UBS AG, Singapore Airlines. *Address:* c/o Supervisory Board, Bayer AG, Kaiser-Wilhelm-Allee 1, Leverkusen, Nordrhein-Westfalen, 51373, Germany.

PANKIN, Boris Dmitriyevich; Russian diplomatist (retd) and essayist; b. 20 Feb. 1931, Frunze (now Bishkek); m.; two s. one d.; ed Moscow State Univ.; journalist and literary critic 1957–; Ed. Komsomolskaya Pravda 1965–73; Chair. Bd USSR Copyright Agency 1973–82; USSR Amb. to Sweden 1982–90, to Czechoslovakia 1990–91; Foreign Minister Aug.–Dec. 1991; Russian Amb. to UK 1991–94; now living in Stockholm, Sweden; Award of the Union of Journalists 1974, USSR State Prize in Literature 1982, Russian National Media Award 'Elite' 2003. *Publications include:* Severe Literature, Time and Word, Boundaries and Books, The Last 100 Days of the Soviet Union, Four I of Konstantin Simonov. *Telephone:* (46) 880-7871.

PANNENBERG, Wolfhart Ulrich, DTheol, FBA; German academic; *Professor Emeritus, University of Munich;* b. 2 Oct. 1928, Stettin; s. of Kurt B.S. Pannenberg and Irmgard Pannenberg; m. Hilke Sabine Schütte 1954; ed Univ. of Heidelberg; ordained as Lutheran Minister 1956; Privatdozent, Heidelberg 1955–58; Prof. of Systematic Theology, Univ. of Wuppertal 1958–61; Prof., Univ. of Mainz 1961–67; Prof., Univ. of Munich 1967–94, Prof. Emer. 1994–; fmr Head, Inst. of Ecumenical Theology; mem. Bavarian Acad. of Sciences; Hon. DD (Glasgow) 1972, (Manchester) 1977, (Trinity Coll. Dublin) 1979, (St Andrews) 1993, (Cambridge) 1997, (Comillas, Madrid) 1999. *Publications include:* Offenbarung als Geschichte (translated as Revelation as History) 1961, Was ist der Mensch?: Die Anthropologie der Gegenwart im Lichte der Theologie (translated as What is Man?) 1962, Grundzüge der Christologie (translated as Jesus: God and Man) 1964, Grundfragen systematischer Theologie (two vols, translated as Basic Questions in Theology) 1967, 1980, Theology and the Kingdom of God 1969, Spirit, Faith and Church (with Carl E. Braaten and Avery Dulles) 1970, Thesen zur Theologie der Kirche 1970, Das Glaubensbekenntnis (translated as The Apostles' Creed in the Light of Today's Questions) 1972, Gottesgedanke und menschliche Freiheit (translated as The Idea of God and Human Freedom) 1972, Wissenschaftstheorie und Theologie (translated as Theology and the Philosophy of Science) 1973, Glaube und Wirklichkeit (translated as Faith and Reality) 1975, Ethik und Ekklesiologie 1977, Human Nature, Election and History 1977, Anthropologie in Theologischer Perspektive (translated as Anthropology in Theological Perspective) 1983, Christian Spirituality 1983, Christentum in Einer Säkularisierten Welt (translated as Christianity in a Secularized World) 1988, Systematische Theologie (three vols, translated as Systematic Theology) 1988–93, Metaphysik und Gottesgedanke (translated as Metaphysics and the Idea of God) 1988, An Introduction to Systematic Theology 1991, Toward a Theology of Nature: Essays on Science and Faith 1993, Grundlagen der Ethik 1996, Theologie und Philosophie 1996, Problemgeschichte der neueren Evangelischen Theologie in Deutschland 1997, Beiträge zur systematischen Theologie (three vols) 1999–2000, Beiträge zur Ethik 2004, Analogie und Offenbarung 2007. *Leisure interests:* history, music, philosophy. *Telephone:* (89) 21803482 (office); (89) 855915 (home).

PANNI, Marcello; Italian conductor and composer; *Musical Director, Orchestra Sinfonica Tito Schipa, Lecce;* b. 24 Jan. 1940, Rome; s. of Arnaldo Panni and Adriana Cortini; m. Jeanne Colombier 1970; one d.; ed Accad. di Santa Cecilia, Rome under Goffredo Petrassi and Conservatoire Nat. Supérieur, Paris under Manuel Rosenthal; conducting debut, Festival of Contemporary Music, Venice 1969; has since achieved renown in field of avant-garde music conducting first performances of works by Berio, Bussotti, Cage, Feldman, Donatoni, Clementi, Sciarrino, Glass and others at all major European festivals and for Italian Radio; regular guest conductor for Accad. di Santa Cecilia, the Italian radio orchestras and other European orchestras performing full range of baroque, classical and modern works; opera debut with The Barber of Seville, Hamburg 1977 and has since conducted opera in all the principal opera houses in Europe; American debut with Elisir d'amore, Metropolitan Opera, New York 1988; conducted world premiere of Bussotti's Cristallo di Rocca (opera) at La Scala 1983; Bolshoi debut with Macbeth, Moscow 2003; Musical Dir Bonn Opera House 1994–97, Nice Opera House 1997–2001; Artistic Dir San Carlo Opera House, Naples 2001–02; Artistic Dir Accad. Filarmonica Romana 2001–04, 2007–09; Musical Dir Orchestra Sinfonica Tito Schipa, Lecce 2008–; Milhaud Prof. of Composition and Conducting, Mills Coll., Oakland, Calif. 1980–84; mem. Accad. di Santa Cecilia 2003–. *Works include* symphonic and chamber music and music for experimental theatrical works; operas: Hanjo (one act) 1994, Il giudizio di Paride (one act) 1996, The Banquet (one act) 1998, Garibaldi in Sicile (two acts) 2005, Apokàlypsis (oratorio) 2009. *Leisure interests:* arts, sport. *Address:* 3 Piazza Borghese, 00186 Rome, Italy (home). *Telephone:* (06) 6873617 (home). *Fax:* (06) 6873617 (office). *E-mail:* marcellopanni@yahoo.it (office).

PANNICK, Baron (Life Peer), cr. 2008, of Radlett in the County of Hertfordshire; **David Philip Pannick,** QC, BCL, MA; British barrister; b. 7 March 1956, London, England; s. of Maurice A. Pannick and Rita L. Pannick; m. Denise Sloam 1978 (died 1999); two s. one d.; m. Nathalie Trager-Lewis 2003; one s. two d.; ed Bancroft's School, Essex and Hertford Coll., Oxford; called to the Bar 1979, QC 1992; Fellow, All Souls Coll. Oxford 1978–; Jr Counsel to the Crown (Common Law) 1988–92; columnist on law, The Times 1991–; Bencher of Gray's Inn 2001; mem. (Crossbench), House of Lords 2008–, mem. Constitution Cttee 2008–13; Chair. British Legal Friends of the Hebrew Univ. 2008–; Hon. Fellow, Hertford Coll., Oxford, Hebrew Univ. of Jerusalem; Hon. LLD (Hertfordshire) 1998. *Publications:* Sex Discrimination Law 1985, Judges 1987, Advocates 1992, Human Rights Law and Practice (co-author with Lord Lester of Herne Hill) 1999, 2004, 2009. *Leisure interests:* theatre, cinema, Arsenal Football Club. *Address:* House of Lords, Westminster, London, SW1A 0PW (office). Blackstone Chambers, Temple, London, EC4Y 7BH, England (office). *Telephone:* (20) 7219-3107 (House of Lords) (office); (20) 7583-1770 (Blackstone Chambers) (office). *Fax:* (20) 7219-5353 (House of Lords) (office); (20) 7822-7222 (Blackstone Chambers) (office). *E-mail:* davidpannick@blackstonechambers.com (office). *Website:* www.parliament.uk/ biographies/lords/lord-pannick/3870 (office).

PANNONE, Rodger John, DL, FRSA; British solicitor; b. 20 April 1943, Minehead, Somerset; s. of Cyril Pannone and Violet Weeks; m. Patricia Todd 1966; two s. one d.; ed St Brendan's Coll. Bristol and Coll. of Law, London and Manchester Polytechnic; articled clerk, Casson & Co. Salford; joined W.H. Thompson 1969, later partner; joined Conn Goldberg (now Pannone & Partners) 1973, Sr Partner 1991–2003, consultant 2003–; lecturer and broadcaster on legal affairs; mem. Lord Chancellor's Advisory Cttee on Civil Justice; fmr mem.

Supreme Court Rule Cttee; Chair. Forensic Science Service; Chair. Gov. Coll. of Law, Council Manchester Univ.; Fellow, Manchester Metropolitan Univ.; mem. Council Law Soc. of England and Wales, Pres. 1993–94; DL Greater Manchester; Hon. Mem. Canadian Bar Asscn; Hon. Fellow, Soc. of Chiropodists, Univ. of Birmingham 1998; Hon. DLitt (Salford); Hon. LLD (Nottingham Trent); Hon. LittD (Manchester). *Publications:* legal articles. *Leisure interests:* walking slowly, food and drink. *Address:* Pannone & Partners, 123 Deansgate, Manchester, M3 2BU, England. *Telephone:* (161) 909-3000. *Fax:* (161) 909-4444. *E-mail:* law@pannone.co.uk (office). *Website:* www.pannone.com (office).

PANOV, Alexander Nikolayevich, CandHistSc; Russian diplomatist; *Rector, Diplomatic Academy, Ministry of Foreign Affairs;* b. 6 July 1944, Moscow; m. 1967; one d.; ed Moscow Inst. of Int. Relations; diplomatic service 1968–; trans., attaché Embassy in Tokyo 1968–71; teacher, Asst Prof., Moscow Inst. of Int. Relations 1971–77; Third, Second Sec., Perm. Mission to UN, New York 1977–82; First Sec., Second Far East Dept USSR Ministry of Foreign Affairs 1982–83; First Sec., Counsellor, Embassy in Tokyo 1983–88; Deputy Chief, Chief of Div., Deputy Chief, Dept of Countries of Pacific Ocean and SE Asia, USSR Ministry of Foreign Affairs 1988–90, Chief 1990–92; Amb. to Repub. of Korea 1992–94; Deputy Minister of Foreign Affairs 1994–96; Amb. to Japan 1996–2003, to Norway 2004–06; Rector of the Diplomatic Acad., Ministry of Foreign Affairs 2006–; Order of Merit. *Publications:* Postwar Reforms in Japan 1945–52, Japanese Diplomatic Service, Beyond Distrust to Trust; articles in periodicals. *Leisure interest:* photography. *Address:* Diplomatic Academy, Ministry of Foreign Affairs, 119992 Moscow, Ostozhenka street, 53/2, Russia (office). *Telephone:* (495) 245-33-86 (office). *Fax:* (495) 244-1878 (office). *E-mail:* Alexander.Panov@dipacademy.ru (office). *Website:* www.dipacademy.ru/english (office).

PANSIERI, Flavia, PhD; Italian diplomatist and UN official; *Deputy High Commissioner for Human Rights, United Nations;* ed Milan and Venice Univs; began UN career with UNDP in China 1983, responsible for UN Volunteers (UNV) and TOKTEN programmes, as well as for projects in energy sector, continued with UNDP in Bangladesh 1987–90 and Myanmar 1990–93, posted to Laos as Dir UN Office on Drugs and Crime (UNODC), served at UNOCD HQ in Vienna 1995–98, Deputy Exec. Dir UNIFEM, New York 1998–2001, took charge of Country Div. of Regional Bureau for Arab States at UNDP 2001–04, UN Resident Co-ordinator and Resident Rep. of UNDP in Yemen 2004–08, Exec. Co-ordinator UNV 2008–13; Deputy High Commr for Human Rights 2013–. *Address:* Office of the United Nations High Commissioner for Human Rights (OHCHR), Palais des Nations, 1211 Geneva 10, Switzerland (office). *Telephone:* (22) 9179220 (office). *E-mail:* infodesk@ohchr.org (office). *Website:* www.ohchr.org (office).

PANTEV, Plamen Ilarionov, PhD; Bulgarian research institute director and academic; *Founder-Director, Institute for Security and International Studies;* b. 31 July 1952, Gradets, Vidin Dist; s. of Ilarion Pantev and Sofiana Panteva; m. Tatyana Panteva; one d.; ed Sofia Univ. 'St Kliment Ohridsky', Nat. Defence Coll., Stockholm, George C. Marshall Centre for European Security Policy, Garmisch-Partenkirchen; fmr Researcher, Columbia Univ., New York, Johns Hopkins Univ., Washington, DC and Harvard Univ., USA 1988–89, WEU Inst. for Security Studies, Paris, Istituto Affari Internazionali, Rome 1992, Netherlands Inst. for International Relations, Clingendael, The Hague 1993; Founder-Dir Inst. for Security and International Studies, Sofia 1994–; currently Prof. of Law and International Relations, Dir MA Program in International Security and Vice-Dean, Law School, Sofia Univ. 'St Kliment Ohridsky', responsible for Int. Relations Dept 2006–11; Lecturer, NATO Defence Coll., Rome, Italy 2002, Henry L. Stimpson Center, Washington, DC 2003, Diplomatic Acad., Vienna July 2004, Texas A&M Univ. March 2006; Co-Chair. Study Group on Regional Stability in SE Europe 2002–10, Consortium of Defence Acad and Security Study Insts of PfP Countries; mem. Supreme Testimonial Comm.'s Specialized Council in International Relations at Council of Ministers of Bulgaria –2011; Ed.-in-Chief, Balkan and Black Regional Profiles (electronic periodicals) –2005; mem. International Studies Asscn, International Advisory Bd, Journal of International Negotiation –2011, Europe's World Journal, Contemporary Law (in Bulgarian); mem. Acad. of Political Science, New York 2011, IISS, London 2013; Ford Foundation/WEU Inst. for Security Studies Fellow, Istituto Affari Internazionali, Rome, Italy 1992, Erazmus Fellowship, Netherlands Inst. for International Relations, Clingendael, The Hague 1993, NATO Individual Fellow 1995–97, USIA Fellow, Univ. of Michigan 1997, Fellowship, Swedish Nat. Defence Coll. 2000, 2010, Hon. Plaque of Austrian NDA, Individual Coin by the PfP Consortium 2010. *Publications include:* 17 books and more than 150 articles on int. and regional security, int. law, relations and negotiations, foreign policy and civil-mil. relations in Bulgarian, English, Italian, German, French, Russian, Ukrainian, Polish, Bahasa (Indonesian). *Leisure interests:* music, swimming, mountain walking, cinema. *Address:* PO Box 231, Institute for Security and International Studies, 1c Krasno selo bl. 194, ent. B ap. 36, 1618 Sofia (office); 1c 'Buxton', bl. 1, ent. A, ap. 11, 1618 Sofia, Bulgaria (home). *Telephone:* (2) 856-2211 (office); 88-8289605 (mobile) (office). *E-mail:* plamen.pantev@abv.bg (office), isis.pantev@gmail.com (office). *Website:* www.isis-bg.org (office).

PANTÓ, György; Hungarian geochemist and academic; *Research Professor, Institute for Geochemical Research;* b. 1936, Budapest; s. of Endre Pantó and Ilona Botár; m. Márta Juhász; one s. one d.; ed Loránd Eötvös Univ.; mine geologist, Hungarian Mineral and Ore Mines 1959–62; postgraduate scholarship, Hungarian Acad. of Sciences 1962–65, Sr Researcher, Lab. for Geochemical Research 1965–76, Dir 1976–2000, now Research Prof.; Dir-Gen. Hungarian Acad. of Sciences Research Centre for Earth Sciences 1998–2004; mem. Hungarian Acad. of Sciences, Pres. Earth Sciences Section 1999–2005; Foreign mem. Serbian Acad. of Arts and Sciences; mem. Editorial Bd Acta Geologica Hungarica; Szèchenyi Prize 2000. *Publications:* numerous articles, books and contribs on geochemistry. *Leisure interests:* gardening, tourism. *Address:* Hungarian Academy of Sciences, Institute for Geochemical Research, Budaörsi út 45, 1112 Budapest, Hungary (office). *Telephone:* (1) 319-3145 (office). *Fax:* (1) 319-3145 (office). *E-mail:* panto@sparc.core.hu (office). *Website:* www.geochem.hu/people/panto_hu.html (office).

PANTON, Seymour; Jamaican judge; *President, Court of Appeal;* called to the Bar, Lincoln's Inn, London 1968; held posts in Jamaica including Deputy Clerk of Courts, Clerk of Courts, Crown Counsel (Acting) in Dir of Public Prosecutions Office, Resident Magistrate, Puisne Judge; fmr Legal Asst to Attorney Gen., Sr

Counsel and Judge of Grand Court, Cayman Islands; Appeal Judge, Court of Appeal, Jamaica 1999–, Pres. 2007–; fmr mem. Bench and Bar Consultative Cttee, Asscn of Resident Magistrates (Vice-Pres.), Commonwealth Magistrates and Judges Asscn; Assoc. Tutor, Norman Manley Law School 1986–93; Examiner, Deputy Clerk of Courts Qualifying Exams 1986–96; Fulbright Grant 1990, Outstanding Service Awards from Rusea's Old Students' Asscn 1990, Cornwall Bar Asscn 1995, Jamaican Govt 2006. *Address:* Supreme Court of Jamaica, Public Building E, 134 Tower Street, Kingston, Jamaica (office). *Telephone:* 922-8300 (office). *E-mail:* justice.srpanton@sc.gov.jm (office). *Website:* www.sc.gov.jm (office).

PANULA, Jorma; Finnish conductor, composer and academic; b. 10 Aug. 1930, Kauhajoki; ed Sibelius Acad., Helsinki; Artistic Dir and Chief Conductor, Turku Philharmonic Orchestra 1963–65, Helsinki Philharmonic 1965–72, Aarhus Symphony, Denmark 1970–73; Prof. of Orchestral Conducting, Sibelius Acad., Helsinki 1973–94; trains conductors in USA, France, Netherlands, Russia, Sweden, Italy, Australia and UK; fmr Visiting Prof. Music, Stockholm Royal Acad. of Music and Copenhagen Royal Acad. of Music, Yale Univ., Bartók Seminar, Hungary; Music Prize, Royal Swedish Acad. of Science 1997. *Music:* (operas) Jaakko Ilkka, The River Opera; musicals, church music, a violin concerto, a jazz capriccio and vocal music. *Address:* Jorma Panula Foundation, c/o Taco Kooistra, Sloterweg 1188, 1066 Amsterdam, Netherlands (office). *E-mail:* tckooistra@zonnet.nl (office). *Website:* www.jormapanula.com.

PANWAR, Lalit K., BSc, MSc, PhD; Indian government official; *Secretary, Ministry of Minority Affairs;* b. 11 July 1955; City Magistrate, Bikaner 1982–83; Collector and Dist Magistrate, Jaisalmer 1985–88; Dir of Primary and Secondary Educ., Bikaner 1988–91, of Art, Culture and Tourism 1991–95; mem. Bd of Revenue, Ajmer 1995–96; Divisional Commr, Jodhpur 1996–98; Sec. to Chief Minister 1998–2000; Sec., Tourism, Art and Culture Dept 2003–04, Mines and Petroleum Dept 2004; Commr Jaipur Devt Authority 2004–05; Prin. Sec., Urban Devt and Housing Dept 2005, Urban Governance Dept 2005–07, Labour and Employment 2007, School and Sanskrit Educ. 2009–10; Chair. and Man. Dir India Tourism Devt Corpn Ltd 2010–13; Sec., Ministry of Minority Affairs 2013–. *Address:* Ministry of Minority Affairs, Paryavaran Bhavan, 11th Floor, CGO Complex, Lodhi Road, New Delhi 110 003, India (office). *Telephone:* (11) 24364272 (office). *Fax:* (11) 24364285 (office). *E-mail:* secy-mma@nic.in (office). *Website:* minorityaffairs.gov.in (office).

PANYARACHUN, Anand; Thai business executive, fmr diplomatist and fmr politician; *Chairman, Siam Commercial Bank;* b. 9 Aug. 1932, Bangkok; s. of Maha Ammat Tri Phya Prichanusat (Sern Panyarachun) and Khunying Prichanusat (Pruek Chotikasathien); m. M. R. Sodsee Chakrabandh; two d.; ed Bangkok Christian Coll., Dulwich Coll., Univ. of Cambridge, UK; joined Ministry of Foreign Affairs 1955, Sec. to Foreign Minister 1959, First Sec., Perm. Mission to UN, New York 1964, Counsellor 1966, concurrently Amb. to Canada and Acting Perm. Rep. to UN 1967–72 (Perm. Rep. 1972–76), concurrently Amb. to USA 1972–76, Amb. to FRG 1978–79, Head, Ministry of Foreign Affairs 1976; accused of being a Communist after coup, suspended but exonerated and reinstated; fmr Exec. Chair. Saha-Union Group (industrial conglomerate); fmr Chair. Fed. of Thai Industries 1990; Prime Minister of Thailand 1991–92; elected mem. Constitution Drafting Ass. 1997, Chair. Drafting Cttee; Chair. UN High-Level Panel on Threats, Challenges and Change, Steering Cttee Asia Pacific Leadership Forum on HIV/AIDS and Devt; mem. Advisory Group Anti-Corruption Issues for the East Asia and Pacific Region, World Bank; UNICEF Amb. 1996–; Dir Sime Siam Commercial Bank 1984–, currently Chair.; Chair. Thailand Devt Research Inst., Council of Trustees Thailand Environment Inst., Council of Asian Univ. of Science and Tech., Bd of Trustees of Asian Inst. of Tech.; Dir Sime Darby Berhad 1982–98; mem. Int. Advisory Bd American Int. Group, Unocal Asia Pacific Ventures, Toyota Motor Corpn; mem. Asian Advisory Bd The Carlyle Group –2004; Hon. KBE 1996; Kt Grand Commdr (Second Class, higher grade) of the Most Illustrious Order of Chula Chom Klao 1968, Order of Diplomatic Service Merit (South Korea) 1970, Ringtang Jasa (First Class) Indonesia 1971, Kt Grand Cordon (Special Class) of the Most Noble Order of the Crown of Thailand 1988, Grand Officier de l'Ordre de la Couronne, 2nd class (Belgium) 1990, Kt Grand Cordon (Special Class) of the Most Exalted Order of the White Elephant 1991, Grand Cordon of the Order of the Rising Sun (Japan) 1991, Commdr, Grand Cross of the Royal Order of the Polar Star (Sweden) 2007; 25 hon. degrees from univs in Thailand, USA, Canada, Hong Kong and Japan; Royal Cypher Medal (Third Class), Ramon Magsaysay Award for Government Service 1997. *Address:* Siam Commercial Bank PCL, 9 Ratchadaphisek Road, SCP Park, Chatuchak, Bangkok 10900, Thailand (office). *Telephone:* (2) 544-4222 (office). *Fax:* (2) 937-7931 (office). *E-mail:* anand.panyarachun@scb.co.th (office). *Website:* www.scb.co.th (office).

PAOCHINDA, Gen. Anupong; Thai army officer; *Commander in Chief, Royal Thai Army;* b. 10 Oct. 1949, Bangkok; m. Kunlaya Paochinda; two c.; ed Amnuay Silpa School, Armed Forces Acads Preparatory School, Bangkok, Chulachomklao Royal Mil. Acad., Nakhon Nayok Prov., Ramkhamhaeng Univ., Nat. Inst. of Devt Admin, Bangkok; fmr commdr of several army divs including 21st Infantry Regt (Queen's Guard), 2nd Infantry Div. (King's Guards), 1st Infantry Div. (King's Guards); fmr Commdr 1st Army Area; Deputy Sec.-Gen., Council for Nat. Security 2006; Deputy Commdr in Chief, Royal Thai Army 2006–07, Commdr in Chief 2007–. *Address:* Ministry of Defence, Thanon Sanamchai, Bangkok 10200, Thailand (office). *Telephone:* (2) 222-1121 (office). *Fax:* (2) 226-3117 (office). *Website:* www.mod.go.th (office).

PAOLILLO, Felipe; Uruguayan lawyer, diplomatist and UN official; *Co-Chair, Open-ended Informal Consultative Process on Oceans and the Law of the Sea, United Nations;* b. 8 Oct. 1931; Prof. of Int. Public Law, Univ. of Uruguay 1967–74, 1985–87; Assoc. Prof. New York Univ. School of Law 1977–84; Perm. Rep. to UN, New York 1987–90, 2000–01, 2003, to Holy See and FAO 1996–2000; Chair. UN Gen. Ass. Credentials Cttee 2002; Vice-Pres. Ass. of States Parties, Int. Criminal Court, The Hague 2002–05; currently Co-Chair. UN Open-ended Informal Consultative Process on Oceans and the Law of the Sea (UNICPOLOS); mem. Inst. of Int. Law; mem. Interamerican Judicial Council. *Address:* Office of the Co-Chair, United Nations Open-ended Informal Consultative Process on Oceans and the Law of the Sea, United Nations, New York, NY 10017, USA (office). *Telephone:* (212) 963-1234 (office). *Fax:* (212) 963-4879 (office). *Website:* www.un.org (office).

PAOLINELLI, Alysson; Brazilian agronomist and academic; b. 1936, Bambuí, Minas Gerais; ed Fed. Agricultural Univ. of Lavras; Prof. of Agric., Fed. Agricultural Univ. of Lavras 1960–67, Dean 1967–71; Sec. of Agric. for Minas Gerais 1971–74; Minister of Agric. for Brazil 1974–79; currently consultant in agribusiness; Pres. Brazilian Asscn for Agricultural Educ. 1970–71; Personality of the Year in Agrobusiness, Ministry of Agriculture 2006, World Food Prize 2006. *Address:* c/o Brazilian Agribusiness Association, Avenida Paulista 1754, 14° andar, Conj. 147–148, 01310-920 São Paulo, Brazil.

PAOLUCCI, Antonio; Italian art historian and museum director; *Director, Vatican Museums;* b. 1939, Rimini; ed student of Roberto Longhi; began his career at Soprintendenza per i Beni Culturali for Venice Region 1969–80; fmr Supt Polo Museale Fiorentino; worked for Mantova-Brescia-Cremona Region 1984–86; Dir Office of Hard Stones and the restoration laboratory in Florence 1986–88, Dept of Artistic Affairs of Tuscany 1988; Minister of Culture 1995–96; supervised comm. in charge of restoration of Basilica of St Francis of Assisi after the earthquake in 1997; was at centre of controversy concerning restoration of Michelangelo's David in Florence 2003; Dir Museums in Florence 2004–06, Vatican Museums 2007–; Pres. Accad. Carrara, Bergamo. *Publications:* more than 300 articles in various journals, including Paragone, Bollettino d'Arte, and of monographic studies on Palmezzano, Signorelli, as well as other Florentine artists and monuments. *Address:* Musei Vaticani, Città del Vaticano, 00120 Città del Vaticano, Rome, Italy (office). *E-mail:* info@mv.vatican.va (office). *Website:* mv.vatican.va (office).

PAPACONSTANTINOU, Georgios, BSc, MA, PhD; Greek economist and politician; *Minister of the Environment, Energy and Climate Change;* b. 1961, Athens; m. Jacoline Vinke; two s.; ed London School of Econs, UK, New York Univ., USA; Sr Economist, OECD, Paris 1988–98; Adviser on Information Soc. issues to fmr Prime Minister Costas Simitis 1998–2000; Special Sec. for the Information Society, Ministry of Economy and Finance 2000–02; mem. Council of Econ. Advisors 2002–04; mem. Bd OTE (telecoms co.) 2002–04; Greek Rep. to EU Econ. Policy Cttee 2002–04; co-ordinated 'Lisbon Strategy' for econ. and social reforms during Greek Presidency of EU 2003; econ. adviser to Panhellenic Socialist Movt (PASOK) Pres. George Papandreou 2004–07; mem. Bd Inst. for Strategic and Devt Studies (PASOK's think-tank) 2005–08; mem. Nat. Council of PASOK 2005–, Press Spokesman 2008–09; taught Econs at Athens Univ. of Econs and Business 2003–07; advised EC on research and information society issues, participating in various int. research projects 2003–07; mem. Vouli (Parl.) for Pref. of Kozani 2007–; mem. European Parl. 2009; Minister of Finance 2009–11, of the Environment, Energy and Climate Change 2011–. *Address:* Ministry of the Environment, Energy and Climate Change, Odos Amalia 17, 115 23 Athens, Greece (office). *Telephone:* (210) 1515000 (office). *Fax:* (210) 6447608 (office). *E-mail:* service@dorg .minenv.gr (office). *Website:* www.minenv.gr (office); www.gpapak.gr (office).

PAPACOSTAS, Costas; Cypriot fmr police officer and politician; b. 12 Nov. 1939, Agia Triada of Yialousa, Famagusta District; m. Chryso Mammidou; one s. one d.; ed War Coll. and Nat. Defence Coll. of Greece, attended further special police training in crisis nan. and int. terrorism matters in Germany and USA; served in Cyprus Army and Nat. Guard for 18 years, reaching rank of Col; seconded to Auxiliary Police Force to fight against illegal activities of EOKA B' 1973, participated in resistance against coup of 15 July 1974; seconded again to Police Force to establish and command Mobile Immediate Action Unit to fight terrorism and organized crime 1974; transferred to Police Force with rank of Chief Supt 1984, attained rank of Deputy Chief of Police, resgnd comm. in protest at state of affairs in the Force 1996; elected mem. House of Reps (AKEL-Left-New Forces) for Famagusta 1996–, Chair. House Standing Cttee on Crime and on the Fight against Drugs and Addictive Substances, Deputy Chair. House Standing Cttee on Refugees-Enclaved-Missing-Adversely Affected Persons. mem. House Standing Cttee on Defence Affairs, House Standing Cttee on Legal Affairs; Minister of Defence 2008–11 (resgnd); Hon. Diploma and Resistance Medal for his actions towards the defence of the Repub. and the defence of law and order against the coup of 15 July 1974, Govt of Cyprus 2004, Hon. Diploma and Medal for his participation in the liberation struggle of EOKA 1955–1959, Govt of Cyprus 2006. *Publications:* two extended essays, 'The Legal and Historical Truth on the Cyprus Problem' 1985, and 'Today's Turkey-trends and Prospects' (in Greek). *Address:* c/o Ministry of Defence, 4 Emmanuel Roides Avenue, 1432 Nicosia, Cyprus (office).

PAPACOSTEA, Serban, DHist; Romanian historian and academic; b. 25 June 1928, Bucharest; s. of Petre G. Papacostea and Josefina Papacostea; ed Univ. of Bucharest; scientific researcher and Dir 'Nicolae Iorga' Inst. of History, Bucharest; mem. editorial Bd Revue Roumaine d'Histoire, Studii si materiale de istorie medie (Studies and Materials of Medieval History), Il Mar Nero (Rome); Corresp. mem. Romanian Acad., Accad. Ligure di Scienze e Lettere; Prize of the Roman Acad. 1971. *Publications:* Istoria României (The History of Romania) (in collaboration) 1964, 1998, 2002, Istoria poporului român (History of the Romanian People) (in collaboration) 1970, Nochmals Wittenberg und Byzanz: die Moldau im Zeitalter der Reformation 1970, Oltenia sub stăpînirea austriacă, 1718–1739 (Oltenia under Austrian Rule, 1718–1739) 1971, Venise et les Pays Roumains au Moyen Age, in Venezia e il Levante fino al secolo XV, 1973, Stephan der Grosse, Fürst der Moldau 1975, Kilia et la politique orientale de Sigismond de Luxembourg 1976, Die politischen Voraussetzungen für die wirtschaftliche Vorherrschaft des Osmanischen Reiches im Schwarzmeergebiet 1453–1484 1978, La fondation de la Valachie et de la Moldavie et les Roumains de Transylvanie 1978, 'Quod non iretur ad Tanam': Un aspect fondamental de la politique génoise dans la Mer Noire au XIVe siècle 1979, Începuturile politicii comerciale a Tării Românesti și Moldovei (The Beginnings of Trade Policy in Wallachia and Moldavia) 1983, La fin de la domination génoise à Licostomo 1985, La Valachie et la crise de structure de l'Empire Ottoman (1402–1413) 1986, La Mer Noire: du monopole byzantin à la domination des Latins aux Détroits 1988, La première crise des rapports byzantino-génois après Nymphaion: le complot de Guglielmo Guercio (1264) 1988, Geneza statului in Evul mediu Românesc (The Formation of the Medieval Romanian State) 1988, Gênes, Venise et la Mer Noire à la fin du XIIIe siècle 1990, Byzance et la Croisade au Bas-Danube à la fin du XIVe siècle 1991, Jews in the Romanian Principalities during the Middle Ages 1993, Romanii in Secolul XIII intre Cruciata și Imperial Mongol 1993, Une révolte antigénoise en Mer Noire et la riposte de Gênes (1432–1434) 1994, Captive Clio: Romanian Historiography under Communist Rule 1996, Un tournant de la politique génoise en Mer Noire au

XIVᵉsiècle 1997, Gênes, Venise et la Croisade de Varna 1997, Between the Crusades and the Mongol Empire 1998, Evul Mediu românesc (The Romanian Middle Ages) 2001, Welthandel und Weltpolitik im Spätmittealter 2001, Byzance et les Detroits sous les Premiers Paléologues 2003, Les Génois et la Horde d'Or: le tournant de 1313 2004. *Leisure interest:* pre-classical music. *Address:* Institutul de Istorie 'Nicolae Iorga', Blvd Aviatorilor 1, Bucharest (office); Caragea Vodă 19, 71149 Bucharest, Romania (home). *Telephone:* (21) 6509045 (office); (21) 2114455 (home). *E-mail:* spap@b.astral.ro (home).

PAPADEMOS, Lucas Demetrios, PhD; Greek economist, banker and politician; b. 11 Oct. 1947, Athens; m. Sana Ingram 1977; ed Athens Coll., Massachusetts Inst. of Tech., USA; Asst Prof., then Assoc. Prof. of Econs, Columbia Univ., New York, USA 1975–84; Prof. of Econs, Univ. of Athens 1988–; Sr Economist, Fed. Reserve Bank of Boston, USA; Econ. Adviser, Bank of Greece 1985–93, Head of Econ. Research Dept 1988–92, Deputy Gov. 1993–94, Gov. 1994–2002; Vice-Pres. European Cen. Bank 2002–10; adviser to Prime Minister George Papandreou Jan.–Nov. 2011; Prime Minister of Greece (following resignation of Papandreou to allow formation of a provisional coalition govt to avert political crisis caused by country's debt crisis) 2011–12; mem. Cttee of Alts of Govs of EC Cen. Banks 1985–93, Council of Econ. Advisers 1985–88, 1991–94, Trilateral Comm. 1998–, EMI and various bds; Visiting Prof. of Public Policy, Kennedy School of Govt, Harvard Univ., USA; mem. Acad. of Athens 2006; Grand Commdr, Order of Honour 1999. *Publications:* numerous articles on macroeconomic theory, the structure and functioning of financial markets, monetary analysis and policy as well as on subjects concerning the economic performance, financial stability and economic policy in the EU. *Address:* c/o Office of the Prime Minister, Maximos Mansion, Herodou Atticou 19, 106 74 Athens, Greece. *E-mail:* primeminister@ primeminister.gr.

PAPADONGONAS, Alexandros; Greek politician and naval officer; b. 11 July 1931, Tripolis; s. of Dionisios Papadongonas and Vasiliki Papadongonas; m. Niki Maidonis 1976; one s. one d.; ed Greek Naval Acad., Naval War Coll., US Naval Schools, NATO Defence Coll.; has served on Greek fleet vessels and submarines and has held staff positions; organized with other Navy officers Movt of Navy against the dictatorship; arrested May 1973 and removed from service; returned to Navy July–Nov. 1974; mem. Vouli (Parl.) 1974–93; Minister of Merchant Shipping 1974–77, 1992–93, of Communications 1977–80; Deputy Minister of Defence 1990–91; mem. Council of Europe 1982–89, 1991; Pres. Greek Del. to Parl. Ass. of OSCE 1993–; mem. North Atlantic Ass.; mem. Bd of Dirs Yacht Club of Greece 2012–; New Democracy Party; Medal of Mil. Valour; Commdr, Order of the Phoenix; Officer Order of George I. *Leisure interests:* sailing, scuba diving, underwater archaeology. *Address:* Yacht Club of Greece, 18 Karagiorgi Servias str. 185 33 Piraeus (office); 11 Nikis Street, Athens 105 57, Greece (home). *Telephone:* (210) 417-9730 (office); (210) 325-5150 (home). *E-mail:* noe@ycg.gr (office). *Website:* www.ycg.gr (office).

PAPAIOANNOU, Miltiades; Greek politician and lawyer; b. 1946, Kalavryta, Achaia; ed Panteio Univ., Law Faculty of Athens; Panhellenic Socialist Movt (PASOK) MP; Deputy Minister, Ministry of Internal Affairs 1982–85, Minister of Justice 1985, Deputy Minister, Prime Minister's Dept and Govt Spokesman 1985–86, Gen. Sec. Ministry of Nat. Economy 1993–96; Minister of Labour and Social Security 1998–2000; Minister of State 2000–02; mem. Exec. Bureau and Cen. Cttee PASOK. *Publications:* numerous articles on politics, econs, public admin, local govt and regional devt. *Address:* c/o Ministry of Labour and Social Security, Odos Pireos 40, 104 37 Athens, Greece.

PAPALOIZOU, John Christopher Baillie, DPhil, FRS; British astrophysicist, applied mathematician and academic; *Professor, Department of Applied Mathematics and Theoretical Physics, University of Cambridge;* b. 4 May 1947, London, England; ed Univ. Coll., London, Univ. of Sussex, Brighton; fmr Prof. of Math. and Astronomy and Dir Astronomy Unit, Queen Mary, Univ. of London; currently Prof., Dept of Applied Math. and Theoretical Physics, Univ. of Cambridge; Brouwer Award Winner 2004, asteroid 17063 Papaloizou named after him. *Achievements include:* co-discovered, with Jim E. Pringle, the Papaloizou-Pringle instability 1984. *Publications:* numerous scientific papers in professional journals on the theory of accretion disks, with particular application to the formation of planets, radial-orbit instability, toroidal modes in stars and different instabilities in accretion disks. *Address:* Department of Applied Mathematics and Theoretical Physics, Centre for Mathematical Sciences, Wilberforce Road, Cambridge, CB3 0WA, England (office). *Telephone:* (1223) 760390 (office). *Fax:* (1223) 765900 (office). *E-mail:* jcbp2@damtp.cam.ac.uk (office); pavfsec@damtp.cam.ac.uk (office). *Website:* damtp.cam.ac.uk (office).

PAPANDREOU, Georgios (George) A., BA, MSc; Greek politician; *President, Socialist International;* b. 16 June 1952, Saint Paul, Minn., USA; s. of Andreas Papandreou and Margaret Papandreou (née Chant); m. 1st Evanthia Zissmidides 1976–87; one s.; m. 2nd Ada Papapanos; one d.; ed King City Secondary School, Canada, Athens Coll., Amherst Coll. and York High School, Elmhurst, Ill., USA, Stockholm Univ., Sweden, London School of Econs, UK; mem. Parl. (Panhellenic Socialist Movt—PASOK) for Achaia (Patrias) 1981–96, for First Dist of Athens 1996–2012, for Achaea 2012–; Under-Sec. for Cultural Affairs 1985–87; Minister of Educ. and Religious Affairs 1988–89, 1994–96; Deputy Minister of Foreign Affairs 1993–94, Alt. Minister of Foreign Affairs 1996–99, Minister of Foreign Affairs 1999–2004, 2009–10; unsuccessful presidential cand. 2004; Leader of the Opposition 2004–09; Prime Minister and Chair. of the Govt 2009–11 (resgnd to allow formation of a provisional coalition govt to avert political crisis caused by country's debt crisis); mem. Cen. Cttee PASOK 1984–, Exec. Cttee 1987–88, mem. Exec. Office and Political Bureau 1996–, Leader, PASOK 2004–12; Govt Co-ordinator for 2004 Athens Olympic bid 1997; mem. Socialist International (Vice-Pres. 2005–06, Pres. 2006–); mem. Bd Foundation of Mediterranean Studies for Research and Self-Educ., Cambridge Foundation for Peace; Fellow, Center for Int. Affairs, Harvard Univ. 1992–93; Distinguished Prof., Center for Hellenic Studies, Georgia State Coll. of Arts and Science 2006; decorations from numerous countries, including Commdr, Order of Prince Yaroslav the Wise (Ukraine) 1996, Grand Cross, Order of the Lion (Finland) 1996, Grand Commdr, Order of the Polish Repub. 1996, Grand Cross, Order of Civil Merit (Spain) 1998, Grand Cross, Order of the Polar Star (Sweden) 1999, Grand Cross, Order of the White Star (Estonia) 1999, Grand Cross, Order of Honour, First Class (Austria) 1999, Grand Cross,

Order of Merit (Germany) 2000, Grand Cross, Order of Isabella the Catholic (Spain) 2001, Grand Cross, Order of the Crown (Belgum) 2001, Grand Cross, Order of Infante Dom Henrique (Portugal) 2002, Grand Cross, Order of Pius IX (Vatican) 2002, Grand Commdr, Order of Merit (Hungary) 2003, Grand Cross, Order of Merit (Italy), Gran Cruz El Sol de Peru 2003; Hon. LLD (Amherst Coll.) 2002; Botsis Foundation for Promotion of Journalism Award 1988, SOS against Racism Award 1996, Abdi Ipekci Special Award for Peace and Friendship (Turkey) 1997, Statesman of the Year Award, Eastwest Inst. (USA) 2000, Jackie Robinson Humanitarianism Award, US Sport Acad. 2002, Defender of Democracy, Parliamentarians for Global Action 2003, Open Fields Award, Truce Foundation (USA) 2006, Quadriga Award, Werkstatt Deutschland (Germany) for The Power of Veracity (transparency regarding the state of the Greek economy) 2010. *Address:* Panhellenic Socialist Movement (PASOK), Odos Hippocrates 22, 106 80 Athens, Greece (office); Socialist International, Maritime House, Old Town, Clapham, London, SW4 0JW, England. *Telephone:* (210) 3665000 (office); (20) 7627-4449. *Fax:* (210) 3665209 (office); (20) 7720-4448. *E-mail:* pasok@pasok.gr (office); dialogue@politicalforum.gr (office); secretariat@socialistinternational.org. *Website:* www.pasok.gr (office); www.socialistinternational.org; www.papandreou.gr.

PAPANDREOU, Vasiliki (Vasso), PhD; Greek politician; b. 1944, Valimitika nr Aeghiou; ed School of Econ. and Trade Sciences, Univ. of Athens, Univs of London and Reading, UK; Lecturer, Univ. of Athens; Research Asst, Univs of Exeter and Oxford, UK; Dir Hellenic Org. of Small and Medium-sized Businesses, Athens 1981–85; Founder-mem. Panhellenic Socialist Party (PASOK) 1974, mem. Cen. Cttee Exec. Bureau 1984–88, 1996–; MP 1985–89, 1993–; Deputy Minister for Industry, Energy and Tech. 1985–89, Alt. Minister 1986–87; Alt. Minister for Trade 1988–89; Commr for Social Affairs, Employment, Educ., Comm. of European Communities 1989–92; Head of Greek Del. Council of Europe Parl. Ass. 1993–96, Vice-Pres. 1995–96; Minister for Devt 1996–99, of the Interior, Public Admin and Decentralization 1999–2001, of the Environment, Physical Planning and Public Works 2001–04; Chevalier Légion d'honneur 1993, Grand-Croix, Belgium 1993, Great Cross of the Order of the North Star 1999; Hon. LittD (Sheffield) 1992; Dr hc (CNAA, London) 1992, (P. Sabatier, Toulouse) 1993. *Publications:* Multinational Companies and Less Developed Countries: The Case of Greece 1981; numerous papers on politics and econs. *Address:* c/o Ministry of the Environment, Physical Planning and Public Works, Odos Amaliados 17, 115 23 Athens; 15 Omirou Street, 10672 Athens, Greece. *Telephone:* (210) 6431461 (office). *Fax:* (210) 6432589 (office).

PAPANTONIOU, Ioannis, PhD; Greek politician; b. 1949, Paris, France; m.; two s. one d.; ed Univ. of Athens, Univ. of Wisconsin, USA, Univ. of Paris, France and Univ. of Cambridge, UK; Lecturer, Dept of Econs, Univ. of Athens, Researcher Centre of Planning and Econ. Research 1977–78; staff mem. Econs Dept OECD, Paris 1978–81; Panhellenic Socialist Movt (PASOK) MEP 1981–84; Special Adviser to Prime Minister on EC Affairs; Deputy Minister for Nat. Economy 1985–89, Minister of Trade 1989; mem. Parl. for first Dist of Athens 1989–; Deputy Minister for Nat. Economy 1985–86, 1987–89; Minister for Commerce 1993–94; Minister for Nat. Economy 1994–96, for Nat. Economy and Econs 1996–2001, of Nat. Defence 2001–04.

PAPARIGA, Alexandra (Aleka), BA; Greek politician; b. 5 Nov. 1945, Athens; widowed; one d.; ed Univ. of Athens; joined CP of Greece (KKE) in 1968 during mil. dictatorship (1967–74), mem. Cen. Cttee, KKE 1978–, mem. Politburo 1986–, Gen. Sec. Cen. Cttee 1991–2013; mem. of the Vouli (Parl.) 1993–; mem. Bureau of City Cttee of Athens Party Org. (KOA), then active in women's movt; Founding mem. Women's Fed. of Greece (OGE), helped organize nat. events for Int. Women's Day; leading cadre of women's movt –1981, then active in KOA –1991; participated in int. congresses of World Women Democratic Fed. and UNO. *Publications:* two books on women's emancipation. *Address:* Communist Party of Greece (KKE), Leoforos Irakliou 145, Nea Ionia, 142 31 Athens, Greece (office). *Telephone:* (210) 2592111 (office). *Fax:* (210) 2592298 (office); (210) 3232821 (office). *E-mail:* cpg@int .kke.gr (office); cpg.kke@gmail.com (office). *Website:* inter.kke.gr (office); www.kke .gr (office).

PAPATHANASIOU, Ioannis; Greek business executive and politician; b. 1 Jan. 1954, Athens; m. Ileana Iliopoulou; two d.; ed Tech. Univ. of Athens; Pres. and Man. Dir J.D. Papathanassiou SA –2002; mem. Bd of Dirs Athens Chamber of Commerce and Industry 1982–88, Sec.-Gen. 1988–93, Pres. 1994–2000; adviser to Minister of Commerce, Industry and Energy 1991–92; Vice-Pres. DEPA (Public Gas Enterprises) 1992–93; mem. New Democracy party; mem. Vouli (Parl.) 2002– (re-elected 2004, 2007, 2009); Deputy Minister of Devt 2004–07, of the Economy and Finance 2007–09, Minister of the Economy and Finance 2009–. *Address:* Ministry of the Economy and Finance, Odos Nikis 5–7, 101 80 Athens, Greece (office). *Telephone:* (210) 3332000 (office). *E-mail:* ypetho@mnec.gr (office); info@ papathanassiou.gr. *Website:* www.mnec.gr (office); www.papathanassiou.gr.

PAPAZIAN, Vahan; Armenian politician, diplomatist, historian and orientalist; *Professor of Political Sciences, Yerevan State University;* b. 26 Jan. 1957, Yerevan; s. of Hagop Papazian and Ophelia Papazian; m. Anahit Papazian; two s.; ed Yerevan State Univ.; researcher, Inst. of History, Armenian Acad. of Sciences 1980–91; Counsellor to Pres. of Armenia 1991–92; Chargé d'Affaires of Armenia to France 1992–93; Minister of Foreign Affairs 1993–96; on staff, Acad. of Sciences 1996–98; Amb. to France 1997–98; Prof. of Political Sciences, Yerevan State Univ. 1998–. *Publications:* works on history of Armenian-Iranian relations and trade routes in Middle Ages, politics. *Address:* Yerevan State University, 1 Alek Manukian, 375025 Yerevan (office); 1st Pass, Av. Baghramian 1, Apt 30, Yerevan, Armenia (home). *Telephone:* (10) 551804 (office); (10) 542980 (home). *E-mail:* vahanpapazian@yahoo.com (home).

PAPOULIAS, Karolos, PhD; Greek politician, lawyer and head of state; *President;* b. 4 June 1929, Ioannina, Epirus; s. of the late Maj.-Gen. Gregorios Papoulias; m. May Panou Papoulia; three d.; ed Nat. and Kapodistrian Univ. of Athens, Univ. of Madrid, Spain, Ludwig Maximilian Univ. of Munich and Univ. of Cologne, Germany; fmr pole-vault and volleyball champion; fmr practising lawyer in Athens; lived in Germany 1962–74; Founding mem. Socialist Democratic Union which mobilized Greeks living in Western Europe against the mil. coup 1967; worked for Greek radio programme of Deutsche Welle; mem. Greek democratic del.

at Gen. Ass. of Council of Europe during period of mil. dictatorship in Greece; mem. Parl. 1977–2004; mem. Cen. Cttee Panhellenic Socialist Movt (PASOK); Sec.-Gen. Centre for Mediterranean Studies, Athens; Deputy Minister for Foreign Affairs 1981–84, Alt. Minister 1984–85, Minister of Foreign Affairs 1985–89, 1993–96; Alt. Minister for Defence 1989–90; Pres. of Greece 2005–; Founder and fmr Pres. Asscn for Greek Linguistic Heritage; Chair. Nat. Sports Asscn 1985–; fmr Pres. Ethnikos athletic union; Kt, Order of the Elephant (Denmark), Kt Grand Cross with Grand Cordon, Order of Merit of the Italian Repub. 2006, Grand Star of the Decoration of Honour for Services to the Repub. of Austria 2007, Kt Grand Cross, Grand Order of King Tomislav (Croatia) 2007, Kt, Order of the Seraphim (Sweden) 2008, Kt, Order of the White Eagle (Poland) 2013. *Address:* Office of the President, Odos Vassileos Georgiou 2, 100 28 Athens, Greece (office). *Telephone:* (210) 7283111 (office). *Fax:* (210) 7248938 (office). *E-mail:* publicrelationsoffice@presidency.gr (office). *Website:* www.presidency.gr (office).

PAPOUTSIS, Christos; Greek economist and politician; b. 11 April 1953, Larissa; m.; one d.; ed Univ. of Athens; Pres. Greek Nat. Union of Students 1978–80; Special Adviser on Public Admin, Ministry of Presidency of Govt 1981–84; mem. Exec. Bureau Pan-Hellenic Socialist Movt (PASOK), Leader PASOK Del. to European Parl., mem. Political Council for Foreign Affairs, Security and Defence Policy; mem. European Parl. 1984–95, Vice-Pres. Socialist Group 1987–89; mem. Presidium, Party of European Socialists 1988–; Commr for Energy and Euratom Supply Agency, Small and Medium Enterprises (SME) and Tourism, European Comm. 1995–99; Minister of Mercantile Marine 2000–01; mem. Parl. 2000–, PASOK Parl. Spokesman 2007–; Highest Mark of Distinction with Cross (Austria), Gran Official, Orden Libertador Bernardo O'Higgins (Chile). *Publications:* European Journeys 1994, The Colour of the Future 1998, For Europe in the 21st Century 1999. *Address:* Lykavittou 5, 106 72 Athens, Greece (office). *Telephone:* (210) 3387700 (office). *Fax:* (210) 3387709 (office). *E-mail:* papoutsi@ otenet.gr (office). *Website:* www.cpapoutsis.gr.

PAPPANO, Sir Antonio (Tony), Kt; British conductor and pianist; *Music Director, The Royal Opera, Covent Garden;* b. 30 Dec. 1959, Epping, London; m. Pam Bullock 1995; ed studied in USA with Norma Verrilli, Arnold Franchetti and Gustav Meier; Répétiteur and Asst Conductor New York City Opera, Gran Teatro del Liceo, Barcelona, Frankfurt Opera, Lyric Opera of Chicago early to mid-1980s; asst to Daniel Barenboim for Tristan und Isolde, Parsifal and the Ring cycle at Bayreuth Festival 1986; opera conducting debut with Norwegian Opera, Oslo 1987; Music Dir, Norwegian Opera 1990–92; Covent Garden debut conducting La Bohème 1990; Vienna Staatsoper debut conducting new production of Wagner's Siegfried 1993; season 1996 included the original Don Carlos in Brussels and at the Paris Théâtre du Châtelet; season 1997 Salome at Chicago and Eugene Onegin at the Metropolitan; Prin. Guest Conductor Israel Philharmonic Orchestra 1997–2000; seasons 1999–2001 Lohengrin at Bayreuth; Music Dir, Théâtre Royal de la Monnaie, Brussels 1992–2002, conducting a wide variety of titles; Music Dir, Royal Opera, Covent Garden 2002–; new productions of Ariadne auf Naxos, Wozzeck, Madama Butterfly and Pagliacci, revival of Falstaff 2002–03; Don Giovanni, Aida, Lady Macbeth of Mtsensk, Faust and Peter Grimes in 2003–04; Das Rheingold and Die Walküre 2005; 2008 performances at ROH included Don Giovanni, La fanciulla del West, Les contes d'Hoffmann; 2009 included Lulu, La Traviata, Il barbiere di Siviglia, Tristan und Isolde; 2010 Simon Boccanegra, Les Pêcheurs de perles; 2011 Turnage's new opera Anna Nicole, Werther, Macbeth and Tosca, among others; 2012 Die Meistersinger von Nürnberg, Le nozze di Figaro, Les Troyens, Otello; Music Dir Orchestra dell' Accad. Nazionale di Santa Cecilia, Rome 2005–; has conducted major orchestras, including Berlin Philharmonic Orchestra, Boston Symphony Orchestra, Chicago Symphony Orchestra, Cleveland Orchestra, London Symphony Orchestra, Los Angeles Philharmonic Orchestra, Orchestre de Paris, Oslo Philharmonic Orchestra, Munich Philharmonic Orchestra; Commendatore of Italian Repub. 2008, Cavaliere di Gran Croce, Order of Merit of Italian Repub. 2012; Olivier Award for Outstanding Achievement in Opera 2003, Royal Philharmonic Soc. Award for best conductor 2005, Assoc. Naz. Critici Musicali Premio Abbiati Prize for Conductor 2006, Inc. Soc. of Musicians Distinguished Musician Award 2012, Int. Opera Awards Best Conductor 2013. *Recordings include:* many recordings as conductor including Puccini's La Rondine (Gramophone Award for Best Opera Recording and Record of the Year 1997), Il Trittico 1999, Britten's The Turn of the Screw (Choc du Monde de la Musique, Prix de l'Acad. du Disque Lyrique, Grand Prix Int., Orphées d'Or) 1999, Werther 1999, Manon (Gramophone Award for Best Opera Recording) 2001, Rachmaninov's Piano Concertos 1 & 2 2005, Madame Butterfly 2009, Verdi's Messa da Requiem 2009, Wagner: Tristan and Isolde 2011, Rossini: William Tell 2011; recordings as pianist with Rockwell Blake, Barbara Bonney and Han-Na Chang. *Address:* c/o Peter Wiggins, IMG Artists, 31–33 rue du Temple, 75004 Paris, France (office); Royal Opera House, Bow Street, Covent Garden, London, WC2E 9DD, England (office). *Telephone:* 1-44-31-00-10 (office); (20) 7240-1200 (office). *Fax:* 1-44-31-44-40 (office). *E-mail:* pwiggins@imgartists.com (office); info@roh.org.uk (office). *Website:* www.imgartists.com (office); www.roh.org.uk (office).

PAPPAS, Spyros; Greek lawyer, judge, academic, civil servant and EU official; *Managing Partner, Pappas & Associates;* b. (Spyridon Pappas), 1 Jan. 1953, Athens; m. Frady Karkanis; one s. one d.; ed Univ. of Athens, Panteios School of Econ. and Political Studies, Univ. of Paris, Directorate for European Affairs, Institut Européen d'Admin des Affaires (INSEAD), Brookings Inst., Washington, DC, USA; fmr naval Petty Officer; barrister, Athens 1976; Auditor Council of State 1978, Judge in Supreme Admin. Court 1983; Special Adviser in Prime Minister's Legal Office 1981; mem. Cen. Comm. for Drafting of Laws 1982; est. Nat. Centre of Public Admin., Sec.-Gen. 1985; est. Inst. of Permanent Training 1985; Assoc. Prof., European Inst. of Public Admin, Maastricht 1988, Dir of Faculty 1989, Dir-Gen. 1990, Prof. of European Law 1992; Dir-Gen. for Consumer Policy, EC 1995, for Information, Communication, Culture and Audiovisual Media 1997–99, for Educ. and Culture 2000; Founder and Man. Partner, Pappas & Associates (legal practice), Brussels 2004–; Chair. Centre of European Culture 2010, Centre of Social Responsibility in the Digital Age 2011; Chair. Bd of Govs Int. East-West Acad.; mem. Supreme Council Church of Greece 1984, Comm. of Information on National Affairs, Inst. for Admin. Studies, Asscn of the Judges of the Council of State, Inst. of Public Admin., Cttee for Drafting of the Encyclopedia of Admin., Centre for European Policy Studies Int. Advisory Council, Scientific Council of Academia Istropolitana Bratislava Inst. of Advanced Studies, Foundation for

Hellenic Culture; assoc. mem. Asscn of European Magistrates for Democracy and Liberty (MEDEL); Substitute Bd mem. Open Univ., Athens; cr. European Centre of Judges and Lawyers 1992; Hon. title of State Scholar 1971–73; Hon. Fellow, European Coll. of Sport Science, Univs of Cologne and Jyväskylä 2000; Hon. mem. Asscn of European Journalists, The Hague 2000; Officer Order of Merit (Luxembourg) 1994; Distinction of the Pan-Greek Dissertation 1968, First Prize, Foundation for Admin. Law 'Michel Stassinopoulos' 1976, Scholar of the Council of Europe 1977, Medal of Honour, European Inst., Łódź 1998. *Publications:* La constitution de la Grèce de 1975 1976, Le régime de planification en Grèce 1977, Le Tribunal de Première Instance 1990, Tendances actuelles et évolution de la jurisprudence de la cour de justice des Communautés européennes: suivi annuel (ed.) Vol. I 1993, Vol. II 1995, Procédures administratives nationales: préparation et mise en oeuvre des décisions communautaires: études comparatives (ed.) 1994, EC Competition Law: Financial Aspects (Co-Ed.) 1994, The Changing Role of Parliaments in the European Union (co-ed.) 1995, The European Union's Common Foreign and Security Policy: The Challenges of the Future 1996, Politiques publiques dans l'Union européenne 1996, Digital Television and EU Audiovisual Policy 1999, The New European Governance 2001, The Institutional Alteration of the Right of Initiative of the European Commission 2003, A New Era of Competition Policy? – Competition DG and the Control of the Court of Justice of the European Communities 2004, Morale and Change in the EU 2005, Pro-Action versus Reaction within the EU 2005, Competitiveness and Data Protection 2005, The Lisbon Strategy and its Implementation 2006, When Competition Law is a Commercial Tool 2006, Implementation of Competition Rules in Mergers and Protection of Personal Data 2007, Is European Audiovisual Policy a Driver to European Identity or a Carrier to Further Globalization? 2007, La crise grecque: dégénérescence ou régénération de l'intégration européenne? 2010, Case law of the European Civil Service Tribunal: Restarting or Continuation?, in The European Union Civil Service Tribunal (CST) 2005–2010, Proceedings of the Colloquium organized on the occasion of the 5th Anniversary of the CST, Luxembourg, 1 Oct. 2010, Human Rights Law Journal, Vol. 31 No. 1 2011, Google and the Credibility of EU Data Protection Laws 2012, Towards EU State Aid Modernisation: What Role Do Member States and the Market Play in State Aid Cases? 2012. *E-mail:* spyridonapappas@gmail.com (office); info@pappaslaw.eu (office). *Address:* Pappas & Associates, 49–51 rue Stévin, 1000 Brussels, Belgium (office). *Telephone:* (2) 23-15-704-5 (office). *Website:* www.pappaslaw.eu (office).

PAPUC, Gheorghe; Moldovan politician and military officer; *Minister of Internal Affairs;* b. 6 May 1954, Frăsineşti; m.; three c.; ed Inst. of Econs and Law, Moscow, Legal Inst., Ministry of Internal Affairs of Russian Fed.; various military positions in Soviet and Moldovan armed forces to brigade command level 1973–97; Head of Advanced Courses, Ministry of the Interior, fmr USSR 1989–92; Minister of Internal Affairs 2002–. *Address:* Ministry of Internal Affairs, 2012 Chişinău, bd Ştefan cel Mare 75, Moldova (office). *Telephone:* (22) 22-45-47 (office). *Fax:* (22) 22-27-43 (office). *E-mail:* mai@mai.md (office). *Website:* www.mai.md (office).

PARADIS, The Hon. Christian; Canadian politician; *Minister of International Development and Minister for La Francophonie;* b. 1 Jan. 1974, Thetford Mines, Québec; MP Parl. for Mégantic—L'Érable 2006–; Parl. Sec. to Minister of Natural Resources 2006–07, Sec. of State for Agric. and Agri-food 2007–08, Minister of Public Works and Govt Services 2008–10, of Natural Resources 2010–11, of Industry 2011–13, of International Devt 2013–, also Minister for La Francophonie 2013–; mem. Conservative Party of Canada. *Address:* Department of Foreign Affairs, Trade and Development, Lester B. Pearson Building, 125 Sussex Dr., Ottawa, ON K1A 0G2, Canada (office). *Telephone:* (613) 944-4000 (office). *Fax:* (613) 996-9709 (office). *E-mail:* enqserv@international.gc.ca (office). *Website:* www .international.gc.ca (office).

PARAMONOVA, Tatyana Vladimirovna, CandSci; Russian banker; b. 24 Oct. 1950; one s.; ed G.V. Plekhanov Inst. of Nat. Economy, Moscow; economist, later Head of Div., USSR State Bank 1972–92; Deputy Chair. Cen. Bank of Russian Fed. 1992–94, 1995–97, Acting Chair. 1994–95, First Deputy Chair. 1998–2007, mem. Bd of Dirs 2002–, also IMF Alt. Gov. for Russian Fed. 2000–; worked in various Moscow commercial banks 1992, 1997–98; Adviser to Pres. of JSC Russian Railways; CEO JSC JASO (insurance co) 2009; Dr hc (G.V. Plekhanov Inst. of Nat. Economy); Order of Merit 2000; Merited Economist of the Russian Fed. 1999. *Publications:* more than 120 research papers on economics. *Address:* c/o Central Bank of Russian Federation, Neglinnaya str. 12, 107016 Moscow, Russia (office).

PARAS BIR BIKRAM SHAH DEV; Nepalese royal; b. 30 Dec. 1971, Kathmandu; s. of King Gyanendra Bir Bikram Shah Dev and Queen Komal Rajya Laxmi Devi Shah; m. Himani Rajya Laxmi Devi Shah 2000; one s. two d.; ed St Joseph's Coll., Darjeeling, India, Budhanilkantha School, Schiller Int. Univ., UK; proclaimed Crown Prince of Nepal 26 Oct. 2001, heir-apparent to throne of Nepal until monarchy was abolished and replaced by secular fed. repub. May 2008; Chair. Council of Royal Reps during state visits; Coordinator, Zoo Devt Cttee, King Mahendra Trust for Nature Conservation –2001, Chair. King Mahendra Trust for Nature Conservation 2001–; conferred title of Grand Master of all Orders of the Kingdom of Nepal 2006; Shubha Rajyabhisheka Padaka 1975, Gaddi Aarohan Ko Rajat Mahotsav Padaka, 2028–2053 B.S. 1997, Vishista Seva Padaka 1999, Birendra-Aishwarya Seva Padaka 2001, Suprasiddha Prabala Gorkha Dakshina Bahu 2001, Daivi Prakopa Piditoddhara Padaka 2003, Maha Ujjvala Keertimaya Nepal-Shreepada (First Class) 2004, Birendra-Mala 2006, Ati Maha Gauravamaya Supradeepta Birendra Prajatantra Bhaskara 2006. *Leisure interests:* horse riding, music, composing poems.

PARASKEVA, Rt Hon Janet, BA, JP; British civil servant; *Chairman, Child Maintenance and Enforcement Commission;* b. 28 May 1946; d. of Antonis Paraskeva and Doris Paraskeva (née Fowler); m. Alan Hunt 1967 (divorced 1983); two d. two step s.; ed Worcester Coll. of Educ., Open Univ., UK; teacher 1967–71; self-employed toy maker 1970–73; several positions in youth work 1972–78; Head of Youth Work Unit, Nat. Youth Bureau 1978–81; HM Insp. of Schools Dept of Educ. and Science (now Dept for Educ. and Employment) 1983–88; Dir Nat. Youth Bureau 1988–91; CEO Nat. Youth Agency 1991–95; Dir Nat. Lotteries Charities Bd, England 1995–2000; CEO Law Soc. of England and Wales 2000–06; First Civil Service Commr 2006–10; Chair. Olympic Lottery Distributor 2006–; Chair. Child Maintenance and Enforcement Comm. 2007–; mem. UK Govt Torture Inquiry 2010–. *Publications:* articles in youth, educ. and law journals and periodicals and

in Times Education Supplement. *Leisure interests:* golf, riding, gardening. *Address:* Office of the Chairman, Child Maintenance and Enforcement Commission, London, SW1P 9NT, England (office). *Telephone:* (20) 7853-8001 (office). *E-mail:* cmec@dwpdevelopment.net (office). *Website:* www.childmaintenance.org (office).

PARAVAĆ, Borislav; Bosnia and Herzegovina politician; b. 18 Feb. 1943, Kostajnica; m.; two c.; ed Univ. of Zagreb; certified accountant and financial auditor; fmr Mayor of Doboj; mem. Republika Srpska Parl. 1996–2002; First Deputy Chair. Parl. House of Reps 2002; Serb mem. Presidency (tripartite) of Bosnia and Herzegovina 2003–06, Chair. April–June 2003, Oct. 2004–June 2005. *Address:* c/o Social Democratic Party of Bosnia and Herzegovina (SDP BiH) (Socijaldemokratska Partija BiH), 71000 Sarajevo, Alipašina 41, Bosnia and Herzegovina.

PARAYRE, Jean-Paul-Christophe; French building and civil engineering executive; b. 5 July 1937, Lorient; s. of Louis Parayre and Jeanne Parayre (née Malarde); m. Marie-Françoise Chaufour 1962; two s. two d.; ed Lycées in Casablanca (Morocco) and Versailles, Ecole Polytechnique, Paris, Ecole Nat. des Ponts et Chaussées; Engineer, Dept of Highways 1963–67; Tech. Adviser, Ministry of Social Affairs 1967, Ministry of Econ. and Finance 1968; Dir of Mech. Industries at Ministry of Industry and Research 1970–74; Chief Adviser to Pres. and Gen. Man. Banque Vernes et Commerciale 1974; Man. of Planning, Automobile Div. of Peugeot 1975; Man. Automobile Div. of Peugeot-Citroën 1976, Chair. Bd of Dirs Peugeot SA 1977–84, mem. advisory Bd 1984; mem. Supervisory Bd Soc. Dumez 1977–84 (Dir-Gen. 1984, Chair. 1988–90, Pres. 1991–92); Pres., Dir-Gen. Fidel Financière (affil. to Dumez) 1985; Vice-Pres., Dir-Gen. Lyonnaise des Eaux-Dumez 1990–92, Vice-Pres. 1990–93; Pres. Supervisory Bd Razel 1991; Pres. Bolloré Technologies Jan.–Sept. 1994, Scac-Delmas-Vieljeux 1994, Pres. Saga 1996–99; Vice-Pres. Bolloré Group 1994–99; Dir Bolloré Investissement 1994, Carillion PLC 1999, Stena UK 1999; Chair. Advisory Bd Vallourec 2000; Officier, Légion d'honneur, Commdr Ordre nat. du Mérite. *Leisure interests:* golf, tennis.

PARDEE, Arthur Beck, BS, MA, PhD; American biochemist and academic; *Professor Emeritus of Biological Chemistry and Molecular Pharmacology, Harvard Medical School;* b. 13 July 1921, Chicago, Ill.; s. of Charles A. Pardee and Elizabeth Beck; m. Ruth Sager (died 1997); three s. from previous m.; m. Ann Goodman; ed Univ. of California, Berkeley, California Inst. of Tech.; Postdoctoral Fellow, Univ. of Wisconsin 1947–49; Instructor, Asst and Assoc. Prof., Univ. of Calif., Berkeley 1949–61; Sr Postdoctoral Fellow, Pasteur Inst. 1957–58; Prof. of Biochemical Sciences and Donner Prof. of Science, Princeton Univ. 1961–75; Prof. of Biological Chem. and Molecular Pharmacology, Harvard Medical School, Boston 1975–97, Prof. Emer. 1997–; Prof. Emer., Harvard Univ. 1998–; Chief, Div. Cell Growth and Regulation, Dana Farber Cancer Inst. 1975–98; mem. ACS, American Soc. of Biological Chemists (Treasurer 1964–70, Pres. 1980), American Asscn for Cancer Research (Pres. 1985), American Acad. of Arts and Sciences, American Soc. of Microbiologists, Japanese Biochemical Soc.; mem. Council American Cancer Soc. 1967–71; Fellow, Int. Inst. for Advanced Studies Nara, Japan 1999, American Philosophical Soc. 2001; Hon. Faculty mem. Nanjing Univ. 1999; Dr hc (Paris) 1993; ACS Paul Lewis Award 1960, Krebs Medal, Fed. of European Biochemical Socs 1973, Rosensteil Award, Brandeis Univ. 1975, Princess Takamatsee Award (Japan) 1990, Boehringer Bioanalytica Award 1998, Ludwig Award 2002, and numerous other honours and awards. *Publications:* Experiments in Biochemical Research Techniques (co-author) 1957; more than 500 articles on subjects including bacterial physiology and enzymology in synchronous cultures, cell division cycle events, growth regulation in cancer and normal cells, enzymology of DNA synthesis, repair of damaged DNA. *Leisure interests:* music, tennis, travel, art. *Address:* Dana Farber Cancer Institute, 44 Binney Street, Boston, MA 02115 (office); 987 Memorial Drive, Unit 271, Cambridge, MA 02138 (home). *Telephone:* (617) 632-3372 (office). *Fax:* (617) 632-4680 (office). *E-mail:* arthur-pardee@fci .harvard.edu (office). *Website:* hms.harvard.edu/hms/home.asp (office).

PARDO, Jorge, BFA; Cuban sculptor; b. 1963, Havana; ed Art Center Coll. of Design, Univ. of Illinois, USA; collections at Museum of Contemporary Art, Los Angeles, Museum of Modern Art, New York, Tate Gallery, London, Cooper-Hewitt, Nat. Design Museum, New York, Harvard Univ. Art Museums, Mildred Lane Kemper Art Museum, St Louis, Stedelijk Museum voor Actuele Kunst, Belgium, Smithsonian American Art Museum, Washington, DC; Fellow, John D. and Catherine T. MacArthur Foundation 2010–. *Telephone:* (323) 225-4700. *E-mail:* jps@jorgepardosculpture.com. *Website:* www.jorgepardosculpture.com.

PARED PÉREZ, Vice-Adm. Sigfrido; Dominican Republic government official and military officer; *Minister for Armed Forces;* twice Head of Nat. Investigations Directorate; Sec. of State for Armed Forces 2004–08; Dir of Migration/Immigration Dept 2009–11; Minister for Armed Forces 2012–. *Address:* Ministry for the Armed Forces, Plaza de la Bandera, Avda 27 de Febrero, esq. Avda Luperón, Santo Domingo, Dominican Republic (office). *Telephone:* 530-5149 (office). *Fax:* 531-0461 (office). *E-mail:* directorrev@j2.mil.do (office). *Website:* www.fuerzasarmadas.mil .do (office).

PAREDES RANGEL, Beatriz Elena; Mexican politician; b. 18 Aug. 1953, Tlaxcala; ed Nat. Autonomous Univ. of Mexico (UNAM); Tlaxcala state deputy (Partido Revolucionario Institucional—PRI) 1974–77; adviser to Gov. of Tlaxcala 1978–80; Under-Sec. for Agrarian Reform 1982; Gov. of Tlaxcala (first woman) 1987–92; Amb. to Cuba 1993; unsuccessful cand. for presidency of PRI 2002; unsuccessful campaign for mayoralty of Mexico City, representing alliance of PRI and Partido Verde Ecologista de Mexico (PVEM) 2006; Pres. PRI Nat. Exec. Cttee 2007–11; fmr mem. Chamber of Deputies and Senate; fmr Pres. Nat. Comm. of Integral Devt and Social Justice for Indigenous Peoples; fmr Pres. Colosio Trust Fund; Vice-Pres. Socialist Int.; fmr Pres. Parlatino (Latin American Parl.), currently mem. Consulting Council; Orden de la Solidaridad (Cuba) 1994, Gran Cruz, Orden del Soberano Congreso Nacional de Guatemala 2001, Gran Cruz de Isabel la Católica (Spain) 2002, Ordem Nacional do Cruzeiro do Sul (Brazil) 2003. *Music:* two CDs: El Loco Afán, Corazón Gemelo. *Publications:* Acaso la Palabra, Con la Cabeza Descubierta; regular contrib. to journal El Universal. *Leisure interests:* music and poetry. *Address:* Partido Revolucionario Institucional (PRI), Insurgentes Norte 59, Col. Buenavista, Del. Cuauhtémoc, CP 06359, México, DF,

Mexico (office). *Telephone:* (55) 55-41-91-22 (office). *Fax:* (55) 55-41-91-34 (office). *E-mail:* beatrizparedes@pri.org.mx (office). *Website:* www.pri.org.mx (office).

PAREKH, Deepak Shantilal, BCom, CA; Indian business executive and banker; *Chairman, Housing Development Finance Corporation Ltd;* b. 18 Oct. 1944; ed Sydenham Coll., Mumbai, Inst. of Chartered Accountants in England & Wales; began career with Ernst & Young Management Consultancy Services, New York 1970; worked with Grindlays Bank for three years; Asst Rep. for South Asia, Chase Manhattan Bank for three years; Deputy Gen. Man., Housing Development Finance Corpn Ltd 1978–85, Man. Dir 1985–93, Chair. 1993–; Chair. (non-exec.) Infrastructure Development Finance Co. Ltd 1997, GlaxoSmithkline Pharmaceuticals Ltd, Siemens Ltd; mem. Bd of Dirs Mahindra & Mahindra Ltd, Indian Hotels Co. Ltd amongst others; mem. Int. Bd WNS (Holdings) (USA), DP World (UAE); mem. Advisory Bd of several Indian and multinational corpns; Chevalier, Légion d'honneur 2010; Businessman of the Year, Business India 1996, JRD Tata Corp. Leadership Award, All India Man. Asscn, Padma Bhushan 2006, Lifetime Achievement Award, Econ. Times 2006, Best Non-Exec. Dir, Asian Centre for Corp. Governance 2006, IMC Juran Quality Medal 2008, Outstanding Business Leader of the Year 2008, NDTV Business Leader of the Year Award 2008, Lifetime Achievement Award, CNBC Awaaz Crisil Real Estate Awards 2008, Priyadarshni Acad. Award 2008, Qimpro Platinum Award, Corp. Award for Lifetime Achievement, Econ. Times, AIMA Man. India Award 2010, Most Inspiring Business Leader Award, NDTV Profit, Lifetime Achievement Award, Confed. of Real Estate Developers Asscn 2010, Lifetime Achievement Award, Finance Asia magazine, Hong Kong, first int. recipient of Outstanding Achievement Award, Inst. of Chartered Accountants in England and Wales 2010. *Address:* Housing Development Finance Corporation Ltd, Ramon House 169, Backbay Reclamation, H T Parekh Marg, Churchgate, Mumbai 400 020, India (office). *Telephone:* (22) 66316000 (office). *Fax:* (22) 22048834 (office). *Website:* (office).

PARENT, Mary Campbell; American film industry executive; *President, Disruption Entertainment;* b. 1968, Santa Barbara, Calif.; began career as agent trainee, Int. Creative Man. (ICM); Dir of Devt then Production Vice-Pres. New Line Cinema 1994–97; Sr Vice-Pres. of Production Universal Pictures 1997–2000, Exec. Vice-Pres. of Production 2000–01, Co-Pres. of Production 2001–03, Vice-Chair. Worldwide Production 2003–05; Producer Stuber/Parent 2006–08; Chair. Worldwide Motion Picture Group Metro-Goldwyn-Mayer Inc. 2008–10, also mem. Office of CEO; currently Pres. Disruption Entertainment (subsidiary of Paramount Pictures). *Films produced include:* Set It Off 1996, Trial and Error 1997, Pleasantville 1998, You, Me and Dupree 2006, The Kingdom 2007, Welcome Home, Roscoe Jenkins 2008, Role Models 2008, Love Happens 2009, Pacific Rim 2013. *Address:* Disruption Entertainment, 5555 Melrose Avenue, Swanson Bldg, 4th Floor, Los Angeles, CA 90038, USA (office).

PARET, Peter, PhD, DLit, LittD, DH, DPhil; American historian and academic; *Andrew W. Mellon Professor Emeritus in the Humanities, Institute for Advanced Study;* b. 13 April 1924, Berlin, Germany; s. of Dr Hans Paret and Suzanne Aimée Cassirer; m. Isabel Harris 1961; one s. one d.; ed Univ. of California, Berkeley, Univ. of London, UK; Research Assoc. Center of Int. Studies, Princeton Univ. 1960–62; Visiting Asst Prof., Univ. of Calif., Davis 1962–63, Assoc. Prof. 1963–66, Prof. of History 1966–69; Prof. of History, Stanford Univ. 1969–77, Raymond A. Spruance Prof. in Int. History 1977–86; Andrew W. Mellon Prof. in the Humanities, Inst. for Advanced Study, Princeton 1986–97, Andrew W Mellon Prof. Emer. 1997–; Lees Knowles Lecturer, Univ. Cambridge 2008; mem. American Philosophical Soc., Historische Kommission zu Berlin; Fellow, American Acad. of Arts and Sciences, Leo Baeck Inst.; Hon. Fellow, LSE, Clausewitz Gesellschaft; Great Cross, German Order of Merit; four hon. degrees; Thomas Jefferson Medal, Samuel Eliot Morison Medal, Moncado Prizes. *Publications:* Guerrillas in the 1960s (with John Shy) 1961, French Revolutionary Warfare 1964, Yorck and the Era of Prussian Reform 1966, The Berlin Secession 1980, Makers of Modern Strategy (ed.) 1986, Art as History 1988, Carl von Clausewitz: On War (ed. and trans. with Michael Howard) 1976, 1984, Clausewitz and the State 1985, Carl von Clausewitz, Historical and Political Writings (ed. and trans.) 1991, Understanding War 1992, Persuasive Images (with Beth Lewis and Paul Paret) 1992, Sammler, Stifter und Museen (ed. with Ekkehard Mai) 1993, Imagined Battles 1997, German Encounters with Modernism 2001, An Artist against the Third Reich: Ernst Barlach, 1933–38 2003, 1806: The Cognitive Challenge of War 2009. *Address:* School of Historical Studies, Institute for Advanced Study, Einstein Drive, Princeton, NJ 08540, USA (office). *Telephone:* (609) 734-8344 (home). *Fax:* (609) 683-5027 (home). *E-mail:* paret@ias.edu (office). *Website:* www.hs.ias.edu (office).

PARETSKY, Sara N., MBA, PhD; American writer; b. 8 June 1947, Ames, Ia; d. of David Paretsky and Mary E. Edwards; m. Courtenay Wright 1976; three c.; ed Univs of Kansas and Chicago; Man. Urban Research Center, Chicago, Ill. 1971–74, CNA Insurance Co., Chicago 1977–85; writer of crime novels 1982–; Pres. Sisters in Crime, Chicago 1986–88; Dir Nat. Abortion Rights Action League, Ill. 1987–90; mem. Crime Writers' Asscn; four hon. degrees; Ms Magazine Woman of the Year 1987, CWA Silver Dagger Award 1988, Diamond Dagger for Lifetime Achievement, British Crime Writers Asscn 2002. *Publications include:* Indemnity Only 1982, Deadlock (Friends of American Writers Prize 1985) 1984, Killing Orders 1986, Bitter Medicine 1987, Toxic Shock (British Crime Writers' Asscn Silver Dagger for Fiction 1988) 1987, Blood Shot 1988, Burn Marks 1990, Guardian Angel 1992, A Woman's Eye (ed.) 1992, Tunnel Vision 1994, Women on the Case 1997, Hard Time 2000, Total Recall 2002, Blacklist 2003 (British Crime Writers' Asscn Gold Dagger for Fiction 2004), Fire Sale 2006, Writing in an Age of Silence 2007, Bleeding Kansas 2008, Hardball 2009, Body Work 2010, Breakdown 2012; numerous short stories and articles. *Leisure interests:* walking, singing, making the perfect cappuccino. *Address:* c/o Dominick Abel Literary Agency, Inc., 146 West 82nd Street, Apartment 1A, New York, NY 10024, USA (office). *Telephone:* (212) 877-0710 (office). *E-mail:* dominick@dalainc.com (office); viwarshawski@mindspring.com (office). *Website:* www.saraparetsky.com.

PARFIT, Derek, MA, FBA; British philosopher and academic; *Senior Research Fellow Emeritus, All Souls College, Oxford;* b. 11 Dec. 1942, Chengtu, China; s. of Norman Parfit and Jessie Parfit (née Browne); m. Janet Radcliffe Richards; ed Balliol Coll., Oxford; Harkness Fellow, Columbia and Harvard Univs, USA 1964–67; Prize Fellow, All Souls Coll., Oxford 1967–74, Jr Research Fellow 1974–81, Research Fellow 1981–84, Sr Research Fellow 1984–2010, Emer. 2010–; Visiting Prof. of Philosophy, Harvard, Princeton, New York and Rutgers Univs; Fellow, American Acad. of Arts and Sciences. *Publications:* Eton Microcosm (co-ed.) 1964, Reasons and Persons 1984, On What Matters 2011; papers in professional journals on problems of personal identity, rationality and ethics. *Leisure interest:* architectural photography. *Address:* All Souls College, Oxford, OX1 4AL, England. *Telephone:* (1865) 279379. *Website:* www.all-souls.ox.ac.uk/people.php?personid=49.

PARFITT, David John; British film and television producer; *Director/Partner, Trademark Films Limited;* b. 8 July 1958, Reading, Berks., England; s. of the late William Parfitt and Maureen Collinson; m. 1st Susan Coates (divorced 1993); one s.; m. 2nd Elizabeth Barron 1996; two s.; ed Bede Grammar School, Sunderland, Barbara Speake Stage School, London; actor 1970–88; producer 1985–; Man. Dir Renaissance Theatre Co. 1987–, Trademark Films Ltd 1999–; mem. Bd Chicken Shed Theatre Trust 1997–2011; mem. Council BAFTA 2000–, mem. Bd of Trustees 2006–11, Chair. of Film 2004–07, Deputy Chair. BAFTA 2007–08, Chair. 2008–10; Chair. Film London 2010–; Dr hc (Sunderland) 2000, Hon. Dr of Drama (Royal Scottish Acad. of Music and Drama) 2001. *Plays (as producer):* Public Enemy, John Sessions' Napoleon, Twelfth Night, Much Ado About Nothing, Hamlet, As You Like It, Scenes from a Marriage, A Midsummer Night's Dream, King Lear, Travelling Tales, Uncle Vanya, Coriolanus, Les Liaisons Dangereuses, Elling, A Bunch of Amateurs. *Films include:* Henry V 1989, Peter's Friends 1992, Swan Song 1992, Much Ado About Nothing 1993, Mary Shelley's Frankenstein 1994, The Madness of King George (BAFTA Best British Film 1995) 1994, Twelfth Night 1996, The Wings of the Dove 1997, Shakespeare in Love (BAFTA Best Film 1998, Golden Globe Award for Best Musical or Comedy 1998, Academy Award for Best Film 1998) 1998, Gangs of New York (production consultant) 2001, I Capture the Castle 2003, Chasing Liberty 2004, My Talks with Dean Spanley (exec. producer) 2008, A Bunch of Amateurs 2008, My Week with Marilyn 2011, The Truth About Stanley (short) (exec. producer) 2012. *Television (as producer):* Twelfth Night 1988, Look Back in Anger 1989, Parade's End (series) 2012, Wipers Times 2013. *Address:* Trademark Films, 14A Goodwin's Court, London, WC2N 4LL, England (office). *Telephone:* (20) 3322-8900 (office). *E-mail:* mail@trademarkfilms.co.uk (office). *Website:* www.trademarkfilms.co.uk (office).

PARISI, Arturo Mario Luigi; Italian politician and academic; b. 13 Sept. 1940, San Mango Piemonte; ed Nunziatella Mil. School, Univ. of Sassari; worked as forester and teacher at training centre for industrial workers while attending univ.; Sec., then Nat. Vice-Pres. Youth Dept, Azione Cattolica, also mem., Exec. Cttee, Int. Fed. of Catholic Youth Movt 1963–68; academic posts have included Asst Lecturer of Statistics, Univ. of Sassari, Researcher, Cattaneo Inst., Bologna 1968, Asst Prof. of Ecclesiastical Law, Univ. of Parma, Asst Prof. of History of Religious Insts, Univ. of Florence; First Prof. of Sociology of Religions, then full Prof. of Sociology of Political Phenomena, Cattaneo Inst., Bologna 1971–, also currently Dir Cattaneo Inst.; mem. Chamber of Deputies for Bologna 1999–2001, for Sardinia 2001–; mem. Partito Democratico 2007–; Minister of Defence 2006–08; political adviser to Romani Prodi; Under-Sec., Presidency of Council of Ministers 1996; active in I Democratici movt 1999; Co-founder and Nat. Vice-Pres. Democrazia è Libertà – La Margherita 2001, Pres. of party in Fed. Ass. 2004–07; Vice-Pres. Il Mulino Asscn, also ed. of journal; fmr Pres. Italian Soc. of Electoral Studies; served as expert to govt cttee and parl. comm. on domestic terrorism 1987–88; active in movt for Institutional Reforms and Ulivo movt. *Address:* Partito Democratico, Piazza Sant'Anastasia 7, 00186 Rome, Italy (office). *Telephone:* (06) 675471 (office). *Fax:* (06) 67547319 (office). *E-mail:* info@partitodemocratico.it (office). *Website:* www.partitodemocratico.it (office).

PARISI, Giorgio, PhD; Italian theoretical physicist and academic; *Professor, University of Rome;* b. 4 Aug. 1948, Rome; m.; two c.; ed Univ. of Rome; Researcher, Laboratori Nazionali di Frascati 1971–81, on leave of absence to Columbia Univ., USA 1973–74, to Institut des Hautes Études Scientifiques 1976–77, to École Normale Supérieure, Paris 1977–78; Prof., Univ. of Rome 1981–; Prof. of Theoretical Physics, Univ. of Roma II, 'Tor Vergata' 1981–92; currently also Prof. of Quantum Theories, Univ. of Rome I, 'La Sapienza'; mem. or fmr mem. various editorial bds and of various scientific cttees, including Scientific Cttee, INFM, French Nat. Research Panel; Head of Italian Del. to IUPAP; Dir CNR-INFM Research and Devt Centre SMC (Statistical Mechanics and Complexity), Rome; Fellow, Accad. dei Lincei, Acad. des sciences, Accad. dei XL, NAS; Laurea hc in Philosophy (Urbin Univ.); Feltrinelli Prize for Physics, Accad. dei Lincei 1986, Boltzmann Medal 1992, Italgas Prize 1993, Dirac Medal and Prize, Inst. of Physics (UK) 1999, Italian Prime Minister's Prize 2002, Enrico Fermi Prize 2003, Dannie Heineman Prize 2005, Nonino Prize 2005, Galileo Prize 2006, Microsoft Award 2007, Lagrange Prize 2009, Max Planck Medal, Deutsche Physikalische Gesellschaft 2011. *Publications:* Statistical Field Theory 1988, Spin Glass Theory and Beyond 1988, Field Theory, Disorder and Simulations (co-author) 1992; more than 500 papers in professional journals. *Address:* Piazzale Aldo Moro n° 2, Rome 00185, Italy (office). *Telephone:* (06) 49913481 (office). *Fax:* (06) 4463158 (office). *E-mail:* giorgio.parisi@roma1.infn.it (office). *Website:* chimera.roma1.infn.it/GIORGIO/index.html (office).

PARISOT, Laurence; French business executive; *Vice-Chairman, IFOP;* b. 31 Aug. 1959, Luxeuil-les-Bains; d. of Michel Parisot and Janine Parisot; ed Institut d'études politiques de Paris, Univ. of Nancy 11, Sciences Po, Paris; inherited Optimum (France's leading maker of cupboard doors) from her father; Asst to Alain Lancelot, Pres. Centre d'Etudes de la Vie Politique Française (CEVIPOF) 1983–85; Dir-Gen. Louis Harris France (polling co.) 1986–90; Chair. and CEO IFOP (polling co.) 1990–2007, Vice-Chair. 2008–; mem. Exec. Council, Medef, le Mouvement des Entreprises de France 2003, Pres. 2005–13; mem. Bd of Dirs BNP-Paribas 2006–, Coface 2007–; mem. Comité des Sages, Samu Social; mem. Bd of Trustees, Michelin SCA 2005–; Chevalier, Légion d'honneur, Officier, Ordre nat. du Mérite, Commdr du Ouissam Al Alaoui (Morocco). *Publications:* Besoin d'Air 2007, Un piège Bleu Marine 2012. *Address:* IFOP, Le Milénaire 2, 35 rue de la Gare, 75019 Paris, France (office). *Telephone:* 1-45-84-14-44 (office). *Fax:* 1-45-84-93-36 (office). *Website:* www.ifop.com (office).

PARIVODIĆ, Milan, LLM, PhD; Serbian lawyer, academic and politician; b. 1966, Belgrade; m. Alexandra Parivodić; two d.; ed Faculty of Law, Univ. of Belgrade, University College London, UK; Lecturer in Civil Law and Property

Law, Faculty of Law, Univ. of Belgrade 1991–2004; pvt. law practice 2004–06; Minister of Int. Econ. Relations 2006, Co-ordinator Ministry of Finance 2006; mem. Editorial Advisory Bd Journal of International Franchising; Sec. Gen. Serbian chapter of Association Internationale pour la Protection de la Propriété Intellectuelle—Int. Asscn for Protection of Intellectual Property; mem. Democratic Party of Serbia. *Publications:* Exclusive Distribution in the Laws of Yugoslavia and the European Community 1996, Law of International Franchising 2003; numerous articles on int. trade law, contract law, intellectual property law, competition law, distribution law in professional journals. *Address:* c/o Ministry of International Economic Relations, 11000 Belgrade, Gračanička 8, Serbia (office).

PARIZEAU, Jacques, PhD; Canadian fmr politician; b. 9 Aug. 1930, Montreal; s. of Gérard Parizeau and Germaine Parizeau (née Biron); m. 1st Alicja Poznanska 1956, one s. one d.; m. 2nd Lisette Lapointe 1992; ed Ecole des Hautes Etudes Commerciales, Montreal, Institut d'Etudes Politiques, Paris, London School of Econs, UK; Adviser to Govt of Québec 1961–65; elected Deputy for Assomption, Montreal 1976–84, 1989–; fmr Minister of Finance, Prov. of Québec (resgnd 1985); mem. Exec. Cttee Parti Québecois 1969, Pres. 1988–96; Premier of Québec 1994–95 (resgnd). *Publications:* The Terms of Trade of Canada 1966, Initiation à l'économie du Québec 1975, Pour un Québec souverain 1997, numerous articles. *Leisure interests:* reading, music.

PARK, Bong-heum, MA (Econ); South Korean business executive; *Chairman, Samsung Life Insurance Company Limited;* ed Duke Univ., USA; fmrly worked for Bank of Korea; Ind. Dir (non-exec.), Samsung Life Insurance Co. Ltd 2011–, currently also Chair.; Ind. Dir, SK Gas Ltd. *Address:* Samsung Life Insurance Co. Ltd, 150 Taepyung-ro 2-ga, Jung-gu, Seoul 100-716, South Korea (office). *Telephone:* (2) 1588-3114 (office). *Fax:* (2) 751-8021 (office). *E-mail:* info@samsunglife.com (office). *Website:* www.samsunglife.com (office).

PARK, Chan-wook; South Korean filmmaker; b. 23 Aug. 1963, *Films directed:* Simpan (Judgement) (also screenplay) 1999, Gongdong gyeongbi guyeok JSA (Joint Security Area) (also screenplay) 2000, Boksuneun naui geot (Sympathy for Mr Vengeance) (also screenplay) 2002, Yeoseot gae ui siseon (If You Were Me) (also screenplay) 2003, Oldboy (also screenplay) (Grand Prix, Cannes Film Festival 2004) 2003, Three… Extremes (also screenplay) 2004, Chinjeolhan Geumja-ssi (Sympathy for Lady Vengeance) (Bangkok Film Festival Golden Kinaree Award for Best Director 2006) 2005, I'm A Cyborg 2006, Crush and Blush 2008, Bak-jwi (Thirst) (Jury Prize, Cannes Film Festival) 2009. *Film screenplays:* Anarchists 2000, The Humanist 2001.

PARK, Charles Rawlinson, AB, MD; American biochemist and academic; *Professor Emeritus of Physiology, School of Medicine, Vanderbilt University;* b. 2 March 1916, Baltimore, Md; s. of Edwards A. Park and Agnes Bevan Park; m. Jane Harting 1953; one s.; ed Harvard Coll. and Johns Hopkins Univ. School of Medicine; Intern in Medicine, Johns Hopkins Univ. 1942; Asst Resident then Chief Resident, Harvard Univ. 1943–44; served in US Army 1944–47; Welch Fellow in Biochemistry, Wash. Univ. 1947–52; Prof. of Physiology and Chair. of Dept, Vanderbilt School of Medicine 1952–84, Prof. of Molecular Physiology and Biophysics, Prof. Emer. 1984–; Adjunct Prof. of Biochemistry, Meharry Medical Coll., Nashville 1993–; mem. Bd of Dirs Life Insurance Fund, Howard Hughes Medical Inst. 1964–84, Juvenile Diabetes Foundation, Int. Inst. of Cellular and Molecular Pathology, Nat. Inst. of Heart, Lung and Blood (NIH); mem. Editorial Bd Journal of Biological Chemistry; mem. American Physiological Soc., American Soc. of Biological Chemists, American Soc. of Clinical Investigation (Vice-Pres. 1961), Asscn of American Physicians, NAS; Branscomb Distinguished Prof. Award, Vanderbilt Univ. 1968–69, Banting Medal for Research, American Diabetes Asscn, Nat. Acad. of Sciences 1979. *Publications include:* approx. 120 scientific papers in journals of biochemistry and physiology 1942–; major topics concern action of hormones, diabetes, metabolic regulation, sugar and fat transport into mammalian cells. *Leisure interests:* music, reading, outdoor sports. *Address:* 5325 Stanford Drive, Nashville, TN 37215, USA (home). *Telephone:* (615) 665-1228 (home). *E-mail:* charles.park@vanderbilt.edu (office).

PARK, Geun-hye; South Korean politician and head of state; *President;* b. 2 Feb. 1952, Gumi, northern Gyeongsang Prov.; d. of the late Park Chung-hee (Pres. of South Korea 1961–79); ed Sogang Univ.; worked for Yukyoung Foundation and Saemaeum Hosp.; served as dir in sr citizen welfare centre; Dir Korean Cultural Foundation 1993; Dir Jeongsu Scholarship Fund 1994; mem. Grand Nat. Party (GNP) (renamed Saenuri Party 2012) 1998–2012, Vice-Pres. 2000–02, Chair. 2004–06, 2011–12; mem. Nat. Ass. for Daegu 1998–2012, as Proportional Representation mem. Parl. May–Dec. 2012; Pres. of South Korea (first woman) 2012–; Chair. Preparatory Cttee Korean Coalition for the Future 2001, Leader 2002 (merged with GNP 2003); mem. Korean Literature Asscn 1994; Hon. Pres. Korean Girl Scouts 1974; ranked by Forbes magazine amongst The World's 100 Most Powerful Women (11th) 2013, and amongst The World's Most Powerful People (52nd) 2013. *Publications include:* six books on family and literature. *Address:* Office of the President, Chong Wa Dae (The Blue House), 1, Sejong-no, Jongno-gu, Seoul, South Korea (office). *Telephone:* (2) 770-0055 (office). *Fax:* (2) 770-0344 (office). *E-mail:* president@cwd.go.kr (office). *Website:* english.president.go.kr; www.park2013.com.

PARK, Keun-hee; South Korean business executive; currently Vice-Chair. and CEO Samsung Life Insurance Co. Ltd. *Address:* Samsung Life Insurance Co. Ltd, 150 Taepyung-ro 2-ga, Jung-gu, Seoul 100-716, South Korea (office). *Telephone:* (2) 1588-3114 (office). *Fax:* (2) 751-8021 (office). *E-mail:* info@samsunglife.com (office). *Website:* www.samsunglife.com (office).

PARK, (Nicholas Wulstan) Nick, CBE, BA; British animated film director; b. 6 Dec. 1958, Preston, Lancs., England; ed Sheffield Art School and Nat. Film and TV School, Beaconsfield; joined Aardman Animations 1985, Partner 1995–; best known as the creator of Wallace and Gromit and Shaun the Sheep. *Films include:* Wallace & Gromit: A Grand Day Out (BAFTA Awards for Best Short Animated Film) 1989, Creature Comforts (Academy Award for Best Animated Short Film) 1990, Wallace & Gromit: The Wrong Trousers (Academy Award for Best Animated Short Film) 1993, Wallace & Gromit: A Close Shave (Academy Award for Best Animated Short Film) 1995, Chicken Run (co-dir) 2000, Wallace & Gromit: The Curse of the Were-Rabbit (BAFTA Best British Film 2006, Academy Award for Best Animated Feature Film 2006) 2005, Wallace & Gromit's Grand Adventures:

Fright of the Bumblebees (video game) 2009. *Television:* Creature Comforts (series) 2003–05, Shaun the Sheep (series) 2007–09, Wallace & Gromit in A Matter of Loaf and Death (short; writer) 2008, Wallace and Gromit's World of Invention (series) 2010. *Website:* www.aardman.com.

PARK, Seung, PhD; South Korean fmr central banker, economist and academic; b. 16 Feb. 1936; ed Seoul Nat. Univ. and State Univ. of New York, USA; economist at Bank of Korea 1961–76, Gov. 2002–06, fmr mem. Monetary Bd; Assoc. Prof., Chung-Ang Univ. 1976, Prof. 1982–88, 1990–, Dean Coll. of Politics and Econs 1984–87, Dean Grad. School 1988; Sr Sec. for Econs, Presidential Secr. 1988; Minister of Construction 1988–89; Chief Dir Korea Nat. Housing Corpn 1993–96; Chief Dir Korea Transport Inst. 1997; Chair. Korea Econ. Asscn 1999; Head, Public Funds Man. Cttee –2002; Pres. Korea Int. Econ. Asscn 1986. *Address:* c/o Bank of Korea, 110, 3-ga, Namdaemun-no, Jung-gu, Seoul 100-794, Republic of Korea (office).

PARK, Tae-hwan; South Korean swimmer; b. 27 Sept. 1989, Seoul; ed Kyunggi High School, Dankook Univ.; began swimming aged five, began competitive swimming aged 17, won several medals in junior competitions; selected by Korean Swimming Fed. as mem. of nat. team based in Taereung, Seoul 2003; Asian Games Doha, 2006: gold medal, 200m freestyle, 400m freestyle, 1,500m freestyle, bronze medal, 4×100m freestyle relay, 4×200m freestyle relay, 4×100m medley relay; Pan Pacific Championships, Victoria 2006: gold medal, 400m freestyle, 1,500m freestyle, silver medal, 200m freestyle; Olympic Games, Beijing 2008: gold medal, 400m freestyle, silver medal, 200m freestyle; World Championships, Shanghai 2011: gold medal, 400m freestyle; Olympic Games, London 2012: silver medal, 200m freestyle, 400m freestyle; trains in Melbourne, Australia; Goodwill Amb. for 'Dynamic Korea'; coach Michael Bohl 2010–; voted Most Valuable Player at Asian Games, Doha 2006, World Pacific Rim Swimmer of the Year 2006. *Address:* Korea Swimming Federation, RM 510 Olympic Center #88, Ohryun-Dong Songpa-ku, 138-749 Seoul, South Korea. *Telephone:* (2) 4204236. *Fax:* (2) 4206934. *E-mail:* korswim@chol.com. *Website:* swimming.sports.or.kr.

PARK, Y. H., BA, MA, PhD; South Korean surgeon and business executive; *Chairman, Doosan Corporation;* ed Kyunggi High School, Dept of Surgery, School of Medicine, Seoul Nat. Univ.; full-time medical doctor at Brigham and Women's Hosp., Harvard Medical School, Boston; apptd Pres. 11th and 12th Seoul Nat. Univ. Hosp. 1998, Chair. Hosp. Man. Cttee, Korean Red Cross 2005; Chair. Yonkang Foundation 2005–; Chair. Doosan Corpn 2007–; Vice-Chair. Fed. of Korean Industries 2007–; mem. Bd of Trustees, Chung-Ang Univ. Foundation 2008–; Chair. Korea Arts and Culture Educ. Centre 2009–. *Address:* Doosan Corporation, Doosan Tower 18-12, Euljiro 6-ga, Jung-gu, Seoul 100-730, South Korea (office). *Telephone:* (2) 3398-0114 (office). *Fax:* (2) 3398-1135 (office). *E-mail:* info@doosan.com (office). *Website:* www.doosan.com (office).

PARK, Yong-sung, MBA; South Korean business executive and international organization official; *Chairman, Doosan Heavy Industries and Construction Company;* b. 11 Sept. 1940, Seoul; ed School of Commerce, Seoul Nat. Univ., Leonard N. Stern School of Business, New York Univ., USA; fmr mem. Exec. Bd ICC 1998–2003, Vice-Chair. 2003–05, Chair. 2005–06; currently Chair. Doosan Heavy Industries and Construction Co.; Chair. Korean Chamber of Commerce and Industry (KCCI); fmr mem. Int. Olympic Cttee, Pres. South Korea Olympic Cttee 2008–13; Pres. Int. Judo Fed. 1995–2007. *Address:* Doosan Heavy Industries and Construction Company, 1303–22 Seocho-Dong, Seocho-Gu, Seoul 137-920, South Korea (office). *Telephone:* (2) 513-6114 (office). *Fax:* (2) 513-6200 (office). *Website:* www.doosanheavy.com.

PARK, Yongmaan, BA, MBA; South Korean business executive; *CEO, Doosan Corporation;* ed Kyunggi High School, Seoul National University, Boston University, USA; joined Doosan Engineering and Construction 1982, Pres. and CEO Doosan Corpn 1998–2000, 2001–09, Chair. and CEO Doosan Infracore 2007–, CEO Doosan Corpn 2009–; Vice-Chair. Seoul Chamber of Commerce and Industry 2009–; Chair. for Korea, Korea-Spain Econ. Cooperation Council 2000–. *Address:* Doosan Corpn, Doosan Tower 18-12, Euljiro 6-ga, Jung-gu, Seoul 100-730, South Korea (office). *Telephone:* (2) 3398-0114 (office). *Fax:* (2) 3398-1135 (office). *E-mail:* info@doosan.com (office). *Website:* www.doosan.com (office).

PARK, Young-ho, MBA; South Korean business executive; *Vice-Chairman, SK China;* ed Seoul Nat. Univ.; worked at Posco Research Inst. –2000; joined SK Holdings Co. Ltd 2000, Pres. and Co-CEO SK Holdings Co. Ltd 2007–10, Vice-Chair. SK China 2010–. *Address:* SK China, SK Holdings Co. Ltd, 99 Seorin-Dong, Jongru-Gu, Seoul 110-110, South Korea (office). *Telephone:* (2) 2121-5114 (office). *Fax:* (2) 2121-7001 (office). *E-mail:* Byc778@sk.com (office). *Website:* www.sk.com.cn (office).

PARKANOVÁ, Vlasta, JUDr; Czech lawyer and politician; *Vice-Chairman, Chamber of Deputies;* b. 21 Nov. 1951, Prague; m. Zdeněk Parkan; one d.; ed Charles Univ.; began legal career specialising in commercial law 1975–88; co-f. Civic Forum, Tábor 1989; mem. Fed. Ass. 1990–93; various positions within Ministry of Foreign Affairs and Ministry of Interior 1992–96; mem. Parl. 1996–, Vice-Chair. Chamber of Deputies 2011–; Minister of Justice 1997–98, Deputy Chair. Cttee on Defence and Security 1998–2002, Minister of Defence 2007–09; Vice-Chair. Constitution and Legal Cttee 1998–2002, Chair. 2003–06; mem. Perm. Del. of Parl. of Czech Repub. to NATO 1998–2006; mem. Civic Democratic Alliance (ODA) 1991–98; mem. Christian Democratic Party (KDU-CSL) 2001–09. *Address:* Sněmovní 4, 118 26 Prague 1, Czech Republic (office). *Telephone:* (2) 57173085 (office). *E-mail:* parkanova@psp.cz (office). *Website:* www.psp.cz (office).

PARKER, Sir Alan William, Kt, CBE; British film director, producer and writer; b. 14 Feb. 1944, Islington, London, England; s. of William Leslie Parker and Elsie Parker; m. 1st Annie Inglis 1966 (divorced 1992); three s. one d.; m. Lisa Moran; ed Dame Alice Owen's School, Islington; advertising copywriter 1965–67; TV commercials dir 1968–78; wrote screenplay Melody 1969; Founding mem. and Chair. Directors Guild of GB 1982–86; Chair. British Film Inst. 1998–99, Film Council 1999–2010; mem. British Screen Advisory Council 1985–, Jury, Cannes Film Festival 1991; Hon. Fellow, Nat. Film and Television School; Officier des Arts et des Lettres 2005; Hon. DArts (Sunderland) 2005; BAFTA Michael Balcon Award for Outstanding Contrib. to British Film, Directors Guild of GB Lifetime Achievement Award, BAFTA Fellowship 2013. *Screenplay:* Melody (also original story) 197. *Wrote and directed:* Our Cissy (short) 1974, Footsteps (short) 1974, Bugsy Malone 1976, No Hard Feelings (TV film) 1976, Angel Heart 1987, A Turnip Head's Guide to the British Cinema, Come See the Paradise 1990, The Road to Wellville (also producer) 1994, Evita (also actor and producer) 1996, Angela's Ashes (also actor and producer) 1999. *Directed:* The Evacuees (TV film) 1974, Midnight Express (also actor) 1978, Fame 1980, Shoot the Moon 1982, Pink Floyd The Wall 1982, Birdy 1984, Mississippi Burning (Nat. Review Bd Best Dir Award) 1988, Renegade MTV Special (TV film) 1990, The Commitments (also actor) (BAFTA Award for Best Dir) 1991 The Life of David Gale (also actor and producer) 2003. *Produced:* I Really Hate My Job (exec. producer) 2007. *Publications:* (novels) Bugsy Malone 1976, Puddles in the Lane 1977, The Sucker's Kiss 2003; (cartoon) Hares in the Gate 1983, Making Movies 1998. *Leisure interest:* cartooning. *Address:* c/o Creative Artists Agency, 2000 Avenue of the Stars, Los Angeles, CA 90067, USA. *Telephone:* (424) 288-2000. *Fax:* (424) 288-2900. *Website:* www.caa .com; www.alanparker.com.

PARKER, Cornelia, OBE, BA (Hons), MFA, RA; British artist; b. 14 July 1956, Cheshire, England; m.; one d.; ed Gloucestershire Coll. of Art and Design, Wolverhampton Polytechnic, Univ. of Reading; Int. Artist-in-Residence, Two Rooms, Auckland 2010, Artist-in-Residence, Jupiter Artland, Edinburgh 2009, Brontë Parsonage Museum, Yorks. 2006, part of Illuminate festival 2006, For-site Residency, Nevada City, Calif. 2005, Artist-in-Residence, Science Museum, London 1998–99, Int. Artist-in-Residence, ArtPace Foundation for Contemporary Art, San Antonio, Tex., 1997, Koopman Chair, Jose Loff Gallery, Hartford Art School, Conn. 1997, Sr Fellow in Fine Art, Cardiff Inst. 1992–95, Henry Moore Sculpture Residency, Wimbledon School of Art 1991–92, Sculpture Residency and Commission, Forest of Dean, Gloucestershire 1988, Artist-in-Residence, Crewe & Alsager Coll., Cheshire 1980; Dr hc (Univ. of Wolverhampton) 2000, (Univ. of Birmingham) 2005, (Univ. of Gloucestershire) 2008; First Prize, Midland View Stoke City Art Gallery & Museum 1980, Southern Arts Award 1983, Greater London Arts Award 1985, British School at Rome Award 1989, Henry Moore Scholarship, Wimbledon School of Art 1991–92, Int. Asscn of Art Critics Prize (USA) 1998, Best Show by an Emerging Artist, for Mass: Colder Darker Matter at Deitch Projects, New York 1998, The Hugh Casson Drawing Prize, RA Summer Exhbn 2011. *Television:* Date With An Artist – 1997 Turner Prize (Channel 4) 1997, Artist ties up Rodin's lovers (BBC News) 2003, Tate Modern: Different Dimensions, Tate Modern and Nat. Gallery, Series 1 Episode 5 (Channel 4) 2008, Vic Reeves' Turner Prize Moments (Channel 4) 2011, Cornelia Parker Night (Sky Arts) 2011. *Publications:* Cold Dark Matter: An Exploded View, Essay by Adrian Searl, London: Chisenhale Gallery 1991, Avoided Object (with Guy Brett, Stuart Cameron, Antonia Payne and Jonathon Watkins) 1996, Contemporary Art 1992, Cornelia Parker (with Bruce Ferguson and Jessica Morgan) 2000, On Second Thoughts – Cornelia Parker 2003, Brontean Abstracts 2006. *Address:* c/o Frith Street Gallery, 59–60 Frith Street, London, W1D 3JJ, England (office). *Telephone:* (20) 7494-1550 (office). *Fax:* (20) 7287-3733 (office). *E-mail:* info@frithstreetgallery .com (office). *Website:* www.frithstreetgallery.com (office).

PARKER, Sir Eric Wilson, Kt, FCA; British business executive; *Owner, Crimbourne Stud Farm;* b. 8 June 1933, Shrewsbury, Shropshire, England; s. of Wilson Parker and Gladys Edith Wellings; m. Marlene Teresa Neale 1955; two s. two d.; ed The Priory Grammar School for Boys, Shrewsbury; articled clerk with Wheeler, Whittingham & Kent, Shrewsbury 1950–55; nat. service, Pay Corps 1956–58; Taylor Woodrow Group 1958–64; joined Trafalgar House Group 1965, Finance/Admin. Dir 1969, Deputy Man. Dir 1973, Group Man. Dir 1977, Group Chief Exec. 1983–92, Deputy Chair. 1988–93; Chair. Caradon PLC 1998–99; Dir Racehorse Owners Asscn 1994–, Pres. 1998–2001; Trustee, Trafalgar House Pension (fmrly Kvaerner Trustees (KPF) Ltd) 2002–12; Dir (non-exec.) Int. Real Estates 1997–2009, Ministry of Defence Quartermaster Gen. Bd 1997–2000, British Borneo PLC 1998–2000, British Horseracing Bd 1999–2004, Horserace Betting Levy Bd 2000–04, Job Partners 2000–02; Horserace Totalisator Bd 2002–08, Albert Goodwin PLC 2003–10, National Stud 2005–08, Nameco (No. 346) Ltd 2009–; Cttee mem. Teenage Cancer Trust; mem. Lloyds; Owner Crimbourne Stud Farm. *Leisure interests:* golf, horse racing, wines. *Address:* Crimbourne Stud Farm, Crimbourne Lane, Wisborough Green, nr Billingshurst, West Sussex, RH14 0HR, England. *Telephone:* (1403) 700400. *Fax:* (1403) 700776. *E-mail:* office@crimbournestud.com. *Website:* www.crimbournestud.co.uk.

PARKER, Eugene N., PhD; American physicist (retd) and academic; b. 10 June 1927, Houghton, Mich.; s. of Glenn H. Parker and Helen M. Parker; m. Niesje Meuter 1954; one s. one d.; ed Michigan State Univ. and California Inst. of Tech.; Instructor, Dept of Math. and Astronomy, Univ. of Utah 1951–53, Asst Prof., Dept of Physics 1953–55; joined Univ. of Chicago 1955, Prof., Dept of Physics 1962–95, Prof., Dept of Astronomy 1967–95, now S. Chandrasekhar Distinguished Service Prof. Emer.; mem. NAS 1967–, Norwegian Acad. of Sciences 1988–; Hon. DSc (Michigan State Univ.) 1975; Dr hc (Utrecht) 1986; Space Science Award, AIAA 1964, John Adam Fleming Award, American Geophysical Union 1968, Henryk Arctowski Medal, NAS 1969, Henry Norris Russell Lecture, American Astronomical Soc. 1969, George Ellery Hale Award, Solar Physics Div. American Astronomical Soc. 1978, Sydney Chapman Medal, Royal Astronomical Soc. 1979, Distinguished Alumnus Award, Calif. Inst. of Tech. 1980, James Arthur Prize Lecture, Harvard Smithsonian Center for Astrophysics 1986, US Nat. Medal of Science 1989, William Bowie Medal, American Geophysical Union 1990, Karl Schwarzschild Medal (FRG) 1990, Gold Medal, Royal Astronomical Soc. 1992, Bruce Medal, Astronomical Soc. of the Pacific 1997, ADION Medal, Observatoire de Nice 1997, James Clark Maxwell Prize, American Physical Soc. 2003, Kyoto Prize, Inamori Foundation 2003, Outstanding Alumni Award, Michigan State Univ. 2004. *Publications include:* Interplanetary Dynamical Processes 1963, Cosmical Magnetic Fields 1979, Spontaneous Current Sheets in Magnetic Fields 1994. *Leisure interests:* hiking, history, wood-carving. *Address:* Department of Physics, University of Chicago, 5720 South Ellis Avenue, Chicago, IL 60637, USA. *Website:* physics.uchicago.edu.

PARKER, Franklin, BA, MS, EdD; American writer and educationalist; b. 2 June 1921, New York, NY; m. Betty June Parker 1950; ed Berea Coll., Univ. of Illinois, Peabody Coll., Vanderbilt Univ.; Librarian and Speech Teacher, Ferrum Coll., Va 1950–52, Belmont Coll., Nashville, Tenn. 1952–54, Peabody Coll., Vanderbilt Univ. 1955–56; Assoc. Prof. of Educ., State Univ. Coll., New Paltz, NY

1956–57, Univ. of Texas 1957–64; Prof., Univ. of Oklahoma 1964–68; Claude Worthington Benedum Prof. of Educ., West Virginia Univ., Morgantown 1968–86; Distinguished Prof. Emer., Center for Excellence in Educ. 1986–89; Visiting Distinguished Prof., Western Carolina Univ. 1989–94; consultant, Macmillan Merrill (Publrs), Teachers Coll. Press, William C. Brown 1988–; several visiting professorships; Sr Fulbright Research Scholar, Zambia 1961–62; Distinguished Alumnus Award, Peabody Coll., Vanderbilt Univ. 1970, Berea Coll. 1989. *Publications include:* African Development and Education in Southern Rhodesia 1960, Government Policy and International Education 1965, Church and State in Education 1966, Strategies for Curriculum Change: Cases from 13 Nations 1968, International Education: Understandings and Misunderstandings 1969, George Peabody: A Biography 1971, American Dissertations on Foreign Education: Abstracts of Doctoral Dissertations (20 vols) 1971–91, What We Can Learn from China's Schools 1977, Education in Puerto Rico and of Puerto Ricans in the USA Vol. 1 1978, Vol. 2 1984, British Schools and Ours 1979, Women's Education (two vols) 1979–81, US Higher Education: Guide to Information Sources 1980, Education in the People's Republic of China, Past and Present: Annotated Bibliography 1986, Education in England and Wales: Annotated Bibliography 1991, Academic Profiles in Higher Education 1993, Tennessee Encyclopaedia of History and Culture (mem. Editorial Bd) 1998; numerous articles, contribs to encyclopaedias. *E-mail:* bfparker@frontiernet.net.

PARKER, Mark G., BS; American business executive; *President and CEO, Nike, Inc.;* b. Poughkeepsie, NY; ed Pennsylvania State Univ.; Designer and Devt Man., Nike, Inc., Exeter, NH 1979–80, Man. Advanced Product Design, Exeter 1980–81, Dir Design Concepts and Eng 1981–82, Dir Footwear Design 1982–83, Man. Running and Fitness Footwear Marketing 1983–85, Head Special Design Project Teams 1985–87, Divisional Vice-Pres. Footwear Research, Design and Devt 1987–88, Corporate Vice-Pres. Research, Design and Devt 1988–93, Vice-Pres. Consumer Product Marketing 1993–98, Vice-Pres. and Gen. Man. Global Footwear 1998–2001, Pres. Nike Brand 2001–06, CEO and Pres. Nike Inc. 2006–. *Address:* Nike, Inc., 1 Bowerman Drive, Beaverton, OR 97005-6453, USA (office). *Telephone:* (503) 671-6453 (office). *Fax:* (503) 671-6300 (office). *E-mail:* info@nikebiz.com (office). *Website:* www.nikebiz.com (office).

PARKER, Michael D., CBE, BChemEng, MBA; American/British business executive; m. Noreen Parker; one s. one d.; ed Univ. of Manchester and Manchester Business School, UK; joined Dow Chemical Co. 1968, later served with Dow Int. Research and Devt, Freeport, Tex., field sales post, Birmingham, UK 1972, Dist Sales Man. 1975, Product Marketing Man. for Epoxy Resins, Dow Europe, later Dir Marketing for Inorganic Chemicals, then Dir Marketing for Organic Chemicals, Commercial Dir Functional Products Dept, Dow Europe 1983, Gen. Man. Specialty Chemicals Dept, Dow USA, Midland, Mich. 1984, Commercial Vice-Pres. Dow Pacific, Hong Kong 1987, Pres. 1988–93, Group Vice-Pres. (Chemicals and Hydrocarbons) 1993–95, Pres. Dow N America 1995–96, mem. Bd of Dirs 1995, mem. Exec. Cttee Bd, Chair. Corp. Operating Bd, Exec. Vice-Pres. 1996–2000, Pres. and CEO 2000–02, also mem. Bd of Dirs and Exec. Cttee Dow Corning Corpn 2000–02, mem. Mems Cttee of Dow Agrosciences; CEO British Nuclear Fuels plc 2003–09; mem. Bd of Dirs SNC-Lavalin, PV Crystalox Solar PLC, Invensys PLC, Tianhe Chemicals PLC (Sr Ind. Dir); Chair. Liverpool Vision, Street League (charity); Trustee Royal Soc. for the Prevention of Accidents; mem. Manchester Business School Advisory Bd. *Address:* c/o Liverpool Vision, 10th Floor, The Capital, 39 Old Hall Street, Liverpool, L3 9PP, England.

PARKER, Robert M., Jr, BA, LLB; American writer and wine critic; *Publisher, The Wine Advocate;* b. 23 July 1947, Baltimore, Md; m. Patricia Parker 1969; one d.; ed Univ. of Maryland; attorney, Sr Attorney and later Asst Gen. Counsel for Farm Credits, Bank of Baltimore 1973–84; Founder, Writer and Publr The Wine Advocate 1978–; Contributing Ed. Food and Wine Magazine; wine critic for L'Express magazine (first non-French holder of post); Hon. Citizen of Châteauneuf du Pape 1995; Chevalier, Ordre nat. du Mérite 1993, Chevalier, Légion d'honneur 1999; Loyola Coll. Marylander of the Year Award 1992, James Beard Foundation Wine and Spirits Professional of 1997. *Publications include:* Bordeaux (Glenfiddich Award 1986, Int. Asscn of Cooking Professionals Award for second edn 1992, Goldene Feder Award (Germany) for third edn 1993, Moët-Hennessy Wine and Vine Communication Award for French edn 1993) 1985, Parker's Wine Buyer's Guide 1987, The Wines of the Rhône Valley and Provence (Tastemaker's Award, USA 1989, Wine Guild's Wine Book of the Year Award, UK 1989) 1987, Burgundy (Moët-Hennessy Wine and Vine Communication Award for French edn 1993) 1990; contribs to The Field. *Address:* The Wine Advocate, Inc., PO Box 311, Monkton, MD 21111, USA (office). *Telephone:* (410) 329-6477 (office). *Fax:* (410) 357-4504 (office). *E-mail:* wineadvocate@erobertparker.com (office). *Website:* www .erobertparker.com.

PARKER, Sarah Jessica; American actress and fashion designer; b. 25 March 1965, Nelsonville, Ohio; m. Matthew Broderick (q.v.) 1997; one s. two d.; best known for leading role as Carrie Bradshaw on HBO TV series Sex and the City 1998–2004; played same role in feature film based on the show, Sex and the City: The Movie 2008, and its sequel, Sex and the City 2 2010; ranked by Forbes magazine amongst The World's 100 Most Powerful Women (45th) 2010. *Stage appearances include:* The Innocents 1976, The Sound of Music 1977, Annie 1978, The War Brides 1981, The Death of a Miner 1982, To Gillian on Her 37th Birthday 1983–84, Terry Neal's Future 1986, The Heidi Chronicles 1989, How To Succeed in Business Without Really Trying 1996, Once Upon A Mattress 1996, Wonder of the World 2001. *Films include:* Rich Kids 1979, Somewhere Tomorrow 1983, Firstborn 1984, Footloose 1984, Girls Just Want to Have Fun 1985, Flight of the Navigator 1986, LA Story 1991, Honeymoon in Vegas 1992, Hocus Pocus 1993, Striking Distance 1993, Ed Wood 1994, Miami Rhapsody 1995, If Lucy Fell 1996, Mars Attacks! 1996, The First Wives Club 1996, Extreme Measures 1996, A Life Apart: Hasidism in America 1997, 'Til There Was You 1997, Isn't She Great 1999, Dudley Do-Right 1999, State and Main 2000, Life Without Dick 2001, Strangers with Candy 2005, Family Stone 2005, Failure to Launch 2006, Slammer 2007, Smart People 2008, Sex and the City: The Movie 2008, Did You Hear About the Morgans? 2009, Sex and the City 2 2010, New Year's Eve 2011. *Television includes:* Equal Justice 1990–91, The Sunshine Boys (film) 1995, Sex and the City (four Golden Globe Awards for Best Actress in a TV series 2000, 2001, 2002, 2004, three Screen Actors Guild Awards for Outstanding Performance by a Female Actor in a Comedy

Series 2001, 2002, 2004, Emmy Award for Outstanding Comedy Series 2001, Emmy Award for Outstanding Lead Actress in a Comedy 2004) 1998–2004, Stories from My Childhood (series, narrator) 1998, Sex and the Matrix (short) 2000, Who Do You Think You Are? 2010. *Address:* c/o Jane Berliner, Creative Artists Agency, 2000 Avenue of the Stars, Los Angeles, CA 90067, USA. *Telephone:* (424) 288-2000. *Fax:* (424) 288-2900. *Website:* www.caa.com.

PARKER, Sir (Thomas) John, Kt, GBE, DSc (Eng), FREng; British business executive; *Non-Executive Chairman, Anglo American plc;* b. 8 April 1942, Downpatrick, Northern Ireland; s. of Robert Parker and Margaret Elizabeth Parker (née Bell); m. Emma Elizabeth Blair 1967; one s. one d.; ed Belfast Coll. of Tech., Queen's Univ., Belfast; Ship Design Staff, Harland and Wolff PLC 1963–69, Ship Production Man. 1969–71, Production Drawing Office Man. 1971–72, Sales and Projects Dept Gen. Man. 1972–74; Man. Dir Austin & Pickersgill 1974–78; mem. Bd for Shipbuilding (Marketing and Operations), British Shipbuilders 1978–80, Corpn Deputy Chief Exec. 1980–83; Chair. and CEO Harland and Wolff Holdings PLC 1983–93, Dir (non-exec.) 1993–94; Chair. Harland-MAN Engines 1983–93; mem. Industrial Devt Bd for NI 1983–87; mem. Gen. Cttee Lloyds Register of Shipping 1983– (Chair. Tech. Cttee 1996–); mem. Bd QUBIS 1984–93, British Coal 1986–93; Deputy Chair. Babcock Int. Group PLC 1993–94, Chief Exec. 1993–2000, Chair. 1994–2001; Jt Chair. (non-exec.) Mondi Group (following its demerger from Anglo American plc) –2009; Deputy Chair. DP World (Dubai); Chair. (non-exec.) Lattice Group PLC (merged with National Grid Group to become National Grid Transco PLC 2002, renamed National Grid PLC 2005) 2000–11, Firth Rixson PLC 2001–04, Anglo American plc 2009–; Chair. RMC Group plc 2002–05; Sr Non-Exec. Dir (Chair.) Court of the Bank of England 2005–09; Dir (non-exec.) GKN PLC 1993–2008, BG PLC 1997–2000, Carnival PLC and Carnival Corpn, Inc. 2003–, P&O Princess Cruises PLC (Chair. P&O Group PLC 2005–08), European Aeronautic Defence and Space Co. (EADS) NV 2007–; fmr Dir (non-exec.) British Coal Corpn Brambles Industries plc; Pres. Royal Acad. of Eng; Vice-Pres. Royal Inst. of Naval Architects 1985–93, Pres. 1996–99; Chair. Council of European Shipbuilders Asscn 1993; Chancellor Univ. of Southampton –2011; Visiting Fellow, Univ. of Oxford; Fellow, Inst. of Marine Engineers; Hon. Fellow, Inst. of Marine Eng, Science and Tech. (IMarEST), Royal Inst. of Naval Architects; Hon. DSc (Trinity Coll. Dublin, Ulster, Abertay), Hon. ScD, Hon. DUniv; Man. of the Year Award, Ireland 1986, Inst. of Energy Melchett Medal 2003, and other awards. *Publications:* A Profile of British Shipbuilders 1979, British Shipbuilders – A Period of Constructive Change (Marintec Conf., Shanghai) 1981, The Challenge of Change in Shipbuilding Today (ICCAS '85 Conf., Trieste) 1985. *Leisure interests:* reading, music, ships, sailing. *Address:* Anglo American plc, 20 Carlton House Terrace, London, SW1Y 5AN, England (office). *Telephone:* (20) 7968-8888 (office). *Fax:* (20) 7968-8500 (office). *E-mail:* info@angloamerican.com (office). *Website:* www.angloamerican.com (office).

PARKER, Trey; American screenwriter, film director and producer; b. (Randolph Severn Parker III), 19 Oct. 1969, Conifer, Colo; collaborated with Matt Stone on short animation, Jesus vs Frosty 1992, later remade as animated Christmas card for FoxLab, titled The Spirit of Christmas 1995; Co-creator and Exec. Producer, South Park animation (with Matt Stone) 1997–, and other films and TV series. *Films include:* Jesus vs Frosty (writer, dir, producer) 1992, American History (writer, dir) (Student Acad. Award) 1992, Your Studio and You (writer, dir) 1995, The Spirit of Christmas (writer, dir, producer) 1995, For Goodness Sake II (dir) 1996, Alferd Packer: The Musical (aka Cannibal! The Musical) (writer, dir, producer) 1996, Orgazmo (writer, dir, producer) 1997, South Park: Bigger Longer & Uncut (writer, dir, producer) (Los Angeles Film Critics Award, New York Film Critics Award, MTV Movie Award) 1999, How's Your News? (exec. producer) 1999, Team America: World Police (writer, dir, producer) 2004. *Film appearances include:* BASEketball 1998, provides voices for many characters in his animation films and television series. *Television includes:* South Park (series writer, dir, producer) 1997–, That's My Bush! (series writer, dir, producer) 2001, Kenny vs. Spenny (producer) 2007. *Recordings include:* albums: Chef Aid: The South Park Album, South Park: Bigger, Longer and Uncut (soundtrack), Mr Hankey's Christmas Classics, Timmy and the Lords of the Underworld, The Book of Mormon (Grammy Award for Best Musical Theater Album 2012) 2011. *Play:* The Book of Mormon (Tony Award for Best Musical 2011, WhatsOnStage Award for Best New Musical 2014, Olivier Award for Best New Musical 2014) 2011. *Address:* c/o Paramount Studios, 5555 Melrose Avenue, Hollywood, CA 90038, USA. *E-mail:* news@southparkstudios.com. *Website:* www.southparkstudios.com.

PARKER, W(illiam) Douglas (Doug), BA, MBA; American airline executive; *CEO, American Airlines Group, Inc. and American Airlines;* m. Gwen Parker; three c.; ed Albion Coll., Owen Grad. School of Man. at Vanderbilt Univ.; held several financial management positions with American Airlines 1986–91; Vice-Pres. and Asst Treas., and Vice-Pres. of Financial Planning and Analysis, Northwest Airlines 1991–95; Sr Vice-Pres. and Chief Financial Officer, America West Airlines from 1995, later Exec. Vice-Pres. (Corporate Group) and COO, CEO 2001–05, apptd Chair., Pres. and CEO (merged with US Airways 2005), Chair. and CEO US Airways 2005–13, CEO American Airlines Group, Inc. and American Airlines (following merger of US Airways and American Airlines) 2013–; mem. Bd of Dirs, Valley of the Sun United Way. *Address:* American Airlines Group, PO Box 619616, Dallas/Fort Worth Airport, TX 75261-9616, USA (office). *Telephone:* (817) 963-1234 (office). *Website:* www.aa.com (office).

PARKHOMENKO, Sergey Borisovich; Russian journalist; b. 13 March 1964, Moscow; m.; two s.; ed Moscow State Univ.; Head of Div. Teatre (magazine) 1985–90; political observer, Nezavisimaya Gazeta 1990–92; mem. Bd Segodnya (newspaper) 1993–95; Co-founder Moscow Charter for Journalists 1994; Ed.-in-Chief Itogi (magazine) 1996–2001, IT Weekly (journal) 2002, Real Itogi 2002, Yezhenedel'ny zhurnal 2003; Co-founder League of Voters (opposition movt) 2012.

PARKIN, Stuart S. P., MA, PhD, FRS; British physicist; *IBM Fellow, IBM Almaden Research Center;* b. 9 Dec. 1955, Watford, Herts., England; ed Univ. of Cambridge; Research Student, Cavendish Lab., Cambridge 1977; Research Fellow, Trinity Coll., Cambridge 1979–85; Royal Soc. European Exchange Fellowship, Univ. Paris-Sud, Lab. de Physique des Solides, France 1980–81, Visiting Prof. 1988; IBM World Trade Fellowship, IBM Research Lab., Almaden Research Center, San José, Calif., USA 1982, Adjunct Research Staff Mem. 1983, Research Staff Mem. 1984, mem. IBM Acad. of Tech. 1997–, IBM Fellow 1999–;

Consulting Prof., Dept of Applied Physics, Stanford Univ. 1997–, Nat. Taiwan Univ. 2007; Visiting Chair Prof., Taipei, Taiwan 2007; Distinguished Visiting Prof., Dept of Electrical and Computer Eng, Nat. Univ. of Singapore 2007; Distinguished Research Chair Prof., Nat. Yunlin Univ. of Science and Tech., Douliou, Taiwan; Distinguished Visiting Prof., Eindhoven Univ. of Tech. 2008–; mem. Advisory Bd Journal of Physics: Condensed Matter 1993–96; Assoc. Ed. Materials Letters 1993–2006; Chief Ed. Spin Journal 2010–; mem. Editorial Advisory Bd Advanced Materials 2008–; mem. Admin. Cttee IEEE Magnetics Soc. 2010–, Scientific Advisory Bd IFW Dresden, Germany 2010–, Standing Cttee on Tech. Insight (TIGER), Nat. Acads 2009–, Condensed Matter and Materials Research Cttee, Nat. Acads 2010–; mem. NAS 2008–, Nat. Acad. of Eng 2009–; Fellow, American Physical Soc., Cambridge Philosophical Soc., Inst. of Physics, London, Materials Research Soc., IEEE, AAAS, American Acad. of Arts and Sciences; Dr hc (RWTH Aachen Univ.) 2007, (Eindhoven Univ. of Tech.) 2008; numerous IBM Patent Achievement Awards, Inst. of Physics Charles Vernon Boys Prize 1991, American Physical Soc. Int. Prize for New Materials 1994, European Physical Soc. Hewlett-Packard Europhysics Prize 1997, American Inst. of Physics Prize for Industrial Application of Physics 1999–2000, R&D Magazine's first Innovator of the Year 2001, Economist Magazine's 'No Boundaries' Award for Innovation 2007, IEEE Daniel E. Noble Award 2008, Johannes Gutenberg Research Award 2008, IUPAP Magnetism Prize and Neel Medal 2009, Dresden Barkhausen Award 2009. *Publications:* more than 380 scientific papers in refereed journals; 83 issued patents. *Address:* IBM Almaden Research Center, Room D1-306, 650 Harry Road, San José, CA 95120-6099, USA (office). *Telephone:* (408) 927-2390 (office). *Fax:* (845) 489-9710 (office). *E-mail:* parkin@almaden.ibm.com (office). *Website:* www.almaden.ibm.com/spinaps (office).

PARKINSON, Bradford W., BS, SM, PhD; American engineer, inventor and academic; *Edward C. Wells Professor of Aeronautics and Astronautics, Stanford University;* b. 1935, Wis.; m. Virginia Parkinson; ed US Naval Acad., MIT, Stanford Univ.; served in USAF 1957–78, retiring with rank of Col; instructor, Air Foce Test Pilot School, Edwards Air Force Base, Calif.; Head, Dept of Astronautics and Computer Science, USAF Acad. Colo; cr. and managed NAVSTAR GPS Jt Program Office 1972–78; Edward C. Wells Prof. of Aeronautics and Astronautics, W. W. Hansen Experimental Physics Lab., Stanford Univ. 1984–; fmr Prof., Colo State Univ.; Chair. Bd of Trustees The Aerospace Corpn; co-Chair. JPL Advisory Council; mem. AAAS, IEEE, Pres. Comm. on Air Safety and Security, Royal Inst. of Navigation (RION); Legion of Merit; Defense Dept Superior Performance Award for Best Program Dir in USAF 1977, Discover Innovation Award, NASA Distinguished Public Service Medal, IEEE Simon Ramo Award, Von Karman Lectureship and Aerospace Contrib. to Soc. Medal, AIAA, Thurlow Award ION, Gold Medal RION, Draper Prize (jtly) 2003. *Invention:* Global Positioning System (GPS) (co-inventor). *Address:* W. W. Hansen Experimental Physics Laboratory, Stanford University, Stanford, CA 94305-4085, USA (home). *Website:* einstein .stanford.edu.

PARKINSON, Baron (Life Peer), cr. 1992, of Carnforth in the County of Lancashire; *Cecil Edward Parkinson,* PC, MA; British politician and chartered accountant; b. 1 Sept. 1931; s. of Sidney Parkinson; m. Ann Mary Jarvis 1957; three d.; one d. by Sarah Keays; ed Royal Lancaster Grammar School and Emmanuel Coll., Cambridge; joined Metal Box Co. as man. trainee; joined West, Wake, Price & Co. (chartered accountants) as articled clerk 1956, Partner 1961–71; f. Parkinson Hart Securities Ltd 1967, Chair. 1967–79, Dir 1967–79, 1984–; Dir several other cos 1967–79; Branch Treas. Hemel Hempstead Conservative Asscn 1961–64, Constituency Chair. 1965–66, Chair. and ex-officio mem. all cttees 1966–69; Chair. Herts. 100 Club 1968–69; Pres. Hemel Hempstead Young Conservatives 1968–71, Northampton Young Conservatives 1969–71; contested Northampton, Gen. Election 1970; MP for Enfield West 1970–74, for Hertfordshire South 1974–83, for Hertsmere 1983–92; Sec. Conservative Backbench Finance Cttee 1971–72; Parl. Pvt. Sec. to Minister for Aerospace and Shipping 1972–74; Asst Govt Whip 1974, Opposition Whip 1974–76; Opposition Spokesman on Trade 1976–79; Minister of State for Trade 1979–81; Paymaster-Gen. 1981–83; Chair. Conservative Party 1981–83, 1997–98; Sec. of State for Trade and Industry June–Oct. 1983, for Energy 1987–89, for Transport 1989–90; Chair. Conservative Way Forward Group 1991–; Chancellor of the Duchy of Lancaster 1982–83; Leader, Inst. of Dirs. Parl. Panel 1972–79; Sec. Anglo-Swiss Parl. Group 1972–79, Chair. 1979–82; Chair. Anglo-Polish Conservative Soc. 1986–98, Chemical Dependency Centre Ltd 1986–, Jarvis (Harpenden) Holdings, Usborne 1991–, Midland Expressway Ltd 1993–, Dartford River Crossing Ltd 1993–; Dir Babcock Int. 1984–87, Sports Aid Foundation, Save and Prosper 1984–87, Tarmac 1984–87, Sears PLC 1984–87. *Publication:* An Autobiography: Right at the Centre 1992. *Leisure interests:* skiing, reading, golf. *Address:* House of Lords, London, SW1A 0PW, England. *Telephone:* (20) 7219-5353.

PARKINSON, Mark Vincent, BA, JD; American lawyer, politician and business executive; *President and CEO, American Health Care Association and National Center for Assisted Living (AHCA/NCAL);* b. 24 June 1957, Wichita, Kan.; s. of Henry Filson and Barbara Ann Horton (née Gilbert); m. Stacy Abbott 1983; three s.; ed Wichita Heights High School, Wichita State Univ., Univ. of Kansas; Assoc., Payne & Jones (law firm), Olathe, Kan. 1984–86; Co-founder and Partner, Parkinson, Foth & Reynolds (law firm) 1986–96; mem. Kan. State House of Reps 1990–92, Kan. State Senate 1992–96; Chair. Kan. Republican Party 1999–2003; mem. Democratic Party 2006–; Lt-Gov. of Kan. 2007–09, Gov. of Kan. 2009–11; Pres. and CEO American Health Care Asscn and Nat. Center for Assisted Living (AHCA/NCAL) 2011–; Chair. Shawnee Area Chamber of Commerce 2004–05; mem. ABA, Kansas Bar Asscn, Johnson Co. Bar Foundation (fmr Pres.), Kansas Mentors Leadership Council; named by Topeka Capital Journal as Kansan of the Year 2009. *Leisure interests:* travel, running, films. *Address:* American Health Care Association, 1201 L Street NW, Washington, DC 20005, USA (office). *Telephone:* (202) 842-4444 (office). *Fax:* (202) 842-3860 (office). *E-mail:* info@ahcancal.org (office). *Website:* www.ahcancal.org (office).

PARKINSON, Sir Michael, Kt, CBE; British television and radio presenter and writer; b. 28 March 1935, Barnsley; m. Mary Heneghan 1959; three s.; ed Barnsley Grammar School; began career as journalist with local paper, then worked on The Guardian, Daily Express, Sunday Times, Punch, The Listener etc.; joined Granada TV as interviewer/reporter 1965; joined 24 Hours (BBC) as reporter; Exec.

Producer and Presenter, London Weekend TV 1968; Presenter Cinema 1969–70, Tea Break, Where in the World 1971, host own chat show 'Parkinson' 1971–82, 1998–2004, The Boys of '66 1981, Presenter TV-AM 1983–84, Give Us a Clue 1984–92, All Star Secrets 1984–86, The Skag Kids 1985, Desert Island Discs (BBC Radio 4) 1986–88, The Help Squad 1991–92, Ghostwatch 1992, Parkinson on Sport (BBC Radio 5) 1994–97, Going for a Song 1995–99, A League Apart, 100 Years of Rugby League (BBC 2) 1995, Parkinson: The Interviews 1995–97, Parkinson's Sunday Supplement (BBC Radio 2) 1996–2007, Auntie's All-Time Greats 1997, Parkinson's Choice (BBC Radio 2) 1999–2004; columnist for Daily Mirror 1986–90, for Daily Telegraph 1991–2007; Parkinson One-to-One 1987–88; Parkinson (ITV) 2004–07; Ed. Catalyst 1988–; has worked extensively on Australian TV; founder and Dir Pavilion Books 1980–97; Dr hc (Lincs. and Humberside) 1999; Sports Feature Writer of the Year, British Sports Journalism Awards 1995, 1998, Fellow, BFI for contrib. to TV 1997, Yorks. Man of the Year 1998, Sony Radio Award 1998, Sports Writer of the Year, British Press Award 1998, BAFTA Award for Best Light Entertainment (for 'Parkinson') 1999, Media Soc. Award for Distinguished Contrib. to Media 2000. *Publications include:* Football Daft 1968, Cricket Mad 1969, Sporting Fever 1974, George Best: An Intimate Biography 1975, A–Z of Soccer (Jt author) 1975, Bats in the Pavilion 1977, The Woofits 1980, Parkinson's Lore 1981, The Best of Parkinson 1982, Sporting Lives 1992, Sporting Profiles 1995, Michael Parkinson on Golf 1999, Michael Parkinson on Football 2001, Parky: My Autobiography 2008. *Leisure interests:* cricket, golf. *Website:* www .michaelparkinson.tv.

PARKS, Suzan-Lori, BA; American playwright; b. 10 May 1963, Fort Knox, Ky; m. Paul Oscher; ed John Carroll School, Mount Holyoke Coll.; Guggenheim Foundation Fellow 2000; Master Writer Chair., Public Theater, New York 2008–; Visiting Arts Prof., Tisch School of the Arts, New York Univ. 2008–; MacArthur Foundation Award 2001, Eugene McDermott Award in the Arts, Council for the Arts at MIT 2006, Academy of Achievement Golden Plate Award 2007. *Plays include:* The Sinner's Place 1984, Imperceptible Mutabilities in the Third Kingdom (Obie Award for Best New American Play) 1989, Betting on the Dust Commander 1990, The Death of the Last Black Man in the Whole Entire World 1990, Devotees in the Garden of Love 1992, The America Play 1994, Venus 1996, In the Blood 1999, Fucking A 2000, Topdog/Underdog (Pulitzer Prize for Drama 2002) 2001, 365 Days/365 Plays 2006, Ray Charles Live! A New Musical (NAACP Theatre Award 2008) 2007, Father Comes Home from the Wars 2009, The Book of Grace 2010. *Plays for radio:* Pickling 1990, Third Kingdom 1990, Locomotive 1991. *Screenplays:* Girl 6 1996, Their Eyes Were Watching God 2005, The Great Debaters (cowriter) 2007. *Publication:* Getting Mother's Body: A Novel 2003. *Address:* c/o Jesse Alick, The Public Theater, 425 Lafayette Street, New York, NY 10003, USA. *Telephone:* (212) 539-8500 (home). *E-mail:* jalick@publictheater.org; press@ publictheater.org (office). *Website:* www.publictheater.org (office); www .suzanloriparks.com.

PARKS, Timothy Harold, BA, MA; British writer, educator and translator; *Professor of English Literature, Università IULM, Milan;* b. 19 Dec. 1954, Manchester, England; m. Rita Baldassare; three d.; ed Univ. of Cambridge, Harvard Univ., USA; teacher of trans. studies, Università IULM, Milan, Prof. of English Literature 2006–; mem. Authors' Soc.; Somerset Maugham Award 1986, Betty Trask Prize 1986, Rhys Prize 1986, John Floria Prize for Best Trans. from Italian. *Publications include:* novels: Tongues of Flame 1985, Loving Roger 1986, Home Thoughts 1987, Family Planning 1989, Cara Massimina 1990, Goodness 1991, Italian Neighbours 1992, Juggling the Stars 1993, Shear 1993, Mimi's Ghost 1995, An Italian Education 1996, Europa 1997, Adultery and Other Diversions 1999, Destiny 2000, A Season with Verona 2002, Judge Savage 2003, Rapids 2005, Cleaver 2006, Dreams of Rivers and Seas 2008, Sex is Forbidden (The Server) 2012; short stories: Keeping Distance 1988, The Room 1992; non-fiction: Translating Style: The English Modernists and their Italian Translations 1999, Hell and Back: Reflections on Writers and Writing from Dante to Rushdie 2001, Medici Money: Banking, Metaphysics and Art in Fifteenth-Century Florence 2005, The Fighter 2007, Teach Us to Sit Still 2010, Italian Ways: On and Off the Rails from Milan to Palermo 2013; numerous trans. from Italian; contrib. of numerous articles, reviews and talks to BBC Radio 3. *Address:* Istituto di Anglistica, Università IULM, Via Carlo Bo, 20143 Milan, Italy (office). *Website:* tim-parks .com.

PARMIGGIANI, Claudio; Italian artist; b. 1 March 1943, Lussara, Reggio Emilia; ed Istituto Statale di Belle Arti, Modena; first solo exhbn at Libreria Feltrinelli, Bologna 1965; progression from conceptual works, including installations, photo-works and books, towards use of assemblage; first Delocazioni appear 1970, works realized with use of powder, fire and smoke; realized series of works using plaster models of ancient works of art early 1960s; among the more significant later works are the Iconostasi of statues and veiled canvases 1980s (presented for the first time at Galleria Stein, Milan 1989); realized Il faro d'Islanda (perm. work) in most deserted part of Iceland 2000; realized Teatro dell'arte e della guerra in Teatro Farnese in Parma (labyrinth of shattered crystals); most recent work includes Ex-voto at Louvre Museum; lives and works in Bologna. *Address:* c/o Galerie Serge Leborgne, 108 rue Vieille-du-Temple, Paris - 3, France (office). *Telephone:* 1-42-74-53-57 (office).

PARNELL, Sean R., BBA, JD; American lawyer and politician; *Governor of Alaska;* b. 19 Nov. 1962, Hanford, Calif.; s. of Pat Parnell and Thelma Parnell; m. Sandra Parnell 1987; two d.; ed East Anchorage High School, Pacific Lutheran Univ., Univ. of Puget Sound School of Law (now Seattle Univ. School of Law); family moved to Alaska aged 10; attorney 1987–, admitted to practise law in Alaska and Washington, DC; owned small law practice in Anchorage for many years; mem. Alaska State House of Reps 1992–96 (re-elected 1994), mem. Finance Cttee; mem. Alaska State Senate 1996–2000, mem. Energy Council, served on and then co-chaired Senate Finance Cttee and numerous budget sub-cttees; left Senate to become Dir of Governmental Relations in Alaska for Conoco Phillips oil co.; joined lobbying firm Patton Boggs (had earlier represented Exxon Mobil in Exxon Valdez oil spill litigation) 2005–06; adviser on oil and gas issues to Gov. Sarah Palin 2006–09; Lt Gov. of Alaska 2008–09; campaigned to be elected to US House of Reps 2008; Gov. of Alaska 2009–; Republican. *Leisure interest:* outdoor activities. *Address:* Office of the Governor, Alaska State Capitol Building, Third Floor, PO Box 110001, Juneau, AK 99811-0001, USA (office). *Telephone:* (907) 465-3500

(office). *Fax:* (907) 465-3532 (office). *E-mail:* info@gov.state.ak.us (office). *Website:* gov.state.ak.us (office); gov.alaska.gov (office).

PAROLIN, HE Cardinal Pietro; Italian ecclesiastic and diplomatist; *Secretary of State, Roman Curia;* b. 17 Jan. 1955, Schiavon, Prov. of Vicenza; ed Pontifical Gregorian Univ., Pontifical Ecclesiastical Acad.; ordained priest of Vicenza 1980; entered diplomatic service of Holy See 1986, served for three years in Nunciature of Nigeria, in Nunciature of Mexico 1989–92, Country Dir for Spain, Andorra, Italy, San Marino, Apostolic Nuncio to Venezuela 2009–13; Undersecretary for Relations with States 2002–09; consecrated by Pope Benedict XVI 2009; Titular Archbisop of Aquipendium 2009–; Pres. Interdicasterial Comm. on Particular Churches 2013–, Interdicasterial Comm. for the Church in Eastern Europe 2013–; Protector of Pontifical Ecclesiastical Acad. 2013–; Sec. of State 2013–; cr. Cardinal (Cardinal-Priest of Santi Simone e Giuda Taddeo a Torre Angela) 2014–; Kt Grand Cross, Order of Merit of the Italian Repub. 2005. *Address:* Secretariat of State, Palazzo Apostolico Vaticano, 00120 Città del Vaticano, Rome, Italy (office). *Telephone:* (06) 69883913 (office). *Fax:* (06) 69885255 (office). *Website:* www .vatican.va/roman_curia/secretariat_state (office).

PAROUBEK, Jiří, MA; Czech politician; b. 21 Aug. 1952, Olomouc; m. 1st Zuzana Paroubková 1979 (divorced 2007); m. 2nd Petra Paroubková 2007; one s. one d.; ed Prague School of Econs; economist, pvt. sector 1976–90; Sec.-Gen. Czechoslovak Social Democrats 1990; financial consultant 1991–98; various positions in the Czech Social Democratic Party (CSSD) Prague Regional Exec. 1993–95, Vice-Chair. 2001–03, Vice-Chair. CSSD 2005–06, Chair. 2006–10; Deputy Mayor for Finance, Prague 1998–2004; Minister of Regional Devt 2004–05; Prime Minister of Czech Repub. 2005–06; Chair. Editorial Bd, Trend; contrib. to several daily newspapers. *Address:* Czech Social Democratic Party (Česká strana sociálně demokratická), Lidový dům, Hybernská 7, 110 00 Prague 1, Czech Republic (office). *Telephone:* (2) 96522218 (office). *Fax:* (2) 24222190 (office). *E-mail:* jparoubek@socdem.cz (office). *Website:* www.socdem.cz (office); www.paroubek.cz.

PARR, Robert Ghormley, AB, PhD; American theoretical chemist and academic; *Research Professor of Chemical Physics, University of North Carolina;* b. 22 Sept. 1921, Chicago, Ill.; s. of Leland Wilbur Parr and Grace Ghormley; m. Jane Bolstad 1944; one s. two d.; ed Western High School, Washington, DC, Brown Univ., Univ. of Minnesota; Asst Prof. of Chem., Univ. of Minn. 1947–48; Asst Prof. to Prof. of Chem., Carnegie Inst. of Tech. 1948–62, Chair. of Gen. Faculty 1960–61; Prof. of Chem., Johns Hopkins Univ. 1962–74, Chair. of Dept of Chem. 1969–72; William R. Kenan, Jr Prof. of Theoretical Chem., Univ. of NC 1974–90, Wassily Hoeffding Prof. of Chemical Physics 1990–2000, Research Prof. 2000–; Guggenheim Fellow and Fulbright Scholar, Univ. of Cambridge 1953–54; Sloan Fellow 1956–60; Visiting Prof., Univ. of Ill. 1962, State Univ. of New York at Buffalo and Pa State Univ. 1967, Japan Soc. for Promotion of Sciences 1968, 1979; Firth Prof., Univ. of Sheffield 1976; Visiting Prof., Univ. of Berlin 1977, Duke Univ. 1996–97; Fellow, Univ. of Chicago 1949, Research Assoc. 1957; NSF Sr Postdoctoral Fellow, Univ. of Oxford and CSIRO, Melbourne 1967–68; fmr mem. editorial bd of numerous specialist magazines and reviews; mem. of numerous academic and scientific socs including AAAS, American Physical Soc., ACS, NAS, American Acad. of Arts and Sciences, Int. Acad. of Quantum Molecular Science (Vice-Pres. 1973–79, Pres. 1991–97); Trustee, Inst. for Fundamental Chem., Kyoto 1988–2000; Dr hc (Louvain) 1986, (Jagiellonian) 1996; NC Inst. of Chemists Distinguished Chemists Award 1982, Langmuir Award in Chemical Physics, ACS 1994, North Carolina Award in Science 1999, Nat. Acad. of Sciences Award in Chemical Sciences 2004, ACS Award in Theoretical Chem. 2009. *Publications:* The Quantum Theory of Molecular Electronic Structure 1963; Density: Functional Theory of Atoms and Molecules 1989; more than 200 scientific articles in specialist publs. *Address:* Department of Chemistry, Kenan Laboratory C440, University of North Carolina, Chapel Hill, NC 27599-3290 (office); 701 Kenmore Road, Chapel Hill, NC 27514, USA (home). *Telephone:* (919) 962-1577 (office); (919) 929-2609 (home). *Fax:* (919) 962-2388 (office). *E-mail:* rgparr@email.unc.edu (office). *Website:* www.chem.unc.edu/people/faculty/parrrg/rgpindex.html (office).

PARRA, Nicanor; Chilean poet; b. 5 Sept. 1914, San Fabián; s. of Nicanor P. Parra and Clara S. Navarrete; m. 1st Ana Troncoso 1948; m. 2nd Inga Palmen; seven c.; ed Univ. de Chile, Brown Univ., USA, Univ. of Oxford, UK; Prof. of Theoretical Mechanics, Univ. de Chile 1964–; has given poetry readings in LA, Moscow, Leningrad, Havana, Lima, Ayacucho, Cuzco; Premio Municipal de Poesía, Santiago 1937, 1954, Premio Nacional de Literatura 1969, Miguel de Cervantes Prize 2011. *Publications include:* poetry: Cancionero sin nombre 1937, Poemas y antipoemas 1954, La cueca larga 1958, Antipoems 1958, Versos de salón 1962, Discursos (with Pablo Neruda) 1962, Manifiesto 1963, Deux Poèmes (bilingual) 1964, Antología (also in Russian) 1965, Antología de la Poesía Soviética Rusa (bilingual) 1965, Canciones Rusas 1967, Defensa de Violeta Parra 1967, Artefactos 1972, Sermones y prédicas del Cristo de Elqui 1977, Nuevos sermones y prédicas del Cristo de Elqui 1979, El anti-Lázaro 1981, Poema y antipoema de Eduardo Frei 1982, Cachureos, ecopoemas, guatapiques, últimas prédicas 1983, Chistes para desorientar a la policía 1983, Coplas de Navidad 1983, Poesía política 1983, Hojas de Parra 1985, Poemas para combatir la calvicie 1993, Páginas en blanco 2001, Lear Rey & Mendigo 2004, Discursos de Sobremesa 2006; scientific works: La Evolución del Concepto de Masa 1958, Fundamentos de la Física (trans. of Foundation of Physics by Profs Lindsay and Margenau) 1967, Obra Gruesa 1969, Los profesores, 1971. *Address:* Julia Bernstein, Parcela 272, Lareina, Santiago, Chile. *Website:* www.nicanorparra.uchile.cl.

PARRA-ARANGUREN, Gonzalo; Venezuelan judge; b. 5 Dec. 1928, Caracas; m. María Trinidad Pulido Santana; ed Cen. Univ. of Venezuela, Inter-American Law Inst., Univ. of New York, USA, Ludwig-Maximilians Univ., Munich, Germany; Prof., Cen. Univ. of Venezuela, Caracas 1956–96, Andrés Bello Catholic Univ., Caracas 1957–96, The Hague Acad. of Int. Law 1988; Judge, Second Court of First Instance (commercial matters), Fed. Dist and State of Miranda, Caracas 1958–71; First Assoc. Judge, Chamber of Cassation (civil, commercial and labour matters) of Supreme Court of Justice 1988–92, elected Alt. Judge 1992; mem. nat. group for Venezuela, Perm. Court of Arbitration, The Hague 1985–; Judge, Int. Court of Justice 1996–2009; has acted as arbitrator in Venezuela and abroad on pvt. commercial matters; mem. Legal Advisory Cttee of Ministry of Foreign Affairs 1984–96, of Nat. Congress 1990–96; mem. Acad. of Political and Social Sciences of Caracas 1966– (Pres. 1993–95), Inst. of Int. Law 1979–; rep. Venezuela at several sessions of The Hague Conf. on Pvt. Int. Law. *Publications:* Die Regel "Locus Regit Actum" und die Formen der Testamente 1955, La Nacionalidad Venezolana Originaria, Vols I and II 1964, La Constitución de 1830 y los Venezolanos por Naturalización 1969, Codificación del Derecho Internacional Privado en América, Vol. I 1982, Vol. II 1998, La Nacionalidad Venezolana: I. Antecedentes Históricos 1983, La Influencia del Matrimonio sobre la Nacionalidad de la Mujer en la Legislación Venezolana 1983, La Nacionalidad Venezolana: II. Problemas Actuales 1983, Monografías Selectas de Derecho Internacional Privado 1984, Ensayos de Derecho Procesal Civil Internacional 1986, Curso General de Derecho Internacional Privado (Problemas Selectos) 1991, Curso General de Derecho Internacional Privado. Problemas Selectos y Otros Estudios 1992, Curso General de Derecho Internacional Privado. Problemas Selectos y Otros Estudios, Tercera Edición 1998, Estudios de Derecho Procesal Civil Internacional 1998, Escritos Diversos de Derecho Internacional Privado 1998, Estudios de Derecho Mercantil Internacional 1998, El Régimen de los Bienes en el Matrimonio en el Derecho Internacional Privado Venezolano 2007, Padrino de la Promoción de abogados que lleva su nombre del año 1963 de la Universidad Central de Venezuela, Caracas, Padrino de la Promoción de abogados que lleva su nombre del año 1979 de la Universidad Católica Andrés Bello, Caracas, Venezuela; numerous articles in Venezuelan and foreign journals on law of nationality, pvt. int. law and int. civil procedural law. *Address:* c/o International Court of Justice, Peace Palace, Carnegieplein 2, 2517 KJ The Hague, Netherlands. *Telephone:* (70) 302-2323. *E-mail:* information@icj-cij.org.

PARRA GIL, Antonio; Ecuadorean lawyer, politician and diplomatist; ed Univ. of Salamanca; fmr Asst Sec. of State in Ministries of Educ. and Public Works; Minister of Foreign Affairs 2004–05; Amb. to Spain 2005–07. *Address:* c/o Ministry of Foreign Affairs, Avda 10 de Agosto y Carrión, Quito, Ecuador (office).

PARRATT, James Roy, DSc, DSc (Med), PhD, FRSE, FESC, FRCPath, FRPharmS; British professor of cardiovascular pharmacology; *Professor Emeritus, University of Strathclyde;* b. 19 Aug. 1933, London, England; s. of James J. Parratt and Eunice E. King; m. Pamela J. Lyndon 1957; two s. one d.; ed St Clement Danes Holborn Estate Grammar School, London and Univ. of London; Nigerian School of Pharmacy 1958–61; Dept of Physiology, Univ. Coll. Ibadan, Nigeria 1961–67; Univ. of Strathclyde, Glasgow 1967–, Reader 1970, Personal Prof. 1975, Prof. of Cardiovascular Pharmacology 1983–, now Prof. Emer., Head, Dept of Physiology and Pharmacology 1986–90, Chair. School of Pharmacy and Pharmacology 1988; Visiting Prof. Albert-Szent-Györgyi Medical Univ., Szeged 1995–; Vice-Pres. European Shock Soc.; mem. Council, Int. Soc. for Heart Research (European Section); Emer. Fellow, Leverhulme Trust 2002–03; Szent-Györgyi Research Fellow, Szeged Univ. 2003; Fellow, Royal Pharmacology Soc., Inst. of Biology, Int. Soc. for Heart Research; Hon. mem. Hungarian Pharmacological Soc., Slovak Medical and Cardiological Socs, Czech Cardiological Soc.; Hon. MD (Albert-Szent-Gyorgyi Univ. Medical School); Gold Medal, Univ. of Szeged, Hungary, Gold J.E. Purkyne Medal, Acad. of Sciences of the Czech Repub. *Leisure interests:* active within Baptist denomination in Scotland and in Christian mission, music. *Address:* Strathclyde Institute of Pharmacy and Biomedical Sciences, University of Strathclyde, 161 Cathedral Street, Glasgow, G4 0RE (office); 16 Russell Drive, Bearsden, Glasgow, G61 3BD, Scotland (home). *Telephone:* (141) 548-2125 (office); (141) 942-7164 (home). *E-mail:* j.r.parratt@strath.ac.uk (office). *Website:* spider .science.strath.ac.uk/sipbs/staff.php?limit=emeritus (office).

PARRIKAR, Manohar, B. Tech.; Indian politician; *Chief Minister of Goa;* b. 13 Dec. 1955, Mapusa, Goa; m. Medha Parrikar (died 2000); two s.; ed Indian Inst. of Tech., Bombay (now Mumbai); started industrial unit in specialized hydraulic eng; elected to Legis. Ass. 1994, Leader of the Opposition June–Nov. 1999, 2005–12; Chief Minister of Goa 2000–07, 2012–; instrumental in setting up perm. centre for International Film Festival of India in Goa; started unique Cyberage scheme for providing computers to students in Goa, initiated and implemented various devt schemes in Goa; fmr Chair. Goa State Infrastructure Devt Corpn; Distinguished Alumnus Award, Indian Inst. of Tech., Bombay (now Mumbai) 2001. *Leisure interests:* reading, watching cricket, movies. *Address:* Office of the Chief Minister, Secretariat, Panaji, 403 001 (office); House Number 12/182, Khorlim, Mapusa 403 507, India (home). *Telephone:* (832) 2223970 (office); (832) 2250905 (home). *Fax:* (832) 2223648 (office). *E-mail:* manohar.parrikar@gmail.com; cmgoa@goa.nic.in (office). *Website:* www.goa.gov.in (office).

PARRIS, Matthew Francis, BA, MA; British author, broadcaster and fmr politician; b. 7 Aug. 1949, Johannesburg, S Africa; s. of Leslie F. Parris and Theresa E. Parris (née Littler); civil partnership with Julian Glover; ed Waterford School, Swaziland, Clare Coll., Cambridge and Yale Univ.; FCO 1974–76; with Conservative Research Dept 1976–79; MP (Conservative) for W Derbyshire 1979–86; Parl. Sketch Writer for The Times 1988–2001; columnist, the Times 1988–, The Spectator 1992–; mem. Broadcasting Standards Council 1992–97; various awards for writing and journalism. *Radio:* presenter, Great Lives series (BBC Radio 4) 2007–. *Television:* presenter, Weekend World (LWT) 1986–88. *Publications:* Inca Kola (travel) 1990, Chance Witness (memoir) 2001, expanded and updated edn 2013, Great Parliamentary Scandals (with Kevin Maguire) 2004, A Castle in Spain 2005, Mission Accomplished (with Phil Mason) 2007, Scorn 2008, Parting Shots (with Andrew Bryson) 2010, The Spanish Ambassador's Suitcase, and Other Stories (with Andrew Bryson) 2012; various books about politics, insult and scandal; various collections of journalism. *Address:* The Spout, Gratton, Bakewell, Derbyshire, DE45 1LN; c/o The Times, Pennington Street, London, E1 9XN, England.

PARROTT, Andrew Haden, BA; British conductor and musicologist; b. 10 March 1947, Walsall, W Midlands, England; s. of R. C. Parrott and E. D. Parrott; m. 1st Emma Kirkby 1971; m. 2nd Emily Van Evera 1986; one d.; ed Queen Mary's Grammar School, Walsall, Merton Coll., Oxford; Dir of Music, Merton Coll., Oxford 1969–71; Founder, Conductor and Dir Taverner Choir, Taverner Consort and Taverner Players 1973–; Music Dir and Prin. Conductor London Mozart Players 2000–06; Music Dir New York Collegium 2002–10; BBC Promenade Concerts debut 1977; fmr musical asst to Sir Michael Tippett; freelance orchestral and operatic conductor; occasional writer, lecturer and continuo player; Open Postmastership, Merton Coll. 1966–69; Leverhulme Fellowship 1984–85; Hon. Research Fellow, Royal Holloway, Univ. of London 1995; Hon. Sr Research Fellow, Univ. of Birmingham 2000–. *Recordings include:* more than 60 recordings of

medieval and renaissance music and major works by Monteverdi, Purcell, Vivaldi, Bach, Handel, Mozart, Beethoven and 20th-century composers. *Publications include:* New Oxford Book of Carols (co-ed.) 1992, The Essential Bach Choir 2000 (German edn 2003); articles in Early Music and other journals. *Address:* c/o Rayfield Allied, Southbank House, Black Prince Road, London, SE1 7SJ, England (office); Mill Farm, Stanton St John, Oxford, OX33 1HN, England. *Telephone:* (20) 3176-5500 (office). *E-mail:* info@rayfieldallied.com (office).

PARROTT, Jasper William, BA; British impresario and agent; *Executive Chairman and Head of Tours/Projects, Harrison/Parrott Limited;* b. 8 Sept. 1944, Stockholm, Sweden; s. of the late Prof. Sir Cecil Parrott and of Lady Parrott; m. Cristina Ortiz; two d.; ed Tonbridge School, Peterhouse Cambridge; joined Ibbs & Tillett Ltd 1965–69; f. Harrison Parrott Ltd 1969, Chair. and Jt Man. Dir 1987–2013, Exec. Chair. and Head of Tours/Projects 2013–; Dir Japan Festival 1991, Swiss Festival in UK 1991; Dir Rambert Dance Co. 1993–98; Hon. Trustee Kew Foundation, Royal Botanical Gardens 1991–; Co-Dir Simdi Now, Turkish Festival of Arts, Berlin 2004; Int. Adviser, Sakip Sabanci Museum, Istanbul 2005–07; Dir Polyarts UK 2004–; consultant, The Icelandic Nat. Concert and Conf. Centre 2007–11. *Publication:* Beyond Frontiers: Vladimir Ashkenazy. *Leisure interests:* reading, theatre, history, tennis, landscape and water gardening, languages. *Address:* Harrison/Parrott Ltd, 5–6 Albion Court, Albion Place, London, W6 0QT, England (office). *Telephone:* (20) 7313-3527 (office). *Fax:* (20) 7221-5042 (office). *E-mail:* jp@harrisonparrott.co.uk (office). *Website:* www .harrisonparrott.com (office).

PARRY, Eric Owen, MA, RA, RIBA; British architect; *Principal, Eric Parry Architects;* b. 24 March 1952, Kuwait; s. of the late Eric Parry and of Marion Parry; ed Univ. of Newcastle upon Tyne, Royal Coll. of Art, London, Architectural Assen, London; Founder and Prin. Eric Parry Architects 1983–, est. Eric Parry Assocs 1983, including Eric Parry Architects Ltd 1990; Lecturer, Univ. of Cambridge 1983–97, Harvard Univ. Grad. School of Design 1988, Univ. of Houston 1988, 1990, Tokyo Inst. of Tech. 1996; mem. RIBA Awards Group 2001–04, Chair. 2002–04; mem. Arts Council of England (ACE) Architecture Unit 1991–2003, ACE Lottery Architecture Advisory Cttee 1991–99, ACE Visual Arts Panel 1996–2003; mem. Council, Architectural Assen 1995– (Pres. 2005–07); mem. Royal Acad. Architecture Cttee, RIBA Library Cttee, Canterbury Cathedral Fabric Advisory Cttee, Council of the British School at Rome, Mayor's Design Advisory Group; External Examiner, Univ. of Kent at Canterbury, John Moore's Univ., Cardiff Univ. and Univ. Coll., London; Hon. mem. Librarian Architectural Assen; Hon. Dr of Arts. *Architectural works include:* Artists' Studio, London 1986–88, Stockley Park Office Bldg W3, London 1989–91, Foundress Court, Pembroke Coll. Cambridge (RIBA Award 1998) 1993–98, Damai Suria Luxury Apartments, Kuala Lumpur 1996–97, Southwark Information Centre, London Bridge (RIBA Award 1999) 1997–99, Mandarin Oriental, Hyde Park, London (FX Int. Interior Award for the Spa 2001) 1997–2000, 30 Finsbury Square, London 1999–2002, King Edward Court, Paternoster Square (HQ for London Stock Exchange) 2000–03, St Martin-in-the-Fields, London 2002–08. *Publications include:* On Certain Possibilities of the Irrational Embellishment of a Town (co-author with Peter Carl) 1999, Eric Parry Architects Vol. 1 2002 Eric Parry Architects Vol. 2 2012. *Leisure interests:* walking, drawing, general cultural pursuits. *Address:* Eric Parry Architects Ltd, 28–42 Banner Street, London, EC1Y 8QE, England (office). *Telephone:* (20) 7608-9600 (office). *Fax:* (20) 7608-9601 (office). *E-mail:* eric.p@ericparryarchitects.co.uk (office). *Website:* www.ericparryarchitects.co.uk (office).

PARRY, Martin, OBE, PhD; British environmentalist and academic; *Climate Scientist, Met Office;* b. 12 Dec. 1945; s. of John Fyson Parry and Frances Joan Stewart; m. Cynthia Jane Mueller 1968; two d.; ed Durham and West Indies Univs; Prof. of Environmental Man. and Dir Oxford Univ. Environmental Change Unit 1991–94; Prof. of Environmental Man., Dept of Geography, Univ. Coll. London 1996–99; apptd Prof. of Environmental Sciences and Dir Jackson Environment Inst., Univ. of East Anglia 1996; later Climate Scientist with Met Office; Co-Chair. Working Group II, Intergovernmental Panel on Climate Change (IPCC) 2002–08; fmrly with Univ. of Birmingham; Chair. UK Climate Change Review Group; Royal Geographical Soc. Peek Award 1991, WMO Gerbier-Mumm Int. Award 1993. *Publications:* Climatic Change, Agric. and Settlement 1976, Climate Change and World Agriculture 1990, Economic Implications of Climate Change in Britain 1995. *Leisure interests:* riding, sailing. *Address:* Technical Support Unit, Hadley Centre, Met Office, Fitzroy Road, Exeter, EX1 3PB, England (office). *Telephone:* (1392) 886695 (office). *Fax:* (1392) 885681 (office). *E-mail:* martin.parry@metoffice .gov.uk (office); parryml@aol.com. *Website:* www.metoffice.gov.uk (office).

PARSONS, Charles Dacre, PhD; American philosopher and academic; *Professor Emeritus of Philosophy, Harvard University;* b. 13 April 1933, Cambridge, Mass; s. of Talcott Parsons and Helen Walker Parsons; m. Marjorie Louise Wood 1968; one s. one d.; ed Harvard Coll., King's Coll., Cambridge, UK, Harvard Univ.; Jr Fellow, Soc. of Fellows, Harvard Univ. 1958–61, Santayana Fellow 1964–65; Asst Prof. of Philosophy, Cornell Univ. 1961–62, Harvard Univ. 1962–65; Assoc. Prof. of Philosophy, Columbia Univ. 1965–69, Prof. 1969–89, Chair. Dept of Philosophy 1976–79, 1985–89; Prof. of Philosophy, Harvard Univ. 1989–91, Edgar Pierce Prof. of Philosophy 1991–2005, Prof. Emer. 2005–; Visiting Prof. of Philosophy, UCLA 2002, 2005, 2007, 2009; Ed. The Journal of Philosophy 1966–90, Consulting Ed. 1990–; Sec. Assen for Symbolic Logic 1971–76, Vice-Pres. 1986–89, Pres. 1989–92; Vice-Pres. Institut Int. de Philosophie 2012–; Foreign mem. Norwegian Acad. of Science and Letters 2002–; Fellow, Nat. Endowment for the Humanities 1979–80, American Acad. of Arts and Sciences 1982–, Center for Advanced Study in The Behavioral Sciences 1994–95; Guggenheim Fellow 1986–87. *Publications:* Mathematics in Philosophy 1983, Kurt Gödel, Collected Works, Vols III–V (co-ed.) 1995, 2003, Mathematical Thought and its Objects 2008, Hao Wang, Logician and Philosopher (co-ed.) 2011, From Kant to Husserl 2012, Philosophy of Mathematics in the Twentieth Century 2014; articles on logic and philosophy. *Address:* Department of Philosophy, Emerson Hall, Harvard University, Cambridge, MA 02138 (office); 22 Hancock Street, Cambridge, MA 02139, USA (home). *Telephone:* (617) 495-2191 (office). *E-mail:* parsons2@fas.harvard.edu (office). *Website:* www .fas.harvard.edu/~phildept (office).

PARSONS, Nigel; British media executive; *CEO, Continental Broadcasting Ltd;* b. 27 May 1951; Lt Col Parsons and Mrs F. A. Parsons; m. Zoulfia Parsons; four c.; ed Framlingham Coll., Suffolk, Portsmouth Univ. (Certificate of Journalism);

previous roles as journalist/producer at BBC Radios 1–4, BBC World Service Radio and TV and WTN (Worldwide Television News), conceived and oversaw launch of global broadcaster Al Jazeera English, also managed TV start-up news network teams, EBC in Switzerland, Middle East Broadcasting and Telecampione in Italy; Vice-Pres. (Eastern European and fmr USSR markets), WTN; Dir of Associated Press TV News (APTN, cr. when Associated Press bought WTN); Man. Dir Al Jazeera English, Doha, Qatar 2004–09; Sr Partner, NZN Media Consultants 2009–11; CEO Continental Broadcasting Ltd, Lagos, Nigeria 2011–. *Leisure interests:* reading, skiing, diving. *Address:* 456 Merton Road, London, SW18 5AE, England (office). *Telephone:* 7768-728234 (mobile) (office). *E-mail:* nigel.parsons@gmail.com (home).

PARSONS, Peter John, MA, FBA; British academic; b. 24 Sept. 1936, Surbiton, Surrey, England; s. of Robert John Parsons and Ethel Ada Parsons (née Frary); m. Barbara Montagna Macleod 2006; ed Raynes Park County Grammar School and Christ Church, Oxford; Lecturer in Documentary Papyrology, Univ. of Oxford 1960–65, Lecturer in Papyrology 1965–89, Regius Prof. of Greek 1989–2003; Student (Fellow), Christ Church Oxford 1964–2003; J. H. Gray Lecturer, Univ. of Cambridge 1982; Hon. PhD (Berne) 1985, (Athens) 1995; Hon. DLitt (Milan) 1994. *Publications:* The Oxyrhynchus Papyri (jtly) Vols XXXI 1966, XXXIII and XXXIV 1968, LIV 1987, LIX 1992, LX 1994, LXVI 1999, LXVIII 2003, (solely) Vol. XLII 1973, Supplementum Hellenisticum (with H. Lloyd-Jones) 1983, City of the Sharpnosed Fish 2007; articles in learned journals. *Leisure interests:* music, cinema, cooking, eating. *Address:* Christ Church, Oxford, OX1 1DP, England (home). *Telephone:* (1865) 422132 (home). *E-mail:* peter.parsons@classics.ox.ac.uk (office).

PARSONS, Richard (Dick) Dean, JD; American lawyer and business executive; b. 4 April 1948, Brooklyn, NY; m. Laura Ann Bush; three c.; ed Univ. of Hawaii, Albany Law School, Union Univ.; began career with various positions in state and fed. service, including counsel for NY Gov. Nelson Rockefeller and Sr White House aide under Pres. Gerald Ford; Founder and Man. Partner, Patterson, Belknap, Webb & Tyler 1979–88; COO Dime Bancorp Inc. 1988–90, Chair. 1990–94; joined Time Warner Inc., mem. Bd of Dirs 1991–2008, apptd Pres. 1995, Co-COO –2002, CEO 2002–07, Chair. 2003–08; mem. Bd of Dirs Citigroup Inc. 1996–2012, Lead Dir and Chair. Nomination and Governance Cttee –2009, Chair. Citigroup Inc. 2009–12; mem. Bd of Dirs Estée Lauder; Co-Chair. Pres.'s Comm. to Strengthen Social Security 2001–, Mayor's Comm. on Econ. Opportunity in New York; Dir and Chair. Emer., New York City Partnership; Chair. Apollo Theatre Foundation, Exec. Bd of the Jazz Foundation of America 2007–; Co-Chair. Advisory Bd Smithsonian Inst. of African American History and Culture, New York City Comm. for Econ. Opportunity; econ. adviser on Pres. Barack Obama's transition team 2008–09; mem. Pres.'s Council on Jobs and Competitiveness; mem. Bd of Dirs Comm. on Presidential Debates; Trustee, Museum of Modern Art, American Museum of Natural History, Rockefeller Foundation. *Address:* Jazz Foundation of America, 322 West 48th Street, 6th Floor, New York, NY 10036, USA (office). *Telephone:* (212) 245-3999 (office). *E-mail:* info@jazzfoundation.org (office). *Website:* jazzfoundation.org (office).

PARSONS, Roger, PhD, DSc, FRS; British chemist and academic; *Professor Emeritus of Chemistry, University of Southampton;* b. 31 Oct. 1926, London, England; s. of Robert H. A. Parsons and Ethel Fenton; m. Ruby M. Turner 1953; three s. one d.; ed King Alfred School, London, Strathcona High School, Edmonton, Alberta, Canada and Imperial Coll., London; Asst Lecturer, Imperial Coll. London 1948–51; Deedes Fellow, Univ. Coll., Dundee 1951–54; Lecturer, Univ. of Bristol 1954–63, Reader 1963–79; Dir Lab. d'Electrochimie Interfaciale du CNRS, Meudon, France 1977–84; Prof. of Chem., Univ. of Southampton 1985–92, Prof. Emer. 1992–; Pres. Faraday Div., Royal Soc. of Chem. 1991–93; Hon. DUniv (Buenos Aires) 1997; Prix Pascal, Palladium Medal, Breyer Medal, Galvani Medal, Frumkin Memorial Medal, Royal Soc. Davy Medal 2003. *Publications include:* Electrochemical Data 1956, Electrical Properties of Interfaces (with J. Lyklema), Standard Potentials in Aqueous Solution (co-ed.) 1985, Electrochemistry in Research and Development 1985; more than 200 scientific papers. *Leisure interests:* listening to music, going to the opera. *Address:* 16 Thornhill Road, Bassett, Southampton, SO16 7AT, England. *Telephone:* (23) 8079-0143. *E-mail:* roger.parsons@care4free.net.

PARSURAMEN, Armoogum (Dassen), GOSK, BA (Hons); Mauritian politician and international organization official; *Founder-President, Global Rainbow Foundation;* b. 30 June 1951; m.; ed Friendship Coll., Goodlands, Univ. of Mauritius; fmr Chair. Parti Socialiste Mauricien (PSM); Vice-Pres. MSM from 1986; mem. MSM/PMSD/Labour Party Govt –1990, MSM/MMM Govt from 1990; mem. Legis. Ass. 1982–95, Chair. Public Accounts Cttee 1982–83; Minister of Educ., Arts and Culture 1983–92, of Educ. and Science 1992–95; Sr Adviser, The World Bank 1997–98; Dir Div. for Secondary Educ., UNESCO, Paris 1998–2000, Dir and Rep., Regional Bureau for Educ. in Africa 2000–04, Sec. Exec. Bd and Gen. Conf. 2004–09, Dir and Rep., Cluster Office, New Delhi 2009–11; Founder-Pres. Global Rainbow Foundation (charitable trust) 2011–; Chair. Advisory Bd Amity Inst. of Higher Educ. 2012–; fmr Chair. Mauritius Ex-Servicemen Welfare Fund; mem. Local Govt Comm., Select Cttee on Industrial Relations Act; Hon. Freedom of the Dist of Pamplemousses-Riviere du Rempart 1984; Hon. Chair. Gandhi Ashram, Petit-Raffray 2012; Grand Officer of the Star and Key of the Indian Ocean 2010; Officier des Arts et des Lettres 2011; Outstanding Int. Leader in Tech. Vocational Educ. and Training, Wolansky Award Fund and Int. Vocational Educ. and Training Asscn 2002, honoured by UNESCO Exec. Bd Decision 182 EX/PLEN/DR.3 2009. *Address:* Global Rainbow Foundation, Old Mill Road, Morc Swan, Pereybere, Mauritius (office). *Telephone:* 2691501 (office); 591-83767 (mobile). *E-mail:* chairman@globalrainbowfoundation.org (office). *Website:* www.grftrust.org (office).

PÄRT, Arvo; Estonian composer; b. 11 Sept. 1935, Paide; m. Eleonora Pärt; ed composition studies with Heino Eller at Tallinn Conservatory; sound engineer, Estonian Radio 1958–67; freelance composer 1967–; first creative period starting with neoclassicist piano music 1958–68; experiments with serial techniques, aleatoricism ("incorporation of chance into the process of creation"), collage and sonic fields; his piece Credo from this period caused scandal in Soviet Estonia and was immediately banned 1968; new artistic re-orientation 1968–76; studied Gregorian chant, Notre Dame School and classic vocal polyphony; long silence broken by Symphony No. 3 1971 (sole work from this period); Für Alina 1976, first

composition in tintinnabuli technique; emigrated to Vienna, Austria 1980; contract with Universal Edition; grant from German Academic Exchange Service (DAAD) 1981, moved to Berlin; began collaboration with ECM label and producer Manfred Eicher 1984; Int. Arvo Pärt Centre est. in Laulasmaa, Estonia 2010 (holds composer's personal archive); returned to Estonia where he resides 2011–; mem. Estonian Acad. of Sciences 2011, Pontifical Council for Culture, Vatican City 2011; Academician for Music, Tallinn 2011; Hon. Citizen of Rakvere 1995, Paide 2009; Hon. mem. Royal Swedish Acad. of Music 1991, American Acad. of Arts and Letters 1996, Royal Acad. of Sciences, Letters and Fine Arts (Belgium) 2001, Royal School of Church Music (UK) 2003, Accad. Nazionale di Santa Cecilia (Italy) 2004; Hon. title 'Borderlander' from Borderland Foundation, Sejny, Poland 2003; Second Class Order, Nat. Coat of Arms 1998, Commdr, Ordre des Arts et des Lettres 2001, Estonian Nat. Honour First Class 2006, Cross of Honour for Science and Art First Class (Austrian) 2008, Coat of Arms of Tallinn 2011, Chevalier, Légion d'honneur 2011; Dr hc (Estonian Acad. of Music) 1990, (Sydney) 1996, (Tartu) 1998, (Durham) 2002, (Nat. Univ. of Gen. San Martín, Argentina) 2003, (Freiburg) 2007, (Liège) 2009, (St Andrews) 2009, (Pontifical Inst. for Sacred Music) 2011, (Lugano) 2012; DAAD Fellowship (German Academic Exchange Service), Berlin 1981, Ind. Russian Arts Award 'Triumph', Moscow 1997, Culture Award (Estonia) 1998, Herder Prize (Germany) 2000, Composition Award for choral work, C.A. Seghizzi, Gorizia, Italy 2003, Composer of the Year, Musical America 2005, European Church Music Prize (Germany) 2005, Int. Prize 'Baltic Star', St Petersburg 2007, Int. Brückepreis Award, European City of Görlitz/Zgorzelec 2007, Léonie Sonning Music Prize (Denmark) 2008, Lifelong Achievement Award (Estonia) 2009, Lifelong Achievement Award, Int. Istanbul Music Festival 2010, Baltic Image Enhancement Award (USA) 2010, Homage to Arvo Pärt by Konrad Adenauer Fund (Germany) 2011, Prize of Int. Festival Cervantino (Mexico) 2012, Estonian Music Council Composition Award 2012. *Compositions include:* for chamber or symphony orchestra: Symphony No. 1 (Polyphonic) 1963, Symphony No. 2 1966, Symphony No. 3 1971, Symphony No. 4 (Classic Brit Award – Composer of the Year 2011) 2008, Nekrolog 1960, Perpetuum mobile 1963, Collage über B-A-C-H 1964, Pro et contra (concerto for violoncello and orchestra) 1966, Wenn Bach Bienen gezüchtet hätte . . . 1976–2001, Cantus in Memory of Benjamin Britten 1977–80, Fratres for different ensembles 1977, Tabula rasa for two violins or one violin and one viola, prepared piano and orchestra 1977, Silouan's Song, 'My Soul Yearns after the Lord . . .' 1991, Trisagion 1992–94, Orient & Occident (Classical Brit Award – Contemporary Music Award 2003) 2000, Lamentate, Homage to Anish Kapoor and His Sculpture 'Marsyas' for piano and orchestra 2002, La Sindone 2005–13, Für Lennart in memoriam 2006, Silhouette, Hommage à Gustave Eiffel 2009–10, Swan-Song, Littlemore Tractus 2013; for choir and orchestra: Our Garden (First Prize, Composers Forum, Moscow 1962) 1959, Credo 1968, Stabat Mater 1985–2008, Te Deum 1985–92, Miserere 1989–92, Berliner Messe for different instrumentation 1990–2002, Litany, Prayers of St John Chrysostom for each hour of the day and night 1994–96, Como cierva sedienta 1998–2002, Cantique des degrés 1999–2002, Cecilia, vergine romana 2000–02, Salve Regina 2011, In principio 2003, Adam's Lament 2010; chamber music: Quintettino 1964, Sarah Was Ninety Years Old 1976–89, In spe (later: An den Wassern zu Babel. . . for different ensembles) 1976, Pari intervallo (later for different ensembles) 1976, Arbos for different ensembles 1977, Spiegel im Spiegel for different ensembles 1978, De profundiis 1980, Passio (Edison Classical Music Award 1989) 1982, Ein Wallfahrtslied/Pilgrims' Song 1984, Psalm for different ensembles 1985, Mozart-Adagio 1992–2005, My Heart's in the Highlands 2000, Salve Regina 2001, Estonian Lullaby for different ensembles 2002, Christmas Lullaby for different ensembles 2002, L'abbé Agathon for different ensembles 2004, Vater unser 2005–11, Sei gelobt, du Baum 2007, Alleluia-Tropus 2008, Missa brevis 2009; for choir a cappella: Solfeggio 1963, Missa syllabica for different ensembles 1977, Summa for different ensembles 1977, Sieben Magnificat-Antiphonen 1988–91, Magnificat 1989, Dopo la vittoria 1996–98, Kanon pokajanen 1997, Triodion 1998, Zwei Beter 1998, Which Was the Son of . . . 2000, Peace upon You, Jerusalem 2002, Most Holy Mother of God 2003, Da pacem Domine for different ensembles (Estonian Philharmonic Chamber Choir, conductor Paul Hillier, Grammy Award – Best Choral Performance2007) 2004, Habitare fratres in unum 2012, Virgencita 2012–13; for piano: Partita 1958, Two Sonatinas 1958–59, Diagramme 1964, Für Alina 1976, Variations for the Healing of Arinushka 1977; for organ: Trivium 1976, Pari intervallo 1976–80, Annum per annum 1980, Mein Weg hat Gipfel und Wellentäler 1989. *Address:* c/o Universal Edition AG, Boesendorferstrasse 12, 1010 Vienna, Austria (office). *Telephone:* (1) 337-23-0 (office). *Fax:* (1) 337-23-400 (office). *E-mail:* office@universaledition.com (office); info@arvopart.ee (office). *Website:* www.universaledition.com/paert (office); www.arvopart.ee.

PARTON, Dolly Rebecca; American singer, songwriter and actress; b. 19 Jan. 1946, Sevier County, Tenn.; d. of Robert Lee Parton and Avie Lee Parton (née Owens); m. Carl Dean 1966; Owner, Dollywood Entertainment Complex, including Dollywood Theme Park; CMA Vocal Group of the Year (with Porter Wagoner) 1968, Vocal Duo of the Year 1970, 1971, Female Vocalist of the Year 1975, 1976, Country Star of the Year 1978, Nashville Metronome Award 1979, People's Choice 1980, ACM Female Vocalist of the Year 1980, ACM Vocal Event of the Year and Video of the Year (both for When I Get Where I'm Going, with Brad Paisley) 2006, Kennedy Center Honor 2006, US Songwriters' Hall of Fame Johnny Mercer Award 2007. *Films include:* Nine to Five 1980, The Best Little Whorehouse in Texas 1982, Rhinestone 1984, Steel Magnolias 1989, Straight Talk 1991, The Beverly Hillbillies 1993, Frank McKlusky, C.I. 2002, Miss Congeniality 2: Armed and Fabulous 2005, Joyful Noise 2012. *Stage:* as score writer: Nine to Five: The Musical, Broadway 2009. *Recordings include:* albums: Here You Come Again (Grammy Award 1978), Real Love 1985, Just the Way I Am 1986, Heartbreaker, Great Balls of Fire, Rainbow 1988, White Limozeen 1989, Home for Christmas 1990, Eagle When She Flies 1991, Slow Dancing with the Moon 1993, Honky Tonk Angels 1994, The Essential Dolly Parton 1995, Just the Way I Am 1996, Super Hits 1996, I Will Always Love You and Other Greatest Hits (with others) 1996, Hungary Again 1998, Grass is Blue 1999, Best of the Best-Porter 2 Doll 1999, Halos and Horns 2002, Those Were The Days 2006, Backwoods Barbie 2008. *Composed numerous songs including:* Nine to Five (Grammy Award 1981). *Radio includes:* Grand Ole Opry, WSM Radio, Cass Walker Program. *Publication:* Dolly: My Life and Other Unfinished Business 1994. *Address:* c/o Sugar Hill Records, 120 31st Avenue North, Nashville, TN 37203, USA. *E-mail:* info@sugarhillrecords.com. *Website:* www.dollypartonmusic.net.

PARTRIDGE, Frank David Peregrine; British art dealer; b. 14 Sept. 1955, London, England; s. of John Arthur Partridge and The Hon. Caroline Elizabeth Maud Cust; m. Susan Anne Hince 1982; three d.; ed Elstree and Harrow Schools; Dir Partridge Fine Arts Plc 1989–2006, Fine Arts Holdings Ltd 2005–, Partridge Fine Art Ltd 2006–; mem. British Antique Dealers' Assn 2002–, BADA Fair Cttee (fmr Council mem.). *Leisure interests:* shooting, tennis, skiing, golf, bridge. *Address:* 7 Thurloe Square, London, SW7 2TA, England. *Telephone:* (20) 7225-3654. *Fax:* (20) 7581-9387. *E-mail:* mail@frankpartridge.co.uk. *Website:* www .frankpartridge.co.uk.

PARTRIDGE, John Albert, CBE, RA, FRIBA; British architect; b. 26 Aug. 1924, London, England; s. of George Partridge and Gladys Partridge; m. Doris Foreman 1953 (died 2000); one s. one d.; ed Shooter's Hill Grammar School, Woolwich and Polytechnic School of Architecture, London; London County Council Housing Architects' Dept 1951–59; Sr and Founding Partner, Howell, Killick, Partridge & Amis (HKPA) 1959–95; John Partridge Consultancy 1995–; Vice-Pres. RIBA 1977–79, Concrete Soc. 1979–81; RIBA Hon. Librarian 1977–81; Chair. RIBA Architectural Research Steering Cttee 1978–84, Clients Advisory Steering Cttee 1990–94; Gov. Building Centre, London 1981–96; Chair. Trustees Eric Lyons Memorial Fund 1982–; Chair. Asscn of Consultant Architects 1983–85; mem. NEDO Construction Research Strategy Cttee 1983–86; Architect mem. FCO Advisory Bd on the Diplomatic Estate 1985–94; External Examiner in Architecture, Univ. of Bath 1975–78, 1992, Thames Polytechnic 1978–86, Univ. of Cambridge 1979–81, Univ. of Manchester 1982–, South Bank Polytechnic (London) 1981–86, Brighton Polytechnic 1987–91, RCA 1991–94; Asscn of Consultant Architects Award 2005. *Major work include:* Wolfson Rayne and Gatehouse Bldg, St Anne's Coll., Oxford, New Hall and Common Room, St Antony's Coll., Oxford, Weston Rise Housing, Islington, Wells Hall, Univ. of Reading, Middlesex Polytechnic Coll. of Art, Cat Hill, Medway Magistrates Court, The Albany, Deptford, Hall of Justice, Trinidad & Tobago, in Asscn with ACLP, Trinidad; Warrington Crown Courthouse, Basildon Courthouse, Haywards Heath Magistrates Courthouse, Chaucer Coll., Univ. of Kent; exhbns of HKPA work at Heinz Gallery, London 1983, Puck Bldg, New York 1983; 35 Nat. Design Awards for HKPA 1965–93. *Publications:* articles in the tech. press and architectural papers to conferences. *Leisure interests:* looking at buildings and gardens, travel, sketching and water colours, photography, music. *Address:* Cudham Court, Cudham, nr Sevenoaks, Kent, TN14 7QF, England. *Telephone:* (1959) 571294. *E-mail:* john.partridge1@btinternet.com.

PARTRIDGE, Dame Linda, DBE, CBE, BA, DPhil, FRS, FRSE, FMedSci; British biometrist and academic; *Director, Institute of Healthy Ageing, University College London;* b. 18 March 1950, Bath, England; d. of George Albert Partridge and Ida Partridge (née Tucker); m. 1st Vernon French (divorced 1989); m. 2nd Michael John Morgan 1996; ed Convent of Sacred Heart, Tunbridge Wells, Univ. of Oxford; NERC Post-doctoral Fellow, Univ. of York 1974–76; Demonstrator then Lecturer, Reader, Prof. of Evolutionary Biology, Univ. of Edinburgh 1976–1993; Weldon Prof. of Biometry, Univ. Coll. London 1993–, NERC Research Prof. 1997–2002, Biotechnology and Biological Sciences Research Council Professorial Fellowship 2002–07, Dir Inst. of Healthy Ageing 2008–; Founding Dir Max Planck Inst. for Biology of Ageing, Cologne; mem. European Acad. of Sciences 2005, European Molecular Biology Org. 2006; Hon. DSc (St Andrews) 2004; London Zoological Soc. Frink Medal 2000, American Soc. of Naturalists Sewall Wright Award 2002, Sewall Wright Award, American Soc. of Naturalists 2003, Longevity Prize, Fondation IPSEN 2004, The Lord Cohen Medal, British Soc. for Research on Ageing 2004, Medal of the Asscn for the Study of Animal Behaviour 2005, Living Legend, Help the Aged 2008, Thomassen a Thuessink Medal, Univ. of Groningen, Netherlands 2009, Darwin-Wallace Medal, Linnean Soc. of London 2009, Women of Outstanding Achievement Award for Science Discovery, Innovation and Entrepreneurship, UKRC for Women 2009, Royal Soc. Croonian Prize Lecturer 2009. *Leisure interests:* sailing, gardening, tennis, natural history. *Address:* Department of Genetics, Evolution and Environment, Darwin Building, University College London, Gower Street, London, WC1E 6BT, England (office). *Telephone:* (20) 7679-4380 (office). *Fax:* (20) 7679-7096 (office). *Website:* www.ucl .ac.uk/iha (office).

PARTRIDGE, Sir Michael John Anthony, KCB, MA, CB; British civil servant; b. 29 Sept. 1935, Stourbridge, Worcs.; s. of Dr John Henry Partridge and Ethel Green; m. Joan Elizabeth Hughes 1968; two s. one d.; ed Merchant Taylors' School, St John's Coll., Oxford; joined Home Civil Service (Ministry of Pensions and Nat. Insurance–MPNI) 1960, Pvt. Sec. to Perm. Sec. 1962–64, Prin. MPNI 1964–71, Asst Sec. 1971–76, UnderSec. 1976–81, Deputy Sec. 1981–83; Deputy Under-Sec. of State, Home Office 1983–87; Second Perm. Sec. Dept of Health and Social Security 1987–88; Perm. Sec. Dept of Social Security 1988–95; Sr Treas. Methodist Church Finance Div. 1980–96; Hon. Fellow St John's Coll. Oxford 1991–; Dir (non-exec.) Methodist Ministers' Pensions Trust 1992–2010, Epworth Investment Man. 1995–2011, Commercial Gen. and Norwich Union and Aviva 1996–2003, Stationery Office 1997–99; Gov. Middx Univ. 1992–, Chair. Bd of Govs 1996–2002, Pro-Chancellor 2001–; Vice-Chair. Magdi Yacoub Research Foundation 2001–; mem. Council Sheffield Univ. 2001–03; Gov. Merchant Taylors' School 1992–99; Chair. Stationery Office Pension Scheme 2002–; Chair. Bd of Govs Heathfield School 2004–11; Pres. Old Merchant Taylors' Soc. 2002–03; Trustee Harefield Hosp. Heart Transplant Trust 1992–2003; Liveryman Merchant Taylors' Co. 1987. *Publication:* Serta Scissorum 2012. *Leisure interests:* do-it-yourself, Greece, reading, skiing. *Address:* 27 High View, Pinner, Middx, HA5 3NZ, England (home). *Telephone:* (20) 8868-0657 (home). *E-mail:* michael@partridges.org.uk (home).

PARTS, Juhan, BL; Estonian politician; *Minister of Economic Affairs and Communications;* b. 27 Aug. 1966, Tallinn; m.; one s. one d.; ed Tallinn First Secondary School, Univ. of Tartu; Deputy Sec.-Gen., Ministry of Justice 1992–98; Auditor Gen. 1998–2002; Chair. Res Publica Party 2002–05; Prime Minister of Estonia 2003–05 (resgnd); Minister of Econ. Affairs and Communications 2007–. *Leisure interest:* football (mem. FC Toompea). *Address:* Ministry of Economic Affairs and Communications, Harju 11, Tallinn 15072 (office); Res Publica, Narva mnt. 7, Tallinn 10117, Estonia (office). *Telephone:* 625-6342 (Ministry) (office); 610-9244 (Res Publica) (office). *Fax:* 631-3660 (Ministry) (office); 610-9243 (Res

Publica) (office). *E-mail:* juhan.parts@mkm.ee (office); respublica@respublica.ee (office). *Website:* www.mkm.ee (office); www.respublica.ee (office).

PARVANOV, Georgi Sedefchov, MA, PhD; Bulgarian historian and fmr head of state; b. 28 June 1957, Sirishnik, Pernik Dist; m. Zorka Petrova; two s.; ed Secondary School of Math., Pernik, St Clement of Ohrid Univ. of Sofia; researcher, Inst. of History, Bulgarian CP (BCP—became Bulgarian Socialist Party—BSP 1990) 1981–91, conducted research on the nat. question and history of social democracy in Bulgaria, Sr Research Assoc. 1989–92, Dir Centre for History and Policy Studies with the Supreme Council of the Bulgarian Socialist Party (BSP) 1992–96; joined BCP 1981 first party post 1991, Deputy Chair. Supreme Council 1994–96, Chair. 1996–2001; mem. Narodno Sobraniye (Parl.) for Kurdjali (Southern Bulgaria) 1994–2001, Chair. Parl. Group for Friendship with Greece and mem. Parl. Cttee on Radio and Television 1994–97, Parl. Group of the Democratic Left, Parl. Group of Coalition for Bulgaria 1997–2001; Pres. of Bulgaria 2002–12; fmr Chair. Parl. Group on Friendship between Bulgaria and Greece; initiated Bulgarian Christmas Charity Campaign 2003–08; Heydar Aliyev Order (Azerbaijan); Grand Cordon of the Leopold (Belgium); Grand Cross, Order of the Southern Cross (Brazil); Collar of the Order of the Cross of Terra Mariana (Estonia); First Class with Chain, Order of the Three Stars (Latvia); Grand Cross with Golden Chain, Order of Vytautas the Great (Lithuania); Grand Cross, Order of Saint-Charles (Monaco) 2004; Kt Grand Cross, Order of St Olav (Norway); Dr hc (Prešov Univ., Baku Univ., Yerevan State Univ.); Grand Gold Medal, Tomáš Garrigue Masaryk Univ., Brno, Czech Repub. *Publications:* numerous scientific articles, monographs and books, including Dimitar Blagoev and the Bulgarian National Problem 1879–1917 1988, From Bouzloudja to the Corona Theatre–An Attempt at a New Reading of Pages from the BSP's Social Democratic Period 1995, The Bulgarian Social Democracy and the Macedonian Issue at the End of the 19th Century up to 1918 1997, November 10: Before and After 2001. *Address:* Bulgarian Socialist Party (Balgarska Sotsialisticheska Partiya), 1000 Sofia, ul. Positano 20, Bulgaria (office). *Telephone:* (2) 810-72-00 (office). *Fax:* (2) 981-21-85 (office). *E-mail:* bsppress@bsp.bg (office). *Website:* www.bsp.bg (office); georgiparvanov.bg.

PARVEEN, Abida; Pakistani singer; b. 1954, Larkana, Sindh; d. of Ghulam Haider; m. Ghulam Hussain Sheikh (deceased); one s. two d.; ed attended father's music school; studied classical music with Salamat Ali Khan; debut on Hyderabad Radio Station; repertoire includes classical music, ghazals, traditional Sufiana kalaam and Punjabi folk music; worldwide tours and performances before heads of state; made recordings of original works of Sufi poets; President's Award for Pride of Performance 1982, Sitara-i-Imtiaz Award 2005, Lifetime Achievement Award, Kaladharmi Begum Akhtar Academy of Ghaza, India 2012. *Recordings include:* Pakistani Sufi Songs 1995, The Best of Abida Parveen 1997, Ho Jamalo 2000, Songs of the Mystics 2000, Tere Ishq Nachaya 2001, Raqs-e-Bismil 2001, Faiz by Abida 2001, Jahan E. Khusrau 2001, Visal – The Meeting Mystic Poets from the Hind & Mind 2002, Baba Bulleh Shah 2003, Mere Dil Se 2005, Ishq: l'Amour Absolu (Supreme Love) 2005, Svar Utsav 2006, Abida Parveen-The Sufi Queen 2011.

PASANELLA, Giovanni, FAIA; American architect; b. 13 Jan. 1931, New York; two s.; ed Cooper Union, New York, Yale Univ.; designer, Edward L. Barnes, New York 1959–64; Prin. Giovanni Pasanella, New York 1964–76; co-owner Pasanella & Klein, New York 1976–; Architecture Critic, Univ. of Ky, Lexington 1963, Yale Univ. 1964; Adjunct Prof. of Architecture, Columbia Univ. 1965–87, Project Dir Inst. of Urban Environment 1965–68; Visiting Fellow Urban Studies, Inst. of Architecture 1975; Consultant Architect to Chair. New York City Planning Comm. 1967; mem. Bd of Trustees Il Piccolo Teatro dell'Opera, Brooklyn, New York 1986; Yale Univ. Travelling Fellow 1958–59; mem. Soc. of Architectural Historians; Architecture Award, Architectural Record 1974, 1975. *Address:* 115 South Street, New York, NY 10038, USA (home); Villa Cannizzaro, via Fondi Camaiore, Lucca, Italy. *Telephone:* (584) 989297 (office); (212) 566-2352 (home). *Fax:* (212) 566-2481 (home). *E-mail:* marcopasanella@verizon.net (home).

PASCAL, Amy Beth; American film industry executive; *Chairman, Sony Pictures Entertainment Motion Picture Group and Co-Chairman, Sony Pictures Entertainment;* b. 25 March 1958, Los Angeles, Calif.; m. Bernard Weinraub; ed Univ. of California, Los Angeles; worked for producer Tony Garnett at Kestral Films (affiliated to Warner Bros); Vice-Pres. of Production, 20th Century Fox 1986–87; Studio Exec., Columbia Pictures 1987–94, Pres. 1996–99, Chair. 1999–2003, Vice-Chair. Sony Pictures Entertainment 2002–06, Chair. Sony Pictures Entertainment Motion Picture Group 2003–, Co-Chair. Sony Pictures Entertainment 2006–; Pres. of Production, Turner Pictures 1994–96; mem. Exec. Bd UCLA School of Theater, Film and Television; Trustee, RAND Corpn, American Film Inst.; named by The Hollywood Reporter on Women in Entertainment Power 100 list (first) 2003, 2006, Hollywood Leadership Award Honoree 2003, ranked by Fortune magazine amongst the 50 Most Powerful Women in Business in the US (21st) 2004, (42nd) 2005, (41st) 2006, (46th) 2007, (49th) 2009, (47th) 2010, (50th) 2011, ranked by Forbes magazine amongst The World's 100 Most Powerful Women (66th) 2004, (50th) 2005, (59th) 2006, (35th) 2007, (54th) 2008, (60th) 2009, (87th) 2010, (28th) 2011, (36th) 2012–13. *Films:* appeared in Intimate Portrait: Jennifer Lopez (TV documentary) 2002; Peter Pan (co-producer) 2003. *Address:* Sony Pictures Entertainment, 10202 W Washington Boulevard, Culver City, CA 90232, USA (office). *Telephone:* (310) 244-4000 (office). *Fax:* (310) 244-2626 (office). *Website:* www.sonypictures.com (office).

PASCAL, Jean-Baptiste Lucien, LenD; French banker; b. 26 Nov. 1930, Bordeaux; s. of Ernest Pascal and Paule de Battisti; m. Christiane Gardelle 1962; three s. (one deceased); ed Univ. of Paris; attached to Banque Nat. pour le Commerce et l'Industrie 1954; Head of Supplies Mission for the Devt of Algeria and Jt Govt Commr for Crédit Populaire de France in Algeria 1959; Head of Bureau for Financial Co-operation to Sec. of State for Algerian Affairs 1963; mem. Crédit Commercial de France (CCF) 1965, Deputy Dir Cen. Admin. CCF 1967, Dir-Gen. d'Interbail 1971, Dir Gen. Admin. 1973–, Admin. Dir-Gen. 1974, Vice-Pres. Dir-Gen. d'Interbail 1978–96; Dir Crédit Commercial de France 1977; Pres. Dir-Gen. Banque Hervet 1986–89; Pres. Admin. Council SOFEC 1991; Pres. GOBTP 1993–97, Pres. Conseil de Surveillance du GOBTP 1997–99, Interbail 1996– (Chair. Bd of Dirs 1996–97); Dir French Assocn of Financial Cos, Vice-Pres. 1995–97; Chevalier, Légion d'honneur. *Publication:* La Décolonisation de l'Europe:

Querelle des Continents 1964. *Leisure interests:* alpinism, hunting. *Address:* 14 rue Jules Claretie, 75116 Paris, France (home).

PASCHKE, Fritz, DTechSc; Austrian electrical engineer and academic; *Professor Emeritus, Technical University of Vienna;* b. 2 March 1929, Graz/Goesting; s. of late Eduard Paschke and Stefanie Mittellehner; m. Gertrud P. Kutschera 1955; two d.; ed Tech. Univs of Graz and Vienna; Asst, Tech. Univ. Vienna 1953–55; consultant, New York 1955–56; mem. tech. staff, RCA David Sarnoff Research Center 1956–61; Components Div. Siemens AG, Munich 1961–66; Prof. of Gen. Electronics, Tech. Univ. Vienna 1965–97, Prof. Emer. 1997–, Dean, School of Electrical Eng 1970–71, Rector/Pro-Rector 1971–76, Head, Inst. für Allgemeine Elektrotechnik und Elektronik 1980–97; Vice-Pres. Austrian Nat. Science Foundation 1974–82; Dr hc (Budapest) 1974; Ludwig Boltzmann Award 1977, HE Cardinal Innitzer Award 1984, Erwin Schrödinger Award (Austrian Acad.) 1988, City of Vienna Award for Science and Tech. 1988, Leonardo da Vinci Medal, Soc. Européenne pour la Formations des Ingénieurs 1996. *Leisure interests:* art, hiking, swimming. *Address:* Technical University of Vienna, Karlsplatz 13, 1040 Vienna, Austria (office). *Telephone:* (1) 58801-36653 (office). *Fax:* (1) 58801-36699 (office). *E-mail:* fritz.paschke@tuwien.ac.at (office); fritz.paschke@chello.at (home). *Website:* www.isas.tuwien.ac.at (office).

PASCHKE, Karl Theodor; German diplomatist, UN official and academic; b. 12 Nov. 1935, Berlin; s. of Adolf Paschke and Adele Cornill; m. Pia-Irene Schwerber 1963; one s. one d.; ed Univs of Munich and Bonn; Consul, New Orleans, La, USA 1964–68; Deputy Chief of Mission, Embassy in Kinshasa 1968–71; Dean, Foreign Office Training School, Bonn 1972–77; Press Counsellor, Washington, DC 1977–80; Spokesman, German Foreign Office, Bonn 1980–84; Amb. to UN Orgs, Vienna 1984–86; Minister, Embassy in Washington, DC 1987–90; Dir-Gen. for Personnel and Man., Foreign Office, Bonn 1990–94; Under-Sec.-Gen. for Internal Oversight Services, UN, New York 1994–99, Special Insp., Foreign Office 2000, Special Envoy for UN Secr. and Managerial Reform 2006; fmr Chair. Cttee on Budget and Finance, Ass. of States Parties, Int. Criminal Court; fmr mem. Bd of Advisors, Comprehensive Nuclear-Test-Ban Treaty Org.; Lecturer, Erfurt Univ. School of Public Policy. *Publication:* Reform der Attache-Ausbildung 1975. *Leisure interest:* music, especially jazz. *Address:* Denglerstrasse 46, 53173 Bonn, Germany (home). *Telephone:* (228) 9562032 (home). *Fax:* (228) 9562083 (home). *E-mail:* kpaschke@t-online.de.

PASCO, Richard Edward, CBE; British actor; b. 18 July 1926, Barnes; s. of Cecil George Pasco and Phyllis (née Widdison) Pasco; m. 1st Greta Watson 1956 (divorced 1964); one s.; m. 2nd Barbara Leigh-Hunt 1967; ed Colet Court and King's Coll. School, Wimbledon, Cen. School of Speech and Drama; first appearance on stage, Q Theatre 1943; served in HM forces 1944–48; Old Vic Co. 1950–52; Birmingham Repertory Co. 1952–55; played Fortinbras in Hamlet (Moscow and London) 1955; English Stage Co. 1957, played in The Member of the Wedding, Look Back in Anger, The Entertainer, Man from Bellac and The Chairs; toured USA and Europe 1967 (with RSC), Japan, Australia 1970, Japan 1972; joined RSC 1969, Nat. Theatre 1987; now Hon. Assoc. Artist RSC; has made broadcasts and recordings of plays and verse, including complete sonnets of Shakespeare. *Roles include:* The Entertainer (New York) 1958, Moscow Youth Festival in Look Back in Anger 1959, Teresa of Avila (Dublin Theatre Festival and Vaudeville) 1961, Henry V, Love's Labour's Lost (Bristol Old Vic, Old Vic and tour to Europe) 1964; Hamlet, Bristol Old Vic, 1965, Measure for Measure, Peer Gynt, Man and Superman, Hamlet 1966, Polixenes in The Winter's Tale, Proteus in The Two Gentlemen of Verona, Buckingham in Henry VIII 1969, Major Barbara, Richard II, Duchess of Malfi 1971, Becket in Murder in the Catherdral, Medraut in the Island of the Mighty 1972, Richard and Bolingbroke in Richard II 1973–74; The Marrying of Ann Leete 1975, Jack Tanner in Man and Superman 1977, Trigorin in The Seagull 1978, Timon in Timon of Athens 1980, Clarence in Richard III 1980, Arkady Schatslivtses in The Forest 1981, La Ronde 1982, Father in Six Characters in Search of an Author 1987, Pavel in Fathers and Sons 1987, Charlie Southwark in Racing Demon, Sir Peter Edgcombe in Murmuring Judges, Mr Birling in An Inspector Calls, Malcolm Pryce in Absence of War, Boss Findley in Sweet Bird of Youth 1994, Sorin in The Seagull, Stratford, Barbican 2000. *Television appearances include:* Henry Irving, The Three Musketeers, Savages, As You Like It, Julius Caesar, British in Love, Trouble with Gregory, Philby, The House Boy, Number 10—Disraeli, The Plot to Murder Lloyd George, Let's Run Away to Africa, Sorrell and Son, Drummonds, etc. *Films include:* Room at the Top, Yesterday's Enemy, The Gorgon, Rasputin, Watcher in the Woods, Wagner, Arch of Triumph, Inspector Morse, etc. *Publications:* Time and Concord: Aldeburgh Festival Recollections (contrib.) 1997, Acting in Stratford (contrib.) 1997. *Leisure interests:* music, gardening, preservation of rural England. *Address:* c/o Michael Whitehall Ltd, 10 Lower Common South, London, SW15 1BP, England.

PASCOE, B. Lynn, BA, MA; American diplomatist and UN official; b. 1943, Missouri; m. Diana Pascoe; two d.; ed Univ. of Kansas, Columbia Univ.; served on Soviet and China Desks; postings to embassies in Moscow, Hong Kong, Bangkok, Beijing (twice) and Taiwan; Prin. Deputy Asst Sec., East Asian and Pacific Bureau, State Dept; Deputy Chief of Mission, Embassy in Beijing; Deputy Exec. Sec., US Dept of State; Special Asst to Deputy Sec. of State; Dir American Inst., Taiwan 1993–96; Sr Adviser, Bureau of E African and Pacific Affairs and at US Mission to UN; Special Negotiator for Nagorno-Karabakh and Regional Conflicts; Co-Chair. OSCE Minsk Group; apptd Amb. to Malaysia 1999; Deputy Asst Sec. for European and Eurasian Affairs, US Dept of State 2001–04; Amb. to Indonesia 2004–07; Under-Sec.-Gen. for Political Affairs, UN 2007–12. *Address:* c/o Department of Political Affairs, United Nations, New York, NY 10017, USA.

PASCUA CERRATO, Marlon; Honduran business executive and politician; fmr Vice-Pres. Comisión para la Defensa y Promoción de la Competencia (Nat. Comm. for the Defence of Competition); mem. Congreso Nacional (Parl.) for Francisco Morazán constituency 2002–06; Minister of Defence 2010–14; mem. Partido Nacional. *Address:* c/o Ministry of Defence, Tegucigalpa, Honduras (office).

PASCUAL, Ramon, PhD; Spanish physicist and academic; *Professor of Theoretical Physics, Universitad Autónoma de Barcelona;* b. 4 Feb. 1942, Barcelona; s. of Josep Pascual and Montserrat Pascual; m. Maria Lluisa Roca 1966; two s. one d.; Junta de Energía Nuclear, Madrid 1963–64; Teaching Asst Univ. of Valencia 1964–67; Asst Prof. of Quantum Mechanics, Univ. Complutense de Madrid

1967–70; Prof. of Math. Physics, Univ. of Zaragoza Jan.–Sept. 1970; Prof., Univ. Autónoma de Madrid 1970–71; Prof. of Theoretical Physics, Univ. Autónoma de Barcelona 1971–, Dean, Faculty of Science 1976–79, Vice-Rector for Academic Affairs 1979–80, Rector 1986–90; Visiting Scientist, CERN, Geneva, Switzerland 1969, 1970, 1977, 1978, 1981, 1983, 1986, Faculty of Science, Paris (Orsay) 1972, 1975, Rutherford Appleton Lab., Oxford, UK 1975; Chair. Exec. Cttee of the Synchrotron Light Source Alba; mem. Real Sociedad Española de Física y Química, European Physical Soc.; mem. and Pres. Reial Acadèmia Ciencies i Artes de Barcelona. *Publications:* more than 40 articles in scientific journals etc. *Address:* Universitat Autónoma de Barcelona, Edificio C, 08193 Bellaterra, Barcelona, Spain (office). *Telephone:* (93) 581-1307 (office); (93) 592-4444 (office). *Fax:* (93) 581-3213 (office). *E-mail:* pascual@ifae.es (office). *Website:* www.ifae.es (office); www.cells.es.

PASHA, Lt-Gen. Ahmed Shuja; Pakistani military officer and intelligence official; b. 18 March 1952; Second Lt, Frontier Force Regiment, PMA Long Course 1974; Chief Instructor, Command and Staff Coll.; Contingent and Sector Commdr, UN Mission in Sierra Leone 2001–02; promoted to Maj. Gen., posted as GOC 8th Infantry Div., Sialkot 2003; Commdt, Command and Staff Coll., Quetta 2005; Dir-Gen. of Mil. Operations 2006–08; Dir-Gen. Inter-Services Intelligence 2008–12 (retd); Hilal-e-Imtiaz (Mil.). *Address:* c/o Inter-Services Intelligence, c/o Ministry of Defence, Pakistan Secretariat, No. II, Rawalpindi 46000, Pakistan.

PASHTUN, Mohammad Yousef, BSc, MA; Afghan politician and engineer; b. 15 Nov. 1946, Kandahar; s. of Brig. Mohammad Ghani Khan; m. Qamar Angaar Pashtun; ed Ahmad Shah Baba High School, Kabul Univ., American Univ. of Beirut, Lebanon; worked in Dar-ul-Handasa Design & Construction Co.; took refuge in Pakistan during Soviet occupation 1980s; fmr Lecturer, Eng Faculty, Kabul Univ.; Minister of Urban Affairs 2002–03; Gov. of Qandahar Prov. 2003–04; Minister of Urban Devt and Housing 2004–10. *Address:* c/o Ministry of Urban Development and Housing, Microrayon 3, Kabul, Afghanistan. *Telephone:* 79-9682833 (mobile). *E-mail:* info@moud.gov.af.

PASIARDIS, Christodoulos; Cypriot politician and diplomatist; b. 31 Jan. 1944, Tseri; m. Ava Pasiardis; two c.; ed Pancyprian Gymnasium and Univ. of Athens; worked in Political Affairs Dept, Ministry of Foreign Affairs 1974–75, 1978–84; Dir Office of the Minister of Foreign Affairs 1975–78, 1992–93; Diplomatic Adviser to the Pres. 1984–88; First Counsellor and Chargé d'Affaires, Embassy in Athens 1989–92; High Commr to Australia 1994–96; Political Dir, Ministry of Foreign Affairs 1996–98; Amb. to Greece (also accred to Bulgaria and Romania) 1998–2001; Perm. Sec., Ministry of Foreign Affairs 2001–03; Deputy Minister to the Pres. and Govt Spokesperson 2003–07; Minister of Defence 2007–08. *Address:* c/o Ministry of Defence, 4 Emmanuel Roides Avenue, 1432, Nicosia, Cyprus (office).

PASINETTI, Luigi Lodovico, MA, PhD; Italian economist and academic; *Professor Emeritus of Economics, Università Cattolica del Sacro Cuore, Milan;* b. 12 Sept. 1930, Zanica (Bergamo); s. of Giovanni Pasinetti and Romilda Arzuffi; m. Carmela Colombo 1966; one s.; ed Università Cattolica del Sacro Cuore, Milan, Univ. of Cambridge, UK, Harvard Univ., USA, Univ. of Oxford, UK; Research Fellow, Nuffield Coll., Oxford 1960–61; Fellow and Lecturer in Econs, King's Coll., Cambridge 1961–73; Lecturer, then Reader in Econs, Univ. of Cambridge 1961–76; Prof. of Econs, Università Cattolica del Sacro Cuore 1976–2007, Prof. Emer. 2007–, Chair. 1980–83; Wesley Clair Mitchell Visiting Research Prof. of Econs, Columbia Univ., New York 1971, 1975; Visiting Research Prof., Indian Statistical Inst., Calcutta and New Delhi 1979; Visiting Prof. of Econs, Univ. of Ottawa, Carleton Univ. 1981, Kyoto Univ. 1984, Univ. of Southern California 1985; Visiting Fellow, Gonville & Caius Coll., Cambridge 1989; McDonnell Distinguished Scholars Fellow, WIDER, the UN Univ., Helsinki 1991, 1992; Visiting Prof., Univ. of Sydney 1993; Visiting Fellow, Trinity Coll. Cambridge 1997, 1999; mem. Council and Exec. Cttee, Int. Econ. Asscn 1980–99, Hon. Pres. 2005; Pres. Italian Econ. Asscn 1986–89, Confed. of European Econ. Asscns 1992–93, European Soc. for the History of Econ. Thought 1995–97; Fellow, Econometric Soc. 1978–; mem. Accad. Nazionale dei Lincei, Rome 1986–, Inst. Lombardo Accad. di Scienze e Lettere, Milan 1995–; Hon. Fellow, Gonville & Caius Coll., Cambridge 1999–, Hon. Pres. European Asscn for Evolutionary Political Economy 1989, European Soc. for the History of Economic Thought 2003–, Int. Econ. Asscn 2005–; Dr hc (Univ. of Fribourg, Switzerland) 1986; St Vincent Prize for Econs 1979, 2002, Gold Medal (First Class) for Educ., Culture and Arts 1982, 'La Madonnina' Int. Prize (Econs section), Milan 1987, Special Prize for Culture (Econs section), Presidency of the Council of Ministers 1996, Invernizzi Prize for Econs 1997. *Publications include:* Growth and Income Distribution 1974, Lectures on the Theory of Production 1977, Structural Change and Economic Growth 1981, Structural Change and Adjustment in the World Economy (with P. Lloyd) 1987, Structural Economic Dynamics 1993, Economic Growth and the Structure of Long-Term Development (with R. M. Solow) 1994, The Impact of Keynes in the 20th Century (with B. Schefold) 1999, Keynes and the Cambridge Keynesians – A 'Revolution in Economics' to be Accomplished 2007; as contrib.: Structural Dynamics and Economic Growth (ed by R. Arena and P.L. Porta) 2012; numerous articles on income distribution, capital theory, econ. growth and structural econ. dynamics, and on the econ. crisis of 2011–12. *Leisure interests:* tennis, climbing, music, reading. *Address:* Faculty of Economics, Università Cattolica del Sacro Cuore, Largo A. Gemelli 1, 20123 Milan, Italy (office). *Telephone:* (02) 72342470 (office). *Fax:* (02) 72342406 (office). *E-mail:* llp@unicatt.it (office). *Website:* docenti.unicatt.it/eng/luigi_lodovico_pasinetti (office); www.unicatt.it/docenti/pasinetti (office).

PAŠKA, Pavol, BA; Slovak politician; *Chairman (Speaker), National Council of the Slovak Republic;* b. 23 Feb. 1958, Košice; m.; two s.; ed Comenius Univ., Bratislava; several roles at State Co. Zdroj, Educ. and Culture Centre, Self-Admin Office and Municipal Dist Admin KVP, Košice; Co-founder Direction (later SMER – Sociálna demokracia (Direction – Social Democracy)) 1999, Vice-Pres. 2003–; mem. Národná rada Slovenskej republiky (Nat. Council of the Slovak Repub.— Parl.) 2002– (re-elected 2006), Chair. (Speaker) 2006–10, 2012–, Chair. Foreign Relations Cttee 2004–06, mem. Health Care Cttee 2002–04, Special Oversight Cttee for the SIS 2002–04; Chair. Conf. of Speakers of EU Parls 2006. *Address:* Office of the Chairman, National Council of the Slovak Republic (Národná rada Slovenskej republiky), nám. Alexandra Dubčeka 1, 812 80 Bratislava, Slovakia (office). *Telephone:* (2) 5972-1111 (office). *Fax:* (2) 5441-9529 (office). *E-mail:* pavol_paska@nrsr.sk (office). *Website:* www.nrsr.sk (office); www.pavolpaska.sk.

PASKAI, HE Cardinal László, OFM; Hungarian ecclesiastic; *Archbishop Emeritus of Esztergom-Budapest;* b. 8 May 1927, Szeged; joined Minor Franciscan Order, professed his vows 1949; assumed diocesan service 1950; ordained priest 1951; Episcopal liturgist 1952–55, Szeged; Prof. of Philosophy, Theological Acad., Szeged 1955–65, simultaneously Prefect 1955–62, Spiritual 1962–65; Spiritual Prefect, Central Seminary of Budapest 1965–69; commissioned lecturer 1965–67, leading Prof. of Philosophy, Theological Academy, Budapest 1967–78; Rector of Seminary 1973–78; apptd Titular Bishop of Bavagaliana and Apostolic Gov. of Veszprém 1978; Diocesan Bishop of Veszprém 1979, Coadjutor Archbishop of Kalocsa-Kecskemét 1982; Archbishop of Esztergom (now Esztergom-Budapest) and Primate of Hungary 1987–2002, Archbishop Emer. 2002–; cr. Cardinal (Cardinal-Priest of S. Teresa al Corso d'Italia) 1988; Chair. Hungarian Episcopal Conf. 1986–90. *Address:* Prímasi es Erseki Hivatal, Mindszenty hercegprimas ter 2, Pf. 25, 2501 Esztergom; Uri u. 62, 1014 Budapest, Hungary. *Telephone:* (1) 202-5611. *Fax:* (1) 202-5458.

PASLOSKI, Darrell, BPharm; Canadian pharmacist and politician; *Premier of Yukon;* m. Tammie Pasloski; four c.; ed Univ. of Saskatchewan; propr of two pharmacies, Whitehorse 1991–; mem. Yukon Party, Leader 2011–; Premier of Yukon 2011–, also Minister responsible for Exec. Council Office, Minister of Finance, Minister responsible for Yukon Energy Corpn and for Yukon Devt Corpn; fmr Dir MacBride Museum, Swim Yukon, Mountainview Golf Course; Yukon Chamber of Commerce Business Person of the Year 2009. *Leisure interests:* ice hockey, hiking, fishing, hunting, camping. *Address:* Government of Yukon, Box 2703, Whitehorse, YK Y1A 2C6, Canada (office). *Telephone:* (867) 667-5811 (office). *Fax:* (867) 393-6252 (office). *E-mail:* premier@gov.yk.ca (office). *Website:* www.yukonpremier.ca (office).

PASQUA, Charles Victor; French politician; b. 18 April 1927, Grasse; s. of André Pasqua and Françoise Rinaldi; m. Jeanne Joly 1947; one s.; ed College de Grasse, Inst. d'Etudes Juridiques, Nice and Faculté de Droit, Aix-en-Provence; Rep. Société Ricard 1952, Insp. 1955, Regional Dir 1960, Dir French Sales 1962, Dir-Gen. French Sales and Export 1963; Pres.-Dir-Gen. Société Euralim 1967–71; Commercial Consultant 1972–; Deputy to Nat. Ass. (UDR) 1968–73; Sec.-Gen. UDR 1974–76; Senator, Hauts de Seine 1977–86, 1988–93, 1995–99, 2004–; Pres. RPR Group in Senate 1981–86, 1988–93; Minister of the Interior and Administration 1986–88, 1993–95; Political adviser Exec. Comm. of RPR 1998–99; Co-founder and Pres Rassemblement pour la France et l'Indépendance de l'Europe 1999–; mem. European Parl. 1999–2004; Chevalier, Légion d'honneur; Médaille de la France libre. *Publications:* La libre entreprise – un état d'esprit 1964, L'ardeur nouvelle 1985, Que demande le peuple 1992, Demain, la France (Vol. I): la priorité sociale (jtly) 1992, Tous pour la France 1999. *Address:* Sénat, Palais du Luxembourg, 75291 Paris Cedex 06, France.

PASQUAL, Lluís; Spanish theatre and opera director; b. 5 June 1951, Reus, Catalonia; ed Universitat Autònoma de Barcelona, Institut del Teatre, Barcelona; founder and Dir Lliure Theatre, Barcelona 1976, co-Dir 1998–2000; worked in Poland; Asst to Giorgio Strehler, Italy 1978; Dir Centro Dramático Nacional, Teatro María Guerrero, Madrid 1983–89; Dir Odéon, Théâtre de l'Europe, Paris 1990–96; Dir Venice Theatre Biennale 1995–96; Commr Projecte Ciutat del Teatre, Barcelona City Council 1997–99; Officier des Arts et des Lettres; Nat. Theatre and Dance Prize 1984, Ciutat de Barcelona Prize 1985, Generalitat de Catalunya Prize 1988, Nat. Theatre Prize, Spanish Ministry of Culture 1991, Paris Chamber of Commerce Prize 1995, Egyptian Ministry of Culture's Hon. CIFET Prize 1995, Comunidad de Madrid Prize 2002, Max de Teatro Award 2003. *Plays directed include:* Luces de Bohemia (Valle Inclán) 1984, Sans Titre (Lorca) 1990, Le Balcon (Genet) 1991, Tirano Banderas (Valle Inclán) 1992; Le Chevalier d'Olméido (Lope de Vega) 1992, El Público (Lorca) 1986. *Operas directed include:* (Teatro de la Zarzuela, Madrid); Samson et Dalila (Saint-Saëns) 1982, Falstaff (Verdi) 1983, Don Carlo (Verdi) 1985, Il Trittico (Puccini) 1987, Il Turco in Italia (Rossini) 1990; La Vera Storia (Berio), Paris 1985, Maggio Musicale, Florence 1986, Falstaff, Bologna 1987. *Address:* c/o Teatre Lliure, plaça margarida xirgu, 1, 08004 Barcelona, Spain; c/o Matthias Vogt Artistic Management, 211 Gough Street, Suite 115, San Francisco, CA 94102, USA.

PASSACANTANDO, Franco, DEcon; Italian economist; *Managing Director for Relations with International Institutions, Banca d'Italia (Bank of Italy);* b. 7 Aug. 1947, Rome; m. Miriam Veronesi 1987; three s. one d.; ed Rome and Stanford Univs; Head, Money Market Div., Research Dept, Banca d'Italia (Bank of Italy) 1981–85, Task Force on the Reform of the Italian Payment System 1986–89, Dir Monetary and Financial Sector, Research Dept 1990–95, Head of Asset Man. Dept 2003–06, Man. Dir Cen. Banking, Markets and Payment Systems Area 2006–12, Man. Dir for Relations with Int. Insts 2012–; Exec. Dir World Bank Group 1995–2003, Chair. Budget Cttee, Audit Cttee, Steering Cttee; mem. T2S Project Steering Cttee, Cen. European Bank; mem. Cttee on Payment and Settlement Systems, BIS; mem. Econ. and Financial Cttee, EC; mem. Working Party 3, OECD; G7 Deputy; G20 Deputy; Chair. OTC Derivatives Regulators' Forum 2013–; Fulbright, Einaudi and Stringher fellowships. *Publications:* White Paper on the Payment System in Italy 1988, Le Banche e il Finanziamento delle Imprese 1997, Governance Reforms at the World Bank 2002, Building an International Framework for Monetary Stability: The Case of Italy 1979–1994 1996, The Loss of Confidence in Bank Money in the Great Depression; and articles on monetary policy in professional journals. *Leisure interests:* making movies, art. *Address:* Banca d'Italia, Via Nazionale, 91, 00184 Rome, Italy (office). *Telephone:* (06) 47923515 (office). *Fax:* (06) 47923883 (office). *E-mail:* franco.passacantando@bancaditalia.it (office). *Website:* www.bancaditalia.it (office).

PASSERA, Corrado, MBA; Italian banking executive and government official; b. 30 Dec. 1954, Como; m. Cecilia Canepa; one s. one d.; ed Bocconi Univ., Milan, Wharton School, Univ. of Pennsylvania; Sr Engagement Man., McKinsey & Co., Milan 1980–85; with CIR SpA, Milan 1985–86, COO 1988–90; Deputy Chair. Credito Romagnolo 1988–95; COO Arnoldo Mondadori Editore SpA 1990–91; Deputy Chair. and CEO Gruppo Espresso–Repubblica, Rome 1991–92; Man. Dir and Co-CEO Olivetti SpA, Ivrea 1992–96; Man. Dir and CEO Banco Ambrosiano Veneto 1996–98; Man. Dir and CEO Poste Italiane 1998–2002; Man. Dir and CEO Banca Intesa SpA (fmrly IntesaBci) 2002–06, Man. Dir and CEO Intesa Sanpaolo (following merger between Banca Intesa and Sanpaolo IMI) 2007–11; Minister of Econ. Devt, Infrastructure and Transport (in Mario Monti's 'govt of technocrats')

2011–13; Dir RCS MediaGroup, Bocconi Univ.; Dir and mem. Exec. Cttee Italian Bankers' Asscn (ABI); mem. Advisory Bd Scuola Normale, Pisa, Int. Advisory Bd Wharton School, Gen. Council Fondazione Giorgio Cini; Int. Business Hon. Degree (MIB School of Man. of Trieste) 2001, Man. Eng Hon. Degree (Politecnico of Bari) 2004. *Address:* c/o Ministry of Infrastructure and Transport, Piazzale Porta Pia 1, 000198 Rome, Italy.

PASSOS COELHO, Pedro Manuel Mamede; Portuguese economist and politician; *Prime Minister;* b. 24 July 1964, Coimbra; s. of António Passos Coelho and Maria Rodrigues Santos Mamede; m. 1st Fátima Padinha, two d.; m. 2nd Laura Ferreira, one d.; ed Univ. of Lisbon, Lusíada Univ.; mem. Assembleia da República (Parl.) for Lisbon 1991–99, for Vila Real 2011–; mem. Partido Social Democrata (PSD), Vice-Chair. PSD Parl. Group 1996–99, Vice-Pres. PSD 2005–06, Pres. 2010–; Prime Minister 2011–; consultant, Tecnoforma 2000–04. *Publication:* Mudar 2010. *Address:* Office of the Prime Minister, Presidency of the Council of Ministers, Rua da Imprensa à Estrela 4, 1200-888 Lisbon, Portugal (office). *Telephone:* (21) 3923500 (office). *Fax:* (21) 3951616 (office). *E-mail:* pm@pm.gov.pt (office). *Website:* www.portugal.gov.pt (office).

PASSY, Solomon Isaac, MS, PhD; Bulgarian politician and academic; b. 22 Dec. 1956, Plovdiv; m.; two s. one d.; ed Sofia Univ. 'St Kliment Ohridski'; in opposition to anti-Muslim policy of the Communist regime 1985–89; Asst Prof. of Math. Logic and Computer Science, Sofia Univ. 'St Kliment Ohridski' and at Bulgarian Acad. of Sciences 1984–94; participant in Nat. Round Table for transition to democracy 1989–90; activist of Ecoglasnost opposition movt 1989; Co-founder and mem. Coordinating Council of UDF 1990–91; Founding Pres. and CEO Atlantic Club of Bulgaria (first pro-Atlantic NGO in a non-NATO mem. state) 1991–2001; Founder and Spokesman, Green Party of Bulgaria 1989; Mem. Grand Nat. Ass. (Green Party, Union of Democratic Forces—UDF) 1990–91, (Nat. Movt Simeon II) 2005–, Chair. Foreign Affairs, Defence and Security Cttee, 39th Nat. Ass. July 2001, Foreign Affairs Cttee, 40th Nat. Ass. 2005–, Bulgaria–USA caucus, 40th Nat. Ass. 2005–; Minister of Foreign Affairs 2001–05; Vice-Pres. Nat. Movt Simeon II 2005, mem. Political Council 2002–05; Special Adviser on NATO accession to Govt of Macedonia 2007–; mem. 2nd, 3rd, 4th and 13th Bulgarian Antarctic Expeditions to Livingston Island, Antarctica 1993–2005; Leader, Bulgarian Del. for the Audience with Pope John Paul II 1994; Vice-Chair. Atlantic Treaty Asscn, Paris 1996–99; Hon. Citizen of Nedelino 2003, of State of Tex., USA 2004; Orden Infante Don Enrique (Grã-Cruz) (Portugal) 2002; Orden del Mérito Civil (Gran Cruz) (Spain) 2003; Order of Léopold II (Grand Cross) (Belgium) 2004; Ordine della Stella della Solidarieta' Italiana (I classe) (Italy) 2006; Orden de Isabel la Catolica (Gran Cruz) (Spain) 2006; Dr hc (South-West Univ. of Bulgaria) 2005; Balkan Peace Award 2004. *Publications:* numerous scientific articles on math. logic and computer science. *Address:* Foreign Affairs Committee, Bulgarian National Assembly, 1 Al. Battenberg Square, 1169 Sofia (office); National Movement Simeon II, 23 Vrabcha Street, 1000 Sofia, Bulgaria. *Telephone:* (2) 9861133 (office). *Fax:* (2) 9818568 (office). *E-mail:* kvp@parliament.bg; ndsv@ndsv.bg. *Website:* www.parliament.bg/kvp (office).

PASTERNAK, Anne, MA; American gallery director; *President and Artistic Director, Creative Time;* b. 1965; m. Mike Starn; one d.; ed Univ. of Massachusetts, Hunter Coll., New York; fmr Dir Stux Galleries, Boston and New York; fmr Curator, Real Art Ways, Hartford, Conn.; Co-founder and Dir BRAT (arts org.); Pres. and Artistic Dir Creative Time, New York 1994–; Advisor, Nat. Asscn of Artists Orgs, Public Art Seminar (SESC), São Paulo, Brazil, Artists' Museum, Negev, Israel, Hallwalls Contemporary Arts Center; fmr guest critic, Yale Univ.; Lecturer, School of Visual Arts, New York; panel mem. Pew Center for Arts and Heritage 2002, Philadelphia Exhbns Initiative 2009; mem. Bd White Columns (gallery) 1994–97. *Publications:* numerous essays in cultural publs; Creative Time: The Book 2007; contribs to Columbia Journal of American Studies, New York Times Magazine, Art New England, Journal of Contemporary Art. *Address:* Creative Time, 59 East 4th Street, 6th Floor, New York, NY 10003, USA (office). *Telephone:* (212) 206-6674 (office). *Fax:* (212) 255-8467 (office). *E-mail:* info@creativetime.org (office). *Website:* www.creativetime.org (office).

PASTORELLI, Jean, LenD; Monegasque civil servant, diplomatist and politician; *President, Telemontecarlo (TMC);* b. 20 June 1942, Monaco; m.; two c.; ed Institut d'Etudes Politiques, Diplome d'Etudes Supérieures de la Faculté de Droit de Paris, Ecole Nationale d'Admin (Fonctionnaire Etranger), Paris; joined Secr., Dept of Finance and Economy 1969; Dir Budget and Treasury 1978–88; Govt Counsellor for Finance and the Economy 1988–95; Pres. Radio Monte Carlo 1995–2000, Monaco Telecom 1997–99; Perm. Del. to Posteurop 1995–; Perm. Del. to ITU, UPU 1995–2004; Pres. Tele Monte Carlo 1995–, Monte Carlo Radiodiffusion (MCR) 1995–; Minister Plenipotentiary 1995; Perm. Del. to UNESCO 2003, to French-speaking community 2003; Perm. Rep. at IAEA 2003; Nat. Authority for Principality of Monaco to Org. for Prohibition of Chemical Weapons 2003, Perm. Rep. 2003–; Pres. EUTELSAT Ass. of Parties 2001–04, INTELSAT Ass. of Parties (ITSO) 2002–04; Amb. to Belgium, the Netherlands and Grand Duchy of Luxembourg 2003–07; Head of Mission to European Communities 2003–07, Observer within Int. Criminal Court 2003–; Govt Counsellor for External Relations 2007–08; Amb. to France 2008–11; Pres. Telemontecarlo (TMC) 2011–; Commdr, Ordre de Saint-Charles. *Address:* Telemontecarlo (TMC), 6 quai Antoine 1er, 98000 Monte Carlo, Monaco (office). *Telephone:* 93151415 (office). *Fax:* 93151436 (office). *Website:* www.tmc.tv (office).

PASTRANA ARANGO, Andrés, LLD; Colombian journalist, diplomatist and fmr head of state; b. 17 Aug. 1954, Bogotá; s. of Misael Pastrana Borrero (fmr Pres. of Colombia) and María Cristina Arango de Pastrana; m. Nohra Puyana Bickenbach; one s. two d.; ed Colegio San Carlos de Bogotá, Colegio Mayor de Nuestra Señora del Rosario Law School, Harvard Univ.; Founder and Man. Dir Revista Guión (political magazine) 1978–79; Man. Dir Datos y Mensajes SA News Broadcasting Co. 1979–80; Dir TV Hoy News 1980–87; Councillor Bogotá City Council 1982–86, Chair. Jan.–April 1983, 1984–85; Mayor of Bogotá 1988–90; Senator 1991–93; Founder and Presidential Cand. of Nueva Fuerza Democrática 1994; Pres. of Colombia 1998–2002; Amb. to USA 2005–06 (resgnd); mem. Int. Union of Local Authorities, Exec. Cttee 1989, Pres. Latin American Chapter 1988–89; Vice-Pres. Latin American Union of Capital Cities; Co-Dir World Mayors' Conf. on Drug Addiction, New York 1989, Madrid 1990; Sec. Gen. Union of Latin American Parties 1992, now Hon. Pres.; Adviser to UN Univ., Tokyo 1994; Founder and Dir

UN Leadership Acad., Jordan; fmr Chair. Bogotá Telephone Co., Bogotá Aqueduct and Sewerage Co., Electricity and Public Utilities Co. of Bogotá, Inst. for Urban Devt, Dist Planning; mem. Bd of Dirs Int. Foundation for Electoral Systems; Nat. Police Distinguished Service Order, UNESCO Order, Grand Cross, Civilian Order of Merit 1988, Order of Merit, Colombian Publishing Industry 1988, Civilian Defence Order 1989, Order of Santa Bárbara, Colombian Navy 1990, José María Córdova Order of Mil. Merit 1990; Colombian Jr Chamber Exec. of the Year 1981, King of Spain Int. Journalism Award 1985, Simón Bolívar Nat. Journalism Award 1987, King of Spain Nat. Journalism Award 1987, Bogotá Circle of Journalists Nat. Award 1987. *Publication:* Hacia la formulación de un derecho ecológico (Towards the formulation of an ecological law). *Address:* c/o Ministry of Foreign Affairs, Palacio de San Carlos, Calle 10a, No 5-51, Bogotá, DC, Colombia.

PASTUKHOV, Boris Nikolayevich; Russian politician; b. 10 Oct. 1933, Moscow; m. Janna Pastukhova; two d.; ed Bauman Higher Tech. Coll., Moscow; mem. CPSU 1959–91; First Sec. Bauman Regional Komsomol Cttee, Moscow 1959–61; Second Sec. Moscow City Komsomol Cttee 1961–62, First Sec. 1962–64; Second Sec. All-Union Komsomol Cttee 1964–77, First Sec. 1977–82; Chair. USSR State Cttee for Publishing, Printing and Bookselling, USSR Goskomizdat 1982–86; mem. Presidium, Supreme Soviet of the USSR 1978–83; USSR Amb. to Denmark 1986–89, to Afghanistan 1989–92; Deputy Foreign Minister of Russia 1989–96; First Deputy Foreign Minister 1996–98; mediator in negotiations between Georgia and Abkhazia; Minister for CIS Affairs 1998–99; Chair. Govt Cttee on CIS; mem. State Duma (Otechestvo) 1999–, re-elected 2003 (United Russia); mem. Cttee on Connections with Compatriots 2000–. *Address:* State Duma, Okhotny Ryad 1, 103265, Moscow, Russia. *Telephone:* (495) 292-59-95. *Fax:* (495) 292-41-90.

PASTUSIAK, Longin, PhD; Polish politician and academic; *Professor, Vistula University;* b. 22 Aug. 1935, Łódź; s. of Josef Pastusiak and Sabina Pastusiak; m. Anna Ochab; one s. one d.; ed Warsaw Univ., American Univ., Univ. of Virginia, USA; Prof. and Head Dept, Polish Inst. of Int. Affairs 1963–93; Deputy to Sejm (Parl.) 1991–2001, Vice-Chair. Foreign Affairs Cttee 1993–2001; Head, Polish Del. to WEU Ass. 1993–; Head, Polish Del. to NATO Parl. Ass. 1993–, Vice-Pres. 2002–; Senator 2001–05, Pres. of the Senate 2001–05; Prof. of Int. Relations, Gdansk Univ. 1994–2005; Prof., Vistula Univ., Warsaw 2005–, Higher School of Communications and Mass Media, Warsaw 2005–; Visiting Prof., Appalachian State Univ., USA; Silver Cross of Merit 1972, Kt's Cross 1985, Order of Merit (Lithuania) 2004, Grand Commdr's Cross (Lithuania) 2004; Dr hc (Naval Mil. Acad. Gdynia, Poland) 2003, Hon. DHumLitt (Appalachian State Univ.) 2004; Parliamentarian of the Year 1997, numerous scholarly awards. *Television:* various programmes on Polish public and pvt. TV. *Publications:* more than 80 books including Poland–Canada 1945–1961 1994, United States Diplomacy, 18th and 19th Century 1997, Chicago: Portrait of the City 1997, Will the World Come to an End? 1999, From the Secrets of the Diplomatic Archives: Polish–American Relations 1948–1954 1999, Ladies of the White House 2000, Presidents of the USA 2002; 800 scholarly publs and more than 3,000 articles in daily and weekly journals on American history and foreign policy, German studies, East–West relations, Polish foreign policy, Polish–American relations and theoretical aspects of int. relations. *Leisure interest:* tennis. *Address:* al. Niepodleglosci 151, Apt 21, 02-555 Warsaw, Poland. *Telephone:* (22) 8495044. *Fax:* (22) 8495044. *E-mail:* longin.pastusiak@mac.com.

PASWAN, Ram Vilas, BL, MA; Indian politician; *President, Lok Jan Shakti Party;* b. 5 July 1946, Shaharbanni, Bihar; s. of the late Jamun Paswan and Siya Devi; m. 1st Raj Kumari; two d.; m. 2nd Reena Sharma-Paswan; one s. one d.; ed Kosi Coll., Khagaria, Patna Univ.; mem. Bihar Legis. Ass. 1969; Gen. Sec. Lok Dal, Bihar 1974; mem. Lok Sabha 1977–, Leader of the House 1996; Gen. Sec. Janata Party 1987–88, Janata Dal 1988–90; Sec. Nat. Front 1988–90; Minister of Labour and Welfare 1989–90, of Railways 1996–98, of Communications 1999–2001, of Coal and Mines 2001–02, of Chemicals and Fertilizers and of Steel 2004–09; Pres. Lok Jan Shakti Party (formed following split from Janata Dal (United) 2000–; mem. Court of Jawaharlal Nehru Univ. 1998–99. *Leisure interests:* playing chess, social work. *Address:* Shaharbanni, Tola, Bellai, Khagaria 851 204 (home); Lok Jan Shakti Party, 14 Janpath, Firozshah Marg, New Delhi 110 001, India (office). *Telephone:* (11) 23017681 (office). *Fax:* (11) 23015249 (office). *E-mail:* info@lokjanshaktiparty.com (office). *Website:* www.lokjanshaktiparty.com (office).

PATABENDIGE DON, HE Cardinal Albert Malcolm Ranjith, BTh; Sri Lankan ecclesiastic; *Archbishop of Colombo;* b. 15 Nov. 1947, Polgahawela; s. of Don William and Mary Winifreeda; ed De La Salle Coll., Mutwal, St Aloysius Seminary, Borella, Nat. Seminary, Kandy, Pontifical Urbanian Univ. and Pontifical Biblical Inst., Rome, Hebrew Univ. of Jerusalem, Israel; ordained priest, Diocese of Colombo 1975; Asst Pastor in Pamunugama 1978, later served as Pastor in Payagala and Kalutara; est. Seth Sarana (centre for poor relief), Archdiocese of Colombo; named Nat. Dir Pontifical Mission Socs 1983; revived Soc. of the Holy Childhood; also served as Diocesan Co-ordinator for Human Devt; Auxiliary Bishop of Colombo 1991–95; Titular Bishop of Cabarsussi 1991–2004; Vicar Gen. in charge of Parochial Apostolate and Lay Apostolate 1991–95; Sec. Gen. Catholic Bishops' Conf. of Sri Lanka, Chair. Organizing Cttee for the Beatification of Venerable Joseph Vaz; first Bishop of Ratnapura 1995–2001; Adjunct Sec. Congregation for the Evangelisation of Peoples 2001–04; Pres. Pontifical Mission Socs 2001–04; Apostolic Nuncio (first Sri Lankan) to Indonesia and Timor-Leste 2004–05; Titular Archbishop of Umbriatico 2004–; Sec. Congregation for Divine Worship and the Discipline of the Sacraments 2005–09; Archbishop of Colombo 2009–; cr. Cardinal (Cardinal-Priest of San Lorenzo in Lucina) 2010; participated in Papal Conclave 2013. *Address:* Archbishop's House, 976 Gnanartha Pradeepaya Mawatha, Colombo 8, Sri Lanka (office). *Telephone:* (11) 2695471 (office). *Fax:* (11) 2692009 (office). *E-mail:* info@archdioceseofcolombo .com (office). *Website:* www.archdioceseofcolombo.com (office).

PATAIL, Hon. Tan Sri Abdul Gani, LLB (Hons); Malaysian lawyer; *Attorney-General;* b. 6 Oct. 1955; m. 1st YBhg. Puan Sri Datin Seri; m. 2nd Panglima Maimun Datuk Haji Arif; ed Univ. of Malaya; began legal career as a Deputy Public Prosecutor in Kota Kinabalu, Sabah 1980; promoted to Sr Fed. Counsel for Sabah 1985; moved to Attorney-Gen.'s Chambers, Kuala Lumpur 1994, Sr Public Prosecutor 1994–95, 2000–01, Head of Advisory and Int. Div. 1995–97, Commr of Law Revision 1997–2000, Attorney-Gen. 2002–; involved in numerous high-profile cases, led prosecution of fmr Deputy Prime Minister Anwar Ibrahim in trials involving corruption and sodomy 1998. *Address:* Attorney-General's Chambers, 45

Persiaran Perdana, Precint 4, 62100 Putrajaya, Malaysia (office). *Telephone:* (603) 8872-2000 (office). *Fax:* (603) 8890-5670 (office). *E-mail:* pro@agc.gov.my (office). *Website:* www.agc.gov.my (office).

PATAKI, George E., BA, JD; American lawyer, politician and fmr state official; *Counsel, Chadbourne & Parke LLP;* b. 24 June 1945, Peekskill, NY; m. Elizabeth Rowland; two s. two d.; ed Yale Univ., Columbia Univ. Law School; Assoc. Dewey Ballantine PC (law firm), New York 1970–74; Pnr, Plunkett & Jaffee PC (law firm), White Plains and New York; Co-Owner, Pataki's Farm, Peekskill, NY; Mayor of Peekskill 1981–84; mem. New York State Ass. 1985–92; mem. New York State Senate 1993–94; Gov. of New York State 1994–2007; Counsel, Chadbourne & Parke LLP (law firm), New York 2007–; Republican. *Address:* Chadbourne & Parke LLP, 30 Rockefeller Plaza, New York, NY 10112, USA (office). *Telephone:* (212) 408-5145 (office). *E-mail:* gpataki@chadbourne.com (office). *Website:* www .chadbourne.com (office).

PATCHETT, Ann, BA, MFA; American writer; b. 2 Dec. 1963, Los Angeles; ed Sarah Lawrence Coll. and Univ. of Iowa Writers' Workshop; Writer-in-Residence, Allegheny Coll. 1989–90; Yaddo Fellow 1990; Millay Fellow 1990; Resident Fellow, Fine Arts Work Center, Provincetown 1990–91; Visiting Asst Prof., Murray State Univ. 1992; Bunting Fellow, Mary Ingram Bunting Inst., Radcliffe Coll. 1993; Guggenheim Fellowship 1994; Nashville Banner Tenn. Writer of the Year Award 1994. *Publications:* The Patron Saint of Liars (Univ. of Iowa James A. Michener/ Copernicus Award for a book in progress 1989, American Library Asscn Notable Book 1992) 1992, Taft (Janet Heidinger Kafka Prize) 1994, The Magician's Assistant 1997, Bel Canto (PEN/Faulkner Award 2002, Orange Prize 2002) 2001, Truth and Beauty (biog.) 2004, Run 2007, What Now? 2008, State of Wonder 2011; contribs to anthologies and to periodicals, including The New York Times Magazine, Chicago Tribune, Boston Globe, Vogue, GQ, Elle, Gourmet. *Address:* c/o Author Mail, 11th Floor, Harper Collins Publishers, 10 East 53rd Street, New York, NY 10022, USA (office). *Website:* www.annpatchett.com (office).

PATE, John Stewart, DSc, PhD, FAA, FRS; British scientist and academic; *Emeritus Professor of Botany, University of Western Australia;* b. 15 Jan. 1932; s. of H. S. Pate and M. M. Pate; m. Elizabeth L. Sloan 1959 (died 2004); three s.; ed Campbell Coll. Belfast and Queen's Univ. Belfast; lecturer in Botany, Univ. of Sydney 1957–60; lecturer in Botany, Queen's Univ. Belfast 1960–65, then Reader, Personal Chair. in Plant Physiology 1970–83; Prof. of Botany, Univ. of W Australia 1974–2001, Emer. Prof. 2001–; Hon. DSc (Univ. of W Australia); Australian Minerals and Energy Research Foundation Award 1999, Commonwealth Centenary Medal 2003. *Publications:* Restionaceae and Allied Families of Australia 1999 (co.-ed.); over 350 books, research articles, reviews, chapters for textbooks and conf. proceedings. *Leisure interests:* music, reading, nature study, writing nature books, committed Christian. *Address:* Department of Plant Sciences, University of Western Australia, Nedlands, WA 6009 (office); 681 Mount Shadforth Road, Denmark, WA 6333, Australia. *Telephone:* (9) 848-1096.

PATEL, A. K., MB; Indian politician and medical practitioner; b. 1 July 1931, Vadu, Mehsana Dist, Gujarat; s. of Kalidas Patel; m. Divaben Patel; two s. one d.; ed B. J. Medical Coll., Ahmedabad; mem. Gujarat Legis. Ass. –1984; mem. for Mehsana, Lok Sabha 1984–, Minister of State for Chemicals and Fertilizers 1998–99; Pres. Bharatiya Janata Party, Gujarat 1982–85; mem. Rajya Sabha; Man. Trustee, SRST Gen. Hosp., Vijapur, Asha Educ. Trust, Girls' Coll., Vijapur; Trustee St Joseph Public School, Vijapur. *Leisure interests:* reading, swimming, riding, sports. *Address:* 30 Canning Lane, New Delhi 110 001 (office); nr T. B. Hospital, Bhavsor, Vijapur 384 001, India (home). *Telephone:* (11) 3722922; (27) 6320080 (home).

PATEL, Dev; British actor; b. 3 April 1990, Harrow, Middx, England; s. of Raj Patel and Anita Patel; partner Freida Pinto 2009–; ed Longfield Middle School, Whitmore High School, Rayners Lane Acad. of Taekwon-do. *Films include:* Slumdog Millionaire (Black Reel Award for Best Actor 2008, Black Reel Award for Best Breakthrough Performance 2008, British Ind. Film Award for Most Promising Newcomer 2008, Chicago Film Critics Asscn Award for Most Promising Performer 2008, Nat. Board of Review Award for Best Breakthrough Performance 2008, Phoenix Film Critics Soc. Award for Break Out On Camera 2008, Washington, DC Area Film Critics Asscn Award for Best Breakthrough Performance 2008, Critics' Choice Award for Best Young Performer (Actor/Actress) 2009, Richard Attenborough Film Award for Best Breakthrough 2009, Richard Attenborough Film Award for Rising Star of the Year 2009) 2008, The Last Airbender 2010, The Commuter (short) 2010, The Best Exotic Marigold Hotel 2011, Cherry 2012. *Television includes:* Skins (series) 2007–08, Mister Eleven (mini-series) 2009, True Jackson, VP (series) 2010, The Newsroom (series) 2012–13. *Achievements include:* competed regularly in both nat. and int. Taekwon-do championships, including Action Int. Martial Arts Asscn World Championships, Dublin 2004, won a bronze medal; bronze medal, World Championships 2004; gained a 1st dan black belt 2006. *Address:* c/o Sarah Spear, Curtis Brown Ltd, 28–29 Haymarket, London, SW1Y 4SP, England (office). *Telephone:* (20) 7393-4466 (office). *Fax:* (20) 7393-4401 (office). *E-mail:* spearclissoldoffice@curtisbrown.co.uk (office). *Website:* www.curtisbrown.co.uk (office).

PATEL, Dinsha Jhaverbhai; Indian politician; *Minister of Mines;* b. 25 May 1937, Itola, Baroda Dist, Gujarat; s. of the late Jhaverbhai Patel and Hiraben J. Patel; m. Kundanben Dinsha Patel; started political career as youth leader 1956; mem. Nagar Palika (municipal council), Nadiad, Gujarat 1972–82; mem. Gujarat Legis. Ass. 1975–96; Minister of Public Works and Parl. Affairs, Govt of Gujarat 1990–95; elected to 11th Lok Sabha (lower house of Parl.) for Kheda constituency (Gujarat) 1996–98, re-elected to 12th Lok Sabha 1998–99, 13th Lok Sabha 1999–2004, 14th Lok Sabha 2004–09, 15th Lok Sabha 2009–; Union Cabinet Minister of State for Petroleum and Natural Gas 2006–09, Minister of State (Ind. Charge) for Micro, Small and Medium Enterprises 2009–11, Minister of State for Mines 2011–12, Minister of Mines 2012–; mem. Exec. Cttee Gujarat Cricket Asscn. *Leisure interests:* hockey, cricket. *Address:* Ministry of Mines, 'A' Wing, 3rd Floor, Shastri Bhavan, Dr Rajendra Prasad Road, New Delhi, India (office). *Telephone:* (11) 23385173 (office). *Fax:* (11) 23384682 (office). *E-mail:* secy-mines@nic.in (office). *Website:* mines.nic.in (office).

PATEL, Lilian; Malawi politician; b. 21 Feb. 1951; four d.; ed Malawi Polytechnic, Univ. of New Delhi, India; sec. 1970–80; Man. Dir Holiday Motel and Budu Estate, Mangochi 1981; Ward Counsellor Mangochi Town Council 1989–92, Chair. (acting) 1991–92; elected MP for Mangochi South 1994; Sec. Women's Parl. Caucus 1995–99; Minister of Gender, Youth and Community Services 1996–99, of Health and Population 1999–2000, of Foreign Affairs and Int. Co-operation 2000–04, of Labour and Vocational Training 2004–05; Chair. Cabinet Cttee on Gender, Youth and Persons with Disabilities 1999; mem. United Democratic Front. *Address:* United Democratic Front (UDF), PO Box 5446, Limbe, Malawi (office).

PATEL, Praful Raojibhai Chaturbhai; British campaigner and business executive; *President, Que Capital Limited;* b. 7 March 1939, Jinja, Uganda; s. of Raojibhai Chaturbhai Patel and Maniben Jivabhai Lalaji Patel; ed Govt Secondary School and London Inst. of World Affairs, Univ. Coll., London; Gen. Sec. Uganda Students' Union 1956–58; Del. to Int. Youth Ass., New Delhi 1958; arrived in UK as student, then commenced commercial and financial services activities 1962; Pres. Nava Kala India Socio-Cultural Centre, London 1962–75; Hon. Sec. All-Party Parl. Cttee on UK Citizenship 1968–82; Founder and Council mem. UK Immigration Advisory Service 1970–82; Chair. Bd of Trustees, Swaminarayan Hindu Mission, UK 1970–76; mem. Uganda Resettlement Bd 1972–74; Hon. Sec. Uganda Evacuees Resettlement Advisory Trust 1974–2000; Jt Convener Asian Action Cttee 1976; mem. Indian Govt Consultative Cttee on Non-Resident Indian Investments 1986–91; adviser to His Holiness Pramukh Swami Maharaj on NGO activities, continues to support the activities of Worldwide Swaminarayan Fellowship; initiator of many inter-faith dialogues with spiritual leaders in India and abroad, including organizing many recitations of Hindu scriptures; fmr Gov. City Lit Coll., London; cand. (Labour) for Brent N constituency 1986; organized historic trip of His Holiness Sant Shri Morari Bapu to Kailas Manasarovar, Tibet, China in 1997; Dir Indo-British Cultural Exchange 2002–; Chair. 40th Anniversary British Uganda Asian Celebration Cttee 2012–; Pres. Que Capital Ltd 2013–; fmr Chair. Asia Fuel Ltd; Chair. and Trustee, Manava Trust 1979–; Trustee and Gen. Sec. Int. Ayurveda Foundation, UK 2002–; involved in industrial, cultural and educational projects affecting immigrants in UK; spokesman for Asians in UK following restrictions of immigration resulting from Commonwealth Immigrants Act 1968; active campaigner for civil and human rights issues, co-operation between Third World countries and investments in India; mem. British Labour Party, Charter '88 Movt, UK Democratic Audit; UK Del. to Indo-British Conf. on Democracy and Human Rights organized by Rajiv Gandhi Foundation, New Delhi; specialist on immigration, citizenship and race-relation issues; Trustee, The Charutar Arogya Mandal Trust, UK 1980, India Overseas Trust 2002–, Kailas Manasarovar Trust 2002–; Queen's Scout 1956, Asian Times Award for achievement 1986, Neasden Swaminarayan Mandir Award. *Dance:* Nritya Natika Ramayana (producer) 1982. *Film:* Kailas Manasarovar Yatra (producer). *Publications:* numerous articles in newspapers and journals on political, immigration, race relations and business related issues. *Leisure interests:* cricket, campaigning and lobbying, current affairs, promoting traditional Ayurveda medicines, inter-faith co-operation, passionate about his unique collection of more than 3,000 Ganesh Murtis (idols) and Hindu artifacts. *Address:* 60 Bedford Court Mansions, Bedford Avenue, London, WC1B 3AD, England (home); Praful Patel Associates, Readymoney Mansion, 3rd Floor, 43 Veer Nariman Road, Mumbai, 400023 India (office); Que Capital Ltd, Office 1905, INDEX Tower, Dubai International Financial Centre, PO Box 506581, Dubai, United Arab Emirates (office). *Telephone:* (20) 7580-0897 (London) (home); (22) 22049248 (India) (office); (4) 818-4014 (Dubai) (office). *Fax:* (20) 7436-2418 (London) (home); (22) 22048938 (India) (office); (4) 432-5783 (Dubai) (office). *E-mail:* prcpatel@vsnl.com (home); praful.patel@quecap.com (office). *Website:* www.quecap.com (office); www .prafulpatel.co.uk.

PATERSON, David Alexander, BA, JD; American academic, politician and fmr state governor; *Guest Lecturer, New York University;* b. 20 May 1954, Brooklyn, NY; s. of Basil Paterson and Portia Paterson (née Hairston); m. Michelle Paige 1992; one s. one step-d.; ed Hempstead High School, Columbia Univ., New York, Hofstra Law School; born legally blind; worked for Queens Dist Attorney's Office (failed NY Bar examination); joined campaign staff of David Dinkins for Manhattan Borough Pres. 1985; won selection process to serve remainder of term in NY State Senate for 30th Senate Dist following death of Senator Bogues 1985, youngest senator when elected aged 31, won seat for first full term representing 29th Dist 1986–2007; ran in Democratic primary for office of New York Public Advocate 1993; elected by Democratic Caucus of Senate as Minority Leader (first non-white state legis. leader and highest-ranking black elected official in history of NY State) 2002; mem. Democratic Nat. Cttee, Bd Democratic Legis. Campaign Cttee; selected as running mate by NY Attorney Gen. and Democratic Party nominee Eliot Spitzer in NY gubernatorial election 2006; Lt-Gov. of NY (first legally blind lt-gov.) 2006–08, Gov. of NY (first African American) 2008–10; Guest Lecturer, New York Univ. 2011–; fmr Adjunct Prof., Columbia Univ. School of Int. and Public Affairs; mem. Bd of Dirs Achilles Track Club; mem. Nat. Asscn for the Advancement of Colored People (mem. Bd of Dirs Mid-Manhattan Br.), Allen Black Bar Asscn, New York State Bar Asscn, Metropolitan Cttee of 100 (legal adviser), Martin Luther King Democratic Club; mem. Bd of Trustees, American Foundation for the Blind; Community Service Award, New Hampshire Hairston Clan 1984, Achievement Award, Courtsman A.A., Inc. 1986, named Senator of Year, New York State Nat. Org. of Women 1989, Migel Award, American Foundation for Blind 1996, named to The Power 150, Ebony magazine 2008. *Achievement:* ran New York City Marathon 1999. *Publications:* numerous articles in professional journals. *Leisure interests:* playing basketball, fan of New York sports teams, theatre, history. *Address:* College of Arts and Science, New York University, The Silver Center, 100 Washington Square East, New York, NY 10003, USA (office). *Website:* cas.nyu.edu (office).

PATERSON, Sir Dennis Craig, Kt, MB, BS, MD, FRCS, FRACS; Australian orthopaedic surgeon; b. 14 Oct. 1930, Adelaide, S Australia; s. of Gilbert Charles Paterson and Thelma Drysdale Paterson; m. Mary Mansell Hardy 1955 (died 2004); one s. three d.; m. Katalin Clara Maria Line 2006; ed Collegiate School of St Peter, Adelaide, Univ. of Adelaide; Resident Medical Officer, Royal Adelaide Hosp. 1954, Adelaide Children's Hosp. 1956; Registrar, Robert Jones and Agnes Hunt Orthopaedic Hosp., Oswestry, Shropshire, England 1958–60; Sr Registrar, Royal Adelaide Hosp. 1960–62; Consultant Orthopaedic Surgeon, Repatriation Gen.

Hosp., Adelaide 1962–70; Asst Hon. Orthopaedic Surgeon, Adelaide Children's Hosp. 1964–66, Sr Hon. Orthopaedic Surgeon 1966–70, Dir and Chief Orthopaedic Surgeon 1970–95, mem. Bd of Man., Chair. Medical Advisory Cttee, Medical Staff Cttee 1976–84; Sr Hon. Orthopaedic Surgeon, Queen Victoria and Modbury Hosps, Adelaide 1970–95; Sr Visiting Consultant Orthopaedic Surgeon, Royal Adelaide Hosp. 1962–85; Clinical Assoc. Prof. Orthopaedic Surgery Univ. of Adelaide 1990–; mem. Bd of Orthopaedic Surgery, Royal Australasian Coll. of Surgeons 1974–82, 1984–87, Chair. 1977–82, mem. Court of Examiners 1974–84; Censor-in-Chief, Australian Orthopaedic Asscn 1976–80, Dir Continuing Educ. 1982–86; Pres. Crippled Children's Asscn of S. Australia 1970–84; Pres. Int. Soc. of Orthopaedic Surgery and Traumatology 1987–90; Chair. S Australia Road Safety Consultative Council 1994–99, Trauma Systems Cttee of S Australia 1994–2000; mem. Bd Man. McLaren Vale and Fleurian Visitor Centre 1995–2001, Chair. 1998–2001; Chair. Southern Partnership 1997–2000; mem. Archbishops' Appeal Cttee 1993–2005, Cttee of the Commonwealth Club of South Australia (currently Vice-Pres.), Probus Club of Glen Osmond (currently Vice-Pres.), South Australian Cricket Asscn, Royal Adelaide Golf Club; Queen's Jubilee Medal 1977, L.O. Betts Medal in Orthopaedic Surgery 1980. *Publications:* Electrical Stimulation and Osteogenesis (thesis) 1982; more than 80 articles in peer-reviewed scientific journals. *Leisure interests:* golf, tennis, gardening. *Address:* 26 Queen Street, Glenunga, South Australia 5064, Australia (home). *Telephone:* (8) 8379-2669 (home). *Fax:* (8) 8379-6449 (home). *E-mail:* paterson@awam.com.au (home).

PATERSON, Rt Rev. John Campbell, BA, LTh; New Zealand ecclesiastic; b. 4 Jan. 1945, Auckland; s. of Thomas Paterson and Mary Paterson; m. Marion Reid Anderson 1968; two d.; ed King's Coll., Univ. of Auckland, St John's Coll.; asst curate, Whangarei 1969–71; vicar, Waimate N Maori pastorate 1971–76; Priest-in-Charge, Hokianga 1973–74, Bay of Islands 1974–75; Chaplain, Queen Victoria School 1976–82; Asst Priest, Maori Mission 1976–82; Sec. Bishopric of Aotearoa 1978–87; Prov. Sec. 1986–92; mem. Anglican Consultative Council 1990–96, Chair. 2002; Gen. Sec. of Anglican Church, Aotearoa, Polynesia and NZ 1992–95, Presiding Bishop and Primate of Anglican Church, Aotearoa, Polynesia and NZ 1998–2004; Bishop of Auckland 1995–2010; Outstanding Old Collegian Award King's Coll. 2000, Univ. of Auckland Distinguished Alumni Award 2004. *Publications:* He Toenga Whatiwhatinga 1984. *Leisure interests:* literature, music. *Address:* Bishopscourt, PO Box 37242, Parnell 1033, New Zealand (home). *Telephone:* (9) 302-7202 (home). *Fax:* (9) 377-6962 (home). *E-mail:* bishop .auckland@xtra.co.nz (office).

PATERSON, Katherine Womeldorf; American children's writer; b. 31 Oct. 1932, Qing Jiang, People's Republic of China; m. John Paterson 1962; four c.; ed King Coll., Union Theological Seminary; Nat. Amb. to Young People's Literature, Library of Congress 2010–; Drr hc (St Mary of the Woods), (Univ. of Maryland), (Hope Coll.), (Otterbein Coll.), (Presbyterian Coll.), (King Coll.), (Norwich Univ.), (Saint Michael's Coll.), (Shenandoah Coll. and Conservatory), (Washington and Lee Univ.), (Mount Saint Vincent Univ., Canada); Union Theological Seminary Union Medal, New York, Univ. of Southern Mississippi Medallion 1983, Univ. of Minnesota Kerlan Award 1983, Keene State Coll. Children's Literature Award 1987, Catholic Library Asscn Regina Medal 1988, New England Book Award 1992, Tulsa Public Library Anne V. Zarrow Award 1993, Education Press Friend of Education Award 1993, Hans Christian Andersen Medal for Writing 1998, New York Public Library Lion 1998, Library of Congress Living Legend Award 2000, Boston Public Library Literary Light 2000, Astrid Lindgren Memorial Award 2006, NSK Neustadt Prize for Children's Literature 2007, Laura Ingalls Wilder Medal 2013. *Publications include:* novels: Bread and Roses, Too, Bridge to Terabithia (Newbery Medal 1978, Lewis Carroll Shelf Award 1978, Janusz Korczak Medal, Poland 1981, Silver Pencil Award, Netherlands 1981, Grand Prix des Jeunes Lecturs, France 1986, Colorado Blue Spruce Young Adult Book Award 1986), Come Sing, Jimmy Jo, The Day of the Pelican, Flip-Flop Girl, The Great Gilly Hopkins (Nat. Book Award 1979, Newbery Honor Award 1979, Jane Addams Children's Book Award 1979, Christopher Award 1979), Jacob Have I Loved (Newbery Medal 1981), Jip, his Story (Scott O'Dell Award for Historical Fiction 1997), Lyddie (Int. Bd of Books for Young People Honor Book 1994, IBBY Honor Book), The Master Puppeteer (Nat. Book Award for Childrens Literature 1977, MWA Edgar Allen Poe Special Award 1977), Of Nightingales that Weep (Children's Literature Asscn Phoenix Award 1994), Park's Quest, Preacher's Boy (Jefferson Cup of Virginia Library Asscn), Rebels of the Heavenly Kingdom, The Same Stuff as Stars (Paterson Prize 2003, Jane Addams Award 2003, Judy Lopez Memorial Award 2003), Sign of the Chrysanthemum; picture books: The Angel and the Donkey, Blueberries for the Queen, Celia and the Sweet, Sweet Water, The King's Equal, The Tale of the Mandarin Ducks (Boston Globe/Horn Book Picture Book Award 1991), The Wide-Awake Princess; non-fiction: Consider the Lilies, Gates of Excellence, Images of God, The Invisible Child, A Sense of Wonder, The Spying Heart, Who Am I?. *Address:* c/o Harper Collins Publishers, Elsinore House, 77 Fulham Palace Road, London, W6 8JB, England. *Website:* www.terabithia.com.

PATERSON, Mervyn Silas, FAA, ScD; Australian geophysicist; *Visiting Fellow and Emeritus Professor, Research School of Earth Sciences, Australian National University;* b. 7 March 1925, South Australia; s. of Charles Paterson and Edith M. Michael; m. Katalin Sarosy 1952; one s. one d.; ed Adelaide Technical High School, Univs of Adelaide and Cambridge; research, Aeronautical Research Labs, Melbourne 1945–53; ANU, Canberra 1953–, Prof. Research School of Earth Sciences 1987–90, Visiting Fellow and Emer. Prof. 1990–; Consultant Australian Scientific Instruments Pty Ltd; Fellow American Mineralogical Soc., American Geophysical Union; Hon. Fellow Geological Soc. of America 1987, Walter H Bucher medal of American Geophysical Union 2004. *Publications:* Experimental Rock Deformation: The Brittle Field 1978; about 110 research papers in rock deformation and materials science. *Leisure interests:* walking, reading. *Address:* Research School of Earth Sciences, Australian National University, Canberra 0200, Australia. *Telephone:* (2) 6125-2497 (office). *Fax:* (2) 6125-0738.

PATERSON, Rt Hon. Owen William, PC, MA; British politician; *Secretary of State for Environment, Food and Rural Affairs;* b. 24 June 1956, Whitchurch, Salop., England; m. The Hon. Rose Ridley 1980; two s. one d.; ed Abberley Hall School, Radley Coll., Corpus Christi Coll., Cambridge, Nat. Leathersellers Coll. (now British School of Leather Tech. at Univ. of Northampton); joined British Leather Co. (family leather business) 1979, Sales Dir 1983–94, Man. Dir 1994–99;

Dir, Parsons & Sons (leather co.), Halesowen 1990s; contested Wrexham constituency 1992; MP for N Shropshire 1997–, mem. (Select Cttees), Welsh Affairs 1997–2001, European Standing Cttee A 1998–2001, Welsh Grand Cttee 1998–2000, European Scrutiny 1999–2000, Agric. 2000–01; Opposition Whip 2000–01; Parl. Pvt. Sec. to Iain Duncan Smith as Leader of the Opposition 2001–03; Shadow Minister for Environment, Food and Rural Affairs 2003–05, for Transport 2005–07; Shadow Sec. of State for NI 2007–10; Sec. of State for NI 2010–12, for Environment, Food and Rural Affairs 2012–; Vice-Pres. Conservatives Against a Fed. Europe 1998–2001; mem. 92 Group 1997–, Conservative Friends of Israel 1997–, Conservative Way Forward 1997–, Conservative 2000 1997–, No Turning Back Group 1998–, Exec. 1922 Committee 2000; Pres. Cotance (European Tanners' Confed.) 1996–98; mem. Inter-Parl. Union 1997–, Commonwealth Parl. Asscn 1997–, Advisory Bd European Foundation 1998–; Conservative; Liveryman of the Leathersellers' Co. *Leisure interests:* horses, racing and eventing, trees, architecture, history. *Address:* Department for Environment, Food and Rural Affairs, Nobel House, 17 Smith Square, London, SW1P 3JR (office); House of Commons, Westminster, London, SW1A 0AA, England. *Telephone:* (20) 7238-5339 (Dept) (office); (20) 7219-5185 (Westminster). *Fax:* (20) 7238-6465 (Dept) (office); (20) 7219-3955 (Westminster). *E-mail:* owen.paterson@defra.gsi .gov.uk (office); patersono@parliament.uk; owen@shellbrook.demon.co.uk. *Website:* www.defra.gov.uk (office); www.owenpaterson.org.

PATERSON, William Edgar, OBE, MSc, PhD, FRSE, FRSA; British academic; *Honorary Professor of German and European Politics, Aston University;* b. 26 Sept. 1941, Blair Atholl, Scotland; s. of William Edgar Paterson and Winnie Paterson (née McIntyre); m. 1st Jacqueline Cramb 1964 (died 1974); two s.; m. 2nd Phyllis MacDowell 1979; one d. one step-s. one step-d.; ed Morrison's Acad., Univ. of St Andrews, London School of Econs; Lecturer in Int. Relations, Univ. of Aberdeen 1967–70; Volkswagen Lecturer in German Politics, Univ. of Warwick 1970–75, Sr Lecturer 1975–82, Reader 1982–89, Prof. and Chair. of Dept 1989–90; Salvesen Prof. and Dir of Europa Inst., Univ. of Edin. 1990–94; Dir Inst. for German Studies, Univ. of Birmingham 1994–2008, now Emer. Prof. in German Politics; currently Hon. Prof. in German and European Politics, Aston Centre for Europe, Aston Univ.; Chair. Asscn for the Study of German Politics 1974–76, Univ. Asscn for Contemporary European Studies 1989–94; Vice-Chair. German-British Forum 1996, Chair. 2005–13; mem. Econ. and Social Research Council Research Priorities Bd 1994–99, British Königswinter Cttee 1995–, Kuratorium Allianz Kulturstiftung 2001–04; Co-Ed. German Politics 1991–2001, Journal of Common Market Studies 2003–08; Academician, Acad. of Learned Socs in Social Sciences 2000; Bundesverdienstkreuz (Germany) 1999; Lifetime Award, Asscn for the Study of German Politics 2004, Lifetime Award, Univ. Asscn for Contemporary European Studies 2007, Special Recognition Award for excellence in German politics, European integration and the study of German-British relations, Political Studies Asscn. *Publications include:* The Federal Republic of Germany and the European Community (with Simon Bulmer) 1987, Government and the Chemical Industry (with Wyn Grant) 1988, Developments in German Politics II 1996, The Kohl Chancellorship (with Clay Clemens) 1998, The Future of the German Economy (with Rebecca Harding) 2000, Developments in German Politics 3 2003, Governance in Contemporary Germany: The Semisovereign State Revisited (co-ed.) 2005, Germany's Gathering Crisis (co-ed) 2009, Research Agendas in European Union Studies (co-ed) 2010, Developments in German Politics 4 2014; 20 other books and over 120 articles in learned journals. *Leisure interest:* walking. *Address:* 220 Myton Road, Warwick, CV34 6PS, England (home). *Telephone:* (1926) 492492 (home). *E-mail:* w.paterson@aston.ac.uk (office).

PATHMANATHAN, Selvarasa, (Shanmugam Kumaran Tharmalingam); Sri Lankan rebel leader; *Leader, Liberation Tigers of Tamil Eelam (LTTE);* b. 6 April 1955, Kankesanthurai, Jaffna Dist; ed Nadeswara Coll., Kankesanthurai, Mahajana Coll., Thellipalai, Jaffna Univ.; left Sri Lanka and fled to India after outbreak of civil war in 1983, began procuring arms and equipment for Liberation Tigers of Tamil Eelam (LTTE) (Tamil separatist group), in exile in Malaysia 1987–90, in Thailand 1990; apptd Head of Dept of Int. Relations, Jan. 2009, Chief LTTE Int. Spokesman during last months of civil war in 2009, Leader, LTTE July 2009–, arrested Aug. 2009.

PATIASHVILI, Jumber Ilich; Georgian politician; *Co-Chair, Unity Alliance (Ertoba);* b. 5 Jan. 1940, Lagodekhi, Kakheti Oblast; m.; two c.; ed Tbilisi Agricultural Inst.; worked for the Komsomol (V. I. Lenin Young Communist League) from 1966, subsequently for Communist Party; Dir Land Inst. of Georgia 1980–2000; apptd First Sec. Communist Party of Georgian SSR 1985–89 (resgnd after Soviet troops killed demonstrators in Tbilisi); cand. for presidency 1995, 2000; Founder and Leader of Unity Alliance (Ertoba) (social-democratic party which contested gen. election as part of Jumber Patiashvili-Unity bloc 2003), currently Co-Chair. *Address:* Unity Alliance (Ertoba), Svobodi pl., Tbilisi, Georgia (office). *Telephone:* (32) 92-30-65 (office). *Fax:* (32) 93-46-94 (office). *E-mail:* ertoba@post.com (office).

PATIL, Dnyandeo Yashwantrao, MA, LLB, PhD; Indian educationalist and government official; *Governor of Bihar;* b. 22 Oct. 1935, Ambap village, Kolhapur, Maharashtra; ed Shivaji Univ., Kolhapur; mem. Kolhapur Municipal Council (Indian Nat. Congress) 1957–62; mem. Maharashtra Vidhan Sabha (state legis. ass.) for Panhala Vidhan Sabha constituency 1967–78; Founding Pres. D. Y. Patil Educational Acad., Ramrao Adik Educ. Soc., Dr D. Y. Patil Pratishthan, D. Y. Patil Educ. Soc., Continental Medicare Foundation; Gov. of Tripura 2009–13, of Bihar 2013–; mem. Indian Nat. Congress party; Dr hc (Nottingham Trent Univ.) 2000; Padma Shri 1991, Manapatra Award, Kolhapur Municipal Corpn 2000, Special Award, Fourth Zorostasian Dental Congress 2000, Vocational Excellence Award, Rotary Int. Dist 3140 2000, Rajiv Gandhi Award 2007. *Address:* Office of the Governor, Raj Bhavan, Patna, India (office). *Telephone:* (612) 2221230 (office). *Fax:* (612) 2232868 (office). *E-mail:* governorbihar@nic.in (office); governor.bih.nic.in.

PATIL, Pratibha Devisingh, LLB, MA; Indian politician and fmr head of state; b. 19 Dec. 1934, Jalgaon, Mahar; d. of Narayanrao and Gangaji Patil; m. D. R. Shekhawat; one s. one d.; ed Mooljee Jetha Coll., Jalgaon, Govt Law Coll., Mumbai; mem. Maharashtra Legis. Ass. 1962–85, Deputy Minister 1967–72, Cabinet Minister for Social Welfare 1972–74, for Public Health and Social Welfare 1974–75, for Prohibition, Rehabilitation and Cultural Affairs 1975–76, for Educ. 1977–78, for Urban Devt and Housing 1982–83; Deputy Chair. Rajya Sabha

(Council of States, Parl.) 1986–88; mem. Lok Sabha 1991; Gov. of Rajasthan 2004–07; Pres. of India 2007–12; Vice-Chair. Nat. Fed. for Co-operative Urban Banks and Credit Soc.; Chair. Bhartiya Granin Mahila Sangh, Mahar; Organizer, Women Home Guards, Jalgaon Dist 1962; mem. Standing Cttee, All India Women's Council; Convener, Women's Conf., Delhi. *Leisure interest:* social service. *Address:* 57 New Congress Nagar, Opposite. Government Milk Scheme, Amravati 444 601, India (home).

PATIL, Shivraj Vishwanath, BS, LLM; Indian politician; *Governor of Punjab, Administrator of Chandigarh;* b. 12 Oct. 1935, Chakur, Latur dist (Marathwada region) of Bombay State, British India; s. of the late Vishwanath Rao and of Bhagiriti Bai; m. Vijaya Patil (deceased); one s. one d.; ed Osmania Univ., Hyderabad, Univ. of Bombay (now Mumbai); Pres. Latur Municipality 1967–69, 1971–72; mem. Maharashtra Legis. Ass. 1972–79; mem. Lok Sabha (Parl.) 1980, Speaker, Lok Sabha 1991–96; Minister of State, including Defence, Commerce, Science and Tech., Space and Tourism portfolios 1980–89; Minister of Home Affairs 2004–08 (resgnd); Gov. of Punjab and Admin. of Chandigarh 2010–; Acting Gov. of Rajasthan 2010–12; mem. Indian Nat. Congress party; Hon. Prof. of Law. *Leisure interests:* reading, painting, farming, swimming, horse-riding, shooting. *Address:* Office of the Governor of Punjab, Raj Bhavan, Vigyan Path, Chandigarh 760 001, India (office). *Telephone:* (172) 2740740 (office). *Fax:* (172) 2741058 (office). *Website:* www.punjabgovt.nic.in (office).

PATIL, Shriniwas Dadasaheb, BA, MA, LLB; Indian politician and fmr civil servant; *Governor of Sikkim;* b. 11 April 1941, Tehsil Patan, Maharashtra; s. of Dadasaheb Ramchandra Patil and Anusaya Dadasaheb Patil; m. Rajanidevi Patil; one s.; ed Univ. of Poona, Govt Law Coll., Bombay; joined Maharashtra Public Service Comm. as Deputy Collector (Dist Commr) 1965, served as sub-divisional officer in several dists 1965–71, 1973–75, seconded as Man. Dir, Sangamner Cooperative Sugar Factory 1971–73 and as Sr Personnel Man., Hindustan Antibiotics Ltd 1975–77; CEO Pimpri Chinchwad Municipality 1977–78; promoted to Indian Admin. Services 1979; Dir of Sugar, Maharashtra State 1985–87; Collector and Dist Magistrate, Beed 1987–88, Pune 1988–92, Commr, Pimpri Chinchwad Municipal Corpn and Chair., Pimpri Chinchwad New Township Devt Authority 1992–95; Chair., Nagpur Improvement Trust 1996–99; mem. Lok Sabha (Parl.) for Karad constituency 1999–2009; Gov. of Sikkim 2013–; mem. Nationalist Congress Party 1999–. *Address:* Raj Bhavan, Gangtok 737 103, India (office). *Telephone:* (3592) 222400 (office). *Fax:* (3592) 222742 (office). *E-mail:* governorpatil@gmail.com (office). *Website:* www.rajbhavansikkim.gov.in (office); www.shriniwaspatil.com.

PATIÑO AROCA, Ricardo Armando, PhD; Ecuadorean economist and politician; *Minister of Foreign Relations, Trade and Integration;* b. 1955, Guayaquil; m. Miriam Alcívar; one d.; ed Autonomous Metropolitan Univ. of Iztalapa, Mexico, Univ. of Guayaquil and Int. Univ., Andalucía, Spain; Head, Econ. Planning Dept Nat. Agrarian Reform Inst. in southern Nicaragua 1980–81; mem. Econs Dept, Univ. of Guayaquil; fmr Coordinator Inter-Ministerial Comm. on Employment; fmr consultant ILO; Deputy Minister of the Economy 2005–07, Minister of the Economy and Finance 2007, of Coastal Affairs 2007, Co-ordinating Minister for Politics 2007–10, Minister of Foreign Relations, Trade and Integration 2010–; Dir Acción Política del Movimiento Patria Altiva y Soberana (PAIS) 2006. *Address:* Ministry of Foreign Relations, Trade and Integration, Avda 10 de Agosto y Carrión, Quito, Ecuador (office). *Telephone:* (2) 299-3200 (office). *Fax:* (2) 256-4873 (office). *E-mail:* webmast@mmrree.gov.ec (office). *Website:* www.mmrree.gov.ec (office).

PATNAIK, Janaki Ballav, MA; Indian politician; *Governor of Assam;* b. 3 Jan. 1927, Khurda District, Orissa; s. of Gokulanand Devi and Rambha Devi; m. Jayanti Patnaik; one s. two d.; ed Banaras and Utkal Univs; Sub-Ed. Eastern Times 1949, Jt Ed. 1950, Ed. (also for Prajatantra) 1952–67; Ed. Paurusha; led tenants' agitation in Madhupur, Cuttack District 1953; mem. Sahitya Akademi, Orissa 1956–57, Lok Sabha 1971–77; Minister of State for Defence, Govt of India 1973–77; Minister of Tourism, Civil Aviation and Labour Jan.–Dec. 1980; Chief Minister of Orissa State 1980–89, 1995–99; Pres. Pradesh Congress Cttee, Orissa 1978–80, 1992–98, 1999–2001, Jan.–June 2004; Leader of the Opposition, Orissa Legislative Ass., Bhubaneswar 2004; Gov. of Assam 2009–; Dr hc (Jagannath Sanskrit Univ.); Hon. DLitt (Tirupati Sanskrit Univ.); Orissa Sahitya Akademi Award, Bankim Chandra Sahitya Samman. *Publications:* Life History of the Lord Buddha; collections of poems and essays: Gautama Buddha, Swapna O'Sankalpa, Sindhu Upatyaka, Mahabharat, Ramayana, Niti Sataka, Srungar Sataka, Bairagya Staka, Gokulananda Granthavali, Novels of Bankimchandra, Prabandha Sankalan, Srimad Bhagabat, Swadhinata Sangramara Smruti. *Leisure interests:* reading, writing creative literature. *Address:* Office of the Governor, Raj Bhavan, Guwahati 781 004 (office); 201, Forest Park, Bhubaneswar 751 009, India (home). *Telephone:* (361) 2540250 (office); (674) 2536789 (office). *Fax:* (361) 2540500 (office); (674) 2536957 (home).

PATNAIK, Naveen, BA; Indian politician; *Chief Minister of Orissa;* b. 16 Oct. 1946, Cuttack; s. of the late Biju Patnaik and Gyan Patnaik; ed Doon School, Dehradun, Univ. of Delhi; mem. Lok Sabha 1997–; State Minister of Steel and Mines 1998–99, of Mines and Minerals 1999–2000, of Water Resources, Information and Tech. 2000–02, of Home, Agric. and Admin 2000–, of Works, Parl. Affairs, Housing, Health, Families and Rural Devt 2001–02, of Finance, Planning and Co-ordination 2002–, mem. Library Cttee, Standing Cttee on Commerce, Gen. Purpose Cttee; Chief Minister of Orissa 2000–; Founder and Pres. Biju Janata Dal; Founding mem. Indian Nat. Trust for Art and Cultural Heritage. *Publications:* A Second Paradise, A Desert Kingdom, The Garden of Life. *Leisure interests:* reading, watching programmes on culture, history and environment. *Address:* Office of the Chief Minister, Government of Orissa, Bhubaneswar, (office); Naveen Nivas, Aerodrome Rd, Bhubaneswar, District Khurda, 751 001, India (home). *Telephone:* (674) 2590299 (office); (674) 2531100 (office). *E-mail:* cmo@ori.nic.in (office). *Website:* orissagov.nic.in (office).

PATON, Borys Yevgenovych, DTechSc; Ukrainian metallurgist; *President, Ukraine National Academy of Sciences;* b. 27 Nov. 1918, Kyiv; s. of Yevgen Oskarovych Paton and Natalya Viktorivna Paton; m. Olga Borysivna Milovanova 1948; one d.; ed Kiev Polytechnic Inst.; Dir E. O. Paton Electric Welding Institute of Ukrainian SSR (now Ukraine) Acad. of Sciences 1953–; Corresp. mem.

Ukrainian SSR (now Ukraine) Acad. of Sciences 1951–58, mem. 1958–, Pres. 1962–; mem. USSR (now Russian) Acad. of Sciences 1962, mem. Presidium 1963–91; Pres. Int. Engineering Acad. 1991–; mem. CPSU 1952–91, cand. mem. Cen. Cttee of CPSU 1961–66, mem. 1966–91; mem. Central Cttee of CP of Ukraine 1960–91; Deputy to USSR Supreme Soviet 1962–89; Vice-Chair. Soviet of the Union USSR Supreme Soviet 1966–89; Deputy to Ukrainian SSR Supreme Soviet 1959–90, mem. of Pres. 1963–80; People's Deputy of the USSR 1989–91; mem. of editorial bd and ed.-in-chief of several scientific and tech. journals; Foreign mem. of Acads of Science of 10 countries; Honoured Scientist of Ukrainian SSR 1968, Honoured Inventor of USSR 1983; more than 10 hon. doctorates; State Prize of the USSR 1950, Lenin Prize 1957, State Prize of the Ukraine 2004, Order of Liberty 2012, numerous other awards. *Publications include:* numerous books and articles in professional journals; more than 1,000 patents 1942–2004. *Leisure interest:* swimming. *Address:* E.O. Paton Electric Welding Institute, 11 Bozhenko Street, Kyiv 150, 03680, Ukraine. *Telephone:* (44) 287-31-83. *Fax:* (44) 528-04-86. *E-mail:* office@paton.kiev.ua. *Website:* www.paton.kiev.ua.

PATRICIU, Dan Costache (Dinu), MA; Romanian architect, academic, politician and business executive; *Chairman and CEO, Rompetrol Group NV;* b. 1950; m.; two d.; ed Bucharest Inst. of Architecture; Prof., Bucharest Inst. of Architecture 1975–; fmr Chair. Investment Cttee, Romania and Moldova Direct Fund LP (pvt. equity investment fund); mem. Parl. and Leader, Romanian Liberal Party Parl. Group 1990–96, 2000–03; led investor buyout of Rompetrol SA 1998, mem. Supervisory Bd 1998–, Chair. and CEO 2001–; f. Free Initiative Foundation; shareholder in several real estate cos and investment funds; First Prize, Abu Dhabi City Centre Architecture Contest 1984, Runner up, Nat. Contest for Urban Dwellings, Romania. *Achievements:* has designed more than 40 residential and commercial projects in Romania and more than 25 residential complexes, offices and hotels in UAE. *Address:* Rompetrol Building, 222 Calea Victoriei, 010099 Bucharest, Romania (office). *Telephone:* (21) 3030800 (office). *Fax:* (21) 3122490 (office). *E-mail:* office@rompetrol.com (office). *Website:* www.rompetrol.ro (office).

PATRICK, Danica Sue; American racing driver and model; b. 25 March 1982, Beloit, Wis.; d. of T. J. Patrick and Beverly Patrick; m. Paul Edward Hospenthal 2005; grew up in Roscoe, Ill.; began go-karting competitively aged ten, won first World Karting Asscn championship aged 12; moved to Milton Keynes, UK aged 16 to advance her racing career, racing in British nat. series events against drivers including future Formula 1 world champion Jenson Button (q.v.); raced in Formula Ford, Formula Vauxhall and earned a second-place in Formula Ford Festival (highest finish by a woman) 1998–2001; finished 2nd Formula Ford Festival, Brands Hatch, UK 2000; winner Pro Div. Long Beach Grand Prix Toyota Pro-Celebrity Race 2002; third in Toyota Atlantic Championship; with Rahal Letterman Racing –2006; with Andretti Green Racing 2007–10, Andretti Autosport 2010–; earned ten top-five finishes in 12 races including best finish (second) at Portland 2004; finished fourth Indianapolis (Indy) 500 2005; won Indy Japan 300 2008 (first woman to win an Indy car race); came third in Indianapolis 500 2009 (personal best and highest finish by a woman in event's history); currently drives #7 GoDaddy.com Honda/Dallara for Andretti Autosport; began racing in NASCAR Nationwide Series, driving #7 GoDaddy.com Chevrolet Impala for JR Motorsports part-time 2010; also has equity stake in her #7 team; has hosted several shows on Spike TV, including the Powerblock 2004; featured in Girl Racers documentary 2005; Gorsline Scholarship Award for top upcoming road racing driver 2001, Indianapolis 500 Rookie of the Year 2005, IndyCar Series Rookie of the Year 2005, IndyCar Most Popular Driver 2005–07, 2009, ranked by Forbes magazine amongst The World's 100 Most Powerful Women (93rd) 2010. *Television:* acting debut in episode of CSI: New York Feb. 2010 (played a racing driver suspected of murder). *Publication:* Danica: Crossing the Line 2006. *Address:* Andretti Green Racing, 7615 Zionsville Road, Indianapolis, IN 46268, USA (office). *Telephone:* (317) 872-2700 (office). *E-mail:* DanicaMedia7@GoDaddy.com. *Website:* www.andrettigreenracing.com; www.danicaracing.com.

PATRICK, Deval Laurdine, JD; American lawyer, business executive, politician and state official; *Governor of Massachusetts;* b. 31 July 1956, Chicago, Ill.; s. of Pat Patrick and Emily Patrick; m. Diane Bemus 1984; two d.; ed Milton Acad., Harvard Coll., Harvard Law School; worked with UN in Africa 1978; Pres. Legal Aid Bureau, Harvard Law School; worked as law clerk for Judge Stephen Reinhardt, US Court of Appeals for the Ninth Circuit; attorney for Nat. Asscn for the Advancement of Colored People (NAACP) Legal Defense and Educational Fund, New York City; attorney, Hill & Barlow 1986–90, Pnr 1990; apptd Asst Attorney Gen. for Civil Rights 1994; adviser to post-apartheid S Africa and helped to create their civil rights laws; attorney, Day, Berry & Howard 1997; apptd by Fed. Dist Court to serve as Chair. Task Force to oversee implementation of terms of race discrimination settlement at Texaco, apptd Vice-Pres. and Gen. Counsel, Texaco, New York City; Exec. Vice-Pres., Gen. Counsel and Corp. Sec. Coca-Cola Co., Atlanta 2000–04 (resgnd); Gov. of the Commonwealth of Massachusetts 2007– (first African-American state gov. and only second in US history); mem. Bd of Dirs United Airlines 2004–06; Democrat. *Address:* Office of the Governor, Room 360, State House, Boston, MA 02133 (office); Office of Federal-State Relations, Commonwealth of Massachusetts, 444 North Capitol Street, Suite 208, Washington, DC 20001, USA (office). *Telephone:* (617) 725-4005 (Boston) (office); (202) 624-7713 (DC) (office). *Fax:* (617) 727-9725 (Boston) (office); (202) 624-7714 (DC) (office). *Website:* www.mass.gov/governor (office); www.devalpatrick.com.

PATRIOTA, Antonio de Aguiar; Brazilian diplomatist and politician; *Permanent Representative, United Nations;* b. 27 April 1954, Rio de Janeiro; m. Tania Cooper Patriota; two s.; ed Univ. of Geneva, Switzerland and Rio Branco Inst.; Adviser to Head of UN Div., Ministry of Foreign Affairs 1980–82, mem. Perm. Mission to Int. Orgs, Geneva 1983–87, Political Counsellor, Embassy in Beijing 1987–88, Head of Econ. Section, Embassy in Caracas 1988–90, Adviser to Sec.-Gen. for Political Affairs, Ministry of Foreign Affairs 1990–92, Deputy Diplomatic Adviser to Pres. of Brazil 1992–94, Political Counsellor, Perm. Mission to UN, New York 1994–99, mem. Brazilian del. to UN Security Council 1995, 1998–99, Minister Counsellor, Perm. Mission to Int. Orgs, Geneva 1999–2003, Deputy Perm. Rep. to WTO 2001–02, Sec. for Diplomatic Planning, Office of the Minister of Foreign Affairs 2003, Chief of Staff 2004, Under-Sec.-Gen. for Political Affairs 2005–07, Amb. to USA 2007–09, Sec.-Gen., Ministry of Foreign Affairs 2009–10, Minister of Foreign Affairs 2011–13 (resgnd), Amb. and Perm. Rep. to UN, New

York 2013–; several decorations from Brazil, France, Norway and Morocco. *Address:* Permanent Mission of Brazil, 747 Third Avenue, 9th Floor, New York, NY 10017, USA (office). *Telephone:* (212) 372-2607 (office); (212) 372-2600 (office). *Fax:* (212) 371-5716 (office). *E-mail:* delbrasonu@delbrasonu.org (office); distri .delbrasonu@itamaraty.gov.br (office). *Website:* www.un.int/brazil (office).

PATRONI GRIFFI, Filippo; Italian lawyer and government official; *Secretary of State to the Prime Minister and Secretary, Council of Ministers;* b. 27 Aug. 1955, Naples; Judge, Admin. Court of Basilicata 1984; Legal Adviser to Minister of State Holdings 1987, to Minister for Social Affairs 1989, to Minister of the Budget and Econ. Planning 1989–92, to Prime Minister and later Head, Legis. Office of Minister for Public Admin 1993–98, Chef de Cabinet of Minister for Institutional Reforms 1998–99, Legal Adviser to Minister for Heritage 2002, Legal Adviser, Nat. Centre for Information Tech. in Public Admin (CNIPA) 2003–05; Head, Dept for Legal Affairs of Presidency of the Council of Ministers 2006–08; Chef de Cabinet of Minister for Public Admin Reforms and Innovation 2008–09; Minister for Public Admin 2011–13; Sec. of State to the Prime Minister and Sec., Council of Ministers 2013–; mem. Central Tax Comm. 2007; mem. editorial bd several journals including Giurisdizione amministrativa, Rivista italiana di diritto pubblico comunitario, Rivista dello sport, Federalismi.it, Il lavoro nelle pubbliche amministrazioni. *Publications:* contributions to various legal journals. *Address:* Office of the Prime Minister, Palazzo Chigi, Piazza Colonna 370, 00187 Rome, Italy (office). *Telephone:* (06) 67791 (office). *Website:* www.governo.it (office).

PATRUSHEV, Col-Gen. Nikolai Platonovich, PhD; Russian government security official; *Secretary of the Security Council;* b. 11 July 1951, Leningrad (now St Petersburg); m.; two s.; ed Leningrad Inst. of Vessel Construction (now the State Marine Tech. Univ. of St Petersburg); on staff KGB, Kareliyan ASSR 1974; in Leningrad Oblast 1974–92; Minister of Security, Repub. of Kariliya 1992–94; Head Dept of Self-Security, Fed. Security Service 1994–98, Deputy Dir, then Head, Dept of Econs 1998–99, Dir 1999–; Head of Presidential Control Dept May–Aug. 1998; Deputy Head Admin. of Russian Presidency Aug.–Oct. 1998; Deputy Dir Fed. Security Service of Russia (FSB), Head of Econ. Security Dept 1998, First Deputy Dir April–Aug. 1999, Dir Aug. 1999–2008; Sec. Security Council of Russian Fed. 2008–; Hon. Citizen of the Repub. of Karelia; Hero of the Russian Fed., Order of Merit for the Fatherland (First Class) 2006, (Second Class, Third Class and Fourth Class), Order of Courage, Order of Mil. Merit, Order of Naval Merit, Order of Honour, Jubilee Medal '300 Years of the Russian Navy', Medal 'In Commemoration of the 850th Anniversary of Moscow', Jubilee Medal '60 Years of the Armed Forces of the USSR', Jubilee Medal '70 Years of the Armed Forces of the USSR', Medal Anatoly Koni, Medal for Strengthening Mil. Cooperation (Defence) three times, Medal 'Diligence in carrying out engineering tasks' (Defence), Medal for distinction in military service (MOD) (First Class), Meritorious Service (Second Class), Medal of Honour (Belarus) 2001, Order of Bogdan Khmelnitsky (Third Class) (Ukraine) 2001, Medal 'For Services to Stavropol Krai' (Stavropol Krai) 2003, Order of the Cross (First Class) (Armenia) 2003, Order of Saint Blessed Prince Dimitry Donskoy Great (First Class) (Russian Orthodox Church) 2005. *Achievements include:* joined expedition of polar explorer, Arthur Chilingarov, that flew on two helicopters to Antarctica and visited S Pole and Amundsen-Scott station Jan. 2007. *Address:* Security Council of Russian Federation, 103132 Moscow, Ipatyevskii per. 4/10, Russia (office). *Telephone:* (495) 206-35-96 (office). *Website:* www.scrf.gov.ru (office).

PATRY, Gilles G., CM, MASc, PhD; Canadian engineer, academic and university administrator; *Professor and President Emeritus, University of Ottawa;* ed Univ. of Ottawa, Univ. of California, Davis; began career as consulting engineer 1971–78; Prof. of Civil Eng, École Polytechnique de Montréal 1978–83; Prof. of Civil Eng, McMaster Univ. 1983–93; f. Hydromantis Inc. 1985; Dean, Faculty of Eng, Univ. of Ottawa 1993, Vice-Pres. (Academic) 1997, Pres. and Vice-Chancellor 2001–08, Prof. and Pres. Emer. 2008–; Pres. and CEO Canada Foundation for Innovation 2010–; Assoc. Ed. Journal of Environmental Engineering and Science 2001–05; Fellow, Canadian Acad. of Eng 2002–; mem. Bd Canadian Merit Scholarship Foundation 2006–, Audit Cttee Nat. Research Council of Canada 2006–, Bd Canadian Water Network (Réseau canadien de l'eau) 2009–, Advisory Bd Canadian Research Knowledge Network 2009–; Chevalier, Ordre de la Pléiade 2009, mem. Order of Canada 2010, Order of Ontario 2011; Hon. DSc (McMaster) 2009; Hon. LLD (Waterloo) 2008; co-author of paper selected as one of the 10 most significant ground-breaking papers in the 40-year history of Water Research 2006, Alumnus of the Year Award, Faculty of Eng, Univ. of Ottawa 2008, Community Builder Award, United Way Ottawa 2009, 26th John W. Hodgins Memorial Lecturer, McMaster Univ. 2009, Water Research Award. *Publications:* more than 125 journal and conf. papers. *Address:* University of Ottawa, 800 King Edward (4050), Ottawa, ON K1N 6N5, Canada (office). *Telephone:* (613) 562-5870 (office). *Fax:* (613) 562-5664 (office). *E-mail:* patry@uottawa.ca (office). *Website:* www .gillespatry.ca (office).

PATSEV, Aleksander Konstantinovich; Russian fmr diplomatist; b. 29 June 1936, Moscow; m.; two c.; ed Moscow State Inst. of History and Archives, Higher Diplomatic School at Ministry of Foreign Affairs; Komsomol functionary 1959–66; mem. staff Ministry of Foreign Affairs 1966–69; Head of Sector, Dept of Information 1985–87, Deputy Head Gen. Secr. 1987–89; Amb. to Oman 1990–96, to Uzbekistan 1997–99, Amb. to Finland 1999–2003. *Address:* c/o Ministry of Foreign Affairs, Smolenskaya-Sennaya pl. 32/34, 119200 Moscow, Russia (office).

PATTAMA, Noppadon, LLB (Hons), BA, LLM, MA; Thai lawyer and politician; b. 23 April 1961, Nakorn Rachasima; ed Thammasat Univ., Univs of Oxford and London, UK; practised as barrister in Bangkok 1983–; called to the Bar, Lincoln's Inn, London 1991; Sec. to Leader of the Opposition Chuan Leekpai 1995–96; mem. Parl. (Democrat Party) 1996–2000, mem. Standing Cttee on Foreign Affairs, House of Reps 1996–2000; Parl. Sec. to Minister of Foreign Affairs 1999–2001; defected to Thai Rak Thai party 2006; Vice-Minister of Natural Resources and Environment 2006; legal adviser to fmr Prime Minister Thaksin Shinawatra (deposed in mil. coup Sept. 2006) Nov. 2006; mem. People's Power Party (successor to Thai Rak Thai) –2008, Pheu Thai Party 2008–; Minister of Foreign Affairs 2008; Pres. Thai Students' Asscn in UK (Samaggi Samagom) 1988–89; participant in The Ship for Southeast Asian Youth Programme 1981; Fulbright Scholarship to study in USA 1982, Ananda Mahidol Scholarship to study law in UK, King of Thailand 1984. *Publications:* book: I'm Not a Traitor. *Address:* c/o Pheu Thai Party, 1770

Thanon Petchaburi Tat Mai, Bang Gapi, Huay Kwang, Bangkok 10310, Thailand (office). *Telephone:* (2) 686–7000 (office). *Website:* www.ptp.or.th (office).

PATTEN, Brian, FRSL; British poet and author; b. 7 Feb. 1946, Liverpool, Merseyside, England; s. of Ireen Stella Bevan; Regents Lecturer, Univ. of California, San Diego; performance work and lectures worldwide for British Council; Freedom of the City of Liverpool 2000; Hon. Fellow, John Moores Univ. 2002; Hon. DLitt (Liverpool) 2006; Cholmondeley Award for Poetry 2002. *Radio:* various, including History of 20th-Century Poetry for Children, BBC Radio 2000, The Dittisham Nativity, BBC Radio 2005, Lost Voices, BBC Radio 2009, 2010, 2011. *Publications include:* poetry: The Mersey Sound 1967, Little Johnny's Confession 1967, The Home Coming 1969, Notes to the Hurrying Man 1969, At Four O'Clock in the Morning 1971, Walking Out: The Early Poems of Brian Patten 1971, Love Poems 1981, New Volume 1983, Gargling With Jelly 1985, Storm Damage 1988, Grinning Jack: Selected Poems 1990, Thawing Frozen Frogs 1990, Armada 1996; (ed) Clare's Countryside: A Book of John Clare 1981, Selected Poems 2007, New Collected Love Poems 2007, View From The Boathouse Window 2010; children's fiction: Grizzelda Frizzle and Other Stories 1992, The Magic Bicycle 1993, Impossible Parents 1994, Frognapped! and Other Stories 1994, The Utter Nutters 1995, The Blue and Green Ark 1999, Juggling with Gerbils 2000, Little Hotchpotch 2000, The Impossible Parents Go Green 2001, View From The Boathouse Window 2009, The Big Snuggle-up 2011; (ed) The Puffin Book of 20th Century Children's Verse 1991, The Story Giant 2001, Ben's Magic Telescope 2003, The Puffin Book of Modern Children's Verse 2006, The Big Snuggle-Up 2011. *Leisure interests:* river cruising/travel. *Address:* c/o Rogers, Coleridge & White Literary Agency, 20 Powis Mews, London, W11 1JN, England (office). *Telephone:* (20) 7221-3717 (office). *Fax:* (20) 7229-9084 (office). *E-mail:* info@rcwlitagency.co.uk (office); happydaze@uku.co.uk (office). *Website:* www.rcwlitagency.co.uk (office); www.brianpatten.co.uk.

PATTEN OF BARNES, Baron (Life Peer), cr. 2005, of Barnes in the London Borough of Richmond; **Christopher Francis Patten,** CH, PC; British politician and government official; b. 12 May 1944, Cleveleys, Lancs., England; s. of the late Francis Joseph Patten and Joan McCarthy; m. Mary Lavender Thornton 1971; three d.; ed St Benedict's School, Ealing, Balliol Coll., Oxford; worked in Conservative Party Research Dept 1966–70, Dir 1974–79; seconded to Cabinet Office 1970; at Home Office, then personal asst to Lord Carrington, Party Chair. 1972–74; MP for Bath 1979–92; Parl. Pvt. Sec. (PPS) to Leader of the House 1979–81, to Social Services Sec. 1981–83; Parl. Under-Sec. for Northern Ireland 1983–85; Minister of State for Educ. 1985–86; Overseas Devt Minister 1986–89; Sec. of State for the Environment 1989–90; Chancellor of the Duchy of Lancaster and Chair. of the Conservative Party 1990–92; Gov. of Hong Kong 1992–97; Chair. Comm. charged with reform of Royal Ulster Constabulary 1998–99; EU Commr for External Relations 1999–2004; Chancellor, Newcastle Univ. 1999–2009, Univ. of Oxford 2003–; Chair. BBC Trust 2011–14 (resgnd); Co-Chair. UK-India Round Table, Int. Crisis Group 2004–11; Pres. Medical Aid for Palestinians 2010–11; mem. Bd of Dirs Russell Reynolds Assocs; mem. Int. Advisory Bd BP; mem. European Advisory Bd Bridgepoint; European Adviser, Hutchinson Whampoa Ltd; Int. Adviser to Praemium Imperiale, Japan Art Asscn; mem. Bd of Overseers, Sabanci Univ.; mem. (Crossbench) House of Lords 2005–; Hon. FRCP (Edin.) 1994; Hon. Fellow, Balliol Coll., Oxford 1999; several hon. degrees from British and foreign univs, including Hon. DCL (Newcastle) 1999; Coolidge Travelling Scholarship, USA 1965. *Publications:* The Tory Case 1983, Letters to Hong Kong 1997, East and West: The Last Governor of Hong Kong on Power Freedom and the Future 1998, Not Quite the Diplomat: Home Truths About World Affairs 2005, Cousins and Strangers: America, Britain, and Europe in a New Century 2006, What Next? Surviving the 21st Century 2008. *Leisure interests:* reading, tennis, gardening. *Address:* House of Lords, Westminster, London, SW1A 0PW, England. *Telephone:* (20) 7219-5353. *Fax:* (20) 7219-5979.

PATTERSON, Gavin E.; British business executive; *CEO, BT Group plc;* b. 1967, Altrincham, Greater Manchester; m. Karen Patterson; four c.; ed Emmanuel Coll., Cambridge; with Procter and Gamble 1991–2000, rose to become European Marketing Dir; with Telewest (now Virgin Media) 2000–04, latterly as Man. Dir Consumer; joined BT as Group Man. Dir BT Retail's Consumer div. 2004, Chief Exec. BT Retail May 2008–13, mem. Bd of Dirs BT Group plc June 2008–; launched BT Infinity, led BT as Founder-Partner in YouView, cr. BT Sport 2013, CEO BT Group plc 2013–; Pres. Advertising Asscn 2011–; Dir (non-exec.) British Airways; Trustee, British Museum; mem. Advisory Bd, Cambridge Judge Business School; mem. Thirty Club; Fellow, Marketing Soc. *Leisure interest:* Liverpool Football Club. *Address:* BT Group plc, BT Centre, 81 Newgate Street, London, EC1A 7AJ, England (office). *Telephone:* (20) 7356-5000 (office). *E-mail:* info@btplc.com (office). *Website:* www.btplc.com (office).

PATTERSON, Henry (Harry), (Martin Fallon, James Graham, Jack Higgins, Hugh Marlowe), BSc, FRSA; British/Irish novelist; b. 27 July 1929, Newcastle upon Tyne; s. of Henry Patterson and Rita Higgins Bell; m. 1st Amy Margaret Hewitt 1958 (divorced 1984); one s. three d.; m. 2nd Denise Leslie Ann Palmer 1985; ed Roundhay School, Leeds, Beckett Park Coll. for Teachers, London School of Econs; NCO, The Blues 1947–50, tried numerous jobs including clerk and circus tent hand 1950–58; schoolmaster, lecturer in liberal studies, Leeds Polytechnic, Sr Lecturer in Educ., James Graham Coll. and Tutor in School Practice, Leeds Univ. 1958–72; full-time writer from age of 41; Hon. DUniv (Leeds Metropolitan Univ.) 1995. *Publications include:* as Martin Fallon: The Testament of Caspar Schultz 1962, Year of the Tiger 1963, The Keys to Hell 1965, Midnight Never Comes 1966, Dark Side of the Street 1967, A Fine Night for Dying 1969, Day of Judgement 1979; as Hugh Marlowe: Seven Pillars to Hell 1963, Passage by Night 1964, A Candle for the Dead (aka The Violent Enemy) 1966; as James Graham: A Game for Heroes 1970, The Wrath of God 1971, The Khufra Run 1972, The Run to Morning 1974; as Harry Patterson: Sad Wind from the Sea 1959, Cry of the Hunter 1960, The Thousand Faces of Night 1961, Comes the Dark Stranger 1962, Wrath of the Lion 1963, Pay the Devil 1963, The Dark Side of the Island 1963, A Phoenix in Blood 1964, Thunder at Noon (aka Dillinger) 1964, The Graveyard Shift 1965, Iron Tiger 1966, Brought in Dead 1967, Hell is Always Today 1968, Toll for the Brave 1971, To Catch a king (aka The Judas Gate) 1979; as Jack Higgins: East of Desolation 1968, In the Hour Before Midnight 1969, Night Judgement at Sinos 1970, The Last Place God Made 1971, The Savage Day 1972, The Eagle has Landed 1975, Storm

Warning 1976, The Valhalla Exchange 1976, A Prayer for the Dying 1977, Solo (aka The Cretan Lover) 1980, Luciano's Luck 1981, Touch the Devil 1982, Exocet 1983, Confessional 1985, Night of the Fox 1986, Walking Wounded (play) 1987, Memoirs of a Dance Hall Romeo 1989, A Season in Hell 1989, Cold Harbour 1989, The Eagle Has Flown 1990, Eye of the Storm (aka Midnight Man) 1992, Thunder Point 1993, On Dangerous Ground 1994, Angel of Death 1995, Sheba 1995, Drink With the Devil 1996, The President's Daughter 1996, The Violent Enemy 1997, Flight of Eagles 1998, The White House Connection 1999, Day of Reckoning 1999, Midnight Runner 2001, Edge of Danger 2001, The Keys of Hell 2002, Bad Company 2003, Without Mercy 2005, Death Run (with Justin Richards) 2007, Sure Fire (juvenile, with Justin Richards) 2007, The Killing Ground 2008, Rough Justice 2008, A Darker Place 2009, Wolf at the Door 2009, The Judas Gate 2011, A Devil is Waiting 2012. *Leisure interests:* tennis, old movies. *Address:* Ed Victor Ltd, 6 Bayley Street, London, WC1B 3HE, England (office). *Telephone:* (20) 7304-4100 (office). *Fax:* (20) 7304-4111 (office). *E-mail:* ed@edvictor.com (office). *Website:* www.edvictor.com (office).

PATTERSON, James, BA, MA; American writer and fmr advertising executive; b. 22 March 1947, Newburgh, NY; m.; one s.; ed Manhattan Coll., Vanderbilt Univ.; wrote first novel 1976; joined J. Walter Thompson as jr copywriter 1971, subsequently Exec. Creative Dir, CEO, Chair. 1990–96. *Publications:* The Thomas Berryman Number (MWA Edgar Award) 1976, The Season of the Machete 1977, The Jericho Commandment (aka See How They Run) 1979, Virgin 1980, Black Market 1986, The Midnight Club 1989, The Day America Told the Truth: What People Really Believe About Everything that Matters (non-fiction, with Peter Kim) 1991, Along Came a Spider 1993, The Second American Revolution 1994, Kiss the Girls 1995, Hide & Seek 1996, Jack & Jill 1996, Miracle on the 17th Green (with Peter de Jonge) 1996, Cat & Mouse 1997, When the Wind Blows 1998, Pop Goes the Weasel 1999, Cradle and All (revised version of Virgin) 2000, Roses are Red 2000, Suzanne's Diary for Nicholas 2001, 1st to Die 2001, Violets are Blue 2001, 2nd Chance (with Andrew Gross) 2002, Four Blind Mice 2002, The Beach House (with Peter de Jonge) 2002, The Jester 2003, The Lake House 2003, The Big Bad Wolf 2003, 3rd Degree 2003, Sam's Letters to Jennifer 2004, London Bridges 2004, Honeymoon 2005, 4th of July 2005, Mary Mary 2005, Maximum Ride: The Angel 2005, The 5th Horseman (with Maxine Paetro) 2006, Judge and Jury 2006, Lifeguard (with Andrew Gross) 2006, Thriller (short stories) (ed) 2006, Maximum Ride: School's Out Forever (with Peter De Jonge) 2006, Cross 2006, Step on a Crack (with Michael Ledwidge) 2007, The Beach Road (with Peter De Jonge) 2007, The 6th Target (with Maxine Paetro) 2007, Maximum Ride: Saving the World and Other Extreme Sports (children's fiction) 2007, The Quickie (with Michael Ledwidge) 2007, Double Cross 2007, You've Been Warned 2007, 7th Heaven 2008, Maximum Ride: The Final Warning 2008, Sundays at Tiffany's 2008, Sail 2008, The Dangerous Days of Daniel X 2008, Against All Odds (non-fiction), Cross Country 2008, 8th Confession (with Maxine Paetro) 2009, Max: A Maximum Ride Novel 2009, Swimsuit 2009, Alex Cross's Trial 2009, Run for Your Life 2009, The Murder of King Tut (with Martin Dugard) 2009, I, Alex Cross 2009, Worst Case 2010, 9th Judgement (with Maxine Paetro) 2010, Private (with Maxine Paetro) 2010, Daniel X: Demons and Druids 2010, The Postcard Killers (with Liza Marklund) 2010, Don't Blink 2010, The Gift (with Ned Rust) 2010, Tick Tock 2011, The Christmas Wedding 2011, Kill Alex Cross 2011, Witch and Wizard: The Fire (with Jill Dembowski) 2011, Private Games (with Mark Sullivan) 2012, Private: #1 Suspect (with Maxine Paetro) 2012, 11th Hour (with Maxine Paetro) 2012, Guilty Wives (with David Ellis) 2012, Middle School: Get Me Out of Here (with Chris Tebbetts) 2012, I, Michael Bennett (with Michael Ledwidge) 2012, Nevermore: The Final Maximum Ride Adventure 2012, Zoo (with Michael Ledwidge) 2012, Confessions of a Murder Suspect (with Maxine Paetro) 2012, NYPD Red (with Marshall Karp) 2012, Daniel X: Armageddon (with Chris Grabenstein) 2012, I Funny (with Chris Grabenstein) 2012, Merry Christmas, Alex Cross 2012, Private Berlin (with Mark Sullivan) 2013, The Kiss (with Jill Dembowski) 2013. *Address:* c/o Author Mail, Hachette Book Group USA, 237 Park Avenue, New York, NY 10017, USA (office). *Website:* www.jamespatterson.com.

PATTERSON, The Most Hon. Percival James, BA, LLB, ON, PC, QC; Jamaican international consultant; *President, Heisconsults;* b. 10 April 1935, Cross Road, St Andrew; s. of Henry Patterson and Ina James; m. (divorced); one s. one d.; ed Univ. of West Indies, London School of Econs; called to Bar, Middle Temple 1963, Jamaican Bar 1963; party organizer, People's Nat. Party (PNP) 1958–60, mem. party exec. 1964–2006, Vice-Pres. 1969–82, Chair. 1983–92, Pres. 1992–2006; mem. nominated to Senate 1967; Leader of Opposition Business in Senate 1969–70; mem. House of Reps for S.E.Westmoreland 1969–80, 1989–2006; Minister for Industry and Tourism 1972–77, Deputy Prime Minister 1978–92, also Minister of Foreign Affairs and Foreign Trade 1978–80, Minister for Devt, Planning and Production 1989–90, for Finance and Planning 1990–91, of Defence 1992–2006; Prime Minister 1992–2006; Adviser to Govt of Belize 1982; currently Pres. Heisconsults; Pursell Trust Scholarship, Leverhulme Scholarship; Gran Cruz Placa De Oro, Order of Francisco Morazán (Honduras) 1990, Order of Águila Aztec (Mexico) 1990, Order of San Martín (Argentina) 1992, Great Cross of the Order of Bernado O'Higgins (Chile) 1992, Order of the Liberator Simon Bolivar (Venezuela) 1992, Order of Gran Cruz Gonzalo Jiménez de Quesada (Colombia) 1994, Order of Jose Marti (Cuba) 1997, Order of the Volta (Ghana) 1999, Gran Cruz Placa, Order Juan Mora Fernández (Costa Rica) 2001, Grand Cross, Nat. Order of Civil Merit (Spain) 2006, Order of Excellence (Guyana) 2006, Order of Belize 2006, Grand Cross, Order of Cruzeiro do Sul (Brazil) 2006, Order of the Caribbean Community 2009, Order of the Companions of O.R. Tambo (Gold) (South Africa) 2012; Hon. DLitt (Northeastern, Boston) 1994, (Connecticut) 2003, (Igbinedion Univ., Nigeria) 2007, Hon. LLD (Brown) 1998; FAO Agricola Medal 2001, Distinguished Service Award, Caribbean Tourism Org. 2005, Diggs Award for Foreign Affairs (Congressional Black Caucus) 2005, Chancellor's Medal, Univ. of the West Indies 2006, Living Legends Award, Economic Community of West African States, African Communications Agency, Ghana 2007, Andrew Young Medal for Capitalism and Social Progress 2007, Northern California Caribbean-American Heritage Month Cttee Award 2007, Jamaican Bar Asscn Award 2007, Caribbean Bar Asscn Govt Service Award 2007, Pinnacle Award, Org. of Nat. Coalition on Caribbean Affairs 2007, Lifetime Achievement Award, Hanover Homecoming Foundation 2008, EC Honour 2009. *Leisure interests:* jazz, Jamaican music, spectator sports including cricket, boxing, track and field events, tennis.

Address: Heisconsults, Sagicor Life Jamaica Centre (10th Floor), 28-48 Barbados Avenue, Kingston 5, Jamaica (office). *Telephone:* 929-57014 (office). *Fax:* 929-5705 (office). *E-mail:* pjpatterson@heisconsults.com (office).

PATTERSON, Walter Cram, MSc; Canadian/British energy analyst and writer; *Associate Fellow, Chatham House;* b. 4 Nov. 1936, Winnipeg, Man., Canada; s. of Walter Thomas Patterson and Thirza Helen Cram; m. Cleone Susan Davis 1966; two d.; ed Kelvin High School, Winnipeg, Univ. of Manitoba; Ed. Your Environment 1970–73, European Ed. Bulletin of the Atomic Scientists 1979–81; First 'Energy Campaigner' Friends of the Earth 1972–78; ind. analyst, writer 1978–93; with Gorleben Int. Review 1978–79; course tutor, Open Univ. 1981–91; series adviser, BBC TV Drama Edge of Darkness 1984–85; specialist adviser, House of Commons Select Cttee on Environment 1985–86, on Energy 1991–92; Assoc. Fellow, Energy and Environmental Programme, Royal Inst. of Int. Affairs (now Chatham House) 1991–93, Sr Research Fellow 1993–2000, Assoc. Fellow 2001–; Visiting Fellow, Sussex Energy Group, Univ. of Sussex 2006–; Fellow, Energy Inst.; Companion, Inst. of Energy 1991; Melchett Medal, Inst. of Energy 2000, Scientific American 50 Energy Policy Leader 2004. *Publications:* Nuclear Power 1976–86, The Fissile Society 1977, Coming to a Boil 1978, The Plutonium Business 1984, Going Critical 1985, Advanced Coal-Use Technology 1987, The Energy Alternative 1990, Coal-Use Technology in a Changing Environment 1990, Coal-Use Technology: New Challenges, New Responses 1993, Power from Plants 1994, Rebuilding Romania: Energy, Efficiency and the Economic Transition 1994, Electric Futures 1997, Transforming Electricity 1999, Keeping the Lights On 2007, 2009, Managing Energy: Rethinking The Fundamentals 2007–, The Fire Age: What We Do, How We Do It, How We Can Do Better 2014. *Leisure interests:* baseball, beer, computers, languages, music, orchids, playing with the family, travel. *Address:* Little Rushmoor, High Bois Lane, Amersham, Bucks., HP6 6DQ (home); Chatham House, St James's Square, London, SW1Y 4LE, England (office). *Telephone:* (1494) 726748 (home); 7971-840036 (mobile) (office). *E-mail:* waltpattersn@gn.apc.org (home); walt@waltpatterson.org (home). *Website:* www .waltpatterson.org (home); www.chathamhouse.org.uk (office).

PATTISON, Jim, OC; Canadian business executive; *Managing Director, Chairman and CEO, The Jim Pattison Group;* b. Luseland, Sask.; m.; three c.; ed Univ. of BC; paid univ. tuition fees washing cars and selling cars to fellow students; bought General Motors automobile dealership 1961, Owner, Man. Dir, Chair. and CEO The Jim Pattison Group 1961–; bought CJOR radio station 1965; Owner Ripley's Believe It or Not!, Overwaitea Food Group (including Save-On-Foods) and Buy-Low Foods grocery stores, Canadian Fishing Co., News Group; Dir The Toronto Dominion Bank, Canadian Pacific Ltd, Livent Inc.; Chair. and Pres. Vancouver EXPO '86; mem. Bd Trustees Ronald Reagan Presidential Foundation; Order of British Columbia 1990; Gov. Gen.'s Commemorative Medal 1992; inducted into Canadian Business Hall of Fame 1996, one of eight inaugural laureates of Canadian Professional Sales Asscn Sales Hall of Fame. *Leisure interests:* playing the piano, organ and trumpet. *Address:* The Jim Pattison Group, 1055 W. Hastings Street, Suite 1600, Vancouver, BC V6E 2H2, Canada (office). *Telephone:* (604) 688-6764 (office). *Fax:* (604) 687-2601 (office). *Website:* www .jimpattison.com (office).

PATTISON, Sir John Ridley, BSc, MA, DM, FRCPath, FMedSci; British fmr medical scientist; b. 1 Aug. 1942; s. of Tom Frederick Pattison and Elizabeth Pattison; m. Pauline Evans 1965; one s. two d.; ed Barnard Castle School, Univ. Coll. Oxford, Middlesex Hosp. Medical School; Asst Lecturer in Pathology, later Lecturer in Virology, Middx Hosp. Medical School 1970–75; Lecturer, later Sr Lecturer in Virology, St Bartholomew's and London Hosp. Medical Colls 1976–77; Prof. of Medical Microbiology, King's Coll. Hosp. Medical School 1977–84, Univ. Coll. London 1984–2004, Dean 1990–98, Vice-Provost 1994–99; Dir of Research and Devt, Dept of Health and Nat. Health Service 1999–2004; consultant, GlaxoSmithKline, Legal & General; mem. MRC 1992–2004, Sr Medical Advisor 1996–99; mem. Spongiform Encephalopathy Advisory Cttee 1994–95, Chair. 1995–99; mem. Council, International Journal of Experimental Pathology 1979–2001, Soc. of Gen. Microbiology 1981–87; mem. Bd Inst. of Child Health 1992–96, Inst. of Neurology 1995–97; mem. Man. Cttee King's Fund 1993–, Deputy Chair. 1994–99; Founder-fellow, Acad. of Medical Science 1998; Ed.-in-Chief Epidemiology and Infection 1980–94; Hon. Fellow, Imperial Coll. London, Univ. Coll. London; hon. degrees (Middlesex, Southampton, Durham). *Publications include:* Principles and Practice of Clinical Virology (co-ed. five edns) 1987–2006, Practical Guide to Clinical Virology (co-ed.) 1989, Practical Guide to Clinical Bacteriology (co-ed.) 1995; numerous papers on medical virology. *Address:* 17 Broadwater Lane, Towcester, NN12 6YF, England (home). *Telephone:* (1327) 352116 (home); 7747-441313 (mobile). *E-mail:* portsea200@btopenworld.com.

PATTISON, Seamus, DipSocEconSc; Irish trade union official and politician (retd); b. 19 April 1936, Kilkenny; s. of James Pattison and Ellen Fogarty; ed St Kieran's Coll., Kilkenny, Univ. Coll., Dublin; mem. Dáil Eireann 1961–2007; MEP 1981–83; Minister of State Dept of Social Welfare 1983–87; mem. British–Irish Parl. Body 1991–97; Chair. Select Cttee on Social Affairs 1993–97; Speaker Dáil Eireann 1997–2002, Father of the Dáil 1995–2007, Deputy Speaker 2002–07; fmr Labour Party spokesman on Educ. 1963–67, on Justice 1967–72, 1991–92, on Lands 1972–73, on Defence and Marine Affairs 1987, on Energy and Forestry 1989–91; mem. Parl. Ass. of Council of Europe 1989–90, 1996–97; mem. Kilkenny Co. Council 1964–97 (Chair. 1975–76 and 1980–81); Alderman Kilkenny Corpn 1964–97; Mayor of Kilkenny 1967–68, 1976–77, 1992–93; mem. Kilkenny Vocational Educ. Cttee 1964–97 (Vice-Chair. 1990–97), South Eastern Health Bd 1971–84. *Leisure interests:* reading, theatre, travel and sport. *Address:* 6 Upper New Street, Kilkenny, Ireland (home). *Telephone:* (56) 7721295 (home). *Fax:* (56) 7752533 (home).

PATTON, Paul E., BEng; American politician, government official and university administrator; *President, Pikeville College;* b. Fallsburg; ed Univ. of Kentucky; early career as owner of coal co. –1979; Judge Exec., Pike Co. 1981; Lt.-Gov. of Ky 1991–95, Gov. of Ky 1995–2003; Chair. Ky Democrats 1981–83; Chair. Ky Council on Postsecondary Educ. 2009–; Pres. Pikeville Coll. 2009–, also Distinguished Visiting Lecturer in Public Policy and Leadership; served numerous terms Pike Co. Democrats Exec. Comm.; mem. Bd Overseers Bellarmine Coll., Bd Trustees Pikeville Coll. *Address:* Office of the President, Pikeville College, 147 Sycamore

Street, Pikeville, KY 41501, USA (office). *Telephone:* (606) 218-5250 (office). *Website:* www.pc.edu (office).

PATTULLO, Sir (David) Bruce, Kt, CBE, BA, FCIBS, FRSE; British banker (retd); b. 2 Jan. 1938, Edinburgh; s. of late Colin Pattullo and Elizabeth Bruce; m. Fiona Nicholson 1962; three s. one d.; ed Rugby School and Hertford Coll. Oxford; Gen. Man. Bank of Scotland Finance Co. Ltd 1973–77; Dir British Linen Bank Ltd 1977–98, Chief Exec. 1977–78; Deputy Treas. Bank of Scotland 1978, Treas. and Gen. Man. (Chief Exec.) 1979–88, Dir 1980–98, Group Chief Exec. 1988–96, Deputy Gov. 1988–91, Gov. 1991–98; Chair. Cttee of Scottish Clearing Bankers 1981–83, 1987–89; three hon. degrees; Bilsland Prize, Inst. of Bankers in Scotland 1964. *Leisure interests:* tennis, hill walking. *Telephone:* (131) 339-6012 (home).

PATZIG, Günther, DPhil; German philosopher and academic; *Professor Emeritus, Philosophisches Seminar, Universität Göttingen;* b. 28 Sept. 1926, Kiel; s. of Admiral Conrad Patzig and Gertrud Patzig (née Thomsen); m. Christiane Köhn 1948; one s. one d.; ed Gymnasiums in Kiel and Berlin-Steglitz, Univs of Göttingen and Hamburg; Asst, Philosophisches Seminar, Göttingen 1953–60, Privatdozent 1958–60, Prof. of Philosophy 1963–91, now Emer.; Prof. of Philosophy, Univ. of Hamburg 1960–63; Christian-Wolff Prof., Univ. of Halle-Wittenberg 2002; UNESCO Fellowship in Philosophy 1951–52; mem. Göttingen Acad. of Sciences 1971– (Pres. 1986–90), Wissenschaftskolleg, Berlin 1984–85, J. Jungius-Gesellschaft, Hamburg 1989–, Oslo Acad. of Sciences 1997–; Hon. DPhil (Saarbrücken) 2003; Howison Memorial Lecturer, Berkeley 1971, Lower Saxony Prize for Science 1983, Keeling Lecturer, London 1992, Heisenberg Medal 1998, Ernst-Hellmut-Vits-Preis 2000. *Publications:* Die aristotelische Syllogistik 1959, Sprache und Logik 1970, Ethik ohne Metaphysik 1971, Tatsachen, Normen, Sätze 1980, Aristoteles Metaphysik Z: Text, Übersetzung, Kommentar (with M. Frede) 1988, Gesammelte Schriften Vols I–IV 1993–96, Die Rationalität der Moral 1996, Gottlob Frege: Logische Untersuchungen (Hrsg.) 2003, Wie geht man mit bioethischen Grundkonflikten um? In: Kaminsky/Hallich. Verantwortung für die Zukunft 2006, Immanuel Kant und das 'kategoriale Gefängnis' unserer Sinne: In: Bilderwelten. Vom farbigen Abglanz der Natur, hrsg. von Elsner, Wallstein 2007, 19 S., Herausgeber von 'Gottlob Frege. Funktion, Begriff, Bedeutung. Vandenhoeck und Ruprecht 2008, Philosophische Aspekte der Sterbehilfe-Problematik. In: Jahrbuch der Akademie der Wissenschaften zu Göttingen 2007, Walter de Gruyter 2008 S. 90-101. *Address:* Philosophisches Seminar, Universität Göttingen, Humboldtallee 19, 37073 Göttingen (office); Otfried-Müller-Weg 6, 37075 Göttingen, Germany (home). *Telephone:* (551) 394742 (office); (551) 42929 (home). *Fax:* (551) 399607 (home). *E-mail:* ikaraku@gwdg.de (office). *Website:* www.uni -goettingen.de/de/70432.html (office).

PAU, Louis-François, DSc, MBA, PhD; French communications industry executive and academic; *Professor of Mobile Business, Rotterdam School of Management;* b. 29 May 1948, Copenhagen, Denmark; s. of Louis Pau and Marie-Louise Von Jessen; m. 1st Miki Miyamoto 1983 (divorced 1990); one d.; m. 2nd Maria Joukovskaia; one d.; ed Ecole Nat. Supérieure de l'Aéronautique et de l'Espace (renamed Institut Supérieur de l'Aéronautique et Espace), Paris Univ. (VI and IX), Inst. d'Etudes Politiques, Paris, Int. Inst. for Man. Devt, Lausanne, Switzerland, Institut Européen d'Admin des Affaires (INSEAD); dancer, Royal Ballet, Copenhagen 1957–66; served in Air Force 1970–72; Asst Prof., Tech. Univ., Denmark 1972–74; Prof. and Dept Head, Ecole Nat. Supérieure Télécommunications, Paris 1974–82; Assoc. Prof., MIT, USA 1977–78; Science and Tech. Counsellor, French Embassy, Washington, DC 1979–82; Professorial Lecturer, Univ. of Maryland, College Park, Md 1980–82; Sr Scientist, Battelle Memorial Inst. 1982–86; Research Prof., Tech. Univ., Denmark 1986–90; CSK Prof., Univ. of Tokyo 1988–90; Tech. Dir, Digital Equipment Corpn (Europe) (later Hewlett Packard (Europe)) 1990–95; Chief Tech. Officer, Ericsson Network Systems Div., Sweden 1995–2011; Prof. of Mobile Business, Rotterdam School of Man. 2001–; Adjunct Prof., Copenhagen Business School 2003–; Vodacom Chair Prof., Gordon Inst. of Business, Johannesburg, SA 2010–11; mem. Bd of Dirs SCF Technologies A/S 2006–12; consultant to several int. corpns; adviser to several govts and govt agencies in USA, Asia and Europe; mem. Nat. Research Foundation Scientific Advisory Bd, Singapore, ASTRI Tech. Advisory Bd, People's Repub. of China, review bds in EU and USA; Vice-Pres. (Tech.) Int. Fed. of Automatic Control 1982–86; Fellow, IEEE, Japan Soc. of Promotion Sciences, British Computer Soc.; many awards and prizes. *Publications:* 10 authored and 12 edited books; more than 350 papers on computers and communications, management science, aerospace tech. and financial/econ. models. *Leisure interests:* ballet, flying, travel. *Address:* T-9, Rotterdam School of Management, PO Box 1738, 3000 DR Rotterdam, The Netherlands (office). *Telephone:* (10) 590-13-39 (office). *E-mail:* lpau@nypost.dk (office).

PAUDYAL, Leela Mani, MBA; Nepalese government official; *Chief Secretary;* b. 9 May 1962, Baletaksar-5, Gulmi; m.; two c.; ed Tribhuwan Univ.; joined Civil Service 1988; Accounts Officer, Office of the Comptroller-Gen. 1988–96; Under-Sec. (Admin), Ministry of Local Devt 1996–97; Jt Sec., Ministry of Industries, Commerce and Supplies 1997–2000; Dir-Gen., Dept of Cottage and Small Industries 2000–03; Jt Sec., Ministry of Industries, Commerce and Supplies May–Oct. 2003; Consular-Gen. for Tibet Autonomous Region of China, Lhasa 2003–07; Jt Sec., Ministry of Gen. Admin (Reserve) 2007–08; Sec., Ministry of Culture, Tourism and Civil Aviation 2007–08, Ministry of Information and Communications 2008–09, Office of Prime Minister and Council of Ministers 2009–12, Ministry of Home Affairs May–Sept. 2011; Chief Sec. 2012–. *Leisure interests:* travelling, yoga, meditation. *Address:* Office of the Prime Minister and Council of Ministers, Singh Durbar, PO Box 23312, Kathmandu, Nepal (office). *Telephone:* (1) 4211000 (office). *Fax:* (1) 4256909 (office). *E-mail:* info@opmcm.gov .np (office). *Website:* www.opmcm.gov.np (office).

PAUGAM, Anne; French civil servant and international organization official; *CEO, Agence Française de Développement;* b. Oct. 1966; ed Institut d'études politiques de Paris (Sciences Po), Ecole nationale d'admin; joined Inspectorate Gen. of Finance 1993, Insp. Gen. of Finances 2010–13; joined World Bank, Washington, DC via Young Professionals' Program 1997, held positions related to strategic management, then operational functions, in charge of public sector reform projects at World Bank's office in Rabat; Tech. Adviser, then Deputy Dir, Cabinet of Minister for Co-operation and Francophonie 2001–02, worked on devt finance issues (Inter-ministerial Cttee on Int. Co-operation and Devt, Monterrey

Conf.); joined Agence Française de Développement (AFD) 2002, held positions in strategic management (creation and management of the Strategic Steering and Forward-looking Dept) and operations (Dir Dept that finances projects in the education, vocational training and health sectors), later apptd Sec. Gen. and mem. Exec. Cttee responsible for budget, resources, finance and risks, CEO (first woman) 2013–. *Address:* Agence Française de Développement, 5 rue Roland Barthes, 75598 Paris Cedex 12, France (office). *Telephone:* 1-53-44-31-31 (office). *Fax:* 1-44-87-99-39 (office). *E-mail:* site@afd.fr (office). *Website:* www.afd.fr (office).

PAUGET, Georges, MA, PhD; French banking executive; *Chairman, Amundi Group;* b. 1947, Rumilly, Haute-Savoie; ed Univs of Lyon and Bordeaux; joined Groupe Crédit Agricole SA 1973, early man. positions with Aude Regional Bank and Caisse Nationale de Crédit Agricole, then internal auditor and then project leader in Group Control and Audit, Cen. Sec. then Sr Gen. Man. Unicrédit; CEO Haute Saône et du Territoire de Belfort Regional Bank 1985–87, Pyrénées-Atlantique 1987–92, Pyrénées-Gascogne Regional Bank 1992–2002; Deputy CEO Crédit Agricole SA 2003–05, CEO and Chair. Exec. Cttee 2005–10, Perm. Rep. on Supervisory Bd of Fonds de Garantie des Dépôts, and COO, mem. Exec. Cttee and Dir Regional Banks Div.; Chair. and CEO Le Crédit Lyonnais 2003–10; Chair. Calyon –2010; Chair. Amundi Group 2009–; mem. Bd of Dirs Paris-Europlace, Valeo; mem. Exec. Cttee Fédération Bancaire Française, Chair. –2009; fmr Chair. Union des Assurances Fédérales. *Publication:* Faut-il brûler les banquiers? 2009. *Address:* Amundi, 90 boulevard Pasteur, 75730 Paris Cedex 15, France (office). *Telephone:* 1-76-33-30-30 (office). *E-mail:* info@amundi.com (office). *Website:* www .amundi.com (office).

PAUK, György; British (b. Hungarian) violinist; *Professor of Violin, Royal Academy of Music;* b. 26 Oct. 1936, Budapest, Hungary; s. of Imre Pauk and Magdolna Pauk; m. Susan Mautner 1959; one s. one d.; ed Franz Liszt Acad. of Music, Budapest under Ede Zathureczky, Leo Weiner and Zoltán Kodály; concerts all over Eastern Europe 1952–58 and rest of world; settled in Western Europe 1958, The Netherlands 1958–61, England 1961–; Prof. of Violin, RAM 1987–; Artistic Dir Mozart Bicentenary Festival, London 1991; Prof. of Violin, Winterthur-Zürich Konservatorium of Music 1994–2000; Prof. Emer., Franz Liszt Acad. of Music, Budapest; jury mem. at int. violin competitions; master classes world-wide; Hon. mem. and Prof., Guildhall School of Music and Drama, London 1987; Hon. RAM 1990; highest civilian award, Hungarian Govt 1998; Paganini Prize 1956, Sonata Competition Prize, Munich 1957, Jacques Thibaud Prize 1959, Grand Prix for Bartók Records (Ovation Magazine, USA) 1982, Best Record of 1983 (Gramophone Magazine), Bartók-Pasztory Prize (Hungary). *Recordings include:* numerous concertos, the complete violin/piano music of Mozart and Schubert, Handel and Brahms sonatas, Mozart string quintets, all Bartók's music for solo, duo and sonatas; first performances of Penderecki's violin concerto, UK, Japan, Sir Michael Tippett's Triple Concerto, London 1980, Lutosławski's Chain 2, UK, Netherlands, Hungary, with composer conducting, Sir Peter Maxwell Davies' violin concerto, Switzerland, Germany, William Mathias violin concerto, England. *Leisure interests:* football, tennis, theatre, reading, swimming, grandchildren. *Address:* Royal Academy of Music, Marylebone Road, London, NW1 5HT, England (office). *Telephone:* (20) 7873-7395 (office). *E-mail:* strings@ram.ac.uk (office). *Website:* www.ram.ac.uk (office).

PAUL, Christian; French politician; b. 23 March 1960, Clermont-Ferrand (Puy-de-Dôme); Deputy to Nat. Ass. for Nièvre (3ème) 1997–, mem. Comm. des affaires sociales; Sec. of State for Overseas, Ministry of the Interior 2000–02; Founding mem. Nouveau Parti Socialiste (New Socialist Party); left party, along with Arnaud Montebourg, to create Rénover Maintenant (Renew Now) within Socialist party; Pres. Parc Régional du Morvan; mem. Comm. nationale des comptes de la formation professionnelle, Comm. du dividende numérique; temporary mem. Conseil d'admin de l'Ecole nationale admin; mem. Municipal Council of Lormes, Nièvre 1995–2008, Gen. Council of Nièvre 1994–2004; Vice-Pres. Regional Council of Burgundy 2004–10; mem. Communauté de communes des Portes du Morvan. *Publications:* Le défi numérique des territoires 2007, Pour la République européenne (with Stéphane Collignon) 2008. *Address:* Assemblée nationale, 126 rue de l'Université, 75355 Paris 07 SP (office); 1 rue des Teureaux, 58140 Lormes, France. *Telephone:* 1-40-63-68-11 (office); (3) 86-22-89-50. *Fax:* (3) 86-22-58-32. *E-mail:* christian.paul@orange.fr (office); cpaul@christianpaul.fr (office). *Website:* www .assemblee-nationale.fr (office); www.christianpaul.fr.

PAUL, Krishan Kant, MSc, PhD; Indian politician and fmr police commissioner; *Governor of Meghalaya;* b. 8 July 1948; m. Omita Paul; ed Punjab Univ.; joined Indian Police Service 1970, allocated to Arunachal Pradesh–Goa–Mizoram–Union Territories Div., Superintendent of Police, Andaman and Nicobar Islands, later Chief of Police, Arunachal Pradesh, served in Intelligence Bureau and Research and Analytical Wing, Commr Delhi Police 2004–07 (retd); mem. Union Public Service Comm. 2007–13; Gov. of Meghalaya 2013–; Special Duty Medal (Andaman and Nicobar), Pres.'s Police Medal for Distinguished Services, Sangram Medal, Paschim Star. *Leisure interest:* cricket. *Address:* Raj Bhavan, 793 001 Shillong, India (office). *Telephone:* (364) 2223001 (office). *Fax:* (364) 2223338 (office). *Website:* meghalaya.gov.in (office).

PAUL, Randal (Rand) Howard, BS, MD; American ophthalmologist and politician; *Senator from Kentucky;* b. 7 Jan. 1963, Pittsburgh, Pa; s. of Ronald Ernest Paul and Carolyn (Carol) Paul (née Wells); m. Kelley Ashby 1990; three s.; ed Baylor Univ., Duke Univ. School of Medicine; internship, Georgia Baptist Medical Center 1989; resident in ophthalmology, Duke Univ. Medical Center 1990–93; staff mem. Greenview Regional Hosp., Bowling Green, Ky, Bowling Green Medical Center, Logan Co. Memorial Hosp., Russellville, TJ Sampson Hosp., Glasgow; ophthalmologist, Graves-Gilbert Clinic; practising ophthalmologist in Bowling Green 1993–, est. own clinic 2007; Founder and Chair. Kentucky Taxpayers United 1994–; Founder Southern Kentucky Lions Eye Clinic, 1995; Senator from Kentucky 2011–, mem. Energy and Natural Resources Cttee 2011–, Homeland Security and Governmental Affairs Cttee 2011–, Small Business and Entrepreneurship Cttee 2011–; mem. Lions Clubs International (fmr Pres.); Republican; Melvin Jones Fellow Award for Dedicated Humanitarian Services, Lions Clubs International, Lion of the Year Award, Bowling Green Lions, Fines E. Davis Fellow Award for Dedicated Humanitarian Service, Gov.'s Appreciation Award for Sight Conservation, Outstanding Service and Commitment to Seniors, Twilight Wish Foundation 2002. *Address:* 208 Russell Senate Office Building,

Washington, DC 20510, USA (office). *Telephone:* (202) 224-4343 (office). *Website:* www.senate.gov (office).

PAUL, Baron (Life Peer), cr. 1996, of Marylebone in the City of Westminster; **Swraj Paul,** MSc, FRSA; British business executive; b. 18 Feb. 1931, India; s. of Payare Paul and Mongwati Paul; m. Aruna Vij 1956; three s. one d. (and one d. deceased); ed Punjab Univ., Massachusetts Inst. of Tech., USA; joined family-owned Apeejay Surrendra Group as Partner 1953; moved to UK and est. Natural Gas Tubes Ltd 1966; Founder-Chair. Caparo Group Ltd 1978–, Caparo Industries PLC 1981–; Chair. Caparo Inc., USA 1988–, Armstrong Equipment Ltd 1989–, CREMSA, Spain 1989–, ENSA, Spain 1989–; Founder-Chair. Indo-British Asscn 1975–; Pres. Family Service Unit 1997–; Chancellor, Univ. of Wolverhampton 1999–, Univ. of Westminster; Deputy Speaker, House of Lords 2008–10, Deputy Chair. of Cttees 2008–10, suspended from membership Oct. 2010–Feb. 2011; Resigned Labour Whip Oct. 2010; Chair. PiggyBankKids Projects Ltd (charity); mem. London Devt Agency 2000–08, London 2012 2003–05; mem. Parliamentarians for Global Action; Chair. of Trustees, Ambika Paul Foundation; Trustee, Police Foundation 1997–; Hon. PhD (American Coll. of Switzerland, Leysin) 1986; Hon. DSc (Econ.) (Hull) 1992; Hon. DLitt (Westminster) 1996; Hon. DHL (Chapman) 1996; Hon. DUniv (Bradford) 1997, (Central England) 1999; Hon. DSc (Buckingham) 1999; Padma Bhushan 1983, Corp. Leadership Award, MIT 1987. *Publications:* Indira Gandhi 1984, Beyond Boundaries 1998. *Address:* House of Lords, Westminster, London, SW1A 0PW, England (office). *Telephone:* (20) 7219-5016 (office). *Website:* www.parliament.uk/biographies/lords/swraj-paul/ 26477 (office).

PAUL, Vivek, BE, MBA; American (b. Indian) business executive; b. 1958; m.; three c.; ed BITS, Pilani, Univ. of Massachusetts; fmrly with Pepsi and Bain & Co.; joined Gen. Electric (GE) 1989, Pres. and CEO medical equipment joint venture in India, then global head Computerized Tomography business 1995–99, Pres. and CEO Wipro GE Medical Systems Ltd 1993–95, Vice-Chair. Wipro, Bangalore, India 1999–2005, Pres. and CEO global IT, product engineering, and business process services; Pnr, Texas Pacific Group (TPG), Man. Dir Ventures 2005–2008; Founder KineticGlue (cloud-based software co. 2008, sold co. 2013; Consulting Professor of Radiology, Molecular Imaging Program, Stanford Univ.; Dir Electronic Arts, Inc. 2008–. *Address:* c/o Molecular Imaging Program, Stanford University, The James H Clark Center 318 Campus Drive, East Wing, 1st Floor, Stanford, CA 9 4305-5427, USA (office).

PAULA, Alejandro Felippe "Jandi"; Curaçao politician and librarian; Govt Librarian 1973–93; Prime Minister of Netherlands Antilles 1993–94. *Address:* c/o Office of the Prime Minister, Willemstad, Curaçao.

PAULA GUTIÉRREZ, Francisco de, MA, PhD; Costa Rican economist, academic, fmr politician and fmr central banker; *Professor of Economics and Finance, INCAE Business School;* ed Univ. of Costa Rica, Univ. of Pennsylvania, USA; Lecturer in Econs, Univ. of Costa Rica 1972–86; Economist, Banco Centroamericano de Integración Económico, Tegulcigalpa, Honduras 1973–74; Adviser to Pres. of Costa Rica 1974–76, to Exec. Cttee, Banco Central de Costa Rica 1974–76; Economist, Wharton Econometric Forecasting Associates, Philadelphia, Pa 1981–84; Dir Consejeros Económicos y Financieros SA (CEFSA) 1984; mem. Comisión Internacional para la Reconstrucción y el Desarrollo de Centroamérica 1987–89; Minister of Finance 1996–98; Dir Banco Central de Costa Rica 1989–90, 1996–98, Pres. 2002–10; Prof. of Econs and Finance, INCAE Business School 1986–; Pres. Grupo Financiero SAMA 1998–; Dir Banco de Fomento Agrícola 1985–87, Productos de Concreto 1985–86, RICALIT SA 1986–96, Atlas Eléctrica 1990–96, ACORDE 1993–95, FUNDES 1993–96, Banco de COFISA 1993–96, Corporación INCSA 1998–, El Financiero (periodical) 1998–. *Publications:* numerous specialist papers on economics. *Address:* INCAE Business School, Campus Walter Kissling, 960-4050 Alajuela, Costa Rica (office). *Telephone:* 243-72153 (office). *Fax:* 433-9820 (office). *E-mail:* Francisco.Gutierrez@incae.edu (office). *Website:* www.incae.edu/ES/facultad/Francisco.Gutierrez (office).

PAULAUSKAS, Artūras; Lithuanian politician; b. 23 Aug. 1963; m. Jolanta Paulauskienė; one s. one d. (and two s. from previous m.); ed Vilnius State Univ.; Deputy Prosecutor, Kaisiadoris 1979–82; Prosecutor, Varena 1982–87; instructor, Cen. Cttee CP 1987; Deputy Prosecutor-Gen. of Lithuania 1987–90, Prosecutor-Gen. 1990–95; barrister 1997–2000; cand. in presidential elections 1997, 1998; est. The New Union (Social Liberals) Party, Leader 2006–; mem. Seimas (Parl.) of Lithuania 2000–08, Speaker 2000–06; Acting Pres. of Lithuania 6 April–12 July 2004; Minister of Environment Jan.–Nov. 2008. *Leisure interests:* sport, reading. *Address:* New Union (Social Liberals), Gedimino pr. 10/1, Vilnius 01103, Lithuania (office). *Telephone:* (5) 210-7600 (office). *Fax:* (5) 210-7602 (office). *E-mail:* arturas .paulauskas@lrs.lt (office); centras@nsajunga.lt (office). *Website:* www.nsajunga.lt (office); www.paulauskas.lt.

PAULIN, Pierre; French designer; b. 1927, Paris; ed Ecole Camondo; first exhbn of furniture in section entitled Le Foyer d'aujourd'hui, Salon des Arts ménagers 1953; influenced by Scandinavian furniture and American productions of Charles Eames and Florence Knoll; first revealed to general public in article by New York Times 1967; recognized by Museum of Modern Art, New York as world-class designer; commissioned by French Govt to redesign Pres. Georges Pompidou's pvt. apartments 1968; participates in devt of Denon Wing of Louvre Museum 1968–72; also asked by Pres. François Mitterrand to design his furniture 1984; participated in devt of Airbus aircraft 1986; works in collections of Museum of Modern Art, New York, Fonds nat. d'art contemporain, Centre Nat. d'art et de culture Georges-Pompidou, Musée des Arts Décoratifs, Paris, Victoria and Albert Museum, London, etc.; Chicago Design Award for the Ribbon Chair 1969, Grand Prix Nat. de la Création industrielle 1987. *Address:* c/o Gallerie des Gobelins, 42 avenue des Gobelins, Paris - 13, France. *Telephone:* 1-44-08-53-49.

PAULIN, Thomas (Tom) Neilson, BA, BLitt; British poet, critic and academic; *G. M. Young Lecturer in English Literature, Hertford College, University of Oxford;* b. 25 Jan. 1949, Leeds, Yorkshire; m. Munjiet Kaut Khosa 1973; two s.; ed Univ. of Hull, Lincoln Coll., Oxford; Lecturer, Univ. of Nottingham 1972–89, Reader in Poetry 1989–94; G. M. Young Lecturer in English Literature, Hertford Coll., Univ. of Oxford 1994–; Fellow, Hertford Coll., Oxford 1994–; Co-founder Field Day Theatre Co., Derry; Eric Gregory Award 1978, Faber Memorial Prize 1982, Fulbright Scholarship 1983–84. *Television:* panel mem. Newsnight Review (BBC

2). *Publications include:* poetry: Theoretical Locations 1975, A State of Justice (Somerset Maugham Award 1978) 1977, Personal Column 1978, The Strange Museum 1980, The Book of Juniper 1981, Liberty Tree 1983, The Argument at Great Tew 1985, Fivemiletown 1987, Selected Poems 1972–90 1993, Walking a Line 1994, The Wind Dog 1999, The Invasion Handbook 2002, The Road to Inver 2004; non-fiction: Thomas Hardy: The Poetry of Perception 1975, Ireland and the English Crisis 1984, The Faber Book of Political Verse (ed.) 1986, Hard Lines 3 (co-ed.) 1987, Minotaur: Poetry and the Nation State 1992, Writing to the Moment: Selected Critical Essays 1996, The Day Star of Liberty: William Hazlitt's Radical Style (biog.) 1998, Crusoe's Secret: The Aesthetics of Dissent 2005, The Secret Life of Poems 2008, Love's Bonfire 2012. *Address:* Hertford College, Catte Street, Oxford, OX1 3BW (office); c/o Faber and Faber, Bloomsbury House, 74–77 Great Russell Street, London, WC1B 3DA, England (office). *Website:* www.faber.co.uk (office).

PAULS, Raymond; Latvian composer and jazz pianist; b. 12 Jan. 1936, Riga; ed Latvian Conservatory; Artistic Dir and Chief Conductor of Latvian State Radio and TV 1985–88; Chair. Latvian State Cttee for Culture, later Minister of Culture 1988–93 (first non-communist minister in USSR since 1920s); Counsellor to Pres. 1993–97; mem. Parl. (Saeima) 1998–; Latvian State Prize 1979, USSR People's Artist 1985. *Compositions include:* musicals Sister Kerry, Sherlock Holmes; many popular songs, jazz pieces. *Recordings include:* Cinema 1982, U morya zhizn' moya 1995, Na Rozhdestvo 1995, Izbrannoe 1995, Nostal'giya. Instrumental'naya muzika 1996, Dva maestro 1997. *Address:* Veidenbaum Str. 41/43, Apt 26, 6001 Rīga, Latvia. *Telephone:* 6227-5588.

PAULSON, Henry (Hank) Merritt, Jr, BA, MBA; American investment banker and fmr government official; *Distinguished Visiting Scholar, Paul H. Nitze School of Advanced International Studies, Johns Hopkins University;* b. 28 March 1946, Palm Beach, Fla; s. of Henry Merritt and Marianna Paulson (née Gallaeur); m. Wendy Judge 1969; one s. one d.; ed Dartmouth Coll., Harvard Univ. Business School; Staff Asst to Asst Sec. of Defense (Comptroller), Pentagon, Washington, DC 1970–72; Staff Asst to Pres.'s Domestic Council, The White House, Washington, DC 1972–73; Assoc. Goldman Sachs & Co., Chicago 1974–77, Vice-Pres. 1977–82, Pnr, Investment Banking Dept 1982–, pnr in charge of investment banking, Midwest Region 1984–90, Man. Cttee Co-Head Investment Banking Div., Vice-Chair., COO 1990–99, CEO and Chair. 1999–2006; US Sec. of the Treasury 2006–09; Distinguished Visiting Scholar, Johns Hopkins School of Advanced Int. Studies, Washington, DC 2009–, Fellow, Bernard Schwartz Forum on Constructive Capitalism; Trustee Chicago Symphony Orchestra; Dir The Peregrine Fund Inc.; Vice-Chair. Nature Conservancy and co-Chair. of Nature Conservancy Asia-Pacific Council. *Publication:* On the Brink: Inside the Race to Stop the Collapse of the Global Financial System 2010. *Leisure interests:* skiing, fishing, canoeing, tennis, visiting wildlife habitats. *Address:* Paul H. Nitze School of Advanced International Studies, The Johns Hopkins University, 1740 Massachusetts Avenue, NW, Washington, DC 20036 (office); 101 West 67th Street, Apt 50A, New York, NY 10023, USA (home). *Telephone:* (202) 663-5600 (office). *Fax:* (202) 663-5656 (office). *Website:* www.sais-jhu.edu (office).

PAULY, Daniel, PhD; French marine biologist and academic; b. 2 May 1946, Paris; ed Univ. of Kiel, Germany; Project Asst, German Soc. for Technical Cooperation (GTZ) 1974–76; Research Asst, Dept of Fishery Biology, Inst. for Marine Sciences, Kiel 1978–79; Post-Doctoral Fellow, Int. Center for Living Aquatic Resources Man. (ICLARM), Manila 1979–80, Assoc. Scientist 1980–85, Sr Scientist 1985–94; Prof. of Fisheries, Univ. of British Columbia, Vancouver 1994–, Project Leader of Sea Around Us Project, Dir Fisheries Centre 2003–08; mem. Bd of Oceana; earned place in Scientific American 50 2003, labelled by New York Times as an "iconoclast" 2003, Int. Cosmos Prize 2005, Volvo Environment Prize, Volvo Environment Foundation (co-recipient) 2006, ECI Prize 2007, Ted Danson Ocean Hero Award 2007, Ramon Margalef Prize in Ecology 2008. *Achievements include:* early in his career, worked in tropics and developed new methods for estimating fish populations; developed concept of shifting baselines in 1995; published seminal paper on Fishing Down Marine Food Webs in Science 1998; developed important models and tools, including the Marine Trophic Index, Ecopath Modelling Model, and global database FishBase. *Publications:* author of several books and more than 500 scientific papers in professional journals on studies of human impacts on global fisheries. *Address:* AERL Room 333, Fisheries Centre, Aquatic Ecosystems Research Laboratory, University of British Columbia, 2202 Main Mall, Vancouver, BC V6T 1Z4, Canada (office). *Telephone:* (604) 822-1201 (office). *E-mail:* d.pauly@fisheries.ubc.ca (office). *Website:* www.fisheries.ubc.ca (office).

PAUZE, Jean-Charles, BEng, MSc (Econ), MBA; French business executive; *Chairman of the Management Board and CEO, Rexel SA;* b. 1947; ed IDN-EC Lille, Institut Européen d'Admin des Affaires (INSEAD); began career with Total 1971–74; joined Alfa Laval Group 1974, held several positions, CEO Alfa Laval France 1981–84, CEO Brand & Luebbe (subsidiary in Germany) 1984–86; Chair. and CEO Clestra-Hauserman, Strafor Facom Group 1986–91, Chair. and CEO Steelcase Strafor 1991–98; Chair. Man. Bd Guilbert (PPR Group) 1998–2002; CEO Rexel 2002–, Chair. Man. Bd 2007–. *Address:* Rexel SA, 25 rue de Clichy, 75009 Paris, France (office). *Telephone:* 1-42-85-85-00 (office). *Fax:* 1-45-26-25-83 (office). *E-mail:* info@rexel.com (office). *Website:* www.rexel.com (office).

PAVLOPOULOS, Prokopis K., PhD; Greek politician, lawyer and academic; b. 10 July 1950, Kalamata; m. Sissy Peltsemi; one s. two d.; ed Univ. of Athens, Univ. of Paris II; Sec. to Pres. 1974; Alt. Minister for the Presidency and Govt Spokesman 1989; legal adviser to Pres. 1990–95; political adviser to Chair. New Democracy (ND—Nea Demokratia) party 1995, Press and Information Officer 1996; mem. Parl. (ND) 1996–, ND Parl. Spokesman 2000–, mem. Standing Cttee on Public Admin., Public Order and Justice, Special Standing Cttee on Institutions and Transparency, Cttee for Revision of Constitution, Cttee on Public Enterprises, Banks and Public Utilities; Minister of the Interior, Public Admin and Decentralization 2004–07, of the Interior and Public Order 2007–09; Visiting Prof., Univ. of Paris II 1986; Prof. of Admin. Law, Univ. of Athens 1989; fmr mem. Bd Greek Culture Foundation; fmr Vice-Chair. Greek State Radio and TV Co. (ERT SA). *Publications include:* The Constitutional Safeguard for Plea in Abatement, The Civil Responsibility of the Government. *Address:* 36 Michalako-poulou str., 115 28, Athens; c/o New Democracy Party (Nea Demokratia), Odos

Rhigillis 18, 106 74 Athens, Greece. *Telephone:* (210) 3390201 (office); (210) 3616926 (office). *Fax:* (210) 3390507 (office). *E-mail:* ppavlopoulos@prokopispavlopoulos.gr (office); pavp@hellasnet.gr. *Website:* www.nd.gr.

PAVLOVSKY, Gleb Olegovich; Russian journalist and historian; b. 5 March 1951, Odessa; m.; one s. four d.; ed Odessa State Univ.; with Samizdat 1972–86; co-f., mem. Bd Poiski (magazine) 1978–80; Chair. Bd of Dirs Postfactum (information agency) 1988–93; mem. ed. bd Obshchaya Gazeta 1993–; Ed.-in-Chief Twentieth Century and World; Co.-Publr Sreda (Russian-European review) 1993–95; took part in election campaign of Pres. Vladimir Putin 2000; Founder and Pres. Fund of Efficient Policy 1995–. *Address:* Fund of Efficient Policy, Zubovsky blvd 4 entr. 8, 119021 Moscow, Russia (office). *Telephone:* (495) 745-52-25 (office).

PAVĻUTS, Daniels, BA, MPA; Latvian politician and academic; b. 14 May 1976, Jūrmala; ed Jāzeps Vītols Latvian Acad. of Music, City Univ., London, UK, John F. Kennedy School of Govt, Harvard Univ., USA; Exec. Dir Int. Boys' Choir Festival 'Rigas Doms' 1997–2001; Adviser to the Dir on Man. and Communication, Latvian Nat. Opera 2001; Brand Dir, DDB LATVIJA Ltd 2001–03; State Sec., Ministry of Culture 2003–06; mem. Bd, ZENO Consulting 2007–11, Latvian Chamber of Commerce and Industry 2008–10; mem. Man. Team and Head of Corp. Affairs, Swedbank AS 2010–11; Minister of the Economy 2011–14; Visiting Lecturer, Stockholm School of Econs, Rīga 2007–. *Address:* Stockholm School of Economics, Strelnieku iela 4A, Rīga 1010, Latvia (office). *Telephone:* 6701-5800 (office). *Fax:* 6783-0249 (office). *E-mail:* office@sseriga.edu (office). *Website:* www.sseriga.edu (office).

PAVLYCHKO, Dmytro Vasylovych; Ukrainian poet and politician; b. 28 Sept. 1929, Ivano-Frankivsk; s. of Vasyl Pavlychko and Paraska Bojchuk; ed Lviv Univ.; started publishing in early 1950s; mem. CPSU 1954–88; keen advocate of de-Stalinization from 1962; f. Taras Shevchenko Ukrainian Language Soc. 1988, for protection of language; Chair. Inaugural Congress of the Popular Movt of the Ukraine for Perestroika (Rukh); Deputy to Ukrainian Supreme Soviet 1990–95; Chair., Parl. Cttee for Int. Affairs 1991–95; Amb. to Slovakia 1995–98, to Poland 1999–2003; Pres., Ukrainian World Coordinating Council 2006–11. *Publications include:* poems: My Land 1955, The Day 1960, Bread and Banner 1968, Sonnets 1978, Turned to the Future 1986, Repentance Psalms 1994, Nostalgia 1998, Thimble 2002, Memory 2004, Three Verses 2007, Autodaphe 2008; trans.: C. Baudelaire, Poems 2001, José Martí, Poesías 2001, W. Shakespeare, Sonnets 2001; contrib. to anthologies. *Address:* Khreshchatyk str. 13, Apt 42, 01001 Kiev, Ukraine (home). *Telephone:* (44) 278-79-75 (home).

PAWAR, Sharad; Indian politician and sports administrator; *Minister of Agriculture and of Food Processing Industries;* b. (Sharadchandra Govindrao Pawar), 12 Dec. 1940, Baramati, Pune, Maharashtra; m. Pratibha Pawar; one d.; became mem. State Ass. 1968, joined State Cabinet 1973; apptd Chief Minister of Maharashtra 1978 (then youngest Chief Minister of the country, held post four times); elected Leader of Opposition in Lok Sabha 1998; Union Cabinet Minister for Agric., Consumer Affairs, Food and Public Distribution 2004–11, for Agric. and of Food Processing Industries 2011–; Pres. Maharashtra Olympic Asscn 1990–, Mumbai Cricket Asscn 2001–, Bd of Control for Cricket in India (BCCI) 2005–08; Vice-Pres. Int. Cricket Council (ICC) 2008–10, Pres. 2010–12, Pres. Organizing Pres. of ICC Cricket World Cup 2011. *Address:* Ministry of Agriculture, Krishi Bhavan, Dr Rajendra Prasad Road, New Delhi 110 001 (office); Ministry of Food Processing Industries, Panchsheel Bhavan, August Kranti Marg, New Delhi 110 049, India (office). *Telephone:* (11) 23383370 (Agric.) (office); (11) 26492475 (Food Processing) (office). *Fax:* (11) 23384129 (Agric.) (office); (11) 26493228 (Food Processing) (office). *E-mail:* ajitji@nic.in (office). *Website:* india.gov.in/sectors/agriculture/ministry_agriculture.php (office); mofpi.nic.in (office).

PAWAR, Sharadchandra Govindrao, BCom; Indian politician; *Minister of Agriculture and of Food Processing Industries;* b. 12 Dec. 1940, Baramati, Pune; s. of Govindrao Jijaba Pawar and Shardabai G. Pawar; m. Pratibha Pawar 1967; one d.; ed Brihan Maharashtra Coll. of Commerce, Pune; Head, State Level Youth Congress; Gen. Sec. Maharashtra Pradesh Congress Cttee; elected to State Legis. 1967, held Portfolios of Home and Publicity and Rehabilitation, Minister of State and Educ. and Youth Welfare, Home, Agric. and Industries and Labour; Chief Minister of Maharashtra 1978–80, 1993–95; Minister of Defence 1991–93; Minister of Agric. 2004–; Minister of Consumer Affairs, Food and Public Distribution 2004–11, of Food Processing Industries 2011–; Pres. Nat. Congress (opposition) 1981–86; rejoined Congress (I) 1986; fmr Pres. Congress Forum for Socialistic Action; Sec. Defence Cttee; mem. Lok Sabha 1996–; Leader of Opposition 1998–99; Founder-Pres. Nationalist Congress Party 1999–; Pres. Maharashtra Kabbadi Asscn, Maharashtra Olympic Asscn, Agricultural Devt Foundation, Mumbai Cricket Asscn, Garware Club House, Maharashtra Kustigir Parishad, Nehru Centre, Vasantdada Sugar Inst., Bd of Control for Cricket in India 2005–08; Vice-Pres. Int. Cricket Council; Dr hc (Lawrence Technological Univ., USA); Outstanding Parliamentarian Award 2003. *Leisure interests:* sports, reading, travelling. *Address:* Ministry of Agriculture, Krishi Bhavan, Dr Rajendra Prasad Road, New Delhi 110 001 (office); Govind Bagh, Baramati, Pune 413 002 (home); Ramalayan, 44-A Pedder Road, Mumbai 400 026, India (home). *Telephone:* (11) 23383370 (office); (22) 23659191 (Mumbai) (home). *Fax:* (11) 23384129 (office). *E-mail:* sharadpawar.sp@gmail.com. *Website:* agricoop.nic.in (office).

PAWLAK, Waldemar, MSc; Polish politician and business executive; b. 5 Sept. 1959, Model, Mazowieckie Voivodship; m. Elżbieta Pawlak; two s. one d.; ed Warsaw Univ. of Tech.; computer teacher in Pacyna 1984; farm man. 1984; mem. United Peasant Party (ZSL) 1984–90; Deputy to Sejm (Parl.) 1989–; mem. Polish Peasant Party (PSL) 1992– (Chair. 1992–97, 2005–12); Chair. Council of Ministers (Prime Minister) June–July 1992, 1993–95; Chair. Union of Volunteer Fire Brigades with rank of Brig.-Gen. 1992–; Pres. Warszawska Gielda Towarowa Spolka Akcyjna (WGT) S.A. (commodity exchange) Warsaw 2001–05; Deputy Prime Minister and Minister of the Economy 2007–12. *Leisure interests:* philosophy, information science, computers. *Address:* Polish People's Party (PSL), 00-924 Warsaw, ul. Kopernika 36/40, Poland (office). *Telephone:* (22) 6206020 (office). *Fax:* (22) 6543583 (office). *E-mail:* biuronkw@psl.org.pl (office). *Website:* www.psl.pl (office).

PAWLENTY, Timothy James (Tim), BA, JD; American politician and fmr state governor; b. 27 Nov. 1960, St Paul, Minn.; s. of Eugene Pawlenty and Virginia

Pawlenty (née Oldenburg); m. Mary Elizabeth Anderson 1987; two d.; ed South St Paul High School, Univ. of Minnesota; fmr labour law attorney, Rider Bennett, LLP, Minneapolis for 15 years, served as Lead Counsel for Minneapolis School Dist for ten years, later Partner; fmr prosecutor, Hennepin Co.; fmr Vice-Pres. Wizmo Inc.; Chair. Eagan Planning Comm. 1988–89; mem. Eagan City Council 1990–92; mem. for Dist 38B, Minnesota House of Reps 1993–2003, Majority Leader 1999–2003; Gov. of Minn. 2003–11; unsuccessful cand. for Republican US presidential nomination 2011; Chair. Nat. Govs Asscn 2007–08; Republican. *Publications:* Minnesota's Capitol: A Centennial Story (contrib.), Courage to Stand: An American Story 2011. *Address:* c/o Office of the Governor, 130 State Capitol Building, 75 Rev. Dr Martin Luther King Jr Blvd, St Paul, MN 55155, USA.

PAWLIK, Kurt, PhD, PrivDoz; Austrian academic; *Professor Emeritus of Psychology, University of Hamburg;* b. 16 March 1934, Vienna; ed Univ. of Vienna; Prof. of Psychology and Dept Dir, Univ. of Hamburg, Germany 1966–, now Emer.; Founder and Ed.-in-Chief European Psychologist journal; Ed. Methods of Psychology monograph series; Co-Ed. Research Texts in Psychology monograph series (more than 60 vols) and several scientific journals including American Psychologist; Pres. German Soc. of Psychology 1972–74, Int. Social Science Council 1998–2000, J. Jungius Soc. of Science 1999–; Sec.-Gen. Int. Union of Psychological Science 1984–92, Pres. 1992–96, 2000–02; Hon. mem. German Soc. of Psychology 2002–, Acad. of Sciences, Hamburg; Fellow, Chinese Psychological Soc. 2004–; Asscn of Psychological Sciences; Austrian Cross of Honours (First Class) in Science and Arts 1999; Outstanding Psychologist Award, American Psychological Asscn 2012. *Publications include:* International Handbook of Psychology (co-ed.) 2000; 17 books and more than 180 research papers. *Leisure interests:* music, theatre, skiing. *Address:* University of Hamburg, Department of Psychology, Von Melle Park 11, LD 20146 Hamburg, Germany (office). *Telephone:* (40) 428384722 (office); (40) 6072210 (home). *Fax:* (40) 428386591 (office); (40) 6072334 (home). *E-mail:* pawlik@uni-hamburg.de (office); kfpawlik@aol.com (home).

PAWSON, John; British architect; b. 6 May 1949; s. of the late Jim Pawson and Winifred Ward; m. Catherine Berning 1989; two s.; ed Eton; lived three years in Japan before studying architecture; pvt. architectural practice 1981–; pvt. bldgs designed include Neundorf House, Majorca, Klein Apartment, NY; commercial bldgs designed include Calvin Klein Store, Madison Avenue, NY, Jigsaw clothes store, Bond St, London, Cathay Pacific Lounges, Chek Lap Kok Airport, Hong Kong, Novy Dvur Monastery, Czech Rep., Sackler Crossing, Royal Botanic Gardens, Kew. *Publications:* Minimum 1996, Living and Eating (with Annie Bell) 2001, Themes and Projects 2002, Leçons du Thoronet 2006, John Pawson: Plain Space (with Alison Morris) 2010. *Address:* Unit B, 70–78 York Way, London, N1 9AG, England (office). *Telephone:* (20) 7837-2929 (office). *Fax:* (20) 7837-4949 (office). *E-mail:* email@johnpawson.com (office). *Website:* www.johnpawson.com.

PAXMAN, Jeremy Dickson, MA; British broadcast journalist, writer and television presenter; *Presenter, University Challenge;* b. 11 May 1950, Leeds, Yorks., England; s. of Arthur Keith Paxman and the late Joan McKay Dickson; one s. two d.; ed Malvern Coll., St Catharine's Coll., Cambridge; journalist, NI 1973–77; reporter, BBC TV Tonight and Panorama programmes 1977–85, presenter, Breakfast Time (BBC 1) 1986–89, Newsnight (BBC 2) 1989–2014, Univ. Challenge 1994–, Start the Week, Radio 4, 1998–2002; Fellow, St Edmund Hall, Oxford; Vice-Pres. The Wild Trout Trust 2004–, The London Library; Patron Sustrans; Hon. Fellow, St Catharine's Coll. Cambridge 2001; Dr hc (Leeds) 1999, (Bradford) 1999, (Open Univ.) 2006; TV Soc. Award for Int. Reporting, Richard Dimbleby Award, BAFTA 1996, 2000, Royal TV Soc. Interview of the Year 1997, Presenter of the Year 2001, 2007, Voice of the Viewer and Listener Presenter of the Year 1994, 1997, 2005, Variety Club Media Personality of the Year 1999. *Publications:* A Higher Form of Killing (co-author) 1982, Through the Volcanoes: A Central American Journey 1985, Friends in High Places: Who Runs Britain? 1990, Fish, Fishing and the Meaning of Life 1994, The Compleat Angler 1996, The English: A Portrait of a People 1998, The Political Animal: An Anatomy 2002, On Royalty 2006, The Victorians: Britain Through the Paintings of the Age 2009, Empire: What Ruling the World Did to the British 2011, Great Britain's Great War 2013; numerous articles in newspapers and magazines. *Leisure interests:* fly-fishing, daydreaming. *Address:* c/o Capel & Land, 29 Wardour Street, London, W1V 6PS, England (office). *Website:* www.bbc.co.uk/programmes/b006t6l0.

PAXSON, Christina Hull, BA, MA, PhD; American economist, academic and university administrator; *President, Brown University;* ed Swarthmore Coll., Columbia Univ.; Lecturer, Princeton Univ. 1986–87, Asst Prof. 1987–94, Assoc. Prof. 1994–97, Prof. of Econs and Public Affairs 1997–2012, Hughes-Rogers Prof. of Econs and Public Affairs 2007–12, Faculty Chair. MPA Program, Woodrow Wilson School 1997–99, Founding Dir Center for Health and Wellbeing 2000–09 (included directorship of Princeton's Health Grand Challenges programme 2007–09), Assoc. Chair. Dept of Econs 2005–08, Chair. 2008–09, Dean of Woodrow Wilson School of Public and Int. Affairs 2009–12; Prof. of Econs and Public Policy and Pres. Brown Univ. 2012–; Visiting Prof., Wharton School, Univ. of Pennsylvania 1999; Sr Ed. The Future of Children 2004–12; mem. Bd of Assoc. Eds, Journal of Development Economics 1995–99; mem. Bd of Eds, American Economic Review 1996–2000; Vice-Pres. American Econs Asscn 2012, mem. Exec. Cttee 2012–13; mem. Council on Foreign Relations 2012–, Bd of Trustees, MDRC 2011–12, Bd of Trustees, Center for Health Care Strategies 2002–12 (Chair. 2010–12); Sr Fellow, Bureau for Research and Econ. Analysis of Devt 2005–; teaching awards from Woodrow Wilson School MPA students 1991/92, 1992/93, 1993/94, 1994/95, 1995/96, H. Gregg Lewis Prize for best paper published in Journal of Labor Economics (co-recipient) 1996–97, Kenneth Arrow Award for best paper in health economics (co-recipient) 2003. *Publications:* numerous papers in professional journals. *Address:* Office of the President, Brown University, Box 1860, 1 Prospect Street, Providence, RI 02912, USA (office). *Telephone:* (401) 863-2234 (office). *Fax:* (401) 863-7737 (office). *E-mail:* president@brown.edu (office). *Website:* www.brown.edu/about/administration/president (office).

PAYNE, Alexander, BA, MFA; American film director and screenwriter; b. 10 Feb. 1961, Omaha, Neb.; s. of George Payne and Peggy Payne (née Constantine); m. Sandra Oh 2003; ed Stanford Univ. and Univ. of California, Los Angeles; fmr employee at Universal Pictures; completed several shorts for Propaganda Films and screened on Playboy Channel; feature film debut with Citizen Ruth (co-wrote screenplay with Jim Taylor) 1996. *Films include:* Carmen (short) 1985, Inside Out 1991, The Passion of Martin (thesis film, dir) 1989, Inside Out (dir and screenwriter) 1992, Citizen Ruth (dir and screenwriter) (First Prize, Munich Film Festival) 1996, Election (dir and co-screenwriter with Jim Taylor) (Best Screenplay Award: WGA, New York Film Critics' Circle and Ind. Spirit, Best Film and Best Dir, Ind. Spirit Awards) 1999, Jurassic Park III (screenplay) 2001, About Schmidt (dir and co-screenwriter with Jim Taylor) (Best Movie of the Year, Los Angeles Film Critics' Asscn 2002, Golden Globe for Best Screenplay 2003) 2002, Sideways (dir) (Los Angeles Film Critics' Asscn Best Movie of the Year, Golden Globe Award for Best Screenplay 2005, BAFTA Award for Best Adapted Screenplay 2005, Writers' Guild of America Award for best adapted screenplay 2005, Acad. Award for Best Writing, Adapted Screenplay2005), Independent Spirit Awards for Best Dir, Best Screenplay 2005) 2004, Paris, je t'aime (segment) 2006, I Now Pronounce You Chuck and Larry (co-screenwriter) 2007, The Descendants (dir) (Dallas-Fort Worth Film Critics Asscn Award for Best Dir and Best Screenplay 2011, Florida Film Critics Circle Award for Best Adapted Screenplay 2011, Acad. Award for Best Writing, Adapted Screenplay 2012) 2011, Nebraska 2013. *Television includes:* Hung (also exec. producer 2009–11) 2009. *Address:* c/o David Lonner, WME, 9601 Wilshire Boulevard, Beverly Hills, CA 90210, USA (office).

PAYNE, Anthony Edward, BA, FRCM; British composer; b. 2 Aug. 1936, London, England; s. of the late Edward Alexander Payne and (Muriel) Margaret Payne; m. Jane Manning (q.v.) 1966; ed Dulwich Coll., London and Durham Univ.; freelance musical journalist, musicologist, lecturer, etc. with various publs and BBC Radio, active in promoting new music, serving on Cttee of Macnaghten Concerts (Chair. 1967) and Soc. for the Promotion of New Music (Chair. 1969–71), composed part-time 1962–73; full-time composer 1973–; Composition Tutor, London Coll. of Music 1983–85, Sydney Conservatorium 1986, Univ. of Western Australia 1996; Milhaud Prof., Mills Coll., Oakland, Calif., USA 1983; Artistic Dir Spitalfields Festival; Creative Arts Fellow, Royal Coll. of Music 2007–08; Professorial Fellow, Univ. of East Anglia; mem. Cttee Asscn Frank Bridge Trust; Vice-Pres. Delius Trust; Hon. mem. Royal Philharmonic Soc. 1999; Hon. DMus (Birmingham) 2000, (Kingston) 2002, (Durham) 2007; Radcliffe Award 1975, South Bank Show Award 1998, Evening Standard Classical Music Award 1998, New York Critics' Circle Nat. Public Radio Award 1999, Classical CD Award 1999, Elgar Medal 2011. *Compositions:* Paraphrases and Cadenzas 1969, Paean for solo piano 1971, Phoenix Mass 1972, The Spirits Harvest for full orchestra 1972, Concerto for Orchestra (Int. Jury Choice for Int. Soc. for Contemporary Music Festival 1976) 1974, The World's Winter for soprano and ensemble 1976, String Quartet 1978, The Stones and Lonely Places Sing (septet) 1979, Song of the Clouds for oboe and orchestra 1980, A Day in the Life of a Mayfly (sextet) 1981, Evening Land for soprano and piano 1981, Spring's Shining Wake for orchestra 1981, Songs and Seascapes for strings 1984, The Song Streams in the Firmament (sextet) 1986, Fanfares and Processional 1986, Half Heard in the Stillness for orchestra 1987, Consort Music for string quintet 1987, Sea Change (septet) 1988, Time's Arrow for orchestra 1990, The Enchantress Plays bassoon and piano 1990, Symphonies of Wind and Rain for chamber ensemble 1991, A Hidden Music 1992, Orchestral Variations: The Seeds Long Hidden 1993, Empty Landscape–Heart's Ease (sextet) 1995, Break, Break, Break for unaccompanied chorus 1996, Elgar's Third Symphony (commissioned by Elgar Trust to complete Elgar's sketches) 1997, Piano Trio 1998, Scenes from The Woodlanders for soprano and ensemble 1999, Of Knots and Skeins for violin and piano 2000, Betwixt Heaven and Charing Cross for unaccompanied chorus 2001, Visions and Journeys for orchestra (British Composers Award 2003) 2001, Poems of Edward Thomas for soprano and piano quartet 2003, Horn Trio 2005, Elgar's Sixth Pomp & Circumstance March (commissioned by Elgar Trust to complete Elgar's sketches) 2006, Windows on Eternity 2007, Piano Quintet 2007, Out of the Depths Comes Song for cello and piano 2008, From a Mouthful of Air for quintet 2009, The Period of Cosmographie for orchestra 2009, Second String Quartet (British Composer Award Chamber category 2011) 2010, Arrangement of Bruckner's Second Symphony for Chamber Ensemble 2012, The Undiscovered Country (octet) 2012. *Recordings include:* The Music of Anthony Payne (Gramophone Critics' Choice) 1977, Time's Arrow 1996, A Day in the Life of a Mayfly 1998, The Stones and Lonely Places Sing 2007, My Own Country (Warlock arrangements) 2008, Elgar/Payne Symphony No. 3 (six recordings), Elgar/Payne Pomp & Circumstance March No. 6 (three recordings), Elgar (orchestrated Payne) Crown of India. *Radio:* frequent talks for BBC Radio 3 (music matters, Proms, etc.). *Television:* appearances, BBC documentaries by John Bridcut on Elgar, Vaughan Williams, Parry and Delius. *Publications:* Schoenberg 1968, The Music of Frank Bridge 1984, Elgar's Third Symphony: The Story of the Reconstruction 1998; contrib. to Musical Times, Tempo, Music and Musicians, The Listener, Daily Telegraph, The Times, The Independent, Country Life. *Leisure interests:* English countryside, cinema. *Address:* 2 Wilton Square, London, N1 3DL (home); c/o Boosey & Hawkes, 295 Regent Street, London, W1B 2JH; c/o Chester Music, Music Sales Ltd, 14–15 Berners Street, London, W1T 3LJ, England. *Telephone:* (20) 7359-1593 (home). *E-mail:* paynecomp@gmail.com (office). *Website:* classical-artists.com/anthonypayne (office).

PAYNE, Sir David Neil, Kt, CBE, PhD, FRS, FREng; British professor of photonics, academic and entrepreneur; *Professor and Director, Optoelectronics Research Centre, University of Southampton;* b. 13 Aug. 1944; currently Prof. and Dir Optoelectronics Research Centre, Univ. of Southampton, also directs Photonics Hyperhighway research project; f. SPI Lasers PLC (acquired by Trumpf Corpn); Chair. Marconi Soc.; Foreign mem. Russian Acad. of Sciences; Queens Award for Industry 1986, Rank Prize for Optics 1991, Tyndall Award 1991, Japanese Computers and Communications Prize 1993, Benjamin Franklin Medal for Eng 1998, Eduard Rhein Foundation Laureate (Germany), Mountbatten Medal of IEE 2001, Kelvin Medal 2004, IEEE Photonics Award (first time awarded outside USA) 2007, Marconi Prize 2008, Asscn of Laser Users Award 2010. *Publications:* more than 650 papers in professional journals. *Address:* Optoelectronics Research Centre, University of Southampton, Highfield, Southampton, Hants., SO17 1BJ, England (office). *Telephone:* (23) 8059-3583 (office). *Fax:* (23) 8059-3142 (office). *E-mail:* dnp@soton.ac.uk (office). *Website:* www.orc.soton.ac.uk (office).

PAYNE, Julien David, OC, CM, LSM, QC, LLD, FRSC; Canadian/British lawyer; *President, Danreb Incorporated;* b. 4 Feb. 1934, Nottingham, England; s. of

Frederick Payne and Kathleen Payne (née Maltby); m. Marilyn Ann Payne; five c.; ed Univ. of London; Asst Lecturer, Queen's Univ., Belfast 1956–60; Prof. of Law in various Canadian univs 1960–2001; Simon Sr Fellowship, Univ. of Manchester 1968; admitted as solicitor and barrister, Prov. of Ont. 1965; served as advocate, mediator and arbitrator of family law disputes across Canada (pioneer of no-fault divorce and Unified Family Courts); adviser to fed. and prov. govts on family and law reform 1966–; Dir Family Law Project, Law Reform Comm. of Canada 1972–75; Prof., Common Law Section, Univ. of Ottawa 1974–99; Chair. Law Foundation of Saskatchewan 1999–2001; Pres. Danreb Inc. 1985–; Founding mem. Int. Soc. on Family Law 1972; visiting univs. fellowships or chairs include Manchester, Santa Clara, Calif., Victoria, British Columbia, Hong Kong Univ., City Univ. of Hong Kong, Saskatchewan; Hon. Life mem. Bd of Dirs, Ont. Asscn of Family Mediation, Ottawa 1992; Hon. Life Fellow, Canadian Inst. for Conflict Resolution, St Paul's Univ., Ottawa; Law Soc. of Upper Canada, Medal for Contribs to Legal Profession 2002. *Publications include:* Power on Divorce 1964, Conceptual Analysis of Unified Family Courts, Law Reform Commission of Canada 1973, Payne on Divorce 1996, Child Support Guidelines in Canada 2004, Canadian Family Law 2006. *Address:* 1188 Morrison Drive, Ottawa, ON K2H 7L3, Canada (home). *Telephone:* (613) 829-1905 (home). *E-mail:* j_d_payne@sympatico.ca (office); julien.payne@gmail.com (home).

PAYNE, Nicholas; British opera company director; *Director, Opera Europa; b.* (Geoffrey John Nicholas Payne), 4 Jan. 1945, Bromley, Kent, England; s. of the late John Laurence Payne and of Dorothy Gwendoline Payne (née Attenborough); m. Linda Jane Adamson 1986; two s.; ed Eton Coll. and Trinity Coll. Cambridge; worked for Paterson Concert Management 1967; Arts Council administration course 1967–68; joined finance dept Royal Opera House, Covent Garden 1968–70; Subsidy Officer, Arts Council 1970–76; Financial Controller, Welsh Nat. Opera 1976–82; Gen. Admin. Opera North 1982–93; Dir of Opera, Royal Opera House 1993–98; Gen. Dir ENO 1998–2002; Dir Opera Europa 2003–; Hon. mem. Guildhall School of Music and Drama, Royal Northern College of Music; Dr hc (Leeds Metropolitan Univ.). *Address:* Opera Europa, 23 rue Léopold, 1000 Brussels, Belgium (office). *Telephone:* (2) 217-67-05 (office). *E-mail:* nicholas.payne@opera-europa.org (office). *Website:* www.opera-europa.org (office).

PAZ, George, BS; American business executive; *Chairman and CEO, Express Scripts Inc.; b.* 27 Aug. 1955, St Louis, Mo.; s. of Geronimo Paz and Collen May Hart; m. Georgene Marie Wade 1974; three c.; ed Univ. of Missouri; Jr Accountant, Gen. Am. 1980–82, Sr Accountant 1982–83, Accounting Admin. 1983–85, Tax Planning Analyst 1985–87, Dir of Tax Planning 1987–, mem. Bd of Dirs Gen. Am. Employees Fed. Credit Union 1985–; Partner, Coopers & Lybrand 1988–93, 1996–98; Exec. Vice-Pres. and Chief Financial Officer, Life Partners Group 1993–95; Sr Vice-Pres. and Chief Financial Officer, Express Scripts Inc. 1998–2003, Pres. 2003–05, CEO 2005–, Chair. 2006–; mem. Bd of Dirs Honeywell, Inc.; mem. Pharmaceutical Care Man. Asscn, American Inst. of Certified Public Accountants; Fellow, Life Office Man. Asscn. *Leisure interests:* golf, running, softball. *Address:* Express Scripts Inc., 1 Express Way, St Louis, MO 63121, USA (office). *Telephone:* (314) 996-0900 (office). *E-mail:* info@express-scripts.com (office). *Website:* www.express-scripts.com (office).

PAZ DE MELLO, Bernardo; Brazilian mining industry executive and art collector; b. 1949, Belo Horizonte, Minas Gerais; m. 6th Adriana Varejão (divorced); six c. (one from each m.); began by buying land and setting up mining cos; sold Itaminas (Itaminas Comércio de Minérios SA) (pig iron producer) to East China Mineral Exploration and Development Bureau, Nanjing (Chinese state-owned co.) 2010; Founder and mem. Bd of Dirs Centro de Arte Contemporânea Inhotim (or Instituto Inhotim) 2006–, botanical garden and contemporary art museum located on one of his properties. *Address:* Inhotim, Rua B 20, Brumadinho, Minas Gerais, 35460-000, Brazil (office). *Telephone:* (31) 32270001 (office). *E-mail:* info@inhotim.org.br (office). *Website:* www.inhotim.org.br (office).

PAZ ZAMORA, Jaime; Bolivian politician, academic and fmr head of state; b. 15 April 1939, Cochabamba; ed Colegio Jesuita, Sucre, Seminario Mayor de Villa Allende en Córdoba, Argentina and Catholic Univ. of Louvain, Belgium; fmr Pres. de la Fed. de Estudiantes Latino-Americanos, Belgium; Prof. of Sociology, Univ. Mayor de San Andrés; f. Movimiento de la Izquierda Revolucionaria, currently Leader; cand. for Vice-Pres. of Bolivia 1978 and 1980; first Vice-Pres. of the Andean Parl.; Vice-Pres. of Bolivia and Pres. Nat. Congress 1982–84; Pres. of Bolivia 1989–93; unsuccessful presidential cand. 2002; mem. Exec. Cttee Assoc. Latino-Americana de Derechos Humanos; mem. Movimiento de la Izquierda Revolucionaria. *Address:* Movimiento de la Izquierda Revolucionaria, Avda América 119, 2°, La Paz, Bolivia (office).

PAZNIAK, Zianon Stanislavavich; Belarusian politician; *Chairman, Conservative Christian Party of the Belarusian Popular Front; b.* 24 April 1944; fmr anti-Communist dissident; founder mem. Belorussian Popular Front (BPF) Oct. 1988, Leader 1989–99, Chair. Conservative Christian Party of the BPF (breakaway faction) 1999–; elected to Supreme Soviet as mem. Belorussian Democratic Bloc 1990–; cand. in presidential elections 1994; lives in Warsaw. *Address:* c/o Conservative Christian Party of the BPF, PO Box 208, 220040 Minsk, Belarus.

PEACE, Sir John Wilfred, Kt, FRSA; British retail executive; *Chairman, Standard Chartered PLC; b.* 2 March 1949; m. Christine Blakemore; three d.; ed Royal Mil. Acad., Sandhurst; joined Great Universal Stores (now GUS) PLC 1970, held several sr IT man. positions 1970–80, Co-founder CCN (market information services co.) 1980, CEO CCN 1991–2000, mem. Bd GUS PLC 1997–2006, Group CEO 2000–06; Chair. Burberry Group PLC 2002–; Chair. Experian plc 2006–; Ind. Dir (non-exec.) Standard Chartered PLC, Deputy Chair. Standard Chartered PLC 2007–09, Chair. 2009–; Chair. Bd Govs Nottingham Trent Univ. for ten years; Chair. The Work Foundation, Nottingham Econ. Resilience Forum; East Midlands Amb. for Business in the Community; mem. Bd Companions of the Chartered Man. Inst.; Trustee, Djanogly City Acad., Nottingham 1999–; DL Notts., High Sheriff 2011–; Dr hc (Nottingham). *Leisure interests:* horse riding, golf, watching Manchester United Football Club. *Address:* Standard Chartered PLC, 1 Basinghall Avenue, London, EC2V 5DD, England (office). *Telephone:* (20) 7885-8888 (office). *Fax:* (20) 7885-9999 (office). *E-mail:* info@standardchartered.com (office). *Website:* www.standardchartered.com (office).

PEACOCK, Sir Alan, Kt, DSC, MA, FBA, FRSE; British economist and academic; *Research Professor in Public Finance, Heriot-Watt University; b.* 26 June 1922, Ryton-on-Tyne, Tyne and Wear; s. of Alexander D. Peacock and Clara M. Peacock; m. Margaret Martha Astell-Burt 1944; two s. one d.; ed Grove Acad., Dundee High School, Univ. of St Andrews; RN 1942–45; Lecturer in Econs, Univ. of St Andrews 1947–48; lecturer in Econs, LSE 1948–51, Reader in Public Finance 1951–56; Prof. of Econ. Science, Univ. of Edinburgh 1956–62; Prof. of Econs, Univ. of York 1962–78; Prof. of Econs and Prin. Univ. Coll. at Buckingham 1980–83, Vice-Chancellor 1983–84, Prof. Emer. 1985–; Research Prof. in Public Finance, Heriot-Watt Univ. 1987–; Chief Econ. Adviser, Dept of Trade and Industry 1973–76; Pres. Int. Inst. of Public Finance 1966–69, Hon. Pres. 1975–; mem. Royal Comm. on Constitution 1970–73, Social Science Research Council 1971–72; Trustee, Inst. of Econ. Affairs; mem. Council, London Philharmonic Orchestra 1975–79; Chair. Arts Council Enquiry into Orchestral Resources 1969–70, Cttee on Financing the BBC 1985–86, Scottish Arts Council 1986–92; mem. Bd of Dirs English Music Theatre Ltd 1975–77; Chair. Hebrides Ensemble 1994–2000; mem. Council of Man., Nat. Inst. of Econ. and Social Research 1977–86; Dir (non-exec.) Economist Intelligence Unit 1977–84, Caledonian Bank PLC 1989–96; Exec. Dir David Hume Inst. 1985–90, Hon. Pres. 2002–05; Foreign mem. Accad. Naz. dei Lincei, Rome 1996–; Hon. Pres. Atlantic Econ. Soc. 1981–82; Hon. Fellow, LSE 1980–; Hon. mem. Royal Soc. of Musicians 1999–; Dr hc (Stirling) 1974, (Catania) 1991, (Brunel) 1989, (York) 1997, (Lisbon) 2000, (Turin) 2001; Hon. DEcon (Zürich) 1984; Hon. DSc (Buckingham) 1986; Hon. DSocSc (Edinburgh) 1990; Hon. LLD (St Andrews, Dundee) 1990; Scottish Free Enterprise Award 1987, Keynes Lecturer, British Acad. 1994, Royal Soc. of Edinburgh (Royal Medal) 2002. *Publications include:* Economics of National Insurance 1952, Growth of Public Expenditure in United Kingdom (with J. Wiseman) 1961, Economic Theory of Fiscal Policy (with G. K. Shaw) 1971, The Composer in the Market Place (with R. Weir) 1975, Welfare Economics: A Liberal Reinterpretation (with Charles Rowley), The Credibility of Liberal Economics 1977, The Political Economy of Taxation (ed. with Francesco Forte) 1980, The Regulation Game (ed.) 1984, Public Expenditure and Government Growth (ed. with F. Forte) 1985, Corporate Takeovers and the Public Interest (with G. Bannock) 1991, Paying the Piper: Culture, Music and Money 1993, Cultural Economics and Cultural Policies (ed. with Ilde Rizzo), The Political Economy of Economic Freedom 1997, The Political Economy of Heritage (ed.) 1998, What Price Civil Justice (with B. Main) 2000, Calling the Tune 2001, The Enigmatic Sailor 2003, The Political Economy of Sustainable Development 2003, Public Service Broadcasting without the BBC? 2004; numerous articles in professional journals on economics, public finance and public policy. *Leisure interest:* trying to write music, wine spotting. *Address:* David Hume Institute, 25 Buccleuch Place, Edinburgh, EH8 9LD (office); 5/24 Oswald Road, Edinburgh, EH9 2HE, Scotland (home). *Telephone:* (131) 667-9609 (office); (131) 667-5677 (home). *Fax:* (131) 667-9609 (office). *E-mail:* hume.institute@ed.ac.uk (office); peacock@ebs.hw.ac.uk (home). *Website:* www.ed.ac.uk/~hume (office).

PEACOCK, Hon. Andrew Sharp, AC, GCL, LLB; Australian diplomatist and fmr politician; b. 13 Feb. 1939, Melbourne, Vic.; s. of A. S. Peacock and Iris Peacock; m. 1st Susan Renouf (divorced), three d.; m. 2nd Margaret Ingram 1983 (divorced); m. 3rd Penne Percy North 2002; ed Scotch Coll., Univ. of Melbourne; Pres., Victorian Liberal Party 1965–66; mem. House of Rep. for Kooyong, Vic. 1966–94; fmr Partner, Rigby and Fielding (solicitors); fmr Chair. Peacock & Smith Pty Ltd (engineers); Minister for the Army and Minister Assisting the Prime Minister 1969–71, Assisting the Treas. 1971–72; Minister for External Territories 1972; mem. Opposition Exec. 1973–75, Spokesman on Foreign Affairs 1973–75; Minister for Foreign Affairs 1975–80, for the Environment Nov.–Dec. 1975, for Industrial Relations 1980–81, for Industry and Commerce 1982–83; Leader Parl. Liberal Party 1983–85; Opposition Spokesman on Foreign Affairs 1985–87; Deputy Leader of the Opposition and Shadow Treas. 1987–89; Leader of the Opposition 1989–90; Shadow Attorney-Gen. and Shadow Minister for Justice 1990–92; Shadow Minister for Trade 1992–93, for Foreign Affairs 1993–94; Chair. Parl. Political Strategy Cttee 1994; Amb. to USA 1997–2000; Chair. Int. Democrat Union 1989–92, Australian Horse Council 1996; Pres. Boeing Australia 2002–07; Dir, Orbital Engine Corpn Ltd 2001–02; Chief Grand Companion, Order of Logohu (New Guinea) 2006. *Leisure interests:* horse racing, Australian Rules Football, surfing, reading. *Address:* 19 Queens Road, Melbourne, Vic. 3004, Australia.

PEACOCK, William James, AC, PhD, FRS, FAA, FAIAS, FTSE; Australian research scientist; *Fellow, Commonwealth Scientific and Industrial Research Organisation (CSIRO); b.* 14 Dec. 1937, Leura, NSW; s. of William Edward Peacock and Evelyn Alison Peacock; m. Margaret Constance Woodward 1961; one s. two d.; ed Univ. of Sydney; Visiting Research Scientist, Genetics, CSIRO, Canberra 1963; Fellow, Dept of Biology, Univ. of Oregon 1963–64, Visiting Assoc. Prof. 1964–65; Research Consultant, Biology Div., Oak Ridge Nat. Lab., USA 1965; Sr Research Scientist, Div. of Plant Industry, CSIRO, Canberra 1965–69, Prin. Research Scientist 1969–73, Sr Prin. Research Scientist 1973–77, Chief Research Scientist 1977–78, Chief 1978–2003, now CSIRO Fellow; Distinguished Prof., Univ. of Technology, Sydney 2012–; Pres. Australian Acad. of Science 2002–06; Chief Scientist of Australia 2006–08; Adjunct Prof. of Biology, Univ. of California, San Diego, USA 1969–70; Visiting Prof. of Biochemistry, Stanford Univ., USA 1970–71; Visiting Distinguished Prof. of Molecular Biology, UCLA, USA 1977; Scientific Adviser, Australian Genetic Eng Ltd; Foreign Assoc., NAS 1990; Fellow, Australian Acad. of Technological Sciences; Foreign Fellow, Indian Nat. Science Acad. 1990; Hon. DSc (Charles Sturt Univ., Wagga Wagga) 1996, (Ghent) 2004, (Sydney) 2008, Hon. DScAg (Sydney) 2002; Edgeworth David Medal, Royal Soc. of NSW 1967, Lemberg Medal, Australian Biochemical Soc. 1978, N.I. Vavilov Medal 1987, BHP Bicentennial Prize 1988, Burnet Medal, Australian Acad. of Science 1989, CSIRO Medal 1989, Farrer Memorial Medal 1999, Prime Minister's Prize for Science 2000, Rabobank Leadership Award 2012, ACT Sr Australian of the Year 2013. *Publications:* 350 research papers on molecular biology, cytogenetics and evolution; ed. of six books. *Leisure interests:* bush-walking. *Address:* 16 Brassey Street, Deakin, ACT 2600, Australia (home). *Telephone:* (2) 6246-5250 (office); (2) 6281-4485 (home). *Fax:* (2) 6246-4866 (home). *E-mail:* jim.peacock@csiro.au (office).

PEACOCKE, Christopher Arthur Bruce, MA, DPhil, FBA; British academic; *Johnsonian Professor of Philosophy and Chairman, Department of Philosophy, Columbia University; b.* 22 May 1950, Birmingham, England; s. of Arthur

Peacocke and Rosemary Peacocke; m. Teresa Rosen 1980; one s. one d.; ed Magdalen Coll. School, Exeter Coll., Oxford and Harvard Univ. (Kennedy Scholar), USA; Sr Scholar, Merton Coll. Oxford 1972–73; Jr Research Fellow, Queen's Coll. Oxford 1973–76; Visiting Lecturer, Univ. of California, Berkeley 1975–76; Prize Fellow, All Souls Coll. Oxford 1975–79; Visiting Prof., Univ. of Mich. 1978; Fellow, New Coll., Oxford and Common Univ. Fund Lecturer in Philosophy, Univ. of Oxford 1979–85; Visiting Prof., UCLA 1981; Visiting Fellow, ANU, Canberra 1981, 1998; Fellow, Center for Advanced Study in Behavioural Sciences, Stanford 1983–84; Susan Stebbing Prof. of Philosophy, King's Coll. London 1985–88; Pres. Mind Asscn 1986; Waynflete Prof. of Metaphysical Philosophy, Univ. of Oxford and Fellow Magdalen Coll. Oxford 1989–2000; Leverhulme Research Professorship 1996–2000; Visiting Prof., New York Univ. 1996–2000, Prof. of Philosophy 2000–04; Prof. of Philosophy, Columbia Univ., New York 2004–, Johnsonian Prof. 2013–, Chair. Philosophy Dept 2013–; Richard Wollheim Chair of Philosophy, Univ. Coll. London 2007–; Fellow, American Acad. of Arts and Sciences 2010; Hon. DLitt (Warwick) 2007; Wilde Prize 1971, Webb-Medley Prize 1971, John Locke Prize 1972; Whitehead Lecturer, Harvard Univ. 2001, Immanuel Kant Lecturer, Stanford Univ. 2003, Gareth Evans Memorial Lecturer, Univ. of Oxford 2010, Context and Content Lecturer, Institut Jean Nicod, École Nat. Supérieure, Paris 2010, Kohut Lecturer, Univ. of Chicago 2011. *Publications:* Holistic Explanation: Action, Space, Interpretation 1979, Sense and Content 1983, Thoughts: An Essay on Content 1986, A Study of Concepts 1992, Being Known 1999, The Realm of Reason 2004, Truly Understood 2008, The Mirror of the World 2014; papers in Mind, Philosophical Review, Journal of Philosophy etc. *Leisure interests:* music, visual arts. *Address:* Department of Philosophy, MC 4971, Columbia University, 1150 Amsterdam Avenue, New York, NY 10027, USA (office). *Telephone:* (212) 854-3384 (office). *Fax:* (212) 854-4986 (office). *E-mail:* cp2161@columbia.edu (office). *Website:* philosophy.columbia.edu/directories/faculty/christopher-ab-peacocke (office).

PEAKE, Karolína; Czech lawyer and politician; *Chairman, LIDEM—Liberal Democrats;* b. (Karolína Kvačková), 10 Oct. 1975, Prague; m. Charles Peake 1999; two s.; ed Faculty of Law, Charles Univ.; mem. Civic Democratic Party while studying at univ. 1997–98; worked as trainee lawyer in Czech br of Baker & McKenzie; co-f. a maternal centre, along with other mothers from Prague 1; became involved in local politics, including campaigns to save a local park and extend local children's playgrounds 2005; elected to town council of Prague 1 as ind. 2006; mem. Public Affairs (Věci veřejné—VV) party 2007–12 (left with seven other MPs); mem. Chamber of Deputies 2010–, Chair. Constitutional Law Cttee, Chair. VV Parl. Group April–July 2011, Chair. Govt Anti-corruption Cttee 2011, Legis. Council of Govt 2011–12; Deputy Prime Minister 2011–13; Founder and Leader, LIDEM—Liberal Democrats 2012–; Minister of Defence 12–20 Dec. 2012. *Address:* LIDEM—Liberal Democrats, Štěpanská 611/14, 110 00 Prague, Czech Republic (office). *Telephone:* 777756704 (office). *E-mail:* info@lidem.cz (office). *Website:* www.lidem.cz (office); www.karolinapeake.cz.

PEARCE, Sir (Daniel Norton) Idris, Kt, CBE, TD, DL, FRICS; British chartered surveyor; b. 28 Nov. 1933, Neath, W Glam., Wales; s. of Lemeul George Douglas Pearce and Evelyn Mary Pearce; m. Ursula Helene Langley 1963 (divorced 1997); two d.; ed West Buckland School, Coll. of Estate Man.; joined Richard Ellis 1959, Partner 1961–92, Man. Partner 1981–87, Consultant 1992–2000; Chair. English Estates 1989–94; Chair. Higher Educ. Funding Council for Wales 1992–96; mem. Advisory Panel for Institutional Finance in New Towns 1974–80; mem. Property Services Agency Advisory Bd 1981–86; Property Adviser to Nat. Health Service Man. Bd 1985–90; mem. FCO Advisory Panel on Diplomatic Estate 1982–90, Financial Reporting Review Panel 1991–92, UFC 1991–93; Vice-Chair. Greater London TA & VRA 1991–94; mem. Gen. Council The Royal Inst. of Chartered Surveyors 1989–95, mem. Exec. Cttee 1984–91, Pres. 1990–91, Chair. Int. Assets Valuation Standards Cttee 1981–86; mem. Higher Educ. Funding Council for England 1992–96; Deputy Chair. Urban Regeneration Agency 1993–2000; Dir (non-exec.) Swan Hill 1993–2002, Nat. Mortgage Bank 1992–97, Innisfree Man. Ltd 1996–, Redburgh Ltd 1996–98, Millennium and Copthorne Hotels PLC 1996–; Gov. Peabody Trust 1992–2003; Pro-Chancellor Univ. of Surrey 1994–2003, Chair. Council 1997–2000, Pro-Chancellor Emer. 2003–; Sr Fellow, RCA 2012; Hon. Fellow, Coll. of Estate Man., Univ. of Wales, Cardiff 1997; Hon. Col, 135 Independent Topographic Squadron Royal Engineers (V); Hon. DSc (City Univ., London, Salford, Oxford Polytechnic); Hon. DTechSc (Univ. of E London); Hon. DEng (Bristol, Univ. of W of England); Hon. DUniv (Surrey), (Glamorgan); Thames Polytechnic, Centenary Fellowship 1991, Companion, De Monfort Univ. *Publications:* Profession of the Land – A Future; articles on valuation and property matters. *Leisure interests:* reading, opera, ballet, travel.

PEARCE, Reynold, BA, MA; British fashion designer; ed Nottingham Trent Univ., Central St Martin's Coll. of Art and Design; worked for John Galliano (q.v.); design asst for Roland Klein; Co-founder, with Andrew Fionda (q.v.), and Man. Dir Pearce Fionda 1994–, first capsule collection for Spring/Summer 1995 shown in New Generation show during London Fashion Week; also designs PIIF collection for Designers at Debenhams range 1997–, duo now concentrate on eveningwear range and children's bridesmaid creations; with Andrew Fionda received Newcomers Award for Export, British Knitwear Clothing Export Council and Fashion Weekly 1994, New Generation Award, Lloyds Bank British Fashion Awards 1995, World Young Designers Award, Int. Apparel Fed. 1996, Glamour Award, Lloyds Bank British Fashion Awards 1997. *Address:* Pearce Fionda, The Loft, 27 Horsell Road, Highbury, London, N5 1XL, England. *Telephone:* (20) 7609-6470. *Fax:* (20) 7609-6470. *E-mail:* info@pearcefionda.com. *Website:* pearcefionda.com.

PEARL, Judea, BS, MS, PhD; Israeli/American computer scientist, philosopher and academic; *Professor of Computer Science and Statistics and Director, Cognitive Systems Laboratory, University of California, Los Angeles;* b. 1936, Tel-Aviv; m. Ruth Pearl; three c. (one s. deceased); ed Technion, Haifa, Israel, Rutgers Univ. and Polytechnic Inst. of Brooklyn, USA; worked at RCA Research Labs, Princeton, NJ –1970; joined UCLA 1970, currently Prof. of Computer Science and Statistics and Dir Cognitive Systems Lab.; Distinguished Visiting Prof. of Computer Science, Inst. of Tech., Technion, Israel 2013; mem. Nat. Acad. of Eng 1995, American Acad. of Arts and Sciences 2012; Corresp. mem. Spanish Acad. of Eng 2002; Fellow, IEEE 1988, American Asscn of Artificial Intelligence 1990, Cognitive Science Soc. 2011; Hon. DSc (Toronto) 2007; Hon. DHumLitt (Chapman

Univ.) 2008; RCA Labs Achievement Award 1965, Nat. Sr Fellowship in Science 1975, UCLA 81st Faculty Research Lecturer 1996, IJCAI Research Excellence Award in Artificial Intelligence 1999, AAAI Classic Paper Award 2000, Lakatos Award 2001, Pekeris Memorial Lecturer 2003, 2003 Allen Newell Award 2004, Purpose Prize 2006, Benjamin Franklin Medal in Computers and Cognitive Science 2008, Festschrift and symposium in honour of Judea Pearl 2010, IEEE AI's Hall-of-Fame Aug. 2011, Rumelhart Prize Symposium 2011, Rumelhart Lecturer, Cognitive Science Soc. 2011, David E. Rumelhart Prize 2011, Harvey Prize 2012, A.M. Turing Award, Asscn for Computing Machinery 2012, Special Issue honouring Judea Pearl, Cognitive Science Journal Aug. 2013, Medallion Lecturer, Inst. of Math. Statistics 2013. *Achievements include:* pioneered use of Bayesian networks and probabilistic approach to artificial intelligence. *Publications:* Heuristics 1984, Probabilistic Reasoning in Intelligent Systems 1988, I Am Jewish: Personal Reflections Inspired by the Last Words of Daniel Pearl 2004, Causality: Models, Reasoning, and Inference (second edn) 2009; numerous papers in professional journals. *Leisure interests:* music: tenor, guitar, choir conducting; early printed books: science, philosophy, Judaica; history of science. *Address:* 4532 Boelter Hall, Computer Science Department, Cognitive Systems Lab, University of California, Los Angeles, CA 90024-1596, USA (office). *Telephone:* (310) 825-3243 (office). *Fax:* (310) 825-2273 (office). *E-mail:* judea@cs.ucla.edu (office). *Website:* bayes.cs.ucla.edu/jp_home.html (office).

PEARL, Valerie Louise, DPhil, FRHistS, FSA; British historian, academic and university administrator; b. 31 Dec. 1926, Newport, Mon.; d. of the late C. R. Bence, MP and F. Bowler; m. Morris L. Pearl 1949; one d.; ed King Edward VI High School, Birmingham and St Anne's Coll. Oxford; Sr Research Studentship, Westfield Coll. London 1962; Leverhulme Research Award 1962; Graham Research Fellow, lecturer in History, Somerville Coll. Oxford 1965–68; Reader in History of London, Univ. Coll. London 1968–76, Prof. 1976–81; Pres. New Hall, Cambridge 1981–1995; Founder and Ed.-in-Chief, The London Journal 1973–77; McBride Visiting Prof., Bryn Mawr Coll., USA 1974; Woodward Lecturer, Yale Univ. 1974; Literary Dir Royal Historical Soc. 1975–77; Gov. Museum of London 1978–92; Stow Commemorative Lecturer 1979; Ford Special Lecturer, Oxford 1980; Syndic, Univ. of Cambridge Library, Cambridge Univ. Press 1982–92; Commr Royal Comm. on Historical Manuscripts 1983–92; Hon. Fellow, St Anne's Coll. Oxford 1992. *Publications:* London and the Outbreak of the Puritan Revolution 1625–43 1961, contrib. to The Interregnum; Puritans and Revolutionaries, co-ed. and contrib. to History and Imagination (vol. in honour of Hugh Trevor-Roper) 1981, Stow's Survey of London (ed.) 1985, Change and Continuity in 17th-Century London 1981 (Japanese edn 1992); articles and contribs to books, encyclopedias and learned journals. *Leisure interests:* walking, gardening, swimming. *Address:* c/o New Hall, Cambridge, CB3 0DF, England.

PEARLSTEIN, Philip, MA; American artist; b. 24 May 1924, Pittsburgh; s. of David Pearlstein and Libbie Kalser; m. Dorothy Cantor 1950; one s. two d.; ed Carnegie Inst. of Tech. and New York Univ.; Instructor Pratt Inst. 1959–63; visiting critic, Yale 1962–63; Asst Prof. then Prof., Art Dept Brooklyn Coll. 1963–82, now Distinguished Prof. Emer.; participant in numerous group exhbns at Whitney Museum of American Art and elsewhere; work in perm. collections including Whitney Museum and Museum of Modern Art, New York; mem. American Acad. of Arts and Letters; Fulbright Fellow 1958–59; Guggenheim Fellow 1971–72. *Address:* c/o Forum Gallery, New York, 745 Fifth Avenue, New York, NY 10151, USA.

PEARLSTINE, Norman, LLB; American journalist, editor and publishing executive; b. 4 Oct. 1942; s. of Raymond Pearlstine and Gladys Pearlstine; ed Haverford Coll., Univ. of Pennsylvania; staff reporter, Wall Street Journal, Dallas, Detroit, LA 1968–73, Tokyo Bureau Chief 1973–76, Man. Ed. Asian Wall Street Journal, Hong Kong 1976–78; Exec. Ed. Forbes Magazine, LA 1978–80; Nat. News Ed. Wall Street Journal, New York 1980–82, Ed. and Publr Wall Street Journal Europe, Brussels 1982–83, Man. Ed. and Vice-Pres. Wall Street Journal, New York 1983–91, Exec. Ed. 1991–92; Pres. and CEO Friday Holdings L.P., New York 1993–94; Ed.-in-Chief Time Inc. 1995–2006, then Sr Advisor to Time Warner; Sr Advisor to global telecommunications and media team, The Carlyle Group 2006–08; Chief Content Officer, Bloomberg L.P. 2008–11; Pres. and CEO The American Acad. in Berlin 2006–11; mem. New York Historical Soc., Council on Foreign Relations; Ed. of Year Award, Nat. Press Foundation 1989, Loeb Lifetime Achievement Award for Distinguished Business and Financial Journalism 2000, American Soc. of Magazine Editors Lifetime Achievement Award 2005. *Publication:* Off the Record 2007. *Website:* www.normanpearlstine.com.

PEARSE, Sir Brian, Kt, FCIB; British banker; *Chairman of Trustees, Centre for the Study of Financial Innovation;* b. 23 Aug. 1933; s. of Francis Pearse and Eileen Pearse; m. Patricia M. Callaghan 1959; one s. two d.; ed St Edward's Coll., Liverpool; joined Martin's Bank Ltd 1950; joined Barclays Bank 1969, Local Dir, Birmingham 1972, Gen. Man. 1977, CEO, N America 1983, Finance Dir Barclays Bank PLC 1987–91; Chief Exec. Midland Bank 1991–94; Pres. Chartered Inst. of Bankers 1993–94; Chair. Housing Corpn 1994–97, British Invisibles 1994–97, Lucas Industries PLC 1994–96, LucasVarity PLC 1996–98; mem. and fmr Chair. Governing Council, Centre for the Study of Financial Innovation, currently Chair. of Trustees; Dir British American Chamber of Commerce 1987–98; Dir (non-exec.), Smith & Nephew 1993–; Dir, British Overseas Trade Bd 1994–97; Gov. Univ. of Plymouth 1997– (Vice-Chair. 1999–); Deputy Chair. Britannic Assurance PLC 1997–; mem. Bd of Banking Supervision 1998–. *Leisure interests:* rugby, opera. *Address:* Centre for the Study of Financial Innovation, First Floor, 73 Leadenhall Market, London, EC3V 1LT (office); Flat 7, 14 Gloucester Street, London, SW1V 2DN, England (home). *Telephone:* (20) 7621-1056 (office). *E-mail:* info@csfi.org (office). *Website:* www.csfi.org (office).

PEARSON, Ralph Gottfried, PhD; American chemist and academic; *Professor Emeritus of Chemistry, University of California, Santa Barbara;* b. 12 Jan. 1919, Chicago, Ill.; s. of Gottfried Pearson and Kerstin Pearson (née Larson); m. Lenore Johnson 1941 (died 1982); two s. one d.; ed Lewis Inst., Northwestern Univ.; First Lt in USAF 1944–46; Asst Prof., Chem. Dept, Northwestern Univ. 1946–52, Assoc. Prof. 1952–57, Prof. 1957–76; Prof. of Chem., Univ. of Calif., Santa Barbara 1976–89, Prof. Emer. 1989–; mem. NAS 1974–; fmr Guggenheim Fellow; Inorganic Award, ACS, Chemical Pioneer Award, American Inst. of Chemists 1995. *Publications:* Kinetics and Mechanism 1953, Mechanisms of Inorganic Reactions

1958, Hard and Soft Acids and Bases 1974, Symmetry Rules for Chemical Reactions 1976, Chemical Hardness 1997. *Leisure interest:* classical music. *Address:* 4619 Physical Sciences Building North, Chemistry Department, University of California, Santa Barbara, CA 93106 (office); 715 Grove Lane, Santa Barbara, CA 93105, USA (home). *Telephone:* (805) 893-3745 (office); (805) 687-7890 (home). *Fax:* (805) 893-4120 (office). *Website:* www.chem.ucsb.edu (office).

PEARSON WRIGHT, Stuart, BA; British portrait artist; b. 1975, Northampton, England; m. Polly Pearson Wright; one s.; ed Slade School of Fine Art, Univ. Coll. London; grew up in Eastbourne; award-winning portrait painter; noted persons depicted in paintings include six past-Presidents of the British Acad., Charles Saumerez Smith (Dir Nat. Gallery, London), HRH The Duke of Edinburgh, Mike Leigh (film dir), Brenda Blethyn, Richard E. Grant, John Hurt, David Thewlis (actors), J. K. Rowling (author); co-ran a project space on Vyner Street called Five Hundred Dollars 2009; curated a group drawing exhbn called Kunskog which featured the work of Gillian Wearing, Michael Landy, Paul Noble and Ged Quinn, amongst others; has working on a series of set designs: one for an opera, Dido and Aeneas by Jevington Nat. Opera and also for his wife, the singer/songwriter The Tiger's Bride, who performed at the Nat. Portrait Gallery 2012; lives and works in East London; Travel Award, BP Portrait Award 1998, Third Prize, Singer & Friedlander/Sunday Times Watercolour competition 1999, British Finalist, Windsor & Newton Millennium Competition 2000, Grant Award, Elizabeth Greenshield Foundation 2000, Third Prize, Garrick/Milne Prize 2000, Winner, BP Portrait Award 2001, Travel Award, Discerning Eye (Sri Lanka) 2003, Printmaking Award, Joseph Webb Commemorative Fund 2004, Purchase Prize, Univ. of Wales, Aberystwyth 2004, First Prize, Singer & Friedlander/Sunday Times Watercolour competition 2004, First Prize, Garrick/Milne Prize 2005. *Works in public collections:* Aberdeen Art Gallery, Aldo Coronelli Collection, Ashmolean Museum, Oxford, British Academy, British Museum, Daniel Radcliffe Collection, David Roberts Art Foundation, David Thewlis Collection, London, Frank Cohen Collection, Manchester Garrick Club, London, Govt Art collection, House of Commons, London, Graham Fink Collection, Beijing, Index ventures Collection, Geneva, ING Barings Bank, Brussels, Jerwood Foundation, London, J. K. Rowling Collection, Edinburgh, John Hurt Collection, London, Keira Knightley Collection, London, Nat. Portrait Gallery, London, Nick Candy Collection, London, Omer Koç Collection, Istanbul, Philip Mould Collection, London, Rhode Island School of Design Museum, USA, School of Art Gallery & Museum, Aberystwyth, Wales, Singer and Friedlander Bank, Singer and Friedlander PLC, Sir Paul Smith Collection, London, Scheringa Museum, Netherlands, Taylor Thomson Collection, Los Angeles. *Telephone:* 7794-629188 (mobile, Riflemaker). *E-mail:* info@riflemaker.org. *Website:* www.stuartpearsonwright.com.

PEART, Sir (William) Stanley, Kt, MB, BS, MD, FRCP, FRS; British academic and physician; *Professor Emeritus of Medicine, St Mary's Hospital, London;* b. 31 March 1922, South Shields; s. of J. G. Peart and M. Peart; m. Peggy Parkes 1947 (died 2002); one s. one d.; ed King's Coll. School, Wimbledon and St Mary's Hosp. Medical School, London; Lecturer in Medicine, St Mary's Hosp., London 1950–56, Prof. of Medicine 1956–87, Prof. Emer. 1987–; Master, Hunterian Inst. Royal Coll. of Surgeons 1988–92; Chair. Medical Research Soc. 1968, Beit Trust Advisory Bd 1980, Northwick Park Inst. for Medical Research 1994–; mem. Medical Research Council 1969; mem. Advisory Bd for the Research Councils 1973; Trustee Wellcome Trust 1975–94 (Deputy Chair. 1991–94, Consultant 1994–99); Councillor, Royal Coll. of Physicians 1977; Stouffer Prize 1968, Buchanan Medal, Royal Soc. 2000. *Publications:* Clinical Atlas of Hypertension 1991; articles in The Biochemical Journal, Journal of Physiology, The Lancet; chapters in textbooks on renal disease and high blood pressure. *Leisure interests:* reading, photography, astronomy. *Address:* 17 Highgate Close, London, N6 4SD, England (home). *Telephone:* (20) 8341-3111 (home). *E-mail:* stanleypeart@blueyonder.com (home).

PÉBEREAU, Georges Alexandre; French engineer and business executive; b. 20 July 1931, Digne, Basses-Alpes; s. of Alexandre Pébereau and Yvonne Raybaud; m. Bernadette Potier 1954; three d.; ed Lycées Buffon, Saint-Louis, Paris, Ecole Polytechnique; engineer of roads and bridges in various wards 1955–64; Pres. Assen des ingénieurs des ponts et chaussées 1964; teacher of Urban Man. Ecole nat. des ponts et chaussées 1964; Chief-Eng, Dept Seine-St-Denis 1965, Tech. Counsellor to Ministry of Equipment 1966, Dir Office Ministry of Equipment and Housing 1967–68; Dir Land and Urban Man. 1966–68; Vice-Pres. Cttee action concertée Urbanisation 1967–68; at Cie industrielle des télécommunications (Cit) 1968–70, Jt Dir-Gen. 1968–69, Dir-Gen. 1969–70; Admin.-Dir-Gen. Cie industrielle des télécommunications (Cit-Alcatel) 1970–83, Pres., Dir 1982–86, Hon. Pres. 1986–; at Cie Gén d'électricité 1970–86, Dir then Jt Dir-Gen. 1970–72, Admin. 1971, Dir-Gen. 1972, then Chair., Pres. and CEO Admin., Dir –1986; Hon. Pres. 1986; Co-owner Cie Privée de Banque 1987; Founder and Chair. Marceau Investissements 1997–, Indra Finance 1987–95; Pres. Délia Finance 1997–; mem. Cttee de direction et de conseil d'admin 1970–; mem. conseil d'admin de la Soc. des sucreries de Bourbon 1995–, of Musée du Louvre 1996; Commdr Légion d'honneur, Commdr, Ordre nat. du Mérite. *Address:* Marceau Investissements, 10–12 Avenue de Mesine, 75008 Paris (office); 19 avenue Charles Floquet, 75007 Paris, France (home). *Telephone:* 1-40-74-25-06 (office). *Fax:* 1-40-74-25-10 (office). *E-mail:* contact@marceau-finance.fr (office). *Website:* www.marceau-finance.fr (office).

PÉBEREAU, Michel Jean Denis; French banker; *Honorary Chairman, BNP Paribas;* b. 23 Jan. 1942, Paris; s. of Alexandre Pébereau and Yvonne Raybaud; m. Agnès Faure 1962; two s. two d.; ed Lycées Buffon and Louis-le-Grand, Paris, Ecole Polytechnique and Ecole Nat. d'Admin; various appointments in Ministry of Economy and Finance 1970–81; Man. Dir Crédit Commercial de France 1982–87, Chair. and CEO 1987–93; Chair. and CEO Banque Nationale de Paris (BNP) 1993–2000, apptd Chair. Paribas 1999, Chair. and CEO BNP Paribas 2000–03, Chair. 2006–11, Hon. Chair. 2011–, mem. Bd of Dirs BNP Paribas SA (Switzerland); Dir, SA des Galeries Lafayette (non-voting), Lafarge, Cie de Saint-Gobain, Total, European Aeronautic Defence and Space Co. (EADS) NV, Pargesa Holding SA (Switzerland); Comm. for Selective Aid for Film Distribution 1987–88; Lecturer, Inst. d'Etudes Politiques Paris 1967–78, Prof. 1980–, mem. Man. Cttee 1984–; Lecturer, Ecole Nat. de Statistiques et d'Admin Economique 1968–79; Inspecteur Général des Finances; mem. Supervisory Bd Dresdner Bank 1997–2009, AXA, Banque Marocaine pour le Commerce et l'Industrie (Morocco); mem. Int. Capital Markets Advisory Cttee Fed. Reserve Bank, New York 1998;

Pres. Comm. d'exploitation bancaire de l'Asscn française des banques 2000; Censor, Galeries Lafayette SA; mem. Bd AXA, Lafarge, Cie de Saint-Gobain, Total, BNP Paribas SA (Switzerland), EADS NV (Netherlands), Pargesa Holding SA (Switzerland); Chair. Investment Banking and Financial Markets Cttee, Fédération Bancaire Française, Man. Bd of Institut d'Etudes Politiques de Paris, Supervisory Bd of Institut Aspen, France, Institut de l'Entreprise, European Financial Round Table; mem. Acad. des sciences morales et politiques, Exec. Cttee Mouvement des Entreprises en France, Haut Conseil de l'Educ., European Financial Round Table, Institut Int. d'Etudes Bancaires, Int. Advisory Panel of Monetary Authority of Singapore, Int. Capital Markets Advisory Cttee of Fed. Reserve Bank of New York, Int. Business Leaders' Advisory Council for the Mayor of Shanghai, Supervisory Bd of Banque Marocaine pour le Commerce et l'Industrie (Morocco); Non-voting Dir, Soc. Anonyme des Galeries Lafayette; Grand Officier, Légion d'honneur; Commdr, Ordre nat. du Mérite. *Publications:* La politique économique de la France (three vols); science fiction book reviews magazine Le Journal du dimanche. *Leisure interest:* piano. *Address:* BNP Paribas, 16 boulevard des Italiens, 75009 Paris, France (office). *Telephone:* 1-40-14-45-46 (office). *Fax:* 1-40-14-69-73 (office). *Website:* www.bnpparibas.com (office).

PECCERELLI, Fredy, BA; Guatemalan forensic anthropologist; *Executive Director, Guatemalan Forensic Anthropology Foundation;* b. 1971; m.; several c.; ed Brooklyn Coll., City Univ. of New York, USA and Univ. of Bournemouth, UK; went into exile with his family to New York aged nine; led forensic archeological investgations of war crimes in Bosnia and Herzegovina for Int. Criminal Tribunal for the Fmr Yugoslavia; founding mem. Fundación de Antropología Forense de Guatemala (FAFG–Guatemalan Forensic Anthropology Foundation) 1996, responsible for investigating human rights abuses committed during 36-year civil war, now Exec. Dir FAFG; currently studying for MSc degree in UK; chosen by Time magazine as one of 50 Latin American Leaders for the New Millennium 1999, named by Guatemalan Youth Comm. an Icon for Youth of Guatemala 1999. *Address:* c/o AAAS Science and Human Rights Program, 1200 New York Avenue, NW, Washington, DC 20005, USA (office).

PECINA, Martin, MBA; Czech engineer, business executive and politician; b. 9 July 1968, Ostrava; m.; two c.; ed Mechanical Eng High School, Karviná, Faculty of Mechanical Eng, VSB-Tech. Univ. of Ostrava, Masaryk Inst. of Higher Educ., Prague, Sheffield Business School, UK; sales dir of pvt. co. 1992–96; employee, Hutní projekt Frýdek-Místek 1996–99; CEO Hutní projekt Frýdek-Místek Jt-Stock Co. 1999–2003; Deputy Minister of Industry and Trade 2003–05; Chair. Office for the Protection of Competition 2005–09; Minister of the Interior 2009–10; Deputy Prime Minister and Minister of the Interior 2013–14; mem. Civic Democratic Party (ODS) –1997, Czech Social Democratic Party (ČSSD) 2001–05. *Address:* c/o Ministry of the Interior, Nad Štolou 3, PO Box 21, 170 34 Prague 7, Czech Republic. *E-mail:* public@mvcr.cz.

PECKER, David J., CPA; American publishing executive; *Chairman and CEO, American Media, Inc.;* b. 24 Sept. 1951; m. Karen Balan 1987; ed Pace and New York Univs; fmrly Sr Auditor, Price Waterhouse & Co.; fmrly Man. Financial Reporting, Diamandis Communications Inc., also Dir Financial Reporting, Dir Accounting, Asst Controller; Exec. Vice-Pres. Hachette Magazines Inc. 1990–91, Pres. 1991–92, Pres., CEO 1992–99, Chair. and CEO American Media Inc. 1999–; mem. Fashion Group's Int. Advisory Bd, NY City Partnership Cttee, American Man. Asscn; mem. Bd Dirs Pace Univ., Drug Enforcement Agents Foundation 1995–. *Address:* American Media Inc., 4 New York Plaza, New York, NY 10004, USA (office). *Telephone:* (212) 545-4800 (office). *Website:* www.americanmediainc .com.

PECKER, Jean-Claude, (Jean-Claude Pradel); French astronomer; *Honorary Professor, Collège de France;* b. 10 May 1923, Reims, Marne; s. of Victor-Noel Pecker and Nelly Catherine Herrmann; m. 2nd Annie A. Vormser 1974 (died 2002); one s. two d. (by previous m.); ed Lycée de Bordeaux, Univs of Grenoble and Paris (Sorbonne) and Ecole Normale Supérieure; Research Asst, CNRS 1946–52; Assoc. Prof., Univ. of Clermont-Ferrand 1952–55; Assoc. Astronomer, Paris Observatory 1955–62, Astronomer 1962–69; Dir Nice Observatory 1962–69; Dir Inst. of Astrophysics, Paris 1972–79; Prof., Collège de France 1963–89, Hon. Prof. 1989–; Asst Gen. Sec. Int. Astronomical Union 1961–63, Gen. Sec. 1964–67; Pres. Comité Nat. Français d'Astronomie 1970–73; Dir Inst. Astrophysique, Paris 1971–78; Pres. Soc. Astronomique de France 1973–76; Pres. French Asscn for Advancement of Science 1978; Chair. Orientation Cttee, Sciences-Industries Museum, La Villette 1983–85; Chair. Nat. Cttee Scientific and Tech. Culture 1985–87; Vice-Chair. French Comm. for UNESCO 1991–96; Perm. Rep. to UNESCO of Int. Humanist and Ethical Union; Vice-Chair. Scientific Cttee Musées de France 1988–; Pres. Asscn française d'information scientifique 1999–2001; Assoc. Royal Soc. of Science, Liège 1967; Corresp., Bureau des Longitudes 1968; Assoc. Royal Astronomical Soc. 1968; Corresp. mem. Acad. des Sciences, France 1969, mem. 1977; mem. Acad. Nat. Bordeaux 1977, Acad. Royale Belgique 1979, Acad. European of Science, Arts and Letters 1982, Int. Acad. of Humanism 1983 (Sec.), Acad. Europaea 1988 (Council mem., Vice-Pres. 1989–92; Commdr, Légion d'honneur, des Palmes académiques, Grand Croix, Ordre nat. du Mérite; Prix Forthuny, Inst. de France, Prix Stroobant Acad. des Sciences de Belgique 1965, Prix Manley-Bendall de l'Acad. de Bordeaux 1966, Prix des Trois Physiciens 1969, Janssen Medal Astronomical Soc., France 1967, Prix Jean Perrin, Soc. Française de Physique 1973, Medal Univ. de Nice 1972, Adion Medal 1981, Prix Union Rationaliste 1983, Personnalité de l'année 1984, Janssen Medal, Photographic Soc. of France 1989, Lodén Prize, Royal Astronomical Soc. of Sweden 1996. *Radio includes:* many programmes on popular astronomy 1957–. *Television includes:* many programmes on popular astronomy. *Publications include:* L'astronomie au jour le jour (with P. Couderc and E. Schatzman) 1954, Astrophysique générale (with E. Schatzman) 1959, Le ciel 1959, L'astronomie expérimentale 1969, Les laboratoires spatiaux 1969, Papa, dis-moi: L'astronomie, qu'est-ce que c'est? 1971, L'astronomie nouvelle (ed.) 1971, Clefs pour l'astronomie 1981, Sous l'étoile soleil 1984, Astronomie (ed.) 1985, Pour comprendre l'univers (with Delsemme and Reeves) 1988, L'avenir du soleil 1990, Le promeneur du ciel 1992, Le soleil est une étoile 1992, Débat sur les phénomènes paranormaux 1997, Understanding the Universe 2001, L'Univers exploré, peu à peu expliqué 2003, La photographie astronomique 2003, Lalanduana I (with S. Dumont) 2007. *Leisure interests:* painting, poetry, swimming. *Address:* Annexe du Collège de France, 3 rue d'Ulm, 75005 Paris (office); Pusat-Tasek, Les Corbeaux, 85350 L'Île d'Yeu, France (home). *Telephone:* 1-44-27-16-95 (office); (2) 51-58-58-27 (home). *E-mail:* j.c.pecker@wanadoo.fr (home).

PECKHAM, Sir Michael John, Kt, MA, MD, FRCP, FRCPath, FRCR, FRCS; British physician and academic; b. 2 Aug. 1935, Panteg, Wales; s. of William Stuart Peckham and Gladys Mary Peckham (née Harris); m. Catherine Stevenson King 1958; three s.; ed St Catharine's Coll. Cambridge, Univ. Coll. Hosp. Medical School; Sr Lecturer, Inst. of Cancer Research 1972–74, Prof. and Hon. Consultant, Inst. of Cancer Research and Royal Marsden Hosp. 1974–86, Dean Inst. of Cancer Research 1984–86; Dir British Post grad. Medical Fed. 1986–90; Ed.-in-Chief European Journal of Cancer 1990–95; Dir of Research and Devt, Dept of Health 1991–95; Dir School of Public Policy, Univ. Coll. London 1996–2000; Vice-Chair. Imperial Cancer Research Fund 1987–90; Chair. Office of Science and Tech. Healthcare Foresight Programme 1999–2000, Nat. Educational Research Forum 2000, Devt Forum 2000; Founding Pres. British Oncological Asscn 1986–88; Pres. Fed. of European Cancer Socs 1989–91, European Soc. for Therapeutic Radiology and Oncology 1983–85; Foreign Assoc. mem. NAS Inst. of Medicine 1994–; Hon. Fellow, St Catharine's Coll., Cambridge 1998; Dr hc (Besançon), (Catholic Univ. of Louvain) 1993; Hon. DSc (Loughborough), (Exeter) 1996. *Publications:* Oxford Textbook of Oncology (co-author) 1995, Clinical Futures 1999, A Model for Health: Innovation and the Future of Health Services 2000. *Address:* 6 Crescent Place, London, SW3 2EA, England (home). *E-mail:* michael.peckham@yahoo.com (home).

PECKOVÁ, Dagmar; Czech singer (mezzo-soprano); b. 4 April 1961, Chrudim; m. 1st J. Vejvoda; m. 2nd Aleš Kasprík 1997; one s.; m. 3rd Klaus Schiesser; one d.; ed Prague Conservatory; soloist at Karlín Musical Theatre, Prague 1982–85; soloist with numerous cos including Czech Philharmonic 1985–, with Semper Opera, Dresden 1985–88, with State Opera Berlin 1989–92; guest appearances in Tokyo, Paris 1992, Bregenz Festival, Austria 1992, 1993, Hamburg 1993, Salzburg Festival 1993, 1995, 1996, Basel 1994, Zürich 1994, London 1995, Tel-Aviv 1996, La Corona Festival, Spain 1996, San Sebastien Festival, Spain 1996, Prague Spring Festival 1996, Frankfurt 1996; concert tours Austria, Switzerland, Germany, UK 1993, France, Japan 1990, 1994, USA 1997–99; charity concerts after floods in Czech Repub. 2002; roles include Leonora (Basel), Cherubino in The Marriage of Figaro (London), Rosina in The Barber of Seville (Berlin, Dresden), Carmen (Prague), Varvara in Katya Kabanova (Salzburg, Barcelona); First Prize, Antonin Dvořák Competition 1982, Second Prize, Brno Vocal Competition 1985, Czech Music Fund Award (for role of Eliza Doolittle in My Fair Lady) 1985, First Prize, Prague Spring Vocal Competition 1986, Berlin Critics' Prize (for role of Dorabella in Così fan tutte) 1989, European Foundation for Music Prize 1993, Thalia Prize (for Carmen) 2000. *Recordings include:* Martinů—Nipponari 1991, Mozart—Che Bella 1994, Janáček—Moravian Folk Poetry in Song 1994, Mahler—Adagietto, Kindertotenlieder 1996, Songs of Mahler and Berio 1997, Janáček—Kátá Kabanová 1997, Janáček—Diary of One Who Disappeared 1999, recital of music by Wagner, Schoenberg, Zemlinsky and Brahms 2000, Lieder by Strauss, Schoeck, Berg 2001, Lieder by Dvořák 2001, Arias (live) 2002. *Leisure interests:* reading, driving. *Address:* c/o Austroconcert, Gluckgasse 1, 1010 Vienna, Austria.

PÉCRESSE, Valérie; French politician; b. 14 July 1967, Neuilly-sur-Seine (Hauts-de-Seine); d. of Dominique Roux; m.; two s. one d.; ed Haute École de Commerce, École Nat. d'Admin; auditor, Conseil d'État 1992–98; adviser, French Presidency 1998; Deputy for Yvelines, Nat. Ass. 2002–07, mem. Comm. on Cultural, Family and Social Affairs, Rapporteur, Mission of Information on the Family and the Rights of Children, Pres. Study Group on the Applications of Biotechnologies in Genetics and Ethical Problems, Vice-Pres. Study Group on the Internet, Information Technologies and of Communication and e-Commerce, mem. Del. on the Rights of Women and Gender Equality, Organizer, Union pour un Mouvement Populaire (UMP) Working Group on the Family; Spokesman for UMP; Regional Councillor, Île-de-France 2004–; Minister of Higher Educ. and Research 2007–11, of the Budget, Public Finances, Civil Service and State Reform 2011–12; spokeswoman for the Govt 2011–12. *Address:* Conseil régional d'Île-de-France, 33 rue Barbet de Jouy, 75007 Paris, France (office). *Telephone:* 1-53-85-53-85 (office). *E-mail:* contact@valeriepecresse.fr (office). *Website:* www.iledefrance.fr (office). www.valeriepecresse.fr.

PEDDER, Anthony P. (Tony), OBE, MSc; British company director and fmr steel industry executive; *Chairman, Sheffield Forgemasters International Limited;* b. 1949; m.; two. s.; ed Univ. of London; joined steel industry 1972; several sr man. positions in British Steel (now Corus), mem. bd British Steel 1992, mem. bd Corus Group (after merger with British Steel) 1999, CEO 2001–03; Chair. Sheffield Forgemasters International Ltd 2005–; Dir (non-exec.), Metalysis Ltd 2005–, JSW (India) Ltd 2005–, HCF International Ltd 2006–, EEF Ltd 2008; Chair. Sheffield Teaching Hospitals Trust 2012–, Council of Univ. of Sheffield 2013–; DL, South Yorks. 2007; Master Cutler 2013–14. *Address:* Sheffield Forgemasters International Ltd, PO Box 286, Brightside Lane, Sheffield, S9 2RW, England (office). *Website:* www.sheffieldforgemasters.com (office).

PEDERSEN, Helga; Norwegian politician; b. 13 Jan. 1973; ed Univ. of Tromsø, Univ. of Bergen; teacher, Boftsa School, Tana 1992–93; Civil Servant, Econ. Devt and Transport Dept, Finnmark County 1998–2000, County Council Rep. 1999–2005, Chair. County Council 2003–05; Political Adviser to Minister of Trade and Industry 2001; part-time project worker, UNEP/GRID, Arendal 2001–02; Head of Project to Promote Econ. and Cultural Devt, Tanafjord Area 2002–03; Minister of Fisheries and Coastal Affairs 2005–09; mem. Det norske Arbeiderparti (Norwegian Labour Party). *Address:* Storting, Karl Johansgt. 22, 0026 Oslo, Norway (office). *Telephone:* 23-31-30-50 (office). *E-mail:* info@stortinget.no (office). *Website:* www.stortinget.no (office).

PEDERSEN, K(nud) George, OC, O.Ont, OBC, PhD, FRSA, FCCT; Canadian university president (retd) and academic; b. 13 June 1931, Peace River, Alberta; s. of Hjalmar Pedersen and Anna Jensen; m. 1st Joan Vanderwarker 1953 (died 1988); m. 2nd Penny Jones 1988; one s. one d.; ed Chilliwack Sr High School and Univs of BC, Washington and Chicago; school teacher, N Vancouver school system 1952–56; Vice-Prin., North Star Elementary School 1956–59; Prin. Carisbrooke Elementary School 1959–61; Vice-Prin., Handsworth Secondary School 1961–63; Prin., Balmoral Secondary School 1963–65; Research Assoc. Univ. of Chicago 1965–68; Asst Prof., Ont. Inst. for Studies in Educ. and Univ. of Toronto 1968–70;

Assoc. Dir Midwest Admin. Center, Univ. of Chicago 1970–72; Dean, Faculty of Educ. Univ. of Vic. 1972–75, Vice-Pres. (Academic) 1975–78; Pres. and Vice-Chancellor Simon Fraser Univ. 1979–83, Univ. of British Columbia 1983–85, Univ. of Western Ontario 1985–94, Univ. of Northern British Columbia 1995–2004, Royal Roads Univ. 1995–96; Chancellor Univ. of Northern British Columbia 1998–2004; Chair. Bd Govs, Emily Carr Univ. of Art and Design 2004–10; Fellow, Canadian Coll. of Teachers; Commemorative Medal 1992, Order of Canada 1993, Order of Ont. 1994, Order of BC 2002, Queen's Golden Jubilee Medal 2002, Queen's Diamond Jubilee Medal 2012; Hon. LLD (McMaster) 1996, (Simon Fraser Univ.) 2003, (Univ. of Northern British Columbia) 2005; Hon. DLitt (Emily Carr Univ. of Art and Design) 2003, (Univ. of the Fraser Valley) 2007; ten major scholarships, including Univ. of Chicago Scholarships 1965–68, Canada Council Scholarships 1966–68, Ford Foundation Fellowship 1967–68. *Publications:* The Itinerant Schoolmaster 1973; book chapters and numerous articles. *Leisure interests:* fishing, golf, gardening, cooking, carving. *Address:* 2232 Spruce Street, Vancouver, BC V6H 2P3, Canada. *Telephone:* (604) 733-2400; (360) 371-7071. *Fax:* (604) 733-2400; (360) 371-7071. *E-mail:* pgpedersen@telus.net; pgpedersen@comcast.net.

PEDERSEN, Roger A., PhD; American embryologist and academic; *Professor of Regenerative Medicine and Director of Research in Regenerative Medicine, Department of Surgery and the Anne McLaren Laboratory for Regenerative Medicine, University of Cambridge;* Prof., Univ. of California, San Francisco –2001, Prof. Emer. 2001–; Prof. of Regenerative Medicine, Dept of Surgery, Univ. of Cambridge School of Clinical Medicine, UK 2001–, Dir Cambridge Stem Cell Inst. (fmrly Cambridge Centre for Stem Cell Biology and Medicine) 2004–, Prin. Collaborator, Cambridge Inst. of Medical Research 2004–, currently Dir of Research in Regenerative Medicine, Dept of Surgery and the Anne McLaren Lab. for Regenerative Medicine; sabbatical, Inst. for Stem Cell Biology and Regenerative Medicine, Stanford Medical School 2012–13. *Publications:* Experimental Approaches to Mammalian Embryonic Development 1988, Current Topics in Developmental Biology 1998, Embryonic Stem Cells for Medicine: A Scientific American article 2002, Handbook of Stem Cells –Vol. 1: Embryonic Stem Cells, Vol. 2: Adult and Fetal Stem Cells 2004; numerous articles in medical and scientific journals on stem cell research. *Address:* Anne McLaren Laboratory for Regenerative Medicine, Cambridge Stem Cell Institute, University of Cambridge, Cambridge, CB2 2XY, England (office). *Telephone:* (1223) 763236 (office). *E-mail:* ralp2@cam.ac.uk (office). *Website:* www.stemcells.cam.ac.uk/researchers/principal -investigators/rpedersen (office).

PEDERSEN, Thor; Danish politician; *President of the Folketing;* b. 14 June 1945, Gentofte; s. of Laurits Pedersen; ed Copenhagen Univ.; fmr mem. staff, Assessments Div.; fmr Man. Dir of a construction co., North Zealand; fmr Mayor of Helsinge; mem. Folketing (Parl.) 1985–, Pres. 2007–; Minister of Housing 1986–87, of the Interior 1987–93, of Nordic Affairs 1988, of Econ. Affairs 1992–93, of Finance 2001–07. *Address:* Graudebjerggaard, Nakke Øst Vej 49, 4500 Nykøbing Sjælland, Denmark (office). *E-mail:* thor.pedersen@ft.dk (office). *Website:* www.folketinget .dk (office).

PEDLEY, Timothy John, ScD, FRS; British academic; *G. I. Taylor Professor Emeritus of Fluid Mechanics, University of Cambridge;* b. 23 March 1942, Leicester; s. of Richard Rodman Pedley and Jeanie Mary Mudie Pedley; m. Avril Jennifer Martin Uden 1965; two s.; ed Rugby School, Trinity Coll., Cambridge; Postdoctoral Fellow, Johns Hopkins Univ., USA 1966–68; Research Assoc. and lecturer, Imperial Coll. London 1968–73; Lecturer, Dept of Applied Math. and Theoretical Physics, Univ. of Cambridge 1973–89, Reader in Biological Fluid Dynamics 1989, G. I. Taylor Prof. of Fluid Mechanics 1996–2009, Prof. Emer. 2009–, Head, Dept of Applied Math. and Theoretical Physics 2000–05; Fellow, Gonville & Caius Coll. Cambridge 1973–89, 1996–; Prof. of Applied Math., Univ. of Leeds 1990–96; Ed. Journal of Fluid Mechanics 2000–06; Pres. Inst. of Math. and its Applications (IMA) 2004–05; Int. Union of Theoretical and Applied Mechanics 2008–12; Chair. World Council for Biomechanics 2002–06; mem. Eng and Physical Sciences Research Council 2009–; Fellow, American Inst. of Medical and Biological Eng 2001, American Physical Soc. 2005; Adams Prize, Univ. of Cambridge 1977, IMA Gold Medal 2008. *Publications:* The Mechanics of the Circulation (co-author) 1978, Scale Effects in Animal Locomotion (ed.) 1977, The Fluid Mechanics of Large Blood Vessels 1980, Biological Fluid Dynamics (co-ed.) 1995. *Leisure interests:* bird-watching, running, reading. *Address:* Department of Applied Mathematics and Theoretical Physics (DAMTP), Centre for Mathematical Sciences, University of Cambridge, Wilberforce Road, Cambridge, CB3 0WA (office); Oakhurst Farm, 375 Shadwell Lane, Leeds, LS17 8AH, England (home). *Telephone:* (1223) 339842 (office); (113) 266-2854 (home). *Fax:* (1223) 760497 (office). *E-mail:* t.j.pedley@damtp.cam.ac.uk (office). *Website:* www.damtp.cam.ac.uk (office).

PEDNYCYA, Kazys; Lithuanian lawyer; b. 16 Nov. 1949, Plaskunai, Kaisiadoriai Region, Lithuania; m. Viktorija Pednycienė; two s.; ed Vilnius State Univ.; interrogator, Kedainai Regional Public Prosecutor's Office 1972–76; Asst Public Prosecutor, Panevezys City 1976–84; Supervision Prosecutor, Lithuanian Repub. Reformatories 1984–91; Judge, Lithuanian Repub. Supreme Court 1991–92; Sr Customs Official, Lithuanian Repub. 1992–93; Asst Dir-Gen. Lithuanian Nat. Security Dept 1993–97; Gen. Public Prosecutor 1997–2001. *Address:* Justiniskiu 36-20, 2000 Vilnius, Lithuania (home). *Telephone:* (2) 22-83-38 (home).

PEDRAZA RODRÍGUEZ, Lina, BSc; Cuban politician; *Minister of Finance and Prices;* b. 15 Sept. 1955, Villa Clara prov.; head of Central Bank in Villa Clara prov. in the early 1990s; Deputy, Nat. Ass. of People's Power; elected to Central Cttee, Communist Party of Cuba 1991, Head of Econs Div. 2006–09, mem. CP Secr. 2006–09; Minister of Auditing and Control 2001–06, of Finance and Prices 2009–. *Address:* Ministry of Finance and Prices, Calle Obispo 211, esq. Cuba, Habana Vieja, Havana, Cuba (office). *Telephone:* (7) 867-1920 (office). *Fax:* (7) 33-8050 (office). *E-mail:* bhcifip@mfp.gov.cu (office). *Website:* www.mfp.cu (office).

PEDROSO, Iván; Cuban fmr track and field athlete; b. 17 Dec. 1972, Havana; long jumper; jumped more than 8m for the first time aged 17 July 1990; winner Pan American Junior Championships, Kingston, Jamaica 1991, Ibero-American Championships, Seville 1992, World Cup, Havana 1992, Pan American Games, Mar del Plata, Argentina 1995, IAAF Grand Prix Final, Monte Carlo 1995, Central American and Caribbean Championships, San Juan, Puerto Rico 1997, Universiade, Catania, Italy 1997, IAAF Grand Prix Final, Fukuoka, Japan 1997, World Cup, Johannesburg 1998, Central American and Caribbean Games, Maracaibo, Venezuela 1998, Goodwill Games, Uniondale, USA 1998, Pan American Games, Winnipeg 1999, IAAF Grand Prix Final, Munich 1999, Goodwill Games, Brisbane 2001, Pan American Games, Santo Domingo, Dominican Repub. 2003; gold medallist, World Indoor Championships, Toronto 1993, Barcelona 1995, Paris 1997, Maebashi 1999, Lisbon 2001; gold medallist, World Championships Gothenburg 1995, Athens 1997, Seville 1999, Edmonton 2001; gold medallist, Olympic Games, Sydney 2000; best jump officially 8.71m, in Salamanca 1995; announced retirement Sept. 2007; coach of 2013 triple jump world champion, Teddy Tamgho; Flagbearer for Cuba, Olympic Summer Games, Athens 2004, London 2012; voted Best Cuban Sportsman 1998. *Address:* c/o Cubadeportes SA, 710 Calle 20 no. 710 e/ 7ma y 9na, Miramar, Havana, Cuba. *Website:* www.iaaf.org/athletes/cuba/ivan-pedroso-4205.

PEEBLES, Phillip James E., BS, PhD, FRS, FRSC; American (b. Canadian) cosmologist and academic; *Albert Einstein Professor Emeritus of Science, Princeton University;* b. 25 April 1935, Winnipeg, Man.; m. Alison Peebles; one s. two d.; ed Univ. of Manitoba, Princeton Univ.; Instructor, Princeton Univ. 1961–62, Research Assoc. 1962–64, Research Staff mem. 1964–65, faculty mem. Physics Dept 1965–, Asst Prof. to Prof. 1965–84, Albert Einstein Prof. of Science 1984–2000, Albert Einstein Prof. Emer. of Science 2000–; Fellow, American Acad. of Arts and Sciences, American Physical Soc., American Philosophical Soc.; mem. NAS (Foreign Asscn), American Astronomical Soc., AAAS, Int. Astronomical Union; Hon. DSc (Toronto) 1986, (Chicago) 1986, (McMaster) 1989, (Manitoba) 1989, (Newcastle-upon-Tyne, Catholic Univ. of Louvain); numerous hon. lectureships including Henry Norris Russell Lectureship (American Astronomical Soc.), Silliman Lectureship (Yale Univ.), de Vaucouleurs Lectureship (Univ. of TX), Jansky Lectureship (Nat. Radio Astronomy Observatory, NRAO), Feshbach Lectureship (MIT), McPherson Lectureship (McGill Univ.), Klein Lectureship (Univ. of Stockholm); Danz Prof., Univ. of Washington; New York Acad. of Sciences A.C. Morrison Award in Nat. Science 1977, Royal Astronomical Soc. Eddington Medal 1981, Gold Medal 1998, American Astronomical Soc. Heineman Prize 1982, Univ. of Newcastle Robinson Prize, Astronomical Soc. of the Pacific Bruce Medal 1995, Université catholique de Louvain Lemaître Award, Peter Gruber Foundation Cosmology Prize 2000, ADION Medal (France) 2003, Shaw Prize in Astronomy (Hong Kong) 2004, Royal Swedish Acad. of Sciences Crafoord Prize 2005. *Publications:* Physical Cosmology 1971; numerous scientific papers in professional journals. *Leisure interest:* gardening. *Address:* Department of Physics, Princeton University, 216 Jadwin Hall, Princeton, NJ 08544-0001, USA (office). *Telephone:* (609) 258-4386 (office). *Fax:* (609) 258-6853 (office). *E-mail:* pjep@princeton.edu (office); pjep@pupgg.princeton.edu (office). *Website:* www.phy.princeton.edu/cosmology (office); www.physics.princeton.edu (office).

PEERS, Most Rev. Michael Geoffrey, BA, zert.dolm., LTh; Canadian ecclesiastic (retd); b. 31 July 1934, Vancouver, BC; s. of Geoffrey H. Peers and Dorothy E. Mantle; m. Dorothy E. Bradley 1963; two s. one d.; ed Univs of British Columbia and Heidelberg and Trinity Coll. Toronto; ordained priest 1960; Curate, Ottawa 1959–65; Univ. Chaplain, Diocese of Ottawa 1961–66; Rector, St Bede's, Winnipeg 1966–72, St Martin's, Winnipeg with St Paul's Middlechurch 1972–74; Archdeacon of Winnipeg 1969–74; Rector, St Paul's Cathedral, Regina 1974–77; Dean of Qu'Appelle 1974–77; Bishop of Qu'Appelle 1977–82; Archbishop of Qu'Appelle and Metropolitan of Rupert's Land 1982–86; Primate, Anglican Church of Canada 1986–2004; Ecumenist-in-Residence, Toronto School of Theology 2004–06; mem. Cen. Cttee World Council of Churches (WCC) 1991–98, Jt Standing Cttee of Anglican Communion 1994–2003, WCC Special Comm. on relations with Orthodox Churches 1999–2006; Hon. DD (Trinity Coll. Toronto) 1978, (Wycliffe Coll. Toronto) 1981, (St John's Coll. Winnipeg) 1981, (Univ. of Kent) 1988, (Montreal Diocesan Coll.) 1989, (Coll. of Emmanuel and St Chad, Saskatoon) 1990, (Thorneloe Univ. Sudbury) 1993, (Huron Coll., London, Ont.) 1998, (Huron Univ. Coll.) 1998, (Lutheran Theological Seminary Saskatoon) 2001, (Episcopal Divinity School, Cambridge USA) 2004; Hon. DCL (Bishop's Univ., Lennoxville) 1993. *Publications:* Grace Notes: Journeying with the Primate 1995–2004 2005. *Address:* 195 Westminster Avenue, Toronto, Ont., M6R 1N9, Canada. *Telephone:* (416) 531-8958. *E-mail:* mpeers@sympatico.ca.

PEERTHUM, Satteeanund; Mauritian diplomatist; b. 15 March 1941; m.; three c.; ed People's Friendship Univ., Moscow; Sr Research Fellow, Inst. of Oriental Studies, Moscow, USSR 1973–74; Head of History Dept, Bhojoharry Coll., Mauritius several times between 1975 and 1987; Sr Research Fellow, School of Mauritian Asian and African Studies, Mahatma Gandhi Inst. 1985–87; Founding mem. Mouvement Socialiste Militant; mem. Mauritian Parl. and Minister of Labour and Industrial Relations 1982–83; Chair. Sugar Industry Devt Fund Bds of Mauritius 1984–87; Amb. and Perm. Rep. to UN, New York 1987–96; Chair. Nat. Steering Cttee for the Teaching of Mauritian History; mem. Advisory Cttee, African Cultural Centre of Mauritius 1986–87; fmr mem. Court, Nat. Univ. of Mauritius. *Address:* c/o Ministry of Foreign Affairs, Regional Integration and International Trade, Newton Tower, 9th–11th Floors, Sir William Newton Street, Port Louis, Mauritius. *E-mail:* mfa@mail.gov.mu.

PEFANIS, Harry N.; American petroleum industry executive; *President and Chief Operating Officer, Plains All American Pipeline LP;* b. 1957, Buffalo, NY; ed Univ. of Oklahoma; has worked with Plains All American Pipeline LP and its predecessors since 1983, Special Asst for Corp. Planning, Plains Resources 1983–87, Products Marketing Man. 1987–88, Vice-Pres. Products Marketing 1988–96, Sr Vice-Pres. 1996–98, Exec. Vice-Pres., Midstream of Plains Resources 1998–2001, Pres. and COO Plains All American Pipeline LP 1998–; mem. Bd of Dirs PAA/Vulcan. *Address:* Plains All American Pipeline LP, 333 Clay Street, Suite 1600, Houston, TX 77002, USA (office). *Telephone:* (713) 646-4100 (office). *Fax:* (713) 646-4572 (office). *E-mail:* info@paalp.com (office). *Website:* www.paalp.com (office).

PÉGARD, Catherine; French journalist and government official; *President, Public Establishment of the Palace, Museum and National Estate of Versailles;* b. 5 Aug. 1954, Le Havre; began career in journalism at daily J'informe 1977; worked in Political Dept of Quotidien de Paris (Groupe Quotidien) 1978–82; joined weekly Le Point 1982, becoming Asst Ed.-in-Chief, later Ed.-in-Chief; Co-host Les Femmes et les Patrons d'abord, Paris Première 2004–07; adviser to Pres. Sarkozy 2007–08, in charge of 'pôle politique' at Elysée Palace 2008–11; Pres. Public Establishment of the Palace, Museum and Nat. Estate of Versailles 2011–; Chevalier, Légion d'honneur 2012. *Address:* Établissement Public du château, du musée et du domaine national de Versailles, Ministry of Culture and Communication, 3 rue de Valois, 75033 Paris Cedex 01, France (office). *Telephone:* 1-40-15-80-00 (office). *Fax:* 1-40-15-85-30 (office). *E-mail:* point.culture@culture.fr (office). *Website:* www.culturecommunication.gouv.fr (office).

PEH, Joanne; Singaporean actress; b. 1983; ed Nanyang Technological Univ. *Television includes:* Beautiful Connection 2002, To Mum With Love 2004, The Ties That Bind 2004, A Life of Hope 2005, Yours Always 2006, Like Father, Like Daughter 2007, Path of Gold 2007, The Truth 2008, The Little Nyonya (Star Awards Best Actress Award) 2008, Your Hand in Mine 2009, Love in a Cab (film) 2010, C.L.I.F. 2 (series) 2013. *Films:* City Beat 2002, High on Life 2005, Tua Seh Kai 2011. *Address:* Artiste Management Division, MediaCorp Studios Pte Ltd, Caldecott Broadcast Centre, Andrew Road, East Wing Building, Level 3, 29939 Singapore (office). *E-mail:* joannepeh.email@gmail.com (office). *Website:* joannepeh.com (office).

PEI, I(eoh) M(ing), MArch, FAIA, RIBA; American architect; b. 26 April 1917, Canton, China; s. of Tsu Yee Pei and Lien Kwun Chwong; m. Eileen Loo 1942; three s. one d.; ed Shanghai Univ., Massachusetts Inst. of Tech., Harvard Univ.; moved to USA 1935, became naturalized citizen 1954; est. architectural practice 1939; Nat. Defense Research Cttee 1943–45; Asst Prof. Harvard Graduate School of Design 1945–48; Webb and Knapp Inc. 1948–55, Pei, Cobb, Freed & Pnrs (fmrly I. M. Pei & Pnrs) 1955–90; Wheelwright Traveling Fellowship, Harvard Univ. 1951; MIT Traveling Fellowship 1940; Fellow AIA; mem. Nat. Council on the Humanities 1966–70, American Acad. of Arts and Sciences, Nat. Acad. of Design, American Acad. of Arts and Letters (Chancellor 1978–80), Nat. Council on the Arts 1981–84, RIBA, Urban Design Council (New York), Corpn of MIT 1972–77, 1978–83, American Philosophical Soc., Institut de France (Foreign Assoc.); Commdr, Ordre des Arts et des Lettres, Officier, Légion d'honneur 1988; Hon. DFA (Pennsylvania) 1970, (Rensselaer Polytechnic Inst.) 1978, (Northeastern Univ.) 1979, (Univs of Mass., Rochester, Brown) 1982, (New York Univ.) 1983; Hon. LLD (Chinese Univ. of Hong Kong) 1970, Hon. DHL (Columbia Univ., Univs of Colorado, Rochester, Hong Kong, American Univ. of Paris); Hon. Prof. Tonji Univ., Shanghai 1985; Brunner Award, Nat. Inst. of Arts and Letters 1961; Medal of Honor NY Chapter AIA 1963, The Thomas Jefferson Memorial Medal for Architecture 1976, Gold Medal (American Acad. of Arts and Letters) 1979, Gold Medal (American Inst. of Architects) 1979, La Grande Medaille d'Or (Académie d'Architecture) 1981, Pritzker Architecture Prize 1983, Asia Soc. Award 1984, Medal of Liberty 1986, Nat. Medal of Arts 1988, Praemium Imperiale (Japan Art Asscn) 1989, Univ. of Calif. Gold Medal 1990, Calbert Award for Excellence 1991, Presidential Medal of Freedom 1992, Edward MacDowell Medal 1998, BZ Kulturpreis (Germany) 1999, Historic Landmarks Preservation Center, New York Cultural Laureate 1999, Erwin Wickert Foundation Orient und Okzident Preis 2006, Royal Gold Medal for Architecture, RIBA 2010. *Address:* Pei Cobb Freed & Partners, 88 Pine Street, New York, NY 10005, USA (office). *Telephone:* (212) 872-4010 (office). *Fax:* (212) 872-4222 (office). *E-mail:* information@pcf-p.com (office). *Website:* www.pcf-p.com (office).

PEI, Yanling; Chinese actress; b. Aug. 1947, Shuning Co., Hebei Prov.; Vice-Chair. Hebei Fed. of Literary and Art Circles 1993–, China Fed. of Literary and Art Circles 2001–; Chair. Hebei Professional Dramatists' Asscn; Dir Pei Yanling Co. of Hebei Prov. Peking Opera Theatre; mem. 7th CPPCC 1987–92, 8th CPPCC 1992–97; Excellent Performing Artist Award, Ministry of Culture 1992, Plum Blossom Award. *Performances include:* The Man and the Ghost, Lotus Lantern, Ren gui qing (Woman-Demon-Human) 1987 and others. *Address:* Hebei Federation of Literary and Art Circles, Shijiazhuang City, People's Republic of China (office).

PEICHL, Gustav; Austrian architect and caricaturist; b. 18 March 1928, Vienna; Prof., Acad. of Fine Arts, Vienna; major works include Austrian Broadcasting Stations in Salzburg, Linz, Innsbrück, Dornbirn 1970–72, Graz 1979–80, Eisenstadt 1981–83; EFA Radio Satellite Station, Aflenz 1976–79; PEA-Phosphate Elimination Plant, Berlin-Tegel; design for Papal visit to Vienna 1984; art and exhbn centre, Bonn 1986–92; extension to Städel Museum, Frankfurt am Main; ÖMV-Center, Vienna 1991–; rehearsal stage of Burgtheater, Vienna 1991–93; Co-founder Peichl & Partner ZT GmbH 2002; caricaturist under alias Ironimus; Verleihung der Grossen Verdienst-Kreuzes des Verdienstordens 1996; Award of City of Vienna for Architecture, Austrian State Award, Reynolds Memorial Award, Styria Award for Architecture, Mies van der Rohe Award, Berlin Architectural Award. *Address:* Atelier Peichl, Opernring 4/2/19, 1010 Vienna, Austria (office). *Telephone:* (1) 512-32-48 (office). *Fax:* (1) 512-32-48-71 (office). *E-mail:* g.peichl@cehl.at (office).

PEILLON, Vincent Benoît Camille, PhD; French politician; b. 7 July 1960, Suresnes, Paris; Lecturer in Philosophy 1984–97; Econ. Research Dir, CNRS 2002–04; Sec. Socialist Party's (PS—Parti socialiste) group of experts 1993–94, seconded to First Sec. of PS 1995–97, Nat. Research Sec. 1997–2000, PS Nat. Spokesman 2000–02, mem. PS Nat. Bureau 1994–; Deputy to Nat. Ass. 1997–2002, Chair. Nat. Ass.'s inquiry into money laundering 1999–2002; mem. European Parl. for North West France (Group of the Progressive Alliance of Socialists and Democrats in the European Parl.) 2004–, mem. Cttee on Foreign Affairs, Del. for relations with the Maghreb countries and the Arab Maghreb Union, Del. to Parl. Ass. of the Union for the Mediterranean; Minister of Nat. Educ. 2012–14. *Address:* c/o Ministry of National Education, Hôtel de Rochechouart, 110 rue de Grenelle, 75357 Paris SP 07, France (office).

PEIMBERT, Manuel, BS, MA, PhD; Mexican astronomer and academic; *Professor Emeritus, Instituto de Astronomía, Universidad Nacional Autónoma de México;* b. 9 June 1941, Mexico City; s. of Gonzalo Peimbert and Catalina Sierra; m. Silvia Torres-Peimbert 1962; one s. one d.; ed Universidad Nacional Autónoma de México (UNAM) and Univ. of California, Berkeley, USA; Research Asst, Instituto de Astronomía, UNAM 1960–63, Prof., Faculty of Sciences 1968–2006, Prof. Emer. 2006–, Instituto de Astronomía 1970–2006, mem. Academic Bd of Govs 2000–10; Research Asst, Univ. of California, Berkeley 1963–64, Postdoctoral Fellow 1967–68; on sabbatical leave at Kitt Peak Nat. Observatory, USA 1975–76,

Univ. Coll., London, UK 1976, Tokyo Astronomical Observatory 1986; Emer. Researcher, Nat. System of Researchers 2007–; Vice-Pres. Int. Astronomical Union 1982–88; mem. Science Advisory Council of the Presidency of the Repub.; Assoc. Ed. Journal of the National Autonomous University of Mexico 1994–2001; Foreign Assoc., NAS 1987; Assoc., Royal Astronomical Soc. 1989; mem. Nat. Coll. (Mexico) 1992; Foreign mem. American Philosophical Soc. 2002; Fellow, Third World Acad. of Sciences (TWAS) 1987 (Vice-Pres. 1998–2003), Acad. of Sciences of Latin America 1996; Investigador al Honorem, Francisco J. Duarte Centre for Astronomy, Venezuela 1981; Luis G. León Medal, Sociedad Astronómica de México, Science Prize, Academia Mexicana de Ciencias 1971, Guillaume Budé Medal, Coll. de France 1974, Premio Nacional de Ciencias y Artes en el área de Ciencias Físico-Matemáticas y Naturales en 1978, Mexican Nat. Prize in Science and Arts 1981, UNAM Science Prize 1988, Academic Medal, Mexican Soc. of Physics 1991, Medal and Lecture, TWAS 1996. Publications: Selected Topics in Astrophysics (ed.) 1984, Frontiers of the Universe (ed.) 2000, The Evolution in Astronomy (ed.) 2006; more than 200 research papers in int. journals of astronomy and astrophysics; more than 50 popular articles and book chapters. Address: Instituto de Astronomía, Universidad Nacional Autónoma de México, Apartado Postal 70-264, 04510 México DF, Mexico. Telephone: (5) 622-3906. Fax: (5) 616-0653. E-mail: peimbert@astroscu.unam.mx. Website: www.astroscu.unam.mx/~peimbert.

PEINEMANN, Edith; German concert violinist; b. 3 March 1939, Mainz; d. of Robert Peinemann and Hildegard (née Rohde) Peinemann; ed studied under her father and later with Heinz Stauske and Max Rostal; has performed with leading orchestras and conductors worldwide; orchestral debut, Carnegie Hall 1965; performed at Salzburg, Lucerne, Ravinia, Mozart, Marlboro Chamber Music Festivals; Prof. of Violin, Hochschule für Musik, Frankfurt 1976–; Int. Pres., European String Teachers' Asscn 2005–; First Prize, ARD competition, Munich 1956, Plaquette Eugène Ysaye 1858–1958. Leisure interests: art, hiking, cooking, cross-country skiing. Address: Oberlindau 15, 60323 Frankfurt, Germany (office). E-mail: info@esta-int.com (office). Website: www.esta-int.com (office).

PEIRANO, Miguel Gustavo; Argentine economist and government official; ed Universidad de Buenos Aires; began career at Banco Sudameris 1989; worked for Techint Group 1990–92; various posts at Argentine Industrial Union (UIA) 1993–2004; Prof. of Political Economy, Colegio Nacional de Buenos Aires 1995–97; served as econ. adviser to Dir-Gen. of Industry of the City of Buenos Aires, Bd of Bank of the Province of Buenos Aires, Nat. Sub-secretariat of Small and Medium Enterprise and Regional Devt; fmr Pres. Econs Dept, Buenos Aires City Industrial Union; Sr Vice-Pres. Bank of Investment and Foreign Trade (BICE) –2007; Minister of Economy and Production July–Dec. 2007–. Address: c/o Ministry of Economy and Production, Hipólito Yrigoyen 250, C1086AAB Buenos Aires, Argentina.

PEIRIS, Gamini Lakshman, DPhil, PhD; Sri Lankan politician and academic; Minister of External Affairs; b. 13 Aug. 1946, Colombo; s. of Glanville S. Peiris and Lakshmi C. Salgado; m. Savitri N. Amarasuriya 1971; one d.; ed St Thomas' Coll., Mount Lavinia, Univ. of Ceylon and New Coll., Oxford, UK; Prof. of Law, Univ. of Colombo 1979, Dean, Faculty of Law 1982–88; Vice-Chancellor, Univ. of Colombo –1994; Dir Nat. Film Corpn of Sri Lanka 1973–78; Commr Law Comm. of Sri Lanka 1986–; mem. Inc. Soc. of Legal Educ. 1986–; Visiting Fellow, All Souls Coll. Oxford 1980–81; Butterworths Visiting Fellow, Inst. of Advanced Legal Studies, Univ. of London 1984; Distinguished Visiting Fellow, Christ's Coll. Cambridge, UK 1985–86; Smuts Visiting Fellow in Commonwealth Studies, Univ. of Cambridge 1985–86; Chair. Cttee of Vice-Chancellors of the Univs of Sri Lanka; Minister of Justice, Constitutional Affairs, Ethnic Affairs and Nat. Integration and Deputy Minister of Finance 1994–99; Minister of Enterprise Devt, Industrial Policy and Investment Promotion and of Constitutional Affairs 1999–2004, of Export Devt and Int. Trade 2007–10, of External Affairs 2010–; mem. United People's Freedom Alliance (UPFA) 2007–; Vice-Chair. Janasaviya Trust Fund; mem. Securities Council of Sri Lanka 1987–; mem. Pres. Comm. on Youth Unrest 1989; mem. Nat. Educ. Comm., Exec. Cttee of Asscn of Teachers and Researchers in Intellectual Property Law, Bd Govs Inst. of Fundamental Studies; Assoc. mem. Int. Acad. of Comparative Law; Presidential Award 1987. Publications: Law of Unjust Enrichment in South Africa and Ceylon 1971, General Principles of Criminal Liability in Ceylon 1972, Offences Under the Penal Code of Sri Lanka 1973, The Law of Evidence in Sri Lanka 1974, Criminal Procedure in Sri Lanka 1975, The Law of Property in Sri Lanka 1976, Landlord and Tenant in Sri Lanka 1977; numerous articles on comparative and admin. law and law of evidence. Leisure interest: walking. Address: Ministry of External Affairs, Republic Building, Colombo 1 (office); No. 37, Kirula Place, Off Kirula Road, Colombo 05, Sri Lanka (home). Telephone: (11) 2325371 (office). Fax: (11) 2446091 (office). E-mail: publicity@formin.gov.lk (office). Website: www.slmfa.gov.lk (office).

PEIRIS, Mohan, PC; Sri Lankan lawyer, judge and government official; Chief Justice of the Supreme Court; m. Priyanthi Peiris; one d.; ed St Joseph's Coll., Colombo, Royal Coll., Colombo, Sri Lanka Law Coll., Nat. Inst. of Trial Advocacy, Harvard Law School, Centre for Police and Criminal Justice Studies, Jesus Coll., England, George Washington Univ., USA; called to the Bar 1975; began legal practice under sr lawyers D. R. P. Gunatilleke and Daya Perera; enrolled as a solicitor, Supreme Court of England and Wales 1978; joined Attorney-Gen.'s Dept as State Counsel 1981, later became Sr State Counsel and served for more than 15 years; est. pvt. practice in Unofficial Bar, specialized in original and appellate courts in areas of admin. law, commercial law, land law, fundamental rights, industrial law, inquiry and criminal law and as arbitrator; Attorney-Gen. 2009–11; Sr Legal Adviser to Cabinet of Ministers 2011–13; Chief Justice of the Supreme Court 2013–; Chair. Inter Agency Comm. to Implement the Interim Recommendations of the Lessons Learnt and Reconciliation Comm. (LLRC); fmr Chair. Bd of Examiners for Intermediate Examination and Examiner of Sri Lanka Law Coll.; fmr Visiting Lecturer, Faculty of Law, Univ. of Colombo; fmr Deputy Pres. Sri Lanka Bar Asscn; mem. Sri Lankan Del. to Universal Periodic review at Eighth Session of the Human Rights Council of the UN. Address: Supreme Court of Sri Lanka, Superior Court Complex, PO Box 01200, Colombo 12, Sri Lanka (office). Website: www.supremecourt.lk (office).

PEIROTES, Yves Jean-Marie, MSc; French business executive; b. 7 Nov. 1940, Epinal, Vosges; s. of Marcel Georges Peirotes and Germaine Eugénie Schaeffer; m. 1st Victoria Longacre 1968 (divorced 1981); two s.; m. 2nd Viviane France Bastiani

1987; ed Lycée de Belfort, Lycée Kleber, Strasbourg, Ecole Polytechnique, Paris, Ecole Nat. Supérieure du Génie Maritime, Paris, Univ. of Calif., Berkeley; prin. engineer, Maritime Eng, Del. Ministérielle pour l'Armement 1966–70; Head of Logistics, Strafor, Strasbourg 1971–72, Tech. and Industrial Devt Dir 1972–77; Gen. Man. Industrial Equipment Div., Forges de Strasbourg 1997–81; Man. Dir Air Industrie 1981–84; Chair., Man. Dir Sofiltra Poelman 1981–84; Deputy Man. Dir Cie Industrielle et Financière de Pompey 1984–85; Gen. Man. White Goods Div. Electrolux France 1985–90, White Goods & Floor Care Appliances Div. 1990–94, Man. Dir Electrolux France SA 1995–97, Chair. and Man. Dir 1997–; Chair. Usines et Fonderies Arthur Martin 1985–; Pres. Bureau Départemental d'Industrialisation des Ardennes 1987–91; mem. Advisory Bd Senlis branch, Banque de France 1995–; Chevalier, Ordre nat. du Mérite. Leisure interests: skiing, jogging, swimming. Address: Electrolux France SA, 43 ave. Félix Louat, BP 20139, 60300 Senlis (office); 6 place Winston Churchill, 92200 Neuilly sur Seine, France (home). Telephone: (3) 44-62-28-00 (office). Fax: (3) 44-62-21-89 (office). E-mail: yves.peirotes@notes.electrolux.fr (office).

PEISACH, Max, PhD, DSc, FRSSA, FRPSL; South African nuclear analytical chemist; b. 3 Aug. 1926, Birzai, Lithuania; s. of Hyman Peisach and Sonia Kantor; m. Eunice Sheila Glick 1950; one s. three d.; ed Boys' High School, Worcester, Univ. of Cape Town; demonstrator, Univ. of Cape Town 1948–49, Jr lecturer 1949–50, lecturer 1950–53; Research Officer, Nat. Chemical Research Lab., S African Council for Scientific and Industrial Research 1953–57, Sr Research Officer 1957–60; Head, Isotope Production, Israel Atomic Energy Comm. 1960–63; Head Chem. Div., Southern Univs Nuclear Inst. 1963–83; Head Nuclear Analytical Chem. Div., Nat. Accelerator Centre 1983–91, Chief Specialist Researcher 1986–91; mem. Int. Cttee on Modern Trends in Activation Analysis 1969–91, Hon. Life mem. 1994–; Nat. Rep., IUPAC Comm. on Radiochemistry 1985–96; Research Consultant, Witwatersrand Chem. Ion-Beam Analysis Group 1992–98; Research Fellow, Solid State and Materials, Nat. Accelerator Centre 1994; Research Adviser, Dept of Materials and Interfaces, Weizmann Inst., Rehovot, Israel 1995–2004; Assoc. Royal Soc. of Chem. (London) 1951–61, Fellow 1962–86; Fellow, Royal Soc. of SA 1984–, Royal Philatelic Soc. London 1966–; mem. S African Chemical Inst. 1952–96, Sr mem. 1996–98, Life mem. 1998–; Hon. Citizen, State of Tenn., USA 1965; Order of the Postal Stone 1988; AE & CI Gold Medal 1965, Roll of Distinguished Philatelists (South Africa) 1966, Int. Hevesy Medal 1981, South Africa Chemical Inst. Gold Medal 1986. Publications include: Elemental Analysis by Particle Accelerators; many scientific papers; research papers on nuclear analytical chem.; book chapters on specialized analytical topics; research articles on philately of South Africa and Israel. Leisure interests: philately, numismatics, judging philatelic exhbns. Address: Sderot Ye'elim 30/4, Beersheba 84739 (home); PO Box 3581, Beersheba 8413502, Israel. Telephone: 8-6442232. E-mail: mpeisach@bezeqint.net.

PEJANOVIĆ-ĐURIŠIĆ, Milica, BSc, MSc, PhD; Montenegrin electrical engineer, academic, diplomatist and politician; Minister of Defence; b. 27 April 1959, Nikšić; m. Zoran Djurišić; two s.; ed Univ. of Montenegro, Podgorica, Univ. of Belgrade; Teaching/Research Asst, Dept of Electrical Eng, Univ. of Montenegro 1983–88, Asst Prof. 1988–94, Assoc. Prof. 1994–98, Prof. 1998–; mem. State Presidency of Montenegro 1990–92; mem. Ass. of Repub. of Montenegro 1992–2001; Amb. of State Union of Serbia and Montenegro to Belgium and Luxembourg 2004–06, Amb. of Montenegro to France, Monaco and UNESCO 2007–10; Minister of Defence 2012–; consultant to Ericsson ETK, Zagreb 2002–04, Telecom Montenegro 2002–05, Ericsson, Stockholm 2002–04, Agency for Telecommunications, Montenegro 2004–07; mem. Democratic Party of Socialists of Montenegro, Vice-Pres. 1992–97, Pres. 1997–98. Address: Ministry of Defence, 81000 Podgorica, ul. Jovana Tomaševića 29, Montenegro (office). Telephone: (20) 242042 (office). Fax: (20) 224702 (office). E-mail: kabinet@mod.gov.me (office). Website: www.odbrana.gov.me (office).

PEKHTIN, Vladimir Alekseyevich, DrTechSci; Russian politician and engineer; First Deputy, United Russia Parliamentary Group, State Duma; b. 9 Dec. 1950, Leningrad; m.; one s.; ed Leningrad Polytech. Inst.; engineer with Kolymagestroi (power co.), then Kolymaenergo 1974–97; Chair. Magadan Regional Duma 1994; Chair. Council of Feds of Russia 1999–; mem. State Duma (Parl.) 1999–, Head Cttee on Property; Head Yedinstvo Parl. Group in State Duma (Parl.) 2001–07, currently First Deputy, United Russia Parl. Group; Order, Friendship of Peoples, Merited Constructor of Russia, Hon. Power Engineer. Leisure interests: hunting, shooting (Master of Sports). Address: State Duma of Russian Federation, Okhotny Ryad 1, 103265 Moscow, Russia (office). Telephone: (495) 292-83-01 (office). Fax: (495) 292-34-76 (office). Website: www.duma.gov.ru (office).

PEKKANEN, Raimo Oskari, LLD; Finnish judge; Chairman, Sub-Committee on Medical Research Ethics, National Advisory Board on Health Care Ethics; b. 29 July 1927, Kivennapa; m. Eeva Niittyla 1953; two s.; ed Univ. of Helsinki; State Admin. 1950–60; researcher and teacher, Helsinki School of Econ. and Univ. of Tampere 1961–67; Acting Prof. in Labour Law, Univ. of Helsinki 1967–68; Justice, Supreme Admin. Court of Finland 1969–90; Sec.-Gen. Ministry of Justice (on leave of absence from Supreme Admin. Court) 1982–90; Judge, European Court of Human Rights 1990–98; Chair. Sub-Cttee on Medical Research Ethics, Nat. Advisory Bd on Health Care Ethics 2000–; Commdr Order of Finnish Lion, Commdr Order of Finnish White Rose. Publications: Mixed Type Contracts of Employment 1966, On the Commencement and Termination of Employment Relationships 1968, On Participation in Water System Regulation 1968; articles in legal publs. Leisure interests: fly-fishing, skiing. Address: Nyyrikinte 8, 02100 Espoo, Finland (home). Telephone: (9) 4554557 (home). E-mail: raimo.pekkanen@ppl.inet.fi (home).

PEKKARINEN, Mauri, MSc; Finnish politician; b. 6 Oct. 1947, Kinnula; m. Raija Kaarina Pekkarinen 1979; four c.; ed Univ. of Jyväskylä; mem. Jyväskylä Town Council 1977–2004, 2008–; mem. Parl. (Finnish Centre Party) 1979–, Vice-Pres. Finnish Centre Party Parl. Group 1987–91, Chair. 1999–2003, Chair. Finance Cttee 1995–99; Political Sec. Ministry of Labour 1976–77, Ministry of the Interior 1978–79; Minister of the Interior 1991–95, of Trade and Industry 2003–07, of Econ. Affairs 2008–11; Chair. Cen. Finland 1999–2002, Cen. Finnish Sports Fed. 1995–2002, Asscn of Finnish Local Councils 1997–2001; Vice-Pres. Biathlon Asscn 2006–; mem. Cen. Finland Regional Planning Asscn of the Fed. Govt 1981–84; mem. Supervisory Bd Export Credit Agency 1982–86; mem. Supervisory Bd State

Guarantee Fund 1995–96; mem. Supervisory Bd Finnish Broadcasting Company YLE 1982–91, Chair. 1987–91; Bd mem. Cen. Prov. of Finland 1985–90; Chair. Cen. Finland Centre Party constituency 1987–1991; mem. Parliamentary Supervisory Bd, Bank of Finland 1995–2003, Chair. 2003; DSc hc (Lappeenranta) 2008, (Jyväskylä) 2009. *Leisure interests:* music, sport. *Address:* c/o Ministry of Employment and the Economy, Aleksanterinkatu 4, POB 32, 00170 Helsinki, Finland.

PELÉ; Brazilian fmr professional footballer; b. (Edson Arantes do Nascimento), 23 Oct. 1940, Três Corações, Minas Gerais State; s. of João Ramos do Nascimento (Fluminense footballer nicknamed Dondinho) and Maria Celeste Arantes; m. 1st Rosemeri dos Reis Cholby 1966 (divorced 1978); one s. two d.; m. 2nd Assíria Lemos Seixas 1994; one s. one d. (twins); ed Santos Univ.; forward; first played football at Baurú, São Paulo 1952–56; mem. Baurú Atlético Clube; played for Santos Football Club 1956–74 (438 appearances, scored 474 goals, won Campeonato Paulista 1958, 1960, 1961, 1962, 1964, 1965, 1967, 1968, 1969, 1973, Torneio Rio-São Paulo 1959, 1963, 1964, Torneio Roberto Gomes Pedrosa (Taça de Prata) 1968, Taça Brasil 1961, 1962, 1963, 1964, 1965, Copa Libertadores 1962, 1963, Intercontinental Cup 1962, 1963, South-American Recopa 1968, Recopa Intercontinental 1968), Dir 1993–; played for Brazil nat. team 1957–71, first int. game vs Argentina, played in World Cup 1958, 1962, 1966, 1970; finished career with New York Cosmos 1975–77 (NASL Champions 1977); Chair. Pelé Soccer Camps 1978–82; Special Minister for Sports, Govt of Brazil 1994–98; Dir Soccer Clinics; three World Cup winners' medals 1958, 1962, 1970; two World Club Championship medals; Roca Cup winner 1957, 1963; 110 int. caps, 97 goals for Brazil; 1,114 appearances for Santos, 1,088 goals; career total 1,282 goals in 1,364 games, most goals in season 53 (1958); Goodwill Amb. for UN Conf. on Environment and Devt, Rio de Janeiro 1992; Hans Christian Andersen Amb. 2003–; UNESCO Goodwill Amb.; appeared at closing ceremony of Summer Olympics, London Aug. 2012; Hon. Pres. New York Cosmos 2010; Hon. KBE 1997; hon. degree (Univ. of Edinburgh, UK) 2012; FIFA World Cup Golden Ball (Best Player) 1970, BBC Sports Personality of the Year Overseas Personality 1970, Int. Peace Award 1978, Athlete of the Century 1980, WHO Medal 1989, Gold Medal for outstanding services to the sport (Brazil) 1995, elected Athlete of the Century by IOC 1999, elected Athlete of the Century by Reuters News Agency 1999, UNICEF Football Player of the Century 1999, FIFA World Footballer of the Century (with Diego Maradona) 2000, elected Football Player of the Century by France Football's Golden Ball Winners 1999, elected Football Player of the Century by Int. Fed. of Football History and Statistics (IFFHS) 1999, elected South America Football Player of the Century by IFFHS 1999, Laureus World Sports Awards Lifetime Achievement Award from Pres. Nelson Mandela 2000, BBC Sports Personality of the Year Lifetime Achievement Award 2005, World Soccer Greatest XI of All Time 2013, FIFA Ballon d'Or Prix d'Honneur 2013. *Films include:* O Barão Otelo no Barato dos Bilhões 1971, A Marcha 1973, Os Trombadinhas 1978, Escape to Victory 1981, A Minor Miracle 1983, Pedro Mico 1985, Os Trapalhões e o Rei do Futebol 1986, Hotshot 1987, Solidão, Uma Linda História de Amor 1990, Mike Bassett: England Manager 2001, ESPN Sports-Century 2004, Pelé Eterno (documentary about Pelé's career) 2004. *Music:* has composed numerous songs in Samba style. *Television includes:* Os Estranhos (series) 1969. *Publications:* Eu Sou Pelé 1962, Jogando com Pelé 1974, My Life and the Beautiful Game 1977, Pelé Soccer Training Program 1982, The World Cup Murders (novel) 1988, Pelé: The Autobiography 2006. *Address:* 75 Rockefeller Plaza, New York, NY 10019, USA.

PELED, Efrat, BA, MBA, CPA; Israeli business executive; *Chairman and CEO, Arison Investments;* b. 1974; ed Tel-Aviv Univ., Kellogg-Recanati (int. programme of Northwestern and Tel-Aviv Univs); began career as Chief Financial Officer, Ted Arison Family Foundation in Israel and USA –2003, CEO SAFO (Shari Arison's Family Office) LLC, Miami, Fla 2003–, CEO Arison Investments 2006–, Chair. 2010–; Vice-Chair. Miya (part of Arison Group); Dir Miya, Bank Hapoalim 2006–, Shikun & Binui (real estate and infrastructure group), Israel Salt Industries; ranked by Forbes magazine amongst The World's 100 Most Powerful Women (94th) 2009, included by World Econ. Forum among Young Global Leaders under 40 2009, ranked by Fortune magazine amongst the 50 Most Powerful Women in Business outside the US (44th) 2011, (50th) 2012. *Address:* Arison Investments, Golda Center, 23 Shaul Hamelech Boulevard, Tel-Aviv 64367, Israel (office). *Telephone:* (3) 6073100 (office). *Fax:* (3) 6073101 (office). *E-mail:* info@arison.co.il (office). *Website:* www.arison.co.il (office).

PELEVIN, Viktor Olegovich; Russian writer; b. 27 Nov. 1962, Moscow; ed Moscow Power Engineering Inst., Gorky Inst. of Literature, Moscow; army service; corresp., Face-to-Face journal 1989–90; journal Science and Religion; author of numerous novels and stories; Wanderer Prize 1995, Nonino Literary Prize 2001, Robert Schönefeld Prize 2000, 2001, Grigoriev Prize 2004. *Publications include:* (most in trans.) Omon Ra (novel) 1996, Vera Pavlovna's Ninth Dream, Reconstructor, Prince of Gosplan, The Yellow Arrow (novella) 1996, Ivan Kublakhanov, Generation, Babylon, The Blue Lantern (short stories) (Russian Booker Prize 1997), The Life of Insects 1998, Crystal World, A Werewolf Problem in Central Russia (short stories) 1998, Chapayev and Pustota (Buddha's Little Finger, aka Babylon) 2000, The Clay Machine-Gun (novel), Generation P 1999, Homo Zapiens (aka Generation P) 2002, Dialectic for the Transitional Phase From Nowhere to Nowhere 2003, The Sacred Book of the Werewolf 2006, The Helmet of Horror 2006, Empire V 2006, t 2009, S.N.U.F.F 2011. *Address:* c/o Aragi Inc., 143 West 27th Street, #4F, New York, NY 10001, USA (office).

PELHAM, Sir Hugh Reginald Brentnall, Kt, MA, PhD, FRS; British research scientist and institute director; *Director, Medical Research Council Laboratory of Molecular Biology;* b. 26 Aug. 1954, Shawford, nr Winchester, Hants., England; s. of the late Reginald Arthur Pelham and Pauline Mary Pelham; m. Mariann Bienz; one s. one d.; ed Marlborough Coll. and Christ's Coll., Cambridge; Research Fellow, Christ's Coll., Cambridge 1978–84; Postdoctoral Fellow, Carnegie Inst. of Washington, Baltimore, Md 1979–81; mem. Scientific Staff, MRC Lab. of Molecular Biology, Cambridge 1981–, Head of Cell Biology Div. 1995–2006, Deputy Dir 1996–2006, Dir 2006–; mem. European Molecular Biology Org. 1985, Academia Europaea 1990, Acad. of Medical Sciences 1998; Colworth Medal 1988, European Molecular Biology Org. Medal 1989, Louis Jeantet Prize for Medicine 1991, King Faisal Int. Prize for Science 1996, Royal Soc. Croonian Medal 1999. *Publications:* articles on molecular and cell biology in scientific journals. *Address:*

MRC Laboratory of Molecular Biology, Francis Crick Avenue, Cambridge Biomedical Campus, Cambridge, CB2 0QH, England (office). *Telephone:* (1223) 267181 (office). *Website:* www.mrc-lmb.cam.ac.uk (office).

PELL, HE Cardinal George, AC, STL, MEd, DPhil (Oxon.), DD, FACE; Australian ecclesiastic; *Archbishop of Sydney;* b. 8 June 1941, Ballarat, Vic.; s. of George Arthur Pell and Margaret Lillian Burke; ed Loreto Convent and St Patrick's Coll., Ballarat, Corpus Christi Coll., Werribee, Propaganda Fide Coll. and Urban Univ., Rome, Italy, Univ. of Oxford, UK, Monash Univ., Vic.; signed to play professional Australian Rules Football with Richmond Football Club, Melbourne 1959 (currently Vice-Patron), chose to study for priesthood; fmr sports coach in soccer, Aussie Rules and rowing; ordained priest 1966; Asst Priest, Swan Hill 1971–72, Ballarat East 1973–83; Episcopal Vicar for Educ., Diocese of Ballarat 1973–84; Dir Aquinas Campus, Inst. of Catholic Educ. 1974–84, Prin., Inst. of Catholic Educ. (now merged into Australian Catholic Univ.) 1981–84; Rector Corpus Christi Seminary 1985–87; Parish Priest, Mentone and Bishop for the Southern Region of Melbourne 1987–96; Auxiliary Bishop of Melbourne and Titular Bishop of Scala 1987; Apostolic Visitor on behalf of the Congregation for Evangelization of Peoples to the seminaries of NZ 1994, Papua New Guinea and the Solomon Islands 1995, the Pacific 1996, Irian Jaya and Sulawesi 1998; Metropolitan Archbishop of Melbourne 1996; Metropolitan Archbishop of Sydney 2001–; cr. Cardinal (Cardinal Priest of Santa Maria Dominica Mazzarello) 2003; participated in Conclave of Cardinal Electors 2005, 2013; mem. Nat. Catholic Educ. Comm. 1988–97; Sec. Bishops' Cttee for Educ. 1994–97, 2000–03 (Chair. 2003–06), Council of Cardinals for the Study of Admin. and Econ. Problems of the Holy See 2007–; Chair. Caritas Australia 1988–97; Chair. cttee charged with setting up the new Australian Catholic Univ. 1989, served as Univ.'s Foundation Pro-Chancellor 1991–95, Pres. Univ.'s Bd of Owners 1996–; currently Chair. Australian Catholic Bishops' Cttee for Doctrine and Morals; mem. Bishops' Cttee for Justice Devt and Peace 1987–97, Pontifical Council for Justice and Peace 1990–95, 2002–, Vatican Congregation for the Doctrine of the Faith 1990–2000, Vatican Council of the Synod of Bishops 2001–05, 2006–08, 2012–, Supreme Cttee of the Pontifical Missions Socs 2005–, Vatican Congregation for Bishops 2012–; Advisory Group of Cardinals to Pope Francis 2013–; Visiting Scholar, Campion Hall, Oxford 1979, St Edmund's Coll., Cambridge, UK 1983; weekly columnist for Sunday Telegraph, Sydney 2001–; has lectured throughout Australia and in USA, UK, Ireland, NZ and Croatia; Hon. Fellow, St Edmund's Coll., Cambridge 2003–; Grand Prior Equestrian Order of the Holy Sepulchre of Jerusalem, Australian Lieutenancy-Southern 1998–2001, Grand Prior for the Order in NSW 2001, Kt Grand Cross 2003, Grand Cross of Merit, Order of St Lazarus, Nat. Chaplain 2001–07, Ecclesiastic Grand Cross of St Lazarus 2003, Bailiff Grand Cross of Honour and Devotion, Sovereign Mil. Order of Malta 2007, Conventual Chaplain 2007, Thomas Aquinas Medallion, Thomas Aquinas Coll. USA 2008, Bailiff Grand Cross of Justice, Sacred Mil. Constantinian Order of St George 2011, Medal of Gratitude (Poland) 2011; Dr hc (Christendom Coll., USA) 2006, (Univ. of Notre Dame) 2010; Centenary Medal 2003. *Publications:* The Sisters of St Joseph in Swan Hill 1922–72 1972, Catholicism in Australia 1988, Rerum Novarum – One Hundred Years Later 1992, Issues of Faith and Morals 1996, Catholicism and the Architecture of Freedom 1999, Be Not Afraid 2004, God and Caesar: Selected Essays on Religion, Politics and Society 2007, Free for All: Negotiating Freedom in a World of Individuals 2009, Test Everything: Hold Fast to What is Good 2010, One Christian Perspective on Climate Change 2011, Contemplating Christ with Luke 2012. *Leisure interests:* reading, writing, football. *Address:* Archdiocese of Sydney, Polding Centre, 133 Liverpool Street, Sydney, NSW 2000, Australia (office). *Telephone:* (2) 9390-5100 (office). *Fax:* (2) 9261-8312 (office). *E-mail:* cardinal@sydneycatholic.org (office). *Website:* www.sydney.catholic.org.au (office).

PELLEGRINI, Federica; Italian swimmer; b. 5 Aug. 1988, Mirano, Venice; Olympic Games, Athens 2004: silver medal, 200m freestyle; Olympic Games, Beijing 2008: gold medal, 200m freestyle; World Championships (long course): gold medal, 200m and 400m freestyle, Rome 2009, 200m and 400m freestyle, Shanghai 2011, silver medal, 200m freestyle, Montreal 2005, Barcelona 2013, bronze medal, 200m freestyle, Melbourne 2007; World Championships (short course): silver medal, 200m freestyle, Shanghai 2006, bronze medal, 400m freestyle, Shanghai 2006, 400m freestyle, Dubai 2010; European Championships (long course): gold medal, 400m freestyle, Eindhoven 2008, 200m freestyle, Budapest 2010, silver medal, 4×100m freestyle relay, Eindhoven 2008, bronze medal, 4×200m freestyle relay, Eindhoven 2008, 800m freestyle, Budapest 2010; European Championships (short course): gold medal, 200m freestyle, Trieste 2005, 200m freestyle, Rijeka 2008, 200m freestyle, Istanbul 2009, 800m freestyle, Eindhoven 2010, silver medal, 400m freestyle, Helsinki 2006, 400m freestyle, Debrecen 2007, bronze medal, 400m freestyle, Trieste 2005, 4×50m medley relay, Rijeka 2008, 4×50m medley relay, Eindhoven 2010; Summer Universiade: gold medal, 200m freestyle, Bangkok 2007, 400m freestyle, Bangkok 2007; swims for Circolo Canottieri Aniene club; coaches, Alberto Castagnetti –2009, Philippe Lucas 2009–11, Federico Bonifacenti 2011, Claudio Rossetto 2012, Philippe Lucas 2013; World Swimmer of the Year 2009, European Swimmer of the Year 2009, 2010, 2011. *Achievements include:* became the first woman to breach the four-minute barrier in 400m freestyle 2009. *Address:* c/o Circolo Canottieri Aniene a.s.d., Lungotevere dell'Acqua Acetosa 119, Rome, Italy. *Telephone:* (02) 121341008. *E-mail:* info@ccaniene.com. *Website:* www.ccaniene.com.

PELLERIN, Fleur; French (b. South Korean) politician; *Minister Delegate with responsibility for Small and Medium-sized Enterprises, Innovation and the Digital Economy;* b. (Kim Jong-suk), 29 Aug. 1973, Seoul, South Korea; m. Laurent Olléon; one d.; ed École Supérieure des Sciences Économiques et Commerciales, Cergy-Pontoise, Institut d'École Politiques (Sciences Po), Paris, École Nationale d'Admin, Strasbourg; abandoned on streets of Seoul at three or four days old, sent to an orphanage, adopted six months later by a French family; Magistrate of the Court of Auditors 2001–05, Rapporteur to Standing Cttee on Scrutiny of Companies and Perception of Copyright (SPRD); external audit assignments within statutory auditors of UN in Iraq, New York and Geneva 2001–06; Assoc. Dir, Tilder (communication strategy consultancy) 2007–08; Rapporteur, Comm. on Public Ethics 2007–09; Auditor and Counsellor at Court of Auditors 2009–; in charge of societal and digital economy issues in François Hollande's presidential election campaign 2012; Minister Delegate with responsibility for Small and Medium Enterprises, Innovation, and the Digital Economy attached to the Minister for

Econ. Regeneration (fmr Ministry of the Economy, Finance, and Industry) 2012–; fmr mem. Bd and Pres. Club XXIe siècle; fmr mem. Bd and Treas. Entretiens de l'excellence; Dir Unis-Cité asscn; fmr Dir Fondation de Royaumont; fmr mem. Cttee on Sanctions of ARJEL; fmr mem. Bd of Dirs Public Sénat; fmr mem. Diversity Cttee of France Télévisions. *Address:* Ministère du Redressement productif, Télédoc 151, 139 rue de Bercy, 75572 Paris Cedex 12, France (office). *Telephone:* 1-40-04-04-04 (office). *Website:* www.redressement-productif.gouv.fr (office).

PELLI, César, MArch, FAIA, RIBA, JIA; Argentine/American architect and academic; *Senior Principal, Pelli Clarke Pelli Architects;* b. 12 Oct. 1926, Tucumán, Argentina; s. of Victor Vicente Pelli and Teresa S. Pelli (née Suppa); m. Diana Balmori 1950; two s.; ed Universidad Nacional de Tucumán, Univ. of Illinois-Urbana Champaign; emigrated to USA 1952, naturalized 1964; known for designing some of the world's tallest buildings and other major urban landmarks; Project Designer, Eero Saarinen Offices, Mich., Conn. 1954–64; Dir of Design, Daniel, Mann, Johnson & Medenhall 1964–68; Partner in Charge of Design, Gruen Assocs 1968–76; Prof. of Architecture, Yale Univ. 1977–, Dean Yale School of Architecture 1977–84; Sr Prin., César Pelli & Assocs 1977– (now known as Pelli Clarke Pelli Architects); mem. American Acad. of Arts and Letters; 14 hon. doctorates including Hon. Dr of Arts (Yale) 2008; over 200 awards and prizes, including UN City Competition First Prize, Vienna 1969, Arnold W. Brunner Prize, Nat. Inst. Arts and Letters 1978, AIA Honor Award for Fed. Office Bldg, Lawndale, San Bernardino City Hall, Calif., Arnold M. Brunner Memorial Prize, Nat. Acad. of Design 1991, listed by AIA amongst the ten most influential living American architects 1991, AIA Honor Award 1994, AIA Firm Award 1989, and Gold Medal 1995, The Lynn S. Beedle Lifetime Achievement Award, Council on Tall Buildings and Urban Habitat 2008, Diamond Konex Award for Visual Arts, Konex Foundation 2012. *Buildings completed:* Worldway Postal Center, Los Angeles Int. Airport, Calif. 1966, Kukui Gardens housing, Honolulu, HI 1967, San Bernardino City Hall, Calif. 1969, US Embassy, Tokyo 1972, Commons Centre and Mall, Columbus, Ind. 1973, Eaton's Dept Store, Vancouver, BC 1973, Design Center, Los Angeles 1973, 1988 and 2014, Wintergarden Arboretum, Niagara Falls, NY 1977 (demolished 2009), World Financial Center, New York 1981–87, Residential Tower atop Museum of Modern Art, New York 1984, Cleveland Clinic, Cleveland, Ohio 1984–86, Mattatuck Museum Arts and History Center renovation, Waterbury, Conn. 1984, Blumenthal Performing Arts Center, Charlotte, NC 1987, Carnegie Hall Tower, New York 1987–90, Maryland Residence, Bethesda, Md 1987–89, One Canada Square, Canary Wharf, London, UK 1987–91, Wells Fargo Center (fmrly Norwest Center), Minneapolis, Minn. 1988, Gaviidae Common, Minneapolis 1989, Nippon Telegraph and Telephone HQ, Tokyo 1990, Roy Nutt Math., Eng & Computer Science Center, Trinity Coll., Hartford, Conn. 1990, 181 West Madison Street, Chicago, Ill. 1990, Key Tower, Cleveland, Ohio 1991, 777 Tower, Los Angeles 1991, Frances Lehman Loeb Art Center, Vassar Coll., Poughkeepsie, NY 1991, Bank of America Corp. Center, Charlotte, NC 1992, Plaza Tower, Costa Mesa, Calif. 1992, Worrell Professional Center, Wake Forest Univ. School of Law, Winston-Salem, NC 1993, Physics and Astronomy Bldg, Univ. of Washington, Seattle 1994, Aronoff Center for Performing Arts, Cincinnati, Ohio 1995, 100 North Main Street (fmrly Wachovia Center), Winston-Salem, NC 1995, Edificio República, Buenos Aires 1996, Residencial del Bosque, Mexico City 1996, Owens Corning World HQ, Toledo, Ohio 1996, Expansion of Washington Reagan Nat. Airport, Washington, DC (AIA Design Award 1998, Design for Transportation Award 2000) 1997, Overture Center, Madison, Wis. 1998, Petronas Twin Towers, Kuala Lumpur, Malaysia (Aga Khan Award 2004) 1998, Schuster Center, Dayton, Ohio 1998, Cheung Kong Centre, Hong Kong 1999, Zurich tower office bldg in The Hague, Netherlands 1999, Kurayoshi Park Square, Kurayoshi, Japan 2000, Boston Bank Bldg, Buenos Aires 2000, KABC-TV, Los Angeles 2000, Citigroup Centre, 25 Canada Square, Canary Wharf, London 2001, Bucksbaum Center for the Arts, Grinnell Coll., Grinnell, Ia 2001, Athletic and Fitness Center, Grinnell Coll. 2001, The Investment Building, Washington, DC 2001, JP MorganChase Bldg, San Francisco 2002, Weber Music Hall, Univ. of Minnesota, Duluth, Minn. 2002, Former Enron HQ, 1500 Louisiana Street, Houston, Tex. 2002, Gerald Ratner Athletics Center, Univ. of Chicago 2003, Two Int. Finance Centre, Hong Kong 2003, Center for Drama and Film & the Martel Theater, Vassar Coll., Poughkeepsie, NY 2003, 25 Bank Street, Canary Wharf, Docklands, London 2003, 40 Bank Street, Canary Wharf, Docklands, London 2003, Benjamin & Mariam Schuster Performing Arts Center, Dayton, Ohio 2003, Goldman Sachs Tower, Jersey City, NJ 2004, Cira Centre, Philadelphia, Pa 2005, Malone Engineering Center, Yale Univ., New Haven, Conn. 2005, Theodore Roosevelt Fed. Bldg Eastern Dist Courthouse, Brooklyn, NY 2006, Science and Eng Research and Classroom Complex, Univ. of Houston, Tex. 2006, Minneapolis Public Library's Central br., Minneapolis, Minn. 2006, Joe Rosenfield '25 Center, Grinnell Coll., Ia 2006, Renée and Henry Segerstrom Concert Hall, Segerstrom Center For the Arts, Orange County Performing Arts Center, Costa Mesa, Calif. 2006, Thomas E. Golden Jr Center, St Thomas More Catholic Chapel and Center, Yale Univ. 2006, Adrienne Arsht Center for the Performing Arts, Miami, Fla 2006, BOK Center, Tulsa, Okla 2008, One Park West, Liverpool, UK 2008, Torre de Cristal, Madrid, Spain 2008, Repsol-YPF Bldg, Buenos Aires 2008, St Regis Residences and Hotel, Mexico City 2008, Business Instructional Facility, Univ. of Illinois, Urbana-Champaign 2008, Co-operative Arts and Humanities High School, New Haven, Conn. 2009, Connecticut Science Center, Hartford, Conn. 2009, Aria Resort & Casino, the central feature of CityCenter, Las Vegas, NV 2009, Shanghai IFC, Pudong, sister project of Two Int. Finance Centre, Hong Kong 2010, New Airport Terminal Bldg (Phase 1), Winnipeg James Armstrong Richardson Int. Airport, Winnipeg, Manitoba 2011, Iberdrola Tower, office bldg, Bilbao, Spain 2011, The Landmark, Abu Dhabi, UAE 2013. *Publications:* Architecture and Urbanism 1985, César Pelli (monograph) 1991, César Pelli, in The Master Architect series 1993, Cesar Pelli: Recent Themes (co-author) 1995, World Architecture Review 1998, Observations for Young Architects 1999; various articles in specialist journals. *Address:* Pelli Clarke Pelli Architects, 1056 Chapel Street, New Haven, CT 06510, USA (office). *Telephone:* (203) 777-2515 (office). *Fax:* (203) 787-2856 (office). *E-mail:* InfoNH@pcparch.com (office). *Website:* pcparch.com (office).

PËLLUMBI, Servet, PhD; Albanian politician; b. 14 Dec. 1936, Korçë; s. of Ismail Pëllumbi and Hazize Pëllumbi; ed State Univ. of St Petersburg; Prof. of Philosophy 1960–74; Univ. Prof. of Philosophy 1974–91; Vice-Chair. Socialist Party of Albania 1991–96; mem. Parl. 1992–2003; Speaker of Parl. of Albania 2002–05; Academic Dir Inst. of Political and Social Studies; Dir Publishing Bd Policy & Society magazine. *Publications include:* Think Differently, Transition in its Light-Shade, Endeavour in Political Sociology, Sociology Tracing, Dictionary of Philosophy 1974, 1982; univ. text books and numerous articles on policy and society. *Leisure interests:* sports, reading, books, music, community devt activities, writing memories. *Address:* Rruga "Brigada e tetë", Pallati Havari, shk. 2, Ap. 7/1, Tirana, (home); c/o Socialist Party of Albania (SPA) (Partia Socialiste e Shqipërisë) (PSSh), Tirana, Albania. *Telephone:* (5) 4271500 (home).

PELLY, Derek (Derk) Roland, MA, AIB; British banker; b. 12 June 1929, Welwyn Garden City; s. of the late Arthur Roland Pelly and Phyllis Elsie Henderson; m. Susan Roberts 1953; one s. two d.; ed Marlborough Coll. and Trinity Coll., Cambridge; joined Barclays Bank Ltd (various positions) 1952, Local Dir, Chelmsford 1959, Sr Local Dir, Luton 1969; Vice-Chair. Barclays Bank Int. Ltd 1977, full-time Vice-Chair. 1979; Group Vice-Chair. Barclays Bank PLC 1985, Group Deputy Chair. and Chair. Barclays Int. Ltd 1986–88; Gov. London House for Overseas Grads 1985–91; Dir The Pvt. Bank and Trust Co. 1989–94. *Leisure interest:* painting. *Address:* 2 Swallow Field, Earls Colne, Colchester, Essex, CO6 2RW, England (home). *Telephone:* (1787) 223389 (home).

PELOSI, Nancy Patricia D'Alesandro; American politician; *Minority Leader, House of Representatives;* b. 26 March 1940, Baltimore, Md; d. of Thomas D'Alesandro, Jr; m. Paul Pelosi; one s. four d.; ed Trinity Coll., Washington, DC; Democratic Nat. Committeewoman 1976–96, Chair. Democratic Nat. Convention Host Cttee 1984, Chief Fundraiser for Nat. Democratic Senatorial Campaign Cttee 1986, State and Northern Chair. Calif. Democratic Party –1987; Rep. (Democrat) 8th Congressional Dist of Calif. 1987–, mem. House Perm. Select Cttee on Intelligence, House Democratic Whip 2001–03, Democratic Minority Leader 2002–07 (first woman to lead a major party in Congress), 2011–, Speaker (first female speaker) 2007–11; sr mem. House Appropriations Cttee, mem. Appropriations Sub-cttee on Labor, Health and Human Services and Educ.; Chair. Congressional Working Group on China; Co-Chair. AIDS Task Force of House Democratic Caucus, Bio-Medical Research Caucus; fmr Ranking Democrat on Appropriations Sub-cttee on Foreign Operations and Export Financing; fmr mem. House Cttee on Standards of Official Conduct (Ethics); Democrat; ranked by Forbes magazine amongst The World's 100 Most Powerful Women (11th) 2004, (76th) 2005, (48th) 2006, (26th) 2007, (35th) 2008, (35th) 2009, (11th) 2010, (52nd) 2011, (28th) 2012, (22nd) 2013. *Address:* 235 Cannon HOB, Washington, DC 20515, USA (office). *Telephone:* (202) 225-0100 (office); (202) 225-4965 (office). *E-mail:* americanvoices@mail.house.gov (office). *Website:* pelosi.house.gov (office).

PELPOLA, Daya; Sri Lankan lawyer, politician and business executive; fmr sports sub-ed., Ceylon Daily News; fmr mem. Parl.; Vice-Chair. United Nat. Party, also legal adviser to party leader Ranil Wickramasinghe; Chair. Sri Lankan Airlines Ltd 2002–08; judge, Miss Tourism Int. competition 2002. *Leisure interests:* sports, especially hockey and rugby. *Address:* c/o Head Office, Sri Lankan Airlines Ltd, Level 22, East Tower, World Trade Centre, Echelon Square, Colombo 1, Sri Lanka. *Telephone:* (19) 7335555. *Fax:* (19) 7335122. *E-mail:* ulweb@srilankan .aero. *Website:* www.srilankan.aero.

PELTASON, Jack W., PhD; American university president (retd); *President Emeritus, University of California;* b. 29 Aug. 1923, St Louis, Mo.; s. of Walter Peltason and Emma Hartman; m. Suzanne Toll 1945; one s. two d.; ed Univ. of Missouri and Princeton Univ.; Asst Prof., Smith Coll. 1947–51; Asst Prof. of Political Science, Univ. of Illinois, Urbana-Champaign 1951–52, Assoc. Prof. 1953–59, Dean Coll. of Liberal Arts and Sciences 1960–64, Chancellor 1967–77; Vice-Chancellor Univ. of California, Irvine 1964–67, Chancellor 1984–92, Chancellor Emer. 1992–; Pres. Univ. of California 1992–95, Pres. Emer. 1995–; Pres. American Council on Educ. 1977–84, Bren Foundation 1997–; mem. Bd of Dirs The Archstone Foundation, The Irvine Health Foundation, The Irvine Barclay Theater; mem. Bd of Trustees, Soka Univ. of America; Fellow, American Acad. of Arts and Sciences; 22 hon. degrees and other awards. *Publications include:* Federal Courts in the Political Process 1955, Fifty-Eight Lonely Men: Southern Federal Judges and School Desegregation 1961, Understanding the Constitution 1997, Government by the People; co-author of several other books; articles in journals and encyclopedias and book chapters etc. *Leisure interests:* reading, writing, family. *Address:* University of California, 5295 Social Sciences Plaza B, Mail Code: 5100, Irvine, CA 92697 (office); 18 Whistler Court, Irvine, CA 92612, USA (home). *Telephone:* (949) 824-3938. *Fax:* (949) 824-3960. *E-mail:* jwpeltas@uci .edu (office); jwpeltason@aol.com (home); jwpeltason@uci.edu. *Website:* www .faculty.uci.edu/profile.cfm?faculty_id=2462 (office).

PELTIER, Guillaume; French politician and business executive; *Vice-President and National Secretary, Union pour un Mouvement Populaire;* b. 27 Aug. 1976, Paris; f. a business in Tours, and runs Lettre de l'opinion monthly magazine; also involved with Univ. of Orléans; cand. in local elections in Municipality of Tours South (Febvotte, Prébendes and Sanitas) 2011; fmr mem. Nat. Front and fmr leader of youth section; leader La Droite forte (The Strong Right) faction of Union pour un Mouvement Populaire (UMP) 2012–, Vice-Pres. and Nat. Sec. UMP 2013–, Communications Man. UMP Indre-et-Loire. *Address:* UMP, TSA 41557, 75901 Paris Cedex 15, France (office). *Telephone:* 1-40-76-60-00 (office). *E-mail:* info@u-m -p.org (office). *Website:* www.u-m-p.org (office).

PELTOLA, Timo Veikko, MSc; Finnish petroleum industry executive; *Chairman, Neste Oil Oyj;* b. 19 April 1946, Lieto; m. Katariina Helena Toivonen; three c.; Product Man. Huhtamäki Corpn 1971–75, Marketing Dir 1975–81, Pres. Polarcup Div. 1981–83, Corp. Vice-Pres. 1984–86, Exec. Vice-Pres. 1987–89, CEO 1989–2004; Ind. Chair. Neste Oil Oyj 2005–, Chair. Personnel and Remuneration Cttee; Chair. AW-Energy Oy; Chair. Supervisory Bd Ilmarinen Mutual Pension Insurance Co.; Vice-Chair. Nordea AB; mem. Bd of Dirs TeliaSonera AB, SAS AB; mem. Supervisory Bd Finnish Fair Corpn Co-operative; mem. Advisory Bd CVC Capital Pnrs; Hon. DEcon. *Address:* Neste Oil Oyj, Keilaranta 8, PO Box 95, 00095 Espoo, Finland (office). *Telephone:* (10) 45811 (office). *Fax:* (10) 4584442 (office). *E-mail:* info@nestoil.com (office). *Website:* www.nesteoil.com (office).

PEÑA, Federico, LLB; American lawyer, business executive, fmr politician and fmr government official; *Managing Director, Vestar Capital Partners;* b. 15 March 1947, Laredo, Tex.; ed Univ. of Tex.; fmr Pnr, Peña & Peña (law firm); mem. Colo

Legis. 1979–83; Mayor of Denver, Colo 1983–91; f. Peña Investment Advisors Inc. 1991; apptd part-time legal consultant, Brownstein Hyatt Farber & Strickland (law firm), Denver 1992; US Sec. of Transportation 1993–97, of Energy 1997–98; Sr Advisor, Vestar Capital Pnrs (pvt. equity firm), Denver 1998–2000, Man. Dir 2000–; mem. Bd of Dirs Marsico Capital Man., Prin. Financial Group, Sonic Corpn, Valor Telecommunications; mem. Toyota North American Diversity Advisory Bd; Assoc., Harvard Univ. Centre for Law and Educ. *Address:* Vestar Capital Partners, Seventeenth Street Plaza, 1225 17th Street, Suite 1660, Denver, CO 80202 USA.

PEÑA, Paco; Spanish flamenco guitarist, musical director and professor of flamenco guitar; *Director, Paco Peña Flamenco Company;* b. (Francisco Peña Perez), 1 June 1942, Córdoba; s. of Antonio Peña and Rosario Pérez; m. Karin Vaessen 1982; two d.; int. concert artist since 1968; f. Paco Peña Flamenco Co. 1970, Centro Flamenco Paco Peña, Córdoba 1981; Prof. of Flamenco, Rotterdam Conservatory, Netherlands 1985; composed Misa Flamenca 1991; produced Musa Gitana 1999, Voces y Ecos 2002; composed Flamenco Requiem 2004; produced flamenco dance show A Compas! 2006; devised dance productions Flamenco sin Fronteras 2009, Quimeras 2010, Flamenco Vivo 2011, Quimeras 2012; Oficial de la Cruz de la Orden del Mérito Civil; Ramón Montoya Prize 1983, Arts Gold Medal in the Arts, John F. Kennedy Centre for the Performing Arts, Washington, DC 2012. *Publication:* Toques Flamencos. *Address:* c/o MPM London, Suite 20, 1 Prince of Wales Road, London, NW5 3LW, England (office). *Telephone:* (20) 7681-7475 (office). *Fax:* (20) 7681-7476 (office). *E-mail:* MPM@pacopena.com. *Website:* www.pacopena.com.

PEÑA NIETO, Enrique, LicenDer, MBA; Mexican lawyer and politician; *President;* b. 20 July 1966, Atlacomulco, State of Mexico; s. of the late Enrique Peña del Mazo and Maria del Socorro Nieto Sánchez; m. 1st Mónica Pretelini Sáenz 1993 (died 2007); one s. two d.; m. 2nd Angélica Rivera 2010; ed Universidad Panamericana, Instituto Tecnológico y de Estudios Superiores de Monterrey; taught law at Universidad Panamericana; Sec. Citizen Movt of Zone I of State Directive Cttee of Nat. Confed. of Popular Orgs (CNOP) 1990; del. to Org. and Citizen Front in different municipalities of State of Mexico 1991; also served as instructor at Electoral Training Centre of Partido Revolucionario Institucional (PRI—Institutional Revolutionary Party); held admin. positions in state govt during this time; Chief of Staff for Sec. of Econ. Devt of State of Mexico 1993–98; Deputy Sec. of Govt of State of Mexico 1999–2000; exercised different tasks for state's admin: Govt Admin Sec., Pres. Directive Council for Social Security Inst. of State of Mexico and its municipalities, Pres. Internal Council of Health Inst. of State of Mexico and Vice-Pres. for State of Mexico's Govt Bd for the Integral Family Devt System (DIF) 2000–02; mem. Nat. Inst. of Public Admin, Admin. Council for different decentralized public agencies; mem. PRI's Nat. and State Political Council and del. to PRI's XVIII Gen. Ass. 2001; won election for local rep. for XIII Dist in LV Legis.; Co-ordinator PRI's Parl. group in LV Legis. and Chair. Bd of Political Co-ordination of the local congress 2003–04; PRI cand. for governorship 2005; Gov. of State of Mexico 2005–11; involved in Supreme Court case, along with other politicians, charged with abuse of power in events of civil unrest in San Salvador Atenco 2006, exonerated 2009; Pres.-elect July–Nov. 2012, Pres. Dec. 2012–; ranked by Forbes magazine amongst The World's Most Powerful People (54th) 2012, (37th) 2013. *Publication:* México, la gran esperanza: un Estado eficaz para una democracia de resultados (Mexico, The Great Hope: An Efficient State for a Democracy of Results) 2011. *Address:* Office of the President, Los Pinos, Col. San Miguel Chapultepec, 11850 México, DF, Mexico (office). *Telephone:* (55) 5093-5300 (office). *Fax:* (55) 5277-2376 (office). *E-mail:* felipe.calderon@presidencia.gob.mx (office). *Website:* www.presidencia.gob.mx (office).

PEÑALOSA, Antonio; Spanish international organization official; *Special Adviser to President and Management Board, International Organization of Employers;* ed Univ. of Santiago, Coll. of Europe, Brussels, Belgium; staff mem. Industrial Policy Directorate, EC 1977–78; Asst to Sec.-Gen. of Int. Org. of Employers 1978–1983, Exec. Sec. 1983–94, Deputy Sec.-Gen. 1993–99, Sec.-Gen. 1999–2011, Special Adviser to Pres. and Man. Bd 2011–. *Address:* International Organization of Employers, 26 Chemin de Joinville, Cointrin, 1216 Geneva, Switzerland (office). *Telephone:* (22) 9290000 (office). *Fax:* (22) 9290001 (office). *E-mail:* penalosa@ioe-emp.org (office). *Website:* www.ioe-emp.org (office).

PEÑALOSA LONDOÑO, Enrique, BA, MA, DESS; Colombian politician, international organization official and consultant; *President, Board of Directors, Institute for Transportation and Development Policy;* b. 30 Sept. 1954, Washington, DC, USA; s. of Enrique Peñalosa Camargo and Cecilia Londoño; ed Duke Univ., USA, Institut Int. d'Admin Publique and Univ. of Paris II, France; Pres. of the Instituto Colombiano de Ahorro y Vivienda (ICAV); Sec. of Econ. Affairs, Presidency of Colombia 1986–89; mem. Chamber of Reps 1990–91; Mayor of Bogotá 1998–2001; Consultant on Urban Strategy, Vision and Policy 2001–; Visiting Scholar, New York Univ. 2007; Pres. Bd of Dirs, Inst. for Transportation and Devt Policy, New York 2009–; Co-Pres. Colombian Green Party 2010–; Eisenhower Fellowship, Nat. Simon Bolivar Prize for Journalism, Soc. of Economists of Bogotá and Cundinamarca Prize, Göteborg Award for Sustainable Devt 2009. *Publications:* Capitalism: The Better Option 1989, Democracy and Capitalism: The Challenges of the Next Century 1990, Cerros de Bogotá 2003; numerous articles on econ. and urban issues. *Leisure interests:* cycling, reading, going to the movies. *Address:* Board of Directors, Institute for Transportation and Development Policy, 127 West 26th Street, Suite 1002, New York, NY 10001, USA (office); Carrera 11 No. 86-53, Piso 14, Bogotá, Colombia. *Telephone:* (212) 629-8001 (office); (1) 6913323 (ext. 151). *Fax:* (212) 629-8334 (office). *E-mail:* mobility@itdp.org (office). *Website:* www.itdp.org (office); www.enriquepenalosa.com.

PENCE, Michael (Mike) Richard; American lawyer, politician and state governor; *Governor of Indiana;* b. 7 June 1959, Columbus, Ind.; s. of Edward J. Pence, Jr and Nancy Jane Pence (née Cawley); m. Karen Pence; one s. two d.; ed Columbus North High School, Hanover Coll., Indiana Univ. Robert H. McKinney School of Law; mem. US House of Reps for 2nd Congressional Dist of Indiana 2001–03, for 6th Congressional Dist 2003–13, mem. Cttee on Foreign Affairs, Cttee on the Judiciary, mem. Congressional Internet Caucus, Int. Conservation Caucus, Sportsmen's Caucus, Tea Party Caucus; Gov. of Indiana 2013–; fmr Chair. Republican Study Cttee; Republican. *Address:* Office of Governor, State House Room 206, 200 West Washington Street, Indianapolis, IN 46204, USA (office).

Telephone: (317) 232-4567 (office). *Fax:* (317) 232-3443 (office). *E-mail:* mpence@mikepence.com (office). *Website:* www.in.gov/gov (office); www.mikepence.com.

PENCHAS, Shmuel, MD, DIC, MSc; Israeli professor of health administration and physician; *Consultant, Hadassah Medical Organization;* b. 12 Feb. 1939, Romania; s. of Nathan Penchas and Liuba Penchas; four s.; ed Hebrew Univ.-Hadassah Medical School, Jerusalem, Haifa Technion Grad. School, Imperial Coll. and Univ. Coll., London, UK, Harvard Univ., USA; Physician, Hadassah Univ. Hosp., Jerusalem 1967–76, Dir of Computing 1977–78; Lecturer in Medicine, Hebrew Univ.-Hadassah Medical School, Jerusalem 1975, Sr Lecturer 1978, Assoc. Prof. of Internal Medicine 1984, Prof. of Health Care Admin 1993; Research Fellow, Harvard Univ. Medical School 1978; Deputy Dir-Gen. Hadassah Medical Org. 1978, Dir-Gen. 1981–98, now Consultant; Chair. Israel Asscn of Hosp. Dirs 1984–91, Foreign Assoc. mem. US Acad. of Medicine of NAS; Consultant to Hadassah (Women's Zionist Org. of America); Advisor to the Prime Minister of Bosnia (Srbska); mem. Romanian Nat. Acad. of Science; Hon. PhD, Hon. DrSc. *Publications:* articles in professional journals. *Address:* 6 Manger Street, Tel-Aviv 64585, Israel (office). *Telephone:* (3) 5220090 (office). *Fax:* (3) 5220090 (office). *E-mail:* penchas@netvision.net.il (office).

PENDERECKI, Krzysztof; Polish composer and conductor; b. 23 Nov. 1933, Dębica, Kraków Prov.; s. of Tadeusz Penderecki and Zofia Penderecka; m. Elżbieta Solecka 1965; one s. two d.; ed Jagiellonian Univ., Kraków and State Higher Music School (now Music Acad.), Kraków, studied composition first with Skołyszewski, later with Malawski and Wiechowicz, Kraków; Lecturer in Composition, State Higher Music School, Kraków 1958–66, Prof. Extraordinary 1972–75, Prof. 1975–; Rector Kraków Conservatory 1972–87; Prof. of Composition, Folkwang Hochschule für Musik, Essen 1966–68; Musical Adviser, Vienna Radio 1970–71; Prof. of Composition, Yale Univ. Music Dir, Casals Festival, Puerto Rico 1992–2002; Music Man. Sinfonia Varsovia Orchestra 1997–; Guest Conductor China Philharmonic Orchestra 2000–; mem. Presidential Council of Culture 1992–; Corresp. mem. Arts Acad. of GDR, Berlin 1975, Academia Nacional de Bellas Artes, Buenos Aires 1982; Extraordinary mem. Arts Acad. of W Berlin 1975; mem. Royal Acad. of Music, Stockholm 1976, Acad. Nat. de Sciences, Belles-Lettres et Arts, Bordeaux, American Acad. of Arts and Letters 1999, Hong Kong Acad. for the Performing Arts 2001 etc.; Fellow, Royal Irish Acad. of Music; Hon. RAM, London 1974; Hon. mem. Accad. Nazionale di Santa Cecilia, Rome 1976, Acad. Int. de Philosophie et de l'Art, Berne 1987, Musikkreis der Stadt, Duisburg 1999, Gesellschaft der Musikfreunds, Vienna 2000; Hon. Prof., Moscow Conservatory 1997, Cen. Beijing Conservatory 1998, St Petersburg Conservatory 2003, Komitas State Conservatory, Yerevan 2008; Officier, Ordre de Saint-Georges de Bourgogne (Belgium) 1990, Grand Cross Order of Merit (FRG) 1990, Commdr, Ordre des Arts et des Lettres 1996, Ordine al Merito della Repub. Italiana 2000, Commdr of the Three Star Order, Riga (Latvia) 2006, Order of the White Eagle (Poland) 2006; Dr hc (Univ. of Rochester, NY) 1972, (St Olaf Coll., Northfield, Minn.) 1977, (Katholieke Univ., Leuven) 1979, (Univ. of Bordeaux) 1979, (Georgetown Univ., Washington, DC) 1984, (Univ. of Belgrade) 1985, (Univ. Autónoma, Madrid) 1987; Hon. DMus (Glasgow) 1995, (Jagiellonian Univ., Krakow) 1998, (Ukrainian Nat. Tchaikovsky Acad. of Music) 1999, (Pittsburgh) 1999, (Lucerne) 2000, Univ. of St Petersburg, Yale Univ., Univ. of Leipzig 2003, and many others; Fitelberg Prize for Threnody for the Victims of Hiroshima 1960, also UNESCO award 1959, Polish Minister of Culture and Art Prize 1961, (First Class) 1981, Kraków Composition Prize for Canon 1962, North Rhine-Westphalia Grand Prize for St Luke's Passion 1966, also Pax Prize (Poland) 1966, Alfred Jurzykowski Foundation Award, Polish Inst. of Arts and Sciences in America 1966, Prix Italia 1967/68, State Prize (1st Class) 1968, Gustav Charpentier Prize 1971, Gottfried von Herder Prize 1977, Prix Arthur Honegger for Magnificat 1978, Grand Medal of Paris 1981, Sibelius Prize (Wihouri Foundation, Finland) 1983, Order of Banner of Labour (1st Class) 1983, Premio Lorenzo il Magnifico (Italy) 1985, Wolf Foundation Award 1987, Grammy Award Nat. Acad. of Recording Arts and Sciences (for Best Contemporary Composition) 1988, (for Best Instrumental Soloist Performance with Orchestra) 1999, (for Best Choral Composition) 2001, Grawemeyer Award for Music Composition 1992, City of Strasbourg Medal 1995, Crystal Award, World Econ. Forum, Davos 1997, Business Center Club Special Award, Warsaw 1998, AFIM Indie Award 1999, Köhler-Osbahr-Stiftung Music Award 1999, Best Living Composer Award, Midem Classic Award, Cannes 2000, Príncipe de Asturias Award 2001, Roman Guardini Prize, Catholic Acad. of Music 2002, North Rhine-Westphalia Award 2003, Praemium Imperiale 2004, Gold Medal, Ministry of Culture (Armenia) 2009, Lifetime Achievement Award, Int. Classical Music Awards 2012. *Works include:* Psalms of David (for choir and percussion) 1958, Emanations (for two string orchestras) 1958, Strophes (for soprano, speaker and ten instruments) 1959, Anaklasis (for strings and percussion) 1959–60, Dimensions of Time and Silence (for 40-part mixed choir and chamber ensemble) 1959–60, String Quartet no. 1 1960, no. 2 1968, Threnody for the Victims of Hiroshima (for 52 strings) 1960, Polymorphia (for strings) 1961, Psalms (for tape) 1961, Fluorescences (for large orchestra) 1961, Sonata for Cello and Orchestra 1964, St Luke's Passion 1965–66, Capriccio per oboe e 11 archi 1965, De natura sonoris (for large orchestra) 1966, Dies irae (for soprano, tenor, bass, chorus and large orchestra) 1967, Violin Concerto 1967–77, The Devils of Loudun (opera) 1968–69, Cosmogony 1970, De natura sonoris II (for wind instruments, percussion and strings) 1970, Canticum Canticorum Salomonis (for 16 voices and chamber orchestra) 1970–73, Russian Mass Utrenja 1971, Partita (for harpsichord, guitars, harp, double bass and chamber orchestra) 1972, Symphony no. 1 1972–73, Magnificat (for bass solo, voice ensemble, double choir, boys' voices and orchestra) 1973–74, When Jacob Awoke (for orchestra) 1974, Paradise Lost (opera) 1976–78, Christmas Symphony No. 2 1979–80, Te Deum 1979–80, Lacrimosa 1980, Cello Concerto No. 2 1982, Viola Concerto 1983, Polish Requiem 1980–84, Black Mask (opera) 1984–86, Der unterbrochene Gedanke (for string quartet) 1988, Adagio (for orchestra) 1989, Symphony No. 4 (Adagio for orchestra) 1989, Sinfonietta (for orchestra) 1990–91, Symphony No. 5 (for orchestra) 1991–92, Partita (for orchestra, rev. ed.) 1991, Ubu Rex (opera) 1991, Benedicamus Domine 1992, Benedictus 1992, Flute Concerto 1992–93, Quartet for Clarinet and String Trio 1993, Violin Concerto No. 2 1992–95, Divertimento (for cello solo) 1994, Symphony No. 3 1995, Agnus Dei from Versöhnung Messe (a cappella choir) 1995, Seven Gates of Jerusalem (oratorio) 1995–96, Passacaglia (chamber music) 1995–96, Larghetto (chamber music) 1997, Credo 1997–98, Sonata for Violin and Piano

2000, Sextet for Violin, Viola, Cello, Piano, Clarinet and French Horn 2000, Concerto Grosso for Three Cellos 2001, Benedictus 2002, Resurrection Piano Concerto 2002, Largo for violoncello and orchestra 2003, Symphony No. 8 2005–07, Concerto per corno 'Winterreise' 2007–08, Quartetto per archi No. 3 2008, Drei chinesische Lieder 2008, Kaddisz 2009, Prelude for Peace 2009. *Leisure interest:* dendrology. *Address:* c/o Schott Musik International, Weihergarten 5, 55116 Mainz, Germany (office). *Telephone:* (6131) 246812 (office). *Fax:* (6131) 246250 (office). *E-mail:* katja.riepl@schott-music.com (office). *Website:* www.penderecki.de.

PENDLETON, Victoria Louise, CBE, MBE, BSc; British fmr track cyclist; b. 24 Sept. 1980, Stotfold, Beds., England; d. of Max Pendleton and Pauline M. Viney; fiancé Scott Gardner; ed Northumbria Univ.; began cycling aged six, first race, 400m event on grass track at Fordham aged nine; gold medal, 800m, Nat. Grass Track Championship 1998, 1999, 2005; three silver medals, bronze medal, Nat. Track Championship 2001; gold medal, sprint, bronze medal, 500m, World Cup, Manchester 2004; silver medal, sprint, World Championship, Bordeaux 2006; gold medal, sprint, silver medal, 500m trial, Commonwealth Games, Melbourne 2006; gold medal, Nat. Derny Championship 2006; gold medal, sprint, gold medal, Keirin, gold medal, sprint (team), Union Cycliste Internationale Track Cycling World Championship, Palma de Mallorca 2007; gold medal, sprint, silver medal, Keirin, gold medal, sprint (team), Union Cycliste Internationale Track Cycling World Championship, Manchester 2008; gold medal, sprint, Olympic Games, Beijing 2008; gold medal, sprint, Union Cycliste Internationale Track Cycling World Championship, Pruszków 2009; bronze medal, sprint, silver medal, sprint (team), World Championship 2011; gold medal, sprint (team), European Track Championship 2011; gold medal, Keirin, silver medal, sprint, Olympic Games, London 2012; mem. Sky Track Cycling until her retirement from professional cycling Sept. 2012; Dr hc (Northumbria Univ.) 2008; Sunday Times Sportswoman of the Year 2007, Sportswoman of the Year, Sports Journalists' Asscn of Great Britain 2007. *Television:* contestant, series 10 of Strictly Come Dancing, with professional partner Brendan Cole 2012. *Address:* c/o three60 Sports Management, The Studio, Hudson Street, Deddington, OX15 0SW, England. *Website:* victoriapendleton.co.uk.

PENDRY, Sir John Brian, Kt, BA, MA, PhD, FRS, FInstP; British physicist and academic; *Professor of Theoretical Solid State Physics, Imperial College London;* b. 4 July 1943; s. of Frank Johnson Pendry and Kathleen Pendry (née Shaw); m. Patricia Gard; ed Downing Coll., Cambridge; Research Fellowship in Physics, Downing Coll., Cambridge 1969–73, Fellow in Physics and Praelector 1973–75; ICI Post-doctoral Fellow 1969–71; mem. tech. staff, Theoretical Physics Dept, Bell Labs, Murray Hill, NJ, USA 1972–73; Sr Asst in Research, Cavendish Lab., Cambridge 1973–75; Sr Prin. Scientific Officer: Head of Theory Group, Science and Eng Research Council (SERC) Daresbury Lab. 1975–81; Prof. of Theoretical Solid State Physics, Imperial Coll. of Science and Tech. and Head of Condensed Matter Theory Group 1981–, Head of Experimental Solid State Physics Group 1983–85, Assoc. Head of Physics Dept 1984–92, Head of Physics Dept 1998–2001, Prin., Faculty of Physical Sciences 2001–02; mem. SERC Science Bd, SERC Nuclear Physics Bd 1992–93, Council, Royal Soc. 1992–94, Particle Physics and Astronomy Research Council 1998–2002; Dean, Royal Coll. of Science 1993–96; Ed. Proceedings A of the Royal Society 1996–2002; Leverhulme Trust Sr Research Fellowship 1996–97; Eng and Physical Sciences Research Council (EPSRC) Sr Research Five-Year Fellowship 1997–98, (resgnd) 2003; Commonwealth Scholarships Commr 1998–2000; Chair. Physics sub-panel of Research Assessment Exercise (RAE 2008) 2005–08, Inst. of Physics Publishing 2007–11, Cockcroft Inst. BC 2009–12; Visiting mem., Inst. of Advanced Studies, Hong Kong Univ. of Science and Tech. 2011–; Fellow, Optical Soc. of America 2005, AAAS 2009, American Acad. of Arts and Sciences 2012; Hon. Prof., Nanjing South Eastern Univ. 2012; Dr hc (Universität Erlangen, Nürnberg) 2010, (Duke Univ.) 2010; Hon. DSc (Hong Kong Baptist Univ.) 2010; British Vacuum Council Prize and Medal 1994, Dirac Medal and Prize, Inst. of Physics 1996, Int. Surface Structure Prize 1996, Appleton Lecturer 2003, Celsius Lecturer, Univ. of Uppsala, Sweden 2004, Bakerian Lecturer, Royal Soc. 2005, Larmor Lecturer, Queen's Univ. Belfast 2005, Fröhlich Lecturer, Univ. of Liverpool 2005, EU Decartes Prize for "extending electromagnetism through novel artificial materials" 2005, Royal Medal, Royal Soc. 2006, Centenary Kelvin Lecturer, Inst. of Eng and Tech. 2009, UNESCO-Niels Bohr Gold Medal 2009, W.E. Lamb Medal for Laser Science and Quantum Optics 2010, Fred Kavli Distinguished Lectureship in Nanoscience, MRS Fall Meeting 2012, APS McGroddy Prize (co-recipient) 2012, 30th Anniversary Prize, European Materials Research Soc. 2013, Newton Medal, Inst. of Physics 2013. *Publications:* numerous scientific papers in professional journals on condensed matter theory, optics and metamaterials. *Address:* Room 808 Blackett, Department of Physics, Imperial College London, Prince Consort Road, London, SW7 2AZ, England (office). *Telephone:* (20) 7594-7606 (office). *E-mail:* j.pendry@imperial.ac.uk (office). *Website:* www3.imperial.ac.uk/people/j.pendry (office); www.cmth.ph.ic.ac.uk/photonics/Newphotonics (office).

PENG, Liyuan; Chinese singer and actress; *First Lady;* b. 20 Nov. 1962, Yuncheng, Shandong Prov.; d. of Peng Longkun; m. Xi Jinping (Pres. of People's Repub. of China 2013–) 1987; one d.; ed Shandong Acad. of Arts, China Acad. of Music; solo singer, Qianwei Song and Dance Troupe of Ji'nan Mil. Command 1980–84; gained widespread popularity following appearance on China Central TV (CCTV) New Year Gala 1983; solo singer and civilian mem., Song and Dance Troupe, PLA Gen. Political Dept 1984–; nicknamed 'The Peony Fairy'; specializes in traditional Chinese folk music and patriotic songs; frequent appearances on stage and on state TV; has performed overseas in USA, Canada, Japan and Austria; part-time Prof. Central Beijing Conservatory; Ministry of Health Amb. for HIV/AIDS Prevention 2006–; Amb. Chinese Asscn on Tobacco Control 2009–; WHO Goodwill Amb. for Tuberculosis and HIV 2011–; UNESCO Amb. for Women's Education 2014–; mem. CCP 1985–, mem. 11th CPPCC Nat. Cttee; several awards including Plum Blossom Award 1985, Nat. Cultural Projects Award, China Golden Records Award, Lincoln Center for the Arts Distinguished Artist Award, ranked by Forbes magazine amongst The World's 100 Most Powerful Women (54th) 2013. *Works include:* People from Our Village, Mount Everest, On the Plains of Hope, Mountain Song, I Love You Saibei Snow, High Heaven Clouds, We are the Yellow Tarzan, Folks, Exalted, Sunnyway. *Operas include:* White Haired Girl, The Daughter of the Party, Melancholy Dawn, Poems of Mulan. *Television:* regular

appearances on China Central TV (CCTV) New Year Gala. *Address:* Song and Dance Troupe, People's Liberation Army General Political Department, A-16, East Huayuan Road, Haidian District, Beijing 100083, People's Republic of China (office). *Telephone:* (10) 62010693 (office). *Fax:* (10) 62369748 (office).

PENG, Ming-Min; Taiwanese politician; b. 1923; ed in Japan and Nat. Taiwan Univ.; lost left arm during US bombing raid on Nagasaki; fmr Chair. Political Science Dept, Nat. Taiwan Univ.; arrested for activities supporting self-determination for Taiwan 1964 and sentenced to eight years' imprisonment; sentence commuted to house arrest; escaped into exile in USA; returned home 1992; joined Democratic Progressive Party (DDP) 1995; DDP cand., presidential elections March 1996; Sr Adviser to the Office of the President 2001. *Publication:* A Perfect Escape 2009. *Address:* c/o Democratic Progressive Party, 10/F, 30 Beiping East Rd, Taipei 10051, Taiwan.

PENG, Peiyun; Chinese administrator; *Honorary President, All-China Women's Federation;* b. 1929, Liuyang Co., Hunan Prov.; ed Tsinghua Univ., Beijing; joined CCP Communist Youth League 1945, CCP 1946; Sec.-Gen. CCP Party Br., Tsinghua Univ. 1949–78 (also Deputy Sec. CCP Party Cttee); Vice-Chair. CCP Revolutionary Cttee, Beijing Chemical Eng Inst., Beijing 1949–78; Head, 1st Bureau, State Science and Tech. Comm., 1978–79; Vice-Minister of Educ. 1982–88, State Educ. Comm. 1982–88; Sec. CCP Party Cttee, Chinese Univ. of Science and Tech., Anhui Prov. 1982–88; mem. Central Comm. for Discipline Inspection, CCP Cen. Cttee 1982–92; Minister of State Family Planning Comm. 1988–98; State Councillor 1988–98; Del., 12th CCP Nat. Congress 1982–87, 13th CCP Nat. Congress 1987–92; mem. 14th CCP Cen. Cttee 1992–97, 15th CCP Cen. Cttee 1997–2002; Chair. Coordination Cttee for the Handicapped (State Council) 1993–; Chair. Nat. Cttee for Patriotic Public Health Campaign 1994–, Women and Children's Work Cttee of the State Council; Vice-Chair. Standing Cttee of 9th NPC 1998–2003; Pres. Chinese Asscn for Promotion of the Population Culture 1993, Soc. of Population 1994, Exec. Cttee All-China Women's Fed. 1998–2003, Hon. Pres. 2003–; Pres. Red Cross Soc. of China 1999–2009; ranked 47th by Forbes magazine amongst 100 Most Powerful Women 2004. *Website:* www.womenofchina.cn.

PENGO, HE Cardinal Polycarp, DTheol; Tanzanian ecclesiastic; *Archbishop of Dar es Salaam and President of Symposium of Episcopal Conferences of Africa and Madagascar (SECAM);* b. 5 Aug. 1944, Mwazye; ed Kipapala Major Seminary, Tabora, Makerere Univ., Pontifical Lateran Univ.; ordained priest 1971; sec. to Bishop of Sumbawanga 1971–73; Rector Segerea Major Seminary 1977–90; Bishop of Nachingwea 1984–87, of Tunduru-Massai 1987–90; Coadjutor Archbishop of Dar es Salaam 1990–92, Archbishop of Dar es Salaam 1992–; cr. Cardinal (Cardinal-Priest of Nostra Signora de La Salette) 1998; participated in Papal Conclave 2005, 2013; Pres. Symposium of Episcopal Confs of Africa and Madagascar (SECAM) 2007–. *Address:* Archbishop's House, PO Box 167, Dar es Salaam, Tanzania. *Telephone:* (22) 2113223 (office). *Fax:* (22) 2125751 (office). *E-mail:* nyumba@cats-net.com (office). *Website:* www.rc.net/tanzania/tec/dsmweb/contents.htm (office).

PENJO, Daw, MA; Bhutanese diplomatist and government official; b. 7 March 1958; m.; three c.; ed Univ. of Delhi, India, Tufts Univ., USA; joined Ministry of Foreign Affairs 1980; assigned to Perm. Mission to UN, Geneva 1986–90; Head of Bilateral and Multilateral Div., Ministry of Foreign Affairs 1990–94; First Sec. and Deputy Chief of Mission, Dhaka, Bangladesh 1994–97; Counsellor and Deputy Chief of Mission, New Delhi 1997–2000; Dir of Bilateral Dept 2000–03; Amb. and Perm. Rep. to UN, New York 2003–08 (also accred as Amb. to Canada) 2004–08; Foreign Sec., Ministry of Foreign Affairs 2008–13; Vice-Pres. ECOSOC 2004. *Address:* c/o Ministry of Foreign Affairs, Convention Centre, PO Box 103, Gyalyong Tshokhang, Thimphu, Bhutan.

PENJOR, Rinzin, BCom, LLB, LLM; Bhutanese lawyer and government official; b. Kazhi geog, Wangduephodrang; ed Univ. of Delhi, India, Lord Dalhousie Law Coll., Canada; began career with High Court 1989, served as Drangpoen in Tsirang, Sarpang and Punakha Dist Courts; Militia Officer with Royal Bhutan Army 1990–95; Attorney-Gen. 2008–10; currently Judge (Drangpon) Supreme Court; Patang. *Address:* c/o Office of the Attorney General, POB 1045, Thori Lam, Lower Motithang, Thimphu, Bhutan.

PENJORE, Thrizin Namgye, MBA; Bhutanese politician; b. 21 May 1966, Amrimo, Punakha; m. Namgay Lhamo; one s. one d.; elected as mem. Nat. Council (Upper House of bicameral Parl.) from Punakha Dzongkhag (constituency), Chair. Nat. Council 2008–13. *Address:* c/o National Council Secretariat, Langjophakha, PO Box 200, Thimphu, Bhutan. *Telephone:* 17-603532 (mobile).

PENN, Sean; American actor; b. 17 Aug. 1960, Burbank, Calif.; s. of the late Leo Penn and Eileen Penn (née Ryan); m. 1st Madonna (q.v.) 1985 (divorced); m. 2nd Robin Wright 1996 (divorced 2010); two c.; f. Clyde is Hungry Films (production co.); Chair. Cannes Film Festival jury 2008; named Amb. to Haiti 2012–; Modern Master Award, Santa Barbara Int. Film Festival 2002, Donostia Lifetime Achievement Award, San Sebastian Film Festival 2003, John Steinbeck Award 2004, Christopher Reeve First Amendment Award 2006. *Theatre appearances include:* Heartland (Broadway debut), Slab Boys, Hurlyburly 1988. *Films include:* Taps 1981, Fast Times at Ridgemont High 1982, Bad Boys 1983, Crackers 1984, Racing with the Moon 1984, The Falcon and the Snowman 1985, At Close Range 1986, Shanghai Surprise 1986, Colors 1988, Judgement in Berlin 1988, Casualties of War 1989, We're No Angels 1989, State of Grace 1990, Carlito's Way 1993, Dead Man Walking 1996 (Best Actor Award Berlin Film Festival 1996), U Turn 1997, She's So Lovely 1997, Hurlyburly 1998, As I Lay Dying 1998, Up at the Villa 1998, The Thin Red Line 1998, Sweet and Lowdown 1999, The Pledge 2000, Up at the Villa 2000, Before Night Falls 2000, The Weight of Water 2000, I am Sam 2001, It's All About Love 2003, Mystic River (Golden Globe Award, Best Dramatic Actor 2004, Critics' Choice Award Best Actor 2004, Acad. Award, Best Actor 2004) 2003, 21 Grams (Venice Film Festival Best Actor Award 2003) 2003, The Assassination of Richard Nixon 2005, The Interpreter 2005, All the King's Men 2006, Persepolis 2007, What Just Happened? 2007, Milk 2008 (Acad. Award for Best Actor 2009), Fair Game 2010, The Tree of Life 2011, This Must Be the Place 2011, Gangster Squad 2013; dir and writer The Indian Runner 1991, The Crossing Guard 1995, The Pledge 2001, Into the Wild 2007. *Address:* 2049 Century Park East, Suite 2500, Los Angeles, CA 90067-3101, USA (office).

PENNANEACH, Biova-Soumi, MSc; Togolese diplomatist; b. 5 Oct. 1941, Lomé; m. 1972; two s. four d.; ed State Univ. of Moscow, USSR and Laval Univ., Québec, Canada; active trade unionist from 1966; Head, Soils Analysis Labs 1966–74, 1976–80; Dir Agricultural and Land Legislation Service 1980–82; Prefect of Tchaoudjo and the Lakes and Tech. Adviser, Nat. Science Inst. 1982–87; Dir Office of Minister of Rural Devt 1987–90; Under-Sec.-Gen. Nat. Confed. of Workers of Togo 1988–90; Amb. and Perm. Rep. to UN, New York 1990–96, Vice-Pres. 46th session of UN Gen. Ass. 1991. *Publications:* numerous, on conservation and environment protection. *Address:* c/o Ministry of Foreign Affairs and Cooperation, Place du Monument aux Morts, Avenue Georges Pompidou, BP 900, Lomé, Togo. *E-mail:* maeirtgce@yahoo.fr.

PENNANT-REA, Rupert Lascelles, MA; British business executive and journalist; *Chairman, Henderson Group plc;* b. 23 Jan. 1948, Harare, Zimbabwe; s. of Peter A. Pennant-Rea and Pauline E. Pennant-Rea; m. several times; two s. one d.; ed Peterhouse, Zimbabwe, Trinity Coll., Dublin and Univ. of Manchester; with Confed. of Irish Industry 1970–71, Gen. and Municipal Workers' Union 1972–73, Bank of England 1973–77; with The Economist 1977–93, Ed. 1986–93; Deputy Gov. of Bank of England 1993–95; Chair. Henderson Group plc 2005–, The Economist Group 2009–; numerous other appointments; Wincott Prize for Journalism 1984. *Publications:* Gold Foil 1979, Who Runs the Economy? (co-author) 1980, The Pocket Economist (co-author) 1983, The Economist Economics (co-author) 1986. *Leisure interests:* music, tennis, fishing, golf, family. *Address:* Henderson Group plc, 4 Broadgate, London, EC2M 3AE, England (office). *Website:* www.henderson.com (office).

PENNER, Stanford S. 'Sol', PhD; American chemical engineer and academic; *Distinguished Professor of Engineering Physics Emeritus, University of California, San Diego;* b. 1921; ed Univ. of Wisconsin; worked during World War II at Allegany Ballistics Lab. on solid rocket propulsion systems; Research Engineer, Jet Propulsion Lab., Pasadena, Calif. 1946–50; Prof. of Jet Propulsion, California Inst. of Tech. (Caltech) 1950–62; Dir Research and Eng Div., Inst. for Defense Analyses, Washington, DC 1962–64; Founding Chair. Dept of Aerospace and Mechanical Eng Sciences, Univ. of California, San Diego 1964, has also held positions of Vice-Chancellor for Academic Affairs, Dir Inst. for Pure and Applied Physical Sciences, and Founding Dir Energy Center (later named Center for Energy and Combustion Research) 1972–90, now Distinguished Prof. of Eng Physics Emer.; Founding Ed. The Journal of Quantitative Spectroscopy and Radiative Transfer 1960–92, Energy – The International Journal 1974–98, (classified) Journal of Defense Research; mem. Nat. Acad. of Eng, Int. Acad. of Astronautics; Fellow, American Acad. of Arts and Sciences, and of seven learned socs; numerous hon. degrees; numerous nat. and int. awards, including Distinguished Assoc. Award, US Dept of Energy, Edward Teller Award for the Defense of Freedom 1998, three different awards from AIAA for combustion research, thermophysics, and energy-system studies, Founders Award, Nat. Acad. of Eng 2007. *Publications include:* Chemistry Problems in Jet Propulsion (textbook) 1954; numerous scientific papers in professional journals on thermophysics, applied spectroscopy, combustion, propulsion, and energy. *Address:* Irwin & Joan Jacobs School of Engineering, University of California, San Diego, EBU II 559, 9500 Gilman Drive, La Jolla, CA 92093-0403, USA (office). *Telephone:* (858) 534-4284 (office). *E-mail:* spenner@ucsd.edu (office). *Website:* www.jacobsschool.ucsd.edu (office).

PENNIE, Michael William, ARCA; British sculptor; b. 23 Oct. 1936, Wallasey, Cheshire, England; s. of George A. Pennie and Isabel Duff; m. 1st Norah Kimmit 1959 (divorced 1977); m. 2nd Marlene Stride 1985; two s. one d.; ed Bede Collegiate for Boys, Sunderland, Sunderland Coll. of Art and Royal Coll. of Art; Visiting Lecturer, Bath Acad. of Art, Winchester and Wimbledon Schools of Art, Norwich Coll. of Art and Brighton Polytechnic 1962–82; Sr Lecturer, Bath Spa, Univ. Coll. 1985–2001, now Prof.; Co-Organizer, Sculpture in the City, Bath 1986; Consultant, Goodwill Art Service 1992–; Chair. Bath Area Network for Artists 2001–03; Consultant, Horniman Museum and Gardens, Bath Spa Sculpture Garden, Bath Spa Univ. 2005–; 12 research trips to W Africa 1994–2000; Rome Scholar 1962, Gregynog Fellow, Univ. of Wales 1971. *Publications:* Where Shall We Put This One? 1987, Smoke of the Savannah 1989, African Assortment: African Art in Museums in England and Scotland 1991, Friday's Rain Takes a Long Time to Stop 1994, Some Sculptors and African Art 1995, Marriage Poles of the Lobi 1996, Adventures with Lobi – an abc 1998, West African Journeys 2001, Lobi Notes 2002, Across the Board and 2 Other Sculptures 2007. *Leisure interest:* African music. *Address:* 117 Bradford Road, Atworth, Melksham, Wilts., SN12 8HY, England. *Telephone:* (1225) 705409. *Fax:* (1225) 705409. *E-mail:* michael.pennie@btinternet .com. *Website:* www.michaelpennie.net.

PENNINGER, Josef, MD; Austrian biologist and academic; *Scientific Director, Institute for Molecular Biotechnology, Austrian Academy of Sciences;* b. 5 Sept. 1964, Gurten; m. Liqun Zhang 1997; one s. two d.; ed Humanistic Gymnasium, Ried, Univ. of Innsbruck; Post-doctoral Fellow, Ont. Cancer Inst., Princess Margaret Hosp., Toronto, Canada 1990–94, Assoc. Scientist, Dept of Molecular and Cellular Biology 1994–; Prin. Investigator, Amgen Inst., Toronto 1994–; Asst Prof., Depts of Immunology and Medical Biophysics, Univ. of Toronto 1994–99, Full mem. School of Grad. Studies 1998–, Assoc. Prof., Depts of Immunology and Medical Biophysics 1999–2002, Full Prof. 2002–, Adjunct Full Prof. of Immunology 2003–; Assoc. Prof. (Dozent), Dept of Experimental and Gen. Pathology, Univ. of Innsbruck 1998–; Scientific Dir Inst. for Molecular Biotechnology of the Austrian Acad. of Sciences (IMBA), Vienna 2002–; Prof. of Genetics, Univ. of Vienna 2004–; Affiliate Scientist, Keenan Research Centre, Li Ka Shing Knowledge Inst., St Michael's Hosp., Toronto 2010–; Guest Prof., Medical Univ., Vienna 2011–; Corresp. mem. Austrian Acad. of Sciences 2002, mem. 2007; mem. Deutsche Akad. der Naturforscher Leopoldina 2004, European Molecular Biology Org. 2008, Academia Europaea 2009, European Research Inst. for Integrated Cellular Pathology (ERI-ICP), Paris 2009 (Vice-Pres. 2011–), European Acad. for Tumor Immunology 2010; Fellow, AAAS 2012; Hon. Prof., Peking Union Medical Coll., Beijing 2005–; Special fellowship from Austrian Ministry for Arts and Science 1987, Scholarship from European Fed. of Immunological Societies 1988, 'Highest Talented' Award, Rotary Club, Innsbruck 1990, Anton von Eiselsberg Prize for best medical related scientific work in Austria 1991, Erwin Schroedinger Fellowship, Austrian Fonds zür Foerderung der Wissenschaftlichen Forschung

1990–92, Austrotransplant-Biotest Prize, Austrian Soc. of Transplantation, Transfusion and Genetics 1993, Talentefoerderpraemie (talent prize for science and culture), Prov. of Upper Austria 1994, The William E. Rawls Prize, Nat. Cancer Inst. of Canada 1999, included in 'Celebration of Canadian Healthcare Research' of leading historical and contemporary medical scientists in Canada during 20th century selected by Asscn of Canadian Medical Colls, Asscn of Canadian Teaching Hosps, Alumni and Friends of the Medical Research Council and Partners in Research 2000, selected as a 'Young Leader in Medicine in Canada' by the Globe and Mail, Univ. of Toronto 2000, named One of Canada's Top 40 under 40 2001, CIAR Young Canadian Explorer Award 2002, listed among the 10 most promising scientists in all fields in the world by Esquire magazine 2002, Culture Prize for Science, Prov. of Upper Austria 2003, Int. Research Prize in Bone Research 2003, Austrian Scientist of the Year Award 2003, Austria04 Award: Austrian of the Year (in science), Die Presse newspaper 2004, Young Global Leader appointed by World Econ. Forum 2004, Descartes Prize for Research, European Comm. 2007, Ernst Jung Prize, Jung-Stiftung für Wissenschaft and Forschung (co-recipient) 2007, Carus Medal, German Academy of Sciences Leopoldina 2007, Wellenreiter Prize, Austrian Man. Club 2007, Carus-Prize, City of Schweinfurt 2008, included in list of 1,000 most important Austrian immigrant/emigrants in politics, arts, sports, philosophy, business, or music from 1900–2008, Karl Landsteiner Prize, Austrian Soc. of Immunology and Allergology 2008, first ERC Advanced Grant 2009, ESCI Award, European Soc. for Clinical Investigation 2009, Medal of the Australian Soc. for Medical Research 2009, Innovator Award, Era of Hope/DOD 2012. *Publications:* more than 400 scientific papers in professional journals. *Leisure interest:* football. *Address:* IMBA, Institute of Molecular Biotechnology of the Austrian Academy of Sciences, Dr Bohrgasse 3, 1030 Vienna, Austria (office). *Fax:* (1) 79044-4702 (office). *E-mail:* josef.penninger@imba.oeaw .ac.at (office). *Website:* www.imba.oeaw.ac.at (office).

PENNINGTON, (Thomas) Hugh, CBE, MB, PhD, FRCPath, FRCP, FRSE, FMedSci; British microbiologist and academic; *Professor Emeritus of Bacteriology, University of Aberdeen;* b. 19 April 1938, Edgware, London, England; m. Carolyn Beattie 1966; two d.; ed Royal Grammar School, Lancaster, St Thomas's Medical School, Univ. of London; house appointments, St Thomas's Hosp. 1962–63, Asst Lecturer in Medical Microbiology, St Thomas's Hosp. Medical School 1963–67; Postdoctoral Fellow, Univ. of Wisconsin-Madison, USA 1967–68; Lecturer, then Sr Lecturer in Virology, Univ. of Glasgow 1969–79; Prof. of Bacteriology, Univ. of Aberdeen 1979–2003, Prof. Emer. 2003–, Dean of Medicine 1987–92; Gov. Rowett Research Inst. 1980–88, 1996–; Gov. Moredun Research Inst. 2003–; Chair. Expert Group on 1996 E. Coli Outbreak in Cen. Scotland; Vice-Chair. Broadcasting Council for Scotland; Vice-Pres. Chartered Inst. of Environmental Health; mem. Scottish Food Advisory Cttee, Food Standards Agency; Pres. Soc. for Gen. Microbiology 2003–06; Hon. DSc (Lancaster) 1999, (Strathclyde) 2001, (Aberdeen) 2003; Caroline Walker Trust Consumer Advocate Award 1997, John Kershaw Memorial Prize for Notable Services to Public Health 1998, Royal Scottish Soc. of Arts Silver Medal 1999, Thomas Graham Medal, Royal Glasgow Philosophical Soc. 2001, Burgess of Guild, City of Aberdeen 2002. *Publications:* When Food Kills 2003, Food Poisoning, Policy and Politics: Corned Beef and Typhoid in Britain in the 1960s (co-author) 2005; numerous papers, articles and book chapters on viruses and bacteria and on food safety. *Leisure interest:* collecting old books. *Address:* Department of Medical Microbiology, Medical School, University of Aberdeen, Foresterhill, Aberdeen, AB25 2ZD (office); 13 Carlton Place, Aberdeen, AB15 4BR, Scotland (home). *Telephone:* (1224) 55863 (office); (1224) 645136 (home). *Fax:* (1224) 685604 (office). *E-mail:* t.h.pennington@abdn.ac.uk (office). *Website:* www.abdn.ac.uk (office).

PENNY, Gareth, MA; South African business executive; *Executive Chairman, New World Resources plc;* b. 24 Dec. 1962; m. Kate Penny; two c.; ed Diocesan Coll. (Bishops), Cape Town, Eton Coll., Oxford, UK; joined Anglo American Corpn 1988, becoming Man. Anglo American/De Beers Small Business Initiative, SA, Personal Asst to Chair. of Anglo American/De Beers, Dir of Sales and Marketing, Diamond Trading Co. 2001–04, Dir De Beers 2003–, Group Man. Dir and Chair. Exec. Cttee, De Beers Group 2006–10; Exec. Chair. New World Resources plc 2010–; also mem. Bd Julius Baer Holding Ltd, OKD 2012–; mem. Advisory Bd TowerBrook Capital Partners; Vice-Chair. Botswana Economic Advisory Cttee; Hon. Life mem. London Diamond Bourse & Club. *Address:* New World Resources plc, Jachthavenweg 109h, 1081 KM Amsterdam, Netherlands (office). *E-mail:* info@nwrgroup.eu (office). *Website:* www.newworldresources.eu (office).

PENNY, Nicholas, PhD; British art historian, gallery director and academic; *Director, National Gallery, London;* b. 21 Dec. 1949; m. Mary Crettier; ed Shrewsbury School, St Catharine's Coll., Cambridge, Courtauld Inst. of Art, London; academic career began with a research fellowship at Clare Hall, Cambridge; taught art history at Univ. of Manchester 1975–82; Slade Prof. of Fine Art, Univ. of Oxford 1980–81; Sr Research Fellow, King's Coll., Cambridge 1982–84; Keeper of Dept of Western Art, Ashmolean Museum, Oxford 1984–89; Clore Curator of Renaissance Painting, Nat. Gallery, London 1990–2000, identified the Madonna of the Pinks belonging to the Duke of Northumberland as a genuine Raphael, and not a copy of a lost original, as was previously supposed 1991, Keeper 1998–2002, made unsuccessful bid for directorship of Nat. Gallery 2002, Dir 2007–; Andrew W. Mellon Prof., Center for Advanced Study in the Visual Arts, Nat. Gallery of Art, Washington, DC, USA 2000–07, Sr Curator of Sculpture, Nat. Gallery of Art 2002–07. *Publications include:* Church Monuments in Romantic England 1977, Taste and the Antique (co-author, with Francis Haskell) 1981, Raphael (co-author) 1987, Ruskin's Drawings (Ashmolean Handbooks) 1988, Alfred and Winifred Turner: Exhibition Catalogue 1988, Giotto to Dürer: Early Renaissance Painting in The National Gallery (co-author) 1991, three-volume scholarly catalogue of European sculpture in the Ashmolean Museum 1992, The Materials of Sculpture 1993, Tradition and Revolution in French Art, 1700–1880: Paintings and Drawings from Lille 1993, Making and Meaning: the Young Michelangelo: The Artist in Rome, 1496–1501 (Making & Meaning Series) (co-author) 1994, Frames 1997, Saints (National Gallery Pocket Guides) 2000, Dürer to Veronese: Sixteenth-century Painting in the National Gallery (co-author) 2002, Titian (National Gallery Catalogues) 2003, The Sixteenth-Century Italian Paintings, Vol. 1 2004, Desiderio Da Settignano: Sculpture of Renaissance Florence (co-author) 2007, The Sixteenth-Century Italian Paintings, Vol. 2: Venice 1540–1600 2008; regular contrib. to The Burlington Magazine and London Review of Books.

Address: The National Gallery, Trafalgar Square, London, WC2N 5DN, England (office). *Telephone:* (20) 7747-2885 (office). *Fax:* (20) 7747-2423 (office). *E-mail:* information@ng-london.org.uk (office). *Website:* www.nationalgallery.org.uk (office).

PENROSE, Oliver, PhD, FRS, FRSE; British mathematician and academic; *Professor Emeritus, Heriot-Watt University;* b. 6 June 1929, London, England; s. of Lionel S. Penrose and Margaret Leathes; m. Joan L. Dilley 1953; three s. (one deceased) one d.; ed Cen. Collegiate Inst., London, Ont., Canada, Univ. Coll., London, King's Coll., Cambridge; Math. Physicist, English Electric Co., Luton 1952–55; Research Asst, Yale Univ., USA 1955–56; Lecturer, then Reader, Imperial Coll. London 1956–69; Prof. of Math., Open Univ. 1969–86; Prof. of Math., Heriot-Watt Univ. 1986–94, Prof. Emer. 1994–. *Publications:* Foundations of Statistical Mechanics 1969 (reprinted 2005); about 85 papers in scientific journals. *Leisure interests:* music, chess. *Address:* Department of Mathematics, Heriot-Watt University, Riccarton, Edinburgh, EH14 4AS (office); 29 Frederick Street, Edinburgh, EH2 2ND, Scotland (home). *Telephone:* (131) 451-3225 (office); (131) 225-5879 (home). *E-mail:* oliver@ma.hw.ac.uk (office). *Website:* www.ma.hw.ac.uk/~oliver (office).

PENROSE, Sir Roger, Kt, OM, PhD, FRS; British mathematician, writer and academic; *Rouse Ball Professor Emeritus of Mathematics, University of Oxford;* b. 8 Aug. 1931, Colchester, Essex, England; s. of Lionel Sharples Penrose; m. 1st Joan Wedge 1959 (divorced 1981), three s.; m. 2nd Vanessa Thomas 1988; one s.; ed Univ. Coll. School, Univ. Coll. London and St John's Coll. Cambridge; Asst Lecturer, Bedford Coll. London 1956–57; Research Fellow, St John's Coll. Cambridge 1957–60; NATO Research Fellow, Princeton and Syracuse Univs 1959–61; Research Assoc., King's Coll. London 1961–63; Visiting Assoc. Prof., Univ. of Texas, Austin 1963–64; Reader, Birkbeck Coll. London 1964–66, Prof. of Applied Math. 1966–73, Fellow 1998–; Rouse Ball Prof. of Math., Univ. of Oxford 1973–98, Prof. Emer. 1998–, Emer. Fellow, Wadham Coll.; Fellow, Univ. Coll. London 1975; Gresham Prof. of Geometry, Gresham Coll. 1998–2001; Visiting Prof. Yeshiva, Princeton and Cornell Univs 1966–67, 1969; Lovett Prof. Rice Univ. Houston 1983–87; Distinguished Prof. of Physics and Math. Syracuse Univ. 1987–93, Francis and Helen Pentz Distinguished Prof. of Physics and Math., Penn State Univ. 1993–; mem. London Math. Soc., Cambridge Philosophical Soc., Inst. for Math. and its Applications, Int. Soc. for Gen. Relativity and Gravitation; Foreign mem. Polish Acad. of Science, Accad. Nazionale dei Lincei; Foreign Assoc. NAS 1998; Fellow, Inst. of Physics 1999; Distinguished Supporter, British Humanist Assocn; a Patron of the Oxford Univ. Scientific Soc.; Hon. Fellow, St John's Coll. Cambridge 1987; Hon. mem. Royal Irish Acad. of Science 2001; Dr hc (New Brunswick) 1992, (Surrey) 1993, (Bath) 1994, (London) 1995, (Glasgow) 1996, (Essex) 1996, (St Andrew's) 1997, (Santiniketon) 1998, (Warsaw) 2005, (Katholieke Universiteit Leuven) 2005; Hon. DUniv (Open Univ.) 1998, (Southampton) 2002, (Waterloo, Ontario) 2003, (Leiden) 2004, (Athens) 2005, (York) 2006; Adams Prize, Univ. of Cambridge 1966–67, Dannie Heinemann Prize, American Physics Soc. and American Inst. of Physics 1971, Eddington Medal, Royal Astronomical Soc. (with S. W. Hawking) 1975, Royal Medal, Royal Soc. 1985, Wolf Foundation Prize in Physics (with S. W. Hawking) 1988, Dirac Medal and Prize, Inst. of Physics 1989, Einstein Medal 1990, Science Book Prize 1990, Naylor Prize, London Math. Soc. 1991, DeMorgan Medal 2004, Copley Medal, Royal Soc. 2008, Fonseca Prize, Univ. of Santiago de Compostela 2011, Richard R. Ernst Medal, ETH Zurich 2012. *Publications:* Techniques of Differential Topology in Relativity 1973, Spinors and Space-time (with W. Rindler), (Vol. I) 1984, (Vol. II) 1986, The Emperor's New Mind 1989, The Nature of Space and Time (with S. W. Hawking) 1996, The Large, the Small and the Human Mind 1997, White Mars (with B. Aldiss) 1999, The Road to Reality: A Complete Guide to the Laws of the Universe 2004, Cycles of Time: An Extraordinary New View of the Universe 2010; articles in scientific journals. *Leisure interests:* three-dimensional puzzles, doodling at the piano. *Address:* Mathematical Institute, University of Oxford, Andrew Wiles Building, Radcliffe Observatory Quarter, Woodstock Road, Oxford, OX2 6GG, England (office). *Telephone:* (1865) 273525 (office); (1865) 273521 (office). *Fax:* (1865) 273583 (office). *E-mail:* roger.penrose@maths.ox.ac.uk (office). *Website:* www.maths.ox.ac.uk/people/profiles/roger.penrose (office).

PENSKE, Roger S.; American motor racing team owner, business executive and fmr racing driver; *Chairman, Penske Corporation;* b. 20 Feb. 1937, Shaker Heights, Ohio; ed Lehigh Univ.; early career buying, racing and selling race cars, f. Penske Racing 1958–, launched Team Penske 1966; co-f. Championship Auto Racing Teams (CART); Penske Racing has won 12 Indianapolis 500s and 9 CART points titles; Nat. Sports Car Driving Champion 1964; founding Chair. Penske Corpn 1969–; Chair. Penske Truck Leasing Business 1982–; Chair. Bd United Auto Group 1999–; mem. Bd of Dirs Home Depot, Inc., Universal Technical Inst. Inc., Detroit Renaissance, Inc.; Chair. Detroit Super Bowl XL Host Cttee 2004–06; Chair. Downtown Detroit Partnership 2006–; mem. Business Council; Sports Illustrated Driver of the Year 1960, New York Times Driver of the Year 1962, inducted into Int. Motorsports Hall of Fame 1998. *Address:* Penske Corporation, 2550 Telegraph Road, Bloomfield Hills, MI 48302, USA (office). *Telephone:* (248) 648-2000 (office). *Fax:* (248) 648-2005 (office). *Website:* www.penske.com (office).

PENZIAS, Arno Allan, PhD; American astrophysicist; *Venture Partner, New Enterprise Associates;* b. 26 April 1933, Munich, Germany; s. of Karl Penzias and Justine Penzias; m. 1st Anne Barras Penzias 1954; one s. two d.; m. 2nd Sherry Chamovelevit 1996; ed City Coll. of New York, Columbia Univ.; mem. tech. staff Bell Laboratories, Holmdel, NJ 1961–72, Head Radiophysics Research Dept 1972–76, Dir Radio Research Lab. 1976–79, Exec. Dir Research, Communications Sciences Div. 1979–81, Exec. Dir Research, Bell Labs, Murray Hill, NJ 1979–81, Vice-Pres. Research 1981–95, Vice-Pres., Chief Scientist 1995–96; Vice-Pres., Chief Scientist Bell Labs Innovations 1996–98; Venture Partner, New Enterprise Assocs 1998–; Sr Tech Adviser Lucent Technologies 1998–; Lecturer, Princeton Univ. 1967–72, Visiting Prof. Astrophysical Sciences Dept 1972–85; Harvard Coll. Observatory Research Assoc. 1968–80; Adjunct Prof., State Univ. of New York (SUNY) at Stony Brook 1974–84; discovered cosmic microwave background radiation 1965; Assoc. Ed. Astrophysical Journal 1978–82; mem. Editorial Bd Annual Review of Astronomy and Astrophysics 1974–78, AT & TBL Tech. Journal 1978–84 (Chair. 1981–84); mem. Bd of Trustees of Trenton State Coll. 1977–79, Visiting Cttee of Calif. Inst. of Tech. 1977–79; mem. Astronomy Advisory Panel of

NSF 1978–79, Industrial Panel on Science and Tech. 1982–, Bd of Overseers, School of Eng and Applied Science, Univ. of Pa 1983–86; mem. Max Planck Inst. Fachbeirat 1978–85 (Chair. 1981–83); mem. Council on Competitiveness 1989–; Vice-Chair. Cttee Concerned Scientists; mem. NAS, Nat. Acad. Eng, American Astronomical Soc., World Acad. Art and Science; Fellow AAAS, American Physical Soc.; numerous hon. degrees; numerous prizes, awards and lectureships including Henry Draper Medal, NAS 1977, Herschel Medal, Royal Astronomical Soc. 1977, Pender Award 1992, Int. Eng Consortium Fellow Award 1997, Nobel Prize in Physics 1978. *Publications:* Ideas and Information 1989, Digital Harmony 1995; over 100 scientific papers in various journals. *Leisure interests:* swimming, jogging, skiing. *Address:* New Enterprise Associates, 2490 Sand Hill Road, Menlo Park, CA 94025, USA (office). *Telephone:* (650) 854-9499 (office). *Fax:* (415) 544-0833. *E-mail:* apenzias@nea.com (office). *Website:* www.nea.com (office).

PEPPER, Sir David Edwin, Kt, KCMG, MA, DPhil; British civil servant; *Director, Government Communications Headquarters;* b. 1947; m.; two s.; ed St John's Coll., Oxford; joined Govt Communications HQ (GCHQ) 1972, various positions in operational intelligence work, Dir of Personnel 1995–98, Head Corp. Devt Directorate Home Office 1998–2000, Dir of Finance GCHQ 2000–03, Dir GCHQ 2003–(08). *Leisure interests:* music, reading, walking, cooking. *Address:* GCHQ, A3A, Hubble Road, Cheltenham, Glos., GL51 0EX, England (office). *Telephone:* (1242) 221491 (office). *E-mail:* david.pepper@gchq.gsi.gov.uk (office). *Website:* www.gchq.gov.uk (office).

PEPPER, John Ennis, Jr; American business executive; *Presiding Co-Chairman, National Underground Railroad Freedom Center;* b. 2 Aug. 1938, Pottsville, Pa; s. of John Ennis Pepper, Sr and Irma O'Connor; m. Frances Graham Garber 1967; three s. one d.; ed Yale Univ.; joined Procter & Gamble Co. 1963, Gen. Man. Italian subsidiary 1974–77, Vice-Pres. and Gen. Man. packaged soap div. 1977–80, Group Vice-Pres. 1980–84, mem. Bd Dirs 1984–2003, Exec. Vice-Pres. 1984–86, Pres. 1986–95, Chair. and CEO 1995–99, Chair. 2000–02, Chair. Exec. Cttee of the Bd 2000–03 (retd); Vice-Pres. for Finance and Admin, Yale Univ. 2004–05; Chair. The Walt Disney Co. 2007–12; mem. Bd of Dirs Boston Scientific Corpn 2003–10; Co-Chair. Gov.'s Educ. Council of State of Ohio; CEO Nat. Underground Railroad Freedom Center 2005–07, Presiding Co-Chair. 2007–; mem. Advisory Council Yale School of Man., Exec. Cttee Cincinnati Youth Collaborative, Bd Nat. Campaign to Prevent Teen Pregnancy, Partnership for a Drug-Free America; inducted into Junior Achievement US Business Hall of Fame 2008. *Address:* National Underground Railroad Freedom Center, 50 East Freedom Way, Cincinnati, OH 452022, USA (office). *Telephone:* (513) 333-7500 (office). *E-mail:* info@freedomcenter.org (office). *Website:* www.freedomcenter.org (office).

PEPPER, Sir Michael, Kt, ScD, PhD, FRS, FREng; British physicist, academic and business executive; *Professor of Nanoelectronics, University College, London;* b. 10 Aug. 1942, London, England; s. of Morris Pepper and Ruby Pepper; m. Dr Jeannette D. Josse 1973; two d.; ed St Marylebone Grammar School, London, Reading Univ.; physicist, Mullard Research Lab. 1967–69; physicist engaged in solid state device research, Allen Clark Research Centre, Plessey Co. 1969–73; research at Cavendish Lab., Cambridge 1973–, Prof. of Physics, Univ. of Cambridge 1987–2009; Pender Chair of Nanoelectronics, Univ. Coll. London 2009–; Visiting Prof., Univ. of Oxford 2010–; Jt Man. Dir Toshiba Research Europe Ltd 1991–2007; Co-founder and Dir TeraView Ltd 2001–; Warren Research Fellow, Royal Soc. 1978–86; Sr Research Fellow, Trinity Coll., Cambridge 1982–87, Professorial Fellow 1987–; Sr Research Fellow, GEC Hirst Research Centre 1982–87; Visiting Prof., Bar-Ilan Univ., Israel 1984; Fellow, Royal Acad. of Eng, American Physical Soc.; Hon. Prof., Univ. of Otago, NZ 2005–11; Hon. FInstP 2012; Hon. DSc (Bar-Ilan) 1993, (Linköping) 1997, (New South Wales) 2012; Guthrie Prize and Medal, Inst. of Physics 1985, Hewlett-Packard Prize, European Physical Soc. 1985, Hughes Medal, Royal Soc. 1987, Mott Prize, Inst. of Physics 2000, Bakerian Lecturer, Royal Soc. 2004 and various other named lectures, Royal Medal, Royal Soc. 2005, Gold Medal for Business and Innovation, Inst. of Physics 2010, Faraday Medal, Inst. of Eng and Tech. 2013, Silver Dirac Medal, Univ. of New South Wales/Australian Inst. of Physics 2013. *Publications:* numerous papers on solid state physics and semiconductors in scientific journals. *Leisure interests:* travel, music, whisky tasting. *Address:* Department of Electronic and Electrical Engineering, University College, Torrington Place, London, WC1E 6BT, England (office). *Telephone:* (20) 7679-3978 (office). *E-mail:* michael.pepper@ucl.ac.uk (office).

PEPY, Guillaume; French transport industry executive; *Chairman, Société Nationale des Chemins de Fer Français (SNCF);* b. 26 May 1958, Neuilly-sur-Seine (Hauts-de-Seine); ed Alsace School, Paris, Inst. of Political Studies, Paris, Ecole Nat. d'Admin; began career as magistrate Conseil d'Etat (French Admin. Court); Chief of Staff to Chair., Soc. Nat. des Chemins de Fer Français (SNCF–French Nat. Railways) 1988–93, Dir of Strategy 1993–98, apptd mem. Exec. Cttee 1998, Vice-Pres. –2003, CEO 2003–08, Chair. 2008–; Chair. Eurostar Group 2002–10, Assocn pour le Développement du Mécénat Industriel et Commercial (Admical) 2008–; Vice-Chair. Keolis Group, Systra; Officier, Légion d'honneur. *Address:* Société Nationale des Chemins de Fer Français (SNCF), 34 rue du Commandant Mouchotte, 75699 Paris Cedex 14, France (office). *Telephone:* 1-53-25-62-02 (office). *Fax:* 1-53-25-62-25 (office). *E-mail:* guillaume.pepy@sncf.fr (office). *Website:* www.sncf.fr (office).

PEPYS, Sir Mark Brian, Kt, PhD, MD, FRCP, FRCPath, FMedSci, FRS; British physician and academic; *Principal Clinical Research Associate and Director of the Wolfson Drug Discovery Unit, School of Life and Medical Sciences, University College London;* b. 18 Sept. 1944, Cape Town, South Africa; s. of Jack Pepys and Rhoda Pepys; m. Elizabeth Olga Winternitz 1971; one s. one d.; ed Trinity Coll., Cambridge, Univ. Coll. Hosp. Medical School, London, Harvard Medical School; house officer, Univ. Coll. Hosp. London 1968–69; Sr House Officer, Hammersmith Hosp. 1969–70, Asst Lecturer/Hon. Sr Registrar 1974–76, Head of Immunological Medicine and Hon. Consultant Physician 1977–79, Sr Lecturer 1977–81, Reader 1981–84; Prof. of Immunological Medicine 1984–99; MRC Jr Research Fellowship, Cambridge Univ., Research Scholar 1970–73, Fellow (Title A) Trinity Coll. Cambridge 1973–79, Registrar 1973–74; Sr Lecturer/Hon. Consultant and Head of Immunology Dept Royal Free Hosp. School of Medicine, London 1976–77, Prof. and Head of Medicine 1999–2011, Prin. Clinical Research Assoc. 2011–, Hon. Consultant Physician 1999–; Fellow, Univ. Coll., London 2003; Founder Fellow,

Acad. of Medical Sciences 1998; Royal Coll. of Surgeons of England Sir Arthur Sims Commonwealth Travelling Professorship 1991; Royal Coll. of Physicians Goulstonian Lecturer 1982, Lumleian Lecturer 1998, Moxon Trust Medal 1999, Royal Coll. of Pathologists Kohn Lecturer, GlaxoSmithKline Prize 2007, Ernst Chain Prize 2008. *Publications:* Samter's Immunologic Diseases (contrib.) 2001, Oxford Textbook of Medicine (contrib.) 2003; numerous research papers in learned journals. *Leisure interests:* tennis, surfing, skiing, wine. *Address:* Centre for Amyloidosis and Acute Phase Proteins, Department of Medicine, Royal Free Campus, Rowland Hill Street, London, NW3 2PF (office); 22 Wildwood Road, London, NW11 6TE, England (home). *Telephone:* (20) 7433-2801 (office). *Fax:* (20) 7433-2803 (office). *E-mail:* m.pepys@ucl.ac.uk (office); m.pepys@rfc.ucl.ac.uk (office). *Website:* www.ucl.ac.uk/medicine/amyloidosis (office).

PERA, Marcello; Italian politician and professor of philosophy; b. 28 Jan. 1943, Lucca, Tuscany; ed Univ. of Pisa; Full Prof. of Theoretical Philosophy, Univ. of Catania 1989–92; Full Prof. of Philosophy of Science, Univ. of Pisa 1992; Visiting Fellow, Univ. of Pittsburgh, USA 1984, Van Leer Foundation, Jerusalem 1987, MIT Dept of Linguistics and Philosophy, Cambridge, Mass 1990; mem. Steering Cttee Forza Italia Party, Deputy Leader Forza Italia Parl. Group 1996–2001; Head, Judiciary Dept, Nat. Co-ordinator Convention for Liberal Reform; Senator (Forza Italia) 1996–2006, Pres. of Senate 2001–06; mem. Cttee on Justice, Cttee on Educ. and Culture, Jt Cttee on Constitutional Reforms 1996–2001; mem. Advisory Panel Physis – Rivista internazionale di storia della scienza, Epistemologia, Perspectives on Science, Philosophical, Historical, Social; Fellow, Center for the Study of Science in Soc., Univ. of Virginia, USA; mem. Accademia Lucchese di Lettere, Scienze e Arti. *Publications include:* The Ambiguous Frog – The Galvani-Volta Controversy on Animal Electricity 1991, The Discourses of Science 1994; Senza radici (with Cardinal Joseph Ratzinger); ed. or co-ed. several books including Rational Changes in Science 1987, Persuading Science – The Art of Scientific Rhetoric 1991, Scientific Controversies 2000, Without Roots (with Pope Benedict XVI) 2006; numerous articles and essays in learned journals. *Leisure interests:* reading essays and novels. *Address:* c/o Office of the President, Senato della Repubblica, 00186 Rome, Italy (office).

PERAHIA, Murray; American pianist and conductor; b. 19 April 1947, New York, NY; s. of David Perahia and Flora Perahia; m. Naomi (Ninette) Shohet 1980; two s.; ed High School of Performing Arts, Mannes Coll. of Music, studied with Jeanette Haien, Arthur Balsam, Mieczyslaw Horszowski; debut, Carnegie Hall 1968; won Leeds Int. Piano Competition 1972; has appeared with many of world's leading orchestras and with Amadeus, Budapest, Guarneri and Galimir string quartets; regular recital tours N America, Europe, Japan; Co-Artistic Dir Aldeburgh Festival 1983–89; numerous recordings including complete Mozart Piano Concertos; prin. guest conductor, Acad. of St Martin-in-the-Fields; Dr hc (Univ. of Leeds), Hon. FRCM, FRAM; Hon. KBE 2004; Kosciusko Chopin Prize 1965, Avery Fisher Award 1975, Gramophone Record Award 1997, Grammy Award 1999, Gramophone Piano Award 2012. *Recordings include:* Bach Partitas Nos 2, 3, 4 (Midem Classical Award for Solo Instrument Recording 2009) 2008, Bach Partitas Nos 1, 5, 6 2009, Brahms: Händel Variations 2010. *Address:* IMG Artists, Carnegie Hall Tower, 152 W. 57th Street, 5th Floor, New York, NY 10019, USA (office). *Telephone:* (212) 994-3500 (office). *Fax:* (212) 994-3550 (office). *E-mail:* info@imgartists.com (office). *Website:* www.imgartists.com (office); www.murrayperahia.com.

PERAK, HRH The Sultan of; Tuanku Azlan Muhibuddin Shah ibni al-Marhum Sultan Yusuf Izuddin Ghafarullah Shah, GCB, KStJ; Malaysian; b. 19 April 1928, Batu Gajah, Perak, Federated Malay States, British Malaya; s. of Sultan Yusuff Izzuddin Shah ibni al-Marhum Sultan Abdul Jalil Nasshirruddin al-Makhtarram Karamatullah Shah and Toh Puan Dewangsa Khadijah binti Ahmad; m. Tuanku Bainun Mohamed Ali 1954; two s. three d.; ed Govt English School (now Sultan Yussuf School), Malay Coll. and Univ. of Nottingham, UK; called to the Bar, Lincoln's Inn, London 1954; elevated to the Bench of the High Court of Malaya 1965; Magistrate, Kuala Lumpur; Asst State Sec., Perak; Deputy Public Prosecutor; Pres. Sessions Court, Seremban and Taiping; State Legal Adviser, Pahang and Johore; Fed. Court Judge 1973–79; Chief Justice of Malaysia 1979–82; Lord Pres. Fed. Court of Malaysia 1982–83; Raja Kechil Bongsu (sixth-in-line) 1962, Raja Muda (Crown Prince) 1 July 1983; Sultan of Perak 3 Feb. 1984–; Yang di-Pertuan Agong (Supreme Head of State) 1989–94; Pro-Chancellor Universiti Sains Malaysia 1971–84; Chair. Higher Educ. Advisory Council 1974–76; Chancellor Univ. of Malaya 1986–; Hon. Col-in-Chief Malaysian Armed Forces' Engineers Corps; Man. Malaysian Hockey Team 1972; Pres. Malaysian Hockey Fed. –2005, Asian Hockey Fed.; mem. Exec. Bd and fmr Vice-Pres. Int. Hockey Fed.; Patron Malaysian Law Soc. in GB and Éire, British Grads Asscn of Malaysia, Acad. of Medicine of Malaysia, The Rotary Clubs, The Lions Clubs The Royal Ipoh Club, WWF-Malaysia, The Royal Perak Golf Club, The Iskandar Polo Club, Ipoh, The Kuala Kangsar Golf Club, The Perak Veteran Hockey Asscn; Hon. Bencher, Hon. Soc. of Lincoln's Inn 1988; Hon. FRCPI 1991, Hon. FRCSI 1991, Hon. FRCSE 1991, Hon. FRCS 1999; Star of the Repub. of Indonesia, First Class 1990, Collar of the Order of the Rajamitrabhorn (Thailand) 1990, Collar of the Order of the Chrysanthemum (Japan) 1991, Collar of the Order of Honour of the Sudan 1991, Collar of the Civil Order of Oman, First Class 1991, Grand Cross, Order of the Merit of Chile (with Collar) 1992, Special Grand Cordon, Order of Merit of the FRG 1992, Supreme Order of Hibiscus of South Korea 1992, Grand Star of the Decoration for Services to the Repub. of Austria 1992; Hon. DLitt (Univ. of Malaya) 1979; Hon. LLD (Universiti Sains Malaysia) 1980, (Univ. of Nottingham, UK) 1986, (Universitas Gajah Mada, Jogjakarta, Indonesia) 1990, (Universiti Brunei Darussalam) 1990, (Chulalongkorn Univ., Bangkok, Thailand) 1990; annual Sultan Azlan Shah Hockey Tournament named after him.

PERBEN, Dominique; French lawyer, fmr politician and civil servant; b. 11 Aug. 1945, Lyon; s. of Jacques Perben and Agnès Berthier; m. 1st Annick Demoustier 1968; m. 2nd Corinne Garnier 1996; one s. two d. from previous m.; ed Univ. of Paris, Inst. of Political Studies, Paris; Pvt. Sec. to Maine-et-Loire Prefect 1972–75, to Norbert Ségard (Sec. of State for Postal Services and Telecommunications) 1977; Sec.-Gen. Territoire de Belfort 1975–76; Head of Mission Del. of Devt of Belfort Region 1977, Pres.'s Office Regional Council at Rhône-Alpes 1983–86; Admin. Télédiffusion de France 1980; with Ministry of the Interior 1981; Mayor of Chalon-sur-Saône 1983–2002, Deputy Mayor 2002–04; Vice-Pres. Regional Council Saône-

et-Loire 1985–88; mem. Assemblée Nat. (parl) (RPR) for Saône-et-Loire 1986–93, 1995, 1997–2002, for Rhône 2007–12; mem. Regional Council Bourgogne 1992–93; Vice-Pres. Regional Council Rhône 2004–08; RPR Nat. Sec. of Local Elections 1984–86, of General Elections 1986–88, of Communication 1988–89, Asst Sec.-Gen. 1990–93; Minister of Overseas Territories 1993–95, for the Civil Service, Admin. Reform and Decentralization 1995–97; Keeper of the Seals and Minister of Justice 2002–05, Minister of Transport, Capital Works, Tourism and the Sea 2005–07; Chevalier du Mérite agricole. *Leisure interests:* skiing, tennis. *Address:* c/o Mairie, BP 92, Place de l'Hôtel de Ville, 71321 Chalon-sur-Saône Cedex, France (office).

PERDOMO, Carlos; Belizean fmr teacher and politician; m.; five c.; fmr Pres. St John's Coll; fmr Gen. Man. Centre for Employment Training; fmr Cabinet Sec. and Perm. Sec.; mem. United Democratic Party; Minister of Nat. Security 2008–10, of Defence 2010–12. *Address:* c/o Ministry of Defence, Belmopan, Belize (office).

PERDUE, Beverly (Bev) Eaves, BA, MEd, PhD; American politician and fmr state governor; b. (Beverly Marlene Moore), 14 Jan. 1947, Grundy, Va; d. of Alfred P. Moore and Irene Morefield Moore; m. 1st Gary Perdue 1970 (divorced 1994); two s.; m. 2nd Bob Eaves 1997; ed Univ. of Kentucky, Univ. of Florida; Dir of Human Services, Neuse River Council of Governments (now the Eastern Carolina Council) 1975–77; Consultant, Craven Co. Hosp. (now Craven Regional Medical Center) 1982; Pres. The Perdue Co. 1985–; mem. N Carolina State Gen. Ass. Reps 1986–90, N Carolina State Senate 1990–2001; Lt Gov. of N Carolina 2001–09, Gov. of N Carolina (first woman) 2009–13; Democrat.

PERDUE, George Ervin (Sonny), III, DVM; American politician and fmr state governor; b. 20 Dec. 1946, Perry, Ga; s. of Ervin Perdue, Jr and Ophie Perdue; m. Mary Ruff 1972; two s. two d.; ed Warner Robbins High School, Univ. of Georgia Coll. of Veterinary Medicine; Capt., USAF 1971–74; fmr veterinarian, Raleigh, NC; Propr Houston Fertilizer and Grain, Agrowstar Inc.; began public service 1980s serving on Houston County Planning and Zoning Bd; Democratic mem. of State Senate, Ga 1991–98, Chair. Higher Educ. Cttee 1993–94, Majority Leader 1995–96, Pres. Pro Tempore 1997, re-elected as Republican cand. 1998–2002; Gov. of Ga 2003–11. *Leisure interests:* flying, playing sports. *Address:* PO Box 698, Bonaire, GA 31005, USA.

PEREIRA, Raimundo; Guinea-Bissau lawyer and politician; b. 1956; mem. African Party for Independence of Guinea and Cape Verde (PAIGC); mem. Assembléia Nacional Popular (Parl.) 2008–, apptd Speaker 2008; Pres. (interim) of Guinea-Bissau March–Sept. 2009, Acting Pres. Jan.–April 2012 (deposed). *Address:* Assembleia Nacional Popular, Palácio Colinas de Boé, Bissau, Guinea-Bissau (office). *Telephone:* 3201991 (office).

PEREIRA DOS SANTOS VAN-DÚNEM, Gen. Cândido; Angolan army officer and politician; fmr Deputy Minister of Nat. Defence, Minister of Nat. Defence 2010–14; mem. Cen. Cttee Movimento Popular de Libertação de Angola. *Address:* c/o Ministry of National Defence, Rua 17 de Setembro, Luanda, Angola (office).

PEREIRA PUCHY, Gonzalo; Chilean lawyer, academic and international organization official; b. 1967; ed Inst. of Int. Studies, Univ. of Chile; participated in numerous courses, seminars and meetings organized or sponsored by Cepal, FAO, Int. Whaling Comm., Int. Fund for Animal Welfare, Inst. of Int. Studies, Univ. of Chile and other Chilean univs on Law of the Sea, fishing legislation and environment; represented Chile at int. meeting of operating countries of ships of fishing and oceanographic investigation, Barcelona, Spain 1997; visited Spain and Portugal to observe insts and examine fishing legislation 2001; mem. Chilean del. to XXV Ordinary Meeting of Comision Permanente del Pacifico Sur Quito, Ecuador 2001, Chilean del. to VIII Ronda de Negociaciones Chile, EU to obtain Agreement on Free Trade, Brussels, Belgium 2002, Chilean del. to X Round of Chile Negotiations EU 2002; Prof. of Environmental Law, Univ. of the Sea, Valparaiso, Chile 2001–02; worked at Legal Div. of Under-Sec.'s Office of Fishing, Ministry of Economy 1995–98; Head of Legal Dept, Nat. Fishing Service, Ministry of Economy 1998–2002; Under-Sec. Comision Permanente del Pacifico Sur (Perm. Comm. of the South Pacific) 2002–06, Sec.-Gen. 2006–10. *Address:* c/o Comision Permanente del Pacifico Sur, Av. Carlos Julio Arosemena, KM 3 Ed. Classic, 2 piso, Guayaquil, Ecuador (office).

PEREK, Luboš, DrSc; Czech astronomer; b. 26 July 1919, Prague; s. of Zdeněk Perek and Vilemina Perek (née Trapp); m. Vlasta Straková 1945 (died 2007); ed Masaryk Univ., Brno and Charles Univ., Prague; Asst Astronomical Inst., Masaryk Univ., Brno 1946, Head 1953; Head, Stellar Dept, Astronomical Inst. of Czechoslovak Acad. of Sciences, Prague 1956, Dir Astronomical Inst. 1968–75; Vice-Pres. Comm. of the Galactic Structure and Dynamics, Int. Astronomical Union 1961–64, Asst Gen. Sec., Int. Astronomical Union 1964–67, Gen. Sec. 1967–70; Chief, Outer Space Affairs Division, UN Secr. 1975–80; Visiting Prof., Dearborn Observatory, Evanston, Ill. 1964; mem. Czechoslovak Astronomical Soc., Exec. Cttee Int. Council of Scientific Unions 1967–70, Vice-Pres. 1968–70; Chair. Int. Astronautical Fed. 1980–82; mem. Leopoldina Acad., Int. Acad. of Astronautics, Int. Inst. of Space Law, Nat. Acad. of the Air and Space, Toulouse, Czech Learned Soc. 1999; Assoc. mem. Royal Astronomical Soc.; Dr hc (Masaryk Univ., Brno) 1999; Silver Plaque for services to science 1969, Gold Plaque 1989, Janssen Medal, Paris 1992. *Publications include:* Catalogue of Galactic Planetary Nebulae (with L. Kohoutek) 1967, about 80 articles on geostationary orbits, definition of space, space debris and environment of space. *Leisure interest:* collecting seashells. *Address:* Astronomical Institute, Bočni II 1401, 141 31 Prague 4 (office); Kouřimská 28, 130 00 Prague 3, Czech Republic (home). *Telephone:* (267) 103068 (office); (272) 744780 (home). *Fax:* (272) 769023 (office). *E-mail:* perek@ig.cas.cz (office). *Website:* www.galaxy.ig.cas.cz (office); www.asu.cas.cz (home).

PERELLA, Joseph (Joe) Robert, MBA, CPA; American investment banker; *Chairman and CEO, Perella Weinberg Partners LP;* b. 20 Sept. 1941, Newark; s. of Dominic Perella and Agnes Perella; m. Amy Gralnick 1974; ed Lehigh Univ. and Harvard Business School; public accountant, Haskins & Sells, New York 1964–70; consultant, IBRD, Washington, DC 1971; Assoc. The First Boston Corpn New York 1972–74, Asst Vice-Pres. 1974–75, Vice-Pres. 1975-78, Man. Dir 1978–88; Chair. Wasserstein, Perella & Co. New York 1988–93; head of mergers and acquisitions then Chair. Institutional Securities and Investment Banking Group, mem. operating Cttee Morgan Stanley 1993–2005; co-f. Perella Weinberg Pnrs LP (investment banking firm), New York, Chair. and CEO 2006–. *Address:* Perella Weinberg Partners LP, 767 Fifth Avenue, New York, NY 10153, USA (office); Perella Weinberg Partners UK LLP, 20 Grafton Street, London, W1S 4DZ, England (office). *Telephone:* (212) 287-3300 (NY) (office); (20) 7268-2800 (London) (office). *Fax:* (212) 287-3201 (NY) (office); (20) 7268-2900 (London) (office). *Website:* www.pwpartners.com (office).

PERELMAN, Grigori Yakovlevich, CandSci; Russian mathematician; b. 13 June 1966, Leningrad (now St Petersburg); ed Leningrad Secondary School #239, Leningrad State Univ.; worked under Aleksandr Danilovich Aleksandrov and Yuri Dmitrievich Burago at Leningrad Dept of Steklov Math. Inst. of USSR (now Russian) Acad. of Sciences –2003; held posts at several univs in USA late 1980s–early 1990s; invited to spend a semester each at New York Univ. and State Univ. of NY at Stony Brook 1992; held fellowship at Univ. of Calif., Berkeley 1993–95; returned to Steklov Math. Inst. 1995; accepted invitation to visit and give series of talks on his work at MIT, Princeton Univ., State Univ. of NY at Stony Brook, Columbia Univ. and Harvard Univ. 2003; solved affirmatively the famous Poincaré conjecture, posed in 1904, and regarded as one of the most important and difficult open problems in math.; won Gold Medal as mem. USSR team competing in Int. Math. Olympiad 1982, Fields Medal (co-recipient) for "his contributions to geometry and his revolutionary insights into the analytical and geometric structure of the Ricci flow" (declined to accept the award or appear at the congress) 2006, Millennium Prize, Clay Mathematical Inst. 2010. *Publications:* numerous papers in professional journals. *Address:* c/o Steklov Mathematical Institute, Gubkina str. 8, 119991 Moscow, Russia. *Telephone:* (495) 135-22-91. *Fax:* (495) 135-05-55. *E-mail:* steklov@mi.ras.ru. *Website:* www.mi.ras.ru.

PERELMAN, Ronald Owen, MBA; American business executive; *Chairman, Revlon, Inc.;* b. 1944, Greensboro, NC; s. of Raymond Perelman and Claudia (née Cohen) Perelman; m. 1st Faith Golding (divorced); four c.; m. 2nd Claudia Cohen (divorced); one d.; m. 3rd Patricia Duff (divorced); one d.; m. 4th Ellen Barkin (q.v.) 2000 (divorced 2006); ed Univ. of Pennsylvania and Wharton School of Finance; with Belmont Industries Inc. 1966–78; Dir, Chair. and CEO MacAndrews & Forbes Group, Inc., New York City 1978–; Dir, Chair. and CEO Revlon Group, Inc. (later Revlon, Inc.), New York City 1985–; Chair., CEO and Man. REV Holdings LLC; Chair. and CEO MacAndrews & Forbes Holdings, Inc.; Andrews Group Inc., New York 1985–; Chair. Nat. Health Labs, La Jolla, Calif. 1985–; Chair. Technicolor Inc., Hollywood, Calif.; Co-Chair. and CEO Panavision Inc.; Pres. Solomon R. Guggenheim Museum, NY 1995–; Dir Four Star Int. Inc., Compact Video Inc., M&F Worldwide Corpn, Scientific Games Corpn. *Address:* Revlon Inc., 237 Park Avenue, New York, NY 10017 (office); Solomark Guggenheim Museum, 1071 5th Avenue, New York, NY 10128, USA. *Telephone:* (212) 527-4000 (office). *Fax:* (212) 527-4995 (office). *Website:* www.revloninc.com (office).

PERENCHIO, A. Jerrold, BA; American media executive; *Chairman and CEO, Univision Communications Inc.;* b. Fresno, Calif.; m.; three c.; ed UCLA; boxing promoter and talent agent 1960s; pioneer of pay-TV; co-f. Embassy Communications 1974, sold to Coca-Cola 1985; bought Spanish-language broadcaster Univision 1992, floated 1996, added second Spanish-language network Telefutura 2003, currently Chair. and CEO Univision Communications Inc. *Address:* Univision Communications Inc., 1999 Avenue of the Stars, Suite 3050, Los Angeles, CA 90067, USA (office). *Telephone:* (310) 556-7676 (office). *Fax:* (310) 556-7615 (office). *Website:* www.univision.com (office).

PERÉNYI, Miklós; Hungarian cellist and composer; b. 5 Jan. 1948, Budapest; ed Music Acad. of Budapest, studied with Enrico Meinardi in Rome and Ede Bande in Budapest; started playing cello aged five, first public recital aged nine, Budapest; Violoncello Teacher, Franz Liszt Acad. of Music, Budapest 1974–, Prof. 1980–; appearances at int. music festivals including Edinburgh, Lucerne, Prague, Salzburg, Vienna, Hohenems, Warsaw, Berlin, also cello festivals in Kronberg, Winterthur and Manchester, Festival Pablo Casals, Prades, France, as well as in Japan, China and USA; collaborates with pianist András Schiff, including concerts at Schubertiade Festival, Austria, Wigmore Hall, London, Edinburgh and Ruhr Festivals; Prizewinner, Int. Pablo Casals Cello Competition, Budapest 1963, Liszt Prize 1970, Kossuth Prize 1980, Bartók-Pasztory Prize 1987. *Recordings include:* works of Ernö Dohnányi, Ferenc Farkas, Zoltán Kodály, György Ligeti, András Mihály and Sándor Veress (with Dénes Várjon), complete Beethoven Sonatas (with András Schiff), Hungarian Cello Music, complete Music for Piano and Violoncello (with András Schiff) (Cannes Classical Award 2005). *Leisure interests:* swimming, cycling. *Address:* c/o Impresariat Simmenauer GmbH, Kurfürstendamm 211, 10719 Berlin, Germany (office). *Telephone:* (30) 414-781-714 (office). *Fax:* (30) 414-781-713 (office). *E-mail:* oda.caspar@impresariat-simmenauer.de (office). *Website:* www.impresariat-simmenauer.de (office).

PERERA, Air Chief Marshal G. Donald; Sri Lankan diplomatist and air force officer; s. of the late G. Victor Perera and W. Somawathi Perera; ed Nat. Defence Coll., India, Air Command and Staff Coll., Air Univ., Maxwell Air Force Base, Ala, USA; participated in Air Operations in North and East since 1983, Chief of Staff 1998–2002, Commdr Sri Lanka Air Force 2002–06, Chief of Defence Staff 2006–09; Amb. to Israel 2010–13; Vishista Seva Vibhushanaya, Utthama Seva Padakkama, Repub. of Sri Lanka Armed Services Medal, Sri Lanka Air Force 50th Anniversary Medal, Sri Lanka Armed Services Long Service Medal, Presidential Inauguration Medal, 50th Independence Anniversary Commemoration Medal, North and East Operations Medal, Purna Bhumi Padakkama, Vadamarachchi Operations Medal, Riviresa Campaign Service Medal. *Address:* c/o Ministry of External Affairs, Republic Building, Colombo 1, Sri Lanka.

PERES, Shimon; Israeli politician, writer and head of state; *President;* b. 2 Aug. 1923, Poland; s. of Isaac Persky and Sara Persky; m. Sonia Gelman; two s. one d.; ed New York Univ., Harvard Univ.; immigrated to Palestine 1934; fmr Sec. Hano'ar Ha'oved Movt; mem. Haganah Movt 1947; Israel Naval Service, Ministry of Defence 1948; Head of Defence Mission in USA; Deputy Dir-Gen. of Ministry of Defence 1952–53, Dir-Gen. 1953–59, Deputy Minister of Defence 1959–65; mem. Knesset 1959–; mem. Mapai Party 1941–65, founder mem. and Sec.-Gen. Rafi Party 1965, mem. Labour Party after merger 1968, Chair. 1977–92, 1995–97, 2003–05, resgnd from party Nov. 2005; Minister for Econ. Devt in the Administered Areas and for Immigrant Absorption 1969–70, of Transport and Communications 1970–74, of Information March–June 1974, of Defence 1974–77, of Foreign Affairs 1992–95; Acting Prime Minister April–May 1977; Leader of the Opposition 1977–84, 1996–97; Prime Minister of Israel 1984–86, 1995–96; Minister of the Interior and of Religious Affairs 1984–85, of Defence 1995–96; Vice-Premier and Minister of Foreign Affairs 1986–88, Vice-Premier and Finance Minister 1988–90, Minister of Regional Co-operation –2001, of Foreign Affairs 2001–02; Vice-Premier –2005; Vice-Premier and Minister for Devt of the Negev and Galillee 2006–07; Pres. of Israel 2007–; shared Nobel Prize for Peace 1994, Int. Council of Christians and Jews Interfaith Gold Medallion 1997. *Publications:* The Next Step 1965, David's Sling 1970, Tomorrow is Now 1978, From These Men 1979, Witness (autobiography) 1993, The New Middle East 1993, Battling for Peace 1995, For the Future of Israel 1998, The Imaginary Voyage: With Theodor Herzl in Israel 1999, Ben-Gurion: A Political Life 2011; numerous articles in Israeli and foreign publs. *Address:* Office of the President, 3 Hanassi Street, Jerusalem 92188, Israel (office). *Telephone:* (2) 6707211 (office). *Fax:* (2) 5611033 (office). *E-mail:* president@president.gov.il (office). *Website:* www.president.gov.il (office).

PERETSMAN, Nancy B., AB, MPPM; American investment banker; *Executive Vice-President and Managing Director, Allen & Co. LLC;* m. Robert Scully 1988; one d.; ed Woodrow Wilson School, Princeton Univ., Yale School of Man.; joined Salomon Brothers in 1983, Man. Dir 1990–95; Exec. Vice-Pres. and Man. Dir Allen & Co. LLC (fmrly Allen & Co. Inc.) 1995–; mem. Bd Dirs Charter Communications Inc. –2004, Priceline.com 1999–, several privately held cos; mem. Advisory Bd Narad Networks; Vice-Chair. The New School; mem. Bd Teach for America; Trustee Inst. of Advanced Study, Princeton Univ. (Emer.); named by Money magazine one of Smartest Women in the Money Business, Financial Women's Asscn Private Sector Woman of the Year 2001, ranked by Fortune magazine amongst 50 Most Powerful Women in Business in the US 1999–2001, (31st) 2002, (36th) 2003, (37th) 2004, (38th) 2005, (47th) 2006, (43rd) 2008, ranked 44th by The Hollywood Reporter amongst Women in Entertainment Power 100 2013. *Address:* Allen & Co. LLC, 711 5th Avenue, 9th Floor, New York, NY 10022, USA (office). *Telephone:* (212) 832-80000 (office). *Fax:* (212) 832-8023 (office).

PERETZ, Amir; Israeli politician and fmr trade union official; *Minister of Environmental Protection;* b. (Armand Peretz), 1952, Morocco; m. Ahlama; four c.; emigrated to Israel at age of four; fmr Munitions Officer, Paratroopers Div., Israeli Army; fmr farmer; elected Mayor of Sderot 1983; mem. Knesset 1988–; CEO Histadrut Haovdim Haleumit 1995–2005; founder and Leader Am Ehad (One Nation) 1999–2004 (until merger with Israel Labour Party); Chair. Israel Labour Party 2005–07; Deputy Prime Minister and Minister of Defence 2006–07; Minister of Environmental Protection 2013–; mem. Peace Now. *Address:* Ministry of Environmental Protection, POB 34033, 5 Kanfei Nesharim Street, Givat Shaul, Jerusalem 95464 (office); Israel Labour Party, POB 62033, Tel-Aviv 61620, Israel (office). *Telephone:* 2-6553777 (office). *Fax:* 2-6495892 (office). *E-mail:* pniot@environment.gov.il (office). *Website:* www.environment.gov.il (office); www.havoda.org.il (office).

PERETZ, David Lindsay Corbett, CB, MA; British international finance official; b. 29 May 1943; s. of Michael Peretz and April Peretz; m. Jane Wildman 1966; one s. one d.; ed The Leys School Cambridge and Exeter Coll. Oxford; Asst Prin. Ministry of Tech. 1965–69; Head of Public Policy and Institutional Studies, Int. Bank Research Org. 1969–76; Prin. HM Treasury 1976–80, Asst Sec. External Finance 1980–84, Prin. Pvt. Sec. to Chancellor of Exchequer 1984–85, Under-Sec. (Home Finance) 1985–86, (Monetary Group, Public Finance) 1986–90; UK Exec. Dir IMF and IBRD and Econ. Minister, Washington, DC 1990–94; Deputy Dir Int. Finance, HM Treasury 1994–99; UK G7 Financial Sherpa 1994–98; Sr Adviser, World Bank Group 1999–, Exec. Sec. World Bank Joint Task Force on Small States 2001; currently consultant Ind. Evaluation Office of the IMF, Washington, DC 2007–10; Chair. UK Advisory Cttee on Devt Effectiveness. *Leisure interests:* walking, sailing, listening to music. *Address:* Independent Evaluation Office of the International Monetary Fund, 700 19th Street NW, Washington, DC 20431, USA (office). *Telephone:* (202) 623-7312 (office). *Fax:* (202) 623-9990 (office). *E-mail:* dperetz@imf.org (office); dlcperetz@yahoo.co.uk (office). *Website:* www.ieo-imf.org (office).

PEREZ, Antonio M., MBA; American/Spanish business executive; *Special Advisor to the Board, Eastman Kodak Company;* ed Technical Univ. of Madrid, INSEAD, France; fmrly with Hewlett-Packard Co., positions including Corp. Vice-Pres., Pres. Consumer Business, mem. Exec. Council; Pres. and CEO Gemplus Int. 2000–01; COO Eastman Kodak Co. 2003–05, Pres. 2003–06, CEO 2005–14, Chair. 2006–14, Special Advisor to Bd of Dirs 2014–; mem. Bd of Dirs Freescale Semiconductor Inc.; mem. Business Roundtable. *Address:* Eastman Kodak Company, 343 State Street, Rochester, NY 14650, USA (office). *Fax:* (585) 724-1089 (office). *Website:* www.kodak.com (office).

PÉREZ, Jésus Arnaldo; Venezuelan geographer, academic and diplomatist; *Ambassador to France;* ed Univ. of Toulouse II, Univ. of Bordeaux III, Univ. of Paris, France; after studies in France returned to Venezuela 1986, then back to France to teach and work for CNRS; has served as environmental adviser for petroleum exploration in Venezuela and researcher and environmental cooperation project manager with NGOs in both France and Latin America; fmr Lecturer, Univ. of Toulouse I, Univ. of Toulouse II, Univ. of Toulouse III, has also taught at Toulouse Coll. of Agric.; fmr Guest Lecturer,Alcala de Nerares Univ., Madrid; Minister of the Environment and Natural Resources 1999–2000; Amb. to Algeria 2000–02; Amb. to France and Perm. Del. to UNESCO, Paris 2002–04, 2006–; Minister of Foreign Affairs 2004; Amb. to Canada 2005–06. *Address:* Embassy of Venezuela, 11 rue Copernic, 75116 Paris, France (office). *Telephone:* 1-45-53-29-98 (office). *Fax:* 1-47-55-64-56 (office). *E-mail:* info@amb-venezuela.fr (office). *Website:* www.embavenez-paris.com (home).

PEREZ, Thomas Edward, BA, JD; American lawyer and government official; *Secretary of Labor;* b. 7 Oct. 1961, Buffalo, New York; s. of Rafael Perez and Grace Perez (née Brache); m. Ann Marie Staudenmaier; three c.; ed Brown Univ., Harvard Law School, John F. Kennedy School of Govt; law clerk for Judge Zita Weinshienk, US Dist Court, Colo 1987–89; called to the Bar, New York 1988, Washington, DC 1988; Trial Lawyer, Criminal Section, Civil Rights Div., US Dept of Justice, Washington, DC 1989–94, Deputy Chief, Criminal Section 1994–97, Deputy Asst Attorney for Civil Rights 1998–99, Asst Attorney-Gen. for Civil Rights 2009–13; Special Counsel to Senator Edward Kennedy 1995–98; Dir, Office of Civil

Rights, US Dept of Health and Human Services, Washington, DC 1999–2002; Asst Prof. and Dir, Clinical Law Office, Univ. of Maryland School of Law, Baltimore 2001–07; Sec., Dept of Labor, Licensing & Regulation, State of Maryland 2007–09; Sec. of Labor 2013–. *Address:* Department of Labor, Frances Perkins Building, 200 Constitution Avenue, NW, Washington, DC 20210, USA (office). *Telephone:* (202) 693-6000 (office). *Fax:* (202) 693-6111 (office). *E-mail:* contact-ocio@dol.gov (office). *Website:* www.dol.gov (office).

PEREZ, Vincent; Swiss actor; b. 10 June 1964, Lausanne; m. Karine Silla; three c.; ed acting studies in Geneva, Conservatoire Nat. Supérieur d'Art Dramatiqu, Paris, school of the Théâtre Nanterre-Amandiers; best known internationally for playing the title character Ashe Corven in The Crow: City of Angels and for starring in Queen of the Damned, playing Marius de Romanus; Prix Jean Gabin 1992, named one of People magazine's 50 Most Beautiful People in the World 1995. *Films include:* Gardien de la nuit 1986, Hotel de France 1987, La maison de jade 1988, Cyrano de Bergerac 1990, The Voyage of Captain Fracassa 1990, La neige et le feu 1991, Indochine 1992, Cendre d'or (short) 1992, Fanfan 1993, La Reine Margot 1994, Beyond the Clouds 1995, Line of Life 1996, The Crow: City of Angels 1996, Amy Foster 1997, On Guard (Best Actor, Cabourg Romantic Film Festival 1998) 1997, Those Who Love Me Can Take the Train 1998, The Treat 1998, Talk of Angels 1998, Time Regained 1999, Épouse-moi 2000, The Libertine 2000, I Dreamed of Africa 2000, Love Bites 2001, Bride of the Wind 2001, Queen of the Damned 2002, The Pharmacist 2003, Happiness Costs Nothing 2003, Fanfan la Tulipe 2003, I'm Staying! 2003, The Car Keys 2003, Welcome to Switzerland 2004, Battle of the Brave 2004, Kod apokalipsisa (as Vensan Peres) 2007, Arn: The Knight Templar 2007, Tomorrow at Dawn 2009, Bruc, the Manhunt 2010, Inhale 2010, Tempus Fugit (short) 2010, Monsieur Papa 2011, A Butterfly Kiss 2011, Ma première fois 2012, Lines of Wellington 2012, Ce que le jour doit à la nuit 2012, Un prince (presque) charmant 2013, Puppylove 2013; dir: L'échange (short) (also writer) 1992, Rien à dire (short) 1999, Once Upon an Angel (also writer) 2002, The Secret (also producer) 2007. *Television includes:* Série noire (series) 1986, Hamlet (film) 1990, Shot Through the Heart (film) 1998, Frankenstein (film) 2004, Le juge (mini-series) 2005, Avec le temps… (film) 2006, Madame De Pompadour: The King's Favourite (film) 2006, Paris Criminal Inquiries (series) 2007–08, Die Jahrhundertlawine (film) 2008, Lo scandalo della Banca Romana (mini-series) 2010, Trahie! (film) 2010, Arn (mini-series) 2010, Cesare Mori – Il prefetto di ferro (film) 2012, As Linhas de Torres Vedras (mini-series) 2012, Disparus (mini-series) 2014; dir: Scénarios sur la drogue (series) (one episode) 2000. *Address:* c/o Elisabeth Tanner, Artmedia, 20 avenue Rapp, 75007 Paris, France (office). *Telephone:* 1-43-17-33-00 (office). *E-mail:* info@artmedia.fr (office). *Website:* www.artmedia.fr (office).

PEREZ, William (Bill) D., BA; American business executive; *Senior Advisor, Greenhill & Co.;* b. 10 Sept. 1947, Akron, Ohio; m. Catherine A. Perez; two c.; ed Cornell Univ., American Grad. School of Int. Man.; joined S.C. Johnson & Son Inc. 1970, fmr positions include Gen. Man. S.C. Johnson Spain, S.C. Johnson Iberia, Vice-Pres. and Regional Dir of Consumer Products, Latin America, Vice-Pres. Home Care business, Exec. Vice-Pres. of Consumer Products, N America, Pres. and COO Worldwide Consumer Products 1993–96, Pres. and CEO S.C. Johnson & Son Inc. 1996–2004; Pres. and CEO Nike Inc. 2004–06 (resgnd); mem. Bd of Dirs –2006; Pres. and CEO Wm. Wrigley Jr. Co., Chicago 2006–08; Sr Advisor, Greenhill & Co. 2010–; mem. Bd of Dirs Campbell Soup Co., Johnson & Johnson, Whirlpool Corpn, Northwest Memorial Hospital, Boys and Girls Clubs of Chicago; Trustee, Cornell Univ. *Leisure interests:* running. *Address:* Greenhill & Co., 155 North Upper Wacker Drive, #4550, Chicago, IL 60606, USA (office). *Telephone:* (312) 846-4994 (office). *Website:* www.greenhill.com (office).

PÉREZ BALLADARES, Ernesto, MBA; Panamanian fmr head of state; b. 29 June 1946, Panama City; s. of Ernesto Pérez Balladares Sr and María Enriqueta González Revilla; m. Dora Boyd; two s. three d.; ed Univs of Notre Dame and Pennsylvania; Dir and Corp. Credit Official for Cen. America and Panama, Citibank 1971–75; Minister of Finance and the Treasury 1976–81, of Planning and Econ. Policy 1981–82; Founding mem. Partido Revolucionario Democrático (PRD) 1979, Sec.-Gen. 1982, 1992; Dir-Gen. Instituto de Recursos Hidráulicos y Electrificación 1983; Pres. of Panama 1994–99; Pres. Golden Fruit, SA, Inversionista el Torreón, SA; mem. Legislation Comm., PRD Political Comm.; under house arrest during investigation by Special Prosecutor of money laundering charges 2010; Order of Sacred Treasure (1st class) (Japan) 1980, Orden Aguila Azteca in Grado de Bando (Mexico) 1981.

PÉREZ DE BRICIO OLARIAGA, Carlos, Spanish oil industry executive; b. 31 Dec. 1927, Madrid; Vice-Pres. Comm. of Basic Industries of Iron and Steel 1968; Chair. Sub-Cttee on Iron and Steel, OECD 1969; Chief of Directorate of Naval and Iron and Steel Industries 1969–74; Minister of Industry 1975–76, 1976–77; Pres. Sodiex 1981–83; Dir Compañía Española de Petróleos SA (CEPSA) 1991–2008, Exec. Vice-Pres. 1996, Chair. and CEO 1996–2008; Head of Ministry of Public Works 1997; Pres. Union of Iron and Steel Cos (UNESID) 1968; Founder and Pres. Spanish Confed. of Metal Cos (CONFEMETAL) 1978–; Vice-Pres. Spanish Confed. of Enterprise Orgs (CEOE) 1981–98, European Org. of Metallurgical Industries 1990; fmr mem. Advisory Bd Macosa, Carburos Metálicos, Acerinox; mem. Bd Dirs Compañía Logistica de Hidrocarburos CLH SA 2004.

PÉREZ DE CUÉLLAR, Javier; Peruvian politician and diplomatist (retd); b. 19 Jan. 1920, Lima; m. Marcela Temple; two c.; ed Catholic Univ., Lima; joined Foreign Ministry 1940, diplomatic service 1944; served as Sec. in embassies in France, UK, Bolivia, Brazil (later Counsellor); Dir Legal and Personnel Dept, Dir of Admin., of Protocol and of Political Affairs, Ministry of External Relations 1961–63; Amb. to Switzerland 1964–66; Perm. Under-Sec. and Sec.-Gen. Foreign Office 1966–69, Amb. to USSR (concurrently to Poland) 1969–71; to Venezuela 1978; Perm. Rep. to UN 1971–75; mem. UN Security Council 1973–74, Pres. 1974; Special Rep. of UN Sec.-Gen. in Cyprus 1975–77; UN Under-Sec.-Gen. for Special Political Affairs 1979–81; UN Sec.-Gen. 1982–91; Prime Minister of Peru 2000–01; Amb. to France 2001–04; Pres. World Comm. on Culture and Devt UN/UNESCO 1992–, Int. Disability Foundation 1992–, Fondation de l'Arche de la Fraternité 1993–; Dir Repub. Nat. Bank of New York 1992; unsuccessful cand. for Pres. of Peru 1995; fmr Prof. of Diplomatic Law, Acad. Diplomática del Perú and Prof. of Int. Relations, Acad. de Guerra Aérea del Perú; del. to First UN Gen. Ass. 1946–47 and other int. confs; Montague Burton Visiting Prof. of Int. Relations, Univ. of Edinburgh 1985; mem. Acad. Mexicana de Derecho Int. 1988–; Dr hc (Univ. of Nice) 1983, (Jagiellonian, Charles and Sofia Univs, Univ. of San Marcos and Vrije Univ., Brussels) 1984, (Carleton Univ., Ottawa, Sorbonne Univ., Paris) 1985, (Osnabruck) 1986, (Univs of Mich., Coimbra, Mongolian State, Humbolt, Moscow State) 1987, (Univ. of Leiden) 1988, (Cambridge) 1989, (Univ. of Kuwait) 1993, (Oxford) 1993; Olaf Palme Prize for Public Service 1989, Prince of Asturias Prize for Ibero-American Co-operation, Alexander Onassis Foundation Prize 1990, Presidential Medal of Freedom (US) 1991, Four Freedoms Award (Franklin Delano Roosevelt Inst.) 1992. *Publication:* Manual de Derecho Diplomático 1964, Anarchy or Order 1992, Pilgrimage for Peace 1997. *Address:* c/o Ministry of Foreign Affairs, Jirón Lampa 535, Lima 1; Avenida A. Miro Quesada, 1071 Lima, Peru.

PÉREZ ESQUIVEL, Adolfo; Argentine human rights leader, architect and sculptor; b. 26 Nov. 1931, Buenos Aires; m. Amanda Pérez 1956; three s.; ed Nat. School of Fine Arts, Buenos Aires; trained as architect and sculptor; Prof. of Art, Manuel Belgrano Nat. School of Fine Arts, Buenos Aires 1956–71; Prof. Faculty of Architecture and Urban Studies; Univ. Nacional de la Plata; gave up teaching to concentrate on non-violent human rights movt; f. Servicio Paz y Justicia en America Latina, Buenos Aires 1973, Sec.-Gen. 1974–86, Hon. Pres. 1986–; co-founder Ecumenical Movt for Human Rights, Argentina; Pres. Perm. Ass. for Human Rights; arrested 1977, released May 1978; visited Europe 1980; Pres. Int. League for Human Rights and Liberation of Peoples 1987; fmr Rector UN Univ. for Peace; Hon. Citizen of Assisi 1982; Nobel Prize for Peace 1980. *Publication:* Caminando Junto al Pueblo (Walking Together with the People) 1995. *Address:* Servicio Paz y Justicia, Piedras 730, CP 1070, Buenos Aires, Argentina.

PÉREZ-LLORCA, José Pedro; Spanish politician and lawyer; *Partner, Pérez-Llorca law firm;* b. 30 Nov. 1940, Cadiz; s. of José Pérez-Llorca and Carmen Pérez-Llorca; m. Carmen Zamora Bonilla 1965; one s. one d.; ed Madrid Central (Complutense) Univ., Univs of Freiburg and Munich; entered diplomatic service 1964; adviser, Spanish del. to 21st and 22nd Gen. Ass. of UN and 5th extraordinary emergency session; Legal Adviser to Parl. 1968; Higher Council for Foreign Affairs 1970; practised law, Madrid 1970–, pvt. law practice 1983–; mem. Cortes 1977–82; fmr Parl. Leader Unión de Centro Democrático (UCD); mem. Comm. for drawing up Constitution 1978; Minister of the Presidency 1979–80, for Relations with Parl. Jan.–May 1980, for Territorial Admin. May–Oct. 1980, for Foreign Affairs 1980–82; Chair. AEG-Ibérica SA, Urquiso Leasing SA; Dir Robert Bosch Española SA; Prof. of Constitutional Law, School of Diplomacy; Iberian Law Firm of the Year, Chambers Global Awards 2006. *Address:* Alcalá 61, 28014 Madrid, Spain (office). *Telephone:* (914) 360420 (office). *Fax:* (914) 360430 (office). *E-mail:* ppl@perezllorca.com (office). *Website:* www.perezllorca.com (office).

PÉREZ MOLINA, Gen. (retd) Otto Fernando; Guatemalan fmr army officer, politician and head of state; *President;* b. 1 Dec. 1950, Guatemala City; ed School of the Americas (now Western Hemisphere Inst. for Security Cooperation), Fort Benning, Columbus, Ga and Inter-American Defense Coll., Washington, DC, USA; served as Dir of Mil. Intelligence and Insp.-Gen. of the Army, member of group of army officers who backed Defence Minister Óscar Mejía's coup d'état against de facto Pres. Efraín Ríos Montt 1983, also instrumental in restoring normality in aftermath of Pres. Jorge Serrano Elías's abortive 'self-coup' 1993; apptd by incoming Pres. Ramiro de León Carpio as Head of Presidential Gen. Staff (EMP) 1993–95; also represented mil. in negotiations that led to 1996 Peace Accords, ending Guatemala's 30-year-long civil war; represented Guatemala on Inter-American Defense Bd 1998–2000; retd from active mil. duty in Jan. 2000; f. Partido Patriota (Patriotic Party) 2001; elected to Congress 2003–; cand. in presidential elections 2007, 2011; Pres. of Guatemala 2012–. *Address:* Partido Patriota, 11 Calle 11-54, Zona 1, Guatemala City, Guatemala (office). *Telephone:* 2230-5068 (office). *Fax:* 2230-6227 (office). *E-mail:* comunicacion@partidopatriota.org (office). *Website:* www.partidopatriota.com (office).

PÉREZ-REVERTE, Arturo; Spanish journalist and writer; b. 1951, Cartagena, Murcia; fmr journalist, war corresp., Pueblo; war corresp., Spanish nat. TV; now writes fiction full-time; elected to Spanish Royal Acad. 2003; Chevalier, Ordre des Arts et des Lettres 1998, Gran Cruz del Mérito Naval 2005, Chevalier, Ordre nat. du Mérite 2008; Grand Prix for Detective Literature (France) 1993, Asturias Prize for Journalism for his coverage of the war in the fmr Yugoslavia for TV 1993, Ondas Prize for Radio de España's La Ley de la Calle 1993. *Films include:* El Maestro de Esgrima 1992, La Tabla de Flandes 1994, Cachito 1995, Territorio Comanche 1997, La Novena Puerta 1999, Gitano 2000, Alatriste 2006, La Carta Esférica 2007. *Publications include:* El Húsar 1986, El maestro de esgrima (trans. as The Fencing Master) 1988, La tabla de Flandes (trans. as The Flanders Panel) 1990, El club Dumas (trans. as The Dumas Club) 1993, La sombra del águila 1993, Territorio comanche 1994, Un asunto de honor 1995, Obra breve 1995, La piel del tambor (trans. as The Seville Communion; Jean Monnet Prize for European Literature 1997) 1995, El capitán Alatriste (trans. as Captain Alatriste) 1996, Limpieza de sangre (trans. as Purity of Blood) 1997, El sol de Breda (trans. as The Sun Over Breda) 1998, Patente de corso 1998, La carta esférica (trans. as The Nautical Chart) (Prix Beau Livre, Acad. de Marine Française) 2000, El oro del rey (trans. as The King's Gold) 2000, Con ánimo de ofender 2001, La Reina del Sur (translated as The Queen of the South) 2002, El caballero del jubón amarillo (trans. as The Man in the Yellow Doublet) 2003, Cabo Trafalgar 2004, No me cogeréis vivo 2005, El pintor de batallas (trans. as The Painter of Battles) (Premio Vallombrosa-Gregor von Rezzori 2008) 2006, Corsarios de Levante 2006, Un Día de Cólera 2007, Ojos Azules 2009, Cuando éramos honrados mercenarios 2009, El asedio 2010, El puente de los Asesinos 2011, El tango de la Guardia Vieja 2012, El francotirador paciente 2013; contrib. to Spanish periodicals, including XL Semanal (weekly article). *Address:* c/o RDC Agencia Literaria, Fernando VI 13–15, 3° derecha, 28004 Madrid, Spain (office). *Telephone:* (91) 3085585 (office); (91) 3912034 (office). *Fax:* (91) 3085600 (office). *E-mail:* rdc@rdclitera.com (office); RDCprom@rdclitera.com (office). *Website:* www.perezreverte.com; www.perez-reverte.com (office).

PÉREZ RODRÍGUEZ, Florentino; Spanish civil engineer and construction industry executive; *Chairman and CEO, ACS Group;* b. 1947, Madrid; ed Polytechnic Univ. of Madrid; fmr Lecturer in Physical Foundations of Tech., Higher Tech. School of Civil Eng; began career as Dir Spanish Road Asscn 1971; served in various public admin posts 1976–82, including Del. for Sanitation and Environment, Madrid City Council, Gen. Sub-Dir of Promotion, Centre for Devt of Industrial Tech., Ministry of Industry and Energy, Gen. Man. Transport

Infrastructures, Ministry for Transport, Chair. Inst. for Agrarian Reform and Devt (IRYDA), Ministry of Agric.; joined Construcciones Padrós SA as CEO 1983; Chair. OCP Construcciones SA 1993–97; mem. Bd Dirs ACS Group (Actividades de Construcción y Servicios SA) 1989–, Chair. and CEO 1993–; Dir and Second Vice-Chair. Abertis Infraestructuras SA 2007–; mem. Bd Dirs Sanef. *Address:* ACS, Actividades de Construcción y Servicios SA, Avenida Pío XII 102, Madrid 28036, Spain (office). *Telephone:* (91) 3439200 (office). *Fax:* (91) 3439456 (office). *E-mail:* infogrupoacs@grupoacs.com (office). *Website:* www.grupoacs.com (office).

PEREZ ROQUE, Felipe Ramón; Cuban politician; b. 28 March 1965, Havana; m.; two c.; ed Superior Politécnico José A. Echeverría; head univ. students union 1988; fmr electronics engineer; involved with biotechnology complex 1960; mem. Cen. Cttee CP of Cuba 1991–2009; mem. Nat. Ass. 1986–2009, State Council 1993–2009; Pvt. Sec. to Fidel Castro; Minister of Foreign Affairs 1999–2009; José A. Echeverría Medal. *Address:* c/o Ministry of Foreign Affairs, Calzada 360, Vedado, Havana, Cuba.

PÉREZ VERA, Víctor L., MSc; Chilean engineer, university administrator and academic; *Rector, University of Chile;* b. Rancagua; ed liceo Manuel Barros Borgoño de Santiago and studies with Prof. Elisa Gayán, Faculty of Physical Sciences and Math., Univ. of Chile, Univ. of Michigan, USA; Dir Polytechnic Inst. of Santiago 1967–69; Investigator and Prof., Dept of Industrial Eng, Universidad de Chile 1969, Titular Prof. 1986, Dir Dept of Industrial Eng 1980–84, 1988–90, Vice-Dean Faculty 1984–85, mem. Comm. of Academic Evaluation 1991–92, Pro-Rector Universidad de Chile 1993, Dean Faculty of Physical Sciences and Math. 1994–2002, mem. Special Univ. Senate Comm. 2002–05, Rector Universidad de Chile 2006–; Visiting Prof. at several nat. and Latin American univs; mem. Editorial Cttee Information and Management journal; Coordinator Higher Educ. Comm.; mem. Inst. of Engineers of Chile; Premio 'Profesor Enrique Silva a la Trayectoria Docente', Dept of Industrial Eng, Universidad de Chile 1994, Premio 'Ingeniero Civil Industrial del Año', Especialidad Civil Industrial, Coll. of Engineers of Chile, AG 1994, Premio 'Raúl Devés Jullián', Inst. of Engineers of Chile 2001, Premio 'Al Ingeniero por Acciones Distinguidas' 2003. *Publications:* author or co-author of seven books; numerous scientific papers in professional journals on information systems and financial analysis; articles on higher educ. in El Mercurio, La Segunda, El Mostrador, La Tercera. *Address:* Office of the Rector, Universidad de Chile, Avda Libertador Bernardo O'Higgins 1058, Casilla 10-D, Santiago, Chile (office). *Telephone:* (2) 9782000 (office). *Fax:* (2) 6781012 (office). *Website:* ww.uchile.cl (office).

PERHAM, Richard Nelson, MA, PhD, ScD, FRS, FRSA, FMedSci; British biochemist and academic; *Professor Emeritus of Structural Biochemistry, University of Cambridge;* b. 27 April 1937, London, England; s. of Cyril Perham and Helen Thornton; m. Nancy Lane 1969; one s. one d.; ed Latymer Upper School, London and St John's Coll., Cambridge; MRC Scholar, MRC Lab. of Molecular Biology, Cambridge 1961–64; Helen Hay Whitney Fellow, Dept of Molecular Biophysics, Yale Univ. 1966–67; Univ. Lecturer in Biochemistry, Univ. of Cambridge 1969–77, Reader in Biochemistry of Macromolecular Structures 1977–89, Prof. of Structural Biochemistry 1989–2004, Head Dept of Biochemistry 1985–96, Prof. Emer. 2004–; Fellow, St John's Coll., Cambridge 1964–2004, 2007–, Pres. 1983–87, Master 2004–07; Fogarty Int. Scholar, NIH, USA 1990–93; Chair. Editorial Bd FEBS Journal 1998–; Chair. Bd Govs Latymer Upper School 2004–10; Chair. Scientific Advisory Bd Max-Planck-Institut fur Molekulare Physiologie, Dortmund 2002–09; Deputy Pres. Science Cttee, Fondation Louis-Jeantet de Medecine, Geneva 2005–10; mem. Biochemical Soc., Royal Inst. of GB, Academia Europaea, European Molecular Biology Org.; Max Planck Prize 1993, Novartis Medal and Prize 1998, Silver Medal Italian Biochemical Soc. 2000, Pehr Edman Award, Int. Asscn of Protein Structure and Proteomics 2008, Diplome d'Honneur, Fed. of European Biochemical Socs 2011. *Publications:* Instrumentation in Amino Acid Sequence Analysis; more than 250 papers and articles in learned journals. *Leisure interests:* gardening, theatre, opera, rowing, antiques (18th century). *Address:* St John's College, Cambridge, CB2 1TP, England (office). *Telephone:* (1223) 337724 (office). *Fax:* (1223) 337720 (office). *E-mail:* rnp1@cam.ac.uk (office). *Website:* www .joh.cam.ac.uk (office); www.bioc.cam.ac.uk (office).

PERIGOT, François; French business executive; b. 12 May 1926, Lyons; s. of Jean-Paul Perigot and Marguerite de la Tour; m. 2nd Isabelle Paque 1986; one s. one d. from fmr marriage; ed Lycée de Bastia, Faculté de Droit, Paris and Inst. d'Etudes Politiques, Paris; joined Unilever group (France) 1955, Head of Personnel 1966; Pres.-Dir-Gen. Thibaud Gibbs et Cie 1968–70; Dir Unilever (Spain) 1971–75; Pres.-Dir-Gen. Unilever (France) 1976–86; Pres. Campagnie de Plâtre 1987–98; mem. Bd of Sodexho, OENEO, CDC lxis Pvt. Equity, Lever, Astra; mem. Exec. Council, Conseil Nat. du Patronat Français (CNPF) 1981–86, Pres. 1986–94; Vice-Pres. Union des confédératios de l'industrie et des employeurs d'Europe (UNICE) 1988–92, Pres. 1994; mem. Social and Econ. Council (CES) 1989–99; Pres. MEDEF Int. (Int. Br. of French Employers' Asscn) 1997–2005, Hon. Pres. 2005–; Pres. Org. Int. des Employeurs (OIE), Geneva 2001–06, Hon. Pres. 2006–; mem. Bd of Dirs Sodexho; mem. World Comm. on the Social Dimension of Globalization; Commdr, Légion d'honneur; numerous foreign decorations. *Leisure interest:* golf. *Address:* Organisation Internationale des Employeurs, Geneva, Switzerland (office); 9 Avenue Fréderic le Ploy, 75007 Paris, France (home). *Telephone:* 1-53-59-16-12 (office). *Fax:* 1-45-55-03-77 (office). *E-mail:* ioe@ioe-emp.org (office). *Website:* www .ioe-emp.org (office).

PERINETTI, André Louis; French administrator and theatre director; *Honorary President, International Theatre Institute;* b. 7 Aug. 1933, Asnières; m. Fatiha Bel-el-Abbas 1974; two s. one d.; ed Collège Turgot, Law Faculty of Paris, Univ. of Theatre of Nations; theatre dir 1965–83; Gen. Man. Théâtre Cité Universitaire 1968–72, Nat. Theatre of Strasbourg 1972–75, Nat. Theatre of Chaillot, Paris 1974–81; Consultant, UNESCO 1974, Ministry of Culture 1982–83; Sec.-Gen. Int. Theatre Inst. (UNESCO) 1984–2004, Hon. Pres. 2004–; Chevalier, Légion d'honneur, des Arts et des Lettres; Dr hc (Bratislava); UNESCO Picasso Medal. *Leisure interests:* theatre, music, tennis. *Address:* International Theatre Institute—ITI, Maison de l'UNESCO, 1 rue Miollis, 75732 Paris Cedex 15 (office); 109 avenue Charles de Gaulle, 92200 Neuilly, France. *Telephone:* 1-45-68-48-80 (office). *E-mail:* alperinetti@yahoo.fr (home). *Website:* iti-worldwide.org (office).

PERINO, Dana Marie, BA; American journalist, consultant and fmr government official; *Chief Issues Counselor, Burson-Marsteller;* b. 9 May 1972, Evanston, Wy.; d. of Leo Perino and Jan Perino; m. Peter McMahon; ed Ponderosa High School, Parker, Colo, Univ. of Southern Colorado, Univ. of Illinois at Springfield; while attending univ. worked with KTSC (Univ. of Southern Colorado radio station), also host Capitol Journal, weekly TV summary of Colo politics and producer Standoff, a weekly TV public affairs program; worked as daily reporter covering Springfield, Ill. for WCIA-TV; early career in Washington, DC as Staff Asst for US Congressman Scott McInnis of Colo 1995, then Press Sec. for US Congressman Dan Schaefer of Colo; worked in high-tech public affairs, San Diego, Calif.; Spokesperson US Dept of Justice, Washington, DC 2001, then Dir of Communications, White House Council on Environmental Quality; Deputy Asst to the Pres. and Deputy White House Press Sec. 2006–07, White House Press Sec. 2007–09; Chief Issues Counselor, Burson-Marsteller, Washington, DC 2009–; co-host The Five (TV show), Fox News. *Address:* Burson-Marsteller, 1110 Vermont Avenue, NW, Suite 1200, Washington, DC 20005-3554, USA (office). *Telephone:* (202) 530-0400 (office). *Fax:* (202) 530-4500 (office). *Website:* www.burson-marsteller.com (office).

PERIŠIC, Zoran; Serbian film director, writer, producer and visual effects supervisor; b. 16 March 1940, Zemun; Dir Sky Bandits/Gunbus (film) 1986; Producer-Dir The Phoenix and the Magic Carpet 1995; Dir-Writer Captain Cook's Travels (TV, animated series), Magic Fountain (TV, animated series), In Search of the Real Dracula (documentary), etc.; cr. visual and/or special effects for 2001 – A Space Odyssey 1968, Land of the Minotaur 1976, Superman I 1978, Superman II 1980, Superman III 1983, Return to Oz 1985, Sky Bandits 1986, Cliffhanger and other films; several patents, including ZOPTIC front-projection system and 3D cinematography; Acad. Award (Oscar) for Outstanding Achievement in Visual Effects (for Superman – the Movie), BAFTA Award for Outstanding Contrib. to the Cinema, American Acad. Tech. Achievement Award for the invention and devt of the ZOPTIC dual-zoom front-projection system. *Publications:* Special Optical Effects, The Animation Stand, Photoguide to Shooting Animation, Visual Effects Cinematography 2000. *Leisure interest:* flying (pvt. pilot's licence). *E-mail:* zoptic@hotmail.com (office); zoran@zoptic.force9.co.uk (home). *Website:* www.zoptic.com (office).

PERISSICH, Riccardo; Italian/French international civil servant; *Executive Vice-President, Italian Branch, Council for the United States and Italy;* b. 24 Jan. 1942, Milan; m. Anne Treca 1989; one s.; writer on foreign policy for Il Punto (Rome weekly) 1962; with Italconsult SpA (consulting engineers) 1962–64; Head of EC Studies, Istituto Affari Internazionali, Rome 1966–70; joined Comm. of EC, Brussels 1970; Chef de Cabinet of Altiero Spinelli 1970–76, Cesidio Guazzaroni 1976; Dir Directorate A (energy savings and energy forecasts) 1977–81; Chef de Cabinet of Antonio Giolitti (regional policy) 1981–84, of Carlo Ripa di Meana (institutional affairs) 1985–86; Dir, later Deputy Dir-Gen. Directorate-Gen. for Industry 1986, Dir-Gen. 1990–94; Bd mem. and Dir Public and Econ. Affairs Pirelli SpA 1994–2001, Co-ordinator of Institutional Affairs 2001–06; Dir Public and Econ. Affairs, Telecom Italia Group 2001–06, Chair. Telecomitalia Media 2002–07; Chair. Seat Pagine Gialle from 2002; Vice-Chair. Assolombarda from 1995, Unione Industriali di Roma, ASSONIME (Italian Cos Asscns); Exec. Vice-Pres. Italian br. of Council for the United States and Italy (CONSIUSA) 2010–; Bd mem. European Inst. of Oncology; mem. IISS, London, Istituto Affari Internazionali, Aspen Inst. Italia; Chevalier des Arts et des Lettres. *Publications:* Gli eurocrati fra realtà e mitologia 1969, Europa America: materiali per un dibattito (with S. Silvestri) 1970, L'Unione europea, una storia non ufficiale 2008, Le Regole del Gioco (novel) 2012; contrib. to Italian and foreign publs on European and int. politics. *E-mail:* info@consiusa.org. *Website:* www.consiusa.org.

PERISSINOTTO, Giovanni, BEcons, PhD; Italian insurance executive; b. 6 Dec. 1953, Conselice (Ravenna); m.; three c.; ed Università degli Studi di Trieste; chartered accountant 1978; internship at Generali UK Br. Financial Office, London 1979; joined Generali Assicurazioni SpA, Trieste 1980, Cen. Dept of parent co. 1988–89, Deputy Man. responsible for the Italian and foreign market 1989–92, responsible for Admin. Office 1992–93, responsible for co-ordination of corp. assets at Admin and Finance Dept 1993–95, Jt Man. responsible for Accounting and Finance Dept 1995–96, Deputy Gen. Man. with responsibilities a.i. for Admin and Finance Dept 1996–98, Gen. Man. 1998–2001, Group CEO and Jt Man. Dir 2001–12 (resgnd), also Chair. Banca Generali SpA, Generali Properties SpA, Supervisory Bd Generali Investments SpA, Vice-Chair. Banca della Svizzera Italiana SA (BSI SA); mem. Bd Dirs Participatie Maatschappij Graafscap Holland NV, Transocean Holding Corpn, Generali France Holding, Generali España Holding de Entidades de Seguros, Alleanza Toro Assicurazioni SpA, INA Assitalia SpA, Generali Immobiliare Italia SGR SpA, Generali Business Solutions, Pirelli & Co. SpA 2003–12; mem. Supervisory Bd Participatie Maatschappij Transhol BV, Man. Bd Intesa San Paolo, Man. Council Federazione ABl-ANlA, Presidential Cttee Assonime, Exec. Cttee ANIA; Cavaliere del Lavoro 2007. *Publications include:* articles on econs including The Creation of Value through a Specialized Distribution Network 2003. *Address:* c/o Assicurazioni Generali SpA, Piazza Duca degli Abruzzi 2, 34132 Trieste, Italy. *E-mail:* info@generali.com.

PERISSOL, Pierre-André Daniel; French politician and engineer; b. 30 April 1947, Nice; s. of Louis Perissol and Aline Cardiec; ed Lycée Massena, Nice, Ecole Polytechnique, Ecole Nat. des Ponts et Chaussées; Dir of Planning, Saint-Quentin-en-Yvelines new town 1972–74; Adviser to Sec. of State for Housing 1974–76; Chief Eng Ecole Nat. des Ponts et Chaussées 1986; Dir-Gen. Soc. Centrale de Crédit Immobilier 1977–91, Pres., Dir-Gen. 1991–92, Pres. 1993–95; Founder and Dir.-Gen. Groupe Arcade 1980–91, Pres. 1991–95; Pres. Coopérer pour Habiter 1982, Aiguillon Construction 1987, Fed. Nat. (now Chambre Syndicale) des Sociétés de Crédit Immobilier 1988, Caisse Centrale de Crédit Immobilier 1990–93; Regional Councillor, Ile-de-France 1983–86; Councillor, Paris 1983–95; Deputy Mayor of Paris responsible for Educ. 1989–93; RPR Deputy to Nat. Ass. 1993–95; Minister of Housing May–Nov. 1995, Deputy Minister 1995–97; Mayor of Moulins 1995–; Vice-Pres. Regional Council of Auvergne 1998–; UMP Deputy to Nat. Ass. 2002–; Officier, Légion d'honneur, Ordre Nat. du Mérite. *Publications:* Le défi social 1985, En mal de toit 1995, A bonne école 2002. *Leisure interests:* travel, tennis. *Address:* Assemblée Nationale, 126 rue de l'Université, 75007 Paris, France (office).

Telephone: 4-70-48-50-21 (office). *Fax:* 4-70-48-50-84 (office). *E-mail:* paperissol@asemblee.nationale.fr (office).

PERKIN, James Russell Conway, DPhil; British/Canadian university president; b. 19 Aug. 1928, Northants.; s. of William Perkin and Lily Drage; m. Dorothy Bentley 1953; two s. one d.; ed Daventry Grammar School, Northants. and Univ. of Oxford; Minister, Altrincham Baptist Church, Cheshire 1955–62; lecturer in New Testament Greek, New Coll. Edinburgh 1963–65; Assoc. Prof. of New Testament Interpretation, McMaster Divinity Coll. Hamilton, Ont. 1965–69; Prof. of Religious Studies and Head of Dept Acadia Univ. NS 1969–77, Dean of Arts 1977–80, Vice-Pres. (Academic) 1980–81, Acting Pres. 1981–82, Pres. 1982–93; mem. Soc. for New Testament Studies, Canadian Soc. for Study of Religion; Hon. DD (McMaster) 1986; Hon. DLitt (Acadia) 1995; Canada 125th Medal 1992, Queen's Jubilee Medal 2013. *Publications:* Such is Our Story (with E. A. Payne) 1955, Study Notes on Romans 1957, Resurrection in Theology and Life 1966, Handbook for Biblical Studies 1973, Scripture Then and Now 1975, In Season 1978, With Mind and Heart 1979, Crucial Questions 1980, Seedtime and Harvest 1982, Arrows in the Mind 1984, Morning in his Heart: Life and Writings of Watson Kirkconnell (with J. Snelson) 1986, Morning in his Heart: a Biographical Sketch of Watson Kirkconnell 1987, Commonplace Book 1986, Reflections and Insights 1993, Ordinary Magic 1995, Devotional Diary 1998, 1999, 2011; book chapters, essays, articles and reviews. *Leisure interests:* reading, gardening, sailing, classical music. *Address:* 10 Harris Place, Wolfville, NS B4P 1T2, Canada (home). *Telephone:* (902) 542-5501 (home).

PERKINS, Alice Elizabeth, BA, CB; British business executive; *Partner and Executive Coach, JCA Group;* b. 24 May 1949; d. of Derrick Leslie John Perkins and Elsa Rose Perkins (née Rink); m. Jack (John Whitaker) Straw 1978; one s. one d.; ed N London Collegiate School for Girls and St Anne's Coll., Oxford; joined Civil Service in Dept of Health and Social Security (DHSS) 1971, Prin. 1976–84, Asst Sec. DHSS, then Dept of Social Security (DSS) 1984–90, Dir of Personnel 1990–93; Under-Sec. Defence Policy and Material Group, HM Treasury 1993–95, Deputy Dir of Public Spending 1995–98; Dir of Corp. Man., Dept of Health 1998–2000; Head of Civil Service Human Resources and Corp. Devt, Cabinet Office 2000–05; Trustee Whitehall and Industry Group 1993–98; Dir (non-exec.) Littlewoods Org. 1997–2000, Taylor Nelson Sofres 2005–08, BAA 2006; Partner and Exec. Coach JCA Group 2006–; external mem. Oxford Univ. Council 2006; Hon. Fellow, St Anne's Coll., Oxford 2006. *Leisure interests:* gardening, travelling, looking at paintings. *Address:* JCA Group, 55 Baker Street, London, W1N 8EW, England (office).

PERKINS, Donald Hill, CBE, MA, PhD, FRS; British physicist and academic; *Professor Emeritus of Physics, University of Oxford;* b. 15 Oct. 1925, Hull; s. of G. W. Perkins and G. Perkins; m. Dorothy M. Maloney 1955; two d.; ed Imperial Coll., London; Sr 1851 Scholar, Univ. of Bristol 1949–52, G. A. Wills Research Assoc. 1952–55, Lecturer, then Reader in Physics 1956–65; Visiting Scientist, Univ. of California, USA 1955–56; Prof. of Elementary Particle Physics, Univ. of Oxford 1965–93, Prof. Emer. 1993–, Fellow, St Catherine's Coll. 1965–; mem. Science and Eng Research Council 1985–89; Hon. DSc (Sheffield) 1982, (Bristol) 1995; Guthrie Medal, Inst. of Physics 1979, Holweck Medal, Soc. française de physique 1992, Royal Medal, Royal Soc. of London 1997, High-Energy Physics Prize, European Physical Soc. 2001. *Publications:* Study of Elementary Particles by the Photographic Method (with C. F. Powell and P. H. Fowler) 1959, Introduction to High Energy Physics 1972, Particle Astrophysics 2002. *Leisure interests:* squash, skiing, lepidoptera. *Address:* 37 Redan Street, London, W14 0AB, England (home). *Telephone:* (20) 7348-0028 (home). *E-mail:* d.perkins1@physics.ox.ac.uk (office).

PERKINS, Edward J., DPA; American diplomatist and academic; *Professor Emeritus, University of Oklahoma;* b. 8 June 1928, Sterlington, La; s. of Edward Joseph Perkins Sr and Tiny Estella Noble Holmes; m. Lucy Cheng-mei Liu; two d.; ed Univ. of Maryland and Univ. of Southern California; Chief of Personnel, Army and Air Force Exchange Service, Taiwan 1958–62; Deputy Chief, Okinawa, Japan 1962–64, Chief of Personnel and Admin. 1964–66; Asst Gen. Services Officer, Far East Bureau, AID 1967–69, Man. Analyst 1969–70; Deputy Dir Man. US Operations, Mission to Thailand 1970–72; Staff Asst Office of Dir-Gen. of Foreign Service 1972; Personnel Officer 1972–74; Admin. Officer, Bureau of Near Eastern and South Asian Affairs 1974–75; Man. Analysis Officer, Office of Man. Operations, Dept of State 1975–78; Counsellor for Political Affairs, Accra 1978–81; Deputy Chief of Mission, Monrovia 1981–83; Dir Office of W African Affairs, Dept of State 1983–85; Amb. to Liberia 1985–86, to S Africa 1986–89; Dir-Gen. Foreign Service, Washington 1989–92; Perm. Rep. to UN 1992–93; Amb. to Australia 1993–96; William J. Crowe Chair Prof. of Geopolitics and Exec. Dir Int. Programs Center, Univ. of Okla 1996–2007, Prof. Emer. 2007–; Bd Dir Asscn for Diplomatic Studies and Training 1998–; Trustee Lewis and Clark Coll. 1994–, Asia Soc. 1997–2000, Inst. of Int. Educ. 1997–2000; Gov. Jt Center for Political and Econ. Studies 1996–2002; mem. Advisory Council Univ. Office of Int. Programs Pa State Univ. 1997–; mem. Advisory Bd Inst. of Int. Public Policy 1997–; Trustee Woodrow Wilson Fellowship Foundation 1999–; Bd of Visitors, Nat. Defense Univ. 2002–; mem. Pres.'s Advisory Cttee on Trade Policy ad Negotiation 2003–; Distinguished Alumni Award, Univ. of Southern Calif. 1991, Distinguished Honor Award, Dept of State 1992, Statesman of the Year Award, George Washington Univ. 1992, Dept of State Dir-Gen. Cup 2001 and numerous other awards. *Publications include:* Preparing America's Foreign Policy for the 21st Century (ed. with David L. Boren) 1999, Palestinian Refugees: Traditional Positions and New Solutions (ed. with Joseph Ginat) 1999, Democracy, Morality and the Search for Peace in America's Foreign Policy (ed. with David L. Boren) 2002, Middle East Peace Process: Vision versus Reality (ed. with Joseph Ginat and Edwin G. Corr) 2002; contribs to specialized journals and reviews. *Leisure interests:* art, jazz. *Address:* Room 105, 729 Elm Avenue, Norman, OK 73019, USA (office). *Telephone:* (405) 325-1584 (office). *Fax:* (405) 325-7738 (office).

PERKINS, Frederick J., MSc; British business executive; *Founding Chairman and CEO, Information TV Limited;* b. 2 March 1948, Glasgow, Scotland; ed Univs of Strathclyde and Sussex; fmr Vice-Pres., Europe, McGraw-Hill; Chief Exec. and COO The Stationery Office (fmrly Her Majesty's Stationery Office) 1996–2003; Group Dir The Financial Times, Citibank; Chair. Electronic Publrs Forum from 1998, Dept for Trade and Industry's Innovation and Growth Task Force for software, digital content and related services, Public Policy Forum from 2001;

Founding Chair. and CEO Information TV Ltd 2003–; fmr mem. Exec. of the Broadband Stakeholder Group. *Address:* Information TV Ltd, 1 Stephen Street, London, W1T 1AL, England (office). *Telephone:* (20) 7131-6693 (office). *E-mail:* fred.perkins@information.tv (office). *Website:* www.information.tv (office).

PERKINS, Kieren John, OA; Australian fmr swimmer; b. 14 Aug. 1973, Brisbane; s. of Kevin Perkins and Gloria Perkins; m. Symantha Liu 1997; one s. one d.; ed Brisbane Boys' Coll., Univ. of Queensland; gold medal Olympic Games, Barcelona 1992 for 1,500m freestyle (world record), gold medal Olympic Games, Atlanta 1996 for 1,500m (first swimmer to hold Olympic, World, Commonwealth and Pan Pacific titles simultaneously), two gold medals World Championships, Rome 1994 (world and Commonwealth records for 400m freestyle), four gold medals Commonwealth Games, Canada 1994 (world and Commonwealth records for 800m and 1,500m freestyle); set 10 Australian, 11 Queensland and 10 Brisbane records and two Commonwealth and one Australian standard time records; silver medal 1500m freestyle Olympic Games, Sydney 2000; retd; World Oceania Award, LA Amateur Athletic Foundation Award 1992, Australian Sports and Tourism Amb., Australia Tourist Comm. 1993, Advance Australia Award 1993, World Male Swimmer of the Year 1994, FINA Award 1994, Australian flag-bearer Commonwealth Games 1998. *Leisure interests:* music, motorcycling, horse riding, reading, surfing, boating, fishing, jetskiing. *Address:* c/o Swimming Australia, 12/7 Beissel Street, Belconnen, ACT 2617, Australia.

PERKINS, Lawrence Bradford, Jr., BA, BArch, MBA, FAIA, MRAIC, AICP; American architect; b. 13 Jan. 1943, Chicago, Ill.; s. of Lawrence B. Perkins and Margery Perkins; m. Phyllis Friedman 1966; three d.; ed Cornell and Stanford Univs and City Coll. of New York; President, Omnidata Services 1971–73; Man. Pnr, Llewellyn-Davies Assocs 1973–77; Sr Vice-Pres., Pnr, Perkins and Will 1977–81; Pnr Attia & Perkins 1981–83; Pres. Perkins Eastman Architects 1983–; Dir Settlement Housing Fund 1991–, Helen Keller Int. 1993–; Dir New York City AIA, NY Foundation for Architecture; Fellow, American Inst. of Architects, Epsilon Asscn (Pres. 1993–96); various design awards. *Publications:* articles in professional journals and chapters for professional textbooks. *Address:* Perkins Eastman Architects, 115 Fifth Avenue, New York, NY 10003 (office); 4 Rectory Lane, Scarsdale, NY 10583, USA (home). *Telephone:* (212) 353-7200 (office); (914) 723-8875 (home). *Fax:* (212) 353-7676 (office). *Website:* www.perkinseastman.com (office).

PERL, Martin Lewis, PhD; American research physicist, academic and engineer; *Professor of Physics, Stanford Linear Accelerator Center (SLAC), Stanford University;* b. 24 June 1927, New York; three s. one d.; ed Polytechnic Inst. of New York and Columbia Univ.; Chemical Engineer, General Electric Co. 1948–50; Asst, then Assoc. Prof. of Physics, Univ. of Mich. 1955–63; Prof. of Physics, Stanford Linear Accelerator Center, Stanford Univ. 1963–, Prof. of Physics, Stanford Univ. 1970–; research in experimental elementary particle physics 1955–, small drop technology 1995–; discovered the elementary particle tau lepton 1975–78; Hon. DSc (Chicago) 1990, (Polytechnic Univ.) 1997; Wolf Prize in Physics 1982, Nobel Prize in Physics (co-recipient) 1995. *Publications:* High Energy Hadron Physics 1974, Reflections on Experimental Science 1996, articles on science and soc. issues and on physics educ. *Leisure interests:* mechanical antiques, gardening. *Address:* SLAC National Accelerator Laboratory, 2575 Sand Hill Road, Menlo Park, CA 94025 (office); 3737 El Centro Avenue, Palo Alto, CA 94306, USA (home). *Telephone:* (650) 926-4286 (office). *Fax:* (650) 926-4001 (office). *E-mail:* martin@SLAC.Stanford.edu (office). *Website:* www.slac.stanford.edu (office).

PERLE, Richard Norman, BA, MA; American business executive and fmr government official; *Resident Fellow, American Enterprise Institute;* b. 16 Sept. 1941, New York, NY; s. of Jack and Martha Perle; m. Leslie Barr; one s.; ed Univ. of S California, Princeton Univ.; Asst Sec. US Dept of Defense, Int. Security Policy 1981–88; fmr foreign policy adviser; mem. Defense Policy Bd 2001–04, Chair. 2001–03 (resgnd); fmr Dir GeoBiotics; Dir Hollinger Int. Inc. 1994–2005; Resident Fellow, American Enterprise Inst. for Public Policy Research 1987–; Patron, Henry Jackson Soc. *Television:* produced The Gulf Crisis: The Road to War for PBS 1992. *Publications:* Reshaping Western Security (ed.) 1991, Hard Line 1992, An End to Evil (with David Frum) 2004. *Address:* American Enterprise Institute for Public Policy Research, 1150 17th Street, NW, Washington, DC 20036, USA (office). *Telephone:* (301) 656-0390 (office). *Fax:* (202) 862-7177 (office). *E-mail:* rperle@aei.org (office). *Website:* www.aei.org (office).

PERLET, Helmut, PhD; German business executive; *Chairman of the Supervisory Board, Allianz SE;* b. 9 April 1947, Planegg, Munich; ed Ludwig Maximilians Univ., Munich, Univ. of Hamburg; worked for tax office in Munich 1971–72; employee, Allianz Versicherungs-AG, Munich 1973–81, involved in establishment and management of Foreign Tax Dept 1981–90, Head of Finance Dept (Non-domestic) 1990–92, Head of Dept of Group Accounting and Dept Group Planning and Control 1992–97, in addition Head of Tax Dept 1994–97, mem. Man. Bd Allianz SE, Munich 1997–2009, Chair. Supervisory Bd 2012–; mem. Supervisory or Admin. Bd Commerzbank AG, Frankfurt-am-Main, GEA Group AG, Düsseldorf; Hon. Prof., Dr Wolfgang Schieren Inst. of Insurance and Risk Man., Econs Faculty of Humboldt Univ., Berlin. *Publications include:* Rückstellungen für noch nicht abgewickelte Versicherungsfälle in Handels- und Steuerbilanz, Vol. 2 of Veröffentlichungen des Seminars für Versicherungswissenschaft der Universität Hamburg und des Vereins zur Förderung der Versicherungswissenschaft in Hamburg e.V. 1986, Die deutsche Unternehmensbesteuerung im europäischen Binnenmarkt (co-author) 1994 (second edn 2003), Die Hinzurechnungsbesteuerung bei Auslandsbeteiligungen – Mit den neuen Grundsätzen der Finanzverwaltung zur Anwendung des Außensteuergesetzes (co-author) 1996, Solvency II & Risikomanagement: Umbruch in der Versicherungswirtschaft (co-author) 2005. *Address:* Allianz SE, Königinstrasse 28, 80802 Munich, Germany (office). *Telephone:* (89) 3800-5592 (office). *Fax:* (89) 3800-5593 (office). *E-mail:* info@allianz.com (office). *Website:* www.allianz.com (office).

PERLIS, HRH The Raja of; Tuanku Syed Sirajuddin ibni al-Marhum Syed Putra Jamalullail; Malaysian ruler; b. 1943; m.; one s. one d.; ed Sandhurst Mil. Acad., UK; fmr army officer; Raja of Perlis 2000–; elected as twelfth Yang di-Pertuan Agong (Supreme Head of State) 13 Dec. 2001–06.

PERLMAN, Itzhak; Israeli violinist and conductor; b. 31 Aug. 1945, Tel-Aviv; s. of Chaim Perlman and Shoshana Perlman; m. Toby Lynn Friedlander 1967; two s.

three d.; ed Shulamit High School, Tel-Aviv, Tel-Aviv Acad. of Music and Juilliard School, USA, studied with Ivan Galamian and Dorothy De Lay; gave recitals on radio at the age of 10; went to USA 1958; first recital at Carnegie Hall 1963; has played with maj. American orchestras 1964–; has toured Europe regularly and played with maj. European orchestras 1966–; debut in UK with London Symphony Orchestra 1968; toured Poland, Hungary, Far East; played with Israel Philharmonic Orchestra in fmr Soviet Union; appearances at Israel Festival and most European Festivals; Prin. Guest Conductor Detroit Symphony Orchestra 2001–; numerous recordings; Hon. DMus (Univ. of S Carolina) 1982, Dr hc (Yale, Harvard and Yeshivah Univs); several Grammy awards, EMI Artist of the Year 1995, Royal Philharmonic Soc. gold medal 1996; Medal of Liberty 1986, Nat. Medal of Arts 2001. *Leisure interest:* cooking. *Address:* c/o IMG Artists, Carnegie Hall Tower, 152 West 57th Street, 5th Floor, New York, NY 10019, USA (office). *Telephone:* (212) 994-3500 (office). *Fax:* (212) 994-3550 (office). *E-mail:* esobol@imgartists.com (office). *Website:* www.imgartists.com (office).

PERLMUTTER, Saul, BS, PhD; American physicist and academic; *Professor, University of California, Berkeley;* b. 1959; ed Harvard Univ., Univ. of California, Berkeley; currently astrophysicist, Lawrence Berkeley Nat. Lab. and Leader of Int. Supernova Cosmology Project; Prof., Physics Dept, Univ. of California, Berkeley 2004–; Fellow, Ameican Acad. of Arts and Sciences; Henri Chretien Award, American Astronomical Soc. 1996, Lawrence Award in Physics, US Dept of Energy 2002, Calif. Scientist of Year 2003, John Scott Award 2005, Padua Prize 2005, Feltrinelli International Prize, Lincei Acad., Rome 2006, Shaw Prize in Astronomy (co-recipient) 2006, Gruber Cosmology Prize (co-recipient) 2007, Nobel Prize in Physics (jtly) 2011. *Achievements include:* discovery through the study of distant supernovae that the expansion of the universe is speeding up rather than slowing down. *Television:* has appeared in Public Broadcasting System and BBC TV documentaries on astronomy and cosmology. *Publications:* numerous scientific papers in professional journals; has also written popular articles for Sky and Telescope magazine. *Address:* 429 Old LeConte Hall, Department of Physics, University of California, Berkeley, CA 94720, USA (office). *Telephone:* (510) 642-3596 (office). *Fax:* (510) 643-8497 (office). *E-mail:* saul@lbl.gov (office). *Website:* www.physics.berkeley.edu/research/faculty/perlmutter.html (office); supernova .lbl.gov/~saul/home.html (office).

PERMAN, Finley S.; Micronesian auditor and government official; ed Hawaii Pacific Coll.; previous positions include Devt Specialist, Pohnpei Small Business Guarantee and Finance Corpn, Sr Service Asst, Bank of Hawaii, Pohnpei br.; Dir Pohnpei State Dept of Treasury and Admin 2005–07; Sec. Dept of Finance and Admin 2007–10 (resgnd). *Address:* c/o Department of Finance and Administration, PS158, Palikir 96941, Pohnpei State, Federated States of Micronesia.

PERNG, Fai-Nan, MA; Taiwanese central banker and economist; *Governor, Central Bank of the Republic of China (Taiwan);* b. 2 Jan. 1939; m.; two s.; ed Nat. Chung Hsing Univ., Univ. of Minnesota, USA and Int. Monetary Fund Inst.; with Bank of Taiwan 1969; Asst Specialist, Cen. Bank of China (CBC), later Deputy Div. Chief, Div. Chief, Econ. Research Dept 1971–78, Asst Dir-Gen. and Div. Chief, Econ. Research Dept 1978–80, Deputy Dir-Gen. 1980–86, Dir-Gen. 1986–89, Dir-Gen. Foreign Exchange Dept 1989–94, Deputy Gov. CBC 1994–95, mem. Bd of Dirs 1995–, Gov. 1998–, also mem. Exec. Yuan (cabinet); Chair. Cen. Trust of China 1995–97, Int. Commercial Bank of China 1997–98; Gov. for Taiwan, Asian Devt Bank 1998–, Cen. American Bank for Econ. Integration 1998–; Adjunct Prof., Nat. Chung Hsing Univ. 1986–89; Hon. LLD (Univ. of Minnesota) 2006, (Nat. Taipei Univ.) 2009; Office of the Pres. Best Employee Award 1975, Cen. Bank of China Best Essay Award 1982, Excellence Magazine Outstanding Govt Official 1998, Nat. Chung Hsing Univ. Outstanding Alumnus Award 1999, Univ. of Minn. Outstanding Achievement Award 2000, Global Finance Top Central Banker Award 2000, 2005, 2006, 2007, 2008, 2009, 2010, 2011, 2012, 2013, The Banker Central Banker of the Year Asia Award 2009. *Publications include:* Possible Methods for the Liberalization of Foreign Exchange Control 1985, Asian Financial Crisis 1998; numerous articles. *Address:* Central Bank of the Republic of China (Taiwan), 2 Roosevelt Road, Sec. 1, Taipei 100, Taiwan (office). *Telephone:* (2) 2393-6161 (office). *Fax:* (2) 2357-1974 (office). *E-mail:* adminrol@mail.cbc.gov.tw (office). *Website:* www.cbc.gov.tw (office).

PÉROL, François; French civil servant and business executive; *Chairman of the Management Board, Groupe BPCE;* b. 1963; ed Haute École Commerciale School of Man., Institut d'Études Politiques (Sciences Po), École Nationale d'Admin, Paris; began career in Inspection générale des Finances 1990; served as rapporteur and later Asst Sec.-Gen., Comite Interministeriel de Restructuration Industrielle 1994–96; Head, Office of Financial Markets, Treasury Dept 1996–99, Asst Dir of Financial Support and Devt 2001–02; Sec.-Gen. Club de Paris 1999–2001; served as Deputy Chief of Staff to ministers François Mer and Nicolas Sarkozy, Ministry of Economy 2002–05; Gen. Partner, Rothschild Bank 2005–; Deputy Gen. Sec., Office of the Pres. 2007–09; Chair. Man. Bd Caisse Nationale des Caisses d'Epargne (CNCE) and CEO Banque Fédérale des Banques Populaires (BFBP) March–Aug. 2009, Chair. Man. Bd Groupe BPCE (following merger) Aug. 2009–; Chair. Supervisory Bd Natixis. *Address:* Groupe BPCE, 50 avenue Pierre Mendès France, 75201 Paris Cedex 13, France (office). *Telephone:* 1-58-40-41-42 (office). *Website:* www.bpce.fr (office).

PERÓN, María Estela (Isabelita) (see Martínez de Perón).

PEROT, (Henry) Ross; American business executive; b. 27 June 1930, Texarkana, Tex.; s. of Gabriel Ross Perot; m. Margot Birmingham 1956; five c.; ed US Naval Acad.; served in USN 1953–57; with IBM Corpn 1957–62; f. Electronic Data Systems Corpn 1962, Chair. and CEO 1982–86; Dir Perot Group, Dallas 1986; Founder and Chair. Perot Systems Corpn, Washington, DC 1988–2009; Chair. Bd of Visitors US Naval Acad. 1970; unsuccessful cand. for Pres. of USA 1992, 1996, f. Reform Party 1995, Chair. 1995–99. *Publications:* Not For Sale at Any Price 1993, Intensive Care 1995. *Leisure interest:* horses.

PERPIÑA-ROBERT PEYRA, Fernando; Spanish diplomatist; b. 17 April 1937, San Sebastián; s. of Benito Perpiña and Cármen Peyra; m. Alba Navarro Feussier 1964; two s. two d.; ed Univ. of Barcelona; joined Diplomatic Service 1965, Consul Gen. Boston 1978, Minister Counsellor, Bonn 1982–85, Under-Sec. of State, Ministry of Foreign Affairs 1985–88, Sec. Gen. 1988–91, Amb. to Germany 1991–96, to Hungary 1996–2001, Special Rep. for Terrorism Affairs, Ministry of

Foreign Affairs 2001–03, Consul-Gen. to Paris 2003–07; Sec. Gen. Club of Madrid 2010; mem. Group of Experts on NATO's Strategic Concept; numerous Spanish and foreign decorations. *Leisure interest:* bridge. *Address:* c/o Club of Madrid, Palacio del Marqués de Cañete, Calle Mayor 69, Planta 1, 28013 Madrid, Spain. *E-mail:* clubmadrid@clubmadrid.org.

PERRAULT, Dominique; French architect and urban planner; *Principal, Dominique Perrault Architecture;* b. 9 April 1953, Clermont-Ferrand; s. of Jean Perrault and Thérèse Souchon; m. Aude Lauriot-dit-Prévost 1986; three c.; ed Ecole Nationale Supérieure des Beaux-Arts de Paris, Ecole Nationale des Ponts et Chaussées, Ecole des Hautes Etudes en Sciences Sociales; f. architectural practice, Paris 1981; opened offices in Berlin 1992, Luxembourg 2000, Madrid 2006; architect-consultant to City of Nantes 1990–92, Bordeaux 1992–97, Barcelona 2000–03; Pres. Institut français d'architecture 1998–2001; Pres. Bd of Clermont-Ferrand ENSA 2010–; mem. Salzburg Urban Cttee 1994–97, Bd of Cité de l'Architecture et du patrimoine 2004–, Bd of Grand Paris Scientific Council 2008–09; Curator of French Pavilion at 12th Architecture Biennale in Venice 2010 (installation Metropolis); Hon. mem. RIBA; Chevalier, Légion d'honneur; numerous architectural awards and prizes, including Grand prix nat. d'architecture 1993, Grande Médaille d'Or d'Architecture, Acad. d'Architecture. *Major works include:* ESIEE – Electronic Engineers Acad., Marne-la-Vallée 1987, Industrial Hotel Berlier, Paris (Equerre d'Argent Award) 1990, Nat. Library of France, Paris (Mies van der Rohe Pavilion Award for European architecture 1997) 1995, Velodrome and Olympic Swimming Pool, Berlin 1999, Town Hall, Innsbruck 1997, Aplix Factory, Le Cellier 1999, EU Court of Justice, Luxembourg 2008, Ewha Womans Univ., Seoul (Seoul Metropolitan Architecture Award) 2008, Olympic Tennis Centre, Madrid 2009, NH Fieramilano Hotel (four star) 2009, Fukoku Tower, Osaka 2010, Arganzuela Footbridge, Madrid 2011, La Liberté Building, Groningen 2011. *Ongoing projects include:* Piazza Garibaldi, Naples, Congress and Exhbn Hall, Leon, DC Towers, Vienna, rehabilitation/extension of fmr mechanical eng halls and central library and construction of Teaching Bridge of Ecole Polytechnique Fédérale, Lausanne, Grand Theatre, Albi, Dobrée Museum, Nantes, renovation of Pavillon Dufour, Château de Versailles, Sports Palace, Rouen, New European neighbourhood and business centre, Sofia, new FSS train station dist, Locarno. *Publications:* An Atmosphere of Falling Meteors, Perrault Architecte (monograph) Italy 2000, 2004, El Croquis 2001, Mesh A+U 2003, Dominique Perrault by Gilles de Bure 2004, Dominique Perrault Architecture (exhbn catalogue) 2008; several articles in professional journals. *Address:* Dominique Perrault Architecture, 6 rue Bouvier, 75011 Paris, France (office). *Telephone:* 1-44-06-00-00 (office). *Fax:* 1-44-06-00-01 (office). *E-mail:* dpa@d-p-a.fr (office). *Website:* www.perraultarchitecte.com (office).

PERROTIN, Emmanuel; French art dealer and gallery owner; b. May 1968; opened first gallery in his apartment 1992; represented Damien Hirst, Maurizio Cattelan, Takashi Murakami, Mariko Mori, Xavier Veilhan, Sophie Calle and Bernard Frize; opened gallery in Miami, Fla, USA 2004, then in the rue de Turenne, Paris, then in New York 2013; represented artists including Jeff Koons 2008, Xavier Veilhan 2009, Takashi Murakami 2010; other artists represented include Chiho Aoshima, Daniel Arsham, Hernan Bas, Sophie Calle, Maurizio Cattelan, Peter Coffin, Johan Creten, Matthew Day Jackson, Wim Delvoye, Elmgreen & Dragset, Lionel Esteve, Daniel Firman, Bernard Frize, Giuseppe Gabellone, Gelitin, Duane Hanson, Jesper Just, Bharti Kher, Kolkoz, Klara Kristalova, Guy Limone, Jin Meyerson, Mariko Mori, Mr., Jean-Michel Othoniel, Paola Pivi, Claude Rutault, Michael Sailstorfer, Aya Takano, Tatiana Trouve, Piotr Uklanski and Peter Zimmermann. *Publications:* publishes own magazine, Bing. *Address:* Galerie Perrotin, 76 rue de Turenne, 75003 Paris, France (office); Galerie Perrotin, 909 Madison Avenue & 73rd Street, Upper East Side, New York, NY 10021, USA (office). *Telephone:* 1-42-16-79-79 (Paris) (office); (212) 812-2902 (New York) (office). *Fax:* 1-42-16-79-74 (Paris) (office). *E-mail:* paris@perrotin.com (office); newyork@perrotin.com (office). *Website:* www.perrotin.com (office).

PERRY, Grayson, CBE, BA, RA; British artist; b. 24 March 1960, Chelmsford, Essex, England; m. Philippa Perry; one d.; ed Portsmouth Polytechnic; known for his ceramic vases and cross-dressing; curated the Tomb of the Unknown Craftsman at the British Museum 2011; Turner Prize 2003, BAFTA Award for Specialist Factual (mem. production team) 2013. *Works include:* Mother of All Battles 1996, Growing Up As a Boy, Strangely Familiar, Golden Ghosts 2001. *Radio includes:* Playing to the Gallery, Reith Lectures (BBC Radio 4 and BBC World Service) 2013. *Television includes:* BBC: Question Time, Hard Talk, Desert Island Discs, Have I Got News for You, subject of a South Bank Show 2006, of an Imagine documentary 2011; Channel 4: All In The Best Possible Taste with Grayson Perry (series) 2012. *Publication:* Portrait of the Artist as a Young Girl (with Wendy Jones) 2006. *Address:* c/o Tate Britain, Millbank, London, SW1P 4RG, England.

PERRY, James Richard (Rick); American rancher, politician and state governor; *Governor of Texas;* b. 4 March 1950, Paint Creek, Tex.; s. of Joseph Ray Perry and Amelia June Perry (née Holt); m. Anita Thigpen 1982; one s. one d.; ed Paint Creek High School, Texas A&M Univ.; served in USAF 1972–77, rank of Capt.; farmer and rancher 1977–90; mem. Tex. House of Reps 1985–91; Tex. Commr of Agric. 1991–99; Lt-Gov. of Tex. 1999–2000; Gov. of Texas 2000–; cand. for Republican US presidential nomination 2012; Democrat –1989, Republican 1989–; Border Texan of the Year 2001, Govt Leadership Award, Nat. Comm. Against Drunk Driving 2001, Top Cowboy of the Year Award 2001. *Publications include:* On My Honor: Why the American Values of the Boy Scouts are Worth Fighting For 2008, Fed Up! Our Fight to Save America from Washington 2010. *Address:* Office of the Governor, PO Box 12428, Austin, TX 78711-2428, USA (office). *Telephone:* (512) 463-2000 (office). *Fax:* (512) 463-1849 (office). *Website:* www.governor.state.tx.us (office); www.rickperry.org.

PERRY, John Richard, PhD; American professor of philosophy; *Henry Waldgrave Stuart Professor Emeritus of Philosophy, Stanford University;* b. 16 Jan. 1943, Lincoln, Neb.; s. of Ralph R. Perry and Ann Roscow Perry; m. Louise E. French 1962; two s. one d.; ed Doane Coll., Crete, Neb. and Cornell Univ.; Asst Prof. of Philosophy, UCLA 1968–72, Assoc. Prof. 1972–74; Assoc. Prof. of Philosophy, Stanford Univ. 1974–77, Prof. of Philosophy 1977–85, Henry Waldgrave Stuart Prof. of Philosophy 1985–2011, Emer. 2011–, Chair. Dept of Philosophy 1976–82, 1990–91, Dir Center for Language and Information 1982–83,

1985–86, 1993–99; Distinguished Prof. of Philosophy (half-time), Univ. of California, Riverside 2008–; Pres. American Philosophical Asscn 1993–94; Hon. DLitt (Doane Coll.) 1982; Dr hc (Univ. of the Basque Country) 2002, (Ruhr-Universität, Bochum) 2013; Woodrow Wilson Fellow 1964, Danforth Fellow 1964–68, Guggenheim Fellow 1975–76, NEH Fellow 1980–81, Dinkelspiel Teaching Award 1989, Humboldt Prize 1998, Nicod Prize 1999, Ig-Nobel Prize (Literature) 2011, Quinn Prize 2013. *Radio:* Philosophy Talk 2003–. *Publications:* A Dialogue on Personal Identity and Immortality 1978, Situations and Attitudes (with J. Barwise) 1983, The Problem of the Essential Indexical and Other Essays 1993 (second enlarged edn 2000), A Dialogue on Good, Evil and the Existence of God 1999, Knowledge, Possibility and Consciousness 2000, Reference and Reflexivity 2001 (second revised edn 2011), Identity, Personal Identity and the Self 2002, Critical Pragmatics (co-author) 2011, The Art of Procrastination 2011. *Leisure interests:* reading, walking, grandchildren. *Address:* 127 Cordura Hall, CSLI, Stanford University, 210 Panama Street, Stanford, CA 94305, USA (office). *Telephone:* (650) 796-2798 (office). *Fax:* (650) 723-0985 (office). *E-mail:* john@csli.stanford.edu (office); johnperry43@gmail.com (home). *Website:* john.jperry.net.

PERRY, Katy; American singer; b. (Katheryn Elizabeth Hudson), 25 Oct. 1984, Santa Barbara, Calif.; m. Russell Brand 2010 (divorced); as a child sang in local church, at family functions; moved to Nashville to work with professional songwriters and producers, aged 15; solo artist 2007–; UNICEF Goodwill Amb. 2013–; MTV Europe Music Award for Best New Act 2008, for Best Female 2013, People's Choice Award for Favorite Pop Song (for I Kissed a Girl) 2009, BRIT Award for Best Int. Female Artist 2009, People's Choice Award 2012. *Recordings include:* albums: Katy Hudson 2001, One of the Boys 2008, Teenage Dream 2010, Prism 2013. *Address:* Bradford Cobb, Direct Management Group Inc., 947 North La Cienaga Boulevard, Suite G, Los Angeles, CA 90069, USA (office). *Telephone:* (310) 854-3535 (office). *E-mail:* bradford@directmanagement.com (office). *Website:* www.directmanagement.com (office); www.katyperry.com.

PERRY, Matthew Langford; American/Canadian actor; b. 19 Aug. 1969, Williamstown, Mass; s. of John Bennett Perry and Suzanne Perry; ed Ashbury Coll., Ottawa, Canada; mem. Bd of Dirs Ron Clark Acad. *Films:* A Night in the Life of Jimmy Reardon 1988, She's Out of Control 1989, Getting In 1994, Fools Rush In 1997, Almost Heroes 1998, Three To Tango 1999, Imagining Emily (writer) 1999, The Whole Nine Yards 2000, Serving Sara 2002, The Whole Ten Yards 2004, Numb 2007, Birds of America 2008, 17 Again 2009. *Television includes:* Friends (series) 1994–2004, The West Wing (series) 2003, The Ron Clark Story 2006, Studio 60 on the Sunset Strip (series) 2006, The End of Steve 2008, Mr Sunshine (series) 2011. *Play:* Sexual Perversity in Chicago, Comedy Theatre, London 2003. *Leisure interests:* ice hockey, softball. *Address:* c/o CAA, 9830 Wilshire Blvd, Beverly Hills, CA 90212-1825, USA (office). *Telephone:* (310) 288-4545. *Fax:* (310) 288-4800.

PERRY, Sir Michael Sydney, Kt, GBE, MA; British business executive; b. 26 Feb. 1934, Eastbourne, East Sussex; s. of Sydney Albert Perry and Jessie Kate Perry (née Brooker); m. Joan Mary Stallard 1958; one s. two d.; ed King William's Coll., Isle of Man, St John's Coll., Oxford; Chair. Lever Brothers (Thailand) Ltd 1973–77, Centrica 1997–2004, Nippon Lever (Japan) 1981–83, UAC Int. Ltd 1985–87, Unilever PLC 1992–96, Dunlop Slazenger Group 1996–2002; Pres. Lever y Asociados (Argentina) 1977–81; Dir Unilever NV 1985–96 (Vice-Chair. 1992–96), Bass PLC 1991–2001 (Deputy Chair. 1996–2001); Dir (non-exec.) British Gas 1994–97, Marks & Spencer 1996–2001; Pres. Liverpool School of Tropical Medicine 1997–2002; Pres. Advertising Asscn 1993–96; Chair. Leverhulme Trust 2008–; Trustee, Shakespeare Globe Trust 1987– (Chair. 1993–2006), Glyndebourne Arts Trust 1996–2004, Dyson Perrins Museum Trust 2000–, Inst. of Public Policy Research 2003–07, Three Choirs Festival Asscn 2007–; Hon. LLD (London South Bank) 1995, Dr hc (Worcester) 2013; Commdr, Order of Oranje Nassau 1996; Shakespeare's Globe Sam Wanamaker Award 2013. *Leisure interest:* music. *Address:* Bridges Stone Mill, Alfrick, Worcester, WR6 5HR, England (home).

PERRY OF SOUTHWARK, Baroness (Life Peer), cr. 1991, of Charlbury in the County of Oxfordshire; **Pauline Perry;** MA, FRSA, CIMgt; British fmr university administrator; *Conservative Party Whip, House of Lords;* b. (Pauline Welch), 15 Oct. 1931, Wolverhampton, England; d. of John Welch and Elizabeth Welch (née Cowan); m. George W. Perry 1952 (died 2008); three s. one d.; ed Wolverhampton Girls' High School, Girton Coll., Cambridge; Univ. Lecturer in Philosophy, Univ. of Manitoba, Canada, Massachusetts, USA, Exeter and Oxford 1956–59, 1961–63, 1966–70; HM Insp. 1970, Staff Insp. 1975, HM Chief Insp. of Schools 1981–86; Vice-Chancellor South Bank Univ. (fmrly South Bank Polytechnic) 1987–93; Pres. Lucy Cavendish Coll., Cambridge 1994–2001; Pro-Chancellor Univ. of Surrey 2001–06; Chair. Council of Roehampton Univ. 2001–05; Chair. Dept of Trade and Industry Export Group for Educ. and Training Sector 1993–98; Vice-Pres. City and Guilds of London Inst. 1994–99, Chair. City and Guilds Quality and Standards Cttee 2005–10; Chair. Comm. on Free Schools and Academies, Wandsworth Borough 2012–, Kaplan Coll. Governing Body 2014–; Co-Chair. All-Party Univs Group 1996–2010; mem. (Conservative) House of Lords 1991–, mem. House of Lords Select Cttee on Science and Tech. 1992–95, 1997–2000, 2004–07, 2009–14, on Scrutiny of Delegated Powers 1995–98, on Cen. and Local Govt Relations 1995–96, on Religious Offences 2002–03, Conservative Party Whip 2011–; mem. Prime Minister's Advisory Group on the Citizen's Charter 1993–97, Jt Select Cttee on Human Rights 2001–03; Chair. Judges Panel on Citizen's Charter 1997–2003, Church of England Review of the Crown Appointments Comm. 1999–2001, Nuffield Council on Bio-Ethics Inquiry into Animals in Scientific Experiments 2003–05; Co-Chair. Conservative Party Policy Comm. on Public Services 2007–08; mem. Bd of Patrons, Royal Soc. Appeal 1995–2001, Governing Body, Abbey Plus Schools 2013–; Trustee, Cambridge Univ. Foundation 1997–2006; Liveryman, Worshipful Co. of Bakers; Hon. Freeman, Worshipful Co. of Fishmongers; Freeman of the City of London; Hon. Fellow, Coll. of Preceptors, City and Guilds, Girton Coll. Cambridge, Roehampton Univ., Lucy Cavendish Coll. Cambridge, Swedish Acad. of Sciences (Pedagogy); Hon. LLD (Aberdeen, Bath), Hon. DLitt (Sussex, South Bank, City Univ.), Hon. DUniv (Surrey), Hon. DEd (Wolverhampton). *Publications:* The Womb in Which I Lay 2003; four earlier books, several chapters and numerous articles. *Leisure interests:* music, power walking. *Address:* House of Lords, Westminster, London, SW1A 0PW, England (office). *Telephone:*

(20) 7219-5474 (office). *E-mail:* perryp@parliament.uk (office). *Website:* www.parliament.uk/biographies/lords/baroness-perry-of-southwark/3157 (office).

PERRY, Simon Frank, CBE, BA; British film producer; b. 5 Aug. 1943, Farnham; s. of Frank Horace Perry and Brenda Mary Dorothea Perry; ed Eton Coll., King's Coll.; worked in theatre production (RSC, Bristol Old Vic, London West End) 1965–69, TV production (Anglia TV, Yorkshire TV) 1969–74; independent filmmaker 1974–77; entertainment trade journalist (Variety Magazine etc.) 1978–80; Admin. Nat. Film Devt Fund 1980–82; feature film producer 1982–; Chief Exec. British Screen Finance 1991–2000; Chevalier des Arts et Lettres. *Films include:* Knots 1975, Loose Connections 1983, Another Time, Another Place 1983, Nineteen Eighty-Four 1984, Hôtel du paradis 1986, Nanou 1986, White Mischief 1987, The Favour, the Watch and the Very Big Fish 1991, The Playboys 1992, Innocent Lies 1995. *Leisure interests:* cinema-going, cycling, European travel. *Address:* Studio C, Chelsea Studios, 416 Fulham Road, London, SW6 1EB, England. *Telephone:* (20) 7386-5119. *Fax:* (20) 7386-0017.

PERRY, Tyler; American actor, director, producer and screenwriter, author, playwright and songwriter; b. (Emmitt Perry, Jr), 14 Sept. 1969, New Orleans, La; s. of Emmitt Perry, Sr and the late Willie Maxine Perry (née Campbell); wrote a series of letters to himself, which became the basis for the musical, I Know I've Been Changed; moved to Atlanta 1990; wrote and produced numerous stage plays during the 1990s and early 2000s; known for creating, and performing in drag, the character Mabel 'Madea' Simmons; f. The Tyler Perry Foundation; lives and works in SW Atlanta where he operates the Tyler Perry movies and TV studios; Helen Hayes Award for Excellence in Theater 2001, Black Business Professionals Entrepreneur of the Year 2004, Brandon Tartikoff Legacy Award, Nat. Asscn of Television Program Execs 2009, honoured by BET at Second Annual BET Honors 2009, NAACP Chair.'s Award 2010, inaugural Visionary Award, CinemaCon 2011. *Films include:* Madea's Family Reunion (video) 2002, Diary of a Mad Black Woman (video) (Outstanding Actor in a Theatrical Film and Outstanding Writing for Theatrical Film, BET Comedy Awards 2005, Outstanding Achievement in Screenwriting, Black Movie Awards 2005, MTV Movie Award for Breakthrough Male 2005) 2002, I Can Do Bad All by Myself (video) 2002, Madea's Class Reunion (video) 2003, Meet the Browns (video) 2004, Madea's Family Reunion 2006, Madea Goes to Jail (video) 2006, Why Did I Get Married? (video) 2006, Daddy's Little Girls 2007, Why Did I Get Married? 2007, What's Done in the Dark (video) 2008, Meet the Browns 2008, The Family That Preys (Movieguild Award for Most Inspirational Film 2008) 2008, Madea Goes to Jail 2009, I Can Do Bad All by Myself 2009, Why Did I Get Married Too? 2010, For Colored Girls (Best Movie BET Award 2011, NAACP Image Awards for Outstanding Motion Picture and for Outstanding Director 2011) 2010, Madea's Big Happy Family (video) 2010, Madea's Big Happy Family 2011, Laugh to Keep from Crying (video) 2011, A Madea Christmas (video) 2011, Good Deeds 2012, Madea's Witness Protection 2012, Aunt Bam's Place 2012, Alex Cross (actor) 2012, The Marriage Counselor 2013, We the Peeples (producer) 2013. *Television includes:* House of Payne (series) (NAACP Image Awards for Outstanding Comedy Series 2009, 2010, 2011, 2012) 2007–12, Meet the Browns (series) 2009, For Better or Worse (series) 2011. *Publications:* Don't Make a Black Woman Take Off Her Earrings: Madea's Uninhibited Commentaries on Love and Life (novel) (Book of the Year, Best Humor Book, Quill Awards 2006) 2006, Madea's Big Happy Family 2010. *Address:* c/o WME, 1325 Avenue of the Americas, New York, NY 10019, USA (office). *Website:* www.tylerperry.com.

PERRY, William J., BS, MS, PhD; American academic and fmr government official; *Michael and Barbara Berberian Professor, Freeman Spogli Institute for International Studies, Center for International Security and Cooperation, Stanford University;* b. 11 Oct. 1927, Vandergift, Pa; s. of Edward Martin Perry and Mabelle Estelle Dunlop; m. Leonilla Mary Green 1947; three s. two d.; ed Stanford Univ., Pennsylvania State Univ.; served in US Army Corps of Engineers 1946–47, Reserve Officer Training Corps 1948–55; laboratory dir General Telephone and Electronics 1954–64; f. and served as Pres. ESL, Inc. 1964–77; Exec. Vice-Pres. Hambrecht & Quist, Inc. 1981–85; f. and served as Chair. Tech. Strategies & Alliances 1985–93; Prof. (half-time) Stanford Univ. 1988–93, also Co-Dir Center for Int. Security and Arms Control; Under-Sec. of Defense for Research and Eng 1976–81; Mil. Tech. Adviser to Pres. Clinton 1993; Deputy Sec. of Defense 1993–94, Sec. of Defense 1994–97; Sr Fellow, Stanford Univ. 1997–, now also Sr Fellow, Freeman Spogli Inst. for Int. Studies (FSI) and Michael and Barbara Berberian Prof. (FSI and School of Eng), Stanford Univ., also Co-Dir Preventive Defense Project; Chair. Global Tech. Pnrs; mem. Bd of Dirs United Techs Corpn, FMC Corpn, Sylvania/General Telephone's Electronic Defense Labs, Space Foundation, Thomas Jefferson Program in Public Policy, Concord Coalition, Strategic Partnerships LLC, Center for the Study of the Presidency; mem. Pres.'s Foreign Intelligence Advisory Bd, Sec. of State's Arms Control and Nonproliferation Advisory Bd, FBI Dir's Advisory Bd, Iraq Study Group, US Inst. of Peace 2006; fmr Chair. Bd of Visitors, US Naval Acad.; fmr Co-Chair. Pres. Comm. on Intelligence Capabilities of the US Regarding Weapons of Mass Destruction; mem. Nat. Acad. of Eng, NAS Cttee on Int. Security and Arms Control; Fellow, American Acad. of Arts and Sciences; Trustee MITRE Corpn, Carnegie Endowment for Int. Peace; fmr Fellow, Inst. of Politics, Harvard Univ., Marshall Wythe School of Law, Coll. of William and Mary; several nat. and int. honours including Outstanding Civilian Service Medals from the Army 1962, 1997, Air Force 1997, Navy (1997, Defense Intelligence Agency 1977, 1997, NASA 1981, Coast Guard 1997; Dept of Defense Distinguished Service Medal 1980, 1981, American Electronic Asscn Medal of Achievement 1980, Forrestal Medal 1994, Henry Stimson Medal 1994, Arthur Bueche Medal 1996, Eisenhower Award 1996, Marshall Award 1997, Presidential Medal of Freedom 1997. *Address:* CISAC, Encina Hall, Stanford University, Stanford, CA 94305-6165, USA (office). *Telephone:* (650) 725-6501 (office). *Fax:* (650) 725-0920 (office). *E-mail:* dcgordon@stanford.edu (office). *Website:* cisac.stanford.edu (office).

PERSAD-BISSESSAR, Kamla, BA, LLB, MBA; Trinidad and Tobago lawyer, academic and politician; *Prime Minister;* b. 22 April 1952, Penal; m. Dr Gregory Bissessar; one s.; ed Univ. of the West Indies, Norwood Technical Coll., UK, Hugh Wooding Law School, Arthur Lok Jack Grad. School of Business; fmr Social Worker for Church of England Children's Soc., London; taught at St Andrew High School, Jamaica and St Augustine campus of Univ. of the West Indies; fmr Consultant Lecturer, Jamaica Coll. of Insurance; fmr Lecturer, Tertiary Educ.

Inst.; Alderman, St Patrick Co. Council 1987–91; mem. Parl. 1995–; Attorney Gen. and Minister of Legal Affairs 1995–96, Oct.–Dec. 2001; Minister of Legal Affairs 1996–99; Minister of Education 1999–2001; Leader of the Opposition 2006–07, Feb.–May 2010, Prime Minister 2010–; Commonwealth Chair.-in-Office 2010–; fmr Sec. and Vice-Chair. Nat. Org. for Women; Hon. Prof. (China Agricultural Univ.) 2014; *Democracy Medal* 2013. *Leisure interests:* reading, walking. *Address:* Office of the Prime Minister, 13-15 Saint Clair Avenue, Saint Clair, Trinidad and Tobago (office). *Telephone:* 622-1625 (office). *Fax:* 622-2241 (office). *E-mail:* opm@ ttgov.gov (office). *Website:* www.ttparliament.org (office).

PERSEKIAN, Jack; Palestinian art foundation director, gallery curator and producer; *Director, Sharjah Art Foundation;* b. Jerusalem; Founding Dir Anadiel Gallery, Al-Ma'mal Foundation for Contemporary Art, Jerusalem, XEIN Productions; Chief Curator 7th Sharjah Biennial, Sharjah, UAE 2005, Artistic Dir 8th Sharjah Biennial 2007, 9th Sharjah Biennial 2009; Dir Sharjah Art Foundation 2009–. *Films:* several short films and video works. *Address:* Sharjah Art Museum, Arts Area, PO Box 19989, Sharjah, United Arab Emirates (office). *Telephone:* (6) 568-5050 (office). *Fax:* (6) 568-5800 (office). *E-mail:* info@sharjahart.org (office). *Website:* www.sharjahart.org (office).

PERSSON, (Carl) Stefan (Erling); Swedish retail executive; *Chairman, H&M Hennes & Mauritz AB;* b. 4 Oct. 1947, Stockholm; s. of the late Erling Persson; m. Carolyn Denise Persson; three c.; ed Univs of Stockholm and Lund; started working for family-controlled H&M Hennes & Mauritz AB 1967, Country Man. for H&M in UK and responsible for H&M's expansion abroad 1967–82, Man. Dir and CEO 1982–98, Chair. (succeeded on death of his father) 1998–; owns substantial stake in Swedish tech. co., Hexagon AB; owns properties in London, Paris and Stockholm; acquired 21-cottage village of Linkenholt, Hants., UK 2009; Deputy Bd of Dirs Stockholm School of Econs; mem. Bd of Dirs AB Electrolux, Investor AB, Atlas Copco, ABB, Ingka Holding, Mentor Foundation (founder), Stockholm School of Entrepreneurship. *Leisure interests:* downhill skiing, tennis, golf. *Address:* H&M Hennes & Mauritz AB, Mäster Samuelsgatan 46A, 106 38 Stockholm, Sweden (office). *Telephone:* (8) 796-55-00 (office). *Fax:* (8) 796-57-03 (office). *E-mail:* info@hm.com (office). *Website:* www.hm.com (office); about.hm.com/en/About.html (office).

PERSSON, Göran; Swedish politician; b. 20 Jan. 1949, Vingaker; m. Gunnel Persson (divorced); two c.; m. Anitra Steen; ed Orebro Univ.; Org. Sec. Swedish Social Democratic Youth League Sörmland 1971; Studies Sec. Workers' Educ. Asscn Sörmland, 1974–76; Chair. Katrineholm Educ. Authority 1977–79; mem. Parl. 1979–84; Councillor, Chair. Municipal Exec. Bd Katrineholm 1985–89; Minister with special responsibility for schools and adult educ., Ministry of Educ. and Cultural Affairs 1989–91, of Finance 1994–96; Prime Minister of Sweden 1996–2006; Chair. Sveriges Socialdemokratiska Arbetareparti (SAP) (Swedish Social Democratic Party) 1996–2007; Vice-Chair. Bd Oppunda Savings Bank 1976–89, Nordic Museum 1983–89; Chair. Sörmland Co-operative Consumers' Asscn 1976–89; Chair. Sörmland Co. Bd of Educ. 1982–89; Nat. Auditor, Swedish Co-operative Wholesale Soc. 1988–89. *Address:* c/o Sveriges Socialdemokratiska Arbetareparti (SAP) (Swedish Social Democratic Party), Sveavägen 68, 105 60 Stockholm, Sweden. *Telephone:* (8) 700-26-00. *Fax:* (8) 21-93-31. *E-mail:* info@sap .se. *Website:* www.socialdemokraterna.se.

PERSSON, Jörgen; Swedish director of photography; b. 10 Sept. 1936, Helsingborg; s. of Erik W. Persson and Thyra Liljeroth; m. Anne von Sydow 1969; two s.; ed High School and Swedish Film School; Dir of Photography (Features) 1965–; Felix Award, Paris 1989, several Swedish and Danish awards. *Films include:* Elvira Madigan 1967, Adalen-31 1969, My Life as a Dog 1986, Pelle the Conqueror 1988, Best Intentions 1991, Sofi 1991, Young Indy, The House of the Spirits 1993, Jerusalem 1995, Smilla's Sense of Snow 1996, Digging to China 1996, Les Misérables 1997, Faithless 2000, A Song for Martin 2001, Wolf 2008. *Leisure interests:* off-road sport, classic cars. *Address:* Rydbolundsvagen 7, 18531 Vaxholm, Sweden.

PERSSON, Olof, BSc; Swedish business executive; *President and CEO, Volvo Group;* b. 1964; m.; three c.; ed Karlstad Univ.; began career at ABB, held several exec. positions at AdTranz and Bombardier, including Pres., Mainline and Metros Div. 2004–06; mem. Group Exec. Cttee AB Volvo and Pres. Volvo Aero 2006–08, Pres. Volvo Construction Equipment 2008–11, Exec. Vice-Pres. AB Volvo and Deputy CEO May–Aug. 2011, mem. Bd of Dirs, Pres. AB Volvo and CEO Volvo Group 2011–; Chair. German-Swedish Chamber of Commerce; mem. Confed. of Swedish Enterprise, Swedish-American Chamber of Commerce. *Address:* AB Volvo, 405 08 Göteborg, Sweden (office). *Telephone:* (31) 66-00-90 (office). *Fax:* (31) 54-33-72 (office). *E-mail:* olof.persson@volvo.com. *Website:* www.volvogroup.com (office); www.volvo.com (office).

PERT, Geoffrey (Geoff) James, PhD, FRS, FInstP, CPhys; British physicist and academic; *Professor of Physics, University of York;* b. 15 Aug. 1941, Market Harborough, Leics., England; s. of Norman James Pert and Grace W. Pert; m. Janice Ann Alexander 1967; one d.; ed Norwich School, Imperial Coll., Univ. of London; Asst Prof., Univ. of Alberta 1967–70; Lecturer, Univ. of Hull 1970–76, Sr Lecturer, Reader 1976–82, Prof. 1982–87; Prof. of Physics, Univ. of York 1987–. *Publications:* numerous scientific papers. *Leisure interests:* hill-walking, gardening. *Address:* Department of Physics, University of York, Heslington, York, YO10 5DD, England (office). *Telephone:* (1904) 324910 (office). *Fax:* (1904) 432214 (office). *E-mail:* gjp1@york.ac.uk (office). *Website:* www.york.ac.uk/depts/phys (office).

PERTHES, Volker; German political scientist and research institute director; *Director, Stiftung Wissenschaft und Politik (German Institute for International and Security Affairs);* b. 16 May 1958, Homberg/Niederrhein; ed Duisburg Univ.; fmr mem. Faculty, Univs of Duisburg, Munich and Münster; fmr Adjunct Prof., Humboldt Univ.; Asst Prof., American Univ. of Beirut 1991–93; Sr Research Assoc., Stiftung Wissenschaft und Politik (German Inst. for Int. and Security Affairs) and Head of Middle East and Africa Div. 1992–2005, Dir and Exec. Chair. 2005; mem. Trilateral Comm., Int. Spectator, Rome; mem. Advisory Bd, Shanghai Inst. for Int. Studies Studies, Finnish Inst. of Int. Affairs (Chair.), Hellenic Foundation for European and Foreign Policy (ELIAMEP); Verdienstkreuz am Bande der Bundesrepublik Deutschland 2011; Hon. Prof., Free Univ. of Berlin, Humboldt Univ., Berlin. *Publications include:* The Political Economy of Syria

under Assad 1995, Arab Elites: Negotiating the Politics of Change 2004, Orientalische Promenaden: Der Nahe und Mittlere Osten im Umbruch 2006, Of Trust and Security: The Challenge of Iran, a Report to the Trilateral Commission 2008, Iran – Eine politische Herausforderung 2008, Iran – Eine politische Herausforderung 2008, Der Aufstand: Die arabische Revolution und ihre Folgen 2011; numerous research papers and articles. *Address:* Stiftung Wissenschaft und Politik, Ludwigkirchplatz 3–4, 10719 Berlin, Germany (office). *Telephone:* (30) 88007-101 (office); (30) 88007-102 (office). *Fax:* (30) 88007-100 (office). *E-mail:* swp@swp-berlin.org (office); volker.perthes@swp-berlin.org (office). *Website:* www .swp-berlin.org (office).

PERUASHEV, Azat, PhD; Kazakhstani politician; *Leader, Bright Road Democratic Party of Kazakhstan (Ak Jol);* b. 8 Sept. 1967, Rgayty village, Zhambyl (now Taraz) Oblast, Kazakh SSR, USSR; ed Maxim Gorky Ural State Univ., Higher School of Public Admin, Zhetysu Econ. Inst.; worked in various management positions, including in Panfilov Dist Cttee of the party 1991–92, in Taldy-Kurgan Oblast Admin 1992–95, as a consultant and div. man. in Office of Pres. of Kazakhstan 1996–98; Deputy Gen. Dir JSC Aluminium of Kazakhstan 1998–2000, Vice-Pres. 2001–05; First Sec. Cen. Cttee, Civil Party of Kazakhstan 1999–2006, party merged with Otan party 2006, Deputy Chair. Nur Otan party 2006–07, left the party 2011; Chair. 'Atameken' Union of Entrepreneurs and Employers of Kazakhstan 2006–07, Chair. 'Atameken' Union Nat. Chamber of Economy of Kazakhstan 2007–11; mem. Pres.'s Council of Entrepreneurs 2007–11; also acted as an int. election observer and was a mem. of the State Comm. on Democratization under the Pres. of Kazakhstan; Leader, Bright Road Democratic Party of Kazakhstan (Ak Jol) (Kazakstannyn 'Ak Jol' Demokratiyalyk Partiyasy) 2011–; Deputy of the Majlis (Parl.) 2012–; Hon. Prof., South Kazakhstan State Univ. named after M. Auezova, East Kazakhstan State Univ. named after S. Amanzholov, Taldy-Kurgan Inst. of Economy; 'Dostyk' Medal (II Degree), Russian Medal of Community, 'Barys' Medal (III Degree); Young Researchers' Award of Cultural Initiative, Soviet-American Fund, Moscow 1991. *Address:* Bright Road Democratic Party of Kazakhstan (Ak Jol), 010000 Astana, Kazakhstan (office). *Telephone:* (7172) 20-05-85 (office). *Fax:* (7172) 21-37-50 (office). *E-mail:* akzholpress@mail.ru (office). *Website:* www.akzhol.kz (office).

PERVAIZ, Ansar, BSc, MSc, PhD; Pakistani nuclear scientist, educationalist and administrator; *Chairman, Pakistan Atomic Energy Commission;* b. Lahore, British India (now in Pakistan); ed Punjab Univ., Quaid-e-Azam Univ., Islamabad, Rensselaer Polytechnic Inst., USA; joined Pakistan Atomic Energy Comm. (PAEC) late 1960s, was put in charge of nuclear tech. labs, promoted to Jr Scientific Prin. Officer 1986, formed nuclear safety group, later transferred to Karachi nuclear power plant and apptd Head of Nuclear Safety Dept, also est. food processing and agricultural eng labs, apptd Project Dir of nuclear power plant March 2009, Chair. PAEC April 2009–; Visiting Asst Prof. of both Nuclear Physics and Nuclear Tech., Purdue Univ., West Lafayette, Ind., USA 1982–84; Hilal-i-Imtiaz 1998. *Publications:* numerous scientific papers in int. journals and proceedings. *Address:* Pakistan Atomic Energy Commission, POB 1114, Islamabad, Pakistan (office). *Telephone:* (51) 9209032 (office). *Fax:* (51) 9204908 (office). *E-mail:* feedback@paec .gov.pk (office). *Website:* www.paec.gov.pk (office).

PERVYSHIN, Erlen Kirikovich; Russian industrial manager; b. 25 June 1932, Russia; ed Moscow Electrotechnical Inst. of Communications; mem. Int. Engineer Acad.; engineer 1955–, then Head of Ass. Section, Deputy Chief Engineer, Head of Admin., Manager of Design and Ass. Trust, Dir-Gen. All-Union Scientific production Asscn; Deputy USSR Minister of Radio Industry 1970–74, Minister of Communications Equipment Mfg 1974–89, of Communications 1989–91; Chair. Telecom (now Meltelecom Corpn) 1991–; Pres. ORB & TEL Co., Andrew Int. Corpn 1997–; Pres. Mirtelecom Asscn 1999–. *Address:* Mirtelecom, Gubkina str. 8, Moscow 17966, Russia. *Telephone:* (495) 748-00-01. *Fax:* (495) 748-00-02.

PESÁNTEZ BENÍTEZ, Johana Farina, DJur, PhD; Ecuadorean lawyer, academic and politician; *Minister of Justice, Human Rights and Worship;* b. 20 Nov. 1975, Quito; m. Jaime Xavier Cazar Valencia; ed Pontificia Universidad Católica del Ecuador, Universidad Pablo de Olavide, Seville, Spain; served in several positions in legal practice, including as Research Asst responsible for monitoring processes in Supreme Court; fmr Legal Co-ordinator, Nat. Court of Justice; fmr Lecturer, Universidad Católica, Universidad de las Americas, Universidad Tecnológica Indoamérica de Ambato, Universidad Técnica Particular de Loja; consultant on issues of justice to Pres. of Ecuador; Minister of Justice, Human Rights and Worship 2011–. *Publications include:* several works of legal analysis. *Address:* Ministry of Justice, Human Rights and Worship, Avda Amazonas N34-451 y Atahualpa, Quito, Ecuador (office). *Telephone:* (2) 246-3083 (office). *Fax:* (2) 246-4914 (office). *E-mail:* webmaster@minjusticia-ddhh.gov.ec (office). *Website:* www.minjusticia-ddhh.gov.ec (office).

PESCI, Joe; American film actor; b. 9 Feb. 1943, Newark, NJ. *Films include:* Death Collector 1976, Raging Bull 1980, I'm Dancing as Fast as I Can 1982, Easy Money 1983, Dear Mr Wonderful 1983, Eureka 1983, Once Upon a Time in America 1984, Tutti Dentro 1984, Man On Fire 1987, Moonwalker 1988, Backtrack 1988, Lethal Weapon 2 1989, Betsy's Wedding 1990, Goodfellas (Acad. Award for Best Supporting Actor) 1991, Home Alone 1990, The Super 1991, JFK 1991, Lethal Weapon 3 1992, Home Alone II 1992, The Public Eye 1992, My Cousin Vinny 1992, A Bronx Tale 1993, With Honours 1993, Jimmy Hollywood 1994, Casino 1995, 8 Heads in a Duffel Bag 1997, Gone Fishing 1997, Lethal Weapon 4 1998, The Good Shepherd 2006, Love Ranch 2010. *Address:* c/o Fred Specktor, Creative Artists Agency, Inc., 9830 Wilshire Blvd, Beverly Hills, CA 90212-1825, USA.

PESCUCCI, Gabriella; Italian costume designer; b. 1941, Castiglioncello, Tuscany; ed Accademia di Belle Arti, Florence; worked as Asst to Piero Tosi on set of Luchino Visconti's films Death in Venice and Ludwig; solo debut designing costumes for Charlotte Rampling in Italian film adaptation of 'Tis Pity She's a Whore 1971; designed costumes for Maria Callas in Medea, for Sean Connery in The Name of the Rose, Montserrat Caballé in Norma at La Scala, Milan; two Donatello Davids from Italian Acad. of Cinema and two BAFTA Awards. *Films as costume designer include:* I Sette fratelli Cervi 1967, Uomini contro 1970, Addio, fratello crudele 1971, Fatti di gente per bene 1974, Identikit 1974, Divina creatura 1976, L' Eredità Ferramonti 1976, Prova d'orchestra 1978, La Città delle donne 1980, Tre fratelli 1981, Passione d'amore 1981, La Nuit de Varennes 1982, Once

Upon a Time in America 1984, Il Trovatore 1985, Orfeo 1985, The Name of the Rose 1986, La Famiglia 1987, The Adventures of Baron Munchausen 1988, Haunted Summer 1988, Splendor 1989, Che ora è? 1989, Indochine 1992, Per amore, solo per amore 1993, The Age of Innocence (Acad. Award for Best Costume Design 1994) 1993, The Scarlet Letter 1995, Albergo Roma 1996, Dangerous Beauty 1998, Les Misérables 1998, Cousin Bette 1998, Le Temps retrouvé 1999, A Midsummer Night's Dream 1999, Perduto amor 2003, Secret Passage 2004, Van Helsing 2004, Charlie and the Chocolate Factory 2005, The Brothers Grimm 2005, Beowulf 2007, Agora 2009, The First Beautiful Thing 2010, The Jewel 2011.

PEŠEK, Libor; Czech conductor; *Chief Conductor, Czech National Symphony Orchestra;* b. 22 June 1933, Prague; ed Prague Acad. of Musical Arts; studied conducting with Karel Ancerl, Vaclav Neumann and Václav Smetáček; f. Prague Chamber Harmony 1958; Chief Conductor Slovak Philharmonic 1980–81; Conductor-in-Residence Czech Philharmonic Orchestra 1982–90, Germany tour 1998; Prin. Conductor and Artistic Adviser Royal Liverpool Philharmonic Orchestra 1982–97, Hon. Conductor 1997–; Visiting Conductor Prague Symphony Orchestra 1989–; Pres. Prague Spring Festival 1994–; Chief Conductor, Czech Nat. Symphony Orchestra 2007–; mem. Bd of Supervisors OPS Prague European City of Culture 1999–; conducted Royal Liverpool Philharmonic Orchestra, Prague Spring Festival 2000; has conducted Philharmonia, London Symphony, Royal Philharmonic, BBC Philharmonic, Hallé, Oslo Philharmonic, Danish Radio, Los Angeles Philharmonic and Cincinnati, Dallas, Minnesota, Pittsburgh, Cleveland, Montreal, Indianapolis and Philadelphia orchestras, Orchestra of La Scala, Milan and Orchestre de Paris; charity concerts after floods in Czech Repub. 2002; Hon. mem. Preston Univ. 1997; Hon. Fellow, Univ. of Cen. Lancashire 1997; Hon. KBE; Classic Prize for Extraordinary Merit in Musical Culture (Czech Repub.) 1997, Journal Harmonie Lifelong Contrib. to Czech Culture 2002. *Recordings include:* works by Dvořák, Suk, Janáček, Martinů and Britten. *Leisure interests:* physics, Eastern philosophy, literature. *Address:* IMG Artists, The Light Box, 111 Power Road, London, W4 5PY, England (office). *Telephone:* (20) 7957-5800 (office). *Fax:* (20) 7957-5801 (office). *E-mail:* ajamieson@imgartists.com (office). *Website:* www .imgartists.com (office).

PEŠEVSKI, Vladimir, BSc, MBA; Macedonian politician, electrical engineer and business executive; *Deputy Prime Minister, responsible for Economic Affairs;* b. 19 June 1970; m.; three c.; ed SS Cyril and Methodius Univ., Skopje, Univ. of Sheffield, UK; served as CEO of publishing co. that publishes Dnevnik newspaper; Research Asst, Macedonian Inst. for Energy and Computer Science 1993–95; worked as consultant providing gen. man. and financial consulting services to medium and large Macedonian cos, Macedonian Business Resource Centre (USAID-funded project) 1995–98; joined Small Enterprise Assistance Funds (SEAF) South Balkan LLC (US-based pvt. equity investment fund) 1998, Deputy Dir Gen. SEAF Macedonia 2000, Dir Gen. SEAF South Balkan LLC 2000–, Dir in first AmCham Bd in Macedonia 2001; mem. bd of dirs of several cos and regional think-thanks, including Nat. Entrepreneurship and Competitiveness Council, First Bd of Dirs American Chamber of Commerce in Macedonia; Lecturer in MA Studies, Univ. of Sheffield (Program on Strategic Man., City Coll., Thessaloniki); advised Pres. of Macedonia on econ. policies for small and medium enterprises in the troubled regions 2001; Deputy Prime Minister, responsible for Econ. Affairs 2009–; Alt. Gov., EBRD, London. *Address:* Office of the Prime Minister, Ilindenska bb, 1000 Skopje, Former Yugoslav Republic of Macedonia (office). *Telephone:* (2) 3118022 (office); (2) 3115455 (office). *Fax:* (2) 3112561 (office). *E-mail:* primeminister@primeminister.gov.mk (office). *Website:* www.vlada.mk (office).

PESIĆ, Dragiša, MSc(Econ); Montenegrin fmr head of state and business executive; b. 8 Aug. 1954, Danilovgrad; s. of Lazar Pesić and Andja Pesić; m. Lela Savović; one s. one d.; ed Sarajevo Univ.; worked as financial expert; fmr Chair. Exec. Bd Municipal Ass. of Podgorica (twice); Deputy to Fed. Ass., Chair. Budget Cttee, Chamber of Citizens; Minister of Finance 1998–2001; Prime Minister of Serbia and Montenegro (fmr Fed. Repub. of Yugoslavia) 2001–03, Pres. 2003–04; mem. Socialist Nat. Party of Montenegro. *Leisure interests:* music, literature, sports. *Address:* c/o Office of the Federal Government, Belgrade, Serbia (office).

PEŠIĆ, Vesna, BA, MA, PhD; Serbian sociologist, lawyer, diplomatist and politician; b. 6 May 1940, Groska; m.; one s.; ed Univ. of Belgrade; mem. staff, Inst. of Social Sciences 1964–72; Sr Researcher, Inst. of Social Policy 1972–78; Prof., Higher School for Social Workers 1978–91; Sr Researcher, Inst. of Philosophy and Social Theory, Belgrade 1991–2001; Co-f. Union for Yugoslavian Democratic Initiative (IZDI) 1991, Helsinki Cttee for Serbia, Belgrade 1985; Founder and Pres. Center of Peace and Democracy Devt (fmrly Cen. for Antiwar Action); mem. Cttee for Freedom of Speech and Self-Expression; fmr Pres. Civil Alliance of Serbia (now merged into Liberal Democratic Party), currently Pres. Political Council of Liberal Democratic Party; Amb. to Mexico 2001–05; mem. Narodna skupština (Parl.) 1993–97, 2007–12; Int. Policy Fellowship 2006–07; Award for Democracy Nat. Foundation of Democracy, Washington, DC 1993, Andrej Sakharov Freedom Price, Norwegian Sakharov Freedom Fund 1997, W. Averell Harriman Democracy Award, Nat. Democratic Inst. 1997. *Publications include:* Social Traditions and Style of Life 1977, Social Deviations: Criticism of Social Pathology (with I. Jancović) 1981, Ethnomethodology and Sociology 1985, Brief Course of Equality 1988, Theory of Changes and Parsons Concept of Contemporary Soc. 1990, Yugoslavian Military Crisis and World Movement 1992, Nationalism, War and Disintegration of Communist Federation 1993; articles in scientific journals and periodicals.

PESONEN, Jussi, MSc; Finnish paper industry executive; *President and CEO, UPM-Kymmene Corporation;* b. 24 Nov. 1960, Helsinki; ed Univ. of Oulu; joined UPM 1987, various positions including Production Man. Jämsänkoski Mill, Production Unit Dir Kajaani, Kaukas and Shotton Mills, Vice-Pres. Newsprint Product Group, Publ. Papers Div. 2001, Group Sr Exec. Vice-Pres. and COO 2001–04, Pres. and CEO 2004–; Chair. Ilmarinen Mutual Pension Insurance Co. 2012–; mem. Bd of Dirs Outokumpu Ltd 2009–12; mem. Bd, Confed. of European Paper Industries 2004– (Chair. 2012–), mem. Exec. Cttee 2006–), Asscn of European Publ. Paper Producers, Finnish Forest Industries Fed. 2003– (Deputy Chair. 2005, 2009–11, Chair. 2006–08, mem. Exec. Cttee 2004–07), East Office of Finnish Industries Oy; Co-Chair. Forest Solutions Group, World Business Council for Sustainable Devt. *Address:* UPM, Alvar Aallon katu 1, PO Box 380, 00101

Helsinki, Finland (office). *Telephone:* (8) 204-15-111 (office). *Fax:* (8) 204-15-110 (office). *E-mail:* jussi.pesonen@upm.com (office). *Website:* www.upm.com (office).

PESSINA, Stefano; Italian engineer and pharmaceutical industry executive; *Executive Chairman, Alliance Boots plc;* m.; two c.; ed Univ. of Milan; trained as nuclear engineer; fmr Lecturer, Univ. of Milan; Consultant, AC Nielsen 1973–76; f. Gruppo Alliance Santé 1977 (merged with UniChem PLC to form Alliance UniChem Plc 1997), apptd to Bd 1997, Exec. Deputy Chair. 2004–06 (merged with Boots PLC to form Alliance Boots plc), Exec. Deputy Chair. 2006–07, Exec. Chair. 2007–; Dir (non-exec.) Galenica, Walgreen Co. 2012–; mem. Council Int. Fed. of Pharmaceutical Wholesalers (IFPW) 1999–, Chair. 2000–02. *Leisure interest:* yachting. *Address:* Alliance Boots plc, 4th Floor, Sedley Place, 361 Oxford Street, London, W1C 2JL, England (office); Alliance Boots GmbH, Baarerstrasse 78, 6300 Zug, Switzerland (office). *Telephone:* (115) 950-6111 (Nottingham) (office). *Fax:* (20) 7491-0149 (London) (office). *E-mail:* enquiries@allianceboots.com (office). *Website:* www.allianceboots.com (office).

PESSOA PEREIRA DA SILVA PINTO, Ana Maria; Timor-Leste politician; *Prosecutor General;* m. José Ramos-Horta (divorced); one s.; mem. Nat. Political Comm. of Timorese Resistance 1998–2000; mem. Transitional Cabinet for Internal Admin 2000–01; Minister of Justice 2001–03; Deputy Prime Minister and Minister of State and Minister of the Presidency of the Council of Ministers 2003–05; Minister for State and Internal Admin 2005–07, Sr Minister of State 2006; unsuccessful cand. for Prime Minister 2006; mem. Nat. Parl. 2007–; Prosecutor Gen. 2009–; mem. FRETILIN (Frente Revolucionaria do Timor-Leste Independente). *Address:* Ministry of Justice, Av. Jacinto Candido, Dili, Timor-Leste (office). *Telephone:* 3331160 (office). *E-mail:* mj@mj.gov.tl (office). *Website:* www.mj .gov.tl (office).

PESTANA NETO, Enéas César; Brazilian business executive; b. 27 Feb. 1963; ed Pontificia Universidade Católica de São Paulo; worked at GP Investimentos and Carrefour; fmr Vice-Pres., Diagnostics, America SA– Laboratory Delboni Auriemo; Chief Financial Officer, Grupo Pão de Açúcar (trading name of Companhia Brasileira de Distribuição) for seven years, CEO 2012–14.

PESTER, Paul, DPhil; British business executive; *CEO, TSB Bank plc;* ed Univs of Manchester and Oxford; spent ten years in management consultancy, mostly at McKinsey & Co.; Group CEO Virgin Money 2000–05; Man. Dir Consumer Banking, Lloyds TSB 2005–08; joined Santander UK 2008, led acquisition of Bradford & Bingley and subsequent integration of Abbey, Alliance & Leicester and Bradford & Bingley; Man. Dir of Consumer Banking and Payments, Lloyds Banking Group 2010–11, CEO Verde programme 2011–13, led development and establishment of new TSB Bank within Lloyds Banking Group; CEO TSB Bank plc 2013–. *Address:* TSB Bank plc, Henry Duncan House, 120 George Street, Edinburgh, EH2 4LH, Scotland (office). *E-mail:* info@tsb.co.uk (office). *Website:* www.tsb.co.uk (office).

PESTILLO, Peter J., BEcons, LLB; American automotive executive; b. 22 March 1938, Bristol, Conn.; ed Fairfield Univ., Georgetown Univ., Harvard Business School Advanced Management Program; admitted to Bar, Washington, DC; began career in industrial relations, General Electric (GE) Co.; Vice-Pres. Corp. and Employee Relations, B.F. Goodrich –1980; Vice-Pres. Labour Relations Ford Motor Co. 1980–85, Vice-Pres. Employee Relations 1985–86, Vice-Pres. Employee Relations and External Affairs 1986–90, Vice-Pres. Corp. Relations and Diversified Businesses 1990–93, apptd Exec. Vice-Pres. Corp. Relations 1993, Vice-Chair. and Chief of Staff –1999; Chair. and CEO Visteon (following spin-off from Ford Motor Co.) 2000–04, Chair. 2004–05; mem. Bd of Dirs Rouge Industries, Mich. Mfrs Asscn, Nat. Asscn of Mfrs and Sentry Insurance; Hon. Chair. Motorsports Hall of Fame of America 2001.

PESTKA, Sidney, BA, MD; American (b. Polish) molecular geneticist and academic; *Chairman and Professor, Department of Molecular Genetics, Microbiology and Immunology, Robert Wood Johnson Medical School, University of Medicine and Dentistry of New Jersey;* b. 1936; ed Princeton Univ., Univ. of Pennsylvania School of Medicine; worked as intern in medicine and paediatrics; worked at NIH, later at NIH Nat. Cancer Inst. 1966–69; mem. staff, Roche Inst. of Molecular Biology, Nutley, New Jersey 1969; currently Chair. and Prof., Dept of Molecular Genetics, Microbiology and Immunology, Robert Wood Johnson Medical School, Univ. of Medicine and Dentistry of New Jersey; Founder and Chief Scientific Officer, Pestka Biomedical Laboratories (PBL) 1990; Sec. Int. Soc. for Interferon and Cytokine Research 1989–93, 1996–2005, Vice-Pres. 1992–93, Pres. 1994–95; known as the "father of interferon" for work developing antiviral treatments for chronic hepatitis B and C, multiple sclerosis and cancers; Hon. DSc (Rider Univ.) 1987; Mayer Lecturer in the Life Sciences, MIT 1986, Nat. Medal of Tech., Pres. George W. Bush 2001, Warren Alpert Foundation Prize, Harvard Univ. 2004, Lemelson-MIT Lifetime Achievement Award 2006. *Publications include:* more than 270 US and foreign patents; ed five books; more than 400 papers on protein biosynthesis and interferons. *Address:* Department of Molecular Genetics, Microbiology and Immunology, Robert Wood Johnson Medical School, University of Medicine and Dentistry of New Jersey, RWJMS 736, 675 Hoes Lane, Piscataway, NJ 08854-5635, USA (office). *Telephone:* (732) 235-4567 (office). *Fax:* (732) 235-5223 (office). *E-mail:* pestka@rwjms.rutgers.edu (office). *Website:* www2 .umdnj.edu/mgenmweb (office).

PESTON, Robert James Kenneth; British journalist and broadcaster; *Economics Editor, BBC News;* b. 24 April 1960, London; s. of Maurice Peston and Helen Peston (née Conroy); m. Siân Busby (died 2012); one s. one step-s.; ed Balliol Coll., Oxford, Université Libre de Bruxelles, Belgium; began career as stockbroker with Williams de Broë; journalist, Investors Chronicle 1983; City Corresp., The Independent 1986–89; Deputy City Ed., Sunday Correspondent 1989–90; City Ed., Independent on Sunday 1990–91; Banking Ed., Financial Times 1991–93, Head of Investigations 1993–95, Political Ed. 1995–2000, Financial Ed. 2000; Editorial Dir, Collins Stewart Quest 2001–05; columnist, Daily Telegraph 2001; Assoc. Ed., The Spectator 2001; Business Columnist, New Statesman and Sunday Times 2002; City Ed. and Asst Ed., Sunday Telegraph 2002–06; Business Ed., BBC News 2006–13, Econs Ed. 2013–; f. Speakers for Schools (educ. charity); Fellow, Aberystwyth Univ. 2011; Hon. DLitt (Heriot-Watt) 2010; numerous awards including What The Papers Say Investigative Journalist of the Year 1994, Wincott Sr Financial Journalist of the Year 2005, London Press Club Scoop of the Year

2007, Business Journalism Awards Journalist of the Year 2007/08, Royal TV Soc. Journalism Awards TV Journalist of the Year, Specialist Journalist of the Year and Scoop of the Year 2008, Harold Wincott Awards Broadcaster of the Year and Online Media Award 2008, London Press Club Awards Business Journalist of the Year 2009, Political Studies Asscn Political Journalist of the Year 2009, Press Gazette Business Journalist of the Year 2009, Foreign Press Asscn Award Financial/Economic Story of the Year 2012. *Publications include:* Brown's Britain 2005, Who Runs Britain? How the Super-Rich are Changing our Lives 2008, How Do We Fix This Mess? The Economic Price of Having it All and the Route to Lasting Prosperity 2012. *Address:* BBC News, BBC Broadcasting House, London, W1A 1AA, England (office). *Telephone:* (20) 8743-8000 (office). *Website:* www.bbc .co.uk/news (office).

PETERLE, Lojze; Slovenian politician; b. 5 July 1948, Čužnja Vas, Trebnje; ed Ljubljana Univ.; Researcher Urban Planning Inst. 1975–84; environmental protection adviser Social Planning Inst. 1985–89; mem. Nat. Ass. 1990–; Pres. Slovenian Christian Democrats (SKD) 1989–2000 (merged to form Slovenian People's Party 2000); Prime Minister of Slovenia 1990–92; Minister of Foreign Affairs 1993–94, 2000; Chair. Parl. Cttee on European Affairs 1997–; First Vice-Pres. European Union of Christian Democrats 1996–99; Observer European Parl. 2003–04, mem. European Parl. 2004–, mem. Cttee on Foreign Affairs, Subcttee on Human Rights, delegation for relations with countries of Southeast Asia and ASEAN; unsuccessful cand. of Pres. of Slovenia 2007; mem. Praesidium of the Convention on the Future of Europe 2002–03; Vice-Pres. Union of European Federalists 2004–; mem. State Legis. Leaders Foundation 1989; Kt Grand Cross, Papal Order 1993. *Address:* Cankarjeva 11, 1000 Ljubljana, Slovenia; European Parliament, Bât. Altiero Spinelli, 05F366 60, rue Wiertz 60, 1047 Brussels, Belgium (office). *Telephone:* (1) 4223585; (2) 2845638 (Brussels) (office). *Fax:* (1) 4261092; (2) 2849638 (Brussels) (office). *E-mail:* press@peterle.si; alojz.peterle@ europarl.europa.eu (office). *Website:* www.peterle.si.

PETERS, Janis; Latvian writer, poet, essayist, publicist and fmr diplomatist; b. 30 June 1939, Liepāja Region; s. of Janis Peters and Zelma Peters; m. Baiba Kalniņa 1969; one s.; ed Rīga 25 secondary school; started as journalist in Latvian newspapers, later freelance; Chair. Bd of Latvian Writers' Union 1985–89; led historic Latvian Writers' Union conf. against censorship and for freedom of speech 1st and 2nd June 1988; participant democratic movt for independence; Chair. Org. Cttee People's Front of Latvia 1988; signed petition to Pres. of Communist Czechoslovakia to free dissident Vaclav Havel in Copenhagen (with Danish PEN Club members) 1990; USSR People's Deputy 1989–90; Perm. Rep. of Council of Ministers of Latvia to Russia 1990–91, then first Amb. of Repub. of Latvia to Russian Fed. after regaining independence 1992–97; mem. govt del. to negoti-ations with Russia, negotiations del. to Russian Fed. on withdrawal of Russian Fed. troops from Latvia 1992–94; Hon. mem. Latvian Acad. of Sciences 1990–, Latvian Univ. 1991–; Cavaliere di San Marco 1993, Order of Three Stars (Latvia), Order of the Dannebrog (Denmark), Order of Barricades (Latvia), Cross of Recognition (Latvia). *Publications:* more than 20 books of poetry, prose and essays in Latvian, Russian, English, Ukrainian; poems translated also into Lithuanian, Estonian, Finnish, Georgian, Spanish, Bulgarian, German, Danish, etc. *Leisure interests:* gardening, driving. *Address:* Vesetas Str. 8, Apt 12, 1013 Rīga, Latvia (home). *Telephone:* 6733-9350 (home). *E-mail:* peters@apollo.lv (office).

PETERS, Mary E., BA; American consultant and fmr government official; m. Terry Peters; three c.; ed Univ. of Phoenix; joined Ariz. Dept of Transportation 1985, served in several positions including Contract Admin., Deputy Dir for Admin, Deputy Dir –1998, Dir 1998–2001; US Fed. Highway Admin. 2001–05; Nat. Dir for Transportation Policy and Consulting, HDR, Inc., Phoenix 2005–06; US Sec. of Transportation 2006–09; f. Mary E Peters Consulting Group LLC 2009; fmr Chair. Standing Cttee on Planning and Asset Man. Task Force, American Asscn of State Highway Officials; Nat. Woman of the Year Award, Women's Transportation Seminar 2004, ARTBA Award, American Road and Transportation Builders Asscn 2005. *Address:* Mary E Peters Consulting Group LLC, 8323 West Via Montoya Drive, Peoria, AZ 85383, USA (office). *E-mail:* mary@marypetersconsulting.com (office). *Website:* www.marypetersconsulting.com (office).

PETERS, Wallace, MD, DSc, FRCP; British professor of parasitology; *Professor Emeritus of Medical Protozoology, London School of Hygiene and Tropical Medicine;* b. 1 April 1924, London, England; s. of Henry Peters and Fanny Peters; m. Ruth Scheidegger-Frehner 1954; ed Haberdashers Aske's Hampstead School, St Bartholomew's Hosp. Medical Coll., Univ. of London; Physician West and East Africa, including RAMC 1947–53; Scientist-Entomologist and Malarialogist, WHO, in Liberia and Nepal 1953–55; Malariologist, Territory of Papua and New Guinea 1956–61; Research Assoc., CIBA Pharmaceutical Co., Basel 1961–66; Prof. of Parasitology, Liverpool School of Tropical Medicine 1966–79, Dean 1975–78; Prof. of Medical Protozoology, London School of Hygiene and Tropical Medicine 1979–89, now Prof. Emer.; Hon. Consultant in Parasitology, Camden Area Health Authority 1978–89, on malariology, to Army 1986–89; Jt Dir Public Health Lab. Service Malaria Reference Centre 1979–89; Dir Centre for Tropical Antiprotozoal Chemotherapy, Northwick Park Inst. for Medical Research 1999–2004; Hon. Research Fellow Int. Inst. of Parasitology (IIP) (then CABI Bioscience) 1992–99; Pres. Royal Soc. of Tropical Medicine and Hygiene 1987–88 (Vice-Pres. 1982–83, 1985–87); mem. Expert Advisory Panel on Malaria of WHO 1967–2004; Hon. Fellow, Royal Soc. of Tropical Medicine and Hygiene; Hon. mem. American Soc. of Tropical Medicine and Parasitology; Dr hc (Univ. René Descartes, Paris) 1992; King Faisal Int. Prize, Medicine 1983, Rudolf Leuckart Medallist, German Soc. of Parasitology 1980, Le Prince Medallist, American Soc. of Tropical Medicine and Hygiene 1994, Emile Brumpt Prize, Société de Pathologie Exotique 1998. *Publications:* Checklist of Ethiopian Butterflies 1952, Chemotherapy and Drug Resistance in Malaria 1970 (revised edn 1987), Rodent Malaria (co-ed.) 1978, Atlas of Tropical Medicine and Parasitology (with H. M. Gilles) 1977 (sixth edn 2006), Colour Atlas of Tropical Medicine and Parasitology (co-ed.) 1981, Pharmacology of Antimalarials (two vols) (co-ed.) 1984, Leishmaniases in Biology and Medicine (co-ed.) 1987, Atlas of Arthropods in Clinical Medicine 1992, Tropical Medicine and Parasitology (with G. Pasvol) 2001, Four Passions: Conversations with Myself 2012. *Leisure interests:* photography, entomology, writing. *Address:* c/o Northwick Park Institute for Medical Research, Watford Road, HA1 3UJ, England (office).

Fax: (20) 8422-7136 (office); (144) 284-3044 (home). *E-mail:* wallacepeters2@aol .com (home); w.peters@imperial.ac.uk (office).

PETERS, Rt Hon Winston R.; New Zealand politician and lawyer; *Leader, New Zealand First Party;* b. 11 April 1945; MP for Tauranga; fmr Minister of Maori Affairs, Minister in charge of the Iwi Transition Agency, Chair. Cabinet Cttee on Treaty of Waitangi Issues 1990–91; independent MP 1993–, now New Zealand First Party; Leader New Zealand First Party 1993–; Deputy Prime Minister and Treas. 1996–98; Minister of Foreign Affairs and for Racing 2005–08. *Address:* New Zealand First Party, Parliament Buildings, Wellington, New Zealand (office). *Telephone:* (4) 471-9292 (office); (4) 471-9999 (office). *Fax:* (4) 472-8557 (office). *E-mail:* info@nzfirst.org.nz (office). *Website:* www.nzfirst.org.nz (office).

PETERSEN, George Bouet, MSc, MA, DPhil, DSc, FRSNZ; New Zealand scientist and academic; *Professor Emeritus of Biochemistry, University of Otago;* b. 5 Sept. 1933, Palmerston North; s. of George C. Petersen and Elizabeth S. Petersen; m. Patricia J.E. Caughey 1960; four d.; ed Univ. of Otago and Univ. of Oxford, England; scientist, Dept of Scientific and Industrial Research Plant Chem. Div., Palmerston North 1959–60, 1963–67; Departmental Demonstrator in Biochemistry, Univ. of Oxford 1961–63; Head of Dept of Biochemistry, Univ. of Otago 1968–91, Prof. of Biochemistry 1968–99, Prof. Emer. 1999–; Deputy Dean, Otago Medical School 1991–95; Pres. Acad. Council Royal Soc. of New Zealand 1997–2000; Visiting Research Fellow, Harvard Univ., USA 1964; Royal Soc. Commonwealth Bursar, MRC Lab. of Molecular Biology, Cambridge, UK 1973–74, 1981; Carnegie Corpn of New York Travel Grantee 1964; Officer, New Zealand Order of Merit 1997; Hon. DSc (Otago) 2000; Marsden Medal, New Zealand Assocn of Scientists 1995, Rutherford Medal, Royal Soc. of New Zealand 2003. *Publica-tions include:* numerous papers on aspects of nucleic acid chemistry and biochemistry in various scientific journals. *Leisure interests:* music, literature, book collecting. *Address:* Department of Biochemistry, School of Medical Sciences, University of Otago, PO Box 56, Dunedin, New Zealand (office). *Telephone:* (3) 477-0784 (home). *Fax:* (3) 479-7866 (office). *E-mail:* george.petersen@otago.ac.nz (office). *Website:* biochem.otago.ac.nz (office).

PETERSEN, Jan, LLB; Norwegian politician and diplomatist; *Ambassador to Austria;* b. 11 June 1946, Oslo; s. of Kaare Petersen and Elsa Olsen; m. Gerda Mollatt Petersen; two c.; with Norwegian Consumers' Asscn 1974, Norwegian Agency for Devt Co-operation (NORAD) 1975–78; Chair. Unge Høyre (Young Conservatives) 1971–73; Mayor of Oppegård 1976–81; mem. Stortinget (Parl.) for Akershus constituency 1981–2009, mem. Standing Cttee on Local Govt and Environment 1981–84, Standing Cttee on Foreign Affairs 1984–2009 (Chair. 1985–86); Leader Akershus Conservative Party 1992–94, Conservative Party (Høyre) 1994–2004; Chair. NATO Political Cttee 1996–2001; Minister of Foreign Affairs 2001–05; Amb. to Austria 2009–; Commdr with Star, Order of St Olav 2004. *Address:* Embassy of Norway, Reisnerstr. 55–57, 1030 Vienna, Austria (office). *Telephone:* (1) 715-66-92 (office). *Fax:* (1) 712-65-52 (office). *E-mail:* emb.vienna@ mfa.no (office). *Website:* www.norwegen.or.at (office).

PETERSEN, Niels Helveg, LLD; Danish politician; b. 17 Jan. 1939, Odense; s. of Kristen Helveg Petersen and Lilly Helveg Petersen; m. Kirsten Lee; two s.; ed Copenhagen Univ. and Stanford Univ., USA; mem. Folketing (Parl.) 1966–74, 1977–; Chef de Cabinet to Danish Commr for the European Communities 1974–77; mem. Parl. Foreign Affairs Cttee 1968–74, Market Cttee 1972–74, 1977–78, 1982–88, 1990–93, Parl. Politico-Econ. Cttee 1982–84; Social Liberal Party Spokesman on Political Affairs 1968–74, 1977–78, Chair. Parl. Group 1978–88; Minister for Econ. Affairs 1988–90, for Foreign Affairs 1993–2000. *Leisure interests:* football, tennis, chess. *Address:* Folketinget, Christiansborg, 1240 Copenhagen K (office); Drosselvej 72, 2000 Petersen Frederiksberg, Denmark (home). *Telephone:* 33-37-47-10 (office). *E-mail:* niels.helveg.petersen@ft.dk (office).

PETERSEN, Wolfgang; German film director, producer and screenwriter; b. 14 March 1941, Emden; m. 1st Ursula Sieg (divorced 1978); m. 2nd Maria Borgel-Petersen 1978; ed Gelehrtenschule des Johanneums, Hamburg, German Film and TV Acad., Berlin; actor and Asst Stage Dir, Ernst Deutsch Theatre, Hamburg 1964–69; directed six 100-minute episodes for West German TV series Tatort (Scene of the Crime) 1971–76; first feature film, Einer von uns beiden 1973; German Film Award for Best New Direction. *Films include:* Der Eine – Der Andere (short) 1967, Die rote Fahne (documentary short) 1968, Ich nicht (short) 1969, I Will Kill You, Wolf 1971, One or the Other of Us (German Nat. Film Prize for Best New Director 1973) 1974, For Your Love Only, Scene of the Crime, Die Konsequenz 1977, Das Boot (Bavarian Film Award for Best Dir 1983) 1981, The Neverending Story 1984, Enemy Mine 1985, Shattered 1991, In the Line of Fire 1993, Outbreak 1995, Air Force One, The Red Corner 1997, The Perfect Storm 2000, Troy 2004, Poseidon 2006; exec. producer: Instinct 1999, Chicxulub (short) 2006. *Television includes:* Stadt auf Stelzen (film) 1965, Tatort (series) (Prix Italia and Best Dir, Monte Carlo Television Festival 1977) 1971–77, Anna und Totò (film) 1972, Smog (film) (Prix Futura, Berlin Festival 1975), Van der Valk und die Reichen (film) 1973, Aufs Kreuz gelegt (film) 1974, Die Stadt im Tal (mini-series) 1975, Stellenweise Glatteis (film) 1975, Hans im Glück (film) 1976, Vier gegen die Bank (film) 1976, Planübung (film) 1977, Schwarz und weiß wie Tage und Nächte (film) 1978, Das Boot (mini-series) 1985; exec. producer: The Agency (series) 2001, Avenger (film) 2006. *Address:* c/o Creative Artists Agency, 2000 Avenue of the Stars, Los Angeles, CA 90067, USA (office). *Telephone:* (424) 288-2000 (office). *Fax:* (424) 288-2900 (office). *Website:* www.caa.com (office); wolfgangpetersen.net.

PETERSON, Hon. David Robert, PC, CStJ, LLD, QC; Canadian lawyer, business executive and fmr politician; *Senior Partner and Chairman, Cassels Brock & Blackwell LLP;* b. 28 Dec. 1943, Toronto, Ont.; s. of the late Clarence Peterson; m. Shelley Matthews 1974; two s. one d.; ed Univ. of Western Ontario, Univ. of Toronto; called to the Bar 1969; MP for London Centre 1975, re-elected 1977, 1981; elected Leader of Ont. Liberal Party 1982, won election for Liberal Party 1985; Premier of Ont. 1985–90; currently Chair. and Sr Partner, Cassels Brock & Blackwell LLP; Chancellor Univ. of Toronto 2006–12; Chair. Toronto 2015 Pan American Games Organizing Cttee 2013–; numerous directorships; Founding Chair. Toronto Raptors Basketball Club, Chapters Inc.; Dir Young Presidents' Org., Council for Canadian Unity etc.; Adjunct Prof., York Univ.; Liberal; Chevalier, Légion d'honneur 1994, Ordre de la Pléiade, Int. Ass. of French-speaking Parliamentarians 1995, Order of Ontario 2009; several hon. degrees, including Hon. DUniv. *Leisure interests:* theatre, riding, jogging, golf, skiing, tennis, reading, gardening. *Address:* Cassels Brock & Blackwell LLP, 2100 Scotia Plaza, 40 King Street West, Toronto, ON M5H 3C2 (office); 8 Gibson Avenue, Toronto, ON M5R 1T5, Canada (home). *Telephone:* (416) 869-5451 (office); (416) 925-0460 (home). *Fax:* (416) 350-6961 (office). *E-mail:* dpeterson@casselsbrock.com (office). *Website:* www.casselsbrock.com (office).

PETERSON, G. P. (Bud), BS, MS, PhD; American engineer, academic and university administrator; *President, Georgia Institute of Technology;* b. 1 Sept. 1952, San Francisco, Calif.; m. Val Peterson; four c.; ed Kansas State Univ., Texas A&M Univ.; Visiting Research Scientist, NASA Johnson Space Center 1981–82; Lecturer and Researcher, Dept of Mechanical Eng, Texas A&M Univ. 1985–90, Halliburton Prof. of Mechanical Eng 1990, also Tenneco Prof., Coll. of Eng 1991, Head of Dept of Mechanical Eng 1993–96, Exec. Assoc. Dean, Coll. of Eng, also Assoc. Vice-Chancellor for Eng 1996; Provost Rensselaer Polytechnic Inst. 2000–06; Chancellor Univ. of Colorado, Boulder 2006–09; Pres. Georgia Inst. of Tech. 2009–; Program Dir Thermal Transport and Thermal Processing Div., NSF 1993; mem. Nat. Science Bd 2008–; mem. American Asscn of Colls and Univs, Middle States Comm. on Higher Educ., New England Asscn of Schools and Colls; Fellow, ASME, AIAA; Ralph James and the O.L. 'Andy Lewis' Award, ASME, Pi Tau Sigma Gustus L. Larson Memorial Award, ASME, AIAA Thermophysics Award, ASME Memorial Award, AIAA Sustained Service Award, NSF Award for Outstanding Man., Int. Astronautical Fed. Frank J. Malina Astronautics Medal 2005. *Publications:* author or co-author of 14 books and book chapters, 165 refereed journal articles and more than 140 conf. publs. *Address:* Office of the President, Georgia Institute of Technology, North Avenue, Atlanta, GA 30332, USA (office). *Telephone:* (404) 894-5051 (office). *E-mail:* president@gatech.edu (office). *Website:* www.president.gatech.edu (office).

PETERSON, James Scott, DCL, LLM; Canadian lawyer and politician; *Counsel, Fasken Martineau DuMoulin LLP;* b. 30 July 1941, Ottawa; m. Heather Peterson; ed McGill Univ., Columbia Univ., USA, Univ. of West Ontario, Acad. de Droit Int., The Hague, The Netherlands, La Sorbonne, Paris, France; mem. Faculty of Law, Univ. of Toronto 1974–79; pvt. practice, int. tax and business law 1970–80; Chair. Cambridge Acceptance Corpn Ltd 1984–87; MP for Willowdale 1980, re-elected 1988, 1993, 1997; fmr Liberal Party Industry Critic, Treasury Bd Critic, Parl. Sec. to Minister of State for Econ. Devt, Science and Tech. and to Minister of Justice; Chair. Parl. Task Force on Regulatory Reform; Chair. Standing Cttee on Finance 1993–97, Sec. of State (Int. Financial Insts) 1997–2002, Minister of Int. Trade Dec. 2003–06; fmr legal counsel and consultant to UN on jt ventures and major devt projects; Sr Resident Massey Coll., Munk Centre for Int. Studies, Univ. of Toronto 2002–; Co-Chair. Canada/US Law Inst.; mem. Canadian Bar Asscn, Ontario Bar Asscn. *Publications:* numerous works on int. taxation and int. jt business ventures. *Address:* Fasken Martineau DuMoulin LLP, 333 Bay Street, Suite 2400, Bay Adelaide Centre, Box 20, Toronto, ON M5H 2T6, Canada (office). *Telephone:* (416) 865-5489 (office). *Fax:* (416) 364-7813 (office). *E-mail:* jpeterson@fasken.com (office). *Website:* www.fasken.com (office).

PETERSON, Paul E., BA, MA, PhD; American political scientist and academic; *Director, Program on Education Policy and Governance, John F. Kennedy School of Government, Harvard University;* b. 16 Sept. 1940, Montevideo, Minn.; ed Concordia Coll., Moorhead, Minn. and Univ. of Chicago; Asst Prof., then Assoc. Prof. and Prof., Depts of Political Science and Educ., Univ. of Chicago 1967–83, Chair. Cttee on Public Policy Studies 1981–83; Dir Governmental Studies, The Brookings Inst., Washington, DC 1983–87; Benjamin H. Griswold III Prof. of Public Policy, Dept of Political Science, Johns Hopkins Univ. 1987–88; Prof. Dept of Govt, Harvard Univ. 1988–89, Henry Lee Shattuck Prof. of Govt 1989, Dir Centre for American Political Studies 1989–2000, Dir Program on Educ. Policy and Governance 1996–; Acad. Visitor, Dept of Govt, LSE, England 1977–78; John Simon Guggenheim Fellowship, German Marshall Fund of the US Fellowship 1977–78; Fellow, Center for Advanced Study in the Center for the Behavioral and Social Sciences, Stanford 1996; Sr Fellow, Hoover Inst. 2000; mem. Koret Task Force on K-12 Educ., Hoover Inst. 2000, Title I Ind. Review Cttee, US Dept of Educ. 2003, Educ. Research and Devt Center Grants Peer Review Panel, Inst. of Educ. Sciences, US Dept of Educ. 2005; named to Head Florida Educ. Transition Team by Gov.-Elect Charlie Crist 2006; mem. Nat. Acad. of Educ., American Acad. of Arts and Sciences. *Publications:* School Politics Chicago Style 1976 (Gladys Kammerer Award), City Limits 1981 (Woodrow Wilson Foundation Award), The Politics of School Reform, 1870–1940 1985, The New Urban Reality (ed.) 1985, The New Direction in American Politics (co-ed. with J. Chubb) 1985, When Federalism Works (with B. Rabe and K. Wong) 1987, Political Institutions and Effective Government, Can the Government Govern? 1989, Welfare Magnets (with Mark Rom) 1991, The Urban Underclass (with C. Jencks) 1991, The President, the Congress and the Making of Foreign Policy 1994, The Price of Federalism 1995 (Aaron Wildavsky Award 1996), Classifying by Race 1995, The New American Democracy (with M. Fiorina) 2001, Learning from School Choice (co-ed. with B. Hassel) 1998, Earning and Learning (co-ed. with S. Mayer), Charters, Vouchers and Public Education (co-ed. with David E. Campbell) 2001, The Education Gap: Vouchers and Urban Schools (with William Q. Howell) 2002. *Leisure interests:* tennis, piano. *Address:* Taubman 306, John F. Kennedy School of Government, Harvard University, 79 John F. Kennedy Street, T306, Cambridge, MA 02138, USA (office). *Telephone:* (617) 495-8312 (office). *Fax:* (617) 496-4428 (office). *E-mail:* ppeterson@gov.harvard.edu (office). *Website:* www.people.fas.harvard .edu/%7Epepeters/index.htm (office); www.hks.harvard.edu/pepg (office); www .educationnext.org.

PETERSON, Peter G., MBA; American business executive and fmr government official; b. 5 June 1926, Kearney, Neb.; s. of George Peterson and Venetia Peterson (née Paul); m. 1st Sally Hornbogen 1953 (divorced 1979); four s. one d.; m. 2nd Joan Ganz Cooney 1980; ed Northwestern Univ. and Univ. of Chicago; Market Analyst, Market Facts Inc., Chicago 1947–49, Assoc. Dir 1949–51, Exec. Vice-Pres. 1951–53; Dir of Marketing Services, McCann-Erickson (advertising firm) 1953, Vice-Pres. 1954–58, Gen. Man. Chicago Office 1955–57, Dir, Asst to Pres. co-ordinating services regional offices 1957–58; Exec. Vice-Pres. and Dir Bell & Howell 1958–61, Pres. 1961–63, CEO 1963–71, Chair. 1968–71; Asst to Pres. of USA for Int. Econ. Affairs 1971–72, also Exec. Dir Council on Int. Econ. Policy; Sec.

of Commerce 1972–73; Chair. Bd Lehman Bros Kuhn Loeb Inc. (fmrly Lehman Bros Inc.), New York 1973–83; Co-founder and Chair. The Blackstone Group 1985–2008, Chair. Emer. 2008–; Founder and Chair. Peter G. Peterson Foundation 2008–; mem. Pres. Clinton's Bipartisan Comm. on Entitlement Reform 1994; mem. Inst. of Int. Econs, Ind. Comm. on Int. Devt Issues, Trilateral Comm.; Trustee, Museum of Modern Art; Man of Vision Award 1994. *Publications:* Facing Up: How to Rescue the Economy from Crushing Debt and Restore the American Dream, On Borrowed Time (co-author), Readings in Market Organization and Price Policies (ed.), Running on Empty: How the Democratic and Republican Parties are Bankrupting Our Future and What Americans Can Do About It 2004. *Address:* Peter G. Peterson Foundation, 888-C Eighth Avenue, Box #144, New York, NY 10019, USA (office). *Website:* pgpf.org (office).

PETERSON, Sandra E., BA, MPA; American business executive; *CEO, Bayer CropScience;* b. 1959, New York, NY; ed Cornell Univ., Princeton Univ.; received fellowship from Robert Bosch Foundation, Stuttgart, Germany, spent a year serving with Fed. Ministry of Finance and Fed. of German Industries 1984–85; Man. Consultant, McKinsey & Co. 1987–93; held various global exec. positions with Whirlpool Corpn 1993–96; Exec. Vice-Pres. Nabisco 1996–99; Sr Vice-Pres. Merck-Medco's Health Businesses 1999, mem. Exec. Man. team, played role in spin-off of Medco Health from Merck & Co., Inc., latterly serving as Group Pres. Medco Health Solutions, Inc.; mem. Exec. Cttee Bayer HealthCare 2005–, Head of Diabetes Care Div. –2009, Head of Medical Care Div. 2009–10, CEO Bayer CropScience and Chair. Bayer CropScience AG 2010–; mem. Bd of Dirs Dun & Bradstreet; mem. Bd CropLife International; mem. and fmr Chair. Wildlife Trust; mem. Committee of 200, Women's Forum; ranked by Fortune magazine amongst the 50 Most Powerful Women in Business outside the US (13th) 2012. *Address:* Bayer CropScience AG, Alfred-Nobel-Str. 50, 40789 Monheim am Rhein, Germany (office). *Telephone:* (21) 7338-0 (office). *Website:* www.cropscience.bayer.com (office).

PETERSON, Thage G.; Swedish politician; *Senior Adviser, Expandum AB;* b. 1933, Berg, Kronoberg; ed Inst. of Social Studies, Lund; Municipal Treas. Community Centre Asscn 1957–59, head 1967–71; Sec. and Vice-Chair. Social Democratic Youth Union 1964–67; elected to Parl. 1970; Under-Sec. of State to Cabinet 1971–75; Chair. Stockholm County br. of Socialdemokratiska Arbetarepartiet (Social Democratic Labour Party—SDLP) 1974–89; mem. SDLP Exec. Cttee 1975–90; Minister without Portfolio 1975–76; SDLP spokesman for Industrial Policy 1976–82; mem. SDLP Parl. Group Exec. and Head of Research Div.; Minister of Industry 1982–88, of Justice 1988, of Defence 1994–97, Minister in the Prime Minister's Office 1997; Speaker of Parl. 1988–91; Chair. Standing Cttee on the Constitution 1991–94; Sr Adviser Expandum AB. *Address:* Expandum AB, Box 840, 982 28 Gällivare, Sweden (office). *Telephone:* (970) 641-60 (office). *Fax:* (970) 641-05 (office). *E-mail:* info@expandum.se (office). *Website:* www.expandum.se (office).

PETERSSON, Lars-Eric Gustav, BSc; Swedish business executive; b. 21 June 1950, Mönsterås; m.; two s.; Exec. Vice-Pres. Sparbanken/Svenska Sparbanksförmingen 1984–90; Pres., later Pres. and Chair. Pronator 1990–93; with Skandia Insurance Co. Ltd as mem. Man. Group, Head Business Control/Business Devt, Exec. Vice-Pres., mem. Exec. Man., Head Int. Direct Insurance and Reinsurance (IDR), Acting Head, Skandia Investment Man., Deputy Chief Exec. 1993–97, Pres. and CEO Skandia Insurance Co. Ltd 1997–2003.

PETHICA, John Bernard, BA, PhD, FRS; British physicist and academic; *Principal Investigator, School of Physics, Trinity College, Dublin;* ed St Ambrose Coll., Altrincham, Cambridge Univ.; Staff Scientist, Brown Boveri Corp. Research Centre, Baden, Switzerland 1980–82; Oppenheimer Fellow, Univ. of Cambridge 1982–84; Guest Scientist, ABB Research Centre, Baden, Switzerland 1983–87; Royal Soc. Univ. Research Fellow, Cavendish Lab., Cambridge 1984–87; Guest Scientist, Oak Ridge Nat. Lab., Tenn., USA 1985–89; Univ. Lecturer in Physics of Materials and Fellow of St Cross Coll., Oxford 1987–96, Prof. of Materials Science 1996–2003; Visiting Prof., Univ. of Konstanz, Germany 1990, Univ. of Nijmegen, Netherlands 1992, Dept of Materials Univ. of Oxford 2013–; Sabbatical Chair., Sony Corpn, Yokohama, Japan 1993–94; Visiting Fellow, Australian Nuclear Science and Tech. Org., Menai, Australia 1994; SFI Research Prof., Trinity Coll., Dublin, Ireland 2001–, Founding Dir Centre for Research on Adaptive Nanostructures and Nanodevices 2003–05; part-time Chief Science Advisor, Nat. Physical Lab.; Official Guest of Japan Acad. from the Royal Soc. Jan. 2002; IP for SMEs, UK Intellectual Property Conf., Said Business School, Oxford June 2003; Founder and Dir, Nano Instruments Inc., Knoxville, Tenn., USA 1984–98; consultant for several cos.; Physical Sciences Sec. and Vice-Pres. Royal Soc. 2009–; mem. Thin Films & Interfaces Cttee, Inst. of Physics 1987–90 (mem. Tribology Cttee 1991–94), Surface & Interface Science Bd, European Physical Soc. 1988–97, UK-Japan N+N Panels 1990–2003; Elegant Work Prize, Inst. of Materials 1994, Rosenhain Medal and Prize, Inst. of Materials 1997, Royal Soc. Hughes Medal 2001, Holweck Medal, Sociéte Française de Physique 2002. *Address:* Department of Materials, University of Oxford, 16 Parks Road, Oxford, OX1 3PH, England (office); Department of Physics, Trinity College, Dublin 2, Ireland (office). *Telephone:* (1865) 273700 (Oxford, switchboard) (office); (1) 8963036 (Dublin) (office). *Fax:* (1865) 273783 (Oxford) (office). *E-mail:* john.pethica@materials.ox.ac .uk (office); jp12@tcd.ie (office); john.pethica@tcd.ie (office). *Website:* www .materials.ox.ac.uk/peoplepages/pethica.html (office); www.crann.tcd.ie/Research/ Investigators/School-of-Physics/Prof-John-Pethica.aspx (office); people.tcd.ie/jp12 (office).

PETHRICK, Richard Arthur, PhD, CChem, FRSC, FRSE, FIMMM; British physical chemist and academic; *Professor Emeritus of Chemistry, University of Strathclyde;* b. 26 Oct. 1942, Yate, Glos., England; s. of A. T. A. Pethrick and L. M. Pethrick; m. J. Hume 1975; one s.; ed Univs of London and Salford; Lecturer, Dept of Pure and Applied Chem., Univ. of Strathclyde 1970, Sr Lecturer 1978, Reader 1981, Prof. of Chem. 1983–2003, Head of Dept 1992–95, 1999–2005, Burmah Prof. of Physical Chem. 2003–08, Prof. Emer. 2008–; mem. Editorial Bd British Polymer Journal 1979–93, Int. Journal of Polymeric Materials 1990–, Polymer News 1991–, Trends in Polymer Science 1992–, Polymer Int. 1993–; Ed. Polymer Yearbook 1983–; Visiting Prof., Univ. of Punjab 1979; British Council Visiting Lecturer, Australia 1985, 1989; Royal Soc. Visiting Lecturer, UK-China Del., Beijing 1992; mem. Int. Swedish Tech. Review Cttee for Polymer Science 1988, Int. Danish Tech.

Review Cttee for Polymer Science 2003, Polymers and Composites Cttee Science and Eng Research Council 1993–, Large Area Displays Cttee Eng and Physical Sciences Research Council 1994–, IRC Review Cttee 1995–; Chair. Science Sector Scottish Vocational Awards Council 1995–2001; mem. RSC Accreditation Cttee 1996–2002, RSC Educ. Cttee 2005–, NSF Polymers Cttee 2009, Materials Panel, Royal Soc. of Edinburgh 2008–; elected mem. Hon. Craft of Weavers of Glasgow 1991; Fellow, Inst. of Materials, Minerals and Mining 1998. *Publications:* Molecular Motion in High Polymers 1979, Modern Methods of Polymer Characterization 1999, Polymer Characterization – Physical Techniques (with D. Campbell, J. R. White) 2000, Techniques for Polymer Organization and Morphological Characterization 2003, Polymer Structure Characterization – From Nano to Macro Organization 2007, Polymer Science and Technology for Engineers and Scientists 2011, Introduction to Molecular Motion in Polymers (with T. Amornsakchai and A. M. North) 2011; more than 460 scientific papers and numerous book chapters and review articles. *Leisure interests:* walking, painting, photography. *Address:* WestCHEM, Department of Pure and Applied Chemistry, University of Strathclyde, Thomas Building, 295 Cathedral Street, Glasgow, G1 1XL, Scotland (office). *Telephone:* (141) 548-4760 (office); (141) 548-2795 (office). *Fax:* (141) 548-4822 (office). *E-mail:* r.a.pethrick@strath.ac.uk (office).

PETIT, Antoni Marti; Andorran architect and politician; *Head of Government;* b. 1963, Escaldes-Engordany; m.; three c.; ed École Nationale Supérieur d'Architecture de Toulouse, France; mem. Consell Gen. (Parl.) 1994–2003; Mayor of Andorra la Vella 2004–11; Cap de Govern (Head of Govt) 2011–, also Acting Minister of Culture; Leader, Demòcrates per Andorra (Democracy for Andorra). *Address:* Office of the Head of Government, Govern d'Andorra, Carrer Prat de la Creu 62–64, Edif. Administratiu, AD500 Andorra la Vella, Andorra (office). *Telephone:* 875700 (office). *E-mail:* portal@govern.ad (office). *Website:* www.presidencia.ad (office).

PETIT, Christine, MD, PhD; French geneticist, biochemist and academic; *Director, Laboratory of Genetics and Physiology of Hearing, Institut Pasteur;* ed Université Paris V (Medicine), Université Paris XI-Orsay (Sciences); researcher, Immunochemistry Lab., Institut Pasteur 1970s, apptd Dir Sensory Deficit Genetics Unit 1985, now Head of Lab. of Genetics and Physiology of Hearing and of Dept of Neuroscience, mem. Bd of Dirs Institut Pasteur 2003–; postdoctoral researcher, Basel, Switzerland; researcher, CNRS Molecular Genetics Centre, Gif-sur-Yvette; Prof. of Genetics and Cellular Physiology, Collège de France, Paris; Head of INSERM UMRS 587 Lab.; mem. Scientific Council, Université Paris-Descartes, Ecole Normale Supérieure; mem. Council for Teaching, Ecole Supérieure de Physique et de Chimie Industrielles de la Ville de Paris 2007–; Pres. Steering Cttee CTRS/RTRS 'Sensory Handicap' 2007–; mem. Bd of Dirs Institut Carnot 'Seeing and Hearing' 2006–; responsible for co-ordination of European FP6 EuroHear consortium 2004–; mem. Acad. des sciences 2002, European Molecular Biology Org. 1996, Academia Europaea 1998; Chevalier, Légion d'honneur 2002; Prix de thèse de médecine 1974, Prix Janine Courrier de l'Académie des sciences 1992, Charles-Léopold Meyer Award 1999, Ernst Jung für Wissenschaft und Forschung: Medizin Award 2001, Leçon Inaugurale, Collège de France 2002, L'Oréal-UNESCO For Women in Science Award 2004, Rechercher Medecine, ISS 2004, Freedom to Discover in Neuroscience Prize, Bristol-Myers Squibb Inst. 2005, Prix Louis-Jeantet de Médecine 2006, Grand Prix, INSERM 2007, Brain Prize 2012. *Publications:* numerous articles in medical journals on genetic basis of sensory disorders and pathophysiology. *Address:* Institut Pasteur, 25 rue du Dr Roux, 75724 Paris Cedex 15, France (office). *Telephone:* 1-45-68-80-90 (office). *Fax:* 1-40-61-34-42 (office). *E-mail:* cpetit@pasteur.fr (office). *Website:* www.pasteur.fr/ip/easysite/pasteur/en/research/scientific-departments/neuroscience/units-and-groups/genetics-and-physiology-of-hearing (office).

PETKOFF MALEC, Teodoro, BEcons; Venezuelan politician, journalist and economist; *President, TalCual newspaper;* b. 3 Jan. 1932, Maracaibo, Zulia; ed Central Univ. of Venezuela; father was Bulgarian emigrant and mother a Pole; Prof., Central Univ. of Venezuela for 14 years; joined CP of Venezuela (PCV) and formed part of student resistance against dictatorship of Marcos Pérez Jiménez 1950s; served as guerrilla commdr under Douglas Bravo, operating under codenames 'Roberto' and 'Reodulo Perdomo' against govt of Rómulo Betancourt 1960s; escaped from San Carlos prison via tunnel 1967; accepted govt's peace offer 1969; left PCV along with other dissidents; f. Movimiento al Socialismo (MAS) 1971; mem. Congress (MAS) 1974–94; cand. for presidency 1983, 1988; Minister of Central Office of Coordination and Planning (Cordiplan) 1996–99; quit MAS after party's support of candidacy of Hugo Chávez 1998; Dir El Mundo newspaper 1999–2001; Founder and Dir TalCual (evening paper) 2001–; intended to run as ind. cand. in presidential elections Dec. 2006 but dropped out of race to support Manuel Rosales Aug. 2006. *Publications:* Checoslovaquia: El Socialismo como problema 1969, ¿Socialismo para Venezuela? 1970, Razón y pasión del socialismo: el tema socialista en Venezuela 1973, Proceso a la izquierda: O de la falsa conducta revolucionaria 1976, Del optimismo de la voluntad: Escritos políticos 1987, Por qué hago lo que hago 1997, Venezuela en la encrucijada (co-author) 1998, Una segunda opinión: La Venezuela de Chávez: un libro hablado con Ibsen Martínez y Elías Pino Iturrieta 2000, Hugo Chávez, tal cual 2000, Las Dos Izquierdas (The Two Lefts) 2005. *Address:* TalCual, Edif. Menegrande, 5°, Of. 51, Avda Francisco de Miranda, Caracas, Venezuela (office). *Telephone:* (212) 286-7446 (office). *Fax:* (212) 232-7446 (office). *E-mail:* tpetkoff@talcualdigital.com (office). *Website:* www.talcualdigital.com (office).

PETKOV, Petko Danev; Bulgarian politician; b. 2 March 1942, Dobrotich; ed Higher Naval School, Varna; joined Dimitrov Young Communist League 1956, Bulgarian Communist Party (BCP) 1973; worked for 1st Coast Artillery Regt, Varna, radio mechanic for Navigation Maritime Bulgare Shipping Co., designer at Resprom Plant, Varna, Deputy Man., then Man. of Radio Navigation Equipment Works, Varna, Man. Dir of Cherno More Research and Industry Combined Works; First Sec., BCP Municipal Cttee, Varna Sept. 1987–; Alt. mem., BCP Cen. Cttee; Alt. mem., Political Bureau 1989–. *Address:* Bulgarian Communist Party, Sofia, Bulgaria.

PETKOVSKI, Tito; Macedonian politician; b. 23 Jan. 1945, Psacha, Kriva Palanka; m. Tanja Petkovska; two d.; ed Kriva Palanka High School, Skopje Univ.; worked in Municipal court Kriva Palanka, Repub. Bureau on Urban Planning and Communal Issues; political career started as deputy in Karposh Communal Ass.,

deputy City Ass. Skopje; later Vice-Pres. Exec. Council City Ass. Skopje; Sec. Cen. Cttee League of Communists of Macedonia—Party for Democratic Prosperity; mem. Cttee on Constitutional Problems, Ass. Repub. of Macedonia; Vice-Pres. first multi-party Ass. of Macedonia 1994–96; co-ordinator Parl. Group Social-Democratic Union of Macedonia; mem. Council of Inter-Parl. Union; Pres. Ass. (Sobranje) Repub. of Macedonia 1996–98, Pres. Standing Inquiry Cttee for Protection of Citizens' Freedoms and Rights 1998–; cand. in presidential elections 1999. *Publications include:* legal articles on housing policy, town planning and land devt. *Address:* 11 Oktombri blvd, 91000 Skopje, Macedonia. *Telephone:* (91) 112255. *Fax:* (91) 237947 (office).

PETO, Sir Richard, Kt, MSc, MA, FRS; British epidemiologist; *Professor of Medical Statistics and Epidemiology, University of Oxford;* b. 14 May 1943; s. of Leonard Huntley Peto and Carrie Clarinda Peto; m. 1st Sallie Messum 1970 (divorced); two s.; partner Gale Mead (deceased); two s.; ed Tauntons School, Southampton, Trinity Coll., Cambridge, Imperial Coll., London; Research Officer, MRC 1967–69; with Univ. of Oxford 1969–, Lecturer 1972–75, Reader in Cancer Studies 1975–92, Prof. of Medical Statistics and Epidemiology 1992–; Guy Medal in Silver 1986, Royal Medal, Royal Soc. 2002, Charles S. Mott Prize 2002, King Faisal Int. Prize (co-winner) 2005, Dr A.H. Heineken Prize in Medicine 2008. *Publications include:* Natural History of Chronic Bronchitis and Emphysema 1976, Quantification of Occupational Cancer 1981, The Causes of Cancer 1983, Diet, Lifestyle and Mortality in China 1990, Mortality from Smoking in Developed Countries 1950–2000 1994, Emerging Tobacco Hazards in China 1998, Tobacco: The Growing Epidemic 2000, Geographic Study of Mortality, Biochemistry, Diet and Lifestyle in Rural China 2006; more than 500 papers. *Leisure interests:* science, children. *Address:* Clinical Trial Service Unit and Epidemiological Studies Unit (CTSU), Nuffield Department of Clinical Medicine, Richard Doll Building, Old Road Campus, Oxford, OX3 7LF (office); 62 Great Clarendon Street, Oxford, OX2 6AX, England (home). *Telephone:* (1865) 743801 (office). *Fax:* (1865) 743985 (office). *E-mail:* secretary@ctsu.ox.ac.uk (office). *Website:* www.cardioscience.ox.ac.uk/bhf-centre-of-research-excellence/researcher-profiles/sir-richard-peto (office); www.ctsu.ox.ac.uk (office).

PETRAEUS, Gen. (retd) David Howell, BS, MPA, PhD; American government official, academic and fmr army officer; *Visiting Professor of Public Policy, Macaulay Honors College, City University of New York;* b. 7 Nov. 1952, Cornwall-on-Hudson, New York; m. Holly Knowlton 1974; one s. one d.; ed West Point Mil. Acad., Princeton Univ.; commissioned Second-Lt 1974, assigned to 509th Airborne Infantry Bn, Vicenza, Italy, served in various leadership posts in airborne, mechanized and air assault infantry units in Europe and USA including Operations Officer, 3rd Infantry Div. (Mechanized) 1st Bn 1978–79, command of 101st Airborne Div. (Air Assault) 3rd Bn 1991–93, command of 82nd Airborne Div. 1st Brigade 1995–97; staff posts have included Aide to Chief of Staff of the Army, Mil. Asst to Supreme Allied Commdr—Europe, Chief Mil. Operations Officer, UN Mission, Haiti 1995, Exec. Asst to Dir of Jt Staff and subsequently Chair. Jt Chiefs of Staff, Pentagon 1997–99; promoted to Brig.-Gen. 1999; Asst Div. Commdr for Operations, 82nd Airborne Div., Fort Bragg, NC 1999–2000; Chief of Staff, XVIII Airborne Corps 2000–01; promoted to Maj.-Gen. 2001; Asst Chief of Staff for Operations, NATO Stabilization Force and Deputy Commdr, US Jt Interagency Counter-Terrorism Task Force, Bosnia 2001–02; commanded 101st Airborne Div. during Operation Iraqi Freedom, Iraq 2003; promoted to Lt-Gen. 2004; Commdr, Multi-Nat. Security Transition Command and NATO Training Mission, Iraq 2004–05; Commanding Gen. US Army Combined Arms Center and Fort Leavenworth 2005–07; promoted to Gen. 2007; Commdr Multi-Nat. Force-Iraq, overseeing all coalition forces 2007–08; Commdr US Cen. Command 2008–10; Commdr Int. Security Assistance Force (ISAF) and Commdr, US Forces Afghanistan (USFOR-A) 2010–11; Dir CIA 2011–12 (resgnd); Visiting Prof. of Public Policy, Macaulay Honors Coll., CUNY 2013–; Chair. Kohlberg Kravis Roberts (KKR) Global Inst. 2013–; Judge Widney Prof., Univ. of S California 2013–; Sr Fellow, Harvard Univ. 2013–; Sr Vice-Pres., Royal United Services Inst. 2013; Co-Chair. Council on Foreign Relations Task Force on N America 2013–; Hon. Prof., Exeter Univ. 2014; Gold Award of the Iraqi Order of the Date Palm; Gen. George C. Marshall Award 1983, Combat Action Badge, Army Achievement Medal, Defense Distinguished Service Medal, two Distinguished Service Medals, two Defense Superior Service Medals, four Legion of Merit awards, Bronze Star Medal for Valor, State Dept Superior Honor Award, NATO Meritorious Service Medal. *Publication:* US Army Counterinsurgency Field Manual (co-author). *Address:* Macaulay Honors College, City University of New York, 35 West 67th Street, New York, NY 10023, USA (office). *Website:* www.macaulay.cuny.edu (office).

PETRAKOV, Nikolai Yakovlevich, D.ECON.SC.; Russian economist; *Director, Institute for Market Problems;* b. 1 March 1937; m. Tat'yana Aleksandrovna; one s. one d.; ed Moscow Univ.; mem. CPSU 1964–90; mem. staff Inst. of Tech.-Econ. Research 1959–61, Econ. Inst. 1961–65, then Head of Lab.; Deputy Dir, Cen. Mathematics-Econ. Inst., USSR Acad. of Sciences 1965–91; corresp. mem. USSR (now Russian) Acad. of Sciences 1984–90, mem. 1990–; USSR People's Deputy 1989–91; Dir Inst. for Market Problems 1991–; Adviser to Pres. Yeltsin 1994; mem. Political Consultative Council 1991; mem. State Duma (Parl.) 1993–95; Chair. Bd Savings Investment Bank 1996–. *Publications:* papers and articles on the problems of pricing policies and on socialist econs. *Address:* Institute for Market Problems, Krasikova Str. 32, 117418 Moscow (office); Acad. Zelinski Str. 38, korp. 8, Apt 40, 117334 Moscow, Russia (home). *Telephone:* (495) 129-10-00 (office); (495) 135-14-46 (home).

PETRÁŇOVÁ, Ludmila; Czech business executive; *CEO, Lumen Energy a.s.;* ed Faculty of Nuclear and Physical Eng, Czech Tech. Univ., Prague; Chair. and CEO ČEPS a.s. (state-owned transmission grid) 2002–06; mem. Bd Electricity Market Operator (OTE) 2006–09; CEO Lumen Energy a.s. 2009–; mem. energy advisory team, Ernst & Young 2011–; ranked by Fortune magazine amongst 50 Most Powerful Women in Business outside the US (50th) 2004. *Address:* Lumen Energy a.s., Tylovická 372/16, 155 21 Prague 5, Czech Republic (office). *Telephone:* (2) 272655855 (office). *Fax:* (office). *E-mail:* ludmila.petranova@lumen-energy.com (office). *Website:* www.lumen-energy.cz (office).

PETRE, Zoe, PhD; Romanian historian, academic and politician; *Vice-President, Actiunea Populara (Popular Action);* b. 23 Aug. 1940, Bucharest; m. (husband deceased); two s.; ed Univ. of Bucharest; Prof., Head of Dept of Ancient History and

Archaeology and fmr Dean, History Faculty, Univ. of Bucharest 1990–96; worked on presidential campaign of Emil Constantinescu 1996, after election served as Sr Adviser to the Pres. and co-ordinator Dept of Public Policy –2000; Founding mem. and Vice-Pres. Actiunea Populara (Popular Action) 2003–; Assoc. Prof., École des Hautes Études en Sciences Sociales, Centre de Recherches Comparées sur les Sociétés anciennes, Paris 1982, 1991, 1993; mem. Romanian socs of Classical Studies, Historical Sciences and Anthropology, Asscn pour l'encouragement des études grecques (France), East-West Inst., New York, USA; Order of the Dannebrog (Denmark), Commdr, Légion d'honneur; Timotei Ciparius Award of the Romanian Acad., Nicolae Jorga Award, Romanian Ministry of Culture and several other honours and awards. *Publications:* Commentaire aux 'Sept contre Thèbes' d'Eschyle (with Liana Lupas) 1981, Civilizaţia greacă şi originile democratiei 1993–, Virsta de Bronz 2000, Cetatea greacă, între real şi imaginar 2000; and articles in scientific journals specializing in ancient history, culture, philology. *Leisure interests:* literature, music. *Address:* Actiunea Populara (Popular Action), 050093 Bucharest 5, Splaiul Independenţei 17/101 (office); Universitatea Bucureşti, Blvd Regina Elisabeta 4-12, sala 301, 70609 Bucharest Romania. *Telephone:* (21) 3160293 (office). *Fax:* (21) 3160399 (office). *E-mail:* office@actiunea.ro (office). *Website:* www.actiunea.ro (home).

PETRENKO, Aleksey Vasilyevich; Ukrainian actor; b. 26 March 1938, Tchernigov; ed Kharkov Theatre Inst.; acted with various prov. cos in the USSR, including Lensovet Theatre 1967–81, Moscow Art Theatre 1978–83, Moscow Taganka Theatre, Russia 1985–; actor Cen. M. Gorki film studio 1983–; RSFSR People's Artist 1988, United Russia and Belarus Prize for Devt of Russia 1998, Russian Govt Prize 2001. *Films include:* King Lear 1971, Peter the First (title role) 1975, Marriage 1978, Agony (role of Grigoriy Rasputin) 1981, A Cruel Romance 1984, 20 Days Out of War 1987, The Servant 1989, Balthazar's Feasts or The Night with Stalin 1990, The Small Bees 1995, The Barber of Siberia 1998, Fortune 1999, Listen! Isn't it Raining? 2000, Collectioner 2002, Belle occasion 2003, Idiot 2003, Casus belli 2003, The Chess Player 2004, Dr Zhivago 2005, Comrade Chief 2 2005, Not Only With Bread 2005, Wedding. Case. Death 2005, 12 Angry Men 2006, and many others. *Address:* Nikitsky Blvd 9, Apt 39, 121019 Moscow, Russia. *Telephone:* 291-48-51.

PETRESCU, Ioana Maria, BA, MA, PhD; Romanian economist, academic and politician; *Minister of Public Finance;* b. 1980; ed Wellesley Coll. and Harvard Univ., USA; lived in Boston and Washington, DC for 14 years; worked as NRI Fellow at American Enterprise Inst., Washington, DC; Asst Prof., Univ. of Maryland, USA (on temporary leave 2013–14); economic adviser to Prime Minister 2013–14; Minister of Public Finance 2014–; Ind. *Address:* Ministry of Public Finance, 050741 Bucharest 5, Str. Apolodor 17, Romania (office); 4131 Van Munching Hall, University of Maryland, College Park, MD 20742, , USA. *Telephone:* (21) 3199759 (office). *Fax:* (21) 3122509 (office). *E-mail:* presa.mfp@mfinante.gov.ro (office). *Website:* www.mfinante.gov.ro (office).

PETRESKI, Dušan; Macedonian association executive; b. 19 Jan. 1948, Mavrovo; m. Liliana Mirchevska 1973; two s.; ed Skopje Univ.; Sec. and mem. Exec. Bd Econ. Chamber of Macedonia 1984–87, Vice-Pres. 1987–90, Pres. 1990–2005; Vice-Pres. Asscn of Balkan Chambers 1997–98, Pres. 1998; many state and other decorations and awards. *Publications:* professional articles in many magazines and journals. *Leisure interests:* social activities, sport, walking. *Address:* c/o Economic Chamber of Macedonia, Dimitrie Čupovski 13, 1000 Skopje (office); Meksička 7, 1000 Skopje, Macedonia (home).

PETRI, Michala; Danish musician (recorder player); b. 7 July 1958, Copenhagen; d. of Kanny Sambleben and Hanne Petri; m. Lars Hannibal 1992 (divorced 2010); two d.; ed Staatliche Hochschule für Musik und Theater, Hannover; debut aged five, Danish Radio 1964; soloist with Orchestra Tivoli, Copenhagen 1969; over 4,000 concerts in Europe, USA, Japan, China, Korea, Mexico, Canada and Australia; numerous appearances at festivals, performances on TV and radio; performs frequently with orchestras world-wide, also as duo with lutenist and guitarist, Lars Hannibal; has inspired and initiated various contemporary compositions by Malcolm Arnold, Vagn Holmboe, Per Nørgård, Thomas Koppel, Daniel Boertz, Gary Kulesha, Stephen Stucky, Joan Albert Amargos, Chen Yi and others; mem. Presidium, UNICEF Denmark; Vice-Pres. Cancer Asscn (Denmark); Hon. Prof., Royal Danish Acad. of Music; Kt of the Dannebrog 1995, Order Kt of First Grade 2010; Jacob Gade Prize 1969, 1975, Critics' Prize of Honour 1976, Nording Radio Prize 1977, Niels Prize 1980, Tagea Brandts Prize 1980, Maarum Prize 1981, Schroder Prize 1982, Deutscher Schallplattenpreis 1997, 2002, Sonning Music Prize 2000, H. C. Lumbye Prize 2000, European Soloist Prize 'Pro Europa' 2005, Danish Music Award 2006, three ECHO Klassik Awards. *Recordings:* more than 60 albums, including 12 with Academy of St Martin-in-the-Fields, Bach Sonatas and Handel Sonatas with Keith Jarrett, Vivaldi Concertos with Heinz Holliger, Henryk Szeryng, contemporary concerts with English Chamber Orchestra and Danish Nat. Symphony Orchestra, six albums with Lars Hannibal, albums with Chen Yue, Kremerata Baltica, Chinese Recorder Concertos, English Recorder Concertos, Uģis Prauliņš: The Nightingale (ECHO Klassik Award for World Premiere Recording of the Year 2012) 2011, two albums with Danish Nat. Vocal Ensemble. *Publications:* ed. of several works for Wilhelm Hansen and Moeck; Sheet Music Now. *Address:* c/o Lars Hannibal, Borgergade 142, 3rd, 1300 Copenhagen K, Denmark (office); Nordskraenten 3, 2980 Kokkedal, Denmark (office). *Telephone:* 40-15-05-77 (office); 26-13-58-77 (office). *E-mail:* hannibal@michalapetri.com (office); mail@michalapetri.com (office). *Website:* www.ourrecordings.com (office). *Website:* www.michalapetri.com.

PETRIASHVILI, Aleksi, BA; Georgian politician; *State Minister, responsible for European and Euro-Atlantic Integration;* b. 24 Aug. 1970, Tbilisi; ed Tbilisi State Univ., NATO Defence Coll., Rome; Sr Specialist, Foreign Relations Div., State Logistic Service, Staff of the Head of State 1994–95; State Adviser, Foreign Policy Analysis Service, State Chancellery, Staff of Pres. of Georgia 1995–98; Head of Bilateral Relations Div., Politico-Mil. Dept, Ministry of Foreign Affairs May–Sept. 1998, Deputy Dir Politico-Mil. Dept 1998–2001; Sr Counsellor, Embassy in Vienna, Perm. Mission of Georgia to OSCE and other Int. Orgs in Vienna, UN Orgs, UNIDO, UN Office on Drugs and Crime, etc. 2001–02, Sr Counsellor, Embassy in Washington, DC (also accred to Mexico and Canada) 2002–04, Amb. to Turkmenistan (also accred to Afghanistan) 2004–09; mem. Parl. Oct. 2012; Political Sec., Free Democrats party 2009–12; Political Bd mem. Georgian Dream

Coalition 2012–; State Minister, responsible for European and Euro-Atlantic Integration 2012–. *Address:* Ministry of Foreign Affairs, 0108 Tbilisi, Sh. Chitadze 4, Georgia (office). *Telephone:* (32) 294-50-00 (office). *Fax:* (32) 294-50-01 (office). *E-mail:* inform@mfa.gov.ge (office). *Website:* www.mfa.gov.ge (office).

PETRIČ, Ernest, PhD; Slovenian judge, diplomatist and academic; *President, Constitutional Court of the Republic of Slovenia;* b. 18 Nov. 1936, Trzic; s. of Joze Petrič and Angela Godnov; m. Silvestra Rogelj; three d.; ed Univ. of Ljubljana, Univ. of Vienna; Research Asst, Inst. for Ethnic Studies, Ljubljana 1961–65; Asst Prof. of Int. Law, Univ. of Ljubljana 1965–67, Prof. 1972–83; mem. Exec. Council of Slovenia, Minister of Science and Tech. 1967–72; Prof., Univ. of Addis Ababa, Ethiopia 1983–86; Dean Faculty of Social Science, Univ. of Ljubljana 1986–89; Amb. of Yugoslavia to India (also accred to Nepal) 1989–91, to USA (also accred to Mexico) 1991–97; State Sec. Ministry of Foreign Affairs 1997–2000; Amb. and Perm. Rep. to UN, New York (also accred to Brazil) 2000–02; Amb. to Austria and Perm. Rep. to UN, Vienna and to OSCE 2002–09; Judge, Constitutional Court of the Repub. of Slovenia 2008–, Pres. 2010–; Kidric Award 1979, Yugoslav Silver Medal for Achievement 1986, Colorado Meritorious Service Medal, USA 1997. *Publications:* International Legal Protection of Minorities 1977, The International Legal Position of the Slovenian Minority in Italy 1981, The Right to Self-Determination 1984, From Emperor to Leader 1987. *Leisure interests:* literature, skiing, tennis. *Address:* Constitutional Court of the Republic of Slovenia (Ustavno sodišča Republike Slovenije), 1001 Ljubljana, Beethovnova 10, Slovenia (office). *Telephone:* (1) 4776400 (office). *Fax:* (1) 2510451 (office). *E-mail:* info@us-rs.si (office). *Website:* www.us-rs.si (office).

PETRIE, Sir Peter (Charles), 5th Bt, cr. 1918, of Carrowcarden, CMG; British diplomatist; b. 7 March 1932, London; s. of Sir Charles Petrie, Bt, CBE and Lady Petrie; m. Countess Lydwine von Oberndorff 1958; two s. one d.; ed Westminster School and Christ Church, Oxford; Second Sec. UK del. to NATO 1958–62; First Sec. New Delhi 1961–63; Chargé d'affaires, Kathmandu 1963–64; Cabinet Office, London 1965–67; FCO 1967–69; First Sec. later Counsellor, UK Perm. Mission at UN, New York 1969–73; Counsellor, Bonn 1973–76; FCO 1976–79; Minister, Paris 1979–85; Amb. to Belgium 1985–89; Adviser to Gov. of Bank of England on European and Parl. Affairs 1989–2003; mem. Franco-British Council 1995, Chair. British Section 1997–2002; Acad. de Compatibilité (Paris) 1997–; mem. Council, City Univ. 1997–2002. *Leisure interests:* gardening, golf, shooting. *Address:* 16a Cambridge Street, London, SW1V 4QH, England (home); 40 rue Lauriston, 75116 Paris, France (home); 4 Hameau du Jardin, 50310 Lestre, France (home). *Telephone:* (20) 7834-0801 (home). *E-mail:* lydwinepo@aol.fr (home).

PETRIN, Tea, MEconSc; Slovenian economist, academic, politician and diplomatist; *Professor of Economics, University of Ljubljana;* b. 9 July 1944, Celje; ed Univ. of Ljubljana, Louisiana State Univ., USA; Visiting Prof., Univ. of Massachusetts at Amherst, USA 1988–89, Haas School of Business, Univ. of Calif., Berkeley 1992; Head, Research Centre and Centre for Continuous Educ., Faculty of Econs, Univ. of Ljubljana 1989–92, currently Prof., f. Postgrad. Studies in Entrepreneurship Programme 1990; Adviser to Cttee for Small Business Devt, Govt of Slovenia 1987–90, to Agency for Restructuring and Privatization Fund 1990–91, to Govt on Real Sector Structuring 1992–93; Adviser on Devt of Entrepreneurship in Rural Areas, to Foreign Affairs Office (FAO) Regional Office for Europe 1990–93, mem. staff 1994–97; involved in assessment of financial entrepreneurs in Slovenia, World Bank (IBRD) 1993; mem. working group World Bank, UNDP/UNIDO 1988–92, FAO Investment Centre 1996–97, EU Enterprise Enlargement Unit 2000; Minister for Econ. Affairs 1999–2000, of the Economy 2001–04; Amb. to Netherlands 2004–08; mem. Editorial Bd Review of Industrial Org. 1994–; mem. Int. Small Business Council 1992–, Econ. Council of Govt of Slovenia 1992, European Small Business Council 1994–96, European Asscn for Industrial Econs Research 1998–; Bd of Advisers of The Competitiveness Inst.; Fulbright Scholar, Inst. of Int. Studies, Univ. of California, Berkeley 1993–94, Univ. of Massachusetts, Lowell 1994. *Publications include:* over 200 books, monographs and articles in professional journals in fields of industrial policy, competition policy, restructuring of enterprises and entrepreneurship. *Address:* Department of Economics, University of Ljubljana, 1000, Ljubljana, Kardeljeva ploščad 17, Slovenia (office). *Telephone:* (1) 5892-400 (office). *E-mail:* tea.petrin@ef .uni-lj.si (office). *Website:* www.uni-lj.si (office).

PETRITSCH, Wolfgang, PhD; Austrian diplomatist and writer; *Permanent Representative, Organisation for Economic Co-operation and Development;* b. 26 Aug. 1947, Klagenfurt; ed Univs of Vienna and Southern California, USA; Adviser, Press Sec. of Austrian Fed. Chancellor 1977–83; mem. Austrian Mission to OECD, Paris 1983–84; Head Austrian Press and Information Service, New York 1984–92; Acting Head Dept for Multilateral Econ. Co-operation, Ministry of Foreign Affairs 1992–94; Head Dept for Information on European Affairs, Fed. Chancellery 1994; Head Dept for Int. Relations, City of Vienna 1995–97; Amb. to Yugoslavia 1997–99; EU Special Envoy for Kosovo 1998–99, EU Chief Negotiator at Kosovo peace talks, France Feb.–March 1999; High Rep. of the Int. Community in Bosnia and Herzegovina 1999–2002; Perm. Rep. to UN, WTO, Geneva 2002–08, to OECD 2008–; Pres. Mine Ban Convention's First Review Conference (Nairobi Summit) 2004; Chair. Vienna Cluster Munitions Conf. 2007, European Cultural Foundation, Amsterdam, Paul Lazarsfeld Soc. for Social Research, Vienna, Centre for European Integration Strategies, Geneva-Vienna-Sarajevo, Bruno Kreisky Forum for Int. Dialogue, Vienna, Herbert C. Kelman Inst. for Interactive Conflict Transformation, Vienna; Person of the Year, Bosnia and Herzegovina 2002, Friedrich Torberg Medal for Human Rights 2002, Bruno Kreisky Award for Best Political Book 2004, European Award for Human Rights Strasbourg 2006. *Publications include:* Kosovo-Kosova. Mythen, Daten, Fakten, Bosnien und Herzegowina fünf Jahre nach Dayton – Hat der Friede eine Chance? Zielpunkt Europa: Von den Schluchten des Balkan und den Mühen der Ebene, Das Kreisky-Prinzip: Der Mensch im Mittelpunkt 2009, Bruno Kreisky: Die Biografie 2011, Kärnten liegt am Meer: Konfliktgeschichten über Trauma, Macht und Identität 2012. *Address:* Permanent Representation of Austria to the OECD, 3, rue Albéric Magnard, 75116 Paris Cedex 16, France (office). *Telephone:* (1) 53922333 (office). *Fax:* (1) 40508705 (office). *E-mail:* wolfgang.petritsch@bka.gv.at (office). *Website:* www.wolfgangpetritsch.com (office).

PETROV, Aleksander Aleksandrovich; Russian scientist; *Head of Division, Dorodnicyn Computing Centre, Russian Academy of Sciences;* b. 3 Feb. 1934,

Orekchovo-Zuyevo, Moscow Region; s. of late Alexander Vasilyevich Petrov and Evgenia Nikolaevna Petrova; ed Moscow Inst. of Physics and Eng; Head of Div., Dorodnicyn Computation Centre, Russian Acad. of Sciences 1975–; Corresp. mem. Russian Acad. of Sciences 1991, mem. 1997–; main research in problems of evolution of econ. systems and methods of estimating potential possibilities of Econs, math. modelling of complex systems; USSR State Prize 1980, Nat. Peter The Great Prize and Medal 2000, Order of Friendship. *Publications include:* From Gosplan to Market Economy: Mathematics Analysis of the Evolution of the Russian Economic Structures 1999. *Leisure interests:* tennis, music. *Address:* Dorodnicyn Computing Centre, Russian Academy of Sciences, Vavilov str. 40, 119333, Moscow, Russia (office). *Telephone:* (495) 135-30-23 (office). *Fax:* (495) 135-61-59 (office). *E-mail:* petrov@ccas.ru (office).

PETROV, Andrei Borisovich; Russian ballet dancer and choreographer; *Artistic Director, Kremlin Ballet Theatre;* b. 27 Dec. 1945, Moscow; s. of Boris Kholfin and Olga Petrova; m. Olga Polyanskaya; ed Moscow Higher School of Choreography, Moscow Inst. of Theatre Arts; ballet dancer Bolshoi Theatre 1965–86, head of ballet troupe 1987–89, choreographer 1989–90; Founder and Artistic Dir Kremlin Ballet Theatre 1990–; juror and Chair. Organizing Cttee Moscow Int. Ballet Competition; juror Maya (St Petersburg), Benoit de la Dance (UNESCO); Chair. Theatre Artists' League Choreography Cttee; Order of the Great Services to the Native Land, Order of Saint Prince Daniyl of Moscow RSFSR People's Artist 1985. *Ballets include:* Don Quixote, Swan Lake, Fountain of Bakhchisarai, Raimonda, Romeo and Juliet; *Ballets directed include:* Red Snow-ball-Tree, Wooden Prince, Sketches, Knight of a Sorrowful Look, Ruslan and Ludmila, Swan Lake, Nutcracker, Zeus, Napoleon Bonaparte, Nevsky Prospect, Tom Sawyer, Fantastic Symphony, Coppelia. *Address:* Kremlin Ballet Theatre, Kremlin, Palace of Congresses, 03073 Moscow (office); Academician Zelensky str. 6, 41, Moscow, Russia (home). *Telephone:* (495) 917-23-36 (office); (495) 419-44-49 (home). *Fax:* (495) 928-52-32 (office). *Website:* www.kremlin-gkd.ru/index.htm (office).

PETROV, Rem Viktorovich, DrMedSc; Russian immunologist; b. 22 March 1930, Serafimovitch; s. of Victor Ivanovich Petrov and Kutniak Evdokia Emelianovna; m. 1st Tatiana Kuk 1960 (died 1970); m. 2nd Natalia Yemetz 1978; one s. one d.; ed Voronezh Medical Inst.; mem. CPSU 1956–91; research work at various grades in USSR (now Russian) Ministry of Health Inst. of Bio-Physics 1959–83, Head of Lab. 1983–; Pres. USSR (now Russian) Immunology Soc. 1983–; Dir of USSR (now Russian) Ministry of Health Inst. of Immunology 1983–88; mem. of Acad. of Medical Sciences 1978–; concurrently Head of Dept of Immunology of Second Moscow Inst. of Medicine 1974–; mem. Int. Scientific Advisory Bd of UNESCO 1996–; mem. USSR (now Russian) Acad. of Sciences 1984–, Vice-Pres. 1988–; mem. Acad. of Agric. 1991–; Ed. Sciences in Russia 1989; mem. World Acad. of Art and Sciences 1989–, New York Acad. of Sciences 1992–, Washington Acad. of Sciences 1993–, Norwegian Acad. of Sciences 1999–; Dr hc (Bar-Ilan Univ.) 1990, (Madrid Polytechnic Univ.) 1995; L. Mechnikov Gold Medal and Prize, Acad. of Sciences 1987; Hero of Labour 1990, Order of Lenin 1990, Achievements for the Fatherland, Third Degree 1999, State Prize in Science and Tech. 2001. *Publications:* Essays on the New Immunology 1976, Immunology and Immunogenetics 1981, Immunology 1982, Me or Not Me 1983, Suppressor B-lymphocytes 1988, Myelopeptides 1999, Scientific Publicistics 2000. *Leisure interests:* fishing, hunting, woodwork. *Address:* Russian Academy of Sciences, Leninsky pr. 14, 117901 Moscow (office); 38-8-86 Zelinskogo St, 117334 Moscow, Russia (home). *Telephone:* (495) 954-32-76 (office); (495) 135-10-63 (home). *Fax:* (495) 954-32-26 (office). *E-mail:* petrov@pran.ru (office).

PETROVIĆ, Slobodan; Kosovo lawyer and politician; *Deputy Prime Minister and Minister of Local Government;* b. 21 Dec. 1969, Prishtina; m.; one s.; Co-founder and Pres. Ind. Liberal Party (SLS) 2006–; mem. Kosovo Ass. 2008–, signed coalition agreement with Prime Minister Hashim Thaçi Feb. 2011; Dir for Integration in Post and Telecommunications of Kosovo 2007–10; Deputy Prime Minister and Minister of Local Govt 2011–; mem. Steering Council, Kosovo Privatization Agency 2008–; has participated in numerous int. confs and debates, official visits and meetings around the world; named Politician of the Year by Ass. of Non-governmental Orgs in Kosovo 2008, Amb. of Peace Award, Universal Peace Fed. 2012. *Address:* Ministry of Local Government, 10000 Prishtina, Ndërtesa e ish Rilindjes, Katet 10–13, Kosovo (office). *Telephone:* (38) 20035630 (office). *E-mail:* slobodan.petrovic@ks-gov.net (office); blerta.miftari@rks-gov.net (office). *Website:* mapl.rks-gov.net (office).

PETROVSKY, Artur Vladimirovich, PhD; Russian academic; *Professor of Psychology, RAE University;* b. 14 May 1924, Sevastopol; s. of Vladimir Vasilievich Petrovsky and Alexandra Abramovna Petrovskaya; m. Ivetta Sinelnikova; one s., one d.; ed Moscow Pedagogical Inst.; teacher, sr teacher, Vologda Pedagogical Inst. 1947–58; Asst Prof., Moscow State Pedagogical Inst., Prof. 1952–66; Chair. Psychology Dept 1966–92; Prof. RAE Univ. 1998–, Head of Theory and History of Psychology Lab.; Corresp. mem. USSR Acad. of Pedagogical Sciences 1968, mem. 1971; Academician-Sec. Dept of Psychology and Age Physiology 1968–76, 1997–, Vice-Pres. 1976–79, Pres. 1992–97; mem. Russian Acad. of Educ. 1991; Consultant Russian Acad. of Educ. Univ.; Honoured Scientist, Govt Prize of Russian Fed. 1998, Order of Honour 1999. *Publications:* History of Soviet Psychology 1967, General Psychology 1970, 1976–86, Problems of History and Theory of Psychology: selected works 1984. Essays on Psychology 1985, Psychology in USSR 1990, Psychology of Each of Us 1992, History of Psychology (co-author Yaroshevsky) 1994, Foundations of Theoretical Psychology 1996–98, Psychology in Russia: 20th Century 2001, Theoretical Psychology (co-author Yaroshevsky) 2001, Memories of a Psychologist 2001. *Leisure interest:* collecting books of fiction. *Address:* RAE University, Bolshaya Polyanka Str. 58, 119180 Moscow (office); Str. Chernya-khovskogo 4, Apt. 11, 125319 Moscow, Russia (home). *Telephone:* (495) 237-31-51 (office); (045) 151-98-63 (home). *Fax:* (495) 237-45-61 (office). *E-mail:* boris@urao .edu.

PETROVSKY, Vladimir Fyodorovich, DHist; Russian diplomatist; *Senior Research Fellow, United Nations Institute for Training and Research (UNITAR);* b. 29 April 1933, Volgograd; s. of Fyodor Petrovsky and Anna Khritinina; m. Myra Mukhina; one d.; ed Moscow Inst. of Int. Relations; with USSR (now Russian) Ministry of Foreign Affairs 1957–; staff mem. USSR Mission to UN 1957–61, mem. Office of the Foreign Minister, USSR Ministry of Foreign Affairs 1961–64; mem.

UN Secr. 1964–71; with dept of planning of int. policy, USSR Ministry of Foreign Affairs 1971–78, Head of Dept 1978–79, Head Dept of Int. Orgs 1979–86, Deputy Minister 1986–91, First Deputy Minister Aug.–Dec. 1991; Exec. Sec. CSCE Conf. on Human Dimension 1991; UN Under-Sec.-Gen. for Political Affairs 1992; Dir-Gen. UN Office, Geneva 1993–2002; Sec.-Gen. Conf. on Disarmament 1994–2002; Sr Research Fellow, UN Inst. for Training and Research (UNITAR) 2002–; Chair. Asscn for Comprehensive Dialogue Among Civilizations 2003–; mem. Acad. of Natural Sciences of Russian Fed., Mil. Acad. of Russian Fed., Russian Acad. of Outer Space, Int. Acad. of Information; Order of Merit (Russia) 1976, Order of Labour Red Banner 1983, Polish Order of Merit 2001. *Publications:* The Foreign Service of Great Britain 1958, The Diplomacy of 10 Downing Street 1964, US Foreign Policy Thinking: Theories and Concepts 1976, The Doctrine of National Security in US Global Strategy 1980, Disarmament: Concept, Problems, Mechanisms 1983, Security in the Era of Nuclear and Outer Space Technology 1985, The Triad of Strategic Security in the Global Society 2005, The Triad of Strategic Security in the New Global Community 2006. *Leisure interests:* art, memoirs. *Address:* Maly Kozhinsky Perelok 4, Apt 12, 123001 Moscow, Russia (home). *Telephone:* (495) 650-78-12 (home). *E-mail:* vpetrovs@yandex.ru (home).

PETRUCCIOLI, Claudio; Italian journalist, broadcasting executive, politician, writer and essayist; *President, Radiotelevisione Italiana SpA (RAI);* b. 22 March 1941, Terni, Umbria; obtained degree in political science and moved to Rome to become a professional journalist; mem. Partito Comunista Italiano (Italian Communist Party—PCI) 1960s, Municipal and Regional Sec., Terni and Regional Vice-Sec. in Umbria, Pres. Italian Communist Youth Fed. 1966–69, Nat. Dir PCI 1987; contributed to definition of first major reform of broadcasting system, implemented by Law 103 1975; Dir L'Unità 1980–83; elected to Lower House for Democratici di Sinistra (Democrats of the Left—DS) 1992–94; apptd by Parl. Cttee for Supervision of Broadcasting to post of Pres. Radiotelevisione Italiana SpA (RAI) 2005–. *Publications:* Rendi conto 2001, Quale Futuro per Il Servizio Pubblico Radiotelevisivo: Una [i.E. Un] Dibattito a Partire Dal Documento Per Una Discussione Su Televisione E Servizio Pubblico. Dentro E Fuori La Rai Di Claudio Petruccioli 2006. *Address:* Radiotelevisione Italiana SpA, Viale Mazzini 14, 00195 Rome, Italy (office). *Telephone:* (06) 38781 (office). *E-mail:* info@rai.it (office). *Website:* www.rai.it (office).

PETRUSHEVSKAYA, Liudmila Stefanovna; Russian author, playwright and poet; b. 26 May 1938, Moscow; d. of Stefan Antonovitsh Petrushevskij and Valentina Nikolaevna Jakovleva; m. 1st Evgenij Kharatian; one s.; m. 2nd Boris Pavlov; one s. one d.; ed Moscow Univ.; newspaper and radio journalist 1957–73; started writing short stories 1968, plays and folk tales 1971; stage productions and publ. of works were forbidden for many years; first underground performance 1975, first official performance, Tallinn 1979; mem. Bayerische Akad. der Schönen Kunste 1997; Int. A. Pushkin Prize (Germany) 1991, Triumph Award for Lifetime Achievement 2002, Russian State Prize for Arts 2004, Stanislavsky Award 2005, Triumph Prize 2006; prizes for the best short story of the year from Ogoniok 1988, 1989 and Oktiabr 1993, 1996, Grand Prize for play The Time: Night, Annual All-Russian Theatre Festival of Solo Theatre, Perm 1995, Moscow-Penne Prize (Russia/Italy) 1996. *Plays include:* Two Windows 1971, Music Lessons 1973, Cinzano 1973, Love 1974, The Landing 1974, Andante 1975, The Execution, A Glass of Water, Smirnova's Birthday 1977–78, Three Girls in Blue 1980, Colombina's Flat 1981, Moscow Choir 1984, The Golden Goddess 1986, The Wedding Night 1990, The Men's Quarters 1992; co-author of screenplay Tale of Tales (prize for best animated film of all time, Los Angeles 1980). *Publications include:* Immortal Love 1988, Songs of the 20th Century 1988, On the Way to the God Eros 1993, The Mystery of the House 1993; (children's books) Vasilli's Treatment 1991, Once Upon a Time There Was a Trrrr! 1994, Real Fairy Tales 1997, The Alphabet's Tale 1997; Complete Works (5 vols) 1996, The Girl's House 1998, Find Me, My Dream 2000, There Once Lived a Woman Who Tried to Kill Her Neighbor's Baby (World Fantasy Award 2010) 2009. *Leisure interest:* watercolour painting. *Address:* c/o OKNO Literary Agency, Solid Entertainment AB, S. Neptunig. 10C, 211 18 Malmo, Sweden; 107113 Moscow, Staroslobodsky per. 2A, Apt 20, Russia. *Telephone:* (495) 269-74-48. *Fax:* (495) 269-74-48.

PETSALNIKOS, Philippos I.; Greek lawyer and politician; b. 1 Dec. 1950, Mavrochori, Kastoria; m. Mariele Biedehdick; one s. two d.; ed Kastoria High School, Aristotle Univ. of Thessaloniki, Univ. of Bonn, Germany; fmr Scientific Assoc., Univ. of Bonn; Founding mem. Panhellenic Socialist Movt (PASOK), served as Sec. for Sector of Educ. as well as Sec. for PASOK's br. for Greeks living abroad; unsuccessful parl. cand. 1977, 1981; Gen. Sec., Ministry of Nat. Educ. and Religion (section of People's Educ.) 1984–85; mem. Vouli (Parl.) for Kastoria 1985–, Vice-Pres. 2004–09, Pres. (Speaker) 2009–12, Chair. Cttee on Parl. Procedure, Cttee on Public Enterprises, Banks, Public Utilities and Social Security Orgs; Deputy Minister of Educ. and Religious Affairs 1986–87, 1988–89, of Culture (responsible for Youth, for Greeks Living Abroad and for People's Educ.) 1987–88; Alt. Minister of Educ. and Religious Affairs 1994–96; Minister of Macedonia-Thrace 1996–98, of Public Order 1998–99, of Educ. and Religious Affairs 2000–01, of Justice 2001–04. *Address:* Vouli, Parliament Building, Leoforos Vassilissis Sofias 2, 100 21 Athens (office); Ath. Diakou 2, 521 00 Kastoria, Greece. *Telephone:* (210) 3708112 (office); (4670) 81006; (4670) 81444. *Fax:* (210) 3232913 (office). *E-mail:* petsalnikos@parliament.gr (office); petsaln@otenet.gr (office). *Website:* www.hellenicparliament .gr (office); www.petsalnikos.gr.

PETTENGILL, Gordon Hemenway, PhD; American physicist and academic; *Professor Emeritus of Planetary Physics, Department of Earth, Atmospheric and Planetary Sciences, Massachusetts Institute of Technology;* b. 10 Feb. 1926, Providence, RI; s. of Rodney G. Pettengill and Frances Pettengill; m. Pamela Wolfenden 1967; one s. one d.; ed Massachusetts Inst. of Tech., Univ. of California, Berkeley; staff mem., MIT Lincoln Lab. 1954–68, Assoc. Leader, Haystack Observatory 1965–68; Dir Arecibo Observatory, Puerto Rico (operated by Cornell Univ.) 1968–70; Prof. of Planetary Physics, Dept of Earth Atmospheric and Planetary Sciences, MIT 1970–2001, Prof. Emer. 2001–; Dir MIT Center for Space Research 1984–90; Prin. Investigator, Pioneer Venus Radar Mapper 1978–81, Magellan Venus Radar Mapper 1990–93, Mars Orbiting Laser Altimeter 1996–2001; mem. NAS, American Acad. of Arts and Sciences, AAAS, American Physical Soc., American Astronomical Soc., Int. Radio Science Union; Fellow, American Geophysical Union; Guggenheim Fellow 1980–81, Magellan Premium,

American Philosophical Soc. 1994, Charles A. Whitten Medal, American Geophysical Union 1997. *Achievements include:* involved in the study of the solar system using radar and radio techniques; discovered 3/2 spin-orbit resonance of Mercury 1965; pioneered delay-doppler radar mapping of planets; mapped surface of Venus using radar to penetrate the thick cloud layer. *Leisure interests:* ornithology, amateur radio (W1OUN). *Address:* MIT Center for Space Research, Room 37-587, Massachusetts Institute of Technology, 77 Massachusetts Avenue, Cambridge, MA 02139, USA (office). *Telephone:* (617) 253-4281 (office). *Fax:* (617) 253-0861 (office). *E-mail:* ghp@space.mit.edu (office). *Website:* space.mit.edu (office).

PETTIGREW, Pierre S., BA, MPhil; Canadian politician; b. 18 April 1951; ed Univ. du Québec à Trois-Rivières, Balliol Coll., Oxford, UK; Dir Political Cttee NATO Ass., Brussels 1976–78; Exec. Asst to Leader of Québec Liberal Party 1978–81; Foreign Policy Adviser to Prime Minister, Privy Council Office 1981–84; Vice-Pres. Samson Belair Deloitte and Touche Int. (Montreal) 1985–95, Exec. Adviser (Int.), Deloitte Canada 2006–; MP for Papineau 1996–2006; Minister for Int. Co-operation and Minister with special responsibility for La Francophonie 1996–97, Minister of Human Resources Devt 1997–99, of Int. Trade 1999–2003, of Health, of Intergovernmental Affairs, responsible for Official Languages 2003–04, of Foreign Affairs 2004–06; Co-Chair. First Nat. Forum on Canada's Int. Relations 1994. *Publication:* The New Politics of Confidence 1999. *Address:* Deloitte Canada, 33 Yonge Street, 2nd floor, Toronto, ON M5E 1G4, Canada (office). *Website:* www .deloitte.com (office).

PETTIT, Philip Noel, PhD, FAHA, FASSA, FAAAS, FBA, MRIA; Irish/Australian philosopher and academic; *L.S. Rockefeller University Professor of Politics and Human Values, Princeton University;* b. 20 Dec. 1945, Ballinasloe, Co. Galway, Ireland; s. of Michael A. Pettit and Bridget C. Molony; m. Victoria McGeer; two s.; ed Maynooth Coll., Nat. Univ. of Ireland, Queen's Univ. Belfast, Northern Ireland; Lecturer, Univ. Coll. Dublin 1968–72, 1975–77; Research Fellow, Trinity Hall Cambridge, UK 1972–75; Prof. of Philosophy, Univ. of Bradford, UK 1977–83; Professorial Fellow, Research School of Social Sciences, ANU, Canberra, Australia 1983–89, Prof. of Social and Political Theory 1989–2002, Distinguished Prof. of Philosophy 2013–; Visiting Prof. of Philosophy, Columbia Univ., New York, USA 1997–2001; William Nelson Cromwell Prof. of Politics, Princeton Univ., USA 2002, currently L.S. Rockefeller Univ. Prof. of Politics and Human Values Fellow, American Acad. of Arts and Sciences; Hon. mem. Italian Soc. for Analytical Philosophy, Hon. MRIA; Hon. DLitt (Nat. Univ. of Ireland) 2000, (Queen's Univ., Belfast) 2007; Hon. PhD (Crete) 2005, (Montreal) 2006; Hon. DPhil (Lund) 2008; Univ. Medal, Univ. of Helsinki 1992. *Publications:* Concept of Structuralism 1975, Judging Justice 1980, Semantics and Social Science (with G. Macdonald) 1981, Not Just Deserts: A Republican Theory of Criminal Justice (with J. Braithwaite) 1990, The Common Mind: An Essay on Psychology, Society and Politics 1992, Republicanism: A Theory of Freedom and Government 1997, A Theory of Freedom: From the Psychology to the Politics of Agency 2001, Rules, Reasons and Norms: Selected Essays 2002, Penser en Société 2003, Mind, Morality, and Explanation: Selected Collaborations (co-author) 2004, The Economy of Esteem (with Geoffrey Brennan) 2004, Made with Words: Hobbes on Language, Thought and Mind 2008, A Political Philosophy in Public Life (with Jose Marti) 2010, Group Agency (with Christian List) 2011, On the People's Terms 2012. *Leisure interest:* cycling. *Address:* UCHV, 308 Marx Hall, Princeton University, Princeton, NJ 08544-1012 (office); 16 College Road, Princeton, NJ 08540, USA (home). *Telephone:* (609) 258-4759 (office); (609) 924-3664 (home). *E-mail:* ppettit@princeton.edu (office). *Website:* www.princeton .edu/~ppettit (office).

PETTY, Richard; American fmr racing driver; b. 2 July 1937, Level Cross, NC; s. of Lee Petty Lee; m. Lynda Owens Petty; one s. three d.; stock car racing driver 1958–92; Winston Cup Rookie of the Year 1959; total of 200 Career NASCAR Winston Cup Victories, NASCAR Winston Cup Champion 1964, 1967, 1971, 1972, 1974, 1975, 1979; winner Daytona 500 1964, 1966, 1971, 1973, 1974, 1979, 1981; 27 victories in one season 1967; sport's first million-dollar driver; last race in 1992; f. Petty Enterprises LLC (complete stock car racing operation); est. Richard Petty Museum 1988; Most Popular Winston Cup Driver 1962, 1964, 1968, 1970, 1974, 1975, 1976, 1977, 1978; Nat. Motorsports Press Asscn (NMPA) Myers Brothers Award 1964, 1967, 1971, 1992, NMPA Driver of the Year 1974, 1975; Nat. NC Athletic Hall of Fame 1973, Int. Motorsports Hall of Fame 1997, Automotive Hall of Fame 2002; Medal of Freedom 1992; American Auto Racing Writers & Broadcasters Asscn (AARWBA) Man of the Year 1995. *Address:* Petty Enterprises LLC, 311 Branson Mill Road, Randleman, NC 27317-8008, USA. *Telephone:* (336) 498-3745. *Website:* www.pettyracing.com (office).

PETTY, Tom; American singer, songwriter and musician (guitar); b. 20 Oct. 1953, Gainesville, Fla; guitarist with local groups, Sundowners, Epics, Mudcrutch; founder mem., Tom Petty and The Heartbreakers 1975–; mem., the Traveling Wilburys 1988–; regular US and int. tours, concert and festival appearances; MTV Music Video Award (for Don't Come Around Here No More) 1985, Billboard Century Award 2005. *Film appearances:* FM 1978, Made in Heaven 1987, The Postman 1997. *Recordings include:* albums: with the Heartbreakers: Tom Petty and The Heartbreakers 1976, You Gonna Get It! 1978, Damn The Torpedoes 1979, Hard Promises 1981, Long After Dark 1982, Southern Accents 1985, Pack Up The Plantation 1986, Let Me Up (I've Had Enough) 1987, Full Moon Fever 1989, Into The Great Wide Open 1991, Greatest Hits 1993, Take The Highway 1994, She's The One (OST) 1996, Echo 1999, Anthology: Through The Years 2000, The Last DJ 2002, Mojo 2010; with The Traveling Wilburys: Traveling Wilburys 1988, Vol. 2 1989, Vol. 3 1990; solo: Wildflowers 1994, Highway Companion 2006; with Mudcrutch: Mudcrutch 2008. *Address:* East End Management, 12441 Ventura Court, Studio City, CA 91604, USA (office). *Telephone:* (818) 985-5060 (office). *Fax:* (818) 985-5069 (office). *Website:* www.tompetty.com; www.mudcrutchmusic.com.

PEUGEOT, Patrick; French insurance executive; *Chairman, Comité Intermouvements auprès des Évacués;* b. 3 Aug. 1937, Paris; s. of Jacques Peugeot and Edith Peugeot (née Genoyer); m. Catherine Dupont 1963; three s.; ed Lycée Hoche, Ecole Sainte-Geneviève à Versailles, Ecole polytechnique, Ecole nat. d'admin.; auditor, Cour des comptes 1965, Commissariat au plan (Public Enterprises Cttee) 1966–70; Sec.-Gen. Librairie Hachette 1972–74; Sec.-Gen. Groupe des Assurances générales de France (AGF) 1975–83, Dir-Gen. AGF-Réassurance 1979–83; tech. consultant to Ministry of Economy and Finances 1981–83; Dir-Gen. Caisse centrale de

réassurance 1983–84, Pres. Advisory Bd 1984–85, Hon. Pres. 1985–; Pres. Dir-Gen. Société commerciale de réassurance (Scor) 1983–94, Hon. Pres. and Dir. 1994–; Vice-Pres. Dir-Gen. La Mondiale 1995, Chair. and CEO 1996–2005; Pres. Groupement des assurances des personnes (Gap) 1997–99; Pres. Réunion des organismes d'assurance mutuelle 1999–2005; Chair. Asscn Int. des Socs d'Assurance Mutelle 2004–, Comité Intermouvements auprès des Évacués (CIMADE) 2005–; Chevalier, Ordre nat. du Mérite. *Address:* CIMADE, 64 rue Clisson, 75013 Paris (office); 82 rue Notre-Dame-des-Champs, 75006 Paris, France (home). *Telephone:* 1-44-18-60-50 (office). *Fax:* 1-45-56-08-59 (office). *E-mail:* infos@cimade.org (office). *Website:* www.cimade.org (office).

PEUGEOT, Roland; French automotive industry executive; b. 20 March 1926, Valentigney; s. of Jean-Pierre and Colette (née Boillat-Japy) Peugeot; m. Colette Mayesky 1949; two s.; ed Lycées Janson-de-Sailly and Saint-Louis, Paris and Harvard Business School, Mass., USA; Pres. Etablissements Peugeot Frères 1959–; Pres. du Conseil de Surveillance de Peugeot SA 1972–98, advisor to Supervisory Bd 2001–07; mem. Bd Automobiles Peugeot 1982–; Pres. Peugeot Talbot Belgique 1985; Dir of subsidiaries and other cos including L'Union et Le Phénix Espagnol 1974–, Champagne Laurent Perrier 1992–; Officier, Légion d'honneur, Officier, Ordre des Arts et des Lettres 2002. *Address:* 75 avenue de la Grande Armée, 75116 Paris (office); 170 avenue Victor-Hugo, 75116 Paris, France (home).

PEUGEOT, Thierry; French automotive industry executive; *Chairman of the Supervisory Board, PSA Peugeot Citroën SA;* b. 19 Aug. 1957; s. of the late Pierre Peugeot; early career as Export Man. for Middle East, Marrel Group, then Dir of American subsidiary; joined Peugeot 1988, fmrly Regional SE Asia Man., Peugeot, Man. Dir Peugeot do Brasil, Man. Dir SLICA, Vice-Pres. Citroën Large Int. Accounts, Citroën Services and Spare Parts, Chair. Peugeot SA 2002–03, Chair. Supervisory Bd PSA Peugeot Citroën SA 2003–, Chair. Compensation Cttee, mem. Appointments and Governance Cttee, Strategy Cttee; Vice-Chair. and COO Établissements Peugeot Frères; Dir, Soc. Foncière, Financière et de Participations, Soc. Anonyme de Participations, Immeubles et Participations de l'Est, Faurecia, Cie Industrielle de Delle (CIS), Air Liquide; Perm. Rep. of CID on Bd of Dirs of LISI Aerospace. *Address:* PSA Peugeot Citroën SA, 75 avenue de la Grande-Armée, 75116 Paris, France (office). *Telephone:* 1-40-66-55-11 (office). *Fax:* 1-40-66-54-14 (office). *Website:* www.psa-peugeot-citroen.com (office).

PEVTSOV, Dmitry Anatlyevich; Russian actor; b. 8 July 1963, Moscow; m. Olga Drozdova; ed Moscow State Inst. of Theatre Arts; actor Taganka Theatre 1985–91; Moscow Theatre of Leninsky Komsomol (LENKOM) 1991–; European Prize Felix (Glasgow). *Films include:* Mother 1989, The Witches Cave 1989, His Nickname is Beast 1990, I Hope for You 1992, The Possessed 1992, Alice and the Bookseller 1992, The Mafia is Immortal 1993, Line of Life 1996, Queen Margo 1996, The Countess of Monsoreau 1998. *Plays include:* The Marriage of Figaro, The Seagull. *Address:* Teplichny per. 5, Apt 139, 123298 Moscow, Russia (home). *Telephone:* (495) 198-77-69 (home).

PEYRAT, Jérôme, LenD; French civil servant; *Director of Cabinet, Secretariat of State for Cooperation and Francophony;* b. 28 Nov. 1962, Sarlat, Dordogne; m.; three c.; ed Institut d'études politiques de Paris, École nationale d'administration, Institut des Hautes Etudes de la Défense Nationale; served as intern in Embassy in Turkey; joined Dept of Int. Relations, Mayor of Paris 1990; served as foreign press adviser and asst spokesperson to Pres. Jacques Chirac; Dir of Communications to Mayor of Paris 1998–2000; Dir of Communications and Dir of Cabinet to Michèle Alliot-Marie, Pres. Rassemblement pour la République 2000–02; Political Adviser to Minister of Interior, Nicolas Sarkozy 2005–07, to Pres. Nicolas Sarkozy 2007–09; mem. Union pour un Mouvement Populaire (UMP) 2002–09; unsuccessful UMP cand. for parl. elections in Dordogne; currently Mayor, La Roque-Gageac; Dir of Cabinet to Alain Joyandet, Minister of State for Cooperation and Francophony 2009–; Pres. Communauté de Communes du Périgord Noir; Chevalier, Ordre Nat. du Mérite. *Publications:* Les Petits matins: essai sur la pensée politique (with Nathalie Kosciusko-Morizet) 2002. *Leisure interests:* mountaineering, skiing, hiking. *Address:* Mairie, 24250 La Roque-Gageac (office); Secrétariat d'État à la Coopération et à la Francophonie, 20 Rue Monsieur, 75007 Paris, France (office). *Telephone:* 1-53-69-40-02 (office). *Fax:* 1-53-69-43-73 (office). *E-mail:* jerome.peyrat@diplomatie.gouv.fr (office). *Website:* www.jeromepeyrat.org (home); www.diplomatie.gouv.fr (office).

PEYRELEVADE, Jean; French business executive; *Partner, Toulouse et Associés;* b. 24 Oct. 1939, Marseille; s. of Paul Peyrelevade and Nadia Benveniste; m. Anne Chavy 1962; three s. one d.; ed Faculté de droit de Paris, Ecole Nat. de l'aviation civile; fmr armaments and aviation engineer; Dir Dept of Foreign Business, Crédit Lyonnais 1973–82; Asst Dir Cabinet of M. Pierre Mauroy 1982; Pres. Cie Financière de Suez 1983–86; Pres. Banque Stern 1986–88; Chair. Union des Assurances de Paris 1988–93; Dir Bouygues 1994–; Chair. Crédit Lyonnais 1993–2003 (resgnd after bank's acquistion by Crédit Agricole); Govt Rep. on Bd of Renault 1996–2000; mem. Econ. and Social Council 1994–; Partner Toulouse et Assocs 2004–; mem. Supervisory Bd CMA-CGM 2005–; mem. Bd of Dirs Suez. *Publications:* La mort du dollar 1974, L'economie de spéculation 1978, Economie de l'entreprise 1989, Pour un capitalisme intelligent 1993, Le gouvernement d'entreprise 1999. *Leisure interests:* skiing, golf. *Address:* Conseil de surveillance, CMA-CGM Marseille Siège Social 4, quai d'Arenc, 13235 Maresille Cedex 02, France (office). *Telephone:* 4-88-91-90-00 (office). *Fax:* 4-88-91-90-95 (office). *E-mail:* media@cma-cgm.com (office). *Website:* www.cma-cgm.com (office).

PFAFF, Judy, BFA, MFA; American artist; b. 22 Sept. 1946, London, England; ed Wayne State Univ., Southern Illinois Univ., Univ. of Washington and Yale Univ.; numerous visiting faculty positions since 1971 including Calif. Inst. of Arts, Yale Univ., Rhode Island School of Design, Oberlin Coll., Princeton Univ.; mem. of Grad. Faculty, School of Visual Arts, New York 1986–91; Prof. of Visual Arts, Columbia Univ. 1992–94; Guggenheim Fellowship for Sculpture, MacArthur Fellow 2004, Barnett and Annalee Newman Foundation Fellowship 2006, Acad. Member Fellowship, American Acad. of Arts and Sciences 2013; mem. American Acad. of Arts and Letters 2009–; Dr hc (Pratt Inst.) 1999; Award of Merit Gold Medal for Sculpture, American Acad. of Arts and Letters 2002, Lifetime Achievement Award, Southern Graphics Council Int. Conf. 2010. *Address:* c/o Bellas Artes Gallery, 653 Canyon Road, Santa Fe, NM 87501, USA (office).

Telephone: (505) 983-2745 (office). *E-mail:* info@judypfaffstudio.com (office). *Website:* www.judypfaffstudio.com.

PFAFF, William W., III; American author and journalist; b. 29 Dec. 1928, Council Bluffs, Ia; s. of William W. Pfaff, Jr and Adele Keeline Pfaff; m. Carolyn Cleary; one s. one d.; ed Univ. of Notre Dame; Asst Ed. Commonweal magazine, New York 1949–55; Writer, ABC News 1955–57; Exec. Free Europe Cttee 1957–61; Sr mem. Hudson Inst., New York 1961–75, Deputy Dir Hudson Research Europe, Paris 1971–78; freelance writer 1978–; syndicated columnist, International Herald Tribune 1978–2003; contrib. to The New Yorker magazine 1971–92, also New York Review of Books, Harper's Magazine, Foreign Affairs, The National Interest, The Observer (London), Commentaire (Paris) and others; Hon. LLD (Univ. of Notre Dame) 1992; Rockefeller Foundation Grant 1962, Prix de l'Annuaire Français de Relations Internationales 2004, Arthur Ross Award for Distinguished Commentary, American Acad. of Diplomacy 2006. *Publications include:* The New Politics (with Edmund Stillman) 1960, The Politics of Hysteria (with Edmund Stillman) 1964, Power and Impotence (with Edmund Stillman) 1966, Condemned to Freedom 1971, Barbarian Sentiments: How the American Century Ends (Prix Jean-Jacques Rousseau for Best Political Book of 1990, Geneva) 1989, The Wrath of Nations 1993, Barbarian Sentiments: America in the New Century 2000, Fear, Anger and Failure 2004, The Bullet's Song: Romantic Violence and Utopia 2004, The Irony of Manifest Destiny 2010; published in Best American Essays: The Lay Intellectual (autobiographical essay) 1987. *Address:* 23/25 rue de Lisbonne, 75008 Paris, France. *Telephone:* 1-43-59-05-66. *E-mail:* wpfaff@orange.fr. *Website:* www .williampfaff.com.

PFEIFFER, Michelle; American actress; b. 29 April 1957, Santa Ana, Calif.; d. of Dick Pfeiffer and Donna Pfeiffer; m. 1st Peter Horton (divorced 1987); one adopted d.; m. 2nd David E. Kelley 1993; one s.; ed Fountain Valley High School, Golden West Coll., Whitley Coll. *Films include:* Grease 2, Into the Night, The Witches of Eastwick, Sweet Liberty, Married to the Mob, Tequila Sunrise 1989, Dangerous Liaisons 1989, The Fabulous Baker Boys 1989, The Russia House 1989, Love Field, Frankie and Johnny 1991, Batman Returns 1992, The Age of Innocence 1993, Wolf 1994, My Posse Don't Do Homework 1994, Dangerous Minds, Up Close and Personal, To Gillian on Her 37th Birthday, One Fine Day 1997, A Thousand Acres 1997, Privacy 1997, The Prince of Egypt (voice) 1998, The Story of Us 1999, The Deep End of the Ocean 1999, A Midsummer Night's Dream 1999, Being John Malkovich 1999, What Lies Beneath 2000, I am Sam 2001, White Oleander 2002, Sinbad: Legend of the Seven Seas (voice) 2003, I Could Never Be Your Woman 2007, Hairspray 2007, Stardust 2007, Chéri 2009, Personal Effects 2009, Dark Shadows 2012, People Like Us 2012. *Address:* ICM, 8492 Wilshire Blvd, Beverly Hills, CA 90211-1934, USA (office). *Telephone:* (310) 550-4000 (office). *Website:* www.icmtalent.com (office).

PFISTER, Bruno, LLM, MBA; Swiss business executive; *Group CEO, Swiss Life Group;* b. 1959; ed Univ. of Geneva, Grad. School of Man., Univ. of California, Los Angeles, USA; called to the Bar, Geneva; worked for Chase Manhattan Bank in London and Geneva; Man. Consultant, McKinsey & Co. 1988–96; Chief of Staff of Pvt. Banking Div., Liechtenstein Global Trust 1996–98, Chief Financial Officer LGT Group and LGT Bank, Liechtenstein 1998–99; mem. Credit Suisse Group Exec. Bd, Head of Customer Segment Man. and Product Man., Credit Suisse 1999–2002; Chief Financial Officer Swiss Life Group 2002–06, CEO Swiss Life Group International 2006–08, Group CEO Swiss Life Group 2008–; mem. Bd of Dirs Gottex Fund Man. Holdings Ltd, St Peter Port, Guernsey, Swiss Insurance Asscn; Vice-Chair. Admission Bd and Exec. Cttee of Admission Bd of SIX Swiss Exchange. *Address:* Swiss Life Group, General Guisan-Quai 40, 8022 Zürich, Switzerland (office). *Telephone:* (4) 32843253 (office). *Fax:* (4) 33383253 (office). *E-mail:* info@swisslife.ch (office). *Website:* www.swisslife.com (office).

PFLIMLIN, Etienne Alphonse Marie Georges; French banking executive and fmr civil servant; *Chairman of the Supervisory Board, CIC Crédit Industriel & Commercial SA;* b. 16 Oct. 1941, Thonon les Bains, Haute Savoie; s. of Pierre Pflimlin and Marie-Odile Pflimlin (née Heinrich); m. Marie-Sophie Nehlil; two s.; ed Ecole Polytechnique, Ecole Nat. d'Admin, Institut d'Etudes Politiques, Paris; fmr teacher, Univ. Paris-IX Dauphine, Institut d'Etudes Politiques de Paris; Commr, Ministry of Finance 1964–67; Dir of Cabinet, Pref. of Finistère 1968; Counsellor, Cour des Comptes (Nat. Audit Office) 1970–84; with Ministry of Culture 1973–78; Counsellor, Ministry of Budget 1978–79; Dir of Cabinet Ministry of Commerce and Handicrafts 1979–81; joined Crédit Mutuel 1984, became Pres. Banque Fédérative du Crédit Mutuel 1985, Pres. Crédit Mutuel Centre Est Europe 1985, Pres. Confédération Nationale du Crédit Mutuel 1987, Pres. Supervisory Bd Banque de l'Economie du Commerce et de la Monetique 1992, Chair. CIC Crédit Industriel et Commercial SA 1998–; Pres. Groupe L'Alsace 1988–, Le Monde Enterprises 1988–, European Co-operative Bank Group 2002–; Pres. European Cttee Int. Co-operative Banking Assnc; Chevalier, Order nat. du Mèrite, Officier, Légion d'honneur, des Palmes académiques. *Address:* CIC Crédit Industriel & Commercial SA, 6 avenue de Provence, 75452 Paris 9, France (office). *Telephone:* 1-45-96-96-96 (office). *Fax:* 1-45-96-96-66 (office). *E-mail:* filbass@cic.fr (office). *Website:* www.cic.fr/en (office).

PHAM, Binh Minh; Vietnamese diplomatist and politician; *Minister of Foreign Affairs;* b. 26 March 1959, Vu Ban Dist, Nam Dinh Prov.; s. of Nguyen Co Thach (Pham Van Cuong) and Phan Thi Phuc; m. Nguyen Nguyet Nga; two c.; ed Hanoi Inst. of Foreign Relations, Attaché, Embassy in London 1982–86; Officer, Dept of Public Affairs, Ministry of Foreign Affairs (MFA) 1986–91, Deputy Dir, Dept of Int. Orgs 1991, Deputy Perm. Rep., Perm. Mission to UN, New York 1999, Minister and Deputy Amb., Embassy in Washington, DC 2001–03, Dir Dept of Int. Orgs, MFA 2003, Asst Minister of Foreign Affairs 2006, Deputy Minister 2007–11, Minister 2011–; Chair. Vietnam–Cambodia Cooperation Sub-Cttee; mem. Dang Cong San Viet Nam (Communist Party of Viet Nam), alt. mem. Cen. Cttee 1996–2009, official mem. 2009–11, mem. 2011–. *Address:* Ministry of Foreign Affairs, 1 Ton That Dam, Ba Dinh District, Hanoi, Viet Nam (office). *Telephone:* (4) 37992000 (office). *Fax:* (4) 38231872 (office). *E-mail:* banbientap@mofa.gov.vn (office). *Website:* www.mofa.gov.vn (office).

PHAM, Gia Khiem, PhD; Vietnamese politician and government official; b. 6 Aug. 1944, Hanoi; m.; one s. one d.; ed Hanoi Univ. of Tech. and postgraduate studies in Czechoslovakia; Lecturer, Bac Thai Univ. of Mechanical Eng and

Electronics 1968–70; worked at Ministry of Investment and Planning 1976–96, positions included Head, Industrial Div. and Dir Dept of Science, Educ. and Environment, then Deputy Minister of Investment and Planning, Minister of Science, Tech. and Planning 1996–97; Deputy Prime Minister 1997–2011; Minister of Foreign Affairs 2006–11; Deputy, Nat. Ass. 1997–; mem. Cen. Cttee, CP of Viet Nam 1997–2006, Politburo 2006–11. *Address:* c/o Ministry of Foreign Affairs, 1 Ton That Dam, Ba Dinh District, Hanoi, Viet Nam (office).

PHAM, The Duyet; Vietnamese trade union official, economist and fmr politician; fmr mine man.; fmr Pres. Viet Nam Gen. Confed. of Labour; Leader CP of Hanoi, Viet Nam 1987; elected to Politburo of CP of Viet Nam 1991–2001, to Standing Bd 1998. *Address:* Communist Party of Viet Nam, 1 Hoang Van Thu, Hanoi, Viet Nam (office).

PHAM, Gen. Van Tra; Vietnamese army officer and politician; b. 19 Aug. 1935, Que Vo, Bac Ninh, Tonkin; served in army 1953–2006; Chief of the Gen. Staff and Vice-Minister of Defence 1995–97; Minister of Nat. Defence 1997–2006; mem. Politburo, CP of Viet Nam 1996–2006, Vice-Sec. Party Cen. Cttee Mil. Comm.; Deputy, Nat. Ass.; Hero of the People's Armed Forces. *Address:* c/o Ministry of National Defence, 7 Nguyen Tri Phuong, Ba Dinh District, Hanoi, Viet Nam.

PHAM MINH MÂN, HE Cardinal Jean-Baptiste, MEd; Vietnamese ecclesiastic; *Archbishop of Thành-Phô Hô Chí Minh (Hôchiminh Ville);* b. 5 March 1934, Ca Mau; ed Minor Seminary of Cantho, St Joseph's Major Seminary, Saigon (now Ho Chi Minh City, and in USA; ordained priest 1965; Prof., Minor Seminary of Cantho; further studies in USA 1968–71; returned to Viet Nam and again named Prof. at Minor Seminary of Cantho until Communist invasion in 1975; Rector Major Seminary of Can Tho for three dioceses of Can Tho, Vinh Long and Long Xuyen 1989–93; Coadjutor Bishop of My Tho 1993–98; Archbishop of Thành-Phô Hô Chí Minh (Hôchiminh Ville) 1998–; cr. Cardinal (Cardinal Priest of San Giustino) 2003; attended Xth Ordinary Ass. of World Synod of Bishops, Vatican City 2001. *Address:* Archdiocese of Thanh-Pho Ho Chi Minh, Toa Tong Muc, 180 Nguyen Dink Chieu, Q. 3, Thanh-Pho Ho Chi Minh City, Viet Nam (office). *Telephone:* (8) 930-3828 (office). *Fax:* (8) 930-0598 (office).

PHAN, Van Khai; Vietnamese politician; b. 25 Dec. 1933, Thong Hoi village, Cu Chi Dist, Saigon (now Ho Chi Minh City); involved in revolutionary activities from 1947, in N Viet Nam 1954–60; joined CP 1959; student, Moscow Nat. Univ. of Econs 1960–65; fmrly with Gen. Dept of State Planning Cttee, fmr econ. researcher; in communist-controlled areas of S Viet Nam 1973; Deputy Dir Aid Planning Dept of Nat. Reunification Cttee 1974–75; Deputy Dir Planning Dept, Ho Chi Minh City 1976–78, Dir 1979–80; Deputy Mayor, Ho Chi Minh City 1979–80, Perm. Deputy Mayor 1981–84, Mayor 1985–89; Chair. People's Cttee of Ho Chi Minh City 1985–89; Perm. mem. Ho Chi Minh City CP Cttee 1979–80, Deputy Sec. 1981–84; Alt. mem. CP Cen. Cttee 1982–84, mem. 1984–, mem. Political Bureau 1991–; Chair. State Planning Cttee 1989–91; Deputy Chair. Council of Ministers 1991–92; Perm. Deputy Prime Minister of Viet Nam 1992–97; Prime Minister of Viet Nam 1997–2006; currently Chair. Viet Nam Badminton Fed. *Address:* Viet Nam Badminton Federation, 36, Tran Phu Street, Hanoi, Viet Nam (office).

PHANSTIEL, Howard G., MA; American healthcare industry executive; *Chairman, President and CEO, PacifiCare Health Systems Inc.;* ed Syracuse Univ., NY; various exec. and man. positions with Prudential Bache Int. Bank, Marine Midland Bank, Student Loan Marketing Asscn (Sallie Mae), US Dept of Health, Educ. and Welfare, Health Care Financing Administration (HCFA), Citibank, Ill. Bureau of Budget, WI Bureau of Planning and Budget; fmr Exec. Vice-Pres. Finance and Information Services, WellPoint Health Networks Inc., Calif.; Chair. and CEO ARV Assisted Living Inc., Calif. –2000, Exec. Vice-Pres. and Chief Financial Officer, PacifiCare Health Systems July–Oct. 2000, Pres. and CEO Oct. 2000–. *Address:* PacifiCare Health Systems Inc., 5995 Plaza Drive, Cypress, CA 90630, USA (office). *Telephone:* (714) 952-1121 (office). *Fax:* (714) 226-3581 (office). *Website:* www.pacificare.com (office).

PHANTOG; Chinese mountaineer; b. Aug. 1939, Xigazê, Tibet; d. of Cirhen Phantog and Cijiu Phantog; m. Jia-shang Deng 1963; one s. two d.; ed Cen. Coll. of Nationalities; first Chinese woman to climb Everest 1975; Deputy Dir Wuxi Sports and Physical Culture Comm. 1981–. *Leisure interests:* table tennis, badminton. *Address:* Wuxi Sports and Physical Culture Commission, Jiangsu, People's Republic of China (office). *Telephone:* 225810 (office).

PHARAON, Ghaith Rashad, MBA, PhD; Saudi Arabian business executive and financier; b. 7 Sept. 1940, Riyadh; ed Colorado School of Mines, Stanford and Harvard Univs, USA; Founder Saudi Arabia Research and Devt Corpn (Redec) 1965, now Chair. and Dir-Gen.; Chair. Bd Saudi Arabian Parsons Ltd, Saudi Automotive Industries Ltd, Redec Daelim Ltd, Interstal, Saudi Chemical Processors Ltd, Arabian Maritime Co., Saudi Inland Transport, Attock Petroleum, Nat. Refinery Ltd, Attock Cement Pakistan Ltd, Attock Refinery Ltd –2011; Vice-Chair. Jezirah Bank Ltd, Saudi Light Industries Ltd, Arabian Chemical Industries Ltd; mem. Bd Okaz Publications, Pakistan Oilfields, Attock Refinery Ltd, Attock Cement Pakistan Ltd, Nat. Refinery Ltd, Tihama, Bd of Assocs of Harvard Business School, Int. Devt Council of Colorado School of Mines; int. fugitive, wanted by the FBI following collapse of Bank of Credit and Commerce International (BCCI) on charges of fraud, money laundering and racketeering 1992, has travelled the world aboard luxury yacht Le Pharaon; Commendatore (Italy); King Abdul Aziz Award. *Address:* PO Box 1935, Jeddah (office); Ghaith Pharaon Residence, Ruwais, Jeddah, Saudi Arabia (home).

PHAYSITH, Sompao; Laotian economist and central banker; *Governor, Banque de la RDP Lao;* Deputy Gov. Banque de la RDP Lao (central bank) 2006–11, Gov. 2011–; mem. Bd of Govs South East Asian Central Banks 2012–; fmr mem. Lao Securities Exchange Comm. *Address:* Office of the Governor, Banque de la RDP Lao, rue Yonnet, BP 19, Vientiane, Laos (office). *Telephone:* (21) 213109 (office). *Fax:* (21) 213108 (office). *E-mail:* bol@bol.gov.la (office). *Website:* www.bol.gov.la (office).

PHELPS, Edmund Strother, PhD; American economist and academic; *Professor of Political Economics and Director of Center on Capitalism and Society, Columbia University;* b. 26 July 1933, Evanston, Ill.; s. of Edmund S. Phelps and Florence Stone Phelps; m. Viviana Montdor 1974; ed Amherst Coll. and Yale Univ.; Research Economist, RAND Corpn 1959–60; taught Yale Univ. 1960–66; Prof.,

Univ. of Pennsylvania 1966–71; Prof., Columbia Univ. 1971–78, 1979–82, McVickar Prof. of Political Econs 1982–, also Dir, Center on Capitalism and Soc.; Prof., New York Univ. 1977–78; Sr Adviser Brookings Inst. 1976–; Econ. Adviser EBRD 1991–94; mem. NAS 1982; mem. Econ. Policy Panel, Observatoire Français des Conjonctures Economiques 1991–; Sr Adviser Consiglio Nazionale delle Ricerche 1997–2000; Dean, New Huadu Business School of China and Switzerland 2010–; Full Foreign mem. Russian Acad. of Sciences; Distinguished Fellow, American Econ. Asscn 2000; several hon. professorships; Hon. Patron Univ. Philosophical Soc., Trinity Coll.; Hon. DH (Amherst Coll.) 1985, (Univ. of Mannheim) 2001, (Univ. Tor Vergata, Rome) 2001, (Université Paris-Dauphine) 2004, (Institut d'Etudes Politiques) 2006, (Univ. of Buenos Aires) 2007, (Tsinghua Univ.) 2007, (Université Libre de Bruxelles) 2010; Chevalier, Légion d'honneur 2008; Kenan Enterprise Award 1996, Nobel Prize in Econ. Science 2006, Premio Pico della Mirandola for humanism 2008, Kiel Global Economy Prize 2008, Louise Blouin Creative Leadership Award 2011, Mendeleev Medal and Pres.'s Medal, Nat. Univ. of Ireland 2012. *Publications:* Golden Rules of Economic Growth 1966, Microeconomic Foundations of Employment and Inflation Theory (ed.) 1970, Studies in Macroeconomic Theory: Vols 1, 2 1979, 1980, Political Economy: An Introductory Text 1985, The Slump in Europe 1988, Seven Schools of Macroeconomic Thought 1990, Structural Slumps 1994, Rewarding Work 19977, Enterprise and Inclusion in Italy 2002, Designing Inclusion (ed.) 2003, Rethinking Expectations (co-ed.) 2012, Mass Flourishing 2013. *Leisure interest:* music. *Address:* Center on Capitalism and Society, Columbia University, 1126 International Affairs Building, 420 West 118th Street, New York, NY 10027, USA (office). *Telephone:* (212) 854-2060 (office). *Fax:* (212) 854-3735 (office). *E-mail:* esp2@columbia.edu (office). *Website:* www.edmundphelps.com.

PHELPS, Michael Fred; American swimmer; b. 30 June 1985, Baltimore, Md; s. of Fred Phelps and Debbie Davisson Phelps; ed Towson High School, Univ. of Michigan; Olympic Games, Sydney 2000: 5th 200m butterfly; World Championships, Fukuoka 2001: gold medal, 200m butterfly (world record); Pan Pacific Championships, Yokohama 2002: gold medal, 200m individual medley, 400m individual medley, 4×100m medley relay (world record), silver medal, 200m butterfly, 4×200m freestyle relay; World Championships, Barcelona 2003: gold medal, 200m butterfly (world record), 200m individual medley (world record), 400m individual medley (world record), 4×100m medley relay (world record), silver medal, 100m butterfly (broke world record in semi-final, subsequently broken by gold-medallist Ian Crocker), 4×200m freestyle relay; youngest male Olympian since 1932, Olympic Games, Sydney 2000; Olympic Games, Athens 2004: gold medal, 100m butterfly, 200m butterfly, 200m individual medley, 400m individual medley (world record), 4×200m freestyle relay, 4×100m medley relay (world record), bronze medal, 200m freestyle, 4×100m freestyle relay; first in 200m freestyle, World Short Course Championships 2004; World Championships, Montreal 2005: gold medal, 200m freestyle, 200m individual medley, 4×100m freestyle relay, 4×200m freestyle relay, 4×100m medley relay, silver medal, 100m butterfly; three gold medals, US Nat. Championships 2005; Pan Pacific Championships, Victoria 2006: gold medal, 200m butterfly (world record), 200m individual medley (world record), 400m individual medley, 4×100m freestyle relay (world record), 4×200m freestyle relay, silver medal, 200m backstroke; six medals, US Nat. Championships 2006; World Championships, Melbourne 2007: gold medal, 100m butterfly, 200m butterfly (world record), 200m freestyle (world record), 200m individual medley (world record), 400m individual medley (world record), 4×100m freestyle relay, 4×200m freestyle relay (world record); Olympic Games, Beijing 2008: gold medal, 100m butterfly, 200m butterfly (world record), 200m freestyle (world record), 200m individual medley (world record), 400m individual medley (world record), 4×100m freestyle relay (world record), 4×200m freestyle relay (world record), 4×100m medley relay (world record) (five gold medals won in individual events, tying record for individual gold medals at a single Games originally set by Eric Heiden in 1980 Winter Olympics and equalled by Vitaly Scherbo at 1992 Summer Games); World Championships, Rome 2009: gold medal, 100m butterfly (world record), 200m butterfly (world record), 4×100m freestyle relay, 4×200m freestyle relay (world record), 4×100m medley relay (world record), silver medal, 200m freestyle; Pan Pacific Games, Irvine 2010: gold medal, 100m butterfly, 200m butterfly, 4×100m freestyle relay, 4×200m freestyle relay, 4×100m medley relay; World Championships, Shanghai 2011: gold medal, 100m butterfly, 200m butterfly, 4×200m freestyle, 4×100m medley, silver medal, 200m freestyle, 200m individual medley, bronze medal, 4×100m freestyle relay; Olympic Games, London 2012: gold medal, 100m butterfly, 200m individual medley, 4×200m freestyle relay, 4×100m medley relay, silver medal, 200m butterfly, 4×100m freestyle relay; holds record in total career of Olympic medals, with total of 22 medals (18 gold) (the most by any Olympian); only man to win five US Nat. titles at the same Championships, only swimmer to win US Nat. titles in three different strokes at the same Championships 2003; set seven world records and one Olympic record at Beijing Olympics 2008 (only swimmer to break seven world records at one tournament); coach Bob Bowman; swims for North Baltimore Aquatic Club; est. Michael Phelps Foundation 2008; American Swimmer of the Year Award 2001, 2002, 2003, 2004, 2006, 2007, 2008, 2009, FINA Trophy (Best Swimmer, World Championships 2003) 2003, James E. Sullivan Award 2003, World Swimmer of the Year 2003, 2004, 2006, 2007, 2008, 2009, Golden Goggle Male Performance of the Year 2004, 2006, 2007, 2008, 2009, a street in Baltimore re-named The Michael Phelps Way 2004, Golden Goggle Male Athlete of the Year 2004, 2007, 2008, US Olympic Cttee SportsMan of the Year Award 2004, 2008, Golden Goggle Relay Performance of the Year 2006, 2007, 2008, 2009, Sports Illustrated Sportsman of the Year 2008, invited to appear before Maryland House of Delegates and Maryland Senate to be honoured for his Olympic accomplishments 2009. *Address:* c/o Melissa Gagnon, Octagon, 15 Lund Road, Suite 101, Saco, ME 04072, USA (office); PO Box 1734, Olney, MD 20830-1734, USA. *Telephone:* (207) 775-1500 (office). *E-mail:* melissa.gagnon@octagon.com (office); info@michaelphelpsfoundation.org (office). *Website:* www.octagon.com (office); www.michaelphelpsfoundation.org (office).

PHELPS DE CISNEROS, Patricia, BA; Venezuelan philanthropist, art collector and museum trustee; *Founder, Fundación Cisneros and Colección Patricia Phelps de Cisneros;* b. Caracas; m. Gustavo A.Cisneros; ed Wheaton Coll., Mass, USA; began collecting art works from 1970, Co-founder (with husband and brother-in-law, Ricardo Cisneros, in asscn with Cisneros Group of Cos) and

Chair. Fundación Cisneros (pvt. philanthropic org. based in Caracas, Venezuela); runs four main programmes: Colección Patricia Phelps de Cisneros (CPPC), Piensa en arte/Think Art, Cl@se and AME, Professional Devt for Educators; collaboration with Hunter Coll., New York, Bard Graduate Center, Museum of Modern Art (MoMA); exhbn at Museo Reina Sofia in Madrid, La invención concreta: Colección Patricia Phelps de Cisneros, introduced new artists to the European public, including Lygia Clark, Lygia Pape and Hélio Oiticica 2013; Trustee, MoMA; mem. Advisory Cttee David Rockefeller Center for Latin American Studies, London Tate Modern Int. Council and Latin American Acquisition Cttee; mem. Bd Fundación Museo Nacional Centro de Arte Reina Sofia, Fundación Amigos del Museo del Prado, Madrid; mem. Council, Berggruen Museum, Berlin; mem. American Friends of the Beyeler Fondation, New York; Golden Lion of San Marco 2000; Chevalier, Légion d'honneur 2002; Dr hc (Wheaton Coll.) 2003; Gertrude Vanderbilt Whitney Award for Patronage of the Arts 2008, Bard Graduate Center Iris Prize 2010. *Address:* 2 East 78th Street, New York, NY 10075, USA (office). *Telephone:* (212) 717-6080 (office). *Fax:* (212) 717-6183 (office). *E-mail:* info@coleccioncisneros.org (office). *Website:* www.coleccioncisneros.org (office); www.fundacion.cisneros.org (office).

PHILARET, (Kyrill Varfolomeyevich Vakhromeyev); Russian/Belarusian ecclesiastic; *Patriarchal Exarch of All Byelorussia;* b. 21 March 1935, Moscow; s. of Varfolomey and Aleksandra V. Vakhromeyev; ed Moscow Theological Seminary and Moscow Theological Acad.; became monk 1959, ordained as a priest 1961; lecturer, Asst Prof., Moscow Theological Acad. 1961–65, Rector 1966–73; Bishop of Tikhvin 1965, of Dmitrov 1966; Vice-Chair. Dept of External Church Relations, Moscow Patriarchate 1968–71, Chair. 1981–; Archbishop 1971; Archbishop of Berlin and Middle Europe 1973–78; Metropolitan 1975, of Minsk and Byelorussia 1978, of Minsk and Grodno (later Minsk and Slutsk 1992), Patriarchal Exarch of All Byelorussia 1989; Perm. mem. Holy Synod of Russian Orthodox Church 1981–, Chair. Foreign Relations Dept 1987–89, Theological Comm. 1993–; Dean, Theological Faculty of St Methodius & Cyril, European Humanities Univ. 1993–2005; Rector, Theological Inst. of St Methodius & Cyril, Byelorussian State Univ. 2005–; Chair. Editorial Bd Theological Studies 2001–; Hon. mem. Moscow and St Petersburg Theological Acads; Order of St Vladimir 1969, Order of St Sergey of Radonezh 1981, Order of Friendship of the Peoples 1985, 2005, Order of Daniil of Moscow 1990, Order of Fatherland 1998, Cross of St Euphrosyne of Polotsk 1998, Order of St Seraphim of Sarov 2005; D'Theol hc (St Vladimir Seminary, New York), (St Sergey Orthodox Theological Inst., Paris) Medal of Frantsysk Skorina 1995. *Publications:* Russian Orthodox Church Relations to Western Non-Orthodox Churches, St Cyril and Methodius' Works in the Territory of The Russian State in Russian Historical Literature, Patriotic Character of Patriarch Aleksiy, Theology of Neighbourhood 2002, The Vital Way of Life 2004, The Search for the Kingdom 2005; contrib.: Studies of the Minsk Theological Acad. *Address:* 220004 Minsk, 10 Osvobozdeniya Street, Belarus (home). *Telephone:* (172) 03-73-48 (office); (172) 09-42-99 (office). *Fax:* (172) 00-11-19 (office). *E-mail:* press-service@church.by (office). *Website:* www.church.by (office).

PHILBIN, Ann, BA, MA; American museum curator; *Director, Hammer Museum of Art and Cultural Center, University of California, Los Angeles;* b. 21 March 1952, Boston, Mass; ed Univ. of New Hampshire, New York Univ.; Researcher, Frick Art Reference Library, New York 1977–79; Program Coordinator, Artists Space 1979–80; Asst Curatorial Coordinator, The Neue Museum 1980–81; Curator The Ian Woodner Family Collection 1981–83; Asst Dir Grace Borgenicht Gallery 1983–85; Dir Curt Marcus Gallery 1985–88; Dir The Drawing Center, New York 1989–98; Dir UCLA Hammer Museum of Art and Cultural Center 1999–; mem. Bd of Dirs several arts and non-profit orgs, including Vera List Center for Art and Politics at The New School for Social Research, Etant Donne (grant-making agency promoting French-American cultural exchange), Streb/Ringside dance co., HIV Law Project, New York. *Address:* The Hammer Museum, 10899 Wilshire Blvd, Los Angeles, CA 90024, USA (office). *Telephone:* (310) 443-7032 (office). *E-mail:* info@hammer.ucla.edu (office). *Website:* hammer.ucla.edu (office).

PHILEMON, Bart; Papua New Guinea politician; *Minister for Public Service;* Minister for Transport and Civil Aviation –2000, Minister for Foreign Affairs and Bougainville Affairs 2000–02; Caretaker Gov., Minister for Treasury, Finance, Privatisation and Agric. 2002; Minister for Finance and Treasury 2002–06, currently Minister for Public Service; Gov. World Bank for Papua New Guinea. *Address:* Ministry of Public Servie, Vulpindi Haus, Waigani NCD, Papua New Guinea (office).

PHILIP, Danny; Solomon Islands politician; b. 5 Aug. 1953; m.; fmr English teacher; MP for Vona Vona-Rendova-Tetepare 1984–93, for S New Georgia-Rendova-Tetepare 1994–2001, for Rendova Tetepare 2010–, Prime Minister 2010–11 (resgnd); Minister of Foreign Affairs 1995–96, 2000–01; Leader People's Progressive Party 1997–2000; f. Reform and Democratic Party 2010. *Address:* c/o Office of the Prime Minister, PO Box G1, Honiara, Solomon Islands (office).

PHILIPPE, Guy; Haitian rebel leader and fmr police chief; *Secretary-General, Front pour la Reconstruction Nationale;* b. 29 Feb. 1968, Pestel, Nippes; m.; ed Saint-Louis de Gonzague, law degree from Ecuador and studied medicine in Mexico for a year, Escuela Superior de Poilicia General Alberto Enriquez Gallo, Ecuador; fmr mem. FAD'H (Haitian Army); trained by US Special Forces in Ecuador 1991–94; sr security official under Pres. René Preval 1995; when FAD'H was dissolved in early 1995, Philippe incorporated into new Nat. Police Force, served as police chief in Port-au-Prince suburb of Delmas 1997–99, in Cap-Haitien 1999–2000; accused of organizing coup attempt, fled to Ecuador then to Dominican Repub. 2002, remained there until coup d'état that ousted Pres. Jean-Bertrand Aristide Feb. 2004; named commdr of rebel army by Buteur Metayer; Sec.-Gen. Front pour la Réconstruction Nationale 2004–; presidential cand. in general election 2006; wanted by US Govt for drug trafficking. *Address:* Front pour la Réconstruction Nationale, Gonaïves, Haiti.

PHILIPPE I, HM King of the Belgians Philippe Léopold Louis Marie, MA; Belgian; b. 15 April 1960, Brussels; s. of King Albert II and Queen Paola; m. Mathilde d'Udekem d'Acoz 1999; children: HRH Princess Elisabeth, HRH Prince Gabriel, HRH Prince Emmanuel and HRH Princess Eléonore; ed Royal Mil. Acad., Trinity Coll., Oxford, UK and Stanford Univ., USA; apptd Second Lt Belgian armed forces 1980, subsequently obtained fighter pilot's wings and certificates as parachutist and commando, attended Royal Higher Defence Inst. 1989, apptd Col 1989, apptd Maj.-Gen. and Rear-Adm. 2001; Royal Household est. 1992; Pres. Nat. Sustainable Devt Council 1993–97; apptd Senator 1994; Founder Le Fonds Prince Philippe 1998–; succeeded to the throne 21 July 2013; Hon. Pres. Bd of Dirs Foreign Trade Office 1993–, Fed. Sustainable Devt Council 1997–; Hon. Chair. Belgian Investment Co. for Developing Countries 2003–, European Chapter of the Club of Rome 2004–, Int. Polar Foundation 2004–. *Address:* Royal Palace, 16 rue Bréderode, 1000 Brussels, Belgium. *Telephone:* (2) 5512020. *Website:* www .monarchie.be.

PHILIPPOU, Andreas N., PhD; Cypriot politician and university professor; *Member, Republic of Cyprus Tax Tribunal;* b. 15 July 1944, Katokopia; s. of Nicholas Philippou and Maria G. Protopapa; m. Athina Roustani 1984; three d.; ed Pancyprian Gymnasium, Athens Univ., Greece, Univ. of Wisconsin, USA; Teaching and Research Asst, Univ. of Wis., Asst Prof. of Math., Univ. of Tex., El Paso; Asst then Assoc. Prof. of Math., American Univ. of Beirut, Lebanon; Prof. of Business Admin., Beirut Univ. Coll.; Visiting Prof. of Applied Math., subsequently Prof. of Probability and Statistics, Pres. of Math. Dept and Vice-Rector, Univ. of Patras, Greece; Minister of Educ. 1988–90; Pres. Preparatory Cttee for establishment of Univ. of Cyprus, then first Pres. Interim Governing Bd of Univ. 1988–90; mem. House of Reps 1991–2001, mem. House Cttees. on Educ. and the Budget, Council of IPU, Rapporteur for Kosovo 1998, for the Middle East 1991–2001; Founding mem. Cen. Cttee, Social Democratic Movt (EDEK) 2000–; mem., Tax Tribunal 2004–; fmr Vice-Pres. Hellenic Aerospace Industry; Hon. Pres. Math. Asscn of Cyprus 1988; Grande Ufficiale Repub. of Italy. *Publications:* 65 research papers; ed seven books. *Leisure interests:* swimming, sailing. *Address:* Tax Tribunal, 9 Stasandrou, 1648 Nicosia (office); 26 Atlantis Street, 2107 Nicosia, Cyprus (home). *Telephone:* (22) 803405 (office); (22) 336360 (also fax) (home). *Fax:* (22) 803450 (office).

PHILIPS, Dalton, MBA; Irish retail executive; *Chief Executive, William Morrison Supermarkets PLC;* b. 1969, Co. Wicklow; ed Univ. Coll. Dublin, Harvard Univ., USA; began retail career with Jardine Matheson, NZ; with Wal-Mart 1998–2005, various man. positions in Int. Div. including COO in Germany; Chief Exec. Brown Thomas Group Ltd, Dublin 2005–07; COO Loblaw Companies Ltd, Canada 2007–10; Chief Exec. William Morrison Supermarkets PLC 2010–. *Address:* William Morrison Supermarkets PLC, Hilmore House, Gain Lane, Bradford, West Yorks., BD3 7DL, England (office). *Telephone:* (845) 611-5000 (office). *Website:* www.morrisons.co.uk (office).

PHILIPS, Luc; Belgian financial services industry executive; *Chief Financial Officer, KBC Groep NV;* b. 1952; ed Coll. of Man. and Commercial Sciences, Brussels; joined KBC Bank 1971, various positions in Credit Dept and Int. Credit Div., with New York Br., 1981–87, Man.-Dir New York Br. 1987–91, Head of Cen. Man.–Multinationals Div. 1991–93, Gen.-Man. Investment Banking Directorate 1993–97, Man.-Dir and mem. Exec. Cttee KBC Bank and KBC Bank and Insurance Holding Co. 1998–2003; Man.-Dir and mem. Exec. Cttee Kredietbank 1997–98; Man.-Dir and mem. Exec. Cttee Almanij NV 2003–05, mem. Bd of Dirs KBC Bank and Insurance Holding Co., KBC Bank, KBC Insurance, then Chair. KBC Insurance, Deputy Chair. KBC Bank and Dir KBC Group NV (following merger of KBC Bank and Insurance Holding Co. with Almanij in 2005), mem. Exec. Cttee and Chief Financial and Risk Officer KBC Groep May–Sept 2009, mem. Exec. Cttee and Chief Financial Officer KBC Groep NV 2009–. *Address:* KBC Groep NV, Havenlaan 2, Brussels 1080, Belgium (office). *Telephone:* (2) 781-52-154 (office). *Fax:* (2) 429-44-16 (office). *Website:* www.kbc.com (office).

PHILLIPPE, Ryan; American actor; b. 10 Sept. 1974, New Castle, Del.; m. Reese Witherspoon 1999 (divorced 2007); one s. one d. *Films include:* Crimson Tide 1995, Invader 1996, White Squall 1996, Nowhere 1997, I Know What You Did Last Summer 1997, Little Boy Blue 1997, Homegrown 1998, 54 1998, Playing by Heart 1998, Cruel Intentions 1999, Company Man 2000, The Way of the Gun 2000, Antitrust 2001, Igby Goes Down 2002, Gosford Park 2002, The I Inside 2003, Crash 2004, Five Fingers 2005, Chaos 2005, Flags of Our Fathers 2006, Breach 2007, Stop-Loss 2008. *Television includes:* One Life to Live 1992, The Secrets of Lake Success (mini-series) 1993, Natural Enemies 1993, A Perry Mason Mystery: The Case of the Grimacing Governor 1994, Deadly Invasion: The Killer Bee Nightmare 1995. *E-mail:* ryanphillonline@yahoo.com. *Website:* www.ryan-phillippe.com.

PHILLIPS, Caryl, BA, FRSL, FRSA; British/Saint Christopher and Nevis writer and academic; *Professor of English, Yale University;* b. 13 March 1958, St Kitts, West Indies; ed The Queen's Coll., Oxford; Writer-in-Residence, The Factory Arts Centre, London 1980–82, Univ. of Mysore, India 1987, Univ. of Stockholm 1989; visiting writer, Amherst Coll., Mass., USA 1990–92, Writer-in-Residence and Co-Dir Creative Writing Center 1992–94, Prof. of English 1994–97, Prof. of English and Writer-in-Residence 1997–98; Prof. of English and Henry R. Luce Prof. of Migration and Social Order, Barnard Coll., Columbia Univ., New York 1998–2005, Dir of Initiatives in the Humanities 2003–05; Prof. of English, Yale Univ. 2005–; Visiting Prof. of English, Dartmouth Coll., NH 2008, Univ. of Oxford 2009; Writing Instructor, Arvon Foundation, UK 1983–; Visiting Prof. of Humanities, Univ. of the West Indies, Barbados 1999–2000; Exec. Sec., N American Network of Cities of Asylum 2005–09; Consultant Ed., Faber Inc., Boston 1992–94, Graywolf Press, Minneapolis 1994–; Contributing Ed., Bomb Magazine, New York 1993–; Dir Heartland Productions Ltd 1994–2000; Advisory Ed. Wasifiri Magazine, London 1995–; Series Ed. Faber and Faber, London 1996–2000; mem. Arts Council of GB Drama Panel 1982–85, British Film Inst. Production Bd 1985–88, Bd, The Bush Theatre, London 1985–89; mem. English PEN 1997, Writers' Guild of GB 1997, American PEN (Council mem.) 1998; Fellow, New York Public Library 2002–03; Hon. Sr mem. Univ. of Kent 1988–; Hon. Fellow The Queen's Coll., Oxford 2006–; Hon. AM (Amherst Coll.) 1995; Hon. DUniv (Leeds Metropolitan) 1997, (York) 2003; Hon. DLett (Leeds) 2003, (Univ. of the West Indies) 2010, (Univ. of Edinburgh); Hon. MA (Yale) 2006; British Council 50th Anniversary Fellowship 1984, Guggenheim Fellowship 1992, Lannan Literary Award 1994. *Films:* Playing Away 1986, The Mystic Masseur 2001. *Plays:* Strange Fruit 1980, Where There is Darkness 1982, The Shelter 1983, Rough Crossings 2007. *Radio:* plays: The Wasted Years (BBC Giles Cooper Award for Best Radio Play of the Year) 1984, Crossing the River 1985, The Prince of Africa 1987, Writing Fiction 1991, A Kind of Home 2004, Hotel Cristobel 2005, Dinner with Friends 2011; several documentaries. *Television:* The Final Passage (Channel 4) 1996. *Publications:* fiction: The

Final Passage (Malcolm X Prize for Literature) 1985, A State of Independence 1986, Higher Ground 1989, Cambridge (Sunday Times Young Writer of the Year Award) 1991, Crossing the River (James Tait Black Memorial Prize 1994) 1993, The Nature of Blood 1997, A Distant Shore (Commonwealth Writers Prize 2004) 2003, Dancing in the Dark (PEN/Beyond Margins Award 2006) 2005, In the Falling Snow 2009; non-fiction: The European Tribe (Martin Luther King Memorial Prize) 1987, The Atlantic Sound 2000, A New World Order: Selected Essays 2001, Foreigners: Three English Lives 2007, Colour Me English: Selected Essays 2011; editor: Extravagant Strangers 1997, The Right Set: A Tennis Anthology 1999. *Leisure interests:* golf, running. *Address:* c/o Georgia Garrett, Rogers, Coleridge & White Literary Agency, 20 Powis Mews, London, W11 1JN, England (office). *Telephone:* (20) 7221-3717 (office). *Fax:* (20) 7229-9084 (office). *E-mail:* georgia@rcwlitagency.co.uk (office). *Website:* www.rcwlitagency.co.uk (office); www.carylphillips.com.

PHILLIPS, Charles E., Jr, BS, MBA, JD; American business executive; *CEO, Infor;* b. Little Rock, Ark.; ed USAF Acad., Hampton Univ., New York Law School; served as Capt. in US Marine Corps; with Morgan Stanley –2003; joined Oracle in 2003, mem. Bd of Dirs and Pres. Oracle Corpn –2010, responsible for global field operations, including consulting, marketing, sales, alliances and channels, and customer programmes; CEO Infor (software co.) 2010–; mem. Bd of Dirs Jazz at Lincoln Center, New York City, American Museum of Natural History, New York Law School, Viacom Inc., Morgan Stanley. *Address:* c/o Infor, 641 Avenue of the Americas, New York, NY 10011, USA (office). *Telephone:* (646) 336-1700 (office). *Website:* www.infor.com (office).

PHILLIPS, David, CBE, OBE, BSc, PhD, FRSC, FCGI; British chemist and academic; *Professor Emeritus and Senior Research Investigator, Imperial College, London;* b. 3 Dec. 1939, Kendal, Westmorland (now Cumbria); s. of Stanley Phillips and Daphne Ivy Phillips (née Harris); m. Caroline L. Scoble 1970; one d.; ed South Shields Grammar Tech. School and Univ. of Birmingham; Postdoctoral Fellow and Fulbright Scholar, Univ. of Texas, USA 1964–66; Visiting Scientist, Acad. of Sciences of USSR 1966–67; Lecturer, Dept of Chem., Univ. of Southampton 1967–73, Sr Lecturer 1973–76, Reader 1976–80; Wolfson Prof. of Natural Philosophy, Royal Inst. of GB 1980–89, Acting Dir 1986, Deputy Dir 1986–89; Prof. of Physical Chem., Imperial Coll. of Science, Tech. and Medicine 1989–2002, Head of Dept of Chem. 1992–2002, Hofmann Prof. of Chem. 1999–2006, Dean of Life Sciences and Physical Sciences Faculties 2002–05, Sr Dean 2005–06, Prof. Emer. and Sr Research Investigator 2006–, Fellow of Imperial Coll. 2010–; Chair. European Photochemistry Asscn, London Gifted and Talented; mem. Council, RSC, Chair. Educ. and Qualification Bd; Vice-Pres. and Gen. Sec. BAAS 1987–89, Hon. Life Fellow 2006; Pres. RSC 2010–12; Hon. Life Fellow, City and Guilds of London Inst., Royal Inst. of GB 2005, British Science Asscn; Hon. DSc (Birmingham) 2011, (Durham) 2012, (Leicester) 2012; Hon. LLD (Bath) 2012; Spinks Lecturer, Univ. of Saskatchewan 1979, Wilsmore Fellow, Univ. of Melbourne 1983, 1990, RSC Nyholm Lectureship and Medal 1994, Faraday Award for Public Understanding of Science, Royal Soc. 1997, Premio Internazionale Sebetia Ter, Premio Internazionale Sebetia-Ter, Napoli 1999, B.D. Shaw Medal, Univ. of Nottingham 2005, RSC Award for Service 2008, Porter Medal, European Photochemistry Asscn, Inter-American Photochemistry Soc. and Asian Oceanic Photochemistry Asscn 2010. *Radio:* Desert Island Discs (BBC Radio 4) 2011, Private Passions (BBC Radio 3) 2012. *Television:* BBC TV Christmas Lectures for Young People (with J. M. Thomas) 1987. *Publications:* Time-Correlated Single-Photon Counting 1984, Polymer Photophysics 1985, Time-Resolved Laser Raman Spectroscopy 1987, Jet Spectroscopy and Dynamics 1994, Life and Scientific Legacy of George Porter, Nobel Laureate 2008; 593 publns in refereed literature on photochemistry and related topics. *Leisure interests:* music, theatre, popularization of science, tennis. *Address:* Department of Chemistry, Imperial College London, Exhibition Road, London, SW7 2AZ (office); 195 Barnett Wood Lane, Ashtead, Surrey, KT21 2LP, England (home). *Telephone:* (20) 7594-5716 (office); (1372) 274385 (home). *E-mail:* d.phillips@imperial.ac.uk (office); dclphillips@btinternet.com (home). *Website:* www.ch.imperial.ac.uk (office).

PHILLIPS, Douglas George; Canadian politician; *Commissioner, Yukon Territory;* b. 4 Dec. 1946, Toronto; s. of Norm Phillips and Grace Phillips; m. Dale Stokes; five c.; spent several years as small business owner, Yukon Territory; mem. Yukon Legis. Ass. for Riverdale N constituency 1985–2000, becoming Minister of Tourism, Minister of Educ., Minister responsible for the Women's Directorate, Minister of Justice, Minister responsible for the Public Service Comm.; Yukon Admin. 2007–10, Commr of Yukon 2010–; fmr Dir Yukon Sourdough Rendezvous Cttee; fmr mem. and Pres. Yukon Fish and Game Asscn; mem. Yukon Land Use Planning Council 2004–10 (Chair. 2007–10); fmr Chair. Whitehorse Hosp. Close to Your Heart Fund; Dir Yukon Hosp. Foundation. *Leisure interests:* travelling, gardening, fishing, hunting and trapping. *Address:* Office of the Commissioner, 1098 First Avenue, Closeleigh Manor Building, Whitehorse, YT Y1A 0C1, Canada (office). *Telephone:* (867) 667-5121 (office). *Fax:* (867) 393-6201 (office). *E-mail:* commissioner@gov.yk.ca (office). *Website:* www.gov.yk.ca/commissioner (office).

PHILLIPS, Dwight; American track and field athlete and business executive; b. 1 Oct. 1977, Decatur, Ga; m. Valerie Phillips 2004; ed Univ. of Kentucky, Arizona State Univ.; started out in triple jump before switching to long jump; gold medal World Indoor and Outdoor Championships 2003; gold medal Athens Olympics 2004; gold medal World Outdoor Championships 2005, 2009, 2011; gold medal Continental Cup, Split 2011; currently Prin., Rebel Star Media (film production co., Atlanta. *Address:* Rebel Star Media, Suite Ell-2, 500 Bishop Street, Atlanta, GA 30318, USA (office). *Telephone:* (678) 973-0977 (office). *E-mail:* win@rebelstarmedia.com (office). *Website:* www.rebelstarmedia.com (office).

PHILLIPS, Leon Francis, MSc, PhD, ScD, FRSNZ, FNZIC; New Zealand physical chemist, academic and novelist; *Professor of Chemistry, University of Canterbury;* b. 14 July 1935; m. Pamela A. Johnstone 1959; two s.; ed Westport Tech. Coll., Christchurch Boys' High School, Univ. of Canterbury, Univ. of Cambridge, UK; Upper Atmosphere Chem. Group, McGill Univ., Canada 1961; Lecturer, Univ. of Canterbury 1962, Prof. of Chem. 1966–; Pres. NZ Inst. of Chem. 2001; Visiting Prof., Univ. of Washington 1968, Monash Univ. 1969, Univ. of Perugia 2000; Visiting Fellow, Balliol Coll., Oxford 1975, Japan Soc. for Promotion of Science 1984; Visiting Scholar, Rice Univ., Houston, USA 1987; SERC Research Fellow, Univ. Birmingham 1989; Harkness Fellow 1968; Fellow, NZ Inst. of Chem.;

RSC Corday-Morgan Medal 1971, Hector Medal, Royal Soc. of NZ 1979, Fulbright Award 1980, Easterfield and ICI prizes, NZ Inst. of Chem., Research Medal, Univ. of Canterbury 2000, JILA Fellowship, Univ. of Colorado, Boulder 2011. *Publications:* Basic Quantum Chemistry, Electronics for Experimenters, Chemistry of the Atmosphere (with M. J. McEwan), First Year Chemistry (with J. M. Coxon and J. E. Fergusson); over 200 scientific papers; novels: Fire in His Hand 1978, The Phoenix Reaction 1979, Ritual Fire Dance 1980. *Leisure interests:* sailing, skiing, reading, writing. *Address:* Department of Chemistry, University of Canterbury, Private Bag 4800, Christchurch 1 (office); 12 Maidstone Road, Christchurch 4, New Zealand (home). *Telephone:* (3) 364-2425 (office); (3) 366-7001 (home). *Fax:* (3) 364-2110 (office); (3) 364-2999 (home). *E-mail:* leon.phillips@canterbury.ac.nz (office). *Website:* www.chem.canterbury.ac.nz/people/phillips.shtml (office).

PHILLIPS, Leslie Samuel, OBE, CBE; British actor, producer and director; b. 20 April 1924, Tottenham, London; m. four c.; ed Chingford School; early career as child actor; fmr army officer; Vice-Pres. Royal Theatrical Fund, Disabled Living Foundation; Evening Standard Lifetime Achievement in Films Award 1997, Dilys Powell Award, London Film Critics' Circle Awards 2007. *Theatre includes:* Falstaff in The Merry Wives of Windsor (RSC), On the Whole Life's Been Jolly Good (Edin. Festival), Love for Love, Naked Justice, For Better or Worse, Ghosts of Albion, Charley's Aunt, Camino Real, Deadly Game, Diary of a Nobody, Man Most Likely To…, Passion Play, Naked Justice. *Films include:* Lassie From Lancashire (uncredited) 1938, The Citadel (uncredited) 1938, Train of Events 1949, The Woman with No Name 1950, Pool of London 1951, The Galloping Major (uncredited) 1951, The Sound Barrier 1952, Time Bomb (uncredited) 1953, The Fake 1953, The Limping Man 1953, You Know What Sailors Are 1954, Value for Money 1955, As Long as They're Happy 1955, High Flight 1956, The Gamma People 1956, Just My Luck 1957, The Barretts of Wimpole Street 1957, Brothers in Law 1957, Les Girls 1957, The Smallest Show on Earth 1957, I Was Monty's Double 1958, The Big Money 1958, This Other Eden 1959, Please Turn Over 1959, The Night We Dropped a Clanger 1959, The Navy Lark 1959, The Man Who Liked Funerals 1959, The Angry Hills 1959, Carry on Nurse 1959, Carry on Teacher 1959, Ferdinando I. re di Napoli (Ferdinand I: King of Naples) 1959, Watch Your Stern 1960, No Kidding 1960, Inn for Trouble 1960, Carry on Constable 1960, Doctor in Love 1960, Raising the Wind 1961, In the Doghouse 1961, Very Important Person 1961, A Weekend with Lulu 1962, Crooks Anonymous 1962, The Fast Lady 1962, Father Came Too! 1963, You Mus Be Joking! 1965, Doctor in Clover 1966, Maroc 7 (also producer) 1967, Some Will, Some Won't 1969, Doctor in Trouble 1970, The Magnificent Seven Deadly Sins 1971, Don't Just Lie There, Say Something 1973, Not Now Darling 1973, Not Now, Comrade 1976, Spanish Fly 1976, Out of Africa 1985, Empire of the Sun 1987, Scandal 1989, Mountains of the Moon 1990, King Ralph 1991, Carry on Columbus 1992, August 1996, Caught in the Act (video) 1997, The Jackal 1997, Gex: Enter the Gecko (video game; voice) 1998, The Orgasm Raygun 1998, Saving Grace 2000, Lara Croft – Tomb Raider 2001, Harry Potter and the Philosopher's Stone (voice) 2001, Arthur's Amazing Things 2002, Thunderpants 2002, Harry Potter and the Chamber of Secrets (voice) 2002, Collusion 2003, Doctor in Trouble, Pool of London, Churchill: The Hollywood Years 2004, Colour Me Kubrick 2005, With Shadows, Venus 2006, Is Anybody There? 2008. *Radio:* numerous plays including Navy Lark, Les Miserables, Tales From the Backbench, Round the World in 80 Days, Wind in the Willows. *Television includes:* Impasse 1963, Our Man at St. Mark's (series) 1963, The Time and Motion Man 1965, Foreign Affairs (series) 1966, The Suit 1969, The Culture Vultures (series) 1970, Casanova '73 (series) 1973, Monte Carlo 1986, Reluctant Debutante, A Very Fine Line, Casanova 74 (series), You'll Never See Me Again, Rumpole, Summer's Lease (mini-series) 1989, Chancer (series) 1990, The Trials of Oz 1991, Royal Celebration 1993, Two Golden Balls 1994, The Changeling 1994, Bermuda Grace 1994, Honey for Tea (series) 1994, Lovejoy, Boon, The House of Windsor (series) 1994, Love on the Branch Line (mini-series) 1994, Vanity Dies Hard 1995, The Canterville Ghost 1996, Die Katze von Kensington 1996, Das Karussell des Todes 1996, Der Blinde 1996, The Pale Horse 1997, Dalziel and Pascoe: Recalled to Life 1999, Cinderella 2000, Take a Girl Like You 2000, Sword of Honour 2001, Ghosts of Abion: Legacy (voice) 2003, Revolver (series) 2004, Into the Void, Tales of the Crypt, Who Bombed Birmingham?, Holby City, Midsomer Murders, Where the Heart Is, Heartbeat, Marple: By the Pricking of My Thumbs 2006, Harley Street 2008. *Publication:* Hello: The Autobiography 2006. *Leisure interests:* restoring property, chess, poker, racing, gardening. *Address:* c/o Jonathan Lloyd, Curtis Brown Ltd, Haymarket House, 28–29 Haymarket, London, SW1Y 4SP, England (office).

PHILLIPS, (Mark) Trevor, OBE, BSc, ARCS, FRSA; British journalist, broadcaster and public servant; *Chair, Equality and Human Rights Commission;* b. 31 Dec. 1953; s. of George Milton Phillips and Marjorie Eileen Canzius; m. Asha Bhownagary 1981; two d.; ed Queens' Coll., Georgetown, Guyana, Imperial Coll., London; Pres. Nat. Union of Students 1978–80; researcher London Weekend TV 1980–81, producer Black on Black, The Making of Britain 1981–86, Ed. London Programme 1987–92 (presenter 1987–2000), Head of Current Affairs 1992–94; reporter This Week, Thames TV 1986–87; presenter, Crosstalk 1994–2000, The Material World 1998–2000; Dir Pepper Productions 1994–; mem. and Chair. London Ass., GLA 2000–03; columnist, The Independent 1997–99; Chair. Runnymede Trust 1993–98, Hampstead Theatre 1993–97, London Arts Bd 1997–2000; Chair. or Deputy Chair. London Ass. 2000–03; Chair. Comm. for Racial Equality 2003–06, Equality and Human Rights Comm. 2006–; Chevalier, Légion d'Honneur 2007; Hon. DLitt (Westminster, South Bank, Warwick, York, City Univ., Luton, Open Univ.); Hon. MU (London Metropolitan); Journalism Award, Royal TV Soc. 1988, 1993, 1998. *Television:* several series and productions including The London Programme, Windrush. *Publication:* Windrush: The Irresistible Rise of Multi-Racial Britain 1998, Britain's Slave Trade 1999. *Leisure interests:* music, reading, running, crosswords. *Address:* Equality and Human Rights Commission, 3 More London, Riverside, Tooley Street, London, SE1 2RG, England (office). *Telephone:* (20) 3117-0235 (office). *Fax:* (20) 7407-7557 (office). *E-mail:* chair@equalityhumanrights.com (office). *Website:* www.equalityhumanrights.com (office).

PHILLIPS, Peter David, BSc, MSc, PhD; Jamaican economist, politician and academic; *Minister of Finance, Planning and the Public Service;* b. 28 Dec. 1949, Kingston; s. of Aubrey Phillips and Thelma Phillips; m. Sandra Minott; two d.; ed Univ. of the West Indies, State Univ. of New York, Binghampton, USA; Lecturer,

Univ. of the West Indies 1981–89; Gen. Sec. People's Nat. Party 1991–94, Vice-Pres. 1998–2008; elected MP (People's Nat. Party) 1994 (re-elected 1997, 2002, 2007); Minister without Portfolio, Office of the Prime Minister 1993–94, Minister of Special Projects 1994–95, of Health 1995–97, of Transport and Works 1998–2001, of Nat. Security 2001–07, also Minister of Electoral Matters, of Finance, Planning and the Public Service 2012–; Leader, House of Reps 1995–2007, Leader of Opposition Business 2007–08; currently Pnr Belleville Consultants Ltd; mem. Electoral Advisory Cttee, Jt Select Cttee on Constitutional Reform. *Publications:* numerous works on Caribbean devt issues. *Address:* Ministry of Finance and Planning, 30 National Heroes Circle, Kingston 4 (office); Belleville Consultants Ltd, 26 Trafalgar Road, Kingston 10, Jamaica (office). *Telephone:* 922-8600 (Ministry of Finance and Planning) (office); 926-2345 (Belleville Consultants Ltd) (office). *Fax:* 922-7097 (Ministry of Finance and Planning) (office); 960-1944 (Belleville Consultants Ltd) (office). *E-mail:* belleconsults@gmail.com (office); info@mof.gov.jm (office). *Website:* www.mof.gov.jm (office).

PHILLIPS, Ronald Lewis, BS, MS, PhD; American geneticist and academic; *Regents Professor Emeritus and McKnight Presidential Chair in Genomics, University of Minnesota;* b. 1 Jan. 1940, Indiana; s. of Philemon Phillips and Louie Phillips; m. Judith Brett; one d.; ed Purdue Univ., Univ. of Minn., Cornell Univ.; Prof. of Minn. 1967–, currently Regents Prof. Emer. and McKnight Presidential Chair in Genomics, fmr Dir Plant Molecular Genetics Inst. and Center for Microbial and Plant Genomics; specializes in plant biotechnology and genetics related to agric.; Chief Scientist, US Dept of Agric. 1996–98; judge, Beachell-Borlaug Int. Scholars Program; fmr Pres. Crop Science Soc. of America; fmr mem. Scientific Advisory Bd Donald Danforth Plant Science Center; fmr mem. Bd of Trustees, Int. Rice Research Inst. of the Philippines; mem. NAS 1991, fmr Chair. Section on Plant, Soil and Microbial Sciences; fmr Fellow (non-resident), Noble Foundation; Dr hc (Purdue Univ.); Purdue Univ. Agric. Distinguished Alumni Award, Dekalb Genetics Crop Science Distinguished Career Award, Wolf Foundation Prize in Agriculture 2007, Medal of Science, Univ. of Bologna, Italy, Crop Science Soc. of America Presidential Award. *Publications:* over 70 chapters, 130 refereed journal articles and 300 abstracts. *Address:* Department of Agronomy and Plant Genetics, University of Minnesota, 411 Borlaug Hall, 1991 Upper Buford Circle, St Paul, MN 55108-6026, USA (office). *Telephone:* (612) 625-1213 (office). *Fax:* (612) 625-1268 (office). *E-mail:* phill005@umn.edu (office). *Website:* www.umn.edu (office).

PHILLIPS, Siân, CBE, BA (Hons), FRSA; British actress and writer; b. Betws, Carmarthenshire, Wales; d. of D. Phillips and Sally Phillips; m. 1st D. H. Roy 1954; m. 2nd Peter O'Toole 1960 (divorced 1979); two d.; m. 3rd Robin Sachs 1979 (divorced 1992); ed Pontardawe Grammar School, Univ. of Wales (Cardiff Coll.), Royal Acad. of Dramatic Art, London; child actress at BBC Radio Wales and BBC TV Wales; newsreader and announcer and mem. BBC repertory co. 1953–55; toured for Welsh Arts Council with Nat. Theatre Co. 1953–55; Arts Council Bursary to study drama outside Wales 1955; Royal TV Soc. annual televised lecture 1992; Vice-Pres. Welsh Coll. of Music and Drama; mem. Gorsedd of Bards (for services to drama in Wales) 1960; mem. Arts Council Drama Cttee for five years; Gov. St David's Trust; fmr Gov. Welsh Coll. of Music and Drama; Vice-Pres. Actors Benevolent Fund; Patron Restoration of Appearance and Function Trust; Hon. Fellow, Univ. of Cardiff 1981, Polytechnic of Wales 1988, Univ. of Wales, Swansea 1998, Trinity Coll., Carmarthen; Hon. DLitt (Wales) 1984; numerous awards for work in cinema, theatre and on TV, including BAFTA Wales Lifetime Achievement Award 2001. *Stage appearances include:* Hedda Gabler 1959, Ondine and The Duchess of Malfi 1960–61 (first RSC season at Aldwych), The Lizard on the Rock 1961, Gentle Jack, Maxibules and the Night of the Iguana 1964, Ride a Cock Horse 1965, Man and Superman and Man of Destiny 1966, The Burglar 1967, Epitaph for George Dillon 1972, A Nightingale in Bloomsbury Square 1973, The Gay Lord Quex 1975, Spinechiller 1978, You Never Can Tell, Lyric, Hammersmith 1979, Pal Joey, Half Moon and Albery Theatres 1980 and 1981, Dear Liar 1982, Major Barbara, Nat. Theatre 1982, Peg (musical) 1984, Love Affair 1984, Gigi 1986, Thursday's Ladies 1987, Brel (musical) 1987–88, Paris Match 1989, Vanilla 1990, The Manchurian Candidate 1991, Painting Churches 1992, Ghosts, Cardiff and Wales tour 1993, The Lion in Winter 1994, Marlene, An Inspector Calls, Broadway 1995, A Little Night Music, Royal Nat. Theatre 1995–96, Marlene 1996–97, int. tour 1998, concert tour Middle East 1999, Marlene, Broadway 1999, Lettice and Lovage 2001, Divas at The Donmar Season 2001, My Old Lady, Doolittle Theatre, Los Angeles 2002, Promenade Theatre, New York 2002–03, Nat. Tour The Old Ladies 2003, The Dark, Donmar, London 2004, Falling in Love Again, Cabaret, London, Europe, Israel, New York, continuing UK Tour, The Unexpected Man, UK tour 2004, Quartet, New York 2005, Regrets Only, Broadway 2006, Great Expectations, Royal Shakespeare Co., Stratford 2007, Les Liaisons Dangereuses, Broadway 2008, Calendar Girls, UK tour and West End 2009, Juliet and Her Romeo, Bristol Old Vic 2010, A Little Night Music, St Louis Opera 2010, Lovesong Frantic, Assembly Tour and London, Bitter Sweet (USA), Little Dogs, Nat. Theatre Wales, My Fair Lady, Royal Albert Hall, Cabaret (musical), UK tour and West End, solo cabaret, Crossing Borders, London and UK tour. *Films include:* Becket 1963, Goodbye Mr. Chips (Critics' Circle Award, New York Critics' Award and Famous Seven Critics' Award 1969), Laughter in the Dark 1968, Murphy's War 1970, Under Milk Wood 1971, The Clash of the Titans 1979, Dune 1983, Ewok II, The Two Mrs Grenvilles, "Siân" (Cineclaire), Valmont 1988, Dark River 1990, The Age of Innocence 1993, House of America 1997, Coming and Going 2001, The Gigolos 2006, Bella Fleace Gave a Party 2011. *Radio work includes:* Phédre, Oedipus, Henry VIII, Antony and Cleopatra, Bequest to a Nation, The Maids, Henry VIII, All's Well That Ends Well, Leopard in Autumn, Bridge of San Luis Rey, Ghosts, Dance to the Music of Time, Private Lives, The Visits. *Television appearances include:* Shoulder to Shoulder 1974, How Green was my Valley (BAFTA Award) 1975, I, Claudius (Royal Television Soc. Award and BAFTA Award for Best Actress 1978) 1976, Boudicca, Off to Philadelphia in the Morning 1977, The Oresteia of Aeschylus 1978, Crime and Punishment 1979, Tinker, Tailor, Soldier, Spy 1979, Sean O'Casey (RTÉ) 1980, Churchill: The Wilderness Years 1981, How Many Miles to Babylon 1982, Smiley's People 1982, George Borrow 1983, A Painful Case (RTE), Beyond All Reason, Murder on the Exchange, The Shadow of the Noose (BBC series) 1988, Snow Spider (HTV serial) 1988, Freddie & Max, Emlyn's Moon, Perfect Scoundrels 1990, Heidi 1992, The

Borrowers (series) 1992, 1993, The Chestnut Soldier 1992, Huw Weldon TV Lecture 1993, Summer Silence (HTV musical), The Vacillations of Poppy Carew (BBC), Mind to Kill (film series), Ivanhoe (mini-series) 1997, The Scold's Bridle 1998, Alice Through the Looking Glass (feature film) 1998, Aristocrats (mini-series) 1999, La Femme Nikita (series) 1999, The Magician's House 1999, 2000, Cinderella 2000, Attila (film) 2001, Ballykissangel (series) 2001, The Last Detective (series) 2003, The Murder Room 2004, Midsomer Murders (series) 2006, Kitchen (film) 2007, Holby City (series) 2007, Agatha Christie's Poirot 2008, Shortland Street (series) 2008, Missing (series) 2010, New Tricks (series) 2010, Lewis (series) 2011, An Audience with Sian Phillips (S4C) 2013. *Recordings include:* Bewitched, Bothered and Bewildered, Pal Joey, Peg, I Remember Mama, Gigi, A Little Night Music 1990, A Little Night Music (2) 1995, Marlene 1996, Both Sides Now 2002. *Publications:* Needlepoint 1987, Private Faces (autobiog., Vol. I) 1999, Public Places (autobiog., Vol. II) 2001 (USA) 2003. *Leisure interests:* travelling, drawing. *Address:* c/o Simon Beresford, Dalzell Beresford, 26 Astwood Mews, London, SW7 4DE, England (office). *E-mail:* vicki@dbltd.co.uk (office). *Website:* www.sian-phillips-cabaret.com.

PHILLIPS, Tom, CBE, MA, NDD, RA, RE; British artist, writer and composer; b. 24 May 1937, London, England; s. of David John Phillips and Margaret Agnes Arnold; m. 1st Jill Purdy 1961 (divorced 1988), one s. one d.; m. 2nd Fiona Maddocks 1995, two step-d.; ed St Catherine's Coll., Oxford and Camberwell School of Art; solo exhbns: A1A Galleries, Angela Flowers Gallery, Marlborough Fine Art and Waddingtons, London, Galerie Ba Ma, Paris; touring retrospective exhbn, Serpentine Gallery, London, Gemeente Museum, The Hague, Kunsthalle, Basel 1975; 50 years of Tom Phillips, Angela Flowers Gallery, Mappin Art Gallery, Sheffield 1987, British Council Touring Exhbn, Nat. Gallery, Australia 1988; retrospective exhbns: Nat. Portrait Gallery, London 1989, NC Museum of Art, USA 1990, Royal Acad., London 1992, Victoria & Albert Museum, London 1992, Univ. of Pennsylvania 1993, Yale Centre for British Art, USA 1994, Dulwich Picture Gallery 1998, South London Gallery 1998, Modern Art Museum, Forth Worth 2001, Flowers East 2004; publ. music scores 1965–; first performance opera IRMA, York Univ. 1973, revival ICA, London 1983 (CD 1986); collaborations with Jean-Yves Bosseur and John Tilbury on music works/performances 1970–84, Retrospective Concert ICA 1992; Music Works CD 1996, Six of Hearts CD 1997; worked with Peter Greenaway on TV version of Dante's Inferno, as published, translated and illustrated by the artist, broadcast 1990 (1st Prize Montreal TV Festival 1990, Italia Prize 1991); Curator of exhbn Africa: The Art of a Continent, Royal Acad., London, Gropius Bau, Berlin, Guggenheim Museum, New York 1995–96; stage design for A Winter's Tale 1997, Otello 1998, The Entertainer 2003; Vice-Chair. Copyright Council 1985–89; Chair. Royal Acad. Library, Exhbns, Royal Acad., Frua Foundation 1997–2002; Pres. Heatherley's School of Fine Art 2004; Slade Prof. of Fine Art, Univ. of Oxford 2005–06; mem. Royal Soc. of Painter-Etchers and Engravers; Trustee, Nat. Portrait Gallery 1998, British Museum 2000; Hon. mem. Royal Soc. of Portrait Painters 1999, Pastel Soc. 2001; Hon. Fellow, The London Inst. 1999, St Catherine's Coll., Oxford, Univ. of Leeds (Bretton Hall); John Moores Prize 1969, Frances Williams Memorial Prize, Victoria and Albert Museum 1983; *Publications:* Trailer 1971, A Humument 1973, Works and Texts to 1974 1975, Dante's Inferno 1983, Heart of a Humument 1985, Where are They Now? The Class of '47 1990, Works and Texts II 1992, Merely Connect (with Salman Rushdie) 1994, Africa: The Art of a Continent 1995, Aspects of Art 1997, Music in Art 1997, The Postcard Century 2000, We Are The People 2004, A Humument 2005, Merry Meetings 2005. *Leisure interests:* opera, ping pong. *Telephone:* (20) 7701-3978. *Fax:* (20) 7703-2800. *E-mail:* tom@tomphillips.co.uk (home). *Website:* www.tomphillips .co.uk (home).

PHILLIPS, Warren Henry, BA; American publisher and newspaper executive; b. 28 June 1926, New York City; s. of Abraham Phillips and Juliette Phillips; m. Barbara Anne Thomas 1951; three d.; ed Queens Coll.; copyreader, Wall Street Journal 1947–48, Foreign Corresp., Germany 1949–50, Chief, London Bureau 1950–51, Foreign Ed. 1951–53, News Ed. 1953–54, Man. Ed. Midwest Edition 1954–57, Man. Ed. Wall Street Journal 1957–65, Publr 1975–88, Exec. Ed. Dow Jones & Co. 1965–70, Vice-Pres. and Gen. Man. Dow Jones & Co. Inc. 1970–71, Editorial Dir 1971–88, Exec. Vice-Pres. 1972, Pres. 1972–79, CEO 1975–90, Chair. 1978–91, mem. Bd of Dirs 1972–97, Dir Emer. 1997–; Pres. American Council on Educ. for Journalism 1971–73; Co-founder (with wife) and Co-Publr Bridge Works Publishing Co. 1992–; mem. Bd of Dirs Public Broadcasting Service 1991–97; Pres. American Soc. of Newspaper Eds 1975–76; mem. Pulitzer Prizes Bd 1977–87; Trustee, Columbia Univ. 1980–93, Trustee Emer. 1993–; mem. Visitors' Cttee Kennedy School of Govt, Harvard Univ. 1984–90, 1992–97; mem. Corp. Advisory Bd Queens Coll. 1986–90, Foundation Bd of Trustees 1990–97; Hon. LHD (Pace) 1982, (Queens Coll.) 1987, (Long Island) 1987, Hon. JD (Portland) 1973. *Publication:* China: Behind the Mask (with Robert Keatley) 1973. *Address:* Bridge Works Publishing, PO Box 1798, Bridgehampton, NY 11932, USA (office). *Telephone:* (631) 537-3418 (office). *Fax:* (631) 537-5092 (office). *Website:* www .bridgeworksbooks.com.

PHILLIPS, William D., BS, PhD; American physicist and academic; *Physicist, National Institute of Standards and Technology;* b. 5 Nov. 1948, Wilkes-Barre, Pa; s. of William Cornelius Phillips and Mary Catherine Phillips (née Savine); m. Jane Van Wynen 1970; two d.; ed Juniata Coll., Huntington, Massachusetts Inst. of Tech.; mem. tech. staff, Nat. Inst. of Standards and Tech., Gaithersburg, Md 1978–; Distinguished Univ. Prof., Univ. of Maryland 2001–06, Fellow, Jt Quantum Inst. 2006–; Eastman Prof., Univ. of Oxford, UK 2002–03; mem. NAS; Fellow, American Physical Soc., American Acad. of Arts and Sciences; Fellow and Hon. Mem. Optical Soc. of America; Hon. DSc (Williams Coll.) 1998, (Juniata Coll.) 1999; Dr hc (Universidad de Buenos Aires) 1998; shared Nobel Prize for Physics for developing methods of cooling matter to very low temperatures using lasers 1997, Schawlow Prize in Laser Sciences 1998, Pennsylvania Soc. Gold Medal 1999, Service to America Medal, Career Achievement Award 2006. *Publications:* Laser Cooling and Trapping of Neutral Atoms (Nobel Lecture, published in Reviews of Modern Physics, Vol. 70, pp. 721–741 1998); numerous scientific papers in professional journals. *Address:* National Institute of Standards and Technology, 100 Bureau Drive, Stop 8424, Gaithersburg, MD 20899, USA (office). *Telephone:* (301) 975-6554 (office). *E-mail:* william.phillips@nist.gov (office); william.phillips@ physics.umd.edu (office). *Website:* www.physics.umd.edu/amo (office); www.nist .gov (office).

PHILLIPS, Zara Anne Elizabeth, MBE; British equestrian; b. 15 May 1981, London; d. of Capt. Mark Phillips and HRH The Princess Anne, Princess Royal; grand-daughter of HRH Queen Elizabeth II; m. Michael Tindall 2011; one d.; ed Gordonstoun, Univ. of Exeter; victories include Individual Gold Medal, European Eventing Championship 2005, Gold Team Medal; Individual Gold Medal, World Equestrian Games 2006, Silver Team Medal, named Eventing World Champion (third rider in history to hold both European and World titles simultaneously); rides horse ToyTown; Pres. Club 16-24, Cheltenham Racetrack 2000–05; mem. Cheltenham Ladies Hockey Club; Eventing European Champion 2005, Sunday Times Sportswoman of the Year Award 2005, Eventing World Champion 2006, BBC Sports Personality of the Year Award 2006, Equestrian Olympic Athlete of the Year 2006, British Equestrian Writers Assen Personality of the Year 2006. *Address:* The Bothy, Gatcombe Park, Minchinhampton, Stroud, Glos., GL6 9AT, England (home).

PHILLIPS-DAVIES, Alistair, BSc; British chartered accountant and business executive; *Chief Executive, SSE plc;* has worked in energy industry since 1997; joined Southern Electric 1997, apptd to Bd of SSE plc as Energy Supply Dir 2002, Deputy Chief Exec. 2012–13, Chief Exec. SSE plc 2013–. *Address:* SSE plc, Inveralmond House, 200 Dunkeld Road, Perth, PH1 3AQ, Scotland (office). *Telephone:* (1738) 456000 (office). *E-mail:* info@sse.com (office). *Website:* www.sse .com (office). *Website:* www.hydro.co.uk (office).

PHILLIPS OF WORTH MATRAVERS, Baron (Life Peer), cr. 1999, of Belsize Park in the London Borough of Camden; **Nicholas Addison Phillips,** Kt, PC, MA; British judge; *President, The Supreme Court;* b. 21 Jan. 1938; s. of Michael Pennington Phillips and Dora Hassid; m. Christylle Marie-Therese Rouffiac 1972; two d. one step-s. one step-d.; ed Bryanston School, King's Coll. Cambridge; called to the Bar 1962; in practice 1962–87; Jr Counsel to Ministry of Defence and Treasury 1973–78; QC 1978; Recorder 1982–87; Judge, Queen's Bench Div., High Court of Justice 1987–95; Lord Justice of Appeal 1995–98; Chair. BSE Inquiry 1998–2000; Lord of Appeal in Ordinary 1999–2000; Master of the Rolls 2000–05; Lord Chief Justice of England and Wales 2005–08; Sr Law Lord 2008–; Pres. The Supreme Court 2009–; Chair. Law Advisory Cttee, British Council 1991–97; Chair. Council of Legal Educ. 1992–97; Vice-Pres. British Maritime Law Assen 1993–; Gov. Bryanston School 1975–2008, Chair. of Govs 1981–2008; Chancellor Bournemouth Univ. 2009–; Hon. Fellow, Soc. for Advanced Legal Studies 1999, American Coll. of Trial Lawyers 2002–; King's Coll. Cambridge 2003; Hon. LLD (Exeter) 1998, (Birmingham) 2003, (London) 2004; Hon. DCL (City Univ.) 2003. *Leisure interests:* sea, mountains. *Address:* The Supreme Court, Parliament Square, London, SW1P 3BD, England (office). *Telephone:* (20) 7960-1966 (office). *Fax:* (20) 7960-1961 (office). *E-mail:* registry@supremecourt.gsi.gov.uk (office). *Website:* www.supremecourt.gov.uk (office).

PHILO, Phoebe, OBE; British fashion designer; *Creative Director, Céline;* b. 1973, Paris, France; m. Max Wigram; three c.; ed Central St Martin's Fashion Coll.; grew up in London suburb; invited to work at Chloé, Paris (part of Swiss-based Richemont Group) working as Asst to Stella McCartney 1997–2001, Creative Dir 2001–06 (resgnd); presented first collection for Spring/Summer 2002; mem. Bd and Creative Dir, Céline 2008–; Best Dressed Jan. issue of Vogue 2003, British Designer of the Year, British Fashion Council 2005, 2010, Int. Designer of the Year, Council of Fashion Designers of America 2011. *Address:* Céline, 23–25 rue du Pont Neuf, 75001 Paris, France (office). *Telephone:* 1-55-80-12-12 (office). *Website:* www.celine.com (office).

PHOENIX, Joaqin Rafael; American actor; b. 27 Oct. 1974, Puerto Rico; s. of John Bottom Amram and Arlyn Dunitz Jochebed; brother of the late River Phoenix. *Films include:* SpaceCamp 1986, Russkies 1987, Parenthood 1989, Walking the Dog 1991, To Die For 1995, Inventing the Abbotts 1997, U Turn 1997, Return to Paradise 1998, Clay Pigeons 1998, 8MM 1999, The Yards 2000, Gladiator 2000, Quills 2000, Buffalo Soldiers 2001, Signs 2002, It's All About Love 2003, Brother Bear 2003, The Village 2004, Hotel Rwanda 2004, Ladder 49 2004, Walk the Line 2005 (Golden Globe Award for Best Performance by Actor in a Musical or Comedy 2006), We Own the Night 2007, Reservation Road 2007, Two Lovers 2008, I'm Still Here 2010, The Master 2012. *Television includes:* Backwards: The Riddle of Dyslexia 1984, Kids Don't Tell 1985, Morningstar/ Eveningstar 1986, Secret Witness 1988. *Address:* c/o The Endeavour Agency, 9601 Wilshire Blvd, 10th Floor, Beverly Hills, CA, USA. *Telephone:* (310) 248-2000 (office). *Fax:* (310) 248-2020 (office).

PHOSA, Nakedi Mathews, LLB; South African lawyer, business executive and politician; *Treasurer-General, African National Congress (ANC);* b. 1 Sept. 1952, Mbombela township, Nelspruit; m. Pinkie Phosa; three c.; ed Univ. of the North (Turfloop); articled clerk, Godfrey Rabin Attorneys 1979–81; f. Nelspruit (first black-owned legal firm) 1981, Pnr 1981–85 (went into exile); fmr Nat. Organiser Black Lawyers' Assen; fmr Head Legal Div., African Nat. Congress (ANC) Dept of Constitutional and Legal Affairs, mem. ANC Nat. Exec. Cttee 1999–, Treasurer-Gen. ANC 2007–; fmr mem. Nat. Negotiations Comm.; Premier Mpumalanga regional govt 1994–99; Chair. (non-exec.) EOH 2003–; fmr Chair. (non-exec.) Atos KPMG Consulting; Chair. Vuka Alliance (Pty) Ltd, Du Toit-Smuts & Mathews Phosa Inc. (attorneys), Zero Pollution Motors SA (Pty) Ltd, Value Logistics Ltd, Hans Merensky Holdings; Chair. Council Univ. of SA, Special Olympics SA; Hon. PhD (Boston). *Address:* African National Congress, 54 Sauer Street, Johannesburg 2001, South Africa (office). *Telephone:* (11) 3761000 (office). *Fax:* (11) 3761134 (office). *Website:* www.anc.org.za (office).

PHOSIKHAM, Chansy; Laotian politician; *Governor of Vientiane Province;* fmr Gov. Prov. of Luang Prabang; Gov. State Bank –2003; Minister of Finance 2003–07; Gov. Vientiane Prov. 2007–; mem. Seventh Party Cen. Cttee. *Address:* Office of Vientiane Capital, Vientiane, Laos (office). *Telephone:* (21) 412502 (office).

PHOUPHET, Khamphounvong; Laotian fmr central banker and politician; Alt. Gov. for Laos, IFAD 2003, Asian Devt Bank –2007; Deputy Gov., then Gov. Bank of the Lao PDR 2006–11; Minister of Finance 2011–14. *Address:* c/o Ministry of Finance, 23 rue Singha, BP 24, Ban Phonxay, Vientiane, Laos (office).

PHUNG, Gen. Quang Thanh; Vietnamese army officer and government official; *Minister of National Defence;* b. 2 Feb. 1949, Thach Da commune, Me Linh, Hanoi; ed School for Infantry Officers, Acad. of Infantry, Voroshilov Acad., USSR, Mil.

Acad. of Viet Nam; joined army 1967, fought in various battles during the Viet Nam War, notably in Quang Tri campaign and during counterattack of Viet Nam People's Army against Operation Lam Son 719 where he served as co. commdr in 9th Bn, 64th Regt, 320th Div.; apptd Commdr of 9th Bn, 320th Div., 1st Army Corps 1972; continued to hold several positions in 1st Army Corps from Chief of Staff of 64th Regt to Acting Commdr of 312th Div. 1988; promoted to Commdr of 312th Div. 1991; later served in Gen. Staff of Viet Nam People's Army 1993–97; Commdr 1st Mil. Zone 1997–2001; Chief of the Gen. Staff and Deputy Minister of Defence 2001–06; Minister of Nat. Defence 2006–; admitted to CP of Viet Nam, then known as the Vietnam Workers' Party 1968, elected to Politburo 2006; rank of Maj. Gen. 1994, Lt Gen. 1999, Col Gen. 2003, Gen. 2007; Hero of the People's Armed Forces 1971, three Liberation Distinguished Service Medals, 1st Order, three Brave Soldier Titles and other awards. *Address:* Ministry of National Defence, 7 Nguyen Tri Phuong, Ba Dinh District, Hanoi, Viet Nam (office). *Telephone:* (69) 534223 (office). *Fax:* (69) 532090 (office).

PHUVANATNARANUBALA, Thirachai, BEcons; Thai economist and politician; b. 21 Dec. 1951; m.; three c.; ed London School of Econs; fmrly worked at Price Waterhouse, London; worked at Bank of Thailand 1977–2003, Deputy Gov. –2003; Sec.-Gen. Securities and Exchange Comm. of Thailand 2003–11; Minister of Finance 2011–12; Chair. ASEAN Capital Markets Forum 2003–11; fmr Bd mem. Experts for Interpretation of Tax Code, Thai Inst. of Dirs, Bank of Thailand Financial Inst. Policy Bd, Nat. Credit Bureau Co. Ltd, Insurance Comm. *Address:* c/o Ministry of Finance, Rama 6 Road, Phayathai, Bangkok 10400, Thailand (office).

PIACENZA, HE Cardinal Mauro, JCD; Italian ecclesiastic and academic; *Prefect of the Congregation for the Clergy;* b. 15 Sept. 1944, Genoa; ed Major Archiepiscopal Seminary of Genoa, Pontifical Lateran Univ., Rome; ordained priest, Diocese of Genoa 1969; served as a parochial vicar, as Chaplain and later Apostolic Del. to Univ. of Genoa; taught canon law at Theological Faculty of Northern Italy; held several other curial positions and served as the Archbishop's Press Officer; fmr Diocesan Asst of the ecclesial Movt of Cultural Commitment; fmr Prof. of Contemporary Culture and History of Atheism, Ligurian Higher Inst. of Religious Studies as well as Prof. of Dogmatic Theology, Diocesan Inst. of Theology for the Lay 'Didascaleion'; also taught theology at several state lyceums; made a Canon of the Genoa Cathedral 1986; entered Congregation for the Clergy 1990, Undersecretary 2000–07, Sec. 2007–10, Prefect 2010–; Pres. Pontifical Comm. for the Cultural Heritage of the Church 2003–04; Titular Bishop of Victoriana 2003–07, Titular Archbishop 2007–; Pres. Pontifical Comm. for Sacred Archeology 2004–07; cr. Cardinal (Cardinal-Deacon of San Paolo alle Tre Fontane) 2010; participated in Papal Conclave 2013. *Address:* Congregation for the Clergy, Palazzo delle Congregazioni, 00193 Roma, Piazza Pio XII, 3 00120 Città del Vaticano, Rome postcode, Italy (office). *Telephone:* (06) 69884151 (office). *Fax:* (06) 69884845 (office). *Website:* www.vatican.va/roman_curia/congregations/cclergy (office).

PIANO, Renzo; Italian architect; b. 14 Sept. 1937, Genoa; s. of Carlo Piano and Rosa Odone; m. 1st Magda Ardnino 1962; two s. one d.; m. 2nd Emilia Rossato 1992; ed Milan Polytechnic School of Architecture; worked with Louis I. Kahn, Phila, USA, Z.S. Makowsky, London 1965–70, with Richard Rogers (as Piano & Rogers) 1977–, with Peter Rice (as Atelier Piano & Rice) 1977–; currently has offices in Genoa, Paris, Berlin (Renzo Piano Bldg Workshop); mem. Nat. Acad. of Design 2013; Hon. Fellow Union Int. des Architectes 1978, AIA, 1981, RIBA, 1985, American Acad. of Arts and Letters 1994; Dr hc (Stuttgart) 1990, (Delft) 1992; Compasso d'Oro Award, Milan 1981, RIBA Gold Medal 1989, Kyoto Prize, Japan 1990, Neutra Prize, Pomona, Calif. 1991, Goodwill Amb. of UNESCO for Architecture 1994, Premio Michelangelo 1994, Art Prize of Akademie der Künste, Berlin 1995, Praemium Imperiale, Tokyo 1995, Erasmus Prize, Amsterdam 1995, The Pritzker Architecture Prize, Washington, DC 1998, Médaille d'Or, Int. Union of Architects 2002, Gold Medal, American Inst. of Architects 2008, and other prizes and awards; Commdr des Arts et des Lettres, Légion d'honneur, Cavaliere di Gran Croce, Officer, Ordre Nat. du Mérite, Senator for Life (highest Italian honour) 2013–. *Completed projects include:* office bldg for B&B, Como 1973, Georges Pompidou Centre, Paris (with Richard Rogers) 1977, IRCAM Int. for Acoustic Research, Paris 1977, housing, Rigo Dist, Perugia 1982, office bldg for Olivetti, Naples 1984, office bldg for Lowara, Vicenza 1985, museum for Menil Collection, Houston, USA 1988, HQ for Light Metals Experimental Inst., Novara 1988, S. Nicola Football Stadium, Bari 1989, Underground stations for Ansaldo, Genoa 1990, Bercy commercial centre, Paris 1990, Thomson factories, Guyancourt, France 1991, HQ for Credito Industriale Sardo, Cagliari 1992, Lingotto congress and concert hall, Turin 1994, Kansai Int. Airport, Osaka, Japan 1994, Meridien Hotel, Lingotto and Business Centre, Turin 1995, Harbour Authorities HQ, Genoa 1995, cinema, offices, contemporary art gallery, conf. centre, landscaping, Cité Int., Lyon 1996, Ushibuka Bridge, Kumamoto, Japan 1996, Museum of Science and Tech., Amsterdam 1997, Museum of Beyeler Foundation, Basel 1997, Debis Bldg HQ, Daimler Benz, Berlin 1997, Cultural Centre J.-M. Tjibao, Nouméa, New Caledonia 1998, Mercedes-Benz Design Centre, Stuttgart 1998, Daimler-Benz Potsdamer Platz project including Imax theatre, offices, housing, shops, Berlin 1998, Lodi Bank HQ, Milan 1998, Rome Auditorium 2003, Morgan Library extension, NY 2006, NY Times Bldg, Manhattan 2007, Broad Contemporary Art Museum, Los Angeles 2008, California Acad. of Sciences rebuilding, San Francisco 2008, Nichols Bridgeway, Chicago 2009, Modern Wing expansion, Art Inst. of Chicago 2009, Central Saint Giles, London 2010, The Shard, London (tallest skyscraper in Europe) 2000–12, Astrup Fearnley Museum of Modern Art, Tjuvholmen, Oslo 2002–12, Isabella Stewart Gardner Museum wing, Boston 2005–12. *Projects in progress include:* contemporary art gallery, Varnamö, Sweden, office block, Sydney, Australia, PTT Telecom office tower, Rotterdam, Harvard Univ. Art Gallery master plan, renovation and extension, HQ newspaper Il Sole/24 Ore, Milan Padre Pio Basilica Church, Puglia, Italy, Whitney Museum, Centro de Arte Botín, Santander, Spain, Acad. Museum of Motion Pictures, Los Angeles; work shown at exhbns Europe, USA, Australia, Japan 1967–; numerous lectures worldwide. *Publications:* author or co-author of 12 books on architecture. *Leisure interest:* sailing. *Address:* Renzo Piano Building Workshop, Via Rubens 29, 16158 Genoa, Italy; 34, rue des Archives, 75004 Paris, France. *Telephone:* (010) 61711 (Genoa). *Fax:* (010) 6171350 (Genoa). *E-mail:* italy@rpbw.com. *Website:* rpbw.r.ui-pro.com.

PIAT, Jean; French actor and writer; b. 23 Sept. 1924, Lannoy (Nord); m. Françoise Engel (died 2005); ed Conservatoire national; enlisted in Comédie-Française 1947, mem. 1953–72, Hon. mem. 1972–; Prof. of Dramatic Arts of the Simon Course; Commdr, Ordre des Arts et des Lettres; Grand Croix, Ordre nat. du Mérite. *Films include:* Rouletabille joue et gagne 1947, The Lame Devil 1948, Rouletabille contre la dame de pique 1948, Clara de Montargis 1951, Maxim's Porter 1953, Napoléon (uncredited) 1955, Would-Be Gentleman 1958, Marriage of Figaro 1959, Panurge's Sheep 1961, She Lost Her... You Know What 1968, The Milky Way 1969, Rider on the Rain 1970, La rivale 1974, Ciao, les mecs 1979, The Lion King (French version, voice) 1994, The Hunchback of Notre Dame (French version, voice) 1996, A Monkey's Tale (French version, voice) 1999, The Lord of the Rings: The Fellowship of the Ring (French version, voice) 2001, The Lord of the Rings: The Two Towers (French version, voice) 2002, The Lord of the Rings: The Return of the King (French version, voice) 2003, Kaena: The Prophecy (French version, voice) 2003, Tous à l'Ouest: Une aventure de Lucky Luke (voice) 2007, The Golden Compass (French version, voice) 2007, The Hobbit: An Unexpected Journey (French version, voice) 2012. *Television includes:* L'étiquette (film) 1986, L'affaire Saint-Romans (mini-series) 1988, La maison du lac (film) 2009. *Address:* c/o Françoise Salimov, Artmedia, 20 avenue Rapp, 75007 Paris, France (office). *Telephone:* 1-43-17-33-84 (office). *E-mail:* f.salimov@artmedia.fr (office); f.minvielle@artmedia.fr (office). *Website:* www.artmedia.fr (office).

PIĄTAS, Gen. Czesław; Polish army officer and politician; b. 20 March 1946, Germany; m. Danuta Piątas; two c.; ed Armour Officer's School, Acad. of Gen. Staff, USSR, US Nat. War Coll., USA; began career in Polish Armed Forces 1968; served in variety of command and staff positions in armour units 1970s; Chief of Staff, Deputy Commdr of 10th Armoured Div. and Commdr of tank regiment 1980–82; apptd G-3 Dir Silesian Mil. Dist HQ 1982; Commdr 4th Mechanized Div.; Staff Position Silesian Mil. Dist. HQ 1993–94; Chief of Staff DCG, Warsaw Mil. Dist 1995–96; Chief of Operational and Strategic Div., Gen. Staff 1996–99; Deputy Chief of Gen. Staff of Polish Armed Forces 1999–2000, Chief of Gen. Staff Sept. 2000–06; Sec. of State, Ministry of Defence 2008–11; lecturer, Tadeusz Kościuszko Land Forces Military Acad. 2012–; apptd Brig.-Gen. 1992, Maj.-Gen. 1999, Lt-Gen. 2000, Gen. 2000. *Leisure interests:* mil. history, tennis. *Address:* c/o Ministry of National Defence, ul. Klonowa 1, 00-909 Warsaw, Poland (office).

PIBULSONGGRAM, Nitya, MA; Thai diplomatist; b. 30 June 1941; s. of Field Marshal Pibul Songgram and Lady La-iad Bhandhukran; m. Pacharin Pibulsonggram 1965; ed Dartmouth Coll. and Brown Univ.; entered Foreign Service as Third Sec. Foreign News Div. Information Dept June 1968; served in fmr SEATO Div., Thailand's Int. Org. Dept 1969–72; Office of Sec. to Minister of Foreign Affairs 1973, Office of Under-Sec. of State, Policy Planning Div. 1974; Head Southeast Asia Div., Political Dept 1975; First Sec. Perm. Mission to UN 1976–79, Deputy Perm. Rep. 1979–80, Perm. Rep. 1988–96; Deputy Dir-Gen. Information Dept, Foreign Ministry 1980, Political Dept 1981; Amb.-at-Large 1982; Dir-Gen. Dept of Int. Org. 1983–88; Amb. to USA 1996–2001; Adviser and Special Envoy of the Minister of Foreign Affairs, 2002–06, Chief Negotiator for US-Thai Free Trade Agreement 2002–06, Minister of Foreign Affairs 2006–08; Chair. Thailand–US Educational Foundation (TUSEF); Trustee Kenan Inst. Asia; Knight Grand Cross, Order of White Elephant 1984, Special Grand Cordam, Order of Crown of Thailand 1988, Kt Commdr Order of Chula Chom Klao 2000. *Leisure interests:* tennis, golf, skiing. *Address:* c/o Ministry of Foreign Affairs, Thanon Sri Ayudhya, Bangkok, Thailand (office).

PICADO SOTELA, Sonia, LicenD; Costa Rican lawyer, international organization official, academic and fmr politician; *President, Inter-American Institute of Human Rights;* b. 20 Dec. 1936; d. of Antonio de Picado and Odile Sotela; m. (divorced); one s. one d.; ed Univ. of Costa Rica; Prof., Faculty of Law, Univ. of Costa Rica 1972–2003, Dean, Faculty of Law 1980–84, Cathedratical Chair. 1984; Co-Chair. Int. Comm. for Central American Recovery and Devt 1987–89; mem. Cttee of Jurists, World Conf. on Refugees, UNHCR, Geneva 1988–89; Prof., Inter-American Inst. of Human Rights 1985–, Exec. Dir 1988–94, currently Pres.; Vice-Pres. Inter-American Court of Human Rights 1988–94; Co-Chair. Inter-American Dialogue, Washington, DC 1993–94; Amb. to USA 1994–98; Head of UN Comm. of Inquiry on East Timor 1999–2000; mem. Legislative Ass. for San José 1999–2001; Pres. Nat. Liberation Party 1999–2001; mem. Comm. on Human Security; Pres. UN Voluntary Fund for Victims of Torture; Trustee Equal Rights Trust; Dr hc (Elmhurst Coll., Chicago) 2000, (Univ. of Miami) 2002, (Colby Coll.) 2003; Max Planck/Humboldt Award (Germany) 1991, Leonidas Proaño Award (Ecuador) 1991, UN Prize in Human Rights 1993, UNDP Award 1995. *Publications:* Women and Human Rights 1986, Philosophical Fundamentals of Human Rights in Latin America 1987, Religion, Tolerance and Liberty: A Human Rights Perspective 1989, Peace, Development and Human Rights 1989. *Address:* Inter-American Institute of Human Rights, PO Box 10.081-1000, San José, Costa Rica (office). *Telephone:* 234-0404 (office). *Fax:* 234-0955 (office). *E-mail:* instituto@iidh.ed.cr (office). *Website:* (office).

PICARD, Dennis J.; American business executive; *Chairman Emeritus, Raytheon Company;* b. 1932, Rhode Island; m. Dolores M. Petit; five c.; ed LaSalle Acad., Providence, RI, RCA Inst., New York, Northeastern Univ.; served in USAF during Korean War early 1950s; joined Raytheon 1955, Sr Vice-Pres., Gen. Man. Missile Systems Div. Raytheon Co., Lexington, Mass 1985–89, Pres. 1989–90, Chair. 1990–99, CEO 1990–99 (also mem. Bd of Dirs), Chair. Emer. 1999–; Pres. AIAA 2001, Hon. Fellow; mem. Defence Policy Advisory Cttee on Trade, Pres.'s Export Council; fmr Dir, State Street Boston Corpn, Discovery Museums, Acton, Mass; fmr mem. Advisory Cttee, American Red Cross, Armed Services YMCA of the US, Business Council, Defense Policy Advisory Cttee on Trade, Pres.'s Nat. Security Telecommunications Advisory Cttee, Pres.'s Export Council; Trustee, Northeastern Univ.; Trustee Emer., Bentley Coll.; mem. Nat. Acad. of Eng; Life Fellow, IEEE; US Army's Order of Santa Barbara 1991; Dr hc (Northeastern Univ.), (Merrimack Coll.), (Bentley Coll.); Environmental Achievement Award, Nat. Security Industrial Asscn 1996, Adm. Chester W. Nimitz Award, Navy League of the US Fleet 1997, Intrepid Salute Award, Intrepid Museum Foundation 1997, John R. Allison Award, USAF Asscn 1997, John W. Dixon Medal, Asscn of the US Army 1997, New Englander of the Year, New England Council 1997, Ralph Lowell Distinguished Citizen Award, Boston Minuteman Council, Boy Scouts of America 1997, Industrial Leadership Award, Nat. Defense Industrial Asscn 1998,

Semper Fidelis Award, Marine Corps Scholarship Foundation 1998, Rear Adm. John J. Bergen Leadership Medal for Industry, Navy League (New York Council) 1998, IEEE Dennis J. Picard Medal for Radar Technologies and Applications est. in his honour 1999. *Address:* Raytheon Company, 870 Winter Street, Waltham, MA 02451-1449 (office); 1373 Monument Street, Concord, MA 01742, USA (home). *Telephone:* (781) 522-3000 (office). *E-mail:* info@raytheon.com (office). *Website:* www.raytheon.com (office).

PICARDO, Fabian, LLB; Gibraltarian lawyer and politician; *Chief Minister;* b. 18 Feb. 1972; m. 2nd Justine Olivero 2011; ed Oriel Coll., Oxford, Inns of Court School of Law, Gray's Inn, London, UK; called to the Bar 1994; joined Hassans Int. Law Firm 1994, currently Pnr; mem. Gibraltar Socialist Labour Party, Leader 2011–; Chief Minister of Gibraltar Dec. 2011–; mem. Hon. Soc. Middle Temple; mem. Bar in Gibraltar and British Virgin Islands. *Address:* Office of the Chief Minister, 6 Convent Pl., Gibraltar (office). *Telephone:* 20070071 (office). *Fax:* 20076396 (office).

PICASSO, Manuel; Peruvian diplomatist and international organization official; *Secretary-General, Amazon Co-operation Treaty Organization (ACTO);* held various positions with Ministry of External Relations, including in Cabinet of Minister of External Relations, in Directorate for Econ. Affairs and Under-Secr. of Political Affairs, Sec., Embassy in Ottawa 1979–82, Embassy in The Hague 1982–85, Sec. and Counsellor, Embassy in Brasília 1988–92, Counsellor, Embassy in Paris 1992–93, Consul-Gen. in Barcelona 1997–99, Jt Perm. Rep. to UN, New York 1999–2001, Exec. Dir for Peru, Binational Plan for Devt of Peru-Ecuador Transboundary Region 2001–04, also Chair. Binational Plan Governing Bd, Peru-Ecuador Binational Fund for Peace and Devt, Amb. to Finland (also accred to Latvia, Estonia and Lithuania) 2004–08, to India 2008–09; fmr Dir Pro Tempore Secr., Deputy Pro Tempore Sec., Amazon Co-operation Treaty, Sec.-Gen. Amazon Co-operation Treaty Org. 2009–; mem. Peru-Ecuador Binational Business Group; Order of Merit for Distinguished Services (Peru) 1976, Officer, Order of Orange Nassau (Netherlands) 1985, Grand Cross, Order of Merit (Ecuador) 2003, Order of Merit for Distinguished Services, Grand Cross of the Order (Peru) 2004, Grand Cross, Order of Lion of Finland 2008. *Address:* Office of the Secretary-General, Amazon Co-operation Treaty Organization, SHIS – QI 05, Conjunto 16, casa 21, Lago Sul, Brasilia 71615-160, Brazil (office). *Telephone:* (61) 3248-4119/ 4132 (office). *Fax:* (61) 3248-4238 (office). *Website:* www.otca.org.br (office).

PICASSO, Paloma; French designer; b. 19 April 1949, Paris; d. of the late Pablo Ruiz-Picasso and Françoise Gilot; m. Rafael Lopez-Cambil (Lopez-Sanchez) 1978 (divorced 1998); m. 2nd Eric Thevennet 1999; ed Univ. of Paris, Sorbonne; studied jewellery design and manufacture; fashion jewellery for Yves St Laurent 1969; jewellery for Zolotas 1971, costumes and sets for Parisian theatre productions, L'Interprétation 1975, Succès 1978; created Paloma Picasso brand; creations designed by her for the Paloma Picasso brand include jewellery for Tiffany & Co. 1980, fragrance (Paloma Picasso 1984, Minotaure 1992, Tentations 1996) and cosmetics for L'Oréal, eyewear for Metzler Optik Partner AG, bone china, crystal, silverware and tiles for Villeroy & Boch, home linens for KBC, fabrics and wall coverings for Motif; pieces in perm. collections of Smithsonian Inst. (Washington, DC), Musée des Arts Décoratifs (Paris) and Die Neue Zamlang (Munich); f. Paloma Picasso Foundation, Lausanne, Switzerland; Council of Fashion Design of America (CFDA) Accessory Award 1989. *Film:* Contes immoraux 1974. *Address:* Paloma Picasso Foundation, c/o Piaget & De Mitri SA, Avenue Mon-Repos 14, 1000, Lausanne, Switzerland (office).

PICCOLI, Michel; French actor; b. 27 Dec. 1925, Paris; s. of Henri Piccoli; m. 1st Juliette Gréco 1966; m. 3rd Ludivine Clerc 1978; one s. from fmr m.; ed Collège d'Annel, Collège Sainte Barbe, Paris; Man. of the Théâtre de Babylone for two years before joining the Madeleine Renaud and Jean-Louis Barrault Theatre Co.; appeared in Phèdre at the Théâtre Nationale Populaire; jury mem. Cannes Film Festival 2007; Best Actor, Cannes 1980 (for Salto nel Vuoto), European Prize, Taormina Theatre, Sicily 2001; Chevalier Légion d'honneur, Ordre nationale du Mérite. *Films include:* Le point du jour 1946, Parfum de la dame en noire 1949, French Cancan 1955, The Witches of Salem 1956, Le mépris 1963, Diary of a Chambermaid 1964, De l'amour 1965, Lady L 1965, La curée 1965, Les demoiselles de Rochefort 1967, Un homme de trop 1967, Belle de jour 1967, Dillinger is Dead 1968, The Milky Way 1969, Topaz 1969, The Discreet Charm of the Bourgeoisie 1972, Themroc 1972, Blow-out 1973, The Infernal Trio 1974, Le fantôme de la liberté 1974, La faille 1975, Léonar 1975, Sept morts sur ordonnance 1976, La dernière femme 1976, Savage State 1978, Le divorcement 1979, Le saut dans le vide 1979, Le mors aux dents 1979, La città delle donne 1980, Salto nel Vuoto 1980, La passante du sans-souci 1982, Adieu Bonaparte 1985, The Night is Young 1986, L'homme voilé, Maladie d'amour, La rumba 1987, Y a bon les blancs, Blanc de Chine 1988, Milou en mai 1990, Martha et moi 1991, La belle noiseuse 1991, Les equilibristes, Le voleur d'enfants 1991, Le bal des cassepieds 1992, Archipel 1993, Rupture(s) 1993, L'Ange noir 1994, Les cent et une nuits 1995, 2 × 50 Years of French Cinema 1995, Compagna di Viaggio 1996, Beaumarchais l'insolent 1996, Généalogies d'un crime 1997, Alors voilà (dir) 1997, Rien sur Robert 1999, Compagne de voyage 2000, Les acteurs 2000, Je rentre à la maison 2001, La Plague noire 2001, Ce Jour-là 2003, Belle Toujours 2006, Jardins en Automne 2006, We Have a Pope 2011, Holy Motors 2012. *Publication:* Dialogues égoistes 1976. *Leisure interests:* riding, flying. *Address:* 11 rue des Lions Saint-Paul, 75004 Paris, France.

PICEK, Lt-Gen. Vlastimil; Czech military officer and politician; b. 25 Oct. 1956, Turnov; m. Dagmar Picková (divorced); two c.; ed Mil. Acad., Brno, Czech Tech. Univ.; sr radio operator 1975–78; Deputy Battalion Commdr for Tech. Issues 1983–86, Sr Officer, Nat. Air Defence HQ 1986–89; Chief of Signal Br., Fourth Air Defence Corps HQ 1993–94; Section Chief Signal Br., Armed Forces Gen. Staff 1994–95, Deputy Chief 1995–96, Chief of Signal Br. 1996–97, Chief of Operational-Tactical C2 Systems Dept 1997–2000, Chief of Command and Control Div. 2000–03; Security Dir, Ministry of Defence 2001–03; promoted to Brig. 2001; Chief of Mil. Office of Pres. 2003–07; rank of Maj.-Gen. 2003, Lt Gen. 2006; Chief of Gen. Staff 2007–12; rank of Army Gen. 2009; First Deputy Minister of Defence Sept.–13 Dec. 2012, 21 Dec. 2012–13; Minister of Defence 2013–14; Cross of Merit of the Minister of Defence Third Grade, ACR Medal Third Grade, Nat. Service Medal, Hon. Commemorative Badge for Service in Peace Operation in the Balkans, NATO 50th Anniversary Medal. *Leisure interests:* tennis, skiing. *Address:* c/o Ministry of Defence, Tychonova 1, 160 01 Prague 6, Czech Republic. *E-mail:* info@army.cz.

PICHET, Patrice; French entrepreneur and business executive; *CEO, Groupe Pichet;* b. 1959, Bassin d'Arcachon, Bordeaux; has spent his entire career in construction industry, initially as trading and sales man. 1983–87; Founder and CEO Groupe Pichet (nationwide real-estate business) 1988–, now 20 subsidiaries, covering the construction trades, four regional offices: Bordeaux (HQ in Pessac), Biarritz, Nantes and Paris, also partner of Girondins de Bordeaux and Bayonne rugby team; leads a consulting team within IG2P; interests in wine and vineyards of Bordeaux (Château Haut Brion Carmelite); Palm'Elec Nat. Award for Sustainable Devt 2007, Prix Bas Carbone des Trophées Nationaux Habitat Bleu Ciel EDF 2011. *Address:* Pichet Immobilier, Siège social sur Bordeaux, 20–24 avenue de Canteranne, 33600 Pessac, Gironde, France (office). *E-mail:* info@pichet.com (office). *Website:* en.pichet.com (office). www.pichet-immobilier.fr (office).

PICHLER, Joseph A., MBA, PhD; American business executive; b. 3 Oct. 1939, St Louis, Mo.; s. of late Anton Pichler and Anita Pichler; m. Susan Eyerly 1962; two s. two d.; ed Notre Dame Univ. of Chicago, Univ. of Chicago; Prof., School of Business, Univ. of Kan., Dean 1974–80; Exec. Vice-Pres. Dillon Companies Inc. 1980–82, Pres. 1982–84, Pres. and CEO 1984–86, CEO 1986–88; Exec. Vice-Pres. The Kroger Co. 1985–86, Pres. and COO 1986–90, Pres. and CEO 1990–2003, Chair. 1990–2004; mem. Bd of Dirs Macy's Inc. 1997–2012; Woodrow Wilson Fellow 1961, Ford Foundation Doctoral Fellow 1962–64, Standard Oil Industrial Relations Fellow 1964; 1993, Trustee Xavier University 1993–, Chair. 2004–09; mem. Cincinnati Business Comm. 1991, Chair. 1997–98; Dr hc (Univ. of Cincinnati) 2009; Performance Award, US Dept of Labor Manpower Admin. 1969, William Booth Award, The Salvation Army 1998, Horatio Alger Award 1999, Distinguished Service Award, Nat. Conf. Cttee of Justice 2000, 2003, inducted into Grocery Manufacturer's Asscn Grocery Hall of Fame 2003, Great Living Cincinnatian, Cincinnati Regional Chamber of Commerce 2008, Founders' Day Award, Xavier Univ. 2013. *Publications:* Inequality: The Poor and the Rich in America (with Joseph W. McGuire) 1969, Ethics, Free Enterprise and Public Policy (with Richard T. De George) 1978. *Leisure interests:* fly-fishing, music, reading.

PICKARD, Ann, BA, MA; American oil company executive; *Country Chair, Shell in Australia and Executive Vice-President, Upstream Australia, Royal Dutch Shell;* b. Wyo.; m.; two c.; ed Univ. of California, San Diego, Univ. of Pennsylvania; extensive business experience throughout S America, the countries of the fmr Soviet Union, the Middle East and Africa; worked for Mobil, left co. upon merger with Exxon; joined Shell 2000, Dir, Global Businesses and Strategy and mem. Shell Gas & Power Exec. Cttee with responsibility for Global LNG, Power, and Gas & Power Strategy –2005, Regional Exec. Vice-Pres. for Sub-Sahara Africa, based in Lagos, Nigeria, 2005–10, Exec. Vice-Pres. Upstream Australia within Shell Upstream International org. 2010–, also Country Chair Shell in Australia, Dir of Shell Energy Holdings Australia Ltd and its subsidiary cos; mem. Bd Energy & Minerals Inst. of Int., Univ. of Western Australia; ranked by Fortune magazine amongst the 50 Most Powerful Women in Business outside the US (25th) 2009–10, (23rd) 2011, (46th) 2012. *Address:* Shell Australia Ltd, PO Box 872K, Melbourne, Vic. 3000, Australia (office). *Telephone:* (3) 9666-5444 (switchboard) (office). *Fax:* (3) 8823-4800 (office). *E-mail:* info@shell.com.au (office). *Website:* www.shell.com .au (office).

PICKARD, Sir (John) Michael, Kt, FCA, CIMgt; British fmr business executive; b. 29 July 1932, Banstead, Surrey; s. of the late John Stanley Pickard and of Winifred Joan Pickard; m. Penelope Jane Catterall 1959; one d. three s.; ed Oundle School; Finance Dir British Printing Corpn 1965–68, Man. Dir Trusthouses Ltd 1968–70, Trusthouse Forte Ltd 1970–71; Chair. Happy Eater Ltd 1972–86, Grattan PLC 1978–84, Courage Ltd and Imperial Brewing & Leisure Ltd 1981–86; CEO Sears PLC 1988–92; Chair. Freemans PLC 1988–92, Bullough PLC 1996–2002 (Dir 1995–), London Docklands Devt Corpn 1992–98, Servus Holdings Ltd 1997–2001, Nat. House-Building Council 1998–2002, London First Centre 1998–2001; Past Pres. Surrey Co. Cricket Club; Dir (non-exec) Brown Shipley Holdings PLC 1986–93, Electra Investment Trust PLC 1989–2002, Nationwide Bldg Soc. 1991–94, Pinnacle Clubs Ltd 1992–99, Bentalls PLC 1993–2001, United Racecourses (Holdings) Ltd 1995–02; mem. Bd London First 1992–2002 (Deputy Chair. 1998–03); Epsom Downs Racecourse Ltd (Deputy Chair. 2002–06); mem. Cttee The Automobile Asscn 1994–99; Chair. Roedean School Council 1980–90, The Housing Forum 1999–2002, Freeport PLC 2001–03; Gov. Oundle School 1987–2000, Chair. Bd Govs 2004–07; Hon. LLD (East London) 1997. *Leisure interests:* sport, education. *Address:* Kingsbarn, Tothill, Headley, Surrey, KT18 6PU, England (home). *Telephone:* (1372) 377331 (home). *Fax:* (1372) 363350 (home). *E-mail:* jane@michaelpickard.co.uk (home).

PICKARD, Vivian R., BS, MS; American automobile industry executive and philanthropist; *President, General Motors Foundation and Director, Corporate Relations, General Motors Company;* b. Sturgis, Miss.; ed Ferris State Univ., Central Michigan Univ.; joined General Motors 1980, has held several key roles, including admin. and man. positions within the Finance, Human Resources and Public Policy functions, Pres. General Motors Foundation and Dir, Corp. Relations, General Motors Company 2010–; mem. Bd Washington, DC Martin Luther King, Jr Nat. Memorial, Friends of African and African American Art (Detroit Inst. of Arts), Detroit Regional Chamber Foundation, The Parade Company, New Detroit The Coalition, Fifth Third Bank – Eastern Michigan, Michigan Women's Foundation, Council of Michigan Foundations, Cultural Alliance of Southeastern Michigan, Sphinx Org.; Past Pres. The Black Women's Agenda, Inc.; fmr Chair. Inforum; mem. The Executive Leadership Council; Exec. Cttee for The Links, Inc.; Lifetime mem. Nat. Asscn for the Advancement of Colored People (NAACP), Nat. Council of Negro Women, Nat. Black MBA Asscn, Leadership Detroit; Women of Excellence Award, Michigan Chronicle 2009, Inforum Inner Circle Honoree 2010, Alpha Award of Honor, Alpha Phi Alpha Fraternity, Inc. 2011, Bridge Builder Award, Rainbow PUSH Coalition 2011. *Address:* General Motors Corporation, 300 Renaissance Center, Detroit, MI 48265-3000, USA (office). *Telephone:* (313) 556-5000 (office). *Website:* www.gm.com (office).

PICKENS, Thomas Boone, Jr, BS; American business executive; *Chairman and CEO, BP Capital Management LP;* b. 22 May 1928, Holdenville, Okla; s. of Thomas Boone Pickens and Grace Molonson Pickens; m. Beatrice L. Carr 1972 (divorced); m. Madeleine Pickens; ed Oklahoma State Univ.; geologist, Phillips Petroleum Co. 1951–55; Founder, Pres., Chair. Bd Mesa Petroleum Co., Amarillo, Tex.

1956–1996; Gen. Pnr, Mesa Inc. 1985–; Founder, Chair. and CEO BP Capital Man. LP (pvt. investment firm) 1997–; f. Pickens Fuel Corpn (now Clean Energy) 1997; mem. Nat. Petroleum Council 1970–; Founder and Chair. United Shareholders Asscn Washington 1986–93. *Publication:* Boone 1987. *Address:* BP Capital Management, LP, 8117 Preston Road, Suite 260, Dallas TX 75225, USA (office). *Telephone:* (214) 265-4165 (office). *Fax:* (214) 750-0216 (office). *E-mail:* info@bpcap .net (office). *Website:* www.bpcap.net (office).

PICKERING, Thomas Reeve, MA; American diplomatist and business executive; *Vice-Chairman, Hills and Company;* b. 5 Nov. 1931, Orange, NJ; s. of Hamilton Reeve Pickering and Sarah P. Chasteney; m. Alice Jean Stover 1955; one s. one d.; ed Bowdoin Coll., Brunswick, Maine, Fletcher School of Law and Diplomacy, Medford, Mass., Univ. of Melbourne, Australia; Lt Commdr USNR 1956–64; joined Dept of State 1959, Intelligence Research Specialist 1960, Foreign Affairs Officer 1961, Arms Control and Disarmament Agency 1961–62; mem. US Del. to Disarmament Conf., Geneva 1962–64; Prin. Officer, Zanzibar 1965–67; Deputy Chief of Mission, Dar es Salaam 1967–69; Deputy Dir Bureau of Politico-Mil. Affairs 1969–73; Exec. Sec. Dept of State, Special Asst to Sec. of State 1973–74; Amb. to Jordan 1974–78; Asst Sec. of State, Bureau of Oceans, Environment and Science 1978–81; Amb. to Nigeria 1981–83; Amb. to El Salvador 1983–85, to Israel 1985–88; Perm. Rep. to UN 1989–92, Amb. to India 1992–93, to Russia 1993–96; Under-Sec. of State for Political Affairs 1997–2000; named Career Amb.; Pres. Eurasia Foundation 1996–97; fmr Sr Vice-Pres. Int. Relations, The Boeing Co., now consultant; Vice-Chair. Hills and Co. 2006–. *Leisure interests:* archaeology, scuba, photography, carpentry. *Address:* Hills and Company, 901 15th Street, NW, Washington, DC 20006 (office); 2318 Kimbro Street, Alexandria, VA 22307-1822, USA (home). *Telephone:* (202) 822-4912 (office); (903) 660-8929 (home).

PICKETT, John Anthony, CBE, PhD, DSc, CChem, FRS, FRSC, FRES; British research chemist and academic; *Michael Elliott Distinguished Research Fellow and Scientific Leader of Chemical Ecology, Rothamsted Research;* b. 21 April 1945, Leicester, England; s. of Samuel Victor Pickett and Lilian Frances Hoar; m. Ulla Birgitta Skålén 1970; one s. one d.; ed King Edward VII Grammar School, Coalville, Univ. of Surrey; Postdoctoral Fellowship, UMIST (organic chem.) 1970–72; Sr Scientist, Chem. Dept, Brewing Research Foundation, Surrey 1972–76; Prin. Scientific Officer, Dept of Insecticides and Fungicides, Rothamsted Experimental Station 1976–83, Individual Merit (Grade 2) and Head of Dept of Insecticides and Fungicides (now Biological Chem. Div.), Inst. of Arable Crops Research (now Rothamsted Research) 1984–2010, Michael Elliott Distinguished Research Fellow and Scientific Leader of Chemical Ecology, Rothamsted Research 2010–; Pres. Int. Soc. of Chemical Ecology (ISCE) 1995; mem. and current Chair. Int. Centre of Insect Physiology and Ecology Governing Council, Nairobi 2005–; mem. Deutsche Akad. der Naturforscher Leopoldina 2001; Foreign mem. Royal Swedish Acad. of Agric. and Forestry 2005; mem. Bd of Trustees, Int. Inst. of Tropical Agric. 2010–; Hon. Prof., Univ. of Nottingham 1991; Hon. mem. Academic Staff, Univ. of Reading 1995, Chemical Soc. of Ethiopia, Hon. Fellow, Royal Entomological Soc. 2010; Hon. DSc (Aberdeen) 2008; Rank Prize for Nutrition and Crop Husbandry 1995, ISCE Medal 2002, Wolf Prize in Agric. (co-recipient) 2008, Croonian Prize Lecture, Royal Soc. 2008, Millennium Award, Associated Chambers of Commerce and Industry of India 2011. *Research:* chemical ecology and insect pheromones in particular. *Publications:* more than 400 papers, including patents. *Leisure interest:* jazz trumpet playing. *Address:* Biological Chemistry Department, Rothamsted Research, Harpenden, Herts., AL5 2JQ (office); 53 Parkfield Crescent, Kimpton, nr Hitchin, Herts., SG4 8EQ, England (home). *Telephone:* (1582) 763133 (ext. 2321) (office); (1438) 832832 (home). *Fax:* (1582) 762595 (office). *E-mail:* john .pickett@rothamsted.ac.uk (office). *Website:* www.rothamsted.ac.uk/people/ jpickett (office).

PICKETT-HEAPS, Jeremy David, BA, PhD, FAA, FRS; Australian botanist and academic; *Professorial Fellow of Botany, University of Melbourne;* b. 5 June 1940, Bombay, India; m. 1st Charmian Scott 1964; one s. one d.; m. 2nd Julianne Francis 1978; two s.; ed Univ. of Cambridge; Prof., Dept of Molecular, Cellular and Developmental Biology, Univ. of Colorado, Boulder, USA 1970–88; Prof. of Botany, Univ. of Melbourne 1988–, Professorial Fellow 2003–. *Publications:* Green Algae 1975; 180 research publns in peer-reviewed journals. *Address:* School of Botany, University of Melbourne, Parkville, Vic. 3052 (office); PO Box 247, Mallacoota, Vic. 3892, Australia (home). *Telephone:* (3) 5158-0123 (office); (3) 5158-0123 (home). *E-mail:* jeremyph@unimelb.edu.au (office). *Website:* www.cytographics.com (office).

PICKLES, Rt Hon. Eric Jack; British politician; *Secretary of State for Communities and Local Government;* b. 20 April 1952, Keighley, Yorks., England; m. Irene Coates 1976; ed Greenhead Grammar School (later Greenhead High School, now Univ. Acad. Keighley), Leeds Polytechnic; worked as Consultant in Employment Practice; Councillor, Bradford Metropolitan Dist Council 1979–91, Leader, Conservative Group 1988–90; Nat. Chair. Young Conservatives 1980–81; Deputy Leader of Conservative Group, Asscn of Metropolitan Authorities 1989–91; MP for Brentwood and Ongar 1992–2010, for Brentwood and Ongar (revised boundary) 2010–; Opposition Spokesperson for Social Security 1998–2001; Shadow Minister for Transport 2001–02; Shadow Sec. of State for Local Govt and the Regions 2002–03, for Local Govt 2003–05; Shadow Minister for Local Govt 2005–07; Shadow Sec. of State for Communities and Local Govt 2007–09; Sec. of State for Communities and Local Govt 2010–; mem. Conservative Party Nat. Union Exec. Cttee 1975–97; mem. Conservative Party Nat. Local Govt Advisory Cttee 1985–, One Nation Forum 1987–91; Local Govt Ed., Conservative Newsline 1990–92; Vice-Chair. Conservative Party 1993–97, Deputy Chair. (Local Govt) 2005–07, Chair. 2009–10; mem. (Select Cttees), Environment, Transport and Regional Affairs 1997–98, Environment, Transport and Regional Affairs (Transport Sub-Cttee) 1997–98; mem. Yorkshire Regional Health Authority 1982–90; Chair. Jt Cttee Against Racism 1982–87, Nat. Local Govt Advisory Cttee 1992–95; Vice-Pres. Local Govt Asscn 1997–2010; Trustee, Brentwood Foyer, Brentwood Theatre. *Radio:* fmr presenter on The Eric and Brandon Show for local community radio station Phoenix FM (together with the then Leader of Brentwood Council Brandon Lewis). *Leisure interests:* bird watching, opera, film. *Address:* Department for Communities and Local Government, Eland House, Bressenden Place, London, SW1E 5DU (office); House of Commons, Westminster, London, SW1A

0AA, England. *Telephone:* (30) 3444-3450 (Dept) (office); (20) 7219-4428 (Westminster). *Fax:* (20) 7219-2783 (Westminster). *E-mail:* eric.pickles@communities .gsi.gov.uk (office); picklese@parliament.uk. *Website:* www.gov.uk/government/ organisations/department-for-communities-and-local-government (office); www .parliament.uk/biographies/commons/mr-eric-pickles/33; www.ericpickles.com.

PICULA, Tonino; Croatian politician and historian; b. 31 Aug. 1961, Mali Losinj; ed Zagreb Univ.; Assoc. Prof. and Sec. Kulturni Radnik (magazine), Cultural and Educ. Ass. 1987–89; mem. Exec. Cttee, Int. Sec. SDP of Croatia 1993–; Counsellor, SDP Co. Ass. of Zagreb, mem. Cttee for Int. Co-operation for Local Self-Govt Devt, Pres. City Org. SDP for Velika Gorica 1997–2000; mem. Croatian Parl. 2000–; Minister of Foreign Affairs 2000–03; Mayor of Velika Gorica 2005–09. *Address:* c/o Ministry of Foreign Affairs, trg. Nikole Šubića Zrinskog 7-8, 10000 Zagreb, Croatia (office).

PIEBALGS, Andris; Latvian EU official, politician and diplomatist; *Commissioner for Development, European Commission;* b. 17 Sept. 1957, Valmiera; m.; three c.; ed Univ. of Latvia; teacher, Headmaster, Secondary School No. 1, Valmiera 1980–88; desk officer, Head of Dept, Ministry of Educ. 1988–90; Minister of Educ. 1990–93; mem. Parl. 1993–94, Chair. Budget and Finance Cttee; Minister of Finance 1994–95; Amb. to Estonia 1995–97; Perm. Rep. of Latvia to EU 1998–2003; Deputy Sec. of State, Ministry of Foreign Affairs, responsible for relations with EU 2003–04; Head of Cabinet of Commr Kalniete 2004; Commr for Energy, EC 2004–10, for Devt 2010–, mem. Lead Group of the Scaling Up Nutrition Movt 2011–; mem. UN High Level Group on Sustainable Energy for All 2011–, UN High Level Panel on the post-Millennium Devt Goals agenda beyond 2015 2012–. *Leisure interests:* tennis, skiing. *Address:* European Commission, 200 Rue de la Loi, 1049 Brussels, Belgium (office). *Telephone:* (2) 299-05-20 (PA) (office); (2) 299-11-11 (switchboard) (office). *Fax:* (2) 298-86-24 (office). *E-mail:* cab -piebalgs-archives@ec.europa.eu (office). *Website:* ec.europa.eu/commission_2010 -2014/piebalgs (office); blogs.ec.europa.eu/piebalgs (office).

PIËCH, Ferdinand Karl; Austrian automotive executive; *Chairman of the Supervisory Board, Volkswagen AG;* b. 17 April 1937, Vienna; grand-s. of Ferdinand Porsche, founder of Porsche, Stuttgart; ed Eidgenössische Technische Hochschule (ETH), Zürich; joined Porsche KG in engine testing 1963, Tech. Man. 1971; joined Audi NSU Auto Union AG 1972, Divisional Man. Gen. Testing 1973, mem. Bd of Man. 1975, Vice-Chair. Bd of Man. 1983, Chair. Bd of Man. Audi AG 1988; Chair. Bd Dirs Volkswagen AG 1993–2002, Dir, Head of Research and Devt 1995–2000, responsible for Production Optimisation and Purchasing 1996–2001, Chair. Supervisory Bd 2002–; Chair. Supervisory Bd MAN SE; Pres. Asscn of European Automobile Mfrs 1999–2000; Chair. Scania 2000–02; Hon. Citizen of Zwickau 1999, Ingolstadt 2001, Wolfsburg 2002; Hon. Prof., Tech. Univ., Vienna 2002; Hon. DTech (Tech. Univ. Vienna) 1984; Dr hc (Ben Gurion Univ.) 1997, (ETH, Zurich) 1999; Distinguished Service Medal (1st Class) 1984, Automobile Business Manager of the Century 1999, Automobile Magazine Man of the Year 2011. *Address:* Volkswagen AG, Brieffach 1848-2, 38436 Wolfsburg, Germany (office). *Telephone:* (53) 6190 (office). *Fax:* (53) 61928282 (office). *Website:* www .volkswagen.com (office); www.volkswagen.de (office).

PIECHOCIŃSKI, Janusz; Polish politician; *Deputy Prime Minister and Minister of the Economy;* b. 15 March 1960, Pancerne (now Studzianki Pancerne), Mazowieckie Voivodship; m. Halina Piechocińska; one s. two d.; ed Warsaw Univ. of Tech., Warsaw School of Econs; researcher, Dept of Econ. and Social History, Warsaw School of Econs 1987–99; Councillor, Mazowieckie Municipal Ass. 1999–2001, 2006–07; mem. Sejm (Parl.) for Warsaw 20 constituency –2005, 2007–11, 2011–, mem. Parl. Cttee on Finance and Budget 1991–97, Chair. Cttee on Infrastructure 2001–05; Deputy Prime Minister and Minister of the Economy 2012–; Pres. Regional Fund for Environmental Protection and Water Man., Warsaw 1999–2001, Nat. Social Ecological Movt 2005–07; Vice-Pres. Comm. for Economic Reform 1996; mem. Prime Minister's Nat. Council for European Integration 2000–01; mem. Polish People's Party (PSL) 1990–, Pres. 2012–. *Leisure interests:* football (mem. Sejm football team), ecology, politics, history. *Address:* Ministry of the Economy, 00-507 Warsaw, pl. Trzech Krzyży 3/5, Poland (office). *Telephone:* (22) 6935000 (office). *Fax:* (22) 6934048 (office). *E-mail:* mg@mg .gov.pl (office). *Website:* www.mg.gov.pl (office); www.piechocinski.pl.

PIEDRABUENA, Guillermo; Chilean lawyer; *National Public Prosecutor;* b. 18 Jan. 1937, Viña del Mar; m. Isabel Keymer; six c.; ed Saint George's Coll., Santiago, School of Law, Universidad de Chile, Santiago; lawyer, Consejo de Defensa del Estado 1963–76, Lawyer Counsellor 1976–96, Pres. 1990–93; Sub-Sec. Justice Dept 1970; mem. Appeal Court, Santiago 1997, Special Tribunal of Industrial Property 1993–2000; Nat. Public Prosecutor of Chile 2000–. *Publications include:* Breves comentarios a la reforma procesal penal 1998, El Recurso de apelación y la consulta 1999, Introducción a la reforma procesal penal 2000. *Address:* Fiscalía Nacional del Ministerio Publico, Almirante Lorenzo Gotuzzo 124, Piso 11, 650 10 61 Santiago, Chile (office). *Telephone:* (2) 690-9101 (office). *Fax:* (2) 690-9108 (office). *E-mail:* gpiedrabuena@minpublico.cl (office). *Website:* www .ministeriopublico.cl (office).

PIENAAR, Jacobus François, LLB; South African fmr rugby union player; b. 2 Jan. 1967, Vereeniging; s. of Johan Pienaar and Valerie Du Toit; m. Nerene Winter 1996; two s.; ed Patriot High School and Rand Afrikaans Univ.; flanker; capped for S African Schools 1985, S African Under 20 1987, S African Barbarians 1990; Capt. Transvaal 1989–96, won Super 10, Currie Cup and Lion Cup 1993, retained Currie Cup 1994; Capt. S African Rugby Team 1993–96, World Cup winners 1995; holds record for most tests as Capt. of SA (29); played for Saracens, UK 1997–2000, Coach and CEO 2000–02, won Pilkington Cup; captained the Barbarians v. Leicester 1999; involved in South Africa's failed bid to host the 2011 Rugby World Cup 2005; subject of book by John Carlin, Playing the Enemy: Nelson Mandela 2008, filmed as Invictus 2009; pundit for ITV Sport, Rugby World Cup 2007, 2011; motivational speaker; Dr hc (Univ. of Hertfordshire) 2000; voted by Rugby Union Writers' Club as Rugby Personality of the Year 1995, Newsmaker of the Year in South Africa 1995, Lifetime Achievement Award, British Rugby Writers 1995, voted 50th in the Top 100 Great South Africans 2004, inducted into Int. Rugby Hall of Fame 2005, inducted into IRB Hall of Fame 2011. *Publication:* Rainbow Warrior (autobiog., with Edward Griffiths) 1999. *Leisure interests:* golf, spending time at home. *Address:* c/o South African Rugby Union, PO Box 15929, Panorama 7506,

South Africa. *Telephone:* (21) 9287000. *Fax:* (21) 9287181. *Website:* www.sarugby.net.

PIENE, Otto Ludwig Wilhelm Hermann Leonhard; German artist and academic; *Director Emeritus, Center for Advanced Visual Studies, Massachusetts Institute of Technology;* b. 18 April 1928, Laasphe, Westphalia; s. of Otto and Anne (Niemeyer) Piene; m. Elizabeth Olson 1988; one s. three d.; ed Acad. of Fine Arts, Munich and Düsseldorf and Univ. of Cologne; organized Night Exhbns, f. Group Zero, Düsseldorf, with Heinz Mack 1957–66; Visiting Prof., Graduate School of Art, Univ. of Pa 1964; Prof. of Environmental Art, School of Architecture, MIT 1972–, Dir Center for Advanced Visual Studies, MIT 1974–94, Acting Dir 1993–94, Dir Emer. 1994–; Prof. Emer. MIT 1993–; Founder and Dir Sky Art Conf. 1981–; one-man exhbns include: Galerie Heseler, Munich 1971, 1972, 1975, 1977–79, 1981, 1983, Galerie Heimeshoff, Essen 1974, 1977, 1983, 1988, Galerie Schoeller, Düsseldorf 1976, 1977, 1980, 1984, 1987, 1991, 1995, 2000, Galerie Löhrl, Mönchengladbach 1986, 1988, 1991, 1996, Gallery 360°, Tokyo 1991, 1992; retrospective exhbn Museum am Ostwall, Dortmund 1967, Hayden Gallery, MIT 1975, Karlsruhe 1988, Städt. Kunstmuseum, Düsseldorf 1996, City Gallery, Prague 2002; group exhbns. include: Tate Gallery 1964, Düsseldorf 1973, Antwerp 1979, Paris 1983, London, Berlin 1987, New York 1988–89, Copenhagen 1992; performed works include Olympic Rainbow 1972, Sky Events, SAC 1981, 1982, 1983, 1986, Sky Dance, Guggenheim 1984, Dialogue de Têtes, Reims 1990; Les fleurs du mal, Québec 1996; works in museums in many countries; DFA hc (Univ. of Md) 1995; North Rhine-Westphalia Medal of Merit, American Acad. of Arts and Letters Sculpture Prize, Leonardo da Vinci Prize 2003. *Publications:* (with Heinz Mack) Zero 1, Zero 2 1958, Zero 3 1961; More Sky 1973; author and ed. Zero 1973, Art Transition 1975–76, Centerbeam 1980, Sky Art Conference Catalog 1981, 1982, 1983, 1986, Lightsorot 1988, Feuerbilder und Texte 1988, Überblick 1991. *Address:* Center for Advanced Visual Studies, Massachusetts Institute of Technology, N52-373g, 265 Massachusetts Avenue, Cambridge, MA 02139-4307 (office); 383 Old Ayer Road, Groton, MA 01450, USA (Home and Studio); Hüttenstr. 104, Atelier 40215 Düsseldorf, Germany (Studio). *Telephone:* (617) 253-4415 (office); (978) 448-5240 (Home and Studio). *Fax:* (617) 253-1660 (office); (978) 448-6716 (Home and Studio). *Website:* web.mit.edu/cavs/people/piene/piene.html (office).

PIERANTOZZI, Sandra Sumang, BEd; Palauan politician and business executive; b. 9 Aug. 1953, Koror; d. of the late Yechadrechemai Sumang Demei and of Mitsko Wong Sumang; m. Marcello Pierantozzi; ed Palau Mission Acad., Union Coll., USA, Univ. of Hawaii; teacher, Micronesian Occupational Coll. 1974–79; Journal Clerk, First Palau Constitutional Convention 1979; Office Man. Koror Wholesalers 1980; owner pvt. business including MVP Construction & Realty, Belau Business Services, SPACO Finance 1980–; newscaster WALU-TV 1980–82; Clerk of the Senate 1981–91; Minister of Admin. 1991–92; Special Consultant, Nat. Congress 1992–93; Senator, Floor Leader, Chair. Cttee on Health and Social Welfare 1997–2000; Minister of Health 2001–04; Vice-Pres. of Palau 2001–05; Minister of State responsible for foreign and domestic affairs 2009–10; mem. Bd of Dirs Palau Chamber of Commerce; Gov. and Dir Pacific Islands Devt Bank; Senate Rep., Bd of Dirs Asscn Pacific Island Legislatures; Sec. Center for Asia-Pacific Women in Politics; Founding Dir Palau Conservation Soc.; f. Sumang Demei Memorial Scholarship Award 1992. *Leisure interests:* philately, numismatics, environmental conservation, travel.

PIERCE, Mary; French (b. Canadian) professional tennis player; b. 15 Jan. 1975, Montréal, Canada; d. of Jim Pierce and Yannick Pierce; turned professional 1989; moved to France 1990; first career title, Palermo 1991; runner-up French Open 1994; winner Australian Open 1995, Tokyo Nichirei 1995; semi-finalist Italian Open, Canadian Open 1996; finalist Australian Open singles 1997, doubles (with Martina Hingis q.v.), 2000; won singles and doubles (with Martina Hingis) French Open 2000; highest singles ranking No. three; winner of doubles (with Martina Hingis q.v.), Pan Pacific; French Fed. Cup team 1990–92, 1994–97; French Olympic team 1992, 1996; 26 WTA Tour singles and doubles titles; France's (rising star) Burgeon Award 1992, WTA Tour Comeback Player of the Year 1997. *Leisure interests:* hiking, jet skiing, boating, shopping, reading, yoga.

PIERCY, Marge, MA; American novelist, poet and essayist; b. 31 March 1936, Detroit, Mich.; d. of Robert Douglas Piercy and Bert Bernice Piercy (née Bunnin); m. Ira Wood 1982; ed Univ. of Michigan and Northwestern Univ.; instructor, Gary Extension, Indiana Univ. 1960–62; Poet-in-Residence, Univ. of Kansas 1971; Distinguished Visiting Lecturer, Thomas Jefferson Coll., Grand Valley State Coll. 1975, 1976, 1978, 1980; mem. staff, Fine Arts Work Center, Provincetown, Mass 1976–77; Visiting Faculty, Women's Writers' Conf., Cazenovia, NY 1976, 1978, 1980; Fiction Writer-in-Residence, Holy Cross Univ., Worcester, Mass 1976; Purdue Univ. Summer Write-In 1977; Butler Chair of Letters, State Univ. of NY at Buffalo 1977; poetry and fiction workshops at Writers' Conf., Univ. of Indiana, Bloomington 1977, 1980; poetry, Writers' Conf., Vanderbilt Univ., Nashville, Tenn. 1981; Visiting Faculty, Women's Writers' Conf., Hartwick Coll. 1979, 1981, 1984; poetry and fiction, Lake Superior Writers' Conf. 1984; Fiction Writer-in-Residence, Ohio State Univ. 1986; Elliston Poetry Fellow, Univ. of Cincinnati 1986; masterclass in poetry, Omega Inst. for Holistic Studies 1990, 1991, 1994; DeRoy Distinguished Visiting Prof., Univ. of Michigan 1992; Thunder Bay Writers' Conf. 1994; Univ. of North Dakota Writers' Conf. 1995; Florida Suncoast Writers' Conf. 1996; Hassayampa Summer Inst. for Creative Writing, Prescott, Ariz. 1998, 2000, 2002, 2004, 2006; Washington Library Asscn Conf., Spokane 2001; Bilgray Scholar-in-Residence, Temple Emmanuel Residency, Univ. of Arizona 2001; Residency and Silver Memorial Lecture, Temple Israel, Duluth, Minn. 2002; Writer-in-Residence, World Fellowship Center, Conway, NH 2005, World Fellowship Center 2005; mini-residency, Trinity Coll., San Antonio, Tex. 2003, Rowe Camp and Conf. Center 2007, 2009, 2012, Christopher Newport Univ. 2007, St Louis Community Coll. in connection with Nishmah 2007, Wayne State Univ. 2008, State Univ. of NY (SUNY), Brockport 2009, Vermont Studio Center 2009, Lafayette Coll. 2009, Northhampton Community Coll. 2009, 2010, Kripalu Center 2010–11, Univ. of Tennessee 2010, SUNY, Oswego 2011, Univ. of Michigan 2012, Jewish Community of Amherst 2013; Instructor, Juried Intensive Poetry Workshop, Wellfleet 2009–; judge, Leapfrog Press Fiction Contest 2009; mem. Advisory Bd Eastern Massachusetts Abortion Fund 1999–, Advisory Bd FEMSPEC: An Interdisciplinary Feminist Journal 1998–2004, Advisory Bd The Poetry Center at Passaic Co. Community Coll. 2004–, Advisory Bd Carrie A. Seaman Animal

Shelter 2005–, Artists Grants Panel in Poetry 2006; Ed. Leapfrog Press 1997–; Poetry Ed. Lilith 2000–; Fiction Ed. Seattle Review 2003–; Hon. DLitt (Lesley Coll.), (Bridgewater State Coll.); Hon. DHumLitt (Hebrew Union Coll.) 2004, (Eastern Connecticut State Univ.) 2005; Rhode Island School of Design Faculty Asscn Medal, Borestone Mountain Poetry Award (twice), Avery Hopwood Contest, Orion Scott Award in Humanities, Lucinda Goodrich Downs Scholar, James B. Angell Scholar, Sheaffer-PEN/New England Award for Literary Excellence, Calapooya Coll. 1986, 1990, Carolyn Kizer Poetry Prize, Literary Award, Gov. of Mass Comm. on Status of Women 1974, Nat. Endowment for the Arts Award 1978, Golden Rose Poetry Prize 1990, The Golden Rose, New England Poetry Club 1990, May Sarton Award, New England Poetry Club 1991, Barbara Bradley Award, New England Poetry Club 1992, Brit ha-Dorot Award, The Shalom Center 1992, Arthur C. Clarke Award for Best Science Fiction Novel published in UK 1993, American Library Asscn Notable Book Award 1997, Paterson Poetry Prize 2000, Paterson Award for Literary Achievement 2004. *Recording:* Louder We Can't Hear You (Yet!): The Political Poems of Marge Piercy 2004. *Publications:* Breaking Camp 1968, Hard Loving 1969, Going Down Fast 1969, Dance the Eagle to Sleep 1970 (republished with new introduction by Marge Piercy 2012), Small Changes 1973, To Be of Use 1973, Living in the Open 1976, Woman on the Edge of Time 1976, The High Cost of Living 1978, Vida 1980 (republished with new introduction by Marge Piercy 2011), The Moon is Always Female 1980, Braided Lives 1982, Circles on the Water 1982, Stone, Paper, Knife 1983, My Mother's Body 1985, Gone to Soldiers 1988, Available Light (May Sarton Award 1991) 1988, Summer People 1989, He, She and It 1991, Body of Glass (Arthur C. Clarke Award 1993) 1991, Mars and Her Children 1992, The Longings of Women 1994, Eight Chambers of the Heart 1995, City of Darkness, City of Light 1996, What Are Big Girls Made Of? 1997, Storm Tide 1998, Early Grrrl 1999, The Art of Blessing the Day 1999, Three Women 1999, So You Want to Write: How to Master the Craft of Writing Fiction and the Personal Narrative (with Ira Wood) 2001, 2005, Sleeping with Cats, A Memoir 2002, The Third Child 2003, Colors Passing Through Us 2003, Sex Wars 2006, The Crooked Inheritance 2006, Pesach for the Rest of Us 2007, The Hunger Moon, New and Selected Poems, 1980–2010 2011. *Address:* PO Box 1473, Wellfleet, MA 02667, USA (home). *Telephone:* (508) 349-3163 (office). *E-mail:* hagolem@c4.net (office). *Website:* www.margepiercy.com (office).

PIERONEK, Most Rev. Tadeusz; Polish ecclesiastic and professor of theology and canon law; *Auxiliary Bishop Emeritus of Sosnowiec;* b. 24 Oct. 1934, Radziechowy n. Żywiec; ed Jagiellonian Univ., Kraków, Higher Ecclesiastic Seminary, Kraków, Catholic Univ. of Lublin, Lateral Univ., Rome; ordained priest, Kraków 1957; notary, Metropolitan Curia, Kraków; prefect, Higher Ecclesiastic Seminary, Kraków; Lecturer, Catholic Theology Acad., Warsaw 1967–76, Asst Prof. 1975; Lecturer and Head of Dept of Canon Law, Pontifical Acad. of Theology, Kraków 1965–, Prof. 1985; Visiting Prof., Santa Croce Univ., Rome 1985–; Titular Bishop of Cufruta 1992; Auxiliary Bishop of Sosnowiec 1992–98, Auxiliary Bishop Emer. 1998–; Deputy Gen. Sec. Polish Episcopate 1992–93; Gen. Sec. Polish Episcopate Conf. 1993–98; Gen. Sec. Second Plenary Synod, Poland 1987; Rector Pontifical Acad. of Theology, Kraków 1998–; leading mem. Stefan Batory Foundation (a George Soros Foundation br. in Poland); Dr hc (Pedagogical Univ. of Kraków) 2011; Jan Karski Eagle Award 2008. *Publications:* The Church Is Not Afraid of Freedom 1998, and over 100 articles. *Leisure interests:* Polish poetry, landscape tourism, cooking, classical music, painting, folklore. *Address:* Diocese of Sosnowiec, ul. Wawel 19, 41-200 Sosnowiec (office); Papieska Akademia Teologiczna, ul. Kanonicza 25, 31-002 Kraków, Poland. *Telephone:* (32) 293-51-51 (office). *Fax:* (32) 293-51-88 (office). *Website:* www.kuria.sosnowiec.pl (office).

PIEROTH, Elmar; German politician and viticulturist; b. 9 Nov. 1934, Bad Kreuznach; s. of Philip Pieroth; m. Hannelore Ribow 1957; six c.; ed Stefan Georg Gymnasium, Bingen and Univs of Mainz and Munich; has run Weingut Ferdinand Pieroth GmbH since 1955; creator of Pieroth-Modell; devt work in Togo 1960; initiator Bad Kreuznach talks; mem. Bundestag 1969–81, mem. Bd CDU/CSU Parl. Group 1972–81, mem. Parl. Econ. Cttee and Spokesman of CDU/CSU Parl. Group on Econ. Co-operation and Devt Aid 1980; mem. Berlin Chamber of Deputies 1981–96; Senator for Economy and Labour, Berlin 1981–89, 1995–98, for Finance, Berlin 1991–96; fmr Chair. Supervisory Bd Berlin Transport Services (BVG), Berlin City Cleaning Services (BSR), Berlin Water Works (BWB), Wirtschaftsförderung Berlin GmbH, Berliner Hafen- und Lagerhausbetriebe; Rep. for Eastern Europe, Fed. State of Berlin 1999–2001; Founder Bürgermu Foundation, Berlin 2007, Chair. Bd of Trustees; mem. CDU; honorary chairman of the "Most Bridge from Berlin to Central and Eastern Europe eV 2001. *Publications:* Die Union in der Opposition (with G. Golter) 1970, Chancen der Betriebe durch Umweltschutz (with L. Wicke) 1988. *Address:* 105 Martin-Luther-Strasse, 10825 Berlin, Germany.

PIERRE, D. B. C. (Dirty But Clean); British novelist; b. (Peter Finlay), 18 June 1961, Australia; s. of Dr Keith W. Finlay and Lilian Mary Tate; allegorist, cartoonist, photographer, designer, filmmaker; James Joyce Award, Literary & Historical Soc., Univ. Coll., Dublin 2005. *Television:* Imagine, with Alan Yentob (biographical; BBC) 2004, The Last Aztec (Channel 4 two-hour special on the Spanish conquest of Mexico) 2002. *Publications include:* Vernon God Little (Man Booker Prize, Bollinger Everyman Woodhouse Award, Whitbread Prize for first novel) 2003, Ludmila's Broken English 2006, Lights Out in Wonderland 2010. *Leisure interests:* travel, music, cricket. *Address:* c/o Conville & Walsh Ltd, 2 Ganton Street, London, W1F 7QL, England (office); c/o Faber and Faber Ltd, Bloomsbury House, 74–77 Great Russell Street, London, WC1B 3DA, England. *Telephone:* (20) 7287-3030 (office); (20) 7927-3800. *Fax:* (20) 7287-4545 (office); (20) 7927-3801. *E-mail:* info@convilleandwalsh.com (office). *Website:* www.convilleandwalsh.com (office). *Website:* www.faber.co.uk; www.dbcpierre.com.

PIERRE-BROSSOLETTE, Claude, LenD; French civil servant; b. 5 March 1928, Paris; s. of Pierre Brossolette and Gilberte (née Bruel); m. Sabine Goldet 1953; two d.; ed Lycée Henri-IV, Faculty of Law of Paris Univ., Ecole nat. d'admin; Inspecteur adjoint des Finances 1952, Insp. 1955; served under two successive Ministers in Office of Minister of Econ. and Financial Affairs 1956; Asst to Financial Adviser, Embassy in USA 1957; served Direction des Finances Extérieures 1958; Tech. Adviser, Office of Minister of Finance 1960–62, Asst Dir of Office 1962, Deputy Dir 1963; Asst Dir of External Financial Affairs in Direction du Trésor 1964, later Chef de Service 1966; Sec.-Gen. Conseil nat. du Crédit

1967–71; served in office of Valéry Giscard d'Estaing, Minister of Econ. and Financial Affairs 1969–71; Dir du Trésor, Ministry of Econ. and Financial Affairs 1971; Censeur, Banque de France, Crédit nat. 1971; Vice-Chair. Caisse nat. des Télécommunications 1971–74; Dir SNCF (Nat. Railways Bd) 1971–74, Air France 1971–74; Sec.-Gen. of Presidency of the Repub. 1974–76; Chair. Crédit Lyonnais 1976–82, Omnium financier pour l'Industrie nat. (OFINA) 1976, Europartners Securities Corpn, Banque Stern 1982–86 (Vice-Chair. 1986); Assoc. Man. Worms et Cie 1986–92; Admin. Crédit Nat. 1976–81; Pres. Démachy et Assocs 1987; mem. Conseil nat. du Crédit 1976–81, Conseil de Surveillance de la Cie Bancaire 1976, Dir Société Air-liquide, Crédit Foncier de France 1978–82, Générale Occidentale 1979–82, Péchiney Ugine Kuhlmann 1980–82, Lyonnaise des Eaux 1980, BSN 1981, Norsolor 1988; Pres. Supervisory Council Câbles Pirelli 1992–; Vice-Pres. Eurofin 1992–95, Pres. 1995–96; Pres. Caisse de refinancement hypothécaire 1995; Adviser to Pres. of Merrill Lynch Int. 1993–97, Chair. Supervisory Bd Merrill Lynch France 1997–99; fmr Dir GTM-Enterpose; Chair. Bd of Dirs Caisse de Refinancement de l'Habitat SA 1994–2007; Officier, Légion d'honneur, Commdr de l'Ordre nat. du Mérite, Chevalier, Ordre des Palmes académiques; Médaille de la Résistance. *Address:* c/o Caisse de Refinancement de l'Habitat, 35 rue la Boetie, 75008 Paris (office); 37 avenue d'Iéna, 75116 Paris, France (home).

PIERRE-LOUIS, Michèle, MEconSc, DH; Haitian economist and politician; b. 5 Oct. 1947, Jeremie; ed Queens Coll., City Univ. of New York, St Michael's Coll., USA; Operations and Credit Officer, Bank of Nova Scotia 1976–79; Asst Dir Gen. Nat. Airport Authority 1979–82; Admin. Dir Société Financière Haïtienne de Développement (SOFIHDES) 1983–84; Nat. Trainer, Mission Alpha (nat. literacy program) 1986–88; Consultant to Pres. Jean-Bertrand Aristide on land reform 1991; Exec. Dir Knowledge and Freedom Foundation 1995–; Prime Minister of Haiti 2008–09; fmr Dir Karl Leveque Inst., Man. Consultant Haitian Devt Foundation. *Address:* c/o Office of the Prime Minister, Villa d'Accueil, Delmas 60, Musseau, Port-au-Prince, Haiti (office).

PIERRET, Christian; French politician, economist and lawyer; *Mayor of St-Dié-des-Vosges;* b. 12 March 1946, Bar-le-Duc; s. of Jean Pierret and Anne Radet; m. Marie-Odile Schibler 1978; one d. (and three d. from previous marriages); ed Faculty of Law and Econs, Paris, Inst. d'Etudes Politiques de Paris, Ecole Nat. d'Administration; civil servant, Ministry for the Economy and Finance, then Cour des Comptes 1972–78; fmr Lorraine regional councillor and mem. Vosges Gen. Council; Nat. Ass. Deputy for Vosges 1978–93, 1997–; Vice Minister attached to Minister for the Economy, Finance and Industry, with responsibility for Industry 1997–2002; Mayor of St-Dié-des-Vosges 1989–97, 2002–, Deputy Mayor 1997–2002; Chair. Caisse Nat. d'Epargne 1986–93; Vice-Chair. Accor Hotels group 1993–96; Chair. Parl. Study Group on Textile and Clothing industry 1988–, France–Israel Parl. Friendship Group 1988–; Vice-Chair. France–Great Britain Parl. Friendship Group 1988–; Chair. Fédération des Villes Moyennes; Regional councillor of Vosges (Saint Dié Est) 1979–89, of Lorraine 1978–88, 1998–2001; mem. Comité pour l'union monétaire de l'Europe (CUME); lawyer, Paris Bar 2003–; Chevalier de la Légion d'honneur, Chevalier des Palmes Académiques, Chevalier de l'Ordre des Arts et des Lettres. *Publications:* Plan et autogestion, Socialisme et multinationales, Ministre à gauche 2002, France 2012, refusons le déclin! 2011; many articles in various publs. *Address:* Hôtel de Ville, BP 275, 88100 St-Dié, France. *Telephone:* 3-29-52-66-66. *Fax:* 3-29-52-66-89. *E-mail:* contact@christianpierret.net (home). *Website:* www.christianpierret.net.

PIETERS, Bruno; Belgian fashion designer; *Artistic Director, Hugo Boss;* ed Royal Acad. of Antwerp; began career as an asst designer for Martin Margiela, Josephus Thimister and Christian Lacroix Haute Couture 1999; also worked as freelance designer for cos such as New York Industry, Milan and Antonio Pernas, Madrid; presented his first couture collection entitled 'Part I: Daywear. The Suit' during the Paris couture week in 2001; launched his first complete ready-to-wear collection March 2002; Artistic Dir for Hugo Boss 2007–; Swiss Textiles Award 2006. *Address:* c/o MO Communications, 33 avenue de l'Opera, 75002 Paris, France (office). *Telephone:* 1-44-77-93-60 (office). *Fax:* 1-44-77-93-70 (office). *E-mail:* presse@mocommunications.com (office). *Website:* www.mocommunications.com (office); www.brunopieters.com (office).

PIETERSEN, Kevin Peter, MBE; South African-born professional cricketer; b. 27 June 1980, Pietermaritzburg, Natal; s. of Jannie Pietersen and Penny Pietersen (English); m. Jessica Taylor 2007; ed Maritzburg Coll., Univ. of South Africa; moved to England after protesting at racial quota system in SA 2000; right-handed middle order batsman; occasional right-arm off-spin bowler; plays for Natal B 1997–98, KwaZulu-Natal B 1998–99, KwaZulu-Natal 1999–2000, Notts. 2001–04, MCC 2004, Hants. 2005–10, ICC (Int. Cricket Council) World XI 2005, England 2005– (Capt. Test side 2008–09 (resgnd)), Royal Challengers Bangalore (Capt.) 2009–10, Surrey 2010–, Deccan Chargers 2011, Delhi Daredevils 2012–; First-class debut: for Natal B 1997/98; Test debut: England v Australia, Lord's 21–24 July 2005; One-Day Int. (ODI) debut: Zimbabwe v England, Harare, 28 Nov. 2004; T20I debut: England v Australia, Southampton 13 June 2005; has played in 104 Tests, taken 10 wickets and scored 8,181 runs (23 centuries, 35 fifties), highest score 227, average 47.28, best bowling (innings) 3/52, (match) 4/78; ODIs: 136 matches, scored 4,440 runs, average 40.73, highest score 130, took 7 wickets, average 52.85, best bowling 2/22; First-class: 213 matches, 16,053 runs, average 48.79, highest score 254 not out, took 73 wickets, average 51.39, best bowling (innings) 4/31; mem. England Ashes-winning Test team 2009, 2010–11, England ICC Twenty20 World Cup winning team (against Australia), Barbados, West Indies 2010; first batsman to reach 5,000 Test runs in less than five years (taking four years 242 days in Test against Bangladesh, Mirpur 20 March 2010); fastest batsman to reach both 1,000 and 2,000 runs in ODI cricket and has highest average of any England player to have played more than 20 innings of one-day cricket; has second-highest run total from his first 25 Tests, behind only Donald Bradman; only third English batsman to top ICC ODI rankings March 2007; ICC Emerging Player of the Year 2005, ICC One-Day Player of the Year 2005, Wisden Cricketer of the Year 2006, called by The Times "the most complete batsman in cricket" 2008, Player of the Tournament, ICC Twenty20 World Cup 2010. *Publication:* Kevin Pietersen: Crossing the Boundary (autobiog.) 2007. *Address:* c/o Surrey County Cricket Club, The Kia Oval, Kennington, London, SE11 5SS, England. *Telephone:* (20) 7820-5700. *Fax:* (20) 7735-7769. *E-mail:* enquiries@surreycricket.com. *Website:* www.kiaoval.com.

PIETRUSKI, John Michael, BS; American business executive; b. 12 March 1933, Sayreville, NJ; s. of the late John M. Pietruski, Sr and Lillian Christensen Pietruski; m. Roberta Jeanne Talbot 1954; two s. one d.; ed Sayreville High School and Rutgers Univ.; First Lt US Army 1955–57; Mfg Man., Industrial Eng Man., Procter & Gamble Co. 1954–63; Pres. Medical Products and Hosp. Divs, C.R. Bard, Inc. 1963–77; Pres. Pharmaceutical Group, Sterling Drug Inc. 1977–81, Corp. Exec. Vice-Pres. 1981–83, Pres. and COO 1983–85, Chair. and CEO 1985–88, mem. Bd of Dirs 1977–88; Pres. Dansara Co. 1988–; Chair. Bd Encysive Pharmaceuticals Inc. (fmrly Texas Biotech Corp.) 1990–2008; mem. Bd of Dirs Irving Bank Corpn 1985–89, Associated Dry Goods Corpn 1985–88, Hershey Foods Corpn 1987–2003, Cytogen Corpn 1989–94, Gen. Public Utilities Corpn 1989–2001, Lincoln Nat. Corpn 1989–2003, McKesson Corpn 1990–99, PDI Inc. 1998–2010, FirstEnergy Corpn 2001–04, Xylos Corpn 2001–12, Trial Card Inc. 2002–10; mem. Pharmaceutical Mfrs Asscn 1985–88; Trustee Rutgers Univ. Foundation 1985–94; Regent, Concordia Coll. 1993–2003, 2005–; Hon. LLD 1993. *Leisure interests:* boating, fishing, travelling, athletics. *Address:* Suite 3408, One Penn Plaza, New York, NY 10119, USA (home). *Telephone:* (212) 268-5510 (office). *Fax:* (212) 268-5765 (office).

PIGEAT, Henri Michel; French civil administrator and publisher; *President and CEO, Editions de l'Ilissos;* b. 13 Nov. 1939, Montluçon; s. of Eugène Pigeat and Odette Micard; m. Passerose Cyprienne Rueff 1976; one d.; ed Inst. des Sciences Politiques, Paris and Ecole Nat. d'Admin; Civil Servant Office of Gen. Admin. and Public Service 1965–69; Head Office of Sec. of State for Public Service 1969–71, Tech. Adviser 1971–72; Head of Information Services, Office of Sec. of State for Public Service and Information 1973; Sec.-Gen. Interministerial Cttee for Information 1973–74; Asst Gen. Dir Information, Gen. Office of Information 1974, Dir 1975–76; Dir Information and Broadcasting Service 1976–; Deputy Man. Dir Agence France-Presse 1976–79, Chair. and Man. Dir 1979–86; Chair. and Man. Dir IBIS SA: Prof. Univ. of Paris II; Prof. Inst. d'Etudes Politiques de Paris 1986–92; Dir Soc. nat. des entreprises de presse 1974–76; Dir Soc. financière de radiodiffusion (Sofirad) 1972–76; fmr Dir E1, RMC, Sud Radio, SNEP, TDF, Europe 1, Radio Monte Carlo; Maître de conférances, Inst. d'études politiques, Paris 1966–73, Ecole nat. d'admin. 1967–69, Inst. int. d'admin publique 1966–73; CEO Burson Marsteller 1987–89; Pres. Quacom SA; mem. Exec. Cttee Int. Inst. of Communications, London, fmr Pres. of French section; Pres. and Dir Gen. L & A Editions 2000–; Pres. and CEO Editions de l'Ilissos 2002–; mem. Int. Press Inst.; Chevalier, Ordre nat. du Mérite; Commdr Nat. Order of FRG. *Publications:* La France contemporaine, L'Europe contemporaine (both jointly) 1966–70, Saint Ecran ou la télévision par câbles 1974, Du téléphone à la télématique, La télévision par cable commence demain 1983, Le nouveau désordre mondial de l'information 1987, Les agences de presse 1997, Médias et déontologie 1997, Tendences Economiques Internationales de la Presse 2002. *Leisure interest:* tennis. *Address:* Editions de l'Ilissos, 14 rue de la Sourdière, 75001 Paris (office); 23 quai Antatole France, 75007 Paris, France (home). *Telephone:* 1-42-60-11-03 (office); 1-45-51-70-01 (home). *E-mail:* edesc@wanadoo.fr (home).

PIGGOTT, Arnold A., BBA; Trinidad and Tobago diplomatist, politician and fmr banker; m. Allison Wendy Kitson-Piggott; two s. one d.; ed St Francis Coll., Brooklyn, New York; pvt. consultant in electronic banking –2001; mem. Senate (Parl.) 2007–10; Minister of Works and Transport 2001–03; High Commr to Canada 2003–06; Minister of Foreign Affairs and Govt Senator 2006–07, Minister of Agric., Land and Marine Resources 2007–10; Chair. Bd of Man., Bishop Anstey Jr School 1992–97.

PIGGOTT, Lester Keith; British fmr professional jockey and trainer; b. 5 Nov. 1935, Wantage, Oxon., England; s. of Keith Piggott and Iris Rickaby; m. Susan Armstrong 1960; two d.; one s. with Anna Ludlow; rode over 100 winners per year in UK alone in several seasons since 1955; rode 3,000th winner in UK 27 July 1974; Champion Jockey 11 times (1960, 1964–71); frequently rode in France; equalled record of 21 classic victories 1975; retd Oct. 1985; races won include: 1000 Guineas (twice): Humble Duty 1970, Fairy Footsteps 1981; 2000 Guineas (five times): Crepello 1957, Sir Ivor 1968, Nijinsky 1970, Shadeed 1985, Rodrigo de Triano 1992; the Derby (nine times): Never Say Die 1954, Crepello 1957, St Paddy 1960, Sir Ivor 1968, Nijinsky 1970, Roberto 1972, Empery 1976, The Minstrel 1977, Teenoso 1983; St Leger (eight times): St Paddy 1960, Aurelius 1961, Ribocco 1967, Ribero 1968, Nijinsky 1970, Athens Wood 1971, Boucher 1972, Commanche Run 1984; Prix de l'Arc de Triomphe (three times): Rheingold 1973, Alleged 1977, 1978; Breeders' Cup Mile, USA: Royal Academy 1990; Washington, DC Int. on Sir Ivor 1968 (first time since 1922 an English Derby winner raced in USA), Karabas 1969, Argument 1980; trainer 1985–87; sentenced to three years' imprisonment for tax fraud Oct. 1987, released after 12 months, returned to racing Oct. 1990; retd as jockey 1995; achieved a record of 30 classic wins; 4,493 winners in total; nickname The Long Fellow; OBE (withdrawn); British flat racing Champion Jockey 1960, 1964, 1965, 1966, 1967, 1968, 1969, 1970, 1971, 1981, 1982, annual jockey awards, The Lesters, named in his honour 1990–. *Leisure interests:* swimming, water skiing, golf. *Address:* Florizel, Newmarket, Suffolk, CB8 0NY, England. *Telephone:* (1683) 662584.

PIGOTT, Mark C., BA, BS, MS; American business executive; *Executive Chairman, PACCAR Inc.;* b. 1954; s. of Charles McGee Pigott and Yvonne Flood; ed Stanford Univ.; Internal Auditor, PACCAR Inc. 1977–88, Vice-Pres. 1988–90, Sr Vice-Pres. 1990–93, Exec. Vice-Pres. 1993–95, mem. Bd of Dirs 1994–, Vice-Chair. 1995–96, Chair. and CEO 1997–2013, Exec. Chair. 2013–; Chair. PACCAR Foundation Europe; mem. Washington State Roundtable, World Econ. Forum; Hon. OBE 2003, Hon. KBE 2012. *Address:* PACCAR Inc., 777 106th Avenue NE, Bellvue, WA 98004, USA (office). *Telephone:* (425) 468-7400 (office). *Fax:* (425) 468-8216 (office). *Website:* www.paccar.com (office).

PIGOTT-SMITH, Tim; British actor and director; b. 13 May 1946, Rugby, Warwicks., England; s. of Harry Pigott-Smith and Margaret Pigott-Smith; m. Pamela Miles 1972; one s.; ed Univ. of Bristol, Bristol Old Vic Theatre School; began stage career at Bristol Old Vic; mem. RSC 1972–75; Dir Company by Samuel Beckett, Edinburgh Fringe Festival 1988; Artistic Dir Compass Theatre 1989; Dir The Royal Hunt of the Sun 1989, Playing the Wife 1992, Hamlet, Regent's Park 1994; Hon. DLitt (Leicester) 2002; BAFTA Award for Best TV Actor 1984, Broadcasting Press Guild Award for Best TV Actor 1984, TV Times Award for Best Actor on TV 1984. *Stage appearances include:* As You Like it, Major Barbara,

Benefactors, Sherlock Holmes 1973, Broadway 1974, Bengal Lancer 1985, Antony and Cleopatra, Coming into Land 1987, Entertaining Strangers, Cymbeline, The Winter's Tale, The Tempest 1988, Julius Caesar 1990, Amadeus 1991, Old Times, Jane Eyre 1993, The Picture of Dorian Gray 1994, Retreat, The Letter 1995, Mary Stuart 1996, The Alchemist, Heritage 1997, The Iceman Cometh 1998, Broadway 1999, Five Kinds of Silence 2000, Julius Caesar 2001, Christmas Carol 2002, Mourning Becomes Electra 2003. *Film appearances include:* Aces High 1975, Joseph Andrews 1977, Sweet William, Richard's Things 1978, The Day Christ Died 1979, Clash of the Titans 1981, Escape to Victory, State of Emergency, Life Story 1986, The Remains of the Day 1993, Four Feathers 2001, Laissez Passer 2001, Bloody Sunday 2002, Johnny English 2003, Alexander 2004, V for Vendetta 2005, Flyboys 2006, L'entente cordiale 2006, Normal for Norfolk 2006, Quantum of Solace 2008, Alice in Wonderland 2010. *TV appearances include:* Hamlet, Antony and Cleopatra, Glittering Prizes, Wings, Eustace and Hilda, Lost Boys, Measure for Measure, Fame is the Spur, The Hunchback of Notre Dame, The Jewel in the Crown, Dead Man's Folly, Life Story 1990, The Chief 1990, 1991, 1992, The Adventures of Christopher Columbus, Bullion Boys 1993, The Shadowy Third, Calcutta Chronicles 1995, Innocents 2000, The Vice (eight episodes) 2001–03, Kavanagh QC 2001, Dr. Terrible's House of Horrible 2001, Bloody Sunday 2002, Inspector Lynley Mysteries 2002, The Day Britain Stopped (voice) 2003, Pompeii: the Last Day 2003, Eroica 2003, The Private Life of Samuel Pepys 2003, London 2004, North & South (four episodes) 2004, Agatha Christie: Poirot (episode, Taken at the Flood) 2006, The Last Flight to Kuwait 2007, Holby Blue (eight episodes) 2007, Crimes That Shook the World (narrator, The Backpacker Murderer) 2007, Midsomer Murders (episode, Days of Misrule) 2008, On Expenses 2010. *Publication:* Out of India 1986. *Leisure interests:* music, reading. *Address:* c/o Actual Management, 7 Great Russell Street, London, WC1B 3NH, England. *Telephone:* (20) 7631-4422.

PIGOZZI, Jean, BA; Italian photographer and investor; *Owner, Contemporary African Art Collection;* b. 1952, Paris, France; s. of founder of French car manufacturer Simca; ed lycée in Paris, Harvard Univ., USA; sold supermarket carts for uncle in France 1974; worked in Accounting Dept at Gaumont Film Co., Paris and at Fox Studios, Los Angeles, USA 1975–80; venture capital investor, mainly in USA and UK 1981–; est. Contemporary African Art Collection 1992, world's largest collection of contemporary African Art; recently est. Liquid Jungle Lab in Panama working on high-tech ecological research with Smithsonian Tropical Research Inst., Woods Hole Oceanographic Inst., Royal Botanical Garden of Madrid, Yale School of Forestry. *Address:* The Contemporary African Art Collection, Geneva, Switzerland (office). *E-mail:* caacart-contact@cogitel-forum .com (office). *Website:* www.caacart.com (office).

PIHL, Jüri; Estonian lawyer and politician; b. 17 March 1954, Kuressaare; m.; one d. from previous m.; ed Faculty of Law, Univ. of Tartu; served as Criminal Investigation Inspector, Tallinn 1975–86, Head, Criminal Investigation Dept 1986–88, 1990–91; Head, Võru Police 1988–90; Dir of Security, Estonian Police Bd's Security Police 1991–93, Dir-Gen. 1993–2003; Attorney-Gen. of Estonia 2003–05; Sec.-Gen. Ministry of Justice 2005–07; Minister of the Interior 2007–09; Chair. Estonian Social Democratic Party (Sotsiaaldemokraatlik Erakond) 2009–10; Deputy Mayor, Tallinn City Govt 2009–10; Order of the Cross of the Eagle (Third Class), Order of the White Star (Fourth Class), Police Cross of Merit (First Class), Grand Duke Gediminas' Order of the Cross of Commdr, Lithuania, Police Golden Cross of Merit, Finland, Cross of Recognition (Second Class), Latvia. *Address:* Sotsiaaldemokraatlik Erakond, Ahtri 10A, Tallinn 10151, Estonia (office). *Telephone:* 611-6040 (office). *Fax:* 611-6050 (office). *E-mail:* kantselei@ sotsdem.ee (office). *Website:* www.sotsdem.ee (office).

PIKE, Edward Roy, PhD, CPhys, CMath, FRS, FInstP, FIMA, FRMS; British physicist and academic; *Professor Emeritus of Physics, King's College London;* b. 4 Dec. 1929, Perth, Western Australia; s. of Anthony Pike and Rosalind Irene Davies; m. Pamela Sawtell 1955; one s. two d.; ed Southfield Grammar School, Oxford, Univ. Coll., Cardiff; Royal Corps of Signals 1948–50; Instructor, Physics Faculty, MIT 1958–60; Sr Scientific Officer, Royal Signals and Radar Establishment Physics Group 1960, Prin. Scientific Officer 1967, Deputy Chief Scientific Officer 1973, Chief Scientific Officer 1984–91; Visiting Prof. of Math., Imperial Coll. London 1985–86; Clerk Maxwell Prof. of Theoretical Physics, King's Coll. London 1986–2010, Prof. Emer. 2010–; Head, School of Physical Sciences and Eng 1991–94; fmr Fulbright Scholar; Chair. Oval (114) Ltd 1984–85; Vice-Pres. for Publs, Inst. of Physics 1981–85; Chair. Adam Hilger Ltd 1981–85, Stilo Tech. Ltd 1996–2002; Chair. (non-exec.) Stilo Int. PLC 2000–02, Dir (non-exec.) 2002–04; Dir (non-exec.) Richard Clay plc 1985–86, Phonological Ltd 2004–05; Fellow, Royal Microscopical Soc.; Royal Soc. Charles Parsons Medal and Lecture 1975, MacRobert Award (jtly) and Lecture 1977, Worshipful Co. of Scientific Instrument Makers Annual Achievement Award (jtly) 1978, Civil Service Award to Inventors 1980, Guthrie Medal and Prize, Inst. of Physics 1996. *Publications:* The Quantum Theory of Radiation (co-author) 1995, Light Scattering and Photon Correlation Spectroscopy (co-author) 1997, Scattering (co-author) 2002; Jt-Ed.: Photon Correlation and Light-Beating Spectroscopy 1974, High Power Gas Lasers 1975, Photon Correlation Spectroscopy and Velocimetry 1977, Frontiers in Quantum Optics 1986, Fractals, Noise and Chaos 1987, Quantum Measurement and Chaos 1987, Squeezed and Non-classical Light 1988, Photons and Quantum Fluctuations 1988, Inverse Problems in Scattering and Imaging 1992; numerous papers in scientific journals. *Leisure interests:* music, languages, woodwork. *Address:* Physics Department, King's College, Strand, London, WC2R 2LS (office); 22 Mathew Close, North Kensington, London, W10 5YJ, England (home). *Telephone:* (20) 7848-2043 (office). *Fax:* (20) 7848-2420 (office). *E-mail:* roy.pike@kcl.ac.uk (office). *Website:* www.kcl.ac.uk/nms/depts/physics/people/emeritus.aspx (office).

PIKETTY, Thomas, MSc, PhD; French economist and academic; *Professor of Economics, Paris School of Economics;* b. 7 May 1971, Clichy; ed Ecole normale supérieure (ENS), London School of Econs, UK; Asst Prof., Dept of Econs, MIT, USA 1993–95, Visiting Prof. 2000–01; Research Fellow, CNRS and Centre pour la Recherche Économique et ses applications, Paris 1995–2000; Prof. of Econs, Ecole des Hautes Etudes en Sciences Sociales, Paris 2000–; Co-Dir Public Policy Programme, Center for Econ. and Policy Research, London 2002–13; Dir, Dept of Social Sciences, ENS 2004–06; Dir Paris School of Econs 2005–07, Prof. of Econs 2007–; columnist, Libération, Le Monde; CNRS Bronze Medal 2001, Le Monde/Le

Cercle des économistes Best Young Economist 2002, European Econ. Asscn Yrjö Jahnsson Prize 2013. *Publications:* World Top Incomes Database (with F. Alvaredo, A. Atkinson and E. Saez) 2011–14, A Theory of Optimal Inheritance Taxation (with E. Saez) 2013, Capital is Back: Wealth-Income Ratios in Rich Countries 1700–2010 (with G. Zucman) 2014, Le capital au 21e siècle (Capital in the 21st Century) 2014; numerous articles published in journals including Quarterly Journal of Economics, Journal of Political Economy, American Economic Review, Review of Economic Studies. *Address:* Paris School of Economics, Campus Paris-jourdan, 48, boulevard Jourdan, 75014 Paris, France (office). *Telephone:* 1-43-13-62-50 (office). *E-mail:* piketty@ens.fr (office). *Website:* piketty .pse.ens.fr (office).

PIKHOYA, Rudolf Germanovich, D.HIST.SC.; Russian historian; b. 27 Jan. 1947, Polevskoe, Sverdlovsk Region; m.; one s.; ed Ural Univ.; with Ural Univ. 1971–, Sr researcher Ural Scientific Centre, USSR Acad. of Sciences 1981–86; Prorector Ural Univ. 1986–90; Chair. Cttee on problems of archives, Council of Ministers of Russian Fed. 1990–, Chief, Archive Service of Russia 1992–96; participated in movt for making secret documents of the Communist period public; Vice-Pres. Int. Fund for Democracy, Dir of Research Programmes 1996–98; Prof. and Chair. Acad. of State Service 1998–. *Leisure interest:* music. *Address:* Academy of State Service, Vernadskogo prospekt 84, 117606 Moscow, Russia. *Telephone:* (495) 436-98-14.

PIKIS, Georghios M., LLB; Cypriot judge; b. 22 Jan. 1939, Larnaca; s. of Michael I. Pikis and Erini M. Pikis; m. Maria G. Pikis (née Papaneophytou); two s. one d.; ed Univ. of London, UK; called to the Bar, Gray's Inn, London 1961; Advocate of the Cyprus Bar 1961–66; Dist Judge 1966–72; Pres. Dist Court 1972–81; Justice of Supreme Court of Cyprus 1981–95, Pres. Supreme Court 1995–2004; Judge, Appeals Div., Int. Criminal Court, The Hague 2003–09, full-time mem. 2004–09; *ad hoc* judge, European Court of Human Rights 1993, 1997; mem. UN Cttee against Torture 1996–98; mem. Bd of Dirs Int. Asscn of Supreme Admin. Jurisdictions 1999–2004; mem. Circle of Pres of Conf. of European Constitutional Courts 1999–2004, Pres. 2002–04. *Publications:* books: Criminal Procedure in Cyprus (in English, co-author) 1975, Sentencing in Cyprus (in English) 1978, The Common Law and Principles of Equity and Their Application in Cyprus (in Greek) 1981, Basic Aspects of Cyprus Law (in Greek) 2003, Constitutionalism – Human Rights – Separation of Powers, The Cyprus Precedent (in English) 2006; numerous lectures, speeches and reports (including reports to Int., European and Commonwealth Judicial Confs and Asscns) on human rights, constitutional law and the judiciary. *Address:* c/o International Criminal Court, PO Box 19519, 2500 CM The Hague, The Netherlands. *Telephone:* (70) 515-8216. *E-mail:* pio@icc-cpi.int.

PIKRAMMENOS, Panagiotis; Greek judge and government official; b. 26 July 1945, Athens; s. of Otto Pikrammenou; m. Athina Noutsou; one d.; ed German School of Athens, Law School at Kapodistrian Univ. of Athens, Pantheon-Assas Paris II Univ., France; worked as a lawyer in Athens and London, UK; became rapporteur of Council of State 1976, held several sr positions, then Pres. 2009–12; worked on several legis. cttees for Ministry of Justice; special adviser on judicial affairs to Prime Minister Konstantinos Mitsotakis 1991–93; Gen. Man. Nat. School of Judges 2005–09; Prime Minister of Greece 16 May–20 June 2012; Ind. *Address:* c/o Office of the Prime Minister, Maximos Mansion, Herodou Atticou 19, 106 74 Athens, Greece. *E-mail:* primeminister@primeminister.gr.

PĪKS, Rihards; Latvian politician; b. 31 Dec. 1941, Rīga; m.; four c.; ed All-Union Cinematography Inst., Moscow, two-year advanced filmmaking course, Moscow; film dir, producer, cameraman, Rīga Film Studio –1987, Studio Dir 1987–1990; Founder-Dir Nat. Cinematography Centre 1991–93, SIA Baltic Cinema 1993–95; Founder-Pres. Baltic Films asscn 1991–93; Founder, lecturer Cinematography Dept, Latvian Acad. of Culture 1993–95; Deputy Chair. Nat. Radio and TV Council 1995–96; Minister for Culture 1996–97; Pres. SIA Audiovizualie Multimediji Baltija 1997–98; mem. Parl. 1998–, Deputy Speaker 1999–2002, Chair. Foreign Affairs Cttee Feb.–March 2004; Minister of Foreign Affairs 2004; mem. European Parl. 2004–09; mem. People's Party; around 20 int. awards at film festivals; Commdr, Order of Merit (Italy). *Films:* as dir: four full length features, five documentaries; as producer: 35 full length features; as cameraman: 20 documentaries; as dir of photography: 11 full length features. *Publications:* numerous articles in newspapers and magazines. *Leisure interests:* basketball, summer, nature, tourism. *Address:* 29 Balozu prosp., 1024 Rīga, Latvia. *Telephone:* 6799-4803. *Fax:* 6799-4803. *E-mail:* rpiks@inbox.lv; piks.rihards@gmail.com.

PILARCZYK, Most Rev. Daniel Edward, MA, PhD, STD; American ecclesiastic; *Archbishop Emeritus of Cincinnati;* b. 12 Aug. 1934, Dayton, Ohio; s. of Daniel J. Pilarczyk and Frieda S. Hilgefort; ed St Gregory Seminary, Ohio, Pontifical Urban Univ. Rome, Xavier Univ. Cincinnati and Univ. of Cincinnati; ordained Roman Catholic priest 1959; Asst Chancellor, Archdiocese of Cincinnati 1961–63; Faculty, Athenaeum of Ohio (St Gregory Seminary) 1963–74, Vice-Pres. 1968–74, Trustee 1974–; Rector, St Gregory Seminary 1968–74; Synodal Judge, Archdiocesan Tribunal 1971–82; Dir of Archdiocesan Educ. Services 1974–82; Auxiliary Bishop of Cincinnati 1974–82, Archbishop 1982–2009, Emer. 2009–, pleaded no contest on behalf of the Archdiocese to five misdemeanor counts of failing to report a crime during period 1978–82 2003; Vice-Pres. Nat. Conf. of Catholic Bishops 1986–89; Pres. Nat. Conf. of Catholic Bishops 1989–92; mem. Episcopal Bd Int. Comm. on English in Liturgy 1987–97; mem. Jt Cttee of Orthodox and Catholic Bishops 2002; numerous professional appts; Hon. LLD (Xavier Univ.) 1975, (Calumet Coll.) 1982, (Univ. of Dayton) 1990, (Marquette Univ.) 1990, (Thomas More Coll.) 1991, (Coll. of Mount St Joseph) 1994, (Hebrew Union Coll./Jewish Inst. of Religion) 1997. *Publications:* Twelve Tough Issues 1988, We Believe 1989, Living in the Lord 1990, The Parish: Where God's People Live 1991, Forgiveness 1992, What Must I Do? 1993, Our Priests: Who They Are and What They Do 1994, Lenten Lunches 1995, Bringing Forth Justice 1996, Thinking Catholic 1997, Practicing Catholic 1998, Believing Catholic 2000, Live Letters 2001, Twelve Tough Issues and More 2002, Being Catholic 2006, When God Speaks 2006; numerous articles in newspapers and journals. *Address:* 100 East Eighth Street, Cincinnati, OH 45202, USA (office). *Telephone:* (513) 421-3131 (office). *E-mail:* dpilarczyk@catholiccincinnati.org (office).

PILGER, John Richard; Australian journalist, filmmaker and writer; b. Sydney, NSW; s. of Claude Pilger and Elsie Pilger (née Marheine); m. (divorced); one s. one d.; ed Sydney High School, Journalism Cadet Training, Australian Consolidated Press; journalist, Sydney Daily/Sunday Telegraph 1958–62, Reuters, London 1962; feature writer, columnist and Foreign Corresp. (latterly Chief Foreign Corresp.), Daily Mirror, London 1963–86; columnist, New Statesman, London 1991–; freelance contrib., The Guardian, London, The Independent, London, New York Times, Melbourne Age, The Nation, New York, South China Morning Post, Hong Kong, Aftonbladet, Sweden; documentary filmmaker, Granada TV, UK 1969–71, Associated Television 1972–80, Central/Carlton/Granada Television, UK 1980–; credited with alerting much of int. community to horrors of Pol Pot régime in Cambodia, also occupation of Timor-Leste; Visiting Fellow, Deakin Univ., Australia 1995; Frank H. T. Rhodes Visiting Prof., Cornell Univ., USA 2003–; Hon. DLitt (Staffordshire Univ.) 1994, (Lincoln) 2008, Hon. PhD (Dublin City Univ.) 1995, (Kingston) 1999, (Open Univ.), Hon. DArts (Oxford Brookes Univ.) 1997, Hon. DrIur (St Andrews) 1999, Hon. DUniv (Open Univ.) 2001, Hon. DrLaw (Rhodes, SA) 2008; Descriptive Writer of the Year, UK 1966, Journalist of the Year, UK 1967, 1979, Int. Reporter of the Year, UK 1970, Reporter of the Year, UK 1974, BAFTA Richard Dimbleby Award 1991, US Acad. Award (Emmy) 1991, Reporteurs sans frontières, France 1993, George Foster Peabody Award, USA 1992, Sophie Prize for Human Rights 2003, Royal TV Soc. Award 2005, One World Award for Best Documentary 2008, Sydney Peace Prize 2009, Grierson Trust Lifetime Award 2011. *Feature film:* The Last Day 1983. *Documentary films include:* Cambodia: Year Zero 1979 (and four other films on Cambodia), The Quiet Mutiny 1970, Japan Behind the Mask 1986, The Last Dream 1988, Death of a Nation 1994, Flying the Flag: Arming the World 1994, Inside Burma 1996, Breaking The Mirror: The Murdoch Effect 1997, Apartheid Did Not Die 1998, Welcome to Australia 1999, Paying the Price: Killing the Children of Iraq 2000, The New Rulers of the World 2001, Palestine Is Still The Issue 2002, Breaking the Silence: Truth and Lies in the War on Terror 2003, Stealing a Nation 2004, The War on Democracy 2007, The War You Don't See 2010. *Publications include:* The Last Day 1975, Aftermath: The Struggle of Cambodia and Vietnam 1981, The Outsiders 1983, Heroes 1986, A Secret Country 1989, Distant Voices 1992, Hidden Agendas 1998, Reporting the World: John Pilger's Great Eyewitness Photographers 2001, The New Rulers of the World 2002, Tell Me No Lies: Investigative Journalism and its Triumphs (ed) 2004, Freedom Next Time 2006. *Leisure interests:* swimming, running, reading, sunning, mulling. *Address:* 57 Hambalt Road, London, SW4 9EQ, England. *Telephone:* (20) 8673-2848. *Fax:* (20) 8772-0235. *E-mail:* jpilger2003@yahoo.co.uk. *Website:* www.johnpilger.com.

PILIKIAN, Hovhanness Israel, BSc, MA; British theatre director, writer, composer, academic and filmmaker; b. 15 April 1942, Nineveh-Mosul, Iraq; s. of Israel Pilikian and Tefarik Pilikian; m. 1st Gail Rademacher (divorced 1992, died 2000); two s. one d.; m. 2nd Clarice Stephens 1993; one s. two d.; ed Univ. of Munich, Univ. of London, Royal Acad. of Dramatic Art, Open Univ., American Univ. of Beirut; cr. Hanano Mask Theatre Co. 1970, Cervantes Players (first all-black actors' co. in Europe), London 1971; f. Spice of Life Theatre Club 1980, Bloomsbury Theatre Club 1982; Consultant, Cheltenham Int. Guitar Music Festival 2001; mem. Acad. Bd City Lit Inst. 2000–; Fellow, Royal Anthropological Inst., Deutscher Akademischer Austauschdienst; life mem. Swedenborg Soc. of GB, Univ. of London Convocation Governing Bd; mem. Turner Soc.; Visiting Prof., State Univ. of Yerevan, Dutch Drama Center, Slade School of Art, Cen. School of Art and Design, Yerevan Inst. of Literature, Armenian Acad. of Sciences; regular columnist, Gibrahayer weekly internet magazine 2005–; Adamian Award for Lifetime Achievement, Ministry of Culture of Armenian SSR 1985, Calouste Gulbenkian Foundation Scholar (LSE) 1990, Wandsworth Council Business Award 2004. *Films:* The New Supremes in London 1986, A King of Arabia 1987. *Plays directed include:* Euripides' Electra (Greenwich Theatre, London) 1971, Euripides' Medea (Yvonne Arnaud Theatre) 1971, William Alfred's Agamemnon (McCarthur Theater, Princeton Univ.) 1973, Sophocles' Oedipus Tyrannus (Chichester Festival Theatre) 1974, Schiller's Die Räuber (Roundhouse) 1975, King Lear (Nat. Theatre of Iceland) 1977, Fat Hamlet (Shaw Theatre, London) 1993. *Music:* Clarice de Lune 2003, Katya's Baby Or Lenin's Revolution 2005. *Achievements include:* organized and produced first ever season of Armenian Cinema for the Nat. Film Theatre, London 1981; Armenian Cinema weeks in Venice 1983, Paris 1986, Montreal 2000. *Publications include:* My Hamlet 1961, An Armenian Symphony and Other Poems 1980, Armenian Cinema, A Source Book 1981, Flower of Japanese Theatre 1984, Aspects of Armenian History 1986; contrib. to Society Matters (Open Univ. newspaper), Encyclopedia Britannica. *Leisure interests:* book mad –pvt. library of 10,000 books and expanding. *E-mail:* profpilikian@hotmail.com. *Website:* pilikian.blogspot.com.

PILLAY, Navanethem (Navi), BA, LLB, LLM, SJD; South African judge and UN official; *High Commissioner for Human Rights, United Nations Office of the High Commissioner for Human Rights;* b. 23 Sept. 1941, Durban; m. (deceased); two d.; ed Natal Univ., Harvard Univ., USA; first woman to start a law practice in Natal Prov. 1967, Sr Partner 1967–95; first black woman apptd Acting Judge High Court of SA 1995; Judge, UN Int. Criminal Tribunal for Rwanda 1995–2003, Pres. 1999–2003; Judge, Int. Criminal Court 2003–08; UN High Commr for Human Rights, Geneva 2008–; Chair. Equality Now 1990–95, Hon. Chair. 1995–; Pres. Advice Desk for Abused Women 1989–99, Women Lawyers' Asscn 1995–98; Vice-Chair. of Council, Univ. of Durban-Westville 1995–98; Lecturer, Dept of Public Law, Natal Univ. 1980; Trustee, Legal Resources Centre 1995–98, Lawyers for Human Rights 1998–2001; mem. Women's Nat. Coalition 1992–93, Black Lawyers' Asscn 1995–98, UN Expert Groups on Refugees and on Genocide Persecution 1997, Rules Bd for Courts 1997–98, Expert Group on African Perspectives on Universal Jurisdiction, Cairo and Arusha 2001–02; currently mem. Int. Criminal Law Network, Advisory Bd Journal of Int. Criminal Justice, Bd Harvard-South Africa Scholarship Cttee, Bd Dirs Nozala Investments (women's component of Nat. Econ. Initiative); Hon. mem. American Soc. of Int. Law; Unifem and Noel Foundation Life Award (Los Angeles), Award for Leadership in the Fight for Human Rights, California Legislative Assembly, Dr Edgar Brookes Award, Natal Univ., Award for Outstanding contrib. in Raising Awareness of Women's Rights and Domestic Violence, Advice Desk for Abused Women, Award for Dedication to Human Rights, Equality Now, New York, One Hundred Heroines Award, Washington DC, Human Rights Award, Int. Asscn of Women Judges, Award for High Achievement by a Woman in the Legal Profession, Center for Human Rights and Univ. of Pretoria; further awards from Asscn of Law Soc. of SA, Black Lawyers' Asscn, Feminist

Majority Foundation, Int. Bar Asscn, Peter Gruber Foundation; ranked by Forbes magazine amongst 100 Most Powerful Women (64th) 2009. *Publications:* contrib.: Civilians in War 2001, Essays in Memory of Judge Cassese 2003. *Address:* Office of the High Commissioner for Human Rights, Palais Wilson 52 rue des Pâquis, 1201 Geneva, Switzerland (office). *Telephone:* (22) 917-901100 (office). *Fax:* (22) 917-9008 (office). *E-mail:* registry@ohchr.org (office). *Website:* www.ohchr.org (office).

PILLAY, Patrick, MA; Seychelles politician and diplomatist; two s. (one adopted) one d.; fmr Minister of Educ., of Youth and Culture, of Industries and Int. Business; fmr Seychelles Gov. to African Devt Bank; fmr Pres. Seychelles Nat. Comm. for UNESCO; Minister of Health –2005, of Foreign Affairs 2005–10; High Commr to UK 2010–12. *Address:* Ministry of Foreign Affairs, Maison Quéau de Quinssy, PO Box 656, Mont Fleuri, Mahé, Seychelles (office). *Telephone:* 4283500 (office). *Fax:* 4224845 (office). *E-mail:* mfapesey@seychelles.net (office). *Website:* www.mfa.gov.sc (office).

PILON, Jean-Guy, OC, LLB, CQ; Canadian poet; b. 12 Nov. 1930, St Polycarpe; s. of Arthur Pilon and Alida Besner; m. 2nd Denise Viens 1988; two s. from 1st marriage; ed Univ. de Montréal; f. Liberté (review) 1959, Ed. 1959–79; Head of Cultural Programmes and Producer Radio-Canada 1970–88; with Les Ecrits (literary review); mem. Académie des lettres du Québec 1982, Royal Soc. of Canada 1967–; Chevalier, Ordre Nat. du Québec 1987, Officier Ordre des Arts et des Lettres 1992; Prix de Poésie du Québec 1956, Louise Labé (Paris) 1969, France-Canada 1969, van Lerberghe (Paris) 1969, du Gouverneur gén. du Canada 1970, Athanase-David 1984, Prix littéraire int. de la Paix (PEN Club Québec) 1991. *Publications:* poetry: La fiancée du matin 1953, Les cloîtres de l'été 1954, L'homme et le jour 1957, La mouette et le large 1960, Recours au pays 1961, Pour saluer une ville 1963, Comme eau retenue 1969 (enlarged edn 1985), Saisons pour la continuelle 1969, Silences pour une souveraine 1972. *Address:* 5724 Côte St-Antoine, Montréal, PQ H4A 1R9, Canada (home).

PILOT, Sachin, BA, MBA; Indian politician; *Minister of State for Corporate Affairs;* b. 7 Sept. 1977, Uttar Pradesh; s. of Rajesh Pilot and Rama Pilot; m. Sara Abdullah 2004; two s.; ed St Stephen's Coll., Univ. of Delhi, Inst. of Man. Tech., Ghaziabad, Wharton Business School, Univ. of Pennsylvania, USA; began career with Delhi Bureau of BBC; two years with General Motors; elected to 14th Lok Sabha (lower house of Parl.) for Ajmer constituency 2004, re-elected to 15th Lok Sabha 2009–, mem. Cttee on Home Affairs; Union Cabinet Minister of State for Communications and Information Tech. 2009–12, for Corp. Affairs 2012–; mem. Indian Nat. Congress (Congress); named as Young Global Leader by World Econ. Forum 2008. *Leisure interests:* flying (private pilot's licence), shooting, squash, cricket. *Address:* Ministry of Corporate Affairs, 'A' Wing, Shastri Bhavan, Dr Rajendra Prasad Road, New Delhi 110 001, India (office). *Telephone:* (11) 23384660 (office). *Fax:* (11) 23073806 (office). *E-mail:* hq.delhi@mca.gov.in (office). *Website:* www.mca.gov.in (office); www.sachinpilot.gov.in.

PILSWORTH, Michael John, MA; British television executive; b. 1 April 1951, Leeds; s. of Alwyne Pilsworth and Catherine Pilsworth (née Silverwood); m. Stella Frances Pilsworth (née Hore) 1972; one s. one d.; ed King Edward VI Grammar School, Retford, Univ. of Manchester; Research Asst Inst. of Advanced Studies, Manchester Polytechnic 1972–73; Research Associate Univ. of Manchester 1973–75, lecturer 1973–77; Research Fellow, Centre for TV Research 1977–79, Univ. of Leeds 1979–81; researcher, London Weekend 1982–83; Head of Programme Devt TV South 1984–86, Controller Corp. Devt 1987–88; Chief Exec. MGMM Communications Ltd 1988–89; Man. Dir Alomo Productions Ltd 1990–92, Selec TV PLC 1992–93; Chief Exec. Chrysalis TV Group Ltd 1993–2002; currently Chair. Motive Television PLC mem. Advisory Bd MediaWin & Partners. *Publications include:* co-author Broadcasting in the Third World 1977. *Leisure interests:* reading, cinema, gardening. *Address:* Motive Television PLC, 18 Soho Square, London W1D 3QL, England (office). *Website:* www.motivetelevision.co.uk (office).

PIMENTAL VALENZUELA, Josefina; Dominican Republic academic and politician; *Secretary of State for Education;* ed Universidad Autónoma de Santo Domingo; Prof. of Psychology, Universidad Autónoma de Santo Domingo 1977–, Dir, Dept of Educ. and Faculty of Humanities 1987–90; Dir Educational System Guidance Dept, State Secretariat of Educ., Fine Arts and Religion 1975–79, Training Programme Co-ordinator 1992–96; Deputy Sec. of State for Educ. 1996–2000, for Technical Educ. and Pedagogical Affairs 2004–07, Sec. of State for Educ. 2011–; Dir-Gen. Nat. Inst. of Professional and Technical Training 2007–; mem. Partido de la Liberación Dominicana. *Address:* Secretariat of State for Education, Avda Máximo Gómez, esq. Santiago 2, Gazcue, Santo Domingo DN, Dominican Republic (office). *Telephone:* 688-9700 (office). *Fax:* 689-8688 (office). *E-mail:* mlibreacceso@see.gob.do (office). *Website:* www.see.gob.do (office).

PIMM, Stuart Leonard, BA, PhD; American (b. British) ecologist and academic; *Doris Duke Professor of Conservation Ecology, Duke University;* b. 27 Feb. 1949, Derbyshire, England; m. Julia Killeffer 1990; two d.; ed Univ. of Oxford, UK, New Mexico State Univ.; Asst Prof., Clemson Univ. 1974–75; Asst Prof., Texas Tech Univ. 1975–79, Assoc. Prof. 1979–82; Assoc. Prof., Dept of Ecology and Evolutionary Biology, Univ. of Tennessee 1982–86, Prof. 1986–99; Prof., Center for Environmental Research and Conservation, Columbia Univ. 1999–2002; Doris Duke Prof. of Conservation Ecology, Duke Univ. 2002–; Extraordinary Prof., Univ. of Pretoria, SA 2001–; visiting appointments at Griffith Univ., Australia 1983–84, Inst. for Nonlinear Science, Univ. of California, San Diego 1987, School of Ecosystem Man., Univ. of New England, Australia 1987, Centre for Population Biology, Imperial Coll., Silwood Park, UK 1990, Nat. Research Council (Sr Visiting Scholar) 1995, Conservation Ecology Research Unit, Univ. of Pretoria 1996, 2000; Fellow, American Acad. of Arts and Sciences 2004; Distinguished Assoc. in Research, Bernice P. Bishop Museum, Honolulu, Hawaii 1997–; Pew Scholar in Conservation and the Environment 1993, Sigma Xi Nat. Lecturer 1993–95, Kempe Prize for Distinguished Ecologists 1994, Aldo Leopold Leadership Fellow 1999, Marsh Prize, Zoological Soc. of London 2004, Alumnus of the Year, Coll. of Arts and Sciences, New Mexico State Univ. 2005, Edward T. LaRoe III Memorial Award, Soc. for Conservation Biology 2006, Dr A.H. Heineken Prize for Environmental Sciences, Royal Netherlands Acad. of Arts and Sciences 2006, William Proctor Prize for Scientific Achievement, Sigma Xi, The Scientific Research Soc. 2007, Tyler Prize for Environmental Achievement, Univ. of Southern California 2010. *Films:* contrib. to: The 11th Hour 2007, The Planet (dir Michael Stenberg) 2006,

What a Way to Go (dir T. S. Bennett) 2007. *Publications:* Food Webs 1982 (second edn 2003), The Balance of Nature? Ecological Issues in the Conservation of Species and Communities 1991, The Bird Watcher's Handbook: A Field Guide to the Natural History of European Birds (co-author, also of species treatments) 1994, The World According to Pimm: A Scientist Audits the Earth 2001, Sparrow in the Grass 2002; about 240 papers in professional journals. *Address:* Nicholas School of the Environment and Earth Science, Box 90328, Room A301, LSRC Building, Durham, NC 27708, USA (office). *Telephone:* (919) 613-8141 (office). *Fax:* (919) 684-8741 (office). *E-mail:* stuartpimm@me.com (office). *Website:* www.nicholas .duke.edu (office).

PINA-CABRAL, Prof. João de, BA, DPhil Hab; Portuguese social anthropologist and academic; *Research Coordinator, Institute of Social Sciences, University of Lisbon;* b. 9 May 1954; s. of Daniel de Pina Cabral and Ana A. de Pina Cabral; m. Monica Chan; ed Univ. of Witwatersrand, Johannesburg, Univ. of Oxford, Univ. of Lisbon; Auxiliary Prof., Dept of Social Anthropology, ISCTE, Lisbon 1982–84, Assoc. Prof. 1988–; Gulbenkian Fellow in Portuguese Studies, Univ of South-ampton 1984–86; Research Fellow, Inst. of Social Sciences, Univ. of Lisbon 1986–92, Sr Research Fellow 1992–2004, Research Coordinator 2004–, Pres. Scientific Bd 1998–2004; Pres. European Asscn of Social Anthropologists 2003–05; mem. Portuguese Acad. of Sciences 2004–; Corresp. mem. Real Academia de Ciencias Morales y Politicas; Hon. mem. Royal Anthropological Inst.; Malinowski Memorial Lecturer 1992. *Publications:* over 80 papers in refereed journals; books: Death in Portugal (co-ed.) 1983, Sons of Adam, Daughters of Eve 1986, Os Contextos da Antropologia 1991, Europe Observed (co-ed.) 1992, Aromas de Urze e de Lama 1993, Em Terra de Tufões 1993, Elites: Choice, Leadership and Succession (co-ed.) 2000, Between China and Europe 2002, O Homem na Família 2003, A persistência da história: Passado e contemporaneidade em África (co-ed.) 2004, Nomes: Género, Etnicidade e Familia (co-ed.) 2007, On the margins of Religion (co-ed.) 2008. *Address:* Institute of Social Sciences, University of Lisbon, Avenida A. Bettencourt 9, 1600-189 Lisbon, Portugal (office). *Telephone:* (21) 7804700 (office). *Fax:* (21) 7940274 (office). *E-mail:* pina.cabral@ics.ul.pt (office). *Website:* www.ics.ul.pt (office).

PINA TORIBIO, César, PhD; Dominican Republic politician; *Secretary of State for the Presidency;* b. 17 Dec. 1946, Santo Domingo; ed Universidad Autonoma de Santo Domingo; fmr Juridical Consultant of the Presidency; Sec. of State for the Presidency 2008–; mem. Partido de la Liberación Dominicana (PLD), also PLD del. to Cen. Electoral Bd. *Publication:* Temas Notariales. *Address:* Office of the President, Palacio Nacional, Avda México, esq. Dr Delgado, Santo Domingo, The Dominican Republic (office). *Telephone:* 695-8000 (office). *E-mail:* cesar.pina@sep .gob.do (office). *Website:* www.presidencia.gov.do (office); www.minpre.gob.do (office).

PINARD, Hon. Yvon, BA, LLL; Canadian politician and lawyer; *Judge of the Federal Court;* b. 10 Oct. 1940, Drummondville, Québec; s. of Jean-Jacques Pinard and Cécile Chassé; m. Renée Chaput 1964; two d.; ed Immaculate Conception School, Drummondville, Nicolet Seminary, Sherbrooke Univ.; Pres. Sherbrooke Univ. Law Faculty 1963; admitted to Québec Bar 1964; Pres. and founder Drummond Caisse d'Entraide Economique; Pres. Drummond Liberal Asscn 1968–70; mem. Admin. Council Centre Communautaire d'Aide Juridique Mauricie-Bois-Francs region; mem. Commonwealth Parl. Asscn and Canadian Del. Interparl. Union; mem. House of Commons 1974–84; Parl. Sec. to Pres. of Privy Council Oct. 1977; Pres. of HM the Queen's Privy Council for Canada 1980–84; Judge Federal Court of Canada, Trial Div. Judge 1984–; mem. ex-officio Fed. Court of Appeal 1984–, Judge of Fed. Court 2003–; Liberal. *Address:* Federal Court of Canada, Ottawa, ON K1A 0H9, Canada (office). *Website:* www.fct-cf.gc.ca (office).

PINAULT, François; French business executive; b. 21 Aug. 1936, Champs Géraux (Côtes-du-Nord); s. of François Pinault and Eugénie Gabillard; m. Mary Campbell 1970; two s. (including François-Henri Pinault) two d.; ed Collège Saint-Martin, Rennes; worked in father's timber co. aged 16; f. Société Pinault, Rennes 1963, Président-Directeur Général 1970; Pres. Cie. française de l'Afrique occidentale (CFAO) 1990–91; Vice-Pres. Supervisory Bd Groupe Pinault-Printemps-Redoute (renamed PPR SA, now Kering) 1992, led PPR in protracted battle for control of Italian fashion house Gucci against rival co. LVMH and its Chair. Bernard Arnault 1999–2004; Founder, Président-Directeur Général Artémis SA (family holding co.) 1992 owns, amongst others, Christie's, London 1998–, Château Latour vineyard, Vail ski resort in Colo, USA, Converse shoes, luggage mfrs Samsonite and majority shareholding in French real estate investment co. Sefimeg, also owns Executive Life (now Aurora Life) in Calif.; leading modern art collector, acquired ownership of Palazzo Grassi in Venice to display his collection 2006, 'Mapping the Studio' exhbn in Punta della Dogana, a second museum in Venice opened by Pinault 2009, includes 300 works from more than 50 leading artists; Officier, Légion d'honneur, Croix de la Valeur Militaire; ranked in first place by ArtReview magazine in its list of the most powerful people in modern art 2006. *Leisure interests:* cinema, theatre, art collecting, cycling, walking. *Address:* Kering, 10 avenue Hoche, 75381 Paris Cedex 08, France (office); Christie's International PLC, 8 King Street, London, SW1Y 6QT, England (office). *Telephone:* 1-45-64-61-00 (Paris) (office). *Fax:* 1-44-90-62-25 (Paris) (office). *E-mail:* info@kering.com (office). *Website:* www.kering.com (office).

PINAULT, François-Henri; French business executive; *Chairman and CEO, Kering;* b. 28 May 1962, Rennes, Brittany; s. of François Pinault; m. 1st; one s. one d., and one s. with Linda Evangelista; m. 2nd Salma Hayek 2009; one d.; ed HEC (Hautes Etudes Commerciales) business school, Paris; began career as salesman in timber import and retail business at Evreux br. of Pinault Distribution, joined Pinault Group 1987, held positions in several of the Group's operating businesses, established co.'s purchasing group 1988–89, later apptd CEO France Bois Industries and managed co.'s 14 plants, Chair. Pinault Distribution 1990–93, Chair. Co. française de l'Afrique occidentale (CFAO) and mem. Exec. Bd PPR (fmrly Pinault-Printemps-Redoute) 1993–97, Chair. and CEO FNAC 1997–2000, Deputy CEO PPR SA 2000–05, Co-Man. Financière Pinault 2000–, Chair. Artemis Group 2003–05, Chair. and CEO PPR SA 2005– (renamed Kering 2013); Chair. Supervisory Bd Puma AG; Vice-Chair. Supervisory Bd CFAO; mem. Bd of Dirs Bouygues; Zeitz Foundation Amb. for Commerce 2009–. *Address:* Kering, 10 avenue Hoche, 75381 Paris, France (office). *Telephone:* 1-45-64-61-00 (office). *Fax:* 1-44-90-62-25 (office). *E-mail:* info@kering.com (office). *Website:* www.kering.com (office).

PINCAY, Laffit Alejandro, Jr; Panamanian fmr professional jockey; b. 29 Dec. 1946, Panama City; m. 1st Linda Pincay 1967 (died 1985); one s. one d.; m. 2nd Jeanine Pincay; one s.; learned to ride by watching his father racing at numerous tracks in Panama and Venezuela; rode first winner 1964, first US winner 1966, 3,000th winner 1975; Winner Belmont Stakes 1982, 1983, 1984, Kentucky Derby 1984; rode 6,000th winner 1985; broke Willie Shoemaker's record with 8,834 wins 1999; first jockey to reach 9,000 wins; seven Breeders' Cup wins; 9,530 wins in total (passed by Russell Baze 2006), retd 2003; lifesize bust of him erected at Santa Anita Park, US Champion Jockey by earnings 1970–74, 1979, 1985, US Champion Jockey by wins 1971, Eclipse Award for Outstanding Jockey 1971, 1973, 1974, 1979, 1985, inducted into Nat. Museum of Racing and Hall of Fame 1975, Eclipse Special Award 1999, Big Sport of Turfdom Award 2000, Pincay Drive (fmrly 90th Street) at Prairie Avenue, Inglewood, Calif. renamed 2003, Laffit Pincay Jr Award cr. in his honour by Hollywood Park Racetrack 2004.

PINCHUK, Victor Mykhaylovych, PhD; Ukrainian business executive and philanthropist; b. 14 Dec. 1960, Kiev; m. 1st Olena Arshava (divorced); m. 2nd Olena Leonidivna Pinchuk (d. of fmr Pres. of Ukraine, Leonid Kuchma); one s. three d.; ed Dnipropetrovsk Metallurgical Inst.; owner of wide range of businesses, including Interpipe Corpn (industrial conglomerate) 1990, Geo Alliance, Starlight Media TV Group (first nat. commercial TV network in Ukraine that includes ICTV, STB, NOVY, M1, M2, QTV Int.), Fakty i Kommentarii newspaper; Founder EastOne Group Ltd (investment and advisory group); mem. Verkhovna Rada (Parl. of Ukraine) 1998–2006; f. Victor Pinchuk Foundation 2006, PinchukArt-Centre 2007; Founder, Future Generation Art Prize for artists under the age of 35 and awarded biannually 2009; mem. Bd Peterson Inst. for Int. Econs., Int. Advisory Council of Brookings Inst., Bd of Trustees of the Museum of Contemporary Art; Hon. Citizen of Kiev 2009; Chevalier des Arts et des Lettres 2013; one of the TIME 100 – The World's Most Influential People 2010, Trebbia European Award 2011. *Address:* 01601 Kyiv, vul. Mechnikova 2, Ukraine (office). *Telephone:* (44) 490-48-35 (office). *Fax:* (44) 490-48-78 (office). *E-mail:* info@pinchukfund.org (office). *Website:* www.pinchukfund.org (office).

PINCOTT, Leslie Rundell, CBE, FCA; British company director (retd); b. 27 March 1923, London; s. of Hubert George Pincott and Gertrude Elizabeth Pincott (née Rundell); m. 1st Mary Mae Tuffin 1944 (died 1996); two s. one d.; m. 2nd Elaine Sunderland 1997; ed Mercers School, Holborn, London, Harvard Business School, USA; Lt in RNVR 1942–46; qualified as chartered accountant 1948; worked for Esso Petroleum and Exxon 1950–1978, Man. Dir 1970–78; Chair. Oxford Univ. Business Summer School 1975–78; Vice-Chair. Remploy Ltd 1979–87 (Dir 1975–79); Dir British Railways Southern Bd 1977–86, Chair. 1986–89; Pres. Dist Heating Asscn 1977–79; Chair. Canada Perm. Trust (UK) Ltd 1978–80, Dir in Toronto; Dir George Wimpey PLC 1978–85, Brown & Root-Wimpey Highlands Fabricators Ltd 1984–91; Deputy Chair., Chair. Price Comm. 1978–80; Chair. Stone-Platt Industries Ltd 1980–82, Edman Communications Group PLC 1982–87, Nat. Econ. Devt Cttee 1982–88; mem. Investment Cttee, London Devt Capital Devt Fund 1984–99; Chair. The Hurlingham Club 1989–92, Trustee 1996–98; mem. bd Wandle Housing Asscn 1996, Chair. 1997–99; Chair. Hurlingham Court Ltd 1999–2003, 2005–09. *Leisure interests:* walking, travel, swimming, painting, bowls. *Address:* 53 Hurlingham Court, Ranelagh Gardens, London, SW6 3UP, England (home). *Telephone:* (20) 7736-1440 (home). *Fax:* (20) 7736-1440 (home). *E-mail:* l.pincott@sky.com (home).

PINDA, Mizengo Kayanza Peter, LLB; Tanzanian lawyer; *Prime Minister;* b. 12 Aug. 1948, Rukwa Region; ed Univ. of Dar es Salaam; State Attorney, Ministry of Justice and Constitutional Affairs 1974–78; Pres.'s Office 1978–82; Asst Pvt. Sec. to the Pres. 1982–92; State House Clerk to the Cabinet 1996–2000; MP for Mpanda East 2000–05, for Mpanda Mashariki 2005–; Deputy Minister in Prime Minister's Office for Regional Admin and Local Govt 2000–05; Minister of State for Regional Admin and Local Govt 2006–08; Prime Minister 2008–. *Address:* Office of the Prime Minister, PO Box 980, Dodoma, Tanzania (office). *Telephone:* (26) 2322484 (office); (22) 2112847 (office). *Fax:* (26) 2321955 (office); (22) 2116798 (office). *E-mail:* pm@pmo.go.tz (office); mizengopk@gmail.com (home). *Website:* www.pmo.go.tz (office).

PINE, Courtney Fitzgerald, CBE; British jazz musician (saxophone) and composer; b. 18 March 1964, London; m. June Guishard 1997; one s. three d.; founder mem. Jazz Warriors 1985–, The Abiba Jazz Arts 1985–; tours inter-nationally with reggae and acoustic jazz bands; Musical Dir Windrush Gala Concert, BBC TV 1998; organizes free workshops for young people in many countries; regular presenter of radio shows (BBC); bandleader at concerts worldwide; Fellow Leeds Coll. of Music, MOBO for Best Jazz Act 1996, BBC Jazz Award for Best Jazz Act 2001, Acad. of Composers and Songwriters Gold Badge 2002, Urban Music Award for Best Jazz Act 2005, Ronnie Scott Award for Int. Saxophonist 2007, Lifetime Achievement Award, Brecon Jazz Festival 2009. *Recordings include:* albums: Journey to the Urge Within 1986, Destiny's Song and The Image of Pursuance 1988, The Vision's Tale 1989, Closer to Home 1990, Within the Realm of Our Dreams 1991, To the Eyes of Creation 1993, Modern Day Jazz Stories (Mercury Music Prize for Best Album of the Year 1996) 1996, Underground 1997, Another Story 1998, History is Made at Night (soundtrack) 1999, Back in the Day 2000, Devotion 2003. *Television:* soundtrack to BBC documentary Mandela: Living Legend 2002. *Radio:* presented BBC Radio 2 series Millennium Jazz 1999, five series of BBC Radio 2 Jazz Crusade 1999–2004, UK Black 2003, Jazz Makers, weekly show on digital station The Jazz 2007–. *Address:* Collaboration, 33 Montpelier Street, Brighton, BN1 3DL, England (office). *Telephone:* (1273) 730744 (office). *Fax:* (1273) 775135 (office). *E-mail:* nikki@ collaborationuk.com (office). *Website:* www.courtney-pine.com (office).

PINEAU-VALENCIENNE, Didier; French company director; b. 21 March 1931, Paris; s. of Maurice and Madeleine (née Dubigeon) Pineau-Valencienne; m. Guillemette Rident 1964; one s. three d.; ed Lycée Janson-de-Sailly, Paris, Hautes Etudes Commerciales, Paris, Dartmouth Univ. (USA) and Harvard Business School,; Man. Asst Banque Parisienne pour l'Industrie 1958, Prin. Man. Asst 1962, Dir 1964–67, Dir-Gen. 1969 and Admin. 1971; Pres. and Dir-Gen. Carbonisation et Charbons Actifs (CECA) 1972–74, Société Resogil 1975–76; Dir-Gen. Société

Celogil 1975–76; Admin. Isorel 1976; Dir of Admin. and Strategy and Planning Rhone-Poulenc SA 1976–77, Dir-Gen. (Polymer Div.) 1978; Admin. Quartz et Silice; Admin., Vice–Pres., Dir-Gen. Schneider SA 1980–81, Pres.-Dir-Gen. 1981–98; Pres.-Dir-Gen. Jeumont-Schneider 1987–89, Pres. Schneider Industries Services Int. 1991–92, Schneider Electric SA 1993–98; Asst Admin. Société Electrorail SA 1980–; Dir Merlin-Gérin 1981–, Pres.-Dir-Gen. 1989–; Chair. Empain-Schneider Group 1981–, Société Parisienne d'Etudes et de Participations 1982–; Chair. and Man. Dir Creusot-Loire 1982–84; Vice-Chair. Crédit Suisse First Boston, London 1999–; Dir Paribas 1989–98, Whirlpool Corpn 1992–; Pres. Admin. Council, Tech. Univ. of Compiègne 1992–96; Pres. Inst. de L'Entreprise 1993–96, Hon. Pres. 1996–; Pres. Asscn française des entreprises privées 1999–; Vice-Pres. and Pres. Comm. Sociale du Conseil nat. du patronat français (CNPF) 1997; Chair. Advisory Bd Sisie 1997–98; fmr teacher Ecole des Hautes Etudes Commerciales; Officier, Légion d'honneur, Officier Ordre nat. du Mérite; Chair. and Partner SAGARD; Senior Advisor Crédit Suisse First Boston (Europe) Ltd; Manager of the Year (Le Nouvel Economiste) 1991, Falk Award (USA) 1998, Man of the Year (Franco-American Chamber of Commerce). *Leisure interests:* tennis, skiing, collecting books. *Address:* Crédit Suisse First Boston, 1 Cabot Square, London, E14 4QJ, England (office); Schneider Electric, 64 rue de Miromesnil, 75008 Paris, France (office). *Telephone:* 1-42-56-02-88 (office); 1-42-56-60-33 (office). *Fax:* 1-42-56-59-48 (office). *E-mail:* d-pineau-valencienne@wanadoo.fr (office).

PINEL, Sylvia; French politician; *Minister of Territorial Equality and Housing;* b. 28 Sept. 1977, L'Union (Haute-Garonne); d. of the late Michel Pinel; ed Lycée Michelet, Montauban, Univ. of Toulouse 1 Capitole; began in politics as project man. and Chief of Staff to Pres. of Gen. Council of Tarn-et-Garonne; mem. (PRG—Parti Radical de Gauche) Assemblée nationale for Second Dist of Tarn-et-Garonne 2007– (re-elected 2012); Regional Councillor for Midi-Pyrénées 2010–; Chair. Departmental Fed. of PRG of Tarn-et-Garonne and Deputy Del. Gen. of PRG; Vice-Pres. Rights of Citizens, Security and Justice, PRG nat. party 2011–; mem. presidential election campaign team of François Hollande 2012; Minister delegated to Minister of Productive Recovery, responsible for Crafts, Trade and Tourism May–June 2012, Minister for Crafts, Trade and Tourism 2012–14, of Territorial Equality and Housing 2014–. *Address:* Ministry of Territorial Equality and Housing, 92055 La Défense Cedex, France (office). *Telephone:* 1-40-81-21-22 (office). *Website:* www.territoires.gouv.fr (office).

PIÑERA ECHENIQUE, (Miguel Juan) Sebastián, MA, PhD; Chilean engineer, business executive, politician and fmr head of state; b. 1 Dec. 1949, Santiago; s. of the late José Piñera Carvallo and Magdalena Echenique Rozas; m. Cecilia Morel Montes 1973; two s. two d.; ed Pontificia Universidad Católica de Chile, Harvard Univ., USA; fmr Prof. of Econs, Pontificia Universidad Católica de Chile and Adolfo Ibáñez Univ.; Prof. of Econ. Political Theory, Univ. of Chile 1971; Prof., Valparaíso Business School 1972; business interests include 100% ownership of Chilevisión (terrestrial TV channel), LAN Airlines stock, Axxion SA (holding co.); mem. Senado (Senate) for East Santiago 1990–98; mem. Renovación Nacional (RN), Pres. 2001–04; presidential cand. 2005, (unsuccessful) 2009 (elected as Coalición por el Cambio cand.); Pres. of Chile 2010–14; ranked by Forbes magazine amongst The World's Most Powerful People (51st) 2010, (66th) 2011, (49th) 2012. *Address:* c/o Office of the President, Palacio de La Moneda, Santiago, Chile.

PINES, Alexander, BSc, PhD, FRS; American chemist and academic; *Glenn T. Seaborg Professor of Chemistry, University of California, Berkeley;* b. 1945; ed Hebrew Univ. of Jerusalem, Massachusetts Inst. of Tech.; joined Dept of Physics, Univ. of Calif., Berkeley 1972, becoming Faculty Sr Scientist, Lawrence Berkeley Nat. Lab., also Chancellor's Research Prof. in Chem. and Glenn T. Seaborg Prof. of Chem.; mem. NAS 1988–, American Acad. of Arts and Sciences 1999; fmr Pres. Int. Soc. of Magnetic Resonance; numerous hon. lectureships, including Loeb Lecturer, Harvard Univ., Joliot-Curie Prof., Ecole Superieure de Physique et Chemie, Paris 1987, Hinshelwood Prof., Univ. of Oxford 1990, Centenary Lecturer and Medal, Royal Soc. of Chem. 1994, Lord Todd Prof., Cambridge Univ. 1999; Dr hc (Paris VI) 1999; ACS Baekeland Award in Pure Chem. 1985, Univ. of Calif. Distinguished Teaching Award 1986, ACS Nobel Signature Award for Grad. Educ., Pittsburgh Spectroscopy Award 1989, ACS Harrison Howe Award 1991, Royal Soc. of Chem. Bourke Medal, ACS Langmuir Award, Wolf Prize in Chem. 1991, Baylor Univ. Robert Foster Cherry Great Teacher Award 1995, Dept of Energy Ernest O. Lawrence Award 1997, ACS Irving Langmuir Award in Chemical Physics 1998, F. A. Cotton Medal for Excellence in Chemical Research 1998, ACS Remsen Award 2000, Carnegie Mellon Univ. Dickson Prize in Science, Seaborg Medal 2003. *Address:* Department of Chemistry, Room 419, Latimer Hall, University of California, Berkeley, CA 94720-1460, USA (office). *Telephone:* (510) 642-1220 (office). *Fax:* (510) 486-5744 (office). *E-mail:* pines@cchem.berkeley.edu (office). *Website:* chem.berkeley.edu/people/faculty/pines/pines.html (office).

PING, Jean, PhD; Gabonese economist, politician and international organization official; b. 24 Nov. 1942, Omboué; m.; c.; ed Univ. of Paris I (Panthéon-Sorbonne); began career 1972 at UNESCO, Sector for External Relations and Cooperation, Paris; Perm. Rep. to UNESCO 1978–84; Dir Cabinet of the Pres. of Gabon 1984–90; Minister of Information 1990, then Minister of Mines, Energy and Water Resources and Deputy Minister, Ministry of Finance, Economy, Budget and Privatization, then Minister of Planning, Environment and Tourism –1999, Vice-Prime Minister, Minister of Foreign Affairs, Co-operation, Francophonie and Regional Integration 1999–2008; Chair. Comm. of the African Union 2008–12; Pres. 59th session of UN Gen. Ass. 2004–05; mem. French Nat. Asscn of Doctors of Econs; Commdr of the Equatorial Star, Grand Officer of the Equatorial Star, Commdr of the Maritime Merit Order, Commdr of the Gabonese Nat. Order of Merit, Commdr Légion d'honneur, Officer of the Order of the Pleiad and the Order of la Francophonie, Grand Cross of the Order of Merit (Portugal); Dr hc (Inst. of Diplomacy of China), (Inst. of African Studies, Russian Acad. of Sciences). *Address:* c/o African Union, PO Box 3243, Addis Ababa, Ethiopia.

PINKAYAN, Subin, MEng, PhD; Thai engineer and business executive; b. 16 June 1934, Chiang Mai; m. Boonsri Pinkayan; one s. one d.; ed Chulalongkorn Univ., Asian Inst. of Tech., Colorado State Univ., USA; civil engineer, Port Authority of Thailand, Bangkok 1958–60; hydrologist, Royal Irrigation Dept 1967–69; Assoc. Prof. Asian Inst. of Tech. 1969–74; mem. Parl. for Chiang Mai 1983–91; Deputy Leader Social Action Party 1986–91, mem. Exec. Cttee 1981–91,

Registrar 1981–86, Deputy Sec.-Gen. 1979–80; Deputy Minister of Finance 1986, Minister of Univ. Affairs 1986–88, Minister of Commerce 1988–90, Minister of Foreign Affairs 1990; Pres. SEATEC (Southeast Asia Technology Co. Ltd) Group 1974–85, Chair. 1991, now Chief Hon. Advisor; Hon. Advisor, MDX Group, GMS Power Public Co. Ltd; Chair. Bd of Trustees, Asian Inst. of Tech. 2013–; Commdr (Third Class) of the Most Noble Order of the Crown of Thailand 1983, Commdr (Third Class) of the Most Exalted Order of the White Elephant 1985, Kt Grand Cross (First Class) of the Most Noble Order of the Crown of Thailand 1986, Kt Grand Cross (First Class) of the Most Exalted Order of the White Elephant 1987, Kt Grand Cordon (Special Class) of the Most Exalted Order of the White Elephant 1989; Personal Service Award in 'National and International Prestige,' Colorado State Univ. 1991, Outstanding Alumni Award, Asian Inst. of Tech. Alumni Asscn of Thailand 2003, inducted into Asian Inst. of Tech. Hall of Fame 2010. *Leisure interests:* golf, travel, gardening. *Address:* Seatec Group, 281 Soi Phanit Anan 7, Preedee Phanomyong 42, Sukhumvit 71, Bangkok 10110, Thailand (office). *Telephone:* (2) 7133888 (office). *Fax:* (2) 7133889 (office). *E-mail:* seatec@seatecgroup.com (office). *Website:* www.seatecgroup.com (office).

PINKER, Robert Arthur, CBE, MSc; British academic; *Professor Emeritus of Social Administration, London School of Economics;* b. 27 May 1931; s. of Dora Elizabeth Pinker and Joseph Pinker; m. Jennifer Farrington Boulton 1955 (died 1994); two d.; ed Holloway Co. School, London School of Econs; Head of Sociology Dept, Goldsmiths Coll., London Univ. 1964–72, Lewisham Prof. of Social Admin., Goldsmiths Coll. and Bedford Coll. 1972–74; Prof. of Social Studies, Chelsea Coll. 1974–78; Prof. of Social Work Studies, LSE 1978–93, Pro-Dir LSE 1985–88, Prof. of Social Admin. 1993–96, Prof. Emer. 1996–; Pro-Vice-Chancellor for Social Sciences, Univ. of London 1989–90; Chair. Editorial Bd Journal of Social Policy 1981–86; Chair. British Library Project on Family and Social Research 1983–86; mem. Council, Advertising Standards Authority 1988–95, Press Complaints Comm. 1991– (Privacy Commr 1994–2004, Acting Chair. 2002–03), Council, Direct Mail Accreditation and Recognition Centre 1995–97 (Int. Consultant 2002–), Bd of Man. London School of Hygiene and Tropical Medicine 1990–94; Chair. Govs Centre for Policy on Ageing 1988–94; Fellow, Soc. of Eds 2004; Hon. Fellow, Goldsmiths Coll., Univ. of London 1999. *Publications include:* English Hospital Statistics 1861–1938 1964, Social Theory and Social Policy 1971, The Idea of Welfare 1979, Social Work in an Enterprise Society 1990, Privacy and Personality Rights (with Robert Deacon and Nigel Lipton) 2010. *Leisure interests:* reading, writing, travel, unskilled gardening. *Address:* Press Complaints Commission, 1 Salisbury Square, London, EC4Y 8JB (office); 76 Coleraine Road, Blackheath, London, SE3 7PE, England (home). *Telephone:* (20) 7955-7358 (office); (20) 8858-5320 (home). *Fax:* (20) 8293-4770 (home). *E-mail:* rpinker@freenetname.co.uk (home).

PINKER, Steven, BA, PhD; Canadian/American psychologist, scientist, writer and academic; *Johnstone Family Professor of Psychology, Harvard University;* b. 18 Sept. 1954, Montreal, Canada; s. of Harry Pinker and Roslyn Pinker; m. 1st Nancy Etcoff 1980 (divorced 1992); m. 2nd Ilavenil Subbiah 1995 (divorced); ed McGill Univ., Harvard Univ.; Asst Prof., Harvard Univ. 1980–81, Johnstone Family Prof. of Psychology 2003–, Harvard Coll. Prof. 2008–13; Asst Prof., Stanford Univ. 1981–82; Asst Prof., Dept of Psychology, MIT 1982–85, Assoc. Prof., Dept of Brain and Cognitive Sciences 1985–89, Prof. 1989–2000, Peter de Florez Prof. 2000–03, Co-Dir Center for Cognitive Science 1985–94, Dir McDonnell-Pew Center for Cognitive Neuroscience 1994–99; Chair. Usage Panel, American Heritage Dictionary 2008–; Contributing Ed. The New Republic 2008–, Seed 2006–; Exec. Assoc. Ed. Cognition: International Journal of Cognitive Science 1985–2006; Herbert Simon Fellow, American Acad. of Political and Social Science 2006–; Fellow, AAAS 1987–, American Psychological Soc. 1990–, American Psychological Asscn 1992–, American Acad. of Arts and Sciences 1998–, Linguistics Soc. of America 2007–, Académie Internationale de Philosophie des Sciences 2007–; Distinguished Fellow, New England Inst. for Cognitive Science and Evolutionary Psychology 2001–04; Hon. Pres. Canadian Psychological Asscn 2008; Hon. DSc (McGill) 1999, (Newcastle) 2005; Hon. DPhil (Tel-Aviv) 2003; Hon. DUniv (Surrey) 2003; Dr hc (Albion Coll.) 2007, (Univ. of Tromsø, Norway) 2008; Distinguished Scientific Award for Early Career Contribution to Psychology, American Psychological Asscn 1984, Boyd R. McCandless Young Scientist Award, Div. of Developmental Psychology, American Psychological Asscn 1986, Troland Research Award, NAS 1993, Linguistics, Language and the Public Interest Award, Linguistics Soc. of America 1997, Los Angeles Times Book Prize in Science and Technology 1998, Golden Plate Award, American Acad. of Achievement 1999, Humanist Laureate Int. Acad. of Humanism 2001, Henry Dale Prize 2004, Humanist of the Year 2006, Innovation for Humanity Prize, La Ciudad de las Ideas 2008, George Miller Prize, Cognitive Neuroscience Soc. 2010. *Publications include:* Language Learnability and Language Development 1984, Visual Cognition (ed.) 1985, Connections and Symbols (ed. with J. Mehler) 1988, Learnability and Cognition: The Acquisition of Argument Structure 1989, The Language Instinct 1994 (William James Book Prize, American Psychological Asscn 1995), How the Mind Works 1997 (William James Book Prize, American Psychological Asscn 1999), Words and Rules: The Ingredients of Language 1999, The Blank Slate: The Modern Denial of Human Nature (Troland Award 2003, Walter P. Kistler Book Award 2005) 2002, The Stuff of Thought: Language as a Window into Human Nature 2007, The Better Angels of Our Nature 2011; numerous articles in scholarly journals, including Animal Learning and Behavior, Annals of the New York Academy of Sciences, Behavioral and Brain Sciences, Canadian Journal of Psychology, Child Development, Cognition, Cognitive Psychology, Cognitive Science, Communication and Cognition, Journal of Child Language, Journal of Cognitive Neuroscience, Journal of Experimental Psychology, Journal of Mental Imagery, Journal of Psycholinguistic Research, Journal of Verbal Learning and Verbal Behavior, Language and Cognitive Processes, Language, Lingua, Memory and Cognition, Monographs of the Society for Research in Child Development, Nature, New York Times, The New Yorker, Papers and Reports in Child Language, Psychological Science, Science, Slate, Time, Trends in Cognitive Science, Trends in Neurosciences, Visual Cognition. *Leisure interests:* bicycling, photography. *Address:* Department of Psychology, Harvard University, William James Hall 970, 33 Kirkland Street, Cambridge, MA 02138, USA (office). *Website:* pinker.wjh.harvard.edu (office); stevenpinker.com.

PINNOCK, Trevor David, CBE, ARCM, FRAM; British harpsichordist and conductor; b. 16 Dec. 1946, Canterbury, Kent, England; s. of Kenneth Pinnock and Joyce Pinnock; ed Canterbury Cathedral School, Royal Coll. of Music, London; Co-founder Galliard Harpsichord Trio, debut, London 1966, solo debut, London 1968, Dir The English Concert 1973–2003; Artistic Dir, Prin. Conductor Nat. Arts Centre Orchestra, Ottawa 1991–96, Artistic Adviser 1996–; f. European Branden-burg Ensemble 2006–, numerous tours and recordings; has toured Western Europe, USA, S America, Canada, Australia, Japan with The English Concert, as solo harpsichordist and as orchestral/opera conductor; debut at Metropolitan Opera, New York 1988; has worked with Opera Australia, Freiburg Baroque Orchestra, Salzburg Camerata, Salzburg Mozarteum Orchestra, Deutsche Kammerphilharmonie Bremen, Deutsches Symphonie-Orchester Berlin, Amster-dam Concertgebouw Orchestra; Gramophone Award for Bach Partitas BWV 825–30 2001. *Recordings include:* Rameau, Pièces de Clavecin (with Jonathan Manson, J. S. Bach, Sonatas for viola da gamba and obligato harpsichord, and works by Handel, C. P. E. Bach, Vivaldi, Scarlatti, 16th, 17th and 18th-century harpsichord music and most of the standard baroque orchestral/concerto/choral repertoire, Brandenburg Concertos (with European Brandenburg Ensemble) (Gramophone Award for Best Baroque Instrumental Recording 2008). *Website:* www.askonasholt.co.uk (office); www.trevorpinnock.com.

PINÓS, Carmen; Spanish architect; b. 23 June 1954, Barcelona; ed Escuela Superior de Arquitectura de Barcelona, Int. Lab. of Architecture with Urban Design, Urbino, Columbia Univ., USA; Visiting Prof. at Univs of Illinois at Urbana-Champaign, USA 1994–95, Kunstakademie, Dusseldorf, Germany 1994–98, Columbia Univ. 1999, École Polytechnique Federale de Lausanne, Switzerland 2001–02, Escola Tècnica Superior d'Arquitectura del Vallès, Barce-lona 2002, Università degli Studi di Sassari, Alghero, Italy 2002, 2004, Harvard Univ. Grad. School of Design, USA 2003; FAD Prize, La Llauna School, FAD Prize for the Igualada Cemetery, The City of Barcelona Prize for the archery range building for the 1992 Olympic Games, Spanish Nat. Architecture Prize for the boarding school of Morella 1995, Inst. of Architects Award from the Valencia Govt for the public spaces of the Waterfront Juan Aparicio in Torrevieja 2001. *Major works:* El Croquis 1986, Arte Cemento 1987, Baumeister 1989. *Publications:* Carme Pinós: Some Projects (since 1991) 1998, Carme Pinós: An Architecture of Overlay (Ana Maria Torres) 2004. *Address:* Diagonal 490, 3-2, 08006 Barcelona, Spain (office). *Telephone:* (93) 4160372 (office). *Fax:* (93) 2781473 (office). *E-mail:* info@cpinos.com (office). *Website:* www.cpinos.com (office).

PINOTTI, Roberta; Italian politician; *Minister of Defence;* b. 20 May 1961, Genoa; m.; two d.; began career in local govt, including as Dist Councillor for Educ., Youth and Social Policies, Prov. of Genoa 1993–97, Councillor for Educ. Insts, Genoa City Council 1997–99, Councillor, Prov. of Genoa 1999–2011; mem. Chamber of Deputies (Parl.) (Ulivo list) for Genoa 7 constituency 2001–08, Pres. Defence Cttee 2006; elected Senator for Liguria 2008, Vice-Chair. Senate Defence Cttee 2010; Shadow Minister of Defence 2008–09, Deputy Minister of Defence 2013–14, Minister of Defence 2014–; mem. Partito Democratico (PD); Legion d'Honneur 2008, Chancellor and Treasurer, Mil. Order of Italy 2014. *Address:* Ministry of Defence, Palazzo Baracchini, Via XX Settembre 8, 00187 Rome, Italy (office). *Telephone:* (06) 46911 (office). *Fax:* (06) 3236210 (office). *Website:* www .difesa.it (office); www.robertapinotti.it.

PINSENT, Sir Matthew Clive, Kt, CBE, BA; British fmr oarsman; b. 10 Oct. 1970, Norfolk; s. of Rev. Ewen Pinsent and Jean Pinsent; m. Demetra Pinsent 2002; two s.; ed Eton Coll. and Univ. of Oxford; first rep. UK at Jr World Championships 1987, 1988, Gold Medal in Coxless Pairs (with Tim Foster) 1988; competed three times in Univ. Boat Race for Oxford 1990, 1991, 1993, winning twice; Gold Medal, Coxless Pairs (with Steve Redgrave q.v.) World Championships 1991, 1993, 1994, 1995, Olympic Games, Barcelona 1992, Atlanta 1996; Gold Medal, Coxless Fours (with Steve Redgrave, Tim Foster and James Cracknell) World Championships 1997, 1998, 1999, Olympic Games, Sydney 2000; Gold Medal, Coxless Pairs (with James Cracknell) World Championships 2001, 2002 (new world record); Gold Medal, Coxless Fours (with Cracknell, Coode and Williams) Olympic Games, Athens 2004; mem. Int. Olympic Cttee 2002–04; announced retirement Nov. 2004; Int. Rowing Fed. Male Rower of the Year, mem. BBC Sports Team of the Year 2004. *Publication:* A Lifetime in a Race 2004. *Leisure interests:* golf, flying. *Address:* c/o Lu Adams, Professional Sports Partnerships Ltd, The Coach House, 2 Heath Road, Weybridge, KT13 8AP, England. *Website:* www.matthewpinsent.com; www.profsports.com.

PINSKY, Robert Neal, PhD; American poet and academic; *Professor of Creative Writing, Boston University;* b. 20 Oct. 1940, Long Branch, NJ; s. of Milford Simon Pinsky and Sylvia Pinsky (née Eisenberg); m. Ellen Jane Bailey 1961; three d.; ed Rutgers Univ., Stanford Univ.; taught English at Univ. of Chicago 1967–68, Wellesley Coll. 1968–80; Prof. of English, Univ. of Calif., Berkeley 1980–89; Prof., Boston Univ. 1980–89, Prof. of Creative Writing 1989–; Poet Laureate of USA 1997–2000; f. Favorite Poem Project; Visiting Lecturer, Harvard Univ.; Hurst Prof., Washington Univ., St Louis; Poetry Ed. New Republic magazine 1978, Slate Magazine 1994–; Guggenheim Fellow 1980; mem. AAAL (Sec. 2003–06), American Acad. of Arts and Sciences; Chancellor, Acad. of American Poets; Artist's Award, American Acad. of Arts and Letters 1979, Saxifrage Prize 1980, William Carlos Williams Prize 1984, Shelley Memorial Award 1996, Harold Washington Literary Award 1999, Manhae Foundation Prize 2006, Jewish Cultural Foundation Achievement Award 2006, Theodore Roethke Prize 2008. *Publications include:* Landor's Poetry 1968, Sadness and Happiness 1975, The Situation of Poetry 1977, An Explanation of America 1980, History of My Heart 1980, Poetry and the World 1988, The Want Bone 1990, The Inferno of Dante (trans.; Howard Morton Landon Trans. Prize) 1994, The Figured Wheel: New and Collected Poems 1966–96 (Lenore Marshall Award, Amb. Book Award, English Speaking Union) 1996, The Sounds of Poetry 1998, The Handbook of Heartbreak 1998, Americans' Favorite Poems (co-ed.) 1999, Jersey Rain 2000, Democracy, Culture, and the Voice of Poetry 2002, Poems to Read (co-ed.) 2004, Invitation to Poetry (co-ed.) 2004, First Things to Hand 2006, Gulf Music (Theodore Roethke Prize 2008) 2007, The Life of David (Jewish Encounters) 2008, Thousands of Broadways: Dreams and Night-mares of the American Small Town 2009, Essential Pleasures: A New Anthology of Poems to Read Aloud 2009, Death and the Powers (libretto) 2010, Selected Poems 2011. *Address:* Steven Barclay Agency, 12 Western Avenue, Petaluma, CA 94952,

USA (office); Department of English, Boston University, 236 Bay State Road, Boston, MA 02215, USA (office). *Telephone:* (707) 773-0654 (office); (617) 353-2821 (office). *Fax:* (707) 778-1868 (office). *E-mail:* steven@barclayagency.com (office); rpinsky@bu.edu (office). *Website:* www.barclayagency.com (office); www.bu.edu/ english (office).

PINTAT SANTOLÀRIA, Albert, Lic en Sc économiques; Andorran diplomatist and politician; b. 23 June 1943; m.; three c.; ed Catholic Univ. of Friburg, Switzerland; Asst Consul, Sant Julià, Andorra 1982–83; Sec. to Josep Pintat, Head of Govt 1984–85; Counsellor-Gen. 1986–91; Amb. to Benelux countries and EU 1995–97; Minister of Foreign Affairs 1997–2001; Amb. to Switzerland and UK 2001–04; Cap de Govern (Head of Govt) 2005–09; mem. Liberal Party of Andorra (PLA). *Address:* c/o Partit Liberal d'Andorra, Carrer Babot Camp 13, 2°, Andorra la Vella AD500, Andorra (office).

PINTER, Frances Mercedes Judith, PhD; American/British publisher; *Execu-tive Director, Knowledge Unlatched;* b. 13 June 1949, Venezuela; d. of George Pinter and Vera Hirschenhauser Pinter; m. David Percy 1985; ed Univ. Coll., London; Research Officer, Centre for Criminological Research, Univ. of Oxford, UK 1976–79; Man. Dir Pinter Publrs 1979–94; Chair. Ind. Publrs Guild 1979–82, Publrs Assoc E European Task Force 1990–; Man. Dir Cen. European Univ. Press 1994–96; Chair. Bd of Trustees, Int. House 2001, CEO Int. House Trust 2002–06; Deputy Chair. Book Devt Council 1985–89; Publr, Bloomsbury Academic 2008–12; mem. Bd UK Publrs Assoc 1987–92, IBIS Information Services 1988–90, Libra Books 1991–; Exec. Dir Centre for Publishing Devt 1994–, Open Soc. Inst. 1994–99, Knowledge Unlatched; Visiting Fellow, LSE 2000–01, 2006–. *Leisure interests:* reading, travelling, hiking. *Address:* 1 Belsize Avenue, London, NW3 4BL, England (home). *Telephone:* (20) 7431-7849 (office). *E-mail:* frances@pinter.org .uk (office). *Website:* www.pinter.org.uk.

PINTÉR, Sándor; Hungarian politician and police officer (retd); *Minister of the Interior;* b. 3 July 1948, Budapest; driver, Ministry of the Interior 1972–78; rapporteur, Dept of Test Drafts, Nat. Police HQ 1978–85, Head of Criminal Police Dept of the Castle, then in charge of appointments of police station chiefs 1985–88, Head of Investigation Dept, Pest Co. HQ 1988–90, Deputy Prov. Police Chief of Public Security 1990–91, Chief of Budapest Police March–Sept. 1991, Chief of Nat. Police 1991–96 (retd); Minister of the Interior 1998–2002, 2010–; Security Adviser to Preventive Security Inc., OTP Bank Rt 1997–98; Man. Dir P&V Consulting 2002; attained rank of Maj. 1991, Lt-Gen. 1993. *Address:* Ministry of the Interior, 1903 Budapest, Pf. 314 (office); Ministry of the Interior, 1055 Budapest, József Attila u. 2–4, Hungary (office). *Telephone:* (1) 441-1000 (office). *Fax:* (1) 441-1437 (office). *E-mail:* ugyfelszolgalat@bm.gov.hu (office). *Website:* www.kormany.hu/hu/ belugyminiszterium (office).

PINTILIE, Lucian; Romanian director; b. 9 Nov. 1933, Tarutino (Bessarabia); s. of Victor Pintilie and Amelia Pintilie; ed Bucharest Theatrical and Cinemato-graphic Art Inst.; career at Lucia Sturdza Bulandra Theatre, directing The Cherry Orchard by Chekhov, D'ale carnavalului by I. L. Caragiale, The Inspector General by Gogol; staged several plays by Chekhov, Gorki, Ibsen, Eugène Ionesco, Pirandello and Strindberg abroad; also operas such as Rigoletto, Carmen, The Magic Flute etc.; worked for TV, doing reporting and theatrical programs 1956–59; debut as film dir 1965; Commdr des Arts et des Lettres 2001. *Films:* Duminică la ora 6 (At Six O'Clock on Sunday), Reconstituirea (The Reconstruction) 1969, Salonul nr 6 (Ward No. 6) 1973 (Yugoslavia), De ce trag clopotele Mitică? (What Do The Bells Toll For Mitică?) 1980, Balanța (The Oak) 1992, O Vară de Neuitat (An Unforgettable Summer) 1994, Prea tirziu (Too Late) 1996, Terminus Paradis (Last Stop Paradise) (Jury's Special Award, Venice Film Festival 1998) 1998, După-amiaza unui torționar (A Torturer's Afternoon) 2001, Niki et Flo (Niki and Flo) 2003, Tertium Nom Datur 2006. *Publications:* Bricabrac 2004. *Address:* 44 Mihail Kogălniceanu Blvd, Bucharest, Romania. *Telephone:* 3154715; 2320644.

PINTO BALSEMÃO, Francisco José Pereira; Portuguese politician, lawyer and journalist; *Chairman and CEO, Impresa SGPS;* b. 1 Sept. 1937, Lisbon; s. of Henrique Pinto Balsemão and Maria Adelaide C. P. Pinto Balsemão; m. Mercedes Presas Pinto Balsemão 1975; three s. two d.; Ed.-in-Chief review Mais Alto 1961–63; Sec. to Man. Bd Diário Popular, later Man. –1971; f. weekly Expresso 1973; mem. Nat. Ass. during govt of Dr Marcello Caetano; f. Popular Democratic Party (PPD), later renamed Social Democratic Party (PSD), with the late Dr Sá Carneiro and Joaquim Magalhães Mota May 1974; Vice-Pres. Constituent Ass. 1975; Opposition Spokesman on Foreign Affairs 1977; mem. Ass. of the Repub. 1979; Minister Without Portfolio and Deputy Prime Minister 1980; Prime Minister of Portugal 1981–83; Pres. Instituto Progresso Social e Democracia, Francisco dá Carneiro 1983–; Chair. Int. Relations Cttee and mem. Political Cttee PSD, party leader 1980–83; Pres. Sociedad Independente de Comunicação (SIC); Pres. European Inst. for the Media 1990; Chair. Sojornal and Controjornal (Media) Groups; Chair. and CEO Impresa SGPS; Chair. European Publrs Council; Pres. Companhia de Seguros Allianz Portugal SA; Prof. of Communication Science, New Univ., Lisbon; Rafael Calvo Serer Prize, Spain 2007. *Address:* Impresa SGPS SA, Rua Ribeiro Sanches 65, 1200-787 Lisbon, Portugal (office). *Telephone:* (213) 929780 (office). *Fax:* (213) 929787 (office). *Website:* www.impresa.pt (office).

PINTO COELHO SERRA, João António; Cape Verde politician; b. 25 Jan. 1961, Praia, Santiago; fmr Sec. of State for Finance; fmr Pres. Admin Council, Instituto Nacional da Previdência Social; fmr Man. Dir Instituto do Emprego e Formação Profissional; fmr Dir Projecto de Promoção de Microempresas; Minister of Finance and Public Admin 2005, of Finance, Planning and Devt 2006. *Address:* c/o Ministry of Finance and Public Administration, 107 Avda Amílcar Cabral, CP 30, Praia, Santiago, Cape Verde (office).

PINTO MARANHÃO, Rossano, MEconSc; Brazilian banking executive; b. 17 July 1957, São Luís, Maranhão; m.; one s. two d.; ed Univ. of Illinois at Urbana-Champaign, USA, Univ. of Brasília; joined Banco do Brasil 1976, served as Man. Dir for Int. Div., CEO BB Leasing Co., Vice-Pres. for Int. Businesses and Wholesale 2001–04, Vice-Chair., Interim Pres. and CEO 2004–06; mem. Bd of Dirs Telecomunicações do Rio de Janeiro (Telemar Rio) 1998–99, Tele Norte Leste (Telemar) 1999–2003, Banco Latino Americano de Exportações SA (BLADEX) 1999–2000; Ind. Dir Iguatemi Empresa de Shopping Centers SA 2007–; fmr Prof. Instituto Brasileiro de Mercado de Capitais–Ibmec and Universidade Católica de Brasília. *Address:* Iguatemi Empresa de Shopping Centers SA, Avenida Dr Chucri

Zaidan 920, São Paulo 04583-110, Brazil (office). *Telephone:* (11) 3048-7289 (office). *Fax:* (11) 3048-7292 (office). *E-mail:* info@iguatemi.com.br (office). *Website:* www.iguatemi.com.br (office).

PINTO MONTEIRO, Fernando José; Portuguese lawyer and judge; *Chief Public Prosecutor;* b. 5 April 1942, Porto de Ovelha, Almeida; s. of Amílcar Monteiro and Lurdes Monteiro; ed Univ. of Coimbra; Public Prosecutor, Idanha-a-Nova, Anadia, Porto and Lisbon 1966; Judge, Ponta do Sol, Alcácer do Sal, Loures, Torres Vedras and Lisboa; fmr Asst High Commr Higher Authority Against Corruption; Judge Court of Appeals 1990–98; Judge Supreme Court of Justice 1998–2006; Chief Public Prosecutor 2006–; Visiting Prof. of Law, Autonomous Univ. of Lisbon 1992–2006; Pres. Disciplinary Council, Portuguese Football Asscn 1995–97; fmr Sec. Gen. Portuguese Asscn of Judges. *Address:* Procuradoria-Geral da República, Rua da Escola Politécnica, 140, 1269-269 Lisbon, Portugal (office). *Telephone:* (213) 921900 (office). *Fax:* (213) 975255 (office). *Website:* www.pgr.pt (office).

PINTO RUBIANES, Pedro Alfredo; Ecuadorean politician and industrialist; b. 31 Jan. 1931, Quito; ed Univ. Cen. del Ecuador, Vanderbilt Univ.; Gen. Man. Textile San Pedro SA 1967–82, 1984–97, Pres. 1997; Pres. Asscn of Textile Mfrs 1968–70; Dean Faculty of Admin, Univ. Cen. del Ecuador 1970–72; Pres. Chamber of Mfrs of Pichincha 1971–73, Fed. of Industrialists of Ecuador 1972–73; town councillor, Quito 1973–77; Dir Corporación Financiera Ecuatoriana (COFIEC) 1976–82; Minister of Finance and Public Credit 1982–84; Gov. for Ecuador, Banco Interamericano de Desarrollo (BID), IBRD 1983–84; Dir CORDES 1988, Bank of Pichincha 1993–98, Chamber of Mfrs of Pichincha 1997–98; Deputy for Pichincha 1998; apptd Vice-Pres. of Ecuador 2001. *Address:* c/o Office of the Vice-President, Manuel Larrea y Arenas, Edif. Conseyo Provincial de Pichincha, 21°, Quito, Ecuador (office).

PINZÓN BUENO, Juan Carlos; Colombian economist and politician; *Minister of National Defence;* b. 22 Dec. 1971; s. of Rafael Pinzón Rincón and Marlene Bueno; m. María del Pilar Lozano; one s. one d.; ed Universidad Javeriana, Bogota, Paul H. Nitze School of Advanced Int. Studies, Washington, DC, Belfer Center for Science and Int. Affairs, Harvard Univ., Woodrow Wilson School of Public and Int. Affairs, Princeton Univ., USA; Researcher, Federación Nacional de Cafeteros 1996; Researcher, Asociación Bancaria y de Entidades Financieras de Colombia 1996–97, Vice-Pres. 2003–04; Head of Econ. Investigation Dept, Citibank-Citigroup, Bogota 1997–2000, Asst Vice-Pres. of Investment Banking 2002; Private Sec., Ministry of Finance and Public Credit 2000–02; Prof. of Macroeconomics, Universidad Javeriana 2000–04; Sr Adviser to Exec. Dir, World Bank, Washington, DC 2004–06; Deputy Minister of Defence for Strategy and Planning 2006–09, Minister of Nat. Defence 2011–; Dir Admin. Dept of Presidency of Colombia 2010–11; mem. Partido Social de Unidad Nacional. *Address:* Ministry of National Defence, Carrera 54, No 26-25, Centro Administrativo Nacional, 2°, Bogotá DC, Colombia (office). *Telephone:* (1) 266-0296 (office). *Fax:* (1) 315-0111 (office). *E-mail:* usuarios@mindefensa.gov.co (office). *Website:* www.mindefensa.gov.co (office).

PIO DOS SANTOS GOURGEL, Abraão; Angolan economist, politician and fmr central banker; *Minister of the Economy;* fmr Coordinator, Gabinete Técnico dos Projectos dos Programas de Investimento Públicos, Uíge Prov.; Vice Minister of Industry 2005–09; Gov. Nat. Bank of Angola 2009–10; Minister of the Economy 2010–; Central Bank Gov. of the Year for Africa, Banker Magazine 2009. *Address:* Ministry of the Economy, Luanda, Angola (office). *E-mail:* geral@minec.gov.ao (office). *Website:* www.minec.gov.ao (office).

PIOT, Baron; Peter, MD, PhD, FRCP; Belgian international development and public health official; *Professor and Director, Institute of Global Health, Imperial College, London;* b. 17 Feb. 1949, Leuven; m. Greet Kimzeke 1975; two c.; ed Univs of Ghent and Antwerp, Belgium, and Washington, USA; Asst in Microbiology, Inst. of Tropical Medicine, Antwerp 1974–78, Prof., Head Dept of Microbiology 1981–92; NATO Fellow 1978–79; Sr Fellow, Microbiology and Infectious Diseases, Washington Univ. 1978–79; Researcher, Nairobi Univ., STD/AIDS Project, Kenya 1981–92; Supervisor, Project SIDA, Kinshasa 1985–91; Asst Prof. of Public Health, Free Univ. Brussels 1989–94; Assoc. Dir Global Program AIDS, WHO 1995, Exec. Dir Jt UN Program on HIV/AIDS (UNAIDS), Geneva 1995–2008, Under-Sec.-Gen. UN 1995–2008; currently Prof. and Dir, Inst. of Global Health, Imperial Coll. London; Dir WHO Collaborating Centre on AIDS, Antwerp; Chair. King Baudouin Foundation, Brussels; mem. Royal Acad. of Medicine, Int. AIDS Soc. (Pres. 1992–), Inst. of Medicine, Washington, DC, AAAS, and numerous other socs in Europe, USA and Africa; cr. baron by King Albert II 1995; numerous decorations including Officier, Ordre Nat. du Léopard (Zaïre) 1977, Ordre du Lion (Senegal), Nat. Order, Burkina Faso, Madagascar, Vietnam, Grand Official, Order of the Infante Don Enrique (Portugal) 2005, Commandeur, Ordre Nat., Mali 2008; various hon. doctorates; numerous awards including De Kerkheer Prize for Medicine 1989, Health Research Award (Belgium) 1989, Public Health Award, Flemish Community 1990, AMICOM Award for Medicine 1991, H. Breurs Prize 1992, A. Jaunioux Prize 1992, van Thiel Award 1993, Glaxo award for infectious diseases 1995, Nelson Mandela Award 2001, Royal Acad. of Arts and Sciences Gold Medal, Belgium 2002, E. Calderone Medal, Columbia Univ. 2003, Outstanding Physician AMA Chicago, Vlerick Award, Belgium 2004, Congressional Award of Achievement, Philippines 2005, Mother Theresa Award, New Delhi, 2007, Person of the Year, Knack Magazine, Belgium 2008. *Publications:* author and co-author of 16 books and over 500 scientific papers on women's health, AIDS and other sexually transmitted diseases. *Address:* Institute of Global Health, Imperial College, 30 Guilford Street, London, WC1N 1EH, England (office). *Telephone:* (20) 7905-2122 (office). *E-mail:* p.piot@imperial.ac.uk (office). *Website:* www.ucl.ac.uk/global-health (office).

PIOTROVSKY, Mikhail Borisovich, DHist; Russian art researcher; *Director, State Hermitage;* b. 9 Dec. 1944, Yerevan, Armenia; s. of Boris Piotrovsky; m. Irina Leonidovna Piotrovskaya; one s. one d.; ed Leningrad State Univ., Cairo Univ.; researcher Leningrad Inst. of Oriental Studies USSR Acad. of Sciences 1967–91; First Deputy Dir State Hermitage, St Petersburg 1991–92, Dir. 1992–; Corresp. mem. Russian Acad. of Sciences 1997–; mem. Acad. of Humanitarian Sciences; mem. Presidium, Cttee on State Prizes of Russian Presidency, Presidium, Russian Cttee of UNESCO; mem. Int. Council of Museums; consultant to European Parl.;

main research in ancient and medieval history of Near E, Muslim art in archaeology. *Publications:* over 150 scientific works. *Address:* State Hermitage, Dvortsovaya nab. 34, 191186 St Petersburg, Russia (office). *Telephone:* (812) 110-96-01. *Fax:* (812) 311-90-09. *E-mail:* haltunen@hermitage.ru.

PIOVANELLI, HE Cardinal Silvano; Italian ecclesiastic; b. 21 Feb. 1924; ordained priest 1947; consecrated Bishop (Titular Church of Tubune, Mauritania) 1982; Archbishop of Florence 1983–2001, Archbishop Emer. 2001–; cr. Cardinal-Priest S. Maria delle Grazie a Via Tionfale 1985. *Address:* Arcivescovado, Piazza S. Giovanni 3, 50129 Florence, Italy. *Telephone:* (055) 239-88-13.

PIPE, Martin Charles, CBE; British race horse trainer (retd); b. 29 May 1945; s. of D. A. C. Pipe and M. E. R. Pipe; m. Mary Caroline; one s.; ed Queen's Coll., Taunton; first trainer's licence 1977; major wins include: Grand National (with Miinnehoma) 1994, Champion hurdle (twice), Welsh National (six times), Irish National, Scottish National, Midlands National, Hennessy Gold Cup (three times), Mackeson Gold Cup; only British trainer to train 200 winners in a season 1989; 15 times National Hunt champion trainer (1989/90, 1990/91, 1991/92, 1992/93, 1995/96, 1996/97, 1997/98, 1998/99, 1999/2000, 2000/01, 2001/02, 2002/03, 2003/04); four winners at Royal Ascot; 28 winners at Cheltenham Festival including record four winners in consecutive years. *Publications:* Martin Pipe: The Champion Trainer's Story (with Richard Pitman) 1992. *Address:* Pond House, Nicholashayne, nr Wellington, Somerset, TA21 9QY, England (office). *Telephone:* (1884) 840715 (office). *Fax:* (1884) 841343 (office). *E-mail:* martin@martinpipe.co.uk (office); www.martinpipe.co.uk (office).

PIPER, Martha Cook, BSc, MA, PhD, OC, OBC; Canadian/American epidemiologist, academic and university administrator; *Chairman, Board of Trustees, National Institute for Nanotechnology;* b. Lorain, OH; ed Univ. of Michigan, Univ. of Connecticut, McGill Univ.; physical therapist, Sr then Chief Physical Therapist at various US hosps 1967–73; Dir School of Physical and Occupational Therapy, McGill Univ., Montréal 1979–85, Asst Prof. then Assoc. Prof. 1979–84; Dean, Assoc. Prof., then Prof. of Rehabilitation Medicine and Vice Pres. (Research, later Research and External Affairs), Univ. of Alberta, Edmonton 1985–96; Pres. and Vice-Chancellor, Univ. of British Columbia 1997–2006; Chair. Bd of Trustees Nat. Inst. of Nanotechnology 2008–; fmr Dir Canadian Genetic Diseases Network; mem. Bd of Dirs Bank of Montreal 2006–, Transalta Corpn 2006–, Shoppers Drug Mart Corpn 2007–, Grosvenor Americas Ltd, CARE Canada, Inst. for Research on Public Policy, BC Children's Hosp. Foundation; fmr mem. Bd of Dirs Center for Frontier Engineering Research 1993–97, Telecommunications Research Labs 1993–97, Alberta Research Council 1993–97, Canada Israel Industrial Research Foundation 1994–97, The Conf. Bd of Canada, Pierre Elliot Trudeau Foundation, PrioNet Canada; fmr mem. Advisory Council on Science and Tech. 1996–2004, Protein Eng Network Centre of Excellence (PENCE), Canada Foundation for Innovation, Advisory Bd Vancouver Econ. Devt Comm., Distinguished Profs Selection Cttee, Univ. of Manitoba, Canadian-American Business Council, Nat. Univ. of Singapore Council, Steering Cttee, Asscn of Pacific Rim Univs; fmr Chair. Standing Advisory Cttee on Univ. Research, Asscn of Univs and Colls of Canada; fmr Public Gov., Bd of Canadian Acads of Science; Specially Elected Fellow, Royal Soc. of Canada 2009–; Trustee Dalia Lama Center for Peace and Educ., Vancouver; mem. Trilateral Comm., Canadian Insts of Advanced Research; Hon. Fellow, Merton Coll., Oxford 2007; Hon. DSc (McGill) 1998, (Western Ontario) 2002; Hon. LLD (Dalhousie) 1999, (Toronto) 2001, (Melbourne, Australia) 2003, (Saskatchewan) 2005, (St Francis Xavier) 2006, (Calgary) 2006, (Alberta) 2006, (Victoria) 2006, (Simon Fraser) 2008; Educator of the Year, Learning Partnership 2004 and was recently appointed a. *Address:* c/o Board of Trustees, National Institute for Nanotechnology, 11421 Saskatchewan Drive, Edmonton, AB T6G 2M9, Canada. *E-mail:* nintinfo@nrc.gc.ca. *Website:* nint-innt.nrc-cnrc.gc.ca.

PIQUÉ I CAMPS, Josep, LLB, PhD; Spanish economist, politician and business executive; *Chairman, Vueling Airlines SA;* b. 21 Feb. 1955, Barcelona; ed Univ. of Barcelona; Lecturer in Econ. Theory, Univ. of Barcelona 1977–86, 1990; Economist, Studies Dept, La Caixa 1984–85; Gen. Dir of Industry, Catalan Autonomous Govt 1986–88; Gen. Man. of Corp. Strategy, Ercros. SA (pvt. chemicals group) 1989–91, Man. Dir 1992, Chair. and CEO 1992–96, various posts in group including Chair. EMESA 1989–91, ERKIMIA SA 1990–96, FERTIBERIA 1993–96, FYSE 1992–93, LISAC 1992, META 1990–94, Sole Admin. FESA 1992–93, mem. Bd Prisma 1991–96, Río Tinto Minera 1991–93, Erkol 1991–96, Rhodiamul 1991–92; Minister of Industry and Energy 1996–2000; Govt Spokesman 1998–2000; Minister of Foreign Affairs 2000–02, of Science and Tech. 2002–04; Chair. Vueling Airlines SA, Barcelona 2007–. *Address:* Vueling Airlines SA, Parque de Negocios Mas Blau II Pla de l'Estany, 5 El Prat de Llobregat, Barcelona 08820, Spain (office). *Telephone:* (93) 3787878 (office). *Fax:* (93) 3787879 (office). *Website:* www.vueling.com (office).

PIQUET (SOUTO MAIOR), Nélson; Brazilian fmr racing driver; b. 17 Aug. 1952, Rio de Janeiro; s. of Estácio Souto Maior and Clotilde Maior; m. 1st Maria Clara; m. 2nd Vivianne Leao, one s. racing driver Nelson Angelo "Nelsinho" Piquet Jr; first Grand Prix, Germany 1978; mem. Ensign Grand Prix team 1978, BS McLaren team 1978, Brabham team 1978–85, Williams team 1986–87, Lotus team 1988–89, Benetton team 1990; winner of 23 Grand Prix races; Formula One World Champion 1981, 1983, 1987; lives in Monaco; International Motorsports Hall of Fame 2000. *Leisure interest:* sports.

PIRES, Maria Madalena Emília; Timor-Leste politician; *Minister of Finance;* ed La Trobe Univ., Australia; came to Australia as refugee with family aged 14 in 1975; fmr Admin. Nat. Council of Timorese Resistance office, Darwin; fmr Pres. Timorese Asscn of Vic.; mem. World Bank jt assessment mission in Timor-Leste 1999; est. East Timor Devt Office, Melbourne; Head, Nat. Planning and Devt Agency, Timor-Leste 2000–01; joined Ministry of Planning and Finances, held several positions including Sec., East Timor Planning Comm. 2002, Advisor on Planning and External Assistance Man. 2003–04; Sr Coordination Adviser to UN Deputy Special Rep. of the Sec.-Gen. for Int. Compact on Timor-Leste –2007; Minister of Finance 2007–. *Address:* Ministry of Finance, Palácio do Governo, Edif. 5, Av. Presidente Nicolau Lobato, Dili, Timor-Leste (office). *Telephone:* 3339510 (office). *E-mail:* info@mof.gov.tl (office). *Website:* www.mof.gov.tl (office).

PIRES, Gen. Pedro Verona Rodrigues; Cape Verde politician and fmr head of state; *President, Amílcar Cabral Foundation;* b. 29 April 1934, Sant' Ana, Fogo; s.

of Luís Rodrigues Pires and Maria Fidalga Lopes Pires; m. Adélcia Maria da Luz Lima Barreto Pires 1975; two d.; ed Liceu Gil Eanes de São Vicente, Faculty of Science, Lisbon Univ., Portugal; left Portugal to join Partido Africano da Independência da Guiné e Cabo Verde (PAIGC) 1961; mem. PAIGC dels 1961–63; involved in preparation for liberation of Cape Verde 1963–65; mem. Cen. Cttee of PAIGC 1965, of Council of War, PAIGC 1967; re-elected mem. of Commissão Permanente do Comité Executivo da Luta (CEL) and of Council of War 1970; involved in admin. of liberated areas of southern Guinea-Bissau 1971–73; Pres. Nat. Comm. of PAIGC for Cape Verde 1973 (reaffirmed as mem. of Council of War and CEL), appointed an Asst State Commr in first Govt of Repub. of Guinea-Bissau 1973–74; negotiated independence agreements of Cape Verde and Guinea-Bissau 1974; Dir PAIGC policies during transitional govt before independence of Cape Verde 1975; elected Deputy in Nat. Popular Ass. of Cape Verde June 1975–, re-elected 1980; Prime Minister of Cape Verde 1975–91, with responsibility for Finance, Planning and Co-operation; elected Deputy Gen. Sec. Partido Africano da Independência de Cabo Verde (PAICV) 1981, Sec. Gen. 1990–93, fmr Chair. Gen. 1993; Pres. of Cape Verde 2001–11; Pres. Fundação Amílcar Cabral, Cape Verde; mem. Perm. Comm. of CEL 1977; Ordem Amílcar Cabral 1976, Order of the Lion (Senegal), Ordem Infante D. Henrique (Portugal), Orden José Martí (Cuba), Orden de las Islas Canarias (Spain), Nat. Order (Gambia), Grande Colar da Ordem de Timor-Leste 2011, Mo Ibrahim Prize for Achievement in African Leadership 2011; Dr hc (Universidade do Ceará, Brazil), (Universidade Técnica de Lisboa), (ISCSP), (Universidade Lusófona de Humanidades e de Tecnologias, Lisbon). *Leisure interests:* philosophy, sociology, politics. *Address:* Fundação Amílcar Cabral, Praia, Santiago; CP 429, Praia, Santiago; Rua Dr Manuel Duarte, Praia, Santiago, Republic of Cape Verde (home). *Telephone:* 2616585 (home). *E-mail:* pvrodriguespires@gmail.com (home).

PIRIE, Madsen Duncan, MA, PhD, MPhil; British research institute director; *President, Adam Smith Institute;* b. 24 Aug. 1940; s. of Douglas G. Pirie and Eva Madsen; ed Univs of Edinburgh, St Andrews and Cambridge; Republican Study Cttee 1974; Distinguished Visiting Prof. of Philosophy, Hillsdale Coll., Mich. 1975–78; Pres. Adam Smith Inst. 1978–; mem. Citizens' Charter Advisory Panel 1991–95; RC Hoiles Fellow 1975. *Publications:* Freeports 1983, Test Your IQ 1983, Book of the Fallacy 1985, Privatization 1988, Micropolitics 1988, Boost Your IQ 1990, The Sherlock Holmes I.Q. Book 1995, 101 Great Philosophers: Makers of Modern Thought 2009. *Leisure interest:* calligraphy. *Address:* 23 Great Smith Street, London, SW1P 3BL, England. *Telephone:* (20) 7222-4995 (office). *Fax:* (20) 7222-4503 (office). *E-mail:* m.pirie@adamsmith.org (office). *Website:* www .adamsmith.org (office).

PIRINSKI, Georgi Georgiev; Bulgarian politician; b. 10 Sept. 1948, New York, USA; m.; two c.; ed English Language Secondary School No. 114, Sofia, Karl Marx Higher Inst. of Econs, Sofia; moved to Bulgaria 1952; Research Assoc., Int. Relations and Socialist Integration Inst. 1972–74; economist, Int. Orgs Div., Ministry of Foreign Trade 1974–76; Advisor, Council of Ministers 1976–80; fmr Deputy Minister and First Deputy Minister of Foreign Trade 1980–89; Deputy Minister and First Deputy Minister of Foreign Trade 1980–90; Deputy Prime Minister Nov. 1989–Feb. 1990, Aug.–Dec. 1990; mem. Parl. for Blagoevgrad in 7th Grand Nat. Ass. (Parl. Group of Bulgarian Socialist Party—BSP), for Plovdiv in 36th Nat. Ass. (Parl. Union for Social Democracy), for Sofia in 37th, 38th, 39th and 40th Nat. Ass. (Parl. Group of Democratic Left) 1995–2009, Pres. (Speaker) 40th Nat. Ass. 2005–09; Minister of Foreign Affairs 1995–96 (resgnd); mem. Dels of Nat. Ass. to Parl. Ass of OSCE, Council of Europe and WEU; nominated from BSP for Pres. in Oct. 1996 presidential elections but rejected by Constitutional Court on basis of not being a Bulgarian citizen by birth; mem. BSP 1969–2005 (mem. Presidency and Deputy Chair. Supreme Council 1990–2005), Cen. Cttee Bulgarian CP 1989–90, Coalition for Bulgaria (led by BSP) 2005–. *Address:* c/o Office of the Chairman, Narodno Sobranie, 1169 Sofia, pl. Narodno Sobranie 2, Bulgaria. *Telephone:* (2) 939-39. *E-mail:* infocenter@parliament.bg.

PIRK, Jan, MUDr, DSc; Czech heart surgeon; *Head, IKEM Clinic for Heart Surgery;* b. 20 April 1948, Prague; s. of Otto Pirk and Jitka Pirk; m. Blanka Pirk; two s.; ed Charles Univ., Prague; occupied numerous medical and surgical positions; researcher 1978–90; consultant, Odense Univ. Hosp., Denmark 1990–91, Ochsner Hosp., New Orleans, USA 1983–84; Head, Institutu Klinické a Experimentální Medicíny (IKEM) Clinic for Heart Surgery 1991–; Hon. mem. Czech Medical Soc., Czech Cardiology Soc. *Publications include:* The Effect of Antiaggregation Drugs on the Patency of Grafts in the Arterial System 1980, Improved Patency of the Aortocoronary Bypass by Anti-Trombic Drugs (co-author) 1986, Surgery for Ischaemic Heart Disease in Patients Under Forty (co-author) 1989, An Alternative to Cardioplegia (with M. D. Kellovsky) 1995. *Leisure interests:* skiing, biking, long-distance running, theatre, yachting. *Address:* IKEM Clinic for Heart Surgery, Vídeňská 1958, 140 21 Prague 4 (office); V Domově 28, 130 00 Prague 3, Czech Republic (home). *Telephone:* (2) 3605-5014 (office). *Fax:* (2) 3605-2776 (office). *E-mail:* japx@medicon.cz (office). *Website:* www.ikem.cz (office).

PIRUMOV, Vladimir Semenovich, DrMilSc; naval officer, politician and scientist; b. 1 Feb. 1926, Kirovakan, Armenia; m.; two d.; ed Caspian Higher Mil. Marine School, Mil. Marine Acad.; artillery officer, Asst to Commdr of cruiser, Commdr of destroyer Baltic Navy 1948–60; Head of Dept Gen. Staff of Mil. Marine forces 1974–85; teacher, Sr teacher, Head of Chair Mil. Marine Acad. 1963–74; Prof. Mil. Acad. of Gen. Staff 1985–; mem. Russian Acad. of Nat. Sciences; Vice-Pres., Head Section of Geopolitics and Security, Russian Acad. of Sciences 1993; Pres. Cen. of Studies of Problems of Geopolitics and Security at Security Council of Russian Fed. 1993–; First Vice-Pres. Acad. of Geopolitics and Security 2000–; mem. Ed. Bd journals Geopolitica i Besopasnost, Vooruzheniye, Politika, Konversia; P. Kapitsa Silver Medal, Piotr the Great Gold Medal, State Prize of Russian Fed. 1977, Merited Worker of Science of Russian Fed., various scientific awards. *Publications:* over 170 publications including Actual Problems of Security, Regions of Russia and the World, Strategy of Socio-Survival. *Address:* Russian Academy of Natural Sciences, Varshawskoye shosse 8, 113105 Moscow, Russia (office). *Telephone:* (495) 252-55-74 (office). *E-mail:* mediterra@yandex.ru (home).

PIRZADA, Syed Sharifuddin, SPk; Pakistani politician and lawyer; b. 12 June 1923, Burhanpur; s. of S. Vilayat Ali Pirzada and Butul Begum; m. 1st Rafia Sultana (died 1960); m. 2nd Safiya Pirzada; m. 3rd Rashda Pirzada; two s. three d.; ed Univ. of Bombay; Sec. Muslim Students Fed. 1943–45; Hon. Sec. to Quaid-i-

Azam, Jinnah 1941–44; Sec. Bombay City Muslim League 1945–47; Prof., Sind Muslim Law Coll. 1947–54; Adviser to Constitution Comm. of Pakistan 1960–61; Chair. Co. Law Comm. 1962; Pres. Karachi High Court Bar Asscn, Pakistan Br. 1964–67; Attorney-Gen. of Pakistan 1965–66, 1968–72, 1977–89; Minister of Foreign Affairs 1966–68, April–Oct. 1993; Minister of Justice 1979–84; mem. or Pres. several asscns and socs; led Pakistan Del. to Session of UN Gen. Ass. 1966–67; Chair. UN Human Rights Sub-Cttee on Minorities 1977; mem. Panel of Perm. Court of Arbitration; mem. Int. Law Comm. 1981–86; Sec.-Gen. Org. of Islamic Conf. 1984–88; Chair. Heritage Council and Amb.-at-large with rank of Fed. Minister 1989–93; mem. Nat. Security Council of Pakistan 1999–; Hon. Sr Adviser to Chief Exec. on Foreign Affairs, Law, Justice and Human Rights 1999–; Judge (ad-hoc), Int. Court of Justice 2000; Chair. Nat. Cttee on Quaid-i-Azam Year 2001; Sr Adviser (Sr Fed. Minister) to Prime Minister on Foreign Affairs, Law, Justice and Human Rights 2002–08; Sr Advocate, Supreme Court. *Publications include:* Evolution of Pakistan 1962, Fundamental Rights and Constitutional Remedies in Pakistan 1966, Some Aspects of Quaid-i-Azam's Life 1978, Collected Works of Quaid-i-Azam Mohammad Ali Jinnah (Vol. I) 1985, (Vol. II) 1986, (Vol. III) 1987; Dissolution of Constituent Assembly of Pakistan 1996. *Leisure interest:* bridge. *Address:* House No. 25/1–4, Phase-V, Zamzama Street, Clifton, Karachi, Pakistan (home). *Telephone:* (21) 5874183 (home).

PISANI-FERRY, Jean; French economist; *Director, Bruegel;* b. 28 July 1951, Boulogne-Billancourt; ed Ecole Supérieure d'Electricité, Université Paris V, Centre d'études des programmes économiques; Econ. Adviser with EC 1989–92; Dir of CEPII (Centre d'études prospectives et d'informations internationales—French inst. for int. econs) 1992–97; Sr Econ. Adviser to the Minister of Finance 1997–2000; Exec. Pres. of the Prime Minister's Council of Econ. Analysis 2001–02; Prof. of Econs, Université Paris-Dauphine; current research interests include economic policy in Europe and global macroeconomics; regular columns in Le Monde, Handelsblatt, The FT A-List, Project Syndicate and the Chinese magazine Caixin; Chevalier de la Légion d'honneur. *Publications:* recent publications include Economic Policy (co-author) 2010, Le Réveil des Démons 2011, Démons: la crise de l'euro et comment nous en sortir (in French) 2011 (in English 2012), Global Currencies for Tomorrow (co-author) 2011, An Ocean Apart? – Comparing Transatlantic Responses to the Financial Crisis (co-ed.) 2011. *Address:* Bruegel, 33 Rue de la Charité, Brussels 1210, Belgium (office). *Telephone:* (2) 227-4210 (office). *Fax:* (2) 227-4219 (office). *E-mail:* jean.pisani-ferry@bruegel.org (office). *Website:* www.bruegel.org (office); www.pisani-ferry.net.

PISANU, Giuseppe; Italian politician; b. 2 Jan. 1937, Ittiri, Sassari; m.; three s.; Deputy Man. Dir Soc. of Finance and Industry for the Rebirth of Sardinia (SFIRS); Prov. Sec., Regional Sec. (Sardinia), Exec. Sec. to Pres. Democrazia Cristiana (Christian Democrats) 1975–80; elected Deputy 1972–92; Under-Sec. of State for Treasury 1980–83; Under-Sec. of State for Defence 1986–90; Minister of the Interior 2002–06; elected mem. Forza Italia (Sardinia) 1994–; mem. Pres.'s cttee 1994–96, Deputy-Chair. Parl. Group, then Chair. 1996–2001; mem. Defence Cttee; Del. of Italy to CSCE 1998, to WEU 1999. *Address:* c/o Forza Italia, Via dell'Umiltà 36, 00187 Rome, Italy (office). *Telephone:* (06) 67311 (office). *Fax:* (06) 6788255 (office). *E-mail:* lettere@forza-italia.it (office). *Website:* www.forza-italia.it (office).

PISCHETSRIEDER, Bernd Peter, DipEng; German automotive engineer and business executive; *Chairman of the Supervisory Board, Münchener Rückversicherungsgesellschaft AG (Munich Re);* b. 15 Feb. 1948, Munich, Bavaria; ed Technical Univ. Munich; joined BMW AG, Munich as production planning eng 1973; Production Dir BMW South Africa (Pty) Ltd 1982–85; Dir for Quality Control, BMW AG 1985–87, for Tech. Planning 1987–90; Deputy mem. Admin. Bd in charge of Production 1990, mem. Admin. 1991, Chair. Admin. Bd 1993–99; fmr Chair. Rover; Chair. SEAT SA 2000–02; Chair. Bd of Man. Volkswagen AG 2002–06 (resgnd), Advisor to the Bd; Chair. Scania AB 2002–07; mem. Supervisory Bd Münchener Rückversicherungsgesellschaft AG (Munich Re) 2002–, Chair. 2013–; mem. Jt Advisory Council, Allianz Group of Cos –2012; Dr hc (Birmingham) 1996. *Address:* Münchener Rückversicherungs-Gesellschaft AG, Königinstrasse 107, 80802 Munich, Germany (office). *Telephone:* (89) 38910 (office). *Fax:* (89) 399056 (office). *E-mail:* info@munichre.com (office). *Website:* www.munichre.com (office).

PISCHINGER, Franz Felix, Dr Techn.; Austrian scientist, academic and business executive; *Chairman, FEV GmbH;* b. 18 July 1930, Waidhofen; s. of Franz Pischinger and Karoline Pischinger; m. Elfriede Pischinger 1957 (died 2001); m. Elisabeth Pischinger 2003; four s. one d.; ed Graz Univ. of Tech.; tech. asst, Graz Univ. of Tech. 1953–58; Head of Research Dept, Inst. of Internal Combustion Engines, Prof. List (AVL) 1958–62; leading positions in research and devt with Kloeckner-Humboldt-Deutz AG, Cologne 1962–70; Dir Inst. for Applied Thermodynamics, Aachen Tech. Univ. 1970–97; Pres. and CEO, FEV Motorentechnik GmbH (now FEV GmbH), Aachen 1978–2003, Chair. 2003–; Vice-Pres. DFG (German Research Soc.) 1984–90, Acatech German Acad. of Science and Eng 2002–05; Foreign Assoc. mem. Nat. Acad. of Eng (USA) 1997–; Fellow, Soc. of Automotive Engineers 1996–; Österreichischer Ehrenring 1954, Deutsches Bundesverdienstkreuz 1978, Cross of Honour for Science and Art, First Class (Austria) 1998; Dr hc (Graz Univ. of Tech.) 1994; Hon. Prof., Dalian Univ., People's Repub. of China 2005; Herbert Akroyd Stuart Award 1962, Carl-Engler-Medaille, Deutsche Wissenschaftliche Gesellschaft für Erdöl, Erdgas und Kohle (DGMK) 1990, Medal of Honour, Verein Deutscher Ingenieure 1993, Soichiro Honda Medal, ASME 2000, FISITA Medal 2012. *Publications:* articles in professional journals. *Address:* FEV GmbH, Neuenhofstrasse 181, 52078 Aachen, Germany (office). *Telephone:* (241) 5689100 (office). *Website:* www.fev.com (office).

PISTOLETTO, Michelangelo; Italian artist; b. 1933, Biella; worked with his father as painting restorer 1947–58; first solo exhbn at Galleria Galatea, Turin 1960; first solo exhbn in USA at Walker Art Center, Minneapolis 1966; f. Zoo Group of performance artists 1968; associated with Arte Povera movt; works include paintings, sculptures with steel, mirrors and everyday objects, films and video work and performance art; launched his Progetto Arte manifesto 1994, f. Cittadellarte – Fondazione Pistoletto for the study and promotion of creative projects 1998; Grand Prize, Bienale di São Paulo 1967, Belgian Art Critics' Award 1967, Wolf Foundation Prize in the Arts (Painting and Sculpture) 2007. *Works include:* Autoritratto oro 1960, Il Presente – Uomo di schiena 1960–61, Quadri Specchianti (Mirror Paintings), Oggetti in meno (Minus Objects) 1965–66, Venere degli stracci (Venus of the Rags) 1967, Pietra miliare 1967, Opera Ah (performance work) 1979, Anno uno (performance work) 1981. *Publications:* L'uomo nero, il lato insopportabile 1970. *Address:* Cittadellarte – Fondazione Pistoletto, via Serralunga 27, Biella 13900, Italy (office). *Telephone:* (015) 28400 (office). *Fax:* (015) 2522540 (office). *E-mail:* fondazionepistoletto@cittadellarte.it (office). *Website:* www.cittadellarte.it (office).

PISTORIO, Pasquale, M.Electronics; Italian business executive; b. 1936, Sicily; ed Polytechnic of Turin; began career as salesman for Motorola Italy 1967, becoming Dir of Int. Marketing, Phoenix, Ariz. 1977, also Vice-Pres. Motorola Corpn 1977, Gen. Man. Int. Semiconductor Div. 1978–80; Pres. and CEO SGS Group 1980–98 (renamed STMicroelectronics 1998), Pres. and CEO STMicroelectronics 1998–2005, Hon. Chair. 2005–; Chair. Telecom Italia SpA April–Dec. 2007; f. Pistorio Foundation (charity) 2005; Vice-Pres. for Innovation and Research, Confindustria (Confed. of Italian Industrialists); mem. numerous bds including FIAT SpA, Telecom Italia, Atos, Brenbo, STATS ChipPAC; Hon. Citizen of Singapore 2003; Commendatore al Merito 1974, Chevalier, Ordre nat. du Mérite 1990, Cavaliere del Lavoro 1997, Ouissam Alaouite (Morocco) 1999, Public Service Star (Singapore) 1999, Chevalier, Légion d'Honneur 1999, Officier, Légion d'Honneur 2005, Commdr, Ordre nat. du Mérite 2009; Dr hc (Genoa), (Malta), (Pavia), (Catania), (Palermo), (Sannio), (Bicocca), (Bristol); Akira Inoue Award for Outstanding Achievement in Environmental Health and Safety in the Semiconductor Industry 2000, Lifetime Achievement Award, Reed Electronics Group 2003, Prix du Manager d'Entreprise, Prix des Technologies de l'information 2003, Green Hero Lifetime Achievement Award, AnalogZONE magazine 2005, ACE Lifetime Achievement Award, EETimes magazine 2010, IEEE Robert N. Noyce Medal Award 2011, Ellis Island Medal of Honor Award 2012. *Address:* Pistorio Foundation, Associazione Amici della Fondazione Pistorio, Via Lecco, 61, 20059 Vimercate MI, Italy. *Website:* www.pistoriofoundation.org.

PITCHER, Sir Desmond Henry, Kt; British company executive; b. 23 March 1935, Liverpool; s. of George Charles Pitcher and Alice Marion Pitcher (née Osborne); m. 1st Patricia Ainsworth 1961 (divorced 1973); two d.; m. 2nd Carol Ann Rose 1978 (divorced); two s.; m. 3rd Norma Barbara Niven 1991; ed Liverpool Coll. of Tech. and Commerce; Man. Dir then Vice-Pres. Int. Div. The Sperry Corpn 1961–76; Man. Dir British Leyland Truck and Bus Div. 1976–78, Plessey Telecommunications and Office Systems Ltd 1978–83; Group Chief Exec. The Littlewoods Org. PLC 1983–93, Vice-Chair. 1993–95; Chair. The Mersey Barrage Co. Ltd 1986–96, The Merseyside Devt Corpn 1991–98, The North West Water Group PLC (now United Utilities) 1993–98 (Dir 1990–98); Dir Everton Football Club Co. Ltd 1987–90, Deputy Chair. 1990–98; Dir Northern Advisory Bd of Nat. Westminster Bank PLC 1989–92, Dir (non-exec.) Nat. Westminster Bank 1994–98; Dir Liverpool School of Tropical Medicine 1996–; Chair. Royal Liverpool Philharmonic Social Devt Trust 1992–. *Leisure interests:* football, golf, 19th century history, opera, sailing.

PITCHER, Hon. Frederick W., BA, MBA; Nauruan/Australian politician, diplomatist and environmentalist; b. 5 Feb. 1967, Nauru; s. of Graeme Pitcher and Melody Halstead; m. Juliana Pitcher; three c.; ed educated in Australia, Japan and UK; govt statistician/economist 1992–96; Sec. for Finance 1997; Adviser to Exec. Dir, Asian Devt Bank, Manila, The Philippines 1997–99; Deputy Perm. Rep., UN, New York 2000–04; mem. Parl. 2004–, mem. Constitutional Review Cttee 2005; served in second Admin of fmr Pres. Ludwig Scotty; Minister for Island Devt and Industry 2004–07, of Finance and Econ. Planning 2007, of Commerce, Industry and Environment and Minister for Utilities 2007–11; Acting Foreign Minister 2007; elected Pres. of Nauru 10 Nov. 2011, but removed by parl. 15 Nov.; Pres. Nauru Island Basketball Asscn. *Leisure interests:* fishing, music, sports. *Address:* c/o Office of the President, Yaren, Nauru.

PITHART, Petr, JUDr; Czech politician and academic; *First Vice-President of the Senate;* b. 2 Jan. 1941, Kladno; s. of Vilém Pithart and Blažena Pithart (née Krystýnková); m. Drahomíra Hromádková 1964; one s. one d.; ed Charles Univ., Prague (Faculty of Law); Dept of Theory of State and Law, Charles Univ. 1964–70; scholarship Univ. of Oxford, UK 1969–70; labourer 1970–72; co. lawyer 1972–77; signed Charter 77; labourer 1977–79; clerk with Central Warehouses, Prague 1979–89; Spokesman Co-ordination Centre, Civic Forum 1989–90; Prime Minister of Czech Repub. 1990–92; Deputy to Czech Nat. Council 1990–92; mem. and Chair. Senate 1996–98, Vice-Chair. 1998–2000, Chair. 2000, currently Vice-Pres.; mem. Christian and Democratic Union, Czech People's Party (KDU-ČSL) 1999–, cand. presidential election 2003; Sr Research Fellow, Cen. European Univ., Prague 1992–94; teacher, Faculty of Law, Charles Univ., Prague 1994–, Head of Dept of Political Science and Sociology, Faculty of Law 2007–; Ed.-in-Chief The New Presence (periodical) 1992–96; Commdr's Cross with Star (Poland) 2004, Great Gold Cross of Merit (Austria) 2004, Officier, Légion d'honneur 2004; Frantisek Kriegel Prize, Foundation of Chart 77, Prague 1991. *Publications:* The Defence of Politics 1974, The Year Sixty-Eight 1978, 1990, History and Politics 1992, Czechs in the History of Modern Times (co-author) 1992, Who We Are After '89 1997, The Reading on the Resettled History (co-author) 1998, The Year Eighty-Nine 2009; numerous articles and essays. *Leisure interests:* politics, history, hiking, fishing. *Address:* Senate of the Czech Republic, Valdštejnské nám. 4, 118 11 Prague 1, Czech Republic (office). *Telephone:* (2) 57071111 (office). *Fax:* (2) 57534484 (office). *E-mail:* pithartp@senat.cz (office); petr@pithart.cz (home). *Website:* www.pithart .cz.

PITSUWAN, Surin, PhD; Thai politician, diplomatist and international organization official; *Head, Future Innovative Thailand Institute;* b. 28 Oct. 1949, Nakhon Si Thammarat; s. of Ismael Pitsuwan and Sapiya Pitsuwan; m. Alisa Ariya 1983; three s.; ed Claremont McKenna Coll., Harvard Univ., USA; taught at Thammasat Univ. 1975–86, Academic Asst to Dean of Faculty of Political Science and to Vice-Rector for Academic Affairs 1985–86; columnist, The Nation Review and Bangkok Post newspapers 1980–92; fmr corresp. and analyst, ASEAN Forecast; Congressional Fellow, Office of US Rep. Geraldine Ferraro and Senate Republican Conf. 1983–84; mem. Parl. from Nakhon Si Thammarat Prov. 1986–; Sec. to Speaker of House of Reps 1986; Asst Sec. to Minister of Interior 1988; Deputy Minister of Foreign Affairs 1992–95; Minister of Foreign Affairs 1997–2001; adviser to Int. Comm. on Intervention and State Sovereignty 1999–2001; mem. UN Comm. on Human Security 2001–03; served on ILO's World Comm. on the Social Dimension of Globalization 2002–04; Sec.-Gen. ASEAN

2008–13; Head, Future Innovative Thailand Inst. 2013–; mem. Democratic Party (fmr Deputy Leader); mem. Advisory Bd Council on Foreign Relations, New York, Int. Advisory Bd Int. Crisis Group, Advisory Bd UN Human Security Trust Fund, 'Wise Men Group' under auspices of the Henri Dunant Centre for Humanitarian Dialogue, Geneva (advising peace negotiations between Acehnese Independence Movt (GAM) and Govt of Indonesia) 2002–04, Islamic Devt Bank's 1440 AH (2020) Vision Comm. –2005; fmr mem. Nat. Reconciliation Comm.; Int. Academic Advisor, Centre for Islamic Studies, Univ. of Oxford, UK; adviser to the Leaders Project (conf. arm of the Cohen Group of fmr US Sec. of Defense William S. Cohen), Washington, DC. *Leisure interest:* reading. *Address:* Future Innovative Thailand Institute, 67 Sedsiri Road. Samsannai Phayathai, Bangkok 10400, Thailand (office). *Telephone:* (2) 828-1000 (office). *Fax:* (2) 828-1001 (office). *E-mail:* info@fit .or.th (office). *Website:* www.fit.or.th (office).

PITT, Brad; American film actor and producer; b. 18 Dec. 1963, Shawnee, Okla; s. of Bill Pitt and Jane Pitt; m. Jennifer Aniston (q.v.) 2000 (divorced 2005); six c. (with Angelina Jolie); ed Univ. of Missouri; Special Amb. for Nelson Mandela's 46664 campaign against HIV/AIDS 2004. *Films appearances include:* Cutting Glass, Happy Together 1989, Across the Tracks 1990, Contact, Thelma and Louise 1991, The Favor 1992, Johnny Suede 1992, Cool World 1992, A River Runs Through It 1992, Kalifornia 1993, Legend of the Fall 1994, Interview With The Vampire 1994, 12 Monkeys (Golden Globe Award for Best Supporting Actor) 1995, Seven 1996, Sleepers 1996, Tomorrow Never Dies 1996, Seven Years in Tibet 1997, The Devil's Own 1997, Meet Joe Black 1998, Fight Club 1999, Snatch 2000, The Mexican 2001, Spy Game 2001, Ocean's Eleven 2001, Full Frontal 2002, Confessions of a Dangerous Mind 2002, Sinbad: Legend of the Seven Seas (voice) 2003, Troy 2004, Ocean's Twelve 2004, Mr and Mrs Smith 2005, Babel 2006, Ocean's Thirteen 2007, The Assassination of Jesse James by the Coward Robert Ford (Best Actor, Venice Film Festival 2007) 2007, Burn After Reading 2008, The Curious Case of Benjamin Button 2008, Inglourious Basterds 2009, Megamind (voice) 2010, The Tree of Life 2011, Moneyball 2011, Killing Them Softly 2012, World War Z 2013, 12 Years a Slave 2013, The Counsellor 2013. *Films produced include:* The Departed 2006, A Mighty Heart 2007, The Assassination of Jesse James by the Coward Robert Ford 2007, The Time Traveller's Wife 2009, Eat Pray Love 2010, The Tree of Life 2011, Moneyball 2011, Killing them Softly 2012, World War Z 2013, 12 Years a Slave (BAFTA Award for Best Picture, Golden Globe Award for Best Motion Picture, Drama, Academy Award for Best Picture 2014) 2013. *Television appearances include:* Dallas (series), Glory Days (series), Too Young to Die? (film), The Image (film). *Address:* c/o Creative Artists Agency, 2000 Avenue of the Stars, Los Angeles, CA 90067, USA (office).

PITT, Hon. Harvey Lloyd, BA, JD; American lawyer and fmr government official; *CEO, Kalorama Partners LLC;* b. 28 Feb. 1945, Brooklyn, NY; s. of Morris Jacob Pitt and Sara Pitt (née Sapir); m. Saree Ruffin 1984; one s. one d. (and one d. one s. from previous marriage); ed City Univ. of New York (Brooklyn Coll.) and St John's Univ., New York; with SEC, Washington, DC 1968–78, Legal Asst to Commr 1969, Ed. Institutional Investor Study 1970–71, Special Counsel, Office of Gen. Counsel 1971–72, Chief Counsel Market Regulation Div. 1972–73, Exec. Asst to Chair. 1973–75, Gen. Counsel 1975–78, Chair. 2001–03; f. Kalorama Partners LLC, CEO 2002–; called to Bar, NY 1969, US Supreme Court 1972, DC 1979; Man. Pnr, Fried, Frank, Harris, Shriver & Jacobson, Washington, DC 1978–89, Co-Chair. 1997–; Adjunct Prof. of Law, George Washington Univ. Nat. Law Centre 1974–82, Univ. of Pennsylvania Law School 1983–84; Vice-Pres. Glen Haven Civic Asscn, Silver Spring, Md 1972–73, Pres. 1974; mem. ABA, Fed. Bar Asscn, Admin. Conf. of US, American Law Inst.; Hon. LLD (St John's Univ. School of Law) 2002; Outstanding Young Lawyer Award, Fed. Bar Asscn 1975, Learned Hand Award, Inst. for Human Relations 1988, Brooklyn Coll. Pres. Medal of Distinction 2003. *Address:* Kalorama Partners LLC, 1130 Connecticut Avenue, NW, Suite 800, Washington, DC 20036 (office); 2404 Wyoming Ave, NW, Washington, DC 20008-1643, USA (home). *Telephone:* (202) 721-0000 (office). *Fax:* (202) 721-0007 (office). *E-mail:* info@kaloramapartners.com (office). *Website:* www.kaloramapartners.com (office).

PITTMAN, James A., Jr, MD; American medical scientist and academic; *Distinguished Professor of Physiology and Biophysics, and Professor of Medicine, University of Alabama;* b. 12 April 1927, Orlando, Fla; s. of James A. Pittman and Jean C. Garretson; m. Constance Ming Chung Shen 1955; two s.; ed Davidson Coll. and Harvard Medical School; Clinical Assoc., NIH, Bethesda, Md 1954–56; Instructor in Medicine, Univ. of Alabama 1956–59, Asst Prof. 1959–62, Assoc. Prof. 1962–64, Prof. of Medicine 1964–92, Prof. of Physiology and Biophysics 1967–92, Dean, School of Medicine 1973–92, Distinguished Prof. 1992–; Consultant, Children's Hosp. Birmingham, Ala 1962–71; Prof. of Medicine, Georgetown Univ. School of Medicine, Washington, DC 1971–73; Sr Adviser Int. Council on Control of Iodine Deficiency Diseases 1994–96; Master, American Coll. of Physicians, Asscn of American Physicians, American Chemical Soc. etc.; Hon. DSc (Davidson Coll.) 1980, (Alabama) 1984, (Chung Shan Univ., Taiwan) 2005. *Publications:* Diagnosis and Treatment of Thyroid Disease 1963; articles in professional journals. *Leisure interests:* flying, scuba diving, hunting, sailing. *Address:* University of Alabama School of Medicine, SDB 75, 1924 Seventh Avenue South, Birmingham, AL 35294 (office); 5 Ridge Drive, Birmingham, AL 35213, USA (home). *Telephone:* (205) 934-3414 (office); (205) 871-9261 (home). *Fax:* (205) 975-4976 (office). *E-mail:* jap@uab.edu (office); japdoc@msm.com (home). *Website:* main.uab.edu/uasom/show.asp?durki=2023 (office).

PITTMAN, Robert Warren; American media executive; b. 28 Dec. 1953, Jackson, Miss.; s. of Warren E. Pittman and Lanita Pittman (née Hurdle); m. 1st Sandra Hill 1979 (divorced); one s.; m. 2nd Veronique Choa 1997; one c.; ed Millsaps Coll., Oakland, Pittsburg and Harvard Univs; disc jockey WJDX-FM (Miss.) 1970–72; disc jockey WRIT (Milwaukee) 1972; Research Dir WDRQ (Detroit) 1972–73; Programme Dir WPEZ (Pittsburg) 1973–74; with WMAQ-WKQZ (NY) and NBC Radio 1974–77; with WNBC (NY) 1977–79; exec. producer Album Tracks NBC TV 1977–78; Dir, Vice-Pres., Sr Vice-Pres. Warner Amex Satellite Entertainment Co. (now MTV Networks Inc.) 1979–82, Pres., CEO 1985–86; Exec. Vice-Pres., COO MTV Networks Inc. 1983–85; Pres., CEO Quantum Media Inc. 1987–89; Exec. Adviser Warner Communications Inc. 1989–90; Pres., CEO Time Warner Enterprises 1990–95; CEO Six Flags Entertainment 1991–95; Man. Pnr and CEO Century 21 Real Estate 1995–96; Pres.,

CEO America On-Line Networks 1996–97, Pres., COO America On-Line Inc. 1997–2001, Co-COO 2001–02; Co-founder Pilot Group LLC (investment firm), New York 2003; Chair. NY Shakespeare Festival 1987–94; dir numerous cos; Golden Plate Award, American Acad. of Achievement 1990, Lifetime Achievement Int. Monitor Award, Int. Teleproduction Soc. 1993 and many others. *Address:* 47 East Lake Drive, Katonah, NY 10586, USA.

PIVETTI, Irene; Italian politician; b. 4 April 1963; d. of Grazia Gabrielli; m. Paolo Taranta 1988 (separated 1992); ed Catholic Univ. of the Sacred Heart, Milan; journalist; mem. Parl. 1992–2001, Speaker 1995–96; fmr mem. Lega Nord (Northern League); currently Pres. Unione Democratici per l'Europa (UDEUR, f. 1999). *Address:* Unione Democratici per l'Europa, Largo Arenula 34, 00186 Rome; Camera dei Deputati, Rome, Italy; (06) 684241. *Fax:* (06) 6872593. *E-mail:* udeur@udeur.org. *Website:* www.udeur.org.

PIVOT, Bernard; French journalist and writer; *Chairman, Académie Goncourt;* b. 5 May 1935, Lyons; s. of Charles Pivot and Marie-Louise Pivot (née Dumas); m. Monique Dupuisz 1959; two d.; ed Centre de formation des Journalistes; on staff of Figaro littéraire, then Literary Ed.; Figaro 1958–74; Chronique pour sourire, on Europe 1 1970–73; columnist, Le Point 1974–77; producer and presenter of Ouvrez les guillemets 1973–74, Apostrophes, France 2 1975–90, Bouillon de culture 1991–2001, Double Je 2002–05; Ed. Lire 1975–93; Dir Sofica Créations 1986–; mem. Conseil supérieur de la langue française 1989–; Pres. Grévin Acad. 2001–; mem. Acad. Goncourt 2004–, Chair. 2014–; Chevalier du Mérite agricole; Hon. OC 2008; Nat. Order of Québec; Grand Prix de la Critique, Acad. française 1983, Prix Louise Weiss, Bibliothèque Nat. 1989, Prix de la langue française décerné à la Foire 2000. *Publications include:* L'Amour en vogue (novel) 1959, La vie oh là là! 1966, Les critiques littéraires 1968, Beaujolaises 1978, Le Football en vert 1980, Le Métier de lire. Réponses à Pierre Nora 1990, Remontrances à la ménagère de moins de cinquante ans (essay) 1998. *Leisure interests:* tennis, football, gastronomy. *Address:* Grévin, 10 boulevard Montmartre, 75009 Paris (office); Les Jonnerys, 69430 Quincié-en-Beaujolais, France (home). *Telephone:* 1-47-70-85-05 (office). *Website:* www.academie-goncourt.fr.

PIVOVAROV, Yuri Sergeyevich, Dr rer. pol; Russian political scientist; *Director, Institute of Scientific Information on Social Sciences (INION), Russian Academy of Sciences;* b. 25 April 1950, Moscow; m.; one s. one d.; ed Moscow Inst. of Int. Relations; Jr then Sr Researcher, Prof., Head of Div., Deputy Dir Inst. of Scientific Information on Social Sciences (INION), USSR (now Russian) Acad. of Sciences 1976–98, Dir 1998–; mem. Exec. Bd Russian Assen of Political Sciences; mem. Council on Politology, Presidium, Russian Acad. of Sciences; Ed.-in-Chief Gosudarstvo i Pravo (journal), Politicheskaya Nauka (periodical); Corresp. mem. Russian Acad. of Sciences 1997–. *Publications:* Political Culture of Russia after Reforms, Essays on the History of Russian Socio-political Ideas of the 19th and Early 20th Century and over 200 articles. *Address:* INION, Nakhimovsky prosp. 51/21, 117418 Moscow, Russia (office). *Telephone:* (495) 123-88-81 (office). *Website:* www.inion.ru (office).

PIWOWSKI, Marek; Polish/American film director, writer, actor and journalist; b. 24 Oct. 1935, Warsaw; s. of Władysław Piwowski and Jadwiga Piwowska; ed State Acad. of Film, Łódź, Univ. of Warsaw; Visiting Prof., City Univ. of New York; Dir and writer of 17 films which have won 24 int. film festival awards; mem. American Film Inst.; Order of Polonia Restituta. *Films include:* Kirk Douglas 1967, Flybeater 1967, A Cruise 1970, Psychodrama 1972, Corkscrew 1971, Blue Hair 1972, How to Recognize the Vampire 1974, Foul Play 1977, Trouble is My Business 1988, Catch 22 1990, Kidnapping Agata 1993, The Parade Step 1998, The Barracuda's Kiss 1998, The Knife in the Head of Dino Baggio 1999, Olympiad in Zakopane 1999, Executioners 2001, Martin's Law 2001, Body Language 2002, Oskar (dir, scriptwriter) 2005. *Leisure interests:* sailing, skiing, gliders, windsurfing. *Address:* ul. Promenada 21 m 7, 00-778 Warsaw, Poland. *Telephone:* (58) 5858858 (office); 50-1011111 (mobile) (office); (22) 841-80-80; 60-6600000 (mobile). *Fax:* (22) 841-80-80. *E-mail:* wujekpiwek@gmail.com (office); piwek@eranet.pl.

PIZA, Arthur Luiz; Brazilian painter and printmaker; b. 1928, São Paulo; painter and exhibitor 1943–; moved to Paris 1952; works in many important museums and pvt. collections; Purchase Prize 1953 and Nat. Prize for Prints São Paulo Biennale 1959, Prizes at biennales at Ljubljana 1961, Santiago 1966, Venice 1966, Grenchen Triennale 1961, biennales of Norway and Mexico 1980, Puerto Rico 1991, Nat. Assen of Critics Grand Prize, Brazil 1994. *Publications:* Abstract Painting 1962, Larousse of Paintings (Small Larousse of Paintings, Vol. II) 1979, Bénézit Dictionary of Painters, Sculptors and Engravers 1999, Arthur Luiz Piza 2003. *Address:* 16 rue Dauphine, 75006 Paris, France.

PIZARRO, Artur; Portuguese pianist; b. 1968, Lisbon; regular int. performanes with leading conductors including Esa-Pekka Salonen, Sir Andrew Davis, Charles Dutoit, Franz Welser-Most, Ilan Volkov, Tugan Sokhiev, Yakov Kreizberg, Yannick Nezet-Seguin, Libor Pesek, Vladimir Jurowski, Sir Simon Rattle, Sir Charles Mackerras; as recitalist has performed at many of the world's most prestigious venues and festivals including Kennedy Centre, Washington, Wigmore Hall, London, Aldeburgh Festival, Neues Gewandhaus, Leipzig, Frankfurt Alte Oper, Théâtre du Chatelet and Musee D'Orsay, Paris, Zürich Tonhalle, BBC Proms, London, NHK and Orchard Halls, Japan; chamber music appearances have partnered him with Raphael Oleg, Christian Altenburger, Truls Mork, Toby Hoffmann, the St Lawrence, Muir and Petersen quartets; taught at GSMD 1998–2002; performed complete cycle of Beethoven Piano Sonatas, St John Smith's Square, London 2004–05; f. the Pizarro Trio with violinist Raphael Oleg and cellist Josephine Knight 2005; Medal of Cultural Merit, Portugal 2007; winner, Vianna da Motta Int. Piano Competition 1987, Greater Palm Beach Symphony Invitational Piano Competition 1989, Leeds Int. Piano Competition 1990, Bordalo Prize 1998. *Radio:* Performance On 3, BBC Radio 3. *Recordings include:* Milhaud, Music for Two Pianos (with Stephen Coombs) 1997, Vianna da Motta, The Romantic Piano Concerto 1999, Beethoven Piano Sonatas 2003, Beethoven, Last Three Piano Sonatas 2003, Chopin, Reminiscences 2005, Rodrigo, Complete Piano Works (Ed.'s Choice, Gramophone Magazine) 2005, Chopin, Second and Third Sonatas 2006, Lizst, Hungarian Rhapsodies 2006, Ravel, Complete Solo Works 2007, Piano Duo Music, with Vita Panomariovaite 2007, Ravel, Complete Piano Works, Vol. 2 2008. *Address:* c/o Tom Croxon Management, 22 Hurst Road, Buckhurst Hill, Essex IG9 6AB, England (office). *Telephone:* (20) 8279-2516 (office). *Fax:* (20) 8504-2200

(office). *E-mail:* tom@tomcroxonmanagement.co.uk (office). *Website:* www.tomcroxonmanagement.co.uk (office).

PIZARRO MORENO, Manuel, LicenDer; Spanish lawyer, business executive and politician; ed Univ. Complutense de Madrid; Attorney-Gen. (Advocate of the State); apptd mem. Bd of Dirs Endesa SA 1996, mem. Exec. Cttee 1997–98, Vice-Chair. 1998–2002, Chair. 2002–07; mem. Bd of Dirs Telefónica 2007–08; Chair. Ibercaja, Spanish Savings Banks Confed.; Vice-Chair. Madrid Stock Exchange; fmr Vice-Chair. Bolsa de Madrid, Bolsas y Mercados Espaqoles, Sociedad Holding de Mercados y Sistemas Financieros SA; mem. Spanish Royal Acad. of Legislation and Jurisprudence; Chair. Bd of Trustees, Nat. Park of Ordesa and Monte Perdido; Vice-Chair. Bd of Trustees, Nat. Museum of Archeology; mem. Bd of Trustees, Univ. Pontificia de Salamanca; joined Partido Popular 2008, Partido Popular spokesman, Constitutional Comm., Congress of Deputies 2008–. *Address:* Constitutional Commission, Congress of Deputies, Carrera de San Jerónimo s/n, 28071 Madrid, Spain (office). *Telephone:* (91) 3906000 (office). *Fax:* (91) 4298707 (office). *E-mail:* servicio.informacion@sgral.congreso.es (office). *Website:* www.congreso.es (office).

PIZZO, Philip A., BA, MD; American physician and academic; *Dean, School of Medicine, Stanford University;* b. 6 Dec. 1944, New York City; s. of Vito Pizzo; m. Peggy Pizzo; ed Fordham Univ., Univ. of Rochester School of Medicine; intern, Children's Hosp. Medical Center, Boston 1970–71, Jr Asst Resident 1971–72, Sr Asst Resident 1972–73; Clinical Assoc., Nat. Cancer Inst. 1973–75, Investigator 1975–76, Sr Investigator 1976–80, Head of Infectious Disease Section, Pediatric Br., Nat. Cancer Inst. 1980–96, Chief of Pediatrics 1982–96; Thomas Morgan Rotch Prof. and Chair., Dept of Pediatrics, Harvard Univ. Medical School, Children's Hosp., Boston 1996–2001, also Faculty Dean for Academic Programs 1996–99; Dean, Stanford Univ. School of Medicine 2001–, also Carl and Elizabeth Naumann Prof. of Pediatrics 2001–; Attending Physician, NIH, Bethesda, Md 1976–96; Prof. of Pediatrics, F. Edward Hebert School of Medicine, Bethesda 1987–96; mem. Bd of Dirs Lucile Packard Children's Hosp. 2001–, Stanford Hosp. and Clinics 2001–; mem. numerous professional socs including American Pediatric Soc. 1995, NAS Inst. of Medicine 1997, American Assen of Physicians 1998; mem. editorial bd numerous journals; Hon. ScD (Fordham) 1996, Hon. MA (Harvard) 1996; numerous awards including US Public Health Service Meritorious Service Award 1985, Outstanding Service Medal 1995. *Publications include:* over 500 papers in professional journals. *Address:* Office of the Dean, Stanford University School of Medicine, 300 Pasteur Drive, Stanford, CA 94305, USA (office). *Telephone:* (650) 723-4000 (office). *E-mail:* philip.pizzo@stanford.edu (office). *Website:* med.stanford.edu (office).

PLACIDO, Michele; Italian actor and director; b. 19 May 1946, Ascoli Satriano, Foggia; m. Simonetta Stefanelli (divorced); three c.; two c. with other pnrs; ed Centro Sperimentale di Cinematografia, Acad. of Dramatic Arts, Rome; made acting debut 1969, has appeared in more than 70 films and numerous tv series; has worked with dirs including Luigi Comencini, Mario Monicelli, Salvatore Samperi, Damiano Damiani, Francesco Rosi, Walerian Borowczyk, Marco Bellocchio, Carlo Lizzani; made directorial debut 1989; jury mem. Venice Film Festival 2006; Bambi Award 1989, Actor's Mission Award, Art Film Festival 1999. *Television:* actor: Il Picciotto 1973, Moses the Lawgiver 1975, Il Passo falso 1983, La Piovra 1983, La Piovra 2 1985, La Piovra 3 1987, La Piovra 4 1989, Scoop 1991, Drug Wars: The Cocaine Cartel 1992, Racket (also story) 1997, La Missione (also writer) 1998, Padre Pio - Tra cielo e terra 2000, Il Sequestro Soffiantini 2002, Un Papà quasi perfetto 2003, Soraya 2003, Il Grande Torino 2004, Karol, un Papa rimasto uomo 2006, Assunta Spina 2006, L'Ultimo padrino 2007. *Films:* actor: Teresa la ladra 1972, Il Caso Pisciotta 1972, La Mano nera - prima della mafia, più della mafia 1973, Mia moglie, un corpo per l'amore 1973, Mio Dio come sono caduta in basso! 1974, Processo per direttissima 1974, Romanzo popolare 1974, Peccati in famiglia 1975, Orlando Furioso movie, 1975, L'Agnese va a morire 1976, La Orca 1976, Divina creatura 1976, Marcia trionfale (Acting Award, David di Donatello Awards, Best Actor, Silver Ribbon Awards) 1976, Corleone 1977, Fontamara 1977, Kleinhoff Hotel 1977, La Ragazza dal pigiama giallo 1977, Casotto 1977, Un Uomo in ginocchio 1978, Io sono mia 1978, Letti selvaggi 1979, Il Prato 1979, Sabato, domenica e venerdì 1979, Ernesto (Best Actor, Berlin Int. Film Festival) 1979, Lulu 1980, Salto nel vuoto 1980, Cargo film, 1981, Les Ailes de la colombe 1981, Tre fratelli 1981, Sciopèn 1982, Ars amandi 1983, Les Amants terribles 1984, Pizza Connection (Best Actor, Silver Ribbon Awards) 1985, Grandi magazzini 1986, Notte d'estate con profilo greco, occhi a mandorla e odore di basilico 1986, Ti presento un'amica 1987, Via Paradiso 1988, Big Business 1988, Come sono buoni i bianchi 1988, Mery per sempre 1989, Afganskiy izlom 1990, Le Amiche del cuore 1992, Uomo di rispetto 1992, Quattro bravi ragazzi 1993, Padre e figlio 1994, Poliziotti 1994, Lamerica 1994, Un Eroe borghese 1995, La Lupa 1996, Le Plaisir 1998, Del perduto amore (FEDIC Award, Venice Film Festival) 1998, Terra bruciata 1999, Un Uomo perbene 1999, La Balia 1999, Panni sporchi 1999, Liberate i pesci! 2000, Tra due mondi 2001, Searching for Paradise 2002, Il Posto dell'anima 2003, L'Odore del sangue 2004, L'Amore ritorna 2004, Romanzo criminale 2005, Arrivederci amore, ciao 2006, Commediasexi 2006, Le Rose del deserto 2006, La Sconosciuta 2006, Smutek paní Snajdrové 2006, Il Caimano 2006, 2061: Un anno eccezionale 2007, Piano, solo 2007, SoloMetro 2007, Estrenando sueños 2007, Liola 2007; director: Pummarò (writer/dir) 1989, Le Amiche del cuore (writer/dir) 1992, Un Eroe borghese (Special Award, David di Donatello Awards) 1995, Del perduto amore (writer/dir) 1998, Un Altro mondo è possibile 2001, Un Viaggio chiamato amore (writer/dir) 2002, Ovunque sei (writer/dir) 2004, Romanzo criminale (co-writer/dir) (Best Screenplay, David di Donatello Awards (jtly) 2006, Best Director, Silver Ribbon Awards 2006) 2005; writer: L'Uomo giusto (producer and writer) 2007. *Address:* c/o Cattleya S.p.A., Via della Frezza, 59, 00186 Rome, Italy (office). *E-mail:* info@cattleya.it (office).

PLANT OF HIGHFIELD, Baron (Life Peer), cr. 1991, of Weelsby in the County of Humberside; **Raymond Plant,** PhD, DLitt; British academic and politician; *Professor of Jurisprudence, King's College London;* b. 19 March 1945, Grimsby; s. of Stanley Plant and Marjorie Plant; m. Katherine Dixon 1967; three s.; ed Havelock School, Grimsby, King's Coll. London and Univ. of Hull; Lecturer, then Sr Lecturer in Philosophy, Univ. of Manchester 1967–79; Prof. of Politics, Univ. of Southampton 1979–94, Pro-Chancellor 1996–2002, Prof. of European Political Thought 2000–02; Prof. of Jurisprudence, King's Coll. London 2001–; Lay Canon,

Winchester Cathedral 2008–; Master, St Catherine's Coll. Oxford 1994–2000; Pres. Nat. Council of Voluntary Orgs 1997–2002, Acad. of Learned Socs in the Social Sciences; Hon. Fellow, Harris Manchester Coll., Oxford, St Catherine's Coll., Oxford, Univ. of Cardiff; Hon. DLitt (Hull, London Guildhall), Hon. DUniv (York), (Winchester); Stanton Lecturer, Univ. of Cambridge 1989–91, Sarum Lecturer, Univ. of Oxford 1991, Boutwood Lecturer, Univ. of Cambridge 2006, Bampton Lecturer, Univ. of Oxford. *Publications:* Hegel 1973, Community and Ideology 1974, Political Philosophy and Social Welfare 1981, Philosophy, Politics and Citizenship 1984, Conservative Capitalism 1989, Modern Political Thought 1991, Democracy, Representation and Elections 1992, Hegel on Religion 1997, Politics, Theology and History 2000, The Neo-Liberal State 2009. *Leisure interests:* music, opera, politics. *Address:* 6 Woodview Close, Bassett, Southampton, SO16 3PZ, England (home). *Telephone:* (20) 7848-2448 (office); (23) 8076-9529 (home). *E-mail:* raymond.plant@kcl.ac.uk (office).

PLANTIN, Marcus; British broadcasting executive; b. 23 Oct. 1945; s. of Charles P. Plantin and Vera H. Plantin; m. 1980; two s.; ed Surbiton Co. Grammar School, Guildford School of Acting; Producer, BBC TV 1978–84; joined London Weekend TV (LWT), Head Light Entertainment 1985–87, Controller of Entertainment 1987–90, Dir of Programmes 1990–92, 1997, Dir London Weekend Productions and LWT Holdings 1990–92; Network Dir ITV 1992–97, Man. ITV Network Centre 1995–97; Dir of Programmes LWT Productions 1998–2000, LWT/United Productions 2000–01; Dir of Int. Entertainment Formats and Production, Granada TV 2000–01, Dir of Entertainment Content 2001–02; Chief Exec. September Films Ltd 2003–05. *Leisure interests:* gardening, swimming, travel. *Address:* c/o September Films Ltd, Glen House, 22 Glenthorne Road, London, W6 0NG, England. *E-mail:* purdenhoe@msn.com; september@septemberfilms.com.

PLANTUREUX, Jean-Henri, (PLANTU); French artist, cartoonist, journalist and editor; *Editorial Cartoonist, Le Monde, L'Express;* b. (Jean-Henri Plantureux), 23 March 1951, Paris; s. of Henri Plantureux and Renée Seignardie; m. Chantal Meyer 1971; four c.; ed Baccalaureate, Lycée Henri IV, Paris, Saint-Luc Art School, Brussels, Belgium; political cartoonist, Le Monde 1972–, L'Express 1991–; caricaturist, Droit de réponse (TV show) 1981–87; special edition of Le Monde to mark 40 years of collaboration and 19,000 cartoons published, Oct. 2012; Dr hc (Liège) 2013; Mumm Foundation Prize 1988, Black Humour Award 1989, Grand Prix de l'Humour noir Granville 1989, Prix du Festival du Scoop (film on Yasser Arafat) 1991, Int. Gat Perich Caricature Award 1996, UN Political Cartoon Award 2006, Second Prize, UN Best Caricature of the Year 2007, Markiezenaward 2013. *Publications include:* Pauvres chéris 1978, La Démocratie? Parlons-en 1979, Les Cours de caoutchouc sont trop élastiques 1982, C'est le goulag 1983, Pas nette, la planète! 1984, Politic-look 1984, Bonne année pour tous 1985, Ça manque de femmes 1986, Wolfgang, tu feras informatique 1988, Ouverture en bémol 1988, Des fourmis dans les jambes 1989, C'est la lutte finale 1990, Reproche-Orient 1991, Le Président Hip-Hop! 1991, Le Douanier se fait la malle 1992, Ici Maastricht, les Européens parlent aux Européens 1992, Cohabitation à l'Eau de Rose 1993, Le Pire est derrière nous! 1994, Le Petit Mitterrand Illustré 1995, Le Petit Chirac et le Petit Balladur Illustrés 1995, Le Petit Raciste Illustré 1995, Le Petit Communiste Illustré 1995, Le Petit Socialiste Illustré 95, Magic Chirac 1995, Les Années vaches folles 1996, La France dopée 1998, Le Petit Juge Illustré 1999, L'Année PLANTU 1999, Ils pourraient dire merci! 2004, À quoi ça rime 2005, Je ne dois pas dessiner 2006, La Présidentielle 2007, Racaille Le Rouge 2007, Un Boulevard pour Sarko 2008, Parmis de croquer – Un tour du monde du dessin de presse 2008, Petite histoire de la chute du communisme 2008, Sarko Le Best Of 2009, Almaniak 2010, Bas les masques 2009, Tête de Gondole 2010, Les conseils de tonton DSK 2011, On a marché sur les urnes - Présidentielle 2012, Sarko, sors de ce corps !!, 2013. *Address:* Le Monde, 80 blvd Auguste Blanqui, 75707 Paris Cedex 13, France (office). *Telephone:* 1-57-28-25-30 (office). *Fax:* 1-57-28-21-69 (office). *E-mail:* plantu@lemonde.fr (office). *Website:* www.plantu.net (home).

PLASSAT, Georges; French business executive; *Chairman and CEO, Carrefour Group;* b. 1949; ed Ecole hôtelière, Lausanne, Switzerland, Cornell Univ., USA; with Casino Group 1983–97, Marketing Dir and subsequently Chief Exec. of Restaurant Div. 1988–90, Chief Exec. of Casino France 1990–92, Man. Dir 1992–94, Vice-Pres. Man. Bd 1994–96, Chair. Man. Bd Casino Group 1996–97; Exec. Dir for Spain, Carrefour Group and Chief Exec. Pryca 1997–99, COO Carrefour Group April–May 2012, Chair. and CEO May 2012–; Chair. Man. Bd Vivarte Group (fmrly Groupe André) 2000–04, Chair. and CEO 2004–12. *Address:* Groupe Carrefour, 33 avenue Émile Zola, TSA 55 555, 92649 Boulogne-Billancourt Cedex, France (office). *Telephone:* 1-41-04-26-00 (office). *Fax:* 1-41-04-26-01 (office). *E-mail:* info@carrefour.com (office). *Website:* www.carrefour.com (office).

PLASSNIK, Ursula, DrIur; Austrian politician; b. 23 May 1956, Klagenfurt; m. 1st Georg Posch (divorced); m. 2nd Gérard Stoudmann; ed Vienna Univ., Coll. d'Europe, Bruges, Belgium; with Ministry of Foreign Affairs, in int. law office and directorates for security policy and CSCE 1981–84; CSCE Del. to Madrid Follow-up Meeting 1981–83, Vienna 1986–87; at Embassy, Berne 1984–86; Rep. Council of Europe 1987–90; at Directorate Gen. for Econ. Policy and EU Coordination, later head of Directorate for Gen. Affairs Council and the European Council 1994–97; at Fed. Chancellery, Cabinet Chief of Dr Wolfgang Schüssel when Fed. Vice Chancellor 1997–2000, when Chancellor 2000–04; Amb. to Switzerland Jan.–Oct. 2004; Minister for Foreign Affairs 2004–08; mem. Austrian People's Party; Premio Mediterraneo Diplomazia, Fondazione Mediterraneo 2010. *Address:* Austrian People's Party, Lichtenfelsgasse 7, 1010 Vienna, Austria (office). *Telephone:* (1) 401-26-0 (office). *Fax:* (1) 401-26-10-9 (office). *E-mail:* email@oevp.at (office). *Website:* www.oevp.at (office).

PLASTERK, Ronald Hans Anton, PhD; Dutch academic and politician; *Minister of the Interior and Kingdom Relations;* b. 12 April 1957, The Hague; ed Univ. of Leiden, California Inst. of Tech.; Head of Research Group, Netherlands Cancer Inst., Antoni van Leeuwenhoek Hospital, Amsterdam 1987–2000; Chair in Molecular Biology, VU Univ. Amsterdam 1993–97; Prof. of Molecular Genetics, Univ. of Amsterdam 1997–2000; Prof. of Developmental Genetics, Univ. of Utrecht 2000–07; Dir Hubrecht Lab., Netherlands Inst. for Developmental Biology 2000–07; Minister of Educ., Culture and Science 2007–10, Minister of the Interior and Kingdom Relations 2012–; mem. European Molecular Biology Org., Bd of Govs Wellcome Trust, Standing Cttee on Genetics, Dutch Health Council; mem. Royal Netherlands Acad. of Arts and Sciences, Royal Dutch Soc. of Sciences and

Humanities; mem. Labour Party (PvdA). *Address:* Ministry of the Interior and Kingdom Relations, Schedeldoekshaven 200, POB 20011, 2500 EA The Hague, The Netherlands (office). *Telephone:* (70) 4266426. *Fax:* (70) 3639153. *Website:* www.rijksoverheid.nl/ministeries/bzk.

PLASTOW, Sir David Arnold Stuart, Kt, CIMgt, FBIM, FRSA; British business executive; b. 9 May 1932, Grimsby, Lincs., England; s. of James Stuart Plastow and Marie Plastow; m. Barbara Ann May 1954; one s. one d.; ed Culford School, Bury St Edmunds; apprenticed to Vauxhall Motors Ltd 1950; joined Rolls-Royce Ltd, Motor Car Div. Crewe 1958, Marketing Dir Motor Car Div. 1967–71, Man. Dir 1971–72; Man. Dir Rolls-Royce Motors Ltd 1972–74, Group Man. Dir 1974–80; Regional Dir Lloyds Bank 1974–76; Dir Vickers Ltd 1975–92, Man. Dir 1980–86, Chief Exec. 1980–92, Chair. 1987–92; Chair. Inchape PLC 1992–95; Dir GKN Ltd 1978–84, Legal & General 1985–87, Guinness PLC 1986–94 (Deputy Chair. 1987–89, Jt Deputy Chair. 1989–94), Tenneco Automotive Inc. 1985–92, 1996–, F.T. Everard & Sons Ltd 1991–2001, Vinters Engineering Ltd 1992, Genome Research Ltd 1993–96, Lloyds Bank Trustee Services Ltd 1995, Kent Messenger Ltd 2000–03, Norman Court School Ltd 2008–11; Deputy Chair. (non-exec.) TSB Group PLC 1991–95; Dir (non-exec.) Cable and Wireless PLC 1991–93, Lloyds TSB 1996–99; Gov. (non-exec.) BUPA 1990–95 (Deputy Chair. 1992–95); Pres. Soc. of Motor Mfrs and Traders Ltd 1976–78, Deputy Pres. 1978–80; Pres. Motor Industry Research Asscn 1978–81; Vice-Pres. Inst. of Motor Industry 1974–82; Chair. Grand Council, Motor and Cycle Trades Benevolent Fund 1976–78; mem. Eng Council 1981–83, Council CBI, Council, Manchester Business School, Court of Manchester Univ., Council, Regular Forces Employment Asscn, Council, Industrial Soc., Chair. 1983–87, British Overseas Trade Bd 1980–83, British North American Cttee; Chair. MRC 1994–98; Chancellor Univ. of Luton (now Univ. of Bedfordshire) from 1993; Chair. of Govs, Culford School, Bury St Edmunds from 1979; Trustee, Royal Opera House Trust 1992–93 (Chair. 1992–93); Patron, Coll. of Aeronautical and Automobile Eng 1972–79; Liveryman, Worshipful Co. of Coachmakers and Coach Harness Makers; Hon. DSc (Cranfield Inst. of Tech.) 1978; Young Businessman of the Year Award (The Guardian) 1976. *Leisure interests:* golf, music. *Address:* c/o Office of the Chancellor, University of Bedfordshire, University Square, Luton, Beds., LU1 3JU, England.

PLATINI, Michel François; French sports administrator, football coach, broadcaster and fmr footballer; *President, Union of European Football Associations (UEFA);* b. 21 June 1955, Joeuf; s. of Aldo Platini and Anna Pillenelli; m. Christele Bigoni 1977; one s. one d.; attacking midfielder; youth player, AS Joeuf 1966–72; professional footballer, AS Nancy-Lorraine 1972–79 (Ligue 2 Champions 1975, won Coupe de France 1978), AS St-Etienne 1979–82 (Ligue 1 Champions 1981), Juventus, Turin, Italy 1982–87 (scored 68 goals in 147 games, won Coppa Italia 1983, European Cup Winners' Cup Winner 1984, UEFA Super Cup Winner 1984, Serie A 1984, 1986, European Cup 1985, Intercontinental Cup 1985); player with French nat. team 1976–87 (winners European Championship 1984, Artemio Franqui Trophy 1985), Nat. Team Coach 1988–92; co-presenter, ed. and consultant, French TV 1985–88, consultant 1993–; Founder and Pres. Michel Platini Foundation 1987–; Jt Pres. French 1998 World Cup Organizng Cttee; Vice-Pres. French Football Fed.; Adviser to Pres. FIFA; mem. Exec. Cttee Union of European Football Asscns (UEFA) 2002–, Pres. 2007–; mem. Exec. Cttee FIFA, Vice-Pres. 2007–; mem. Laureus World Sports Acad.; Chevalier, Légion d'honneur 1985, Officier 1988; Officier, Ordre nat. du Mérite; France Football French Player of the Year 1976, 1977, L'Équipe French Champion of Champions 1977, selected in FIFA XI to play Argentina 1979, selected in Europe team to face FIFA XI in charity match for UNICEF 1982, Capocannoniere (top scorer) in Italian championship (16 goals) 1983, (20 goals) 1984, (18 goals) 1985, Coppa Super Clubs Payer of the Tounament 1983, Chevron Award (best goal per game ratio in Italian league) 1983, Ballon d'Or (European Footballer of the Year) 1983, 1984, Onze d'Or 1983, 1984, European Championship Payer of the Tournament 1984, European Championship top goal-scorer (nine goals) 1984, Guerin Sportivo magazine's Player of the Italian Championship 1984, L'Equipe French Champion of Champions 1984, World Soccer Player of the Year 1984, 1985, Ballon d'Or (European Footballer of the Year) 1983, 1984, 1985, French Player of the Century 1984, Chevron Award (best goal per game ratio in Italian league) 1985, European Cup top scorer (seven goals) 1985, Intercontinental Cup Man of the Match 1985, Man of the Match, English Football League Centenary Classic Match 1987, El País European Coach of the Year 1991, World Soccer Manager of the Year 1991, lighter of the Olympic Flame with François-Cyrille Grange, Winter Olympics, Albertville, France 1992, Artemio Franchi Prize 2003, named in FIFA 100 2004, inducted into the English Football Hall of Fame and voted All-Time Great European Footballer (only person outside the English game to be honoured by the Museum) 2008. *Publication:* Ma vie comme un match 1987. *Address:* UEFA, Route de Genève 46, Case Postale, 1260 Nyon 2, Switzerland (office). *Telephone:* (848) 042727 (office). *Fax:* (848) 012727 (office). *E-mail:* info@uefa.com (office). *Website:* www.uefa.com (office).

PLATONOV, Vladimir Mikhailovich, CandJurSc; Russian politician; b. 24 Dec. 1954, Moscow; m.; one s. one d.; ed Lumumba Univ. of Peoples' Friendship; worked in machine-construction factory 1972–75; investigator Prosecutor's Office, Deputy Prosecutor Moskvoretsky Dist of Moscow 1983–91; pvt. law practice, Exec. Dir Avtum Co. 1991–94; mem. Moscow City Duma 1993, Chair. (Speaker) 1994–; mem. Party Block Choice of Russia; mem. Russian Council of Fed. 1996–; Chair. Cttee on Constitutional Law Feb. 1996–. *Address:* Moscow City Duma, Petrovka str. 22, 103051 Moscow, Russia (office). *Telephone:* (4095) 923-50-80 (office). *Fax:* (495) 753-71-31 (office). *E-mail:* d29@duma.munic.ru (office).

PLATONOV, Vladimir Petrovich, DSc; Belarusian mathematician and academic; b. 1 Dec. 1939, Staiki, Byelorussian SSR; s. of Petr Platonov and Anna Platonova; m. Valentina Platonova 1974; two d.; ed Byelorussian State University; Asst Prof. Byelorussian State Univ. 1963, Prof. 1968, Head of Algebra Dept 1967–71; corresp. mem. Acad. of Sciences of Byelorussian SSR (now Belarus) 1969, mem. 1972 (Pres. 1987–92); Head Algebra Dept, Inst. of Math. 1971–93, Dir 1977–92, Lecturer; mem. Inst. for Advanced Studies, Princeton, NJ 1991–92; Prof., Univ. of Mich., USA 1993, Univ. of Bielefeld 1994, Univ. of Waterloo, Canada 1995–2001; mem. USSR (now Russian) Acad. of Sciences 1987, Belarus Acad. for Educ. 1995, New York Acad. of Sciences 1995; Foreign mem. Indian Nat. Science Acad.; Hon. mem. Chinese-Henan Acad. of Sciences; People's Deputy of the USSR 1989–91; Lenin Prize 1978, Humboldt Prize 1993. *Publications include:* Algebraic groups and number theory 1991, Finite-dimensional division algebras 1992. *Leisure interest:* literature. *Address:* c/o National Academy of Sciences of Belarus, 66 Franziska Skaryny Praspekt, Minsk 220072, Belarus.

PLATT, Nicholas, Sr, BA, MA; American diplomatist and educational administrator; *President Emeritus, Asia Society;* b. 10 March 1936, New York, NY; s. of Geoffrey Platt; m. Sheila Maynard; three s.; ed Harvard Coll. and Johns Hopkins Univ. School of Advanced Int. Studies; Chinese language student, Taiwan 1963; Political Officer, Hong Kong 1964–68, Beijing 1973–74, Tokyo 1974–77; staff mem. President Nixon's Del. to China 1972, later mem. US Liaison Office, Beijing; Dir for Japanese Affairs, Dept of State 1977–78; Nat. Security Council staff mem. specializing in Asian Affairs 1978–79; Deputy Asst Sec. for Defense 1980–81; Acting Asst Sec. of State for UN Affairs 1981–82; Amb. to Zambia 1982–84, to the Philippines 1987–91, to Pakistan 1991–92; Pres. Asia Soc. 1992–2004, Pres. Emer. 2004–; Special Asst to Sec. of State and Exec. Sec., Dept of State 1985–87; Chair. US-China Educ. Trust Advisory Bd; mem. Bd of Dirs Fiduciary Trust International; mem. New York Council on Foreign Relations, Friends of China Heritage Fund Ltd. *Publication:* China Boys: How U.S. Relations with the PRC Began and Grew. A Personal Memoir 2010. *Address:* 131 East 69th Street, New York, NY 10021, USA. *Telephone:* (212) 772-0724. *Fax:* (212) 772-0732. *E-mail:* info@asiasociety.org; nplatt@attglobal.net.

PLATT, Stephen (Steve), BSc (Econ); British journalist, writer and editor; b. 29 Sept. 1954, Stoke-on-Trent, Staffs., England; s. of Kenneth Platt and Joyce Pritchard; one d. with Diane Louise Paice; ed Longton High School, Stoke On Trent, Wade Deacon School, Widnes and London School of Econs; teacher, Moss Brook Special School, Widnes 1972–73; Dir Self Help Housing Resource Library, Polytechnic of N London 1977–80; co-ordinator, Islington Community Housing 1980–83; freelance writer and journalist 1983–; News Ed., subsequently Acting Ed. New Society 1986–88; Ed. Midweek 1988–89, Enjoying the Countryside 1988–91; Ed. New Statesman and Society 1991–96; Contributing Ed. Channel 4 TV 1996–; Website and Contributing Ed., Time Team 1999–2010 (BAFTA Award for Interactive Entertainment 2002); Dispatches Website Ed. 1999–2010; freelance writer, ed. and consultant 1996–; UKGLO Award for Outstanding Achievement 1999. *Leisure interests:* football, walking, countryside, gardening, breeding frogs, Paddington Bear, archaeology, ancient history, mountains and music. *Address:* 46 Tufnell Park Road, London, N7 0DT, England. *Telephone:* (20) 7263-4185. *E-mail:* mail@steveplatt.net. *Website:* www.steveplatt.net.

PLATT, Trevor, PhD, FRS, FRSC; British/Canadian oceanographer; *Professorial Fellow and Executive Director, Partnership for Observation for the Global Oceans Secretariat, Plymouth Marine Laboratory;* b. 12 Aug. 1942, Salford, England; s. of John Platt and Lily Platt; m. Shubha Sathyendranath 1988; ed Nottingham, Toronto and Dalhousie Univs; research scientist, Bedford Inst. of Oceanography, Canada 1965–72, Head of Biological Oceanography 1972–2008; mem. Professorial Fellow and Exec. Dir Partnership for Observation for the Global Oceans Secr., Plymouth Marine Lab., UK 2008–; Chair. Int. Ocean-Colow Co-ordinating Group 1996–, Jt Global Ocean Flux Study 1991–93; Huntsman Medal 1992 Hutchinson Medal, Rosenstiel Medal, Plymouth Marine Medal 1999, Timothy R. Parsons Award 2006. *Publications:* numerous papers in learned journals. *Leisure interests:* cycling, fly-fishing, languages. *Address:* Plymouth Marine Laboratory, Prospect Place, The Hoe, Plymouth, PL1 3DH, England (office). *Telephone:* (1752) 633164 (office). *Fax:* (1752) 633101 (office). *E-mail:* treatt@pml.ac.uk (office). *Website:* rsg .pml.ac.uk (office).

PLATTER, Günther; Austrian politician; *Governor of Tyrol;* m.; two c.; Minister of Defence 2003–07, of the Interior 2007–08; Gov. of Tyrol 2008–; mem. ÖVP (Austrian People's Party). *Address:* Governor of Tyrol, Eduard-Wallnöfer-Platz 3, 6020 Innsbruck, Tyrol, Austria (office). *Telephone:* (5) 125-08-20-02 (office). *Fax:* (5) 125-08-20-05 (office). *E-mail:* buero.lh.platter@tirol.gv.at (office). *Website:* www .tirol.gv.at (office).

PLATTNER, Hasso; German computer industry executive; *Chairman of the Supervisory Board, SAP AG;* b. 21 Jan. 1944, Berlin; m.; two c.; ed Univ. of Karlsruhe; consultant, IBM 1968–72; Co-founder SAP AG 1972, Chair. SAP America, CEO SAP Markets, Co-Chair. and CEO –2003, Chair. Supervisory Bd 2003–; f. HassoPlattnerVentures (HPV), Potsdam 2005, Hasso Plattner Inst. of Design, Stanford Univ., USA 2005, HPV Africa 2009; investor in San Jose Sports & Entertainment Enterprises (owns San Jose Sharks, HP Pavilion at San Jose and other related properties); bought out two of the partners in SJS&E and began serving as the Sharks' Rep. on Nat. Hockey League's Bd Govs 2013; Hon. Prof., Univ. of Saarbrücken. *Leisure interests:* golf, sailing. *Address:* SAP AG, Dietmar-Hopp-Allee 16, 69190 Walldorf, Germany (office). *Telephone:* (6227) 747474 (office). *Fax:* (6227) 757575 (office). *E-mail:* info@sap.com (office). *Website:* www.sap.com (office).

PLAVINSKY, Dmitri; Russian artist; b. 28 April 1937, Moscow; m. Maria Plavinskaya; three d.; ed Moscow Regional Art Coll.; painter and printmaker. *Publication:* Dmitri Plavinsky 2000. *Address:* c/o Mimi Ferzt Gallery, 81 Greene Street, New York, NY 10012; 370 Fort Washington Avenue #507, New York, NY 10033, USA (office); Arbat str. 51, korp. 2, Apt 97, 121002 Moscow, Russia. *Telephone:* (212) 928-3260; (495) 241-32-29 (Moscow). *E-mail:* plavinsky@aol.com (home).

PLAYER, Gary Jim; South African professional golfer; b. 1 Nov. 1935, Johannesburg; s. of Francis Harry Audley Player and of the late Muriel Marie Ferguson; m. Vivienne Verwey 1957; two s. four d.; turned professional 1953; first overseas player for 45 years to win US Open Championship 1965; Winner, British Open Championship 1959, 1968, 1974; Piccadilly World Match Play Champion 1965, 1966, 1968, 1971, 1973; US Open Champion 1965; US Masters Champion 1961, 1974, 1978; US Professional Golf Asscn Champion 1962, 1972; Winner, South African Open 13 times; South African PGA Champion 1959, 1960, 1969, 1979, 1982; Winner, Australian Open 7 times; Quadel Sr Classic Champion 1985; third player ever to win all four major world professional titles; holds world record for lowest 18-hole score in any Open Championship (59 in the Brazilian Open 1974); Sr Tour victories include: Sr British Open 1988, 1990, 1997, Sr PGA Champion 1986, 1988, 1990, Long Island Sr Classic, Sr Skins Game 2000; Capt. Rest of the World Team, Pres.'s Cup 2003, 2005; f. Gary Player Group, Gary Player Foundation (rural educ.); golf course designer (over 200 projects world-wide);

breeds thoroughbred racehorses; Order of Ikhamanga; Dr hc (Ulster) 1997, (Dundee) 1999; South African Sportsman of the Century 1989, Hilton Hotel Lifetime Achievement Award 1995, Laureus Lifetime Achievement Award 2003, Asia Pacific Golf Humanitarian Award 2009, Canada Lifetime Achievement Award 2009, Asia Pacific Hall of Fame 2010. *Publications include:* Gary Player: The Autobiography 1991, The Golfer's Guide to the Meaning of Life 2001. *Leisure interests:* breeding thoroughbred racehorses, farming, educ., family, health, fitness. *Address:* Blair Atholl Farm, Lanseria, Johannesburg (office); Gary Player Stud, POB 189, Colesberg 9795, South Africa (office); POB 785629, Sandton 2146. *Telephone:* (11) 8833333 (office); (11) 6592800 (home). *Fax:* (11) 8834444 (office). *E-mail:* info@garyplayer.co.za (office). *Website:* www.garyplayer.co.za (office).

PLÉAH, Natie; Malian politician; b. 1953, Moutigué, Ké-Macina Circle; m.; seven c.; ed secondary school in Sévaré, Markala Coll., school in Badalabougou, Ecole Nationale d'Admin, Paris, France; began serving Gov.-Gen. Sikasso 1976, held several posts as an adviser, including Second Deputy Commdr Ansongo Circle, Deputy Commdr Koulikoro then Yanfolila Circles, Commdr Circle then Koulikoro Timbuktu, Admin. Affairs Advisor to Gov. of Timbuktu, Advisor for Admin. Affairs in Ségou, Chief of Staff to Gov. of Mopti and High Commr of Kayes; Acting High Commr First Econ. Region 2002–04, Gov. of Kayes 2004–05; Gov. Dist of Bamako 2005; Minister of Youth and Sports 2005–07, of the Environment and Sanitation May 2007, of Defence and Veterans 2007–12. *Leisure interests:* reading and agricultural activities. *Address:* c/o Ministry of Defence and Veterans, route de Koulouba, BP 2083, Bamako, Mali (office).

PLEISTER, Christopher, Dr rer. pol; German banker; b. 15 May 1948, Hamburg; m.; three s.; ed Ludwig-Maximilians Univ., Munich; with Landesgenossenschaftsbank AG, Hanover 1977–81, Hallbaum, Maier & Co. Landkreditbank AG, Hanover 1981–84; Exec. Man. Norddeutsche Genossenschaftsbank AG 1984, mem. Bd of Man. 1985–90; mem. Bd of Man. DG Bank (now DZ Bank), Frankfurt-am-Main 1990–99, Chair. Supervisory Bd DZ Bank 2001–08; Chair. Bundesverband der Deutschen Volksbanken und Raiffeisenbanken (BVR—Fed. Asscn of German Co-operative Banks) 2000–08; Pres. European Asscn of Cooperative Banks (EACB) 2006–; mem. Man. Cttee Financial Market Stabilization Fund (SoFFin) 2009–. *Address:* Financial Market Stabilization Fund (SoFFin), Taunusanlage 6, 60329 Frankfurt (office). *Telephone:* (69) 2388-3000 (office). *Fax:* (69) 9566-509090 (office). *E-mail:* info@soffin.de (office). *Website:* www.soffin.de (office).

PLENDERLEITH, Ian, CBE, MA, MBA, MSI, FCT; British central banker and economist; *Deputy Governor, South African Reserve Bank;* b. 27 Sept. 1943, York; s. of Raymond William Plenderleith and Louise Helen Plenderleith (née Martin); m. Kristina Mary Bentley; one s. two d.; ed King Edward's School, Birmingham, Christ Church, Oxford, Columbia Business School, New York; joined Bank of England 1965, seconded to IMF, Washington, DC 1972–74, Pvt. Sec. to Gov. Bank of England 1976–79; Alt. Dir EIB 1980–86, Head Gilt-Edged Div. 1982–90, Asst Dir 1986–90, Sr Broker to Commrs for Reduction of Nat. Debt 1989–2002, Assoc. Dir 1990–94; Dir Bank of England Nominees Ltd 1994–2002, Exec. Dir Bank of England and mem. Monetary Policy Cttee 1994–2002; Alt. Dir BIS 1994–2002; Dir London Stock Exchange (fmrly mem. Stock Exchange Council) 1989–2001 (Deputy Chair. 1996), Chair. Stock Borrowing and Lending Cttee 1990–95; Chair. G-10 Gold and Foreign Exchange Cttee 1995–2001; Co-Chair. Govt Borrowers' Forum 1991–94; Chair. Sterling Money Markets Liaison Group 1999–2002; Chair. Corpn for Public Deposits 2003–; Deputy Gov. and mem. Monetary Policy Cttee, South African Reserve Bank 2003–; mem. Editorial Cttee OECD Study on Debt Man. 1990–93, Legal Risk Review Cttee 1991–92, Financial Law Panel 1992–94, G-10 Cttee on Global Financial System 1994–2002; mem. Advisory Bd Inst. of Archaeology Devt Trust, Univ. Coll. London 1987–96, Bd of Overseers Columbia Business School 1991–, Fund-raising Planning Group, St Bartholomew's Hosp. 1992–94, Council, British Museum Friends 1993–99, 2000–03, Fund-raising Planning Cttee St Bartholomew's and The London Hosps 1998–2003, Advisory Bd The Actors Centre 2002–, Devt Council Shakespeare's Globe 2002–, Advisory Bd London Capital Club 2002–; Dir City Arts Trust 1997–2003; Fellow, Asscn of Corp. Treasurers; mem. Securities Inst.; Liveryman Innholders' Co. 1977–; Sec. Tillington Cricket Club 1983–2003; Beta Gamma Sigma Medal 1971. *Leisure interests:* archaeology, theatre, cricket, long-distance walking. *Address:* South African Reserve Bank, POB 427, Pretoria 0001 (office); Suite #686, Private Bag X4, Menlo Park, Pretoria 0102, South Africa (home); Goldneys, River, Petworth, W Sussex, GU28 9AU, England. *Telephone:* (12) 313-3139 (office); (12) 346-8179 (home). *Fax:* (12) 313-4767 (office); (12) 346-8179 (home). *E-mail:* ian .plenderleith@resbank.co.za (office); ianplenderleith@yahoo.co.uk (home). *Website:* www.reservebank.co.za (office).

PLENEL, Edwy; French journalist; b. 31 Aug. 1952, Nantes; s. of Alain Plenel and Michèle Bertreux; m. Nicole Lapierre; one d.; ed Institut d'études politiques, Paris; journalist, Rouge 1976–78, Matin de Paris 1980; joined Le Monde 1980, Educ. Ed. 1980–82, Legal columnist 1982–90, Reporter 1991, Head Legal Dept 1992–94, Chief Ed. 1994–95, Asst Editorial Dir 1995–96, Ed. 1996–2000, Ed.-in-Chief 2000–05 (resgnd); f. Mediapart 2008, currently Ed.-in-Chief. *Publications include:* L'Effet Le Pen 1984, La République inachevée: l'État et l'école en France 1985, Mourir à Ouvéa: le tournant calédonien 1988, Voyage avec Colomb 1991, La République menacée: dix ans d'effet Le Pen 1992, La Part d'ombre 1992, Un temps de chien 1994, Les Mots volés 1997, L'Epreuve 1999, Secrets de jeunesse 2001, La Découverte du monde 2002, Procès 2006. *Website:* www.mediapart.fr; blogs .mediapart.fr/blog/edwy-plenel.

PLEŞCA, Valeriu; Moldovan politician, business executive and economist; b. 8 Nov. 1958, Dumitreni, Floresti Dist; m.; one s. one d.; ed State Univ. of Moldova, Acad. of Econ. Studies; Adviser, Ministry of Social Assistance 1983–86, Office of the Chief Prosecutor 1986–91; Head of Gloria V&A Co. 1990–; mem. Parl. 1998– (ind. 2003–), fmr Deputy Chair. Comm. for Rules and Immunities; Minister of Defence 2004–05, 2005–07; Serghei Radonejskii Award 2006. *Publications include:* numerous articles on defence and security policy. *Leisure interests include:* tennis, skiing, hunting. *Address:* c/o Ministry of Defence, 2021 Chişinău şos. Hîncesti 84, Moldova (office).

PLESHAKOVA, Olga Alexandrovna, CandSci (Eng); Russian airline industry executive; *General Director, Chairperson of the Management Board and CEO,*

Transaero Airlines; b. 1966; d. of T. G. Anodina; m. Alexander Petrovich Pleshakov; ed Moscow Aviation Inst.; currently Gen. Dir, Chair. Man. Bd and CEO Transaero Airlines; Order of the Russian Orthodox Church 2011; CIS Business Leader 2011, Award of the Imperial Orthodox Palestine Soc. 2011, ranked by Fortune magazine amongst the 50 Most Powerful Women in Business outside the US (49th) 2012. *Address:* OJSC Transaero Airlines, 119180 Moscow, 47 Bolshaya Polyanka Street, Building 1, Russia (office). *Telephone:* (495) 788-8080 (office). *E-mail:* info@transaero.com (office). *Website:* www.transaero.com (office).

PLESSNER, Yakir, BS, MS, PhD; Israeli economist and academic; *Associate Professor Emeritus, Department of Agricultural Economics and Management, Hebrew University of Jerusalem;* b. 18 Jan. 1935, Haifa; s. of Martin Plessner and Eva Ester Plessner; m. Ora Ester Frenkel 1959; one s. one d.; ed Iowa State Univ., USA and Hebrew Univ. of Jerusalem; Visiting Lecturer, Univ. of Pennsylvania 1971–73; Sr Lecturer, Hebrew Univ. of Jerusalem 1973–96, now Assoc. Prof. Emer., Dept of Agricultural Econs and Man.; Research Consultant, The World Bank 1977–78; Econ. Adviser to Israel's Minister of Finance 1981–83; Deputy Gov. Bank of Israel 1982–85; mem. Israel's Securities Authority 1982–85; Joseph and Esther Foster Visiting Prof., Brandeis Univ. 1985–86; Visiting Prof., Dartmouth Coll., USA 1987–88; Visiting Assoc. Prof., Dept of Econs, American Univ., Washington, DC, USA 1992–93, 1999–2000; Consultant, Ministry of Defence 1991–2003, Sadan-Lowental 2006–; Fellow and Vice-Chair. Jerusalem Center for Public Affairs 1991–2012, Chair. 2012–; The Oded Levine Prize of the Operations Research Soc. of Israel 1974, Koret Foundation First Prize for best paper on Israel's economy 1998. *Publications:* The Marketing of Israel's Citrus Fruit in Major European Markets 1976; regular columnist for Globes and Hadashot (daily newspapers); several articles in learned society journals. *Leisure interests:* music, tennis. *Address:* Department of Agricultural Economics and Management, Faculty of Agriculture, Hebrew University, PO Box 12, Rehovot 76100, Israel (office). *Telephone:* (8) 9489373 (office); (8) 9468745 (home). *Fax:* (8) 9466267 (office). *E-mail:* yakir.plessner@mail.huji.ac.il (office). *Website:* www.departments.agri .huji.ac.il (office).

PLEŞU, Andrei Gabriel, PhD; Romanian philosopher, college rector and fmr government official; b. 23 Aug. 1948, Bucharest; s. of Radu Pleşu and Zoe Pleşu; m. Catrinel Maria Lăcrămioara 1972; two s.; ed Acad. of Fine Arts and Univ. of Bucharest; Lecturer, Acad. of Fine Arts, Bucharest 1980–82, Prof. 1991–92; Prof., Univ. of Bucharest 1992–, Prof. of Philosophy of Religion 1999–97; Dir of Dilema (weekly); Founder and Rector New Europe Coll., Bucharest 1994–2001; Minister of Culture 1989–91, of Foreign Affairs 1997–99; mem. Romanian Artists' Union 1975, Romanian Writers' Union 1980, World Acad. of Art and Science, Acad. Internationale de Philosophie de l'Art, Geneva, Scientific Advisory Bd Europe Inst., Budapest, Advisory Group for Social Sciences and Humanities in the European Research Area (Research Directorate Gen. of the EU Comm.), Bd of Trustees, Collegium Budapest, Bd of Trustees, Maison des Sciences de l'Homme, Paris, Bd of Trustees and Advisory Bd, Centre for Advanced Study, Sofia; Corresp. mem. Consejo Argentino para las Relaciones Internacionales; Perm. Research Fellow, Wissenschaftskollege, Berlin 1992; Commdr des Arts et des Lettres 1990, Gran Cruz, Orden El Sol del Perú (Peru) 1998, Grand Officier, Légion d'honneur 1999, Grand Officier, Order of Diplomatic Merit, Grand Cross, Order of the Faithful Service; Hon. PhD (Albert-Ludwig Univ., Freiburg) 2000, (Humboldt Univ., Berlin) 2001; Humboldt Research Fellowship, Univ. of Bonn 1975–77, Univ. of Heidelberg 1983–84, Prize for Art Criticism, Romanian Artists' Union 1980, Prize for Essay, Writers' Asscn, Bucharest 1980, Prize, Ateneu review 1991, Prize, Flacara weekly 1993, New Europe Prize 1993, Prize of Brandenburg Acad. of Sciences, Berlin 1996, Humboldt Medal (Germany) 1998, Hannah Arendt Prize 1998, Goethe Medal, Goethe Inst., Weimar 1999, Konstantin Jireček Medal, South-Eastern European Soc., Berlin 2000 and numerous other prizes, two volumes published in his honour, both edited by Mihail Neam?u and Bogdan Tătaru-Cazaban: O filozofie a intervalului: In Honorem Andrei Pleşu (A Philosophy of the Interval: In Honor of Andrei Plesu, in Romanian) and an int. Festschrift in honour of his 60th birthday 2009. *Publications:* Călătorie în lumea formelor (Journey to the World of Forms) 1974, Pitoresc ?i melancolie (The Picturesque and Melancholy) 1980, Francesco Guardi 1981, Ochiul ?i lucrurile (The Eye and Things) 1986, Minima moralia (Moral Minimum) 1988, Dialoguri de seară (Evening Dialogues) 1991, Jurnalul de la Tescani (The Tescany Journal) 1993, Limba păsărilor (The Language of Birds) 1994, Chipuri ?i mă?ti ale tranzi?iei (Faces and Masks of Transition) 1996, Despre îngeri (On Angels) 2003, Obscenitatea publică (Public Obscenity) 2004, Comedii la por?ile Orientului (Comedies at the Gates of the Orient) 2005, Despre bucurie în Est ?i în Vest ?i alte eseuri (About Joy in East and West and other essays) 2006, Despre frumuse?ea uitată a vie?ii (About the Forgotten Beauty of Life) 2011, Parabolele lui Iisus. Adevarul ca poveste (Jesus' Parables. The Truth as Story) 2012, On Angels – Exposition for a Post Modern World (in English) 2012; numerous papers and articles. *Address:* Faculty of Philosophy, University of Bucharest, Splaiul Independentei nr. 204, Sector 6, 060024 Bucharest (office); Str. Paris 14, 71241 Bucharest 1, Romania (home). *Telephone:* (21) 3181556 (office). *E-mail:* filosofie@ ub-filosofie.ro (office). *Website:* www.filosofie.unibuc.ro (office), www.humanitas .ro/andrei-plesu.

PLETNEV, Mikhail Vasilievich; Russian pianist, conductor and composer; *Founder, Russian National Orchestra;* b. 14 April 1957, Arkhangelsk; ed Moscow State Conservatory with Yakov Flier and Lev Vlasenko (piano), Albert Leman (composition); gave recitals and played with orchestras in major cities of Russia, Europe, Japan and America; gained reputation as Russian music interpreter; Founder and Chief Conductor Russian Nat. Orchestra 1990–99, Hon. Conductor 1999–, and head of the Conductor Collegium 2006–; tours with orchestra and as piano soloist in various countries; has performed with Haitink, Maazel, Chailly, Tennstedt, Sanderling, Blomstedt, Järvi, Thielemann; also conducted Philharmonia Orchestra, Deutsche Kammerphilharmonie, Norddeutsche Rundfunk Symphony Orchestra, London Symphony Orchestra, Berlin Philharmonic, Bayerische Rundfunk Symphony, Orchestre Nat. de France, Israel Philharmonic, San Francisco Symphony and Pittsburgh Symphony; teacher in Moscow Conservatory 1981–1992; First Prize Int. Tchaikovsky competition, Moscow 1978, People's Artist of Russia 1990, State Prize of Russia 1982, 1993. *Address:* Opus 3 Artists, 470 Park Avenue South, 9th Floor North, New York, NY 10016, USA (office); Russian National Orchestra, Moscow 117335, Orchestrion, Garibaldi 19, Russia (office).

Telephone: (212) 584-7500 (office); (495) 504-07-81-83 (office). *Fax:* (646) 300-8200 (office); (495) 504-07-88 (office). *E-mail:* info@opus3artists.com (office); info@rno.ru (office). *Website:* www.opus3artists.com (office); www.russianarts.org/rno (office).

PLEVNELIEV, Rosen Asenov; Bulgarian business executive, politician and head of state; *President;* b. 14 May 1964, Gotse Delchev; m. Yuliyana Plevnelieva; three s.; ed Blagoevgrad Math. and Natural Sciences High School, Higher Mechanical-Electrotechnical Inst., Sofia, Technical Univ. of Sofia; Fellow, Inst. for Microprocessing Tech., Pravets 1989; f. and managed several businesses including Iris International JSC 1990, Linbalgariya Ltd 1994, Iris Linder Immobilien Ltd 1998, Business Park Sofia EOOD 1999, Lindner Bulgaria Ltd 2001, Residential Park Sofia Ltd 2003, Lindner Imobilen Management Ltd 2005; Minister of Regional Devt and Public Works 2009–11; Pres. of Bulgaria 2012–; mem. Citizens for European Devt of Bulgaria –2012; Ind. 2012–; mem. Bd Confed. of Employers and Industrialists in Bulgaria 2007, American Chamber of Commerce, Sofia 2008; mem. Bd of Trustees 'For Our Children' (non-profit org.) 2008. *Address:* Office of the President, 1123 Sofia, bul. Dondukov 2, Bulgaria (office). *Telephone:* (2) 923-93-33 (office). *E-mail:* priemna@president.bg (office). *Website:* www.president.bg (office).

PLISETSKAYA, Maya Mikhailovna; Russian ballerina; b. 20 Nov. 1925, Moscow; m. Rodion Shchedrin; ed Moscow Bolshoi Theatre Ballet School; soloist Bolshoi Ballet 1943–90; Artistic Dir Ballet Roma Opera 1984–85, Nat. Ballet of Spain 1987–89; f. Maya Plisetskaya Int. Ballet Competition, St Petersburg 1994; Pres. Imperial Russian Ballet 1996–2005; Hon. mem. Portuguese Dance Centre; Hon. Prof. Moscow Univ. 1993; First Prize, Budapest Int. Competition 1949; People's Artist of the RSFSR 1951; People's Artist of the USSR 1959, Anna Pavlova Prize 1962, Lenin Prize 1964, Hero of Socialist Labour 1985, Légion d'honneur 1986, Triumph Prize 2000, Asturias Prize 2005, Imperial Prize Tokyo, and other decorations. *Main ballet roles:* Odette-Odile (Swan Lake, Tchaikovsky), Raimonda (Raimonda, Glazunov), Zaryema (The Fountain of Bakhchisarai, Asafiev), Kitri (Don Quixote, Minkus), Juliet (Romeo and Juliet, Prokofiev), Girl-Bird, Syunmbike (Shuralye, Yarullin), Laurencia (Laurencia, Krein), Aegina (Spartak, Khachaturian); ballets by R. Shchedrin: Carmen (Carmen Suite), Anna (Anna Karenina) 1972, Nina (The Seagull) 1980, Lady with a Lap-dog 1983, La folle de Chaillot 1992; ballets by M. Béjart: Bolero 1976, Isadora 1977, Leda 1979, Kurazuka 1995, Ave, Maya 2000. *Publication:* I, Maya Plisetskaya. *Address:* Salvator Str. 5, 80333 Munich, Germany (home); 125009 Moscow, Tverskaya 25/9, Apt 31, Russia (home). *Telephone:* (89) 24218991 (Munich); (495) 699-72-39 (Moscow). *Fax:* (89) 24218987 (Munich) (home); (495) 699-72-39 (Moscow). *E-mail:* rshchedrin@aol.com (office). *Website:* www.plisetskaya.de (office).

PLOIX, Hélène Marie Joseph, MA, MBA; French business executive; *Chairman, Pechel Industries;* b. 25 Sept. 1944, Anould; d. of René Ploix and Antoinette Jobert; m. Alexandre Lumbroso 1988; ed Univ. of Paris, Univ. of California, Berkeley; Man. Consultant, McKinsey and Co., Paris 1968–78; Special Asst to Cabinet of Sec. of State for Consumer Affairs 1977–78; Dir Cie Européenne de Publication 1978–82; Chair. Banque Industrielle et Mobilière Privée 1982–84; mem. of Bd Comm. des Opérations de Bourse 1983–84; Adviser to Prime Minister for Econ. and Financial Affairs 1984–86; Exec. Dir IMF and World Bank, representing France 1986–89; Deputy CEO Caisse des dépôts et consignations 1989–95; Chair. Caisse autonome de refinancement 1990–95, CDC Participations 1992–95; Chair. Pechel Industries 1997–; currently mem. Jt Staff Pension Fund Investments Cttee, UN; mem. Bd of Dirs (non-exec.) BNP Paribas 2003–, Ferring Pharmaceuticals, Publicis Groupe 1998–, Lafarge 1999–, The Boots Co. PLC 2000–, Completel; mem. Strategic Advisory Bd Generis Capital Partners; Chevalier Ordre Nat. du Mérite, Chevalier Légion d'honneur. *Publications:* Le dirigeant et le gouvernement d'entreprise 2003, Gouvernement d'enterprise 2006. *Leisure interest:* golf. *Address:* Pechel Industries, 162 rue du Faubourg Saint-Honoré, 75008 Paris (office); 42 quai des Orfèvres, 75001 Paris, France. *Telephone:* 1-56-59-79-59 (office). *Fax:* 1-56-59-79-56 (office). *E-mail:* contact@pechel.com (office). *Website:* www.pechel.com (office).

PLOWDEN, David, BA; American photographer, fmr academic, author and teacher; b. 9 Oct. 1932, Boston, Mass; s. of Roger Stanley Plowden and Mary Plowden (née Butler); m. 1st Pleasance Coggeshall (divorced 1976); m. 2nd Sandra Schoellkopf 1977; three s. one d.; ed Yale Univ.; Asst to Trainmaster, Great Northern Railway 1955–56; self-employed photographer/writer 1962–; Assoc. Prof., Illinois Inst. of Tech. Inst. of Design 1978–85; Lecturer, Univ. of Iowa School of Journalism 1985–88; Visiting Prof., Grand Valley State Univ. 1988–2007 (retd); numerous photographic exhbns; John Simon Guggenheim Memorial Fellowship 1968; Smithsonian Inst. Award 1970–71, 1975–76, Iowa Humanities Award and Nat. Endowment for the Humanities Award 1987–88. *Publications:* Lincoln and His America 1970, The Hand of Man on America 1971, Floor of the Sky, The Great Plains 1972, Commonplace 1974, Bridges: The Spans of North America 1974, revised edn 2002, Tugboat 1976, Steel 1981, An American Chronology 1982, Industrial Landscape 1985, A Time of Trains 1987, A Sense of Place 1988, End of an Era 1992, Small Town America 1994, Imprints 1997, David Plowden: The American Barn 2003, A Handful of Dust 2006, Vanishing Point 2007, Requiem for Steam 2010, Heartland: The Plains and the Prairie 2013; co-author of numerous books. *Address:* 609 Cherry Street, Winnetka, IL 60093, USA (home). *Telephone:* (847) 446-2793 (home). *Fax:* (847) 446-2795 (home). *E-mail:* david@davidplowden .com. *Website:* www.davidplowden.com.

PLOWRIGHT, Dame Joan Ann, DBE; British actress; b. 28 Oct. 1929, Brigg, Lancashire; d. of William Plowright and Daisy Plowright (née Burton); m. 1st Roger Gage 1953 (divorced); m. 2nd Sir Laurence (later Lord) Olivier 1961 (died 1989); one s. two d.; ed Scunthorpe Grammar School and Old Vic Theatre School; mem. Old Vic Company, toured South Africa 1952–53; first leading rôle in The Country Wife, London 1956; mem. English Stage Company 1956; at Nat. Theatre 1963–74; Vice-Pres. Nat. Youth Theatre; Vice-Pres. and mem. Council English Stage Co.; mem. Council, Royal Acad. of Dramatic Art (RADA); Best Actress Soc. of West End Theatre (Filumena) 1978, 18th Crystal Award for Women in Film, USA 1994. *Plays include:* The Chairs 1957, The Entertainer 1958, Major Barbara and Roots 1959, A Taste of Honey (Best Actress (Tony) Award 1960) 1960, Uncle Vanya 1962, 1963, 1964, St Joan (Best Actress (Evening Standard) Award 1964) 1963, Hobson's Choice 1964, The Master Builder 1965, Much Ado About Nothing 1967, Tartuffe 1967, Three Sisters 1967, 1969 (film 1969), The Advertisement 1968,

1969, Love's Labour's Lost 1968, 1969, The Merchant of Venice, 1970, 1971–72, Rules of the Game, Woman Killed with Kindness 1971–72, Taming of the Shrew, Doctor's Dilemma 1972, Rosmersholm 1973, Saturday Sunday Monday 1973, Eden's End 1974, The Sea Gull 1975, The Bed Before Yesterday (Variety Club Award 1976) 1975, Filumena 1977, Enjoy 1980, Who's Afraid of Virginia Woolf? 1981, Cavell 1982, The Cherry Orchard 1983, The Way of the World 1984, Mrs Warren's Profession 1985, Revolution 1985, The House of Bernarda Alba 1986, And a Nightingale Sang 1989, Time and the Conways 1991, Absolutely Perhaps 2003. *Films include:* Equus 1976, Britannia Hospital 1981, Richard Wagner 1982, Brimstone and Treacle 1982, Drowning by Numbers (Variety Club Film Actress of the Year Award 1987) 1987, The Dressmaker 1988, Conquest of the South Pole 1989, I Love You to Death 1989, Avalon 1990, Enchanted April (Golden Globe Award 1993) 1991, Stalin (Golden Globe Award 1993) 1991, Dennis the Menace, A Place for Annie 1992, A Pin for the Butterfly 1993, Last Action Hero 1993, Widow's Peak 1994, On Promised Land 1994, Return of the Natives 1994, Hotel Sorrento 1994, A Pyromaniac's Love Story 1994, The Scarlet Letter 1994, Jane Eyre 1994, If We Are Women 1995, Surviving Picasso 1995, Mr. Wrong 1995, 101 Dalmatians 1996, The Assistant 1996, Shut Up and Dance 1997, Tom's Midnight Garden 1997, America Betrayed 1998, Tea with Mussolini 1999, Return to the Secret Garden 2001, Callas Forever 2002, Global Heresy 2002, Bringing Down the House 2003, I Am David 2003, The Great Goose Caper 2003, George and the Dragon 2004, Goose! 2004, Mrs Palfry at the Claremont (AARP Best Actress Award 2006) 2005, Curious George (voice) 2006, The Spiderwick Chronicles 2007. *Television includes:* Merchant of Venice 1973, Daphne Laureola 1977, Saturday Sunday Monday 1977, The Importance of Being Earnest 1988, It May Be the Last Time 1997, Frankie and Hazel 2000, Bailey's Mistake 2001. *Publication:* And That's Not All (autobiog.) 2001. *Leisure interests:* entertaining, music, reading. *Address:* c/o ICM, 76 Oxford Street, London, W1N 0AX, England (office).

PLOWRIGHT, Jonathan Daniel, Dip RAM, ARAM, FRAM; British pianist and academic; *Professor of Piano, Royal Conservatoire of Scotland;* b. 24 Sept. 1959, Doncaster, S Yorks., England; s. of Cyril James Plowright and Molly Plowright; m. Diane Rosemary Shaw 1990; ed Stonyhurst Coll., Univ. of Birmingham, Royal Acad. of Music, London, Peabody Conservatory of Music, USA; debut at Carnegie Recital Hall, New York 1984, Purcell Room, London 1985; has performed with all major UK orchestras and numerous int. orchestras; solo recitals throughout UK and many int. tours; regular BBC broadcasts and commercial recordings; performed world premiere of Constant Lambert's piano concerto, St John's Smith Square 1988; Head of Keyboard, Univ. of Chichester; currently Prof. of Piano, Royal Conservatoire of Scotland (fmrly Royal Scottish Acad. of Music and Drama); RAM McFarren Gold Medal 1983, Fulbright Scholarship 1983, Countess of Munster Scholarship, Commonwealth Musician of the Year 1983, Gold Medal, Royal Overseas League 1983, winner, Baltimore Symphony Orchestra Awards 1984, winner, European Piano Competition 1989. *Recordings include:* Capital Virtuosi, Brahms Solo Piano, Chopin Solo Piano, Vol. 1, Jonathan Plowright (recital), Paderewski (solo piano), Sigismund Stojowski Piano Concertos, Sigismund Stojowski (solo piano), Constant Lambert Piano Concerto, Rarities of Piano Music at Schloss vor Husum 2003, 2004, 2007, 2010, Paderewski (solo piano), Henryk Melcer Piano Concertos 2008, Hommage à Chopin 2010, Johann Sebastian Bach Piano Transcriptions 2010, Homage to Paderewski 2011, Zelenski & Zarebski Chamber Music 2012, Zelenski Piano Concertos, Brahms Works for Solo Piano Vol. 1 2013. *Leisure interests:* wine, rugby, cricket, fishing. *E-mail:* jonathan@jonathanplowright.com. *Website:* www.jonathanplowright.com.

PLOWRIGHT, Rosalind Anne, OBE, LRAM; British singer (mezzo-soprano); b. 21 May 1949, Worksop, Notts.; d. of Robert Arthur Plowright and Celia Adelaide Plowright; m. James Anthony Kaye 1984; one s. one d.; ed Notre Dame High School, Wigan, Royal Northern Coll. of Music, Manchester; began career at London Opera Centre 1973–75; Glyndebourne Chorus and Touring Co. 1974–77; debut with ENO as Page in Salome 1975, Miss Jessel in Turn of the Screw 1979 (Soc. of West End Theatre Laurence Olivier Award 1980), at Covent Garden as Ortlinde in Die Walküre 1980; Metropolitan Opera debut 2003; has also sung in Argentina, Austria, Chile, Denmark, France, Germany, Greece, Israel, Italy, Japan, Netherlands, Portugal, Spain, Switzerland, USA; wide repertoire as soprano, but has sung mezzo roles since 1999; principal roles (as soprano) include Ariadne, Alceste, Médée, Norma, Tosca, title role and Elizabeth I in Mary Stuart, Maddalena in Andrea Chénier, Antonia in The Tales of Hoffman, Donna Anna in Don Giovanni, Vitellia in La Clemenza di Tito, Madame Butterfly, Manon Lescaut, Suor Angelica, Giorgetta in Il Tabarro, Aida, Abigaille in Nabucco, Desdemona in Otello, Elena in I Vespri Siciliani, Leonora in Il Trovatore, Amelia in Un Ballo in Maschera, Leonora in La Forza del Destino, Violetta in La Traviata; (as mezzo) Kostelnička in Jenufa, Amneris in Aida, Fricka in Das Rheingold and Die Walküre, Gertrude in Hansel & Gretel, Klytemnestra in Elektra, Madame de Croissy in Dialogues des Carmelites, Herodias in Salome; First Prize, 7th Int. Competition for Opera Singers, Sofia 1979, Prix Fondation Fanny Heldy, Acad. Nat. du Disque Lyrique 1985, Grammy 2009. *Television:* House of Elliot 1992, The Man Who Made Husbands Jealous 1997. *Address:* c/o Askonas/Green Artists Management, 104 West 73rd Street, Suite 1, New York, NY 10023, USA (office); 83 St Mark's Avenue, Salisbury, Wilts., SP1 3DW, England (home). *Website:* www.rosalindplowright.com (home); www.ros-sing.co.uk (home).

PLUGCHIEVA, Meglena Ivanova, PhD; Bulgarian diplomatist and politician; *Ambassador to Switzerland;* b. 12 Feb. 1956, Balchik; m.; two c.; ed German Language High School, Varna, Forestry Univ.; worked as an insp. at Regional Environmental Protection Directorate, Varna 1981–84; a Deputy Dir Varna Regional Forestry Directorate 1984–90; Head of Foreign Relations Dept, Nat. Forestry Directorate 1990–95; mem. Parl. (Bulgarian Socialist Party—BSP) 1995–2001, 2009–12; Deputy Minister of Agric. and Forests 2001–04 (resgnd as mem. Supreme Council of BSP to take this position), Deputy Prime Minister, responsible for EU Funds 2008–09; Amb. to Germany 2004–08; to Switzerland 2012–; Rep. of Bulgaria at Rheinland-Pfalz, Germany 1997–2008, mem. Governing Bd Bulgarian-German Forum 1996; Bundesverdienstkreuz. *Address:* Embassy of Bulgaria, Bernastr. 2–4, 3005 Bern, Switzerland (office). *Telephone:* 313511455 (office). *Fax:* 313510064 (office). *E-mail:* bulembassy@bluewin.ch (office). *Website:* www.mfa.bg/embassies/switzerland (office).

PLUMB, Baron (Life Peer), cr. 1987, of Coleshill in the County of Warwickshire; **(Charles) Henry Plumb,** Kt, DL; British politician; b. 27 March 1925; s. of Charles Plumb and Louise Plumb; m. Marjorie Dorothy Dunn 1947; one s. two d.; ed King Edward VI School, Nuneaton; mem. Council Nat. Farmers Union 1959, Vice-Pres. 1964, 1965, Deputy-Pres. 1966–69, Pres. 1970–79; mem. Duke of Northumberland's Cttee of Inquiry on Foot and Mouth Disease 1967–68; Chair. British Agricultural Council 1975–79; Pres. Nat. Fed. of Young Farmers' Clubs 1976–86; Pres. Royal Agricultural Soc. of England 1977, Deputy Pres. 1978; Pres. Int. Fed. of Agricultural Producers 1979–82, Royal Agricultural Benevolent Inst.; MEP (Conservative) 1979–99, Chair. Agricultural Cttee 1979–82, Leader, European Democratic Group (Conservative) 1982–87, 1994–97, Pres. European Parl. 1987–90, Leader British Conservatives in European Parl. 1994–97, Co-Pres. EU/ ACP Jt Ass. for Africa/Caribbean/Pacific Countries 1994–99, Hon. Pres. 1999–; Vice-Pres. EPP Group in European Parl. 1994–97; Chancellor Coventry Univ. 1995–2007; Founder EU lobbying law firm Alber & Geiger; Chair. Agricultural Mortgage Corpn 1994–95; mem. Temporary Cttee of Enquiry into BSE 1996–97; Fellow, Royal Agric. Socs, Duchy; Order of Merit, FRG and decorations from Portugal, Luxembourg, Spain, France, Greece, Italy and others; Hon. DSc (Cranfield) 1983; Hon. DLitt (Warwick Coll.); Royal Agricultural Soc. of England Gold Medal 1983. *Leisure interests:* fishing, shooting, country pursuits. *Address:* House of Lords, Westminster, London, SW1A 0PW (office); The Dairy Farm, Maxstoke, Coleshill, Warwicks., B46 2QJ, England (home). *Telephone:* (20) 7219-1233 (office); (1675) 463133 (Coleshill) (home). *Fax:* (20) 7219-1649 (office); (1675) 464156 (Coleshill). *E-mail:* plumbh@parliament.uk (office).

PLUMBLY, Sir Derek John, KCMG, BA; British diplomatist and UN official; *Special Coordinator of the Secretary-General for Lebanon, United Nations;* b. 15 May 1948, Lyndhurst, Hants.; s. of John Plumbly and Jean Plumbly (née Baker); m. Nadia Youssef Gohar 1979; one d. two s.; ed Brockenhurst Grammar School, Magdalen Coll., Oxford; with VSO, Pakistan 1970–71; joined FCO 1972, Arabic language training, Middle East Centre for Arab Studies, Lebanon 1973–74, Second Sec., Embassy in Jeddah 1975–77, First Sec., Embassy in Cairo 1977–80, at FCO 1980–84, at Embassy in Washington, DC 1984–88, Counsellor, Embassy in Riyadh 1988–92, with Perm. Mission to UN, New York 1992–96, Dir Drugs and Crime Dept, FCO 1996–97, Dir Middle East and North Africa Dept 1997–2000, Amb. to Saudi Arabia 2000–03, to Egypt 2003–07; Chair. Assessment and Evaluation Comm., est. under Sudan Comprehensive Peace Agreement, Khartoum 2008–11; Special Coordinator of the UN Sec.-Gen. for Lebanon 2012–; Dr hc (Loughborough) 2007. *Leisure interests:* family, reading, travel. *E-mail:* unscol-website@un.org (office). *Website:* www.unscol.unmissions.org (office).

PLUMBRIDGE, Robin Allan, MA; South African business executive (retd); b. 6 April 1935, Cape Town; s. of the late C. O. Plumbridge and of the late M. A. Plumbridge; m. Celia Anne Millar 1959; two s. two d.; ed St Andrew's Coll., Grahamstown, Univ. of Cape Town, Univ. of Oxford, UK; joined Gold Fields of South Africa Ltd 1957, Asst Man. 1962–65, Man. 1965–69, Exec. Dir 1969–80, CEO 1980–95, Chair. 1980–97; Chair. World Gold Council 1993–95; Dir Standard Bank Group 1980–2005, Newmont Mining Corpn 1983–2008; Hon. LLD. *Address:* Postnet Suite #107, Private Bag X15, Somerset West 7129; Navarre Farm, Stellenbosch, South Africa (home). *Telephone:* (21) 8551568 (office). *Fax:* (21) 8552170 (office). *E-mail:* rplum@mweb.co.za (home).

PLUMMER, (Arthur) Christopher (Orme), CC; Canadian actor; b. 13 Dec. 1929, Toronto, Ont.; m. 1st Tammy Lee Grimes 1956 (divorced 1960); one d.; m. 2nd Patricia Audrey Lewis 1962 (divorced 1967); m. 3rd Elaine Regina Taylor 1970; ed public and pvt. schools in Montréal, Province of Quebec; studied under Iris Warren and C. Herbertcasari; professional debut as Faulkland in The Rivals, Ottawa Repertory Theatre; Broadway debut in Starcross Story 1954; film debut in Stage Struck 1958; numerous appearances in theatres in USA; played many leading Shakespearean roles in productions by the Stratford Canadian Festival Co.; British debut in title role of Richard III, Stratford on Avon 1961 and then in London as Henry II in Anouilh's Becket; a leading actor in the Nat. Theatre Co. of GB 1971–72; has appeared in Nat. Theatre productions of Amphytrion 38, Danton's Death 1971; many TV roles including Hamlet in BBC TV/Danish TV production, Hamlet in Elsinore, Jesus of Nazareth 1977; Hon. DFA (Juilliard School of Performing Arts) 1993, Dr hc (Ryerson Univ., Toronto) 2002, (Univ. of Toronto) 2003, (Univ. of Western Ontario) 2004, (McGill Univ.) 2006; Theatre World Award 1955, Delia Australian Medal 1973, Australian Golden Badge of Honour 1982, Maple Leaf Award 1982, Edwin Booth Lifetime Achievement Award 1997, Maple Leaf Award, LAFCA 1999, Gov. Gen.'s Performing Arts Award 2001, Jason Robards Award for Excellence in Theatre 2002, The Sir John Gielgud Award for Excellence in the Dramatic Arts (aka The Golden Quill) 2006. *Plays include:* Faulkland in The Rivals 1950, Old Mahon in The Playboy of the Western World 1952, Anthony Cavendish in The Royal Family 1952, Ben in The Little Foxes 1952, Duke Manti in The Petrified Forest 1952, Father in George and Margaret 1952, Hector Benbow in Thark 1952, Bernard Kersal in The Constant Wife 1952, George Phillips in The Starcross Story 1954, Manchester Monaghan in Home Is the Hero 1954, Jason in Medea 1955, Earl of Warwick in Anouilh's The Lark 1955, The Dark is Light Enough 1955, Mark Antony in Julius Caesar 1955, Ferdinand in The Tempest 1955, Henry V 1956, 1981, The Narrator in Stravinsky's L'Histoire du Soldat 1956, Hamlet 1957, Twelfth Night 1957, The Winter's Tale 1958, Much Ado About Nothing 1958, Henry IV Part 1 1958, The Devil in J.B. 1958, Romeo and Juliet 1960, King John 1960, Much Ado About Nothing 1961, Becket (London Evening Standard Award for Best Actor 1961) 1961, Richard III 1961, Macbeth 1962, 1988, The Resistible Rise of Arturo Ui 1965–66, The Royal Hunt of the Sun 1965–66, Anthony and Cleopatra 1967, Danton's Death 1971, Cyrano (Tony Award for Best Leading Actor in a Musical 1974) 1973, The Good Doctor 1973, Iago in Othello 1982, Peccadillo 1985, A Christmas Carol 1990, No Man's Land 1994, Barrymore (Tony Award for Best Leading Actor in a Play 1997) 1996, King Lear 2004, A World or Two, Before You Go 2005, Inherit the Wind 2007, Barrymore (Toronto) 2010. *Films include:* Stage Struck 1958, Wind Across the Everglades 1958, The Fall of the Roman Empire 1964, The Sound of Music 1965, Inside Daisy Clover 1965, Triple Cross 1966, The Night of the Generals 1967, Oedipus the King 1968, Nobody Runs Forever 1968, Lock Up Your Daughters! 1969, Battle of Britain 1969, The Royal Hunt of the Sun 1969, Waterloo 1970, The Pyx 1973, The Happy Prince (short, voice) 1974, The Spiral Staircase 1975, The Return of the Pink Panther 1975, Conduct Unbecoming 1975, Sarajevski atentat 1975, The Man Who

Would be King 1975, Aces High 1976, The Assignment 1977, The Disappearance 1977, International Velvet 1978, The Silent Partner 1978, Starcrash 1978, Murder by Decree (Genie Award for Best Actor 1980) 1979, Hanover Street 1979, Somewhere in Time 1980, The Janitor 1981, Eyewitness 1981, The Amateur 1981, Highpoint 1982, Dreamscape 1984, Lily in Love 1984, Playing for Keeps 1985, Ordeal by Innocence 1985, The Boy in Blue 1986, The Boss's Wife 1986, An American Tail 1986, The Gnomes' Great Adventure (narrator) 1987, I Love N.Y. 1987, Dragnet 1987, Gandahar (voice, English version) 1988, The Man Who Planted Trees (short) 1988, Nosferatu a Venezia 1988, Shadow Dancing 1988, Kingsgate 1989, Souvenir 1989, Mindfield 1989, Where the Heart Is 1990, Red Blooded American Girl 1990, Firehead 1991, Money 1991, Rock-A-Doodle (voice) 1991, Star Trek VI: The Undiscovered Country 1991, Liar's Edge 1992, Impolite (uncredited) 1992, Malcolm X 1992, Wolf 1994, Crackerjack 1994, Dolores Claiborne 1995, Twelve Monkeys 1995, Skeletons 1996, Babes in Toyland (voice) 1997, The First Christmas (narrator) 1998, Blackheart 1998, The Clown at Midnight 1999, Hidden Agenda 1999, Madeline: Lost in Paris (narrator) 1999, The Insider (Boston Society of Film Critics Award 1999, Los Angeles Film Critics Association Award 1999) 1999, All the Fine 1999, Dracula 2001, Lucky Break 2001, A Beautiful Mind 2001, Full Disclosure 2001, Ararat 2002, Nicholas Nickleby 2002, Blizzard 2003, The Visual Bible: The Gospel of John (narrator) 2003, Cold Creek Manor 2003, National Treasure 2004, Alexander 2004, Tma 2005, Must Love Dogs 2005, Syriana 2005, Heidi 2005, The New World 2005, Inside Man 2006, The Lake House 2006, Man in the Chair 2007, Closing the Ring 2007, Emotional Arithmetic 2007, Already Dead 2007, Caesar and Cleopatra 2009, Up (voice) 2009, The Imaginarium of Doctor Parnassus 2009, My Dog Tulip 2009, 9 2009, The Last Station 2009, Beginners (Golden Globe Award for Best Supporting Actor 2012, BAFTA Film Award for Best Supporting Actor 2012, Acad. Award for Best Performance by an Actor in a Supporting Role 2012) 2010, Priest 2011, Barrymore 2011, The Girl with the Dragon Tattoo 2011. Television includes: Ford Television Theatre (series) 1953, Studio One (series) 1953, Suspense (series) 1953, Broadway Television Theatre (series) 1953, The Web (series) 1954, Kraft Television Theatre (series) 1954, Kraft Television Theatre (series) 1955, Producers' Showcase (series) 1955, General Electric Theater (series) 1956, Appointment with Adventure (series) 1956, The Alcoa Hour (series) 1956, Eye on New York (series) 1956, Omnibus (series) 1957–58, The DuPont Show of the Month (series) 1957–61, Hallmark Hall of Fame (series) 1958–62, The Philadelphia Story (film) 1959, Sunday Showcase (series) 1960, Playdate (series) 1961–62, Hamlet at Elsinore (film) 1964, The Secret of Michelangelo (film) 1968, BBC Play of the Month (series) – Don Juan 1971, Witness to Yesterday (series) 1974, After the Fall (film) 1974, Arthur Hailey's The Moneychangers (mini-series) (Emmy Award as Outstanding Lead Actor in a Limited Series 1976) 1976, Jesus of Nazareth (mini-series) 1977, Silver Blaze (short) 1977, Riel (film) 1979, The Shadow Box (film) 1980, Desperate Voyage (film) 1980, When the Circus Came to Town (film) 1981, Dial M for Murder (film) 1981, Little Gloria. . . Happy at Last (film) 1982, The Scarlet and the Black (film) 1983, The Thorn Birds (mini-series) 1983, Parade of Stars (film) 1983, Prototype (film) 1983, The Velveteen Rabbit (film) 1985, Rumpelstiltskin (film) 1985, David el gnomo (series) 1985, Spearfield's Daughter (mini-series) 1986, The Tin Soldier (film) 1986, Crossings (mini-series) 1986, The Nightingale (film) (voice) 1986, The Cosby Show (series) 1987, A Hazard of Hearts (film) 1987, Nabokov on Kafka (short) 1989, Madeline (film) 1989, The Little Crooked Christmas Tree (short) 1990, A Ghost in Monte Carlo (film) 1990, Madeline's Christmas (film, voice) 1990, Madeline's Rescue (film, voice) 1990, Young Catherine (film) 1991, Madeline and the Bad Hat (film, voice) 1991, A Marriage: Georgia O'Keeffe and Alfred Stieglitz (film) 1991, Madeline and the Gypsies (film, voice) 1991, Madeline in London (film, voice) 1991, Berlin Lady (mini-series) 1991, The First Circle (film) 1992, Secrets (film) 1992, Counterstrike (series) 1990–93, A Stranger in the Mirror (film) 1993, Madeline (children's series) (Emmy Award for Outstanding Voice-Over Performance 1994) 1993–94, Harrison Bergeron (film) 1995, The New Adventures of Madeline (series) 1995, We the Jury (film) 1996, The Arrow (film) 1997, The Conspiracy of Fear (film) 1997, Skeletons (film) 1997, Winchell (film) 1998, The Dinosaur Hunter (film) 2000, Possessed (film) 2000, American Tragedy (film) 2000, Leo's Journey (film) 2001, On Golden Pond (film) 2001, Night Flight (film) 2002, Agent of Influence (film) 2002, Odd Job Jack (series) 2003, Our Fathers (film) 2005, Four Minutes (film) 2005, The American Experience (series documentary) 2006, The Summit (mini-series) 2008, The Tempest (film) 2010. Publication includes: In Spite of Myself: A Memoir 2008. Leisure interests: piano, skiing, tennis, old cars. Address: c/o Lou Pitt, The Pitt Group, 9465 Wilshire Boulevard, Suite 480, Beverly Hills, CA 90212, USA (office). Telephone: (310) 246-4800 (office). Fax: (310) 275-9258 (office).

PLUMMER, James D., BS, MS, PhD; Canadian electrical engineer and academic; John M. Fluke Professor of Electrical Engineering and Frederick Emmons Terman Dean of the School of Engineering, Stanford University; b. Toronto, Ont.; m. Patti Plummer; two d.; ed Univ. of California, Los Angeles, Stanford Univ.; research staff member, Integrated Circuits Lab, Stanford Univ. 1971–78, Assoc. Prof. 1978–83, Prof. of Electrical Eng 1983–, served as Dir IC Lab., as Sr Assoc. Dean in School of Eng, and as Chair. Electrical Eng Dept, apptd John M. Fluke Prof. of Electrical Eng, currently the Frederick Emmons Terman Dean of the School of Eng, Dir Stanford Nanofabrication Facility 1994–2000; Co-founder T-RAM; mem. Bd of Dirs and Tech. Advisory Bd several public and start-up cos; mem. Nat. Acad. of Eng, American Acad. of Arts and Sciences 2008; Fellow, IEEE; teaching awards, Stanford Univ. 1991, 1992, 1993, Solid State Science and Tech. Award, Electrochemical Soc. 1991, NSF commendation for nat. leadership in building the NNUN (consortium of five univs who opened their nanofabrication facilities as nat. resources for industry and for students from around the nation) 2000, Semiconductor Industry Asscn Univ. Research Award 2001, IEEE Third Millennium Medal 2001, Aviation Week & Space Technology Laurels Award – Electronics 2003, IEEE J.J. Ebers Award 2003, IEEE Aldert Van der Ziel Award 2003, McGraw-Hill/Jacob Millman Award 2004, IEDM Paul Rappaport Award 2006, IEEE Andrew S. Grove Award 2007; eight conf. and student best paper awards, including two at IEDM and three at ISSCC. Publications: Silicon VLSI Technology – Fundamentals, Practice and Modeling; more than 400 scientific papers in professional journals on the physics governing device operation in silicon integrated circuits and the technology used to fabricate these circuits. Address: Office of the Dean, Terman 214, MC 4027, 380 Panama Mall, Stanford, CA 94305-

4207, USA (office). Telephone: (650) 723-3938 (office). Fax: (650) 725-8545 (office). E-mail: plummer@stanford.edu (office). Website: soe.stanford.edu (office).

PLUMMER, James W.; American engineer; fmr Corona Program Man., Div. of Missiles and Space Co., Lockheed Corpn, served as overall systems engineer for Corona, later Vice-Pres. Lockheed Corpn; fmr Under-Sec. USAF; fmr Dir Nat. Reconnaissance Office; fmr Chair. The Aerospace Corpn; mem. Nat. Acad. of Eng; Hon. Fellow, AIAA; designated as a Space and Missile Pioneer by USAF 1989, honoured by Dir of CIA as a Corona Pioneer 1995, Charles Stark Draper Prize, Nat. Acad. of Eng (co-recipient) 2005. Address: c/o National Academy of Engineering, 500 Fifth Street, NW, Washington, DC 20001, USA. E-mail: NAEMembershipOffice@nae.edu.

PLUSHENKO, Evgeni Viktorovich; Russian figure skater; b. 3 Nov. 1982, Solnechni, Khabarovsk region in Siberia; s. of Viktor Plushenko and Tatiana Vasilievna; m. Maria Erma 2005; one s.; family moved to Volgograd aged three; began skating aged four; sent to St Petersburg to train under Alexei Mishin aged 11; Nat. Champion 1999–2002, 2004–06, 2010, 2012; gold medal, Grand Prix Final 2000, 2001, 2003, 2005, silver medal, 2002, 2004, bronze medal 1999; gold medal, World Jr Championships 1997; silver medal, European Championships 1998, 1999, 2004, gold medal, 2000, 2001, 2003, 2005, 2006, 2010, 2012; bronze medal, World Championships 1998, silver medal, 1999, gold medal, 2001, 2003, 2004; silver medal, Winter Olympics, Salt Lake City 2002, Vancouver 2010, gold medal, Winter Olympics, Turin 2006, team competition, Sochi 2014; first skater in the world to perform a 4-3-2 (quadruple toe loop-triple toe loop-double loop) jump combination and later a 4-3-3 (quadruple toe loop-triple toe loop-triple loop) jump combination at Cup of Russia 2002; youngest male skater to receive perfect score of 6.0 aged 16; received total of 70 6.0s before new Code of Points judging system was introduced; retd from competition following Sochi Winter Olympics Feb. 2014; mem. Ybileiny Sport Club, St Petersburg. Address: c/o Ari Zakaryan. Telephone: 916-968-04-26 (mobile); (917) 434-0424 (USA). E-mail: ari.zakaryan@evgeni -plushenko.com. Website: evgeni-plushenko.com.

PLYUSHCH, Ivan Stepanovich; Ukrainian politician; b. 11 Sept. 1941, Borzna, Chernigov Dist; m.; one d.; ed Ukrainian Agricultural Acad., Acad. of Social Sciences of Communist Party Cen. Cttee; mem. CPSU 1962–91; worked as agronomist, Dir of collective farms, Dir Sovkhoz 1959–74, party work in Kiev Dist Cttee 1975–84; Deputy Chair. Kiev Dist Soviet 1984–90, Chair. 1990; Deputy to Ukrainian Supreme Soviet 1990; Chair. (Speaker) Verkhovna Rada (parl.) 1991–94, 2000–02; mem. Higher Econ. Bd 1997; mem. People's Democratic Party 1998–; mem. All-Ukrainian Union of Democratic Forces 1998–, Chair. 1999–; rep. of presidential cand. Viktor Yushchenko during elections 2004, now adviser to Pres.; Yaroslav Mudzy Order 1996. Address: c/o Office of the President, vul. Bankova 11, 01220 Kiev, Ukraine. Telephone: (44) 291-53-33. Fax: (44) 293-61-61. E-mail: president@adm.gov.ua. Website: www.president.gov.ua.

POCAR, Fausto, LLD; Italian judge, international organization executive and academic; Appeals Judge, International Criminal Tribunal for the former Yugoslavia (ICTY); b. 21 Feb. 1939, Milan; ed Univ. of Milan; Prof. of Int. Law, Univ. of Milan, fmr Dean, Faculty of Political Sciences, fmr Vice-Rector Univ. of Milan; Judge, Int. Criminal Tribunal for the fmr Yugoslavia (ICTY), The Hague 2000–, Appeals Judge 2000–, also Judge of the Appeals Chamber and mem. Int. Criminal Tribunal for Rwanda (ICTR), Vice-Pres. ICTY 2003–05, Pres. 2005–08; mem. Human Rights Cttee under Int. Covenant on Civil and Political Rights 1984–2000, Rapporteur 1989–90, Chair. 1991–92; Special Rep. of UN High Commr for Human Rights for visits to Chechnya and Russian Fed. 1995–96; has chaired informal working group that drafted declaration on the rights of people belonging to nat. or ethnic, religious or linguistic minorities, Comm. on Human Rights 1992; Italian del. to Cttee on the Peaceful Uses of Outer Space and its Legal Sub-cttee; Pres. Int. Inst. of Humanitarian Law, San Remo 2012–; mem. Panel of Arbitrators for Outer Space Disputes, Perm. Court of Arbitration 2012–; has lectured at The Hague Acad. of Int. Law; mem. and Treas. Institut de Droit Int.; mem. several other int. law asscns; Grand Ufficiale 2003; Dr hc (Antwerp) 2007, (Buenos Aires) 2008. Publications: author of numerous publs on int. law, including human rights and humanitarian law, pvt. int. law and European law. Address: International Criminal Tribunal for the Former Yugoslavia, PO Box 13888, 2501 EW The Hague, Netherlands (office). Telephone: (70) 512-5362 (office). Fax: (70) 512-5307 (office). E-mail: pocar.icty@un.org (office). Website: www.un.org/icty (office).

POCHINOK, Aleksander Petrovich, CandEcon; Russian politician; b. 12 Jan. 1958, Chelyabinsk; m.; one d.; ed Chelyabinsk Polytech. Inst., Inst. of Econs Urals br. USSR Acad. of Sciences; with Chelyabinsk Inst. of Econs 1985–89; People's Deputy Russian Fed.; mem. Supreme Soviet, Chair. Comm. on Budget Planning, Taxation and Prices 1990–93; mem. State Duma (Parl.), Deputy Chair., Chair. Subcttee. on Budget, Taxation, Banks and Finance 1993–97; mem. Political Council Democratic Union of Russia 1994; Head State Taxation Service Russian Fed. 1997–98; Head of Financial Dept of Govt admin. 1998; Minister of Taxation 1999–2000, of Labour and Social Devt 2000–04; Dir Fed. Labour and Social Protection Agency 2004; Presidential Aide 2004; Deputy Presidential Envoy to Southern Fed. Dist 2004–. Publications: I Pay Taxes (with S. Shatalov), Principles of Tax Systems (jtly). Leisure interest: sea cruises. Address: Sadovo-Kudrinskaya Str. 19, Apt 23, Moscow, Russia. Telephone: (495) 201-35-05 (home).

POČIATEK, Ján; Slovak economist and government official; b. 19 Sept. 1970; m. Ivana Počiatek; one d.; ed Slovak Tech. Univ., Univ. of Econs, Bratislava, Stockholm School of Econs, Sweden, Telenor Corp. Univ., Oslo, Norway; Project Dir, Satellite Communications Div., Telenor Slovakia 1997–2000, Commercial Dir and Vice-Exec. Dir 2000–01, Exec. Dir 2001–06; mem. Bd Dirs Int. Satellite Communication 2001–06; Minister of Finance 2006–10. Address: c/o Ministry of Finance, PO Box 82, Štefanovičova 5, 817 82 Bratislava, Slovakia (office).

PODBEREZKIN, Aleksei Ivanovich, DHist; Russian historian and politician; President, International Non-Government Research and Education Organization; b. 7 Feb. 1953, Moscow; m.; three d.; ed Moscow State Inst. of Int. Relations; started career as metal worker in Moscow 1968; served in the army; referent Group of Scientific Consultants, USSR Cttee of Youth Orgs 1981–85; Sr Researcher Inst. of World Econs and Int. Relations, Diplomatic Acad., Ministry of Foreign Affairs 1985–90; f. Russian-American Univ. 1990, Pres. 1991–; Pres. Int. Non-Govt Research and Educ. Org. 1992–; adviser to Vice-Pres. of Russia 1991–93;

Founder, Chair. and Sec.-Gen. All-Russian Political Movt Spiritual Heritage (Dukhovnoye Naslediye) 1994–; mem. State Duma (Parl.), mem. Communist Party faction 1995–99; Asst to Pres. Dmitry Medvedev 2005–08; Deputy Chair. Cttee on Int. Issues; Founder People's Patriotic Union of Russia 1996–; ed. Observer (analytical monthly); Ed.-in-Chief Russia: Contemporary Political History (annual) 1998–; several state decorations; Adviser of the Year 1998. *Publications:* over 1,200 publs on problems of int. relations, foreign and defence policy, state construction, ideology of state patriotism, economics and financial control. *Leisure interests:* tennis, swimming. *Address:* Dukhovnoye Naslediye, Bakhrushina str. 32, Building 2, 113054 Moscow (office); B. Serpukovsky str. 62/44, Moscow, Russia (home). *Telephone:* (495) 959-20-45 (office); (495) 635-48-94 (home). *E-mail:* podberezkin_a@nasled.ru (office). *Website:* www.viperson.ru (office).

PODESTA, John David, BS, JD; American lawyer and government official; *Senior Advisor to the President of the United States; b.* 1 Aug. 1949, Chicago, Ill.; s. of John David Podesta and Mary Kokoris; m. Mary Spieczny 1978; one s. two d.; ed Knox Coll., Illinois, Georgetown Univ. Law Center; attorney, Dept of Justice 1976–77; Special Asst to Dir, ACTION 1978–79; Counsel, Senate Judiciary Cttee 1979–81; Chief Minority Counsel, Senate Judiciary Sub-Cttee 1981–86; Chief Counsel, Senate Agric. Cttee 1987–88; Pres., Gen. Counsel, Podesta Assocs Inc. 1988–93; Asst to the Pres. (Staff Sec.) 1993–95; Asst to Pres. (Deputy Chief of Staff) 1997–98; Chief of Staff to the Pres. 1998–2001; Pres. and CEO Center for American Progress 2001–13, Chair. 2013–; Sr Advisor to the Pres., The White House, Washington, DC 2014–; Visiting Prof. of Law, Georgetown Univ. Law Center 1995–98, Adjunct Prof. 1998–. *Publication:* Protecting Electronic Messaging 1990. *Address:* Center for American Progress, 805 15th Street, NW, Suite 400, Washington, DC 20005 (office); 3743 Brandywine Street, Washington, DC 20016, USA (home). *Telephone:* (202) 682-1611 (office). *E-mail:* progress@ americanprogress.org (office). *Website:* www.americanprogress.org (office).

PODHORETZ, John, AB; American writer and editor; *Editor, Commentary; b.* 18 April 1961, New York; s. of Norman Podhoretz (q.v.) and Midge Podhoretz (née Rosenthal); m. 1st Elisabeth Hickey 1996 (divorced); m. 2nd Ayala Cohen; two d.; ed Univ. of Chicago; Exec. News Ed. Insight Magazine 1985–87; contrib. US News and World Report 1987–88; speechwriter for US Pres. Ronald Reagan, Pres. George H.W. Bush 1988–89; Asst Man. Ed. Washington Times 1989–91; Sr Fellow, Hudson Inst. 1991–94; Ed. of editorial page, lead political columnist, arts ed., New York Post, TV critic 1994–95, now political columnist; Co-founder and Deputy Ed. The Weekly Standard 1995–97, now movie critic; Editorial Dir Commentary (magazine) 2007–09, Ed. 2009–; J. C. Penney/Mo. Award for Excellence in Feature Sections 1990. *Publication:* Hell of a Ride: Backstage at the White House Follies 1989–93 1993, Bush Country: How Dubya Became a Great President While Driving Liberals Insane 2004, Can She Be Stopped?: Hillary Clinton Will Be the Next President of the United States Unless...2007. *Address:* Commentary, 165 East 56th Street, New York, NY 10022, USA (office). *E-mail:* letters@ commentarymagazine.com. *Website:* www.commentarymagazine.com (office).

PODHORETZ, Norman, BA, MA, BHL; American writer and editor; b. 16 Jan. 1930, Brooklyn, NY; s. of Julius Podhoretz and Helen Podhoretz (née Woliner); m. Midge R. Decter 1956; one s. (John Podhoretz) three d.; ed Columbia Univ., Jewish Theological Seminary and Univ. of Cambridge, UK; Assoc. Ed. Commentary 1956–58, Ed.-in-Chief 1960–95, Ed.-at-Large 1995–2008; Ed.-in-Chief, Looking Glass Library 1959–60; Chair. New Directions Advisory Comm. US Information Agency 1981–87; Sr Fellow, Hudson Inst. 1995–2003; Fulbright Fellow 1950–51; Kellett Fellow 1950–53; Hon. LLD (Jewish Theological Seminary); Hon. LHD (Hamilton Coll.), (Boston) 1995, (Adelphi) 1996; Hon. DHumLitt (Yeshiva) 1991; Presidential Medal of Freedom 2004. *Publications include:* Doings and Undoings: The Fifties and After in American Writing 1964, Making It 1968, Breaking Ranks: A Political Memoir 1979, The Present Danger 1980, Why We Were in Vietnam 1982, The Bloody Crossroads: Where Literature and Politics Meet 1986, Ex-Friends 1999, My Love Affair with America 2000, The Prophets: Who They Were, What They Are 2002, The Norman Podhoretz Reader 2004, World War IV 2007, Why Are Jews Liberal? 2009. *Leisure interest:* listening to music. *Address:* c/o Commentary, 165 East 56th Street, New York, NY 10022, USA (office). *Telephone:* (212) 891-6735 (office). *Fax:* (212) 891-6700 (office). *E-mail:* nhp30@hotmail.com (office).

PODNAR, Gregor; Slovenian gallery owner; Artistic Dir Galerija Škuc, Ljubljana 1996–2003; est. Galerija Gregor Podnar in Kranj as part of Asscn DUM 2003, gallery moved to Ljubljana 2005; opened second gallery in Berlin 2007; represents established artists mostly from Eastern European centres, including Slovenian collective IRWIN, Yuri Leiderman, Vadim Fiškin, Dan Perjovschi, Goran Petercol and Attila Csörgő, as well as young emerging artists, including Alexander Gutke, Magnus Larsson, Tobias Putrih and Ariel Schlesinger. *Address:* Galerija Gregor Podnar, Lindenstrasse 35, 10969 Berlin, Germany (office); Galerija Gregor Podnar, Kolodvorska 6, 1000 Ljubljana, Slovenia (office). *Telephone:* (30) 25934651 (Berlin) (office); (1) 4304929 (Ljubljana) (office). *Fax:* (30) 25934652 (Berlin) (office); (1) 4304928 (Ljubljana) (office). *E-mail:* berlin@gregorpodnar.com (office); ljubljana@gregorpodnar.com (office). *Website:* www.gregorpodnar.com (office).

PODOLSKY, Daniel K., BA, MD; American physician and university administrator; *President, University of Texas Southwestern Medical Centre; b.* 1953; m. Dr. Carol P. Podolsky; three c.; ed Harvard Coll., Harvard Medical School; Clinical Fellow in Medicine, Harvard Medical School 1978–80, Research Fellow 1980–81, Asst Prof. of Medicine 1982–86, Assoc. Prof. 1986–96, Prof. 1996–2008, Mallinckrodt Prof. of Medicine 1998–2008; Asst Resident, Mass Gen. Hosp. 1978–80, Clinical Research Fellow 1980–81, Asst in Medicine 1982–86, Assoc. Physician 1988–93, Physician 1993–2008, Chief of Gastroenterology 1998–2008; Pres. Univ. of Texas SW Medical Center 2008–; Chair. and Scientific Co-Founder GI Co., Framingham, Mass; Chief Academic Officer, Partners HealthCare System, Boston 2005–08; mem. Bd of Dirs GlaxoSmithKline plc, Antibe Therapeutics, Inc.; Pres. American Gastroenterological Asscn 2003–04; fmr Ed.-in-Chief Gastroenterology (journal); Distinguished Achievement Award, American Gastroenterological Asscn 2007. *Publications:* more than 300 original research and review articles. *Address:* Office of the President, University of Texas Southwestern Medical Center, 5323 Harry Hines Boulevard, Dallas, TX 75235-9002, USA (office). *Telephone:* (214) 648-2508 (office). *Fax:* (214) 648-8690 (office). *E-mail:* daniel

.podolsky@utsouthwestern.edu (office). *Website:* www.utsystem.edu/hea/ Presidents.htm (office).

PODSIADŁO, Andrzej; Polish banking executive; b. 2 Dec. 1950; ed Main School of Econs and Planning, Warsaw (now Warsaw School of Econs); fmr teacher, Main School of Planning and Statistics, Warsaw; Dir, Econ. Analysis Team, Planning Comm. of Council of Ministers 1978–88, Under-Sec. and later Sec. of State, Ministry of Finance 1989–92; Pres., Man. Bd, Powszechny Bank Handlowy Gecobank SA 1994; Vice-Pres., Man. Bd, PKO BP 1994–95; Pres., Man. Bd, Powszechny Bank Kredytowy SA 1995–2002; Pres., Man. Bd, PKO Bank 2002–06; Vice-Pres. Supervisory Bd, Bank Pocztowy SA 2004–; fmr Chair., Gornoslaski Bank Gospodarczy SA, Powszechne Towarzystwo Emerytalne PBK SA, PTE Ergo Hestia SA, Bank Pekao SA, TUiR Warta; mem. Supervisory Bd, Poskie Koleje Panstwowe, Huta Katowice SA, Fabryka Samochodow Malolitrazowych w Bielsku-Bialej, Bank Wschodni SA, Polska Fundacja Promocji Kadr; fmr Pres., Man. Bd Polish Red Cross; mem. Curriculum Bd, Warsaw Banking School; mem. Council of Banks; Polish Rep., Int. Bank of Econ. Co-operation, Moscow, Int. Investment Bank, Moscow; Vice-Pres., Union of Polish Banks; mem. Bd, Nat. Museum, Warsaw.

POE, Jeff; American gallery owner and art dealer; *Co-Owner, Blum & Poe;* worked as dir of Kim Light Gallery, Los Angeles; co-founded (with Tim Blum) small exhbn space in Santa Monica, Calif. 1994; introduced Japanese artists Takashi Murakami and Yoshito Nara in USA; Co-Owner Blum & Poe gallery, expanded to larger space in 2003, renovated and opened new gallery 2009, regularly exhibits local and internationally recognized artists, including Chiho Aoshima, J. B. Blunk, Slater Bradley, Chuck Close, Nigel Cooke, Carroll Dunham, Sam Durant, Kōji Enokura, Anya Gallaccio, Mark Grotjahn, Tim Hawkinson, Drew Heitzler, Julian Hoeber, Zhang Huan, Zhu Jinshi, Matt Johnson, Susumu Koshimizu, Friedrich Kunath, Shio Kusaka, Linder, Sharon Lockhart, Florian Maier-Aichen, Victor Man, Dave Muller, Takashi Murakami, Yoshitomo Nara, Matt Saunders, Hugh Scott–Douglas, Nobuo Sekine, Jim Shaw, Dirk Skreber, Kishio Suga, Henry Taylor, Keith Tyson, Lee Ufan, Chris Vasell and Michael Wilkinson. *Address:* Blum & Poe, 2727 S La Cienega Blvd, Los Angeles, CA 90034, USA (office). *Telephone:* (310) 836-2062 (office). *Fax:* (310) 836-2104 (office). *E-mail:* info@blumandpoe.com (office). *Website:* www.blumandpoe.com (office).

POFALLA, Ronald; German lawyer and politician; b. 15 May 1959; ed Fachhochschule, Kleve, Univ. of Cologne; mem. Christlich-Demokratische Union (Christian Democratic Union—CDU) 1975–, initially engaged in Junge Union (JU), Chair. JU, North Rhine-Westphalia 1986–92, Gen. Sec. CDU 2005–; mem. Bundestag (Parl.) 1990–, Deputy Chair. CDU/CSU (Christlich-Soziale Union) Parl. Group in Bundestag 2004–05; passed Staatsexamen (bar examination) 1991, in legal practice 1991–; Chief of Staff, Fed. Chancellery and Minister for Special Affairs 2009–13. *Address:* c/o Bundeskanzler-Amt, Willy-Brandt Str. 1, 10557 Berlin, Germany (office). *Website:* www.bundeskanzlerin.de (office); www.ronald -pofalla.de.

POGEA, Gheorghe, PhD; Romanian business executive and politician; b. 21 Dec. 1955; m.; two c.; ed Bucharest Polytechnic Inst., École Superieure de Commerce Marseille, France; Dir-Gen. S.C Siderurgica SA 1996–2000, S.C Marmosin SA 2001–04, SC Titan Mar SA 2006–08; mem. Democratic Liberal Party (PDL), Pres. PDL Org. for Hunedoara Co. 2000–06, Coordinator PDL Strategy Comm. 2005–06; Minister of State 2005–06; Minister of Economy and Finance 2008–09; apptd to Supervisory Bd Fondului Proprietatea 2010, Bd of Dirs CEC Bank 2010; Gen. Man. Cris-Tim 2013–. *Address:* Chris-Tim, 012 367 Bucharest, Boulevard Bucurestii Noi no. 140, Sector 1, Romania (office). *Website:* en.cristim.ro (office).

PÖGGELER, Otto, DPhil; German academic; *Professor Emeritus of Philosophy and Director, Hegel-Archiv der Ruhr-Universität; b.* 12 Dec. 1928, Attendorn; m. 1959, two c.; ed Bonn Univ.; Prof. of Philosophy, Ruhr-Universität, Bochum Univ. 1968–94, Prof. Emer. 1994–, Dir Hegel Archives; mem. Rheinland-Westphalia Acad. of Sciences 1977–. *Publications:* Etudes hégéliennes 1985, Martin Heidegger's Path of Thinking 1987, Schritte zu einer Hermeneutischen Philosophie 1994, Heidegger in seiner Zeit 1999, Der Stein hinter Aug. Studien zu Célans Gedichten 2000, Bild und Technik-Heidegger, Klee und die Moderne Kunst 2002, Schicksal und Geschichte. Antigone im Spiegel der Deutungen 2004, Philosophie und Hermeneutische Theologie 2009. *Address:* Hegel-Archiv der Ruhr-Universität, 44780 Bochum (office); Paracelsusweg 22, 44801 Bochum, Germany (home). *Telephone:* (234) 701160 (home).

POGGIO, Albert Andrew, OBE; British diplomatist; *UK Representative for HM Government of Gibraltar; b.* 18 Aug. 1946, Ballymena, Co. Antrim, Northern Ireland; one d.; ed Christian Brothers Coll., Gibraltar and City of London Coll.; UK Rep. for HM Govt of Gibraltar 1988–; Chair. British Overseas Territories Asscn, Vital Health Group of Cop, Westex Group of Cos; Vice-Chair. Calpe House Trust; Dir Friends of Gibraltar Heritage Soc., SVP Medcruise (Asscn of Mediterranean Ports); Freeman, City of London. *Leisure interests:* reading, walking, military memorabilia, sports. *Address:* 150 Strand, London, WC2R 1JA (office); The Old House, Manor Place, Chislehurst, Kent, BR7 5QJ, England (home). *Telephone:* (20) 7836-0777 (office). *Fax:* (20) 7240-6612 (office). *E-mail:* a.poggio@gibraltar.gov.uk (office). *Website:* www.gibraltar.gov.uk (office).

POGORELICH, Ivo; Croatian concert pianist; b. 20 Oct. 1958, Belgrade; s. of I. Pogorelich and D. Pogorelich; m. Aliza Kezeradze 1980 (died 1996); ed Tchaikovsky Conservatoire of Moscow, then studied with Aliza Kezeradze; debut recital in Carnegie Hall, New York, USA 1981; has appeared in major concert halls throughout the world; f. Bad Wörishofen Festival (Germany) 1988; inaugurated Ivo Pogorelich Int. Solo Piano Competition, Pasadena, CA 1993; UNESCO Goodwill Amb. 1988; f. Sarajevo Charitable Foundation (to raise funds for people of Bosnia in fields of medicine and health) 1994; Fellow-Commoner, Balliol Coll. Oxford 1993; First Prize, Casagrande Competition, Terni, Italy 1978, First Prize, Montréal Int. Music Competition, Canada 1980, Special Prize, Int. Chopin Competition, Warsaw 1980. *Recordings:* numerous recordings for Deutsche Grammophon, starting with a Chopin recital in 1981 and including works by Bach, Beethoven, Brahms, Chopin, Haydn, Liszt, Mozart, Mussorgsky, Prokofiev, Ravel, Scarlatti, Schumann and the Tchaikovsky Piano Concerto No. 1. *Address:* c/o Kajimoto Concert Management Co. Ltd, Kahoku Building, 8–6–25 Hinza, Chuiku, Tokyo 104-0061, Japan (office). *Telephone:* (3) 3574-0969 (office). *Fax:* (3) 3574-0980 (office). *Website:* www.kajimotomusic.com (office).

POHAMBA, Hifikepunye Lucas; Namibian politician and head of state; *President;* b. 18 Aug. 1935; Sec. of Finance SWAPO 1977–89, Sec.-Gen. SWAPO 1997–2002, Vice Pres. 2002–07, Pres. 2007–; Minister of Home Affairs 1990–95, of Fisheries and Marine Resources 1995–98, without Portfolio 1998–2000, of Lands, Resettlement and Rehabilitation 2001–04; Pres. of Namibia 2004–; Chancellor Univ. of Namibia 2011–; Swapo Ongulumbashe Medal 1987. *Address:* Office of the President, State House, Robert Mugabe Avenue, PMB 13339, Windhoek, Namibia (office). *Telephone:* (61) 2707111 (office). *Fax:* (61) 221780 (office). *E-mail:* angolo@op.gov.na (office). *Website:* www.op.gov.na (office).

PÖHL, Karl Otto; German economist; b. 1 Dec. 1929, Hanover; m. Dr Ulrike Pesch; two s. two d.; ed Univ. of Göttingen; Head of Dept Ifo-Research Inst., Munich 1955–60; econ. journalist 1961–67; mem. Man. Bd of the Fed. Asscn of German Banks, Cologne 1968–69; Head of Dept Fed. Ministry of Econ. Affairs 1970–71; Head of Econ. and Fiscal Policy Dept, Fed Chancellor's Office 1971–72; State Sec. Fed. Ministry of Finance 1972–77; Vice-Chair. Deutsche Bundesbank 1977–79, Pres. 1980–91; Pnr, Bankhaus Sal Oppenheimer Jr et Cie 1992–98; Dr hc (Georgetown, Ruhr Univ.) 1983, (Tel Aviv Univ.) 1986, (Maryland) 1987, (Buckingham, London) 1992, (Johann-Wolfgang-Goethe Univ.) 2000. *Address:* c/o Frau Janine Helfenstein, Sal. Oppenheim j. & Cie (Schweiz) AG, Uraniastr. 28, 8022 Zürich, Switzerland. *Telephone:* (44) 2142332. *Fax:* (44) 2142241.

POHL, Reimund, MBA; German business executive; *CEO, Phoenix Pharmahandel AG & Co. KG;* b. 1952; mem. Exec. Bd and CEO Phoenix Pharmahandel AG & Co. KG 2005–; mem. Bd of Dirs and Chair. Phoenix-Pharma Einkauf GmbH; mem. Supervisory Bd Amedis-Ue AG; Dir, COMIFAR SpA, Tamro Group 2000–. *Address:* Phoenix Pharmahandel AG & Co. KG, Pfingstweidstr. 10–12, 68199 Mannheim, Baden-Württemberg, Germany (office). *Telephone:* (6) 2185050 (office). *Fax:* (6) 21854031 (office). *E-mail:* info@phoenixgroup.eu (office). *Website:* www.phoenixgroup.eu (office).

POITIER, Sidney; American actor and film director; b. 20 Feb. 1927, Miami; s. of Reginald Poitier and Evelyn Poitier; m. 1st Juanita Hardy; four d.; m. 2nd Joanna Shimkus 1975; two d.; ed Western Senior High School, Nassau, Governors High School, Nassau; army service 1941–45; acted with American Negro Theatre 1946; appeared in Anna Lucasta 1948, A Raisin in the Sun 1959; mem. Bd of Dirs Walt Disney Co. 1994–2003, Pres. 1994–2003; Amb. to Japan from the Commonwealth of the Bahamas; Hon. KBE 1974; Silver Bear Award, Berlin Film Festival 1958; New York Film Critics' Award 1958; Acad. Award Best Actor of 1963 (for Lilies of the Field); Cecil B. De Mille Award 1982, Life Achievement Award American Film Inst. 1992, Kennedy Center Honors 1995, Hon. Acad. Award for Lifetime Achievement 2002, Presidential Medal of Freedom 2009. *Films include:* No Way Out 1950, Cry, the Beloved Country 1951, Red Ball Express 1952, Go, Man, Go! 1954, Blackboard Jungle 1955, Good-bye, My Lady 1956, Edge of the City 1957, Something of Value 1957, Band of Angels 1957, The Mark of the Hawk 1957, Virgin Island 1958, The Defiant Ones 1958, Porgy and Bess 1959, All the Young Men 1960, A Raisin in the Sun 1961, Paris Blues 1961, Pressure Point 1962, The Long Ships 1963, Lilies of the Field 1963, The Bedford Incident 1965, The Greatest Story Ever Told 1965, A Patch of Blue 1965, The Slender Thread 1965, Duel at Diablo 1966), To Sir, with Love 1967, In the Heat of the Night 1967, Guess Who's Coming to Dinner 1967, For Love of Ivy (also writer) 1968, The Lost Man 1969, They Call Me Mister Tibbs! 1970, Brother John 1971, The Organization 1971, Buck and the Preacher (also dir) 1972, A Warm December (also dir) 1973, Uptown Saturday Night (also dir) 1974, The Wilby Conspiracy 1975, Let's Do It Again (also dir) 1975, A Piece of the Action (also dir) 1977, Stir Crazy (dir) 1980, Hanky Panky (dir) 1982, Fast Forward (dir) 1985, Shoot to Kill 1988, Little Nikita 1988, Ghost Dad (dir) 1990, Sneakers 1992, The Jackal 1997, Bicentennial Nigger 2006. *Television includes:* Separate But Equal 1991, Children of the Dust 1995, To Sir, with Love II 1996, Mandela and de Klerk 1997, David and Lisa 1998, Free of Eden (also exec. producer) 1999, The Simple Life of Noah Dearborn 1999, The Last Brickmaker in America 2001. *Publication:* This Life 1981. *Leisure interests:* football, tennis, gardening. *Address:* c/o CAA, 2000 Avenue of the Stars, Los Angeles, CA 90067, USA.

POIVRE D'ARVOR, Patrick, LenD; French journalist and radio and television presenter; b. 20 Sept. 1947, Reims (Marne); s. of Jacques Poivre and Madeleine France Jeuge; m. Véronique Courcoux 1971 (divorced); six c. (two deceased); ed Lycée Georges-Clemenceau, Reims, Instituts d'études politiques, Strasbourg and Paris, Faculties of Law, Strasbourg, Paris and Reims, École des langues orientales vivantes; Special Corresp., France-Inter 1971, journalist 1971–74, Head Political Dept 1975–76, Deputy Chief Ed., Antenne 2 1976–83, Presenter, evening news programme 1976–83, 1987–2008, Deputy Dir News 1989–; Leader writer, Paris-Match, Journal du Dimanche 1983–91; Producer and Compère, A nous deux, Antenne 2 1983–86, A la folie, TF1 1986–88; Compère, Tous en Scène, Canal Plus 1984–85; Compère and Producer Ex libris 1988–99; Compère Vol de nuit 1999–; Presenter and Producer magazine programme Le Droit de savoir, TF1 1990–94; Pres. Prix Bretagne 2001–11, Jury du Grand Prix de l'Héroïne; Commdr, Ordre des Arts et des Lettres; Chevalier, Ordre nat. du Mérite, Légion d'honneur; Prix Interallié 2000, Prix des Lettres du Livre de Poche 2003, Prix Cyrano 2004. *Television:* led a team in the French TV show Fort Boyard 2010. *Publications include:* Mai 68-Mai 78 1978, Les enfants de l'aube 1982, Deux amants 1984, Le Roman de Virginie 1985, Les Derniers trains de rêve 1986, La Traversée du miroir 1986, Rencontres 1987, Les Femmes de ma vie 1988, L'Homme d'images 1992, Lettres à l'absente 1993, Les Loups et la bergerie 1994, Elle n'était pas d'ici 1995, Anthologie des plus beaux poèmes d'amour 1995, Un héros de passage 1996, Lettre ouverte aux violeurs de vie privée 1997, Une trahison amoureuse 1997, La fin du monde (collection) 1998, Petit homme 1999, Les rats de garde (collection) 2000, L'Irrésolu 2000 (Prix Interallié), Un enfant 2001, Courriers de nuit (collection) 2002, J'ai aimé une reine 2003, Coureurs des morts (collection) 2003, La Mort de don Juan (Prix Maurice-Genevoix 2205) 2004, Les Plus Beaux Poèmes d'amour 2004, Chasseurs de trésors et autres flibustiers 2005, Pirates et corsaires 2005, Coureurs des mers 2005, Le Monde selon Jules Verne 2005, Confessions 2005, Disparaître (co-author) 2006, Age d'or du voyage en train 2006, Rêveurs des Mers (co-author) 2007, J'ai tant rêvé de toi 2007, La vie jusqu'à l'excès 2011. *Website:* patrickpoivredarvor.com.

POKHAREL, Bhoj Raj; Nepalese civil servant; has worked for Ministry of Health, of Supply, of Information and Communication as Sec.; associated with Nat. Referendum Comm. 1979; has worked with numerous nat. and int. orgs including Asian Development Bank, UK Dept for Int. Devt, Danish Int. Devt Agency, WHO, UNDP; Chief Election Commr 2006–09; mem. UN panel to monitor Southern Sudan referendum 2010–. *Address:* c/o Election Commission, Kantipath, Kathmandu, Nepal.

POKHMELKIN, Victor Valeryevich, CAND.JUR.; Russian politician and jurist; b. 3 Feb. 1960, Perm; m.; one s.; ed Perm State Univ., Moscow State Univ.; docent, lecturer Higher Courses of USSR Ministry of Internal Affairs, Perm; f. and Scientific Head Research Inst. of Legal Policy; mem. State Duma (Parl.) 1993–, mem. Vybor Rosii 1993–99, Union of Rightist Forces 2000–01, Co-Chair. Liberal Russia 2001–04; Deputy Chair. Comm. on Law and Legal Reform; mem. Political Council Demokratichesky Vybor Rossii 1994–; Founder and Chair. Motorists of Russia 2002–. *Publications:* several monographs and scientific publs. *Address:* State Duma, Okhotny Ryad 1, 103265 Moscow, Russia (office). *Telephone:* (495) 692-77-66 (office). *Fax:* (495) 692-32-87 (office). *E-mail:* pokhmelkin@duma .gov.ru (office). *Website:* www.pokhmelkin.ru (office).

POKHRIYAL, Ramesh (Nishank), MA, PhD; Indian journalist, poet and politician; b. 15 Aug. 1959, Pinani, Pauri dist; s. of Parmanand Pokhriyal and Vishwambhari Devi; m. Kusum Kanta; three d.; fmr teacher; started political career Ram Mandir Movt; elected mem. Vidhan Sabha (Legis. Ass.) of Uttar Pradesh from Karnpryag 1991, re-elected 1993, 1996, elected from Thalisain constituency 2007; fmr Minister of Culture, Arts and Religion, Minister of Uttaranchal Devt 1998, Minister of Finance 2000, Minister of Health 2007–09; Chief Minister of Uttarakhand 2009–11; mem. Bharatiya Janata Party; Chief Ed. Seemant Varta; Dr hc (International Open Univ., Colombo) 2007, Hon. DLitt (International Open Univ., Colombo) 2009; honoured for his literary work by Univ. of Hamburg, Germany 2008. *Publications include:* has written more than 20 books including several collections of poems, among them Samarpan 1983, Navankur 1984, Mujhe Vidhata Banna Hai 1985, Tum Bhee Mera Saath Chalo 1986, Desh Hum Jalne Na Denge 1988, Koi Mushkil Naheen 2005, Ae Vatan Tere Liye 2006, Ek aur Kahani 2007, Nishant 2008, Sangharsh Jaari Hai 2009, Apna Paraya 2010. *Address:* 37/1, Vijay Colony, Rabindranath Tagore Marg, Dehradun 248 001, India (home). *E-mail:* nishankramesh@gmail.com. *Website:* www .rameshpokhriyalnishank.com.

POKORNI, Zoltán, AB; Hungarian politician and academic; *Vice President, FIDESZ Party;* b. 10 Jan. 1962, Budapest; s. of János Pokorni and Klara Vincz; m. Andrea Beck 1992; four s.; ed Loránd Eötvös Univ., Budapest; Lecturer, Toldy Ferenc High School, Budapest 1987–94; Founding mem. 1988, spokesman 1988–93, Ed. Democratic Trades Union of Teachers' paper –1993; joined Fed. of Young Democrats–Hungarian Civic Party (Magyar Polgári Párt–FIDESZ) 1993, Vice-Pres. 1994–2001, 2003–, Leader 2001–02; mem. Parl. 1994–; Deputy Head Parl. Group 1994–97, Head 1997–98, personal rep. of Budapest XIIth Dist 1998–; fmr Head FIDESZ Dept for Educational Politics; (FIDESZ) Minister of Educ. 1998–2001; Vice-Pres. Parl. Cttee for Educ. and Science; Mayor, Budapest XII Dist 2006. *Address:* FIDESZ, Szentkirályi u.18, 1088 Budapest, Hungary. *Telephone:* (1) 327-6100 (office). *Fax:* (1) 441-5414 (office). *E-mail:* sajtoosztaly@fidesz.hu (office). *Website:* www.fidesz.hu (office); www.pokornizoltan.hu.

POKROVSKY, Valentin Ivanovich, DrMed; Russian physician; *Director, Central Scientific Research Institute of Epidemiology; President, Russian Academy of Medical Sciences;* b. 1 April 1929; m. Nina Yakovlevna Pokrovskaya; one s.; ed First Moscow Medical Inst.; mem. CPSU 1959–91; Dir Central Scientific Research Inst. of Epidemiology 1971–; USSR People's Deputy 1989–91; has studied problems of AIDS treatment, meningitis and intestinal diseases; Chair. Scientific Soc. of Microbiologists, Epidemiologists and Parasitologists; mem. Physicians for the Prevention of Nuclear War; mem. WHO Expert Cttee, WHO Global Cttee on AIDS and Diarrhoeal Diseases, Bd Int. Fed. of Infectionists; mem. USSR (now Russian) Acad. of Medical Sciences 1982– (Pres. 1987–), Presidium of USSR (now Russian) Fed. of Space Flight; Hon. mem. Soc. of Microbiologists of Czech Repub.; V. Timakov Prize, D. Ivanovsky Prize. *Publications:* Symptoms, Treatment and Diagnostics of Salmonellesis in Adults 1981, Immuno-ferment Analysis 1985, Symptoms, Pathogenesis and Treatment of Cholera 1988, Small Medical Encylopaedia (ed.) 1991, Encyclopaedia of Health 1992, Epidemiology of Viral Diseases 2000, Cholera in the USSR – Period of the VIIth Pandemia 2000, Social Hygiene Monitoring and Epidemiology Surveillance in Moscow 2000, Cholera – Acute Problems 2000, Manual of Infectious Diseases and Epidemiology 2004, Prion Diseases 2004. *Address:* Russian Academy of Medical Sciences, Solyanka str. 14, 109544 GSP Moscow, Russia (office). *Telephone:* (495) 298-21-37 (home). *Fax:* (495) 921-56-15 (office). *E-mail:* ramn@ramn.ru (office). *Website:* www.ramn.ru (office).

POL, Marek; Polish politician and economist; b. 8 Dec. 1953, Słupsk; m.; one s. one d.; ed Poznań Univ. of Technology and Acad. of Economy, Poznań; mem. staff advancing to Deputy Dir for Financial and Commercial Affairs, Agric. Vehicle Factory, Antoninek, Poznań 1977–93; mem. Polish United Workers' Party (PZPR) 1976–90; Co-Founder Union of Labour (UP) 1992–, Chair. 1998–; Minister of Industry and Trade 1993–95; Govt Plenipotentiary responsible for reforming the cen. econ. admins 1995–97; Deputy Prime Minister and Minister of Infrastructure 2001–04; Deputy to Sjem (Parl.), mem. Social, Health and Family Affairs Cttee, Alternate mem. Cttee on Culture, Science and Educ.; mem. Supervisory Bd Daewoo-FSO 2000–01. *Leisure interests:* walks with family, reading books and journals. *Address:* Sejm, Chancellerie de la Diète, ul. Wiejska 4/6/8, 00-902, Warsaw, Poland (office); Biuro Poselskie Marka Pola, ul. Torowa 2B 62-510 Konin. *Telephone:* (22) 630-1000 (office); (63) 245-3745.

POLAK, Dame Julia Margaret, DBE, MD, DSc, FRCP, FRCPath, FMedSci; British professor and consultant in histopathology; *Professor Emerita, Department of Chemical Engineering, Imperial College School of Medicine;* b. 29 June 1939, Buenos Aires, Argentina; m. Daniel Catovsky; two s. one d.; ed Univ. of Buenos Aires; various hosp. posts, Buenos Aires 1961–67; Asst Lecturer, Dept of Histochemistry, Royal Postgraduate Medical School, London 1968–69, Lecturer 1970–73, Sr Lecturer 1973–79, Reader 1982–84, Prof. 1984–, Chair. Dept 1992–; Hon. Consultant in Histopathology, Hammersmith Hosp. 1979–, Deputy Dir Dept of Histopathology 1988–; Chair. British Endocrine Pathologists Group 1988–;

Chair. Cognate Research Group, Imperial Coll. School of Medicine 1997–, mem. Scientific Advisory Bd Imperial Coll. Inst. of Biomedical Eng, Dir Tissue Eng Centre 1998–2008, now Prof. Emer., Dept of Chemical Eng; Visiting Prof., Univ. of Texas Health Science Center, Houston 2004; Pres. Tissue and Cell Eng Soc. 1998–; mem. Council Tissue Eng Soc. Int. 2002–05, Acad. of Medical Sciences 2002–05, Stem Cell Advisory Bd Panel Jt MRC/UK Stem Cell Foundation Science Advisory Bd 2005, Panel of Eng and Physical Sciences Research Council Peer Review Coll. 2006–, Panel of MRC Coll. of Experts 2006–; Co-founder and Dir Novathera Ltd (Imperial spin-out co.); European Ed. Tissue Engineering –2004; mem. editorial bd 34 journals; mem. 34 scientific and medical socs; Hon. Fellow, Asscn of Clinical Pathologists 2003; Hon. PhD (Univ. Complutense, Madrid); Dr hc (Sheffield) 2005; Benito de Udaondo Cardiology Prize 1967, Medal of Soc. of Endocrinology 1984, The Cable and Wireless Sir Eric Sharpe Prize for Oncology 1987, Medal, Swedish Soc. of Pathology 1998, Ellison-Cliffe Medal, Royal Soc. of Medicine 2004, Pathology Soc. Award for long services to Pathology 2004, Life Time Achievement Award for contribs to Endocrine Pathology 2006, and others. *Publications:* author or ed. of 25 books, more than 120 review articles and about 1,000 research papers. *Address:* 11 Thames Quay, Chelsea Harbour, London, SW10 0UY, England (home). *Website:* www1.imperial.ac.uk/medicine/about/institutes/tissue (office).

POLANČEC, Damir; Croatian business executive and politician; b. 25 June 1967, Koprivnica; ed Univ. of Zagreb, Leeds Metropolitan Univ.; Import-Export Dept, Podravka dd (food co.) 1992–94, Commercial Assoc. 1994–97, Sr Assoc. 1997, Dir of Cen. Buying 1997–2000, mem. Bd 2000–; Deputy Prime Minister 2005–09, Minister of Economy, Labour and Entrepreneurship 2008–09; mem. Man. Cttee, Croatian Handball Asscn; Pres. HC Podravka, Koprivnica 2000–; mem. Croatian Democratic Union (Hrvatska demokratska zajednica—HDZ). *Address:* c/o Ministry of the Economy, Labour and Entrepreneurship, 10000 Zagreb, ul. grada Vukovara 78, Croatia. *Telephone:* (1) 6106111. *E-mail:* info@mingorp.hr.

POLANCO MORENO, Ignacio, BA (Econ), MBA; Spanish media executive; *Chairman, Grupo Prisa;* s. of the late Jesús de Polanco; ed Univ. of Madrid (Complutense), Instituto de Empresa; professional positions at Timón SA and Promotora de Informaciones SA; mem. Bd of Dirs Grupo Prisa 1993–, Corp. Asst to Chair. Prisa –2006, Deputy Chair. Prisa 2006–07, Chair. 2007–; Chair. Timón SA, Promotora de Publicaciones, SL; Pres. El País newspaper. *Address:* Grupo Prisa, Gran Vía 32 28013 Madrid; El País, Miguel Yuste 40, 28037 Madrid, Spain (office). *Telephone:* (91) 337-8200 (El País) (office); (91) 330-1000 (Prisa) (office). *Fax:* (91) 337-7758 (El País) (office); (91) 330-1038 (Prisa) (office). *E-mail:* redaccion@elpais .com (office); sugerencias@prisa.es (office). *Website:* www.elpais.com (office); www .prisa.es (office).

POLAŃSKI, Roman; French film director, writer and actor; b. 18 Aug. 1933, Paris; s. of Ryszard Polański and Bule Katz-Przedborska; m. 1st Barbara Kwiatkowska-Lass (divorced); m. 2nd Sharon Tate 1968 (died 1969); m. 3rd Emmanuelle Seigner; one s. one d.; ed Polish Film School, Łódź; Acad. française Pris René Clair for Lifetime Achievement 1999, European Film Acad. Lifetime Achievement Award 2006, Federico Fellini Prize for lifetime achievement 2006. *Film roles include:* A Generation, The End of the Night, See You Tomorrow, The Innocent Sorcerers, Two Men and a Wardrobe, The Vampire Killers, What? 1972, Blood for Dracula (uncredited) 1974, Chinatown 1974, The Tenant 1976, Chassécroisé 1982, Back in the U.S.S.R. 1992, A Pure Formality 1994, Dead Tired 1994, Tribute to Alfred Lepetit 2000, The Revenge 2002. *Films directed include:* Two Men and a Wardrobe 1958, When Angels Fall, Le Gros et Le Maigre, Knife in the Water (prize at Venice Film Festival 1962), The Mammals (prize at Tours Film Festival 1963), Repulsion (prize at Berlin Film Festival 1965), Cul de Sac (prize at Berlin Film Festival 1966), The Vampire Killers 1967, Rosemary's Baby 1968, Macbeth 1971, What? 1972, Lulu (opera), Spoleto Festival 1974, Chinatown (Soc. of Film and TV Arts Best Dir Award) 1974, Le Prix Raoul-Levy 1975) 1974, The Tenant 1976, Rigoletto (opera) 1976, Tess (Golden Globe Award) 1980, Vampires Ball 1980, Amadeus (play) 1981, Pirates 1986, Frantic 1988, Tales of Hoffmann (opera) 1992, Bitter Moon (Dir, produced, written) 1992, Death and the Maiden 1994, Dance of the Vampire (play) 1997, The Ninth Gate 1999, Icons, A Pure Formality, In Stuttgart 2000, The Pianist (Best Film, Cannes Film Festival 2002, Acad. Award for Best Dir 2003, BAFTA Award for Best Film and Best Dir 2003) 2002, Oliver Twist 2005, The Ghost Writer (European Film Awards for Best Dir, Best Film) 2010. *Publication:* Roman (authobiography) 1984. *Address:* c/o ICM, 8942 Wilshire Boulevard, Beverly Hills, CA 90211-1934, USA (office). *Telephone:* (310) 550-4000 (office). *Website:* www.icmtalent.com (office).

POLANYI, John Charles, CC, PhD, FRS, FRSC, FRSE; Canadian physical chemist and academic; *University Professor of Physical Chemistry, University of Toronto;* b. 23 Jan. 1929, Berlin, Germany; s. of Michael Polanyi and Magda Polanyi (née Kemeny); m. 1st Anne Ferrar Davidson 1958 (died 2013); one s. one d.; m. 2nd Brenda Bury; ed Manchester Grammar School and Univ. of Manchester, UK; Postdoctoral Fellow, Nat. Research Council of Canada 1952–54; Research Assoc., Princeton Univ., USA 1954–56; Lecturer, Univ. of Toronto, Canada 1956–57, Asst Prof. 1957–60, Assoc. Prof. 1960–62, Prof. of Chem. 1962–; numerous visiting lectureships; mem. numerous professional asscns, including American Acad. of Arts and Sciences, Pontifical Acad. of Sciences; Foreign Assoc., NAS; Hon. Foreign mem. AAAS; Hon. FRSC; Hon. FCIC; hon. degrees from over 30 univs; Marlow Medal, Faraday Soc. 1962, British Chemical Soc. Award 1971, Chemical Inst. of Canada Medal 1976, Henry Marshall Tory Medal, Royal Soc. of Canada 1977, Wolf Prize in Chem. (shared with G. Pimentel) 1982, shared Nobel Prize for Chem. 1986, John Charles Polanyi Prizes est. in his honour by Ont. Govt 1986, Izaak Walton Killam Memorial Prize 1988, Royal Medal, Royal Soc. 1989, Gerhard Herzberg Canada Gold Medal for Science and Eng 2007, pictured on Canada Post first class postage stamp issued for the Int. Year of Chem. 2011, John C. Polanyi Award est. by Natural Sciences and Eng Research Council in his honour, Toronto District School Bd changed name of Sir Sandford Fleming Acad. to the John Polanyi Collegiate Inst. 2011. *Film:* produced Concepts in Reaction Dynamics 1970. *Publications:* The Dangers of Nuclear War (co-ed.) 1979; author of over 250 scientific papers and over 100 articles on policy, the impact of science on society and armament control. *Leisure interests:* walking, skiing. *Address:* Department of Chemistry, University of Toronto, 80 St George Street, Toronto, ON M5S 3H6 (office); 142 Collier Street, Toronto, ON M4W 1M3, Canada (home). *Telephone:* (416) 978-3580 (office); (416) 961-6545 (home). *Fax:* (416)-978-7580

(office). *E-mail:* jpolanyi@chem.utoronto.ca (office). *Website:* www.utoronto.ca/ jpolanyi (office); www.chem.utoronto.ca (office).

POLEGATO, Mario Moretti; Italian business executive; *President, Board of Directors, Geox Group;* b. 1952, Crocetta del Montello; m.; one c.; worked in family wine and agricultural business; f. Geox SpA 1995 (now Geox Group), created and developed a range of 'breathable' footwear, currently Pres. Bd of Dirs and leading shareholder; mem. Bd of Dirs Siparex Italia (pvt. equity fund); mem. arbitration panel Confindustria; Founder ONLUS 'Il Ponte del Sorriso' charitable org. 2004; mem. Aspen Inst. Italia; Hon. Consul-Gen. for Northeastern Italy to Romania 2000, Hon. Affiliate Prof. of Entrepreneurship, ESCP-EAP Business School; Cavaliere al Merito dell'Ordine Nazionale di Romania 2002, Cavaliere del Lavoro 2005; Dr hc (Banatului-Timisoara Univ., Romania) 2003, (Ca' Foscari Univ., Venice); Confindustria Award 1994, Ernst & Young/Il Sole 24 Ore/Borse Italiana Entrepreneur of the Year 2002, Ernst & Young Global Best Italian Entrepreneur in the World 2003, Italian Marketing Asscn Award 2004. *Address:* Geox Group, Via Feltrina Centro 16, Montebelluna, Treviso, Italy (office). *Telephone:* (04) 232822 (office). *Website:* www.geox.biz (office).

POLESE, Kim Karin, BS; American computer industry executive; *Chairman, ClearStreet, Inc.;* b. 13 Nov. 1961; ed Univ. of California, Berkeley, Univ. of Washington, Seattle; started career at IntelliCorp, Inc.; Product Man. Sun Microsystems 1988–95 played a role in definition, direction and launch of Java; Co-founder Marimba Inc. 1996, Pres. and CEO 1996–2000, Chair. 1996–2004; Founder and CEO SpikeSource Inc. 2004–11; currently Chair. ClearStreet, Inc.; mem. Exec. Council TechNet; mem. Bd of Dirs Global Security Inst., Univ of Calif. Pres.'s Bd on Science and Innovation, Silicon Valley Leadership Group; Fellow, Center for Engineered Innovation, Carnegie Mellon Univ; mem. Bd Technorati, Inc. 2004–06, Bd Global Security Inst., Bd Long Now Foundation, Univ. of California Pres.'s Bd on Science and Innovation, Exec. Council of TechNet, Silicon Valley Leadership Group; Hon. DHumLitt (California State Univ.) 2011; named one of Top 25 Most Influential People in America 1997, Symons Innovator Award, Nat. Center for Women & Information Tech. 2010. *Website:* myclearstreet.com (office).

POLET, Robert, MBA; Dutch business executive; *CEO, Gucci Group NV;* b. 1955, Kuala Lumpur; m.; two d.; ed Nijenrode and Univ. of Oregon, USA; joined Marketing and Sales Dept, Unilever in 1978, worked in Paris for two years, spent one year in Milan, then moved to Hamburg, Chair. Unilever Malaysia 1990–92, Chair. Van den Bergh's (Dutch subsidiary) 1993–96, Vice-Pres. Home and Personal Care, Unilever HPC Europe, Brussels 1996, Exec. Vice-Pres., later Business Group Pres. and mem. Unilever Exec. Council, Ice Cream and Frozen Foods Europe Business Group, Rotterdam 1997–2001, Pres. Global Business, Ice Cream and Frozen Foods (following merger with Bestfoods and re-org. of Unilever's foods business) 2001–04; CEO Gucci Group NV 2004–; mem. Supervisory Bd Reed Elsevier NV 2007–. *Leisure interests:* spending time with family, sailing, travelling, playing golf. *Address:* Gucci Group NV, Rembrandt Tower, 1 Amstelplein, 1096 HA, Amsterdam, Netherlands (office). *Telephone:* (20) 462-1700 (office). *Fax:* (20) 465-3569 (office). *Website:* www.gucci.com (office).

POLETTI, Alan Ronald, DPhil, FRSNZ; New Zealand physicist; *Professor Emeritus of Physics, University of Auckland;* b. 19 Oct. 1937, New Plymouth; s. of John Poletti and Pearl Poletti; m. 1st Dorothy M. Martin 1961 (died 1994); three s. one d.; m. 2nd Marcia M. Stenson 1996; ed Univ. of Oxford; Prof. of Physics, Univ. of Auckland 1969–98, Head of Dept of Physics 1986–92, now Prof. Emer. *Publications:* over 100 scientific papers. *Leisure interests:* sailing, public history. *Address:* 11 Tole Street, Ponsonby, Auckland, New Zealand (home). *Telephone:* (9) 373-7599 (home).

POLETTO, HE Cardinal Severino; Italian ecclesiastic; *Archbishop Emeritus of Turin;* b. 18 March 1933, Salgareda, Treviso; ordained priest 1957; parish priest St Mary of the Assumption, Casale 1965; f. Diocesan Centre for Family Ministry 1973; Coadjutant Bishop of Fossano 1980; Bishop of Fossano 1980–89, of Asti 1989–99; Archbishop of Turin 1999–2010, Archbishop Emer. 2010–; cr. Cardinal (Cardinal-Priest of San Giuseppe in via Trionfale) 2001. *Address:* Archdiocese of Torino, Via Arcivescovado 12, 10121 Turin, Italy (office). *Telephone:* (011) 5156211 (office). *Fax:* (011) 5156209 (office). *Website:* www.diocesi.torino.it (office).

POLFER, Lydie; Luxembourg lawyer and politician; b. 22 Nov. 1952; d. of Camille Polfer; m. Hubert Wurth (q.v.); one d.; ed Lycée Robert Schuman, Univ. of Grenoble, France, Univ. Centre for Int. and European Research, Grenoble; admitted to Luxembourg Bar 1977; mem. Chamber of Deputies (Parl.) 1979–99; Mayor City of Luxembourg 1982–99; mem. European Parl. 1985–89, 1990–94, 2004–, mem. Group of the Alliance of Liberals and Democrats for Europe, Chair. Del. to ACP-EU Jt Parl. Ass., mem. Cttee on Foreign Affairs; Chair. Democratic Party 1994–2004; Deputy Prime Minister, Minister of Foreign Affairs and External Trade, Minister of Civil Service and Admin. Reform 1999–2005; Großes Goldenes Ehrenzeichen am Bande für Verdienste um die Republik Österreich 2006. *Address:* Bât. Altiero Spinelli, 08G258, 60, rue Wiertz 60, 1047 Brussels, Belgium (office). *Telephone:* (2) 284-56-21 (office). *Fax:* (2) 284-96-21 (office).

POLI, Roberto; Italian energy industry executive and academic; *Chairman, Eni SpA;* b. 1938; Prof. of Corp. Finance, Cattolica di Milano 1966–98; fmr Chair. Rizzoli-Corriere della Sera SpA, Publitania SpA; currently Pres. Poli e Associati SpA (fmrly Poli Morelli & Partners SpA); Chair. Ente Nazionale Idrocarburi (Eni) Group SpA (oil and gas co.) 2002–; mem. Bd of Dirs Fininvest SpA, Mondadori SpA, Merloni Termosanitari SpA, Coesia SpA, Maire Tecnimont SpA, Perennius Capital Partners SGR SpA. *Address:* Eni SpA, Piazzale Enrico Mattei 1, 00144 Rome, Italy (office). *Telephone:* (06) 59821 (office). *Fax:* (06) 59822141 (office). *E-mail:* segreteriasocietaria.azionisti@eni.it (office). *Website:* www.eni.it (office).

POLIAKOFF, Martyn, CBE, BA, PhD, FRS, FRSC, FIChemE; British chemist and academic; *Research Professor of Chemistry, Faculty of Science, University of Nottingham;* b. 16 Dec. 1947; s. of Alexander Poliakoff and Ina Poliakoff (née Montagu); brother of Stephen Poliakoff; one s. one d.; ed Westminster School, King's Coll., Cambridge; Research/Sr Research Officer, Dept of Inorganic Chem., Univ. of Newcastle upon Tyne 1972–79; Lecturer, Dept of Chem., Univ. of Nottingham 1979–85, Reader in Inorganic Chem. 1985–91, Prof. of Chem. 1991–, EPSRC/Royal Acad. of Eng Clean Tech. Fellow 1994–99; Foreign Sec. and Vice-

Pres. Royal Soc. 2011–; mem. Council Inst. of Chemical Enginners 2009–13, Advisory Council for Campaign for Science and Eng; Chair. Editorial Bd RSC journal Green Chemistry; Foreign mem. Russian Acad. of Sciences 2011; Prof. of Chem., Moscow State Univ.; Hon. mem. Chemical Soc. of Ethiopia 2008; RSC Meldola Medal and Prize 1976, Leverhulme Medal, Royal Soc. 2010, Nyholm Prize for Education 2011. *Publications:* numerous papers in professional journals on the chemical applications of supercritical fluids, with particular emphasis on Green Chemistry. *Address:* Room B13A, School of Chemistry, University Park, Nottingham, NG7 2RD, England (office). *Telephone:* (115) 951-3520 (office). *Fax:* (115) 951-3058 (office). *E-mail:* martyn.poliakoff@nottingham.ac.uk (office). *Website:* www .nottingham.ac.uk/chemistry (office).

POLIAKOFF, Stephen, CBE, FRSL; British playwright and film director; b. 1 Dec. 1952, London; s. of the late Alexander Poliakoff and Ina Montagu; m. Sandy Welch 1983; one s. one d.; ed Westminster School and Univ. of Cambridge; Hon. degree (Tavistock Inst.). *Theatre:* Clever Soldiers 1974, The Carnation Gang 1974, Hitting Town 1975, City Sugar 1976, Strawberry Fields (Nat. Theatre) 1978, Shout Across the River (RSC) 1978, The Summer Party 1980, Favourite Nights 1981, Breaking the Silence (RSC) 1984, Coming in to Land (Nat. Theatre) 1987, Playing with Trains (RSC) 1989, Siena Red 1992, Sweet Panic (Hampstead) 1996, Blinded by the Sun (Nat. Theatre) 1996 (Critics' Circle Best Play Award), Talk of the City (RSC) 1998, Remember This (Nat. Theatre) 1999, My City 2011. *Films:* Runners (original story and screenplay) 1983, Hidden City 1988, Close My Eyes (Best British Film Award, Evening Standard) 1991, Century 1993, Glorious 39 2009. *Television:* Stronger Than the Sun 1977, Bloody Kids (aka One Joke Too Many, USA) 1979, Caught on a Train (BAFTA for Best Single Drama) 1980, Soft Targets 1982, She's Been Away (Venice Film Festival Prize) 1989, Frontiers 1996, Food of Love 1998, The Tribe 1998, Shooting the Past (Prix Italia for Best Drama, RTS Award for Best Drama) 1999, Perfect Strangers/Almost Strangers (RTS Award for Best Drama and Best Writer, BAFTA Dennis Potter Award, Peabody Award for Drama) 2001, The Lost Prince (Primetime Emmy for Outstanding Miniseries, Best Costume and Best Production Design) 2004, Friends and Crocodiles 2006, Gideon's Daughter (Peabody Award for Drama) 2007, Joe's Palace 2007, A Real Summer 2007, Capturing Mary 2007, Dancing on the Edge 2013. *Publications:* Plays One 1989, Plays Two 1994, Plays Three 1998, Sweet Panic and Blinded by the Sun, Talk of the City, Shooting the Past, Remember This. *Leisure interests:* watching cricket, going to the cinema. *Address:* Ruby Films, 26 Lloyd Baker Street, London, WC1X 9AW, England (office). *Telephone:* (20) 7833-9990 (office).

POLITI, Mauro; Italian judge and professor of law; b. 13 Sept. 1944, Fabrica di Roma; ed Univ. of Florence; Asst Prof. of Pvt Int. Law, Univ. of Cagliari, Sardinia 1976–79; Asst Prof. of Public Int. Law, Univ. of Urbino 1979–83, Assoc. Prof. of Int. Law 1983–86; Assoc. Prof. of Int. Law, Univ. of Trento 1986–90, Prof. of Int. Law 1990–; began judicial career at Tribunal of Florence 1969; Judge, Tribunal of Oristano 1972, of Milan 1975–83; Deputy Prosecutor, Juvenile Court, Milan 1972–75; Legal Adviser, Perm. Mission to UN, New York, USA 1992–2001; *ad litem* Judge, Int. Criminal Tribunal for Fmr Yugoslavia (ICTY) 2001; Judge, Int. Criminal Court (ICC), The Hague 2003–09; mem. Del. to UN Security Council 1995–96; mem. Del. to Preparatory Cttee for ICC 1995–97, 1999–2002; Chair. Sixth Legal Cttee of UN Gen. Ass. 2000–01. *Publications include:* The Rome Statute of the International Criminal Court: A Challenge to Impunity (co-ed.) 2001, International Criminal Court and National Jurisdictions (co-ed.) 2008; book chapters and articles in professional law journals. *Address:* Università degli Studi di Trento, Facoltà di Giurisprudenza, Dipartimento di Scienze Giuridiche, Via Giuseppe Verdi 53, 38100 Trento, Italy (office). *Telephone:* (0461) 881818 (office). *Fax:* (0461) 881899 (office). *E-mail:* mauro.politi@jus.unitn.it (office). *Website:* www.jus.unitn.it (office).

POLITZER, H. David, BS, PhD; American physicist and academic; *Professor of Physics, California Institute of Technology;* b. 31 Aug. 1949, New York; ed Bronx High School of Science, Harvard Univ.; Visiting Assoc., Calif. Inst. of Tech., Pasadena 1975–76, faculty mem. 1976–, Full Prof. 1979–, Head of Physics Dept 1986–88; Nobel Prize in Physics (jt recipient) 2004. *Films:* appeared in minor role in film Fat Man and Little Boy 1989. *Address:* California Institute of Technology, High Energy Physics, 1201 East California Boulevard, Mail Code 452-48, Pasadena, CA 91106-3368, USA (office). *Telephone:* (626) 395-4252 (office). *E-mail:* politzer@theory.caltech.edu. *Website:* www.pma.caltech.edu.

POLKINGHORNE, Rev. Canon John Charlton, Kt, KBE, MA, PhD, ScD, FRS; British physicist and fmr ecclesiastic; b. 16 Oct. 1930, Weston-super-Mare; s. of George B. Polkinghorne and Dorothy E. Charlton; m. Ruth I. Martin 1955; two s. one d.; ed Perse School, Cambridge, Trinity Coll., Cambridge and Westcott House, Cambridge; Commonwealth Fund Fellow Calif. Inst. of Tech. 1955–56; Lecturer, Univ. of Edin. 1956–58; Lecturer, Univ. of Cambridge 1958–65, Reader 1965–68, Prof. of Math. Physics 1968–79; Fellow, Trinity Coll. Cambridge 1954–86; ordained deacon 1981, priest 1982; Curate, St Andrew's, Chesterton 1981–82, St Michael & All Angels, Bedminster 1982–84; Vicar of St Cosmus and St Damian in the Blean 1984–86; Fellow and Dean, Trinity Hall, Cambridge 1986–89, Hon. Fellow 1989–; Pres. Queens' Coll. Cambridge 1989–96, Fellow 1996–, Hon. Fellow 1996–; Canon Theologian, Liverpool Cathedral 1994–2005; Six Preacher, Canterbury Cathedral 1996–2006; mem. Church of England Doctrine Comm. 1989–95, General Synod 1990–2000, Human Genetics Advisory Comm. 1996–99, Human Genetics Comm. 2000–02; Hon. Fellow, St Edmund's Coll., Cambridge 2002; Hon. Prof. of Theoretical Physics, Univ. of Kent 1984–89; Hon. DD (Kent) 1994, (Durham) 1999, (Gen. Theological Seminary) 2010, (Wycliffe Coll.) 2011; Hon. DSc (Exeter) 1994, (Leicester) 1995, (Marquette) 2003; Hon. DHum (Hong Kong Baptist) 2006; Templeton Prize 2002. *Publications:* The Analytic S-Matrix (jointly) 1966, The Particle Play 1979, Models of High Energy Processes 1980, The Way the World Is 1983, The Quantum World 1984, One World 1986, Science and Creation 1988, Science and Providence 1989, Rochester Roundabout 1989, Reason and Reality 1991, Science and Christian Belief 1994, Quarks, Chaos and Christianity 1994, Serious Talk 1995, Scientists as Theologians 1996, Beyond Science 1996, Searching for Truth 1996, Belief in God in an Age of Science 1998, Science and Theology 1998, Faith, Science and Understanding 2000, The End of the World and the Ends of God (ed with M. Welker) 2000, Faith in the Living God (with M. Welker) 2001, The Work of Love (ed.) 2001, The God of Hope and the End of the World 2002, Quantum Theory: A Very Short Introduction 2002, Living with Hope

2003, Science and the Trinity 2004, Exploring Reality 2005, Quantum Physics and Theology 2007, From Physicist to Priest 2007, Theology in the Context of Science 2008, Questions of Truth (with N. Beale) 2009, Encountering Scripture 2010, Science and Religion in Quest of Truth 2011. *Leisure interest:* gardening. *Address:* Queens' College, Cambridge, CB3 9ET, England (office).

POLLACK, Ilana, BA; Israeli librarian; b. 13 Aug. 1946, Tel-Aviv; d. of Leon Pinsky and Mala First Pinsky (née Ferszt); m. Joseph Pollack 1977 (died 1994); two s.; ed Re'alit High School, Rishon Le Zion, Tel-Aviv Univ. and Hebrew Univ. Jerusalem; served in Israeli Army 1964–66; joined Weizmann Inst. of Science, Rehovot, Asst Librarian 1966, Librarian in charge of Physics Faculty Library 1975, Chief Librarian, Weizmann Inst. of Science 1983–2009 (retd). *Address:* 22 Shenkin Street, Rishon Le-Zion 75282, Israel. *Telephone:* 3-9692186. *Fax:* 8-9344176.

POLLINI, Maurizio; Italian pianist; b. 5 Jan. 1942, Milan; s. of Gino Pollini and Renata Melotti; m. Maria Elisabetta Marzotto 1968; one s.; has played with Berlin and Vienna Philharmonic Orchestras, Bayerischer Rundfunk Orchestra, London Symphony Orchestra, Boston, New York, Philadelphia, LA and San Francisco Orchestras; has played at Salzburg, Vienna, Berlin, Prague Festivals; recordings for Polydor Int; First Prize Int. Chopin Competition, Warsaw 1960, Ernst von Siemens Music Prize, Munich 1996, Edison Classical Music Award for Best Instrumental Solo Recital 2007, Grammy Award for Best Instrumental Soloist Performance 2007, Disco d'Oro 2007, Praemium Imperiale 2010, RPS Instrumentalist Award 2012. *Recordings include:* Chopin's Nocturnes (Prix Victoire for Best Classical Recording) 2007, Bach's The Well-Tempered Clavier, Book 1 2010, Chopin Etudes Opp.10 & 25 (Gramophone Award for Best Historic Recording 2012) 2011, Brahms Piano Concerto No. 1 op.15 (ECHO Klassik Award for Concerto Recording of the Year/Piano – 19th Century 2012). *Address:* Harrison Parrott, 5–6 Albion Court, London, W6 0QT, England (office). *Telephone:* (20) 7229-9166 (office). *Fax:* (20) 7221-5042 (office). *E-mail:* info@harrisonparrott.co.uk (office). *Website:* www.harrisonparrott.com (office).

POLLO, Genc; Albanian politician; *Minister for Innovation and Information and Communication Technologies;* b. 7 April 1963, Tirana; m.; two c.; ed Univ. of Tirana, Univ. of Vienna, Austria; Researcher, Acad. of Sciences 1986–88; adviser to Pres. of Albania 1992–96; Chair. New Democrat Party 2001–; Minister of Educ. and Science 2005–07, Deputy Prime Minister 2007–09, Minister of State and Parliamentary Relations 2009–10, Minister for Innovation and Information and Communication Technologies 2010–. *Address:* Council of Ministers Building, Dëshmoret e Kombit Blvd 1, Tirana, Albania (office). *Telephone:* (4) 2277306 (office). *Fax:* (4) 2248298 (office). *E-mail:* gpollo@km.gov.al (office). *Website:* www .mitik.gov.al (office).

POLLOCK, Shaun MacLean, BCom; South African fmr professional cricketer; b. 16 July 1973, Port Elizabeth, Cape Prov.; s. of Peter Pollock and Inez Pollock; m. Patricia 'Trish' Lauderdale; two d.; ed Northwood High School, Univ. of Natal, Durban; bowling all-rounder: right-hand batsman, right-arm fast-medium bowler; played for KwaZulu-Natal 1992–2004, S Africa 1995–2008 (Capt. Test side 2000–03, ODI side 2000–05), Warwicks. 1996–2002, Dolphins 2004/05, Africa XI 2007, Durham 2008, Mumbai Indians 2008, Natal, ICC (Int. Cricket Council) World XI; First-class debut: Natal B v Western Prov. B, Pietermaritzburg 1991; Test debut: S Africa v England, Centurion 16–20 Nov. 1995; One-Day Int. (ODI) debut: S Africa v England, Cape Town 9 Jan. 1996; S Africa v NZ, Johannesburg 21 Oct. 2005; played in 108 Tests, scored 3,781 runs (average 32.31, highest score 111, 2 hundreds), bowling figures: 421 wickets at an average of 23.11 runs, best bowling (innings) 7/87, (match) 10/147; ODIs: played in 303 matches, scored 3,519 runs, took 393 wickets; First-class: played in 186 matches, scored 7,023 runs (average 33.12), took 667 wickets at an average of 23.25 runs; announced retirement from all forms of int. cricket 11 Jan. 2008; Wisden Cricketer of the Year 2003. *Leisure interests:* music, golf, reading. *Address:* c/o KwaZulu-Natal Cricket Union, PO Box 47266, Greyville, 4023, South Africa. *Website:* dolphinscricket.co.za.

POLMAN, Paul, BBA, BA, MA, MBA; Dutch business executive; *CEO, Unilever NV and Unilever PLC;* b. 1956, Enschede; m.; three c.; ed Univ. of Groningen, Univ. of Cincinnati, USA; began career with Procter & Gamble in finance 1979, assignments in Belgium, the Netherlands, France, Spain, UK and USA, Assoc. Finance position, Procter & Gamble 1979–86, Category Man. and Marketing Dir Baby, FemPro, Cleanser and Beverages, Procter & Gamble France 1986–89, Vice-Pres. and Gen. Man. Procter & Gamble Iberia 1989–95, Vice-Pres. and Gen. Man. Procter & Gamble UK 1995–98, Pres. Global Fabric Care 1998–2001, Group Pres. Procter & Gamble Europe 2001–06; Chief Financial Officer Nestlé SA 2006–08, Exec. Vice-Pres. and Zone Dir for US, Canada, Latin America and The Caribbean 2008, Chair. and Dir Enterprises Maggi SA, Nestlé Finance SA, Nestlé International Travel Retail SA, Nestlé Capital Advisers; Chair. and Dir Intercona Re AG; Exec. Dir, Unilever PLC and Unilever NV 2008–, CEO Unilever NV 2008–, Unilever PLC 2009–; mem. Bd of Dirs Alcon Inc. 2006–10; Dir (non-exec.) Dow Chemical Co. 2010–; Chair. Perkins Int. Advisory Bd; Pres. Kilimanjaro Blindtrust; mem. Exec. Cttee World Business Council for Sustainable Devt, European Round Table, Int. Business Council of the World Econ. Forum, Swiss American Chamber of Commerce, Bd of Consumer Goods Forum (Co-Chair. Bd Strategy and Sustainability Cttees); Trustee, Leverhulme Trust, Asia House; Hon. DCL (Univ. of Northumbria, UK) 2000; WSJ/CNBC European Business Leader of the Year 2003, Carl Lidner Award, Univ. of Cincinnati 2006, Chief Financial Officer of the Year, Investor Magazine 2007, Atlantic Council Award for Distinguished Business Leadership 2012, CK Prahalad Award for Global Sustainability Leadership 2012. *Leisure interests:* running marathons, mountaineering, sailing, reading, travelling. *Address:* Unilever PLC, Unilever House, 100 Victoria Embankment, London, EC4Y 0DY, England (office). *Telephone:* (20) 7822-5252 (office). *Fax:* (20) 7822-5511 (office). *E-mail:* press-office.london@unilever.com (office). *Website:* www.unilever.com (office).

POLOZ, Stephen S., BA, MA, PhD; Canadian economist and central banker; *Governor, Bank of Canada;* b. 1955, Oshawa, Ont.; m. Valerie Poloz; one s. one d.; ed Queen's Univ., Univ. of Western Ontario; served 14 years at Bank of Canada (central bank) 1981–94, becoming Chief of Research Dept 1992–94, Gov. 2013–; economist with BCA Research (ind. investment research firm), Montreal 1994–99; Man. Ed. The International Bank Credit Analyst 1996; Vice-Pres. and Chief Economist, Export Devt Canada 1999–2004, Sr Vice-Pres. of Corp. Affairs

2004–08, Sr Vice-Pres. of Financing 2008–10, Pres. and CEO 2011–13; fmr Visiting Scholar, IMF, Washington, DC and Econ. Planning Agency, Tokyo; fmr Pres. Ottawa Econs Asscn. *Address:* Bank of Canada, 234 Wellington Street, Ottawa, ON K1A 0G9, Canada (office). *Telephone:* (800) 303-1282 (office). *Fax:* (613) 782-7713 (office). *E-mail:* info@bankofcanada.ca (office). *Website:* www.bankofcanada.ca (office).

POLOZKOVA, Lidia Pavlovna; Russian sports official and fmr speed skater; b. 8 March 1939, Zlatoust; d. of Pavel I. Skoblikov and Klavdia N. Skoblikova; m. Alexander G. Polozkov; one s.; six gold medals in Winter Olympic Games 1960 and 1964; all-round world champion 1963–64; won 40 gold medals, 25 at world championships and 15 in USSR; mem. CPSU 1964–91; Head Dept of Physical Educ., Moscow Higher School of the All-Union Trade Union Movt 1974–88; Sr Vice-Pres. of All-Union Trade Unions Soc. for Physical Culture and Sports 1988–92; Vice-Pres. Russian Speed-Skating Fed. 1992–95; Head, Fund for Support of Sports Veterans 1997–; Hon. mem. Russian Speed-Skating Fed. 1995–; Honoured Master of Sports 1960, Olympic Order in Silver 1983, Int. Women's Sports Hall of Fame 1996, Order of Red Banner of Labour. *Publications:* numerous publs on sport and physical culture. *Leisure interests:* reading, theatre, forest walking, sports, knitting. *Address:* c/o Russian Speed-Skating Federation, Luzhnetskaya nab. 8, Moscow, Russia. *Telephone:* (495) 201-10-40.

POLTAVCHENKO, Lt-Gen. Georgy Sergeyevich; Russian politician and engineer; *Governor of St Petersburg;* b. 24 Feb. 1953, Baku, Azerbaijan SSR, Soviet Union (now Azerbaijan); m.; one s.; ed Leningrad Inst. of Aviation Machinery, Higher KGB Courses, St Petersburg Finance Tech. School; constructor, involved in bldg Kama truck plant 1972, worked in unit Leninets, worked in local Comsomol Cttee St Petersburg; on staff in KGB orgs 1979–, with KGB, Leningrad Region 1980–92; People's Deputy of Leningrad Regional Council 1990–93; Head Dept Fed. Service of Tax Police, St Petersburg 1993–99; unsuccessful cand. in Leningrad City Council elections 1998; Rep. of Russian Pres. to Leningrad Region 1999–2000, to Cen. Fed. Okrug (Dist) 2000–11; Gov. of St Petersburg 2011–; Pres. St Petersburg Basketball Fed. *Address:* Office of the Governor, 19000 St Petersburg, Russia (office). *Telephone:* (812) 276-4501 (office). *E-mail:* gov@gov.spb.ru (office). *Website:* http://petersburgcity.com/city/administration/ (office).

POLTORANIN, Mikhail Nikiforovich; Russian politician and journalist; b. 22 Nov. 1939, Leninogorsk, E Kazakhstan Region; m.; two s.; ed Kazakh State Univ., Higher CP School; corresp., Ed.-in-Chief local newspapers in Altai 1966–68, Exec. Sec. Kazakhstanskaya Pravda 1970–75, Corresp. Pravda in Kazakhstan 1975–86, Ed.-in-Chief Moskovskaya Pravda 1986–88, Political Corresp. Press Agency Novosti 1988–90; USSR People's Deputy 1989–91; Minister of Press and Mass Media of Russia 1990–92, Deputy-Chair. of Govt (Deputy Prime Minister) of Russia Feb.–Nov. 1992, Dir Fed. Information Agency 1992–93; mem. State Duma (Parl.) 1993–95; Chair. Cttee on Information Policy and Communications 1994–95; Chair. Bd Moment of Truth Corpn 1994–; mem. Bd of Dirs TV-3 Russia 1998–, Exec. Dir 1999–. *Address:* TV-3, Bersenevskaya nab. 20/2, 109017 Moscow, Russia. *Telephone:* (495) 959-06-37.

POLUNIN, Vyacheslav Ivanovich; Russian mime artist and clown; *Artistic Director, Litsedei;* b. 12 June 1950, Novosil, Orlov Region; s. of Pavlovich Polunin and Nikolayevna Polunina; m. Elena Ushakova; two s.; ed Leningrad Inst. of Culture; f. Theatre of Comic Pantomime Actors Litsedei 1968; f. Leningrad Mime Parade 1982; f. All-Union Festival of Street Theatres 1987, All-Union Congress of Fools 1988, Russian Acad. of Fools; took part in European Caravan of Peace 1989; tours around Europe; lives in UK; Golden Angel Prize of Edin. Festival, Golden Nose Prize, Spain, Lawrence Olivier Prize, England, Triumph Prize, Russia 1999. *Leisure interests:* painting, sculpture, architecture, design. *Address:* Litsedei, Tchaikovskogo ul., 59, St Petersburg, Russia. *Telephone:* (812) 272-8879. *Fax:* (812) 272-2356. *E-mail:* licedei@cityline.spb.ru.

POLVINEN, Tuomo Ilmari, PhD; Finnish historian and professor of history; *Professor Emeritus, Academy of Finland;* b. 2 Dec. 1931, Helsinki; s. of Eino Ilmari Polvinen and Ilona Vihersalo; m. Eeva-Liisa Rommi 1965; two d.; ed Univ. of Helsinki; Docent, Univ. of Helsinki 1965; Prof. of Modern History, Tampere Univ. 1968–70; Dir-Gen. Nat. Archives of Finland 1970–74; Prof. of Modern History, Univ. of Helsinki 1974–92; Research Prof., Acad. of Finland 1979–95, now Prof. Emer.; Urho Kekkonen Prize 1981. *Publications include:* Venäjän vallankuuma ja Suomi 1917–1920, I–II 1967, 1971, Suomi kansainvälisessä politiikassa 1941–47, I–III 1979, 1980, 1981, Between East and West: Finland in International Politics 1944–47 1986, J. K. Paasikivi, Valtiomiehen elämäntyö Vol. 1, 1870–1918 1989, Vol. 2, 1918–39 1992, Vol. 3, 1939–44 1995, Vol. 4, 1944–48 1999, Vol. 5, 1948–56 2003, Imperial Borderland: Bobrikov and the Attempted Russification of Finland, 1898–1904 1995. *Address:* Purotie 3 A 10, 00380 Helsinki, Finland (home). *Telephone:* (9) 408554 (home). *E-mail:* tuomo.polvinen@elisanet.fi.

POLYAKOV, Alexander Markovich, PhD; Russian theoretical physicist and academic; *Joseph Henry Professor of Physics, Princeton University;* b. 27 Sept. 1945, Moscow; fmrly with Landau Inst. for Theoretical Physics, Moscow; now Joseph Henry Prof. of Physics, Princeton Univ., USA; mem. USSR (now Russian) Acad. of Sciences 1984, NAS 2005; Dirac Medal, Int. Centre for Theoretical Physics 1986, Dannie Heineman Prize for Math. Physics 1986, Lorentz Medal 1994, Oskar Klein Medal 1996, Harvey Prize, Technion, Israel 2010, Lars Onsager Prize (co-recipient) 2011, Fundamental Physics Prize 2013. *Publications:* numerous papers in professional journals. *Address:* Department of Physics, Princeton University, 348 Jadwin Hall, Princeton, NJ 08544, USA (office). *Telephone:* (609) 258-4314 (office). *Fax:* (609) 258-1073 (office). *E-mail:* polyakov@princeton.edu (office). *Website:* www.princeton.edu/physics (office).

POLYDORAS, Vyron; Greek lawyer, politician and writer; b. 27 Jan. 1947, Perivolia, Olympia; m.; one s. twin d.; ed Univ. of Athens, Univ. of Nevada, USA, Acad. of Int. Law, The Hague, Netherlands, Univ. of Strasbourg, France, Univ. of Salzburg, Austria; mem. (New Democracy) of the Vouli (Parl. for Athens B 1981–, mem. Standing Cttee on Public Admin, Public Order and Justice, Cttee for the Revision of the Constitution, mem. Parl. Assemblies of the Council of Europe and WEU 1990–2000, elected Dean of the House June and Nov. 1989, Vice-Pres. of the Vouli (Deputy Speaker) 2009–12, Pres. (Speaker) 6 May 2012; Deputy Minister for the Presidency and Govt Spokesman 1990–91, 1991–92; Deputy Minister for Educ. and Religious Affairs Aug.–Dec. 1992; Deputy Minister for Foreign Affairs

(responsible for Greeks Abroad) 1992–93; Minister of Public Order 2006–07; elected onto Admin. Cttee of New Democracy 1979, stood for office of Party Chair. 1997, Head of New Democracy Section on the Interior, Public Admin and Decentralization 2000–01, mem. Cen. Cttee of New Democracy and group co-ordinator for the Standing Cttee on Public Admin, Public Order and Decentralization 2001, Party Officer responsible for trade, medium-sized enterprises and the Cttee for Competition; fmr reserve officer in the Greek Army; Makarios III Medal (highest decoration of the Repub. of Cyprus); Ipektsi Award for Greek-Turkish friendship 1995. *Publications include:* (in Greek): Greek Ideology, In the Ideological Trenches, On Meritocracy, Politics and Art, Positive Logos, Bushido, Greek Political Development; trans. into Greek of John Keats' Eve of St Agnes (awarded Prize for Best Trans.). *Address:* Vouli, Parliament Building, Leoforos Vassilissis Sofias 2, 100 21 Athens (office); 5 Sofokleous str., 10559 Athens, Greece. *Telephone:* (210) 3708112 (office); (210) 3242550. *Fax:* (210) 3733566 (office); (210) 3243650. *E-mail:* vpolydoras@yahoo.gr (office); polydoras@parliament.gr (office). *Website:* www.hellenicparliament.gr (office); www.vyron-polydoras.gr.

POLYE, Don; Papua New Guinea civil engineer and politician; spent several years working in transport infrastructure sector; mem. Nat. Parl. for Kandep Open electorate 2002–09; Minister for Transport and Civil Aviation 2006–09, Deputy Prime Minister July–Dec. 2010, Minister for Foreign Affairs, Trade and Immigration 2010–11 (dismissed), apptd Minister for Finance and Treasury 2011, lost finance portfolio 2012, Minister for Treasury 2012–14; Founding mem. Nat. Alliance Party. *Address:* c/o Department of Finance, Vulupindi Haus, POB 710, Waigani, NCD, Papua New Guinea.

POLZE, Werner, Dr rer. pol; German banker; b. 26 March 1931, Altenburg; m. Margitta Polze 1956; one d.; ed School of Economics, Berlin, Akad. für Staats- und Rechtswissenschafte, Babelsberg (Inst. of Int. Relations); worked for Deutsche Notenbank, Berlin, GDR 1956–66; joined Deutsche Aussenhandelsbank AG 1966, Exec. Vice-Pres. 1969–78, Pres. 1978–91, Spokesman for the Bd from 1991; Deputy Chair. Supervisory Bd, DIHB Deutsche Industrie- und Handelsbank AG, Berlin from 1990.

POMERANTS, Marko, MA; Estonian politician; b. 24 Sept. 1964, Tamsalu, Lääne-Viru Co.; m.; two s.; ed Univ. of Tartu; Deputy Head, Rakvere Nature Protection Admin 1989–90; Head of Nature Protection Service, Lääne-Viru Co. Govt 1990–94, Head of Environment Dept 1994–95, Gov. Lääne-Viru Co. 1995–2003; mem. (Union of Pro Patria and Res Publica) 10th Riigikogu (Parl.) 2003, 2005–07, 11th Riigikogu 2007–09; Minister of Social Affairs 2003–05, of the Interior 2009–11; mem. Union of Pro Patria and Res Publica; Estonian Border Guards Meritorious Service Cross (2nd class) 2000; Memorial Medal for 10 Years of the Re-Established Defence Forces 2001, Golden Cross of the Rescue Service 2002, Border Guards Sword and Lynx Badge 2002. *Leisure interests:* volleyball, nature, family, physical and social environment. *Address:* c/o Ministry of the Interior, Pikk 61, Tallinn 15065, Estonia. *Telephone:* 612-5001.

POMEROL, Jean-Charles; French computer scientist, academic and fmr university administrator; *Professor Emeritus, Université Pierre et Marie Curie;* b. 22 May 1943, Mantes-la-Jolie, Yvelines, Ile-de-France; s. of Charles Pomerol and Marcelle Legay; m. Marie-Jeanne Danjou 1972; three c.; ed Univ. Pierre et Marie Curie, Paris; began career as teacher, Lycée Saint-Quentin; Lecturer, Centre universitaire Saint-Quentin (Aisne); Sr Lecturer, Univ. Pierre et Marie Curie, Paris (UPMC) later Prof. of Computer Science and Dir Teaching and Research Dept, now Prof. Emer., Project Leader CNRS 1995–2000, Dir CNRS-UPMC Lab. for Artificial Intelligence, Vice-Pres. of Science 2002–06, Pres. UPMC 2006–11; Pres. Fondation Voir et Entendre, Fondation des Sciences Mathématiques de Paris; fmr Ed. Revue Française d'Intelligence Artificielle; Founder Journal of Decision Systems; Chevalier, Légion d'honneur. *Publications:* numerous books and publs, including Multicriterion Decision Making for Business 2000, Decision-Making and Action 2012. *Leisure interest:* the mountains. *Address:* Université Pierre et Marie Curie, Tour Zamansky, 19th Floor, 4 place Jussieu, 75252 Paris Cedex 05, France (office). *Telephone:* 1-44-27-38-81 (office). *Fax:* 1-44-27-74-84 (office). *E-mail:* jean-charles.pomerol@upmc.fr (office). *Website:* www.upmc.fr/fr/universite/histoire_et_personnalites/les_presidents_de_l_universite/jean_charles_pomerol_depuis_2006.html (office).

POMMIER, Jean-Bernard; French pianist and conductor; b. 17 Aug. 1944, Beziers; two d. by Irena Podleska; ed Conservatoire de Paris; as pianist has appeared with conductors including: Herbert von Karajan, Bernard Haitink, Pierre Boulez, Riccardo Muti, Gennadi Rozhdestvensky, Leonard Slatkin, Zubin Mehta and Daniel Barenboim; has conducted numerous orchestras including Chamber Orchestra of Europe, Orchestre de Paris; debut with Royal Liverpool Philharmonic Orchestra 1991; Artistic Dir Northern Sinfonia, Newcastle-upon-Tyne 1996–99; Prin. conductor Orchestra Filarmonica di Torino 1997; f. and Artistic Dir Musiké International Acad.; performances world-wide; masterclasses in Chicago, London, Lausanne and Melbourne; Officier, Ordre nat. du mérite; awards include Int. Competition of Young Musicians, Berlin, Prix de la Guilde des artistes solistes Français, Diapason d'Or, Tchaikovsky Prize, Moscow. *Recordings include:* Mozart Piano Concerti (with Sinfonia Varsovia), Poulenc Piano Concerti (with City of London Sinfonia), Brahms Cello Sonatas and Violin Sonatas, Complete Beethoven Piano Sonatas, complete Mozart Sonatas. *Address:* Musiké Académies Productions, Chemin de Praz-Simon 3, 1000 Lausanne, Switzerland. *Website:* www.musike.co.uk.

POMODORO, Arnaldo; Italian sculptor and theatrical designer; b. 23 June 1926, Morciano di Romagna; s. of Antonio Pomodoro and Beatrice Luzzi; has worked as jeweller and goldsmith 1950–; artist-in-residence, Stanford Univ. 1966–67, Univ. of Calif., Berkeley 1968; lecture course, Mills Coll., Oakland, Calif. 1979–82; Grande Ufficiale, Ordine al Merito (Italy) 1986, Cavaliere di Gran Croce dell' Ordine al merito 1996; Hon. DLitt (Dublin) 1992, Hon. DArch (Ancona) 2001; Int. Sculpture Prize, São Paulo Biennale, Brazil 1963, Premio Nazionale di scultura, Venice Biennale 1964, Int. Sculpture Prize (Carnegie Inst., Pittsburgh) 1967, Henry Moore Grand Prize (Hakone Open-Air Museum, Japan) 1981, Praemium Imperiale for Sculpture (Japan Art Asscn) 1990, VII Premio Michelangelo per la Scultura 1998, Ministry of Culture Gold Medal 2005, Premio Lex Spolentina 2006, Guglielmo Marconi Award 2006, ISC Lifetime Achievement in Contemporary Sculpture Award 2008. *Theatrical designs include:* Semiramide, Rome 1982,

Orestea, Gibellina, Sicily 1983–85, Alceste, Genoa 1987, Oedipus Rex, Siena 1988, Cleopatra, Gibellina, Sicily 1989, I Paraventi at Bologna 1990, Nella solitudine dei campi di cotone by Koltès, Rome 1991, Benevento 1998, More Stately Mansions by O'Neill, Rome 1992, Oreste by Alfieri, Rome 1993, Stabat Mater by Tarantino, Rome 1994–95, Moonlight by Pinter, Brescia, Rome 1995, Antigone by Anouilh, Taormina 1996, Il Caso Fedra by di Martino 1997, The Tempest, Palermo 1998, Capriccio by Strauss, Naples 2002, Madama Butterfly by Puccini, Torre del Lago 2004, Un Ballo in Maschera by Verdi, Lipsia 2005. *Publications:* L'arte lunga 1992, Arnaldo Pomodoro 1995, Scritti critici per Arnaldo Pomodoro e opere dell'artista 1955–2000 2000, Arnaldo Pomodoro nei giardini del Palais-Royal di Parigi 2003, Arnaldo Pomodoro e il Museo Poldi Pezzoli, La Sala d'Armi 2004, Corona nella Cattedrale di Milwaukee (with Giuseppe Maraniello) 2004, Catalogo della scultura 2007. *Leisure interests:* photography, theatre, literature. *Address:* Via Vigevano 5, 20144 Milan, Italy. *Telephone:* (02) 58104131. *Fax:* (02) 89401303 (office). *E-mail:* info@arnaldopomodoro.it (office). *Website:* www.fondazionearnaldopomodoro.it (office).

PONCE CEVALLOS, Javier; Ecuadorean journalist and government official; *Minister of National Defence;* b. 28 April 1948, Quito; ed Escuela de Sociología y Ciencias Políticas, Univ. Central del Ecuador; columnist El Tiempo newspaper 1966–70; with Ministry of Agriculture 1973–77; Dir Artes cultural review 1977–78; Sec. Gen. Ecumenical Cttee of Projects 1986–97, Coordinator 1997–; Ed. HOY 1992–99, Ed. de investigaciones 1999–2001, columnist 1989–2001; editorial writer and columnist El Universo 2001–; Ed. Enciclopedia Planeta 2002–03; Personal Sec. to Pres. Rafael Correa 2006–08; Minister of Nat. Defence 2008–. *Address:* Ministry of National Defence, Exposición 208, Quito, Ecuador (office). *Telephone:* (2) 221-6150 (office). *Fax:* (2) 256-9386 (office). *Website:* www.midena.gov.ec (office).

PONCE ENRILE, Juan, LLM; Philippine lawyer and government official; b. 14 Feb. 1924, Gonzaga, Cagayan; s. of Alfonso Ponce Enrile and Petra Furagganan; m. Cristina Castañer 1957; one s. one d.; ed Ateneo de Manila, Univ. of the Philippines and Harvard Law School; practising corp. lawyer and Prof. of Law 1956–64; Under-Sec. of Finance 1966–68; Acting Sec. of Finance; Acting Insurance Commr; Acting Commr of Customs; Sec. of Justice 1968–70; Sec. of Nat. Defence 1970–71 (resgnd), 1972–78, Minister 1978–86 (reappointed under Aquino Govt 1986); Chair. Cttee on Nat. Security, Defense, Peace and Order; mem. Senate and Opposition Leader (Nacionalista Party) 1987–92, 1995–2001, 2004–, Senate Pres. 2008–13; arrested Feb. 1990, released March 1990; mem. House of Reps 1992–95, mem. Finance, Appropriations and Steering Cttees; Chair., Bd of Dirs Philippine Nat. Bank until 1978, Nat. Investment and Devt Co., United Coconut Planters Bank, Nat. Disaster Control Center; Dir Philippine Communications Satellite Corpn; Trustee and Sec., Bd of Trustees, Cultural Centre of the Philippines; Chair. Exec. Cttee, Nat. Security Council; mem. Bd, Nat. Econ. and Devt Authority, Energy Devt, Philippine Nat. Oil Co., Nat. Environmental Protection Council, Philippine Overseas Telecommunications Corpn, Philippine Crop Insurance Corpn; mem. numerous law and commercial asscns; two hon. degrees; Commdr, Philippine Legion of Honour 1986; Mahaputra Adipranada Medal (Indonesia) 1975, People of the Year Award 2010 (Govt Service) 2011. *Publications include:* A Proposal on Capital Gains Tax 1960, Income Tax Treatment of Corporate Merger and Consolidation Revisited 1962, Tax Treatment of Real Estate Transactions 1964, Where There's a Will 1995, Juan Ponce Enrile – A Memoir 2012. *Leisure interests:* reading, golf, tennis, swimming, water-skiing, fishing. *Address:* 2305 Morado Street, Dasmariñas Village, Makati, Metro Manila, Philippines (home). *Website:* www.juanponceenrile.com.

PONCELET, Christian; French politician; b. 24 March 1928, Blaise (now part of Vouziers) in the Ardennes; s. of Raoul Poncelet and Raymonde Poncelet (née Chamillard); m. Yvette Miclot 1949; two d.; ed Coll. Saint-Sulpice, Paris and Nat. Ecole Professionelle des Postes, Télégraphes et Télécommunications; Deputy (Union pour un Mouvement Populaire—UMP) to Nat. Ass. for the Vosges 1962–77; Sec. of State, Ministry of Social Affairs 1972–73, Ministry of Employment, Labour and Population 1973–74; Sec. of State for the Civil Service attached to Prime Minister March–May 1974; Sec. of State for the Budget, Ministry of Econ. Affairs and Finance 1974–77, for Relations with Parl. 1977; Conseiller Général, Remiremont 1963–73; Pres. Conseil Général des Vosges 1976–; Sénateur des Vosges 1977–, Pres. Comm. for Finance, Budgetary Control and Econ. Accounts of the Nation to the Senate 1986–98, Pres. of Senate 1998–2008; mem. European Parl. 1979–80; Mayor of Remiremont 1983–2001; Pres. groupe France-Viet Nam, Groupe français de l'Union Interparlementaire; mem. French Section Assemblée parlementaire de la francophonie; mem. Institut de France, Acad. des Sciences morales et politiques; Grand Cross of the Royal Norwegian Order of Merit 2000. *Leisure interest:* hunting. *Address:* Palais du Luxembourg, 75291 Paris Cedex 06 (office); 17 rue du Etats-Unis, 88200 Remiremont, France (home). *Telephone:* 1-42-34-36-77 (office). *Fax:* 1-42-34-20-94 (office). *E-mail:* c.poncelet@senat.fr (office). *Website:* www.senat.fr (office).

PONDER, Sir Bruce Anthony John, Kt, MB, BChir, PhD, FRS, FRCP, FRCPath, FMedSci; British medical scientist, oncologist and academic; *Professor Emeritus of Oncology, University of Cambridge;* b. 25 April 1944, Haywards Heath, Sussex, England; s. of Anthony West Ponder and Dorothy Mary Ponder (née Peachey); m. Margaret Ann Hickinbotham; four c.; ed Univ. of Cambridge; began career as clinician, St Thomas' Hosp., London; fmr Sr Registrar Oncology Dept, St Bartholomew's Hosp., London; Researcher, Imperial Cancer Research Unit, Mill Hill 1977; Hamilton Fairley Fellowship, Harvard Medical School, USA 1977–78; Researcher, Inst. of Cancer Research, Sutton 1978, also clinical appointment, Royal Marsden Hosp.; Prof. of Oncology, Univ. of Cambridge 1996–, also becoming Head of Dept of Oncology, Li Ka-shing Prof. of Oncology 2007–11, Prof. Emer. 2013–, Dir Li Ka-shing Centre 2007–13; Co-Dir Hutchison/MRC Research Centre; Co-Dir Strangeways Research Labs 1996–2009; Dir Cancer Research UK Cambridge Inst. 2006–13; Founder-Fellow, Acad. of Medical Sciences; Ed.-in-Chief Breast Cancer Research 1999–2009; Pres. British Asscn for Cancer Research 2010–14; mem. Bd of Dirs American Asscn for Cancer Research 2007–11; Founder Faculty, Acad. of the American Asscn for Cancer Research 2013; Hamilton Fairley Award, Eur Soc. for Medical Oncology 2004, MD Anderson Cancer Center Bertner Award 2007, NCI Alfred Knudson Award for Cancer Genetics 2008, Ambuj Nath Bose Prize, Royal Coll. of Physicians 2008, Lifetime Achievement Award in Cancer

Research, Cancer Research UK 2013. *Publications:* more than 500 peer-reviewed scientific papers on cancer research and genetics. *Leisure interests:* photography, gardening, golf, travel, wine. *Address:* Cancer Research UK, Cambridge Research Institute, Li Ka Shing Centre, Robinson Way, Cambridge, CB2 0RE, England (office). *Telephone:* (1223) 761860 (office). *E-mail:* bruce.ponder@cruk.cam.ac.uk (office). *Website:* www.cambridgecancer.org.uk (office).

PONOMAREV, Aleksander Sergeyevich; Russian journalist and manager; b. 13 Oct. 1956; m. Nadezhda Ponomareva; one s. one d.; ed Saratov State Univ.; Komsomol work 1979–87; Deputy Ed.-in-Chief Cen. Youth Programme Section, USSR Cen. TV 1987–88, Ed.-in-Chief 1988–91; Dir Creative Union of Experimental TV, Ostankino 1992–93, First Deputy Dir-Gen. Oskankino 1992–93; co-founder and Vice-Pres. Moscow Ind. Broadcasting Corpn (MNVK), Dir-Gen. 1993–, First Vice-Pres. 1997–2001; Deputy Chair. All-Russian State TV Co.; Dir Cultura Camel 2001–. *Address:* Kultura TV Channel, Leningradsky prosp. 22/2, Moscow, Russia. *Telephone:* (495) 234-89-75 (office).

PONS, Bernard Claude, DenM; French physician and politician; b. 18 July 1926, Béziers, Hérault; s. of Claude Pons and Véronique Vogel; m. Josette Cros 1952; one s. three d.; ed Lycées, Marseilles and Toulouse and Faculté de Médecine, Montpellier; gen. practitioner, Cahors 1954; mem. Union pour la nouvelle République 1967–68, Union des Démocrats pour la République 1968–78, Rassemblement pour la République (RPR) 1978–2002, Union pour un Mouvement Populaire (UMP) 2002–; Deputy to Nat. Ass. 1967–69, 1973–86, 1988–95, 1997–2002, Pres. RPR Group 1988–95; Conseiller-Gen. Cajarc canton 1967–78; Sec. of State, Ministry of Agric. 1969–73; mem. Conseil-Gen. Ile-de-France 1978; Sec.-Gen. RPR 1979–84; Paris City Councillor 1983–; Pres. Admin. Council, Paris Câble 1984–; Rep. to Ass. of EC 1984–85; Minister for Overseas Departments and Territories 1986–88; Minister of Town and Country Planning, Equipment and Transport May–Nov. 1995, for Capital Works, Housing, Transport and Tourism 1995–97. *Address:* Union pour un Mouvement Populaire, 55 rue de La Boétie, 75384 Paris Cedex 08 (office); Paris TV câble, 4 villa Thoréton, 75015 Paris, France. *Telephone:* 1-40-76-60-00 (office). *E-mail:* webmaster@u-m-p.org (home). *Website:* www.u-m-p.org (office).

PONSOLLE, Patrick; French business executive; *Chairman, Morgan Stanley France;* b. 20 July 1944, Toulouse; s. of Jean Ponsolle and Marie-Rose Courthaliac; m. Nathalie Elie Lefebvre 1983; two d.; ed Lycées Janson-de-Sailly and Henry IV, Paris, Ecole normale supérieure de la rue d'Ulm, Ecole Nat. d'Admin; civil servant Ministry of Econs and Finance 1973–77; Financial Attaché Embassy, Washington 1977–79; Head of Mission for Dir of Forecasting, Ministry of Econs and Finance 1980; Sec.-Gen. Nat. Accounts and Budgets Comm. 1980–81; Deputy Chief of Staff to Budget Minister 1981–83; Deputy Dir, Asst Man. Dir Compagnie de Suez 1983–87, Man. Dir 1988, Chief Exec. 1991–93; Vice-Chair., Man. Dir then Chair. and Man. Dir Suez International 1985; Chair. Soc. financière pour la France et les pays d'outre mer (Soffo) 1990–96; Co-Chair. Eurotunnel Group, Chair. Eurotunnel SA 1994–96, Exec. Co-Chair. 1996–2001; Dir Unichem PLC 1998–2006; Dir (non-exec.) Alliance Boots PLC 2006–07; Adviser, Morgan Stanley Dean Witter (now Morgan Stanley) 1999–, Chair. Morgan Stanley France, Vice-Chair. and Man. Dir 2001–; Dir numerous cos, including France Télécom, Banque Indosuez; chair. numerous bodies. *Address:* Morgan Stanley France, 61 rue de Monceau, 75008 Paris (office); 3 rue Danton, 75006 Paris, France (home). *Telephone:* 1-42-90-70-00. *Fax:* 1-42-90-70-99 (office). *Website:* www.morganstanley.com.

PONTA, Victor, BA, MA, PhD; Romanian lawyer and politician; *Prime Minister;* b. 20 Sept. 1972, Bucharest; m. 1st Roxana (divorced 2006); one s.; m. 2nd Daciana Sârbu 2008; one d.; ed Neculce High School, Univ. of Bucharest, Univ. of Catania, Italy, Carol I Nat. Defence Univ., Social Democratic Inst., Bucharest; Lecturer in Criminal Law, Romanian-American Univ. 1996–98, 2002–12; worked as prosecutor handling cases at Sector 1 Courthouse 1995–98; prosecutor at Supreme Court of Justice in anti-corruption div. dealing with econ. and financial crimes 1998–2001; co-ordinated Bureau for Combating Money Laundering 2000–01; held rank of Sec. of State as Head of Govt's Control Dept 2001–04; joined Supervisory Council of Authority for State Assets Recovery 2001, mem. special cttee investigating penal infractions committed by mems of the govt 2001; Minister-Del. for Control of Int. Grant Programmes Implementation and for Monitoring the Application of Acquis Communautaire 2004; mem. Partidul Social Democrat (PSD—Social Democratic Party) 2002–, Head of Interim Nat. Council of Social Democratic Youth (TSD) July–Nov. 2002, mem. Nat. Council of PSD Oct. 2002–, mem. Exec. Bureau Nov. 2002–, Pres. TSD Nov. 2002–06, Vice-Pres. PSD 2006–10, Pres. 2010–; mem. Camera Deputaților (Chamber of Deputies) for Gorj Co. 2004– (re-elected 2008), served as Sec. and Vice-Pres. of its Perm. Bureau; Minister-Del. for Relations with Parl. in Office 2008–09; apptd Vice-Pres. European Community Org. of Socialist Youth 2005; Prime Minister 2012–; Jt Leader Social Liberal Union (Uniunea Social Liberală) 2012–14; Vice-Pres. Socialist International 2012–; Kt, Nat. Order for Faithful Service 2002, Ordine della Stella della Solidarietà Italiana 2004. *Achievements include:* won nat. championships in basketball 1989, auto-racing 2008. *Publications:* several books on criminal law, including one on the International Criminal Court. *Address:* Office of the Prime Minister, 011791 Bucharest 1, Piața Victoriei 1 (office); Partidul Social Democrat (Social Democratic Party), 011346 Bucharest 1, Șos. Kiseleff 10 (office); Birou de avocatură, Bucharest, bl. Dimitrie Cantemir, 2A, bl. P2 sc. 1 et. 1 ap. 3 Sector 4, Romania; 210191, jud Gorj, Târgu Jiu, Str. Victoriei 2–4. *Telephone:* (21) 3143400 (office); (21) 2222953 (office); (21) 3356231; (253) 214224 (Gorj). *Fax:* (21) 3139846 (office); (21) 2223272 (office); (21) 3356231; (353) 810513 (Gorj). *E-mail:* drp@guv.ro (office); pontavictor@ymail.com (office); info@psd.ro (office). *Website:* www.guv.ro (office); www.psd.ro (office); www.victorponta.ro.

PONTAL, Jean-François; French business executive; *Adviser, ING Direct France;* b. 17 April 1943, Chaton; m. Martine Lorain-Broca 1968; two c.; ed Centres d'Etudes Supérieures des Techniques Industrielles; human resources consultant Inst. Bossard; Vice-Pres. of Operations, then of Resources and Markets Carrefour, CEO Pryca (Spanish subsidiary), mem. bd with responsibility for S Europe 1993–96; Head Consumer Services Div. France Télécom 1996–2001, apptd Pres. Wanadoo 2000, Exec. Vice-Pres. France Télécom –2001, CEO Orange (after merger with France Télécom) 2001–03 (retd); Adviser Retail Banking Segment ING Direct France 2003–; mem. Bd of Dirs Sonaecom 2003–, Southwing S.L. 2004–, Investcom LLC 2005–, OTL 2006–; Chevalier, Ordre nat. du Mérite. *Leisure* *interests:* sailing, tennis. *Address:* c/o ING Direct, Service Clientèle, Libre Réponse 70678, 75568 Paris cedex 12, France (office).

PONTI, Michael; German-American concert pianist; b. 29 Oct. 1937, Freiburg, Germany; s. of Joseph Ponti and Zita Wüchner; m. 1st Carmen Wiechmann 1962 (divorced 1971); one s. two d.; m. 2nd Beatrice van Stappen 1984; one s.; studied under Prof. Gilmour McDonald and Prof. Erich Flinsch; debut in Vienna 1964, in New York 1972; has toured extensively world-wide; over 80 recordings; suffered a stroke 2000, now performs concerts for left hand only; Busoni Award, Italy 1964. *Address:* Heubergstrasse 32, 82438 Eschenlohe, Germany. *Telephone:* (8824) 913754.

PONTING, Ricky Thomas, AO; Australian fmr professional cricketer; b. 19 Dec. 1974, Launceston, Tasmania; s. of Graeme Ponting and Lorraine Ponting (née Campbell); m. Rianna Jennifer Cantor 2002; two d.; ed Brooks Sr High School, Launceston; right-handed higher middle-order batsman; occasional right-arm medium-pace and off break bowler; slips and close catching fielder; played for Tasmania 1992–2013 (Capt. 2001–02, 2007–08), Australia 1995–2012 (Vice-Capt. Test side 2000–03, Capt. 2003–11, Capt. ODI side 2002–11), Somerset 2004, Kolkata Knight Riders 2008, Hobart Hurricanes 2011–13, Mumbai Indians (Capt.) 2013, Surrey June–July 2013, Antigua Hawksbills 2013, ICC (Int. Cricket Council) World XI; First-class debut: Nov. 1992; Test debut: Australia v Sri Lanka, Perth 8–11 Dec. 1995; final Test: Australia v South Africa, Perth 30 Nov.–3 Dec. 2012; One-Day Int. (ODI) debut: Australia v S Africa, Wellington, NZ 15 Feb. 1995; T20I debut: NZ v Australia, Auckland, NZ 17 Feb. 2005; played in 168 Tests, took five wickets and scored 13,378 runs (41 centuries, 62 fifties), highest score 257, average 51.85; ODIs: 375 matches, took three wickets and scored 13,704 runs, highest score 164, average 42.03; Capt. of Australia's World Cup winning side 2003 (scored 140 in final against India), 2007; second batsman ever to score more than 1,500 runs in a calendar year 2003; only fourth batsman to score more than 11,000 career runs in Test cricket 2009; highest Australian run-scorer in history of Test cricket 31 July 2009; only the third player and the first Australian (after Sachin Tendulkar and Rahul Dravid) to pass 13,000 career Test runs 2012; most successful Australian capt. of all time; player with Most World Cup matches as capt.; retd from all forms of the game 2013; One-Day Int. Player of the Year 2002, ICC Test Player of the Year 2003, 2004, 2006, Allan Border Medal as Australian Cricketer of the Year 2004, 2006, 2007, 2009 (jtly), Wisden Cricketer of the Year 2006, Compton-Miller Medal (The Ashes Man of the Series) 2006–07, ICC Player of the Year 2006, 2007, voted Cricinfo Player of the Decade 2000–09 2010, inducted into Australian Inst. of Sport 'Best of the Best' 2011. *Leisure interests:* football, golf. *Address:* c/o DSEG, Level 1, 189 Rouse Street, Port Melbourne, Vic. 3207, Australia (office). *Telephone:* (3) 9645-6911 (office). *Fax:* (3) 9646-8470 (office). *E-mail:* jahenderson@dseg.com.au (office). *Website:* www.dseg.com.au (office).

PONTZIOUS, Richard; American conductor and artistic director; *Artistic Director and Conductor, Asian Youth Orchestra;* has conducted orchestras, bands and choirs in Europe and Asia; Founder, Artistic and Exec. Dir and Conductor, Asian Youth Orchestra 1990–; Bronze Bauhina Star, Hong Kong Govt 2000. *Address:* Suite 15A, One Capital Place, 18 Luard Road, Wanchai, Hong Kong Special Administrative Region, People's Republic of China (office). *Telephone:* (852) 28661623 (office). *Fax:* (852) 28613340 (office). *E-mail:* ayo@asianyouthorchestra.com (office). *Website:* www.asianyouthorchestra.com (office).

POO, Murdaya Widyawimarta; Indonesian business executive and politician; b. (Poo Tjie Gwan), 21 Jan. 1941, Blitar, East Java; m. Siti Hartati Murdaya; four c.; f. Berca Group (now Central Cipta Murdaya—CCM), cos include PT Abdibangun Buana, PT Asea Brown Boveri Sakti, PT Intracawood Manufacturing (Intraca), also owns Nike Shoe factories in Indonesia; Dir Metropolitan Kentjana (real estate co.); Commr PT Dharmala Intiland; fmr mem. Partai Demokrasi Indonesia Perjuangan (expelled Dec. 2009), mem. House of Reps (parl.) for Banten –2009; Pres. Dir Pondok Indah Golf Course. *Address:* c/o Metropolitan Kentjana, Jl Metro Pd Indah Bl III-B Pon., Jakarta 12310, Indonesia (office).

POOLE, David James, PPRP, ARCA; British artist; b. 5 June 1931, London; s. of Thomas Herbert Poole and Catherine Poole; m. Iris Mary Toomer 1958; three s.; ed Stoneleigh Secondary School, Wimbledon School of Art, Royal Coll. of Art; Sr Lecturer in Painting and Drawing, Wimbledon School of Art 1961–77; Pres. Royal Soc. of Portrait Painters 1983–91; work in HM The Queen's collection, London and in pvt. collections in Australia, Bermuda, France, Germany, S Africa, Saudi Arabia, Switzerland and USA; solo exhbns in Zurich and London; portraits include: HM Queen Elizabeth II, HRH Prince Philip, HM Queen Elizabeth the Queen Mother, HRH Prince Charles, HRH Prince Andrew, HRH Prince Edward, HRH The Princess Royal, The Duke of Kent, Earl Mountbatten of Burma, mems of royal staff including Sir Alan Lascelles, Sir Michael Adeane, Sir Martin Charteris, Sir Philip Moore, Sir William Heseltine, Sir Robert Fellowes, Sir Robin Janvrin, mems of govt, industry, commerce, medicine and acad. and legal professions. *Leisure interests:* French travel, food and drink. *Address:* Trinity Flint Barn, Weston Lane, Weston, Petersfield, GU32 3NN, England. *Telephone:* (1730) 265075. *E-mail:* david@trinity04.fsnet.co.uk.

POON, Christine A., MS, MBA; American business executive; *Dean, Fisher College of Business;* b. Cincinnati, Ohio; d. of James Poon and Virginia Poon; m. Mike Tweedle; ed Northwestern, St Louis and Boston Univs; joined Bristol-Myers Squibb in 1985, various man. positions including Pres. and Gen. Man. Squibb Diagnostics' Canadian operation 1994, Sr Vice-Pres. for Canada and Latin America, Pharmaceutical Operations –1997, Pres. Medical Devices 1997–98, Pres. Int. Medicines 1998–2000; Co. Group Chair. Pharmaceuticals Group, Johnson & Johnson 2000–01, mem. Exec. Cttee and Worldwide Chair. Pharmaceuticals Group 2001–03, Worldwide Chair. Medicines and Nutritionals 2003–09, Vice-Chair., mem. Office of the Chair. and mem. Bd Dirs Johnson & Johnson 2005–2009; Dir, mem. Finance Cttee and Investment Cttee, Prudential Financial, Inc. 2006–; mem. Advisory Bd Healthcare Businesswomen's Asscn; Dean and John W. Berry, Sr Chair in Business, Ohio State Univ.'s Fisher Coll. of Business 2009–; Dir, mem. Compensation Cttee and Corporate Governance & Compliance Cttee, Regeneron Pharmaceuticals, Inc. 2010–; mem. Bd Dirs Fox Chase Cancer Center, Phila; ranked by Fortune magazine amongst 50 Most Powerful Women in Business in the US (27th) 2003, (15th) 2004, (12th) 2005, (11th) 2006, (14th) 2007, ranked by Forbes magazine amongst 100 Most Powerful Women (17th) 2004, (43rd) 2005,

(26th) 2006, (46th) 2007, (46th) 2008, Healthcare Businesswomen's Asscn Woman of the Year 2004. *Address:* The Fisher College of Business, The Ohio State University, 201 Fisher Hall, 2100 Neil Avenue, Columbus, OH 43210, USA (office). *Telephone:* (614) 292-2666 (office). *Website:* fisher.osu.edu (office).

POON, Chung-Kwong, OBE, BSc, PhD, DSc, CChem, FRSC, JP; Hong Kong chemist, university president and academic; *President Emeritus, The Hong Kong Polytechnic University;* b. 1940, Hong Kong; m.; three c.; ed St Paul's Co-educational Coll., Univ. of Hong Kong, Univ. of London, UK; Post-doctoral Research Fellow, Univ. Coll. London 1967, Calif. Inst. of Tech., USA 1967–68 (Visiting Research Assoc. 1976, 1979); Visiting Research Assoc., Univ. of Southern California 1972; Lecturer in Chem., Univ. of Hong Kong 1968–75, Prof. of Chem. 1982–90, Dean of Faculty of Science 1983–90; Dir Hong Kong Polytechnic 1991–94; Pres. The Hong Kong Polytechnic Univ. 1991–2008, Pres. Emer. 2009–; has chaired or been a mem. of numerous cttees of Hong Kong Govt and of industrial, business and educational sectors, including mem. Legis. Council 1985–91, Preparatory Cttee for Hong Kong Special Admin. Region 1994–97; Founding Chair. Govt's Cttee on Science and Tech. 1988–91; mem. CPPCC Nat. Cttee 1998–; Chair. Radiological Protection Advisory Group 1989–2007; Consultant of Science and Tech. Consulting Cttee, Shenzhen Municipal People's Govt 2000–; mem. Policy Consultative Cttee, Shaanxi Prov. 2000–; mem. Nuclear Safety Consultative Cttee, Guangdong Daya Bay Nuclear Power Station 1986–, Huaqiao Univ. Council 1992–, Shantou Univ. Council 2000–07; Fellow, Univ. Coll. London 1996; Foreign mem. Russian Acad. of Eng 2004; apptd a non-official JP 1989; Hon. Prof. at several univs on Chinese mainland; Gold Bauhinia Star 2002; recipient of UK Commonwealth Scholarship 1964–67, Fulbright Scholarship 1967–68, honoured as one of "Ten Outstanding Young Persons in Hong Kong" 1979. *Address:* Office of the President Emeritus, The Hong Kong Polytechnic University, Yuk Choi Road, Hung Hom, Kowloon, Hong Kong Special Administrative Region, People's Republic of China (office). *Telephone:* 27665381 (office). *Fax:* 27731447 (office). *E-mail:* pckpoon@polyu.edu.hk (office). *Website:* www.polyu.edu.hk (office).

POON, Dickson, CBE; Hong Kong business executive; *Group Executive Chairman, Dickson Concepts (International) Limited;* s. of Poon Kam Kai; m. 1st Marjorie Yang (divorced); one d.; m. 2nd Michelle Yeoh (q.v.) 1988 (divorced 1991); m. 3rd Pearl Yu 1992; ed St Joseph's Coll., Hong Kong, Uppingham School, UK and Occidental Coll., Los Angeles, USA; apprenticeship in watchmaking at Chopard's, Geneva, Switzerland; returned to Hong Kong and opened first Dickson watch and jewellery shop 1980; Co-founder (with Sammo Hung) DMV film co. 1983; Head of Dickson Concepts, Hong Kong, operating more than 240 boutiques and outlets throughout SE Asia and in China; acquired French co. S.T. Dupont label 1987, sold 1997; acquired stake in Harvey Nichols, London 1991, floated co. 1996, pvt. takeover 2002, opened brs in Leeds 1997, Edinburgh 2002, Manchester 2003; bought 85% stake in Hong Kong and Shenzhen brs of Japanese dept store Seibu 1996; sole benefactor of Hong Kong Univ.'s Man. Inst.; The Dickson Poon China Centre, St Hugh's Coll., Oxford named in his honour 2010, The Dickson Poon School of Law, King's Coll., London named in his honour 2012. *Address:* Dickson Concepts (International) Ltd, Fourth Floor, East Ocean Centre, 98 Granville Road, Tsimshatsui East, Kowloon, Hong Kong (office). *Telephone:* 2311-3888 (office). *Fax:* 2311-3323 (office). *E-mail:* info@dickson.com.hk (office). *Website:* www.dickson.com.hk (office).

POOS, Jacques F., Dr.Oec; Luxembourg politician; b. 3 June 1935; m.; three c.; ed Athénée Grand-Ducal, Univ. of Lausanne and Luxembourg Int. Univ.; Ministry of Nat. Economy 1959–62; Service d'Etudes et de Statistiques Economiques (STATEC) 1962–64; Dir Imprimerie Coopérative 1964–76; Pres. SYTRAGAZ 1970–76; MP 1974–76; Minister of Finance, Gov. IBRD, IMF, EIB 1976–79; Dir Banque Continentale du Luxembourg SA 1980–82, Banque Paribas (Luxembourg) SA 1982–84; Vice-Pres. Parti Socialiste 1982; Deputy Prime Minister and Minister of Foreign Affairs, Foreign Trade and Co-operation 1984–99; Pres. EU Council of Ministers 1985, 1991, 1997; mem. European Parl. 1999–2004, mem. Comm. for Foreign Affairs, Human Rights, Public Security and Defence Policy; fmr Pres. Council of European Union; currently mem. Council, Banque Centrale du Luxembourg; mem. various Bds of Dirs in financial sector; Hon. DIur (Athens) 2002. *Publications:* Le Luxembourg dans le Marché Commun 1961, Le Modèle Luxembourgeois 1981, La Crise Economique et Financière: est-elle encore maitrisable? 1984; numerous newspaper and periodical articles. *Address:* 45 Square Mayrisch, 4240 Esch-Alzette, Luxembourg (home). *Telephone:* (352) 556425 (home). *Fax:* (352) 570419 (home). *E-mail:* poosj@pt.lu (home).

POP, Iggy; American singer, musician (guitar) and actor; b. (James Jewel Osterberg), 21 April 1947, Ann Arbor, Mich.; ed Univ. of Michigan; formed high-school band Iguanas 1962, Prime Movers 1966; concerts in Michigan, Detroit and Chicago; formed The Stooges (originally the Pyschedelic Stooges) 1967, re-formed 2007–; solo artist 1976–; collaborations with David Bowie 1972–; numerous tours and TV appearances; inducted into Rock and Roll Hall of Fame 2010. *Film appearances:* Rock & Rule (voice) 1983, Sid and Nancy 1986, The Color of Money 1986, Hardware 1990, Cry-Baby 1990, Atolladero 1995, Tank Girl 1995, Dead Man 1995, The Crow – City of Angels (also known as The Crow II) 1996, The Brave 1997, The Rugrats Movie (voice) 1998, Snow Day 2000, Coffee and Cigarettes 2003, Persepolis (voice) 2007. *Television appearances:* Miami Vice (series), The Adventures of Pete & Pete (series). *Other appearances include:* Driv3r (video game, voice) 2004. *Compositions include:* China Girl (with David Bowie). *Film songs include:* Repo Man (theme song 'Repo Man') 1984, Sid and Nancy (song 'I Wanna Be Your Dog') 1986, Dogs in Space (songs 'Dog Food' and 'Endless Sea') 1987, Slaves of New York (song 'Fall in Love with Me') 1989, Tales from the Crypt (TV series, songs 'Kill City' and 'Five Foot One' for episode 'For Cryin'' Out Loud') 1989, Va mourire (1995), Trainspotting (song 'Nightclubbing') 1996, Space Goofs (series theme song) 1997, Full Blast (song 'Loose') 1997, The Brave 1997, Home to Rent (TV series theme song) 1997, Great Expectations (song) 1998, The Wedding Singer (song 'China Girl') 1998, Velvet Goldmine (song 'T.V. Eye') 1998, Whatever (song 'Gimme Danger') 1998, Lock, Stock and Two Smoking Barrels (song 'I Wanna Be Your Dog', as James Oaterberg, Jr) 1998, Radiofreccia (song 'The Passenger') 1998, Born to Lose (song 'Tight Pants') 1999, The Filth and the Fury (song 'No Fun') 2000, Almost Famous (song 'Search and Destroy') 2000, Dogtown and Z-Boys (song 'I Wanna Be Your Dog') 2001, Intimacy (songs 'Consolation Prizes' and 'Penetration', as J. Osterberg alias I. Pop) 2001, Gran Turismo 3: A-Spec (video game) 2001, Killer

Barbys vs. Dracula (song 'Candy') 2002, Pro BMX 2 (video game) (song 'The Passenger') 2002, Rugrats Go Wild! (song 'Lust for Life') 2003, Wonderland (song 'Search and Destroy') 2003, The School of Rock (song 'T.V. Eye', as James Osterberg) 2003, The Life Aquatic with Steve Zissou (song 'Search and Destroy') 2004. *Recordings:* albums: with The Stooges: The Stooges 1969, Fun House 1970, Jesus Loves The Stooges 1977, I'm Sick of You 1977, Raw Stooges 1988, Raw Stooges 2 1988, The Weirdness 2007; solo: Raw Power 1973, Metallic KO 1976, The Idiot 1977, Lust For Life 1977, TV Eye Live 1978, Kill City 1978, New Values 1979, Soldier 1980, Party 1981, I'm Sick of You 1981, Zombie Birdhouse 1982, I Got The Right 1983, Blah Blah Blah 1986, Rubber Legs 1987, Live At The Whiskey A Go Go 1988, Death Trip 1988, Instinct 1988, Brick By Brick 1990, American Caesar 1994, Naughty Little Doggie 1996, Heroin Hates You 1997, King Biscuit Flower Hour 1997, Your Pretty Face is Going to Hell 1998, Sister Midnight 1999, Avenue B 1999, Iggy Pop 1999, Hippodrome Paris '77 (live) 1999, Beat 'Em Up 2001, Skull Ring 2003, Preliminaires 2009. *Publications:* I Need More (autobiog.), Iggy Pop's A–Z (autobiog.) 2005. *Website:* www.iggypop.com.

POP, Mihai; Moldovan economist and government official; b. 31 Oct. 1955, Apşa de Mijloc, Transcarpathian Oblast, Ukraine; m.; two c.; ed Chişinău Polytechnic Inst.; Head, Dept for Econ. Planning, Făleşti tobacco factory 1977–86; Industry Coordinator, Făleşti Dist Agricultural and Industrial Agency 1986–89; instructor, organisational agency of Făleşti Dist CP Cttee 1989–90, Head of Finance Dept, then Deputy Head of Finance and Econs Dept 1990–94; Head, State Fiscal Inspectorate of Bălţi Dist 1994–99; Head, Ministry of Finance Fiscal Inspectorate 1999–2005, Deputy Minister of Finance, May–Oct. 2005, Minister of Finance Oct. 2005–08. *Address:* c/o Ministry of Finance, str. Cosmonauţilor 7, 2005 Chişinău, Moldova (office).

POPE, Martin, BS, PhD; American physical chemist and academic; *Professor Emeritus of Physical Chemistry, New York University;* b. 22 Aug. 1918, New York City; ed City Coll. of New York, Brooklyn Polytechnic Inst.; parents immigrated to USA from Poland; Scientist, Radiation Lab., Brooklyn Navy Yard 1942; First Lt, US Armed Forces, Pacific theatre, World War II 1945; Research Scientist, Balco Research Lab. 1947–51, Tech. Dir 1951–56; Sr Research Scientist, Radiation and Solid State Physics Lab., New York Univ. 1956–60, Research Assoc. Prof. 1960–65, Assoc. Prof. of Chem. 1965–68, Prof. of Chem. 1968–88, Co-Dir Radiation and Solid State Physics Lab. 1968–83, Dir 1983–88, Prof. Emer. of Physical Chem. 1988–; Visiting Prof. in Puerto Rico 1969–70; Scientific Guest of State and Visiting Prof., China 1978, USSR 1987; Visiting Prof., Univ. of Alexandria, Egypt 1981; Guest Lecturer in Leningrad, Moscow, Kiev, Riga, Israel, Gdansk, Kraków, Puerto Rico, Japan, Czechoslovakia and Germany 1980s; Founder Gordon Conf. on Electronic Processes in Organic Materials 1990; mem. Editorial Bd, Mol. Cryst. Liq. Cryst. 1965–94; Fellow, American Physics Soc., New York Acad. of Sciences, AAAS; Fulbright Scholar 1981, Citation of Honor, US Dept of Energy 1988, Citation of Honor, Gordon Research Confs 1990, Townsend Harris Medal, CUNY 1996, Royal Society Davy Medal for "his pioneering work in the field of molecular semiconductors" 2006, Distinguished Lecturer, CUNY Center for Advanced Tech. 2006. *Publications:* Electronic Processes in Organic Crystals (co-author) 1982, Electronic Processes in Organic Crystals and Polymers (co-author) 1992; more than 100 scientific papers in professional journals. *Address:* Department of Chemistry, New York University, 100 Washington Square East, Room 1001, New York, NY 10003-6688, USA (office). *Telephone:* (212) 998-8414 (office). *Fax:* (212) 252-6605 (office). *E-mail:* martin.pope@nyu.edu (office). *Website:* chemxserver.chem.nyu.edu/MPope/index.htm (office).

POPESCU, Dan Mircea, DJur; Romanian politician; *Vice-President, Senate;* b. 6 Oct. 1950, Bucharest; m.; one c.; ed Faculty of Law, Bucharest Univ.; legal adviser, then researcher at Inst. of Political Sciences, Bucharest and Lecturer in Int. Relations, Acad. of Socio-Political Studies, Bucharest 1975–89; mem. Council Nat. Salvation Front, then mem. of Provisional Council of Nat. Union; Presidential Adviser for matters of domestic policy Dec. 1990; Minister of State for Living Standards and Social Security 1991; Minister of Labour and Social Protection 1991–92, Minister of State, Minister of Labour and Social Protection 1992–96; Deputy Prime Minister 1992–96; Dir Romanian Inst. of Social-Democratic Studies 1999–2001; Vice-Pres. Partidul Social Democrat (PSD), mem. Exec. Bureau 2001–; Senator for Teleorman constituency 1992–; Pres. Labour Comm. of Senate 1996–2000, Econ. Comm. of Senate 2000–, Vice-Pres. Senate 2003–; Minister of Labour, Social Solidarity and Family 2004; mem. Ass. Council of Europe (Socialist Group) 2003–; Nat. Order of Faithful Service 2003; Grosser Verdienstkreuz mit Stern (Germany) 2005. *Publications:* books and studies in the field of political sciences. *Address:* Senatul României, Calea 13 Septembrie 1–3, Bucharest (office); 42–46 Aurel Vlaicu Street, Bucharest, Romania (home). *Telephone:* (21) 3124198 (office). *Fax:* (21) 3158928 (office). *E-mail:* dmpopescu@senat.ro (office).

POPESCU, Dumitru Radu; Romanian writer and editor; *Director General, Editura Academiei Române;* b. 19 Aug. 1935, Păusa Village, Bihor Co.; ed Colls of Medicine and Philology, Cluj; reporter, literary magazine Steaua 1956–69; Ed.-in-Chief literary magazine Tribuna 1969–82, Contemporanul 1982; Dir Gen., Ediţurii Academiei Române 2006–; Alt. mem. Cen. Cttee Romanian CP 1968–89, mem. 1979–90; Chair. Romanian Writers' Union 1980–90; Corresp. mem. Romanian Acad. 1997–; Prize of the Writers' Union 1964, 1969, 1974, 1977, 1980, Prize of the Romanian Acad. 1970, Grand Prize for Balkan Writers 1998, Writers' Union Prize 1994, Writers' Assocn of Bucharest Prize 1997, Grand Prize Camil Petrescu 1995. *Publications include:* collections of short stories: Fuga (Flight) 1958, Fata de la miazăzi (A Girl from the South) 1964, Somnul pământului (The Earth's Sleep) 1965, Dor (Longing) 1966, Umbrela de soare (The Parasol) 1967, Prea mic pentru un război aşa de mare (Too Little for Such a Big War) 1969, Duios Anastasia trecea (Tenderly Anastasia Passed) 1967, Leul albastru (The Blue Lion) 1981, The Ice Bridge 1980, the Lame Hare 1981, God in the Kitchen 1994, Truman Capote and Nicolae 1995; novels: Zilele săptămînii (Weekdays) 1959, Vara oltenilor (The Oltenians' Summer) 1964, F 1944, Vînătoarea regală (Royal Hunt) 1973, O bere pentru calul meu (A Beer for My Horse) 1974, Ploile de dincolo de vreme (Rains beyond Time) 1976, Împăratul norilor (Emperor of the Clouds) 1976; plays: Vara imposibilei iubiri (The Summer of Impossible Love) 1966, Vis (Dream) 1968, Aceşti îngeri trişti (Those Sad Angels) 1969, Pisica în noaptea Anului nou (Cat on the New Year's Eve) 1970, Pasărea Shakespeare (The Shakespeare Bird) 1973, Rezervaţia de pelicani (The Pelican Reservation) 1983, Iepurele şchiop (The Lame

Rabbit) 1980, Orasul îngerilor (The Angel's City) 1985, Powder Mill 1989, The Bride with False Eyelashes 1994, Love is like a Scab 1995; poems: Ciinele de fosfor (The Phosphorus Dog) 1981; essays: Virgule (Commas) 1978, Galaxy 1994, Ophelia's Complex 1998. *Address:* Office of the Director, Editura Academiei Române, 050711 Bucharest 5, Calea 13 Septembrie nr. 13, Romania (office). *Telephone:* (21) 3188146 (office). *Fax:* (21) 3182444 (office). *Website:* www.ear.ro (office).

POPESCU, Ioan-Iovitz (Iovitzu), PhD; Romanian academic; b. 1 Oct. 1932, Burila-Mare, Mehedintzi Co.; s. of Dumitru Popescu and Elvira Popescu; m. Georgeta-Denisa Chiru 1963; ed Univ. of Bucharest; Asst Prof. of Optics and Gaseous Electronics, Univ. of Bucharest 1955–60, Prof., Faculty of Physics 1972–, Dean 1972–77, Rector of Univ. of Bucharest 1981–89; Head of Plasma Physics Lab., Inst. of Physics, Bucharest 1960–67, Scientific Deputy Dir 1970–72; Dir Inst. of Physics and Radiation Tech. 1977–81, Romanian Centre for Induced Gamma Emission 1995–2010; Alexander von Humboldt Dozenten Stipendium, Kiel Univ. 1967–69; Corresp. mem. Romanian Acad. 1974, Full mem. 1990 (Pres. Physics Section 1990–92); Hon. Citizen of Mehedintzi Co. 1997, of Drobeta-Turnu Severin City; Labour Order of Romania 1964, Scientific Merit Order 1981, Commdr Loyal Service Nat. Order 2000; Dr hc (Univ. of Craiova) 1998; Prize for Physics, Romanian Acad. 1966, Romanian Opera Omnia Prize 2009, Grigore Moisil Prize for Exact Sciences 2012. *Publications include:* Ionized Gases 1965, General Physics 1971–75, Plasma Physics and Applications 1981, Plasma Spectroscopy 1987, Optics 1988, The Nobel Prizes for Physics 1901–1998 1998, Word Frequency Studies 2009, The Lambda – Structure of Texts (Grigore Moisil Award for Exact Sciences) 2011; 165 scientific papers cited in about 2,400 foreign works; numerous articles on gas discharges and pioneering works in optogalvanic and multiphoton spectroscopy. *Leisure interests:* linguistics: word frequency studies, quantitative linguistics. *Address:* Str. Fizicienilor 6, Block M4, Apt 6, 077125 Magurele, Bucharest, Romania. *Telephone:* (21) 4574180; 72-4115865 (mobile). *E-mail:* iovitzu@gmail.com. *Website:* www.iipopescu.com.

POPESCU, Gen. Mihail Eugeniu, PhD; Romanian army officer and politician; b. 1 April 1948, Carlogani, Olt County; m.; one d.; ed Artillery Officers Mil. School, Mil. Acad., Nat. Defence Coll.; command position, platoon artillery battalion 1969–82; Deputy Commdr and Artillery Chief of Mechanized Div. 1982–92; Artillery Chief 4th Transylvania Army 1984–92; Insp.-Gen. of Artillery, Artillery Gen. Inspectorate 1992–93; Artillery Insp., Gen. Staff Inspectorate 1993–97; Chief of Instruction and Doctrine Directorate, Chief of Army Staff 1997–2000; Chief of Gen. Staff 2000–04; apptd Gen. 2000; Assoc. Prof. Nat. Defence Coll. 2004–; mem. Senate for Vâlcea 2004–08; mem. Partidul Social Democrat (PSD). *Address:* c/o Ministry of National Defence, 77303 Bucharest, Str. Izvor 13–15, Sector 5, Romania (office).

POPESCU-TĂRICEANU, Călin Constantin Anton, MSc; Romanian politician; *President of the Senate;* b. 14 Jan. 1952; m. 1st Cornelia Tăriceanu (divorced); m. 2nd Livia Tăriceanu (divorced); m. 3rd Ioana Popescu-Tăriceanu; m. 4th Loredana Moise; two s.; ed Inst. of Civil Eng, Univ. of Bucharest; started as engineer, Nat. Water Admin, Argeş Co. 1976–77, Industrial Building Co., Bucharest 1977–79; Prof., Faculty of Hydro-technology, Inst. of Civil Eng, Bucharest 1980–91; f. Radio Contact, Romania's first pvt. radio network 1990, Gen. Man. 1992–96; Founder-mem. Nat. Liberal Party (Partidul Naţional Liberal—PNL) 1990–2014, Exec. Sec. 1990–92, Deputy Chair. 1993–2004, Pres. 2004–09; mem. Constituent Ass. (Parl.) 1990–92, 1996–2012, Leader of PNL Parl. Group 2008–12; Deputy Prime Minister 1996–97; Minister of Industry and Trade 1996–97; Prime Minister of Romania 2005–08; Acting Minister of Foreign Affairs 21 March–5 April 2007; mem. Senate 2012–, Ind. Senator 2014–, Pres. of the Senate 2014–; mem. Economy, Reform and Privatization Comm. 1996–2000; Vice-Pres. Fiscal and Budgetary Policies Comm. 2000–; Assoc. Partner, Automotive Trading Services 1993–; Founding mem. and Chair. Automobile and Importers Asscn 1994–97, 2001–03, Hon. Pres. 2003–. *Publications:* 37 scientific papers and articles on water treatment and distribution. *Address:* Senatul Romaniei (The Senate), 050711 Bucharest 5, Calea 13 Septembrie 1–3, Romania (office). *Telephone:* (21) 3113532 (office). *E-mail:* cabinet.presedinte@senat.ro (office). *Website:* www.senat.ro (office); www.tariceanu.ro (office).

POPHAM, Stuart; British lawyer, business executive and research institute executive; *Chairman, Chatham House;* ed Univ. of Southampton; joined Clifford Chance LLP (law firm) 1976, elected to Partnership 1984, held various roles including leading the Banking and Finance practice areas 1999–2003, Sr Partner (worldwide) 2003–10, Chair. Partnership Council (Supervisory Bd); Chair. TheCityUK 2008–12; joined Citigroup as Vice-Chair. EMEA Banking 2011–; Council mem. Royal Inst. of Int. Affairs (now Chatham House), Chair. 2012–; mem. Bd of Dirs Legal & General Insurance, The Barbican Centre Trust, Council of the Royal Nat. Lifeboat Inst., Birkbeck Univ. of London, Advisory Forum of the Saïd Business School, Univ. of Oxford; mem. CBI, fmr Chair. London Region and fmr mem. Chair.'s and other cttees; Hon. QC 2011. *Address:* Chatham House, 10 St James's Square, London, SW1Y 4LE, England (office). *Telephone:* (20) 7957-5700 (office). *Fax:* (20) 7957-5710 (office). *E-mail:* contact@chathamhouse.org (office). *Website:* www.chathamhouse.org.uk (office).

POPOFF, Frank Peter, AB, MBA; Bulgarian/American business executive and academic; b. 27 Oct. 1935, Sofia, Bulgaria; s. of Eftim Popoff and Stoyanka Kossoroff; m. Jean Urse; three s.; ed Indiana Univ.; family emigrated to USA 1941; with Dow Chemical Co. 1959–2000, Exec. Vice-Pres. 1985–87, Pres. 1987–92, CEO 1987–96, Chair. 1992–2000, Dir Emer. 2000–; Exec. Vice-Pres., then Pres. Dow Chemical European subsidiary, Switzerland 1976–85; Dir, Dow Corning Corpn 1982–, Chemical Bank & Trust Co. 1985–2006, Chemical Financial Corpn 1989–2006 (Chair. 2004–06), American Express Co. 1990–2008, United Technologies Corpn 1996–2008, US West, Inc. 1998–, The Salk Inst., Shin-Etsu Chemical Co. Ltd, Qwest Communications International Inc.; Dir Emer., Indiana Univ. Foundation; mem. ACS, Société de Chimie Industrielle (American Section), Chemical Mfrs Asscn (Bd of Dirs); fmr mem. The Business Roundtable, Business Council; Harold A. 'Red' Poling Chair of Business and Govt, Kelley School of Business, Indiana Univ. from 2001; Kt Commdr, Order of Oranje-Nassau (Netherlands) 1989; Leadership Award, US Council for Int. Business 1992, René Dubos Environmental Award 1993, Palladium Medal 1994. *Address:* c/o Kelley

School of Business, Indiana University, Godfrey Graduate and Executive Education Center, 1275 East 10th Street, Bloomington, IN 47405, USA.

POPOSKI, Nikola, BEcons, MA, MA; Macedonian economist and politician; *Minister of Foreign Affairs;* b. 24 Oct. 1977, Skopje; m.; one c.; ed Univ. of Skopje, Univ. of Nice, France, EU Univ. of Rennes, France, College of Europe, Bruges, Belgium; Man.'s Asst, British Royal Engineers Quality 1999–2001; Analysis and Devt Dept, Rouen Port Authorities, France 2003–04; Sec., Embassy of France to the Fmr Yugoslavia Repub. of Macedonia 2001–04; Client Relationship Man., DEPFA Bank plc HQ, Dublin, Ireland 2005–06; Team Leader, Jt Research Centre, EC, Brussels 2006–09; Amb. and Head of Mission, Mission of the Fmr Yugoslavia Repub. of Macedonia to the EU 2010–11; Minister of Foreign Affairs 2011–; EC-trained internal auditor for implementation of integrated environmental management and health and safety standards; mem. Internal Macedonian Revolutionary Org.– Democratic Party for Macedonian Nat. Unity (VMRO-DPMNE). *Leisure interest:* sports. *Address:* Ministry of Foreign Affairs, 1000 Skopje, Filip II Makedonski 7, Former Yugoslav Republic of Macedonia (office). *Telephone:* (2) 3115266 (office). *Fax:* (2) 3115790 (office). *E-mail:* mailmnr@mfa.gov.mk (office). *Website:* www.mfa.gov.mk (office).

POPOV, Anatolii Aleksandrovich, DEconSci; Russian/Chechen politician; b. 10 July 1960, Sovetskoye village, Volgograd Oblast; m.; one s.; ed Volgograd Agricultural Inst.; fmr researcher, agricultural scientific research inst. and irrigation farming scientific research inst.; Sec. of Gorodishchenskii Raion (dist) Cttee of V.I. Lenin Young Communist League (Komsomol), Volgograd Oblast; Adviser to the Council of Ministers of the USSR; fmr Deputy to Head of Man. MENATEP Bank; Financial Dir Rosoboroneksport (Russian Defence Export) State Corpn April–Sept. 1998; fmr Deputy Leader Dept of Food Resources, Govt of Moscow City; Head Centre for Econ. Strategy, Volgograd Oblast; Dir Centre of School of Investment Man. VAPK, Acad. of Nat. Economy, Govt of Russian Fed.; apptd Gen. Dir Direction for the Works of Construction-Restoration in Chechnya (state firm responsible for rebuilding Chechnya) 2001; Deputy Chair. Comm. for the Reconstruction of Chechnya 2002; Prime Minister of the Govt of Chechnya Feb.–Aug. 2003; Acting Pres. Aug.–Oct. 2003; Presidential Asst in Charge of Domestic Politics Dept from 2004. *Address:* c/o Office of the Government, Krasnopresnenskaya nab. 2, 103274 Moscow, Russia.

POPOV, Gavriil Kharitonovich, DEcon; Russian politician and economist; *President, International University, Moscow;* b. 31 Oct. 1936, Moscow; s. of Khariton Popov and Theodora Popova; m. Irina Popova 1968; two s.; ed Moscow State Univ.; mem. CPSU 1959–90; teacher at Moscow Univ. 1960–89, Dean of Econ. Faculty 1977–80; introduced man. and business studies to Moscow Univ., Prof. 1971–; Ed.-in-Chief of journal Voprosy ekonomiki (Questions of Economics) 1988–90; People's Deputy of USSR 1989–91; Co-Chair. Inter-regional Group of Deputies, pressing for radical change; Chair. Moscow City Soviet 1990–91; Mayor of Moscow 1991–92 (resgnd); mem. Consultative Council 1991–2000 (Chair, Foreign Policy Cttee 1996–2000); Pres., Int. Univ., Moscow 1991–; Pres. Int. Union of Economists 1991–, Free Econ. Soc. of Russia 1991–; M. Lomonosov Prize. *Publications include:* The Wolfhound Century Leaps on my Neck (10-vol. series). *Leisure interest:* bees. *Address:* International University, 125040 Moscow, Russia. *Telephone:* (495) 956-69-90. *Website:* www.interun.ru.

POPOV, Mihai, DHisSc; Moldovan philologist and diplomatist; b. 1949, Chebruchi, Sloboza Region; ed Kishinev State Univ., Diplomatic Acad., Moscow; worked as Komsomol and CSPU functionary in Kishinev 1973–83; joined diplomatic service 1983, First Counsellor, USSR Embassy in Bucharest 1986–92, Minister-Counsellor, Moldovan Embassy in Moscow 1992–93, Amb. to Belgium 1993–94; Minister of Foreign Affairs 1994–96; Amb. to France 1996–2002, Amb. to Belgium and Perm. Rep. to NATO and EU, Brussels 2002–04; currently Special Adviser for Moldova and European Neighbourhood, East West Inst. (EWI), Brussels. *Address:* EWI Brussels Centre, 59-61 Rue de Trèves, 1040 Brussels, Belgium (office). *Telephone:* (2) 743-46-10 (office). *Fax:* (2) 743-46-39 (office). *E-mail:* brussels@ewi.info (office). *Website:* www.ewi.info (office).

POPOV, Vadim Aleksandrovich; Belarusian politician; b. 1940, Demidov, Smolensk Oblast, Russia; m.; two c.; ed Minsk Higher CPSU School, Belarus State Inst. of Agric. Mechanisation; army service 1961–64; Komsomol functionary 1964–71; Dir Sovkhoz Mogilev region 1972–76; party functionary, instructor, Head of Div. Mogilev Regional CP Cttee, First Sec. 1976–92; instructor, Cen. Cttee CP of Belarus 1976–92; worked in agric. roles in complex of Mogilev region 1992–99; First Deputy Minister of Agric. and Food March–July 1999, Minister July–Nov. 2000; mem. Palata Predstaviteley (House of Reps), Nat. Ass. (Parl.) 2000–, Chair. 2000–04, 2007–09; Deputy Prime Minister March–June 2001, Prime Minister June–Nov. 2001; Order, Labour Red Banner, three medals; Hon. Diploma Supreme Soviet Belarus SSR. *Address:* c/o House of Representatives, 220010 Minsk, vul. Savetskaya 11, Belarus. *Website:* www.house.gov.by (office).

POPOV, Yevgeny Anatolyevich; Russian writer; b. 5 Jan. 1946, Krasnoyarsk; m. Svetlana Anatoliyevna Vasilyeva; one s.; ed Moscow Inst. of Geological Survey; worked as geologist in various regions 1968–73; mem. USSR Union of Writers 1978, expelled 1979, readmitted 1988; Assoc. mem. Swedish PEN 1980–; Founder and mem. Bd Russian PEN 1989–; Venets Prize (Corona), Moscow 2000, Triumph Prize, Moscow 2010. *Publications:* The Merriment of Old Russia (short stories) 1981, Awaiting Untreacherous Love (short stories) 1989, Wonderfulness of Life (novel) 1990, A Plane to Cologne (short stories) 1991, On the Eve, On the Eve (novel) 1993, The Soul of a Patriot (novel) 1994, Green Musicians (novel) 1998, Thirteen (essays) 1999, Badly Tempered Piano (play), The Bold Boy (play) 2000, A Quiet Barque Named 'Hope' (short stories) 2001, Master Chaos (novel) 2002, Communists (novel) 2003, The Bold Boy (prose, co-author) 2004, Beggars' Opera (prose) 2006, The Song of a First Love (short stories) 2009, Red-hot Iron (short stories) 2009, A Restaurant 'The Birch' (novel) 2009. *Address:* Leningradsky prospect 26, korp. 2, Apt 52, 125040 Moscow, Russia. *Telephone:* (495) 612-33-97. *Fax:* (495) 612-33-97. *E-mail:* popov1984@yandex.ru.

POPOVIČ, Štěpán, CSc; Czech engineer; b. 28 Dec. 1945, Ústí nad Labem; m. Iva Popovič; one s. one d.; ed Mechanical Eng and Textile Coll., Liberec, Econs Univ., Prague; with Sklo Union Teplice 1968–89, Dir-Gen. 1989; Dir-Gen. Glav Union from 1991; Country Man. for Czech Operations and Gen. Man. Russian Operations, Glaverbel (acquired by AGC and renamed AGC Flat Glass Europe

2007, AGC Glass Europe 2009), CEO –2011; Pres. Union of Industry and Transport 1992–2000; Chair. FC Teplice 2000–01; Man. of the Year 1993, 1998. *Leisure interests:* sport, music, playing the piano. *Address:* AGC Glass Europe Headquarters, Avenue Jean Monnet 4, 1348 Louvain-la-Neuve, Belgium (office). *Telephone:* (2) 409-30-00 (office). *Fax:* (2) 672-44-62 (office). *E-mail:* info@agc-glass .eu (office). *Website:* www.agc-glass.eu (office).

POPPEMA, Sibrand, MD, PhD; Dutch pathologist, academic and university administrator; *President, University of Groningen;* b. 24 July 1949, Emmen; ed Gymnasium, Ubbo Emmius Lyceum Stadskanaal, Univ. of Groningen; Resident in Pathology, Univ. of Groningen 1974–79; Research Fellow, Dept of Pathology, Christian Albrechts Univ., Kiel, Germany 1978; Research Fellow, Massachusetts Gen. Hosp., Harvard Medical School, Boston, USA 1979–80; Pathologist (Asst Prof.), Univ. of Groningen 1979–82, Pathologist (Assoc. Prof.) 1982–85, J.K. de Cock Prof. of Immunopathology 1985–87, Prof. of Gen. and Surgical Pathology and Chair. Dept of Pathology 1995–98, Head, Dept of Pathology, Univ. Hosp., Groningen, Prof. and Chair. Dept of Pathology and Lab. Medicine 1998–2002, Head, Dept of Pathology and Lab., Univ. Hosp., Groningen, Dean, Faculty of Medical Sciences 1999–2005, Pro-Rector Univ. of Groningen, Prof. of Pathology 2005–08, Dean, Faculty of Medical Sciences, Vice-Pres. Univ. Medical Centre, Groningen, Prof. of Pathology and Pres. Univ. of Groningen 2008–; Prof. of Pathology, Univ. of Alberta, Canada 1987–95, Prof. of Oncology and Dir of Lab. Medicine, Cross Cancer Inst. (CCI), Edmonton, Dir Tumor Immunobiology Program, CCI 1992–95, Dir Dept of Experimental Oncology, CCI, Assoc. Dir of Research, CCI Jan.–Sept. 1995; Visiting Professorship, McGill Univ. 1998, Université de Montreal 1998; Co-founder IQ Corpn (biotech co.), Groningen 1985, Alimmune, Del., USA 2001; Chair. Energy Academy Europe, Platform Sensor Universe, AOG (Academic Postgraduate Courses); mem. Supervisory Bd BMM (Biomedical Materials), Bd Netherlands Antillean Foundation for Clinical Higher Educ., Supervisory Bd Energy Delta Inst., Supervisory Bd Energy Valley, Supervisory Bd Energy Delta Gas Research, Supervisory Bd LifeLines Biobank, Supervisory Bd INCAS3, Supervisory Bd Leveste, Advisory Bd Healthy Ageing Network Northern Netherlands, THES Univ. Ranking Expert Platform Group; Special Advisor, Skolkovo Univ.; mem. US and Canadian Acad. of Pathologists, American Soc. of Investigative Pathology, Int. Acad. of Pathologists (British Div.), American Soc. of Hematology, Soc. of Hematopathology, European Asscn of Hematopathology, Royal Coll. of Physicians and Surgeons of Canada 1987; Hon. Consul Gen., Repub. of Korea; Hon. Prof., Peking Union Medical Coll. 2003–, Tianjin Medical Univ. 2006–, Peking Univ. 2007–; Kt, Order of the Netherlands Lion 2007. *Publications:* editor of two books on Hodgkin's disease; 231 papers in professional journals; five US and two int. patents. *Address:* Office of the President, University of Groningen, Oude Boteringestraat 44, 9712 GL Groningen, The Netherlands (office). *Telephone:* (50) 363-5285 (office). *Fax:* (50) 363-4847 (office). *E-mail:* s.poppema@rug.nl (office). *Website:* www.rug.nl/staff/s.poppema (office).

POPPER, Frank Geoffrey, DèsL; British/French art historian; *Professor Emeritus, University of Paris VIII;* b. (Franz Gottfried Popper), 17 April 1918, Prague, Czech Repub.; s. of Otto Popper and Paula Goldmann; m. 1st Hella Guth 1946; m. 2nd Aline Dallier 1973; ed Univ. of Paris IV (Paris-Sorbonne); voluntary service in RAF 1941–46; Dir of shipping and travel agencies 1947–53; mem. research group Inst. of Aesthetics, Paris 1961–68; Asst Prof. of Aesthetics and the Science of Art, Univ. of Paris VIII (Vincennes à St-Denis) 1969–71, Dir of Art Dept 1970–83, Temp. Reader 1971–73, Reader 1973–75, Prof. 1975–76, Full Prof. 1976–85, Prof. Emer. 1985–; also organizes art exhbns, including Electra at Musée d'art moderne de la ville de Paris 1983; Chevalier, Ordre nat. du Mérite 1998, Commdr, Ordre des Arts et des Lettres 2004, Chevalier, Légion d'honneur 2010. *Publications include:* Kunst-Licht-Kunst (exhbn catalogue) 1966, Lumière et Mouvement (exhbn catalogue) 1967, Naissance de l'Art Cinétique 1967, Origins and Development of Kinetic Art 1968, Art, Action and Participation 1975, Agam 1976, Electra, Electricity and Electronics in the Art of the Twentieth Century (exhbn catalogue) 1983, Art of the Electronic Age 1993, Réflexions sur l'Exil, l'Art et l'Europe 1998, From Technological to Virtual Art 2005, Ecrire sur l'art: de l'art optique à l'art virtuel 2007, Collection Frank Popper (exhbn catalogue) 2009. *Leisure interests:* chess, music, literature. *Address:* 6 rue du Marché Saint-Honoré, 75001 Paris, France (home). *Telephone:* 1-42-61-21-38 (home). *E-mail:* fpopper@ club-internet.fr (home). *Website:* www.arpla.univ-paris8.fr (office).

PORAT, Ruth M., BA, MSc (Econ), MBA; American investment banking executive; *Executive Vice-President and Chief Financial Officer, Morgan Stanley;* b. 1958; d. of Dan I. Porat and Freida Porat; m. Anthony Paduano 1983; three c.; ed Stanford Univ., London School of Econs, UK, Wharton School, Univ. of Pennsylvania; early position as man. consultant, Yankelovich, Skelly & White, New York; with Mergers and Acquisitions, Morgan Stanley, New York 1987–90, Chair. Equity Capital Markets 1996–2006, Co-head Global Tech. Group, Vice-Chair. Investment Banking Div. 2003–09 (Chair. Financial Sponsors Group 2004–06), Global Head Financial Insts Group 2006–09, Exec. Vice-Pres. and Chief Financial Officer 2010–; with Smith Barney 1993–96; ranked by Forbes magazine amongst The World's 100 Most Powerful Women (90th) 2011. *Address:* Morgan Stanley & Co. Inc., 1585 Broadway, New York, NY 10036 (office); 1 West 72nd Street, New York, NY 10023-3486, USA. *Telephone:* (212) 761-4000 (office). *Fax:* (212) 761-0086 (office). *Website:* www.morganstanley.com (office).

PORNCHAI, Rujiprapa, BSc, MSc, PhD; Thai business executive and government official; *Chairman, Electricity Generating Public Co. Ltd;* b. 19 April 1952; ed Kasetsart Univ. of Econs, Thammasart Univ., Univ. of Pennsylvania, USA; fmr Deputy Sec.-Gen. Nat. Econ. and Social Devt Bd; fmr Dir Regional Econ. Devt Cooperation Cttee Office (REDCCO); fmr Exec. Dir Office of the E Seaboard Devt Cttee (OESB); fmr Exec. Dir Office of the S Seaboard Devt Cttee (OSSB); Deputy Perm. Sec. of Energy, Ministry of Energy 2003–06, Perm. Sec. of Energy 2006–; Chair. and Dir Electricity Generating Public Co. Ltd (EGCO) 2006–07 (resgnd) 2009–; fmr Chair. PTT Public Co. Ltd; Chair. Electricity Generating Authority of Thailand. *Address:* Electricity Generating Public Co., EGCO Tower, Bangkok 10210, Thailand (office). *Telephone:* (2) 998-5000 (office). *Fax:* (2) 995-0956 (office). *E-mail:* info@egco.com (office). *Website:* www.egco.com (office).

POROKHOVSHCHIKOV, Aleksander Shalvovich; Russian actor, film director and scriptwriter; b. 31 Jan. 1939, Moscow; s. of Mikhail Nikolaevich Dudin and Galina Aleksandrovna Porokhovshchikova; m. Irina Valeryevna Zhukova 1995; ed Chelyabinsk Inst. of Medicine, Shchukin High School of Theatre Art; worked in Satire Theatre 1966–71, Taganka Theatre 1971–81, A. Pushkin Theatre 1981–; f. first Russian pvt. film studio Rodina 1987–, Dir Studio; Pres. Cultural Centre "House of A. A. Porokhovshchikov 1871"; Prof. Russian Acad. of Theatre Art; Main Prize Scochi Film Market (Russia) 1993, Spectators Prize, Tver Film Festival, Golden Sail Prize, St Raphaël Russian Film Festival (France) 1994 (all for Film Memory); People's Artist of Russia. *Roles in drama productions include:* Profitable Position, Inspector, Lighting but not Warming, Optimistic Tragedy. *Roles in films include:* Ring 1973, The Star of Captivating Happiness 1975, Diamonds for the Proletariat Dictatorship 1976, Seek the Wind 1979, Family Circle 1980, Living Target 1989, Heir 1992. *Films directed:* The Ninth of May 1988, dir, scriptwriter and actor: Uncensored Memory 1991. *Leisure interest:* music, piano playing, jazz band, nature, diving. *Address:* Prospekt Mira 180, Apt 169, 129366 Moscow, Russia. *Telephone:* (495) 245-26-47. *Fax:* (495) 245-26-47. *E-mail:* vyatkin@npi.ru (home).

POROSHENKO, Petro Oleksiyovych; Ukrainian business executive and politician; b. 26 Sept. 1965, Bolhrad, Odesa Oblast; m. Maryna Poroshenka; two s. two d.; ed Taras Shevchenko Univ., Kyiv; Deputy Dir-Gen. Respublika Asscn of Small Businesses and Businessmen 1990–91; Pres. Birzhovy Dim Ukraine 1991–93; Pres. and prin. shareholder PJSC Ukrprominvest 1993–98 (holding co. with control of Roshen confectionery, Mriya bank, Radomysh brewery, Leninsak Kuznia Works, Lutsk automobile plant, Cherkasy bus plant, Channel 5 (5 Kanal) TV station, currently Hon. Pres.; mem. Verkhovna Rada (Parl.) 1998–2007, 2012–, Chair. Sub-cttee for Securities, Stock and Investment Markets 2000, Budget Cttee 2002–04, later Chair. Finance and Banking Cttee, mem. Cttee for European Integration 2012–; mem. United Social Democratic Party of Ukraine –2000; f. Solidarnist party 2000, then joined Party of Regions, then joined Our Ukraine party 2001; apptd mem. Pres.'s Coordinating Council for the Securities Market 1998; Deputy Man. Viktor Yushchenko's presidential campaign 2004; Sec. Nat. Security and Defence Council Feb.–Sept. 2005; Chair. Council of Nat. Bank of Ukraine 2007–12, mem. 2012–; Minister of Foreign Affairs 2009–10, of Econ. Devt and Trade March–Dec. 2012; State Prize of Ukraine, Merited Economist of Ukraine, Pylyp Orlyk Int. Prize. *Address:* Verkhovna Rada (Supreme Council), 01008 Kyiv, vul. M. Hrushevskoho 5, Ukraine. *Telephone:* (44) 255-21-25. *Fax:* (44) 253-32-17. *E-mail:* umz@rada.gov.ua. *Website:* www.rada.gov.ua; www .poroshenko.com.ua.

PORRITT, Sir Jonathon Espie, 2nd Bt, cr. 1963, CBE, BA; British environmentalist and writer; *Founding Director, Forum for the Future;* b. 6 July 1950, London; s. of the late Lord Porritt, 11th Gov.-Gen. of New Zealand; m. Sarah Staniforth 1986; two d.; ed Eton Coll. and Magdalen Coll. Oxford; trained as solicitor; English teacher, St Clement Danes Grammar School (later Burlington Danes School), Shepherd's Bush, West London 1975–84; Head of English, Burlington Danes School, London 1980–84; Chair. Ecology Party 1979–80, 1982–84; parl. cand. at gen. elections in 1979, 1983; Dir Friends of the Earth 1984–90; Founder Dir Forum for the Future 1996–; Chair. UK Sustainable Devt Comm. 2000–09; Co-Dir Prince of Wales Business and Environment Programme; currently Dir (non-exec.), Willmott Dixon Holdings Ltd; mem. Bd South West Regional Devt Agency 2000–09; adviser to many bodies on environmental matters, as well as to individuals, including Prince Charles and Chief Exec. of Marks & Spencer; Chancellor, Keele Univ. 2012–; mem. Advisory Bd BBC Wildlife magazine; Patron, Population Matters. *Publications include:* Seeing Green: The Politics of Ecology Explained 1984, Friends of the Earth Handbook 1987, The Coming of the Greens 1988, Save the Earth (ed.) 1990, Where on Earth are We Going? 1991, Captain Eco (for children) 1991, The Reader's Digest Good Beach Guide 1994, Liberty and Sustainability: Where One Person's Freedom is Another's Nuisance 1995, Playing Safe: Science and the Environment (Prospects for Tomorrow) 2000, Making the Net Work: Sustainable Development in a Digital Society 2004, Capitalism: As if the World Matters 2005 (revised edn 2007), The World We Made 2013. *Leisure interests:* walking, cooking. *Address:* 9 Imperial Square, Cheltenham, Glos., GL50 1QB; 9 Lypiatt Terrace, Cheltenham, Glos., GL50 2SX, England (home). *Telephone:* (1242) 262737 (office). *Fax:* (1242) 262757 (office). *E-mail:* jpoffice@forumforthefuture.org (office). *Website:* www .jonathonporritt.com.

PORTAS, Paulo Sacadura Cabral, LLD; Portuguese journalist and politician; *Deputy Prime Minister;* b. 12 Sept. 1962, Lisbon; s. of Nuno Portas and Helena de Sacadura Cabral; ed Univ. Católica de Lisboa; began career as journalist with O Tempo (newspaper); mem. Grupo de Ofir (reform group) 1986; mem. political comm. for presidential candidacy of Freitas do Amaral 1986; f. O Independente (weekly newspaper) 1988, Dir –1995; Jt Founder Instituto de Estudos Políticos 1995; Deputy, Assembleia da República (Parl.), (CDS/Partido Popular) 1995–2002, Parl. Leader 1999–2001; Municipal Deputy, Oliveira de Azeméis 1997; fmr Pres. CDS/Partido Popular (now Partido Popular); Speaker, Câmara Municipal de Lisboa 2001; Minister of State and of Nat. Defence 2002–05; Minister of Foreign Affairs 2011–13; Deputy Prime Minister 2013–; Lecturer, Dept of Politics, Univ. Moderna 1995–97; Distinguished Public Service Award, US Defense Dept 2005. *Address:* c/o Office of the Prime Minister, Rua da Imprensa à Estrela 4, 1200-888 Lisbon, Portugal.

PORTER, Andrew Brian, MA; British music critic; b. 26 Aug. 1928, Cape Town, South Africa; s. of Andrew Ferdinand and Vera Sybil Porter (née Bloxham); ed Diocesan Coll., Rondebosch, Cape Town, Univ. Coll., Oxford; music critic, Financial Times 1950–74; Ed. The Musical Times 1960–67; music critic, The New Yorker 1972–92, Observer 1992–97, Times Literary Supplement 1997–2010; Visiting Fellow, All Souls Coll., Oxford 1973–74; Bloch Prof., Univ. of Calif., Berkeley 1981; Corresp. mem. American Musicological Soc. 1993; ASCAP-Deems Taylor Award 1975, 1978, 1982, Nat. Music Theater Award 1988, Words on Music: Essays in Honour of Andrew Porter on the Occasion of His 75th Birthday (co-ed. by David Rosen and Claire Brook) 2003. *Opera:* librettos for The Tempest 1985, The Song of Majnun 1991 and numerous trans. *Publications:* A Musical Season 1974, Wagner's Ring 1976, Music of Three Seasons 1974–77 1978, Music of Three More Seasons 1977–80 1981, Musical Events: A Chronicle 1980–1983 1987, Musical Events: A Chronicle 1983–1986 1989, Verdi's Macbeth: A Sourcebook (ed. with David Rosen) 1984, A Music Critic Remembers 2000; contrib. to Music & Letters,

Musical Quarterly, Musical Times, Proceedings of the Royal Musical Association, Atti del Congresso Internazionale di Studi Verdiani. *Leisure interest:* architecture. *Address:* 9 Pembroke Walk, London, W8 6PQ, England.

PORTER, Brian Johnston, BCom; Canadian banking executive; *President and CEO, Bank of Nova Scotia (Scotiabank);* b. Calgary, Alberta; m. Megan Porter; three c.; ed Dalhousie Univ.; began career with investment dealer McLeod Young Weir 1981 (co. acquired by Scotiabank 1987), held various sr positions with Scotiabank including exec. roles with Global Banking & Markets Dept, Global Risk Man., Group Treasury and Int. Banking, Chief Risk Officer 2006–08, Group Head of Risk and Treasury 2008–10, Group Head of Int. Banking 2010–12, Pres. 2012–, elected to Bd of Dirs April 2013, CEO Nov. 2013–; Hon. LLD (Dalhousie) 2008. *Address:* The Bank of Nova Scotia (Scotiabank), 44 King Street West, Toronto, ON M5H 1H1, Canada. *Telephone:* (416) 866-6430 (office). *Fax:* (416) 866-3750 (office). *E-mail:* email@scotiabank.com (office). *Website:* www.scotiabank.com (office).

PORTER, Michael E., MBA, PhD; American economist, academic and consultant; *Bishop William Lawrence University Professor and Director, Institute for Strategy and Competitiveness, Harvard Business School;* b. Ann Arbor, Mich.; two d.; ed Princeton Univ., Harvard Business School, Harvard Univ.; currently Bishop William Lawrence Univ. Prof., Harvard Business School, also Dir Inst. for Strategy and Competitiveness 2001–; Advisor to local and nat. govts; mem. Exec. Cttee Council on Competitiveness; Co-chair. Global Competitiveness Report; has led studies for Govts of India, New Zealand, Canada and Portugal; advises on competitive strategy for US and int. cos including DuPont, Procter & Gamble, Royal Dutch Shell, Taiwan Semiconductor Manufacturing Co.; mem. Bd of Dirs Parametric Technology Corpn, Thermo Electron Corpn; Co-founder and Sr Advisor, Center for Effective Philanthropy; Fellow, Acad. of Man., Royal Swedish Acad. of Eng Sciences, Int. Acad. of Man., Royal Soc. of Edinburgh; Creu de St Jordi (Spain), Jose Dolores Estrada Order of Merit (Nicaragua), Hon. FRSE 2005; Dr hc (HHL, Leipzig), (Univ. of Iceland), (Univ. of Los Andres), (Stockholm School of Econs, Sweden), (Erasmus Univ., Netherlands), (Hautes Ecoles Commerciales, France), (Univ. Tech. de Lisboa, Portugal), (Adolfo Ibanez Univ., Chile), (INCAE, Central America), (Johnson and Wales Univ.), (Mount Ida Coll., Universidad del Pacifico, Peru), (Toronto Univ.), (McGill Univ., Canada), (Nyenrode Business Universiteit, Netherlands); six McKinsey Awards (for best Harvard Business Review article of the year), Charles Coolidge Parlin Award, American Marketing Asscn 1991, Richard D. Irwin Outstanding Educator in Business Policy and Strategy, Acad. of Man. 1993, Adam Smith Award, Nat. Asscn of Business Economists 1997, Distinguished Award for contribs in the field of man. 1998, Acad. of Man. Award 2003, John Kenneth Galbraith Medal, American Agricultural Econs Asscn 2005, Lifetime Achievement Award in Economic Devt, US Dept of Commerce 2008. *Publications include:* author of 18 books including Competitive Strategy: Techniques for Analyzing Industries and Competitors 1980, Competitive Advantage: Creating and Sustaining Superior Performance (George R. Terry Book Award Acad. of Man.) 1985, The Competitive Advantage of Nations 1990, On Competition 1998, 2008, Can Japan Compete? 2000, Redefining Health Care 2006; contrib. over 125 essays and articles to magazines, journals and newspapers. *Address:* Institute for Strategy and Competitiveness, Ludcke House, Harvard Business School, Soldiers Field Road, Boston, MA 02163, USA (office). *Telephone:* (617) 495-6309 (office). *Fax:* (617) 547-8543 (office). *E-mail:* mporter@hbs.edu (office). *Website:* www.isc.hbs.edu (office).

PORTER, Robert, AC, MA, DM, DSc, FRACP, FRACMA, FAA; Australian professor of medical research; *Honorary Adjunct Professor, School of Medicine and Dentistry, James Cook University;* b. 10 Sept. 1932, Port Augusta, S Australia; s. of the late William J. Porter and Amy Porter (née Tottman); m. Anne D. Steell 1961; two s. two d.; ed Univ. of Adelaide and Univ. of Oxford, UK; House Physician and House Surgeon, Radcliffe Infirmary, Oxford 1959–60; Univ. Lecturer in Physiology, Oxford 1961–67; Medical Tutor and Fellow, St Catherine's Coll. Oxford 1963–67; Prof. of Physiology, Monash Univ. 1967–80, Dean 1989–98, Deputy Vice-Chancellor 1992–93; Dir John Curtin School of Medical Research and Howard Florey Prof. of Medical Research, ANU 1980–89; Planning Dean (Medicine), James Cook Univ. of N Queensland, Townsville 1998–99, Dir Research Devt 1999–2008, currently Hon. Adjunct Prof., School of Medicine and Dentistry; Rhodes Scholar 1954; Radcliffe Travelling Fellow in Medical Science 1963–64; Sr Fulbright Fellow, Washington Univ. School of Medicine, St Louis 1973; Fogarty Scholar-in-Residence, NIH, Bethesda, Md, USA 1986–87; Chair. Nat. Expert Advisory Group on Safety and Quality in Australian Health Care 1998–2000; Fellow, Royal Australian Coll. of Medical Admins; Hon. DSc (Univ. of Sydney) 2001, (James Cook Univ.) 2009; Centenary Medal 2003. *Publications:* Corticospinal Neurones: Their Role in Movement (with C. G. Phillips) 1977, Corticospinal Function and Voluntary Movement (with R. N. Lemon) 1993; articles on neurophysiology. *Leisure interests:* sport, reading, photography. *Address:* 2 Denison Court, Toomulla, Queensland 4816, Australia (home). *Telephone:* (7) 4781-5330 (office); (7) 4770-7121 (home). *Fax:* (7) 4781-4655 (office). *E-mail:* Robert.Porter@jcu.edu .au (office). *Website:* www.jcu.edu.au/fmhms (office).

PORTES, Richard David, CBE, DPhil, FBA; American/British economist and academic; *Professor of Economics, London Business School;* b. 10 Dec. 1941, Chicago, Ill., USA; s. of Herbert Portes and Abra Halperin Portes; m. 1st Barbara Diana Frank 1963 (divorced); one s. one d.; m. 2nd Helene Mireille Rey 2006; one d.; ed Yale Univ., Balliol and Nuffield Colls, Oxford; Official Fellow and Tutor in Econs, Balliol Coll. 1965–69, Hon. Fellow; Asst Prof. of Econs and Int. Affairs, Princeton Univ. 1969–72; Prof. of Econs, Birkbeck Coll., London Univ. 1972–94, Head Dept 1975–77, 1980–83, 1994; Prof. of Econs, London Business School 1995–; Pres. Centre for Econ. Policy Research, London 1983–; Directeur d'Etudes, Ecole des Hautes Etudes en Sciences Sociales, Paris 1978–2011; fmr Rhodes Scholar, Woodrow Wilson Fellow, Danforth Fellow; Guggenheim Fellow 1977–78; British Acad. Overseas Visiting Fellow 1977–78; Research Assoc., Nat. Bureau of Econ. Research, Cambridge, Mass 1980–; Visiting Prof., Harvard Univ. 1977–78, Univ. of California 1999–2000, Columbia Univ. Business School 2003–04; Vice-Chair. Econs Cttee Social Science Research Council 1981–84; Sec.-Gen. Royal Econ. Soc. 1992–2008; Co-Chair. Bd of Govs and Sr Ed., Economic Policy 1985–; mem. Bd of Dirs Soc. for Econ. Analysis 1967–69, 1972–80 (Sec. 1974–77); mem. Council on Foreign Relations 1978–, Hon. Degrees Cttee, Univ. of London 1984–89, Council, Royal Econ. Soc. 1986–92, 2008– (mem. Exec. Cttee 1987–2008), Bellagio

Group on the Int. Economy 1990–, Council, European Econ. Asscn 1992–96, Franco-British Council 1996–2002, Comm. on the Social Sciences 2000–03; mem. and fmr mem. several editorial bds; Chair. Collegio di Probiviri (Wise Men Cttee), MTS 2001–; Fellow Econometric Soc. 1983–; Hon. DSc (Université Libre de Bruxelles) 2000; Hon. PhD (London Guildhall) 2000, (Paris-Dauphine) 2013. *Publications:* The Polish Crisis 1981, Deficits and Detente 1983, Threats to International Financial Stability (co-author) 1987, Crisis? What Crisis? Orderly Workouts for Sovereign Debtors 1995, Making Sense of Globalization 2002, Crises de la Dette 2003, International Financial Stability 2007; editor: Global Macroeconomics: Policy Conflict and Cooperation 1987, Blueprints for Exchange Rate Management 1989, Macroeconomic Policies in an Interdependent World 1989, The EMS in Transition: a CEPR Report 1989, External Constraints on Macroeconomic Policy: The European Experience 1991, The Path of Reform in Central and Eastern Europe 1991, Economic Transformation of Central Europe 1993, European Union Trade with Eastern Europe 1995, Macroeconomic Stability and Financial Regulation 2009, The Social Value of the Financial Sector 2013; numerous papers and contribs to learned journals. *Leisure interest:* living beyond my means. *Address:* London Business School, Regent's Park, London, NW1 4SA, England (office). *Telephone:* (20) 7000-8424 (office). *Fax:* (20) 7000-8401 (office). *E-mail:* rportes@london.edu (office). *Website:* faculty.london.edu/rportes (office); www.richardportes.eu.

PORTILLO, Rt Hon. Michael Denzil Xavier, PC, MA; British politician, writer and broadcaster; b. 26 May 1953, London; s. of Luis G. Portillo and Cora W. Blyth; m. Carolyn C. Eadie 1982; ed Harrow Co. Boys' School and Peterhouse, Cambridge; Ocean Transport & Trading Co. 1975–76; Conservative Research Dept 1976–79; Special Adviser to Sec. of State for Energy 1979–81; Kerr McGee Oil (UK) Ltd 1981–83; Special Adviser to Sec. of State for Trade and Industry 1983, to Chancellor of Exchequer 1983–84; MP for Enfield, Southgate 1984–97, for Kensington and Chelsea 1999–2005; Asst Govt Whip 1986–87; Parl. Under-Sec. of State, Dept of Health and Social Security 1987–88; Minister of State, Dept of Transport 1988–90; Minister of State for Local Govt and Inner Cities 1990–92; Chief Sec. to the Treasury 1992–94; Sec. of State for Employment 1994–95, for Defence 1995–97; Shadow Chancellor of the Exchequer 2000–01; freelance writer and broadcaster 1997–2001; Theatre Critic, The New Statesman 2004–06; adviser Kerr McGee Corpn 1997–, mem. Bd of Dirs 2006–; Chair. of jury, Man Booker Prize for Fiction 2008; columnist, The Sunday Times 2004–; Dir (non-exec.) BAE Systems PLC 2002–06; mem. Int. Comm. for Missing Persons in Fmr Yugoslavia; Pres. DebRA (charity working on behalf of people with Epidermolysis Bullosa—EB); British Chair. British-Spanish Tertulias; fmr weekly columnist, The Scotsman. *Television includes:* Portillo's Progress (three-part series for Channel 4), programme in BBC 2's Great Railway Journeys series, Art That Shook the World: Richard Wagner's Ring (BBC 2), Portillo in Euroland, Elizabeth I in the series Great Britons (BBC 2), When Michael Portillo Became a Single Mum (BBC 2) 2003. *Publications:* Clear Blue Water 1994, Democratic Values and the Currency 1998. *Address:* Office of The Rt Hon Michael Portillo, Suite 99, 34 Buckingham Palace Road, London, SW1W 0RH, England (office). *Telephone:* (20) 7931-9422 (office). *Fax:* (20) 7931-6549 (office). *E-mail:* michael@michaelportillo.co.uk (office). *Website:* www.michaelportillo.co.uk (office).

PORTILLO CABRERA, Alfonso Antonio; Guatemalan politician and fmr head of state; ed Universidad Autónoma de Guerrero, Mexico, Universidad Autónoma de México; fmr columnist, daily newspaper Siglo Veintiuno; mem. Editorial Bd Suplemento Económico Pulso; Prof. of Law, Econs and Politics in univs in Latin America; fmr Leader of Democracia Cristiana (DC) Deputies in Congress, Chair. Comm. of Econ., Foreign Trade and Integration; Asst Gen. Sec. DC, Dir DC's Centro de Estudios Socio-Políticos (IGESP); Pres. of Guatemala 2000–04; fled to Mexico to escape corruption charges 2004, extradited to Guatemala 2008, now in custody.

PORTISCH, Lajos; Hungarian chess player and singer; b. 4 April 1937, Zalaegerszeg; s. of Lajos Portisch, Sr and Anna Simon; represented Hungary at World Junior Chess Championships, Antwerp 1955; represented Hungary four times at Student Olympiads 1956, 1957, 1958, 1959; to-ranking player of Hungary's selected team from 1962; Hungarian Chess Champion 1958, 1959, 1961, 1964, 1965, 1971, 1975, 1981; holder of Int. Grandmaster title from 1961; European Team Championships bronze medallist 1961, 1965, 1973, team silver medallist 1970, 1977, 1980; Chess Olympiad team bronze medallist 1956, 1966, silver 1970, 1972, 1980, gold 1978; qualified eight times as cand. for the individual chess world title; holder of Master Coach qualification; bass-baritone singer, gives regular concerts; positional style earned him the nickname of the "Hungarian Botvinnik"; mem. MTK-Sport Club; Labour Order of Merit (Golden Degree); Nemzet Sportoloja (highest nat. sports achievement award) 2004. *Publication:* Six Hundred Endings (with B. Sárközi) 1973. *Leisure interest:* music. *Address:* c/o Hungarian Chess Federation, 1055 Budapest, Falk Miksa u. 10, Hungary. *Telephone:* (1) 473-2360. *E-mail:* chess@chess.hu.

PORTMAN, Natalie; American/Israeli actress; b. 9 June 1981, Jerusalem; m. Benjamin Millepied; ed Harvard Univ.; left Israel with her family aged three and moved to USA; discovered by modelling scout at New York pizza parlour aged 11. *Theatre includes:* A Midsummer Night's Dream, Cabaret, Anne of Green Gables (title role), Tapestry, The Seagull 2001. *Films include:* The Professional (also known as Léon) 1994, Developing 1995, Heat 1995, Beautiful Girls 1996, Everyone Says I Love You 1996, Mars Attacks! 1996, The Diary of Anne Frank 1997, Star Wars: Episode I – The Phantom Menace (as Queen Amidala) 1999, Anywhere But Here, Where the Heart Is 2000, The Seagull 2001, Zoolander 2001, Star Wars: Episode II – Attack of the Clones 2002, Cold Mountain 2003, Garden State 2004, True 2004, Closer (Best Supporting Actress, Golden Globe Awards 2005) 2004, Star Wars: Episode III – Revenge of the Sith 2005, V for Vendetta 2006, Paris, je t'aime 2006, Goya's Ghosts 2006, My Blueberry Nights 2007, Hotel Chevalier 2007, The Darjeeling Limited 2007, Mr Magorium's Wonder Emporium 2007, The Other Boleyn Girl 2008, Love and Other Impossible Pursuits 2009, New York, I Love You 2009, Brothers 2009, Hesher 2010, Black Swan (several awards, including Boston Soc. of Film Critics Award for Best Actress, Las Vegas Film Critics Soc. Award for Best Actress, Southeastern Film Critics Asscn Award for Best Actress, Golden Globe Award for Best Actress 2011, BAFTA Award for Leading Actress 2011, Academy Award for Actress in a leading Role 2011) 2010, No Strings Attached 2011, Your Highness 2011, Thor 2011. *Address:* c/o CAA, 2000 Avenue of the Stars, Los Angeles, CA 90067, USA. *Website:* www.natalieportman.com.

PORTMAN, Rachel Mary Berkeley, OBE; British composer; b. 11 Dec. 1960, Haslemere, Surrey, England; m. Uberto Pasolini; three d.; ed Worcester Coll., Oxford; composer of film and TV scores, for US productions 1992–; British Film Inst. Young Composer of the Year Award 1988, Georges Delerue Prize for 'Ratcatcher', Ghent Int. Film Festival 1997, Phoenix Film Critics Soc. Award for Best Original Score (The Legend of Baggar Vance) 1999. *Compositions for film and television:* Experience Preferred... But Not Essential 1982, The Storyteller (TV series) 1986–88, 1990, Life is Sweet 1990, Oranges Are Not the Only Fruit (TV drama) 1990, Antonia and Jane 1991, Where Angels Fear to Tread 1991, Used People 1992, The Joy Luck Club 1993, Benny and Joon 1993, Friends 1993, Sirens 1994, Only You 1994, War of the Buttons 1994, To Wong Foo – Thanks for Everything! 1995, A Pyromaniac's Love Story 1995, Smoke 1995, The Adventures of Pinocchio 1996, Marvin's Room 1996, Emma (Academy Award for Best Music, Original Music or Comedy Score 1997) 1996, Addicted to Love 1997, The Cider House Rules 1999, Chocolat 2000, The Emperor's New Clothes 2001, Hart's War 2002, The Truth About Charlie 2002, Nicholas Nickleby 2002, The Human Stain 2003, Mona Lisa Smile 2003, The Little Prince 2003, Lard 2004, The Manchurian Candidate 2004, Because of Winn-Dixie 2005, Oliver Twist 2006, The Lake House 2006, Miss Potter 2006, Infamous 2006, H2Ohope: The Water Divine's Tale (BBC Proms) 2007, Little House on the Prairie Musical (theatre) 2008, The Duchess 2008, Grey Gardens (TV) 2009, London Assurance (Royal Nat. Theatre) 2010, Never Let Me Go (San Diego Film Critics Soc. Award for Best Score) 2010, Snowflower and the Secret Fan 2011, One Day 2011. *Recordings include:* Rachel Portman Soundtracks (compilation album), numerous soundtrack recordings. *Address:* c/o ChesterNovello, 14–15 Berners Street, London, W1T 3LJ, England (office). *Telephone:* (20) 7612-7549 (office). *Website:* www.chesternovello.com (office); www.rachelportman.co.uk.

PORTMAN, Robert (Rob) Jones, BA, JD; American lawyer, politician and fmr government official; *Senator from Ohio;* b. 19 Dec. 1955, Cincinnati, Ohio; m. Jane D. Dudley 1986; two s. one d.; ed Dartmouth Coll., Univ. of Michigan Law School; Assoc., Patton Boggs law firm, Washington, DC 1984–86; Partner, Graydon, Head & Ritchey, Cincinnati 1986–89, 1991–93; Assoc. Counsel to the Pres., The White House, Washington, DC 1989–91, then Dir White House Office of Legis. Affairs; mem. US Del. to UN Sub-cttee on Human Rights 1992; mem. US House of Reps, 2nd Dist of Ohio 1993–2005, Vice-Chair. Budget Cttee, mem. Ways and Means Cttee, Chair. House Republican Leadership; US Trade Rep., Exec. Office of the Pres. 2005–06, Dir Office of Man. and Budget 2006–07; Of Counsel, Squire, Sanders & Dempsey LLP (law firm), Cincinnati and Washington, DC 2007–09; Senator from Ohio 2011–, mem. Budget Cttee, Energy and Natural Resources Cttee, Homeland Security and Governmental Reform Cttee; Founding Chair. Coalition for a Drug Free Greater Cincinnati; mem. Advisory Bd, John Glenn School of Public Affairs, Ohio State Univ. 2008–; Vice-Chair. Hamilton Co. George Bush for President Campaign 1988, 1992, active in Hamilton Co. Republican Party Exec. Cttee, Hamilton Co. Republican Party Finance Cttee; Chair. Republican Early Bird Campaign Cttee 1992; del., Republican Nat. Convention 1988, 1992; mem. Bd of Trustees, Springer School, The United Way, Hyde Park Community United Methodist Church; Founding Trustee, Cincinnati-China Sister City Cttee; mem. Cincinnati World Trade Asscn; Excellence in Public Service Award, John Glenn School of Public Affairs, Ohio State Univ. 2008, Nelson A. Rockefeller Distinguished Public Service Award, Nelson A. Rockefeller Center, Dartmouth Coll., PLANSPONSOR magazine Legend Award, Nat. Leadership Award, Community Anti-Drug Coalition of America 2008, Leadership on Alcohol & Other Drug Services Award, Hamilton Co. Mental Health & Recovery Services Bd, Albert Gallatin Award, Swiss-American Chamber of Commerce, named as one of The 10 Members to Watch in the 112th Congress, Roll Call 2011. *Publication:* Wisdom's Paradise: The Forgotten Shakers of Union Village (with Cheryl Bauer) 2004. *Address:* 338 Russell Senate Office Building, Washington, DC 20510, USA (office). *Telephone:* (202) 224-3353 (office). *Fax:* (513) 361-1201 (office). *Website:* portman.senate.gov (office).

PORTOS, Michel; French chef and restaurateur; *Director, Le Saint-James Hotel;* ed school leaving certificate in accountancy and vocational training certificate in cooking; two-star Michelin chef; began apprenticeship and worked at Le Rouzic, Gauthier's restaurant in Bordeaux, Dominique Toulousy's restaurant, Les Jardins de l'Opéra, Troisgros in Roanne; owned restaurant in Perpignan; currently Relais & Châteaux Grand Chef and Dir Le Saint-James Hotel, Bordeaux; named by Gault & Millau gastronomy guide as Chef of the Year 2012. *Address:* Le Saint-James, 3 place Camille Hostein, 33270 Bouliac, Gironde, France (office). *Telephone:* (5) 57-97-06-00 (office). *Fax:* (5) 56-20-92-58 (office). *E-mail:* stjames@relaischateaux.com (office). *Website:* www.saintjames-bouliac.com.

PORTZAMPARC, Christian de; French architect; b. 9 May 1944, Casablanca, Morocco; s. of Maurice Urvay de Portzamparc and Annick de Boutray; m. Elizabeth Jardim Neves 1982; two s.; ed Ecole Supérieure des Beaux Arts; worked with Eugene Baudoin and George Candilis; cr. own agency 1980, now has offices in New York and Rio de Janeiro; retrospective exhbn, Pompidou Centre 1996; Artistic Creation Chair, Collège de France (first occupant) 2006–; Commdr des Arts et des Lettres 1989; Great Prize of Architecture of the City of Paris awarded by the Mayor of Paris 1990, Médaille d'Argent, French Acad. of Architecture 1992, Great Nat. Prize of Architecture, Ministry of Urbanism and Transport 1993, Pritzker Prize for Architecture, Hyatt Foundation 1994, Great Urbanism Prize 2004, Créateurs sans Frontières Trophy, Ministry of Foreign Affairs 2008. *Publications include:* La Cité de la musique 1986, Scènes d'atelier, Généalogie des formes 1996, Christian de Portzamparc, Le Dantec 1995, Christian de Portzamparc 1996, Généalogie des formes 1996, Disegno e forma dell'architettura per la città 1996, Voir écrire (with Philippe Sollers) 2005, Architecture: figures du monde, figures du temps, Leçons inaugurales au Collège de France 2006, Rêver la ville (exhbn catalogue) 2007. *Address:* 1 rue de l'Aude, 75014 Paris, France (office). *Telephone:* 1-40-64-80-00 (office). *Fax:* 1-43-27-74-79 (office). *E-mail:* mail@portzamparc.com (office); studio@chdeportzamparc.com (office). *Website:* www.chdeportzamparc.com (office).

POSOKHIN, Mikhail Mikhailovich; Russian architect; b. 10 July 1948, Moscow; s. of Mikhail Vasilyevich Posokhin and Galina Arkadyevna Posokhina; m. 1st (divorced); one s.; m. 2nd Vitalina Kudzyavtseva; two d.; ed Moscow Inst. of

Architecture; Chief Architect Dept of Civil and Residential Construction Mosproyekt-1 1976–80; head of workshop, Dept for Designs of Exemplary Perspective residential area Chertanovo 1980–82; head of workshop, Dept for Designs of Public Bldgs and Edifices Mosproyekt-2 1982–, Gen. Dir 1983; fmr Vice-Chair. Cttee on Architecture and Town-planning of Moscow 1994; mem. Presidium Russian Acad. of Arts, Int. Acad. of Architecture, Acad. Architectural Heritage; The Honour Order, Sergey Radonezhsky Order (2nd and 3rd Degrees), Moscow Daneel Godly Prince Order (2nd Degree), Golden Order of Labour (Bulgary), Golden Order, Russian Acad. of Arts; Merited Architect of Russia, State Prize of Russia, Public Acknowledgement Prize. *Works include:* numerous residential complexes and public edifices including restoration of Cathedral of Christ the Saviour, the Business Centre on Kudrinskaya Square, trade complex on Manege Square, the Gosinny Dvor, reconstruction of the Kremlin and others; 101 projects. *Address:* Mosproyekt-2, 2 Brestskaya str. 5, 123056 Moscow, Russia (office). *Telephone:* (495) 200-56-47 (office).

POSPÍŠIL, Jiří, JUDr; Czech lawyer and politician; b. 24 Nov. 1975, Chomutov; ed Univ. of Western Bohemia, Plzeň; early career as articled clerk in pvt law firm; mem. Civic Democratic Alliance (Občanská demokratická aliance) 1994–98; mem. Civic Democratic Party (Občanská demokratická strana) 1998–, Chair. Regional Asscn for Plzeň 2003–, mem. Exec. Council 2005–; mem. Parl. 2000–, Shadow Minister of Justice 2003–06, Minister of Justice 2006–09, Vice-Chair. Constitutional-Legal Cttee 2002–06, mem. Sub-Cttee for Penal System 2002–06; Expert Asst, Admin. Law Dept, Univ. of Western Bohemia 2002–. *Address:* c/o Civic Democratic Party (Občanská demokratická strana), Jánský vršek 13, 118 00 Prague 1, Czech Republic. *Telephone:* 234707111. *Fax:* 234707101. *E-mail:* hk@ods .cz. *Website:* www.ods.cz.

POSSER DA COSTA, Guilherme; São Tomé and Príncipe politician; b. 1953; Minister of Foreign Affairs and Co-operation 1987–88, 1990–91; Prime Minister 1999–2001; Vice-Pres. Movimento de Libertação de São Tomé e Príncipe–Partido Social Democrata (MLSTP-PSD). *Address:* Movimento de Libertação de São Tomé e Príncipe–Partido Social Democrata, Riboque Cidade Capital, São Tomé e Príncipe (office). *Telephone:* (12) 22253 (office).

POST, Herschel, MBE, MA, LLB; American investment banker; b. 9 Oct. 1939; s. of Herschel E. Post and Marie C. Post; m. Peggy Mayne 1963; one s. three d.; ed Yale and Harvard Univs and New Coll., Oxford, UK; Assoc., Davis, Polk & Wordwell (attorneys) 1966–69; Exec. Dir Parks Council of New York City 1969–72; Deputy Admin., Parks, Recreation and Cultural Affairs Admin, New York 1973; Vice-Pres. and Man. Euro-clear Operations, JPMorgan & Co. Brussels 1974–78; Vice-Pres. and Deputy Head, Int. Investment Dept JPMorgan, London 1978–83; Pres. Posthorn Global Asset Man., London 1984–90; Shearson Lehman Global Asset Man., London 1984–90; Deputy Chair. London Stock Exchange 1988–95, Chair. Trading Markets Man. Bd 1990–95, Euroclear Plc 1992–2000, Euroclear UK and Ireland 2002–12, Earthwatch Europe 1988– (Chair. 1997–2011); COO Lehman Brothers Int. Ltd 1990–94, Coutts & Co. 1994–95 (CEO and Deputy Chair. 1995–2000); Int. Man. Dir of Business Devt, Christie's International PLC 2000–05; Chair. Woodcock Foundation 2000–05; Deputy Chair. EFG Private Bank Ltd 2002–05; Dir (non-exec.), Investors Capital Trust 2000–14; Ahli United Bank BSC 2002–, Notting Hill Housing Group 2002–07; Threadneedle Asset Management SARL 2006–. *Address:* Ahli United Bank BSC, PO Box 2424, Bldg 2495, Road 2832, Al Seef District 428, Manama, Bahrain (office). *Telephone:* (17) 585858 (Manama) (office); (20) 7792-9337 (London) (office). *Fax:* (17) 580589 (Manama) (office); (20) 7243-2775 (London) (office). *E-mail:* info@ahliunited.com (office). *Website:* www.ahliunited.com (office).

POSTE, George, CBE, BVSC, PhD, FRS, FRCVS, FRCPath; American (b. British) research scientist, business executive and academic; *Co-Director and Chief Scientist, Complex Adaptive Systems Network, Arizona State University;* b. 30 April 1944, Polegate, Sussex, England; s. of the late John H. Poste and of Kathleen B. Poste; m. Linda Suhler 1992; one s. two d.; ed Bristol Univ.; Lecturer, Royal Postgraduate Medical School, Univ. of London 1969–72, Sr Lecturer 1974; Assoc. Prof. of Experimental Pathology, State Univ. of New York (SUNY), Buffalo 1972–74, Prin. Cancer Research Scientist and Prof. of Cell and Molecular Biology 1975–80; Vice-Pres. and Dir of Research, Smith Kline & French Labs, Philadelphia, Pa 1980–83, Vice-Pres. Research and Devt Technologies 1983–86, Vice-Pres. Worldwide Research and Preclinical Devt 1987–88, Pres. Research and Devt 1988–89, Exec. Vice-Pres. Research and Devt SmithKline Beecham Pharmaceuticals 1989–91, Pres. Research and Devt 1991–97, Chief Science and Tech. Officer 1997–99; CEO Health Tech. Networks 2000–; Partner, Care Capital, Princeton, NJ 2000–; Research Prof., Univ. of Pennsylvania 1981–, Univ. of Texas Medical Center 1986–; Fleming Fellow, Lincoln Coll. Oxford 1995; William Pitt Fellow, Pembroke Coll. Cambridge 1996–; Distinguished Visiting Fellow, Hoover Inst., Stanford Univ. 2000–; Del E. Webb Distinguished Prof. of Biology and Founder and Dir Biodesign Inst., Arizona State Univ. 2003–09, Regents Prof. 2006–, Co-Dir and Chief Scientist, Complex Adaptive Systems Initiative and Del E. Webb Chair in Health Innovation 2009–; Chair. (non-exec.) Orchid Biosciences, Princeton NJ; mem. Bd of Dirs Exelixis, Monsanto; mem. Defense Science Bd of US Dept of Defense 2003–09, Chair. Task Force on Bioterrorism; mem. NAS Working Group on Defense Against Bioweapons; mem. Human Genetics Advisory Cttee 1996–; mem. Bd of Govs Center for Molecular Medicine and Genetics, Stanford Univ. 1992–; mem. Alliance for Ageing 1992–97; Jt Ed. Cell Surface Reviews 1976–83, New Horizons in Therapeutics 1984–; mem. Council on Foreign Relations 2004–; Fellow, Royal Coll. of Veterinary Surgeons; Hon. FRCP 1993; Hon. Fellow, Univ. Coll. London 1993; Hon. DSc 1987, (Sussex) 1999; Hon. LLD (Bristol) 1995, (Dundee) 1998; R&D Scientist of the Year, R&D Magazine 2004, Albert Einstein Award, Global Business Leadership Council 2006, SCRIP Lifetime Achievement Award 2009. *Publications:* numerous reviews and papers in learned journals. *Leisure interests:* automobile racing, mil. history, photography, desert exploration. *Address:* Complex Adaptive Systems Network, Arizona State University-Skysong 1475 North Scottsdale Road, Ste 361, Scottsdale, AZ 85257, USA (office). *Telephone:* (480) 727-8662 (office). *Fax:* (480) 965-2765 (office). *E-mail:* george .poste@asu.edu (office). *Website:* www.casi.asu.edu (office).

POSTGATE, John Raymond, DPhil, DSc, FRS; British microbiologist and academic; *Professor Emeritus of Microbiology, University of Sussex;* b. 24 June 1922, London, England; s. of Raymond William Postgate and Daisy Postgate (née

Lansbury); m. Mary Stewart 1948 (died 2008); three d.; ed Woodstock School, Kingsbury Co. School, Balliol Coll., Oxford; Sr Research Investigator, Nat. Chemical Lab. 1949–50, Sr Prin. 1950–59; Prin., Sr Prin. Scientific Officer, Microbiology Research Establishment 1959–63; Asst Dir Agricultural and Food Research Council (AFRC) Unit of Nitrogen Fixation, Royal Veterinary Coll. 1963–65; Prof. of Microbiology, Univ. of Sussex 1965–87, Prof. Emer. 1987–, Asst Dir AFRC Unit of Nitrogen Fixation 1965–80, Dir 1980–87; Visiting Prof., Univ. of Illinois 1962–63, Oregon State Univ. 1977–78; Pres. Inst. of Biology 1982–84, Soc. for Gen. Microbiology 1984–87; Fellow, Soc. of Biology; Hon. DSc (Bath), Hon. LLD (Dundee). *Music:* reviewer of jazz recordings 1960–2010. *Publications include:* Microbes and Man 1969, (fourth edn) 2000, Biological Nitrogen Fixation 1972, A Plain Man's Guide to Jazz 1973, Nitrogen Fixation 1978, (third edn) 1998, The Sulphate-Reducing Bacteria 1979, (second edn) 1984, The Fundamentals of Nitrogen Fixation 1982, The Outer Reaches of Life 1994, A Stomach for Dissent: The Life of Raymond Postgate (with Mary Postgate) 1994, Lethal Lozenges and Tainted Tea: A Biography of John Postgate (1820–1881) 2001, Looking For Frankie: A Biodiscography of the Jazz Trumpeter Frankie Newton (with Bob Weir) 2003, Microbes, Music and Me: A Life in Science 2013. *Leisure interests:* listening to jazz and attempting to play it, cookery. *Address:* 1 Houndean Rise, Lewes, Sussex, BN7 1EG, England (home). *Telephone:* (1273) 472675 (home). *E-mail:* johnp@sussex.ac.uk (office).

POTANIN, Vladimir Olegovich; Russian politician, banker and business executive; *CEO, Mining and Metallurgical Company Norilsk Nickel;* b. 3 Jan. 1961, Moscow; m.; two s., one d.; ed Moscow Inst. of Int. Relations; mem. staff, USSR Ministry of Foreign Trade 1983–90; Head Econ. Co. Interros 1991–92; Vice-Pres., Pres. Joint-Stock Commercial Bank International Financial Co. 1992–93; Pres. UNEXIM Bank 1993–98, InterRos Financial and Industrial Group (now Interros Holding Co.) 1994–2012; with partners acquired several govt oil and mineral assets including Norilsk Nickel (world's largest producer of nickel); First Deputy Chair. Govt of Russian Fed. 1996–97; CEO Mining and Metallurgical Co. Norilsk Nickel 2012–; joined Giving Pledge 2013; Officier, Ordre des Arts et des Lettres 2007, Fourth Degree, Order of Merit for the Motherland 2007, Third and Second Degree, Order of St Prince Vladimir Equal-to-the-Apostles, Third and Second Degree, Order of St Sergius of Radonezh, Second Degree, Order of the Holy Prince Daniel of Moscow, First Degree, Order of the St Seraphim of Sarov 2012. *Leisure interests:* travelling, soccer, alpine skiing, various water sports, chess. *Address:* Mining and Metallurgical Company Norilsk Nickel, 22 Voznesensky Pereulok, Moscow, Russia (office). *Telephone:* (495) 787-76-67 (office). *E-mail:* info@nornik.ru (office). *Website:* www.nornik.ru (office).

POTAPOV, Alexander Serafimovich, CandPhil; Russian journalist and newspaper publishing executive; *Director, Izvestia TV News Channel;* b. 6 Feb. 1936, Oktyabry, Kharkov Region, Ukraine; m.; one s.; ed Vilnius State Univ., Lithuania; contrib. Leninskaya Smena (newspaper) 1958–66; Head of Dept, Deputy Ed.-in-Chief Belgorodskaya Pravda (newspaper) 1966–73; Head of Dept Belgorod Regional Exec. CPSU Cttee 1973–75; Ed. Belgorodskaya Pravda 1975–76; instructor, CPSU Cen. Cttee 1976–78, 1981–85; apptd Ed.-in-Chief Trud (Labour) newspaper 1985; Ed.-in-Chief Marker (online business newspaper) 2010–12; Ed.-in-Chief Izvestia 2012–13, also Deputy Editorial Dir Holding News Media, Dir Izvestia TV News Channel 2013–; People's Deputy of Russian Fed., mem. Cttee of Supreme Soviet of Russian Fed. on Problems of Glasnost and Human Rights –1993. *Address:* Izvestia, 127994 Moscow, ul. Tverskaya 18/1, POB 4, Russia (office). *Telephone:* (495) 209-05-81 (office). *Fax:* (495) 933-64-62 (office). *E-mail:* a.potapov@izvestia.ru (office). *Website:* www.izvestia.ru (office).

POTAPOV, Leonid Vasilyevich; Russian politician; b. 4 July 1935, Uakit, Buryatia; m.; two c.; ed Khabarovsk Inst. of Railway Eng, Irkutsk Inst. of Nat. Econs; various positions from engineer to Chief Engineer, Ulan-Ude train factory 1959–76; Head Div. of Industry, then Sec. Buryat Regional CP Cttee 1976–87; Chair. Mary Regional Exec. Cttee Turkmenia 1987–89; Chair. Supreme Soviet Turkmen SSR 1989–90; First Sec. Buryat CPSU Cttee 1990–91; Chair. Supreme Soviet Buryat Autonomous SSR (now Buryatskaya Repub.) 1991–94; Pres. of Buryatskaya Repub. 1994–2007; mem. Council of Fed., Russian Fed. 1993–2001; Hon. Engineer, Buryat Repub.; Order of the Oct. Revolution, Red Banner of Labour, Honour Award, Order of Friendship, Order for Excellent Service to the Native Land (IV degree), Polar Star Order (Mongolia). *Leisure interest:* reading literature on history, philosophy and economics. *Address:* c/o Government House, Sukhe Bator str. 9, 670001 Ulan-Ude, Republic of Buryatia, Russia (office).

POTERBA, James Michael, AB, MPhil, DPhil; American economist and academic; *President and CEO, National Bureau of Economic Research;* b. 13 July 1958, New York, NY; m. Nancy Lin Rose 1984; two s. one d.; ed Harvard Coll., Univ. of Oxford, UK; Jr Research Fellow, Nuffield Coll. Oxford 1982–83; Asst Prof. of Econs, MIT 1983–86, Assoc. Prof. of Econs 1986–88, Prof. of Econs 1988–96, Assoc. Head, Dept of Econs 1994–2000, 2001–06, Mitsui Prof. of Econs 1996–, Head, Dept of Econs 2006–, mem. Program Bd MIT Center for Energy and Environmental Policy Research 1993–, MIT Advisory Cttee on Shareholder Responsibility 2006–; CRSP Visiting Prof. of Finance, Univ. of Chicago GSB 1988; Faculty Research Fellow, Nat. Bureau of Econ. Research (NBER) 1982–85, Research Assoc. 1985–, Assoc. Dir Taxation Research Program, NBER 1989–91, Dir NBER Public Econs Research Program 1991–, Pres. and CEO NBER 2008–; Dir American Finance Asscn 1993–95; Fellow, Center for Advanced Study in Behavioral Sciences 1993–94; George and Karen McCown Distinguished Visiting Fellow, Hoover Inst. 2000–01; Distinguished Scholar, American Council on Capital Formation 2002; CES Distinguished Fellow, Univ. of Munich 2003; TIAA-CREF Inst. Fellow 2004–06; Int. Research Fellow, Inst. for Fiscal Studies, London, UK 2006; Int. Research Fellow, Centre for Business Taxation, Univ. of Oxford 2007–; mem. Research Advisory Bd American Council on Capital Formation 1993–, Advisory Bd Stanford Inst. for Econ. Policy Research 2005–, Econs Advisory Panel Congressional Budget Office 2006–, Retirement Security Task Force, Investment Co. Inst. 2007; First Vice-Pres. Nat. Tax Asscn 2008 (Second Vice-Pres. 2007); mem. Exec. Cttee American Econs Asscn 2001–03, Chair. Honors and Awards Cttee 2006–; Sr Fellow, Inst. for Policy Reform 1992–93; Assoc. Ed. Journal of Finance 1988–2000, Review of Economics & Statistics 1993–2002, Regional Science & Urban Economics 1997–2004; Co-Ed. RAND Journal of Economics 1986–95, Journal of Public Economics 1995–97 (Ed. 1998–2006, Advisory Ed.

2007–); mem. Advisory Bd Journal of Investment Consulting 1998–2005, Journal of Wealth Management 1998–, Retirement Income Review 2002–; mem. Editorial Advisory Bd National Tax Journal 2007–; Fellow, Econometric Soc. 1988, Nat. Acad. of Social Insurance 1992, American Acad. of Arts and Sciences 1996; Trustee, Coll. Retirement Equity Fund (TIAA-CREF) 2006–; John Williams Prize 1980, Marshall Scholarship 1980–83, George Webb Medley MPhil Thesis Prize 1982, Batterymarch Financial Fellowship 1986, James L. Barr Award 1986, Alfred P. Sloan Fellowship 1988, MIT Econs Dept Teacher of the Year 1990, 1993, 1995, Certificate of Excellence, Paul Samuelson Prize, TIAA-CREF 1996, 2004, Woytinsky Lecturer, Univ. of Michigan 1996, Nat. Acad. of Sciences Award for Scientific Reviewing 1999, Duncan Black Prize, Public Choice Soc. 2000, Review of Economics and Statistics Lecturer, Harvard Univ. 2000, Inst. for Fiscal Studies Lecturer, London 2000, David Kinley Lecturer, Univ. of Illinois 2001, MIT Grad. Econs Asscn Teacher of the Year 2002, Watson-Wyatt Lecture, City Univ., London 2002, Hon. Mention, Culp-Wright Book Award, American Risk and Insurance Asscn 2003, Munich Lectures, Centre for Econ. Studies 2003, Marsh & McLennan Lecturer, Furman Univ. 2003, Hahn Lecturer, Royal Econ. Soc. 2003, EFACT Hon. Award, Univ. of Tilburg 2005, Elder Law Journal Lecturer, Univ. of Illinois 2005, American Econs Asscn/American Finance Asscn Jt Luncheon Lecturer 2006, Plenary Lecture, North American Summer Econometric Soc. Meetings 2007. *Publications:* Economic Policy Responses to Global Warming (co-ed.), Tax Policy and the Economy: Vols 6–22 (ed.) 1992–2008, Public Policies and Household Saving (ed.) 1994, Housing Markets in the United States and Japan (co-ed.) 1994, International Comparisons of Household Saving (ed.) 1994), Empirical Foundations of Household Taxation (co-ed.) 1996, Borderline Case: International Tax Policy, Corporate Research and Development, and Investment (ed.) 1998, Fiscal Institutions and Fiscal Performance (co-ed.) 1999, Fiscal Rules and State Borrowing Costs: Evidence from California and Other States (co-author) 1999, The Role of Annuity Markets in Financing Retirement (co-author) 2001, Fiscal Reform in Colombia: Problems and Prospects (co-ed.) 2005; more than 200 book chapters, reviews, articles and papers in professional journals. *Address:* Department of Economics, Massachusetts Inst. of Tech., E17-214, 77 Massachusetts Avenu, Cambridge, MA 02139 (office); National Bureau of Economic Research, Inc., 1050 Massachusetts Avenue, Cambridge, MA 02138-5398, USA. *Telephone:* (617) 253-6673 (MIT) (office); (617) 868-3900 (NBER) (office). *Fax:* (617) 253-1330 (MIT) (office); (617) 868-2742 (NBER) (office). *E-mail:* poterba@mit.edu (office). *Website:* econ-www.mit.edu/faculty/poterba (office); www.nber.org (office).

POTIER, Benoit; French business executive; *Chairman and CEO, Air Liquide;* b. 3 Sept. 1957, Mulhouse; m. Claude Menard; ed Ecole Centrale Paris; joined Research Devt Dept, Air Liquide 1981, positions in Eng and Construction Div. 1993–97, CEO 1997–, mem. Bd 2000–, Chair. 2006–, Chair. and CEO Air Liquide Int., American Air Liquide Inc.; mem. Bd of Dirs Danone Group; mem. Supervisory Bd Michelin; Admin. Ecole Centrale des Arts et Manufactures; mem. Conseil de France, Institut Européen d'Admin des Affaires (INSEAD), European Trilateral Comm.; Chevalier, Légion d'honneur, Officier, Ordre nat. du Mérite. *Address:* Air Liquide, 75 quai d'Orsay, 75321 Paris Cedex 07, France (office). *Telephone:* 1-40-68-55-55 (office). *Fax:* 1-40-68-58-40 (office). *E-mail:* info@airliquide.com (office). *Website:* www.airliquide.com (office).

POTOČNIK, Janez, BA, MA, PhD; Slovenian economist, government official and international organization official; *Commissioner for Environment, European Commission;* b. 22 March 1958, Kropa; m.; two c.; ed Univ. of Ljubljana; Analyst, SDK 1983–84; Asst Dir Inst. of Econ. Analysis and Devt, Ljubljana 1984–87; Sr Researcher, Inst. for Econ. Research, Ljubljana 1988–93; part-time Asst Prof. of Statistics and Economy, Faculty of Law, Univ. of Ljubljana 1991–2004; Dir Inst. of Macroeconomic Analysis and Devt, Ljubljana 1993–2001; Head of negotiating team for Slovenian accession to EU 1998–2004; Minister Counsellor in Prime Minister's Cabinet 2001–02; Minister for European Affairs 2002–04; EC 'Shadow' Commr for Enlargement, sharing portfolio with Commr Günther Verheugen May–Nov. 2004, for Science and Research 2004–10, Commr for Environment 2010–; Hon. DSc (Imperial Coll. London) 2008; Dr hc (Ghent Univ., Belgium) 2009. *Address:* European Commission, Rue de la Loi 200, 1049 Brussels, Belgium (office). *Telephone:* (2) 298-86-70 (office). *Fax:* (2) 298-82-88 (office). *E-mail:* janez .potocnik@ec.europa.eu (office). *Website:* ec.europa.eu/commission_2010-2014/ potocnik (office).

POTRČ, Marjetica; Slovenian artist and architect; *Professor, University of Fine Arts/HFBK, Hamburg;* b. 1953, Ljubljana; d. of Ivan Potrč and Branka Jurca; ed Univ. of Ljubljana; Assoc. Prof., Dept of Design, Acad. of Fine Arts and Design, Ljubljana 1993–2004; taught at MIT, USA 2005, Städelschule Art Acad., Frankfurt am Main, Germany 2006, Fondazione Antonio Ratti, Como, Italy 2006, IUAV Faculty of Arts and Design, Venice 2008, 2010; Prof., Univ. of Fine Arts/HFBK, Hamburg, Germany 2011–; work has been exhibited extensively throughout Europe and the Americas, including Venice Biennial 1993, 2003, 2009, São Paulo Biennial 1996, 2006, Skulptur: Projekte in Münster, Germany 1997; her work 'Soweto House with Prepaid Water Meter' exhibited at Eli and Edythe Broad Art Museum, Michigan State Univ., East Lansing 2013; Pollock-Krasner Foundation Grants 1993, 1999, Hugo Boss Prize 2000, Caracas Case Project Fellowship, Federal Cultural Foundation, Germany and Caracas Urban Think Tank, Venezuela 2002, Vera List Center for Arts and Politics Fellowship, New School in New York 2007. *Publications include:* Urban Negotiation 2003, Next Stop, Kiosk 2003, Urgent Architecture 2003, Fragment Worlds 2006, Florestania 2009; several essays on contemporary architecture and art. *Address:* c/o Galerie Nordenhake, Berlin/Stockholm Lindenstrasse 34, Berlin 10969, Germany. *Telephone:* (30) 206-1483. *Fax:* (30) 2061-4848. *E-mail:* berlin@nordenhake.com. *Website:* www .nordenhake.com; www.potrc.org.

POTRČ, Miran; Slovenian politician and lawyer; b. 27 March 1938, Maribor, Slovenia; s. of Ivan Potrč and Olga Potrč; m. Zdenka Potrč 1992; one d.; ed Univ. of Ljubljana; with Secr. of Justice and Public Admin Maribor 1962–63; Head, Legal Dept Mariborska Livarna (Maribor Foundry) 1963–68; Sec. Communal Cttee of League of Communists of Maribor 1968–73; mem. Presidency of Cen. Cttee League of Communists of Slovenia and Pres. Comm. for Socio-Economic Matters and Social Policy 1973; mem. Exec. Cttee Presidency of Cen. Cttee of League of Communists of Slovenia 1974–78; Vice-Pres. Repub. Council of Trade Unions of Slovenia 1978–80; mem. Presidency, Trade Unions of Yugoslavia 1980–82, Pres.

1980–81; Head, Del. of Skupshtina (Parl.) of SR of Slovenia in Fed. Chamber of Repubs and Provs 1982–86; Pres. Skupshtina of SR of Slovenia 1986–90; mem. Parl. of Repub. of Slovenia, Head of Parl. Group and mem. Presidium, Party of Democratic Reforms of Slovenia 1990–2011; Head of Parl. Group United List of Social Democrats, Vice-Pres. Social Democrats 2009; fnr Pres. Council, Univ. of Maribor. *Address:* c/o Assembly of the Republic of Slovenia, Tomšičeva 5, 61000 Ljubljana, Slovenia. *E-mail:* miran.potrc@dz-ns.si.

POTTAKIS, Yannis A.; Greek politician; b. 1939, Corinth; m. Constantina Alexopoulou; two s. one d.; ed Univs of Athens and Munich, Germany; founding mem. of Pasok; mem. Parl. 1977–; Alt. Minister of Nat. Economy 1982–83, Minister of Finance 1983–84, of Agric. 1985–89, of Justice 1995–96; Alt. Minister of Foreign Affairs; Chair. Council of Budget Ministers of EEC 1983.

POTTER, David Edwin, CBE, PhD, MA, FREng; British business executive; *Chairman, Psion Plc;* b. 4 July 1943, East London, South Africa; s. of Paul James Potter and Mary Agnes Snape; m. Elaine Goldberg 1969; three s.; ed Trinity Coll. Cambridge, Imperial Coll. London; Lecturer, Blackett Lab., Imperial Coll. London 1970–80; Asst Prof., UCLA 1974; Founder, Chair., CEO Psion PLC 1980–; Dir Press Assoc. Ltd 1994–97 (Vice-Chair. 1995–97), London First Centre 1994–, Finsbury Tech. Trust 1995–; Chair. Symbian Ltd 1998–2004; mem. Nat. Cttee of Inquiry into Higher Educ. (Dearing Cttee) 1996–97, Higher Educ. Funding Council for England 1997–2003, Council for Science and Tech., Cabinet Office 1998–2003; Visiting Fellow, Nuffield Coll. Oxford 1998–; Gov. London Business School 2000; Dir Bank of England 2003; Hon. Fellow, Imperial Coll. 1998, London Business School 1998; Hon. DTech (Kingston) 1998, (Brunel) 1998, Hon. DSc (Sheffield) 2000, (Warwick) 2001, (York) 2002, (Edinburgh) 2002; Mountbatten Medal for Outstanding Services to Electronics Industry, Nat. Electronics Council 1994. *Publications:* Computational Physics 1972, contribs to numerous physics journals. *Leisure interests:* flute, gardening, reading, tennis. *Address:* Psion PLC, 10 Park Crescent, London, W1B 1PQ (office); 8 Hamilton Terrace, St John's Wood, London, NW8 9UG, England (home). *Telephone:* (20) 7291-3999 (office). *Fax:* (20) 7291-3991 (office). *E-mail:* david@depotter.net (office). *Website:* www.psion.com (office).

POTTER, John (Jack) E., MA; American business executive; *President and CEO, Metropolitan Washington Airports Authority;* b. 1956, Bronx, New York; m. Maureen Potter; two c.; ed Fordham Univ., Massachusetts Inst. of Tech. (Sloan Fellow); began career as distribution clerk, US Postal Service, Westchester, NY 1977, various exec. and man. positions including Sr Vice-Pres. Labour Relations 1998–99, Sr Vice-Pres. Operations 1999–2000, COO and Exec. Vice-Pres. 2000–01, Postmaster Gen. and CEO 2001–10, mem. Postal Service Bd of Govs; Pres. and CEO Metropolitan Washington Airports Authority 2011–; fmr Vice-Chair. Int. Post Corpn, Chair. Kahala Posts Group; mem. Pres.'s Nat. Hire Veterans Cttee; Republican; American Postal Services Bd of Govs Award 1999, Elmo Zumwalt Legacy Award, Marrow Foundation 2003, J. Edward Day Award, Asscn of Postal Commerce 2003, Tom Tully Award, AM Business Media 2006, Roger W. Jones Award for Executive Leadership, American Univ. 2007. *Address:* Metropolitan Washington Airports Authority, 1 Aviation Circle, Washington, DC 20001-6000, USA (office). *Telephone:* (703) 417-8600 (office). *E-mail:* info@mwaa.com (office). *Website:* www.mwaa.com (office).

POTTER, William C., BA, MA, PhD; American research institute director; *Director, Center for Nonproliferation Studies;* b. 8 July 1947, New Brunswick, NJ; ed Southern Illinois Univ., Univ. of Michigan; started career as Research Assoc., Univ. of Mich; Lecturer, Dept of Political Science, Univ. of Calif. 1973–76; Post-Doctoral Fellow, Stanford Univ. 1976–77; arms control consultant 1976–77; Asst Prof., Tulane Univ.; Asst Dir Center for Int. and Strategic Affairs, UCLA 1979–82, Visiting Assoc. Prof. 1979–88, Assoc. Dir 1982–84, Exec. Dir 1984–89; Exec. Officer Southern Calif Consortium on Int. Studies 1982–83; consultant to Lawrence Livermore Nat. Lab. 1982–89, 1992–, Jet Propulsion Lab. 1984–85, RAND Corpn 1984–86; Program Coordinator RAND/UCLA Center for the Study of Soviet Int. Behaviour 1983–85; Prof., Int. Policy Studies, Monterey Inst. of Int. Studies 1989–, Dir Center for Russian and Eurasian Studies 1989–, Dir Center for Nonproliferation Studies 1992–, Inst. Prof. 1998–; mem. several cttees Nat. Acad. of Sciences; mem. Council on Foreign Relations, Pacific Council on Int. Policy, IISS; mem. Advisory Bds UN Disarmament Matters, Center for Policy Studies in Russia; mem. Bd of Trustees UN Inst. for Disarmament Research. *Publications:* SALT and Beyond: A Handbook on Strategic Weapons and Means for Their Control (jtly) 1977, Nuclear Power and Nonproliferation: An Interdisciplinary Perspective 1982, Verification and Arms Control (ed.) 1985, International Nuclear Trade and Nonproliferation: The Challenge of the Emerging Suppliers (ed.) 1990, Nuclear Profiles of the Soviet Successor States (jtly) 1993, The International Missile Bazaar (co-ed.) 1994, Dismantling the Cold War: US and NIS Perspectives on the Nunn-Lugar Cooperative Threat Reduction Program (co-ed.) 1997, Dangerous Weapons, Desperate States (co-ed.) 1999, The Different Faces of Nuclear Terrorism (jtly) 2004; numerous chapters and articles in over eighty scholarly books and journals. *Address:* Center for Nonproliferation Studies, 460 Pierce Street, Monterey, CA 93940 (office); 52 Cuesta Drive, Monterey, CA 93940, USA (home). *Telephone:* (831) 647-3511 (office); (831) 375-3472 (home). *Fax:* (831) 647-3519 (office). *E-mail:* wpotter@miis.edu (office). *Website:* cns.miis.edu (office).

PÖTTERING, Hans-Gert, PhD; German politician; *Chairman, Konrad-Adenauer-Stiftung;* b. 15 Sept. 1945, Bersenbrueck; two s.; ed Univs of Bonn and Geneva, Institut des Hautes Études Internationales, Geneva; Reserve Officer, Nat. Service 1966–68; European Policy Spokesman, Young Union of Lower Saxony 1974-80; Research Assistant Univ. of Osnabrueck, 1976–79, Lecturer 1989–95, Hon. Prof. 1995–; mem. European Parl. 1979–, Chair. European Parl. Sub-cttee on Security and Defence 1984–94, Vice-Chair. European People's Party–European Democrats Group (EPP–ED) Group 1994–99, Chair. 1999–2007, Leader EPP EU Enlargement Working Group 1996–99, Pres. European Parl. 2007–09; Chair. Europa-Union Deutschland 1997–99, Osnabrueck Dist CDU 1990– (mem. Exec. Cttee and Fed. Exec. CDU 1999–2007), Konrad-Adenauer-Stiftung 2010–; European Hon. Senator; Grand Order of Merit of the FRG, Grand Decoration of the Repub. of Austria, Grand Cross, Order of St Gregory the Great, Grand Order of Queen Jelena with Sash and Star (Croatia); Dr hc (Babeș-Bolyai-Univ., Cluj-Napoca, Romania); Konsul-Penseler P, Artland-Gymnasium, Quakenbrück, Robert Schuman Medal, EPP-Group, Gold Medal of Mérite Européen, Luxembourg, MEP of the Year 2004 (European Voice), Walter Hallstein Prize (Frankfurt am Main) 2007. *Publications:* Adenauers Sicherheitspolitik 1955–1963. Ein Beitrag zum deutsch-amerikanischen Verhältnis (Adenauer's Security Policy 1955–1963. A Contribution to the German-American relationship) 1975, Die vergessenen Regionen: Plädoyer für eine solidarische Regionalpolitik in der Europäischen Gemeinschaft (The Forgotten Regions: for a European Community Regional Policy Based on Solidarity) (with Frank Wiehler) 1983, Europas vereinigte Staaten – Annäherungen an Werte und Ziele (Europe's United States – Approaches to Values and Objectives) (with Ludger Kühnhardt) 1993, Kontinent Europa: Kern, Übergänge, Grenzen (The Continent of Europe: Nucleus, Transitions, Borders) (with Ludger Kühnhardt) 1998, Weltpartner Europäische Union (The European Union as a World Partner) (with Ludger Kühnhardt) 2001, Von der Vision zur Wirklichkeit. Auf dem Weg zur Einigung Europas (From Vision to Reality – Towards a United Europe) 2004. *Address:* European Parliament, Bâtiment Paul-Henri Spaak, 08B043, 60 rue Wiertz, 1047 Brussels, Belgium (office). *Telephone:* (2) 284-57-69 (office). *Fax:* (2) 284-97-69 (office). *E-mail:* hans-gert.poettering@europarl.europa.eu (office). *Website:* www.europarl.europa.eu (office).

POUDEL, Ram Chandra; Nepalese politician; mem. Parl. for Tanahu Dist 1994–99; fmr Deputy Prime Minister; Gen. Sec. Nepali Congress; Minister of Peace and Reconstruction 2007–08; mem. Nepali Nat. Congress party. *Address:* Nepali Congress Party, Bhansar Tole, Teku, Kathmandu, Nepal (office). *Website:* www.nepalicongress.org (office).

POUGATCHEV, Sergueï; Russian politician and banker; b. 1963; f. Mejprombank 1992, Dir and later Pres. –2001; mem. (Senator) Council of the Fed. for Tver Oblast 2001–; acquired numerous properties and cos including Luxe TV, Poljot (watches), Hédiard (French luxury grocer) 2007, France-Soir (French newspaper) 2010; Co-f. Almazi Yakoutil co.

POUND, Richard (Dick) William Duncan, OC, OQ, QC, BCom, BA, BCL, LLD, FCPA; Canadian fmr Olympic swimmer, lawyer, chartered accountant and university administrator; *Of Counsel, Stikeman Elliott LLP;* b. 22 March 1942, St Catharines, Ont.; s. of William Thomas Pound and Jessie Edith Duncan Thom; m. Julie Houghton Keith; ed McGill Univ. and Sir George Williams Univ. (now Concordia Univ.), Montreal; competitor in Olympics Games, Rome 1960, double finalist in 100m freestyle (6th) and 4×100m medley relay (4th); Gold Medal in 110-yard freestyle event, two Silver Medals in 440- and 880-yard freestyle relay, and Bronze Medal in 440-yard medley relay, Commonwealth Games 1962; Canadian Champion in freestyle 1958, 1960–62, butterfly 1961; Sec. Canadian Olympic Asscn 1968–76, Pres. 1977–82; Deputy Chef de Mission, Canadian Olympic Del., Munich 1972; joined IOC in 1978, served on Exec. Bd 1983–91, 1992–2000, Vice-Pres. IOC 1987–91, 1996–2000, Chair. Coordination Comm. for Olympic Games in Atlanta 1996; his investigation of Salt Lake City Winter Olympics scandal led to creation of new ethics watchdog to monitor future interaction between bidding cities and IOC mems; Chair. World Anti-Doping Agency, Lausanne, Switzerland 1999–2007; currently of Counsel, Stikeman Elliott LLP, Montréal; mem. Int. Council Arbitration for Sport 2007–; lectured in taxation matters at Faculty of Law, McGill Univ., Montréal and at McGill Centre for Continuing Educ. in Chartered Accountancy program, Past Pres. Grads' Soc. (now McGill Alumni Asscn), fmr Chair. Alma Mater Fund and McGill's Fund Council, mem. Bd Govs 1986 (Chair. 1994–99), Chancellor McGill Univ. 1999–2009, Chancellor Emer. 2009–; mem. Quebec and Ontario Bars; has been apptd to Fed. Court Bench and Bar Liaison Cttee; Ed. Legal Notes, CGA Magazine; mem. Canadian Tax Foundation, Asscn de planification fiscale et financière, Canadian Bar Asscn, Int. Fiscal Asscn, Int. Asscn of Practising Lawyers, IOC; Chubb Fellow, Timothy Dwight Coll., Yale Univ. 2004; Hon. Consul Gen. of Norway in Montreal; Hon. Lt Col, Canadian Grenadier Guards; several Canadian and foreign decorations; Hon. PhD (United Sports Acad.) 1989; Hon. LLD (Univ. of Windsor) 1997, (Univ. of Western Ontario) 2004; Dr hc (Laurentian Univ.) 2005, (Beijing Sport Univ.) 2006; Carswell Company Prize, McGill Univ. 1967, Laureus Spirit of Sport Prize 2008, inducted into Canada Sports Hall of Fame 2011. *Publications:* Five Rings Over Korea 1994, Chief Justice W. R. Jackett: By the Law of the Land 1999, Stikeman Elliott: The Firts Fifty Years 2002, Inside the Olympics 2004, High Impact Quotations 2004, Canadian Facts and Dates 2004, Inside Dope 2006, Unlucky to the End: The Story of Janise Gamble 2007, Rocke Robertson, Surgeon and Shepherd of Change 2008, Stikeman Elliott: New Millennium, New Paradigms 2012, Quotations for the Fast Lane 2013, Made in Court: Supreme Court Cases That Shaped Canada 2014; Ed.-in-Chief: Annotated Stikeman Income Tax Act (Carswell), Canadian Tax Cases (Carswell), Doing Business in Canada; ed. and author of Pound's Tax Case Notes (Carswell). *Address:* Stikeman Elliott LLP, 1155 René-Lévesque Blvd West, 40th Floor, Montreal, QC H3B 3V2 (office); 87 Arlington Avenue, Westmount, QC H3Y 2W5, Canada (home). *Telephone:* (514) 397-3037 (office). *Fax:* (514) 397-3063 (office). *E-mail:* rpound@stikeman.com (office). *Website:* www.stikeman.com (office).

POUNDS, Kenneth (Ken) Alwyne, CBE, BSc, PhD; British physicist and academic; *Professor Emeritus of Space Physics, University of Leicester;* b. 17 Nov. 1934, Leeds, Yorks., England; s. of Harry Pounds and Dorothy Pounds (née Hunt); m. 1st Margaret Connell 1961; two s. one d.; m. 2nd Joan Mary Millit 1982; one s. one d.; ed Salt High School, Shipley, Yorks. and Univ. Coll., London; Prof. of Space Physics, Univ. of Leicester 1973–2002, Prof. Emer. 2002–, Dir X-ray Astronomy Group 1973–94, Head of Dept of Physics and Astronomy 1986–2002 (on leave of absence 1994–98); Chief Exec. Particle Physics and Astronomy Research Council 1994–98; Pres. Royal Astronomical Soc. 1990–92; mem. Academia Europaea, Int. Acad. of Astronautics; Fellow, University Coll., London 1993, now Hon. Fellow; Leverhulme Research Fellow 2003–05; Trustee, Nat. Space Centre; Hon. DUniv (York), Hon. DSc (Loughborough, Sheffield Hallam, Warwick, Leicester); Gold Medal, Royal Astronomical Soc. 1990, Planetary Scientist of the Year 2007, COSPAR Space Science Award 2008. *Publications:* more than 300 scientific publs. *Leisure interests:* sport, music. *Address:* Department of Physics and Astronomy, University of Leicester, University Road, Leicester, LE1 7RH (office); 12 Swale Close, Oadby, Leics., LE2 4GF, England (home). *Telephone:* (116) 252-3509 (office); (116) 271-9370 (home). *Fax:* (116) 252-3311 (office). *E-mail:* kap@le.ac.uk (office). *Website:* www2.le.ac.uk/departments/physics/research/xroa (office).

POUNGUI, Ange-Edouard; Republic of the Congo politician, economist and banker; *Vice-President, Union panafricaine pour la démocratie sociale;* b. 1942; began career in school, student unions; apptd mem. Nat. Council for Revolution 1968, then mem. Political Bureau, Minister for Finance 1971–73, Vice-Pres. Council of State and Minister for Planning 1973–76; Prime Minister of The Congo 1984–89; fmr Pres. Union pour le Renouveau Démocratique (URD); worked for IMF and African Devt Bank, then Dir-Gen. Cen. African Bank 1976–79, then CEO Congolese Commercial Bank; Dir Cen. Bank of the Congo 1994–2001; currently Vice-Pres. Union panafricaine pour la démocratie sociale (UPADS); selected as UPADS cand. for 2009 presidential election, but ruled ineligible to stand. *Address:* c/o Union panafricaine pour la démocratie sociale, BP 1370, Brazzaville, Republic of the Congo (office). *E-mail:* courrier@upads.org (office). *Website:* www.upads.org (office).

POUNTNEY, David Willoughby, CBE, MA; British opera director; *Artistic Director and Chief Executive, Welsh National Opera;* b. 10 Sept. 1947, Oxford, England; s. of E. W. Pountney and D. L. Byrt; m. 1st Jane R. Henderson 1980; one s. one d.; m. 2nd Nicola Raab 2007; ed St John's Coll. Choir School, Cambridge, Radley Coll. and St John's Coll. Cambridge; first opera production, Scarlatti's Trionfo dell'Onore, Cambridge 1967; Katya Kabanova at Wexford Festival 1972; Dir of Productions, Scottish Opera 1975–80, notably with Die Meistersinger, Eugene Onegin, Jenůfa, The Cunning Little Vixen, Die Entführung and Don Giovanni; Australian debut in Die Meistersinger 1978; world premiere of Philip Glass's Satyagraha, Netherlands Opera 1980; Prin. Prod. and Dir of Productions, ENO 1982–93, notably with The Flying Dutchman, The Queen of Spades, Rusalka, The Valkyrie and Lady Macbeth of Mtsensk; US debut with Houston Opera, Verdi's Macbeth, returning for world premiere of Bilby's Doll by Carlisle Floyd, Katya Kabanova and Jenůfa; produced Weill's Street Scene for Scottish Opera 1989; other productions include From the House of the Dead in Vancouver, Dr Faust in Berlin and Paris, The Fiery Angel at State Opera of South Australia, Adelaide, The Flying Dutchman, Nabucco and Fidelio for Bregenz Festival, The Excursions of Mr Brouček for Munich State Opera, world premiere of Philip Glass's The Voyage at the Met, The Fairy Queen for ENO, Der Kaukasianische Kreidekreis in Zurich, A Midsummer Night's Dream in Venice, Jenůfa, Rienzi and La Forza del Destino for the Vienna Staatsoper 2002, Turandot at Salzburg 2002, Lulu at Welsh Nat. Opera (WNO), world premiere of Philip Glass's Spuren der Verirrten in Linz, Die Zauberflöte in Bregenz; future plans include The Fall of the House of Usher and Guillaume Tell for WNO and The Passenger at Lincoln Center Arts Festival; Intendant and Artistic Dir, Bregenzer Festspiele 2003–13; Chief Exec. and Artistic Dir, Welsh Nat. Opera 2011–; Janáček Medal, SWET Award, Martinu Medal, Olivier Award; Chevalier des Arts et des Lettres; Knight's Cross, Order of Merit of the Repub. of Poland. *Publications:* Powerhouse; The Doctor of Myddfai (libretto for Peter Maxwell Davies), Mr Emmett Takes a Walk (libretto for Peter Maxwell Davies), Kommilitonen (libretto for Peter Maxwell Davies); several trans. from German, Italian, Russian and Czech. *Leisure interests:* gardening, cooking, croquet. *Address:* c/o IMG Artists, The Light Box, 111 Power Road, London, W4 5PY, England (office); c/o Bregenzer Festspiele, Postfach 311, 6900 Bregenz, Austria (office). *Telephone:* (20) 7957-5800 (office). *Fax:* (20) 7957-5801 (office). *E-mail:* bsegal@imgartists.com (office); info@bregenzerfestspiele.com (office). *Website:* www.imgartists.com (office); www.bregenzerfestspiele.com (office); www.wno.org.uk (office).

POUPARD, HE Cardinal Paul; French ecclesiastic; b. 30 Aug. 1930, Bouzillé; s. of Joseph Poupard and Celestine Guéry; ed Catholic Univ., Angers, Ecole Pratique des Hautes Études Sorbonne Univ.; ordained priest 1954; Parochial Minister, Paris and attaché to CNRS 1958; attaché to Sec. of State 1959–71; Rector Institut Catholique de Paris 1971–81; Titular Bishop of Usula 1979, Archbishop 1980; cr. Cardinal 1985; Priest of S. Prassede; Pres. Pontifical Council for Culture 1982–2007, for Inter-Religious Dialogue 2006–07; Commdr, Légion d'honneur, Grand Cross Order of Merit (Germany); Grand Prix Cardinal Crente, Acad. Française, Prix Robert Schuman, Prix Empedocle. *Publications include:* Les Religions 1987, L'Eglise au Défi des Cultures 1989, The Church and Culture 1989, Dieu et la Liberté 1992, Après Galilée, Science et Foi, Nouveau Dialogue 1994, What Will Give Us Happiness 1992, Dictionnaire des Religions 1993, Le Christianisme à l'aube du troisième millénaire 1999, Where is Your God? Responding to the Challenge of Unbelief and Religious Intolerance Today 2004, Que sais-je: Les Religions 2004, Foi et cultures au tournant du nouveau millénaire 2005, Chant Grégorien: Art et Prière de l'Eglise 2005, Foi Catholique 2005, L'affaire Galilée 2005, Le christianisme, ferment de nouveauté en Europe 2005, Lumières de Terre Sainte 2005, Le catholicisme au défi des cultures 2006, Des femmes prêtres? 2006, Paul de Tarse : Navigateur de l'espérance 2006, La Voie de la Beauté: Assemblée plénière de 2006, Voyage apostolique de Benoît XVI à Munich, Altötting et Ratisbonne 2006, Le concile Vatican II 2007. *Address:* Piazza San Calisto, 00120 Vatican City (home). *Telephone:* (6) 69-88-73-93 (office); (6) 69-89-38-11 (office). *Fax:* (6) 69-88-73-68 (office). *E-mail:* cultura@cultr.va (office). *Website:* www.vatican.va (office).

POUSSOT, Bernard; French business executive; *Chairman, President and CEO, Wyeth;* ed Ecole Supérieure de Commerce de Paris; Chair. Students' Council, Ecole Supérieure de Commerce de Paris 1975; mil. service as civil servant in Casablanca, Morocco 1976–77; began career with Merck and Searle in marketing positions in Europe and USA; joined Wyeth Gen. Man. France 1986–91, Head of Europe 1991–93, Exec. Vice-Pres. 1993–96, Pres. Wyeth International 1996–97, Pres. and Vice-Chair. Wyeth 2006–, mem. Bd of Dirs, Vice-Chair., Pres. and COO 2007–08, Vice-Chair., Pres. and CEO Jan.–June 2008, Chair., Pres. and CEO June 2008–; mem. Bd Univ. of Pennsylvania School of Dental Medicine, Eisenhower Fellowships, French American Chamber of Commerce, Opera Co. of Philadelphia; Sabin Lifetime Award 2003, Union League Founders Award for Business Leadership 2006. *Address:* Wyeth, 5 Giralda Farms, Madison, NJ 07940-0874, USA (office). *Telephone:* (973) 660-5000 (office). *Fax:* (973) 660-7026 (office). *E-mail:* info@wyeth.com (office). *Website:* www.wyeth.com (office).

POUZIN, Louis; French computer scientist; *Chairman, Native Language Internet Consortium;* b. 1931, Chantenay-Saint-Imbert (Nièvre); ed École Polytechnique, Paris; on staff, MIT Computer Center 1960s; Dir Cyclades project at Institut de Recherche d'Informatique et d'Automatique, France 1970s; Lecturer, Asscn for

Computing Machinery (ACM); Dean of Information Tech., THESEUS (France Telecom inst.) early 1990s; Project Dir, Eurolinc France; Chair. Native Language Internet Consortium 2006–; Chevalier, Légion d'honneur 2003; Silver Core Award, Int. Fed. for Information Processing, IEEE Internet Award, ACM SIGCOMM Award 1997, inducted into Internet Hall of Fame, Internet Soc. 2012, Queen Elizabeth Prize for Eng (co-recipient) 2013. *Achievements include:* best known as inventor and advocate of datagram, designed the first packet communications network, Cyclades; also created first forms of command-line interface; his work was broadly used by Vinton Cerf in his development of Internet and TCP/IP. *Publications:* one book and 82 articles on computer networks. *Address:* Native Language Internet Consortium, 17 rue Mesnil, 75116 Paris, France (office). *Telephone:* 1-47-55-14-51 (office). *Fax:* 1-47-55-14-51 (office). *E-mail:* Pouzin@ nliconsortium.org (office). *Website:* www.nliconsortium.org (office).

POWATHIL, Most Rev. Joseph, MA, DD; Indian ecclesiastic; *Archbishop Emeritus of Changanacherry;* b. 14 Aug. 1930, Kurumpanadom; s. of Ulahannan Joseph Powathil and Mariyam Joseph Powathil; ed St Berchmans' Coll., Changanacherry, Loyola Coll., Madras, St Thomas Minor Seminary, Parel and Papal Seminary, Pune; ordained RC priest 1962; Lecturer in Econs, St Berchmans's Coll., Changanacherry 1963–72; Auxiliary Bishop of Changanacherry 1972–77, Titular Bishop of Caesarea Philipi, 1972, consecrated Bishop 1972; 1st Bishop of Kanjirappally Diocese, Kerala 1977–85; Archbishop of Changanacherry 1985–2007, Archbishop Emer. 2007–; Chair. Kerala Catholic Bishops' Conf. (KCBC) and Chair. Educational Comm. 1993–96; Pres. Catholic Bishops' Conf. of India (CBCI) 1993–98; Perm. mem. Syro Malabar Bishops' Synod 1993; Chair. CBCI Comm. for Educ. and Clergy, KCBC Comm. for Vigilance 1998–; mem. Comm. for Devt, Justice and Peace; Chair. SMBC Comm. for Ecumenism 1993–; Chair. Inter-Church Council for Educ. 1990–; mem. Asian Synod of Bishops, Post Synodal Council (for Asia) 1998–; mem. Pontifical Comm. for Dialogue with the Orthodox Syrian Church; Chair. Religious Fellowship Foundation 1994; Hon. mem. Pro-Oriente, Vienna 1994. *Address:* Metropolitan Archbishop's House, PO Box 20, Changanacherry, Kottayam 686 101, India (office). *Telephone:* (481) 2420040 (office). *Fax:* (481) 2422540 (office). *E-mail:* abchry@ sancharnet.in (office). *Website:* www.archdiocesechanganacherry.org.

POWELL, Gen. Colin Luther, MBA; American business executive, academic, fmr government official and fmr army officer; *Strategic Limited Partner, Kleiner Perkins Caufield and Byers;* b. 5 April 1937, New York; s. of Luther Powell and Maud A. McKoy; m. Alma V. Johnson 1962; one s. (Michael K. Powell) two d.; ed City Coll. of New York and George Washington Univ.; commissioned US Army 1958, Lt-Gen. 1986; Commdr 2nd Brigade, 101st Airborne Div. 1976–77; Exec. Asst to Sec. Dept of Energy 1979; Sr Mil. Asst to Sec. Dept of Defense 1979–81; Asst Div. Commdr 4th Infantry Div. Fort Carson, Colo 1981–83; Mil. Asst to Sec. of Defense 1983–86; assigned to US V Corps, Europe 1986–87; Nat. Security Adviser, White House, Washington 1987–88; C-in-C US Forces, Fort McPherson, Ga April–Sept. 1989; Chair. Jt Chiefs of Staff 1989–93; Sec. of State 2001–05 (resgnd); public speaker 1993–2000; Strategic Ltd Pnr, Kleiner Perkins Caufield & Byers (venture capital firm) 2005–; investor and mem. Bd Revolution Health Group LLC 2005–; Founder, Advisory Council Chair, Distinguished Scholar, Colin Powell Center for Policy Studies, City Coll. of New York 1997–; Chair. Pres.'s Summit For America's Future 1997–; Founding Chair. America's Promise: The Alliance for Youth 1997–2001; Fellow, American Acad. of Arts and Sciences 2009–; Hon. LLD (Univ. of West Indies) 1994; Legion of Merit, Bronze Star, Air Medal, Purple Heart, Pres. Medal of Freedom, Pres. Citizen's Medal, Hon. KCB 1993, Order of Jamaica. *Publication:* My American Journey (autobiog. with Joseph E. Persico) 1995. *Address:* Kleiner Perkins Caufield and Byers, 2750 Sand Hill Road, Menlo Park, CA 94025, USA (office). *Telephone:* (650) 233-2750 (office). *Fax:* (650) 233-0300 (office). *Website:* www.kpcb.com (office).

POWELL, Dina Habib; American (b. Egyptian) business executive and fmr government official; *Director of Global Corporate Engagement, Goldman Sachs Group;* b. 1973, Cairo, Egypt; d. of Onsi Habib and Hoda Soliman; m. Richard C. Powell; two d.; ed Univ. of Texas; began career as intern for US Senator Kay Bailey Hutchinson and US Rep. Dick Armey, Washington, DC; Dir of Congressional Affairs and Sr Advisor to Chair., Republican Nat. Cttee 1999–2001; Special Asst to Pres. George W. Bush 2001–03, Asst to Pres. for Presidential Personnel 2003–05, Asst Sec. of State for Educational and Cultural Affairs, US State Dept 2005–07; joined Goldman Sachs as Man. Dir 2007, Partner 2010–, Dir of Global Corp. Engagement, Goldman Sachs Group 2007–, also Pres. Goldman Sachs Foundation; mem. Bd of Dirs Center for Global Development; mem. Bd of Trustees American Univ. in Cairo, Vital Voices Global Partnership, Nightingale-Bamford School; mem. Council on Foreign Relations; named Young Global Leader by World Econ. Forum. *Address:* Office of Corporate Engagement, Goldman Sachs Group, 85 Broad Street, 17th Floor, New York, NY 10004, USA (office). *Telephone:* (212) 902-1000 (office). *Fax:* (212) 902-3000 (office). *E-mail:* info@gs.com (office). *Website:* www.goldmansachs.com (office).

POWELL, Earl Alexander, III, AB, AM, PhD; American art museum director; *Director, National Gallery of Art;* b. 24 Oct. 1943, Spartanburg, SC; s. of Earl Alexander Powell, II and Elizabeth Duckworth; m. Nancy Landry 1971; three d.; ed Williams Coll. and Harvard Univ.; Teaching Fellow, Harvard Univ. 1970–74; Curator, Michener Collection, Univ. of Texas, Austin 1974–76, also Asst Prof. of Art History; Museum Curator, Sr Staff Asst to Asst Dir and Chief Curator, Nat. Gallery of Art, Washington, DC 1976–78, Exec. Curator 1979–80, Dir 1992–; Dir LA Co. Museum of Art 1980–92; Trustee, American Fed. of Arts, Morris and Gwendolyn Cafritz Foundation, Nat. Trust for Historic Preservation, White House Historical Asscn, John F. Kennedy Center for Performing Arts, Norton Simon Museum, The Mariner's Museum; Chair. Comm. of Fine Arts; mem. Asscn of Art Museum Dirs, Cttee for the Preservation of the White House, Pres.'s Cttee on the Arts and Humanities, American Philosophical Soc., American Acad. of Arts and Sciences, Friends of Art and Preservation in Embassies; Grand Official, Order of the Infante D. Henrique 1995, Commendatore, Ordine al Merito (Italy) 1998, Chevalier Légion d'honneur 2000, Officier Ordre des Arts et des Lettres 2004, Order of the Aztec Eagle (Mexico) 2007, Officer's Cross of the Order of Merit (Hungary); King Olav Medal 1978, Williams Bicentennial Medal 1995, Mexican Cultural Inst. Award 1996, Centennial Medal, Harvard Graduate School of Arts and Sciences 2008. *Publications:* American Art at Harvard 1973, Selections from

the James Michener Collection 1975, Abstract Expressionists and Imagists: A Retrospective View 1976, Milton Avery 1976, The James A. Michener Collection (catalogue) 1978, Thomas Cole monograph 1990. *Address:* National Gallery of Art, Sixth Street and Constitution Avenue NW, Washington, DC, USA (office). *Website:* www.nga.gov (office).

POWELL, Jonathan Leslie; British television producer and academic; b. 25 April 1947, Faversham, Kent; s. of James Dawson Powell and Phyllis N. Sylvester (née Doubleday); m. Sally Brampton 1990; one d.; ed Sherborne School and Univ. of East Anglia; script and producer of drama, Granada TV 1970–77; producer, drama serials, BBC TV 1977–83, Head of Drama Series and Serials 1983–87; Controller BBC 1 1987–92; Dir Drama and Co-Production, Carlton TV 1993–2004; Prof. of Media, Royal Holloway Coll., Univ. of London 2007–; Royal TV Soc. Silver Award 1979–80. *Television includes:* Testament of Youth 1979 (BAFTA award), Tinker, Tailor, Soldier, Spy 1979, Pride and Prejudice 1980, The Bell 1982, Smiley's People 1982 (Peabody Medal, USA), The Old Men at the Zoo 1983, Bleak House 1985, Tender is the Night 1985, A Perfect Spy 1987. *Leisure interest:* fly-fishing. *Address:* 1 First Avenue, Acton, London, W3 7JP, England (home). *Telephone:* (20) 8740-7853 (home).

POWELL, Jonathan Nicholas, MA; British political adviser; *Managing Director of Investment Banking, Morgan Stanley and Co.;* b. 14 Aug. 1956, Fulbeck; s. of Air Vice-Marshal John Frederick Powell and Geraldine Ysolda Powell; m. Karen Drayne (divorced 1997); two s.; pnr Sarah Helm; two d.; ed Univ. Coll. Oxford, Univ. of Pennsylvania, Univ. with BBC 1978, Granada TV 1978–79; joined FCO 1979, served in Lisbon 1980–83, FCO, London 1983–85, CSCE, Vienna 1985–89, FCO, London 1989–91, Washington 1991–95; Chief of Staff to Leader of the Opposition 1995–97, to Prime Minister 1997–2007; Man. Dir of European Investment Banking, Morgan Stanley and Co. 2008–. *Publication:* Great Hatred, Little Room: Making Peace in Northern Ireland 2008, The New Machiavelli 2010. *Leisure interests:* walking, skiing. *Address:* Morgan Stanley and Co., 25 Cabot Square, Canary Wharf, London E14 4QA, England (office). *Telephone:* (20) 7425-8000 (office). *Fax:* (20) 7425-8990 (office). *Website:* www.morganstanley.com (office).

POWELL, Kendall (Ken) J., BA, MBA; American business executive; *Chairman and CEO, General Mills, Inc.;* b. 1954, Denver, Colo; ed Harvard Univ., Stanford Univ.; joined General Mills, Minneapolis, Minn. 1979, held various positions, helped launch Cereal Partners Worldwide (CPW) joint venture with Nestlé 1990, Pres. Yoplait USA 1996–97, Pres. General Mills Big G cereal div. 1997–99, CEO CPW 1999–2006, Pres. and COO General Mills 2006–07, CEO 2007–, Chair. 2008–; mem. Bd of Dirs Medtronic, Inc. *Address:* General Mills, Inc., PO Box 9452, Minneapolis, MN 55440, USA (office). *Telephone:* (800) 248-7310 (office). *Fax:* (763) 764-8330 (office). *E-mail:* info@generalmills.com (office). *Website:* www .generalmills.com (office).

POWELL, Michael James David, ScD, FRS; British mathematician and academic; *John Harvey Plummer Professor Emeritus of Applied Numerical Analysis, University of Cambridge;* b. 29 July 1936; s. of William James David Powell and Beatrice Margaret Powell (née Page); m. Caroline Mary Henderson 1959; one s. (deceased) two d.; ed Eastbourne Coll. and Peterhouse, Cambridge; mathematician at AERE, Harwell 1959–76; John Humphrey Plummer Prof. of Applied Numerical Analysis, Univ. of Cambridge 1976–2001; Prof. Emer. 2001–, apptd Professorial Fellow, Pembroke Coll. 1978, now Emer. Fellow; Foreign Assoc. NAS 2001–; Corresp. Fellow, Australian Acad. of Science 2007; Hon. DSc (Univ. of East Anglia) 2001; George B. Dantzig Prize in Math. Programming 1982, Naylor Prize, London Math. Soc. 1983, Gold Medal, Inst. of Math. Applications 1996, Sr Whitehead Prize, London Math. Soc. 1999. *Publications:* Approximation Theory and Methods 1981; 171 papers on numerical mathematics, especially approximation and optimization calculations. *Leisure interests:* golf, walking. *Address:* Room F2.04, Department of Applied Mathematics and Theoretical Physics, Centre for Mathematical Sciences, University of Cambridge, Wilberforce Road, Cambridge, CB3 0WA (office); 134 Milton Road, Cambridge, CB4 1LE, England (home). *Telephone:* (1223) 337889 (office). *E-mail:* mjdp@cam.ac.uk (office); m.j.d.powell@ damtp.cam.ac.uk (office). *Website:* www.damtp.cam.ac.uk (office).

POWELL, Michael K.; American lawyer and fmr government official; s. of Gen. Colin L. Powell (q.v.) and Alma V. Powell; m. Jane Knott Powell; two s.; ed Coll. of William and Mary and Georgetown Univ. Law Center; mil. service as Cavalry Platoon Leader and Troop Exec. Officer, 3/2 Armored Cavalry Regt, Amberg, Germany; fmr Policy Adviser to Sec. of Defense; fmr Judicial Clerk to Chief Judge of Court of Appeals for DC Circuit; fmr Assoc. O'Melveny & Myers LLP, Washington; fmr Chief of Staff Antitrust Div., Dept of Justice; Chair. Fed. Communications Comm. Jan. 2001–05 (mem. 1997–), also Defense Chair.; apptd Advisor, Providence Equity Pnrs Inc. 2005; mem. Bd of Visitors, Georgetown Univ. Law Center; Henry Crown Fellow, Aspen Inst. 1999, Sr Fellow Communications and Society Program 2005–; mem. Bd of Dirs, AOL 2009–; Henry Crown Leadership Award, Aspen Inst. 2004. *Address:* Communcations and Society Program, The Aspen Institute, One Dupont Circle, NW, Suite 700, Washington, DC 20036-1133, USA (office). *Telephone:* (202) 736-5800 (office). *Fax:* (202) 467-0790 (office). *Website:* www.aspeninstitute.org (office).

POWELL, Robert; British actor; b. 1 June 1944, Salford, Lancs.; s. of John W. Powell and Kathleen C. Powell; m. Barbara Lord 1975; one s. one d.; ed Manchester Grammar School, Manchester Univ.; first job, Victoria Theatre, Stoke On Trent 1964; Hon. MA (Salford) 1990, Hon. DLitt (Salford) 2000; Best Actor, Paris Film Festival 1980, Venice Film Festival 1982. *Television roles include:* Doomwatch 1970, Jude the Obscure 1971, Jesus of Nazareth 1977, Pygmalion 1981, Frankenstein 1984, Hannay (series) 1988, The Sign of Command 1989, The First Circle 1990, The Golden Years 1992, The Detectives 1992–97, Pride of Africa 1997, Kind Hearts and Coronets 1998, Escape (series, voice) 1998, Marple: The Murder at the Vicarage 2004, Holby City (series) 2005–07. *Theatre roles include:* Hamlet 1971, Travesties (RSC) 1975, Terra Nova 1982, Private Dick 1982, Tovarich 1991, Sherlock Holmes 1992. *Films include:* Walk a Crooked Path 1969, The Italian Job 1969, Secrets 1971, Running Scared 1972, Shelley 1972, Asylum 1972, The Asphyx 1973, Mahler 1974, Tommy 1975, Al di là del bene e del male 1977, The Thirty-Nine Steps 1978, Harlequin 1980, Jane Austen in Manhattan 1980, The Survivor 1981, Imperativ 1982, The Jigsaw Man 1983, What Waits Below 1984, D'Annunzio

1985 Laggiù nella giungla 1986, Shaka Zulu 1987, Romeo-Juliet (voice) 1990, Chunuk Bair 1992, The Mystery of Edwin Drood 1993, Hey Mr DJ 2005, Colour Me Kubrick 2005. *Leisure interests:* golf, tennis, cricket, computers. *Address:* c/o Jonathan Altaras Associates, 11 Garrick Street, London, WC2E 9AR, England. *Telephone:* (20) 7836-8722 (office).

POWELL, Sandy, OBE; British costume and set designer; b. 7 April 1960; ed St Martin's Coll. of Art and Design, Cen. School of Art, London. *Designs:* costume designer for most shows by The Cholmondoleys and The Featherstonehaughs; stage sets include: Edward II (RSC), Rigoletto (Netherlands Opera) and Dr. Ox's Experiment (ENO); costumes for films include: The Last of England 1988, Stormy Monday 1988, Caravaggio 1986, Venus Peter 1989, The Pope Must Die (Best Tech. Achievement Award, Evening Standard Award 1992) 1991, Edward II (Best Tech. Achievement Award, Evening Standard Award 1992) 1991, The Miracle (Best Tech. Achievement Award, Evening Standard Award 1992) 1991, The Crying Game 1992, Orlando (Evening Standard Award 1994) 1992, Being Human 1994, Interview with a Vampire (Saturn Award 1995) 1994, Rob Roy 1995, Michael Collins 1996, The Butcher Boy 1997, The Wings of the Dove 1997, Shakespeare in Love (Academy Award 1999) 1998, Velvet Goldmine (BAFTA Award 1999) 1998, Hilary and Jackie 1998, The End of the Affair 1999, Felicia's Journey 1999, Miss Julie 1999, Gangs of New York 2002, Far From Heaven (OFCS Award 2003) 2002, Sylvia 2003, The Aviator (Academy Award, Sierra Award 2005) 2004, Mrs Henderson Presents (Golden Capital Award 2006) 2005, The Departed 2006, The Young Victoria (PFCS Award 2009, Academy Award, BAFTA Award, CDG Award 2010) 2009, The Tempest 2010, Shutter Island 2010.

POWELL JOBS, Laurene, BA, BSc, MBA; American business executive and philanthropist; *Founder and Chairwoman, Emerson Collective;* b. 6 Nov. 1963, NJ; m. Steve Jobs 1991 (died 2011); one s. two d. one step-d.; ed Univ. of Pennsylvania, Univ. of Pennsylvania Wharton School, Stanford Grad. School of Business; spent several years working in investment banking and later co-f. Terravera (natural foods co.); worked for Merrill Lynch Asset Management and spent three years at Goldman Sachs as a fixed-income trading strategist; fmr angel investor in SocialCam (mobile video sharing start-up); inherited estate of the late Steve Jobs Oct. 2011, maintains control of living trusts under her late husband's name, including the Steven P. Jobs Trust (largest shareholder of Walt Disney Co.); Co-founder, with Carlos Watson, and Pres. of the Bd, College Track 1997–; Founder and Chair. Emerson Collective (works with entrepreneurs to advance education, immigration reform, social justice and conservation); mem. or fmr mem. Bd of Dirs Achieva, Teach for America, Global Fund for Women, KQED (PBS), EdVoice, Stanford Schools Corpn, New Schools Venture Fund, New America Foundation –2012; mem. Advisory Bd Stanford Grad. School of Business; mem. Bd of Trustees, Stanford Univ. 2012–; apptd mem. of White House Council for Community Solutions by Pres. Obama 2010; ranked by Forbes magazine amongst The World's 100 Most Powerful Women (49th) 2012, (39th) 2013. *Address:* College Track, 111 Broadway Avenue, Suite 101, Oakland, CA 94607, USA (office). *Telephone:* (510) 834-3295 (office). *Fax:* (510) 834-3312 (office). *E-mail:* info@collegetrack.org (office). *Website:* www.collegetrack.org (office).

POWELL OF BAYSWATER, Baron (Life Peer), cr. 2000, of Bayswater; **Charles David Powell,** Kt, KCMG, BA; British company director, policy adviser and fmr diplomatist; b. 6 July 1941, Sussex, England; s. of the late Air Vice-Marshal John Frederick Powell OBE; m. Carla Bonardi 1964; two s.; ed King's School, Canterbury, New Coll., Oxford; Diplomatic Service 1963–83; Pvt. Sec. and Foreign Affairs Adviser to the Prime Minister 1983–91; mem. (Crossbench) House of Lords 2000–; mem. Bd of Dirs National Westminster Bank 1991–2000 (also Chair. Int. Advisory Bd), Matheson & Co. 1991–, Jardine Matheson Holdings 1992–2000, Hong Kong Land Holdings 1992–2000, 2006–, Mandarin Oriental Hotel Group 1992–, J. Rothschild Name Co. 1993–2003, LVMH Louis Vuitton-Moet Hennessy 1995– (Chair. LVMH UK), British Mediterranean Airways 1997–2007, Sagitta 2000–06, Caterpillar Inc. 2001–14, Textron Corpn 2001–, Schindler Corpn 2003–14, Northern Trust Global Services 2005–14; mem. Advisory Bd Rolls-Royce (Chair.), Bowmark (Chair.), GEMS (Chair.), Barrick Gold, ACE, Council on Foreign Relations, New York; Co-Chair. Asia Task Force 2005–; Chair. Said Business School Foundation, Oxford; Pres. Singapore-British Business Council 1994–2001, China-Britain Business Council 1995–2007; Trustee, British Museum Trust, Aspen Inst., KRS Foundation, IISS; Singapore Public Service Medal. *Address:* LVMH House, 15 St George Street, London, W1S 1FH, England (office); House of Lords, Westminster, London, SW1A 0PW, England. *Telephone:* (20) 7408-7426 (office); (20) 7219-5451. *Fax:* (20) 7408-7428 (office). *E-mail:* lordpowell@charlespowell.com (office). *Website:* www.parliament.uk/biographies/lords/lord-powell-of-bayswater/2527.

POWER, Samantha, BA, JD; American academic, journalist and diplomatist; *Permanent Representative, United Nations;* b. 21 Sept. 1970, Dungarvan, Co. Waterford, Ireland; m. Cass Sunstein 2008; one s. one d.; ed Lakeside High School, Atlanta, Ga, Yale Univ. and Harvard Law School; emigrated to USA aged nine; early career as staff mem. CBS Sports and Atlanta affiliate; covered wars in fmr Yugoslavia as reporter for US News and World Report, Boston Globe, and the Economist 1993–96; joined Int. Crisis Group (ICG) as political analyst and helped launch ICG in Bosnia 1996; also worked for Carnegie Endowment for Peace, Washington, DC; adviser to fmr Democratic presidential cand. Wesley Clark 2004; Founding Exec. Dir Carr Center for Human Rights Policy, John F. Kennedy School of Govt, Harvard Univ. 1998–2002, Lecturer in Public Policy 2002–05, Anna Lindh Prof. of Practice of Global Leadership and Public Policy 2005–09, took leave of absence to advise US Senator Barack Obama (Democrat from Ill.) on issues of foreign policy 2005–06; Dir for Multilateral Affairs, Nat. Security Council, The White House 2009–13; Amb. and Perm. Rep. to UN, New York 2013–; columnist, Time magazine 2007–. *Publications:* Realizing Human Rights: Moving from Inspiration to Impact (co-ed.) 2000, A Problem from Hell: America and the Age of Genocide (Pulitzer Prize for Gen. Nonfiction 2003, Award for Gen. Nonfiction, Nat. Book Critics' Circle 2003, Arthur Ross Prize, Council on Foreign Relations 2003) 2002, Chasing the Flame: Sergio Vieira de Mello and the Fight to Save the World 2008; new introduction to Hannah Arendt's Origins of Totalitarianism; numerous articles on human rights and public policy. *Address:* United States Mission to the United Nations, 799 United Nations Plaza, New York NY 10017, USA (office).

Telephone: (212) 415-4050 (office). *Fax:* (212) 415-4053 (office). *E-mail:* usunpolfax@state.gov (office). *Website:* www.usunnewyork.usmission.gov (office).

POWER, Simon, BA, LLB; New Zealand lawyer and politician; b. 5 Dec. 1969; m.; ed St Peter's Coll., Victoria Univ.; Assoc. Pnr and Solicitor, Fitzherbert Rowe 1993–97; Solicitor, Kensington Swan 1997; MP for Rangitikei 1999–; mem. Select Cttees on Transport and Industrial Relations 1999–2002, Justice 2002, Educ. and Science 2002–03, Foreign affairs, Defence and Trade 2003–04, Business 2004, Standing Orders 2004–05, Law and Order 2005–08, Chair. Privileges Cttee 2006–08, Sr Whip 2004–05; mem. New Zealand Nat. Party 2003–, Party Spokesman for Labour and Industrial Relations 1999–2002, for Youth Affairs 1999–2004, for Justice 2002–03, for Tertiary Educ. 2002–03, for Defence 2003–04, Veterans' Affairs 2003–04, for Conservation 2004–05, for Law and Order 2005–06, Assoc. Spokesman for Foreign Affairs 2003–04, for Educ. 2004–05; Minister of Justice, of State Owned Enterprises, of Commerce, Minister Responsible for the Law Comm., Assoc. Minister of Finance and Deputy Leader of the House 2008–11. *Address:* c/o Ministry of Justice, POB 180, Wellington, New Zealand.

POWERS, Richard; American writer and academic; *Swanlund Professor of English, University of Illinois;* b. 1957; m. Jane Powers; Swanlund Prof. of English, Univ. of Illinois 1996–; Fellow, American Acad. of Arts and Sciences 1998, American Acad. of Arts and Letters 2010; Rosenthal Award, American Acad. and Inst. of Arts and Letters 1985, John D. and Catherine T. MacArthur Foundation grant 1989, Lannan Literary Award 1999, Corrington Award for Literary Excellence 2001, John Dos Passos Prize For Literature 2002,. *Publications include:* Three Farmers on Their Way to a Dance (Richard and Hinda Rosenthal Foundation Award, American Acad. and Inst. of Arts and Letters, PEN/Hemingway Foundation special citation) 1985, Prisoner's Dilemma 1988, The Gold Bug Variations 1991, Operation Wandering Soul 1993, Galatea 2.2 1995, Gain (American Soc. of Historians James Fenimore Cooper Prize 1999) 1998, Plowing the Dark (American Acad. and Inst. of Arts and Letters Vursell Prize) 2000, The Time of Our Singing (WH Smith Literary Award 2004) 2003, The Echo Maker (Nat. Book Award for Fiction) 2006, Generosity: An Enhancement 2009; contrib. to journals and magazines. *Address:* Department of English, University of Illinois, 608 South Wright Street, Urbana, IL 61801, USA (office). *Telephone:* (217) 244-4958 (office). *E-mail:* rpowers@illinois.edu (office). *Website:* www.english .illinois.edu/people/rpowers (office); www.richardpowers.net.

POWERS, William C., Jr, BA, JD; American lawyer, university administrator and academic; *President, University of Texas at Austin;* b. 30 May 1946, Los Angeles, Calif.; m. Kim Heilbrun; five c.; ed Univ. of California, Berkeley, Harvard Law School; stationed with LTJG USNR, Bahrain Island in the Persian Gulf 1967–70; Ed. Harvard Law Review 1971–72, Man. Ed. 1972–73; law clerk to Judge Eugene Wright, US Court of Appeals (Ninth Circuit) 1973–74; Teaching Fellow, Harvard Coll. 1973; mem. Washington Bar 1974–80 (resgnd), Texas Bar 1980–; Asst Prof., Univ. of Washington School of Law 1974–77, Assoc. Prof. 1977–78; Visiting Prof., Univ. of Texas School of Law Austin 1977–78, Prof. 1978–; James R. Dougherty Chair for Faculty Excellence 1984–85, Assoc. Dean for Academic Affairs 1984–87, Joseph C. Hutcheson Prof. 1985–86, Judge Benjamin Harrison Powell Prof. 1986–89, Bernard J. Ward Centennial Prof. of Law 1986–89, Fondren Foundation Centennial Chair for Faculty Excellence 1987–88, James R. Dougherty Chair for Faculty Excellence 1991–92, Assoc. Dean for Academic Affairs 1994–95, Hines H. Baker and Thelma Kelley Baker Chair in Law 1990–, Univ. Distinguished Teaching Prof. 1997–, John Jeffers Research Chair in Law 2000–05, Dean School of Law 2000–05, Regents' Chair in Higher Educ. Leadership 2006–, Pres. Univ. of Texas at Austin 2006–; Chair. ExploreUT 2005 (mem. Univ of Texas Corp. Governance Inst.) 2005; Visiting Prof., Univ. of Michigan School of Law 1981, Southern Methodist School of Law, Dallas, Texas 1982–83; Of Counsel, Hogan Dubose & Townsend, Houston, Texas (civil appellate practice) 1998–2003, Hogan & Hogan, Houston 2003–04, Beck, Redden & Secrest, Houston 2004–; worked as legal consultant with US Congress, Brazilian legislature and Tex. legislature; mem. Bd of Dirs Enron Corpn 2001–02, Chair. Special Investigation Cttee 2001–02, mem. Special Litigation Cttee 2001–02, subsequent report known as 'Powers Report' 2002; mem. Advisory Bd Southwestern Legal Foundation 1997–, Organizing Cttee Southwestern Legal Foundation Inst. of Litigation 2000–; mem. Bd Trustees Austin Presbyterian Theological Seminary 2005–; mem. American Law Inst. 1992–, Philosophical Soc. of Tex. 2003–; Fellow, Tex. Bar Foundation 1992–, American Bar Foundation 1993– (Life Fellow 2002–); ABA McKay Award 2003. *Publications:* several books, Texas Products Liability Law (second edn) 1992, including Cases and Materials in Torts (co-author) (third edn) 2004, Cases and Materials in Products Liability (co-author) (fourth edn) 2006; articles on tort law and legal philosophy; Co-reporter for Restatement (Third) of Torts: Apportionment of Liability 1993–2000, Restatement (Third) of Torts: Liability for Physical Harm 2001–. *Address:* Office of the President, University of Texas at Austin, PO Box T, Main Building 400 (G3400), Austin, TX 78713-8920, USA (office). *Telephone:* (512) 471-1232 (office). *Fax:* (512) 471-8102 (office). *E-mail:* president@po.utexas.edu (office). *Website:* www.utexas.edu/president (office).

POYNTER, John Riddoch, AO, OBE, PhD, FAHA, FASSA; Australian historian, academic and university administrator; *Professor Emeritus and Professorial Fellow, University of Melbourne;* b. 13 Nov. 1929, Coleraine, Vic.; s. of Robert Poynter and Valetta Riddoch; m. 1st Rosslyn M. Rowell 1954 (divorced 1983); two d.; m. 2nd Marion Davidson 1984; ed Trinity Grammar School, Kew, Victoria, Trinity Coll. Univ. of Melbourne and Magdalen Coll. Oxford; Dean, Trinity Coll., Univ. of Melbourne 1953–64, Ernest Scott Prof. of History 1966–75, Dean, Faculty of Arts 1971–73, Pro-Vice-Chancellor 1972–75, Deputy Vice-Chancellor (Research) 1975–82, Deputy Vice-Chancellor 1982–89, Deputy Vice-Chancellor (Academic) 1989–90, Dean, Faculty of Music, Visual and Performing Arts 1991–93, Asst Vice-Chancellor (Cultural Affairs) 1991–94, Prof. Emer. and Prof. Fellow 1995–; Nuffield Dominion Travelling Fellow, London and Oxford 1959; Visiting Fellow, ANU 1968, Carnegie Fellow, Fulbright Grant, USA 1968; Section Ed. Australian Dictionary of Biography 1972–90; Australian Sec. Rhodes Trust 1974–97; Chair. Melbourne Univ. Press 1976–88; mem. Bd Australian-American Educ. Foundation 1977–84; Rhodes Scholar 1951; Chevalier, Ordre des Palmes Académiques 1981, Centenary Medal 2001; Australian Dictionary of Biography Medal 2004. *Publications:* Russell Grimwade 1967, Society and Pauperism 1969, A Place Apart 1996,

Doubts and Certainties 1997, Mr Felton's Bequests 2003, The Tarnished Swan 2009. *Leisure interest:* music. *Address:* The Australian Centre, University of Melbourne, Parkville, Vic. 3052 (office); 38 Brougham Street, North Melbourne, Vic. 3051, Australia (home). *Telephone:* (3) 8344-2104 (office); (3) 9329-8163 (home). *Fax:* (3) 9329-8276 (home). *E-mail:* j.poynter@unimelb.edu.au (office); johnpoynter@fastmail.com (home).

POYNTZ, Rt Rev. Samuel Greenfield, BD, MA, PhD; Irish ecclesiastic (retd); b. 4 March 1926, Manitoba, Canada; s. of Rev. James Poyntz and Catherine Greenfield; m. Noreen H. Armstrong 1952; one s. two d.; ed Portora Royal School, Enniskillen and Trinity Coll. Dublin; curate, St George, Dublin 1950–52, Bray 1952–55, St Michan and St Paul, Dublin 1955–59; Incumbent, St Stephen, Dublin 1959–67, St Ann, Dublin 1967–70, St Ann with St Stephen, Dublin 1970–78; Archdeacon of Dublin 1974–78; mem. Governing Body, Univ. Coll. Cork 1978–87, Court of the Univ. of Ulster 1987–2006; Examining Chaplain to the Archbishop of Dublin 1974–78; Bishop of Cork, Cloyne and Ross 1978–87; Bishop of Connor 1987–95; Chair. Youth Department, British Council of Churches 1965–70; Chair. Irish Council of Churches 1986–88; Co-Chair. Irish Inter-Church Meeting 1986–88; Vice-Pres. British Council of Churches 1987–90; Hon. Chaplain Boys Brigade, Repub. of Ireland 1978–; DLitt hc (Univ. of Ulster) 1995. *Publications:* The Exaltation of the Blessed Virgin Mary 1953, Journey Towards Union 1975, Our Church – Praying with Our Church Family 1983; contrib. A Tapestry of Beliefs 1998, Mary for Earth and Heaven 2002, Inter Church Relations: Developments and Perspectives 2008. *Leisure interests:* stamp collecting, rugby football, travel, walking. *Address:* 3 The Gables, Ballinteer Road, Dundrum, Dublin 16, Ireland (home). *Telephone:* (1) 2966748 (home).

POŽELA, Juras, DPhys; Lithuanian physicist; *Senior Researcher, Semiconductor Physics Institute;* b. 5 Dec. 1925, Moscow; s. of Karolis Požela and Eugenija Tautkaitė; m. Rima Poželienė 1953; one s. one d.; ed Vilnius State Univ. and Moscow M. Lomonosov Univ.; Researcher, Sr Researcher, Sector Man., Dir Inst. of Physics and Math., Lithuanian Acad. of Sciences 1952–67; Dir Semiconductor Physics Inst. 1967–85, Sr Researcher 1996–; mem. Seimas (Parl.) 1992–96; Academician Lithuanian Acad. of Sciences 1968, Pres. 1984–92; mem. USSR (now Russian) Acad. of Sciences 1984, European Acad. of Sciences and Arts 1991, Academia Europaea 1993; 3rd Order of Grand Duke Gediminas (Lithuania) 1996; Lenin Prize 1978, Hero of Socialist Labour 1985, USSR State Prize 1988, Lithuanian State Prizes 1965, 1982, Lithuanian Merited Scientist 1965. *Publications include:* Plasma and Current Instabilities in Semiconductors 1981, Physics of High Speed Transistors 1993; more than 200 articles, 9 monographs; about 100 inventions. *Leisure interests:* hunting, chess. *Address:* Lithuanian Academy of Sciences, Gedimino Prospect 3, 2600 Vilnius; Semiconductor Physics Institute, A. Goštauto 11, 2600 Vilnius (office); M. Paco 7/2, apt 7, 2055 Vilnius, Lithuania (home). *Telephone:* (2) 62-71-22 (office); (2) 72-70-22 (home). *Fax:* (2) 62-71-23 (office). *E-mail:* pozela@uj.pfi.lt (office).

POZNER, Vladimir Gerald Dmitri Vladimirovich; Russian broadcaster; *President, Russian Television Academy;* b. 1 April 1934, Paris; s. of Vladimir Aleksandrovich Pozner; m. 1st (divorced); one d.; m. 2nd Yekaterina Orlova; ed Moscow Univ.; worked as trans. of medical biological literature, literary sec. of poet Samuel Marshak 1959–61; Sr Ed., Exec. Sec. Soviet Life 1961–67, Sputnik 1967–70; commentator USA and Britain Broadcasting Service of USSR TV and Radio Cttee 1970–86; political observer Cen. TV 1986–91; author of film scripts; Pres. Russian TV Acad. 1996–; mem. Fed. Tenders Comm. 2004–; mem. Bd of Dirs Transatlantic Partners Against AIDS (TPAA); Communicator of the Year Prize of Soviet Journalists' Union 1986; Communicator of the Year Medal of the Better World Soc. (with Phil Donahue). *Television shows:* regular appearances in Pozner-Donahue show, Multimedia Entertainment Inc. (USA) 1991–95; Meetings with Vladimir Pozner (Moscow Channel, Russia) 1991–94, If 1995, We 1995–2000, Man in a Mask 1996–99, Time and US 1998–2000, Times 2000–. *Publications:* Parting with Illusions 1990, Remembering War (with E. Keyssar 1990), Eyewitness 1992, numerous articles in Russian and American newspapers and magazines. *Address:* c/o Board of Directors, Transatlantic Partners Against AIDS (TPAA), Gazetny Pereulok 5, 3rd Floor, 125993 Moscow, Russia. *Telephone:* (495) 202-71-61 (Moscow); (212) 355-3454 (New York). *Fax:* (495) 230-29-41 (Moscow); (212) 644-1193 (New York).

POZO CRESPO, Mauricio, MEconSci; Ecuadorean banker, government official, banker and economist; ed Pontificia Univ. Católica del Ecuador, Univ. of Colorado, Univ. of Notre Dame, USA; Dir Stock Exchange, Quito; Dir Chamber of Commerce, Quito; Dir Seguros Equinoccial; Tech. Co-ordinator, Ecuadorean Sub-cttee, Pacific Econ. Co-operation Council (PECC); Pres. Investments Tech. Cttee, Inst. Ecuatoriano de Seguridad Social (IESS); Dir Tech. Div., Cen. Bank of Ecuador; Pres. Monetary Council 1981–91; Prof. of Econs, Pontificia Univ. Católica del Ecuador 1987–, Monterrey Tech. Inst. 1987–; Pres. Magna Credit Card 1991–93; Vice-Pres. Produbanco 1993–2000; Pres. Multienlace 2001–02; Minister of Economy and Finance 2003–04 (resgnd). *Address:* c/o Ministry of Economy and Finance, Avda 10 de Agosto 1661 y Jorge Washington, Quito, Ecuador (office).

PRADA, Michel André Jean Edmond; French fmr civil servant; *Chairman, Public Sector Accounting Standards Council;* b. 2 April 1940, Bordeaux; s. of Robert Prada and Suzanne Prada (née Bouffard); m. Annick Saudubray 1963; two s. three d.; ed Lycée Montesquieu Bordeaux, Faculté de Droit et Inst. d'Etudes Politiques de Bordeaux, Ecole Nat. d'Admin; Inspecteur des Finances with Ministry of Econ. and Finance 1966–; Chargé de Mission, Inspection Générale des Finances 1969; Chargé de Mission, Direction de la Comptabilité Publique 1970, Asst Dir 1974, Head of Service 1977, Dir de la Comptabilité Publique 1978–85; Dir of Budget, Ministry of the Economy, Finance and the Budget 1986–88; Chair. Bd Dirs Credit d'équipement des petites et moyennes entreprises (CEPME) 1988–95; Chair. Comm. des Opérations de Bourse 1995–2002; Chair. French Financial Markets Authority 2003–09, Orchestre de Paris 1989–2001, Inst. d'Etudes Politiques de Bordeaux 1989–2005, Exec. Cttee Int. Org. of Securities Comms (IOSCO) 1996–98, Tech. Cttee of IOSCO 1998–2001, 2005–08; fmr mem. Econ. and Social Council, Nat. Credit Council; Chair. Public Sector Accounting Standards Council 2009–; Chair. Bd of Trustees, Int. Valuation Standards Council 2009–11; Chair. Bd of Trustees, Int. Financial Reporting Standards Foundation 2012–; Chevalier des Arts et Lettres 1995, Commdr, Légion d'honneur 2002, Grand Officier, Ordre nat. du Mérite 2005, Grand Croix, Ordre nat. du Mérite

2012. *Address:* Immeuble Atrium 5, place des Vins-de-France, 75573 Paris Cedex 12 (office); 2 rue Cart, 94160 Saint-Mandé, France (home). *Telephone:* 1-53-44-22-80 (office); 1-43-74-95-33 (home). *Fax:* 1-53-44-22-97 (office). *E-mail:* michel .prada@finances.gouv.fr (office).

PRADA, Miuccia, PhD; Italian fashion designer; b. (Miuccia Prada Bianchi), 10 May 1949, Milan; d. of Luisa Prada; youngest granddaughter of Prada founder Mario Prada; m. Patrizio Bertelli; two c.; ed Univ. of Milan, Teatro Piccolo, Milan; inherited Prada SpA business from her mother, designer for Prada since 1979, with her husband led co.'s expansion into haute couture, launched collection of women's clothing 1988, Miu Miu collection 1992, men's collection 1994; currently has about 250 stores in 65 countries; opened a contemporary art space, Fondazione Prada 2002; Council of Fashion Designers of America Int. Award 1993, ranked 22nd by the Financial Times amongst Top 25 Businesswomen in Europe 2005, ranked by Forbes magazine amongst The World's 100 Most Powerful Women (79th) 2011, (67th) 2012, (58th) 2013. *Leisure interest:* collecting contemporary art, including several works by Young British Artists (YBAs) such as Damien Hirst. *Address:* Prada SpA, via Andrea Maffei 2, 20135 Milan, Italy (office). *Telephone:* (02) 76001426 (office). *Website:* www.prada.com (office).

PRADA BORDENAVE, Emmanuelle; French government official; *Director General, Agence de la Biomédecine;* ed Institut d'Etudes Politiques de Paris, Ecole Nationale d'Admin, Strasbourg; began career at Admin. Tribunal of Paris 1984–97, now Rapporteur and Govt Commr; Head of Legal Dept, CNRS 1990–92; Master of Requests, Conseil d'État –2008; also served as Rapporteur Général, State Comm. of Public Ethics 2001–04, as Head of Mission of Legal Council of State from Social Ministries 2004–07, as Deputy Rapporteur to Constitutional Council and Govt Commr to Tribunal of Conflicts 2007–08; participated in Gen. Review of Public Policies (RGPP) in the field of justice 2008; Dir Gen. Agence de la Biomédecine 2008–. *Address:* Agence de la Biomédecine, 1 avenue du stade de France, 93212 Saint-Denis la Plaine Cedex, France (office). *Telephone:* 1-55-93-65-50 (office). *Fax:* 1-55-93-65-50 (office). *E-mail:* info@agence -biomedecine.fr (office). *Website:* www.agence-biomedecine.fr (office).

PRADHAN, Mukti Narayan, LLM; Nepalese lawyer and fmr government official; mem. Law and Human Rights Dept, Maoist Party; Attorney-Gen. 2011–13. *Address:* c/o Office of the Attorney-General, Ramshah Path, Kathmandu, Nepal. *E-mail:* info@attorneygeneral.gov.np.

PRADHAN, Lyonpo Om, BA; Bhutanese diplomatist, politician and business executive; *Chairperson, Druk Holding and Investments Ltd;* b. 6 Oct. 1946; m.; three c.; ed Delhi Univ., India; various posts in Ministry of Trade, Industry and Forests 1969–80; Perm. Rep. to the UN 1980–84, 1998–2004; Amb. to India (also accred to Nepal and Maldives) 1984–85, Head of Bhutanese Del. to first and second rounds of boundary talks with China; Deputy Minister, Ministry of Trade and Industry 1985–89, Head of Del. to fifth round of boundary talks with China; Minister for Trade and Industry 1989–98; fmr Chief, Policy Devt and Coordination Monitoring and Reporting Unit, UN Office of High Rep. for the Least Developed Countries, Landlocked Countries and Small Island Developing Sites (UN-OHRLLS); Chair. Druk Holding and Investments Ltd 2007–; mem. Nat. Ass., Council of Ministers; Chair. State Trading Corpn, Chhukha Hydroelectric Project Corpn and Tala Hydroelectric Project Authority; mem. Planning Comm., Nat. Environment Comm. *Address:* Druk Holding and Investments Ltd, POB 1127, Motithang, Thimphu, Bhutan (office). *Telephone:* (2) 336257 (office). *Fax:* (2) 336259 (office). *E-mail:* info@dhi.bt (office). *Website:* www.dhi.bt (office).

PRADHAN, Sahana Devi, MEconSc; Nepalese lawyer, women's rights activist and politician; b. 15 July 1932; m. Pushpa Lal Pradhan (died 1978); ed Patna Univ., Tribhuvan Univ., Kathmandu, Delhi Univ., India; began teaching during the ban on political parties 1960; Chair. United Left Front 1990; Minister of Industry 1990–91, of Women, Children and Social Welfare 1997–98, of Foreign Affairs April 2007–08; Sr Partner, Development Law Assocs 1992–; co-f. Forum for Women, Law and Development, Exec. Dir and Pres. 1995–; fmrly consultant to UN Div. for Advancement of Women to Analyze Impact of Strategies on Violence Against Women; mem. Communist Party of Nepal (Unified Marxist-Leninist— UML). *Address:* Communist Party of Nepal, Kathmandu, Nepal (office).

PRADHAN, Trilochan, MSc, PhD; Indian physicist and academic; *Professor Emeritus, Institute of Physics, Bhubaneshwar;* b. 3 Jan. 1929, Ghanashalia, Orissa; s. of Ramachandra and Ahalya Dakshinaray; m. Sanjukta Pradhan 1959; one s. one d.; ed Utkal Univ., Benares Hindu Univ. and Univ. of Chicago; Research Assoc., Univ. of Chicago 1956–57, Niels Bohr Inst., Copenhagen 1957–58; Lecturer in Physics, Ravenshaw Coll., Cuttack 1951–62; Assoc. Prof., Saha Inst. of Nuclear Physics, Calcutta 1962–67, Prof. and Head, Div. of Theoretical Nuclear Physics 1967–74; Founder Dir, Inst. of Physics, Bhubaneshwar 1974–89, Prof. Emer. 1989–; Visiting Prof., Univ. of Virginia 1985; Vice-Chancellor, Utkal Univ. 1989–91; Visiting Scientist, Int. Centre for Theoretical Physics, Trieste 1966–97, Univ. of Syracuse 1967, Univ. of Texas, Austin 1970, Inst. of Theoretical Physics, Gothenberg 1973, KEK, Japan 1985; Meghnad Saha Award, Univ. Grants Comm. of India 1980, Pres. of India's Padma Bhusan Award 1990. *Publications:* The Photon 2001, Quantum Mechanics 2008; about 60 papers on theoretical physics in the areas of elementary particles, atomic physics, plasma physics. *Leisure interests:* gardening, indoor games. *Address:* Institute of Physics, Sachivalaya Marg, Bhubaneswar 751 005 (office); 71 Gajapatinagar, Bhubaneswar 751 005, India (home). *Telephone:* (674) 2300637 (office); (674) 2300962. *Fax:* (674) 2300142 (office). *E-mail:* pradhan@iopb.res.in (office).

PRADIER, Henri Joseph Marie; French engineer; b. 5 Nov. 1931, Sainte-Colombe-lès-Vienne, Rhône; s. of Camille Pradier and Anne-Marie Côte; m. 1st Marie-France Michot (deceased); two s. and 2nd Brigitte Dapvril 1973; one s. one d.; ed Institution Robin, Vienne, Lycée du Parc, Lyons and Ecole Polytechnique; consulting engineer 1955–58; Shell Française 1958–67 and 1970; Man. Dir Shell du Maroc 1967–79, Vice-Pres. Distribution 1975–84; Man. Dir Shell Française 1984–92, now Hon. Pres.; Dir Soc. pour l'Utilisation Rationnelle des Gaz (Butagaz) 1975, Shell Chimie 1984, Hosp. Works Française de l'Ordre de Malte (OHFOM) 1992–95, St Joseph and St Luke Hospital, Lyon 1994–97, Publicis 1998–; Chevalier Légion d'honneur, Officer, Order of Orange-Nassau (Netherlands). *Leisure interests:* gardening, sailing, swimming. *Address:* 52 rue du Ranelagh, 75016 Paris, France.

PRAKKE, Lucas, LLD; Dutch academic; *Professor Emeritus of Law, University of Amsterdam;* b. 20 Feb. 1938, Groningen; m. Margaretha M. O. de Bruijn Kops 1965; two s.; ed Gemeentelijk Lyceum, Doetinchem, Univ. of Amsterdam and Columbia Univ. Law School, New York; Asst Prof. of Law, Univ. of Amsterdam 1963–72, Prof. of Dutch and Comparative Constitutional Law 1972–2003, Dean, Faculty of Law 1981–83, Prof. Emer. 2003–; Judge, Civil Service Appeal Tribunal 1977–89; mem. Royal Comm. on Constitution 1982–85; mem. Royal Netherlands Acad. *Publications:* Principles of Constitutional Interpretation in the Netherlands 1970, Toetsing in het publiekrecht 1972, Pluralisme en staatsrecht 1974, Het bestuursrecht van de landen der Europese Gemeenschappen 1986, Bedenkingen tegen het toetsingsrecht (Report of Netherlands Lawyers' Asscn) 1992, Swamping the Lords, Packing the Court, Sacking the King: Address on 'dies natalis' of University of Amsterdam 1994, Handboek van het Nederlandse staatsrecht 1995, Het staatsrecht van de landen van de Europese Unie (fifth edn, co-ed.) 1998 (trans. as Constitution Law of 15 EU Member States 2005), Pluralisme van Staatsrecht 2003. *Leisure interests:* history, music, walking. *Address:* Faculteit der Rechtsgeleerdheid, Universiteit van Amsterdam, Postbus 1030, 1000 BA Amsterdam (office); Koedijklaan 15, 1406 KW Bussum, Netherlands (home). *Telephone:* (20) 5253966 (office); (35) 6989520 (home). *Fax:* (35) 6989501 (home).

PRANCE, Sir Ghillean Tolmie, Kt, DPhil, FRS; British botanist; *Director of Research, The Eden Project;* b. 13 July 1937, Brandeston, Suffolk, England; s. of Basil Camden Prance and Margaret Hope Prance (née Tolmie); m. Anne Elizabeth Hay 1961; two d.; ed Malvern Coll., Keble Coll. Oxford; Research Asst, The New York Botanical Garden 1963–66, Assoc. Curator 1966–68, Krukoff Curator of Amazonian Botany 1968–75, Dir of Botanical Research 1975–81, Vice-Pres. 1977–81, Sr Vice-Pres. 1981–88, Dir Inst. of Economic Botany 1981–88; Dir Royal Botanic Gardens, Kew 1988–99; Dir of Research, The Eden Project 1999–; McBryde Prof. Nat. Tropical Botanical Garden 2000–02; Adjunct Prof., City Univ. of New York 1988–99; Dir of Graduate Studies, Instituto Nacional de Pesquisas da Amazônia, Brazil 1973–75; Exec. Dir Org. for Flora Neotropica 1975–88; Visiting Prof. in Tropical Studies, Yale Univ. 1983–88; Visiting Prof., Reading Univ. 1988–; Chair. Bentham-Moxon Trust 1988–99, Brazilian Atlantic Rainforest Trust 1999–, Global Diversity Foundation 1999–2008; Pres. Linnean Soc. of London 1997–2000; Trustee Au Sable Inst. of Environmental Studies 1984–91, Margaret Mee Amazon Trust 1988–96, Worldwide Fund for Nature Int. 1989–93, Horniman Museum 1990–99; Pres. Asscn of Tropical Biology 1979–80, American Asscn of Plant Taxonomists 1984–85, Systematics Asscn 1988–91, Inst. of Biology 2000–02; mem. Bd of Govs Lovaine Trust Co. Ltd 1989–99; Council mem. Royal Horticultural Soc. 1990–2000; Corresp. mem. Botanical Soc. of America 1994; Hon. mem. British Ecological Soc. 1996–; Commendador da Ordem Nacional do Cruzeiro do Sul (Brazil) 2000, Order of the Rising Sun (Japan) 2012; Hon. FilDr (Göteborg) 1983; Hon. DSc (Univ. of Kent at Canterbury) 1994, (Portsmouth) 1994, (Kingston) 1994, (St Andrews) 1995, (CUNY) 1998, Dr hc (Bergen) 1996, (Sheffield) 1997, (Florida) 1997, (Liverpool) 1998, (Glasgow) 1999, (Plymouth) 1999, (Keele) 2000, (Exeter) 2000, (Gloucester) 2006; Henry Shaw Medal, Missouri Botanical Garden 1988, Linnean Medal 1990, Int. Cosmos Prize 1993, Patron's Medal (Royal Geographical Soc.) 1994, Asa Gray Award (American Soc. of Plant Taxonomists) 1998, Int. Award of Excellence (Botanical Research Inst. of Tex.) 1998, Lifetime Discovery Award 1999, Victoria Medal of Honour, Royal Horticultural Soc. 1999, Fairchild Medal for Botanical Exploration 2000, Soc. for Econ. Botany Award 2002, Graziela Barroso Prize Brazilian Botanic Garden Network 2004, Allerton Award, Nat. Tropical Botanical Garden 2005. *Television:* Superteacher (NHK, Japan) 2002. *Publications:* Arvores de Manaus 1975, Extinction is Forever 1977, Biological Diversification in the Tropics 1981, Amazonia–Key Environments 1985, Tropical Forests and World Climate 1986, Leaves 1986, White Gold 1989, Wildflowers for All Seasons 1989, Out of the Amazon 1992, Bark 1993, Rainforests of the World 1998, Rainforest Light and Spirit 2009, Go to the Ant 2013; Ed. 14 books; numerous scientific and gen. articles. *Leisure interests:* bird watching, stamp collecting. *Address:* The Eden Project, Bodelva, Cornwall, PL24 2SG (office); The Old Vicarage, Silver Street, Lyme Regis, Dorset, DT7 3HS, England (home). *Telephone:* (1726) 811900 (office); (1297) 444991 (home). *E-mail:* gprance@edenproject.com (office); siriain01@yahoo.co.uk (home). *Website:* www.edenproject.com (office).

PRASAD, Alok, BA, MA; Indian diplomatist; m. Nandini Prasad; two c.; ed Delhi Univ.; joined Indian Foreign Service 1974, has represented India in various capacities in Germany, UN (New York), the Netherlands, Nepal, Burma and Botswana; also worked in Prime Minister's Office; Jt Sec. for Americas Div., Ministry of External Affairs, New Delhi 1995–2000; Deputy Chief of Mission, Washington, DC 2000–04; High Commr to Singapore 2004–06, to Sri Lanka 2006–09; Deputy Nat. Security Adviser 2009–11; Amb. to Japan 2011–12; Fellow, Center for Int. Affairs, Harvard Univ., USA. *Address:* Ministry of External Affairs, South Block, New Delhi 110 011, India (office). *Telephone:* (11) 23011127 (office). *Fax:* (11) 23013254 (office). *E-mail:* eam@mea.gov.in (office). *Website:* meaindia.nic.in (office).

PRASAD, Ashoka, MD, FRHistS; Indian psychiatrist and university professor; b. 10 May 1955, Patna; s. of the late Judge Jahnavi Prasad and Usha Prasad; ed Colvin Taluqdar's Coll., Lucknow, GSVM Medical Coll., Kanpur, Univs of Oxford and St Andrews, UK, Univ. of North Carolina at Chapel Hill, Harvard Univ. and Brandeis Univ., USA; Resident in Paediatrics and Psychiatry, Castlebar Gen. Hosp., Ireland, Resident in Psychiatry, Royal Edinburgh Hosp., UK 1980–83; Research Fellow, Depts of Biochemistry and Psychiatry, Univ. of Leeds, UK 1983–85; Kate Stillman Lecturer in Psychiatry, Univ. Coll. Hosp. and Queen Charlotte's Hosp., London, UK 1984–86; Consultant Psychiatrist, Whipps Cross Hosp., Claybury Hosp. and Thorpe Coombe Hosp., London 1986–87; Prof., Dalhousie Univ., Canada 1987, Columbia Univ., USA 1989, Univ. of British Columbia, Canada 1990, Univ. of Pennsylvania, USA 1992, Drexel Univ., USA; in charge of Psychopharmacology and Hon. Sr Lecturer, Mental Health Research Inst. and Monash Univ., Melbourne, Australia, Assoc. Dept of Psychiatry, Univ. of Melbourne 1987; Visiting Specialist, Kingseat Hosp., NZ 1988; Consultant Psychiatrist, Claybury Hosp., London and St Margaret's Hosp., Essex 1988–89; at Dept of Psychiatry, Dalhousie Univ., Canada, Dept of Psychology, St Mary's Univ., Canada 1989; J. Ernest Runions Fellow, Dept of Psychiatry, Univ. of British Columbia, Vancouver 1989–90; Prof. of Psychiatry, Hahnemann Univ., Phila, USA 1990–91; Adjunct Prof. of Medical Anthropology, Columbia Univ., USA 1990–91, of

Anthropology, Univ. of Pa 1991; Medical Dir Phila Consultation Center 1990–92; currently hon. consultant to several bodies, including Jain TV, India, for medical programmes, Hon. Adviser 1993–; several visiting professorships including Harvard Univ. 1986, 1991; Visiting Psychiatrist, Sahlgrenska Univ. Hosp., Gothenberg, Sweden 2009; Hon. Foreign mem. American Acad. of Arts and Sciences; Hon. DrMed (Natal, S Africa) 2000; Murphy Award 1987, Blueler Award 1987, delivered Annual Mil. Medicine Oration in Bombay 2012. *Publications:* five books including Biological Basis and Therapy of Neuroses; more than 125 publs in various journals. *Leisure interests:* bird-watching, unravelling Greek myths, cricket, history of science and medicine, naturopathy, medical anthropology, aviation medicine, Jalaluddin Rumi's works, reading, light classical music, collecting cookery books. *Address:* 1 Avas Vikas, Betia Hata, Gorakhpur 273 001, India. *Telephone:* (551) 334020. *Fax:* (551) 332845. *E-mail:* praashok@gmail.com.

PRASAD, H. Rajesh, BCom, MBA, MPM; Indian civil servant and government official; *Administrator of Union Territory of Lakshadweep;* fmr Collector and Dist Magistrate, South Goa; fmr Deputy Commr and Dist Magistrate, West Kamang Dist, Arunachal Pradesh, East and South Delhi; fmr Commr (Lands), Delhi Devt Authority; Admin. of Union Territory of Lakshadweep 2012–. *Address:* Central Secretariat, Kavaratti 682 555, India (office). *Telephone:* (4896) 262255 (office). *Fax:* (4896) 262184 (office). *E-mail:* lk-admin@ hub.nic.in (office). *Website:* lakshadweep.nic.in (office).

PRASAD, Mata; Indian politician; b. 11 Oct. 1925, Machi Shahar; s. of Rajji Devi and Jagarup Ram; m. Lekhraji Mata Prasad; three s. two d.; ed Sahitya Ratna; mem. UP Ass. 1957–77, Legis. Council 1980–92; Gen. Sec. UP Congress Cttee 1971–73, 1980–82; mem. UP Congress Legislature Party 1982–86, Treas. 1986–92; Cabinet mem. 1988–89; Chair. UP Congress Cttee SC/ST 1982–88; Gov. of Arunachal Pradesh 1993–99; Chair. Poorvottar Parishad 1993–99; Vice-Pres. Al Dalit Sahitya Acad.; Sec. UP Dalit Varg Sangh; mem. Housing and Devt Bd and Minority Comm., UP; Hon. DLit (Purvanchal Univ.) 1998 numerous awards including Dr Ambedkar Nat. Award 1988, Keerti Bharti 1994, Sahitya Bhusan 1995, Lok Mitra 1997, Bharat Jyoti Award 2001. *Publications:* more than 20 books including works of poetry and drama; Jhopdi Se Raj Bhawan (autobiog). *Address:* 20/25 Indira Nagar, Lucknow 226 016, (office); PO Box Kacheheri, PS Line Bazar, Shekhpura, Jaunpur District, India (home). *Telephone:* (9415) 207155 (office); (5452) 261835 (home).

PRASAD, Siddheshwar, DLitt; Indian politician, author and journalist; b. 19 June 1929, Bind; s. of Bhikari Mahton; m. Rajkumari Prasad; six c.; Lecturer, Nalanda Coll., Biharsharif 1953–61; mem. Lok Sabha 1962–77; Deputy Minister for Irrigation and Power 1967–71, for Industrial Devt 1971–73, for Heavy Industry Feb.–Nov. 1973, for Irrigation 1973–74, for Energy 1974–77; Minister, Govt of Bihar 1985–88; Gov. of Tripura 1995–99; Chair. Gandhi-Marx Research Inst.; Exec. Chair. Rashtra Bhasha Prachar Samiti; Sec.-Gen. Third World Hindi Conf. *Publications:* Chhayavadottar Kavya, Satyagraha Aur Vigyan, Sahitya Ka Muyankan, Upanishad Chintan Aur Adhunik Jiwan, Ekalavyon Aur Abimanyuon Se, Multi-Dimensional Transformation, Vichar Pravah, New Economic Policy, The Vedic Vision, Kamayni: Vishwa Kavya Ka Abhinava Sarga. *Address:* Sector 7, Block 1, Flat 23, Bahadurpur HIG Cology, Kankarbagh, Patna 800 020, India (office). *Telephone:* (80) 02219902 (office); 98-71669133 (mobile) (office). *E-mail:* siddheshwar_prasad@ymail.com (office).

PRASAD, Sunand, MA, PhD; British (b. Indian) architect; *Partner, Penoyre & Prasad LLP;* b. 22 May 1950, Dehra Dun, India; m. Susan Francis; three c.; ed Cambridge School of Architecture, Architectural Assen, Royal Coll. of Art; Partner, Edward Cullinan Architects 1976–85; Leverhulme Research Fellow, RCA 1985–88; Founding Partner, Penoyre & Prasad LLP 1988–; Vice-Pres. Architectural Assen 1999–2001; Commr, Comm. for Architecture and the Built Environment 1999–; mem. London Mayor's Design Advisory Panel 2009–; Pres. RIBA 2007–09; Trustee, Article 25 2007–, Cycle to Cannes 2007–, Centre for Cities 2009–, Cape Farewell 2010–; Hon. Fellow, Royal Town Planning Inst.; Hon. Dr of Arts (Univ. of East London); Eternit Award for Architecture 1989, RIBA Regional Award 1991, 1992, RIBA Award 1997, 1999, 2000, 2001, 2003, American Inst. of Architects/UK Excellence in Design Award 1998, Design Sense 1999, numerous other architectural awards. *Radio:* 'The Essay' - Architecture the 4th R (BBC Radio 3) 2010. *Publications:* Accommodating Diversity: Housing Design in a Multi-Cultural Society 1998, Paradigms of Indian Architecture 1998, Designing Better Buildings 2003, Contemporary Hospital Design (ed) 2005, Transformations – The Architecture of Penoyre & Prasad 2007, Changing Hospital Architecture (ed) 2008; chapters in Le Corbusier: Architect of the Century 1987. *Leisure interests:* music, cycling. *Address:* Penoyre & Prasad LLP, 28–42 Banner Street, London, EC1Y 8QE, England (office). *Telephone:* (20) 7250-3477 (office). *Fax:* (20) 7250-0844 (office). *E-mail:* s.prasad@penoyreprasad.com (office). *Website:* www.penoyreprasad.com and www.sunandprasad.com (home).

PRASAD SINGH, Balmiki, MA; Indian politician; b. 1 Jan. 1942, Begusarai, Bihar; m. Karuna Singh; three c.; ed Patna Univ., Oxford Univ.; fmr Lecturer in Political Sciences, Patna Univ.; joined Indian Administrative Service 1964; Deputy Sec., Ministry of Defence 1975–79; Sec. for all d epts under the Chief Sec. and Home Sec., Govt of Assam 1980–82, mem. Assam Planning Bd 1982–84, Agricultural Production Commr, Special Commr and Special Sec., Sec. 1990–92; Jt Sec. Ministry of Steel and Mines 1984–89; Jt Sec., then Additional Sec., Ministry of Home Affairs 1992–93; Additional Sec., Ministry of Environment and Forests 1993–95, Chair. Nat. Cttee on Bio-diversity Conservation, Asia Rep. on Ramar Convention on Wetlands, Gland, Switzerland; Union Culture Sec., Govt of India 1995–97, Union Home Sec. 1997–99; Exec. Dir World Bank, representing India, Bangladesh, Bhutan and Sri Lanka 1999–2002; Gov. of Sikkim 2008–13; Jawaharlal Nehru Fellow 1982–84; Queen Elizabeth Fellow, Univ. of Oxford 1989–90; fmr Mahatma Gandhi Nat. Fellow; fmr Chancellor Cen. Inst. of Higher Tibetan Studies, Sarnath; Chancellor Sikkim Manipal Univ. 2008–; fmr Chair. Nat. Comm. for Economically Backward Classes; mem. Indian Nat. Trust for Arts and Cultural Heritage 1995–; Patna Univ. Gold Medals 1960, Gov. of Assam Gold Medal 1991, Gulzarilal Nanda Award 1998, Man of Letters Award from Dalai Lama 2003. *Publications include:* Threads Woven: Ideals, Principles & Administration 1975, The Indian National Congress and Cultural Renaissance, The Problem of Change: A Study of North-East India 1987, India's Culture: the State, the Arts and Beyond 1998, Bahudha and the post-9/11 World 2008, Our India 2011; numerous articles and monographs on culture, poverty, ecology and public admin in India and abroad. *Website:* www.balmikiprasadsingh.com.

PRASHAR, Baroness (Life Peer), cr. 1999, of Runnymede in the County of Surrey; **Rt Hon Usha Kumari Prashar,** CBE, BA, FRSA; British public policy specialist; *Deputy Chair, British Council;* b. 29 June 1948, Nairobi, Kenya; d. of Nauhria Lal Prashar and Durga Devi Prashar; m. Vijay Kumar Sharma 1973; ed Duchess of Gloucester School, Nairobi, Wakefield Girls' High School, Univs of Leeds and Glasgow; Conciliation Officer, Race Relations Bd 1971–75; Asst Dir Runnymede Trust 1975–77, Dir 1977–84; Sr Fellow, Policy Studies Inst. 1984–86 (mem. Council 1992–97); Dir Nat. Council for Voluntary Orgs 1986–91; Vice-Chair. British Refugee Council 1987–89; Civil Service Commr (part-time) 1990–96, First Civil Service Commr 2000–05; Deputy Chair. Nat. Literacy Trust 1992–2000, Chair. 2001–05; Chair. Parole Bd of England and Wales 1997–2000, Judicial Appointments Comm. 2006–10; Dir (non-exec.) Channel 4 1992–99, Unite PLC 2001–04, ITV 2005–; mem. Bd Salzburg Seminar 2000–04, Arts Council of GB 1979–81, Arts Council of England 1994–97, Study Comm. on the Family 1980–83, Social Security Advisory Cttee 1980–83, Exec. Cttee, Child Poverty Action Group 1984–85, Greater London Arts Asscn 1984–86, London Food Comm. 1984–90, BBC Educational Broadcasting Council 1987–89, Advisory Council, Open Coll. 1987–89, Solicitors' Complaints Bureau 1989–90, Royal Comm. on Criminal Justice 1991–93, Lord Chancellor's Advisory Cttee on Legal Educ. and Conduct 1991–97, Bd Energy Saving Trust 1992–98; mem. (Crossbench), House of Lords 1999–; Cttee mem., The Iraq Inquiry 2009–; Chair. English Advisory Cttee, Nat. AIDS Trust 1988–89; currently Deputy Chair., British Council; Chancellor De Montfort Univ. 2000–06 (Gov. 1996–2006); Trustee, King's Fund 1998–2002, Jt Cttee on Human Rights 2001–04, 2008–, Thames Help Trust 1984–86, Charities Aid Foundation 1986–91, Ind. Broadcasting Telethon Trust 1987–92, Acad. of Indian Dance 1987–91, Camelot Foundation 1996–, Ethnic Minority Foundation 2000–; Patron Sickle Cell Soc. 1986–, Elfrida Rathbone Soc. 1988–; Hon. Pres. Community Foundation Network, Royal Commonwealth Soc., UK Council for Int. Student Affairs; Hon. Fellow, Goldsmiths' Coll., Univ. of London 1992; Hon. LLD (De Montfort) 1994, (South Bank) 1994, (Greenwich) 1999, (Leeds Metropolitan) 1999, (Ulster) 2000, (Oxford Brookes) 2000; Asian Women of Achievement Award 2002. *Publications include:* contribs to Britain's Black Population 1980, The System: A Study of Lambeth Borough Council's Race Relations Unit 1981, Scarman and After 1984, Sickle Cell Anaemia, Who Cares? A Survey of Screen, Counselling, Training and Educational Facilities in England 1985, Routes or Road Blocks, A Study of Consultation Arrangements Between Local Authorities and Local Communities 1985, Acheson and After: Primary Health Care in the Inner City 1986. *Leisure interests:* reading, music, golf, current affairs. *Address:* House of Lords, Westminster, London, SW1A 0PW, England (office). *Telephone:* (20) 7219-6792 (office). *E-mail:* prasharu@parliament.uk (office). *Website:* www.parliament.uk/biographies/lords/baroness-prashar/2476 (office).

PRASOLOV, Ihor Nikolayevych; Ukrainian political economist, academic and politician; b. 4 Feb. 1962, Peschanyi, Murmansk Oblast, Russian SFSR, USSR; m. Natalia Prasolova; one s. one d.; ed Rostov State Univ., Donetsk State Univ.; electrical fitter trainee and electrical fitter, Novocherkassk power plant 1979–80; mil. service in Soviet Army, discharged with rank of Staff Sergeant 1980–82; Asst Prof. of Political Economy, Donetsk State Univ. 1987–93; Gen. Dir CJSC Investment Co. Keramet Invest 1993–2000, JSC System Capital Man. 2000–05; mem. Verkhovna Rada (Parl.) (Party of Regions) 2006–, Chair. Cttee on Finance, Banking, Tax and Customs Policy, Subcommittee on Securities and Stock Market, mem. Group for Interparliamentary Relations with Russian Fed., with Repub. of Belarus, with Czech Repub.; Minister of Econ. Devt and Trade 2012–14 (dismissed by Parl.). *Address:* c/o Ministry of Economic Development and Trade, 01008 Kyiv, vul. M. Hrushevskoho 12/2, Ukraine. *E-mail:* meconomy@me.gov.ua.

PRAT-GAY, Alfonso; Argentine economist, business executive and fmr central banker; ed Pennsylvania Univ., USA; worked for macro-econ. consultancy, Buenos Aires –1991; country economist (Argentina), JP Morgan, New York 1994, Head of Emerging Market Proprietary Trading Desk, London –1999, Chief of Currency Strategy (cr. Liquidity and Credit Premia Index), London 1999–2001; Prof., Univ. of Buenos Aires 2001–02; Gov. Cen. Bank of Argentina 2002–04; Chair. Tilton Capital (asset man. firm); mem. Cámara de Diputados (Coalición Cívica Afirmación para una República Igualitaria) 2009–; Pres. Fundación Andares para el desarrollo de las Microfinanzas. *Address:* c/o Coalición Cívica Afirmación para una República Igualitaria, Callao 143, C1022AAB, Buenos Aires, Argentina. *Telephone:* (11) 4384-1268 (office). *E-mail:* arinacional@ari.org.ar. *Website:* www.ccari.org.ar; www.alfonspratgay.com (office).

PRATCHETT, Sir Terence (Terry) David John, OBE; British writer; b. 28 April 1948, Beaconsfield, Bucks.; m. Lyn Marian Purves 1968; one d.; journalist 1965–80; Press Officer, Cen. Electricity Generating Bd 1980–87; Chair. Soc. of Authors 1994–95; Hon. DLitt (Portsmouth) 2001, (Bath) 2003, (Bristol) 2004, (Warwick) 1999, (Bradford) 2009, (Winchester) 2009; Hon. LittD (Dublin) 2008; Dr hc (Bucks New) 2008, (Open) 2014; Galaxy Nat. Book Award for Outstanding Achievement 2010. *Television:* Terry Pratchett's Jungle Quest (documentary) 1995, Terry Pratchett: Living with Alzheimer's (documentary) 2009, Terry Pratchett: Choosing to Die (documentary) (BAFTA Award for Best Single Documentary 2012, Int. Emmy) 2011, Terry Pratchett: Facing Extinction (documentary) 2013. *Publications include:* Discworld series: The Colour of Magic 1983, The Light Fantastic 1986, Equal Rites 1987, Mort 1987, Sourcery 1989, Wyrd Sisters 1988, Pyramids 1989, Eric (illustrated by Josh Kirby) 1989, Guards! Guards! 1989, Moving Pictures 1990, Reaper Man 1991, Witches Abroad 1991, Small Gods 1992, Lords and Ladies 1993, Men at Arms 1993, The Streets of Ankh-Morpork (with Stephen Briggs) 1993, Soul Music 1994, Interesting Times 1994, The Discworld Companion (with Stephen Briggs) 1994, Maskerade 1995, Discworld Mapp (with Stephen Briggs) 1995, Feet of Clay 1996, Hogfather 1996, The Pratchett Portfolio (with Paul Kidby) 1996, Jingo 1997, The Last Continent 1998, Carpe Jugulum 1998, A Tourist Guide to Lancre (with Stephen Briggs and Paul Kidby) 1998, The Fifth Elephant 1999, The Science of Discworld (with Ian Stewart and Jack Cohen) 1999, Death's Domain (with Paul Kidby) 1999, The Truth 2000, Nanny Ogg's Cookbook (with Stephen Briggs, Tina Hannan and Paul Kidby) 2000, The Last Hero (illustrated by Paul Kidby) 2001, Thief of Time 2001, The Amazing

Maurice and His Educated Rodents (Carnegie Medal) 2001, Night Watch 2002, The Science of the Discworld II: The Globe (with Ian Stewart and Jack Cohen) 2002, Monstrous Regiment 2003, The Wee Free Men 2003, A Hat Full of Sky 2004, The Science of Discworld III: Darwin's Watch (with Ian Stewart and Jack Cohen) 2005, Going Postal 2004, Thud! 2005, Where's My Cow 2005, Wintersmith 2006, Making Money 2007, The Folklore of Discworld (with Jacqueline Simpson) 2008, Unseen Academicals 2009, I Shall Wear Midnight 2010, Snuff (P.G. Wodehouse Award) 2011, The Compleat Ankh-Morpork (with Discworld Emporium) 2012, Turtle Recall: The Discworld Companion ...so far (with Stephen Briggs) 2012, Raising Steam 2013; other fiction: The Carpet People 1971, The Dark Side of the Sun 1976, Strata 1981, The Unadulterated Cat (illustrated by Gray Jolliffe) 1989, Truckers 1989, Diggers 1990, Wings 1990, Good Omens: The Nice and Accurate Predictions of Agnes Nutter, Witch (with Neil Gaiman) 1990, Only You Can Save Mankind 1992, Johnny and the Dead 1993, Johnny and the Bomb 1996, Nation (Boston Globe-Horn Book Award 2009) 2008, The Long Earth (with Stephen Baxter) 2012, Dodger 2012, A Blink of the Screen 2012, The Science of Discworld IV: Judgement Day (with Ian Stewart and Jack Cohen) 2013, The Long War (with Stephen Baxter) 2013, The Long Mars (with Stephen Baxter) 2014; screenplay: Terry Pratchett's Hogfather (BAFTA Award 2007) 2006; other: short stories. *Leisure interests:* astronomy, gardening, folklore. *Address:* c/o Colin Smythe Ltd, 38 Mill Lane, Gerrards Cross, Bucks., SL9 8BA, England (office). *Telephone:* (1753) 886000 (office). *Fax:* (1753) 886469 (office). *Website:* www.terrypratchett.co.uk.

PRATT, (John) Christopher, OC, CC, RCA, BFA; Canadian painter and printmaker; b. 9 Dec. 1935, St John's, Newfoundland; s. of John Kerr Pratt and Christine Emily Pratt (née Dawe); m. 1st Mary Frances West 1957 (divorced 2004); two s. two d.; m. 2nd Jeanette Meehan 2007; ed Prince of Wales Coll., St John's, Newfoundland, Memorial Univ. of Newfoundland, Mount Allison Univ., Sackville, NB and the Glasgow School of Art, Scotland; taught as specialist in art, Memorial Univ. 1961–63; freelance artist 1963–; mem. Mount Carmel Town Council 1969–73, Postage Stamp Design Cttee, Ottawa 1970–73, The Canada Council 1976–82, Memorial Univ. Bd of Regents 1972–75; designed prov. flag for Newfoundland and Labrador 1980; Hon. Chair. Bay Roberts Heritage Soc. 1999–; Hon. Fellow, Royal Architectural Inst. of Canada 2012; Hon. DLitt (Memorial) 1972; Hon. LLD (Mount Allison) 1973, (Dalhousie) 1986. *Publications:* Christopher Pratt 1982, The Prints of Christopher Pratt (with Mira Godard) 1991, Christopher Pratt: Personal Reflections on a Life in Art 1995, Christopher Pratt: All My Own Work 2005, A Painter's Poems 2005, Ordinary Things: A Different Kind of Voyage 2009, Christopher Pratt: Six Decades 2013. *Leisure interests:* offshore sailing, walking/hiking and fly-fishing. *Address:* PO Box 87, Mount Carmel, St Mary's Bay, Newfoundland, A0B 2M0, Canada. *Telephone:* (709) 521-2048. *Fax:* (709) 521-2707.

PRATT, Cynthia Alexandria, BSc; Bahamian politician; b. 5 Nov. 1945; d. of the late Herman Mackay and Rose Mackay; m. Joseph Benjamin Pratt; six c.; ed Western Sr School, Princess Margaret Hosp. School of Nursing, Aquinas Coll., Nassau, St Augustine's Coll., Raleigh, NC, USA; surgical nurse, Princess Margaret Hosp., Nassau 1971–79; Head, Dept of Physical Educ., C.C. Sweeting High School 1978–91; part-time Lecturer and Asst Dir of Student Activities, Coll. of the Bahamas 1991–96; MP (Progressive Liberal Party) for St Cecilia, New Providence; fmrly Chief Opposition Whip, House of Ass.; Deputy Prime Minister and Minister of Nat. Security 2002–07; f. St Cecilia's Church Youth and Ladies Club, Dr Keva Bethel Basketball Classic, Coconut Grove Youth Club; recruiter for St Augustine's Coll., Raleigh, NC; Coach and Rep. of Bahamas overseas in softball, volleyball and basketball; mem. Kappa Delta Pi Soc., Alpha Kappa Mu Honour Soc.; Hon. DHumLitt (Raleigh, NC). *Leisure interests:* arranging sporting events, coaching and meeting people, serving the under-privileged. *Address:* Poincianna Avenue and Six Street, Nassau, NP, The Bahamas (home). *Telephone:* 422-5542 (home).

PRAWER, Siegbert Salomon, MA, DLitt, PhD, LittD, FBA; British university teacher (retd) and author; b. 15 Feb. 1925, Cologne, Germany; s. of Marcus Prawer and Eleonora Prawer; brother of Ruth Prawer Jhabvala; m. Helga Alice Schaefer 1949; one s. two d. (and one s. deceased); ed King Henry VIII School, Coventry, Jesus Coll., Christ's Coll. Cambridge; Adelaide Stoll Research Student, Christ's Coll. Cambridge 1947–48; Asst Lecturer, then Lecturer, then Sr Lecturer, Univ. of Birmingham 1948–63; Prof. of German, Westfield Coll., London Univ. 1964–69; Taylor Prof. of German Language and Literature, Oxford 1969–86, Prof. Emer. 1986–; Co-editor, Oxford Germanic Studies 1971–75, Anglica Germanica 1973–79; Fulbright Exchange Scholar, Columbia Univ. 1956; Visiting Prof. City Coll., New York 1956–57, Univ. of Chicago 1963–64, Harvard Univ. 1968, Hamburg Univ. 1969, Univ. of Calif., Irvine 1975, Otago Univ., NZ 1976, Univ. of Pittsburgh 1977, ANU Canberra 1980, Brandeis Univ. 1981–82; Resident Fellow, Knox Coll., Dunedin, NZ 1976, Russell Sage Foundation, New York 1988; Fellow, Queen's Coll. Oxford 1969–86, Supernumerary Fellow 1986–90, Hon. Fellow 1990–, Dean of Degrees 1976–93; Pres. British Comparative Literature Asscn 1984–87, Hon. Fellow 1989; Corresp. Fellow, German Acad. of Literature 1989; Pres. English Goethe Soc. 1992–95, Vice-Pres. 1995–; Hon. Dir London Univ. Inst. of Germanic Studies 1965–68, Hon. Fellow 1986; Hon. mem. Modern Languages Asscn of America 1986; Hon. Fellow, Jesus Coll. Cambridge 1996–; Hon. DPhil (Cologne) 1985; Hon. DLitt (Birmingham) 1988; Goethe Medal 1973, Gold Medal, German Goethe Soc. 1995; Isaac Deutscher Memorial Prize 1977, Gundolf-Prize of the German Acad. 1986. *Publications:* German Lyric Poetry 1952, Mörike und seine Leser 1960, Heine's Buch der Lieder: A Critical Study 1960, Heine: The Tragic Satirist 1962, The Penguin Book of Lieder 1964, The Uncanny in Literature (inaugural lecture) 1965, Heine's Shakespeare, a Study in Contexts (inaugural lecture) 1970, Comparative Literary Studies: An Introduction 1973, Karl Marx and World Literature 1976, Caligari's Children: The Film as Tale of Terror 1980, Heine's Jewish Comedy: A Study of His Portraits of Jews and Judaism 1983, Coalsmoke and Englishmen 1984, A. N. Stencl–Poet of Whitechapel 1984, Frankenstein's Island–England and the English in the Writings of Heinrich Heine 1986, Israel at Vanity Fair: Jews and Judaism in the Writings of W. M. Thackeray 1992, Breeches and Metaphysics, Thackeray's German Discourse 1997, W. M. Thackeray's European Sketch Books: A Study of Literary and Graphic Portraiture 2000, The Blue Angel 2002, Werner Herzog's Nosferatu 2004, Between Two Worlds: The Jewish Presence in German and Austrian Film 1910–1933 2005, A Cultural Citizen of the World: Sigmund Freud's Knowledge and Use of British and American Writings 2009; edited: The Penguin Book of Lieder 1964, Essays in

German Language, Culture and Society (with R. H. Thomas and L. W. Forster) 1969, The Romantic Period in Germany 1970, Seventeen Modern German Poets 1971; screenplay: Das Kabinett des Dr Caligari (ed and introduction); numerous articles on German, English and comparative literature. *Leisure interest:* portrait drawing. *Address:* The Queen's College, Oxford, OX1 4AW (office); 9 Hawkswell Gardens, Oxford, OX2 7EX, England (home). *Telephone:* (1865) 279121 (office); (1865) 557614 (home).

PREBBLE, Mark, CNZM, PhD; New Zealand civil servant and academic; *Adjunct Professor, School of Government, Victoria University of Wellington;* b. 12 May 1951, Auckland; s. of Archdeacon K. R. Prebble and Mary Prebble; brother of Richard William Prebble (q.v.); m. 1st Fenella Druce 1974 (died 1977); m. 2nd Lesley Bagnall 1978; two s. two d.; ed Auckland Grammar School, Auckland Univ. and Victoria Univ. of Wellington; with Treasury, Govt of NZ 1977–82, Dept of Labour 1982–85; Seconded to Prime Minister and Cabinet as Man. Change Team on Targeting Social Assistance 1991–92; Minister (Econ.) NZ High Comm., London 1992–93; Deputy Sec. of Treasury 1993–98; Chief Exec. Dept of Prime Minister and Cabinet 1998–2004; State Services Commr 2004–08 (retd); Adjunct Prof., School of Govt, Victoria Univ. of Wellington 2012–; Companion of the NZ Order of Merit 2009. *Publications:* Smart Cards: Is it Smart to Use a Smart Card? 1990, Information, Privacy and the Welfare State 1990, Incentives and Labour Supply: Modelling Taxes and Benefits (ed. with P. Rebstock) 1992, New Zealand: The Turnaround Economy 1993, With Respect: Parliamentarians, Officials and Judges Too 2010; articles in econ., public policy and educational journals. *Leisure interests:* walking, family and gardening. *Address:* School of Government, Victoria University of Wellington, PO Box 600, Wellington 6140, New Zealand (office).

PREBBLE, Hon. Richard William, CBE, BA, LLB; New Zealand politician and lawyer; b. 7 Feb. 1948, UK; s. of Archdeacon K. R. Prebble; brother of Mark Prebble (q.v.); m. 1st Nancy Prebble 1970; m. 2nd Doreen Prebble 1991; ed Auckland Boys' Grammar School, Auckland Technical Inst. and Auckland Univ.; admitted as barrister and solicitor, NZ Supreme Court 1971; admitted to Bar, Fiji Supreme Court 1973; MP for Auckland Cen. 1975–; Jr Opposition Whip 1978–79; Minister of Transport, of Railways, of Civil Aviation and Meteorological Services, of Pacific Island Affairs, Assoc. Minister of Finance 1984–87; Minister of State-Owned Enterprises, Postmaster-Gen., Minister of Works and Devt and Minister of Pacific Island Affairs 1987–88, of Railways, Police, State-Owned Enterprises and Pacific Island Affairs Jan.–Oct. 1990; Leader ACT New Zealand 1996–2004. *Publications:* I've Been Thinking 1996, What Happens Next 1997, I've Been Writing. *Leisure interests:* Polynesian and Melanesian culture, opera, drama. *Address:* Parliament Buildings, Wellington, New Zealand (office). *Telephone:* (4) 470-6638 (office). *Fax:* (4) 473-3532 (office). *E-mail:* richard.prebble@parliament.govt.nz (office). *Website:* www.act.org.nz (office).

PREBBLE, Stuart; British media executive; *Director, Storyvault Films;* b. April 1951, London, England; s. of the late Dennis Stanley Prebble and Jean McIntosh; m.; one d.; ed Beckenham and Penge Grammar School for Boys, Newcastle Univ.; joined BBC as grad. trainee, worked as regional reporter for BBC TV in Newcastle; presenter for Granada TV; Deputy Ed. of World in Action (ITV) 1987, Ed. 1988 (fmr presenter and producer); Head of Granada's Regional Programmes 1990, Head of Factual Programmes 1992; Controller of Network Factual Programmes, ITV Network Centre 1993; CEO Granada Sky Broadcasting and Man. Dir of Channels and Interactive Media, Granada Media Group; CEO ONdigital PLC 1999–2002, ITV 2001–02; Co-founder and Man. Dir Liberty Bell Productions 2002–11; Founder www.storyvault.com (social history and genealogy networking website) 2009; Co-founder and Dir Storyvault Films 2010–; RTS Award for Best Factual Series 1995. *Television productions include:* as Exec. Producer: Stars Reunited (BBC 1) 2003–04, Grumpy Old Men (BBC 2) 2003–04, Grumpy Old Women (BBC 2) 2005–, He Says, She Says (BBC 2) 2005–, Three Men in a Boat (BBC 2) 2006, Why We Went To War 2006, The Alastair Campbell Diaries, the Widow's Tale. *Publications include:* A Power in the Land 1988, The Lazarus File 1989, Grumpy Old Men – The Official Handbook 2004, Grumpy Old Men – The Secret Diary 2005, Grumpy Old Christmas 2007, Grumpy Old Workers 2007, Grumpy Old Drivers 2008, Secrets of The Conqueror 2012. *Leisure interests:* politics, cinema. *Address:* Storyvault Films, Bridge Studios, 107A Hammersmith Bridge Road, London, W6 9DA, England (office). *Telephone:* (20) 8741-3929 (office). *E-mail:* stuart.prebble@storyvault.tv (office). *Website:* www.storyvault.tv (office).

PREDOIU, Cătălin Marian, PhD; Romanian lawyer and government official; *Minister of Justice;* b. 27 Aug. 1968, Buzău; ed Univ. of Bucharest; commercial and corp. governance lawyer; completed a training programme in commercial law at Caen Bar, France 1994; Lecturer in Commercial Law, Univ. of Bucharest 1994–2007; Assoc. Lawyer, ZRP law partnership 2005–; mem. Council of Bucharest Bar Asscn 2003–; Minister of Justice (ind.) Feb.–Dec. 2008, of Justice Dec. 2008–, also Acting Minister of Foreign Affairs Oct.–Nov. 2009, Interim Prime Minister Feb. 2012; Prize of Romanian Acad. as a co-author of a law treatise. *Publications:* has published several articles and studies about commercial law. *Address:* Ministry of Justice, 050741 Bucharest 5, Str. Apolodor 17, Romania (office). *Telephone:* (21) 3144400 (office). *Fax:* (21) 3101664 (office). *E-mail:* relatiipublice@just.ro (office). *Website:* www.just.ro (office).

PREM, Gen. Tinsulanonda; Thai politician, army officer and government official; *Head of the Privy Council;* b. 26 Aug. 1920, Songkhla, Songkhla; ed Suan Kularb School and Chulachomklao Royal Mil. Acad., Bangkok, US Army Armor School, Fort Knox, USA; started mil. career as Sub-Lt 1941; Commdr Cavalry HQ 1968; Commdr-Gen. 2nd Army Area 1974; Asst C-in-C Royal Thai Army 1977, C-in-C 1978–81; Deputy Minister of Interior, Govt of Gen. Kriangsak Chomanan 1977; Minister of Defence 1979–86; Prime Minister of Thailand 1980–88; Chair. Petroleum Authority of Thailand 1981; Head of the Privy Council 1998–; named as a leading figure in the Thailand political crisis of 2005–06; Chair. Hon. Bd Govs and Hon. Chair. Bd Govs, Prem Tinsulanonda Int. School; Kt Grand Cordon (Special Class) of the Most Noble Order of the Crown of Thailand 1975, Kt Grand Cordon (Special Class) of the Most Exalted Order of the White Elephant 1978, Kt Grand Cross (First Class) of the Most Illustrious Order of Chula Chom Klao 1982, Seri Maharajah Mangku Negara (Malaysia) 1984, Order of Symbolic Propitiousness Ramkeerati Boy Scout Citation Medal (Special Class) 1988, Kt of the Ancient and Auspicious Order of the Nine Gems 1988, Kt Grand Commdr (First Class) of the Hon. Order of Rama 1990, Kt Grand Cross (First Class) of the Most Admirable

Order of the Direkgunabhorn 1996; Victory Medal – Indochina, Victory Medal – World War II, Freemen Safeguarding Medal (First Class), Safeguarding the Constitution Medal, Chakra Mala Medal (15 years military/police service), King Rama IX Royal Cypher Medal, 1st Class 1982, Red Cross Medal of Appreciation. *Address:* HM Privy Council, Grand Palace, Thanon Na Phra Lan, Bangkok 10200 (office); 279 Sri Ayutthaya Road, Sisao Theves, Bangkok 10300, Thailand. *Website:* www.generalprem.com; ptis.threegeneration.org.

PREMAJAYANTHA, A. D. Susil, LLB, MPA; Sri Lankan politician and lawyer; *Minister of the Environment and Renewable Energy;* b. Gangodawila village, Nugegoda; ed St John's Coll., Nugegoda, Univ. of Colombo (external student), Postgraduate Inst. of Man., Univ. of Sri Jayawardenepura; joined Bank of Ceylon while a student; enrolled as an attorney-at-law 1985; resigned from bank and began practice as a defence counsel in Colombo High Courts; Deputy Chair. Urban Council, Sri Jayawardanepura, Kotte 1991–93; mem. Prov. Council, Western Prov. 1993–94, Minister of Western Prov. 1994–95, Chief Minister of Western Prov. 1995–98, 1999–2000; Minister of Educ. 2000–01, 2005–10; MP 2001–04; Minister of Power and Energy 2004–05, of Petroleum Industries 2010–13, of the Environment and Renewable Energy 2013–; Gen. Sec. United People's Freedom Alliance. *Address:* Ministry of Environment and Renewable Energy, 82 Sampath Paya, Rajamalwatte Road, Battaramulla, Colombo, Sri Lanka (office). *Telephone:* (11) 2866617 (office). *Fax:* (11) 2877288 (office). *E-mail:* promotion@menr.lk; susilpremajayantha@hotmail.com. *Website:* www.environmentmin.gov.lk; www.susilpremajayantha.com.

PREMJI, Azim Hashim, BS, BEng; Indian engineer, business executive and philanthropist; *Chairman, Wipro Ltd;* b. 24 July 1945, Bombay (now Mumbai); s. of Mohamed Husain Premji and G. M. H. Premji; m. Yasmeen Premji; two s.; ed Stanford Univ., USA; took over his father's Western India Vegetable Products Ltd (WIPRO) vegetable oil business upon his death 1966; apptd Chair., CEO and Man. Dir Wipro Ltd (IT and software co.), Bangalore 1983, currently Chair.; mem. Prime Minister's Cttee for Trade and Industry, Prime Minister's Advisory Cttee for Information Tech. in India; f. Azim Premji Foundation 2001; Hon. Fellowship, Inst. of Electronics and Telecommunication Engineers 2000; Dr hc (Indian Inst. of Tech.), (Manipal Acad. of Higher Educ.) 2000, (Wesleyan Univ.) 2009, (Visveswaraya Technological Univ.); Hon. DLitt (Aligarh Muslim Univ.) 2008; Sir M. Visvesvaraya Memorial Award 2000, Businessman of the Year, Business India magazine 2000, Business Leader of the Year, Econ. Times 2004, Padma Bhushan, Govt of India 2005, Faraday Medal 2005, Global Vision Award, US-India Business Council, Sir Jehangir Ghandy Medal, XLRI, Jamshedpur, recognized by Business Week as one of the Greatest Entrepreneurs of All Time, Lakshya Business Visionary, Nat. Inst. of Industrial Eng 2006, featured in Business Week's All-Time Top 30 Entrepreneurs of the World 2007, listed by Time magazine among 100 Most Influential People in the World 2004, named by Fortune magazine among the 25 Most Powerful Business Leaders Outside the US 2003, Padma Vibhushan, Govt of India 2011, ranked by Forbes magazine amongst The World's Most Powerful People (61st) 2011. *Leisure interests:* jogging, spending time at hillside resorts. *Address:* Wipro Ltd, Doddakannelli, Sarjapur Road, Bangalore 560 035 (office); Bakhtawar, 229, Nariman Point, Mumbai 400 021, India (home). *Telephone:* (80) 28440011 (office); (80) 5569991 (home). *Fax:* (80) 28440256 (office). *E-mail:* azim.premji@corp.wipro.co.in (office); info@azimpremjifoundation.org. *Website:* www.wipro.com (office); www.wiprocorporate.com (office); www.azimpremjifoundation.org.

PRENDERGAST, Patrick J., BA, BAI, PhD, ScD, MRIA; Irish engineer, academic and university administrator; *Provost and President, Trinity College Dublin;* ed Trinity Coll. Dublin (Univ. of Dublin); post-doctoral positions in Bologna, Italy and Nijmegen, The Netherlands; apptd to Faculty of Eng, Trinity Coll. Dublin 1995, later Prof. of Bioengineering and Dir Trinity Centre for Bioengineering, Dean of Grad. Studies 2004–07, Vice-Provost and Chief Academic Officer 2008–11, Provost and Pres. 2011–; Visiting Prof., Inst. of Fundamental Technological Research, Poland, Erasmus Univ. Rotterdam, Tech. Univ. of Delft, Univ. Politicnic of Catalonia, Barcelona 2008; fmr mem. Bd of Dirs ClearStream Technologies plc; apptd by EC to Governing Bd of European Inst. of Innovation and Tech. 2012–; mem. Bd Tallaght Hosp.; Fellow, Irish Acad. of Eng; Int. Fellow, Royal Acad. of Eng (UK). *Publications:* several hundred articles related to implant design and tissue mechanobiology. *Address:* Office of the Provost, House 1, Trinity College, Dublin, 2, Ireland (office). *Telephone:* (1) 8964362 (office). *Fax:* (1) 8962303 (office). *E-mail:* provost@tcd.ie (office). *Website:* www.tcd.ie/provost (office).

PRENTICE, Rt Hon. James (Jim), PC; Canadian lawyer and politician; *Minister of Government;* b. 20 July 1956, South Porcupine, Ont.; s. of Eric Prentice; m. Karen Prentice; three d.; ed Univ. of Alberta and Dalhousie Univ.; worked in Crowsnest Pass coal mines; as lawyer, specialized in property rights and has handled several relocations, environmental protection suits and cases arising from restricted devt areas; also served as a Commr Indian Claims Comm. of Canada for 10 years; active in Conservative party politics 1976–, cand. for leadership of Progressive Conservative Party of Canada 2003; MP (Conservative Party of Canada) for Calgary Centre-North, Alberta 2004–; Minister of Indian Affairs and Northern Devt and Fed. Interlocutor for Métis and Non-Status Indians 2006–07, of Industry 2007–08, of Environment 2008–; served for seven years on Bd of Dirs Calgary Winter Club, including as Pres. and Chair.; fmr volunteer advocate for learning-disabled children; fmr ice hockey coach. *Address:* Environment Canada, Les Terrasses de la Chaudière, 10 Wellington Street, 28th Floor, Gatineau, PQ K1A 0H3, Canada (office). *Telephone:* (819) 997-1441 (office). *Fax:* (819) 953-0279 (office). *E-mail:* minister@ec.gc.ca (office); prentice.j@parl.gc.ca (office). *Website:* www.ec.gc.ca (office); www.jimprentice.ca; www2.parl.gc.ca/Parlinfo.

PRESCOTT, Edward C., MS, PhD; American economist and academic; *W. P. Carey Chaired Professor, Arizona State University;* ed Swarthmore Coll., Pa, Case-Western Reserve Univ., Cleveland, Carnegie-Mellon Univ., Pittsburgh; Lecturer, Econs Dept, Univ. of Pennsylvania 1966–67, Asst Prof. 1967–71; Asst Prof. of Econs, Grad. School of Industrial Admin, Carnegie-Mellon Univ. 1971–72, Assoc. Prof. 1972–75, Prof. 1975–80; Prof., Dept of Econs, Univ. of Minnesota 1980–98, 1999–2003, McKnight Presidential Chair in Econs 2003; Prof. of Econs, Univ. of Chicago 1998–99; Prof., Dept of Econs, Ariz. State Univ. 2003–, W. P. Carey Chaired Prof. 2003; Sr Advisor, Research Dept, Fed. Reserve Bank of Minneapolis

1980–2003, Sr Monetary Advisor 2003–; Visiting Prof. of Econs, Norwegian School of Business and Econs 1974–75; Ford Visiting Research Prof., Univ. of Chicago 1978–79; Visiting Prof. of Econs, Northwestern Univ. 1979–80, Visiting Prof. of Finance, Kellogg Grad. School of Man. 1980–82; Regents' Prof., Univ. of Minn. 1996; Leader Nat. Bureau of Econ. Research/NSF Workshop in Industrial Org. 1977–84; Research Assoc., Nat. Bureau of Econ. Research 1988–; Pres. Soc. for the Advancement of Econ. Theory 1992–94, Soc. of Econ. Dynamics and Control 1992–95; Assoc. Ed. Journal of Econometrics 1976–82, Int. Econ. Review 1980–90, Journal of Econ. Theory 1990–92; Co-ed. Econ. Theory 1991; Brookings Econ. Policy Fellow 1969–70; Guggenheim Fellow 1974–75; Fellow, Econometric Soc. 1980, American Acad. of Arts and Sciences 1992; Laurea hc in Economica (Univ. of Rome 'Tor Vergata') 2002; First Lionel McKenzie Lecturer 1990, Walras-Pareto Lecturer 1994, First Lawrence R. Klein Lecturer 1997, Sidrauski Lecturer, Latin America Econometric Soc. 1999, Plenary Lecturer, Soc. for Econ. Dynamics 2001, Richard T. Ely Lecturer, American Econ. Asscn Meetings 2002, Erwin Plein Nemmers Prize in Econs, Northwestern Univ. 2002, Bank of Sweden Prize in Econ. Sciences in Memory of Alfred Nobel (Nobel Prize) (jtly) 2004. *Publications:* Contractual Arrangements for Intertemporal Trade (co-ed.) 1987, Recursive Methods in Economic Dynamics (collaborator) 1989, Applied General Equilibrium Symposium (co-ed.) 1995, Great Depressions of the 20th Century (co-ed.) 2002, Barriers to Riches (co-author) 2000; numerous articles in econs journals. *Address:* Department of Economics, W.P. Carey School of Business, Arizona State University, Tempe, AZ 85287-3806 (office); Research Department, Federal Reserve Bank of Minneapolis, 90 Hennepin Avenue, Minneapolis, MN 55401-1804, USA (office). *Telephone:* 480-965-3531 (Tempe) (office); 612-204-5520 (Minneapolis) (office). *Fax:* 480-965-0748 (Tempe) (office); 612-204-5515 (Minneapolis) (office). *Website:* wpcarey.asu.edu (office); www.minneapolisfed.org (office).

PRESCOTT, John Barry, AC, BComm, FAICD, FAIM, FTSE; Australian business executive; *Chairman, Aurizon Holdings Limited;* b. 22 Oct. 1940, Sydney, NSW; s. of John Norman Prescott and Margaret Ellen Brownie; m. Jennifer Mary Louise Cahill; one s. three d. (one deceased); ed North Sydney Boys' High School, Univ. of New South Wales, Northwestern Univ. USA; Gen. Man. Transport, Broken Hill Proprietary Co. Ltd (BHP) 1982–87, Exec. Gen. Man. and CEO BHP Steel 1987–91, Dir BHP 1988–98, Man. Dir and CEO BHP 1991–98; Chair. Horizon Pvt. Equity 1998–2005, ASC Pty Ltd 2000–09, Aurizon Holdings Ltd (fmrly QR National Ltd, fmrly QR Ltd) 2006–; Dir Tubemakers 1988–92, Normandy Mining 1999–2001, Newmont Mining Corpn 2002–13; mem. Advisory Bd Booz Allen 1991–2003; mem. Defence Industry Cttee 1988–93, Bd, Business Council of Australia 1995–97; Chair. Mfg Council 1990–95, Sunshine Coast Business Council, Queensland 2004–07 (Patron 2007–09); mem. Int. Council of JP Morgan 1994–2003, Asia Pacific Advisory Cttee of New York Stock Exchange 1995–2005, Council of World Econ. Forum 1996–98, Bd of The Walter and Eliza Hall Inst. of Medical Research 1994–98; Trustee, The Conf. Bd 1993–2001, Global Counsellor 2001–, mem. Global Advisory Council 2013–; Patron Australian Quality Council 1990–2000; Fellow, Australian Inst. of Co. Dirs, Australian Acad. of Technological Sciences; Hon. LLD (Monash) 1994; Hon. DSc (Univ. of New South Wales) 1995; Centenary Medal 2003. *Leisure interests:* tennis, golf. *Address:* Level 39, 140 William Street, Melbourne, Vic. 3000, Australia (office). *Telephone:* (3) 9642-2518 (office). *Fax:* (3) 9642-2517 (office). *E-mail:* jbp@jbprescott.com (home).

PRESCOTT, Baron (Life Peer), cr. 2010, of Kingston-upon-Hull in the County of East Yorkshire; **John Leslie Prescott,** DipEconPol; British trade union official and politician; b. 31 May 1938, Prestatyn, Denbighshire, North Wales; s. of John Herbert Prescott and Phyllis Prescott; m. Pauline Tilston 1961; two s.; ed WEA correspondence courses, Ruskin Coll. Oxford, Hull Univ.; trainee chef 1953–55; steward in Merchant Navy 1955–63; Recruitment Officer, Gen. & Municipal Workers Union 1965; contested Southport for Labour 1966; full-time official Nat. Union of Seamen 1968–70; MP for Kingston-upon-Hull East 1970–83, for Hull East 1983–2010; mem. Select Cttee Nationalized Industries 1973–79, Council of Europe 1972–75, European Parl. 1975–79; Parl. Pvt. Sec. to Sec. of State for Trade 1974–76; Opposition Spokesman on Transport 1979–81, Regional Affairs and Devolution 1981–83, on Transport 1983–84, on Employment 1984–87, on Energy 1987–89, on Transport 1988–93, on Employment 1993–94; Deputy Prime Minister and Sec. of State for the Environment, Transport and the Regions 1997–2001, Deputy Prime Minister and First Sec. of State, Head of Office of the Deputy Prime Minister 1997–2006, Deputy Prime Minister 2006–07; British Rep. to Parl. Ass., Council of Europe, Strasbourg, France 2007–, also sits on Ass. of Western European Union; mem. Labour Party Nat. Exec. Cttee 1989–, Deputy Leader 1994–2007, contested Labour Party Treas. 2010; mem. Shadow Cabinet 1983–97; mem. Bd Hull Kingston Rovers Rugby League Club; resgnd from Privy Council in protest over its role in the debate surrounding press regulation July 2013; North of England Zoological Soc. Gold Medal 1999, Priyadarshni Award 2002. *Publications:* Not Wanted on Voyage: A Report of the 1966 Seamen's Strike 1966, Alternative Regional Strategy: A Framework for Discussion 1982, Planning for Full Employment 1985, Real Needs–Local Jobs 1987, Moving Britain into the 1990s 1989, Moving Britain into Europe 1991, Full Steam Ahead 1993, Financing Infrastructure Investment 1994, Jobs and Social Justice 1994, Prezza: My Story – Pulling No Punches 2008. *Address:* House of Lords, Westminster, London, SW1A 0PW, England (office). *Telephone:* (20) 7219-5353 (office). *E-mail:* contactholmember@ parliament.uk (office). *Website:* www.parliament.uk/biographies/lords/lord -prescott/374 (office).

PRESS, Frank, PhD; American geophysicist and academic; *Professor Emeritus of Geophysics, Massachusetts Institute of Technology;* b. 4 Dec. 1924, Brooklyn, New York; s. of Solomon Press and Dora Press (née Steinholz); m. Billie Kallick 1946; one s. one d.; ed Coll. of City of New York and Columbia Univ.; Research Associate, Columbia Univ. 1946–49, Instructor, Geology 1949–51, Asst Prof. of Geology 1951–52, Assoc. Prof. 1952–55; Prof. of Geophysics, Calif. Inst. of Tech. 1955–65, Dir Seismological Lab. 1957–65; Co-Ed. Physics and Chemistry of the Earth 1957–; Chair. Dept of Earth and Planetary Sciences, MIT 1965–77, Prof. Emer. 1981–; Dir Office of Science and Tech. Policy, Exec. Office of Pres. and Science and Tech. Adviser to Pres. 1977–81; Consultant to USN 1956–57, US Dept of Defense 1958–62, NASA 1960–62, 1965–70; mem. US del. to Nuclear Test Ban Conf. Geneva 1959–61, Moscow 1963; Pres. Science Advisory Comm. 1961–64; Chair. Bd of Advisors Nat. Center for Earthquake Research of the US Geological Survey

1966–76; Planetology Subcomm. NASA 1966–70; Chair. Earthquake Prediction Panel Office of Science and Tech. 1965–66; Fellow, American Acad. of Arts and Sciences 1966, Royal Astronomical Soc.; mem. Nat. Science Bd 1970–77, NAS 1958, Pres. 1981–93; Cecil & Ida Green Sr Fellow, Carnegie Inst. of Washington 1993–97; Dir Washington Advisory Group 1996–; fmr Pres. American Geophysical Union; Chair. Cttee on Scholarly Communication with People's Repub. of China 1975–77; mem. French Acad. of Science, Japan Acad. of Eng, Royal Soc., London; Hon. LLD (City Univ. of NY) 1972, Hon. DSc (Notre Dame Univ.) 1973, (Univ. of Rhode Island, of Arizona, Rutgers Univ., City Univ. of New York) 1979; Townsend Harris Medal Coll. of the City of New York, Royal Astronomical Soc. Gold Medal (UK) 1971, Day Medal Geological Soc. of America, Interior 1972, NASA Award 1973, Killian Faculty Achievement Award, MIT 1975, Japan Prize 1993, Nat. Medal of Science 1994, Philip Hauge Abelson Prize, AAAS 1995, Lomonosov Gold Medal, Russian Acad. of Sciences 1998. *Publications:* Earth (with R. Siever) 1986, Understanding Earth 2000. *Leisure interests:* skiing, sailing. *Address:* Suite 616 S, 2500 Virginia Avenue, Washington, DC 20037, USA. *E-mail:* fpress@ theadvisorygroup.com (office). *Website:* www.theadvisorygroup.com (office).

PRESS, James (Jim) E., BS; American automotive industry executive; *President, McLarty Global Transportation LLC;* b. 4 Oct. 1946, Los Angeles, Calif.; ed Kansas State Coll. (now Pittsburgh State Univ.); with Ford Motor Co. until 1970; with Toyota Motor Sales, USA Inc., in various positions, since 1970, Sr Vice-Pres. and Gen. Man. Lexus 1995–98, Sr Vice-Pres. Toyota Motor USA Inc. 1998–99, Exec. Vice-Pres. 1999–2001, COO 2001–03, Man. Officer Toyota Motor Corpn 2003–06, Pres. and COO (first non-Japanese) Toyota Motor North America Inc. 2006–07, Bd of Dirs Toyota Motor Corpn (first non-Japanese mem.) 2006–07, mem. Bd of Dirs Toyota Motor Credit Corpn 1999–2007; mem. Bd of Dirs, Vice-Chair. and Pres. Chrysler LLC, Detroit 2007–09, Deputy CEO and Special Advisor June–Dec. 2009, mem. Bd Mans and Vice-Chair. Cerberus Operations and Advisory Co. (COAC) LLC; Pres. McLarty Global Transportation LLC 2011–; mem. Bd of Dirs and mem. Nominating, Corp. Governance and Public Policy Cttee, Best Buy Co. Inc. 2006–07; fmr Chair. Asscn of Automotive Mfrs; mem. Pittsburgh State Univ., Pittsburgh, Kan., Advisory Bd and Switzer Center School, Torrance, Calif.; Gold Medallion, Int. Swimming Hall of Fame, Distinguished Service Citation Award, Automotive Hall of Fame, named an industry All-Star by both Automotive News and Automobile Magazine.

PRESSLER, Larry, MA, JD; American politician and lawyer; *President and CEO, Pressler Group LLC;* b. 29 March 1942, Humboldt, SDak; s. of Antone Pressler and Loretta Claussen; m. Harriet Dent 1982; one d.; ed Univ. of South Dakota, Univ. of Oxford, UK (Rhodes Scholar), Harvard Kennedy School of Govt and Harvard Law School; Lt in US Army, Viet Nam 1966–68; mem. House of Reps 1975–79; Senator from South Dakota 1979–97, mem. several Senate cttees, Chair. Commerce, Science and Transport Cttees 1995–96; Congressional Del. to 47th UN Gen. Ass. 1992; mem. US Comm. on Improving the Effectiveness of the UN 1993; Sec. US Del. to Inter-Parl. Union 1981; Dir USAF Bd of Visitory 1987–; Founder, Pres., CEO Pressler and Assocs (now Pressler Group LLC), Washington 1997–; fmr Visiting Prof. of Govt, Univ. of S Dakota; mem. Adjunct Faculty, Native American Oglala Lakota Coll., S Dakota; Sr Fellow, UCLA 2001; taught American Govt at Fudan Univ., Shanghai, People's Repub. of China 2005; mem. seven Corp. Bds, including Infosys Technologies, Bangalore, India; mem. Council on Foreign Relations, Vietnam Veterans Memorial Educ. Center Advisory Council; mem. US Comm. for the Preservation of America's Heritage Abroad 2009, Jericho Project Veterans Advisory Council 2010; decorations for service as Lt in US Army in Viet Nam. *Publications:* US Senators from the Prairie 1982, Star Wars: The SDI Debates in Congress 1986. *Leisure interests:* running, tennis. *Address:* 800 25th Street, NW, The Plaza, Suite 504, Washington, DC 20037, USA (office). *Telephone:* (202) 210-5330 (office); (202) 546-5959 (home). *Fax:* (202) 333-5854 (office); (202) 333-5854 (home). *E-mail:* lpressler@larrypressler.com (home). *Website:* www .larrypressler.com (office); www.senatorlarrypressler.com.

PRESSLER, Paul S.; American business executive; b. 1956; ed State Univ. of New York at Oneonta; various positions in branding and marketing, Remco Toys, Mego Toys and Kenner-Parker –1987; Sr Vice-Pres. Product Licensing, The Walt Disney Co. 1987–90, Sr Vice-Pres. Consumer Products 1990–93, Pres. The Disney Stores 1993–96, Pres. Disneyland Resort, Anaheim, Calif. 1996–99, Chair. Global Theme Park and Resorts Div. 1999–2002; Pres. and CEO Gap Inc. 2002–07; currently Advisor, Clayton, Dubilier & Rice LLC, (pvt. equity firm), New York; mem. Bd of Dirs Avon Products, Inc., OpenTable, Inc. *Address:* Clayton, Dubilier & Rice LLC, 375 Park Avenue, 18th Floor, New York, NY 10152, USA (office). *Telephone:* (212) 407-5200 (office). *Fax:* (212) 407-5252 (office). *Website:* www.cdr -inc.com (office).

PRESTON, Paul, CBE, MA, DPhil, FRHistS, FBA; British historian, author and academic; *Prince of Asturias Professor of Contemporary Spanish History, London School of Economics;* b. 21 July 1946, Liverpool, England; s. of Charles R. Preston and Alice Hoskisson; m. Gabrielle P. Ashford-Hodges 1983; two s.; ed St Edward's Coll. Liverpool, Oriel Coll. Oxford and Univ. of Reading; Research Fellow, Centre for Mediterranean Studies, Rome 1973–74; Lecturer in History, Univ. of Reading 1974–75; Lecturer in Modern History, Queen Mary Coll. London 1975–79, Reader 1979–85, Prof. of History 1985–91; Prof. of Int. History, LSE 1991–94, Prince of Asturias Prof. of Contemporary Spanish History 1994–; regular contrib. to Times Literary Supplement; columnist in ABC, Diario 16 and El País, Madrid; Comendador, Orden del Mérito Civil (Spain) 1987, Caballero Gran Cruz de la Orden de Isabel la Católica 2006; Yorkshire Post Book of the Year 1994, Así fue – La Historia rescatada Prize 1998, Premi Internacional Ramon Llull, Catalan Govt 2005, Trias Fargas Non-Fiction Prize 2006, Marcel Proust Chair of European Acad. 2006. *Publications:* The Coming of the Spanish Civil War 1978, The Triumph of Democracy in Spain 1986, The Spanish Civil War 1986, The Politics of Revenge 1990, Franco: A Biography 1993, Comrades: Portraits from the Spanish Civil War 1999, Doves of War: Four Women of Spain 2003, Juan Carlos: A People's King 2004, We Saw Spain Die 2008, The Spanish Holocaust: Inquisition and Extermination in Twentieth-Century Spain 2011. *Leisure interests:* classical music, especially opera, modern fiction, supporting Everton Football Club. *Address:* Cañada Blanch Centre for Contemporary Spanish Studies, London School of Economics, London, WC2A 2AE, England (office). *Telephone:* (20) 7955-6508 (office). *Fax:* (20) 7955-6757 (office). *E-mail:* p.preston@lse.ac.uk (office). *Website:* www2.lse.ac.uk/europeanInstitute/research/canadaBlanch/home.aspx (office).

PRESTON, Peter John, MA; British journalist; b. 23 May 1938, Barrow-upon-Soar, Leicestershire; s. of John Whittle Preston and Kathlyn Preston (née Chell); m. Jean Mary Burrell 1962; two s. two d.; ed Loughborough Grammar School and St John's Coll. Oxford; editorial trainee, Liverpool Daily Post 1960–63; Political Reporter, The Guardian 1963–64, Educ. Corresp. 1965–66, Diary Ed. 1966–68, Features Ed. 1968–72, Production Ed. 1972–75, Ed. The Guardian 1975–95, Ed.-in-Chief 1995, Ed.-in-Chief The Observer 1995–96, Editorial Dir Guardian Media Group 1996–98; Co-Dir Guardian Foundation 1997, now columnist; mem. Scott Trust 1976–; Chair. Int. Press Inst. 1995–97, Asscn of British Eds 1996–99; mem. UNESCO Advisory Group on Press Freedom 2000–04; Gov. British Asscn for Cen. and Eastern Europe 2000–; Hon. Fellow, St John's Coll. Oxford 2003; Hon. DLitt (Loughborough) 1982, (E Anglia), (City Univ.) 1997, (Leicester) 2003; What the Papers Say Award for Lifetime Achievement 2006. *Publications:* Dunblane: Reflecting Tragedy 1996, The 51st State 1998, Bess 1999. *Leisure interests:* football, films, four children. *Address:* The Guardian, Kings Place, 90 York Way, London, N1 9GU, England (office). *Telephone:* (20) 3353-2000 (office). *Website:* www.guardian.co.uk (office).

PRESTON, Simon John, CBE, MusB, MA, FRAM, FRCM, FRCO, FRCCO, FRSA; British organist and conductor; b. 4 Aug. 1938, Bournemouth, Dorset, England; m. Elizabeth Hays; ed Canford School, King's Coll., Cambridge; Sub-Organist, Westminster Abbey 1962–67; Acting Organist, St Albans Abbey 1967–68; Organist and Lecturer in Music, Christ Church, Oxford 1970–81; Organist and Master of the Choristers, Westminster Abbey 1981–87; Conductor, Oxford Bach Choir 1971–74; Artistic Dir, Calgary Int. Organ Festival; Patron, Univ. of Buckingham; mem. Royal Soc. of Musicians, Council of Friends of St John's Smith Square; over 30 recordings; Edison Award 1971, Grand Prix du Disque 1979, Performer of the Year Award, American Guild of Organists 1987, Medal of the Royal Coll. of Organists 2014. *Leisure interests:* croquet, theatre, opera. *Address:* 15 St Margaret's Road, Oxford, OX2 6RU, England. *Telephone:* (1865) 512276.

PRESTON, Steven C., BA, MBA; American business executive and fmr government official; *CEO, Livingston International;* b. 4 Aug. 1960; m. Molly Preston; five c.; ed Northwestern Univ., Univ. of Chicago, Ludwig-Maximilians Univ., Germany; Sr Vice-Pres. and Treas., First Data Corpn 1993–97; Chief Financial Officer, then Exec. Vice-Pres. Service Master 1997–2006; Admin., US Small Business Admin, Washington, DC 2006–08; US Sec. of Housing and Urban Devt 2008–09; Pres. and CEO Oakleaf Waste Management 2009–11, Exec. Vice-Pres. for Finance, Recycling and Energy Services, Waste Management (after acquisition of Oakleaf) 2011–12; advisor to Republican Presidential nominee Mitt Romney 2012; CEO Livingston International 2013–; mem. Bd of Dirs Habitat for Humanity, Wheaton Coll.; mem. Bd of Visitors, Weinberg Coll. of Arts and Sciences, Northwestern Univ. *Address:* Livingston International, 150 Pierce Road, Suite 500, Itasca, IL 60143-1222, USA (office). *Website:* www.livingstonintl.com (office).

PRÊTRE, Georges; French conductor; b. 14 Aug. 1924, Waziers; s. of Emile Prêtre and Jeanne Prêtre (née Dérin); m. Gina Marny 1950; one s. one d.; ed Lycée and Conservatoire de Douai, Conservatoire national supérieur de musique de Paris and Ecole des chefs d'orchestre; Dir of Music, Opera Houses of Marseilles, Lille and Toulouse 1946–55; Dir of Music, Opéra Comique, Paris 1955–59; Dir of Music, l'Opéra de Paris 1959, Artistic Dir 1966, Dir-Gen. of Music 1970–71; conductor of the symphonic asscns of Paris and of principal festivals throughout the world; also conducted at La Scala, Milan and major American orchestras; Conductor Metropolitan Opera House, New York 1964–65, La Scala, Milan 1965–66, Salzburg 1966; First Visiting Conductor, Vienna Symphony Orchestra 1986–91, Opéra Bastille (Turandot) 1997, Opéra-Comique (Pelléas et Mélisande) 1998; Turandot at La Scala 2001; concert to celebrate 80th birthday, l'Opéra-Bastille 2004, New Year concert, Vienna 2008; Hon. mem. Gesellschaft der Musikfreunde, Vienna; Officier, Légion d'honneur 1971, Commdr 2003, Chevalier des Palmes Academiques, Haute Distinction République Italienne 1975, Commdr République Italienne 1980; Europa Prize 1982, Victoire de la musique Award for Best Conductor 1997. *Leisure interests:* riding, swimming, aviation, judo. *Address:* Künstleragentur Dr. Raab & Dr. Böhm Gesellschaft m.b.H., Plankengasse 7, 1010 Vienna, Austria (office). *Telephone:* (1) 5120501 (office). *Fax:* (1) 5127743 (office). *E-mail:* office@rbartists.at (office). *Website:* www.rbartists.at (office).

PRETTEJOHN, Nicholas Edward Tucker, BA; British business executive; b. 22 July 1960; s. of Edward Joseph Tucker Prettejohn and Diana Sally Prettejohn; m. 1st Elizabeth Esch 1986 (divorced 1997); m. 2nd Claire Helen McKenna 1997; two d.; ed Taunton School, Somerset and Balliol Coll., Oxford; Research Assoc., Bain & Co. 1982–91, Partner 1988–91; Dir Apax Partners 1991–94; Dir Corp. Strategy, Nat. Freight Corpn PLC 1994–95; Head of Strategy, Lloyd's of London 1995–97, Man. Dir Business Devt Unit 1997–99, N America Business Unit 1998–99, CEO 1999–2006; CEO, Prudential UK and Europe 2006–09; Chair. Brit Insurance 2011–; Dir (non-exec.) Anglo & Overseas Trust PLC 1998–2004, Legal & General 2010–; Chair. Financial Services Practitioner Panel 2007–09; Chair. Britten-Pears Foundation 2009–; mem. Bd of Trustees, Royal Opera House 2005– (Chair. Finance and Audit Cttee 2008–); Chair. Bd Govs, Royal Northern Coll. of Music 2012–; Hon. Fellow, Chartered Insurance Inst. 2004–. *Leisure interests:* opera, music, theatre, horse racing, golf, cricket, rugby, current affairs.

PREUSS, Daphne, BS, PhD; American business executive and academic; *President and CEO, Chromatin, Inc;* m.; ed Univ. of Denver, Massachusetts Inst. of Tech.; performed postdoctoral research at Stanford Univ. –1995; joined Dept of Molecular Genetics, Univ. of Chicago 1995, Asst Prof. then Prof., Albert D. Lasker Prof. in Molecular Genetics 2006–, also Investigator, Howard Hughes Medical Inst.; Co-founder Chromatin, Inc., Chicago 2002, Sr Vice-Pres. then Pres. and Chief Scientific Officer 2007–08, Pres. and CEO 2008–; mem. Bd of Govs Argonne Nat. Lab. 2003–; David and Lucile Packard Fellow; Searle Scholar; Lifetime Nat. Assoc., NAS. *Address:* Chromatin, Inc., 3440 South Dearborn Street, Suite 280, Chicago, IL 60616, USA (office). *Telephone:* (312) 235-3610 (office). *Fax:* (312) 325-3611 (office). *E-mail:* info@chromatininc.com

(office); dpreuss@midway.uchicago.edu (office). *Website:* www.chromatininc.com (office); mgcb.uchicago.edu/phd_program/index.html (office).

PRÉVAL, René; Haitian agronomist, politician and fmr head of state; b. 17 Jan. 1943, Port-au-Prince; m.; two c.; ed Coll. of Jembloux, Belgium; forced to leave Haiti with his family after dispute with Duvalier dictatorship 1963; returned 1975 after five years in USA; worked at Nat. Inst. for Mineral Resources 1975–77; Founding mem. Group for Defence of Constitution; Chair. Cttee Pa Blié investigating disappearance of persons under Duvalier regime 1987–91; Prime Minister Feb.–Sept. 1991; Pres. of Haiti 1996–2001, 2006–11; mem. Lespwa Party. *Address:* c/o La Fanmi Lavalas, blvd 15 Octobre, Tabarre, Port-au-Prince, Haiti.

PREVIN, André George; American conductor, pianist and composer; b. (Andreas Ludwig Priwin), 6 April 1929, Berlin, Germany; s. of Jack Previn and Charlotte Previn (née Epstein); m. 1st Betty Bennett (divorced); two d.; m. 2nd Dory Langan 1959 (divorced 1970); m. 3rd Mia Farrow 1970 (divorced 1979); three s. three d.; m. 4th Heather Hales 1982 (divorced); one s.; m. 5th Anne-Sophie Mutter 2002 (divorced 2006); ed Berlin and Paris Conservatories; began career as film score composer, MGM studios, Los Angeles; Music Dir, Houston Symphony, US 1967–69; Music Dir and Prin. Conductor, London Symphony Orchestra 1968–79, Conductor Laureate 1979–; composed and conducted approx. 50 film scores 1950–65; guest conductor of most major world orchestras, also Royal Opera House, Covent Garden, Salzburg, Edinburgh, Osaka, Flanders Festivals; Music Dir, London South Bank Summer Music Festival 1972–74; Pittsburgh Symphony Orchestra 1976–84, LA Philharmonic Orchestra 1984–89; Music Dir, Royal Philharmonic Orchestra 1985–86, Prin. Conductor 1987–92; Chief Conductor and Music Dir, Oslo Philharmonic Orchestra 2004–06, Conductor Laureate 2006–; Hon. KBE 1996; Television Critics' Award 1972, Acad. Award for Best Film Score 1959, 1960, 1964, 1965, Kennedy Center Honor 1998, Glenn Gould Prize 2005, London Symphony Orchestra Lifetime Achievement Award 2008, Gramophone Award for Lifetime Achievement 2009–, 10 Grammy Awards. *Television:* series of television specials for BBC and for American Public Broadcasting Service. *Major works:* Symphony for Strings 1965, Overture to a Comedy 1966, Suite for Piano 1967, Cello Concerto 1968, Four Songs (for soprano and orchestra) 1968, Two Serenades for Violin 1969, Guitar Concerto 1970, Piano Preludes 1972, Good Companions (musical) 1974, Song Cycle on Poems by Philip Larkin 1977, Every Good Boy Deserves Favour (music, drama, text by Tom Stoppard) 1977, Pages from the Calendar for solo piano 1977, Peaches for flute and strings 1978, Principals 1980, Outings for brass quintet 1980, Reflections 1981, Piano Concerto 1984, Triolet for Brass 1987, Variations for Solo Piano 1991, Six Songs for Soprano and Orchestra on texts by Toni Morrison 1991, Sonata for Cello and Piano 1992, The Magic Number for soprano and orchestra 1995, Trio for Bassoon, Oboe and Piano 1995, Sonata for Violin 1996, Sonata for Bassoon and Piano 1997, Streetcar Named Desire (opera) 1998, The Giraffes Go to Hamburg for soprano, alto, flute and piano, Three Dickinson Songs for soprano and piano, Diversions for orchestra, Violin Concerto Anne-Sophie 2001, Double Concerto for Violin, Double Bass and Orchestra 2004, Double Concerto for Violin, Viola and Orchestra 2009, Brief Encounter (opera) 2009. *Publications:* Music Face to Face 1971, Orchestra (ed.) 1977, Guide to Music 1983, No Minor Chords: My Days in Hollywood 1992. *Leisure interests:* collecting contemporary art, fencing, American folk art. *Address:* c/o Tanja Dorn, IMG Artists, Carnegie Hall Tower, 152 West 57th Street, 5th Floor, New York, NY 10019, USA (office). *Telephone:* (212) 994-3540 (office). *Fax:* (212) 994-3550 (office). *E-mail:* tdorn@imgartists.com (office). *Website:* www.imgartists .com (office); www.andre-previn.com.

PRICE, Antony, MA; British fashion designer; b. 5 March 1945, Yorks.; s. of Peter Price and Joan Price; ed Bradford Coll. of Art and Royal Coll. of Art; designer for Sterling Cooper 1968–72, for Plaza 1972–79; Chair. of own fashion co. 1979–; British Glamour Award 1989. *Leisure interests:* tropical plants, tropical ornithology, modern and classical music. *Address:* 17 Langton Street, London, SW10 0JL, England. *Telephone:* (20) 7376-7250. *Fax:* (20) 7376-4599.

PRICE, Curtis Alexander, AM, PhD, FRCM, FRNCM; American musicologist; *Principal, Royal Academy of Music;* b. 7 Sept. 1945, Springfield, Mo.; ed Southern Illinois Univ., Harvard Univ. with John Ward and Nino Pirotta; teacher, Washington Univ., St Louis 1974–81; teacher, King's Coll. London 1981, Reader 1985, Prof. 1988; Prin. RAM, London 1995–2008; Prof., Univ. of London 2000–; mem. Royal Musical Assc (Pres. 1999–2002); Trustee Musica Britannica and the Handel House Museum; Fellow, King's Coll. London; Hon. RAM; Hon. KBE 2005. *Publications include:* The Critical Decade for English Music Drama 1700–1710 1978, Music in the Restoration Theater: with a Catalogue of Instrumental Music in the Plays 1665–1713 1979, Henry Purcell and the London Stage 1984, H. Purcell: Dido and Aeneas (ed.) 1986, Italian Opera and Arson in Late Eighteenth-Century London 1989, The Impresario's Ten Commandments: Continental Recruitment for Italian Opera in London 1763–4 (with J. Milhous and R. D. Hume) 1992, Man and Music: The Early Baroque Era (ed.) 1993, Purcell Studies (ed.) 1995. *Address:* Royal Academy of Music, Marylebone Road, London, NW1 5HT, England (office). *Telephone:* (20) 7873-7373 (office). *Fax:* (20) 7873-7374 (office). *E-mail:* go@ram.ac .uk (office). *Website:* www.ram.ac.uk (office).

PRICE, Frank; American television and cinema producer and executive; b. 17 May 1930, Decatur, Ill.; s. of William Price and Winifred Price (née Moran); m. Katherine Huggins 1965; four s.; ed Michigan State Univ.; served with USN 1948–49; Writer and Story Ed., CBS-TV, New York 1951–53; with Columbia Pictures, Hollywood 1953–57, NBC-TV 1957–58; Producer, Writer, Universal Television, Calif. 1959–64, Vice-Pres. 1964–71, Sr Vice-Pres. 1971–73, Exec. Vice-Pres. 1973–74, Pres. 1974–78; Pres. Columbia Pictures 1978–79, Chair. and CEO 1979–83; Chair. and CEO MCA Motion Picture Group 1983–86, Price Entertainment 1991–; Chair. Columbia Pictures 1990–91; Dir Sony Pictures Entertainment, Savoy Pictures; Exec. Producer The Virginian 1961–64, Ironside 1965, Kojak, Six Million Dollar Man, Bionic Woman, Rockford Files, Quincy, Rich Man, Poor Man, The Tuskegee Airmen 1996; mem. Writers Guild of America; Peabody Award 1996, NAACP Image Award 1996. *Films include:* Circle of Friends 1995, The Walking Dead 1995, Mariette in Ecstasy 1996, Getting Away with Murder 1996, Texas Rangers 2001, Zeus and Roxanne 1997. *Address:* Price Entertainment Inc., 527 Spoleto Drive, Pacific Palisades, CA 90272, USA (office).

PRICE, James Gordon, BA, MD; American physician and academic; *Professor Emeritus of Medicine, University of Kansas;* b. 20 June 1926, Brush, Colo, USA; s. of John Hoover Price and Laurette (née Dodds) Price; m. Janet Alice McSween 1949; two s. two d.; ed Univ. of Colorado; intern, Denver Gen. Hosp.; pvt. practice, family medicine, Brush, Colo 1952–78; Prof. Dept of Family Practice, Univ. of Kan. 1978–93 (Chair. 1978–90), Dean, School of Medicine 1990–93, Prof. Emer. 1993–; nationally syndicated newspaper column, Your Family Physician 1973–86; Medical Ed., Curriculum Innovations 1973–93; mem. Inst. of Medicine, NAS; Pres. American Acad. of Family Physicians 1973–, American Bd of Family Practice 1980–. *Leisure interest:* computer programming. *Address:* 12205 Mohawk Road, Shawnee Mission, Leawood, KS 66209, USA (home). *Telephone:* (913) 491-3072 (home). *E-mail:* jimtad@sbcglobal.net (home).

PRICE, Leontyne; American singer (soprano); b. 10 Feb. 1927, Laurel, Miss.; d. of James A. Price and Kate Price (née Baker); m. William Warfield 1952 (divorced 1973); ed Central State Coll., Wilberforce, Ohio and Juilliard School of Music, New York; appeared as Bess (Porgy and Bess), Vienna, Berlin, Paris, London, New York 1952–54; recitalist, soloist 1954–; soloist Hollywood Bowl 1955–59, 1966; opera singer NBC-TV 1955–58, San Francisco Opera Co. 1957–59, 1960–61, Vienna Staatsoper 1958, 1959–60, 1961; recording artist RCA-Victor 1958–; appeared Covent Garden 1958–59, 1970, Chicago 1959, 1960, Milan 1960–61, 1963, 1967, Metropolitan Opera, New York 1961–62, 1963–70, 1972, Paris Opéra as Aida 1968, Metropolitan Opera as Aida 1985 (retd); numerous recordings; Fellow, American Acad. of Arts and Sciences; Trustee, International House; Hon. Vice-Chair. US Cttee of UNESCO; Hon. DMus (Howard Univ., Cen. State Coll., Ohio); Hon. DHL (Dartmouth); Hon. DH (Rust Coll., Miss.); Hon. DHumLitt (Fordham); Presidential Medal of Freedom, Order of Merit (Italy), Nat. Medal of Arts 1985, Essence Award 1991, 20 Grammy Awards for classical recordings, Nat. Endowment for the Arts Opera Award 2008.

PRICE, Michael F.; American financial executive; *Managing Partner, MFP Investors LLC;* b. 1952; m. (divorced); three s.; ed Univ. of Okla; joined Heine Securities Corpn as Research Asst 1975, sole owner, CEO 1988–96; sold co. to Franklin Resources 1996 and f. advisory co. Franklin Mutual Advisers Inc., Pres., CEO 1996–2001; f. and Man. Pnr MFP Investors LLC (investment fund) 2001–; founder and Pres. Michael F. Price Foundation; mem. Bd of Dirs Liquidnet Holdings; Sr Advisor, Michael F. Price School of Business, Univ. of Okla; Fund Action Lifetime Achievement Award 2005. *Address:* MFP Investors LLC, 51 JFK Parkway, Short Hills, NJ 07078, USA. *Telephone:* (973) 921-2201. *Fax:* (973) 921-2236. *E-mail:* mprice@mfpllc.com.

PRICE, Nicholas Raymond Leige (Nick); Zimbabwean (b. South African) professional golfer; b. 28 Jan. 1957, Durban, Natal Prov.; m. Sue Price; one s. two d.; turned professional 1977; won Asseng Invitational 1979, Canon European Masters 1980, Italian Open, S African Masters 1981, Vaals Reef Open 1982, World Series of Golf 1983, Trophée Lancôme, ICI Int. 1985, West End S Australian Open 1989, GTE Byron Nelson Classic, Canadian Open 1991, Air New Zealand/Shell Open, PGA Championships, H-E-B Texas Open 1992, The Players' Championship, Canon Greater Hartford Open, Sprint Western Open, Federal Express St Jude Classic, ICL Int., Sun City Million Dollar Challenge 1993, The Open Championship, ICL Int. Honda Classic, Southwestern Bell Colonial, Motorola Western Open, PGA Championship, Bell Canadian Open 1994, Alfred Dunhill Challenge, Hassan II Golf Trophy, Morocco, Zimbabwe Open 1995, MCI Classic 1997, Suntory Open 1999, CVS Charity Classic 2001, MasterCard Colonial 2002, CVS/pharmacy Charity Classic (unofficial event) 2006, CVS Caremark Charity Classic (unofficial event) 2009; reached No. 1 in Official World Golf Ranking mid-1990s; f. Nick Price Golf Course Design 2001, has designed courses in Fla, Dominican Repub., Ireland, South Africa and Mexico; named Amb. of Golf by Northern Ohio Golf Charities 2011; lives in Fla, USA; Sunshine Tour Order of Merit Winner 1982–83, PGA Player of the Year 1993, 1994, PGA Tour Player of the Year 1993, 1994, PGA Tour leading money winner 1993, 1994, Vardon Trophy 1993, 1997, Byron Nelson Award 1997, Payne Stewart Award 2002, inducted into World Golf Hall of Fame 2003, Bob Jones Award, USGA 2005, Old Tom Morris Award, Golf Course Supts Asscn of America 2011. *Publication:* The Swing 1997. *Leisure interests:* water skiing, tennis, fishing, flying. *Address:* c/o PGA Tour, 100 PGA TOUR Boulevard, Ponte Vedra Beach, FL 32082, USA. *Website:* www.pgatour.com/players/player .01968.html; www.nickprice.com.

PRICE, Paul Buford, Jr, BS, PhD; American physicist and academic; *Professor, Graduate School, University of California, Berkeley;* b. 8 Nov. 1932, Memphis, Tenn.; s. of the late Paul Buford Price, Sr and Eva Price (née Dupuy); m. Jo Ann Baum 1958; one s. three d.; ed Davidson Coll., Univ. of Virginia, Univ. of Bristol, Univ. of Cambridge, UK; Physicist, Gen. Electric Research Lab., New York 1960–69; Visiting Prof., Tata Inst. of Fundamental Research, Bombay, India 1965–66; Adjunct Prof. of Physics, Rensselaer Polytechnic Inst. 1967–68; Prof. of Physics, Univ. of Calif., Berkeley 1969–2001, Chair. Dept of Physics 1987–91, William H. McAdams Prof. of Physics 1990–92, Dean, Physical Sciences, Coll. of Letters and Science 1992–2001, Prof., Grad. School 2001–; Dir Space Science Lab. 1979–85; NASA Consultant on Lunar Sample Analysis Planning Team; mem. Bd of Dirs Terradex Corpn 1978–86; mem. Visiting Cttee, Bartol Research Inst. 1991–94, Advisory Cttee, Indian Inst. of Astrophysics 1993–95; Fellow and Chair, Cosmic Physics Div., American Physical Soc.; mem. NAS 1975–, mem. Space Science Bd, Sec. Physical and Math. Sciences Class of NAS 1985–88, Chair. 1988–91, mem. Steering Group on Future of Space Science (NAS) 1994–95, Polar Research Bd (NAS) 1999–2002; Regional Dir Calif. Alliance for Minority Participation 1994–2004; US Ice Core Working Group 2001–03; led a 20-person review of Uppsala Univ., Sweden 2001–02; Chair. Scientific Advisory Bd, Univ. of Vienna, Austria 2006–, Workshop on Antarctic Science Symposium 2011; Co-organizer Conf. and Proceedings of Workshop on Methane on Mars, Frascati, Italy 2009–10; Fellow, American Geophysical Union, American Astronomical Soc.; Hon. Fellow, Indian Inst. of Astrophysics 2000; Hon. mem. Int. Nuclear Track Soc.; Hon. ScD (Davidson Coll.) 1973; Distinguished Service Award, (American Nuclear Soc.) 1964, Ernest O. Lawrence Memorial Award of Atomic Energy Comm. 1971, NASA Medal for Exceptional Scientific Achievement 1973, Scientific Symposium in Honor of P.B. Price's 65th Birthday 1997, Berkeley Citation for outstanding research and leadership 2002, Price Terrace, located at 77°19'40"S, 161°18'00"E, a region of Antarctica named for P. B. Price by US Bd on Geographic Names,

Berkeley Citation, IR-100 Awards for invention of Nuclepore Filter, radon detector and radiation dosimeter). *Achievements include:* scientific inventions: nuclepore filter, fission track dating, radon detector, optical dust logger, Berkeley fluorescent spectrometer. *Publications:* Nuclear Tracks in Solids (co-author); more than 550 research papers in specialized journals. *Leisure interests:* skiing, travel, walking, reading. *Address:* Physics Department, University of California, Berkeley, 335 LeConte Hall, Berkeley, CA 94720 (office); 1056 Overlook Road, Berkeley, CA 94708, USA (home). *Telephone:* (510) 642-4982 (office); (510) 548-5206 (home). *Fax:* (510) 643-8497 (office); (510) 548-5206 (home). *E-mail:* bprice@berkeley.edu (office). *Website:* www.physics.berkeley.edu (office).

PRIDEAUX, Sir Humphrey Povah Treverbian, Kt, OBE, MA; British business executive; b. 13 Dec. 1915, London, England; s. of Walter Treverbian Prideaux and Marion Fenn Prideaux (née Arbuthnot); m. Cynthia V. Birch Reynardson 1939; four s.; ed St Aubyns, Eton Coll. and Trinity Coll., Oxford; Regular army officer 1936–53; Dir Navy, Army & Air Force Insts 1956–63, Chair. 1963–73; Chair. Lord Wandsworth Foundation 1966–92, Trustee 1963–92; Deputy Chair. Liebig's Extract of Meat Co. Ltd 1968–69, Dir 1966–69; Chair. Oxo Ltd 1968–72; Dir WH Smith & Son (Holdings) Ltd 1969, Vice-Chair. 1977–81; Dir Brooke Bond Oxo Ltd 1969–70; Chair. Brooke Bond Liebig 1972–81; Pres. London Life Asscn Ltd 1973–83, Dir 1964–88; Vice-Chair. Morland & Co. 1981–82, Chair. 1983–92; Dir Grindlays (Holdings) PLC 1982–85, Grindlays Bank PLC 1984–85; Hon. DL (Hants.). *Leisure interests:* country pursuits. *Address:* Kings Cottage, Buryfields, Odiham, Hook, Hants., RG29 1NE, England (home). *Telephone:* (1256) 703658 (home). *E-mail:* hptprideaux@aol.com (home).

PRIDIYATHORN, Devakula, BEcons, MBA; Thai government official and fmr central banker; b. 15 July 1947, Bangkok; s. of Prince Prididebyabongs Devakula and Mom Taengthai Devakula; m. Prapapan Devakula Na Ayudhya; two s. one d.; ed Wharton School, Univ. of Pennsylvania, USA, Thammasat Univ.; joined Thai Farmers Bank 1971, Dir and Sr Exec. Vice-Pres. –1990; Govt Spokesperson for Prime Minister Gen. Chatichai Choonhavan 1990–91; Deputy Minister of Commerce 1991–92; Pres. Export-Import Bank of Thailand 1993–2001; Gov. Bank of Thailand 2001–06; Minister of Finance 2006–07 (resgnd); mem. Wharton School Exec. Bd for Asia; Kt Order of The Crown Of Thailand, Kt Grand Cross Order of The White Elephant, Grand Companion Order of Chula Chom Klao; Hon. DBA (Chulalongkorn Univ.) 2002, (Mahasarakam Univ.) 2003, Hon. DEcon (Sripatum Univ.) 2003, Hon. DEcon (Univ. Thai Chamber of Commerce) 2006. *Leisure interest:* golf. *Address:* 33 Soi 6, Serivilla 7, Srinakarin Road, Nhongborn, Praves, Bangkok 10250, Thailand (home). *Telephone:* (2) 399-1599 (home). *Fax:* (2) 399-1745 (home).

PRIESTMAN, Jane, OBE, FCSD; British design management consultant; b. 7 April 1930; d. of the late Reuben Stanley Herbert and Mary Elizabeth Herbert (née Ramply); m. Arthur Martin Priestman 1954 (divorced 1986); two s.; ed Northwood Coll., Liverpool Coll. of Art; design practice 1954–75; Design Man., Gen. Man. Architecture and Design British Airports Authority 1975–86; Dir Architecture and Design British Railways Bd 1986–91; Visiting Prof., De Montfort Univ. 1997–2001; mem. London Regional Transport Design Panel 1985–88, Jaguar Styling Panel 1988–91, Percentage for Art Steering Group, Arts Council 1989–91; mem. Council of Design Council 1996–2000; Gov. Commonwealth Inst. 1987–98, Kingston Univ. 1988–96; Enabler Comm. for Architecture and the Built Environment; Hon. FRIBA, Hon. FRSA; Hon. DrDes (De Montfort) 1994, (Sheffield Hallam) 1998. *Leisure interests:* textiles, city architecture, opera, travel. *Address:* 30 Duncan Terrace, London, N1 8BS, England (home). *Telephone:* (20) 7837-4525 (home). *Fax:* (20) 7837-4525 (home). *E-mail:* jane.priestman@virgin.net.

PRIETO JIMÉNEZ, Abel Enrique; Cuban writer, academic and politician; *Minister of Culture;* b. 11 Nov. 1950, Pinar del Rio; joined Communist Party of Cuba 1978, mem. Cen. Cttee 1991–; Deputy, Nat. Ass. of People's Power 1993–; Minister of Culture 1997–; fmr Prof. of Literature, Univ. of Havana, Ed.-in-Chief and Dir Letras Cubanas, Dir Arte y Literatura, Dir Juan Marinello Cultural Centre; fmr Pres. Unión de Escritores y Artistas de Cuba; Premio Nacional de Literatura. *Publications include:* Los bitongos y los guapos 1980, Noche de sábado 1989, El vuelo del gato 1999. *Address:* Ministry of Culture, Calle 2, No 258, entre 11 y 13, Plaza de la Revolución, Vedado, 10400 Havana, Cuba (office). *Telephone:* (7) 55-2260 (office). *Fax:* (7) 66-2053 (office). *E-mail:* atencion@min.cult.cu (office). *Website:* www.min.cult.cu (office).

PRIFTI, Dritan V., BA, MPA; Albanian politician; m.; three s.; ed Univ. of Tirana, Univ. of New Mexico, John F. Kennedy School of Govt, Harvard Univ., USA; Chief of Staff to Minister of Labour and Social Affairs 1997–98; Chief of Staff to Minister of Finance 1998–99; Dir of Cabinet (Chief of Staff) to Prime Minister July–Oct. 2000; CEO Albanian Electro-Energy Corpn 2000–01; Minister of State for Energy 2001–02; Minister of the Economy, Trade and Energy 2009–10; mem. Socialist Movt for Integration (SMI), currently Deputy Chair.; mem. Kuvendi Popullor (Parl.) for Fier Region (Socialist Party) 2001–05, (SMI) 2005–; Chair. Albanian Devt Council 1998. *Address:* c/o Ministry of the Economy, Trade and Energy, Bulevardi Dëshmorët e Kombit 2, Tirana, Albania (office).

PRIKHODKO, Sergey Eduardovich; Russian diplomatist and government official; *Deputy Chairman of the Government and Head of the Government Administration;* b. 12 Jan. 1957, Moscow; m.; two d.; ed Moscow State Inst. of Int. Relations; mem. of staff, Ministry of Foreign Affairs 1980–93, including as diplomat at Soviet Embassy in Prague, Attaché and Third Sec., Office of European Socialist Countries, Soviet Foreign Ministry 1986–87, Second Sec., later First Sec., Embassy of Russia in Prague 1992–93; Head Div. of Baltic Countries, Deputy Dir Second European Dept 1993–97; Asst to Russian Pres. on Int. Problems 1997–98, Deputy Head of Admin, Russian Presidency 1998–99, concurrently Head, Dept of Admin on Int. Policy 1998; Adviser to the Pres. 2004–12; Deputy Chair. of the Govt and Head of the Govt Admin 2012–; Public Recognition Award 1999. *Leisure interests:* literature, fishing, hunting. *Address:* Office of the Government, 103274 Moscow, Krasnopresnenskaya nab. 2, Russia (office). *Telephone:* (495) 605-53-29 (office). *Fax:* (495) 605-52-43 (office). *E-mail:* duty_press@aprf.gov.ru (office). *Website:* www.government.ru (office).

PRIMAKOV, Yevgeniy Maksimovich, DEcon; Russian politician and economist; b. 29 Oct. 1929, Kiev; m. Laura V. Kharadze (died 1987); one s. one d.; ed Moscow Inst. of Oriental Studies; worked for State Comm. on Broadcasting and

Television 1953–62; mem. CPSU 1959–91; Columnist and Deputy Ed. (Asia and Africa Desk), Pravda 1962–70; Deputy Dir Inst. of World Econ. and Int. Relations, USSR (now Russian) Acad. of Sciences 1970–77, Dir 1985–, Dir Inst. of Oriental Studies 1977–85; elected to Congress of People's Deputies of the USSR 1989; mem. CPSU Cen. Cttee 1989–91; cand. mem. Politburo 1989–90; Chair. Soviet of the Union June 1989–March 1990; mem. Presidential Council 1989–90; Pres. Gorbachev's Special Envoy to the Gulf 1990–91; Dir Central Intelligence Service of USSR 1991, Foreign Intelligence Service of Russian Fed. 1991–96; Minister of Foreign Affairs 1996–98; Chair of Govt (Prime Minister) 1998–99; Chair. Exec. Council of Russia and Belarus Union 1998–99; mem. Security Council 1996–98; mem. State Duma (Parl.) 1999, Head Otechestvo faction 2000; Pres. Russian Fed. Chamber of Commerce and Industry 2001–11; Corresp. mem. USSR (now Russian) Acad. of Sciences 1974, mem. 1979, Acad.-Sec., mem. of Presidium 1988–91; specialist on Egypt and other Arab countries; Chief Ed. of and contributor to a number of collective works, including: International Conflicts 1972, The Energy Crisis in the Capitalist World 1975, Years in Large-Scale Policy 1999; Order of the Red Banner of Labour 1975, Order of Friendship of Peoples 1979, Order of the Badge of Honour 1985, Order of Merit for the Fatherland 3rd Class, Order of Merit for the Fatherland 2nd Class 1998, Order of Friendship (Tajikistan) 1999, Order of Honour 2004, Order of Yaroslav I the Wise 5th Class (Ukraine) 2004, Order of Danaker (Kyrgyzstan), Order of Friendship of Peoples (Belorussia) 2005, Order Of Dostyk 1st Class (Kazakhstan) 2007, Order of Merit for the Fatherland 1st Class 2009; Nasser Prize 1975, USSR State Prize 1980, Avicenna Prize 1983, George F. Kennan Prize 1990, Hugo Grotius Prize 2000, Lomonosov Gold Medal, Russian Acad. of Sciences 2008. *Publications include:* Egypt under Nasser (with I. P. Belyayev) 1975, The War Which Could Be Avoided 1991, Years at the Top Level of Politics 2000, Eight Months Plus 2001. *Address:* c/o Russian Federation Chamber of Commerce & Industry, 103684 Moscow, Ilyinka str. 6, Russia.

PRINCE; American musician, singer, producer and actor; b. (Prince Rogers Nelson), 7 June 1958, Minneapolis, Minn.; s. of John L. Nelson and Mattie Nelson (née Shaw); m. 1st Mayté Garcia 1996 (divorced 1998); one s. (deceased); m. 2nd Manuela Testolini Nelson; alternatively known as The Artist Formerly Known as Prince (AFKAP) and Symbol; fmr lead singer, Prince and The Revolution; singer with own backing group the New Power Generation 1991–; numerous tours, concerts; own recording studio and record label, Paisley Park; three Grammy awards 1985, Nat. Asscn for the Advancement of Colored People Special Achievement Award 1997, Q Award for Best Songwriter 1990, BRIT Awards for Best International Male Artist 1992, 1993, 1995, 1996, BET Award for Best Male R&B Artist 2006, Grammy Award for Best Male R&B Vocal Performance (for Future Baby Mama) 2008. *Recordings include:* albums: For You 1978, Prince 1979, Dirty Mind 1980, Controversy 1981, 1999 1982, Purple Rain (Acad. Award for Best Original Score, BRIT Award for Best Soundtrack 1985) 1984, Around the World in a Day (Best Soul/Rhythm and Blues Album of the Year, Down Beat Readers' Poll) 1985, Parade 1986, Sign O' The Times 1987, Lovesexy 1988, Batman (film soundtrack) (BRIT Award for Best Soundtrack 1990) 1989, Graffiti Bridge (film soundtrack) 1990, Diamonds and Pearls 1991, (symbol as title) 1992, Come 1994, The Black Album (recorded 1987) 1994, The Gold Experience 1995, Emancipation 1996, Chaos and Disorder 1996, New Power Soul 1998, Rave Un2 The Joy Fantastic 1999, The Rainbow Children 2002, One Nite Alone – Live! 2002, Musicology 2004, 3121 2006, Planet Earth 2007, LotusFlow3r 2009, 20Ten 2010. *Films include:* Purple Rain 1984, Under the Cherry Moon 1986, Sign O' The Times 1987, Graffiti Bridge 1990. *Address:* Paisley Park Enterprises, 7801 Audoban Road, Chanhassen, MN 55317, USA (office). *Website:* www.npgmusicclub.com (office).

PRINCE, Charles (Chuck) O., III, MA, LLM; American banker; ed Univ. of Southern California, Georgetown Univ.; began career as attorney US Steel Corpn 1975–79; joined Commercial Credit Co. (later renamed Citigroup Inc.) 1979, Sr Vice-Pres. and Gen. Counsel 1983–86, Exec. Vice-Pres. 1996–2000, Chief Admin. Officer 2000–01, COO 2001–02, CEO and Dir Citigroup Inc. 2003–07, Chair. and CEO 2006–07; Chair. and CEO Global Corp. and Investment Bank 2002–03; mem. Council on Foreign Relations; mem. Bd of Dirs United Negro Coll. Fund, Teachers' Coll., Columbia Univ., New York; fmr mem. Bd of Dirs New York Urban League; mem. various bar asscns and professional asscns. *Address:* c/o Citigroup Inc., 399 Park Avenue, New York, NY 10043, USA (office).

PRINCE, Harold (Hal) Smith, LittD; American theatre director; b. 30 Jan. 1928, New York; s. of Milton A. Prince and Blanche Prince (née Stern); m. Judith Chaplin 1962; one s. one d.; ed Emerson Coll.; co-produced Pajama Game 1954–56 (Antoinette Perry Award), Damn Yankees 1955–57 (Antoinette Perry Award), New Girl in Town 1957–58, West Side Story 1957–59, Fiorello! 1959–61 (Antoinette Perry Award, Pulitzer Prize), Tenderloin 1960–61, A Call on Kuprin 1961, They Might Be Giants 1961, Side by Side by Sondheim 1976; produced Take Her, She's Mine 1961–62, A Funny thing Happened on the Way to the Forum 1962–64 (Antoinette Perry Award), Fiddler on the Roof 1964–72 (Antoinette Perry Award), Poor Bitos 1964, Flora the Red Menace 1965; dir, producer She Loves Me! 1963–64, London 1964, Superman 1966, Cabaret 1966–69 (Antoinette Perry Award), London 1968, Zorba 1968–69, Company 1970–72 (Antoinette Perry Award), London 1972, A Little Night Music 1973–74 (Antoinette Perry Award) (London 1975), Pacific Overtures 1976; co-dir, producer Follies 1971–72; co-producer, dir Candide 1974–75, Merrily We Roll Along 1981; dir A Family Affair 1962, Baker Street 1965, Great God Brown 1972–73, The Visit 1973–74, Love for Love 1974–75, On the Twentieth Century 1978, Evita, London 1978, Broadway 1979, Los Angeles 1980, Chicago 1980, Australia 1980, Vienna 1981, Mexico City 1981, Sweeney Todd, the Demon Barber of Fleet Street 1979–80, London 1980, A Doll's Life 1982, Diamonds 1984, Grind 1985, The Phantom of the Opera (Antoinette Perry Award for Best Dir 1988) 1986, Play Memory, End of the World, Roza 1987, Grandchild of Kings (The O'Casey Project) (author and dir) 1992, Kiss of the Spider Woman (Toronto, London) 1992, (New York, Vienna) 1993, Show Boat (Toronto) 1993, (New York) 1994, (nat. tour) 1996, Candide 1997, Parade 1998; mem. Council, Nat. Endowment of the Arts, League of New York Theatres; Critics Circle awards, Best Music Award, Evening Standard; Commonwealth Award 1982; John F. Kennedy Center Awards 1994. *Films include:* (co-producer) The Pajama Game 1957, Damn Yankees 1958; (dir) Something for Everyone 1970, A Little Night Music 1978. *Operas:* Ashmedai 1976, Silverlake 1980, Don Giovanni 1989 (New York City Opera); Madame Butterfly 1982; Candide 1982; Willie Stark

1982 (Houston Opera Co.); Turandot 1983 (Vienna Staatsoper); Faust 1990, 1991 (Metropolitan Opera), La Fanciulla del West 1991 (Chicago Lyric Opera, San Francisco Opera). *Publication:* Contradictions (autobiography) 1974. *Address:* Suite 1009, 10 Rockefeller Plaza, New York, NY 10020, USA.

PRINCE, Richard; American painter and photographer; b. 6 Aug. 1949, Panama Canal Zone; began career at Time-Life magazine; trained as a figure painter, began creating collages containing photographs 1975. *Works include:* Untitled (Cigarettes) 1978–79, Untitled (Cowboy) 1980–84, Entertainers 1982–83, Spiritual America 1983, Jokes 1986, My Usual Procedure 1988, The Wrong Joke 1989, Untitled (Hoods) 1989, Girlfriends 1992, Second House, Debutante Nurse 2004. *Publications:* numerous articles and reviews in art magazines. *Address:* c/o Gladstone Gallery, 515 West 24th Street, New York, NY 10011, USA (office). *Telephone:* (212) 206-9300 (office). *Fax:* (212) 206-9301 (office). *E-mail:* richardprin@aol.com (office). *Website:* www.richardprinceart.com (office).

PRINCIPI, Anthony J., BS, JD; American business executive, fmr government official and fmr naval officer; b. 16 April 1944, New York City; m. Elizabeth Ann Ahlering 1971; three s.; ed US Naval Acad., Seton Hall Univ.; service with USN in Viet Nam, Chief Defense Counsel, Judge Advocate Gen. Corps, San Diego, Staff Counsel, Commdr US Pacific Fleet; Legis. Counsel, Dept of the Navy 1980; Deputy Sec. of Veterans' Affairs, Acting Sec. 1992, Sec. of Veterans' Affairs 2001–04; Chair. Fed. Quality Inst. 1991; Chief Counsel and Staff Dir, US Senate Cttee on Armed Services 1993; Chair. Comm. on Service Mems and Veterans Transition Assistance; COO Lockheed Martin Integrated Solutions 1995–2001; Principal, Principi Group, LLC; Co-Founder, Pres. and Chair. Fed. Network; Pres. QTC Medical Services (now QTC Management Inc.) 1999–2001, then Exec. Chair.; Sr Vice-Pres. for Government Relations, Pfizer, Inc. 2005–10; Chair. 2005 Defense Base Closure and Realignment Comm. 2005; mem. Bd of Dirs Engility Holdings, Inc., Mutual of Omaha, A.T. Kearney PSDS, Cleveland BioLabs, Lung Cancer Alliance, Wounded Warrior Project; Bronze Star, Vietnamese Cross of Gallantry, Navy Combat Action Medal and other decorations. *Address:* Principi Group, 1850 M Street, NW, Suite 840, Washington, DC 20036, USA (office).

PRINGLE, Dame Anne Fyfe, DCMG, CMG, MA, FRSA; British diplomatist; b. 13 Jan. 1955, Glasgow, Scotland; d. of George Grant Pringle and Margaret Fyfe; m. Bleddyn Glynne Phillips 1987; ed Univ. of St Andrews; joined FCO 1977, Third Sec., Moscow 1980–83, Vice-Consul, San Francisco 1983–85, Brussels 1986–87, First Sec., FCO 1987–91, Brussels 1991–94, African Security Coordination Dept, FCO 1994–96, Head of Common Foreign and Security Policy Dept 1996–98, Head of Eastern Dept 1998–2001, Amb. to Czech Repub. 2001–04, Dir Directorate for Strategy and Information 2004–07, Amb. to Russian Fed. 2008–11; Public Appointments Assessor 2012–; Dir (non-exec.) Ashmore Group PLC 2013–; mem. Bd VSO 1996–97, Czech/Slovak Asscn, Court of Univ. of St Andrews 2012–; Dr hc (Heriot-Watt) 2010. *Address:* Foreign and Commonwealth Office, King Charles Street, London, SW1A 2AH, England (office). *Telephone:* (20) 7008-1500 (office). *E-mail:* webmaster@fco.gov.uk (office). *Website:* www.gov.uk/government/ organisations/foreign-commonwealth-office (office).

PRINGLE, James Robert Henry, MA; British economist and journalist; *Editor-in-Chief, Central Banking Publications Ltd;* b. 27 Aug. 1939, Surrey; s. of John Pringle and Jacqueline (née Berry) Pringle; m. 1st Rita Schuchard 1966 (divorced 1998); m. 2nd Ikuko Hiroe 2003; ed King's School, Canterbury, King's Coll., Cambridge and London School of Econs; Asst to Ed., then Asst Ed. The Banker, London 1963–67, Ed. 1972–79; mem. editorial staff The Economist, London 1968; Asst Dir, later Deputy Dir Cttee on Invisible Exports 1969–72; Exec. Dir Group of Thirty, Consultative Group on Int. Econ. and Monetary Affairs, New York 1979–86; Sr Fellow, World Inst. for Devt Econs Research of the UN Univ. 1986–89; Sr Research Fellow, David Hume Inst., Edinburgh 1989–91; Dir Graham Bannock and Pnrs 1989–97; Ed.-in-Chief Central Banking Publications Ltd 1990–; fmr Man. Dir Public Policy, The World Gold Council. *Publications:* Banking in Britain 1973, The Growth Merchants 1977, The Central Banks (co-author) 1994, International Financial Institutions 1998. *Leisure interests:* classical music, the theatre. *Address:* 9 Northwood Lodge, Oakhill Park, London, NW3 7LL (home); Central Banking Publications, Tavistock House, Tavistock Square, London, WC1H 9JZ, England (office). *Telephone:* (20) 7388-0006 (office); (20) 7786-4721 (home). *Fax:* (20) 7388-9040 (office). *E-mail:* info@centralbanking.co.uk (office). *Website:* www.centralbanking.co.uk (office).

PRINGUET, Pierre; French business executive; *CEO, Pernod Ricard;* b. 1950; m.; two c.; ed École Polytechnique and École des Mines, Paris; began career with French civil service, adviser to Govt Minister Michel Rocard 1981–85, responsible for farming and food-processing industries at Ministry of Agric. 1985–87; joined Pernod Ricard as Devt Dir 1987, positions include Man. Dir of Soc. pour l'Exportation des Grandes Marques 1987–96, Chair. and CEO Pernod Ricard Europe 1997–2000, together with Richard Burrows at corp. HQ served as one of Pernod Ricard's two jt Man. Dirs 2000–05, mem. Bd of Dirs 2004–, led acquisition of Allied Domecq 2005, sole Man. Dir Dec. 2005–08, led acquisition of Vin & Sprit and its vodka brand Absolut 2008, CEO Pernod Ricard 2008–; Chair. Comité Sully (promotes French food-processing industry); Chevalier, Ordre nat. du Mérite; Officier du Mérite agricole. *Leisure interests:* skiing, golf, opera. *Address:* Pernod Ricard, 12 place des Etats-Unis, 75783 Paris Cedex 16, France (office). *Telephone:* 1-41-00-41-00 (office). *E-mail:* info@pernod-ricard.com (office). *Website:* www .pernod-ricard.com (office).

PRINZ, Birgit; German professional footballer; b. 25 Oct. 1977, Frankfurt am Main; centre forward; trained to become a physiotherapist; youth player, SV Dörnigheim FC 1986–88, FC Hochstadt 1988–92; sr player for FSV Frankfurt 1992–98 (won Bundesliga 1995, 1998), 1. FFC Frankfurt 1998–2002, 2002– (won Bundesliga 1999, 2001, 2002, 2003, 2005, German Cup 2000, 2001, 2002, UEFA Cup 2002), Carolina Courage (Women's United Soccer Asscn, won Founders Cup 2003 (Most Valuable Player in the final), won WUSA Championship 2003) 2002; mem. German nat. team 1994–, represented Germany at World Cup 1995 (silver medal), 2003 (gold medal), European Championship 1995, 1997, 1999, 2001 (won 1995, 1997, 2001), Olympic Games 2000 (bronze medal), 2004 (bronze medal), 2008, 198 int. caps, 125 goals; became all-time leading scorer in FIFA Women's World Cup history with 13 career goals in World Cup play 17 Sept. 2007, extended this record to 14 career goals in final; mem. Deutschen Olympischen Sportbund

2006–; Player of the Match, UEFA Cup 2002, German Female Player of the Year 2001, 2002, 2003, 2004, 2005, 2006, 2007, 2008, FIFA Female Player of the Year 2003, 2004, 2005. *Leisure interests:* badminton, squash, walking her dog. *Address:* c/o 1. FFC Frankfurt, Stadion am Brentanobad, Rödelheimer Parkweg 39, 60489 Frankfurt am Main, Germany. *Website:* www.ffc-frankfurt.de; www.birgitprinz .de.

PRIOR, Baron (Life Peer), cr. 1987, of Brampton in the County of Suffolk; **James Michael Leathes Prior,** PC; British politician and farmer; b. 11 Oct. 1927, Norwich; s. of the late C. B. L. Prior and A. S. M. Prior; m. Jane P. G. Lywood 1954; three s. one d.; ed Charterhouse and Pembroke Coll., Cambridge; MP for Lowestoft 1959–83, for Waveney 1983–87; Parl. Pvt. Sec. to Pres. of Bd of Trade 1963, to Minister of Power 1963–64, to Rt Hon. Edward Heath 1965–70; Vice-Chair. Conservative Party 1965, 1972–74; Minister of Agric., Fisheries and Food 1970–72, Lord Pres. of Council 1972–74; Shadow Spokesman on Home Affairs March–June 1974, on Employment June 1974–79; Sec. of State for Employment 1979–81, for Northern Ireland 1981–84; Chair. GEC 1984–98; Dir Barclays PLC 1984–89, J. Sainsbury PLC 1984–92, United Biscuits 1974–79, 1984–94; mem. Tenneco European Advisory Council 1986–97, AIG Advisory Council; Dir Arab-British Chamber of Commerce; Chair. Royal Veterinary Coll. –1998; Chancellor Anglia Polytechnic Univ. 1992–99; Deputy Chair. MSI Cellular Investments BV 1999–2005, Ascot Underwriting Ltd 2001–06. *Publication:* A Balance of Power 1986. *Leisure interests:* cricket, tennis, golf, gardening. *Address:* House of Lords, Westminster, London, SW1A 0PW (office); Old Hall, Brampton, Beccles, Suffolk NR34 8EE, England (home). *Telephone:* (1502) 575278 (home).

PRIORY, Richard B., MSc; American energy executive; b. 1946, Lakehurst, NJ; m. Joan Priory; one s., one d.; ed West Virginia Univ. Inst. of Tech., Princeton Univ., Univ. of Michigan; registered professional engineer in NC and SC; design and product engineer, Union Carbide Corpn 1969–72; Asst Prof. of Structural Eng, Univ. of NC at Charlotte 1973–76; joined Duke Power Corpn as design engineer 1976, various positions including Vice-Pres. Design Eng 1984–91, Exec. Vice-Pres. Power Generation Group 1991–94, Pres. and COO 1994–97, Chair. and CEO 1997–2003 (retd); fmr Dir Dana Corpn; mem. Bd Edison Electric Inst., Asscn of Edison Illuminating Cos; mem. NC Govs Business Council of Man. and Devt, The Conf. Bd, The Business Roundtable, Pres's Advisory Group, US Chamber of Commerce, Business Council; fmr Chair. Inst. of Nuclear Power Operations; Chair. Charlotte Research Inst. and Foundation Dir Univ. of NC at Charlotte; mem. Nat. Acad. of Eng 1993–; Hon. DSc (West Virginia Univ. Inst. of Tech.); Distinguished Service Award, Charlotte Engineers Club 1998, Alumnus of the Year Award, WV Univ. Inst. of Tech. 1998, Ellis Island Medal of Honor 1999. *Address:* c/o Charlotte Research Institute, 9201 University City Blvd, Charlotte, NC 28223-0001, USA (office).

PRITCHARD, David E., PhD; American physicist, academic and education consultant; *Cecil and Ida Green Professor of Physics, Massachusetts Institute of Technology;* b. 15 Oct. 1941, New York, NY; s. of Edward M. Pritchard and Blanche M. Allen Pritchard; m. Andrea Hasler Pritchard; two s.; Postdoctoral Fellow, MIT, Cambridge, Mass 1968, Instructor 1968–70, Asst Prof. 1970–75, Assoc. Prof. 1975–80, Cecil and Ida Green Prof. of Physics 1980–; Div. Assoc. Ed. Physics Review Letters 1983–88; Distinguished Traveling Lecturer, LSTG/American Physical Soc. 1991–93; f. Effective Educational Technologies (online educ. co.); mem. NAS; Fellow, AAAS, American Physical Soc., Optical Soc. of America, American Acad. of Arts and Sciences; Broida Prize, American Physical Soc. 1991, Arthur L. Schawlow Prize, American Physical Soc. 2003, Max Born Award Optical Soc. of America 2004, IUPAP Precision Measurements Medal and numerous other awards and honours. *Achievements:* mentored four Nobel Prize winners and four Nat. Thesis Award winners. *Publications:* numerous scientific papers, articles and contribs to books. *Leisure interests:* piano playing, sailing. *Address:* Department of Physics, Bldg 26-241, Massachusetts Institute of Technology, 77 Massachusetts Avenue, Cambridge, MA 02139 (office); 88 Washington Avenue, Cambridge, MA 02140, USA (home). *Telephone:* (617) 253-6812 (office). *Fax:* (617) 253-4876 (office). *E-mail:* dpritch@mit.edu (office). *Website:* web.mit.edu/physics/people/faculty/ pritchard_david.html (office); www.relate.mit.edu.

PRITZKER, Penny S., BA, MBA, JD; American lawyer and business executive; *Secretary of Commerce;* b. 2 May 1959, Chicago; d. of Donald N. Pritzker and Sue Ann Pritzker (neé Sandel); m. Bryan Traubert 1988; one s. one d.; ed Harvard and Stanford Univs; fmr Chair. Superior Bank (now defunct); Chair. Classic Residence by Hyatt 1987–, TransUnion LLC (credit reporting firm) 2005–; Pres. Pritzker Realty Group 1990–; Pnr, Pritzker & Pritzker 1987–; Sec. of Commerce 2013–; mem. Bd of Dirs William Wrigley Jr Co.; fmr Chair. Chicago Museum of Contemporary Art; mem. Women's Issues Network 1991–, The Chicago Network 1992–, Int. Women's Forum, Council on Foreign Relations, Econ. Recovery Advisory Bd 2009–; mem. Harvard Bd of Overseers 2002–; served as Nat. Finance Chair for Barack Obama's presidential campaign 2008; ranked by Forbes magazine amongst 100 Most Powerful Women (89th) 2005, (82nd) 2009. *Leisure interests:* competing in marathons and recreational ski races. *Address:* Department of Commerce, 1401 Constitution Avenue, NW, Washington, DC 20230 (office); Trans Union LLC, 555 West Adams Street, 6th Floor, Chicago, IL 60661-3614, USA (office). *Telephone:* (202) 482-2000 (Washington) (office); (312) 258-1717 (Chicago) (office). *E-mail:* thesec@doc.gov (office). *Website:* www.commerce.gov (office); www.transunion.com (office).

PRITZKER, Thomas J., MBA, JD; American business executive; *Executive Chairman, Hyatt Hotels Corporation;* b. 6 June 1950; s. of the late Jay A. Pritzker and Marian Pritzker; m.; four s.; ed Claremont McKenna Coll., Univ. of Chicago; Exec. Chair. Hyatt Hotels Corpn, Chair. and CEO The Pritzker Organization; Chair. Marmon Group; Chair., Man. Dir and Co-founder Bay City Capital; Co-founder First Health Group Corpn, Chair. 1990–2001, mem. Bd of Dirs 1985–86, 1990–2002; Founder Triton Container; Founding Gen. Pnr, GKH; Dir Pritzker Philanthropic Fund, Royal Caribbean Cruise Lines; mem. Bd of Trustees, Univ. of Chicago; mem. Interdisciplinary Biosciences Advisory Cttee (Bio-X program), Stanford Univ. *Address:* Hyatt Hotels Corporation, 71 South Wacker Drive, Suite 4700, Chicago, IL 60606, USA (office). *Telephone:* (312) 750-1234 (office). *Fax:* (312) 750-8550 (office). *Website:* www.hyatt.com (office).

PRIX, Wolf D.; Austrian architect and academic; *Design Principal and CEO, Coop Himmelb(l)au;* b. 13 Dec. 1942, Vienna; ed Tech. Univ., Vienna, Architectural Asscn, London, UK, Southern California Inst. of Architecture, USA; Co-founder (with Helmut Swiczinsky and Michael Holzer) Coop Himmelb(l)au 1968, now Design Prin. and CEO; Prof. of Architecture, Univ. of Applied Arts, Vienna 1993–, Head, Inst. for Architecture, Head, Studio Prix and Vice-Rector, Univ. of Applied Arts 2003–; Visiting Prof., Architectural Asscn, London 1984, Harvard Univ., USA 1990; Adjunct Prof., Southern Calif. Inst. of Architecture, LA 1985–95; Faculty mem. Columbia Univ., New York 1998–; Harvey Perloff Prof., UCLA 1999, Adjunct Prof. 2001; mem. Architectural Council, Fed. Ministry of Science, Research and the Arts 1995–97; mem. Austrian Art Senate, European Acad. of Sciences and Arts, Advisory Cttee for Building Culture, Architectural Asscn of Austria, Architectural Union Santa Clara, Cuba, Architectural Asscn of Italy, Union of German Architects (BDA); Int. FRIBA 2006, AIA; Hon. mem. League of German Architects 1989, Hon. FAIA 2006; Officier des Arts et des Lettres 2002; Dr hc (Universidad de Palermo, Buenos Aires) 2001; numerous awards including Berlin Prize for Building Art 1982, Austrian Architectural Asscn (AAA) Award 1985, PA Award 1991, European Industrial Architecture Award 1992, Erich-Schelling-Architecture Prize 1992, Tau Sigma Delta Award 1993, Grosser Österreichischer Staatspreis 1999, Gold Medal for Merits to the Fed. State of Vienna 2002, Annie Spink Award for Excellence in Architectural Education 2004, Jencks Award: Visions Built 2008. *Architectural works include:* Rooftop Remodelling Falkestrasse (City of Vienna Award for Architecture 1989) 1983–88, Funder Factory 3 (State of Carinthia Award for Superior Architecture 1989, AAA Award 1990) 1988–89, Los Angeles Art Park (PA Award 1989), Open House (PA Award 1990), Groninger Museum (Dutch Nat. Steel Prize 1992) 1993–94, Seibersdorf Office and Research Centre (AAA Prize 1996) 1993–95, UFA Cinema Centre, Dresden (Neuer Sächsicher Kunstverein Prize 1996, German Architecture Prize 1999, Concrete Architectural Prize 1999, European Steel Design Award 2001) 1993–98, SEG Apt Tower (AAA Award 1999) 1994–98, SEG Remise (Austrian Cement Industry Award 2001) 1994–2000, Wassertum Hainburg (Anerkennungspreis für Architektur des Landes Niederösterreich 2002) 1999, Akron Art Museum (American Architecture Award 2005) 2001–07, Busan Cinema Complex, S Korea 2005–11, Acad. of Fine Arts, Munich 1992, 2002–05, Space of Contemporary Artistic Creation, Cordoba, Spain 2005, The Great Egyptian Museum, Cairo, Egypt (Int. Architecture Award 2007) 2002, BMW Welt (RIBA European Award 2008, Preis des Deutschen Stahlbaues 2008, World Architecture Festival Award: Production, Wallpaper Design Award 2009: Best New Public Building, Detail Prize 2009 – Innovation Steel) 2001–07; works in progress: Musée des Confluences, Lyon, France 2001–(13), European Central Bank, Frankfurt, Germany 2014, Busan Cinema Center 2011, House of Music, Aalborg, Denmark, Museum of Contemporary Art & Planning Exhbn, Shenzhen, China 2007–10, Dalian Int. Conf. Centre, China 2008–12, Cloud Roof, Riva del Garda, Italy (2014). *Publications include:* Coop Himmelb(l)au – Sie leben in Wien 1975, Coop Himmelb(l)au: Architecture is Now 1983; The Vienna Trilogy and One Cinema 1999, Blue Universe: Architectural Manifestos by Coop Himmelb(l)au 2002, Get Off of My Cloud 2005, Dynamic Forces 2007, Coop Himmelb(l)au: Beyond the Blue 2007, I Maestri dell'Architettura: Coop Himmelb(l)au 2011, Coop Himmelb(l)au Complete Works 1968–2010 (ed. Peter Gössel) 2010, Himmelblau no es ningún color – Wolf D. Prix, Coop Jimmelb(l)au (ed. Thomas Kramer) 2010, Coop Himmelb(l)au: Pavillon 21 MINI Opera Space 2010, Coop Himmelb(l)au: HS#9, Central Los Angeles Area High School #9 for the Visual and Performing Arts 2010. *Address:* Coop Himmelb(l)au, Wolf D. Prix & Partner ZT GmbH, Spengergasse 37, 1050 Vienna, Austria (office). *Telephone:* (1) 546-60-0 (office). *Fax:* (1) 546-60-600 (office). *E-mail:* office@coop-himmelblau.at (office). *Website:* www.coop -himmelblau.at (office).

PRLIĆ, Jadranko, DSc; Bosnia and Herzegovina politician and academic; b. 10 June 1959, Djakovo; m. Ankica Prlić; two d.; ed Univs of Mostar and Sarajevo; worked as a journalist; joined teaching staff, Univ. of Mostar 1987, Prof. Emer. 1999–; Mayor of Mostar 1987–88; fmr Gen. Man. Apro-Mostar agricultural enterprise; Vice-Pres. Govt of Bosnia and Herzegovina 1989–91; Deputy Prime Minister and Minister of Defence following signing of Washington (1994) and Dayton (1995) Agreements; mem. Parl. of Bosnia and Herzegovina and Minister of Foreign Affairs 1996–2001; mem. Council of Ministers 2001–03; Deputy Minister of Foreign Trade and Econ. Relations 2001–03; Founder and Pres. European Movt in Bosnia and Herzegovina; fmr IMF Gov. for Bosnia and Herzegovina; Pres. Pro-European People's Party; indicted by Int. Criminal Tribunal for the Fmr Yugoslavia for crimes against humanity and war crimes against the non-Croat population 2005, surrendered voluntarily to Tribunal. *Publications:* Policy of Fluctuating Foreign Exchange Rates 1990, Imperfect Peace 1998, Fuga Della Storia 2000, Return to Europe 2002, Unfinished Game 2002; numerous articles in field of int. economy, particularly finance and political issues. *Leisure interests:* tennis, soccer, econ. and political literature, etc. *Address:* Srosmeyorova 6, 71000 Sarajevo (office); Grbavička 21C, 71000 Sarajevo, Bosnia and Herzegovina. *Telephone:* (33) 213001 (home). *Fax:* (33) 679275 (office). *E-mail:* jprlic@bih.net .ba (office). *Website:* www.jprlic.ba (home).

PRODI, Romano, LLB; Italian academic, politician and UN official; *Special Envoy of the Secretary-General for the Sahel, United Nations;* b. 9 Aug. 1939, Scandiano; s. of Mario Prodi and Enrica Prodi; m. Flavia Franzoni; two s.; ed Catholic Univ. of Milan, London School of Econs; Prof. of Econs and Industrial Policy, Univ. of Bologna 1971–99, Prof. of Industrial Org. and Policy, 1990–93; Minister of Industry 1978–79; Chair. Scientific Cttee Econ. Research Inst. Nomisma, Bologna 1981–95; Chair. Istituto per la Ricostruzione Industriale (IRI) 1982–89, 1993–94; Founder l'Ulivo (The Olive Tree coalition of centre-left parties) 1995–2007 (evolved into Partito Democratico 2007), Pres. Partito Democratico 2007–08; Pres. Council of Ministers (Prime Minister) 1996–98; Pres. European Comm. 1999–2004; Prime Minister of Italy 2006–08; apptd Jt Chair. UN–African Union Peacekeeping Panel 2008; Special Envoy of the Sec.-Gen. for the Sahel, UN 2012–; unsuccessful cand. in Italian presidential election 2013; mem. Club de Madrid; mem. Asscn di cultura e politica, Il Mulino, Bologna, Asscn Italiana degli Economisti, Rome; Hon. mem. Real Academia de Ciencias Morales y Políticas, Madrid, Hon. Fellow, LSE; Knight Grand Cross, Order of Merit (Italy), 1993, Knight Grand Cross, Order of Merit (Poland) 1997, Knight Grand Cross, Order of the Star of Romania, Order of the Rising Sun, Grand Cordon

2012; numerous hon. degrees. *Publications include:* author of numerous scientific publs with particular reference to questions of European industrial policies, public enterprises in Italy and comparative analysis of econ. systems. *Address:* Office of the Secretary-General, United Nations, New York, NY 10017, USA (office). *Telephone:* (212) 963-1234 (office). *Fax:* (212) 963-4879 (office). *Website:* www.un .org/sg (office).

PROFUMO, Alessandro; Italian banking executive; *Chairman, Banca Monte dei Paschi di Siena SpA;* b. 17 Feb. 1957, Genoa; m. Sabina Ratti; ed Luigi Bocconi Univ., Milan; commercial and exec. positions Banco Lariano 1977–87; financial consultant, McKinsey & Co. 1987; marketing consultant, Bain, Cuneao & Associati 1988–91; Gen. Man. Banking and Parabanking, Riunione Adriatica di Sicurtà (RAS) 1991–94; Deputy Gen. Man. Planning and Group Control, Credito Italiano SpA 1994–95, Chief Gen. Man. 1995–96, CEO 1997–99, Man. Dir and CEO UniCredit Group 1997–2010 (resgnd); Chair. Supervisory Bd Bank Pekao SA –2005, Unicredit Bank AG (Bayerische Hypo- und Vereinsbank AG) 2005–09, UniCredit Bank Austria AG (Bank Austria Creditanstalt) 2006–11; Deputy Chair. UniCredit Banca Mobiliare (UBM); Chair. Banca Monte dei Paschi di Siena SpA 2012–; mem. Bd of Dirs and Exec. Cttee Asscn Bancaria Italiana; Pres. European Banking Fed., Brussels; mem. Supervisory Bd Deutsche Boerse AG 2004–07, Sberbank 2011–; mem. European Financial Services Round Table, London, Steering Cttee of The Group of Thirty, New York, Italian Group of the Trilateral Comm., Investment Advisory Council for Turkey, Istanbul, Man. Cttee Harvard Business School European Advisory Bd, Boston, Asscn for the Devt and Study of Banks and the Stock Exchange, Exec. Bd of AIRC (Italian Asscn for Cancer Research), Bd of Arnaldo Pomodoro Foundation, Bd Teatro alla Scala Foundation; Cavaliere al Merito del Lavoro 2004. *Publications include:* Plus Valori (with Giovanni Moro) (co-eds Baldini & Castoldi) 2003; numerous articles and studies. *Address:* Banca Monte dei Paschi di Siena S.p.A., Piazza Salimbeni, 3 53100 Siena, Italy (office). *Telephone:* (02) 94111 (office). *E-mail:* info@banca.mps .it (office). *Website:* www.english.mps.it (office).

PROGLIO, Henri; French business executive; *Chairman and CEO, EDF Group;* b. 29 June 1949, Antibes; ed École des Hautes Études Commerciales, Paris; began career with Compagnie Générale des Eaux 1972, Chair. and CEO of waste man. and transportation subsidiary 1990–91, Sr Exec. 1991–90, CEO Vivendi Water, Chair. Générale des Eaux and Sr Exec. Vice-Pres. Vivendi 1999–2000, Chair. (non-exec.) Veolia Environnement (fmrly Vivendi Environnement) 2000–10, CEO 2003–09; Dir (non-exec.) EDF Group 2004–, Chair. and CEO 2009–; Dir (non-exec.) CNP Assurances, Dassault Aviation, Natixis; mem. Exec. Cttee Vinci, Elior, Fomento de Construcciones y Contratas, Madrid; Commdr, Ordre nat. du Mérite, Légion d'honneur. *Address:* EDF Group, 22–30 avenue de Wagram, 75382 Paris, Cedex 8, France (office). *Telephone:* 1-40-42-22-22 (office). *Fax:* 1-40-42-79-40 (office). *E-mail:* info@edf.fr (office). *Website:* www.edf.fr (office).

PROKEŠ, Jozef, DSc; Slovak politician; b. 12 June 1950, Nitra; s. of Jozef Prokeš and Elena Manicová; m. 1979; one s. one d.; ed Komenský Univ., Bratislava; research student with Inst. of Physics, Slovak Acad. of Sciences, Bratislava 1973–82; worked for Heavy Current Electrotechnical Works, Čab 1982–85; research worker Inst. of Measurements, Slovak Acad. of Sciences, Bratislava 1985–89; co-f. Forum of Co-ordinating Cttees of Workers in Slovakia 1989; Chair. Independent Trade Unions 1990; Chair. Trade Union of Research Workers of Slovak Acad. of Sciences 1990; Deputy to Slovak Nat. Council 1990–92; Chair. Slovak Nat. Party (SNP) 1991–92, Hon. Chair. 1992–; Vice-Pres. Slovak Nat. Council 1992–93; Deputy Premier of Slovak Govt 1993–94; Deputy to Nat. Council 1994–2003; Vice-Chair. Foreign Cttee of Nat. Council 1994–98; Mayor of Nitra 1998–2002, unsuccessful cand. 2006; Head, Slovak Del. to CSCE 1993–94; mem. Slovak del. to WEU 1995. *Address:* c/o National Council of the Slovak Republic, Námestie Alexandra Dubčeka 1, 812 80 Bratislava 1, Slovakia. *E-mail:* info@nrsr .sk.

PROKHOROV, Mikhail Dmitriyevich; Russian business executive and politician; *Founder, ONEXIM Group;* b. 3 May 1965, Moscow; s. of the late Dmitry Prokhorov and Tamara Prokhorova; brother of Irina Prokhorova; ed Moscow Finance Inst. (now the Finance Acad. under the Govt of the Russian Fed.); Head of Man. Bd Dept, Int. Bank for Econ. Co-operation 1989–92; Chair. International Finance Co. (jt stock commercial bank) 1992–93; Chair. ONEXIM Bank 1993–, Chair. and Pres. 1998–2000, Pres. ONEXIM Group 2007–11; Pres. Rosbank (jt stock commercial bank) 2000–01; Gen. Dir and Chair. MMC Norilsk Nickel 2001–07, mem. Bd of Dirs June–Dec. 2008; Chair. OJSC Polyus Gold 2006, CEO 2010–11; Chair. JSCB IFC Bank 2010, Soglasiye Insurance Co. LLC 2010–; Prin. Owner, New Jersey Nets (professional basketball team) and shareholder of Barclays Center (team's arena in Brooklyn, NY) 2010–; mem. Bd of Dirs JSC Int. Airport Sheremetyevo 2009; f. Cultural Initiatives Charitable Foundation (Mikhail Prokhorov Foundation) 2004; Pres. Russian Biathlon Union 2008–; Amb. for Peace and Sport (Monaco-based int. org.) 2011–; Leader of Right Cause party June–Sept. 2011 (forced to resign); Leader Platform (Grazhdanskaya Platforma) 2012–13; ind. cand. in presidential election 2012; Order of Friendship 2006, Chevalier, Légion d'honneur 2011. *Leisure interest:* martial arts. *Address:* ONEXIM Group, 123104 Moscow, Tverskoi bulv. 13/1, Russia (office). *Telephone:* (495) 229-29-39 (office). *E-mail:* info@onexim.org (office). *Website:* www.onexim .org (office); www.polyusgold.com (office); md-prokhorov.livejournal.com; mprokhorov.com.

PROKHOROVA, Irina, PhD; Russian editor, literary critic, cultural historian and politician; *Leader, Civic Platform (Grazhdanskaya Platforma);* b. 3 March 1956, Moscow; d. of the late Dmitry Prokhorov and Tamara Prokhorova; sister of Mikhail Prokhorov; one d.; ed Moscow State Univ.; fmr Ed., Literaturnoe Obozrenie (Literary Review) magazine; Founder, Novoe Literaturnoe Obozrenie (New Literary Observer) magazine and publishing house 1992, currently Ed.-in-Chief; Leader Civic Platform (Grazhdanskaya Platforma) 2013–; Co-founder, Mikhail Prokhorov Fund 2004; Chevalier, Ordre des Arts et des Lettres, France 2005, Chevalier, Légion d'Honneur 2012; honoured by Govt of Russian Fed. (for New Literary Observer Magazine) 2002, Liberty Award 2003, Laureate of Andrey Bely Prize for Literature 2006. *Publication:* 1990: Russians Remember a Turning Point (ed.) 2013. *Address:* Civic Platform (Grazhdanskaya Platforma), 123104 Moscow, bul. Tverskoi 13, Russia (office). *Telephone:* (495) 787-11-10 (office). *E-mail:* feedback@civilplatform.ru (office). *Website:* www.civilplatform.ru (office).

PROKOPOVICH, Petr Petrovich; Belarusian engineer, politician and fmr central banker; *Economic Adviser to the President;* b. 3 Nov. 1942, Rovno, Brest Region; s. of Petr Prokopovich and Evgeniya Prokopovich; m. Ludmila Prokopovich; one s. one d.; ed Dnepropetrovsk Eng and Construction Inst.; Dir-Gen. Brest Regional Planning and Construction Asscn 1976–96; mem. Supreme Soviet 1990–95; Deputy Head of Admin. of Pres. of Belarus 1996; First Deputy Prime Minister of Belarus 1996–98; Chair. Nat. Bank of the Repub. of Belarus 1998–2011; Econ. Adviser to Pres. 2011–; Order of Labour Red Banner, Order of Honour; Honoured Constructor of the USSR Award, Diploma of the Supreme Soviet of Belarus. *Publications:* various articles in Belarusian and foreign edns. *Leisure interests:* billiards, tennis. *Address:* c/o Office of the President, 220016 Minsk, vul. K. Marksa 38, Dom Urada, Belarus (office).

PRÖLL, Josef; Austrian politician; b. 14 Sept. 1968, Stockerau; m.; three c.; ed Univ. of Natural Resources and Applied Life Sciences, Vienna; Official at Chamber of Agric., Fed. Prov. of Lower Austria 1993–98; Official in charge of econ. policy, Austrian Farmers' Fed. 1998–2000, Dir 2001–03; Dir Vienna Farmers' Fed. 1999–2000; Head of Cabinet, Fed. Ministry of Agric., Forestry, Environment and Water Man. 2000–01; Fed. Minister of Agric., Forestry, Environment and Water Man. 2003–08, Vice-Chancellor and Fed. Minister for Finance 2008–11 (resgnd); mem. Austrian People's Party, Chair. 2008–. *Address:* c/o Federal Ministry of Finance, Hintere Zollamtsstrasse 2b, 1030 Vienna, Austria.

PRONK, Johannes (Jan) Pieter; Dutch international organization official, academic and fmr politician; *Professor of Theory and Practice of International Development, Institute of Social Studies;* b. 16 March 1940, The Hague; m.; one s. one d.; ed Erasmus Univ., Rotterdam; Lecturer, Devt Programming Centre, School of Econs and Netherlands Econ. Inst. 1965–71; mem. Second Chamber (Parl.) 1971–73, 1978–80, 1986–89; Minister for Devt Co-operation 1973–77, 1989–98; Treas., Brandt Comm. 1978–81; Prof. of Int. Devt Policy, Inst. of Social Studies, The Hague 1979–80; Deputy Sec.-Gen. UNCTAD 1980–85, Asst Sec.-Gen. UN 1985–86; Deputy Chair. Dutch Labour Party 1986–89; Den Uyl Chair, Univ. of Amsterdam 1989; Minister of Housing, Spatial Planning and the Environment 1998–2002; Pres. UN Conf. of Parties of the Convention on Climate Change, The Hague 2000, Bonn 2001, Special Envoy of the Sec.-Gen. for the World Summit on Sustainable Devt, Johannesburg 2002; Chair. Water Supply and Sanitation Collaborative Council 2002–04, Int. Inst. for Environment and Devt, London 2002–04; Prof. of Theory and Practice of Int. Devt, Inst. of Social Studies, The Hague 2003–; Visiting Prof., UN Univ. for Peace, Costa Rica 2009–; Assoc. Fellow and Guest Lecturer, Univs of Amsterdam and Nijmegen 2012–; Special Rep. of the Sec.-Gen. for Sudan 2004–06; Pres. Soc. for Int. Devt 2008–11, Netherlands Interpeace Council 2008–11; Grootlint Orde Palm (Suriname) 1977, Ridder Orde Nederlandse Leeuw (Netherlands) 1978, Gran Cruz Orden Bernardo O'Higgins (Chile) 1993, 26th September Medal (Yemen) 1996, Officier, Légion d'honneur 2001, Officier, Orde Oranje Nassau (Netherlands) 2002; Dr hc (San Marcos Univ., Lima) 1974, (Inst. of Social Studies) 2002; US Business Council for Sustainable Energy Climate e-Award 2001. *Publications:* De Kritische Grens 1994, Catalysing Development? 2004, Willens en Wetens 2005, Het Pantser Afleggen 2007. *Leisure interests:* jogging, skiing. *Address:* Institute of Social Studies, PO Box 29776, 2502 LT The Hague, The Netherlands (office). *Telephone:* (70) 4260460 (office). *Fax:* (70) 4260799 (office). *E-mail:* pronk333@gmail.com (office). *Website:* www.iss.nl (office); www.janpronk.nl (home).

PROPPER, Carol, CBE, PhD; British economist and academic; *Professor of Economics and Head of Healthcare Management Group, Business School, Imperial College London;* ed Univs of Bristol, Oxford and York, Univ. of Toronto, Canada; Community Worker, Islington, London 1977–79; Research Officer, Nuffield Coll., Oxford 1981–82; Research Economist, New Zealand Inst. of Econ. Research 1983–84; Research Fellow, Centre for Health Econs, Univ. of York 1986–87, Visiting Fellow 1987–96; Lecturer in Econs, Brunel Univ. 1987–88; Lecturer, Univ. of Bristol 1988–93, Reader 1993–94, Prof. of Econs of Public Policy 1995–2007, Deputy Dir Centre for Market and Public Organisation 1998– (part-time 2007–); Prof. of Econs and Head of Healthcare Man. Group, Imperial Coll. Business School, London 2007–; Visiting Prof., La Follette Inst. for Public Affairs, Univ. of Wisconsin, USA 1993; Research Assoc., Welfare State Programme, LSE 1987–94; Sr Econ. Adviser to NHS Exec. on Regulation of NHS Internal Market 1993–94, Incentives Sanction Group, Dept of Health 1999–, Adding It Up Implementation Group, HM Treasury 2000–; Research Fellow, CEPR 1998–; Co-Dir Centre for Social Exclusion, LSE 1997–2007; EC Expert on Social Protection in Europe (DGV) 1991–93; Research Team mem. ECuity Project on Health Care Reform 1992–, COMAC–HSR Project on Equity in Healthcare Finance and Delivery 1992–94; Chair. Cttee on Women in Econs, Royal Econ. Soc. 1998–2001, mem. Council 2000–, Chair. Conf. Programme 2001; Ed. Economic Journal Conference Supplement 2002; mem. Editorial Bd Journal of Health Economics, Health Economics, Fiscal Studies. *Publications include:* The Economics of Social Policy (co-author) 1992, Quasi-Markets: The Emerging Findings (co-ed.) 1994, Who Pays For, Who Gets Health Care: Equity in the Finance and Delivery of Health Care in the UK 1998, Private Welfare and Public Policy (co-ed.) 1999; numerous chapters in books, articles in professional journals and reports. *Address:* Imperial College London, South Kensington Campus, London, SW7 2AZ, England (office). *Telephone:* (20) 7594-9291 (office). *Website:* www3.imperial.ac.uk/business -school (office).

PROSOR, Ron; Israeli diplomatist; *Permanent Representative, United Nations;* m. Hadas Prosor; served in USA and in major European capitals, served as spokesman in London and Bonn, as Minister-Counsellor for Political Affairs, Embassy in Washington, DC; mem. Israeli del. to Wye River Plantation talks, Md 1998; Sr Deputy Dir-Gen., Ministry of Foreign Affairs and Chief of Policy Staff to the Minister –2004, Dir-Gen., Ministry of Foreign Affairs 2004–06; Amb. to UK 2007–11, Perm. Rep. to UN, New York 2011–. *Address:* Permanent Representative of Israel to United Nations, 800 Second Avenue, New York, NY 10017, USA (office). *Telephone:* (212) 499-5510 (office). *Fax:* (212) 499-5516 (office). *E-mail:* info-un@ newyork.mfa.gov.il (office); un@israel.org (office). *Website:* www.israel-un.org (office).

PROSPER, Pierre-Richard, BA, JD; American lawyer and fmr government official; *Counsel, Arent Fox LLP;* b. 1963, Denver, Colo.; ed Boston Coll., Pepperdine Univ.; Deputy Dist Attorney, LA County 1989–94; Asst US Attorney for Cen. Dist. of Calif. 1994–96; war crimes prosecutor UN Int. Criminal Tribunal for Rwanda 1996–98; Special Asst to Asst Attorney Gen. for Criminal Div., US Justice Dept, seconded to US State Dept as Special Counsel and Policy Advisor on War Crimes Issues 1999–2001, Amb.-at-Large, War Crimes Issues, US State Dept 2001–05; Counsel, Arent Fox LLP (law firm), Los Angeles 2005–; mem. UN Cttee on the Elimination of Racial Discrimination, Geneva 2007–; Trustee, Boston Coll. Bd of Trustees. *Address:* Arent Fox LLP, Gas Company Tower, 555 West Fifth Street, 48th Floor, Los Angeles, CA 90013, USA (office). *Telephone:* (213) 629-7400 (office). *Fax:* (213) 629-7401 (office). *E-mail:* prosper.pierre@arentfox.com (office). *Website:* www.arentfox.com (office).

PROSSER, Sir David J., Kt, BSc, FIA; British fmr insurance executive; b. 1944; s. of Ronald Prosser and Dorothy Prosser; m. Rosemary Snuggs 1971; two d.; ed Ogmore Grammar School, Univ. of Wales, Aberystwyth; with Sun Alliance and London Assurance Co. 1965–69; Hoare Govett & Co. 1969–73; joined Superannuation Investments Dept, Nat. Coal Bd 1973, Head of Stock Market Activities –1981; Man. Dir Venture Capital CIN Industrial Investments 1981–85, CEO 1985–88; Group Dir Investments, Legal & Gen. PLC 1988–91, Deputy CEO Jan.–Sept. 1991, Group CEO Sept. 1991–2006 (retd); Dir (non-exec.) InterContinental Hotels Group 2003–08, Epsom Downs Racecourse 2003–, Investec 2006–; Chair. Royal Automobile Club 2007–12. *Address:* 206 Gilbert House, The Barbican, London, EC2Y 8BD, England (office). *Telephone:* (1306) 731113 (office). *E-mail:* sirdavid.prosser@btconnect.com (office).

PROSSER, Sir Ian Maurice Gray, Kt, BComm, FCA; British business executive; b. 5 July 1943, Bath, Avon, England; s. of Maurice Prosser and Freda Prosser; m. 1st Elizabeth Herman 1964 (divorced 2003); two d.; m. 2nd Hilary Prewer 2003; ed King Edward's School, Bath, Watford Grammar School, Univ. of Birmingham; with Cooper Bros (chartered accountants) 1964–69; with Bass Charrington Ltd 1969–82, Financial Dir 1978; Vice-Chair. and Financial Dir Bass PLC 1982–84, Vice-Chair. and Group Man. Dir 1984–87, Chair. and CEO 1987–2000, Exec. Chair. 2000, co. then de-merged into Intercontinental Hotels Group PLC, Chair. 2000–03 (retd); Chair. The Brewers' Soc. 1992–94; Chair. Exec., World Travel and Tourism Council 2001–04; Chair. Navy, Army and Air Force Insts 2008–, Aviva Staff Pension Fund 2013–; Dir (non-exec.) The Boots Co. 1984–96, Lloyds TSB Group PLC 1988–99, BP (later BP Amoco now BP PLC) 1997–2010 (Deputy Chair. 1999–2010, Dir, BP Pension Fund 2010–), Glaxo SmithKline PLC 1999–2009, Sara Lee Inc. 2004–12, Hillshire Brands 2012–; Hon. DUniv. *Leisure interests:* bridge, gardening, golf. *Address:* BP Pensions Ltd, 1 St James's Square, London, SW1Y 4PD, England (office). *Telephone:* (20) 7496-4000 (office). *Fax:* (20) 7496-4630 (office). *E-mail:* ian.prosser@imgp.co.uk (office).

PROST, Alain Marie Pascal; French motor racing team owner and fmr racing driver; b. 24 Feb. 1955, Saint-Chamond; s. of André Prost and Marie-Rose Karatchian; m. Anne-Marie Prost; two s.; ed Coll. Sainte-Marie, Saint-Chamond; joined Marlboro MacLaren Group 1980, Renault team 1981–83, McLaren TAG team 1984–87, McLaren Honda 1988–89, Ferrari 1990–91, Williams Renault 1993; winner Formula 1 Grand Prix races in France 1981, 1983, 1988, 1989, 1990, 1993, Netherlands 1981, 1984, Italy 1981, 1985, 1989, Brazil 1982, 1984, 1985, 1987, 1988, 1990, South Africa 1982, 1993, Austria 1983, 1985, 1986, Britain 1985, 1989, 1990, 1993, Belgium 1983, 1987, Europe 1984, Monte Carlo 1984, 1985, 1986, 1988, San Marino 1984, 1986, 1993, Portugal 1984, 1987, 1988, Germany 1984, 1993, Australia 1986, 1988, Mexico 1988, 1990, Spain 1988, 1990, 1993, USA 1989, Canada 1993; Formula 1 World Champion 1985, 1986, 1989, 1993; total 51 Grand Prix wins, 106 podium finishes; technical consultant to McLaren Mercedes 1995; founder and Pres. Prost Grand Prix Team 1997–2002; Hon. OBE 1994; Trophée du champion automobile du siécle en Autriche 1999; Officier, Légion d'honneur. *Publications:* Vive ma vie 1993.

PROT, Baudouin Daniel Claude; French banker; *Chairman, BNP Paribas SA;* b. 24 May 1951, Paris; s. of André Prot and Marguerite Le Febvre; m. Viviane Abel 1981; one s. one d.; ed Inst. de Sainte-Croix, Neuilly, Ecole Saint-Louis des hautes études commerciales, Ecole nat. d'admin.; Inspecteur, Inspection générale des finances, Paris 1976; Deputy Dir Gen. Energy and Raw Materials, Ministry of Industry 1982–83; joined Banque Nat. de Paris (BNP) 1983, managerial positions depts for Europe 1985–87, metropolitan networks 1987–92, France 1992–96, Deputy Dir-Gen. BNP 1992–96, apptd Dir-Gen. 1996, mem. Bd of Dirs BNP Paribas SA 2000–, CEO 2005–11, Chair. 2011–; Chair. Carte bleue group 1991–97; Dir, Pinault-Printemps-Redoute, Veolia Environnement, Erbé SA (Belgium), Pargesa Holding SA (Switzerland); mem. Exec. Bd Fédération Bancaire Française; Inspecteur générale des finances 1993; Chevalier, Légion d'honneur, Ordre nat. du Mérite. *Publications:* Armée-Nation, le Rendez-vous manqué 1975, Nationalisations 1977, Réduire l'impôt 1985, Dénationalisation 1986, La Jeunesse inégale 1987, Le Retour de capital 1990. *Leisure interests:* tennis, skiing, sailing. *Address:* BNP Paribas SA, 16 boulevard des Italiens, 75009 Paris (office); 21 rue Monsieur, 75007 Paris, France (home). *Telephone:* 1-40-14-45-46 (office). *Fax:* 1-40-14-69-73 (office). *E-mail:* baudouin.prot@bnpparibas.com (office). *Website:* www.bnpparibas .com (office).

PROULX, (Edna) Annie, MA; American writer; b. 22 Aug. 1935, Norwich, Conn.; d. of George Napoleon Proulx and Lois Nellie Gill; m. 1st H. Ridgeley Bullock 1955 (divorced); one d.; m. 2nd James Hamilton Lang 1969 (divorced 1990); three s.; ed Univ. of Vermont and Sir George Williams (now Concordia) Univ., Montréal; freelance journalist, Vt 1975–87; f. Vershire Behind the Times newspaper, Vershire, Vt; short stories appeared in Blair & Ketchums Country Journal, Esquire, etc.; Vt Council Arts Fellowship 1989, Ucross Foundation Residency, Wyo. 1990, 1992; mem. PEN; Guggenheim Fellow 1993; active anti-illiteracy campaigner; Hon. DHumLitt (Maine) 1994; Alumni Achievement Award, Univ. of Vt 1994, New York Public Library Literary Lion 1994, Dos Passos Prize for Literature 1996, American Acad. of Achievement Award 1998. *Publications:* Heart Songs and Other Stories 1988, Postcards (novel) (PEN/Faulkner Award for Fiction 1993) 1992, The Shipping News (Chicago Tribune Heartland Prize for Fiction, Irish Times Int. Fiction Prize, Nat. Book Award for Fiction, Pulitzer Prize for Fiction 1994) 1993, Accordion Crimes 1996, Best American Short Stories (ed.) 1997, Brokeback Mountain (short story, Nat. Magazine Award 1998, O. Henry Awards Prize 1998) 1998, Close Range: Wyoming Stories (New Yorker Book Award Best Fiction 1999, English-Speaking Union's Amb. Book Award 2000, Borders Original Voices Award in Fiction 2000) 1998, That Old Ace in the Hole (Best

Foreign Language Novels of 2002/Best American Novel Award, Chinese Publishing Asscn and Peoples' Literature Publishing House 2002) 2002, Bad Dirt: Wyoming Stories 2 2004, Fine Just the Way It Is: Wyoming Stories 3 2008, Bird Cloud: A Memoir 2011. *Leisure interests:* fly-fishing, canoeing, playing the fiddle. *Address:* PO Box 230, Centennial, WY 82055; c/o Simon & Schuster Inc., 1230 Avenue of the Americas, New York, NY 10020, USA (office). *Fax:* (307) 742-6159. *Website:* authors.simonandschuster.com/Annie-Proulx/8544.

PROVOPOULOS, Georgios A., BA, MA, PhD; Greek economist, academic and central banker; *Governor, Bank of Greece;* b. 20 April 1950, Pireaus; m.; three c.; ed Univ. of Athens, Univ. of Essex, UK; Assoc. Prof., Dept of Econs, Univ. of Athens 1979–2007; Chair. Centre for Planning and Econ. Research (KEPE) 1989–90; Chair. Council of Econ. Experts, Ministry of Economy and Finance July–Nov. 1989, April–Oct. 1990, mem. –1992; Deputy Gov. Bank of Greece and Alt. Gov. for Greece in IMF 1990–93, Gov. Bank of Greece 2008–; Gen. Man. Foundation of Econ. and Industrial Research (IOBE) 1993–97; Econ. Adviser, Alpha Bank 1994–2004; Chair. and CEO Emporiki Bank 2004–06; Vice-Chair. and Man. Dir Piraeus Bank 2006–08, Chair. Piraeus Bank's subsidiaries in Romania, Albania, Bulgaria, Serbia and Egypt 2007–08; Vice-Chair. Hellenic Banks' Asscn 2007–08; mem. EU Monetary Cttee 1990–93; Chair. Cttee for reform of Greek tax system 1989; Chair. Piraeus AEEAP 2006–08, Piraeus Real Estate 2006–08, Marathon Banking Corpn 2007–08, Marathon Nat. Bank of New York 2007–08, Alpha Investment Portfolio 2000–03, Alpha Mutual Fund Man. Co. 2000–04, ICAP 2000–05; Vice-Chair. Hellenic Postbank 1992–93, Hellenic Banks' Asscn (Rep. of Asscn at European Banking Fed.) 2004–06; mem. Bd of Dirs TITAN Cement Co. 1996–2004, Foundation of Econ. and Industrial Research 1998–2006, Hellenic Centre for Investment (ELKE) 1999–2004, European Cen. Bank Governing Council; mem. Co-ordination Cttee, Ministry of Finance for reform of taxation system 2001; Greek State Scholarship's Foundation (IKY). *Publication:* The Dynamics of the Financial System (with P. Kapopoulos) (Award of the Class of Ethical and Political Sciences, Acad. of Athens 2003). *Address:* Bank of Greece, Leoforos E. Venizelos 21, 102 50 Athens, Greece (office). *Telephone:* (210) 3202001 (office). *Fax:* (210) 3241500 (office). *E-mail:* gprovopoulos@bankofgreece.gr (office). *Website:* www.bankofgreece.gr (office).

PRUAITCH, Patrick; Papua New Guinea politician; *Minister of Treasury;* mem. Parl. for Aitape-Lumi; Minister of Finance and the Treasury 2007–10 (suspended by Supreme Court May 2010), 2011; Minister of Forestry and Climate Change 2012–14, of Treasury 2014–; mem. Nat. Alliance Party. *Address:* Department of Treasury, POB 542, Waigani, 131, National Capital District, Papua New Guinea. *Telephone:* 3128817 (office). *Fax:* 3128844 (office). *E-mail:* enquiries@treasury.gov .pg (office). *Website:* www.treasury.gov.pg (office).

PRUDNIKOV, Gen. Victor Alexeyevich; Russian army officer (retd); b. 4 Feb. 1939, Rostov-on-Don; m.; two s.; ed Armavir Higher Mil. Aviation School of Pilots, Gagarin Mil. Aviation Acad., Mil. Acad. of Gen. Staff; pilot, instructor aviation regt 1959–65; Commdr of squadron, Regt Commdr, Deputy Div. Commdr 1968–75; Commdr Anti-Aircraft Defence Div. 1975–78; Deputy C-in-C 1978–81, First Deputy C-in-C 1981–83; Commdr Anti-Aircraft Defence Army 1983–89; C-in-C Moscow Mil. Command 1989–91; C-in-C Anti-Aircraft Defence Forces of Russia 1991–97; Head of Staff on Co-ordination of Mil. Co-operation CIS Cos 1998–2001. *Leisure interests:* tennis, swimming. *Address:* Ministry of Defence, Myasnitskaya str. 37, 103175 Moscow, Russia (office). *Telephone:* (495) 296-18-00 (office).

PRUEHER, Adm. Joseph W., MS; American diplomatist, naval officer and academic; *Consulting Professor, Center for International Security and Cooperation, Stanford University;* b. 25 Nov. 1942, Nashville, Tenn.; m. Suzanne Prueher; one s. one d.; ed Montgomery Bell Acad., US Naval Acad., Annapolis, Md, Naval War Coll., Newport, RI and George Washington Univ.; started naval career as Command Ensign, USN, advanced through grades to Adm., C-in-C US Pacific Command, Camp HM Smith, Hawaii 1996–99; Amb. to People's Repub. of China 1999–2001; Consulting Prof., Center for International Security and Cooperation, Stanford Univ. 2001–; mem. Bd of Dirs Merrill Lynch 2001–; decorations from govts of Singapore, Thailand, Japan, Korea, Philippines, Indonesia and Australia; multiple awards for combat flying as well as naval and jt service. *Publications include:* numerous articles on leadership, mil. readiness and Pacific region security issues. *Address:* Center for International Security and Cooperation, Stanford University, 616 Serra Street, E200, Stanford, CA 94305-6165, USA (office). *Telephone:* (650) 723-9625 (office). *Fax:* (650) 724-5683 (office). *E-mail:* dcgordon@stanford.edu (office). *Website:* cisac.stanford.edu (office).

PRUNARIU, Maj.-Gen. (retd) Dumitru-Dorin, PhD; Romanian airspace engineer, cosmonaut and diplomatist; *President, Romanian Association for Space Technology and Industry;* b. 27 Sept. 1952, Brasov; s. of Simion Prunariu and Elena Prunariu; m. Crina Prunariu; two s.; ed Airspace Eng Faculty at Polytechnic Univ., Bucharest, Cosmonaut Training Course, Star City, Russia, Int. Aviation Man. Training Inst. (IAMTI/IIFGA), Montreal, Canada, Nat. Defence Coll., Bucharest, course on applied diplomacy within Ministry of Foreign Affairs; engineer at IAR-BRASOV (aircraft co.) 1976–77; Romanian Air Force 1977–2007; crew member, Soyuz 40 space mission 1981, Chief Inspector for Airspace Activities 1981–89; Deputy Minister to Ministry of Transportation and Chief of Romanian Civil Aviation Dept 1990–91; Co-leader World Bank Project on reorganization of the higher educ. and research system in Romania 1992–93; Sec. Romanian Space Agency 1992–95, mem. Admin. Council 1995–98, Pres. 1998–2004, Pres. Bd 2005–, Pres., Scientific Bd 2008–; Amb. to Russian Fed. 2004–05; Dir Romanian Office for Science and Tech. to the EU, Nat. Authority for Scientific Research 2006–08; Vice-Pres. European Inst. for Risk Man., Security and Communication (EURISC) Foundation 1995–; Chair. S&T Sub-cttee, UN COPUOS 2004–06, Chair. UN COPUOS 2010–12; Pres. Romanian Asscn for Space Tech. and Industry 2013–; Assoc. Prof. of Geopolitics, Faculty of Int. Business and Econs, Acad. of Econ. Studies, Bucharest 1995–; mem. Astronautic Comm., Romanian Acad. 1981–; Founder-mem. Asscn of Space Explorers, Paris 1985, mem. Exec. Cttee 1995–2001, Pres. 2011–14; mem. Romanian Nat. COSPAR Cttee 1994–, Group of Govt Experts on outer space transparency and confidence-building measures, in accordance with UN Gen. Ass. Resolution 65/68 2012–13; mem. Bd, TAROM air co. 2012–13; mem. Int. Astronautic Acad. 1992, first Rotary Club of Bucharest 1997; hon. citizen of several cities; Hon. mem. American Romanian Acad. of Arts and Sciences, registered in Calif., USA 2002, Romanian Acad. 2011; Hero of Romania 1981,

Golden Star and Hero of the Soviet Union 1981, Grand Officer of the Order Steaua României (Star of Romania) 2000, mil. orders; Yuri Gagarin Medal, Int. Astronautic Fed. 1982, Hermann Oberth Gold Medal, German Rocket Soc. Hermann Oberth-Wernher von Braun, Germany 1984, Medal for Merits in Space Exploration, Pres. of Russian Fed. 2011 and others. *Publications:* author or co-author of several books and numerous scientific papers on space tech. and space flight; studies on security, risk and communication man., geopolitics accomplished within the EURISC Foundation; articles on scientific topics published in Romanian and foreign publs. *Leisure interest:* photography. *Address:* Romanian Space Agency, Mendeleev Str. 21–25, 010632 Bucharest, Romania (office). *Telephone:* (21) 3168722 (office). *Fax:* (21) 3128804 (office). *E-mail:* dorin52@ yahoo.com (home). *Website:* www.rosa.ro (office); www.eurisc.org (office).

PRUNSKIENĖ, Kazimiera Danutė, DEconSci; Lithuanian politician; b. 26 Feb. 1943, Švenčionėliai Region; d. of Ona Stankevičienė and Pranas Stankevičius; m. 1st Povilas Prunskus 1961; m. 2nd Algimantas Tarvydas 1990 (divorced); one s. two d.; ed Vilnius State Univ.; teacher, then Dean of Faculty, Vilnius State Univ. 1965–85; Deputy Dir Inst. of Econ. Agric. 1986–88; People's Deputy of the USSR 1989–90, mem. USSR Supreme Soviet 1989–90; Deputy Chair. Council of Ministers of Lithuania 1989–90, Chair. 1990–91; mem. Lithuanian Parl. 1990–92, 1996–; Minister of Agric. 2005–08; Pres. Lithuanian-European Inst. 1991–; Pres. pvt. consulting firm K. Prunskienė-Consulting 1993–96; Prof. of Econs, Vilnius Gediminas Tech. Univ. 1996–2000; Founder and Pres. Lithuanian Women's Party (later New Democracy Party) 1995–; Chair. Lithuanian Peasant Nationalists' Union (fmrly Peasants' and New Democracy Union 2001–06) 2001–09; mem. CEPS Int. Advisory Council 1992–, Int. Cttee for Econ. Reform and Co-operation 1994–; Pres. Baltic Women's Basketball League 1994–; mem. Council of Women World Leaders 1997–; Order of Grand Duke of Lithuania Gediminas (2nd Degree) and Medal of the Order of Gediminas 2000, Medal of the Independence of Lithuania 2000, Medal of the FRG, Order of Merit 2000, Grand Cross of Merit with Star 2001; Alexander von Humboldt Foundation Scholarship, Minerva Prize (Italy). *Publications:* Amber Lady's Confession 1991, Leben für Litauen 1992, Behind the Scenes 1992, Challenge to Dragon 1992, Price of Liberation 1993, Markt Balticum 1994, Transformation, Co-operation and Conversion 1996, Science and Technology Policy of the Baltic States and International Co-operation 1997, Intellectual Property Rights in Central and Eastern Europe: the Creation of Favourable Legal and Market Preconditions 1998. *Leisure interests:* sports, music, literature, knitting, cooking, walking in the forest. *Address:* Lithuanian Peasant Nationalists' Union (Lietuvos Valstiečių Liaudininkų Sajunga), Paménkalnio g. 28, Vilnius 01114 (office); Krivių g. 53a-13, Vilnius 02007, Lithuania (home). *Telephone:* (5) 261-3704 (office). *Fax:* (5) 212-4518 (office). *E-mail:* k.prunskiene@gmail.com (office). *Website:* www.lvls.lt (office); www.prunskiene.lt.

PRUSAK, Mikhail Mikhailovich, DEcon; Russian politician and economist; b. 23 Feb. 1960, Ivano-Frankovskaya region, Ukraine; m.; one s. one d.; ed Higher Komsomol School, Acad. of National Econs; Sec. Novgorod regional Komsomol Cttee –1988; Dir Sovkhoz Trudovik Novgorod region 1988–91; People's Deputy, mem. USSR Supreme Soviet, mem. Interregional Deputies' Group 1989–91; Gov. of Novgorod Region 1991–2007 (resgnd); mem. Council of Federal Ass. of Russian Fed. 1996–2001; Chair. Democratic Party of Russia; Vice-Pres. Parl. Ass. Council of Europe 1999–2001; author of numerous works; Corresp. mem. St Petersburg Acad. of Eng; recipient of awards. *Leisure interest:* hunting. *Address:* c/o Office of the Governor, Sophiiyskaya pl. 1, 173005 Veliky Novgorod, Russia (office).

PRUSINER, Stanley B., AB, MD; American neuroscientist, neurologist and academic; *Professor of Neurology, University of California, San Francisco;* b. 1942; ed Walnut Hills High School, Cincinnati, Ohio, Univ. of Pennsylvania, Univ. of California, San Francisco; US Public Health Service, NIH 1968–71; Internship in Medicine, Univ. of California, San Francisco 1968–69, Residency in Neurology 1972–74, Asst Prof. of Neurology in Residence 1974–80, Lecturer, Dept of Biochemistry and Biophysics 1976–78, Assoc. Prof. of Neurology in Residence 1980–81, Assoc. Prof. of Neurology 1981–84, Prof. of Neurology 1984–, Prof. of Biochemistry 1988–2010; Asst Prof. of Virology in Residence, Univ. of California, Berkeley 1979–83, Prof. of Virology in Residence 1984–; Potamkin Prize for Alzheimer's Disease Research, American Acad. of Neurology 1991, NIH Christopher Columbus Quincentennial Discovery Award in Biomedical Research 1992, Metropolitan Life Foundation Award for Medical Research 1992, Dickson Prize for Distinguished Scientific Accomplishments, Univ. of Pittsburgh 1992, Charles A. Dana Award for Pioneering Achievements in Health 1992, NAS Richard Lounsbery Award for Extraordinary Scientific Research 1993, Gairdner Foundation Award for Outstanding Achievement in Medical Science 1993, Bristol-Myers Squibb Award for Distinguished Achievement in Neuroscience Research 1994, Albert Lasker Award for Basic Medical Research 1994, Paul Ehrlich Prize, Paul Ehrlich Foundation and FRG 1995, Wolf Prize in Medicine, Wolf Foundation and State of Israel 1996, Keio Int. Award for Medical Science, Keio Univ., Tokyo 1996, Nobel Laureate in Physiology or Medicine (for his discovery of prions) 1997, Nat. Medal of Science 2009. *Publications:* The Molecular and Genetic Basis of Neurological Disease, Prions Prions Prions (Current Topics in Microbiology and Immunology, Vol. 207), Prions – Novel Infectious Pathogens Causing Scrapie and Creutzfeldt-Jakob Disease, Prion Diseases of Humans and Animals, Slow Transmissible Diseases of the Nervous System, Clinical Companion to the Molecular and Genetic Basis of Neurological Disease 1998, Prion Biology and Diseases 2003, The Molecular and Genetic Basis of Neurologic and Psychiatric Disease 2003. *Address:* University of California, San Francisco, 513 Parnassus Avenue, HSE-774, San Francisco, CA 94143-0518, USA (office). *Telephone:* (415) 476-4482 (office).

PRYCE, Jonathan, CBE; British actor; b. 1 June 1947, Holywell, North Wales; s. of Isaac Price and Margaret Ellen Price (née Williams); partner Kate Fahy; two s. one d.; ed Royal Acad. of Dramatic Art; Patron Friends Works, Saving Faces; Dr hc (Liverpool); Tony and Drama Desk Awards, Best Actor, Cannes Film Festival 1995. *Stage appearances include:* Comedians (Tony Award 1976), Nottingham Old Vic 1975, New York 1976, Hamlet (Olivier Award 1980), Royal Court Theatre, London 1980, The Caretaker, Nat. Theatre 1981, Accidental Death of an Anarchist, Broadway 1984, The Seagull, Queen's Theatre 1985, Macbeth, RSC 1986, Uncle Vanya 1988, Miss Saigon (Olivier and Variety Club Awards 1991),

Drury Lane 1989, New York 1991, Nine – The Concert 1992, Under Milk Wood 1992, Cabaret 1994, Oliver!, London Palladium 1995, Hey! Mr Producer 1998, My Fair Lady, Nat. Theatre and Drury Lane, London 2001, A Reckoning, Soho Theatre 2003, The Goat, Almeida Theatre 2004, Dirty Rotten Scoundrels, New York 2005, Glengarry Glen Ross, Apollo Theatre 2007–08, Dimetos, Donmar Warehouse 2009, The Caretaker, Liverpool Everyman, Theatre Royal Bath, Trafalgar Studios, London 2011, The Caretaker, World Tour 2012, King Lear, Almeida Theatre 2012. *Films include:* Something Wicked This Way Comes 1982, The Ploughman's Lunch 1983, Brazil 1985, The Doctor and the Devils 1986, Haunted Honeymoon 1986, Jumpin' Jack Flash 1987, Consuming Passions 1988, The Adventures of Baron Munchausen 1988, The Rachel Papers 1989, Glengarry Glen Ross 1992, Barbarians at the Gate 1992, Great Moments in Aviation 1993, The Age of Innocence 1993, A Business Affair 1993, Deadly Advice 1994, Carrington (Best Actor, Evening Standard Film Awards 1996) 1995, Evita 1996, Tomorrow Never Dies 1997, Regeneration 1997, Ronin 1998, Stigmata 1999, Taliesin Jones 2000, The Suicide Club 2000, Very Annie Mary 2001, The Affair of the Necklace 2001, Bride of the Wind 2001, Unconditional Love 2002, Mad Dogs 2002, What a Girl Wants 2003, Pirates of the Caribbean: The Curse of the Black Pearl 2003, De-Lovely 2004, The Brothers Grimm 2005, The New World 2005, Pirates of the Caribbean 2: Dead Man's Chest 2006, Brothers of the Head 2006, The Moon and the Stars 2007, Pirates of the Caribbean: At the World's End 2007, Leatherheads 2007, Bedtime Stories 2008, G.I. Joe: The Rise of Cobra 2009, Hysteria 2011, City State 2011, Dark Blood 2012, GI Joe: Retaliation 2013, Listen Up Philip 2014, The Ghost and the Whale 2014, Dough 2014, The Salvation 2014, Narcopolis 2014. *Radio:* HR (BBC Radio 4) 2007–. *Television includes:* Roger Doesn't Live Here Anymore (series) 1981, Timon of Athens 1981, Martin Luther 1983, Praying Mantis 1983, Whose Line Is It Anyway? 1988, The Man from the Pru 1990, Selling Hitler 1991, Mr Wroe's Virgins 1993, Barbarians at the Gate 1993, Thicker than Water 1993, Great Moments in Aviation 1993, David 1997, Hey, Mr Producer! The Musical World of Cameron Mackintosh 1998, The Union Game: A Rugby History (series) (voice) 1999, Victoria & Albert 2001, Confessions of an Ugly Stepsister 2002, HR (film) 2007, Sherlock Holmes and the Baker Street Irregulars (film) 2007, My Zinc Bed (film) 2008, Clone (series) 2008, Cranford (series) 2009. *Recordings include:* Miss Saigon 1989, Nine – The Concert 1992, Under Milk Wood 1992, Cabaret 1994, Oliver! 1995, Hey! Mr Producer 1998, My Fair Lady 2001. *Leisure interests:* painting, drawing. *Address:* c/o Julian Belfrage Associates, 3rd Floor, 9 Argyll Street, London, W1F 7TG, England (office).

PRYOR, David Hampton, LLB; American lawyer, politician and academic; b. 29 Aug. 1934, Camden, Ark.; s. of Edgar Pryor and Susan Pryor (née Newton); m. Barbara Jean Lunsford 1957; three s. including Mark Pryor (q.v.); ed Henderson State Univ., Univ. of Arkansas; admitted to Ark. Bar 1964; mem. Ark. House of Reps 1961–66; mem. US House of Reps 1966–73; Gov. of Ark. 1974–79; Senator from Ark. 1979–97, Chair. Senate Special Cttee on Aging 1989–95, Democratic Conf. Sec. of the US Senate 1989–95; Chair. Arkansas Democratic Party 2008–09; mem. ABA, Ark. Bar Asscn; Fellow, Inst. of Politics, School of Govt, Harvard Univ. 1999; Dir Inst. of Politics, Kennedy School of Govt, Harvard Univ. 2000; fmr Dean, Clinton School of Public Service, Univ. of Arkansas, taught a political science course at Univ. of Arkansas, Fayetteville 2008; mem. Bd Corpn for Public Broadcasting 2006–12; Democrat. *Address:* c/o University of Arkansas Clinton School of Public Service, Sturgis Hall, 1200 President Clinton Avenue, Little Rock, AR 72201; 2701 Kavanaugh Boulevard, Suite 300, Little Rock, AR 72205, USA (office). *E-mail:* info@clintonschool.uasys.edu.

PRYOR, Mark, BA, LLB; American politician and lawyer; *Senator from Arkansas;* b. 10 Jan. 1963, Fayetteville, Ark.; s. of David Hampton Pryor (q.v.); m. Jill Pryor; one s. one d.; ed Univ. of Arkansas; practised law with Wright, Lindsey & Jennings, Little Rock 1982–90; elected to Ark. State House of Reps (Democrat) for two terms 1990; Attorney-Gen. of Ark. 1999–2003, Senator from Arkansas 2003–, mem. Appropriations Cttee, Commerce, Science, and Transportation Cttee, Homeland Security and Governmental Affairs Cttee, Small Business and Entrepreneurship Cttee, Senate Rules Cttee, Senate Ethics Cttee; served as campaign chair. in Ark. for Vice-Pres. Al Gore 2000; Democrat. *Address:* 255 Dirksen Senate Office Building, Washington, DC 20150, USA (office). *Telephone:* (202) 224-2353 (office). *Fax:* (202) 228-0908 (office). *Website:* pryor.senate.gov (office).

BENAKI-PSAROUDA, Anna, PhD; Greek politician, lawyer and academic; b. 12 Dec. 1934, Athens; m. Linos Benakis 1957; ed Pierce Coll. of Athens, Univ. of Athens, Univ. of Bonn, Germany; attorney-at-law 1962–; Researcher, Max Planck Inst. for Int. Criminal Law, Freiburg 1962–78; Asst Prof., Prof. of Criminal Law, Univ. of Athens 1978–2002, currently Prof. Emer.; mem. Vouli (Parl.) 1981–2009, Alt. Minister of Education 1989, of Culture 1990–92, of Justice 1992–93; Vice-Pres. Vouli 2002–04, Pres. 2004–07; mem. Acad. of Athens 2010–; Grand Cross, Royal Norwegian Order of Merit 2004, Grand Cross, Order of Honour of Hellenic Repub. 2005, Grand Cross, Order of Dannebrog (Denmark) 2006, Grand Decoration of Honour for Services (Austria) 2007. *Publications include:* four books and several articles on criminal matters; political articles. *Leisure interests include:* swimming, classical music, literature. *Address:* Didotou 25, 106 80 Athens (office); Sina 58, 106 72 Athens, Greece (home). *Telephone:* (210) 3636818 (home). *Fax:* (210) 3602633 (office); (210) 3636681 (home). *E-mail:* benaki@parliament.gr (office); benakis@hol.gr. *Website:* benakianna.gr (office).

PSY; South Korean rapper, dancer, songwriter and record producer; b. (Park Jaesang), 31 Dec. 1977, Gangnam Dist, Seoul; s. of Park Won-ho; m. Yoo Hye-yeon 2006; two d.; ed Berklee Coll. of Music, Boston, USA; released debut album 2001; served in military 2003–05, 2007–09; signed to YG Entertainment label 2010; released Gangnam Style 2012, first single by South Korean artist to chart at number one on the iTunes Music Video Charts; Goodwill Amb., UNICEF 2012; Military Grand Award 2009, Dept of Defense Plaque of Appreciation 2011, Okgwan Order 2012; Mnet Asian Music Awards for Best Video Performer 2005, for Best Music Video 2006, for Best Producer 2010, Seoul Music Award for Best Performance 2010, Melon Music Award for Best Performance 2010, 1st Korea Music Copyright Target Singer Awards for Songwriting and Composition 2011, Cyworld Digital Music Award for Song of the Month 2012, MTV Europe Music Award for Best Video 2012, American Music Award New Media Award 2012, Billboard Music Award for Top Streaming Song (Video) 2013. *Films:* Mong Jung Gi

2002, Mong Jung Gi 2 2005. *Television includes:* Superstar K4 (as regular judge) 2012–; numerous guest appearances. *Recordings include:* albums: PSY from the PSYcho World! 2001, Sa 2 2002, 3 PSY 2003, Sa Jib 2006, PSY Five (Seoul Music Award for Record of the Year 2011) 2010, PSY 6 (Six Rules) 2012; single: Gentleman 2013. *Address:* c/o YG Entertainment, 397-5 YG Building, Hapjeong-Dong, Mapo-Gu, Seoul, 121-886, South Korea (office). *Website:* www.psypark.com.

PSZONIAK, Wojciech Zygmunt; Polish actor; b. 2 May 1942, Lvov, Poland (now Lviv, Ukraine); m.; ed State High Theatre School, Kraków; Asst State High Theatre School, Kraków 1967–72, lecturer 1972–; prin. theatrical roles at Stary Theatre, Kraków 1968–72, Narodowy Theatre, Warsaw 1972–74, Powszechny Theatre, Warsaw 1974–80; presenter TV show Wojtek Pszoniak – pytania do siebie (Pszoniak – Questions to Himself) 1995–96; Gold Cross of Merit 1975, Kt's Cross, Order of Polonia Restituta 1997; Prize of Ministry of Culture (2nd Class) 1975, Masters Award, Montréal Film Festival 1982. *Films:* Wesele (The Wedding) 1973, Ziemia obiecana (The Promised Land) 1975, Austeria 1981, Danton 1982, Je huis les acteurs 1986, Les années-sandwiches 1987, Czerwona Wenecja (Red Venice) 1988, Korczak 1990, Gawin 1991, Le Bal des Casse-Pieds 1992, Coupable d'innocence 1992, Le Vent d'Est 1993, La Chica 1995, Wielki Tydzien 1996, Our God's Brother 1997, L'Atelier (TV) 1999, Deuxième vie 2000, Bajland 2000, Chaos 2001, Le Pacte du silence 2003, Là-haut, un roi au-dessus des nuages (Above the Clouds) 2003, Vipère au poing 2004, Hope 2007. *Plays:* Poskromienie złośnicy (The Taming of the Shrew) 1969, Sen nocy letniej (A Midsummer Night's Dream) 1970, Wszystko dobre, co się dobrze kończy (All's Well That Ends Well) 1971, Biesy 1971, Makbet (Macbeth) 1973, Les gens déraisonnables sont en voie de disparition, Théâtre des Amandiers, Nanterre 1978, Zemsta (Revenge) 1980, Czekając na Godota (Waiting for Godot) 1989, Król Ubu (King Ubu) 1992, The Deep Blue Sea, Apollo Theatre, London 1993, Atelier, Théâtre Hébertot, Paris 1999, Pracownia krawiecka (Tailor's Shop – actor and dir) 2000, Kolacja dla głupca (Supper for Fools) 2001, La boutique au coin de la rue, Théâtre Montparnasse, Paris 2001. *Publication:* Pszoniak & Co. czyli Towarzystwo Dobrego Stołu 1993. *Leisure interests:* classical music, jazz, cooking.

PTASHNE, Mark Stephen, PhD; American biochemist and academic; *Ludwig Chair of Molecular Biology, Sloan-Kettering Cancer Center;* b. 5 June 1940, Chicago, Ill.; s. of Fred Ptashne and Mildred Ptashne; ed Reed Coll. and Harvard Univ.; Jr Fellow, Harvard Soc. of Fellows 1965–68; Lecturer, Dept of Biochem. and Molecular Biology, Harvard Univ. 1968–71, Prof. 1971, Chair. Dept of Biochem. and Molecular Biology 1980–83, Herchel Smith Prof. of Molecular Biology 1993; mem. Faculty, Molecular Biology Program, Memorial Sloan-Kettering Cancer Center, Ludwig Chair of Molecular Biology 1997–; Guggenheim Fellow 1973–74; Fellow American Acad. of Arts and Sciences; mem. NAS; Feodor Lynen Lecturer 1988; Prix Charles-Léopold Mayer, Acad. des Sciences, Inst. de France (with W. Gilbert and E. Witkin) 1977; Eli Lilly Award 1975; shared Louisa Gross Horwitz Prize 1985; Gairdner Foundation Int. Award (with Charles Yanofsky) 1985; Cancer Research Foundation Award 1990, Lasker Award 1997. *Publications:* A Genetic Switch 1986, A Genetic Switch: Phage (Lambda) and Higher Organisms 1992, Genes and Signals 2002, Genetic Switch: Phage Lambda Revisited 2004; 122 papers in scientific journals 1950–89. *Leisure interests:* classical music, opera. *Address:* Molecular Biology Program, Memorial Sloan-Kettering Cancer Center, 1275 York Avenue, New York, NY 10021, USA. *Telephone:* (212) 639-2297 (office); (212) 639-5183 (office). *Fax:* (212) 717-3627 (office). *E-mail:* m-ptashne@ski.mskcc .org (office). *Website:* www.mskcc.org/mskcc/html/5781.cfm (office).

PU, Haiqing; Chinese politician; *Director, Three Gorges Project Construction Committee, Office of the State Council;* b. 1941, Nanbu, Sichuan Prov.; ed Chongqing Univ.; joined CCP 1973; Man. Chongqing Iron and Steel Co.; Vice-Gov. Sichuan Prov.; Acting Mayor of Chongqing Municipality 1996–97, Mayor 1997–99, Deputy Sec. CCP Chongqing Municipal Cttee 1997–99; Dir Nat. Metallurgical Industry Bureau 1999–2001 (Sec. CCP Leading Party Group); Deputy Dir Three Gorges Project Construction Cttee, Office of the State Council 2001–03 (Deputy Sec. CCP Leading Party Group), Dir 2003– (Sec. CCP Leading Party Group); Del., 14th CCP Cen. Cttee 1992–97, mem. 15th CCP Cen. Cttee 1997–2002, 16th CCP Cen. Cttee 2002–07. *Address:* Three Gorges Project Construction Committee, Office of the State Council, Beijing, People's Republic of China.

PUAPUA, Rt Hon. Sir Tomasi, Kt, GCMG, KBE, PC; Tuvaluan physician and politician; b. 10 Sept. 1938; s. of Fitilau Puapua and Olive Puapua; m. Riana Tabokai 1971; two s. two d.; ed Fiji School of Medicine and Univ. of Otago, NZ; Prime Minister of Tuvalu 1981–90, also Minister for Civil Service Admin., Local Govt and Minister for Foreign Affairs; Speaker of Parl. 1993–98; Gov. Gen. of Tuvalu 1998–2005. *Leisure interests:* athletics, rugby, tennis, volleyball, cricket, soccer, fishing, pig and poultry farming, gardening. *Address:* c/o Government House, Vaiaku, Funafuti, Tuvalu (office).

PUCCIO HUIDOBRO, Osvaldo, LLB, PhD; Chilean fmr diplomatist; b. 21 Dec. 1952; three c.; ed Univ. of Chile, Humboldt Univ., Berlin; consultant, Latin-American Faculty of Social Sciences (FLASCO) 1984–86; Assoc. Researcher, Centre for Devt Studies (CED) 1986–88; consultant, UNDP 1987–88, 2000–03; Founder mem. Chilean Asscn of Political Sciences 1988; Dir Centro de Estudios Sociales AVANCE 1988–94; political advisor to Minister Sec. Gen. of the Presidency 1990–94, 2000–03; Amb. to Austria 1994–2000, to Brazil 2003–05, to Spain 2006–08; Vice-Chair. Int. Cooperation Agency of Chile (AGCI) 2000–03; Minister Sec. Gen. of the Presidency 2005–06; mem. Bd of Dirs Victoria de Lebu-Carville (coal co.) 1990–92, SACOR-CORFO (agric. co.) 1992–93; mem. Academic Cttee, Santo Tomás Univ. 1992–94; Dir for Latin America, Acciona SA 2008–. *Address:* Acciona SA, Avenida Apoquindo, nº 4499-piso 14, Las Condes, 7580575 Santiago, Chile (office).

PÚCIK, Brig.-Gen. Vladimir; Slovak air force officer; b. 20 June 1952, Lazisko; m. Viera Púciková; two c.; ed Mil. Acad., Liptovský Mikuláš, Air Defence Mil. Acad., Tver, Royal Coll. Defence Studies, London; promoted to Lt 1976; Deputy Commdr, 52nd Air Surveillance Unit, Stod 1976–77, Commdr 1977–79; promoted to First Lt 1979; Chief of Staff, 54th Air Surveillance Battalion, Nepolisy 1979–81, Commdr 1981–83; promoted to Capt. 1982, to Maj. 1985; Sr Officer, Air Surveillance Branch 3rd AD Div., Žatec 1986–87; Sr Officer, Air Surveillance Dept, HQ of AF and Air Defences, Stará Boleslav 1987–91; promoted to Lt Col 1989; Chief Air Surveillance Branch 1st AD Div., Zvolen 1991–93; Deputy Chief of

AD Dept, HQ AF and Air Defence of SR, Trencín 1993–94; promoted to Col 1994; Deputy Commdr in Chief, 3rd AF and Air Defence Corps, Zvolen 1994–98; promoted to Col of Gen. Staff 2000; Deputy Commdr in Chief, Slovak AFs, Zvolen 2000-02; promoted to Brig.-Gen. 2002; Mil. Rep. of Slovakia to NATO and EU 2002–06; Medal for Homeland Service, Medal for Merit of Homeland Defence, Medal for Merit of Czechoslovak Armed Forces, Memorial Medal of Ministry of Defence of Slovak Repub., Mil. Badge of Honour, Slovak Armed Forces. *Leisure interests:* downhill skiing, hiking. *Address:* Ministry of Defence, Kutuzovova 7, 832 47 Bratislava, Slovakia. *Telephone:* (2) 4425-0320. *Fax:* (2) 4425-3242. *E-mail:* iveta.viragova@mod.gov.sk. *Website:* www.mosr.sk.

PUDDEPHATT, Andrew Charles, OBE, BA; British company director; b. 2 April 1950, Luton, Beds., England; s. of Andrew Ross Puddephatt and Margaret Deboo; two c.; ed Kingsbury School, Dunstable and Sidney Sussex Coll., Cambridge; Deputy Leader Hackney Council 1984–85, Leader 1986–89; Dir Nat. Council for Civil Liberties 1989–95; Dir Charter 88 1995–99; Exec. Dir Article 19 1999–2004; Visiting Fellow, Centre for the Study of Human Rights, LSE 2004–08; Dir, Hackney Empire Preservation Trust 1992–93, Global Dialogue 2006, 2008, Crarg Trading Ltd 2006–12; Chair. Bd of Trustees, Coordinated Action Against Domestic Abuse –2011; Vice-Chair. Int. Media Support, Denmark; mem. Int. Steering Cttee, Bibliotheca Alexandrina database, Norway; Int. Bd mem. Open Democracy Centre, South Africa; fmr Expert mem. Council of Europe and Commonwealth Expert working groups on freedom of information and freedom of expression. *Publications include:* Freedom of expression, Association and Assembly 2003, Post Conflict Intervention (working paper for UNESCO and Swedish Devt Agency) 2003, The Right to Information (for UNDP) 2004. *Leisure interests:* music, literature, cinema, walking. *Address:* c/o CAADA, Third Floor, Maxet House, 28 Baldwin Street, Bristol, BS1 1NG, England. *E-mail:* queries@caada.org.uk.

PUDDEPHATT, Richard John, OC, PhD, FRS, FRSC; British/Canadian chemist and academic; *Professor of Chemistry, University of Western Ontario;* b. 10 Oct. 1943; s. of Harry Puddephatt and Ena Puddephatt; m. Alice Poulton 1969; one s. one d.; ed Univ. Coll. London; Teaching Postdoctoral Fellow Univ. of Western Ontario 1968–70, Prof. of Chem. 1978–; Lecturer, Univ. of Liverpool 1970–77, Sr Lecturer 1977–78; currently Chair. Chemical Inst. of Canada; Nyholm Award 1997, CIC Medal 1998, Queen's Diamond Jubilee Medal 2012. *Publications include:* The Chemistry of Gold 1978, The Periodic Table of the Elements 1986. *Leisure interest:* gardening. *Address:* Department of Chemistry, Chemistry Building, University of Western Ontario, London, Ont., N6A 5B7, Canada (office). *Telephone:* (519) 679-2111 (office). *Fax:* (519) 661-3022 (office). *E-mail:* pudd@uwo .ca (office). *Website:* www.uwo.ca/chem/Tpuddr (office).

PUENZO, Luis; Argentine film director; b. 24 Feb. 1949, Buenos Aires; worked as storyboard designer in advertising, becoming advertising dir; f. Historias Cinematograficas Cinemania (film production co.) 1974. *Films include:* Luces de mis zapatos (Lights of my Shoes) 1973, Cinco años de vida (Five Years of Life) 1975, The Official Story 1985 (Palme d'Or, Cannes, Acad. Award for Best Foreign Film 1986 and 47 other int. awards), Gringo viejo (Old Gringo) 1989. *Address:* c/o Instituto Nacional de Cinematografía, Lima 319, 1073 Buenos Aires, Argentina.

PUGACHEV, Sergey Victorovich; Russian politician and business executive; b. 4 Feb. 1963, Kostoma; m.; two c.; ed Leningrad State Univ.; credit inspector, Head of Div., mem. Bd of Dirs USSR Promstroibank 1985–90; mem. Bd of Dirs N Trade Bank 1990–92; Chair. Bd of Dirs Int. Industrial Bank (Mezhprombank) 1992–2002; mem. Bureau Russian Union of Businessmen and Entrepreneurs 2002–; mem. Council of Feds, Rep. of Govt, Tuva Repub. 2001–; mem. Cttee on Problems of Fed. and Regional Policy Council of Feds; mem. Russian Acad. of Eng. *Publications include:* Commercial Bank in Conditions of Free Market Relations Formation: Economic and Financial Analysis 1998. *Address:* House of Government, Chuldum str. 18, 667000 Kyzyl (office); Council of Federation, Bolshaya Dmitrovka 26, 103426 Moscow, Russia (office). *Telephone:* (839422) 11284 (Kyzyl) (office); (495) 925-65-19 (Moscow) (office). *Fax:* (839422) 11354 (Kyzyl) (office); (495) 292-14-85 (Moscow) (office). *E-mail:* council@gov.ru (office).

PUGACHEVA, Alla Borisovna; Russian singer; b. 15 April 1949, Moscow; m. 1st Mykolas Orbakas 1969 (divorced 1973); m. 2nd Alexander Stefanovich 1976 (divorced 1980); m. 3rd Yevgeniy Boldin 1985 (divorced 1993); m. 4th Filipp Kirkorov 1994 (divorced 2005); one d.; ed M. Ippolitov-Ivanov Music High School, A. Lunacharsky State Inst. of Theatre Art; debut as soloist of Lipetsk vocal-instrumental group 1970; with O Lundstrem Jazz orchestra 1971; soloist, Veselye Rebyata Ensemble 1973–78; f. Song Theatre 1988; numerous prizes and awards including 3rd prize All-Union Contest Moscow, 1974; Grand Prix Int. Competition Golden Orpheus Bulgaria 1975, Int. Festival Sopot 1978; acted in films; tours in USA, Germany, Switzerland, India, France, Italy and other countries; f. Theatre of Songs 1988, Alla Co. 1993, Alla Magazine 1993; toured Russia and other countries in honour of her 60th birthday 2009; Order of Merit for the Fatherland, 2nd degree 1999, 3rd degree 2009, Order of Dostlugn (Friendship) (Azerbaijan) 2009, Order of St Mesrop Mashtots (Armenia) 2009; USSR People's Artist 1991, Ovation Prize 1994, State Prize of Russia 1995. *Repertoire includes:* numerous songs by popular Soviet composers such as R. Pauls, A. Muromtsev, A. Zatsepin and others, also songs of her own; albums: Alla 1990, Yes! 1998, River Tram 2001, Was There a Boy? 2002, Live Peacefully, My Country! 2003, Invitation to a Sunset 2008. *Address:* Tverskaya-Yamskaya str., Apt 57, Moscow, Russia (home). *Telephone:* (495) 250-95-78 (home).

PUGIN, Nikolai Andreyevich; Russian industrialist; b. 30 June 1940; ed Gorky Polytechnic Inst.; worker, foreman at car factory 1958–75; chief engineer at gearbox factory 1975–81; Tech. Dir 1981–83, Gen. Dir of Gorky Automobile Works 1983–86; Minister of Automobile Industry 1986–88, of Automobile and Agricultural Machines Industry 1988–91; mem. Russian Eng Acad. 1991–; mem. Russian Acad. of Natural Science 1992–; Pres. ASM Holding Inc. (mfrs of motor vehicles and farm machinery in CIS) 1992–; Chair. Bd GAZ Co. (Nizhny Novgorod); Pres. Ind. Financial Group Nizhegorodskiye Automobili 1994–; Chair. Bd of Dirs Autobank 1996–2002; mem. Nizhny Novgorod Regional Ass. 2002–. *Address:* ASM Holding, 21/5 Kuznetsky Most, 103895 Moscow; GAZ, Lenina prosp. 9, 603046, Nizhny Novgorod; Oblastnaya Duma, Kremlin, korp. 2, 603082 Nizhny Novgorod,

Russia. *Telephone:* (495) 921-68-21; (495) 924-53-85; (8312) 56-10-70 (Nizhny Novgorod). *Fax:* (495) 924-39-00. *Website:* www.asm-holding.ru.

PUIG, Lluis de Maria; Spanish historian and politician; *President, Parliamentary Assembly, Council of Europe;* b. 29 July 1945, Bascara, Gerona; m.; two c.; ed Autonomous Univ. of Barcelona, Ecole des Hautes Etudes de la Sorbonne, Paris; worked in anti-Franco opposition as active mem. of underground Catalan and socialist orgs; Prof. of Contemporary History, Autonomous Univ. of Barcelona; Socialist mem. Cortes for Gerona 1979–2004; mem. Catalonian Socialist Party Bureau 1986–; Pres. Gerona Fed. of Socialist Party 1993–; mem. Parl. Ass. of Council of Europe (PACE) 1983–97, Chair. Sub-Cttee on European Social Charter 1984–89, Vice-Pres. PACE 1993–96, Chair. PACE Cttee on Culture, Science and Educ. 2002–05, Chair. Spanish del. to PACE 2004–, Pres. PACE 2008–; mem. Spanish del. to WEU Ass. 1990–, Vice-Chair. Socialist Group 1992–96, Defence Cttee 1992–94, Chair. Political Cttee 1995–97, mem. Presidential Cttee 1994, Pres. WEU Ass. 1997–2000; elected Senator for Girona 2004; Sec. Alexander Cirici Inst. for European Co-operation 1986–96, Pres. 1996–; Vice-Pres. Ernest Lluch Foundation 2002–; Dr hc (Ovidius Univ. of Constanta, Romania) 1998. *Publications:* author of 15 books on history and contemporary politics; has written 100 academic studies on history, culture and politics and frequent articles in Spanish and int. press. *Address:* Office of the President, Parliamentary Assembly, Council of Europe, Avenue de l'Europe, 67075 Strasbourg Cedex, France (office). *Telephone:* 3-88-41-20-00 (office). *Fax:* 3-88-41-27-81 (office). *Website:* assembly .coe.int (home).

PUISSOCHET, Jean-Pierre, LLD, PhD; French lawyer and international judge; *Judge, Court of Justice of the European Union;* b. 3 May 1936, Clermont-Ferrand; s. of René Puissochet and Hélène Puissochet (née Brengues); m. Eliane Millet 1973; one d.; ed Lycée du Parc, Lyon, Inst. for Political Studies, Lyon, School of Law, Lyon, Ecole Nat. d'Admin., Paris; Auditeur, Conseil d'Etat 1962, Maître des Requêtes 1968, Conseiller 1985; Dir Legal Service, Council of EC 1968–70, Dir-Gen. 1970–73; Dir-Gen. Agence Nat. pour l'Emploi 1973–75; Dir Ministry of Industry and Research 1977–79; Dir of Legal Affairs, OECD 1979–85; Dir Int. Inst. of Public Admin. 1985–87; Legal Adviser, Dir of Legal Affairs, Ministry of Foreign Affairs 1987–94; Judge, Court of Justice of the European Communities (now EU) 1994–; mem. Perm. Court of Arbitration, The Hague 1990–; Officier, Légion d'honneur, Grand Officier Ordre nat. du Mérite, Officier du Mérite agricole, Grand'Uffiziale dell Ordine al Merito (Italy). *Publications:* The Enlargement of the EC 1974; numerous articles on Community and int. law. *Address:* Court of Justice of the European Union, Plateau du Kirchberg, 2925 Luxembourg (office); 15 rue Jean-Pierre Brasseur, 1258, Luxembourg (home). *Telephone:* 43-03-22-46 (office). *Fax:* 43-03-20-00. *E-mail:* jean-pierre.puissochet@curia.eu.int (office). *Website:* www.curia.eu.int (office).

PUJATS, HE Cardinal Jānis; Latvian ecclesiastic; *Archbishop of Rīga;* b. 14 Nov. 1930, Nautrani, Rezekne Dist; ed Catholic Seminary, Riga; ordained priest 1951; taught art history and liturgy at Catholic Theological Seminary, Rīga; Vicar General, Metropolitan Curia in Rīga 1979–84; KGB declared him persona non grata 1984; consecrated Bishop 1991; Archbishop of Rīga 1991; cr. Cardinal (in pectore—secretly) 1998, (openly) 2001; Pres. Latvian Bishops' Conf.; mem. Congregation for the Causes of Saints. *Address:* Metropolijas Kurija, Mazā Pils iela 2/a, 1050 Rīga, Latvia (office). *Telephone:* 6222-7266 (office); 6222-0775 (home). *Fax:* 722-0060 (office); 782-0274 (home). *E-mail:* sacerdos@inbox.lv (home).

PUJOL I SOLEY, Rt Hon. Jordi, MD; Spanish politician, pharmacologist and business executive; *President, Centre Estudis Jordi Pujol;* b. 9 June 1930, Barcelona; s. of Florenci Pujol i Brugat and Maria Soley i Mas; m. Marta Ferrusola 1956; seven s.; ed Faculty of Medicine, Univ. of Barcelona; worked in pharmaceutical industry 1953–60; f. Banca Catalana group 1959, Man. Dir 1959–76; f. Convergència Democratica de Catalunya 1974; Councillor, provisional Generalitat 1977–80; mem. Congress, Madrid 1977, 1979; Head Convergència i Unió Parl. Group in Congress 1977–80; mem. Catalan Parl. 1980–; Pres. Generalitat de Catalunya 1980–2003; Vice-Pres. Ass. of European Regions 1988–92, Pres. 1992–96; Pres. Centre Estudis Jordi Pujol 2005–; Dr hc (Brussels, Toulouse, Lyon, Rosario, Argentina, Barcelona). *Publications include:* Una política per Catalunya 1976, Construir Catalunya 1980, Als joves de Catalunya 1988, La Força serena i constructiva de Catalunya 1991, Pensar Europa 1993, Passió per Catalunya 1999, El Libre Roig de Jordi Pujol 2003, Sobre Europa (i altres coses) 2004, Una reflexió necessària 2006, Memòries Història d'una convicció (1930–1980) 2007, Memòries Temps de construir (1980–2003) 2009. *Leisure interests:* reading, walking, cycling. *Address:* Passeig de Gràcia, 39, pral. 08007 Barcelona, Spain (office). *Telephone:* (93) 5529110 (office). *Fax:* (93) 5529114 (office). *E-mail:* jordipujol@gencat.cat (office). *Website:* www.jordipujol.cat (home).

PUJOLS ALCÁNTARA, José Alberto (Albert); American (b. Dominican Repub.) professional baseball player; b. 16 Jan. 1980, Santo Domingo; s. of Bienvenido Pujols; m. Deidre Pujols 2000; three c.; ed Fort Osage High School, Independence, Mo., Maple Woods Community Coll., Kansas City; emigrated to USA 1996; played in Jayhawk League, Kan. 1999; signed with St Louis Cardinals professional baseball team 1999, assigned to minor leagues 1999–2000; played for Peroia Chiefs 2000, then Potomac Cannons, Memphis Redbirds, first baseman St Louis Cardinals 2001–11; signed as free agent with Los Angeles Angels of Anaheim 2011–; Co-f. Pujols Family Foundation 2005; Nat. League Batting Champion (average .359) 2003, Nat. League Rookie of the Year 2001, Sporting News Player of the Year 2003, 2008, Gold Glove Award 2006, Roberto Clemente Award 2008, Nat. League Most Nat. League Valuable Player 2005, 2008, 2009, Hank Aaron Award 2003, 2009, nine times All-star selection 2001, 2003–10. *Address:* Angels Baseball LP, 2000 Gene Autry Way, Anaheim, CA 92806, USA (office). *Telephone:* (714) 940-2000 (office). *Website:* losangeles.angels.mlb.com (office).

PULAT, Abdurakhim; Uzbekistani politician; Chair. Unity People's Movt Party ('Birlik' Xalq Harakati Partiyasi—Birlik) founded in 1988; leading opposition group, banned in 1992; registered as social movt; refused registration as political party 2004), living in self-imposed exile in USA c. 2003. *Address:* Unity People's Movement Party ('Birlik' Xalq Harakati Partiyasi—Birlik), c/o Union of Writers of Uzbekistan, Neru ko'ch. 1, 100000 Tashkent, Uzbekistan (office). *Telephone:* (71)

233-63-74 (office). *E-mail:* webmaster@birlik.net (office). *Website:* www.birlik.net (office).

PULATOV, Timur Iskhakovich; Uzbekistani writer; b. 1939, Bukhara; ed Bukhara Pedagogical Inst., High School of Scriptwriters and Film Directors; freelance writer 1974–; First Sec., Co-ordinator Exec. Bd Int. Soc. of Writers' Unions 1992–; Ed. Literary Eurasia; Order, Friendship of Peoples for devt of lit. and art and strengthening of int. relations 1994. *Publications:* Life Story of a Naughty Boy from Bukhara 1984, Other Populated Points, Properties, Passions of the Bukhara House, Tortoise Tarasi, Swimming Eurasia. *Address:* Moscow City Organization of Russian Writers' Union, B. Nikitskaya str. 50a/5, 121069 Moscow, Russia (office). *Telephone:* (095) 202-87-83 (office).

PULIKOVSKY, Lt-Gen. Konstantin Borisovich; Russian army officer and politician; b. 9 Feb. 1948, Ussuriysk, Primorsk Territory; ed M. Frunze Mil. Acad., Mil. Acad. of Gen. Staff; mil. posts to rank of Army Commdr 1972; took part in conflict in Chechnya 1994–96; Commdr group of Fed. forces in Chechen Repub. 1996, Deputy Commdr., N Caucasus Mil. District 1997; leader Krasnodar Org. All-Russian Movt of veterans of local wars and mil. conflicts Boyevoye Bratstvo; Rep. of Russian Pres. to Far Eastern Fed. Dist 2000–04; head of Rostekhnadzor (Fed. Service for Environmental, Tech. and Nuclear Supervision) 2005–08. *Publications include:* The Eastern Express: Through Russia With Kim Jong Il 2002. *Address:* c/o Rostekhnadzor, 105066 Moscow ul. A. Lukyanov, 4, Russia (office). *Website:* .

PULJIĆ, HE Cardinal Vinko; Bosnia and Herzegovina ecclesiastic; *Archbishop of Vrhbosna;* b. 8 Sept. 1945, Prijećani, Banja Luka; s. of Ivan Puljić and Kaja Puljić (née Pletikosa); ed seminary of Salata, Zagreb and at Đakovo; ordained priest Đakovo 1970; Parish Vicar, Banja Luka, Parish Priest Sasina, then Ravska; Pedagogue, Zmajević seminary, Zadar 1978–87; Parish Priest, Bosanska Gradiška 1987–90; Vice-Rector Catholic Theological Seminary of Vrhbosna, Sarajevo 1990; Archbishop of Vrhbosna 1990–; cr. Cardinal (Cardinal Priest of Santa Chiara a Vigna Clara) 1994; participated in Papal Conclave 2005, 2013; travelled to many countries in Europe and N America to publicise the suffering caused by the war in Bosnia and Herzegovina and discuss possible solutions; Hon. Dr of Humanitarian Science (Grand Valley State Univ., Mich., USA) 1995; Hon. Dr of Pastoral Theology (Catholic Univ. Santa Maria in Apartade, Peru) 2001; Humanist of the Decade and Golden Diploma of Humanism, Int. League of Humanists, Sarajevo 1995. *Publications:* Suffering With Hope: Appeals, Addresses, Interviews 1995, Non cancellato l'uomo – Un grido di speranza da Sarajevo 1997, Per amore dell'uomo–Testimone di pace a Sarajevo 1999. *Address:* Nadbiskupski Ordinarijat, Kaptol 7, BiH 71000 Sarajevo, Bosnia and Herzegovina (office). *Telephone:* (33) 225501 (office); (33) 218823 (office). *Fax:* (33) 218824 (office). *E-mail:* kartolka@bih.nct.ba (office).

PULLEN, Roderick (Rod) Allen, BA, DPhil; British diplomatist; b. 11 April 1949; m. Karen Sketchley; four s. one d.; ed Mansfield Coll. and Univs of Oxford and Sussex; with Ministry of Defence 1975–78, 1980–81; Second Sec. UK Del. to NATO 1978–80, First Sec., Del. to CSCE 1981–82, FCO 1982–84, 1988–90, Deputy High Commr, Suva 1984–88, Nairobi 1994–97, Abuja 1997–2000, High Commr to Ghana 2000–04, Amb. to Zimbabwe 2004–06, UK Special Rep. at Inter-Sudanese Peace Talks on Darfur 2006; Junior Bursar, Trinity Coll. ., Cambridge 2006–. *Address:* Office of the Junior Bursar, Trinity College, Cambridge, CB2 1TQ, England. *Website:* www.trin.cam.ac.uk.

PULLMAN, Bill; American actor; b. 17 Dec. 1953, Hornell, NY; m. Tamara Pullman; three c.; ed Univ. of Massachusetts; fmr drama teacher, bldg contractor, dir of a theatre group; started acting in fringe theatres, New York; f. Big Town Productions (film production co.). *Films include:* Ruthless People, A League of Their Own, Sommersby, Sleepless in Seattle, While You Were Sleeping, Caspar, Independence Day, Lost Highway 1997, The End of Violence 1997, The Thin Red Line 1998, Zero Effect 1998, A Man is Mostly Water 1999, History is Made at Night 1999, The Guilt 1999, Brokedown Place 1999, Lake Placid 1999, Coming To Light: Edward S. Curtis and the North American Indians (voice) 2000, Titan A.E. 2000, Lucky Numbers 2000, Ignition 2001, A Man Is Mostly Water 2001, Igby Goes Down 2002, 29 Palms 2002, Rick 2003, The Grudge 2004, The Orphan King 2005, Dear Wendy 2005, Scary Movie 4 2006, You Kill Me 2007, Nobel Son 2007, Bottle Shock 2008, Phoebe in Wonderland 2008, Surveillance 2008, Your Name Here 2008, The Killer Inside Me 2010, Peacock 2010, Rio Sex Comedy 2010, Bringing Up Bobby 2011, Lola Versus 2012. *Address:* c/o One Talent Management, 9220 Sunset Blvd, Los Angeles, CA 90069, USA (office). *E-mail:* billpullman.org@gmail.com (office); ceres21@juno.com (office). *Website:* www.billpullman.org (office).

PULLMAN, Philip, CBE, BA, FRSL; British writer; b. 19 Oct. 1946, Norwich, Norfolk; m. Jude Speller 1970; two s.; ed Exeter Coll., Oxford; teacher in Oxford 1972–86; part-time Lecturer, Westminster Coll., Oxford 1986–96; Hon. Fellow, Univ. of Wales, Bangor; Hon. DLitt (Univ. of East Anglia), (Oxford Brookes Univ.), (Oxford Univ.) (Exeter Univ.) 2010, Hon. DUniv (Univ. of Surrey Roehampton); Booksellers' Asscn/Book Data Author of the Year Award 2001, Booksellers' Asscn Author of the Year 2001, 2002, British Book Awards Author of the Year Award 2002, Whitbread Book of the Year Award 2002. *Publications:* Count Karlstein 1982, The Ruby in the Smoke (Sally Lockhart series) 1985, The Shadow in the Plate 1986, The Shadow in the North (Sally Lockhart series) 1987, Spring-Heeled Jack 1989, The Tiger in the Well (Sally Lockhart series) 1990, The Broken Bridge 1990, The White Mercedes 1992, The Tin Princess (Sally Lockhart series) 1994, The New Cut Gang: Thunderbolt's Waxwork 1994, The New Cut Gang: The Gas-fitter's Ball 1995, The Wonderful Story of Aladdin and the Enchanted Lamp 1995, The Firework-Maker's Daughter 1995, Northern Lights (aka The Golden Compass, Vol. I, His Dark Materials trilogy) (Carnegie Medal 1996, Guardian Children's Fiction Prize 1996, British Book Awards Children's Book of the Year 1996, CILIP Carnegie Medal 2007) 1995, Clockwork 1996, The Subtle Knife (Vol. II, His Dark Materials trilogy) 1997, The Butterfly Tattoo 1998, Mossycoat 1998, Detective Stories (ed.) 1998, I Was a Rat! 1999, The Amber Spyglass (Vol. III, His Dark Materials trilogy) (British Book Awards WH Smith Children's Book of the Year, Whitbread Children's Book of the Year Prize 2001, Whitbread Book of the Year Award 2001) 2000, Puss-in-Boots 2000, Sherlock Holmes and the Limehouse Horror 2001, Lyra's Oxford 2003, The Scarecrow and his Servant 2004, A Word or Two About Myths 2005, The Good Man Jesus and the Scoundrel Christ 2010, Grimm Tales for Young and Old 2012; contrib. reviews to

Times Educational Supplement, The Guardian. *Address:* c/o Caradoc King, AP Watt at United Agents LLP, 12–26 Lexington Street, London, W1F 0LE, England (office). *Telephone:* (20) 3214-0800 (office). *Fax:* (20) 3214-0801 (office). *E-mail:* info@unitedagents.co.uk (office). *Website:* www.apwatt.co.uk (office); www.philip -pullman.com.

PULTE, William J.; American construction industry executive; m.; 14 c.; started house-building co. William J. Pulte Inc. (now Pulte Home Corpn) 1956, Pres. and Chair. Exec. Cttee 1972–90, Chair. of the Bd 1990–98, 2002–09, currently mem. Bd of Dirs. *Address:* c/o Pulte Homes Inc., 100 Bloomfield Hills Parkway, Suite 300, Broomfield Hills, MI 48304, USA (office). *Telephone:* (248) 647-2750 (office). *Fax:* (248) 433-4598 (office). *Website:* www.pulte.com (office).

PUN, Barsha Man (Ananta); Nepalese politician; fmr Deputy Commdr Maoist People's Liberation Army (PLA); mem. Unified Communist Party of Nepal (Maoist), mem. Cen. Secr.; mem. Constituent Ass. for Lalitpur No 1 constituency; Minister for Peace and Reconstruction March–Aug. 2011, Minister of Finance 2011–13; fmr Chair. Indigenous Peoples' Caucus; Chair. Nat. Council of Nepal Scouts. *Address:* c/o Ministry of Finance, Singha Durbar, Kathmandu, Nepal.

PUNA, Henry; Cook Islands lawyer and politician; *Prime Minister;* s. of Tupuariki Puna; m. Akaiti Puna; ed Univ. of Auckland, New Zealand, Univ. of Tasmania, Australia; fmr pearl farmer; pvt. practise as lawyer; MP for Manihiki 2005–06, 2010–, Prime Minister 2010–, also Minister for the Public Service Comm., Attorney-Gen., Parl. Services, Police, Minister of Justice, Ombudsman, Nat. Environment Service, Energy and Renewable Energy, and Emergency Man.; mem. Cook Islands Party, Leader 2006–. *Address:* Office of the Prime Minister, Government of the Cook Islands, Private Bag, Avarua, Rarotonga, Cook Islands (office). *Telephone:* 25494 (office). *Fax:* 20856 (office). *E-mail:* coso@pmoffice.gov.ck (office). *Website:* www.pmoffice.gov.ck (office).

PURCELL, James (Jim) Nelson, Jr, MPA; American international official and international consultant; *Chairman, US Association for International Migration;* b. 16 July 1938, Nashville, Tenn.; s. of James Nelson Purcell, Sr; m. Walda Primm 1961; two d.; ed Furman Univ., Syracuse Univ.; Budget Analyst, US Atomic Energy Comm. 1962–66; Man. Analyst, Agency for Int. Devt 1966–68; Deputy Dir Budget Preparation Staff, Office of Man. and Budget (OMB) 1968–72, Sr Examiner, Int. Affairs Div. OMB 1972–74, Chief Justice, Treasury Br. OMB 1974–76; Chief Resources Programming and Man. Div., Bureau for Educ. and Cultural Affairs, Dept of State 1976–77; Deputy Budget Dir, Dept of State 1977–78; Exec. Dir Bureau of Admin., Dept of State 1978–79; Deputy Asst Sec., Programmes and Budget, Bureau for Refugee Programs, Dept of State 1979–82, Dir, Asst Sec., Bureau for Refugee Programmes 1982–87; Dir-Gen. Int. Org. for Migration 1988–98; int. consultant 1998–; Chair. US Asscn for Int. Migration 2009–; mem. Council for Community of Democracies, Columbia Housing Corpn; mem. American Soc. of Public Admin.; Order of the Phoenix (Greece) 1993; Distinguished Honor Award, State Dept 1987, Meritorious Executive Award, US Sr Exec. Service 1985, Golden Medal of Pres. of Hungary 1995, Immigration and Refugee Policy Award, Centre for Migration Studies 1998, Wings of Hope Award, US Asscn for Int. Migration 1992, Helping Hands Award, World Relief 1987, Special Commendation Award, Inst. for Int. Humanitarian Law, San Remo, Italy 1998, Appreciation Award, Pres. of Armenia 1994. *Publication:* The Perils of Unresolved Humanitarian Problems: A Region of Crisis-the Middle East 2001. *Address:* 5113 West Running Brook Road, Columbia, MD 21044, USA (home). *Telephone:* (443) 745-1004 (office). *Fax:* (410) 730-1353 (office). *E-mail:* jpurcell7@ verizon.net (office). *Website:* www.iom.int (office).

PURCELL, Philip James, MSc, MBA; American business executive; *President, Continental Investors, LLC;* b. 5 Sept. 1943, Salt Lake City, Utah; m. Anne Marie McNamara 1964; seven s.; ed Univ. of Notre Dame, London School of Econs, UK, Univ. of Chicago; Man. Dir McKinsey & Co. Inc., Chicago 1967–78; Vice-Pres. Planning and Admin., Sears, Roebuck & Co., Chicago 1978–82; Pres., CEO then Chair., CEO Dean Witter Discover & Co., New York 1982–97, Chair. and CEO Morgan Stanley, Dean Witter & Co. (after merger with Morgan Stanley), New York 1997–2005 (co. name changed to Morgan Stanley 2001); Pres. Continental Investors, LLC 2006–; Dir New York Stock Exchange 1991–96 (Vice-Chair. 1995, 1996, later mem. Exec. Bd), AMR Corpn –2013, American Airlines –2013; Founder and Chair. Financial Services Forum; Trustee, Univ. of Notre Dame, Chair. Athletic Affairs Cttee. *Address:* Continental Investors, LLC, 227 West Monroe Street, Suite 5045, Chicago, IL 60606, USA (office). *Telephone:* (312) 628-2451 (office). *E-mail:* ellie@continv.com (office). *Website:* www.continentalinvestors.com (office).

PURI, Balraj; Indian human rights campaigner, author and academic; *Director, Institute of Jammu and Kashmir Affairs;* b. 5 Aug. 1928; columnist and activist; Founding mem. People's Union for Civil Liberties, Convenor Jammu and Kashmir State Br.; currently Dir Inst. of Jammu and Kashmir Affairs, Jammu; several hon. appointments in academic and govt orgs and non-governmental orgs (NGOs); numerous awards, including M.A. Thomas Human Rights Award 1995, Mother Teresa Communal Harmony Award 1995, Padma Bhushan 2005, Indira Gandhi Award for Nat. Integration 2009. *Publications include:* author and co-author of 40 books including Jammu: A Clue of Kashmir Tangle 1966, Abdullah Era 1983, Jammu and Kashmir: Triumph and Tragedy of Indian Federalism 1991, Kashmir towards Insurgency 1995, 5000 years of Kashmir (ed.) 1997, JP on Kashmir 2005, Kashmir Insurgency and After 2008, Muslims of India Since Partition 2008. *Address:* Karan Nagar, Jammu 180 005, India (office). *Telephone:* (191) 254-2687 (home). *Fax:* (191) 254-3556 (home). *E-mail:* balraj_puri1@rediffmail.com (office). *Website:* www.humanrightsjournal.com (office).

PURI, Om, OBE; Indian actor; b. (Om Prakash Puri), 18 Oct. 1950, Ambala; s. of Tek Chand Puri and Tara Devi; m. Nandita C. Puri; one s.; ed Film and TV Inst. of India, Nat. School of Drama; Hon. OBE 2004; Padma Shri 1990, Grand Prix Special des Amériques, Montréal World Film Festival 1998, Filmfare Lifetime Achievement Award 2009. *Films include:* Ghashiram Kotwal 1976, Bhavani Bhavai 1980, Sadgati 1981, Arohan (Nat. Film Award for Best Actor 1982), Ardh Satya (Nat. Film Award for Best Actor 1984, Karlovy Vary Int. Film Festival Best Actor Award 1984) 1982, Jaane Bhi Do Yaaro 1983, Aaghat 1986, Mirch Masala 1986, Genesis 1986, Spices 1986, Dharavi 1992, In Custody 1993, Target 1995, Ghatak 1996, Brothers in Trouble 1996, Ghost and the Darkness 1996, Maachis

1997, My Son the Fanatic (Brussels Int. Film Festival Best Actor 1998) 1997, East is East (BAFTA Award 2000) 1999, Hera Pheri 2000, The Zookeeper 2001, Bollywood Calling 2001, Happy Now 2001, Indian 2001, The Mystic Masseur 2001, The Parole Officer 2001, Pitaah 2002, Maa Tujhhe Salaam (voice) 2002, Ansh: The Dangerous Part 2002, Pyaar Diwana Hota Hai 2002, Murder (TV) 2002, Awara Paagal Deewana 2002, Shararat 2002, Chor Machaye Shor 2002, White Teeth 2002 (TV mini-series), Ghaav: The Wound 2002, Ghaav: The Wound 2002, Aapko Pehle Bhi Kahin Dekha Hai 2003, Kash… Aap Hamare Hote 2003, Ek Aur Ek Gyarah 2003, Code 46 2003, Maqbool 2003, The Canterbury Tales, Chupke Se 2003, Second Generation (TV) 2003, Dhoop 2003, Kagaar 2003, Dev 2004, Lakshya 2004, Charlie Wilson's War 2007, Singh Is Kinng (sic) 2008, Billu Barber 2009, London Dreams 2009, Kurbaan 2009, Bolo Raam 2009, Khap 2010, Na Ghar Ke Na Ghaat Ke 2010, Kushti 2010, Dabangg 2010, West Is West 2010, Action Replayy (sic) 2010, Society Kaam Se Gayi 2011, Little Terrors 2011. *Publication:* Unlikely Hero: Om Puri (biog. by Nandita C. Puri). *Address:* 703, Trishul-2, Seven Bungalows, Andheri-W, Mumbai 400 061, India (home). *Telephone:* (22) 26342902 (home); (98) 20060766 (mobile). *E-mail:* ompuri50@gmail.com (office).

PURICELLI, Arturo Antonio; Argentine politician; *Minister of Security;* b. 1948, Río Gallegos, Santa Cruz Prov.; Gov. Santa Cruz Prov. 1983–87; mem. Partido Justicialista, Pres. Santa Cruz chapter 1987; elected to Cámara de Diputados (Parl.) 1989; Head of Encotesa (state postal service) 1996; elected to Prov. Lower House, Santa Cruz 1997; Vice-Pres. Nat. Airports Regulatory Agency –1999; Sec. of Provincial Affairs 2001–03; Head of Fabricaciones Militares (state-owned defence contractor) 2006–10; Minister of Defence 2010–13, of Security 2013–. *Address:* Ministry of Security, Gelly y Obes 2289, C1425EMA Buenos Aires, Argentina (office). *Website:* www.minseg.gob.ar (office).

PURISIMA, Cesar V., BSc, MBA; Philippine politician; *Secretary of Finance;* ed De la Salle Univ., Manila, JL Kellogg Grad. School of Man., Northwestern Univ., USA; fmr Chair. and Man. Pnr, SGV & Co.; fmr mem. Global Exec. Bd and Global Practice Council, Ernst & Young; Chair. Exec. Cttee, Ciba Capital 2006; Sec., Dept of Trade and Industry 2004–05, Sec., Dept of Finance Feb.–July 2005, Sec. of Finance 2010–; mem. Bd Trustees Makati Business Club 2008; Ind. Dir Energy Devt Corpn 2009–10; fmr mem. Monetary Bd Bangko Sentral ng Pilipinas. *Address:* Department of Finance, DOF Bldg, BSP Complex, Roxas Blvd, 1004 Metro Manila, Philippines (office). *Telephone:* (2) 5236051 (office). *Fax:* (2) 5268474 (office). *E-mail:* cpurisima@dof.gov.ph (office). *Website:* www.dof.gov.ph (office).

PURNELL, James Mark Dakin, BA; British broadcasting executive and fmr politician; *Director, Strategy and Digital, British Broadcasting Corporation;* b. 2 March 1970; s. of John Purnell and Janet Purnell; ed Royal Grammar School, Guildford, Balliol Coll., Oxford; researcher for Shadow Employment Sec. Tony Blair 1989–92; researcher, Hydra Assocs (media consultants), London 1992–94; Research Fellow, Inst. for Public Policy Research 1994–95; Head of Corp. Planning, BBC 1995–97, Dir Strategy and Digital 2013–; Special Adviser to Prime Minister Tony Blair 1997–2001; Labour MP for Stalybridge and Hyde 2001–10, Parl. Pvt. Sec. to Ruth Kelly 2003–04, Asst Govt Whip 2004–05, Parl. Under-Sec. of State, Dept for Culture, Media and Sport 2005–06, Minister of State for Pensions Dept for Work and Pensions 2006–07, Sec. of State for Culture, Media and Sport 2007–08, Sec. of State for Work and Pensions 2008–09 (resgnd); mem. Bd of Dirs Open Left Project, Demos (think-tank), London 2009, Royal Nat. Theatre, British Film Inst.; Chair. of Trustees, Inst. for Public Policy Research (think-tank) 2010. *Leisure interests:* film, music, theatre and football. *Address:* BBC Broadcasting House, Portland Place, London, W1A 1AA, England (office). *Website:* www.bbc.co .uk (office).

PURPURA, Dominick Paul, AB, MD; American neuroscientist and academic; *Distinguished Professor Emeritus and Dean Emeritus, Albert Einstein College of Medicine, Yeshiva University;* b. 2 April 1927, New York, NY; s. of John R. Purpura and Rose Ruffino; m. Florence Williams 1948; three s. one d.; ed Columbia Univ. and Harvard Medical School; mem. Faculty, Coll. of Physicians and Surgeon, Columbia Univ. 1957–67; Chair. and Prof., Dept of Anatomy, Albert Einstein Coll. of Medicine, Yeshiva Univ. 1967–74, Dept of Neuroscience 1974–82, Prof. and Chair. of Neuroscience 1974–82, Dean, Albert Einstein Coll. of Medicine and Vice-Pres. for Medical Affairs 1984–2006, Distinguished Prof. Emer. and Dean Emer. 2006–; Dir Rose F. Kennedy Center for Research in Mental Retardation and Human Devt 1972–82; Dean, Stanford Univ. School of Medicine 1982–84; Pres. Soc. for Neuroscience 1982–83, Int. Brain Research Org. 1987–98, Vice-Pres. for Medical Affairs UNESCO from 1961; Chief Ed. Brain Research for 25 years; mem. NAS, Inst. of Medicine; Fellow, New York Acad. of Sciences; first annual Nat. Medical Research Award, Nat. Health Council (co-recipient) 1983, Lifetime Achievement Award for Research, American Epilepsy Society 1993, Presidential Award, Soc. of Neuroscience 1996, New York City Mayor's Lifetime Achievement Award for Excellence in the Medical and Biological Sciences 2001. *Publications:* about 200 scientific papers. *Address:* Albert Einstein College of Medicine, Yeshiva University, Room 912D, Rose F. Kennedy Center, 1410 Pelham Parkway South, Bronx, NY 10461, USA (office). *Telephone:* (718) 430-3617 (office). *E-mail:* dominick.purpura@einstein.yu.edu (office). *Website:* www.einstein.yu.edu/ departments/neuroscience/dominick-purpura.aspx (office).

PURRYAG, Rajkeswur (Kailash); Mauritian attorney and head of state; *President;* b. 12 Dec. 1947, Camp Fouquereaux; m. Aneetah Purryag; one d.; ed Mauritius Coll., Curepipe; has worked as attorney since 1973; mem. Vacoas/ Phoenix Municipal Comm. 1974–76; elected mem. Nat. Ass. (Parl.) 1976, Speaker 2005–12; Minister of Social Security 1980–82, of Health 1984–86, of Econ. Planning, Information and Telecommunications 1995–97, Deputy Prime Minister and Minister of Foreign Affairs and Int. Trade 1997–2000; Pres. of Mauritius 2012–; mem. Mauritius Labour Party, Sec.-Gen. 1987–91, Pres. 1991–96; Hon. Freedom of the City of Port Louis 2007; Grand Officer, Order of the Star and Key of the Indian Ocean 1998, Grand Commdr, Order of the Star and Key of the Indian Ocean 2009. *Address:* Office of the President, State House, Le Réduit, Port Louis, Mauritius (office). *Telephone:* 454-3021 (office). *Fax:* 464-5370 (office). *E-mail:* president@mail.gov.mu (office). *Website:* www.gov.mu/portal/site/president (office).

PURUSHOTHAMAN, Vakkom B.; Indian politician; *Governor of Mizoram;* b. 12 April 1928, Vakkom, Kerala; s. of Bhanu Panicker and Smt Bhavani; m. Lilly

Purushothaman; two s. one d.; mem. Indian Nat. Congress Party, fmr Pres. Thiruvananthapuram Dist Congress Cttee, Gen. Sec. and Vice-Pres., Kerala Pradesh Congress Cttee, mem. All-India Congress Cttee for 25 years; elected to Kerala Legis. Ass. from Attingal constituency 1970, 1977, 1980, 1982, Speaker 1982–84, 2001–04, State Minister of Agric. and Labour 1971–77, for Health and Tourism 1980–81, Minister of Finance and Excise 2004; mem. Lok Sabha (lower house of nat. parl.) 1984–89, 1989–91; Lt-Gov. of Andaman and Nicobar Islands 1993–96; Gov. of Mizoram 2011–. *Address:* Office of the Governor, Raj Bhavan, Aizawl 796 001, India (office). *Telephone:* (389) 2322262 (office). *Fax:* (389) 2323344 (office).

PURVES, Sir William, Kt, KStJ, CBE, DSO; British banker (retd); b. 27 Dec. 1931, Kelso, Roxburghshire, Scotland; s. of Andrew Purves and Ida Purves; m. 1st Diana T. Richardson 1958 (divorced 1988); two s. two d.; m. 2nd Rebecca Jane Lewellen 1989; ed Kelso High School; with Nat. Bank of Scotland, Kelso 1948–54; joined the Hongkong and Shanghai Banking Corpn 1954, Chief Accountant 1970–74, Man., Tokyo 1974–76, Sr Man. Overseas Operations 1976–78, Asst Gen. Man. Overseas Operations 1978–79, Gen. Man. Int. 1979–82, Exec. Dir 1982–84, Deputy Chair. 1984–86, Chair. and CEO 1986–92, Exec. Chair. HSBC Holdings PLC 1992–98; Pres. Int. Monetary Conf. 1992, mem. Exec. Council Hong Kong 1987–93; Chair. British Bank of the Middle East 1979–98, Midland Bank PLC 1994–97 (Dir 1987–98); Dir HBSC Americas Inc. 1984–88; Deputy Chair. (non-exec.) Alstom SA 1998–2003; Dir (non-exec.) Shell Transport and Trading Co. PLC 1993–2002, Trident Safeguards Ltd 1999–2003, World Shipping and Investment Ltd 1998–2004, Reuters Founders Share Co. Ltd 1998–2009, Scottish Medicine Ltd 1999–2003, Interpacific Holding Ltd 2000–08, Aquarius Platinum 2004–12, BW Group Ltd 2004–12; Chair. Hakluyt & Co. 2000–09; Chair. Royal Hong Kong Jockey Club 1992–93; Fellow, Chartered Inst. of Bankers; Trustee, Gurkha Welfare Trust 1993–2006; Gov. Queenswood School 1997–2007; Pres. Penguin Rugby Football Club 2006–08; Hon. DUniv (Stirling) 1987; Hon. DLaws (Sheffield) 1993; Hon. LLD (Nottingham) 1997; Hon. Dr Business Admin. (Hong Kong Polytechnic) 1993, (Strathclyde) 1996; Dr hc (Hong Kong) 1997, (Napier) 1998, (Hong Kong Open) 1998, (Manchester Science and Tech.) 2000; Grand Bauhinia Medal (Hong Kong). *Leisure interests:* golf, rugby. *Address:* One Ebury House, 39 Elizabeth Street, London, SW1W 9RP, England (home). *Telephone:* (20) 7823-6775 (home). *Fax:* (20) 7824-8351.

PURVIS, Stewart Peter, CBE, BA; British media executive and journalist; *Chair of Television Journalism, City University;* b. 28 Oct. 1947, Isleworth; s. of the late Peter Purvis and the late Lydia Purvis; m. Mary Presnail 1972 (divorced 1993); one d.; two s. with Jacqui Marson; ed Dulwich Coll., Exeter Univ.; fmr presenter Harlech TV; news trainee BBC 1969; Ind. TV News producer 1972, Programme Ed. News at Ten 1980, Ed. Channel 4 News 1983; Deputy Ed. Ind. TV News 1986, Ed. 1989, Ed.-in-Chief 1991, CEO 1995–2003; Pres. EuroNews 1997; Dir Travel News Ltd 1995, London News Radio 1996; Chair of TV Journalism, City Univ. London 2003–; Deputy Chair . King's Cross Partnership (Dir TV) (non-exec) Royal Marsden Nat. Health Service Trust; mem. council European Journalism Centre 1996–; Fellow Royal TV Soc.; recipient of two Royal TV Soc. Awards, BAFTA Award for Best News or Outside Broadcast 1987, 1988, Broadcasting Press Guild Award for Best News or Current Affairs Programme 1988. *Leisure interests:* being at home, keeping fit, yoga. *Address:* Department of Journalism, City University, Northampton Square, London, EC1V 0HB, England (office). *Telephone:* (20) 7040-8783 (office). *Fax:* (20) 7040-8562 (office). *Website:* www.city.ac.uk (office).

PURWAR, A(run) K(umar), MCom; Indian banker; *Executive Chairman, India Venture Advisors;* ed Allahabad Univ.; fmr Man. Dir State Bank of Patiala; fmr Lecturer in Commerce, Business Admin Dept, Allahabad Univ.; joined State Bank of India 1968, held numerous positions including CEO Tokyo Br. 1995–98, Chair. State Bank of India 2002–06 (retd); Exec. Chair. India Venture Advisors; fmr Chair. Fed. of Indian Chambers of Commerce and Industry (FICCI) Banking and Financial Insts, later Chair. FICCI Diaspora Div.; Dir (non-exec.) Caparo Group 2007; Ind. Dir India Infoline Investment Services Ltd 2009–; mem. Bd of Dirs Apollo Tyres Ltd; CEO of the Year Award, Inst. for Tech. & Man. 2004, Outstanding Achiever of the Year Award, Indian Banks Asscn 2004, Finance Man of the Year Award, Bombay Man. Asscn 2006. *Address:* Office of the Board of Directors, Apollo Tyres Ltd, Apollo House, 7 Institutional Area, Sector 32, Gurgaon 122 001, India (office). *Telephone:* (124) 2721000 (office). *E-mail:* info@apollotyres.com (office). *Website:* www.apollotyres.com (office).

PUSIĆ, Vesna, DSc; Croatian sociologist, academic and politician; *First Deputy Prime Minister and Minister of Foreign and European Affairs;* b. 25 March 1953, Zagreb; d. of Eugen Pusić and Višnja Pusić; m.; one d.; ed Univ. of Zagreb; Faculty mem. Dept of Sociology, Univ. of Zagreb 1978–, Prof. 1988–; Founding mem. Croatian People's Party (Hrvatska narodna stranka—HNS) 1990– (Pres. 2000–08, 2013–); Co-founder and Dir Erasmus Guild (think-tank) 1993–98; mem. Sabor (Parl.) 2000–11, Deputy Speaker 2003–07, Chair. HNS parl. group 2008–11; fmr Vice-Pres. European Liberal Democrat and Reform Party; Minister of Foreign and European Affairs 2011–; First Deputy Prime Minister 2012–. *Publications include:* Industrial Democracy and Civil Society 1986, Rulers and Administrators 1992, Democracies and Dictatorships 1998; more than 50 scientific articles in Croatian and int. journals. *Address:* Ministry of Foreign and European Affairs, 10000 Zagreb, trg Nikole Šubića Zrinskog 7–8, Croatia (office). *Telephone:* (1) 4569964 (office). *Fax:* (1) 4569988 (office). *E-mail:* ministrica@mvep.hr (office). *Website:* www.mvpei.hr (office); vesna-pusic.hns.hr.

PUSKA, Pekka, MD, PhD, MPolSci; Finnish epidemiologist and academic; *Director General, National Institute for Health and Welfare;* b. 18 Dec. 1945, Vaasa; m. Arja Puska; one s. one d.; ed Univ. of Turku, Univ. of Kuopio; Prin. Investigator, N Karelia Project, Univ. of Kuopio 1972–78; Visiting Prof., Stanford Univ., USA 1983; Research Prof. and Dir Dept of Epidemiology and Health Promotion, Nat. Public Health Inst. 1978–, Dir Div. of Health and Chronic Diseases 1992–2000, Deputy to Dir-Gen. 1995–2000, Dir-Gen. 2000–01, Dir Dept of Noncommunicable Disease Prevention and Health Promotion WHO, Geneva, Switzerland 2001–03, Dir Gen. Nat. Public Health Inst. 2004–08, Nat. Inst. for Health and Welfare (THL) 2009–; mem. Parl. 1987–91; Elector of Presidents of Repub. 1988; Pres. Centre for Health Educ. 1989–95; mem. City Council, Joensuu 1993–97; mem. WHO panel of experts on cardiovascular diseases 1978–2001; Dir

International Quit and Win 1994–2006; Vice-Chair. ALKO Ltd (nat. alcohol monopoly) 2007–13; Chair. several organizing cttees of int. confs on tobacco and health 1996–; Pres. Finnish Heart Asscn 2004–09; Chair. Nat. Nutrition Council 2005–11, UKK Inst. 2005–10 (Pres.-Elect 2007–08, Pres. 2009–10), World Heart Fed. (Vice-Pres. 2006–12, Pres. 2013–), Int. Asscn of Nat. Public Health Insts, Governing Council WHO IARC (Lyon) (Vice-Chair. 2008–10, Chair. 2010–13); Chancellor Univ. of Turku 2010–13; mem. Russian Acad. of Natural Sciences 1997; Hon. mem. Hungarian Soc. of Hygiene 2000; Hon. DSc (St Andrews, Scotland) 1999, Hon. DMed (Turku) 2009, Hon. DPhil l (Kuopio) 2010; WHO Annual Health Educ. Award 1990, Int. Union for Health Educ. AMIE Award 1991, WHO Tobacco Free World Award 1999, Nordic Public Health Award 2005, Rank Prize 2008. *Publications:* 10 books on public health; contrib. of numerous articles to journals. *Address:* National Institute for Health and Welfare (THL), Mannerheimintie 166, 00300 Helsinki, Finland (office). *Telephone:* 40-7715571 (office). *Fax:* (2) 95246020 (office). *E-mail:* pekka.puska@thl.fi (office). *Website:* www.thl.fi (office).

PUSTOVOITENKO, Valery Pavlovich, CandTechSc; Ukrainian politician; *Leader, People's Democratic Party of Ukraine;* b. 23 Feb. 1947, Adamivka, Nikolayev Region; m.; two c.; ed Dnipropetrovsk Inst. of Construction Eng; worked as mechanical eng.; head of trusts in Odessa and Dnipropetrovsk 1965–87; People's Deputy of Ukraine; Chair. Dnipropetrovsk City Soviet 1987–93; mem. Higher Econ. Council, Security Council 1997–; Head election campaign of Pres. Kuchma 1994; mem. Ukrainian Cabinet of Ministers 1994–97; Head of Ukrainian Football Fed. 1996–; mem. People's Democratic Party of Ukraine, currently Leader; mem. Parl.; mem. Political Exec. Council 1996–; Prime Minister of Ukraine 1997–99; Minister of Transport 2000–02. *Address:* c/o Government Offices, M. Hrushevskoga 12/2, 252008 Kiev, Ukraine. *Telephone:* (44) 226 2204.

PUTILIN, Nikolai Georgiyevich; Russian singer (baritone); b. 1954; ed Krasnoyarsk Inst. of Arts; lessons with Nikola Nikolov in Bulgaria; started as singer of Variety Theatre; soloist of Syktyvkar Musical Theatre, Komi Repub. 1983–85; Kazan Opera Theatre 1985–92; Kirov (Mariinsky) Theatre in St Petersburg 1992–; Prizewinner Int. Chaliapin Competition 1989. *Repertoire includes:* over 40 leading roles toured Metropolitan Opera, La Scala, Teatro Comunale di Firenze, Covent Garden, Bolshoi Theatre and others. *Address:* c/o Mariinsky Theatre, 1 Theatre Square, St Petersburg, 190000, Russia (office). *Telephone:* (812) 3264141 (office). *Website:* www.mariinsky.ru/en (office).

PUTIN, Col Vladimir Vladimirovich, PhD; Russian politician and head of state; *President;* b. 7 Oct. 1952, Leningrad (now St Petersburg); s. of Vladimir Spiridonovich Putin and Mariya Ivanovna Putin; m. Lyudmila Aleksandrovna Shkrebneva 1983 (divorced 2013); two d.; ed Law Dept, Leningrad State Univ.; assigned to work on staff of KGB, USSR 1975–91, with First Chief Dept of KGB and in GDR 1985–90; asst to Pro-Rector, Leningrad State Univ. 1990; adviser to Chair. of Leningrad City Exec. Cttee 1990–91; Chair. Cttee on Foreign Relations, St Petersburg City Council 1991–96, then also First Deputy Chair. St Petersburg City Govt (First Deputy Mayor) 1994–96; Deputy Head, Admin. of Russian Presidency, Property Man. Directorate 1996–98, then also Deputy Head, Exec. Office of Pres. (Presidential Admin) and Head, Cen. Supervision and Inspections Directorate 1997–98; First Deputy Head, Presidential Admin May–July 1998; Dir Fed. Security Service of Russian Fed. 1998–99; Sec. Security Council of Russia March–Aug. 1999; Chair. of Govt (Prime Minister) 1999–2000, 2008–12; Acting Pres. of Russian Fed. 1999–2000, Pres. of Russian Fed. 2000–08, 2012–; Chair. Group of 8 (G8) 2006, excluded from the G8 group as a result of what it called his "illegal" invasion and annexation of Crimea 2014; Chair. United Russia (Yedinaya Rossiya) party 2008–12; Grand Cross Bundesverdienstkreuz (Germany) 2001, Grand Croix, Légion d'honneur 2006, King Abdul Aziz Award (Saudi Arabia) 2007, Order of Zayed (UAE) 2007; Dr hc (Univ. of Belgrade) 2011; named Person of the Year by TIME magazine 2007, named Person of the Year by Expert magazine 2007, ranked by Forbes magazine amongst The World's Most Powerful People (third) 2009, (fourth) 2010, (second) 2011, (third) 2012, (first) 2013, Confucius Peace Prize, China Int. Peace Research Centre 2011. *Leisure interests:* judo, biking, supports FC Zenit Saint Petersburg. *Address:* Office of the President, 103132 Moscow, Staraya pl. 4, Russia (office). *Telephone:* (495) 625-35-81 (office). *Fax:* (495) 606-07-66 (office). *E-mail:* president@gov.ru (office). *Website:* www .kremlin.ru (office); www.state.kremlin.ru (office). putin.kremlin.ru.

PUTINA, Lyudmila; Russian teacher; b. 6 Jan. 1958, Kaliningrad; m. Vladimir Vladimirvich Putin 1983; two d.; ed Leningrad State Univ.; early career as airline hostess, Kaliningrad; accompanied husband living in E Germany 1986–90; taught German language advanced courses for teachers at Leningrad State Univ. 1990–94; initiated creation of Center for the Devt of Russian Language. *Leisure interests:* theatre, music, tennis, downhill skiing. *Address:* c/o Office of the Government, 103274 Moscow, Krasnopresnenskaya nab. 2, Russia.

PUTNAM, Hilary, PhD; American philosopher, mathematician and academic; *Cogan University Professor Emeritus, Department of Philosophy, Harvard University;* b. 31 July 1926, Chicago, Ill.; s. of Samuel Putnam and Riva Sampson; m. 1st Erna Diesendruck 1948 (divorced 1962); one d.; m. 2nd Ruth A. Hall 1962; two s. one d.; ed Cen. High School of Philadelphia, Univ. of Pennsylvania, Harvard Univ. and Univ. of California, Los Angeles; Asst Prof. of Philosophy, Princeton Univ. 1953–60, Assoc. Prof. of Philosophy and of Math. 1960–61; Prof. of Philosophy of Science, MIT 1961–65; Prof. of Philosophy, Harvard Univ. 1965, Walter Beverly Pearson Prof. of Mathematical Logic and Modern Math. 1976–, then Cogan Univ. Prof., Emer. 2000–; Corresp. mem. British Acad., Acad. des Sciences Morales et Politiques; many other fellowships; ten hon. degrees; Guggenheim Fellow 1960–61, Rolf Schock Prize in Logic and Philosophy 2011. *Publications:* Meaning and the Moral Sciences 1978, Reason, Truth and History 1981, Philosophical Papers (three vols) 1975–83, The Many Faces of Realism 1987, Representation and Reality 1989, Realism with a Human Face 1990, Renewing Philosophy 1992, Words and Life 1994, Pragmatism: an Open Question 1995, The Threefold Cord 1999, Enlightenment and Pragmatism 2001, The Collapse of the Fact/Value Dichotomy 2002, Ethics without Ontology 2004, Philosophy in an Age of Science 2012. *Leisure interests:* travel, cooking, languages. *Address:* Department of Philosophy, Emerson 207, Harvard University, Cambridge, MA 02138 (office); 31 Cleveland Street, Arlington, MA 02174, USA (home). *Telephone:* (617) 495-2191 (office). *Fax:* (617) 495-2192 (office). *E-mail:* hputnam@fas.harvard.edu (office). *Website:* www.fas.harvard.edu/~phildept/putnam.html (office).

PUTS, Kevin, MMus; American composer, pianist and academic; b. 1972, St Louis, Mo.; ed Eastman School of Music, Yale Univ.; works commissioned and performed throughout North America, Europe and the Far East; commissions from New York Philharmonic, Nat. Symphony Orchestra, Tonhalle Orchester Zurich, symphony orchestras of Baltimore, Cincinnati, Detroit, Atlanta, Colorado, Houston, Forth Worth, Utah, St Louis, Boston Pops, Minnesota Orchestra and chamber ensembles including Mirò Quartet, Eroica Trio, eighth blackbird, Pittsburgh New Music Ensemble and Chamber Music Soc. of Lincoln Center; Concerto for Everyone premiered at Carnegie Hall 1999; premieres performed by artists including Evelyn Glennie, Yo-Yo Ma, Bill Jackson and Makoto Nakura; Composer-in-Residence, Young Concert Artists and California Symphony 1996, Forth Worth Symphony and Bravo! Vail Valley Music Festival 2007; Assoc. Prof. of Composition, Univ. of Texas at Austin 1999–2005; mem. Composition Faculty, Peabody Inst., Johns Hopkins Univ., Baltimore 2006–; grants and awards from ASCAP, BMI, Charles Ives Scholarship, Barlow Int. Prize for Orchestral Music 1999, Guggenheim Fellowship, Rome Prize 2001–02, American Acad. of Arts and Letters Benjamin H. Danks Award for Excellence in Orchestral Composition 2003. *Compositions:* numerous orchestral, chamber and ensemble works including four symphonies and several concertos; works for solo instruments with and without orchestra; other: Silent Night (opera) (Pulitzer Prize for Music 2012). *Recordings:* works included on CDs including Violinguistics: American Voices, Alternating Current 2010, Playing the Edge: Music for Violin and Percussion 2010, River of Light 2011, Sound the Bells! 2011, American Portraits 2011. *Address:* Peabody Institute of The Johns Hopkins University, 1 East Mount Vernon Place, Baltimore, MD 21202, USA (office); Bill Holab Music, 377 Sterling Place, No. 4, Brooklyn, NY 11238, USA. *Website:* www.peabody.jhu.edu (office); www.kevinputs.com.

PUTTNAM, Baron (Life Peer), cr. 1997, of Queensgate in the Royal Borough of Kensington and Chelsea; **David Terence Puttnam,** Kt, CBE, FRGS, FRSA; British film producer and educationalist; b. 25 Feb. 1941, London, England; s. of Leonard Arthur Puttnam and Marie Beatrix Puttnam; m. Patricia Mary Jones 1961; one s. one d.; ed Minchenden Grammar School, London; in advertising 1958–66, photography 1966–68, film production 1968–2000; Chair. Enigma Productions Ltd 1978–, Spectrum Strategy Consultants 1999–2008; Dir Nat. Film Finance Corpn 1980–85, Anglia TV Group 1982–99, Village Roadshow Corpn 1989–99, Survival Anglia 1989–99, Chrysalis Group 1993–96; Chair., CEO Columbia Pictures, USA 1986–88; Pres. Council for Protection of Rural England 1985–92; Visiting Lecturer, Univ. of Bristol, Visiting Industrial Prof. 1986–96; Gov. and Lecturer, LSE 1997–; Gov. Nat. Film and TV School 1974–87, (Chair. 1988–96); Chair. Teaching Council 2000–02; mem. Governing Council Royal Photographic Soc., Bd Landscape Foundation; Trustee Tate Gallery 1985–92, Science Museum 1994–2003, IPPR, Royal Acad. of Arts; Chancellor Univ. of Sunderland 1998–2007; Chair. Nat. Endowment for Science, Tech. and the Arts 1998–2003, Nat. Museum of Photography 1994–2003, Film and Television, Teaching Awards Trust; mem. Bd BECTA; Vice-Pres. BAFTA 1995–2002; mem. Educ. Standards Task Force 1997–2001, Arts Council Lottery Panel 1993–97; Pres. UNICEF 2002–09; Chair. QCA 2000–03; Lay Canon Durham Cathedral; Chancellor Open Univ. 2006–; BAFTA Acad. Fellowship 2006, Fellow, British Film Inst.; Hon. FCSD, Officier, Ordre des Arts et des Lettres 1986; ; Hon. degrees (Bristol, Keele, Leicester, Manchester, Leeds, Birmingham, Southampton, Bradford, Heriot-Watt Edin., Westminster, Humberside, Sunderland, Cheltenham and Glos., Kent, Queens Belfast, London Guildhall Univs, North London, London (City), Royal Scottish Acad., Imperial Coll. London, Sheffield Hallam, American Int. Univ., Richmond, Nottingham, Winchester, Surrey, Navarra, Abertay, Leicester, Middlesex, Brunel, Greenwich); Special Jury Prize for The Duellists, Cannes 1977, two Acad. Awards and four BAFTA Awards for Midnight Express 1978, four Acad. Awards (including Best Film), three BAFTA Awards (including Best Film) for Chariots of Fire 1981, three Acad. Awards and nine BAFTA Awards for The Killing Fields 1985; Michael Balcon Award for outstanding contrib. to the British Film Industry, BAFTA 1982; Palme d'Or (Cannes), one Acad. Award and three BAFTA Awards for The Mission 1987. *Films:* producer of around 50 feature films including Bugsy Malone 1976, The Duellists 1977, Midnight Express 1978, Chariots of Fire 1981, Local Hero 1983, The Killing Fields 1984, Cal 1984, The Mission 1986, Memphis Belle 1990, Meeting Venus 1991. *Television:* 15 films including A Dangerous Man, Josephine Baker (Emmy Awards), P'tang, Yang, Kipperbang 1982, Without Warning (Golden Globe Award) 1991. *Publications:* Rural England: Our Countryside at the Crossroads 1988, Undeclared War: The Struggle to Control the World's Film Industry 1997. *Address:* Enigma Productions, PO Box 54828, London, SW1A 0WZ, England (office). *Telephone:* (20) 7219-6822 (office). *E-mail:* puttnam@enigma.co.uk (office).

PUYOL ANTOLIN, Rafael; Spanish professor of geography and university rector; *Executive Vice-President, IE University;* b. 26 Feb. 1945, Gijón, Asturias; m. Dolores Martínez-Ferrando; four c.; ed Colegio de la Inmaculada, Gijón, Universidad Complutense de Madrid; Asst Prof. of Human Geography, Faculty of Geography and History, Universidad Complutense de Madrid 1975–78, Assoc. Prof. 1978–82, Prof. 1982–, Chair. Dept of Geography 1981–82, Dean, Faculty of Geography and History 1986–87, Vice-Chancellor for Academic Affairs 1988–95, Rector of Univ. 1995–2003; currently Exec. Vice-Pres., IE Univ., Vice-Pres. of Institutional Relations, IE Business School, Chair. IE Univ.; mem. editorial bds of various journals; fmr mem. Pres. and current mem. Population Group, Asociación de Geógrafos Españoles 1986–; Vice-Pres. Exec. Cttee Real Sociedad Geográfica; fmr Vice-Pres. Gen. Foundation of the UCM; mem. Exec. Cttee and Bd of Dirs Portal Universia; mem. Jury, Prince of Asturias Award for scientific and technical research 1996–2006; Vice-Pres. Conf. of Rectors of Spanish Universities 1997–; fmr Pres. Instituto Universitario Ortega y Gasset 1996–98, Inst. of Musical Studies 1999–2003; mem. Bd Spanish Chapter of the Club of Rome, Club of the Hague; Trustee, five foundations; Academician, Royal Acad. of Physicians, Acad. of Social Sciences at the European Acad. of Sciences and Arts, Salzburg; Hon. mem. UNICEF; Commdr's Cross, Order of Merit (FRG), Grand Cross of Aeronautical Merit and Naval Merit with White Distinctive, Order of Honour Nuñez de Balboa (Panama), Order Grand Duke Gediminas (Lithuania); Dr hc (Universidad Anáhuac, Mexico), (Universidad del Norte, Paraguay), (Nat. Univ. of Cuzco, Peru), (Universidad Ricardo Palma, Peru), (Inter American Univ. of Puerto Rico), (Univ. Rodríguez Ureña, Dominican Repub.), (Univ. of Panama);

UNICEF Commemorative Medal, Gold Medal, Universidad Complutense de Madrid. *Publications include:* Emigración y desigualdades regionales en España 1979, Población y Espacio 1982, Población y recursos 1984, Población española 1988, Los grandes problemas demográficos 1993, La Unión Europea 1995, Estructura demográfica de la población española. Un ejercicio de prospectiva 2006, Aspectos demográficos de la inmigración 2006, Población y Dinámica demográfica 2006, El futuro de la población española 2007, Demografía y sanidad 2008, El reto demográfico. El verdadero sentido de la emigración 2008, El envejecimiento de la población y sus repercusiones sobre el mercado de trabajo 2008, Población e inmigración en España 2009, Las consecuencias demográficas de la crisis económica 2011, Crecemos, pero menos 2011, Demografía y políticas demográficas para una nueva década 2011; more than 200 articles in professional journals on migration and demographic aging; regular columnist for several national newspapers. *Leisure interests:* music, reading. *Address:* IE University, María de Molina 11, 28006 madrid (office); C/ Marbella 50, 28034 Madrid, Spain (home). *Telephone:* (91) 5689600 (office); (91) 3720480 (home). *Fax:* (91) 3943472 (home). *E-mail:* university@ie.edu (office). *Website:* www.ie .edu (office).

PUZANOV, Col-Gen. Igor Yevgenyevich; Russian army officer; *Deputy Minister of Defence;* b. 31 Jan. 1947, Tyumen; ed Omsk Gen. Army Command School, M. V. Frunze Mil. Acad., Mil. Acad. of Gen. Staff; Commdr platoon Siberian Mil. Command –1976, Deputy Div. Commdr, then Commdr 1981–88; Deputy Regt Commdr, then Commdr Karpaty Mil. Command 1976–79; served in Afghanistan 1979–81; Head of Gen. Staff Baltic Mil. Command 1988–90; Army Commdr N Caucasian Mil. Command 1990–92; First Deputy Commdr Moscow Mil. Command 1992–2001, Statistics-Sec.; Deputy Minister of Defence 2001–; Merited Mil. Specialist. *Address:* Ministry of Defence, 105175 Moscow, ul. Myasnitskaya 37, Russia (office). *Telephone:* (495) 293-38-54 (office). *Fax:* (495) 296-84-36 (office). *Website:* www.mil.ru (office).

PYAVKO, Vladislav Ivanovich; Russian singer (tenor); b. 4 Feb. 1941, Krasnoyarsk; s. of Nina Piavko and step-s. of Nikolai Bakhin; m. Irina Arkhipova (died 2010); four s. two d.; ed State Inst. of Theatrical Art, Moscow; studied under S. Rebrikov, Moscow, R. Pastorino, La Scala, Milan; mem. CPSU 1978–89; soloist with Bolshoi Opera 1965–89, Berliner Staatsoper 1989–96; teacher of singing and dramatic art, State Inst. of Theatrical Art 1980–89, Dean of School 1983–89; producer at Mosfilm 1980–83; Prof., Moscow State Conservatory 2000–; Pres. Int. Union of Musicians 2010–, The Arkhipova Foundation 2010–; has also sung at Teatro Colón, Buenos Aires, Teatro Comunale, Florence, Opéra Bastille, Paris, Nat. and Smetana Operas, Prague, Metropolitan, New York, Kirov, St Petersburg and in many other houses; also at many int. festivals; mem. Acad. of the Arts 1992; Hon. Prof., Lomonosov Moscow State Univ. 2004–; Gold Medal in tenor section, Vervier Int. Competition 1969, Silver Medal, Tchaikovsky Int. Competition 1970, Gold Medal and Pietro Mascagni Silver Medal, Livorno 1984, Gold Plank of Cisternino, Italy 1993; People's Artist of USSR 1983, of Kyrgyzstan 1993, Prize of Moscow 2004 and other awards. *Major roles include:* Hermann in Queen of Spades, Andrei in Mazeppa, Dmitry and Shuisky in Boris Godunov, Andrei and Golitsin in Khovanshchina, Radames, Otello, Manrico in Il Trovatore, Cavaradossi in Tosca, Pinkerton in Madam Butterfly, Don José in Carmen, Turiddu in Cavalleria Rusticana, Guglielmo Ratcliff, Sergei in Katerina Izmailova, Canio in Pagliacci and many other roles. *Film:* You're My Delight My Suffering... (Mosfilm) 1983. *Recordings:* numerous recordings for leading int. labels including EMI, HMV, Philips, Chant du Monde, Columbia. *Publication:* Tenor, Vladislav Pyavko. *Leisure interests:* poetry, photography, cars. *Address:* Bryusov, per. 2/14, stroenie 2, Apt 26, 125009 Moscow, Russia. *Telephone:* (495) 629-43-07 (home); (495) 629-60-29 (office). *Fax:* (495) 629-60-29 (office). *E-mail:* amguem@gmail.com (home).

PYE, William Burns, ARCA, FRBS; British sculptor; *President, Hampshire Sculpture Trust;* b. 16 July 1938, London, England; s. of Sir David Pye and Virginia Pye; m. Susan Marsh 1963; one s. two d.; ed Charterhouse School, Wimbledon School of Art, Royal Coll. of Art; Visiting Prof., California State Univ. 1975–76; kinetic sculpture Revolving Tower 1970; sculpture 'Zemran' on South Bank, London 1971; currently Pres. Hampshire Sculpture Trust; introduction of tensioned cables with less emphasis on volume 1972; combined working on comms with smaller work and installations 1972–75; water an integral element of sculptures since mid-1970s in public, private and corporate comms internationally; works include: Slipstream and Jetstream (water sculptures) for Gatwick Airport 1988, Balla Frois (30m long water sculpture) comm. for Glasgow Garden Festival 1988, Chalice water sculpture for 123 Buckingham Palace Road, London 1990, cr. Water Wall and Portico for British Pavilion, Expo '92, Seville, Spain, Cristos at St Christopher's Place, London, Downpour at British Embassy, Oman, Cascade at Market Square, Derby 1994, Water Cone at Antony House, Cornwall for Nat. Trust 1996, bronze of Lord Hurd for Nat. Portrait Gallery 1996, Cader Idris at Cen. Square, Cardiff 1998, Prism for Cathay Pacific at Hong Kong Airport 1999, Aquarena Millennium Square, Bristol 2000, Cornucopia at Millfield School; St John's Innovation Park, Cambridge, Millennium Fountain for Wilton House and Sunderland Winter Garden 2001, Jubilee Fountain, Lincoln's Inn, London 2003, eight Water Sculptures for Serpent Garden, Alnwick Castle 2004, three sculptures at Mariinsky Concert Hall, St Petersburg, 8m high water piece nr Athens 2006, stone and bronze font for Salisbury Cathedral 2008, Sakirin Mosque fountain, Istanbul, 2009, Hypanthium for British Columbia Botanical Gardens, Vancouver 2010, Water Pavilion in Drammen nr Oslo 2011, Vortex water sculptures in Campinas, Brazil & Muscat, Oman, 2012; Hon. FRIBA 1993; Prix de Sculpture, Budapest 1981, Vauxhall Mural Prize 1983, Peace Sculpture Prize 1984, ABSA award for best commission of new art in any medium 1988, Art at Work award for best site-specific comm. 1988, Royal Ueno Museum Award (Japan) 1989. *Film:* Reflections 1972. *Publication:* William Pye – His Work and His Words 2010. *Leisure interest:* playing the flute. *Address:* The Studio, Rear of 31 Bellevue Road, London, SW17 7EF (office); 43 Hambalt Road, London, SW4 9EQ, England (home); The Hampshire Sculpture Trust, St Thomas Centre, Southgate Street, Winchester, SO23 9EF, England (office). *Telephone:* (20) 8682-2727 (Studio) (office). *Fax:* (20) 8682-3218 (office). *E-mail:* william.pye@btconnect.com (office); hst@soton.ac .uk (office). *Website:* www.williampye.com (office); www.hampshiresculpturetrust .co.uk (office).

PYETSUKH, Vyacheslav Alekseyevich; Russian writer; b. 18 Nov. 1946, Moscow; ed Moscow State Pedagogical Inst.; history teacher Moscow Pedagogical Inst.; work first published in Selskaya Molodezh magazine; freelance writer 1970s–; Emily Clark Balach Prize 1999. *Publications:* Alphabet 1983, New Times 1988, History of the Town of Glupov in New and Newest Times, New Moscow Philosophy 1989, Rommat, I and Others 1990, Cycles 1991, State Child 1997. *Address:* c/o Vagrius Publishers, Troitskaya str. 7/1, building 2, 129090 Moscow, Russia (office). *Telephone:* (495) 785-09-03 (office).

PYNCHON, Thomas Ruggles, Jr, BA; American novelist; b. 8 May 1937, Glen Cove, NY; s. of Thomas R. Pynchon; ed Cornell Univ.; fmr editorial writer, Boeing Aircraft Co.; Fellow, American Acad. of Arts and Sciences 2009–; John D. and Catherine T. MacArthur Foundation Fellowship 1988; American Acad. of Arts and Letters Howells Medal 1975. *Publications include:* V (Faulkner Prize for Best First Novel) 1963, The Crying of Lot 49 (Rosenthal Foundation Award 1967) 1965, Gravity's Rainbow (Nat. Book Award) 1973, Mortality and Mercy in Vienna 1976, Low-Lands 1978, Slow Learner (short stories) 1984, In the Rocket's Red Glare 1986, Vineland 1989, Deadly Sins 1994, Mason & Dixon 1996, Against the Day 2006, Inherent Vice 2009, Bleeding Edge 2013; contrib. short stories to various publs, including Saturday Evening Post. *Address:* Melanie Jackson Agency, 41 West 72nd Street, Suite 3-F, New York, NY 10023, USA (office); c/o Penguin Books, 375 Hudson Street, New York, NY 10014, USA (office). *E-mail:* m.jackson@mjalit.com (office).

PYNZENYK, Viktor Mikhailovich, DEcon; Ukrainian politician and economist; *Leader, Reforms and Order Party (Partiya 'Reformy i poryadok');* b. 15 April 1954, Smologovitsa; s. of Mikailo Vasilyevich Pynzenyk and Maria Ivanovna Pynzenyk; m. 1st; two d.; m. 2nd Mariya Romanivna Pynzenyk; two s.; ed Lviv State Univ.; Asst, then Docent, Sr Researcher, Prof., Chair. Lviv State Univ. 1975–92; mem. Vakhovna Rada (Parl.) 1991–2001; Deputy Chair. Bd on Problems of Econ. Policy 1992; Minister of Economy 1992–93, Deputy Prime Minister 1992–97; Pres. Foundation of Support to Reforms 1993; Chair. Council on Econ. Reforms 1994; Chair. Nat. Council on Statistics 1995; Head, State Comm. on Admin. Reform 1997–99; Head, Partiya 'Reformy i poryadok' (Reforms and Order Party) 1998–; Minister of Finance 2005–06, 2007–09 (resgnd); Dir Inst. of Reforms; Hon. Prof., Mohyla Acad.—Nat. Univ. of Kyiv 1996–, Econs Inst. of Ternopil; named an Honoured Economist of Ukraine 2004. *Publications:* more than 400 papers in professional journals. *Leisure interests:* tourism, music, playing the preferans card game. *Address:* Reforms and Order Party (Partiya 'Reformy i poryadok'), 01021 Kyiv, vul. Instytutska 28, Ukraine (office). *Telephone:* (44) 585-41-16 (office). *Fax:* (44) 585-41-17 (office). *E-mail:* ref_ord@i.com.ua (office). *Website:* www.prp.org.ua (office).

Q

QABOOS BIN SAID AS-SAID, Sultan of Oman; *Prime Minister and Minister of Foreign Affairs, Defence and Finance;* b. 18 Nov. 1940, Salalah; s. of the late HH Said bin Taimur; m. Sayyidah Nawwal bint Tariq 1976 (divorced 1977); ed privately in UK, Royal Mil. Acad. Sandhurst; 14th descendant of the ruling dynasty of Albusaid Family; Sultan of Oman (following deposition of his father) 23 July 1970–, also Prime Minister, Minister of Foreign Affairs, Defence and Finance; Hon. KCMG. *Leisure interests:* reading, horse-riding, classical music. *Address:* Diwan of the Royal Court, PO Box 632, Muscat 113, Sultanate of Oman. *Telephone:* 738711. *Fax:* 739427.

QADIR, Irfan; Pakistani lawyer and government official; served in numerous govt legal positions including Prosecutor-Gen. Nat. Accountability Bureau, Consultant (Legal Affairs), Pres.'s Secr., Sec. of Law, Justice and Parl. Affairs; Attorney-Gen. 2012–13. *Address:* c/o Office of the Attorney-General, Supreme Court of Pakistan, Constitution Avenue, Islamabad, Pakistan. *E-mail:* mail@supremecourt.gov.pk.

QAHTAN, Maj.-Gen. Abd al-Qader; Yemeni army officer and politician; Minister of the Interior 2011–14. *Address:* c/o Ministry of the Interior, POB 4991, Sana'a, Yemen.

QAHTANI, Sheikh; Tareq Abdel Hadi Al-; Saudi Arabian business executive; *Chairman, Abdel Hadi Abdullah Al-Qahtani Group of Companies;* Chair. Abdel Hadi Abdullah Al-Qahtani Group of Companies, activities involve petrochemicals, oil and gas sectors, manufacturing, contracting and services, insurance, travel, tourism, transportation and custom clearance, est. an office in Texas, USA 1970s, subsequently est. offices in Europe and elsewhere. *Address:* Abdel Hadi Abdullah Al-Qahtani & Sons Co., Al Qahtani Building, Street 9, Al Adami Area, PO Box 20, Dammam 31411, Saudi Arabia (office). *Telephone:* (3) 8261477 (office). *Fax:* (3) 8269894 (office). *E-mail:* info@ahqsons.com (office). *Website:* www.ahqsons.com (office).

QAMAR, Syed Naveed, BSc, MS, MBA; Pakistani politician; b. 22 Sept. 1955, Karachi; m.; one s. three d.; ed Univ. of Manchester, UK, California State Univ., USA; mem. Computer Science faculty, FAST-NU (then called FAST-ICS) 1988–89; sr mem. Pakistan People's Party, currently mem. Cen. Exec. Cttee; elected mem. Prov. Ass., Sindh 1988–90, mem. Nat. Ass. 1990–93, 1993–96, 1997–99, elected from NA-222 (Tando Muhammad Khan-cum-Hyderabad-cum-Badin) constituency in gen. elections 2008; Prov. Minister (Sindh) for Information 1990; Chair. Privatization Comm. 1993; apptd Fed. Minister for Finance and Privatization 1996, for Privatization and Investment (with additional charge of Finance, Revenue, Econ. Affairs and Statistics) 2008, for Petroleum and Natural Resources (with additional charge of Ministry of Privatization) 2009–11, for Privatization (with additional charge of Ministry of Water and Power) 2011, of Defence 2012–13. *Address:* c/o Ministry of Defence, Pakistan Secretariat, No. II, Rawalpindi 46000, Pakistan.

QÄMBÄR, İsa Yunis oğlu; Azerbaijani politician and historian; *Chairman, Müsavat (Equality) Party;* b. 24 Feb. 1957, Baku, Azerbaijan SSR, USSR; s. of Yunis Qämbärov and Tahira Qämbärov; m. Prof. Aida Bağrova 1986; two s.; ed Baku High School No. 62, Baku State Univ.; researcher, Azerbaijan Acad. of Sciences 1979–82, Inst. of Oriental Studies 1982–90; active participant in democratic movt in late 1980s, head of organizational div. of Popular Front 1990–, Deputy Chair. 1990–91; mem. Supreme Soviet of Azerbaijan 1990–95, Chair. Milli Mäclis (Parl.) and Acting Pres. of Azerbaijan 1992–93 (resgnd); Chair. Comm. on Foreign Affairs 1991–92; Chair. Müsavat (Equality) Party 1992–; Co-founder and Chair. Democratic Congress 1999, 2001–03; joined United Opposition Alliance 2002; presidential cand. 2003; played a major part in organizing demonstrations inspired by other protests throughout the Middle East Spring 2011; 'A Friend of Journalists' Prize 2000. *Address:* Müsavat (Equality) Party (Müsavat Partiyası), 1025 Baku, Därnägül qasabasi 30/97, Azerbaijan (office). *Telephone:* (12) 448-23-82 (office); (12) 461-15-00 (home). *Fax:* (12) 448-23-81 (office); (12) 498-31-66 (home). *E-mail:* info@musavat.org (office); isa.gambar@gmail.com (home). *Website:* isagambar.blogspot.com (office); www.isagambar.az (home).

QANDIL, Hisham Mohamed, BEng, PhD; Egyptian water resources engineer and politician; b. 17 Sept. 1962, Beni Suef; m.; five d.; ed Univ. of Cairo, Utah State Univ., North Carolina State Univ., USA; began career with Nat. Water Research Centre, Ministry of Water Resources and Irrigation, becoming Chief of Staff for Minister of Water Resources 1999–2005; worked for ADB, Tunisia, becoming Chief Water Resources Engineer; Minister of Water Resources and Irrigation 2011–12; Prime Minister 2012–13 (dismissed); fmr Pres. African Ministers Council on Water; fmr Observer, Jt Egyptian–Sudanese Nile Water Authority; mem. Nile Basin Initiative Council of Ministers; Egyptian Order of the Repub., Second Class 1995. *Address:* c/o Office of the Prime Minister, 2 Sharia Majlis al-Sha'ab, Cairo, Egypt.

QANOONI, Younis; Afghan politician; b. 1957, Panjshir Valley; ed Kabul Univ.; joined mujahidin troops fighting against Soviet occupation forces 1979–89; apptd Jt Minister of Defence 1993; co-f. Defence of the Motherland and United Nat. Islamic Front for the Salvation of Afghanistan (Unifsa–Northern Alliance) 1996; political head of NA's main Jamiat-i Islami party 2001; Leader NA Del. to Future of Afghanistan Govt Talks, Bonn Nov. 2001; Minister of the Interior, Afghan Interim Authority Dec. 2001–02; Minister of Educ. 2002–04 (resgnd); apptd Head of Nizzat-i-Milli Party 2002; presidential cand. 2004; Founder and Leader Hizb-i Afghanistan-i Nawin (New Afghanistan Party) 2005–; Chair. Nat. Understanding Front (opposition coalition) 2005; Speaker of Wolasi Jirga (House of Representatives) –2011. *Address:* Hizb-i Afghanistan-i Nawin (New Afghanistan Party), Kabul, Afghanistan (office).

QARABALİN, Uzaqbay Süleymenulı; Kazakhstani politician and government official; *Minister of Oil and Gas;* b. 14 Oct. 1947, Qossağil village, Embi dist, Guriyev (now Atiraw) Oblast; ed Moscow Gubkin Inst. of Oil and Gas; tech. engineer in exploration of South Embi gas and oil fields 1973–74, head of labs of

drilling technologies, Kazakh Research Inst. of Oil Geology and Prospecting 1974–81; Deputy Dir for Academic Work 1981–88; Head of Dept for Devt of Technological Progress and Deep Drilling, 'Prikaspiigeologiya' territorial management, Oral 1988–90; Chair. Guriyev br. of Kazakh Lenin Polytechnical Inst. 1990; Sr Officer, Dept of Industry in apparatus of Pres. and Cabinet of Ministers of Kazakhstan 1991–92; Head of Oil and Gas Dept, Ministry of Energy and Fuel Reserves 1992–94; Deputy Man. of Energy and Fuel Resources, Deputy Man. of the Oil and Gas Industry 1994–95; secondment to Agip, Italy 1995–97; Vice-Pres. for Corp. Devt, Dir for Devt of Prospecting, Vice-Pres. of Dept, first Vice-Pres. 'Kazakhoil' Oil & Gas Co. 1997–2000, Acting Pres. 'Kazakhoil' Aug.–Oct. 1999; Pres. 'KazTransGaz' Co. 2000–01; Deputy Minister of Energy and Mineral Resources 2001–03; Pres. 'KazMunaiGaz' Nat. Co. 2003–08; Pres. 'Mangistaumunaigaz' 2008–, Acting Gen.-Dir 2008–09, Gen.-Dir 2010–13; Minister of Oil and Gas 2013–; Badge for excellence in exploring natural resources of the USSR 1998, Qurmet 2000, Leader of the Russian Economy 2005, Baris, Third Degree 2005; '10 Years of Constitution of Kazakhstan' 2005, '10 years of Parl. of Repub. of Kazakhstan' 2006, Award for Honoured Explorer of Natural Resources of Repub. of Kazakhstan 2003, Honoured Sportsman of Repub. of Kazakhstan 2007, awarded titles of 'Person of the Year' and 'Golden Prometheus', KazEnergy Eurasian Energy Forum 2009, 'Kazakstanyn Enbek Eri' Award 2011. *Publications:* more than 40 academic and literary works and publs, articles and books. *Address:* Ministry of Oil and Gas, 010000 Astana, Kabanbai batyr kosh. 19, Kazakhstan (office). *Telephone:* (7172) 97-68-83 (office). *Fax:* (7172) 97-68-88 (office). *E-mail:* bogdanova@mgm.gov.kz (office). *Website:* mgm.gov.kz (office).

QARADAWI, Ilham Yousef al-, PhD, CPhys, FInstP; Qatari physicist and academic; *Professor of Nuclear Physics, Qatar University;* ed Univ. of Qatar, Bedford Coll. and Royal Holloway Coll., London, UK; Teaching Asst, Physics Dept, Qatar Univ. 1981–84, Lecturer 1984–91, Assoc. Prof. 2003–08, Prof. of Physics 2009–; Asst Prof., Physics Dept, Univ. of Qatar 1991–2002; Research Fellow, Dept of Physics and Astronomy, Univ. Coll. London 1998–99; Adjunct Prof. of Physics, Texas A&M Univ. Qatar, Doha 2011–; mem. Advisory Cttee for World Nuclear Univ. School on Radiation Technologies, World Council on Isotopes; mem. AAAS, American Physical Soc., American Asscn of Physics Teachers, American Nuclear Soc., European Physical Soc., Women in Nuclear, World Nuclear Asscn; Chevening Scholarship (UK) 1998, Merit Award for Excellence in Research, Univ. of Qatar 2004, honoured by Arab World Inst. (Institut du Monde Arabe), Paris 2005, Fellowship of the World Nuclear Univ. 2007, Ahmad Badeeb Prize for Arab Women in Science (Paris) 2008, Women Innovation in Science and Eng Leadership Program, US Dept of State 2011, Outstanding Contrib. to Science Award, CEO Middle East 2012, named by CEO Middle East as one of the 100 Most Powerful Arab Women for 2012, named by Arabian Business magazine as one of the 50 most influential people in the State of Qatar 2012, ranked by Arabian Business amongst the Power 500: The Worlds's Most Influential Arabs (65th) 2012. *Achievements include:* est. a positron lab and successfully built the first variable energy slow positron beam in the Middle East; has also est. a radiation measurement lab carrying out research in the area of environmental radiation physics. *Publications:* numerous papers in professional journals on positron physics and its applications, environmental nuclear and radiation physics, and recent trends in physics education. *Address:* Physics Department, Qatar University, PO Box 2713, Doha, Qatar (office). *Telephone:* 4852126 (office); 44034634 (office). *Fax:* 4852221 (office). *E-mail:* ilham@qu.edu.qa (office); ilham@ilhamalqaradawi.com. *Website:* faculty.qu.edu.qa/ilhamq (office); www.ilhamalqaradawi.com.

QARASE, Laisenia, BCom; Fijian politician; *Leader, Soqosoqo Duavata ni Lewenivanua (Fiji United Party);* b. 4 Feb. 1941; m.; four s. one d.; ed Ratu Kadavulevu School, Queen Victoria School, Suva Boys' Grammar School, Univ. of Auckland, NZ, British Co-operative Coll., UK, Auckland Tech. Inst.; exec. cadet, Fijian Affairs Bd 1959–66, financial adviser 1979–99; joined Civil Service 1967, Co-operative Officer 1, Co-operatives Dept 1967–68, Asst Registrar of Co-operatives 1969–70, Sr Asst Registrar 1971–72, Chief Asst Registrar 1973–75, Registrar 1976–78; Deputy Sec. of Finance 1978–79; Perm. Sec. for Commerce and Industry 1979–80; Sec. of the Public Service Comm. 1980–83; Prime Minister and Minister for Nat. Reconciliation and Unity July 2000–06 (resigned following Court of Appeal ruling that his Govt was illegal March 7th 2001, reappointed March 15th 2001, dismissed by Acting Pres. Commodore Voreqe Bainimarama in mil. takeover of Govt Dec. 2006), also fmrly Minister for Fijian Affairs, Culture and Heritage, Multi-Ethnic Affairs and Reform of the Sugar Industry; Founder and Leader, Soqosoqo Duavata ni Lewenivanua (SDL) (Fiji United Party) 2001–; Man. Dir Fiji Devt Bank 1983–97, Merchant Bank of Fiji 1997–2000; Chair. South Pacific Fertilizers Ltd 1985–86, Fiji Post & Telecommunications Ltd 1990–91, Fiji TV Ltd 1994–98; Dir Fiji Int. Telecommunication Ltd (FINTEL) 1978–79, Foods Pacific Ltd 1985–86, Fiji Forest Industries Ltd 1988–97, Carlton Brewery (Fiji) Ltd 1989–99, Unit Trust of Fiji 1990–99, Voko Industries Ltd 1993–97, Air Pacific Ltd 1996–98, Colonial Advisory Council 1996–99; Chair. Mavanu Investments Ltd, Qalitu Enterprises Ltd; Dir Mualevu Tikina Holdings Ltd, Yatu Lau Co. Ltd. *Address:* Soqosoqo Duavata ni Lewenivanua (Fiji United Party), c/o House of Representatives, Suva, Fiji (office).

QASEM, Subhi, PhD; Jordanian agriculturalist, politician and academic; *Professor Emeritus, University of Jordan;* b. 1934, Palestine; ed Kansas State Univ., Univ. of Minnesota, USA; worked in Ministry of Agric.; Prof. of Agric., Univ. of Jordan, Dean Faculty of Grad. Studies 1986, Founding Dean Faculties of Sciences, Agric. and Grad. Studies; Minister of Agric. 1991, now Prof. Emer.; consultant in scientific and tech. educ., research and devt, agric. policy and the environment; Fellow Islamic Acad. of Sciences; Medal of the Kawkab (Star) Award, Istiqlal (Independence) Medal. *Address:* PO Box 13300, Amman 11942 (office); Villa No. 7, University District, Abdul Rahim Omar Street, Amman, Jordan (home). *Telephone:* (6) 5346746 (office); (6) 5155200 (home). *Fax:* (6) 5346740 (office). *E-mail:* ubcc@go.com.jo (office).

QASIMI, Sheikha Lubna bint Khalid bin Sultan al-, BSc, MBA; United Arab Emirates information technology manager, business executive and government official; *Minister of Development and International Co-operation;* ed Al Zahra Secondary School, Sharjah, California State Univ., Chico, USA, American Univ. of Sharjah; computer programmer with Datamation 1981; fmr Dubai br. man. for Gen. Information Authority; Sr Man. Information Systems Dept, Dubai Ports Authority 1993–2000; apptd CEO Tejari.com (online business-to-business marketplace) 2000; headed Dubai e-Govt Exec. team responsible for instituting e-govt initiatives throughout public sector 2001; Minister of Economy and Planning (first woman minister) 2004, of Foreign Trade 2004–13, of Devt and Int. Co-operation 2013–; mem. Bd of Dirs Dubai Chamber of Commerce and Industry, Dubai Autism Centre, Simsari.com; mem. Bd of Trustees Dubai Univ. Coll., Electronic-Total Quality Man. Coll., Thunderbird, The American Grad. School of Int. Man., Phoenix, Ariz., Zayed Univ., UAE; volunteer for Friends of Cancer Patients' Soc.; Hon. Kentucky Col, Commonwealth of Kentucky 2003; Hon. mem. Bd of Dirs Nat. US-Arab Chamber of Commerce; Hon. DSc (California State Univ.); Distinguished Govt Employee Award 1999, Dubai Quality Group Award For Support to Leadership, Quality, and Change 2000, ITP Best Personal Achievement Award 2000, Datamatix IT Woman of the Year 2001, Business.com Personal Contribution Award 2001, Datamatix Outstanding Contrib. 2002, World Summit Award for .com 2003, UK House of Lords Special Entrepreneurship Award 2004, ranked by Forbes magazine amongst The World's 100 Most Powerful Women (99th) 2007, (95th) 2009, (70th) 2010, (92nd) 2012, (67th) 2013, ranked by Arabian Business amongst the Power 500: The World's Most Influential Arabs (tenth) 2012, (12th) 2013. *Address:* Ministry of Development and International Co-operation, PO Box 110555, Abu Dhabi, United Arab Emirates (office). *Telephone:* (2) 4956000 (office). *Fax:* (2) 4499164 (office); (2) 449-9164 (office). *Website:* www.micad.gov.ae (office).

QASIMI, HH Sheikh Saud ibn Saqr al-, BSc; United Arab Emirates ruler; *Ruler of Ras al-Khaimah;* b. 10 Feb. 1956, Dubai; s. of the late Sheikh Saqr bin Mohammad al-Qasimi, fmr Ruler of Ras al-Khaimah; ed American Univ. of Beirut, Lebanon, Univ. of Michigan, USA; Chief of the Ruler's Court, Ras al-Khaimah 1979, named Crown Prince 14 June 14 2003, mem. Supreme Council and Ruler of Ras al-Khaimah 27 Oct. 2010–; Chair. Ras al-Khaimah Municipal Council 1986; f. Ras al-Khaimah Investment Authority 2005; Chancellor Ras al-Khaimah Medical and Health Sciences Univ.; Dr hc (Univ. of Bolton–Ras al-Khaimah) 2010. *Address:* The Ruler's Palace, Ras al-Khaimah, United Arab Emirates (office).

QASIMI, HH Sheikh Sultan bin Muhammad al-, (Ruler of Sharjah), PhD; United Arab Emirates; b. 1 July 1939; ed Cairo Univ. and Univs of Exeter and Durham, UK; Minister of Educ., UAE 1972; Ruler of Sharjah 1972–; Chair. Sharjah Human Soc., Arab/African Symposium; mem. Arab Historians' Union; Fellow Durham Univ.; Hon. Fellow Centre for Middle Eastern and Islamic Studies 1992; Hon. LLD (Khartoum); Hon. DSc (Univ. of Agric., Faisalabad) 1983; Distinguished Personality Prize, Univ. of Exeter 1993. *Publications:* The Myth of Arab Piracy in the Gulf, The Division of the Omani Empire, The Occupation of Aden, French-Omani Relations, The Arabian Documents in the French Archives, The White Shaikh, The Rebellious Prince, The Return of Holako, Power Struggles and Trade in the Gulf, The Gulf in Historic Maps. *Leisure interest:* reading. *Address:* Ruler's Palace, Sharjah, United Arab Emirates.

QASIMOV, Gen. Qalmuxanbet Nurmuxanbetulı; Kazakhstani army officer and government official; *Minister of Internal Affairs;* b. 18 May 1957, Dmitrievka Ili dist, Almatı Oblast; m.; three c.; ed Kazakh State Univ.; Investigator, Sr Investigator, Head of Investigation Dept, Deputy Chief ATC, ATS Ili dist, Almatı Oblast 1979–88, Deputy Head of Public Order ATC, Almatı Oblast 1988–89; Head of Police Dept, Kapchagai, Almatı Oblast 1989–92, Head of Criminal Police, Deputy Chief of Police, Almatı Oblast 1992–97; Head of Criminal Police, Ministry of Internal Affairs March–July 1997, Head of Main Dept of Internal Affairs of Almatı 1997–2003, Head of Main Dept of Internal Affairs, Dept of Internal Affairs, Almatı Oblast 2003–05; First Deputy Minister, Deputy Minister of Internal Affairs 2005–09; Head of Dept of Internal Affairs, East Kazakhstan Oblast 2009–11; Minister of Internal Affairs 2011–; Maj.-Gen. of the Militia; several state decorations and medals, including 'Dank' Order of Second Degree, Astana Medal, Honoured Worker of Internal Affairs Badge. *Address:* Ministry of Internal Affairs, 010000 Astana, Tauelsizdik d-ly 1, Kazakhstan (office). *Telephone:* (7172) 71-32-30 (office); (7172) 71-40-10 (office). *Fax:* (7172) 34-17-38 (office). *E-mail:* kense@mvd .kz (office). *Website:* www.mvd.kz (office).

QASSEM, Sheikh Naim; Lebanese politician; *Deputy Secretary-General, Hezbollah;* b. 1953; fmr Prof. of Chem.; Founding mem. Hezbollah (Party of God) 1982, Deputy Sec.-Gen. 1991–. *Publication:* Hizbullah: The Story from Within 2005. *E-mail:* info@moqawama.net. *Website:* www.moqawama.org.

QASSEMI, HH Sheikh Sultan Sooud al-, BSc, MA; United Arab Emirates business executive and political commentator; ed European Business School, London, American Univ. of Paris; Founder and Chair. Barjeel Geojit Securities 2001–; Man. Dir Al-Saud Co. Ltd 1998–; Lecturer in Middle Eastern History and Entrepreneurship, Dubai Men's Coll.; non-resident Fellow, Dubai School of Govt 2009–; Columnist The National (English language newspaper, Abu Dhabi) 2008–; widely recognised for posts on Twitter; columns have appeared in The New York Times, Financial Times, Foreign Policy, Open Democracy, the Independent, the Guardian and Gulf News; Founder Barjeel Art Foundation 2010; Sheikh Rashid Award for Academic Excellence 2006, Patrons of the Arts Award, Dubai Culture 2010; listed by TIME magazine in the 140 Best Twitter Feeds of 2011, ranked by Arabian Business amongst the Power 500: The World's Most Influential Arabs (66th) 2012, (35th) 2013. *Address:* Barjeel Geojit Securities LLC, PO Box 32313, Suite No #403, United Bank Ltd Building, Bank Street, Bur Dubai, Dubai, United Arab Emirates (office). *Telephone:* (4) 3555900 (office). *Fax:* (4) 3555903 (office). *E-mail:* dubai@barjeel.ae (office). *Website:* www.barjeel.ae (office); sultanalqassemi.com/Sultan_Sooud_Al_Qassemi.

QASSIS, Nabil, PhD; Palestinian physicist, academic and politician; b. 1945; ed Mainz Univ., Germany, American Univ. of Beirut; worked in France and Italy 1972–80, returned to Palestine 1980; Prof. of Theoretical Physics, Birzeit Univ., Ramallah 1982–, Chair. Dept of Physics 1982–84, Univ. Vice-Pres. for Academic Affairs 1984–89; sr mem. of Palestinian dels to several sets of negotiations, including Madrid Conf. 1991–93, Deputy Head of del. to Washington talks 1993–94, mem. perm. status negotiating team 1999; frequent participant in unofficial negotiations with Israeli leaders, including at Harvard Univ. Jt Working Group on the right of return 1998, in South Africa 2002, Stafford, UK 2002; Co-founder Palestine Econ. Research and Policy Inst. 1996, Dir 1996–98; Minister and Coordinator-Gen., Bethlehem 2000 project 1998–; Chair. Yasser Arafat Foundation –2012; Minister of Finance 2012–13 (resgnd). *Address:* c/o Ministry of Finance, POB 795, Sateh Marhaba, al-Birah, Ramallah, Palestinian Autonomous Areas (office).

QAWASMI, Hani-al; Palestinian academic and fmr government official; m.; four c.; fmr admin. Islamic University of Gaza; fmr judge; Sr Admin., Ministry of the Interior and Civil Affairs –2007, Minister of Interior and Civil Affairs 2007 (resgnd). *Address:* c/o Ministry of the Interior and Civil Affairs, Gaza, Palestinian Autonomous Areas (office).

QAYYUM, Malik Muhammad; Pakistani lawyer, judge and government official; b. 18 Dec. 1944; s. of the late Justice Muhammad Akram; Sr Advocate, Supreme Court; began career as legal practitioner 1964; elected Sec., Bar Asscn, Lahore 1970, Pres. Dist Bar Asscn, Lahore 1980; mem. Punjab Bar Council 1984–88; Deputy Attorney-Gen. of Pakistan 1984–88; Judge, Lahore High Court 1988–2001 (resgnd); Attorney-Gen. of Pakistan 2007–08; mem. Pakistan Law Comm.; Chief Ed. Pakistan Supreme Court Cases. *Address:* c/o Office of the Attorney General, Supreme Court of Pakistan, Constitution Avenue, Islamabad, Pakistan. *Telephone:* (51) 9220581. *E-mail:* info@supremecourt.gov.pk.

QAZIXANOV, Erjan, PhD; Kazakhstani diplomatist and politician; b. 21 Aug. 1964; m.; two c.; ed St Petersburg State Univ.; Second Sec., later First Sec., Protocol-Political Div., Ministry of Foreign Affairs 1989–92, Head of Div., Deputy Chief of State Protocol Service 1992–95; First Sec. and Counsellor, Perm. Mission of Kazakhstan to UN, New York 1995–2000; Dir Dept of Multilateral Cooperation, Ministry of Foreign Affairs 2000–03; Amb. and Perm. Rep. to UN 2003–07 (also accred as Amb. to Cuba); Asst to the Pres. of Kazakhstan Feb.–Dec. 2008; Amb. to Austria and Perm. Rep. to the Int. Orgs, Vienna 2009–11; Deputy Minister of Foreign Affairs Feb.–April 2011; Minister of Foreign Affairs 2011–12; Chair. OIC Conf. 2011; Medals 'For Valorous Work' 2005, '10 Years of Independence of the Repub. of Kazakhstan' 2001, '10 Years of the Constitution of Kazakhstan' 2005, '10 Years of the Parl. of the Repub. of Kazakhstan' 2006, '10 Years of Astana' 2008. *Publications:* numerous articles and publs in Kazakh and foreign periodicals on multilateral diplomacy issues and the UN. *Address:* c/o Ministry of Foreign Affairs, 010000 Astana, Soljagaw, Tauelsizdik kosh. 31, Kazakhstan.

QI, Huaiyuan; Chinese diplomatist and state official; *President, Chinese People's Association for Friendship with Foreign Countries;* b. 1930, Ezhou City, Hubei Prov.; ed North China People's Univ., Harbin Foreign Languages Coll.; joined CCP 1948; Counsellor, Chinese Embassy, Bonn, FRG 1974–77; Asst to Minister of Foreign Affairs 1984–86, Vice-Minister of Foreign Affairs 1986–91, Dir Foreign Affairs Office of State Council 1991–94; Alt. mem. 13th CCP Cen. Cttee 1987–92, mem. 14th CCP Cen. Cttee 1992–97; Del., 15th CCP Nat. Congress 1997–2002; Pres. Chinese People's Asscn for Friendship with Foreign Countries (CPAFFC) 1994–; mem. Standing Cttee, 9th Nat. Cttee of CPPCC 1998–2003, Vice-Chair. Foreign Affairs Sub-cttee 1998–2003. *Address:* Chinese People's Association for Friendship with Foreign Countries, 1 Taijichang Dajie, Beijing 100740, People's Republic of China (office). *Telephone:* (10) 65125505 (office).

QIAN, Guanlin; Chinese politician; b. Oct. 1946, Funing, Jiangsu Prov.; ed Shanghai Foreign Trade Inst.; joined CCP 1973; Deputy Head, Customs Dept, Guangzhou City, Guangdong Prov. 1984–86; Deputy Dir, later Dir Prov. Br., Gen. Admin of Customs, Guangdong Prov. 1987–90; Deputy Dir Gen. Admin of Customs 1990–93, Dir 1993–2001; Deputy Dir Nat. Narcotics Control Comm. 1993–2001; Deputy Dir State Admin of Taxation 2001–12 (Deputy Sec. CCP Leading Party Group); mem. CCP 14th Cen. Cttee for Discipline Inspection 1992–97, Alt. mem. CCP 15th Cen. Cttee 1997–2002. *Address:* c/o State Administration of Taxation, Beijing 100038, People's Republic of China (office).

QIAN, Gen. Guoliang; Chinese army officer; b. 1940, Wujiang, Jiangsu Prov.; ed Mil. Acad. of the Chinese PLA; joined PLA 1958, CCP 1960; Squad Leader, Combat Training Section, Army (or Ground Force), PLA Services and Arms, Staff Officer and Deputy Section Chief 1966, Div. Commdr, PLA 1979–83, Chief of Staff, Army (or Ground Force) 1983–85, Commdr Group Army 1985; rank of Maj.-Gen. 1988–95, Lt-Gen. 1995–2002, Gen. 2002–; Chief of Staff, PLA Jinan Mil. Region 1993–96; Deputy Mil. Region C-in-C 1996, C-in-C 1996–99 (Deputy Sec. CCP Party Cttee); C-in-C PLA Shenyang Mil. Region 1999–2004; Alt. mem. 13th CCP Cen. Cttee 1987–92, 14th CCP Cen. Cttee 1992–97, mem. 15th CCP Cen. Cttee 1997–2002, 16th CCP Cen. Cttee 2002–07. *Address:* c/o People's Liberation Army, Ministry of National Defence, Jingshanqian Jie, Beijing, People's Republic of China (office).

QIAN, Liren; Chinese party official; b. 20 Aug. 1924, Jiaxing Co., Zhejiang Prov.; s. of Qian Xunyi and Hu Suxian; m. Zheng Yun 1952; one s. one d.; joined CCP 1940; Deputy Sec.-Gen. All-China Fed. of Democratic Youth 1953; Sec.-Gen. All-China Students' Fed. 1956; Dir Int. Liaison Dept Communist Youth League 1959–64; Vice-Chair. All-China Fed. of Youth 1962; Dept Dir Foreign Affairs Office, State Council of People's Repub. of China 1964–65; mem. Standing Council Chinese People's Asscn for Friendship with Foreign Countries 1974–78; Amb. and Perm. Rep. UNESCO 1978–81; Deputy Dir Int. Liaison Dept, Cen. Cttee CCP 1982–83, Dir 1983–85; Pres. Renmin Ribao (People's Daily) 1985–89; mem. CCP Cen. Cttee 1985–92, mem. Propaganda and Ideological Work Leading Group 1988–89; mem. Standing Cttee 8th Nat. Cttee 1993–98; Chair. CPPCC Foreign Affairs Cttee 1995–98; Vice-Pres. Chinese Asscn for Int. Understanding 1995–2003, Adviser 2003–; Hon. Pres. Newspaper Operation and Man. Asscn 1988. *Leisure interests:* reading, swimming. *Address:* c/o Chinese Association for International Understanding, 4 Fuxing Road, Beijing 100860, People's Republic of China. *Telephone:* (10) 83907341. *Fax:* (10) 83907342.

QIAN, Qichen; Chinese diplomatist and state official; b. Jan. 1928, Tiading Co., Shanghai; m. Zhou Hanqiong; one s. one d.; ed Shanghai Datung Middle School and Communist Youth League School, USSR; joined CCP 1942; mem. CCP Communist Youth League, Shanghai Municipality 1949, Researcher, Gen. Office 1953; Second Sec. Embassy, Moscow, USSR 1955–63, Deputy Section Chief 1955–64, Counsellor 1972–74; Section Chief, Ministry of Higher Educ. 1963, Deputy Dir External Relations Dept 1963; Amb. to Guinea and Guinea-Bissau

1974–76; Dir Information Dept, Ministry of Foreign Affairs 1977–82, later Spokesman, Vice-Minister of Foreign Affairs and Special Envoy to 2nd–11th Round Sino-Soviet Consultations 1982–88, Minister of Foreign Affairs 1988–98; Head of Chinese Del., First Round Sino-Soviet Border Talks 1987; Deputy Dir Comm. for Commemorating 40th Anniversary of UN 1985; Vice-Chair. Organizing Cttee for Int. Year of Peace 1985; State Councillor 1991–93, Vice-Premier of State Council 1993–2003; Leader Special Admin. Region Preparatory Cttee (to establish post-1997 govt in Hong Kong) 1993–97; Chair. Macao Special Admin. Region Preparatory Cttee 1998, mem. Govt Del., Macao Hand-Over Ceremony 1999; Alt. mem. 12th CCP Cen. Cttee 1982–87, mem. 1985, mem. 13th Cen. Cttee 1987–92, 14th Cen. Cttee 1992–97, 15th CCP Cen. Cttee 1997–2002, Deputy Head Cen. Foreign Affairs Leading Group; mem. Politburo CCP 1992–2002. *Address:* c/o State Council, Beijing, People's Republic of China (office).

QIAN, Gen. Shugen; Chinese army officer; b. Feb. 1939, Wuxi City, Jiangsu Prov.; ed Chongqing Artillery School, PLA Mil. Acad. and Univ. of Nat. Defence; mem. CCP 1956–; entered army 1954; Deputy Div. Commdr 47th Army 1981; Div. Commdr 139th Div. 1983; Deputy Army Commdr 47th Army 1984; Army Commdr 47th Group Army 1985; Chief of Staff, Lanzhou Mil. Region 1992; Deputy Political Commissar, Lanzhou Mil. Region 1993; rank of Lt-Gen. 1993; Asst to Chief of Gen. Staff 1994; Deputy Chief, PLA Gen. Staff 1995; rank of Gen. 2000; Alt. mem. 13th CCP Cen. Cttee 1987–92, 14th CCP Cen. Cttee 1992–97, mem. 15th CCP Cen. Cttee 1997–2002, 16th CCP Cen. Cttee 2002–07. *Address:* c/o Ministry of National Defence, Jingshanqian Jie, Beijing, People's Republic of China (office). *Telephone:* (10) 6370000 (office).

QIAN, Yi, BS, MS; Chinese environmental scientist and academic; *Professor, Department of Environmental Science and Engineering, Tsinghua University;* b. 1936, Suzhou, Jiangsu Prov.; d. of Qian Mu; ed Tongji Univ., Shanghai, Tsinghua Univ., Beijing; Teaching Asst, Lecturer, Assoc. Prof., then Prof., Dept of Environmental Science and Eng, Tsinghua Univ. 1959–; Dir State Key Jt Lab. of Environmental Simulation and Pollution Control; science consultant, Environmental Protection Comm. of State Council; Vice-Chair., Gen. Cttee of ICSU; Vice-Chair. Eng and Environment Cttee of the World Fed. of Eng Orgs; Deputy, 7th NPC 1988–93, mem. Standing Cttee 8th NPC 1993–98, 9th NPC 1998–2003, Vice-Chair. Cttee of Environment and Resource Protection; mem. Exec. Cttee All-China Women's Fed. 1993; mem. Chinese Acad. of Eng 1994–; Nat. Science and Tech. Advancement Award (2nd Class), State Educ. Comm. Science and Tech. Advancement Award (1st Class) 1987, 2nd Award of Nat. Science and Tech. Progress 2003. *Publications:* Modern Wastewater Treatment Technology; The Prevention and Control of Industrial Environmental Pollution; Water Pollution Volume of Environmental Engineering Handbook; more than 100 research papers. *Address:* Department of Environmental Engineering, Tsinghua University, Beijing 100084, People's Republic of China (office). *Telephone:* (10) 62785684 (office). *Fax:* (10) 62595687 (office). *E-mail:* qiany@tsinghua.edu.cn (office). *Website:* www.tsinghua.edu.cn (office).

QIAN, Yongchang; Chinese politician; *President, China Communication & Transportation Association;* b. 1933, Shanghai City; joined CCP 1953; Vice-Minister of Communications 1982–84, Minister 1984–91; Chair. Bd of Dirs, Hong Kong China Merchants Group 1985–; fmr Chair. China Ocean Shipping Company (COSCO); Pres. China Communications and Transportation Asscn; Alt. mem. 12th Cen. Cttee CCP 1982–87, mem. 13th Cen. Cttee 1987–92. *Address:* China Communication & Transportation Association, Beijing, People's Republic of China (office).

QIAN, Yunlu; Chinese politician; b. Oct. 1944, Dawu Co., Hubei Prov.; ed Hubei Univ.; joined CCP 1965; sent to do manual labour, Sanli Commune 1968–70; Sec. Publicity Dept, CCP Dawu Co. Cttee, Hubei Prov. 1970–73, later Deputy Sec. Co. Cttee; Sec. Org. Dept CCP Xiaogan Prefectural Cttee, Hubei Prov. 1970–73; fmr Sec. CCP Party Cttee, Xinhe People's Commune, Hanchuan Co., Hubei Prov., later Deputy Sec. CCP Co. Cttee; fmr Magistrate, Dawu Co. (Dist) People's Court; Sec. CCP Communist Youth League Hubei Prov. Cttee 1973–83; Deputy Sec. CCP Hubei Prov. Cttee and mem. Standing Cttee 1983–91; Sec. CCP Wuhan City Cttee 1991–95; Chair. Hubei Prov. Cttee CPPCC 1995–98; Vice-Gov. Guizhou Prov. 1998–99, Gov. 1999–2001; Deputy Sec. CCP Guizhou Prov. Cttee 1998–2000, Sec. 2000–05; Chair. Standing Cttee Guizhou Prov. People's Congress 2003–05; Sec., CCP Heilongjiang Prov. Cttee 2005–08; Alt. mem. 14th CCP Cen. Cttee 1992–97, 15th CCP Cen. Cttee 1992–97, mem. 16th CCP Cen. Cttee 2002–07, 17th CCP Cen. Cttee 2007–12; Sec.-Gen. 11th CPPCC Nat. Cttee 2008–13. *Address:* c/o Guizhou Provincial People's Congress, Guiyang, Guizhou Province, People's Republic of China.

QIAN, Zhengying; Chinese engineer and government official; b. 1923, Jiaxing Co., Zhejiang Prov.; m. Huang Xinbai; ed Dadong Univ., Shanghai; joined CCP 1941; Section Chief, Water Conservancy Bureau (Jiangsu-Anhui Border Regional Govt) 1945–48; Dir Front Eng Div., Dept of Army Service Station (E China Mil. Command) 1945–48; Sec. and Deputy Dir Yellow River Man. Bureau, Shandong Prov. 1948–50; Deputy Head, E China Mil. Admin. Cttee, Dept of Water Conservancy 1949; Deputy Head, Cttee for Harnessing Huaihe River 1950–52; Vice-Minister of Water Conservancy 1952–67, Minister of Water Conservancy and Electrical Power 1970–88; Adviser to State Council 1981–82, mem. 1982–; Vice-Chair. CCP Nat. Comm., Chair. Women, Youth and Legal Affairs Cttee; Adviser to State Flood Control HQ 1988–; mem. 10th Cen. Cttee of CCP 1972–77, 11th Cen. Cttee of CCP 1977–82, 12th Cen. Cttee 1982–87, 13th Cen. Cttee 1987–92, 14th Cen. Cttee 1992–97; Vice-Chair. 7th CPPCC Nat. Cttee 1988–93, 8th CPPCC Nat. Cttee 1993–98, 9th CPPCC Nat. Cttee 1998–2003; Pres. Red Cross Soc. of China 1994–, China-India Friendship Asscn, China Award Foundation for Teachers of Middle and Primary Schools and Kindergartens; Gold Medal (Somalia), China Eng Science and Tech. Prize 2000. *Address:* National Committee of Chinese People's Political Consultative Conference, 23 Taipingqiao Street, Beijing, People's Republic of China (office).

QIAO, Baoping, BA; Chinese economist and business executive; *Chairman, China Guodian Corporation;* ed Nankai Univ., Party School of CCP Cen. Cttee; fmr Deputy Sec.-Gen. All-China Students Fed. and Deputy Dir of Gen. Office of All-China Students Fed.; Man. Dir Standing Cttee and Org. Dept at Cen. Cttee of Communist Youth League 1998–2000; Man. Dir Mass Work Dept of Cen. Work for Cen. Govt-led Enterprises 2000–03, Sec. of Cttee of Communist Youth League for Cen. Govt-led Enterprises; Man. Dir Mass Work Bureau and United Front Work Dept of SASAC 2003–05; Disciplinary Officer/Chief of Discipline Inspection Group, China Power Investment Corpn 2005–08; fmr Deputy Gen. Man. and Party Sec., China Guodian Group, Exec. Vice-Pres. China Guodian Corpn –2013, Chair. 2013–; Supervisor, China Longyuan Power Group Corpn Ltd 2011–13, Chief Supervisor of 2012–13, Chair. Bd of Supervisors 2013–; Chair. Bd of Supervisors, Guodian Technology and Environment Group Corpn Ltd 2011–13; fmr mem. Exec. Cttee China Power Investment Corpn. *Address:* China Guodian Corporation, 6–8 Fuchengmen Bei Street, Beijing 100034, People's Republic of China (office). *Telephone:* (10) 58682000 (office). *Fax:* (10) 58553900 (office). *E-mail:* cgdcb@cgdc.com.cn (office). *Website:* www.cgdc.com.cn (office).

QIAO, Shi; Chinese party official (retd); b. Dec. 1924, Dinghai Co., Zhejiang Prov.; m. Yu Wen; joined CCP 1940; Sec. CP br., Shanghai Middle School 1942; Deputy Sec. Shanghai Dist CP; Sec. Youth Cttee, Hangzhou CP 1950–; Dir Designing Inst. of Jiuquan Iron and Steel Co. 1960–63; Sec. Afro-Asian Solidarity Cttee 1965– Cultural Revolution; Deputy Dir Int. Liaison Dept, CCP Cen. Cttee 1978–82, Dir 1982–83; mem. 12th Cen. Cttee, CCP 1982–87, 13th Cen. Cttee 1987–92, 14th Cen. Cttee 1992–97; mem. Politburo 1985 and Standing Cttee of Politburo 1987–; Vice-Premier, State Council 1986–88; Alt. mem. Secr., Cen. Cttee 1982–85, mem. 1985; Dir Org. Dept, CCP Cen. Cttee 1984–85; Sec. Cen. Cttee of Political Science and Law 1985–87; Sec. Cen. Comm. for Discipline Inspection 1987–93; mem. Politburo, Standing Cttee of Politburo, Secr. CCP Cen. Cttee 1989–92; Perm. mem. Politburo 14th Cen. Cttee 1992–97; Chair. Standing Cttee 8th NPC 1993–98. *Address:* c/o International Liaison Department, Central Committee, Communist Party, Beijing, People's Republic of China.

QIAO, Shibo, BA; Chinese business executive; *President and Managing Director, China Resources (Holdings) Co. Ltd;* ed Jilin Univ.; worked as section dir in Ministry of Foreign Trade and Econ. Co-operation (MOFTEC, now the Ministry of Commerce); joined China Resources (Holdings) Co. Ltd 1992, currently Man. Dir and also Pres. China Resources Nat. Corpn, also Chair. and Exec. Dir China Resources Enterprise Ltd, CEO China Resources Medications Group Ltd; Vice-Chair. China Vanke Co. Ltd. *Address:* China Resources (Holdings) Co. Ltd, Floor 49, CRC Building, 26 Harbour Road, Wanchai, Hong Kong Special Administrative Region, People's Republic of China (office). *Telephone:* 28797888 (office). *Fax:* 28275774 (office). *E-mail:* crc@crc.com.hk (office). *Website:* www.crc.com.hk (office).

QIAO, Shiguang; Chinese artist; b. 5 Feb. 1937, Guantao Co., Hebei Prov.; s. of Qiao Lu De and Wang Hao Ling; m. Luo Zhen Ru 1961; two d.; Prof., Cen. Acad. of Arts and Design; Founder-Chair. Chinese Soc. of Lacquer Painting 1990 (group exhbn, Beijing 1990); Dir Chinese Artists Asscn; Dir Int. Culture of Lacquer 1992–; Founder Korea-China Lacquer Art Exchange Exhbn, Seoul 1994. *Publications:* Selected Lacquer Paintings of Qiao Shiguang 1993, The Skill and Artistic Expression of Lacquer Painting 1995, Collection of Qiao Shiguang's Lacquer Paintings 1996. *Leisure interests:* calligraphy, writing poetry. *Address:* QIAO Gallery, Seven Star Street, 798 Art Zone Jiuxianqiao Rd.4, Chaoyang District, Beijing 100015 (office); 3 602 Building, 6 Hong Miao Bei Li, Chao Yang District, Beijing 100025, People's Republic of China (home).

QIN, Huasun; Chinese diplomatist (retd); b. Sept. 1935, Jiangsu Prov.; Counsellor and Deputy Perm. Rep. to Office of UN and other int. orgs Geneva 1984–87; Perm. Rep. Vienna 1987–90; Dir-Gen. Dept of Int. Orgs and Confs Ministry of Foreign Affairs 1990–93; Asst Minister of Foreign Affairs 1993–95; Perm. Rep. to UN 1995–97; mem. CPPCC Nat. Cttee 1998; retd 2004. *Address:* c/o Ministry of Foreign Affairs, 2 Chaoyangmennei Dajie Dongsi, Beijing 100701, People's Republic of China (office).

QIN, Jiaming; Chinese railway executive; b. 1945, Guilin, Guangxi Prov.; ed Changsha Railway Univ.; fmr Dir-Gen. China Railway Construction Soc.; fmr Deputy Pres. China Construction Enterprise Man. Asscn; Pres. China Railway Engineering Corpn 1996; Ministry of Railways Educ. Medal 1989, Henan Provincial Award for Excellent Constructors 1990, Ministry of Railways Excellent Zhigong-Zhi-You 1997, Ministry of Railways Huo-Che-Tou (Locomotive) Medal 1998, State Award for Excellent Constructors 1999. *Address:* China Railway Engineering Corporation, CREC Mansion, Southern Square, Beijing West Railway Station, Beijing 100055, People's Republic of China (office). *Telephone:* (10) 51845159 (office). *Fax:* (10) 51844877 (office). *Website:* www.crecg.com (office).

QIN, Wencai; Chinese energy industry executive; b. Feb. 1925, Shanxi; s. of Qin Wanrong and Qin Wangshi; m. Zhang Huang 1950; one s. three d.; Vice-Minister, Minister of Petroleum Industry 1979–82; Pres. China Nat. Offshore Oil Corpn 1982–87; Chair. Consultative Cttee 1987–; Chair. Capital Entrepreneurs Club 1991–2001, now consultant; consultant and Vice-Chair. China Entreprises Man. Asscn 1991–2003. *Publications:* Facts About China National Offshore Oil Corporation, Oil People in the Chinese Petroleum Industry, A Century's Journey in the China Sea, Oil People in CNOOC, Oil People in Yumen. *Leisure interests:* reading, sports. *Address:* PO Box No. 25, Chaoyangmenbei Dajie, Dongcheng District, Beijing 100010, People's Republic of China (office). *Telephone:* (10) 84521002 (office). *Fax:* (10) 64602600 (office). *E-mail:* quinwc@cnooc.com.cn (office). *Website:* www.cnooc.com.cn (office).

QIN, Xiao, PhD; Chinese business executive; *Chairman, Boyuan Foundation;* b. April 1947; ed Univ. of Cambridge, UK; joined China Int. Trust and Investment Corpn (CITIC) 1986, becoming Vice-Pres. 1994–95, Pres. 1995, Vice-Chair., fmr Deputy Party Sec. and Chair. CITIC Industrial Bank; Chair. China Merchants Group 2001–10, China Merchants Bank Co. Ltd 2001–10; Chair. Boyuan Foundation 2010–; Chair. Hong Kong Chinese Enterprises Asscn; mem. Toyota Int. Advisory Bd, Asia Business Council; Adviser and Sr Research Fellow, Hong Kong and Macao Research Inst. of State Council Devt and Research Centre; Guest Prof., School of Econs and Man., Tsinghua Univ. and Grad. School of the People's Bank of China; mem. 10th CPPCC; Deputy, 16th Nat. Congress of CCP 2002–07; Rep. 9th NPC 1998–2003; mem. 10th Nat. Cttee CPPCC, 11th Nat. Cttee CPPCC; adviser on Foreign Currency Policy of State Admin of Foreign Exchange. *Publications:* several papers and books in the fields of economics and management. *Address:* Boyuan Foundation, Hong Kong Special Administrative Region, People's

Republic of China (office). *E-mail:* info@boyuan.hk (office). *Website:* www.boyuan .hk (office).

QIRBI, Abu Bakr Abdallah al-, BSc, MB, ChB, FRCP, FRCPath, FRCP (C); Yemeni medical consultant and politician; *Minister of Foreign Affairs;* b. 6 June 1941, Aden; s. of Abdulla al-Qirbi and Fatoom al-Qirbi; m.; two s.; ed Aden Coll.; Edinburgh Univ. and Univ. of London, UK; Prof. of Clinical Pathology, San'a Univ., Dean Faculty of Science 1979–83, Faculty of Medicine 1982–87, Univ. Vice-Rector 1982–83; Minister of Educ. 1993–94; mem. Consultative Council 1997–2001; Minister of Foreign Affairs 2001–, of Immigrants' Affairs 2006–07; Chair. People's Charitable Soc. 1995–; has made several radio and TV programmes on educ., scientific research, non-governmental work, charity and medical topics; Yemen Unification Medal; WHO Scholarship for Postgraduate Study. *Publications:* author of book on political and development issues in Yemen; more than 40 papers on the biological effects of clinical chemistry, renal disease, gastro-intestinal diseases and numerous papers on politics and social affairs. *Leisure interests include:* tennis, billiards, swimming. *Address:* PO Box 11351, San'a, Yemen (office). *Telephone:* (1) 276555 (office). *Fax:* (1) 276618 (office). *E-mail:* aqirbi@hotmail.com (office). *Website:* www.mofa.gov.ye (office).

QIU, Bojun; Chinese business executive; *Chairman, Zhuhai Jinshan Computer Co. Ltd;* b. 1964, Hebei Prov.; ed Univ. of Science and Tech. for Nat. Defence; developed the Chinese word-processing system WPS; f. Kingsoft Corpn 1988, Dir 1988–, est. Zhuhai Kingsoft Computer Co. Ltd 1993; designed and developed Pangu Office System 1994, WPS97 Chinese processing system 1997; received funds from Legend and reconstructed Kingsoft 1998, establishing two e-commerce websites www.joyo.com and www.xoyow.myrice.com 2000; currently Chair. Zhuhai Jinshan Computer Co. Ltd. *Publications:* A WPS Course, WPS User Guide. *Address:* Zhuhai Jinshan Computer Co., Ltd., No.8, Lianshan Lane, Lianhuashan, Jida Town, Xiangzhou, Zhuhai 519015, Guangdong, People's Republic of China (office). *Telephone:* (756) 3335688 (office).

QIU, Chunpu; Chinese business executive; b. 1930; joined CCP 1958; Chair. of Bd of Dirs, China Nat. Nonferrous Metals Industry Corpn 1993–; fmr Chair. China Packing Technique Asscn. *Address:* China National Nonferrous Metals Industry Corporation, 9 Xizhang Hutong, Xicheng District, Beijing 100814, People's Republic of China (office).

QU, Xing, BA, MA, PhD; Chinese political scientist and diplomatist; *President, China Institute of International Studies;* b. May 1956; ed Beijing Foreign Studies Univ., China Foreign Affairs Univ., Paris Inst. of Political Studies; teacher at China Foreign Affairs Univ. 1985–, Vice-Pres. 1995–2006; fmr Dir Teaching and Research Section, Dept of Diplomacy, fmr Deputy Dean; Minister, Embassy in Paris 2006–09; Pres. China Inst. of Int. Studies 2010–. *Publications include:* A Diplomatic History of China 1979–1994 1995, Diplomacy of the Contemporary China 1997, New Dimensions of China's Diplomacy 1998, The Art of Diplomacy of Deng Xiaoping 1999, 50 Years of China's Diplomacy 2000, Le temps de soupecon, relations franco-chinoises 1949–1955 2006, China's Diplomacy in Decades of Reform and Opening to the Outside World 1978–2008 2008; numerous articles. *Address:* China Institute of International Studies, No. 3 Toutiao, Taijichang, Beijing 100005, People's Republic of China (office). *Telephone:* (10) 85119547 (office). *Fax:* (10) 65123744 (office). *Website:* www.ciis.org.cn (office).

QUADEN, Baron; Guy, PhD; Belgian economist and banker; b. 5 Aug. 1945, Liège; ed Univ. of Liège, Univ. of the Sorbonne, Paris, France; Prof. of Econs, Univ. of Liège 1978–; Pres. High Council for Econ. Affairs 1984–88; Exec. Dir Nat. Bank of Belgium 1988–99, Gov. 1999–2011; Belgian Govt Gen. Commr for the Euro 1996–99; mem. Governing Council, European Central Bank 1999–2011; Officier, Légion d'honneur 2001. *Publications include:* Le budget de l'état belge 1980, La crise des finances publiques 1984, L'économie belge dans la crise 1987, Politique économique 1991. *Leisure interests:* soccer, modern art. *E-mail:* pressoffice@nbb.be (office).

QUADRIO CURZIO, Alberto, PhD; Italian economist and professor of political economy; *Professor Emeritus of Political Economy of Institutions, Università Cattolica del Sacro Cuore, Milan;* b. 25 Dec. 1937, Tirano-Valtellina; ed Faculty of Political Sciences, Catholic Univ., Milan, St John's Coll., Cambridge, UK; Assoc. Prof. of Econs, Univ. of Cagliari 1965–68; Assoc. Prof. of Econs, Univ. of Bologna 1968–72, Prof. 1972–75, Chair., Faculty of Political Sciences 1974–75; Prof. of Econs, Università Cattolica del Sacro Cuore, Milan 1976–2010, apptd Prof. of Political Economy of Insts 2010, now Prof. Emer., Dir Centre of Econ. Analysis 1977–2010, Chair. Faculty of Political Sciences 1989–2010, Pres. Scientific Bd, Centre of Econ. Analysis 2010–; Distinguished Academic Visitor, Queens' Coll., Cambridge and Visiting Research Fellow, Centre for Financial Analysis and Policy, Judge Business School, Cambridge, UK 2010–11; Dir Economia Politica – Journal of Analytical and Institutional Economics (quarterly review) 1984–; mem. Italian Nat. Research Council 1977–88, 2006–; Pres. Italian Econs Asscn 1995–98, Bd for Donato Menichella scholarships, Bank of Italy 2004–07, Scientific Bd for Paolo Baffi Lectures, Bank of Italy 2003–07, Centesimus Annus Foundation 2003–; mem. Reflection Group on Spiritual and Cultural Dimension of Europe est. by Pres. of EC 2002–04, Bd for European Investment Bank Prize 1995–2000; has delivered lectures at many Italian and foreign univs; speaker at many confs and seminars in Italy and abroad; mem. Istituto Lombardo-Accad. di Scienze e Lettere, Accad. Naz. dei Lincei (Vice-Pres. 2009–); St Vincent Award 1984, W. Tobagi Award 1996, Cortina Ulisse Int. Award 1997, Gold Medal for contribs to Science and Culture, Pres. of Italian Repub. 2000, Capri-San Michele for Econs 2003, Targa alla coerenza Zoli Foundation 2004, Cardano-Beccaria Int. Prize Rotary Pavia 2004, Associazione Nuova Spoleto Award for Economy 2005, Economia Internazionale Chamber of Commerce and Univ. of Genoa 2009, Canova Award 2010, Gozzo d'Argento Int. Prize (with R. Prodi) 2011, Scanno Prize for Economy 2011, Gold Medal "Ambrogino d'Oro" City of Milan 2011, Guido Carli Award 2012, Basilicata Award 2012. *Publications:* about 350, including Reddito e Saggio di Interesse nelle Decisioni di Consumo e Risparmio nell'ipotesi di comportamento razionale 1965, Rendita e distribuzione in un modello economico plurisettoriale 1967, Investimenti in istruzione e sviluppo economico 1973, Protagonisti del pensiero economico 1977, Rent, Income Distribution, Order of Efficiency and Rentability 1980, The Gold Problem: Economic Perspectives 1982, Planning Manpower Education and Economic Growth 1983, Sui Momenti costitutivi della

Economia Politica (co-author) 1983–84, The Exchange-Production Duality and the Dynamics of Economic Knowledge (co-author) 1986, Industrial Raw Materials: A Multi-Country, Multi-Commodity Analysis (co-author) 1986, The Agro-Technological System towards 2000: A European perspective (co-ed.) 1988, Rent, Distribution and Economic Structure 1990, Structural Rigidities and Dynamic Choice of Technologies (co-author) 1991, Issues on International Development and Solidarity 1992, On Economic Science: Its Tools and Economic Reality 1993, Innovation, Resources and Economic Growth (co-ed.) 1994, Risorse, Tecnologie, Rendita (co-author) 1996, Noi, l'Economia e l'Europa 1996, Production and Efficiency with Global Technologies 1996, Rent Resources, Technology (co-author) 1999, Il Made in Italy oltre il 2000 2000, La Società Italiana degli Economisti 2000, Profili della Costituzione Europea 2001, Complexity and industrial clusters (co-ed.) 2002, Il Gruppo Edison: 1993–2003 (co-ed) 2003, Technological Scarcity: An Essay on Production and Structural Change 2003, La globalizzazione e i rapporti Nord-Est-Sud 2004, Rent, Technology, and the Environment (co-author) 2004, Research and Technological innovation (co-ed.) 2005, Research and Technological Innovation: The Challenge for a New Europe (co-ed.) 2006, Industria e Distretti. Un Paradigma di perdurante competitività italiana (co-ed.) 2006, Economisti ed Economia. Per un'Italia europea: paradigmi tra il XVIII e il XX secolo 2007, Intrapresa, sussidiarietà, sviluppo (co-ed.) 2007, Valorizzare un'economia forte. L'Italia e il ruolo della sussidiarietà (co-ed.) 2007, The EU and the Economies of the Eastern European Enlargement (co-ed.) 2008, Democracy, Institutions and Social Justice (co-ed.) 2008, Historical Stylizations and Monetary Theory (co-author) 2008, Fondazioni, enti e reti nello spazio europeo della ricerca. La sussidiarietà in atto (co-ed.) 2009, I fondi sovrani (co-author) 2009, Social Capital and Human Development (co-ed.) 2009, Nuove polarità nella geo-economia. Globalizzazione, crisi ed Italia (co-ed.) 2010, Values and Rules for a New Model of Development (co-ed.) 2010, Sovereign Wealth Funds – A Complete Guide to State-Owned Investment Funds (co-author) 2010, La Facoltà di Scienze Politiche della Università Cattolica 1989–2010, Profili istituzionali e internazionali nella interdisciplinarietà 2011, Economia oltre la crisi 2012, L'industria nei 150 anni dell'Unità d'Italia. Paradigmi e Protagonisti (co-ed.). *Leisure interest:* skiing. *Address:* CRANEC, Università Cattolica del Sacro Cuore, Largo Gemelli, 20123 Milan (office); Via A. Saffi 31, 20123 Milan, Italy (home). *Telephone:* (02) 72342474 (office). *Fax:* (02) 72342475 (office). *E-mail:* alberto.quadriocurzio@unicatt.it (office). *Website:* www.unicatt.it (office); docenti.unicatt.it/ita/ alberto_quadrio_curzio (office).

QUAH, Danny, AB, PhD; British (b. Malaysian) economist and academic; *Professor of Economics and Head, Department of Economics, London School of Economics;* b. 26 July 1958, Penang; m. Kathleen Tyson; two s.; ed Princeton Univ., Harvard Univ.; Asst Prof. of Econs, MIT 1985–91; Prof. of Econs, LSE 1996–, Head of Dept of Econs 2006–; fmr consultant to World Bank, Bank of England, Monetary Authority of Singapore; Gov. Nat. Inst. of Econ. and Social Research 2002–; mem. Editorial Bd Journal of Global Policy 2009–; Fellow, European Econ. Asscn 2004. *Leisure interest:* Taekwon-do. *Address:* Department of Economics, London School of Economics, Houghton Street, London, WC2A 2AE, England (office). *Telephone:* (20) 7955-7535 (office). *E-mail:* dq@econ.lse.ac.uk (office). *Website:* econ.lse.ac.uk/~dquah (office).

QUAID, Dennis; American actor; b. 9 April 1954, Houston, Tex.; s. of William Rudy Quaid and Juanita B. Quaid; m. 2nd Meg Ryan (q.v.) 1991 (divorced); one s.; m. 3rd Kimberly Buffington 2004; one s. one d.; ed Univ. of Houston; appeared on stage in Houston before moving to Hollywood; appeared on stage in New York with brother, Randy Quaid, in True West; performs with rock band The Electrics; wrote songs for films The Night the Lights Went Out in Georgia, Tough Enough, The Big Easy. *Films:* September 30 1955, 1978, Crazy Mama, Our Winning Season, Seniors, Breaking Away, I Never Promised You a Rose Garden, Gorp, The Long Riders, All Night Long, Caveman, The Night the Lights Went Out in Georgia, Tough Enough, Jaws 3-D, The Right Stuff, Dreamscape, Enemy Mine, The Big Easy, Innerspace, Suspect, D.O.A., Everyone's All-American, Great Balls of Fire, Lie Down With Lions, Postcards From the Edge, Come See the Paradise, A 22 Cent Romance, Wilder Napalu, Flesh and Bone, Wyatt Earp, Something To Talk About 1995, Dragonheart 1996, Criminal Element 1997, Going West 1997, Gang Related 1997, Savior 1997, Switchback 1997, The Parent Trap 1998, Any Given Sunday 1999, Frequency 2000, Traffic 2000, The Rookie 2002, Far From Heaven 2002, Cold Creek Manor 2003, The Alamo 2004, The Day After Tomorrow 2004, Flight of the Phoenix 2004, Synergy 2004, In Good Company 2004, Yours, Mine and Ours 2005, American Dreamz 2006, Smart People 2007, Vantage Point 2008, The Express 2008, Playing for Keeps 2012, Beneath the Darkness 2012, What to Expect When You're Expecting 2012, At Any Price 2012, Playing for Keeps 2012. *Television includes:* Amateur Night at the Dixie Bar and Grill 1979, Johnny Belinda 1982, Bill: On His Own 1983, Everything That Rises 1998, Dinner with Friends 2001, Vegas (series 2012–13). *Address:* William Morris Agency, 1 William Morris Place, Beverly Hills, CA 90212; c/o Hansen Jacobson Teller Hoberman Newman, Warren, Sloane & Richman, LLP, 450 North Roxbury Drive, 8th Floor, Beverly Hills, CA 90210-4222, USA.

QUAKE, Stephen R., BS, MS, DPhil; American biophysicist and academic; *Professor of Bioengineering, Stanford University;* ed Stanford Univ., Univ. of Oxford, UK; Postdoctoral Assoc., Steven Chu group, Stanford Univ. 1994–96, Prof. of Bioengineering 2004–; Asst Prof. of Applied Physics, California Inst. of Tech. 1996–99, Assoc. Prof. 1999–2002, Assoc. Prof. of Applied Physics and Physics 2002–03, Prof. 2003–04, Thomas E. and Doris Everhard Prof. of Applied Physics and Physics 2004–05; Investigator, Howard Hughes Medical Inst. 2006–; Visiting Scholar, Univ. of Minnesota 1996; mem. Quake Group, California Inst. of Tech., Pasadena, CSULA-California Inst. of Tech. partnerships for Research and Educ. in Materials (PREM) Collaborative 2004–; Co-founder, fmr Dir and Chair. Scientific Advisory Bd Fluidigm Corpn 1999–, Helicos, Inc. 2003–; consultant, Pharma Genomix 2000–, Axon Instruments 2003, Intel Corpn 2003, Molecular Technologies, Inc. 2004–05; participant in Nat. Acad. of Eng Symposium for Frontiers in Eng 1999; Firestone Prize, Stanford Univ. 1991, Apker Award, American Physical Soc. 1991, Marshall Scholar 1991, NSF Grad. Fellow 1993, NIH R29 'FIRST' Award 1997, NSF Career Award 1997, Packard Fellow 1999, named by Popular Science magazine one of Brilliant 10 2003, named to TR100 'Young Innovators that will create the Future', Massachusetts Inst. of Tech. Tech. Review magazine 2002, NIH Dir's Pioneer Award 2004. *Publications:* numerous papers in professional journals on fundamental and applied topics in biophysics, especially single molecule science. *Address:* Department of Bioengineering, Stanford University, James H Clark Center, Room E300, 318 Campus Drive, Stanford, CA 94305, USA (office). *Telephone:* (650) 736-7890 (office). *E-mail:* quake@stanford.edu (office). *Website:* thebigone.stanford.edu (office).

QUAM, Lois E., BA, MA, MHCA; American business executive and government official; *Executive Director, Global Health Initiative, US Department of State;* b. 21 June 1961; m. Matt Entenza; two s.; ed Macalaster Coll., Univ. of Oxford, UK; Pres. and CEO Penrose-St Francis Health System, Colo −1989; Dir Research and Evaluation, UnitedHealth Group 1989–93, Vice-Pres. Public Sector Services and Dir Research and Evaluation 1993, Corp. Vice-Pres. Man. Process 1996, CEO American Asscn of Retired Persons (AARP) Health Care Options Div. 1996–98, CEO Ovations, UnitedHealth Group 2002–06, Exec. Vice-Pres. Public and Sr Markets Group 2006–07; Man. Dir of Alternative Investments, Piper Jaffray and Co., Minneapolis 2007–09; Founder Tysvar, LLC 2009–; Sr Fellow, Center for American Progress, Washington, DC 2009; Exec. Dir Global Health Initiative, US Dept of State, Washington, DC 2011–; Sr Advisor to White House Task Force on Nat. Health Care Reform 1993–96; Chair. Minn. Health Care Access Comm. 1989–91; mem. Bd of Dirs General Mills Inc. 2007–11 (resgnd); mem. Council on Foreign Relations; Trustee, Macalaster Coll.; fmr Trustee, George C. Marshall Foundation, National Wildlife Federation; Rhodes Scholar; ranked by Fortune magazine amongst 50 Most Powerful Women in Business in the US (43rd) 2003, (42nd) 2004, (36th) 2005, (24th) 2006. *Publication:* Wills, Trusts & Estate Planning (co-author) 2001. *Address:* Office of the Executive Director, Global Health Initiative, Department of State, 2201 C St, NW, Washington, DC 20520, USA (office). *Telephone:* (202) 647-4000 (office). *E-mail:* ghi_comments@state.gov (office). *Website:* www.ghi.gov (office).

QUAN, Shuren; Chinese party and government official; b. 1930, Ximing Co., Liaoning Prov.; joined CCP 1949; mem. Standing Cttee CCP Cen. Cttee, Fushun City, Liaoning Prov. 1969–79; Mayor of Fushun 1980–82; Sec. CCP Fushun City Cttee 1980–82; Gov. of Liaoning Prov. 1983–86; Sec. 7th CCP Liaoning Prov. Cttee 1983–85, Deputy Sec. 1985–86, Sec. 1986–93; Chair. Standing Cttee 8th Liaoning Prov. People's Congress 1993–; Alt. mem. 12th CCP Cen. Cttee 1982–87, mem. 13th Cen. Cttee 1987–92, mem. 14th Cen. Cttee 1992–97; Del., 15th CCP Nat. Congress 1997–2002; mem. Standing Cttee 9th CPPCC Nat. Cttee 1998–2003. *Address:* Liaoning Provincial Committee, Shenyang, Liaoning Province, People's Republic of China (office).

QUAN, Zhenghuan; Chinese muralist, painter and university professor; b. 16 June 1932, Beijing; d. of Quan Liang-Su and Qin Xiao-Qing; m. Li Hua-Ji 1959; two d.; ed Cen. Acad. of Fine Arts, Beijing; Asst Lecturer, Cen. Acad. of Fine Arts 1955–56, Cen. Acad. of Applied Arts 1956–59, Lecturer 1959–78, Asst Prof. 1978–87, Prof. and mem. Academic Cttee 1987–; mem. Standing Cttee Artists' Asscn of China. *Murals include:* The Story of the White Snake (Beijing Int. Airport) 1979, Jin Wei filled the Ocean (Beijing Yian Jing Hotel), Dances of China (Beijing Opera House) 1984. *Leisure interests:* Beijing Opera, old movies of 1930–1940s, football. *Address:* Central Academy of Applied Arts, Beijing (office); 3-601, 6/F Hongmiao Beili, 100025, Beijing, People's Republic of China. *Telephone:* (1) 5963912 (office); (1) 5015522.

QUANT, Mary, OBE, FSIA; British fashion, cosmetic and textile designer; *Joint Chairperson, Mary Quant Ltd.;* b. 11 Feb. 1934, London; d. of Jack Quant and Mildred Quant (née Jones); m. Alexander Plunket Greene 1957 (died 1990); one s.; ed Goldsmiths Coll. of Art, London; started career in Chelsea, London 1954; Dir Mary Quant Group of cos 1955–, Jt Chair. Mary Quant Ltd; Dir (non-exec.) House of Fraser 1997–; mem. Design Council 1971–74, UK-USA Bicentennial Liaison Cttee 1973, Advisory Council Victoria and Albert Museum 1976–78; retrospective exhbn of 1960s fashion, London Museum 1974; Sr Fellow, Royal Coll. of Art 1991; Hon. Fellow, Goldsmiths Coll., Univ. of London 1993; Hon. FRSA 1995; Dr hc (Winchester Coll. of Art) 2000; Sunday Times Int. Fashion Award, Rex Award (USA), Annual Design Medal, Soc. of Industrial Artists and Designers, Piavolo d'Oro (Italy), Royal Designer for Industry, Hall of Fame Award, British Fashion Council (for outstanding contrib. to British fashion) 1990. *Publications:* Quant by Quant 1966, Colour by Quant 1984, Quant on Make-up 1986, Mary Quant Classic Make-up and Beauty Book 1996. *Address:* Mary Quant Ltd, 1st Floor, Lynton House, 7–12 Tavistock Square, London, WC1H 9LT (office); 34 Dalby Road, London, SW18 1AW, England (home). *Telephone:* (20) 7383-2518 (office). *Fax:* (20) 7383-0814 (office). *E-mail:* mqltdldn@ma.kew.net. *Website:* www.maryquant.co.uk (office).

QUARRIE, Donald (Don); Jamaican fmr athlete; b. 25 Feb. 1951, Kingston; ed Univ. of Southern California, USA; competed at Olympic Games, Munich 1972, reaching semifinal of 200m; Montreal 1976, won gold medal at 200m and silver medal at 100m; Moscow 1980, won bronze medal at 200m; Los Angeles 1984, won silver medal 4×100m relay; competed at Commonwealth Games, Edinburgh 1970, won gold medals at 100m, 200m and 4×100m relay; Christchurch, NZ 1974 won gold medals at 100m and 200m; Edmonton 1978, won gold medal at 100m; coach in Calif., runs sprint clinics in Calif. and world-wide; Donald Quarrie High School named in his honour. *Address:* c/o Jamaica Athletics Administrative Association, PO Box 272, 6 Tremaine Road, Kingston 6, Jamaica, West Indies. *E-mail:* athleticsja@cwjamaica.com.

QUARTA, Roberto; American (b. Italian) business executive; *Partner and Chairman, Clayton, Dubilier & Rice Europe;* b. May 1949; ed Coll. of the Holy Cross, Mass; served for six years in US Army; Pnr, Clayton, Dubilier & Rice (CD&R), Inc. (pvt. equity group) 2001–, Chair. CD&R Europe, London; CEO BBA Group 1993–2001 (renamed BBA Aviation following demerger of Fiberweb 2006), Chair. −2007, Chair. Supervisory Bd Rexel SA (owned by CD&R) 2007–, Chair., Pres., Man. Dir and mem. Exec. Cttee ItalTel SpA (owned by CD&R); Chair. IMI plc 2011–, Smith & Nephew PLC 2014–; mem. Bd of Dirs Foster Wheeler AG; mem. Country Advisory Bd Institut Européen d'Admin des Affaires (INSEAD); mem. Bd of Trustees Coll. of the Holy Cross. *Address:* Clayton, Dubilier & Rice Ltd, Cleveland House, 33 King Street, London, SW1Y 6RJ, England (office). *Telephone:* (20) 7747-3800 (office). *Fax:* (20) 7747-3801 (office). *E-mail:* info@cdr-inc.com (office). *Website:* www.cdr-inc.com (office).

QUAYES, Mohamed Mijarul, BA, MPA; Bangladeshi academic, diplomatist and government official; *High Commissioner to UK;* b. 2 April 1960, Kishoregonj; m. Naeema Chaudhury Quayes; two d.; ed Univ. of Dhaka, Kennedy School of Govt, Harvard Univ., USA; joined Foreign Service 1982, Asst Sec. (Desk Officer), South Asia Wing, Ministry of Foreign Affairs 1982–85, Second Sec., Embassy in Tokyo 1985–90, Sec., 7th SAARC Summit Cell, Ministry of Foreign Affairs, Dir, Personnel Directorate 1991–94, Counsellor, Perm. Mission to UN Office and other Int. Orgs, Geneva, Perm. Mission to UN Office, Vienna 1994–98, Counsellor and Deputy Chief of Mission, Singapore 1998–2000, Dir Gen., Ministry of Foreign Affairs 2001–05, High Commr to the Maldives 2005–08, Amb. to Russia 2008–09, Foreign Sec. 2009–12, High Commr to UK 2012–; Edward S. Mason Fellow in Public Policy and Man., Harvard Inst. for Int. Devt; lecturer in aesthetics and history of art, Nat. Acad. of the Arts, Dhaka. *Leisure interest:* collecting works of art. *Address:* Bangladesh High Commission, 28 Queen's Gate, London, SW7 5JA, England (office). *Telephone:* (20) 7584-0081 (office). *Fax:* (20) 7581-7477 (office). *E-mail:* hc@bhclondon.org.uk (office). *Website:* www.bhclondon.org.uk (office).

QUAYLE, James Danforth (Dan), BS, JD; American international business consultant and fmr politician; *Chairman, Cerberus Global Investments LLC;* b. 4 Feb. 1947, Indianapolis, Ind.; s. of the late James C. Quayle and of Corinne Quayle (née Pulliam); m. Marilyn Tucker 1972; two s. one d.; ed DePauw Univ., Indiana Univ.; served in Indiana Nat. Guard; court reporter, Huntington Herald Press, Ind. 1965–69, Assoc. Publr and Gen. Man. 1974–76; mem. Consumer Protection Div., Office of Ind. Attorney-Gen. 1970–71; Admin. Asst to Gov. of Ind. 1971–73; Dir Ind. Inheritance Tax Div. 1973–74; admitted to Indiana bar 1974; teacher of business law, Huntington Coll. 1975; mem. US House of Reps 1977–79; Senator from Ind. 1981–88; Vice-Pres. of USA 1989–93; with Circle Investors 1993; currently Chair. Cerberus Global Investments, LLC; Distinguished Visiting Prof., American Grad. School of Int. Man. 1997–99; f. J. D. Quayle & Co. 2000; mem. Huntington Bar Asscn; mem. Hoosier State Press Asscn; Chair. Council on Competitiveness; Republican. *Publications include:* Standing Firm 1994, The American Family 1995, Worth Fighting For 1999. *Address:* Cerberus Global Investments LLC, c/o Cerberus Capital Management, L.P., 875 Third Avenue, New York, NY 10022; c/o Kathleen Murphy, 7001 N. Scottsdale Road, Suite 2010, Scottsdale, AZ 85253, USA (office). *Telephone:* (212) 891-2100 (office); (480) 922-5700 (office). *E-mail:* info@cerberuscapital.com (office). *Website:* www .vicepresidentdanquayle.com.

QUBAISI, Khadem Abdulla al-, BEcons; United Arab Emirates business executive; *Managing Director, International Petroleum Investment Company;* b. 27 Sept. 1971; Sr Financial Analyst, N America Equities Dept, Abu Dhabi Investment Authority 1994–99; Investment Man. Div. Man., Int. Petroleum Investment Co. 2000–07, currently Man. Dir; Chair. Aabar Investments PJSC 2008–, Borealis 2010–, Nat. Central Cooling Co. (Tabreed), Abu Dhabi Nat. Takaful Co. (Takaful), I-Media Newspaper (Alrroya Aleqtisadiya), Hyundai Oilbank Co. Ltd, S Korea, Gulf Energy Maritime PJSC −2008, Arabtec Holding PJSC; Dir Compañia Española de Petróleos SA, First Gulf Bank, Emirates Investment Authority, Aldar Properties PJSC −2010; voted Arabian Businessman of the Year 2009, ICIS Power Player of the Year 2009, ranked by Arabian Business amongst the Power 500: The Worlds's Most Influential Arabs (76th) 2012. *Address:* International Petroleum Investment Company, PO Box 7528, Sheikh Zayed the 1st Street, Al Muhairy Centre, Office Tower, 10th Floor, Abu Dhabi, United Arab Emirates (office). *Telephone:* (2) 6336555 (office). *Fax:* (2) 6330111 (office). *E-mail:* info@ipic.ae (office). *Website:* www.ipic.ae (office).

QUBAYSI, Sheikha Munira al-; Syrian educator; *Founder and Director, Al-Qubaysiat;* b. 1933, Damascus; Founder of Al-Qubaysiat (female-only quasi-Sufi movt, the largest women-only Islamic movt in the world), offers Islamic educ. exclusively to girls and women, banned by Syrian Govt until 2006; directs approx. 80 schools in Damascus with 75,000 students; ranked by the Royal Islamic Strategic Studies Centre as the 24th most influential Muslim in the world and the most influential Muslim woman 2011, ranked by Arabian Business amongst the 100 Most Powerful Arab Women (94th) 2011, and amongst the Power 500: The Worlds's Most Influential Arabs (42nd) 2012.

QUDAH, Adel, BA, MA; Jordanian government official; b. Al-Salt; m.; four c.; ed Cairo Univ., Egypt, Univ. of Southern Calif., USA; Gen. Dir Customs Dept, Ministry of Finance 1982–91, Income Tax Dept 1990–91; Pres. Audit Bureau 1991–94; Minister of Supply 1996–2005; Chair. Exec. Privatization Comm. 1996–2005; Minister of Finance July–Nov. 2005; convicted of bribery by military court July 2010, sentenced to three years' imprisonment; Order of the Jordan Star of the First Order, Order of the Repub. of Egypt of the First Order.

QUE AZCONA, Vivian; Philippine business executive; b. 1 Sept. 1955; d. of Mariano Que; m. Edward Azcona; ed Univ. of Santo Tomas; Pres. Mercury Drugs Inc. (f. by father 1945) 1998–. *Address:* Mercury Drugs Inc., 7 Mercury Avenue, Corner E. Rodriguez Jr, Bagumbayan, Quezon City 1110, Philippines (office). *Telephone:* (2) 9115071 (office). *Fax:* (2) 9110673 (office). *Website:* www .mercurydrug.com (office).

QUEEN LATIFAH; American rap artist and actress; b. (Dana Owens), 18 March 1970, East Orange, NJ; d. of Lance Owens and Rita Bray; worked with female rap act, Ladies Fresh; recorded with producers Dady-O, KRS-1, DJ Mark the 45 King and mems of De La Soul; moved to Motown Records; began acting career with sitcom Living Single; established management company, Flavor Unit Entertainment and label, Flavor Unit Records 1993–; guest appearance on Shabba Ranks' single, Watcha Gonna Do; other recording collaborations with De La Soul and Monie Love; Grammy Award for Best Rap Solo Performance 1994. *Films:* Living Single, Jungle Fever 1991, House Party 2 1991, Juice 1992, My Life 1993, Set It Off 1996, Hoodlum 1997, Sphere 1998, Living Out Loud 1998, The Bone Collector 1999, Bringing Out the Dead 1999, The Country Bears 2002, Brown Sugar 2002, Chicago 2002, Bringing Down the House (also exec. producer) 2003, Scary Movie 3 2003, Barbershop 2: Back in Business 2004, The Cookout (also writer and producer) 2004, Beauty Shop (also producer) 2005, Last Holiday 2006, Ice Age: The Meltdown (voice) 2006, Stranger Than Fiction 2006, Hairspray 2007, The Perfect Holiday 2007, Mad Money 2008, What Happens in Vegas 2008, The Secret Life of Bees 2008, Joyful Noise 2012. *Television includes:* Living Single (series) 1993, Mama Flora's Family 1998, Queen Latifah Show 1999, Living with the Dead (mini series) 2002, The Muppets' Wizard of Oz 2005, Life Support (Golden Globe Award for Outstanding Performance by a Female Actor in a Television Movie or Miniseries 2008) 2007. *Recordings include:* albums: All Hail The Queen 1989, Latifah's Had It Up 2 Here 1989, Nature Of A Sista 1991, Black Reign 1993, Queen Latifah and Original Flava Unit 1996, Order In The Court 1998, The Dana Owens Album 2004, Trav'lin' Light 2008, Persona 2009. *Publications:* Ladies First 2000, Queen of the Scene 2006, Put On Your Crown 2010. *Website:* www.queenlatifah .com.

QUEFFÉLEC, Anne; French concert pianist; b. 17 Jan. 1948, Paris; d. of Henri Queffélec and Yvonne Pénau; m. Luc Dehaene 1983; ed Conservatoire Nat., Paris; since 1968 has played in tours of Europe, Japan, Israel, Africa, Canada and USA; has played with BBC Symphony, London Symphony, Royal Philharmonic, Bournemouth Symphony, Hallé, Scottish Chamber, City of Birmingham Symphony, Miami Symphony, NHK Tokyo, Tokyo Symphony orchestras, Nouvel orchestre philharmonique de Radio-France, Orchestre nat. de Radio-France, Orchestre de Strasbourg, Ensemble Intercontemporain, etc., under conductors including Zinman, Groves, Leppard, Marriner, Boulez, Semkow, Skrowaczewski, Eschenbach, Gardiner, Pritchard, Atherton, etc.; has played at numerous festivals including Strasbourg, Dijon, Besançon, La Roque d'Anthéron, La Grange de Meslay, Bordeaux, Paris, King's Lynn, Bath, Cheltenham, London Proms; judge in several int. piano competitions; master-classes in France (including Ecole normale de musique, Paris), England and Japan; Pres. Asscn des amis d'Henri Queffélec, Asscn musicale 'Ballades'; Chevalier, Légion d'honneur 1998, Officier, Ordre nat. du Mérite 2001; First Prize for Piano 1965, for Chamber Music 1966, Conservatoire Nat., Paris; First Prize, Munich Int. Piano Competition 1968, Prizewinner, Leeds Int. Piano Competition 1969, Best Classical Artist of the Year, Victoires de la Musique 1990. *Recordings:* more than 30 records of music by Scarlatti, Handel, Chopin, Schubert, Fauré, Ravel (complete piano works), Debussy, Liszt, Hummel, Beethoven, Mendelssohn, Bach, Satie, complete piano works of Henri Dutilleux 1996 and Mozart and Haydn recitals. *Radio:* numerous appearances on BBC Radio 3, France Musique and Japanese radio. *Television:* numerous appearances on musical, but also literary and religious, programmes. *Leisure interests:* children, literature, cycling, theatre, friends, humour, art. *Address:* c/o Christine Talbot-Cooper, International Artists, Stoneville Cottage, Gretton Fields, Cheltenham, Glos. GL54 5HH, England (office); 15 avenue Corneille, 78600 Maisons-Laffitte, France. *Telephone:* (1242) 620736 (office); 1-39-62-25-64. *Fax:* (1242) 620736 (office); 1-39-62-25-64. *E-mail:* talbotcooper@onetel.com (office). *Website:* www .ctcinternationalartists.com (office).

QUEK, Tan Sri Leng Chan; Malaysian barrister and business executive; *Executive Chairman and CEO, Hong Leong Group Malaysia;* b. 1941; m.; three c.; called to Bar, Middle Temple, UK; has extensive business experience in financial services, manufacturing and real estate; Co-founder, Exec. Chair. and CEO Hong Leong Group Malaysia (includes semiconductor cos, automotive assembly, materials, newsprint, furniture); Exec. Chair. Guoco Group Ltd 1990–; Chair. HL Holdings Sdn Bhd. *Address:* Hong Leong Group Malaysia, Wisma Hong Leong, 18 Jalan Perak, 50450 Kuala Lumpur, Malaysia (office). *Telephone:* (3) 2164-1818 (office). *Fax:* (3) 2164-2477 (office). *E-mail:* info@hongleong.com (office). *Website:* www.hongleong.com (office).

QUELCH, John Anthony, CBE, MA, MBA, MS, DBA, CIMgt, FRGS; British/American academic; *Dean, Vice-President and Distinguished Professor of International Management, China Europe International Business School;* b. 8 Aug. 1951, London, England; s. of Norman Quelch and Laura Sally Quelch (née Jones); m. Joyce Ann Huntley 1978; ed Exeter Coll., Oxford, Wharton School, Univ. of Pennsylvania, Harvard Univ., USA; Asst Prof., Univ. of Western Ontario, Canada 1977–79; Asst Prof., then Assoc. Prof., then Prof., then Sebastian S. Kresge Prof. of Marketing, Harvard Univ., USA 1979–98; Sr Assoc. Dean and Lincoln Filene Prof. of Business Admin., Harvard Business School 2001–11; Dean of London Business School 1998–2001; Dean, Vice-Pres. and Distinguished Prof. of Int. Man., China Europe Int. Business School, Shanghai 2011–; Chair. Massachusetts Port Authority 2002–11; Dir (non-exec.) WPP plc, Alere, Inc., Americans For Oxford 2002–11; Fellow, Int. Acad. of Man. 2000; HM Fellow, London Business School 2009; Hon. Fellow, Exeter Coll. Oxford 2002, Hon. Consul Gen., Kingdom of Morocco, Hon. Chair. British American Business Council of New England; Dr hc (Vietnam Nat. Univ.) 2011; Leadership Award, British American Business Council of New England 2008, World Boston International Citizens Award 2010. *Publications:* How to Market to Consumers 1989, Sales Promotion Management 1989, Cases in Advertising and Promotion Management 1995, Marketing Management 2004, Global Marketing Management 2004, The Global Market 2004, The New Global Brands 2005, Business Solutions for the Global Poor 2007, Greater Good: How Good Marketing Makes for Better Democracy 2009, All Business Is Local 2011. *Leisure interests:* squash, tennis. *Address:* China Europe International Business School, 699 Hongfeng Road, Pudong, Shanghai 201206, People's Republic of China (office); 57 Baker Bridge Road, Lincoln, MA 01773, USA (home). *Telephone:* (21) 28905890 (office); (21) 28905101 (switchboard) (office); (781) 259-0594 (home). *Fax:* (21) 28905678 (office). *E-mail:* jquelch@ceibs.edu (office); jaquelch@yahoo.com (home). *Website:* www.ceibs.edu (office).

QUESTROM, Allen I., BA; American retail executive; *Senior Advisor, Lee Equity Partners LLC;* m. Kelli Questrom; ed Boston Univ.; began career with Federated Dept Stores Inc. 1964, apptd Chair. and CEO Rich Div. 1980, Chair. and CEO fmr Bullock Div. 1984–88, Exec. Vice-Pres. 1988, Chair. and CEO 1990–97; Pres. and CEO Neiman Marcus 1988–90; joined Barneys New York Inc. 1997, Chair., Pres. and CEO 1999–2000; Chair. and CEO J. C. Penney Co. Inc. 2000–04; Prin. AEA Investors Inc.; Partner Mellon Ventures; Sr Advisor, Lee Equity Partners LLC 2006–; mem. Bd Dirs Barneys New York Inc.; Dir Nat. Retail Fed.; mem. Nat. Cttee Whitney Museum of American Art, New York; mem. Business Council; Trustee, Boston Univ. *Address:* Lee Equity Partners, 767 5th Avenue, New York, NY 10153, USA. *Telephone:* (212) 888-1500.

QUEYRANNE, Jean-Jack; French politician; b. 2 Nov. 1945, Lyon; s. of Maurice Queyranne and Jeanne Bonavent; First Deputy Mayor of Villeurbanne (Rhône) 1977–88; Parti Socialiste (PS) mem. Rhône Gen. Council 1979–90, Regional Council Rhône-Alps 1986–2002, Pres. 2004–; Nat. Ass. Deputy (alt.) for Rhone 1981–93; mem. PS Steering Cttee, Deputy Nat. Sec. responsible for cultural policy 1983, for press and culture 1985, Party Spokesman 1985, Nat. Del. and Spokesman

1987, Nat. Sec. responsible for audiovisual policy 1988, mem. Nat. Council 1993–94; Mayor of Bron (Rhône) 1989–97, Deputy Mayor 1997–2004; Nat. Ass. Deputy for Rhône 1997–; Minister of State attached to Minister of the Interior, with responsibility for Overseas Depts and Territories 1997–2000; Minister of Relations with Parliament 2000–02. *Leisure interests:* theatre, music, cinema. *Address:* 1 rue Roger Salengro, 69500 Bron (office); Assemblée nationale, 126 rue de l'Université, 75355 Paris 07 SP, France (office). *Telephone:* 4-72-37-50-99 (office). *Fax:* 4-72-37-58-87 (office). *E-mail:* jjqueyranne@assemblee-nationale.fr (office). *Website:* www.assemblee-nationale.fr (office).

QUIGLEY, Michael (Mike), BSc, BEE; British/Australian business executive; b. 1953; m.; three d.; ed Univ. of New South Wales; joined ITT Australia (now Alcatel Australia) 1971, positions including research and devt, manufacturing, sales and marketing, Gen. Man. for Australia and NZ 1996–99, COO Alcatel USA 1999, later CEO Alcatel USA, Pres. Alcatel N America, mem. Exec. Cttee, Pres. Fixed Communications Activities 2003, Pres. and COO Alcatel 2005–06, COO joint Alcatel-Lucent techs co. after Alcatel acquisition of Lucent 2006–07 (resgnd), also fmr mem. Exec. Bd; CEO NBN (National Broadband Network) Co Ltd 2009–13; mem. Bd Alliance for Telecommunications Industry Solutions; Charles Todd Medal for outstanding services to telecommunications in Australia 2013.

QUIGNARD, Pascal Charles Edmond, LicenFil; French writer; b. 23 April 1948, Verneuil-sur-Avre, Eure; s. of Jacques Quignard and Anne Quignard (née Bruneau); one s.; ed Lycée de Havre, Lycée de Sèvres and Faculté des Lettres de Nanterre; Lecturer 1969–77; mem. Cttee of Lecturing 1977–94; Sec.-Gen. for Editorial Devt, Editions Gallimard; Pres. Int. Festival of Opera and Baroque Theatre, Château de Versailles 1990–94; Pres. Concert des Nations 1990–93; Chevalier, Légion d'honneur; Prix de la Soc. des gens de lettres for his collected works 1998, Grand prix du roman de la Ville de Paris 1998, Prix de la fondation Prince Pierre de Monaco for his collected works 2000. *Publications include:* L'être du balbutiement 1969, Alexandra de Lycophron 1971, La parole de la Délie 1974, Michel Deguy 1975, Echo 1975, Sang 1976, Le lecteur 1976, Hiems 1977, Sarx 1977, Inter aerias fagos 1977, Sur le défaut de terre 1979, Carus 1979, Le secret du domaine 1980, Petits traités (tome I à VIII) 1990, Les tablettes de buis d'Apronenia Avitia 1984, Le vœu de silence (essay) 1985, Une gêne technique à l'égard des fragments 1986, Ethelrude et Wolframm 1986, Le salon de Wurtemberg 1986, La leçon de musique 1987, Les escaliers de Chambord 1989, La raison 1990, Albucius 1990, Tous les matins du monde 1991, Georges de La Tour 1991, La Frontière 1992, Le nom sur le bout de la langue 1993, Le sexe et l'effroi 1994, L'occupation américaine 1994, Rhétorique spéculative 1995, L'amour conjugal 1995, Les septante 1995, La haine de la musique 1996, Vie secrète 1998, Terrasse à Rome (Grand Prix du roman de l'Acad. française 2000) 2000, Albucius 2001, Les ombres errantes (Prix Goncourt 2002) 2002, Sur le jadis 2002, Abîmes 2002, Les Paradisiaques 2005, Sordidissimes 2005, Écrits de l'éphémère 2005, Pour trouver les Enfers 2005, Villa Amalia 2006, L'Enfant au visage couleur de la mort 2006, Triomphe du temps 2006, Ethelrude et Wolframm 2006, Le Petit Cupidon 2006, Requiem 2006, La Nuit sexuelle 2007, Boutès 2008, La Barque Silencieuse 2009, Assises du roman 2009. *Address:* c/o Éditions du Seuil, 25 boulevard Romain Rolland, 75993 Paris, France (office). *Website:* www.seuil.com.

QUIJANO CAPURRO, José Manuel; Uruguayan economist and international organization official; Dir Consultora Alianza Cooperativa Internacional, ACI, Uruguay; Advisor, Perm. Secr., Sistema Economico Latinoamericana (SELA) c. 2001; fmr consultant with Integración AFAP, Montevideo; mem. Mercosur Sectoral Comm., Exec. Dir Mercosur Secr. 2008–09. *Address:* c/o Secretaría del Mercosur, Código Postal 11.200, Dr Luis Piera 1992, 1º Piso – Edificio MERCOSUR, Montevideo, Uruguay. *Telephone:* (2) 412-9024. *E-mail:* secretaria@mercosur.org.uy.

QUILÈS, Paul; French politician; *Mayor of Cordes-sur-Ciel (Tarn);* b. 27 Jan. 1942, St Denis du Sig, Algeria; s. of René Quilès and Odette Tyrode; m. Josephe-Marie Bureau 1964; three d.; ed Ecole Polytechnique, Paris; engineer, Shell Française 1964–78; Socialist Deputy to Nat. Ass. 1978–83, 1986–88, 1993–2007; Minister of Town Planning and Housing 1983–85, of Transport 1984–85, of Defence 1985–86, of Posts, Telecommunications and Space 1988–91, of Public Works, Housing, Transportation and Space Research 1991–92, of the Interior and Public Security 1992–93; Chair. Nat. Defence and Armed Forces Comm. 1997–2002; Mayor of Cordes-sur-Ciel (Tarn) 1995–; mem. Econ. and Social Council 1974–75; mem. Parl. Foreign Affairs Comm. 2002, Vice-Pres. 2004–07. *Publications:* La Politique n'est pas ce que vous croyez 1985, Nous vivons une époque intéressante 1992, Les 577, Un parlement pour quoi faire 2001, Face aux désordres du monde 2005, 18 mois chrono 2010, On a repris la Bastille 2011, Nucléaire: un mensonge français 2012, Arrêtez la bombe 2013. *Address:* Mairie, 34 Grande Rue Raymond VII, 81170 Cordes-sur-Ciel, (Tarn) France (office). *Website:* paul.quiles.over-blog.com.

QUINLAN, Michael (Mike) R., BS, MBA; American business executive; *Chairman Emeritus, McDonald's Corporation;* b. 9 Dec. 1944, Chicago; s. of Robert Joseph Quinlan and Kathryn Quinlan (née Koerner); m. Marilyn DeLashmutt 1966; two s.; ed Loyola Univ.; started career as part-time mailroom worker, McDonald's Corpn 1963, Asst Buyer 1966, Pres. (USA) 1980–82, CEO 1987–98, Chair. 1989–97, Dir 1979–2002 (retd), now Chair. Emer.; mem. Bd of Dirs Dun & Bradstreet Corpn 1989–, May Dept Stores Co., Warren Resources, Inc. *Leisure interest:* racquetball. *Address:* c/o Board of Directors, Dun & Bradstreet Corporation, 103 JFK Pkwy, Short Hills, NJ 07078, USA.

QUINN, Aidan; American actor; b. 8 March 1959, Chicago; m. Elizabeth Bracco; two d.; worked with various theatre groups in Chicago before moving to New York; off-Broadway appearances in Sam Shepard's plays Fool for Love and A Lie of the Mind; appeared in Hamlet, Wisdom Bridge Theater, Chicago, numerous other plays. *Films:* Reckless 1984, Desperately Seeking Susan 1985, The Mission 1986, Stakeout 1987, Crusoe 1989, The Handmaid's Tale 1990, The Lemon Sisters 1990, Avalon 1990, At Play in the Fields of the Lord 1991, The Playboys 1992, Benny & Joon 1993, Blink 1994, Legends of the Fall 1994, Mary Shelley's Frankenstein 1994, The Stars Fell on Henrietta 1995, Haunted 1995, Michael Collins 1996, Looking For Richard 1996, Commandments 1997, The Assignment 1997, This is My Father 1998, Practical Magic 1998, In Dreams 1999, Music of the Heart 1999, Songcatcher 2000, Stolen Summer 2002, Evelyn 2002, Song for a Raggy Boy 2003

Cavedweller 2004, Shadow of Fear 2004, Bobby Jones, Stroke of Genius 2004, Plainsong 2004, Return to Sender 2004, Proud 2004, Nine Lives 2005, Dark Matter 2007, Wild Child 2008, The Eclipse 2009, The 5th Quarter 2009, Flipped 2010, Jonah Hex 2010. *Stage appearances include:* Fool for Love 1983, A Streetcar Named Desire (Theatre World Award) 1988. *Television includes:* An Early Frost 1985, Perfect Witness 1989, Lies of the Twins 1991, A Private Matter 1992, Forbidden Territory: Stanley's Search for Livingstone 1997, The Prince and the Pauper 2000, See You in My Dreams 2000, Two of Us 2000, Benedict Arnold: A Question of Honor 2003, Plainsong 2004, Cavedweller 2004, Miracle Run 2004, Third Watch (series) 2004–05, The Exonerated 2005, Empire Falls 2005, Mayday 2005, The Book of Daniel (series) 2006, Bury My Heart at Wounded Knee 2007, Canterbury's Law 2008, White Collar 2010. *Address:* Framework Entertainment, 9057 Nemo Street, Suite C, West Hollywood, CA 90069; c/o ICM, 8942 Wilshire Boulevard, Beverly Hills, CA 90211, USA.

QUINN, Aidy; Irish singer; b. Co. Tyrone; s. of Tom Quinn and Philomena Quinn; ed St Patrick's Coll., Dungannon; country music singer; Irish World Award for Most Promising New Act 2006, Irish Entertainment Award for Best New Artist 2007. *Recordings include:* albums: Born and Bred on Country Music (Irish Country Music Award for Best New Album) 2006. *Address:* c/o Purple Heather Promotions, 8 Forthill Road, Enniskillen, BT74 6AW, Northern Ireland (office); Millbrook House, Galbally, BT70 2NR, Northern Ireland (home). *Telephone:* (28) 6632-3238 (office); (28) 8775-8526 (home). *Fax:* (28) 6632-3225 (office). *E-mail:* erneproms@btinternet.com (office). *Website:* www.aidyquinn.com.

QUINN, Brian, CBE, MA (Hons), MA (Econ), PhD; British banker, economist and consultant; *Chairman, Bvalco Limited;* b. 18 Nov. 1936, Glasgow, Scotland; s. of Thomas Quinn and Margaret Cairns; m. Mary Bradley 1961; two s. one d.; ed Univs of Glasgow and Manchester, Cornell Univ., USA; economist, African Dept, IMF, Washington, DC 1964–70; Rep. of IMF in Sierra Leone 1966–68; joined Bank of England 1970, Econ. Div. 1970–74, Chief Cashier's Dept 1974–77, Head of Information Div. 1977–82, Asst Dir 1982–88, Head of Banking Supervision 1986–88, Exec. Dir 1988–96, Acting Deputy Gov. 1995; Chair. Nomura Bank Int. PLC 1996–99; Vice-Chair. Celtic PLC 1996–2000, Chair. 2000–07; Chair. Bvalco Ltd; mem. Club Financial Control Body, Union of European Football Assocns (UEFA) 2009–; Dir (non-exec.) Bankgesellschaft Berlin UK PLC 1996–2001, Britannic Asset Man. 1998–2004, Nomura Holdings Europe 1998–99; Man. Dir Brian Quinn Consultancy 1997–; Chair. Financial Markets Group, LSE 1996–2001; consultant, World Bank 1997–; Fellow, Chartered Inst. of Bankers in Scotland; Hon. Prof. of Econs and Finance, Univ. of Glasgow 2006–. *Publications:* contribs to various books and journals. *Leisure interests:* fishing, watching football, reading, walking. *Address:* Bvalco Ltd, Munro House, Portsmouth Road, Cobham, Surrey, KT11 1PP (office); 14 Homewood Road, St Albans, Herts., AL1 4BH, England (home). *Telephone:* (1727) 853900. *Fax:* (1727) 866646. *E-mail:* bqconns@aol.com. *Website:* www.bvalco.com (office).

QUINN, Patrick (Pat) Joseph, III, BA, JD; American lawyer, politician and state governor; *Governor of Illinois;* b. 16 Dec. 1948, Hinsdale, Ill.; m. (divorced); two s.; ed Georgetown Univ., Northwestern Univ. School of Law; Commr Cook Co. Bd of (Property) Tax Appeals 1982–86; Revenue Dir, City of Chicago 1986; Treas. State of Illinois 1991–95; Lt Gov. of Illinois 2003–09; Gov. of Illinois 2009–; Chair. Blackout Solutions Task Force, Mississippi River Coordinating Council, Illinois Green Govts Coordinating Council, Illinois Biofuels Investment and Infrastructure Working Group, Broadband Deployment Council; Democrat; Commdr's Cross, Order of Merit (Poland) 2012. *Publication:* How to Appeal Your Property Taxes . . . Without a Lawyer. *Address:* Office of the Governor, 207 State House, Springfield, IL 62706, USA (office). *Telephone:* (217) 782-0244 (office). *Fax:* (217) 524-4049 (office). *Website:* www2.illinois.gov/gov (office).

QUINN, Ruairi, BArch, RIBA; Irish politician, architect and town planner; b. 2 April 1946, Dublin; s. of Malachi Quinn and Julia Quinn; m. 1st Nicola Underwood 1969 (divorced), one s. one d.; m. 2nd Liz Allman 1990, one s.; ed Blackrock Coll. and Univ. Coll., Dublin, Athens Center of Ekistics, Greece; Athens Center of Ekistics, Greece 1970–71; Architects' Dept, Dublin Corpn 1971–73; Pnr, Burke-Kennedy Doyle and Pnr 1973–82; mem. Dublin Corpn 1974–77, 1981–82; mem. Seanad Éireann 1976–77, 1981–82; mem. Dáil Éireann for Dublin SE constituency 1977–81, 1982–; Minister of State, Dept of the Environment 1982–83; Minister for Labour and Minister for the Public Service 1983–87; Deputy Leader Irish Labour Party 1989, Leader 1997–2002; Treas. Party of European Socialists 2000–, also Vice-Pres.; Dir of Elections for Pres. Mary Robinson (q.v.); Labour Spokesperson on Finance and Econ. Affairs 1990, on European Affairs, on Enterprise, Trade and Employment 2006–; Minister for Enterprise and Employment 1993–94, for Finance 1994–97; mem. Royal Inst. of the Architects of Ireland. *Publication:* Straight Left: A Journey in Politics 2005. *Leisure interests:* athletics, reading, hill walking. *Address:* Dáil Éireann, Kildare Street, Dublin 2 (office); 23 Strand Road, Sandymount, Dublin 4, Ireland (home). *Telephone:* (1) 6183434 (office). *Fax:* (1) 6184153 (office). *E-mail:* ruairi.quinn@oireachtas.ie (office). *Website:* www.ruairiquinn.ie (office).

QUIÑONES AMEZQUITA, Mario Rafael; Guatemalan lawyer and diplomatist; b. 4 June 1933, Quezaltenango; s. of the late Hector Quiñones and of Elisa de Quiñones; m. Yolanda de Quiñones 1963; two s. two d.; ed Univ. of San Carlos and Univ. of Rio Grande do Sul, Brazil; lawyer and notary with law firm of Viteri, Falla, Quiñones, Umaña, Orellana y Cáceres 1959–; Prof. of Law, Rafael Landívar Univ. 1962–, Dean Dept of Legal and Social Sciences 1974–82; Vice-Pres. of Landívar Univ. 1978–82, Pres. March–Oct. 1982; Amb. and Perm. Rep. to UN 1982–84; Minister of Foreign Affairs 1986–87; Vice-Pres. N and Cen. American Region, Union of Latin Notaries 1978; Pres. Assocn of Lawyers and Notaries of Guatemala 1977; mem. Guatemalan Del. UN Comm. on Int. Trade Law 1974; Orden de Malta, Orden dell Quetzal, Orden de los Cinco Volcanes and decorations from govts of Spain, Peru, Germany, Argentina and Mexico; Dr hc (Univ. Rafael Landivar) 1998. *Leisure interests:* reading, music. *Address:* 6A Calle 5-47, Zona 9 –3er. Nivel, Guatemala City 01009 (office); 8 Avenida 5-55, Zona 14, Condominio Villalbosque Torre Norte, Apartamento 1501, Guatemala (office). *Telephone:* (2) 2331-1721 (office); (2) 2368-1449 (home). *Fax:* (2) 2337-0186 (home). *E-mail:* mrqamz20@gmail.com (office).

QUIÑÓNEZ, Alfonso, MA; Guatemalan lawyer, diplomatist and international organization executive; *Secretary for External Relations, Organization of American States;* ed Francisco Marroquín Univ. of Guatemala, Georgetown Univ., Washington, DC, Univ. of Maryland, Inter-American Defense Coll., Washington, DC; mem. Guatemalan Foreign Service for 10 years, held positions of Counsellor in Spain, Minister Counsellor in USA, Amb. and Perm. Rep. to OAS 1998–2000; Exec. Dir Alvaro Arzú Foundation for Peace, Guatemala and Adviser to Mayor of Guatemala City –2001; Dir Dept of Co-operation Policies, OAS 2001, later Dir Office of Policies and Programs for Devt, OAS Exec. Secr. for Integral Devt, later Chief of Staff to Asst Sec.-Gen., Acting Exec. Sec. for Integral Devt and Acting Dir-Gen. Inter-American Agency for Integral Devt 2004–05, Exec. Sec. for Integral Devt and Dir-Gen. Inter-American Agency for Co-operation and Devt 2005, currently Sec. for External Relations, OAS; Prof., Schools of Law and Int. Relations, Francisco Marroquín Univ. 2001–02. *Address:* Organization of American States, corner of 17th Street and Constitution Avenue, NW, Washington, DC 20006, USA (office). *Telephone:* (202) 458-3000 (office). *Website:* www.oas.org (office).

QUINTANILLA SCHMIDT, Carlos, BSc; Salvadorean lawyer and politician; b. 5 Aug. 1953, San Miguel; m. Alexandra Rodríguez; two s.; ed José Matías Delgado Univ., San Salvador, American Univ., Washington, DC, USA; Pnr, Guandique-Segovia-Quintanilla, San Salvador (law firm) 1981–; Prof. of Commercial Law, José Matías Delgado Univ. 1985–, Dean, School of Law 1986–92, Deputy Dean of Univ. 1992–; Legal Counsel to Alianza Republicana Nacionalista (ARENA) party 1988–97, mem. Exec. Body 1997–; Vice-Pres. of El Salvador 1999–2004; Vice-Pres. Canadian Chamber of Commerce of El Salvador; mem. Bd of Dirs Fundación Salvadoreña para el Desarrollo Económico y Social (think tank) 2005–. *Address:* Guandique-Segovia-Quintanilla, Pasaje Senda Florida Norte #124, Colonia Escalón, San Salvador, El Salvador (office). *Telephone:* 2245-3444 (office). *Fax:* 2298-6613 (office). *E-mail:* cquintanilla@gsqlaw.com (office). *Website:* www.gsqlaw.com (office).

QUINTON, Sir John Grand, Kt, MA, FCIB; British fmr banker; b. 21 Dec. 1929, Norwich, Norfolk, England; s. of William Grand Quinton and Norah May Quinton (née Nunn); m. Jean Margaret Chastney 1954; one s. one d.; ed Norwich School, St John's Coll. Cambridge; Asst Gen. Man. Barclays Bank Ltd 1968, Local Dir Nottingham Dist Barclays Bank Ltd 1969–71, Regional Gen. Man. 1971–75, Gen. Man. Barclays Bank Ltd and Dir Barclays Bank UK Ltd 1975–84, Dir Barclays Bank PLC and Sr Gen. Man. 1982–84, Deputy Chair. Barclays Bank PLC 1985–87, Chair. 1987–92; Chair. (non-exec.) Wimpey 1993–95; Chair. Motability Finance Ltd 1978–84, Gov. Motability 1985– (Hon. Treas. 1998–2003); Chair. Cttee of CEOs, Cttee of London Clearing Bankers 1982–83; Chair. Office of the Banking Ombudsman 1987–92, Cttee of London and Scottish Bankers 1989–91; Dir (non-exec.) Norwich and Peterborough Bldg Soc. 1993–99 (Deputy Chair. 1996–99); Treas. Inst. of Bankers 1980–86; mem. City Capital Markets Cttee 1981–86; mem. NE Thames Regional Health Authority 1974–87; mem. Accounting Standards Cttee 1982–85; Gov. Royal Shakespeare Theatre 1986–2000; Pres. Chartered Inst. of Bankers 1989–90; Chair. Botanic Gardens Conservation Int. 1988–99; Chair. Football Assocn Premier League 1992–99, Metropolitan Police Cttee 1995–2000; mem. Metropolitan Police Authority 2000–04; Trustee, RA 1987–93, Thrombosis Research Inst. 1993–2001. *Leisure interests:* gardening, music, golf. *Address:* Chenies Place, Chenies, Bucks., WD3 6EU, England (home). *Telephone:* (1923) 284002 (home). *Fax:* (1923) 285579 (home).

QUIRK, James Patrick, AO, PhD, DSc, FAA; Australian agricultural scientist and academic; *Professor Emeritus, Faculty of Natural and Agricultural Sciences, University of Western Australia;* b. 17 Dec. 1924, Sydney; s. of J. P. Quirk; m. Helen M. Sykes 1950; one s. one d.; ed Christian Brothers High School, Lewisham, St John's Coll., Univ. of Sydney and Univ. of London; Research Scientist, CSIRO Div. of Soils, Soil Physics Section 1947; CSIRO Sr Postgraduate Studentship, Physics Dept, Rothamsted Experimental Station, England 1950; Research Scientist, Sr Research Scientist, CSIRO 1952–56; Reader in Soil Science, Dept of Agricultural Chem., Waite Agricultural Research Inst., Univ. of Adelaide 1956–62; Carnegie Travelling Fellow, USA 1960; Foundation Prof. and Head, Dept of Soil Science and Plant Nutrition, Univ. of WA 1963–74, Emer. Prof. 1974–, Dir Inst. of Agric. 1971–74, Dir, Waite Agricultural Research Inst. and Prof. 1974–89, Emer. Prof. and Hon. Research Fellow, Univ. of WA 1990–; Prof. Fellow, Dept Applied Math., ANU 1990–96, Hon. Prof. Fellow 1996–; Commonwealth Visiting Prof., Oxford Univ. 1967; Fellow, Australian Acad. of Science (Sec. Biological Sciences 1990–94), Australian Inst. of Agricultural Science, Australian Acad. of Technological Sciences and Eng (mem. Council 1996–), American Soc. of Agronomy, Australian and NZ Assocn for the Advancement of Science; Hon. mem. Int. Union of Soil Science 1998; Hon. DSc Agric. (Louvain, Belgium) 1978, (Melbourne) 1990, (Western Australia) 1991, (Sydney) 1997; Prescott Medal for Soil Science 1975, Medal of the Australian Inst. of Agricultural Science 1980, Farrer Memorial Medal 1982, Mueller Medal 1988, Brindley Lecturer (USA) 1992, Distinguished Service Award (Soil Science Soc. of America) 1996. *Publications:* about 200 scientific publs. *Leisure interests:* reading, tennis. *Address:* School of Earth and Geographical Sciences (South), University of Western Australia, 35 Stirling Highway-M087, Crawley 6009, Western Australia (office); 70 Archdeacon Street, Nedlands 6009, Western Australia (home). *Telephone:* (8) 6488-2503 (office); (8) 9386-5948 (home). *Fax:* (8) 9380-2504. *E-mail:* jquirk@agric.uwa.edu.au (office). *Website:* www.are.uwa.edu.au (office).

QUIRK, Baron (Life Peer), cr. 1994, of Bloomsbury in the London Borough of Camden; **(Charles) Randolph Quirk,** Kt, CBE, PhD, DLitt, LLD, FBA; British academic; b. 12 July 1920, Isle of Man; s. of the late Thomas Quirk and Amy Randolph Quirk; m. 1st Jean Williams 1946; two s.; m. 2nd Gabriele Stein 1984; ed Cronk y Voddy School, Douglas High School, Isle of Man, Univ. Coll., London; served in RAF 1940–45; Lecturer in English, Univ. Coll. London 1947–54; Commonwealth Fund Fellow, Yale Univ. and Univ. of Mich., USA 1951–52; Reader in English Language and Literature, Durham Univ. 1954–58, Prof. of English Language 1958–60; Quain Prof. of English, Univ. Coll. London 1960–81; Dir, Univ. of London Summer School of English 1962–67; Survey of English Usage 1959–83; mem. Senate, Univ. of London 1970–85 (Chair. Academic Council 1972–75), Court 1972–85; Vice-Chancellor, Univ. of London 1981–85; Pres., Inst. of Linguists 1983–86, British Acad. 1985–89, Coll. of Speech Therapists 1987–91; Gov., British

Inst. of Recorded Sound, English-Speaking Union; Chair., Cttee of Enquiry into Speech Therapy Services, British Council English Cttee 1976–80, Hornby Educational Trust 1979–93; mem. BBC Archives Cttee 1975–79, British Council 1983–91; Trustee, Wolfson Foundation 1987–2013; Lee Kwan Yew Fellow, Singapore 1985–86; Vice-Pres., Foundation of Science and Tech. 1986–90; mem. House of Lords Select Cttee on Science and Tech. 1999–2002; Fellow, King's Coll. London, Queen Mary Coll. London, Univ. Coll. London, Imperial Coll. London, Academia Europaea; Foreign Fellow, Royal Belgian Acad. Sciences 1975, Royal Swedish Acad. 1986, Finnish Acad. of Sciences 1992, American Acad. of Arts and Sciences 1995; Hon. Fellow, Coll. of Speech Therapists, Inst. of Linguists, Hon. Master, Gray's Inn Bench 1983; numerous hon. degrees (Lund, Uppsala, Poznań, Nijmegen, Paris, Liège, Helsinki, Prague, Reading, Leicester, Salford, London, Newcastle, Bath, Durham, Essex, Open Univ., Glasgow, Bar-Ilan, Brunel, Bucharest, Sheffield, Richmond Coll., Aston, Copenhagen, Queen Margaret); Jubilee Medal, Inst. of Linguists 1973. *Publications:* The Concessive Relation in Old English Poetry 1954, Studies in Communication (with A. J. Ayer and others) 1955, An Old English Grammar (with C. L. Wrenn) 1955, Charles Dickens and Appropriate Language 1959, The Teaching of English (with A. H. Smith) 1959, The Study of the Mother-Tongue 1961, The Use of English (with supplements by A. C. Gimson and J. Warburg) 1962, Prosodic and Paralinguistic Features in English (with D. Crystal) 1964, A Common Language (with A. H. Marckwardt) 1964, Investigating Linguistic Acceptability (with J. Svartvik) 1966, Essays on the English Language–Medieval and Modern 1968, Elicitation Experiments in English (with S. Greenbaum) 1970, A Grammar of Contemporary English 1972 (with S. Greenbaum, G. Leech, J. Svartvik) 1972, The English Language and Images of Matter 1972, A University Grammar of English (with S. Greenbaum) 1973, The Linguist and the English Language 1974, Old English Literature: A Practical Introduction (with V. Adams, D. Davy) 1975, A Corpus of English Conversation 1980; contrib. to many others including Charles Dickens (ed. S. Wall) 1970, A New Companion to Shakespeare Studies 1971, The State of the Language (with J. Svartvik) 1980, Style and Communication in the English Language 1982, A Comprehensive Grammar of the English Language (with S. Greenbaum, G. Leech and J. Svartvik) 1985, Words at Work: Lectures on Textual Structure 1986, English in Use (with Gabriele Stein) 1990, A Student's Grammar of the English Language (with S. Greenbaum) 1990, Grammatical and Lexical Variance in English 1995, Cronk y Voddy (with V. Cottle) 2010; papers in linguistic and literary journals. *Leisure interest:* music. *Address:* University College London, Gower Street, London, WC1E 6BT, England (office). *Telephone:* (20) 7219-2226 (office). *Fax:* (20) 7219-5979 (office).

QUIROGA RAMÍREZ, Jorge Fernando, BEng, MBA; Bolivian engineer and politician; *Leader, Acción Democrática Nacionalista (ADN);* b. 5 May 1960, Cochabamba; m. Virginia Gillum 1989; four c.; ed La Salle Coll., Santa Cruz de la Sierra, Texas A&M Univ. and St Edward's Univ., Austin, Tex.; with IBM, Austin, Tex. 1981–88; returned to Bolivia 1988; Econometrician, Mintec 1988; Vice-Pres. Banco Mercantil de Bolivia 1988; mem. Acción Democrática Nacionalista (ADN) 1988–, apptd Deputy Leader 1995, currently Leader; Under-Sec. for Public Investment and Int. Co-operation, Ministry of Planning 1989–90; Minister of Finance 1990–93; Gov. Cooperación Financiera de Inversiones –1993; Dir Andean Devt Corpn –1993; Nat. Sec. Política Social –1993; led electoral campaign of ADN 1993 then worked in pvt. sector; Vice-Pres. of Bolivia 1997–2001, Acting Pres. July–Aug. 2001, Pres. of Bolivia 2001–02; fmr Gov. IBRD and IMF. *Leisure interests:* football, basketball, mountain-climbing. *Address:* Acción Democrática Nacionalista (ADN), La Paz, Bolivia (office). *Website:* www.bolivian.com/adn.

QUJAUKITSOQ, Vittus; Greenlandic politician; *Minister for Finance and Domestic Affairs;* b. 5 Oct. 1971, Qaanaaq; m. Naja Kreutzmann Qujaukitsoq; one d.; ed Nuuk Trade and Business School; Head of Secr. of Trade and Industrial Council, Sisimiut 1997; Private Asst to Minister of Social Affairs, Labour and Public Works 1997–99, to Minister of Fisheries, Hunting, Agric. and Industry 2000–01; Corp. Sec., Royal Greenland A/S (fishing co.) 2001–05; Corp. Sec. and Communications Officer, Nukissiorfiit (state-owned energy co.) 2005; Communication Dir KNI A/S (trading group) 2005–06; Private Asst to MP Lars-Emil Johansen 2007–10, to Minister of Culture, Educ., Church and Research 2008, to Minister of Housing, Transportation and Infrastructure 2009; Mineral Resources Adviser, SIK (trade union) 2010–13; mem. Inatsisartut (parl.) 2013–; Minister for Finance and Domestic Affairs 2013–; mem. Siumut party, Organizational Sec. 1994–95, Organizational Vice-Chair. 2011–. *Address:* Grønlands Selvstyre (Naalakkersuisut), Imaneq 4, POB 1015, 3900 Nuuk, Greenland (office). *Telephone:* 345000 (office). *Fax:* 325002 (office). *E-mail:* info@gh.gl (office). *Website:* www.nanoq.gl (office).

QURAISHI, Abdul Aziz Bin Said Al, MBA, FIBA; Saudi Arabian government official and business executive; *CEO, Ali Zaid Al-Quraishi & Brothers Company Limited;* b. 1930, Hail; s. of Zaid al-Quraishi and Sheikhah Abdul Aziz; m. Amal Abdul Aziz al-Turki 1965; one s. two d.; ed Univ. of Southern California, USA; Gen. Man. State Railways 1961–68; Pres. Gen. Personnel Bureau 1968–74; Minister of State 1971–74; Gov. Saudi Arabian Monetary Agency 1974–83; fmr Gov. for Saudi Arabia, IMF, Arab Monetary Fund; fmr Alt. Gov. for Saudi Arabia, Islamic Devt Bank; fmr mem. Bd of Dirs Supreme Council for Petroleum and Mineral Affairs, Gen. Petroleum and Mineral Org., Public Investment Fund, Pension Fund; CEO Ali Zaid Al-Quraishi & Brothers Co. Ltd, Riyadh 1983–; Co-Chair. US-Saudi Arabian Business Council 1993–; fmr Chair. Nat. Saudi Shipping Co., Riyadh 1983; Vice-Chair. Saudi Int. Bank, London 1983–; mem. Int. Advisory Bd, Security Pacific Nat. Bank of LA 1983–; King Abdul Aziz Medal (Second Class), Order of Brilliant Star with Grand Cordon (Taiwan), Order of Diplomatic Merit, Gwan

Ghwa Medal (Repub. of Korea), King Leopold Medal, Commdr Class (Belgium), Emperor of Japan Award, Order of Sacred Treasure (First Class) 1980. *Address:* Ali Zaid Al-Quraishi & Brothers Co. Ltd, PO Box 339, Dammam 31411 (office); PO Box 1848, Riyadh 11441, Saudi Arabia (home). *Telephone:* (3) 833-3339 (office). *Fax:* (3) 834-3402 (office). *E-mail:* info@alquraishi.com (office). *Website:* www.alquraishi.com (office).

QURAISHI, Shahabuddin Yaqoob, PhD; Indian fmr government official; b. 11 July 1947; ed St Stephen's Coll., Delhi; joined Indian Admin. Services 1971, has held numerous positions including Special Sec. (Health), Sec., Sports and Youth Affairs –2006; Chief Election Commr 2010–12; served as consultant to UNICEF, Dir-Gen. Nat. AIDS Control Org., Doordarshan, Nehru Yuva Kendra Sangathan; Founder-Dir Rajiv Gandhi Nat. Inst. of Youth Devt, Sriperumbudur, Dir 1993–97; fmr Dir Women and Child Devt; nominated as Specialist and Resource Person for Int. Conf. on Islam and Family Planning, Ankara 1995. *Publication:* Social Marketing for Social Change. *Address:* c/o Election Commission of India, Ashoka Road, New Delhi 110 001, India.

QURAY, Ahmad, (Abu Ala); Palestinian diplomatist and politician; b. 1937, Abu Dis; joined Fatah 1968, currently mem. Revolutionary Council Cen. Cttee; fmr Minister of Economy and Trade and Minister of Industry, Palestinian Authority; Chief Palestinian Negotiator, Oslo Agreement 1993 and all subsequent Israeli–Palestinian talks including Taba, Cairo, Wye River, and talks in 2007; Deputy and Speaker Palestinian Legis. Council 1996–2003; Prime Minister, Palestinian Authority (PA) 2003–05 (resgnd), Head Nat. Security Council 2004–05; mem. Palestinian Nat. Council; mem. Bd Palestinian Econ. Policy Research Inst., Peres Center for Peace; mem. Bd of Advisers Gleitsman Foundation; Norwegian Royal Order of Merit 1994, Seeds of Peace Foundation Award 1996, Gleitsman Foundation Int. Activist Award 1999. *Publications include:* Hanging Peace; numerous economic essays. *Address:* c/o Palestinian Authority, Jericho Area, West Bank, Palestinian Autonomous Areas. *E-mail:* info@gov.ps. *Website:* www.pna.net.

QURBONOV, Abdusalom; Tajikistani politician; *Minister of Finance;* Head, Construction Dept of Presidential Admin –2013; Minister of Finance 2013–. *Address:* Ministry of Finance, 734025 Dushanbe, Xiyoboni Rajabov 3, Tajikistan (office). *Telephone:* (372) 21-14-17 (office). *Fax:* (372) 21-33-29 (office). *E-mail:* min_fin@tojikiston.com (office). *Website:* www.minfin.tj (office).

QURESHI, Ashraf; Pakistani diplomatist and public servant; ed Fletcher School of Law and Diplomacy, Tufts Univ., USA, Quaid-e-Azam Univ.; joined Foreign Service 1977, served in numerous positions including Section Officer 1978–80, Dir 1985–87, 1995–97, Dir-Gen. 1997–98, 2003–04, Additional Sec., Prime Minister's Secr. 2004–05; diplomatic assignments include postings in Tunis 1980–85, New York 1988–93, Kuala Lumpur 1993–95, Brussels 1998–2001, High Commr to Sri Lanka 2001–03, to South Africa 2006–10, to Bangladesh 2010–11, Amb., Ministry of Foreign Affairs 2011–12 (retd); mem. Punjab Public Service Comm., Govt of Punjab 2012–. *Address:* Punjab Public Service Commission, 2 Agha Khan (Davis Road), Lahore, Pakistan (office). *Telephone:* (42) 99202762 (office). *Fax:* (42) 99202766 (office). *E-mail:* ppsc@punjab.gov.pk (office). *Website:* www.ppsc.gop.pk (office).

QURESHI, Moeen Ahmad, MA, PhD; American (b. Pakistani) economist, international organization official and business executive; *Chairman and Managing Partner, EMP Global LLC;* b. 26 June 1930, Lahore, Pakistan; s. of Mohyeddin Ahmad Qureshi and Khursheed Jabin; m. Lilo Elizabeth Kreter 1958; two s. two d.; ed Islamia Coll. and Govt Coll., Univ. of Punjab and Indiana Univ., USA; social science consultant, Ford Foundation, Pakistan 1953; Hon. Lecturer, Univ. of Karachi 1953–54; Asst Chief, Planning Comm., Govt of Pakistan 1954–56, Deputy Chief 1956–58; Economist, IMF 1958–61, Div. Chief 1961–65, Adviser Africa Dept 1965–66, Resident Rep. Ghana 1966–68, Sr Adviser 1968–70; Econ. Adviser IFC 1970–74, Vice-Pres. 1974–77, Exec. Vice-Pres. 1977–81; Vice-Pres. Finance, World Bank 1979–80, Sr Vice-Pres. Finance 1980–87, Sr Vice-Pres. Operations 1987–91; Prime Minister of Pakistan July–Oct. 1993; currently Chair. and Man. Pnr EMP Global LLC, Washington DC; mem. Bd Global Trade and Political Risk Insurance Co., American Int. Group; mem. Advisory Bd, American International Group (AIG); mem. Bd Educ. for Employment Foundation; Trustee, Bibliotheca Alexandria, Egypt; Hon. Co-Chair. American Pakistan Foundation; Hilal-i-Imtiaz 1992. *Publications:* various articles in econ. journals. *Leisure interests:* tennis, collecting antiques. *Address:* EMP Global LLC, 1901 Pennsylvania Avenue, NW, Suite 300, Washington, DC 20006, USA (office). *Telephone:* (202) 331-9051 (office). *Fax:* (202) 331-9250 (office). *E-mail:* qureshim@empglobal.com (office). *Website:* www.empglobal.com (office).

QURESHI, Makhdoom Shah Mehmu, BA, MA; Pakistani politician; b. 22 June 1966, Murree; m.; one s. two d.; ed Aitchison Coll., Lahore, Forman Christian Coll., Lahore, Corpus Christi Coll., Cambridge, UK; grew up in Multan; returned to Pakistan following law studies in UK 1983; mem. Punjab Ass. 1985–93; Chair. Dist Council, Multan 1987–91; contested and won local, prov. and nat. elections from his home constituency in Multan; served as Minister for Planning and Devt Punjab; Minister of Finance, Punjab 1990–93; Fed. Minister for Parl. Affairs 1994–96; Dist Nazim, Multan 2001–02; represented Pakistan People's Party (PPP) Punjab as their prime ministerial cand. 2002; sr mem. PPP and Pres. PPP Punjab; Minister of Foreign Affairs 2008–11; Chair. Farmers Asscn Pakistan 1991; Co-Chair. S.O.S. Children's Village, Multan 1997; mem. Bd of Govs Aitchison Coll.; Life Patron Al-Shifa Trust. *Leisure interests:* reading, watching television. *Address:* c/o Ministry of Foreign Affairs, Constitution Avenue, Islamabad, Pakistan.

R

RA, Jong-yil, BA, MA, PhD; South Korean academic, university administrator and fmr diplomatist; *President, Woosuk University;* b. 5 Dec. 1940, Seoul; m. Hong Jae-ja; one s. three d.; ed Seoul Nat. Univ., Trinity Coll., Univ. of Cambridge, UK; held teaching posts at several univs including Kyunghee, Southern California, Mich. and Stanford, USA, Cambridge and Sussex, UK; Dir Nat. Intelligence Service 1998–99; fmr mem. Exec. Cttee and fmr Dir-Gen., Millennium Democratic Party (MDP); fmr Special Asst to Pres. for Foreign and Security Affairs; Amb. to UK 2001–03; Sr Adviser to Pres. for Nat. Security 2003; Amb. to Japan 2004–07; Pres. Woosuk Univ. 2007–. *Publications include:* Politics of Western Europe 1982, Cooperation and Conflict 1986, The New Right 1990, Perestroika and its Impacts 1991, Points of Departure 1992, Unfinished War 1994, Man and Politics 1995, In Preparation for the New Millennium 1999, Advantage of Hindsight 2001, Conflict and Resolution in the Korean Church 2002. *Leisure interest:* playing tennis. *Address:* Office of the President, Woosuk University, 490 Hujeong-ri, Samrye-eup, Wanju-kun, Jeollabuk-do, 565-701, Republic of Korea (office). *Telephone:* (63) 290-1003 (office). *Fax:* (63) 290-1004 (office). *Website:* www.woosuk.ac.kr (office).

RAAD, Walid, BFA, MA, PhD; Lebanese artist and academic; *Associate Professor of Art, Cooper Union School of Art;* b. (Walid Ra'ad), 1967, Chbanieh; ed Boston Univ., Mass, Rochester Inst. of Tech. and Univ. of Rochester, NY, USA; works include mixed media, installations, performance, video and photography, and literary essays; f. The Atlas Group (imaginary foundation whose objective is to research and document Lebanon's contemporary history, especially the Lebanese wars 1975–91) 1999, with work presented through films, photography exhbns, videos and documents; has co-curated, with Akram Zaatari, the exhbn Mapping Sitting: On Portraiture and Photography, an investigation in Arab photography and its relationship to questions of identity; Instructor, Dept of Art and Art History, Univ. of Rochester 1991–95, Instructor, Dept of Film Studies 1994–95; Asst Prof., School of Humanities, Cultural Studies and Arts, Hampshire Coll. 1995–98; Asst Prof., Dept of Media Studies, Queen's Coll., CUNY 1998–2002; Asst Prof. of Art, Cooper Union School of Art, New York 2002–05, Assoc. Prof. of Art 2005–; Fellow, Vera List Center for Art and Politics, New School 2004–05; mem. Arab Image Foundation; Best Conceptual Innovation Award, New England Film and Video Festival, Boston 1997, Award of Accomplishment Experimental, Missouri Video Festival, St Louis, Mo. 1998, Director's Citation, Black Maria Film and Video Festival, NJ 1999, Best Short Film and Best Scenario for a Short Film, Beirut Film Festival 1999, Grand Prize, 8th Biennial of the Moving Image, Switzerland 1999, First Prize, VideoEx, Zurich 2000, 2001, Special Jury Prize, 5th Biennial of Arab Cinemas, Institut du Monde Arabe, Paris 2000, Certificate of Merit, San Francisco Int. Film Festival 2000, Rhineland Award, Oberhausen Film and VideoFest, Oberhausen, Germany 2001, Juror Citation Award, Black Maria Festival 2002, Special Prize, Media Arts Awards, ZKM, Karlsruhe, Germany 2002, First Prize, Oneiras Film and Video Festival, Lisbon 2002, First Prize, Vidarte Festival, Mexico City 2002, First Prize, Onion City Experimental Film and Video Festival 2002, Rockefeller Fellowship, NYSCA 2003, Rockefeller Fellowship 2003, Camera Austria Award 2005, Lauréat d'Aide au projet, Rencontres d'Arles, Arles, France 2006, First Prize, Deutsche Börse Photography Prize, London 2007, Alpert Award for Visual Arts, Herb Alpert Foundation 2007, Hasselblad-Prize 2011. *Video works include:* Talaeen a Junuub (Up to the South) 1993, I Think It Would Be Better If I Could Weep, a collection of video shorts titled The Dead Weight of a Quarrel Hangs 1996–99, Hostage: The Bachar Tapes 2000; mixed-media projects include The Atlas Group: Documents from The Atlas Group Archive (1999–), The Loudest Muttering Is Over: Documents from The Atlas Group Archive (2001–), My Neck Is Thinner Than A Hair 2004. *Publications:* The Truth Will be Known When the Last Witness is Dead, My Neck is Thinner than a Hair, Scratching on Things I Could Disavow, Let's Be Honest, The Weather Helped. *Address:* The Cooper Union School of Art, Room 236, 7 East 7th Street, New York, NY 10003, USA (office). *Telephone:* (212) 353-4214 (office); (917) 345-0065 (office). *E-mail:* wraad@earthlink.net (office); info@walidraad.com (office). *Website:* www.walidraad.com (office); www.theatlasgroup.org (office).

RÄÄTS, Jaan; Estonian composer and teacher; *Professor Emeritus of Composition, Estonian Academy of Music;* b. 15 Oct. 1932, Tartu; s. of Peeter Rääts and Linda Rääts; m. 1st Marianne Rääts 1958; m. 2nd Ebba Rääts 1983; three c.; ed Tartu Music School with Aleksandra Sarv, Tallinn Conservatory with Mart Saar, Heino Eller; mem. CPSU 1964–90; recording engineer, Estonian Radio 1955–66, Chief Dir Music Programmes, Estonian TV 1966–74; Teacher of composition, Tallinn Conservatory (later Estonian Acad. of Music) 1968–70, 1974–, Prof. 1990–2003, Prof. Emer. 2003–; initiated Estonian Music Days 1979; Vice-Chair. Estonian Composers' Union 1964–74, Chair. 1974–93; Order of the White Star (3rd Class) 2002; People's Artist of the Estonian SSR 1977. *Compositions include:* Symphony No. 1 1957, Symphony No. 2 1958, Symphony No. 3 1959, Symphony No. 4 Cosmic 1959, Concerto for chamber orchestra No. 1 1961, Violin Concerto No. 1 1963, Symphony No. 5 1966, Symphony No. 6 1967, Piano Concerto No. 1 1968, 24 Preludes 1968, Toccata 1970, Symphony No. 7 1973, 24 Estonian Preludes 1977, Violin Concerto No. 2 1979, 24 Marginalia 1979, 24 Marginalia for two pianos 1982, Piano Concerto No. 2 1983, Symphony No. 8 1985, Concerto for two pianos and symphony orchestra 1986, Concerto for chamber orchestra No. 2 1987, Piano Concerto No. 3 1990, Concerto for guitar and orchestra 1992, Concerto for trumpet and piano 1994, Concerto for violin and chamber orchestra 1995, Violin Concerto No. 3 1995, Five Sketches for Requiem for symphony orchestra 1999, Concerto for flute, guitar and symphony orchestra 2001, Symphony No. 9, Symphony No. 10, 10 piano sonatas, seven piano trios –2004, six string quartets. *Film scores:* Roosa kübar 1963, Null kolm 1965, Tütarlaps mustas 1966, Supernova 1966, Viini postmark 1967, Gladiaator 1969, Tuulevaikus 1971, Väike reekviem suupillile 1972, Ohtlikud mängud 1974, Aeg elada, aeg armastada 1976, Pihlakaväravad 1982. *Leisure interests:* technology, science. *Address:* c/o Estonian Composers' Union, A. Lauteri Street 7c, 10145 Tallinn, Estonia. *Telephone:* 646-6536 (office); 645-4395 (office); 520-3339 (home); 648-5744 (home). *E-mail:* heliloojate.liit@gmail .com (office); emie@emie.ee; ebba@hot.ee. *Website:* www.zzz.ee/edition49 (office).

RABAN, Jonathan Mark Hamilton Priaulx, BA, FRSL; British author and critic; b. 14 June 1942, Fakenham, Norfolk; s. of Rev. Peter J. C. P. Raban and

Monica Sandison; m. 1st Bridget Johnson (divorced 1970s); m. 2nd Caroline Cuthbert 1985 (divorced 1992); m. 3rd Jean Cara Lenihan 1992 (divorced 1997); one d.; ed King's School, Worcester, Peter Symonds School, Winchester, Brockenhurst Grammar, Univ. of Hull; Asst Lecturer, Univ. Coll. of Wales, Aberystwyth 1965–67; Lecturer in English and American Literature, Univ. of East Anglia 1967–69; professional writer 1969–; emigrated to USA 1990; Hon. DLitt (Univ. of Hull); Thomas Cook Award, Pacific Northwest Booksellers Asscn Award, Murray Morgan Prize, Gov.'s Award of the State of Washington, Nat. Book Critics' Circle Award, Heinemann Award, Royal Soc. of Literature, PEN/West Award for Creative Nonfiction. *Publications include:* The Technique of Modern Fiction 1969, Mark Twain: Huckleberry Finn 1969, The Society of the Poem 1971, Soft City 1973, Robert Lowell's Poems (ed.) 1974, Arabia Through the Looking Glass 1979, Old Glory (RSL Heinemann Award and Thomas Cook Award 1982) 1981, Foreign Land (novel) 1985, Coasting 1986, For Love and Money 1987, God, Man & Mrs Thatcher 1989, Hunting Mister Heartbreak (Thomas Cook Award 1991) 1990, The Oxford Book of the Sea (ed.) 1992, Bad Land: An American Romance (Nat. Book Critics Circle Award and PEN/West Creative Nonfiction Award 1997) 1996, Passage to Juneau 1999, Waxwings (novel) 2003, My Holy War: Dispatches from the Home Front 2005, Surveillance (novel) 2006, Driving Home: An American Journey 2011; contribs to Harper's, Esquire, New Republic, Atlantic Monthly, New York Review of Books, London Review of Books, Outside, Granta, New York Times Book Review, Vogue, The Guardian, Independent, Financial Times, Wall Street Journal. *Leisure interest:* sailing. *Address:* c/o Aitken Alexander Associates Ltd, 18–21 Cavaye Place, London, SW10 9PT, England (office). *Telephone:* (20) 7373-8672 (office). *Fax:* (20) 7373-6002 (office). *E-mail:* reception@aitkenalexander.co .uk (office). *Website:* www.jonathanraban.com (office).

RABASSA, Gregory, PhD; American academic and translator; *Distinguished Professor Emeritus of Romance Languages and Comparative Literature, Queens College, City University of New York;* b. 9 March 1922, Yonkers, NY; s. of Miguel Rabassa and Clara Macfarland; m. 1st Roney Edelstein 1957 (divorced 1966); one d.; m. 2nd Clementine Christos 1966; one d.; ed Dartmouth Coll. and Columbia Univ.; mil. service 1942–45; Instructor in Spanish, Columbia Univ. 1947–52, Assoc. Instructor 1952–58, Asst Prof. 1958–63, Assoc. Prof. of Spanish and Portuguese 1963–68; Prof. of Romance Languages, Queens Coll., Flushing, NY 1968–86, Distinguished Prof. 1986–2008, Emer. 2008–; Assoc. Ed. Odyssey Review 1961–64; mem. Renaissance Soc. of America, PEN Club and other professional asscns; Fulbright-Hays Fellow, Brazil 1965–66; Guggenheim Fellow 1988–89; Croce al Merito di Guerra (Italy), Order of San Carlos (Colombia), Gabriela Mistral Medal (Chile) 1996, Ordem do Rio Branco (Brazil) 2008, Order of Prince Henry the Navigator (Portugal) 2011; Dr hc (Dartmouth Coll.) 1982, (Hartford) 2005; Hon. DLitt (Univ. of Mass, Dartmouth) 2008; Nat. Book Award for trans. 1967, New York Gov.'s Arts Award 1985, Wheatland Translation Prize 1988, Literature Award, American Acad. and Inst. of Arts and Letters 1989, Sandrof Award (Nat. Book Critics Circle) 1993, New York Public Library Literary Lion Award 1993, Gregory Kolovakos Award, PEN 2001, John Steinbeck Award, Southhampton Coll. 2002, Nat. Medal of Arts 2006, PEN/Martha Albrand Memoir Award 2006, Thornton Wilder Translation Award, American Acad. of Arts and Letters 2009, Brazilian Acad. of Letters 2010. *Publications:* O Negro na Ficção Brasileira 1965; A Cloudy Day in Gray Minor (poetry) 1995, If This Be Treason: Translation and its Dyscontents 2005. *Leisure interests:* hiking, birding, jazz. *Address:* 140 East 72nd Street, New York, NY 10021, USA (home). *Telephone:* (212) 439-6636 (home).

RABBANI, Salahuddin, BA, MBA, MIA; Afghan politician and diplomatist; *Chairman, High Peace Council;* b. 1971, Kabul; s. of Burhanuddin Rabbani; m.; four c.; ed King Fahd Univ. of Petroleum and Minerals, Saudi Arabia, Kingston Univ., UK, Columbia Univ., USA; started career in Financial Accounting Dept, Aramco, Saudi Arabia; apptd interpreter and adviser, Presidential Palace 1998; joined Ministry of Foreign Affairs 2002, Political Consular, Perm. Mission to UN, New York 2003–06; Deputy Head for Political Affairs, Jamiat-i-Islami Party 2008, Acting Leader 2011–, also Man. Noor TV (party's TV channel); apptd Amb. to Turkey 2010; Chair. High Peace Council 2012–. *Address:* Jamiat-i Islami Party, Karte Parwan, Phase 2, Badaam Bagh, Kabul, Afghanistan (office). *Website:* www .hpc.org.af/english (office).

RABE, Thomas, BA, MBA, Dr rer. pol; Luxembourg business executive; *Chairman and CEO, Bertelsmann SE & Co. KGaA;* b. 6 Aug. 1965; ed École Européenne, Brussels, Belgium, Rheinisch-Westfaelische Technische Hochschule Aachen and Univ. of Cologne, Germany; with Directorate-Gen. for Financial Insts and Corp. Law, EC, Brussels 1989–90; Assoc., Forrester Norall & Sutton law firm (now White & Case), Brussels 1990–91; joined Treuhandanstalt, Berlin 1991, Dir Controlling 1993; Head of Acquisitions, Beteiligungsgesellschaft New Länder, Berlin 1993–98; Chief Financial Officer (CFO) Clearstream International 1996–98, mem. Bd of Dirs 1998–2000; CFO RTL Group, Luxembourg 2000–06, Head of Corp. Centre 2003–06; CFO and Head of Corp. Centre, Bertelsmann AG, Gütersloh 2006–12, Head of Bertelsmann Music Group 2006–08, Chair. and CEO Bertelsmann SE & Co. KGaA 2012–. *Address:* Bertelsmann SE & Co. KGaA, Carl-Bertelsmann-Str. 270, 33311 Gütersloh, Germany (office). *Telephone:* (5241) 80-0 (office). *Fax:* (5241) 80-62321 (office). *E-mail:* info@bertelsmann.com (office). *Website:* www.bertelsmann.com (office).

RABEA, Abdullah ibn Abd al-Aziz al-, MD, FRCS; Saudi Arabian surgeon and politician; *Minister of Health;* m. Huda al-Ghunaim; eight c.; ed King Saud Univ., Riyadh, Univ. of Alberta, Canada, Dalhousie Univ. Faculty of Medicine; began training in surgery in Riyadh, moved to Edmonton, Canada 1981 for residency in gen. surgery, then paediatric surgery in Edmonton and at Dalhousie 1987; started as Asst Lecturer, King Saud Univ.; spent 14 years with Nat. Guard Health Affairs (medical complex) becoming Exec. Dir, later CEO and also Pres. King Saud Univ. for Medical Sciences; Minister of Health 2009–; mem. several nat. cttees; Dir King Faisal Specialist Hosp. and Research Center, King Saud bin Abdulaziz Univ., also Pres. Faculty of Nursing and Allied Health Sciences; King Abdul Aziz Medal of the First Order. *Achievements include:* as head of surgical team at Abdulaziz Medical City, Riyadh, became world renowned for surgery separating conjoined twins.

Address: Ministry of Health, Airport Rd, Riyadh 11176, Saudi Arabia (office). **Telephone:** (1) 401-2220 (office). **Fax:** (1) 402-9876 (office). **Website:** www.moh.gov.sa (office).

RABEE, Hayder K. Gafar, BA; Iraqi teacher of calligraphy; *Head, Calligraphy Department, Institute of Fine Arts;* b. 22 Feb. 1962, Najaf; m. Ahalam A. al-Zahawi 1986; two s. one d.; ed Coll. of Fine Arts; calligrapher, Baghdad TV 1982–88; worked as designer, newspapers and magazines 1989–91; teacher, Inst. of Fine Arts, Baghdad 1992–, Head, Calligraphy Dept (evening classes) 1995–; teacher of Arabic Calligraphy, Jordanian Calligraphers' Soc. 1998; Gen. Sec. Iraqi Calligraphers' Soc. 1998–99; mem. Iraqi Plastic Arts Soc. 1996–2002, Iraqi Union of Artists, Iraqi Soc. for Calligraphy Jordanian Calligraphers' Soc., Egyptian Calligraphers' Soc.; State Trophy for Plastic Arts and Calligraphy 1989, 1999, Gold Medal, 2nd World Festival 1992, Third World Festival 1993, Gold Medal for Creativity, Dar Es-Salaam 1st Nat. Festival 1993, Appreciation Prize, 4th Baghdad Nat. Festival 1998, Appreciation Prize in 5th Int. Competition for Calligraphy, Turkey 2001, a main prizewinner, Int. Meeting for Calligraphy of the Islam World, Tehran 2002, Certificate in first contest of the miniatures and decoration, Algeria 2008, Certificate in Festival of the Holy Quran, Dubai 2009/2011, Certificate, Second Int. Festival of Culture and Arts, Greece 2010, Certificate in Calligraphy, Sharjah Biennial 2012. *Publication:* Proposed Alphabetic Study for Arabic Calligraphy in Printing 1989. *Leisure interest:* chess. *Address:* al-Waziria, Sector 301, Street 13 Ho. 50, Baghdad (home); Department of Calligraphy, Institute of Fine Arts, al-Mansur, Baghdad, Iraq (office).

RABEE, Mohammed al-; Yemeni economist and international organization official; Asst Sec.-Gen. Council of Arab Econ. Unity (CAEU) 2005–10, Sec.-Gen. CAEU 2010–. *Address:* Council of Arab Economic Unity, 1113 Corniche en-Nil, 4th Floor, PO Box 1, 11518 Cairo, Egypt (office). *Telephone:* (2) 25755045 (office). *Fax:* (2) 25754090 (office). *E-mail:* caeu@idsc.net.eg (office). *Website:* www.caeu.org.eg (office).

RABEMANANJARA, Gen. Charles; Malagasy politician; b. June 1947, Antananarivo; fmr senior police officer, later Head of Gen. Armoured Corps; Dir Presidential Security Cabinet 2004–05; Minister of the Interior and Admin. Reform 2005–09, Prime Minister 2007–09. *Address:* c/o Office of the Prime Minister, BP 248, Mahazoarivo, 101 Antananarivo, Madagascar (office).

RABIN, Oskar Yakovlevich; Russian painter; b. 1928, Moscow; m. Valentina Kropovnitskaya; one s.; student of artist and teacher Yevgeny Kropovnitsky; worked in Riga 1946–48; thereafter student of Surikov Art Inst., Moscow; later expelled for unorthodox views; worked until 1958 as loader on railways and on construction sites, painting clandestinely; employed in arts and design centre 1958–67; f. Leonozovo group in Moscow; exhibited in 'Festival of Youth' Exhbn, Moscow 1957; forced to emigrate 1977; now lives in Paris. *Publication:* Memoirs: Three Lives 1986.

RABINOVICH, Itamar, PhD; Israeli university administrator, historian, academic and fmr diplomatist; *Senior Research Fellow, Moshe Dayan Center for Middle Eastern and African Studies, Tel-Aviv University;* b. 1942, Jerusalem; ed UCLA; joined faculty Tel-Aviv Univ. 1971, Dir Moshe Dayan Center for Middle Eastern and African Studies 1980–88, now Sr Research Fellow and Ettinger Prof. of Contemporary Middle Eastern History, Dean of Humanities, Tel-Aviv Univ. 1989–90, Rector 1990–92, Pres. 1999–2007; Israel's Chief Negotiator with Syria and Amb. to USA 1992–96; A.D. White Prof. at Large, Cornell Univ. 1997–2002; fmr Visiting Prof. Univ. of Pa, Univ. of Toronto, Woodrow Wilson Int. Center for Scholars, Inst. of Advanced Studies, Princeton; mem. Trilateral Comm.; Chair. Advisory Council, Wexner Israel Program; Chair. Heseg Project; Foreign Hon. Fellow, American Acad. of Arts and Sciences 2009. *Publications:* Syria Under the Ba'th, The War for Lebanon, The Road Not Taken, Early Arab–Israeli Negotiations, The Brink of Peace: Israel and Syria, Waging Peace: Israel and the Arabs at the End of the Century; numerous articles, essays and chapters in books and journals. *Address:* Moshe Dayan Center for Middle Eastern and African Studies, Tel-Aviv University, Ramat Aviv, Tel-Aviv 69978, Israel (office). *Telephone:* (3) 6409646 (office). *Fax:* (3) 6415802 (office). *E-mail:* efratal@post.tau.ac.il (office). *Website:* www.dayan.org (office).

RABINOVITCH, B(enton) Seymour, PhD, FRS; Canadian chemist and academic; *Professor Emeritus of Chemistry, University of Washington, Seattle;* b. 19 Feb. 1919, Montreal, PQ; s. of Samuel Rabinovitch and Rachel Shachter; m. 1st Marilyn Werby 1949 (deceased); m. 2nd Flora Reitman 1980; two s. two d. from 1st m.; ed McGill Univ.; Royal Soc. of Canada Research Fellow 1946–47; Milton Research Fellow, Harvard Univ. 1947–48; Asst Prof., Univ. of Washington, Seattle 1948–53, Assoc. Prof. 1953–57, Prof., Dept of Chem. 1957–85, Prof. Emer. 1985–; Fellow, American Acad. of Arts and Sciences, American Physics Soc.; mem. Silver Soc.; Guggenheim Fellowship 1961; Hon. Liveryman, Worshipful Co. of Goldsmiths, London 2000; Hon. DSc (Technion Univ., Haifa) 1991; Peter Debye Award, Michael Polyani Medal, Sigma Xi Award for Outstanding Research. *Publications:* Textbook of Physical Chemistry 1964, Antique Silver Servers 1991, Contemporary Silver 2000, Contemporary Silver, Part II 2005; Ed. Annual Reviews of Physical Chemistry 1975–85; 220 research papers. *Leisure interest:* silversmithing, decorative silver. *Address:* Department of Chemistry, Box 351700, University of Washington, Seattle, WA 98195, USA (office).

RABINOVITCH, Robert, BComm MA, PhD; Canadian broadcasting executive; *Chairman, Board of Governors, McGill University;* b. 1943, Montréal; m.; one s. one d.; ed McGill Univ., Univ. of Pennsylvania; held various positions with Fed. Govt, including Deputy Minister of Communications 1982–85, Under-Sec. of State 1985–86, also held several positions within Privy Council Office, including Deputy Sec. to the Cabinet and Sr Asst Sec. to the Cabinet for Priorities and Planning; Exec. Vice-Pres. and COO Claridge Inc. 1987–99; Pres. and CEO CBC/Radio Canada 1999–2007, Acting Chair. March–Sept. 2005, Sept. 2006; fmr mem. Bd of Dirs Cineplex Odeon, NetStar Communications; Special Advisor, MaxLink Communications, Loews Cineplex; fmr mem. Govt of Canada Direct-to-Home Satellite Broadcasting Policy Review Panel; fmr mem. Canadian Exec. Service Org., CRB Foundation, Samuel and Saidye Bronfman Family Foundation, Canadian Film Centre; Chair. Exec. Cttee Canadian Jewish Congress (Québec) –1999; mem. Bd of Govs McGill Univ. 1997–, Chair. 1999–; mem. Advisory Bd Sauvé Scholars Foundation, McGill Univ., Nunavut Trust Investment Advisory

Cttee; Hon. LLD (York Univ.) 2003. *Address:* c/o Board of Governors, McGill University, Room 313, James Administration Building, 845 Sherbrooke Street West, Montréal, PQ H3A 2T5, Canada. *Telephone:* (514) 398-3215. *Fax:* (514) 398-4758. *E-mail:* jennifer.oneil@mcgill.ca. *Website:* www.mcgill.ca/boardofgovernors.

RABINOWITZ, Cay Sophie, MA, PhD; American curator, editor and arts executive; *Artistic Director, Art Basel;* b. 1965, Norfolk, Va; d. of Jeanne and Ralph Rabinowitz; m. Christian Rattemeyer; ed Tufts Univ., Reed Coll., Univ. of Calif., Berkeley, Emory Univ.; DAAD Fellow, Hochschule der Künste, Berlin 1995–96; curator or co-curator for numerous exhbns including Lauretta Rix's Paint and Graphic, Atlanta 1996, Splendid Isolation, Berlin 1997, Patterns of Intention, OSMOS, Berlin 1998, Thinking Loud/Cutting Through, Space 1181, Atlanta 1999, Tonal Bliss, Marietta/Cobb Museum of Art, Atlanta 2001, Scarlett Hooft-Graafland and Jeff Feld, Mary Goldman Gallery, Los Angeles 2003, Erik Schmidt, Henry Urbach Gallery, New York 2004, APEX Summer show, New York 2004; curatorial asst, Venice Biennial 1999; Art Basel–Parkett Publishers 1999–2008; faculty mem. Parson School of Fine Art, New York 1999–; fmr Faculty mem. Emory Univ., Calif. Inst. of the Arts; Artistic Dir Art Basel and Art Basel Miami Beach 2008–; Contributing Ed., Art Papers Magazine 1998. *Publications include:* Escape 1994, Thomas Schutte (co-author) 2001, Julie Mehretu: Black City (co-author) 2007, Fiona Banner's work as work-in-progress 2007; contribs to Financial Times, Artforum, Grand Street, Afterall, Boiler, Self Service; other: numerous exhbn catalogues. *Address:* Art Basel, c/o MCH Swiss Exhibition (Basel) Ltd, 4005 Basel, Switzerland (office). *Telephone:* 582062703 (office). *Fax:* 582063130 (office). *E-mail:* info@artbasel.com (office). *Website:* www.artbasel.com (office).

RABINOWITZ, Harry, (Henry Oliver, Andy Thurlow), MBE; British composer and conductor; b. 26 March 1916, Johannesburg, S Africa; s. of Israel Rabinowitz and Eva Rabinowitz (née Kirkel); m. 1st Lorna T. Anderson 1944 (divorced); one s. two d.; m. 2nd Mitzi Scott 2001; ed Athlone High School, Johannesburg, Univ. of the Witwatersrand and Guildhall School of Music, London; Conductor, BBC Radio 1953–60; Musical Dir BBC TV Light Entertainment 1960–68; Head of Music, London Weekend TV 1968–77; freelance composer and conductor 1977–; appeared with London Symphony and Royal Philharmonic Orchestras in UK and with the Los Angeles Philharmonic and Boston Pops Orchestras and Orchestra of St Luke's in USA; Musical Dir for world premieres of Cats and Song & Dance; composed and conducted several TV scores including The Charlie Drake Show (series) 1960, BBC Top of the Pops Theme, The Marquise 1980, The Sign of Four 1983, Reilly: The Ace of Spies (mini-series) 1983, The Ewok Adventure 1984, The Insurance Man 1986, Agatha Christie Hour 1987, In a Glass Darkly (aka Agatha Christie's In a Glass Darkly) 1987, L'Amérique en otage 1991, Memento Mori 1992, Alien Empire (BBC); mem. British Acad. of Songwriters, Composers and Authors, Composers' Guild (BASCA); Freeman of the City of London 1995; BASCA Gold Badge for Services to British Music 1985, Radio and TV Industries Award for Best TV Theme 1984, All-Music Gold Award 1991. *Television:* Musical Dir: Julia and Friends 1986, Paul Nicholas and Friends 1987, New Faces 1987. *Films:* Musical Dir: Funeral in Berlin 1966, Puppet on a Chain 1970, Inside Out 1975, All This and World War II 1976, The Greek Tycoon 1978, Roberte 1979, Hanover Street 1979, Goldengirl 1979, La mort en direct 1980, Mon oncle d'Amérique 1980, Chariots of Fire 1981, Time Bandits 1981, Heat and Dust 1983, The Bostonians 1984, Electric Dreams (also actor) 1984, Nemo 1984, Revolution 1985, Return to Oz 1985, Lady Jane 1986, F/X 1986, The Manhattan Project 1986, RoboCop 1987, Masters of the Universe 1987, Maurice 1987, Mangeclous 1988, Camille Claudel 1988, Queen of Hearts 1989, Shirley Valentine 1989, L'Argent, Lord of the Flies 1990, La Voix, Les Carnassiers, Le Petit Garçon, La Baule-les Pins, La Fille des Collines, Eve of Destruction, Jesuit Joe, Jeanne, Putain du Roi, The Ballad of the Sad Café 1991, J'embrasse pas 1991, Howards End 1992, The Remains of the Day 1993, A Business Affair 1994, Gross Fatigue 1994, La Fille d'Artagnan, Death and the Maiden 1994, Jefferson in Paris 1995, Secret Agent 1996, The Proprietor 1996, The Stupids, The English Patient 1996, Tonka, Surviving Picasso 1996, Wings of the Dove, Amour Sorcier, My Story So Far, City of Angels 1998, A Soldier's Daughter Never Cries 1998, Message in a Bottle 1999, My Life So Far 1999, Cotton Mary 1999, The Talented Mr. Ripley 1999, Place Vendome, The Golden Bowl 2000, Possession 2002, Bon Voyage 2003, Le Divorce 2003, Cold Mountain 2003. *Leisure interests:* listening to others making music, edible fungi hunting, wine-tasting. *Address:* Yellow Cottage, Walking Bottom, Peaslake, Surrey, GU5 9RR, England (home). *Telephone:* (1306) 730674 (home); (503) 224-2541 (USA) (home); (4) 90-75-89-47 (France) (home). *E-mail:* mitziscott@aol.com (home).

RABIU, Abdulsamad, CON; Nigerian business executive; *Chairman and CEO, BUA Group;* s. of Isyaku Rabiu; m.; four c.; ed Govt Coll., Kano; started career by importing basic commodities such as rice, sugar, cement during 1980s; est. BUA International Ltd (now BUA Group) 1988, currently Chair. and CEO; Chair. Nigeria's Bank of Industry 2010–, Cement Co. of Northern Nigeria Plc. *Leisure interests:* squash, polo. *Address:* BUA Group, 35 Saka Tinubu Street, Victoria Island, Lagos, Nigeria (office). *Telephone:* (1) 4610669 (office). *Fax:* (1) 2623535 (office). *E-mail:* info@buagroup.com (office). *Website:* www.buagroup.com (office).

RABKIN, Mitchell T., MD; American physician, academic and hospital administrator; *Professor of Medicine, Harvard Medical School;* b. 27 Nov. 1930, Boston, Mass; s. of Morris A. Rabkin and Esther Quint Rabkin; m. Adrienne M. Najarian 1956; one s. one d.; ed Harvard Coll. and Harvard Medical School, Massachusetts Gen. Hosp., Boston; US Public Health Service, NIH, Bethesda, Md 1957–59; Chief Resident in Medicine, Massachusetts Gen. Hosp. 1962, medical staff 1963–66, Bd Consultation 1972–80, Hon. Physician 1981–; Gen. Dir Beth Israel Hosp., Boston 1966–80, Pres. 1980–96, now CEO Emer.; Prof. of Medicine, Harvard Medical School 1983–, Pres. Harvard Medical Alumni Council 2000–01; CEO CareGroup, Boston 1996–98; Distinguished Inst. Scholar, Inst. for Educ. and Research, Beth Israel Deaconess Medical Center, Boston 1998–; mem. Bd of Dirs Duke Univ. Health System 1998–2003; Dir Washington Advisory Group, LECG; mem. Bd of Trustees, New York Univ. School of Medicine Foundation 2000–07, Vice-Chair. 2006–07; mem. NAS Inst. of Medicine; Fellow, AAAS, ACP; Hon. DSc (Brandeis), (Curry Coll., Milton, Mass.), (Mass. Coll. of Pharmacy) 1983, (Northeastern Univ.) 1994; Distinguished Service Award, American Hosp. Asscn 1999, Distinguished Service Medal, Asscn of American Medical Colls 1999. *Publications:* numerous articles in academic journals. *Leisure interests:* sailing, gardening, travel. *Address:* Carl J. Shapiro Institute for Education and Research at Harvard Medical School and Beth Israel Deaconess Medical Center, 330 Brookline Avenue, Boston, MA 02186, USA (office); 124 Canton Avenue, Milton, MA 02186, USA (home). *Telephone:* (617) 667-9400 (office); (617) 696-6614 (home). *Fax:* (617) 667-9122 (office); (617) 696-1008 (home). *E-mail:* mtrabkin@caregroup.harvard.edu (office); mtrabkin@mindspring.com (home). *Website:* www.bidmc.harvard.edu (office).

RABUKA, Maj.-Gen. Sitiveni Ligamamada, OBE, MSc; Fijian politician and army officer; b. 13 Sept. 1948, Nakobo; s. of Kolinio E. V. Rabuka and Salote Lomaloma; m. Suluweti Camamaivuna Tuiloma 1975; two s. two d.; ed Prov. School Northern, Queen Victoria School, NZ Army schools, Indian Defence Services Staff Coll. and Australian Jt Services Staff Coll.; Sr Operational Plans Officer, UN Interim Force in Lebanon (UNIFIL) 1980; Commdr Fiji Bn UNIFL Lebanon 1980–81; Chief of Staff, Fiji July–Dec. 1981; SO 1 Operations and Training, Fiji Army 1982–83, 1985–87; Chief of Mil. Personnel MFO, Sinai, Egypt 1983–84; Commdr Fiji Bn MFO, Sinai, Egypt 1984–85; staged coup 14 May 1987; Adviser on Home Affairs and Head of Security May–Sept. 1987; staged second coup 25 Sept. 1987; declared Fiji a Repub. 7 Oct. 1987; Commdr and Head of Interim Mil. Govt of Fiji Sept.–Dec. 1987; Commdr Fiji Security Forces 1987–91; Minister for Home Affairs, Nat. Youth Service and Army Auxiliary Services 1987–90; Commdr Republic of Fiji Military Forces 1991; Deputy Prime Minister 1991, Minister for Home Affairs 1991; elected Founding Pres. Fijian Political Party 1991; Prime Minister of Fiji 1992–99, fmrly Minister for Home Affairs, Immigration, Fijian Affairs and Rural Devt and Foreign Affairs, fmrly with special responsibility for the Constitutional Review and the Agricultural, Landlords and Tenants Act; Commonwealth Rep. to Solomon Islands 1999–2000; Chair. Cakaudrove Prov. Council 2001–08; Pres. Fijian Political Party (SVT); Commdr, Légion d'honneur 1980, Grand Officier 1997, Meritorious Service Decoration 1987, Officer, Order of St John of Jerusalem 1987, Companion of the Order of Fiji 1998, Order of Tahiti Nui 1998; Dr hc (Cen. Queensland Univ.) 1997. *Film:* Operation Surprise (documentary on Fiji coup d'etat) 1987. *Publications:* No Other Way 1988, Rabuka of Fiji 2000. *Leisure interests:* golf, rugby, weightlifting. *Address:* Box 2437, Government Buildings, Savusavu, Fiji (office). *Telephone:* (9) 3323753 (home); (9) 9937023 (mobile) (home). *Fax:* (9) 3323753 (office). *E-mail:* leo@connect.com.fj (home). *Website:* blighwatershipping.com.fj (office).

RABY, Geoffrey William, BEc, MEc, PhD; Australian fmr diplomatist; b. Sept. 1953, Melbourne; ed La Trobe Univ.; fmr Sr Tutor in Econs, La Trobe Univ.; trade policy adviser, Office of Nat. Assessments 1984–86, to Minister for Trade 1993; served twice as Head, Econ. Section, Embassy in Beijing 1986–91; est. Northeast Asia Analytical Unit, Dept of Foreign Affairs and Trade (DFAT) 1991, Head of Unit 1991–93; other sr positions at DFAT include First Asst Sec., Trade Negotiations Div. 1995–98, First Asst Sec., Int. Orgs and Legal Div. 2001–02, Deputy Sec. DFAT 2002–06; Head, Trade Policy Issues Div., OECD, Paris 1993–95, Perm. Rep. to WTO, Geneva 1998–2001; Amb. to APEC, Singapore 2002–04; Amb. to People's Repub. of China (also accred to Mongolia and North Korea) 2007–11; Chair and CEO Geoff Raby and Associates, Beijing. *Address:* Geoff Raby and Associates, Suite 2425, Tower 3, China Central Place, Beijing 100025, People's Republic of China (office). *Website:* www.geoffraby.com (office).

RACHDI, Allal; Moroccan civil servant and international organization executive; b. 17 June 1951; ed Grande Ecole of Public Admin, Faculty of Law (Political Sciences), Certificate of Trade Policy, GATT, Geneva; sr civil servant at Ministry of Foreign Trade since 1978, participated in devt and implementation of Structural Adjustment programmes, also took part in bilateral and multilateral trade negotiations, particularly in negotiations for accession of Morocco to GATT, co-operation and asscn agreements of Morocco with EU, Uruguay Round negotiations as well as negotiations of several free trade agreements, Dir Foreign Trade Policy, Ministry of Foreign Trade 1994–2000, Co-ordinator at Gen. Secr.; Chair. Nat. Comm. of Foreign Trade Facilitation 1986–2000, Nat. Imports Consultative Comm. 1992–2000; Admin., Common Fund for Commodities, Amsterdam 1998–2000, Moroccan Exports Asscn; mem. Jt Cttee of Pvt./Public Sector; Dir-Gen. Islamic Centre for the Devt of Trade, OIC 2000–11; D Dir-Gen. AS3M (investment co.) 2011–. *Address:* c/o Islamic Centre for the Development of Trade, Tours des Habous, Avenue des FAR, BP 13545, Casablanca – Principal 20000, Morocco.

RACHMAT, Theodore (Teddy) Permadi; Indonesian business executive; b. 1943; m.; ed Bandung Inst. of Tech.; Pres. Dir PT Astra International Tbk (Indonesian car mfr) 1984–98, 2000–02, Commr 1998–2000, Pres. Commr 2002–05; f. Triputra Group 1998, has interests in agribusiness, manufacturing, mining, trading and services; Pres. Commr Adira Finance 2004–; Vice-Pres. PT Adaro Energy Tbk; fmr Commr PT Unilever Indonesia Tbk; fmr Chair. Indonesian Business Execs Asscn (Apindo); Adviser, Protocol One; mem. Nat. Econs Bd. *Address:* Triputra Group, Menara Kadin 23rd Floor, H.R. Rasuna Said Kav. 2&3, Jakarta 12950, Indonesia (office). *Telephone:* (21) 5274323 (office). *E-mail:* info@triputra-group.com (office). *Website:* www.triputra-group.com (office).

RACICOT, Marc F., BA, JD; American lawyer, association executive and fmr politician; *President, American Insurance Association;* b. 24 July 1948, Thompson Falls, Mont.; s. of William E. Racicot and Patricia E. Racicot (née Bentley); m. Theresa J. Barber 1970; two s. three d.; ed Carroll Coll., Helena, Mont., Univ. of Montana; called to Bar, Mont. 1973; served US Army 1973–76, Chief Trial Counsel US Army, Kaiserslautern, FRG 1975–76, resgnd 1976; Deputy Co. Attorney, Missoula (Mont.) Co. 1976–77; Asst Attorney-Gen. State of Mont. 1977–88, Attorney-Gen. 1988–93; Gov. of Montana 1993–2001; Pnr, Bracewell & Patterson LLP (now Bracewell & Giuliani, LLP), Washington, DC 2001–03; Chair. Republican Nat. Cttee 2002–04; Chair. Bush-Cheney re-election campaign 2004; Pres. American Insurance Asscn 2005–. *Address:* American Insurance Association, 1130 Connecticut Avenue, NW, Suite 1000, Washington, DC 20036, USA (office). *Telephone:* (202) 828-7100 (office). *Fax:* (202) 293-1219 (office). *E-mail:* mracicot@aiadc.org (office). *Website:* www.aiadc.org (office).

RACIONERO GRAU, Luis; Spanish librarian, academic and writer; b. 1940, Seu d'Urgell, Lleida; ed Univ. of California, Berkeley, USA, Churchill Coll., Cambridge, UK; industrial engineer, Barcelona 1965; Prof. of Microeconomics, Faculty of Econ. Sciences and Urban Studies, School of Architecture, Barcelona; fmr Dir Spanish Coll., Paris; Dir-Gen. Biblioteca Nacional, Madrid 2001–04. *Publications include:* Taoista textos de estética 1991, Atenas de Pericles 1993, El arte de escribir

1995, La sonrisa de la Gioconda: Memorias de Leonardo 1999, Filosofias del Underground 2000, El pecado original 2001, Oriente y Occidente 2001, El progreso decadente (Espasa de Ensayo Prize) 2001, El alquimista trouador 2003, The Book Of Small Pleasures 2005, Complexes Of The Right 2006, Leonardo Da Vinci: Renaissance Genius 2006, Surviving a Great Love Six Times-Memories 2009. *Address:* c/o Editorial Planeta, Córcega 273-277, 08008 Barcelona, Spain.

RACZKO, Andrzej, DEcons; Polish economist; b. 27 Feb. 1953, Kutno; m.; two c.; ed Univ. of Łódź; early career as Asst, then Asst Prof., Inst. of Econs, Univ. of Łódź 1977–86; Chief Specialist on Foreign Cooperation, Łódźkie Towarzystwo Kredy-towe Bank SA 1992–93; Econ. Dir Petrobank SA 1993–97, mem. Man. Bd LG Petro Bank SA 1995–97, Dir 1997–99; Man. Mortgage Team, PKO Bank Polski SA 1999–2001; Under-Sec. of State, Ministry of Finance 2001–02, Minister of Finance 2003–04; mem. Bd of Dirs Bank Gospodarki Żywnościowej SA 2002–03; fmr mem. EU negotiating team; fmr Vice-Gov. IMF, Alt. Exec. Dir (Poland) 2004; fmr Chief Economist and Dir of Research Dept, Polish Financial Supervision Authority; mem. Bd of Man. National Bank of Poland 2010–; fmr Co-Chair. Public Debt Cttee. *Address:* National Bank of Poland, 00-919 Warsaw, ul. Świętokrzyska 11/21, Poland (office). *Website:* www.nbp.pl (office).

RADAVIDSON, Benjamin Andriamparany; Malagasy politician; b. religious leader; Minister of the Economy, Finance and the Budget 2002–07, of Nat. Educ. and Scientific Research 2007–08; fmr mem. Bd of Govs IMF; Nat. Pres. Laics FJKM Reformed Church of Madagascar. *Address:* FJKM Reformed Church of Madagascar, BP 623, Antananarivo, Madagascar (office). *E-mail:* fjkm@fjkm.mg (office). *Website:* www.fjkm.mg (office).

RADCLIFFE, Daniel Jacob; British actor; b. 23 July 1989, London; s. of Alan Radcliffe and Marcia Gresham; ed Sussex House School, London, City of London School. *Films include:* The Tailor of Panama 2001, Harry Potter and the Philosopher's Stone 2001, Harry Potter and the Chamber of Secrets 2002, Harry Potter and the Prisoner of Azkaban 2004, Harry Potter and the Goblet of Fire 2005, Harry Potter and the Order of the Phoenix 2007, December Boys 2007, Harry Potter and the Half-Blood Prince 2009, Harry Potter and the Deathly Hallows: Part 1 2010, Harry Potter and the Deathly Hallows: Part 2 2011, The Woman in Black 2012, Kill Your Darlings 2013, Horns 2013, The F Word 2013. *Television appearances include:* David Copperfield 1999, My Boy Jack 2007, The Simpsons (voice) 2010, 2014, A Young Doctor's Notebook (series) 2012–13. *Theatre appearances include:* The Play What I Wrote 2002, Equus (London and Broadway) 2007, The Cripple of Inishmaan (WhatsOnStage Award for Best Actor in a Play) 2014. *Address:* Artists Rights Group, 4 Great Portland Street, London, W1W 8PA, England (office). *Telephone:* (20) 7436-6400 (office). *E-mail:* Vanessa.Davies@organic-marketing.co.uk (office). *Website:* argtalent.com (office).

RADCLIFFE, Paula Jane, MBE, BA; British athlete; b. 17 Dec. 1973, North-wich, Cheshire, England; d. of Peter Radcliffe and Pat Radcliffe; m. Gary Lough; one s. one d.; ed Univ. of Loughborough; distance runner; World Jr Cross Country Champion 1992; started sr career 1993; fifth place, 5,000m, Olympic Games 1996; won Fifth Avenue Mile, New York 1996, 1997; third place, Int. Asscn of Athletics Feds (IAAF) World Cross Challenge series 1997; fourth place, 5,000m, World Championships 1997; European Cross Country Champion 1998; second place, 10,000m, European Challenge 1998; silver medal, 10,000m World Championships, 1999; fourth place, 10,000m Olympic Games 2000; World Half Marathon Champion 2000, 2001; World Cross Country Champion 2002; gold medallist, 5,000m, Commonwealth Games 2002; gold medallist, 10,000m, European Championships 2002; won London Marathon 2002, 2003, 2005, Chicago Marathon 2002, New York City Marathon 2004, 2007, 2008; set world best time for 5,000m in Flora Light 5km 2003; won Great North Run Half Marathon in world best time 2003; won World Championship's marathon 2005; world record holder for 10,000m, 20,000m and marathon; Capt. GB's Women's Athletic Team 1998–; Hon. DLitt (De Montfort, Loughborough); British Female Athlete of the Year 1999, 2001 and 2002, IAAF World Female Athlete of the Year 2002, BBC Sports Personality of the Year 2002, Sunday Times Sportswoman of the Year 2002, Laureus World Comeback of the Year 2008. *Publication:* Paula: My Story So Far 2004. *Leisure interests:* dining out, languages, reading, music, cinema, travel, spending time with family and friends. *Address:* c/o Bedford and County Athletics Club, 3 Regent Close, Bedford, MK41 7XG, England (office). *Website:* www.paularadcliffe.com (office).

RADCLIFFE, Father Timothy Peter Joseph, OP, MA; British RC ecclesiastic and Dominican friar; b. 22 Aug. 1945, London, England; s. of Hugh Radcliffe and Marie-Therese Pereira; ed Downside School, Le Saulchoir, Paris and St John's Coll., Oxford; entered Dominican Order 1965; Chaplain to Imperial Coll.; Prior of Blackfriars, Oxford 1982–88; Chair. New Blackfriars 1983–88; Provincial of Prov. of England 1988–92; Pres. Conf. of Major Religious Superiors of England and Wales 1991–; Grand Chancellor, Pontifical Univ. of St Thomas (The Angelicum), Rome 1992–2001, Univ. of Santo Tomas, Manila 1992–2001, Ecole Biblique, Jerusalem 1992–2001, Faculty of Theology, Fribourg 1992–2001; Master, Order of Preachers 1992–2001; Hon. Citizen of Augusta (Italy) and Sepahua (Peru); Hon. Fellow, St John's Coll. Oxford, Sarum Canon of Salisbury Cathedral; Hon. DD (Oxford), (Pontifical Univ. of St Thomas), Hon. STD (Providence Coll. RI), Hon. LLD (Barry Univ., Fla) 1996, Hon. DHumLitt (Ohio Dominican Coll.) 1996 (Dominican Univ., Chicago) 2007, (Aquinas Inst., St Louis), Dr hc (Université Catholique de l'Ouest, Angers) 2007; Prix de Littérature Religieuse 2001, Prix Spiritualités d'aujourd'hui 2001, Premio Ecumenico San Nicola 2004, Prix des lecteurs du Procure 2005, Michael Ramsey Award for Theological Writing 2007. *Publications:* El Manantial de la Esperanza 1998, Sing a New Song: The Christian Vocation 1999, I Call You Friends 2001, Seven Last Words of Christ 2004, What is the Point of Being a Christian? 2005, Just One Year – A Global Treasury of Prayer and Worship 2007, Why Go to Church? The Drama of the Eucharist 2008, Take the Plunge 2012. *Leisure interests:* walking, reading long novels. *Address:* Blackfriars, St Giles, Oxford, OX1 3LY, England (home). *Telephone:* (1865) 278422 (home). *Fax:* (1865) 278403 (home). *E-mail:* timothy.radcliffe@english.op.org (office).

RADDA, Sir George Karoly, Kt, CBE, MA, DPhil, FRS; British medical research director and academic; *Chairman, Singapore Bioimaging Consortium, Singapore A*Biomedical Research Council;* b. 9 June 1936, Gyor, Hungary; s. of Gyula Radda and Anna Bernolak; m. 1st Mary O'Brien 1961 (divorced 1995), two s. one d.; m. 2nd Sue Bailey 1995; ed Pannonhalma and Eötvös Univ., Budapest and Merton

Coll. Oxford; Research Assoc., Univ. of Calif., USA 1962–63; Lecturer in Organic Chem., St John's Coll., Oxford Univ. 1963–64, Fellow and Tutor in Organic Chem., Merton Coll. 1964–84, Lecturer in Biochem, Oxford Univ. 1966–84, British Heart Foundation Prof. of Molecular Cardiology 1984–2003, Prof. Emer. 2003, Prof. and Head, Dept of Physiology, Anatomy and Genetics 2006–08; Professorial Fellow, Merton Coll. 1984–2008, Head Dept of Biochem. 1991–96; Chair. MRC Cell. Bd 1988–92; mem. MRC Council 1988–92, Chief Exec. MRC (on leave from Oxford Univ.) 1996–2003; Chair. Nat. Cancer Research Inst. 2001–, Singapore Bioimaging Consortium 2006–, Singapore A* Biomedical Research Council 2009–; mem. Council, Royal Soc. 1990–92, ICRF 1991–96; Ed. Biochemical and Biophysical Research Communications 1977–84; Man. Ed. Biochimica et Biophysica Acta 1977–, Chair. 1989–95; Founder mem. Oxford Enzyme Group 1970–87, Acad. of Medical Sciences 1998; Pres. Soc. for Magnetic Resonance in Medicine 1985–86, Fellow 1994–; Fellow, Int. Soc. of Magnetic Resonance in Medicine 1995–; mem. European Molecular Biology Org. 1997– (Fellow 2008–), Academia Europaea 1999–; Hon. Dir MRC Biochemical and Clinical Magnetic Resonance Unit 1988–96; Hon. FRCR 1985; Hon. Fellow, American Heart Asscn and Citation for Int. Achievement 1987; Hon. FRCP 1997; Hon. mem. European Soc. of Magnetic Resonance in Medicine and Biology 2007; Hon. DrMed (Berne) 1985, (London) 1991; Hon. DSc (Stirling) 1997, (Sheffield) 1999, (Debrecen, Hungary) 2001, (Birmingham) 2003, (Univ. de la Mediterranée) 2003, (Aberdeen) 2004, (Heinrich Heine Univ., Düsseldorf) 2004, (Semmelweis, Hungary) 2004, (Hull) 2005, (Leicester) 2006; Colworth Medal, Biochemical Soc. 1969, CIBA Medal and Prize 1983, Feldberg Prize 1982, British Heart Foundation Prize and Gold Medal for cardiovascular research 1982, Gold Medal, Soc. for Magnetic Resonance in Medicine 1984, Buchanan Medal, Royal Soc. 1987, Rank Prize in Nutrition 1990, Medal of Merit, Int. Acad. of Cardiovascular Sciences 2006, Public Service Medal, Friends of Singapore 2008. *Publications:* articles in books and scientific journals. *Leisure interests:* opera, jazz, swimming. *Address:* Agency for Science Technology and Research, Singapore Bioimaging Consortium, 11 Biopolis Way, #02-02 Helios, Singapore, 138667, Singapore (office). *Telephone:* 64788721 (office). *E-mail:* george .radda@sbic.a-star.edu.sg (office).

RADEBE, Bridgette, BA; South African mining industry executive; *Executive Chairman, Mmakau Mining (Pty) Ltd;* b. 26 Feb. 1960, Johannesburg; sister of Patrice Motsepe; m. Jeff Radebe; ed Univ. of Botswana; Founder and Executive Chair. Mmakau Mining (Pty) Ltd 1995–; Pres. South African Mining Devt Asscn; fmr Vice-Chair. Minerals and Mining Devt Bd; Co-founder and Trustee, New Africa Mining Fund; participated in the design of the SA Mining Charter; mem. Bd of Dirs Sappi Ltd 2004–, Nat. Research Foundation, Leadership Foundation, Int. Women's Forum Washington, DC; Business Person of the Year Award, Global Foundation for Democracy 2008. *Address:* Mmakau Mining (Pty) Ltd, PO Box 2236, Houghton, 2041, South Africa (office). *Telephone:* (11) 268 6780 (office). *Fax:* (11) 268 0186 (office). *E-mail:* info@mmakau.co.za (office). *Website:* www .mmakaumining.co.za (office).

RADEBE, Jeffrey (Jeff) Thamsanqa, LLB; South African politician; *Minister of Justice and Constitutional Development;* b. 18 Feb. 1953, Cato Manor; m. Bridget Radebe; three c.; ed Isibonelo High School, Univ. of Zululand, Leipzig Univ., Germany, Lenin Int. School, Moscow; joined Black Consciousness Movt 1970; Co-founder Kwamashu Youth Org. 1972; articled clerk with A. J. Gumede & Phyllis Naidoo, E. S. Mchunu & Co. 1976–77; with Radio Freedom 1977–78; Deputy Chief African Nat. Congress (ANC) Rep., Tanzania 1981; headed clandestine political movt of ANC and South African Communist Party (SACP) 1986, Head of Political Dept and Co-ordinator of 12 day hunger strike on Robben Island; arrested and sentenced to ten years on Robben Island 1986, sentence reduced to six years, released 1990; Sec. interim leadership group of SACP 1990–91; Deputy Chair. ANC Southern Natal Region 1990–91, Chair. 1991–94; Minister of Public Works, Govt of Nat. Unity 1994–99, of Public Enterprises 1999–2004, of Transport 2004–09, of Justice and Constitutional Devt 2009–, also currently mem. ANC Nat. Exec. Cttee (NEC) and Nat. Working Cttee, Head ANC Policy Unit and NEC Convener in North West Prov.; Hon. LLM (Leipzig); Dr hc (Chicago State Univ.) 1996. *Address:* Ministry of Justice and Constitutional Development, Momentum Centre, 329 Pretorius St, cnr Pretorius and Prinsloo Sts, Pretoria 0001, South Africa (office). *Telephone:* (12) 313578217 (office). *Fax:* (12) 3151749 (office). *E-mail:* znqayi@justice.gov.za (office). *Website:* www.doj.gov.za (office).

RADER, Gen. Paul Alexander, BA, BD, MTh, DMiss; American religious leader and fmr university administrator; b. 14 March 1934, New York, NY; s. of Lyell M. Rader and Gladys Mina Damon; m. Kay Fuller 1956; one s. two d.; ed Asbury Theological Seminary, Southern Baptist Theological Seminary, Salvation Army's School for Officers' Training, New York, Fuller Theological Seminary; mem. staff Salvation Army Training School, Seoul, S Korea 1962–67, Vice-Prin. 1967–71, Training Prin., then Educ. Officer, then Asst Chief Sec. Salvation Army in S Korea 1973–77, Chief Sec. with rank of Lt-Col 1977–84; Prin. School for Officers' Training, Suffern, NY 1984–87, Div. Leader 1987–89; Chief Sec. USA Eastern Territory 1989; rank of Commr 1989; Commdr USA Western Territory 1989–94; Pres. The Salvation Army Calif. Corps 1989–94; rank of Gen. of The Salvation Army 1994–99; Pres. Asbury Coll. 2000–06 (retd); Hon. DD (Asbury Theological Seminary, Roberts Wesleyan Coll.), Hon. LHD (Asbury Coll.); Order of Diplomatic Service Merit, Gwanghwa Medal "for distinguished service in the field of mission to the Repub. of Korea and the world" 1998. *Address:* 3953 Rock Ledge Lane, Lexington, KY 40513, USA. *E-mail:* paularader@aol.com.

RADHAKRISHNAN, K., BSc, MBA, PhD; Indian scientist; *Chairman, Indian Space Research Organisation (ISRO);* b. 29 Aug. 1949, Irinjalkuda, Kerala; m. Padmini Radhakrishnan; ed Univ. of Kerala, Indian Inst. of Man., Bangalore, Indian Inst. of Tech.; started career as Avionics Engineer, Vikram Sarabhai Space Centre 1971, Dir 2007–09; Dir, Budget and Economic Analysis, Indian Space Research Org. (ISRO) 1987–97, Chair. 2009–; Dir Nat. Natural Resources Man. System-Regional Remote Sensing Service Centres 1989–97; Mission Dir Integrated Mission for Sustainable Devt 1997–2000; Deputy Dir Nat. Remote Sensing Agency, Hyderabad 1997–2000, Dir 2005–08; Founder-Dir Indian Nat. Centre for Ocean Information Services 2000–05; Vice-Chair. Intergovernmental Oceanographic Comm. 2001–05; Founder-Dir Regional Alliance in Indian Ocean for Global Ocean Observing System (IOGOOS) 2002–06; Pres. Indian Soc. of Remote Sensing 2005–07; Vice-Pres. Indian Geophysical Union 2007–09; mem. Space

Comm. 2008–09, Chair. 2009–; Sec., Dept of Space, Govt of India 2009–; currently Pres. Astronautical Soc. of India, Chair. Scientific Advisory Bd, B M Birla Science Centre, Hyderabad; mem. International Acad. of Astronautics; leads Indian del. to UN Cttee on Peaceful Use of Outer Space; Fellow, Indian Nat. Acad. of Eng, Andhra Pradesh Acad. of Sciences, Indian Soc. of Remote Sensing, Systems Soc. of India, Indian Geophysical Union; Hon. Life Fellow, Inst. of Engineers, Hon. Fellow, Inst. of Electrical and Telecommunication Engineers; Dr hc (Sri Venkateswara Univ.), (Rajasthan Technical Univ.), (GITAM Univ.), (Tumkur Univ.), (SRM Univ.) 2010, (KIIT Univ.) 2010. *Leisure interest:* Kathakali dance. *Address:* Office of the Chairman, Indian Space Research Organisation, Antariksh Bhavan, New BEL Road, Bangalore 560 231, India (office). *Telephone:* (80) 23415275 (office). *Fax:* (80) 23511984 (office). *E-mail:* chairman@isro.gov.in (office). *Website:* www.isro.gov.in (office).

RADHAKRISHNAN, S., BTech (Mech), MBA; Indian mechanical engineer and business executive; ed Univ., Indian Inst. of Tech., Chennai, Indian Inst. of Man., Bangalore; Man. Dir Bharat Shell Ltd –1977; joined Bharat Petroleum 1977, Dir (Marketing), Bharat Petroleum Corpn Ltd 2002–11, Chair. and Man. Dir Aug.–Dec. 2010; Ind. Dir (non-exec.) Indraprastha Gas Ltd –2005, Additional Dir 2007–, Chair. 2009–; Dir, Numaligarh Refinery Ltd 2002–, Kochi Refineries Ltd, Sabarmati Gas Ltd, Bharat Stars Services Pvt. Ltd, Petronet India Ltd. *Address:* Bharat Petroleum Corpn Ltd, 4–6 Currimbhoy Road, Ballard Estate, Mumbai 400 001, India (office). *Telephone:* (22) 2271-3000 (office). *E-mail:* info@ bharatpetroleum.com (office). *Website:* www.bharatpetroleum.com (office).

RADICE, Vittorio; Italian retail executive; *CEO, La Rinascente;* b. 1957, Como; m. Gemma Radice; two s.; ed Univ. of Milan; home furnishings buyer, Associated Merchandising Corpn; Buying Dir Habitat Int., then Man. Dir Habitat UK 1990–96; Man. Dir Selfridges PLC 1996–98, CEO 1998–2003; Exec. Dir and Head of Home Furnishings, Marks and Spencer PLC 2003–04; CEO La Rinascente, Milan 2005–; Dir (non-exec.) Shoppers Stop India 2000–06, McArthurGlen 2005–, Ishaan plc 2006–. *Leisure interests:* travel, India, art, music. *Address:* la Rinascente s.r.l., Via Washington 70, 20146 Milan (office); Strada 8, Palazzo N, 20089 Rozzano-Milano, Italy (office). *Telephone:* (2) 57583922 (office). *Fax:* (2) 57982015 (office). *E-mail:* vittorio.radice@lu.centralretail.com (office). *Website:* www.rinascente.it (office).

RADIČOVÁ, Iveta, PhDr, PhD; Slovak politician, political scientist and academic; b. 7 Dec. 1956, Bratislava; m. Stano Radič (died 2005); one d.; ed Comenius Univ., Bratislava, Slovak Acad. of Sciences, Bratislava, Univ. of Oxford, UK; Research Team Coordinator for Family Policy, Inst. for Sociology 1979–83, Dir of Inst. 2005; Univ. Lecturer, Dept of Sociology, Comenius Univ. 1990–93, Reader 1997, Univ. Lecturer, Dept of Political Science 1997–2005, Prof. 2005–, Univ. Lecturer, Dept of Social Work 2007–; Exec. Dir SPACE Foundation – Centre for Social Policy Analysis, Bratislava 1992–2005; Deputy Dir Academia Istropolitana, Bratislava 1993–97; Sociology Dept Supervisor, Dept of Sociology, Univ. of Constantine the Philosopher, Nitra 2005–07; Visiting Prof. at univs in USA, UK, Sweden, Finland, Austria while EC's expert on social policy; Minister of Labour, Social and Family Affairs 2005–06; Prime Minister (first female) 2010–12, Minister of Defence 2011–12; mem. Slovak Democratic and Christian Union-Democratic Party (Slovenská demokratická a kresťanská únia-Demokratická strana—SDKU-DS); mem. Parl. (SDKU-DS) 2006–09, Chair. Parl. Cttee for Social Affairs and Housing; led SDKU-DS party list in 2010 parl. elections. *Publications:* For People and People: Issues Shaping Social Policy in Slovakia 1995, Cross-Roads of Social Knowledge 1996, We Reject What We Know and What We Want? Environmental Strategy of Slovak Citizens 1998, Social Policy in Slovakia 1998, Social Policy in Bohemia and Slovakia after ROCE 1989 (co-ed.) 1998, Health, Work, Retirement (with H. Woleková and J. Nemec) 1999, Hic Sunt Romales 2001, S.O.S.: Social Protection in Slovakia 2003. *Address:* c/o Office of the Government, nám. Slobody 1, 813 70 Bratislava, Slovakia. *E-mail:* iveta.radicova@sdkuonline .sk.

RADIŠIĆ, Živko; Bosnia and Herzegovina politician; *Chairman, Socialist Party;* b. 15 Aug. 1937, Prijedor; m.; two c.; ed Univ. of Sarajevo; Mayor of Banja Luka 1977–82; Minister of Defence of the Fmr Socialist Repub. of Bosnia and Herzegovina 1982–85; Man. Cajavec Holding Co., Banja Luka 1985–92; Chair. Ass., Banja Luka; Pres. and Chair. of the Presidency of Bosnia and Herzegovina 1998–99, 2000–01, Co-Pres. 1999–2001, Mem. of the Presidency 2002; Founding mem. Socialist Party (fmrly Socialist Party of Republika Srpska) 1996–, currently Chair. *Address:* Socialist Party (Socijalistička Partija) (SP), 78000 Banja Luka, Bana Lazarevića 7, Bosnia and Herzegovina (office). *Telephone:* (51) 328750 (office). *Fax:* (51) 328753 (office). *E-mail:* sprs@inecco.net (office).

RADMANOVIĆ, Nebojša; Bosnia and Herzegovina politician; *Member of the State Presidency;* b. 1 Oct. 1949, Gračanica; m.; two c.; ed high school in Banja Luka, Faculty of Philosophy, Univ. of Belgrade; has held numerous positions in culture and state admin including Dir Bosanska Krajina Archives and Archives of Republika Srpska, Dir Nat. Theatre of Republika Srpska, Banja Luka, Dir and Ed.-in-Chief GLAS, Pres. Exec. Bd Banja Luka Urban Municipality, Rep. Nat. Ass., Republika Srpska and Minister of Admin and Local Self-Man.; Serb mem. State Presidency 2006–, Chair. (Pres. of Bosnia and Herzegovina) 2006–07, 2008–09, 2010–11, 2012–13; mem. Alliance of Ind. Social Democrats. *Publications include:* several books and scientific papers. *Address:* Office of the State Presidency, 71000 Sarajevo, Maršala Tita 16, Bosnia and Herzegovina (office). *Telephone:* (33) 567510 (office). *Fax:* (33) 555620 (office). *E-mail:* press@ predsjednistvobih.ba (office). *Website:* www.predsjednistvobih.ba (office).

RADNER, Roy, PhD; American economist, applied mathematician and academic; *Professor of Business, Leonard N. Stern School of Business, New York University;* b. 29 June 1927, Chicago; s. of Ella Radner and Samuel Radner; m. 1st Virginia Honoski (died 1976); one s. three d. (one d. deceased); m. 2nd Charlotte V. Kuh 1978; ed Hyde Park High School, Chicago and Univ. of Chicago; served US army 1945–48; Research Assoc., Cowles Comm., Univ. of Chicago 1951–54, Asst Prof. 1954–55; Asst Prof. of Econs Yale Univ. 1955–57; Assoc. Prof. of Econs and Statistics, Univ. of Calif., Berkeley 1957–61, Prof. 1961–79, Chair. Dept of Econs 1965–69; Distinguished mem. tech. staff, AT&T Bell Labs 1979–95; Research Prof. of Econs New York Univ. 1983–95, Prof. of Econs and Information Systems 1995–96, Stern School Prof. of Business 1995–; Guggenheim Fellow 1961–62 and

1965–66; Overseas Fellow, Churchill Coll. Cambridge, UK 1969–70, 1989; Assoc. Ed. Journal of Econ. Theory 1968–, Games and Economic Behavior 1989–, Review of Economic Design 1994–, Information Systems Frontiers, 1999–; mem. NAS; Fellow, American Acad. of Arts and Sciences, Econometric Soc. (Pres. 1973); Distinguished Fellow, American Econ. Asscn, AAAS; Woytinsky Award, Univ. of Mich. 1998. *Publications:* Notes on the Theory of Economic Planning 1963, Optimal Replacement Policy (with others) 1967, Decision and Organization (co-ed.) 1972, Economic Theory of Teams (with J. Marschak) 1972, Demand and Supply in U.S. Higher Education (with L. S. Miller) 1975, Education as an Industry (co-ed.) 1976, Mathematicians in Academia (with C. V. Kuh) 1980, Information, Incentives and Economic Mechanisms (co-ed.) 1987, Perspectives on Deterrence 1989 (co-ed.), Bargaining with Incomplete Information (co-ed.) 1992; and many articles. *Leisure interests:* music, hiking, cross-country skiing. *Address:* Stern School of Business, Kaufmann Management Center, Room 8–87, New York University, 44 W Fourth Street, New York, NY 10012 (office); 3203 Davenport Street, NW, Washington, DC 20008, USA (home). *Telephone:* (212) 998-0813 (office). *Fax:* (212) 995-4228 (office). *Website:* www.stern.nyu.edu/~rradner (office).

RADOJIČIĆ, Igor, MEng; Bosnia and Herzegovina (Republika Srpska) engineer, politician and academic; *President of the National Assembly;* b. 13 Sept. 1966, Banja Luka; m.; two c.; ed Faculty of Electrical Eng, Banja Luka; on staff, Faculty of Electrical Eng, Banja Luka 1991–; mem. Savez nezavisnih socijaldemokrata (Alliance of Ind. Social Democrats), Sec.-Gen. 2003–; Deputy in Nat. Ass., Pres. Nat. Ass. 2006–; Acting Pres. of Republika Srpska Oct.–Dec. 2007. *Publications:* 14 scientific works on signal processing. *Address:* National Assembly, Vuka Karadzica 2, Banja Luka (office); c/o Savez nezavisnih socijaldemokrata, Petra Kočića 5, 78000 Banja Luka, Republika Srpska. *Telephone:* (51) 338117 (office); (51) 318492. *Fax:* (51) 338141 (office); (51) 318495. *E-mail:* predsjednik@snsd.org. *Website:* www.narodnaskupstinars.net (office); www.snsd.org.

RADOŠ, Jozo, MSc; Croatian academic, engineer and politician; b. 3 Nov. 1956, Seonica, Tomislavgrad, Bosnia-Herzegovina; m.; one s. two d.; ed Zagreb Univ.; Prof. of History and Electrical Eng, Osijek and Dakovo 1983–86; Devt Planner, Rade Kondar Co., Zagreb 1986–90; engineer, Zagreb Electric Bulb factory 1990–92; mem. House of Reps 1992–2000, 2002–08, 2011–; Observer in European Parl. 2012–13; mem. Zagreb City Ass. 1995–97, 2005–; mem. Croatian Parl. Del. to Parl. Ass. of Council of Europe 1998–2000, to Parl. Ass. of WEU 2004–08; Minister of Defence 2000–02; Acting Chair. Croatian Social Liberal Party (HSLS) 2001–02; Chair. Party of Liberal Democrats (Libra) 2002–05 (merged with Croatian People's Party to form Croatian People's Party–Liberal Democrats 2005), Vice-Pres. 2005–12; Homeland War Memorial Certificate. *Leisure interests:* mountaineering, bowling. *Address:* Hrvatska narodna stranka—Liberalni demokrati, 10000 Zagreb, Kneza Mislava 8, Croatia (office). *Telephone:* (1) 4629111 (office). *Fax:* (1) 4629110 (office). *E-mail:* hns@hns.hr (office). *Website:* www.hns.hr (office).

RADOVANOVIĆ, Nikola; Bosnia and Herzegovina government official; ed Ground Forces Acad., GHQ School, King's Coll. London and Univ. of Oxford, UK; Head of Office for Peace and Stability, Ministry of Foreign Affairs –2004; Minister of Defence 2004–07. *Address:* c/o Ministry of Defence, Hamdije Kresevljakovica 98, 71000 Sarajevo, Bosnia and Herzegovina (office).

RADWAN, Samir, BSc, MSc, PhD; Egyptian economist, international organization official and government official; ed Cairo Univ., School of Oriental and African Studies, Univ. of London; spent nearly 30 years with ILO, positions included Adviser to Dir-Gen. on Devt Policies and Counsellor on Arab Countries 2001–03; Man. Dir Econ. Research Forum, Egypt 2003–06; fmr Adviser and mem. Bd of Trustees, Gen. Authority for Investment, Egypt; fmr Exec. Dir Egyptian Nat. Competitiveness Council; fmr Lecturer, Faculty of Econs, Cairo Univ.; Minister of Finance Feb.–July 2011. *Publications:* several publications on labour markets, industrialization, development and agrarian systems and poverty. *Address:* c/o Ministry of Finance, Ministry of Finance Towers, Nasr City, Cairo, Egypt (office).

RADZIKHOVSKY, Leonid; Russian journalist and political analyst; fmr sr columnist for liberal daily newspaper, Segodnya (now defunct); currently with Rossiyskaya Gazeta; mem. RIA Novosti Expert Council. *Publications:* numerous articles in newspapers and journals. *Address:* c/o Rossiiskaya Gazeta, PO Box 40, ul. Pravdy 24, 125993 Moscow, Russia. *Telephone:* (495) 257-52-52. *Fax:* (495) 973-22-56. *E-mail:* sekretar@rg.ru. *Website:* www.rg.ru.

RADZINSKY, Edvard Stanislavovich; Russian dramatist; b. 23 Sept. 1936, Moscow; s. of Stanislav Radzinsky and Sofia Radzinsky; m. 2nd Yelena Timofeyevna Denisova; ed Inst. of History and Archival Science, Moscow. *Plays include:* My Dream is India 1960, You're All of Twenty-Two, you Old Men! 1962, One Hundred and Four Pages on Love 1964, Kolobashkin the Seducer 1967, Socrates 1977, Lunin 1980, I Stand at the Restaurant 1982, Theatre of the Time of Nero and Seneca 1984, Elderly Actress in the Role of Dostoevsky's Wife 1986, Sporting Scenes 1987, Our Decameron 1989. *Television:* author and narrator of TV series Mysteries of History 1997–. *Publications include:* novels: The Last of the Romanovs 1989, Our Decameron 1990; non-fiction: The Last Tsar: The Life and Death of Nicholas II 1992, God Save and Restrain Russia 1993, Stalin 1996, Mysteries of History 1997, Mysteries of Love 1998, Fall of Gallant Century 1998, Collected Works (7 Vols) 1998–99, Rasputin 1999, The Theatrical Novel (memoirs) 1999, Alexander II, The Last Great Tsar 2005. *Address:* Usiyevicha Street 8, Apartment 96, 125319 Moscow, Russia (home). *E-mail:* edvard@radzinski.ru (office). *Website:* www.radzinski.ru (office).

RADZIWILL, John S. A., MA; British lawyer and business executive; *Chairman, INTL FCStone Inc.;* ed Univ. of Oxford; mem. Bar of England and Wales; with Markman Securities (British investment banking firm) 1973–74; Pres. Radix Organization Inc. 1976–97, Radix Ventures Inc. 1979–95; mem. Bd of Dirs International Assets Holding Corpn (INTL) 2002– (merged with FCStone Sept. 2009), Chair. 2012–; Chair. New York Holdings Ltd, Co-founder and Chair. (non-exec.) Acquisitor PLC, fmr Chair. Acquisitor Holdings (Bermuda) Ltd; mem. Bd of Dirs Baltimore PLC 2006–, Oryx International Growth Fund Ltd 2007–, Lionheart Group, Inc., USA Micro Cap Value Co. Ltd, Goldcrown Group Ltd (and subsidiaries), New York Holdings Ltd (parent of Lionheart Advisors, Inc.); fmr mem. Bd of Dirs Interequity Capital Corpn, GP, Air Express International Corpn 1995–2000; registered rep. associated with Cohmad Securities Corpn –1997. *Address:* INTL FCStone Inc., 708 Third Avenue, 15th Floor, New York, NY 10017,

USA (office). *Telephone:* (212) 485-3500 (office). *Fax:* (212) 485-3505 (office). *E-mail:* info@intlfcstone.com (office). *Website:* www.intlfcstone.com (office).

RAE, Barbara, CBE, RA, RE, RSA, RSW, RGI, FRSE; Scottish painter and printmaker; b. 10 Dec. 1943, Falkirk, Scotland; d. of James Rae and Mary Young; one s.; ed Morrison's Acad., Crieff, Perthshire, Edinburgh Coll. of Art; Lecturer, Glasgow School of Art 1975–96; mem. Bd, Royal Fine Art Comm. 1995–; solo exhbns annually in Edinburgh, London, Bath, Dublin, Belfast and selected European and US cities; numerous group exhbns UK, USA, Germany, Norway, Netherlands, Spain, Ireland; artwork in numerous public and pvt. collections, including Scottish Nat. Gallery of Modern Art, Univs of Edinburgh, Glasgow, Aberdeen, St Andrews and York, Royal Bank of Scotland, Bank of England, Lloyds TSB Group, Robert Fleming Holdings, HRH the Duke of Edinburgh; mem. Royal Scottish Soc. of Painters and Watercolour (RSW), Royal Glasgow Inst. of the Fine Arts, Soc. of Scottish Artists, Royal Soc. of Painter-Printmakers (RE); Trustee, British School, Rome 1997–2000; Hon. Fellow, RCA, London 2003–; Dr hc (Napier Univ., Edinburgh) 2000; Hon. DLitt (Aberdeen) 2003, (St Andrews) 2008; awards include Guthrie Award, RSA 1977, May Marshall Brown Award, RSW Centenary Exhbn 1979, Sir William Gillies Travel Award 1983, Calouste Gulbenkian Printmaking Award 1983, Alexander Graham Munro Award, RSW 1989. *Publications:* Barbara Rae – Paintings 2008, Barbara Rae – Prints 2010, Barbara Rae – Sketchbooks 2011. *Leisure interest:* travel. *Address:* Royal Academy of Arts, Burlington House, Piccadilly, London, W1J 0BD, England. *Telephone:* (20) 7300-8000. *E-mail:* garethwardell@hotmail.com (office). *Website:* www.barbararae.com.

RAE, Hon. Robert (Bob) Keith, PC, OC, O.Ont., QC, BA, BPhil, LLB; Canadian lawyer, arbitrator and politician; b. 2 Aug. 1948, Ottawa; s. of Saul Rae and Lois George; m. Arlene Perly 1980; three d.; ed public school in Washington, DC, Int. School of Geneva, Univ. of Toronto and Balliol Coll., Oxford; fmr volunteer, legal aid clinics in Toronto and Asst counsel for United Steelworkers of America and Union of Injured Workers; mem. Canadian Fed. Parl. 1978–82; Prov. Leader, New Democratic Party (NDP), Ont. 1982–96; mem. Ont. Prov. Legis. 1982–95; Premier of Ontario 1990–95; Partner Goodman Phillips & Vineberg (now Goodmans LLP) 1996–2007; MP for Toronto Centre 2008–; mem. Security Intelligence Review Cttee; mem. Bd of Dirs Hydro One Inc., Niigon Technologies Ltd, Iter Canada Inc., Tembec Ltd, Trojan Technologies; Chair. Forum of Federations, Toronto Symphony Orchestra, Ivesprint, Inc., Inst. for Research on Public Policy; Chancellor Wilfrid Laurier Univ.; Adjunct Prof., Univ. of Toronto; Sr Fellow, Massey Coll.; Dr hc (Law Soc. of Upper Canada), (Univ. of Toronto), (Assumption Univ.). *Publications include:* From Protest to Power 1996, The Three Questions: Prosperity and the Public Good 1998, Ontario, A Leader in Learning 2005, Air India, Lessons to be Learned 2005. *Leisure interests:* tennis, golf, fishing, reading, music. *Address:* 514 Parliament Street, Toronto, ON M4X 1P4 (office); House of Commons, Ottawa, ON K1A 0A6, Canada (office). *Telephone:* (416) 954-2222 (office). *Fax:* (416) 954-9649 (office). *E-mail:* info@bobrae.ca (office). *Website:* www.bobrae.ca; www.bobrae .liberal.ca.

RAFAJLOVSKA, Vera, BEcons; Macedonian economist and government official; b. 26 Feb. 1947, Bitola; ed Univs of Bitola and Skopje; Asst Dir and Pnr, V&F Centre for Econ. and Legal Consulting, Skopje 1991–98; Dir Rafajlovski Consulting DOO 1998–2000, Rafajlovski Revizija DOO 2000–; Minister of the Economy 2006–08; fmr Ed.-in-Chief, Economic and Legal Adviser magazine; mem. NSDP party; also functions as a consultant in implementation of IFRS and IAS as well as a tax, accounting and financial consultant. *Publications:* author and co-author of several books in accounting, taxation, int. financial reporting. *Address:* Rafajlovski Consulting, str. Orce Nikolov 190, Skopje, Macedonia (office). *Telephone:* (2) 3088900 (office). *Fax:* (2) 3088912 (office). *E-mail:* info@rafajlovski.com.mk (office). *Website:* www.rafajlovski.com.mk (office).

RAFELSON, Bob; American film director; b. 21 Feb. 1933, New York. *Films directed include:* Head 1968, Five Easy Pieces 1970 (New York Film Critics Award), The King of Marvin Gardens 1972, Stay Hungry 1976, The Postman Always Rings Twice 1981, Black Widow 1987, Mountains of the Moon 1990, Man Trouble 1992, Wet 1993, Armed Response 1994, Blood and Wine 1997, Poodle Springs 1998, Erotic Tales-Porn.com 2002, House on Turk Street 2002, No Good Deed 2002. *Television:* The Monkees 1966–68, Modesty 1981, All Night Long 1983, Afterthoughts 2002.

RAFFARIN, Jean-Pierre; French politician; b. 3 Aug. 1948, Poitiers (Vienne); s. of Jean Raffarin and Renée Michaud; m. Anne-Marie Perrier 1980; one d.; ed Lycée Henri IV, Poitiers, Faculté de Droit, Paris-Assas, Ecole Supérieure de Commerce, Paris; Marketing Dept Cafés Jacques Vabre 1973–76; Adviser, Office of Minister of Labour 1976–81; Pres. Crédit Immobilier Rural de la Vienne 1978–95; Lecturer, Inst. d'Etudes Politiques, Paris 1979–88; Dir-Gen. Bernard Krief Communication 1981–88; Gen. Del. Inst. Euro-92 1988–89; Nat. Del., Deputy Sec.-Gen. and mem. Political Bureau, Parti Républicain 1977–2002; City Councillor, Poitiers 1977–95; Conseiller Régional 1986–88; Pres. Conseil Régional, Poitou-Charentes 1988–2002; mem. European Parl. 1989–95; Deputy Sec.-Gen. and Spokesman for Union pour la Démocratie Française 1993, Sec.-Gen. 1995–2002; Pres. Comm. Arc Atlantique 1994–1998; Minister of Small and Medium-Sized Businesses, Commerce and Craft Industry 1995–97; mem. Senate (for Vienne) 1995, 1997–2002, 2005–; Vice-Mayor of Chasseneuil-du-Poitou 1995–2001; Vice-Pres. Démocratie Libérale 1997–2002 (merged with Union pour un Mouvement Populaire, UMP 2002), First Vice-Pres. UMP 2002–; Pres. Asscn des régions de France 1998–2002; Prime Minister of France 2002–05; Grand Officier, Légion d'honneur, Grand Croix, Ordre nat. du Mérite 2002, Officier, Ordre nat. du Québec 2003, Grand Cross, Order of the Star of Romania 2004. *Publications:* La vie en jaune 1977, La publicité nerf de la communication 1983, L'avenir a ses racines 1986, Nous sommes tous les régionaux 1988, Pour une morale de l'action 1992, Le livre de l'Atlantique 1994, Notre Contrat pour l'Alternance 2001, La Nouvelle Gouvernance 2002, La France de Mai 2003, La dernière marche 2007. *Leisure interests:* contemporary painting, regional literature. *Address:* Senat, 15 rue de Vaugirard, 75291 Paris Cedex 06; Union pour un Mouvement Populaire, 55 rue La Boétie 75384 Paris Cedex 08 (office); 7 route de Saint-Georges, 86360 Chasseneuil-du-Poitou, France (home). *Telephone:* 1-42-34-20-00 (Senat) (office); 1-40-76-60-00 (UMP) (office). *Fax:* 1-42-34-26-77 (office). *E-mail:* jpr@carnetjpr.com (office). *Website:* www.senat.fr (office); www.carnetjpr.com (office).

RAFFENNE, Gen. Jean-Paul; French army officer (retd); b. 1944; Liaison Officer, Fort Leavenworth, USA 1990–92; Deputy Defence Attaché, Embassy in Washington, DC 1994–96; Head, French Del. to EU Mil. Cttee 2001; Chief French Liaison Officer in unit directing Operation Enduring Freedom (mil. campaign in Afghanistan), Tampa, Fla., USA 2001; Head, Direction du renseignement militaire (mil. intelligence agency) 2002; currently Prof. and Dir, Sr Exec. Seminar, George C. Marshall Center European Center for Security Studies, Germany. *Address:* George C. Marshall Center, Gernackerstrasse 2, 82467 Garmisch-Partenkirchen, Germany (office). *Telephone:* (8821) 750-2680 (office). *E-mail:* cisscontact@ marshallcenter.org (office). *Website:* www.marshallcenter.org (office).

RAFINI, Brigi; Niger government official and politician; *Prime Minister;* b. 7 April 1953, Iférouane, Agadez Dist; ed École nat. d'admin, Niamey, Inst. Int. d'admin publique and École nat. d'admin, Paris, France; mem. Mouvement nat. pour la société de développement—Nassara 1989–91, left to join Alliance nigérienne pour la démocratie et le progrès social—Zaman Lahiya (breakaway faction) 1993–96, co-f. Rassemblement pour la démocratie et le progrès—Djamaa; currently mem. Parti nigérien pour la démocratie et le socialisme—Tarayya; spent several years as civil servant; served several terms as mayor of Iferouane Dist; Minister of Agriculture in late 1980s; elected mem. Assemblée Nat. (Parl.) for Agadez region 2004, Fourth Vice-Pres., Assemblée Nat. 2004–09, Prime Minister 2011–. *Address:* Office of the Prime Minister, BP 893, Niamey, Niger (office). *Telephone:* 20-72-26-99 (office). *Fax:* 20-73-58-59 (office).

RAFIQUE, Muhammad; Pakistani trade union official; *President, National Trade Union Federation of Pakistan;* b. 3 Oct. 1942, Delhi, India; s. of Muhammad Umer; m.; three s. two d.; technician Karachi Water and Sewerage Bd 1971; currently man. of tech. affairs, water treatment plant; joined local union 1972; Treas. Nat. Trade Union Fed. (NTUF), Pres. 1999–; Pres. KMC United Workers Housing Soc.; Best Trade Unionist Award, NTUF-SINDH. *Leisure interest:* singing. *Address:* National Trade Union Federation Pakistan, Bharocha Bldg. 2-B/6, Commercial Area, Nazimabad No. 2, Karachi 74600, Pakistan (office). *Telephone:* (21) 6622361 (office). *Fax:* (21) 6622529 (office). *E-mail:* ntuf@super .netpak (office).

RAFSANJANI, Hojatoleslam Ali Akhbar Hashemi; Iranian ecclesiastic and politician; b. 25 Aug. 1934, Rafsanjan, Kerman prov.; ed Qom; Speaker, Islamic Consultative Ass. 1980–89; MP –2000; Founding mem. Islamic Repub. Party; Acting C-in-C of the Armed Forces 1988–89; Vice-Chair. Cttee to revise the Constitution 1989; Pres. of the Islamic Repub. of Iran 1989–97; Chair. Expediency Council of Iran 2002–; mem. Ass. of Experts (Majlis-E-Khobregan) representing Tehran, Vice Chair. and First Deputy Speaker 2006–07, Chair. 2007–11. *Address:* Expediency Council, POB 13165-311, Pastor Street, Tehran, Iran. *E-mail:* info@ maslahat.ir. *Website:* www.maslehat.ir; www.hashemirafsanjani.ir.

RAFTER, Patrick Michael; Australian fmr professional tennis player; b. 28 Dec. 1972, Mount Isa, Queensland; s. of Jim Rafter and Jocelyn Rafter; pnr Lara Feltham; one s.; turned professional 1991; Grand Slam highlights: semi-finalist French Open 1997; winner US Open 1997, 1998; semi-finalist Wimbledon 1999, finalist 2000, 2001; semi-finalist Australian Open 2001; winner Australia Open Doubles title (with Jonas Bjorkman) 1999; sustained serious shoulder injury and took extended break from tennis following Australia's Davis Cup defeat in Dec. 2001; winner of 11 singles titles, 10 doubles titles; announced retirement Jan. 2003; brief comeback (doubles only) 2004; f. Patrick Rafter Cherish the Children Foundation 1999; ATP Newcomer of the Year 1993, Awarded Diploma of Honor International Committee for Fair Play by International Olympic Committee 1997, ATP Tour Stefan Edberg Sportsmanship Award 1997, Australian Sports Personality of the Year Award 1997, Media Sports Personality of the Year Award 1997, ATP Arthur Ash Humanitarian Award 1998, Australian People's Choice Award - Male Sports Star 1998, Awarded Honorary Ambassador for Queensland (presented with the keys to city of Brisbane) 1998, Queensland Young Achiever Award 1998, ATP Tour Stefan Edberg Sportsmanship Award 1998, ATP Tour's Web site Star of the Year Award 1999, Australian People's Choice Award - Male Sports Star 1999, ATP Tour Stefan Edberg Sportsmanship Award 2000, ANSVAR The Bill Brown Community Award 2000, ATP Tour Stefan Edberg Sportsmanship Award 2001, Australian Of The Year 2002. *Leisure interests:* golf, fishing. *Address:* c/o Patrick Rafter Cherish the Children Foundation, POB 1855, Noosa Heads, Queensland 4567, Australia (office). *Fax:* (7) 5455 4433 (office). *Website:* www .cherishthechildren.com.au (office).

RAGHAVAN, T.C.A. (Tirumallai Cunnuvakum Anandanpillai), MA, PhD; Indian diplomatist; *High Commissioner to Pakistan;* b. Dec. 1955, Nagpur; m. Ranjana Raghavan; two d.; ed St Stephen's Coll., Jawaharlal Nehru Univ.; with Embassy in Kuwait 1983–86, Embassy in Bhutan 1992–95, High Comm. in UK 1995–98, Deputy High Commr to Pakistan 2003–07, Head, Ministry of External Affairs Div. for Pakistan, Afghanistan and Iran –2009, High Commr to Singapore 2009–13, High Commr to Pakistan 2013–. *Address:* Indian High Commission, G-5, Diplomatic Enclave, Islamabad, Pakistan (office). *Telephone:* (51) 2206950 (office). *Fax:* (51) 2823102 (office). *E-mail:* info2.islamabad@mea.gov.in (office). *Website:* www.india.org.pk (office).

RAGHEB, Ali Abu, BSc; Jordanian politician; b. 1946, Amman; ed Univ. of Tennessee, USA; Pnr and Man. Dir National Engineering and Contracting Co. 1971–91; Minister of Industry and Trade 1991, 1995, Minister of Energy and Mineral Resources 1991–93; elected mem. Nat. Ass. 1993; Prime Minister of Jordan and Minister of Defence 2000–03 (resgnd); Grand Cordon of the Order of Al-Kawkab Al-Urduni, Grand Cordon of the Order of Al-Nahda, Kt Grand Cross (Italy), GCMG (UK). *Address:* c/o National Assembly, 72 Amman 11118, Jordan (office).

RAGNEMALM, Hans, LLD; Swedish judge; b. 30 March 1940, Laholm; m. Vivi Ragnemalm 1961; Assoc. Prof. of Public Law, Univ. of Lund 1970–75; Prof. of Public Law, Univ. of Stockholm 1975–87, Dean, Faculty of Law 1984–87; Parl. Ombudsman 1987–92; Judge, Supreme Admin. Court 1992–94, Justice 1999, Pres. 2000–05; currently Juris Ombudsman; Judge, European Court of Justice 1995–99; Alt. Mem. Court of Conciliation and Arbitration, OSCE. *Publications:* Appealability of Administrative Decisions 1970, Extraordinary Remedies in Administrative Procedure Law 1973, Elements of Administrative Procedure Law 1977, The Constitution of Sweden 1980, Administrative Justice in Sweden 1991; numerous

other books and articles. *Address:* c/o Regeringsrätten, PO Box 2293, 103 17 Stockholm, Sweden. *Telephone:* (8) 6176212 (office). *Fax:* (8) 6176234 (office).

RAGON, Michel, Dr d'Etat-ès-Lettres; French writer and lecturer; b. 24 June 1924, Marseille; s. of Aristide Ragon and Camille Sourisseau; m. Françoise Antoine 1968; worked in manual jobs from the age of 14; lived in Paris 1945–, bookseller on the Seine embankments 1954–64; art critic, architectural historian, novelist; Lecturer, l'Ecole Nat. Supérieure des Arts Décoratifs, Paris 1972–85; Chevalier, Ordre du Mérite, Légion d'honneur, Commdr des Arts et des Lettres; Prix de l'Acad. Française et de l'Acad. d'Architecture. *Publications:* Histoire mondiale de l'architecture et de l'urbanisme modernes 1971–78, L'homme et les villes 1975, L'espace de la mort 1981, L'art abstrait 1973–74, L'art pour quoi faire? 1971, 25 ans d'art vivant 1969, Histoire de la littérature prolétarienne en France 1974, L'accent de ma mère 1980, Ma soeur aux yeux d'Asie 1982, Les mouchoirs rouges de Cholet 1984, La louve de Mervent 1985, Le marin des sables 1988, La mémoire des vaincus 1990, Le Cocher du Boiroux 1992, Journal de l'Art Abstrait 1992, Le roman de Rabelais 1994, Les Coquelicots sont revenus 1996, Un si bel espoir 1999, Georges et Louise 2000, Un rossignol chantait 2001, Cinquante ans d'art vivant 2001, Un amour de Jeanne 2003, La ferme d'en haut 2005, Le prisonnier 2007, Dictionnaire de l'Anarchie 2009, Ils se croyaient illustres et immortels 2011, Journal d'un critique d'art désabusé 2013. *Address:* 4 rue du Faubourg Poissonnière, 75010 Paris, France. *Telephone:* 1-48-24-66-47.

RAGOUSSIS, Yiannis; Greek politician; *Minister of Infrastructures;* b. 11 Dec. 1965, Athens; m. Katerina Roussou; one s. two d.; ed Aristotle Univ. of Thessaloniki, Univ. of Sussex, UK; joined Panhellenic Socialist Movt (PASOK) 1983, mem. Cen. Cttee 1994–96, Spokesman 2007–08, Gen. Sec. Political Council of PASOK 2008–09; Gen. Dir Research Centre for Equality Issues (KETHI) 1994–95, Special Adviser to European Commr Christos Papoutsis 1995–98; elected Mayor of Paros Island 2002 (re-elected) 2006, mem. Bd in Cyclades Pref.'s Local Union of Municipalities and Communities; mem. Parl. (PASOK) 2007–; Minister of the Interior, Decentralization and e-Governance 2009–11, of Infrastructures 2011–. *Address:* Ministry of Infrastructures, Odos Anastaseos 2, 101 91 Athens (office); 37 Harilaou Trikoupi Street, 106 80 Athens, Greece. *Telephone:* (210) 6508000 (office); (210) 3665401. *Fax:* (210) 6508088 (office); (210) 3665409. *E-mail:* ragoussis@pasok.gr (office); press@yme.gov.gr (office). *Website:* www.yme.gr (office); www.hellenicparliament.gr (office).

RAHBANI, Ziad; Lebanese composer, singer and playwright; b. 1956, Antelias; s. of Assi Rahbani and Nuhad Haddad (née Fairuz); m. Dalal Karam (divorced); composer of numerous songs for mother Fairuz (successful Lebanese singer); contributor to several political radio shows including Bazdna Taybeen Oulou Allah and El Akl Zeeneh; columnist, Al-Akhbar (daily newspaper) 2006–; well known as satirist of Lebanese politics. *Recordings:* solo albums: Belly Dance 1972, Bil Afrah 1972, Sahrieh - Songs 1973, Abou Ali 1979, Ana Mosh Kafer 1985, Hodou' Nisbi 1985, Bema Enno 1996, Amrak Seedna 2000, Bnisba la boukra shou Monodose 2001, Live at Damascus Citadel 2009. *Plays:* Sahriyyeh 1973, Nazl el Sourour 1974, Bennesbe La Boukra Shou? 1978, Film Ameriki Taweel 1980, Shi fashel 1983, Bikhsous el Karameh wel Shaab el aaneed 1993, Lawla Fos'hat el Amali 1994. *Address:* c/o Al-Akhbar, POB 5963-113, 6th Floor, Concorde Centre, rue Verdun, Beirut, Lebanon (office).

RAHEEN, Sayed Makhdoom, MA, PhD; Afghan diplomatist, politician and writer; *Minister of Information and Culture;* b. 1946, Kabul; ed Tehran Univ., Iran; apptd Lecturer, Kabul Univ. 1973; fmr Head of Bureau of Afghan Culture and Art, Ministry of Information, Culture and Tourism; fmr mem. Drafting Cttee of Constitution of Afghanistan; mem. Grand Nat. Ass. (Loya Jirga) 1976; put under house arrest following Communist coup d'etat April 1978; moved to Pakistan after Soviet invasion; apptd mem. High Council and Chair. Cttee of Culture and Publicity, Islamic Unity of Afghanistan Mujahedeen 1982; selected as Head of Radio Free Kabul by Mujahidin parties; served as adviser with rank of Minister to Pres. of Afghan Interim Govt; co-f. Nat. Islamic Movt of Afghanistan in Peshawar, Pakistan 1988; abandoned Afghan resistance and left for USA following disagreements with Jihad leaders 1991; Co-founder and first Chair. Asscn for Peace and Democracy for Afghanistan 1996; mem. Exec. Cttee Loya Jirga, Rome 1998; selected as Minister of Information, Culture and Tourism of Interim Admin, Bonn Conf. 2002; Chair. Kabul City Council 2003; Amb. to India 2007–09; Minister of Information and Culture Dec. 2009–; Medal for serving the freedom of speech and promoting cultural activities, presented by HM Zahir Shah 2004. *Publications include:* Tears of Khorasan, The Mourners, Reply to Khalili (poetry), Today's Muslims (in Pashto); several books and articles on culture, literature, history and Islamic Sufism, the works of Sayed Jamaludeen Afghani, Daqiqi Nama, research on Amir Khosrow, and the relations of Afghanistan and the subcontinent; f. and published resistance magazines and papers, in Dari, Pashto, Urdu, Arabic and English. *Address:* Ministry of Information and Culture, Mohammad Jan Khan Wat, Kabul 110 021, Afghanistan (office). *Telephone:* (20) 2101301 (office). *Fax:* (20) 2101301 (office). *Website:* moic.afghanistan.af (office).

RAHIM, Arbab Ghulam, MB BS; Pakistani physician and politician; b. 15 Sept. 1956, Mirpurkhas Dist, Sindh Prov.; s. of Arbab Taj Muhammad; m.; ed Cadet Coll. Petaro, Sind Medical Coll., Karachi; Chair. Dist Council, Mirpurkhas 1984–87; Public Health Eng and Rural Devt Adviser to Chief Minister of Sindh 1988; elected to Nat. Ass. 1993, 1996, 1999, Chair. Steering Cttee for Ind. Mems, Standing Cttee on Commerce, Parl. Sec. for Water and Power; Prov. Minister of Sindh for Local Govt, Katchi Abadis and Public Health Eng 2000, for Works and Services 2003–04; Chief Minister of Sindh and Leader of the House 2004–07; Founding Pres. Sindh Democratic Alliance 1999–2000; beaten with shoes by mob of political activists and fmr servants 7 April 2008. *Address:* Khetlari, Tehsil Diplo, District Tharparkar, Sindh, Pakistan (home). *Telephone:* (21) 5383114 (home).

RAHIMOV, Saidahmad Borievich, PhD; Uzbekistani politician and banker; *Chairman, National Bank for Foreign Economic Activity;* b. 1960; m.; three c.; ed Tashkent Inst. of Agriculture; Asst Sr Teacher, Tashkent Econ. Inst. 1989–93; fmr Presidential Adviser for Socioeconomic Affairs; fmr Chair., Auditing Comm.; fmr Man. Asaka Bank; Minister of Finance 2004–05; currently Chair. Nat. Bank for Foreign Economic Activity; Dustlik Medal 2010. *Address:* National Bank for Foreign Economic Activity, 100047 Tashkent, Uzbekistan (office). *Telephone:* (71)

133-62-87 (office). *Fax:* (71) 132-01-72 (office). *E-mail:* webmaster@central.nbu .com (office). *Website:* www.eng.nbu.com (office).

RAHMAN, A. S. F.; Bangladeshi business executive; *Chairman, Beximco Group;* Chair. Beximco Group, including Beximco Pharmaceutical Ltd, Beximco Holdings Ltd, Beximco Agro-Chemicals Ltd, Beximco Foods Ltd, Beximco Synthetics Ltd, Comtrade Beximco Apparels Ltd, Sonali Ansh., Beximco Infusions Ltd; Dir IPDC; mem. Bd of Govs Bangladesh Enterprise Inst. *Address:* Beximco Pharmaceuticals Ltd, 17 Dhanmondi R/A, Road 2, Dhaka 1205, Bangladesh (office). *Telephone:* (2) 9127721 (office). *Fax:* (2) 8613470 (office). *Website:* www.beximco.net (office).

RAHMAN, Allah Rakha (A. R.); Indian musician (keyboards), singer and composer; b. (A. S. Dileep Kumar), 6 Jan. 1967, Chennai; s. of the late R. K. Sekhar and of Kareema Begum; m. Saira Banu; three c.; ed Padma Seshadri Bal Bhavan, Madras Christian Coll. and Trinity Coll. of Music, London; studied piano aged four; began musical career aged 11 as keyboard player, performing with Illaiyaraja's troupe, later with orchestras of M. S. Vishwanathan and Ramesh Naidu; mem. local rock bands, including Roots, Magic and Nemesis Avenue; began composing 1987–; f. Panchathan Record Inn studio 1989; performances and recordings with many artists, including Nusrat Fateh Ali Khan, Apache Indian, Zakir Hussein, Dr L. Shankar, Talvin Singh, Dominic Miller, David Byrne and Michael Jackson (Friends of the World, Munich 2002); has created music for many TV and radio advertisements as well as scores for corp. videos and documentaries; fuses music of different traditions (Western classical, reggae, rock and Karnatic music); apptd Global Amb. of WHO Stop TB Partnership project 2004; UN Amb. for 2015 Millennium Devt Goals; f. A R Rahman Foundation, KM Music Conservatory, Chennai; Dr hc (Aligarh Muslim Univ.), (Middlesex Univ.); SuMu Music Award 1993, R. D. Burman Awards 1993, 1995, Telega Purashkar Award 1992, 1993, 1994, Filmfare Awards 1992–2002, Padma Shree 2000, Awadh Sammaan UP govt 2001, Al-Ameen Educ. Soc. Community Award 2001, Amir Khusro Sangeet Nawaz Award 2002, Lata Mangeshkar Samman, MP govt 2005, Mahavir Mahatma Award, Oneness Foundation 2005, Stanford Univ. Award for contrib. to Global Music 2006, Bommai Nagi Reddy Award, Rajiv Gandhi Award, Padma Bhushan 2010; several other nat. and int. awards. *Selected film soundtracks include:* Roja (Nat. Film Award 1993, Cinema Express Award 1993) 1992, Gentleman (Cinema Express Award 1994) 1993, Kadhalan (Cinema Express Award 1995) 1994, Kadhal Desam (Screen-Videocon Awards 1997, Cinema Express Award 1997) 1996, Minsaara Kanavu (Nat. Film Award for Best Music Direction 1998, Screen-Videocon Award 1998) 1997, Dil Se… (Zee Sangeet Award, MTV-VMA Award 1999) 1998 Jeans (Cinema Express Award 1999) 1998, Taal (Screen-Videocon Award 2000, Zee Cine Award 2000, Zee Gold Bollywood Award 2000, Int. India Film Award 2000) 1999, Lagaan (Nat. Film Award) 2001, Elizabeth – The Golden Age 2007, Slumdog Millionaire (Golden Globe Award for Best Musical Score 2009, BAFTA Award for Best Film Music 2009, Academy Award for Best Original Score 2009, Academy Award for Best Original Song (music) 2009, Grammy Awards for Best Compilation Soundtrack Album for Motion Picture 2010, Best Song Written for Motion Picture 2010) 2008, Vinnaithaandi Varuvaayaa (Filmfare Best Music Dir Award (Tamil), Vijay Best Music Dir Award) 2010, Ye Maaya Chesave (CineMAA Award for Best Music Dir, Filmfare Best Music Dir Award (Telugu) 2010, 127 Hours (Denver Film Critics Soc. Award) 2010, Rockstar (Filmfare Best Music Dir Award, Zee Cine Best Music Dir Award, Screen Best Music Dir Award) 2011, Ekk Deewana Tha 2012. *TV soundtracks include:* Vande Mataram (Screen-Videocon Award 1998) 1997. *Musicals include:* Bombay Dreams (with Don Black) 2001, The Lord of the Rings (with Varttina) (Princess of Wales Theatre, Toronto) 2006. *Recordings include:* Deen Isai Malai (Muslim devotional songs) 1988, Set Me Free (launch album of Malgudi Subha) 1992, Vande Mataram 1997, Jana Gana Mana 2000, Pray For Me Brother 2007, Thenvandhu Paayedhu, Connections, Andhi Maalai, Gurus of Peace, Harem, Indian Mantra. *Leisure interest:* singing. *Address:* c/o The Really Useful Group, 22 Tower Street, London, WC2H 9TW, England. *E-mail:* info@arrahman.com. *Website:* www.arrahman.com.

RAHMAN, Atiur, BA (Hons), MA, PhD; Bangladeshi economist, academic and central banker; *Governor and Chairman, Bangladesh Bank (Central Bank of Bangladesh);* b. 1951; m. Prof. Shahana Rahman; three d.; ed Mirzapur Cadet Coll., Univ. of Dhaka, School of Oriental and African Studies, Univ. of London, UK (Commonwealth Scholarship); Chair. Bd of Trustees Shamunnay (centre for devt research); also served as Chair. Unnayan Shamannay (non-profit org. for research, devt and cultural learning); fmr Sr Research Fellow, Bangladesh Inst. of Devt Studies; Commonwealth Devt Fellowship, Univ. of Manitoba, Canada 1989, Ford Foundation Post-doctoral Fellowship, Univ. of London 1991–92, Visiting Research Fellowship, Inst. of South-East Asian Studies, Singapore 1998–99; Prof. of Econs, Dept of Devt, Univ. of Dhaka 2006–09; Gov. and Chair. Bangladesh Bank (Cen. Bank of Bangladesh) 2009–; fmr visiting/adjunct prof. at several univs; fmr Dir several socio-cultural orgs, including Biswa Sahitya Kendra and Monajatuddin Smriti Sangsad; Project Dir/Team Leader on 22 int. and 58 nat. socio-econ. devt projects; participated in 75 int. and more than 250 nat. workshops; fmr Chair. Janata Bank, Credit Devt Forum; fmr mem. Bd of Dirs Sonali Bank; fmr Gen. Sec. Bangladesh Econ. Asscn; Life mem. Asiatic Soc. (Bangladesh), Bangla Acad.; Atish Dipankar Gold Medal 2000, Chandrabati Gold Medal 2008. *Publications:* 45 books (16 in English and 29 in Bangla); numerous papers in nat. and int. journals. *Address:* Office of the Governor, Bangladesh Bank, Motijheel C/A, PO Box 325, Dhaka 1000, Bangladesh (office). *Telephone:* (2) 7120106 (office). *Fax:* (2) 9566212 (office). *E-mail:* governor@bangladeshbank.org.bd (office); governor@bangla.net (office). *Website:* www.bangladeshbank.org.bd (office); www.bangladesh-bank.org (office).

RAHMAN, Atta-Ur, BSc, MSc, PhD, FRS, FRSC; Pakistani politician, chemist and academic; *President, Pakistan Academy of Sciences;* b. 20 Sept. 1942, Delhi, India; s. of Jameel-Ur-Rahman and Amtul Subhan; m. Nargis Begum; ed Coventry Univ. and Univ. of Cambridge, UK, Karachi Univ.; Lecturer in Chem., Karachi Univ. 1964–69, Asst Prof. 1969–74, Assoc. Prof. 1974–81, Prof. 1981–2011, Prof. Emer. 2011–; Fellow, King's Coll. Cambridge 1969–73, Hon. Life Fellow 2007–; Co-Dir Husein Ebrahim Jamal Research Inst. of Chem. 1977–81, apptd Dir 1990; Co-ordinator-Gen., Org. of Islamic Conf. (OIC) Standing Cttee on Scientific and Technological Co-operation (COMSTECH) 1996–2012; Fed. Minister for Science and Tech. 1999–2002, for Educ. 2002; Chair. Higher Educ. Comm. (rank of Fed. Minister) 2002–08; Adviser to Prime Minister and Minister, Ministry of Science

and Tech. 2003–04, Adviser to Prime Minister on Science and Tech. 2002–08; Pres. Chem. Soc. of Pakistan 1992, Network of Acads of Science in the Countries of the Org. of Islamic Conf. (NASIC) 2007–; Vice-Pres. Pakistan Acad. of Sciences 1997–2001, Pres. 2003–06, 2011–; Chair. Working Group on Science and Tech. (Pakistan) 1998–2003; Scientific Adviser to CIBA Foundation, London 1995; mem. Nat. Comm. for Science and Tech. 1985, Steering Cttee for Establishment of Chem. Centre in Trieste, Italy; mem. editorial bds of several int. journals, Advisory Bd Journal of Pharmacy of Istanbul Univ., Turkey 1998; mem. ACS, American Soc. of Pharmacognosy, Swiss Chemical Soc., New York Acad. of Sciences, Russian Acad. of Sciences, Repub. of Uzbekistan Acad. of Natural Sciences; Fellow, Third World Acad. of Sciences 1985 (Vice-Pres. (Cen. and S Asia) Council), Islamic Acad. of Sciences 1988; Foreign Fellow, Korean Acad. of Science and Tech. 2004; Commonwealth Scholar 1985–86; Hon. Fellow, Chinese Chemical Soc. 2012–; Tamgha-I-Imtiaz 1983, Sitara-I-Imtiaz 1991, Hilal-I-Imtiaz 1998, Nishan-I-Imtiaz 2002, Grand Decoration of Honour in Gold with Sash (Austria); Hon. ScD (Cambridge) 1987, Hon. DEduc (Coventry) 2007; several awards, including Pakistan Acad. of Sciences Gold Medal 1977, 1984, 1996, Gold Medal, Govt of Kuwait 1980, Best Scientist of the Year Award, Govt of Pakistan 1986, FPCCI Prize for Technological Innovation (Pakistan) 1985, Scientist of the Year (Pakistan) 1987, Islamic Org. Prize for Science (Kuwait) 1988, First Prize at Sixth Khwrazmi Festival, Pres. of Iran 1993, Baba-I-Urdu Award (Pakistan) 1994, Salimuzzaman Siddiqui Gold Medal, Pakistan Intellectuals Forum 1995, Prime Minister's Gold Medal 1995, Pakistan Acad. of Sciences-INFAQ Foundation Prize in Science 1995, Fed. of Asian Chemical Socs Award (Japan) 1997, Third World Acad. of Sciences Award 1999, UNESCO Science Prize (first Muslim scientist) 1999, ECO Prize 2000, ISESCO Chem. Award 2001, Gold Medal of the Scientific Partnership Charitable Foundation, Inter Bio Screen Ltd, Russia 2004, Int. Scientific Cooperation Award, Chinese Acad. of Sciences 2013. *Achievements:* 27 patents. *Publications:* has written or edited 116 books, 65 book chapters, 701 research papers in leading int. scientific journals. *Leisure interests:* reading, cricket, table tennis. *Address:* Pakistan Academy of Sciences, 3-Constitution Avenue, Sector G-5/2, Islamabad (office); House No. 35, Ministers' Enclave, Islamabad, Pakistan (home). *Telephone:* (21) 9202603 (home) *Fax:* (51) 2823850 (home). *E-mail:* pas.editor@gmail.com (office); attast@comsats.net.pk. *Website:* www.paspk.org (office).

RAHMAN, Latifur, LLB, MA; Bangladeshi judge (retd); b. 1 March 1936, Jessore Town; s. of the late Khan Bahadur Lutfor Rahman; ed Jessore Zilla School, Dhaka Coll. and Dhaka Univ.; Lecturer in English, Jagannath Coll. and Suhrawardy Coll., Dhaka; Advocate of the Dhaka High Court 1960; Advocate of the then Supreme Court of Pakistan 1965; Additional Judge, Supreme Court of Bangladesh, High Court Div. 1979, Permanent Judge 1981, Judge of the Appellate Div. 1990; Chief Justice of Bangladesh 2000–01; Chief Adviser of the Caretaker Govt of Bangladesh July–Oct. 2001; Head Interim Govt which conducted elections –2002. *Address:* Dhanmondi, Dhaka, Bangladesh (office).

RAHMAN, Mir Shakil-ur-; Pakistani media executive and philanthropist; *CEO, Jang Group;* s. of Mir Khalil-ur-Rahman; Founder and CEO GEO TV (24-hour news network), CEO Jang Group (part-owner of Independent Media Corpn which publishes several newspapers and magazines in Urdu and English and also owns GEO TV); Pres. Council of Pakistan Newspapers Eds 1995–96, 2003–04, All Pakistan Newspapers Soc., Pakistan Broadcasters' Asscn; selected as one of 25 Stars of Asia by Business Week magazine 2005. *Address:* Jang Group of Newspapers, Printing House, I.I. Chundrigar Road, Karachi 74200, Pakistan (office). *E-mail:* groupeditor@janggroup.com.pk (office). *Website:* www.jang.com.pk (office); www.jang.net (office); www.geo.tv (office).

RAHMAN, Air Marshal (retd) Shah Mohammad Ziaur; Bangladeshi air force officer; b. 1955, Gopalgonj; m. Shameema Parveen; one s. one d.; ed Univ. Defence Services Command & Staff Coll., Dhaka, Pakistan Air Force Air War Coll., Nat. Defence Coll., Pakistan, Exec. Course seminars, USA Asia Pacific Centre for Security Studies, Mil. and Peace Keeping Operations in Accordance with Rule of Law course, RI, USA; guerrilla fighter in Dhaka area during Liberation War of Bangladesh 1971; joined Bangladesh Air Force (BAF) as flight cadet 1975, commissioned in Gen. Duties (Pilot) br. 1976; qualified fighter pilot and Qualified Flying Instructor of BAF with more than 2,400 flying hours; has flown almost all types of fighter aircraft in BAF, including MiG-21MF, A-5IIIA, F-6, F-7MB, L-39ZA, FT-5, FT-6, FT-7B as well as Bell Helicopters; has held command positions with most of the air squadrons of BAF; commanded BAF's two fighter squadrons, 25 Squadron and 35 Squadron; Directing Staff and Sr Instructor in Defence Services, Command and Staff Coll., Mirpur 1994–98; commanded Flying Wing of BAF Base Bashar, Dhaka 1999; Deputy Commdt BAF Acad. 2000; also held several staff command positions, including Air Officer Commdg, Paharkanchanpur, Air Officer Commdg, Bashar and Air Officer Commdg, Jahurul Huq 2001–05; Asst Chief of Air Staff (Operations and Training) at Air HQ 2005–07; promoted from Air Cdre to Air Vice-Marshal and apptd Chief of Air Staff 2007–12; promoted to Air Marshal (first ever) 2007; Pres. Nat. Hockey Fed. *Leisure interest:* golf. *Address:* c/o Directorate of Communication & Electronics, Air Force Headquarters, Dhaka Cantonment, Bangladesh. *E-mail:* dce@baf.mil.bd.

RAHMANI, Chérif, PhD; Algerian politician; *Minister of Industry, Small and Medium-sized Enterprises and Investment Promotion;* b. 16 Jan. 1945, Aïn Oussera; s. of Caïd Bouamama; m.; four c.; ed Ecole Nat. d'Admin; fmr Prof., Univ. of Poitiers; fmr Prof., Ecole Nat. d'Admin; fmr Sub-Man. Local Communities, Ministry of the Interior, also Dir Admin and Local Finances and Gen. Man. Local Communities; fmr Inspector Gen., Presidency of the Repub.; fmr Wali de Tébessa; fmr Wali of Algiers; fmr Sec. Gen. to the Ministry of the Interior; Minister of Youth and Sport 1988–89, of Equipment 1989–90, for Equipment and Regional Planning, Minister Gov. of Greater Algiers, on Mission Extraordinary in Charge of Admin of Wilaya of Algiers; fmr Minister of Territorial Planning and the Environment; currently Minister of Industry, Small and Medium-sized Enterprises and Investment Promotion; UNEP Champion of the Earth Laureate 2007. *Address:* Ministry of Industry, Small and Medium-sized Enterprises and Investment Promotion, Immeuble de la Colisée, 2 rue Ahmed Bey, el-Biar, Algiers, Algeria (office). *Telephone:* (21) 23-91-43 (office). *Fax:* (21) 23-94-88 (office). *Website:* www.mipi.dz (office).

RAHMON, Emomali, BEcons; Tajikistani politician and head of state; *President and Chairman of the Government;* b. (Imamali Rahmonov), 5 Oct. 1952, Dangar, Kulob Oblast; m. Azizmo Asadullayeva; nine c.; ed Lenin Tajikistan State Univ.; served in USSR army; early jobs as electrician, salesman, as trade union sec. and on various CP cttees; Dir Dangarin Sovkhoz (Soviet farm), Kulob Oblast 1982–92, Chair. Union Cttee 1976–88; Chair. Kulob Oblast Exec. Cttee 1992; Chair. Majlisi Oli (Supreme Ass.) 1992–94; Pres. of Tajikistan and Chair. of the Govt 1994–; Leader, People's Democratic Party of Tajikistan; Dr hc (Taras Shevchenko Kyiv Univ.) 2008, (Inst. of Oriental Studies, Russian Acad. of Sciences) 2009; World Peace Corps Acad. Gold Medal 2000, Anniversary Award '10 Year Old Astana', Olympic Award of Asia 2009, Golden Medal of FIAS 2009, Golden Medal of UNESCO by Jalolidinni Rumi 2009. *Address:* Office of the President, 734023 Dushanbe, Xiyoboni Rudaki 80, Tajikistan (office). *Telephone:* (372) 21-25-20 (office). *Fax:* (372) 21-25-20 (office). *E-mail:* mail@president.tj (office). *Website:* www.president.tj (office).

RAHMOUNI, Hassan, LLM, PhD; Moroccan lawyer, academic and politician; b. 10 Dec. 1949; m.; four c.; ed Fairfax High School, Va, USA, Mohammed V Univ., Rabat, Univ. of Paris (Sorbonne), France; Chief of Legal Service, Office for Industrial Devt, Ministry of Industry 1975–77; Asst Prof., Lecturer and Chair Prof., School of Law and Econs, Mohammed V Univ., Rabat 1977–98; Prof. of Admin. Law, Moroccan Royal Mil. Acad. 1977–80, Prof. of English Terminology in Law 1983–85; Prof. and Staff Coordinator, US Peace Corps, Michigan State Univ. 1981; Prof. of Law, Institut Nat. d'Aménagement et d'Urbanisme, Ministry of Urban Devt 1981–82; Counsellor to Cabinet of Minister of Admin. Affairs 1987–88; Dir of Gen. Matters, Ministry of Communication 1989–92; Gov. of Mohammedia, apptd by King Hassan II 1992–93; Gov. of Mohammedia (Casablanca) 1994–98; Prof. of Constitutional Law, Political Science and Local Admin, Hassan II Univ. 1998–2005, Vice-Pres. of Hassan II Univ. 2002–03; currently attorney and legal consultant, Casablanca; Visiting Prof., Indiana State Univ. 2000–04, Wayne State Univ. 2000, Purdue Univ. 2001; Program Dir Indiana State Univ., funded by USAID 2003; consultant to Govt of Equatorial Guinea 1992, Govt of Congo 1992; Vice-Pres. Moroccan Nat. Asscn for Governance; mem. Casablanca Order of Lawyers, Moroccan Fulbright Asscn, Nat. Union of Univ. Profs, Nat. Asscn of Civil Service; Trustee, Mohammedia School of Law and Social Sciences; Chevalier, Order of the Throne 1994; Green March Medal 1975, Fulbright Scholar, George Washington Univ. 1985, Fulbright Visiting Specialist, Harvard Univ. 2004. *Publications:* English for Economists (co-author) 1985, Droit Administratif et Sciences Administratives (co-author) 1990; numerous book chapters, scholarly articles and conf. papers. *Address:* Quartier Alsace Lorraine, Mers Sultan, Casablanca, Morocco. *Telephone:* (522) 541515. *Fax:* (522) 541717. *E-mail:* hr@hassanrahmouni.com. *Website:* www.hassanrahmouni.com.

RAÏ, HE Cardinal Béchara Boutros, OMM, PhD; Lebanese ecclesiastic; *Patriarch of Antioch (Maronite);* b. (Bechara al-Rahi), 25 Feb. 1940, Himlaya, Matn Dist; ed Collège Notre Dame de Jamhour, Lateran Univ., Rome; ordained priest, Archdiocese of Ar-Rouhbanyat Al-Marounyat Liltoubawyat Mariam Al-Azra 1967; responsible for Arabic transmissions of Vatican Radio 1967–75; Titular Bishop of Caesarea Philippi 1986–; Auxiliary Bishop of Antioch (Maronite) 1986–90; Bishop of Jbeil (Maronite) 1990–2011; Patriarch of Antioch (Maronite) 2011–; cr. Cardinal 2012; participated in Papal Conclave (one of four cardinal-electors from outside the Latin Church) 2013; Sec. Maronite Synod 2003–09; Pres. Lebanese Episcopal Comm. for the Media 2009–11; mem. Congregation for Oriental Churches 2012–, Supreme Tribunal of Apostolic Signatura 2013–, Pontifical Council for Pastoral Care of Migrants and Itinerants 2013–, Pontifical Council for Social Communications 2013–; Nat. Order of the Cedar 2007; Grand Croix, Légion d'honneur 2011. *Address:* See of the Maronite Catholic Patriarchate, Bkerké, Lebanon (office).

RAI BACHCHAN, Aishwarya, (Aish); Indian actress and model; b. 1 Nov. 1973, Mangalore, Karnataka; d. of Krishnaraj Rai and Vrinda Rai; m. Abhishek Bachchan 2007; one d.; studied architecture in Bombay (now Mumbai); worked as model for advertising campaigns and major fashion shows; won Miss Catwalk, Miss Photogenic and Miss Perfect 10 competitions; runner-up in Miss India Contest 1994; winner Miss World Contest 1994; Ordre des Arts et des Lettres 2009; Discovery of the Year (Screen) 1998, Rajiv Gandhi Award 2002, GR8! Women Award 2004, 2010, Next Step World Diversity Champion Award, UK Govt 2005, Padma Shri 2009, India Today Women Award 2010; listed among 100 Most Influential People in the World, Time Magazine; several nat. and int. awards. *Films include:* Mamagari 1991, Iruvar (also known as Duo, Iddaru) 1997, Aur Pyar Ho Gaya 1997, Jeans 1998, Aa Ab Laut Chalen 1999, Hum Dil De Chuke Sanam 1999, Taal 1999, Mela – The Great Entertainer 2000, Kandukondain Kandukondain 2000, Josh 2000, Mohabbatein 2000, Dhai Akshar Prem Ke 2000, Hamare Dil Aapke Paas Hai 2000, Sanam Tere Hain Hum 2000, Albela 2001, Devdas (Filmfare Awards, Best Actress 2003) 2002, Hum Tumhare Hain Sanam 2002, Hum Kisi Se Kum Nahin 2002, 23rd March 1931: Shaheed (song) 2002, Shakthi: The Power 2002, Dil Ka Rishta 2003, Kyon Ho Gaya Na 2003, Khakee 2003, Chokher Bali 2003, Kuch Naa Kaho 2003, Khakee 2004, Bride and Prejudice 2004, The Mistress of Spices 2005, Provoked 2006, Umrao Jaan 2006, Guru 2007, The Last Legion 2007, Jodhaa Akbar 2007, The Pink Panther 2009, Raavan 2010, Enthiran 2010, Action Replay 2010, Guzaarish 2010. *Address:* Pratiksha, 10th Road, JVPD Scheme, Mumbai 400 049 (home); 402 Ramlaxmi Niwas, 16th Road, Khar (West), Mumbai 400 054, India. *Telephone:* (22) 6207579 (home); (22) 6206162 (home).

RAIDI; Chinese politician; *Vice-Chairman, 10th Standing Committee, National People's Congress;* b. 1938, Biru Co., northern Tibet; ed Cen. Nationalities Inst., Cen. Political Science and Law Cadre School, Beijing, CCP Cen. Cttee Cen. Party School; Sec. Public Security Div., Nagqu Prefectural Admin. Office, Tibet Autonomous Region 1962–66; worker, Mil. Control Comm., Nagqu Prefecture, PLA Tibet Mil. Region 1966–68, CCP Revolutionary Cttee 1968–72; Sec. CCP Nagqu Autonomous Prefectural Cttee 1972–75; Sec. CCP Tibet Autonomous Regional Cttee 1977–85, Deputy Sec. 1985–2002, Sec. Comm. for Discipline Inspection 1979–85; Chair. Peasants' Fed. of Tibet 1975; Vice-Chair. Revolutionary Cttee, Tibet Autonomous Region 1977–79; Vice-Chair. Standing Cttee Tibet Autonomous Regional People's Congress 1979–83, Chair. 1986–93; Chair. Standing Cttee Tibet Autonomous Regional 6th People's Congress 1993–; Deputy, 8th NPC, Tibet Autonomous Region; Alt. mem. 11th CCP Cen. Cttee 1977–82, mem. 12th CCP Cen. Cttee 1982–87, 13th CCP Cen. Cttee 1987–92, 14th CCP Cen. Cttee 1992–97, 15th CCP Cen. Cttee 1997–2002, 16th CCP Cen. Cttee 2002–07; Vice-Chair. 10th Standing Cttee of NPC 2003–. *Address:* Chinese Communist Party, Tibet Autonomous Region, Lhasa, Tibet, People's Republic of China (office).

RAIDL, Claus J.; Austrian economist, business executive and central banker; *President, Oesterreichische Nationalbank;* b. 6 Nov. 1942, Kapfenberg, Styria; m.; three c.; ed Vienna Univ. of Int. Trade; Asst. Inst. for Applied Social and Econ. Research, Vienna 1970–71; worked at bank and accounting firm, also consultant to OECD on issues of int. taxation on multinational enterprises 1971–74; with Österreichische Volksfürsorge Allgemeine Versicherung AG (insurance co.) 1974–81; mem. Bd of Man. Wiener Holding GmbH 1981–82; mem. Bd of Man. ÖIAG (Österreichische Industrieverwaltungs AG) 1982–86; Deputy Chair. Voest Alpine AG 1986–88, mem. Bd of Man. 2007–10; Deputy Chair. Voest Alpine Stahl AG 1988–92; Chair. Boehler-Uddeholm AG 1991–2010; mem. Bd of Man. Austrian Industries AG 1993–94; Pres. Oesterreichische Nationalbank 2008–; Chair. Bd of Trustees IST Austria (Inst. of Science and Tech.); Vice-Pres. European Forum Alpbach; mem. Bd Technical Museum Vienna; mem. Supervisory Bd Flughafen Wien AG. *Publications:* Mehrwertsteuer und Preisniveau 1971; numerous contribs to specialist publs on econ., tax, business and budgetary issues. *Address:* Office of the President, Oesterreichische Nationalbank, Otto-Wagner-Pl. 3, 1090 Vienna, Austria (office). *Telephone:* (1) 404-20 (office). *Fax:* (1) 404-23-99 (office). *E-mail:* oenb.info@oenb.co.at (office). *Website:* www.oenb.at (office).

RAIGETAL, Larry; Micronesian civil servant and business executive; *President, Waa'gey Inc.;* b. 4 July 1968, Lamotrek Atoll; two d.; ed Univ. of Oxford, UK, Univ. of San Francisco, USA; Dean of Students, Xavier High School, Chuuk 1992–93; diplomatic functions 1993–2001; Chair. FSM Banking Bd 1998; Chief of Manpower, Yap State Govt 2001–04; Dir, Dept of Youth and Civic Affairs, Yap State Govt 2007–; currently Pres. Waa'gey Inc. *Leisure interest:* fishing. *Address:* Waa'gey Inc., PO Box 254, Colonia Yap, FM 96943 (office); Box 254, Colonia Yap, 96943, Micronesia (home). *Telephone:* 952-6346 (office). *Fax:* 950-1151 (office). *E-mail:* larry@waagey.org (home); contact@waagey.org (office). *Website:* www .waagey.org (office).

RAIKIN, Konstantin Arkadyevich; Russian actor and theatre director; *Artistic Director, Theatre Satirikon;* b. 8 July 1950, Leningrad; s. of Arkady Raikin and Roma M. Joffe; m. Elena Butenko; one d.; ed M. Shchukin Theatre High School, Moscow; theatre Sovremennik 1971–81, debut in Valentin and Valentina; 38 roles including 15 leading, acted in plays of Shakespeare and Russian classics; actor State Theatre of Miniatures (renamed Theatre Satirikon 1987) under Arkady Raikin 1981–87, actor and Artistic Dir 1988–; Prize for Best Acting, Belgrade Festival 1990, People's Artist of Russia 1992, State Prize 1996, Gold Mask Prize 1996, Stanislavsky Prize 1998, Order of the Fatherland 2000. *Films:* Sensation is Anything 1971, Friends Among Strangers, Strangers Among Friends 1972. *TV Films:* Truffaldino from Bergamo 1976, The Island of Dead Ships 1988, Shadow 1990, Failure Puaro 2002. *Stage appearances include:* Cyrano de Bergerac (Cyrano) 1992, The Magnanimous Cuckold (Bruno) 1994, Metamorphosis (Gregor Zamza) 1995, The Threepenny Opera (Mack the Knife) 1996, Jacques and His Master (Jacques) 1998, Hamlet (Hamlet) 1998, Double Bass 2000. *Plays directed include:* Mowgli 1990, Butterflies Are Free 1993, Romeo and Juliet 1995, The Chioggian Squabbles 1997, Quartet 1999, Chanticleer 2001. *Address:* Theatre Satirikon, Sheremetyevskaya str. 8, 129594 Moscow, Russia. *Telephone:* (495) 289-87-07 (office). *Fax:* (495) 284-49-37 (office). *E-mail:* theatre@satirikon.msk.ru (office). *Website:* www.satirikon.ru (office).

RAIKOV, Gennady Ivanovich; Russian engineer and politician; b. 8 Aug. 1939, Khabarovsk; m.; one s.; ed Omsk State Machine Construction Inst.; mechanical engineer, docent, Omsk State Machine-Construction Inst. 1956–63; lawyer Russian Acad. of Civil Service; engineer, Head of workshop, Deputy Chief Engineer, Branch Dir Omsk Machine Construction production corpn 1961–77; Chief Engineer, Dir-Gen. Tumen Motor Mfg plant 1977–90; Head of City Admin., Tumen City Soviet 1990–93; Deputy Chief Tumenneftegazstroy Co. 1993, Deputy Dir-Gen. 1995–; Deputy Dir-Gen. Siberian Wood Co., Sweden 1993–95; mem. State Duma of Russian Fed. representing Tyumen dist 1995–, Leader People's Deputy faction 2000, mem. Duma Security Cttee, Mandate Comm., currently Head, Credentials and Ethics Comm.; mem. Perm. Del. of Fed. Ass. of Russian Fed. to Ass. of WEU; Rep. of State Duma to Perm. Comm. of Parl. Ass. Union of Belarus and Russian Fed.; mem. Governmental Comm. of Russian Fed. for participation in APEC forum; Chair. People's Party of the Russian Fed. 2001–04, now mem. United Russia party; Order Sign of Honour, Order of Red Banner of Labour, Order of October Revolution, Order for Service to Motherland (Fourth Degree), Order of Saint Sergei of Radonezh (Second Degree); several medals. *Leisure interest:* ice hockey. *Address:* State Duma, Okhotny Ryad 1, 103265 Moscow, Russia (office). *Telephone:* (495) 292-87-01 (office). *Fax:* (495) 292-87-15 (office).

RAIMI, Samuel (Sam) Marshall; American film director, producer and screenwriter; b. 23 Oct. 1959, Franklin, Mich.; ed Michigan State Univ. *Films include:* The Evil Dead (also producer/writer) 1981, Evil Dead II (also producer/writer) 1987, Darkman 1990, Army of Darkness (also producer/writer) 1993, The Quick and the Dead 1995, A Simple Plan 1998, For Love of the Game 1999, The Gift 2000, Spider-Man 2002, Spider-Man 2 2004, Spider-Man 3 (also writer) 2007, Oz the Great and Powerful 2013; as producer: Hard Target 1993, Timecop 1994, The Hudsucker Proxy (writer) 1994, The Grudge 2004, Boogeyman 2005, Rise 2007, 30 Days of Night 2007, Drag Me to Hell 2009, Oz the Great and Powerful 2013. *Television series:* as producer: M.A.N.T.I.S. 1994, Hercules: The Legendary Journeys 1994, American Gothic 1995, Xena: Warrior Princess 1995, Spy Game 1997, Young Hercules 1998, Jack of All Trades 2000, Cleopatra 2525 2000, Legend of the Seeker 2008–09, 13: Fear is Real 2009. *Address:* c/o Creative Artists Agency, 9830 Wilshire Boulevard, Beverly Hills, CA 90212-1825, USA.

RAIMONDI, Ruggero; Monegasque singer (bass) and director; b. 3 Oct. 1941, Bologna, Italy; m. Isabel Maier 1987; operatic debut in La Bohème, Spoleto Festival 1964; debut at Metropolitan Opera, New York in Ernani 1970; engagements include Don Giovanni, Le Nozze di Figaro, Faust, Attila, Nabucco, Don Carlos, Boris Godunov, Don Quichotte, Don Pasquale, Otello, Contes d'Hoffmann, Carmen, Il Viaggio a Rheims, Falstaff, I Vespri Siciliani, I Lombardi, L'Italiana in

Algieri, Il Turco in Italia, Tosca, Assassinio nella Cattedrale, Così fan tutte and others; Commdr des Arts et des Lettres, Officier de la Légion d'honneur, Kt, Order of Malta, Grand Ufficiale della Repubblica Italiana, Citizen of Honour, Athens, Commdr du Mérite Culturel (Monaco). *Opera productions include:* Don Giovanni, The Barber of Seville, Don Carlos. *Films:* Don Giovanni 1979, Six Characters in Search of a Singer 1981, La Truite 1982, Life is a Bed of Roses 1983, Carmen 1984, Boris Godunov 1989, Tosca 2001. *Television:* Boris Godunov staged by Joseph Losey at Opéra Nat. de Paris 1980, Six personnages en quête d'un chanteur by Maurice Béjart 1981, Verdi's Requiem 1982, Ernani directed by Kirk Browning (with Milnes and Pavarotti) 1983, Le nozze di Figaro directed by Jonathan Miller 1992, Tosca: In the Settings and at the Times of Tosca, directed by Brian Large (with Malfitano and Domingo) 1992, Il Turco in Italia with Cecilia Bartoli at Zurich Opera House 2001, Così fan tutte staged by Patrice Chéreau 2005. *Recordings include:* Verdi: Aida 1983, 2005, Rossini: L'Italiana in Algeri 1989, Puccini: Turandot 1990, Rossini: Il Viaggio a Reims 1990, Verdi: Don Carlos 1990, Rossini: Il barbiere di Siviglia 1993, Verdi: Un Ballo in Maschera 1998, Mozart: Le Nozze di Figaro 2003, Rossini: La Cenerentola 2003, Rossini: Il Barbiere di Siviglia (DVD) 2005, Verdi: Attila 2005. *Address:* 140 bis rue Lecourbe, 75015 Paris, France (office).

RAINE, Craig Anthony, BA, BPhil; British writer; b. 3 Dec. 1944, Shildon, Co. Durham; s. of Norman Edward and Olive Marie Raine; m. Ann Pasternak Slater 1972; three s. one d.; ed Exeter Coll., Oxford; Lecturer, Exeter Coll., Oxford 1971–72, 1975–76, Lincoln Coll. 1974–75, Christ Church 1976–79; Books Ed. New Review 1977–78; Ed. Quarto 1979–80; Poetry Ed. New Statesman 1981; Poetry Ed. Faber and Faber Ltd 1981–91; Fellow in English, New Coll., Oxford 1991–2010; Ed. Areté 1999–; Kelus Prize 1979, Southern Arts Literature Award 1979, Cholmondeley Poetry Award 1983, Sunday Times Award for Literary Excellence 1998. *Publications include:* The Onion, Memory 1978, A Martian Sends a Postcard Home 1979, A Free Translation 1981, Rich 1984, The Electrification of the Soviet Union (opera) 1986, A Choice of Kipling's Prose (ed.) 1987, The Prophetic Book 1988, '1953' (play) 1990, Haydn and the Valve Trumpet: Literary Essays 1990, Rudyard Kipling: Selected Poetry (ed.) 1992, History: The Home Movie 1994, Clay. Whereabouts Unknown 1996, New Writing 7 1998, A la recherche du temps perdu 1999, In Defence of T.S. Eliot: Literary Essays (Vol. 2) 2000, Collected Poems 1978–1999 2000, Rudyard Kipling: The Wish House and Other Stories (ed.) 2002, T.S. Eliot 2006, Heartbreak (novel) 2010, How Snow Falls (poems) 2010, The Divine Comedy (novel) 2012, More Dynamite (essays) 2012. *Leisure interests:* music, skiing. *Address:* New College, Oxford, OX1 3BN, England (office).

RAINES, Howell, MA; American journalist and editor; b. 5 Feb. 1943; ed Birmingham-Southern Coll. and Univ. of Alabama; journalist, Birmingham Post-Herald 1964, Birmingham (Ala) News 1970; Political Ed. Atlanta Constitution 1971–76, St Petersburg (Fla) Times 1976–78; Nat. Corresp. in Atlanta, NY Times 1978, Atlanta Bureau Chief 1979–81, White House Corresp. 1981–84, Nat. Political Corresp. 1984, Deputy Washington Ed. 1985–87, London Bureau Chief 1987–88, Washington Bureau Chief 1988–93, Editorial Page Ed. 1993–2001, Exec. Ed. 2001–03 (resgnd); currently columnist, The Guardian (UK); Pulitzer Prize for feature writing 1992, Davis Lecturer, Auburn Univ. 2013. *Publications include:* My Soul Is Rested 1977, Whiskey Man 1977, Fly Fishing Through the Midlife Crisis 1993, The One That Got Away 2006.

RAIS, Abdul Qader al-; United Arab Emirates artist; b. 1951, Kuwait; ed United Arab Emirates Univ.; began career as legal adviser, Ministry of Labour; became full-time painter in mid-1990s; works often include Arabic writing; co-f. Emirates Fine Arts Soc.; works held in numerous public collections; several awards including First Prize, Arab Painters' Exhbn, Kuwait, Gold Medal, Abu Dhabi Spring Exhbn, Golden Palm Leaf, GCC Exhbn 1999, Sheikh Khalifa Emirates Appreciation Award for Science, Arts and Literature 2006. *Publication:* The Colours of My Life 2008. *Address:* c/o Majlis Gallery, Al Musalla Roundabout, Al Fahidi Street, Bastakiya, Bur Dubai, POB 42885, Dubai, United Arab Emirates (office).

RAIS, Amien; Indonesian politician; b. 26 April 1944, Solo, Java; m. Kusnariyati Sri Rahayu; three s. two d.; ed Gadjah Mada Univ., Al Azhar Univ., Cairo, Egypt, Univ. of Notre Dame and Univ. of Chicago, USA; joined Muhammadiyah (Muslim group) 1985, Vice-Chair 1990–95, 1995–98; Chair. People's Consultative Ass. (MPR) 1999–2004; co-f. Partai Amanat Nasional (PAN) (National Mandate Party), Gen. Chair. 1998–2004; helped found Asscn of Indonesian Muslim Intellectuals (ICMI); Prof., Gadjah Mada Univ., Jogjakarta. *Address:* Partai Amanat Nasional, Jalan H. Nawi 15, Jakarta Selatan 12420, Indonesia (office). *Telephone:* (21) 72794535 (office). *Fax:* (21) 7268695 (office). *Website:* www.geocities.com/CapitolHill/Congress/6678 (office).

RÄISÄNEN, Heikki Martti, MA, DTheol; Finnish professor of New Testament exegesis; *Professor Emeritus, University of Helsinki;* b. 10 Dec. 1941, Helsinki; s. of Martti Olavi Räisänen and Saara Ilona Itkonen; m. Leena Marjatta Wright 1974; three s. one d.; ed Univ. of Helsinki; Lecturer in New Testament Exegesis, Univ. of Helsinki 1969–74, Acting Assoc. Prof. in Biblical Languages 1971–74, Prof. of New Testament Exegesis 1975–2006; Research Prof., Acad. of Finland 1984–94, Acad. Prof. 2001–06, Prof. Emer. 2006–; Dir Exegetical Inst., Univ. of Helsinki 1975–84, 1995–96, Vice-Dean of the Theological Faculty 1978–80, Dir Centre of Excellence 1994–2005; Chief Ed. Vartija 1989–2000; mem. Cttee Finnish Exegetical Soc. 1969–85, Chair. 1980–85; mem. Finnish Acad. of Sciences 1978–, Cttee Soc. for New Testament Studies 1986–89, Academia Europaea 2004; Fulbright Visiting Scholar, Harvard 1970–71; Visiting Scholar, Univ. of Cambridge 1978; Humboldt Visiting Scholar, Tübingen 1980–82; Hon. DD (Edin.) 1990, (Uppsala) 2002; Edward Cadbury Lectures, Univ. of Birmingham 1996, Prize of the Finnish Cultural Foundation 2005, Gad Rausing Prize, Acad. of Letters, Vitterhetsakademi, Stockholm 2006. *Publications:* Die Mutter Jesu im Neuen Testament 1969, Das koranische Jesusbild 1971, The Idea of Divine Hardening 1972, Das 'Messiasgeheimnis' im Markusevangelium 1976, Paul and the Law 1983, The Torah and Christ 1986, The 'Messianic Secret' in Mark's Gospel 1990, Beyond New Testament Theology 1990, Jesus, Paul and Torah 1992, Marcion, Muhammad and the Mahatma 1997, Neutestamentliche Theologie? 2000, Challenges to Biblical Interpretation 2001, The Rise of Christian Beliefs 2009; numerous books in Finnish; numerous articles on early Christianity. *Address:* Vantaanjänne 1 B 11,

01730 Vantaa, Finland (home). *Telephone:* (9) 898422 (home). *E-mail:* heikki.raisanen@helsinki.fi (office). *Website:* www.helsinki.fi/teol/hyel (office).

RAISANI, Nawab Muhammad Aslam Khan, MA; Pakistani politician and farmer; b. 5 July 1955, Sarawan, Balochistan; s. of Nawab Ghaus Bakhsh Khan Raisani (fmr Gov. of Balochistan and fed. minister); ed Univ. of Balochistan; Tumandar of Raisani Tribe; became Chief of Sarawan and Raisani tribe following his father's assassination; fmr Deputy Man., BDA; fmr Purchase Officer, PASCO, Jacobabad; apptd as DSP in Balochistan police force following graduation; Minister for Agric., Cooperative, Labour and Manpower in caretaker Prov. Govt Cabinet 1988; Minister for Food and Fisheries in caretaker Prov. Cabinet; elected mem. Prov. Ass. from PB-27 Mastung; mem. Prov. Ass. of Balochistan 1988, 1990, 1993, 2002; joined Pakistan Nat. Party (PNP) 1989, elected Parl. Leader of PNP in Prov. Ass.; apptd Pres. PNP of Balochistan 1990; Minister for Finance in Prov.; joined Pakistan People's Party 1999, mem. Cen. Exec. Cttee; Chief Minister of Balochistan 2008–13 (dismissed); Pres. Chamber of Agric., Balochistan; Founder and fmr Pres. Fed. of Chambers of Agric. Pakistan. *Leisure interests:* farming, angling, hiking. *Address:* Pakistan Peoples Party (PPP), 8, Street 19, F-8/2, Islamabad, Pakistan (office). *Telephone:* (51) 2255264 (office). *Fax:* (51) 2282741 (office). *E-mail:* ppp@comsats.net.pk (office). *Website:* www.ppp.org.pk (office).

RAISER, Konrad; German theologian, academic and fmr organization official; *Visiting Professor, Ecumenical Institute, Château de Bossey;* b. 25 Jan. 1938, Magdeburg; m. Bertha Elisabeth von Weizsaecker 1967; Study Sec., Comm. on Faith and Order, WCC 1969–73, Deputy Gen. Sec. WCC, Gen. Sec. 1992–2004 (retd); Prof. of Systematic Theology and Ecumenics, Univ. of the Ruhr, Bochum 1983–93; currently Visiting Prof., Ecumenical Inst., Château de Bossey, Switzerland; mem. Evangelical Church in Germany (EKD); investor in Oikocredit (microfinance and microcredit org.). *Publications:* Identität und Sozialität 1971, Ökumene im Übergang (Ecumenism in Transition) 1989, Wir stehen noch am Anfang 1994, To Be the Church 1997, For a Culture of Life 2002; more than 200 articles and essays on theological and ecumenical subjects. *Address:* Ecumenical Institute, Château de Bossey, PO Box 1000, 1299 Crans-près-Céligny, Switzerland (office). *Telephone:* (22) 960-7300 (office). *Fax:* (22) 960-7367 (office). *Website:* www.oikoumene.org (office).

RAISMAN, John Michael, CBE, CBIM, MA; British business executive; b. 12 Feb. 1929, Lahore, India; s. of Sir Jeremy Raisman and Renee Mary Raisman (née Kelly); m. Evelyn Anne Muirhead 1953; one s. three d. (one deceased); ed Rugby School, Queen's Coll., Oxford; joined Shell Int. Petroleum Co. Ltd 1953, served in Brazil 1953–60; Gen. Man., Shell Panama 1960–62; Asst to Exploration and Production Co-ordinator, Shell Int. Petroleum, Maatschappij 1963–65; Gen. Man., Shell Co. of Turkey Ltd 1965–69; Pres. Shell Sekiyu KK 1970–73; Head of European Supply and Marketing, Shell Int. Petroleum 1974–77; Man. Dir, Shell UK Oil 1977–78; Deputy Chair. and CEO Shell UK Ltd 1978–79, Chair. and CEO 1979–85; Chair. Shell Chemicals UK Ltd 1979–85; Dir Vickers 1981–90, Glaxo Holdings PLC 1982–90, Lloyds Bank 1985–95, Lloyds TSB 1996–98, Lloyds Merchant Bank Holdings 1985–87, Candover 1990–98, Tandem Computers 1991–97, British Biotech. 1993–98 (Chair. 1995–98); Deputy Chair. British Telecom 1987–91; mem. Pres.'s Cttee of Confed. of British Industry (CBI), Chair. Europe Cttee of CBI 1980–88, Council of Industry for Man. Educ. 1981–85, Oil Industry Emergency Cttee (OIEC) 1981–85, Advisory Council, London Enterprise Agency 1979–85, Investment Bd Electra Candover Pnrs 1985–95, Electronics Industry EDC 1986–88, Business Forum of European Movt, Council for Industry and Higher Educ. 1991–98; Deputy Chair. Nat. Comm. on Educ. 1991–95; Gov. Nat. Inst. of Econ. and Social Research 1981–; mem. Governing Council of Business in the Community 1982–85; mem. Council, Inst. for Fiscal Studies 1982–; mem. Royal Comm. on Environmental Pollution 1986–87; Chair. Bd of Trustees RA 1986–96; Pro-Chancellor Univ. of Aston 1987–93; Chair. British Empire and Commonwealth Museum Trust 2002–06; Hon. DUniv (Stirling) 1983, Hon. LLD (Aberdeen) 1985, (Manchester) 1986, (UWE) 1994; Hon. DSc (Aston) 1992. *Leisure interests:* golf, travel, opera, theatre. *Address:* Netheravon House, Netheravon Road South, London, W4 2PY, England (home). *Telephone:* (20) 8994-3731 (home). *Fax:* (20) 8742-1000 (home).

RAISS, Sid Ahmed Ould; Mauritanian politician and central banker; *Governor, Banque Centrale de Mauritanie;* b. 9 Sept. 1964, Atar; ed Univ. de Nouakchott, Univ. de Tunis, Ecole Nat. d'Admin., Paris, France; Asst lecturer, Dept of Law, Univ. de Nouakchott 1991–95; lawyer, Comm. for Food Security 1993–94; Auditor, Court of Auditors 1994–2002; Minister of Trade and Industry 2007–08, of Finance 2008–09; Gov. Banque Centrale de Mauritanie 2009–. *Address:* Banque Centrale de Mauritanie, ave de l'Indépendance, BP 623, Nouakchott, Mauritania (office). *Telephone:* 45-25-22-06 (office). *Fax:* 45-25-27-59 (office). *E-mail:* info@bcm.mr (office). *Website:* www.bcm.mr (office).

RAITT, Bonnie Lynn; American blues singer and musician (guitar, piano); b. 8 Nov. 1949, Burbank, Calif.; d. of the late John Raitt; m. Michael O'Keefe 1991 (divorced 1999); ed Radcliffe Coll.; performer in blues clubs on American E Coast; numerous concert tours and live appearances. *Recordings include:* albums: Bonnie Raitt 1971, Give It Up 1972, Takin' My Time 1973, Streetlights 1974, Home Plate 1975, Sweet Forgiveness 1977, The Glow 1979, Green Light 1982, Nine Lives 1986, Nick of Time (Grammy Awards for Best Female Rock Vocal Performance, Best Female Pop Vocal Performance, Album of the Year 1990) 1989, I'm in the Mood (with John Lee Hooker) (Grammy Award for Best Blues Traditional Record 1990), The Bonnie Raitt Collection 1990, Luck of the Draw (Grammy Award for Best Female Rock Vocal Performance, Best Duet 1992) 1991, Longing in Their Hearts (Grammy Award for Best Pop Album) 1994, Road Tested 1995, Fundamental 1998, Silver Lining 2002, Souls Alike 2005, Bonnie Raitt and Friends 2006, SlipStream (Grammy Award for Best Americana Album 2013) 2012. *Address:* PO Box 626, Los Angeles, CA 90078, USA. *Website:* www.bonnieraitt.com.

RAITT, Lisa, PC, BSc, MSc, LLB; Canadian politician; *Minister of Transport;* m.; two s.; ed St Francis Xavier Univ., Univ. of Guelph, Osgoode Hall Law School; fmr Corp. Sec., Toronto Port Authority, then Gen. Counsel, Harbourmaster, Pres. and CEO; MP for Halton 2008–; Minister of Natural Resources 2008–10, of Labour 2010–13, of Transport 2013–; mem. Conservative Party of Canada. *Address:* Department of Transport, 330 Sparks Street, Ottawa, ON K1A 0N5, Canada (office). *Telephone:* (613) 990-2309 (office). *Fax:* (613) 954-4731 (office). *E-mail:* questions@tc.gc.ca (office). *Website:* www.tc.gc.ca (office).

RAJABOV, Safarali; Tajikistani lawyer and politician; b. 2 Sept. 1955, Fayzabad Dist; m. 1976; two s. six d.; ed Dushanbe State Pedagogical Inst.; Dir Special Training Centre, Fayzabad Dist 1980–86; Tech. Coll. N2U, Fayzabad Dist 1986–90; Deputy of Tajikistan Supreme Soviet 1990–95; Sec., Deputy Chair., Chair. Cttee on Legislation and Human Rights 1990–95; Chair. Majlisi Oli (Parl.) of Tajikistan 1995–2000; Minister of Educ. 2000–05; Dr hc (Tajik State Agrarian Univ.) 1998. *Publications:* Independence is Sacred 1997, Majlisi Oli 1998. *Address:* c/o Ministry of Education, Nisor Mukhammad 13A, 734024 Dushanbe, Tajikistan.

RAJAN, Raghuram G., BTech, MBA, PhD; Indian academic, central banker and fmr international organization official; *Governor, Reserve Bank of India;* b. 3 Feb. 1963, Bhopal; ed Indian Inst. of Tech., Delhi, Indian Inst. of Man., Ahmedabad, MIT, USA; Officer, Tata Admin. Service 1987; fmr consultant to US Fed. Reserve Bd, World Bank, IMF, Swedish Parl. Comm., Indian Finance Ministry; Asst Prof. of Finance, Booth School of Business, Univ. of Chicago 1991–95, Prof. of Finance 1995–96, Joseph L. Gidwitz Prof. of Finance 1997–2003, Eric J. Gleacher Distinguished Service Prof. of Finance 2006–13 (currently on leave of absence); Gov. Reserve Bank of India 2013–; Visiting Prof. of Finance, Kellogg School, Northwestern Univ. 1996–97; Bertil Daniellson Visiting Prof. of Banking, Stockholm School of Econs 1996–97; Fischer Black Visiting Prof., MIT 2000–01; Econ. Counselor and Dir of Research, IMF 2003–07; Program Dir for Corp. Finance, Nat. Bureau of Econ. Research; Dir Int. School of Business, Hyderabad; Dir American Finance Asscn 2001–04, then Vice-Pres.; Dir Chicago Council on Global Affairs; Program Dir (Corp. Finance) Nat. Bureau of Econ. Research 1998; mem. Advisory Bd US Comptroller Gen.; mem. Int. Advisory Bd Indian Inst. of Man., Ahmedabad; Adviser Securities and Exchange Bd of India; Founding mem. Academic Council, Indian School of Business; mem. Academic Advisory Council, Moodys Investor Services; mem. Int. Advisory Bd Itau-Unibanco Bank; Assoc. Ed. American Economic Review, Journal of Financial Intermediation, Review of Financial Studies, Journal of Finance, Quarterly Journal of Economics, Financial Management (various times); Fellow, American Acad. of Arts and Sciences 2009–; fmr Sr Advisor, Booz and Co.; Hon. Econ. Advisor to Indian Prime Minister 2008–; Western Finance Asscn Treffstz Prize for Outstanding Academic Achievement 1991, Smith Breeden Prize 1992, 1994, Fifth Annual Small Firm Research Symposium Best Paper Award 1993, Michael Brennan Award 1997, Brattle Prize 2000, 2001, 2002, Fischer Black Prize, American Finance Asscn 2003, Fama/DFA Prize 2003, Jensen Prize 2006. *Publications:* Saving Capitalism from the Capitalists (co-author) 2003, Fault Lines: How Hidden Fractures Still Threaten the World Economy (Financial Times/Goldman Sachs Business Book of the Year) 2010. *Leisure interests:* tennis, squash, history, Indian politics. *Address:* Office of the Governor, Reserve Bank of India, POB 601, Main Building Mumbai 400 001, India (office). *Telephone:* (22) 22601000 (office). *Website:* www.rbi.org.in (office).

RAJAONARIMAMPIANINA, Hery Martial, CPA; Malagasy accountant, politician and head of state; *President;* ed Université des Trois Rivières, Canada; fmr Prof., Institut Nat. des Sciences Comptables et de l'Admin d'Entreprises, Antananarivo; Chair. Ordre des Experts Comptables et Financiers de Madagascar (Chartered Accountants and Financial Experts Asscn) –2009; Minister of Finance 2009–11 (resgnd), of Finance and the Budget 2011–13; cand. in presidential election 2013; elected Pres. 2014–; Founder Cabinet Auditeurs Associés (Accounting Expertise and Auditing); Commdr, Ordre Nat. Malagasy 2010. *Address:* Office of the President, BP 955, 101 Antananarivo, Madagascar (office). *Telephone:* (20) 2254703 (office). *Fax:* (20) 2256252 (office). *E-mail:* communication@presidence .gov.mg (office). *Website:* www.presidence.gov.mg (office).

RAJAPAKSA, Basil Rohana; Sri Lankan politician; *Minister of Economic Development;* s. of D. A. Rajapaksa; brother of Mahinda Rajapaksa; m. Pushpa Rajapaksa; three c.; ed Ananda Coll.; apptd MP 2007, elected MP for Gampaha 2010–; fmr Sr Adviser to Pres. of Sri Lanka; Minister of Econ. Devt 2010–; mem. Sri Lanka Freedom Party; fmr mem. United Nat. Party. *Address:* Ministry of Economic Development, 177 Galle Road, Colombo 03 (office); C 79, Gregory Avenue, Colombo 07, Sri Lanka (home). *Telephone:* (11) 2394764 (office). *Fax:* (11) 2394763 (office). *E-mail:* secedip@sltnet.lk (office). *Website:* www.med.gov.lk (office); www.basilrajapaksa.lk.

RAJAPAKSA, Chamal Jayantha; Sri Lankan politician; *Speaker of the Parliament;* b. 30 Oct. 1942; s. of D. A. Rajapaksa, fmr Minister of Agric. and Land; elder brother of Mahinda Rajapaksa, Pres. of Sri Lanka; m. Chandra Rajapaksa; two s.; mem. Sri Lanka Freedom Party (now part of United People's Freedom Alliance); MP for Hambantota; Minister of Ports, Aviation, Irrigation and Water Man. –2010; Speaker of the Parl. 2010–. *Address:* Office of the Speaker, Parliament of Sri Lanka, Sri Jayewardenepura Kotte, Colombo; No. C 79, Gregory's Avenue, Colombo 07, Sri Lanka. *Telephone:* (11) 2777100 (office). *Fax:* (11) 2777564 (office). *E-mail:* webmaster@parliament.lk (office). *Website:* www .parliament.lk (office).

RAJAPAKSA, Lt-Col (retd) Gotabhaya; Sri Lankan government official and fmr army officer; *Permanent Secretary, Ministry of Defence;* b. Palatuwa, Matara Dist; s. of D. A. Rajapaksa; brother of Mahinda Rajapaksa (Pres. of Sri Lanka); m. Ioma Rajapaksa; one s.; ed Ananda Coll., Colombo; joined Sri Lanka Army as Cadet Officer 1971, rank of Second Lt 1972, becoming Officer, Ceylon Signals Corps, served with Sri Lanka Sinha Regt and Rajarata Rifles, transferred to Gajaba Regt 1983, Second-in-Command, 1st Gajaba Regt, Commdr 1983–90, promoted to Lt-Col, Commdt, Kotelawala Defence Acad. –1992 (retd); worked as Unix System Admin., Loyola Law School, Los Angeles, USA –2005; Perm. Sec., Ministry of Defence 2005–; Hon. DLitt (Colombo) 2009; several awards for gallantry including Rana Wickrama Padakkama (Combat Gallantry Medal), Rana Sura Padakkama (Combat Excellence Medal). *Address:* Ministry of Defence, 15/5 Baladaksha Mawatha, POB 322, Colombo 3, Sri Lanka (office). *Telephone:* (11) 2430860 (office). *Fax:* (11) 2446300 (office). *E-mail:* webinfo@defence.lk (office). *Website:* www .defence.lk (office).

RAJAPAKSA, Mahinda; Sri Lankan politician, lawyer and head of state; *President, Minister of Defence, of Highways and Road Development, of Finance and Planning, and of Ports and Aviation;* b. 18 Nov. 1945, Weerakatiya, Hambantota, British Ceylon; s. of D. A. Rajapaksa; m. Shiranthi Wickramasinghe;

three s.; ed Richmond Coll., Galle, Nalanda and Thurstan Colls, Colombo, Sri Lanka Law Coll.; fmr lawyer, Tangalle; mem. Parl. for Beliatta 1970; fmr Minister of Labour, of Fisheries, of Ports and Shipping; Leader of the Opposition 2002–04; Prime Minister of Sri Lanka 2004–05; Pres. of Sri Lanka Nov. 2005–, Minister of Defence and of Finance and Planning 2005–07, of Defence, Public Security, Law and Order, Religious Affairs, Nation Building and Finance and Planning 2007–10, of Highways and Road Devt, of Finance and Planning, and of Ports and Aviation 2010–; mem. United People's Freedom Alliance; Pres. Sri Lankan Cttee for Solidarity with Palestine; Chair. Sri Lanka Freedom Party 2006–; Sri Rohana Janaranjana 2000. *Address:* President's Secretariat, Republic Square, Colombo 1, Sri Lanka (office). *Telephone:* (11) 2324801 (office). *Fax:* (11) 2331246 (office). *E-mail:* gosl@presidentsl.org (office). *Website:* www.president.gov.lk (office); www .mahindarajapaksa.com.

RAJAVI, Maryam, BSc; Iranian politician; b. (Maryam Qajar-Azedanllo), 3 Dec. 1953, Tehran; m. Massoud Rajavi 1985; one s. one d.; ed Sharif Univ. of Tech., Tehran; leader anti-Shah student movt; joined Mojahedin-e Khalq Org. (People's Mojahedin of Iran, leading Iranian opposition group) 1970s, parl. cand. for Tehran in first post-revolutionary parl. elections 1979; official in social dept 1980–81, organized demonstrations against Khomeini Govt 1980–1981; left Iran for Paris 1982; elected jt-leader of Mojahedin 1985, Sec.-Gen. 1989–93; Deputy C-in-C Nat. Liberation Army of Iran (NLA) 1987–93, launched programme for introduction of women in front-line combat and combat pilots 1987, transformed NLA from infantry to armoured force 1989–93; Pres.-Elect, Nat. Council of Resistance of Iran (540-mem. Parl. in exile) 1993–; proposed platform for women's int. alliance against fundamentalism 1993; prominent int. campaigner for women's rights 1993–; Guest Speaker, European Parl. 2004, Int. Human Rights Conf., Paris 2004, Int. Conf. of Jurists, Paris 2004, Parls of Norway and UK 1995–96; numerous lectures, TV appearances, interviews in int. media; awards include Medal of Honour for contrib. to emancipation of women, Nat. Comm. for Gender Equality, Italy 1993, one of The Times 100 Most Powerful Women, UK 1996. *Publications include:* Charter of Fundamental Freedoms in Post-dictatorship Iran 1995, Message to Fourth Int. Women's Conf., Beijing 1995, A Message of Tolerance 1995, Women, Islam and Fundamentalism 1996, Women, Voice of the Oppressed 1996, United Against Fundamentalism 1996, Message to Women in Frontline (conf.) 1997, Misogyny, Pillar of Religious Fascism 2003, Message to Int. Federation of Women against Fundamentalism and for Equality (conf.) 2004, Women and Islamic Fundamentalism 2004, Women Empowerment 2005, Women in Leadership 2006, Ten-Point Platform for Future Iran 2006; contrib.: Le Monde, De Welt, Le Figaro, International Herald Tribune. *Leisure interest:* reading. *Website:* www.ncr-iran.org; www.maryam-rajavi.com/en.

RAJE, Vasundhara; Indian politician; *Chief Minister of Rajasthan;* b. 8 March 1953, Mumbai; d. of Jiwaji Rao and Vijayaraje Scindia; m. Hemant Singh; one s.; ed Sofia Coll., Mumbai Univ.; mem. Bhartiya Janata Party (BJP), mem. Nat. Exec. 1984, Vice-Pres. Yuva Morcha BJP 1985–87, 1987–89, mem. state and nat. execs 1989–2002, State BJP Pres. 2002–03, 2013–; mem. Rajasthan Legis. Ass. 1985–90, 2003–08, 2008–13, 2013–, State Leader of Opposition 2009–10; mem. Lok Sabha (lower house of Parl.) from Jhalawar constituency 1989–2003; Union Minister of State, External Affairs 1998–99, Small Industries, Personnel & Training, Pension & Pensioners Welfare 1999–2001; Chief Minister of Rajasthan (first woman) 2003–08, 2013–. *Leisure interests:* reading, music, horse-riding, gardening. *Address:* Office of the Chief Minister, Government of Rajasthan, 8 Civil Lines, Jaipur, India (home). *Telephone:* (141) 2227351 (office). *Fax:* (141) 2381687 (office). *E-mail:* cmraj@rajasthan.gov.in (office). *Website:* cmo.rajasthan.gov.in (office).

RAJE SCINDIA, Vasundhara, BA; Indian politician; *Chief Minister of Rajasthan;* b. 8 March 1953, Bombay (now Mumbai); d. of the late Jivaji Rao Scindia and of Rajmata Vijya Raje Scindia; m. Raja Hemant Singh 1972; one s.; ed Presentation Convent, Kodaikanal, Sophia Coll., Mumbai Univ.; MLA for Dholpur 1984–89; Vice-Pres. Bharatiya Janata Party (BJP) Yuva Morcha 1984–89; Vice-Pres. Rajasthan State BJP 1985–88, Pres. 2002–; mem. Lok Sabha 1989–2003; Jt Sec. BJP Parl. Cttee 1997; Union Minister for Foreign Affairs 1998–99; Minister for Small Scale Industries and Agric. and Rural Industries (Ind. charge) 1999–2003; State Minister for Personnel and Training, Pensions and Welfare, Personnel, Public Grievance and Pension Ministry, Atomic Energy and Space Dept 1999–2003; Chief Minister of Rajasthan 2003–08, 2013–; mem. Rajasthan Legis. Ass. 2008–, Leader of Opposition 2009–10, 2011–13; UN Women Together Award 2007. *Leisure interests:* reading, music, horse riding, gardening. *Address:* Chief Minister's Office, Secretariat, Government of Rajasthan, Jaipur 302 005, Rajasthan (office); 13, Civil Lines, Jaipur 302 006, Rajasthan, India. *Telephone:* (11) 2220320 (office); (11) 2224400 (home). *E-mail:* cmraj@rajasthan.gov.in (office); cmo-rj@nic.in (office).

RAJESWAR, Thanjavelu, BA (Hons), MA; Indian police officer and government official; b. 28 Aug. 1926, Salem, Tamil Nadu; m. Mahalaxmi Rajeswar; one s. one d.; ed Presidency Coll., Univ. of Madras; joined Indian Police Service in 1949, posted to erstwhile Hyderabad State, later to Andhra Pradesh, served as Supt of Police in Dist of Nizamabad, Raichur and Guntur and as Deputy Commr of Police in the twin cities of Hyderabad and Secunderabad; joined Intelligence Bureau (IB) in 1962 as Asst Dir, served in Sikkim and Bhutan as OSD and Advisor, respectively 1963–67, Deputy Dir and Jt Dir IB HQ 1967–80, Dir 1980–83; Lt Gov. Arunachal Pradesh (first ever IPS Officer to be apptd to a constitutional post) 1983–85; Gov. of Sikkim 1985–89, of West Bengal 1989–90 (resgnd), of Uttar Pradesh 2004–09. *Address:* 9 Anand Lok Colony, New Delhi 110 049, India.

RAJHI, Sheikh; Sulaiman bin Abdul Aziz Al-, BA; Saudi Arabian banking executive and philanthropist; *Chairman, Al Rajhi Bank;* b. 1920; m.; at least 23 c.; ed King Abdulaziz Univ.; grew up in Nejd desert; began business with brother Saleh changing money for pilgrims in camel caravans crossing the desert to Mecca and Medina; Co-founder (with brother) and Chair. Al Rajhi Bank; diversified family investments into gypsum, agriculture, steel and other industrial sectors; opened office in Kuwait 2010, opened branches in Jordan 2011; holds stakes in several Saudi firms, including Yanbu Cement Co. and National Agricultural Development Co. (Nadec); f. SAAR Foundation; launched Sulaiman Al Rajhi Univ. *Address:* Al Rajhi Bank, Aakaria 3rd Building, 7th Floor, Olaya Street, Riyadh, 11411, Saudi Arabia (office). *Telephone:* (1) 4603333 (office). *Fax:* (1) 4600705 (office). *E-mail:* ContactCenter1@alrajhibank.com.sa (office). *Website:* www .alrajhibank.com.sa (office).

RAJINIKANTH; Indian actor and producer; b. (Shivaji Rao Gaekwad), 12 Dec. 1950, Bangalore; s. of Ramoji Rao Gaekwad and Rambhai Gaekwad; m. Latha Rajinikanth 1981; two d.; ed Acharya Patasala, Ramakrishna Mission, Bangalore; worked with Bangalore Transport Service; moved to Chennai, joined Madras Film Inst. 1973; Kalaimamani Award, Tamil Nadu Govt 1984, MGR Award, Tamil Nadu Govt 1989, Kalaichelvam Award, Nadigar Sangam 1995, Oshobismit Award, Rajinish Ashram Award 1995, Padma Bhushan 2000, Raj Kapoor Award 2007, Vijay Award 2010. *Films include:* Apoorva Raagangal (Nat. Award, Filmfare Award, Arima Sangam Award, Filmfans Award) 1975, Moondru Mudichu 1976, Tholireyi Gadichindi 1977, Bhuvana Oru Kelvikkuri (Tamil Nadu Govt Award, Filmfans Award) 1977, 16 Vayathinile (Filmfans Award, ThiraiKadhir, Arima Sangam Award) 1977, Vayasu Pilichindi 1978, Ilamai Oonjal Aadukirathu (Tamil Nadu Govt Award) 1978, Mullum Malarum (Tamil Nadu Govt Award, Filmfans Award, Filmfare Award, Cinema Express Award) 1978, Tiger 1979, Thayillamal Nannilai 1979, Dharma Yuddham 1979, Ram Robert Rahim 1980, Mr. Rajanikant 1980, Anbukku Naan Adimai 1980, Ranuva Veeran 1981, Netri Kann 1981, Thanikkattu Raja 1982, Pudhu Kavithai 1982, Agni Sakshi 1982, Engeyo Ketta Kural (Tamil Nadu Govt Award, Filmfans Award) 1982, Thudikkum Karangal 1983, Thanga Magan 1983, Tiger Rajani 1984, Takkaridonga 1984, Naan Mahaan Alla 1984, Bhooka Sher 1984, Unn Kannil Neer Vazhindal 1985, Nyayam Meere Cheppali 1985, Mera Inteqam 1985, Viduthalai 1986, Maaveran 1986, Dosti Dushmani 1986, Uttar Dakshin 1987, Bloodstone 1988, Siva 1989, Raajadhi Raaja 1989, Adisaya Piravi 1990, Hum 1991, Shanti Kranti 1991, Pandian 1992, Chor Ke Ghar Chorni 1992, Valli 1993, Badsha 1995, Peda Rayudu (Filmfans Award, Cinema Express), Arunachalam (Tamil Nadu Govt Award) 1997, Padaiyappa (Tamil Nadu Govt Award) 1999, Bulandi 2000, Baba (writer, producer) 2002, Chandramukhi 2005, Sivaji 2007, Kuselan 2008, Endhiran 2010. *Address:* 18, Raghava Veera Avenue, Poes Garden, Chennai 600 086, India. *Fax:* (44) 24838890. *Website:* www.rajinikanth.com.

RAJNA, Thomas, DMus, ARCM; British composer, pianist and teacher (retd); b. 21 Dec. 1928, Budapest, Hungary; s. of Dr Nandor Rajna and Hella Riser; m. Anthea Valentine Campion 1967; one s. two d.; ed Nat. Musical School, Budapest, Franz Liszt Acad. of Music, Budapest and Royal Coll. of Music, London; freelance composer, pianist and teacher, London 1951–63; Prof. of Piano, Guildhall School of Music 1963–70; Lecturer, Univ. of Surrey 1967–70; Sr Lecturer in Piano, Faculty of Music, Univ. of Cape Town 1970–89, Assoc. Prof. 1989–93; launched own record label Amarantha Records 2001; Fellow, Univ. of Cape Town 1981; DMus (Cape Town) 1985; Liszt Prize, Budapest 1947, Artes Award (SABC) 1981, UCT Book Award 1996, Cape Tercentenary Foundation Merit Award 1997. *Compositions include:* film and ballet music, orchestral and chamber music, two piano concertos, Harp Concerto 1990, Amarantha (opera in 11 scenes) 1991–94, Video Games (for orchestra) 1994, Rhapsody for clarinet and orchestra 1995, Fantasy for violin and orchestra 1996, Suite for violin and harp 1997, Stop All the Clocks (four songs on poems by W. H. Auden) 1998, The Creation – A Negro Sermon for unaccompanied choir 2000, Valley Song (opera) 2002–04, Tarantulla for violin and piano 2001, Violin Concerto 2007. *Recordings:* works by Stravinsky (complete piano works), Messiaen: Vingt regards sur l'Enfant-Jesus; Scriabin, Granados (complete piano works), Liszt (Transcendental Studies), Schumann (A minor Piano Concerto and Piano Quintet and Quartet), Dohnanyi (Nursery Variations), The Hungarian Connection: Instrumental Works by Dohnányi and Rajna, Bach Harpsichord Concertos, Bartok 2nd and 3rd Piano Concertos, Stravinsky Capriccio, Prokofiev 3rd Piano Concerto, Barber Piano Concerto, A Garland of Spanish Songs; own compositions: Amarantha (opera), Valley Song (opera), Suite for violin and harp, Rhapsody for clarinet and orchestra, 1st Piano Concerto, Piano Preludes and Capriccio, 2nd Piano Concerto and Harp Concerto, Video Games and other orchestral works, The Creation – A Negro Sermon for chorus and orchestra, Violin Concerto. *Publications:* Dialogues for Clarinet and Piano 1970, Piano Preludes 1988, Music for Violin and Piano 1990, Concerto for Harp and Orchestra 1990; publs by Amarantha Music: Video Games for Orchestra 1994, Rhapsody for Clarinet and Orchestra 1995, Amarantha (opera) 1995, Fantasy for Violin and Orchestra 1996, Suite for Violin and Harp 1998, Stop All the Clocks – Four Songs on Poems by W. H. Auden 1998, Tarantulla for Violin and Piano 2001, Valley Song (opera) 2004, The Creation – A Negro Sermon for Chorus and Orchestra 2006, Violin Concerto 2007. *Leisure interests:* chess, swimming. *Address:* 10 Wyndover Road, Claremont, Cape Town, West Cape 7708, South Africa (home). *Telephone:* (21) 6713937 (home). *Fax:* (21) 6713937 (home). *E-mail:* trajna@telkomsa.net (home). *Website:* www.lib.uct.ac.za/mss/composers/rajna.

RAJOELINA, Andry Nirina; Malagasy politician and broadcasting and media executive; b. 30 May 1974, Antananarivo; m. Mialy Rajoelina; worked as disc jockey around Antananarivo early 1990s; gained prominence after establishing own radio station, Viva Radio, and a successful advertising co.; Mayor of Antananarivo 2007–09; opposed Pres. Marc Ravalomanana, led protests that, together with mil. intervention, opposed a free electoral vote, plotted a coup and resulted in Ravalomanana's resignation, dissolved Parl., changed high court judges and was installed by mil. as head of state 19 March 2009, sworn in as Head of the High Authority of Transition 21 March 2009–25 Jan. 2014, presidency not recognised by Southern African Devt Community. *Address:* c/o Office of the President of the Haute Autorité de la Transition, Antananarivo, Madagascar.

RAJOUB, Jibril; Palestinian government official; b. 1953, Dura; m.; three c.; spent 17 years in Israeli prison 1968–85; exiled to Lebanon 1988, returned to West Bank 1994; Chief West Bank Preventive Security Service 1994–2002; Nat. Security Adviser to Yasser Arafat and Head of Nat. Palestinian Security Council 2003–04; mem. Fatah-Revolutionary Council. *E-mail:* fateh@fateh.org. *Website:* www.fateh.net.

RAJOY BREY, Mariano; Spanish politician and property registrar; *Prime Minister and President of the Government;* b. 27 March 1955, Santiago de Compostela (La Coruña); m.; two s.; ed Universidad de Santiago de Compostela; fmr Prof. of Law, Univ. of Santiago de Compostela; Vice-Chair. Governing Council Alianza Popular (People's Alliance) in Galicia, Chair. Local and Prov. Council of Alianza Popular in Pontevedra, mem. Perm. Cttee of Alianza Popular; mem. Regional Parl. of Galicia 1981, fmr Dir-Gen. for Institutional Relations of Regional

of Galicia; Pres. Prov. Council of Pontevedra 1983–86; Vice-Pres. Regional Govt of Galicia 1986–87; mem. Nat. Exec. Cttee Partido Popular (People's Party—PP) 1989–, Deputy Gen. Sec. PP 1990–2003, Gen. Sec. PP 2003–04, Pres. 2004–; mem. Parl. during 3rd, 4th, 5th, 6th, 7th, 8th and 9th Legislatures; Minister for Public Admin Services 1996–99, for Educ. and Culture 1999–2000; First Vice-Pres. of the Govt and Minister for Home Affairs 2001–02; First Vice-Pres. of the Govt, Govt Spokesperson and Minister for the Presidency 2002–03; cand. for presidency of the govt 2004, 2008; Prime Minister and Pres. of the Govt 2011–; Vice-Pres. Int. Democratic Union 2005–, Centrist Democrat International 2006–; Trustee, Foundation for Social Studies and Analysis (FAES); Order of Charles III 2003, Order of the Aztec Eagle (Mexico) 2012; Dr hc (Sergio Arboleda Univ., Bogotá, Colombia) 2012. *Address:* Prime Minister's Chancellery, Complejo de la Moncloa, Avenida de Puerta de Hierro s/n, 28071 Madrid, Spain (office). *Telephone:* (91) 3353535 (office). *Fax:* (91) 3900217 (office); (91) 5492739 (office); (91) 3085642 (office). *E-mail:* secretariapresidente@presidencia.gob.es (office); presidencia@pp .es (office). *Website:* www.la-moncloa.es (office); www.pp.es (office).

RAJU, B(yrraju) Ramalinga, BCom, MBA; Indian business executive; b. 16 Sept. 1954, Bhimavaram, Andhra Pradesh; m. Nandini Raju; two s.; ed Loyola Coll., Vijayawada, Ohio Univ., USA; Co-founder and Chair. Satyam Computer Services Ltd, Satyam Infoway Ltd and VisionCompass, Inc. 1987–2009 (resgnd), jt ventures include Satyam–GE Software Services Ltd, Satyam Venture Eng Services Pvt. Ltd, Satyam Manufacturing Technologies Ltd, Satyam ideaEdge Technologies Pvt. Ltd, CA Satyam ASP Pvt. Ltd; f. several trusts and charities including Alambana, Naandi and the Byyrajju Foundation; Chair. Nat. Asscn of Software and Service Cos 2006–07; held in Hyderabad's Chanchalguda jail on criminal charges of corp. fraud July 2009, granted bail 2010; Dr hc (Andhra Univ.) 2007; Ernst & Young Entrepreneur of the Year Award 2000, 2007, Dataquest IT Man. of the Year Award 2001, Asia Business Leader Award for Corp. Citizen of the Year, Hong Kong 2002. *Leisure interests:* reading, snooker.

RAJU, M. Mangapati Pallam, BE, MBA; Indian business executive and politician; *Minister of Human Resource Development;* b. 31 Aug. 1962, Pithapuram, East Godavari Dist, Andhra Pradesh; s. of M. S. Sanjeevi Rao and Rama Rajeshwari; m. Mamatha Raju 1989; one s. one d.; ed Andhra Univ., Visakhapatnam, Temple Univ., Philadelphia, USA; Research Asst Temple Univ., USA 1985–86; Research Assoc. Federal Group Inc. (man. consulting firm), South Natick, Mass, USA 1986–87; Dir Air India & Indian Airlines 1994–97; Man. Dir TTM (India) Private Limited (ASIC Design Services), Secunderabad 1999–; elected to 9th Lok Sabha (lower house of Parl.) for Kakinada constituency 1989–91, 14th Lok Sabha 2004, 15th Lok Sabha 2009–; Gen.-Sec. Andhra Pradesh Congress Cttee 1995–2000; mem. All India Congress Cttee 1997–2000; Union Cabinet Minister of State for Defence 2006–12, Minister of Human Resource Devt 2012–; Life mem. Equestrian Fed. of India; Fellow, Inst. of Electronics & Telecommunications Engineers, New Delhi. *Leisure interests:* athletics, football, swimming, horse riding, music, photography and travelling. *Address:* Ministry of Human Resource Development, Shastri Bhavan, Dr Rajendra Prasad Road, New Delhi 110 001, India (office). *Telephone:* (11) 23383936 (office). *Fax:* (11) 23381355 (office). *E-mail:* dsel-mhrd@nic.in (office). *Website:* mhrd.gov.in (office).

RAKE, Sir Michael Derek Vaughan, Kt, FCA; British accountant and business executive; *Chairman, BT Group plc;* b. 17 Jan. 1948; s. of Derek Shannon Vaughan Rake and Rosamund Rake (née Barrett); m. 1st Julia Rake Cook 1970; three s.; m. 2nd Caroline Thomas 1986; one s.; ed Wellington Coll.; with Turquands Barton Mayhew, London and Brussels 1968–74; accountant KPMG (Peat Marwick Mitchell Continental Europe), Brussels 1974, Pnr 1979–, Pnr in charge of Audit, Belgium and Luxembourg 1983–86, Sr Resident Pnr, ME 1986–89, Pnr, London office 1989–, mem. UK Bd 1991–, Regional Man. Pnr, SE Region 1992–94, Chief Exec. London and SE Region 1994–96, COO, UK 1996–98, Sr Pnr, UK and Chair. UK Bd 1998–, Chair. KPMG Europe 1999–2002, Chair. KPMG International 2002–07; Chair. BT Group plc 2007–; Deputy Chair. EasyJet June–Dec. 2009, Chair. 2010–; Chair. Business in the Community 2004–07, Guidelines Monitoring Cttee (pvt. equity oversight group), UK Comm. for Employment and Skills 2007–10; mem. Bd of Dirs Barclays PLC, McGraw Hill Inc., Financial Reporting Council 2008–11; mem. Bd Prince of Wales Int. Business Leaders' Forum 1998–2007, Britain in Europe Business Leaders' Group 2000–, CBI Pres.'s Cttee 2001–, TransAtlantic Business Dialogue, CBI Int. Advisory Bd, Chartered Man. Inst., DTI's US/UK Regulatory Taskforce, Advisory Council for Business for New Europe, Ethnic Minority Employment Taskforce, SOAS Advisory Bd, Advisory Bd of Judge Inst. at Univ. of Cambridge 2004, Nat. Security Forum 2009–10, Prime Minister's Business Advisory Group 2010–12; Vice-Pres. Royal Nat. Inst. of Blind People 2003–, Reviseur d'Entreprise (Luxembourg); Leader, Advisory Bd HBS Global Leadership Forum 2003–; Assoc. mem. BUPA; Sr Adviser, Chatham House, Global Advisory Bd of Univ. of Oxford Centre for Corp. Reputation; Vice-Pres. and Chair. of Govs of Wellington Coll.; mem. Bd Guards Polo Club; Trustee, Prince of Wales' Charitable Foundation; William Pitt Fellow, Pembroke Coll., Cambridge. *Leisure interests:* polo, skiing. *Address:* BT Group plc, BT Centre, 81 Newgate Street, London, EC1A 7AJ, England (office). *Telephone:* (20) 7356-5000 (office). *Fax:* (20) 7356-5520 (office). *E-mail:* btgroup@bt.com (office). *Website:* www.btplc .com (office).

RAKHIMOV, Murtaza Gubaidullovich; Russian politician; b. 7 Feb. 1934, Tavakanovo, Bashkiria; s. of Gubaidulla Zufarovich Rakhimov and Galimya Abdullovna Rakhimova; m. Luiza Galimovna Rakhimova; one s.; ed Ufa Oil Inst.; operator, then Chief of Oil Rig, Chief Chemist, Chief Engineer, Dir Ufa Oil Processing Plant 1956–90; USSR People's Deputy 1990–92; Chair. Supreme Soviet Repub. of Bashkortostan 1990–93, Pres. 1993–2010; mem. Russian Council of Fed. (Parl.) 1993–2001; Public Services to Repub. of Bashkortostan, Order of Peter the Great, Labour Red Banner, People's Friendship Order, Honour Symbol, Order of Salavat Yulayev. *Leisure interests:* sports, music, literature. *Address:* c/o The Republic House, 46 Tukayev Street, 450101, Ufa, Bashkortostan, Russia (home).

RAKHMONOV, Imamali Sharipovich (see Rakhmon, Imamali Sharipovich).

RAKOTOARIMASY, Lt-Gen. André Lucien; Malagasy army officer and politician; b. 12 Feb. 1953, Ambohimanga Rova, Antananarivo; s. of Alphonse Rakotofiringa and Marie Jeanne Raveloharimanana; m.; four c.; ed Univ. of Antananarivo, Mil. Acad., Antsirabe, Malagasy Inst. for Planning Techniques,

Antananarivo, Collège Interarmées de Défense, Paris, France, Centre for Strategic and Diplomatic Studies, Antananarivo; Dir of Human Resources, Ministry of Defence 2004–06, Gen. Man. of Operations and Planning 2007–08; Chief of the Gen. Staff of the Malagasy Army 2008–09; Dir of Mil. Cabinet at the Presidency of the High Authority of the Transition 2009–10; Minister of the Armed Forces 2010–14; Kt of the Malagasy Nat. Order 1994, Officer 1999; Kt of the Madagascar Order of Merit 1996, Officer; Commdr, Malagasy Nat. Order, Grand Officer. *Leisure interest:* tennis practice. *Address:* c/o Ministry of Defence, BP 08, Ampahibe, 101 Antananarivo, Madagascar (office). *E-mail:* rakotoarimasyal@yahoo.fr (office).

RAKOTONANDRASANA, Gen. Noël; Malagasy army officer and government official; fmrly with Parachute Regt; Commdr, Corps d'Armée du Personnel et des Services Administratif et Technique (Capsat) 2009; led army faction during coup d'état of March 2009; Minister of the Armed Forces 2009–10 (dismissed). *Address:* c/o Ministry of the Armed Forces, BP 08, Ampahibe, 101 Antananarivo, Madagascar. *Telephone:* (20) 2222211. *E-mail:* mdn@wanadoo.fr. *Website:* www.defense.gov.mg.

RAKOTONIAINA, Justin; Malagasy politician, academic and diplomatist; b. 1933, Betsileo; fmr Prof. of Law, Univ. of Madagascar; Amb. to Algeria, also accred to Tunisia and Guinea 1973–75; Minister of Nat. Educ. 1975–76; Prime Minister of Madagascar 1976–77; mem. Supreme Revolutionary Council; currently Prof., Faculty of Law, Univ. of Fianarantsoa and Head, Department DEA Peace, Democracy and Devt. *Address:* Department DEA Peace, Democracy and Development, Law Faculty of Law, University of Fianarantsoa, BP 1264–301, Fianarantsoa, Madagascar (office). *Telephone:* (20) 7550849 (office). *Fax:* (20) 7550619 (office). *E-mail:* ufianara@syfed.refer.mg (office). *Website:* www.refer.mg/edu (office).

RAKOTOVAHINY, Emmanuel; Malagasy politician; *Vice-President;* b. Aug. 1938, Toliara; fmr Chair. Union nat. pour la démocratie et le développement; fmr Minister of State for Rural Devt and Land Reform; Prime Minister of Madagascar 1995–96; Pres. Comité pour la Réconciliation Nationale 2009; Vice-Pres. of Madagascar 2009–. *Address:* Comité pour la Réconciliation Nationale, Villa la Franchise, Lot II-I 160 A, Alarobia, Antananarivo, Madagascar (office). *Telephone:* (20) 2242022 (office).

RALPH, Richard Peter, CMG, CVO, MSc (Hons); British diplomatist (retd) and consultant; *Director, Foro Consulting Ltd;* b. 27 April 1946, London, England; s. of the late Peter Ralph and Evelyn Marion Ralph; m. 1st Margaret Elisabeth Coulthurst 1970 (divorced 2001); one s. one d.; m. 2nd Jemma Victoria Elizabeth Marlor 2002; one d.; ed The King's School, Canterbury, Univ. of Edin.; served at Embassy in Vientiane, Laos 1970–73, Lisbon 1974–77; at FCO 1977–81; High Comm. to Zimbabwe 1981–84, Councillor, Embassy in Washington, DC 1989–93, Amb. to Latvia 1993–95, Gov. Falkland Islands 1996–99, concurrently Commr S Georgia and S Sandwich Islands, Amb. to Romania (also accred to Moldova) 1999–2002, to Peru 2003–06 (retd); Chair. Monterrico Metals plc 2006–08; Dir, British-Peruvian Infrastructure Development Co. plc, Foro Consulting Ltd, Latin-American business consultancy; fmr Chair. Anglo-Peruvian Soc., South Georgia Asscn. *Leisure interests:* reading, int. relations, theatre, music, art, travel, tennis. *Address:* 29 Surrey Lane, Battersea, London, SW11 4PA, England (home). *Telephone:* (20) 7924-4188 (office). *E-mail:* r.ralph@foroconsulting.com (office); richardralph87@hotmail.com (home). *Website:* www.foroconsulting.com (office).

RALSTON, Gen. Joseph W.; American air force officer (retd); *Vice-Chairman, Cohen Group;* b. 4 Nov. 1943, Hopkinsville, Ky; m. Diane Dougherty; two s. two d.; ed Miami Univ., Ohio, Cen. Michigan Univ., Army Command and Gen. Staff Coll., Nat. War Coll., Harvard Univ.; mem. reserve officer training program USAF 1965; Vice-Chair. of Jt Chiefs of Staff 1996–2000; concurrently Chair. Jt Requirements Oversight Council, Planning, Programming and Budgeting Systems; Vice-Chair. Defense Acquisition Bd; mem. Nat. Security Council Deputies Comm., Nuclear Weapons Council; Supreme Allied Commdr, Europe 2000–03; C-in-C, US European Command 2000–03; Vice Chair. The Cohen Group 2003–; numerous mil. decorations including Defense Distinguished Service Medal (two awards), Distinguished Service Medal. *Address:* The Cohen Group, 1200 19th Street, NW, Suite 400, Washington, DC 20036, USA (office). *Telephone:* (202) 689-7900 (office). *Fax:* (202) 689-7910 (office). *E-mail:* jralston@cohengroup.net (office). *Website:* www.cohengroup.net/team-jwr.html (office).

RAMA, Carlos M., PhD; Uruguayan writer, lawyer, academic and editor; b. 26 Oct. 1921, Montevideo; s. of Manuel Rama and Carolina Facal; m. Judith Dellepiane 1943; one s. one d.; ed Univ. de la República and Univ. de Paris; journalist 1940–48, 1972–; Exec. Sec. of Uruguayan Bar Asscn 1940–49; Prof. of Universal History in secondary schools 1944–48; Ed. Nuestro Tiempo 1954–56, Gacetilla Austral 1961–73; Prof. of Sociology and Social Research, Prof. of Contemporary History, Prof. of Theory and Methodology of History, Univ. de la República 1950–72; Prof. of Latin American History, Univ. Autónoma de Barcelona 1973–; Pres. PEN Club Latinoamericano en España; Sec. Gen. Grupo de Estudios Latinoamericanos de Barcelona; Commdr, Order of Liberator (Spain), Officier des Palmes académiques (France). *Publications:* La Historia y la Novela 1947, 1963, 1970, 1974, Las ideas socialistas en el siglo XIX 1947, 1949, 1963, 1967, 1976, Ensayo de Sociología Uruguaya 1956, Teoría de la Historia 1959, 1968, 1974, 1980, Las clases sociales en el Uruguay 1960, La Crisis española del siglo XX 1960, 1962, 1976, Itinerario español 1961, 1977, Revolución social y fascismo en el siglo XX 1962, Sociología del Uruguay 1965, 1973, Historia del movimiento obrero y social latinoamericano contemporáneo 1967, 1969, 1976, Los afrouruguayos 1967, 1968, 1969, 1970, Garibaldi y el Uruguay 1968, Uruguay en Crisis 1969, Sociología de América Latina 1970, 1977, Chile, mil días entre la revolución y el fascismo 1974, España, crónica entrañable 1973–77, 1978, Historia de América Latina 1978, Fascismo y anarquismo en la España contemporánea 1979. *Leisure interest:* gardening. *Address:* c/o Monte de Orsá 7, Vallvidrera, Barcelona 17, Spain.

RAMA, Edi Kristaq; Albanian politician and artist; *Prime Minister;* b. 4 July 1964, Tirana; s. of Kristaq Rama (sculptor) and Aneta Rama (née Koleka); m. 1st Matilda Makoci; one s.; Lindita Xhillari Rama (née Basha); two c.; ed Albanian Acad. of Arts, Tirana; player for Dinamo (basketball team) and Albanian nat. basketball team in early 1980s; following collapse of Communism, became active in democracy movt in early 1990s; Prof., Albanian Acad. of Arts; emigrated to France

and lived as an artist 1994, returned to Albania 1998; Founding mem. Movt for Democracy 1996; Minister of Culture, Youth and Sports 1998–2000; Mayor of Tirana 2000–11; Prime Minister 2013–; mem. Socialist Party of Albania 2003–, Chair. 2005–; Robert C. Wood Visiting Prof. of Public and Urban Affairs, Univ. of Massachusetts, USA 2003; mem. Regional Advisory Bd of UNDP; Pres. Albanian Municipalities Asscn; fmr Bd mem. Open Society Foundation; UN Poverty Eradication Award 2002, World Mayor 2004, included in TIME magazine's European Heroes list 2005. *Publications:* Refleksione (with Ardian Klosi) 1991, Edi Rama 2009, Kurban 2011; numerous articles in Albanian and int. magazines and newspapers. *Address:* Office of the Prime Minister, Bulevardi Dëshmorët e Kombit 1, 1000 Tirana (office); Socialist Party of Albania (Partia Socialiste e Shqipërisë), Tirana, Albania (office). *Telephone:* (4) 2227409 (office). *Fax:* (4) 2227417 (office). *E-mail:* info@ps.al (office). *Website:* www.km.gov.al (office); www.ps.al (office); www.edirama.al.

RAMACHANDRAN, Dato C(herubala) P(athayapurayil), MSc, DrMedSc, DAP&E, FIBiol; Malaysian medical scientist and academic; *Chairman, Programme Review Group, Pacific Island Countries, Global Programme to Eliminate Lymphatic Filariasis, World Health Organisation;* b. 3 June 1936, Kuala Lumpur; s. of KK Madhavan Nair and Kamalam M. Nair; m. Githa Priya Darshini 1966; one s. one d.; ed St John's Inst., Kuala Lumpur, Christian Coll., Madras, India, Univ. of London, UK, Univ. of Liverpool, UK, Tulane Univ., USA, Univ. of Tokyo, Japan; Wellcome Trust Research Scholar and Demonstrator in Medical Parasitology, Liverpool School of Tropical Medicine 1959–62, Research Fellow in Tropical Medicine, Inst. for Medical Research, Kuala Lumpur 1962–63, Head Filariasis Research Div. 1967–70; Asst Prof. in Medical Parasitology Faculty of Medicine, Univ. of Malaya, Kuala Lumpur 1963–67; Assoc. Prof. in Medical Parasitology and Head, School of Biological Sciences, Universiti Sains Malaysia, Penang 1970–72, Prof. and Dean 1972–79, now Prof. Emer.; Sr Scientist Human Resource Devt Tropical Disease Research WHO, Geneva, Switzerland 1979–87, Man. Research and Devt Filariasis Research Programme, Tropical Disease Research, WHO, Switzerland 1987–92; Chief Filariasis Research and Control, WHO, Geneva 1992–96, Chair., Programme Review Group, Pacific Island Countries, Global Programme to Eliminate Lymphatic Filariasis; Prof. of Clinical Parasitology, Universiti Putra, Malaysia 1996–2005; Adjunct Prof., Faculty of Medicine, Universiti Technologi MARA, Malaysia; Adjunct Prof., MAHSA Univ.; Visiting Prof., Faculty of Tropical Medicine, Mahidol Univ., Bangkok, Thailand; Pres. Int. Civil Service Asscn of Malaysia-Singapore and Brunei Darasalam; fmr Pres. Malaysian Soc. of Parasitology and Tropical Medicine, mem. Council, World Fed. of Parasitologists, Council; mem. Council and Vice-Pres. UN Asscn Malaysia; Fellow, Liverpool School of Tropical Medicine, UK, Malaysian Scientific Asscn, Acad. of Medicine (Malaysia), Australian Coll. of Tropical Medicine; Academician, Acad. of Sciences, Malaysia; Sandosham Medal (Malaysia) 1974, Mary Kingsley Medal for Tropical Medicine (UK) 1998, Darjah Setia Pangkuan Negeri (Malaysia) 1999, Johan Setia Mahota (Malaysia), Gold Medal, Rotary International, Life Time Achievement Award, Indian Council for Medical Research. *Publications:* numerous scientific papers in learned journals. *Leisure interests:* squash, photography, music. *Address:* Apt-8A-4-4, Belvedere, off Jalan Tunku, Bukit Tunku, 50480 Kuala Lumpur, Malaysia (home). *Telephone:* 26987275 (home). *Fax:* 26986152 (home). *E-mail:* ramacp@hotmail.com (home).

RAMACHANDRAN, Vilayanur Subramanian, MD, PhD; Indian neuroscientist, psychologist, physician and academic; *Director, Center for Brain and Cognition and Professor Psychology Department and Neurosciences Program, University of California, San Diego;* b. 1951, Madras; ed Stanley Medical Coll., Trinity Coll., Cambridge; currently Dir Center for Brain and Cognition, Prof. of Psychology, Dept and Neurosciences Program, Univ. of Calif., San Diego; Adjunct Prof. of Biology, Salk Inst.; Ed.-in-Chief Encyclopedia of Human Behavior; Fellow, Neurosciences Inst., La Jolla, Inst. for Advanced Studies in Behavioral Sciences, Stanford; lectures worldwide including BBC Reith Lectures 2003; Trustee San Diego Museum of Art; mem. Nat. Acad. of Sciences (India); Visiting Prof., Stanford Univ., Harvard Univ. 2008, Columbia Univ.; Fellow, Stanford Univ., Neurosciences Inst., Calif., Athenaeum Club, London; Hon. Fellow, Royal Inst. of GB; Dr hc (Conn. Coll.); Gold Medal, ANU, Ariens Kappers Medal, Royal Netherlands Acad. of Sciences, Presidential Lecture Award, American Acad. of Neurology, Chancellor's Award for excellence in research, Univ. of Calif., Henry Dale Medal 2005, Padma Bhushan 2007, Ramony Cajal Award, Int. Neuropsychiatry Soc. *Publications:* Phantoms in the Brain (co-author) 1998; over 180 papers in scientific journals. *Address:* Center for Brain and Cognition, University of California, 9500 Gilman Drive, #0109, La Jolla, CA 92093-0109, USA (office). *Telephone:* (858) 534-6240 (office). *Fax:* (858) 534-7190 (office). *E-mail:* vramachandran@ucsd.edu (office). *Website:* www.ucsd.edu (office).

RAMADAN, Tariq, MA, PhD; Swiss academic; *Professor of Contemporary Islamic Studies, St Antony's College, University of Oxford;* b. 26 Aug. 1962, Geneva; ed Univ. of Geneva; fmr Prof. of Islamic Studies and Philosophy, Freiburg Univ.; Prof. of Islamic Studies and Luce Prof. of Religion, Conflict and Peacebuilding, Kroc Inst., Univ. of Notre Dame, USA Aug.–Dec. 2004 (visa revoked); Sr Research Fellow, Lokahi Foundation 2004–, Doshisha Univ., Kyoto 2007–; Prof. of Contemporary Islamic Studies, St Antony's Coll., Oxford, UK 2004–; Chair Citizenship and Identity, Erasmus Univ., Rotterdam, Netherlands 2007–; Chair. European Muslim Network, Brussels; One of the Seven Innovators of the 21st Century, Time magazine 2000, One of the 100 People of the Year 2004, European of the Year, European Voice 2006, The Muslim News Special Award for Excellence (Faith and Action) for academic and intellectual contrib. to Islamic thought 2007. *Publications:* Islam, le face à face des civilisations, Quel projet pour quelle modernité? 1995, Les Musulmans dans la Laïcité, responsabilités et droits des musulmans dans les sociétés occidentales 1994, To be a European Muslim 1999, Muslims in France: The Way Towards Coexistence 1999, Islam, the West, and the Challenges of Modernity 2001, Jihad, Violence, War and Peace in Islam (in French) 2002, Western Muslims and the Future of Islam 2004, Globalisation: Muslim Resistances 2004, Radical Reform, In the Footsteps of the Prophet 2007, Radical Ijtihad 2008, The Quest for Meaning: Developing a Philosophy of Pluralism 2010, Islam and the Arab Awakening 2012; contrib. of more than 850 articles, reviews and chapters in books and magazines. *Leisure interest:* literature. *Address:* St Antony's College, 62 Woodstock Road, Oxford, OX2 6JF, England (office); 39 rue de la boulangerie, 93200 Saint Denis, France (home). *Telephone:* (1865) 612302 (Oxford) (office); 1-49-22-01-12 (Saint Denis) (home). *Fax:* (1865) 612844 (Oxford) (office); 1-49-22-00-39 (Saint Denis) (home). *E-mail:* office@tariqramadan.com (office); cisoq@sant.ox.ac.uk (office). *Website:* www.tariqramadan.com (office).

RAMADHANI, Rt Rev. John Acland, BA; Tanzanian ecclesiastic (retd); b. 1 Aug. 1932, Zanzibar; s. of Augustine Ramadhani and Mary Majaliwa; ed Dar es Salaam Univ., Queen's Coll., Birmingham and Univ. of Birmingham, UK; Prin. St Andrew's Teacher Training Coll., Korogwe 1967–69; Warden, St Mark's Theological Coll., Dar es Salaam 1977–79; Bishop of Zanzibar and Tanga 1980–2000; Archbishop of the Prov. of Tanzania 1984–97; Bishop of Zanzibar 2001–02; Chair. Christian Council of Tanzania –2002; Patron Misufini Leprosy Centre. *Leisure interest:* reading. *Address:* c/o Anglican Church of Tanzania, Diocese of Zanzibar, PO Box 5, Mkunazini, Zanzibar, Tanzania. *E-mail:* zanbishop@hotmail.com.

RAMADORAI, Subramaniam, CBE, BSc, BEng, MSc; Indian business executive; *Adviser to Prime Minister for the National Skill Development Council;* b. 6 Oct. 1944, Nagpur; m. Mala Ramadorai; ed Univ. of Delhi, Indian Inst. of Science, Bangalore, Univ. of California and Massachusetts Inst. of Tech., USA; jr engineer, Tata Consultancy Services (TCS) 1972, later set up TCS's operations in New York 1979, CEO and Man. Dir TCS 1996–2009, currently Vice-Chair.; Adviser to Prime Minister for the Nat. Skill Devt Council 2011–; Chair. Tata Technologies Ltd, TATA Elxsi (India) Ltd, Computational Research Laboratories Ltd, CMC Ltd; Ind. Dir (non-exec.) Hindustan Lever Ltd 2002–; mem. Bd of Dirs Nicholas Piramal, TATA Ltd (India), TATA Infotech Ltd (India), TATA Internet Services Ltd, Nelito Systems Ltd; IT Adviser to Qingdao City and Hangzhou City, People's Repub. of China; Fellow, Inst. of Electrical and Electronics Engineers, Indian Nat. Acad. of Engineers; Vice-Chair. Nat. Asscn of Software Companies; mem. Nat. Council of the Confed. of Indian Industry, Corporate Advisory Bd, Marshall School of Business; Dr hc (Anna Univ., Tamil Nadu) 2004, Hon. DrSc (Sastra Univ.) 2006; Asia Business Leader of the Year Award, Hong Kong 2002, Business India Businessman of the Year 2004, UK Trade and Investment Special Recognition Award 2005, Padma Bhushan 2006, Int. CEO of the Year, LT Bravo Business Awards 2008, Nayudamma Award 2008. *Address:* Prime Minister's Office, National Skill Development Council, South Blk, Raisina Hill, New Delhi 110 011, India (office). *Telephone:* (11) 23012312 (office). *Fax:* (11) 23016857 (office). *Website:* www.pmindia.nic.in (office).

RAMADOSS, Anbumani, MD; Indian physician and politician; b. 9 Oct. 1968, Puducherry; s. of Dr S. Ramadoss and Shrimati R. Saraswathi; m. Sowmya Anbumani 1991; three d.; ed Madras Medical Coll., London School of Econs, UK; fmr medical practitioner, Tamil Nadu; Leader, Pattali Makkal Katchi; mem. Rajya Sabha (Parl.) 2004–; Minister of Health and Family Welfare 2004–09 (resgnd); Co-f. Nat. Rural Health Mission 2005; Pres. Pasumai Thayagam (Green Mother Land); Luther L. Terry Award, American Cancer Soc. 2006. *Address:* 30/34, 4th Cross St, Kasturibai Nagar, Raja Anamalai Puram, Chennai 600 028, India (home).

RAMAHATRA, Maj.-Gen. (retd) Victor; Malagasy international business strategy consultant, fmr politician and fmr army officer; *International Business Consultant and Board Member, Vision Madagascar Group;* b. 6 Sept. 1945, Antananarivo; s. of Pierre Longin Ramahatra and Marie Lucile Ratsimandresy; m. Nivonirina Rajoelson 1971 (deceased); two s. one d.; ed Saint-Cyr Mil. Acad. and Ecole Supérieure du Génie Militaire, France; officer in Corps of Engineers 1967; mil. engineer 1972; Minister of Public Work 1982–87; Prime Minister of Malagasy Repub. 1987–91; man. locust plague control campaign 1998–2000; Special Adviser to Pres. of Malagasy Repub. in econs and int. affairs 1997–2001; Int. Business Consultant and mem. Bd Vision Madagascar (VIMA) Group 2009–, HFF Group; Adviser, UBP Group (Mauritius), Bd Adviser 2005; mem. Supervisory Bd Henri Fraise Fils Group 2010–; mem. Asscn des Ingénieurs Diplômés de l'Ecole Supérieure du Génie Militaire d'Angers, Asscn des Anciens Elèves de Saint-Cyr (Madagascar), Asscn des Anciens de Saint-Cyr dans la Vie Civile (France); mem. Supervisory Bd Henri fraise Holding (Madagascar), Bd mem., Vision Madagascar Group; Adviser, United basalt Products group of Mauritius; Grand-Croix, Ordre nat. du Mérite 1990, Officier, Légion d'honneur 2000, Grand Officier de l'Ordre nat. (Madagascar) 2000. *Leisure interests:* reading, march/walking, swimming. *Address:* VR. 104P, Fenomanana, 101 Antananarivo (home); PO Box 6004, 101 Antananarivo, Madagascar. *Telephone:* (202) 223767 (home); 33-18147 (mobile). *Fax:* (202) 2453088 (office). *E-mail:* ramfan@moov.mg (home).

RAMAKRISHNAN, T. V., BSc, MSc, PhD; Indian physicist and academic; *TIFR-NCBS Distinguished Research Professor, Banaras Hindu University;* b. 14 Aug. 1941, Madras (now Chennai); s. of T. R. Venkatachala Murti and Jayalakshmi Murti; m. Meera Rao; one s. one d.; ed Banaras Hindu Univ., Columbia Univ., USA; CSIR Junior Research Fellow, Banaras Hindu Univ., Varanasi 1961–62; Lecturer in Physics, Indian Inst. of Tech. (IIT), Kanpur 1966–67, Asst Prof. 1967, 1970–77, Prof., 1977–80; Asst Research Physicist, Univ. of California, San Diego, USA 1968–70; Consultant, Bell Laboratories, Murray Hill, NJ 1980–81, 1990–91; Coordinator, Research Programme on Disorder, Inst. for Theoretical Physics, Univ. of Calif., Santa Barbara 1983; Prof. of Physics, Banaras Hindu Univ., Varanasi 1984–86, DAE Homi Bhabha Prof. 2003–12, TIFR-NCBS Distinguished Research Prof. 2012–; Visiting Prof., Dept of Physics, Indian Inst. of Science, Bangalore 1981–84, Prof. of Physics 1986–2003, Distinguished Assoc., Centre for Condensed Matter Theory 2003–; INSA Srinivasa Ramanujan Research Prof. 1997–2002; Visiting Fellow, Princeton Univ., USA 1978–81, Visiting Prof. and Visiting Research Physicist 1990–91; Rothschild Visiting Prof., Isaac Newton Inst. for Math. Sciences, Univ. of Cambridge, UK 2000, Visiting Fellow Commoner, Trinity Coll. and Visiting Prof. 2004; Pres. Indian Acad. of Sciences 2004–06; Vice-Pres. Indian Nat. Science Acad. 2000–03; Fellow, Indian Acad. of Sciences (Bangalore) 1980, Indian Nat. Science Acad. (New Delhi) 1984, American Physical Soc. 1984, Third World Acad. of Sciences (Trieste, Italy) 1991, Nat. Acad. of Sciences, Allahabad 1993, Royal Soc., London 2000, Inst. of Physics (UK) 2000; Foreign Assoc., Acad. of Sciences, Paris 2005; mem. Indian Asscn for Cultivation of Science, Kolkata 2004–, Science Advisory Council to the Prime Minister 2005–; mem. Union of Concerned Scientists (USA) 1994–; Hon. Prof., Jawaharlal Nehru Centre for Advanced Scientific Research, Bangalore 1993–, Hon. Fellow, TIFR, Mumbai 2004–, Hon. Distinguished Prof., IIT Kanpur 2004–; Hon. Assoc., Tata Inst. of Fundamental Research, Mumbai; Padma Shri 2001; Dr hc (Banaras Hindu Univ.) 2004; numerous awards including Devasthale Prize in Physics 1959, Shanti

Swarup Bhatnagar Award for Physical Sciences, CSIR 1982, Third World Acad. of Sciences Award in Physics 1990, Jawaharlal Nehru Award for Science, MP Council for Science and Technology 1999, C.V. Raman Centenary Medal, Indian Science Congress 2001, Meghnad Saha Medal, Asiatic Soc. 2002, Distinguished Materials Scientist of the Year, Materials Research Soc. of India 2004, Goyal Prize in Physics, Kurukshetra 2004, Trieste Science Prize 2005, G.M. Modi Award 2008, H.K. Firodia Award 2012. *Address:* Department of Physics, Faculty of Science, Banaras Hindu University, Varanasi 221 005 (office); Department of Physics, Indian Indian Institute of Science, Bangalore 560 012, India (office). *Telephone:* (542) 2367005 (Varanasi) (office); (80) 23600228 (Bangalore) (office). *Fax:* (542) 2368468 (Varanasi) (office); (80) 23602602 (Bangalore) (office). *E-mail:* tvrama@physics.iisc.ernet.in (office). *Website:* www.physics.iisc.ernet.in (office).

RAMAKRISHNAN, Sir Venkatraman, Kt, BSc, PhD, FRS; American/British (b. Indian) biologist and academic; *Senior Scientist and Group Leader, MRC Laboratory of Molecular Biology, University of Cambridge;* b. 1952, Chidambaram, Tamil Nadu, India; ed Maharaja Sayajirao Univ., Baroda, India, Ohio Univ., Univ. of California, San Diego; Postdoctoral Fellow, Dept of Chem., Yale Univ. 1978–82; mem. Research Staff, Oak Ridge Nat. Lab. 1982–83; Asst Biophysicist, Biology Dept, Brookhaven Nat. Lab. 1983–85, Assoc. Biophysicist 1985–88, Biophysicist 1988–90, Biophysicist with tenure 1990–94, Sr Biophysicist 1994–95; Visiting Scientist, MRC Lab. of Molecular Biology, Cambridge, UK 1991–92, Sr Scientist and Group Leader, Structural Studies Div. 1999–, Sr Research Fellow, Trinity Coll., Cambridge 2008–, Fellow, Trinity Coll. 2008–; Prof., Biochemistry Dept, Univ. of Utah, also Faculty mem., Grad. Programs in Biological Chem. and Molecular Biology 1995–99; mem. Scientific Advisory Cttee, EMBL 2002–06, IMP, Vienna 2008–; mem. Scientific Advisory Bd Rib-X Pharmaceuticals, New Haven, Conn., USA; mem. European Molecular Biology Org. 2002, NAS 2004; Foreign mem., Indian Nat. Science Acad. 2008; Rolf-Sammet Professorship, Univ. of Frankfurt 2009; Guggenheim Fellowship 1991–92, Datta Medal and Lecture, FEBS annual meeting, Vienna 2007, Louis Jeantet Prize for Medicine 2007, Heatley Medal, British Biochemical Soc. 2008, Nobel Prize in Chem. (with Thomas A. Steitz and Ada E. Yonath) 2009. *Address:* Structural Studies Division, MRC Laboratory of Molecular Biology, Hills Road, Cambridge, CB2 0QH, England (office). *Telephone:* (1223) 402213 (office); (1223) 248011 (office). *Fax:* (1223) 213556 (office). *E-mail:* ramak@mrc-lmb.cam.ac.uk (office). *Website:* www.mrc-lmb.cam.ac.uk/ribo/homepage/ramak/index.html (office).

RAMALHO, Ivan, PhD; Brazilian economist and international organization official; *High Representative, Mercosur;* Head of Dept, Banco do Brasil (Cacex) 1973–2003; Sec. of Foreign Trade, Ministry of Devt, Industry and Foreign Trade 2003–06, Exec. Sec. 2006–10; Pres. Brazilian Foreign Trade Asscn 2011–12; High Rep. Mercosur 2012–; mem. Bd of Dirs BNDES Participações SA (BNDESPar); mem. Brazilian Foreign Trade Chamber, Foundation Council, Centre for the Study of Foreign Trade (Funcex); served as Pres. Exports Guarantee and Finance Cttee, Orientation Council of Devt Nat. Fund; fmr Dir Dept of Foreign Trade Operations (Decex), served as coordinator of technical group responsible for devt and implementation of Integrated Foreign Trade System (Siscomex). *Address:* Mercosur, Dr. Luis Piera 1992, Floor 1, 11200 Montevideo, Uruguay (office). *Telephone:* (2) 4129024 (office). *Fax:* (2) 4100958 (office). *Website:* www.mercosur.int (office).

RAMANATHAN, Veerabhadran (Ram), BE, MSc, PhD; American (b. Indian) scientist and academic; *Victor Alderson Professor of Applied Ocean Sciences and Distinguished Professor of Climate and Atmospheric Sciences, University of California, San Diego;* b. 24 Nov. 1944, Madras, India; m. Girija (Giri) Ramanathan; one s. two d.; ed Annamalai Univ., Indian Inst. of Science, State Univ. of New York (SUNY) at Stony Brook (Planetary Atmospheres); engineer, Shri Ram Refrigeration Industries, Secunderabad, India 1965–67; Nat. Research Council Post Doctoral Fellow, NASA Langley Research Center and George Washington Univ., Hampton, Va 1975–76; Scientist, Nat. Center for Atmospheric Research (NCAR), Boulder, Colo 1976–82; Prin. Investigator, NASA Earth Radiation Budget Experiment 1979–; Sr Scientist, Nat. Center for Atmospheric Research (NCAR), Boulder, Colo 1985–88; Affiliate Prof., Colorado State Univ., Fort Collins 1985–88; Visiting Prof., Université Catholique de Louvain, Belgium 1985–88; Prof., Dept of Geophysical Sciences, Univ. of Chicago, Ill. 1986–90; Victor C. Alderson Prof. of Applied Ocean Sciences, and Prof. of Climate and Atmospheric Sciences, Scripps Inst. of Oceanography, Univ. of California, San Diego 1990–, Dir Center for Clouds, Chem. and Climate 1991–, Dir Center for Atmospheric Sciences 1996–, Distinguished Prof. of Atmospheric and Climate Sciences 2004–; mem. Bd Dirs Tata Energy Research Inst., Arlington, Va 1992–; Chief Scientist, Cen. Equatorial Pacific Experiment (CEPEX) 1993; Co-Chief Scientist, Indian Ocean Experiment (INDOEX) 1996–2002, Chair. Int. Steering Cttee 1996–2002; First K.R. Ramanathan Visiting Prof., Physical Research Lab., India 1998; Chair. US Climate Change Science Program 2006–; mem. Science Editorial Bd NASA Earth Observatory 1999–, Atmospheric Brown Cloud Project (ABC) 2002– (Chair. 2005–), Geophysical Inst. Review Panel for Atmospheric Sciences 2002–, Advisory Bd World Clean Air Congress 2005–, NCAR Earth Observing Lab. External Advisory Cttee 2005–, Strategic Advisory Bd, Inst. for Advanced Sustainability Studies, Potsdam, Germany, US Climate Change Science Program 2011–; mem. Royal Swedish Acad. of Sciences 2011; numerous awards, including NASA Special Achievement Award 1975, NCAR Outstanding Publication Award 1981, Distinguished Alumnus Award, SUNY 1984, NASA Medal for Exceptional Scientific Achievement 1989, Buys Ballot Medal, Royal Netherlands Acad. of Sciences 1995, Volvo Environment Prize (co-recipient) 1997, elected to Stonybrook 40, SUNY 1998, W.S. Jardetzky Lecturer, Lamont Doherty Observatory, Columbia Univ. 2000, Rossby Medal, American Meteorological Soc. 2002, NSF Pioneer Award 2003, Johannes Gutenberg Lecturer 2004, Cozzarelli Prize 2007, Zayed Int. Prize for the Environment, Category II: Scientific/Technological Achievements in Environment, H.H. Sheikh Mohammad Bin Rashid Al Maktoum (co-recipient) 2007, Henry W. Kendall Memorial Lecturer, MIT 2008, Tyler Prize for Environmental Achievement, Univ. of Southern California (co-recipient) 2009. *Publications:* numerous scientific papers in professional journals on mitigation of climate change, climate dynamics, the greenhouse effect, air pollution, clouds, aerosols, satellite radiation measurements and global climate models. *Address:* Center for Clouds, Chemistry and Climate, Scripps Institution of Oceanography, University of California, San Diego, 9500 Gilman Drive, MC 0221, La Jolla, CA 92093-0221,

USA (office). *Telephone:* (858) 534-8815 (office). *Fax:* (858) 822-5607 (office). *E-mail:* vram@ucsd.edu (office). *Website:* www.ramanathan.ucsd.edu (office).

RAMANDIMBIARISON, Zaza Manitranja; Malagasy politician and engineer; b. 12 Dec. 1953, Ambatosoratra; s. of André Ramandimbiarison and Delphine Razanamanarivo; m.; one s. two d.; ed France and USA; Deputy Prime Minister in charge of Econ. Programmes, Minister of Transport, Public Works and Regional Planning 2002–07. *Leisure interests:* tennis, football, reading. *Address:* Villa Manarivo, Lot MC, 1209 Mandrosoa, Ivato, 105 Antananarivo, Madagascar (home). *Telephone:* (20) 22-455-77 (home).

RAMAPHOSA, Matamela Cyril, BProc; South African business executive and fmr politician; *Executive Chairman, Shanduka Group;* b. 17 Nov. 1952, Johannesburg; s. of Samuel Ramaphosa and Erdmuth Ramaphosa; m. Tshepo Motsepe; two s. two d.; ed Sekano-Ntoane High School, Soweto, Univ. of Turfloop and Univ. of S Africa; Chair. Univ. br. S African Students' Org. 1974; imprisoned under Section Six of Terrorism Act for 11 months, then for 6 months in 1976; returned to law studies and qualified 1981; apptd legal adviser, Council of Unions of S Africa; Gen. Sec. Nat. Union of Mineworkers 1982–91; Sec.-Gen. African National Congress (ANC) 1991–, nominated for ANC Pres. 2007; Visiting Prof. of Law, Stanford Univ. 1991; mem. Parl. 1994–96; Chair. of Constitutional Ass. 1994–96; Weapons Inspector N Ireland 2000; Deputy Exec. Chair. New Africa Investments Ltd 1996–99; with Nat. Empowerment Consortium 1996–; Chair. and CEO Molope Group 1999–2000; Chair. Rebserve Ltd 2000–03; Chair. Millennium Consolidated Investments (MCI) 2003; currently Exec. Chair. Shanduka Group; Dr hc (Univs of Natal, Port Elizabeth, Mass., Cape Town, Lesotho, Galway, Ireland); Olaf Palme Prize (Sweden) 1987. *Address:* Shanduka Group, Suite 167, Private Bag X9924, Sandton 2146, South Africa (office). *Telephone:* (11) 3058900 (office). *Fax:* (11) 3058999 (office). *E-mail:* cramaphosa@shanduka.co.za (office). *Website:* www.shanduka.co.za (office).

RAMAROSON, Vice-Adm. Hyppolite Rarison; Malagasy naval officer and politician; b. 28 Sept. 1951, Antananarivo; m.; three c.; ed Collège Saint Michel, Institution Sainte Famille, Académie Militaire, Antsirabe, Ecole Navale de Brest, France, Ecole supérieure de guerre navale, Paris, France; naval officer, responsibilities include fmr Coast Guard Officer, Fanantenana, Commdr, Antsiranana Naval Base, Head of Int. Relations, Ministry of Nat. Defence, Dir of Cabinet, Ministry of Nat. Defence; took part in NATO jt operations; apptd Pres. of Madagascar for one day 17 March 2009; Deputy Prime Minister and Minister of Foreign Affairs 2010–11 (resgnd). *Address:* c/o Ministry of Foreign Affairs, BP 836, Anosy, 101 Antananarivo, Madagascar (office).

RAMATHLODI, Ngoako, LLB, MSc; South African politician; b. 21 Aug. 1955, Potgietersrus (Tauatswala); m. Mathuding Ouma Ramatlhodi; one s. one d.; fmr Chair. African Nat. Congress (ANC), Northern Prov.; Deputy Registrar (student affairs), Exec. Asst to Vice-Chancellor Univ. of the N; in exile 1979, Commdr Unkhonto weSizwe; Head Political and Mil. ANC Council, Zimbabwe 1986; Political Sec., Asst to Oliver Tambo and Nelson Mandela 1988–91; Premier of Northern Prov. 1994–2002, of Limpopo Prov. 2002–04; mem. ANC Nat. Exec. Cttee 2007–; Hon. LLD (Univ. of the North, Limpopo). *Publications:* History of the ANC, Charade of Social Emanicipation and National Liberation, Ethnicity: How The ANC Must Govern. *Leisure interests:* music, reading, writing. *Address:* c/o National Executive Committee, African National Congress, PO Box 61884, Marshalltown 2107,, South Africa (office). *Website:* www.anc.org.za (office).

RAMAZANI BAYA, Raymond; Democratic Republic of the Congo politician and diplomatist; b. 17 June 1943; fmr Minister of Information; Amb. to France 1990–96 (resgnd); joined Congolese Liberation Movt (rebel group based in Gbadolite) following fall of Pres. Mobutu 1997, group entered into transitional govt with other rebel groups and govt of Pres. Joseph Kabila 2003; Minister of Foreign Affairs and Int. Co-operation 2004–07. *Address:* c/o Ministry of Foreign Affairs and International Co-operation, place de l'Indépendence, BP 1700, Kinshasa-Gombe, Democratic Republic of the Congo (office).

RAMBARRAN, Jwala, BSc; Trinidad and Tobago economist and central banker; *Governor, Central Bank of Trinidad and Tobago;* b. 1967; ed Univ. of the West Indies, Univ. of London, UK, Kennedy School of Govt, Harvard Univ., USA, IMF Inst., Washington, DC, Fed. Reserve Bank of New York; Research Asst, Dept of Econs, Univ. of the West Indies 1989–90; Economist, Research Dept, Central Bank of Trinidad and Tobago 1990–98, Economist/Man., Money and Finance Unit, Research Dept 1998–2001, Sr Economist, Monetary and Financial Policy 2003–04, Gov. and Chair. Bd of Dirs 2012–; Asst to Exec. Dir, IMF 2001–03; Chief Economist, Caribbean Money Market Brokers 2004–07; f. own business, Cap-M Research; CEO Infinity Financial Engineering 2010; Chair. Bd of Govs Nat. Inst. of Higher Educ., Research, Science and Tech., Trinidad 2010–12; mem. Bd of Dirs NOVO Technology 2010–; mem. Latin American & Caribbean Econs Asscn 2010–, Nat. Comm. for Higher Educ. 2011–, mem. World Future Soc., McKinsey Online Quarterly Panel. *Address:* Office of the Governor, Central Bank of Trinidad and Tobago, Eric Williams Plaza, Brian Lara Promenade, POB 1250, Port of Spain, Trinidad and Tobago (office). *Telephone:* 625-4835 (office). *Fax:* 627-4696 (office). *E-mail:* info@central-bank.org.tt (office). *Website:* www.central-bank.org.tt (office).

RAMBAUD, Patrick; French writer; b. 21 April 1946, Paris; s. of François Rambaud and Madeleine de Magondeau; m. Pham-thi Tieu Hong 1988; mil. service with French AF 1968–69; co-f. Actual magazine 1970–84; mem. Acad. Goncourt 2008–; Prix Alexandre Dumas 1976, Prix Lamartine 1981, Prix de l'Insolent 1988, Grand Prix du roman, Acad. Française 1997, Prix Goncourt 1997, Napoleonic Soc. of America Literary Award 2000, Prix Ciné-Roman 2001, Prix Rabelais 2005. *Plays:* Fregoli (with Bernard Haller) (Théâtre nat. de Chaillot 1991. *Publications:* La Saignée 1970, Les Aventures communautaires de Wao-le-Laid (with Michel-Antoine Burnier) 1973, Les Complots de la liberté: 1832 (with Michel-Antoine Burnier) (Prix Alexandre Dumas) 1976, Parodies (with Michel-Antoine Burnier) 1977, 1848 (with Michel-Antoine Burnier) 1977, Le Roland Barthes sans peine (with Michel-Antoine Burnier) 1978, Comme des rats 1980, La Farce des choses et autres parodies (with Michel-Antoine Burnier) 1982, Fric-Frac 1984, La Mort d'un ministre 1985, Frontière suisse (with Jean-Marie Stoerkel) 1986, Comment se tuer sans en avoir l'air 1987, Virginie Q (Prix de l'Insolent) 1988, Le Visage parle (with Bernard Haller) 1988, Bernard Pivot reçoit… 1989, Le Dernier voyage de San Marco 1990, Ubu Président ou L'Imposteur 1990, Les Carnets secrets d'Elena

Ceaucescu (with Francis Szpiner) 1990, Les Mirobolantes aventures de Frégoli 1991, Mururoa mon amour 1996, Le Gros secret 1996, Oraisons funèbres des dignitaires politiques qui ont fait leur temps et feignent de l'ignorer (with André Balland) 1996, La Bataille (Grand Prix du Roman de l'Acad. française 1997, Prix Goncourt 1997, Napoleonic Soc. of America Literary Award 2000) 1997, Le Journalisme sans peine (with Michel-Antoine Burnier) 1997, Les Aventures de Mai 1998, Il neigeait (Prix Ciné-Roman 2001) 2000, L'Absent 2003, L'Idiot du village (Prix de la dédicace sonore 2005) 2004, Le Chat botté 2006, La Grammaire en s'amusant 2007, Chronique du règne de Nicolas I 2008, Deuxième Chronique du règne de Nicolas I 2009, Troisième Chronique du règne de Nicolas I 2010, Quatrième Chronique du règne de Nicolas I 2011, Cinquième Chronique du règne de Nicolas I 2012, Tombeau de Nicolas I et avènement de François IV 2013. *Leisure interests:* writing, cooking, walking. *Address:* c/o Editions Grasset, 61 rue des Saints-Pères, 75006 Paris, France. *Telephone:* (06) 03-97-72-52 (home).

RAMDEV, Baba; Indian yoga teacher; b. (Ram Krishn Yadav), 11 Jan. 1971, Ali Saiyad Pur, Mahendragarh dist, Haryana; s. of Ram Nivas Yadav and Gulabo Devi; ed Aarsh (Arya) Gurukul, Gurukul Kangri Vishwavidyalaya; f. Patanjali Yogpeeth 2006, Divya Yog Mandir Trust, Patanjali Ayurved Coll., Patanjali Chikitsalaya, Yog Gram, Go-Shala, Patanjali Herbal Botanical Garden, Organic Agriculture Farm, Patanjali Food and Herbal Park Ltd; conducts yoga training camps in India and abroad; Host, Divya Yog on Aastha TV; Dr hc (Kalinga Inst. of Industrial Tech., Bhubaneswar) 2007, (Amity Univ.) 2010, (Dr D. Y. Patil Deemed Univ.) 2010; Sri Chandrashekharendra Saraswati Nat. Eminence Award 2011. *Address:* Patanjali Yogpeeth, Maharshi Dayanand Gram, Delhi-Haridwar National Highway, Near Bahadarbad, Haridwar 249 402, India (office). *Telephone:* (13) 34240008 (office). *Fax:* (13) 34244805 (office). *E-mail:* divyayoga@rediffmail .com (office). *Website:* www.divyayoga.com (office).

RAMDIN, Albert R.; Suriname diplomatist and international organization executive; *Assistant Secretary-General, Organization of American States (OAS);* b. 27 Feb. 1958; m. Charmaine Baksh; one s. one d.; ed schools in Paramaribo and the Netherlands, Univ. of Amsterdam and Free Univ.; career diplomat in public service at nat. and int. level, served as Sr Adviser to Minister of Trade and Industry; worked for two years in pvt. sector before returning to public service; apptd Adviser to Minister of Foreign Affairs and Minister of Finance; Amb. and Perm. Rep. to OAS 1997, Chair. Perm. Council Jan.–March 1998, Inter-American Council for Integral Devt 1999, coordinated Caribbean Community (CARICOM) Ambs' Caucus during Suriname's chairmanship of sub-regional group; apptd to serve concurrently as non-resident Amb. to Costa Rica 1999; Asst Sec.-Gen. for Foreign and Community Relations, CARICOM Secr. 1999; served as Amb. at Large and Special Adviser to Govt of Suriname on Western Hemispheric Affairs –2005; Adviser to OAS Sec.-Gen. with special attention to the Caribbean 2001–05, Asst Sec.-Gen. OAS 2005–. *Address:* Organization of American States, 17th Street & Constitution Avenue, NW, Washington, DC 20006, USA (office). *Telephone:* (202) 458-3000 (office). *Fax:* (202) 458-6319 (office). *E-mail:* OASWeb@oas.org (office). *Website:* www.oas.org (office).

RAMDORAI, Sujatha, BSc, MSc, PhD; Indian mathematician and academic; *Canada Research Chair, University of British Columbia;* b. 23 May 1962, Bangalore; d. of Parthasarathy Rangarajan and Srimathi Rangarajan; m. Srinivasan Ramdorai; one d.; ed St Joseph's Coll., Bangalore, Annamalai Univ. and Tata Inst. of Fundamental Research; Research Fellow, Univ. of Regensburg, Germany 1992–93, Ohio State Univ., USA 1993–95; Assoc. Prof. of Math., Tata Inst. of Fundamental Research 2000–06, Prof. of Math. 2006–; Vaidyanathaswamy Visiting Chair Prof., Chennai Mathematical Inst. 2008–11; Canada Research Chair, Univ. of British Columbia, Vancouver 2010–; mem. Nat. Knowledge Comm. 2007–09, Prime Minister's Scientific Advisory Council 2009; Alexander von Humboldt Fellow 1997–98; Man. Ed. International Journal of Number Theory; Ed. Journal of Ramanujan Mathematical Society; mem. Nat. Innovation Council; Fellow, Indian Acad. of Sciences 2003; Young Scientist Award 1993, Shanti Swarup Bhatnagar Prize, Council of Scientific & Industrial Research 2004, Ramanujan Prize, Int. Centre for Theoretical Physics 2006. *Leisure interests:* education, research. *Address:* Mathematics Department, 1984 Mathematics Road, University of British Columbia, Vancouver, BC V6T 1Z2, Canada (office). *Telephone:* (604) 822-3627 (office). *E-mail:* sujatha@math.ubc.ca (office). *Website:* www.math.ubc.ca/~sujatha (office).

RAMESH, Jairam; Indian politician; *Minister of Rural Development and of Panchayati Raj;* b. 9 April 1954, Chikmagalur, Karnataka; s. of C. K. Ramesh and Shrimati Sridevi Rameshat; m. K. R. Jayashree; two s.; ed Indian Inst. of Tech., Mumbai, Carnegie Mellon Univ., Massachusetts Inst. of Tech., USA; Adviser to Prime Minister 1991, to Deputy Chair., Planning Comm. 1992–94, to Finance Minister 1996–98; mem. Rajasthan Devt Council 1999–2003; Deputy Chair. Karnataka Planning Bd 2000–02; Econ. Adviser to govt of Chattisgarh 2001–03; mem. Rajya Sabha (Council of States) for Andhra Pradesh constituency 2004–; Minister of State for Commerce and Industry 2006–09, for Power 2008–09, for Environment and Forests 2009–11; Minister of Rural Devt and of Panchayati Raj 2011–; chief negotiator for India at UN Climate Change Conf., Copenhagen, Denmark 2009; mem. Nat. Advisory Council; Founding mem. Indian School of Business, Hyderabad; mem. Indian Nat. Congress party; Hon. Fellow, Inst. of Chinese Studies, New Delhi 2002–; Distinguished Alumnus Award, Indian Inst. of Tech., Mumbai 2001. *Publications:* Kautilya Today 2002, Making Sense of Chindia 2006. *Address:* Ministry of Rural Development, Krishi Bhavan, Dr Rajendra Prasad Rd, New Delhi 110 001, India (office). *Telephone:* (11) 23382230 (office). *Fax:* (11) 23382408 (office). *E-mail:* secyrd@nic.in (office); jairam@jairam-ramesh .com. *Website:* www.rural.nic.in (office); www.jairamramesh.in.

RAMGOOLAM, Hon. Navinchandra, LLB, LRCP; Mauritian physician, barrister and politician; *Prime Minister and Minister of Defence, Home Affairs and External Communications;* b. 14 July 1947, Mauritius; s. of the late Sir Seewoosagur Ramgoolam (first Prime Minister of Mauritius) and Lady Sushil Ramgoolam; m. Veena Ramgoolam 1979; ed Royal Coll. of Surgeons, Dublin, Ireland, London School of Econs and Inns of Court School of Law, London, UK; called to the Bar, Inner Temple 1993; Leader, Mauritius Labour Party (MLP) 1991–, Pres. 1991–92; Leader of Opposition and mem. Nat. Ass. 1991–95; Prime Minister 1995–2000, also Minister of Defence and Home Affairs, External Communications; leader of opposition 2000–2005; Prime Minister 2005–, also

Minister of Defence and Home Affairs, of Defence, Home Affairs and External Communications 2010–; acting Minister of Foreign Affairs 2008; mem. Int. Advisory Bd Center for Int. Devt, Harvard Univ. 1999–; Licentiate, Royal Coll. of Surgeons in Ireland; Hon. Fellow, London School of Econs 1998; Dr hc (Mauritius) 1998, (Aligarh Muslim Univ.) 1998, (Jawaharlal Nehru Univ.) 2005. *Leisure interests:* reading, music, water skiing, chess. *Address:* Prime Minister's Office, New Treasury Building, Intendance Street, Port Louis, Mauritius (office). *Telephone:* 207-9595 (office). *Fax:* 208-8619 (office). *E-mail:* primeminister@mail .gov.mu (office). *Website:* pmo.gov.mu (office).

RAMIA, José Serulle; Dominican Republic academic and diplomatist; *Ambassador to Trinidad and Tobago;* b. 11 June 1950, San Francisco de Macoris; m. Jacqueline Boin; fmr Vice-Rector, teacher of int. economy, Univ. of Santo Domingo; Amb. to Haiti 2005–08, to Trinidad and Tobago 2009–; Founder Fundación Ciencia y Arte Inc., fmr Pres. *Publications include:* 14 books including as co-author (with wife) El proceso del capitalism en la República Dominicana 1979, Inversion de capitales imperialistas en la República Dominicana: elementos de crítica a la "teoría de la dependencia" 1981, Fondo Monetario Internacional: deuda externa y crisis mundial 1984. *Address:* Embassy of Dominican Republic, Suite 101, 10b Queen's Park West, Port of Spain, Trinidad and Tobago (office). *Telephone:* 624-7930 (office). *Fax:* 623-7779 (office). *E-mail:* embdomtrinidadytobago@serex.gov.do (office).

RAMIREZ, Manuel Aristides (Manny); American (b. Dominican Republic) professional baseball player; b. 30 May 1972, Santo Domingo; s. of Aristides Ramirez and Onelcida Ramirez; m.; ed George Washington High School, NY; left fielder; moved to USA 1985; drafted in first round of amateur draft (13th overall) by Cleveland Indians 1991, debuted 2 Sept. 1993 versus Minnesota; runner-up Rookie of the Year 1994; signed as free agent with Boston Red Sox 2002; led American League in runs-batted-in with 165 in 1999; American League batting champion 2002 with .349 average; led American League in home runs with 43 in 2004; 1,000th career run versus Texas Rangers 23 Aug. 2002; hit 500th home run in 2008; traded to Los Angeles Dodgers 2008; American League All-Star Team 1995, 1998–2007; inducted into New York City Public Schools Athletic Hall of Fame 1999; voted Most Valuable Player, World Series 2004. *Address:* Los Angeles Dodgers, 1000 Elysian Park Ave., Los Angeles, CA 90012-1199, USA. *Telephone:* (323) 224-1500. *Fax:* (323) 224-1269. *Website:* losangeles.dodgers.mlb.com.

RAMÍREZ ACUÑA, Francisco Javier; Mexican politician; b. 22 April 1952, Jamay, Jalisco; m. María de la Paz Verduzco; two s. two d.; ed Universidad de Guadalajara; joined Partido Acción Nacional (PAN) 1969; Congressional Deputy for Jalisco State 1974–77, 1980–83; Local Rep. to Municipal Pres. of Zapopan 1983–85; Dir Gen. Sistecozome (public transport system of Jalisco) 1995–97; Mayor of Guadalajara 1998–2000; Gov. of Jalisco 2001–2006; Sec. of the Interior 2006–08 (resgnd). *Address:* Partido Acción Nacional, Avda Coyoacán 1546, Col. del Valle, Juárez 03100, Mexico (office). *Telephone:* (55) 5200-4000 (office). *E-mail:* correo@cen.pan.org.mx (office). *Website:* www.pan.org.mx (office).

RAMÍREZ CARREÑO, Rafael Darío; Venezuelan engineer and politician; *Minister of Petroleum and Mining and President and CEO, Petróleos de Venezuela SA (PDVSA);* ed Univ. of the Andes, Universidad Central de Venezuela; worked for eng firms Inelectra and Intevep; fmr Head, Enegas (nat. gas regulatory body) –2002; Minister of Energy and Mines (renamed Ministry of Energy and Petroleum 2005, further renamed Ministry of Petroleum and Mining) 2002–; Pres. and CEO Petróleos de Venezuela SA (PDVSA) 2004–. *Address:* Ministry of Petroleum and Mining, Edif. Petróleos de Venezuela, Torre Oeste, Avenida Libertador, La Campiña, Apdo 169, Caracas 1010-A (office); Petróleos de Venezuela SA, Edif. Petróleos de Venezuela, Torre Oeste, Avenida Libertador, La Campiña, Apdo 169, Caracas 1010-A, Venezuela (office). *Telephone:* (212) 708-7581 (Ministry) (office); (212) 708-4743 (PDVSA) (office). *Fax:* (212) 708-7598 (Ministry) (office); (212) 708-4661 (PDVSA) (office). *E-mail:* atencionalpublico@menpet.gob.ve (office); dazaroy@hotmail.com (office). *Website:* www.menpet.gob.ve (office); www.mem .gov.ve (office); www.pdvsa.com (office).

RAMÍREZ CODINA, Pedro Jeta; Spanish journalist and newspaper executive; *Director, El Mundo (del Siglo Veintiuno);* b. 26 March 1952, Logroño; m. 1st Rocío Fernández Iglesias; m. 2nd Agatha Ruíz de la Prada; one s. one d.; ed Univ. of Navarre; Prof. of Contemporary Spanish Literature, Lebanon Valley Coll., Pa, USA 1973–74; with La Actualidad Económica 1974–76; wrote weekly column for ABC newspaper; corresp. for El Noticiero Universal, Madrid; Dir of Diario 16 1980; Co-founder (with Alfonso de Salas, Balbino Fraga and Juan González) El Mundo (del Siglo Veinte, now Veintiuno) 1989, Publr and Ed. 1989–; Medalla de Oro de la Rioja 1997, Premio Montaigne de la Fundación Alemana Alfred Toepfer Stiftung 2005, Isaiah Berlin International Prize for Journalism 2007. *Address:* El Mundo, Pradillo 42, 28002 Madrid, Spain (office). *Telephone:* (91) 5864800 (office). *Fax:* (91) 5864848 (office). *E-mail:* editor@elmundo.es (office). *Website:* www.elmundo.es (office).

RAMÍREZ CORZO, Luis, MSc; Mexican petroleum industry executive; ed Nat. Univ. of Mexico, Univ. of Louisiana, USA Instituto Tecnológico Autónomo de México; fmr teacher Eng Dept, Nat. Univ. of Mexico; Dir Gen. PEMEX Exploration and Production 2001–04, Dir Gen. PEMEX 2004; mem. Academia de Ingeniería, Asociación de Ingenieros Petroleros de México, Soc. of Petroleum Engineers of American Inst. of Mechanical Engineers; Nat. Petroleum Eng Prize 2000. *Address:* c/o PEMEX, Avenida Marina Nacional 329, Colonia Huasteca, 11311 México DF, Mexico.

RAMÍREZ DE RINCÓN, Marta Lucía, PhD; Colombian politician and lawyer; b. Bogotá; m.; ed Javeriana Pontifical Univ., Univ. of the Andes, Harvard Univ., USA; fmr Prof., Univ. of the Andes; fmr Prof. of Foreign Trade, Faculty of Law, Javeriana Pontifical Univ.; Exec. Pres. Inversiones de Gases de Colombia SA, Federación Colombiana de Compañías Leasing, Nat. Asscn of Finance Insts, Financiera Mazda Crédito SA; fmr Vice-Minister of External Trade, Minister of External Trade 1998–2002; Amb. to France Feb.–Oct. 2002; Minister of Nat. Defence 2002–03; Gen. Man. and Pnr Ramirez and Orozco Int. Strategy Consultants 2004–06; Senator (Partido Social de Unidad Nacional) 2006–; Dir-Gen. Instituto de Comercio Exterior; Fellow, Center for Int. Affairs, Harvard Univ. *Publications include:* El Contrato de Descuento y la Apertura de Crédito Antecedentes y Perspectivas del Negocio Fiduciario en Colombia, Régimen Legal

de las Compañías de Financiamiento Comercial, Los Avances del Proceso de Interación Andina entre 1990 y 1991, El Programa Especial de Cooperación de la CEE para los Países Andinos. *Address:* Senado, Bogotá DC, Colombia (office). *E-mail:* martha.ramirez.derincon@senado.gov.co (office). *Website:* martaluciaramirez .com.

RAMÍREZ LEZCANO, Rubén, MA, MBA; Paraguayan economist, diplomatist and government official; b. 11 Jan. 1966; m. Adriana Cabelluzzi; two s.; ed Univ. of Buenos Aires, Univ. of Paris, Sorbonne, Univ. of California, Los Angeles, USA; with Int. Econ. Affairs Counselling Dept, Pres.'s Office 1989; Sec. Embassy in Buenos Aires, in charge of Commercial Dept 1989–92; Dir Dept of Foreign Trade, Ministry of Foreign Affairs (MFA) 1994–96; Exec. Sec. Nat. Council for Foreign Trade 1994–96; Counsellor Embassy in Paris and Standing Rep. at UNESCO 1996–98; Consul Gen. Los Angeles, Calif. 1998–99; Gen. Dir Export and Promotion Dept, MFA 1999–2000; Embassy Minister and Standing Rep. Latin American Integration Asscn, Montevideo, Uruguay 2000; Standing Rep. UN Special Orgs, Geneva, Switzerland 2001–04; Vice Minister for Econ. Relations and Integration 2004–06; Minister of Foreign Affairs 2006–08; mem. Asoc. Nacional Republicana–Partido Colorado (Nat. Republican Asscn–Colorado Party). *Address:* Asociación Nacional Republicana–Partido Colorado, Casa de los Colorados, 25 de Mayo 842, Asunción, Paraguay (office). *Telephone:* (21) 44-4137 (office). *Fax:* (21) 49-7857 (office). *Website:* www.anr.org.py (office).

RAMÍREZ MERCADO, Sergio; Nicaraguan author and politician; b. 5 Aug. 1942, Masatepe, Masaya; s. of late Pedro Ramírez Gutiérrez and Luisa Mercado Gutiérrez; m. Gertrudis Guerrero Mayorga 1964; one s. two d.; ed Univ. Autónoma de Nicaragua, León; was active in revolutionary student movt and founding mem. of Frente Estudiantil Revolucionario 1962; mem. Cen. American Univ. Supreme Council (CSUCA), Costa Rica 1964, Pres. 1968; mem. Int. Comm. of FSLN (Sandinista Liberation Front) 1975; undertook tasks on diplomatic front, propaganda and int. work on behalf of FSLN leading to overthrow of regime 1979; mem. Junta de Nat. Reconstruction Govt 1979; Vice-Pres. of Nicaragua 1984–90; minority leader, Speaker, Nat. Ass. 1990–94; Pres. Movimiento de Renovación Sandinista (MRS) 1994, MRS pre-cand. for presidency 1996; Co-founder literary journal Ventana; Pres. Int. Jury, Festival de Cine de Cartagena de Indias 1993, Jury, Festival Iberoamericano – de Cine de Huelva 2002, Premio Internacional de Novela Alfaguara 2008; mem. Jury, Premio Internacional de Periodismo Rey de España 1995, Premio Ulises de relato periodístico, Letra Internacional, Berlin 2005, 2006; mem. Governing Council, Fundación Nuevo Periodismo, Steering Cttee, Julio Cortazar Chair, Univ. of Guadalajara; Perm. mem. Iberoamerican Forum; columnist for numerous newspapers and journals; mem. Nicaraguan Acad. of Language; Corresp. mem. Royal Spanish Acad.; Hon. Prof., Faculty of Humanities, Universidad Pedagógica Francisco Morazán, Honduras 2007; Chevalier des Arts et des Lettres 1993, Orden Mariano Fiallos Gil del Consejo Nacional de Universidades de Nicaragua 1994, Medalla Presidencial del centenario de Pablo Neruda, otorgada por el gobierno de Chile 2004, Order of Merit, First Class (Germany) 2007; Dr hc (Universidad Central del Ecuador) 1984, (Université Blaise Pascal de Clermont-Ferrand, France) 2000, (Universidad der Catamarca, Argentina) 2007, (Universidad Latina, Panamá) 2011; De Tropeles y Tropelías 1971. *Publications include:* Cuentos 1963, El cuento centroamericano 1974, Charles Atlas también muere 1976, El cuento nicaragüense 1976, ¿Te dio miedo la sangre? (Premio Latinoamericano de Cuento, revista Imagen, Caracas) 1978, Castigo divino (Premio Dashiel Hammett 1990) 1988, Confesión de amor 1991, Clave de sol 1992, Cuentos 1994, Oficios compartidos 1994, Un baile de máscaras (Premio Laure Bataillon for Best Foreign Book translated in France 1998) 1995, Margarita, Está Linda la Mar (Premio Internacional de Novela Alfaguara 1998, Premio Latinoamericano de Novela José María Arguedas 2000) 1998, Adiós muchachos 1999, Mentiras Verdaderas 2001, Catalina y Catalina 2001, Sombras nada más 2002, El viajo arte de menir 2004, Mil y una muertes 2004, El reino animal 2006, Tambor Olvidado 2007, Juego perfecto 2008, El cielo llora por mi 2008, Cuando todos hablamos 2008, Perdón y olvido: Antología de cuentos (1960–2009) 2009, Casa de las Américas (Premio Iberoamericano de Letras José Donoso) 2011, La Fugitiva 2011, Abiertos/Puertas Abiertas 2011, La manzana de oro 2012, La viuda Carlota y otros cuentos 2012, Por qué cantan los pájaros y otros cuentos 2012, Historias para ser contadas 2012. *Leisure interests:* classical music, reading. *Address:* Apdo Postal LM-280, Managua, Nicaragua (office). *Telephone:* (22) 771718 (office). *Fax:* (22) 660548 (office). *E-mail:* srm@ibw .com.ni (office); sergioramirezm@gmail.com (office). *Website:* www.sergioramirez .org.ni (office); www.sergioramirez.com (office)

RAMÍREZ VALDIVIA, Avil; Nicaraguan fmr lawyer and government official; b. 1964, El Jicaral, León; m.; three c.; ed Universidad Nacional Autónoma de Nicaragua; joined Juventud Democrática Nicaragüense, Movimiento Democrático Nicaragüense 1979; moved to USA 1982, with AmeriFirst Bank, Miami 1983–89; returned to Nicaragua 1989; with USAID 1989; Sub-Dir for Europe, Ministry of Foreign Affairs 1994; Sec. to the Presidency 2001; Deputy Minister of the Interior, Dir of Immigration and Foreign Services 2004; Minister of Nat. Defence 2005–06. *Address:* c/o Ministry of National Defence, Casa de la Presidencia, Managua, Nicaragua (office).

RAMIRO DE LA FUENTE BLOCH, Gen. Carlos; Bolivian army officer; *Commander of the Armed Forces;* Gen. Commdr of the Army 2009–10, Commdr Armed Forces Jan. 2010–. *Address:* Ministry of National Defence, Plaza Avaroa, esq. Pedro Salazar y 20 de Octubre 2502, La Paz, Bolivia (office). *Telephone:* (2) 232-0225 (office). *Fax:* (2) 243-3153 (office). *E-mail:* correomaster@mindef.gov.bo (office). *Website:* www.mindef.gov.bo (office).

RAMKALAWAN, Rev. Wavel John Charles, BTheol; Seychelles theologian and politician; *Leader, Seychelles National Party;* b. 15 March 1961, Mahé; m.; three s.; ed Seychelles Coll., St Paul's Theological Coll., Univ. of Birmingham, UK; Founder and Leader of Parti Seselwa 1991–94; mem. Nat. Ass. 1993–97; Leader of Seychelles Nat. Party; Leader of the Opposition 1998–. *Address:* Seychelles National Party, Arpent Vert, Mant Fleuri, PO Box 81, Victoria (office); St Louis, Mahé, Seychelles (home). *Telephone:* (248) 224124 (office); (248) 516465 (home). *Fax:* (248) 225151 (office). *E-mail:* wavel24@hotmail.com (office).

RAMLI, Rizal, MA, PhD; Indonesian economist, business executive and fmr government official; *President, Board of Commissioners, PT Semen Gresik (Persero) Tbk;* b. 10 May 1953, Padang, West Sumatra; ed Bandung Inst. of Tech., Sophia Univ., Tokyo, Boston Univ., USA; econ. analyst; imprisoned for one year for writing white paper exposing failings of 'trickle-down' econs 1980s; ran ind. consultancy, Jakarta 1990s; Chair. Nat. Logistics Agency (Bulog) 2000; Chief Econs Minister –2001; Coordinating Minister for the Economy, Finance and Industry 2000; Minister of Finance June–July 2001; fmr Sr Consultant Van Zorge, Heffernan and Assocs, Jakarta; Pres. Bd of Comms PT Semen Gresik (Persero) Tbk 2006–. *Address:* PT Semen Gresik (Persero) Tbk, Gedung Utama Semen Gresik, Jl. Veteran, Gresik, 61122, Indonesia (office). *Telephone:* (31) 3981732 (office). *Fax:* (31) 3983209 (office). *Website:* www.semengresik.com (office).

RAMO, Simon, BS, PhD; American engineering executive (retd); b. 7 May 1913, Salt Lake City, Utah; s. of Benjamin Ramo and Clara Ramo (née Trestman); m. Virginia Smith 1937; two s.; ed Univ. of Utah and California Inst. of Tech.; with General Electric Co. 1936–46; Vice-Pres. Operations, Hughes Aircraft Co. 1946–53; with Ramo-Woolridge Corpn 1953–58; Dir US Intercontinental Ballistic Missile Program 1954–58; Dir TRW Inc. 1954–85, Exec. Vice-Pres. 1958–61, Vice-Chair. 1961–78, Chair. 1969–78, consultant 1978–, Chair. TRW-Fujitsu Co. 1980–83; Pres. The Bunker-Ramo Corpn 1964–66; Chair. Aetna, Jacobs & Ramo Venture Capital 1987–90, Allenwood Ventures, Inc. 1987–; adviser, Axiom Venture Pnrs 1997–; Visiting Prof. of Man. Science, California Inst. of Tech. 1978–; Regents Lecturer, UCLA 1981–82, Univ. of California, Santa Cruz 1978–79; Chair. Center for Study of American Experience, Univ. of Southern California 1978–80; Faculty Fellow, John F. Kennedy School of Govt, Harvard Univ. 1980–84; mem. White House Energy Research and Devt Advisory Council 1973–75; Chair. Pres.'s Comm. on Science and Tech. 1976–77; mem. Bd of Advisors for Science and Tech., Repub. of China 1981–84; Life Trustee, California Inst. of Tech., Nat. Symphony Orchestra Asscn 1973–83; Trustee Emer., California State Univ.; Pres. Bd Govs Performing Arts Council Music Center, LA 1976–77; Co-Chair. Bd Overseers Keck School of Medicine, Univ. of Southern California (USC) 1999–; mem. Bd of Dirs W.M. Keck Foundation 1983–, LA World Affairs Council 1973–85, Music Center Foundation, LA, LA Philharmonic Asscn 1981–84, Arco Power Technologies; Fellow, American Acad. of Political Science, American Acad. of Arts and Sciences, IEEE; mem. Nat. Acad. of Eng, Int. Acad. of Astronautics, Pacific Council on Int. Policy, Council on Foreign Relations, Inst. for the Advancement of Eng, American Philosophical Soc., American Physical Soc., New York Acad. of Sciences; Hon. DSc (Utah) 1961, (Union Coll.) 1963, (Worcester Polytechnic Inst.) 1968, (Akron) 1969, (Cleveland State) 1976, Hon. DEng (Case Western Reserve) 1960, (Michigan) 1961, (Polytechnic Inst., New York) 1971, Hon. LLD (Carnegie-Mellon) 1970, (USC) 1972, (Gonzaga) 1983, (Occidental Coll.) 1984, (Claremont) 1985; IEEE Electronic Achievement Award 1953, IAS Award 1956, American Inst. of Electronic Engineers Award 1959, American Iron and Steel Inst. Award 1968, Medal of Achievement, American Electronics Asscn 1970, Distinguished Service Medal, Armed Forces Comm. and Electronics Asscn 1970, Medal of Achievement, Western Electronics Mfrs Asscn 1970, USC Award 1971, 1979, Kayan Medal, Columbia Univ. 1972, American Construction Engineers Council Award 1974, IEEE Golden Omega Award 1975, IEEE Founders' Medal 1980, IEEE Centennial Medal 1984, named to Business Hall of Fame 1984, Nat. Medal of Science 1976, 1979, Franklin Inst. Medal 1978, Pres.'s Medal of Science 1981, UCLA Medal 1982, Presidential Medal of Freedom 1983, Aesculapian Award, UCLA 1984, Durand Medal, American Asscn of ind. Architects 1984, John Fritz Medal 1986, Henry Townley Heald Award, IIlinois Inst. of Tech. 1988, Nat. Eng Award, American Asscn of Eng Socs 1988, Franklin-Jefferson Medal 1988, Howard Hughes Memorial Award 1989, Air Force Space and Missile Pioneers Award 1989, Pioneer Award, Int. Council on Systems Eng 1997, NASA Distinguished Public Service Medal 1999, Lifetime Achievement Trophy, Smithsonian Inst. 1999, John F. Kennedy Astronautics Award, American Astronautical Soc. 2000, John R. Alison Award for Industrial Leadership, Air Force Asscn 2000, USC Presidential Medallion 2002, Founders' Award, USC Thornton School of Music 2003, Space Foundation Lifetime Space Achievement Award 2007, Dr Robert H. Goddard Memorial Trophy 2011. *Publications include:* Fields and Waves in Modern Radio (with J. R. Whinnery) 1944, 1953, Introduction to Microwaves 1945, Fields and Waves in Communication Electronics (with J. R. Whinnery and Theodore Van Duzer) 1965, Cure for Chaos 1969, Century of Mismatch 1970, Extraordinary Tennis for the Ordinary Player 1970, The Islands of E, Cono and My 1973, The Business of Science 1988, Meetings, Meetings and More Meetings (non-fiction) 2005. *Address:* 9200 Wesst Sunset Boulevard, Suite 801, Los Angeles, CA 90069-3603, USA (office). *Telephone:* (310) 550-8360 (office).

RAMON, Haim, BA; Israeli politician and lawyer; b. 10 April 1950, Jaffa; s. of Asher Vishnia and Bina Vishnia; m. 1st Prina Tenenbaum (divorced); one s. one d.; m. 2nd Vered Ramon Rivlin; ed Tel-Aviv Univ.; fmr Capt. in Israeli Air Force; Chair. Public Council for Youth Exchanges; Nat. Sec. Labour Party's Young Guard 1978–84; co-ordinator Finance Cttee, Labour Party 1984–88, Chair. Labour Party 1988–92; Minister of Health 1992–94, of the Interior 1995–96, 2000–01; apptd mem. Foreign Affairs and Defence Cttee 2001; Minister responsible for Jerusalem Affairs, Prime Minister's Office –2001; Minister without Portfolio 2005–06, of Justice 2006 (resgnd); Vice-Premier of Israel and Minister in Prime Minister's Office 2007; mem. Knesset 1983–2009; served on numerous cttees 1983–92 (Labour); fmr Sec.-Gen. Histadrut (Gen. Fed. of Labour in Israel); joined Kadima Party 2005; Chair. Int. Inst.—Histadrut; convicted of indecent assault 2007, sentenced to community service. *Address:* c/o The Knesset, Kiryat Ben-Gurion, Jerusalem, 91950, Israel (office).

RAMOS, Gen. Fidel Valdez; Philippine fmr head of state and army officer; *Chairman, Ramos Peace and Development Foundation;* b. 18 March 1928, Lingayen, Pangasinan; s. of Narciso Ramos and Angela Valdez; m. Amelita Martinez; five d.; ed Nat. Univ. Manila, US Mil. Acad., West Point and Univ. of Illinois; active service in Korea and Viet Nam; Deputy Chief of Staff 1981–84; Acting Chief of Staff, Philippines Armed Forces 1984–86, Chief of Staff 1986–88; Sec. of Nat. Defence 1988–91, cand. for Pres. May 1992; Pres. of the Philippines 1992–98; Chair. Emer. Lakas-Christian Muslim Democrats Party (CMD); Chair. Bd of Dirs Boao Forum for Asia; mem. ASEAN Eminent Persons Group 2005–; f. and Chair. Ramos Peace and Devt Foundation; Légion d'honneur 1987; numerous hon. degrees; Peace Prize Award, UNESCO 1997 and numerous other awards.

Address: c/o Ramos Peace and Development Foundation, 26th Floor, Export Bank Plaza, Corner Senator Gil Puyat and Chino Roces Avenues, 1200 Makati City (office); 120 Maria Cristina Street, Ayala Alabang Village, Muntinlupa City, Philippines (home). *Telephone:* (2) 8878964 (office). *Fax:* (2) 8878966 (office). *E-mail:* fvr@rpdev.org (office); rpdev@skyinet.net (home). *Website:* www.rpdev .org (office). www.boaoforum.org.

RAMOS, Maria Da Conceiçao Das Neves Calha, BCom, MSc; South African business executive; *Group Chief Executive, Absa Group Ltd;* b. 22 Feb. 1959, Lisbon, Portugal; m. Trevor Andrew Manuel; ed Univ. of the Witwatersrand, Univ. of London, UK, Inst. of Bankers Diploma (CAIB); emigrated to S Africa as a child; various positions, First Nat. Bank 1978–89; Lecturer in Econs, Univ. of South Africa 1989–91; Co-ordinator Econ. Study Cttee, Centre for Devt Studies 1989–90; mem. Transitional Exec. Council, Sub-Council on Finance 1989–95; Economist, Dept of Econ. Planning, African Nat. Congress (ANC) 1990–94, Project Leader, Inflation Project, Macro Econ. Research Group 1992–93; Research Assoc., Centre for Study of South African Econs and Int. Finance, LSE 1990–94, Research Officer, Centre for Research into Econs and Finance 1994–95; Lecturer in Econs, Univ. of the Witwatersrand 1991–94; Deputy Dir-Gen., Financial Planning, Dept of Finance 1995–96; joined Nat. Treasury, Pretoria as jr 1992, Dir-Gen. 1996–2003; Group Chief Exec. Transnet Ltd (state-owned transport group) 2004–09; Group Chief Exec. Absa Group 2009–, mem. Barclays Group Exec. Cttee; Dir (non-exec.) South African Airways (Pty) Ltd, Sanlam Ltd 2004–; Ind. Dir (non-exec.) Remgro 2007–; mem. World Bank Chief Economist Advisory Panel; Global Leader for Tomorrow, World Econ. Forum, British Council Scholarship (Helen Suzman Award) 1991, 1992, Santambank Marketing Prize, Inst. of Bankers Marketing Prize, Barclays Bank Grad. Scholarship, Senbank Prize for Honours Dissertation, Econ. Soc., Nedbank/Old Mutual Budget Competition, Business Women of the Year, Leader of the Year, Sunday Times Business Times, South Africa's Businesswoman of the Year 2001, ranked by Fortune magazine amongst the 50 Most Powerful Women in Business outside the US (29th) 2004, (28th) 2005, (16th) 2006, (14th) 2007, (22nd) 2008, (ninth) 2009, (11th) 2010, (seventh) 2011, (11th) 2012, Outstanding Businesswoman of the Year, African Business Awards 2009, ranked by Forbes magazine amongst The World's 100 Most Powerful Women (32nd) 2010, (93rd) 2011. *Address:* Absa Group Banks, Absa Towers West, 15 Troye Street, Johannesburg 2001 (office); Absa Group Banks, PO Box 7735, Johannesburg 2000, South Africa (office). *Telephone:* (11) 350-0304 (office). *Fax:* (86) 584-9760 (office). *E-mail:* Michelle.Buthelezi@absa.co.za (office). *Website:* www.absa.co .za (office).

RAMOS-HORTA, José, MA; Timor-Leste politician, UN official and fmr head of state; *Special Representative of the Secretary-General and Head, United Nations Integrated Peace-building Office in Guinea-Bissau (UNIOGBIS);* b. 26 Dec. 1949, Dili; s. of the late Francisco Horta and of Natalina Ramos Filipe Horta; m. Ana Pessoa 1978 (divorced); one s.; ed Hague Acad. of International Law, The Netherlands, Int. Inst. of Human Rights, Strasbourg, France, Columbia Univ., Antioch Univ., USA; journalist and broadcaster 1969–74; Minister for External Affairs and Information, Timor-Leste 1975; Perm. Rep. of Fretilin to UN, New York 1976–89; Public Affairs and Media Dir Mozambican Embassy, Washington, DC 1987–88; Exec.-Dir Lecturer Diplomacy Training Programme, Univ. of New South Wales 1990–, Visiting Prof. 1996–; Special Rep. Nat. Council of Maubere Resistance 1991–; returned to Timor-Leste Dec. 1999; Vice-Pres. Nat. Council of Resistance 1999–; Sr Minister for Foreign Affairs and Co-operation 2000–06 (resgnd), apptd Acting Defence Minister June 2006; Prime Minister of Timor-Leste 2006–07, also Minister of Defence; Pres. of Timor-Leste 2007–12; served in Timor-Leste Transitional Admin. 2000–02; Special Rep. of the Sec.-Gen. and Head of Integrated Peacebuilding Office in Guinea-Bissau (UNIOGBIS), UN 2013–; Bd mem. Timor-Leste Human Rights Centre, Melbourne; Sr Assoc. Mem. St Antony's Coll., Oxford 1987–; Order of Freedom (Portugal) 1996; Prof. Thorolf Rafto Human Rights Prize 1993, Gleitzman Foundation Award 1995, received Unrepresented Nations and People's Org. Award 1996, shared Nobel Peace Prize 1996 (with Mgr Carlos Ximenes Belo q.v.) 1996. *Publications include:* Funu: The Unfinished Saga of East Timor 1987, Timor Amanha em Dili, Dom Quixote 1994; articles in numerous publs worldwide. *Leisure interest:* tennis. *Address:* United Nations Integrated Peacebuilding Office in Guinea-Bissau (UNIOGBIS), Predio das Nações Unidas, Rua Rui Djassi, CP 179, PO Box 1011, Bissau, Guinea-Bissau (office). *E-mail:* blackman@un.org (office). *Website:* uniogbis.unmissions.org (office).

RAMOS ROSA, António; Portuguese poet and literary critic; b. 17 Oct. 1924, Faro; m. Agripina Costa Marques 1962; one d.; Dir literary reviews, Árvore 1951–53, Cassiopeia 1955, Cadernos do Meio-Dia 1958–60; Grand Oficial, Order of Santiago da Espada; Great Cross, Order of Infante Dom Henrique; Prize of Portuguese Centre of Int. Asscn of Literary Critics 1980, PEN Club's Poetry Prize 1980, 2006, Portuguese Asscn of Writers' Grand Prize 1989, Pessoa Prize 1988, International Poetry Prize of Liège Poetry Biennial 1991, European Poet of the Decade (Collège de l'Europe) 1991, Jean Malrieu Prize (Marseille) 1992, Grande Prémio Sophia de Mello Breyner Andresen 2005, Luís Miguel Nava Poetry Prize 2006. *Publications include:* poetry: Delta seguido de Pela Primeira Vez 1996, Nomes de Ninguém 1997, A Mesa do Vento seguido de As Espirais de Dioniso 1997, A Imobilidade Fulminante 1998; essays: Poesia, Liberdade Livre 1962, A Poesia Moderna e a Interrogação do Real 1979, Incisões Oblíquas 1987, A Parede Azul 1991, As Palavras 2001, Génese 2005. *Address:* c/o Roma Editora, Avenida Roma, 129 r/c Esq., 1700-346 Lisbon, Portugal.

RAMOTAR, Donald; Guyanese politician and head of state; *President;* b. 22 Oct. 1950, Caria Caria, Essequibo Islands, West Demerara region; ed Govt Tech. Inst., Univ. of Guyana, sent to USSR to study political science; worked for Guyana Import Export Co. (Gimpex) 1966–75; joined People's Progressive Party (PPP) 1967, numerous party positions including Man. of Freedom House (party HQ) 1975–79, elected to PPP Cen. Cttee 1979, Exec. Cttee 1983, Exec. Sec. of PPP 1993–97, Gen.-Sec. 1997–2013, mem. Editorial Bd Thunder (PPP newspaper) 2008–; Deputy, Nat. Ass. 1992–2011; Political Adviser to Pres. Bharrat Jagdeo April–Dec. 2011; Pres. of Guyana 2011–; mem. Editorial Council, Problems of Peace and Socialism magazine 1983–88; represented Guyana as mem. of ACP (African, Caribbean and Pacific States)–EU Jt Parl. Ass. *Address:* Office of the President, New Garden Street, Bourda, Georgetown, Guyana (office). *Telephone:*

225-7051 (office). *Fax:* 226-3395 (office). *E-mail:* opmed@op.gov.gy (office). *Website:* www.op.gov.gy (office).

RAMPHAL, Sir Shridath Surendranath, GCMG, OE, OM, ONZ, AC, QC, SC, LLM, FRSA; Guyanese international organization official, barrister and politician; b. 3 Oct. 1928, New Amsterdam; s. of James I. Ramphal and Grace Ramphal (née Abdool); m. Lois Winifred King 1951; two s. two d.; ed Queen's Coll., Georgetown, King's Coll., London, Harvard Law School; Crown Counsel, British Guiana 1953–54; Asst to Attorney-Gen. 1954–56; Legal Draftsman 1956–58; Solicitor-Gen. 1959–61; Legal Draftsman, West Indies 1958–59; Asst Attorney-Gen., West Indies 1961–62; Attorney-Gen., Guyana 1965–73; mem. Nat. Assembly 1965–75; Minister of State for External Affairs 1967–72, Minister of Foreign Affairs 1972–75, of Justice 1973–75; Commonwealth Sec.-Gen. 1975–90; Chancellor Univ. of Guyana 1988–92, Univ. of Warwick 1989–2001, Univ. of West Indies 1989–; Queen's Counsel 1965 and Sr Counsel, Guyana 1966; mem. Int. Comm. of Jurists, Ind. Comm. on Int. Devt Issues, Ind. Comm. on Disarmament and Security Issues, Ind. Comm. on Int. Humanitarian Issues, World Comm. on Environment and Devt, South Comm., Carnegie Comm. on Deadly Conflict, Bd of Govs Int. Devt Research Center, Canada, Exec. Cttee of Int. Inst. for Environment and Devt, Council of Int. Negotiation Network Carter Center, Georgia, USA 1991–97; Patron One World Broadcasting Trust; Chair. UN Cttee for Devt Planning 1984–87, West Indian Comm. 1990–92, Bd Int. Inst. for Democracy and Electoral Assistance (IDEA) 1995–2001, Advisory Cttee Future Generations Alliance Foundation 1995–97; Pres. World Conservation Union—IUCN 1990–93; Int. Steering Cttee Leadership for Environment and Devt Program Rockefeller Foundation 1991–98; Co-Chair. Comm. on Global Governance 1992–2000; Adviser to Sec.-Gen. of UNCED 1992; Chief Negotiator on Int. Econ. Issues for the Caribbean Region 1997–2001; Facilitator Belize–Guatemala Dispute 2000–02; John Simon Guggenheim Fellowship 1962; Hon. Bencher of Gray's Inn 1981; Fellow, King's Coll., London 1975, LSE 1979, RSA 1981, Magdalen Coll., Oxford 1982; Order of the Repub. (Egypt) 1973; Grand Cross, Order of the Sun (Peru) 1974; Grand Cross, Order of Merit (Ecuador) 1974, Order of Nishaan Izzuddeen (Maldives) 1989, Grand Commdr, Order of Niger 1990, Grand Commdr, Order of the Companion of Freedom (Zambia) 1990, Nishan-e-Quaid-i-Azam (Pakistan) 1990, Order of the Caribbean Community 1991, Commdr Order of the Golden Ark 1994; Hon. LLD (Panjab Univ.) 1975, (Southampton) 1976, (Univ. of The West Indies) 1978, (St Francis Xavier Univ., Halifax, Canada) 1978, (Aberdeen) 1979, (Cape Coast, Ghana) 1980, (London) 1981, (Benin, Nigeria) 1982, (Hull) 1983, (Yale) 1985, (Cambridge) 1985, (Warwick) 1988, (York Univ., Ont., Canada) 1988, (Malta) 1989, (Otago, NZ) 1990; Hon. DHL (Simmons Coll., Boston) 1982; Hon. DCL (Oxon.) 1982, (East Anglia) 1983, (Durham) 1985; Dr hc (Surrey) 1979, (Essex) 1980; Hon. DHumLitt (Duke Univ., USA) 1985; Hon. DLitt (Bradford) 1985, (Indira Gandhi Nat. Open Univ.) 1989; Hon. DSc (Cranfield Inst. of Tech.) 1987; Arden and Atkin Prize, Gray's Inn 1952, Int. Educ. Award (Richmond Coll., London) 1988, RSA Albert Medal 1988, Medal of Friendship, Cuba 2001, Pravasi Bharata Samman Award 2003. *Publications:* One World to Share: Selected Speeches of the Commonwealth Secretary-General 1975–79, Nkrumah and the Eighties (1980 Kwame Nkrumah Memorial Lectures), Sovereignty and Solidarity (1981 Callander Memorial Lectures), Some in Light and Some in Darkness: The Long Shadow of Slavery (Wilberforce Lecture) 1983, The Message not the Messenger (STC Communication Lecture) 1985, The Trampling of the Grass (Econ. Comm. for Africa Silver Jubilee Lecture) 1985, For the South, a Time to Think 1986, Making Human Society a Civilized State (Corbishley Memorial Lecture) 1987, Inseparable Humanity: An Anthology of Reflections of Shridath Ramphal 1988, An End to Otherness (six speeches) 1990, Our Country, The Planet 1992, No Island is an Island and contribs to journals of legal, political and int. affairs, including International and Comparative Law Quarterly, Caribbean Quarterly, Public Law, Guyana Journal, The Round Table, Royal Society of Arts Journal, Foreign Policy, Third World Quarterly, International Affairs. *Leisure interests:* photography, cooking. *Address:* 31 St Mathew's Lodge, 50 Oakley Square, London, NW1 1NB (home); 1 The Sutherlands, 188 Sutherland Avenue, London, W9 1HR, England. *Telephone:* (20) 7266-3409. *Fax:* (20) 7286-2302. *E-mail:* ssramphal@msn.com (office).

RAMPHELE, Mamphela Aletta, MB, ChB, BCom, DPH, PhD; South African physician, anthropologist, business executive and fmr international organization official; *Chairperson, Circle Capital Ventures;* b. 28 Dec. 1947, Pietersburg; d. of Pitsi Eliphaz Ramphele and Rangoato Rahab Ramphele (née Mahlaela); two s.; ed Setotolwane High School, Pietersburg, Univ. of Natal, Univ. of Capetown; community health worker Black Community Programmes, Ktown 1975–77, Ithuseng Community Health Programme, Tzaneen 1978–84; Sr Researcher Dept Social Anthropology, Univ. of Cape Town 1986, Deputy Vice-Chancellor 1991–95, Vice-Chancellor 1996–2000; Researcher and Consultant to Western Cape Hostel Dwellers' Asscn 1986–92; Man. Dir World Bank 2000–05; Chair. Ind. Devt Trust, Circle Capital Ventures; Co-Chair. Global Comm. on Int. Migration 2004–05; mem. Bd of Dirs (non-exec.) Anglo-American Corpn of SA 1992–95, Old Mutual 1993–, Anglo American 2006–; played key role in formation of Black Consciousness Movt 1969; Patron, Cape Town Opera 2006–; mem. NAMDA 1985–; Hon. DHumLitt (Hunter Coll., New York), 1984, New York Univ.) 2007; Hon. MD (Natal) 1989, (Sheffield) 1998; Dr hc for Distinguished Career (Tufts Univ., Mass.) 1991; Hon. DSc (Univ. Coll., London) 1997; Hon. LLD (Princeton) 1997, (Brown Univ.) 1998, (Mich.) 1998; Dr hc (Inst. of Social Studies, Netherlands) 1997; Hon. DPhil (Univ. of Orange Free State); Barnard Medal of Distinction, Barnard Coll., New York 1991. *Publications:* Children on Frontline (UNICEF report) 1987, Uprooting Poverty: The South African Challenge (with David Philip) 1989 (Noma Award for publishing in Africa 1991), A Bed Called Home: Life in Migrant Labour Hostels of Cape Town (with David Philip) 1993, Mamphela Ramphele: A Life (with David Philip) 1995, Across Boundaries: The Journey of a South African Woman Leader 1996. *Leisure interests:* reading, walking. *Address:* Circle Capital Ventures, 28th Floor, #1 Thibault Square, Cape Town 8001, South Africa (office). *Telephone:* (21) 4252231 (office). *Fax:* (21) 4215541 (office). *Website:* www.circlecapitalventures.co.za (office).

RAMPL, Dieter; German/Austrian banking executive; b. 5 Sept. 1947, Munich; m.; one s.; ed studies in econs in Munich; traineeship with Bayerischen Vereinsbank AG, Munich –1966, positions in Düsseldorf, Frankfurt and NY, 1968–83, mem. Exec. Cttee 1968–87, 1994–98, 1998–2006, Head of Regional Office, Munich 1995–97, Man. Dir Bayerische HypoVereinsbank Aktiengesellschaft

(HVB group, cr. through merger between Vereinsbank and Bayerischen Hypotheken und Wechselbank 1998) 1998, Spokesman Group Bd of Man. Dirs 2003–05; Chair. UniCredit SpA 2006–07, Unicredit Group (following merger of Unicredit and Capitalia) 2007–10, Oct. 2010–12, Chair. and Interim CEO Sept. 2010, Chair. Perm. Strategic Cttee, Corp. Governance, HR and Nominations Cttee, Remuneration Cttee, mem. Internal Control and Risks Cttee; with Société de Banque Suisse, Geneva 1966–68; with N American Div., BHF-Bank AG 1983–94; Chair. Supervisory Bd Koenig & Bauer AG, Bayerische Börse AG –2010; Chair. Man. Bd Hypo-Kulturstiftung; Vice-Chair. Mediobanca SpA; mem. Supervisory Bd FC Bayern München AG; mem. Bd Dirs Bode Hewitt Beteiligungs AG –2009, ABI (Italian Banking Asscn), ICC; mem. Bd of Dirs KKR Management LLC (New York), mem. Audit Cttee and mem. Conflicts Cttee –2011; Ind. Dir and Chair. Audit Cttee KKR Guernsey GP Ltd –2010; Dir (non-exec.) Babcock and Brown; Vice-Chair. Inst. for Int. Political Studies; mem. Bd Dirs AIRC (Italian Asscn for Cancer Research), Gen. Council of Aspen Inst. Italia, Trilateral Comm.– Gruppo Italia; Trustee, European School of Man. and Tech. –2009. *Address:* c/o UniCredit Group, Piazza Cordusia, 20123 Milan, Italy. *E-mail:* info@unicreditgroup.eu.

RAMPLING, Charlotte, OBE; British actress; b. 5 Feb. 1945, Sturmer, England; m. 2nd Jean-Michel Jarre 1978; two s. (one s. from previous marriage); one step-d.; film debut 1963; Chevalier, Ordre des Arts et Lettres 1986; César d'honneur 2001; Chevalier, Légion d'honneur 2002. *Films include:* The Knack 1963, Rotten to the Core, Georgy Girl, The Long Duel, Kidnapping, Three, The Damned 1969, Skibum, Corky 1970, 'Tis Pity She's a Whore, Henry VIII and His Six Wives 1971, Asylum 1972, The Night Porter, Giordano Bruno, Zardoz, Caravan to Vaccares 1973, The Flesh of the Orchid, Yuppi Du 1974–75, Farewell My Lovely, Foxtrot 1975, Sherlock Holmes in New York, Orca The Killer Whale, The Purple Taxi 1976, Stardust Memories 1980, The Verdict 1983, Viva la vie 1983, Beauty and Sadness 1984, He Died with His Eyes Open 1985, Max mon Amour, Max My Love 1985, Angel Heart 1987, Paris by Night 1988, Dead on Arrival 1989, Helmut Newton, Frames from the Edge, Hammers Over the Anvil 1991, Time is Money 1992, La marche de Radetzky (TV film) 1994, Asphalt Tango 1995, The Wings of the Dove 1997, The Cherry Orchard 1999, Signs and Wonders 2000, Hommage à Alfred Lepetit 2000, Aberdeen 2000, The Fourth Angel 2001, Under the Sand 2001, Superstition 2001, Spy Game 2001, See How They Run 2002, Summer Things 2003, I'll Sleep When I'm Dead 2003, Swimming Pool 2003, The Statement 2003, Jerusalem 2003, Vers le sud 2004, Lemming 2005, Basic Instinct 2 2006, Angel 2006, Deception 2007, The Duchess 2008, Babylon AD 2008, Never Let Me Go 2010, The Eye of the Storm 2011, I, Anna 2010, Cleanskin 2012, Tutto parla di te 2012, Night Train to Lisbon 2013, Young & Beautiful 2013, The Sea 2013. *Television includes:* numerous appearances including La Femme abandonnée 1992, Murder In Mind 1994, Radetzkymarsch (mini-series) 1995, Samson le magnifique 1995, La Dernière fête 1996, Great Expectations 1999, My Uncle Silas (series) 2000, Imperium: Augustus (film) 2003, Le grand restaurant 2010, Restless 2012, Dexter (series) 2013. *Address:* c/o Artmédia, 20 avenue Rapp, 75007 Paris, France. *Telephone:* 1-43-17-33-00.

RAMQVIST, Lars Henry, PhD; Swedish business executive; *Honorary Chairman, Telefonaktiebolaget L. M. Ericsson;* b. 2 Nov. 1938, Grängesberg; s. of Henry Ramqvist and Alice Ramqvist; m. Barbro Pettersson 1962; one s. one d.; ed Univ. of Uppsala; Section Head, Stora Kopparberg AB 1962–65; with Axel Johnson Inst. 1965–80, Pres. 1975–80; joined L. M. Ericsson Telephone Co. as Vice-Pres. and Head of Information Systems Div. 1980, Pres. and CEO 1990–98, Chair. 1998–2002, Hon. Chair. 2002–; Pres. subsidiary RIFA AB 1984–86, Ericsson Radio AB 1988–90; Vice-Chair. AB Volvo 1998, Chair. 1999–2004 (resgnd); Chair. Skandia Insurance Co. Ltd 1999–2003; mem. Bd of Dirs Svenska Cellulosa Aktiebolaget SCA (publ) 1994–2004, Astra Zeneca; mem. Bd Swedish Eng Employers' Asscn, Asscn of Swedish Eng Industries and Fed. of Swedish Industries (Chair. 1999), European Round Table of Industrialists 1994–2002; mem. Prime Minister's Special Industry Advisory Cttee 1994–; mem. Royal Swedish Acad. of Science, Royal Swedish Acad. of Eng Sciences; Hon. mem. IEEE; Dr hc (Technical Univ. Beijing), (Technical Univ. Moscow).

RAMS, Dieter; German industrial designer; b. 30 May 1932, Wiesbaden; m. Ingeborg Rams; ed Wiesbaden Werkkunstschule (School of Art); worked for Otto Apel (architect), Frankfurt 1953–55; joined Braun AG as architect and interior designer 1955, Chief of Design 1962–95, Exec. Dir, Corp. Identity Affairs 1995–97 (retd after designing, co-designing and overseeing designs of more than 400 products, including audiovisual equipment, coffee makers, calculators, radios and office products as well as a shelving system for Vitsœ); mem. Supervisory Bd German Design Council (Rat für Formgebung) 1976, Chair. 1988–98, Hon. Chair. 1998–; Prof., Acad. of Fine Arts, Hamburg 1980; Hon. Royal Designer for Industry, RSA, UK 1968, Hon. Foreign mem. Academia Mexicana de Diseno, Mexico 1985, Hon. Int. Faculty mem., Ontario Coll. of Art, Toronto, Canada 1986; Hessian Order of Merit 1997, Verdienstkreuz des Verdienstordens der Bundesrepublik Deutschland 2002; Dr hc (RCA, UK) 1989; UK Soc. of Industrial Artists and Designers Medal 1978, Industrial Designers Soc. of America World Design Medal 1996, ONDI Design Award, Havana, Cuba 2003, Design Prize of FRG 2007, Raymond Loewy Foundation Lucky Strike Designer Award 2007. *Address:* c/o Vitsœ, Centric Close, London, NW1 7EP, England (office). *Website:* www.vitsoe.com/en/gb/about/dieterrams (office).

RAMSAMY, Pakereesamy (Prega), BA, MBA, PhD; Mauritian economist and international organization official; *Director General, Economic Development Board of Madagascar;* b. 1950, Rose Hill; m. Novia Ramsamy; two d.; with Preferential Trade Area for Eastern and Southern Africa, then Common Market for Eastern and Southern Africa for 14 years; Chief Economist, Southern African Devt Community 1997–98, Deputy Exec. Sec. 1998–2000, Acting Exec. Sec. 2000, Exec. Sec. 2001–05; Dir Gen. Econ. Devt Bd of Madagascar 2006–. *Leisure interests:* reading, indoor games, swimming, fishing. *Address:* Projet Pôles Intégrés de Croissance, Immeuble Ex-Maison de La Réunion, 2ème étage ISORAKA, Antananarivo 101, Madagascar (office). *Telephone:* (20) 2236777 (office). *Fax:* (20) 2230172 (office). *E-mail:* pic@wanadoo.mg (home).

RAMSAUER, Peter, Dr.oec.publ; German politician; b. 10 Feb. 1954, Traunwalchen, Bavaria; m.; four d.; ed Ludwig-Maximilians-Universität, Munich; Propr, Ramsauer Talmühle eK (milling co.), Traunwalchen; mem. Junge Union (JU) 1972, Chair., JU Traunwalchen 1973–75, JU Traunreut 1977–79, Deputy Dist

Chair., JU Upper Bavaria 1979–81, Dist Chair., JU Dist Div., Traunstein 1983–87; Deputy State Chair., JU Bavaria 1983–89; mem. CSU 1973–, Local Chair., CSU Traunreut 1985–91; mem. Traunreut City Council 1978–91, Traunstein Dist Council 1984; mem. Bundestag (parl.) for Traunstein/Berchtesgadener Land constituency 1990–, Parl. Sec., CSU Regional Group 1998–2005, Chair. 2005–; Fed. Minister of Transport, Building and Urban Affairs 2009–13. *Leisure interests:* playing piano, jogging. *Address:* c/o Federal Ministry of Transport, Building and Urban Affairs, Invalidenstr. 44, 10115 Berlin, Germany (office). *E-mail:* peter .ramsauer@wk.bundestag.de (office). *Website:* www.peter-ramsauer.de (office).

RAMSAY, Lynne; British film director and writer; b. 5 Dec. 1969, Glasgow, Scotland; m. Rory Kinnear 2010; ed Nat. Film and Television School; trained as a camera operator; directed promotional video for Manchester-based indie-rock band Doves' single Black and White Town 2005; Carl Foreman Award for Newcomer in British Film, BAFTA Awards 2000, Sutherland Trophy, London Film Festival, Silver Hugo for Best Dir, Chicago Int. Film Festival, ranked No. 12 in the Guardian Unlimited's list of the world's 40 best directors working today 2007. *Films include:* Small Deaths (short) (Prix de Jury, Cannes Film Festival 1996), Kill the Day (short) (Clemont Ferrand Prix du Jury) 1996, Gasman (short) (Prix de Jury, Cannes Film Festival, Scottish BAFTA for Best Short Film) 1998, Ratcatcher (debut feature) (numerous awards, including the Guardian New Dirs Prize, Edinburgh Int. Film Festival) 1999, Morvern Callar (Award of Confédération Internationnale des Cinémas d'Art et d'Essai, Award of The Youth, Cannes Film Festival) 2002, We Need to Talk about Kevin (BBC Films-produced adaptation) 2011.

RAMSEY, Paul Glenn, AB, MD; American physician and academic; *CEO of UW Medicine and Dean of the School of Medicine, University of Washington;* b. 1949, Pittsburgh; m. Bonnie Ramsey; ed Harvard Coll., Harvard Medical School; Residency in Internal Medicine, Mass Gen. Hosp., Boston 1975–78; Acting Instructor, Dept of Medicine, Univ. of Washington 1980–81, Acting Asst Prof. 1981–82, Asst Prof. 1982–86, Assoc. Prof. 1986–91, Prof. 1991–, Assoc. Chair. Dept of Medicine 1988–90, Chair. 1992–97, Robert G. Petersdorf Endowed Chair. in Medicine 1990, Vice Pres. for Medical Affairs and Dean, School of Medicine 1997–, also CEO UW Medicine and Exec. Vice Pres. of Medical Affairs 2006–; mem. Assn of American Physicians, NAS Inst. of Medicine; Univ. of Washington School of Medicine Distinguished Teacher Award 1984,1986, 1987, Margaret Anderson Award 1989, Nat. Bd of Medical Examiners John P. Hubbard Award 1999. *Address:* Office of the Dean, UW School of Medicine, University of Washington, 325 Ninth Avenue, Seattle, WA 98104-2499, USA (office). *Telephone:* (206) 744-3000 (office). *Website:* uwmedicine.washington.edu (office).

RAMZI, Rashid; Bahraini (b. Moroccan) athlete; b. 17 July 1980, Morocco; middle-distance runner; competes internationally for Bahrain in 800m, 1,500m and 5,000m; only Bahraini Olympic medallist; raised in Safi, Morocco; competed internationally for Morocco until he joined Bahraini armed forces and gained citizenship in 2002; Silver Medal, 800m, World Indoor Championships 2004; became first athlete in history to win gold medals in 800m and 1,500m at same World Championships and first man to perform this feat in a global championship (World Championships or Olympic Games) since Peter Snell in 1964, World Championships, Helsinki 2005; Silver Medal, 1,500m, World Championships, Osaka 2007; Gold Medal, 1,500m, Olympic Games, Beijing 2008. *Address:* c/o Bahrain Amateur Athletics Federation, PO Box 29269, 12344 Manama, Bahrain. *Telephone:* 684905. *Fax:* 687506. *E-mail:* athletic@batelco.com.bh.

RANA, Gen. Gaurav Shamsher Jung Bahadur, BA, MA; Nepalese army officer; *Chief of the Army Staff;* b. 12 Dec. 1955; s. of the late Maj. Gen. Aditya S. J. B. Rana and Rani Sunita Rana; m. Rohini Rana; two d.; ed Tribhuvan Univ., Quaid-E-Azam Univ. of Pakistan, Royal Mil. Acad. Sandhurst, UK, US Army Command and Gen. Staff Coll., Fort Leavenworth, USA, Nat. Defence Univ., Pakistan; commissioned into Purano Gorakh Bn 1974, commanded Shree Taradal Gulma (Ind. Infantry Co.) and Shree Purano Gorakh Bn, led bn in active operational duty in UNIFIL, Lebanon 1994, served as Commdt of Nepalese Mil. Acad., Kharipati, active operational commands include Brigade Commdr in 5th and 9th Infantry Brigades in counter-insurgency environment in far western and central Nepal, respectively, commanded Western Div., headquartered in Pokhara, major staff appointments at the Army HQs include Chief of Gen. Staff, Chief of Staff, Dir of Recruitment, Dir of Logistics, Dir of Army Research and Devt, Insp. Gen. of the Army and Dir Gen. of Mil. Operations, as the latter during the Koshi floods of 2008, he represented the Nepalese Army in the Cen. Natural Disaster Relief Cttee and was the gen. officer in charge of rescue and relief operations, attained rank of Gen. 2012, Chief of the Army Staff 2012–, Col Commdt Purano Gorakh Bn; Suprabal Jana Sewa Shree; other decorations, medals and insignias include the Tri Shakti Patta, Disaster Rescue Award, UN Medal with Bar, Remote Area Service Medal (Mountain Warfare) and Parachutist Wings. *Leisure interests:* military history, golfer, bird watching, mountain biking. *Address:* Office of the Chief of Army Staff, Ministry of Defence, Singha Durbar, Kathmandu, Nepal (office). *Telephone:* (1) 4211290 (office). *Fax:* (1) 4211294 (office). *E-mail:* mod@mos .com.np (office).

RANA, Kipkorir Aly Azad, MPolSci, PhD; Kenyan international civil servant and trade consultant; *Managing Director, Mabwa Enterprise Ltd;* ed Univ. of Nairobi, Univ. of California, Los Angeles, USA; Deputy Head of Mission, Tokyo 1993–96; Deputy Perm. Rep. and Alt. Del./ Co-ordinator to Security Council, UN, New York 1997; Perm. Sec. (Devt Co-ordination), Office of the Pres. of Kenya 1998; Amb. and Perm. Rep. UN, Geneva 1998–2000; Co-ordinator of African Dels to WTO and Sr Trade Policy Adviser, Minister for Trade and Industry 1999–2001; Deputy Dir-Gen. WTO 2002–05; Fulbright Hays Fellow 1973–79; Man. Dir Mabwa Enterprise Ltd (agro-business) 2006–. *Address:* Mabwa Enterprise Ltd, POB 761-40100, 1211 Kisumu, Kenya (office). *E-mail:* info@mabwa-ent.com (office). *Website:* www.mabwa-ent.com (office).

RANA, Madhukar Shumshere J. B., BA, MA; Nepalese economist, academic and fmr government official; *Adjunct Professor, South Asian Institute of Management;* b. 1941, Jawalakhel, Lalitpur; ed McMaster Univ., Canada, Univ. of Manchester, UK, Univ. of Geneva, Switzerland, Delhi Univ., India; Manpower Economist, Govt of Canada 1967; fmr Lecturer in Econs, Nippising Univ.; fmr Assoc. Teaching Master, Cambrian Coll. of Applied Arts and Tech.; Assoc. Prof.,

Centre for Econ. Devt and Admin, Tribhuvan Univ. 1971, then became Exec. Dir; Chief Econ. Adviser to Ministry of Finance 1983–84; Sr Regional Programme Man. for South Asia, UNDP 1994–95; Special Adviser to Ministry of Foreign Affairs 1996–98; Minister of Finance Jan.–Dec. 2005; currently Adjunct Prof., South Asian Inst. of Man., Kathmandu; Commr SAARC Ind. Comm.; Pres. Shaligram Apartment-Hotel; fmr Pres. Rotary Jawalakhel, Man. Asscn of Nepal; mem. South Asian Ind. Comm. on Poverty Allevation 1991–2001. *Address:* South Asian Institute of Management, Lagankhel, Lalitpur, Kathmandu, Nepal (office). *Telephone:* (1) 5522044 (office). *Fax:* (1) 5522044 (office). *E-mail:* info@saim.edu .np (office). *Website:* www.saim.edu.np (office).

RANA, Pashupati S. J. B. R., BA; Nepalese politician; *Chairman, Rashtriya Prajatantra Party;* b. 7 May 1941, Laxmi Niwas, Kathmandu; s. of the late Gen. Bijaya Shumsher Jung Bahadur Rana and Rani Sarla Devi Rana; m. Rani Usha Rajya Laxmi Devi Rana (Princess of Gwailor); two d.; ed Haileybury, ISC and New Coll., Oxford, UK; mem. Parl. 1973–; Minister of Educ., Transport, Civil Aviation and Tourism 1979, Minister of Water Resources 1983–86, 1995–98, Minister of Panchayat and Local Devt 1986–88, Minister of Foreign Affairs, Finance, Water Resources and Communications 1990, Gen. Sec. Rashtriya Prajatantra Party (Nat. Democratic Party) 1991–97, Chair. 2003–; mem. India-Int. Centre, Int. Council Asia Soc.; Pres. Alliance française. *Leisure Interests:* reading, European classical music, writing, shooting, trekking. *Address:* Central Secretariat, Rashtriya Prajatantra Party, Charumati Bahal, Chabahil, Kathmandu (office); Bijaya Bas, PO Box 271, Maharaj Gunj, Kathmandu, Nepal (home). *Telephone:* (1) 4471071 (office); (1) 4437902 (home). *Fax:* (1) 4435173 (office); (1) 4423384 (home). *E-mail:* info@rppnepal.com (office); p-rana@ntc.net.np (home). *Website:* www.rppnepal.org (office).

RANA, Rukma Shumsher, MA; Nepalese business executive and diplomatist; b. 12 March 1936, Kolkata, India; s. of Suvarna Shumsher Rana; ed St Xavier's Coll., Darjeeling, India, Univ. of Kolkata; fmr Pres. Nepal Taekwondo Asscn, Pres. Nepal Olympic Cttee 1998–2006; fmr Man. Dir Dabur Nepal Pvt. Ltd; fmr Pres. Nepal-India Chamber of Commerce and Industry; Amb. to India 2009–11. *Address:* Ministry of Foreign Affairs, Narayanhiti, Kathmandu, Nepal (office). *Telephone:* (1) 4416011 (office). *Fax:* (1) 4416016 (office). *E-mail:* adm@mofa.gov.np (office). *Website:* www.mofa.gov.np (office).

RANA, Sushil Jungbahadur; Nepalese business executive; fmr Sec., Ministry of Commerce and Supplies; Chair. Nepal Oil Corpn –2013. *Address:* c/o Nepal Oil Corporation, GPO Box 1140, Babarmahal, Kathmandu, Nepal. *E-mail:* info@ nepaloil.com.np.

RANATUNGE, Prasanna; Sri Lankan politician; *Chief Minister of Western Province;* b. 1 Jan. 1967, Colombo; fmr Leader, United People's Freedom Alliance, Gampaha Dist; Chief Minister of Western Prov. 2009– (Educ., Finance and Planning, Law and Order, Land, Prov. Admin, Human Resources and Employ-ment, and Econ. Devt portfolios). *Address:* Office of the Chief Minister of Western Province, 'Srawasthi Mandiraya', 32 Sri Marcus Fernando Mawatha, Colombo 07, Sri Lanka (office). *Telephone:* (11) 2698410 (office). *E-mail:* chiefminist@sltnet.lk (office). *Website:* www.wpc.gov.lk (office).

RANCHOD, Bhadra, BA, LLB, LLM, LLD; South African diplomatist, lawyer and academic; *Member of Faculty, Department of Private and Roman Law, University of Stellenbosch;* b. 11 May 1944, Port Elizabeth; s. of Ghalloo Ranchod and Parvaty Ranchod; m. Vibha M. Desai 1980; two d.; ed Univs of Cape Town, Oslo, Norway and Leiden, The Netherlands; Sr Lecturer, Dept of Pvt. Law, Univ. of Durban-Westville 1972, Prof. of Pvt. Law 1974, Dean, Faculty of Law 1976–79; Advocate of Supreme Court 1973–; mem. Bd of Govs S African Broadcasting Corpn; mem. S African Law Comm.; mem. Human Sciences Research Council, numerous cttees and public bodies etc.; Visiting Scholar, Columbia Univ., New York, USA 1980–81; Amb. and Head of S African Mission to European Communities 1986–92; Minister of Tourism 1993–94; Chair. Minister's Council in House of Dels 1993–94; MP 1994–96; Deputy Speaker, Nat. Ass. 1994–96; High Commr in Australia (also accred to NZ and Fiji Islands) 1996–2001; Faculty of Dept of Pvt. and Roman Law 2001–; Vice-Chair. Bd Christel House Cape Town; Dir Maritime Mutual Insurance Co. (NZ); mem. Advisory Cttee Children's Rights Int. *Publications:* Foundations of the South African Law of Defamation (thesis) 1972, Law and Justice in South Africa 1986; about 100 papers on human rights issues. *Leisure interests:* jogging, reading, travel. *Address:* Department of Private and Roman Law, University of Stellenbosch, Private Bag X1, Matieland, 7602 Stellenbosch (office); 3 Eldorado Street, 7600 Stellenbosch, South Africa (home). *Telephone:* (82) 2906099 (mobile) (office); (21) 8878844 (home). *E-mail:* branchod@sun.ac.za (office). *Website:* law.sun .ac.za/DepartmentofPrivateLaw.htm (office).

RANCIÈRE, Jacques; French social historian, philosopher, literary critic, author and academic; *Professor Emeritus, Université de Paris St Denis;* b. 1940, Algiers, Algeria; currently Prof. Emer. Univ. de Paris St Denis; Prof. of Philosophy (Intensive Summer Seminar), European Graduate School, Saas-Fee, Switzerland. *Publications include:* in trans.: Reading Capital (co-author) 1968, The Nights of Labor: The Workers' Dream in Nineteenth-Century France 1989, The Ignorant Schoolmaster 1991, Five Lessons in Intellectual Emancipation 1991, The Names of History 1994, On the Poetics of Knowledge 1994, On the Shores of Politics 1995, Disagreement: Politics and Philosophy 1998, The Politics of Aesthetics: The Distribution of the Sensible 2004, The Future of the Image 2007, Hatred of Democracy 2007, The Aesthetic Unconscious 2009, The Emancipated Spectator 2009. *Address:* c/o European Graduate School, Alter Kehr 20, 3953 Leuk-Stadt, Switzerland (office).

RANDALL, Jeff William, BA; British journalist; *Editor-at-Large, The Daily Telegraph;* b. 3 Oct. 1954, London; s. of Jeffrey Charles Randall and Grace Annie Randall (née Hawkridge); m. Susan Diane Fidler 1986; one d.; ed Royal Liberty Grammar School, Romford, Univ. of Nottingham, Univ. of Florida, USA; with Hawkins Publrs 1982–85; Asst Ed. Financial Weekly 1985–86; City Corresp. Sunday Telegraph 1986–88; Deputy City Ed. The Sunday Times 1988–89, City Ed. 1989–94, City and Business Ed. 1994–95, Asst Ed. and Sports Ed. 1996–97; Ed. Sunday Business 1997–2001; Business Ed. BBC 2001–05; Ed.-at-Large The Daily Telegraph 2005–; host Jeff Randall Live (Sky News) 2007–; freelance contrib. Daily Telegraph, Euromoney; Dir Times Newspapers 1994–95; Deputy Chair. Financial Dynamics Ltd 1995–96; Dr hc (Anglia Ruskin Univ.) 2001, (Univ. of Nottingham)

2006; Financial Journalist of the Year, FT-Analysis 1991, Business Journalist of the Year, London Press Club 2000, Sony Gold Award 2003, Communicator of the Year 2004, Business Broadcaster of the Year, Wincott Awards 2004. *Publications:* The Day That Shook the World (co-author). *Leisure interests:* golf, horse racing, football. *Address:* The Daily Telegraph, 111 Buckingham Palace Road, London, SW1W 0DT, England (office). *Website:* www.telegraph.co.uk/finance/comment/jeffrandall (office).

RANDEL, Don Michael, MFA, PhD; American musicologist, foundation executive and fmr university administrator; *President, The Andrew W. Mellon Foundation;* b. Panama; m. Carol Randel; four d.; ed Princeton Univ.; Asst Prof., Dept of Fine Arts, Syracuse Univ. 1966–68; Asst Prof. of Music, Cornell Univ. 1968–71, Assoc. Prof. 1971–75, Chair. Dept of Music 1971–76, Prof. of Music 1975–2000, Vice-Provost 1978–79, Assoc. Dean, Coll. of Arts and Sciences 1989–91, Harold Tanner Dean 1991–95, Provost 1995–2000; Pres. Univ. of Chicago 2000–06; Pres. Andrew W. Mellon Foundation 2006–; Vice-Pres. American Musicological Soc. 1977–78 (Ed.-in-Chief Journal of the American Musicological Soc. 1972–74); Fellow, American Acad. of Arts and Sciences 2001–; mem., AAAS, Modern Language Asscn, American Philosophical Soc. 2002–; mem., Bd of Trustees Chicago Symphony Orchestra Assocn 2001–, Music and Dance Theater Chicago 2001; mem., Bd of Govs Partnership for Public Service 2001–; mem., Bd of Dirs Chicago Council on Foreign Relations 2001–, CNA Financial Corpn 2002–. *Publications:* New Harvard Dictionary of Music (Ed.) 1986, Harvard Biographical Dictionary of Music (Ed.) 1996, Harvard Concise Dictionary of Music and Musicians (Ed.) 1999; author of numerous articles in musical journals. *Address:* The Andrew W. Mellon Foundation, 140 East 62nd Street, New York, NY 10065, USA (office). *Telephone:* (212) 838-8400 (office). *Fax:* (212) 500-2302 (office). *E-mail:* inquiries@mellon.org (office). *Website:* www.mellon.org (office).

RANDERSON, Baroness (Life Peer), cr. 2011, of Roath Park in the City of Cardiff; **Jenny Randerson;** British politician; m.; several c.; began career in politics in Cardiff late 1970s; Cyncoed Councillor 1983–99; Leader of Opposition, Cardiff Co. Council 1994–99; contested Cardiff Cen. seat 1997; MLA (Liberal Democrat) for Cardiff Cen. in newly est. Welsh Ass. 1999–; Minister for Culture, Sport and the Welsh Language 2003–07; Welsh Liberal Democrat Spokesperson for Health, Social Care, Finance and Local Govt 2007–08; Welsh Liberal Democrat Shadow Minister for the Economy, Educ. and Transport 2008–; introduced into law first ever Pvt. Mems Bill in Wales. *Address:* National Assembly for Wales, Cardiff Bay, Cardiff, CF99 1NA, Wales (office); House of Lords, Westminster, London, SW1A 0PW, England. *Telephone:* (29) 2089-8355 (office); (20) 7219-5353; (29) 2089-8356 (office). *Fax:* (20) 7219-5979. *E-mail:* jenny@jennyranderson.com (office). *Website:* www.jennyranderson.com (office).

RANDT, Clark Thorp, Jr, BA, JD; American lawyer and diplomatist; b. 1 Jan. 1945, Conn.; m. Sarah A. Talcott; two s. one d.; ed Hotchkiss School, Yale Univ., Univ. of Michigan Law School; served with USAF Security Service 1968–72; China rep. Nat. Council for US-China Trade 1974; First Sec. and Commercial Attaché, US Embassy, Beijing 1982–84; pvt. law practice as Partner, Shearman & Sterling, Hong Kong; Amb. to People's Repub. of China 2001–09; Special Advisor, Hopu Investment Man. Co., Beijing 2009–; mem. NY and Hong Kong Bars; fmr Gov. and First Vice-Pres. American Chamber of Commerce, Hong Kong; mem. Council on Foreign Relations;. *Address:* Hopu Investment Management Co., Suite 203-205, North Tower Winland Financial Center, 7 Financial Street, Beijing 100140, People's Republic of China (office).

RANE, Pratapsingh Raoji, BSc, BBA; Indian politician; *Speaker, Goa Legislative Assembly;* b. 28 Jan. 1939; s. of Raoji Rane; m.; Chief Minister of Goa 1980–85, 1985–89, 1990, 1994–99, Feb.–March 2005, June 2005–07; Speaker, Goa Legis. Ass. Speaker 2007–;; mem. Indian Nat. Congress, fmr Leader of the Opposition, Chair. Public Accounts Cttee, Business Advisory Cttee 2002–03. *Leisure interests:* outing, camping, nature study, listening to classical music, reading, drama, reading, watching TV. *Address:* Office of the Speaker, Goa Legislature Secretariat, Alto-Porvorim 403 521 (office); Golden Acres, Kulan, Sanquelim 403 505, India (home). *Telephone:* (832) 2410915 (office); (832) 2362229 (home). *Fax:* (832) 2411066 (office). *E-mail:* assembly@sancharnet.in (office); mla-pori.goa@nic.in. *Website:* www.goavidhansabha.gov.in (office).

RANGARAJAN, Chakravarthi, PhD; Indian economist, academic and politician; *Chairman, Prime Minister's Economic Advisory Council;* b. 5 Jan. 1932, Ariyalur; s. of B. R. Chakravarty and Rangam Chakravarty; m. Haripriya Chakravarty; one s. one d.; ed Madras Univ., Univ. of Pennsylvania, USA; Lecturer, Loyola Coll. Chennai 1954–58, Wharton School of Finance and Commerce, Univ. of Pennsylvania 1963–64; Reader, Raj Univ. 1964–65; Prof., Indian Statistical Inst., New Delhi 1965–66; Visiting Assoc. Prof., New York Univ. 1966–68, Visiting Prof. 1972–73; Prof., Indian Inst. of Managaement, Ahmedabad 1968–81; Deputy Gov. Reserve Bank of India 1982–91, Gov. 1992–97; Gov. of Andhra Pradesh 1997–2003; mem. Planning Comm., Indian Govt 1991–92; Chair. Tenth Finance Comm., Ministry of Finance 2003, Twelfth Finance Comm. 2005, Prime Minister's Econ. Advisory Council 2005–; Chair. Task Force on Jammu and Kashmir; Pres. Indian Econ. Assocn 1982, 1994; Hon. Fellow, Indian Inst. of Man., Ahmedabad 1997; Businessman of the Year, Madras Man. Assocn 1997, Bank of India Award of Excellence 1998, Finance Man of the Decade, Bombay Man. Assocn 1998, Financial Express Award for Economics 1998, Padma Vibhushan 2002, Wharton India Econ. Forum Alumni Award 2002. *Publications include:* author or co-author: Short-Term Investment Forecasting 1974, Principles of Macro-Economics 1979, Strategy for Industrial Development in the 80s 1982, Innovations in Banking 1982, Agricultural Growth and Industrial Performance in India 1982, Structural Reforms in Industry Banking and Finance 2000; contrib.: Indian Economy: Essays on Money and Finance 1998, Perspectives on Indian Economy 2000, Select Essays on Indian Economy; and more than 40 papers. *Address:* Economic Advisory Council to the Prime Minister, Vigyan Bhawan Annex E Hall, Maulana Azad Road, New Delhi 110 011, India (office). *Telephone:* (11) 23022311 (office). *Fax:* (11) 23022318 (office). *E-mail:* c.rangarajan@nic.in (office). *Website:* eac.gov.in (office).

RANGASAMY, N.; Indian politician; *Chief Minister of Puducherry;* b. 4 Aug. 1950, Puducherry; has held several positions in Puducherry govt including Minister of Agric. 1991, of Public Works Dept 1996, of Educ. 2000; Chief Minister of

Puducherry 2001–08, 2011–; mem. Indian Nat. Congress party –2011, left to found new party All India N.R. Congress 2011, currently Pres. *Address:* Chief Minister's Secretariat, Goubert Salai (Beach Rd), Puducherry 605 001, India (office). *Telephone:* (413) 2333399 (office). *Fax:* (413) 2333135 (office). *E-mail:* cm@pondy.pon.nic.in (office).

RANGEL SILVA, Gen.-in-Chief Henry de Jesús; Venezuelan army officer and government official; b. 1961, Santiago, Trujillo State; ed Bolivarian Military Acad., Caracas; took part in military coup with the late Hugo Chávez 1992; fmr Head of Nat. Housing Council; Dir Directorate of Intelligence and Prevention Services 2005–09; Dir CANTV (public telecommunications co.) 2009; attained rank of Maj.-Gen. 2008, of Gen.-in-Chief 2010; Strategic Operational Commdr of the Armed Forces 2010; Minister of Defence Jan.–Oct. 2012. *Address:* c/o Ministry of Defence, Edif. 17 de Diciembre, planta baja, Base Aérea Francisco de Miranda, La Carlota, Caracas, Venezuela.

RANGEL BRICEÑO, Gen.-in-Chief Gustavo; Venezuelan military officer and government official; b. 16 Aug. 1955, Maracaibo; served as Commdr of Army Infantry Div. 2004–05, Reserve and Nat. Mobilization –2007; Minister of Nat. Defence 2007–09. *Address:* c/o Ministry of National Defence, Edif. 17 de Diciembre, planta baja, Base Aérea Francisco de Miranda, La Carlota, Caracas, Venezuela (office).

RANGEL VALE, José Vicente; Venezuelan politician; b. 10 July 1929, Caracas; s. of José Vicente Rangel Cárdenas and Leonor Vale de Rangel; m. Ana Avalos; one s.; ed Colegio La Salle, Barquismeto, Universidad de los Andes, Cen. Univ. of Venezuela, Univ. of Chile, Univs of Salamanca and Santiago de Compostela, Spain; joined Unión Republicana Democrática aged 16; fmr TV Presenter, Televen, Canal 10; fmr columnist, El Universal, El Informadro, La Tarde, El Regional and Bohemia; cand. in presidential elections 1973, 1978, 1983; elected Deputy to Congress for Estado Miranda; fmr Co-ordinator Movimiento Independientes (with Hugo Chávez); Minister of Foreign Affairs 1999–2001, of Defence 2001–02; Vice-Pres. of Venezuela 2002–07. *Publications include:* Tiempo de Verdades, Socialismo y Democracia, Expediente Negro, La Administración de La Justica en Venezuela. *Address:* c/o Central Information Office of the Presidency, Torre Oeste, 18, Parque Central, Caracas 1010, Venezuela (office).

RANJEVA, Gen. Marcel; Malagasy politician and army officer (retd); b. 15 Jan. 1944, Antananarivo; s. of the late Rene Ranjeva Raolosoa and Eugenie Raolosoa; m. Michele Rajaonera; two c.; ed Paris I (Sorbonne), France; mem. Christian Students Youth 1960–64; assigned to Army Staff Tech. Bd 1975, then to Dept of Econ. Affairs of Ministry of Defence 1976; apptd Dir of Mil. Operations, Office of Mil. Agricultural Production 1982; Commdr Mil. Acad. 1986; Sec. Gen. Office Malagasy des Tabacs 1992; Chief of Staff, Office of the Pres. 1995–96; Minister of Defence 1996–2002 (resgnd); Minister of Foreign Affairs 2002–09; mem. Assocn des Anciens Elèves de Coëtquidan; Grand Croix de 2ème Classe de la République Malgache, Grand Officier, Légion d'Honneur, Commandeur de la Légion d'honneur, Officier, Ordre Nat. de Mérite. *Address:* c/o Ministry of Foreign Affairs, BP 836, Anosy, 101 Antananarivo, Madagascar (office).

RANJEVA, Raymond, BA, LLD; Malagasy lawyer, judge, academic and international official; b. 31 Aug. 1942, Antananarivo; m. Yvette Madeleine R. Rabetafika 1967; five c.; ed Univ. of Madagascar, Madagascar Nat. School of Admin., Univ. of Paris, France; trainee, Judicial Div., Conseil d'Etat, Paris; Civil Admin., Univ. of Madagascar 1966, Asst Lecturer 1966–72, Lecturer 1972, Dir Dept of Legal and Political Science 1973–82, Prof. 1981–91, Dean of Faculty of Law, Econs, Man. and Social Sciences 1982–88; Lecturer, Hague Acad. of Int. Law 1987–97; Prof., Madagascar Mil. Acad., Madagascar School of Admin.; Dir Public Law and Political Science Study Centre; First Rector, Univ. of Antananarivo 1988–90; Man. Dir Jureco (econ., financial and legal databank for advisory and research bodies) 1986–90, Ed. Lettre mensuelle de Jureco 1986–88; Conciliator, IBRD Int. Centre for Settlement of Investment Disputes 1970–; Attorney to Mali, Border Dispute (Burkina Faso/Mali); Consultant on transfer to the State of activities of Eau-Electricité de Madagascar and Electricité de France 1973; Judge, Int. Court of Justice, The Hague 1991–2009, Vice-Pres. 2003–06; Founder-mem. Malagasy Human Rights Cttee 1971; mem. and Vice-Pres. Malagasy Acad. 1974, Pres. Ethics and Political Science section 1975–91; mem. Nat. Constitutional Cttee 1975; mem. Court of Arbitration for Sport 1995–; legal adviser to Catholic Bishops' Conf., Madagascar; mem. Governing Body of African Soc. of Int. and Comparative Law, French Soc. of Int. Law, Québec Soc. (Canada); Sec.-Gen. Malagasy Legal Studies Soc.; mem. Pontifical Comm. 'Justice et Paix' 2002–, Curatorium de l'Acad. de Droit Int. 2002–; Commdr, Ordre Nat. Malgache of Madagascar, Chevalier, Ordre de Mérite of Madagascar, Officier, Ordre Nat. of Mali, Grand-Croix nat. malgache 2003. *Address:* c/o International Court of Justice, Peace Palace, Carnegieplein 2, 2517 KJ The Hague, Netherlands. *Telephone:* (70) 302-2323. *E-mail:* information@icj-cij.org.

RÁNKI, Dezsö; Hungarian pianist; b. 8 Sept. 1951, Budapest; s. of József Ránki and Edith Jecsmen; m. Edit Klukon 1979; two c.; ed Ferenc Liszt Music Acad., Budapest (under Pál Kadosa); has given recitals and appeared with several leading orchestras throughout Europe, including Berlin Philharmonic, Concert-gebouw and London Philharmonic; regular concert tours N America and Japan; four-hands piano recitals with Edit Klukon in many European cities 1982–; has taught piano at Budapest Music Acad. since 1973; First Prize, Int. Schumann Competition, Zwickau, GDR 1969, Grand Prix Int. du Disque (Paris) 1972, Liszt Prize 2nd Degree 1973, Kossuth Prize 1978. *Recordings include:* works by Bartók, Brahms, Haydn, Kadosa, Mozart, Ravel and Schumann. *Leisure interests:* gramophone records, sound tapes, books, gardening. *Address:* Béla Simon Artist Management, 29 Goldhurst Terrace, London NW6 3HB, England (office); Ördögorom Lejtö 11/B, 1112 Budapest, Hungary (home). *Telephone:* (20) 7624-7291 (office); (1) 246-4403 (home). *E-mail:* bs@zene91.freeserve.co.uk (office).

RANQUE, Denis; French business executive; *Chairman, Airbus Group;* b. 1952, Marseille; ed École Polytechnique, Ecole des Mines, Paris; began career at Ministry for Industry where he held various positions in the energy sector; joined Thomson group as Dir of Planning 1983, CEO Thomson Tubes Electroniques 1989–92, Chair. and CEO Thomson Sintra ASM 1992–96, CEO Thomson Marconi Sonar 1996–98, Chair. and CEO Thomson-CSF group (now called Thales) 1998–2009; Chair. École Nationale Supérieure des Mines de Paris 2001–12,

Cercle de l'Industrie (French Industrial Asscn) 2002–12; Chair. (non-exec.) Technicolor 2010–12; Chair. Airbus Group 2013–; Dir, CMA CGM 2009–12, CGG VERITAS 2010–12, Fonds Stratégique d'Investissement 2011–12, Saint Gobain; Pres. Bd Scilab Enterprise; Chair. Fondation PARISTECH; Chevalier, Légion d'honneur 1999, Officier 2009; Officier, Ordre nat. du Mérite 2003; Hon. CBE 2004; Verdienstkreuz am Bande. *Leisure interest:* music, sailing. *Address:* Airbus Group, 37 boulevard de Montmorency, 75781 Paris Cedex 16, France (office). *E-mail:* chairman@eads.net (office). *Website:* www.eads.com (office).

RANTANEN, Juha Ilari, MSc, MBA; Finnish business executive; b. 25 Jan. 1952, Helsinki; m. Eija Jaaskelainen 1975; three s. one d.; ed Helsinki School of Econs, Int. Man. Inst., Geneva; Man., Internal Accounting, Neste Oy 1977–78, Planning Man. 1979–81, Exec. Vice-Pres., Gas 1986–89, Chemicals 1989–92, Chief Financial Officer 1992–94; Product Line Man., Covering Materials, Partek Oy 1981–84, Vice-Pres., Insulations 1984–86; CEO Borealis A/S 1994–97; Exec. Vice-Pres. Ahlstrom Corpn 1997–98, Pres., CEO 1998–2004; CEO Outokumpu Oyj 2004–11; mem. Bd of Dirs Yara International 2012–; Vice-Chair. Moventas Group 2007; Chair. Finpro 2005–09; Vice-Pres. European Confed. of Iron and Steel Industries (Eurofer); fmr Chair. Forest Industries Fed.; Vice-Chair. Confed. of Finnish Industry and Employers; Pres. Asscn of Plastics Manufacturers in Europe 1994–96; mem. Supervisory Bd Varma-Sampo Mutual Pension Insurance Co. *Address:* c/o Board of Directors, Yara International ASA, PO Box 2464, Solli Bygdøy allé 2, 0202, Oslo, Norway.

RANTZEN, Esther, CBE, OBE, MA, FRTS; British journalist, television presenter, producer and writer; b. 22 June 1940, Berkhamsted, Herts., England; d. of Harry Barnato Rantzen and Katherine Flora Rantzen (née Leverson); m. Desmond Wilcox 1977 (died 2000); one s. two d.; ed North London Collegiate School and Somerville Coll., Oxford; studio man. making dramatic sound effects, BBC Radio 1963; presenter and producer, That's Life, BBC TV 1973–94; scriptwriter 1976–94; producer, The Big Time (documentary series) 1976–80; regular contrib., Daily Mail, Daily Telegraph, Sunday Times; unsuccessful parl. cand. for Luton South 2010; mem. Nat. Consumer Council 1981–90, Health Educ. Authority 1989–95; Chair. ChildLine (charity) 1986–2006, Pres. (following merger with Nat. Soc. for the Prevention of Cruelty to Children—NSPCC) 2006–; Pres. Asscn of Youth with ME 1996–; numerous charitable activities; Trustee, NSPCC; six hon. doctorates, including Hon. DLitt (South Bank Univ.) 2000; BBC TV Personality of 1975, Variety Club of GB, Richard Dimbleby Award, BAFTA 1988, Snowdon Award for Services to Disabled People 1996, Royal TV Soc. Hall of Fame Award 1997, Champion Community Legal Service 2000. *Television includes:* presenter: That's Life 1973–94, Esther Interviews ..., 1988, Hearts of Gold 1988–96, Drugwatch (BBC 1), Childwatch (BBC 1), The Lost Babies (also producer), Esther (talk show) 1994–, The Rantzen Report 1996–, That's Esther (ITV) 1999–, Children in Need (BBC 1), Hearts of Gold (BBC 1), Loose Women (guest presenter), Winton's Children (ITV 1), Excuse My French (BBC 2), Old Dogs, New Tricks (BBC 2), How to Have a Good Death (BBC) 2006; other: All Star Family Fortunes (contestant, ITV 1), I'm a Celebrity Get Me Out of Here (contestant; ITV 1), Who Do You Think You Are (BBC 1), Would Like To Meet – Celebrity Episode, Prostitute (mini-series) 1998, Grumpy Old Women (guest; BBC 2), Strictly Come Dancing (contestant; BBC 1). *Publications:* Kill the Chocolate Biscuit (with D. Wilcox) 1981, Baby Love 1985, The Story of Ben Hardwick (with S. Woodward) 1985, Once Upon a Christmas 1996, Esther: The Autobiography 2001, A Secret Life (novel) 2003, Running Out of Tears (25 Years of Childline) 2011. *Leisure interests:* work and fantasy. *Address:* c/o Billy Marsh Associates, 76A Grove End Road, St John's Wood, London, NW8 9ND, England (office). *Telephone:* (20) 7449-6930 (office). *Fax:* (20) 7449-6933 (office). *E-mail:* talent@billymarsh.co.uk (office). *Website:* www .billymarsh.co.uk (office).

RAO, A. Janardhana; Indian government official; *Managing Director, India Ports Association;* fmr Financial Advisor and Chief Accounts Officer, Kandla Port Trust, apptd Chair. 2004; currently Man. Dir India Ports Asscn. *Address:* Indian Ports Association, First Floor, South Tower, NBCC Place, Bhisham Pitamah Marg, Lodi Road, New Delhi 110 003, India (office). *Telephone:* (11) 24365632 (office). *Fax:* (11) 24365866 (office). *E-mail:* md.ipa@nic.in (office). *Website:* www.ipa.nic.in (office).

RAO, Calyampudi Radhakrishna, MA, ScD, FRS; American/Indian statistician; *Professor Emeritus of Statistics, Pennsylvania State University;* b. 10 Sept. 1920, Hadagali, Karnataka State; s. of C. D. Naidu and A. Laxmikanthamma; m. Bhargavi Rao 1948; one s. one d.; ed Andhra and Calcutta Univs; Research at Indian Statistical Inst. 1943–46, Univ. of Cambridge, UK 1946–48; Prof. and Head of Div. of Theoretical Research and Training 1949–64; Dir Research and Training School, Indian Statistical Inst. 1964–71, Sec. and Dir 1972–76, Jawaharlal Nehru Prof. 1976–84; Univ. Prof., Univ. of Pittsburgh 1979–88; Nat. Prof., 1981–92; Eberly Prof. of Statistics, Pennsylvania State Univ. 1988–91, Dir Center for Multivariate Analysis 1988–2009, Prof. Emer. 2009–; Ed. Sankhya 1964–80, Journal of Multivariate Analysis 1988–92; Fellow, Inst. of Mathematical Statistics, USA, Pres. 1976–77; Treas. Int. Statistical Inst. 1961–65, Pres. 1977–79; Pres. Int. Biometric Soc. 1973–75, Forum for Interdisciplinary Math.; mem. NAS; Foreign mem. Lithuanian Acad. of Sciences; Fellow, American Statistical Asscn, Econometric Soc., Nat. Acad., Third World Acad. of Sciences; Hon. Life Fellow, King's Coll. Cambridge, Hon. Fellow, Royal Statistical Soc., European Acad. of Sciences, Hon. mem. Int. Statistical Inst., Inst. of Combinatorics and Applications, Finnish Statistical Soc., Portuguese Statistical Soc., Hon. Foreign mem. American Acad. Arts and Sciences, Hon. Life mem. Biometric Soc.; Hon. DSc (31 univs), Hon. DLitt (Delhi); Emanuel and Carol Parzen Prize for Statistical Innovation; Bhatnagar Memorial Award for Scientific Research 1963, Guy Silver Medal Royal Statistical Soc. 1965, Meghnad Saha Medal 1969, Nat. Science Acad., J.C. Bose Gold Medal, Wilks Memorial Medal 1989, Calcutta Univ. Gold Medal, Mahalanobis Birth Centenary Gold Medal, Army Wilks Medal, Padma Vibhushan 2001, Nat. Science Acad. Ramanujan Medal 2003, Int. Statistics Inst. Mahalanobis Prize 2003, Sankhyiki Bhushan, Pres.'s Nat. Medal for Science, USA 2002, India Science Award 2010, Guyn Medal in Gold, Royal Statistical Soc. 2011. *Publications include:* Advanced Statistical Methods in Biometric Research, Linear Statistical Inference and its Application, Generalized Inverse of Matrices and its Applications, Linear Statistical Inference, Characterization Problems of Mathematical Statistics (with A. Kagan and V. Linmik) 1973, Estimation of Variance Compon-

ents and its Applications (with J. Kleffe) 1988, Statistics and Truth 1989, Choquet Deny Type Functional Equations with Applications to Stochastic Models (with D. N. Shanbhaq) 1994, Linear Models: Least Squares and Alternatives (with H. Toutenburg) 1995, Matrix Algebra and Its Applications to Statistics and Econometrics (with M. B. Rao) 1998; more than 350 research papers in math. statistics. *Leisure interest:* writing humorous essays. *Address:* 29 Old Orchard Street, Williamsville, NY 14229, USA (home). *Telephone:* (716) 639-0902 (home). *E-mail:* crr1@psu.edu (office). *Website:* www.stat.psu.edu/~crrao (office).

RAO, Chintamani Nagesa Ramachandra, PhD, DSc, FRS, FNA; Indian chemist and academic; *National Research Professor, Linus Pauling Research Professor and Honorary President, Jawaharlal Nehru Centre for Advanced Scientific Research;* b. 30 June 1934, Bangalore; s. of H. Nagesa Rao; m. Indumati Rao 1960; one s. one d.; ed Banaras Univ., Purdue Univ., USA, Mysore Univ.; Lecturer, Indian Inst. of Science, Bangalore 1959–63, Chair. Solid State and Structural Chem. Unit and Materials Research Lab. 1977–84, Dir Indian Inst. of Science 1984–94; Prof., later Sr Prof., Indian Inst. of Tech., Kanpur 1963–77, Dean of Research and Devt 1969–72; Albert Einstein Research Prof. and Pres. Jawaharlal Nehru Centre for Advanced Scientific Research 1995–99, Linus Pauling Research Prof. and Hon. Pres. 1999–; Visiting Prof., Purdue Univ. 1967–68, Univ. of Oxford, UK 1974–75; Prof., Indian Inst. of Science, Bangalore; Fellow, King's Coll., Cambridge, UK 1983–84; Chair. Science Advisory Council to Prime Minister of India 1985–89 (and currently), Indo-Japan Science Council, Scientific Advisory Cttee to Union Cabinet 1997–98; fmr Chair. Advisory Bd of Council of Scientific and Industrial Research (India); mem. Atomic Energy Comm. of India; mem. editorial bds of 15 leading scientific journals; Pres. St Catherine's Coll. Oxford 1974–75, Indian Nat. Science Acad. 1985–86, IUPAC 1985–87, Indian Science Congress Asscn 1987–88, Indian Acad. of Sciences 1988–91, Materials Research Soc. of India 1989–91; Nehru Visiting Prof., Univ. of Cambridge, Linnett Visiting Prof. 1998; Gauss Professorship, Acad. of Sciences, Göttingen, Germany 2003; Distinguished Visiting Prof., Univ. of California, USA, Univ. of Cambridge, UK; Albert Einstein Prof., Chinese Acad. of Sciences 2012; mem. Editorial Bd of 15 leading scientific journals; Founding mem. and Pres. Third World Acad. of Sciences; mem. Pontifical Acad. of Sciences; Titular mem. European Acad. of Arts, Sciences and Humanities; Corresp. mem. Brazilian Acad. of Sciences; Foreign mem. Academia Europaea, Serbian and Slovenian Acads of Science, Yugoslavia, Russian, Czech and Polish Acads of Sciences, American Acad. of Arts and Sciences, Royal Spanish Acad. of Sciences, French Acad. of Sciences, American Philosophical Soc., African Acad., Materials Socs of Japan and Korea, Int. Acad. of Ceramics; Foreign Assoc. NAS; Foreign Fellow, RSC; Hon. Foreign mem. Korean Acad. of Science and Tech., Hon. mem. Japan Acad., Hon. FRSC 1989, Hon. Fellow, Inst. of Physics, London 2006, St Catherine's Coll. Oxford 2007; Albert Einstein Prof., Chinese Acad. of Sciences 2012; Commdr, Nat. Order of Lion (Senegal) 1999, Karnataka Ratna 2001, Officier des Palmes académiques 2002, Grand-Cross, Order of Scientific Merit (Brazil) 2002, Commdr, Order of Rio Branco (Brazil) 2002, Chevalier, Légion d'honneur 2005, Order of Friendship, Pres. of Russia 2009; Dr hc from 60 univs, including Purdue, Bordeaux, Banaras, Mysore, Indian Inst. of Tech., Bombay, Indian Inst. of Tech., Kharagpur, Notre Dame, Novosibirsk, Université Joseph Fourier, Uppsala, Wales, Wrocław, Caen, Khartoum, Calcutta and Sri Venkateswara Univ.; Marlow Medal, Faraday Soc. 1967, Bhatnagar Award 1968, Jawaharlal Nehru Fellowship, Indian Inst. of Tech. 1973, Padma Shri 1974, Sir C. V. Raman Award 1975, ACS Centennial Foreign Fellowship 1976, Fed. of Indian Chamber of Commerce and Industry Award for Physical Sciences 1977, S.N. Bose Medal, Indian Nat. Science Acad. 1980, Royal Soc. of Chem. (London) Medal 1981, Padma Vibhushan 1985, Jawaharlal Nehru Award 1988, Hevrovsky Gold Medal, Czechoslovak Acad. 1989, Saha Medal, Indian Nat. Science Acad. 1990, Blackett Lecturer, Royal Soc. 1991, CSIR Golden Jubilee Prize 1991, NAS Int. Science Lecture, USA 1993, Sahabdeen Int. Award of Science, Sri Lanka 1994, Third World Acad. of Sciences Medal in Chem. 1995, Albert Einstein Gold Medal, UNESCO 1996, Autosh Mookerjee Medal 1996, Shatabdi Puraskar, Indian Scientific Congress 1999, Hallim Distinguished Lecturer, Korean Acad. of Science and Tech. 1999, Centenary Lectureship and Medal, Royal Soc. of Chem. 2000, Hughes Medal, Royal Soc. 2000, Millennium Plaque of Honour, Indian Science Congress 2001, Somiya Award, Int. Union of Materials Research Socs 2004, Dan David Prize 2005, Chemical Pioneer, American Inst. of Chemists 2005, India Science Award, Govt of India 2005, Nat. Research Professorship, Govt of India 2006, Nikkei Asia Prize for Science, Tech. and Innovation from Japan 2008, Royal Medal (Queen's Medal), Royal Soc., London 2009, August Wilhelm von Hoffmann Medal for outstanding contribs to chem., German Chemical Soc. 2010, Ernesto Illy Trieste Science Prize for materials research 2011, Award for Int. Science Co-operation, Chinese Acad. of Sciences 2012, Bharat Ratna 2014. *Publications include:* 45 books, including Ultraviolet Visible Spectroscopy 1960, Chemical Applications of Infra-red Spectroscopy 1963, Spectroscopy in Inorganic Chemistry 1970, Modern Aspects of Solid State Chemistry 1970, Solid State Chemistry 1974, Educational Technology in Teaching of Chemistry 1975, Phase Transitions in Solids 1978, Preparation and Characterization of Materials 1981, The Metallic and Non-Metallic States of Matter 1985, New Directions in Solid State Chemistry 1986, Chemistry of Oxide Superconductors 1988, Chemical and Structural Aspects of High Temperature Oxide Superconductors 1988, Bismuth and Thallium Superconductors 1989, Chemistry of Advanced Materials 1992, Chemical Approaches to the Synthesis of Inorganic Materials 1994, Transition Metal Oxides 1995, Colossal Magnetoresistance 1998, Understanding Chemistry 1999; more than 1,500 original research papers. *Leisure interests:* gourmet cooking, general reading, music. *Address:* Jawaharlal Nehru Centre for Advanced Scientific Research, Jakkur PO, Bangalore 560 064 (office); JNC President's House, Indian Institute of Science Campus, Bangalore 560 012, India (home). *Telephone:* (80) 23653075 (office); (80) 23601410 (home). *Fax:* (80) 22082760 (office); (80) 23602468 (office). *E-mail:* cnrrao@jncasr.ac.in (office). *Website:* www .jncasr.ac.in/cnrrao (office).

RAO, G. M. (Grandhi Mallikarjuna), BE; Indian mechanical engineer and business executive; *Group Chairman, GMR Group;* b. 14 July 1950, Rajam, Andhra Pradesh; m. Varalakshmi Rao; three c.; ed Vizag Eng Coll.; began career with single jute mill, Rajam 1978; Founder GMR Group, Chair. and Man. Dir 1978–2007, Group Chair. 2007–; infrastructure interests in India and abroad including power plants, airports (Hyderabad, Delhi and Istanbul); Chair. Emer.

ING Vysya Bank; f. GMR Varalakshmi Foundation; mem. Central Bd of Dirs Reserve Bank of India 2011–; Dr hc (Jawaharlal Nehru Technological Univ.) 2005, (York Univ., Canada) 2011; Hon. DLitt (Andhra Univ.) 2010; Economic Times Awards for Corp. Excellence Entrepreneur of theYear 2006/07, Indian Business Leader Award, CNBC TV 18 2007, Sir M. Visveswaraiah Award, Fed. of Karnataka Chamber Of Commerce and Industry 2008, Most Inspiring Entrepreneur of the Year Award, Nat. Inst. of Industrial Eng Mumbai 2008, Infrastructure Person of the Year Award 2009, First Generation Entrepreneur of the Year Award, CNBC TV18 2009. *Address:* GMR Group, Skip House, 25/, Museum Road, Bangalore 560 025, India (office). *Telephone:* (80) 22070100 (office). *Fax:* (80) 22213091 (office). *E-mail:* info@gmrgroup.in (office). *Website:* www.gmrgroup.co.in (office).

RAO, Kalvakuntla Chandrasekhar, MA; Indian politician; b. 17 Feb. 1954, Chintamadaka; m. Kalvakuntla Shobha 1969; one s. one d.; ed Osmania Univ., Hyderabad; mem. AP Legis. Ass. 1985–2004, Chair. Cttee on Public Undertakings 1992–93, Deputy Speaker 1999–2001; Minister of State, Govt of AP 1987–88, Cabinet Minister 1997–99; mem. Lok Sabha from Karimnagar, AP constituency 2004–06 (resgnd), 2006– (re-elected in bye election); Minister without Portfolio May–Nov. 2004, Minister of Labour and Employment 2004–06; Founder and Pres. Telangana Rashtra Samithi 2001–09. *Address:* 8-2-220/110/1/3, Road 14, Banjara Hills, Hyderabad,; Telangana Rashtra Samithi, Karimnagar, India (office). *Telephone:* (40) 23555798.

RAO, Kamini A., MCh, FRCOG; Indian gynaecologist; *Medical Director, BACC Healthcare Private Ltd;* b. 2 July 1953, Hyderabad, Andhra Pradesh; m. Dr Arvind Rao; one s. one d.; ed St John's Medical Coll., Bangalore Univ., Royal Coll. of Physicians, Ireland, Univ. of Liverpool, UK; worked at King's Coll. School of Medicine, St Bartholomew's Hospital, UK; est. Bangalore Assisted Conception Centre (now BACC Healthcare Private Ltd), currently Medical Dir; Sr Vice-Pres. Fed. of Obstetric and Gynaecological Societies (FOGSI) 1997–98, Pres. 2000–01; Sec., Bangalore Soc. of Obstetricians and Gynecologists 1992–94, Pres. 1998–99; mem. Exec. Cttee Indian Soc. for Assisted Reproduction; Chair. Cttee for Genetics and Fetal Medicine 1991–96; Vice-Pres. Karnataka Asscn for Sexual and Reproductive Medicine 1997–, Soc. for Fetal Medicine and Genetics 1998–; Co-Chair. Int. Fed. of Obstetrics and Gynecology (FIGO) Women's Sexual and Reproductive Rights (WSRR) Cttee and Coordinator for WSRR project; FOGSI Rep. to Asia Oceania Fed. of Obstetrics and Gynecology 2003; FOGSI Rep. to FIGO 2004; Fellow, Indian Coll. of Obstetricians and Gynecologists, Bangalore, Royal Coll. of Obstetricians and Gynecologists, UK; mem. Royal Coll. of Physicians, Ireland, Royal Coll. of Surgeons, Ireland, Indian Soc. of Prenatal Diagnosis and Therapy, Indian Asscn of Gynaecological Endoscopists, Indian Menopause Soc., Indian Soc. of Health Admins, Indian Asscn of Human Reproduction, Medical Ultrasound Soc., Karnataka, Tech. Advisory Cttee, Nat. Abortion Assessment Project, Task Force for Health and Family Welfare, Govt of Karnataka; Rajyotsava Award, Govt of Karnataka 1997, Vidya Ratan Award 1998, Lifetime Achievement Honours Tribute Award, Vivekananda Inst. of Human Excellence, Padma Shri 2014. *Publications include:* An Introduction to Genetics and Fetal Medicine, Chorionic Villus Sampling (co- author), Reproductive Medicine and Prenatal Diagnosis, Diagnosis and Management of Infertility, Amniotic Fluid (co- author), The Infertility Manual (co- author), Current Concepts in Perinatologyl, A Handbook on Obstetric Emergencies. *Address:* BACC Healthcare Private Limited, No 6/7, Kumarakrupa Road, High Grounds, Bangalore 560 001, India (office). *Telephone:* (80) 22260880 (office); (80) 41138255 (office). *Fax:* (80) 2250465 (office). *E-mail:* kambacc@vsnl.com (office); drkaminirao@gmail.com (office). *Website:* www .baccweb.com (office).

RAO, Nirupama Menon, MA; Indian diplomatist and civil servant; b. 6 Dec. 1950, Malappuram, Kerala; m. Shri Sudhakar Rao; two s.; ed Univ. of Mysore, Marathwada Univ., Maharashtra; joined Indian Foreign Service 1973, First Sec. (Agreement), Mission in Colombo 1981–83, Desk Officer, Southern Africa and Nepal Desks, Ministry of External Affairs, then with East Asia Div. 1984–92, Minister for Press Affairs, Embassy in Washington, DC 1993–95, Amb. to Peru 1995–98, Deputy Chief of Mission, Embassy in Moscow 1998–99, Head of Div. in charge of Multilateral Econ. Relations, Ministry of External Affairs 2000–01, Jt Sec. for External Publicity and Official Spokesperson 2001–02, Additional Sec. Human Resources Div. 2002–04, Foreign Service Inspector 2004, High Commr to Sri Lanka 2004–06, Amb. to People's Repub. of China (first woman) 2006–09, Foreign Sec. (second woman) 2009–11, Amb. to USA 2011–13; fmr Fellow specializing in Asia-Pacific Security, Center for Int. Affairs (now Weatherhead Center), Harvard Univ., USA; Distinguished Int. Exec. in Residence, Univ. of Maryland, USA 1999–2000. *Publication:* Rain Rising (book of poetry; translated into Chinese and Russian) 2004. *Leisure interests:* fine arts, classical music, literature. *Address:* Ministry of External Affairs, South Block, New Delhi 110 011, India (office). *Telephone:* (11) 23011127 (office). *Fax:* (11) 23013254 (office). *E-mail:* eam@mea.gov.in (office). *Website:* www.mea.gov.in (office).

RAO, Yi, PhD; Chinese neuroscientist and academic; *Professor and Dean, School of Life Sciences, Peking University;* mem. Faculty, Washington Univ., St Louis, USA –2000; apptd first Elsa A. Swanson Research Prof., Feinberg School of Medicine, Northwestern Univ., USA 2000; Chair Prof. and Dean, Peking Univ. School of Life Sciences 2007–; Investigator, Nat. Inst. of Biological Sciences, Beijing; mem. Editorial Bd The Journal of Neuroscience, Developmental Brain Research, NeuroSignals, Neuroscience Research; ad hoc referee for Biochemical Journal, Journal of Molecular Biology, Journal of Cell Biology and other publs; Esther A. and Joseph Lingenstein Fellowship in Neuroscience 2000, Charles B. Wilson Brain Tumor Research Excellence Award in Neuroscience. *Publications:* numerous papers in professional journals on molecular studies of neuronal polarity and genetic analysis of social behaviour. *Address:* New Life Sciences Building, Peking University, 5 Yiheyuan Road, Beijing 100871, People's Republic of China (office). *Telephone:* (10) 80726672 (office). *Fax:* (10) 80726673 (office). *E-mail:* raoyi@nibs.ac.cn (office). *Website:* www.bio.pku.edu.cn (office).

RAO, Zihe, BSc, MSc, PhD; Chinese biologist, biophysicist, virologist and academic; *President, Nankai University;* b. 6 Sept. 1950, Nanjing, Jiangsu Prov.; ed Univ. of Science and Tech. of China, Inst. of Biophysics, Chinese Acad. of Sciences, Melbourne Univ., Australia; Postdoctoral Fellow, Lab. of Molecular Biophysics, Univ. of Oxford, UK 1989–92, Researcher with Prof. David Stuart FRS

1992–96; returned to China to found Lab. of Structural Biology, Tsinghua Univ., Beijing 1996–; Dir-Gen. Inst. of Biophysics (IBP), Chinese Acad. of Sciences, Beijing 2003–07; Pres. Nankai Univ., Tianjin 2006–; Prof. and Head, Tsinghua-Nankai-IBP Jt Lab. for Structural Biology 2006–; mem. Chinese Acad. of Sciences 2003–, Third World Acad. of Sciences 2004–; Qiushi Outstanding Scientist Prize in Life Sciences, Hong Kong 1999, Yangtze River Distinguished Scholar, Ministry of Educ. 2000, He Liang Heli Foundation Science and Tech. Prize 2003. *Publications:* more than 130 papers in int. scientific journals, including Cell, Nature, PNAS, Journal of Molecular Biology, Journal of the American Chemistry Society, on proteins related to human health and disease. *Address:* Laboratory of Structural Biology, Rooms 201–218, Life Science Building, Tsinghua University, Beijing 100084, People's Republic of China (office). *Telephone:* (10) 62771493 (office). *Fax:* (10) 62773145 (office). *E-mail:* raozh@xtal.tsinghua.edu.cn (office). *Website:* xtal .tsinghua.edu.cn (office).

RAOULT, Éric, LèsScEcon; French politician; *Mayor of Raincy;* b. 19 June 1955, Paris; m. Corinne Sapet 2002; ed Inst. d'Etudes Politiques, Paris and Inst. Français de Presse; Parl. Asst to Claude Labbé; Town Councillor, Raincy 1977; Deputy Mayor of Raincy 1983–95, Mayor 1995–; mem. Cen. Cttee of RPR 1982–; Deputy to Nat. Ass. 1986–1995, 2002–, Vice-Pres. 1993–95, 2002–07; mem. Comm. on Foreign Affairs; Regional Councillor, Île de France 1992–2004; Minister of Integration and the Fight against Exclusion May–Nov. 1995, Deputy Minister with responsibility for Urban Affairs and Integration 1995–97; Nat. Sec. with responsibility for elections 1998–99, with responsibility for Feds and Dom-Tom (RPR) 1999–2002, Union pour un Mouvement Populaire 2007–; French mem. OSCE 2011–; Chevalier de la Légion d'honneur. *Publication:* S.O.S Banlieues 1994. *Address:* Casier de la Poste, Palais Bourbon, 75355 Paris 07 (office); Mairie, 121 avenue de la Résistance, 93340 Le Raincy, France (office). *Telephone:* 1-43-02-52-94 (office); 1-40-63-69-93 (office). *Fax:* 1-43-01-24-01 (office). *E-mail:* eraoult@assemblee-nationale.fr (office); ericraoult2007@yahoo.fr (home). *Website:* www .ericraoult.typepad.fr.

RAPACZYNSKI, Wanda, MPPM, PhD; Polish business executive; b. 1947; m.; one d.; ed City Univ. of New York and Yale Univ. School of Org. and Man.; began her career as a prof. of psychology, lectured at several univs in New York and Conn.; Post-doctoral Fellow, Educational Testing Service, Princeton, NJ –1980; Researcher and Project Dir, Yale Univ. Family TV Research and Consultation Center 1980–82; fmr Exec., Vice-Pres. and Head of Project Devt Citibank (NY) –1992; apptd Pres. and CEO Agora SA (media corpn) 1992, Pres. Man. Bd, Head of Finance and Radio Divs, Pres. Supervisory Bd AMS SA (subsidiary) 2002–07, currently mem. Bd Agora Foundation and Supervisory Bd; Pres. Supervisory Bd of Polish Union of Pvt. Employers in Media and Advertising 2003–; mem. Advisory Bd of Centre for European Reform, Polish Group in Trilateral Comm. 2002; represents Agora in Polish Confed. of Pvt. Employers; mem. Bd of Dirs and Corp. Governance Cttee, Adecco SA 2008–; ranked by Fortune magazine amongst 50 Most Powerful Women in Business outside the US (26th) 2001, (47th) 2002, (50th) 2003, (48th) 2004, (45th) 2005, named by Wall Street Journal Europe as one of 30 Most Influential Women in Europe 2001, included by BusinessWeek in list of 50 Stars of Europe 2001, ranked 22nd on list of Europe's 25 Most Successful Businesswomen 2002, placed by BusinessWeek on list of 30 Most Influential People in the Polish Economy 2002, Media Trend Person of the Year statuette 2002, Person of the Year 2002 in the Advertising Industry, Impactor Awards 2003, ranked first by IR Magazine in the Best IR by a CEO/CFO in CEE region category 2003, ranked by the Financial Times amongst Top 25 Businesswomen in Europe (eighth) 2004, (seventh) 2005, (fifth) 2006. *Address:* Agora SA, Czerska 8/10, 00-732 Warsaw, Poland (office). *Telephone:* (22) 5554002 (office). *Fax:* (22) 5554850 (office). *Website:* www.agora.pl (office).

RAPANOS, Vassilis, PhD; Greek economist, politician and fmr central banker; b. 1947, Kos; ed Athens Univ. of Econs and Business, Queen's Univ., Kingston, Canada; imprisoned for more than four years for participating in resistance against mil. regime ruling Greece 1969; fmr Assoc. Prof., Athens Univ. of Econs and Business; financial adviser to Prime Minister Costas Simitis 2000–04, to Perm. Greek Del. to EU, Brussels; fmr Deputy Head of Greek Del. to OECD, Paris; Chair. Hellenic Telecommunications Org. (OTE) 1998–2000; fmr Gov. Nat. Mortgage Bank of Greece (merged with Nat. Bank of Greece 1998), Chair. Nat. Bank of Greece 2009–12, Hellenic Bank Asscn 2009–12; Minister of Finance (designate) following formation of coalition govt with Panhellenic Socialist Movt (PASOK) and Democratic Left (Dimokratiki Aristera) 20–25 June 2012 (resgnd due to ill health); Research Assoc., Inst. of Econ. and Industrial Research (IOBE) 2007–09. *Address:* c/o Ministry of Finance, Odos Nikis 5–7, 101 80 Athens, Greece.

RÂPEANU, Valeriu; Romanian literary critic, historian and editor; b. 28 Sept. 1931, Ploiestiori, Prahova Co.; s. of Gheorghe Râpeanu and Anastasia Râpeanu; m. Sanda Marinescu 1956; one s.; ed Univ. of Bucharest; journalist 1954–69; Vice-Chair. of Romanian Cttee of Radio and TV 1970–72; Dir Mihai Eminescu Publishing House, Bucharest 1972–90; fmr Prof., Faculty of Journalism and Philosophy, Spiru Haret Univ., Bucharest; mem. Romanian Writers' Union; fmr mem. Cen. Cttee Romanian CP; mem. Int. Assoc. of Literary Critics. *Publications:* the monographs George Mihail-Zamfirescu 1958, Al. Vlahuţă 1964, Noi şi cei dinaintea noastră (Ourselves and Our Predecessors) 1966, Interferenţe spirituale (Spiritual Correspondences) 1970, Călător pe două continente (Traveller on Two Continents) 1970, Pe drumurile tradiţiei (Following Traditions) 1973, Interpretări si înţelesuri (Interpretations and Significances) 1975, Cultură si istorie (Culture and History) (two vols) 1979, 1981; Tărâmul unde nu ajungi niciodată (The Land You Could Never Reach) 1982, Scriitori dintre cele două războaie (Writers between the two World Wars) 1986, La vie de l'histoire et l'histoire d'une vie 1989, N. Iorga: Opera, Omul, Prietenii 1992, N. Iorga, Mincea Eliade, Nae Ionescu 1993, N. Iorga 1994; vols by Nicolae Iorga, Gh. Brătianu, Al. Kiriţescu, Cella Delavrancea, Marcel Mihalovici, I. G. Duca, Gh.I. Brătianu, George Enescu, C. Rădulescu-Motru, C. Brâncuşi; anthology of Romanian drama; essays on François Mauriac, Jean d'Ormesson, Marcel Proust, Aaron Copland, André Malraux, Jean Cocteau. *Leisure interests:* music, art. *Address:* Str. Mecet 21, Bucharest, Romania.

RAPHAEL; Spanish singer; b. (Rafael Martos), 5 May 1942, Linares, Jaén; m. Natalia Figueroa 1972; two s. one d.; first prize winner at Salzburg Festival children's singing competition aged nine; subsequently won numerous other competitions; began professional career in Madrid nightclub 1960; rep. of Spain,

Eurovision Song Contest 1966, 1967; US debut 1967; toured USSR 1968, Japan 1970, Australia 1971; Broadway debut 1974; celebrated 25th anniversary as professional singer with open-air concert at Bernabé Stadium, Madrid 1985. *Films include:* Las gemelas 1963, Cuando tú no estás 1966, Al ponerse el sol 1967, Digan lo que digan 1968, El Angel 1969, El golfo 1969, Sin un adiós 1970, Volveré a nacer 1973, Ritmo, amor y primavera 1981. *Television include:* Donde termina el camino (series) 1978, Horas doradas (series) 1980. *Recordings include:* Los hombres lloran también 1964, Sigo siendo aquel 1985, Toda una vida 1985, Las apariencias engañan 1988, Maravilloso corazón 1989, El monstruo de la canción 1990, Andaluz 1990, Fantasia 1994, Brillantes 1994, Monstruo 1995, Desde el fondo de mi alma 1995, Raphael 1998, Dama Dama 1999, Sentado a la vera del camino 1999, Hotel de l'universe 2001, Yo soy aquel 2001, Maldito Raphael 2001, Realite 2003, De vuelta 2003, Vuelve Por Navidad 2004, A Que No Te Vas 2006, Cerca de tí 2006, 50 Años Despues 2008, Viva Raphael! 2009, Te Llevo En El Corazón 2010, El Reencuentro 2012. *Address:* Arie Kaduri Agency, Inc., 16125 NE 18th Avenue, North Miami Beach, FL 33162, USA (office). *Website:* www.raphaelnet.com (office).

RAPHAEL, Farid; Lebanese banker and politician; *Chairman and General Manager, Executive Committee, Banque Libano-Française SAL;* b. 28 Oct. 1933, Dlebta, Kesrouan; s. of Elie Raphael and Evelyne Khalife; m. Ilham Abdel Ahad 1970; one s. three d.; ed Univ. of St Joseph, Beirut, Univ. of Lyons, France; with Cie Algérienne de Crédit et de Banque, Beirut 1956–67; Founder and Gen. Man. Banque Libano-Française SAL 1967–79, Chair. and Gen. Man. Exec. Cttee 1979–; Founder and Vice-Pres. Banque Libano-Française (France) SA (now Banque Française de l'Orient SA), Paris 1976–85, Chair. and Gen. Man. 1985–89, Adviser to BFO-France 1989–; Minister of Justice, Finance, Posts, Telephones and Telecommunications 1976–79; Pres. Lebanese Bankers' Asscn 1997–2001; Officier, Légion d'Honneur 1999. *Address:* Banque Libano-Française, BP 11-808, Tour Liberty, rue de Rome, Beirut 1107-2804 (office); Rue St Charles, Imm. Colette Eddé, Brazilia, Hazmieh, Beirut, Lebanon (home). *Telephone:* (1) 753460 (office). *Fax:* (1) 753461 (office). *E-mail:* farid.raphael@eblf.com (office). *Website:* www.eblf.com (office).

RAPHAEL, Frederic Michael, MA, FRSL; American writer; b. 14 Aug. 1931, Chicago, Ill.; s. of Cedric Michael Raphael and Irene Rose Mauser; m. Sylvia Betty Glatt 1955; two s. one d.; ed Charterhouse, St John's Coll., Cambridge (major scholar in Classics); Lippincott Prize 1961, Prix Simone Genevois 2000. *Radio plays:* The Daedalus Dimension 1982, The Thought of Lydia 1988, The Empty Jew 1993, Final Demands 2010, Couples 2010. *Television plays:* The Glittering Prizes (Royal TV Soc. Writer of the Year Award) 1976, From the Greek 1979, Oxbridge Blues 1984, After the War 1989, A Thousand Kisses 2011, Jake Liebowitz, A Life in Film 2013. *Publications include:* novels: Obbligato 1956, The Earlsdon Way 1958, The Limits of Love 1960, A Wild Sunrise 1961, The Graduate's Wife 1962, The Trouble with England 1962, Lindmann 1963, Orchestra and Beginners 1967, Like Men Betrayed 1970, April, June and November 1972, The Glittering Prizes 1976, Heaven and Earth 1985, After the War 1988, A Wild Surmise 1991, A Double Life 1993, Old Scores 1995, All His Sons 1999, Fame and Fortune 2007, Final Demands 2010, Private Views 2014; short stories: Sleeps Six 1979, Oxbridge Blues 1980, Think of England 1986, The Hidden I (illustrated by Sarah Raphael) 1990, The Latin Lover and Other Stories 1994; biography: Somerset Maugham and his World 1977, Byron 1982, A Jew among the Romans, Flavius Josephus and His Legacy 2013; essays: Cracks in the Ice 1979, Of Gods and Men (illustrated by Sarah Raphael) 1992, The Necessity of Anti-Semitism 1997, Historicism and its Poverty 1998, Karl Popper 1998, Eyes Wide Open 1999, Personal Terms 2001, The Benefits of Doubt 2002, Rough Copy (Personal Terms II) 2004, Cuts and Bruises (Personal Terms III) 2006, Ticks and Crosses (Personal Terms IV) 2008, Ifs and Buts (Personal Terms V) 2011, There and Then (Personal Terms VI) 2013, J. R. Oppenheimer, for example (e-book essay) 2013; translations: Catullus (with K. McLeish) 1976, The Oresteia of Aeschylus 1978, Aeschylus (complete plays, with K. McLeish) 1991, Euripides' Medea (with K. McLeish) 1994, Euripides: Hippolytus, Bacchae (with K. McLeish) 1997, Sophocles Aias (with K. McLeish) 1998, Bacchae 1999, The Satyrica of Petronius 2009; screenplays: Nothing But the Best 1964 (Writers' Guild Best Comedy), Darling (US Acad. Award for Best Original Screenplay, Writer's Guild Best Screenplay, British Film Acad. Award) 1965, Far from the Madding Crowd 1967, Two for the Road 1968, Daisy Miller 1974, Rogue Male 1976, School Play 1978, Richard's Things 1980, The Man in the Brooks Brothers Shirt (ACE Award 1991), Armed Response 1995, Eyes Wide Shut 1998, Coast to Coast 2002. *Leisure interests:* tennis, bridge, having gardened. *Address:* Ed Victor Ltd, 6 Bayley Street, Bedford Square, London, WC1B 3HE, England (office).

RAPLEY, Christopher G., CBE, PhD; British museum director, earth system scientist and academic; *Director, Science Museum, London;* b. 8 April 1947, West Bromwich; s. of Ronald Rapley and Barbara Helen Rapley (née Stubbs); m. Norma Rapley; two d. (twins); ed King Edward's School, Bath, Jesus Coll. Oxford, Victoria Univ. of Manchester, Univ. Coll., London; Head of Remote Sensing, Mullard Space Science Lab., Univ. Coll. London 1982–94, Prof. of Remote Sensing 1991–97, Hon. Prof. 1998–; Exec. Dir Int. Geosphere-Biosphere Programme, Stockholm 1994–97; Dir British Antarctic Survey 1998–2007 (retd); Dir Science Museum, London 2007–; Fellow, St Edmund's Coll. Cambridge 1999–; mem. American Geophysical Union; Chair. Int. Polar Year 2007–08 Planning Group 2003–04; Hon. Prof., Univ. of East Anglia 1999–, Univ. Coll. London 1999–; Edinburgh Medal 2008. *Publications:* more than 120 articles and papers in professional scientific literature. *Leisure interests:* digital photography, jogging. *Address:* Science Museum, Exhibition Road, South Kensington, London, SW7 2DD (office); Flat 3, 51 Bateman Street, Cambridge, CB2 1LR, England (home). *Telephone:* (20) 7942-4000 (office). *E-mail:* christopher.rapley@ntlworld.com (home); feedback@nmsi.ac.uk (office). *Website:* www.sciencemuseum.org.uk (office).

RAPOSO, Mario; Portuguese lawyer and politician; b. Jan. 1929, Coimbra; s. of Mário da Silva Raposo and Adélia Ferreira Bastos; m. Catarina Pera; two s.; ed Univ. of Coimbra; Sub-Insp. for Social Assistance and Sec. to Minister of Finance, resgnd to practise law 1955; mem. Gen. Council, Ordem dos Advogados (Law Soc.) 1972–74, Chair. 1975–77; mem. Exec. Cttee First Nat. Congress of Lawyers 1972, Cttee for Judicial Reform, High Court of Justice 1974; Minister of Justice 1978, 1980–81, 1985–87; mem. Ass. of the Repub. 1978–79, for Social Democratic Party (PSD) Dec. 1979–90; Nat. Ombudsman 1990–91; mem. Council of State 1990–91,

Perm. Court of Arbitration; First Pres. Ibero–American Inst. of Maritime Law; Nat. Council of Ethics for Life Sciences 1991–93; Pres. Friendship Asscn Portugal –Repub. of Korea 1990–2000. *Publications:* five books and around 80 studies on commercial law, maritime law and arbitration. *Address:* Rua Rodrigo da Fonseco, 149-1, Dt, 1070–242 Lisbon (office); Rua de São Gabriel 7, Alto do Lagoal, 2760–107 Caxias, Portugal (home). *Telephone:* (21) 3826200 (office). *Fax:* (21) 3826209 (office). *E-mail:* marioraposoadvogado@sapo.pt (office); marioraposo.advogado@gmail.com (home).

RAPOTA, Lt-Gen. Grigory Alekseyevich; Russian government official and fmr intelligence officer; b. 5 Feb. 1944, Moscow; m.; three c.; ed Moscow Bauman Higher School of Tech., Inst. of Intelligence Service; mem. First Chief Dept of KGB; worked in USA and Finland; Deputy Dir Intelligence Service Russian Fed. 1994–98; Deputy Sec., Security Council April–Nov. 1998; Dir Gen. Rosvooruzheniye state co. 1998–99; First Deputy Minister of Econ. Devt and Trade 1999–2000; First Deputy Minister of Industry, Science and Tech. 2000–01; Sec.-Gen. Eurasian Econ. Community—EurAsEC 2002–07; Presidential Rep. to Southern Fed. Okrug (Dist) 2007–08, to Volga Fed. Okrug 2008–11. *Address:* c/o Office of the Presidential Representative, 603082 Nizhnii Novgorod, Kreml, kor. 1, Russia.

RAPPENEAU, Jean-Paul; French film director and screenwriter; b. 8 April 1932, Auxerre, Yonne; s. of Jean Rappeneau and Anne-Marie Rappeneau (née Bornhauser); m. Claude-Lise Cornély 1971; two s.; ed Lycée Jacques-Amyot, Auxerre, Faculté de droit, Paris; asst dir 1953–57; dir and screenwriter 1958–; Officier, Légion d'honneur, Officier, Ordre Nat. du Mérite, Commdr des Arts et Lettres; 10 César Awards 1990 (including Best Dir, Best Picture), Golden Globe Award for best foreign film 1990, US Nat. Review Bd Best Foreign Film 1990, Grand Prix Nat. du Cinéma 1994. *Films include:* as director: La Maison sur la place, Chronique provinciale 1958; wrote and directed La Vie de château 1966 (Prix Louis-Delluc), Les Mariés de l'An Deux 1970, Le Sauvage 1975, Tout feu, tout flamme 1982; as dir and jt adaptor Cyrano de Bergerac 1990, Le Hussard sur le toit 1995, Bon Voyage (Best Dir Cabourg Romantic Film Festival) 2002; as screenwriter: Signé Arsène Lupin 1959, Le Mariage (in La Française et l'Amour) 1959, Zazie dans le métro 1960, Vie privée 1961, Le Combat dans l'île 1961, L'Homme de Rio 1962, La Fabuleuse aventure de Marco Polo 1965, Les Survivants (TV) 1965, Le Magnifique 1973, Le Sauvage 1975. *Address:* c/o Artmédia, 20 avenue Rapp, 75007 Paris (office); 24 rue Henri Barbusse, 75005 Paris, France (home). *E-mail:* info@artmedia.fr (office).

RARAWA, Denton, MSc; Solomon Islands central banker; *Governor, Central Bank of Solomon Islands;* ed Australian Nat. Univ., Cardiff Business School, Univ. of Wales, UK; joined Central Bank of Solomon Islands as Research Officer, Econs Dept 1983, Asst Man., Econs Dept 1988–92, Man. 1992–98, Deputy Gov., Central Bank of Solomon Islands 1998–2008, Gov. 2008–. *Address:* Office of the Governor, Central Bank of Solomon Islands, POB 634, Honiara, Solomon Islands (office). *Telephone:* 21791 (office). *Fax:* 23513 (office). *E-mail:* info@cbsi.com.sb (office). *Website:* www.cbsi.com.sb (office).

RASHED, Mahmoud Aboul Leil; Egyptian politician; b. 24 Sept. 1935, Minia; m.; one s. two d.; ed Cairo Univ.; Pres. State High Security Court 1988–90, Giza Primary Court 1990–96; Gov. Kafr El Sheikh 1996–2000, Giza Governorate 2000–04; Minister of Justice 2004–06 (resgnd). *Address:* c/o Ministry of Justice, Justice and Finance Building, Sharia Majlis ash-Sha'ab, Lazoughli Square, Cairo, Egypt (office).

RASHEED, Mohamed; Maldivian politician; fmr Dir, Ministry of Health; Minister of Econ. Devt 2008–10 (resgnd); mem. Nat. Planning Council 2009–. *Address:* c/o Ministry of Economic Development, Ghaazee Building, Ameer Ahmed Magu, Malé 20-05, Maldives. *Telephone:* 3323668. *E-mail:* info@trade.gov.mv.

RASHID, Shaikh Ahmed, MA, LLB; Pakistani politician; b. 6 Nov. 1950, Balra Bazar, Rawalpindi; ed Polytech. Coll., Rawalpindi, Gordon Coll., Punjab Univ.; mem. (Ind.) Nat. Ass. 1985–2008; fmr Minister of Labour and Manpower, of Industries and Production, of Culture and Sports, of Tourism and Investment; Fed. Minister of Information and Broadcasting 2002, for Railways 2006–08; participated in Geneva Accords, Moscow Conf.; Head of Gulf War Monitoring Programme; Rep. of Pakistan to UN and numerous int. confs. *Publications include:* Farzand-I -Pakistan, Suboatta Hai. *Address:* c/o Ministry of Railways, Block D, Pakistan Secretariat, Islamabad, Pakistan.

RASHID, Ahmed; Pakistani journalist and author; b. 1948, Rawalpindi; m.; two c.; ed Malvern Coll., UK, Government Coll., Lahore, Fitzwilliam Coll., Univ. of Cambridge, UK; fmr Pakistan, Afghanistan and Cen. Asia Corresp. Far Eastern Economic Review; now writes regularly for Daily Telegraph, London, International Herald Tribune, New York Review of Books, BBC Online, The Nation, Lahore and other academic and foreign affairs journals as well as several Pakistani newspapers and magazines; appears on TV and radio including BBC World Service, ABC Australia, Radio France Int. and German Radio; mem. Advisory Bd Eurasia Net of the Soros Foundation; Scholar, Davos World Economic Forum; mem. Int. Advisory Bd Central Asia Survey; consultant for Human Rights Watch; mem. Bd of Advisers Int. Cttee of the Red Cross, Geneva 2004–08; f. Open Media Fund for Afghanistan (charity) 2002; Nisar Osmani Award for Courage in Journalism, Human Rights Soc. of Pakistan 2001. *Publications include:* The Resurgence of Central Asia: Islam or Nationalism, Fundamentalism Reborn: Afghanistan and the Taliban, Jihad: The Rise of Militant Islam in Central Asia, Taliban: Islam, Oil and the New Great Game in Central Asia 2000, Descent into Chaos 2008, Pakistan on the Brink: The Future of America, Pakistan, and Afghanistan 2012, Afghanistan Revealed (jtly) 2012. *Address:* c/o The Daily Telegraph, 111 Buckingham Palace Road, London, SW1W 0DT, England (office). *Website:* www.ahmedrashid.com.

RASHID, Tan Sri Hussain; Malaysian business executive and banker; fmrly with London Stock Exchange; est. brokerage house 1983; est. Rashid Hussain Berhad group of financial services companies 1996, ceded control 1998; Chair. Exec. Cttee Khazanah Govt holding co. *Address:* c/o D.C.B. Bank Bhd., Menara T.R., 18th Floor, 161B Jalan Ampang, PO Box 10145, 50907 Kuala Lumpur, Malaysia. *Telephone:* (3) 2612444. *Fax:* (3) 2619541. *E-mail:* webmaster@moe.gov.sa (office). *Website:* www.moe.gov.sa (office).

RASHID, Muhammad ibn Ahmad ar-, PhD; Saudi Arabian politician and academic; b. 1944, Al-Majma'a; m.; five s. two d.; ed Imam Mohammed Bin Saud Islamic Univ., Riyadh, Univ. of Indiana, Univ. of Oklahoma; teacher Inst. of Religious Studies, Riyadh 1964–65; Grad. Asst Coll. of Shari'a and Islamic Studies, Makkah 1965–66; sent on mission to USA by King Abdulaziz Univ. 1966–72; Asst Prof. King Saud Univ. 1972–79, Assoc. Prof. 1979–89, Vice-Dean Coll. of Educ. 1974–76, Dean 1976–79; Dir-Gen. Arab Bureau of Educ. for Gulf States 1979–88; Founder of Arab Gulf States Univ. and Vice-Pres. of Founding Cttee 1979–88; Prof. of Educ. King Saud Univ. 1989–94; mem. Saudi Nat. Council 1994–95; Minister of Educ. 1995–2004; Distinguished Fulbright Fellow 1988–89, Distinguished Fellow, World Council for Teacher Training 1989; Gold Medal of Merit (Arab League Educ. Cultural and Scientific Org.). *Publications:* numerous articles and research papers in professional journals. *Leisure interests:* walking, swimming, reading. *Address:* c/o Ministry of Education, PO Box 3734, Airport Road, Riyadh 11481, Saudi Arabia.

RASIZADÄ, Artur Tahir oğlu; Azerbaijani politician and engineer; *Prime Minister;* b. 26 Feb. 1935, Gäncä, Transcaucasian SSR (now Azerbaijan), USSR; m.; one d.; ed Azerbaijan Inst. of Industry; engineer, Deputy Dir Azerbaijan Inst. of Oil Machine Construction 1957–73, Dir 1977–78; Chief Engineer, Trust Soyuz-neftemash 1973–77; Deputy Head Azerbaijan State Planning Cttee 1978–81; Head of Section Cen. Cttee of Azerbaijan CP 1981–86; First Deputy Prime Minister 1986–92; adviser, Foundation of Econ. Reforms 1992–96; Asst to Pres. Heydär Äliyev Feb.–May 1996; First Deputy Prime Minister May–July 1996, Acting Prime Minister July–Nov. 1996, Prime Minister Nov. 1996–Aug. 2003, demoted and apptd Deputy Prime Minister when İlhäm Äliyev assumed office, continued to act as Prime Minister for Äliyev, formally returned to the post when Äliyev elected as Pres. Nov. 2003–; Istiglal Order 2005. *Address:* Office of the Prime Minister, 1066 Baku, Lermontov küç. 68, Azerbaijan (office). *Telephone:* (12) 492-84-19 (office). *Fax:* (12) 492-91-79 (office). *E-mail:* nk@cabmin.gov.az (office). *Website:* www .cabmin.gov.az (office).

RASMUSSEN, Anders Fogh, MSc; Danish politician and international organization official; b. 26 Jan. 1953, Ginnerup, Jutland; s. of Knud Rasmussen and Martha Rasmussen (née Fogh); m. Anne-Mette Rasmussen; three c.; ed Viborg Cathedral School, Univ. of Arhus; consultant to Danish Fed. of Crafts and Small Industries 1978–87; mem. Folketing (Parl.) 1978–2009, mem. Econ. and Political Affairs Cttee 1982–87, Vice-Chair. 1993–98; Vice-Chair. Housing Cttee 1981–86; Minister for Taxation 1987–92, also for Econ. Affairs 1990–92; Vice-Chair. Econ. and Political Affairs Cttee 1993–98; Prime Minister of Denmark 2001–09; Sec.-Gen. NATO 2009–Oct. 2014; mem. Venstre (Liberal Party), Vice-Chair. Nat. Org. Venstre 1985–98, mem. Man. Cttee Parl. Party 1984–87, 1992–2001, Spokesman for Venstre 1992–98, Vice-Chair. Foreign Policy Bd 1998–2001, Chair. Venstre 1998–2009; Grand Cross of the Portuguese Order of Merit 1992, Commdr (First Degree) of the Order of the Dannebrog 2002, Danish Gold Medal of Merit 2002, Grand Cross of the German Order of Merit 2002, Grand Cross of the Order of Merit of Poland 2003, Grand Cross of the Order of the Oak Crown of Luxembourg 2003, Grand Cross of the Order of Nicaragua 2003, Great Cross of the Pedro Joaquín Chamorro Order 2003, Ordinul Steaua României Mare Cruce 2004, Grand Cross of the Order of the Lithuanian Grand Duke Gediminas 2004, Three Star Order of Latvia 2005, Order of Stara Planina, First Class (Bulgaria) 2006, Grand Cross of the Nordstjärneorden (Sweden) 2007, Grand Cross of the Order of the South Cross (Brazil) 2007, Grand Cross of Order of Dannebrog 2009, Estonian Order of Cross of Terra Mañana 2009; Dr hc (George Washington Univ.) 2002, Hon. DIur (Hampden-Sydney Coll., Virginia) 2003, Hon. Alumni (Arhus) 2009; Adam Smith Award 1993, Politician of the Year (Dansk Markedsfuringsforbund) 1998, Netherlands Youth Org. for Freedom and Democracy Liberal of the Year 2002, European Leader Award, Polish Leaders Forum 2003, Danish European Movt European of the Year 2003, Robert Schumann Medal 2003, Pedro Joaquin Chamorro Medal, Nicaragua 2003, Best Leader in Denmark 2005, Politician of the Year 2005, Chevalier du St-Chinian 2007. *Publications include:* Oprør med skattesystemet 1979, Den truede velstand (co-author) 1980, Kampen om boligen 1982, Fra Socialstat til Minimalstat 1993, I Godvejr og storm (interviews) 2001. *Leisure interests:* cycling, kayaking. *Address:* c/o Office of the Secretary-General, North Atlantic Treaty Organization, Blvd Léopold III, 1110 Brussels, Belgium.

RASMUSSEN, Lars Løkke; Danish politician; b. 15 May 1964, Vejle; m. Sólrun Løkke Rasmussen; three c.; ed Copenhagen Univ.; Nat. Chair. Young Liberals 1986–89, Vice-Chair. Liberal Party (Venstre) 1998; mem. Folketing (Parl.) for Frederiksborg Co. Constituency 1994; mem. Græsted-Gilleleje Municipal Council 1986–97; Co. Mayor of Frederiksborg Co. 1998–2001; Minister of the Interior and Health 2001–07, of Finance 2007–09; Prime Minister of Denmark 2009–11; Commdr, Order of the Dannebrog 2003, Commdr (First Class), Order of the Dannebrog 2009, Grand Cross, Order of the Phoenix (Greece) 2009. *Address:* c/o Prime Minister's Office, Christiansborg, Prins Jørgens Gård 11, 1218 Copenhagen K, Denmark.

RASMUSSEN, Michael Pram, LLB; Danish business executive; *Chairman, A.P. Møller-Mærsk A/S;* b. 14 Jan. 1955; m. Anne Pram Kjølbye; ed Univ. of Copenhagen; began career with Nye Danske Lloyd 1979; Asst Man.-Dir Baltica Forsikring A/S 1982–84, Man.-Dir 1984–86, Vice-Pres. 1986–88, Pres. 1988–95; Pres. Tryg Forsikring A/S (later renamed Tryg-Baltica Forsikring A/S) 1995–96; CEO TopDanmark Forsikring A/S (insurance co.) 1996–; Chair. Mærsk Olie & Gas A/S; Vice-Chair. Forsikring & Pension 2000–03; Vice-Chair. A.P. Møller-Mærsk A/S June–Dec. 2002–03, Chair. 2003–; mem. Bd Dirs Baltica Forsikring A/S 1982–85, William Demant Holdings A/S 1999–, Oticon A/S 1999–, Danmark-Amerika Fondet 2002–, Coloplast A/S 2005–; Dir (non-exec.) Øresundsbro Konsortiet 2001–03. *Address:* A.P. Møller-Mærsk A/S, Esplanaden 50, 1098 Copenhagen K (office); TopDanmark Forsikring A/S, Borupvang 4, 2750 Ballerup, Denmark (office). *Fax:* 33-63-33-63 (office). *Fax:* 33-63-36-05 (office). *E-mail:* info@maersk.com (office). *Website:* www.maersk.com (office). www.topdanmark.dk (office).

RASMUSSEN, Stephen S. (Steve), BBA; American insurance company executive; *CEO, Nationwide Mutual Insurance Company;* ed Univ. of Iowa; joined Allied Insurance 1974, later Exec. Vice-Pres. for Product Man., Vice-Pres. for Under-writing and Regional Vice-Pres. for the Pacific Coast Region, Pres. and COO Allied Insurance –2003, held same positions with CalFarm Insurance (affiliated co.)

–2003; Pres. and COO Property and Casualty Operations, Nationwide Mutual Insurance Co. 2003–09, CEO 2009–; mem. Bd Nat. Urban League, Insurance Inst. for Highway Safety, OhioHealth Bd of Dirs, Columbus Metropolitan Library; mem. Columbus Partnership; fmr Trustee Grand View College, Des Moines, Ia; fmr Co-Chair. United Way of Cen. Ohio Alexis de Tocqueville Vingt-Cinq Soc. campaign; holds the Chartered Property Casualty Underwriter designation; Co-Chair. 2012 United Way of Central Ohio campaign. *Address:* Nationwide Mutual Insurance Co., One Nationwide Plaza, Columbus, OH 43215-2220, USA (office). *Telephone:* (614) 249-7111 (office). *Fax:* (614) 249-7705 (office). *E-mail:* info@nationwide.com (office). *Website:* www.nationwide.com (office).

RASMUSSEN, Hon. Wilkie Olaf Patua, BA, LLB, MA (Hons); Cook Islands lawyer, politician, writer and artist; *Leader of the Opposition;* b. (Wilkie Olaf Patua Rakoroa Matara), 21 March 1958, Omoka, Penrhyn; s. of Rakoroa Matara (birth father) and Christmas Matara (née Gifford) (birth mother), raised by Dane Isidor Wilkie Rasmussen and Anna Rasmussen (née Page); m. Tungane Rasmussen (née Woonton); one s. one d.; ed Univ. of Auckland, NZ; odd jobs as labourer, steel worker, freezing worker, kitchen hand; artist/painter 1980–87; journalist for New Zealand Herald 1988–89; practised as sole barrister/solicitor 1996–99, 2011–; fmr Man. Dir Northern Traders Ltd; Cabinet Sec. 1999–2000; High Commr to NZ 2000–02; mem. Parl. for Penrhyn 2002–, Chair. Media Select Cttee 2007, mem. Property Law Select Cttee 2007, Parl. Privileges Select Cttee 2007, 2011, CPA Cook Islands Cttee, Employment Relations Bill Select Cttee 2011, Family Law Bill Select Cttee 2011; Minister of Foreign Affairs and Immigration, Tourism, Cultural Devt, Marine Resources and Natural Environment Resources 2005–09, Minister of Finance and Econ. Man., Financial Intelligence Unit, Public Expenditure and Review Cttee, Business, Trade and Investment Bd, Commerce Comm., Nat. Superannuation, Pearl Authority and Attorney-Gen. 2009–10; Panellist, Pacific Ministers for Post-Forum Dialogue 2006–; fmr Acting Prime Minister; Deputy Leader Democratic Party 2007–09, 2010–12, Leader 2012–; Deputy Leader of the Opposition 2010–12, Leader of the Opposition 2012–; Pres. African Caribbean Pacific Parl. (ACP); Co-Pres. ACP-EU Jt Parl. Ass. 2007–09; Chair. Pacific Forum Trade Ministers Meeting 2008; Pres. Tongareva (Penrhyn) Island Cttee; Deacon of Avarua CICC (Cook Islands Christian Church); Maori and Pacific Islands Univ. Scholarship, Univ. of Auckland Scholarship. *Achievements include:* Cook Islands Bantamweight Boxing Champion. *Publications:* poetry published in Diplomats Journal, Wellington. *Leisure interests:* golden oldies rugby, golf, cricket, reading, photography, compiling genealogies, staying fit and healthy. *Address:* Tongareva (Penrhyn) MP's Office, PO Box 534, Punanga Nui Market, Ruatonga, Avarua, Rarotonga, Cook Islands (office). *Telephone:* 21726 (office). *Fax:* 21725 (office). *E-mail:* mpwilkie@tongareva.net.ck (office); wilkie@oyster.net.ck (home). *Website:* www.wilkierasmussen.com.

RASOOL, Ali Mahmoud Abd al-; Sudanese politician; b. Rahid al-Bardi, Southern Darfur Prov.; ed Univ. of Khartoum; worked on agricultural projects with World Bank; served within Ministry of Finance of Southern Darfur Prov., becoming state Minister of Finance; Gov. Southern Darfur Prov. 2008; Minister of Finance and Nat. Economy 2010–13; mem. Nat. Congress Party. *Address:* c/o Ministry of Finance and National Economy, POB 735, Khartoum, Sudan (office).

RASPUTIN, Valentin Grigoriyevich; Russian writer; b. 15 March 1937, Ust-Uda (Irkutsk); ed Irkutsk Univ.; first works published 1961; elected People's Deputy 1989; mem. Presidential Council 1990–91; USSR State Prize 1977, 1987, Hero of Socialist Labour 1987, Solzhenitsyn Prize 2000. *Publications:* I Forgot to Ask Lyosha 1961, A Man of This World 1965, Bearskin for Sale 1966, Vasilii and Vasilisa 1967, Deadline 1970, Live and Remember, Stories, 1974, Parting with Matera 1976, Live and Love 1982, Fire 1985, Collected Works (2 vols) 1990, Siberia, Siberia 1991. *Address:* 5th Army Street 67, Apt 68, 664000 Irkutsk, Russia. *Telephone:* (3952) 4-71-00.

RASSOUL, Zalmai, MD; Afghan physician and government official; b. 1923, Kabul; ed Estiqlal High School, Univ. of Paris, France; worked at Research Inst. of Cardiac Diseases, Paris, Mil. Hosp. of Saudi Arabia; served as Chief of Staff of HM King Mohammad Zahir Shah, Rome; worked for Haqiqat e Afghan publ. regarding Jihad in Afghanistan, Paris; Minister of Civil Aviation and Tourism and Nat. Security Adviser, Interim Govt of Afghanistan; Nat. Security Adviser, Govt of Afghanistan –2010; Minister of Foreign Affairs 2010–13; cand. in presidential election 2014; mem. American Soc. of Nephrology. *Publications:* more than 30 medical books and booklets published in Europe and USA. *Address:* c/o Ministry of Foreign Affairs, Malek Azghar Street, Kabul, Afghanistan (office).

RASULZODA, Qohir; Tajikistani politician and fmr engineer; *Prime Minister;* b. 8 March 1961, Bobojonghafurov Region, Sughd Dist; m.; three c.; ed Agricultural Inst. of Tajikistan (now Tajikistan Agrarian Univ.); began career as technician supervisor, Tajikirsovkhozstroy Asscn Building Lab., Bobojonghafurov Region 1982; fmr engineer, Production Dept, later chief engineer and Head, Tajikirsov-khozstroy, Khujand; Minister of Land Reclamation and Water Resources 2000–06; Chair. Sughd Region 2006–13; Prime Minister 2013–; mem. Majlisi Milliy (Nat. Ass.), First Vice-Chair. 2007–13; Honoured Worker of Repub. of Tajikistan. *Address:* Secretariat of the Prime Minister, 734023 Dushanbe, Xiyoboni Rudaki 80, Tajikistan (office). *Telephone:* (372) 21-18-71 (office). *Fax:* (372) 21-51-10 (office).

RATANARAK, Krit; Thai business executive; *Chairman, Bangkok Broadcasting & Television Company;* b. 19 April 1946; s. of Chuan Ratanarak and Sasithorn Ratanarak; divorced; one s.; ed Husson Univ., USA; joined Bank of Ayudhya 1972, becoming Pres. 1982, CEO 1990, Chair. and CEO 1993; Chair. Bangkok Broadcasting & Television Co. (BBTV) 1993–; Chair. Siam City Cement 1993–, Ayudhya Insurance 1993–; Owner Tonson Property; mem. Woothi Sapha (Senate) 1981–2005. *Address:* Bangkok Broadcasting & Television Company, 998/1 Soi Sirimitr, Phaholyothin, Talad Mawchid, POB 456, Bangkok 10900, Thailand (office). *Telephone:* (2) 272-0201 (office). *Fax:* (2) 272-0010 (office). *E-mail:* prdept@ch7.com (office). *Website:* www.ch7.com (office).

RATCLIFFE, James A., BSc (ChemEng), MBA; British business executive; *Chairman, Ineos Group Holdings PLC;* ed Univ. of Birmingham, London Business School; qualified as an accountant; began career with Exxon Chemicals before moving to Courtaulds; joined Advent International 1989, led successful buyout of Inspec Group plc 1992, floated co. 1994, left Inspec to lead acquisition of Ineos PLC (now Ineos Oxide) from Inspec 1998; Dir and Chair. Ineos Group Holdings PLC and Chair. Ineos Capital 1998–; Hon. FIChemE 2009. *Leisure interests:* skiing, sailing. *Address:* Ineos Group Holdings PLC, Hawkslease, Chapel Lane, Lyndhurst, SO43 7FG, Hants., England (office); 58 Rue Charles Martel, Luxembourg Ville 2134, Luxembourg (office). *Telephone:* (23) 8028-7067 (Lyndhurst) (office). *Fax:* (23) 8028-7054 (Lyndhurst) (office). *E-mail:* info@ineos.com (office). *Website:* www .ineos.com (office).

RATHER, Dan, BA; American broadcast journalist; b. Oct. 1931, Wharton, Tex.; m. Jean Goebel; one s. one d.; ed Sam Houston State Teachers Coll., Univ. of Houston, South Texas School of Law; writer and sports commentator with KSAM-TV; taught journalism for one year at Houston Chronicle; with CBS 1962; with radio station KTRH, Houston for about four years; News and Current Affairs Dir CBS Houston TV affiliate KHOU-TV late 1950s; joined CBS News 1962; Chief London Bureau 1965–66; worked in Viet Nam; White House 1966; anchorman CBS Reports 1974–75; co-anchorman 60 Minutes CBS-TV 1975–81; anchorman Dan Rather Reporting CBS Radio Network 1977–2006; co-ed. show Who's Who CBS-TV 1977; anchor, Midwest desk CBS Nat. election night 1972–80; CBS Nat. Political Consultant 1964–2006; anchor, Man. Ed. CBS Evening News with Dan Rather 1981–2005, co-anchor 1993–2005; f. News and Guts 2006; anchor and Man. Ed. Dan Rather Reports, HDNet (now AXS TV) 2006–; anchored numerous CBS News Special Programmes, including coverage of presidential campaigns in 1982 and 1984; as White House corresp. accompanied Pres. on numerous travels, including visits to Middle East, USSR, People's Repub. of China; numerous acad. honours; 10 Emmy awards; Distinguished Achievement for Broadcasting Award, Univ. of Southern Calif. Journalism Alumni Asscn, Bob Considine Award 1983. *Publications:* The Palace Guard 1974 (with Gary Gates), The Camera Never Blinks Twice (with Mickey Herskowitz) 1977, I Remember (with Peter Wyden) 1991, The Camera Never Blinks Twice: The Further Adventures of a Television Journalist 1994. *Address:* c/o AXS TV, 320 South Walton Street, Dallas, TX 75226, USA (office). *Telephone:* (214) 698-3800 (office). *Website:* www.axs.tv/programs/ danrather (office); www.danrather.com.

RATHKE, Most Rev. Heinrich Karl Martin Hans, DTheol; German ecclesiastic; *Bishop and Pastor Emeritus, Evangelical-Lutheran Church of Mecklenburg;* b. 12 Dec. 1928, Mölln, Kreis Malchin; s. of Paul Rathke and Hedwig Rathke (née Steding); m. Marianne Rusam 1955; six s. one d.; ed Univs of Kiel, Erlangen, Tübingen and Rostock; parish priest, Althof bei Bad Doberan 1954–55, Warnkenhagen, Mecklenburg 1955–62, Rostock Südstadt 1962–70; Priest in charge of community service and people's mission, Mecklenburg 1970–71; Bishop of the Evangelical-Lutheran Church of Mecklenburg 1971–84; Presiding Bishop of the United Evangelical Lutheran Church of the GDR 1977–81; Pastor in Crivitz/ Mecklenburg 1984–91; Bishop and Pastor Emer. 1991–; Asst Bishop, Evangelical-Lutheran Church of Australia 1991–93; Hon. DTheol (Rostock) 1999. *Publications:* Ignatius von Antiochien und die Paulusbriefe 1967, Gemeinde heute und morgen 1979, Einstehen für Gemeinschaft in Christus 1980, Kirche unterwegs 1995, Predigthilfen (three vols) 1998–2000, Märtyrer, Vorbilder für das Widerstehen 2002, Mitmenschlichkeit, Zivilcourage, Gottvertrauen – Opfer des Stalinismus 2003. *Address:* Pfaffenstr. 3, 19055 Schwerin, Germany. *Telephone:* (385) 562887.

RATMANSKY, Alexei; Russian ballet dancer and choreographer; *Resident Choreographer, New York City Ballet;* b. St Petersburg; ed Ballet School of the Bolshoi Theatre, Moscow; has danced with Ukrainian Nat. Ballet, Kiev Ballet, Royal Winnipeg Ballet; joined Royal Danish Ballet as soloist 1997–2000, Prin. Dancer 2000–04; Artistic Dir Bolshoi Ballet 2004–08; Resident Choreographer, New York City Ballet 2009–; has performed leading roles, including Basil in Don Quixote, Prince Siegfried in Swan Lake, Albrecht in Giselle, James in La Sylphide, and Copain in Gaité Parisienne; has also danced soloist roles in Grass, Mahler's 5th Symphony, A Folk Tale and Suite en Blanc; cr. first ballet, Betwix, as participant in Choreographer Workshop at Royal Danish Ballet 1999; other works include Turandot's Dream, performed as part of the Shaken – Not Stirred program at Old Stage of the Royal Theatre, The Nutcracker and Anna Karenina for The Royal Danish Ballet, Poem of Ecstasy, The Fairy's Kiss, Middle Duo and Cinderella for The Maryinsky Ballet, as well as Capriccio, Dreams About Japan, The Bright Stream, Leah, and Bolt for the Bolshoi Ballet; First Prize, Ukrainian Ballet Competition 1998, Gold Medal, Moscow Diaghilev Competition 1992, Nijinsky Prize 1992. *Address:* New York Choreographic Institute, New York City Ballet, David H. Koch Theater, 20 Lincoln Center, New York, NY 10023, USA (office). *Telephone:* (212) 870-4060 (office). *E-mail:* NYChoreoInst@nycballet.com (office). *Website:* www.nycballet.com (office).

RATNAM, Anita, MA; Indian dancer and choreographer; *Director, Arangham Trust;* b. 21 May 1954, Madurai, Tamil Nadu; m.; two c.; ed Univ. of New Orleans; trained in Bharatanatyam 1969–78, Mohiniattam 1968–78, Kathakali 1968–78; Founder-Dir Arangham Trust 1992–; f. Arangham Dance Theatre 1993; co-f. The Other Festival 1998–2007; f. Narthaki.com 2000, now Consulting Ed.; Observer, Post Modern Dance Festival Germany 2002; columnist, New Indian Express; mem. Int. Advisory Bd Pangea World Theatre USA, Preaksha Dance Canada; Hon. mem. The Duchess Club; Nritya Choodamani, Sri Krishna Gana Sabha 1996, Chennai Kalaimamani, Govt of Tamil Nadu 1998, Media Achievement Award 1991, Mahatma Gandhi Award for Cultural Harmony 1986, Lalithakalaratna, Lalithakala Acad. Foundation Trust 2003, Natya Ratna, Sri Shanmukhananda Sangeeta Sabha 2003, Price Award, Shakespeare Millennium Club Chennai 2004, Natya Kireeta Ratnam Award 2005. *Achievements include:* created unique dance style called Neo Bharat Natyam. *Dance:* 7 Graces New York 2007 (solo). *Films include:* Kandukondain Kandukondain 2000, Boys 2003. *Address:* Arangham Trust, #10, Cenotaph 2nd Lane, Chennai 600018, India (office). *Telephone:* (44) 28522224 (office); 9841026123 (mobile). *Fax:* (44) 28522224 (office). *E-mail:* anita@arangham .com (office); aratnam@vsnl.com. *Website:* www.arangham (office); www .anitaratnam.com.

RATNAM, Mani, BCom, MBA; Indian film director and screenwriter; b. (Gopala Ratnam Subramaniam), 1956, Madurai; s. of Gopal Ratnam Iyer; m. Suhasini Hassan 1988; one s.; ed Univ. of Madras, Jamnalal Bajaj Inst., Mumbai; fmr man. consultant; worked for TVS Sudaram; f. Madras Talkies film production co. *Films include:* Pallavi Anu Palavi 1983, Mauna Ragam 1986, Nayakan 1987, Agni Nakshatram 1988, Gitanjali 1989, Anjali 1990, Roja 1992, Thiruda Thiruda 1993,

Bombay 1994, Dalpati 1995, Chor Chor 1996, Iruvar 1996, Dil Se 1998, Alay Payuthe 2000, Kannathil Muthamittal (A Peck on the Cheek) 2002, Saathiya 2002, Yuva (The Youth) 2004, Ayitha Ezhuthu 2004, Guru 2007. *Address:* 1 Murrey Gate Road, Alwarpet, Chennai 600 018, India (office). *Telephone:* (44) 456998.

RATNAYAKE, Susantha Chaminda; Sri Lankan business executive; *Chairman, John Keells Holdings PLC;* ed Trinity Coll., Kandy, Royal Coll., Colombo; joined Mackinnons Travel as a trainee exec. working under mentorship of Tyrell Mutthiah, rose rapidly within the John Keells Group, apptd a Dir of main group 1992, Deputy Chair. John Keells Holdings PLC 2004–05, Chair. 2006–, Chair. of all subsidiary cos of the Group; mem. Council of Employers Fed. of Ceylon, Cttee of Ceylon Chamber of Commerce, Tourism, Sovereign Rating and Investment Promotion Clusters of Nat. Council of Econ. Devt. *Address:* John Keells Holdings PLC, 130 Glennie Street, Colombo 2, Sri Lanka (office). *Telephone:* (11) 2306000 (office). *E-mail:* jkh@keells.com (office). *Website:* www.keells.com (office).

RATNER, Gerald Irving; British business executive; *Chief Executive, GeraldOnLine;* b. 1 Nov. 1949, Richmond, Surrey, England; s. of Leslie Ratner and Rachelle Ratner; m. 1st (divorced 1989); two d.; m. 2nd Moira Ratner; one s. one d.; ed Hendon County Grammar School, London; Man. Dir Ratners Group 1984, Chair. 1986–91, CEO 1986–92, Dir –1992; Chief Exec. GeraldOnline (online jewellery retailer) 2003–; Dir (non-exec.) Norweb 1991; consultant, Tobacco Dock 1993–; Dir Workshop Health and Fitness Club 1997–. *Radio:* On the Ropes (Stephen Nolan). *Television:* Celebrity Apprentice, Trouble at the Top. *Publication:* Gerald Ratner – The Rise and Fall… and Rise Again (illustrated) 2007. *Leisure interests:* cycling, music. *Telephone:* (1628) 770270 (home); 7710-032619 (mobile). *Fax:* (1628) 770270 (home). *E-mail:* gerald@geraldonline.com (office); gerald.ratner@btinternet.com. *Website:* www.geraldonline.com.

RATNER, Mark A., BA, PhD; American chemist and academic; *Professor of Chemistry and Lawrence B. Dumas Distinguished University Professor, Northwestern University;* b. 1942, Cleveland, Ohio; ed Harvard and Northwestern Univs; postdoctoral work in Aarhus, Denmark and Munich, Germany; taught Chem. at New York Univ. 1970–74; fmr Visiting Prof., Nat. Sciences Research Council, Odense Univ., Denmark; Chair. Dept of Chem., Northwestern Univ. 1988–91, Assoc. Dean, Coll. of Arts and Sciences 1980–84, now Prof. of Chem. and Lawrence B. Dumas Distinguished Univ. Prof.; mem. American Acad. of Arts and Sciences 2001, NAS 2002, Int. Acad. of Quantum Molecular Science 2003; Fellow, AAAS; Hon. ScD (Hebrew Univ. of Jerusalem) 2005, (Copenhagen) 2010; ACS Langmuir Award 2004, John Stauffer Lecturer, Stanford Univ. 2009, Willard Gibbs Medal Award, ACS Chicago Local Section 2012. *Achievements include:* proposed, with Arieh Aviram, the first unimolecular electronic rectifier 1974. *Publications:* Molecular Electronics II (Annals of the New York Academy of Sciences) 1998, Same (co-ed.) 2002, Introduction to Quantum Mechanics in Chemistry (co-author) 2000, Quantum Mechanics in Chemistry (co-author) 2002, Nanotechnology: A Gentle Introduction to the Next Big Idea (co-author) 2002, Nanotechnology and Homeland Security: New Weapons for New Wars (co-author) 2003; numerous papers in professional journals. *Address:* Ryan 4015, Department of Chemistry, Northwestern University, 2145 Sheridan Road, Evanston, IL 60208-3113, USA (office). *Telephone:* (847) 491-5652 (office). *Fax:* (847) 491-7713 (office). *E-mail:* ratner@northwestern.edu (office). *Website:* www.chemistry.northwestern .edu (office); chemgroups.northwestern.edu/ratner/ratner.html (office).

RATO Y FIGAREDO, Rodrigo, JD, MBA, PhD; Spanish international banker and fmr government official; *President, Caja Madrid;* b. 18 March 1949, Madrid; m.; two d.; ed Complutense Univ. Madrid, Univ. of California, Berkeley, USA; mem. Exec. Cttee Partido Popular party 1979–, mem. Parl. for Cádiz 1982–89, for Madrid 1989–2004; co-f. party's Econ. Comm., Parl. Sec.-Gen., 1982–84, Econ. Spokesman 1984–86, Sec.-Gen. for Electoral Action 1988, apptd Vice-Sec. 1996; Second Deputy Prime Minister and Minister of Economy and Finance 1996–2000, First Deputy Prime Minister for Econ. Affairs and Minister of Economy 2000–04, including posts as Gov. for Spain on Bds IMF, World Bank, IDB, EIB and EBRD, also in charge of foreign trade relations for Spain; Man. Dir IMF 2004–07 (resgnd); Sr Man. Dir of Investment Banking, Lazard Ltd 2008; Pres. Caja Madrid 2010–, Bankia 2010–12. *Address:* Caja Madrid, Plaza de Celenque 2, 28013 Madrid, Spain (office). *Website:* www.cajamadrid.com (office).

RATOVONDRAHONA, Guy; Malagasy central banker; *Acting Governor, Banque Centrale de Madagascar;* fmr Sec.-Gen. Commission de supervision bancaire et financière; Dir Fonds de garantie malgache –2011; Dir-Gen. Banque Centrale de Madagascar 2011–12, Acting Gov. 2012–. *Address:* Office of the Governor, Banque Centrale de Madagascar, rue de la Révolution Socialiste Malgache, BP 550, 101 Antananarivo, Madagascar (office). *Telephone:* (20) 2221751 (office). *Fax:* (20) 2234532 (office). *E-mail:* sbu@bfm.mg (office). *Website:* www.banque-centrale.mg (office).

RATSIRAHONANA, Norbert; Malagasy lawyer and politician; *Leader, Ny asa vita no ifampitsara (AVI) Party;* b. 18 Nov. 1938, Antsiranana; Pres. Constitutional High Court –1996; Prime Minister of Madagascar 1996–97; Leader Ny asa vita no ifampitsara (AVI—People are judged by the work they do) Party 1997–. *Address:* c/o Office of the Prime Minister, BP 248, Mahazoarivo, 101 Antananarivo, Madagascar.

RATTLE, Sir Simon, Kt, CBE; British conductor; *Artistic Director and Chief Conductor, Berlin Philharmonic Orchestra;* b. 19 Jan. 1955, Liverpool, England; m. 1st Elise Ross 1980 (divorced 1995); two s.; m. 2nd Candace Allen 1996; partner Magdalena Kožená; one s.; ed Royal Acad. of Music, London; won John Player Int. Conducting Competition 1973; has conducted Bournemouth Symphony, Northern Sinfonia, London Philharmonic, London Sinfonietta, Berlin Philharmonic, LA Philharmonic, Stockholm Philharmonic, Vienna Philharmonic, Philadelphia Orchestra, Boston Symphony orchestras, etc.; debut at Queen Elizabeth Hall, London 1974, Royal Festival Hall, London 1976, Royal Albert Hall, London 1976; Asst Conductor, BBC Symphony Orchestra 1977–80; Assoc. Conductor, Royal Liverpool Philharmonic Soc. 1977–80; Glyndebourne debut 1977, Royal Opera, Covent Garden debut 1990; Artistic Dir, London Choral Soc. 1979–84; Prin. Conductor and Artistic Adviser, City of Birmingham Symphony Orchestra (CBSO) 1980–90, Music Dir 1990–98; Artistic Dir South Bank Summer Music 1981–83; Jt Artistic Dir Aldeburgh Festival 1982–93; Prin. Guest Conductor, LA Philharmonic 1981–94, Rotterdam Philharmonic 1981–84; Prin. Guest Conductor Orchestra of the Age of Enlightenment 1992–; Artistic Dir and Chief Conductor Berlin Philharmonic Orchestra 2002–; Hon. Fellow, St Anne's Coll. Oxford 1991; Officier, Ordre des Arts et des Lettres 1995, Order of Merit of the FRG, Chevalier, Légion d'honneur 2010; Hon. DMus (Liverpool) 1991, (Leeds) 1993; Edison Award (for recording of Shostakovich's Symphony No. 10) 1987, Grand Prix du Disque (Turangalîla Symphony) 1988, Grand Prix Caecilia (Turangalîla Symphony, Jazz Album) 1988, Gramophone Record of the Year Award (Mahler's Symphony No. 2) 1988, Gramophone Opera Award (Porgy and Bess) 1989, Int. Record Critics' Award (Porgy and Bess) 1990, Grand Prix de l'Acad. Charles Cros 1990, Gramophone Artist of the Year 1993, Montblanc de la Culture Award 1993, Shakespeare Prize, Toepfer Foundation, Hamburg 1996, Gramophone Award for Best Concerto recording (Szymanowski Violin Concertos Nos 1 and 2), RSA Albert Medal 1997, Choc de l'Année Award (for recording of Brahms Piano Concerto Op. 15) 1998, Outstanding Achievement Award, South Bank Show 1999, Diapason Recording of the Year Award (complete Beethoven Piano Concertos) 1999, Gramophone Award for Best Opera Recording (Szymanowski's King Roger) 2000, Gramophone Awards for Best Orchestral Recording and Record of the Year (Mahler's Symphony No. 10) 2000, Comenius Prize (Germany) 2004, Classical BRIT Award (for Beethoven Symphonies) 2004, Schiller Special Prize, City of Mannheim 2005, Classical BRIT Award for Classical Recording of the Year (Holst's The Planets) 2007, Gramophone Award for Best Choral Recording (Brahms' Ein deutsches Requiem) 2007, Gold Medal 'Gloria Artis', Premio Don Juan de Borbón de la Música 2009, Wolf Prize in Music (shared with Plácido Domingo) 2012, ECHO Klassik Award for Symphonic Recording of the Year – 20th/21st Century (for Schönberg CD) 2012, Léonie Sonning Music Prize 2013. *Address:* Berlin Philharmonic Orchestra, Herbert-von-Karajan-Str. 1, 10785 Berlin, Germany (office). *Telephone:* (30) 25488999 (office). *Website:* www.berliner-philharmoniker.de (office).

RATTNER, Steven (Steve) Lawrence, BA; American journalist, financial industry executive and fmr government official; b. 5 July 1952, New York; s. of George Seymour Rattner and Selma Ann Silberman; m. P. Maureen White 1986; three s. one d.; ed Brown Univ.; Asst to James Reston, New York Times Corresp., Washington, DC New York and London 1974–82; Assoc. Vice-Pres. Lehman Brothers Kuhn Loeb, New York 1982–84; Assoc. Vice-Pres., Prin., Man. Dir then Head communications group Morgan Stanley and Co., New York 1984–89; Man. Dir then Head communications group Lazard Frères and Co. 1989–97, Deputy CEO and Deputy Chair. 1997–99; Man. Prin. Quadrangle Group LLC 2000–09; Counselor to the Sec. of the Treasury, US Dept of the Treasury, Washington, DC 2009 (resgnd); Dir Falcon Cable Holding Group 1993–98; mem. Bd of Dirs Cablevision, ProSiebenSat.1 Media AG, InterActiveCorp; mem. Man. Cttee Access Spectrum LLC, Global Energy Decisions, GT Brands; Dir New York Outward Bound Center 1990–2001, mem. Advisory Council 2001–; Harvey Baker Fellow, Brown Univ. 1974; Poynter Fellow, Yale Univ. 1979; mem. Council on Foreign Relations; Assoc. mem. Royal Inst. for Int. Affairs; Trustee Brown Univ. 1987–93, 1994–2000 (Fellow 2000–), Educational Broadcasting Corpn 1990– (Vice-Chair. 1994–98, Chair. 1998–), Metropolitan Museum of Art 1996–, Brookings Inst. 1998–, New America Foundation, 2003–; Chair. Mayor's Fund to Advance NYC 2003–. *Publications:* Overhaul: An Insider's Account of the Obama Administration's Emergency Rescue of the Auto Industry 2010; contrib. to various news publs including New York Times, Wall Street Journal, Los Angeles Times, Newsweek and Financial Times. *Address:* c/o Quadrangle Group LLC, 375 Park Avenue, New York, NY 10152, USA.

RATZINGER, Joseph Alois (see BENEDICT XVI).

RAUCH, Neo; German artist; b. 1960, Leipzig; ed Hochschule für Grafik und Buchkunst, Leipzig; Asst Lecturer, Hochschule für Grafik und Buchkunst, Leipzig 1993–98; Vincent Award 2002. *Works include:* Das geht alles von ihrer Zeit ab, Stereo, Falle, Schwieriges Gelände 1997, Handel 1999, Weiche 1999, Quiz 2002, Hatz 2002, Haus des Lehrers 2003, Scheune 2003, Gold 2003, Schmerz 2004. *Address:* Wächterstrasse 11, 04107 Leipzig, Germany (office). *Telephone:* (3) 412135–0 (office). *Website:* www.hgb-leipzig.de (office).

RAUH, Markus, DrScTech; Swiss telecommunications industry executive; b. 1939, St Gallen; ed Swiss Fed. Inst. of Tech. (ETH), Zürich; began career as Sales Man., Sperry Univac 1971–78; Head of Data Systems Dept, Philips AG 1978–83; appttd mem. Corp. Exec. Cttee, Philips Kommunikations Industrie AG 1983, Chair. 1985–88; Pres. Wild Leitz 1988–90; CEO Leica Group 1990–98; apptd Dir Leica Geosystems 1998, Vice-Chair. 2000; Chair. Swisscom AG 1998–2006 (retd); Chair. Synthes Chur AG, Anova Holding AG; Chair. Bd of Dirs AO Foundation; Vice-Chair. Dietiker AG; mem. Bd of Dirs Unaxis Holding AG, The Generics Group AG, Madison Man. AG, Cantonal Bank of St Gallen AG, Sagentia Group 2000–, Madison Pvt Equity Holding Ltd 2002–; mem. Exec. Bd Economiesuisse; Chair. AO ASIF Foundation; Pres. Bd of Trustees, Inst. of Tech. Man., Univ. of St Gallen; Hon. Senator, Univ. of St Gallen 2005. *Address:* c/o AO Foundation, Clavadelerstrasse 8, 7270 Davos Platz, Switzerland. *Telephone:* 814142801. *Fax:* 814142280. *E-mail:* foundation@aofoundation.org. *Website:* www.aofoundation.org.

RAÚL; Spanish professional footballer; b. (Raúl González Blanco), 27 June 1977, Madrid; m. María del Carmen 'Mamen' Redondo Sanz; four s. one d.; centre forward; youth player, San Cristóbal de los Ángeles 1987–90, Atlético Madrid 1990–92, Real Madrid 1992–94; sr player, Real Madrid C 1994, Real Madrid B 1994, Real Madrid 1994–2010 (won La Liga 1994/95, 1996/97, 2000/01, 2002/03, 2006/07, 2007/08, Spanish Super Cup 1997, 2001, 2003, 2008, UEFA Champions League 1997/98, 1999/2000, 2001/02, UEFA Super Cup 2002, Intercontinental Cup 1998, 2002, All-time top scorer with 321 official goals, All-time highest with 726 official matches, Capt. 2003–10), Schalke 04 2010–; mem. Spain U-18 team 1994, Spain U-20 team 1995, Spain U-21 team 1995–96, Spain U-23 team 1996–97, Spain 1996–2006 (102 appearances, 44 goals (All-time top scorer), Capt. 2002–06); Royal Order Gold Medal for Sports Merit 2006; Don Balón Award for Breakthrough Player in La Liga 1995, IFFHS World Goalgetter 1999, Euro 2000 Team of the Tournament 2000, ESM Team of the Year 1996/97, 1998/99, 1999/2000, Pichichi Trophy 1999, 2001, UEFA Champions League Top Scorer 1999/2000, 2000/01, FIFA World Player of the Year Bronze Award 2001, European Footballer of the Year Silver Award 2001, UEFA Club Forward of the Year 1999/2000, 2000/01, 2001/02, Premio Don Balón for Best Spanish Player in La Liga 1996/97, 1998/99, 1999/2000, 2000/01, 2001/02, named in FIFA 100 2004, Trofeo Alfredo Di Stéfano 2008, Madrid Gold Medal 2009, Second Place, Golden Foot 2009. *Leisure*

interests: reading (especially the books of Arturo Pérez Reverte), listening to Spanish music. *Address:* c/o FC Schalke 04, Ernst-Kuzorra-Weg 1, 45891 Gelsenkirchen, Germany. *Telephone:* (209) 36180. *Fax:* (209) 3618109. *E-mail:* post@schalke04.de. *Website:* www.schalke04.com.

RAUSCH, Jean-Marie Victor Alphonse; French politician; b. 24 Sept. 1929, Sarreguemines, Moselle; s. of Victor Rausch and Claire Hessemann; m. 2nd Nadine Haven 1980; two s. by first m.; ed Lycée de Sarreguemines and Ecole française de meunerie, Paris; Dir Moulin Rausch, Woippy 1953–76; Admin. Soc. Anonyme des Moulins Rausch, Woippy 1976–77; Pres. departmental milling syndicate 1967–81; Pres. Millers' Union of Moselle 1974–80; Conseiller-Gen. Metz III 1971, 1976, 1982–88, Pres. of Council 1979–82; Mayor of Metz 1971–2008; mem. Lorraine Regional Council 1974–92, Pres. 1982–92; mem. Nat. Statistical Council 1979, Conseil Nat. du Crédit 1984; numerous other civic, public and professional appointments; Minister of Foreign Trade 1988–91, of Foreign Trade and Tourism 1990–91, of Posts and Telecommunications 1991–92; Deputy Minister attached to Minister of Econ. and Finance in charge of Commerce and Labour April–Oct. 1992; Senator (Moselle) 1974–83, 1983–88, 1992–2001; Pres. Fed. des Asscns de maires de la Moselle 1977–2005, Institut Lorrain de Participation 1984–88, Médiaville 1995–, Metz-interactive 1995–2000, Communauté Numérique Interactive de l'Est 2000–02; Hon. mem. Metz Rotary Club, Acad. de Metz; Chevalier, Légion d'honneur, Commdr, Ordine della Stella della Solidarietà Italiana. *Publication:* Le laminoir et la puce: la troisième génération industrielle 1987 (Grand Prix de la littérature micro-informatique). *Leisure interests:* photography, skiing. *Address:* Médiaville, 42 rue Notre Dame des Champs, 75006 Paris (office); 4 rue Chanoine Collin, 57000 Metz, France (home). *Telephone:* 1-44-39-34-56 (office); 3-87-55-50-00 (home). *E-mail:* hotline@si.mairie-metz.fr (office).

RAUSING, Hans Anders; Swedish business executive; *Honorary Chairman, Ecolean AB;* b. 26 March 1926; s. of Ruben Rausing and Elisabeth Rausing; m. Märit Norrby; one s. two d. including Sigrid Rausing; ed Univ. of Lund; Man. Dir Tetra Pak 1954–83, moved to UK 1983, Chair. and CEO Tetra Pak 1983–91, Chair. Bd of Dirs 1985–91, Chair. and CEO Tetra Laval 1991–93, Hon. Chair. 1993–95; Hon. Chair. and majority investor Ecolean AB, Helsingborg, Sweden 2001–; f. Märit and Hans Rausing Charitable Foundation 1996, Hans and Märit Rausing Charitable Trust 2002; mem. Russian Council on Business Devt 1995; Hon. mem. Royal Swedish Acad. of Eng Sciences, Russian Acad. of Natural Sciences; Hon. Fellow, Isaac Newton Inst., Univ. of Cambridge; Order of People's Friendship 1994; Hon. KBE 2006; Dr hc (Univ. of Lund) 1979, (Royal Inst. of Tech., Stockholm) 1985, (Stockholm School of Econs) 1987, (American Univ. in London) 1991, (Imperial Coll. London) 2005, (Mälardalens Högskola) 2004, (Dubna, Russia). *Address:* Wadhurst Park, Wadhurst, East Sussex, TN5 6NT, England (office). *Website:* www.ecolean.com.

RAUSING, Sigrid, BA, MSc, PhD; Swedish anthropologist, philanthropist and publisher; b. 1962, Lund; d. of Hans Anders Rausing and Märit Rausing; m. 1st Dennis Hotz; one s.; m. 2nd Eric Abraham 2003; ed Univ. of York, Univ. Coll. London, UK; wealth derived from family-owned co. Tetra-Pak (manufacturer of drink cartons); f. Ruben and Elisabeth Rausing Trust 1995 (changed name to Sigrid Rausing Trust 2003); co-f. Portobello Books 2005; acquired Granta (magazine and publishing house) 2005; mem. Bd of Dirs Human Rights Watch, now Emer. Mem.; Trustee, Charleston (musuem), Sussex; Hon. Fellow, LSE 2010–; Int. Service Human Rights Award, Global Human Rights Defender Category 2004, Beacon Special Award for Philanthropy 2005, Changing Face of Philanthropy Award, Women's Funding Network 2006. *Publications include:* History, Memory, and Identity in Post-Soviet Estonia 2004; articles inewspapers and academic journals.

RAVALOMANANA, Marc; Malagasy business executive, politician and fmr head of state; b. 12 Dec. 1949, Imerikasina; m. Lalao Rakotonirainy; three s. one d.; ed in Imerikasina and in Sweden; f. TIKO (dairy and oil producing co.); owns Malagasy Broadcasting System (TV and radio stations), MAGRO (supermarket chain), FANAMBY (rice-producing co.); elected Mayor of Antananarivo 1999; following disputed victory in presidential elections Dec. 2001, declared himself Pres. of Madagascar Feb. 2002, High Constitutional Court ruled that he had won by an overall majority May 2002, Pres. of Madagascar 2002–09 (resgnd); Vice-Pres. Protestant Church of Madagascar; in exile in South Africa; sentenced in absentia to four years in jail for alleged abuse of office June 2009; Dr hc (Univ. of Antananarivo) 2007 Grand Commdr, Order of the Star and Key of the Indian Ocean (Mauritius), Sonderstufe des Großkreuzes (Germany) 2006;; Prix Louise Michel 2005.

RAVASI, HE Cardinal Gianfranco; Italian ecclesiastic and academic; *President of the Pontifical Council for Culture;* b. 18 Oct. 1942, Merate, Prov. of Lecco; ed seminary of Milan, Pontifical Gregorian Univ. and Pontifical Biblical Inst., Rome; ordained priest, Diocese of Milan 1966; spent summers in Syria, Jordan, Iraq and Turkey working as an archaeologist with Kathleen Kenyon and Roland de Vaux; later served as Prof. of Exegesis of the Old Testament at Theological Faculty of Northern Italy, Milan; Prefect of the Ambrosian Library 1989–2007; collaborated with Cardinal Carlo Maria Martini, SJ; Titular Archbishop of Villamagna in Proconsulari 2007–; Pres. Pontifical Council for Culture 2007–, Pontifical Comm. for the Cultural Heritage of the Church 2007–, Pontifical Comm. for Sacred Archeology 2007–; cr. Cardinal (Cardinal-Deacon of San Giorgio in Velabro) 2010; participated in Papal Conclave 2013; Laurea hc specialistica in Antropologia ed Epistemologia delle Religioni (Urbino Univ.); Socio onorario dell' Accad. delle Belle Arti, Brera and Diploma di Secondo Livello in Comunicazione e Didattica dell'Arte hc 2010; Dr hc (Bucharest) 2011, (Lublin) 2012, (Pontifical Lateran Univ.) 2012. *Address:* Pontifical Council for Culture, 00120 Città del Vaticano, Rome, Italy (office). *Telephone:* (06) 69893811 (office). *Fax:* (06) 69887368 (office). *E-mail:* cultura@cultura.va (office). *Website:* www.cultura.va (office).

RAVEN, Abbe, BA, MA; American television executive; *President and CEO, A&E Television Networks;* b. New York, NY; m.; one s.; ed Univ. of Buffalo, Hunter Coll. (Brookdale Fellow); currently Pres. and CEO A&E Television Networks (jt venture of The Hearst Corpn, The Walt Disney Co.'s Disney-ABC Television Group and General Electric's NBCUniversal), oversees History Channel and A&E; fmr Fellow, Center for Theater Research, Univ. of Buffalo; inducted into Hunter Coll. Hall of Fame 1997, Distinguished Alumnus Award, Univ. of Buffalo 2001, ranked by Fortune magazine amongst the 50 Most Powerful Women in Business in the US (40th) 2011, (37th) 2012. *Address:* A&E Television Networks, 235 East 45th Street, Suite 2, New York, NY 10017-3379, USA (office). *Telephone:* (212) 210-1400 (office). *E-mail:* info@aetv.com (office). *Website:* www.aetv.com (office).

RAVEN, Peter Hamilton, BS, PhD; American botanist, administrator and academic; *President Emeritus, Missouri Botanical Garden;* b. 13 June 1936, Shanghai, China; s. of Walter Raven and Isabelle Raven (née Breen); m. 1st Tamra Engelhorn 1968; one s. three d.; m. 2nd Patricia Duncan 2001; ed Univ. of California, Berkeley, Univ. of California, Los Angeles; Nat. Science Foundation Postdoctoral Fellow, British Museum, London 1960–61; Taxonomist, Rancho Santa Ana Botanical Garden, Claremont, Calif. 1961–62; Asst Prof., then Assoc. Prof. of Biological Sciences, Stanford Univ. 1962–71; Pres. Mo. Botanical Garden 1971–2011, Pres. Emer. 2011–; Engelmann Prof. of Botany, Washington Univ., St Louis, Mo. 1973–, currently Prof. Emer.; Adjunct Prof. of Biology, Univ. of Missouri, St Louis 1973–; John D. and Catherine T. MacArthur Foundation Fellow, Univ. of Missouri 1985–90; Chair. Nat. Museum Services Bd 1984–88; mem. Nat. Geographic Soc. Comm. on Research and Exploration 1981, Governing Bd Nat. Research Council 1983–86, 1987–88, Bd World Wildlife Fund (USA) 1983–88, NAS Comm. on Human Rights 1984–87, Smithsonian Council 1985–90; Home Sec. NAS 1987–99; Pres. Org. for Tropical Studies 1985–88; apptd Pres.'s Cttee on the Nat. Medal of Science 2004; mem. Bd of Trustees Nat. Geographic Soc.; Foreign mem. Royal Danish Acad. of Sciences and Letters, Royal Swedish Acad. of Sciences; Fellow, American Acad. of Arts and Sciences, Calif. Acad. of Sciences, AAAS (fmr Pres.), Linnean Soc. of London; Hon. mem. American Soc. of Landscape Architects; several hon. degrees; Distinguished Service Award, American Inst. of Biological Sciences 1981, Int. Environmental Leadership Medal of UNEP 1982, Int. Prize in Biology, Japanese Govt, Pres.'s Conservation Achievement Award 1993, inducted into St Louis Walk of Fame 1995, Field Museum of Natural History Centennial Merit Award 1994, Nat. Medal of Science 2000, Tyler Prize for Environmental Achievement, Int. Cosmos Prize 2003, Gold Veitch Memorial Medal, RHS 2004, Botanical Soc. of America Centennial Award 2006, World Ecology Award 2007, BBVA Foundation Award for Scientific Research in Ecology and Conservation 2008. *Publications:* Papers on Evolution (with Ehrlich and Holm) 1969, Biology of Plants 1970, Principles of Tzeltal Plant Classification 1974, Modern Aspects of Species (with K. Iwatsuki and W. J. Bock) 1986, Understanding Biology (with G. Johnson) 1988; more than 400 professional papers; Ed.: Coevolution of Animals and Plants 1975, Topics in Plant Population Biology 1979, Advances in Legume Systematics 1981, Biology (with G. B. Johnson) 1986, Understanding Biology 1988; contrib. to many other publs. *Leisure interests:* reading, collecting plants. *Address:* Missouri Botanical Garden, PO Box 299, St Louis, MO 63166-0299, USA (office). *Telephone:* (314) 577-5111 (office). *Fax:* (314) 577-9595 (office). *E-mail:* peter.raven@mobot.org (office). *Website:* www.mobot.org (office).

RAVENSDALE, 3rd Baron, cr. 1911, 7th Baronet; **Sir Nicholas Mosley,** Bt, MC; British writer; b. 25 June 1923, London; s. of the late Sir Oswald Mosley and Lady Cynthia Curzon; m. 1st Rosemary Salmond 1947 (divorced 1974, died 1991); three s. one d.; m. 2nd Verity Bailey (née Raymond) 1974; one s.; ed Eton, Balliol Coll., Oxford. *Publications:* novels: Spaces of the Dark 1951, The Rainbearers 1955, Corruption 1957, African Switchback 1958, The Life of Raymond Raynes 1961, Meeting Place 1962, Accident 1964, Assassins 1966, Impossible Object (also screenplay) 1968, Natalie, Natalia 1971, Catastrophe Practice (three plays and a novella) 1979, Imago Bird 1980, Serpent 1981, Judith 1986, Hopeful Monsters (Whitbread Book of the Year) 1990, Children of Darkness and Light 1996, The Hesperides Tree 2001, Inventing God 2003, Look at the Dark 2005, God's Hazard 2009; non-fiction: Experience and Religion: A Lay Essay in Theology 1965, The Assassination of Trotsky (also screenplay) 1972, Julian Grenfell: His Life and the Times of his Death 1988–1915 (biog.) 1976, Rules of the Game: Sir Oswald and Lady Cynthia Mosley 1896–1933 (biog.) 1982, Beyond the Pale: Sir Oswald Mosley and Family 1933–1980 (biog.) 1983, Efforts at Truth (autobiog.) 1994, Time at War: A Memoir 2006, Paradoxes of Peace 2009. *Address:* 5 Hungerford Road, London, N7 9LA, England (home). *Telephone:* (20) 7607-3579 (home).

RAVI, Vayalar, BA, BL, MA; Indian politician; *Minister of Overseas Indian Affairs;* b. 4 June 1937, Vayalar, Alappuzha Dist, Kerala; s. of M. K. Krishnan and Devaky Krishnan; m. Mercy Ravi (died 2009); one s. two d.; ed Sanatana Dharma Coll., Alappuzha, Maharajas Coll., Ernakulam, Kerala, Ernakulam Law Coll.; elected to Fifth Lok Sabha (lower house of Parl.) for Chirayinkil constituency 1971–77, Sixth Lok Sabha 1977–79; mem. Kerala Legis. Ass. 1982–91, Minister of Home Affairs, Govt of Kerala 1982–86; elected to Rajya Sabha (upper house of Parl.) 1994, re-elected 2003, mem. Cttee on Transport, Tourism and Culture 2003–04, Cttee on Petitions 2003–04, Chair. Parl. Standing Cttee on Human Resource Devt 2004–06; mem. Rubber Bd 2003–06; mem. Consultative Cttee, Ministry of Civil Aviation 2004–06; Union Cabinet Minister of Overseas Indian Affairs 2006–, also Minister of Civil Aviation 2011, of Micro, Small and Medium Enterprises Aug.–Oct. 2012, of Science and Tech. and Earth Sciences Aug.–Oct. 2012; fmr Pres. Kerala Pradesh Congress Cttee; attended UN Gen. Ass., New York as mem. Indian Parl. Del. 1986, 1988, 1994, 2004. *Address:* Ministry of Overseas Indian Affairs, Akbar Bhavan, Chanakya Puri, New Delhi 110 021, India (office). *Telephone:* (11) 24197900 (office). *Fax:* (11) 24197919 (office). *E-mail:* info@moia.nic.in (office). *Website:* moia.gov.in (office).

RAVIER, Paul-Henri, LenD; French international organization official and civil servant; *Senior Counsellor, French Court of Audit;* b. 9 Sept. 1948, Lyon; s. of the late Philibert André Ravier and of Roselyne Marie Bellon; m. Martine Caffin; one s.; ed Inst. d'Etudes Politiques, Ecole Nat. d'Admin.; joined Trade Dept, Ministry of the Economy and Finance, in charge of bilateral trade relations with SE Asia and Middle East, later Head of Trade Finance Policy Unit, Asst Dir responsible for man. of bilateral trade relations with Eastern Europe, Asia, the Pacific and the Middle East 1985–90, Deputy Sec. 1991–99; adviser on int. econ. issues to Prime Minister Raymond Barre 1980; Jt Deputy Head World Trade Org. 1999–2002; Sr Counsellor, French Court of Audit (Cour des Comptes) 2006–; mem. Bd Agence Française de Développement 1993–99, SNECMA 1994–99, Pechiney 1993–97; Chevalier, Ordre nat. du Mérite 1993, Légion d'honneur 1998. *Leisure interests:* golf, skiing, mountain climbing, cooking, wine tasting. *Address:* Cour des Comptes, 13 rue Cambon, 75001 Paris (office); 16 rue Théodore de Banville, 75017 Paris,

France (home). *Telephone:* 1-42-98-95-00 (office); 1-45-55-42-46 (home). *Fax:* 1-45-56-10-15 (home). *E-mail:* phravier@ccomptes.fr (office); phravier@noos.fr (home). *Website:* www.ccomptes.fr (office).

RAVINET DE LA FUENTE, Jaime; Chilean politician; b. 17 Oct. 1946, Abogado; ed Univ. of Chile; Pres. Fed. of Students of Univ. of Chile 1968–69, Univ. Council 1967–72; Exec. Sec. Presidential Command of Pres. Patricio Azócar 1989; Mayor of Santiago 1990–2000; Pres. Union of Municipalities and Local Govts 1995–97, Union of Latin American Capital Cities 1995–96, World Asscn of Cities and Local Authorities Coordination 1996–97, Latin American Centre of Urban Strategic Devt 1995–97; Vice-Pres. Latin American Org. of Inter-municipal Co-operation; Minister of Housing and Urban Planning 2000–04; Minister of Nat. Defence 2004–06, 2010–11 (resgnd); mem. Exec. Bureau Worldwide Fed. of United Cities 1992–95; mem. Bd of Dirs Universidad Mayor 2006–; mem. Partido Demócrata Cristiano (PDC) –2010 (resgnd). *Address:* c/o Ministry of National Defence, Villavicencio 364, 22°, Edif. Diego Portales, Santiago, Chile.

RAVITCH, Diane Silvers, PhD; American education scholar and academic; *Research Professor of Education, New York University;* b. 1 July 1938, Houston, Tex.; d. of Walter Cracker and Ann Celia Silvers (née Katz); m. Richard Ravitch 1960 (divorced 1986); three s. (one deceased); partner, Mary Butz; ed Wellesley Coll., Mass, Columbia Univ., New York; Adjunct Asst Prof. of History and Educ., Teachers Coll., Columbia Univ. 1975–78, Assoc. Prof. 1978–83, Adjunct Prof. 1983–91; Dir Woodrow Wilson Nat. Fellowship Foundation 1987–91; Chair. Educational Excellence Network 1988–91; Asst Sec. Office of Research and Improvement, US Dept of Educ., Washington, DC 1991–93, also Counsellor to Sec. of Educ.; Visiting Fellow, Brookings Inst. 1993–94, Brown Chair in Educ. Policy 1997–2012; Sr Research Scholar, New York Univ. 1994–98, Research Prof. in Educ. 1998–; Sr Fellow, Progressive Policy Inst. 1998–2002, Hoover Inst. 1999–2009; Adjunct Fellow, Manhattan Inst. 1996–99; Pres. Network for Public Educ. 2013–; Trustee, New York Historical Soc. 1995–98, New York Council on the Humanities 1996–2004; Hon. DHumLitt (Williams Coll.) 1984, (Reed Coll.) 1985, (Amherst Coll.) 1986, (State Univ. of NY) 1988, (Ramopo Coll.) 1990, (St Joseph's Coll., NY) 1991; Hon. LHD (Middlebury Coll.) 1997, (Union Coll.) 1998, (Siena Coll.) 2012; Leadership Award, Klingenstein Inst., Teachers Coll. 1994, Horace Kidger Award, New England History Teachers Asscn 1998, Leadership Award, New York City Council of Supervisors and Admins 2004, John Dewey Award, United Fed. of Teachers of New York City 2005, Gaudium Award, Breukelein Inst. 2005, Uncommon Book Award, Hoover Inst. 2005, Kenneth J. Bialkin/Citigroup Public Service Award 2006, Friend of Educ., Nat. Educ. Asscn 2010, Distinguished Service Award, Nat. Asscn of Secondary School Prins 2010, Charles W. Eliot Award, New England Asscn of Schools and Colls 2010, American Educ. Award, American Asscn of School Admins 2011, Outstanding Friend of Educ. Award, Horace Mann League 2011, Distinguished Alumni Award, Teachers Coll., Columbia Univ. 2011, Daniel Patrick Moynihan Prize, American Acad. of Political and Social Science 2011. *Publications include:* The Great School Wars: New York City 1805–1973 1974, The Revisionists Revised 1977, Educating an Urban People (co-author) 1981, The Troubled Crusade: American Education 1945–1980 1983, The School and the City (co-author) 1983, Against Mediocrity (co-author) 1984, The Schools We Deserve 1985, Challenges to the Humanities (co-author) 1985, What Do Our 17-Year-Olds Know? (with Chester E. Finn Jr) 1987, The American Reader (co-ed.) 1990, The Democracy Reader (ed. with Abigail Thernstrom) 1992, National Standards in American Education 1995, Debating the Future of American Education (ed.) 1995, Learning from the Past (ed. with Maris Vinovskis) 1995, New Schools for a New Century (ed. with Joseph Viteretti) 1997, Left Back 2000, City Schools (ed.) 2000, The Language Police 2003, Forgotten Heroes of American Education (co-ed.) 2006, The English Reader (co-ed.) 2006, Edspeak 2007, The Death and Life of the Great American School System 2010, Reign of Error 2013; contrib. of. articles and reviews to scholarly books and professional journals. *Address:* New York University, 82 Washington Square East, New York, NY 10003, USA (office). *E-mail:* dr19@nyu.edu (office); gardendr@gmail.com (home). *Website:* dianeravitch.com; dianeravitch.net.

RAVONY, Francisque; Malagasy politician and barrister; fmr First Deputy Prime Minister, Transitional Govt; Prime Minister of Madagascar 1993–95, also Minister of Finance and Budget; Minister of Defence 2002–07; Leader Cttee for the Support of Democracy and Devt in Madagascar; fmr Chair. Union des Forces Vives Démocratiques. *Address:* Union des Forces Vives Démocratiques, Antananarivo, Madagascar.

RAWABDEH, Abd ar-Raouf ar-, BSc; Jordanian politician; *President of the Senate;* b. 13 Feb. 1939, Es-Sarih, Irbid; m. Fandieh Rawabdeh; 11 c.; ed American Univ. of Beirut, Univ. of Jordan; Inspector of Pharmacies, Ministry of Health 1962–64, Head, Pharmacy Section 1964–68, Dir Dept of Pharmacy and Supplies 1968–75, Dept of Planning and Foreign Relations 1975–76; Dir Dept of Admin. and Services, Univ. of Yarmouk April–July 1976; Minister of Communications 1976–77, of Communications and Health 1977–78, of Health 1978–79, of Public Works and Housing 1989–91, of Educ. 1994–95, 1995–96, Deputy Prime Minister 1995–96, Prime Minister and Minister of Defence 1999–2000; mem. Nat. Consultative Council 1978–83 (Vice-Pres. 1978–83); mem. House of Reps (Lower House of Parl.) 1989–2001, 2003–10; mem. Senate (Upper House of Parl.) 2001–03, 2010–, Vice-Pres. 2011–13, Pres. 2013–; Chair. Bd of Dirs, Jordan Phosphate Mining Co. 1982–85; Vice-Chair., Jordan Fertilizer Co. 1982–85, Zetuna Co. 1982–92; Lecturer, School of Pharmacy, Univ. of Jordan 1982–89; Mayor of Amman 1983–86, of Greater Amman 1987–89; Chair. Amman Devt Corpn 1983–89; Sec.-Gen. Awakening Party (Al-Yakza) 1993–96; Vice-Chair., Bd of Trustees, Jordan Univ. of Science and Tech. 1998–99, Jadara Univ. 2006–; Deputy Sec.-Gen. Nat. Constitutional Party 1996–97; mem. Bd of Dirs Al-Aqsa Schools 1964– (Vice-Chair. 1992–94); mem. Jordan Pharmaceutical Asscn 1962–, Royal Soc. for the Conservation of Nature 1994–; Pres., Bd of Trustees, King Abdallah II Prize for Innovation 2001–; Pres. Jordan Football Asscn 1984–85; mem. Jordan Olympic Cttee 1984–85; Great Cross, Spanish Order of Isabella the Catholic 1999, Royal Norwegian Order of Merit 2000; Jordan Al-Kawkab Medal (First Degree) 1976, Italian Medal of Honour (Sr Officer) 1983, German Medal of Merit 1984, Austrian Grand Silver Medal of Honour 1987, Jordan Education Medal (Excellent Degree) 1997, Al-Nahda Medal (First Degree) 1999, French Medal of Merit (First Degree) 2000. *Publications include:* An Outline of Pharmacology 1965, Pharmacy

1965, Microbiology 1965, Physiology 1965, Democracy, Theory and Application 1992, Parliamentary Elections 1992, Education and the Future 1996, Tribes of Jordan 2010. *Leisure interests:* reading. *Address:* Office of the President of the Senate, PO Box 72, Amman 11101 (office); El-Sarih Street, Abu-Nusair, Amman, Jordan (home). *Telephone:* (6) 5664121 (office); (6) 523855 (home). *Fax:* (6) 5676981 (office); (6) 523877 (home). *E-mail:* info@senate.jo (office); alizy_67@yahoo.com. *Website:* www.senate.jo (office).

RAWAL, Tilak, MA, MS, PhD; Nepalese economist, banker and academic; b. 6 Dec. 1950; ed Trihhuvan Univ., Univ. of the Philippines, Dhaka Univ.; Deputy Exec. Dir Agric. Projects Services Centre (APROSC) 1990–91; CEO Agricultural Devt Bank of Nepal 1991–94; Exec. Chair. Rastriya Banijya Bank 1995–99; Gov. Nepal Rastra Bank 2000–05; consultant for several int. orgs, including World Bank, ADB, OECD, FAO, UN, ESCAP; mem. Faculty of Econs, Global Coll. of Man., Kathmandu; mem. Nepal Econ. Asscn. *Publications include:* Corporate Governance and Financial Sector Reform in Nepal 2006; numerous articles. *Address:* c/o Global College of Management, Basuki Marga, Mid-Baneshwor, PO Box No. 24855, Kathmandu, Nepal. *Telephone:* (1) 4488312. *E-mail:* info@proed.edu.np.

RAWASHDEH, Mazen, BS; American internet industry executive; *Vice-President, Infrastructure Operations Engineering, Twitter, Inc.;* ed Chapman Univ.; began career in various technical roles at Oracle and OPSWARE; Vice-Pres. of Technical Operations, eBay, Inc. 2004–11; Vice-Pres. Infrastructure Operations Eng, Twitter, Inc. 2011–. *Address:* Twitter, Inc., 1355 Market Street, Suite 900, San Francisco, CA 94103, USA (office). *Telephone:* (415) 222-9670 (office). *Website:* twitter.com (office).

RAWAT, Harish, BA, LLB; Indian trade unionist and politician; *Chief Minister of Uttarakhand;* b. 27 April 1948, Mohanari, Almora Dist, Uttarakhand; s. of the late Rajendra Singh Rawat and Devaki Devi; m. Renuka Rawat; ed Lucknow Univ.; held various posts in Indian Youth Congress including Nat. Jt Sec. and Gen. Sec.; elected to 7th Lok Sabha (lower house of Parl.) for Almora constituency 1980–84, 8th Lok Sabha 1984–89, 9th Lok Sabha 1989, 15th Lok Sabha for Hardwar constituency 2009–; mem. Rajya Sabha (upper house of Parl.) for Uttarakhand 2002–08; Pres. Uttarakhand Pradesh Congress Cttee 2001–07; Union Cabinet Minister of State for Labour and Employment 2009–11, for Agric. and Food Processing Industries Jan.–June 2011, for Parl. Affairs 2011–12, Minister of Water Resources 2012–; Chief Minister of Uttarakhand 2014–. *Address:* Office of the Chief Minister, Government of Uttarakhand, Civil Secretariat, Dehradun 248 001, India (office). *Telephone:* (135) 2665090 (office). *Fax:* (135) 2665722 (office). *E-mail:* cm-uk@nic.in (office). *Website:* cm.uk.gov.in (office).

RAWI, Najih Mohamed Khalil ar-, MSc, PhD; Iraqi civil engineer, educationalist and fmr government official; b. 4 April 1935, Rawa; m.; one s. two d.; ed Univ. of Wales, Purdue Univ., Oklahoma State Univ.; instructor, Univ. of Baghdad 1967, Asst Prof. of Civil Eng 1971, Prof. 1980; Prof. Emer. 1990–; Dean Higher Inst. of Industrial Eng, Univ. of Baghdad 1968–69; Dean Coll. of Industry (now Tech. Univ.) 1969–70; mem. Bureau of Educ. Affairs, Revolutionary Command Council 1973–74, Council of Higher Educ. 1970–74, 1980–85; Deputy Minister of Municipalities 1974, of Public Works and Housing 1974–77; Minister of Industry and Minerals 1977–78; Vice-Pres. Iraqi Engineers Syndicate 1969–71; Pres. Iraqi Teachers Syndicate 1970–74, Iraqi–Soviet Friendship Soc. 1979–88, Nat. Cttee Tech. and Transfer 1984–89, Man and the Biosphere 1980–89, Int. Geological Correlation Programme 1980–89, Geophysics and Geodesy 1982–89, Council of Scientific Research 1980–89, Iraqi Acad. of Sciences 1996–2001 (mem. 1996–); Head Union of Arab Educators 1983–86; mem. Bd of Trustees, Al-Mustansiryah Univ. 1970–74, Arabian Gulf Univ. 1986–89, Teachers' Union Univ. Coll. 1990–96; mem. Iraq Eng Soc. 1959, American Soc. of Civil Engineers 1967, Council of the World Fed. of Educators 1973–74, 1979–82; Founding Fellow, Islamic Acad. of Sciences 1986; Corresp. mem. Syrian Acad. of Language, Damascus 2001. *Publications:* On Science and Technology (in Arabic) 2003; 65 papers in scientific journals 1960–2003. *Address:* Iraqi Academy of Sciences, Waziriya, A'Adamiah, Baghdad (office); 2/40/635 Hai Al-Jamea, Baghdad, Iraq (home). *Telephone:* (1) 4224202 (office); (1) 5559635 (home). *E-mail:* aos@uruklink.net (office); ahmedelrawi@yahoo.com (home).

RAWLINGS, Hunter R., III, PhD; American academic and fmr university administrator; *Professor, Classics Department, Cornell University;* b. Norfolk, Va; m. Elizabeth Trapnell Rawlings; four c.; ed Haverford Coll., Princeton Univ.; Asst Prof. Univ. of Colo 1970–80, Dept Chair. 1978–88, Prof. 1980–88, Assoc. Vice Chancellor for Instruction 1980–84, Vice-Pres. for Academic Affairs and Research Dean of the System Graduate School 1984–88; Pres. and Prof. of Classics Univ. of Iowa 1988–95; Pres. and Prof. of Classics, Cornell Univ. 1995–, Pres. Emer. 2003–, Interim Pres. 2005–06; fmr Chair. Ivy Council of Presidents; mem. Bd of Dirs American Council on Educ., Exec. Cttee Asscn of American Univs, Nat. Cttee for Selection of Mellon Fellows in Humanities; mem. American Acad. of Arts and Sciences; Woodrow Wilson Fellow, Nat. Defense Educ. Act Fellow, Univ. of Colo Teaching Excellence Award 1979. *Publications:* The Structure of Thucydides' History 1981, The Classical Journal (Ed.); numerous monographs and articles. *Address:* Department of Classics, Cornell University, 120 Goldwin Smith Hall, Ithaca, NY 14853-3201, USA (office). *Telephone:* (607) 255-3354 (office). *Fax:* (607) 254-8899 (office). *E-mail:* sp18@cornell.edu (office). *Website:* www.arts.cornell.edu/classics (office).

RAWLINGS, Flight-Lt Jerry John; Ghanaian fmr head of state and fmr air force officer; b. 22 June 1947, Accra; s. of John Rawlings and Madam Victoria Agbotui; m. Nana Konadu Agyeman; one s. three d.; ed Achimota School and Ghana Military Acad., Teshie; commissioned as Pilot Officer 1969, Flight-Lt 1978; arrested for leading mutiny of jr officers May 1979; leader mil. coup which overthrew Govt of Supreme Mil. Council June 1979; Chair. Armed Forces Revolutionary Council (Head of State) June–Sept. 1979; retd from armed forces Nov. 1979, from air force Sept. 1992; leader mil. coup which overthrew Govt of Dr Hilla Limann Dec. 1981; Head of State 1982–2001; Chief of the Defence Staff 1982–2001; Chair. Provisional Nat. Defence Council 1981–93; Pres. of Ghana 1993–2001. *Leisure interests:* boxing, deep-sea diving, swimming, horse riding, carpentry. *Address:* c/o PO Box 1627, Osu, Accra, Ghana.

RAWLINS, Peter Jonathan, MA, FCA, FRSA; British business executive and management consultant; b. 30 April 1951, London; s. of Kenneth Raymond Ivan Rawlins and Constance Amande Malzy; m. 1st Louise Langton 1973 (divorced 1999); one s. one d.; m. 2nd Christina Conway 2000; two s. one d.; ed St Edward's School and Keble Coll. Oxford; with Arthur Andersen & Co., Chartered Accountants, London 1972–85, partner 1983–85; seconded as Personal Asst to CEO and Deputy Chair. Lloyd's of London 1983–84; Dir Sturge Holdings PLC 1985–89, Man. Dir R. W. Sturge & Co. 1985–89; Dir Sturge Lloyd's Agencies Ltd 1986–89; Dir Wise Speke Holdings Ltd 1987–89; CEO The London Stock Exchange 1989–93 (resgnd); consultant, Rawlins Strategy Consulting 1994–; Man. Dir (Europe, Middle East and Africa) Siegel & Gale Ltd 1996–97; Dir Scala Business Solutions NV 1998–2000, Oyster Prtrs Ltd 2001–02; Chair. (non-exec.) Higham Group 2004–05; fmr Chair. Asscn for Research into Stammering in Childhood 1995; Chair. Spitalfields Festival 1998–2003. *Leisure interests:* the performing arts, tennis, shooting, travelling, national heritage. *Address:* Ramley House, Ramley Road, Lymington, Hants., SO41 8LH, England (home). *Telephone:* (1590) 689661 (home). *Fax:* (1590) 689662 (home). *E-mail:* peter@rawlinsp.fsnet.co.uk (home).

RAWNSLEY, Andrew Nicholas James, MA, FRSA; British journalist, broadcaster and author; *Associate Editor and Chief Political Commentator, The Observer;* b. 5 Jan. 1962, Leeds, Yorks., England; s. of Eric Rawnsley and Barbara Rawnsley (née Butler); m. Jane Leslie Hall 1990; three d.; ed Lawrence Sheriff Grammar School, Rugby, Rugby School, Sidney Sussex Coll., Cambridge; with BBC 1983–85, The Guardian 1985–93 (political columnist 1987–93); Assoc. Ed. and Chief Political Commentator, The Observer 1993–; Ed.-in-Chief, politicsho-me.com (political website) 2008–09; Presenter Channel 4 TV series A Week in Politics 1989–97, ITV series The Agenda 1996, Channel 4 series Bye Bye Blues 1997, Blair's Year 1998, BBC 2 series What The Papers Say and Review of the Year 2002–07, ITV series The Sunday Edition 2006–08, BBC Radio 4 series The Westminster Hour 1998–2006, The Unauthorised Biography of the United Kingdom 1999, The Rise and Fall of Tony Blair 2007, Gordon Brown: Where Did it All Go Wrong? 2008, Crash Gordon: The Inside Story of the Financial Crisis 2009, Cameron Uncovered 2010; Student Journalist of the Year, Guardian/NUS Media Awards 1983, Young Journalist of the Year, British Press Awards 1987, Columnist of the Year, What the Papers Say Award 2000, Book of the Year Award, Channel 4 Political Awards 2001, Political Journalist of the Year, Channel 4 Political Awards 2003, Commentator of the Year, Public Affairs Awards 2005, Commentator of the Year, House Magazine Awards 2008. *Publications:* Servants of the People: The Inside Story of New Labour (Channel 4 Book of the Year 2001) 2000 (revised edn 2001), The End of the Party: The Rise and Fall of New Labour 2010. *Leisure interests:* skiing, scuba diving, mah jong, books, cinema, food and wine. *Address:* The Observer, Kings Place, 90 York Way, London, N1 9GU, England (office). *Telephone:* (20) 7278-2332 (office). *E-mail:* a.rawnsley@observer.co.uk (office). *Website:* www.observer.co.uk (office).

RAWSON, Dame Jessica Mary, DBE, MA, DLitt, FBA; British archaeologist, college warden and writer; *Professor of Chinese Art and Archaeology, Institute of Archaeology, University of Oxford;* b. 20 Jan. 1943; d. of Roger Quirk and Paula Quirk; m. John Rawson 1968; one d.; ed New Hall, Cambridge and Univ. of London; Asst Prin. Ministry of Health 1965–67; Asst Keeper II, Dept of Oriental Antiquities, British Museum 1967–71, Asst Keeper I 1971–76, Deputy Keeper 1976–87, Keeper 1987–94; Warden, Merton Coll. Oxford 1994–2011, currently Prof. of Chinese Art and Archaeology, Inst. of Archaeology, Univ. of Oxford; Visiting Prof., Kunsthistorisches Inst. Heidelberg 1989, Univ. of Chicago 1994; Chair. Oriental Ceramic Soc. 1993–96; Vice-Chair. Bd Govs, SOAS, Univ. of London 1999–2003; mem. British Library Bd 1999–2003; Gov. St Paul's Girls' School 2009–, Compton Verney House Trust; Hon. DSc (St Andrews) 1997, Hon. DLitt (Sussex) 1998, (Royal Holloway, London) 1998, (Newcastle) 1999. *Publications:* Chinese Jade Throughout the Ages (with J. Ayers) 1975, Animals in Art 1977, Ancient China, Art and Archaeology 1980, Chinese Ornament: The Lotus and the Dragon 1984, Chinese Bronzes: Art and Ritual 1987, The Bella and P.P. Chiu Collection of Ancient Chinese Bronzes 1988, Western Zhou Ritual Bronzes from the Arthur M. Sackler Collections 1990, Ancient Chinese and Ordos Bronzes (with E. Bunker) 1990, The British Museum Book of Chinese Art (ed.) 1992, Chinese Jade from the Neolithic to the Qing 1995, The Mysteries of Ancient China (ed.) 1996, Cosmological Systems and Sources of Art, Ornament and Design 2002, China: The Three Emperors, 1662–1795 (co-ed. with Evelyn Rawski) 2005, Treasure from Shanghai 2009. *Leisure interest:* gardening. *Address:* Institute of Archaeology, University of Oxford, 36 Beaumont Street, Oxford, OX1 2PG, England (office). *Telephone:* (1865) 278240 (office). *Website:* www.arch.ox.ac.uk/institute.html (home).

RAY, Pratibha, BSc, MEd, PhD; Indian academic, writer and poet; b. 21 Jan. 1943, Alabol, Cuttack Dist, Orissa; d. of the late Parashuram Das and the late Manorama Devi; m. Akshaya Chandra Ray; two s. one d.; ed Balikuda High School, Ravenshaw Coll., Cuttack; Oriya writer; school teacher at various Orissa State Govt colls for 30 years; mem. Public Service Comm., Orissa State 1998–2004; f. Bhashyan Literary Foundation 2004; mem. Exec. Bd Sahitya Akademi; DLit (Utkal Univ. of Bhubaneswar) 2011; Jhankara Award 1989, Saptarshi Award, Sambalpur Univ. 1989, Katha Prize 1994, 1999, Bisuva Award for Lifetime Achievement 1995, Rastriya Ekta Puruskar 1999, Kapilash Award 2000, Katha Bharati Title 2000, Rajiv Gandhi Sacbhawana Nat. Puraskar 2002, Chitrapuri Samman 2006, Amrita Keerti Award 2006, Padma Shri 2007, Gopichand Nat. Award for Literature 2008, Guru Pranam Samman 2009, Pathaka Sammana 2010, Jnanpith Award 2011, Utkal Pragyan, Bhubaneswar Doordarshan Kendra 2012. *Publications:* novels: Barsha Basanta Baishakha 1974, Aranya 1977, Nishidha Prithivi 1978, Parichaya 1979, Aparichita 1979, Punyatoya 1979, Meghamedura 1980, Ashabari 1980, Ayamarambha 1981, Nilatrishna 1981, Samudrara Swara 1982, Shilapadma (trans. as Stone Lotus, Orissa Sahitya Akademi Award 1985) 1983, Yajnaseni (Sarla Award 1990, Moorti Devi Bharatiya Jnanpath Award 1991) 1984, Dehatit 1986, Uttarmarg 1988, Aadibhoomi (trans. as Primal Land) 1993, Maha Moha 1998, Magnamati (trans. as The Tranced Earth) 2004; short stories: Samanya Kathana 1978, Gangashiuli 1979, Asamapta 1980, Aikatana 1981, Anabana 1983, Hatabaksa 1983, Ghasa o Akasha 1984, Chandrabhaga o Chadrakala 1984, Shrestha Galpa 1984, Abyakta 1986, Itibut 1987, Haritpatra 1989, Prithak Ishwar 1991, Bhagabanara Desha (trans. as Land of God) 1991, Manushya Swara 1992, Sasthasati 1996, Moksha 1996, Ullanghana (Sahitya

Akademi Award 2000) 1998, Nivedanamidam 2000, Gandhinka 2002, Jhoti paka Kantha 2006. *Leisure interest:* philanthrophy. *Website:* www.pratibharay.org.

RAY, Rachael Domenica; American television presenter, author and chef; b. 25 Aug. 1968, Glens Falls, NY; d. of James Ray and Elsa Scuderi; m. John Cusimano (lawyer and lead singer of rock band The Cringe) 2005; raised in Cape Cod, Mass where family owned four restaurants; family moved to Lake George, NY 1976, then moved to New York City 1995; first job at candy counter at Macy's, later managed fresh foods dept; later helped open a New York City market; moved back to upstate NY and managed Mister Brown's Pub at The Sagamore (hotel), Lake George; became a buyer at Cowan & Lobel (gourmet market in Albany); cr. concept of 30 Minute Meals for people who were reluctant to cook, taught course showing how to make meals in less than 30 minutes; asked by WRGB (local CBS TV affiliate) to appear in weekly segment on their newscasts; led to Today show spot and her first Food Network contract 2001; signed deal with Oprah Winfrey and King World Productions to host syndicated daytime TV talk show, Rachael Ray 2006; f. Rachael's Rescue (charity to help at-risk animals); launched Yum-O! charity to help children eat more healthily 2006; hosts syndicated talk and lifestyle programme Rachael Ray and three Food Network series, 30 Minute Meals, Rachael Ray's Tasty Travels and $40 a Day; wrote cookbooks based on the 30 Minute Meals concept, and launched a magazine, Every Day with Rachael Ray 2006; ranked 92nd on FHM-U.S.'s 100 Sexiest Women 2004, ranked 71st on FHM-U.S.'s 100 Sexiest Women 2006, named one of Time magazine's Top 100 influential people 2006, named by Forbes magazine as the 79th Most Powerful Celebrity in the World 2009, ranked by Forbes magazine amongst The World's 100 Most Powerful Women (78th) 2010. *Television includes:* has appeared on The View, The Today Show, The Tonight Show with Jay Leno, The Late Show with David Letterman, Nightline, Late Night with Conan O'Brien, and Larry King Live; appeared in episode of Sesame Street's 38th season; 30 Minute Meals (Daytime Emmy Award for Outstanding Service Show 2006), The Rachael Ray Show (Daytime Emmy Award for Outstanding Talk Show/Entertainment 2008, 2009) 2002–, Rachael's Vacation (series) premiered on the Food Network 2008, producer of a Latin cooking show on the Food Network called Viva Daisy! 2008, appeared as herself on Who Wants to Be a Millionaire for charity for Yum-O! and her own charity for animal rescue with Regis Philbin 2009, appeared on the hidden camera show I Get That a Lot, Rachael Ray's Week In a Day on the Cooking Channel 2010. *Publications:* 30 Minute Meals 1999, Rachael Ray's Open House Cookbook 2000, Comfort Foods 2001, Veggie Meals 2001, 30-Minute Meals 2 2003, Get Togethers: Rachael Ray 30 Minute Meals 2003, Cooking Rocks!: Rachael Ray 30-Minute Meals for Kids 2004, $40 a Day: Best Eats in Town 2004, Rachael Ray's 30-Minute Meals: Cooking 'Round the Clock 2004, Rachael Ray's 30-Minute Meals for Kids: Cooking Rocks! 2004, Rachael Ray's 30-Minute Get Real Meals: Eat Healthy Without Going to Extremes 2005, Rachael Ray 365: No Repeats: A Year of Deliciously Different Dinners 2005, Rachael Ray 2, 4, 6, 8: Great Meals for Couples or Crowds 2006, Rachael Ray's Express Lane Meals 2006, Rachael Ray: Just In Time 2007, Yum-O! The Family Cookbook 2008, Rachael Ray's Big Orange Book 2008, Rachael Ray's Book Of 10: More Than 300 Recipes To Cook Every Day 2009; Reader's Digest Association launched eponymous magazine, Every Day with Rachael Ray 2005, seven issues 2006, ten issues 2007. *Website:* www .rachaelrayshow.com (office); www.foodnetwork.com/rachael-ray (office); www .rachaelray.com.

RAY, Robert Francis, BA; Australian politician; *Senator for Victoria;* b. 8 April 1947, Melbourne; m. Jane Ray; ed Rusden State Coll., Monash Univ.; fmr tech. school teacher; Senator for Victoria 1980–, Minister for Home Affairs and Deputy Man. of Govt Business in the Senate 1987–88, for Transport and Communications Jan.–Sept. 1988, for Immigration, Local Govt and Ethnic Affairs and Minister assisting Prime Minister for Multicultural Affairs 1988–90, for Defence 1990–96, currently mem. Finance and Admin Estimates Cttee, Deputy Leader of Govt in Senate 1993–96; mem. Australian Labor Party (ALP) Nat. Exec. 1983–98. *Leisure interests:* films, billiards, tennis, watching Australian Rules football, golf and cricket. *Address:* Office of Senator Robert Ray, Suite 3, Level 2, Illoura Plaza, 424 St Kilda Road, Melbourne, VIC 3004, Australia (home). *Telephone:* (2) 6277-3775 (office). *Fax:* (2) 6277-3086 (office). *E-mail:* senator.ray@aph.gov.au (office). *Website:* www.alp.org.au/people/vic/ray_robert.php (office).

RAYAMAJHI, Rt Hon. Min Bahadur; Nepalese judge; b. 1944, Helaunchha, Bhojpur dist; joined the judiciary as section officer, Supreme Court 1970; served as Dist Judge in Khotang, Parbat, Kapilvastu, Mugu, has also served in Janakpur and Bagmati Zonal Courts; served in Hetauda, Janakpur and Patan Appellate Courts 1991–2001; Justice of the Supreme Court of Nepal 2001–10, Chief Justice April 2001, 2009–10 (retd); Chair. Nat. Judicial Acad. *Address:* c/o Supreme Court of Nepal, Ramashah Path, Kathmandu, Nepal (office).

RAYKHELHAUS, Iosif Leonidovich; Russian theatre director; b. 2 June 1947, Odessa, Ukraine; m. Maria Khazina; two d.; ed Moscow Inst. of Theatre Arts; stage Dir Moscow Stanislavsky Theatre 1973; founder and Artistic Dir School of Contemporary Play theatre 1989–; teacher All-Union Inst. of Cinematography 1997–; Prize of Moscow Festival of Chamber Productions Martenitsa 1991; Merited Worker of Arts 1993. *Productions include:* Salute, Don Juan!, A Man Came to a Woman, The Seagull. *Address:* Moscow Theatre School of Contemporary Play, Neglinnaya str. 29/14, 103031 Moscow, Russia (office). *Telephone:* (495) 200-09-00 (office). *Fax:* (495) 200-30-87 (office).

RAYKOV, Marin; Bulgarian government official, politician and diplomatist; b. 17 Dec. 1960, Washington, DC, USA; s. of Rayko Nikolov and Lydia Nikolova; m.; two c.; ed Univ. for Nat. and World Economy; joined Ministry of Foreign Affairs 1987, served as Intern Attaché, then Attaché, later Third Sec., Balkan Countries Dept 1987–92, Third, then Second, then First Sec., Embassy in Belgrade 1992–95, Political and Social Issues Expert, Dept for Human Rights, Humanitarian and Social Cooperation, Council of Europe 1995–97; Deputy Perm. Rep., Council of Europe, Strasbourg 1997–98, Deputy Minister of Foreign Affairs 1998–2001, Amb. to France and Perm. Rep. to UNESCO 2001–05, also personal envoy of Head of State to Org. Internationale de la Francophonie; Head of Common European Foreign Policy and Strategic Issues Sections, Foreign Policy Coordination and Planning Directorate 2005–08, Sr Diplomatic Official, Political Issues Directorate 2008–09, Deputy Minister of Foreign Affairs 2009–10, Amb. to France 2010–13; Prime Minister and Minister of Foreign Affairs in caretaker govt March–May

2013; mem. Union of Bulgarian Journalists, Bulgarian Asscn of Int. Law, Bd of Govs, Bulgarian Foreign Policy Asscn; teaches at New Bulgarian Univ.; Grand Officer, Ordre nat. du Mérite; Grand Commdr, Order of Phoenix (Greece). *Address:* c/o Council of Ministers, 1594 Sofia, bul. Dondukov 1 (office); Ministry of Foreign Affairs, 1113 Sofia, ul. Al. Zhendov 2, Bulgaria (office).

RAYMOND, Lee R., PhD; American oil industry executive (retd); b. 13 Aug. 1938, Watertown, South Dakota; m. Charlene Raymond 1960; ed Univ. of Wisconsin, Univ. of Minnesota; various eng positions Exxon Corpn (now Exxon Mobil Corpn), Tulsa, Houston, New York and Caracas, Venezuela 1963–72, Man. Planning, Int. Co. Div., New York 1972–75, Pres. Exxon Nuclear Co. Div. 1979–81, Exec. Vice-Pres. Exxon Enterprises Inc. Div. 1981–83, Sr Vice-Pres. and Dir Exxon Corpn 1984–86, Pres. and Dir 1987–93, Chair. and CEO 1993–99, Chair. and CEO Exxon Mobil Corpn 1999–2005 (retd), Pres. 1999–2003; Vice-Pres. Lago Oil, Netherlands Antilles 1975–76, Pres. and Dir 1976–79; Pres. and Dir Esso Inter-American Inc., Coral Gables, Fla 1983–84, Sr Vice-Pres. and Dir 1984; mem. Bd Dirs J. P. Morgan & Co. Inc., New York, Morgan Guaranty Trust Co. of New York, American Petroleum Inst.; mem. Bd Dirs Nat. Action Council for Minorities in Eng Inc., New York 1985, New American Schools Devt Corpn 1991, Project Shelter PRO-AM 1991; mem. American Petroleum Inst. (mem. Bd of Dirs 1987), The Business Roundtable, American Council on Germany 1986, British-N American Cttee 1985, Singapore-US Business Council, Visitors' Cttee Univ. of Wis. Dept of Chem. Eng 1987, Dallas Cttee on Foreign Relations 1988, The Conf. Bd 2001; mem. Bd of Govs, Dallas Symphony Asscn; Trustee American Enterprise Inst.; Public Service Star (Distinguished Friends of Singapore Award) 2004, Hon. Citizen of Singapore 2006.

RAYMOND, Réal, MBA; Canadian banker; *Special Adviser, National Bank of Canada;* ed Univ. of Quebec, Montreal; joined National Bank 1970, Sr Vice-Pres. Treasury and Financial Markets 1992–99, Sr Exec. Vice-Pres. Corporate Financing Lévesque Beaubien Geoffrion (now National Bank Financial) 1997–99, Pres. Personal and Commercial Bank 1999–2001, Pres. and COO National Bank of Canada 2001–02, Pres. and CEO 2002–07 (retd), Special Adviser 2007–; Pres. Montreal Museum of Fine Arts Foundation; mem. Bd of Dirs Fondation de l'Univ. du Québec à Montréal, St Mary's Hosp. Foundation, Montreal Symphony Orchestra. *Address:* National Bank of Canada, National Bank Tower, 600 de la Gauchetière West, Montreal, PQ H3B 4L2, Canada (office). *Telephone:* (514) 394-5000 (office). *Fax:* (514) 394-8434 (office). *E-mail:* real.raymond@bnc.ca. *Website:* www.nbc.ca (office).

RAYMUND, Steven A., BS, MA; American computer industry executive; *Chairman, Tech Data Corporation;* b. 16 Nov. 1955, Van Nuys, Calif.; s. of Edward C. Raymund and Annette Leah Raymund; ed Univ. of Oregon, George-town Univ. School of Foreign Service, Washington, DC; early position with Manufacturers Hanover Corpn, New York 1980–81; Operations Man. Tech Data Corpn (distributor of computer products f. by Edward Raymund 1974) 1981–84, COO 1984–86, mem. Bd of Dirs 1986–, CEO 1986–2006, Chair. 1991–2006, Chair. (non-exec.) 2006–; mem. Bd of Dirs Jabil Circuit Inc. 1996– (Chair. Audit Cttee), WESCO International, Inc. 2006–, PopCap Games, Inc. 2010–11; Chair. St Petersburg Area Chamber of Commerce 2009; named to Industry Hall of Fame, Computer Reseller News (CRN) 1999. *Address:* Tech Data Corpn, 5350 Tech Data Drive, Clearwater, FL 33760-3122, USA (office). *Telephone:* (727) 539-7429 (office). *Fax:* (727) 538-7803 (office). *E-mail:* info@techdata.com (office). *Website:* www .techdata.com (office).

RAYNAUD, Jean-Pierre; French sculptor; b. 20 April 1939, Courbevoie; s. of André Raynaud and Madeleine Dumay; ed Ecole d'Horticulture du Chesnay; first one-man exhbn Galerie Larcade, Paris 1965; numerous other one-man shows in France, Europe, USA, Japan, Israel; retrospective exhbns. The Menil Collection, Houston, Museum of Contemporary Art, Chicago and Int. Centre of Contemporary Art, Montreal 1991, CAPC, Bordeaux 1993, Paume 1998, Jérôme de Noirmont Gallery, Paris 2001; Grand Prix Nat. de Sculpture 1983; Prix Robert Giron, Palais des Beaux Arts, Brussels 1985; Grand Prix de Sculpture de la Ville de Paris 1986, Prix d'honneur de la Biennale de Venise 1993; Officier des Arts et des Lettres, Chevalier du Mérite, Légion d'honneur. *Work includes:* windows at Cistercian Abbey at Noirlac, Cher 1976–77, large sculpture in gardens of Fondation Cartier pour l'Art Contemporain, Jouy-en-Josas 1985, Autoportrait for City of Québec 1987, Container Zero, Pompidou Centre, Paris 1988, Carte du Ciel, Grande Arche, Paris La Défense 1989. *Address:* 12 avenue Rhin et Danube, 92250 La Garenne-Colombes, France.

RAYNER, Steve, BA, PhD, FRSA; British social scientist and academic; *James Martin Professor of Science and Civilization, Saïd Business School, University of Oxford;* ed Univ. of Kent at Canterbury, Univ. Coll. London; began career as Sr Research Assoc., Centre for Occupational and Community Research, Middx Polytechnic; Deputy Dir, Global Environmental Studies Center, Oak Ridge Nat. Lab., USA –1991; Chief Scientist, Pacific NW Nat. Lab., Richland, Wash. 1991–96; Prof. of Environment and Public Affairs and Prof. of Sociology, Columbia Univ. –2002, also Chief Social Scientist, Int. Research Inst. for Climate Prediction; James Martin Prof. of Science and Civilization, Saïd Business School, Univ. of Oxford 2002–, also Dir Inst. for Science, Innovation and Soc.; Professorial Fellow, Keble College, Oxford; fmr Visiting Scholar, Columbia Univ., Boston Univ. School of Public Health; Fellow, Royal Anthropological Inst., Soc. for Applied Anthropology, AAAS 2003; mem. Royal Comm. on Environmental Pollution; Honorary Prof. of Climate Change and Soc., Univ. of Copenhagen, Denmark. *Publications:* co-author or ed. of seven books, three special issues of journals, more than 50 articles and papers, and 20 technical reports. *Address:* Institute of Science, Innovation and Society, University of Oxford, 64 Banbury Road, Oxford, OX2 6PN, England (office). *Telephone:* (1865) 288938 (office). *E-mail:* Steve.Rayner@insis.ox.ac.uk (office). *Website:* www.insis.ox.ac.uk (office).

RAYNES, Edward Peter, MA, PhD, DSc, FRS; British physicist and academic; *Professor of Optoelectronic Engineering, University of Oxford;* b. 4 July 1945, York, Yorks., England; s. of Edward Gordon Raynes and Ethel Mary Raynes; m. Madeline Ord 1970; two s.; ed St Peter's School, York, Gonville and Caius Coll. and the Cavendish Lab., Cambridge; with Royal Signals and Radar Establishment, Malvern 1971–92, Deputy Chief Scientific Officer 1988–92; Chief Scientist Sharp Laboratories of Europe Ltd 1992–98, Dir of Research 1995–98; Visiting Prof., Dept of Eng Science, Univ. of Oxford 1996–98, Prof. of Optoelectronic Eng 1998–2010;

Leverhulme Emer. Research Fellow, Dept of Chem., Univ. of York 2010–12, Hon. Visiting Prof. 2010–; Rank Opto-Electronic Prize 1980, Paterson Medal, Inst. of Physics 1986, Special Recognition Award, Soc. of Information Display 1987, G.W. Gray Medal, British Liquid Crystal Soc. 2001, Jan Rajchman Prize, Soc. of Information Display 2009. *Publications:* numerous scientific publs and patents; The Physics, Chemistry and Applications of Liquid Crystals (co-ed.). *Leisure interests:* choral and solo singing. *Address:* Department of Chemistry, University of York, York, YO10 5DD, England (office). *Telephone:* (1904) 322607 (office). *E-mail:* peter.raynes@york.ac.uk (office). *Website:* www.york.ac.uk/chemistry (office).

RAYNSFORD, Rt Hon. Wyvill Richard Nicolls (Nick), PC, MA; British politician; b. 28 Jan. 1945, Northampton, Northants.; s. of the late Wyvill Raynsford and Patricia Raynsford (née Dunn); m. Anne Jelley 1968; three d.; ed Repton School, Sidney Sussex Coll. Cambridge, Chelsea School of Art and Design; mem. staff, Soc. of Co-operative Dwellings, AC Nielen, Market Research; Dir SHAC, The London Housing Aid Centre 1976–86, Raynsford & Morris, Housing Consultants 1987–92; Councillor, London Borough of Hammersmith and Fulham 1971–75; MP for Fulham 1986–87, for Greenwich 1992–97, for Greenwich and Woolwich 1997–; mem. House of Commons Environment Select Cttee 1992–93; Front Bench Spokesperson for London 1993–94; Shadow Minister for Housing and Construction, Spokesperson for London 1994–97; Parl. Under-Sec. of State, Minister for London and Construction 1997–99; Minister of State for Housing, Planning and London July–Sept. 1999, for Housing and Planning 1999–2001, for Local Govt and the Regions 2001–04; mem. Nat. Energy Foundation 1989–93. *Publications:* A Guide to Housing Benefits 1982, Making Sense of Localism 2004, Choice Cuts 2004. *Leisure interests:* walking, photography. *Address:* House of Commons, Westminster, London, SW1A 0AA, England (office). *Telephone:* (20) 7219-2773 (office). *Fax:* (20) 7219-2619 (office). *E-mail:* raynsfordn@parliament.uk (office).

RAZ, Joseph, MA, MJr, DPhil, FBA; British (b. Israeli) philosopher and academic; *Thomas M. Macioce Professor of Law, Columbia University;* b. 21 March 1939, Haifa; ed Hebrew Univ., Jerusalem and Univ. of Oxford; Lecturer, Faculty of Law and Dept of Philosophy, Hebrew Univ. 1967–71, Sr Lecturer 1971–72; Research Fellow, Nuffield Coll., Oxford 1970–72; Fellow and Tutor in Law, Balliol Coll., Oxford 1972–85, also mem. Sub-faculty of Philosophy 1977–2009, Prof. of Philosophy of Law and Fellow, Balliol Coll. 1985–2006, Research Prof., Univ. of Oxford 2006–09, Fellow Emer., Balliol Coll. 2006–; Visiting Prof., School of Law, Columbia Univ., New York 1995–2002, Thomas M. Macioce Prof. of Law 2002–; Research Prof. (part time) King's Coll., London 2011–; Visiting Prof., Rockefeller Univ. 1974, ANU 1979, Univ. of California, Berkeley 1984, Univ. of Toronto 1987, Yale Law School 1988, Univ. of Southern California 1989; British-Hispanic Prof., Complutensa Univ., Madrid 2007; Philosopher-in-Residence, Univ. of Michigan 2001; Co-Ed. (with Prof. A. M. Honoré) The Clarendon Law Series 1984–92; Fellow, Humanities Research Inst., Univ. of California, Irvine 1989; Visiting Mellon Fellow, Princeton Univ. 1993; Foreign Hon. mem. American Acad. of Arts and Sciences; Dr hc (Katholieke Univ. Brussels) 1993; Hon. DJur (King's Coll., London) 2009; first Hector Fix-Zamudio Int. Prize for Legal Research (Univ. Nacional Autonoma de Mexico) 2005. *Publications:* The Concept of a Legal System 1970, Practical Reason and Norms 1975, The Authority of Law 1979 (second edn 2009), The Morality of Freedom (W.J.M. Mackenzie Book Prize, Political Studies Asscn of the UK, Elaine and David Spitz Book Prize, Conf. for the Study of Political Thought, New York) 1986, Ethics in the Public Domain 1994, Engaging Reason 2000, Value, Respect and Attachment 2001, The Practice of Value 2003, Between Authority and Interpretation 2009, From Normativity to Responsibility 2011. *Address:* Columbia Law School, 435 West 116th Street, JGH, Room 518, New York, NY 10027, USA (office). *Telephone:* (212) 854-5191 (office). *Fax:* (212) 854-7946 (office). *E-mail:* jr159@columbia.edu (office). *Website:* sites.google.com/site/josephnraz.

RAZA, Syed Salim, MA; Pakistani banking executive; b. 16 Feb. 1946, Lucknow, Uttar Pradesh, India; s. of Syed Hashim Raza; ed Univ. of Oxford, UK; has worked in int. banking since 1973; Country Head for Citibank in Pakistan 1983–87, various positions with Citibank, N.A. (Nat. Asscn), including Country and Regional Man. across the Middle East, Africa and UK, Cen. and Eastern Europe, based in London 1989–2006; CEO Pakistan Business Council 2006–09; Gov. State Bank of Pakistan 2009–10. *Address:* c/o State Bank of Pakistan, Central Directorate, I.I. Chundrigar Road, PO Box 4456, Karachi 2, Pakistan.

RAZAK, Dato' Seri Mohamad Najib bin tun Haj Abdul, BA; Malaysian politician; *Prime Minister and Minister of Finance;* b. 23 July 1953, Kuala Lipis, Pahang; m. 2nd Toh Puan Indera Datin Sri Rosmah Mansor; five c.; ed Univ. of Nottingham; Exec. Patronas 1974–76; Pengerusi Majuternak 1977–78; mem. Parl. 1976–; Deputy Minister of Energy, Telecommunications and Posts 1978–80, of Educ. 1980–81, of Finance 1981–82; mem. State Ass. for Pakan constituency 1982–86; Menteri Besar Pahang 1982–86; Minister of Culture, Youth and Sports 1986–87, of Youth and Sports 1987–90, of Defence 1990–95, 1999–2008, of Educ. 1995–99, of Finance 2008–; Deputy Prime Minister 2004–09, Prime Minister 2009–; mem. UMNO Supreme Council 1981–; Vice-Pres. UMNO Youth 1982–; Chair. Pahang Foundation 1982–86; Grand Order of Youth (Korea) 1988, Kt Grand Cross, First Class (Thailand), Bintang Yudha Dharma Utama (Indonesia) 1994, Distinguished Service Order (Singapore) 1994, DUBC (Thailand) 1995; Hon. PhD (US Acad. of Sports) 1992, (Nottingham) 2004; Orang Kaya Indera Shahbandar 1976, Darjah Sultan Ahmad Shah 1978, Seri Indera Mahkota Pahang 1983, Darjah Kebesaran Seri Sultan Ahmad Shah 1985, Man of the Year Award, New Straits Times 1990, Panglima Bintang Sarawak 1990, Dato Paduka Mahkota Selangor 1992, Seri Panglima Darjah Kinabalu (SPDK) 2002. *Address:* Prime Minister's Office, Federal Government Administration Center, Bangunan Perdana Putra, 62502 Putrajaya, Malaysia (office). *Telephone:* (3) 88888000 (office). *Fax:* (3) 88883444 (office). *E-mail:* ppm@pmo.gov.my (office). *Website:* www.pmo.gov.my (office).

RAZALEIGH, Tan Sri Tengku Hamzah, PSM, SPMK; Malaysian politician and fmr company executive; b. c. 1936; s. of late Tengku Mohamed Hamzah bin Zainal Abidin (fmr Chief Minister of Kelantan); ed Queen's Univ., Belfast and Lincoln's Inn, London; Chair. of Kelantan Div. of United Malays' Nat. Org. (UMNO) in early 1960s; mem. Kelantan State Assembly for some years; Exec. Dir Bank Bumiputra

1963, Chair., Man. Dir 1970; mem. Parl. for Gua Musang 1969–; Exec. Dir PERNAS 1971–74; Chair. Malaysian Nat. Insurance; led trade mission to Beijing 1971; a Vice-Pres. UMNO 1975; Pres. Assoc. Malay Chambers of Commerce until Oct. 1976; Chair. PETRONAS (Nat. Oil Co.) 1974–76; Minister of Finance 1976–84, of Trade and Industry 1984–87; Chair. IMF Meetings 1978, Asram Devt Bank 1977–, Islamic Devt Bank 1977; mem. United Malays National Organization (Pertubuhan Kebangsaan Melayu Bersatu) (UMNO Baru) (New UMNO). *Address:* United Malays National Organization (Pertubuhan Kebangsaan Melayu Bersatu) (UMNO Baru) (New UMNO), Menara Dato' Onn, 38th Floor, Jalan Tun Ismail, 50480 Kuala Lumpur, Malaysia. *Telephone:* (3) 40429511. *Fax:* (3) 40412358. *E-mail:* email@umno.net.my. *Website:* www.umno-online.com.

RAZBOROV, Alexander A., DPhysMathSci; Russian mathematician, computational theorist and academic; *Leading Researcher, Department of Mathematical Logic, Steklov Mathematical Institute, Russian Academy of Sciences;* b. 16 Feb. 1963; Leading Researcher, Dept of Math. Logic, Steklov Math. Inst., Russian Acad. of Sciences, Moscow; Corresp. mem. Russian Acad. of Sciences; Nevanlinna Prize, Univ. of Helsinki 1990, Tarski Lecturer, Univ. of Calif., Berkeley 2000, Gödel Prize, Asscn for Computing Machinery (with Steven Rudich) 2007. *Publications:* numerous articles in math. journals. *Address:* Steklov Mathematical Institute, Gubkina str.8, 119991 Moscow, Russian Federation (office). *Telephone:* (495) 938-37-44 (office). *Fax:* (495) 135-05-55 (office). *E-mail:* razborov@mi.ras.ru (office). razborov@genesis.mi.ras.ru (office). *Website:* www.mi.ras.ru/~razborov (office).

RAZEE, Mahmoud; Maldivian politician; fmr Chair. Privatization Cttee; fmr Exec. Dir Civil Aviation Dept; Minister of State, Ministry of Civil Aviation and Communication –2009, Minister 2009–10; Minister of Econ. Devt and of Transport and Communication 2010–12; mem. Maldivian Democratic Party; Owner Lintel Investment Maldives. *Address:* c/o Ministry of Economic Development, Ghaazee Bldg, Ameer Ahmed Magu, Malé 20–125, Maldives (office).

RAZI, Syed Sibtey, BCom, LLB; Indian politician; b. 7 March 1939, Jais, Rai Bareli Dist, UP; s. of the late Syed Wirasat Husain and Razia Begum; m. Chand Farhana 1973; two s. two d.; ed Husainabad Higher Secondary School, Shia Coll., Lucknow Univ.; began political career as student leader, elected Pres. Commerce Asscn, Lucknow Univ.; Pres. Shia Coll. Student Union 1958–59; joined Congress Party 1969, Gen. Sec. UP Youth Congress 1971–73; Vice-Pres. Youth Welfare Bd, UP Govt 1975–77; mem. Parl. (Rajya Sabha) 1980–85, 1988–98, Vice-Chair. Rajya Sabha (Panel of Presiding Officers) 1993–95; Gen. Sec. UP Congress Cttee 1980–84, Vice-Pres. 2000–02; mem. UP Legis. Council 1985–88; Minister of Educ. and Muslim Waqf, UP Govt 1985–88; mem. All India Congress Cttee 1985–2004, Jt Sec. 1984–85, Spokesperson 2002–04; mem. Indian Del. led by Prime Minister Indira Gandhi to 9th Non-Aligned Movt Summit, New Delhi 1983, Indian Del. to 42nd UN Gen. Ass. 1986; Vice-Chair. UP Institutional Finance Corpn, UP Govt July–Dec. 1988; Deputy Leader Parl. Congress Party 1993–95; Union Minister of State for Home Affairs 1995–96; Gov. of Jharkhand 2004–09, of Assam July–Nov. 2009; mem. Exec. Cttee CPP 1992–94; Chair. Sarvodaya Degree Coll., Salon, Rai Bareli 1999–2004; mem., NGO del. to Human Rights Comm., Geneva 2000–01, Aligarh Muslim Univ. Court 2002–04, Exec. Council Maulana Azad Urdu Univ., Hyderabad 2002–04; Repertoire of Social Justice Cttee, All India Congress Cttee, Simla Camp 2003. *Leisure interests* reading, philanthrophy. *Address:* D2/3, River Bank Colony, Lucknow, India. *Telephone:* 98-10864830 (mobile).

RAZIN, Aharon, PhD; Israeli biochemist and academic; *Dr Jacob Grunbaum Professor Emeritus of Medical Science, The Hebrew University of Jerusalem;* b. Tel-Aviv; ed The Hebrew Univ. of Jerusalem; Lecturer, The Hebrew Univ. of Jerusalem 1967–71, Sr Lecturer 1971–76, Assoc. Prof. 1976–82, Dr Jacob Grunbaum Prof. of Medical Science 1982–2003, Prof. Emer. 2003–; Visiting Scientist, Univ. of Cambridge, UK 1971, City of Hope Medical Center, Calif., USA 1977; Fogarty Scholar, Fogarty International Center, NIH, USA 1984–86; mem. Israel Acad. of Sciences and Humanities, Human Genome Org. (HUGO), European Molecular Biology Org.; Israel Prize 2004, Wolf Prize in Medicine (with Howard Cedar) 2008, EMET Prize in Life Sciences 2009, Canada Gairdner Award (with Howard Cedar), Gairdner Foundation 2011. *Publications:* numerous papers in professional journals. *Address:* Department of Developmental Biology and Cancer Research, Faculty of Medicine, The Hebrew University of Jerusalem, Ein Kerem, PO Box 12272, 91120 Jerusalem, Israel (office). *Telephone:* 2-6758172 (office). *Fax:* 2-6415848 (office). *E-mail:* aharonr@ekmd.huji.ac.il (office). *Website:* research.ekmd.huji.ac.il (office).

RAZOV, Sergey Sergeyevich, PhD; Russian diplomatist and economist; *Ambassador to People's Republic of China;* b. 28 Jan. 1953, Sochi, Krasnodar Territory; m.; one s. one d.; ed Moscow Inst. of Int. Relations; economist, sr economist USSR Trade Mission to Repub. of China 1975–79; head of div., head of group Cen. CPSU Cttee 1979–90; Head Dept of Far East Countries and Indochina, USSR Ministry of Foreign Affairs 1990–92; Amb. to Mongolia 1992–96; Dir Third Dept of CIS Countries, Russian Ministry of Foreign Affairs 1996–99; Amb. to Poland 1999–2002, to People's Repub. of China 2005–; Deputy Minister of Foreign Affairs 2002–05; state awards. *Publications:* The People's Republic of China 1991, Foreign Policy of Open Doors of People's Republic of China 1985; articles and other publs. *Address:* Embassy of the Russian Federation, 4 Dong Zhi Men Nei, Bei Zhong Jie, Beijing 100600, People's Republic of China (office). *Telephone:* (10) 65322051 (office). *Fax:* (10) 65324851 (office). *E-mail:* embassy@russia.org.cn (office). *Website:* (office).

RE, HE Cardinal Giovanni Battista; Italian ecclesiastic; *Prefect Emeritus of the Congregation for Bishops;* b. 30 Jan. 1934, Borno, Brescia; ordained priest 1957; consecrated Bishop 1987; Titular Archbishop of Vescovio; Asst Sec. of State, General Affairs; Prefect of the Congregation for Bishops, 2000–05, 2005–10, currently Prefect Emer.; Pres. Pontifical Comm. for Latin America 2000–05, 2005–10; cr. Cardinal (Cardinal-Priest of Santi XII Apostoli) 2001, (Cardinal Bishop of Sabina-Poggio Mirteto) 2002; participated in Papal Conclave 2005, 2013. *Address:* Palazzina dell'Arciprete, 00120 Vatican City. *Telephone:* (06) 69883942. *Fax:* (06) 69885303 (office). *Website:* www.vatican.va/roman_curia/congregations/cbishops/index.htm (office).

REA, Stephen James; Irish actor; b. 1949, Belfast, Northern Ireland; s. of James Rea and Jane Rea (née Logue); m. Dolours Price 1983; two s.; ed Queen's Univ., Belfast; formed (with Brian Friel q.v.) Field Day Theatre Co. 1980; Hon. DLitt

(Univ. of Staffs.) 1999, (Univ. of Ulster) 2004, Hon. DUniv (Queen's Univ., Belfast) 2004. *Stage appearances include:* The Shadow of a Gunman, The Cherry Orchard, Miss Julie, High Society, Endgame, The Freedom of the City, Translations, Communication Card, St Oscar, Boesman and Lena, Hightime and Riot Act, Double Cross, Pentecost, Making History, Someone Who'll Watch Over Me 1992 (Broadway, New York), Uncle Vanya 1995; at Nat. Theatre: Ashes to Ashes 1997, Playboy of the Western World, Comedians, The Shaughraun, Cyrano de Bergerac (Nat. Theatre) 2004. *Directed:* Three Sisters, The Cure at Troy, Northern Star 1998. *Films include:* Angel 1982, Company of Wolves 1985, The Doctor and the Devils 1985, Loose Connections 1988, Life is Sweet 1991, The Crying Game 1992, Bad Behaviour 1993, Princess Caraboo 1993, Angie 1994, Interview with the Vampire 1994, Prêt-à-Porter 1994, All Men are Mortal 1994, Citizen X 1994, The Devil and the Deep Blue Sea 1994, Michael Collins 1995, Trojan Eddie 1995, A Further Gesture 1995, The Butcher Boy 1998, Guinevere 1999, The End of the Affair 2000, I Could Read the Sky 2000, Fear Dot Com 2002, Proud 2003, Bloom 2003, The Halo Effect 2004, Romeo and Me 2004, The Good Shepherd 2004, Fluent Dysphasia 2004, Proud 2004, Breakfast on Pluto 2005, River Queen 2005, V for Vendetta 2006, Sixty Six 2006, Until Death 2007, The Reaping 2007, Stuck 2007, The Devil's Mercy 2008, The Heavy 2009, Espion(s) 2009, Ondine 2009. *TV appearances include:* Four Days in July, Lost Belongings, Scout, St Oscar, Not with a Bang, Hedda Gabler, Crime of the Century, Copenhagen 2002, I Didn't Know You Cared. *Address:* c/o ICM, 76 Oxford Street, London, W1N 0AX, England (office). *Telephone:* (20) 7636-6565 (office).

READ, Ian C., BSc, CA; British/American chartered accountant and pharmaceutical industry executive; *Chairman and CEO, Pfizer Inc.;* b. Scotland, UK; ed Imperial Coll., London; earned certification from Inst. of Chartered Accountants of England and Wales 1978; began career with Pfizer as operational auditor 1978, worked in Latin America until 1995, held numerous positions including Chief Financial Officer, Pfizer Mexico and Country Man., Pfizer Brazil, Pres. Int. Pharmaceuticals Group, with responsibility for Latin America and Canada 1996–2000, Exec. Vice-Pres., Europe 2000–06, Corp. Vice-Pres. 2001–06, assumed additional responsibility for Canada 2002, later responsible for Africa/Middle East region and Latin America, Sr Vice-Pres., Pfizer Inc. 2006–10, Pres. Worldwide Pharmaceutical Operations 2006–09, Group Pres. Worldwide Biopharmaceutical Businesses 2009–10, oversaw Primary Care, Specialty Care, Oncology, Established Products and Emerging Markets global business units, mem. Bd of Dirs, Pres. and CEO Pfizer Inc. 2010–11, Chair. and CEO 2011–, Chair. Exec. Cttee, mem. Exec. Compliance Exec.; Pfizer's Rep. on Int. Section Exec. Cttee of PhRMA and fmr Chair. Europe Cttee; mem. Bd of Dirs Kimberly-Clark Corpn 2007–, Pharmaceutical Research and Mfrs of America, US Council for Int. Business, European Fed. of Pharmaceutical Industries and Asscns; fmr Dir Brazilian Anglo American Pharmaceutical Asscn (CIFAB), Brazilian Asscn of the Pharmaceutical Industry (ABIFARMA); fmr Chair. PhRMA's Latin America Regional Cttee; fmr Vice-Chair. Intellectual Property Coordination Cttee section of Int. Fed. of Pharmaceutical Mfrs and Asscns. *Address:* Pfizer Inc., 235 East 42nd Street, New York, NY 10017-5755, USA (office). *Telephone:* (212) 733-2323 (office). *Fax:* (212) 573-7851 (office). *E-mail:* info@pfizer.com (office). *Website:* www.pfizer.com (office).

READ, Sir John Emms, Kt, FCA, FIB; British business executive (retd); b. 29 March 1918, Brighton, Sussex, England; s. of William E. Read and Daysie E. Read (née Cooper); m. Dorothy M. Berry 1942 (died 2004); two s.; ed Brighton, Hove and Sussex Grammar School and Admin. Staff Coll., Henley-on-Thames; Commdr RN 1939–46; Adm.'s Sec. to Asst Chief of Naval Staff, Admiralty 1942–45, Naval Sec., British Admiralty Tech. Mission, Ottawa 1945–46; Ford Motor Co. 1946–64, Dir of Sales 1961–64; Exec. Dir EMI Ltd 1965, Man. Dir 1966–69, CEO 1969–79, Deputy Chair. 1973–74, Chair. 1974–79; Deputy Chair. Thorn EMI Ltd 1979–80, Dir 1981–87; Chair. Trustee Savings Bank Cen. Bd 1980–88, Trustee Savings Banks (Holdings) Ltd 1980–86, TSB England and Wales 1983–86, TSB Group PLC 1986–88, (Dir TSB England and Wales PLC 1986–88), United Dominions Trust Ltd 1981–85; Dir Dunlop Holdings Ltd 1971–84, Thames Television Ltd 1973–84 (Deputy Chair. 1981–88), Capitol Industries-EMI Inc., USA 1970–83, Wonderworld PLC 1986–97, FI Group PLC 1989–94, Nat. Youth Film Foundation 1987–90, Cadmus Investment Man. Ltd 1993–98, Cafman Ltd (now Cafcash) 1994–2000, Cafinvest Ltd 1994–96; mem. P.O. Bd 1975–77, Royal Naval Film Corpn 1975–83, British Overseas Trade Bd 1976–79; Chair. Electronics Econ. Devt Comm. 1976–80, Armed Forces Pay Review Body 1976–83, Nat. Electronics Council 1977–80, Gov. Admin. Staff Coll., Henley 1974–92; mem. Council of CBI 1977–89, Pres.'s Cttee 1977–84, Chair. Finance Cttee 1978–84; Trustee, Westminster Abbey Trust 1978–87, Charity Aid Foundation 1985–98 (Chair. 1990–94, Pres. 1994–98), Crimestoppers Trust 1987–2001; Chair. Cttee of Man. Inst. of Neurology 1980–97, Brain Research Trust 1982–2001 (Pres. 2002–); Pres. Sussex Asscn of Boys' Clubs 1982–97, Cheshire Homes, Seven Rivers, Essex 1979–85, Essex Blind 2004–; Vice-Pres. Inst. of Bankers 1982–89; mem. Cttee of London and Scottish Bankers 1986–88, Governing Body, British Postgraduate Medical Fed. 1982–96; Fellow, RSA 1975–90; Hon. Fellow, Henley Man. Coll. 1993, Univ. Coll. London 1999; Companion, Inst. of Radio Engineers, Chartered Man. Inst.; Hon. DUniv (Surrey) 1987; Hon. DBA (Buckingham) 1988. *Leisure interests:* music, the arts, sport, various charities. *Address:* Flat 68, 15 Portman Square, London, W1H 6LL, England (home). *Telephone:* (20) 8617-9400 (home).

READ, Piers Paul, MA, FRSL; British author; b. 7 March 1941, Beaconsfield, Bucks., England; s. of Herbert Edward Read and Margaret Ludwig; m. Emily Albertine Boothby 1967; two s. two d.; ed Ampleforth Coll., York and St John's Coll., Cambridge; Artist-in-Residence, Ford Foundation, West Berlin, Germany 1964; Sub-Ed. Times Literary Supplement, London 1965; Harkness Fellow, Commonwealth Fund, New York 1967–68; Council mem. Inst. of Contemporary Arts (ICA), London 1971–75; Cttee of Man. Soc. of Authors, London 1973–76; mem. Literature Panel Arts Council, London 1975–77; Adjunct Prof. of Writing, Columbia Univ., New York 1980; Chair. Catholic Writers' Guild 1992–97; mem. Bd Aid to the Church in Need 1991–2012; Trustee, Catholic Library 1997–2011; mem. Council RSL 2001–07; Sir Geoffrey Faber Memorial Prize 1968, Somerset Maugham Award 1969, Hawthornden Prize 1969, Thomas More Award (USA) 1976, James Tait Black Memorial Prize 1988. *Publications include:* Game in Heaven with Tussy Marx 1966, The Junkers 1968, Monk Dawson 1969, The Professor's Daughter 1971, The Upstart 1973, Alive: The Story of the Andes

Survivors 1974, Polonaise 1976, The Train Robbers 1978, A Married Man 1979, The Villa Golitsyn 1981, The Free Frenchman 1986, A Season in the West 1988, On the Third Day 1990, Quo Vadis? The Subversion of the Catholic Church 1991, Ablaze: The Story of Chernobyl 1993, A Patriot in Berlin 1995, Knights of The Cross 1997, The Templars 1999, Alice in Exile 2001, Alec Guinness: The Authorised Biography 2003, Hell and Other Essays 2006, The Death of a Pope 2009, The Misogynist 2010. *Leisure interest:* family life. *Address:* c/o Aitken Alexander Associates, 18–21 Cavaye Place, London, SW10 9PT, England (office); 50 Portland Road, London, W11 4LG, England (home). *Telephone:* (20) 7373-8672 (office); (20) 7460-2499 (office); (20) 7727-5719 (home). *Fax:* (20) 7373-6002 (office). *Website:* www.aitkenalexander.co.uk (office); www.pierspaulread.co.uk. *E-mail:* piersread@dial.pipex.com (office).

REAGAN, Nancy Davis, BA; American actress and fmr First Lady; b. (Anne Francis Robbins), 6 July 1921, New York; d. of Kenneth Robbins and Edith Robbins (née Luckett), step-d. of Loyal Davis; m. Ronald Reagan 1952 (died 2004); one s. one d., one step-s. one step-d.; ed Smith Coll., Mass.; contract actress Metro-Goldwyn-Mayer 1949–56; fmr author syndicated column on prisoners-of-war and soldiers missing in action; civic worker active on behalf of Viet Nam war veterans, sr citizens, disabled children and drug victims; First Lady 1981–89; mem. Bd of Dirs Revlon Group Inc. 1989–; Hon. Nat. Chair. Aid to Adoption of Special Kids 1977; Dr hc (Eureka Coll.) 2009; one of Ten Most Admired American Women, Good Housekeeping Magazine 1977, Woman of Year, LA Times 1977, perm. mem. Hall of Fame of Ten Best Dressed Women in US, Lifetime Achievement Award, Council of Fashion Designers of USA 1988, Congressional Gold Medal 2002, Presidential Medal of Freedom 2002, numerous awards for role in fight against drug abuse. *Films include:* The Doctor and the Girl 1949, East Side, West Side 1949, Shadow on the Wall 1950, The Next Voice You Hear 1950, Night Into Morning 1951, It's a Big Country 1951, Talk About a Stranger 1952, Donovan's Brain 1953, Hellcats of the Navy 1957, Crash Landing 1958. *Publications include:* Nancy 1980, To Love A Child (with Jane Wilkie), My Turn (memoirs) 1989. *Address:* 2121 Avenue of the Stars, 34th Floor, Los Angeles, CA 90067, USA.

REARDON, Raymond (Ray), MBE; British fmr professional snooker player; b. 8 Oct. 1932, Tredegar, Monmouthshire, Wales; s. of Benjamin Reardon and Cynthia Jenkins; m. 1st Susan Carter (divorced); one s. one d.; m. 2nd Carol Lovington 1987; ed Georgeton Secondary Modern School, Tredegar; fmr coal miner and police officer; Welsh Amateur Champion 1950–55; English Amateur Champion 1964; invited to tour South Africa; turned professional 1967; Pot Black Champion 1969, 1979; World Snooker Champion 1970, 1973, 1974, 1975, 1976, 1978; Benson & Hedges Masters Champion 1976; Welsh Champion 1981, 1983; Professional Players Tournament Champion 1982; Yamaha International Masters Champion 1983; team wins: World Cup (with Wales) 1979, 1980; ranked World No. 1 for six years; retd 1992; advised Ronnie O'Sullivan on his way to World Championship victory 2004; active in running World Professional Billiards and Snooker Asscn; occasional appearances on BBC TV's Big Break show; Pres. Churston golf club, Devon; lives in Torquay, Devon. *Publications:* Classic Snooker 1974, Ray Reardon (autobiog.) 1982. *Leisure interest:* golf.

REBE, Bernd Werner, DrIur; German academic and fmr university president; b. 5 Sept. 1939, Braunlage; s. of Werner Rebe and Liselotte Rebe; m. 1st Bärbel Bonewitz 1964 (died 1993); two s.; m. 2nd Katharina Ribe (née Becker) 1999; ed Univ. of Kiel, Freie Univ. Berlin and Univ. of Bielefeld; Prof. of Civil Law, Commercial Law, Competition Law and Corpn Law, Univ. of Hannover 1975, Vice-Pres. Univ. of Hannover 1979–81; Pres. Tech. Univ. of Braunschweig 1983–99, Prof. of Constitutional and Media Law 1999–2005; mem. Senate W German Rectors' Conf. 1988; Pres. Rectors' Conf. of Lower Saxony 1989; Hon. Citizen Otto-von-Guericke-Universität Magdeburg. *Publications:* Die Träger der Pressefreiheit nach dem Grundgesetz 1970, Privatrecht und Wirtschaftsordnung 1978, Arbeitslosigkeit—unser Schicksal? 1983, Neue Technologien und die Entwicklung von Wirtschaft und Gesellschaft 1984, Verfassung und Verwaltung des Landes Niedersachsen 1986, Nutzen und Wahrheit: Triebkräfte der Wissenschaftsentwicklung 1991, Die Universität heute—Leitinstitution ohne Leitbild? 1991, Umweltverträgliches Wirtschaften—Wettbewerbsvorteile, Marktchancen, Wohlstandssicherung 1993, Denkerkundungen. Reden wider die Vordergründigkeit 1995, Die unvollendete Einheit. Bestandsaufnahme und Perspektiven für die Wirtschaft 1996, Vision und Verantwortung 1999, Humanität—Wandel—Utopie 2000; Medienrecht als Paradigma "modernen" Rechts? in: FS für Rehbinder, 2002, Die Tyrannei der Fresskette—Wie das Weltfinanzsystem die Fähigkeit zur Selbstzerstörung hervorgebracht hat und weiter hervorbringen kann 2010, Die geschönte Reformation—Warum Martin Luther uns kein Vorbild mehr sein kann 2012. *Leisure interests:* swimming, skiing, tennis, history, politics. *Address:* Weisser Kuhl 13, 38162 Cremlingen, Germany (home). *Telephone:* (531) 8669292 (home).

REBEK, Julius, Jr, BA, PhD; American chemist and academic; *Director, Skaggs Institute for Chemical Biology, Scripps Research Institute;* b. (Gyula Rebek), 11 April 1944, Beregszasz, Hungary; s. of Julius Rebek, Sr and Eva Racz; m. (divorced); two d.; ed Univ. of Kansas and Massachusetts Inst. of Tech.; lived in Austria 1945–49; Asst Prof., UCLA 1970–76; Assoc. Prof., Univ. of Pittsburgh 1976–80, Prof. 1980–89; Prof., Dept of Chem., MIT 1989–96, Camille Dreyfus Prof. of Chem. 1991–96; Dir Skaggs Inst. for Chemical Biology, Scripps Research Inst. 1996–; mem. ACS, NAS; Fellow, American Acad. of Arts and Sciences; Dr hc (Bonn) 2010; NSF Fellow 1967–70, Sloan Fellow 1977, von Humboldt Fellow 1981, Guggenheim Fellow 1986, Cope Scholar Award 1991, James Flack Norris Award in Physical Organic Chem. 1997, Chemical Pioneer Award, American Inst. of Chemists 2002, Ronald Breslow Award for Achievement in Biomimetic Chem., ACS 2004, Medal of the Acad. of Sciences (Czech Repub.) 2005, Medal of the Nat. Acad. of Sciences, Letters and Arts (Italy) 2005, Distinguished Scientist Award, ACS 2006, Evans Award, Ohio State Univ. 2006, Univ. of Oregon Creativity Award in Chem., Dance and Music 2007, Humboldt Sr Scientist Award (Germany) 2008, Tau-Shue Chou Award, Academia Sinica 2008, Nichols Medal, ACS 2011, Prelog Medal, ETH 2012. *Publications:* 500 publs in scientific journals. *Leisure interest:* tennis. *Address:* Rebek Laboratory, Skaggs Institute for Chemical Biology, Scripps Research Institute, 10550 North Torrey Pines Road, La Jolla, CA 92037 (office); 2330 Calle del Oro, La Jolla, CA 92037, USA (home). *Telephone:* (858) 784-2250 (office). *Fax:* (858) 784-2876 (office). *E-mail:* jrebek@scripps.edu (office). *Website:* www.scripps.edu/skaggs/rebek (office).

REBELO PINTO CHICOTI, George; Angolan academic and politician; *Minister of Foreign Affairs;* b. 15 June 1955, Dondi, Huambo Prov.; s. of Mateus Pinto Chikoti and Catarina Chikoti Kanjila; m. Elisabeth Apoque Chikoti; four c.; ed Univ. of Abidjan, Côte d'Ivoire, Univ. de Paris XII, France, Univ. of Ottawa, Canada; in exile with family in Zambia 1964–75; Prof. of English, Escola Industrial do Huambo 1975–76; Asst Prof., Univ. of Abidjan, Côte d'Ivoire 1983–85; with Credit and Int. Investment Dept, Canadian Imperial Bank of Commerce, Toronto, Canada 1987–89; Asst Prof., Univ. of Ottawa 1989–90; mem. Conselho da República de Angola 1992–; Deputy Minister, Ministry of Foreign Affairs 1992, rank of Amb. 1994, Minister of Foreign Affairs 2010–; Pres. Fórum Democrático Angolano 1990–. *Address:* Ministry of Foreign Affairs, Rua Major Kanhangulo, Luanda, Angola (office). *Telephone:* 222394827 (office). *Fax:* 222393246 (office). *E-mail:* geral@mirex.gov.ao (office). *Website:* www.mirex.gov.ao (office).

REBUCK, Dame Gail Ruth, DBE, BA, FRSA; British publishing executive; *Chairman, Penguin Random House UK;* b. 10 Feb. 1952, London; d. of Gordon Rebuck and Mavis Rebuck; m. Philip Gould 1985 (died 2011); two d.; ed Lycée Français de Londres, Univ. of Sussex, Wharton Business School; Production Asst, Grisewood & Dempsey (children's book packager) 1975–76; Ed., later Publr Robert Nicholson Publs London Guidebooks 1976–79; Publr Hamlyn Paperbacks 1979–82; Founder Partner Century Publishing Co. Ltd, Publishing Dir Non-Fiction 1982–85, Publr Century Hutchinson 1985–89, Chair. Random House Div., Random Century 1989–91, Chair. and Chief Exec. Random House UK Ltd (now The Random House Group Ltd) 1991–2013, Chair. Penguin Random House UK 2013–; mem. Group Man. Cttee, Bertelsmann 2012–; mem. COPUS 1995–97, Creative Industries Task Force 1997–2000, Court of Univ. of Sussex 1997–, Council of RCA 1999–, Advisory Bd Cambridge Judge Inst. 2004–08, Govt Fair Access to the Professions panel 2010; Dir (non-exec.) Work Foundation 2001–09, BSkyB 2002–, Skillset 2009–11; Trustee, Inst. for Public Policy Research 1993–2003, Nat. Literacy Trust 2007–; Chair. Quick Reads Charity 2006–; ranked 25th by the Financial Times amongst Top 25 Businesswomen in Europe 2005, Veuve Clicquot Businesswoman of the Year 2009, ranked ninth by the Guardian amongst top people in British books industry 2011. *Leisure interests:* reading, travel. *Address:* Penguin Random House UK, 20 Vauxhall Bridge Road, London, SW1V 2SA, England (office). *Telephone:* (20) 7840-8400 (office). *Fax:* (20) 7233-6120 (office). *E-mail:* grebuck@randomhouse.co.uk (office). *Website:* www .penguinrandomhouse.com (office).

RECCHI, Giuseppe; Italian business executive; *Chairman, Eni SpA;* b. 1964; ed Politechnic of Turin; began career at Recchi SpA (construction co.) 1989, Exec. Chair. Recchi America Inc. 1994–99; joined General Electric (GE) 1999, held several managerial positions in Europe and USA, served as Dir of GE Capital Structure Finance Group, Gen. Man. for Industrial M&A and Business Devt for GE EMEA, Pres. and CEO GE Italy, Pres. and CEO GE South Europe –2011, Vice-Chair. GE Capital SpA; Chair. Eni SpA 2011–; mem. Bd of Dirs, Compensation and Audit Cttees, Exor SpA; mem. European Advisory Bd, Blackstone; mem. Exec. Cttee, Confindustria (Italian Corp. Asscn); mem. Hon. Cttee for the Rome Candidacy to 2020 Olympic Games, Bd of Permasteelisa SpA; Visiting Prof. in Structured Finance, Turin Univ.; occasional editorial commentator for financial papers, national dailies and Harvard Business Review. *Address:* Eni SpA, Piazzale Enrico Mattei 1, 00144 Rome, Italy (office). *Telephone:* (06) 59821 (office). *Fax:* (06) 59822141 (office). *E-mail:* segreteriasocietaria.azionisti@eni.it (office); ufficio .stampa@eni.it (office). *Website:* www.eni.com (office).

REDDY, Jaipal Sudini, BJ, MA; Indian agriculturalist and politician; *Minister of Science and Technology and of Earth Sciences;* b. 16 Jan. 1942, Madgul, Mahbubnagar Dist, Andhra Pradesh; s. of the late Durga Reddy and Yashodamma Reddy; m. Lakshmi Reddy; two s. one d.; ed Osmania Univ., Hyderabad; Pres. AP Youth Congress 1965–71; Gen.-Sec. AP Congress Cttee 1969–72; mem. AP Legis. Ass. 1969–84; mem. Nat. Exec. Janata Party 1979–88, Gen.-Sec. 1985–88; elected to 8th Lok Sabha (lower house of Parl.) (in alliance with Telugu Desam Party, TDP) 1984, 12th Lok Sabha 1998, 13th Lok Sabha for Miryalaguda constituency (Congress Party) 1999, 14th Lok Sabha 2004, 15th Lok Sabha for Chelvella constituency 2009–, mem. Cttee on Finance 1998–99, Chair. Cttee of Privileges 1999–2000; mem. Rajya Sabha (upper house of Parl.) 1990–96, 1997–98, Leader of Opposition 1991–92; Union Cabinet Minister of Information and Broadcasting 1997–98, of Information and Broadcasting and Culture 2004–05, of Urban Devt and Culture 2005–06, of Urban Devt 2006, 2009–11, of Petroleum and Natural Gas 2011–12, of Science and Tech. and of Earth Sciences 2012–; Indian Parl. Group Outstanding Parliamentarian Award 1998. *Address:* Ministry of Science and Technology, Technology Bhavan, New Mehrauli Road, New Delhi 110 016, India (office). *Telephone:* (11) 26567373 (office). *Fax:* (11) 26864570 (office). *E-mail:* dstinfo@nic.in (office). *Website:* dst.gov.in (office); www.sjaipalreddy.com.

REDDY, K. Srinath, MSc, MD; Indian cardiologist, epidemiologist and academic; *President, World Heart Federation;* ed Osmania Medical Coll., Hyderabad, All India Inst. of Medical Sciences, New Delhi, McMaster Univ., Canada; Prof. of Cardiology, All India Inst. of Medical Sciences, New Delhi; coordinator Cardio-vascular Health Research Initiative in Developing Countries; Pres. Public Health Foundation of India; Bernard Lown Visiting Prof. of Cardiovascular Health, Harvard School of Public Health; Adjunct Prof., Rollins School of Public Health, Emory Univ.; Chair. Scientific Council on Epidemiology and Prevention, World Heart Fed. 2003–06, mem. Advisory Bd 2007–10, Pres. World Heart Fed. 2013–; mem. WHO Scientific Advisory Cttee on Tobacco Product Regulation; Foreign Assoc. NAS Inst. of Medicine 2004; Ed. National Medical Journal of India; Fellow, Nat. Acad. of Medical Sciences 2000; Hon. Fellow, London School of Hygiene and Tropical Medicine 2009; WHO Dir-Gen.'s Award for Outstanding Contrib. to Global Tobacco Control 2003, Queen Elizabeth Medal Royal Soc. for Promotion of Health 2005, Padma Bhushan 2005, Luther L Terry Award, American Cancer Society 2009. *Publications:* contrib. over 200 papers and articles in scientific journals. *Address:* Office of the President, PHD House, 2nd Floor, 4/2 Sirifort Institutional Area, August Kranti Marg New Delhi 110 016, India (office). *Telephone:* (11) 46046000 (office). *Fax:* (11) 41648513 (office). *E-mail:* contact@phfi .org (office). *Website:* www.phfi.org (office).

REDDY, Nallari Kiran Kumar, LLB; Indian lawyer and politician; b. 13 Sept. 1969, Hyderabad; s. of the late Amarnatha Reddy and of Sarojamma Reddy; m. Radhika Reddy; one s. one d.; ed Nizam Coll., Hyderabad, Osmania Univ.; mem. Andhra Pradesh Legis. Ass. for Vayalpadu constituency, Chittoor Dist 1989–94, 1999–2009, for Pileru constituency 2009; Govt Chief Whip 2004–09; Speaker, 13th AP Ass. 2009; Chief Minister of Andhra Pradesh 2010–14 (resgnd); fmr mem. Indian Nat. Congress party; f. Jai Samaikyandhra party 2014. *Achievements include:* represented Hyderabad in cricket in Ranji Trophy.

REDDY, Preetha, MD; Indian hospital administrator and business executive; *Managing Director, Apollo Hospitals;* d. of Prathap C. Reddy; ed Annamalai Univ.; joined Apollo Group 1989, currently Man. Dir Apollo Hospitals, Chennai (largest pvt. healthcare provider in Asia and third largest in the world); ranked by Fortune magazine amongst the 50 Most Powerful Women in Business outside the US (46th) 2009, (48th) 2010–11. *Address:* Apollo Hospitals, 21 Greams Lane, off Greams Road, Chennai 600 006, Tamilnadu, India (office). *Telephone:* (44) 28290200 (office), (44) 28293333 (office). *Fax:* (44) 28293524 (office), (44) 28296022 (office). *E-mail:* enquiry@apollohospitals.com (office). *Website:* www.apollohospitals.com (office).

REDDY, Y(aga) Venugopal, MA, PhD; Indian central banker and academic; b. 17 Aug. 1941, Kadapa, Andhra Pradesh; ed Madras Univ., Osmania Univ., Hyderabad, Inst. of Social Studies, Netherlands; joined Indian Admin. Service in 1964, has held several key positions including Sec. (Banking), Ministry of Finance, Additional Sec., Ministry of Commerce, Jt Sec., Ministry of Finance, Prin. Sec., Govt of Andhra Pradesh; Deputy Gov. Reserve Bank of India 1996–2002, Gov. 2003–08; Exec. Dir for India, Sri Lanka, Bangladesh and Bhutan, IMF 2002; Visiting Prof., Osmania Univ.; Visiting Faculty in Admin. Staff, Coll. of India; fmr Visiting Fellow, LSE, London, UK; currently Prof. Emer., Univ. of Hyderabad; Chair. Bank for Int. Settlements 2007–09, Asian Consultative Council 2007–09; fmr Chair. of South Asian Association for Regional Cooperation (SAARC) SAARCFINANCE; Founder mem. and mem. Bd of Govs Centre for Econ. and Social Studies; mem. Advisory Bd, Inst. for New Economic Thinking; Hon. Sr Fellow, Centre for Econ. and Social Studies, Hyderabad, Hon. Fellow, LSE 2008; Hon. DLitt (Sri Venkateswara Univ.), Hon. DCL (Univ. of Mauritius); Padma Vibhushan 2010. *Publications include:* India and the Global Financial Crisis: Managing Money and Finance 2008, Global Crisis, Recession and Uneven Recovery 2011; numerous publs on finance, planning and public enterprises. *Address:* Plot No. 297, Road No. 25, Jubilee Hills, Hyderabad 500 033, India (home). *Telephone:* (40) 23553292 (home). *E-mail:* yvenureddy@yahoo.com.

REDFORD, Alison, QC, MLA; Canadian lawyer and politician; b. 7 March 1965, Kitimat, BC; m. Glen Jermyn; one d.; ed Bishop Carroll High School, Calgary, Univ. of Saskatchewan Coll. of Law; worked as tech. adviser on constitutional and legal reform issues in various parts of Africa for EU, Commonwealth Secr., Canadian Govt and Govt of Australia 1990s; employed by Govt of Alberta as Communications Officer on Cttee for Justice Reform 1999; apptd by Sec.-Gen. of UN as one of four Int. Election Commrs to administer Afghanistan's first parl. elections held Sept. 2005; also assignments in Bosnia and Herzegovina, Serbia, Namibia, Uganda, Zimbabwe, Mozambique and the Philippines; managed a judicial training and legal reform project for Ministry of Justice and Supreme People's Court in Viet Nam; served as Sr Policy Advisor to Rt Hon. Joe Clark, Sec. of State for External Affairs and in Office of Prime Minister 1988–90; organized series of nat. foreign policy consultations facilitating input on Govt of Canada's White Papers on Foreign Affairs and Defence; MLA for Calgary-Elbow 2008–, mem. Cabinet Policy Cttee on Public Safety and Services and Standing Cttee for Private Bills; Minister of Justice and Attorney Gen. 2008–11; led Govt of Alberta's Safe Communities Secr. (SafeComm); Leader of Progressive Conserva-tive Ass[cn of Alberta Oct. 2011–; Premier of Alberta 2011–14 (resgnd); mem. Lycee Louis Pasteur Soc., Heritage Park Foundation, Calgary Winter Club; Progressive Conservative. *Address:* Constituency office, Suite 205, 5005 Elbow Drive SW, Calgary, AB T2S 2T6, Canada (office). *Telephone:* (403) 252-0346 (office). *Fax:* (403) 252-0520 (office). *E-mail:* calgary.elbow@assembly.ab.ca (office). *Website:* www .redford.mypcmla.ca (office).

REDFORD, (Charles) Robert, Jr; American actor and director; *President, Sundance Group;* b. 18 Aug. 1936, Santa Monica, Calif.; s. of Charles Robert Redford, Sr and Martha W. Redford (née Hart); m. 1st Lola Van Wegenen 1958 (divorced 1985); two s. (one s. died 1959) two d.; m. 2nd Sibylle Szaggars 2009; ed Van Nuys High School, Univ. of Colorado, Boulder, Pratt Inst. of Design, American Acad. of Dramatic Arts, New York; Founder and Pres. The Sundance Group 1981–, includes Sundance Channel, Sundance Ski Resort, Utah, Sundance Catalog, Sundance Cinemas, North Fork Preservation Alliance, and Sundance Inst., sponsor of Sundance Film Festival; Légion d'Honneur 2010; Hon. DHumLitt (Bard Coll.) 1995; hon. degrees from Univ. of Colorado, Boulder 1983, Brown Univ. 2008; Audubon Medal 1989, Dartmouth Film Soc. Award 1990, Screen Actors' Guild Award for Lifetime Achievement 1996, Hon. Acad. Award 2002, Kennedy Center Honor 2005, Americans for the Arts Lifetime Achievement Award 2009. *Films include:* Tall Story 1960, War Hunt 1961, Situation Hopeless But Not Serious 1965, Inside Daisy Clover 1965, The Chase 1965, This Property is Condemned 1966, Barefoot in the Park 1967, Tell Them Willie Boy is Here 1969, Butch Cassidy and the Sundance Kid 1969, Downhill Racer 1969, Little Fauss and Big Halsy 1970, Jeremiah Johnson 1972, The Candidate 1972, How to Steal a Diamond in Four Uneasy Lessons 1972, The Way We Were 1973, The Sting 1973, The Great Gatsby 1974, The Great Waldo Pepper 1974, Three Days of the Condor 1975, All the President's Men 1976, A Bridge Too Far 1977, Ordinary People (dir; Acad. Award and Golden Globe Award for Best Dir 1981) 1980, The Electric Horseman 1980, Brubaker 1980, The Natural 1984, Out of Africa 1985, Legal Eagles 1986, Milagro Beanfield War 1988 (also producer), Promised Land (exec. producer) 1988, Havana 1991, Sneakers 1992, A River Runs Through It (also dir) 1992, Quiz Show (dir) 1994, The River Wild 1995, Up Close and Personal 1996, The Horse Whisperer (also dir and producer) 1997, The Legend of Bagger Vance (also dir and producer) 2000, How to Kill Your Neighbour's Dog (exec. producer) 2000, The Last Castle 2001, Spy Game 2001, The Motorcycle Diaries (exec. producer) 2004, The Clearing 2004, Sacred Planet (narrator) 2004, An Unfinished Life 2005, Charlotte's Web (voice) 2006, The Unforeseen (exec. producer) 2006, Lions for Lambs (also dir) 2007, The Conspirator (dir) 2010, The Company You Keep (also producer and dir) 2012, All is Lost 2013. *Television includes:* Skinwalkers (exec. producer) 2002, Coyote Waits (exec. producer) 2003, A Thief of Time (exec. producer) 2004, Iconoclasts (documentary series) 2005–07. *Address:* c/o Sundance Institute, PO Box 684429, Park City, UT 84068 (office); c/o Sundance Institute, 8530 Wilshire Blvd, 3rd Floor, Beverly Hills, CA 90211-3114 (office); c/o David O'Conner, Creative Artists Agency, 9830 Wilshire Boulevard, Beverly Hills, CA 90212, USA (office). *Telephone:* (801) 328-3456 (Sundance) (office). *Fax:* (801) 575-5175 (Sundance) (office). *E-mail:* institute@sundance.org (office); la@sundance.org (office). *Website:* institute.sundance.org (office).

REDGRAVE, Sir Steven Geoffrey (Steve), Kt, CBE; British fmr oarsman; b. 23 March 1962, Marlow, Bucks., England; m. Elizabeth Ann Redgrave; one s. two d.; ed Marlow Comprehensive School; rep. UK at Jr World Championships 1979, 1980, silver medal (with Clift) rep. Marlow Rowing Club 1976–2000, Leander 1987–2000; stroke, British coxed four, gold medal winners, Los Angeles Olympic Games 1984; gold medals, single scull, coxless pair (with Andy Holmes) and coxed four, Commonwealth Games 1986, coxed pair (with Holmes), World Championships 1986; coxless pair gold medal and coxed pair silver medal (with Holmes), World Championships 1987; gold medal (with Holmes), coxless pair and bronze medal, coxed pair, Olympic Games, Seoul 1988; silver medal (with Simon Berrisford), coxless pairs, World Championships 1989; bronze medal, coxless pair (with Matthew Pinsent q.v.) World Championships, Tasmania 1990; gold medal, coxless pair (with Pinsent), World Championships, Vienna 1991; gold medal, Olympic Games, Barcelona 1992; gold medal, World Championships, Czech Repub. 1993; gold medal, Indianapolis, 1994; gold medal, Finland 1995; gold medal, Olympic Games, Atlanta 1996; gold medal, coxless four (with Pinsent, Foster, Cracknell), Aiguebelette 1997; gold medal, coxless four, Cologne 1998; gold medal, coxless four (with Pinsent, Coode, Cracknell), St Catherines 1999; gold medal, Olympic Games, Sydney 2000; holds record for most consecutive Olympic gold medals won in an endurance event (five); f. Sir Steve Redgrave Charitable Trust, Steve Redgrave Fund (with Comic Relief); Vice-Pres. SPARKS, Steward Henley Royal Regatta; active in raising money for children's charities; launched own Fairtrade Cotton Brand of Clothing, FiveG; Hon. Pres. Amateur Rowing Asscn; Hon. Vice-Pres. British Olympic Asscn, Diabetes UK; Hon. DCL (Durham) 1996, Hon. DSc 2001, (Buckingham) 2001, (Hull), Hon. DLitt (Reading, Nottingham), Hon. DUniv (Buckingham Chiltern, Heriot-Watt, Oxford Brookes, Open Univ.); Hon. DTech (Loughborough), Hon. LLD (Aberdeen) 2007; BBC Sports Personality of the Year 2000, British Sports Writers' Asscn Sportsman of the Year 2000, Laureus Lifetime Achievement Award 2001, BBC Golden Sports Personality 2003, BBC Sports Personality of the Year Lifetime Achievement Award 2011. *Publications:* Steven Redgrave's Complete Book of Rowing 1992, A Golden Age (autobiog., with Nick Townsend) 2000, You Can Win at Life! (with Nick Townsend) 2005. *Leisure interest:* golf, skiing. *Address:* c/o IMG, McCormack House, Hogarth Business Park, Burlington Lane, London, W4 2TH, England (office). *Telephone:* (20) 8233-5300 (office). *Fax:* (20) 8233-5301 (office). *E-mail:* katie.leggate@img.com (office). *Website:* www.img.com (office); www.steveredgrave.com.

REDGRAVE, Vanessa, CBE; British actress; b. 30 Jan. 1937; d. of the late Sir Michael Redgrave and Rachel Kempson; sister of the late Lynn Redgrave; m. Tony Richardson 1962 (divorced 1967, died 1991); two d.; one s. by Franco Nero; ed Queensgate School, London and Cen. School of Speech and Drama; actress 1957–; co-f. Moving Theatre 1974; mem. Workers' Revolutionary Party (Cand. for Moss Side 1979); Fellow, BFI 1988, BAFTA 2010; Chevalier, Légion d'Honneur; Dr hc (Mass.) 1990; Ibsen Centennial Award 2006. *Stage appearances include:* A Midsummer Night's Dream 1959, The Tiger and the Horse 1960, The Taming of the Shrew 1961, As You Like It 1961, Cymbeline 1962, The Seagull 1964, 1985, The Prime of Miss Jean Brodie 1966, Daniel Deronda 1969, Cato Street 1971, Threepenny Opera 1972, Twelfth Night 1972, Antony and Cleopatra 1973, 1986, Design for Living 1973, Macbeth 1975, Lady from the Sea 1976 and 1979 (Manchester), The Aspern Papers (Laurence Olivier Award 1984) 1984, Ghosts 1986, A Touch of the Poet 1988, Orpheus Descending 1988, A Madhouse in Goa 1989, The Three Sisters 1990, Lettice and Lovage 1991, When She Danced 1991, Isadora 1991, Heartbreak House 1992, The Master Builder 1992, Maybe 1993, The Liberation of Skopje 1995, John Gabriel Borkman 1996, The Cherry Orchard 2000, The Tempest 2000, Long Day's Journey into Night 2003; Dir and acted in Antony and Cleopatra, Houston, Tex. 1996, John Gabriel Borkman 1996, Song at Twilight 1999, Lady Windermere's Fan 2002, Long Day's Journey Into Night (Tony Award for Best Actress in a Play) 2003, The Year of Magical Thinking 2007, Driving Miss Daisy 2010. *Television includes:* Second Serve 1986, A Man for All Seasons 1988, Orpheus Descending 1990, Young Catherine 1991, What Ever Happened to Baby Jane? 1991, Great Moments in Aviation 1993, They 1993, Down Came a Blackbird 1995, The Wind in the Willows 1995, Two Mothers for Zachary 1996, The Willows in Winter 1996, Bella Mafia 1997, If These Walls Could Talk 2 (Emmy Award for Outstanding Lead Actress, Golden Globe Award for Best Supporting Actress) 2000, Jack and the Beanstalk: The Real Story 2001, The Gathering Storm (Broadcasting Press Guild Award for Best Actress) 2002, The Locket 2002, Byron 2003, Nip/Tuck (series) 2004–05, The Shell Seekers 2006, The Day of the Triffids (mini-series) 2009, Call the Midwife (voice) (series) 2012–13. *Films include:* Morgan—A Suitable Case for Treatment (Cannes Film Festival Award, Best Actress 1966) 1965, Sailor from Gibraltar 1965, Camelot 1967, Blow Up 1967, Charge of the Light Brigade 1968, Isadora (US Nat. Soc. of Film Critics Award) 1968, The Seagull 1968, A Quiet Place in the Country 1968, Dropout, The Trojan Women 1970, The Devils 1971, The Holiday 1971, Mary Queen of Scots 1971, Katherine Mansfield (BBC TV) 1973, Murder on the Orient Express 1974, Winter Rates 1974, 7% Solution 1975, Julia (Academy Award for Best Supporting Actress 1978) 1977, Agatha 1978, Yanks 1978, Bear Island 1979, Playing for Time (CBS TV) 1979, Playing for Time 1980, My Body My Child (ABC TV) 1981, Wagner 1982, The Bostonians 1983, Wetherby 1984, Prick Up Your Ears (New York Film Critics Circle Award for Best Supporting Actress) 1987, Comrades 1987, Consuming Passions 1988, King of the Wind 1989, Diceria dell'intore 1989, The Ballad of the Sad Cafe 1990, Howards End 1992, Breath of Life, The Wall, Sparrow, They, The House of the Spirits, Crime and Punishment, Mother's Boys, Little Odessa, A Month by the Lake 1996, Mission Impossible 1996, Looking for Richard 1997, Wilde 1997, Mrs Dalloway 1997, Bella Mafia (TV) 1997, Deep Impact 1998, Cradle Will Rock 2000, The Pledge 2001, The Gathering Storm (TV) 2002, Crime and Punishment 2002, The Fever 2004, The Keeper 2005, Short Order 2005, The White

Countess 2005, Thief Lord 2006, Venus 2006, How About You 2007, The Riddle 2007, Atonement (London Film Critics Circle Award for British Supporting Actress of the Year) 2007, Evening 2007, Gud, lukt och henne 2008, Letters to Juliet 2010, The Whistleblower 2010, Coriolanus 2011, Anonymous 2011, Song for Marion 2012, The Last Will and Testament of Rosalind Leigh 2012, The Butler 2013; produced and narrated documentary film The Palestinians 1977. *Publications:* Pussies and Tigers 1963, An Autobiography 1991. *Leisure interest:* changing the status quo. *Address:* c/o Gavin Barker Associates, 2d Wimpole Street, London, W1M 7AA, England (office).

REDHEAD, Michael Logan Gonne, PhD, FBA; British professor of philosophy; *Co-director, Centre for Philosophy of Natural and Social Science, London School of Economics;* b. 30 Dec. 1929, London, England; s. of Robert Arthur Redhead and Christabel Lucy Gonne Browning; m. Jennifer Anne Hill 1964 (died 2010); three s.; ed Westminster School, Univ. Coll. London; Prof. of Philosophy of Physics, Chelsea Coll., London 1984–85; King's Coll. London 1985–87; Prof. of History and Philosophy of Science, Cambridge Univ. 1987–97; Fellow, Wolfson Coll. Cambridge 1988–, Vice-Pres. 1992–96; Co-Dir Centre for Philosophy of Natural and Social Science, LSE 1998–, Centennial Prof. 1999–2002; Fellow, King's Coll. London 2000; Tarner Lecturer, Trinity Coll. Cambridge 1991–94; Visiting Fellow, All Souls Coll. Oxford 1995; Pres. British Soc. for Philosophy of Science 1989–91; Lakatos Award for Philosophy of Science 1988. *Publications:* Incompleteness, Nonlocality and Realism 1987, From Physics to Metaphysics 1995. *Leisure interests:* poetry, music, tennis. *Address:* Centre for Philosophy of Natural and Social Science, Lakatos Building, Room T111, London School of Economics, Houghton Street, London, WC2A 2AE (office); 119 Rivermead Court, London, SW6 3SD, England (home). *Telephone:* (20) 7955-6552 (office); (20) 7736-6767 (home). *Fax:* (20) 7955-6869 (office); (20) 7731-7627 (home). *E-mail:* mlr1000@cam.ac.uk (office). *Website:* www.lse.ac.uk/collections/CPNSS (office).

REDING, Viviane, PhD; Luxembourg journalist, politician and EU official; *Vice-President and Commissioner for Justice, Fundamental Rights and Citizenship, European Commission;* b. 27 April 1951, Esch-sur Alzette; ed Sorbonne, Paris; journalist, Luxemburger Wort 1978–99; mem. Parl. 1979–89; communal councillor, City of Esch 1981–99; Pres. Luxembourg Union of Journalists 1986–98; Nat. Pres. Christian-Social Women 1988–93; mem. European Parl. 1989–99; Pres. Cultural Affairs Cttee 1992–99; Vice-Pres. Parti Chrétien-Social 1995–99; Vice-Pres. Civil Liberties and Internal Affairs Cttee 1997–99; EU Commr for Educ. and Culture 1999–2004, for Information Soc. and Media 2004–10, Vice-Pres. EC and Commr for Justice, Fundamental Rights and Citizenship 2010–; mem. Benelux Parl., N Atlantic Ass. (Leader Christian Democrat/Conservative Group); Officier, Légion d'honneur; Dr hc (Hu Chen Univ. of Taiwan) 2004, (Genoa) 2004, (Turin) 2004; St George's Cross, Generalitat of Catalunya 1992, Gold Medal of European Merit 2001, Robert Schuman Medal 2004, Prince of Asturias Int. Co-operation Prize 2004, Gloria Artins Medal of Honour (Poland) 2005. *Address:* European Commission, 200 rue de la Loi, 1049 Brussels, Belgium (office). *Telephone:* (2) 298-16-00 (office). *Fax:* (2) 299-92-01 (office). *E-mail:* viviane.reding@ec.europa.eu (office). *Website:* ec.europa.eu/commission_2010-2014/reding/index_en.htm (office).

REDRADO, Martín; Argentine economist and fmr central banker; ed Harvard Univ., USA; fmrly with Salomon Brothers, USA; fmr Man. Dir Security Pacific Bank; Pres. Nat. Securities Comm. 1991; fmr Chair. Emerging Markets Cttee, Int. Org. of Securities Comms (IOSCO); est. Fundación Capital 1994, Chief Economist –2001; Sec. of State, Technological Educ. Section, Ministry of Educ. 1996; Sec. for Trade and Int. Econ. Relations 2002–04; Gov. Banco Central de la República Argentina 2004–10. *Publications include:* Cómo sobrevivir a la Globalización (How to Survive Globalization) 2002, Exportar para crecer (Exports for Growth) 2003. *Address:* c/o Banco Central de la República Argentina, Reconquista 266, C1003ABF Buenos Aires, Argentina (office).

REDSTONE, Sumner Murray, BA, LLB; American lawyer and business executive; *Executive Chairman, Viacom Inc.;* b. (Sumner Murray Rothstein), 27 May 1923, Boston; s. of Michael Redstone and Belle Redstone (neé Ostrovsky); m. Phyllis Redstone (divorced 2002); one s. one d.; ed Harvard Univ.; served as 1st Lt, US Army 1943–45; called to Bar of Mass. 1947; Special Asst to US Attorney-Gen., Washington, DC 1948–51; Pnr, Ford, Bergson, Adams, Borkland & Redstone (law firm), Washington, DC 1951–54; Pres. and CEO Nat. Amusements Inc., Dedham, Mass. 1967–, Chair. Bd 1986–87, Chair. Viacom Inc., New York 1987–2006, CEO 1996–2006, Exec. Chair. Viacom 2006–, Exec. Chair. CBS Corpn 2006–; Prof., Boston Univ. Law School 1982, 1985–86; Chair. Corp. Comm. on Education Tech. 1996–; mem. Corpn, New England Medical Center 1967–, Mass. Gen. Hosp.; Sponsor, Boston Museum of Science; mem. Bd of Dirs Boston Arts Festival, John F. Kennedy Library Foundation; mem. Nat. Asscn of Theatre Owners, Theatre Owners of America, Motion Picture Pioneers (mem. Bd of Dirs), Boston Bar Asscn, Mass. Bar Asscn; mem. Exec. Cttee Will Rogers Fund; mem. Bd of Overseers Boston Museum of Fine Arts; mem. Exec. Bd Combined Jewish Philanthropies; Hon. LLD (Boston Univ.) 1994; Hon. LHD (New York Inst. of Tech) 1996; Army Commendation Medal, Legends in Leadership Award, Emory Univ. 1995, Lifetime Achievement Award American Cancer Society 1995, Trustees Award Nat. Acad. of TV Arts and Sciences 1997, Robert F. Kennedy Memorial Ripple of Hope Award 1998, Int. Radio and TV Gold Medal Award 1998, Nat. Conf. of Christians and Jews Humanitarian Award 1998, numerous other awards. *Publications:* A Passion to Win (autobiog.) 2001. *Address:* Viacom Inc., 1515 Broadway, New York, NY 10036 (office); National Amusements Inc., 200 Elm Street, Dedham, MA 02026 (office); 98 Baldpate Hill Road, Newton, MA 02159, USA (home); CBS Corporation, 51 West 52nd Street, New York, NY 10019-6188 (office). *Telephone:* (212) 258-6000 (Viacom) (office); (212) 975-4321 (CBS) (office). *Fax:* (212) 258-6464 (Viacom) (office); (212) 975-4516 (CBS) (office). *Website:* www.viacom.com (office); www.national-amusements.com (office); www.cbscorporation.com (office).

REDWOOD, Rt Hon. John Alan, PC, MA, DPhil, CISI, IFA; British politician; b. 15 June 1951, Dover, Kent, England; s. of William Charles Redwood and Amy Emma Champion; m. Gail Felicity Chippington 1974 (divorced 2004); one s. one d.; ed Kent Coll., Canterbury and Magdalen and St Antony's Colls, Oxford; Fellow, All Souls Coll., Oxford 1972–85, 2003–05; Investment Adviser, Robert Fleming & Co. 1973–77; Dir (fmrly Man.) N.M. Rothschild & Sons 1977–87; Dir Norcros PLC 1985–89, Jt Deputy Chair. 1986–87, Chair. (non-exec.) 1987–89; Head, Prime

Minister's Policy Unit 1983–85; MP for Wokingham 1987–; Parl. Under-Sec. of State, Dept of Trade and Industry 1989–90, Minister of State 1990–92, Minister of State, Dept of Environment 1992–93; Sec. of State for Wales 1993–95; unsuccessful cand. for leadership of Conservative Party 1995; Opposition Front Bench Spokesman on Trade and Industry 1997–99, on the Environment 1999–2000; Shadow Sec. of State for Deregulation 2004–05; Chair. Econ. Policy Review, Conservative Party 2005–10; Chair. Concentric PLC 2002–07, Investment Cttee Evercore Pan Asset 2007–, Conservative Econ. Affairs Cttee 2010–; Visiting Prof., Univ. of Middlesex Business School; Parliamentarian of the Year Awards 1987, 1995, 1997, 2013. *Publications:* Reason, Ridicule and Religion 1976, Public Enterprise in Crisis 1980, Value for Money Audits (with J. Hatch) 1981, Controlling Public Industries (with J. Hatch) 1982, Going for Broke 1984, Equity for Everyman 1986, Popular Capitalism 1989, The Global Marketplace 1994, The Single European Currency (with others) 1996, Our Currency, Our Country 1997, The Death of Britain? 1999, Stars and Strife 2001, Just Say No 2001, Third Way – Which Way? 2002, Singing the Blues 2004, I Want to Make a Difference – But I Don't Like Politics 2006, After the Credit Crunch – No More Boom and Bust? 2008. *Leisure interests:* water sports, village cricket. *Address:* House of Commons, Westminster, London, SW1A 0AA, England (office). *Telephone:* (20) 7219-4205 (office). *Fax:* (20) 7219-0377 (office). *E-mail:* redwoodj@parliament.uk (office); john .redwood.mp@parliament.uk (office). *Website:* wwww.johnredwoodsdiary.com (office).

REED, Bruce; American government official; *Chief of Staff to Vice-President;* b. Coeur d'Alene, Ida; ed Princeton Univ., Univ. of Oxford, UK; served as chief speechwriter for US Senator Al Gore 1985–89; Policy Dir Democratic Leadership Council, Washington, DC 1990–91; Deputy Campaign Man. for Policy, Clinton-Gore Presidential Campaign 1992, then Asst to Pres. and Head of Domestic Policy Council 1997–2001; Pres. Democratic Leadership Council, Washington, DC 2001–11, also Ed.-in-Chief Blueprint (journal); Exec. Dir Nat. Comm. on Fiscal Responsibility and Reform (Bowles-Simpson Comm.) 2010; Chief of Staff to Vice-Pres. of the US, Washington, DC 2011–. *Publication:* The Plan: Big Ideas for Change in America (with Rahm Emanuel) 2009. *Address:* Office of the Vice-President, The White House, 1600 Pennsylvania Ave., NW, Washington, DC 20501, USA USA (office). *Telephone:* (202) 456-1414 (office). *Website:* www .whitehouse.gov/administration/vice-president-biden (office).

REED, Charles Bass, BS, MS, EdD; American academic and university administrator; *Chancellor, California State University System;* b. 29 Sept. 1941, Harrisburg, Pa; s. of the late Samuel Ross Reed and Elizabeth Johnson Reed; m. Catherine A. Sayers 1964; one s. one d.; ed George Washington Univ.; Asst Prof., then Assoc. Prof., George Washington Univ. 1963–70; Asst Dir Nat. Performance-based Teacher Educ. Project 1970–71; Co-ordinator, Research and Devt in Teacher Educ., Fla Dept of Educ. 1971–72, Assoc. for Planning and Co-ordination 1972–74, Dir Office of Educational Planning, Budgeting and Evaluation 1974–79; Educ. Policy Co-ordinator, Exec. Office of Fla Gov. Bob Graham 1979–80, Dir of Legis. Affairs 1980–81, Deputy Chief of Staff 1981–84, Chief of Staff 1984–85; Chancellor, State Univ. System of Fla 1985–98, Calif. State Univ. System 1998–; mem. Pres.'s Roundtable, Nat. Bd for Professional Teaching Standards 2005–, mem. Bd of Dirs Policy Consensus Initiative 2005–, ACT, Inc 2002–, Council for Higher Educ. Accreditation 2004–, Nat. Center for Educational Accountability 2002–,; Chair. Bd of Dirs Regional Tech. Strategies Inc.; Fulbright 50th Anniversary Distinguished Fellow, Peru 1996; mem. Council on Foreign Relations, Hispanic Asscn of Colls and Univs 1998–, Nat. Business-Higher Educ. Forum 1992–, American Council on Educ. (Joint Editorial Board 2003–),; mem. Advisory Cttee New Voters Project 2003–; mem. Exec. Advisory Council, Systems & Computer Tech. Corpn 1998–; Trustee Long Beach Memorial Medical Center 1998–; mem. Mayor's Blue Ribbon Task Force on Infrastructure, City of Los Angeles 2003, Nat. Alliance of Business 2001–03, Nat. Advisory Council, Hope for Kids 1995–98; Dr hc (Stetson Univ.) 1987, (George Washington Univ.) 1987, (St. Thomas Univ.) 1988, (Waynesburg Coll.) 1990, (Fla State Univ.) 1997, (British Open Univ.) 2000; George Washington Univ. Football Hall of Fame 1990, Floridian of the Year, Orlando Sentinel 1990, Southern Regional Education Bd's Lamar R. Plunkett Award 2001. *Address:* Office of the Chancellor, California State University System, 401 Golden Shore, Suite 641, Long Beach, CA 90802-4210, USA (office). *Telephone:* (562) 951-4700 (office). *Fax:* (562) 951-4986 (office). *E-mail:* creed@ calstate.edu (office). *Website:* www.calstate.edu (office).

REED, David Patrick, BS, MS, PhD; American computer scientist and academic; *Adjunct Professor of Media Arts and Sciences, Massachusetts Institute of Technology Media Laboratory;* b. 30 Jan. 1952, Portsmouth, Va; ed Massachusetts Inst. of Tech.; Asst Prof. of Computer Science and Eng, MIT Lab. for Computer Science –1983; apptd Vice-Pres. Research and Devt and Chief Scientist, Software Arts (creator of VisiCalc, the first electronic spreadsheet) 1983; spent seven years as Vice-Pres. and Chief Scientist for Lotus Development Corpn; spent four years at Interval Research Corpn; working at Viewpoints Research Inst. 2001–; Visiting Scientist, MIT Media Lab., Adjunct Prof. of Media Arts and Sciences 2002–; HP Fellow, Hewlett-Packard Labs 2003–; has acted as strategic adviser to small and large tech.-based businesses and consultant on advanced computing and communications tech.; has played key role on Advisory Bd of Vanguard research and advisory programme (now part of Technology Transfer Inst.); Fellow, Diamond Technology Pnrs Diamond Exchange Program; World Tech. Award in Communication Tech., The World Tech. Network 2004. *Achievements include:* pioneer in design and construction of internet protocols, distributed data storage and PC software systems and applications; co-inventor of the end-to-end argument, often called the fundamental architectural principle of the internet; discovered Reed's Law, a scaling law for group-forming network architectures; along with Metcalfe's Law, Reed's Law has significant implications for large-scale network business models. *Publications:* numerous scientific papers in professional journals on densely scalable, mobile and robust RF network architectures and highly decentralized systems architectures. *Address:* The Media Laboratory, Building E15-492, 77 Massachusetts Avenue, Cambridge, MA 02139-4307, USA (office). *Telephone:* (617) 253-6469 (office). *Fax:* (617) 258-6264 (office). *E-mail:* dpreed@mit.edu (office). *Website:* www.media.mit.edu (office); www.reed.com (office).

REED, Debra L., BEng; American business executive; *CEO, Sempra Energy;* ed Univ. of Southern California; Pres. San Diego Gas & Electric (SDG&E) and Chief Financial Officer SDG&E and Southern California Gas Co. (SoCalGas) –2004, Pres. and COO SDG&E and SoCalGas 2004–06, Pres. and CEO 2006–10, Exec. Vice-Pres. Sempra Energy –2011, Pres. and CEO 2011–; mem. Bd of Dirs Halliburton Co.; Chair. San Diego Regional Econ. Devt Corpn; mem. Advisory Council, Jacobs School of Eng, Univ. of California, San Diego, Precourt Energy Efficiency Center, Stanford; mem. The Trusteeship (affiliate of Int. Women's Forum); fmr mem. Bd of Dirs Genentech, Dominguez Services Corpn, Avery Dennison Corpn; fmr mem. Bd of Councilors, Univ. of Southern California; ranked by Fortune magazine amongst the 50 Most Powerful Women in Business in the US (45th) 2011, (39th) 2012. *Address:* Sempra Energy, 101 Ash Street, San Diego, CA 92101-3017, USA (office). *Telephone:* (619) 696-2000 (office). *E-mail:* info@www .sempra.com (office). *Website:* www.sempra.com (office).

REED, Ishmael Scott; American writer and poet; b. 22 Feb. 1938, Chattanooga, Tenn.; s. of Bennie S. Reed and Thelma Coleman; m. 1st Priscilla Rose 1960 (divorced 1970); two s.; m. 2nd Carla Blank; one d.; ed Univ. of Buffalo; Co-founder and Dir Reed, Cannon & Johnson Co. 1973–; Assoc. Fellow, Calhoun House, Yale Univ. 1982–; Founder (with Al Young) and Ed., Quilt magazine 1981; Guest Lecturer, Univ. of Calif., Berkeley 1968, then Sr Lecturer, now Lecturer Emer.; f. Konch Magazine 1998; mem. usage panel, American Heritage Dictionary; Assoc. Ed. American Book Review; Exec. Producer, Personal Problems (video soap opera); collaborator in multimedia Bicentennial mystery, The Lost State of Franklin (winner Poetry in Public Places contest 1975); Chair. Berkeley Arts Comm.; Advisory Chair. Co-ordinating Council of Literary Magazines; Pres. Before Columbus Foundation 1976–; Nat. Endowment for Arts Writing Fellow 1974; Guggenheim Fellow 1975; mem. Authors' Guild of America, PEN; Publr Konch magazine; Nat. Inst. of Arts and Letters Award 1975, Rosenthal Foundation Award 1975, Michaux Award 1978, ACLU Award 1978. *Publications include:* fiction: The Free-Lance Pallbearers 1967, Yellow Back Radio Broke Down 1969, Mumbo Jumbo 1972, The Last Days of Louisiana Red 1974, Flight to Canada 1976, The Terrible Twos 1982, Reckless Eyeballing 1986, Cab Calloway Stands in for the Moon 1986, The Terrible Threes 1989, Japanese By Spring 1993, Juice!, 2011; poetry: Catechism of a Neoamerican Hoodoo Church 1970, Conjure: Selected Poems 1963–1970 1972, Chattanooga 1973, A Secretary to the Spirits 1978, Calafia: The California Poetry (ed.) 1979, New and Collected Poems 1988, New and Collected Poems 1964–2006 2006; non-fiction: The Rise, Fall and…? of Adam Clayton Powell (with others) 1967, 19 Necromancers from Now (ed.) 1970, Yardbird Reader (five vols, ed.) 1971–77, Yardbird Lives! (ed., with Al Young) 1978, Shrovetide in Old New Orleans 1978, Quilt 2–3 (ed., with Al Young, two vols) 1981–82, God Made Alaska for the Indians 1982, Writin' is Fightin': Thirty-Seven Years of Boxing on Paper (ed.) 1988, Ishmael Reed: An Interview 1990, The Before Columbus Foundation Fiction Anthology: Selections from the American Book Awards 1980–1990 (ed., with Kathryn Trueblood and Shawn Wong) 1992, Airin' Dirty Laundry 1993, Multi-America 1996, The Reed Reader (ed.) 2000, Blues City: A Walk in Oakland 2003, Barack Obama and the Jim Crow Media 2010, Going Too Far: Essays About America's Nervous Breakdown 2012. *Address:* c/o Lowenstein Associates, 121 West 27th Street, Suite 501, New York, NY 10001, USA. *Telephone:* (212) 206-1630. *E-mail:* uncleish@aol.com. *Website:* www.ishmaelreed .org; www.ishmaelreedpub.com.

REED, John C., MD, PhD; American clinical scientist; *President and CEO, Professor and Donald Bren Presidential Chair, The Burnham Institute for Medical Research;* b. 11 Oct. 1958, New York; ed Univ. of Virginia, Univ. of Pennsylvania School of Medicine; Postdoctoral Fellow in Molecular Biology, Wistar Inst. of Anatomy and Biology, Philadelphia 1986–88; Resident in Clinical Pathology, Dept of Pathology and Lab. Medicine, Univ. of Pennsylvania Hosp. 1986–89, Research Assoc., Dept of Pathology and Laboratory Medicine, Univ. of Pennsylvania 1988–89, Asst Prof. 1989–92, Asst Dir Lab. of Molecular Diagnosis, Univ. of Pennsylvania Hosp. 1989–92; Dir Oncogene and Tumor Suppressor Gene Program, The Burnham Inst. for Medical Research, La Jolla, Calif. 1992–95, then Assoc. Prof. and Leader Apoptosis and Cell Death Research Program, Scientific Dir Burnham Inst. 1995–2003, Deputy Dir NCI Cancer Center 1994–2003, Pres. and CEO The Burnham Inst. 2003–, also Prof. and Donald Bren Presidential Chair; Assoc. mem. Univ. of California, San Diego Cancer Center 1993–; Adjunct Prof., Dept of Biology, San Diego State Univ. 1996–; Adjunct Prof., Dept of Molecular Pathology, Univ. of California, San Diego School of Medicine 1997–; Chair. Translational Apoptosis Research Cttee for Prostate Cancer, CaP-CURE 1999–; mem. Advisory Cttee, Specialized Center of Research on Leukemia and Lymphoma, Univ. of California, San Diego 2001–; mem. Editorial Bd Antisense Research and Development 1993–96, Oncology Reports 1993–99, Cell Death and Differentiation 1994–99, Clinical Cancer Research 1994–99, Molecular Carcinogenesis 1994–, Cancer Gene Therapy 1994–, Advances in Leukemia and Lymphoma 1995–, Cancer Research 1995–, Journal of Inflammation 1996–97, Receptors and Signal Transduction 1996–98, Molecular and Cellular Differentiation 1996–98, Journal of Immunology 1996–98, Journal of Clinical Investigation 1996–, Antisense and Nucleic Acid Drug Development 1996–, Frontiers in Bioscience 1996–, Journal of Biological Chemistry 1996–, BLOOD 1997–, Current Opinion in Oncologic and Endocrine and Metabolic Drugs 1998–2000, Neoplasia 1998–, International Journal of Oncology 1998–, Tumor Targeting 1999–, Nature Reviews 2000–, Current Opinion in Investigational Drugs 2000–, Expert Opinion on Therapeutic Targets 2001–, Cell Cycle 2001–; William R. Drell Chair in Molecular Biology 1995; mem. AAAS 1981, American Soc. for Microbiology 1986, American Asscn for Cancer Research 1990, American Asscn of Univ. Pathologists 1991, Acad. of Clinical Lab. Physicians and Scientists 1991–93, Eastern Cooperative Oncology Group 1991, Clinical Cancer Research 1992, American Hematology Soc. 1992, CALGB 1994, American Soc. for Investigative Pathology 1995, Fed. of American Socs for Experimental Biology 1996, Int. Forum for Corp. Dir 1998; Presidential Award, Reticuloendothelial Soc. 1985, Sheard Stanford Award, American Soc. of Clinical Pathologists 1985, Upjohn Achievement Award 1986, Stohlman Memorial Scholar Award, Leukemic Soc. of America 1994, Local Hero in the Fight Against Breast Cancer Award, Susan G. Komen Foundation 1998, 1st Inaugural D. Wayne Calloway Memorial Lecturer, Memorial Sloan-Kettering Cancer Center 1999, 35th Annual Harold G. Pritzker Memorial Lecture Presenter, Mount Sinai Hosp., Univ. of Toronto 1999, ranked

No. 1 Hottest Researcher in Life Sciences WorldWide Inst. for Scientific Information 1999, 2000, 2000 Decade of the Brain Award, American Acad. of Neurology 2000, Warner-Lambert/Parke Davis Award, American Soc. for Investigative Pathology 2000, Harry B. Van Dyke Award, Columbia Univ. 2001. *Publications:* more than 750 articles in scientific journals. *Address:* The Burnham Institute for Medical Research, 10901 N Torrey Pines Road, La Jolla, CA 92037, USA (office). *Telephone:* (858) 795-5301 (office). *Fax:* (858) 646-3199 (office). *E-mail:* president@burnham.org (office). *Website:* www.burnham.org (office).

REED, John Francis (Jack), BS, JD; American politician; *Senator from Rhode Island;* b. 12 Nov. 1949, Cranston, RI; s. of Joseph Reed and Mary Monahan; m. Julia Hart; one d.; ed LaSalle Acad., Providence, RI, US Mil. Acad., Kennedy School of Govt, Harvard Univ.; commissioned, 2nd Lt US Army 1971, served with 82nd Airborne Div. 1973–77; Asst Prof., US Mil. Acad., West Point, NY 1977–79; resgnd from Army 1979; called to the Bar, DC 1982, Rhode Island 1983; Assoc. Sutherland, Asbill & Brennan, Washington, DC 1982–83, Edwards & Angelli, Providence 1983–89; mem. RI State Senate 1984–90; mem. 102–104th US Congresses 1990–96; Senator from Rhode Island 1996–, mem. Appropriations Cttee, Armed Services Cttee, sr mem. Banking, Housing and Urban Affairs Cttee; Vice-Chair. NE-Midwest Congressional Coalition; Democrat. *Leisure interests:* reading, hiking. *Address:* 728 Hart Senate Office Building, Washington, DC 20510, USA (office). *Telephone:* (202) 224-4642 (office). *Fax:* (202) 224-4680 (office). *Website:* reed.senate.gov (office).

REED, John Shepard, MS; American business executive; b. 7 Feb. 1939, Chicago; m. 1st (divorced), four c.; m. 2nd Cindy McCarthy 1994; ed Washington and Jefferson Coll., Mass Inst. of Tech., Alfred P. Sloan School of Man. (MIT); served with US Army Eng Corps, Korea; fnr Trainee Goodyear Tire & Rubber; joined Citicorp/Citibank 1965, fmrly responsible for operating group, consumer business, fmr Sr Vice-Pres., Chair. and Chief Exec. 1984–98; Jt Chair. and CEO Citigroup (merger between Citicorp and Travelers Group) 1998–2000; Interim Chair. NY Stock Exchange (NYSE) 2003 then Chair. 2004–05; Chair. Coalition of Service Industries, Services Policy Advisory Cttee to the US Trade Rep.; mem. Bd of Dirs Altria Group Inc. (fmly Philip Morris Inc.) 1979–2003, 2004–, Manpower Demonstration Research Corpn; fmr mem. Bd of Dirs Monsanto Co.; mem. Business Council, Business Roundtable Policy Cttee; mem. Corpn of MIT; fmr mem. Bd Memorial Sloan-Kettering Cancer Center, Rand Corpn, Spencer Foundation, American Museum of Natural History; Trustee Center for Advanced Studies in Social and Behavioral Sciences. *Address:* c/o Board of Directors, Altria Group Inc., 120 Park Avenue, New York, NY 10017, USA (office).

REED, Joseph Verner, BA; American diplomatist and UN official; *Special Adviser to the Secretary-General, United Nations;* b. 17 Dec. 1937, Greenwich, Conn.; s. of Joseph Verner Reed and Permelia Pryor; m. Marie Byers 1959; two d.; ed Yale Univ.; Pvt. Sec. to Pres., World Bank 1961–63; Asst to Dir, Chase Manhattan Bank 1963–68, Vice-Pres. and Exec. Asst to Chair. 1969–81; Amb. to Morocco 1981–85; US Rep., UN Econ. and Social Council 1985–87, Under-Sec.-Gen. for Political and Gen. Ass. Affairs 1987–89, Under-Sec.-Gen. and Special Rep. for Public Affairs 1992–97, Under-Sec.-Gen. and Pres., Staff-Man. Coordination Cttee 1997–2004, Under-Sec.-Gen. and Special Adviser to the Sec.-Gen. 2005–; Chief of Protocol to Pres. George Bush, White House 1989–91. *Address:* Office of the Secretary-General, UN Headquarters, First Avenue at 46th Street, New York, NY 10017, USA (office). *Website:* www.un.org (office).

REEDER, Franklin S., BA; American consultant and fmr government official; *President, The Reeder Group;* b. 25 Oct. 1940, Philadelphia, Pa; s. of the late Simon Reeder and Hertha Strauss; m. Anna Marie Seroski 1962; one s. two d.; ed Univ. of Pennsylvania and George Washington Univ.; with US Treasury Dept 1961–64; Defense Dept 1964–70; Office of Man. and Budget, Exec. Office of Pres. of USA 1970–71, 1980–97, Dir 1995–97; currently Pres. The Reeder Group; Deputy Dir House Information System, US House of Reps 1971–80; fmr Chair. Computer Systems Security and Privacy Advisory Bd (now Information Security and Privacy Advisory Bd), Nat. Inst. of Standards and Tech. (NIST); Chair. Center for Internet Security; columnist and Contributing Ed. Government Executive magazine; Fellow, Nat. Acad. of Public Admin; Hon. Certified Information Security Man. (CISM) 2003; numerous awards including Presidential Rank Award as Meritorious Sr Exec.; mem. Govt Computer News Information Resources Man. Hall of Fame. *Leisure interests:* running, swimming, bicycling, watching baseball. *Address:* The Reeder Group, 3200 N Nottingham Street, Arlington, VA 22207 (office); c/o The Center for Internet Security, POB 433, Hershey, PA 17033, USA. *Telephone:* (703) 536-6635 (office). *Fax:* (703) 536-1774 (office). *E-mail:* reeder@bellatlantic.net. *Website:* csrc.nist.gov/ispab; www.cisecurity.org.

REES, Sir Dai (David Allan), Kt, PhD, DSc, FIBiol, FRSC, FRS; British scientist and academic (retd); b. 28 April 1936, Silloth, Cumbria; s. of James A. Rees and Elsie Bolam; m. Myfanwy Owen 1959; two s. one d.; ed Hawarden Grammar School, Clwyd and Univ. Coll. of North Wales, Bangor; joined staff at Univ. of Edin. 1960, Asst Lecturer in Chem. 1961, Lecturer 1962–70, Section Man. 1970–72; Prin. Scientist, Unilever Research, Colworth Lab. 1972–82; Assoc. Dir (part-time) MRC Unit for Cell Biophysics Kings Coll., London 1980–82; Dir Nat. Inst. for Medical Research 1982–87; Sec., then Chief Exec. MRC 1987–96, MRC scientist 1996; Chair. European Medical Research Councils 1989, Pres. European Science Foundation 1994–2001; Visiting Professorial Fellow, Univ. Coll., Cardiff 1972–77; mem. Royal Soc. Council 1985–87; Hon. FRCP 1986; Hon. FRCPE 1998; Hon. Fellow, King's Coll., London 1989, Univ. Coll. of N Wales 1988; Hon. DSc (Edin.) 1989, (Wales) 1991, (Stirling) 1995, (Leicester) 1997, (York) 2007; Colworth Medal, Biochemical Soc. 1970, Carbohydrate Award, Chemical Soc. 1970, Philips Lecturer, Royal Soc. 1984. *Publications:* articles on carbohydrate biochemistry and cell biology. *Leisure interests:* river cruising, reading, listening to music. *Address:* Ford Cottage, 1 High Street, Denford, Kettering, Northants., NN14 4EQ, England. *E-mail:* drees@nimr.mrc.ac.uk.

REES, Roger; British actor; b. 5 May 1944, Aberystwyth, Wales; ed Camberwell and Slade Schools of Art; with RSC 1967–; Assoc. Dir Bristol Old Vic Theatre Co. 1986–. *Stage appearances include:* Hindle Wakes 1964, The Taming of the Shrew, Othello, Major Barbara, Macbeth, Twelfth Night, The Suicide, The Adventures of Nicholas Nickleby, Hapgood, Hamlet, Love's Labours Lost, The Real Thing, Double Double (also writer), Indiscretions, The End of the Day. *Film appearances*

include: Star 80 1983, God's Outlaw 1986, Mountains of the Moon 1990, If Looks Could Kill 1991, Stop! Or My Mom Will Shoot 1992, Robin Hood: Men in Tights 1993, The Substance of Fire 1996, Sudden Manhattan 1997, Trouble on the Corner 1997, Next Stop Wonderland 1998, A Midsummer Night's Dream 1999, The Bumblebee Flies Away 1999, BlackMale 2000, 3 A.M. 2001, Return to Never Land (voice) 2002, The Scorpion King 2002, Frida 2002, The Emperor's Club 2002, Crazy Like a Fox 2003, Garfield 2 (voice) 2006, The Prestige 2006, The Treatment 2006, East Broadway 2007, The Invasion 2007. *Television appearances include:* Under Western Eyes 1975, Bouquet of Barbed Wire (mini-series) 1976, The Comedy of Errors 1978, Macbeth 1979, The Voysey Inheritance 1979, The Adventures of Nicholas Nickleby (mini-series) 1982, Saigon: The Year of the Cat 1983, A Christmas Carol 1984, The Ebony Tower 1984, The Return of Sam McCloud 1989, Imaginary Friends (mini-series) 1987, The Modern World: Ten Great Writers (mini-series) 1988, Singles (series) 1988–89, The Finding 1990, Charles and Diana: Unhappily Ever After 1992, The Tower 1993, M.A.N.T.I.S (series) 1994, The Possession of Michael D. 1995, Cheers 1989–91, Boston Common (series) 1996, Titanic 1996, LIBERTY! The American Revolution (mini-series) 1997, Damian Cromwell's Postcards from America (series) 1997, The Crossing 2000, Double Platinum 1999, The West Wing 2000–05, Grey's Anatomy 2007.

REES OF LUDLOW, Baron (Life Peer), cr. 2005, of Ludlow in the County of Shropshire; **Martin John Rees,** OM, MA, PhD, FRS; British astronomer and academic; *Astronomer Royal;* b. 23 June 1942, York, Yorks., England; s. of Reginald J. Rees and Joan Rees; m. Caroline Humphrey 1986; ed Shrewsbury School and Trinity Coll., Cambridge; Fellow, Jesus Coll., Cambridge 1967–69; Research Assoc. Calif. Inst. of Tech. 1967–68, 1971; mem. Inst. for Advanced Study, Princeton 1969–70, Prof. 1982–96; Visiting Prof., Harvard Univ. 1972, 1986–87; Prof., Univ. of Sussex 1972–73; Plumian Prof. of Astronomy and Experimental Philosophy, Univ. of Cambridge 1973–91, Royal Soc. Research Prof. 1992–2002, Prof. of Cosmology and Astrophysics 2004–09, now Prof. Emer.; Astronomer Royal 1995–; Master, Trinity Coll., Cambridge 2004–12; Fellow, King's Coll., Cambridge 1969–72, 1973–2003; Visiting Prof., Imperial Coll., London 2001–, Univ. of Leicester 2001–; Dir Inst. of Astronomy 1977–82, 1987–91; Regents Fellow, Smithsonian Inst., Washington, DC 1984–88; mem. Council of Royal Soc. 1983–85, 1993–95, Pres. 2005–10; mem. Council of Royal Inst. of GB –2010; Pres. Royal Astronomical Soc. 1992–94, BAAS 1994–95, Asscn for Science Educ. 2012–; Trustee, British Museum 1996–2002, Inst. for Advanced Study, Princeton, USA 1998–, Nat. Endowment for Sciences, Tech. and Arts 1998–2001, Kennedy Memorial Trust 1999–2004, Inst. for Public Policy Research 2001; Foreign Assoc. NAS; mem. Academia Europaea 1989, Pontifical Acad. of Sciences 1990; Foreign mem. American Philosophical Soc., Royal Swedish Acad. of Science, Russian Acad. of Sciences, Norwegian Acad. of Arts and Science, Accad. Lincei (Rome), Royal Netherlands Acad., Finnish Acad. of Arts and Sciences; mem. (Crossbench) House of Lords 2005–; Hon. Fellow, Trinity Coll., Darwin Coll. and Jesus Coll., Cambridge, Indian Acad. of Sciences, Univ. of Wales, Cardiff 1998, Inst. of Physics 2001, British Acad.; Foreign Hon. mem. American Acad. of Arts and Sciences; Officier, Ordre des Arts et des Lettres; Hon. DSc (Sussex) 1990, (Leicester) 1993, (Copenhagen, Keele, Uppsala, Newcastle) 1995, (Toronto) 1997, (Durham) 1999, (Oxford) 2003, (Yale) 2008, (McMaster) 2009; Heinemann Prize, American Inst. of Physics 1984, Gold Medal (Royal Astronomical Soc.) 1987, Guthrie Medal, Inst. of Physics 1989, Balzan Prize 1989, Robinson Prize for Cosmology 1990, Bruce Medal, Astronomical Soc. of Pacific 1993, Science Writing Award, American Inst. of Physics 1996, Bower Award, Franklin Inst. 1998, Rossi Prize, American Astronomical Soc. 2000, Cosmology Prize of Peter Gruber Foundation 2001, Einstein Award, World Cultural Congress 2003, Michael Faraday Prize 2004, Crafoord Prize, Royal Swedish Acad. (jtly) 2005, Niels Bohr Medal, UNESCO 2005, Caird Medal, Nat. Maritime Museum 2007, BBC Reith Lecturer 2010, Templeton Prize 2011, Newton Prize, Inst. of Physics 2012, Asteroid 4587 Rees named after him. *Achievements include:* his studies of the distribution of quasars led to final disproof of Steady State Theory. *Television:* What We Still Don't Know (documentary series, Channel 4) 2004. *Publications:* Perspectives in Astrophysical Cosmology 1995, Gravity's Fatal Attraction (with M. Begelman) 1995, Before the Beginning 1997, Just Six Numbers 1999, Our Cosmic Habitat 2001, Our Final Century? 2003, From Here to Infinity: Scientific Horizons 2011; edited books; more than 500 articles and reviews in scientific journals on the origin of the cosmic microwave background radiation, as well as on galaxy clustering and formation, and numerous gen. articles. *Address:* Trinity College, Cambridge, CB2 1TQ (office); Institute of Astronomy, Madingley Road, Cambridge, CB3 0HA, England (office). *Telephone:* (1223) 338412 (office). *E-mail:* mjr@ast.cam.ac.uk (office). *Website:* www.ast.cam.ac.uk/IoA/staff/mjr (office).

REESE, Colin Bernard, MA, PhD, ScD, FRS; British chemist and academic; *Professor Emeritus of Chemistry, King's College London;* b. 29 July 1930, Plymouth, Devon, England; s. of the late Joseph Reese and Emily Reese; m. Susanne L. Bird 1968; one s. one d.; ed Dartington Hall School and Clare Coll., Cambridge; Research Fellow, Clare Coll. 1956–59, Harvard Univ., USA 1957–58; Official Fellow and Dir of Studies in Chem., Clare Coll. 1959–73; Univ. Demonstrator in Chem., Univ. of Cambridge 1959–63, Asst Dir of Research 1963–64, Univ. Lecturer in Chem. 1964–73; Daniell Prof. of Chem., King's Coll. London 1973–98, Fellow 1989–, Prof. of Organic Chem. 1999–2003, Prof. Emer. 2003–. *Publications:* scientific papers mainly in chem. journals. *Address:* 21 Rozel Road, London, SW4 0EY, England. *Telephone:* (20) 7498-0230. *E-mail:* colin.reese@kcl.ac.uk (office); reese156@btinternet.com (home).

REESE, Stuart Harry, BA, MBA; American business executive; *Chairman and CEO, C.M. Life Insurance Company;* b. 3 May 1955, Richmond, Va; s. of Allison Reese and Virginia Saul; m. Elizabeth Garr 1976; three d. one s.; ed Gettysburg Coll., Dartmouth Coll.; Securities Analyst Aetna 1979–81, Sr Securities Analyst 1981–82, Dir Treas. Investment Planning 1982–83, Sr Investment Officer 1983–84, Asst Vice-Pres. 1984–85, Man. Dir 1985–89, Vice-Pres., Man. Dir Capital Markets 1989–93; Chair. and CEO Babson Capital Man., Massachusetts Mutual Life Insurance Co. (MassMutual) 1993–99, Exec. Vice-Pres. and Chief Investment Officer Massachusetts Mutual Life Insurance Co. (MassMutual) 1999–2005, Pres. 2005–08, CEO 2005–09, Chair. 2007–09, Chair. Exec. Cttee, mem. Corp. Governance Cttee, Investment and Operations Cttee, Chair. (non-exec.) MassMutual Jan.–Dec. 2010, Chair. and CEO C.M. Life Insurance Co. (subsidiary) 2011–; fmr Chair. Advisory Bd LRN-RAND Center for Corp. Ethics, Law and Governance;

mem. Bd of Trustees Gettysburg Coll.; fmr mem. Bd American Council of Life Insurers, Fed. Reserve Bank of Boston, Massachusetts Gov.'s Council of Econ. Advisors. *Address:* C.M. Life Insurance Company, 100 Bright Meadow Boulevard, Enfield, CT 06082, USA (office). *Telephone:* (413) 788-8411 (MassMutual) (office). *Fax:* (413) 744-6005 (MassMutual) (office). *E-mail:* info@massmutual.com (office). *Website:* www.massmutual.com (office).

REETZ, Manfred T., BA, MS, PhD; German chemist and academic; *Hans Meerwein Research Professor, Philipps-Universität Marburg;* b. 13 Aug. 1943, Hirschberg; ed Washington Univ., St Louis, Mo., Univ. of Michigan, Ann Arbor, USA, Göttingen Univ.; Postdoctoral Fellow, Univ. Marburg 1971–72, Asst Prof. 1973–78, Prof. 1980–91; Guest Prof., Univ. of Wisconsin, Madison, USA 1978; Assoc. Prof., Univ. of Bonn 1978–80; Guest Prof., Florida State Univ. 1991–; Dir Max-Planck-Institut für Kohlenforschung 1991–2002, Man. Dir 1993–2002, External (Emer.) Group Leader 2011–, Chair. Studiengesellschaft Kohle mbH 1993–2011; Hans Meerwein Research Prof., Philipps-Universität Marburg 2011–; mem. Advisory Bd, Inst. für Organische Katalyseforschung, Rostock 1993–; Catalysis Nat. Research School Combination (NRSC), Leeuwenhorst, Netherlands 1999–2000; mem. Int. Advisory Bd, Chem. Dept, Nagoya Univ. 2006–07; Senator, Chem. Section, Deutsche Akad. der Naturforscher Leopoldina 2007–11; Associate Ed. Chemistry and Biology 2009–; mem. Editorial Advisory Bd Nachrichten aus Chemie, Technik und Laboratorium 1994–99, Topics in Organometalic Chemistry 1997–, Advanced Synthesis and Catalysis 2000–05, Russian Journal of Organic Chemistry 2000–, Bulletin of the Chemical Society of Japan 2005–; mem. Advisory Bd, Topics in Stereochemistry 2006–, Karl-Ziegler-Foundation 2010–; mem. German Chemical Soc. (Dir 1990–95, Vice-Pres. 1995); mem. Deutsche Akad. der Naturforscher Leopoldina 1997, Nordrheinwestfälischen Akad. der Wissenschaften 2001; Foreign mem. Royal Netherlands Acad. of Arts and Sciences 2005; Hon. Prof., Ruhr-Univ. Bochum 1992–2010, Shanghai Inst. of Organic Chem. 2007; Chemical Industries Prize 1976, Jacobus van't Hoff Prize 1977, Chem. Prize, Göttingen Acad. of Sciences 1978, Otto-Bayer Prize 1986, Leibniz Prize, Deutsche Forschungsgemeinschaft 1989, Nagoya Gold Medal of Organic Chem. 2000, Hans Herloff Inhoffen Medal 2003, Cliff S. Hamilton Award in Organic Chem. (USA) 2005, Karl-Ziegler-Prize, German Chemical Soc. 2005, Ernst Hellmut Vits-Prize 2006, Prelog Medal (Switzerland) 2006, Ruhr-Prize for Arts and Science 2007, Lilly Distinguished Lectureship Award 2009, ACS Arthur C. Cope Award 2009, Yamada-Koga Prize (Japan) 2009, Tetrahedron Prize for Creativity in Organic Chem. 2011, Otto-Hahn-Prize 2011. *Publications:* numerous scientific papers in professional journals. *Address:* Room E 5238, Chemistry Building, Philipps-Universität Marburg, Hans-Meerwein-Straße 4, 35032 Marburg, Germany (office). *Telephone:* (6421) 2825500 (office). *Fax:* (6421) 2825620 (office). *E-mail:* reetz@mpi-muelheim.mpg.de (office). *Website:* www.uni-marburg .de/fb15/fachgebiete-en/organisch/prof-dr-dr-h-c-manfred-t-reetz (office). www .kofo.mpg.de/en/research/organic-synthesis (office).

REEVE, Sir Anthony, Kt, KCMG, KCVO, BA, MA; British business executive and diplomatist (retd); *Chairman, The Curzon Corporation;* b. 20 Oct. 1938, Wakefield, W Yorks., England; s. of Sidney Reeve and Dorothy Reeve (née Mitchell); m. 1st Pamela Margaret Angus 1964 (divorced 1988); one s. two d.; m. 2nd Susan Doull (née Collins) 1997; ed Queen Elizabeth Grammar School, Wakefield, Marling School, Stroud, Open Univ., Merton Coll., Oxford; joined Lever Bros and Assocs 1962–65; entered Diplomatic Service 1965, with Middle East Centre for Arab Studies 1966–68, Asst Political Agent, Abu Dhabi 1968–70, First Sec., FCO 1970–73, First Sec., later Counsellor, Embassy in Washington, DC 1973–78, Head of Arms Control and Disarmament Dept, FCO 1979–81, Counsellor, Embassy in Cairo 1981–84, Head of Southern Africa Dept, FCO 1984–86, Asst Under-Sec. of State 1986–88, Amb. to Jordan 1988–91, Amb. to, later High Commr in South Africa 1991–96; Dir (non-exec.) Barclays Pvt. Bank 1997–2001; Chair. The Curzon Corpn 1998–. *Leisure interests:* music, golf. *Address:* Box Tree Cottage, Horsley, Stroud, Glos., GL6 0QB, England. *Telephone:* (1453) 832891. *E-mail:* anthony.reeve@btinternet.com.

REEVE, Michael David, MA, FBA; British academic; *Emeritus Fellow, Pembroke College, Cambridge;* b. 11 Jan. 1943, Bolton, Lancs., England; s. of Arthur Reeve and Edith Mary Barrett; m. Elizabeth Klingaman 1970 (divorced 1999); two s. one d.; one s. with Emma Gee; ed King Edward's School, Birmingham, Balliol Coll., Oxford; Harmsworth Sr Scholar, Merton Coll., Oxford 1964–65; Woodhouse Research Fellow, St John's Coll., Oxford 1965–66; Tutorial Fellow, Exeter Coll., Oxford 1966–84, Emer. Fellow 1984–; Kennedy Prof. of Latin, Univ. of Cambridge 1984–2006, Dir of Research, Faculty of Classics 2006–07, Fellow, Pembroke Coll. 1984–2007, Emer. Fellow 2008–; Visiting Prof., Univ. of Hamburg 1976, McMaster Univ. 1979, Univ. of Toronto 1982–83; Ed. Classical Quarterly 1981–86; Ed.-in-Chief Cambridge Classical Studies –2007, Cambridge Classical Texts and Commentaries 1984–; Chair. Advisory Council, Warburg Inst. 2008–13; Sandars Reader in Bibliography 2012; Corresp. mem. Akad. der Wissenschaften, Göttingen 1990–; Foreign mem. Istituto Lombardo, Milan 1993–. *Publications:* Longus, Daphnis and Chloe 1982, contributions to Texts and Transmission 1983, Cicero, Pro Quinctio 1992, Vegetius 2004, Geoffrey of Monmouth 2007, Manuscripts and Methods 2011; articles in European and American journals. *Leisure interests:* chess, music, gardening, mountain walking. *Address:* Pembroke College, Cambridge, CB2 1RF, England. *Fax:* (1223) 335409 (office). *E-mail:* mdr1000@cam.ac.uk (office).

REEVES, Keanu; Canadian actor; b. 2 Sept. 1964, Beirut, Lebanon; s. of Samuel Nowin Reeves and Patricia Reeves; ed Toronto High School for Performing Arts; training at Second City Workshop, Toronto; Toronto stage debut in Wolf Boy; other stage appearances in For Adults Only, Romeo and Juliet; bass guitarist, rock band Dogstar 1996–2002. *Television films:* Letting Go 1985, Act of Vengeance 1986, Babes in Toyland 1986, Under the Influence 1986, Brotherhood of Justice 1986, Save the Planet (TV special) 1990. *Films:* Prodigal, Flying 1986, Youngblood 1986, River's Edge 1987, Permanent Record 1988, The Night Before 1988, The Prince of Pennsylvania 1988, Dangerous Liaisons 1988, 18 Again 1988, Bill and Ted's Excellent Adventure 1988, Parenthood 1989, I Love You to Death 1990, Tune In Tomorrow 1990, Bill and Ted's Bogus Journey 1991, Point Break 1991, My Own Private Idaho 1991, Bram Stoker's Dracula 1992, Much Ado About Nothing 1993, Even Cowgirls Get the Blues, Little Buddha 1993, Speed 1994, Johnny Mnemonic 1995, A Walk in the Clouds 1995, Chain Reaction, Feeling Minnesota, The Devil's

Advocate 1996, The Last Time I Committed Suicide 1997, The Matrix 1999, The Replacements 2000, The Watcher 2000, The Gift 2000, Sweet November 2001, The Matrix Reloaded 2003, The Matrix Revolutions 2003, Something's Gotta Give 2003, Thumbsucker 2005, Constantine 2005, A Scanner Darkly 2006, The Lake House 2006, Street Kings 2008, The Day the Earth Stood Still 2008, The Private Lives of Pippa Lee 2009, Henry's Crime 2010. *Address:* c/o Kevin Houvane, CAA, 9830 Wilshire Boulevard, Beverly Hills, CA 90212-1825; 581 North Crescent Heights Boulevard, Los Angeles, CA 90048, USA.

REFALO, Michael A., BA, LLD, FRSA; Maltese politician, lawyer and diplomatist; b. 25 Feb. 1936; s. of Edward Refalo; m. Blanche Smith; one s. three d.; ed St Aloysius Coll., Univ. of Malta; lawyer 1961; fmr Pres. of Students' Council; MP 1971–; Parl. Sec. for Tourism 1987–94; Minister for Youth and the Arts 1994–95, for Justice and the Arts 1995–96; Shadow Minister and Opposition Spokesman on Tourism 1996–98; Minister for Tourism 1998–2005; High Commr to UK 2005–09; currently bringing several state and pvt. cos together to work on promoting a corp. image for Malta; Ed. for nine years of Sunday Nationalist Party newspaper; mem. Nationalist Party; Companion of Honour, Nat. Order of Merit 2007. *Publications:* editorials and articles in other newspapers. *Address:* c/o Ministry of Foreign Affairs, Palazzo Parisio, Merchants Street, Valletta VLT 1171, Malta (office). *Telephone:* 21242191 (office). *Fax:* 21235032 (office). *E-mail:* info.mfa@gov.mt (office). *Website:* www.mfa.gov.mt (office).

REGÀS, Rosa, BPhil; Spanish writer and journalist; b. 1933, Barcelona; m.; five c.; ed Univ. of Barcelona; mem. editorial staff with Seix Barral 1964–70, with Edhasa; Founder and Publisher, La Gaya Ciencia 1970–, journals Arquitectura Vis, Cuadernos de la Gaya Ciencia 1976–; trans. for UN 1983–94; Head of Culture Dept of Casa de América, part of Foreign Affairs Ministry 1994–98; Gen. Dir Biblioteca Nacional de España 2004–07 (resgnd); Chevalier de la Legion d'Honneur 2005, Creu de Sant Jordi, Generalitat de Catalunya 2005; Premio Grandes Viajeros 2005. *Publications include:* fiction: Memoria de Almator (novel) 1991, Azul (novel) (Premio Nadal) 1994, Pobre corazón (short stories) 1996, Barcelona, un día (short stories) 1998, Luna Lunera (novel) (Premio Ciudad de Barcelona) 1999, La canción de Dorotea (novel) (Premio Planeta) 2001, contrib. short stories to anthologies, including Relatos para un fin de milenio 1998, Cuentos solidarios 1999, Mujeres al alba 1999, La paz y la palabra 2003; non-fiction: La cuina de l'ampurdanet (leaflet) 1985, Ginebra (leaflet) 1988, Canciones de amor y de batalla: 1993–1995 (articles) 1995, Viaje a la luz del Cham 1995, Una revolución personal 1997, Desde el mar 1997, España: una nueva mirada (leaflet) 1997, Más canciones 1995–1998 (articles) 1998, La creación, la fantasía y la vida (essay) 1998, Sangre de mi sangre (essay) 1999, Diario de una abuela de verano (biog.) 2004, El valor de la protesta (articles) 2004, La hora de la verdad 2010, La desgracia de ser mujer 2011; contrib. essays to collections, including Retratos literarios 1997, Ser mujer 2000, and to numerous journals and periodicals. *E-mail:* arcano@rosaregas .net. *Website:* www.rosaregas.net.

REGESTER, Michael; British crisis management consultant; *Director, Regester Larkin Ltd;* b. 8 April 1947, Godalming, Surrey, England; s. of Hugh Regester and Monique Levrey; m. 1st Christine Regester 1969 (divorced 1993); two d.; m. 2nd Leanne Moscardi 1994 (divorced 2003); one s. one d.; ed St Peter's School, Guildford; Man. Public Affairs, Gulf Oil Corpn, Europe, W Africa and Middle East 1975–80; Co-founder and Jt Man. Dir Traverse-Healy and Regester Ltd 1980–87; Man. Dir Charles Barker Traverse-Healy Ltd 1987–89; Man. Dir Regester PLC 1990–94; Dir Regester Larkin Ltd 1994–. *Publications:* Crisis Management 1987, Investor Relations (with N. Ryder) 1990, Issues and Crisis Management (with J. Larkin) 2008. *Leisure interests:* sailing, golf, tennis, opera, cooking. *Address:* Regester Larkin Ltd, 16 St Martin's le Grand, London, EC1A 4EN, England (office). *Telephone:* (20) 3179-6000 (office). *Fax:* (20) 3179-6001 (office). *E-mail:* mregester@regesterlarkin.com (office). *Website:* www.regesterlarkin.com (office).

REGIS, John, MBE; British fmr athlete; b. 13 Oct. 1966, Lewisham; s. of Antony Regis and Agnes Regis; winner, UK 200m 1985 (tie), 100m 1988, Amateur Athletics Asscn 200m 1986–87; UK record for 200m, World Championships 1987; World Championships bronze medallist 200m, silver medal, Olympic Games Seoul 1988, 300m indoor record holder Commonwealth Games 1990; silver medal 200m 1991, gold medal 4×100m relay 1991; gold medal 200m, 4×100m relay, 4×400m relay 1993; gold medal World Cup 1994, mem. British team Olympic Games, Atlanta 1996; retd 2000; mem. GB bobsleigh training team 2000; Head Athletics Div., Stellar Group Ltd (athletics man. team) 2000–; coach UK Athletics sprint-relay team 2001–. *Leisure interests:* golf, tennis, martial arts. *Address:* The Stellar Group Limited, 16 Stanhope Place, London, W2 2HH, England. *Telephone:* (20) 7298-0080. *Fax:* (20) 7298-0099. *E-mail:* JRegis1@aol.com. *Website:* www .stellargroup.co.uk.

REGMI, Drona Raj; Nepalese lawyer and government official; *Attorney-General;* fmr Deputy Attorney Gen., Attorney Gen. 2013–. *Address:* Office of the Attorney-General, Ramshah Path, Kathmandu, Nepal (office). *Telephone:* (1) 4240210 (office). *Fax:* (1) 4262582 (office). *E-mail:* info@attorneygeneral.gov.np (office). *Website:* www.attorneygeneral.gov.np (office).

REGMI, Khil Raj, BA, BL, MA; Nepalese judge and politician; b. 31 May 1949, Palpa; m.; three c.; ed Tribhuvan Univ.; Kathmandu Section Officer, Supreme Court of Nepal 1972–74; Judge, Dist Court 1974–85; Kathmandu Deputy Registrar 1985–91; Judge, Appellate Court 1991–96, Chief Judge 1996–2003; Justice, Supreme Court 2003–11, Chief Justice 2011–14; Chair. Council of Ministers, and Minister of Defence, and of Co- operatives and Poverty Alleviation (in interim govt) 2013–14. *Address:* c/o Office of the Chief Justice, Supreme Court, Ramashah Path, Kathmandu, Nepal.

REGO, Paula; British (b. Portuguese) artist; b. 26 Jan. 1935, Lisbon, Portugal; d. of José Figueiroa Rego and Maria de San José Paiva Figueiroa Rego; m. Victor Willing (died 1988); one s. two d.; ed St Julian's School, Carcavelos, Portugal, Slade School of Fine Art, Univ. Coll., London; Assoc. Artist to Nat. Gallery 1990; Sr Fellow, RCA 1989; Dr hc (St Andrews), Univ. of E Anglia), (Rhode Island School of Design) 2000, (London Inst.) 2002, (Univ. Coll. London) 2004, (Oxford) 2005, (Univ. of Roehampton) 2005, (Royal Coll. of Art) 2008. *Television:* The South Bank Show 1992, Artsworld 'The Passion of Paula Rego' 2001, Paula Rego (BBC Four) 2002. *Publications:* Monograph Phaidon 1992, 1997, Peter Pan (etchings) 1992, Nursery Rhymes (etchings) 1994, Pendle Witches (etchings) 1996, Children's Crusade (etchings) 1999, Monograph 2002, Complete Graphic Work 2003, Jane Eyre 2003. *Address:* c/o Marlborough Fine Art, 6 Albemarle Street, London, W1X 4BY, England.

REGY, Claude, LLB; French theatre director; *Artistic Director, Les Ateliers Contemporains;* b. 1 May 1923, Nîmes; s. of Marcel Régy and Suzanne Picheral; ed Univs of Algiers, Lyon and Paris; dir of plays by Marguerite Duras, Harold Pinter, James Saunders, Tom Stoppard, Edward Bond, David Storey 1960–70, by Nathalie Sarraute, Peter Handke, Botho Strauss 1970–80, by Maurice Maeterlinck, Wallace Stevens, Leslie Kaplan, Victor Slavkine 1980–90, by Gregory Motton, Henri Meschonnic, Charles Reznifoff, Jon Fosse, David Harrower 1990–2000; dir Ivanov (Chekhov) 1985, Huis-Clos (J. P. Sartre) 1990 (both at Comédie Française), Melancholia Théâtre (J. Fosse) 2001, 4.48 Psychose (S. Kane) 2002, Variations sur la mort (J. Fosse) 2003, Comme un chant de David (H. Meschonnic) 2005, Homme sans but (A. Lygre) 2007, Ode maritime (F. Pessoa) 2009, Brume de Dieu (T. Vesaas) 2010; dir operas Die Meistersinger von Nürnberg (Wagner), Théâtre du Chatelet 1990, Jeanne d'Arc au Bûcher (Honegger), Opéra Bastille 1992, Carnet d'un Disparu (Janacek), Kunsten Festival des Arts, Festival d'Aix-en-Provence 2001; Artistic Dir Les Ateliers Contemporains 1976–; Officier des Arts et des Lettres; Grand Prix Nat. du Théâtre 1992, Grand Prix des Arts de la Scène de la Ville de Paris 1994. *Film:* Conversation avec Nathalie Sarraute 1989. *Publications:* Espaces Perdus 1991, L'Ordre des Morts 1999, L'Etat d'Incertitude 2002, Au-delà des larmes 2007, La Brulure du monde 2011, Dans le désordre 2011. *E-mail:* clregy@gmail.com (office); atelierscontemporains@gmail.com (office). *Address:* Les Ateliers Contemporains, 68 rue J.J. Rousseau, 75001 Paris, France. *Telephone:* 1-48-87-95-10 (office); 1-42-33-34-11 (home).

REHMAN, Maulana Fazlur; Pakistani politician; b. 21 Aug. 1953, Abdulkhel Banyala area in Dera Ismail Khan dist, North-West Frontier Prov.; s. of Mufti Mehmood; ed Dar-al-Ulum Haqania, Akura, Khatak; Sec.-Gen. Jamiat-e-Ulema-e-Islam 1974–2007, now heads own faction of JUI, Jamiat-e-Ulema-e-Islam—Fazl 2007–, also Sec.-Gen. Muttahida Majlis-e-Amal political coalition; mem. Nat. Ass., fmr Leader of the Opposition. *Address:* c/o Jamiat-e-Ulema-e-Islam (JUI), Jamia al-Maarf, al-Sharia, Dera Ismail Khan, Pakistan.

REHMAN, Shehrbano (Sherry); Pakistani journalist, politician and diplomatist; b. 21 Dec. 1960, Karachi; d. of Hassanally A. Rahman Zubedi; m. Nadeem Hussain; one c.; ed Smith Coll., Mass, USA, Univ. of Sussex, UK; journalist for nat. and int. newspapers and journals, including fmr Ed.-in-Chief The Herald (monthly news magazine); mem. Nat. Ass. (Parl.) 2002–07, 2008; Minister for Information and Broadcasting 2008–09; Amb. to USA 2012–13; Guest Lecturer, School of Advanced Int. Studies, Johns Hopkins Univ., Univ. Now 2004; mem. Pakistan Peoples Party (PPP); mem. Council of Pakistan Newspaper Editors 1988–98; Chair. Lady Dufferin Foundation Trust; Founding Chair. Jinnah Inst. (think-tank); fmr mem. Parliamentarians Network for Conflict Prevention at East West Inst., Brussels, Parliamentarians for Global Action, New York; awarded title of Democracy's Hero, Int. Republican Inst. 2009. *Publication:* The Kashmiri Shawl: From Jamawar to Paisley (co-author) 2006. *Address:* Ministry of Foreign Affairs, Constitution Avenue, Islamabad, Pakistan (office). *Telephone:* (51) 9210335 (office). *Fax:* (51) 9207600 (office). *E-mail:* sadiq@mofa.gov.pk (office). *Website:* www.mofa.gov.pk (office).

REHME, Robert; American film producer; b. 5 May 1935, Cincinnati, Ohio; m.; two d.; ed Univ. of Cincinnati; Pres. and CEO Avco Embassy Pictures 1978–81; Pres. Worldwide Distribution and Marketing, Universal Pictures, then Pres. Theatrical Motion Picture Group 1981–83; Co-Chair. and CEO New World Entertainment Inc. 1989; Co-Founder and Pnr Neufeld/Rehme Productions 1989; currently Head Rehme Productions, Los Angeles; Pres. Acad. of Motion Picture Arts and Sciences 1992–93, 1997–2001; mem. Bd of Trustees American Film Inst., Chair Center for Advanced Film and TV Studies (CAFTS–AFI Conservatory) 2000–; mem. BAFTA. *Films:* Vice Squad 1982, Flight of the Intruder 1991, Necessary Roughness 1991, Patriot Games 1992, Beverly Hills Cop 3 1994, Clear and Present Danger 1994, Blind Faith 1998, Lost in Space 1998, Black Dog 1998, Bless the Child 2000, Gods and Generals 2003. *Television:* Lightning Force (series) 1991, Woman Undone 1996, Gridlock 1996, For the Future: The Irvine Fertility Scandal 1996, Escape: Human Cargo 1998, Love and Treason 2001, Conviction 2002, Deacons for Defense 2003. *Address:* Rehme Productions, 10956 Weyburn Avenue, Los Angeles, CA 90024, USA (office).

REHN, Elisabeth, BSc, DSc; Finnish politician and international organization official; b. (Elisabeth Carlberg), 6 April 1935, Helsinki; m. Ove Rehn 1955 (deceased); two s. two d.; ed Grankulla Samskola Swedish School of Econs, Helsinki; mem. Parl. 1979–95; Minister of Defence 1990–95, Minister for Equality 1991–95; cand. in Finnish Presidential election 1994, 2000; mem. European Parl. 1995–96; UN Special Rapporteur for Human Rights in Fmr Yugoslavia 1995–98; UN Under-Sec.-Gen., Special Rep. of UN Sec.-Gen. in Bosnia and Herzegovina 1998–99; UNIFEM Ind. Expert on impact of war on women 2001–02; Chair. Working Table I (Human Rights and Democratisation), Stability Pact for SE Europe, Brussels 2003–04; Chair. Finnish Asscn for Educ. and Training of Women in Crisis Prevention 1997; mem. UN Dept of Peacekeeping Review Bd, Court of Conciliation and Arbitration, OSCE 1994, Int. Steering Cttee of Engendering The Peace Process; mem. UNICEF Finnish Cttee 1982–94, Chair. 1988–93; Vice-Chair. Finnish Red Cross 1984–88; Chair. Bd of Trustees, WWF Finland 2000–06; Vice-Chair. Suomen Unifem ry 2003–05; mem. Bd of Dirs Trust Fund for Victims, Int. Criminal Court, The Hague; mem. Advisory Bd Femmes Africa Solidarité 2005–, Global Leadership Foundation (Switzerland) 2006–, Advisory Bds of European Leadership Network, Women In Int. Security, Women's Regional Lobby (Balkans); Patron United World Coll. project in Bosnia and Herzegovina 2005–; Hon. mem. UNICEF Finland 1994, Zonta International 1996; Commdr, Order of the White Rose of Finland 1992, Cross of Liberty, First Class with Grand Star (Finland) 2002, First Class Order, Cross of Terra Mariana (Estonia) 2003, Vuoden Lotta 2011; Hon. DSc (Swedish School of Econs and Business Admin) 1994; Hon. DEcon. *Publication:* Women, War, Peace (with Ellen Johnson-Sirleaf) 2002. *Leisure interests:* int. politics, sports, nature. *Address:* Saarentie 22, 02400 Kirkkonummi, Finland (home). *Telephone:* 40-5149369 (mobile); (9) 2952842 (home). *E-mail:* elisabeth.rehn@kolumbus.fi (home). *Website:* www.elisabethrehn.com.

REHN, Olli, DPhil; Finnish politician and international organization official; *Vice-President for Economic and Monetary Affairs and the Euro, European Commission;* b. 31 March 1962, Mikkeli; m. Merja Rehn; one c.; ed Macalester Coll., USA, Univ. of Helsinki, Univ. of Oxford, UK; Chair. Centre Youth of Finland 1987–89; Deputy Chair. Centre Party of Finland 1988–94; mem. Helsinki City Council 1988–94; mem. Parl. 1991–95; Special Adviser to Prime Minister 1992–93, Econ. Policy Adviser 2003–04; mem. European Parl. 1995–96; Head of Cabinet, EC 1998–2002, Commr for Enterprise and the Information Soc. July–Nov. 2004, for Enlargement 2004–10, Vice-Pres. for Econ. and Monetary Affairs and the Euro 2010–; Prof. and Dir of Research, Dept of Political Science and Centre for European Studies, Univ. of Helsinki 2002–03; columnist in several newspapers and magazines; Commissioner of Year, European Voice 2006, Alumnus of Year, Univ. of Helsinki 2011. *Publications:* Europe's Next Frontiers 2006, Suomen eurooppaiainen valinta ei ole suhdannepolitiikkaa 2006. *Leisure interests:* football, reading, rock and jazz. *Address:* European Commission, 200 rue de la Loi, 1049 Brussels, Belgium (office). *Telephone:* (2) 295-79-57 (office). *Fax:* (2) 295-85-61 (office). *E-mail:* cab-rehn-web-feedback@ec.europa.eu (office). *Website:* ec.europa.eu/commission_2010-2014/rehn (office).

REICH, Otto Juan; Cuban-American consultant and fmr government official; *President, Otto Reich Associates LLC;* b. 1945, Cuba; ed Univ. of N Carolina, Georgetown Univ.; Lt, 3rd Civil Affairs Detachment, Panama Canal Zone, US Army 1967–69; Asst Admin. Econ. Assistance to Latin America and the Caribbean, USAID 1981–83; Special Adviser to Sec. of State 1983–86; Founder and Man. Office of Public Diplomacy for Latin America, the Caribbean and US Dept of State 1983–86; Amb. to Venezuela 1986–89; Alt. Rep. to UN Human Rights Comm., Geneva 1991–92; Asst Sec. of State for Western Hemisphere Affairs 2001–02, Special Envoy Nov. 2002–Jan. 2003; Presidential Special Envoy for Latin America, Nat. Security Council 2003–04; Pnr, later Pres. Brock Group (consulting firm) 1989–2001; currently Pres. Otto Reich Assocs LLC (consulting firm), Washington, DC; co-host CNN Int.'s Choque de Opiniones public affairs programme 1998–2001; Dir Center for a Free Cuba, Washington, DC; lobbyist for numerous cos including Bacardi and Lockheed Martin; fmr Washington Dir Council of the Americas; fmr Community Devt Co-ordinator for City of Miami, FL; fmr Int. Rep. of FL Dept of Commerce; fmr staff asst, US House of Reps; Meritorious Honour Award, Dept of State. *Address:* Otto Reich Associates LLC, 1101 30th Street, NW, Suite 200, Washington, DC 20007, USA (office). *Telephone:* (202) 333-1360 (office). *E-mail:* ora@ottoreichassociates.com (office). *Website:* www.ottoreichassociates.net (office).

REICH, Robert Bernard, BA, MA, JD; American political economist, academic and fmr government official; *Professor of Public Policy, Goldman School of Public Policy, University of California, Berkeley;* b. 24 June 1946, Scranton, Pa; s. of Edwin Saul Reich and Mildred Dorf Reich (née Freshman); m. Clare Dalton 1973; two s.; ed Dartmouth Coll., Univ. of Oxford, UK, Yale Univ.; Asst Solicitor-Gen., Dept of Justice, Washington, DC 1974–76; Dir of Policy Planning Fed. Trade Comm., Washington 1976–81; mem. Faculty, John F. Kennedy School of Govt, Harvard Univ. 1981–92; fmr Econ. Adviser to Pres. Bill Clinton (q.v.); Sec. of Labor 1993–97; Univ. Prof., Maurice B. Hexter Prof. of Social and Econ. Policy, Brandeis Univ. Grad. School for Advanced Studies in Social Welfare 1997–2006; Prof. of Public Policy, Goldman School of Public Policy, Univ. of California, Berkeley 2006–; Chair. Biotechnology Section, US Office Tech. Assessment, Washington, DC 1990–91; Co-founder and Chair. Editorial Bd The American Prospect 2002–03; mem. Nat. Governing Bd, Common Cause 1982–88; mem. Mass Comm. on Mature Industries 1985–87; mem. Bd of Dirs Business Enterprise Trust 1986–93, Econ. Policy Inst. 1988–93, 2002–03; Trustee, Dartmouth Coll. 1988–93; Contributing Ed. The New Republic 1982–93; Rhodes Scholar 1968; Dr hc (Dartmouth Coll.) 1994, (Univ. of New Hampshire) 1997, (Wheaton Coll.) 1998, (Emory Univ.) 1999, (Bates Coll.) 2001, (Grinnell Coll.) 2002; Mass Teachers Asscn Award for Excellence 1997, Lifetime Achievement Award, Nat. Ass. of Voluntary Health and Social Welfare Orgs 1997, Eleanor Roosevelt Award for Public Service, Americans for Democratic Action 2001, Vaclav Havel Humanitarian Prize 2003. *Films:* Inequality for All (documentary) 2013. *Publications include:* The Next American Frontier 1983, Tales of a New America 1987, The Power of Public Ideas (co-author) 1987, The Work of Nations 1991, Putting People First 1997, Locked in the Cabinet 1997, The Future of Success 2001, Reason: Why Liberals Will Win the Battle for America 2004, Supercapitalism: The Transformation of Business, Democracy and Everyday Life 2007, Aftershock: The Next Economy and America's Future 2010, Beyond Outrage 2012. *Address:* Richard & Rhoda Goldman School of Public Policy, University of California Berkeley, 301 GSPP Main, 2607 Hearst Avenue, Berkeley, CA 94720-7320, USA (office). *Telephone:* (510) 642-0551 (office). *E-mail:* rreich@berkeley.edu (office); bob@RobertReich.org. *Website:* gspp.berkeley.edu/directories/faculty/robert-reich (office); www.robertreich.org.

REICH, Steve, MA; American composer; b. 3 Oct. 1936, New York; s. of Leonard Reich and June Carroll; m. Beryl Korot 1976; two s.; ed Cornell Univ., Juilliard School of Music, Mills Coll.; studied composition with Berio and Milhaud; also studied at the American Soc. for Eastern Arts and in Accra and Jerusalem; f. own ensemble 1966; Steve Reich and Musicians have completed numerous tours world-wide 1971–; his music performed by maj. orchestras and ensembles in United States and Europe; recipient of three Rockefeller Foundation Grants 1975–81 and a Guggenheim Fellowship; mem. American Acad. of Arts and Letters 1994–, Bavarian Acad. of Fine Arts 1995; Regent Lectureship, Univ. of Calif., Berkeley 2000; Montgomery Fellowship, Dartmouth Coll.; Commdr des Arts et Lettres 1999; Dr hc (Calif. Inst. of the Arts) 2000; Koussevitzky Foundation Award 1981, Schumann Prize, Columbia Univ. 2000, Praemium Imperiale Music Laureate, Japan 2006. *Major works include:* It's Gonna Rain (tape) 1965, Come Out (tape) 1966, Melodica (tape) 1966, Piano Phase for two pianos or two marimbas 1967, Violin Phase for violin and tape or four violins 1967, My Name Is for three tapes recorders and performers (manuscript only) 1967, Pendulum Music for 3 or 4 microphones, amplifiers and loudspeakers 1968, Four Organs for four electric organs and maracas 1970, Phase Patterns for four electric organs 1970, Drumming for 4 pairs of tuned bongo drums, 3 marimbas, 3 glockenspiels, 2 female voices, whistling and piccolo 1970–71, Clapping Music for two musicians clapping 1972, Music for Pieces of Wood for five pair of tuned claves 1973, Music for Mallet Instruments, Voices, and Organ 1973, Six Pianos 1973, Music for 18 Musicians (Grammy Award for Best Contemporary Composition 1995) 1974–76, Music for a Large Ensemble 1978, Variations for Winds, Strings, and Keyboards

1979, Octet 1979, Tehillim for voices and ensemble 1981, Vermont Counterpoint for amplified flute and tape 1982, The Desert Music for 10 singers (amplified) and reduced orchestra 1984, Eight Lines for ensemble 1983, Sextet for percussion and keyboards 1984, New York Counterpoint for amplified clarinet and tape, or 11 clarinets 1985, Six Marimbas (transcription of Six Pianos 1973) for 6 marimbas 1986, Three Movements for orchestra 1986, Electric Counterpoint for electric guitar or amplified acoustic guitar and tape, amplified guitar soloist and tape, or guitar ensemble 1987, The Four Sections for orchestra 1987, Different Trains for string quartet and tape (orchestrated 2000) (Grammy Award for Best Contemporary Composition 1990) 1988, The Cave (with Beryl Korot) for amplified voices and ensemble 1993/2003, Duet for two solo violins and string ensemble 1993, Typing Music 1993, Nagoya Marimbas for two marimbas 1994, City Life for amplified ensemble 1995, Proverb for voices and ensemble 1995, Triple Quartet for amplified string quartet (with pre-recorded tape), or three string quartets, or string orchestra 1998, Know What Is Above You for four women's voices and 2 percussion 1999, Electric Guitar Phase for electric guitar and pre-recorded tape (arrangement of Violin Phase 1967) 2000, Tokyo/Vermont Counterpoint for KAT MIDI mallet and pre-recorded tape (arrangement of Vermont Counterpoint 1981) 2000, Three Tales (video opera, video by Beryl Korot) 2002, Dance Patterns for 2 xylophones, 2 vibraphones, 2 pianofortes 2002, Cello Counterpoint for amplified cello and multi-channel tape 2003, You Are (Variations) (text by Rabbi Nachman of Breslov (English), Psalms (Hebrew), Wittgenstein (English) and Pirke Avot (Hebrew) for amplified ensemble and voices, no brass, 2 marimbas, 2 vibraphones, 4 pianofortes, strings, and voices 2004, The Daniel Variations 2006, Double Sextet (Pulitzer Prize in Music 2009) 2008. *Recordings include:* Come Out, Violin Phase, It's Gonna Rain, Four Organs, Drumming, Six Pianos, Music for Mallet Instruments, Voices and Organ, Music for a Large Ensemble, Octet and Variations for Winds, Strings and Keyboards, Music for 18 Musicians, The Desert Music, Electric Counterpoint, Different Trains, The Four Sections, Nagoya Marimbas, City Life, Proverb, Hindenburg (in collaboration with Beryl Korot), Double Sextet. *Address:* c/o Elizabeth Sobol, IMG Artists, Carnegie Hall Tower, 152 West 57th Street, 5th Floor, New York, NY 10019, USA (office); c/o Andrew Rosner, Allied Artists 42, Montpelier Square, London, SW7 1JZ, England (office). *Telephone:* (212) 994-3500 (New York) (office); (20) 7589-6243 (London) (office). *Fax:* (212) 994-3550 (New York) (office); (20) 7581-5269 (London) (office). *E-mail:* esobol@imgartists.com (office). *Website:* www.imgartists.com (office); www.alliedartists.co.uk (office); www.stevereich.com.

REICHARDT, Robert Heinrich, DPhil; Austrian/Swiss sociologist and academic; b. 2 May 1927, Basel; s. of Heinrich Reichardt and Magdalena Reichardt (née Bachlehner); m. Dr Isolde Dünhofen; ed Univ. of Basel; Research Assoc., Princeton Univ. 1960–61; Asst Inst. for Social Sciences, Univ. of Basel 1962–64; Dir Dept for Sociology, Inst. for Higher Studies, Vienna 1964–66; Prof., Univ. of Vienna 1966–; Exec. Dir Inst. for Research on Socio-Econ. Devt, Austrian Acad. of Sciences 1977–84, Head Comm. for Sociology of Arts and Music 1990–; mem. Austrian Acad. of Sciences 1978–; Fellow, Collegium Ramazzini Carpi, Italy 1990, Academia Artium et Scientiarum Europaea 1991; Co-operative Prize, Univ. of Basel 1960, Gold Medal of Honour, City of Vienna 1993. *Publications:* Die Schallplatte als kulturelles und ökon. Phänomen, Bedürfnisforschung im Dienste der Stadtplanung, Überleben wir den technischen Fortschritt (with others), Einführung in die Soziologie für Juristen. *Leisure interests:* composition, playing the piano.

REICHS, Kathleen (Kathy) J., BA, MA, PhD; American writer and forensic anthropologist; *Professor Emeritus, University of North Carolina;* b. 1950, Chicago; m. Paul Reichs; two d. one s.; ed American Univ., Northwestern Univ.; Asst Prof., Northern Illinois Univ. 1974–78; Instructor, Stateville Correctional Facility, Joliet, Ill. 1975–78; Asst Prof., Davidson Coll. 1981–83; Lecturer, Univ. of North Carolina at Charlotte 1978–81, 1983–87, Asst Prof. 1987–88, Assoc. Prof. 1988–96, then Prof., now Prof. Emer.; works as forensic anthropologist at Office of the Chief Medical Examiner, State of North Carolina and Laboratoires des Sciences Judiciaires et de Médecine Légale, Canada; Visiting Prof., Univ. of Pittsburgh 1987, Visiting Assoc. Prof., Concordia Univ. 1988–89, McGill Univ. 1988–97 (summers); mem. American Acad. of Forensic Sciences, Sec. Physical Anthropology Section 1994–95, Chair, Physical Anthropology Section 1995–96, mem. Bd of c 1996–2002, mem. Exec. Cttee 2000–; mem. Bd of Dirs American Bd of Forensic Anthropology 1986–93, Vice-Pres. 1989–93; mem. Canadian Nat. Police Services Advisory Council; producer, Bones (TV series); named one of Canada's 100 Most Powerful Women 2004, Premio Piemonte Grinzane Noir, Vincitore Sezione Giallo Internazionale Award, Italy 2007. *Publications:* Déjà Dead (Ellis Award for Best First Novel) 1997, Death du Jour 1999, Deadly Decisions 2000, Fatal Voyage 2001, Grave Secrets 2002, Bare Bones 2003, Monday Mourning 2004, Cross Bones 2005, Bones to Ashes 2007, Devil Bones 2008, 206 Bones 2009, Spider Bones 2010, Mortal Remains 2010, Flash and Bones 2011, Virals 2011, Seizure 2011, Bones Are Forever 2012. *Address:* c/o Simon & Schuster, Inc., 1230 Avenue of the Americas, New York, NY 10020, USA. *E-mail:* kjreichs@aol.com. *Website:* www.kathyreichs.com.

REICHSTUL, Henri Philippe; Brazilian business executive; *CEO, Brenco (Brazilian Renewable Energy Company);* b. 12 April 1949; Vice-Pres. Banco Interamerican Express –1999; Pres. Petrobras 1999–2002; CEO Globopar SA 2002–03; Founding Pnr, G&R Gestao Empresarial (consulting firm); currently CEO Brenco (Brazilian Renewable Energy Co.); mem. Bd of Dirs Ashmore Energy Int., REPSOL-YPF, PSA-Peugeot Citroen; mem. Consulting Bd Lhoist Brazil; mem. Admin. Council, Grupo Pão de Açúcar 2003–; mem. Admin. Council, Vivo Participações 2006–. *Address:* Brenco, Avenida Brigadeira Faria Lima, 1309 4° andar, São Paulo CEP 01452-002, Brazil (office). *Telephone:* (11) 3095-2250 (office). *E-mail:* brenco@brenco.com.br (office). *Website:* www.brenco.com.br (office).

REID, Allen (Alan) Forrest, AM, PhD, DSc, FAA; Australian scientist and artist; b. 26 March 1931, New Zealand; s. of V. C. Reid and L. E. Reid; m. Prudence M. Little; two s. one d. two step-d.; ed Univ. of New Zealand, Christchurch, Australian Nat. Univ., Canberra, Cornell Univ., USA; joined CSIRO 1959, Research Scientist 1972–82, Chief Research Scientist 1972–82, Chief of Div. of Mineral Eng 1982–84, Dir Inst. of Energy and Earth Resources 1984–87, Inst. of Minerals, Energy and Construction 1988–97; Chair. Australia Environmental Resources NL 1996–97, Australian Petroleum Co-operative Research Centre 1991–2003; Dir Australian Minerals and Energy Environmental Foundation 1991–; mem. Bd of Govs Adelaide Cen. School of Art 2004–; CSIRO Rivett Medal 1970, high pressure mineral Reidite, found in meteor impact debris, named after him 2001, Ian Wark Medal "for outstanding scientific contributions to Australia's prosperity", Australian Acad. of Science 2008. *Publications:* Urban Air Pollution in Australia (ed) 1997; more than 80 scientific papers on solid state chemistry, mineral processing, commercial solar energy panels and the computer-based image and x-ray analysis techniques on which automated mineral analysis is based; six patents. *Leisure interests:* art collecting, oil painting. *Address:* 178 Ward Street, North Adelaide, South Australia 5006, Australia (home). *E-mail:* alan.reid@kern.com.au (home).

REID, Sir David Edward, Kt, CA; British business executive and chartered accountant; *Chairman, Kwik-Fit Group;* b. 5 Feb. 1947, Zambia; two d.; ed Fettes Coll., Univ. of Aberdeen; qualified as chartered accountant; worked for Peat Marwick Mitchell 1970, Philips Industries and BAT Industries –1985; fmr Chief Accountant, Philips Video, then for International Stores –1985; Dir of Finance, Tesco plc 1985–97, Deputy Chair. 1997–2004, Chair. (non-exec.) 2004–11; Chair. Kwik-Fit Group; Dir (non-exec.) Reed Elsevier Group PLC; fmr Dir (non-exec.) Legal & General, Westbury, De Vere Group; Chair. Whizz-Kidz (charity); Dir, Tesco Charity Trust; apptd one of Prime Minister David Cameron's Business Ambassadors 2010–; Founder and Trustee, The Fettes Foundation; mem. Inst. of Chartered Accountants (Scotland). *Address:* Kwik-Fit (GB) Ltd, 216 East Main Street, Broxburn, West Lothian, EH52 5AS, Scotland (office). *E-mail:* info@kwik-fit.com (office). *Website:* www.kwik-fit.com (office).

REID, Harry Mason, JD; American lawyer and politician; *Senator from Nevada;* b. 2 Dec. 1939, Searchlight, Nev.; s. of Harry Reid and Inez Reid; m. Landra Joy Gould; four s. one d.; ed Southern Utah Univ., Utah State Univ., George Washington Univ.; City Attorney, Henderson, Nev. 1964–66; Trustee, Southern Nev. Memorial Hosp. Bd 1967–69, Chair. Bd of Trustees 1968–69; mem. Nev. Ass. 1969–70; Lt-Gov. of Nev. 1970–74; Chair. Nev. Gaming Comm. 1977–81; Congressman, US House of Reps, Washington, DC 1983–87; Senator from Nevada 1987–, Minority Whip 1999–2001, Jan.–June 2001, 2003–05, Majority Whip Jan. 2001, June 2001–03, Minority Leader 2005–07, Majority Leader 2007–; mem. numerous Senate cttees; mem. Bd of Dirs of American Cancer Soc., of Legal Aid Soc., of YMCA; Democrat; Hon. LLD (Southern Utah State Coll.) 1984; Nat. Jewish Hosp., Humanitarian Award 1984. *Address:* 522 Hart Senate Office Building, Washington, DC 20510, USA (office). *Telephone:* (202) 224-3542 (office). *Fax:* (202) 224-7327 (office). *Website:* reid.senate.gov (office).

REID, Sir Robert Paul (Bob), Kt, MA; British business executive; *Chairman, ICE Futures Europe;* b. 1 May 1934, Cupar, Fife, Scotland; m. Joan Mary Reid 1958; three s.; ed St Andrews Univ.; joined Shell 1956, Sarawak Oilfields 1956–59, Head of Personnel Nigeria 1959–67; Africa and S. Asia Regional Org. 1967–68, Personal Asst and Planning Adviser to Chair. Shell & BP Services, Kenya 1968–70, Man. Dir Nigeria 1970–74, Man. Dir Thailand 1974–78; Vice-Pres. Int. Aviation and Products Training 1978–80, Exec. Dir Downstream Oil, Shell Co. of Australia Int. Petroleum Co. 1984–90, Chair. and Chief Exec. Shell UK 1985–90; Chair. Foundation for Man. Educ. 1986–2003; Chair. British Railways Bd 1990–95, London Electricity PLC 1994–97, Sears PLC 1995–99, Rosyth 2000 1995–, ICE Futures Europe (fmrly Int. Petroleum Exchange of London) 1999–, Milton Keynes Partnership Cttee 2004–08; Deputy Gov. Bank of Scotland 1997–2004; mem. Bd of Dirs The Merchants Trust 1995–2008, Siemens plc 1998–2006, CHC Helicopter Corpn 2004–08, Benella Ltd 2004–, Diligenta Ltd 2005–, Avis 1997–2003, Sun Life Assurance Co. of Canada 1997–2004, HBOS 2001–04, Intercontinental Exchange Inc. 2001–, EEA Helicopter Operations 2008–; Chancellor Robert Gordon Univ. 1993–2004; Hon. LLD (St Andrews) 1987, (Aberdeen) 1988, (Sheffield Hallam) 1995, (South Bank) 1995, (Kent) 2003. *Leisure interests:* golf, opera. *Address:* ICE Futures Europe, Milton Gate, 60 Chiswell Street, London, EC1Y 4SA (office); 24 Ashley Gardens, London, SW1P 1QD, England (home). *Telephone:* (20) 7065-7710 (office). *Fax:* (20) 7065-7813 (office). *E-mail:* kathleen.murray@theice.com (office). *Website:* www.theice.com (office).

REID, Timothy (Tim) Escott Herriot, BA, MA, MLitt; Canadian business executive, public servant and university administrator; *Governor, Governing Council, University of Toronto;* b. 21 Feb. 1936, Toronto, Ont.; s. of Escott Meredith Reid and Ruth Reid (née Herriot); m. Julyan Fancett 1962; one s. one d.; ed Univ. of Toronto, Yale Univ., Univ. of Oxford (Rhodes Scholar), Advanced Man. Program, Harvard Grad. School of Business; Exec. Sec. Canadian Inst. of Public Affairs 1962–63; Asst to Pres., Asst Prof. of Econs, Research Assoc. for Public Policy, York Univ. 1963–72; mem. Ont. Legis. Ass. 1967–71; Prin. Admin., Manpower and Social Affairs, OECD, Paris 1972–74; joined Public Service of Canada 1974, subsequently Deputy Sec. Treasury Bd, Office of Comptroller-Gen. of Canada, Asst Deputy Minister, Dept of Regional Econ. Expansion, Exec. Dir Regional and Industrial Program Affairs, Dept of Regional Industrial Expansion, Asst Deputy Minister responsible for Tourism Canada 1984–85; Referee, NSF (USA) 1979–82; Chair. Research Cttee, Inst. of Public Admin of Canada 1985–87; Dir and mem. exec. Cttee Canada Mortgage and Housing Corpn 1980–82, Canadian Labour Market and Productivity Centre 1989 (Co-Chair. Bd of Dirs 1993–97); Chair. Working Party on Regional Devel, OECD 1982–84, headed 18-nation OECD study visit to Japan 1984; Prof. of Business Man. and Dean, Faculty of Business, Ryerson Polytechnical Inst. 1985–89; Commr Ont. Securities Comm. 1987–89; Prime Minister's Business Rep., Pacific Business Forum APEC 1994, 1995; Pres. Canadian Chamber of Commerce 1989–98; Chair. Advisory Cttee, Faculty of Admin. Studies, Univ. of Ottawa 1992–94, Trade and Security Advisory Cttee, Toronto Bd of Trade 2001–03; Founding mem. and Venture Investor XPV Capital Corpn 2001–; Chair. Bd of Dirs Ontario Lottery and Gaming Corpn 2004–06; mem. Bd of Dirs Canadian Exec. Service Org. 1991–95, Inst. of Corp. Dirs 1999–2003, VIA Rail Canada Corpn 2000–07; mem. Provisional Council, Co. of Young Canadians 1966–70, Int. Trade Advisory Cttee, Govt of Canada 1991–97; Gov., Univ. of Toronto Governing Council 2002– (Exec. Cttee 2006–); Patron, Canadian Inst. of Int. Affairs 1999–2003; Ford Management Fellowship, 125 Anniversary Commemorative Medal, Canada 1992, Queen's Golden Jubilee Medal 2002. *Publications:* Contemporary Canada: Reading in Economics 1969, Student Power and the Canadian Campus (with Julyan Reid) 1969. *Leisure interests:* tennis, swimming, pilates, weight training. *Address:* 25 Scrivener Square, Suite 904, Toronto, ON M4W 3Y6, Canada (home).

REID OF CARDOWAN, Baron (Life Peer), cr. 2010, of Stepps in Lanarkshire; **John Reid,** PC, PhD; British politician and sports administrator; *Chairman, Celtic Football Club;* b. 8 May 1947, Bellshill, Lanarkshire; s. of the late Thomas Reid and Mary Reid; m. 1st Catherine McGowan (died 1998); two s.; m. 2nd Carine Adler 2002; ed St Patrick's Sr Secondary School, Coatbridge and Stirling Univ.; Research Officer, Labour Party 1979–83; Political Adviser to Neil Kinnock 1983–85; Organizer, Scottish Trade Unionists for Labour 1985–87; MP for Motherwell N 1987–97, for Hamilton N and Bellshill 1997–2005, for Airdrie and Shotts 2005–10; Opposition Spokesman on Children 1989–90, on Defence 1990–97; Minister of State for Defence 1997–98; Minister for Transport 1998–99; Sec. of State for Scotland 1999–2000; Sec. of State for NI 2000–02; Chair. of the Labour Party and Minister without Portfolio 2002–03; Leader of the House of Commons and Pres. of the Privy Council April–June 2003; Sec. of State for Health 2003–05, for Defence 2005–06, for the Home Department 2006–07 (resgnd); Chair. Celtic Football Club, Glasgow 2007–; mem. Armed Forces Cttee and Reserved Forces Cttee 1996–97. *Leisure interests:* football, reading history, crossword puzzles. *Address:* Celtic FC Ltd, Celtic Park, Glasgow, G40 3RE, Scotland (office). *Telephone:* (871) 226-1888 (office). *Website:* www.celticfc.net (office).

REIDY, Carolyn Kroll, AB, MA, PhD; American publishing executive; *President and CEO, Simon and Schuster, Inc.;* b. (Carolyn Judith Kroll), 2 May 1949, Washington, DC; d. of Henry Kroll and Mildred Kroll; m. Stephen K. Reidy 1974; ed Middlebury Coll., Vt and Indiana Univ.; various positions, Random House, New York 1975–83; Dir of Subsidiary Rights, William Morrow & Co., New York 1983–85; Vice-Pres. Assoc. Publr, Vintage Books, Random House, New York 1985–87; Assoc. Publr, Random House (concurrent with Assoc. Publr and Publr of Vintage Books) 1987–88; Publr, Vintage Books 1987–88, Anchor Books, Doubleday, New York 1988; Pres. and Publr, Avon Books, New York 1988–92; Pres. and Publr, Simon and Schuster Trade Div. 1992–2001, Pres. Adult Publishing Div., Simon and Schuster 2001–08, Pres. and CEO 2008–; Dir NAMES Project 1994–98, New York Univ. Center for Publishing 1997–2008, Literacy Partners, Inc. 1999–2011, Nat. Book Foundation 2000–; Matrix Award 2002, Distinguished Alumna, Indiana Univ. 2011. *Address:* Simon and Schuster, Inc., 1230 Avenue of the Americas, New York, NY 10020, USA (office). *Telephone:* (212) 698-7323 (office). *Fax:* (212) 698-1258 (office). *E-mail:* carolyn.reidy@simonandschuster.com (office). *Website:* simonandschuster.com (office).

REIF, Rafael, PhD; American computer scientist, academic and university administrator; *President, Massachusetts Institute of Technology;* ed Stanford Univ.; mem. Faculty, MIT 1980–, held the Analog Devices Career Devt Professorship in Electrical Eng and Computer Science (EECS) Dept and an IBM Faculty Fellowship from MIT's Center for Materials Science and Eng, served as Dir MIT's Microsystems Tech. Labs, as Assoc. Dept Head for Electrical Eng, EECS Dept and as EECS Dept Head, named Fariborz Maseeh Prof. of Emerging Tech. 2004, Provost of MIT 2005–12, Pres. 2012–; Asst Prof., Universidad Simón Bolívar, Caracas for four years; fmr Visiting Asst Prof., Stanford Univ.; mem. American Acad. of Arts and Sciences, Electrochemical Soc.; Trustee, Carnegie Endowment for Int. Peace; Fellow, IEEE 1993; Ingeniero Eléctrico (Universidad de Carabobo, Valencia, Venezuela); US Presidential Young Investigator Award 1984, Aristotle Award, Semiconductor Research Corpn 2000, Tribeca Disruptive Innovation Award 2012. *Publications:* numerous papers in professional journals on three-dimensional integrated circuit technologies and on environmentally benign microelectronics fabrication; inventor or co-inventor on 15 patents; has edited or co-edited five books. *Address:* Office of the President, Massachusetts Institute of Technology, 77 Massachusetts Avenue, Building 3-208, Cambridge, MA 02139-4307, USA (office). *Telephone:* (617) 253-0148 (office). *Fax:* (617) 253-3124 (office). *E-mail:* president@mit.edu (office). *Website:* president.mit.edu (office).

REIJNDERS, Lucas, PhD; Dutch scientist and academic; *Professor of Environmental Science, University of Amsterdam;* b. 4 Feb. 1946, Amsterdam; s. of C. Reijnders and C. M. Reijnders-Spillekom; one c.; ed Univ. of Amsterdam; Dir Environmental Inst. Univ. of Groningen 1974–80, mem. staff Nat. Environmental Office 1980–, Prof. of Environmental Science Univ. of Amsterdam 1988–; Prof. of Environmental Science, Open Univ., Heerlen 1999–; Winner, Gouden Ganzeveer 1990, Erewimpel ONRI 1992. *Publications:* Food in the Netherlands 1974, A Consumer Guide to Dutch Medicines 1980, Plea for a Sustainable Relation with the Environment 1984, Help the Environment 1991, Environmentally Improved Production and Products 1995, Agriculture in the Low Countries 1997, Travel Through the Ages 2000, Eating Patterns 2005, Energy 2006, Principles of Environmental Science 2008, Biofuels for Road Transport 2009, Design Issues for Improved Performance of Dye-sensitized and Organic Nanoparticulate Cells 2010, Recycling of Elastomeric Nanocomposites 2011, Human Health Hazards of Persistent Inorganic and Carbon Nanoparticles 2012, The Production of Algal Biofuels 2013. *Leisure interest:* 19th-century literature. *Address:* Science Park 904, PO Box 94248, 1090 GE Amsterdam, Netherlands. *Telephone:* (20) 525-62-69. *Fax:* (20) 525-74-31. *E-mail:* l.reijnders@uva.nl. *Website:* www.uva.nl.

REILLY, (David) Nicholas (Nick), CBE, MA, FIMI; British automotive executive; *President, GM Europe;* b. 17 Dec. 1949, Anglesey, N Wales; s. of the late John Reilly and of Mona (née Glynne Jones) Reilly; m. Susan Haig 1976; one s. two d.; ed Harrow School, St Catharine's Coll. Cambridge; investment analyst 1971–74; joined Gen. Motors 1975, Finance Dir Moto Diesel Mexicana 1980–83, Supply Dir Vauxhall Motors 1984–87, Mfg Dir Vauxhall Ellesmere Port 1990–94, Vice-Pres. Quality Gen. Motors Europe 1994–96, Chair., Man. Dir Vauxhall Motors 1996–2001, Chair. (non-exec.) 2001, Vice-Pres. European Sales and Marketing, Gen. Motors Europe 2001, Pres. and CEO GM Daewoo Auto and Technology Co. 2002–06, Pres. GM Asia Pacific and GM Group Vice Pres. 2006–09, also Chair. GM Daewoo Auto and Technology Co. Bd of Dirs, Pres. GM Int. Operations July–Dec. 2009, Pres. GM Europe Dec. 2009–; Vice-Pres. IBC 1987–90, Chair. IBC Vehicles 1996–; mem. Bd Saab GB 1996; Chair. Chester, Ellesmere, Wirral Training and Enterprise Council 1990–94, Training Standards Council 1997–2001, Adult Learning Inspectorate 2001; Pres. Soc. of Motor Mfrs and Traders 2001–02; Global CEO Grand Prize, Korean Acad. of Int. Business 2006. *Leisure interests:* skiing, swimming, sailing, golf, watching sports, music, opera, theatre. *Address:* GM Europe, Stelzenstrasse 4, 8152 Glattbrugg, Switzerland

(office). *Telephone:* 448282828 (office). *Fax:* 448282155 (office). *Website:* www.gm.com (office).

REILLY, Kevin P., BA, MA, PhD; American university administrator; *President, University of Wisconsin System;* m. Kate Reilly; three c.; ed Univ. of Notre Dame, Indiana Univ. of Minn.; teaching assoc. Dept of English, Univ. of Minn. 1974–79; various posts NY State Bd of Regents 1979–92; Assoc. Provost for Acad. Programs State Univ. of NY System 1992–95, Sec. 1995–96; Provost and Vice Chancellor Univ. of Wis. (UW)-Extension 1996–2000, Chancellor 2000–04, Pres. UW System 2004–; Chair. American Council of Educ.'s Comm. on Adult Learning and Educational Credentials; mem. Steering Cttee of four statewide Wis. econ. summits. *Publications:* has written and edited books and articles on higher education policy, accreditation, biography and Irish studies. *Address:* University of Wisconsin System, Office of the President, 1720 Van Hise Hall, 1220 Linden Drive, Madison, WI 53706, USA (office). *Telephone:* (608) 262-2321. *Fax:* (608) 262-3985. *E-mail:* kreillly@uwsa.edu. *Website:* www.uwsa.edu.

REIMAN, Leonid Dododjonovich; Russian engineer, government official and business executive; b. 12 July 1957, Leningrad (now St Petersburg); m.; one s. one d.; ed Leningrad Inst. of Electro-Tech. Communications; engineer, head of workshop Leningrad Telephone Exchange 1979–85; posts at Leningrad City Telephone Network 1985–88, later Deputy Head, Chief Eng, Dir of Int. Relations, Dir of Investments, First Deputy Dir-Gen. Jt Stock Co. Peterburgskaya Telefonnaya Set 1988–99; First Deputy Chair. State Cttee on Telecommunications Russian Fed. July–Aug. 1999; Chair. 1999–2000; Minister of Communications and Information Tech. 1999–2004; Deputy Minister for Transport and Communications April 2004; Minister of Information and Communications Techs April 2004–08; Adviser to Pres. and Sec., Presidential Council of Information Soc. Devt 2008–10; Pres. Supervisory Bd Mandriva SA 2011–. *Address:* Mandriva SA, 32 rue de Trévise, 75009 Paris, France (office). *Website:* www.mandriva.com (office).

REIN, Jeffrey A., BS; American retail executive; b. 28 Feb. 1952, New Orleans, La; ed Univ. of Arizona; joined Walgreens as Asst Man., Tucson 1982–84, Store Man., Tex. 1984–90, Dist Man., New Mexico 1990–96, Divisional Vice-Pres. and Treas. 1996–2000, Vice-Pres., Marketing Systems and Services 2000–01, Exec. Vice-Pres., Marketing 2001–03, Pres. and COO 2003–06, Pres. 2003–07, CEO 2006–08, Chair. 2007–08; mem. Bd of Dirs Stat Health Services 2012–, Nat. Asscn of Chain Drugstores, Midwest Young Artists, Midtown Educational Foundation, Retail Industry Leaders Asscn; Chair. American Cancer Soc., Illinois Div. of CEOs Against Cancer. *Address:* c/o Walgreen Co., 200 Wilmot Road, Deerfield, IL 60015, USA. *E-mail:* info@walgreens.com.

REINEMUND, Steven S., MBA; American business executive; b. 1949; ed US Naval Acad., Univ. of Va; served as officer US Marine Corps 1970–75, achieved rank of Capt. 1975; joined PepsiCo 1984, Pres. and CEO Pizza Hut Div. 1986–91, Pres. and CEO Pizza Hut Worldwide 1991–92, Pres. and CEO Frito-Lay N America 1992–96, Chair. and CEO Frito-Lay Inc. 1996–1999, Pres. and COO PepsiCo Inc. 1999–2001, Chair. and CEO PepsiCo Inc. 2001–06 (retd); mem. Bd of Dirs Johnson & Johnson 2003–, Exxon Mobil Corpn 2007–, Marriott International Inc. 2007–, American Express Co., Business Council of New York State Inc.; fmr Chair. Nat. Minority Supplier Devt Council; mem. Nat. Advisory Bd The Salvation Army 1990–99, Chair. 1996–99; fmr mem. Nat. Council of La Raza; Trustee US Naval Acad. Foundation; Exec. Fellow, The Exec. Program, Darden School of Business, Univ. of Virginia 2007; Pres.'s Award, Nat. Council of La Raza 1997, Excellence in Bd Leadership Award, Nat. Ass. of Nat. Voluntary Health and Social Welfare Orgs 1998, Order of Auxiliary Service Medal, Salvation Army 1998, William Booth Award 1999. *Address:* c/o PepsiCo Inc., 700 Anderson Hill Road, Purchase, NY 10577-1444, USA (office).

REINER, Rob; American actor, writer, director and producer; b. 6 March 1947, New York, NY; s. of Carl Reiner and Estelle Reiner (née Lebost); m. 1st Penny Marshall 1971 (divorced); m. 2nd Michele Singer 1989; three c.; ed Univ. of California, Los Angeles; co-f. Castle Rock Entertainment (now subsidiary of Warner Bros. Entertainment); has appeared with comic improvisation groups The Session and The Committee; Chair. First 5 Calif. Children and Families Comm. 1995–2006 (resgnd). *Films:* Enter Laughing 1967, Halls of Anger 1970, Where's Poppa 1970, Summertree 1971, How Come Nobody's on Our Side? 1975, Fire Sale 1977, This is Spinal Tap (also dir and writer) 1984, The Sure Thing (dir) 1985, Stand By Me (dir) 1986, Throw Momma from the Train 1987, The Princess Bride (dir and prod.) 1987, When Harry Met Sally (dir and prod.) 1989, Postcards from the Edge 1990, The Spirit of '76 1990, Misery (also dir and prod.) 1990, A Few Good Men (dir and prod.) 1992, Sleepless in Seattle 1993, Bullets Over Broadway 1994, Mixed Nuts 1994, North (dir and prod.) 1994, Bye Bye Love 1995, The American President (dir and prod.) 1995, For Better or Worse 1996, The First Wives Club 1996, Mad Dog Time 1996, Ghosts of Mississippi (dir and prod.) 1996, Primary Colors 1998, Spinal Tap: The Final Tour (dir, writer and prod.) 1998, EdTV 1999, The Story of Us (also dir and prod.) 1999, The Majestic 2001, Alex & Emma (also dir and prod.) 2003, Rumor Has It... (dir) 2005, Everyone's Hero (voice) 2006, The Bucket List (dir and prod.) 2007, Flipped (writer, dir and producer) 2010. *Television includes:* The Glen Campbell Goodtime Hour (writer, series) 1969, All in the Family (series) 1971–78, The Super (prod.) 1972, Thursday's Game 1974, Free Country (series, also prod.) 1978, More Than Friends (also writer and prod.) 1978, The T.V. Show (also writer and prod.) 1979, Million Dollar Infield (also writer and prod.) 1982, Morton & Hayes (series, writer and prod.) 1991, But Seriously (exec. prod.) 1994, I Am Your Child (dir, writer) 1997, Everyday Life 2004. *Address:* c/o Castle Rock Entertainment, 335 North Maple Drive, Suite 350, Beverly Hills, CA 90210, USA.

REINESCH, Gaston, MSc(Econ); Luxembourg central banker; *Governor, Luxembourg Central Bank;* b. 17 May 1958; ed London School of Econs, UK; fmr Pres. Société Nationale de Crédit et d'Investissement, Nat. Post and Telecommunication Co., Luxembourg Econ. and Social Council; fmr Chair. BGL BNP Paribas SA, Dir 2008–; Prof. of Econs, Legal and Econs Dept, Univ. of Luxembourg; Dir Gen., Ministry of Finance 1995–2012; Gov. Luxembourg Cen. Bank 2012–; fmr Vice-Chair. Banque et Caisse d'Epargne de l'Etat; mem. Bd Nat. State and Savings Bank; mem. Bd of Dirs Cargolux Airlines International SA, Entreprise des Postes et Télécommunications, SES SA 1998–, Cegedel SA, European Investment Bank; fmr Dir, Paul Wurth SA; fmr Alt. Bd mem. European Investment Fund. *Address:*

Banque Centrale du Luxembourg, 2 boulevard Royal, 2983 Luxembourg (office). *Telephone:* 4774-1 (office). *Fax:* 4774-4901 (office). *E-mail:* info@bcl.lu (office). *Website:* www.bcl.lu (office).

REINFELDT, Fredrik, BS; Swedish politician; *Prime Minister;* b. 4 Aug. 1965, Stockholm; m. Filippa Reinfeldt (née Holmberg) 1992 (divorced); three c.; ed Stockholm Univ.; Chair. Swedish Conscripts Council, Swedish Defence Staff 1986; with Skandinaviska Enskilda Banken, Täby 1986–87; Deputy Chair. Regional Section, Young Moderates, Stockholm 1988–90, Chair. 1990–92, Chair. Exec. Cttee 1992–95; mem. Regional Section, Moderate Party, Stockholm 1992–2003, mem. Bd 1995–2002, mem. Exec. Cttee Moderate Party Group in Riksdag (Parl.) 1999–2003, Group Leader and First Deputy Chair. 2002–03, Chair. 2003–, mem. Bd Moderate Party 2002–, Party Chair. 2003–; Deputy Sec. Stockholm City Commr 1990–91, Sec. 1991; mem. Riksdag (Parl.) 1991–, Alt. Riksdag Cttee on Taxation 1991–94, mem. Cttee on Finance 1994–2001, Alt. Cttee on EU Affairs 2001–02, Chair. Cttee on Justice 2001–02, Alt. Advisory Council on Foreign Affairs 2002–03; Deputy Chair. Cttee on Finance 2002–03, mem. Advisory Council on Foreign Affairs 2003–06, Prime Minister 2006–; Deputy Chair. Swedish Central Conscripts Council 1985–86; Chair. Democratic Youth Community of Europe 1995–97; mem. Bd Swedish Nat. Union of Students 1989–90; Pres. Youth of European People's Party 1997–99. *Address:* Prime Minister's Office, Rosenbad 4, 103 33 Stockholm (office); Moderata Samlingspartiet (MS) (Moderate Party), Stord Nygatan 30, POB 2080, 113 12 Stockholm, Sweden. *Telephone:* (8) 405-10-00 (office); (8) 676-80-00 (MS). *Fax:* (8) 723-11-71 (office); (8) 21-61-23 (MS). *E-mail:* registrator@primeminister.ministry.se (office). *Website:* www.sweden.gov.se/sb/d/ 577 (office); www.moderat.se.

REINHARD, Keith Leon; American advertising executive; *Chairman Emeritus, DDB Worldwide Communications Group Inc.;* b. 20 Jan. 1935, Berne, Ind.; s. of Herman Reinhard and Agnes Reinhard; m. Rose-Lee Simons 1976; two d.; four s. one d. by previous m.; ed public schools in Berne; commercial artist, Kling Studios, Chicago 1954–56; man. tech. communications Dept Magnavox Co., Fort Wayne, Ind. 1957–60; creative/account exec., Biddle Co., Bloomington, Ill. 1961–63; Exec. Vice-Pres., Dir Creative Services and Pres. Needham, Harper & Steers Inc., Chicago 1964; then Chair. and CEO Needham, Harper & Steers/USA, Chicago; also Dir Needham, Harper & Steers Inc.; Chair. and CEO DDB Needham Worldwide Inc. (later DDB Worldwide Communications Group Inc.) New York 1986–2001, Chair. 2001-06, Chair. Emer. 2006–. *Address:* c/o DDB Worldwide Communications Group Inc., 437 Madison Avenue, New York, NY 10022, USA.

REINHARDT, Klaus, DrPhil; German army officer (retd); b. 15 Jan. 1941, Berlin, m. Heide-Ursula Reinhardt (née Bando) 1966; two c.; ed Univ. of Freiburg; joined army as officer cadet, Mountain Infantry; Commdr Mountain Infantry 1986–88; Commdr Army Führungsakademie 1990–93; Commdg Gen. III Corps 1993–94; Gen.-Lt, Commdr German Army, Koblenz 1994–96; Commdg Gen. of NATO Peace-keeping Unit in Kosovo (Kfor) 1999–2000; Commdr NATO Forces, Heidelberg 2000; retd 2001; currently Lecturer, Univ. of Augsburg and Univ. of Munich; fmr Vice Pres. Clausewitz Soc., now Pres.; mem. Int. Advisory Bd World Security Network Foundation. *Publication:* Wende vor Moskau 1998. *Leisure interests:* classical music, skiing, mountaineering, travel. *Address:* Karthäuserhofweg 10, 56075 Koblenz, Germany. *Telephone:* (261) 55690.

REINHOUDT, David N.; Dutch chemist and academic; *Professor of Applied Chemistry, Radboud University, Nijmegen;* b. 1942; ed Delft Univ. of Tech.; Researcher, Shell NV 1970–75; part-time Prof. (extraordinarius), Univ. Twente 1975–78, Full Prof. 1978–2012, Prof. Emer. 2012–, Scientific Dir, MESA+ Research Inst., Enschede 1999–2007; Chair. NanoNed (Dutch network for nanotechnology) 2002–11; Prof. of Applied Chem., Radboud Univ., Nijmegen 2012–; Chair. Nat. Foundation for Supramolecular Chemistry, European Supramolecular Science and Tech. Foundation; Vice-Chair. Nat. Org. for Applied Science (STW) 1996–; mem. Editorial Bd several journals, including European Journal of Organic Chemistry, Journal of Supramolecular Chemistry, New Journal of Chemistry; mem. Royal Dutch Acad. of Sciences (KNAW), ACS, Royal Dutch Chemical Soc.; Fellow, AAAS 1997–, Inst. of Physics; Kt, Order of the Dutch Lion 2002; Dr hc (Parma), (Pecs); Izatt-Christensen Award 1995, Simon Stevin Meesterschap 1998. *Publications:* more than 1,000 scientific publs, patents, review articles, and books. *Address:* Faculty of Science and Technology/SMCT, Universiteit Twente, Postbus 217, 7500 AE Enschede, Netherlands (office). *Telephone:* (53) 4892980 (office). *Fax:* (53) 4894645 (office). *E-mail:* d.n .reinhoudt@utwente.nl (office). *Website:* www.utwente.nl/tnw/mnf/ Former_members/prof_reinhoudt (office).

REINICHE, Dominique; French business executive; *President and Chief Operating Officer, Europe Group, The Coca-Cola Company;* b. 13 July 1955; one d. two step-d.; ed ESSEC Business School, Cergy-Pontoise; began career as Brand Man. at Procter & Gamble France, promoted to Assoc. Advertising Man.; worked for Kraft Jacobs Suchard; joined Coca-Cola Enterprises in 1992, Group Vice-Pres. and Gen. Man. (France) Coca-Cola Enterprises 1998–2003, Sr Vice-Pres. and Pres. Coca-Cola Enterprises Europe 2003–05, Pres. and COO Europe Group, The Coca-Cola Co. 2005–; mem. Bd Dirs The AXA Group 2005–; Pres. Union des annonceurs (French advertiser asscn), UNESDA (European Soft Drink Asscn); mem. Bd ECR (Efficient Consumer Response) Europe; mem. Advisory Bd ING Direct; mem. Exec. Bd Medef (French employers' org.); Chevalier, Legion d'honneur 2002; ranked by Fortune magazine amongst the 50 Most Powerful Women in Business outside the US (22nd) 2003, (39th) 2004, (25th) 2005, (40th) 2006, (44th) 2007, (30th) 2008, (21st) 2009, (22nd) 2010, (15th) 2011, (16th) 2012, ranked by the Financial Times amongst the Top 25 Businesswomen in Europe (20th) 2007. *Address:* The Coca-Cola Co., PO Box 1734, Atlanta, GA 30301, USA (office). *Telephone:* (404) 676-2121 (office). *Fax:* (404) 676-6792 (office). *Website:* www.coca-cola.com (office).

REINIG, Gen. Gaston Charles-Marie; Luxembourg military officer; *Chief of Defence;* b. 17 Nov. 1956, Diekirch; two d.; ed Ecole Royale Militaire, Brussels, Ecole d'Application d'Infanterie, Montpellier, Ecole d'Etat-major, Compiègne, Ecole Supérieure de Guerre Interarmées, Paris, Institut des Hautes Etudes de Défense Nationale, Strasbourg, JF Kennedy School, Harvard Univ., USA; rifle peloton Commdr, Rifle and Recce Co. Commdr, Commdr Luxembourg contingent, NATO Allied Command Europe Mobile Force Land (AMF (L)) 1981–89; Logistics Staff Officer, Personnel 1989–94; Deputy Commdr Mil. Centre, Diekirch (Armed

Forces Operational Centre) 1994–98, Commdr 2002–08; Perm. Mil. Rep. to NATO, Brussels 1998–2002, Mil. Del. to WEU 2000–02; Chief of Defence of Luxembourg 2008–; numerous decorations including Grand Officier, Ordre du Mérite, Commdr, Ordre de la Couronne de Chêne, Croix d'Honneur et de Mérite militaire, Commdr, Ordre du Mérite, Commdr, Ordre de Mérite civil et militaire Adolphe de Nassau, Commdr, Ordre de Mérite civil et militaire de la Couronne de Chêne, Verdienstkreuz am Bande des Verdienstordens der Bundesrepublik Deutschland, ECMM Medal for Service with EC Monitor Mission, Army Commendation Medal, Commandant, Ordre du Lion de Finlande, Grande Ufficiale, Ordine Al Merito della Repubblica Italiana, Commdr, Légion d'Honneur. *Leisure interests:* military history, mountain trekking, swimming, biking; plays the clarinet (several prizes). *Address:* Etat-Major de l'Armée, 34–38 rue Goethe, BP 1873, 1018 Luxembourg, Luxembourg (office). *Telephone:* 26-84-82-1 (office). *Fax:* 26-84-56-06 (office). *E-mail:* patrice.strasser@armee.etat.lu (office). *Website:* www.armee.lu (office).

REINO, Fernando, LicenDr; Portuguese diplomatist (retd); b. 5 Aug. 1929, Felgar, Moncorvo; s. of Abel Reino and Julia Janeiro Reino; m. Maria Gabriela Vaz Reino 1962; two d.; ed Univ. of Coimbra, Univ. of Strasbourg, NATO Defence Coll.; entered the Foreign Service 1958, Political and NATO Depts, Lisbon 1958–60, Portuguese del. to NATO, Paris 1960–61, Portuguese Embassy, Tokyo 1961–62, Chargé d'affaires titular, Antananarivo 1962–63, Consul-Gen. Cape Town 1963–66, Chargé d'affaires, Tunis 1966–71, Deputy Head of Mission to the EEC 1971–73; Dir Int. Econ. Org. Dept, Lisbon 1973–74; Head of Co-operation and Tech. Assistance Dept and Co-ordinator Nat. Decolonization Comm. 1974–75; Amb. to Norway and Iceland 1977–80, Head of Civilian Staff of the Pres. 1980–81; Perm. Rep. to the UN and other Int. Orgs, Geneva 1981–85; Amb. to Spain 1985–88; Perm. Rep. to UN 1989–92; fmr Prof., Universidade Nova and Univs of Coimbra and Lusiada; decorations from Portugal, Spain, Brazil, Italy, the Vatican, Germany, Norway, Iceland, Greece, Venezuela. *Leisure interests:* writing, reading, music, gardening, trekking. *Address:* Quinta do Rio Touro, Azóia, Cabo da Roca, 2705-001 Colares, Sintra, Portugal (home). *Telephone:* (21) 929-2862 (home). *Fax:* (21) 929-2360 (home). *E-mail:* f.reino@mail.telepac.pt.

REINSALU, Urmas; Estonian politician; *Minister of Defence;* b. 22 June 1975, Tallinn; m.; two d.; ed 37th High School, Univ. Law Faculty; Chair. Univ. Student Body Foundation 1994–95; public law specialist, Ministry of Justice 1996–97; legal expert, Assessment Cttee, Constitution of the Govt of Estonia 1996–97; domestic policy adviser to the Pres. 1997–98; Dir Office of the Pres. 1998–2001; Political Sec., Res Publica 2001–02, Chair. 2002–06, Chair. Union of Pro Patria and Res Publica (Isaamaa ja Res Publica Liit—IRL) (following merger of Pro Patria Union and Res Publica in 2006) 2012–; Lecturer, Service Acad. 2002–03; mem. Riigikogu (Parl.) 2003–; Minister of Defence 2012–; Order of Merit (Second Class), Union of Former Forest Brothers 2013. *Address:* Ministry of Defence, Sakala 1, Tallinn 15094 (office); Union of Pro Patria and Res Publica (Isamaa ja Res Publica Liit), Paldiski mnt. 13, Tallinn 10137, Estonia (office). *Telephone:* 717-0022 (Ministry) (office); 624-0400 (IRL) (office). *Fax:* 717-0001 (Ministry) (office); 669-1071 (IRL) (office). *E-mail:* info@kmin.ee (office); info@irl.ee (office). *Website:* www.mod.gov.ee (office); www.irl.ee (office).

REINSHAGEN, Gerlind; German writer; b. 4 May 1926, Königsberg; d. of Ekkehard Technau and Frieda Technau; m. 1949; ed studies in pharmacy and art, Berlin; freelance author of novels, theatre and radio plays, screenplays, poetry, essays and criticism; mem. German PEN; mem. Deutsche Akad. der darstellenden Künste; Fördergabe Schillerpreis, Baden Württemberg 1974, Mühlheimer Dramatikerpreis 1977, Roswitha von Gandersheim Medaille 1984, Ludwig Mülheims Preis 1993, Niedersächsischer Kunstpreis 1997, Niedersächsischer Staatspreis 1999, Kritikerpris 2008. *Plays:* Doppelkopf 1968, Leben und Tod der Marilyn Monroe 1971, Himmel und Erde 1974, Sonntagskinder 1976, Frühlingsfest 1980, Eisenherz 1982, Die Clownin 1988, Feuerblume 1987, Tanz, Marie! 1989, Die fremde Tochter 1993, Die grüne Tür 1999. *Television:* Doppelkopf 1972, Himmel und Erde 1976, Sonntagskinder 1981. *Radio:* 12 radio plays. *Publications:* novels: Rovinato 1981, Die flüchtige Braut 1984, Zwölf Nächte 1989, Jäger am Rand der Nacht 1993, Am grossen Stern 1996, Göttergeschichte 2000, Nachts 2011; Gesammelte Stücke (collected pieces) 1986, Joint Venture 2003, Vom Feuer 2006, Die Frau und die Stadt 2007; contribs to theatrical journals and yearbooks etc. *Address:* Rheingaustrasse 2, 12161 Berlin, Germany. *Telephone:* (30) 8217171.

REISMAN, Heather; Canadian publishing executive; *CEO, Indigo Books & Music Inc.;* b. Montreal; m. Gerald Schwartz; four c.; ed McGill Univ.; Co-founder and Man. Dir Paradigm Consulting 1979–92; Pres. Cott Corpn 1992–96; Founder, Pres. and CEO Indigo Books, Music and Café, Inc. 1996–2001, Pres. and CEO Indigo Books & Music Inc. (following merger with Chapters Inc. 2001) 2001–; mem. Bd of Dirs Onex Corpn, Right to Play; fmr mem. Bd of Dirs Magna International, Suncor, Rogers Communications, Inc., Williams-Sonoma Inc.; Dir and Officer Mount Sinai Hosp.; fmr Gov. McGill Univ., Toronto Stock Exchange; mem. Bilderberg Steering Cttee; Dr hc (Ryerson Univ.) 2006; Int. Distinguished Entrepreneur Award, Univ. of Manitoba, John Molson School of Business Award of Distinction, Concordia Univ.; inducted into Waterloo Entrepreneur Hall of Fame, Univ. of Waterloo. *Publications include:* numerous articles on media, communications, manufacturing and retailing. *Address:* Indigo Books & Music Inc., 468 King Street West, Suite 500, Toronto, ON M5V 1L8, Canada (office). *Telephone:* (416) 364-4499 (office). *Fax:* (416) 364-0355 (office). *Website:* www .chapters.indigo.ca (office).

REISS, Timothy James, BA, MA, PhD, FRSC; British/Canadian/American academic; *Professor Emeritus of Comparative Literature and Distinguished Scholar in Residence, New York University;* b. 14 May 1942, Stanmore, Middx, England; s. of James Martin Reiss and Margaret Joan Ping; m. 2nd Patricia J. Hilden 1988; two s. one d. from previous m.; ed Hardye's School, Dorchester, Univ. of Manchester, Univ. of Paris (Sorbonne), France, Univ. of Illinois, USA; Instructor to Asst Prof., Yale Univ. 1968–73; Assoc. Prof., Univ. de Montréal 1973–79, Prof. and Chair. of Comparative Literature 1974–84; Prof. of Comparative Literature, Modern Languages and Philosophy, Emory Univ. 1983–86, Samuel C. Dobbs Prof. of Comparative Literature and French 1986–87; Prof. and Chair. of Comparative Literature New York Univ. 1987–94, 2005–06, Prof. 1994–2005, Prof. Emer. and Distinguished Scholar in Residence 2007–; Visiting Prof., Univ. of Toronto 1976–77, Univ. of British Columbia 1979, New York Univ. 1982, Univ. of Montreal 1984–87, Grad. Center, CUNY 1985, State Univ. of NY, Binghamton 1990, Univ. of

California, Berkeley 1996–97, Univ. of Oregon 1999–2000, Stanford Univ. 2001, 2002–03, 2004; Visiting Scholar, Univ. of Arizona, 2007–12; Visiting Scholar, Univ. of California, Davis 2012; Visiting Prof., Stanford Univ. 2014; mem. Acad. of Literary Studies 1986; Morse Fellowship, Paris 1971–72, Canada Council Sr Fellowship, Oxford 1977–78, Social Sciences Research Council of Canada Sr Fellowship, Oxford 1983–84, ACLS Sr Fellowship 1986–87, Guggenheim Fellowship, Cambridge 1990–91, Outstanding Academic Book 1983, 1993, Forkosch Prize in Intellectual History 1992, various other fellowships and awards. *Publications:* Toward Dramatic Illusion 1971, Science, Language and the Perspective Mind (ed.) 1973, Tragedy and Truth 1980, De l'ouverture des disciplines (ed.) 1981, The Discourse of Modernism (Choice Best Academic Book Award) 1982, Tragique et tragédie dans la tradition occidentale (ed.) 1983, The Uncertainty of Analysis 1988, The Meaning of Literature (Forkosch Prize, Choice Best Academic Book Award) 1992, Knowledge, Discovery and Imagination in Early Modern Europe 1997, For the Geography of a Soul (ed.) 2001, Against Autonomy: Global Dialectics of Cultural Exchange 2002, Sisyphus and Eldorado (ed.) (second revised edn) 2002, Mirages of the Selfe 2003, Music, Writing and Cultural Unity in the Caribbean (ed.) 2005, Topographies of Race and Gender: Mapping Cultural Representations, two vols (co-ed.) 2008–09; more than 160 essays and book chapters. *Address:* 1139 Shevlin Drive, El Cerrito, CA 94530 (home); Department of French and Italian, Stanford University, Piggott Hall, 450 Serra Mall, Stanford, CA 94305, USA (office). *Telephone:* (510) 847-9570 (home). *Fax:* (650) 723-0482 (office). *E-mail:* timothy.reiss@nyu.edu (office). *Website:* complit.as.nyu.edu (office).

REITEN, Eivind Kristofer; Norwegian energy and light metal industry executive and fmr politician; b. 2 April 1953, Midsund; m.; two c.; ed Univ. of Oslo; jr exec. officer, Ministry of Fisheries 1979–82; Sec. to Centre Party's Parl. Group 1982–83; State Sec. Ministry of Finance 1983–; Minister of Fisheries 1985–86, of Petroleum and Energy 1989–90; Man. Hydro Agri Div., Norsk Hydro 1986–88, Asst Gen. Man. Hydro Agri 1988, Pres. Energy Div. 1988, Dir Special Projects 1991–92, Pres. Refining and Marketing Div. 1992–96, Pres. Hydro Aluminium Metal Products 1996–98, Exec. Vice-Pres. and mem. Corp. Man. Bd, Norsk Hydro ASA 1999–2001, Pres. and CEO 2001–10 (resgnd), Chair. StatoilHydro (after acquisition of Norsk Hydro by Statoil) 1–4 Oct. 2007 (resgnd); Chair. Bd Norwegian Postal Service 1995–99, Int. Primary Aluminium Inst. 1998–2000, Telenor 2000–01; mem. Bd Cen. Bank of Norway 1988–94, Norske Skog 1995–2000; mem. Green Tax Comm. 1994–95. *Address:* c/o Norsk Hydro ASA, Drammensveien 264, 0283, Oslo, Norway.

REITER, Janusz; Polish diplomatist and international affairs scholar; *President, Center for International Relations, Warsaw;* b. 6 Aug. 1952, Kościerzyna; s. of Stanisław Reiter and Hilda Reiter; m. Hanna Reiter 1975; two d.; ed Warsaw Univ.; foreign affairs commentator, Życie Warszawy (daily) 1977–81 (dismissed during martial law); Co-founder Foundation for Int. Ventures and Centre for Int. Studies in Warsaw; mem. Dziekania Club of Political Thought; staff writer, Przegląd Katolicki (weekly) 1984–89, Gazeta Wyborcza (daily) and Polish TV 1989–90, Rzeczpospolita (daily); Amb. to FRG 1990–95; f. Center for Int. Relations, Warsaw 1996, Pres. 2010–; Amb. to USA 2005–07; Co-founder Council for Foreign Policy; mem. Council on European Integration; Great Cross of Merit with the Star and Ribbon (Germany); Hon. Award, European Univ., Viadrina, Germany; hon. degree from Coll. of the Atlantic, USA. *Publications:* several books, policy papers, and articles on Europe, the transatlantic relations, European security policy and other international topics, including Roads to Europe. *Leisure interests:* music, travelling, literature. *Address:* Center for International Relations, Emilii Plater 25, 00-688 Warsaw, Poland (office). *Telephone:* (22) 646-52-67 (office). *E-mail:* info@reiter.org.pl (office). *Website:* csm.org.pl/pl (office).

REITH, Gen. Sir John, Kt, KCB, CBE; British army officer; commissioned into Parachute Regiment 1969; fmr Chief of Staff, 20 Armoured Brigade, Detmold, W Germany; fmr co. commdr, 3rd Battalion, Parachute Regiment, fmr Commdr, 1st Battalion; Chief of Staff, 1 (UK) Armoured Div., Verden, W Germany 1988; deployed to Gulf for Operation Granby 1990–91; Commdr 4th Armoured Brigade, Munster and Osnabruck 1992; fmr Commdr, British Forces, fmr Commdr, UN Sector SW; Supervisor, Washington Agreement –1994; Dir Int. Orgs, Ministry of Defence, London 1994–95, Dir of Mil. Operations 1995–97; Commdr, Allied Command Europe Mobile Force (Land) 1997–2000; Asst Chief of Defence Staff (Policy), Cen. Staff, Ministry of Defence 2000–01; Chief of Jt Operations, Perm. Jt HQ, Northwood 2001–04; Deputy Supreme Allied Command Europe (DSACEUR), NATO 2004– 07 (retd).

REITH, Peter, BEcons, LLB; Australian company director, consultant, international organization official and fmr politician; b. 15 July 1950, Melbourne; s. of A. C. Reith and E. V. Reith (née Sambell); m. Julie Treganowan 1971; four s.; ed Monash Univ.; Supreme Court 1975; worked as solicitor 1976–82; mem. Westernport Waterworks Trust and Cowes Sewerage Authority 1977–82; Councillor Shire of Phillip Island 1976–81, Pres. 1980–81; mem. various cttees and authorities; MP for Flinders 1982–83, 1984–2001; Deputy Leader of the Opposition 1990–93; Shadow Special Minister of State 1993, responsible for Mabo 1994; Shadow Minister for Defence Jan.–Sept. 1994, Shadow Minister with responsibility for Mabo Jan.–May 1994; Shadow Minister for Defence May–Sept. 1994; Shadow Minister for Foreign Affairs 1994–95, for Industrial Relations and Man. of Opposition Business in the House 1995–96; Minister for Industrial Relations and Leader of the House of Reps and Minister Assisting the Prime Minister for the Public Service 1996–97; Minister for Workplace Relations and Small Business and Leader of the House of Reps 1997–98, Minister for Employment, Workplace Relations and Small Business and Leader of the House of Reps 1998–2001; Minister for Defence 2001; Dir representing Australia, Repub. of Korea, New Zealand and Egypt, EBRD 2003–06, Alt. Dir 2006–; mem. Asscn of Christian Community Colls.; co-ordinator Free Legal Aid Services; Founding Sec. and mem. Newhaven Coll. *Publication:* The Reith Papers. *Leisure interests:* golf, reading. *Address:* European Bank for Reconstruction and Development (EBRD), One Exchange Square, 175 Bishopsgate, London, EC2A 2JN, England (office); 1A Camperdown Street, Brighton East, Vic. 3187, Australia (home). *Telephone:* (20) 7338-6000 (office). *Fax:* (20) 7338-6100 (office). *E-mail:* australiaoffice@ebrd.com (office); peterreith@bigpond.com.au. *Website:* www.ebrd.com (office).

REITHOFER, Norbert, Dr-Ing; German automotive industry executive; *Chairman of the Board of Management, BMW AG;* b. 29 May 1956, Penzberg; ed Technische Universität München; joined BMW 1987, has served in numerous sr man. positions including Dir Body-in-White Production Div. 1991–94, Tech. Dir BMW South Africa 1994–97, Pres. BMW Mfg Corpn, USA, SC 1997–2000, mem. Bd of Man. with responsibility for production 2000–06, Chair. Bd of Man. BMW AG 2006–; Grand Decoration of Honour in Gold (Grosses Goldenes Ehrenzeichen) for Services to the Repub. of Austria 2005, Bayerischen Verdienstorden 2010; Hon. Dr-Ing. *Address:* BMW AG, 130 Petuelring, Munich 80788, Germany (office). *Telephone:* (89) 382-0 (office). *Fax:* (89) 382-258-58 (office). *E-mail:* info@bmwgroup .com (office). *Website:* www.bmwgroup.com (office); www.bmw.com (office).

REITMAN, Ivan, MusB; Canadian film director and producer; b. 27 Oct. 1946, Komarmo, Czechoslovakia; s. of Leslie Reitman and Clara R. Reitman; m. Genevieve Robert 1976; one s. two d.; ed McMaster Univ.; moved to Canada 1951; Hon. LLD (Toronto); Dir of the Year, Nat. Asscn of Theater Owners 1984, Canadian Genie Special Achievement Award 1985, Star on Hollywood Walk of Fame 1997. *Stage shows produced:* The Magic Show 1974, The National Lampoon Show 1975, Merlin 1983 (also Dir). *Films:* (dir and exec. producer) Cannibal Girls 1973; (producer) They Came From Within 1975, Death Weekend 1977, Blackout 1978, National Lampoon's Animal House 1978 (People's Choice Award 1979), Heavy Metal 1981, Stop! Or My Mom Will Shoot 1992, Space Jam 1996, Private Parts 1996; (producer and dir) Foxy Lady 1971, Meatballs 1979, Stripes 1981, Ghostbusters 1984, Legal Eagles 1986, Twins 1988 (People's Choice Award 1989), Ghostbusters II 1989, Kindergarten Cop 1990, Dave 1993, Junior 1994, Father's Day 1996, Six Days/Seven Nights 1998, Doomsday Man 1999; (exec. producer) Rabid 1976, Spacehunter: Adventures in the Forbidden Zone 1983, Big Shots 1987, Casual Sex? 1988, Feds 1988, Beethoven 1992, Beethoven's 2nd 1993, Commandments 1996, Road Trip (exec. producer) 2000, Evolution (exec. producer and dir) 2001, Killing Me Softly (exec. producer) 2002, Old School (exec. producer) 2003, Eurotrip (exec. producer) 2004, Trailer Park Boys: The Movie (exec. producer) 2006, Disturbia (exec. producer) 2007. *TV series:* (producer and dir) Delta House 1978, Alienators: Evolution Continues (exec. producer) 2001. *TV films:* (exec. producer) The Late Shift 1996; mem. Dirs Guild of America. *Address:* Building 489, 100 University City Plaza, Universal City, CA 91608, USA (office).

REITMAN, Jason; Canadian film director; b. 19 Oct. 1977, Montreal; s. of Ivan Reitman and Geneviève Robert; m. Michele Lee 2004; one c.; ed Univ. of Southern California; began career as production asst on father's films; co-f. Hard C Productions (production co.) 2006; named best debut dir by Nat. Bd of Review and US Comedy Arts 2006. *Films:* Operation 1998, In God We Trust 2000, Gulp 2001, Consent 2004, Thank You for Smoking 2006, Juno 2007, Jennifer's Body 2008, Up in the Air (also producer and screenplay) 2009, Chloe 2009, Ceremony 2010. *Address:* c/o Fox Searchlight Pictures, 10201 W. Pico Blvd, Bldg. 38, Los Angeles, CA 90035, USA (office). *Telephone:* (310) 369-4402 (office).

REITZ, Edgar; German film director; b. 1 Nov. 1932, Morbach; m. Salome Kammer 1995; one s.; co-f. Institut für Filmgestaltung 1963; co-f. (with son Christian Reitz) Reitz & Reitz Media, Munich; f. Edgar Reitz Filmproduktion GmbH; Prof. of Film, Staatliche Hochschule für Gestaltung (State Univ. of Design), Karlsruhe; numerous awards including Konrad-Wolf Prize and Hans Abich Prize (for Heimat Trilogy) 2007 Bundesverdienstkreuz 1993, Großes Verdienstkreuz des Verdienstordens der Bundesrepublik Deutschland 2006, Officier, Ordre des arts et des lettres 2010. *Films include:* Mahlzeiten (appeared in UK as Lust for Love) 1966–67, Die Reise nach Wien 1973, Picnic 1975, Stunde Null 1976, Deutschland im Herbst (with others) 1977–78, Der Schneider von Ulm 1978, Heimat 1980–84, Die zweite Heimat 1991, Die Nacht der Regisseure 1995, Heimat 3: Chronik einer Zeitenwende (TV) 2004, Heimat-Fragmente: Die Frauen 2006. *Address:* Reitz & Reitz Medien, Rottmannstraße 11, 80333 Munich (office); Edgar Reitz Filmproduktion GmbH, Studio, Rottmannstraße 11, 80333 Munich, Germany. *Telephone:* (89) 2724524 (office); (89) 2723276. *Fax:* (89) 2719760 (office). *E-mail:* kontakt@reitz-medien.de (office); mail@erfilm.de. *Website:* www.edgar -reitz.de.

RELE, Kanak Y., LLB, PhD; Indian dancer and academic; b. 1937; ed Univ. of Mumbai; Mohini Attam dancer; f. Nalanda Dance Research Centre Mumbai 1996; f. Nalanda Nritya Kala Mahavidyalaya 1973; fmr Dean, Faculty of Fine Arts, Univ. of Mumbai; fmr Convenor Expert Cttee School of Performing and Visual Arts, Indira Gandhi National Open Univ.; Sarangdev Fellowship 1995; Gaurav Puraskar of Gujarat 1989, Padma Shri 1990, Kalidas Samman, Sangeet Natak Akademi Award 1994, M. S. Subbulakshmi Award. *Publications include:* Mohini Attam–The Lyrical Dance, A Handbook of Classical Dance Terminology, Bhaavaniroopanna–On Indian System of Abhinaya. *Address:* Plot number A-7/1 NS Road-10, JVPD Scheme Vile Parle West, Mumbai 400 049, India (home). *Telephone:* (22) 26206326 (home); 9821025843 (mobile). *Website:* drkanakrele.com.

RELL, M(ary) Jodi; American politician and fmr state governor; b. (Mary Carolyn Reavis), 16 June 1946, Norfolk, Va; m. Lou Rell; one s. one d.; ed Old Dominion Univ., Western Conn. State Univ.; served in Conn. House of Reps for ten years, fmr Asst Minority Leader and Deputy Minority Leader; Lt-Gov. of Conn. 1994–2004, presided over Senate, mem. Prison and Jail Overcrowding Comm., Gov.'s Law Enforcement Council, State Finance Advisory Cttee; est. Lt-Gov.'s Comm. on State Mandate Reform 1995; Gov. of Conn. 2004–11; apptd Chair. Hartford Econ. Devt Advisory Group 1998; fmr Vice-Chair. Brookfield Rep. Town Cttee; mem. Women Execs in State Govt, Nat. Order Women Legislators (fmr Vice-Pres. and Nat. Pres.), Brookfield Business and Professional Women's Club, Brookfield Rep. Women's Club (fmr Pres.); fmr mem. Nat. Conf. of Lt-Govs; mem. Bd Trustees, Regional YMCA of Western Conn., Candlewood Lions Club; Republican; Hon. LLD (Hartford) 2001, (New Haven) 2004; honoured by Uniformed Professional Fire Fighters, AmeriCares, Arthritis Foundation, CT Race for the Cure, Conn. Library Asscn, Conn. Chapter of American Coll. of Health Care Admins, Conn. Preservation Council, Conn. Fed. of Business and Professional Women, Arnold Markle Public Service Award, Connecticut Voices for Children, First Kids Policy Leadership Award 2001, Impact Award, Connecticut Tech. Council 2001, named a Melvin Jones Fellow, Lions Club Int. Foundation 2003, Nathan Davis Award for outstanding govt service, American Medical Asscn 2008, Leadership Award, Nat. Order of Women Legislators, among others. *Address:* c/o Office of the Governor, State Capitol, 210 Capitol Avenue, Hartford, CT 06106, USA.

RELYVELD, Steven S.; Suriname lawyer and politician; *Minister of Finance;* b. 12 July 1964, Paramaribo; ed Anton de Kom Univ., Paramaribo; civil servant, Ministry of Labour 1990–95, later becoming Dir and Perm. Sec., Ministry of Labour, Tech. Devt and the Environment 2011; Minister of Physical Planning, Land and Forestry June–Nov. 2013, Minister of Finance 2013–; mem. Mega-combinatie. *Address:* Ministry of Finance, Tamarindelaan 3, Paramaribo, Suriname (office). *Telephone:* 472610 (office). *Fax:* 476314 (office). *E-mail:* secmin@finance.gov.sr (office). *Website:* www.gov.sr/sr/ministerie-van-financiën.aspx (office).

REMEDIOS, Alberto Telisforo, CBE; British singer (tenor); b. 27 Feb. 1935, Liverpool; s. of Albert Remedios and Ida Remedios; brother of Ramon Remedios; m. 1st Shirley Swindells 1958; one s.; m. 2nd Judith Hosken 1965; one s. one d.; studied with Edwin Francis, Liverpool; joined Sadler's Wells Opera Co. 1955; now sings regularly with ENO and Royal Opera House, Covent Garden; has made numerous appearances in USA, Canada, Argentina, Germany, France and Spain and appeared in concert with major British orchestras; Queen's Prize, Royal Coll. of Music; First Prize, Int. Singing Competition, Sofia, Bulgaria; Sir Reginald Goodall Award Wagner Soc. 1995. *Recordings include:* Wagner's Der Ring des Nibelungen and Tippett's A Midsummer Marriage. *Leisure interests:* football, motoring, record collecting. *Address:* c/o Stuart Trotter, 21 Lanhill Road, London, W9 2BS, England. *Telephone:* (20) 7289-6315.

REMENGESAU, Tommy Esang, Jr, BS; Palauan politician and head of state; *President;* b. 28 Feb. 1956, Koror; s. of Thomas O. Remengesau, Sr and Ferista Esang Remengesau; m. Debbie Mineich; two s. two d.; ed Grand Valley State Univ., Mich., Michigan State Univ., USA; Admin./Planner, Palau Bureau of Health Services 1980–81; Public Information Officer, Palau Legislature 1981–84; Senator, Nat. Congress 1984–92; Vice-Pres. and Minister of Admin. 1993–2001, Pres. of Palau 2001–09, 2013–; Senator 2009–; rep. to IMF 1997; led several official dels to Taiwan (Repub. of China); hosted first Taiwan-Pacific Allies Summit 2006; named by Time magazine a Hero of the Environment 2007. *Leisure interests:* fishing (twice Grand Champion All-Micronesia Fishing Derby). *Address:* Office of the President, POB 6051, Koror, PW 96940, Palau (office). *Telephone:* 488-2403 (office). *Fax:* 488-1662 (office). *E-mail:* pres@palaunet.com (office). *Website:* www.kotedlbelau.com.

REMNICK, David J., AB; American journalist, editor and writer; *Editor-in-Chief, The New Yorker;* b. 29 Oct. 1958, Hackensack, NJ; s. of Edward C. Remnick and Barbara Remnick (née Seigel); m. Esther B. Fein; two s. one d.; ed Princeton Univ.; reporter, The Washington Post 1982–91; staff writer, The New Yorker 1992–, Ed.-in-Chief 1998–; Livingston Award 1991, George Polk Award 1994, Helen Bernstein Award 1994, Editor of the Year, Advertising Age 2000. *Publications include:* Lenin's Tomb: The Last Days of the Soviet Empire (Pulitzer Prize for General Non-fiction 1994) 1993, The Devil Problem (and other true stories) 1996, Resurrection: The Struggle for a New Russia 1997, King of the World: Muhammad Ali and the Rise of an American Hero 1998, Life Stories: Profiles from The New Yorker (ed.) 1999, Wonderful Town: Stories from The New Yorker (ed.) 1999, Reporting: Writings from The New Yorker 2006, The Bridge: The Life and Rise of Barack Obama 2010; contrib. to newspapers and periodicals. *Address:* The New Yorker, 4 Times Square, New York, NY 10036, USA (office). *E-mail:* themail@newyorker.com (office). *Website:* www.newyorker.com (office).

REN, Fuyao; Chinese business executive; *Chairman, Shanxi Coking Coal Group;* b. Dec. 1953, Shanxi Xiaxian; joined CCP 1983; with Huozhou Mining bureau 1996–2000, Sec. of Party Cttee and Chair. Huozhou Coal Group Co. 2000–01, Gen. Man. Shanxi Coking Coal Group 2001–05; Deputy Dir State-owned Assets Supervision and Admin Comm., Shanxi Prov. 2005–07; Sec. of Party Cttee and Chair. Yangquan Coal Industry Group 2007–11; Sec. of Party Cttee and Chair. Shanxi Coking Coal Refco Group Ltd 2011–; awarded title of 'model worker' by Govt of Shanxi Prov. 1998. *Address:* Shanxi Coking Coal Group, 1 Xinjinci Road, Taiyuan 30024, People's Republic of China (office). *Telephone:* (351) 8305000 (office). *Fax:* (351) 8305101 (office). *E-mail:* webmaster@sxcc.com.cn (office). *Website:* en.sxjh.com.cn (office); www.sxcc.com.cn (office).

REN, Hongbin; Chinese business executive; *Chairman, China National Machinery Industry Corporation (Sinomach);* Pres. China Nat. Construction & Agricultural Machinery Import & Export Corpn 1991–2001; currently Chair. China Nat. Machinery Industry Corpn (Sinomach), also Deputy Sec. CCP. *Address:* China National Machinery Industry Corporation, 3 Danling Street, Haidian District, Beijing, 100080, People's Republic of China (office). *Telephone:* (10) 82688888 (office). *Fax:* (10) 82688811 (office). *E-mail:* office@sinomach.com.cn (office). *Website:* www.sinomach.com.cn (office).

REN, Jianxin, BA, MA; Chinese business executive; *President and General Manager, China National Chemical Corporation (ChemChina);* b. 1958; ed Lanzhou Univ.; worked as farmer in Dunhuang Co., Gansu Prov. during China's Cultural Revolution; with seven colleagues, co-f. China BlueStar Chemical Cleaning (China's first industrial-cleaning co.) 1984, has acquired more than 100 state-owned enterprises, brokered merger between BlueStar and other cos affiliated to fmr Ministry of Chemical Industry to create China Nat. Chemical Corpn (ChemChina) 2004, currently Pres. and Gen. Man., Sec. Party Cttee; Communist Youth League Sec., Chemical Machinery Research Inst. of original Chemical Industry Ministry 1984; Annual Best China Overseas Investor 2012. *Address:* China National Chemical Corporation (ChemChina), 62 Beisihuan West Road, Haidian District, Beijing 100080, People's Republic of China (office). *Telephone:* (10) 82676988 (office). *Fax:* (10) 82677088 (office). *E-mail:* info@chemchina.com (office). *Website:* www.chemchina.com (office); www.chemchina.com.cn (office).

REN, Jianxin; Chinese judge; b. Aug. 1925, Fencheng (now Xiangfen) Co., Shanxi Prov.; ed Eng Coll., Beijing Univ.; joined CCP 1948; Sec., Secr. N China People's Govt 1948–49; Sec. Gen. Office, Cen. Comm. for Political Science and Law, Sec. Cen. Comm. for Legis. Affairs 1949–54; Sec. Legis. Affairs Bureau, State Council 1954–59; Section Leader, Div. Chief, China Council for the Promotion of Int. Trade (CCPIT) 1959–71, Dir Legal Dept, CCPIT, lawyer 1971–81, Vice-Chair. CCPIT 1981–83; Vice-Pres. Supreme People's Court 1983–88, Pres. 1988–98; Sec.-Gen. Leading Group of Cen. Cttee for Political Science and Law 1989, Deputy Sec. and Sec.-Gen. Cen. Cttee 1990; Chair. Soc. of Chinese Judges 1994–; Hon. Chair China

Law Soc. (fmr Vice-Pres.), China Foreign Econ. Trade and Arbitration Cttee, China Maritime Arbitration Cttee (fmr Chair.); Hon. Pres. China Int. Law Soc. (fmr Vice-Pres.); Dir China Training Centre for Sr Judges; Prof. (part-time) Beijing Univ.; mem. 13th CCP Cen. Cttee 1987–92, 14th CCP Cen. Cttee 1992–97, Sec. Secr. 14th CCP Cen. Cttee 1992–97; Del., 15th CCP Nat. Congress 1997–2002; Sec. CCP Cen. Comm. for Political Science and Law 1992–98; Vice-Chair. 9th Nat. Cttee CPPCC 1998–2003. *Address:* National Committee of Chinese People's Political Consultative Conference, 23 Taipingqiao Street, Beijing, People's Republic of China (office).

REN, Zhengfei; Chinese business executive; *Deputy Chairman and CEO, Huawei Technologies Company Ltd;* b. 1944, Jiangsu; ed Chongqing Inst. of Civil Eng and Architecture; employed in civil eng industry until 1974, joined military's Eng Corps as a soldier tasked to establish the Liao Yang Chemical Fibre Factory 1974, took positions as technician, engineer, promoted as a Deputy Dir (equivalent to a Deputy Regimental Chief but without mil. rank), invited to attend Nat. Science Conf. 1978 and 12th Nat. Congress of CCP 1982, retd from army 1983; worked in logistics service base of Shenzhen South Sea Oil Corpn; left job to co-f. Huawei Technologies Co. Ltd 1987, Deputy Chair. and CEO 1988–; joined CCP 1978, mem. 12th Nat. Congress of CCP; included by TIME magazine in its list of 100 Most Influential People of 2005. *Address:* Huawei Technologies Co. Ltd, Bantian, Longgang District, Shenzen, 518129, China (office). *Telephone:* (755) 28780808 (office). *E-mail:* hwtech@huawei.com (office). *Website:* www.huawei.com (office).

RENARD, Ian Andrew, AM, BA, LLM; Australian lawyer, company director and fmr university chancellor; *Director and Chairman, Remuneration Committee, SP AusNet;* b. 8 Aug. 1946, Melbourne, Vic.; s. of Roy Renard and Dorothy Renard; m. Diana Renard; four d.; ed Univ. of Melbourne; Partner, Arthur Robinson & Hedderwicks 1979–2001, Man. Partner 1989–91; Deputy Chancellor Univ. of Melbourne 2001–05, Chancellor 2005–09, Chair. Univ. of Melbourne Archives; Dir, SP AusNet (Chair. Remuneration Cttee), Hillview Quarries Pty Ltd; fmr Chair. Melbourne Theatre Co.; fmr Pres. Library Bd of Vic.; fmr Treas. Free Kindergarten Asscn; fmr Dir CSL Ltd, AMP Ltd, Newcrest Mining Ltd, Nth Broken Hill Ltd, Royal Children's Hosp.; Trustee, R.E. Ross Trust; fmr Trustee, The Queen's Fund; Hon. LLD; Supreme Court Prize 1969, Australian Library and Information Asscn Redmond Barry Award. *Publication:* Takeovers and Reconstructions in Australia (co-author). *Address:* Allens Linklaters, GPO Box 1776, Melbourne, Vic. 3001, Australia (office). *Telephone:* (3) 9613-8917 (office). *Fax:* (3) 9614-4661 (office). *E-mail:* ian.renard@allens.com.au (office). *Website:* www.allens.com.au (office).

RENAUD, Lerner; Haitian politician; Minister of Nat. Defence 2014–. *Address:* Ministry of National Defence, 2 rue Bazelais, Delmas 60, BP 1106, Pétionville, Haiti (office). *Telephone:* 3454-0501 (office). *E-mail:* haitidefense@gmail.com (office). *Website:* www.md.gouv.ht (office).

RENDELL, Edward (Ed) Gene, BA, JD; American lawyer, politician and fmr state governor; *Partner, Ballard Spahr LLP;* b. 5 Jan. 1944, New York; s. of Jesse T. Rendell and Emma Rendell (née Sloat); m. Marjorie Osterlund 1971; one s.; ed Riverdale Country School, Univ. of Pennsylvania, Villanova Univ. Law School; 2nd Lt, US Army Reserve 1968–74; called to Bar of Pennsylvania 1968, US Supreme Court 1981; Asst Dist Attorney, Chief Homicide Unit, Phila 1968–74, Deputy Special Prosecutor, Phila 1976, Dist Attorney 1978–86; Partner, Ballard Spahr Andrews & Ingersoll LLP 2000–03, Ballard Spahr LLP 2011–; Mayor of Phila 1992–2000; Gen. Chair. Democratic Nat. Cttee 1999–2000; Gov. Commonwealth of Pa 2003–11; Chair. Nat. Govs Asscn 2008–09; Lecturer in Law, Univ. of Pennsylvania; political analyst, NBC News 2011–; mem. Advisory Bd ThinkEco Inc. 2011–; mem. ABA, Phila Bar Asscn, Pennsylvania Dist Attorneys' Asscn, B'nai B'rith, United Jewish Org., Jewish War Vets; Democrat; Man of the Year Award, VFW 1980, American Cancer League 1981, Distinguished Public Service Award, Pa Co. Detectives Asscn 1981. *Leisure interest:* sports. *Address:* Ballard Spahr LLP, 1735 Market Street, 51st Floor, Philadelphia, PA 19103, USA (office). *Telephone:* (215) 864-8401 (office). *Fax:* (215) 933-3995 (office). *E-mail:* rendell@ballardspahr.com (office). *Website:* www.ballardspahr.com (office).

RENDELL OF BABERGH, Baroness (Life Peer), cr. 1997, of Aldeburgh in the County of Suffolk; **Ruth Barbara Rendell,** (Barbara Vine), CBE, FRSL; British crime novelist; b. 17 Feb. 1930; d. of Arthur Grasemann and Ebba Kruse; m. Donald Rendell 1950 (divorced 1975), remarried 1977 (died 1999); one s.; ed Loughton County High School; Dr hc (Essex) 1990; Arts Council Nat. Book Award for Genre Fiction 1981, Sunday Times Award for Literary Excellence 1990, Mystery Ink Gumshoe Award for Lifetime Achievement 2004, and other awards. *Publications include:* From Doon with Death 1964, To Fear a Painted Devil 1965, Vanity Dies Hard 1965, A New Lease of Death (aka Sins of the Father) 1967, Wolf to the Slaughter 1967, The Secret House of Death 1968, The Best Man to Die 1969, A Guilty Thing Surprised 1970, No More Dying Then 1971, One Across, Two Down 1971, Murder Being Once Done 1972, Some Lie and Some Die 1973, The Face of Trespass 1974, Shake Hands Forever 1975, A Demon in My View 1976, A Judgement in Stone 1976, A Sleeping Life 1978, Make Death Love Me 1979, The Lake of Darkness 1980, Put on by Cunning (aka Death Notes) 1981, Master of the Moor 1982, The Speaker of Mandarin 1983, The Killing Doll 1984, The Tree of Hands 1984, An Unkindness of Ravens 1985, Live Flesh 1986, Heartstones 1987, Talking to Strange Men 1987, The Veiled One 1988, The Bridesmaid 1989, Mysterious 1990, Going Wrong 1990, The Strawberry Tree 1990, Walking on Water 1991, Kissing the Gunner's Daughter 1992, The Crocodile Bird 1993, Simisola 1994, Blood Lines 1996, The Keys to the Street 1997, Road Rage 1997, A Sight for Sore Eyes 1998, Harm Done 1999, Babes in the Wood 2002, The Rottweiler 2003, Thirteen Steps Down 2004, End in Tears 2005, The Water's Lovely 2006, Not in the Flesh 2007, Portobello 2008, The Monster in the Box 2009, Tigerlily's Orchids 2010, The Vault 2011, The Saint Zita Society 2012; as Barbara Vine: A Dark-Adapted Eye 1986, A Fatal Inversion 1987, The House of Stairs 1988, Gallowglass 1990, King Solomon's Carpet 1991, Asta's Book 1993, The Children of Men 1994, No Night is Too Long 1994, The Keys to the Street 1996, The Brimstone Wedding 1996, The Chimney Sweeper's Boy 1998, Grasshopper 2000, The Blood Doctor 2002, The Minotaur 2005, The Water's Lovely 2007, The Birthday Present 2008, The Child's Child 2012; short story collections: The Fallen Curtain 1976, Means of Evil 1979, The Fever Tree 1982, The New Girlfriend 1985, Collected Short Stories 1987, Undermining the Central Line (with Colin Ward) 1989, The Copper Peacock 1991, Blood Lines 1995, Piranha to Scurfy and Other Stories 2001;

other: A Warning to the Curious: The Ghost Stories of M. R. James (ed.) 1987, Ruth Rendell's Suffolk 1989, The Reason Why: An Anthology of the Murderous Mind (ed.) 1995, Harm Done (ed.) 2000. *Leisure interests:* reading, walking, opera. *Address:* House of Lords, London, SW1A 0PW (office); 26 Cornwall Terrace Mews, London, NW1 5LL, England. *Telephone:* (20) 7219-2185 (office).

RENÉ, (France) Albert; Seychelles politician; *Leader, Seychelles People's Progressive Front;* b. 16 Nov. 1935, Mahé; s. of Price René and Louisa Morgan; m. 1st Karen Handley 1956; one d.; m. 2nd Geva Adam 1975; one s.; m. 3rd Sarah Zarquani 1993; one d.; ed St Louis Coll., Victoria, Seychelles Coll., St Maurice, Switzerland, St Mary's Coll., Southampton, UK, King's Coll., London; called to Bar 1957; Founder and Leader Seychelles People's United Party (later Seychelles People's Progressive Front) 1964–; mem. Parl. 1965; Minister of Works and Land Devt 1975–77; Prime Minister 1976–77; Pres. of Seychelles 1977–2004, also C-in-C, Minister of Econ. Devt and Housing 1977–78, of Internal Affairs and Finance 1977–79, of Finance 1977–78, of Youth and Community Devt 1978–80, of Finance and Industries 1981–89, of Planning and External Relations 1984–89, of Industry 1986–93, of Community Devt 1993, of Defence 1986–93, of Tourism 1988–89, of Internal Affairs, Defence and Legal Affairs; Order of the Golden Ark 1982. *Leisure interests:* gardening, fishing. *Address:* Seychelles People's Progressive Front (SPPF), PO Box 1242, Victoria, Seychelles (office). *Telephone:* 324622 (office). *Fax:* 225070 (office). *E-mail:* people@sppf.sc (office). *Website:* www.sppf.sc (office).

RENFREW, Magnus Archibald, MA; British exhibition organiser; *Director, ART HK;* b. 5 Nov. 1975, Winchester; s. of Colin Renfrew, Lord Renfrew of Kaimsthorn and Jane Renfrew; m. Emma Louise Renfrew; one s.; ed Univ. of St Andrews; Specialist in contemporary art, Bonhams 1999–2008; Fair Dir ART HK 2008–. *Address:* ART HK 11, 6/F Luk Kwok Centre, 72 Gloucester Road, Wanchai, Hong Kong Special Administrative Region, People's Republic of China (office). *Telephone:* 2918-8791 (office); 2918-8793 (office). *Fax:* 2918-8794 (office). *E-mail:* magnus@hongkongartfair.com (office); info@magnusrenfrew.com. *Website:* www .hongkongartfair.com (office); magnusrenfrew.com.

RENFREW OF KAIMSTHORN, Baron (Life Peer), cr. 1991, of Hurlet in the District of Renfrew; **Andrew Colin Renfrew,** PhD, ScD, FBA, FSA; British archaeologist and academic; *Senior Fellow, McDonald Institute for Archaeological Research, University of Cambridge;* b. 25 July 1937, Stockton-on-Tees; s. of the late Archibald Renfrew and Helena D. Renfrew; m. Jane M. Ewbank 1965; two s. one d.; ed St Albans School, St John's Coll., Cambridge and British School of Archaeology, Athens; Lecturer in Prehistory and Archaeology, Univ. of Sheffield 1965–70, Sr Lecturer 1970–72, Reader in Prehistory and Archaeology 1972; Prof. of Archaeology and Head of Dept, Univ. of Southampton 1972–81; Disney Prof. of Archaeology, Univ. of Cambridge 1981–2004, Dir McDonald Inst. for Archaeological Research 1990–2004, Fellow 2004–, currently Sr Fellow, Fellow, St John's Coll. 1981–86, Hon. Fellow 2004–, Master of Jesus Coll., Cambridge 1986–97, Professorial Fellow 1997–2004, Fellow Emer. 2004–; Visiting Lecturer, UCLA 1967; mem. Ancient Monuments Bd for England 1974–84, Royal Comm. on Historical Monuments 1977–87, Historic Buildings and Monuments Comm. for England 1984–86, Ancient Monuments Advisory Cttee 1984–2002, British Nat. Comm. for UNESCO 1984–86; Trustee, British Museum 1991–2001; Foreign mem. American Philosophical Asscn 2006; Foreign Assoc. NAS; Hon. FSA (Scotland); Hon. FRSE 2001; Hon. LittD (Sheffield) 1990, (Southampton) 1995, (Edinburgh) 2004, (Liverpool) 2004, (St Andrews) 2006, (Kent) 2007, (London) 2008; Dr hc (Faculty of Letters, Univ. of Athens) 1991; Rivers Memorial Medal, British Anthropological Inst. 1979, Sir Joseph Larmor Award 1961, Huxley Memorial Medal, Royal Anthropological Inst. 1991, Prix Int. Fyssen, Fondation Fyssen, Paris 1997, Language and Culture Prize, Univ. of Umeå, Sweden 1998, Rivers Memorial Medal, European Science Foundation Latsis Prize 2003, Balzan Prize 2004. *Publications:* The Emergence of Civilization 1972, Before Civilization 1973, The Explanation of Culture Change (ed.) 1973, British Prehistory (ed.) 1974, Transformations: Mathematical Approaches to Culture Change 1979, Problems in European Prehistory 1979, An Island Polity 1982, Theory and Explanation in Archaeology (ed.) 1982, Approaches to Social Archaeology 1984, The Archaeology of Cult 1985, Peer, Polity Interaction and Socio-Political Change (ed.) 1986, Archaeology and Language: The Puzzle of Indo-European Origins 1987, The Idea of Prehistory (co-author) 1988, Archaeology: Theories, Methods and Practice (co-author) 1991, The Cycladic Spirit 1991, The Archaeology of Mind (co-ed. with E. Zubrow) 1994, Loot, Legitimacy and Ownership 2000, Archaeogenetics (ed.) 2000, Figuring It Out 2003, Archaeology, The Key Concepts (co-ed.) 2005, Phylogenetic Methods and the Prehistory of Languages (co-ed.) 2006, Prehistory: the Making of the Human Mind 2007; contribs to Archaeology, Scientific American. *Leisure interests:* contemporary arts, coins, travel. *Address:* c/o Curtis Brown Ltd, Haymarket House, 28–29 Haymarket, London, SW1Y 4SP, England (office); Room 3.2, West Building, McDonald Institute for Archaeological Research, Downing Street, Cambridge, CB2 3ER, England (office). *Telephone:* (20) 7393-4400 (office); (1223) 333521 (office). *Fax:* (20) 7393-4401 (office); (1223) 333536 (office). *E-mail:* acr10@cam.ac.uk (office). *Website:* www.mcdonald.cam.ac.uk (office); www.parliament.uk/biographies/lords/lord-renfrew-of-kaimsthorn/3234.

RENGIFO RUIZ, Marciano; Peruvian government official and fmr army general; b. 25 Sept. 1934, Bellavista, San Martin; ed Escuela Militar de Chorrillos, Lima, Ecole Militaire St Cyr, France, Univ. de Piura, Centro de Altos Estudios Nacionales; numerous sr positions in Peruvian Army 1973–91; Mil. Rep. at OAS 1991; co-founder and mem. Perú Posible political party, mem. Manifesto Cttee 1999–2001; mem. Congress for San Martin 2000–, Pres. Defence Cttee 2000–02; First Vice-Pres. of Congress 2003–04; Minister of Defence 2005–06. *Address:* c/o Ministry of Defence, Avenida Arequipa 291, Lima 01, Peru (office).

RENHŌ; Japanese/Taiwanese politician, journalist and fmr model; *Minister for Electricity Conservation Promotion and Minister of State for Consumer Affairs and Food Safety and for Government Revitalization;* b. (Hsieh Lien-fang), 28 Nov. 1967, Tokyo, Japan; m. Murata Nobuyuki 1993; one s. one d. (twins); ed Faculty of Law, Aoyama Gakuin Univ., Tokyo, Beijing Univ., People's Repub. of China; born a Taiwanese citizen, also became Japanese citizen when Nationality Law amended 1985; adopted her mother's surname, Saitō; began being known simply as Renhō to avoid name confusion in her career; debut as a Clarion Girl 1988, appeared on several TV and radio programmes as commentator; newscaster on TBS and TV Asahi 1993, returned to television, anchoring and reporting on several TBS

programmes 2000; Councillor for Tokyo's At-large dist 2004–; mem. (Democratic Party of Japan—DPJ) for Tokyo, House of Councillors 2004–, Chair. Cttee on Educ., Culture and Science 2006, Cttee on Health, Welfare and Labour 2007, Cttee on Educ., Culture and Science 2009; Vice-Minister of State for Pensions in the Next Cabinet, DPJ 2009; Minister of State for Govt Revitalization (Kan Cabinet) 2010–; Minister for Civil Service Reform (reshuffled Kan Cabinet) 2010–11; Minister of State for Govt Revitalization 2010–; Minister of State for Consumer Affairs and Food Safety 2011–; Minister for Electricity Conservation Promotion 2011–. *Address:* Cabinet Office, 1-6-1, Nagata-cho, Chiyoda-ku, Tokyo 100-8914, Japan (office). *Telephone:* (3) 5253-2111 (office). *Website:* www.cao.go.jp/minister/1101_renho/profile_en/index.html (office); www.renho.jp; ameblo.jp/renho-blog.

RENNEMO, Svein; Norwegian economist and business executive; *Chairman, Statoil ASA;* b. 1947; ed Univ. of Oslo; analyst and monetary policy and econs adviser with Norges Bank (Norwegian cen. bank), OECD Secr., Paris and Ministry of Finance 1972–82; held various man. positions in Statoil 1982–94, latterly as Head of Petrochemical Div., mem. Bd of Dirs and Chair. StatoilHydro ASA (formed from merger of Statoil and Norsk Hydro 2007) 2008–, Chair. Statoil ASA 2008–, mem. Compensation Cttee; Deputy CEO and Chief Financial Officer Borealis 1994–97, CEO 1997–2001; CEO Petroleum Geo Services ASA 2002–08; Chair. Tomra Systems ASA, Pharmaq AS; mem. Bd of Dirs Norske Skogindustrier ASA. *Address:* Statoil ASA, Forusbeen 50, 4035 Stavanger, Norway (office). *Telephone:* 51-99-00-00 (office). *Fax:* 51-99-00-50 (office). *E-mail:* statoil@statoil.com (office). *Website:* www.statoil.com (office).

RENNER, Jeremy; American actor and musician; b. 7 Jan. 1971, Modesto, Calif.; s. of Lee Renner and Valerie Cearley; UN Goodwill Peace Amb. *Television includes:* Deadly Games 1995, A Nightmare Come True 1997, Time of Your Life 1999, CSI: Crime Scene Investigation 2001, House 2007, The Unusuals 2009. *Films include:* National Lampoon's Senior Trip 1995, Fish in a Barrel 2001, Dahmer 2002, A Little Trip to Heaven 2005, Neo Ned 2005, The Assassination of Jesse James by the Coward Robert Ford 2007, 28 Weeks Later 2007, Taken 2007, The Hurt Locker (Boston Soc. of Film Critics Award for Best Actor, Chicago Film Critics Asscn Award for Best Actor, Las Vegas Film Critics Soc. Award for Best Actor, Nat. Bd of Review Award for Best Breakthrough Performance – Male, Nat. Soc. of Film Critics Award for Best Actor, Online Film Critics Soc. Award for Best Actor) 2009, The Town 2010, Mission: Impossible – Ghost Protocol 2011, Avengers Assemble 2012, The Bourne Legacy 2012, American Hustle 2013. *Address:* c/o Untitled Entertainment, 1801 Century Park East, Suite 700, Los Angeles, CA 90067, USA (office).

RENNIE, Heughan Bassett (Hugh), CBE, BA, LLB, QC; New Zealand barrister, company director and arbitrator; b. 7 April 1945, Wanganui; s. of the late W. S. N. Rennie and of Reta Rennie; m. 1st Caroline Jane Harding 1967 (died 1992); three s.; m. 2nd Penelope Jane Ryder-Lewis 1998; ed Wanganui Collegiate School and Victoria Univ., Wellington; part-time law clerk, Wanganui 1960–67, legal officer, NZ Electricity, Wellington 1967–70; barrister and solicitor, Macalister Mazengarb Parkin and Rose, Wellington 1970–71, Partner 1972–91, Sr Litigation Partner 1982–91, Chair. 1989–91; sole barrister, Wellington 1991–95; QC 1995–; Chair. Fourth Estate Group 1970–88, Broadcasting Corpn of NZ (BCNZ) 1984–88, Govt Cttee on Restructuring BCNZ 1988, Chatham Is. Enterprise Trust 1990–2001, Policy Cttee, Dictionary of NZ Biography 1991–2001, Ministerial Inquiry into Auckland Power Supply Failure 1998, Royal NZ Ballet 1999–2003, The Marketplace Co. Ltd 1999–2009, M-co International Ltd 2001–10; Deputy Chair. Rugby World Cup Authority (NZ) 2010–11; Dir Fletcher Challenge Ltd 1992–99, BNZ Finance Ltd 1993–97, Bank of NZ 1997–2010, Fisher & Paykel Finance 2010–; Ed. Wellington Dist Law Soc. newspaper 1973–84; mem. NZ Law Soc. Cttees on Professional Advertising and Public Affairs 1981–84, NZ Council for Law Reporting 1983–87, Govt Advisory Cttee to statutory mems of Equiticorp 1989–, Sir David Beattie Chair of Communications Trust Bd (VUW) 1986–90, Scientific Cttee, Nat. Heart Foundation 1988–94, Bd NZ Inst. of Chartered Accountants 2009–; Trustee, Broadcasting History Project Trust Bd 1988–2004; NZ Medal 1990. *Leisure interests:* history, travel, writing, cycling, reading. *Address:* Harbour Chambers, 10th Floor, Equinox House, 111 The Terrace, PO Box 10-242, Wellington 6143, New Zealand (office). *Telephone:* 499-2684 (office); 472-9053 (home). *Fax:* 499-2705 (office). *E-mail:* hughrennie@legalchambers.co.nz (office). *Website:* www.harbourchambers.co.nz (office).

RENO, Janet, BA, LLB, JD; American lawyer, politician and fmr government official; b. 21 July 1938, Miami, Fla; d. of Henry Reno and Jane Wood; ed Cornell and Harvard Univs; admitted to Florida Bar 1963; Assoc., Brigham & Brigham 1963–67; Pnr, Lewis & Reno 1967–71; Staff Dir Judiciary Comm., Fla House of Reps 1971–72; Admin. Asst, State Attorney, 11th Judicial Circuit Fla, Miami 1973–76, State Attorney 1978–93; Pnr, Steel, Hector & Davis, Miami 1976–78; US Attorney-Gen. (first woman) 1993–2001; unsuccessful Democratic cand. for Gov. of Fla 2002; mem. Bd of Dirs Innocence Project; mem. ABA, American Law Inst., American Judicature Soc.; Democrat; Women First Award, YWCA 1993, National Women's Hall of Fame 2000, Lindy Boggs Award (Stennis Center) 2003. *Music includes:* exec. producer Song of America (compilation) 2007. *Address:* 11200 North Kendall Drive, Miami, FL 33176, USA.

RENO, Jean; French actor; b. (Juan Moreno Jederique y Jimenez), 30 July 1948, Casablanca, Morocco; four c.; m. 3rd Zofia Borucka 2006; Nat. Order of Merit 2003. *Films include:* L'Hypothèse du tableau volé 1979, Claire de femme 1979, Voulez-vous un bébé Nobel? 1980, L'Avant dernier 1981, Les bidasses aux grandes manoeuvres 1981, La passante du Sans-Souci 1982, Ballade sanglante 1983, Le dernier combat 1983, Subway 1985, Signes Extérieurs de Richesse 1983, Ne quittez pas 1984, Alea 1984, Notre Histoire 1984, Le téléphone sonne toujours deux fois 1985, Subway 1985, Strictement personnel 1985, Zone rouge 1986, I Love You 1986, The Big Blue 1988, La Femme Nikita 1990, L'homme au Masque d'Or 1990, L'Opération Corned Beef 1991, Loulou Graffiti (also wrote screenplay) 1991, Kurenai no buta (aka Porco rosso) 1992, La vis (The Screw) 1993, Paranoïa 1993, Les Visiteurs (The Visitors) 1993, The Professional (Léon) 1994, Les truffes 1995, French Kiss 1995, Beyond the Clouds 1995, Mission: Impossible 1996, Le jaguar 1996, For Roseanna 1997, Un amour de sorcière (Witch Way Love) 1997, Le soeurs soleil 1997, Couloirs du temps: Les visiteurs 2 1998, Godzilla 1998, Ronin 1998, Tripwire 1999, The Crimson Rivers (Les Rivières pourpres) 2000, Just Visiting 2001, Wasabi 2001, Rollerball 2002, The Quiet American 2002, Jet Lag (Décalage horaire) 2002, Ruby & Quentin (Tais-toi!) 2003, Crimson Rivers 2: Angels of the Apocalypse 2004, L'Enquête corse 2004, Hotel Rwanda 2004, L'Empire des loups 2005, La tigre e la neve (The Tiger and the Snow) 2005, The Pink Panther 2006, The Da Vinci Code 2006, Flyboys 2006, Flushed Away (voice) 2006, Ca$h 2008, The Pink Panther 2 2009, Inside Ring 2009, Couples Retreat 2009, Armoured 2009, The Round Up 2010, 22 Bullets 2010, Margaret 2011, You Don't Choose Your Family 2011, The Chef 2012. *Television includes:* L'Aéropostale, courrier du ciel (mini-series) 1980, Quelques hommes de bonne volonté (mini-series) 1983, Et demain viendra le jour 1984, Un homme comblé 1985, Tender Is the Night (mini-series) 1985, Pour venger Pépère 1986, Monsieur Benjamin 1987, Flight from Justice 1993, Les grandes occasions (film) 2006. *Address:* Chez les Films du Dauphin, 25 rue Yves-Toudic, 75010 Paris, France.

RENSCHLER, Andreas; German automotive industry executive; *Member, Board of Management, Daimler AG;* b. 1958, Stuttgart; joined Daimler-Benz 1988, fmrly Asst to Chair., led projects in Latin America and developing four-wheel drive vehicles, later Pres. Mercedes-Benz US Int., Inc., Pres. Smart Car Unit, DaimlerChrysler AG (now Daimler AG) 2004, now Head, Daimler Trucks Div., mem. Bd of Man., Daimler AG 2005–; Pres. Commercial Vehicle (CV) Bd of Dirs, European Automobile Mfrs Asscn 2008–; mem. Bd of Dirs Unaxis Holding AG 2005. *Address:* Daimler AG, Epplestrasse 225, 70546 Stuttgart, Germany. *Telephone:* (711) 17-0 (office). *Fax:* (711) 17-22244 (office). *Website:* www.daimler.com (office).

RENTCHNICK, Pierre, MD; Swiss physician (retd) and editor; b. 17 July 1923, Geneva; s. of Jacques Rentchnick and Blanche (Spiegel) Rentchnick; m. Paule Adam 1948; one s.; ed Univs of Geneva and Paris; Ed.-in-Chief, Médecine et Hygiène, Geneva 1956–93, Recent Results in Cancer Research; Ed. Springer, Heidelberg and New York 1962–83, Bulletin de l'Union int. contre le cancer, Geneva 1962–80; f. Kiwanis-Club, Geneva 1966, Pres. 1976–77; f. Int. Soc. for Chemotherapy 1959; Fellow, New York Acad. of Sciences, Medical Soc. of Prague, French Soc. of Infectious Pathology; Prix Littré (France) 1977. *Publications:* Esculape chez les Soviets 1954, Klinik und Therapie der Nebenwirkungen 1963, Esculape chez Mao 1973, Ces malades qui nous gouvernent 1976, Les orphelins mènent-ils le monde? 1978, Ces malades qui font l'Histoire 1983, Ces nouveaux malades qui nous gouvernent 1988–96; numerous publs on antibiotics in infectious diseases, on ethical problems, euthanasia etc.; numerous pathographies. *Leisure interests:* skiing, golf, swimming, art (Netzuke). *Address:* La Rose des Vents, 74160 Saint-Julien-en-Genevois, France (home). *Telephone:* (4) 50-37-85-47 (home).

RENTON OF MOUNT HARRY, Baron (Life Peer), cr. 1997, of Offham in the County of East Sussex; **(Ronald) Tim(othy) Renton,** PC, MA, DL; British politician, business executive and author; b. 28 May 1932, London; s. of R. K. D. Renton CBE and Mrs Renton MBE; m. Alice Fergusson 1960; two s. three d.; ed Eton Coll., Magdalen Coll., Oxford; joined C. Tennant Sons & Co. Ltd 1954, with Tennants subsidiaries in Canada 1957–62, Dir 1964–73, Man. Dir Tennant Trading Ltd 1964–73; Dir Silvermines Ltd 1967–84, Australia and New Zealand Banking Group 1967–76, J. H. Vavasseur & Co. Ltd 1971–74; mem. BBC Gen. Advisory Council 1982–84; contested (Conservative) Sheffield Park 1970; MP for Mid-Sussex 1974–97; Parl. Pvt. Sec. to Rt Hon. John Biffen, MP 1979–81, to Rt Hon Geoffrey Howe, MP 1983–84; Parl. UnderSec. of State FCO 1984–85, Minister of State FCO 1985–87; Parl. Sec. to HM Treasury and Govt Chief Whip 1989–90, Minister for the Arts and for the Civil Service 1990–92; mem. Select Cttee on Nationalized Industries 1974–79, Vice-Chair. Conservative Parl. Trade Cttee 1974–79, Chair. Conservative Foreign and Commonwealth Council 1982–84; mem. Select Cttee on Nat. Heritage 1995–97; mem. House of Lords European Communities Cttee 1997–; Chair. House of Lords European Cttee on Agric. and Environment 2004–; Vice-Pres. Conservative Trade Unionists 1978–80, Pres. 1980–84; Chair. Outsider Art Archive 1995–2000, Sussex Downs Conservation Bd 1997–2005, South Downs Jt Cttee 2005–; Vice-Chair. British Council 1992–98; Dir (non-exec.) Fleming Continental European Investment Trust PLC, Chair. 1999–2002; Parl. Consultant Robert Fleming Holdings 1992–97; mem. Council Sussex Univ. 2000–; Fellow Industry and Parl. Trust 1977–79; mem. Advisory Bd, Know-How Fund for Cen. and Eastern Europe 1992–99; mem. APEX, Council Roedean School 1982–2005 (Pres. 1998–2005), Devt Council, Parnham Trust, Criterion Theatre Trust; Trustee Mental Health Foundation 1985–89; Founding Pres. (with Mick Jagger) of Nat. Music Day 1992–97; Green Ribbon Political Award for Environmental Campaigning 2000, Bowland Award, Asscn of Areas of Outstanding Natural Beauty 2000. *Publications:* The Dangerous Edge 1994, Hostage to Fortune 1997, Chief Whip 2004. *Leisure interests:* writing, mucking about in boats, listening to opera, growing vines. *Address:* House of Lords, London, SW1A 0PW; Mount Harry House, Offham, Lewes, East Sussex, BN7 3QW, England. *Telephone:* (1273) 471450 (office); (20) 7219-3308. *Fax:* (1273) 471450 (office). *E-mail:* rentont@parliament.uk (office).

RENTZEPIS, Peter M., PhD; American chemist, electrical engineer and academic; *Presidential Chair and Professor of Chemistry and Electrical and Computer Engineering, University of California, Irvine;* b. 11 Dec. 1934, Kalamata, Greece; s. of Michael Rentzepis and Leuci Rentzepis; m. Alma Elizabeth Keenan; two s.; ed Denison, Syracuse and Cambridge Univ.; mem. Tech. Staff Research Labs Gen. Electric Co., New York, then mem. Tech. Staff, Bell Labs, New Jersey, Head, Physical and Inorganic Chem. Research Dept; Presidential Chair. and Prof. of Chem. and Electrical and Computer Eng, Univ. of California, Irvine 1986–, Dir CX (IT) 2; Adjunct Prof. of Chem., Univ. of Pennsylvania, of Chem. and Biophysics, Yale Univ. 1980–; Visiting Prof., Rockefeller Univ. 1971, MIT –1975, of Chem. Univ. of Tel Aviv; mem. numerous academic cttees and editorial bds including US Army Cttee on Energetic Materials Research and Tech. 1982–83; Dir NATO Advanced Study Inst. 1984–; Co-founder and Chair. Bd Call/Recall Inc. 1996–; mem. Bd of Dirs KRIKOS—Science and Tech. for Greece, Bd of Dirs The Quanex Corpn 1984; mem. Advisory Bd Uniloc Corpn, Physical Chem. Div. Nat. Inst. of Science and Tech.; mem. US AmCCOM Advisory Cttee, US Army ARRACOM Exec. Science Advisory Cttee, NATO Advanced Study Insts (Dir), International Science Foundation; mem. NAS 1978, American Physical Soc., AAAS, Nat. Acad. of Greece 1980; Hon. ScD (Denison) 1981, (Carnegie-Mellon) 1983, Hon. DPhil (Syracuse) 1980, Hon. DSc (Nat. Tech. Univ., Greece) 1990; American Chem. Soc. Peter Debye Prize in Physical Chemistry, American Physical Soc. Irving Lungmuize Prize in Chemical Physics, Scientist of the Year 1978, New York

Acad. of Sciences Cressy Morison Award in Natural Sciences, Scientist of the Year 1988, ACS Tolman Award 1995, ISCO Award for Biological Research 1999, and other awards. *Publications include:* more than 400 on lasers, photochemistry, picosecond spectroscopy; 68 patents. *Address:* Department of Chemistry, University of California, 579, 580A Rowland Hall, Mail Code 2025, Irvine, CA 92697 (office); Call/Recall, Inc. Sytems Division, 6160 Lusk Blvd., Suite C-206, San Diego, CA 92121, USA (office). *Telephone:* (949) 824-5934 University of California (office); (858) 550-0596 (Call/Recall) (office). *Fax:* (949) 824-2761 University of California (office); (858) 550-0917 (Call/Recall) (office). *E-mail:* pmrentze@uci.edu (office); info@call-recall.com (office). *Website:* www.chem.uci.edu/people/faculty/pmrentze (office); www.call-recall.com (office).

RENWICK, Glenn M., BS, MEng; American insurance industry executive; *President and CEO, The Progressive Corporation;* b. 22 May 1955; ed Univ. of Canterbury, Christchurch, NZ, Univ. of Florida at Gainesville; joined The Progressive Corpn (automobile insurance co.) 1986, Auto Product Man. for Fla 1986–88, Pres. of Mid-Atlantic, then Calif. Divs, sr positions in Consumer Marketing Dept –1998, Business Tech. Process Leader 1998–2000, Dir 1999–, CEO Insurance Operations 2000–01, Pres. and CEO 2001–. *Address:* The Progressive Corporation, 6300 Wilson Mills Road, Mayfield Village, OH 44143, USA (office). *Telephone:* (440) 461-5000 (office). *Fax:* (440) 603-4420 (office). *Website:* www.progressive.com (office).

RENWICK OF CLIFTON, Baron (Life Peer), cr. 1997, of Chelsea in the Royal Borough of Kensington and Chelsea; **Robin William Renwick,** KCMG, MA; British diplomatist and business executive; *Vice-Chairman, Investment Banking, JP Morgan; Vice-Chairman, JPMorgan Cazenove;* b. 13 Dec. 1937; s. of Richard Renwick and Clarice Renwick; m. Annie Colette Gidicelli 1965; one s. one d.; ed St Paul's School, Jesus Coll., Cambridge and Univ. of Paris (Sorbonne); France; served in army 1956–58; entered Foreign Service 1963, served in Dakar 1963–64, at Foreign Office 1964–66, Embassy in New Delhi 1966–69, Pvt. Sec. to Minister of State, FCO 1970–72, First Sec., Embassy in Paris 1972–76, Counsellor, Cabinet Office 1976–78, Head of Rhodesia Dept, FCO 1978–80; Political Adviser to Gov. of Rhodesia 1980; Visiting Fellow, Center for Int. Affairs, Harvard Univ. 1980–81; Head of Chancery, Washington, DC 1981–84, Asst Under-Sec. of State, FCO 1984–87, Amb. to S Africa 1987–91, to USA 1991–95; Chair. Save and Prosper 1996–98, Fluor Ltd 1996–2010; Dir British Airways 1996–2006, Robert Fleming (Deputy Chair. Robert Fleming Holdings Ltd 1999–2001), BHP Billiton plc 1997–2005, Fluor Corpn 1997–2010, SAB Miller 1999–2009, Compagnie Financière Richemont AG 1995–, Kazakhmys plc 2005–; Vice-Chair. (Investment Banking) JPMorgan, Vice-Chair. JPMorgan Cazenove 2004–; Deputy Chair. Fleming Family and Partners 2000–; Trustee The Economist 1996–2011; Hon. LLD (Witwatersrand) 1991, (American Univ. in London) 1993; Hon. DLitt (Coll. of William and Mary) 1993. *Publications:* Economic Sanctions 1981, Fighting with Allies 1996, Unconventional Diplomacy 1997, A Journey with Margaret Thatcher 2013. *Leisure interests:* tennis, fly fishing, islands. *Address:* House of Lords, London, SW1A 0PW; JPMorgan Cazenove, 10 Aldermanbury, London, EC2V 7RF, England (office). *Telephone:* (20) 7219-5353 (House of Lords); (20) 7325-6375 (office). *Website:* www.jpmorgancazenove.com (office).

RENYI, Thomas A., BA, MBA; American banking executive; *Executive Chairman, Bank of New York Mellon Corporation;* b. 1946; m. Elizabeth Renyi; two s. one d.; ed Rutgers Univ.; joined The Bank of New York Co. Inc. 1971, Pres. 1992–98, Vice Chair. 1992–98, CEO 1997–2007, Chair. 1998–2007, Exec. Chair. Bank of New York Mellon Corpn (after merger with Mellon Financial Corpn) 2007–; fmr Chair. New York Bankers Asscn; mem. Bd of Dirs Public Service Enterprise Group Inc., The Clearing House, World Trade Center Memorial Foundation; Chair-elect The Financial Services Roundtable; mem. Bd of Mans New York Botanical Garden; mem Bd of Trustees Bates Coll., Rutgers Univ., Catholic Charities of the Archdiocese of New York. *Address:* Bank of New York Mellon Corporation, 1 Wall Street, 10th Floor, New York, NY 10286, USA (office). *Telephone:* (212) 495-1784 (office). *Fax:* (212) 809-9528 (office). *Website:* www.bnymellon.com (office).

RENZI, Matteo; Italian politician; *Prime Minister;* b. 11 Jan. 1975, Florence; s. of Tiziano Renzi and Laura Bovoli; m. Agnese Landini; three c.; ed Univ. degli Studi, Florence; began career with CHIL Srl (family-owned communications and marketing co.); Pres., Prov. of Florence 2004–09; Mayor of Florence 2009–; Pres., Council of Ministers (Prime Minister) 2014– (youngest ever Italian Prime Minister); mem. Partito Popolare Italiano 1996–2002, Democrazia è Libertà - La Margherita 2002–07; mem. Partito Democratico (PD) 2007–, Sec. 2013–. *Publications include:* Fuori! 2011, Stilnovo 2012, Oltre la rottamazione 2013. *Address:* Office of the Prime Minister, Palazzo Chigi, Piazza Colonna 370, 00187 Rome, Italy (office). *Telephone:* (06) 67791 (office). *Website:* www.governo.it (office); www.matteorenzi.it.

REPIN, Vadim Viktorovich; Russian violinist; *Artistic Director, Trans-Siberian Arts Festival;* b. 31 Aug. 1971, Novosibirsk, Siberia; s. of Viktor Antonovich Repin and Galina Georgievna Repina; ed Novosibirsk Music School, Hochschule für Musik, Lübeck with Zakhar Bron; began playing violin aged five; first stage performance six months later; won gold medal in all age categories in Wienawski Competition, Poznań aged 11; debut recitals in Moscow and St Petersburg; debuts in Tokyo, Munich, Berlin, Helsinki 1985, Carnegie Hall 1986; has performed with all major orchestras and greatest conductors; regularly collaborates with Nikolai Lugansky and Itamar Golan in recital; other chamber music partners include Martha Argerich, Evgeny Kissin and Mischa Maisky; Season 2009–10: concerts with Muti in New York, with Thielemann in Tokyo, with Chailly in Leipzig, tour of Australia with London Philharmonic Orchestra and Vladimir Jurowski, and première of a violin concerto written for him by James MacMillan, performed with London Symphony Orchestra and Valery Gergiev; Artistic Dir Trans-Siberian Arts Festival 2013–; Chevalier des Arts et des Lettres 2010; Tibor Varga competition winner, Sion 1985, winner, Reine Elisabeth Concours, Brussels (youngest ever winner) 1990, Victoire d'honneur (France) 2010. *Television:* Vadim Repin – A Magician of Sound (film documentary by Claudia Willke) 2010. *Recordings include:* Shostakovich No. 1 and Prokofiev No. 2 with the Hallé Orchestra under Nagano 1995, Prokofiev Violin Sonatas and Five Melodies with Berezovsky 1995, Tchaikovsky and Sibelius Concertos with the London Symphony under Krivine 1996, Tchaikovsky and Shostakovich piano trios with Berezovsky and Yablonsky

1997, Lalo Symphonie Espagnole with the London Symphony Orchestra under Nagano 1998, Tutta Bravura (with Markovich) 1999, Vadim Repin au Louvre (with Berezovsky, Barachovsky, Lakatos, Gothoni) 1999, Tchaikovsky and Myaskovsky violin concertos with the Kirov Orchestra under Gergiev 2002, A Night of Encores (recorded live with the Berlin Philharmonic under Jansons) 2004, Taneyev Piano Quintet and Trio (Gramophone Award for Best Chamber Recording 2006), Beethoven Violin Concerto (with Vienna Philharmonic and Riccardo Muti, coupled with Beethoven's Kreutzer Sonata with Martha Argerich) 2008, Brahms Violin Concerto and Brahms Double Concerto (Truls Mørk, cello, with Gewandhaus Orchester Leipzig and Riccardo Chailly) 2009, Tchaikovsky and Rachmaninov trios with Mischa Maisky and Lang Lang (Echo Award) 2009, recital recording with Nikolai Lugansky 2010. *Leisure interests:* chess, swimming, skiing. *Address:* c/o Interclassica Music Management, Schönburgstrasse 4, 1040 Vienna, Austria (office). *Telephone:* (1) 585-3980 (office). *E-mail:* eleanorhope@interclassica.com (office). *Website:* www.interclassica.com (office); www.vadimrepin.com.

REPŠE, Einars, MS; Latvian politician, fmr central banker, computer scientist and investor; *Chairman, Latvijas Attistibai;* b. 9 Dec. 1961, Jelgava; s. of Aivars-Rihards Repše and Aldona Repše (née Krasauska); m. Ruta Raginska Repse 1985; three s. one d.; ed Latvia State Univ.; engineer, Latvian Acad. of Sciences 1986–90; entered politics as Co-founder of Latvian Nat. Independence Movt (LNNK) 1988; mem. Parl. 1990–91, 2003–; Gov. Bank of Latvia 1991–2001; Founder and Chair. New Era (Jaunais laiks) 2002; Prime Minister of Latvia 2002–04; Minister of Defence 2004–05 (resgnd), of Finance 2009–10; Chair. Artificial Intelligence Foundation 2010–, Latvijas Nakotnes Forums 2012–; Founder and Chair. Latvijas Attistibai 2013–; Commdr, Order of the Three Stars 1997. *Leisure interest:* aviation, art, alpine skiing, mountaineering, music, natural horsemanship. *Address:* Ozolu 40, Ikskile 5052, Latvia (office). *Telephone:* 2925-8135 (home). *E-mail:* einars@apollo.lv (home). *Website:* www.attistibai.lv (office).

RESCHER, Nicholas, PhD, FRSC, FRAS; American philosopher and author; *Distinguished University Professor of Philosophy, University of Pittsburgh;* b. 15 July 1928, Hagen, Germany; s. of Erwin Hans Rescher and Meta Anna Rescher; m. 1st Frances Short 1951 (divorced 1965); one d.; m. 2nd Dorothy Henle 1968; two s. one d.; ed Queens Coll., New York, Princeton Univ.; Assoc. Prof. of Philosophy, Lehigh Univ. 1957–61; Distinguished Univ. Prof. of Philosophy, Univ. of Pittsburgh 1961–, Dir Center for Philosophy of Science 1982–89, Chair. 1989–; consultant, RAND Corpn 1954–66, Encyclopaedia Britannica 1963–64, North American Philosophical Publs 1980–; Ed. American Philosophical Quarterly 1964–94; Sec.-Gen. Int. Union of History and Philosophy of Science 1969–75; visiting lectureships at Univs of Oxford, Munich, Konstanz, Western Ontario and others; Pres. American Philosophical Asscn (Eastern Div.) 1989–90, American Catholic Philosophical Asscn 2003–04, American Metaphysical Soc. 2004–05; mem. Academia Europea, Institut Int. de Philosophie, Acad. Int. de Philosophie des Sciences; Fellow, American Acad. of Arts and Sciences 2009; Hon. mem. Corpus Christi Coll. Oxford; Bundesverdienstkreuz; eight hon. degrees; Guggenheim Fellow 1970–71, Alexander von Humboldt Prize 1983, Aquinas Medal, Cardinal Mercier Prize. *Publications:* more than 100 books, including The Coherence Theory of Truth 1973, Methodological Pragmatism 1977, Scientific Progress 1978, The Limits of Science 1984, Ethical Idealism 1987, Rationality 1988, A System of Pragmatic Idealism (three vols) 1992–94, Pluralism 1993, Predicting the Future 1997, Paradoxes 2001, Philosophical Reasoning 2001, Metaphysics 2005, Epistemetrics 2006, Free Will 2009, Aporetics 2009; numerous articles in many areas of philosophy. *Leisure interests:* reading history and biography. *Address:* 1012 Cathedral of Learning, University of Pittsburgh, Pittsburgh, PA 15260 (office); 1033 Milton Avenue, Pittsburgh, PA 15218, USA (home). *Telephone:* (412) 624-5950 (office); (412) 243-1290 (home). *Fax:* (412) 383-7506 (office). *E-mail:* rescher@pitt.edu (office). *Website:* www.pitt.edu/~rescher (office).

RESIN, Vladimir Iosifovich, PhD; Russian politician and civil engineer; *Adviser to the Mayor of Moscow;* b. 21 Feb. 1936, Minsk, Byelorussian SSR, USSR; s. of Josif Gilimovich Resin and Roza Volfovna Sheydlina; m. Marta Yakovlevna Chadaeva 1958; one d.; ed Moscow Mining Inst.; began working as a mining engineer in Ukraine 1958, then worked at construction sites in Murmansk, Kaluga and Smolensk, transferred to the building orgs of Moscow 1965, held various positions up to Man. of the Trust Tunnelling Works, worked in orgs of USSR Ministry of Coal Industry and Ministry of Ass. and Special Construction; Deputy, First Deputy, then Head, Moscow Dept of Eng and Construction 1974–; Head, Moscow Industrial Construction Dept 1985–; Chair. Moscow Construction Cttee 1989–91; Deputy Chair. Exec. Cttee, Moscow City Council 1989–91; Deputy Premier, Moscow City Govt 1991–92, First Vice-Premier 1992–; Head, Dept of Moscow Architecture, Construction, Prospective Devt Complex and Reconstruction 1992–2000, Head of Complex of Architecture, Construction, Devt and Reconstruction of City (CACDR) 2000–02, Head of Dept, City-Planning Policy, Devt and Reconstruction of City 2002–; First Deputy Mayor of Moscow 2000–02, Acting Mayor of Moscow Sept.–Oct. 2010, Adviser to the Mayor of Moscow 2011–; Deputy (Yedinaya Rossiya) of State Duma, Fed. Ass. of Russian Fed. 2011–, mem. Cttee for Land and Construction; Advisor for Construction to the Patriarch of Moscow and All Russia 2012–; Prof. G.V. Plekhanov Russian Univ. of Econs 1996–, Moscow Int. Univ.; Corresp. mem. and mem. Presidium, Russian Acad. of Architecture and Construction Sciences, Russian Eng Acad.; mem. Russian Union of Architects, and of 21 int. and Russian acads; Sr Fellow, Inst. of Civil Engineers 2000; Hon. Citizen of Yerevan and Gyumri (Armenia), Balakhna (Russia), Honoured Builder of the USSR, Honoured Engineer of Russia, Distinguished Constructor of Russian Fed., Honoured Constructor of Moscow, Hon. Prof., Moscow State Lomonosov Univ., Moscow Int. Univ. 2000, Russian Acad. of Sciences 2005; 60 USSR and Russian State Awards (17 orders, 33 medals, insignias), including Order for Services to the Fatherland of the II, III and IV Ranks 1995, 2005, 2008, Order of Honour 2000, Order of Friendship 2011, Order 'The Symbol of Honor' 1971, Order of Nations' Friendship 1984, Insignia for Services to the City of Moscow; Hon. PhD of leading univs in Russia; six times Laureate of the Pres. of Russian Fed. 1993, 1995, 1996, 1997, 2003, 2006, Hon. Letter of the Pres. of Russian Fed. 2009, 14 awards from Russian Orthodox Church, 250 departmental, public and non-governmental orgs awards. *Publications include:* 26 monographs and books, including Managing the Development of a Large City: A Systems Approach, Development of Large Cities in the Conditions of

a Transitional Economy (System Approach), Probabilistic Technologies in Development Management of the City, Vladimir Resin – Moscow's Foreman-in-Chief 1999, Vladimir Resin – Roads of Moscow-Builder 2006, The Working Foreman of Moscow – Roads of Vladimir Resin 2010; 116 scientific publs in the fields of economy and construction (many translated) and 34 inventions. *Leisure interest:* work. *Address:* State Duma of the Federal Assembly of the Russian Federation, Okhotny Ryad, Building 1, 103265 Moscow (office); 121609 Moscow, Osennyaya Street 4/2-6, Russia (home). *Telephone:* (495) 692-90-09 (office); (495) 956-80-98. *Fax:* (495) 692-43-95 (office); (495) 956-64-90. *E-mail:* resin@duma.gov.ru (office); alexandro.khomenko@gmail.com. *Website:* www.duma.gov.ru (office).

RESTAD, Gudmund; Norwegian politician; b. 19 Dec. 1937, Smøla; s. of Ola Restad and Olga Marie Restad; m. Britt Jorun Wollum 1959; three c.; ed officers' training school (anti-aircraft artillery), business school, Nat. Police Acad.; sergeant at Ørland airport 1959–61, country police Ørland and Orkdal 1961–67; detective constable/inspector Crime Police Centre 1967–73; training in police investigation in Denmark and Germany 1967; Lecturer, Nat. Police Training School 1973–75; sergeant in Smøla 1975–85; mem. Parl. 1985–2001; Chair. Local Council, Smøla 1980–85, mem., Chair., Deputy Chair. Nordmøre Interkommunale Kraftlag (Nordmøre Electricity Bd) 1982–91; mem. Bd Central Police Org. 1969–73, Møre og Romsdal Centre Party 1982–83, The Centre Party 1983–89; mem. Judiciary Cttee Storting (Parl.) 1985–89; mem., Deputy Chair. Finance Cttee 1989–97; Minister of Finance and Customs 1997–2000; Deputy Chair. Defence Cttee 2000–01. *Address:* c/o Stortinget, 0026 Oslo, Norway.

RÉTORÉ, Guy; French theatre director; b. 7 April 1924; s. of Hervé Rétoré and Aline Henry; ed Univ. of Paris; Public Relations Dept, SNCF until 1955; actor and producer, Théâtre de Boulevard until 1955; f. La Guilde (theatrical company), Menilmontant, East Paris 1954; opened Théâtre de Menilmontant 1958; Dir Maison de la Culture, Menilmontant 1962; Dir Théâtre de l'Est Parisien (TEP) 1963–2001 (also gives concerts, ballets, films and confs); Chevalier, Légion d'honneur, Officier Ordre nat. du Mérite, Officier des Arts et des Lettres. *Plays produced include:* La fille du roi (Cosmos) 1955, Life and Death of King John 1956, Grenadiers de la reine (Farquhar, adapted by Cosmos) 1957, L'avare (Molière), Les caprices de Marianne (Musset), La fleur à la bouche (Pirandello), Le médecin malgré lui (Molière), Le manteau (Gogol, adapted by Cosmos) 1963, La Locandiera (Goldoni), Arden of Faversham 1964, Monsieur Alexandre (Cosmos) 1964, Macbeth (Shakespeare) 1964, Turcaret (Lesage) 1965, Measure for Measure (Shakespeare) 1965, Le voyage de Monsieur Perrichon (Labiche) 1965, Live Like Pigs (Arden), The Silver Tassie (O'Casey) 1966–67, Les 13 soleils de la rue St Blaise (A. Gatti), La machine (Jean Cosmos) 1968–69, Lorenzaccio (Musset), The Threepenny Opera (Brecht), Major Barbara (Shaw) 1969–70, Les ennemis (Gorki), L'âne de l'hospice (Arden) 1970–71, Sainte Jeanne des abattoirs (Brecht) 1971–72, Macbeth (Shakespeare) 1972–73, Androclès et le lion 1974–75, Coquin de coq (O'Casey) 1975–76, L'ôtage (Claudel) 1976–77, Le camp du drap d'or 1980, Fin de partie, tueur sans gage 1981, Le Chantier 1982, Clair d'usine 1983, 325000 francs 1984, Entre passions et prairie (Denise Bonal) 1987, Arturo Ui 1988, Clair de Terre 1989, Chacun pleure son Garabed 1991.

RETZER, Michael L., BA; American business executive, politician and fmr diplomatist; *Chairman, Retzer Resources Inc.;* b. 1946, Greenville, Miss.; s. of Karl Retzer and Betty Retzer; ed Honors Coll., Univ. of Oregon; served as Capt. in USAF; Founder and Chair. Retzer Resources Inc., chain of fast food restaurants located in Miss. and Ark.; fmr mem. Bd of Dirs and Exec. Cttee Planters Bank of Miss.; elected several times as Chair. Miss. Republican Party since 1978; elected Republican Nat. Cttee-man for Miss. 2001, Treas. Nat. Republican Party 2002, Treas. Republican Nat. Convention, New York City 2004; career mem. Sr Foreign Service with rank of Minister-Counselor, Amb. to Tanzania 2005–07; fmr mem. Chamber of Commerce, Greenville, Industrial Foundation, South Delta Planning Council; Founding mem. Delta Wildlife Foundation, Miss. Wildlife Foundation; fmr Trustee Nat. Symphony Orchestra, Washington, DC. *Address:* Retzer Resources Inc., 61 South Street, Cleveland, MS 38732, USA (office). *Telephone:* (662) 846-6736 (office). *Fax:* (662) 746-6386 (office).

REUBER, Grant Louis, OC, PhD, LLD, FRSC; Canadian economist; *Senior Advisor, Sussex Circle;* b. 23 Nov. 1927, Mildmay, Ont.; s. of Jacob Daniel Reuber and Gertrude Catherine Reuber; m. Margaret Louise Julia Summerhayes 1951 (deceased); three d.; ed Walkerton High School, Univ. of W Ontario, Harvard Univ., Sidney Sussex Coll., Cambridge; with Econ. Research Dept Bank of Canada 1950–52; Econ. and Int. Relations Div. Dept of Finance 1955–57, Deputy Minister of Finance Govt of Canada 1979–80; at Univ. of W Ontario 1957–78, Asst Prof. 1957–59, Assoc. Prof. 1959–62, Prof. Econ. Dept 1962–78, Dean of Social Science 1969–74, Acad. Vice-Pres. and Provost, mem. Bd of Govs 1974–78; Chair. Ont. Econ. Council 1973–78; Sr Vice-Pres. and Chief Economist Bank of Montreal 1978–79, Exec. Vice-Pres. 1980–81, Dir, Deputy Chair. and Deputy Chief Exec. 1981–83, Pres. 1983–87, Deputy Chair. 1987–90; Chancellor Univ. of Western Ont. 1988–93; Lecturer, Grad. School of Business, Univ. of Chicago 1992–93; Chair. Canada Deposit Insurance Corpn 1993–99 (Dir 1999–), Canada Merit Scholarship Foundation 1994–; Dir Hermitage Museum Foundation of Canada Inc. 2000–; Sr Adviser and Dir Sussex Circle (consulting firm); Gov. Royal Ont. Museum 2000–03; Pres. and Dir Ditchley Foundation of Canada 1989–; Sr Fellow, C.D. Howe Inst. 2000–; Hon. LLD (Wilfred Laurier Univ.) 1983, (Simon Fraser Univ., Univ. of W Ont.) 1985, (McMaster Univ.) 1994. *Publications:* The Cost of Capital in Canada (with R. J. Wonnacott) 1961, (with R. E Caves): Canadian Economic Policy and the Impact of International Capital Flows 1970, Private Foreign Investment in Development 1973, Canada's Political Economy 1980. *Leisure interests:* tennis, reading. *Address:* Sussex Circle, 50 O'Connor Street, Suite 1424, Ottawa, ON K1P 6L2 (office); 90 Glen Edyth Drive, Toronto, ON M4V 2V9, Canada (home). *Telephone:* (613) 567-3200 (office); (416) 924-4971. *Fax:* (613) 567-4627 (office). (416) 924-4784 (home). *Website:* www.sussexcircle.com (office).

REUS GONZÁLEZ, María Esther, LLB; Cuban lawyer and politician; *Minister of Justice;* b. 23 May 1962; fmr Pres. Nat. Electoral Comm.; Vice-Minister of Justice –2007, Minister 2007–. *Address:* Ministry of Justice, Calle O, No 216, entre 23 y 25, Plaza de la Revolución, Apdo 10400, Havana 4, Cuba (office). *Telephone:* (7) 838-3450 (office). *E-mail:* apoblacion@oc.minjus.cu (office). *Website:* www.minjus.cu (office).

REUTERSWÄRD, Carl Fredrik; Swedish artist, writer and sculptor; b. 4 June 1934, Stockholm; s. of Wilhelm Reuterswärd and Thérèse Ingeström; m. 1st Anna Tesch 1958 (divorced 1968); two s. two d.; m. 2nd Mona Moller-Nielsen 1974; one s.; m. 3rd Tonie Lewenhaupt 1997; ed Ecole de Fernand Léger, Paris and Royal Coll. of Art, Stockholm; first artist to use lasers 1965; Prof., Royal Coll. of Art, Stockholm 1965–70; since 1952 active in drawing, painting, sculpture, holography, scenography, graphics, design and architectural comms; prin. themes: Nonsens 1952–58; Cigars and Games 1958–63; Exercise 1958–64; Lazy Lasers and Holy Holos 1965–74; a trilogy: Kilroy (anybody) 1962–72, CAVIART (a somebody) 1972–82; works in public collections in Sweden, USA, Germany, France, England, Switzerland, Netherlands, Norway and Denmark, including Nat. Museum, Stockholm, Museum of Modern Art and Metropolitan Museum of Art, New York, MIT Museum, Cambridge, Mass, Städtische Kunsthalle, Düsseldorf, Musée Nat. d'Art Moderne, Paris, Tate Modern, London and Stedelijk Museum, Amsterdam; Prins Eugen Medal bestowed by King Carl Gustaf XVI 1984, Lifetime Achievements Award 1997. *Works include:* Non-Violence, bronze sculpture on perm. display in front of UN Bldg, New York since 1988 (UN Award of Honour 1999, Daily Points of Right Award 2000), Non-Violence, bronze sculpture on perm. display in Chaoyang Park, Beijing 2008. *Publications:* Kafka, Wahlstrom and Widstrand 1981, Caviart 1982, Making Faces 1984, Mes Autres Moi 1989, Carl Fredrik Reuterswärd, Das Graphische Werk 1993, Style is Fraud 2004, Non-Violence och andra offentliga verk 2005, Skuggor och Glas 2006, From One Side to the Other 2006. *Address:* 6 rue Montolieu, 1030 Bussigny/Lausanne, Switzerland (home). *Telephone:* (21) 7010514 (home). *Fax:* (21) 7012675 (home). *E-mail:* cf .reutersward@gmail.com (office).

REVIGLIO, Franco; Italian economist and academic; b. 3 Feb. 1935, Turin; ed Univ. of Turin; asst in Faculty of Law, Univ. of Turin 1959–64, currently Prof. of Financial Science; economist, IMF, Washington, DC 1964–66; Prof., Univ. of Urbino 1966–68; mem. Cen. Tax Comm. and Tech. Cttee for Tax Reform, Ministry of Finance 1976–79, Minister of Finance 1979–81; mem. Municipal Council of Turin 1981–83; Chair. Tech. Comm. on Public Expenditure Ministry of Treasury 1981–83; mem. Tech. Cttee for Econ. Programming Ministry of the Budget 1981–89, Minister of the Budget 1992–93; Chair. Ente Nazionale Idrocarburi 1983–89; Sr Advisor, Wasserstein Perella 1990–92; Senator 1992–94; Chair. and Man. Dir Azienda Energetica Metropolitana Torino 2000–06; Sr Advisor, Lehman Brothers 2002–07; St Vincent Prize for Econs 1998, Walter Tobagi Prize 1998. *Publications:* La finanza della sicurezza sociale (co-author) 1969, Spesa pubblica e stagnazione dell'economia italiana 1975, Le chiavi del 2000 1990, Meno Stato più mercato: Come ridurre lo Stato per risanare il Paese 1994, Lo Stato imperfetto 1996, Come siama entrati in Europa 1998, Sanità senza vincoli di spesa? 1999; contrib. of numerous essays and articles to journals and newspapers. *Address:* Departimento di Scienze Economiche e Finanziarie G. Prato, Facoltà di Economia – Università di Torino, Corso Unione Sovietica 218bis, 10134 Turin, Italy (office). *Telephone:* (011) 6706080 (office); (02) 645750 (home). *Fax:* (011) 6706062 (office). *E-mail:* franco.reviglio@unito.it (home). *Website:* www.econ.unito.it (office).

REXHEPI, Bajram; Kosovo politician and surgeon; *Minister of Internal Affairs;* b. 3 June 1954, Kosovska Mitrovica (Mitrovicë); m. Shpresa Rexhepi; one d.; ed Faculty of Medicine, Univs of Priština and Zagreb; postgraduate studies in Zagreb 1985; worked as gen. surgeon and endoscopic specialist at regional hosp., Kosovska Mitrovica 1985–90; mem. 'Kosovo Assembly'; joined separatist ethnic Albanian Kosovo Liberation Army March–June 1999, spent three months serving as field doctor in operating zone of Shala; Pres. Kosovska Mitrovica Municipal Council and Mayor of divided town's southern section 1990; mem. Democratic Party of Kosovo (PDK) and Head of PDK br. in the town; first elected post-war Prime Minister of Kosovo 2002–04; mem. Parl. 2004–07; Mayor of Mitrovicë Municipality 2007–10; Pres. Asscn of Kosovo Municipalities 2008–10; Minister of Internal Affairs 2011–. *Address:* Ministry of Internal Affairs, 10000 Prishtina, Rruga Luan Haradinaj, Kosovo (office). *Telephone:* (38) 213007 (office); (38) 20019001 (office). *Fax:* (38) 20019640 (office). *E-mail:* merita.vidishiqi@ks-gov.net (office). *Website:* www.mpb -ks.org (office).

REY, Marie Michèle; Haitian politician; Minister of Finance and Econ. Affairs 1991 (until Oct. 1991 coup), also Rep. for Haiti to Caricom, UNCTAD and other int. orgs; Minister of Foreign Affairs and Religion 2009–11. *Address:* c/o Ministry of Foreign Affairs and Religion, blvd Harry S Truman, Cité de l'Exposition, Port-au-Prince, Haiti (office).

REY, Rafael; Peruvian business executive, diplomatist and politician; b. 26 Feb. 1954, Lima; ed Univ. Católica del Perú, INCAE, Costa Rica, Univ. de Piura; Man. RANSA Comercial SA 1979–82; Man. Dir Crowley Peru SA (fmrly Crowley Caribbean Transport Inc.) 1982–90; Deputy, Congreso de la Republica (parl.) 1990–2006; Minister of State for Production 2006–08; Amb. to Italy 2008–09; Minister of Defence 2009–10; Dir Crowley Perú SA, Diario La Prensa Perú, S.A.M Trading SA, Corporación ACME; mem. Consultative Cttee, Ministry of Foreign Affairs; mem. Partido Renovación Nacional, Pres. 1992–; unsuccessful cand. for Deputy of Keiko Fujimori in general election 2011; mem. Exec. Council, Instituto de Formación para la Acción Política, Instituto Peruano de Economía de Mercado. *Leisure interests:* swimming, jogging. *Address:* Renovación Nacional, Avda Camino Real 1206, 2°, San Isidro, Lima 1, Peru (office). *Telephone:* (1) 5673798 (office).

REYES-HEROLES GONZÁLEZ GARZA, Jesús, BEcons, PhD; Mexican civil servant and petroleum industry executive; b. 1950, Mexico City; ed Instituto Autónomo de México (ITAM), Massachusetts Inst. of Tech., USA; began career as Research Asst, Banco de México; served in various civil service roles including Dir-Gen. Treas. Planning 1983–88, Gen. Coordinator of Foreign Affairs Secr. Advisers 1989–90; Dir-Gen. GEA Grupo de Economistas y Asociados (consultancy firm) 1991–94; Mexican mem. Asia-Pacific Econ. Cooperation (APEC) Group of Eminent Persons 1993–94; Dir-Gen. Banco Nacional de Obras y Servicios Públicos (Banobras) 1994–95; Mexican Sec. of Energy 1995–97; Amb. to USA 1997–2000; Exec. Pres. GEA StructurA (consultancy) 2001–06; Dir-Gen. Petróleos Mexicanos (PEMEX) 2006–09; mem. PRI (Institutional Revolutionary Party) 1972–, Pres. PRI Nat. Comm. on Ideology 1994; fmr mem. Bd of Dirs Banamex, Citigroup, Wal-Mart Mexico; fmr Trustee Gonzalo Río Arronte Foundation, Universidad Iberoamericana (FICSAC). *Publications:* several articles in academic journals. *Address:* c/o Petróleos Mexicanos (PEMEX), Marina Nacional 329, Colonia Huasteca, CP 11311, México, DF, Mexico.

REYES LÓPEZ, Juan Francisco; Guatemalan politician and business executive; b. 10 July 1938; m.; three c.; ed John Carroll High School, Birmingham, Ala, USA, Escuela Militar del General de Armas Bernardo O'Higgins, Santiago de Chile, Universidad Rafael Landivar, Guatemala City; primary school teacher; army officer 1960–61; in pvt. business 1961–89; Pres. Comité Coordinador de Asociaciones Agrícolas, Comerciales, Industriales y Financieras (CACIF) 1979–80, Pres. 1980; Man. Instituto Guatemalteco de Seguridad Social 1982; mem. Frente Republicano Guatemalteco (FRG) party, mem. Nat. Exec. Cttee 1991–99; Deputy to Congreso (Parl.) 1990–94, Chair. Comm. on Foreign Relations 1990, mem. Comm. on Finance 1990–94, First Vice-Pres. Exec. Bd 1994; Vice-Pres. of Guatemala 2000–04; Orden del General O'Higgins 1989, Orden de la Estrella Brillante 1995. *Address:* c/o Office of the President, Guatemala City, Guatemala (office).

REYES RENDÓN, Samuel Armando; Honduran engineer and politician; *Minister of National Defence;* b. Lempira; fmr Presidential Appointee in Congreso Nacional (Parl.); Second Vice-Pres. of Honduras 2010–14; Minister of Nat. Defence 2014–; mem. Partido Nacional. *Address:* Ministry of National Defence, Boulevard Suyapa, Col. Florencia Sur, frente a Iglesia Colegio Episcopal, Tegucigalpa, Honduras (office). *Telephone:* 2239-2330 (office). *E-mail:* transparencia@sedena .gob.hn (office). *Website:* www.sedena.gob.hn (office).

REYN, Evgeny Borisovich; Russian poet and writer; b. 29 Dec. 1935, Leningrad; m. Nadejda Reyn 1989; one s.; ed Leningrad Tech. Inst.; freelance poet published in samizdat magazine Sintaksis and émigré press abroad in magazines Grani, Kovcheg; participated in publication of almanac Metropol; literary debut in Russia 1984; Prof., Moscow M. Gorky Inst. of Literature; mem. Writers' Union, Union of Moscow Writers, Russian PEN Centre; Peterburg Prize of Arts 'Tsarskoye Selo' 1995, State Prize of Russia in Literature and Art 1996, Ind. Alexander Block Literature Award 1999, Alfred Tepfer Foundation Pushkin Prize (Hamburg, Germany) 2003, State Pushkin Prize in Literature and Art 2004, Grinzane Cavour Prize (Turin, Italy) 2004, Petropol Prize in Literature and Arts, St Peterburg 2005, Kiev Laura 2010, Prize Anton Delvig 2010, Nord South Prize 2011, The Poet Prize 2012. *Television:* Kuprin 1967, The Thcukokkala 1969, The Tenth Chapter 1970, Journeys with Josef Brodsky 1993, Josef Brodsky: The Hatchings to Portrait 1996. *Publications:* The Names of Bridges 1984, Shore Line 1989, The Darkness of Mirrors 1989, Breda 1995, Irretrievable Day 1991, Counter-Clockwise 1992, Nezhnosmo 1993, Selected Poems 1993, The Prognostication 1994, The Top-booty 1995, The Others 1996, The News Stages of the Life of The Moscow Beau Monde 1997, Balkony 1998, Arch over Water 2000, The Remarks of Marathon Man: Inconclusive Memoirs 2003, The Overground Transition 2004, After Our Age 2005, My Best Addressman… 2005, The Poems, Prose, Essays 2006, Balcone e altri poesie 2008, The Memory of the Journey 2011, Labyrinth 2013. *Address:* Leningradsky Prospect, 75, Apt 167, 125057 Moscow, Russia (home). *Telephone:* (499) 157-20-14 (home); (7985) 9976858 (cell). *E-mail:* NADIA_REYNE@mail.ru (home).

REYNDERS, Didier, LLB; Belgian politician; *Deputy Prime Minister and Minister of Foreign Affairs, Foreign Trade and European Affairs;* b. 6 Aug. 1958, Liège; ed Inst. St Jean Berchmans, Liège, Univ. of Liège; lawyer 1981–85; Gen. Man. Ministry of Wallonia Region 1985–88; Chair. Belgian Nat. Railway Co. (SNCB) 1986–91; Chef de Cabinet of Deputy Prime Minister, Minister of Justice and Inst. Reform 1987–88; Chair. Nat. Airways Co. 1991–93; Vice-Chair. Parti Réformateur Libéral (PRL) 1992; Deputy, House of Reps 1992; Head PRL Group in Liège Council 1995, Chair. PRL-FDF (Front Démocratique des Francophones) Group 1995; Chair. Fed. Provinciale et d'Arrondissement de Liège of PRL 1995–; Lecturer, Hautes Ecoles Commerciales, Liège; Minister of Finance 1999–2007 (resgnd), reappointed Deputy Prime Minister and Minister of Finance and of Institutional Reform 2008–11, Deputy Prime Minister and Minister of Foreign Affairs, Foreign Trade and European Affairs 2011–; Pres. Mouvement Réformateur (MR) (Reformist Movt) 2004–; Chevalier, Ordre de Léopold 2000. *Leisure interest:* golf. *Address:* Federal Public Service of Foreign Affairs, Foreign Trade and Development Co-operation, 15 rue des Petits Carmes, 1000 Brussels (office); Mouvement Réformateur, 84–86 avenue de la Toison d'Or, 1060 Brussels (office); En Jonruelle 27, 4000 Liège, Belgium (home). *Telephone:* (2) 501-81-11 (office); (2) 500-35-11 (office). *Fax:* (2) 501-81-70 (office); (2) 500-35-00 (home); (4) 227-08-63 (home). *E-mail:* contact@diplobel.fed.be (office); mr@mr.be (office). *Website:* www .diplomatie.be (office); www.mr.be (office); www.didier-reynders.be.

REYNOLDS, Albert; Irish politician and business executive; b. 3 Nov. 1935, Rooskey, Co. Roscommon; m. Kathleen Coén; two s. five d.; ed Summerhill Coll., Sligo; fmr Chair. C & D Petfoods; mem. Longford Co. Council 1974–79; elected mem. Dáil 1977; Minister for Posts and Telegraphs and Transport 1979–81, for Industry and Energy March–Dec. 1982, for Industry and Commerce 1987–88, for Finance and the Public Service 1988–89, of Finance 1989–91; Taoiseach (Prime Minister) 1992–94; Vice-Pres. Fianna Fáil 1983–92, Pres. 1992–94; mem. Bd of Govs European Investment Bank; Gov. for Ireland, Bd of Govs World Bank, IMF; apptd Dir Jefferson Smurfit 1996; Hon. LLD (Univ. Coll., Dublin) 1995; Dr hc from one Irish, three British, four US and one Australian univs. *Leisure interests:* racing, swimming. *Address:* Apt 4, Four Seasons Hotel, Ballsbridge, Dublin 4, Ireland (home). *Fax:* (1) 6601998 (home).

REYNOLDS, Burt; American actor; b. 11 Feb. 1936, Waycross, Ga; s. of Burt Reynolds, Sr; m. 1st Judy Carne (divorced 1965); m. 2nd Loni Anderson 1988 (divorced 1994); one adopted s.; ed Florida State Univ.; mem. Dirs Guild of America. *Stage appearances include:* Mister Roberts, Look, We've Come Through, The Rainmaker. *Films include:* Angel Baby 1961, Operation CIA 1965, Navajo Joe 1967, Impasse 1969, Skullduggery 1970, Deliverance 1972, Everything You've Always Wanted to Know about Sex But Were Afraid to Ask 1972, The Man Who Loved Cat Dancing 1973, Hustle 1975, Silent Movie 1976, Gator (also dir) 1976, Nickelodeon 1976, Smokey and the Bandit 1977, Hooper (also producer) 1978, Starting Over 1979, The Cannonball Run 1981, Sharky's Machine (also dir) 1981, City Heat 1984, Stick (also dir) 1984, Rent A Cop 1987, Switching Channels 1988, Physical Evidence 1989, Breaking In 1989, B. L. Stryker 1989, Modern Love 1990, Alby's House of Bondage 1990, Cop and a Half 1993, Striptease 1996, Mad Dog Time 1996, Boogie Nights (Golden Globe for Best Supporting Actor) 1997, Raven 1997, Waterproof 1998, Mystery Alaska 1998, The Hunter's Moon 1998, Pups 1999, Big City Blues (also producer) 1999, Mystery Alaska 2000, The Crew 2000,

The Last Producer 2000, The Hermit of Amsterdam 2001, Driven 2001, Tempted 2001, Hotel 2001, The Hollywood Sign 2001, Auf Herz und Nieren 2001, Snapshots 2002, Time of the Wolf 2002, The Librarians 2003, Gumball 3000: The Movie 2003, The Librarians 2003, Without a Paddle 2004, Grilled 2005, The Longest Yard 2005, Delgo 2005, The Dukes of Hazzard 200, Forget About It 2005, Legend of Frosty the Snowman (video, voice) 2005, Cloud 9 2006, End Game 2006, Broken Bridges 2006, In the Name of the King: A Dungeon Siege Tale 2007, Deal 2007, Randy and the Mob 2007. *Television appearances include:* Riverboat 1959–60, Pony Express, Gunsmoke 1962–65, Hawk 1966, Dan August 1970, B. L. Stryker: The Dancer's Touch 1989, Evening Shade 1990–94, The Cherokee Kid 1996, Johnson County War (mini-series) 2002, Miss Lettie and Me 2002, Hard Ground 2003, Ed (episode) 2003, The King of Queens (episode) 2005, Duck Dodgers (episode) 2005, Freddie (episode) 2006. *Other work includes:* Grand Theft Auto: Vice City (video game, voice) 2002. *Publication:* My Life (autobiog.) 1994. *Address:* William Morris Agency, 1 William Morris Place, Beverly Hills, CA 90212; Jeffrey Lane & Associates, 8380 Melrose Avenue, Suite 206, Los Angeles, CA 90069, USA. *Website:* www.burtreynolds.com (office).

REYNOLDS, Debbie Mary Frances; American actress and singer; b. 1 April 1932, El Paso, Tex.; m. 1st Eddie Fisher 1955 (divorced 1959) one d. (Carrie Fisher (q.v.)) one s.; m. 2nd Harry Karl 1960 (divorced 1973); m. 3rd Richard Hamlett 1985 (divorced 1994); film debut in June Bride 1948; stage debut at Blis-Hayden Theater 1952; nightclub act mid-1960s–; founder Debbie Reynolds Professional Rehearsal Studios, North Hollywood late 1970s; Prin. Debbie Reynolds Hotel/ Casino and Hollywood Motion Picture Museum, Las Vegas 1993–; Nat. Hon. presented by Girl Scouts USA 1966–69, Nat. Film Soc. Humanitarian Award. *Theatre includes:* Irene 1973, Annie Get Your Gun, Woman of the Year 1983, The Unsinkable Molly Brown (nat. tour) 1989. *Films:* June Bride 1948, The Daughter of Rosie O'Grady 1950, Three Little Words 1950, Two Weeks with Love 1950, Mr Imperium 1951, Singin' in the Rain 1952, I Love Melvin 1953, The Affairs of Dobie Gillis 1953, Give a Girl a Break 1953, Susan Slept Here 1954, Athena 1954, Hit the Deck 1955, The Tender Trap 1955, The Catered Affair 1956, Bundle of Joy 1956, Tammy and the Bachelor 1957, This Happy Feeling 1958, The Mating Game 1959, Say One for Me 1959, It Started with a Kiss 1959, The Gazebo 1959, The Rat Race 1960, The Pleasure of his Company 1961, The Second Time Around 1961, How the West Was Won 1962, Mary, Mary 1963, My Six Loves 1963, The Unsinkable Molly Brown 1964, Goodbye Charlie 1964, The Singing Nun 1966, Divorce American Style 1967, How Sweet It Is! 1968, What's the Matter with Helen? 1971, Charlotte's Web (voice) 1973, Kiki's Delivery Service (voice) 1989, Heaven & Earth 1993, Mother 1996, In & Out 1997, Zack and Reba 1998, Rudolph the Red-Nosed Reindeer: The Movie (voice) 1998, Rugrats in Paris: The Movie – Rugrats II (voice) 2000. *Television:* The Debbie Reynolds Show 1969, Aloha Paradise (series) 1981, Sadie and Son 1987, Perry Mason: The Case of the Musical Murder 1989, Battling for Baby 1992, Halloweentown 1998, The Christmas Wish 1998, A Gift of Love: The Daniel Huffman Story 1999, Virtual Mom 2000, Rugrats (series, voice) 2000–04, These Old Broads 2001, Halloweentown II: Kalabar's Revenge 2001, Halloweentown III: Halloweentown High 2004, Lolo's Cafe (voice) 2006, Will & Grace (series) 1999–2006, Return to Halloweentown 2006. *Publication:* Debbie: My Life (with David Patrick Colombia) 1987. *Address:* William Morris Endeavor, 1 William Morris Place, Beverly Hills, CA 90212 (office); Debbie Reynolds Studios, 6514 Lankershim Blvd, North Hollywood, CA 91606-2409, USA (office). *Telephone:* (818) 985-3193 (office). *Fax:* (818) 985-6927 (office). *E-mail:* DRStudios@sbcglobal .net (office).

REYNOLDS, Francis Martin Baillie, QC, DCL, FBA; British barrister, legal scholar, academic and consultant; *Professor Emeritus of Law, University of Oxford;* b. 11 Nov. 1932, St Albans, Herts., England; s. of Eustace Baillie Reynolds and Emma Holmes; m. Susan Shillito 1965; two s. one d.; ed Winchester Coll. and Worcester Coll., Oxford; Bigelow Teaching Fellow, Univ. of Chicago, USA 1957–58; Lecturer, Worcester Coll. Oxford 1958–60, Fellow 1960–2000, Fellow Emer. 2000–; Barrister, Inner Temple 1960, Hon. Bencher 1979; Reader in Law, Univ. of Oxford 1977, Prof. of Law 1992–2000, Prof. Emer. 2000–; Ed. The Law Quarterly Review 1987–; Visiting Lecturer, Univ. of Auckland, NZ 1971, 1977; Visiting Prof., Nat. Univ. of Singapore 1984, 1986, 1988, 1990–92, 1994, 1996, 1997, 2000, 2003, 2005, 2007, 2009, Univ. Coll. London 1987–89, Univ. of Melbourne, Australia 1989, Monash Univ., Australia 1989, Univ. of Otago, NZ 1993, Univ. of Sydney, Australia 1993, Univ. of Auckland, NZ 1995, Univ. of Hong Kong 2002, 2010, 2011, 2012, 2013; Titular mem. Comité Maritime Int.; Ed. Law Quarterly Review 1988–; Hon. QC; Hon. Prof., Int. Maritime Law Inst., Malta. *Publications:* Bowstead and Reynolds on Agency, 13th–18th edns 1965–2006, Benjamin's Sale of Goods, 1st–8th edns (co-author) 1974–2010, English Private Law (co-author) 2000 (revised edn 2006), Carver on Bills of Lading (with Sir G. Treitel) 2001 (revised edn 2010). *Leisure interests:* music, walking. *Address:* 61 Charlbury Road, Oxford, OX2 6UX, England. *Telephone:* (1865) 559323. *E-mail:* francis.reynolds@law.ox.ac.uk.

REYNOLDS, Paula Rosput, BA; American business executive; *Vice-Chairman and Chief Restructuring Officer, American International Group Inc. (AIG);* b. Newport, RI; m. Stephen P. Reynolds; ed Wellesley Coll., Mass; Chair., Pres. and CEO AGL Resources, Atlanta, Ga 2000–05; Pres., CEO and mem. Bd of Dirs Safeco Corpn 2006–08, Chair. 2008; Vice-Chair. and Chief Restructuring Officer American International Group Inc. (AIG) 2008–; mem. Bd of Dirs Coca-Cola Enterprises (Chair. Audit Cttee), Delta Air Lines, United Way of Metropolitan Atlanta; ranked 40th by Fortune magazine amongst 50 Most Powerful Women in Business in the US 2006, ranked by Forbes magazine amongst 100 Most Powerful Women (58th) 2006, (48th) 2007, (100th) 2008, (23rd) 2009. *Address:* American International Group Inc. (AIG), 70 Pine Street, New York, NY 10270, USA (office). *Telephone:* (800) 433-8880 (office). *Website:* www.aig.com (office).

REYNOLDS, Sir Peter William John, Kt, CBE; British business executive; b. 10 Sept. 1929, Singapore; s. of Harry Reynolds and Gladys Reynolds; m. Barbara Anne Johnson 1955; two s.; ed Haileybury Coll.; with Unilever Ltd 1950–70, Trainee, Man. Dir, then Chair., Walls Ltd; Asst Group Man. Dir Ranks Hovis McDougall 1971, Group Man. Dir 1972–81, Chair. 1981–89, Deputy Chair. 1989–93; mem. Consultative Bd for Resources Devt in Agric. 1982–84; Deputy Chair. AvisEurope PLC 1988–; Dir of Industrial Devt Bd for Northern Ireland 1982–89, Guardian Royal Exchange Assurance PLC 1986–99; Chair. of Resources Cttee of Food and Drink Fed. 1983–86; mem. Bd of Dirs Boots Co. PLC 1986–2000,

Guardian Royal Exchange PLC 1986–99, Avis Europe PLC 1988–2001, Cilva Holdings PLC 1989, Nationwide Anglia Bldg Soc. 1990–92; Chair., Pioneer Concrete (Holdings) 1990–99; mem. Peacock Cttee 1985–86; High Sheriff of Buckingham 1990–91. *Leisure interests:* beagling, riding (occasionally), watching rugby football, reading, gardening. *Address:* Rignall Farm, Rignall Road, Great Missenden, Bucks., HP16 9PE, England. *Telephone:* (1240) 64714.

REZA, (Evelyne Agnès) Yasmina; French novelist, dramatist, screenwriter and actress; b. 1 May 1959, Paris; d. of Jean Reza and of Nora Reza (née Heltaï); one s. one d.; ed Lycée de St-Cloud, Paris Univ. X, Nanterre, Ecole Jacques Lecoq; Chevalier, Ordre des Arts et des Lettres; Prix du jeune théâtre Beatrix Dussane-André Roussin de l'Acad. française 1991. *Stage appearances include:* Le Malade imaginaire 1977, Antigone 1977, Un Sang fort 1977, La Mort de Gaspard Hauser 1978, L'An mil 1980, Le Piège de Méduse 1983, Le Veilleur de nuit 1986, Enorme changement de dernière minute 1989, La Fausse suivante 1990. *Plays directed include:* Birds in the Night 1979, Marie la louve 1981. *Plays written include:* Conversations après un enterrement (Molière Award for Best Author, Prix des Talents nouveaux de la Soc. des auteurs et compositeurs dramatiques, Johnson Foundation prize) 1987, La Traversée de l'hiver 1989, La Métamorphose (adaptation) 1988, 'Art' 1994, L'Homme du hasard 1995, Trois versions de la vie 2000, Une pièce espagnole 2004, Le Dieu du carnage 2007, Comment Vous Racontez la Partie 2011. *Screenplays written include:* Jusqu'à la nuit (also dir) 1984, Le Goûter chez Niels 1986, A demain 1992, Le Pique-nique de Lulu Kreutz 2000. *Publications:* novels: Hammerklavier 1997, Une Désolation (trans. as Desolation) 1999, Adam Haberberg 2003, Nulle part 2005, Dans la luge d'Arthur Schopenhauer 2005; non-fiction: L'aube le soir ou la nuit (trans. as Dawn, Dusk or Night) 2007. *Address:* c/o Marta Andras (Marton Play), 14 rue des Sablons, 75116 Paris, France.

REZAZADEH, Hossein; Iranian weightlifter; b. 12 May 1978, Ardabil; m.; competes in 105 kilogrammes and over (heaviest category); won snatch (world record of 212.5 kilogrammes) and clean and jerk (world record of 260.5 kilogrammes, combined world record of 472.5 kilogrammes) for gold medal Olympic Games, Sydney 2000; gold medals in snatch, clean and jerk, combined (world record of 472.5 kilogrammes) World Weightlifting Championships, 2002; gold medals in snatch and combined, bronze medal in clean and jerk World Weight Lifting Championships, Canada 2003; won snatch and clean and jerk (world record of 262.5 kilogrammes) for gold medal Olympic Games, Athens, 2004; mem. Saipa club; Iranian Badge of Courage in 2000 Int. Weightlifting Fed. World's Best Weightlifter 2000, 2002, voted Champion of Champions of Iran 2002. *Leisure interests:* cooking. *Address:* c/o Weightlifting Federation of Iran, POB 15745-175, Varzandeh Street, Shiroudi Stadium, Tehran, Iran. *Website:* www.iriwf.com.

REZEK, Francisco, LLD, JSD; Brazilian lawyer, fmr judge and fmr politician; *Counsel, Francisco Rezek Sociedade de Advogados;* b. 18 Jan. 1944, Cristina, Minas Gerais; s. of Elias Rezek and Baget Baracat Rezek; ed Fed. Univ. of Minas Gerais, Sorbonne, France, Univ. of Oxford, UK, Harvard Univ., USA, The Hague Acad. of Int. Law, The Netherlands; Attorney of the Repub., Supreme Court 1972–79; Prof. of Int. and Constitutional Law Univ. of Brasília 1971–, Chair. Law Dept 1974–76, Dean, Faculty of Social Studies 1978–79; Prof. of Int., Law Rio Branco Inst. 1976–; Justice of Supreme Court 1983–90, 1992–97; Foreign Minister 1990–92; mem. Perm. Court of Arbitration 1987–2004; Judge, Int. Court of Justice, The Hague 1997–2006; currently lawyer and Counsel, Francisco Rezek Sociedade de Advogados (law firm), São Paulo. *Publications:* Droit des traités: particularités des actes constitutifs d'organisations internationales 1968, La conduite des relations internationales dans le droit constitutionnel latino-américain 1970, Reciprocity as a Basis of Extradition 1980, Direito dos Tratados 1984, Public International Law 1989. *Address:* Francisco Rezek Sociedade de Advogados, Rua Dr. Renato Paes de Barros, 717 - 8 andar, Itaim Bibi, São Paulo SP, 04530-001, Brazil (office). *E-mail:* contato@franciscorezek.adv.br (office).

REZNIK, Genry Markovich, Cand.Jur.; Russian barrister; b. 11 May 1938, Leningrad; m. Larissa Yulianovna Reznik; one s.; ed Kazakhstan Univ., Moscow Inst. of Law; various positions at Acad. of Ministry of Internal Affairs 1975–82, including Internal Investigator, Investigation Dept, Kazakh Repub.; Lecturer in Law, All-Union Legal Acad. 1982–98; f. Reznik, Gagarin, Abushakhmin and Pnrs, Moscow (law firm); Dir Inst. of Bar Int. Union of Advocates; mem. Moscow Helsinki Group 1989–; Chair. Moscow Bar Asscn; mem. of Council, Fed. Chamber of Lawyers 2004. *Achievements include:* mem. USSR volleyball youth team. *Publications:* over 100 articles on criminal law. *Address:* Reznik, Gagarin, Abushakhmin and Partners, Schmidtovskiy pr. 3, 123100 Moscow, Russia (office). *Telephone:* (495) 205-27-09 (office). *Fax:* (495) 256-72-52 (office).

RHEINGOLD, Arnold Lange, BS, MS, PhD; American chemist and academic; *Professor, Department of Chemistry and Biochemistry, University of California, San Diego;* b. 6 Oct. 1940, Chicago, Ill.; s. of Joseph Cyrus Rheingold and Harriet Lange Rheingold; m. Janice F. Rheingold; ed Case Western Reserve Univ., Univ. of Maryland; Project Man., Glidden Co., Cleveland 1963–65; Research Assoc., Virginia Polytechnic Inst. and State Univ., Blacksburg, Va 1969–70; Prof. of Chem., State Univ. of NY (SUNY), Plattsburgh 1970–82, Visiting Scholar, SUNY, Buffalo 1980–81; Visiting Prof. and Sr Scientist, Univ. of Delaware, Newark 1981–84, Assoc. Prof. 1984–87, Prof. 1987–2003; Prof., Univ. of California, San Diego 2003–; Councillor, ACS 1998–2001, Chair.-elect Inorganic Div. 2001, Chair. 2002; mem. Editorial Bd ACS Journal – Organometallics 1990–, Journal of Cluster Science 1993–95, ACS Journal – Inorganic Chemistry 1994–96, 2001–, Organometallic Synthesis 1995–, Inorganica Chimica Acta 2003–; mem. Jt Bd-Council, Chemical Abstracts 1998–2001; mem. American Crystallographic Asscn, Int. Council on Main Group Chem.; Fellow, AAAS, ACS 2011; ACS Nat. Award of Distinguished Service in the Advancement of Inorganic Chem. *Publications:* more than 2,000 articles in peer-reviewed scientific journals. *Address:* Department of Chemistry and Biochemistry, University of California, San Diego, 9500 Gilman Drive, La Jolla, CA 92093-0358, USA (office). *Telephone:* (858) 822-3870 (office). *Fax:* (858) 822-3872 (office). *E-mail:* arheingold@ucsd.edu (office). *Website:* www -chem.ucsd.edu (office).

RHINES, Peter Broomell, PhD; American scientist and academic; *Professor of Oceanography and Atmospheric Sciences, University of Washington, Seattle;* b. 23 July 1942, Hartford, Conn.; s. of Thomas B. Rhines and Olive S. Rhines; m. 1st Marie Lenos 1968 (divorced 1983); m. 2nd Linda Mattson Semtner 1984; one s.; ed

Loomis School, Massachusetts Inst. of Tech., Trinity Coll., Cambridge, UK; Sloan Scholar, MIT 1960–63, NSF Fellow 1963–64, Asst Prof. of Oceanography 1967–71; Marshall Scholar, Univ. of Cambridge 1964–67, Research Scientist 1971–72, Guggenheim Fellow, Christ's Coll. Cambridge 1979–80; mem. Scientific Staff, Woods Hole Oceanographic Inst. 1972–84, Dir Center for Analysis of Marine Systems 1979–82, oceanographic research cruises 1968–2009; Prof. of Oceanography and Atmospheric Sciences, Univ. of Washington, Seattle 1984–; mem. NAS; Fellow, American Geophysical Union, American Meteorological Soc., American Acad. of Arts and Sciences, Queen's Fellow in Marine Sciences, Australia; Founding mem. Washington State Acad. of Sciences; Fulbright Arctic Chair 2014–15; De Florez Award, MIT 1963, Creativity Award, NSF 1996, Stommel Research Award, American Meteorological Soc. 1998, Haurwitz Lecturer, American Meteorological Soc. 2005, Gledden Fellow, Univ. of Western Australia 2005, Fulbright Scholar, Univ. of Concepción, Chile 2011, Albatross Award, American Miscellaneous Soc. 2012, 2, Nobel Lecturer, Univ. of Toronto 2014. *Television:* contribs to climate programmes on BBC, PBS, History Channel, Discovery Channel, National Geographic Channel. *Publications:* research papers and edited vols on general circulation of the oceans and atmosphere, waves and climate. *Leisure interests:* classical guitar, conversations about the global environment, wandering the out-of-doors. *Address:* School of Oceanography, University of Washington, Box 357940, Seattle, WA 98195 (office); 5753 61st Avenue NE, Seattle, WA 98105, USA (home). *Telephone:* (206) 543-0593 (office); (206) 522-5753 (home). *E-mail:* rhines@uw.edu (office). *Website:* www.ocean.washington.edu/people/faculty/rhines/rhines.html (office).

RHOADS, James Berton, PhD; American archivist; *Professor Emeritus of History, Western Washington University;* b. 17 Sept. 1928, Sioux City, Ia; s. of James H. Rhoads and Mary K. Rhoads; m. S. Angela Handy 1947; one s. two d.; ed Univ. of California, Berkeley and The American Univ., Washington, DC; held various positions at Nat. Archives 1952–65; Asst Archivist, Civil Archives 1965–66; Deputy Archivist of USA 1966–68, Archivist of USA 1968–79; Pres. Rhoads Assocs Int. 1980–84; Dir Grad. Program in Archives and Records Man., Western Washington Univ. 1984–94, Prof. of History 1987–94, Prof. Emer. 1994–, Dir Center for Pacific Northwest Studies 1994–97; mem. Cttee on Soviet-American Archival Co-operation 1986–91, Bd of Trustees Washington State Historical Soc. 1986–95, Washington State Historical Records Advisory Bd 1990–97, Acad. of Certified Archivists 1989– (Pres. 1992–94); Pres. Int. Council on Archives 1976–79; Vice-Pres. Intergovernmental Council on Gen. Information Program, UNESCO 1977–79, and mem. numerous other related orgs; Fellow, Soc. of American Archivists, Pres. 1974–75. *Publications:* numerous articles in professional journals. *Leisure interests:* reading, philately. *Address:* 3613 Illinois Lane, Bellingham, WA 98226, USA. *Telephone:* (360) 676-1235.

RHODES, Frank Harold Trevor, DSc, PhD; American geologist, academic and fmr university president; *President Emeritus, Cornell University;* b. 29 Oct. 1926, Warwickshire, England; s. of Harold C. Rhodes and Gladys Rhodes (née Ford); m. Rosa Carlson 1952; four d.; ed Univ. of Birmingham; Post-doctoral Fellow, Fulbright Scholar, Univ. of Illinois 1950–51, Visiting Lecturer in Geology during summers of 1951–52, Asst Prof., Univ. of Illinois 1954–55, Assoc. Prof. 1955–56, Dir Univ. of Illinois Field Station, Wyoming 1956; Lecturer in Geology, Durham Univ. 1951–54; Prof. of Geology and Head Dept of Geology, Univ. of Wales, Swansea 1956–68, Dean Faculty of Science 1967–68; Prof. of Geology and Mineralogy, Coll. of Literature, Science and Arts, Univ. of Michigan 1968–77, Dean 1971–74, Vice-Pres. for Academic Affairs 1974–77; Pres. Cornell Univ. 1977–94, Prof. of Geology 1977–95, Pres. Emer. 1995–; Dir John Heinz III Center for Science, Econs and the Environment 1996–98; Vice-Pres. Dyson Charitable Trust 1996–98; Prin. Washington Advisory Group 1997–; mem. Atlantic Philanthropics 1995 (Chair. 2000–05); mem. Nat. Science Bd 1987–98 (Chair. 1994–96), American Philosophical Soc. 1991– (Pres. 1999–), Johnson Foundation Bd 2000–, Goldman Sachs Foundation Bd 2000–; mem. Int. Advisory Panel King Abdullah Univ. of Science and Tech.; Trustee, Andrew W. Mellon 1984–99; 36 hon. degrees; Bigsby Medal, Geological Soc. 1967, Higher Educ. Leadership Award, Comm. on Ind. Colls and Univs 1987, Justin Smith Morrill Award 1987, Clark Kerr Medal, Univ. of Calif., Berkeley 1995, Jefferson Lecturer, Univ. of Calif., Berkeley 1999. *Publications:* The Evolution of Life 1962, Fossils 1963, Geology 1972, Evolution 1974, Language of the Earth 1981, (Ed.) Successful Fund Raising for Higher Education: The Advancement of Learning 1997, The Creation of the Future: The Role of the American University 2001; over 70 maj. scientific articles and monographs and some 60 articles on educ. *Address:* 603 Cayuga Heights Road, Ithaca, NY, 14850 (home); Cornell University, 3104 Snee Hall, Ithaca, NY 14853, USA. *E-mail:* mjw11@cornell.edu.

RHODES, Richard Lee, BA; American writer; b. 4 July 1937, Kansas City, Kan.; s. of Arthur Rhodes and Georgia Collier Rhodes; m. Ginger Untrif 1993; two c. by previous m.; ed East High School, Kansas City, Yale Univ.; Trustee, Atomic Heritage Foundation 2004–; fmr Assoc., Center for Int. Security and Cooperation, Stanford Univ.; Hon. mem. American Nuclear Soc. 2001; Hon. DHumLitt (Westminster Coll., Fulton, Mo.) 1988; Hon. DLitt (Colby Coll., Me) 2010; Fellowships: John Simon Guggenheim Memorial Foundation 1974–75, Nat. Endowment for the Arts 1978, Ford Foundation 1981–83, Alfred P. Sloan Foundation 1985, 1993, 1995, 2001, 2010, 2012, MacArthur Foundation Program on Peace and Int. Co-operation 1990–91, 2008–09. *Play:* Reykjavik 2010. *Publications include:* non-fiction: The Inland Ground: An Evocation of the American Middle West 1970, The Ozarks 1974, Looking for America: A Writer's Odyssey 1979, The Making of the Atomic Bomb (Nat. Book Critics' Circle Award for Gen. Non-fiction, Nat. Book Award for Non-fiction 1987, Pulitzer Prize for Non-fiction 1988) 1987, Farm: A Year in the Life of an American Farmer 1989, A Hole in the World: An American Boyhood 1990, Making Love: An Erotic Odyssey 1992, Nuclear Renewal: Common Sense about Energy 1993, Dark Sun: The Making of the Hydrogen Bomb 1995, How To Write 1995, Trying To Get Some Dignity: Stories of Triumph Over Childhood Abuse (with Ginger Rhodes) 1996, Deadly Feasts: Tracking the Secrets of a Terrifying New Plague 1997, Visions of Technology (ed) 1999, Why They Kill 1999, Masters of Death 2001, John James Audubon: The Making of an American (biog.) 2004, The Audubon Reader (ed) 2006, Arsenals of Folly: Nuclear Weapons in the Cold War 2007, The Twilight of the Bombs 2010, Hedy's Folly 2011; fiction: The Ungodly 1973, Holy Secrets 1978, The Last Safari 1980, Sons of Earth 1981. *Address:* c/o Janklow & Nesbit Assocs, 455

Park Avenue, New York, NY 10021, USA (office). *Telephone:* (212) 421-1700 (office). *E-mail:* rhodes.today@comcast.net (office). *Website:* www.richardrhodes.com.

RHODES, William Reginald (Bill), BA; American banking executive; *Senior Advisor, Citigroup;* b. 15 Aug. 1935, New York, NY; s. of Edward R. Rhodes and Elsie Rhodes; ed Northfield Mount Hermon, Brown Univ., Providence, RI; joined Citibank 1957, served in various sr positions, Latin America and Caribbean 1957–77, Head, Latin American corp. business and Sr Exec., Int. Citibank NA, New York 1977–91, Vice-Chair. 1991–2001, mem. Bd of Dirs 1991–, Sr Vice-Chair. 2001–03, apptd Chair. 2003, apptd Pres. and CEO 2005, apptd Sr Vice-Chair. Citigroup, Inc. 1999, apptd Chair. and CEO Citicorp Holdings, Inc. 2003, apptd Pres. 2005, later Sr Int. Officer, currently Sr Advisor; fmr chair. several advisory cttees which negotiated debt-restructuring agreements for Argentina, Brazil, Jamaica, Mexico, Peru and Uruguay during 1980s, and S Korea 1998; Dir, Banamex, Private Export Funding Corpn, US-Russia Business Council, US-Hong Kong Business Council, Foreign Policy Asscn; First Vice-Chair. Inst. of Int. Finance; Chair. Emer. Americas Soc., Council of the Americas; Chair. US-Korea Business Council; Vice-Chair. Nat. Cttee on US-China Relations; mem. Inter-American Devt Bank's Pvt. Sector Advisory Bd, Int. Policy Cttee of US Chamber of Commerce, Council on Foreign Relations, Group of Thirty Consultative Group on Int. Econ. and Monetary Affairs, Inc. (G-30), Washington, DC, Econ. Club of New York; Founding mem. US Nat. Advisory Council to the Int. Man. Centre, Budapest, Hungary; Gov. and Trustee, New York Presbyterian Hosp.; mem. Lincoln Center Consolidated Corp. Fund Leadership Cttee; Vice-Chair. Metropolitan Museum of Art Business Cttee and Chair.'s Cttee; mem. Bd of Overseers Watson Inst. for Int. Studies, Rhodes Center for Int. Econs and Finance at Brown Univ.; Chair. Emer. Bd of Trustees, Northfield Mount Hermon School; Officier, Légion d'honneur; decorations from South Korea, Brazil, Mexico, Argentina, Panama, Venezuela, Jamaica and Poland; Hon. DHumLitt (Brown Univ.); numerous awards from not-for-profit orgs for contribs to int. banking and finance. *Address:* Citigroup Inc., 399 Park Avenue, New York, NY 10022, USA (office). *Telephone:* (212) 559-1000 (office). *Website:* www.citibank.com (office).

RHYS-JAMES, Shani, MBE, BA; Australian artist and painter; b. 2 May 1953, Melbourne, Vic.; d. of Harold Marcus Rhys-James and Jeannie James-Money Vine; m. Stephen West 1977; two s.; ed Parliament Hill Girls School, Loughborough Coll. of Art and Cen. St Martin's Coll. of Art and Design; came to London from Australia aged nine, lived in London 1963–84, moved to mid-Wales with family 1984; regular exhbns with Martin Tinney Gallery, Cardiff 1991–2013, Stephen Lacey Gallery, London, Connaught Brown, Mayfair 2007–13, J. Cacciola Gallery, New York, Hillsboro Fine Art, Dublin; work in art collections of Arts Council of England, Nat. Museum of Wales, Newport Museum and Art Gallery, Cyfartha Castle, Merthyr Tydfil, Usher Gallery, Lincoln, Gallery of Modern Art, Glasgow, Wolverhampton Art Gallery, Birmingham Museum and Art Gallery, Nat. Library of Wales, London Borough of Tower Hamlets, BBC Wales, Glyn Vivian Museum and Art Gallery, Murray Edwards Coll. (fmrly New Hall), Cambridge, Jerwood Foundation; featured artist, Carlow Festival 2000, and at Visual 2010, Royal Cambrian Acad. three-person show 2001; invited artist, Discerning Eye 2004; Artist Advisor, Derek Williams Trust 2007–12; Creative Council mem. for Design and Artists Copyright Soc. 2007–10; frequent radio and TV appearances; mem. Royal Cambrian Acad. 1994; Hon. Fellow, Hereford Coll. of Art 2008, Univ. of Wales Inst., Cardiff 2007; numerous prizes, including First Prize, Mostyn Open, Llandudno 1991, Gold Medal for Fine Art, Royal Nat. Eisteddfod, Ceredigion 1992, First Prize, Hunting/Observer Art Prizes 1993, BBC Wales Visual Artist Award 1994, Second Prize, BP Nat. Portrait Award 1994, Jerwood Painting Prize 2003, Welsh Woman of the Year in Culture 2003, Creative Wales Award, Arts Council of Wales to develop concept of making automata – Cassandra's Rant 2006, Glyndwr Award, MOMA 2007, production grant from the Arts Council of Wales to make an installation collaborating with poets: Florilingua 2012. *Radio:* Relative Values, BBC Wales 2008. *Television includes:* The Slate: Blood Ties 1993, Painting the Dragon 2000, The Little Picture 2000, Paintings from Paradise 2000, Shani Rhys-James: A Conversation 2004, Framing Wales (interviewer Kim Howells) 2011, featured artist on Rolf on Welsh Art 2011, What Do Artists Do All Day? (BBC 4) 2013. *Publications:* Art Today – Edward Lucie-Smith 1997, Facing the Self (essay Andrew Patrizzio), Imagine Wales – Hugh Adams 2003, The Black Cot 2004, Edward Lucie-Smith (monograph essay) 2005, Imaging the Imagination 2005, Shani Rhys-James Pixel Foundry (DVD), Cassandra's Rant Artists book 2006, Azart 10 ans 2002–12, The Life History of Five Contemporary Welsh Woman Artists 2012, The Rivalry of Flowers (essays by William Packer, Francesca Rhydderch and Edward Lucie-Smith), Florilingua artists book collaboration with four poets (monograph to accompany the exhbn) 2013. *Leisure interests:* music, films, plays, books, writing, restoring our Welsh farm and French house and studio. *Address:* Dolpebyll, Llangadfan, Welshpool, Powys, SY21 0PU, Wales. *Telephone:* (1938) 820469. *Fax:* (1938) 820469. *E-mail:* shanirhysjames@btinternet.com. *Website:* www.artwales.com; www.connaught-brown.com.

RI, Kwang-gun; North Korean government official and fmr central banker; *Chairman, Joint Venture and Investment Commission;* began career at Ministry of Foreign Affairs 1977, Chief Econ. Counsellor, Embassy in Berlin mid-1990s; Minister of Foreign Trade 2001–04; Deputy Dir, KWP United Front Dept; Pres, Central Bank of the DPRK 2009–11; Chair Joint Venture and Investment Comm. 2012–; fmr Chair., North Korean Football Asscn. *Address:* Joint Venture and Investment Commission (JVIC), Pyongyang, Democratic People's Republic of Korea (office).

RI, Su-yong; North Korean government official and fmr diplomatist; *Minister of Foreign Affairs;* ed Kim il-Sung Univ., Pyongyang Univ. of Foreign Study; Bureau Dir, Ministry of Foreign Affairs 1972, Dir-Gen., Bureau of Protocol and Bureau of Int. Orgs 1974, Amb. to Switzerland 1998–2010; mem. Supreme People's Ass. (Parl.) 2003–; Chair. DPRK Investment Cttee Jt Venture 2011–12; Minister of Foreign Affairs 2014–; mem. Korean Workers' Party (KWP), Alt. mem. Cen. Cttee 2010–, Deputy Dir, KWP Org. Guidance Dept; Order of Kim Jong-il 2012. *Address:* Ministry of Foreign Affairs, Pyongyang, Democratic People's Republic of Korea (office).

RIADY, Mochtar, (Lie Mo Tie); Indonesian business executive; *Chairman, Lippo Group;* b. 12 May 1929, Malang, East Java; m.; six c.; f. Lippo Group (conglomerate) 1950s, currently Chair.; Pres. Commr Lippo Bank 1997–2008; fmr Chair. Asian Bankers Asscn; Sr Adviser Ma Chung Univ.; fmr Chair. Bd of Trustees, Univ. of Indonesia; f. Mochtar Riady Inst. for Nanotechnology (centre for cancer research), Karawaci, Banten 2008. *Publications:* Searching For Opportunities Amid Crisis 1999, Nanotechnology Management Style: How to Heal a Company from Old Illnesses and Save a Family Company 2004, Ancient Philosophy and Modern Management 2006. *Address:* Lippo Group, 78 Shenton Way, #17-01/02, 079120 Singapore, Singapore (office). *Telephone:* 62273613 (office). *Fax:* 62273106 (office). *Website:* www.lipporealty.com (office).

RIBAR, Monika; Swiss business executive; *President and CEO, Panalpina Group;* b. 1959; ed Univ. of St Gallen, Exec. Program of Grad. School of Business at Stanford Univ., USA; Financial Controller, BASF Vienna, Austria 1984–86; Head of Strategic Planning, Fides Group (KPMG), Zürich 1986–90; Controlling and IT Dept, Panalpina Group (freight forwarding and logistics services provider) 1991–92, SAP Global Project Man. 1992–95, Corp. Controller 1995–2000, mem. Exec. Bd 2000–, Chief Information Officer 2000–05, Chief Financial Officer 2005–06, Pres. and CEO 2006–; mem. Bd of Dirs Bank Julius Bär Ltd, Zurich 2001–, Logitech International SA 2004–, Romanel/Morges; ranked by Fortune magazine amongst the 50 Most Powerful Women in Business outside the US (18th) 2008, (28th) 2009, (43rd) 2010, (39th) 2011, (43rd) 2012. *Address:* Panalpina World Transport (Holding) Ltd, Viaduktstrasse 42, 4002 Basel, Switzerland (office). *Telephone:* (61) 226-11-11 (office). *Fax:* (61) 226-11-01 (office). *E-mail:* info@panalpina.com (office). *Website:* www.panalpina.com (office).

RIBEIRO, Baron (Life Peer), cr. 2010, of Achimota in the Republic of Ghana and of Ovington in the County of Hampshire; **Bernard Ribeiro,** Kt, CBE, FRCS; British surgeon; m. Elisabeth Ribeiro; ed Dean Close School, Cheltenham, Glos., Middlesex Hosp. Medical School, London; began career in surgery 1967; Consultant Gen. Surgeon, Basildon Hosp. (now Basildon Univ. Hosp.) 1979–2008 (retd), helped establish Basildon & Thurrock Univ. Hosps NHS Foundation Trust's advanced laparoscopic unit; examiner in surgery for three univ. medical schools; elected to Council of Royal Coll. of Surgeons 1988, Pres. 2005–08; mem. Health Policy Research Advisory Bd of American Coll. of Surgeons; Gov., Dean Close School; Patron Achimota Trust; Hon. DSc (Anglia Ruskin Univ.) 2008; Officer of Order of the Volta (Ghana) 2008. *Achievements include:* special interest in urology, colorectal and laparoscopic surgery. *Publications:* scientific papers on colorectal cancer. *Address:* House of Lords, Westminster, London, SW1A 0PW, England (office). *Telephone:* (20) 7219-5353 (office). *Fax:* (20) 7219-5979 (office).

RIBEIRO, Inacio; Brazilian fashion designer; m. Suzanne Clements 1992; one s.; ed Cen. St Martin's Coll. of Art and Design, London; fmrly designer, Brazil; design consultant in Brazil (with wife) 1991–93; f. Clements Ribeiro (with wife), London 1993; first collection launched Oct. 1993, numerous collections since; first solo show London Fashion Week March 1995; Creative Dir (with wife) Cacharel, Paris 2000–07; fashion shows since in London, Paris, Brazil, Japan; consultant to cos in UK and Italy; winners, Designer of the Year New Generation Category 1996. *Address:* BCPR, Unit 18, Archer Street Studios, 10–11 Archer Street, London, W1D 7AZ (office); Clements Ribeiro Trading Ltd, 17 Alexander Street, London, W2 5NT, England. *Telephone:* (20) 7229-9680 (office). *E-mail:* inacioribeiro@hotmail.com (office). *Website:* www.clementsribeiro.com.

RIBEIRO, João Ubaldo Osório Pimentel, LLB, MS; Brazilian writer and journalist; b. 23 Jan. 1941, Itaparica, Bahia; s. of Manoel Ribeiro and Maria Felipa Osório Pimentel Ribeiro; m. 1st Maria Beatriz Moreira Caldas 1962; m. 2nd Mônica Maria Roters 1971; m. 3rd Berenice de Carvalho Batella Ribeiro 1982; one s. three d.; ed Fed. Univ. of Bahia Law School and School of Admin. and Univ. of Southern California, USA; reporter, Jornal da Bahia, Salvador 1958–59, City Ed. and columnist 1960–63; Chief Ed. Tribuna da Bahia 1968–73; columnist, O Globo, Rio de Janeiro, O Estado de São Paulo, São Paulo; editorial writer, Folha de São Paulo 1969–73; Prof. of Political Science, Fed. Univ. of Bahia 1965–71, Catholic Univ. of Bahia 1967–71; mem. Brazilian Acad. of Letters; Jabuti Prize (Brazilian Book Chamber) 1971, 1984, Golfinho de Ouro (Govt of Rio) 2008, Premio Camões 2008, and many other awards. *Publicationsinclude:* novels: Setembro Não Tem Sentido 1968, Sargento Getúlio 1971, Vila Real 1980, Viva o Povo Brasileiro 1984, O Sorriso do Lagarto 1989, O Feitiço da Ilha do Pavão 1997, Miséria e Grandeza do Amor de Benedita 2000, Diário do Farol 2002; short stories: Vencecavalo e o Outro Povo 1973, Livro de Histórias 1983, Ein Brasilianer in Berlin (autobiog.) 1994, Você me mata, Mãe gentil 2004, A gente se acostuma a tudo 2006, O rei da noite 2008. *Leisure interests:* microscopy (protozoa), music (Bach), sports (soccer, fishing). *Address:* c/o Academia Brasileira de Letras, Av. Presidente Wilson 203, Castelo, CEP 20030-021, Rio de Janeiro RJ; c/o Editora Nova Fronteira SA, Rua Bambina 25, 22251-050 Rio de Janeiro, R.J.; Rua General Urquiza, 147/401, 22431-040 Rio de Janeiro, R.J., Brazil (home). *Telephone:* (21) 537-8770 (office); (21) 239-8528 (home). *Fax:* (21) 286-6755. *Website:* www.academia.org.br.

RIBEIRO CONSTÂNCIO, Vítor Manuel, BEcons; Portuguese economist, international organization official and fmr central banker; *Vice-President, European Central Bank;* b. 12 Oct. 1943, Lisbon; ed Instituto Superior de Ciencias Económicas e Financeiras (later Instituto Superior de Economia e Gestao—ISEG), Universidade Técnica de Lisboa, Univ. of Bristol, UK; Asst Prof. of Econs, ISEG 1965–73, Guest Prof. of Econs 1989–94, 1995–99, 2000–09; Head of Dept, Econ. Models and Global Programming, Centre of Planning Studies 1972–73; Prof., Instituto Superior do Serviço Social 1972–73; Sec. of State, Planning in I and II Provisional Govts 1974–75; Head of Research Dept, Banco de Portugal 1975, Deputy Gov. 1977, 1979, 1981–84, Gov. 1985–86, 2000–10, Sr Adviser 1989–94; Sec. of State, Budget and Planning 1976; Pres., Comm. for European Integration 1977, 1979; Minister of Finance 1978; Prof., Universidade Católica Portuguesa 1980–81; Pres., Portuguese section of European Movt 1980–81; mem. Parl. 1980–81, 1987–88; Pres., Parl. Comm. on European Affairs 1980–81; Guest Prof., Universidade Nova de Lisboa 1982–84; mem. Conselho de Estado 1995–99; Bd mem. and Exec. Dir Banco Portugues de Investimento 1995–99; mem. Governing Council and Gen. Council, European Cen. Bank (ECB) 2000–09, Vice-Pres. 2010–; Order of Christ, Ordem do Infante Dom Henrique. *Address:* European Central Bank, Eurotower (Main Building), Kaiserstrasse 29, 60311 Frankfurt am Main, Germany (office). *Telephone:* (69) 13447455 (office). *Fax:* (69) 13447404 (office). *E-mail:* info@ecb.europa.eu (office). *Website:* www.ecb.europa.eu (office).

RIBEIRO PEREIRA, Lt-Gen. Augusto Heleno; Brazilian military officer (retd); served in Brazilian mil. mission, Paraguay 1981–83; Mil. Attaché to France 1996–98; Head, Centro de Comunicação do Exército 2002–04; C-in-C UN Stabilization Mission in Haiti (MINUSTAH) 2004–05; Head of Cabinet for Mil. Command 2006; retd from army 2011; consultant to Grupo Bandeirantes de Comunicação. *Address:* c/o Quartel General do Exército, Bloco B Térreo, Setor Militário Urbano, 70630-901 Brasília, DF, Brazil (office).

RIBOUD, Franck; Swiss food industry executive; *Chairman and CEO, Groupe Danone;* b. 7 Nov. 1955; ed École Polytechnique Fédérale de Lausanne; joined BSN Group (renamed Groupe Danone 1994) 1981, various positions in man. control div., sales and marketing div. and business div. including Brand Man., Sales Rep., Regional Sales Force Trainer, Regional Man., Sales Man., Key Account Sales Man., Dept Man., involved in acquisition of Nabisco's European activities 1989, Gen. Man. Evian Water 1990–92, Gen. Man. Devt BSN 1992–94, Vice-Pres. and Gen. Man. Groupe Danone 1994–96, Chair. and CEO 1996–, Chair. danone.communities mutual fund (SICAV) 2007–, Chair. Steering Cttee of Fonds Danone pour l'Écosystème 2009–; mem. Bd of Dirs Fiat SpA –2000, Scottish & Newcastle PLC 2000–03, Accor 2001–, Lacoste France (Chair. 2006–), L'Oréal SA 2002–, Renault SAS 2000–, Bagley Latinoamerica SA, Rolex SA, Rolex Holding SA, Global Alliance for Improved Nutrition; mem. Supervisory Bd Fondation Ela; mem. representing Danone, Conseil Nat. du Développement Durable; Dir, Asscn Nationale des Industries Agroalimentaires, Int. Advisory Bd HEC business school. *Address:* Groupe Danone, 17 boulevard Haussmann, 75009 Paris, France (office). *Telephone:* 1-44-35-20-20 (office). *Fax:* 1-42-25-67-16 (office). *E-mail:* info@danone.com (office). *Website:* www.danone.com (office).

RICARD, Alexandre; French business executive; *Deputy CEO and Chief Operating Officer, Pernod Ricard SA;* joined Pernod Ricard SA (distiller) in Audit & Business Devt Dept 2003, Finance and Admin Dir of Irish Distillers div. 2004–06, CEO Pernod Ricard Asia Duty Free 2006–08, Chair. and CEO Irish Distillers 2008–11, Man. Dir Distribution Network 2011–12, Deputy CEO and COO Pernod Ricard SA 2012–. *Address:* Pernod Ricard SA, 12 place des États-Unis, 75783 Paris Cedex 16, France (office). *Telephone:* 1-41-00-41-00 (office). *E-mail:* media.relations@pernod-ricard.com (office). *Website:* pernod-ricard.com (office).

RICARD, François, BA, MA, DLit, FRSC; Canadian author and professor of literature; *James McGill Research Chair in Quebec Literature, McGill University;* b. 4 June 1947, Shawinigan, PQ; ed Laval Univ., McGill Univ., Univ. of Aix-Marseille, France; apptd Prof., Dept of French Language and Literature, McGill Univ., Montréal 1971, Prof. Emer. 2009–, James McGill Research Chair in Quebec Literature 2002–; Dir Liberté (literary journal) 1980–86; Founder Papiers collés; columnist, L'Atelier du Roman (journal), Paris, L'Inconvénient, Montréal; Hon. DèsL (Manitoba) 2009; awards include Grande Médaille de la Francophonie 2001, Prix André-Laurendeau 2005, Canada Council for the Arts Killam Prize 2009; Kt, Nat. Order of Quebec. *Publications include:* Histoire du Québec contemporain 1986, La génération lyrique 1992, Gabrielle Roy, Une Vie (Prix Jean-Éthier-Blais 1997, Prix Maxime-Raymond, Drainie-Taylor Biog. Prize) 1996, Le dernier après-midi d'Agnès 2003, La littérature contre elle-même (Gov.-Gen.'s Literary Award 1985) 2002, Chroniques d'un temps loufoque 2005. *Address:* McGill University, Department of French Language and Literature, 853 rue Sherbrooke ouest, Bureau Arts W130A, Montréal, PQ H3A 0G5, Canada (office). *E-mail:* francois.ricard@mcgill.ca (office). *Website:* litterature.mcgill.ca/ricard.html (office).

RICARD, HE Cardinal Jean-Pierre Bernard, BA, PhD; French ecclesiastic; *Archbishop of Bordeaux (-Bazas);* b. 26 Sept. 1944, Marseille; s. of Georges Ricard and Jeanine Ricard; ed Lycée de Saint-Charles, Lycée Périer, Marseille, and Thiers, Major Seminary of Marseille, Séminare des Carmes and Institut Catholique de Paris; spent one year of Nat. Service of Co-operation in Bamako, Mali; ordained priest, Archdiocese of Marseille 1968; asst pastor of Parish of Sainte-Émilie de Vialoar 1970–78; responsible for Mistral Centre of Religious Culture 1975–81, diocesan del. for seminarians 1975–85; Pastor of Parish of Sainte-Marguerite 1981–88, assoc. del. for ecumenism and episcopal vicar for zone of South Marseille 1984–88; regional theologian for pastoral affairs 1986–93; Gen. Sec. Diocesan Synod of Marseille 1988–91; Vicar Gen. to Cardinal Robert Coffy, Archbishop of Marseille 1988–93; Titular Bishop of Pulcheriopolis 1993–; Auxiliary Bishop of Grenoble 1993–96; Coadjutor Bishop of Montpellier (-Lodève-Béziers-Agde-Saint-Pons-de-Thomières) July–Sept. 1996, Bishop of Montpellier (-Lodève-Béziers-Agde-Saint-Pons-de-Thomières) 1996–2001; Archbishop of Bordeaux (-Bazas) 2001–; cr. Cardinal (Cardinal-Priest of Sant'Agostino) 2006; Vice-Pres. French Episcopal Conf. 1999–2001, Pres. 2001–07; participated in Tenth Ordinary Ass. of World Synod of Bishops, Vatican City, Sept.–Oct. 2001; attended 11th Gen. Ordinary Ass. of the World Synod of Bishops, Vatican City, Oct. 2005; mem. Pontifical Comm. Ecclesia Dei (deals with issue of Tridentine rite) 2006–, Pontifical Council for Culture 2009–, Pontifical Council for Promoting Christian Unity 2010–, Congregation for Divine Worship and the Discipline of the Sacraments 2010–, Congregation for Catholic Educ. 2012–. *Address:* Archevêché, 183 cours de la Somme, 33077 Bordeaux Cedex, France (office). *Telephone:* (5) 56-91-81-82 (office). *Fax:* (5) 56-92-12-98 (office). *E-mail:* accueil@catholique-bordeaux.cef.fr (office). *Website:* catholique-bordeaux.cef.fr (office).

RICCI, Christina; American actress; b. 12 Feb. 1980, Santa Monica, Calif.; d. of Ralph Ricci and Sarah Ricci; began acting career in commercials. *Films:* Mermaids 1990, The Hard Way 1991, The Addams Family 1991, The Cemetery Club 1993, Addams Family Values 1993, Casper 1995, Now and Then 1995, Gold Diggers: The Secret of Bear Mountain 1995, That Darn Cat 1996, Last of the High Kings 1996, Bastard Out of Carolina 1996, Ice Storm 1997, Little Red Riding Hood 1997, Fear and Loathing in Las Vegas 1998, Desert Blue 1998, Buffalo 66 1998, The Opposite of Sex 1998, Small Soldiers 1998, Pecker 1999, 200 Cigarettes 1999, Sleepy Hollow 1999, The Man Who Cried 2001, All Over the Guy 2001, Prozac Nation 2001, Pumpkin 2002, Miranda 2002, The Laramie Project 2002, Anything Else 2003, Monster 2003, I Love Your Work 2003, Cursed 2005, Penelope 2006, Home of the Brave 2006, Black Snake Moan 2006, Speed Racer 2008, New York, I Love You 209, All's Faire in Love 2009, After Life 2009, Alpha and Omega (voice) 2010, War Flowers 2011, Bucky Larson: Born to Be a Star 2011, Bel Ami 2012. *Television:* Ally McBeal (series) 2002, Saving Grace (series) 2009, Pan Am (series) 2011–12.

Address: c/o Toni Howard, ICM, 8942 Wilshire Boulevard, Beverly Hills, CA 90211, USA.

RICCI, Nino, BA, MA; Canadian writer; b. 23 Aug. 1959, Leamington; s. of Virginio Ricci and Amelia Ricci (née Ingratta); m. Erika de Vasconcelos 1997; ed York Univ., Toronto, Concordia Univ., Montreal; taught Creative Writing and Canadian Literature at Concordia Univ.; Pres. Canadian Centre, Int. PEN 1995–96; Writer-in-Residence, Univ. of Windsor 2005–06; Alistair MacLeod Award for Literary Achievement, Writers' Trust Engel/Findley Prize 2012. *Publications:* Lives of the Saints (Books in Canada First Novel Award, Gov. Gen's Award for Fiction, Betty Trask Award, Winifred Holtby Prize for Best Regional Novel, F.G. Bressani Prize) 1990, In a Glass House 1993, Where She Has Gone 1997, Testament 2003 (Trillium Book Award), The Origin of Species (Gov. Gen's Award for Fiction, Canadian Authors Asscn Award) 2008. *Address:* c/o Anne McDermid & Associates, 83 Willcocks Street, Toronto, ON M5S 1C9, Canada (office). *Telephone:* (416) 324-8845 (office). *Fax:* (416) 324-8870 (office). *E-mail:* info@mcdermidagency.com (office); saverio@ninoricci.com (office). *Website:* www.mcdermidagency.com (office); www.ninoricci.com.

RICCIOTTI, Rudy; French architect; b. 1952, Algiers, Algeria; ed School of Engineers, Geneva, UPAM, Marseille; freelance architect in Bandol 1980; Prof., Inst. of Art, Marseille-Luminy 1995–; Visiting Prof., Ecole Spécial d'Architecture Paris 1997–98; Scientific Adviser, Ecole d'architecture de Grenoble 2000–; has participated in numerous publs, confs and exhbns; Officier des Arts et des Lettres, Chevalier, Légion d'honneur, Officier, Ordre nat. du Mérite; competition entries for remodelling for arte TV station in Strasbourg and Quai de Brainly Museum of Early History in Paris were both awarded prizes, won competitions, including Salle de Musique Actuelle et Contemporaine, Boulogne-Billancourt 2007, Siège d'ITER, Cadarache 2007, Stade Jean Bouin, Paris 2007, Ecole Internationale ITER, Manosque 2007, Grand prix nat. d'architecture. *Works include:* Bibliothèque de prêt de Draguignan 1986, Centre des loisirs de jeunes, Bandol 1986, Ecole Jean de Florette, St Cyr 1991, city centre pedestrian redevelopment, Bandol 1991, highway information and control centre, Marseille 1992, Salle de spectacles et de cinéma, Pierrelatte (prize winner) 1993, Salle des Fêtes, Port Saint Louis du Rhône 1994, Base nautique, Bandol 1995, Aire ludique, Lyon-Gerland 1996, Villa Gros, Gémenos 1997, Collège 600, Saint Ouen 1997, beach redevelopment, Lecques, St Cyr-sur-Mer 1998, Great Hall, Faculty of Science, Marseille 1998, Foyer restaurant of CREPS, Boulouris 1998, Villa Lyprendi, Toulon 1998, Salle de spectacles, Manosque (prize winner) 1999, Musée des Arts Premiers, Quai Branly, Paris (competition) 1999, Cinéma-casino, St Cyr-sur-Mer 1999, urban redevelopment of Celle Ligure, Italy 1999, Villa and Marmonier swimming pool, La Garde 1999, Villa and Le Goff swimming pool, Marseille 1999, Salle de musique actuelle, Nîmes (prize winner) 2000, project for seaside railway station, Marseille (competition) 2000, Concert Room, Potsdam, Germany 2000, Collection Yvon Lambert, Avignon (with A. Putman) 2000, Nat. Photographic Centre, Paris 2001, Pôle santé Hosp., Carpentras (with J.-P. Cassulo) 2001, concert and event halls of Les Tanzmatten, Selesteatt (with G. Heintz) 2001, Nat. Choreographic Centre, Aix-en-Provence 2004, Social Centre Consolat-Mirabeau, Marseille 2004, underground car park, Brussels 2004, reuse and redevelopment of Grands moulins, Université Paris VII 2005, Rive Gauche, Paris 13ème 2005, Navy Testing and Survey Centre at Le Mourillon, Toulon 2005, Pavillon Noir, Aix-en-Provence 2006, Palais du cinéma, Venice 2011, Pavillon Blanc Médiathèque and Centre d'art contemporain, Colomiers 2011, Site of Int. Thermonuclear Experimental Reactor, Cadarache 2012, Museum of European and Mediterranean Civilisations, Marseilles 2013, Educational Complex, La Bouilladisse, Stade Jean Bouin, Paris 2013, Centre des Arts et de la Culture, Douchy-les-Mines 2013. *Leisure interest:* collecting contemporary art. *Address:* Rudy Ricciotti Architecte, 17 blvd Victor Hugo, 83150 Bandol, France (office). *Telephone:* (4) 94-29-52-61 (office). *Fax:* (4) 94-32-45-25 (office). *E-mail:* rudy.ricciotti@wanadoo.fr (office). *Website:* www.rudyricciotti.com (office).

RICE, Anne, (Anne Rampling, A. N. Roquelaure), BA, MA; American writer; b. 4 Oct. 1941, New Orleans, La; m. Stan Rice 1961; one s. one d. (deceased) ed Texas Women's Univ., San Francisco State Coll., Univ. of California, Berkeley; mem. Authors' Guild. *Publications include:* Interview with the Vampire 1976, The Feast of All Saints 1979, Cry to Heaven 1982, The Claiming of Sleeping Beauty (as A. N. Roquelaure) 1983, Beauty's Punishment (as A. N. Roquelaure) 1984, The Vampire Lestat 1985, Exit to Eden (as Anne Rampling) 1985, Beauty's Release (as A. N. Roquelaure) 1985, Belinda (as Anne Rampling) 1986, The Queen of the Damned 1988, The Mummy, or Ramses the Damned 1989, The Witching Hour 1990, The Tale of the Body Thief 1992, Lasher 1993, Taltos 1994, Memnoch the Devil 1995, Servant of the Bones 1996, Violin 1997, Pandora 1998, Armand 1998, Vittorio the Vampire 1999, Merrick 2000, Blood and Gold 2001, The Master of Rampling Gate (short story) 2002, Blackwood Farm 2002, Blood Canticle 2003, Christ the Lord: Out of Egypt 2005, Christ the Lord: The Road to Cana 2008, Called out of Darkness: A Spiritual Confession (auto-biog.) 2008, Angel Time: The Songs of the Seraphim 2009, The Wolf Gift 2012, The Wolves of Midwinter 2013. *Address:* c/o Alfred A. Knopf Inc., 1745 Broadway, Suite B1, New York, NY 10019-4305, USA (office). *E-mail:* anneobrienrice@gmail.com (office). *Website:* www.annerice.com (office).

RICE, Condoleezza, PhD; American academic and fmr government official; *Thomas and Barbara Stephenson Senior Fellow on Public Policy, Hoover Institution, Stanford University;* b. 14 Nov. 1954, Birmingham, Ala; ed Univ. of Denver, Univ. of Notre Dame; teacher at Stanford Univ., Calif. 1981–2001, Provost 1993–99, Thomas and Barbara Stephenson Sr Fellow on Public Policy, Hoover Inst. and Prof. of Political Science 2009–; Special Asst to Dir of Jt Chiefs of Staff 1986; Dir, then Sr Dir of Soviet and East European Affairs, Nat. Security Council 1989–91; Special Asst to Pres. for Nat. Security Affairs 1989–91; primary foreign policy adviser to presidential cand. George W. Bush 1999–2000; Asst to Pres. for Nat. Security Affairs and Nat. Security Advisor 2001–04; Sec. of State 2005–09; fmr mem. Bd of Dirs Chevron Corpn, Charles Schwab Corpn, William and Flora Hewlett Foundation, KiOR Inc. 2011–, and numerous other bds; Sr Fellow, Inst. for Int. Studies, Stanford; Fellow, American Acad. of Arts and Sciences; Trustee John F. Kennedy Center for the Performing Arts, Washington, DC; Dr hc (Morehouse Coll.) 1991, (Univ. of Alabama) 1994, (Univ. of Notre Dame) 1995, (Mississippi Coll. School of Law) 2003, (Univ. of Louisville) 2004; ranked by Forbes

magazine amongst 100 Most Powerful Women (first) 2004, (first) 2005, (second) 2006, (fourth) 2007, (seventh) 2008. *Publications:* Uncertain Allegiance: The Soviet Union and the Czechoslovak Army 1984, The Gorbachev Era (co-author) 1986, Germany Unified and Europe Transformed (co-author) 1995, Extraordinary, Ordinary People: A Memoir of Family 2010, No Higher Honor (autobiog.) 2011; numerous articles on Soviet and East European foreign and defence policy. *Address:* Hoover Institution, 434 Galvez Mall, Stanford University, Stanford, CA 94305-6010, USA (office). *Telephone:* (650) 723-1754 (office). *Fax:* (650) 723-1687 (office). *Website:* www.hoover.org (office).

RICE, Dorothy P., BA; American academic and fmr government official; *Professor Emerita, Institute for Health and Aging, University of California, San Francisco;* b. 11 June 1922, Brooklyn, NY; d. of Gershon Pechman and Lena Schiff; m. John D. Rice 1943; three s.; ed Brooklyn Coll., New York, Univ. of Wisconsin; Dept of Labor 1941–42; War Production Bd 1942–44; Nat. War Labor Bd 1944–45; Nat. Wage Stabilization Bd 1945–47; Health Economist, Public Health Service 1947–49, Public Health Analyst 1960–62, 1964–65; Social Science Analyst, Social Security Admin. 1962–64, Chief, Health Insurance Research Branch 1965–72, Deputy Asst Commr Office of Research and Statistics 1972–76; Dir Nat. Center for Health Stats. Hyattsville, Md 1976–82; Prof.-in-Residence, Dept of Social and Behavioral Sciences, Inst. for Health and Aging, Univ. of Calif., San Francisco 1982, Inst. for Health Policy Studies, Univ. of Calif., San Francisco 1982–94, Prof. Emer. 1994–; numerous honours and awards. *Publications:* more than 250 articles in professional journals. *Address:* Institute for Health and Aging, Department of Social and Behavioral Sciences, School of Nursing, University of California, 3333 California Street, Suite 340, San Francisco, CA 94118 (office); 13895 Campus Drive, Oakland, CA 94605, USA (home). *Telephone:* (415) 476-2771 (office); (510) 428-9506 (home). *Fax:* (415) 502-5208 (office); (510) 638-1429 (home). *E-mail:* dorothy.rice@ucsf.edu (office); dorothy.rice@comcast.net (home). *Website:* nurseweb.ucsf.edu/iha (office).

RICE, Sir (Charles) Duncan, Kt, BA, PhD, FRSE, FRSA, FRHistS; British historian, academic and university vice-chancellor; b. Aberdeen, Scotland; m. Susan Rice; three c.; ed Univ. of Aberdeen, Univ. of Edinburgh; Lecturer, Univ. of Aberdeen 1966–69, Prin. 1996–2010; Asst Prof. of History, Yale Univ., USA 1975–79, Assoc. Prof. 1970–75; Prof. of History and Dean of Coll., Hamilton Coll., Clinton, NY, USA 1979–85; Vice-Chancellor New York Univ., USA 1985–96; mem. Bd Trust for Scotland –2003, BT Scotland –2003, Scottish Ballet –2004, Scottish Opera –2005, Rowett Research Inst. –2006, Scottish Enterprise Grampian –2006, Nat., Univs and Colls Employers Asscn –2006; Chair. Circumpolar Universities Asscn 1997–99, UK Socrates-Erasmus Council –2007, Council for the Advancement and Support of Educ. –2009; mem. Heritage Lottery Fund Cttee for Scotland –2009; Burgess, Guild of City of Aberdeen; Hon. Fellow, UHI Millennium Inst.; Hon. Vice-Pres. Scottish Opera; hon. degrees from New York Univ., Robert Gordon Univ., Univ. of Aberdeen, Univ. of Edinburgh; Fellowships at Harvard and Yale Univs. *Publications:* The Rise and Fall of Black Slavery 1975, The Scots Abolitionists 1831–1961 1982; numerous papers in professional journals. *Leisure interests:* hill walking, contemporary literature, opera, studio ceramics. *Address:* c/o Principal's Office, King's College, University of Aberdeen, Aberdeen, AB24 3FX, Scotland (office).

RICE, Jerry Lee; American fmr professional football player; b. 13 Oct. 1962, Starkville, Miss.; s. of Joe Nathan; m. Jacqui Rice; three c.; ed Miss. Valley State Coll.; wide receiver; played receiver for Miss. Valley State Coll. 1980–84; drafted in first round by San Francisco 49ers, Nat. Football League (NFL) 1985, played with 49ers 1985–2000, Oakland Raiders 2001–03, Seattle Seahawks 2004, Denver Broncos 2005 (retd in pre-season); holds 38 NFL records including most touchdowns receiving (197), most passes received (1,549) and most yards receiving (22,895); only player in NFL history to catch three touchdown passes in two Super Bowl games; currently broadcast commentator and radio talk show host; co-host Sports Sunday (prime time sports show shown in San Francisco Bay Area); selected to Pro Bowl 1986–96, 1998, 2002, named All-Pro 10 times in 20 NFL seasons, Sporting News NFL Player of the Year 1987, 1990, Sports Illustrated NFL Player of the Year 1986, 1987, 1990, 1993. *Television includes:* competed in reality show Dancing with the Stars, paired with dancer Anna Trebunskaya 2005–06, appeared as backup dancer in season two episode of Fox's Don't Forget the Lyrics!, appeared in first episode of Spike TV's Pros vs Joes challenge show, appeared in episode of CW's One Tree Hill, appeared on episode of reality show The Biggest Loser: Families as coach putting contestants through football drills, portrayed Hal Gore in film Without a Paddle: Nature's Calling 2009. *Publications:* Rice 1996, Go Long!: My Journey Beyond the Game and the Fame (autobiography) 2007. *Leisure interest:* golf. *Address:* c/o Sports Sunday, NBC11, 2450 North First Street, San Jose, CA 95131, USA. *Telephone:* (408) 432-6221. *Website:* www.nbc11.com/sportssunday; www.jerryricefootball.com.

RICE, Keren D., PhD; Canadian professor of linguistics; *Professor in Linguistics and Founding Director, Centre for Aboriginal Initiatives, University of Toronto;* apptd Asst Prof., Faculty of Arts and Science, Univ. of Toronto 1984, Prof. in Linguistics 1990, Canada Research Chair in Linguistics and Aboriginal Studies 2003–, also Founding Dir Centre for Aboriginal Initiatives; Ed. International Journal of American Linguistics, has also served on editorial bds of several journals; Pres. Canadian Linguistics Asscn 1998–2000; mem. Bd Social Sciences and Humanities Research Council (mem. Standing Cttee, Standing Cttee on Ethics and Integrity); Fellow, Linguistic Soc. of America 2008 (Pres., first from univ. outside of USA), AAAS 2005; Bloomfield Book Award, Linguistic Soc. of America, Killam Research Fellowship for the study of Athapaskan languages 1993–94, Faculty of Arts and Science Outstanding Teacher Award 1998, Connaught Research Leave Fellowship 2001–02, recognized in an Honours Ceremony at First Nations House 2005, Killam Prize in Humanities, Canada Council for the Arts 2011, Canadian Linguistics Asscn Nat. Achievement Award 2013. *Publications include:* Hare Noun Dictionary, Current Issues in Athapaskan Linguistics: Current Perspectives on a Language Family, Morpheme Order and Semantic Scope: Word Formation in the Athapaskan Verb, Athabaskan Prosody (co-ed.) 2005, Featural Markedness, A Grammar of Slave; numerous articles in linguistics and Aboriginal studies. *Address:* Department of Linguistics, Sidney Smith Hall, 4th Floor, University of Toronto, 100 St George Street, Toronto, ON M5S 3G3, Canada (office). *Telephone:* (416) 978-4029 (office). *Fax:* (416) 971-2688 (office). *E-mail:* rice@chass.utoronto.ca (office). *Website:* linguistics.utoronto.ca (office).

RICE, Stuart Alan, SB, AM, PhD; American chemist and academic; *Frank P. Hixon Distinguished Service Professor Emeritus, James Franck Institute, University of Chicago;* b. 6 Jan. 1932, New York, NY; s. of Laurence Harlan Rice and Helen Rayfield; m. 1st Marian Coopersmith 1952 (died 1994); two d.; m. 2nd Ruth O'Brien 1997; one s.; ed Brooklyn Coll. and Harvard Univ.; Asst Prof., Dept of Chem. and Inst. for the Study of Metals, Univ. of Chicago 1957–59, Assoc. Prof., Inst. for the Study of Metals (later James Franck Inst.) 1959–60, 1960–69, Louis Block Prof. of Chem. 1969, Louis Block Prof. of Physical Sciences 1969–71, Chair. Dept of Chem. 1971–77, Frank P. Hixon Distinguished Service Prof. 1977–81, now Emer., Dean, Div. of Physical Sciences, Univ. of Chicago 1981–95; NSF Sr Postdoctoral Fellow and Visiting Prof., Univ. Libre de Bruxelles 1965–66; NIH Special Research Fellow and Visiting Prof., H. C. Ørsted Inst., Univ. of Copenhagen 1970–71; Fairchild Distinguished Scholar, California Inst. of Tech. 1979; Newton-Abraham Prof., Univ. of Oxford, UK 1999–2000; lecturer, numerous univs in USA and abroad; mem. Nat. Science Bd 1980–; Jr Fellow, Soc. of Fellows 1955–57; Fellow, American Acad. of Arts and Sciences, NAS, American Philosophical Soc.; Foreign mem. Royal Danish Acad. of Science and Letters 1976; Hon. DSc (Brooklyn Coll., Notre Dame Coll.) 1982; A. Cressy Morrison Prize in Natural Sciences, New York Acad. of Sciences 1955, Alfred P. Sloan Fellow 1958–62, Guggenheim Fellow 1960–61, ACS Award in Pure Chem. 1962, Marlow Medal, Faraday Soc. 1963, Bourke Lecturer, Faraday Soc. 1964, Llewellyn John and Harriet Manchester Quantrell Award 1970, Leo Hendrik Baekeland Award 1971, Peter Debye ACS Prize 1985, Baker Lecturer, Cornell Univ. 1985–86, Centenary Lecturer, Royal Soc. of Chem. 1986–87, John Howard Appleton Lecturer, Brown Univ. 1995, Joel Henry Hildebrand Award, ACS, Centennial Medal, Harvard Univ. 1997, Nat. Medal of Science 1999, Hirschfelder Prize in Theoretical Chem. 2002, Wolf Prize in Chem. (jtly) 2011. *Publications:* Poly-electrolyte Solutions (with Mitsuru Nagasawa) 1961, Statistical Mechanics of Simple Liquids (with Peter Gray) 1965, Physical Chemistry (with R. S. Berry and John Ross) 1980, Optical Control of Molecular Dynamics (with Meishan Zhao) 2000; and 650 papers on chemical physics in scientific journals. *Leisure interests:* reading, carpentry, collecting antique scientific instruments. *Address:* The James Franck Institute, University of Chicago, GCIS E 235, 929 East 57th Street, Chicago, IL 60637 (office); 5517 South Kimbark Avenue, Chicago, IL 60637, USA (home). *Telephone:* (773) 702-7199 (office); (773) 667-2679 (home). *Fax:* (773) 702-5863 (office); (773) 667-0454 (home). *E-mail:* sarice@harper.uchicago.edu (office); s-rice@uchicago .edu (office). *Website:* jfi.uchicago.edu (office).

RICE, Susan Elizabeth, BA, MPhil, DPhil; American government official and diplomatist; *National Security Advisor;* b. 17 Nov. 1964, Washington, DC; m.; two c.; ed Stanford Univ. (Truman Scholar), New Coll., Oxford, UK (Rhodes Scholar); Man. Consultant, McKinsey and Co., Toronto, Canada 1991–93; Dir for Int. Orgs and Peacekeeping, Nat. Security Council, Washington, DC 1993–95, Special Asst to the Pres. and Sr Dir for African Affairs 1995–97; Asst Sec. of State for African Affairs, US State Dept 1997–2001; Sr Fellow, Foreign Policy and Global Economy and Devt Program, Brookings Inst., Washington, DC 2002–09; Sr Advisor for Nat. Security Affairs on Kerry-Edwards presidential campaign 2004, on Obama for America Campaign 2007–08, Sr Foreign Policy Advisor on Obama presidential campaign 2008; served on Advisory Bd of Obama-Biden Transition and as Co-Chair. of its Policy Working Group on Nat. Security 2009; Amb. and Perm. Rep. to UN, New York 2009–13; Nat. Security Advisor, The White House 2013–; Chatham House-British Int. Studies Asscn Prize for the most distinguished doctoral dissertation in the UK in the field of Int. Relations. *Address:* Office of the National Security Advisor, The White House, 1600 Pennsylvania Avenue, NW, Washington, DC 20500, USA (office). *Website:* www.whitehouse.gov/administration/eop/nsc (office).

RICE, Thomas Maurice, PhD, FRS; American/Irish scientist and academic; b. 26 Jan. 1939, Dundalk, Ireland; s. of James Rice and Maureen Rice; m. Helen D. Spreiter 1966; one s. two d.; ed Univ. Coll. Dublin and Univ. of Cambridge; asst lecturer, Dept of Mathematical Physics, Univ. of Birmingham 1963–64; Research Assoc. Dept of Physics, Univ. of Calif. at San Diego, La Jolla 1964–66; Bell Laboratories, Murray Hill, NJ 1966–81; Prof. of Theoretical Physics, ETH, Zürich 1981–2004; mem. NAS; Hon. MRIA; Hewlett-Packard Europhysics Prize 1998, John Bardeen Prize 2000. *Address:* Theoretische Physik, ETH-Hönggerberg, 8093 Zürich, Switzerland. *Telephone:* (1) 6332581. *Fax:* (1) 6331115 (office). *E-mail:* rice@itp.phys.ethz.ch (office). *Website:* www.itp.phys.ethz.ch/staff/rice (office).

RICE, Sir Timothy (Tim) Miles Bindon, Kt; British songwriter; b. 10 Nov. 1944, Amersham; s. of Hugh Gordon Rice and Joan Odette Rice; m. Jane Artereta McIntosh 1974, one s. one d.; pnr Nell Sully, one d.; ed Lancing Coll.; with EMI Records 1966–68, Norrie Paramor Org. 1968–69; founder and fmr Dir GRRR Books Ltd 1978, Pavilion Books Ltd 1981; Chair. Foundation for Sport and the Arts 1991–; mem. Main Cttee MCC 1992–94, 1995– (Pres. 2002–03); Dr hc (Univ. of Sunderland) 2006; 12 Ivor Novello Awards, three Tony Awards, six Grammy Awards, British Acad. of Songwriters, Composers and Authors Fellowship 2010. *Lyrics for musicals:* (music by Andrew Lloyd Webber q.v. unless otherwise specified) The Likes of Us 1965, Joseph and the Amazing Technicolor Dreamcoat 1968, Jesus Christ Superstar 1970, Evita 1976, Blondel (music by Stephen Oliver) 1983, Chess (music by Benny Andersson and Bjorn Ulvaeus) 1984, Cricket 1986, Starmania/Tycoon (with music by Michael Berger) 1989–90, Aladdin (film musical, music by Alan Menken) 1992, The Lion King (film musical, music by Elton John) 1993 (theatre version 1997), Beauty and the Beast (music by Alan Menken) 1994 (some lyrics for stage version), Heathcliff (music by John Farrar) 1995, King David (music by Alan Menken) 1997, Aida (music by Elton John) 1998, The Road to El Dorado (music by Elton John) 1999; songs include: Don't Cry For Me Argentina, I Know Him So Well, Can You Feel The Love Tonight? (Acad. Award, Golden Globe, with Elton John 1994), I Don't Know How To Love Him, A Winter's Tale, Circle Of Life, Any Dream Will Do, A Whole New World (Acad. Award, Golden Globe, with Alan Menken 1992), All Time High (from film Octopussy), You Must Love Me (Acad. Award, Golden Globe, with Andrew Lloyd Webber 1996), One Night In Bangkok; lyrics for songs with composers, including Paul McCartney, Mike Batt, Freddie Mercury, Graham Gouldman, Marvin Hamlisch, Rick Wakeman, John Barry. *Publications:* Evita (with Andrew Lloyd Webber) 1978, Joseph and the

Amazing Technicolor Dreamcoat 1982, Treasures of Lords 1989, Oh, What a Circus (autobiog.) 1995, The Complete Eurovision Song Contest Companion (jtly) 1998, founder and original author, with Paul Gambaccini, Jonathan Rice and Mike Read, of the Guinness Book of Hit Singles and related titles. *Leisure interests:* cricket, history of popular music, chickens. *Address:* Lewis & Golden, 40 Queen Anne Street, London, W1M 0EL, England (office). *Website:* www.timrice.co.uk (office).

RICH, Alexander, MD; American molecular biologist and academic; *William Thompson Sedgwick Professor of Biophysics, Massachusetts Institute of Technology;* b. 15 Nov. 1924, Hartford, Conn.; s. of Max Rich and Bella Shub; m. Jane Erving King 1952; two s. two d.; ed Harvard Coll. and Harvard Medical School; served in USN 1943–46; Research Fellow, Gates and Crellin Labs, Calif. Inst. of Tech. 1949–54; Chief of Section on Physical Chem., Nat. Inst. of Mental Health, Bethesda, Md 1954–58; Visiting Scientist, Cavendish Lab., Cambridge, UK 1955–56; Assoc. Prof. of Biophysics, MIT 1958–61, Prof. 1961–, William Thompson Sedgwick Prof. of Biophysics 1974–; Fairchild Distinguished Scholar, Calif. Inst. of Tech., Pasadena 1976; Visiting Prof., Coll. de France, Paris 1987; Sr Consultant, Office of Science and Tech. Policy, Exec. Office of the Pres. 1977–81; Chair. Perm. Science Cttee, American Acad. of Arts and Sciences 1967–71, Basic Research Cttee of Nat. Science Bd 1978–82, Biotechnology Programme of NAS Cttee on Scholarly Communication with the People's Republic of China 1986–93; Co-Chair. Scientific and Academic Advisory Cttee of Weizmann Inst. of Science, Israel 1987–93; mem. or fmr mem. numerous cttees etc., including Marine Biological Lab., Woods Hole, Mass, 1965–77, 1987–96, Advisory Bd NAS Acad. Forum 1975–82, Scientific Advisory Bd Stanford Synchrotron Radiation Project 1976–80, US-USSR Jt Comm. on Science and Tech. 1977–82, Council Pugwash Confs on Science and World Affairs 1977–82, Bd of Dirs Medical Foundation, Boston, Mass 1981–90, Governing Bd Nat. Research Council 1985–88, Cttee on USSR and Eastern Europe of Nat. Research Council 1986–92, Exec. Cttee, Council of NAS 1985–88, External Advisory Cttee of Center for Human Genome Studies, Los Alamos, NM 1989–97, Nat. Critical Technologies Panel of Office of Science and Tech. Policy, Washington, DC 1990–91; mem. Visiting Cttee, Calif. Inst. of Tech., Pasadena 1999–2005; on editorial bds of numerous publs, including Journal of Molecular Evolution 1983–94, Proteins, Structure, Function and Genetics 1986–91, Genomics 1987–, Journal of Biotechnology 1987–92, EMBO Journal 1988–90; mem. ACS and other socs, NAS 1970– (mem. Exec. Cttee 1985–88), Pontifical Acad. of Sciences, The Vatican 1978, American Philosophical Soc. 1980; Sr mem. Inst. of Medicine, Washington, DC 1990; Foreign mem. French Acad. of Sciences 1984; Assoc. mem. European Molecular Biology Org. 1984; Fellow, Nat. Research Council 1949–51, American Acad. of Arts and Sciences 1959, AAAS 1965; Hon. mem. Japanese Biochemical Soc. 1986; Dr hc (Rio de Janeiro) 1981; Hon. PhD (Weizmann Inst.) 1992; Hons DSc (ETH, Zurich) 1993, (Freie Universität Berlin) 1996; Guggenheim Fellow 1963, Skylab Achievement Award, NASA 1974, Theodore von Karmen Award 1976, Presidential Award, New York Acad. of Sciences 1977, James R. Killian Faculty Achievement Award, MIT 1980, Jabotinsky Medal, New York 1980, Nat. Medal of Science, Washington, DC 1995, Linus Pauling Medal, ACS 1995, Merck Award, American Soc. for Biochemistry and Molecular Biology, Washington 1998, Bower Award for Achievement in Science, Franklin Inst. Pa 2000, Passano Award, Passano Foundation 2002, Lomonosov Large Gold Medal, Russian Acad. of Sciences 2002, Lifetime Achievement Award, Inst. of Human Virology, Baltimore 2002, Biotechnology Achievement Award, New York Univ. School of Medicine 2003. *Publications:* Structural Chemistry and Molecular Biology (co-ed.) 1968; Primary and Tertiary Structure of Nucleic Acids and Cancer Research (co-ed.) 1982; more than 500 publications in the fields of molecular structure of nucleic acid components, nucleic acids and polynucleotides, physical chem. of nucleotides and polynucleotides, molecular structure of proteins, mechanism of protein synthesis, molecular biology of the nucleic acids, X-ray crystallography, origin of life. *Leisure interests:* ocean sailing in small boats, growing tomato plants, collecting fossils. *Address:* Department of Biology, Room 68-233, Massachusetts Institute of Technology, 77 Massachussetts Avenue, Cambridge, MA 02139 (office); 2 Walnut Avenue, Cambridge, MA 02140, USA (home). *Telephone:* (617) 253-4715 (office); (617) 547-1637 (home). *Fax:* (617) 253-8699 (office). *E-mail:* cbeckman@mit.edu (office). *Website:* biology.mit.edu/people/ alexander_rich (office).

RICH, Frank Hart, Jr, BA; American journalist, critic and writer; b. 2 June 1949, Washington, DC; s. of Frank Hart Rich and Helene Aaronson; m. 1st Gail Winston 1976; two s.; m. 2nd Alexandra Rachelle Witchel 1991; ed Harvard Univ.; Film Critic and Sr Ed. New Times Magazine 1973–75; Film Critic, New York Post 1975–77; Film and TV Critic, Time Magazine 1977–80; Chief Drama Critic, New York Times 1980–93, Op-Ed Columnist 1994–2011, also Sr Adviser to Culture Ed.; Writer-at-Large, New York Magazine 2011–; Assoc. Fellow, Jonathan Edwards Coll., Yale Univ. 1998; George Polk Award 2005. *Publications include:* Hot Seat: Theater Criticism for the New York Times 1980–93 1998, Ghost Light 2000, The Greatest Story Ever Sold 2006. *Address:* New York Media, 75 Varick Street, New York, NY 10013, USA (office). *Website:* nymag.com/frank-rich (office); www .frankrich.com (office).

RICH, Patrick Jean Jacques; French/Swiss/Canadian business executive (retd); b. 28 March 1931, Strasbourg, France; s. of the late Henri Rich and Marguerite Rich; m. Louise Dionne 1961; two s. one d.; ed Univ. of Strasbourg and Harvard Univ., USA; worked for Alcan Aluminium Ltd in Guinea, France, UK, Argentina, Spain and Italy 1959–70, Area Gen. Man. for Latin America 1971–75, Exec. Vice-Pres. Europe, Latin America and Africa 1976–77, mem. Bd 1978–86; Exec. Vice-Pres. Alcan Aluminium Ltd and CEO Aluminium Co. of Canada 1978–81; Exec. Vice-Pres. Europe, Africa, Middle East and Chair. Alcan Aluminium SA 1978–86; CEO Société Générale de Surveillance Holding SA, Geneva 1987–89; Deputy Chair. BOC Group PLC 1990–91, Chief Exec. 1991–92, Chair. 1992–94 (non-exec. 1994) and Chief Exec. 1992–94; Chair. Royal Packaging Industries Van Leer, Netherlands 1988–95, IMEC Research Project 1995–; Gov. Van Leer Group Foundation 1982–99, Van Leer Jerusalem Inst. 1995–99; mem. (non-exec.) Bd, La Farge Cement (Canada) 1977–81, Bekaert 1978–87, IMI Geneva 1977–81; Trustee, Bernard van Leer Foundation 1982–99; Croix de la Valeur Militaire, Army Corps citation, Médaille Commémorative Combattants d'Algérie. *Leisure interests:* opera, walking, skiing, piano playing, reading, sailing. *Address:* Terrazas de Marbella 4C, Los Sueños, Playa Herradura Canton Garabito,

Pcia, Puntarenas, Costa Rica (home). *Telephone:* (22) 3466643 (Switzerland) (office); 8545-8937 (home). *E-mail:* pjj.rich@gmail.com (home).

RICHARD, Alain; French government official; *Mayor of Saint-Ouen-l'Aumône;* b. 29 Aug. 1945, Paris; m. Elisabeth Couffignal 1988; one s. one d. and one s. by previous m.; ed Lycée Henri IV, Paris, Institut d'Etudes Politiques, Ecole Nat. d'Admin; Auditor, Conseil d'Etat 1971, Maître des requêtes 1978, Conseiller d'Etat 1993–95; Mayor, Saint-Ouen-l'Aumône 1977–97, 2001–; Deputy, Val d'Oise 1978–93, Senator 1995–97; Vice-Pres. Commission des lois 1981–86, Nat. Ass. 1987–88; Minister of Defence 1997–2001; Founder and Vice-Pres. Forum for Man. of Towns 1985–97; mem. Nat. Office, Parti Socialiste Unifié 1972–74; mem. Cttee Parti Socialiste 1979, Exec. Bd 1988; mem. Bd Inst. for Int. Relations 1991–97. *Address:* Hôtel de Ville, 2 place Pierre Mendès-France, Saint-Ouen l'Aumône, 95318 Cergy-Pontoise Cedex (office); 28 rue René Clair, 95310 Saint-Ouen-l'Aumône, France (home). *Telephone:* 1-34-21-25-00 (office). *Fax:* 1-34-64-35-65 (office). *E-mail:* courrier@ville-saintouenlaumone.fr (office). *Website:* www.ville-saintouenlaumone.fr (office).

RICHARD, Dame Alison Fettes, DBE, MA, PhD; British university administrator and professor of anthropology and environmental studies; *Vice-Chancellor Emerita, University of Cambridge;* b. 1 March 1948, Kent, England; d. of Gavin Sharp Richard and Joyce Napier Matthews; m. Robert E. Dewar; one s. (deceased) two d.; ed Newnham Coll., Cambridge and King's Coll., London; joined Faculty of Yale Univ., USA 1972, Dir of Grad. Studies 1980–86, Prof. of Anthropology 1986–2003, Chair. Dept of Anthropology 1986–90, Prof. of Environmental Studies, Yale School of Forestry and Environmental Studies 1990–2003, Dir Peabody Museum of Natural History 1991–94, Provost Yale Univ. 1994–2002, Franklin Muzzy Crosby Prof. of the Human Environment 1998, Prof. Emer. 2003–; Vice-Chancellor Univ. of Cambridge 2003–10, Vice-Chancellor Emer. 2010–; mem. Bd World Wildlife Fund International, Liz Claiborne/Art Ortenberg Foundation, Howard Hughes Medical Inst.; Officier, Ordre Nat. (Madagascar) 2005; Dr hc (Peking Univ.) 2004, (Univ. of Antananarivo, Madagascar) 2005, (York Univ., Toronto) 2006, (Univ. of Edinburgh) 2006, (Queen's Univ., Belfast) 2008, (Anglia Ruskin Univ.) 2008, (Yale Univ.) 2009, (Ehwa Woman's Univ., S Korea) 2009, (Chinese Univ. of Hong Kong) 2009, (Univ. of Exeter) 2010, (Univ. of Cambridge) 2011, (Univ. of London) 2011. *Publications include:* Primates in Nature 1985, Behavioral Variation: Case Study of a Malagasy Lemur 1978; numerous articles in scientific journals. *Address:* PO Box 201, Middle Haddam, CT 06456, USA (home). *Telephone:* (860) 267-2732 (office).

RICHARD, Sir Cliff, Kt, OBE; British singer, musician (guitar) and actor; b. (Harry Rodger Webb), 14 Oct. 1940, India; s. of Rodger Webb and the late Dorothy Webb; ed Riversmead School, Cheshunt, Herts.; leader, Cliff Richard and The Shadows; later, solo artist; regular int. concert tours, various repertory and variety seasons; own TV series on BBC and ITV; numerous radio and TV interviews and performances since 1958; mem. Equity; Hon. DUniv (Middlesex) 2003; numerous awards. *Films include:* Serious Charge 1959, Expresso Bongo 1960, The Young Ones 1961, Summer Holiday 1962, Wonderful Life 1964, Finders Keepers 1966, Two a Penny 1968, His Land, Take Me High 1973. *Stage appearances include:* musicals Time, Dominion Theatre, London 1986–87, Heathcliff, UK tour and Hammersmith Apollo, London 1996–97. *Recordings include:* albums: Cliff 1959, Cliff Sings 1959, Me And My Shadows 1960, Listen To Cliff 1961, 21 Today 1961, The Young Ones 1961, 32 Minutes And 17 Seconds With Cliff Richard 1962, Summer Holiday 1963, Cliff's Hit Album 1963, When In Spain 1963, Wonderful Life 1964, Aladdin And His Wonderful Lamp 1964, Cliff Richard 1965, More Hits By Cliff 1965, When In Rome 1965, Love Is Forever 1965, Kinda Latin 1966, Finders Keepers 1966, Cinderella 1967, Don't Stop Me Now 1967, Good News 1967, Cliff In Japan 1968, Two A Penny 1968, Established 1968, The Best Of Cliff 1969, Sincerely 1969, It'll Be Me 1969, Cliff Live At The Talk of The Town 1970, About That Man 1970, His Land 1970, Tracks 'n' Grooves 1970, The Best Of Cliff Vol. Two 1972, Take Me High 1973, Help It Along 1974, The 31st February Street 1974, I'm Nearly Famous 1976, Every Face Tells A Story 1977, 40 Golden Greats 1977, Small Corners 1978, Green Light 1978, Thank You Very Much (Cliff & The Shadows) 1979, Rock 'n' Roll Juvenile 1979, I'm No Hero 1980, Love Songs 1981, Wired For Sound 1981, Now You See Me… Now You Don't 1982, Dressed For The Occasion 1983, Silver 1983, Rock 'n' Roll Silver 1983, Cliff & The Shadows 1984, Always Guaranteed 1987, Private Collection 1988, Stronger 1989, From A Distance – The Event 1990, Together 1991, Cliff Richard: The Album 1993, The Hit List 1994, Songs From Heathcliff 1995, Heathcliff Live 1996, Cliff Richard At The Movies 1996, The Rock 'n' Roll Years 1997, Real As I Wanna Be 1998, The Whole Story 2001, Wanted 2001, The Singles Collection 2002, Cliff At Christmas 2003, Something's Goin' On 2004, Two's Company: The Duets 2006, Love: The Album 2007, 50th Anniversary Album 2008, Reunited (with The Shadows) 2009, Bold As Brass 2010, Soulicious 2011, The Fabulous Rock 'N' Roll Songbook 2013. *Publications include:* Questions 1970, The Way I See It 1972, The Way I See It Now 1975, Which One's Cliff? 1977, Happy Christmas from Cliff 1980, You, Me and Jesus 1983, Mine to Share 1984, Jesus, Me and You 1985, Single-Minded 1988, Mine Forever 1989, My Story: A Celebration of 40 Years in Showbusiness 1998, My Life, My Way (with Penny Junor) 2008. *Leisure interest:* tennis. *Address:* Cliff Richard Organisation, PO Box 46C, Esher, Surrey, KT10 0RB, England (office). *Telephone:* (1372) 467752 (office). *Fax:* (1372) 462352 (office). *E-mail:* general@cliffrichard.org (office). *Website:* www.cliffrichard.org (home).

RICHARD, Baron (Life Peer), cr. 1990, of Ammanford in the County of Dyfed; **Ivor Seward Richard,** PC, MA, QC; British politician, lawyer and diplomatist; b. 30 May 1932, Cardiff; s. of Seward Thomas and Isabella Irene Richard; m. 1st Geraldine Moore 1956 (divorced 1961); one s.; m. 2nd Alison Mary Imrie 1962 (divorced 1984); one s. one d.; m. 3rd Janet Armstrong Jones 1989; one s.; ed Cheltenham Coll., Pembroke Coll., Oxford; called to the Bar 1955; MP for Barons Court 1964–74; Parl. Pvt. Sec. to Sec. of State for Defence 1966–69; Under-Sec. of State for Defence for Army 1969–70; QC 1971; Perm. Rep. to UN 1974–79; EC Commr for Social Affairs, Employment, Educ. and Vocational Training Policy 1981–84; Leader of Opposition in the House of Lords 1992–97; Lord Privy Seal and Leader of the House of Lords, 1997–98; Chair. World Trade Centre Wales Ltd (Cardiff) 1985–97; Chair. Richard Comm. on the Welsh Ass. 2002–04; Chair. Rhodesia Conf., Geneva 1976; Counsel to Chadbourne, Parke, Whiteside and Wolff, New York 1979–81; Labour; Hon. Fellow, Pembroke Coll. 1981–. *Publica-*

tions: Europe or the Open Sea 1971, We, the British 1983, Unfinished Business: Reforming the House of Lords 1998; and articles in various political journals. *Leisure interests:* playing piano, watching football, talking. *Address:* House of Lords, Westminster, London, SW1A 0PW, England. *Telephone:* (20) 7219-1495. *E-mail:* richardi@parliament.uk.

RICHARD, Jean Barthélemy, DèsL; French historian and academic; b. 7 Feb. 1921, Kremlin-Bicêtre; s. of Pierre Richard and Amélie Grandchamp; m. Monique Rivoire 1944; three s. two d.; ed Ecole des Chartes, Ecole Française de Rome and Sorbonne, Paris; Asst Archivist, Dijon 1943–55; Prof., Univ. of Dijon 1955–88, Dean, Faculté des Lettres 1968–71; mem. Acad. des Inscriptions, Inst. de France and other learned socs; Commdr, Légion d'honneur, Grand Officier, Ordre du Mérite, Commdr des Palmes académiques; Dr hc (Cyprus Univ.) 2006; Gold Medal for Altaic Studies, Indiana Univ. *Publications:* The Latin Kingdom of Jerusalem 1953, Les ducs de Bourgogne 1954, L'Esprit de la Croisade 1969, La papauté et les missions d'Orient 1977, Histoire de la Bourgogne 1978, St Louis 1983, Le livre des remembrances de la secrète du royaume de Chypre 1983, Histoire des Croisades 1996, Au-delà de la Perse et de l'Arménie 2005, Lettres papales relatives à Chypre 1314–1378 2013; five vols in Variorum Reprints on Crusades and Oriental History 1976–2003. *Leisure interests:* garden and forest activities. *Address:* 12 rue Pelletier de Chambure, 21000 Dijon (home); Les Billaudots, 71540 Igornay, France. *Telephone:* (3) 80-66-10-28 (home); (3) 85-82-82-98 (home).

RICHARD, Pierre, BEng; French business executive; b. 9 March 1941, Dijon; s. of Henri Richard and Marguerite Richard (née Genty); m. Aleth Sachot 1966; three c.; ed Univ. of Dijon and Univ. of Pennsylvania, USA; teacher, Inst. of Urbanism, Paris 1967–68; Asst Dir-Gen. Public Devt Corpn, new town of Cergy-Pontoise 1967–72; Tech. Adviser to Sec. of State for Housing 1972–74, to Gen. Secr. for the Pres. of the Rep. 1974–78; Dir Gen. for Local Communities, Ministry of the Interior 1978–82; Asst Dir-Gen. of Treasury, Dept of Local Devt 1983–90; Man. Dir Crédit Local de France (CLF) 1993–, Co-Chair. Dexia Group (after merger between CLF and Crédit Communal de Belgique) 1996–99, Deputy Dir 1999, Pres. Supervisory Bd Dexia Crédit Local de France 2000, Group CEO and Chair. Exec. Bd Dexia Group 2000–05, Chair. Bd of Dirs 2006–08; Pres. Group of Specialized Financial Insts 1991–93; Pres. Inst. of Decentralization 1993–95; Pres. Admin. Bd, Ecole Nat. des Ponts et Chaussées 1994–; Dir Municipal Bond Investors Assurance 1990–, Air France 1995–, Banque européenne d'investissement 1994–, Le Monde 1995–; Chevalier, Légion d'honneur; Officier, Ordre nat. du Mérite. *Publications:* Les Communes françaises d'aujourd'hui, Le Temps des citoyens pour une démocratie décentralisée 1995. *Leisure interest:* horseriding. *Address:* c/o Dexia Group, Square de Meeûs 1, 1000 Brussels, Belgium (office).

RICHARD, Stéphane; French business executive; *Chairman and CEO, France Télécom-Orange;* b. 24 Aug. 1961, Caudéran (Gironde); ed École des Hautes Etudes Commerciales, Paris, École Nationale d'Admin, Strasbourg; assigned to French Inspectorate of Public Finances 1987–91; apptd as tech. adviser for the electronics and IT industries in cabinet of Dominique Strauss-Kahn, Minister for Industry and Foreign Trade 1991–92; joined Compagnie Générale des Eaux 1992, first as Deputy to group's Chief Financial Officer, before being appointed CEO Compagnie Immobilière Phénix 1994–97, Chair. Compagnie Générale d'Immobilier et de Services (now Nexity) 1997–2003, Exec. Vice-Pres. Veolia Environnement and Chief CEO Veolia Transport 2003–07; Chief of Staff to French Minister for the Economy, Industry and Employment 2007–09; mem. Bd of Dirs France Télécom SA, UGC SA, Nexity SA, all until 2007, mem. Exec. Bd and Deputy CEO in Charge of Operations in France, France Télécom-Orange 2009–10, CEO Del. Jan.–March 2010, CEO March 2010–11, Chair. and CEO France Télécom-Orange 2011–; Chevalier, Légion d'honneur 2007, Ordre nat. du Mérite. *Address:* France Télécom-Orange, 6 place d'Alleray, 75505 Paris Cedex 15, France (office). *Telephone:* 1-44-44-22-22 (office). *Fax:* 1-44-44-95-95 (office). *E-mail:* info@francetelecom.com (office). *Website:* www.francetelecom.com (office); www.orange.com (office); www.orange-business.com (office).

RICHARDS, Gen. Sir David, Kt, GCB, CBE, DSO, ADC; British army officer; *Chief of the Defence Staff;* b. 1952; m. Caroline Richards; two d.; ed Eastbourne Coll., Royal Artillery, Univ. Coll., Cardiff; regimental duty (29 Commando Regt, RA, C Anti-Tank Battery, Royal Horse Artillery, 11th Armoured Brigade) in the Far East, Germany and UK, including three tours of NI 1974–83; Commdr field battery in 47th Field Regt 1985–86, Chief of Staff, Berlin Infantry Brigade 1986–88; Instructor, Staff Coll., Camberley 1989–91; CO 3rd Regt Royal Horse Artillery 1991–94; Col Army Plans, Ministry of Defence 1994–96; promoted to Brig. 1996; Commdr 4th Armoured Brigade 1996–98; Chief Jt Force Operations, Perm. Jt HQ 1998–2001; promoted to Maj. Gen. 2001; Chief of Staff Allied Rapid Reaction Corps 2001–02; Asst Chief of Gen. Staff 2002–04; Commdr Allied Rapid Reaction Corps 2005–07, Commdr Int. Stabilisation and Assistance Force in Afghanistan 2006–07; C-in-C Land Forces 2008–09; Chief of Gen. Staff 2009–10; Chief of the Defence Staff 2010–. *Address:* Ministry of Defence, Main Building, Whitehall, London, SW1A 2HB, England (office). *Telephone:* (20) 7218-9000 (office). *E-mail:* public@ministers.mod.uk (office). *Website:* www.mod.uk (office).

RICHARDS, Gen. Sir David Julian, Kt, GCB, CBE, DSO, ADC Gen., BA; British army officer; *Chief of the Defence Staff;* b. 1952; m. Caroline Richards; two d.; ed Eastbourne Coll., Univ. Coll., Cardiff; commissioned into Royal Artillery as Second Lt 1971, served as Capt. 1977–89, Lt-Col 1989–94; Col Army Plans, Ministry of Defence 1994–95, Commdr 4th Armoured Brigade, Germany 1995–98, Chief of Jt Force Operations, Perm. Jt HQ 1998–2000, Chief of Staff, Allied Rapid Reaction Corps, NATO 2001–06, Commdr Int. Stabilisation and Assistance Force in southern Afghanistan 2006–07, C-in-C of Land Forces 2008, Chief of the Gen. Staff 2009–10, Chief of the Defence Staff 2010–; Adm. Army Sailing Asscn, British Kiel Yacht Club; Pres. Army Tennis; Chair. Gurkha Welfare Trust; Hon. Col of the Royal Rifle Volunteers 2003, Hon. Col Commdt of the Royal Artillery 2005, Col Commdt of the Brigade of Gurkhas 2007; campaign medals for NI, East Timor (Int. Force for East Timor—INTERFET) and Operational Service Medals for Sierra Leone and Afghanistan, Golden Jubilee Medal 2002. *Address:* CIO Access, 1st Floor, Zone N Main Building, Whitehall, London, SW1A 2HB, England (office). *E-mail:* CIO-FOI@mod.uk (office). *Website:* www.mod.uk (office).

RICHARDS, Ed; British government official; *CEO, Office of Communications (Ofcom);* began career as researcher with Diverse Production Ltd; worked with

London Economics Ltd (consultancy firm); fmr adviser to Gordon Brown MP; served as Controller of Corporate Strategy at BBC; fmr Sr Policy Adviser to Prime Minister Tony Blair for media, telecoms, internet and e-govt; Sr Pnr, Strategy and Market Devts, Ofcom 2003–05, COO 2005–06, CEO 2006–; mem. Bd of Dirs Donmar Warehouse Ltd. *Address:* Ofcom, Riverside House, 2a Southwark Bridge Road, London, SE1 9HA, England (office). *Telephone:* (20) 7981-3000 (office). *Fax:* (20) 7981-3333 (office). *Website:* www.ofcom.org.uk (office).

RICHARDS, Emma, MBE; British yachtswoman; winner Mobil North Sea Race, Banff–Stavanger, Sigma 400 1998, Fastnet Open 60 Team Group Four, Class One; Round Isle of Wight Race, 60 ft Trimaran Fujicolor 1999, Transat Jacques Vabre, double-handed Transatlantic, Open 50 Pindar, Class 2 Monohull 1999, Europe One New Man Star, single-handed Transatlantic race, Open 50 Pindar, Class Two Monohull 2000, RORC 75th Anniversary Round Britain and Ireland Race, Open 50 Pindar, double-handed 2000, OOPS! Cup eight-race series, Scandinavia, 60 ft Trimaran Toshiba 2001; joined Nautor Challenge Amer Sports Too for start of leg four of Volvo Ocean Race 2002; became first woman to sail single-handed across the Atlantic from west to east in a monohull boat 2002; first British woman and youngest competitor to complete Around Alone race May 2003. *Publication:* Around Alone 2004. *Address:* c/o Camilla Green/Victoria Fuller, Pitch PR, First Floor, 39–43 Brewer Street, London, W1F 9UD, England (office). *Telephone:* (20) 7494-1616 (office); (7775) 585437 (Mobile). *Fax:* (20) 7287–0773. *E-mail:* victoria@pitchpr.co.uk; camilla@pitchpr.co.uk. *Website:* www.pindar.com; www.emmarichards.com.

RICHARDS, Sir Francis Neville, Kt, KCMG, CVO, DL, MA; British fmr diplomatist and museum administrator; *Chairman, Imperial War Museums;* b. 18 Nov. 1945; s. of Sir Francis Brooks Richards; m. Gillian Bruce Nevill 1971; one s. one d.; ed Eton Coll. and King's Coll., Cambridge; with Royal Green Jackets 1967, served with UN Force in Cyprus (invalided 1969); joined FCO 1969, served in Moscow 1971; UK Del. to Mutual and Balanced Force Reducations negotiations, Vienna 1973; FCO 1976–85 (Asst Pvt. Sec. to Sec. of State 1981–82); Econ. and Commercial Counsellor, New Delhi 1985–88; FCO 1988–90 (Head S Asian Dept); High Commr to Namibia 1990–92; Minister, Moscow 1992–95; Dir (Europe) FCO 1995–97, Deputy Under-Sec. of State 1997–98; Dir Govt Communications HQ (GCHQ) 1998–2003; Gov. and C-in-C of Gibraltar 2003–06; Hon. Prof., School of Social Sciences and Dir Centre for Studies in Security and Diplomacy, Univ. of Birmingham 2007–10; Chair. Insight Certification Ltd, Int. Advisory Bd Altimo SA; Chair. Bletchley Park Trust 2007–12; Trustee, Imperial War Museum, London 2007 (Deputy Chair. 2009–11, Chair. 2011–); Glos. Co. Pres., SSAFA Forces Help 2011–; Pres. Friends of Gloucester Cathedral 2007–; DL for Glos. 2007–; Hon DUniv (Birmingham) 2012; KStJ 2003. *Leisure interests:* walking, travelling, riding. *Address:* Imperial War Museum, Lambeth Road, London, SE1 6HZ, England (office). *Telephone:* (1452) 813328 (home). *E-mail:* frichards@iwm.org.uk (office). *Website:* www.iwm.org.uk (office).

RICHARDS, George Maxwell, MSc, PhD; Trinidad and Tobago professor of chemical engineering, politician and fmr head of state; b. 1931, San Fernando; m.; two c.; ed Queen's Royal Coll., Port of Spain, Univs of Manchester and Cambridge, UK; staff trainee, United British Oilfields of Trinidad, Ltd 1950–51; held several managerial posts at Shell Trinidad Ltd 1957–65; Sr Lecturer in Chemical Eng, Univ. of the West Indies (UWI), St Augustine 1965–70, Prof. 1970, later Dean Faculty of Chemical Eng, Deputy Prin. and Pro-Vice-Chancellor UWI 1980–85, Acting Prin. 1984–85, Prin. and Pro-Vice-Chancellor 1985–86, currently Prof. Emer.; Chair. Salaries Review Comm. 1977–2003; Pres. 2003–13; Pres. Chair. Nat. Training Bd, Inst. of Marine Affairs; fmr mem. Bd of Dirs Trinidad Publishing Co., TRINTOC, Nat. Gas Co.; fmr mem. Bd of Dirs Nat. Advisory Council; mem. Asscn of Professional Engineers of Trinidad and Tobago, Inst. of Chemical Engineers, London, UK, Inst. of Petroleum, London, Royal Soc. of Chem., UK; Chaconia Medal of the Order of the Trinity (CMT), Class 1 (gold) for public service. *Address:* c/o Office of the President, President's House, Circular Road, St Ann's, Port of Spain, Trinidad.

RICHARDS, Sir Isaac Vivian (Viv) Alexander, KGN, OBE; Antiguan fmr cricketer; b. 7 March 1952, St John's; s. of Malcolm Richards; m. Miriam Lewis; one s. one d.; one d. with Neena Gupta; ed Antigua Grammar School; right-hand batsman, off-break bowler, cover-point fielder; played for Leeward Islands 1971–91 (Capt. 1981–91), Somerset 1974–86, Queensland 1976–77, Glamorgan 1990–93; Test debut: India v West Indies, Bangalore 22–27 Nov. 1974; One-Day Int. (ODI) debut: Sri Lanka v West Indies, Manchester 7 June 1975; played in 121 Tests for W Indies 1974–91, 50 as Capt., scoring 8,540 runs (average 50.23, highest score 291) including 24 hundreds and holding 122 catches; scored record 1,710 runs in a calendar year (11 Tests in 1976); played in 187 ODIs, scoring 6,721 runs (average 47.00, highest score 189 not out) including 11 hundreds; scored 36,212 First-class runs (average 49.40, highest score 322) including 114 hundreds, only W Indian to score 100 hundreds; toured England 1976, 1979 (World Cup), 1980, 1983 (World Cup), 1984, 1988 (as Capt.), 1991 (as Capt.); one of only four non-English cricketers to have scored 100 first-class centuries; only West Indies capt. never to lose a Test series; Chair. Selectors, W Indies Cricket Bd 2002–04; frequently heard on BBC's Test Match Special; Kt of the Order of the Nat. Hero (Antigua) 1999; Dr hc (Exeter) 1986; Wisden Cricketer of the Year 1977, one of Wisden's Five Cricketers of the Century 2000, inducted into Cricket Hall of Fame 2001. *Publications:* (with David Foot) Viv Richards (autobiography) 1982, Cricket Masterclass 1988, Hitting Across The Line (autobiography) 1991, (with Bob Harris) Sir Vivian (autobiography) 2000. *Leisure interests:* music, football, golf, tennis. *Address:* c/o West Indies Cricket Board, PO Box 616 W, St John's, Antigua. *Telephone:* 481-2450. *Fax:* 481-2498. *E-mail:* wicb@windiescricket.com. *Website:* www.windiescricket.com.

RICHARDS, Sir John (Charles Chisholm), KCB, KCVO; British military officer (retd); b. 21 Feb. 1927, Wallasey; s. of Charles Richards and Alice Milner; m. Audrey Hidson 1953; two s. one d.; ed Worksop Coll. Notts.; joined Royal Marines 1945; served in commando units and HM ships worldwide; Canadian Army Staff Coll. 1959–61; Naval Staff in Ministry of Defence 1963–64; Instructor, Army Staff Coll., Camberley 1965–67; CO 42nd and 45th RM Commandos; Chief of Staff, British Defence Staff, Washington, DC and del. to UN 1972–74; Brig. Commdg 3rd Commando Brigade 1975–77; Maj.-Gen. 1977; Commdt-Gen. Royal Marines (with rank of Lt-Gen.) 1977–81; Rep. Col Commdt Royal Marines 1989–90; HM Marshal

of the Diplomatic Corps 1982–92; Dir (non-exec.) DSC Communications (Europe) Ltd 1986–93, Andrew Ltd 1987–94; Extra Equerry to HM The Queen 1992; Freeman, City of London 1982; numerous foreign awards including decorations from FRG, France, Netherlands, Spain, Mexico, Italy, Norway, Senegal, UAE, Malawi, Bahrain, Qatar and Oman. *Leisure interests:* golf, gardening, swimming, military history. *Address:* c/o NatWest Bank, 5 Market Place, Kingston-upon-Thames, KT1 1JX, England.

RICHARDS, Keith; British musician (guitar), singer and songwriter; b. (Keith Richard), 18 Dec. 1943, Dartford, Kent; s. of Bert Richards and Doris Richards; m. 1st Anita Pallenberg; two s. (one deceased) one d.; m. 2nd Patti Hansen 1983; two d.; ed Sidcup Art School; Founder mem., The Rolling Stones 1962–; composer (with Mick Jagger) of numerous songs 1964–; Nordoff-Robbins Silver Clef 1982, Grammy Lifetime Achievement Award 1986, Ivor Novello Award for Outstanding Contribution to British Music 1991. *Films:* Sympathy for the Devil 1970, Gimme Shelter 1970, Ladies and Gentlemen, the Rolling Stones 1974, Let's Spend the Night Together 1983, Hail Hail Rock 'n' Roll 1987 (with Chuck Berry, Eric Clapton and Friends), Flashpoint 1991, Voodoo Lounge 1994, Pirates of the Caribbean: At World's End (actor) 2007, Shine a Light 2007. *Recordings include:* albums: with The Rolling Stones: The Rolling Stones 1964, The Rolling Stones No. 2 1965, Out Of Our Heads 1965, Aftermath 1966, Between The Buttons 1967, Their Satanic Majesties Request 1967, Beggar's Banquet 1968, Let It Bleed 1969, Get Yer Ya's Out 1969, Sticky Fingers 1971, Exile On Main Street 1972, Goat's Head Soup 1973, It's Only Rock And Roll 1974, Black And Blue 1976, Some Girls 1978, Emotional Rescue 1980, Tattoo You 1981, Still Life 1982, Undercover 1983, Dirty Work 1986, Steel Wheels 1989, Flashpoint 1991, Voodoo Lounge 1994, Stripped 1995, Bridges to Babylon 1997, Forty Licks 2002, Live Licks 2004, A Bigger Bang 2005; solo: Hail Hail Rock 'n' Roll (with Chuck Berry) 1987, Talk Is Cheap 1988, Live At The Hollywood Palladium 1991, Main Offender 1992. *Publications:* According to the Rolling Stones (jt autobiography) 2003, Life 2010. *Address:* Munro Sounds, 5 Wandsworth Plain, London, SW18 1ES, England (office). *Telephone:* (20) 8877-3111 (office). *Fax:* (20) 8877-3033 (office). *Website:* www.rollingstones.com; www.keithrichards.com.

RICHARDS, Peter, MA, MD, PhD, FRCP, FMedSci; British professor of medicine (retd); *Honourary Fellow, Hughes Hall, University of Cambridge;* b. 25 May 1936, London; s. of Dr William Richards and Barbara Taylor; m. 1st Anne Marie Larsen 1959 (divorced); one s. three d.; m. 2nd Carol Anne Seymour 1987; ed Monkton Combe School, Emmanuel Coll., Cambridge, St George's Hosp. Medical School and Royal Postgrad. Medical School; MRC Clinical Research Fellow and Tutor in Medicine, Royal Postgrad. Medical School 1964–67; Lecturer, St Mary's Hosp. Medical School 1967–70; Consultant Physician, NW Surrey Hosps 1970–73; Sr Lecturer and Consultant Physician, St George's Hosp. and Medical School 1973–79; Dean, St Mary's Hosp. Medical School 1979–95; Prof. and Hon. Consultant Physician, St Mary's Hosp. 1979–95; Pro-Rector (Medicine), Imperial Coll. of Science, Tech. and Medicine, London 1988–95; Medical Dir and Consultant Physician, Northwick Park and St Mark's NHS Trust 1995–99; Pres. Hughes Hall, Cambridge 1998–2006, now Hon. Fellow; Medical Adviser to Parl. Health Service Commr 1999–2001; mem. Gen. Medical Council (GMC) 1994, Deputy Chair. GMC Professional Conduct Cttee 1999–2001; Chair. Fulbright Award, Univ. of Calif., San Francisco 1990; Hon. Fellow, Emmanuel Coll., Cambridge 2002; Kt, Order of the White Rose of Finland 2001. *Achievements:* responsible (with Prof. Sir Eric Ash) for the introduction of medicine to Imperial Coll. *Publications:* The Medieval Leper 1977, Understanding Water, Electrolytes and Acid/Base Metabolism 1983, Learning Medicine 1983, Living Medicine 1990, Student's Guide to Entry to Medicine 1996, New Learning Medicine 1997; scientific papers on renal disease, metabolism, student selection and educ. *Leisure interests:* social history, music, cycling, mountain walking, Finland. *Address:* Hughes Hall, Cambridge, CB1 2EW, England (office). *Telephone:* (1223) 334890 (office). *Fax:* (1223) 311179 (office). *E-mail:* pr229@cam.ac.uk (office). *Website:* www.hughes.cam.ac.uk (office).

RICHARDS, Sir Rex Edward, Kt, DSc, FRS, FRSC; British chemist and university administrator (retd); b. 28 Oct. 1922, Colyton, Devon, England; s. of H. W. Richards and E. N. Richards; m. Eva Edith Vago 1948; two d.; ed Colyton Grammar School, Devon, St John's Coll., Oxford; Fellow, Lincoln Coll., Oxford 1947–64; Dr Lee's Prof. of Chem., Oxford 1964–70; Fellow, Exeter Coll., Oxford 1964–69; Warden Merton Coll., Oxford 1969–84; Vice-Chancellor Univ. of Oxford 1977–81; Chancellor Univ. of Exeter 1982–98; Tilden Lecturer 1962; Research Fellow, Harvard Univ., USA 1955; Assoc. Fellow, Morse Coll., Yale, USA 1974–79; Chair. Oxford Enzyme Group 1969–83; Dir Oxford Instruments Group 1982–91; Dir Leverhulme Trust 1985–93; Pres. Royal Soc. of Chem. 1990–92; mem. Chem. Soc. Council 1957, 1988, Faraday Soc. Council 1963, Royal Soc. Council 1973–75, Advisory Bd for Research Councils 1980–82, Advisory Council for Applied Research and Devt 1984–87; Dir IBM United Kingdom Holdings, IBM (UK) 1978–82; Chair. British Postgraduate Medical Fed. 1986–93, Nat. Gallery Trust 1995–99; Commr Royal Comm. for Exhbn of 1851 1984–97; Foreign Assoc. Acad. des Sciences, Inst. de France 1995–; Trustee, CiBA Foundation 1978–97, Nat. Heritage Memorial Fund 1979–84, Tate Gallery 1982–88, 1991–93, Nat. Gallery 1982–93, Henry Moore Foundation 1989–2002 (Vice-Chair. 1993–94, Chair. 1994–2001); Hon. Fellow, St John's Coll., Lincoln Coll., Oxford 1968, Merton Coll., Oxford 1984, Thames Polytechnic 1991; Hon. FRCP 1987; Hon. FBA 1990; Hon. FRAM 1991; Hon. DSc (East Anglia) 1971, (Exeter) 1975, (Leicester) 1978, (Salford) 1979, (Edin.) 1981, (Leeds) 1984, (Birmingham) 1993, (London) 1994, (Oxford Brookes) 1998, (Warwick) 1999; Hon. DLitt (Dundee) 1977, (Kent) 1987; Hon. ScD (Cambridge) 1987; Corday-Morgan Medal, Chemical Soc. 1954, Davy Medal, Royal Soc. 1976, Award in Theoretical Chem. and Spectroscopy, Chemical Soc. 1977, Epic Award 1982, Medal of Honour, Bonn Univ. 1983, Royal Medal, Royal Soc. 1986, Pres.'s Medal, Soc. of Chemical Industry 1991. *Publications:* numerous contribs to scientific journals. *Leisure interests:* painting and sculpture. *Address:* Suite 4, West Hanham, Buckland Filleigh, Beaworthy, Devon, EX21 5PJ, England. *Telephone:* (1409) 821985. *E-mail:* rex.richards@merton.ox.ac.uk.

RICHARDSON, Annette; American consultant and UN official; *Senior Advisor, United Nations Office for Partnerships;* ed Université Jussieu Paris VII, France; Exec. Asst to Chair. and CEO of Sithe Energies 1996–2000; Chief of Staff to Chair. and CEO of Vivendi Universal 2000–02; Dir of Int. Relations for the New York City 2012 Olympic Bid Cttee in charge of African Affairs and the UN 2002–05; ind.

consultant 2005–09; Founder and Man. Partner, Richardson Rogers & Assocs LLC, Washington, DC 2005–; Sr Advisor, UN Office for Partnerships 2011–; Vice-Pres. UN Women for Peace; mem. Bd of Dirs UN Women for Peace, Health and Climate Foundation; mem. Bd of Advisors, Powered By Professionals; mem. PTTOW!, Nat. Asscn of Professional Women; Hon. Amb., Univ. for Peace (UPeace); Global Citizen Award 2010, Professional Woman of the Year Award, Nat. Asscn of Professional Women 2010. *Address:* The United Nations Office for Partnerships, 1 United Nations Plaza, Room DC1-1330, New York, NY 10017, USA (office). *Telephone:* (212) 963-1000 (office). *Fax:* (212) 963-1486 (office). *E-mail:* partner@un.org (office). *Website:* www.un.org/partnerships (office).

RICHARDSON, David John; South African lawyer, sports administrator and fmr professional cricketer; *CEO, International Cricket Council;* b. 16 Sept. 1959, Johannesburg, Transvaal; m.; several s.; right-hand batsman, fmr South African Test wicket-keeper, also represented Eastern Prov. and Northern Transvaal in various domestic competitions; played 42 Test matches and 122 One Day Ints (ODIs), taking 152 dismissals, scored a maiden and only Test century (109) against New Zealand at Cape Town 1994–95, 1,359 Test runs, batting average 24.26, retd from int. cricket 1998; Business Dir with Octagon SA (co. responsible for negotiating player employment contracts with United Cricket Bd of South Africa); first Gen. Man. of Cricket, Int. Cricket Council (ICC) 2002–12, relocated with ICC to Dubai 2005, CEO ICC 2012–. *Address:* International Cricket Council, Street 69, Dubai Sports City, Emirates Road, PO Box 500 070, Dubai, United Arab Emirates (office). *Telephone:* (4) 382-8800 (office). *Fax:* (4) 382-8600 (office). *E-mail:* enquiry@icc-cricket.com (office). *Website:* icc-cricket.yahoo.net (office).

RICHARDSON, George Barclay, CBE, MA; British economist and fmr publisher; b. 19 Sept. 1924, London, England; s. of George Richardson and Christina Richardson; m. Isabel A. Chalk 1957 (divorced 1999); two s.; ed Aberdeen Cen. Secondary School and other schools in Scotland, Univ. of Aberdeen and Corpus Christi Coll., Oxford; Admiralty Scientific Research Dept 1944; Lt RNVR 1945; Intelligence Officer, HQ Intelligence Div., British Army of the Rhine 1946–47; Third Sec. HM Foreign Service 1949; student, Nuffield Coll., Oxford 1950; Fellow, St John's Coll. Oxford 1951–88; Univ. Reader in Economics, Univ. of Oxford 1969–73; Warden, Keble Coll. Oxford 1989–94; Pro-Vice-Chancellor, Univ. of Oxford 1988–94; Del. Oxford Univ. Pres. 1971–74, Chief Exec. 1974–88; mem. Econ. Devt Cttee for Electrical Eng Industry 1964–73, Monopolies Comm. 1969–74, Royal Comm. on Environmental Pollution 1973–74; Econ. Adviser, UKAEA 1968–74; mem. Council, Publishers' Asscn 1981–87; Hon. DCL (Oxford), Hon. LLD (Aberdeen). *Publications include:* Information and Investment 1960, 1991, Economic Theory 1964, The Economics of Imperfect Knowledge 1998; articles in academic journals. *Leisure interests:* reading, music, swimming. *Address:* 33 Belsyre Court, Observatory Street, Oxford, OX2 6HU, England (home). *Telephone:* (1865) 510113 (home). *Fax:* (1865) 510113 (home). *E-mail:* george.richardson@keble.ox.ac.uk (home).

RICHARDSON, George Taylor, CM, OM, BComm, LLD; Canadian business executive (retd); *Honorary Chairman, James Richardson & Sons Ltd;* b. 22 Sept. 1924, Winnipeg, Man.; s. of the late James A. Richardson and Muriel Richardson (née Sprague); m. Tannis Maree Thorlakson 1948; two s. one d.; ed Grosvenor and Ravenscourt Schools, Winnipeg and Univ. of Manitoba; joined family firm of James Richardson & Sons, Ltd (grain trader), Winnipeg 1946, Vice-Pres. 1954, Pres. 1966–93, Chair. 1993–2000 (retd), Hon. Chair. and Dir Emer. 2000–; fmr mem. Bd of Dirs Dupont Canada Inc., Canada Packers Inc., Inco Ltd, Tundra Oil & Gas Ltd; fmr Vice-Pres. Canadian Imperial Bank of Commerce; fmr Chair. Great-West Life Assurance Co.; fmr Gov. (first Canadian-born) Hudson's Bay Co.; fmr mem. Bd of Govs Univ. of Manitoba (Chair. 1960–64); Patron, Western Canada Aviation Museum; Hon. LLD (Manitoba, Winnipeg). *Leisure interests:* hunting, helicopter flying. *Address:* James Richardson & Sons Ltd, Richardson Building, 1 Lombard Place, Winnipeg, MB R3B 0Y1 (office); Briarmeade, 850 PR 200, St Germain South, MB R5A IE8, Canada (home). *Telephone:* (204) 253-4221 (home). *Fax:* (204) 942-6339 (office). *E-mail:* george.richardson@jrsl.ca (office).

RICHARDSON, Graham; Australian politician, broadcaster and journalist; b. 27 Sept. 1949, Kogarah, Sydney; s. of Frederick James Richardson and Catherine Maud Richardson; m. Cheryl Gardener 1973; one s. one d.; ed Marist Brothers Coll., Kogarah; state organizer Australian Labor Party, NSW 1971–76, Gen. Sec. 1976–94, State Campaign Dir 1976; Vice-Pres. Nat. Labor Party 1976, Del. to Nat. Conf. 1977–94, convenor Nat. Industrial Platform Cttee; Senator for NSW 1983–94; Minister for the Environment and the Arts 1987–90, for Sports, Tourism and Territories 1988–90, for Social Security 1990, of Transport and Communications 1991–92, of Health 1993–94; political commentator on election coverage and journalist, The Nine Network 1994–; journalist, The Bulletin 1994–; fmr Chair. Senate Estimates Cttee 1986, Senate Select Cttee on TV Equalization; mem. several senate cttees and three ministerial cttees; fmr mem. Bd Sydney Organizing Cttee for the Olympic Games. *Leisure interests:* golf, reading, skiing, tennis. *Address:* Macquarie Radio Network, Level 8, 368 Sussex Street, Sydney, NSW 2000 (office); 24 Artarmon Road, Willoughby, NSW 2028, Australia.

RICHARDSON, Joely; British actress; b. 9 Jan. 1965, London; d. of the late Tony Richardson and of Vanessa Redgrave (q.v.); m. Tim Bevan 1992 (divorced); one d.; ed Lycée Français de Londres, St Paul's Girls' School, London, Pinellas Park High School, Fla, The Thacher School, Ojai, Calif. and Royal Acad. of Dramatic Art. *Plays include:* Steel Magnolias 1989, Lady Windermere's Fan 2002. *Films include:* The Charge of the Light Brigade (uncredited) 1968, The Hotel New Hampshire 1984, Wetherby 1985, Drowning by Numbers 1988, A proposito di quella strana ragazza (About That Foreign Girl) 1989, King Ralph 1991, Shining Through 1992, Rebecca's Daughters 1992, I'll Do Anything 1994, Sister, My Sister 1995, Believe Me 1995, Loch Ness 1996, Hollow Reed 1996, 101 Dalmatians 1996, Event Horizon 1997, Wrestling with Alligators 1998, Under Heaven 1998, Toy Boys 1999, Return to Me 2000, Maybe Baby 2000, The Patriot 2000, The Affair of the Necklace 2001, Shoreditch 2003, The Fever 2004, The Last Mimzy 2007, The Christmas Miracle of Jonathan Toomey 2007, Anonymous 2011, The Girl with the Dragon Tattoo 2011, Red Lights 2012. *Television appearances include:* Body Contact 1987, Behaving Badly 1989, Heading Home 1991, Lady Chatterley's Lover 1993, The Tribe 1998, The Echo 1998, Nip/Tuck (series) 2003–10, Fallen Angel 2003, Lies My Mother Told Me 2005, Wallis & Edward 2005, Fatal Contact: Bird Flu in America 2006, Day of the Triffids (mini-series) 2009, The Tudors 2010, Titanic: Blood and Steel

2012. *Address:* c/o Finch and Partners, First Floor, 6 Heddon Street, London, W1B 4BR (office); c/o ICM London, 4-6 Soho Square, London, W1D 3PZ, England (office). *Telephone:* (20) 7851-7140 (office); (20) 7432-0800 (ICM) (office). *Fax:* (20) 7287-6420 (office). *Website:* www.finchandpartners.com (office). www.icmtalent.com (office).

RICHARDSON, Miranda; British actress; b. 3 March 1958, Southport, Lancs.; d. of William Alan Richardson and Marian Georgina Richardson (née Townsend); ed Old Vic Theatre School, Bristol. *Theatre appearances include:* Moving 1980–81, All My Sons, Who's Afraid of Virginia Woolf?, The Life of Einstein, A Lie of the Mind 1987, The Changeling, Mountain Language 1988, Etta Jenks, The Designated Mourner 1996, Orlando 1996, Aunt Dan and Lemon 1999, Grasses of a Thousand Colours 2009. *Film appearances:* Dance with a Stranger (debut 1985; Best Actress Award, Evening Standard), The Innocent, Empire of the Sun, The Mad Monkey, Eat the Rich, Twisted Obsession, The Bachelor 1992, Enchanted April 1992 (Golden Globe Award for Best Comedy Actress 1993), The Crying Game 1992, Damage (BAFTA Award for Best Supporting Actress 1993), Tom and Viv 1994, La Nuit et Le Moment 1994, Kansas City, Swann 1995, Evening Star 1996, The Designated Mourner 1996, The Apostle 1996, All For Love, Jacob Two Two and the Hooded Fang 1998, The Big Brass Ring 1998, Sleepy Hollow 1999, Blackadder Back and Forth 1999, Chicken Run (voice) 2000, Get Carter 2000, The Hours 2001, Spider 2002, The Hours 2002, The Actors 2003, The Rage in Placid Lake 2003, Falling Angels 2003, The Prince and Me 2004, Churchill: The Hollywood Years 2004, The Phantom of the Opera 2004, Wah-Wah 2005, Harry Potter and the Goblet of Fire 2005, Merlin's Apprentice 2005, Starry Night 2005, Provoked 2006, Paris, je t'aime 2006, Southland Tales 2006, Spinning into Butter 2007, Puffball 2007, Fred Claus 2007, The Young Victoria 2009, Made in Dagenham 2010, Harry Potter and the Deathly Hallows: Part 1 2010. *Television appearances include:* The Hard Word, Sorrel and Son, A Woman of Substance, Blackadder II 1985, After Pilkington 1987, Underworld, Death of the Heart, Blackadder the Third 1987, Blackadder Goes Forth 1989, Die Kinder (mini-series) 1990, Sweet as You Are (Royal TV Soc.'s Best Actress Award), Fatherland (Golden Globe Award), Saint X 1995, Magic Animals, Dance to the Music of Time 1997, The Scold's Bridle, Merlin 1997, Alice 1998, Ted and Ralph 1998, The Miracle Maker (voice) 2000, Snow White 2001, The Lost Prince 2003, Gideon's Daughter 2006, Final Chance to Save 2006, The Life and Times of Vivienne Vyle 2007, Dagenham Girls 2009, World Without End 2011, Parade's End 2012. *Leisure interests:* gardening, junkshops, music, occasional art, reading, softball, walking. *Address:* c/o Independent Talent Group Ltd, Oxford House, 76 Oxford Street, London, W1D 1BS, England (office). *Telephone:* (20) 7636-6565 (office). *Fax:* (20) 7323-0101 (office).

RICHARDSON, Peter Damian, BSc, DSc, PhD, FRS, FCGI, DIC; British mechanical engineer, physiologist and academic; *Professor of Engineering and Physiology, Brown University;* b. 22 Aug. 1935, West Wickham; s. of the late Reginald W. Richardson and Marie S. Richardson; one s.; ed Imperial Coll. London, Brown Univ., USA; demonstrator Dept of Mechanical Eng, Imperial Coll. 1955–58; went to USA 1958; Visiting Lecturer Brown Univ. 1958–59, Research Assoc. 1959–60, Asst Prof. of Eng 1960–65, Assoc. Prof. 1965–68, Prof. 1968–84, Prof. of Eng and Physiology 1984–, Chair. Univ. Faculty 1987–; Chair. Exec. Cttee Center Biomedical Eng 1972–; Consultant to Industry US Govt Agencies; Fellow, ASME, Life Fellow 2001; mem. American Soc. of Artificial Internal Organs; Founding Fellow, American Inst. of Medical and Biological Eng 1991; Fellow of the City and Guilds of London Inst. 2003; Inaugural Fellow, Biomedical Eng Soc. 2005;; Sr Scientist Award, Alexander Von Humboldt Foundation 1976, Laureate in Medicine, Ernst Jung Foundation 1987. *Publications:* Principles of Cell Adhesion (with M. Steiner) 1995; contribs to many professional journals. *Leisure interests:* country life. *Address:* Division of Engineering and Department of Molecular Pharmacology, Physiology and Biotechnology, Box D, Brown University, Providence, RI 02912-9104, USA. *Telephone:* (401) 863-2687.

RICHARDSON, Sir Tom, KCMG, MA; British diplomatist; b. 6 Feb. 1941, Manchester; s. of Arthur Legh Turnour Richardson and Penelope Margaret Richardson (née Waithman); m. Alexandra Frazier Wasiqullah (née Ratcliff) 1979; ed Westminster School, Christ Church, Oxford; postings in Ghana, Tanzania, Milan, New York, mem. Cen. Policy Review Staff 1980–81, Counsellor, Embassy in Rome 1982–86, Head of Econ. Relations Dept, FCO 1986–89, Deputy Perm. Rep. to UN, New York 1989–94, Deputy Political Dir FCO 1994–96, Amb. to Italy 1996–2000; Chair. Governing Body, British Inst. of Florence 2003–08; Pres. British–Italian Soc. 2007–; mem. Council, British School of Rome 2002–06; Trustee, Monte San Martino Trust 2003–; Patron, Venice in Peril. *Leisure interests:* reading, music, walking, Italy.

RICHARDSON, William Blaine (Bill), BA, MA; American politician, diplomatist, fmr government official and fmr state governor; *Special Envoy, Organization of American States;* b. 15 Nov. 1947, Pasadena, Calif.; d. of William Blaine Richardson Jr and María Luisa López-Collada Márquez; m. Barbara Flavin 1972; ed Tufts Univ., Fletcher School of Law and Diplomacy; staff mem., US House of Reps 1971–72, Dept of State 1973–75, US Senate Foreign Relations Cttee 1975–78; Exec. Dir NM State Democratic Cttee 1978, Bernalillo Co. Democratic Cttee 1978; Chair. Democratic Nat. Convention 2004, fmr Chair. Democratic Gov.'s Assoc.; business exec. in Santa Fe 1978–82;; consultant, Salomon Smith Barney; mem. US House of Reps from 3rd Dist of NM 1982–97; Perm. Rep. to UN, New York 1997–98; US Sec. of Energy 1998–2001; Sr Man. Dir Kissinger McLarty Assocs 2001; Adjunct Prof. of Public Policy, Harvard Univ. 2001; Gov. of NM 2003–11; unsuccessful cand. for Democratic party nomination for US Pres. 2007; nominated as US Sec. of Commerce 2008, requested that nomination be withdrawn Jan. 2009; Special Envoy, OAS, Washington, DC 2011–; mem. Council Foreign Relations, Santa Fe Chamber of Commerce, Santa Fe Hispanic Chamber of Commerce, Big Brothers-Big Sisters, Presidential Consolidate-Dew Party 2008; fmr mem. NATO 2000 Bd; named by TIME magazine as one of 25 Most Influential Hispanics 2005. *Publications:* Between Worlds: The Making of an American Life (autobiog., with Mike Ruby) 2005, Leading by Example: How We Can Inspire an Energy and Security Revolution 2007. *Address:* Organization of American States, 17th Street and Constitution Avenue NW, Washington, DC 20006, USA (office). *Telephone:* (202) 458-3000 (office). *E-mail:* pi@oas.org (office). *Website:* www.oas.org (office).

RICHARDSON, William Chase, MBA, PhD; American university administrator and foundation executive; b. 11 May 1940, Passaic, NJ; s. of Henry B. Richardson and Frances Richardson (née Chase); m. Nancy Freeland 1966; two d.; ed Trinity Coll., Hartford, Conn. and Univ. of Chicago; Research Assoc. and Instructor, Univ. of Chicago 1967–70; Asst Prof., Univ. of Washington, School of Public Health and Community Medicine 1971–73, Assoc. Prof. 1973–76, Prof. of Health Services 1976–84, Chair. Dept of Health Services 1973–76, Graduate Dean, Vice-Provost for Research, 1981–84; Exec. Vice-Pres., Provost and Prof. Dept of Family and Community Medicine, Pennsylvania State Univ. 1984–90; Pres. Johns Hopkins Univ. 1990–95, Pres. Emer. 1995–, Prof., Dept of Health Policy Man. 1990–95, Prof. Emer. 1995–; Pres. and CEO W.K. Kellogg Foundation, Battle Creek, Mich. 1995–2005; mem. Inst. of Medicine, NAS, American Acad. of Arts and Sciences; Fellow, American Public Health Asscn; Kellogg Fellow; mem. Bd of Dirs Exelon Corpn 2005–, CSX Corpn, Bank of NY (now Bank of New York Mellon Corpn); Dr hc (Univ. of Michigan) 2006; Trinity Whitlock Award, Mary H. Bachmeyer Award, Univ. of Chicago. *Publications:* numerous articles in professional journals. *Address:* c/o W.K. Kellogg Foundation, One Michigan Avenue East, Battle Creek, MI 49017-4058, USA (office).

RICHIE, Laurel J., BA; American advertising executive and sports administrator; *President, Women's National Basketball Association;* ed Dartmouth Coll., Hanover, NH; worked at Leo Burnett Worldwide (advertising agency), Chicago 1981–83, worked on several Procter & Gamble campaigns; moved to Ogilvy and Mather 1984, clients included American Express, Pepperidge Farm and Unilever, among others, promoted to Sr Partner, Exec. Group Dir with responsibility for portfolio of global brands, continues to work with Ogilvy as Founding mem. of its Diversity Advisory Bd; Sr Vice-Pres. and Chief Marketing Officer for Girl Scouts of the USA –2011; Pres. Women's Nat. Basketball Asscn 2011–; YMCA Black Achiever's Award, Ebony magazine's Outstanding Women in Marketing and Communications, named by The Network Journal as one of the 25 Influential Black Women in Business 2011. *Address:* Women's National Basketball Association, Olympic Tower, 645 Fifth Avenue, New York, NY 10022, USA (office). *Telephone:* (212) 688-9622 (office). *Fax:* (212) 750-9622 (office). *E-mail:* info@wnba .com (office). *Website:* www.wnba.com (office).

RICHIE, Lionel, BS (Econs); American singer, songwriter and musician; b. 20 June 1949, Tuskegee, Ala; m. Diane Alexander 1996; ed Tuskegee Univ.; mem. The Commodores 1968–82; various tours, concerts; solo artist 1982–; ASCAP Songwriter Awards 1979, 1984–96, numerous American Music Awards 1979–, Grammy Awards include: Best Pop Vocal Performance 1982, Album of the Year 1985, Producer of the Year (shared) 1986; Lionel Richie Day, Los Angeles 1983, two Nat. Asscn. for the Advancement of Colored People (NAACP) Image Awards 1983, NAACP Entertainer of the Year 1987, Acad. Award for Best Song 1986, Golden Globe Award for Best Song 1986. *Compositions include:* with The Commodores: Sweet Love 1975, Just To Be Close To You 1976, Easy 1977, Three Times A Lady 1979, Sail On 1980, Still 1980, Oh No 1981; for Kenny Rogers: Lady 1981; for Diana Ross: Missing You 1984; solo hits: Endless Love, film theme duet with Diana Ross 1981, Truly 1982, All Night Long 1983, Running With The Night 1984, Hello 1984, Stuck On You 1984, Penny Lover (with Brenda Harvey) 1984, Say You Say Me 1986, Dancing On The Ceiling 1987, Love Will Conquer All 1987, Ballerina Girl 1987, My Destiny 1992, Don't Wanna Lose You 1996; contrib. We are the World (with Michael Jackson), USA for Africa 1985. *Recordings include:* albums with The Commodores: Machine Gun 1974, Caught In The Act 1975, Movin' On 1975, Hot On The Tracks 1976, Commodores 1977, Commodores Live! 1977, Natural High 1978, Greatest Hits 1978, Midnight Magic 1979, Heroes 1980, In The Pocket 1981; solo: Lionel Richie 1982, Can't Slow Down 1983, Dancing On The Ceiling 1986, Back To Front 1992, Louder Than Words 1996, Time 1998, Encore 2002, Coming Home 2006, Just Go 2009. *Address:* John Reid Management, 505 South Beverly Drive, Suite 1192, Beverly Hills, CA 90212 (office); c/o Island Records, 825 Eighth Avenue, New York, NY 10019, USA (office). *Website:* www6.islandrecords .com/site/artist_home.php?artist_id=342 (office).

RICHMOND, Sir Mark Henry, Kt, ScD, FRS; British academic and scientist; *Member of Staff, School of Public Policy, University College London;* b. 1 Feb. 1931, Sydney, Australia; s. of Harold Sylvester Richmond and Dorothy Plaistowe Tegg; m. 1st Shirley Jean Townrow 1958 (divorced); one s. one d. (and one d. deceased); m. 2nd Sheila Travers 2000; ed Epsom Coll., Clare Coll., Univ. of Cambridge; mem. scientific staff, Medical Research Council 1958–65; Reader in Molecular Biology, Univ. of Edin. 1965–68; Prof. of Bacteriology, Univ. of Bristol 1968–81; Vice-Chancellor and Prof. of Molecular Bacteriology, Victoria Univ. of Manchester 1981–90; mem. Public Health Laboratory Service Bd 1976–85; Chair. Cttee of Vice-Chancellors and Prins of the UK 1987–89, Microbiological Food Safety Cttee 1989–90, Science and Eng Research Council 1990–94; Group Head of Research, Glaxo 1993–95, Science Adviser 1995–96; mem. staff School of Public Policy, Univ. Coll. London 1996–; mem. Int. Science Advisory Cttee, UNESCO 1996–2001; mem. and fmr mem. numerous bds; Robert Koch Award 1977. *Publications:* numerous scientific articles. *Leisure interests:* gardening, hill walking, opera. *Address:* School of Public Policy, The Rubin Building, University College London, 29 Tavistock Square, London, WC1H 9QU, England (office). *Telephone:* (20) 7679-4968 (office). *Fax:* (20) 7679-4969 (office). *E-mail:* m.richmond@ucl.ac.uk (office). *Website:* www .ucl.ac.uk/spp (office).

RICHTER, Burton, PhD; American physicist and academic; *Senior Fellow, Freeman Spogli Institute for International Studies, Stanford University;* b. 22 March 1931, Brooklyn, New York; s. of Abraham Richter and Fannie (Pollack) Richter; m. Laurose Becker 1960; one s. one d.; ed Massachusetts Inst. of Tech.; joined Stanford Univ. 1956, Research Assoc. in Physics, High Energy Physics Lab., Stanford Univ. 1956–59; mem. group building first electron storage ring and conducting a colliding beam experiment extending validity of quantum electrodynamics; Asst Prof., Stanford Univ. 1959–63, Assoc. Prof. 1963–67, Prof. 1967–2006, Paul Pigott Prof. in Physical Sciences 1980–2006, Sr Fellow, Freeman Spogli Inst. for Int. Studies 2005–; worked at Stanford Linear Accelerator Center (SLAC) 1963–99, Tech. Dir 1982–84, Dir 1984–99, Dir Emer. 1999–2006; est. group that built a high-energy electron positron machine (SPEAR) and has continued to develop new accelerator and detector techniques including most recently the SLAC linear collider; fmr Pres. IUPAP; fmr mem. Bd of Dirs Varian Assocs, AREVA; mem. Bd of Dirs Litel Instruments; mem. Visiting Cttee Commissairat à l'Energie Atomique; sabbatical year at CERN, Geneva 1975–76; Loeb Lecturer, Harvard Univ. 1974, DeShalit Lecturer, Weizmann Inst. 1975; mem. NAS 1977; Fellow,

American Acad. of Arts and Sciences 1989, American Physical Soc. (Pres. 1994), AAAS; E. O. Lawrence Medal 1976, Nobel Prize for Physics (jtly with Samuel Ting q.v.) for discovery of the heavy, long-lived 'psi' particle 1976. *Publications:* more than 300 articles in various scientific journals 1963–89. *Address:* Stanford Linear Accelerator Center, 2575 Sand Hill Road, Menlo Park, CA 94025, USA (office). *Telephone:* (650) 926-2601 (office). *E-mail:* brichter@slac.stanford.edu (office). *Website:* www-group.slac.stanford.edu/do/people/richter.html (office).

RICHTER, Gerhard; German artist; b. 9 Feb. 1932, Dresden; s. of Horst Richter and Hildegard Richter; m. 1st Marianne Richter (née Eufinger); m. 2nd Isa Richter (née Genzken) 1982; m. 3rd Sabine Richter (née Moritz) 1995; one s. two d.; ed Hochschule für Bildende Künste, Dresden, Kunstakademie Düsseldorf; emigrated to West Germany 1961; Visiting Prof., Kunstakademie Hamburg 1967, Coll. of Art, Halifax, Canada 1978; Prof., Staatliche Kunstakademie Düsseldorf 1971–; mem. Akad. der Künste, Berlin; solo exhbns in galleries and museums all over world 1964–; paintings in public collections in Berlin, Cologne, Basle, Paris, New York, Chicago, Toronto, London, etc.; retrospective exhbn at Museum of Modern Art, New York 2002; designed a stained-glass window in Cologne Cathedral that was unveiled in 2007; mem. Acad. of Arts, Berlin; Dr hc (Université catholique de Louvain-la-Neuve, Belgium) 2001; Kunstpreis Junger Westen 1966, Arnold Bode Preis 1981, Oskar Kokoschka Prize (Austria) 1985, Wolf Prize 1994–95, Venice Biennial Art Festival Jury Prize 1997, Praemium Imperiale, Japan 1997, Wexner Prize 1998, Nordrhein-Westfalen State Prize 2000. *Address:* Osterrietweg 22, 50996 Cologne, Germany; c/o Marian Goodman, 24 West 57th Street, New York, NY 10019, USA. *Website:* www.gerhard-richter.com.

RICHTHOFEN, Hermann, Freiherr von, DJur; German diplomatist; b. 20 Nov. 1933, Breslau; s. of Herbert Freiherr von Richthofen and Gisela Freifrau von Richthofen (née Schoeller); m. Christa Gräfin von Schwerin 1966; one s. two d.; joined diplomatic service 1963; served in Saigon and Djakarta, Head of Dept of Perm. Rep. Office of FRG for GDR 1975–78, Dir German and Berlin Dept Ministry of Foreign Affairs 1978–80; Dir Working Party on German Policy, Fed. Chancellery 1980–86; Dir Gen. Legal Dept Ministry of Foreign Affairs 1986, Political Dept 1986–88, Amb. to UK 1988–93, Amb. and Perm. Rep. to NATO, Brussels 1993–98; Gov. Ditchley Foundation; Hon. Prof., Cen. Connecticut State Univ., hon. mem. Deutsch-Britische Gesellschaft, Berlin; Officer's Cross Order of Kts of Malta, Commdr's Cross Order of Merit (Italy), Commdr, Légion d'honneur, Grand Officer's Cross Order of Infante D. Henrique (Portugal), Grand Cross Order of Merit (Luxemburg), Kt Commdr's Cross 2nd Class (Austria), Hon. GCVO, Grand Cross Order of Merit (Germany), Commdr's Cross Order of Merit (Poland) 2003; Hon. LLD (Birmingham). *Leisure interests:* literature, history, arts, music. *Address:* Beckerstrasse 6A, 12157 Berlin, Germany.

RICKE, Kai-Uwe; German telecommunications executive; *Member, Supervisory Board, Kabel Baden-Württemberg GmbH & Co. KG;* b. Oct. 1961, Krefeld; ed European Business School, Schloss Reichartshausen, Germany; began career as asst to Bd of Bertelsmann, Guetersloh, later Head of Sales and Marketing, Scandinavian Club (subsidiary); CEO Talkline and Talkline PS Phone Service, Elmshorn 1990–95, Chair. and CEO 1995–98; Chair. Bd Man. DeTeMobil Deutsche Telekom Mobilnet (now T-Mobile Deutschland) 1998–2000, Chair. T-Mobile Int. 2000–01, COO and mem. Bd of Man. Deutsche Telekom AG 2001, Chair. Bd of Man. and CEO 2002–06 (resgnd); mem. Supervisory Bd Kabel Baden-Württemberg GmbH & Co. KG, Heidelberg 2007–. *Address:* Supervisory Board, Kabel Baden-Württemberg GmbH & Co. KG, m Breitspiel 2-4, 69126 Heidelberg, Germany (office). *Telephone:* (6221) 3330 (office). *Website:* www.kabelbw.de (office).

RICKETTS, Sir Peter Forbes, Kt, GCMG, KCMG, MA; British diplomatist; *Ambassador to France;* b. 30 Sept. 1952; m.; two c.; ed Univ. of Oxford; joined FCO 1974, with Mission in New York 1974–75, Desk Officer, Cen. and Southern Africa Dept 1975–76, Third, then Second Sec., Embassy in Singapore 1976–78, Second, then First Sec., Del. to NATO, Brussels 1978–81, Desk Officer, Near East and N Africa Dept 1982–83, Asst Pvt. Sec., Office of Sec. of State 1983–86, First Sec., Chancery, Embassy in Washington, DC 1986–89, Deputy Head of Security Policy Dept 1989–91, Head of Hong Kong Dept 1991–94, Counsellor, EC and Finance, Embassy in Paris 1994–97, Deputy Political Dir 1997–99, Dir for Int. Security 1999–2000; Chair. Jt Intelligence Cttee and Intelligence Coordinator, Cabinet Office 2000–01; Dir-Gen. (Political) FCO 2001–03, Perm. Rep. to NATO, Brussels 2003–06, Perm. Under-Sec. and Head of Diplomatic Service 2006–10; Nat. Security Adviser to HM Govt 2010–11; Amb. to France (also accred to Monaco) 2012–; Hon. LLD (Bath), (Kent). *Address:* British Embassy, 35 rue du Faubourg Saint Honoré, 75363 Paris Cedex 08, France (office). *Telephone:* 1-44-51-31-00 (office). *Fax:* 1-44-51-32-34 (office); 1-44-51-31-09 (office). *E-mail:* public.paris@fco .gov.uk (office). *Website:* ukinfrance.fco.gov.uk (office).

RICKMAN, Alan; British actor, film director and theatre director; b. 21 Feb. 1946, London, England; ed Chelsea Coll. of Art, Royal Coll. of Art and Royal Acad. of Dramatic Art (RADA); repertory theatre in Manchester, Leicester, Sheffield and Glasgow; spent two seasons with RSC at Stratford; later appeared at Bush Theatre, Hampstead and Royal Court Theatre; Time Out Award 1991, Evening Standard Film Actor of the Year 1991, Variety Club Award 2002. *Stage appearances include:* Les Liaisons Dangereuses (RSC Stratford, London and Broadway), The Lucky Chance, The Seagull (Royal Court), Tango at the End of Winter (Edin. Festival and West End London) 1991, Hamlet (Riverside Studios) 1992, Antony and Cleopatra (Nat. Theatre) 1998, Private Lives (West End and Broadway) 2001–02, John Gabriel Borkman, Dublin 2010. *Plays directed:* The Winter Guest (W Yorkshire Playhouse and Almeida, London) 1997, My Name is Rachel Corrie (Royal Court, London) 2005, (Playhouse, London) 2006, New York 2006, Creditors (Donmar Warehouse, London) 2008, (New York) 2010. *Radio includes:* The Seagull, A Good Man in Africa, A Trick to Catch the Old One. *Films include:* Die Hard 1988, The January Man 1989, Close My Eyes 1991, Truly, Madly, Deeply 1991, Closetland 1991, Robin Hood: Prince of Thieves (BAFTA Award for Best Actor in a Supporting Role) 1991, Bob Roberts 1992, Mesmer 1993, An Awfully Big Adventure 1994, Sense and Sensibility 1995, Michael Collins 1996, Rasputin (Golden Globe Award 1996, Emmy Award 1996) 1996, Dark Harbour 1997, The Judas Kiss 1997, Dogma 1998, Galaxy Quest 1999, Blow Dry 1999, Play 2000, The Search for John Gissing 2000, Harry Potter and the Philosopher's Stone 2001, Harry Potter and the Chamber of Secrets 2002, Love Actually 2003, Harry

Potter and the Prisoner of Azkaban 2003, Harry Potter and the Goblet of Fire 2005, Snowcake 2006, Perfume: The Story of a Murderer 2006, Nobel Son 2007, Harry Potter and the Order of the Phoenix 2007, Sweeney Todd 2007, Bottle Shock 2008, Harry Potter and the Half-Blood Prince 2009, Alice in Wonderland (voice) 2010, Harry Potter and the Deathly Hallows: Part I 2010. *Television includes:* The Barchester Chronicles 1982, Pity in History 1984, Revolutionary Witness, Spirit of Man 1989, Rasputin (USA) 1995, Something the Lord Made 2004, The Song of Lunch 2010. *Film directed:* The Winter Guest 1997 (Best Film, Chicago Film Festival 1997). *Address:* c/o Independent, Oxford House, 76 Oxford Street, London, W1D 1BS, England (office). *Telephone:* (20) 7636-6565 (office). *Fax:* (20) 7323-0101 (office). *E-mail:* info@independenttalent.com (office). *Website:* www .independenttalent.com (office).

RICKS, Sir Christopher Bruce, Kt, BA, BLitt, MA, FBA; British academic and writer; *William M. and Sara B. Warren Professor of the Humanities, Boston University;* b. 18 Sept. 1933, London; s. of James Bruce Ricks and Gabrielle Roszak; m. 1st Kirsten Jensen 1956 (divorced 1975); two s. two d.; m. 2nd Judith Aronson 1977; one s. two d.; ed King Alfred's School, Wantage, Oxon., Balliol Coll., Oxford; 2nd Lt Green Howards 1952; Andrew Bradley Jr Research Fellow, Balliol Coll. Univ. of Oxford 1957, Fellow, Worcester Coll. 1958–68; Prof. of English, Bristol Univ. 1968–75; Fellow, Christ's Coll., Prof. of English, Univ. of Cambridge 1975–86, King Edward VII Prof. of English Literature 1982–86; Prof. of English, Boston Univ. 1986–98, William M. and Sara B. Warren Prof. of the Humanities 1998–, Co-Dir Editorial Inst. 1999–; Prof. of Poetry, Univ. of Oxford 2004–09; Visiting Prof., Univ. of California, Berkeley and Stanford Univ. 1965, Smith Coll. 1967, Harvard Univ. 1971, Wesleyan 1974, Brandeis 1977, 1981, 1984, USA; Distinguished Visiting Fellow in Residence, Columbia Univ. 2006; Vice-Pres. Tennyson Soc.; mem. Asscn of Literary Scholars, Critics, and Writers (Pres. 2007–08); Fellow, American Acad. of Arts and Sciences 1991; Hon. Fellow, Balliol Coll. 1989, Worcester Coll. 1990, Christ's Coll. Cambridge 1993; Hon. DLitt (Oxford) 1998, (Bristol) 2003; George Orwell Memorial Prize 1979; Beefeater Club Prize for Literature 1980, Distinguished Achievement Award Andrew W. Mellon Foundation 2004. *Publications include:* Milton's Grand Style 1963, Tennyson 1972, Keats and Embarrassment 1974, The Force of Poetry 1984, T. S. Eliot and Prejudice 1988, Beckett's Dying Words 1993, Essays in Appreciation 1996, Reviewery 2002, Allusion to the Poets 2002, Decisions and Revisions in T. S. Eliot 2003, Dylan's Visions of Sin 2003, True Friendship: Geoffrey Hill, Anthony Hecht and Robert Lowell under the Sign of Eliot and Pound 2010; editor: Poems and Critics: An Anthology of Poetry and Criticism from Shakespeare to Hardy 1966, A. E. Housman: A Collection of Critical Essays 1968, Alfred Tennyson: Poems 1842 1968, John Milton: Paradise Lost and Paradise Regained 1968, The Poems of Tennyson 1969, The Brownings: Letters and Poetry 1970, English Poetry and Prose 1540–1674 1970, English Drama to 1710 1971, Selected Criticism of Matthew Arnold 1972, The State of the Language (with Leonard Michaels) 1980, The New Oxford Book of Victorian Verse 1987, Collected Poems and Selected Prose of A. E. Housman 1988, The Faber Book of America (with William Vance) 1992, Inventions of the March Hare: Poems 1909–1917 by T. S. Eliot 1996, The Oxford Book of English Verse 1999, Selected Poems of James Henry 2002, Samuel Menashe: New and Selected Poems (ed.) 2006, Allusion to the Poets 2002, Reviewery 2002, Decisions and Revisions in T. S. Eliot 2003, Dylan's Visions of Sin 2004, True Friendship: Geoffrey Hill, Anthony Hecht, and Robert Lowell under the Sign of Eliot and Pound 2010; contribs to professional journals. *Address:* Editorial Institute, Boston University, 143 Bay State Road, Boston, MA 02215 (office); 39 Martin Street, Cambridge, MA 02138, USA (home); Lasborough Cottage, Lasborough Park, Tetbury, Glos., GL8 8UF, England (home). *Telephone:* (617) 358-2895 (USA) (office); (617) 354-7887 (USA) (home); (1666) 890252 (England) (home). *E-mail:* cricks@bu.edu (home).

RICKSON, Ian, BA, PGTC; British theatre and film director; ed Essex Univ., Goldsmiths' Coll., London Univ.; freelance Dir King's Head, The Gate, Chichester Festival Theatre; Special Projects Dir Young People's Theatre 1991–92; Assoc. Dir Royal Court Theatre 1993–98, Artistic Dir 1998–2006. *Plays:* Royal Court Theatre productions: Killers 1992, SAB 1992, Wildfire 1992, Ashes and Sand 1994, Some Voices 1994, Pale Horse 1995, Mojo 1995, The Lights 1996, The Weir 1997, Dublin Carol 2000, Mouth to Mouth 2001, Boy Gets Girl 2001, The Night Heron 2002, Fallout 2003, The Sweetest Swing in Baseball 2004, Alice Trilogy 2005, The Winterling 2006, Krapp's Last Tape 2006, The Seagull 2006; other productions: Rinty (Group Theatre, Belfast) 1990, Who's Breaking (Battersea Arts Centre) 1990, First Strike (Soho Poly) 1990, Queer Fish (Battersea Arts Centre) 1991, Me and My Friend (Chichester Festival Theatre) 1992, The House of Yes (Gate Theatre) 1993, La Serva Padrona (Broomhill) 1993, Mojo (Chicago) 1996, The Day I Stood Still (Cottesloe Theatre) 1997, The Hothouse (Lyttelton) 2007, The Seagull (New York) 2008, Hedda Gabler (Broadway) 2009, Parlour Song (Almeida) 2009, Jerusalem (Royal Court Theatre) 2009, Apollo Theatre, West End and Broadway) 2010, (Apollo Theatre) 2011, The Children's Hour (West End) 2011, Betrayal (West End) 2011, Hamlet (Young Vic) 2011, The River (Royal Court) 2012, Old Times (West End) 2013, Mojo (West End) 2013. *Films:* Krapp's Last Tape (BBC Four) 2007, Fallout (Channel 4) 2008, The Clear Road Ahead (FilmFour) 2010. *Address:* c/o Judy Daish Associates Ltd, 2 St Charles Place, London, W10 6EG, England (office).

RICO, Francisco, PhD; Spanish academic; *Professor Emeritus of Medieval Hispanic Literature, Universidad Autónoma de Barcelona;* b. 28 April 1942, Barcelona; s. of the late Cipriano Rico and María Manrique; m. Victoria Camps 1966; three s.; ed Univ. of Barcelona; Prof. of Medieval Hispanic Literature, Universidad Autónoma de Barcelona 1971–2012, Prof. Emer. 2012–; Visiting Prof., The Johns Hopkins Univ., USA 1966–67, Princeton Univ., USA 1981, Scuola Normale Superiore di Pisa, Italy 1987; Gen. Dir Centre of Spanish Letters, Ministry of Culture 1985–86; Ed. Book Series: Letras e ideas, Filología, Biblioteca clásica; mem. Royal Spanish Acad. 1986–; Foreign mem. British Acad. 1992, Accad. dei Lincei 2000, Accad. della Crusca 2003, Acads des Inscriptions et belles Lettres 2010; Commdr, Ordre des Palmes académiques 1994; Dr hc (Università di Napoli) 1992, (Université de Bordeaux) 1994, (Universidad de Valladolid) 1996; Premio Internacional Menéndez Pelayo 1998, Premio Nacional de Investigación 2004, Premio Natalino Sapegno 2005, Premio Alfonso Reyes del Colegio De México 2013, Premio Internacional de Ensayo Caballero Bonald 2013. *Publications:* El pequeño mundo del hombre 1970, The Spanish Picaresque Novel and the Point of

View 1970, Vida u obra de Petrarca (Vol. 1) 1974, Historia y crítica de la literatura española (eight vols) 1980–84, Breve biblioteca de autores españoles 1990, El sueño del humanismo (De Petrarca a Erasmo) 1993, Critical Edition of Cervantes' Don Quixote 1998, El texto del Quijote 2005, Gabbiani 2008, Mil años de poesía europea 2009, Lazarillo de Tormes (ed. crit.) 2012, Ritratti allo specchio (Boccaccio, Petrarca) 2012. *Leisure interest:* contemporary literature. *Address:* Santa Teresa 38, 08172 St Cugat del Vallès, Barcelona; Apartado 1, Universidad Autónoma de Barcelona, Barcelona 08193 Bellaterra-Barcelona, Spain. *Telephone:* (93) 674-07-08; 6-49960695 (mobile). *E-mail:* ilfhf@telefonica.net (office); francisco.rico@rae.es (office). *Website:* bib.cervantesvirtual.com/bib_autor/franciscorico (office).

RICÚPERO, Rubens, LLB; Brazilian international organization official, fmr diplomatist and politician; b. 1 March 1937, São Paulo; m. Marisa Parolari; four c.; ed Univ. of São Paulo and Rio Branco Inst.; Prof. of Theory of Int. Relations, Univ. of Brasília 1979–95; Prof. of History of Brazilian Diplomatic Relations, Rio Branco Inst. 1980–95; with Ministry of Foreign Relations 1981–93, Minister of the Environment and Amazonian Affairs 1993–94, of Finance March–Sept. 1994; Perm. Rep. to UN, Geneva 1987–91; Chair. GATT Council of Reps 1989–91, Contracting Parties 1989–91, GATT Cttee on Trade and Devt 1989–91, GATT Informal Group of Developing Countries 1989–91 (also Spokesman); Amb. to USA 1991–93, to Italy 1995; led Brazilian dels to UN Comm. on Human Rights and Conf. on Disarmament, Geneva; Chair. Finance Cttee, UN Conf. on Environment and Devt, Rio de Janeiro 1992; Sec.-Gen. UNCTAD 1995–2004; Dir Fundação Armando Alvares Penteado 2005–; Pres. Consultative Comm. Conversando com as Nações Unidas (CNU)-Brasil 2006–; Lifetime Achievement Award, World Summit of Young Entrepreneurs of the World Trade Univ. 2004. *Publications:* several books on int. relations, econ. devt problems, int. trade and diplomatic history. *Address:* c/o CNU-Brasil, Rua Plínio Barreto, 285, São Paulo Brazil (office). *Telephone:* (11) 3254-1677. *Fax:* (11) 3254-1675. *Website:* www.cnu-brasil.org.br.

RIDDELL, Clayton (Clay) H., BSc; Canadian geologist and business executive; *Chairman and CEO, Paramount Resources Limited;* b. Winnipeg; ed Univ. of Manitoba; Founder Paramount Resources Ltd, currently Chair. and CEO; fmr Pres. Canadian Soc. of Petroleum Geologists; fmr Chair. Canadian Asscn of Petroleum Producers; co-owner Calgary Flames ice hockey team; Dr hc (Univ. of Man.). *Address:* Paramount Resources Limited, 4700 Bankers Hall, West 888 3rd Street SW, Calgary, AB T2P 5C5, Canada (office). *Telephone:* (403) 290-3600 (office). *Fax:* (403) 262-7994 (office). *Website:* www.paramountres.com

RIDDICK, Frank Adams, Jr., MD; American physician; *CEO Emeritus and Director, Ochsner Clinic Foundation;* b. 14 June 1929, Memphis; s. of Frank Adams Riddick Sr and Falba Crawford Riddick; m. Mary Belle Alston 1952; two s. one d.; ed Vanderbilt and Washington Univs; Staff Physician, Ochsner Clinic, New Orleans 1961–, Asst Medical Dir 1969–73, Assoc. Medical Dir 1973–75, Medical Dir 1975–92, Trustee, Alton Ochsner Medical Foundation 1973–, CEO 1991–2001, now CEO Emer.; Clinical Prof. of Medicine, Tulane Univ., New Orleans 1977–; Chair. Council on Medical Educ., American Medical Asscn 1982–84, Council of Ethical and Judicial Affairs 1995–; mem. NAS Inst. of Medicine; mem. Bd of Govs American Bd of Internal Medicine; Master, American Coll. of Physicians; Distinguished Physician Award, American Soc. of Internal Medicine 1980; Physician Exec. Award, American Coll. of Medical Group Admins 1984; Distinguished Alumnus Award, Vanderbilt Univ. School of Medicine 1988. *Publications:* 56 scientific papers. *Leisure interest:* travel. *Address:* Ochsner Clinic, 1516 Jefferson Highway, New Orleans, LA 70121; 1923 Octavia Street, New Orleans, LA 70115, USA (home). *Telephone:* (504) 838-4001 (office); (504) 897-1737 (home). *Website:* www.ochsner.org (office).

RIDGE, Thomas (Tom) Joseph, BA, JD; American consultant and fmr politician; b. 26 Aug. 1945, Munhall, Pa; m. Michele Moore 1979; one s. one d.; ed Harvard Univ. and Dickinson School of Law, Carlisle, Pa; admitted to Pa Bar 1972; practising lawyer, Erie, Pa 1972–82; Asst Dist Attorney, Erie, Pa 1979–82; mem. US House of Reps 1983–95; Gov. of Pa 1995–2001; Dir US Office of Homeland Security 2001–03, Sec. Dept of Homeland Security 2003–05 (resgnd); Founder, Pres. and CEO Ridge Global LLC (consulting firm), Washington, DC 2006–; mem. Bd of Dirs Home Depot Inc. 2005–; Nat. Co-Chair. Flight 93 Memorial Fundraising Campaign; numerous awards including Bronze Star for Valor, Woodrow Wilson Award, Veterans of Foreign Wars Dwight D. Eisenhower Award, John F. Kennedy Nat. Award, Ellis Island Medal of Honor, ABA John Marshall Award, US Nat. Guard Harry S. Truman Award, Pa Wildlife Fed. Conservationist of the Year Award, US-Mexico Chamber of Commerce Good Neighbor Award, American Cancer Soc. Nat. Medal of Honor, Mister Rogers Award, Champion of Public TV Award, Intrepid Freedom Award, Esperanza Leadership Award. *Address:* Ridge Global LLC, 1101 16th Street, NW, Suite 308, Washington, DC 20036, USA (office). *Telephone:* (202) 833-2008 (office). *Fax:* (202) 833-2009 (office). *E-mail:* press@ridgeglobal.com (office). *Website:* www.ridgeglobal.com (office).

RIDHA, Yasser; Egyptian diplomatist; *Ambassador to Israel;* joined Ministry of Foreign Affairs, postings abroad include to People's Repub. of China, Cyprus, Iraq, Germany, Italy; Deputy Dir-Gen. Office of the Minister of Foreign Affairs –2008; Amb. to Israel 2008–. *Address:* Embassy of Egypt, 54 Basel St, Tel-Aviv 62744, Israel (office). *Telephone:* 3-5464151 (office). *Fax:* 3-5441615 (office). *E-mail:* egypem.ta@zahav.net.il (office).

RIDI, Rashika Ahmed Fathi El, DSc, PhD; Egyptian immunologist and academic; *Professor of Immunology, Cairo University;* ed Cairo Univ., Inst. of Molecular Genetics, Czech Acad. of Science, Prague; Lecturer, Zoology Dept, Faculty of Science, Cairo Univ. 1976–81, Assoc. Prof. of Immunology 1981–86, Prof. of Immunology 1986–; Dir of Schistosomiasis Research, Biomedical Research Center, Egyptian Org. for Sera and Vaccines 1990–2000; Visiting Scientist, Dept of Infectious Diseases, Harvard School of Public Health, USA 1995; Egyptian State Award of Excellence in High Tech. Sciences 2002, Cairo Univ. Award for Recognition in Applied Sciences 2002, Egyptian State Award of Merit in High Tech. Sciences 2010, Laureate for Africa and Arab States, L'Oréal-UNESCO Awards for Women in Science 2010. *Publications:* numerous papers in professional journals. *Address:* Department of Zoology, Faculty of Science, Cairo University, Giza, Egypt (office). *E-mail:* rashika_elridi@yahoo.com (office). *Website:* www.cu.edu.eg (office).

RIDLEY, Brian Kidd, PhD, FRS, FInstP, CPhys; British physicist and academic; *Professor Emeritus of Physics, University of Essex;* b. 2 March 1931, Newcastle upon Tyne, England; s. of Oliver Archbold Ridley and Lillian Beatrice Ridley; m. Sylvia Jean Ridley; one s. one d.; ed Yorebridge (Askrigg) and Gateshead Grammar Schools, Durham Univ.; Research Physicist, Mullard Research Labs 1956–64; Lecturer to Reader, Dept of Physics, Univ. of Essex 1964–86, Prof. of Physics 1986–91, Research Prof. 1991–2007, Prof. Emer. 2007–; several visiting professorial appointments including Cornell, Stanford and Princeton Univs, USA; Paul Dirac Medal and Prize, Inst. of Physics 2001. *Publications:* Time, Space and Things 1976 (revised edn 1994), The Physical Environment 1979, Quantum Process in Semiconductors 1982 (revised edn 1999), Electrons and Phonons in Semiconductor Multilayers 1997 (revised edn 2009), On Science 2001, Reforming Science: Beyond Belief 2010. *Leisure interests:* piano, writing. *Address:* School of Computing Science and Electronic Engineering, University of Essex, Colchester, CO4 3SQ, England (office). *Telephone:* (1206) 872873 (office). *Fax:* (1206) 872900 (office). *E-mail:* bkr@essex.ac.uk (office). *Website:* www.essex.ac.uk/dces/people/profile.aspx?id=63 (office).

RIEBER-MOHN, Georg Fredrik; Norwegian lawyer; *Justice, Supreme Court;* b. 13 Aug. 1945, Lillehammer; m. Kari Nergaard 1967; two s. one d.; ed Univ. of Oslo; Deputy Gov. Western Prison Dist 1971–74; Asst Judge, Magistrates' Court of Stavanger 1975–76; Dist Attorney (Regional Head of Prosecutions) 1976–80; Gen. Dir Prison and Probation Service 1980–85; Judge, Appeal Court 1985–86; Gen. Dir of Public Prosecutions 1986–97 (resgnd); Justice, Supreme Court of Norway 1997–; Commdr, Order of St Olav. *Publications:* numerous articles on law issues and wild salmon conservation efforts. *Leisure interests:* fly fishing, hunting, literature. *Address:* Høyesterettsplass 1, Oslo 1 (office); Somdalen, 3525 Hallingby, Norway (home). *Telephone:* 22-03-59-15 (office); 32-13-00-08 (home). *Fax:* 22-33-23-55 (office). *E-mail:* georg.fr.rieber.mohn@hoyesterett.no (office).

RIEDLBAUCH, Václav; Czech composer; *Professor, Academy of Performing Arts;* b. 1 April 1947, Dýšina; m.; two s.; ed Prague Conservatoire; Lecturer, Prague Conservatory 1970–78; Lecturer, Prague Acad. of Performing Arts 1971, later Sr Lecturer, Head Dept of Composition 1990–2004, Prof. 2000–; Artistic Dir Nat. Theatre Opera 1987–89; Programme Dir, Prague Congress Centre 1990–93; Ed.-in-Chief, Panton Publishers 1993–95, Dir 1996; Dir Gen., Czech Philharmonic Orchestra 2001–09; Minister of Culture 2009–10; Chair. Young Composers Section, Czech Composers' and Performing Artists' Union 1982–; Artist of Merit 1987. *Compositions include:* musical dramatic works: Macbeth (ballet for soloist and group dancers and large orchestra) 1979–82; symphonic works: The Rozmberk Sonata for Winds and Percussion Instruments 1971, Symphony 1972, Symphony with Refrain 1973, Concerto-Battle for Organ and Orchestra 1973, Deadly Rondo for Orchestra 1975, The Story – Symhonic narration 1983, Snake's Skin Shedding for trombone 1986, Preludes to the Exhibition's Openings for flute 1990; chamber instrumental music: Sonatina for James for Violin and Piano 1971, Cathedrals – Organ toccata 1972, The Picture (Still Life with a Dead Nightingale) for flute and piano 1974, Tale for Flute, Violin, Violoncello and Piano 1974, Lamento for Clarinet and Piano 1975, Ballads for Violin and Piano 1975, Stories for Bass-clarinet and Piano 1975, Allegri e Pastorali for wind quintet 1976, Luring for Flute and Piano 1977, Canons for Piano 1977, Parade for Organ 1978, Pastorali e Concerti for brass quintet 1978, Concertie Trenodi for wind octet 1979, The Curtain – Movement for organ 1982, Conjunction – Game for two organs or other keyboard instruments 1983, Epilogue: A Movement for bassoon and piano 1986, String Quartet No. 1 1986, A New Year Meditation for trumpet and organ 1989, Trio for violin, cello and piano 1981, A Small Stone Dance 1993, Wind Quintet No. 2 1999; vocal works: Touzenec pisni – Songs for Tenor and Piano After Verses by R. Tagore 1975, Songs from Rejdova for Soprano, Contralto, Violin and Piano 1976, Tesknice (nostalgic songs) – Three folk songs for two flutes-a-bec and three-part children's choir 1976, Wedding Singing for girls, female or male choirs after Sappho 1978, Rather-Or Cycle for Children – Seven children's choirs to words by R. Steindl 1978, Songs and Games to Excerpts from Shakespeare for six singers, two violins, oboe and violoncello 1979, Teachers Song (celebration of Bohemian baroque) for organ and children's choir to words by V. Fischer 1980, The Primer – Excerpts from beginnings at school – Four polyphonic pieces for children's choir 1980, Daidalos the Creator, for male choir with barytone solo after Ovid 1982; instructive works: Special Book of Prague – A book of polyphonic compositions for accordion 1972, Pastorale for Three Flutes-a-bec 1973, The Wizard – Accordion school for children 1973–76, SU South Bohemian Nocturnes, for two violins, violoncello, accordion and trumpet 1979, Reversals for children's accordion 1980, SU 2' Povidacky (talks) – Eight polyphonic pieces for two violins 1982. *Address:* Academy of Performing Arts, Malostranské nám. 12, 110 00 Prague 1 (office); Revoluční 6, 110 00 Prague 1, Czech Republic (home). *Telephone:* (2) 57533956 (office); (2) 22310710 (home). *Fax:* (2) 57530405 (office). *E-mail:* vaclav.riedlbauch@hamu.cz (office). *Website:* www.amu.cz (office).

RIEKSTIŅŠ, Māris; Latvian lawyer, diplomatist and politician; *Permanent Representative, NATO;* b. 8 April 1963, Rīga; m.; two c.; ed Univ. of Latvia; teacher, Faculty of Pedagogy, Latvian Sports Inst. 1982–85; Deputy Chair. and Desk Officer, Cttee of Latvian Youth Orgs 1987–91; lawyer, Faculty of Law, Univ. of Latvia 1989–93; Chair. Control Cttee of Strategic Goods of Repub. of Latvia 1995–2004, Diplomatic Service Agency's Shareholders' Council 1996–2004, Advisory Council for Membership of Latvia in WTO 1999–2004, Supervisory Cttee on Org. of NATO Aspirant Countries Summit in Rīga Jan.–July 2002; several positions within Ministry of Foreign Affairs, including Desk Officer, Political Dept of Europe Div. and Dir Western Europe and Europe Divs Jan.–Nov. 1992, Under-Sec. of State 1992–93, Sec. of State 1993–2004, Head of Latvian del. for accession negotiations with NATO 2002–04; Amb. to USA 2004–07 (also accred to Mexico 2006–07); Chief of Staff to Prime Minister Jan.–Nov. 2007; Minister of Foreign Affairs Nov. 2007–10 (resgnd); Amb. and Perm. Rep. to NATO, Brussels 2011–; Commdr, Royal Norwegian Order of Merit 1998, Grand Officer, Royal Norwegian Order of Merit 2000, Grand Officier, Ordre nat. du Mérite 2001, Order of the Lithuanian Grand Duke Gediminas (Fourth Class) 2001, Order of the Cross of Terra Mariana (Third Class, Estonia) 2003, Ordem do Infante D. Henrique Grande Oficial (Portugal) 2003, Commdr, Three Star Order of Latvia 2003, Grand Official, Order of Merit of the Italian Repub. 2004. *Address:* Permanent Delegation of Latvia, NATO HQ, Blvd Léopold III, 1110 Brussels, Belgium (office). *Telephone:* (2) 707-97-62 (office); (2) 707-28-86 (office). *Fax:* (2) 707-28-89 (office). *E-mail:*

delegation.nato@mfa.gov.lv (office). *Website:* www.mfa.gov.lv/en/mission/?lv=1&code=48 (office).

RIEMSCHNEIDER, Burkhard; German art critic and gallery curator; *Co-Director, Neugerriemschneider Kunstgalerie;* Co-founder and Co-dir (with Tim Neuger) Neugerriemschneider Kunstgalerie, Berlin, represents artists including Franz Ackermann, Keith Edmier, Olafur Eliasson, Isa Genzken, Sharon Lockhart, the late Michel Majerus, Antje Majewski, Jorge Pardo, Elizabeth Peyton, Tobias Rehberger, Simon Starling, Thaddeus Strode, Wolfgang Tillmans, Rirkrit Tiravanija, Pae White and Jorge Pardo. *Publications include:* Albert Oehlen (co-author) 1995, Twentieth-Century Erotic Art (co-ed.) 1996, Art at the Turn of the Millennium (co-ed.) 1999, Art Now: 137 Artists at the Rise of the New Millennium 2002, 1000 Tattoos (25th Edn) (co-ed.) 2005, Art Now: Artists at the Rise of the New Millennium (25th Edn) (co-ed.) 2005, Studio Olafur Eliasson: An Encyclopedia (ed.) 2008. *Address:* Neugerriemschneider Kunstgalerie, Linienstraße 155, 10115 Berlin, Germany (office). *Telephone:* (30) 288772-77 (office). *E-mail:* mail@neugerriemschneider.com (office). *Website:* (office).

RIES, Col Nico; Luxembourg army officer (retd); b. 30 July 1953; m.; two c.; ed Royal Mil. Acad., Brussels, Belgium, Staff Coll., Compiegne and Ecole Supérieure de Guerre Interarmées, Paris, France; joined Luxembourg Army 1973; apptd to Mil. Instruction Centre 1978–94, held positions successively as Infantry Platoon Leader, Co. Commdr, Personnel Officer, Deputy Commdr; Logistics Officer, Army Staff 1994–98; Asst Chief of Staff 1998–2002, Chief of Staff 2002–08; Chargé de la planification, Ministry of Defence 2008–; participated in EC Monitor Mission in the Fmr Yugoslavia 1991, 1997; Verdienstkreuz 1st Class (Germany) 1988, Officier, Ordre grand-ducal de la Couronne de Chêne 1994, Croix d'honneur et de Mérite militaire en bronze 1998, Croix de 25 ans de service 1999, Meritorious Service Medal (USA) 1998, Medal of EC Monitor Mission in the Fmr Yugoslavia 1998, Grand Officier, Ordre du Mérite of Grand Duchy of Luxembourg 2004, Commdr, Légion d'honneur 2005, Grande Oficial da Ordem Militar de Avis (Portugal) 2005, Grand Officier, Ordre de Viesturs (Latvia) 2006, Commdr, Ordre de Mérite civil et militaire d'Adolphe de Nassau 2007. *E-mail:* nicories@pt.lu.

RIESENHUBER, Heinz Friedrich, Dr rer. nat; German politician; *President, German Parliamentary Society;* b. 1 Dec. 1935, Frankfurt; s. of Karl Riesenhuber and Elisabeth Riesenhuber (née Birkner); m. Beatrix Walter 1968; two s. two d.; ed Gymnasium in Frankfurt and Univs of Frankfurt and Munich; with Erzgesellschaft mbH, c/o Metallgesellschaft, Frankfurt 1966–71; Tech. Man. Synthomer-Chemie GmbH, Frankfurt 1971–82; joined CDU 1961, mem. CDU Hesse Presidium 1968–, Chair. Frankfurt Br. 1973–78, Untermain Br. 1978–; mem. Bundestag 1976–, mem. Cttee on Econ and Tech. 1993– (Chair. 2001–02); Fed. Minister for Research and Tech. 1982–93; Pres. Deutsche Parlamentarische Gesellschaft (German Parl. Soc.) 2006–; Chair. and mem. of numerous supervisory bds and advisory panels; Hon. Prof., Univ of Frankfurt; Fed. Great Cross of Merit with Star, Commdr, Légion d'honneur and numerous other decorations; Dr hc (Weizmann Inst., Israel, Berg Acad., Poland, Univ. of Surrey, UK), (Göttingen) 1997; Cicero Speaker's Award 1995, Golden Ring of Honour, Deutsches Museum, Munich. *Publications:* Japan ist offen; articles in specialist journals. *Leisure interests:* reading, golf. *Address:* Bundestag, Platz der Republik 1, 11011 Berlin, Germany (office). *Telephone:* (30) 22777381 (office). *Fax:* (30) 22776381 (office). *E-mail:* heinz.riesenhuber@bundestag.de (office). *Website:* www.bundestag.de (office).

RIESS, Adam G., BS, AM, PhD; American astrophysicist and academic; *Professor of Astronomy and Physics, Johns Hopkins University;* b. 1969; ed Massachusetts Inst. of Tech., Harvard Univ.; Miller Fellow, Univ. of California, Berkeley 1996–99; mem. Sr Science Science Staff, Space Telescope Science Inst., Baltimore, Md 1999–2005; Prof. of Physics and Astronomy, Johns Hopkins Univ., Baltimore 2006–; led study for High-z Team which provided first direct and published evidence that expansion of Universe was accelerating and filled with Dark Energy 1998; Prin. Investigator of Higher-z SN Team that found and measured 20 most distant type Ia supernovae known through competitive awarding of more than 800 orbits of Hubble Space Telescope Time in five cycles and $2million in grants 2002–; mem. Jt Dark Energy Mission Science Definition Team 2004, Jt Dark Energy Mission Science Working Group 2008; Founding mem. science team for four active dark energy programmes: ESSENCE, ADEPT, SDSS II SN Survey and Pan-STARRS; Fellow, American Acad. of Arts and Sciences 2008; Margaret Weyerhaeuser Jewett Memorial Fellowship 1993, Distinction in Teaching Award, Harvard Univ. 1994, GSAS Merit Fellow, Harvard Univ. 1995, Science Magazine's Research 'Breakthrough of the Year' 1998, Trumpler Award, Astronomical Soc. of the Pacific 1999, Time Magazine Innovator Award 2000, AURA Science Award 2000, STScI Science Merit Award 2000, 2001, Bok Prize, Harvard Univ. 2001 Time Magazine 'Six Who Probed Cosmos', Esquire Magazine 'Best and Brightest' Award 2003, Helen B. Warner Prize, American Astronomical Soc. 2003, Raymond and Beverly Sackler Prize, Tel-Aviv Univ. 2004, Laurels for Achievement Award, Int. Acad. of Astronautics 2004, Townes Prize in Cosmology, Univ. of California, Berkeley 2005, ISI Most Highly Cited 2006, Shaw Prize in Astronomy (co-recipient) 2006, Kavli Frontier of Science Fellow 2007, Gruber Prize in Cosmology (co-recipient) 2007, MacArthur Fellow 2008, Discover Magazine Twenty Under 40 2008, Nobel Prize in Physics (jtly) 2011. *Publications:* more than 80 scientific papers in professional journals on measurements of the cosmological framework with supernovae (exploding stars) and Cepheids (pulsating stars); more than 20 tech. reports. *Address:* Department of Physics and Astronomy, 207 Bloomberg Center, The Johns Hopkins University, 3400 North Charles Street, Baltimore, Baltimore, MD 21218-2686, USA (office). *Telephone:* (410) 516-4474 (office). *Fax:* (410) 516-7239 (office). *E-mail:* ariess@pha.jhu.edu (office). *Website:* physics-astronomy.jhu.edu (office); www.stsci.edu/~ariess (office).

RIESS, Susanne; Austrian lawyer, business executive and fmr politician; *General Director, Bausparkasse Wüstenrot AG;* b. 3 Jan. 1961, Braunau; ed Univ. of Innsbruck; joined Freedom Party as Press Officer 1987, succeeded Jörg Haider as leader 2000–02; Vice-Chancellor and Minister for Public Affairs and Sports 2000–02; Gen. Dir Bausparkasse Wüstenrot AG 2004–; Deputy Chair. Bundestheater Holding. *Address:* Bausparkasse Wüstenrot AG, Alpenstraße 70, 5033 Salzburg, Austria (office). *Telephone:* 57070-110 (office). *Fax:* 57070-109 (office). *Website:* www.wuestenrot.at (office).

RIESTER, Walter; German politician and trade union official; b. 27 Sept. 1943, Kaufbeuren; ed Labour Acad. Frankfurt; apprentice tiler 1957–60; tiler 1960–68; youth training officer German TU Fed. Baden-Württemberg Region 1970, Departmental Gen. Sec. for Youth Questions Stuttgart Region 1970–77; Admin. Sec. IG Metall Geislingen 1977–78, Second Deputy 1978–79, Sec. Dist HQ IG Metall Stuttgart 1980–88, Dist Man. 1988–93, Second Chair. IG Metall Germany 1993–98; Fed. Minister of Labour and Social Affairs 1998–2002; mem. (SPD) Bundestag (Parl.) 2002–. *Address:* Willi-Bleicher-Straße 3, Schillerbau II, 73033 Göppingen; Deutscher Bundestag, Platz der Republik 1, 11011 Berlin, Germany (office). *Telephone:* (30) 22772041 (office). *Fax:* (30) 22776042 (office). *E-mail:* walter.riester@bundestag.de (office). *Website:* walterriester.de (office).

RIFAI, Samir Zaid ar-, MA; Jordanian politician; b. 1 July 1966; s. of Zaid ar-Rifai; ed Harvard Univ., USA, Univ. of Cambridge, UK; Sec. Gen. Royal Hashemite Court and Head, Royal Press Office 1999–2003; Minister of the Royal Court 2003–05; Adviser to King Abdullah 2005; CEO Jordan Dubai Capital (financial group) 2005–09, also Chair. Energy Arabia (Enara); Prime Minister 2009–11, also Minister of Defence Jan. 2010; Grand Cordon, Order of Al-Kawkab Al Urduni, Grand Cordon, Order of Al-Istiqlal. *Address:* c/o The Prime Ministry of Jordan, POB 80, Amman 11180, Jordan.

RIFAI, Taleb, BSc, MSc, PhD; Jordanian architect, academic, government official and international organization official; *Secretary-General, World Tourism Organization;* b. 1949; m.; five c.; ed Univ. of Cairo, Illinois Inst. of Tech., Chicago and Univ. of Pennsylvania, USA; Prof. of Architecture, Planning and Urban Design, Univ. of Jordan 1973–93; Head of Jordan's first Econ. Mission to USA, Washington, DC 1993–95; Dir Gen. Investment Promotion Corpn 1995–97; CEO Jordan Cement Co. 1997–99; held several sr govt portfolios, as Minister of Tourism and Antiquities (Chair. Exec. Council World Tourism Org. (UNWTO) 2002–03) 1999–2003, Minister of Information and Minister of Planning and Int. Co-operation; Asst to Dir-Gen. and Regional Dir for Arab States, ILO 2003–06; Deputy Sec.-Gen. UNWTO 2006–Jan. 2009, Sec.-Gen. a.i. Jan.–Oct. 2009, Sec.-Gen. Oct. 2009–; fmr Chair. Jordan Tourism Bd; fmr Pres. Ammon School for Tourism and Hospitality. *Achievements include:* responsible for founding Jordan's first Arch-aeological Park in ancient city of Petra in collaboration with UNESCO and World Bank, along with other projects in Jerash, the Dead Sea and Wadi Rum. *Address:* World Tourism Organization, Capitán Haya 42, 28020 Madrid, Spain (office). *Telephone:* (91) 567-81-00 (office). *Fax:* (91) 571-37-33 (office). *E-mail:* omt@unwto.org (office). *Website:* www.unwto.org (office).

RIFBJERG, Klaus; Danish author and academic; *Adjunct Professor of Languages, Copenhagen Business School;* b. 15 Dec. 1931, Copenhagen; s. of Thorvald Rifbjerg and Lilly Nielsen; m. Inge Merete Gerner 1955; one s. two d.; ed Princeton Univ., USA and Univ. of Copenhagen; Literary Critic, Information 1955–57, Politiken 1959–65 (Copenhagen daily newspapers); Literary Dir Gyldendal Publrs 1984–92, mem. Bd of Dirs 1992–98; Prof. of Aesthetics, Laererhøjskole, Copenhagen 1986; Adjunct Prof. of Languages, Copenhagen Business School 2003–; Grant of Honour from the Danish Dramatists 1966, Grant of Honour from the Danish Writers' Guild 1973; Dr hc (Lund) 1991, (Odense) 1996; Aarestrup Medal 1964, Danish Critics' Award 1965, Danish Acad. Award 1966, Golden Laurels 1967, Soren Gyldendal Award 1969, Nordic Council Award 1970, PH Prize 1979, Holberg Medal 1979, H. C. Andersen Prize 1988, Johannes V. Jensen Prize 1998, Prize for Nordic Writers, Swedish Acad. 1999, Danish Publicists' Award 2001, Danish Language Soc. Award 2001, Rungstedlund Award 2009. *Publications include:* novels: Den Kroniske Uskyld 1958, Operaelsken 1966, Arkivet 1967, Lonni Og Karl 1968, Anna (Jeg) Anna 1970, Marts 1970 1970, Leif den Lykkelige JR. 1971, Til Spanien 1971, Lena Jorgensen, Klintevej 4, 2650 Hvidovre 1971, Brevet til Gerda 1972, R.R. 1972, Spinatfuglene 1973, Dilettanterne 1973, Du skal ikke vaere ked af det Amalia 1974, En hugorm i solen 1974, Vejen ad hvilken 1975, Tak for turen 1975, Kiks 1976, Twist 1976, Et Bortvendt Ansigt 1977, Tango 1978, Dobbeltgœnger 1978, Drengene 1978, Joker 1979, Voksdugshjertet 1979, Det sorte hul 1980, De hellige aber 1981, Mænd og Kvinder 1982, Jus 1982, En omvej til Klostret 1983, Falsk Forår 1984, Borte tit 1986, Engel 1987, Rapsodi i blåt 1991, Divertimento i mol 1996, Billedet 1999, Regnvejr 2001, Nansen og Johansen 2002; short stories: Og Andre Historier 1964, Rejsende 1969, Den Syende Jomfru 1972, Sommer 1974, Det. Svage Køn 1989; non-fiction: I Medgang Og Modgang 1970, Deres Majestæt! 1977; plays: Gris Pa Gaflen 1962, Hva Skal Vi Lave 1963, Udviklinger 1965, Hvad en Mand Har Brug For 1966, Voks 1968, Ar 1970, Narrene 1971, Svaret Blaeser i Vinden 1971, Det Korte af det lange 1976; poems: Livsfrisen 1979 and several other vols of poetry; 20 radio plays, essays, several film and TV scripts. *Address:* Copenhagen Business School, Nørre Voldgade 34, 1358 Copenhagen, Denmark (office).

RIFKIN, Joshua, BS, MFA; American conductor, musicologist and composer; b. 22 April 1944, New York; s. of Harry H. Rifkin and Dorothy Helsh; m. Helen Palmer 1995; one d.; ed Juilliard School and New York, Göttingen and Princeton Univs; Musical Adviser, Assoc. Dir Nonesuch Records 1963–75; Asst, Assoc. Prof. of Music, Brandeis Univ. 1970–82; Dir The Bach Ensemble 1978–; Visiting Prof. New York Univ. 1978, 1983, 2000, Yale Univ. 1982–83, Princeton Univ. 1988, Stanford Univ. 1989, King's Coll. London 1991, Univ. of Basel 1993, 1997, Ohio State Univ. 1994, Univ. of Dortmund 1996, Schola Cantorum Basiliensis 1997, 2001, Univ. of Munich 2000; Fellow, Inst. for Advanced Study, Berlin 1984–86; guest conductor English Chamber Orchestra, Los Angeles Chamber Orchestra, St Louis Symphony Orchestra, St Paul Chamber Orchestra, Scottish Chamber Orchestra, BBC Symphony Orchestra, Bayerische Staatsoper, San Francisco Symphony Orchestra, City of Glasgow Symphony Orchestra, Jerusalem Symphony Orchestra, Prague Chamber Orchestra; contributed to the revival of interest in the ragtime music of Scott Joplin; as a musicologist has researched Renaissance and Baroque music; recreated J. S. Bach's Wedding Cantata BWV 216 (fragment, originally 1728) 2005; Dr hc (Dortmund) 1999; Gramophone Award 1983. *Recordings:* Bach Mass in B minor 1982, Bach Magnificat 1983, numerous Bach cantatas 1986–2001, Rags and Tangos 1990, Haydn Symphonies 1994, Silvestre Revueltas 1999, rags by Scott Joplin, Mozart Posthorn Serenade, fanfares and sonatas by Pezel and Hammerschmidt, sonatas by Biber, vocal music by Busnois, Josquin. *Publications:* articles on Haydn, Schütz, Bach and Josquin in The Musical Times, Musical Quarterly and other journals, and in the New Grove Dictionary of Music and Musicians. *Leisure interests:* food and wine, cinema, his

daughter. *Address:* 100 Montgomery Street, Cambridge, MA 02138, USA. *Telephone:* (617) 876-4017 (office). *Fax:* (617) 441-5572 (office). *E-mail:* jrifkin@compuserve.com.

RIFKIND, Rt Hon. Sir Malcolm Leslie, Kt, KCMG, PC, QC, LLB, MSc; British politician and business executive; b. 21 June 1946, Edinburgh, Scotland; s. of the late E. Rifkind; m. Edith Steinberg 1970; one s. one d.; ed George Watson's Coll. and Univ. of Edinburgh; Lecturer, Univ. of Rhodesia 1967–68; called to Scottish Bar 1970; MP for Edin., Pentlands 1974–97; Parl. Under-Sec. of State, Scottish Office 1979–82, FCO 1982–83; Minister of State, FCO 1983–86; Sec. of State for Scotland 1986–90, for Transport 1990–92, for Defence 1992–95, for Foreign and Commonwealth Affairs 1995–97; Pres. Scottish Conservative and Unionist Party 1998–; MP for Kensington and Chelsea 2005–, for Kensington 2010–, Shadow Work and Pensions Sec. 2005, mem. Jt Cttee on Conventions 2006–, Chair. Cttee on Standards and Privileges 2009–10; UK Rep., Eminent Persons Group 2010–11; Chair. Intelligence and Security Cttee 2010–; mem. Queen's Bodyguard for Scotland, Royal Co. of Archers; Patron, Tory Reform Club; Hon. Col 162 Movt Control Regt, Royal Logistic Corps (V); Commdr, Order of Merit (Poland); Hon. LLD (Napier) 1998. *Leisure interests:* walking, field sports, reading. *Address:* c/o Ms Christine Shaylor, House of Commons, Westminster, London, SW1A 0AA (office). *Telephone:* (20) 7219-5683 (office). *Fax:* (20) 7219-4213 (office). *E-mail:* shaylorc@parliament.uk (office). *Website:* www.parliament.uk/biographies/commons/sir-malcolm-rifkind/1191 (office); www.malcolmrifkind.com.

RIGALI, HE Cardinal Justin Francis, BSacTheol, DCL; American ecclesiastic and diplomatist; *Archbishop Emeritus of Philadelphia;* b. 19 April 1935, Los Angeles, Calif.; s. of Henry Alphonsus Rigali and Frances Irene Rigali (née White); ed Holy Cross School, preparatory seminary in Hancock Park, Los Angeles Coll., Our Lady Queen of Angels Seminary, San Fernando, St John's Seminary, Camarillo, Catholic Univ. of America, Pontifical North American Coll. and Pontifical Gregorian Univ., Rome; ordained priest, Archdiocese of Los Angeles 1961; asst during first two sessions of Second Vatican Council 1962–63; returned to USA summer 1964, served as assoc. pastor in Pomona; returned to Rome to study at Pontifical Ecclesiastical Acad. in preparation for diplomatic work for the Vatican 1964–66; began service in English section of Secr. of State 1964, Sec. of Apostolic Nunciature to Madagascar (also served as apostolic delegation for Réunion and Mauritius) 1966–70; named a Papal Chamberlain 1967; Dir English section of Secr. of State and English trans. to Servant of God Pope Paul VI 1970, subsequently accompanied Pope Paul on several int. trips; also chaplain at a Carmelite monastery and Prof. at Pontifical Ecclesiastical Acad.; apptd Titular Archbishop of Volsinium 1985; Pres. Pontifical Ecclesiastical Acad. 1985–89; serving in Council for Public Affairs of the Church and Pontifical Council for the Laity 1985–90; mem. Order of the Holy Sepulchre 1986–; Sec., Congregation for Bishops 1989–90, Coll. of Cardinals 1990–94; served on Perm. Interdicasterial Comm., Pontifical Comm. for Latin America, Congregation for Doctrine of the Faith; also engaged in pastoral service to several parishes and seminaries in Rome; Archbishop of Saint Louis, Mo. 1994–2003; Archbishop of Philadelphia, Pa 2003–11, Archbishop Emer. 2011–; cr. Cardinal (Cardinal-Priest of Santa Prisca) 2003; mem. Congregation for Bishops 2007–13; apptd Pope Benedict XVI's special envoy to celebrations at Prachatice in Czech Repub. for 200th anniversary of the birth of St John Neumann 2011; Apostolic Admin. (sede vacante) to Diocese of Scranton 2009–10; mem. Kts of Columbus 1994; Hon. Council mem. Wings of Hope; Prelate of Honour of His Holiness 1980; Magistral Chaplain, Order of Kts of Malta 1984. *Address:* 805 S. NorthShore Drive, Knoxville, TN 37919, USA (office). *Telephone:* (865) 862-5748 (office). *Fax:* (865) 583-3836 (office).

RIGBY, Jean Prescott, ARAM, ARCM, ABSM; British singer (mezzo-soprano); b. Fleetwood, Lancs.; d. of Thomas Boulton Rigby and Margaret Annie Rigby; m. James Hayes 1987; three s.; ed Elmslie Girls' School, Blackpool, Birmingham School of Music, RAM and Opera Studio; studied piano and viola at Birmingham then singing at RAM with Patricia Clark, with whom she continues to study; Prin. Mezzo-Soprano, ENO 1982–90, roles include Mercedes, Marina, Lucretia, Dorabella, Octavian, Penelope, Jocasta, Helen (King Priam), Rosina; debut Covent Garden 1983, roles have included Tebaldo, Mercedes, Hippolyta, second Lady, Magic Flute and Olga, Eugene Onegin, Nicklausse (Hoffman), Irene in Theodora, Emelia in Otello, Geneviève in Pelléas and Mélisande, Edwige in Rodelinda; Glyndebourne debut 1984, sang Nancy in Albert Herring and Mercedes in Carmen 1985; American debut 1993; TV appearances in Così fan tutte and film on Handel; videos of Xerxes, Rigoletto, Lucretia, Carmen, Albert Herring; also sings concert repertoire and has made recordings with Giuseppe Sinopoli; Hon. FRAM 1989; Hon. Assoc., Birmingham Conservatoire 1996, Hon. Fellow 2007; numerous prizes and scholarships at RAM including Countess of Munster, Leverhulme, Peter Stuyvesant, RSA scholarships and the Prin.'s Prize; Royal Overseas League and Young Artists' Competition 1981. *Recordings:* more than 50 recordings, ranging from Bach, Handel, Vivaldi and Debussy to Birtwistle and McMillan. *Leisure interests:* theatre, sport, British heritage. *Address:* c/o Hyperion Records, PO Box 25, London, SE9 1AX, England (office). *Telephone:* (20) 8318-1234 (office). *Fax:* (20) 8463-1230 (office). *E-mail:* info@hyperion-records.co.uk (office). *Website:* www.hyperion-records.co.uk (office).

RIGBY, Peter William Jack, MA, PhD; British medical research scientist and academic; *Professor of Developmental Biology and Chief Executive, Institute of Cancer Research, University of London;* b. 7 July 1947, Savernake; s. of Jack Rigby and Lorna Rigby; m. 1st Paula Webb 1971 (divorced 1983); m. 2nd Julia Maidment 1985; one s.; ed Lower School of John Lyon, Harrow and Jesus Coll. Cambridge; mem. scientific staff, MRC Lab. of Molecular Biology, Cambridge 1971–73; Helen Hay Whitney Foundation Research Fellow, Stanford Univ. Medical School 1973–76; Lecturer, Sr Lecturer in Biochemistry, Imperial Coll. London 1976–83; Reader in Tumour Virology, Univ. of London 1983–86; Head, Genes and Cellular Controls Group and Div. of Eukaryotic Molecular Genetics, MRC Nat. Inst. for Medical Research 1986–2000; Chief Exec. Inst. of Cancer Research, Univ. of London 1999–, also Dir of Research, Prof. of Developmental Biology 2001–; mem. Science Council, Celltech Therapeutics 1982–2003; European Ed. Cell 1984–97; mem. Scientific Advisory Bd Somatix Therapy Corpn 1989–97, KuDos Pharmaceuticals 1999–; Scientific Cttee Cancer Research Campaign 1983–88, 1996–99; non-exec. Dir, Royal Marsden NHS Foundation Trust 2001–; mem. of Council, Acad. of Medical Sciences 2002–04, St George's Hospital Medical School 2003–;

mem. Bd of Govs, Beatson Inst. for Cancer Research, Glasgow 2003–; mem. Nat. Council and Chair. of Medical Research Cttee, Muscular Dystrophy Campaign 2003–; Chair. Principal Research Fellowship Interviewing Cttee, Wellcome Trust 2004–; mem. Strategy Bd, Biotechnology and Biological Sciences Research Council 2005–; Chair. Hexagen Tech. Ltd 1996–99; Chair. Scientific Advisory Bd Proflix 1996–2004; Fellow, Acad. of Medical Sciences 1999; Carter Medal, Clinical Genetics Soc. 1994. *Publications:* papers on molecular biology in scientific journals. *Leisure interests:* narrow boats, listening to music, sport. *Address:* Chester Beatty Laboratories, Institute of Cancer Research, 237 Fulham Road, London, SW3 6JB, England (office). *Telephone:* (20) 7153-5125 (office). *Fax:* (20) 7352-0272 (office). *E-mail:* peter.rigby@icr.ac.uk (office). *Website:* www.icr.ac.uk (office).

RIGG, Dame (Enid) Diana Elizabeth, DBE; British actress; b. 20 July 1938, Doncaster, Yorks.; d. of Louis Rigg and Beryl Rigg (née Helliwell); m. 1st Menahem Gueffen 1973 (divorced 1976); m. 2nd Archibald Hugh Stirling 1982 (divorced 1993); one d.; ed Fulneck Girls School, Pudsey, Yorks., Royal Acad. of Dramatic Art; professional début as Natella Abashwilli (The Caucasian Chalk Circle), York Festival 1957; repertory Chesterfield and Scarborough 1958; Chair. MacRobert Arts Centre, Univ. of Stirling, Chancellor Univ. of Stirling 1997–2008; Prof. of Theatre Studies, Oxford Univ. 1998–; Dir United British Artists 1982–; a Vice-Pres. Baby Life Support Systems (BLISS) 1984–; Visiting Prof. of Contemporary Theatre Oxford Univ. 1999; mem. Arts Council Cttee 1986; mem. British Museum Devt Fund, Assen for Business Sponsorship of the Arts; Assoc. Artist of RSC, Stratford and Aldwych 1962–79; mem. Nat. Theatre 1972; Dr hc (Stirling Univ.) 1988; Hon. DLitt (Leeds) 1992, (South Bank) 1996; Plays and Players Award for Best Actress (Phaedra Britannica 1975, Night and Day 1978), BAFTA Award for Best Actress in Mother Love 1990, Evening Standard Award for Best Actress (Medea 1993, Mother Courage and Her Children 1996, Who's Afraid of Virginia Woolf? 1996), Tony Award for Best Actress in Medea 1994, Special Award for The Avengers, BAFTA 2000. *Roles with RSC include:* Andromache (Troilus and Cressida), 2nd Ondine, Violanta and Princess Bertha (Ondine), Philippe Trincant (The Devils), Gwendolen (Becket), Bianca (The Taming of the Shrew), Madame de Tourvel (The Art of Seduction), Helena (A Midsummer Night's Dream), Adriana (Comedy of Errors), Cordelia (King Lear), Nurse Monika Stettler (The Physicists), Lady Macduff (Macbeth); toured Eastern Europe, USSR, USA in King Lear, Comedy of Errors 1964; Viola (Twelfth Night), Stratford 1966. *National Theatre roles include:* Dottie Moore (Jumpers) 1972, Hippolita ('Tis Pity She's A Whore) 1972, Lady Macbeth (Macbeth) 1972, Célimène (The Misanthrope), Washington and New York 1973, 1975, The Governor's Wife (Phaedra Britannica) 1975; rejoined Nat. Theatre at the Lyttelton to play Ilona in The Guardsman 1978. *Other stage appearances include:* Abelard and Heloise (London) 1970, (LA, New York) 1971, Pygmalion (London) 1974, Night and Day (London) 1978, Colette (Seattle and Denver) 1982, Heartbreak House (London) 1983, Rita in Little Eyolf (London) 1985, Antony and Cleopatra (Chichester) 1985, Wildfire (London) 1986, Follies 1987, Love Letters (San Francisco) 1990, All for Love (London) 1991, Berlin Bertie 1992, Medea 1993 (London and Broadway), Mother Courage and Her Children (London) 1995, Who's Afraid of Virginia Woolf? (London) 1996–97, Phèdre 1998, Britannicus 1998, Humble Boy 2001, Suddenly Last Summer (Theatregoers' Award for Best Actress 2005) (Sheffield) 2004, Honour (London) 2006, All About My Mother (London) 2007, The Cherry Orchard (Chichester Festival Theatre) 2008, Hay Fever (Chichester Festival Theatre) 2009. *Films include:* A Midsummer Night's Dream 1969, The Assassination Bureau 1969, On Her Majesty's Secret Service 1969, Julius Caesar 1970, The Hospital 1971, Theatre of Blood 1973, A Little Night Music 1977, The Great Muppet Caper 1981, Evil under the Sun 1982, Snow White 1988, Cannon Movie Tales: Cinderella 1988, A Good Man in Africa 1994, Parting Shots 1999, Heidi 2005, The Painted Veil 2006. *Television appearances include:* Sentimental Agent 1963, A Comedy of Errors 1964, The Hothouse 1964, The Avengers (series) 1965–67, Women Beware Women 1965, Married Alive 1970, Diana (series) 1973, In This House of Brede 1975, Three Piece Suite 1977, Clytemnestra in The Serpent Son 1979, The Marquise 1980, Hedda Gabler 1981, Rita Allmers in Little Eyolf 1982, Regan in King Lear 1983, Witness for the Prosecution 1983, Bleak House 1984, Host, Held in Trust, A Hazard of Hearts 1987, Worst Witch 1987, Unexplained Laughter 1989, Mother Love (BAFTA Award for Best actress) 1989, Host, Mystery! 1989 (USA), Running Delilah 1994, Zoya 1995, The Haunting of Helen Walker 1995, The Fortunes and Misfortunes of Moll Flanders 1996, Samson and Delilah 1996, Rebecca 1997 (Emmy Award for Best Supporting Actress 1997), The Mrs Bradley Mysteries: Speedy Death 1998, The Mrs. Bradley Mysteries (series) 1999, In the Beginning (mini-series) 2000, The American 2001, The 100 Greatest TV Characters (Mrs Peel) 2001, Victoria & Albert 2001, Charles II: The Power and the Passion (mini-series) 2003. *Publications:* No Turn Unstoned 1982, So To The Land 1994. *Leisure interests:* reading, writing, cooking, travel. *Address:* c/o ARG, 4 Great Portland Street, London, W1W 8PA, England.

RIGGIO, Leonard S.; American business executive; *Chairman, Barnes & Noble, Inc.;* b. 1941, New York; m. (divorced); two d.; ed Brooklyn Tech. High School, New York Univ.; fmrly with New York Univ. campus bookstore; opened Waverly Student Book Exchange 1965; f. Barnes & Noble Bookstores 1971, Chair., CEO Barnes & Noble Inc. 1986–, now Chair., also Chair. barnesandnoble.com inc.; Chair. of Bd, Prin. Beneficial Owner Software Etc. Stores, Mpls, MBS Textbook Exchange, Inc.; Chair. Bd Dia Art Foundation; mem. Bd of Dirs Children's Defense Fund, Black Children's Community Crusade, Brooklyn Tech Foundation, Italian American Foundation; Ellis Island Medal of Honor, Frederick Douglas Medallion, Anti-Defamation League Americanism Award Dr. hc (Baruch College, Bentley College). *Address:* Barnes & Noble, Inc., 122 5th Avenue, New York, NY 10011, USA (office). *Telephone:* (212) 633-3300 (office). *Fax:* (212) 675-0413 (office). *Website:* www.barnesandnobleinc.com (office).

RIGILLO, Maurizio; Italian gallery director; *Co-Director and Partner, Galleria Continua;* co-f. (with Mario Cristiani and Lorenzo Fiaschi) Galleria Continua in San Gimignano, Tuscany 1990, other locations include Beijing 2004 and Boissy-le-Châtel, France 2007–; represents several major artists, including Daniel Buren, Kendell Geers, Anish Kapoor and Hans Op de Beeck. *Address:* Galleria Continua, Via del Castello 11, 53037 San Gimignano, Italy (office). *Telephone:* (0577) 943134 (office). *E-mail:* info@galleriacontinua.com (office). *Website:* www.galleriacontinua .com (office).

RIIS, Povl, MD, DM, FRCP; Danish physician, academic and editor; *Chairman, AgeForum;* b. 28 Dec. 1925, Copenhagen; s. of Lars Otto Riis and Eva Elisabeth Riis (née Erdmann); m. Else Harne 1954 (died 1997); one s. three d.; ed Univ. of Copenhagen; specialist in internal medicine 1960, gastroenterology 1963; Head of Medical Dept B, Gentofte Univ. Hosp. 1963–76; Prof. of Internal Medicine, Univ. of Copenhagen 1974–96, Vice-Dean Faculty of Medicine 1979–82; Head of Gastro-enterological Dept C, Herlev Co. Hosp. 1976–96; Asst Ed. Journal of the Danish Medical Asscn 1957–67, Chief Ed. 1967–90; Ed. Bibliothek for Laeger 1965–90, Danish Medical Bulletin 1968–90, Nordic Medicine 1984–91; mem. Bd, Danish Soc. for Internal Medicine 1962–67, Danish Anti-Cancer League 1970–75, Danish Soc. for Theoretical and Applied Therapy 1972–77, Int. Union against Cancer 1978–86; mem. Danish Medical Research Council 1968–74, Chair. 1972–74; mem. Danish Science Advisory Bd 1972–74, Co-Chair. 1974; mem. Nordic Scientific Co-ordination Cttee for Medicine 1968–72, Chair. 1970–72; Vice-Pres. European Science Foundation (ESF) 1974–77, mem. Exec. Council 1977–83; mem. Council for Int. Org. of Medical Sciences Advisory Cttee 1977; mem. Trustees Foundation of 1870 1976, Trier-Hansen Foundation 1977–, Hartmann Prize Cttee 1986–2002, Buhl Olesen Foundation 1982–, Madsen Foundation 1978–, Jakobsen Foundation 1989–, Brinch Foundation 1990–96; Chair. Danish Central Scientific-Ethical Cttee 1979–98, Nat. Medical Bd Danish Red Cross 1985–94, Int. Org. of Inflammatory Bowel Diseases 1986–89; Danish Foreign Office del. Helsinki negotiations, Hamburg 1980; mem. Nuffield Foundation Working Party on Ethics 1999–2002, Ethical Collegial Council, Ethical Collegial Council, Danish Medical Asscn 2000–03; mem. Medical Advisory Bd NetDoktor 1999–; mem. Int. Cttee of Medical Journal Eds 1980–90, Editorial Bd, Acta Medica Scandinavica, Journal Int. Medicine 1980, Ethics Bd, Danish Medical Asscn 1980–82, WHO European Advisory Cttee for Medical Research 1980–85, Scientific Bd, Danish Nat. Encyclopaedia 1991–2001, Editorial Bd JAMA 1994–; Chair. Nat. Center for First Aid and Health Promotion 1991, AeldreForum (AgeForum) 1996–, Bd Epidemi-ological Research, Univ. of Arhus 2004–; mem. Preid. Cttee Foundation of Psychiatry 1996–; Hon. mem. Icelandic Medical Asscn 1978, Swedish Medical Soc., Finnish Medical Soc., Danish Soc. of Gastroenterology 1995 and 2004; Hon. MRCP (UK) 1991; Hon. DMed (Univ. of Odense) 1996, (Gothenburg); Alfred Benzon Prize, August Krogh Prize 1974, Christensen-Ceson Prize 1976, Klein-Prize 1980, Barfred-Pedersen Prize 1980, Hagedorn Prize 1983, Nordic Gastro Prize 1983, Nordic Language Prize in Medicine 1993, Danish Prize of Honour in Research Ethics 2003, National Prize of Honour, JL-Foundation 2005, Medal of Honour, Icelandic Medical History Soc. 2005. *Television:* several contribs to Danish Broadcasting System for radio and TV. *Publications include:* contrib.: Handbook of Scientific Methodology (in Danish) 1971–, World Medical Association Helsinki Declaration 1975, We Shall All Die – But How? (in Danish) 1977; author: Handbook of Internal Medicine (in Danish) 1968, Grenzen der Forschung 1980, Community and Ethics (in Danish) 1984, Medical Ethics (in Danish) 1985, Ethical Issues in Preventive Medicine 1985, Bearing and Perspective 1988, Face Death 1989, Ethics in Health Education 1990, The Future of Medical Journals 1991, Research on Man: Ethics and Law 1991, Scientific Misconduct – Good Scientific Practice 1992, The Culture of General Education 1996, Drugs and Pharmacother-apy 1997, The Time That Followed (in Danish) 1998, Ethics and Clinical Medicine (in Danish) 1998, Can Our Nat Heritage Survive? (in Danish) 1999, Frailty in Aging (in Danish) 1999, Ethics and Evidence-based Pharmacotherapy 2000, Can We Not Do It A Little Better? 2000, In That We Believe 2001, Fraud and Misconduct in Biomedical Research 2001, The Ethics of Research Related to Health Care in Developing Countries 2002; 48 AgeForum publs 1996–2007; Council of Europe, Ethical Eye: Biomedical Research 2004; many articles in medical journals; lyrics to contemporary Danish compositions, trans of lyrics. *Leisure interests:* tennis, music, mountain walking, botany, linguistics. *Address:* Alice Hansen, AeldreForum, Edisonsvej 18, 1, 5000, Odense C (office); Nerievej 7, 2900 Hellerup, Denmark (home). *Telephone:* 72423990 (office); 39629688 (home). *Fax:* 72423991 (office); 39629588 (home). *E-mail:* aef@aeldreforum.dk (office). *Website:* www.aeldreforum.dk (office).

RIIS-JØRGENSEN, Birger, MA; Danish diplomatist; *Ambassador to Italy;* b. 13 Jan. 1949, Odense; m. Karin Riis-Jørgensen; ed Univ. of Copenhagen; Grad. Fellow, Center for Latin American Studies, Univ. of New Mexico, USA 1974–75; Research Librarian, Royal Library, Copenhagen 1975–76; Lecturer in Int. Politics, Univ. of Copenhagen 1975–76; joined Danish Foreign Service 1976, posted to Danish del. to NATO 1979, served as Denmark's Rep. on Political Cttee and subsequently on NATO's Defence Review Cttee and Exec. Working Group; Head of Western Hemisphere and Nordic Countries Section, Political Dept, Ministry of Foreign Affairs and Sec. to Foreign Affairs Cttee of Parl. 1983–87; mem. team of officials who started Secr. for European Political Cooperation, Brussels 1987–89; with DANIDA (Danish DfID) 1989–91; Head of Africa Dept, Ministry of Foreign Affairs 1991–94, Head of Middle East Dept 1994–96, Under-Sec., responsible for Africa, Asia and Latin America and all Danish bilateral devt assistance 1996–2000, State Sec. (Foreign Trade) and given task of merging trade promotion orgs of four ministries into one (Trade Council of Denmark) in the Foreign Service 2000–06, also joined Four Member Sr Man. Group; Amb. to UK 2006–11, to Italy (also accred to Malta and San Marino) 2011–; Commdr (First Degree), Order of Dannebrog. *Leisure interests:* tennis, swimming, sea kayaking, classical music, reading contemporary history and fiction. *Address:* Royal Danish Embassy, Via dei Monti Parioli 50, 00197 Rome, Italy (office). *Telephone:* (06) 9774831 (office). *Fax:* (06) 97748399 (office). *E-mail:* birrii@um.dk (office); romamb@um.dk (office). *Website:* italien.um.dk (office).

RILEY, Bridget Louise, CH, CBE, ARCA; British artist; b. 24 April 1931, London; d. of John Fisher and the late Bessie Louise Riley (née Gladstone); ed Cheltenham Ladies' Coll., Goldsmiths Coll. of Art and Royal Coll. of Art, London; first one-woman exhbn in London at Gallery One 1962, followed by others in England, USA, Italy, Germany, Ireland, Switzerland, Australia and Japan; has exhibited in group shows in Australia, Italy, France, Netherlands, Germany, Israel, USA, Japan and Argentina; represented GB at Biennale des Jeunes, Paris 1965, at Venice Biennale 1968; retrospective exhbn Europe and UK 1970–72; second retrospective exhbn touring America, Australia and Japan 1978–80; Arts Council Touring Exhbn 1984–85; retrospective exhbn Tate Britain 2003; solo exhbn Museum of Contemporary Art, Sydney 2004–05; paintings, drawings and prints in public collections in England, Ireland, Switzerland, Netherlands,

Austria, Germany, Japan, Israel, USA, Australia and NZ; Founder-mem. and fmr Dir SPACE Ltd; mem. RSA; Trustee, Nat. Gallery 1981–88; Dr hc (Manchester) 1976, (Exeter) 1997, (Ulster) 1986, (Oxford) 1993, (Cambridge) 1995, (De Montfort) 1996; Hon. DLitt (Cambridge) 1995; AICA Critics Prize 1963, Prize in Open Section, John Moores Liverpool Exhbn 1963, Peter Stuyvesant Foundation Travel Bursary to USA 1964, Maj. Painting Prize, Venice Biennale 1968, Prize at Tokyo Print Biennale 1971, Gold Medal at Grafikk-bienniale, Fredrikstad, Norway 1980, Praemium Imperiale 2003. *Address:* c/o Karsten Schubert, 47 Lexington Street, London, W1R 3LG, England (office). *Telephone:* (20) 7734-9002 (office). *Fax:* (20) 7734-9008 (office). *E-mail:* mail@karstenschubert.com (office). *Website:* www.karstenschubert.com (office).

RILEY, Richard Wilson, LLB; American lawyer and fmr politician; *Partner, Nelson Mullins Riley & Scarborough LLP;* b. 2 Jan. 1933, Greenville, South Carolina; s. of E. P. Riley and Martha Dixon Riley; m. Ann Yarborough 1957; three s. one d.; ed Greenville Sr High School, Furman Univ. and SC School of Law; Lt in USN Legal Counsel to US Senate Cttee of Olin D. Johnston 1960; with family law firm 1961–62; mem. SC House of Reps 1962–66, S Carolina Senate 1966–76; S Carolina State Chair. for Jimmy Carter's Presidential Election Campaign 1976; Gov. of S Carolina 1979–87; Personnel Dir for Pres. Bill Clinton's Transition Team 1991–92; US Sec. of Educ. 1993–2001; Pnr, Nelson, Mullins, Riley & Scarborough LLP (law firm) 1987–93, 2001–; mem. Bd of Trustees, Carnegie Corpn of NY; mem. Bd ACT Inc., Knowledge Works Foundation, Furman Univ.; Distinguished Visiting Prof., Univ. of S Carolina 2001–, Distinguished Prof. of Govt, Politics, and Public Leadership, Richard W. Riley Inst., Furman Univ. *Address:* Nelson, Mullins, Riley & Scarborough, Suite 900, Poinsett Plaza, 104 South Main Street, Greenville, SC 29601-2122, USA (office). *Telephone:* (864) 250-2290 (office). *Fax:* (864) 232-2925 (office). *Website:* www.nelsonmullins.com (office).

RILEY, Robert Renfroe (Bob), BBA; American politician, real estate executive and fmr state governor; b. 3 Oct. 1944, Ashland, Clay Co., Ala; m. Patsy Adams; one s. three d. (one deceased); ed Clay Co. High School, Univ. of Alabama; fmr propr of poultry and egg business, automobile dealership, trucking co. grocery story and pharmacy; mem. Ashland City Council 1972–76; mem. from 3rd Alabama Dist, US House of Reps 1997–2002, Asst Whip, House-Senate conferee on FY 1998 Defense Authorization Bill 1997; Gov. of Ala 2003–11; fmr Chair. Finance Cttee, Clay Co. Hosp.; Pres. Alabama State Bd of Educ.; men's Sunday school teacher, First Baptist Church; Republican; named Public Official of Year by Governing magazine 2003, Eagle Award, US Distance Learning Asscn 2010. *Address:* c/o Office of the Governor, State Capitol, 600 Dexter Avenue, Suite N104, Montgomery, AL 36130-2751; c/o Bob Riley For Governor, PO Box 59708, Birmingham, AL 35209, USA. *Website:* www.bobrileyforgovernor.com.

RILEY, Terence; American museum curator; ed Univ. of Notre Dame and Columbia Univ., New York; f. architectural practice with John Keenen, Keenen/ Riley Architects; curator of 'Paul Nelson Filter of Reason' inaugural exhbn at Arthur Ross Architectural Galleries, Columbia Univ. 1989, Dir –1991; directed exhbns on work of Iacov Chernikhov and restaging of Museum of Modern Art's (MoMA) first exhbn on architecture: 'Exhibition 15: The International Style and The Museum of Modern Art', New York; adjunct faculty mem. 1987–; joined MoMA 1991, Chief Curator of Architecture and Design 1992–2006, organized exhbns on the works of, amongst others, Frank Lloyd Wright, Rem Koolhaas 1994, Bernard Tschumi, Mies van der Rohe 2001; Instructor, Harvard Design School 2001–; Dir Miami Art Museum 2006–09, consultant 2009–10; Chief Curator, Shenzhen and Hong Kong Biennale of Urbanism/Architecture 2011. *Publications include:* The Un-Private House (jtly with Glenn D. Lowry) 2002, MoMA QNS Box Set 2002; The Changing of the Avant-garde (Ed.) 2002. *Address:* Keenen/Riley Architects, 526 West 26th Street, 9A, New York, NY 10001, USA (office). *Telephone:* (212) 645-9210 (office). *Fax:* (212) 645-9211 (office). *E-mail:* jk@krnyc.com (office). *Website:* www.krnyc.com (office).

RIM, Choe-yong, BE; North Korean politician; *Premier;* b. 20 Nov. 1930, Ryanggang; one s. one d.; ed Kim Il-sung Univ., Univ. Lomonosov and Moscow State Univ.; served in various positions in Cen. Cttee of the Workers' Party of Korea including Instructor, Section Chief, Vice-Dept Dir and Dept Dir; Dir Chief Public Prosecutor's Office 1998–2003; mem. Kim Jong-il's Special Operations Command Group 2004; Sec. Gen. Presidium of Supreme People's Ass. 2005–10; Chief Sec., Pyongyang City Cttee of the Workers' Party of Korea 2010–; Premier of North Korea 2010–; Chair. Gen. Defence Comm. *Address:* Supreme People's Assembly (Choe Ko In Min Hoe Ui), Pyongyang, North Korea (office).

RIMAWI, Fahid Nimer ar-, BA; Jordanian journalist; *Publisher and Editor-in-Chief, Al Majd;* b. 1942, Palestine; m.; two s. five d.; ed Cairo Univ., Egypt; Ed. Difa (newspaper) 1965–67; Ed.-in-Chief, Jordan News Agency 1968–70; Sec. Editorial Bd, Afkar (magazine) 1970–73; Dir Investigating Dept, Al-Raiue (newspaper) 1975–76, Political Writer 1981–85; writer, Al-Destour (newspaper) 1978–81; Corresp., al Talie'ah (magazine) Paris 1982–85; political writer 1985–94; Publr and Ed.-in-Chief, Al Majd (weekly). *Publications:* Mawaweel Fi al Layl Al Taweel, short stories in Arabic 1982. *Address:* PO Box 926856, Amman 11190 (office), Dahiyat al-Rashid, Amman, Jordan. *Telephone:* (6) 5530553 (office); (6) 5160615 (home). *Fax:* (6) 553 0352. *E-mail:* almajd@almajd.net (office). *Website:* almajd.net (office).

RIMINGTON, Dame Stella, DCB, MA; British author and fmr civil servant; b. (Stella Whitehouse), 1935, London; m. John Rimington 1963; two d.; ed Nottingham High School for Girls, Univs of Edinburgh and Liverpool (Diploma Archive Admin); joined Security Service (MI5) 1969 after working part-time in New Delhi office, numerous positions and responsibilities including recruitment 1986–88, Dir counter espionage 1988–91, Dir counter terrorism 1991–92, Deputy Dir-Gen. 1992–96, Dir-Gen. 1992–96; Dir (non-exec.) Marks and Spencer 1997–2004, BG PLC 1997–2000, BG Group 2000–05, GKR Group (now Whitehead Mann) 1997–2001; Chair. Inst. of Cancer Research 1997–2001; Trustee, Royal Marsden Hosp. 1997–2001, Refuge (charity), Int. Spy Museum, Washington, DC, USA; Gov. St Felix School, Southwold 1998–2002, Town Close House Preparatory School, Norwich 1999–2005; Hon. Air Cdre 7006 (VR) Squadron Royal Auxiliary Air Force 1997–2001; Dame Commdr of the Bath 1996; Hon. LLD (Nottingham) 1995, (Exeter) 1996, (London Metropolitan) 2004, (Liverpool) 2006, Hon. DSocS (Nottingham Trent) 2009; Spirit of Everywoman Award 2007. *Publications*

include: Intelligence, Security and the Law (non-fiction) 1994, Open Secret (autobiog.) 2001; novels: At Risk 2004, Secret Asset 2006, Illegal Action 2007, Dead Line 2008, Present Danger 2009, Geneva Trap 2012. *Address:* PO Box 1604, London, SW1P 1XB, England. *Website:* www.stellarimington.com.

RIMŠĒVIČS, Ilmārs, BA, MBA; Latvian economist and central banker; *Governor, Bank of Latvia;* b. 30 April 1965, Rīga; ed Rīga High School No. 6, Rīga Tech. Univ., St Lawrence Univ. and Clarkson Univ., USA; Deputy Chair. Econs Cttee, Popular Front of Latvia 1989–90; Man. Foreign Operations Dept and Head of Securities Dept, Latvijas Zemes banka 1990–92; Deputy Gov. Bank of Latvia 1992–2001, Chair. Bd 1992–2001, Gov. 2001–. *Address:* Bank of Latvia (Latvijas Banka), K. Valdemāra iela 2A, Rīga 1050, Latvia (office). *Telephone:* 6702-2300 (office). *Fax:* 6702-2420 (office). *E-mail:* info@bank.lv (office). *Website:* www.bank.lv (office).

RINDLER, Wolfgang, PhD; British physicist and academic; *Professor of Physics, University of Texas at Dallas;* b. 18 May 1924, Vienna; s. of Dr Ernst Rindler; m. 1st Phyllis Berla 1959 (died 1966); m. 2nd Linda Veret 1977; two s. one d.; ed Ruthin Grammar School, Liverpool Univ., Imperial Coll., London; Asst Lecturer, Univ. of Liverpool 1947–49; Lecturer, Sir John Cass Coll., London 1949–56; Asst Prof., Cornell Univ., USA 1956–63; Assoc. and Full Prof., Southwest Center for Advanced Studies, Dallas, Tex. 1963–69, Prof. of Physics, Univ. of Texas at Dallas 1969–; Visiting Prof., Univ. of Vienna, Univ. of Rome, Max-Planck Inst. at Munich and Potsdam, King's Coll. London; Visiting Fellow, Churchill Coll., Cambridge 1990; mem. Foreign Editorial Bd Rendiconti di Matematica 1984–; Assoc. Ed. American Journal of Physics 1988–91; Foreign mem. Acad. of Sciences of Turin, Italy 2000; Hon. mem. Austrian Acad. of Sciences 2002; Gold Medal of Honour, City of Vienna 1996. *Publications:* Special Relativity 1960, Essential Relativity 1969, Introduction to Special Relativity 1982, Spinors and Space-Time (with R. Penrose) Vol. I 1984, Vol. II 1986, Relativity: Special, General, and Cosmological 2001; numerous research and encyclopedia articles on special and gen. relativity and cosmology. *Address:* Physics Department, University of Texas at Dallas, Richardson, TX 75080-3021 (office); 7110 Spring Valley Road, Dallas, TX 75254, USA (home). *Telephone:* (972) 883-2880 (office); (972) 387-9768 (home). *E-mail:* rindler@utdallas.edu (office). *Website:* www.utdallas.edu/dept/physics (office).

RINEHART, Georgina (Gina) Hope; Australian business executive; *Chairman, Hancock Prospecting Pty Ltd;* b. 9 Feb. 1954, Perth, WA; d. of Lang Hancock; m. 1st (divorced), two c.; m. 2nd Francis Rinehart (deceased), two c.; ed Univ. of Sydney; joined Hancock Group as personal asst to her father 1973, Exec. Chair. Hancock Prospecting Pty Ltd and Hancock Prospecting Pty Ltd Group 1992–; ranked by Forbes magazine amongst The 100 Most Powerful Women in the World (84th) 2007, (98th) 2008, (19th) 2011, (35th) 2012, (16th) 2013. *Address:* Hancock Prospecting Pty Ltd, 28–42 Ventnor Avenue, West Perth 6005, WA, Australia (office). *Telephone:* (8) 9429-8222 (office). *Fax:* (8) 9429-8268 (office). *E-mail:* mail@hancockprospecting.com.au (office). *Website:* www.hancockprospecting.com.au (office).

RINGEL, Johannes; German banking executive; b. 1941, Breslau; ed Volks-wirtschafts-Studium; joined WestLB (Westdeutsche Landesbank Girozentrale) 1969, Dir Dept of Planning 1974–84, Dir Cen. Control Bureau 1984–87, mem. Exec. Cttee 1987–03, CEO WestLB 2002–04; mem. Exec. Bd Steag AG 2001–. *Address:* c/o WestLB, Herzogstrasse 15, 40217 Düsseldorf, Germany (office).

RINGHOLM, Bosse; Swedish politician; *Chairman, Stockholm Branch, Social Democratic Party;* b. 18 Aug. 1942, Kalköping; m. Kerstin Pehrsson; three c.; Chair. Social Democratic Youth 1967–72; Political Adviser, Ministries of Interior and Labour 1973–76; mem. Stockholm Co. Council 1973–97; Alt. mem./mem. Riksdag 1976, 1982; Dir Ministry of Educ. and Science 1976–82; Lead Co. Councillor for Transport 1983–85, for Finance 1989–91, 1994–97, Opposition Lead Co. Councillor 1986–88, 1991–94; Dir Gen. Nat. Labour Market Bd 1997–99; Minister for Finance 1999–2004; Deputy Prime Minister 2004–06, temp. Minister of Foreign Affairs March 2006; mem. Exec. Cttee Social Democratic Party (Sveriges Socialdemokratiska Arbetareparti—SAP), Chair. Stockholm Br., Social Democratic Party 2001–. *Address:* Sveriges Socialdemokratiska Arbetareparti, Sveavägen 68, 105 60 Stockholm (office); Källv. 33, 122 62, Enskede, Sweden (home). *Telephone:* (8) 786-40-00 (office); (8) 649-00-26 (home). *Fax:* (8) 204257 (office). *E-mail:* info@sap.se (office). *Website:* www.socialdemokraterna.se (office).

RINGIER, Michael; Swiss publishing and media executive; *Chairman, Ringier AG;* b. 30 March 1949, Zofingen; s. of Hans Ringier and Eva Ringier (née Landolt); ed Hochschule St Gallen; est. himself professionally outside of family-owned firm Ringier working as a journalist, travelled to Germany to work for Grüner + Jahr and H. Bauer; joined Ringier 1985 working with brother, Christoph, becoming CEO 1985, two brothers were Co-Chair. –1991, Pres. Bd of Dirs 1991–97, took over operational man. of Ringier AG as mem. Bd of Dirs 1997–2000, COO Ringier AG 2000–03, Chair. Ringier Holding AG (largest media corpn in Switzerland) 2003–, Chair. Publishing Cttee. *Address:* Ringier AG, Dufourstrasse 23, 8008 Zürich, Switzerland (office). *Telephone:* (44) 259-61-11 (office). *Fax:* (44) 259-86-35 (office). *E-mail:* info@ringier.ch (office). *Website:* www.ringier.com (office).

RINI, Snyder; Solomon Islands politician; b. 27 July 1948; ed Univ. of Papua New Guinea, Univ. of Technology, Lae, Papua New Guinea; Financial Controller, Brewer Solomons Agriculture Ltd. 1975–80; Perm. Sec. for Ministry of Natural Resources 1989, for Ministry of Nat. Planning and Devt 1994–95, for Ministry of Agric. and Fisheries 1997; mem. Parl. for Marovo, Western Prov. 1997–; Minister for Finance and Treasury 2000–01, Deputy Prime Minister for Nat. Planning and Devt 2001–02, Deputy Prime Minister and Minister for Finance and Treasury 2002–03, Deputy Prime Minister and Minister for Educ. and Human Resources Devt 2003–06, Prime Minister April–May 2006 (resgnd), Minister of Finance and Treasury 2007–10 (resgnd); mem. Bd of Dirs Devt Bank of Solomon Islands 1976–84, Central Bank of Solomon Islands 1982–84, 1990–96, Solomon Islands Port Authority 1982–84, Nat. Provident Fund 1976–86 (Chair. 1990–96), Solomon Islands Electricity Authority 1988–89. *Address:* c/o Ministry of Finance and Treasury, POB 26, Honiara, Solomon Islands (office).

RINKĒVIČS, Edgars, BA, MSc; Latvian politician; *Minister of Foreign Affairs;* b. 21 Sept. 1973, Jūrmala; ed Univ. of Latvia, Univ. of Groningen, Industrial Coll. of the Armed Forces /Nat. Defense Univ., Washington, DC, USA; early career as journalist covering foreign policy and int. relations for Latvian Radio 1993–94; Sr Desk Officer, Defence Policy Dept, Ministry of Defence 1995–96, Dir March–Sept. 1996, Acting Sec. of State 2005–08, Sec. of State 1997–2008, Head of Chancery of Pres. 2008–11; Deputy Head, Latvian Del. to negotiations on accession to NATO 2002–03; Minister of Foreign Affairs 2011–; mem. Latvian Way 1998–2004, Zatlers Reform Party 2012–; Commdr, Great Cross of the Order of Viesturs 2004, Commdr, Order of Merit of the Repub. of Poland 2005, Order of Merit of the Italian Repub. 2005, Order of Merit of Estonia 2005, Kt, Order of Orange-Nassau (Netherlands) 2006, Grand Officer, Order of Three Stars 2007; Minister of Defence Award – Medal of Hon. Merit for Contrib. to Armed Forces Devt 2000, Minister of Defence Award – Commemorative Medal for Advancing Latvia's Accession to NATO 2004, NATO Award for Meritorious Service 2007. *Address:* Ministry of Foreign Affairs, K. Valdemāra iela 3, Riga 1395, Latvia (office). *Telephone:* 6701-6201 (office). *Fax:* 6782-8121 (office). *E-mail:* mfa.cha@mfa.gov.lv (office). *Website:* www.mfa.gov.lv (office).

RINNE, Risto, MEng; Finnish petroleum industry executive; b. 1949; with Fortum Corpn (later Neste Oil Oyj) 1975, Pres. Neste Oyj Finland 1999–2004, Pres. Oil Sector Finland 2004, Pres., CEO and Chair. Exec. Team Neste Oil Oyj 2004–08; Chair. Bd of Dirs Chemicals Industry Fed. Finland, Finnish Oil and Gas Fed.; mem. Bd of Dirs European Petroleum Industry Asscn (EUROPIA).

RINNERT, Jan; German business executive; *Chairman of the Board of Management, Heraeus Holding GmbH;* b. 1968, Oldenburg/Holstein; worked for State Govt of Bremen as Sr Political Advisor to Senator of Econ. Affairs; moved to pvt. sector, gaining professional experience as man. consultant at leading int. man. consulting firm; Man. Dir Titan-Aluminium-Feinguß GmbH, Bestwig 2002–04; Man. Dir Heraeus Kulzer GmbH 2004–07, mem. Bd of Man., Heraeus Holding GmbH and Chief Financial Officer 2007–10, Vice-Chair. Bd of Man. 2010–13, Chair. 2013–, also Labour Dir. *Address:* Heraeus Holding GmbH, Postfach 1561, 63405 Hanau (office); Heraeus Holding GmbH, Heraeusstrasse 12–14, 63450 Hanau, Germany (office). *Telephone:* (6181) 35-0 (office). *Fax:* (6181) 35-35-50 (office). *E-mail:* pr@heraeus.com (office). *Website:* www.heraeus.com (office).

RINPOCHE, Samdhong; Tibetan academic and politician; *Chief Minister of Tibetan Government in Exile;* b. (Lobsang Tenzin), 5 Nov. 1939, Nagdug, Tibet; ed monastic studies, Univ. of Drepung, Tibet (rehoused in India after Chinese occupation), Monastery of Gyuto, Dalhousie, India; various positions in Tibetan colls in Simla, Darjeeling and Dalhousie, India; Vice-Pres. Congress of Tibetan Youth 1970–73; Prof. Cen. Inst. of Higher Tibetan Studies, Benares (now Varanasi), India 1971–2001, apptd Dir 1988; mem. Standing Cttee Asscn of Indian Univs 1994–, Pres. 1998–; fmr Pres. Tibetan Parl. in Exile; elected Kalon Tripa (Chief Minister) of Tibetan Govt in Exile 2001; Vice-Pres. Library of Tibetan Works and Files, Dharamsala, India; Adviser World Peace Univ., USA; mem. Cttee for Charter of Tibetans in Exile and Future Constitution of Tibet; mem. Bd of Dirs Tibetan Schools, New Delhi, India; mem. Bd of Dirs Asiatic Soc., Calcutta; mem. Bd of Dirs Foundation for Universal Responsibility, New Delhi; mem. Directorate of Indian Council for Philosophical Research; mem. Directorate Krishnamurti Foundation, India; advisory mem. Inst. of Asian Democracy, NY, USA. *Publications include:* numerous academic essays and newspaper articles. *Address:* Kashag Secretariat, Central Tibetan Administration, Dharamsala 176215, Dist Kangra, H.P., India (office). *Telephone:* (18) 92222218 (office). *Fax:* (18) 92224914 (office). *E-mail:* kadrung@gov.tibet.net (home). *Website:* www.tibet.net (office).

RINTZLER, Marius Adrian; German singer; b. 14 March 1932, Bucharest, Romania; m. Sanda Dragomir 1964; ed Acad. of Music, Bucharest; soloist with Bucharest Philharmonic 1959; debut in opera in Bucharest as Don Basilio in Il Barbiere di Siviglia 1964; went to Germany 1966; leading bass at Düsseldorf's Deutsche Oper am Rhein 1968–; guest singer with major opera cos, including Metropolitan, San Francisco, Glyndebourne, Paris, Brussels, Munich; repertoire includes various roles in Richard Strauss' Rosenkavalier (Ochs), Capriccio (La Roche), Schweigsame Frau (Morosus), in Rossini's La Cenerentola (Don Magnifico), Il Barbiere (Bartolo), in Richard Wagner's Ring (Alberich), in Mozart's Don Giovanni (Leporello), Die Entführung (Osmin); appears with major symphony orchestras in Europe and USA, including Philharmonia (London), Berlin Philharmonic, Cleveland Symphony; also gives recitals, TV appearances in England, Germany and France; Kammersänger. *Address:* Friedingstrasse 18, 40625 Düsseldorf, Germany (home). *Telephone:* (211) 297083 (home).

RIO, Neiphiu, BA; Indian politician; *Chief Minister of Nagaland;* b. 11 Nov. 1950, Tuophema village, Kohima Dist; s. of the late Guolhoulie Rio; m.; one s. five d.; ed St Joseph's Coll., Darjeeling and Kohima Arts Coll.; mem. Nagaland Legis. Ass. 1989–2002, 2004–; State Minister of Sports and School Educ. 1989–91, of Higher and Tech. Educ., Arts and Culture 1991–93, of Works and Housing 1993–98, of Home Affairs 1998–2002; Chair. Nagaland Industrial Devt Corpn (NIDC), Nat. Khadi and Village Industries Bd (NKVIB), Devt Authority of Nagaland; Chief Minister of Nagaland 2003–; Leader Democratic Alliance of Nagaland 2004–; Hon. Vice-Pres. Indian Red Cross Soc. *Leisure interests* games, sports, reading, music. *Address:* Office of the Chief Minister, Government of Nagaland, Civil Secretariat, Kohima 797 001, India (office). *Telephone:* (370) 2270097 (office); (370) 2241734 (home). *Fax:* (370) 2243163.

RIORDAN, Richard, BA, JD; American business executive, lawyer and fmr politician; *Of Counsel, Bingham McCutchen LLP;* b. 1930, Flushing, NY; m. 1st Eugenia Riordan; six c. (two deceased); m. 2nd Jill Riordan; ed Univ. of Calif., Santa Clara, Princeton Univ., Univ. of Mich. Law School; served in US Army in Korean War; after law school f. Riordan and McKinzie (law firm); Mayor of LA 1993–2001; Co-founder LEARN 1991; f. Riordan Foundation; Sec. for Educ. for Calif. 2003–05; Of Counsel, Bingham, McCutchen LLP 2005–; mem. Republican Party; Business Person of the Year, Los Angeles Business Journal 2005. *Address:* Bingham McCutchen LLP, 355 South Grand Avenue, Los Angeles, CA 90071-3106, USA (office). *Telephone:* (213) 680-6400 (office). *Fax:* (213) 680-6499 (office). *E-mail:* richard.riordan@bingham.com (office). *Website:* www.bingham.com (office).

RÍOS MONTT, Gen. Efraín; Guatemalan politician and army officer (retd); b. 1927; joined army 1943; defence posting, Washington, DC 1973; contested presidential election for Christian Democratic coalition 1974; Mil. Attaché, Madrid; fmr Commdr Honour Guard Brigade; Dir Mil. Acad.; installed as leader of mil. junta after coup March 1982; Minister of Nat. Defence March–Sept. 1982; Pres. of Guatemala, also C-in-C of the Army 1982–83; overthrown Aug. 1983; Sec.-Gen. Frente Republicano Guatemalteco (FRG) 1988; Pres. of Guatemalan Congress 1995–96, 2001–03; unsuccessful presidential cand. (FRG) 2003; mem. Parl. (FRG) 2007–12; indicted for genocide and crimes against humanity 2012, convicted and sentenced to 80 years in prison May 2013, conviction soon overturned by Constitutional Court and proceedings ordered to return to trial phase.

RIPA DI MEANA, Carlo; Italian politician and journalist; b. 15 Aug. 1929, Marina di Pietrasanta, Lucca; m. 1st Gae Aulenti (divorced); m. 2nd Marina Punturieri; journalist on Il Lavoro (weekly journal of the Confederazione Generale Italiana del Lavoro) and on L'Unità (Italian daily) 1950–53; co-f. and ran weekly Nuova Generazione 1953–56; co-f. and Ed. magazine Passato e Presente 1957; publisher's ed. for Feltrinelli and Rizzoli 1958–66; resgnd from Italian CP 1957, joined Italian Socialist Party (PSI) 1958; Sec.-Gen. Club Turati, Milan 1967–76; Regional Councillor, Lombardy, Leader, Socialist Party group in the Council 1970–82; mem. Bd La Scala Theatre, Milan 1970–74; Chair. Venice Biennale 1974–79; head of int. relations, Italian Socialist Party 1979–80; MEP 1979–84, –1999; Comm. of the European Communities (responsible for Citizen's Europe, information, culture and tourism) 1985–89, (responsible for communication) 1986–89, (responsible for environment, nuclear safety and civil protection) 1989–93; Minister for the Environment 1992–93, leader Green Party 1993–98 (left PSI); Pres. Italia Nostra (environmental org.) 2005–07; apptd Chair. Istituto per la Cooperazione economica internazionale e i problemi dello sviluppo 1983. *Publications:* Un viaggio in Viet Nam 1956, Dedicato a Raymond Roussel e alle sue impressioni d'Africa 1965, Il governo audiovisivo 1973. *Address:* c/o Italia Nostra, Via Sicilia 66, 00187 Rome, Italy.

RIPKEN, Calvin (Cal) Edward, Jr; American business executive and fmr professional baseball player; b. 24 Aug. 1960, Havre de Grace, Md; s. of the late Cal Ripken Sr; m. Kelly Ripken; one s. one d.; ed Aberdeen High School, Md; player minor league teams in Bluefield, Miami, Charlotte, Rochester 1978–81; shortstop Baltimore Orioles 1978–2001; highest single season fielding percentage 1990; maj. league record for consecutive games played (breaking Lou Gehrig's record of 2,130 in 1995), 2,632 ending in 1998; 4,000 home runs, 3,000 hits (2000); retd 2001; purchased Utica Blue Sox Class A minor league team 2002, renamed to Aberdeen IronBirds (affiliate of Baltimore Orioles); f. The Kelly and Cal Ripken, Jr Foundation (now Cal Ripkin Sr Foundation) 1992; currently Pres. and CEO Ripken Baseball Inc., also Pres. and CEO Ripken Baseball Group; mem. Bd of Dirs ZeniMax Media Inc.; Dr hc (Delaware) 2008, (Maryland) 2013; Rookie of the Year, Int. League 1981, Rookie of the Year, Baseball Writers Asscn, American League 1982, Silver Slugger Award 1983–86, 1989, 1991, 1993–94, Golden Glove Award 1991–92, Sportsman of the Year, Sports Illustrated 1995; elected to Baseball Hall of Fame 2007. *Publications:* Play Baseball The Ripken Way (with Bill Ripken) 2004, Parenting Young Athletes the Ripken Way 2006. *Address:* Ripken Baseball, 1427 Clarkview Road, Suite 100, Baltimore, MD 21209, USA (office). *Telephone:* (410) 823-0808 (office). *Fax:* (410) 823-0850 (office). *Website:* www.ripkenbaseball .com (office).

RIPPON, Angela, OBE; British broadcaster and journalist; b. 12 Oct. 1944, Plymouth, Devon; d. of John Rippon and Edna Rippon; m. Christopher Dare 1967 (divorced); ed Plymouth Selective School for Girls; Presenter and Reporter, BBC TV Plymouth 1966–69; Ed., Producer, Dir and Presenter, Westward TV (ITV) 1969–73; Reporter, BBC TV Nat. News 1973–75, Newsreader 1975–81; Founder and Presenter TV-am Feb.–April 1983; Arts Corresp. for WNETV (CBS), Boston, 1983; Reporter and Presenter BBC and ITV 1984–; Vice-Pres. Int. Club for Women in TV 1979–, British Red Cross, NCH Action for Children, Riding for the Disabled Asscn; Dir Nirex 1986–89; Chair. English Nat. Ballet 2000–04; Amb. Altzheimer's Soc.; Dr hc (American Int. Univ.) 1994, Hon. Dr of Arts (Plymouth) 2012; New York Film Festival Silver Medal 1973, Newsreader of the Year (TV and Radio Industries Club) 1975, 1976, 1977, TV Personality of the Year 1977, Emmy Award 1984 (Channel 7 Boston), Sony Radio Award 1990, New York Radio Silver Medal 1992, Royal TV Soc. Hall of Fame 1996, European Woman of Achievement 2002 and other awards. *Dance:* National Tour 'Anything Goes' 2007. *Musical:* Side by Side with Sondheim 2008. *Radio series include:* Angela Rippon's Morning Report for LBC 1992, Angela Rippon's Drive Time Show, LBC 1993, The Health Show (BBC Radio 4), Friday Night with Angela Rippon (BBC Radio 2), LBC Arts Programme 2003–05. *TV appearances include:* Angela Rippon Meets (documentary), Antiques Roadshow, In the Country, Compere, Eurovision Song Contest 1976, The Morecambe and Wise Christmas Show 1976, 1977, Top Gear 1977–79, Royal Wedding 1981, Masterteam (BBC) 1985, 1986, 1987, Come Dancing 1988–91, What's My Line? 1988–90, Healthcheck, Holiday Programme, Simply Money (Family Finance Channel) 2001–02, Channel 5 News 2003–04, Live with Angela Rippon (ITV) 2004–06, Sun, Sea & Bargain Spotting, Cash in the Attic, Rip Off Britain, Holiday Hit Squad 2013. *Publications:* Riding 1980, In the Country 1980, Mark Phillips – The Man and his Horses 1982, Victoria Plum (eight children's books) 1983, Angela Rippon's West Country 1982, Badminton: A Celebration 1987, Fabulous at 50 – And Beyond 2005. *Leisure interests:* cooking, tennis, reading, theatre. *Address:* c/o Knight Ayton Management, 35 Great James Street, London, WC1N 3HB, England (office). *Telephone:* (20) 7836-5333 (office). *Fax:* (20) 7836-8333 (office). *E-mail:* info@knightayton.co.uk (office). *Website:* www.knightayton .co.uk (office).

RISBY, Baron (Life Peer), cr. 2010, of Haverhill in the County of Suffolk; **Richard John Grenville Spring,** MA; British politician and business executive; b. 24 Sept. 1946, Cape Town, South Africa; m. Hon. Jane Henniker-Major 1979 (divorced 1993); two c.; ed Rondebosch Boys' High School, Cape, Univ. of Cape Town, Magdalene Coll., Cambridge; began career at Merrill Lynch and spent 15 years before becoming a Vice-Pres.; joined E.F. Hutton International Associates as Jt Man. Dir 1986 (taken over by Lehman Brothers), Exec. Dir, ran US equities Div.; Man. Dir Furman Selz (Xerox subsidiary), with responsibility for European operations –1992; fmr Chair. Westminster Conservative Political Centre; unsuccessful Parl. cand. for Ashton-under-Lyne in Gen. Election 1983; MP (Conservative) for Bury St Edmunds 1992–97, for West Suffolk 1997–2010; Parl. Pvt. Sec. to Sir Patrick Mayhew 1994–95, to defence ministers 1996–97, to Tim Eggar 1996–2005; Opposition Spokesman on Culture, Media and Sport 1998–2000, for

Foreign and Commonwealth Affairs, with responsibility for Europe and the Middle East 2000–04; Shadow Minister for the Treasury 2004–05; Vice-Chair. Conservative Party 2005–10, responsible for business links in the City of London and Co-Chair. Conservative City Circle; mem. (Conservative), House of Lords 2010–; Vice-Chair. All-Party Parl. Group for East Asian Business 2011–; announced as one of nine prime ministerial trade envoys, with responsibility for Algeria 2012; Chair. British Ukrainian Soc. 2007–; Dir British Syrian Soc. 2003–11; Patron City Future. *Address:* House of Lords, Westminster, London, SW1A 0PW, England (office). *Telephone:* (20) 7219-8996 (office). *E-mail:* risbyr@parliament.uk (office). *Website:* www.parliament.uk/biographies/lords/lord-risby/139 (office).

RISCH, James (Jim) Elroy, BS, JD; American politician, lawyer and rancher; *Senator from Idaho;* b. 3 May 1943, Milwaukee, Wis.; s. of Elroy A. Risch and Helen B. Risch (née Levi); m. Vicki Risch 1968; three s.; ed Univ. of Wisconsin-Milwaukee, Univ. of Idaho and Univ. of Idaho Coll. of Law; began career in public service as Ada Co. Prosecuting Attorney 1970; Pres. Idaho Prosecuting Attorneys Asscn –1975; served on Law Review and Coll. of Law Advisory Cttee, Univ. of Idaho; taught criminal law at Boise State Univ.; mem. Idaho Senate 1975–88, 1995–2002, Majority Leader, Pres. pro tempore 1982–88; Lt Gov. of Idaho 2003–06, 2007–09; Gov. of Idaho 2006–07; small business owner, rancher/farmer and Sr Partner, Risch Goss Insinger Gustavel (law firm) –2008; Senator from Idaho 2009–, mem. Energy and Natural Resources Cttee, Select Cttee on Intelligence, Small Business and Entrepreneurship Cttee, Cttee on Foreign Relations, Select Cttee on Ethics; Republican. *Address:* 483 Russell Senate Office Building, Washington, DC 20510, USA (office). *Telephone:* (202) 224-2752 (office). *Fax:* (202) 224-2573 (office). *Website:* risch.senate.gov (office).

RISDAHL JENSEN, Tom; Danish diplomatist; b. 28 Sept. 1947, Hjørring; m. Helle Bundgaard; Amb. to UK 2001–06, to Sweden 2006–10, to Russia 2010–13; Commdr, Order of the Dannebrog 2005. *Address:* c/o Royal Danish Embassy, 119034 Moscow, Prechistensky Per. 9, Russian Federation (office).

RISHTON, John; British business executive; *Chief Executive, Rolls Royce Group Plc;* b. 21 Feb. 1958; ed Univ. of Nottingham; worked for Ford Motor Co. in various exec. positions, qualified as an accountant and later became Finance Dir of co.'s Portuguese and Spanish operations; joined British Airways Plc as Head of Finance for US Div. 1994, Chief Financial Officer 2001–05; Exec. Vice-Pres. and Chief Financial Officer Royal Ahold NV 2006–07, mem. Corp. Exec. Bd 2006–, Acting Pres. and CEO July–Nov. 2007–, Pres. and CEO Nov. 2007–11; Dir (non-exec.) Rolls Royce Group Plc 2007–, Chief Exec. 2011–; fmr Dir (non-exec.) Allied Domecq. *Address:* Rolls-Royce Plc, 65 Buckingham Gate, London, SW1E 6AT, England (office). *Telephone:* (20) 7222-9020 (office). *Fax:* (20) 7227-9178 (office). *E-mail:* info@rolls-royce.com (office). *Website:* www.rolls-royce.com (office).

RISSEEUW, A. H. J. (Ton), MSc; Dutch business executive; *Chairman of the Supervisory Board, Koninklijke KPN NV;* b. 9 Nov. 1936; Founder and Chair. Exec. Bd Getronics NV 1976–99; Chair. Supervisory Bd Koninklijke KPN NV 2001–, Groeneveld Groep BV, Intergamma BV; mem. Supervisory Bd Heineken Nederlands Beheer BV –2000, Heineken NV 2000–07, Samas-Groep NV 1999–2006, TNO 1997–2007, Blokker Holding BV; mem. Bd of Dirs Stichting ING Aandeeln (ING Trust Office) 2002–06, Chair. 2005–06; mem. Advisory Council Deloitte Netherlands. *Address:* Koninklijke KPN NV, Maanplein 5, 2516 CK The Hague, Netherlands (office). *Website:* www.kpn.com (office).

RISTE, Olav, DPhil (Oxon.); Norwegian historian and academic; *Professor Emeritus and Senior Consultant, Norwegian Institute for Defence Studies;* b. 11 April 1933, Volda; s. of Olav Riste and Bergliot Meidell; m. Ruth Pittman 1964; ed Univ. of Oslo, Univ. of Oxford, UK; Lecturer, Volda Gymnas 1963–64; Historian, Office of Mil. History (with leaves of absence) 1964–79, Dir 1979–80; Research Fellow, Charles Warren Center, Harvard Univ. 1967–68; Visiting Scholar, LSE 1971, 1986; Visiting Prof., Freie Univ., Berlin, Germany 1972–73; Dir Research Centre for Defence History (with leaves of absence) 1980–87; Adjunct Prof. of History, Univ. of Bergen 1980–2003, Univ. of Oslo 1998–2003; Guest Scholar, Woodrow Wilson Center, Washington, DC, USA 1982; Dir Norwegian Inst. for Defence Studies 1988–95, Research Dir 1996–2003, Prof. Emer. and Sr Consultant 2003–; Fellow, Norwegian Acad. of Science and Letters 1984; Kt (First Class), Royal Order of St Olav 2003, Defence Medal with Three Stars. *Publications include:* The Neutral Ally 1965, Norway and the Second World War (ed.) 1966, Norway 1940–45: The Resistance Movement 1970, London-regjeringa: Norge i krigsalliansen 1940–45 I-II 1973–79, Western Security: The Formative Years (ed.) 1985, Norge i Krig: Utefront 1987, Otto Ruge: Felttoget (ed.) 1989, Fredsgeneralen (ed.) 1995, 'Strengt hemmelig.' Norsk etterretningsteneste 1945–70 (with A. Moland) 1997, The Norwegian Intelligence Service 1945–1970 1999, Norway's Foreign Relations: A History 2001 (revised edn 2003). *Leisure interests:* classical music, skiing. *Address:* Husarveien 18, 1396 Billingstad, Norway. *Telephone:* 66-84-63-05; 9-2250280 (mobile). *E-mail:* olavr2010@hotmail.no.

RITBLAT, Sir John Henry, Kt, FSVA, FRICS, FRSA; British business executive; *Chairman, European Real Estate Private Equity Advisory Council;* b. 3 Oct. 1935; m. 1st Isabel Paja 1960 (died 1979); two s. one d.; m. 2nd Jill Rosemary Zilkha (née Slotover) 1986; ed Dulwich Coll., Coll. of Estate Management, Univ. of London; Chair. The British Land Co. PLC 1970 (Man. Dir 1971–2004), Chair. and Chief Exec. The British Land Corpn 1991–2006, Hon. Pres. 2006–; Chair. European Real Estate Pvt. Equity Advisory Council, Lehman Brothers 2006–; Founder and Chair. Conrad Ritblat & Co., Consultant Surveyors and Valuers 1958, Man. Dir 1970, Chair. Conrad Ritblat Group PLC 1993–; Chair. Colliers Conrad Ritblat Erdman 2000–; Man. Dir Union Property Holdings (London) Ltd 1969, Crown Estates Paving Commn. 1969–; mem. Bd of Govs Weizmann Inst. 1991–, London Business School 1991– (Hon. Fellow 2000, Deputy Chair. 2005); Dir and Gov. RAM 1998– (Deputy Chair. 1999–, Hon. Fellow 2000); mem. Council, Business in the Community 1987–, Prince of Wales' Royal Parks Tree Appeal Cttee 1987–, Patrons of British Art (Tate Gallery), Nat. Art. Collections Fund, British Library Bd 1995–; Pres. British Ski Fed. 1994–; Trustee, The Wallace Collection 2003– (Chair. 2005); Life mem. Royal Inst. of GB; Hon. FRIBA 2006; Hon. DLitt (London Metropolitan Univ.) 2003. *Leisure interests:* golf, skiing, real tennis, books, architecture. *Address:* 10 Cornwall Terrace, Regent's Park, London, NW1 4QP; Lehman Brothers, European Headquarters, 25 Bank Street, London, E14 5LE, England. *Telephone:* (20) 7486-4466. *Fax:* (20) 7935-5552.

RITCHIE, Guy; British film director; b. 10 Sept. 1968, Hatfield, Herts.; s. of John Ritchie and Amber Mary Ritchie; m. Madonna Ciccone 2000 (divorced 2008); one s. one step-d.; ed Standbridge Earls School; directed numerous pop videos 1980s; British Ind. Film Award 1998, London Film Critics Circle Award 1999. *Films include:* The Hard Case 1995, Lock, Stock and Two Smoking Barrels 1998, Snatch 2000, What it Feels Like For a Girl (video) 2001, The Hire: Star 2001, Swept Away 2002, Mean Machine (supervising producer) 2002, Revolver 2005, RocknRolla 2008, Sherlock Holmes 2009, Sherlock Holmes: A Game of Shadows 2011. *Television includes:* The Hard Case 1995, Lock, Stock and Two Smoking Barrels (series exec. producer) 2000, Suspect 2007. *Leisure interests:* karate, judo. *Address:* c/o Creative Arts Agency, 2000 Avenue of the Stars, Los Angeles, CA 90201, USA (office).

RITCHIE, Ian, CBE, DipArch (Dist), RIBA, RIAI, FRSA; British architect; *Principal, Ian Ritchie Architects Ltd;* b. 24 June 1947, Hove, Sussex, England; s. of Christopher Ritchie and Mabel Long; pnr Jocelyne van den Bossche; one s.; ed Polytechnic of Central London (now Univ. of Westminster); project architect, Foster Assocs 1972–79; in pvt. practice, France 1976–78; ind. consultant 1979–81; Founder-Partner Chrysalis Architects 1979–81; Co-founder Rice Francis Ritchie 1981, Dir 1981–87, Consultant 1987–89; Prin. Ian Ritchie Architects Ltd 1981–; mem. Royal Inst. of the Architects of Ireland; Hon. Prof. of Architecture, Univ. of Liverpool; Hon. AIA; Hon. mem. Royal Incorporation of Architects in Scotland; Hon. DLitt (Westminster); numerous awards including Architectural Design Silver Medal 1983, Iritecna Prize for Europe (Italy) 1991, Eric Lyons Memorial Award for Housing in Europe 1992, Commonwealth Asscn of Architects Robert Matthews Award 1994, AIA Awards 1997, 2003, 2008, Civic Trust Award 1997, RIBA Awards 1998 (two), 2000, 2003, 2004, 2007, RIBA Stephen Lawrence Award 1998, Arts Building of the Year, Royal Fine Arts Comm. (RFAC) 1998, Sports Building of the Year, RFAC 2000, Building of the Year, RFAC 2003, two Design Council Millennium Product Awards 1999, Int. Outstanding Structure Award, IABSE 2000, Regeneration of Scotland Supreme Award 2000, British Construction Industry Special Award 2000, Copper Building of the Year 2000, Innovation in Copper Award, Copper Devt Asscn 2000, 2003, Abercrombie Awards: Best New Building and Overall Abercrombie Architectural Design Award 2004. *Commissions include:* Eagle Rock House, Sussex, several projects for the Louvre, Paris, including work on the Louvre Pyramids and Sculpture Courts, Nat. Museum of Science, Tech. and Industry, La Villette, Pharmacy Boves, France, Jeu de Paume cultural centre, Albert, France, Ecology Gallery, Natural History Museum, London, Stockley Business Park offices, Oxford Science Park offices, Glass Towers, Reina Sofia Museum of Modern Art, Madrid, Glass Hall, Leipzig Int. Exhbn Centre, Bermondsey and Wood Lane Stations for London Underground, EdF HV electricity pylons, France, Royal Opera House Theatre, Tower Bridge, London, Crystal Palace Concert Platform, White City redevelopment, Theatre Royal Production Centre, Plymouth, Scotland's Home of Tomorrow, Glasgow, Spire of Dublin Nat. Monument, 3rd Millennium Light Monument, Milan, Hayward Gallery Exhbns, London, British Museum masterplan, RSC Courtyard Theatre, Stratford upon Avon, King Solomon Acad., London, Wood Lane Station, London, Central Line Underground Sidings, Laureate Nat. Grid Pylon competition, Sainsbury Wellcome Centre at University Coll., London. *Films:* La cité en lumière (co-scripted/dir) 1986, The Spire of Dublin 2003. *Television:* (scripted, directed or produced) Sandcastles (BBC) 1990, Architect and Engineer 1995, Skyscrapers 1999, Surveillance (Channel 4) 2001. *Publications:* (Well) Connected Architecture 1994, The Biggest Glass Palace in the World 1997, Ian Ritchie: Technoecology 1999, Plymouth Theatre Royal Production Centre 2003, The Spire 2004, RSC Courtyard Theatre 2006, Leipzig Glass Hall (construction drawings) 2007, Lines (poetry) 2010, Being: An Architect 2013. *Leisure interests:* art, swimming, reading, writing, poetry, wild places. *Address:* Ian Ritchie Architects Ltd, 110 Three Colt Street, London, E14 8AZ, England (office). *Telephone:* (20) 7338-1100 (office). *Fax:* (20) 7338-1199 (office). *E-mail:* mail@ianritchiearchitects.co.uk (office). *Website:* www.ianritchiearchitects.co.uk (office).

RITCHIE, Ian Russell, MA; British barrister, business executive and sports administrator; *CEO, Rugby Football Union;* b. 27 Nov. 1953, Leeds; s. of Hugh Ritchie and Sheelah Ritchie; m. Jill Middleton-Walker 1982; two s.; ed Leeds Grammar School, Trinity Coll. Oxford; Barrister (Middle Temple) 1976–77; Industrial Relations Adviser, Eng Employers' Fed. 1978–79; joined Granada TV 1980, Head Production Services 1987–88; Dir of Resources, Tyne-Tees TV 1988–91, Man. Dir 1991–93, Group Deputy Chief Exec. Yorkshire Tyne-Tees TV PLC 1993; Man. Dir Nottingham Studios, Cen. TV 1993–94; Man. Dir London News Network 1994–96; CEO, subsequently COO Channel 5 Broadcasting 1996–97; Man. Dir Russell Reynolds Assocs 1997–98; Chief Exec. Middle East Broadcasting Centre 1998–2000; CEO Assoc. Press (AP) TV News 2000–04, Vice-Pres. Global Business and Man. Dir AP Int. 2003; CEO All England Lawn Tennis Club 2005–11; CEO Rugby Football Union 2012–; mem. Bd of Dirs Football League 2004–12, Wembley National Stadium Ltd 2008–11. *Leisure interests:* golf, tennis, theatre. *Address:* Rugby Football Union, Rugby House, Twickenham Stadium, 200 Whitton Road, Twickenham, Middx, TW2 7BA, England (office). *Fax:* (20) 8892-9816 (office). *Website:* www.rfu.com (office).

RITHAUDDEEN AL-HAJ BIN TENGKU ISMAIL, Y.M. Tengku Ahmad, PMN, SPMP, SSAP, PMK, LLB; Malaysian politician and barrister; *Pro-Chancellor, National University of Malaysia;* b. 24 Jan. 1932, Kota Bharu; s. of Y. M. Tengku Ismail and Y. M. Besar Zabidah Tengku abd Kadir; m. Y. M. Tengku Puan Sri Datin Noor Aini 1957; three s. two d.; ed Nottingham Univ. and Lincoln's Inn, UK; mem. of royal family of Kelantan; Circuit Magistrate in Ipoh 1956–58, Pres. of Sessions Court 1958–60; Deputy Public Prosecutor and Fed. Counsel 1960–62; mem. Council of Advisers to Ruler of State of Kelantan (MPR); resgnd to enter pvt. practice; Chair. East Coast Bar Cttee of Malaya; Chair. Sri Nilam Co-operative Soc., Malaysia; mem. Malayan Council 1967, 1968, 1969, 1970; Sponsor, Adabi Foundation, Kelantan Youth; Adviser, Kesatria; Chair. Farmers' Org. Authority; Minister with Special Functions Assisting Prime Minister on Foreign Affairs 1973–75; mem. Supreme Council, United Malays' Nat. Org. 1975–; Minister for Foreign Affairs 1975–81, 1984–86, for Trade and Industry 1981–83, for Information 1986, of Defence 1986–90; Jt Chair. Malaysia-Thailand Devt Authority (Gas and Oil); Chair. Kinta Kellas Investments PLC 1990–, Idris Hydraulic (Malaysia) Berhad 1991–, Concrete Eng Products Berhad, Road Builder (Malaysia) Holdings Berhad; Pres. UN Asscn of Malaysia (UNAM); Adviser,

KPMG Peat Marwick Malaysia; Pro-Chancellor Nat. Univ. of Malaysia; Chair. Univ. of Nottingham Malaysia Campus; Deputy Pres. Football Asscn of Malaysia. *Leisure interest:* golf. *Address:* c/o Office of Public Relations, Universiti Kebangsaan Malaysia, 43600 UKM, Bangi, Selangor Darul Ehsan, Malaysia. *Telephone:* (3) 89250651. *Fax:* (3) 89254890. *E-mail:* puspa@pkrisc.cc.ukm.my. *Website:* www.ukm.my.

RITOÓK, Zsigmond, PhD; Hungarian professor of Latin; *Professor Emeritus, University of Budapest;* b. 28 Sept. 1929, Budapest; s. of Zsigmond Ritoók and Ilona Ritoók (née Gaylhoffer); m. Agnes Ritoók (née Szalay); one s. two d.; ed Univ. of Budapest; teacher 1958–1970; Research Fellow, Centre of Classical Studies of Hungarian Acad. of Sciences 1970–86; Prof. of Latin, Univ. of Budapest 1986–99, Prof. Emer. 2000–; Corresp. mem. Acad. of Sciences 1990–93, mem. 1993–, Vice-Pres. Section of Linguistics and Literary Scholarship 1990–96, Pres. 1996–99; mem. Academia Latinitati Fovendae, Rome 1984–, Academia Europaea 1991–; Corresp. mem. Österreichische Akad. der Wissenschaften 1998–; Gen. Sec. Hungarian Soc. of Classical Studies 1980–85, Co-Pres. 1985–91, Pres. 1991–97; Dr hc (Miskolc), (Eötvös Loránd Univ., Budapest); Hungarian Order of Merit Cross of the Star 2008; Albert Szent-Gyorgyi Prize (1992, Pázmány Péter Award 1997, Széchenyi Prize 2001, Bolyai Prize 2009, Prima Prize 2012. *Publications:* Everyday Life in Ancient Greece 1960, The Golden Age of Greek Culture (co-author) 1968, (revised and enlarged) 1984, 2006, Theatre and Stadium 1968, Greek Singer of Tales 1973, Sources for the History of Greek Musical Aesthetics 1982, Desire, Poetry, Cognition, Selected Papers 2010 (all in Hungarian); Griechische Musikästhetik (in German) 2004; more than 130 papers in Hungarian and foreign periodicals. *Address:* ELTE Latin Tanszék, Múzeum Körut, 1088 Budapest (office); Mátyás u. 20, 1093 Budapest, Hungary (home). *Telephone:* (1) 217-4033 (home). *E-mail:* latintanszek@freemail.hu (office).

RITTENMEYER, Ronald Allen, BSc, MBA; American business executive; *President and CEO, Electronic Data Systems Corpn (EDS);* b. 22 May 1947, Wilkes-Barre, Pa; m. Hedy Rittenmeyer; two c.; ed Wilkes Univ., Pa, Rockhurst Univ., Mo.; Vice-Pres. of Operations, Frito-Lay Inc. 1974–76; fmr Vice-Pres. Middle East and Worldwide Operations, PepsiCo Food Int.; fmr Pres. and COO Merisel; COO Burlington Northern Railroad 1994; Pres. and COO Ryder TRS Inc. 1997–98; Chair., CEO and Pres. RailTex Inc. 1998–2000; CEO and Pres. AmeriServe 2000; Chair., CEO and Pres. Safety-Kleen Inc. 2001–04; Man. Dir The Cypress Group, NY 2004–05; Co-COO and Exec. Vice-Pres. Global Service Delivery Div., Electronic Data Systems Corpn (EDS) 2005, Pres. and COO 2006–07, Pres. and CEO 2007–, Chair. 2007–08 (following acquisition of EDS by Hewlett-Packard Aug. 2008); fmr mem. Bd of Dirs AmeriServe, RailTex, Ryder TRS, Groceryworks.com, Sterling Chemicals, Merisel, Safety-Kleen, US Chamber of Commerce, American Heart Asscn; fmr Chair. ExcellerateHRO; mem. Bd of Dirs Nat. Kidney Foundation of N Texas; mem. Exec. Bd Southern Methodist Univ. Cox School of Business; mem. Business Council, Gov.'s Business Council; mem. Bd of Visitors US Army War Coll. *Address:* Electronic Data Systems Corpn, 5400 Legacy Drive, Plano, TX 75024-3199, USA (office). *Telephone:* (972) 604-6000 (office). *Fax:* (972) 605-6033 (office). *E-mail:* info@eds.com (office). *Website:* www.eds.com (office).

RITTER, August William (Bill), Jr, BA, JD; American lawyer and politician; *Director, Center for the New Energy Economy and Senior Scholar, School of Global Environmental Sustainability, Colorado State University;* b. 6 Sept. 1956, Denver, Colo; s. of August William Ritter and Ethel Ritter; m. Jeannie L. Ritter 1983; three s. one d.; ed Gateway High School, Aurora, St Anthony Catholic High School, San Antonio, Colorado State Univ., Univ. of Colorado School of Law, Boulder; Deputy Dist Attorney for City and Co. of Denver 1981–87, 1992–93, Dist Attorney 1993–2006; moved with his wife Jeannie to Zambia as missionaries for RC Church 1987–89, opened food distribution and educ. centre; held post in US Attorney's office 1990–92; advised US Attorney Gen. John Ashcroft following attack on World Trade Center 11 Sept. 2001; Gov. of Colo 2007–11; Dir Center for the New Energy Economy and Sr Scholar, School of Global Environmental Sustainability, Colorado State Univ., Fort Collins 2011–; Pres. Colorado Dist Attorneys Council 1999–2000, 2003–04; Vice-Pres. Nat. Asscn of Dist Attorneys 1995–2004; Chair. Bd Promoting Alternatives to Violence through Educ. 1992–2003; American Prosecutors Research Inst. 1998–2003; mem. Bd Nat. Asscn of Drug Court Professionals 1995–2002, Mile High United Way 1999–2004; fmr mem. Denver Foundation's Human Services Cttee, Mile High United Way Bd, Denver Public Schools' Comm. on Secondary School Reform; Democrat. *Address:* School of Global Environmental Sustainability, Mail-Stop 1036, 108 Johnson Hall, Colorado State University, Fort Collins, CO 80523-1036, USA (office). *Telephone:* (970) 492-4215 (office). *Fax:* (970) 492-4130 (office). *Website:* soges.colostate.edu (office).

RITTER, Gerhard A., DPhil; German historian and academic; *Professor Emeritus of Modern History, University of Munich;* b. 29 March 1929, Berlin; s. of Wilhelm Ritter and Martha Ritter (née Wietasch); m. Gisela Kleinschmidt 1955; two s.; ed Arndt.-Oberschule, Berlin, Univ. of Tübingen, Free Univ., Berlin; research, Univ. of Oxford, UK 1952–54; Asst. Free Univ., Berlin 1954–61, Prof. of Political Science 1962–65; Prof. of Modern History, Univ. of Münster 1965–74; Prof. of Modern History, Univ. of Munich 1974–94, Prof. Emer. 1994–; fmr Guest Prof., Washington Univ., St Louis, Mo., USA, Univ. of Oxford, Univ. of California, Berkeley, USA, Tel-Aviv Univ., Israel; mem. Senate and Main Cttee, Deutsche Forschungsgemeinschaft (German Research Soc.), Bonn 1973–76; Chair. Asscn of Historians of Germany 1976–80; mem. Bavarian Acad. of Sciences, Munich, Comm. for History of Parliamentarism and Political Parties, Historische Kommission, Berlin; Hon. Fellow, St Antony's Coll. Oxford; Dr hc (Univ. Bielefeld) 1994, (Humboldt Univ., Berlin) 1999. *Publications:* Die Arbeiterbewegung im Wilhelminischen Reich 1959, Parlament und Demokratie in Grossbritannien 1972, Deutsche Sozialgeschichte 1870–1914 (with Jürgen Kocka) 1982, Arbeiterbewegung, Parteien und Parlamentarismus 1976, Die II. Internationale 1918/19. Protokolle, Memoranden, Berichte und Korrespondenzen 1980, Staat, Arbeiterschaft und Arbeiterbewegung in Deutschland 1980, Die deutschen Parteien 1830–1914 1985, Social Welfare in Germany and Britain 1986, Der Sozialstaat 1991 (third edn 2010), Wahlen in Deutschland 1946–91 (with M. Niehuss) 1991, Das Deutsche Kaiserreich 1871–1914 1992, Arbeiter im Deutschen Kaiserreich 1871–1914 (with Klaus Tenfelde) 1992, Grossforschung und Staat in Deutschland 1992, Der Umbruch von 1989/91 und die Geschichtswissenschaft 1995, Arbeiter-

bewegung und soziale Ideen in Deutschland 1996, Soziale Frage und Sozialpolitik in Deutschland seit Beginn des 19. Jahrhunderts 1998, Über Deutschland, Die Bundesrepublik in der deutschen Geschichte 2000, Continuity and Change. Political and Social Developments in Germany after 1945 and 1989/90 2000, Friedrich Meinecke. Akademischer Lehrer und emigrierter Schüler 2006, Der Preis der deutschen Einheit. Die Wiedervereinigung und die Krise des Sozialstaats 2007, Wir sind das Volk! Wir sind ein Volk! Geschichte der deutschen Einigung 2009, German Refugee Historians and Friedrich Meinecke 2010, Friedrich Meinecke, Neue Briefe und Dokumente (co-ed.) 2012, Hans-Dietrich Genscher, das Auswärtige Amt und die deutsche Vereinigung 2013. *Leisure interests:* sailing, tennis. *Address:* Windscheidstrasse 41, 10627 Berlin, Germany. *Telephone:* (30) 31015794. *Fax:* (30) 31019614. *E-mail:* garitter@web.de.

RITTER, Jorge Eduardo, PhD; Panamanian lawyer, politician and diplomatist; b. 1950, Panama City; s. of the late Eduardo Ritter Aislán; m.; two c.; ed Pontificia Univ. Javeriana, Colombia; Clerk to Legis. Comm. 1973–77; Lecturer in Constitutional and Civil Law, Univ. of Panama; fmr mem. Governing Council, Inst. for Human Resources Training and Devt; Vice-Minister of Labour and Social Welfare 1977–78; Pvt. Sec. and Adviser to Pres. of Panama 1978–81; Minister of Foreign Affairs (desig.) 1981; teacher, Nat. Political Training Coll. of the Guardia Nacional 1981; Minister of Interior and Justice 1981–82; Amb. to Colombia 1982–86; Perm. Rep. to UN 1986–88; Minister of Foreign Affairs 1988–89, 1998–99; Minister for Canal Affairs 1998–99; Vice-Chair. Bd Panama Canal Comm. 1998–99; Chair. Exec. Council Nat. Telecommunications Inst. 1981; Chair. Bd Civil Aviation Authority 1981–82, Panama Canal Authority 1998–99; mem. Bd Banco Ganadero 1980–90; Pnr Ritter, Díaz y Ahumada 1982–; mem. Academia Panameña de la Lengua 2007–. *Publication:* Los Secretos de la Nunciatura 1990. *Address:* Calle José Gabriel Duque, La Cresta, Las Torres (C-6), PO Box 0819-08253, Panamá, Panama (office). *Telephone:* (507) 264-0521 (office). *Fax:* (507) 264-0524 (office). *E-mail:* jritter@cwpanama.net (home).

RITTERMAN, Dame Janet Elizabeth, DBE, MMus, PhD; British/Australian music college director (retd); b. (Janet Elizabeth Palmer), 1 Dec. 1941, Sydney, NSW, Australia; d. of Charles Eric Palmer and Laurie Helen Palmer; m. Gerrard Peter Ritterman 1970; ed North Sydney Girls' High School and New South Wales State Conservatorium of Music, Australia, Univ. of Durham and King's Coll. London, UK; pianist, accompanist, chamber music player, music educator; Sr Lecturer in Music, Middx Polytechnic 1975–79, Goldsmiths, Univ. of London 1980–87; Head of Music, Dartington Coll. of Arts 1987–90, Dean Academic Affairs 1988–90, Acting Prin. 1990–91, Prin. 1991–93; Visiting Prof. of Music Educ., Univ. of Plymouth 1993–2005; Dir Royal Coll. of Music 1993–2005; Chair. Assoc. Bd Royal Schools of Music (Publishing) Ltd 1993–2005, The Mendelssohn and Boise Foundations 1996–98, 2002–04, Advisory Council, Arts Research Ltd 1997–2005, Fed. of British Conservatoires 1998–2003; Vice-Pres. Nat. Asscn of Youth Orchestras 1993–, Royal Coll. of Music 2005–; mem. Music Panel, Arts Council of England 1992–98, Council Royal Musical Asscn 1994–2004 (Vice-Pres. 1998–2004), Bd ENO 1996–2004, Exec. Cttee Inc. Soc. of Musicians 1996–99, Arts and Humanities Research Bd 1998–2004 (Postgraduate Panel 1998–2002, Chair. Postgraduate Cttee 2002–04), Nominating Cttee Arts and Humanities Research Council 2005–07, Bd Nat. Youth Orchestra 1999–2007, Steering Cttee, London Higher Educ. Consortium 1999–2005, Arts Council of England 2000–02, Dept for Educ. and Skills Advisory Group, Music and Dance Scheme 2000–05, Council of Goldsmiths, Univ. of London 2002–07, Bd Anglo-Austrian Soc. 2005–11, Bd The Voices Foundation 2005–11, Advisory Bd Inst. for Advanced Studies in the Humanities, Univ. of Edinburgh 2005–, Advisory Council Inst. of Germanic and Romance Studies 2005–10 and Inst. of Musical Research, Univ. of London 2006–12, Educ. Advisory Group Nuffield Foundation 2007–09; Trustee, Countess of Munster Musical Trust 1993–, Prince Consort Foundation 1993–2005, Plymouth Chamber Music Trust 2006–10; Gov. Associated Bd Royal Schools of Music 1993–2005, Purcell School 1996–2000, Heythrop Coll., Univ. of London 1996–2006, Dartington Coll. of Arts 2005–08, Middlesex Univ. 2005–, Univ. Coll. Falmouth 2008–, Royal Welsh Coll. of Music and Drama 2010–; mem. Österreichischer Wissenschaftsrat 2002–12; mem. Court, Worshipful Co. of Musicians 2005–11; Fellow, Royal Northern Coll. of Music 1996, Dartington Coll. of Arts 1997, Univ. Coll., Northampton 1997, Guildhall School of Music and Drama 2000, Higher Educ. Acad. 2007, Heythrop Coll. 2008, Goldsmiths, Univ. of London 2009; Sr Fellow, RCA 2004; Assoc. Fellow, Inst. of Musical Research, Univ. of London 2006–; Chair. Int. Advisory Bd, Programme for Arts-based Research, Austrian Science Fund 2009–; mem. Conseil de fondation, Haute Ecole de Musique de Genève, Switzerland 2009–; Hon. RAM 1995; Hon. FGSM 2000; Hon. DUniv (Birmingham City) 1996, (Middlesex) 2005; Hon. DLitt (Ulster) 2004; Hon. DMus (Sydney) 2010. *Publications:* articles in learned journals in France, Germany, Australia and UK. *Leisure interests:* reading, theatre-going, country walking.

RITTNER, Luke Philip Hardwick; British arts administrator; *Chief Executive, Royal Academy of Dance;* b. 24 May 1947, Bath; s. of Stephen Rittner and Joane Rittner; m. Corinna Frances Edholm 1974; one d.; ed Blackfriars School, Laxton, City of Bath Tech. Coll., Dartington Coll. of Arts and London Acad. of Music and Dramatic Art; Asst Admin. Bath Festival 1968–71, Jt Admin. 1971–74, Admin. Dir 1974–76; Founder and Dir Asscn for Business Sponsorship of the Arts 1976–83; Sec.-Gen. Arts Council of Great Britain 1983–90; UK Cultural Dir Expo '92 1990–92; Chair. English Shakespeare Co. 1990–94; Dir Marketing and Communications, Sotheby's Europe 1992–99; Chief Exec. Royal Acad. of Dance 1999–; Chair. London Chorus (fmrly The London Choral Soc.) 1994–, Exec. Bd London Acad. of Music and Dramatic Art 1994–; Artistic Adviser to Spanish Arts Festival, London 1991–94; Gov. Urchfont Manor, Wiltshire Adult Educ. Centre 1982–83; mem. Music Panel, British Council 1979–83, Council Victoria and Albert Museum 1980–83, J. Sainsbury Arts Sponsorship Panel 1990–96, Olivier Awards Theatre Panel 1992, Council Almeida Theatre 1997–2001; non-exec. mem. Bd Carlton Television 1991–93; Trustee Bath Preservation Trust 1968–73, Theatre Royal, Bath 1979–82; Foundation Trustee Holburne Museum, Bath 1981–83; mem. Dance Panel, Olivier Awards 2003; Hon. Doctorate (Bath) 2004. *Leisure interest:* the arts. *Address:* Royal Academy of Dance, 36 Battersea Square, London, SW11 3RA, England (office). *Telephone:* (20) 7326-8000 (office). *Fax:* (20) 7924-3129 (office). *E-mail:* info@rad.org.uk (office). *Website:* www.rad.org.uk (office).

RITZ, Gerry, PC; Canadian politician; *Minister of Agriculture and Agri-Food, Minister for the Canadian Wheat Board;* b. 19 Aug. 1951, Delisle, Sask.; m. Judy Ritz; two s.; mem. Reform Party of Canada 1997–2000, Canadian Alliance 2000–03, Conservative Party of Canada 2003–; MP for Battlefords-Lloydminster 1997–; Sec. of State for Small Business and Tourism 2007; Minister of Agric. and Agri-Food 2007–, also Minister for the Canadian Wheat Bd. *Address:* Department of Agriculture and Agri-Food, 1341 Baseline Road, Ottawa, ON K1A 0C5, Canada (office). *Telephone:* (613) 773-1000 (office). *Fax:* (613) 773-1081 (office). *E-mail:* info@agr.gc.ca (office); ritzg@sasktel.net. *Website:* www.agr.gc.ca (office); www.gerryritzmp.com.

RITZEN, Jozef (Jo) Maria Mathias, MSc, PhD; Dutch politician, economist and university administrator; *Professor, Maastricht University;* b. 3 Oct. 1945, Heerlen, Limburg Prov.; m. Hanneke Smulders; four c.; ed Univ. of Tech., Delft, Erasmus Univ., Rotterdam; Project Asst, The Ford Foundation, Dacca 1970; Lecturer, Univ. of California, Berkeley 1971–75, Section Leader, Social and Cultural Planning Office 1975–81; Prof. of Educ. Econs, Nijmegen Univ. 1981–83; Prof. of Public Sector Econs, Erasmus Univ., Rotterdam 1983–89; sometime adviser to Minister of Social Affair, to Minister of Health, Welfare and Sports 1975; Minister of Educ., Culture and Science 1989–99; Special Adviser to the Human Devt Network, IBRD (World Bank) 1998, Vice-Pres. for Devt Policy 1999–2003; Pres. Maastricht Univ. 2003–11, Prof. 2011–; Sr Policy Adviser, Inst. for the Study of Labour (IZA), Bonn 2011–; Chair. Empower European Univs 2011–; mem. Int. Advisory Bd, King Abdul Aziz Univ., Jeddah 2011–, Russian Acad. for Nat. Economy and Public Admin 2011–, Univ. Siegen 2011–; Kt, Order of Orange-Nassau, High Merit Cross (Germany), Kt, Order of Leopold (Belgium); Dr hc (Chinese Acad. of Social Sciences); Winkler Prins Prize for best dissertation 1977. *Publications:* 13 books; numerous articles in peer-reviewed and other journals on education, policy, economics, public sector and finance. *Address:* Kloosterweg 54, 6241 GB Bunde, Netherlands (home). *Telephone:* (43) 3261113 (office). *E-mail:* j.ritzen@maastrichtuniversity.nl (office). *Website:* www.empowereu.org (office).

RIVA, Emmanuelle; French actress and poet; b. (Paulette Germaine Rivat), 24 Feb. 1927, Cheniménil, Vosges; d. of Alfredo Rivat and Jeanne Rivat (née Nourdin); started work as seamstress before moving into acting; first theatre success in Shaw's Arms and the Man, Paris 1954; keen photographer; has published three books of poetry. *Films include:* Hiroshima, Mon Amour 1959, Adua et ses compagnes 1960, Léon Morin, prêtre 1961, Climats 1962, Thérèse Desqueyroux (Venice Film Festival Volpi Cup for Best Actress) 1962, Caterina 1963, Les Heures de l'amour 1963, Le Coup de grâce 1964, Fruits amers 1967, Les Risques du métier 1967, L'Homme de désir 1971, Le Diable au cœur 1976, Liberté, la nuit 1983, Les Tribulations de Balthasar Kober 1988, La Passion de Bernadette 1989, Three Colours: Blue 1993, C'est la vie 2001, Mon fils à moi 2006, Le Grand Alibi 2008, Je ne dis pas non 2009, Amour (Boston Soc. of Film Critics Award for Best Actress, European Film Award for Best Actress, London Film Critics Circle Award for Actress of the Year, Los Angeles Film Critics Asscn Award for Best Actress, Lumières de la presse étrangère Award for Best Actress, Nat. Soc. of Film Critics Award for Best Actress) 2012, Tu honoreras ta mère et ta mère 2013. *Address:* Anne Alvares Correa, 34, rue Jouffroy d'Abbans, 75017 Paris, France (office). *Telephone:* 1-42-67-80-85 (office). *Website:* www.agence-annealvarescorrea.com (office).

RIVALDO; Brazilian professional footballer; b. (Rivaldo Vitor Borba Ferreira), 19 April 1972, Paulista, Pernambuco; s. of the late Romildo Borreira; one s. one d.; played with Paulista, Santa Cruz 1989–91, Magi-Mirim 1992–93, Corinthians 1993–94, Palmeiras 1994–96 (won Brazilian Série A 1994, São Paulo State Championship 1994, 1996, Euro-America Cup 1996), Deportivo La Coruña, Spain (21 goals in 41 matches) 1996–97, FC Barcelona, Spain 1997–2002 (won La Liga 1998, 1999, Copa del Rey 1998, European Super Cup 1997), AC Milan, Italy 2002–03 (won UEFA Champions League 2003, Coppa Italia 2003, European Super Cup 2003), signed for Cruzeiro Jan. 2004 but left team 90 days later, with Olympiakos 2004–07 (won Greek League 2005, 2006, 2007, Greek Cup 2005, 2006), AEK Athens 2007–08, Bunyodkor, Uzbekistan 2008–10 (won Uzbek League 2008, 2009, Uzbekistani Cup 2008), Mogi Mirim, Brazil 2010–; played for Brazil nat. team 1993–2003, scored eight goals in 14 World Cup finals games, runner-up 1998, winner 2002, winner Confederations Cup 1997, Copa América 1999; Pres. Mogi Mirim Esporte Clube; Brazilian Bola de Prata 1993, 1994, named in FIFA World Cup All-Star Team 1998, 2002, FIFA World Player of the Year 1999, Ballon d'Or (European Footballer of the Year) 1999, World Soccer Player of the Year 1999, Onze d'Or 1999, Copa América Top Scorer 1999, Copa América MVP 1999, Spanish League Footballer of the Year 1999, UEFA Champions League Top Scorer 2000, named by Pelé as one of 125 Greatest Living Footballers, FIFA Awards Ceremony 2004, named in FIFA 100 2004, Greek Championship Best Foreign Player 2006, 2007, Uzbek League Top Scorer 2009. *Address:* c/o Mogi Miram, Rua Dr. Ferreira Lima, 150, Centro Mogi Mirim /SP, Brazil. *Website:* www.mogimirim.com.br; www.rivaldo-10.gr.

RIVAS FRANCHINI, Eda Adriana; Peruvian lawyer and politician; *Minister of Foreign Affairs;* b. 23 March 1952, Lima; ed Pontificia Universidad Católica del Perú, Univ. of Las Palmas Gran Canaria, Spain, Univ. of Castilla La Mancha, Toledo; several years' experience in public sector bodies including Comm. for Promotion of Private Investment, Private Investment Promotion Agency, Empresa Nacional de Puertos SA, Organismo Supervisor de la Inversión en Infraestructura de Transporte de Uso Público; worked in Presidency of Council of Ministers; fmr mem. Cabinet of Advisers, Ministry of Justice, fmr Deputy Minister of Justice, Minister of Justice and Human Rights 2012–13, of Foreign Affairs 2013–. *Address:* Ministry of Foreign Affairs, Jirón Lampa 535, Lima 1, Peru (office). *Telephone:* (1) 2042400 (office). *E-mail:* informes@rree.gob.pe (office). *Website:* www.rree.gob.pe (office).

RIVAS-MIJARES, Gustavo, MSc, DrIng; Venezuelan environmental engineer and academic; b. 7 Nov. 1922, Valencia; s. of J. A. Rivas-Montenegro and Amparo Mijares de Rivas; m. Ligia Cardenas 1946; four c.; ed Liceo Pedro Gual, Valencia, Univ. Cen. de Venezuela, Caracas and Univs of Michigan and California, USA; Prof. of Sanitary Eng, Faculty of Eng, Univ. Cen. de Venezuela 1945–85, Dean, Grad. School 1973–76, Prof. Emer. 1985–; Pres. Nat. Acad. of Physics, Math. and Natural Science 1981–85; Dir Nat. Council of Scientific and Tech. Research 1968–72; fmr Dir Venezuela Inst. of Scientific Research; Pres. Superior Council,

Universidad Simón Bolívar, Caracas, Venezuela 1988–91; Chair. Pan-American Eng Acad. 1998; mem. Nat. Acad. of Sciences, Venezuela, Nat. Acad. of Eng (USA), Nat. Acad. of Eng (Mexico), Nat. Acad. of Guatemala, Royal Acad. of Sciences (Spain), Academia Panamericana de Ingenieri, TWAS (fmrly Third World Acad. of Sciences); Fellow, Third World Acad. of Sciences 1988; Foreign Assoc., Nat. Acad. of Eng (USA, Mexico, Spain); Nat. Science Prize (Venezuela) 1986; several awards including Libertador Bolívar 1989. *Publications:* several books, including Supply Water and Sewerage 1957, Treatment of Purification of Water 1963, Wastewater 1967; 136 research papers. *Address:* Department of Sanitary Engineering, Faculty of Engineering, Universidad Central de Venezuela, Ciudad Universitaria, Los Changuaramos, Zona Postal 104, Caracas 1051 (office); Urb. Santa Rosa de Lima, Calle C, Res. Jarama, Apt. 7–A, Caracas, Venezuela (home). *Telephone:* (2) 991-7156 (home). *Fax:* (2) 484-6611 (office). *E-mail:* acfmn@ccs.internet.ve (office).

RIVERA, Chita; American actress, singer and dancer; b. (Dolores Conchita Figueroa del Rivero), 23 Jan. 1933, Washington, DC; d. of Pedro Julio Figuerva del Rivero and Katherine Anderson del Rivero; m. Anthony Mordente (divorced); one d.; ed American School of Ballet, New York; performs in nightclubs and cabarets around the world; Kennedy Center Honor 2002, Presidential Medal of Freedom 2009, League of Professional Theatre Women's Lifetime Achievement Award 2010. *Stage appearances include:* Call Me Madam, Guys and Dolls, Can-Can, Seventh Heaven, Mister Wonderful, West Side Story, Father's Day, Bye Bye Birdie, Threepenny Opera, Flower Drum Song, Zorba, Sweet Charity, Born Yesterday, Jacques is Alive and Well and Living in Paris, Sondheim–A Musical Tribute, Kiss Me Kate, Ivanhoe, Chicago, Bring Back Birdie, Merlin, The Rink 1984 (Tony Award 1984), Jerry's Girls 1985, Kiss of the Spider Woman 1993 (Tony Award for Best Actress in a Musical), Chita Rivera: The Dancer's Life, Chita Rivera: My Broadway 2010. *Films:* Chicago 2002, Kalamazoo? 2005. *Television includes:* Kojak and the Marcus Nelson Murders 1973, The New Dick Van Dyke Show 1973–74, Kennedy Center Tonight–Broadway to Washington!, Pippin 1982, The Mayflower Madam 1987. *Recordings include:* And Now I Swing 2009. *Address:* c/o William Morris Agency, 1325 Avenue of the Americas, New York, NY 10019, USA (office). *Website:* www.wma.com (office); www.chitarivera.com.

RIVERA, Geraldo, BS, JD; American broadcaster and journalist; b. 4 July 1943, New York; s. of Cruz Allen Rivera and Lillian Friedman; m. 3rd Sheri Rivera (divorced 1984); m. 4th C. C. Dyer 1987; two s. two d.; ed Univ. of Arizona, Brooklyn Law School, Univ. of Pennsylvania; with Eyewitness News WABC-TV, New York 1970–75; reporter, Good Morning America programme ABC-TV 1973–76; corresp. and host, Good Night America programme 1975–77; corresp. and Sr Producer, 20/20 Newsmagazine 1978–85; host, syndicated talk show The Geraldo Rivera Show, New York 1987–98; host, CNBC Rivera Life Show 1994, investigative show on cable CNBC Upfront Tonight 1998–2000, Travel Channel documentaries: Voyager – Sail to the Century, NBC 1994–2001, Geraldo Rivera Specials; war reporter in Afghanistan, Somalia, Lebanon, Israel and Sudan, Fox News Channel 2001–02, currently host Geraldo at Large; ten Emmy awards, three Peabody Awards, Kennedy Journalism Award 1973, 1975, Columbia DuPont Award and numerous other awards. *Publications:* Willowbrook 1972, Miguel 1972, Island of Contrasts 1974, A Special Kind of Courage 1976, Exposing Myself 1991. *Address:* Geraldo at Large, FOX News Media, LLC, 1211 Avenue of the Americas, New York, NY 10036, USA (office). *Telephone:* (212) 852-7002 (office). *Fax:* (212) 301-8588 (office). *E-mail:* Atlarge@foxnews.com (office). *Website:* www.foxnews.com (office).

RIVERA CARRERA, HE Cardinal Norberto, DD; Mexican ecclesiastic; *Archbishop of México, Federal District and Archbishop Primate of Mexico;* b. 6 June 1942, La Purísima, Durango; s. of Ramón Rivera Cháidez and Soledad Carrera de Rivera; ed Conciliary Seminary, Durango, Gregorian Univ., Rome; ordained priest 1966; Prof. of Dogmatic Theology Seminario Mayor, Durango 1967–85; Prof. of Ecclesiology, Pontificia Universidad de México 1982–85, mem. sr council 1993–95, vice-grand councillor 1995–; Bishop of Tehuacán 1985; Archbishop of México, DF and Archbishop Primate of Mexico 1995–; cr. Cardinal (Cardinal-Priest of San Francesco d'Assisi a Ripa Grande) 1998; participated in Papal Conclave 2005, 2013; mem. numerous cttees and councils, including the perm. Sinod of Bishops; Pres. Episcopal Comm. for Culture, Inter-religion Council of Mexico, Ecumenical Council of Mexico, Exec. Council of Mexico City Historic Centre. *Address:* Curia Arzobispal, Aptdo Postal 24-433, Durango 90, 5°, Col Roma, CP 06700 México, DF, Mexico (office). *Telephone:* (5) 208-3200 (office). *Fax:* (5) 208-5350 (office). *E-mail:* arzobisp@arquidiocesismexico.org.mx (office). *Website:* www.arzobispadomexico.org.mx (office).

RIVERA SALAZAR, Rodrigo; Colombian lawyer and politician; b. 20 April 1963, Pereira; s. of Rodrigo Rivera Correa and Edilma Salazar; m. Claudia Carrasquilla; two c.; ed Coll. of Law, American Univ., Washington, DC, USA; fmr columnist for La Tarde, Pereira, El Espectador; elected mem. Cámara de Representantes 1989, mem. Senado 1998–2002; Minister of Defence 2010–11 (resgnd); mem. Partido Liberal Colombiano, Pres. Dirección Nacional Liberal 2003. *Publications:* Hacia un nuevo federalismo para Colombia 2001, Colombia Fragmentada 2004. *Address:* c/o Ministry of National Defence, Carrera 54, No 26–25, Centro Administrativo Nacional 2°, Bogotá, DC, Colombia.

RIVERO CASTAÑEDA, Raúl Ramón; Cuban journalist and poet; b. 1945, Morón, Camagüey; m. Blanca Reyes Castañón; ed Univ. of Havana School of Journalism; Co-founder satirical magazine Caimán Barbudo 1966; Moscow correspondent, Prensa Latina (govt press agency) 1973–76, then worked for science and culture service, Cuba; independent journalist 1988–; Co-founder and Dir Cuba Press news agency 1995–2003, contribs to newspapers and journals abroad, including El Nuevo Herald, The Miami Herald, Encounter magazine; correspondent for French press agency, Reporters sans frontières; fmr regional vice-chair. for Cuba, Inter-American Press Asscn Cttee on Freedom of the Press and Information; accused of collaborating with the USA and sentenced to 20 years' imprisonment by govt April 2003, released Nov. 2004; mem. Manuel Márquez Sterling Journalists Asscn; Reporters sans frontières Fondation de France Prize 1997, Inter-American Press Asscn Grand Prize for Press Freedom, Columbia Univ. Graduate School of Journalism Maria Moors Cabot Prize 1999, World Press Freedom Prize 2004. *Publications:* poems include: Suite de la muerte, Patria 1994, Orden de registro, Oración de septiembre, Foto en La Habana, Ensayo sobre la tiranía.

RIVETTE, Jacques; French film director; b. 1 March 1928, Rouen; s. of André Rivette and Andrée Rivette (née Amiard); ed Lycée Corneille, Rouen; began career as journalist and film critic for Cahiers du Cinéma, Gazette du Cinema et Arts 1953–82; worked as cameraman on short films by Eric Rohmer and François Truffaut; asst to Jacques Becker on Ali Baba and the Forty Thieves, Jean Renoir on French Cancan; began directing short films 1949, made first feature film 1960; known as one of the originators of the Nouvelle Vague (New Wave) style of French cinema; Chevalier, Ordre nat. du Mérite; Grand Prix Nat. 1981, Leopard of Honour, Locarno Int. Film Festival 1991, Prix Friedrich Wilhelm Murnau for Outstanding Lifetime Achievement 1998. *Films:* Aux quatre coins (short) 1949, Le Quadrille (short) 1950, Le Divertissement (short) 1952, Le Coup du berger (short) 1956, Paris nous appartient (Sutherland Trophy, London Film Festival) 1960, La Religieuse 1966, L'Amour fou (Sutherland Trophy, London Film Festival) 1969, Out 1: noli me tangere 1971, Out 1: Spectre 1972, Essai sur l'agression 1974, Naissance et mont de Prométhée 1974, Céline et Julie vont en bateau (Special Prize of the Jury, Locarno) 1974, Noroît 1976, Duelle (une quarantaine) 1976, Paris s'en va (short) 1981, Le Pont du Nord 1981, Merry-Go-Round 1981, L'Amour par terre 1984, Hurlevent 1985, La Bande des quatre (FIPRESCI Prize 1989) 1988, La Divertimento 1991, La Belle noiseuse (Grand Jury Prize, Cannes, Best Film, César Awards, French Syndicate of Cinema Critics Award, Kinema Junpo Best Foreign Language Film) 1991, Jeanne la Pucelle I: Les batailles 1994, Jeanne la Pucelle II: Les prisons 1994, Haut bas fragile 1995, Secret défense 1998, Va savoir (Jury Special Prize, Valladolid) 2001, Histoire de Marie et Julien 2003, Ne touchez pas la hache 2007, 36 vues du Pic Saint Loup 2009. *Address:* c/o VMA, 20 avenue Rapp, 75007 Paris, France (office). *Telephone:* 1-43-17-37-00 (office). *E-mail:* d.leprestre@vma.fr (office). *Website:* www.vma.fr (office).

RIVIERE, Francis Osborne, BSc, MSc; Dominican politician and economist; ed Univ. of the West Indies, Trinity Coll., Dublin; Minister of Foreign Affairs and of Trade and Marketing, Dominica 2001–05; Acting Prime Minister Nov. 2003–Jan. 2004; currently consultant, Save the Children (charity). *Leisure interests* volunteer work, sport, light classical music, jazz. *Address:* c/o Save the Children, Bath Estate, PO Box 169, Roseau (office); 6 Francis Lane, Roseau, Dominica (home). *Telephone:* 4482090 (office); 4484872 (home). *Fax:* 4482090 (office).

RIVKIN, Charles H.; American business executive and diplomatist; s. of the late William R. Rivkin; m. Susan Tolson; two c.; ed Yale Univ., Harvard Univ.; internships with Renault and Columbia Pictures; financial analyst, Salomon Brothers 1984–86; Dir of Planning, Jim Henson Co. 1988–90, mem. Bd of Dirs 1990–2005, Vice-Pres. 1990–91, Sr Vice-Pres. and COO 1991–94, Exec. Vice-Pres. and COO 1994–95, Pres. and COO 1995–2000, Pres. and CEO 2000–03; Pres. and CEO Wildbrain entertainment co. 2005–09; Amb. to France (also accred to Monaco) 2009–13; mem. Young Presidents' Org. 1996–2009, Pacific Council on Int. Policy 2007–, Homeland Security Advisory Council, Business Execs for Nat. Security 2008–09; Chair. Bel-Air 2004–05; Dir Chrysalis-Changing Lives through Jobs 1996–2002, Save the Children 1997–2003; served as an at-large California del. to Democratic Nat. Convention for Senator John Kerry 2004, for Senator Barack Obama 2008; BAFTA Award for Best Int. Children's Television Show, Spirit of Chrysalis Award. *Address:* US Department of State, 2201 C Street NW, Washington, DC 20520, USA (office). *Telephone:* (202) 647-4000 (office). *Fax:* (202) 647-6738 (office). *Website:* www.state.gov (office).

RIVLIN, Alice Mitchell, MA, PhD; American economist and fmr government official; *Director, Greater Washington Research Program, Brookings Institution;* b. 4 March 1931, Philadelphia; d. of Allan Mitchell and Georgianna Fales; m. 1st Lewis A. Rivlin 1955 (divorced 1977); two s. one d.; m. 2nd Sidney G. Winter 1989; ed Bryn Mawr Coll. and Radcliffe Coll.; mem. staff, Brookings Inst. Washington, DC 1957–66, 1969–75, 1983–93, Dir of Econ. Studies 1983–87, apptd Sr Fellow, Johnson Chair. 1999, currently Dir Greater Washington Research Program; Dir Congressional Budget Office 1975–83; Prof. of Public Policy, George Mason Univ. 1992; Deputy Dir US Office of Man. and Budget 1993–94, Dir 1994–96; Vice-Chair Fed. Reserve Bd 1996–99; Chair. Dist of Columbia Financial Control Bd 1998–2001; Visiting Prof. Public Policy Inst., Georgetown Univ.; mem. Bd of Dirs BearingPoint, Washington Post Co.; mem. American Econ. Assn (Nat. Pres. 1986); MacArthur Fellow 1983–88. *Publications:* The Role of the Federal Government in Financing Higher Education 1961, Microanalysis of Socioeconomic Systems (jtly) 1961, Systematic Thinking for Social Action 1971, Economic Choices (jtly) 1986, The Swedish Economy (jtly) 1987, Caring for the Disabled Elderly: Who Will Pay? 1988, Reviving the American Dream 1992, The Economic Payoff from the Internet Revolutioin 2001, Beyond the Dot.coms 2001, Restoring Fiscal Sanity 2004. *Address:* Brookings Institution, Center on Urban and Metropolitan Policy, 1755 Massachusetts Avenue, NW, Washington, DC 20036-2188, USA (office). *Telephone:* (202) 797-6026 (office). *Fax:* (202) 797-2965 (office). *E-mail:* ARivlin@brookings.edu (office). *Website:* www.brookings.edu (office).

RIZA, Iqbal, MA; Pakistani UN official; *Special Adviser to the Secretary-General, United Nations;* b. 20 May 1934, Lonavla, India; s. of Sharif Alijan; m. 1959; two s.; ed Univ. of Punjab, Lahore, Fletcher School of Int. Law, Boston; Pakistan Foreign Service 1958–77; served in Madrid 1959–61, Bonn 1962–64, Khartoum 1964–66, London 1966–68; Dir Foreign Service Acad., Lahore 1968–71; Deputy Chief of Mission, Paris and Deputy Perm. Rep. to UNESCO 1972–76; joined UN 1978, Sec. Cttee on the Exercise of the Inalienable Rights of the Palestinian People 1978–80, Prin. Officer, UN Dept of Public Information 1980–82; assigned to negotiations on Iran–Iraq war 1981–87; Dir Office for Special Political Affairs 1983–88, Div. for Political and Gen. Ass. Affairs 1988–89; Chief, UN Observer Mission for verification of the electoral process in Nicaragua (ONUVEN) 1989–90; Chief of Mission of UN Transition Team in El Salvador March–Aug. 1990; Special Rep. of UN Sec.-Gen. and Chief of UN Observer Mission in El Salvador (ONUSAL) 1991–93; Asst Sec.-Gen. for Peace-keeping Operations 1993–96, Coordinator of UN operations in Bosnia-Herzegovina Feb.–Dec. 1996, Under-Sec.-Gen., Chef de Cabinet in Exec. Office of Sec.-Gen. Kofi Annan 1997–2005 (retd); currently Special Adviser to UN Sec.-Gen.; mem. UN Advisory Bd on Human Security. *Leisure interests:* reading, music, riding. *Address:* c/o Executive Office of the UN Secretary-General, United Nations Plaza, New York, NY 10017, USA (office).

RIZAYEV, Ramiz Gasangulu oglu, DrChemSc; Azerbaijani chemist and diplomatist; b. 2 Nov. 1939, Nakhichevan; m.; one s. one d.; ed Azerbaijan State Univ.; corresp. mem. Azerbaijan Acad. of Sciences 1983; Dir Inst. of Inorganic and

Physical Chem. Azerbaijan Acad. of Sciences 1985–93; Plenipotentiary Rep., then Amb. of Azerbaijan to Russian Fed. 1993–2006; numerous inventions in the field of oil extraction and oil processing, 36 patents in various cos; mem. Scientific Council on Catalysis, Russian Acad. of Sciences; mem. Int. Acad. of Eng Sciences 2000–; mem. Ed. Bd Neftekhimiya (journal); Honoured Engineer of Russian Fed. 2000. *Publications:* 250 scientific articles on problems of oil chem. and chemical catalysis. *Address:* c/o Ministry of Foreign Affairs, 1009 Baku, S. Qurbanov küç. 4, Azerbaijan.

RIZO CASTELLÓN, José; Nicaraguan lawyer and politician; ed Catholic Univ. of Chile; Vice-Pres. of Nicaragua 2002–05 (resgnd); mem. Partido Liberal Constitucionalista (PLC), unsuccessful cand. for Pres. of Nicaragua 2006. *Address:* c/o Partido Liberal Constitucionalista (PLC), Semáforos Country Club 100 m al este, Apdo 4569, Managua, Nicaragua. *Telephone:* 278-8705. *Fax:* 278-1800.

RIZZOLI, Angelo, Jr; Italian film producer and publisher; b. 12 Nov. 1943, Como; s. of Andrea Rizzoli and Lucia Rizzoli (née Solmi); m. Eleonora Giorgi 1979; one c.; fmr Pres. and Man. Ed. Rizzoli Editore, Pres. Cineriz Distributori Associati; Pres. Rizzoli Film 1978–. *Films produced include:* Per grazia ricevuta 1971, Paura e amore 1988, Acque di primavera 1989, Stanno tutti bene 1990, Pore aperte 1990, La Settimana della sfinge 1990, In nome del popolo sovrano 1990, The Comfort of Strangers 1990, To Meteoro vima tou pelargou 1991, Paris s'eveille 1991, Il Ladro di bambini 1992, Un Altra vita 1992, Padre e figlio 1994, Anche i commercialisti hanno un'anima 1994,. *Television productions include:* Le Ragazze di Piazza di Spagna (TV series) 1998, Le Ali della vita 2000, Padre Pio 2000, Gioco di specchi 2000, Piccolo mondo antico 2001, Le Ali della vita 2 2001, Cuccioli 2002, Tutti i sogni del mondo 2003, Ferrari 2003, I Ragazzi della via Pal 2003, Al di la delle frontiere (miniseries) 2004, Il Bell'Antonio (miniseries) 2005, 48 ore (series) 2006, La Provinciale 2006, La Freccia nera (miniseries) 2006, Capri (series) 2006, Mafalda di Savoia (miniseries) 2006, Le Ragazze di San Frediano 2007, Il Giudice Mastrangelo (series) 2005–07. *Address:* Via Angelo Rizzoli 2, 20132 Milan, Italy (office). *Telephone:* (02) 25841.

RO, Tu-chol; North Korean politician; *Vice-Premier and Chairman of the State Planning Commission;* Deputy, Supreme People's Ass.; Vice-Chair State Planning Comm. –2003, Chair. 2009–; Vice Premier 2003–. *Address:* Office of the Vice Premier of the Cabinet, Pyongyang, Democratic People's Republic of Korea.

ROBB, Andrew; British business executive; *Chairman, Tata Steel Europe Limited;* m.; two c.; earlier career with Unilever Ltd; various financial positions at P&O Steam Navigation Co. 1971–89, Finance Dir 1983–89; Finance Dir Pilkington plc 1989–2001, Exec. Dir 1989–2003; mem. Bd of Dirs Corus Group plc and Chair. Audit Cttee 2003– (Corus taken over by Tata Steel March 2007), Dir (non-exec.) Tata Steel Ltd 2007– (remained Chair. Audit Cttee and certain other bd cttees of Tata Steel Europe), Chair. Tata Steel Europe Ltd 2009–; Dir (non-exec.) Kesa Electricals plc, Laird plc, Paypoint plc; Fellow, Chartered Inst. of Cost and Man. Accountants, Inst. of Corp. Treas; mem. Urgent Issues Task Force of the Accounting Standards Bd 1991–97. *Address:* Corus Group PLC, 30 Millbank, London, SW1P 4WY, England (office). *Telephone:* (20) 7717-4444 (office). *Fax:* (20) 7717-4455 (office). *E-mail:* feedback@corusgroup.com (office). *Website:* www .corusgroup.com (office).

ROBB, Charles Spittal, BBA, JD; American lawyer, academic and fmr politician; *Distinguished Professor of Law and Public Policy, George Mason University;* b. 26 June 1939, Phoenix, Ariz.; s. of James Spittal Robb and Frances Howard Robb (née Woolley); m. Lynda Johnson (d. of late Pres. Lyndon B. Johnson) 1967; three d.; ed Cornell Univ., Univ. of Wisconsin and Univ. of Virginia; admitted to Va Bar 1973; law clerk to John D. Butzner, Jr, US Court of Appeals 1973–74; admitted to US Supreme Court Bar 1976; Attorney, Williams, Connolly and Califano 1974–77; Lt-Gov. of Va 1978–82, Gov. 1982–86; Pnr, Hunton and Williams 1986–89; Senator from Virginia 1989–2001; Chair. Democratic Govs' Assocn 1984–85, Democratic Leadership Council 1986–88; Chair Educ. Comm. of the States, Educ. Sub-Cttee of the Nat. Govs Assocns' Standing Cttee on Human Resources; Chair. Southern Govs' Assocn 1984–85; Pres. Council of State Govts 1985–86; Distinguished Prof. of Law and Public Policy, George Mason Univ. 2001–; mem. Pres.'s Foreign Intelligence Advisory Bd, Sec. of State's Arms Control and Nonproliferation Advisory Bd, FBI Dir's Advisory Bd; mem. Bd of Dirs Space Foundation, Thomas Jefferson Program in Public Policy, Concord Coalition, Center for the Study of the Presidency; MITRE Corpn (Vice Chair. 2006–); mem. American, Va Bar Assocns, Va Trial Lawyers' Assocn; Co-Chair. Pres.'s Comm. on Intelligence Capabilities 2004; mem. Iraq Study Group, Inst. of Peace 2006; Bronze Star, Viet Nam Service Medal with four stars, Vietnamese Cross of Gallantry with Silver Star; Raven Award 1973; Seven Socs. Org. Award, Univ. of Va. *Address:* School of Law, George Mason University, Room 415, 3301 North Fairfax Drive, Arlington, VA 22201, USA (office). *Telephone:* (703) 993-8000 (office). *Fax:* (703) 993-8088 (office). *Website:* www.law .gmu.edu (office).

ROBB, Graham Macdonald, PhD, FRSL; British writer; b. 2 June 1958, Manchester, England; m. Margaret Hambrick 1986; ed Univ. of Oxford, Gold-smiths Coll., London and Vanderbilt Univ., Nashville, Tenn., USA; British Acad. Fellowship 1987–90; Chevalier, Ordre des Arts et des Lettres, Grande Médaille de la ville de Paris 2012; New York Times Book of the Year 1994, 1999 and 2001, Whitbread Biography of the Year Award 1997, R.S.L. Heinemann Award 1998. *Publications include:* Le Corsaire – Satan en Silhouette 1985, Baudelaire Lecteur de Balzac 1988, Scènes de la Vie de Bohème (ed.) 1988, Baudelaire (trans.) 1989, La Poésie de Baudelaire et la Poésie Française 1993, Balzac 1994, Unlocking Mallarmé 1996, Victor Hugo: A Biography 1998, Rimbaud 2000, Strangers: Homosexual Love in the 19th Century, The Discovery of France (Duff Cooper Prize, Ondaatje Prize, Royal Soc. of Literature 2008) 2007, Parisians: An Adventure History of Paris 2010; contribs to Times Literary Supplement, Daily Telegraph, London Review of Books, Sunday Times, New York Times. *Leisure interest:* cycling. *Address:* c/o Rogers, Coleridge & White Ltd, 20 Powis Mews, London, W11 1JN, England (office). *Telephone:* (20) 7221-3717 (office). *Fax:* (20) 7229-9084 (office). *E-mail:* info@rcwlitagency.com (office). *Website:* www .rcwlitagency.com (office).

RÖBBELEN, Gerhard Paul Karl, Dr rer. nat; German professor of plant breeding; *Professor Emeritus, University of Göttingen;* b. 10 May 1929, Bremen; s. of Ernst Röbbelen and Henny Röbbelen; m. Christa Scherz 1957; two s. one d.; ed

Univs of Göttingen and Freiburg; Asst Prof. Inst. of Agronomy and Plant Breeding, Univ. of Göttingen 1957–67, Prof. and Head Div. of Cytogenetics 1967–70, Dir of Inst. 1970–94, Dean Faculty of Agric. 1971–72, Prof. Emer. 1994–; Visiting Prof. Univ. of Mo., USA 1966–67; Ed. Plant Breeding 1976–2000; mem. German Soc. for Genetics (Pres. 1969–70, 1977–79), European Asscn for Research in Plant Breeding–EUCARPIA (Chair. Section for Oil and Protein Crops 1978–86, Pres. 1986–89), German Botanical Soc., Asscn for Applied Botany, Genetics Soc. of Canada, German Soc. Fat Research (Pres. 1989–92), German Soc. of Plant Breeding (Pres. 1991–96), Acad. of Sciences, Göttingen 1981, Acad. Leopoldina 1990; Order of Merit 1st Class (Germany) 2001; Hon. DAgric. (Kiel) 1976, (Halle/Saale) 1997, (Brno Czech Repub.) 2001; Norman Medal, German Soc. of Fat Science 1984, Chevreul Medal, Asscn Française pour l'Etude des Corps Gras 1989, Eminent Scientist Award, Paris 1999. *Publications:* more than 300 articles on research into plant genetics and breeding. *Leisure interests:* music, mountain climbing, gardening. *Address:* 8 Von Sieboldstrasse, 37075 Göttingen (office); 9 Tuckermannweg, 37085 Göttingen, Germany. *Website:* www.uni-goettingen.de (office).

ROBBINS, John B., MD; American immunologist and academic; *Head, Laboratory of Developmental and Molecular Immunity, National Institute of Child Health and Human Development;* Chief, Lab. of Developmental and Molecular Immunity, Nat. Inst. of Child Health and Human Devt, NIH 1983–; fmr Chair. WHO Ad Hoc Cttee; Albert Lasker Award for Clinical Research (jtly) 1996, Albert B. Sabin Gold Medal Award 2001. *Publications:* Bacterial Vaccines (ed.) 1987, The Awakened Heart 1997, Diet for a New America – How Your Food Choices Affect Your Health, Happiness, and the Future of Life on Earth 1998, Internal Medicine on Call (co-author) 2002, Reclaiming Our Health – Exploding the Medical Myth and Embracing the Sources of True Healing 2004. *Address:* Office of the Chief, Laboratory of Developmental and Molecular Immunity, National Institute of Child Health and Human Development, 6A/2A06, 31 Center Drive, Bethesda, MD 20892, USA (office). *Telephone:* (301) 496-0850 (office). *E-mail:* robbinsj@nichd.nih.gov (office). *Website:* www.nichd.nih.gov (office).

ROBBINS, Keith Gilbert, DPhil, DLitt, FRSE, FLSW; British historian, academic and fmr university vice-chancellor; b. 9 April 1940, Bristol, England; s. of Gilbert Henry John Robbins and Edith Mary Robbins; m. Janet Carey Thomson 1963; three s. one d.; ed Bristol Grammar School, Magdalen Coll. Oxford, St Antony's Coll. Oxford; Lecturer, Univ. of York 1963–71; Prof. of History, Univ. Coll. of N Wales, Bangor 1971–79; Prof. of Modern History, Univ. of Glasgow 1980–91; Vice-Chancellor of Wales, Lampeter 1992–2003; Sr Vice-Chancellor Univ. of Wales 1995–2001; Pres. Historical Asscn 1988–91; Winston Churchill Travelling Fellow 1990; Fellow, Learned Soc. of Wales. *Publications:* Munich 1938, 1968, Sir Edward Grey 1971, The Abolition of War 1976, John Bright 1979, The Eclipse of a Great Power: Modern Britain 1870–1975 1983, 1870–1992 (second edn) 1994, The First World War 1984, Nineteenth-Century Britain: Integration and Diversity 1988, Appeasement 1988, Blackwell Dictionary of Twentieth-Century British Political Life (ed.) 1990, Churchill 1992, History, Religion and Identity in Modern Britain 1993, Politicians, Diplomacy and War in Modern British History 1994, Bibliography of British History 1914–1989 1996, Great Britain: Identities, Institutions and the Idea of Britishness 1997, The World Since 1945: a Concise History 1998, The British Isles 1901–1951 2002, Britain and Europe 1789–2005 2005, England, Ireland, Scotland, Wales: The Christian Church 1900-2000 (ed.) 2008, The Dynamics of Religious Reform in Northern Europe 1780–20, Political and Legal Perspectives (ed.) 2010; Religion and Diplomacy: Religion and British Foreign Policy 1815 to 1941 2010, Pride of Place: A Modern History of Bristol Grammar School 2010, Transforming the World: Global Political History since World War II 2013. *Leisure interests:* walking, music. *Address:* Rhyd y Fran, Cribyn, Lampeter, Ceredigion, SA48 7NH, Wales. *Telephone:* (1570) 470349. *E-mail:* profkgr@clara.co.uk.

ROBBINS, Tim, BA; American actor, director and screenwriter; b. 16 Oct. 1958, West Covina, Calif.; s. of folk singer Gil Robbins; fmr pnr Susan Sarandon (q.v.); three c.; ed Univ. of California, Los Angeles; began career as mem. Theater for the New City; Founding Artistic Dir The Actors' Gang 1981–; Founder Havoc Inc. (production co.). *Theatre includes:* as actor: Ubu Roi 1981; as dir: A Midsummer Night's Dream 1984, The Good Woman of Setzuan 1990; as writer, with Adam Simon: Alagazam, After the Dog Wars, Violence: The Misadventures of Spike Spangle, Farmer, Carnage – A Comedy (rep. USA at Edin. Int. Festival, Scotland); as writer: Embedded 2004. *Films include:* No Small Affair 1984, Toy Soldiers 1984, The Sure Thing 1985, Fraternity Vacation 1985, Top Gun 1986, Howard the Duck 1986, Five Corners 1987, Bull Durham 1988, Tapeheads 1988, Miss Firecracker 1989, Eric the Viking 1989, Cadillac Man 1990, Twister 1990, Jacob's Ladder 1990, Jungle Fever 1991, The Player 1992, Bob Roberts (also writer and dir) 1992, Amazing Stories: Book Four 1992, Short Cuts 1993, The Hudsucker Proxy 1994, The Shawshank Redemption 1994, Prêt-à-Porter 1994, I.Q. 1994, Dead Man Walking (writer and dir) 1995, Nothing to Lose 1997, Arlington Road 1999, Cradle Will Rock (also writer and dir) 1999, Austin Powers: The Spy Who Shagged Me 1999, Mission to Mars 2000, High Fidelity 2000, Antitrust 2001, Human Nature 2001, The Truth About Charlie 2002, The Day My God Died 2003, Mystic River (Golden Globe for Best Supporting Actor 2004, Critics' Choice Award for Best Supporting Actor 2004, Screen Actors Guild Best Supporting Actor Award 2004, Acad. Award for Best Supporting Actor 2004) 2003, Code 46 2003, The Secret Life of Words 2005, War of the Worlds 2005, La Vida secreta de las palabras 2005, Zathura: A Space Adventure 2005, Catch a Fire 2006, Tenacious D: The Pick of Destiny 2006, Noise 2007, The Lucky Ones 2008, City of Ember 2008, Green Lantern 2011. *Television:* Queens Supreme (pilot episode and series dir) 2003, Cinema Verite (movie) 2011. *Address:* c/o Elaine Goldsmith Thomas, ICM, 40 West 57th Street, New York, NY 10019 (office); Havoc Inc., 16 West 19th Street, 12th Floor, New York, NY 10011; The Actors' Gang at The Ivy Substation, 9070 Venice Blvd., Culver City, CA 90232, USA. *Website:* www.theactorsgang.com.

ROBBINS, Tom, BA; American writer; b. 22 July 1936, Blowing Rock, NC; s. of George T. Robbins and Katherine Robinson Robbins; m. 1st Terrie Lunden 1967 (divorced 1972); one s.; m. 2nd Alexa d'Avalon 1987; ed Virginia Commonwealth Univ. and Univ. of Washington; operated black market ring in S Korea 1956–57; int. news Times-Dispatch, Richmond, Va 1959–62; Art Critic, The Seattle Times and contrib. to Artforum and Art in America etc. 1962–65; Art Critic, Seattle

Magazine 1965–67; Bumbershoot Golden Umbrella for Lifetime Achievement 1998, Writers' Digest 100 Best Writers of the 20th Century 2000. *Films:* Even Cowgirls Get the Blues 1994. *Publications:* novels: Another Roadside Attraction 1971, Even Cowgirls Get the Blues 1976, Still Life With Woodpecker 1980, Jitterbug Perfume 1984, Skinny Legs and All 1990, Half Asleep in Frog Pajamas 1994, Fierce Invalids Home from Hot Climates 2000, Villa Incognito 2003, Wild Ducks Flying Backward 2005, B is for Beer 2009. *Leisure interests:* volleyball, white magick, psychedelic plants, art, pop culture and religions. *Address:* PO Box 338, La Conner, WA 98257, USA (home).

ROBBINS, Trevor William, CBE, PhD, FRS, FMedSci; British neuroscientist and academic; *Professor of Cognitive Neuroscience and Director, Behavioural and Clinical Neuroscience Institute, University of Cambridge;* Prof. of Cognitive Neuroscience, Univ. of Cambridge 1997–, elected to Chair of Experimental Psychology and Head of Dept of Experimental Psychology 2002–, Dir Behavioural and Clinical Neuroscience Inst. 2011–, Fellow of Downing Coll.; Pres. European Behavioural Pharmacology Soc. 1992–94, British Asscn of Psychopharmacology 1996–97; Ed. Psychopharmacology 1980–; mem. Editorial Bd Science 2003–; mem. MRC, Chair. Neuroscience and Mental Health Bd 1995–99; Fellow, British Psychological Soc.; inaugural Distinguished Scientist Award, European Behavioural Pharmacology Soc. 2001. *Publications:* Psychology for Medicine: The Prefrontal Cortex (co-ed.), Executive and Cognitive Function (co-ed.), Disorders of Brain and Mind (co-ed.); more than 600 papers in professional journals. *Address:* Behavioural and Clinical Neurosciences Institute, Department of Experimental Psychology, University of Cambridge, Downing Site, Cambridge, CB2 3EB, England (office). *E-mail:* t.robbins@psychol.cam.ac.uk (office); twr2@cam.ac.uk (office). *Website:* research.psychol.cam.ac.uk/~bcni (office); www.neuroscience.cam.ac.uk (office).

RÖBEL, Udo; German editor; b. 20 Jan. 1950, Neustadt, Weinstrasse; Restaurant Ed. for Rheinpfalz and Mil. Service Corresp. for DPA and AP 1969–71; mem. editorial staff Bild newspaper, Frankfurt, Kettwig, and Aachen-zum-Schluss 1972–82; Deputy Ed.-in-Chief Express newspaper, Cologne 1983–89; journalistic adviser Heinrich-Bauer-Verlag 1989–92; mem. Chief Editorial Staff Bild 1993–97, Ed.-in-Chief Bild 1998–2000, Ed.-in-Chief Bild.de 2001–04; freelance writer and media consultant 2004–; Man. Apptory.eu GmbH (app developer) 2011–; Wächter-Preis, Deutschen Tagespresse 1985. *Publications include:* Tod eines Engels 2002, Schattenbrüder 2005, Der rote Reiter 2011.

ROBERT, Jacques Frédéric, DenD; French professor of law; *President, Centre français de Droit comparé;* b. 29 Sept. 1928, Algiers, Algeria; s. of Frédéric Robert and Fanny Robert; m. Marie-Caroline de Bary 1958; two s. two d.; ed Lycée E. F. Gautier, Algiers, Univs. of Algiers and Paris, CNRS; Prof. of Law, Univs of Algiers 1956–60, Rabat, Morocco 1960–62, Grenoble 1962–65; Dir Maison franco-japonaise, Tokyo 1965–68; Prof. of Law, Univ. of Nanterre 1968–69, Univ. of Paris II 1969–; Contributor, Le Monde and La Croix 1970–; Dir Revue de droit public 1977–; Pres. Univ. of Paris II (Panthéon) 1979–85; Pres. of Centre français de Droit comparé 1985–; mem. Conseil Constitutionnel 1989–98; mem. Japan Acad. 1997; Commdr Légion d'honneur, Ordre nat. du Mérite, Order of Honour Austria; Order of the Sacred Treasure (Japan), Officier, Ordre des Palmes académiques; Prix Paul Deschanel 1954. *Publications:* Les violations de la liberté individuelle 1954, La monarchie marocaine 1963, Le Japon 1970, Introduction à l'Esprit des Lois 1973, Libertés publiques 1988, L'Esprit de défense 1988, Libertés et droits fondamentaux (5th edn) 2002, Droits de l'homme et Libertés fondamentales (7th edn) 1999, Le juge constitutionnel, juge des libertés 1999, La Garde de la République 2000, Enjeux du siècle: nos libertés 2002, La fin de la Laicité 2004, Les richesses du droit 2005. *Leisure interests:* music, photography, swimming. *Address:* Centre français de Droit comparé, 28 rue Saint-Guillaume, 75007 Paris (office); 105 Boulevard Murat, 75016 Paris, France (home). *Telephone:* 1-44-39-86-24 (office); 1-40-71-87-05 (home). *Fax:* 1-44-39-86-28 (office); 1-46-51-37-29 (home). *E-mail:* cfdc@legiscompare.com (office).

ROBERT, Lorin S.; Micronesian diplomatist; *Secretary of Foreign Affairs;* ed American Univ. School of Int. Service, Washington, DC, Univ. of Oxford, UK; joined Dept of Foreign Affairs 1984, posts have included Deputy Chief of Mission for Embassy in Tokyo, Deputy Asst Sec. for Asian Affairs, Asst Sec. Asia Pacific and Multilateral Affairs Div., Deputy Sec. for the Dept 2001–07, Sec. of Foreign Affairs 2007–; Chair. Bd of Trustees Micronesian Fisheries Authority; fmr Alternate Gov. IBRD and Asian Devt Bank; has represented Micronesia on various UN panels. *Address:* Department of Foreign Affairs, PS123, Palikir, Pohnpei State, 96941, Federated States of Micronesia (office). *Telephone:* 320-2641 (office). *Fax:* 320-2933 (office). *E-mail:* foreignaffairs@mail.fm (office).

ROBERTO CARLOS; Brazilian professional footballer; b. (Roberto Carlos da Silva Rocha), 10 April 1973, Garça, São Paulo; s. of Oscar and Vera Lúcia; m. to Alexandra; three d.; ed Colonel José Levy School, São Paulo; left wing-back; played for União São João 1990–92 (professional debut 1992), Atlético Mineiro 1992, Palmeiras 1993–95 (45 matches, four goals, won Brazilian League 1993, 1994, Rio-São Paulo Tournament 1993, São Paulo State Championship 1993, 1994), Internazionale, Italy 1995–96 (30 matches, five goals), Real Madrid, Spain 1996–2007 (370 matches, 47 goals, won La Liga 1996/97, 2000/01, 2002/03, 2006/07, Spanish Super Cup 1997, 2001, 2003, UEFA Champions League 1997/98, 1999/2000, 2001/02, UEFA Super Cup 2002, UEFA Super Cup, Intercontinental Cup 1998, 2002), Fenerbahçe, Turkey 2007–10 (101 matches 12 goals, won Turkish Super Cup 2007, 2009), Corinthians, São Paulo 2010–11, Anzhi Makhachkala, Dagestan (caretaker man. 2011) 2011–; played for Brazil nat. team (debut vs USA), 125 int. caps, 11 goals 1992–2006, bronze medal, Olympic Games, Atlanta 1996; Winner, Copa America 1997, 1999, World Cup 2002 (runner-up 1998); UEFA Team of the Year 2002, 2003. *Address:* Dinamo Stadium, 367025 Makhachkala, Dakhadaev street, 23, Dagestan, Russia. *Telephone:* (8722) 67-85-20. *Fax:* (8722) 68-20-08,. *E-mail:* info@fc-anji.ru. *Website:* www.fc-anji.ru; www.robertocarlos .com.br.

ROBERTS, Brian L., BS; American business executive; *Chairman and CEO, Comcast Corporation;* b. 28 June 1959, Philadelphia, Pa; s. of Ralph J. Roberts and Suzanne F. Roberts; m. Aileen Kennedy 1985; one s. two d.; ed Wharton School of Finance Univ. of Pennsylvania; Vice-Pres. Operations, Comcast Cable Communications Inc. 1985–86, Exec. Vice-Pres. Comcast Corpn 1986–90, Pres. 1990, CEO

2001–, Chair. 2004–, also mem. Bd of Dirs (acquired AT&T Broadband 2002); mem. Bd of Dirs Nat. Cable & Telecommunications Asscn, Chair. 1995–96, 2005–07; Chair. CableLabs 1999–2001, 2003–05, 2009–11, Dir Emer. 2011–; Vice-Chair. Walter Katz Foundation; mem. Bd of Dirs Turner Broadcasting System, QVC Network, Bank of NY, Simon Wiesenthal Center, Viewer's Choice; Co-Chair. Resource Devt Campaign for United Way of Southeastern Pennsylvania 2003; Founding Co-Chair. Philadelphia 2000 (nonpartisan host cttee for Republican Nat. Convention) 2000; mem. Business Roundtable, Washington, DC; honoured by The Police Athletic League of Philadelphia 2002, Steven J. Ross Humanitarian Award, UJA Fed. of New York 2003, Humanitarian Award, Simon Wiesenthal Center 2004, named by Institutional Investor magazine as one of America's top CEOs 2004–09, honoured by Nat. Asscn for Multi-ethnicity in Communications 2005, honoured by Partnership for a Drug-Free America 2005, inducted into Cable Television Hall of Fame 2006, Distinguished Vanguard Award for Leadership 2007, recognized by Big Brothers and Big Sisters for outstanding leadership in the community and for serving as a role model to youth 2008, Amb. for Humanity Award, Univ. of Southern California Shoah Foundation Inst. 2011, Fred Dressler Achievement Award, S.I. Newhouse School of Public Communications at Syracuse Univ. 2011 inducted into Babson Coll.'s Acad. of Distinguished Entrepreneurs Hall of Fame 2011, recognized by Fortune magazine as a Businessperson of the Year 2012, Joseph Wharton Award for Leadership 2012. *Achievements include:* earned Silver Medals with US squash team at Maccabiah Games, Israel 1981, 1985, 1997, Gold Medal 2005. *Address:* Comcast Corporation, One Comcast Center, 1701 JFK Blvd, Philadelphia, PA 19103, USA (office). *Telephone:* (215) 286-1700 (office). *Website:* corporate.comcast.com (office).

ROBERTS, (Charles) Patrick; American politician; *Senator from Kansas;* b. 20 April 1936, Topeka, Kan.; s. of Wes Roberts and Ruth Roberts (née Patrick); m. Franki Fann 1970; one s. two d.; ed Holton High School, Kansas State Univ.; served with US Marine Corps 1958–62; Publr Litchfield Park, Ariz. 1962–67; Admin. Asst to US Senator F. Carlson 1967–68, to US Congressman Keith Sebelius 1968–70; mem. 97th–104th US Congresses 1980–97; Senator from Kansas 1997–, fmr Chair. Select Cttee on Intelligence, mem. Cttee on Agric., Nutrition, and Forestry, Cttee on Ethics, Cttee on Finance, Cttee on Health, Educ., Labor, and Pensions, Cttee on Rules and Admin; Republican. *Address:* 109 Hart Senate Office Building, Washington, DC 20510-1605, USA (office). *Telephone:* (202) 224-4774 (office). *Fax:* (202) 224-3514 (office). *Website:* roberts.senate.gov (office).

ROBERTS, Sir Derek Harry, Kt, CBE, BSc, FRS, FEng; British physicist, business executive, fmr university provost and fmr university president; b. 28 March 1932, Manchester; s. of Harry Roberts and Alice Roberts (née Storey); m. Winifred Short 1958; one s. one d.; ed Manchester Cen. High School and Manchester Univ.; Research Scientist, Plessey Co. 1953–67; Gen. Man. Plessey Semiconductors 1967–69; Dir Plessey Allen Clark Research Centre 1969–73; Man. Dir Plessey Microsystems Div. 1973–79; Dir of Research, The General Electric Co. PLC 1979–83, Tech. Dir 1983–85, Jt Deputy Man. Dir (Tech.) 1985–88, Dir 1988–; Visiting Prof., Univ. Coll., London 1979, Provost and Pres. 1989–99, 2002–03; Pres. BAAS 1996–97, Sr Research Fellow, School of Public Policy 1999–; mem. Bd of Dirs Ludwig Inst. for Cancer Research; Hon. Fellow, Univ. Coll. London, British Asscn for the Advancement of Science; Hon. DSc (Bath) 1982, (Loughborough) 1984, (City) 1985, (Lancaster) 1986, (Manchester) 1987, (Queens Univ., Belfast) 1990; Hon. DUniv (Open) 1984, (Salford), (Essex), (London) 1988. *Publications:* about 30 tech. papers in learned soc. journals. *Leisure interests:* gardening, reading. *Address:* The Old Rectory, Maids Moreton, Buckingham, England (home). *Telephone:* (1280) 813470 (home).

ROBERTS, Dorothy Elizabeth, AMusA, LMus; pianist and abstract painter; b. 1930, Brisbane, Qld, Australia; m. (divorced); one s.; ed Sydney Conservatorium of Music, studied with Adelina de Lara in London, also with Clara Schumann; concerts at Balliol Coll., Oxford, Purcell Room, South Bank, London; performed Liszt's Piano Concerto in E Flat with London Symphony Orchestra at Royal Albert Hall, London; other concerto performances with the Hallé Orchestra, Northern Sinfonia Orchestra and London Bach Players; recitals in the UK, Germany, Australia, France, The Netherlands, Canada; television appearance with the Hallé Orchestra; other television appearances with Richard Bonynge, including playing with the BBC Orchestra; Hon. DLit (Univ. of Bradford) 1995. *Address:* Alveley House, 17 Lindum Road, Lincoln, LN2 1NS, England (home).

ROBERTS, Sir Ivor Anthony, Kt, KCMG, CMG, MA, FCIL; British diplomatist (retd) and college principal; *President, Trinity College, Oxford;* b. 24 Sept. 1946, Liverpool, England; s. of Leonard Moore Roberts and Rosa Maria Roberts (née Fusco); m. Elizabeth Bray Bernard Smith 1974; two s. one d.; ed St Mary's Coll., Crosby, Keble Coll., Oxford; entered diplomatic service 1968, with Middle East Centre for Arab Studies 1969, Third, then Second Sec. Paris 1970–73, Second, then First Sec. FCO 1973–78, First Sec. Canberra 1978–82, Deputy Head of News Dept FCO 1982–86, Head Security Co-ordination Dept, FCO 1986–88, Minister and Deputy Head of Mission, Madrid 1989–93, Chargé d'affaires Belgrade 1994–96; Amb. to Yugoslavia 1996–97, to Ireland 1999–2003, to Italy 2003–06 (retd); Chair. Council of British School, Rome; Sr Assoc. mem. St Antony's Coll., Oxford 1998–99; Pres. Trinity Coll. Oxford 2006–; mem. Advisory Bd MacKinder Forum; Fellow, Chartered Inst. of Linguists 1991–; Patron Venice in Peril Fund; Hon. Fellow, Keble Coll. Oxford 2017; Freeman, City of London 2009. *Publication:* Satow's Diplomatic Practice (ed.) 2009. *Leisure interests:* opera, theatre, skiing, golf, photography. *Address:* Trinity College, Broad Street, Oxford, OX1 3BH, England (office). *Telephone:* (1865) 279900 (office). *Fax:* (1865) 279902 (office). *E-mail:* ivor.roberts@trinity.ox.ac.uk (office). *Website:* www.trinity.ox.ac.uk (office).

ROBERTS, John D., PhD, FRSC; American chemist and academic; *Institute Professor Emeritus of Chemistry, California Institute of Technology;* b. 8 June 1918, Los Angeles, Calif.; s. of Allen Andrew Roberts and Flora Dombrowski; m. Edith M. Johnson 1942; three s. one d.; ed Univ. of California, Los Angeles; Instructor, UCLA; Nat. Research Fellow in Chem., Harvard Univ. 1945–46, Instructor 1946; Instructor, MIT 1946–47, Asst Prof. 1947–50, Assoc. Prof. 1950–53; Guggenheim Fellow, California Inst. of Tech. 1952–53, Prof. of Organic Chem. 1953–72, Inst. Prof. of Chem. 1972–88, Prof. Emer. 1988–, Lecturer 1988–, Chair. Div. of Chem. and Chemical Eng 1963–68, Acting Chair. 1972–73, Dean of the Faculty 1980–83, Vice-Pres. and Provost 1980–83; Visiting Prof., Ohio State Univ. 1952, Harvard Univ. 1959–60, Univ. of Munich 1962; Distinguished Visiting

Prof., Univ. of Iowa 1967; Visiting Prof., Stanford Univ. 1973; Noyce Visiting Prof. of Science, Grinnell Coll. 2001; Distinguished Grad. Lecturer, Scripps Research Inst. 1996; mem. NAS, Chair. Section of Chem. 1968–71, of Math. and Physical Sciences 1976–78, Class I 1977–79, Counsellor 1980–83; mem. American Philosophical Soc. 1974, Counsellor, Class I 1983–86; Fellow, ACS 2009; Hon. Alumnus, California Inst. of Tech. 1993; Hon. Dr rer. nat (Munich) 1964; Hon. DSc (Temple Univ.) 1989, (Wales) 1996, (Scripps Research Inst.), Hon. ScD (Notre Dame) 1993; numerous awards, including Nat. Medal of Science 1990, Welch Award 1990, Arthur C. Cope Award 1994, NAS Award in Chemical Sciences 1999, Nakanishi Prize 2001, Pauling Legacy Award 2006, NAS Award for Chem. in Service of Society 2009, American Inst. of Chemists Gold Medal 2013. *Publications:* Nuclear Magnetic Resonance 1958, Spin-Spin Splitting in High Resolution Nuclear Magnetic Resonance Spectra 1961, Molecular Orbital Calculations 1961, Basic Principles of Organic Chemistry 1965, Modern Organic Chemistry 1967, Organic Chemistry, Methane to Macromolecules 1971, At the Right Place at the Right Time (autobiography) 1990, ABC's of FT NMR 2000; numerous articles 1940–. *Leisure interests:* tennis, skiing, sailing, classical music, colour photography. *Address:* California Institute of Technology, 358 Crellin Laboratory, Pasadena, CA 91125, USA (office). *Telephone:* (626) 395-6036 (office). *E-mail:* robertsj@caltech.edu (office). *Website:* www.cce.caltech.edu (office).

ROBERTS, John G., Jr, AB, JD; American lawyer and judge; *Chief Justice of the United States;* b. 27 Jan. 1955, Buffalo, NY; m. Jane Marie Sullivan 1996; one s. one d.; ed Harvard Coll., Harvard Law School; served as a law clerk for Judge Henry J. Friendly, US Court of Appeals for the Second Circuit 1979–80, to then-Assoc. Justice William H. Rehnquist, US Supreme Court 1980–81; Special Asst to the Attorney Gen., US Dept of Justice 1981–82; Assoc. Counsel to Pres. Ronald Reagan, White House Counsel's Office 1982–86; practised law in Washington, DC 1986–89, 1993–2003; Prin. Deputy Solicitor Gen., US Dept of Justice 1989–93; Judge, US Court of Appeals for DC Circuit 2003–05; Chief Justice, Supreme Court of the US 2005–. *Address:* Supreme Court of the United States, 1 First Street NE, Washington, DC 20543, USA (office). *Telephone:* (202) 479-3000 (office). *Website:* www.supremecourt.gov (office).

ROBERTS, Julia; American actress; b. (Julie Fiona Roberts), 28 Oct. 1967, Smyrna, Ga; m. 1st Lyle Lovett 1993 (divorced 1995); m. 2nd Daniel Moder 2002; two s. one d.; ed Campbell High School; UNICEF Goodwill Amb. 1995; f. film production co. Red Om Films Inc. (fmrly Shoelace Productions); American Cinematheque Award 2007. *Films include:* Firehouse (uncredited) 1987, Satisfaction 1988, Mystic Pizza 1988, Blood Red 1989, Steel Magnolias (Golden Globe Award 1990) 1989, Flatliners 1990, Pretty Woman 1990, Sleeping with the Enemy 1991, Dying Young 1991, Hook 1991, The Player 1992, The Pelican Brief 1993, I Love Trouble 1994, Prêt à Porter 1994, Something to Talk About 1995, Mary Reilly 1996, Michael Collins 1996, Everyone Says I Love You 1996, My Best Friend's Wedding 1997, Conspiracy Theory 1997, Stepmom 1998, Notting Hill 1999, Runaway Bride 1999, Erin Brockovich (Acad. Award for Best Actress 2001) 2000, The Mexican 2001, America's Sweethearts 2001, Ocean's Eleven 2001, Grand Champion 2002, Full Frontal 2002, Confessions of a Dangerous Mind 2002, Mona Lisa Smile 2003, Closer 2004, Ocean's Twelve 2004, The Ant Bully (voice) 2006, Charlotte's Web (voice) 2006, Charlie Wilson's War 2007, Fireflies in the Garden 2008, Duplicity 2009, Valentine's Day 2010, Eat Pray Love 2010, Love, Wedding, Marriage (voice) 2011, Larry Crowne 2011, Mirror Mirror: The Untold Adventures of Snow White 2012, August: Osage County 2013. *Television:* Crime Story (series) 1987, Baja Oklahoma (film) 1988, Miami Vice (series) 1988, Friends (series) 1996, Law & Order (series) 1999, Freedom: A History of Us (series documentary) 2003, The Normal Heart (film) 2014. *Address:* c/o Red Om Films Inc., 145 West 57th Street, 19th Floor, New York, NY 10019 (office); c/o Creative Artists Agency, 2000 Avenue of the Stars, Los Angeles, CA 90067, USA (office). *Telephone:* (212) 243-2900 (Red Om) (office); (310) 288-2000 (CAA) (office). *Fax:* (212) 243-2973 (Red Om) (office); (310) 288-2900 (CAA) (office). *Website:* www.caa.com (office).

ROBERTS, Julian V. F., BA, FCA, MCT; British accountant and business executive; *Group Chief Executive, Old Mutual plc;* m. Marion Roberts; three s. one d.; ed Univ. of Stirling; qualified as accountant at PricewaterhouseCoopers 1983; with C E Heath 1987–93; mem. Bd of Dirs and Chief Financial Officer Aon UK Holdings Ltd 1993–98; Group Finance Dir Sun Life & Provincial Holdings plc 1998–2006; Group Finance Dir Old Mutual plc 2000–06, Chief Exec. Skandia 2006–08, Group Chief Exec. Old Mutual plc 2008–. *Leisure interests:* watching sports, playing golf, supporting his children at their rugby, football and hockey fixtures. *Address:* Old Mutual plc, 5th Floor, Old Mutual Place, 2 Lambeth Hill, London, EC4V 4GG, England (office). *Telephone:* (20) 7002-7000 (office). *Fax:* (20) 7002-7200 (office). *E-mail:* matthew.gregorowski@omg.co.uk (office). *Website:* www.oldmutual.com (office).

ROBERTS, Kevin John; British advertising executive; *CEO, Saatchi & Saatchi Worldwide Inc.;* b. 20 Oct. 1949, Lancaster; s. of John Roberts and Jean Roberts (née Lambert); m. 1st Barbara Beckett; one d.; m. 2nd Rowena Joan Honeywill 1974; two s. one d.; Brand Man. Gillette Co., London 1972–74; Group Marketing Man., Procter & Gamble, Geneva 1975–82; Vice-Pres. Pepsico, Nicosia 1982–86; Pres. and CEO Pepsi Cola Canada, Toronto 1987–89; COO Lion Nathan, Auckland 1990–96; CEO Saatchi & Saatchi Worldwide Inc., New York City 1997–, Publicis Groupe SA, Superscape Group PLC; Prof. of Sustainable Enterprise and Sr Fellow, Waikato Man. School, Univ. of Waikato, New Zealand; inaugural CEO in Residence, Judge Inst. of Man., Cambridge Univ. UK; Chair.USA Rugby Bd 2006–; Hon. Prof., Peruvian Univ. of Applied Sciences 2007; Dr hc (Univ. of Waikato) 1998; New Yorker for New York Award 2004. *Publication:* Peak Performing Organisations (co-author) 2000, Lovemarks: The Future Beyond Brands 2004, sisomo: The Future on Screen 2005, Lovemarks Effect: Winning in the Consumer Revolution 2006. *Leisure interests:* rugby, tennis, art, travel, music. *Address:* Saatchi & Saatchi Worldwide Inc., 375 Hudson Street, New York, NY 10014-3620, USA (office); Waikato Management School, The University of Waikato, Private Bag 3105, Hamilton, New Zealand. *Telephone:* (212) 463-2000 (office); (7) 858-5013 (NZ). *Fax:* (212) 463-2367 (office). *E-mail:* kevin_roberts@mngt.waikato.ac.nz. *Website:* www.saatchi.com/worldwide (office); www.saatchikevin.com; www.mngt.waikato.ac.nz.

ROBERTS, Matthew Vernon, MA, MPhil, DipMassComm; Saint Lucia journalist, educator and fmr politician; *Resident Tutor and Head, School of Continuing*

Studies, University of the West Indies; b. 29 July 1954, Castries; m. Catherine (Kate) Regis 1980; one s. three d.; ed Univ. of the West Indies, Jamaica, City Univ., London, UK; primary school teacher 1969–72; Asst Ed. The Voice newspaper 1972–80; fmr Public Relations Officer, Saint Lucia Tourist Bd; fmr Regional Communications Consultant, Caribbean Family Planning Affiliation; fmr Chief Information Officer Govt Information Service; currently Resident Tutor and Head, School of Continuing Studies, Univ. of West Indies; Speaker of House of Ass. –2003. *Leisure interests:* reading, swimming, gardening. *Address:* University of the West Indies, School of Continuing Studies, The Morne, Castries (office); Clavier Ridgeway, Entrepot Summit, PO Box 927, Castries, Saint Lucia (home). *Telephone:* 453-6486 (office); 452-7282 (home). *Fax:* 452-4080 (office). *E-mail:* uwislu@candw.lc (office).

ROBERTS, Michèle Brigitte, MA (Oxon.), ALA, FRSL; British novelist, poet and academic; *Professor of Creative Writing Emerita, University of East Anglia;* b. 20 May 1949, Herts.; d. of Reginald Roberts and Monique Caulle; m. 1st Howard Burns 1984 (divorced 1987); m. 2nd Jim Latter 1991 (divorced 2004); two step-s.; ed Convent Grammar School, Somerville Coll., Oxford and University Coll. London; British Council Librarian, Bangkok 1973–74; Poetry Ed. Spare Rib 1974, City Limits 1981–83; Visiting Fellow, Univ. of East Anglia 1992, Univ. of Nottingham Trent 1994; Visiting Prof., Univ. of Nottingham Trent 1996–2001; Prof. of Creative Writing, Univ. of East Anglia 2002–07, Prof. Emer. 2008–; Chair. Literary Cttee British Council 1998–2002; judge, Booker Prize 2001; mem. Soc. of Authors; Chevalier, Ordre des Arts et des Lettres 2001; Hon. MA (Nene) 1999; WHSmith Literary Award 1993. *Plays:* The Journeywoman 1988, Child-Lover 1995. *Television film:* The Heavenly Twins (Channel 4) 1993. *Publications include:* novels: A Piece of the Night 1978, The Visitation 1983, The Wild Girl 1984, The Book of Mrs Noah 1987, In the Red Kitchen 1990, Daughters of the House 1992, Flesh and Blood 1994, Impossible Saints 1997, Fair Exchange 1999, The Looking-Glass 2000, The Mistressclass 2003, Reader, I Married Him 2005, Ignorance 2012; Paper Houses (auto-biog.) 2007; Mind Readings (co-ed.) 1996; short stories: During Mother's Absence 1993, Playing Sardines 2001, Mud: Stories of Sex and Love 2010, Wooing Mr Wickham: Stories Inspired by Jane Austen and Chawton House 2011; essays: Food, Sex and God 1998; poetry: The Mirror of the Mother 1986, Psyche and the Hurricane 1991, All the Selves I Was 1995; plays: The Journeywoman 1987, Child Lover 1993. *Leisure interests:* reading, talking with friends, cooking, gardening, looking at art. *Address:* Aitken Alexander Associates Ltd, 18–21 Cavaye Place, London, SW10 9PT, England (office). *Telephone:* (20) 7373-8672 (office). *Fax:* (20) 7373-6002 (office). *E-mail:* reception@aitkenalexander.co.uk (office). *Website:* www.aitkenalexander.co.uk (office); www.micheleroberts.co.uk (office).

ROBERTS, Nora, (J. D. Robb); American writer; b. 10 Oct. 1950, Silver Spring, Md; f. Nora Roberts Foundation; Co-owner, Inn BoonsBoro, Boonsboro, Md; mem. Romance Writers of America, Novelists Inc.; various Romance Writers of America Awards, named as one of 100 People Who Shape Our World, Time magazine 2007. *Publications:* Irish Thoroughbred 1981, Blithe Images 1982, Song of the West 1982, Search for Love 1982, Island of Flowers 1982, The Heart's Victory 1982, From This Day 1983, Her Mother's Keeper 1983, Reflections 1983, Once More with Feeling 1983, Untamed 1983, Dance of Dreams 1983, Tonight and Always 1983, This Magic Moment 1983, Endings and Beginnings 1984, Storm Warning 1984, Sullivan's Woman 1984, Rules of the Game 1984, Less of a Stranger 1984, A Matter of Choice 1984, The Law is a Lady 1984, First Impressions 1984, Opposites Attract 1984, Promise Me Tomorrow 1984, Partners 1985, The Right Path 1985, Boundary Lines 1985, Summer Desserts 1985, Dual Images 1985, Night Moves 1985, Playing the Odds 1985, Tempting Fate 1985, All the Possibilities 1985, One Man's Art 1985, The Art of Deception 1986, One Summer 1986, Treasures Lost, Treasures Found 1986, Risky Business 1986, Lessons Learned 1986, Second Nature 1986, A Will and a Way 1986, Home for Christmas 1986, Affaire Royale 1986, Mind Over Matter 1987, Temptation 1987, Hot Ice 1987, Sacred Sins 1987, For Now, Forever 1987, Command Performance 1987, The Playboy Prince 1987, Brazen Virtue 1988, Local Hero 1988, Irish Rose 1988, The Name of the Game 1988, Rebellion 1988, The Last Honest Woman 1988, Dance to the Piper 1988, Skin Deep 1988, Sweet Revenge 1989, Loving Jack 1989, Best Laid Plans 1989, Gabriel's Angel 1989, Lawless 1989, Public Secrets 1990, Taming Natasha 1990, Night Shadow 1991, Genuine Lies 1991, With This Ring 1991, Night Shift 1991, Without a Trace 1991, Luring a Lady 1991, Courting Catherine 1991, A Man for Amanda 1991, For the Love of Lilah 1991, Suzannah's Surrender 1991, Carnal Innocence 1992, Unfinished Business 1992, The Welcoming 1992, Honest Illusions 1992, Divine Evil 1992, Captivated 1992, Entranced 1992, Charmed 1992, Second Nature 1993, Private Scandals 1993, Falling for Rachel 1993, Time Was 1993, Times Change 1993, Boundary Lines 1994, Hidden Riches 1994, Nightshade 1994, The Best Mistake 1994, Night Smoke 1994, Born in Fire 1994, Born in Ice 1995, True Betrayals 1995, Born in Shame 1996, Montana Sky 1996, From the Heart 1997, Sanctuary 1997, Holding the Dream 1997, Daring to Dream 1997, Finding the Dream 1997, The Reef 1998, The Winning Hand 1998, Sea Swept 1998, Homeport 1999, The Perfect Neighbor 1999, Megan's Mate 1999, Enchanted 1999, Rising Tides 1999, Inner Harbor 1999, Carolina Moon 2000, The Villa 2001, Heaven and Earth 2001, Three Fates 2002, Chesapeake Blue 2002, Key of Knowledge 2003, Key of Light 2003, Once Upon a Midnight 2003, Birthright 2003, Remember When 2003, Blue Dahlia 2004, Key of Valor 2004, Northern Lights 2005, Blue Smoke (Quill Award for Romance) 2006, Angels Fall (Quill Award for Book of the Year and for Romance 2007) 2006, Heart of the Sea 2007, Divine Evil 2007, The Hollow 2008, High Noon 2008, Tribute 2008, The Pagan Stone 2008, Black Hills 2009, Vision in White 2009, Bed of Roses 2009, Hot Rocks 2010, The Search 2010, Savour the Moment 2010, Happy Ever After 2010, The Next Always 2011; as J. D. Robb: Only Survivors Tell Tales 1990, Naked in Death 1995, Glory in Death 1995, Rapture in Death 1996, Ceremony in Death 1997, Vengeance in Death 1997, Holiday in Death 1998, Immortal in Death 1998, Silent Night 1998, Loyalty in Death 1999, Conspiracy in Death 1999, Witness in Death 2000, Judgment in Death 2000, Seduction in Death 2001, Out of this World 2001, Betrayal in Death 2002, Reunion in Death 2002, Purity in Death 2002, Imitation in Death 2003, Remember When 2003, Portrait in Death 2003, Once Upon a Midnight 2003, Divided in Death 2004, Visions in Death 2004, Memory in Death 2006, Born in Death 2006, Innocent in Death 2007, Strangers in Death 2008, Creation in Death 2008, Salvation in Death 2008, Kindred in Death 2009, Fantasy in Death 2010, Savor the Moment 2010, The Search 2010, Indulgence in Death 2010, Happy Ever After 2010, Treachery in

Death 2011, Chasing Fire 2011, New York to Dallas 2011, The Next Always 2011, Celebrity in Death 2012, The Witness 2012, The Last Boyfriend 2012, Delusion in Death 2012. *Address:* Inn BoonsBoro, 1 North Main Street, Boonsboro, MD 21713 (office); Writers' House Inc., 21 West 26th Street, New York, NY 10010, USA (office). *Telephone:* (212) 685-2400 (office). *Fax:* (212) 685-1781 (office). *E-mail:* write2nora@msn. com. *Website:* www.noraroberts.com; www.innboonsboro.com.

ROBERTS, Sir Richard John, Kt, BSc, PhD, FRS; British scientist; *Chief Scientific Officer, New England Biolabs;* b. 6 Sept. 1943, Derby, England; s. of John Walter Roberts and Edna Wilhelmina Roberts; m. 1st Elizabeth Dyson 1965 (deceased); one s. one d.; m. 2nd Jean Tagliabue 1986; one s. one d.; ed Univ. of Sheffield; Research Fellow, Harvard Univ. 1969–70, Research Assoc. in Biochemistry 1971–72; Sr Staff Investigator, Cold Spring Harbor Lab. Research Inst., Long Island 1972–86, Asst Dir for Research 1986–92; Research Dir New England Biolabs 1992–2005, Chief Scientific Officer 2005–; Chair. NCI Bd of Scientific Counselors 1996–2000; Chair. Scientific Advisory Bd Celera 1998–2002, Multi-Gene Biotech 1998–; Chair. Steering Cttee on Genetics and Biotechnology, Int. Council for Science 1998–2001; mem. Editorial Bd Bioinformatics 1985–2002, Current Opinions in Chemical Biology 1997–2001; mem. Scientific Advisory Bd Genex Corpn 1977–85, Molecular Tool 1994–2000, Oxford Molecular Group 1996–99, Conservation Law Foundation 1998–, PubMed Central 2000–03, Orchid Biosciences 2000–03, Center for Functional Genomics, State Univ. of NY, Albany 2002–, Diversa Corpn 2003–05, PubChem 2004–, Rain Dance Techs 2004–, Int. Centre for Genetic Eng and Biotechnology 2005–, InVivo Therapeutics 2007–; mem. Bd Albert Schweitzer Acad. of Medicine 1998–2003, Vice-Pres. 2003–; Exec. Ed. Nucleic Acids Research 1987–; Patron Oxford Int. Biomedical Centre 1994–; Adviser to Dir NASA Astrobiology Program 2000–; Vice-Chair. Int. Science Advisory Bd, JDW Inst. of Genome Sciences, Hangzhou, China 2003–; Distinguished Scientist, Research Scholar, Boston Univ. 2003–; Trustee, Gaddafi Int. Charity and Devt Foundation 2009–11; Fellow, American Soc. of Arts and Sciences 1997, American Acad. of Microbiology 1997, Science Museum, London 2009; Hon. Prof., Chinese Univ. of Hong Kong 2006–, Nankai Univ. 2006–; Hon. MD (Uppsala) 1992, (Bath) 1994, (Sheffield) 1994, (Derby) 1995, (Chinese Univ. of Hong Kong) 2005, Dr hc (Athens) 2009; Nobel Prize in Physiology or Medicine (for the discovery of 'split genes') 1993, American Acad. of Achievement Golden Plate Award 1994, Univ. of Sheffield Convocation Award 1994, Gabor Medal of the Royal Soc. 2007. *Publications:* Nucleases (co-ed.) 1982, The Applications of Computers to Research on Nucleic Acids (co-ed.) 1982. *Leisure interest:* croquet. *Address:* New England Biolabs, 240 County Road, Ipswich, MA 01938, USA (office). *Telephone:* (978) 380-7405 (office). *Fax:* (978) 380-7406 (office). *E-mail:* roberts@neb.com (office). *Website:* www.neb.com (office).

ROBERTSON, Dawn, BA; American retail executive; *President, Old Navy;* b. Birmingham, Ala; m. Tom Robertson; two c.; ed Auburn Univ.; held several sr positions at May Company 1983–96; Pres and CEO McRae's (div. of Saks Inc.) Jackson, Miss. 1997–98; Exec. Vice Pres. Federated Merchandising Group 1998–2000, Pres. and Chief Merchandising Officer Federated Direct (online and catalog business div. for Macy's and Bloomingdale's) 2000–02; Man. Dir Myer (fmrly Myer Grace Bros), Melbourne, Australia 2002–06; Pres. Old Navy Div., Gap Inc., San Francisco 2006–; ranked by Fortune magazine amongst 50 Most Powerful Women in Business outside the US (30th) 2004, (37th) 2005. *Address:* Old Navy, 2 Folsom Street, San Francisco, CA 94105, USA (office). *Telephone:* (650) 952-4400 (office). *Fax:* (415) 427-2553 (office). *Website:* www.oldnavy.com (office).

ROBERTSON, Geoffrey Ronald, QC, BA, LLB, BCL; Australian/British judge and barrister; *Head, Doughty Street Chambers;* b. 30 Sept. 1946, Sydney, NSW; s. of Francis Robertson and Bernice Beattie; m. Kathy Lette (q.v.) 1990; one s. one d.; ed Epping Boys' High School and Univs of Sydney and Oxford; Rhodes scholar; solicitor, Allen, Allen & Hemsley 1970; called to the Bar, Middle Temple, London 1973; QC 1988; Visiting Prof., Univ. of New South Wales 1979, Univ. of Warwick 1981, Univ. of London 2008; leader, Amnesty missions to S Africa 1983–90; consultant on Human Rights to Govt of Australia 1984; Founding mem. and Head, Doughty Street Chambers 1990–; Counsel to Royal Comm. on gun-running to Colombian drug cartels 1991; Asst Recorder 1993–99, a Recorder 1999–2012; Master of Bench, Middle Temple 1997–; Chief Counsel Comm. on Admin. of Justice in Trinidad and Tobago 2000; Appeal Judge, UN Special Court for War Crimes in Sierra Leone 2002–07; Chair. Staff Panel on Reform of UN Justice 2006; mem. Exec. Council Justice; Jurist mem. UN Internal Justice Council 2008–12, Bar Council inquiry into impeachment of the Chief Justice of Sri Lanka 2013, Govt of Mauritius inquiry into Media Law Reform 2013; Hon. LLD (Sydney) 2006, (Bucharest) 2009, (Brunel) 2010; Freedom of Information Award 1992, Award for Distinction in Int. Law and Affairs, New York Bar Asscn 2011. *Radio:* Chair. You the Jury (BBC Radio 4). *Plays:* The Trials of Oz (BBC) 1992. *Television series:* Hypotheticals, Granada TV, ABC and Channel 7 (Australia). *Publications:* Reluctant Judas 1976, Obscenity 1979, People Against the Press 1983, Geoffrey Robertson's Hypotheticals 1986, Does Dracula Have AIDS ? 1987, Freedom, The Individual and The Law 1989, The Justice Game 1998, Crimes Against Humanity 1999 (fourth edn 2012), Media Law (with A. Nicol) 2002 (fifth edn 2006), The Tyrannicide Brief 2006, The Levellers – The Putney Debates 2007, Statute of Liberty 2009, The Case of the Pope 2010, Mullahs without Mercy: Human Rights and Nuclear Weapons 2012, Dreaming Too Loud 2013, Stephen Ward Was Innocent, OK 2013. *Leisure interests:* tennis, opera, fishing. *Address:* Doughty Street Chambers, 11 Doughty Street, London, WC1N 2PL, England (office). *Telephone:* (20) 7404-1313 (office); (20) 7624-3268 (home). *Fax:* (20) 7404-2283 (office). *E-mail:* g.robertson@doughtystreet.co.uk (office). *Website:* www .doughtystreet.co.uk (office).

ROBERTSON, Lloyd, OC; Canadian broadcast journalist; b. 19 Jan. 1934, Stratford, Ont.; m. Nancy; four d.; with CJCS radio, Stratford 1952, CJOY, Guelph 1953; with CBC 1954, positions in Winnipeg, Ottawa, Anchor Nat. News 1970–76; joined CTV 1976, Chief Anchor and Sr Ed. CTV News 1983–11, co-host weekly magazine series W5 2011–; Hon. Chair. Terry Fox Run 1992; Hon. LLD (Royal Roads Univ.) 2006; Gemini Award 1992, 1994, 1997, Cen. Canadian Broadcasters Asscn Broadcaster of the Year 1992, Radio TV News Dirs' Asscn Pres.'s Award 1993, Toronto Sun Reader's Voice Award for Favourite TV Anchor 1994, Canadian Asscn of Broadcasters (CAB) Gold Ribbon Award for Broadcast Excellence 1995–96, CAB Hall of Fame 1998, Canada's Favourite News Anchor, TV Times

Readers' Choice Awards 1998, 1999. *Address:* CTV News, CTV Television Network, PO Box 9, Station O, Scarborough, ON M4A 2M9, Canada (office). *Telephone:* (416) 332-5000 (office). *Website:* www.ctv.ca (office).

ROBERTSON, Marion Gordon (Pat), BA, MDiv; American minister and broadcasting executive; *Chairman and CEO, Christian Broadcasting Network;* b. 22 March 1930, Lexington, Va; s. of A. Willis Robertson and Gladys Churchill; m. Adelia Elmer; two s. two d.; ed Washington and Lee Univ., Yale Univ., New York Theology Seminary; founder and CEO Christian Broadcasting Network, Va Beach, Va 1960–; ordained Minister Southern Baptist Convention 1961–87; founder and Chancellor Regent Univ. (fmrly CBN Univ.) 1977–; founder and Chair. Operation Blessing Int. Relief and Devt Inc. 1978–, Int. Family Entertainment Inc. 1990–97, Asia Pacific Media Corpn 1993–; Chair. Starguide Digital Networks Inc. 1995–, Porchlight Entertainment Inc. 1995–; founder and Pres. Christian Coalition 1989–, American Center for Law and Justice 1990–; cand. for Republican nomination for Pres. 1988; Dir United Va Bank, Norfolk; mem. Nat. Broadcasters (Dir 1973–); Knesset Medallion, Israel Pilgrimage Cttee, Faith and Freedom Award, Religious Heritage America, Bronze Halo Award, Southern Calif. Motion Picture Council, George Washington Honor Medal, Freedom Foundation at Valley Forge 1983. *Publications:* Shout it from the Housetops: The Story of the Founder of the Christian Broadcasting Network (jtly) 1972, My Prayer for You 1977, The Secret Kingdom 1982, Answers to 200 of Life's Most Probing Questions 1984, Beyond Reason 1984, America's Dates with Destiny 1986, The Plan 1989, The New Millennium 1990, The New World Order 1991, The End of the Age 1995. *Address:* The Christian Broadcasting Network, 977 Centreville Turnpike, Virginia Beach, VA 23463, USA (office). *Telephone:* (757) 226-7000 (office). *Website:* www .patrobertson.com; www.cbn.com (office).

ROBERTSON, Paul Douglas, BSc (Econ.), MA, PhD; Jamaican politician; b. 7 July 1946, St Andrew; m.; two d.; ed Univ. of the West Indies (UWI), Univ. of Michigan, USA; teacher, Oberlin High School 1965–68; teaching asst, Dept of Govt, UWI 1968–69, Lecturer 1976; Research Fellow, Inst. of Social and Econ. Research 1973–74; Research Assoc., Inst. of Urban Affairs, Asst Prof., Dept of Political Science, Howard Univ. 1974–76; Chair. JAMAL Foundation 1977–78; Special Adviser, Ministry of Justice 1977; Special Asst to Prime Minister 1978, 1980; Deputy Gen. Sec. for Admin, People's Nat. Party 1978–80, Gen. Sec. 1983–91, nat. campaign dir 2007; Deputy Leader of Govt Business in Senate 1989–93; MP for SE St Catherine 1993–2007; Minister without Portfolio 1989, of Information and Culture 1989, of Public Services and Information 1991, of Foreign Affairs 1992–93, of Foreign Affairs and Foreign Trade 1993–95, of Industry, Investment and Commerce 1995–97, of Industry and Investment 1997–2000, of Foreign Affairs 2000–01, Minister of Devt 2001. *Address:* c/o People's National Party, 89 Old Hope Rd, Kingston 6, Jamaica. *Telephone:* 978-1337. *Fax:* 927-4389. *E-mail:* information@pnpjamaica.com. *Website:* www.pnpjamaica.com.

ROBERTSON, Shirley, OBE; British sailor; b. 15 July 1968, Dundee, Scotland; m. Jamie Boag 2001; ed Heriot-Watt Univ.; sailed in Yngling class 2001–, previously sailed in Europe class; position: helm; Olympic results include ninth Barcelona 1992, fourth Atlanta 1996, gold medal Sydney 2000, gold medal Athens 2004; results in other competitions include silver medal Europe World Championships 1998, bronze medal Europe World Championships 1999, silver medal Europe European Championships 1999, bronze medal Pre-Olympic Regatta 1999, silver medal Europe World Championships 2000, 14th Yngling World Championships 2001, 16th Yngling World Championships, bronze medal Olympic Test Event 2002, gold medal Olympic Class Week 2003, gold medal Princess Sophia Trophy 2003, fourth Olympic Class Week 2003, bronze medal SPA Olympic Class Regatta 2003, gold medal Pre-Olympic regatta 2003; took one year break from sailing 2005; host Mainsail (monthly CNN TV show); mem. London Organising Cttee of the Olympic Games (LOCOG) Sport Advisory Group; BBC South Sports Personality of the Year 2000, Int. Sailing Fed. World Sailor of the Year 2000, Sailor of the Year 2002, Yachtsman of the Year 2004, Spirit of Scotland Top Scot award 2004. *Leisure interests:* cycling, films, dancing, socializing with friends. *Telephone:* (1983) 299202. *E-mail:* jogrindley@wight365.net. *Website:* www.shirleyrobertson.com; edition.cnn.com/CNNI/Programs/main.sasl.

ROBERTSON, Thomas S., PhD; British academic; *Reliance Professor of Management and Private Enterprise and Dean, Wharton School, University of Pennsylvania;* b. 16 Nov. 1942, Gourock, Scotland; m. Diana Robertson; three c.; ed Wayne State Univ., Northwestern Univ.; Asst Prof., Anderson School, UCLA 1966–68; Asst Prof., Harvard Business School 1968–70; Assoc. Prof., Wharton School, Univ. of Pennsylvania 1971–76, Prof. 1976–94, Chair. of Marketing Dept 1978–84, 1988–94, Assoc. Dean for Exec. Educ. 1984–88, Pomerantz Prof. of Marketing 1987–94, Reliance Prof. of Man. and Pvt. Enterprise 2007–, Dean, Wharton School 2007–; Deputy Dean, London Business School 1994–98; Dean, Goizueta Business School, Emory Univ. 1998–2004, Exec. Faculty Dir Inst. for Developing Nations 2006–07; Planning Forum Award 1993, Best Paper Award, European Marketing Acad. 1995, Best Paper Award, Winter Conf., American Marketing Asscn 1996. *Publications include:* Handbook of Consumer Behavior (co-ed.) 1991, Perspectives on Consumer Behavior (co-ed.) 1991. *Address:* Wharton School, University of Pennsylvania, 1000 SH-DH, Philadelphia, PA 19104, USA (office). *Telephone:* (215) 898-4715 (office). *Fax:* (215) 573-5001 (office). *E-mail:* Robertson@wharton.upenn.edu (office). *Website:* wharton.upenn.edu (office).

ROBERTSON OF PORT ELLEN, Baron (Life Peer), cr. 1999, of Islay in Argyll and Bute; **George Islay MacNeill Robertson,** PC, KT, GCMG, FRSA, LRPS; British business executive; b. 12 April 1946, Port Ellen, Isle of Islay, Argyll, Scotland; s. of George P. Robertson and Marion Robertson; m. Sandra Wallace 1970; two s. one d.; ed Dunoon Grammar School and Univ. of Dundee; Scottish Organizer, Gen. & Municipal Workers' Union 1968–78; MP for Hamilton 1978–97, for Hamilton South 1997–99; Parl. Pvt. Sec. to Sec. of State for Social Services 1979; Opposition Spokesman on Scottish Affairs 1979–80, on Defence 1980–81, on Foreign and Commonwealth Affairs 1981–93; Prin. Spokesman on European Affairs 1984–94; Shadow Spokesman for Scotland 1994–97; Sec. of State for Defence 1997–99; Sec.-Gen. of NATO 1999–2003; Chair. Scottish Labour Party 1977–78; Vice-Chair. Bd British Council 1985–94; Exec. Deputy Chair. Cable & Wireless (C&W) 2003–06, Chair. Cable & Wireless International 2006–07, Sr Int. Adviser Cable and Wireless PLC 2007–; mem. Bd of Dirs Smiths Group 2004–06, Weir 2004–, Western Ferries (Clyde) Ltd 2004–, Scottish Devt Agency 1975–78,

Scottish Tourist Bd 1974–76; Sr Counsellor, The Cohen Group, Washington, DC 2004–; Chair. Comm. on Global Road Safety 2004–; mem. Steering Cttee Königswinter Conf. 1983–92; mem. Council, Royal Inst. of Int. Affairs 1984–91, Jt Pres. 2001–11; Deputy Chair. TNK-BP 2006–13, Chair. Audit Cttee 2006–13; Jt Pres. Chatham House 2002–12; Chair. Comm. on Global Road Safety 2004–, Council of Man., Ditchley Foundation 2011–; Elder Brother, Trinity House 2001–; Pres. Hamilton Burns Club 2002; Chancellor, Order of St Michael and St George 2011–; Trustee, Queen Elizabeth Diamond Jubilee Trust 2012–, Advisory Bd, World War One Commemoration 2014; Licentiate, Royal Photographic Soc.; Hon. Regimental Col London Scottish (Volunteers) 2001; Hon. FRSE; Hon. Academician, Nat. Acad. of Sciences, Kyrgyz Repub.; Hon. Prof. of Politics, Univ. of Stirling 2009–; Grand Cross, Order of Merit (Germany, Italy, Poland, Hungary, Luxembourg), Grand Cross, Order of Star of Romania, Order of Jesus (Portugal), Order of Isabel the Catholic (Spain), Order of Leopold (Belgium), Order of Oranje-Nassau (Netherlands), Order of the Cross of Terra Mariana (First Class) 2004; Hon. LLD (Dundee, Bradford, St Andrews, Baku State Univ., Azerbaijan, Glasgow Caledonian, Stirling, West of Scotland), Hon. DSc (Cranfield – Royal Mil. Coll. of Science); Dr hc (European Univ., Armenia), (Acad. of Sciences, Azerbaijan), (School of Political and Admin. Studies, Bucharest); Winston Churchill Medal of Honour (English Speaking Union) 2003, Transatlantic Leadership Award (European Inst., Washington, DC) 2003, Award for Distinguished Int. Leadership (Atlantic Council of USA) 2003, Presidential Medal of Freedom (USA) 2003, Distinguished Service Medal, US Dept of Defense 2003, Wallace Award, American-Scottish Foundation 2009, Hanno R. Ellenbogen Citizenship Award. *Publications:* Islay and Jura: Photographs by George Robertson 2006, Dunblane – Its People in a Century of Change (with John Fraser) 2012. *Leisure interests:* photography, golf, walking, family, reading. *Address:* House of Lords, Westminster, London, SW1A 0PW (office); BP plc, 1 St James's Square, London, SW1Y, England (office). *Telephone:* (20) 7219-3000 (office). *E-mail:* robertsong@parliament.uk (office). *Website:* www.parliament.uk/biographies/lords/lord-robertson-of-port-ellen/672 (office); www.bp.com (office).

ROBINS, Sir Ralph Harry, Kt, DL, BSc, FREng; British business executive; b. 16 June 1932, Heanor, Derbyshire, England; s. of Leonard Haddon and Maud Lillian Robins; m. Patricia Maureen Grimes 1962; two d.; ed Imperial Coll., Univ. of London; Devt Engineer, Rolls-Royce 1955–66, Exec. Vice-Pres. Rolls-Royce Inc. 1971, Man. Dir Rolls-Royce Industrial and Marine Div. 1973, Commercial Dir Rolls-Royce Ltd 1978, Man. Dir Rolls-Royce PLC 1984–89, Deputy Chair. 1989–92 and Chief Exec. 1990–92, Chair. Rolls Royce 1992–2003; Chair. Defence Industries Council 1986–, Alter Technology Group; Deputy Lt Derbyshire 2002–; Pres. Soc. of British Aerospace Cos. 1986–87, Deputy Pres. 1987–88; Dir (non-exec.) Standard Chartered 1988–2004, Schroders 1990–2002, Marks & Spencer 1992–2001, Cable & Wireless 1994– (Chair. (non-exec.) 1998–2003), Marshall Holdings; mem. Council for Science and Tech. 1993–98; Fellow of Imperial Coll.; Hon. FRAeS; Hon. FIMechE 1996; Commdr Order of Merit (Germany) 1996; Hon. DSc (Cranfield) 1994, (Cambridge) 2008; Hon. DBA (Strathclyde) 1996; Hon. DEng (Sheffield) 2001, (Nottingham) 2003. *Leisure interests:* tennis, golf, music, classic cars. *Address:* 33 Godfrey Street, Chelsea, London, SW3 3SX, England (home). *Telephone:* (20) 7352-9858 (home). *E-mail:* ralphrobins@mac.com (home).

ROBINSON, (Francis) Alastair Lavie; British banker; b. 19 Sept. 1937, London; s. of Stephen Robinson; m. Lavinia Napier 1961; two d.; ed Eton Coll.; Gen. Man. Mercantile Credit Co. 1971–78; Chair. Exec. Cttee then CEO and Pres. Barclays America Corpn, USA 1981–83; Regional Gen. Man. Barclays Bank Int. 1983–87; Dir Personnel, Barclays Bank PLC 1987–90, Exec. Dir 1990–96, Group Vice-Chair. 1992–96; Dir RMC PLC 1996–2005; Dir Marshall of Cambridge (Holdings) Ltd 1996–2006, Portman Bldg Soc. 1998–2006; apptd Chair. St Nicholas Hospice (Suffolk). *Leisure interests:* music, country pursuits, golf. *Address:* c/o St Nicholas Hospice (Suffolk), Hardwick Lane, Macmillan Way, Bury St Edmunds, IP33 2QY, England (office).

ROBINSON, Anne Josephine; British journalist and broadcaster; b. 26 Sept. 1944; m. 1st Charles Wilson; one d.; m. 2nd John Penrose; ed Farnborough Hill Convent and Les Ambassadrices, Paris, France; reporter Daily Mail 1967–68, Sunday Times 1968–77; Women's Ed. Daily Mirror 1979–80, Asst Ed. 1980–93, columnist 1983–93; columnist Today 1991–95, The Times 1993–95, 1998–2001, The Sun 1995–97, Daily Express 1997–98, The Daily Telegraph 2003–; Hon. Fellow, John Moores Univ. 1996. *Radio work includes:* Anne Robinson Show (BBC Radio 2) 1988–93. *Television:* presenter and writer (BBC) Points of View 1988–98, Watchdog 1993–2001, 2009–, Going for a Song 1999–2000, The Weakest Link 2000–12 (also US version 2001–02), Great Britons 2002, Test the Nation 2002–, Guess Who's Coming to Dinner? 2003, Outtake TV 2003–, Travels with My Unfit Mother 2004, What's the Problem? 2005. *Publication:* Memoirs of an Unfit Mother (autobiog.) 2001. *Leisure interests:* walking her dogs. *Address:* CSS Presenters, Drury House, 34–43 Russell Street, London, WC2B 5HA, England (office). *Telephone:* (20) 7078-1457 (office). *Fax:* (20) 7078-1401 (office). *E-mail:* tracey .chapman@css-stellar.com (office). *Website:* www.bbc.co.uk/weakestlink (office).

ROBINSON, Sir Anthony (Tony), Kt; British actor, comedian, amateur historian and television presenter; b. 15 Aug. 1946, Homerton, London, England; m. 1st Mary Shepherd (divorced); m. 2nd Louise Hobbs 2011; two c.; ed Wanstead High School, Central School of Speech and Drama, London; performed in first professional acting role as mem. of Fagin's gang in original production of musical Oliver! aged 12, including a stint as Artful Dodger; appeared in several West End shows, in film and on TV 1958–63; spent four years in repertory theatre, most notably at West Yorkshire Playhouse, Leeds; won an Arts Council bursary to work as a dir at Midland Arts Centre, Birmingham; f. Avon Touring Co. (Bristol-based community theatre co.) with writer David Illingworth; also wrote and narrated several Jackanory-style children's programmes; presenter, Codex (TV quiz for Channel 4) 2006–; mem. Labour Party, mem. Nat. Exec. Cttee 2000–04; Vice-Pres. actors' union Equity 1996–2000; Patron Street Child Africa charity; Hon. Pres. Young Archaeologists' Club of the Council for British Archaeology; Hon. MA (Bristol) 1999, (East London) 2002; Hon. LLD (Exeter) 2005; Dr hc (Open Univ.) 2005, (Oxford Brookes) 2006, (Chester) 2011; James Joyce Award, Literary and Historical Soc. of Univ. Coll. Dublin 2008. *Films include:* Brannigan 1975, Neverending Story III: Return to Fantasia 1994, Faeries (voice) 1999, Blackadder Back & Forth (short) 1999, Mrs Caldicot's Cabbage War 2002. *Radio includes:*

presented Classic FM's Friendly Guide to Classical Music (series). *Television includes:* as actor: Doctor in Charge (series) 1972–73, Soap Opera in Stockwell (film) 1973, Horizon (series documentary) 1974, Lieutenant Kije (film) 1979, Follow the Star (film) 1979, Chronicle (series documentary) – The Crime of Captain Colthurst 1981, The Black Adder (series) 1983, Who Dares Wins (series) 1983–88, Jackanory (series) 1985–91, Black-Adder II (series) 1986, Black Adder the Third (series) 1987, Blackadder: The Cavalier Years (short) 1988, Blackadder's Christmas Carol (film) 1988, Blackadder Goes Forth (series) 1989, Maid Marian and Her Merry Men (series) 1989–94, Blood and Honey (film) 1991, Licence to Live (film) (also assoc. producer) 1994, My Wonderful Life (series) 1997–99, Tales from the Madhouse (mini-series) – The Best Friend 2000, Hogfather (film) 2006, Tony Robinson's Time Walks (series) 2012; as assoc. producer: Time Team (series documentary) 1994–2014, Time Team Digs (series documentary) 2002, Tony Robinson and... (series documentary) 2008; as writer: Jackanory (series) – Theseus the Hero 1985, – Odysseus: The Greatest Hero of Them All 1986, Tales from Fat Tulip's Garden (series) 1985–87, Comic Relief (film) (uncredited) 1991, Blood and Honey (film) 1991, Maid Marian and Her Merry Men (series) 1993–94, Tales from the Madhouse (mini-series) – The Best Friend 2000, The Real Macbeth (documentary) 2001, Behind the Scenes at 'Time Team' (documentary) 2001, Time Team (series documentary) – Coventry's Lost Cathedral 2001, Fact or Fiction: Braveheart (special) 2001, Fact or Fiction: Boudica (special) 2002, The Worst Jobs in History (series documentary) 2004, Tony Robinson's Cunning Night Out (video) (also dir) 2007. *Publications:* has written 16 children's books. *Leisure interests:* supports Bristol City and Valencia football clubs, fan of the rock band Genesis. *Address:* Time Team, Channel 4, 124 Horseferry Road, London, SW1P 2TX, England (office). *Telephone:* (20) 7396-4444 (office). *E-mail:* info@channel4.com (office). *Website:* www.channel4.com/programmes/time-team (office).

ROBINSON, Dame Carol Vivien, DBE, MSc, PhD, FRS; British chemist and academic; *Royal Society Research Professor and Dr Lee Professor of Physical and Theoretical Chemistry, University of Oxford;* b. (Carol Vivien Bradley), 10 April 1956; m.; two s. one d.; ed Canterbury Coll. of Tech., Medway Coll. of Tech. Grad. of the Royal Soc. of Chem., Univ. of Wales, Swansea, Univ. of Cambridge, Univ. of Keele; began as Research Technician, Pfizer 1972–79; MRC Training Fellowship, Univ. of Bristol Medical School 1982–83; career break, birth of three children 1983–91; Postdoctoral Research Fellow, Univ. of Oxford 1991–95, Royal Soc. Univ. Research Fellow 1995–2001, Research Fellow, Wolfson Coll., Oxford 1998–2001, Titular Prof., Univ. of Oxford 1999–2001, Royal Soc. Research Prof. 2006–, Dr Lee's Prof. of Physical and Theoretical Chem. 2009–, Professorial Fellow, Exeter Coll. 2009–, Assoc. Head, Math., Physics and Life Sciences Div., Univ. of Oxford 2012–; Prof. of Mass Spectrometry, Dept of Chem., Univ. of Cambridge 2001–09, Sr Research Fellow, Churchill Coll. 2003–09; Assoc. Ed. Journal of the American Society for Mass Spectrometry 2000–; mem. Editorial Bd Journal of Molecular and Cellular Proteomics 2002–, Current Opinion in Structural Biology 2012–; mem. Nomination Cttee of Royal Soc. 2011–, ERC Synergy Grant Panel responsible for selection and evaluation of grants 2012–, Govt Blackett Review Panel for Biosecurity 2012–; Hon. Fellow, Churchill Coll., Cambridge 2012; Dr hc (Kent) 2009, (York) 2010, (Bristol) 2013; RSC Silver Medal 2002, Biemann Medal, American Soc. for Mass Spectrometry 2003, Rosalind Franklin Award, Royal Soc. 2004, Christian B. Anfinsen Award, Protein Soc. 2007, Prelog Medal, ETH Zurich 2010, Davy Medal, Royal Soc. 2010, Women in Science Award, European Molecular Biology Org./Fed. of European Biochemical Socs 2011, RSC Interdisciplinary Prize 2011, Aston Medal from the British Mass Spectrometry Society 2011, HUPO Award for Distinguished Achievement in Proteomic Sciences 2012, Anatrace Award for Membrane Proteins, American Biophysical Soc. 2013. *Achievements include:* pioneering work in the devt of mass spectrometry as a tool for investigating structure and dynamics of protein complexes. *Publications:* more than 320 articles in scientific journals. *Leisure interests:* sport, gardening. *Address:* Department of Physical and Theoretical Chemistry Laboratory, University of Oxford, South Parks Road, Oxford, OX1 3QZ (office); Exeter College, Oxford, OX1 3DP, England (home). *Telephone:* (1865) 275473 (office). *E-mail:* carol .robinson@chem.ox.ac.uk (office). *Website:* research.chem.ox.ac.uk/carol-robinson .aspx (office); robinsonweb.chem.ox.ac.uk (office).

ROBINSON, Geoffrey; British politician; b. 25 May 1938; s. of Robert Norman Robinson and Dorothy Jane Robinson (née Skelly); m. Marie Elena Giorgio 1967; one s. one d.; ed Emanuel School, Univ. of Cambridge, Yale Univ.; Research Asst, Labour Party 1965–68; Sr Exec., Industrial Reorganization Corpn 1968–70; Financial Controller, British Leyland 1971–72; Man. Dir Leyland Innocenti, Milan 1972–73; Chief Exec. Jaguar Cars 1973–75, Meriden Motor Cycle Workers' Co-operative 1978–80 (Dir 1980–82); MP (Labour) for Coventry NW 1976–; HM Paymaster Gen. 1997–98; Opposition Spokesman on Science 1982–83, on Regional Affairs and Industry 1983–86. Chair. TransTec PLC 1986–97; Dir West Midlands Enterprise Bd 1980–84; mem. Bd of Dirs Coventry City Football Club 1996, 2002–, Acting Chair. 2005–07. *Publications:* The Unconventional Minister (autobiog.) 2000. *Leisure interests:* reading, architecture, gardens. *Address:* House of Commons, Westminster, London, SW1A 0AA (office); Constituency Office, Transport House, Short Street, Coventry, CV1 2LS, England. *Telephone:* (20) 7219-4083 (office). *Fax:* (20) 7219-0984 (office). *E-mail:* robinsong@parliament.uk (office); geoffrey@newstatesman.co.uk (office).

ROBINSON, Sir Gerrard Jude, Kt, FCMA; British business executive; *Chairman, Moto Hospitality Ltd;* b. 23 Oct. 1948; s. of Antony Robinson and Elizabeth Ann Robinson; m. 1st Maria Ann Borg 1970 (divorced 1990); one s. one d.; m. 2nd Heather Peta Leaman 1990; one s. one d.; ed St Mary's Coll., Castlehead; started work as a cost clerk in a Matchbox toy factory aged 16; Works Accountant, Lesney Products 1970–74; Financial Controller Lex Industrial Distribution and Hire 1974–80; Finance Dir Coca-Cola 1980–83; Sales and Marketing Dir 1981–83, Man. Dir 1983–84; Man. Dir Grand Metropolitan (GrandMet) Contract Services 1984–87; led a man. buy-out of GrandMet catering div. 1987; Chief Exec. Compass GP PLC 1987–91, Granada Group PLC 1991–95, Chair. 1995–2001; Chair. London Weekend Television 1994–96, ITN 1995–97, BSkyB 1995–98, Arts Council 1998–2004, Allied Domecq 2002–05, Moto Hospitality Ltd 2006–; Hon. DLitt (Ulster), Hon. DSc (Econs) (Queen's) 1999. *Television:* I'll Show Them Who's Boss (series), Can Gerry Robinson Fix the NHS?, Can Gerry Robinson Fix Dementia?. *Publication:* I'll Show Them Who's Boss 2004. *Leisure interests:* golf, opera, chess, skiing, reading, music.

ROBINSON, Sir Ian, Kt, BSc, FREng, FIChemE, FRSE; British business executive; *Chairman, Ladbrokes PLC;* b. 3 May 1942, East Boldon, Durham; s. of Thomas Robinson and Eva Robinson; m. Kathleen Crawford Robinson (née Leay) 1967; one s. one d.; ed Leeds Univ., Harvard Business School, MA, USA; chartered engineer; fmr Chair. and Man.-Dir of Eng Div., Trafalgar House PLC; Chair. Amey PLC 2001–03; CEO Scottish Power 1995–2001; Chair. Hilton Group PLC 2001–06, Chair. Ladbrokes PLC (after restructuring of Hilton Group) 2006–; Chair. Scottish Advisory Task Force for Welfare to Work 1997–2000; Chair. Scottish Enterprise 2001–03; Dir (non-exec.) Scottish & Newcastle PLC 2004–, Compass Group PLC 2006–; mem. Advisory Bd Siemens UK; mem. Dept of Trade and Industry Overseas Project Bd 1993–97, Offshore Industry Advisory Bd 1993–95, CBI Scottish Business Council 1995–98, Take Over Panel 2004–; Scottish Businessman of the Year, Business Insider's Corp. Elite Awards 1996, George E. Davis Medal for Outstanding Contribution to Chemical Eng 1998. *Leisure interests:* golf, gardening. *Address:* Ladbrokes PLC, Imperial House, Imperial Drive, Rayners Lane, Harrow, Middx, HA2 7JW, England (office). *Telephone:* (20) 8868-8899 (office). *Fax:* (20) 8868-8767 (office). *Website:* www.ladbrokesplc.com (office).

ROBINSON, James D., III, BS, MBA; American business executive; *Co-founder and General Partner, RRE Ventures LLC;* b. 19 Nov. 1935, Atlanta, Ga; s. of James D. Robinson Jr and Josephine Crawford; m. 1st Bettye Bradley (divorced); one s. one d.; m. 2nd Linda Gosden 1984; two s. two d.; ed Georgia Inst. of Tech., Harvard Graduate School of Business Admin.; Officer, US Naval Supply Corps 1957–59; various depts of Morgan Guaranty Trust Co. 1961–66, Asst Vice-Pres. and Staff Asst to Chair. and Pres. 1967–68; Gen. Partner, White, Weld & Co. 1968–70; Pres., CEO American Express Int. Banking Corpn 1970–73; Exec. Vice-Pres. American Express Co. 1970–75, Pres. 1975–77, Dir 1975–93, Chair. Bd 1977–93; Chair. American Express Credit Corpn 1973–75; Pres. J. D. Robinson Inc. 1993–; Chair. and CEO RRE Investors 1994, Gen. Partner, RRE Ventures LLC 1999–; Dir Bristol-Meyers Squibb Co., Chair. 2005–08; Dir The Coca-Cola Co., Novell Inc.; Dir and Chair. Emer. New York City Partnership, Chamber of Commerce Inc.; Hon. Chair. Memorial Sloan-Kettering Cancer Center; mem. Council on Foreign Relations, US Japan Business Council, Comm. for Econ. Devt; Hon. mem. Bd of Trustees, The Brookings Inst. *Address:* RRE Ventures, 130 East 59th Street, 17th Floor, New York, NY 10022, USA (office). *Telephone:* (212) 418-5100 (office). *Fax:* (212) 688-0289 (office). *Website:* www.rre.com (office).

ROBINSON, Janet L., BA; American newspaper executive; b. 11 June 1950, Fall River, Mass; ed Salve Regina Coll., Newport, RI, Exec. Educ. Program at Amos Tuck School, Dartmouth, Hanover, NH; public school teacher 1972–83; joined The New York Times in 1983, served in a variety of sr advertising positions for the newspaper as well as for The New York Times Co. Women's Magazine Group and Sports Magazine Group, Sr Vice-Pres. Advertising of The Times 1995–96, Pres. and Gen. Man. The New York Times newspaper 1996–2004, Sr Vice-Pres. Newspaper Operations 2001–04, Exec. Vice-Pres. and COO The New York Times Co. 2004, Pres. and CEO 2004–11; mem. Bd The Advertising Council 1997, Vice-Chair. 2001–04, 2004–05 Chair. Bd of Trustees, Carnegie Corpn of New York, Presidential Bd of Trustees of Salve Regina Univ.; Hon. DBA (Salve Regina Univ.) 1998; ranked by Fortune magazine amongst 50 Most Powerful Women in Business in the US (48th) 2003, (34th) 2004, ranked by Forbes magazine amongst The World's 100 Most Powerful Women (77th) 2005, (74th) 2006, (45th) 2007, (83rd) 2008, (49th) 2009, (85th) 2010. *Address:* c/o Board of Trustees, Carnegie Corporation of New York, 437 Madison Avenue, New York, NY 10022, USA (office).

ROBINSON, John Harris, BSc, CEng, FREng, FIChemE, FRSA; British business executive; *Chairman, The Abbeyfield Society;* b. 22 Dec. 1940; s. of Thomas Robinson and Florence Robinson; m. Doreen Alice Gardner 1963; one s. one d.; ed Woodhouse Grove School, Univ. of Birmingham; with ICI PLC 1962–65, Fisons PLC 1965–70, PA Consulting Group 1970–75, Woodhouse and Rixson 1975–79; Man. Dir Healthcare Div., Smith & Nephew PLC 1979–82, Dir 1982–89, Deputy CEO 1989–90, CEO 1990–97, Chair. 1997–99; Chair. Bonar PLC 1997–2001, UK Coal (fmrly RJB Mining) 1997–2003, George Wimpey PLC 1999–2007 (Dir (non-exec.) 1999–2007), Railtrack June–Nov. 2001, Paragon Healthcare Group 2002–06, Consort Medical plc 2004–08, Affinity Healthcare 2005–, Oasis Healthcare 2007–, The Abbeyfield Soc.; Operating Partner, Duke Street Capital 2000–; Dir (non-exec.) Delta PLC 1993–2001, Esporta Group Ltd 2006–07; Chair. Healthcare Sector Group, Dept of Trade and Industry 1996–2001, mem. Industrial Devt Advisory Bd 1998–2001; mem. Council CBI 1991– (Chair. Tech. and Innovation Cttee 1998–2001), mem. Pres.'s Cttee 2001–; Chair. Council and Pro-Chancellor Univ. of Hull 1998–2006; mem. Cttee of Univ. Chairmen 1998–2006; Pres. Inst. of Chemical Engineers 1999, Inst. of Man. 2002; Liveryman, Engineers Co. Ltd (Jr Warden) 2005; Hon. DEng (Birmingham) 2000; Hon. DUniv (Bradford) 2000; Hon. DBA (Lincoln) 2002, Hon. DSc (Hull) 2006. *Leisure interests:* theatre, cricket, golf. *Telephone:* (1732) 760359 (office). *Fax:* (1732) 763951 (office). *E-mail:* terri@jrconsultants.org (office).

ROBINSON, Mary, LLM, DCL, SC, MRIA; Irish academic, international civil servant, UN official and fmr head of state; *Special Envoy of the Secretary-General for the Great Lakes Region of Africa, United Nations;* b. 21 May 1944, Ballina, Co. Mayo; d. of Aubrey Bourke and Tessa O'Donnell; m. Nicholas Robinson 1970; two s. one d.; ed Mount Anville, Trinity Coll. Dublin, King's Inns, Dublin, Harvard Univ., USA; Barrister 1967, Sr Counsel 1980; called to English Bar (Middle Temple) 1973; Reid Prof. of Constitutional and Criminal Law, Trinity Coll. Dublin 1969–75, Lecturer in European Community Law 1975–90; Founder-Dir Irish Centre for European Law 1988–90; Senator 1969–89; Pres. of Ireland 1990–97; UN High Commr for Human Rights and Under-Sec.-Gen. 1997–2002; Chancellor, Univ. of Dublin 1998–; mem. Dublin City Council 1979–83; mem. New Ireland Forum 1983–84; mem. Irish Parl. Jt Cttee on EC Secondary Legislation 1973–89; mem. Vedel Cttee on Enlargement of European Parl., EC 1971–72, Saint-Geours Cttee on Energy Efficiency, EC 1978–79, Advisory Bd of Common Market Law Review 1976–90, Irish Parl. Jt Cttee on Marital Breakdown 1983–85, Editorial Bd of Irish Current Law Statutes Annotated 1984–90, Advisory Cttee of Interights, London 1984–90, Int. Comm. of Jurists, Geneva 1987–90, Cttee of Man., European Air Law Asscn 1989–90, Scientific Council of European Review of Public Law 1989–90, Euro Avocats, Brussels 1989–90; Gen. Rapporteur, Human Rights at the Dawn of the 21st Century, Council of Europe, Strasbourg 1993; Prof. of Practice, School of Int. and Public Affairs, Columbia Univ., New York 2004–; Pres. Cherish (Irish

Asscn of Single Parents) 1973–90; Founder-Pres. Realizing Rights: The Ethical Globalization Initiative 2002–; Founding mem. and Chair. Council of Women World Leaders 2002–; mem. Club of Madrid (fmr Vice-Pres.); Special Envoy of the Sec.-Gen. for the Great Lakes Region of Africa, UN 2013–; mem. American Philosophical Soc.; mem. Bd of Dir Vaccine Fund; mem. Leadership Council UN Global Coalition on Women and AIDS; mem. Advisory Bd Earth Inst.; Hon. mem. New York Bar Asscn, American Soc. of Int. Lawyers, Bar of Tanzania, Hon. Fellow, Trinity Coll. Dublin, Inst. of Engineers of Ireland, Royal Coll. of Physicians in Ireland, Hertford Coll. Oxford, LSE, Royal Coll. of Psychiatrists, London, Royal Coll. of Surgeons, Ireland, Royal Coll. of Obstetricians and Gynaecologists, London, Hon. Bencher King's Inns, Dublin, Middle Temple, London; Kt, Military and Hospitaller Order of St Lazarus of Jerusalem 2010; Dr hc (Nat. Univ. of Ireland, Cambridge, Brown, Liverpool, Dublin, Montpellier, St Andrews, Melbourne, Columbia, Nat. Univ. of Wales, Poznań, Toronto, Fordham, Queens Univ. Belfast, Northeastern Univ., Rennes, Coventry, Dublin City, Essex, Harvard, Leuven, London, Seoul, Univ. of Peace, Costa Rica, Uppsala, Yale, Basle, Nat. Univ. of Mongolia, A. Schweitzer Univ. Berne); Berkeley Medal, Univ. of California, Medal of Honour, Univ. of Coimbra, Medal of Honour, Ordem dos Advogados (Portugal), Gold Medal of Honour, Univ. of Salamanca, Andrés Bello Medal, Univ. of Chile, New Zealand Suffrage Centennial Medal, Freedom Prize, Max Schmidheiny Foundation (Switzerland), UNIFEM Award, Noel Foundation (USA), Marisa Bellisario Prize (Italy) 1991, European Media Prize (Netherlands) 1991, CARE Humanitarian Award (USA) 1993, Int. Human Rights Award, Int. League of Human Rights 1993, Liberal Int. Prize for Freedom 1993, Stephen P. Duggan Award (USA) 1994, Council of Europe North South Prize (Portugal) 1997, Collar of Hussein Bin Ali (Jordan) 1997, F. D. Roosevelt Four Freedoms Medal 1998, Erasmus Prize (Netherlands) 1999, Fulbright Prize (USA) 1999, Garrigues Walker Prize (Spain) 2000, William Butler Prize (USA) 2000, Indira Gandhi Peace Prize (India) 2000, Sydney Peace Prize, Amnesty International Amb. of Conscience Award 2004, Presidential Medal of Freedom 2009. *Publication:* Everybody Matters (memoir) 2012. *Address:* Office of the Secretary-General, United Nations, New York, NY 10017, USA (office). *Telephone:* (212) 963-1234 (office). *Fax:* (212) 963-4879 (office). *Website:* www.un.org/sg (office).

ROBINSON, Nick; British journalist; *Political Editor, BBC;* b. 5 Oct. 1963, Macclesfield, Cheshire; ed Cheadle Hulme School, Univ. Coll., Oxford; trainee producer on programmes, including Brass Tacks, Newsround, Crimewatch 1986, then Deputy Ed. On the Record, Panorama; fmr presenter Late Night Live and Weekend Breakfast (both on BBC Radio Five Live), Westminster Live (BBC 2); fmr Chief Political Corresp., BBC News 24, presenting Straight Talk and One to One –2002; Political Ed. ITV News 2002–05; columnist of political 'Notebook' in the Times 2003–; Political Ed., BBC 2005–. *Publication:* Live from Downing Street 2012. *Leisure interest:* sailing. *Address:* BBC Westminster, 4 Millbank, London, SW1P 3JA, England (office). *Telephone:* (20) 7973-6100 (office). *Fax:* (20) 7973-6336 (office). *Website:* www.bbc.co.uk/nickrobinson (office).

ROBINSON, Rt Hon. Peter David, MLA; British politician; *First Minister of Northern Ireland;* b. 29 Dec. 1948, Belfast, NI; s. of David McCrea Robinson and Sheila Robinson; m. Iris Collins, MP 1970; two s. one d.; ed Annadale Grammar School, Castlereagh Coll. of Further Educ.; fmr estate agent; Founding mem. Ulster Democratic Unionist Party (DUP) and mem. Cen. Exec. Cttee 1973– (Sec. 1974–79), Gen. Sec. DUP 1975–79, Deputy Leader 1980–, Spokesman on Constitutional Affairs; MP for Belfast E, House of Commons 1979–2010 (resgnd seat Dec. 1985 in protest against Anglo-Irish Agreement; re-elected Jan. 1986); mem. for Belfast E, NI Ass. 1982–86 (Chair. Environment Cttee 1982–86), mem. NI Select Cttee 1994, Shipbuilding Group 1997, MLA for Belfast E 1998– (Ass. suspended 11 Feb. 2000, restored 30 May 2000); Minister for Regional Devt 1999–2000, 2001–02, for Finance and Personnel 2007–08; First Minister of NI 2008– (suspended active role 11 Jan.–3 Feb. 2010); Leader DUP 2008–; mem. Castlereagh Borough Council 1977–2008, Alderman 1978–2008, Deputy Mayor 1978, Mayor 1986; mem. NI Forum 1996–98, NI Sports Council; Democratic Unionist; Hon. Dir Voice Newspaper Ltd, Crown Publications; Freedom of Borough of Castlereagh. *Publications:* Ulster – The Facts 1982 (co-author); booklets: Give Me Liberty, Hands Off the UDR, IRA/Sinn Fein, The North Answers Back 1970, Capital Punishment for Capital Crime 1978, Ulster the Prey, Carson Man of Action, A War to Be Won, It's Londonderry, Self-inflicted 1981, Ulster in Peril 1981, Savagery and Suffering 1981, Their Cry Was "No Surrender" 1989, The Union Under Fire 1995, Victims. *Leisure interests:* breeding Japanese Koi, bowling, golf. *Address:* Strandtown Hall, 96 Belmont Avenue, Belfast, BT4 3DE (office); 51 Gransha Road, Dundonald, BT16 2HB, Northern Ireland (home). *Telephone:* (28) 9047-3111 (office). *Fax:* (28) 9047-1797 (office). *E-mail:* peter .robinson.mp@btconnect.com (office); info.cmu@ofmdfmni.gov.uk (office). *Website:* www.ofmdfmni.gov.uk (office); www.peterrobinson.org (office).

ROBINSON, William (Smokey), Jr; American R&B and soul singer, songwriter and producer; b. 19 Feb. 1940, Detroit, Mich.; m. 1st Claudette Robinson 1959; two c.; m. 2nd Frances Robinson; fmr singer with The Matadors; singer with The Miracles 1954–72, also billed as Smokey Robinson and The Miracles 1967–72; solo artist 1973–; Vice Pres. Motown 1961–88; Exec. Producer and composer on film, Big Time 1977; numerous TV appearances; f. SFGL Foods, Inc.; Dr hc (Howard Univ.) 2006, (Berklee Coll. of Music) 2009; Grammy Award for Best R&B Vocal Performance 1988, Grammy Living Legend Award 1989, Soul Train Heritage Award 1991, Motor City Music Award for Lifetime Achievement 1992, Grammy Lifetime Achievement Award 1999, Kennedy Center Honor 2006, Q Award for Outstanding Contribution to Music 2006, Ivor Novello Special Int. Award 2009. *Compositions include:* most recordings with The Miracles –1968; also The Way You Do The Things You Do (recorded by The Temptations) 1964, My Guy (co-writer, recorded by Mary Wells) 1964, My Girl (recorded by The Temptations) 1965. *Recordings include:* albums: with The Miracles: The Fabulous Miracles 1963, The Miracles On Stage 1963, Doin' Mickey's Monkey 1964, Going To A Go-Go 1966, Make It Happen 1967, Special Occasion 1968, Time Out For... 1969, What Love Has Joined Together 1970, A Pocketful Of Miracles 1970, One Dozen Roses 1971, Flying High Together 1972; solo: Smokey 1973, Pure Smokey 1974, A Quiet Storm 1975, Smokey's Family Robinson 1976, Deep In My Soul 1977, Big Time (OST) 1977, Love Breeze 1978, Smokin' Motown 1979, Where There's Smoke 1979, Warm Thoughts 1980, Being With You 1981, Yes It's You Lady 1982, Touch The Sky 1983, Essar 1984, Smoke Signals 1986, One Heartbeat 1987, Love Songs 1988,

Love, Smokey 1990, Double Good Everything 1991, Ballads 1995, Our Very Best Christmas 1999, Intimate 1999, Food For The Spirit 2004, Timeless Love 2006, Time Flies When You're Having Fun 2009. *Address:* c/o WME, 9601 Wilshire Blvd, Beverly Hills, CA 90201, USA (office). *Website:* www.smokeyrobinson.com.

ROBLES, Dayron; Cuban athlete; b. 19 Nov. 1986, Guantánamo; sprinter and hurdler; world record holder in 110m hurdles of 12.87 seconds, set at Golden Spike Ostrava meet 12 June 2008; finished sixth in 110m hurdles at World Youth Championships, Sherbrooke, Canada 2003; Silver Medal, World Jr Championships, Grosseto, Italy 2004, Cen. American and Caribbean Championships, Nassau, Bahamas, 60m hurdles, World Indoor Championships, Moscow 2006 (personal best time of 7.46 seconds); Gold Medal, 110m hurdles, Cen. American and Caribbean Games, Cartagena, Colombia 2006, Panamerican Games, Rio de Janeiro 2007, Int. Asscn of Athletics Feds (IAAF) World Athletics Final, Stuttgart 2007, Olympic Games, Beijing 2008 (12.93 seconds); finished fourth in 110m hurdles, World Championships, Osaka 2007. *Address:* c/o Federacion Cubana de Atletismo, 13 y 3 Vedado 601, C/o Comite Olimpico Cubano, 14000 Havana, Cuba. *Telephone:* (7) 952103. *Fax:* (7) 335310. *E-mail:* estadio@inder.co.cu.

ROBLES, Josue (Joe), Jr, BBA, MBA; Puerto Rican/American business executive; *President and CEO, United Services Automobile Association;* b. Rio Piedras, Puerto Rico; m. Patty Robles; three c.; ed Kent State Univ., Indiana State Univ.; joined US Army 1966, served in a variety of command and staff positions, including active duty posts in Korea, Viet Nam, Germany and Operations Desert Shield/Desert Storm in the Middle East 1966–94, served as Dir of Army Budget and as Commdg Gen. of 1st Infantry Div.; mem. Bd of Dirs United Services Automobile Association (USAA) while on active duty 1990–94, joined USAA as Special Asst to the Chair. after retiring from US Army as Maj. Gen. 1994, Chief Financial Officer and Controller 1994–2007, Corp. Treas. 1995–2007, Pres. and CEO 2007–, includes USAA's Property and Casualty Insurance Group, Fed. Savings Bank, Life Insurance Co. of New York, Investment Man. Co., Alliance Services Co., Financial Planning Services; mem. Bd of Dirs DTE Energy, CHRISTUS Santa Rosa Hosp., CHRISTUS Santa Rosa Children's Hosp. Foundation, P16Plus Council of Greater Bexar Co. Foundation; mem. Advisory Bd FM Global, Texas Gov.'s Business Council; Distinguished Service Medal with Oak Leaf Cluster, Legion of Merit with two Oak Leaf Clusters, Bronze Star with Oak Leaf Cluster, Meritorious Service Medal with Oak Leaf Cluster; named by Christian Science Monitor as No. 1 Veteran in Business 2009, named by American Banker as Innovator of the Year 2009. *Address:* United Services Automobile Association, 9800 Fredericksburg Road, San Antonio, TX 78288, USA (office). *Telephone:* (210) 498-2211 (office). *E-mail:* info@usaa.com (office). *Website:* www.usaa.com (office).

ROBLES ORTEGA, HE Cardinal Francisco; Mexican ecclesiastic; *Archbishop of Guadalajara, Jalisco;* b. 2 March 1949, Mascota, Jalisco; ed studies in Mexico and at Pontifical Gregorian Univ., Rome; ordained priest of Autlán, Jalisco 1976; Parish Priest in Menor de Autlan 1979–91; Auxiliary Bishop of Toluca and Titular Bishop of Bossa 1991–96; Bishop of Toluca 1996–2003; Archbishop of Monterrey, Nuevo León 2003–11; cr. Cardinal (Cardinal-Priest of Santa Maria della Presentazione) 2007; Archbishop of Guadalajara, Jalisco 2011–; participated in Papal Conclave 2013; represented Mexico at Special Ass. of the Synod of Bishops for America 1997. *Address:* Arzobispado, Apartado 1-331, Calle Liceo 17, 44100 Guadalajara, Jalisco, Mexico (office). *Telephone:* (33) 3614-5504 (office). *Fax:* (33) 3658-2300 (office). *E-mail:* info@arquidiocesisgdl.org.mx (office). *Website:* ww .arquidiocesisgdl.org.mx (office).

ROBSON, Alan David, AM, BAgrSc, PhD, FTSE, FACE, FACEL, FAIAS; Australian professor of agriculture and fmr university administrator; *Professor Emeritus of Agriculture, University of Western Australia;* ed Univ. of Melbourne, Univ. of Western Australia; several positions at Univ. of Western Australia, including Dean of Faculty of Agric., Head of School of Agric., Prof. of Agric. (Soil Science), now Emer., Foundation Dir Co-operative Research Centre for Legumes in Mediterranean Agric. (CLIMA), Deputy Vice-Chancellor and Provost 1993–2004, Vice-Chancellor 2004–12, also currently Hackett Prof. of Agric.; mem. Premier's Science Council; Chair. Group of Eight 2007–10; Deputy Chair. Council of the Nat. Library 1998–2005, Universities Australia 2009–11; mem. Western Australian Science Council 2003–09, CSIRO Bd 2003–08; Foundation Chair. Grain Legumes Research Council; Deputy Chair. Research Grants Cttee of the Australian Research Council; mem. Cttee for Univ. Training and Staff Devt 1998–99, Australian Teaching and Learning Cttee 2000–04, Bd of Dirs Australian Univs Quality Agency; Fellow, Acad. of Tech. Sciences and Eng (Australia) 1987; Citizen of Western Australia 2009; Australian Medal of Agric. Science 1987, Centenary Medal 2003. *Address:* Adjunct and Honorary Staff (Earth and Environment), The University of Western Australia (M087), 35 Stirling Highway, Crawley, WA 6009, Australia (office). *Telephone:* (8) 6488-3466 (office). *E-mail:* alan.robson@uwa.edu (office). *Website:* www.uwa.edu.au/people/alan.robson (office).

ROBSON, Bryan, OBE; British professional football manager and fmr professional footballer; b. 11 Jan. 1957, Chester-le-Street, County Durham, England; s. of Brian Robson and Maureen Lowther; m. Denise Brindley 1979; one s. two d.; ed Birtley Lord Lawson Comprehensive; midfielder; youth player, West Bromwich Albion 1972–74, sr team 1974–81; played for Manchester United 1981–94 (Capt. 1982–94, won Premier League 1992/93, 1993/94, FA Cup 1983, 1985, 1990, 1994, Football League Cup 1992, FA Charity Shield 1983, 1990, 1993, UEFA Cup Winners' Cup 1991, UEFA Super Cup 1991); only British capt. to lead a side to four FA Cup wins; longest serving capt. in club history; mem. England U-21 team 1979–80, England B team 1979–80, England nat. team (90 int. caps (65 as capt. 1982–91), scoring 26 goals) 1980–91, Asst Man. 1994–96; player/Man. Middlesbrough Football Club 1994–2001 (won Football League First Div. 1994/95), Man. 1996–2000, Jt Man. with Terry Venables 2000–01; Man. Bradford City 2003–04, West Bromwich Albion 2004–06, Sheffield United FC 2007–08; Global Amb. for Manchester United 2008–; Man. Thailand nat. team 2009–11 (resgnd); formed Robson Lloyd Consultancy Ltd (specialist sports co.) 2007–; Hon. BA (Salford) 1992, (Manchester) 1992; named in list of Football League 100 Legends, an Inaugural Inductee of English Football Hall of Fame 2002, named as one of West Bromwich Albion's 16 greatest players in poll organized as part of club's 125th anniversary celebrations 2004. *Publications:* United I Stand 1983, Robbo: My Autobiography 2006. *Leisure interests:* golf, horse racing. *Address:* Robson Lloyd

Consultancy Ltd, Malthouse Business Centre, 48 Southport Road, Ormskirk, Lancs., L39 1QR, England (office). *Telephone:* (1695) 586040 (office).

ROBUCHON, Joël; French chef and restaurateur; b. 7 April 1945, Poitiers; s. of Henri Robuchon and Julienne Douteau; m. Janine Pallix 1966; one s. one d.; ed Petit séminaire de Mauléon sur Sèvre; Apprenti 1960–63, Commis 1963–64, Chef de Partie 1965–69, Chef 1969–73, Chef de Cuisine 1974–78, Dir Hotel Nikko de Paris 1978–81, Propr and Chef, Restaurant Jamin, Paris 1981–93, Restaurant Laurent, Paris 1992–2001, Restaurant Joël Robuchon 1994–96, Man. Restaurant l'Astor, Paris 1996–, L'Atelier de Joël Robuchon, Paris 2003–, L'Atelier de Joel Robuchon and Joel Robuchon at The Mansion, Las Vegas 2005–; Man. Relais du Parc 1992; numerous demonstrations overseas; Compagnon du Tour de France des Devoirs Unis; Titular mem. Acad. Culinaire de France; Pres. du Salon SIREST 1998–2002, (Cuisine Section) Meilleurs Ouvriers de France Competition 1991, Chaîne Thématique Gastronomique GOURMET TV 2002–; Conseiller de la marque 'Reflets de France' (Groupe Carrefour) 1996; mem. Council, Ordre du Mérite Agricole 1998–; Head Editorial Cttee Larousse Gastronomique; Commdr dans l'Ordre du Mérite Agricole; Officier des Arts et des Lettres; Chevalier, Ordre Nat. du Mérite; Chevalier, Légion d'honneur; professional awards include: Prix Prosper Montagné 1969, Prix Pierre Taittinger 1970, Trophée National de l'Académie Culinaire de France 1972, Meilleur Ouvrier de France 1976, Lauréat du Prix Hachette 1985, Chef de l'Année 1987, Chef of the Century, Gault Millau Guidebook 1990, Int. Herald Tribune Best Restaurant in the World 1994, 3 Stars Michelin Guide; also some 15 gold, silver and bronze medals. *Television:* Cuisinez Comme un Grand Chef (TF1) 1996–99, Bon Appétit Bien Sûr (FRANCE 3) 2000–. *Publications:* Ma cuisine pour vous, Simply French, Le meilleur et le plus simple de Robouchon, Les dimanches de Joël Robuchon, Le meilleur et le plus simple de la pomme de terre, Recettes du terroir d'hier et d'aujourd'hui, Le carnet de route d'un compagnon cuisinier, L'atelier de Joël Robuchon, Le meilleur et le plus simple de la France, Cuisinez comme un grand chef (Grand Prix du Meilleur Ouvrage, Acad. Nat. de Cuisine 1999), Le meilleur et le plus simple pour maigrir, Bon appétit bien sûr (Best Book of Cuisine Award, 7th Salon Int. du Livre Gourmand de Périgueux 2002), The Complete Robuchon 2008. *Leisure interest:* tennis. *Address:* c/o La Table de Joel Robuchon, 16, Avenue Bugeaud, 75016 Paris, France. *Website:* www .joel-robuchon.com; www.robuchon.com.

ROCARD, Michel Louis Léon, LèsL; French politician; b. 23 Aug. 1930, Courbevoie (Hauts-de-Seine); s. of Yves Rocard and Renée Favre; m. 2nd Michèle Legendre 1972 (divorced); two s.; one s. one d. from 1st m.; m. 3rd Sylvie Geoffroy-Emmanuelli; ed Lycée Louis-le-Grand, Paris, Institut d'Études Politiques, Paris, École Nat. d'Admin; Nat. Sec. Assocn des Étudiants socialistes, French Section of Workers' Int. (Socialist Party) 1955–56; Insp. des Finances 1958, Econ. and Financial Studies Service 1962, Head of Budget Div., Forecasting Office 1965, Insp. Gen. des Finances 1985; Sec.-Gen. Nat. Accounts and Budget Comm. 1965; Nat. Sec. Parti Socialiste unifié (PSU) 1967–73; cand. in first round of presidential elections 1969; Deputy (Yvelines) to Nat. Ass. 1969–73, 1978–81; left PSU to join Parti Socialiste (PS) 1974, mem. Exec. Bureau 1975–81, 1986–, Nat. Sec. in charge of public sector 1975–79, First Sec. 1993–94; Mayor of Conflans-Sainte-Honorine 1977–94; Minister of State, Minister of Planning and Regional Devt 1981–83, of Agric. 1983–85; Prime Minister 1988–91; mem. Parl. for Yvelines 1986–88; mem. European Parl. 1994–2009; Amb. in charge of int. negotiations concerning the polar regions 2009–; mem. Senate 1995–97; Chair. Cttee on Devt and Co-operation 1997–99, Employment and Social Affairs 1999–2001, Culture, Educ. and Youth Matters 2001–03; Dr hc (Laval) 2013; Grand-Croix, Ordre nat. du Mérite 1988, Commdr du Mérite agricole 1989, Grand Cross, Order of Christ (Portugal), Grand Officer, Order of the Tunisian Repub., Commdr Ordres des Palmes Académiques 2007, Grand Officier, Legion d'honneur 2008, and numerous other decorations. *Publications:* Le PSU et l'avenir socialiste de la France 1969, Des militants du PSU présentés par Michel Rocard 1971, Questions à l'Etat socialiste 1972, Un député, pourquoi faire? 1973, Le marché commun contre Europe (with B. Jaumont and D. Lenègre) 1973, L'inflation au cœur (with Jacques Gallus) 1975, Parler vrai 1979, À l'épreuve des faits: textes politiques (1979–85) 1986, Le cœur à l'ouvrage 1987, Un pays comme le nôtre, textes politiques 1986–89 1989, Les Moyens d'en sortir 1996, L'art de la paix (essay) 1998, Mes idées pour demain 2000, Pour une autre Afrique 2001, Entretiens 2001, Si la gauche savait 2005. *Leisure interests:* skiing, sailing, gliding. *Address:* 66 Champs Elysées, Batiment D1, 75008 Paris (office); 36 route de la Grange aux Moines, 78460 Choisel, France (home). *Telephone:* 1-47-05-25-00 (office). *Fax:* 1-45-51-42-04 (office). *E-mail:* michel@rocard.fr (office).

ROCCA, Costantino; Italian professional golfer; b. 4 Dec. 1956, Bergamo; m. Antonella Rocca 1981; one s. one d.; fmr factory worker and caddie; turned professional 1981; qualified for PGA European Tour through 1989 Challenge Tour; won Open V33 Da Grand Lyon and Peugeot Open de France; first Italian golfer to be mem. European Ryder Cup team 1993; mem. European Ryder Cup team 1995, 1997; plays on European Seniors Tour 2007–. *Leisure interests:* fishing, football. *Address:* c/o Golf Club Bergamo, L'Albenza, Via Longoni 12, 24030 Almenno S.Bartolomeo BG, Italy. *Telephone:* (035) 640707. *Fax:* (035) 640028. *Website:* www .europeantour.com.

ROĆEN, Milan; Montenegrin diplomatist and politician; *Chief Political Adviser to the Prime Minister;* b. 23 Nov. 1950, Žabljak; m. Stana Roćen; one s.; ed Faculty of Political Science, Univ. of Belgrade; journalist, Ekonomska Politika magazine 1976–79; worked in Information and Propaganda Dept of Pres. of Cen. Cttee of League of Communists of Montenegro 1979–82, Political Chief of Staff 1982–88; Deputy Minister of Foreign Affairs 1988–92; Minister-Counsellor for Political Affairs, Fed. Repub. of Yugoslavia Embassy, Moscow, Russia 1992–97; Foreign Policy Adviser to Prime Minister of Repub. of Montenegro 1997–98, to Pres. 1998–2003; Chief Political Adviser to Prime Minister of Montenegro 2003, Feb.–Sept. 2006, 2012–; Amb. of Serbia and Montenegro to Russian Fed. (also accred to Kazakhstan, Uzbekistan, Turkmenistan, Tajikistan, Kyrgyzstan and Georgia) 2003–06; Co-ordinator Pro-independence Bloc and Gen. Man. of campaign for referendum on independence Feb.–May 2006; Minister of Foreign Affairs 2006–12, also of European Integration 2010–12; mem. Presidium of Democratic Party of Socialists of Montenegro. *Address:* c/o Office of the Prime Minister, Government of Montenegro, 81000 Podgorica, Karadorđeva BB, Montenegro (office). *Telephone:* (20) 482812 (office). *Fax:* (20) 224076 (office). *E-mail:* milan .rocen@gsv.gov.me (office). *Website:* www.gov.me (office).

ROCHA, John, CBE; British fashion designer; b. 1953, Hong Kong; m. Odette Rocha; ed Croydon Coll. of Design and Technology, London Coll. of Fashion; moved to London 1970; opened a design business in Kilkenny, Ireland 1977, later moved to Dublin; worked briefly in Milan 1987–89 then returned to Dublin; menswear line 1993, jeans line 1997; regular collections at all major int. fashion shows; has also designed interiors for hotels and office blocks including The Morrison Hotel, Dublin; launched John Rocha at Waterford Crystal collection 1997; f. Three Moon Design Studio, Dublin; British Designer of the Year 1994. *Address:* Three Moon Design Studio, 10 Ely Place, Dublin 2, Ireland (office). *Telephone:* (1) 662-9225 (office). *Fax:* (1) 662-9226 (office). *E-mail:* info@johnrocha.ie (office). *Website:* www .johnrocha.ie (office).

ROCHA, José Luis; Cape Verde diplomatist and government official; *Deputy Minister of Foreign Affairs;* b. 6 Aug. 1956, São Vicente; ed Univ. of Louvain, Belgium; joined Ministry of Planning and Co-operation 1981, Chief of Div. and Dir of Int. Co-operation Dept 1982–95; Amb. to Belgium and Luxembourg 1995–99; Perm. Rep. of Org. Int. de la Francophonie to EU 2000; Dir-Gen. Political Affairs, Ministry of Foreign Affairs, Co-operation and Communities 2007–09; Nat. Dir for Political Affairs 2009; currently Deputy Minister of Foreign Affairs. *Address:* Ministry of External Relations, Palácio das Comunidades, Achada de Santo António, Praia, Santiago, Cape Verde (office). *Telephone:* (260) 7866 (office). *Fax:* (261) 3952 (office). *E-mail:* jose.l.rocha@mirex.gov.cv (office). *Website:* www.mirex .gov.cv (office); www.governo.cv (office).

ROCHA VIEIRA, Lt-Gen. Vasco Joaquim, MA; Portuguese administrator and army officer; b. 16 Aug. 1939, Lagoa; s. of João da Silva Vieira and Maria Vieira Rocha e Vieira; m. Maria Leonor de Andrada Soares de Albergaria 1976; three s.; ed Tech. Univ. of Lisbon; Prof., Mil. Acad. Lisbon 1968–69; Army Staff course 1969–72; engineer, Urbanization Dept, Urban Council, Lisbon 1973; Ass. for Public Works and Communications, Govt of Macao 1974–75; Dir Engineers Branch, Portuguese Army 1975–76; Army Chief-of-Staff 1976–78; Mil. Rep. of Portugal, SHAPE, Mons, Belgium 1978–82; Army War Coll. course 1982–83; Nat. Defence course 1983–84; Prof., Army War Coll., Lisbon 1983–84; Deputy Dir Nat. Defence Inst., Lisbon 1984–86; Minister for Portuguese Autonomous Region of the Azores 1986–91; Gov. of Macao 1991–99; Chancellor Portuguese Chancery for Honours 2006; Grand Cross, Mil. Order of Christ 1996; Grand Cross, Order of Prince Henry; Kt Commdr, Mil. Order of Aviz; Grand Cross, Order of Infante D. Henrique; service medals; decorations from Brazil, France, Belgium, USA and Japan. *Leisure interests:* tennis, golf. *Address:* c/o Chancelaria das Ordens Honoríficas Portuguesas, Presidência da República, Palácio Nacional de Belém, Calçada da Ajuda, 1340-022 Lisbon (office); Quinta Patino Lote 52, Alcoitão, 2645-143 Alcabideche, Portugal (home). *Telephone:* (21) 3614695 (office); (21) 4693232 (home). *Fax:* (21) 4607258 (home). *E-mail:* vascojrv@yahoo.com (home). *Website:* www.ordens.presidencia.pt (office).

ROCHE, (Eamonn) Kevin; American (b. Irish) architect; *Principal, Kevin Roche John Dinkeloo and Associates LLC;* b. 14 June 1922, Dublin, Ireland; s. of Eamon Roche and Alice Roche (née Harding); m. Jane Tuohy 1963; two s. three d.; ed Univ. Coll. Dublin and Illinois Inst. of Tech.; with Eero Saarinen & Assocs 1950–66, Chief Designer 1954–66; Pnr, later Prin. Kevin Roche John Dinkeloo and Assocs LLC 1966–; Pres. American Acad. of Arts and Letters 1994–97; Academician, Nat. Inst. of Arts and Letters, American Acad. in Rome 1968–71; mem. Fine Arts Comm., Washington, DC, Acad. d'Architecture; Academician Nat. Acad. of Design; mem. Bd of Trustees, Woodrow Wilson Int. Center for Scholars, Smithsonian Inst. Accad. Nazionale di San Luca 1984; Hon. LLD (Ireland Nat. Council for Educational Awards); Brunner Award, Nat. Acad. of Arts and Letters 1965, Brandeis Univ. Creative Arts Award 1967, ASID 1976 Total Design Award, Acad. d'Architecture 1977 Grand Gold Medal, Pritzker Architecture Prize 1982, Gold Medal Award for Architecture, American Acad. of Arts and Letters 1990, Gold Medal AIA 1993, AIA 25 Year Award 1995, and other awards. *Major works include:* IBM World Fair Pavilion, New York, Oakland Museum, Rochester Inst. of Tech., Ford Foundation HQ, New York, Fine Arts Center, Univ. of Massachusetts, Power Center for the Performing Arts, Univ. of Michigan, Creative Arts Center, Wesleyan Univ., Middletown, Conn., Coll. Life Insurance Co. of America HQ, Indianapolis. Master Plan, Galleries and Wings, Metropolitan Museum of Art, New York, Office Complex, UN Devt Corpn, New York, Denver Center for the Performing Arts, Denver, Colo, John Deere & Co., West Office Bldg, Moline, Ill., Union Carbide Corpn World HQ, Conn., General Foods Corpn HQ, Rye, NY, John Deere Insurance Co. HQ, Moline, Ill., Bell Telephone Labs, Holmdel, NJ, Morgan Bank HQ, New York, Northern Telecom HQ, Atlanta, Ga, E.F. Hutton HQ, New York, Bouygues HQ, Paris, IBM Hudson Hills Computer Research Lab., New York, UNICEF HQ, New York, Leo Burnett Company HQ, Chicago, Corning Glass Works HQ, Corning, NY, Merck and Co. HQ, Readington, NJ, Dai Ichi-Seimei Norinchukin Bank HQ, Tokyo, The Jewish Museum, New York, Museum of Jewish Heritage Holocaust Memorial, New York, Nations Bank Plaza, Atlanta, Ga, Tata Cummins, India, Menara Maxis, Kuala Lumpur, Malaysia, Pontiac Marina Hotel and Office Bldg, Singapore, Total System Services Corpn HQ, Columbus, Ga, MIT Cen. Athletic Facility, Cambridge, Mass, Shiodome Block B Devt, Tokyo, Research and Devt Facilities, Lucent Technologies, Lisle, Naperville, Ill., Denver, Co., Allentown, Pa, Nuremberg, Germany, New York Univ. Palladium Student Dormitory, New York Univ. Kimmel Center, Santander Cen. Hispano HQ, Madrid, Bouygues SA Holding Co. HQ, Paris, S.E.C. HQ, Washington, DC, 1101 New York Avenue, Washington, DC, Lafayette Tower, Convention Centre, Dublin, Ireland. *Address:* Kevin Roche John Dinkeloo and Associates, 20 Davis Street, PO Box 6127, Hamden, CT 06517, USA (office). *Telephone:* (203) 777-7251 (office). *Fax:* (203) 776-2299 (office). *E-mail:* kroche@krjda.com (office). *Website:* www.krjda.com (office).

ROCHEFORT, Jean; French actor; b. 29 April 1930, Dinan (Côtes-du-Nord); s. of Celestin Rochefort and Fernande Guillot; m. 3rd Françoise Vidal 1989; one s. one d.; two s. one d. from previous marriages; ed Conservatoire nat. d'art dramatique; mem. Jury, Cannes Int. Film Festival 2003; Chevalier de la Légion d'honneur; Officier des Arts et Lettres; Trophée Dussane 1970, César 1975 (for Que la fête commence), 1978 (for Best Actor of the Year, in Le Crabe-tambour), best actor awards Montreal 1982, Brussels 1982, Locarno 1984, César d'honneur 1999. *Films include:* 20,000 Leagues Under the Sea 1960, La Porteuse de pain 1964, Qui êtes-vous Polly Magoo? 1967, Les Dimanches de la vie 1967, Le Temps de mourir 1970,

Céleste 1970, L'Œuf 1971, l'Héritier 1972, Le Fantôme de la liberté 1974, Un divorce heureux 1975, Isabelle devant le désir 1975, Que la fête commence 1975, Les Magiciens 1976, Un éléphant ça trompe énormément 1976, Le Crabe-tambour 1977, Chère inconnue 1980, Un étrange voyage 1981, l'Indiscrétion 1982, Le grand frère 1982, Un dimanche de flic 1983, L'Ami de Vincent 1983, Réveillon chez Bob, Frankenstein 90 1984, La Galette du roi 1986, Tandem 1987, Le Moustachu 1987, Je suis le seigneur du château 1989, Le Mari de la coiffeuse 1990, Le Château de ma mère 1990, Le Bal des casse-pieds 1992, La prochaine fois le feu 1993, Tombés du ciel 1994, Tom est tout seul 1995, Les grands ducs 1996, Ridicule 1996, Barracuda 1997, Le Vent en emporte autant 1999, Rembrandt 1999, Le Placard 2001, Honolulu Baby 2001, La Vie sans secret de Walter Nions 2001, L'Homme du train 2002, Blanche 2002, Fanfan la tulipe (voice) 2003, Il était une fois Jean-Sébastien Bach (voice) 2003, Saint-Germain ou La négociation (TV) 2003, Les Clefs de bagnole 2003, RRRrrrr!!! 2004, La Dernière minute 2004, Les Dalton 2004, Akoibon 2005, L'Enfer 2005, Ne le dis à personne 2006, Désaccord parfait 2006, Mr. Bean's Holiday 2007, J'ai toujours rêvé d'être un gangster 2007. *Television:* Le Scénario défendu 1984, L'Enigme blanche 1985, Eleveur de chevaux, Nosferatu (mini-series) (voice) 2002. *Leisure interest:* riding. *Address:* c/o Artmédia, 20 avenue Rapp, 75007 Paris, France.

ROCHER, Guy, CC, OQ, PhD, FRSC; Canadian sociologist and academic; *Professor of Sociology, University of Montréal; b.* 20 April 1924, Berthierville, PQ; s. of the late Barthélemy Rocher and Jeanne Magnan; m. 1st Suzanne Cloutier 1949; m. 2nd Claire-Emmanuèle Depocas 1985; four d.; ed Univ. of Montréal, Univ. Laval and Harvard Univ.; Asst Prof. Univ. Laval 1952–57, Assoc. Prof. 1957–60; Prof. of Sociology, Univ. of Montréal 1960–; Deputy Minister of Cultural Devt Govt of Québec 1977–79, of Social Devt 1981–82; mem. Royal Comm. on Educ. in Québec 1961–66; Vice-Pres. Canada Council of Arts 1969–74, Cttee on Univ. Research, Royal Soc. of Canada 1989–90; Pres. Radio-Québec 1979–81; mem. American Acad. of Arts and Sciences; Hon. LLD (Laval) 1996; Dr hc Sociology (Moncton) 1997, (Univ. of Québec at Montréal) 2002; Prix Marcel-Vincent (ACFAS) 1989, Prix Léon-Gérin (Québec Govt) 1995, Prix Molson 1997, Prix Esdras-Minville 1998; Outstanding Contrib. Award (Canadian Asscn Sociology and Anthropology) 1988, Médaille Pierre Chauveau (Royal Soc. of Canada) 1991, Prix William Dawson, Royal Soc. of Canada 1999. *Films:* subject of film by Anne-Marie Rocher: Guy Rocher, Sociologist as Protagonist. *Publications:* Introduction à la sociologie générale 1969, Talcott Parsons et la sociologie américaine, Le Québec en mutation 1973, Ecole et société au Québec 1975, Entre les rêves et l'histoire 1989, Le Québec en jeu 1992, Entre droit et technique 1994, Etudes de sociologie du droit et de l'éthique 1996, Théories et emergence du droit 1998, May Weber, Rudolf Stammler et le matérialisme historique 2001, Le Droit à l'égalité 2001; and numerous articles on sociology, on sociology of law, of education and of health and on the evolution of Québec society. *Leisure interests:* tai-chi, skiing, swimming, concerts, reading. *Address:* Faculté de Droit, Université de Montréal, C.P. 6128, Succursale Centre-Ville, Montréal, PQ, H3C 3J7 (office); 4911 Chemin de la Côte-des-Neiges, Apt. 409, Montréal, PQ, H3V 1H7, Canada (home). *Telephone:* (514) 343-5993 (office); (514) 344-0882 (home). *Fax:* (514) 343-7508 (home). *E-mail:* guy.rocher@umontreal.ca (office).

ROCK, Allan, BA, LLB, QC; Canadian lawyer, fmr politician and fmr diplomatist; *Attorney, Sutts Strosberg LLP; b.* 30 Aug. 1947, Ottawa; m. Deborah Hanscom; three s. one d.; ed Univ. of Ottawa; pvt. practice –1993; MP for Etobicoke Centre 1993–2004; Minister of Justice and Attorney Gen. 1993–97, Minister of Health 1997–2002, Minister of Industry 2002–03; Perm. Rep. to UN Jan. 2004–06; attorney, Sutts Strosberg LLP, Windsor, Ont. 2006–; Special Advisor on Sri Lanka to UN on subject of Children and Armed Conflict; Chair. Trust Fund for War-Affected Children in Northern Uganda; mem. Security Council Report's Int. Advisory Group; Fellow, American Coll. of Trial Lawyers; fmr Treas. (CEO) Law Soc. of Upper Canada. *Address:* Sutts Strosberg LLP, 600 Westcourt Place, 251 Goyeau Street, Windsor, ON N9A 6V4, Canada (office). *Telephone:* (519) 561-6219 (office). *Fax:* (519) 561-6203 (office). *E-mail:* arock@strosbergco.com (office). *Website:* www.strosbergco.com (office).

ROCKBURNE, Dorothea; American artist; *b.* 18 Oct. 1932, Montreal, Canada; m. 1951 (divorced); one d.; ed Ecole des Beaux-Arts, Montreal, Black Mountain Coll., NC, Montreal Museum School; work in many public collections, including Whitney Museum, Museum of Modern Art, Metropolitan Museum of Art, Guggenheim Museum, Nat. Museum of Women in Art, Corcoran Gallery, MoCA LA, Philadelphia Museum of Art, Brooklyn Museum of Art, Nat. Galleries - Washington, Houston Museum of Fine Arts, Carnegie Museum, Museum of Fine Arts - Boston, Cranbrook Art Museum, LACMA, Nat. Acad. of Design Museum, Parrish Art Museum; Artist-in-Residence, American Acad. in Rome 1991, Bellagio Study Centre, Italy 1997; secco frescoes at Hilton Hotel, San Jose, Calif. 1992, Sony HQ, New York 1993, Edward T. Grignoux US Courthouse, Portland, Me 1996, Univ. of Michigan 1997, secco frescoes at US Embassy in Kingston, Jamaica 2009; Visiting Artist, Skowhegan School of Painting and Sculpture 1984; Avery Distinguished Prof., Bard Coll. Annandale-on-Hudson, NY 1986, mem. Dept of Art, American Acad. of Arts and Letters 2001; Hon. DFA (Coll. for Creative Studies) 2002; Guggenheim Fellow 1972, Art Inst. of Chicago Witowsky Painting Award 1972, Nat. Endowment for the Arts 1974, Creative Arts Award, Brandeis Univ. 1985, Lifetime Achievement Award, American Acad. of Arts and Letters 1999, American Acad. of Arts and Letters, Dept of Art 2001, Pollock-Krasner Foundation Grant 2002, Nat. Acad. of Design, Pike Award for Watercolour 2002, Art Omi Int.,. Francis J. Greenberger Award 2003, Pollock-Krasner Foundation Lee Krasner Award 2003 and 2007, Lifetime Achievement Award, Nat. Acad. Museum 2009. *Leisure interests:* astronomy, music, mathematics, theatre, poetry, friends. *Address:* 140 Grand Street, 2WF, New York, NY 10013, USA (home). *Telephone:* (212) 226-4471 (home). *Fax:* (866) 351-4234 (home). *E-mail:* drockburne@gmail.com (office). *Website:* www.dorothearockburne.com (office).

ROCKEFELLER, David, PhD; American banker; *b.* 12 June 1915, New York; s. of John Davison Rockefeller, Jr and Abby Greene Rockefeller (née Aldrich); brother of Laurance Rockefeller; m. Margaret McGrath 1940 (died 1996); two s. four d.; ed Harvard Coll., London School of Econs, Univ. of Chicago; Sec. to Mayor Fiorello H. La Guardia, New York 1940–41; Asst Regional Dir US Office of Defense, Health and Welfare Services 1941–42; served in US Army (Capt.) 1942–45; Foreign Dept Chase Nat. Bank 1946–48, Second Vice-Pres. 1948–49,

Vice-Pres. 1949–51, Sr Vice-Pres. 1951–55; Exec. Vice-Pres. Chase Manhattan Bank 1955–57, Vice-Chair. Bd 1957–61, Pres and Chair. Exec. Cttee 1961–69, CEO 1969–80, Chair. of Bd 1969–81, Chair. Chase Int. Investment Corpn 1961–81, Chase Int. Advisory Cttee 1980–99; Chair. Bd Rockefeller Group Inc. 1981–95, Rockefeller Center Properties, Inc. 1996–, Rockefeller Center Properties Inc. Trust; Chair. Rockefeller Univ. 1950–75, Chair Exec. Cttee 1975–, Council on Foreign Relations 1970–85, Americas Soc. 1981–92, Rockefeller Brothers Fund Inc. 1981–87 and numerous other chairmanships; Trustee Rockefeller Family Fund, Carnegie Endowment for Int. Peace, Museum of Modern Art, Chicago Univ., etc.; Grand-Croix, Légion d'honneur; Hon. LLD from 13 univs; Hon. DEng (Colorado School of Mines) 1974, (Notre Dame Univ.) 1987; Hadrian Award, World Mathematics Fund 1994, Presidential Medal of Freedom 1998, numerous American and foreign awards. *Publications:* Unused Resources and Economic Waste 1940, Creative Management in Banking 1964, Memoirs 2002. *Leisure interest:* sailing. *Address:* 30 Rockefeller Plaza, Room 5600, New York, NY 10112, USA.

ROCKEFELLER, John (Jay) Davison, IV, BA; American politician; *Senator from West Virginia; b.* 18 June 1937, New York, NY; s. of John Davison Rockefeller, III and Blanchette F. Rockefeller (née Hooker); m. Sharon Percy 1967; three s. one d.; ed Harvard and Yale Univs and Int. Christian Univ., Tokyo; mem. Nat. Advisory Council, Peace Corps 1961, Special Adviser to Dir 1962, Operations Officer in Charge of work in Philippines until 1963; Bureau of Far Eastern Affairs, US State Dept 1963, later Asst to Asst Sec. of State for Far Eastern Affairs; consultant, President's Comm. on Juvenile Delinquency and Youth Crime 1964, White House Conf. on Balanced Growth and Econ. Devt 1978, Pres.'s Comm. on Coal 1978–80; field worker, Action for Appalachian Youth Program 1964; mem. W Virginia House of Dels 1966–68; Sec. of State, W Va 1968–72; Pres. West Virginia Wesleyan Coll., Buckhannon 1973–75; Gov. of W Va 1977–85, Senator from West Virginia 1984–, Chair. Cttee on Commerce, Science, and Transportation, mem. Cttee on Finance, Cttee on Intelligence, Cttee on Veterans' Affairs, Jt Cttee on Taxation, Co-Chair. Senate Steel Caucus, US Trade Advisor; Democrat. *Publications:* articles in magazines. *Address:* 531 Hart Senate Office Building, Washington, DC 20510, USA (office). *Telephone:* (202) 224-6472 (office). *Fax:* (202) 224-7665 (office). *Website:* rockefeller.senate.gov (office).

ROCKWELL, John Sargent, PhD; American journalist and author; *b.* 16 Sept. 1940, Washington, DC; s. of Alvin John and Anne Hayward; m. Linda Mevorach; one d.; ed Harvard Univ., Univ. of Munich, FRG and Univ. of Calif., Berkeley; music and dance critic, Oakland (Calif.) Tribune 1969; Asst Music and Dance Critic, Los Angeles Times 1970–72; freelance music critic, New York Times 1972–74, staff music critic 1974–91, Ed. Arts and Leisure section 1998–; European Cultural Corresp. and Prin. Classical Recordings Critic, New York Times, Paris 1992–94, Sr Cultural Corresp. and Columnist 2002–04, Dance Critic 2005–06; Dir Lincoln Center Festival, Lincoln Center for the Performing Arts, New York 1994–98; Chevalier de l'ordre des Arts et Lettres. *Publications:* All American Music: Composition in the Late 20th Century 1983, Sinatra: An American Classic 1984, The Idiots 2003, Outsider: John Rockwell on the Arts 1967–2006 2006. *Address:* 543 Broadway, #10, New York, NY 10012, USA (home). *Telephone:* (212) 334-5073 (home). *Fax:* (212) 334-5073 (home). *E-mail:* rockwell.johnse@mac.com (home).

ROCKWELL, Sam; American actor; *b.* 5 Nov. 1968, Daly City, Calif. *Films include:* Clownhouse 1989, Last Exit to Brooklyn 1989, Teenage Mutant Ninja Turtles 1990, Strictly Business 1991, In the Soup 1992, Light Sleeper 1992, Jack and His Friends 1992, Happy Hell Night 1992, Dead Drunk 1992, Somebody to Love 1994, The Search for One-eye Jimmy 1994, Drunks 1995, Basquiat 1996, Box of Moon Light 1996, Glory Daze 1996, Mercy 1996, Bad Liver and a Broken Heart 1996, Prince Street (TV series) 1997, Subway Stories: Tales from the Underground (TV) 1997, Lawn Dogs 1997, Arresting Gena 1997, Jerry and Tom 1998, Louis & Frank 1998, Safe Men 1998, Celebrity 1998, The Call Back 1998, A Midsummer Night's Dream 1999, The Green Mile 1999, Galaxy Quest 1999, Charlie's Angels 2000, BigLove 2001, Heist 2001, Pretzel 2001, D.C. Smalls 2001, 13 Moons 2002, Running Time 2002, Welcome to Collinwood 2002, Stella Shorts 1998–2002 (video) 2002, Confessions of a Dangerous Mind 2002, Matchstick Men 2003, Piccadilly Jim 2004, The Hitchhiker's Guide to the Galaxy 2005, The F Word 2005, Robin's Big Date 2005, Snow Angels 2007, Joshua 2007, The Assassination of Jesse James by the Coward Robert Ford 2007, Woman in Burka 2008, Choke 2008, Frost/Nixon 2008, The Winning Season 2009, Moon 2009, G-Force 2009, Gentlemen Broncos 2009, Everybody's Fine 2009, Iron Man 2 2010, Conviction 2010, Cowboys & Aliens 2011, The Sitter 2011, Seven Psychopaths 2012. *Address:* c/o The Gersh Agency, 130 West 42nd Street, New York, NY 10036, USA (office).

RODAS, Armando, MA, DJur; Ecuadorean lawyer and politician; *b.* 1966; fmr lawyer; adviser to Pres. of Ecuador; Vice-Minister of Economy and Deputy Sec. of Public Admin –2006, Minister of Economy and Finance 2006 (resgnd). *Address:* c/o Ministry of the Economy and Finance, Avda 10 de Agosto 1661 y Jorge Washington, Quito, Ecuador (office).

RODAS MELGAR, (Róger) Haroldo; Guatemalan civil servant and politician; fmr Adviser, Ministry of Economy; Sec.-Gen. Secretaría de Integración Económica Centroamericana (SIECA) 1997–2007; Minister of Foreign Affairs 2008–12. *Publications:* articles in professional journals. *Address:* c/o Ministry of Foreign Affairs, 2a Avda La Reforma 4-47, Zona 10, Guatemala City, Guatemala (office).

RODAT, Robert, MFA; American screenwriter; *b.* 1953, NH; ed Univ. of Southern California Film School. *Film screenplays include:* Tall Tale 1995, Fly Away Home 1996, Saving Private Ryan 1998, The Patriot 2000. *Television:* TV screenplays include The Comrades of Summer 1992, The Ripper 1997, 36 Hours to Die 1999. *Address:* c/o Hohman Maybank Lieb, 9229 Sunset Blvd., Suite 700, Los Angeles, CA 90069, USA. *Telephone:* (310) 274-4600. *Fax:* (310) 274-4741. *E-mail:* info@hmllit.com.

RODDICK, Andrew (Andy) Stephen; American fmr professional tennis player; *b.* 30 Aug. 1982, Omaha, Neb.; s. of Jerry Roddick and Blanche Roddick; number one US jr 1999–2000 and number one world jr 2000, won six world jr singles and seven doubles titles, including US and Australian Open jr singles titles; turned professional 2000; singles titles: Atlanta 2001, Houston 2001, 2002, 2005, Washington, DC 2001, 2005, 2007, Memphis 2002, 2009, Montreal TMS 2003, Indianapolis 2003, 2004, Queen's Club, London 2003, 2004, 2005, 2007, Cincinnati

TMS 2003, 2006, St Poelten 2003, US Open 2003, Miami 2004, 2010, San José 2004, 2005, 2008, Lyon 2005, Dubai 2008, Beijing 2008, Eastbourne 2012; singles finalist: Wimbledon 2004, 2005, 2009, US Open 2006; doubles titles: Delray Beach (with Jan-Michael Gambill) 2001, Houston (with Mardy Fish) 2002, Indianapolis (with Bobby Reynolds) 2006, Indian Wells (with Mardy Fish) 2009; 612 career singles wins, 212 defeats, 32 singles titles, highest ranking No. 1 3 Nov. 2003; 67 career doubles wins, 50 defeats, four doubles titles, highest ranking No. 50 11 Jan. 2010; mem. winning US Davis Cup team 2007; fmrly coached by Brad Gilbert; announced retirement from tennis during US Open 2012; f. Andy Roddick Foundation charity for children 2001. *Leisure interests:* music, films, skydiving. *Address:* c/o Andrew S. Roddick Foundation, Inc., Helping Children Today For Tomorrow, 2901 Clint Moore Road, #109, Boca Raton, FL 33496, USA (office). *Telephone:* (561) 392-2652 (office); (954) 340-7471 (office). *Fax:* (561) 392-6883 (office). *Website:* www.andyroddick.com (office); www.arfoundation.org (office).

RODÉ, HE Cardinal Franc, CM, DTheol; Slovenian ecclesiastic, academic and diplomatist; *Prefect Emeritus of the Congregation for Institutes of Consecrated Life and Societies of Apostolic Life;* b. 23 Sept. 1934, Rodica, nr Ljubljana, Yugoslavia (now Slovenia); ed Pontifical Gregorian Univ., Rome, Catholic Inst. of Paris; family fled to Austria 1945, to Argentina 1948; ordained priest of the Congregation of the Mission (Lazarists) 1960; returned to Yugoslavia to work as vice-pastor, director of studies and prov. visitor of the Lazarists and Prof. of Fundamental Theology and Missionology, Theological Faculty of Ljubljana 1965; consultor of Secr. for Non-Believers in Roman Curia 1978, transferred to that dicastery 1981, Under-sec. 1982–87, Sec. 1987–93; Sec., Pontifical Council for Culture 1993–97; Archbishop of Ljubljana 1997–2004; Prefect of Congregation for Insts of Consecrated Life and Socs of Apostolic Life 2004–05, 2005–11, Prefect Emer. 2011–; cr. Cardinal (Cardinal-Deacon of San Francesco Saverio alla Garbatella) 2006; mem. Congregation of Divine Worship and Discipline of the Sacraments, Congregation for Bishops, Congregation for Evangelization of Peoples, Congregation for Catholic Educ., Pontifical Council for Culture, Pontifical Comm. Ecclesia Dei. *Address:* Congregation for Institutes of Consecrated Life and Societies of Apostolic Life, Palazzo della Congregazioni, Piazza Pio XII 3, 00193 Rome, Italy (office). *Telephone:* (06) 69892511 (office); (06) 69884128 (office). *Fax:* (06) 69884526 (office). *Website:* www.vatican.va/roman_curia/congregations/ccscrlife (office).

RODGERS, Jimmie, MD; Solomon Islands physician and international organization executive; holds degree in health admin; Under-Sec., later Perm. Sec. for Health, Ministry of Health and Medical Services, Solomon Islands 1990–96; joined Secr. of the Pacific Community (SPC) as Dir of Programmes in 1996, later re-designated as Deputy Dir-Gen. based in Noumea, Head of SPC Suva Regional Office 1998, later Sr Deputy Dir-Gen., Dir-Gen. SPC 2005–14. *E-mail:* drjimmier@gmail.com.

RODGERS, Joan, CBE, BA, FRNCM; British singer (soprano); b. 4 Nov. 1956, Whitehaven, Cumbria; d. of the late Thomas Rodgers and of Julia Rodgers; m. Paul Daniel (q.v.) 1988 (divorced); two d.; ed Whitehaven Grammar School, Univ. of Liverpool and Royal Northern Coll. of Music, Manchester; first maj. professional engagement as Pamina in The Magic Flute, Aix-en-Provence Festival 1982; début at Metropolitan Opera House, New York, in same role 1995; other appearances include title role of Theodora at Glyndebourne, The Governess in Turn of the Screw for Royal Opera House, Blanche in Dialogues des Carmélites for ENO and in Amsterdam, Marschallin in Der Rosenkavalier for Scottish Opera and title role of Alcina for English Nat. Opera; regular appearances at Royal Opera House, English Nat. Opera, Glyndebourne, Promenade Concerts and with leading British and European cos; concert engagements in London, Europe and USA with conductors including Solti, Barenboim, Mehta, Rattle, Harnoncourt and Salonen; numerous recordings; Kathleen Ferrier Memorial Scholarship 1981; Dr hc (Liverpool); Royal Philharmonic Soc. Award as Singer of the Year 1997, Evening Standard Award for Outstanding Individual Performance in Opera 1997. *Leisure interests:* walking, cooking, horse riding. *Address:* c/o Ingpen and Williams Ltd, 7 St George's Court, 131 Putney Bridge Road, London, SW15 2PA, England (office). *Telephone:* (20) 8874-3222 (office). *Fax:* (20) 8877-3113 (office). *Website:* www.ingpen.co.uk/ (office).

RODGERS, Patricia Elaine Joan, MA, DPolSc; Bahamian diplomatist; b. Nassau; ed School of St Helen & St Catherine, Abingdon, Univ. of Aberdeen, Graduate Inst. of Int. Relations, St Augustine, Trinidad, Inst. Universitaire des Hautes Etudes Int., Univ. of Geneva; Counsellor and Consul, Washington, DC 1978–83; Alt. Rep. to OAS 1982–83; Deputy High Commr (Acting High Commr) to Canada 1983–86, High Commr 1986–88; High Commr to UK (also Accred to France, Belgium and Germany) 1988–92; mem. Bahamas Del. to UN Conf. on Law of the Sea 1974, 1975, OAS Gen. Ass. 1982, Caribbean Co-ordinating Meeting (Head of Del.), OAS 1983, Canada/Commonwealth Caribbean Heads of Govt Meeting 1985, Commonwealth Heads of Govt Meeting Nassau 1985, Vancouver 1987; Adviser to Bahamas Del., Annual Gen. Meetings of World Bank and IMF 1978–82; mem. Commonwealth Observer Group, Gen. Elections Lesotho 1993; apptd. Perm. Sec., Ministry of Tourism 1995; currently Perm. Sec., Ministry of Foreign Affairs. *Publications:* Mid-Ocean Archipelagos and International Law: A Study of the Progressive Development of International Law 1981. *Leisure interests:* folk art, theatre, gourmet cooking, gardening. *Address:* Ministry of Foreign Affairs and Public Service, East Hill Street, POB N-3746, Nassau, Bahamas (office). *Telephone:* 302-9300 (office). *Fax:* 328-8212 (office). *E-mail:* mfabahamas@batelnet.bs (office); carridad68@yahoo.com (home).

RODGERS OF QUARRY BANK, Baron (Life Peer), cr. 1992, of Kentish Town in the London Borough of Camden; **William Thomas Rodgers,** PC, MA; British politician and administrator; b. 28 Oct. 1928, Liverpool; s. of William Arthur Rodgers and Gertrude Helen Rodgers; m. Silvia Szulman 1955 (died 2006); three d.; ed Sudley Road Council School, Quarry Bank High School, Liverpool and Magdalen Coll., Oxford; Gen. Sec. Fabian Soc. 1953–60; Labour Cand. for Bristol West 1957; Borough Councillor, St Marylebone 1958–62; MP for Stockton-on-Tees 1962–74, for Stockton Div. of Teesside 1974–83; Parl. Under-Sec. of State, Dept of Econ. Affairs 1964–67, Foreign Office 1967–68; Leader, UK del. to Council of Europe and Ass. of WEU 1967–68; Minister of State, Bd of Trade 1968–69, Treasury 1969–70; Chair. Expenditure Cttee on Trade and Industry 1971–74; Minister of State, Ministry of Defence 1974–76; Sec. of State for Transport 1976–79; Opposition Spokesman for Defence 1979–80; left Labour Party March 1981; Co-founder Social Democratic Party March 1981, mem. Nat. Cttee 1982–87,

Vice-Pres. 1982–87; Dir-Gen. RIBA 1987–94; Chair. Advertising Standards Authority 1995–2000; Leader Liberal Democratic Peers 1998–2001; Liberal Democrat; Hon. Fellow, Liverpool John Moores Univ. 2008; Hon. DLL (Liverpool Univ.) 2008. *Publications:* Hugh Gaitskell 1906–1963 (Ed.) 1964, The People Into Parliament (co-author) 1966, The Politics of Change 1982, Government and Industry (Ed. and co-author) 1986, Fourth Among Equals 2000. *Leisure interests:* reading, walking, cinema. *Address:* House of Lords, London, SW1A 0PW (office); 43 North Road, London, N6 4BE, England (home). *Telephone:* (20) 7219-3607 (office); (20) 8341-2434 (home).

RODIĆ, Nebojša; Serbian lawyer and politician; b. 1953, Šabac; Sec., Electoral Comm. of the Repub. of Serbia 1996, 1997; Sec., Referendum Comm. on foreign mediation in settlement of Kosovo crisis 1998; fmr Deputy Sec. People's Ass. (Parl.); fmr Asst Sec.-Gen., Ministry of the Interior; fmr Amb.; Sec.-Gen. to Pres. of Serbia Tomislav Nikolić May–Aug. 2012; Dir BIA (Security Information Agency) 2012–13; Minister of Defence 2013–14. *Address:* c/o Ministry of Defence, 11000 Belgrade, Birčaninova 5, Serbia (office).

RODIER, Jean-Pierre; French business executive and mining engineer; *Advisor, CVC Capital Partners (France) SA;* b. 4 May 1947, Reims; s. of Pierre Rodier and Gabrielle Sayen; m. Michèle Foz 1969; ed Lycée de Saumur, Lycée de Pamiers, Lycée de Pierre-en-Fermat, Toulouse; Asst Sec.-Gen. Mines Directorate, Ministry of Industry 1975–78, Sec.-Gen. 1978; Head of Econs and Budget mission of Dir-Gen. of Energy and Raw Materials 1979; Head of Raw Material and Subsoil Dept 1981–83; tech. adviser to Prime Minister's Office 1983–84; Dir of Gen. Man. Penarroya mining and metallurgy Co. 1984–85, Asst Dir-Gen. 1985–86, Pres. and Dir Gen. 1986–88; Pres. Bd Dirs Metaleurop 1988–91; Deputy Admin. Mining Union 1991–94; Pres. Asscn of Enterprise and Personnel 2001–; Pres. and Dir-Gen. Pechiney 1994–2003; Advisor, CVC Capital Pnrs (France) SA 2004–; mem. Bd of Dirs Vedanta Resources 2004–; Pres. Bd Dirs Ecole nat. supérieure des techniques industrielles et des mines d'Alès 1992–95; Chevalier de la Légion d'Honneur. *Address:* CVC Capital Partners (France) SA, 40 rue La Pérouse, 75116 Paris, France (office). *Telephone:* 1-45-02-23-00 (office). *Fax:* 1-45-02-23-01 (office). *Website:* www.cvceurope.com (office).

RODIN, Judith, PhD; American physician, foundation executive and fmr university president; *President, The Rockefeller Foundation;* b. 9 Sept. 1944, Philadelphia, Pa; d. of Morris Rodin and Sally (Winson) Seitz; m. 1st 1978; one s.; m. 2nd Paul Verkuil 1994; ed Univ. of Pennsylvania and Columbia Univ.; NSF Postdoctoral Fellow, Univ. of California 1971; Asst Prof. of Psychology, New York Univ. 1970–72; Asst Prof., Yale Univ. 1972–75, Assoc. Prof. 1975–79, Prof. of Psychology 1979–83, Dir of Grad. Studies 1982–89, Philip R. Allen Prof. of Psychology 1984–94, Prof. of Medicine and Psychiatry 1985–94, Chair. Dept of Psychology 1989–91, Dean Grad. School of Arts and Sciences 1991–92, Provost 1992–94; Prof. of Psychology, Medicine and Psychiatry, Univ. of Pennsylvania 1994–2004, Pres. Univ. of Pennsylvania 1994–2004; Pres. Rockefeller Foundation 2005–; Chair. John D. & Catherine T. MacArthur Foundation Research Network on Determinants and Consequences of Health-Promoting and Health-Damaging Behavior 1983–93; Chair. Council of Pres.'s, Univs Research Asscn 1995–96; has served on numerous Bds of Dirs, including Int. Life Sciences Inst. 1993–, Aetna Life & Casualty Co. 1995–, AMR Corpn, Comcast Corpn, Citigroup; has served as mem. of numerous professional cttees, including Pres. Clinton's Cttee of Advisors on Science and Tech., Pa Women's Forum 1995–; Chief Ed. Appetite 1979–92; has served on numerous editorial bds; mem. Bd of Trustees, Brookings Inst. 1995–; Fellow, AAAS, American Acad. of Arts and Sciences; 17 hon. doctorates, including Hon. DHumLitt (New Haven) 1994, (Medical Coll. of Pennsylvania, Hahnemann Univ.) 1995; numerous awards and prizes, including 21st Century Award, Int. Alliance, Glass Ceiling Award, American Red Cross, ranked by Forbes magazine amongst The World's 100 Most Powerful Women (71st) 2011, (98th) 2012, (99th) 2013. *Publications include:* author or co-author of 12 books on the relationship between psychological and biological processes in human health and behaviour, including The University & Urban Renewal: Out of the Ivory Tower and Into the Streets; more than 200 articles in academic journals. *Leisure interests:* tennis, travel, reading. *Address:* The Rockefeller Foundation, 420 Fifth Avenue, New York, NY 10018-2702, USA (office). *Telephone:* (212) 869-8500 (office). *Fax:* (212) 764-3468 (office). *Website:* www.rockfound.org (office).

RODIONOV, Gen. Igor Nikolayevich; Russian politician and army officer (retd); b. 1 Dec. 1936, Kurakino, Penza Region; m.; one s.; ed Orel Tank Higher Mil. School, Mil. Acad. of Armoured Units, Mil. Acad. of Gen. Staff; Asst to Commdr, master sgt's student's co. Orel Tank Higher School 1965–67; in Group of Soviet Troops in Germany 1957–64; Commdr tank co., Deputy Commdr tank bn 1964–67; Deputy Commdr tank regt, Commdr Regt, Deputy Commdr, Commdr div. Carpathian Mil. Command 1970–78; Commdr Army corps Cen. Group of Troops 1980–83; Commdr 5th Army Far E. Mil. Command 1983–85; Commdr Army of Turkestan Mil. Command, participant of war in Afghanistan 1985–86; First Deputy Commdr Moscow Mil. Command 1986–88; Commdr Caucasian Mil. Command, involved in dispersal of demonstration in Tbilisi 1989; Chief Mil. Acad. of Gen. Staff 1989–96; Minister of Defence of Russian Fed., mem. Security Council and Defence Council 1996–97; discharged by Pres. Yeltsin; joined CP of Russian Fed. 1998; mem. State Duma (Parl.), CP faction 1999–2003, Rodina (Homeland) faction 2003–. *Address:* State Duma, Okhotny Ryad 1, 103265 Moscow, Russia. *Telephone:* (495) 292-50-14.

RODIONOV, Piotr Ivanovich; Russian politician; b. 26 Jan. 1951, Przhevalsk, Kyrgyz SSR; m.; three c.; ed Leningrad Inst. of Vessel Construction, Leningrad Inst. of Finance and Econs, Higher School of Commerce, Acad. of Nat. Econs; with USSR Ministry of Gas Industry; Chief Technologist, Head of Div., with Lentransgas 1984–88; Dir-Gen. Lentransgas 1989–96; mem. Bd of Dirs Russian Jt Gazprom 1994; First Deputy Chair. 2001–06; currently investor Severneftegazdobyca (oil and natural gas co.); rep. of Russian Govt to Gazprom 1996, to United Energy System of Russia 1996; Minister of Oil and Gas Industry 1996–97; mem. Govt Comm. for Operational Problems 1996–97; Chair. Bd of Dirs Menatep St Petersburg Bank 1998–; Hon. Worker of Gas Industry. *Address:* c/o Gazprom, Nametkina str. 16, 117884 Moscow, Russia.

RODKIN, Gary M., BEcons, MBA; American food industry executive; *President and CEO, ConAgra Foods Inc.;* b. 6 April 1952; m. Barbara Rodkin; one s. one d.; ed

Rutgers Univ., Harvard Business School; held marketing and man. positions General Mills 1979–95 including Pres. Yoplait-Colombo 1992–95; Pres. Tropicana N America 1995–98; Pres. and CEO Pepsi Cola N America 1999–2002, Pres. PepsiCo Beverages and Foods 2002–03, Chair. CEO 2002–05; Pres. and CEO ConAgra Foods Inc., Omaha 2005–; mem. Bd of Dirs United Industries Corpn 2005–. *Address:* ConAgra Foods Inc., 1 ConAgra Drive, Omaha, NE 68102-5001, USA (office). *Telephone:* (402) 595-4000 (office). *Fax:* (402) 595-4707 (office). *Website:* www.conagra.com (office).

RODRIGO, Nihal; Sri Lankan diplomatist and international organization official; *Adviser to the President on Foreign Affairs;* b. Kandy; ed Trinity Coll., Kandy; Asst Lecturer, Univ. of Ceylon; with Foreign Service, including diplomatic missions in Australia, Germany, India, Switzerland and USA; Deputy Perm. Rep. to UN, New York, Perm. Rep., Geneva; Dir-Gen. for S Asia, SAARC, Sec.-Gen. 1999–2002; co-ordinated activities of Non-Aligned Movt under Sri Lanka's chairmanship 1976–79, del. to summit confs 1976–, Chair. Political Cttee 1995; mem. Advisory Bd on Disarmament of UN Sec.-Gen.; mem. several presidential cttees, including Acquisition of Art Works for State Collections, Foreign Affairs, Human Rights and Information Strategy; mem. Man. Bd Bandaranaike Centre for Int. Studies; Amb. to China, Mongolia and People's Repub. of China 2004–07; Adviser to Pres. of Sri Lanka on Foreign Affairs 2007–. *Address:* c/o President's Secretariat, Republic Square, Colombo 1, Sri Lanka. *Telephone:* (11) 2324801. *Fax:* (11) 2331246. *E-mail:* gosl@presidentsl.org. *Website:* www.presidentsl.org.

RODRIGUES, Christopher John, CBE, MA, MBA, FRSA; British business executive and government official; *Chairman, VisitBritain;* b. 24 Oct. 1949; s. of Alfred John Rodrigues and Joyce Margaret Rodrigues (née Farron-Smith); m. Priscilla Purcell Young 1976; one s. one d.; ed Univ. of Cambridge, Harvard Univ., USA; fmr man. trainee Spillers; fmrly with McKinsey, American Express; fmr COO, fmr Chief Exec. Thomas Cook; Chief Exec. Bradford & Bingley Bldg Soc. (now Bradford & Bingley PLC) 1996–2004; Pres. and CEO Visa International 2004–06; Chair. VisitBritain 2007–, Int. Personal Finance 2007, Windsor Leadership Trust 2007, Almeida Theatre 2008; Founder-Dir Financial Services Authority 1997–2003; Dir (non-exec.) Energis PLC 1997–2003, Ladbrokes plc (fmrly Hilton Group) 2003–13; Chair. British Bobsleigh & Skeleton Asscn 2013–, Openwork Holdings Ltd 2014–; mem. Exec. Cttee World Travel and Tourism Council; mem. Council and Trustee, National Trust; Hon. DUniv (Surrey) 2013. *Leisure interests:* cooking, rowing, opera. *Address:* VisitBritain, Sanctuary Buildings, 20 Great Smith Street, London, SW1P 3BT, England (office). *Telephone:* (20) 7578-1298 (office). *Website:* www.visitbritain.com (office).

RODRIGUES, Gen. (retd) Sunith Francis, MA; Indian fmr army officer and government official; b. 19 Sept. 1933, Bombay (now Mumbai); m. Jean Rodrigues; two s. one d.; ed St Xavier's High School, Bombay, Defence Services Staff Coll., Royal Coll. of Defence Studies, UK; joined Jt Services Wing, Indian Mil. Acad. 1949, commissioned into Regt of Artillery 1952, commanded mountain artillery regt 1970–71, served as Gen. Staff Officer during Indo-Pak War at a Corps HQ 1971, of a Div. 1973–75, commanded mountain brigade at high altitude 1975–77, Chief Instructor (Army) at Defence Services Staff Coll. (DSSC) 1978–81, commanded div. deployed at high altitude on becoming Maj.-Gen. 1981, Chief of Staff of a corps 1983–85, Dir-Gen. Mil. Training and promoted to rank of Lt-Gen. 1985–86, commanded corps in northern sector 1986–89, apptd Hon. ADC to Pres. 1987, served as Vice-Chief of Army Staff 1987–89, GOC-in-C Cen. Command April–Oct. 1989, GOC-in-C Western Command 1989–90, Chief of Army Staff 1990–93; Dir Int. Centre, Goa 1993–99; served two terms on Nat. Security Advisory Bd; mem. Exec. Council Goa Univ. for seven years, Man. Cttee Goa Chamber of Commerce and Industry; Gov. of Punjab and Admin. of Union Territory of Chandigarh 2004–10; mem. Goa Planning Bd, Bd Govs Goa Inst. of Man.; Vishisht Seva Medal (VSM) for distinguished service 1972, Param Vishisht Seva Medal (PVSM) 1988; Hon. DLitt (Goa Univ.); Mother Teresa's Lifetime Achievement Award 2009. *Leisure interests:* social and literary pursuits. *Address:* c/o Punjab Raj Bhawan, Sector 6, Chandigarh, India.

RODRIGUES-BIRKETT, Carolyn; Guyanese politician; *Minister of Foreign Affairs;* b. 16 Sept. 1973, Santa Rosa, Region One; m.; two c.; ed Saskatchewan Federated Coll., Canada, Univ. of Guyana; began career as teacher, Santa Rosa Primary School; Asst Co-ordinator, later Co-ordinator for Amerindian Projects, Social Impact Amelioration Program 1993–2001; Minister of Amerindian Affairs 2001–08, of Foreign Affairs 2008–. *Address:* Ministry of Foreign Affairs, Takuba Lodge, 254 South Road and Shivnarine Chanderpaul Drive, Bourda, Georgetown, Guyana (office). *Telephone:* 226-9080 (office). *Fax:* 223-5241 (office). *E-mail:* minister@minfor.gov.gy (office). *Website:* www.minfor.gov.gy (office).

RODRIGUEZ, Alexander (Alex) Emmanuel; American professional baseball player; b. 27 July 1975, New York, NY; m. Cynthia Scurtis 2002; one d.; ed Westminster Christian High School, Miami, Fla; shortstop and third baseman; Maj. League teams: Seattle Mariners 1994–2000, Texas Rangers 2001–2003, NY Yankees 2004–; first high school player to trial for Team USA 1993; represented US Junior National Squad 1993; Maj. League debut 8 July 1994 (third 18-year-old shortstop to play Maj. Leagues since 1900); est. Seattle record for average, runs, hits, doubles and total bases 1996; traded to NY Yankees 2004; led American League (AL) in home runs 2001, 2002 (with 57 home runs, sixth highest in AL history), 2003, 2005, 2007; youngest player ever to hit 500 home runs; f. Alex Rodriguez Foundation 1998; USA Baseball Junior Player of the Year 1993, National Baseball Student Athlete of the Year 1993, finalist for USA Baseball Golden Spikes Award for top amateur player 1993 (while still at school), AL batting champion 1996, Sporting News Maj. League Player of the Year 1996, 2002 2007, Associated Press Maj. League Player of the Year 1996, All-Star 1996–98, 2000–08, 2010, 2011, Silver Slugger 1996, 1998–2003, 2005, 2007, 2008, AL hits leader 1998, Baseball America Maj. League Player of the Year 2000, 2002, AL Hank Aaron Award winner 2001–03, 2007, Rawlings Gold Glove 2002, 2003 for shortstop, AL RBI leader 2002, 2007, American League Most Valuable Player 2003, 2005, 2007, Babe Ruth Award 2009. *Leisure interests:* basketball, golf, boating. *Address:* New York Yankees, Yankee Stadium, 1 East 161st Street, Bronx, New York, NY 10451, USA (office). *Telephone:* (718) 293-4300 (office). *Fax:* (718) 293-8431 (office). *Website:* newyork.yankees.mlb.com (office).

RODRÍGUEZ, Maria Isabel, MD; Salvadorean physician and politician; *Minister of Public Health and Social Welfare;* b. 5 Nov. 1922, San Salvador; ed Univ. of El Salvador; began career as cardiovascular physiologist and biomedical researcher; Dean, Faculty of Medicine, Univ. of El Salvador 1967–71, Adviser and Hon. Prof. 1995–99, Rector, Univ. of El Salvador 1999–2003; in exile 1972, worked for Pan-American Health Org. and WHO; consultant to US Health Educ. Program, Washington, DC 1985–94; Minister of Public Health and Social Welfare 2009–; Dr hc (Guadalajara) 2005, (Universidad Centroamericana José Simeón Cañas) 2006, (Córdoba) 2007, (San Carlos, Universidad Cayetano Heredia) 2008, (Universidad de El Salvador) 2009. *Publications include:* more than 100 articles on science and education. *Address:* Ministry of Public Health and Social Welfare, Calle Arce 827, San Salvador, El Salvador (office). *Telephone:* 2221-0966 (office). *Fax:* 2221-0991 (office). *E-mail:* webmaster@mspas.gob.sv (office). *Website:* www .mspas.gob.sv (office).

RODRÍGUEZ, Narciso; American fashion designer; b. 27 Jan. 1961, New Jersey; ed Parsons School of Design, New York; Women's Designer Asst, Anne Klein under Donna Karan 1985–91, Women's Ready-to-Wear, Calvin Klein 1991–95; Women's and Men's Design Dir TSE, New York, Women's Creative Dir Cerruti, Paris 1995–97; Women's Design Dir Loewe, Spain 1997; Narciso Rodriguez signature collection presented Milan 1997; Best New Designer, VH1 Fashion Awards 1997, Perry Ellis Award, Council of Fashion Designers of America (CFDA) 1997, Hispanic Designers Moda Award 1997, New York Magazine Award 1997, Womenswear Designer of the Year, CFDA 2002, 2003. *Address:* Narciso Rodriguez LLC, 30 Irving Place, # 9, New York, NY 10003, USA (office); 22-32 ave. Victor Hugo, 75116 Paris, France. *Telephone:* (212) 677-2989 (office). *Fax:* (212) 677-2475 (office). *Website:* www.narcisorodriguez.com.

RODRÍGUEZ ARAQUE, Ali; Venezuelan politician, lawyer, diplomatist and international organization official; *Secretary-General, Union of South American Nations;* b. 9 Sept. 1937, Ejido, Venezuela; ed Univ. Cen. de Venezuela, Univ. de los Andes; practised law; mem. Parl. 1983; mem. Nat. Council of Energy; Chair. Chamber of Deputies Comm. of Energy and Mines 1994–97; Vice-Chair., Bicameral Comm. of Energy and Mines; Senator 1999–2004; Minister of Energy and Mines 1999–2000; Pres. of OPEC Conf. 2000, Sec.-Gen. 2001–02; Pres. and CEO Petróleos de Venezuela SA (PDVSA) 2002–04; Minister of Foreign Affairs 2004–06, of Finance 2008–10, of Electric Energy 2010–12; Amb. to Cuba 2006–08; Sec.-Gen. Union of South American Nations 2012–. *Publications include:* various articles on public policy in the field of energy, including Privatisation Process of the Oil Industry in Venezuela 1997. *Address:* Union of South American Nations, December 6th Avenue, N24-04 and President Wilson, Quito, Ecuador (office). *Telephone:* (2) 4010400 (office). *Website:* www.unasursg.org (office).

RODRÍGUEZ ECHEVERRÍA, Miguel Ángel, PhD; Costa Rican economist, lawyer, business executive, international organization official and fmr head of state; b. 9 Jan. 1940, San José; m.; ed Univ. de Costa Rica, Univ. of California, Berkeley; Lecturer and Economist, Univ. of Costa Rica 1963; Research Asst, Univ. of Calif., Berkeley 1965–66; Dir of Planning Office and Presidential Adviser on Political Econs and Planning 1966–68; Dir Cen. Bank 1967–70; columnist for La Nación 1967–68; with Ministry of Planning 1968–69; Visiting Economist, Univ. of Calif.; with Ministry of the Presidency 1970; exec. with Empacadora de Carne de Cartago and Abonos Superior SA 1970–71; Pres. Agrodinámica Int. SA and subsidiaries 1974–87; Lecturer in Econs, Univ. of Costa Rica and Univ. Autónoma de Centro América 1978; mem. of Counsel (legal and econ. advisers) 1982; mem. nat. political directorate Partido Unidad Social Cristiano 1984, mem. Exec. 1994; Dir Banco Agro Industrial y de Exportaciones SA 1986–87; gen. adviser Grupo Ganadero Int. de Costa Rica SA 1989–90; Deputy Legis. Ass. 1991–92; Vice-Pres. (for Cen. America), Christian Democratic Org. of Latin America 1991, Pres. 1995; Pres. of Costa Rica 1998–2002; Sec.-Gen. OAS Sec.–Oct. 2004 (resgnd and returned to Costa Rica to face allegations of financial wrongdoing during his presidency; currently awaiting trial for corruption charges). *Publications:* El mito de la Racionalidad del Socialismo 1963, El Orden Jurídico de la Libertad 1967, Contributions to Economic Analysis. Production Economics: A Dual Approach to Theory and Applications 1978, Nuestra Crisis Financiera: Causas y Soluciones 1979, De las Ideas a la Acción 1988, Al Progreso por la Libertad 1989, Libertad y Solidaridad: Una Política Social para el Desarrollo Humano 1992, Una Revolución Moral: Democracia, Mercado y Bien Común 1992, Por una Vida Buena, Justa y Solidaria 1993; numerous articles and contribs on econs. *Address:* c/o Organization of American States, 17th Street & Constitution Avenue, NW, Washington, DC 20006, USA.

RODRÍGUEZ GARCÍA, José Luis, PhD; Cuban politician; b. 18 March 1946, Havana; mem. Cen. Cttee, CP of Cuba 1997–; Deputy, Nat. Ass. of People's Power 1998–; Minister of Economy and Planning 1998–2009; fmr Vice-Pres. Council of Ministers; mem. Scientific Council, Inst. of Int. Relations, Cuban Acad. of Sciences. *Address:* c/o Ministry of Economy and Planning, 20 de Mayo, entre Territorial y Ayestarán, Plaza de la Revolución, Havana, Cuba (office).

RODRÍGUEZ GIAVARINI, Adalberto; Argentine politician and economist; *Chairman, Argentine Council for International Relations;* ed Univ. of Buenos Aires; fmr Comptroller Gen. Trust of State Cos.; Pres. and owner macroecons analysis co.; Chair. Microecons, Univ. of Buenos Aires 1972–78; Co-ordinator Postgrad. Studies in Econs, Univ. of Salvador 1980–83; Sec. of State for Budget, Ministry of Economy 1983–85, for Planning, Ministry of Defence 1986–89; elected mem. Chamber of Deputies 1995; Minister of Foreign Affairs, Int. Trade and Religion 1999–2001; mem. Bd of Dirs and Exec. Cttee Fundación Carolina de Argentina, fmr Pres.; Visiting Prof., Univ. of Belgrano 1994; Prof. of Econs, School of Econs and Business Admin. 1995; Chair. Argentine Council for Int. Relations 2007–; mem. various academic insts and advisory bds; guest columnist maj. daily newspapers in Argentina and abroad. *Address:* Argentine Council for International Relations, Uruguay 1037, piso 1° C1016ACA, Buenos Aires, Argentina (office). *E-mail:* cari@cari.org.ar (office). *Website:* www.cari.org.ar (office).

RODRIGUEZ GÓMEZ, Jorge, PhD; Venezuelan psychologist and politician; b. 9 Nov. 1965, Caracas; s. of Jorge Rodríguez; ed Luis Razetti School of Medicine, Central Univ. of Venezuela and Andrés Bello Catholic Univ.; Pres. Student Union, Luis Razetti School of Medicine 1987–88; Pres. Venezuelan Fed. of Univs. 1988–92; Resident Doctor, Venezuelan Inst. of Social Security 1995; joined Movimiento

Quinto República (MVR) 2000; in pvt. medical practice 2002–03; Pres. Nat. Electoral Team 2003–05; Pres. Nat. Electoral Council 2005–06; Vice–Pres. of Venezuela 2007. *Address:* Movimiento Quinto República, Calle Lima, cruce con Avda Libertador, Los Cabos, Caracas, Venezuela (office). *Telephone:* (212) 782-3808 (office). *Fax:* (212) 782-9720 (office).

RODRÍGUEZ HERRER, Elvira; Spanish politician and government official; *President, Comisión Nacional del Mercado de Valores;* b. 15 May 1949; m.; four c.; ed Universidad Complutense de Madrid; lawyer; Inspector and State Auditor 1972–74; Head of Fiscal Section, Seville Property Del. 1974–75; Chief of Finance Unit, Directorate of the Treasury 1975–78; Asst Dir-Gen. Social Security 1978–84; Asst Dir-Gen. Nat. Audit Office 1984–96; Dir-Gen. of Budgets 1996–2000; Sec. of State for Budgets and Expenditure, Ministry of Property 2000; Minister of the Environment 2003–04; Minister of Transport, Community of Madrid 2006–07; Pres. Ass. of Madrid 2007–11; mem. Parl. for Jaén 2011–12; Pres. Comisión Nacional del Mercado de Valores (nat. comm. for stock markets) 2012–; mem. Comms preparing first Gen. Plan of Public Accounts 1981, 1983; Nat. Audit Office Rep. on Comm. of Principles and Public Norms 1991–94. *Address:* Comisión Nacional del Mercado de Valores, Edison, 4, 28006 Madrid, Spain (office). *Telephone:* (91) 5851500 (office). *Fax:* (91) 3193373 (office). *Website:* www.cnmv .es (office).

RODRÍGUEZ IGLESIAS, Gil Carlos, PhD; Spanish judge and professor of law; b. 26 May 1946, Gijón; m. Teresa Diez Gutiérrez 1972; two d.; ed Univ. of Oviedo and Univ. Autónoma de Madrid; Asst, Univers of Oviedo, Freiburg, Autónoma of Madrid and Complutense of Madrid 1969–77; Lecturer, Univ. Complutense of Madrid 1977–82, Prof. 1982–83, Prof. of Int. Law 2003–; Prof., Univ. of Granada 1983–2003, Dir Dept of Int. Law 1983–86; Judge, Court of Justice of European Communities 1986–2003, Pres. 1994–2003; Jean Monnet Chair of European Community Law, Dir Dept of European Studies, Instituto Universitario Ortega y Gasset 2004–05; Co-Dir Revista de Derecho Comunitario Europeo; mem. Bd of Dirs Fundación Real Instituto Elcano; mem. Editorial Bd of several law reviews; mem. Curatorium, Max Planck Inst. for Int. Public Law and Comparative Law, Heidelberg; Hon. Bencher Gray's Inn 1995, King's Inns, Dublin; Hon. Fellow, Soc. of Advanced Legal Studies, London; Hon. mem. Academia Asturiana de Jurisprudencia; Orden de Isabel la Católica, Orden de San Raimundo de Peñafort; Dr hc (Turin) 1996, (Babeș-Bolyai Cluj-Napoca, Romania) 1996, (Sarre Univ.), (Univ. of Ohrid, Bulgaria); Walter-Hallstein Prize 2003. *Publications:* El régimen jurídico de los monopolios de Estado en la Comunidad Económica Europea 1976; numerous articles and studies on EC law and int. law. *Address:* c/o Board of Directors, Fundación Real Instituto Elcano, Príncipe de Vergara, 51, 28006 Madrid, Spain. *E-mail:* maresteban@rielcano.org. *Website:* www .realinstitutoelcano.org.

RODRÍGUEZ MARADIAGA, HE Cardinal Oscar Andrés, SDB; Honduran ecclesiastic; *Archbishop of Tegucigalpa;* b. 29 Dec. 1942, Tegucigalpa; ordained priest of Salesians of Saint John Bosco 1970; Auxiliary Bishop of Tegucigalpa, Honduras 1978; Titular Bishop of Pudentiana 1978; Sec. Gen. Latin American Episcopal Conf. 1987–91, Pres. Econ. Cttee 1991–95; Archbishop of Tegucigalpa 1993–; Pres. Conf. of Latin American Bishops 1995–99; cr. Cardinal (Cardinal-Priest of Santa Maria della Speranza) 2001; participated in Papal Conclave 2005, 2013; served as Vatican spokesperson to IMF and World Bank on Third World debt; Pres. Caritas Internationalis, Caritas Confed. (network of Catholic relief and devt orgs) 2007–. *Address:* Conferencia Episcopal de Honduras, Los Lavreles, Comayagüela, Apdo 3121, Tegucigalpa, Honduras (office). *Telephone:* 2370353 (office); 2372366 (home). *Fax:* 2222337 (office). *Website:* www.cardinalrodriguez .info; www.caritas.org.

RODRÍGUEZ MENDOZA, Miguel; Venezuelan international organization official, lawyer and diplomatist; *Senior Associate, International Centre for Trade and Sustainable Development;* ed Cen. Univ. of Venezuela, Univ. of Manchester, UK, Ecole des Hautes Etudes en Sciences Sociales, France; First Sec. Perm. Mission of Venezuela to UN 1978–81; Dir for Consultation and Co-ordination, Latin American Econ. System 1982–88; Special Adviser to Pres. on int. econ. affairs 1989–91; Minister of State, Pres. Inst. of Foreign Trade 1991–94; Pres. Comm. of Cartagena Agreement 1993; Chief Trade Adviser, OAS –1998; Visiting Scholar, Georgetown Univ., Washington, DC 1998–; Jt Deputy Dir-Gen. WTO 1999–2002; Of Counsel Van Bael & Bellis, Geneva 2002–04; Transatlantic Fellow, German Marshall Fund of the US 2005–; Sr Assoc. Int. Centre for Trade and Sustainable Devt, Geneva; apptd Chair. WTO panel to decide US challenge on EU system of protecting products with geographical names 2004. *Publications:* numerous articles in books and journals; has edited numerous books. *Address:* International Centre for Trade and Sustainable Development, International Environment House 2, Chemin de Balexert 7, 1219 Châtelaine, Geneva, Switzerland (office). *Telephone:* (22) 917-8492 (office). *Fax:* (22) 917-8093 (office). *Website:* www.ictsd.org (office).

RODRÍGUEZ PARRILLA, Bruno, LLB; Cuban diplomatist and government official; *Minister of Foreign Relations;* b. 22 Jan. 1958, Mexico City, Mexico; m.; one s.; mem. Cen. Cttee, CP of Cuba 1990–, Head of Cultural Policy Matters 1992–; Deputy Perm. Rep. to UN, New York 1993–95, Perm. Rep. 1995–2003; Deputy Minister for Foreign Relations in charge of Latin America and the Caribbean and for information and communication 2003–04; First Deputy Minister for Foreign Relations 2004–09, Minister of Foreign Relations 2009–. *Address:* Ministry of Foreign Relations, Calzada 360, esq. G, Vedado, Havana, Cuba (office). *Telephone:* (7) 55-3537 (office). *Fax:* (7) 33-3460 (office). *E-mail:* cubaminrex@minrex.gov.cu (office). *Website:* www.cubaminrex.cu (office).

RODRÍGUEZ VELTZÉ, Eduardo, MPA; Bolivian lawyer, judge and fmr head of state; b. 2 March 1956, Cochabamba; m. Fanny Elena Arguedas Calle; four c.; ed Universidad Mayor de San Simón, Harvard Univ., USA; fmr Resident Co-ordinator, UN Latin American Inst. for the Prevention of Crime and the Treatment of Offenders (ILANUD); fmr Lecturer, Universidad Andina Simón Bolívar, Universidad Mayor de San Andrés; Pres. of the Supreme Court 2004–05; Interim Pres. of Bolivia 2005–06. *Address:* c/o Ministry of the Presidency, Palacio de Gobierno, Plaza Murillo, La Paz, Bolivia (office).

RODRÍGUEZ ZAPATERO, José Luis; Spanish politician and lawyer; b. 4 Aug. 1960, Valladolid; m. Sónsoles Espinosa 1990; two d.; ed Univ. of León; worked as a

teacher of law; joined Partido Socialista Obrero Español (PSOE) 1978, Leader, Socialist Youth Org., León 1982, mem. Parl. for León and Madrid 1986–2011, Leader, PSOE Regional Chapter for León 1988, mem. PSOE Fed. Exec. Cttee 1997, Sec.-Gen. 2000–12; Prime Minister of Spain and Pres. of the Council 2004–11. *Leisure interests:* jogging, trout fishing. *Address:* Fundación IDEAS, Gobelas 31, 28023, Madrid, Spain (office). *Telephone:* (91) 5820091 (office). *Fax:* (91) 5820090 (office). *Website:* www.fundacionideas.es (office).

RODRIQUEZ, Julián Isaias, PhD; Venezuelan lawyer, poet and politician; ed Univs of Santa Maria and Zulia and Cen. Univ. of Venezuela; legal adviser to Ministry of Agric. 1969; fmr Attorney-Gen.; Chief Attorney of Aragua 1990–91; Senator for Aragua 1998; First Vice-Pres. Nat. Constituency Ass. 1999–2000; Vice-Pres. of Venezuela 2000; Attorney-Gen. 2001–07; Prof., Univ. of Carabobo; regular columnist for El Siglo; consultant to Veterinary Asscn 1971; mem. Movimiento Quinta República. *Publications:* legal: New Labour Procedures 1987, Legal Stability in Labour Laws 1993; poetry: Pozo de cabrillas, Con las aspas de todos los molinos, Los tiempos de la sed; contrib. numerous articles.

ROED-LARSEN, Terje, PhD; Norwegian diplomatist, politician and UN official; *Under-Secretary-General and Special Envoy for the Implementation of Security Council Resolution 1559 (on Lebanon), United Nations;* b. 22 Nov. 1947, Bergen; m. Mona Juul; taught sociology and philosophy at Univs of Bergen and Oslo –1981; Founder and Exec. Dir Inst. of Applied Social Sciences (FAFO) 1991, Hon. Chair. Programme for Int. Co-operation and Conflict Resolution; fmr Deputy Foreign Minister; facilitated negotiations between reps of Israel's Labour Govt and Palestine Liberation Org. (PLO) leading to signing of Declaration of Principles, Washington, DC 13 Sept. 1993; Amb. and Special Adviser to Norwegian Foreign Minister for the Middle East Peace Process 1993, 1998–; UN Deputy Sec.-Gen. and Special Co-ordinator in the Occupied Territories, Gaza 1994–96; Minister of Planning 1996–98; Special Co-ordinator for the Middle East Peace Process and Personal Rep. of the UN Sec.-Gen. to the PLO and Palestinian Authority 1999–2005; Under-Sec.-Gen. and Special Envoy for the Implementation of UN Security Council Resolution 1559 (calling for Syrian withdrawal from Lebanon and disarmament of Hezbollah) 2005–; Pres. Int. Peace Acad., New York 2005–. *Address:* International Peace Academy, 777 United Nations Plaza, New York, NY 10017-3521 (office); Executive Office of the UN Secretary-General, United Nations Plaza, New York, NY 10017, USA (office). *Telephone:* (212) 687-4300 (office); (212) 906-5791 (UN) (office). *Fax:* (212) 983-8246 (office); (212) 906-5778 (UN) (office). *E-mail:* ipa@ipacademy.org (office). *Website:* www.ipacademy.org (office); www.un .org (office).

ROEDER, Robert Gayle, BA, MS, PhD; American biologist and academic; *Arnold O. and Mabel S. Beckman Professor and Head, Laboratory of Biochemistry and Molecular Biology, The Rockefeller University;* b. 3 June 1942, Boonville, Ind.; s. of Frederick Roeder and Helene Roeder (née Bredenkamp); m. 1st Suzanne Himsel 1964 (divorced 1980); one s. one d.; m. 2nd Cun Jing Hong 1990; one d.; ed Wabash Coll., Univ. of Illinois, Urbana, Univ. of Washington, Seattle; Postdoctoral Fellow, Dept of Embryology, Carnegie Inst. of Washington, Baltimore, Md 1971; Asst Prof. of Biological Chem., Washington Univ. School of Medicine, St Louis, Mo. 1971–75, Assoc. Prof. 1975–76, Prof. 1976–82, James S. McDonnell Prof. of Biochemical Genetics 1979–82; Prof. and Head, Lab. of Biochemistry and Molecular Biology, The Rockefeller Univ., New York 1982–, Arnold O. and Mabel S. Beckman Prof. 1985–; Chair. Gordon Research Conf. on Nucleic Acids 1982; mem. Research Grant Review, NIH Molecular Biology Study Section 1975–79; mem. Scientific Advisory Bd Roche Inst. of Molecular Biology 1992–95, Second Int. Review, Karolinska Inst. Center for Biotechnology 1993, Scientific Review Bd, Howard Hughes Medical Inst. 1994–99, Nat. Inst. of Child Health and Human Devt 1995–2000; mem. Editorial Bd Journal of Biological Chemistry 1979–84, Nucleic Acids Research 1980–82, Molecular and Cellular Biology 1980–85, Cell 1990–93, Biological Chemistry Hoppe-Seyler 1994–99, Molecular Cell 1999–; mem. NAS 1988, ACS, American Soc. for Biochemistry and Molecular Biology, American Soc. for Microbiology, American Soc. for Virology, Soc. for Developmental Biology, The Harvey Soc. of New York (Pres. 1994–95), The New York Acad. of Sciences, The Protein Soc.; Fellow, AAAS 1992, American Acad. of Microbiology 1992, American Acad. of Arts and Sciences 1995; Assoc. mem. European Molecular Biology Org. 2003; Hon. DSc (Wabash Coll.) 1990, (Washington Univ.) 2005; Gilbert Scholar, Wabash Coll., US Public Health Service Predoctoral Fellowship 1965–69, Outstanding Biochemistry Grad. Student Award, Univ. of Washington 1967, American Cancer Soc. Postdoctoral Fellow 1969–71, NIH Research Career Devt Award 1973–78, Dreyfus Foundation Teacher-Scholar Award 1976–81, ACS Eli Lilly Award in Biological Chem. 1977, US Steel Award in Molecular Biology, NAS 1986, Outstanding Investigator Award, Nat. Cancer Inst. 1986–2000, Harvey Soc. Lecturer 1988, Passano Award 1995, Lewis S. Rosenstiel Award for Distinguished Work in Basic Medical Sciences 1995, Louisa Gross Horwitz Prize 1999, Alfred P. Sloan Prize, General Motors Cancer Research Foundation 1999, Gairdner Foundation Int. Award 2000, Dickson Prize in Medicine, Univ. of Pittsburgh 2001, ASBMB-Merck Award 2002, Albert Lasker Award for Basic Medical Research 2003, Salk Inst. Medal for Scientific Excellence 2010, Prize in Medicine and Biomedical Research, Albany Medical Center 2012. *Publications:* more than 500 papers in scientific journals. *Address:* Laboratory of Biochemistry and Molecular Biology, Rockefeller University, 1230 York Avenue, New York, NY 10021, USA (office). *Telephone:* (212) 327-7600 (office). *Fax:* (212) 327-7949 (office). *E-mail:* roeder@rockefeller.edu (office). *Website:* www.rockefeller.edu/labheads/ roeder/roeder.html (office).

ROEG, Nicolas Jack, CBE; British film director; b. 15 Aug. 1928, London; s. of Jack Nicolas Roeg and Mabel Roeg; m. 1st Susan Rennie Stephen 1957 (divorced); four s.; m. 2nd Theresa Russell 1982 (divorced); two s.; m. 3rd Harriett Harper 2004; ed Mercers School; started in film industry as clapper-boy; Fellow, BFI 1994; Hon. DLitt (Hull) 1995; Hon. DFA (Brooklyn Coll., City Univ. of New York) 2004. *Films include:* as cinematographer: The Caretaker 1963, The Masque of the Red Death, Nothing but the Best 1964, Fahrenheit 451 1966, Far from the Madding Crowd 1967, Petulia 1968; as dir: Performance (with Donald Cammell) 1968, Walkabout 1970, Don't Look Now 1972, The Man who Fell to Earth 1975, Bad Timing 1979, Eureka 1983, Insignificance 1984, Castaway 1985, Track 29 1987, Aria (Sequence) 1988, Cold Heaven 1989, The Witches 1989, Sweet Bird of Youth 1989, Without You I'm Nothing (exec. producer) 1990, Young Indy – Paris 1916

1991, Cold Heaven 1991, Heart of Darkness 1993, Two Deaths 1994, Full Body Massage 1995, Hotel Paradise 1995, Samson and Delilah 1996, The Sound of Claudia Schiffer 2001, Puffball 2007; co-writer film script for Night Train 2002. *Address:* c/o Independent, 32 Tavistock Street, London, WC2E 7PB, England (office). *Telephone:* (20) 7257-8734 (office). *Fax:* (20) 7240-9029 (office). *E-mail:* mail@independentfilmcompany.com (office). *Website:* independentfilmcompany .com (office).

ROELL, Stephen A., BSc; American business executive; *Chairman, President and CEO, Johnson Controls Inc.;* ed St Ambrose Univ., Northeastern Univ.; began career as accountant Arthur Young & Co. 1971; Div. Controller, FMC Corpn 1975–82; joined Johnson Controls Inc. 1982, Operations Controller, Systems and Services Div. 1982, becoming Div. Controller, later Treas. and Corp. Controller, Sr Vice-Pres. and Chief Financial Officer 1991–2004, Exec. Vice-Pres. 2004, Vice-Chair. 2005–07, CEO 2007–, Chair. 2008–; mem. Bd of Dirs Interstate Battery System of America Inc., Wheaton Franciscan Healthcare-Southeast Wis., Hunger Task Force; mem. Business Roundtable; Chair. United Way of Greater Milwaukee 2013–14; Trustee, Boys & Girls Club of Greater Milwaukee, Medical Coll. of Wisconsin; mem. Financial Execs Inst. *Address:* Johnson Controls Inc., 5757 North Green Bay Avenue, Milwaukee, WI 53209, USA (office). *Telephone:* (414) 524-1200 (office). *Fax:* (414) 524-2077 (office). *E-mail:* info@johnsoncontrols.com (office). *Website:* www.johnsoncontrols.com (office).

ROELS, Harry J. M.; Dutch energy industry executive; b. 26 July 1948; ed Univ. of Leiden; began career as oil engineer, Royal Dutch/Shell 1972, various eng and man. positions including Head Exploration and Production Offices, Chief Engineer in Turkey, Tech. Man. Norske Shell, Norway, Dir Enterprise Devt, Shell Int. Petroleum Inst., The Hague, Dir Offshore Bureau then Gen. Man. Aardolie Maatschappij, The Netherlands, Office Coordinator for Latin America, Shell Int. Petroleum Co., London, UK, Regional Business Dir for Middle E and Africa, sr man. positions in Malaysia and Brunei, apptd Man. Dir Royal Dutch Petroleum Co. 1999; Pres. and CEO RWE AG 2003–07, Chair. RWE Energy, RWE Thames Water –2006. *Address:* c/o RWE AG, Opernplatz 1, 45128 Essen, Germany (office).

ROEMER, John E., AB, PhD; American economist and academic; *Elizabeth S. and A. Varick Stout Professor of Political Science and Economics, Yale University;* b. 1 Feb. 1945, Washington, DC; s. of Milton I. Roemer and Ruth Rosenbaum Roemer; m. Carla Natasha Muldavin 1968; two c.; ed Harvard Univ., Univ. of California, Berkeley; math. teacher, Lowell High School and Pelton Jr High School, San Francisco 1969–74; consultant UNCTAD, Geneva 1978; Asst Prof. of Econs, Univ. of Calif., Davis 1974–78, Assoc. Prof. 1978–81, Prof. of Econs 1981–2000; Elizabeth S. and A. Varick Stout Prof. of Political Science and Econs, Yale Univ. 2000–; Visiting Prof., Harvard Univ. 1994, Univ. de Cergy-Pontoise 1995, New York Univ. 1999, Ecole Polytechnique, Paris 2004, EHESS, Marseilles 2005, Univ. de Paris I 2006; Dir Program on Economy, Justice and Society 1988–2000; Guggenheim Fellow; Fellow, Econometric Soc. 1985, American Acad. of Arts and Sciences 2006; Russell Sage Fellow 1998–99; Corresponding Fellow, British Acad. 2005. *Publications:* A General Theory of Exploitation and Class 1982, Free to Lose 1988, Egalitarian Perspectives 1994, A Future for Socialism 1994, Theories of Distributive Justice 1996, Equality of Opportunity 1998, Political Competition 2001, Democracy, Education and Equality 2006. *Address:* Department of Political Science, 124 Prospect Street, Room 208, Box 208301, Yale University, 124 Prospect Street, New Haven, CT 06520, USA (office). *Telephone:* (203) 432-5249. *Fax:* (203) 432-6196. *E-mail:* john.roemer@yale.edu (office). *Website:* www.yale.edu/polisci (office).

ROESKY, Herbert Walter, DrSc; German chemist and academic; *Professor Emeritus, Institute of Inorganic Chemistry, Georg-August University of Göttingen;* b. 6 Nov. 1935, Laukischken; s. of Otto Roesky and Lina Roesky; m. Christel Roesky 1964; two s.; ed Univ. of Göttingen; Lecturer 1970, Univ. of Frankfurt, Prof. of Inorganic Chem. 1970–80; Dir Inst. of Inorganic Chem., Georg-August Univ. of Göttingen 1980, now Prof. Emer., Dean Dept of Chem. 1985–87; Visiting Prof., Auburn Univ., USA 1984, Tokyo Inst. of Tech. 1987; mem. Gesellschaft Deutscher Chemiker (Vice-Pres. 1995), ACS, Chemical Soc., London, Gesellschaft Deutscher Naturforscher und Ärzte, Deutsche Bunsen-Gesellschaft für Physikalische Chemie, Göttinger Akad., Akad. Leopoldina, Austrian Acad. of Sciences, Russian Acad. of Sciences 1999; Foreign Assoc., Acad. des Sciences, France, Romanian Acad. of Sciences, Indian Acad.; mem. Selection Bd, Alexander von Humboldt-Stiftung 1973–84, numerous editorial bds; Hon. FRSC 2007; Wöhler Prize 1960, French Alexander von Humboldt Prize 1986, Leibniz Prize 1987, Alfred-Stock-Gedächtnispreis 1990, Georg Ernst Stahl Medal 1990; Manfred and Wolfgang Flad Prize 1994, Grand Prix Fondation de la maison de la chimie, Carus Prize 1998, Wilkinson Award 1999, ACS Inorganic Award 2004, Wittig-Grignard Prize 2005, Moissan Award 2009, Rössler Prize 2012. *Publications:* seven books and more than 1,100 learned papers and articles. *Leisure interest:* antique collecting. *Address:* Institute of Inorganic Chemistry, University of Göttingen, Tammannstrasse 4, 37077 Göttingen, Germany (office). *Telephone:* (551) 393001 (office). *Fax:* (551) 3933373 (office). *E-mail:* hroesky@gwdg.de (office). *Website:* www.roesky.chemie .uni-goettingen.de (office).

ROGÉ, Pascal; French pianist; b. 6 April 1951, Paris; m. Ami Rogé; two s.; ed Paris Conservatoire, private studies with Lucette Descaves, Pierre Pasquier and Julius Katchen; début Paris 1969, London 1969; specialist in Ravel, Poulenc, Debussy, Satie; soloist with leading orchestras; exclusive recording contract with Decca, London; Premiers Prix for Piano and Chamber Music at the Paris Conservatoire 1966, First Prize Marguerite Long-Jacques Thibaud Int. Competition 1971, Grand Prix du Disque and Edison Award 1984, Gramophone Award for Best Instrumental Recording 1988, Best Chamber Music Recording 1997. *Leisure interests:* reading, tennis, riding, golf. *Address:* Clarion/Seven Muses, 47 Whitehall Park, London, N19 3TW, England (office); Lorentz Concerts, 3 rue de la Boétie, 75008 Paris, France; 17 avenue des Cavaliers, 1224 Geneva, Switzerland. *Telephone:* (20) 7272-4413 (office). *E-mail:* admin@c7m.co.uk (office). *Website:* www.c7m.co.uk (office); www.pascalroge.com.

ROGEL, Steven R., BS; American business executive; *Chairman, Weyerhaeuser Company;* ed Univ. of Washington, Seattle, Dartmouth Coll., Massachusetts Inst. of Tech.; began career with Regis Paper Co. 1966–70; Asst Man. St Anne-Nackawic Pulp and Paper, Nackawic, NB, Canada 1970–72; Tech. Dir Wilamette Industries,

Inc., Albany, Ore. 1972, Pres. and COO 1991–95, Pres. and CEO 1995–97; mem. Bd Dirs, Pres. and CEO Weyerhaeuser Co. 1997–2008, Chair. 1999–2008, Chair. (non-exec.) 2008–; mem. Bd of Dirs Kroger Co., Union Pacific Corpn; fmr Chair. American Forest & Paper Assen, Nat. Council for Air and Stream Improvement, Inc.; fmr Co-Chair. Wood Promotion Network; fmr Vice-Pres. Admin Western Region Boy Scouts of America, mem. Nat. Exec. Bd Boy Scouts of America; Trustee, Pacific Univ. *Address:* Weyerhaeuser Co., 33663 Weyerhaeuser Way South, Federal Way, WA 98063-9777, USA (office). *Telephone:* (253) 924-2345 (office). *Fax:* (253) 924-2685 (office). *E-mail:* PubRelations@weyerhaeuser.com (office). *Website:* www.weyerhaeuser.com (office).

ROGER, Bruno; French banking executive; *Chairman and CEO, Lazard Frères Banque SA;* ed Institut d'Études Politiques, Paris; fmr CEO Compagnie Financière Lazard Frères SAS, now Chair., Chair. Lazard Frères SAS, currently Chair. and CEO Lazard Frères Banque SA; fmr CEO Azeo; mem. Bd of Dirs, Euroazeo SA 1969–, Chair. Emer., fmr Chair. Supervisory Bd Eurazeo (non-voting Bd mem.), now Hon. Chair.; fmr Dir of Finance, Cap Gemini SA; fmr CEO and Vice-Chair. EuraFrance; fmr Chair. Global Investment Banking, Lazard Ltd; fmr Co-Chair. European Advisory Bd; Dir, Saint-Gobain 1987–2005, Sidel SA 1987–, Cap Gemini SA 2000–, Paris Europlace, Ernst & Young, Thalès; fmr Dir, Sofina SA (Belgium); mem. Pinault-Printemps-Redoute SA (PPR SA) 1994–, Supervisory Bd AXA 1997–2005; Admin. and Treas., Les Arts Décoratifs 1999–2013, Chair. 2013–; Chair. Festival d'art lyrique d'Aix-en-Provence 2005–, Fondation Martine Aublet (univ. scholarships and the Atelier Martine Aublet at Musée du Quai Branly); mem. Acquisitions Comm., Musée du Quai Branly. *Address:* Lazard Frères SAS, 121 boulevard Haussmann, 75382 Paris Cedex 08, France (office). *Telephone:* 1-44-13-01-11 (office). *Fax:* 1-44-13-01-00 (office). *E-mail:* info@lazard.com (office). *Website:* www.lazard.com (office).

ROGER, Michel; French lawyer; *Minister of State, Monaco;* b. 9 March 1949, Poitiers; called to the Bar, Poitiers; several ministerial roles in France including Keeper of the Seals 1975–76, with Ministry of Planning and Works 1976–77; Regional Councillor, Poitiers 1983–2001; Adviser to cabinet of Prime Minister Jean-Pierre Raffarin 2002; fmr Insp. Gen., French nat. educ. system; Judge, Tribunal suprême, Monaco 2007–10; Minister of State, Monaco Council of Govt 2010–. *Address:* Ministry of State, place de la Visitation, 98000 Monte Carlo, Monaco (office). *Telephone:* 98-98-80-00 (office). *Fax:* 98-98-82-17 (office). *E-mail:* sgme@gouv.mc (office). *Website:* www.gouv.mc (office).

ROGERS, George Ernest, AO, PhD, DSc, FAA; Australian biochemist and academic; *Professor Emeritus and Honorary Visiting Research Fellow, School of Molecular and Biomedical Science, University of Adelaide;* b. 27 Oct. 1927, Melbourne, Vic.; s. of Percy Rogers and Bertha Beatrice Rogers (née Baxter); m. 2nd Racheline Aladjem 1972; two d.; ed Caulfield Grammar School, Univ. of Melbourne and Trinity Coll., Cambridge, England; Scientist, Wool Research, CSIRO 1951–53, Research Scientist, Div. of Protein Chem. 1957–62; Research Scientist, Univ. of Cambridge, England 1954–56; Reader in Biochem., Univ. of Adelaide 1963–77, Prof. of Biochem. 1978–92 and Chair. Dept of Biochem. 1988–92, now Prof. Emer., Hon. Visiting Research Fellow 1993–; Visiting Fellow, Clare Hall Cambridge 1970; Program Man., Premium Quality Wool CRC 1995–2000; Visiting Scientist, Univ. de Grenoble, France 1977; Guest Scientist, NIH, Bethesda, USA 1985; CSIRO studentship 1954–56; Bourse Scientifique de Haut Niveau 1977; mem. Australian Soc. of Biochemistry and Molecular Biology, New York Acad. of Sciences; Eleanor Roosevelt Int. Cancer Research Fellow 1985; Fellow, Australian Acad. of Science 1977; Hon. Prof., Dept of Medicine, Univ. of Melbourne; Centenary Fed. Medal 2003; Lemberg Medal, Australian Biochemical Soc. 1976. *Publications:* The Keratins (co-author) 1972, The Biology of Wool and Hair (co-author) 1989; 170 publs in scientific journals on wool and hair growth, hair structure and sheep transgenesis. *Leisure interests:* family activities, swimming, golf, gardening. *Address:* School of Molecular and Biomedical Science, University of Adelaide, Adelaide, SA 5005 (office); 1 Gandys Gully Road, Stonyfell, SA 5066, Australia (home). *Telephone:* (8) 8303-4624 (office); (8) 8332-4143 (home). *Fax:* (8) 8303-7532 (office). *E-mail:* george.rogers@adelaide.edu.au (office). *Website:* www.mbs.adelaide.edu.au/people/biochem/grogers (office).

ROGERS, Grant Simon, BA; British artist, art historian and lecturer; *Educator, Imperial War Museum;* b. 4 March 1964, Singapore; s. of Keith Rogers and Diane Rogers; ed Crofton School, Price's Coll., and Portsmouth Coll. of Art, Hampshire, England; founder mem. Cubit Street Artists 1986–1992; lecturer at Nat. Gallery, Nat. Portrait Gallery, Wallace Collection, Victoria and Albert Museum, British Museum, Imperial War Museum 1990–2002; Family and Informal Educ. Co-ordinator Imperial War Museum 2002–. *Television:* BBC television and radio, Channel 4 TV. *Films:* animated: TVC cartoons; Father Christmas; Grandpa; When the Wind Blows. *Publications:* numerous articles in UK press. *Leisure interests:* hedonism and futile introspection. *Address:* 66–68 Camberwell Road, London, SE5 0EG, England (home). *Telephone:* (20) 7416-5329 (office); (7977) 010477 (office). *E-mail:* grogers@iwm.org. *Website:* www.iwm.org.uk (office).

ROGERS, James E., BBA, JD; American energy industry executive; *Chairman, President and CEO, Duke Energy Corporation;* b. 1947, Birmingham, Ala; m. Mary Anne Rogers; one s. two d.; ed Emory Univ., Univ. of Ky; fmr Asst Attorney-Gen. Commonwealth of Ky; fmr Deputy Gen. Counsel for Litigation and Enforcement and Asst to Chief Trial Counsel FERC (Fed. Energy Regulatory Comm.); fmr Pnr Akin, Gump, Strauss, Hauer & Feld (law firm), Dallas, Tex.; Exec. Vice-Pres. Enron Corpn, Houston, TX –1988; Chair., Pres. and CEO PSI Energy Inc. (renamed Cinergy Corpn) 1988, Pres. and CEO Duke Energy (after merger of Cinergy and Duke Corpns) 2006–, Chair. 2007–; Dir Fifth Third Bancorp and Fifth Third Bank, Duke Realty Corpn; Gen. Chair. Greater Cincinnati-N Ky United Way Campaign 1997; Hon. LLD (Indiana State Univ.) 1991; named to Univ. of Ky Coll. of Business and Econs Hall of Fame; Ellis Island Medal of Honor 2007. *Address:* Duke Energy Corporation, 526 South Church Street, Charlotte, NC 28202-1803, USA (office). *Telephone:* (704) 594-6200 (office). *Fax:* (704) 382-3814 (office). *Website:* www.duke-energy.com (office).

ROGERS OF RIVERSIDE, Baron (Life Peer), cr. 1996, of Chelsea in the Royal Borough of Kensington and Chelsea; **Richard George Rogers,** Kt, CH, AADipl, MArch, RA; British architect; *Chairman, Rogers Stirk Harbour + Partners;* b. 23 July 1933, Florence, Italy; s. of Nino Rogers and Dada Geiringer; m. 1st Su

Brumwell 1961; three s.; m. 2nd Ruth Elias 1973; two s.; ed Architectural Asscn, London, Yale Univ., USA; Fulbright, Edward D. Stone and Yale Scholar; worked with Italian architect Renzo Piano; Chair. Rogers Stirk Harbour + Partners (fmrly Richard Rogers Partnership); Pres. Nat. Communities Resource Centre; Chief Advisor to the Mayor on Architecture and Urbanism; Dir River Café Ltd; Saarinen Prof., Yale Univ. 1985; has also taught at Architectural Asscn, London, at Cambridge, Princeton, Columbia, Harvard, Cornell, McGill and Aachen Univs and at UCLA; Vice-Chair. Arts Council of England 1994–97; mem. (Labour) House of Lords 1996–, Hon. Chair. Architecture and Planning Group 2006–; mem. UN Architects' Cttee, Barcelona Urban Strategy Council; Trustee, Tate Gallery 1981–89 (Chair. 1984–88), London First 1993–98, UK Bd Médecins du Monde; Hon. FRIBA, FAIA 1986; Chevalier, Légion d'honneur 1986; Hon. DSc (Bath) 1994; Hon. DLitt (University Coll., London) 1997; Dr hc (Westminster) 1993, (RCA) 1994, (South Bank) 1996, (Alfonso X El Sabio Univ., Madrid), (Oxford Brookes), (Kent), (Czech Tech. Univ., Prague), (Open Univ.); 38 RIBA Awards 1969–, RIBA Royal Gold Medal 1985, 12 Civic Trust Awards 1986–2010, Constructa Prize 1986, 1992, Eternit Int. Prize 1988, Reith Lecturer 1995, Thomas Jefferson Memorial Foundation Medal in Architecture 1999, Praemium Imperiale Award 2000, Golden Lion for Lifetime Achievement, 10th Mostra di Architettura di Venezia 2006, Laureate of the Pritzker Architecture Prize (architecture's highest honour) 2007, Minerva Medal, Chartered Soc. of Designers 2007, Freedom of the City of London 2014 and many other awards. *Works include:* major int. work: Pompidou Centre, Paris, France (with Renzo Piano) 1971–77, masterplanning: Royal Docks, London 1984–86, Potsdamer Platz, Berlin 1991, Shanghai Pu Dong Financial Dist 1992, Greenwich Peninsula Masterplan 1997–98; airports and HQ bldgs: PA Tech., Cambridge 1975–83, PA Tech., Princeton, NJ, USA 1984, European Court of Human Rights, Strasbourg 1990–95, Marseille Airport 1992, Law Courts, Bordeaux, France 1992–98, VR Techno offices and lab., Gifu, Japan 1993–98, Channel 4 HQ 1991–94; recent projects: masterplanning and design of Heathrow Airport Terminal 5 1989–2008, Montevetro Housing, Battersea, London 1994–2000, ParcBIT Devt, Majorca 1994–, Lloyd's Register of Shipping HQ, London 1995–99, 88 Wood Street, London 1995–99, Minami Yamashiro Primary School 1995–2003, Millennium Dome, London 1996–99, masterplanning of Piana di Castello, Florence 1997–, New Area Terminal, Barajas Airport, Madrid (RIBA Stirling Prize 2006) 1997–2005, Nat. Ass. for Wales 1998–2006, Senedd (Nat. Assembly for Wales), Cardiff 1999–2005, Law Courts, Antwerp 1999–2006, Maggie's Centre, London (RIBA Stirling Prize 2009) 2001–08, Mossbourne Community Acad. 2002–04, 122 Leadenhall Street 2002–, Central Park Station (R9), Kaohsiung Mass Rapid Transit system, Kaohsiung City, Taiwan 2003–07, 300 New Jersey Avenue, Washington, DC, USA 2004–09, Ching Fu Group HQ, Kaohsiung City 2005–07, Campus Palmas Altas, Seville, Spain (Abengoa HQ) 2005–09, 175 Greenwich Street, New York 2006–, Capodichino Underground Station, Naples, Italy 2006–, Santa Maria del Pianto Underground Station, Naples 2006–, One Hyde Park, London 2007–10, new city centre and tram station, Scandicci, Italy 2007–, British Museum, Northwest Devt, London 2007–, 360-London 2007–, Bodegas Protos, Peñafiel, Valladolid, Spain 2008, Greater Paris/Grand Paris 2008–, Barangaroo, Sydney, Australia 2009–, Oxley Woods, Milton Keynes, UK (Govt-sponsored 'Design for Manufacture (DfM)' 2010, Las Arenas, Barcelona, remodelling of the bullring into a shopping mall 2011, Neo Bankside, London 2012, Leadenhall bldg ('The Cheesegrater'), London 2014. *Publications:* Richard Rogers and Architects 1985, A+U: Richard Rogers 1978–88 1988, Architecture: A Modern View 1990, A New London (with Mark Fisher) 1992, Reith Lecturer 1995, Cities for a Small Planet 1997, Richard Rogers The Complete Works (Vols I–III) 1999, Cities for a Small Country 2000, Richard Rogers: Architecture of the Future 2006, Richard Rogers 2006, Richard Rogers Architects: From the House to the City 2009. *Leisure interests:* friends, food, travel, art, architecture. *Address:* Rogers Stirk Harbour + Partners, Thames Wharf, Rainville Road, London, W6 9HA (office); House of Lords, Westminster, London, SW1A 0PW, England (office). *Telephone:* (20) 7385-1235 (office); (20) 7219-5353 (House of Lords) (office). *Fax:* (20) 7385-8409 (office). *E-mail:* enquiries@rsh-p.com (office). *Website:* www.rsh-p.com (office); www.parliament.uk/biographies/lords/richard-rogers/27043 (office).

ROGERS, T. Gary; American business executive; *Chairman, Safeway Inc.;* Chair. and CEO Dreyer's Grand Ice Cream, Inc. 1977–2007; fmr Chair. Levi Strauss & Co., Fed. Reserve Bank of San Francisco; mem. Bd of Dirs Safeway Inc. 2011–, Chair. 2013–; mem. Advisory Bd Shorenstein Properties, Stanislaus Food Products. *Address:* Safeway Inc., 5918 Stoneridge Mall Road, Pleasanton, CA 94588-3229, USA (office). *Telephone:* (925) 467-3000 (office). *Fax:* (925) 467-3321 (office). *E-mail:* info@safeway.com (office). *Website:* www.safeway.com (office).

ROGERS, Thomas (Tom) Sydney, BA, JD; American media executive and lawyer; *Vice-Chairman, Tivo, Inc.;* b. 19 Aug. 1954, New Rochelle, NY; s. of Sydney Michael Rogers Jr and Alice Steinhardt; m. Sylvia Texon 1983; two s. one d.; ed Wesleyan Univ., Columbia Univ.; attorney with Wall Street law firm 1979–81; called to New York Bar 1980; Sr Counsel US House of Reps Sub cttee on Telecommunications, Consumer Protection and Finance 1981–86; Vice-Pres. Policy Planning and Business Devt, NBC 1987–88; Pres. NBC Cable 1988–89, NBC Cable and Business Devt 1989–99; Exec. Vice-Pres. NBC 1992–99; Vice-Chair. NBC Internet 1999; Chair. and CEO Primedia Inc. 1999–2003; Chair. TRget Media LLC 2003–05; Sr Operating Exec. for media and entertainment, Cerberus Capital Man. (private equity firm) 2004–05; mem. Bd of Dirs Tivo, Inc. 2003, Vice-Chair. 2004–05, CEO and Pres. 2005–; mem. Bd of Dirs Teleglobe, Chair. 2004–; Pres. and CEO Int. Council, Nat. Acad. of TV Arts and Sciences 1994–97, Chair. 1998–99; mem. New York State Bar Asscn, Int. Radio and TV Soc. *Address:* Tivo Inc., 2160 Gold Street, POB 2160, Alviso, CA 95002-2160, USA (office). *Telephone:* (408) 519-9100 (office). *Fax:* (408) 519-5330 (office). *Website:* www.tivo.com (office).

ROGERSON, Philip Graham, FCA, FCT; British business executive; *Chairman, Carillion plc;* b. 1 Jan. 1945, Manchester, England; s. of Henry Rogerson and Florence Rogerson; m. Susan Janet Kershaw 1968; one s. two d.; ed William Hulme's Grammar School, Manchester; with Dearden Harper, Miller & Co. Chartered Accountants 1962–67; with Hill Samuel & Co. Ltd 1967–69; with Thomas Tilling Ltd 1969–71; with Steetley Ltd 1971–72; with J.W. Chafer Ltd 1972–78; joined ICI 1978, Gen. Man. Finance 1989–92; Man. Dir Finance British Gas PLC 1992–94, Exec. Dir 1994–96, Deputy Chair. 1996–98; Deputy Chair. (non-

exec.) Aggreko PLC 1997–2002, Chair. 2002–12; Chair. (non-exec.) Pipeline Integrity Int. 1998–2002, Bertram Group Ltd 1999–2001, British Biotech 1999–2003, Octopus Capital PLC 2000–01, Copper Eye Ltd 2001–03; Chair. Project Telecom PLC 2000–03, Thus Group plc 2004–08, Carillion plc 2004–, Davis Service Group PLC 2004–10, Bunzl PLC 2010–, KBC Advanced Technologies PLC, De La Rue plc 2012–; Deputy Chair. Viridian Group PLC 1998, Chair. 1999–2005; Dir (non-exec.) Halifax Building Society (now Halifax PLC) 1995–98, LIMIT PLC 1997, Int. Public Relations 1997–98, Wates City of London Properties 1998–2001; Chair. Central YMCA 2011–; Trustee, Changing Faces 1997–2011. *Leisure interests:* golf, tennis, theatre. *Address:* Carillion plc, 1 Providence Tower, Bermondsey Wall West, London, SE16 4US, England (office). *Telephone:* (20) 7237-8962 (office). *Website:* www.carillionplc.com (office).

ROGGE, Count; Jacques; Belgian surgeon, international organization official and fmr sports administrator; b. 1942, Ghent; m. Anne Rogge; two c.; ed Univ. of Ghent; fmr orthopaedic surgeon and sports medicine lecturer; participated as sailing competitor at Summer Olympics in Mexico City, 1968, Munich 1972, Montreal (team gold medal) 1976; also played on Belgian nat. rugby union team; gold medal, Finn-class World Championships, silver medal twice, Belgian champion 16 times; also won Yachting World Cadet Trophy and took part in the regatta Ton Cup; Pres. Belgian Olympic Cttee 1989–92, European Olympic Cttee 1989–2001, Chef de mission, two winter and three summer Olympic Games (Chief Co-ordinator, Olympic Games 2000, 2004), mem. IOC 1991–, mem. Exec. Bd 1998–2013, Pres. 2001–13, Hon. Pres. 2013–; UN Special Envoy for Youth Refugees and Sport 2014–; knighted in 1992, made a Count in the Belgian nobility by King Albert II 2002, Officier, Légion d'honneur 2011; UNEP Champion of the Earth Laureate 2007, ranked by Forbes magazine amongst The World's Most Powerful People (60th) 2009, (67th) 2010, (68th) 2011, FIFA Presidential Award 2013. *Leisure interests:* modern art, avid reader of historical and scientific literature. *Address:* United Nations High Commissioner for Refugees, Case Postale 2500, 2 Dépôt, 1211, Geneva, Switzerland (office). *Telephone:* 227398111 (office). *Fax:* 227397377 (office). *Website:* www.unhcr.org (office).

ROGOFF, Ilan; Israeli concert pianist and conductor; b. 26 July 1943, Tel-Aviv; s. of Boris Rogoff and Sofija Rogoff; m. Vesna Zorka Mimiça 1985; two d.; ed Tel-Aviv Acad. of Music, Royal Conservatoire, Brussels, Belgium, Mannes Coll. and Juilliard School, New York, USA; has performed all over Israel, Europe, N America, Latin America, S Africa, Japan and Far East with Israel Philharmonic Orchestra and many other orchestras; recognized for his interpretation of the Romantic composers, including Beethoven, Schumann, Brahms, Chopin, Liszt, César Franck, Rachmaninov, Tchaikovsky, Piazzolla; has performed twentieth-century and contemporary works including world premiere of concerti by John McCabe and by Ivan Erod; performs with various chamber music groups, including Enesco Quartet, Orpheus Quartet, Amati Trio, Festival Ensemble, Matrix Quintet, Sharon Trio and Quartet, soloists of Vienna Chamber Orchestra and Vienna Philharmonic Orchestra; conducting debut 1985, with Israel Philharmonic 1988; radio performances and TV appearances in UK, Spain, Austria, Germany, Israel, Canada, USA, SA, Colombia, Ecuador, Venezuela and Argentina; lectures and recital/lectures, master classes; juror at various int. music competitions; various int. awards. *Recordings include:* Chopin Concerti (version for piano and string quintet edited by him), transcriptions for piano solo of 12 works by Astor Piazzolla; 'Portraits' by Schumann; complete works by Chopin while in Mallorca; numerous works by Bach-Busoni, Beethoven, Schumann, Schubert, Beethoven, Liszt, Schubert/Liszt and César Franck. *Publications:* Transcriptions for Piano Solo of Works by Astor Piazzolla, edited both Chopin Concerti for Piano and String Quintet; articles on music published in Scherzo magazine, Madrid, Piano magazine, London. *Leisure interests:* water sports, reading, visual arts, theatre, cinema and music research. *Address:* Estudio/Taller, Calle Bartomeu Fons 13, 07015 Palma de Mallorca, Spain (office). *Telephone:* (971) 707016 (home); 6-10980906 (mobile). *E-mail:* ilanrogoff@gmail.com (home). *Website:* www.ilanrogoff.com.

ROGOFF, Kenneth S., BA, MA, PhD; American economist, academic and international finance official; *Thomas D. Cabot Professor of Public Policy, Harvard University;* b. 22 March 1953, Rochester, NY; s. of Stanley Miron Rogoff and June Beatrice Rogoff; m. Natasha Lance; one s. one d.; ed Yale Univ., Massachusetts Inst. of Tech., Cambridge, Mass; Economist, Int. Finance Div., Fed. Reserve Bd of Govs 1980–83; economist, Research Dept, IMF 1982–83, Chief Economist and Dir of Research 2001–03; Assoc. Prof. of Econs, Univ. of Wisconsin 1985–88; Prof. of Econs, Univ. of California, Berkeley 1989–92; Prof. of Econs and Int. Affairs, Princeton Univ. 1992–94, Charles and Marie Robertson Prof. of Int. Affairs 1995–99; Prof. of Econs, Harvard Univ. 1999–, Thomas D. Cabot Prof. of Public Policy 2004–, Dir Harvard Center for Int. Devt 2003–04; Vice-Pres. American Econ. Asscn 2007; Research Assoc., Nat. Bureau of Econ. Research 1985–; mem. Econ. Advisory Panel, Fed. Reserve Bank of New York 2004–, Academic Advisory Panel, Cen. Bank of Sweden 2005–, Advisory Cttee, Inst. for Int. Econs 2001–; mem. Council on Foreign Relations 2004–, Trilateral Comm. 2003–, Group of Thirty Consultative Group on Int. Econ. and Monetary Affairs, Inc. (G-30), Washington, DC; Assoc. Ed. Review of Economics and Statistics 1993–, Economics Letters 1993–96, Journal of International Economics 1995–, Quarterly Journal of Economics 1984–95, Journal of Economic Perspectives 1987–90; mem. NAS 2010; Nat. Science Fellowship, MIT 1975–78; Alfred P. Sloan Research Fellow 1986; Nat. Fellow, The Hoover Inst. 1986; German Marshall Foundation Fellow 1991; Econometric Soc. Fellow 1991–; Guggenheim Fellow 1998; American Acad. of Arts and Sciences Fellow 2001–; World Econ. Forum Fellow 2003–; Hon. Advisor, Inst. for Monetary and Econ. Studies, Bank of Japan 2001. *Achievements include:* Int. Grandmaster of Chess, World Chess Fed. 1978– (inactive). *Publications include:* Foundations of International Macroeconomics (with Maurice Obstfeld) 1996, Workbook for Foundations of International Macroeconomics 1998, This Time is Different: Eight Centuries of Financial Folly (with Carmen M. Reinhart) 2009; numerous contribs to learned journals and newspapers. *Leisure interests:* swimming, chess, cinema. *Address:* Harvard University, Department of Economics, Littauer Center 216, Cambridge, MA 02138-3001 (office); 3723 Harrison Street NW, Washington, DC 20015, USA (home). *Telephone:* (617) 495-4022 (office); (202) 363-4529 (home). *Fax:* (617) 495-7730 (office). *E-mail:* krogoff@harvard.edu (office). *Website:* www.economics.harvard.edu/faculty/rogoff (home).

ROGOV, Sergey Mikhailovich, Dr. Hist.; Russian political scientist and academic; *Director, Institute for USA and Canadian Studies, Russian Academy of Sciences;* b. 22 Oct. 1948, Moscow; m.; one s. one d.; ed Moscow State Inst. of Int. Relations; jr, sr researcher, head of sector Inst. for USA and Canadian Studies, Russian Acad. of Sciences 1976–84, Rep. of Inst. for USA and Canadian Studies to USSR Embassy, Washington, DC 1984–87, Leading Research Fellow, Moscow 1987–89, Chief Dept of Mil. and Political Studies 1989–91, Deputy Dir 1991–95, Dir 1995–; mem. Scientific Council of Ministry of Foreign Affairs, of Security Council; counsellor Cttee on Foreign Relations of State Duma; mem. Russian Acad. of Nat. Sciences; Corresp. mem. Russian Acad. of Sciences 2002–. *Publications:* 16 books on foreign policy of USSR and Russian Fed., Russian-American relationship, mil. aspects of foreign policy, problems of nat. security and over 300 scientific publs and articles. *Address:* Institute for USA and Canadian Studies, Russian Academy of Sciences, 121814 Moscow, Khlebny Pereulok 2/3, Russia (office). *Telephone:* (495) 290-58-75 (office). *Fax:* (495) 200-12-07 (office). *E-mail:* srogov@rambler.ru (office). *Website:* iskran.iip.net/engl/index-en.html (office).

ROGOZHKIN, Aleksandr Vladimirovich, Russian scriptwriter and film director; b. 3 Oct. 1950, Leningrad; ed Leningrad State Univ., All-Union Inst. of Cinematography; worked in TV cos in Leningrad; cinema debut in 1980s. *Films directed include:* Ryzhaya, ryzhaya 1981, Radi neskolkikh strochek 1985, Miss millionersha 1988, Karaul (FIPRESCI Prize for Best Film Moscow Int. Film Festival, Alfred Bauer Prize, Berlin Festival 1989) 1989, The Guard 1990, Tretya planeta (also writer) 1991, Chekist 1992, Akt (also writer) 1993, Zhizn s idiotom (also writer) 1993, Osobennosti natsionalnoy okhoty (also writer, Nika Award for Best Dir) 1995, Blokpost (story, Silver Dolphin for Best Dir Tróia Int. Film Festival 1998, Best Dir Karlovy Vary Int. Film Festival 1998) 1998, Osobennosti natsionalnoy rybalki (also writer) 1998, Boldino Fall 1999, Osobennosti natsionalnoy okhoty v zimniy period 2000, Kukushka (also writer, Grand Prix Honfleur Festival of Russian Cinema, Dialog Prize 2002, Silver Dolphin for Best Dir Tróia Int. Film Festival 2002, FIPRESCI Prize for Best Film Moscow Int. Film Festival, Nika Award for Best Film and Best Dir) 2002, Sapiens (also writer) 2004, Peregon (also writer) 2006. *Address:* Gertsena str. 21, apt 8, 191065 St Petersburg, Russia (home). *Telephone:* (812) 311-76-81 (home).

ROGOZIN, Dmitrii Olegovich, DrPhil; Russian politician and diplomatist; *Deputy Chairman of the Government and Presidential Representative to the 'Transnistrian Moldovan Republic';* b. 21 Dec. 1963, Moscow; s. of Oleg Konstantinovich Rogozin and Tamara Vasilevna Rogozina (née Prokofieva); m. Tatyana Gennadyevna Serebryakova; one s.; ed Moscow State Univ.; worked in USSR Cttee of Youth Orgs and as a journalist; Co-founder Research and Educ. Co. RAU Corp. 1986–90; one of Party of People's Freedom 1990; Pres. Assen of Young Political Leaders of Russia Forum-90; f. Congress of Russian Communities 1993; active in nat. movt; took part in re-establishment of numerous churches; mem. State Duma (Regions of Russia, Motherland) 1997–; Co-founder and Leader Motherland pre-election bloc 2003, Leader Motherland—People's Patriotic Union faction 2004–06; Chair. Cttee on Int. Affairs 2000–03, Deputy Chair. 2003–04; Chief Negotiator with EU on problems of Kaliningrad Region 2002–04; Deputy Chair. Cttee on Nationalities, State Duma 2007–08; Amb. to NATO and Head of Perm. Mission 2008–11; Special Rep. of the Pres. of Russian Fed. for Interaction with NATO in Missile Defence Feb.–Dec. 2011; Deputy Chair. of the Govt in charge of Defence Industry 2011–, Presidential Rep. to the 'Transnistrian Moldovan Republic' 2012–; placed under exec. sanction by US Pres. Barack Obama following the Crimean status referendum, freezing his assets in the USA and banning him from entering the USA March 2014. *Publications include:* Russian Answer 1996, War and Peace (glossary), Enemy of the People 2007, Hawks of Peace 2009; numerous articles in the western and Russian press. *Leisure interests:* master of sports, handball. *Address:* Office of the Government, 103274 Moscow, Krasnopresnenskaya nab. 2, Russia (office). *Telephone:* (495) 605-53-29 (office). *Fax:* (495) 605-52-43 (office). *E-mail:* duty_press@aprf.gov.ru (home). *Website:* www.government.ru (office); www.rogozin.ru (office).

ROH, Tae-woo; South Korean politician; b. 4 Dec. 1932, Daegu; m. Roh (née Kim) Ok Sook 1959; one s. one d.; ed Taegu Tech. School, Kyongbuk High School, Korean Mil. Acad., US Special Warfare School, Repub. of Korea War Coll.; served in Korean War 1950; Commanding Gen. 9th Special Forces Brigade 1974–79, 9th Infantry Div. Jan.–Dec. 1979, Commdr Capital Security Command 1979–80, Defence Security Command 1980–81, Four-Star Gen. 1981, retd from army July 1981; Minister of State for Nat. Security and Foreign Affairs 1981–82, Minister of Sports 1982, of Home Affairs 1982; Pres. Repub. of Korea 1988–93; mem. Nat. Ass. 1985; Chair. Democratic Justice Party 1985–87, Pres. 1987–90, Jt Pres. Democratic Liberal Party (DLP) 1990–92 (had to quit the ruling party by agreement); Pres. Seoul Olympic Organizing Cttee 1983, Korean Amateur Sports Assen 1984, Korean Olympic Cttee 1984; arrested Nov. 1995, charged with aiding Dec. 1979 Coup Dec. 1995; also charged with taking bribes; convicted of mutiny and treason, sentenced to 22½ years' imprisonment Aug. 1996; numerous decorations. *Publications:* Widaehan pot'ougsaram ui shidae 1987, Korea: A Nation Transformed 1990. *Leisure interests:* tennis, swimming, golf, music, reading.

ROHATYN, Felix George; American investment banker and diplomatist; *Special Advisor to the Chairman and CEO, Lazard Ltd;* b. 29 May 1928, Vienna, Austria; s. of Alexander Rohatyn and Edith Rohatyn (née Knoll); m. 1st Jeannette Streit 1956; three s.; m. 2nd Elizabeth Fly 1979; ed Middlebury Coll., Vt; moved to USA 1942; joined Lazard Freres & Co. (investment bankers, now Lazard Ltd) 1948, Gen. Pnr 1961–97, Special Advisor to Chair. and CEO 2010–; Amb. to France 1997–2000; Founder and Pres. Rohatyn Assocs LLC 2001–; Sr Advisor Lehman Brothers Holdings Inc. 2006–09; mem. Bd of Govs NY Stock Exchange 1968–72; Chair. Municipal Assistance Corpn (MAC) 1975–93; mem. Bd of Dirs LVMH (Moet Hennessy Louis Vuitton), Publicis Groupe SA, Rothschild Continuation Holdings AG, Lagardere; Trustee, Center for Strategic and Int. Studies; mem. Council on Foreign Relations; mem. American Acad. of Arts and Sciences; eight hon. degrees; Commdr, Légion d'honneur. *Publications:* The Twenty-Year Century: Essays on Economics and Public Finance 1983, Money Games: My Journey Through American Capitalism 1950–2000 2003, Bold Endeavors: How our Government Built America, and Why it Must Rebuild Now 2009, Dealings: A Political and Financial Life 2010. *Address:* Rohatyn Associates LLC, 280 Park Avenue, 27th Floor, New York, NY 10017 (office); Lazard Ltd, 30 Rockefeller Plaza, New York,

NY 10112-5900, USA (office). *Telephone:* (212) 984-2975 (office); (212) 632-5540 (Lazard) (office). *Fax:* (212) 984-2976 (office). *E-mail:* felix.rohatyn@rohatyn.com (office). *Website:* www.lazard.com (office).

ROHDE, Bruce C., BBA, JD; American lawyer and food industry executive; *Chairman and CEO Emeritus, ConAgra Foods Inc.;* b. 17 Dec. 1948, Sidney, Neb.; ed Creighton Univ., Omaha, NE Creighton School of Law; with McGrath, North, Mullin and Kratz (law firm) 1973–96; Pres. and Vice-Chair. ConAgra Foods Inc. 1996–97, CEO 1997–98, Chair. and CEO 1998–2005, now Chair. and CEO Emer.; mem. Bd of Dirs Grocery Mfrs of America, Preventive Medicine Research Inst.; Vice-Chair. Bd of Dirs Creighton Univ., Nat. Campaign Chair. Willing to Lead: The Campaign for Creighton Univ. 2005–; Chair. Bd Dirs Strategic Air and Space Museum; mem. Pvt. and Public, Scientific, Academic and Consumer Food Policy Cttee (PAPSAC), Harvard Univ.; mem. STRATCOM (US Strategic Command) Consultation Cttee; mem. Nat. Infrastructure Advisory Council, US Dept of Homeland Security; Business Information Professional of the Year Award 2000, Frost & Sullivan Food and Beverage CEO of the Year 2004. *Address:* c/o Willing to Lead: The Campaign for Creighton University, Development Office, 2500 California Plaza, Omaha, NE 68178, USA (office).

ROHNER, Marcel, PhD; Swiss banker; b. 4 Sept. 1964; m.; two c.; ed Univ. of Zurich; research and teaching asst, Inst. for Empirical Research in Econs, Univ. of Zurich 1990–92; Asst to the Global Head of Derivatives, Union Bank of Switzerland 1992–93; Int. Finance Div. Controlling, Market Risk Control, SBC Zürich 1993–95; Head, Market Risk Control Europe, Warburg Dillon Read 1995–98; Head, Market Risk Control UBS AG 1998–99, Group Chief Risk Officer 1999–2001, COO and Deputy CEO Pvt. Pvt. Banking unit of UBS Switzerland 2001–02, mem. Group Exec. Bd 2002–, CEO Wealth Man. and Business Banking 2002–04, Chair. and CEO Wealth Man. and Business Banking 2004–05, Deputy Group CEO 2006–07, Group CEO 2007–09 (resgnd), Chair. and CEO Investment Bank 2007–08; Vice-Chair. Swiss Bankers Asscn –2008, Bd of Trustees, Swiss Finance Inst. *Address:* c/o UBS AG, Postfach 8098, Zurich, Switzerland. *E-mail:* info@ubs.com.

ROHNER, Urs; Swiss lawyer and business executive; *Chairman, Credit Suisse Group AG;* b. 1959; ed Univ. of Zurich; lawyer, Lenz & Staehelin, Attorneys at Law, Zurich 1983–88, Partner 1990–99; admitted to Bar of Canton of Zurich 1986, Bar of State of NY, USA 1990; lawyer, Sullivan & Cromwell LLP, New York 1988–89; CEO ProSieben Media AG Jan.–Sept. 2000, Chair. Exec. Bd and CEO 2000–04; mem. Exec. Bd Credit Suisse Group AG and Credit Suisse AG 2004–09, Gen. Counsel of Credit Suisse Group AG 2004–09, COO and Gen. Counsel of Credit Suisse AG 2006–09, Vice-Chair. Credit Suisse Group AG 2009–11, Chair. 2011–, mem. Chair.'s and Governance Cttee and Risk Cttee; mem. Bd of Dirs Inst. for Int. Finance, Institut Int. d'Etudes Bancaires, Zurich Opera House; mem. Bd of Trustees Lucerne Festival; mem. Exec. Bd Zurich Chamber of Commerce. *Address:* Office of the Chairman, Credit Suisse Group AG, PO Box 1, 8070 Zurich (office); Credit Suisse Group, Paradeplatz 8, 8001 Zurich, Switzerland (office). *Telephone:* (44) 212-16-16 (office). *Fax:* (44) 333-25-87 (office). *E-mail:* info@credit-suisse.com (office). *Website:* www.credit-suisse.com (office).

ROHOVIY, Vasyl Vasylyovich, CandEcons; Ukrainian politician and economist; b. 2 March 1953, Mirivka, Kiev region; s. of Vasyl Loginovich and Zinaida Mikhailivna Rohoviy; m. Svetlana Mikhailivna Rogovaya; one s.; ed Kiev Inst. of National Econs, Ukrainian Acad. of Sciences; engineer and economist Kiev Artem Production co. 1974–75, 1976–77; sr mechanic Odessa Mil. Command 1975–76; jr researcher Inst. of Econs, then Scientific Sec. Dept of Econs, Ukrainian Acad. of Sciences 1980–88; Chief Expert, Head of Sector, then Head of Div. Ukrainian Council of Ministers 1988–94; First Deputy Minister of Econs 1994–98, Minister 1998–99, 2000–01; First Deputy Head of Admin., Office of the Pres. 2000; Deputy Prime Minister for Econ. Policy 2001–02; Presidential Adviser 2002; fmr Deputy Sec. of Econ, Social and Environmental Security Council, Nat. Security and Defense Council of Ukraine; apptd mem. Supervisory Council UkrExImBank JSC—State Export-Import Bank of Ukraine 2003. *Address:* c/o Council of National Security and Defense of Ukraine, 11 Bankova str., 01220 Kiev, Ukraine (office). *Telephone:* (44) 254-40-25. *Website:* www.rainbow.gov.ua.

ROHR, Hans Christoph von, Dr jur.; German lawyer and business executive; b. 1 July 1938, Stettin; s. of Hansjoachim von Rohr; m.; two c.; ed Univs of Heidelberg, Vienna, Bonn, Princeton Univ.; joined Klöckner-Werke AG, Bremen; subsequently held leading position with Klöckner subsidiary in Argentina; worked for Fisser & van Doornum, Emden; Partner, TaylorWessing Lawyers, Düsseldorf; mem. Bd Klöckner & Co. Duisburg 1984; Chair. Exec. Bd Klöckner-Werke AG 1991–96; Man. Chair. Industrial Investment Council GmbH 1997–2002; Chair. (non-exec.) ING Barings (Germany) 1996–2001; Chair. Supervisory Bd, Balfour Beatty GmbH, Munich, mem. Bd Balfour Beatty plc, London 2002–09; mem. Bd Underwriters Laboratories Inc., Chicago 2002–12, Advisory Bd UL International GmbH, Frankfurt; Hon. Chair. German Inst. for Competition and Market Economy (FIW), Cologne; German Order of Merit 2002. *Publications:* Ein Konservativer Kämpfer: Der NS-Gegner und Agrarpolitker Hansjoachim von Rohr 2010, Paritätische Mitbestimmung: Deutschland einsam auf seinem Sonderweg 2010. *Address:* Semmelweisstrasse 34, 45470 Mülheim, Ruhr, Germany.

ROHR, James E., BA, MBA; American business executive; *Chairman and CEO, PNC Financial Services Group;* ed Univ. of Notre Dame, Ohio State Univ.; joined PNC Financial Services Group through its man. devt programme 1972, proceeded through various marketing and man. responsibilities in several Corp. Banking areas, Vice-Chair. PNC 1989, mem. Bd of Dirs 1990–, Pres. 1992–98, COO 1998–2000, CEO 2000–Chair. 2001–; mem. Bd of Dirs BlackRock, Inc., Federal Reserve Bank of Cleveland, Allegheny Technologies Inc., Equitable Resources, Inc., RAND Bd of Trustees, Int. Monetary Conf.; fmr Chair. Pennsylvania Business Roundtable; mem. Financial Services Roundtable, Dir and fmr Chair. BITS (tech. group for Financial Services Roundtable); fmr Chair. Allegheny Conf. on Community Devt, Pittsburgh Cultural Trust; Bd mem. and fmr Chair. Greater Pittsburgh Council of the Boy Scouts of America; Dir Cttee Encouraging Corp. Philanthropy, Carnegie Mellon Univ., Univ. of Pittsburgh's McGowan Inst. for Regenerative Medicine, Heinz Endowments; mem. Bd of Trustees Univ. of Notre Dame, mem. Notre Dame's Coll. of Business Advisory Council; Woodrow Wilson

Award for Corp. Citizenship 2006, Sesame Workshop Corp. Honoree Award 2007, Women's Inst. for a Secure Retirement (WISER) Hero Award, Heinz Family Philanthropies 2008, named American Banker's Banker of the Year for 2007. *Address:* PNC Financial Services Group, 249 Fifth Avenue, Pittsburgh, PA 15222, USA (office). *Telephone:* (412) 762-2000 (office). *Fax:* (412) 762-7829 (office). *E-mail:* info@pnc.com (office). *Website:* www.pnc.com (office).

ROISS, Gerhard; Austrian business executive; *Chairman of the Executive Board and CEO, OMV Group;* b. 2 April 1952, Linz; m.; three c.; ed Univ. of Vienna, Univ. of Linz, Stanford Univ., USA; Head of OMV Marketing, OMV Group 1990, apptd to Man. Bd of PCD Polymere GmbH 1990–97, transferred to Bd of OMV Group and was responsible for Plastics and Chemicals 1997–2000, also assumed responsibility for the Exploration and Production business 2000–02, Deputy CEO OMV Group responsible for Refining and Marketing including Petrochemicals 2002–11, Chair. Exec. Bd and CEO OMV AG 2011–; Chair. Nova Chemicals Corpn 2009–11. *Address:* OMV AG, Trabrennstrasse 6–8, 1020 Vienna, Austria (office). *Telephone:* (1) 40440-21950 (office). *Fax:* (1) 40440-27900 (office). *E-mail:* gerhard.roiss@omv .com (office). *Website:* www.omv.com (office).

ROIZMAN, Bernard, ScD; American scientist and academic; *Joseph Regenstein Distinguished Service Professor of Virology, Departments of Microbiology, Molecular Genetics and Cell Biology and Biochemistry and Molecular Biology, University of Chicago;* b. 17 April 1929, Romania; m. Betty Cohen 1950; two s.; ed Temple Univ., Johns Hopkins Univ.; Instructor of Microbiology, Johns Hopkins Univ. 1956–57, Research Assoc. 1957–58, Asst Prof. 1958–65; Assoc. Prof. of Microbiology, Univ. of Chicago 1965–69, Prof. 1969–84, Prof. of Biophysics 1970–, Chair. Interdepartmental Cttee on Virology 1969–85, 1988–, Joseph Regenstein Prof. of Virology 1981–83, Joseph Regenstein Distinguished Service Prof. of Virology 1984–; Chair. Dept of Molecular Genetics and Cell Biology 1985–88; fmr Ed. of numerous specialist scientific publs and mem. Editorial Bd Journal of Virology 1970–, Intervirology 1972–85, Virology 1976–78, 1983–; Ed.-in-Chief Infectious Agents and Diseases 1992–96; mem. or fmr mem. numerous grant review panels, int. panels, including Chair. Herpes Virus Study Group, Int. Cttee for Taxonomy of Viruses 1971–94 (Chair. 1991–), Scientific Advisory Bd, Showa Univs Center 1983–; mem. Int. Microbial Genetics Comm., Int. Asscn of Microbiological Sciences 1979–86; numerous nat. panels on vaccines, cancers; Scholar in Cancer Research at American Cancer Soc., Inst. Pasteur (with Andre Lwoff), Paris 1961–62; Travelling Fellow, Int. Agency for Research Against Cancer (with Dr Klein), Stockholm, Sweden 1970; mem. NAS, Inst. of Medicine, American Asscn of Immunologists, Soc. for Experimental Biology and Medicine, American Soc. for Microbiology (ASM), for Biological Chemists, Soc. for Gen. Microbiology (UK), American Soc. for Virology, Chinese Acad. of Eng, Hungarian Acad. of Science; Fellow, Japanese Soc. for Promotion of Science, American Acad. of Arts and Sciences, American Acad. of Microbiology; Hon. DHumLitt (Govs State Univ., Ill.) 1984; Hon. MD (Ferrara) 1991; Hon. DSc (Paris) 1997, (Valladolid, Spain) 2001; J. Allyn Taylor Int. Prize in Medicine 1997, Bristol-Myers Squibb Award for Distinguished Achievement in Infectious Disease Research 1998, ICN Int. Prize in Virology 1988, NIH Outstanding Investigator Award 1988–2001, NIH-NCI Merit Award 2003, ASM Lifetime Achievement Award 2008, Brilliant Achievement Award, Chinese Biopharmaceutical Asscn 2012. *Publications:* author or co-author of approx. 600 papers in scientific journals and books; ed. or co-ed. of 20 books. *Address:* Marjorie B. Kohler Viral Oncology Laboratories, University of Chicago, 910 East 58th Street, Chicago, IL 60637 (office); 5555 South Everett Avenue, Chicago, IL 60637, USA (home). *Telephone:* (773) 702-1898 (office); (773) 493-2986 (home). *Fax:* (773) 702-1631 (office); (773) 493-9042 (home). *E-mail:* bernard.roizman@bsd.uchicago.edu (office). *Website:* microbiology.uchicago.edu/ page/bernard-roizman (office).

ROJAS DE MORENO DÍAZ, María Eugenia; Colombian politician; b. 6 Oct. 1934, Vélez, Santander; d. of the late Gen. Gustavo Rojas Pinilla (Pres. of Colombia 1953–57); m. Samuel Moreno Díaz; two s.; mem. of the Senate; Majority Leader, Bogotá City Council; Leader Alianza Nacional Popular 1975. *Address:* Alianza Nacional Popular, Carrera 18, No 33-95, Santa Fe de Bogotá, DC, Colombia (office). *Telephone:* (1) 287-7050 (office). *Fax:* (1) 245-3138 (office). *E-mail:* anapo@neutel .net.co (office).

ROJAS GUTIERREZ, Francisco José; Mexican accountant, politician and business executive; *Director-General, Comisión Federal de Electricidad;* b. 15 Sept. 1944, Mexico City; ed Nat. Autonomous Univ. of Mexico (UNAM); mem. Institutional Revolutionary Party (PRI) since early 1960s, Nat. Pres. of Colosio Foundation, AC 2007–10, mem. Nat. Political Council and Perm. Political Cttee, held various positions, including Sec. of Finance of Nat. Exec. Cttee, Co-ordinator of Nat. Priorities Political Campaign for Presidency of Miguel de la Madrid, Co-ordinator of PRI in LXI Legislature; fmr Deputy Dir Gen. of Expenditures and Chief of Staff, Ministry of Finance; fmr Gen. Co-ordinator of Man. Control, Ministry of Planning and Budget; first Holder of Gen. Secr. of Fed. 1983–87; Dir Gen. Petroleos Mexicanos 1987–94; retd from politics but returned as Deputy (PRI) in LIX Legislature 2003–; Chair. Cttee on Budget and Public Accounts 2003–06, Co-ordinator of PRI Parl. Group 2009; Dir-Gen. Comisión Federal de Electricidad (Fed. Electricity Comm.) 2012–; Pres. Alumni Asscn, School of Accounting and Admin, UNAM 1992–2003, Pres. UNAM 1995–2003, Chair. UNAM Philharmonic Orchestra 1994–2005, Hon. Pres. Foundation UNAM; Exec. Chair. Mexican Industry Consumer Products, AC 1996–2003; Pres. Corp. Council of Mexican American Solidarity Foundation, AC; Chair. Mexico-Israel Cultural Inst., AC; columnist, El Universal and El Sol de Mexico newspapers 2003–; Nat. Political Council mem. and Chair. Bd of Trustees, Luis Donaldo Colosio; mem. Advisory Bd, Inst. of Political, Econ. and Social IEPES; mem. Nat. Inst. of Public Admin, Mexican Inst. of Public Accountants, Mexican Acad. of Comprehensive Audit, Inst. of Chartered Accountants of Mexico, Forum of Sr Man., Cultural Inst. Mexico-Israel; several awards from professional and social insts and awards from various countries. *Publications include:* political essays in various publs. *Address:* Federal Electricity Commission, Avenida Paseo de la Reforma 164, Mexico City 6600, Mexico (office). *Telephone:* (55) 5229-4400 (office). *E-mail:* frojas.dg@cfe.gob.mx (office). *Website:* www.cfe.gob.mx (office).

ROJAS IRIGOYEN, Germán Hugo, MBA; Paraguayan banker and government official; *Minister of Finance;* b. 1958; m.; three c.; ed Universidad Católica Nuestra Señora de la Asunción; served several years with Central Bank of Paraguay,

becoming Man., Int. Operations, Pres. 2007; fmr Project Dir UNDP; various man. positions with Bank of Parana SA, including Head of Financial Man.; Pres. Banco Nacional de Fomento, Asuncion 2003–07; Minister of Finance 2013–. *Address:* Ministry of Finance, Chile 252, entre Palma y Presidente Franco, Asunción, Paraguay (office). *Telephone:* (21) 44-0010 (office). *Fax:* (21) 44-8283 (office). *E-mail:* info@hacienda.gov.py (office). *Website:* www.hacienda.gov.py (office).

ROJAS RAMÍREZ, José Alejandro, PhD; Venezuelan politician and economist; *Executive Director, World Bank Group;* b. 3 Sept. 1959, Caracas; s. of José Alejandro Rojas Leon and Carmen Ramírez Tovar; m.; one s.; ed Universidad Central de Venezuela, Inst. of Petroleum and Univ. of Paris II (Sorbonne), France; fmr Sr Economist, Office of Programming and Macroeconomic Analysis, IDB, also Gov. (for Venezuela), IDB; Exec. Dir for Panama and Venezuela, Inter American Devt Bank, Washington, DC; Deputy Minister, then Minister of Finance 1999–2001; fmr Adviser to Pres. and Bd of Dirs, Cen. Bank of Venezuela; fmr Vice-Pres. Petroleos de Venezuela (PDVSA) 2004; Pres. Ass. of Fondo Latinoamericano de Reservas (FLAR), Consultant Council, Andean Community of Nations; Alt. Exec. Dir (representing Mexico, Costa Rica, El Salvador, Guatemala, Honduras, Nicaragua, Venezuela and Spain), World Bank, Washington, DC –2008, Exec. Dir 2008–; mem. Bd of Dirs Compañía de Energía Eléctrica del Estado Venezolano (CADAFE), Electrificación del Caroni (EDELCA) CA; consultant several cos and orgs; Dir Quantitative Methods Dept, Universidad Central de Venezuela, mem. Postgrad. Scientific Cttee; Prof. of Econometrics and Math. Econs, Universidad Católica Andrés Bello, Caracas, of Operational Research, Instituto Politécnico de las Fuerzas Armadas, Caracas; mem. Colegio de Estadístico de Venezuela, Royal Econometric Soc., UK. *Publications:* numerous research papers. *Address:* MC12-1211, World Bank Group, 1818 H Street, NW, Washington, DC 20433, USA (office). *Telephone:* (202) 458-2095 (office). *Fax:* (202) 522-1575 (office). *E-mail:* jrojasramirez@worldbank.org (office). *Website:* www .worldbank.org (office).

ROJO GARCÍA, Francisco Javier; Spanish politician; *President of the Senate;* b. 2 March 1949, Pamplona; m.; two d.; early political work with Gen. Workers Union 1976–79; Prov. Councillor, Alava 1979–83, City Councillor for Vitoria-Gasteiz (Álava) 1983–84; mem. Gen. Ass. of Álava 1983–87; Councillor of the Presidency of Alava 1987–93, Deputy Mayor of Vitoria-Gasteiz 1991–96; Senator for Alava 1993–2004, Pres. of the Senate 2004–; mem. Basque Parl. 2001–02, mem. Human Rights Cttee and Basque Radio and TV Control Cttee; Sec.-Gen. Basque Socialist Party-Basque Left (PSE-EE), Álava 2000–05, Pres. 2005–; Sec. of Institutional Relations, Spanish Socialist Workers' Party (PSOE) Fed. Exec. Comm. 2002–04; Grand Cross, Order of Civil Merit, Grand Cross, Isabel la Católica; Dr hc (Piura Public Univ., Peru) 2006. *Address:* Office of the President of the Senate, Plaza de la Marina Española 8, 28071 Madrid, Spain (office). *Telephone:* (91) 5381000 (office). *Fax:* (91) 5381003 (office). *E-mail:* webmaster@ senado.es (office). *Website:* www.senado.es (office).

ROKITA, Jan, LLM; Polish politician and lawyer; b. 18 June 1959, Kraków; s. of Tadeusz Rokita and Adela Rokita; m. Nelli Arnold 1994; one d.; ed Jagiellonian Univ., Pontifical Acad. of Theology, Kraków; fmr active mem. of Independent Students' Union (NZS) 1980–82; interned under Martial Law 1982; banned by the Communist authorities from practising law 1983–89; co-founder and participant Freedom and Peace Movt 1985–88; founder and mem. Intervention and Law-abidingness Comm. of Solidarity Trade Union 1986–89; mem. Civic Cttee attached to Lech Wałęsa (q.v.) 1988–90; organizer and Chair. Int. Conf. on Human Rights, Kraków 1988; participant Round Table negotiations 1989; Chair. Special Parl. Comm. of Inquiry in respect of archives of the former Communist Security Service (Rokita Comm.) 1989–90; Deputy Chair. Civic Parl. Caucus 1989–90, Deputy Chair. Democratic Union Parl. Caucus 1991–96, Deputy Chair. Freedom Union Parl. Caucus 1996–97, mem. Solidarity Election Action Parl. Caucus 1997–2001; Deputy Chair. Civic Platform Parl. Caucus 2001–03, Chair. 2003–05; Chair. Parl. Comm. for Admin. and Internal Affairs 1997–2000; Minister-Chief of Office of Council of Ministers 1992–93; Chair. Conservative People's Party (SKL) 1998–2001; mem. Special Parl. Comm. of Inquiry into the Rywin Affair 2003–04; mem. Civic Platform (PO) (Platforma Obywatelska); Commdr, Order of Polonia Restituta 2008; POLCUL Foundation Award (Australia) 1988, Stefan Kisielewski Award 2003, Edward J. Wende Award 2003, Man of the Year (Wprost weekly magazine, Poland) 2003, Top Parliamentarian (Polityka weekly magazine, Poland) 2003. *Publications:* political and historical journalism; Alfabet Rokity 2004. *Leisure interests:* classical music, jazz, ancient Greek philosophy, bicycle riding. *Address:* Biuro Posła Jana Rokity, 31-143 Kraków, ul. Basztowa 15/10, Poland. *Telephone:* (12) 4300186. *Fax:* (12) 4263560. *Website:* www.janrokita.pl.

ROLANDIS, Nikos A.; Cypriot politician, business executive and barrister; b. 10 Dec. 1934, Limassol; m. Lelia Aivaliotis; one s. two d.; ed Pancyprian Gymnasium Nicosia, Middle Temple, London; called to the bar, Middle Temple 1956; practised law in Cyprus for short time before entering business; owner of industrial and commercial cos; Founding mem. Democratic Group (now Democratic Party); f. Liberal Party 1986, Pres. 1986–98; Minister of Foreign Affairs 1978–83; mem. House of Reps 1991–96; Vice-Pres. Liberal Int. 1994–99; Minister of Commerce, Industry and Tourism 1998–2003. *Publications include:* numerous articles. *Address:* 13 Ayias Agapis, Strovolos, Nicosia, Cyprus (home). *Telephone:* 22591900 (office); 22353811/2 (home). *Fax:* 22591700 (office); 22353100 (home). *E-mail:* nikos@yolandis.com (home).

ROLDÓS AGUILERA, Leon; Ecuadorean lawyer, university administrator and politician; b. 21 July 1942, Guayaquil; ed Vicente Rocafuerte High School, Univ. of Guayaquil; practised as lawyer in Guayaquil; Lecturer, Prof. Vicente Rocafuerte Lay Univ. Law School 1967, later Dean; Chair. Monetary Bd 1979–81; Vice-Pres. of Ecuador 1981–83; presidential cand. (Partido Socialista Ecuatoriano (PSE) 1992; Rector, Univ. of Guayaquil 1994–2004; presidential cand. (ind.) 2002, (Red Ética y Democratica-Izquierda Democrática coalition) 2006; currently mem. Partido Roldosista Ecuatoriano (PRE). *Address:* c/o Partido Roldosista Ecuatoriano (PRE), Quito, Ecuador. *Telephone:* (2) 246-8227. *Fax:* (2) 246-8229. *E-mail:* info@ viviendolademocracia.org.

ROLET, Xavier, MBA; French financial services industry executive; *Chief Executive, London Stock Exchange;* b. 12 Nov. 1959, Aix-les-Bains; ed Columbia Univ., New York, Hautes Etudes de Defense Nationale, Paris; Second Lt and

Instructor, French Air Force Acad. 1981; joined Goldman Sachs & Co., New York 1984, becoming Co-Head, European Equity Sales and Trading, Goldman Sachs Int. Ltd, London 1990–94; Global Head of European Equities, Credit Suisse First Boston 1994–97; Global Head of Risk and Trading and Deputy Head of Global Equities, Dresdner Kleinwort Benson 1997; Deputy Co-Head of Global Equity Trading, Lehman Brothers, New York 2000, Co-Head Global Equity Trading 2000–01, Head of European and Asian Cash Equities and mem. Global Investment Banking Operating Cttee, Lehman Brothers, London 2001–03, Head of Sr Relationship Man. for Europe 2003–07, CEO Lehman Brothers, France 2007–09; Dir London Stock Exchange Group PLC 2009–, CEO London Stock Exchange 2009–, fmr Chair., London Stock Exchange Strategic Advisory Group; fmr mem., Conseil d'Orientation, Euronext Paris; fmr mem. EC European Securities Markets Expert Group. *Leisure interests:* cars, skiing, scuba-diving, fly-fishing. *Address:* London Stock Exchange, 10 Paternoster Square, London, EC4M 7LS, England (office). *Telephone:* (20) 7797-1000 (office). *Website:* www.londonstockexchange .com (office).

RÖLLER, Lars-Hendrik, BS, MSc, MA, PhD; German economist and academic; *Head of Economic and Financial Department, Federal Chancellery.;* m.; three c.; ed Texas A&M Univ. and Univ. of Pennsylvania, Phila, USA; Research Asst, Dept of Econs, Univ. of Pennsylvania 1983–86, Inst. for Law and Econs 1986–87, Lecturer, Dept of Econs 1986; Asst Prof. of Econs, Institut Européen d'Admin des Affaires (INSEAD), Paris, France 1987–91, Assoc. Prof. 1991–95, Prof. 1995–99; Prof. of Econs and Chair. Inst. of Industrial Econs, Humboldt Univ., Berlin 1995–; Dir Centre for Econ. Policy Research, London 1992, Co-Dir Industrial Org. Programme 1995–2003; Dir Inst. for Competitiveness and Industrial Change Wissenschafts-zentrum Berlin für Sozialforschung 1994–2007, now Research Prof.; Research Fellow, Forschungsinstitut zur Zukunft der Arbeit (IZA), Bonn 1999–2006; Prof. (part-time), Norwegian School of Econs and Business Admin 2003; Chief Competition Economist, EC 2003–06; Pres. European School of Man. and Tech., Berlin 2006–11; Head, Economic and Financial Dept, Federal Chancellery 2011–; Visiting Prof., Dept of Applied Econs, Univ. Autonoma, Barcelona, Spain 1989; Visiting Scholar, Starr Center for Applied Econs, New York Univ., USA 1992, Grad. School of Business, Stanford Univ. 1993; mem. Exec. Bd European Asscn for Research in Industrial Econs 1999–2004 (Pres. 2005–07), Scientific Cttee of INSEAD Foundation 1999–, Advisory Bd, Centre for Competition Policy, Univ. of East Anglia, Norwich 2004–, Conselho Consultativo, Universidade Nova de Lisboa, Portugal 2005–, Alexander von Humboldt Foundation, Scientific Council for Transatlantic Cooperation (TransCoop) 2003–, American Econ. Asscn, Exec. Bd Vereins für Socialpolitik 2001–03, German-French Council of Econ. Advisers, 2003–06; Ed. Managerial and Decision Economics 1993–98, International Journal of Industrial Organization 1999–2004; mem. editorial bds of several int. journals; Fellow, European Econ. Asscn 2004; Best Teacher Award, INSEAD 1998, Gossen Award Verein für Socialpolitik 2002. *Publications:* Situation und Perspektiven der deutschen Raumfahrtindustrie 1998, The Corporate Structure of UK and German Manufacturing Firms 1999, Europas Nätverksindustrier: Telekommunikationer Avregleringen i Europa 1999, The Political Economy of Industrial Policy: Does Europe Have an Industrial Policy? 2000, Die Soziale Marktwirtschaft in der neuen Weltwirtschaft 2001; contrib. of numerous articles to professional journals. *Address:* Federal Chancellery, Bundeskanzler-Amt, Willy-Brandt Str. 1, 10557 Berlin, Germany (office). *Telephone:* (30) 40000 (office). *Fax:* (30) 40002357 (office). *E-mail:* internetpost@bpa.bund.de (office). *Website:* www.bundeskanzlerin.de (office).

RÖLLER, Wolfgang, Dr rer. pol; German bank executive; *Honorary Chairman, Dresdner Bank AG;* b. 20 Oct. 1929, Uelsen, Lower Saxony; m.; three s.; ed Univs of Berlin and Frankfurt; joined Dresdner Bank AG, Frankfurt am Main, Deputy mem. Bd of Man. Dirs 1971–73, Full mem. 1973–85, Chair. Man. Bd 1985–93, Chair. Supervisory Bd 1993–97, now Hon. Chair.; Chair. Supervisory Bd ABD Securities Corpn, New York, Metallgesellschaft AG, Deutscher Investment-Trust Gesellschaft für Wertpapieranlagen mbH, Frankfurt, Dresdnerbank Investment Man. Kapitalanlage GmbH, Frankfurt, Heidelberger Zementwerke AG; mem. Supervisory Bd Allianz AG Holding, Munich, Daimler-Benz AG, Stuttgart, Degussa AG, Frankfurt, Henkel KGaA, Düsseldorf –2005, Hoechst AG, Frankfurt, Fried. Krupp GmbH, Essen, Rheinisch-Westfälisches Elektrizitätswerk AG (fmr Chair. Supervisory Bd), Essen; fmr Chair. of the Supervisory Bd Deutsche Lufthansa AG, now Hon. Chair. *Address:* c/o Dresdner Bank AG, Jürgen-Ponto-Platz 1, 60329 Frankfurt am Main, Germany.

ROLLIER, Michel, MA; French business executive; *Chairman of the Supervisory Board, Michelin;* b. 19 Sept. 1944, Annecy, Haute Savoie; s. of François Rollier; m.; three c.; ed Institut d'Etudes Politiques, Université de Droit, Paris; with Aussedat-Rey (int. paper group) 1971–96, Controller, facilities, divs and group 1973–82, Unit Operational Man. 1982–87, Chief Financial Officer 1987–94, Deputy Man. Dir 1994–96; Chief Legal Officer and Dir for Financial Operations, Compagnie Générale des Etablissements Michelin 1976, mem. Michelin Group Exec. Council and Chief Financial and Legal Officer 1999–, Co-Man. Partner 2005–06, Sole Man. Partner 2006–07, Man. Gen. Partner and CEO 2007–12 (retd), Chair. Supervisory Bd 2012–; Chair. Plateforme de la Filière Automobile; Officier, Légion d'honneur 2009. *Address:* Compagnie Générale des Etablissements Michelin, 12 cours Sablon, 63000 Clermont-Ferrand, France (office). *Telephone:* (4) 73-98-59-00 (office). *Fax:* (4) 73-98-59-04 (office). *E-mail:* info@michelin.com (office). *Website:* www.michelin.com (office).

ROLLINS, Kevin B., BA, MBA; American business executive; *Senior Advisor, TPG Capital LP;* b. 15 Nov. 1952; ed Brigham Young Univ.; Vice-Pres. and Pnr, Bain & Co. (man. consultants) –1996; joined Dell Inc. and held positions successively as Pres. Dell Americas, Vice-Chair. Dell Inc., Pres. and COO, Pres., CEO and Dir 2004–07 (resgnd); Sr Advisor, TPG Capital LP 2007–; Chair. American Enterprise Inst.; mem. Bd of Dirs Avaya, Inc., Deseret Management Corpn; mem. US Pres.'s Advisory Cttee for Trade Policy and Negotiation, US Business Council, Computer Systems Policy Project; mem. Pres.'s Leadership Council, Brigham Young Univ., Marriott School Nat. Advisory Council; inducted into Hall of Fame, Utah Information Tech. Asscn (UITA) 2004. *Address:* TPG Capital LP, 301 Commerce Street, Suite 3300, Fort Worth, TX 76102, USA (office). *Telephone:* (817) 871-4000 (office). *Fax:* (817) 871-4010 (office). *Website:* www .texaspacificgroup.com (office).

ROLLINS, Theodore Walter (Sonny); American jazz musician (tenor saxophone); b. 7 Sept. 1930, New York, NY; s. of Walter Rollins and Valborg Solomon; m. 1st Dawn Finney 1956 (divorced); m. 2nd Lucille Pearson 1959 (died 2004); ed High School, New York; began rehearsing while in high school, with Thelonious Monk; recorded with Bud Powell 1949; wrote standards 'Airegin' and 'Oleo' recorded with Miles Davis 1953; played and recorded with Clifford Brown/Max Roach 1955; took sabbatical playing on Williamsburg Bridge, New York 1959–61; scored and played music for film Alfie 1966; has appeared in Jazz Heritage series, Smithsonian Inst. and at Newport Jazz Festival; numerous concert tours in Europe and Far East; annual concert tours of Europe, Japan, USA with Concert Orchestra 1973–; mem. American Acad. of Arts and Sciences 2010–; Dr hc (Bard Coll.) 1993, Hon. DMus (Long Island Univ.) 1998, (New England Conservatory of Music) 2002, Hon. DArts (Wesleyan Univ.) 1998, Hon. DFA (Duke Univ.) 1999; Guggenheim Fellow 1972, Lifetime Achievement Award, Tufts Univ. 1996, Lifetime Achievement Award, Nat. Asscn of Recording Arts and Science 2005, Grammy Award for Best Jazz Instrumental Solo (for Why Was I Born?) 2006, Edward MacDowell Medal 2010, Honoree, 34th Annual Kennedy Center Honors 2011, Jazz Journalists Asscn Award 2011. *Recordings include:* albums: Sonny Rollins with the Modern Jazz Quartet 1953, Moving Out 1954, Work Time 1955, Sonny Rollins Plus 4 1956, Tenor Madness 1956, Saxophone Colossus 1956, Rollins Plays for Bird 1956, Tour de Force 1956, Sonny Boy 1956, Sonny Rollins, Vol. 1 1957, Way Out West 1957, Sonny Rollins, Vol. 2 1957, The Sound of Sonny 1957, Newk's Time 1957, A Night at the Village 1957, Sonny Rollins Plays/Thad Jones Plays 1957, Freedom Suite 1958, Brass/Trio 1958, Sonny Rollins and the Big Brass 1958, Sonny Rollins and the Contemporary Leaders 1958, Sonny Rollins 'At Music Inn' (split LP with Teddy Edwards At Falcon Lair with Joe Castro) 1959, The Bridge 1962, What's New? 1962, Our Man in Jazz 1962, Sonny Meets Hawk! 1963, Now's the Time 1964, The Standard Sonny Rollins 1964, There Will Never Be Another You 1965, Sonny Rollins on Impulse! 1965, Alfie 1966, East Broadway Run Down 1966, Next Album 1972, Horn Culture 1973, Sonny Rollins in Japan 1973, The Cutting Edge 1974, Nucleus 1975, The Way I Feel 1976, Easy Living 1977, Don't Stop the Carnival 1978, Don't Ask 1979, Love at First Sight 1980, No Problem 1981, Reel Life 1982, Sunny Days, Starry Nights 1984, The Solo Album 1985, G-Man 1986, Dancing in the Dark 1987, Falling in Love with Jazz 1989, Here's to the People 1991, Old Flames 1993, Sonny Rollins + 3 1996, Global Warming 1998, This Is What I Do 2000, Without a Song: The 9/11 Concert 2001, Sonny, Please 2006, Road Shows 2008, Road Shows Vol. 2 2011. *Address:* c/o Ted Kurland Associates, 173 Brighton Avenue, Boston, MA 02134-2003, USA (office); Route 9G, Germantown, NY 12526, USA. *Telephone:* (617) 254-0007 (office); (518) 537-6112 (office). *E-mail:* ted@tedkurland.com (office). *Website:* www.tedkurland .com (office). www.sonnyrollins.com. *Fax:* (518) 537-4342 (office).

ROMAHI, Seif al-Wady, PhD; Jordanian diplomacy expert and human resources development consultant; b. 28 Dec. 1938, Muzera, Palestine; s. of Ahmed al-Hajj Abdul-Nabi; m. Zaka al-Masri 1971; one s. two d.; ed Lebanese State Univ., Univ. Coll. London, Southern Illinois Univ., USA and Univ. of Birmingham, UK; Admin. Adviser to Cabinet of Prime Minister of Jordan Wasfi al-Tall; Area Educ. Supt, Ministry of Educ., Qatar 1960–64; seconded to Office of the Ruler of Abu Dhabi, Pres. UAE 1968–73; Rep. League of Arab States in USA 1970–72; Assoc. Prof. of Middle East Studies and Political Science, Southern Ill. Univ., USA 1971–72; Minister Plenipotentiary, Foreign Ministry, UAE 1973–91, set up UAE Embassies in Beijing, Tripoli, Tokyo and Seoul; Founder and Prof., Diplomatic Training Centre, UAE 1980–82; Co-founder and Chief Rep. Nat. Bank of Abu Dhabi in Japan 1982–86; Prof. of Int. Law, Diplomacy and Islamic Civilization, Int. Univ. of Japan, Sophia Univ., Tokyo; Founder, Gen. Man. Arab Int. Co. for Investment and Educ. 1988–91, Chair. 1990–94; founder Applied Science Univ., Amman, Jordan, Prof. of Diplomacy and Int. Law 1990–95, American Univ. of the Middle East in Jordan, House of Euro-Arab Experts in Jordan 1992– (also Chair.); Co-Founder Islamic-American Univ. Coll., Chicago; planner Jordan Women's Univ. (now Petra Univ.), Zaitouneh Jordanian Univ., Graduate Studies Univ. in Jordan, Middle East Acad. for Aviation; contrib. (with HE Dr Abdul-Razzaq al-Sanhouri) to writing the Constitution of UAE; co-author Abu Dhabi Public Service Code; Co-Chair. Planning Cttee for British Univ. of Dubai; consultant for establishment of RAK British Univ., UAE 2002–; mem. Acad. of Islamic Research (India), Japanese Acad. of Middle East Studies, Middle East Studies Asscn of USA and Canada, Middle East Inst., Washington, DC, British Soc. for Middle East Studies, Japanese Assoc. for Middle Eastern Studies; Order of Independence (Jordan) 1979; Hon. PhD (World Univ.) 1985. *Publications:* Economics and Political Evolution in Arabian Gulf States 1973, The Palestinian Question and International Law 1979, Studies in International Law and Diplomatic Practice 1980, Arab Customs and Manners 1984; contribs to professional and scientific journals. *Leisure interests:* calligraphy, art, travel, poetry, listening to music, painting and drawing, reading, research. *Address:* PO Box 35087 Hotel Jordan, Amman 11185, Jordan. *Telephone:* (6) 5537028 (home). *Fax:* (6) 5528328 (home). *E-mail:* seif-romahi@yahoo.co.uk.

ROMAN, Martin, LLB; Czech business executive; b. 1969, Havířov; ed Faculty of Law, Charles Univ., Prague, St Gallen Univ., Switzerland, Karl-Ruprechtsuniversität, Heidelberg, Germany; Sales Dir Wolf Bergstrasse ČR s.r.o. 1992–94; CEO Janka Radotín a.s. 1994–99, Chair. 1998–99; Chair. and Gen. Dir ŠKODA a.s., Pilsen 1999–2000, Chair. and CEO ŠKODA Holding 2000–04; Dir, Chair. and CEO, ČEZ a.s. 2004–13.

ROMAN, Petre, PhD, DTech; Romanian academic and politician; b. 22 July 1946, Bucharest; s. of Valter Roman and Hortensia Roman; m. Mioara Georgescu; two d.; ed Petru Groza High School, Bucharest, Bucharest Polytechnic Inst. and Nat. Polytechnic Inst. of Toulouse, France; fmrly Prof. and Head of Dept Hydraulics Dept, Faculty of Hydroenergy, Bucharest Polytechnic Inst.; Founding mem. Nat. Salvation Front 1989, Pres. 1992–93, renamed Democratic Party (PD) 1993–2003, Pres. 1993–2001; Prime Minister 1989–91; mem. Parl. 1992–, Chair. Defence, Public Order and Nat. Security Cttee, Chamber of Deputies 1992–96; Special Rapporteur of North Atlantic Ass. 1993–96; Co-Pres. Union of Social Democrats (USD=PD+PSDR—Party of Social Democracy in Romania) 1995–97; Senator for Bucharest (USD), Chair. of Senate 1996–97, Senator for Bucharest (PD), Chair. of Senate 1997–99, Senator 2000–; cand. in presidential elections 1996; Acting Pres. Parl. Ass. of the Black Sea Econ. Cooperation 1997–98; Deputy Prime Minister, Minister of Foreign Affairs 1999–2000; Founder and Chair. Democratic Force of Romania (Forţa Democrâta din România) (FDR) 2004; mem. Partidul Naţional

Liberal (PNL); Grand Cross of Merit (France), Grand Cross of Nat. Order of Repub. of Ecuador, High Award of Repub. of Colombia; Traian Vuia Award, Romanian Acad. 1990. *Publications:* The Nuclear Energy File: Risk and Security (co-author) 1978, Water and Pollution (co-author) 1978, Introduction to the Physics of Fluid Pollution 1981, The Movement of the Compressible Fluids with Heat Transfer 1982, Special Problems in Hydromechanics (co-author) 1985, Hydrology and the Protection of Water Quality 1989, Fluid Mechanics 1989, Dynamic Hydrology (co-author) 1990, Le devoir de liberté 1992, Freedom as Duty 1994, Romania incotro? 1995, Political Notebook: A Political Vision on Romania's Development Strategy at the Threshold of Centuries 1999. *Leisure interests:* sports, hunting, reading, hiking. *Address:* Senatul României, Piata Revolutiei nr. 1, sector 1, Bucharest, Romania (office). *Telephone:* (21) 3150200 (office). *E-mail:* webmaster@senat.ro (office).

ROMANEK, Mark; American music video director and film director; b. 18 Sept. 1959, Chicago; ed Ithaca Coll., New York,; early directing experience as second Asst Dir for Brian De Palma on Home Movies 1980; worked on numerous music videos with Satellite Films; music videos Closer (Nine Inch Nails) and Bedtime Story (Madonna) now held in perm. collection of Museum of Modern Art, New York; also dir of numerous TV commercials; Dir Anonymous Content (production co.). *Music videos include:* Free Your Mind (En Vogue) 1992, Are You Gonna Go My Way (Lenny Kravitz) 1993, Rain (Madonna) 1993, Closer (Nine Inch Nails) 1994, Scream (Michael and Janet Jackson) (Grammy Award for Best Short Form Video 1996) 1995, Got 'Til It's Gone (Janet Jackson) (Grammy Award for Best Short Form Video 1998) 1997, Hurt (Johnny Cash) 2002, 99 Problems (Jay-Z) 2004, Speed of Sound (Coldplay) 2005. *Films:* Static 1985, One Hour Photo 2002, Never Let Me Go 2010. *Address:* Anonymous Content, 3532 Hayden Ave, Culver City, CA 90232, USA (office). *Telephone:* (310) 558-3667 (office). *E-mail:* mark@markromanek.com (office). *Website:* www.anonymouscontent.com (office); www.markromanek.com (office).

ROMANI, Roger; French politician; *Senator of Paris (Ile-de-France);* b. 25 Aug. 1934, Tunis, Tunisia; s. of Dominique Romani and Madeleine Santelli; m. Joelle Fortier 1971; began career as an asst dir with ORTF; various positions in pvt. offices of Govt Ministers of Posts and Telecommunications, of Information, of State, of the Prime Minister 1967–71; Conseiller de Paris (Paris-Majorité-2ème secteur, then UDP-3ème, then RPR-5ème secteur) 1971–2001; adviser, Office of Jacques Chirac (Minister of Agric. and of Devt 1973, of Interior 1974, Prime Minister 1974–76); Deputy to Mayor of Paris 1977–2001; mem. Conseil Régional, Ile-de-France 1977; Senator of Paris (Ile-de-France) 1977–93, 2002–, Vice-Pres. RPR Group in Senate 1983–86, Pres. 1986–88, Vice-Pres. Group of RPR, later of Union pour un Mouvement Populaire 2002–, mem. Comm. of Foreign Affairs, of Defence and the Armed Forces, Titular mem. Higher Council of the Mil. Reserve 2004–; Vice-Pres. Conseil général de Paris (Departmental Ass.) 1982–2001; Pres. Group 'Rassemblement pour Paris' 1983–2001; Nat. Sec. RPR 1984–86, mem. Political Cttee 1998–2000; adviser to fmr Prime Minister Chirac 1986–88; Minister-Del. for Relations with the Senate 1993–95; Minister for Relations with Parl. 1995–97; adviser to Pres. Chirac 1997–2002; Hon. Pres. Mouvement nat. des élus locaux. *Address:* Sénat, Palais du Luxembourg, Casier postal, 75291 Paris Cedex 06, France (office). *Telephone:* 1-42-34-20-00 (office). *Fax:* 1-42-34-26-77 (office). *E-mail:* r.romani@senat.fr (office). *Website:* www.senat.fr/senfic/romani_roger59312e.html (office).

ROMANO, Sergio, LLD; Italian diplomatist and historian; b. 7 July 1929, Vicenza; s. of Romano Romano and Egle Bazzolo; m. Mary Anne Heinze 1954; two s. one d.; ed Liceo C. Beccaria, Milan, Univ. of Milan, Univ. of Chicago; foreign corresp. and film critic for Italian radio and newspapers, Paris, London and Vienna 1948–52; entered Italian Foreign Service 1954, Vice-Consul, Innsbruck, Austria 1955, Sec., Embassy in London 1958–64, Pvt. Sec. to Minister of Foreign Affairs 1964; mem. Diplomatic Staff of the Pres. of the Repub. 1965–68; Counsellor (later Minister), Embassy in Paris 1968–77, Dir-Gen. of Cultural Relations, Ministry of Foreign Affairs 1977–83; Guest Prof., Faculty of Political Sciences, Univ. of Florence 1981–83; Perm. Rep. to Atlantic Council, Brussels 1983–85, Amb. to USSR 1985–89 (resgnd); currently columnist for Corriere della Sera (newspaper) and Corriere del Ticino (newspaper), also contributes opinion articles to Aspenia, Il Politico, Corriere del Ticino; fmr Visiting Prof., Harvard Univ., Univ. of California, Berkeley; Prof. of History of Int. Relations, Bocconi Univ. 1992–98; mem. Ateneo Veneto, Venice, Accad. Olimpica, Vicenza; Corresp. mem. Royal Acad. of Brussels; Pres. Balzan Foundation Prize Cttee –2009; Cavaliere di Gran Croce, Commdr Légion d'honneur, other European and Latin-American honours; Dr hc (Inst. d'Etudes Politiques, Paris, Univ. of Macerat, Inst. of World History, Russian Acad. of Sciences). *Publications include:* Crispi, Progetto per una Dittatura 1973, 1986, La Quarta Sponda 1977, Histoire de l'Italie du Risorgimento à nos jours 1977, Italie 1979, Giuseppe Volpi, Industria e Finanza tra Giolitti e Mussolini 1979, La Francia dal 1870 ai nostri giorni 1981, Benedetto Croce, La Philosophie comme histoire de la Liberté (ed.) 1983, La Lingua e il Tempo 1983, Giovanni Gentile, La Filosofia al Potere 1984, Florence, Toscane 1988, Giolitti, Lo Stile del Potere 1989, Disegni per una Esposizione 1989, L'Italia scappata di mano 1993, Cinquant'anni di storia mondiale: La pace e le guerre da Yalta ai nostri giorni 1995 (Romanian edn 1999), Lo scambio ineguale: Italia e Stati Uniti da Wilson a Clinton 1995, Le Italie parallele 1996, Lettera ad un amico ebreo 1997 (Lithuanian edn 2001, German edn 2007), Storia d'Italia dal Risorgimento ai nostri giorni 1998 (Serbian edn 2007), Confessioni di un revisionista 1998, I luoghi della storia 2000, La pace perduta 2001, Un'amicizia difficile, conversazioni con Gilles Martinet su due secoli di relazioni italo-francesi 2001, I volti della storia 2001, Memorie di un conservatore 2002, Il rischio americano 2003, Giovanni Gentile 2004, Anatomia del terrore. Colloquio con Guido Olimpio 2004, Europa, storia di un'idea (Serbian edn 2009), Dall'impero all'unione 2004 (Serbian edn 2009), La quarta sponda: La guerra di Libia 1911–1912 2005, Libera Chiesa. Libero Stato? 2005 (French edn 2007), Saremo moderni? Diario di un anno 2007 (French edn 2007), Con gli occhi dell'Islam 2007, Vademecum di storia dell'Italia, 2009 unita 2009. *Address:* via P. Verri 6, 20121 Milan, Italy. *Telephone:* (02) 76000870. *Fax:* (02) 76014719. *E-mail:* romanoser@gmail.com.

ROMANOV, Piotr Vasilyevich, DTechSc; Russian politician; b. 21 July 1943, Kansk, Krasnoyarsk territory; m.; three c.; ed Siberia Inst. of Tech.; engineer, then chief of workshop, Chief Engineer, Dir-Gen. Krasnoyarsky Production Unit of Mil.

Chemical Enterprise Enisey 1967–96; mem. Russian Council of Fed. 1993; Co-Chair. Russian Nat. Sobor 1992–93, mem. Org. Cttee All-Russia Congress of Russian Communists, Co-Chair. Co-ordination Council All-Russia Congress of Russian Communists 1994–; mem. State Duma 1995–, currently First Deputy Chair. of State Cttee on Ecology, mem. Comm. on Problems of North Caucasus; Sec. Cen. Cttee CP of Russian Fed. 1997–; mem. Russian Acad. of Eng Sciences; Hero of Socialist Labour; Distinguished Chemist of Russian Fed.; Order of Lenin; Sergei Radonezhsky Medal. *Publications:* I Am Piotr Romanov: About the Times and Myself 1995, With a Son's Care about Russia 1995, The Sovereign Cross 1997. *Leisure interests:* winter sports, gathering mushrooms and berries, gardening. *Address:* State Duma, Okhotny Ryad 1, 103265 Moscow (office); pr. Mira 108, 660017 Krasnoyarsk, Russia. *Telephone:* (495) 292-18-10 (office). *Fax:* (495) 292-40-58 (office). *Website:* www.duma.gov.ru (office).

ROMEO, HE Cardinal Paolo, STL, JCD; Italian ecclesiastic and diplomatist; *Archbishop of Palermo;* b. 20 Feb. 1938, Acireale, Prov. of Catania, Sicily; ed Pontifical Gregorian Univ. and Pontifical Lateran Univ., Rome; ordained priest, Diocese of Acireale 1961; carried out pastoral ministry as Asst to the Scouts Group 'Roma IX' in Collegio San Giuseppe in Piazza di Spagna and Diocesan Asst of Silenziosi Operai della Croce asscn; called to Pontifical Ecclesiastical Acad. 1964, entered diplomatic service of the Holy See 1967, worked in nunciatures in the Philippines, Belgium and Luxemburg and EC, Venezuela, and Rwanda and Burundi, called to Council for Public Affairs of the Church in Secr. of State 1967; worked as director of Casa Internazionale del Clero and was Regional Asst for the Lazio of the Associazione Genitori Scuole Cattoliche (AGESC); recalled to Vatican Secr. of State to monitor the life of the Catholic community in countries of Latin America and activities of Latin American Episcopal Conf. 1976–83; Titular Archbishop of Vulturia 1983–; Apostolic Nuncio to Haiti 1983–90, to Colombia 1990–99, to Canada 1999–2001, to Italy and San Marino 2001–06; Archbishop of Palermo, Sicily 2006–; Pres. Sicilian Episcopal Conf. 2007–; cr. Cardinal (Cardinal-Priest of Santa Maria Odigitria dei Siciliani) 2010; participated in Papal Conclave 2005, 2013. *Address:* Archdiocese of Palermo, Corso Vittorio Emanuele 461, 90134 Palermo, Italy (office). *Telephone:* (091) 6077111 (office). *Fax:* (091) 6113642 (office). *E-mail:* info@diocesipa.it (office). *Website:* www.diocesipa.it (office).

ROMER, Christina Duckworth, BA, PhD; American economist, academic and fmr government official; *Professor of Economics, University of California, Berkeley;* b. 25 Dec. 1958, Alton, Ill.; m. David Romer; three c.; ed Glen Oak High School, Canton, Ohio, Coll. of William and Mary, Massachusetts Inst. of Tech.; Asst Prof. of Econs, Woodrow Wilson School, Princeton Univ. 1985–88; Acting Assoc. Prof. of Econs, Univ. of California, Berkeley 1988–90, Assoc. Prof. of Econs 1990–93, Class of 1957 Prof. of Econs 1997–2009, 2010–; Chair., Council of Econ. Advisers, The White House 2009–10; Fellow, American Acad. of Arts and Sciences 2004; Research Assoc., Program in Monetary Econs, Nat. Bureau of Econ. Research 1990–, Co-Dir 2003–; mem. Cttee on Honors and Awards, American Econ. Asscn 2004–, Vice-Pres. 2006; Grad. Fellowship Research Grant, NSF 1981–84, Alfred P. Sloan Doctoral Fellowship 1984–85, Research Grant 1987–90, Nat. Bureau of Econ. Research Olin Fellowship 1987–88, Alfred P. Sloan Research Fellowship 1989–91, Presidential Young Investigator Award 1989–94, John Simon Guggenheim Memorial Foundation Fellowship 1998–99, Faculty Award for Women Scientists and Engineers 1991–96, Research Grant 2000–03, 2006–09, Distinguished Teaching Award, Univ. of California, Berkeley 1994, Social Science Research Council Grant 1985–86. *Publications:* as co-ed.: Reducing Inflation: Motivation and Strategy 1997. *Address:* Department of Economics, University of California, 549 Evans Hall #3880, Berkeley, CA 94720-3880, USA (office). *Telephone:* (510) 642-4317 (office). *Fax:* (510) 642-6615 (office). *E-mail:* cromer@econ.berkeley.edu (office). *Website:* www.econ.berkeley.edu/econ (office).

ROMER, Paul Michael, BA, PhD; American economist and academic; *Professor of Economics, Stern School of Business, New York University;* b. 7 Nov. 1955, Denver, Colo; s. of Roy Romer and Beatrice Romer (née Miller); m. Virginia Langmuir; one s. one d.; ed Univ. of Chicago; Asst Prof. of Econs, Univ. of Rochester 1982–88; Prof. of Econs, Univ. of Chicago 1988–90; Fellow, Center for Advanced Study in Behavioral Sciences, Stanford Univ. 1989–90, Prof., Stanford Univ. Grad. School of Business 1996–2007, Ralph Landau Sr Fellow, Stanford Inst. for Econ. Policy Research 1997–, Sr Fellow, Hoover Inst. 1995–; Prof. of Econs, Univ. of California, Berkeley 1990–96; Henry Kaufman Visiting Prof., Stern School of Business, New York Univ. 2010–, Prof. of Econs 2011–; Founder, Aplia Inc. 2000–; Research Assoc., Nat. Bureau of Econ. Research 1987; Fellow, Econometric Soc. 1990; mem. American Econs Asscn, American Acad. of Arts and Sciences 2000; Horst Claus Recktenwald Prize in Econs 2002. *Address:* NYU Stern School of Business, Henry Kaufman Management Center, 44 West Fourth Street, New York, NY 10012, USA (office). *Telephone:* (212) 998-0100 (office). *E-mail:* promer@stern.nyu.edu (office). *Website:* www.stern.nyu.edu (office).

ROMER, Roy R., BS, LLB; American education administrator and fmr politician; *Special Advisor, College Board Advocacy and Policy Center;* b. 31 Oct. 1928, Garden City, Kan.; s. of Irving Rudolph and Margaret Elizabeth Romer (née Snyder); m. Beatrice Miller 1952; five s. two d.; ed Colo State Univ., Univ. of Colo, Yale Univ.; farmed in Colo 1942–52; admitted to Colo Bar 1952; ind. practice, Denver 1955–66; mem. Colo House of Reps 1958–62, Colo Senate 1962–66; Commr for Agric. for Colo 1975; State Treas. 1977–86; Gov. of Colo 1987–98; Supt of Schools, LA Unified School Dist 2001–06; Chair. Strong American Schools (non-profit) 2007–09; Special Advisor, Coll. Board Advocacy and Policy Center 2009–; Owner, Arapahoe Aviation Co., Colo Flying Acad., Geneva Basin Ski Area, Chain Farm Implement and Industrial Equipment Stores in Colo, Fla and Va; Gov. Small Business Council; fmr mem. Agric. Advisory Cttee, Colo Bd of Agric., Colo Bar Asscn; Chair. Nat. Educ. Goals Panel, Democratic Govs' Asscn 1991, Democratic Nat. Cttee. *Address:* College Board Advocacy and Policy Center, 45 Columbus Avenue, New York, NY 10023, USA (office). *E-mail:* cbadvocacy@collegeboard.org (office). *Website:* www.advocacy.collegeboard.org (office).

ROMERO, Pepe; American classical guitarist; b. 3 Aug. 1944, Málaga, Spain; s. of Celedonio Romero and Angelita Romero (née Gallego); m. 1st Kristine Eddy 1965; m. 2nd Carissa Sugg 1987; one s. three d.; ed various music acads in USA, including Music Acad. of the West; began career in Seville, Spain, as part of Romero Quartet 1951, re-formed in USA 1960; averages 200–250 concerts a year world-wide; recordings number more than 50 solos, plus others with the Romero

Quartet and various orchestras; Artist-in-Residence, Univ. of Southern Calif. 1972, Univ. of Calif., San Diego 1984. *Publications:* Guitar Method, Guitar Transcriptions for 1, 2 and 4 guitars. *Leisure interests:* photography, chess. *Address:* c/o Tim Fox, Columbia Artists Management, Inc., 1790 Broadway, New York, NY 10019, USA (office). *E-mail:* TFox@cami.com (office). *Website:* www.peperomero.com (office).

ROMERO-BARCELÓ, Carlos Antonio, BA, LLB, JD; American politician, lawyer and real estate executive; b. 4 Sept. 1932, San Juan, Puerto Rico; s. of Antonio Romero-Moreno and Josefina Barceló-Bird; m. 1st; two s.; m. 2nd Kathleen Donnelly 1966; one s. one d.; ed Phillips Exeter Acad., NH, Yale Univ., Univ. of Puerto Rico; admitted to the Bar, San Juan, Puerto Rico 1956; Pres. Citizens for State 51 1965–67; Mayor of San Juan 1969–77; Pres. New Progressive Party 1974–86, Chair. 1989; Pres. Nat. League of Cities 1974–75; Gov. of Puerto Rico 1977–85; Chair. Southern Govs Conf. 1980–81; Resident Commr in Washington, DC 1993–2001 (serving in US Congress); in pvt. practice 2001–; mem. Council on Foreign Affairs 1985–, Int. Platform Asscn 1985–, League of United Latin American Citizens (LULAC); Hon. LLD (Univ. of Bridgeport, Conn.) 1977; James J. and Jane Hoey Award for Interracial Justice, Catholic Interracial Council of NY 1977; Special Gold Medal Award, Spanish Inst., New York 1979; US Attorney-General's Medal 1981. *Publications:* Statehood is for the Poor 1973, Statehood for Puerto Rico, Vital Speeches of the Day 1979, Puerto Rico, USA: The Case for Statehood, Foreign Affairs 1980, The Soviet Threat to the Americas, Vital Speeches of the Day 1981. *Leisure interests:* reading, horse riding, tennis, swimming, water sports, golf. *Address:* Centro de Seguros, Building 701, Ponce de León Avenue # 412, Miramar, PR 00907 (office); PO Box 364351, San Juan, PR 00936, Puerto Rico. *Telephone:* (787) 724-0526; (787) 724-0511. *Fax:* (787) 724-0959 (office). *E-mail:* rbarcelo@prtc.net (office).

ROMERO MENA, Gen. Carlos Humberto; Salvadorean army officer and fmr head of state; b. Chalatenango; s. of late José María Romero and of Victoria Mena de Romero; m. Gloria Guerrero de Romero; two s. two d.; ed Capitán General Gerardo Barrios Mil. School, Escuela de Armas y Servicios, Escuela de Comando y Estado Mayor Manuel Enrique Araujo; Section Commd., Adjutant and Paymaster, Capt.-Gen. Gerardo Barrios Mil. School and other mil. bodies; Regt Commdr Cavalry; Second Officer 1st Infantry Regt; Sub-Dir Escuela de Armas y Servicios and Head Dept Personnel, Gen. Staff Armed Forces; Mil. Attaché to Embassy, Mexico; Head of Staff of Presidency of Repub.; Minister of Defence and Public Security; Pres. Cen. American Defense Council 1973–77; Pres. of Repub. of El Salvador 1977–79 (overthrown in coup); del. 7th Conf. of American Armies 1966, 2nd Conf. of Cen. American Defense Council 1960, 6th Conf. of American Intelligence Officials 1967; Partido de Conciliación Nacional.

ROMERO ORELLANA, Gen. Otto Alejandro; Salvadorean politician and army officer; b. 4 April 1955, Chalatenango; ed Escuele Militar Capt. Gen. Gerardo Barrios; fmr Section Commdr, First Bn, Oscar Osorio Artillery Brigade; Exec. Sec., Ministry of Nat. Defence 1994; Commdr, Third Military Zone, Infantry Brigade, Domingo Monterrosa 2002; Gen. Inspector of Armed Forces 2002, Minister of Nat. Defence –2007; several nat. and int. decorations. *Address:* c/o Ministry of National Defence, Alameda Dr Manuel Enrique Araújo, Km 5, Carretera a Santa Tecla, San Salvador, El Salvador (office).

ROMETTY, Virginia (Ginni) M., BSc; American business executive; *Chairman, President and CEO, International Business Machines Corporation;* b. 1958; ed Robert R. McCormick School of Eng and Applied Science, Northwestern Univ.; began career with General Motors Corpn; joined International Business Machines Corpn (IBM), becoming Gen. Man. Global Insurance and Financial Services Sector, Gen. Man. IBM Global Services, Americas, later becoming Man. Partner, Business Consulting Services –2005, Sr Vice-Pres. Enterprise Business Services 2005–10, Group Exec., IBM Sales, Marketing and Strategy 2010–11, Pres. and CEO Jan. 2012–, Chair. Oct. 2012–; mem. Bd of Dirs American International Group (AIG); mem. Council on Foreign Relations, Bd of Trustees Northwestern Univ., Bd of Overseers Memorial Sloan-Kettering Cancer Center, Bd of Dirs APQC (not-for-profit business research organization); Columbia Business School's Deming Cup Cttee; named by Time magazine amongst Global Business Influential 2002, ranked by Fortune magazine amongst the 50 Most Powerful Women in Business in the US (15th) 2005, (16th) 2006, (17th) 2007, (14th) 2008, (11th) 2009, (eighth) 2010, (seventh) 2011, (first) 2012, Carl Sloane Award, Asscn of Man. Consulting Firms 2006, ranked by Forbes magazine amongst The World's 100 Most Powerful Women (97th) 2008, (70th) 2009, (82nd) 2011, (15th) 2012, (12th) 2013, and amongst The World's Most Powerful People (56th) 2013. *Leisure interest:* scuba diving. *Address:* International Business Machines Corporation (IBM), Somers, NY 10589, USA (office). *Telephone:* (914) 766-2100 (office). *E-mail:* grometty@us.ibm.com (office). *Website:* www.us.ibm.com (office).

ROMNEY, (Willard) Mitt, BA, JD, MBA; American business executive, politician and fmr state official; b. 12 March 1947, Detroit, Mich.; s. of the late George W. Romney (fmr Gov. of Mich.) and Lenore Romney; m. Ann Romney 1969; five s.; ed Cranbrook School, Bloomfield Hills, Mich., Stanford Univ., Brigham Young Univ., Harvard Univ. Business School, Harvard Law School; served as a Mormon missionary in France; Vice-Pres. Bain & Co. (man. consulting firm) 1978–84, Co-founder Bain Capital (investment firm) 1984–99, CEO (interim) Bain & Co. 1990–92; CEO Salt Lake City Organizing Cttee for 2002 Winter Olympics 1999–2002; Gov. of Mass. 2003–07; unsuccessful cand. for Republican Party presidential nomination 2007–08, unsuccessful cand. (Republican) for Pres. of US 2012; Chair. Exec. Cttee Solamere Capital LLC, Boston 2013–; f. Free and Strong America PAC, Inc. 2008; mem. Bd of Dirs Marriott International 1992–2002, 2009–; Hon. Dr of Business (Univ. of Utah) 1999, Hon. LLD (Bentley Coll.) 2002, Hon. Dr of Public Admin (Suffolk Univ. Law School) 2004, Hon. Dr of Public Service (Hillsdale Coll.) 2007; inaugural Truce Ideal Award for his role in the 2002 Winter Olympics 2004, Canterbury Medal, The Becket Fund for Religious Liberty (shared with his wife) 2008. *Publications:* Turnaround: Crisis, Leadership, and the Olympic Games (with Timothy Robinson) 2004, No Apology: The Case for American Greatness 2010. *Address:* Solamere Capital LLC, 137 Newbury Street, Seventh Floor, Boston, MA 02116, USA (office). *Telephone:* (857) 362-9205 (office). *Website:* www.solameregroup.com (office); www.mittromney.com.

ROMULO, Alberto (Bert) G., BSc, BL; Philippine politician; *Secretary of Foreign Affairs;* b. Camiling, Tarlac province; s. of Carlos P. Romulo; m. Rosie Lovely Tecson; five c.; ed De La Salle Univ., Universidad de Madrid, Spain; fmr Sec. of Budget and Man., Chair. Devt Budget Co-ordinating Cttee, mem. Monetary Bd; fmr Senator, Majority Leader; Exec. Sec. –2004; Sec. of Foreign Affairs 2004–; Gintong Ama Award, Philippines Free Press Most Outstanding Senator. *Address:* Department of Foreign Affairs, DFA Building, 2330 Roxas Blvd, Pasay City, 1330 Metro Manila, The Philippines (office). *Telephone:* (2) 8344000 (office). *Fax:* (2) 8321597 (office). *E-mail:* webmaster@dfa.gov.ph (office). *Website:* www.dfa.gov.ph (office).

RONALD, Mark H., BA, BS, MS; American aerospace and defence industry executive; ed Bucknell Univ., Polytechnic Inst. of New York; served as Vice-Pres., Program Man. Litton Industries, Amecon Div.; fmr mem. Bd of Dirs, Pres. and COO AEL Industries; mem. Bd of Dirs and COO BAE Systems plc, Pres. and CEO BAE Systems, Inc., USA 2003–06, Chair. 2007; mem. Bd of Dirs Cobham plc, Alliant Tech Systems (ATK), DynCorp International LLC 2007–10; mem. Exec. Cttee and Bd of Govs, Aerospace Industries Asscn; mem. Bd of Govs Electronic Industries Alliance; Hon. CBE 2005; Distinguished Engineering Alumni Awards (Bucknell Univ., Polytechnic Inst. of New York), Marine Corps Scholarship Foundation Semper Fidelis Award 2005, John Curtis Sword Award 2006. *Address:* c/o BAE Systems, Inc., 1101 Wilson Blvd, Suite 2000, Arlington, VA 22209, USA.

RONALDINHO GAÚCHO, (Ronaldinho); Brazilian/Spanish professional footballer; b. (Ronaldo de Assis Moreira), 21 March 1980, Pôrto Alegre, Rio Grande do Sul; s. of the late João de Assis Moreira and of Miguelina de Assis Moreira; winger/attacking midfielder; youth player, Grêmio de Pôrto Alegre 1987–98; won World Youth Cup with Brazil Under-17 team (voted Player of the Tournament), Egypt 1997; sr career with Grêmio de Pôrto Alegre (44 appearances, 21 goals) 1998–2001, Paris Saint-Germain, France (55 appearances, 17 goals) 2001–03, FC Barcelona, Spain (145 appearances, 70 goals) 2003–08 (won La Liga 2005, 2006, Supercopa de España 2005, 2006, UEFA Champions League 2006), AC Milan, Italy 2008–11 (43 appearances, 11 goals), Clube de Regatas do Flamengo 2011–; more than 87 caps and 32 goals for Brazil 1999–, won Copa America 1999 (scoring six goals), World Cup 2002, FIFA Confederations Cup 2005, bronze medal, Olympic Games, Beijing 2008; mem. Bronze Medal-winning team, Men's Football, Olympic Games, Beijing 2008; wears No. 80 shirt; became Spanish citizen Jan. 2007; FIFA Confederations Cup Top Scorer 1999, FIFA Confederations Cup Golden Ball 1999, Rio Grande do Sul State Championship Top Scorer 1999, FIFA World Cup All-Star team 2002, named in FIFA 100 2004, EFE Trophy (best South American player in Spanish leagues) 2004, Don Balón Award (Best Foreign Player in La Liga) 2004, 2006, FIFA World Footballer of the Year 2004, 2005, UEFA Team of the Year 2004, 2005, 2006, Ballon d'Or (European Footballer of the Year) 2005, FIFPro (int. professional football players' union) World Player of the Year 2005, 2006, UEFA Club Footballer of the Year 2005–06, FIFPro World XI 2005, 2006, 2007, FIFA Club World Cup Bronze Ball Award 2006. *Address:* c/o Clube de Regatas do Flamengo, Av. Borges de Medeiros 997, Lagoa, Rio de Janeiro, RJ 22430-041, Brazil (office). *Telephone:* (21) 2159-0100 (office). *Website:* www.flamengo.com.br (office); www.ronaldinhogaucho.com (home).

RONALDO; Brazilian/Spanish professional footballer (retd); b. (Ronaldo Luiz Nazário de Lima), 22 Sept. 1976, Bento Ribeiro, Rio de Janeiro; s. of Nelio Nazário de Lima and Sonia Nazário de Lima; m.; striker; youth player, Tennis Club Valqueire 1986–89, Social Ramos Club (12 games, eight goals) 1989–90, São Cristóvão, Rio Second Div. (54 games, 36 goals) 1990–93; sr player, Cruzeiro (14 games, 12 goals) 1993–94 (won Campeonato Mineiro 1994, Brazil Cup 1993), PSV Eindhoven, Netherlands (46 games, 42 goals) 1994–96 (won Dutch Cup 1996), Barcelona, Spain (37 games, 34 goals) 1996–97 (won Copa del Rey 1997, UEFA Cup Winners' Cup 1997, Supercopa de España 1996), Inter Milan (68 games, 49 goals) 1997–2002 (won UEFA Cup 1998), Real Madrid (127 games, 83 goals) 2002–07 (won La Liga 2003, 2007, Intercontinental Cup 2002, Supercopa de España 2003), AC Milan (20 games, nine goals) 2007–08, Corinthians (31 games, 18 goals) 2009–11 (won Campeonato Paulista 2009, Copa do Brasil 2009), retd 2011; mem. Brazilian nat. team (97 int. caps, 62 goals) 1994–2006, won World Cup (aged 17) 1994, 2002 (winner Golden Boot), Bronze medal, Summer Olympics, Atlanta 1996, won Copa America 1997, 1999, FIFA Confederations Cup 1997; Supercopa Libertadores Top Scorer 1993/94, Campeonato Mineiro Top Scorer 1993/94, Campeonato Mineiro Team of The Year 1994, Eredivisie Top Scorer 1994/95, La Liga Top Scorer 1996/97, 2003/04, European Golden Boot 1996/97, Don Balón Award (La Liga Foreign Player of the Year) 1996/97, Copa América Final Most Valuable Player (MVP) 1997, Copa América MVP 1997, Confederations Cup All-Star Team 1997, Cup Winners' Cup Final MVP 1997, Cup Winners' Cup Top Goal Scorer 1996/97, IFFHS World's Top Goal Scorer of the Year 1997, UEFA MVP 1997/98, Serie A Player of the Year 1997/98, Serie A Foreign Player of the Year 1997/98, UEFA Best Forward 1997/98, Bravo Award 1995, 1997, 1998, FIFA World Cup Golden Ball 1998, UEFA Cup Final MVP 1998, Copa América Top Scorer 1999, Copa América All-Star Team 1997, 1999, FIFA World Player of the Year 1996, 1997, 2002, Ballon d'Or 1997, 2002, World Soccer Magazine World Player of The Year 1996, 1997, 2002, Onze d'Or 1997, 2002, FIFA World Cup Silver Ball 2002, named in FIFA 100 2004, FIFA World Cup All-Star Team 1998, 2002, FIFA World Cup Final MVP 2002, FIFA World Cup Top Scorer 2002, Intercontinental Cup MVP 2002, UEFA Team of the Year 2002, Laureus Comeback of the Year 2002, Strogaolo De Legendary Award 2002, BBC Sports Personality of the Year Overseas Personality 2002, La Liga South American Player of the Year 1996/97, 2002/03, Golden Foot 2006, inducted into Brazilian Nat. Hall of Fame Class of 2006, Serie A Player of the Decade 1997–2007, France Football Magazine Starting in 11 of all time 2007, FIFA World Cup All-Time Scoring Leader 2008, Campeonato Paulista Best Player 2009, Goal.com Player of the Decade 2000–09 2010. *Address:* c/o Sport Club Corinthians Paulista, Estádio do Pacaembu, São Paulo, Brazil. *E-mail:* ronaldo@fobazo.com. *Website:* www.ronaldo.com.

RONALDO DOS SANTOS AVEIRO, Cristiano; Portuguese professional footballer; b. 5 Feb. 1985, Funchal, Madeira; s. of the late José Dinis Aveiro and of Maria Dolores dos Santos Aveiro; winger/striker; began career as youth player with Andorinha 1993–95, CD Nacional, Madeira 1995–97, Sporting Clube de Portugal 1997–2001; sr career with Sporting Clube de Portugal 2001–03, Manchester United (196 appearances, 84 goals) 2003–09 (won Premier League

2006/07, 2007/08, 2008/09, FA Cup 2003/04, League Cup 2005/06, 2008/09, FA Community Shield 2007, UEFA Champions League 2007/08, FIFA Club World Cup 2008), Real Madrid 2009–; mem. Portugal nat. team (68 appearances, 22 goals) 2003–; represented Portugal at Summer Olympics, Athens 2004, World Cup, Germany 2006; opened fashion boutique with one of his sisters under the name CR7 (his initials and shirt number), one in Lisbon and other in Madeira; took over from David Beckham as spokesmodel for Emporio Armani men's underwear and jeans 2010–; Officer, Order of Infante Dom Henrique, Medal of Merit, Order of the Immaculate Conception of Vila Viçosa (House of Braganza); UEFA Euro 2004 Team of the Tournament, FIFPro Special Young Player of the Year 2004–05, 2005–06, Portuguese Footballer of the Year 2007–08, UEFA Team of the Year 2003–2004, 2006–07, 2007–08, FIFPro World XI 2006–07, 2007–08, Professional Footballers' Asscn (PFA) Young Player of the Year 2006–07, PFA Players' Player of the Year 2006–07, 2007–08, PFA Fans' Player of the Year 2006–07, 2007–08, PFA Premier League Team of the Year 2005–06, 2006–07, 2007–08, 2008–09, Football Writers' Asscn Footballer of the Year 2006–07, 2007–08, Premier League Player of the Season 2006–07, 2007–08, Premier League Player of the Month Nov. 2006, Dec. 2006, Jan. 2008, March 2008, Premier League Golden Boot 2007–08, Barclays Merit Award 2007–08, European Golden Shoe 2007–08, UEFA Club Footballer of the Year 2007–08, UEFA Club Footballer of the Year 2007–08, FIFPro World Player of the Year 2007–08, Ballon d'Or 2008, 2013, FIFA Team of the Year 2008, World Soccer Player of the Year 2008. *Publication:* Moments (autobiography) 2007. *Address:* c/o FC Real Madrid, Estadio Santiago Bernabeu, Paseo de la Castellana 104, Madrid, Spain. *E-mail:* info@realmadrid.com. *Website:* www .cristianoronaldo.com; www.realmadrid.com.

RONCAGLIOLO ORBEGOSO, Rafael, MA, PhD; Peruvian political scientist, academic and politician; b. 14 Nov. 1944, Lima; s. of Nicolás Roncagliolo Aste and Susana Orbegoso; three c.; ed Pontifical Catholic Univ. of Peru; fmr Prof., Academia Diplomática del Perú; Dir Communication Studies Div., Latin American Inst. for Transnational Studies, Mexico City 1976–82; Pres. Inst. for Latin America, Lima 1982–94; Sr Policy Adviser for Andean Countries and Head of Mission to Peru, Intergovernmental Inst. for Democracy and Electoral Assistance (Int. IDEA) 2009–11; Minister of Foreign Affairs 2011–13 (resgnd); fmr consultant to numerous int. bodies including UNESCO, UNDP, IDB, Sistema Económico Latinoamericano y del Caribe, OAS and govts of USA, Italy and Germany. *Publications include:* numerous books and articles on communication, political systems and electoral analysis. *Address:* c/o Ministry of Foreign Affairs, Jirón Lampa 535, Lima 1, Peru.

RONČEVIĆ, Berislav; Croatian politician; b. 23 June 1960, Borovik; m.; Vlatka Cindori; four c.; ed Secondary Law School, Našice, Univ. of Zagreb; joined Croatian Democratic Union (Hrvatska demokratska zajednica—HDZ) 1990, mem. Našice br., HDZ 1992, Chair. 1998, Man. City Council, Našice 1992, HDZ Pres. in local parl., Našice 1998, Vice-Chair. and mem. Osijek and Baranja Ço. Subsidiary of HDZ 2000–; Head of Legal and Personnel Service, Hrvatske Šume (Forests of Croatia, forest man. co.), Našice 1990, Asst Dir Regional Dept 1995; Deputy Mayor Našice 1998–2002, Mayor 2003; mem. Sabor (Parl.) 2000–; Minister of Defence 2003–07, of Interior 2008; sentenced to four years in jail in 2010 for mismanaging state funds and abuse of power while Minister of Defence in 2004; Chair. Našice Handball Club 2000–; mem. Doris Pejačević folklore orchestra of Našice 2002–. *Leisure interests:* handball, cycling, tennis. *Address:* Croatian Democratic Union, 10000 Zagreb, trg Žrtava fašizma 4, Croatia (office). *Telephone:* (1) 4553000 (office). *Fax:* (1) 4552600 (office). *E-mail:* hdz@hdz.hr (office). *Website:* www.hdz.hr (office).

RONG, Zhijian, (Larry Yung Chi Kin); Chinese business executive; b. 1942, Shanghai; s. of Rong Yiren; m., three c.; ed Tianjin Univ.; began career as intern in hydraulic power plant near Changbai Mountain, Jilin Prov.; co-founded Elcap Electronics Plant, Hong Kong 1978; co-founded Automation Design Co. Ltd, Calif., USA 1982; joined CITIC Pacific Ltd as Vice-Pres., Hong Kong 1986, Dir 1990, Chair., Pres. and Man. Dir, also Chair. Audit Cttee, Exec. Dir CITIC Group –2009 (resgnd); mem. CPPCC; Steward, Hong Kong Jockey Club; mem. Gov.'s Business Council 1994–97; Dr hc (Hong Kong Univ. of Science and Tech.) 1998. *Address:* c/o CITIC Pacific Limited, 32 Floor, CITIC Tower, 1 Tim Mei Avenue, Central, Hong Kong Special Administrative Region, People's Republic of China (office).

RONIS, Aivis; Latvian journalist, diplomatist and politician; b. 20 May 1968, Kuldīga; m. Dace Rone; one c.; ed Latvian State Univ.; Sr Ed. Informative Daily News Broadcast Program, Latvian State Television 1989–91; joined Diplomatic Service 1991, Chief Desk Officer, Asst to Minister of Foreign Affairs and Press Sec., Ministry of Foreign Affairs 1991–93, First Sec., Embassy in Stockholm 1993–95, Under-Sec. of State for Foreign Affairs 1995–2000; Amb. to Turkey (non-resident) 1999–2000, to USA 2000–04 (also accred to Mexico 2002–04), Perm. Rep. to NATO, Brussels 2004–05; mem. Foreign Policy Council, Ministry of Foreign Affairs 2005–07; Chair. Latvian-American Financial Forum, Riga 2005–10; Minister of Foreign Affairs April–Nov. 2010; Co-Chair. NATO Riga Summit Support Cttee 2006; mem. Strategic Analysis Comm. of the Pres. of Latvia 2008–; Expert in Group of Experts for Devt of new NATO Strategic Concept 2009–; Research Fellow and Fullbright Scholar, Columbia Univ., New York 1999–2000. *Achievements include:* Latvian Youth Chess Champion. *Address:* c/o Ministry of Foreign Affairs, K. Valdemāra iela 3, Riga 1395, Latvia.

RONTÓ, Györgyi, DSc; Hungarian biophysicist and academic; *Professor Emeritus of Biophysics, Semmelweis University;* b. 13 July 1934, Budapest; d. of György Rontó and Erzsébet Lanczkor; m. Dr Dezső Holnapy 1961; two s.; ed Semmelweis Univ. of Medicine, Budapest; Prof. of Biophysics, Semmelweis Univ. 1980, now Prof. Emer., Dir Semmelweis Univ. Inst. of Biophysics 1982–99; Head of Research Group for Biophysics of the Hungarian Acad. of Sciences 1982–; Gen. Sec. Hungarian Biophysical Soc. 1969–90, Vice-Pres. 1990–98, Hon. Pres. 2002–; Vice-Pres. Asscn Int. de Photobiologie 1988–92; officer, European Soc. for Photobiology; mem. Nat. Cttee of COSPAR (Cttee on Space Research); specialises in effects of environmental physical and chemical agents on nucleo-proteins; special interest in biological dosimetry of environmental and artificial UV radiations and in exo/astrobiology; Medal of the Hungarian Biophysical Soc. 1990, 2004, Apáczai Csere János Award 1994, Environment Award 1996, Gold Ring, Semmelweis Univ. 1999. *Publications:* A biofizika alapjai (An Introduction to Biophysics With Medical Orientation) (co-author) 1981 (also English and German edns), Light in Biology and Medicine (Vol. 2) 1991; more than 140 articles. *Leisure interests:* arts,

architecture, gardening. *Address:* 1094 Budapest, Tűzoltó-u. 34–47 (home); PO Box 263, 1444 Budapest, Hungary (home). *Telephone:* (1) 267-6261 (home); (1) 252-0895 (home). *Fax:* (1) 266-6656 (home). *E-mail:* ronto.gyorgyi@med.semmelweis-univ.hu (office).

ROOCROFT, Amanda, FRNCM; British singer (soprano); b. 9 Feb. 1966, Coppull, Lancs.; d. of Roger Roocroft and Valerie Roocroft (née Metcalfe); m. 2nd David Gowland 1999; two s.; ed Royal Northern Coll. of Music; appearances include Sophie in Der Rosenkavalier, Welsh Nat. Opera 1990, Pamina in The Magic Flute, Covent Garden 1991, 1993, Fiordiligi in Così fan tutte, Glyndebourne 1991, European tour with John Eliot Gardiner 1992, Bavarian State Opera 1993, 1994, Covent Garden 1995, Giulietta in I Capuleti e I Montecchi, Covent Garden 1993, Ginevra in Ariodante, ENO 1993, Donna Elvira in Don Giovanni, Glyndebourne 1994, New York Metropolitan Opera 1997, Amelia in Simon Boccanegra, Bavarian State Opera 1995, Mimi in La Bohème, Covent Garden 1996, Countess in Marriage of Figaro, Bavarian State Opera 1997, New York Metropolitan Opera 1999, Cleopatra in Giulio Cesare, Covent Garden 1997, Desdemona in Otello, Bavarian State Opera 1999, Covent Garden 2001, Jenůfa, Glyndebourne 2000, Berlin 2002, Katya Kabanova, Glyndebourne 1998, Covent Garden 2000, Meistersinger, Royal Opera House 2002; Jenůfa for ENO 2009, for Teatro Real Madrid 2009; title role in Katya Kabanova for WNO 2011; Feldmarschallin in Rosenkavalier for ENO 2012; debut at BBC Promenade Concert and Edin. Festival 1993; regular concert engagements and recitals; Fellow, Univ. of Cen. Lancs. 1992; Hon. DMus (Manchester) 2003; Kathleen Ferrier Prize 1988, Silver Medal, Worshipful Co. of Musicians 1988, Royal Philharmonic Soc./Charles Heidsieck Award 1990, Barclay Opera Award 2000, Outstanding Achievement In Opera, Laurence Olivier Awards 2007 (for Jenůfa, ENO 2006). *Recordings include:* Vaughan Williams Serenade to Music (with Matthew Best) 1990, Così fan tutte (with John Eliot Gardiner) 1993, Amanda Roocroft (solo album) 1994, Mozart and his Contemporaries 1996, Schoenberg String Quartet No. 2 (with Britten Quartet) 1994, Vaughan Williams Sea Symphony (with Andrew Davies), Mahler Symphony No. 4 (with Simon Rattle) 1998, Vaughan Williams Pastoral Symphony (with Bernard Haitink) 1998, Elgar, Complete Songs for Voice and Piano Vol 1 2007, Steve Nieve, Welcome to the Voice 2007, Vaughan Williams, Choral Works 2008, Beethoven: Symphony No. 9 2011. *Television documentaries include:* The Girl from Coppull, The Debut (Granada TV), Hard Pressed for Signals (Channel 4), Jenufa (BBC Wales). *Leisure interests:* theatre, cinema, reading, cooking.

ROOD, Johannes (Jon) Joseph Van, PhD, MD; Dutch immunologist and academic; b. 7 April 1926, The Hague; s. of Albert van Rood and Rientje Röell; m. Sacha Bsse. van Tuyll van Serooskerken 1957; one s. two d.; ed Univ. of Leiden; worked in bloodbanking 1952–; in charge of Bloodbank and foundation of Dept of Immunohaematology, Univ. Hosp., Leiden 1957; work in tissue typing 1958–; worked on antibody synthesis in Public Health Research Inst., New York 1962; Lecturer in Immunohaematology, Univ. of Leiden 1965–1991, Prof. in Internal Medicine 1969–1991; Founder Eurotransplant 1967, Stichting Europdonor 1970 (Chair. –2000); fmr Pres. World Marrow Donor Asscn. *Publications:* Leukocyte Antibodies in Sera of Pregnant Women 1958, Platelet Survival 1959, Erythrocyte Survival with DFP 32 1961, Leukocyte Groups, the Normal Lymphocyte Transfer Test and Homograft Sensitivity 1965, Platelet Transfusion 1965, The Relevance of Leukocyte Antigens 1967, A Proposal for International Co-operation: EURO-TRANSPLANT 1967, Transplantation of Bone-marrow cells and Fetal Thymus in an Infant with Lymphonenic Immunological Deficiency 1969, The 4a and 4b Antigens: Do They or Don't They? 1970, Anti HL-A 2 Inhibitor in Normal Human Serum 1970, HL-A Identical Phenotypes and Genotypes in Unrelated Individuals 1970, HL-A and the Group Five System in Hodgkin's Disease 1971, The (Relative) Importance of HL-A Matching in Kidney Transplantation 1971, Simultaneous Detection of Two Cell Populations by Two Colour Fluorescence and Application to the Recognition of B Cell Determinants 1976, HLA-linked Control of Susceptibility to Tuberculoid Leprosy and Association with HLA-DR types 1978. *Leisure interest:* sailing. *Address:* c/o Europdonor Foundation, Plesmanlaan 1b, 2333 BZ Leiden, Netherlands.

ROONEY, Daniel (Dan) Milton, BA; American sports executive and fmr diplomatist; *Chairman, Pittsburgh Steelers Sports, Inc.;* b. 20 July 1932, Pittsburgh, Pa; s. of Arthur Rooney and Kathleen Rooney; m. Patricia Rooney; nine c.; ed North Catholic High School, Pittsburgh, Duquesne Univ., Pittsburgh; worked in various exec. positions for Pittsburgh Steelers (professional American football team) 1955–75, Pres. Pittsburgh Steelers 1975–2002, Chair. 2003–; Amb. to Ireland 2009–12; mem. Bd of Dirs Nat. Football League (NFL) Trust Fund, NFL Ventures Cttee, Chair. Expansion Cttee 1973, Negotiating Cttee 1976, Diversity Cttee, mem. NFL Econ. Cttee; mem. Bd of Dirs United Way of America, American Diabetes Asscn, Presbyterian University Hospital, Pittsburgh History and Landmarks Foundation; Co-founder American Ireland Funds; funded annual Rooney Prize for Irish Literature for Irish writers under the age of 40; inducted into Pro Football Hall of Fame 2000, Francis Reds Bagnell Award, Jack Horrigan Memorial Award 2009. *Publication:* Dan Rooney: My 75 Years with the Pittsburgh Steelers and the NFL (co–author) 2008. *Address:* Office of the Chairman, Pittsburgh Steelers Sports, Inc., 3400 South Water Street, Pittsburgh, PA 15203-2349, USA (office). *Telephone:* (412) 432-7800 (office). *Fax:* (412) 432-7878 (office). *Website:* www.steelers.com (office).

ROOS, Björn O., PhD; Swedish chemist and academic; *Professor of Theoretical Chemistry, University of Lund;* b. 28 June 1937, Malmö; m.; four d.; ed Univ. of Stockholm; Sarskild Forskartjanst (Sr Scientist Fellowship), Swedish Natural Science Research Council 1972–78, Asst Prof. 1978–83; Prof. and Head, Dept of Theoretical Chemistry, Univ. of Lund 1983–; Ed. Theoretica Chimica Acta 1985–96; mem. Editorial Bd ChemPhysChem, International Journal of Quantum Chemistry, Molecular Physics, Chemistry Physics Letter; mem. Nobel Cttee for Chemistry 1986–91, Ordinary mem. 1992–2000; mem. Int. Acad. of Quantum Molecular Sciences 1991– (Treas. 1997–2005); mem. ACS, Swedish Asscn of Chemists, Danish Asscn of Chemists, Finnish Asscn of Chemists; Swedish Asscn of Chemists Nordblad-Ekstrand Gold Medal 1977, Univ. of Bratislava Comenius Gold Medal 1996, Royal Soc. of Sciences Celsius Gold Medal 1996, Swedish Asscn of Chemists Bror Holmberg Medal 1997, World Asscn of Theoretically Oriented Chemists (WATOC) Schrodinger Medal 1999, Tokyo Univ. Morino Prize 2001.

Publications: more than 300 articles in scientific journals. *Leisure interests:* stamp collecting, fishing. *Address:* Department of Theoretical Chemistry, University of Lund, Chemical Center, PO Box 124, 221 00 Lund (office); Protokollgr. 12, 226 47, Lund, Sweden (home). *Telephone:* (46) 222-82-51 (office); (46) 46-120692 (home). *Fax:* (46) 222-45-43 (office). *E-mail:* Bjorn.Roos@teokem.lu.se (office). *Website:* www.teokem.lu.se/~roos (office).

ROOS, John Victor, JD; American lawyer, diplomatist and consultant; *Global Adviser, Mitsubishi UFJ Financial Group, Inc.;* b. 14 Feb. 1955, San Francisco, Calif.; m. Susan Roos; one s. one d.; ed Lowell High School, Stanford Univ., Stanford Law School; f. Stanford Speech and Debate Inst., also developed and taught speech and debate course to Stanford undergraduate students; admitted to practise law in Calif. 1980; litigation assoc., O'Melveny & Myers, Los Angeles 1980–84; joined Wilson Sonsini Goodrich & Rosati, Palo Alto, Calif. 1985, Partner 1988–, mem. Bd of Dirs and Man. Dir of Professional Services 2000–05, CEO Wilson Sonsini Goodrich & Rosati 2005–09; Amb. to Japan 2009–13; Global Adviser, Mitsubishi UFJ Financial Group, Inc. 2013–; Special Asst to Nat. Co-Chair. for Walter Mondale's presidential campaign 1984; Sr Advisor to nat. campaign and Chair. Calif. campaign for Bill Bradley's presidential bid 2000, also Treas. Time Future, Inc., Senator Bradley's multi-cand. cttee 2000; Chair. Northern Calif. Finance Cttee for Senator John Kerry's presidential campaign 2004; fmr mem. Nat. Finance Cttee; fmr Co-Chair. Calif. Finance Cttee for the Obama for America presidential campaign and mem. campaign's tech. cttee; mem. San Mateo/Foster City Elementary School Bd 1991–98, Pres. 1995; mem. Stanford Law School Dean's Advisory Council, Stanford School of Educ. Dean's Advisory Bd. *Address:* Mitsubishi UFJ Financial Group, Inc., 7-1, Marunouchi 2-chome, Chiyoda-ku, Tokyo 100-8330, Japan (office). *Telephone:* (3) 3240-8111 (office). *Fax:* (3) 3240-8203 (office). *E-mail:* info@mufg.jp (office). *Website:* www.mufg.jp (office).

ROOSEN, Gustavo; Venezuelan politician and business executive; ed Andrés Bello Catholic Univ., Caracas, New York Univ., USA; Vice-Pres. Venezuelan Banking Asscn 1981–83; Pres. Caracas Chamber of Commerce 1986–88; Minister of Educ. 1989–92; Pres. Petróleos de Venezuela 1992–95; Pres. CANTV (CA Nacional Teléfonos de Venezuela) 1995–, CEO 2002–07 (resgnd). *Address:* c/o CANTV, Final Av. Libertador, Centro Nacional de Telecomunicaciones, Nuevo Edf. Administrativo, Planta Baja, Caracas, Venezuela (office).

ROOTS, Ott, PhD; Estonian environmental scientist; *Director and Leading Research Scientist, Estonian Environmental Research Institute, Estonian Environmental Research Centre;* b. 9 May 1946, Tallinn; s. of Dr Otto Roots and Ida Roots (née Lass); m. Marika Voit; one s.; ed Tallinn Technological Univ., Inst. of Chem., Estonian Acad. of Sciences; Engineer-Lt, Co. Vice-Commdr, 537 Soviet Army Bldg Bn 1969–71; scientist, Inst. of Zoology and Botany, Estonian Acad. of Sciences 1971–74, Baltic Sea Dept, Inst. of Thermo- and Electrophysics 1974–84; Chief Researcher Baltic Br., Inst. of Applied Geophysics 1984–90; Chief Researcher Water Protection Lab., Tallinn Tech. Univ. 1990–92; Sr Scientist Dept of Environmental Carcinogenesis, Inst. of Experimental and Clinical Medicine 1992–94; Monitoring Counsellor, Environment Information Centre, Ministry of the Environment 1993–2000, Councillor, Dept of Environmental Man. and Tech., Ministry of the Environment 2000–02; Monitoring Co-ordinator, Estonian Environmental Research Centre (EERC) 2002–05, Dir and Leading Research Scientist, Estonian Environmental Research Inst. (under EERC) 2005–, mem. Scientific Council of EERC; Sr Researcher, Estonian Marine Inst., Univ. of Tartu 2007–09, 2010–12, Extraordinary Sr Researcher 2012–14; Del. Helsinki Comm. (HELCOM) (expert on persistent organic contaminants) 1974–, UN ECE ICP (expert on monitoring) 1994–; Co-ordinator Finnish-Estonian Training Project (environmental monitoring) 1996–2002; mem. Estonian Chem. Soc. 1995–, Nat. Geographic Soc., Washington 1996–, New York Acad. of Sciences 1997–, Estonian Nature Fund 1998–2002, Estonia Chemicals Safety Comm. 2000–02, Estonian Toxicological Comm., Ministry of Educ. 2001–, Steering Cttee on the Support Project of Chemicals Control in Estonia 2002–05, Estonian Science Soc. 2004–, American Scientist Soc. 2006–, European Lysimeter Research Group, Estonian Co-ordinator –2007, Advisory Bd Scientific Journal Ecological Chemistry (St Petersburg Univ. and Thesa), Estonian Soc. of Toxicology 2009–; Estonian EERC Focal Point – EFSA Article 36; Amb. Int. HCH and Pesticides Asscn 2003–; Second Prize, Tallinn Tech. Univ. students' scientific works competition 1969, Bronze Medal, Environmental Protection Exhbn (Russia) 1982, honoured by Ministry of the Environment, Estonia, for work in environmental protection 1996, by Ministry of Social Affairs for work on Govt Chemical Safety Comm. 2003, by Ministry of the Environment (Honour Certificate) for great and long-term contrib. to Estonian environmental protection 2006, Cen. European Univ. Foundation Individual Research Support Scheme Grant 1993, 1997–99, Estonian Science Foundation Grant 1994–96, 1997–2000, John D. and Catherine T. Mac Arthur Foundation Grant (USA) 2001–02, Honour Certificate for ten years conscientious and successful work in EERC Scientific Grants 2012. *Publications include:* Polychlorinated Biphenyls and Chlororganic Pesticides in the Ecosystem of the Baltic Sea 1992, Toxic Chlororganic Compounds in the Ecosystem of the Baltic Sea 1996, The Effect of Environmental Pollution on Human Health in the Baltic States 1999, UNEP Persistent Bioaccumulative and Toxic Chemicals in Central and Eastern European Countries (co-author) 2000, UNEP Regionally Based Assessment of Persistent Toxic Substances (co-author) 2003, Persistent Organic Pollutants in our Environment, Ministry of the Environment, Estonian Environmental Research Center 2006; more than 230 scientific articles in learned journals. *Leisure interests:* environmental protection, sport (especially basketball), music. *Address:* Estonian Environmental Research Centre, Marja Str. 4D, Tallinn 10617 (office); Karulaugu tee 9–10, 74001 Tallinn, Estonia (home). *Telephone:* (2) 611-2964 (office). *Fax:* (2) 611-2901 (office). *E-mail:* ott.roots@klab.ee (office); ott.roots@ut.ee (office); roots@smail.ee (home). *Website:* www.klab.ee (office); www.sea.ee (office).

ROP, Anton, MA; Slovenian economist and politician; *Vice President, European Investment Bank;* b. 27 Dec. 1960, Ljubljana; ed Univ. of Ljubljana; Asst Dir Slovene Inst. for Macroeconomic Analysis and Devt 1985–92; State Sec. Ministry of Econ. Relations and Devt 1993; Minister of Labour, Family and Social Affairs 1996–2000, of Finance 2002; Prime Minister 2002–04; Pres. Liberal Democratic Party (Liberalna Demokracija Slovenije—LDS) 2002–05, Leader, Parl. Group 2004–07; Vice-Pres. European Investment Bank 2010–. *Leisure interests:* reading,

sport. *Address:* European Investment Bank, 98-100, boulevard Konrad Adenauer, 2950 Luxembourg, Luxembourg (office). *Telephone:* 43-79-1 (office). *Fax:* 43-77-04 (office). *Website:* www.eib.org (office).

ROPAC, Thaddaeus; Austrian gallery owner; b. 1960, Klagenfurt; served first internship with Joseph Beuys 1982; became acquainted with young artists including Jean-Michel Basquiat, Keith Haring and Robert Mapplethorpe in New York; organized exhbns of their work in opening his first gallery in Salzburg 1983; owns Galerie Thaddaeus Ropac, Salzburg, Austria and Paris, France; opened space in Halle, represents more than 50 major artists, ranging from Rosenquist, Baselitz, Kiefer and the Kabakovs to Fleury, Gormley, Violette, Slominski and Erwin Wurm; Pres. Bd of Trustees, Salzburg Foundation 2009–; mem. Advisory Bd Museum of Contemporary Art, Vienna, Museum of Applied Arts (MAK), Vienna, European Univ. of Science & Art, Salzburg, Salzburg Int. Festival; Officier, Ordre des Arts et des Lettres 2005, Verleihung Goldenes Verdienstkreuz der Republik Österreich im Bundeskanzleramt 2006; Kunst und Kulturpreis der Salzburger Wirtschaft 2007. *Address:* Galerie Thaddaeus Ropac, Mirabelle Platz 2, 5020 Salzburg, Austria (office). *Telephone:* (662) 881393 (office). *Fax:* (662) 8813939 (office). *E-mail:* thaddaeus.ropac@ropac.at (office). *Website:* www.ropac.net (office).

ROPER, Warren Richard, MSc, PhD, FRS, FRSNZ; New Zealand chemist and academic; b. 27 Nov. 1938, Nelson; s. of Robert J. Roper and Nancy L. Robinson; m. Judith D. C. Miller 1961; two s. one d.; ed Nelson Coll., Univ. of Canterbury and Univ. of North Carolina, USA; Lecturer, Univ. of Auckland 1966, Prof. of Chem. 1984–2007; Visiting Lecturer, Univ. of Bristol, UK 1972; Visiting Prof., Univ. of Leeds, UK 1983, Univ. of Rennes, France 1984, 1985, Stanford Univ., USA 1988; Visiting Prof., Univ. of Sydney 2001; Fellow, New Zealand Inst. of Chem., Japan Soc. for Promotion of Science 1992; Hon. DSc (Canterbury) 1999; RSC Award in Organometallic Chem. 1983, ICI Medal, NZ Inst. of Chem., 1984, RSC Centenary Lecturer 1988, Hector Medal, Royal Soc. of NZ 1991, Inorganic Chem. Award, Royal Australian Chemical Inst. 1992, G.T. Seaborg Lecturer, Univ. of California, Berkeley 1995, Dwyer Medal, Univ. of NSW 2000, Stone Lecturer, Univ. of Bristol 2003, Arthur D. Little Lecturer, MIT 2005. *Publications:* more than 200 original papers and reviews in scientific journals. *Leisure interests:* listening to music (especially opera), walking. *Address:* 26 Beulah Avenue, Auckland 0630, New Zealand (home). *Telephone:* (9) 478-6940 (home). *E-mail:* w.roper@auckland.ac.nz (office).

RORSTED, Kasper; Danish business executive; *CEO, Henkel AG;* b. 24 Feb. 1962, Arhus; m.; four c.; ed Int. Business School, Copenhagen, Exec. Summer Program, Harvard Business School, USA; various man. positions in marketing and distribution with Oracle and Digital Equipment Corpn –1995; various man. positions at Compaq, including Head of Compaq Enterprise Business Group in Europe, Middle East & Africa (EMEA) 1995–2001, Vice-Pres. and Gen. Man. Compaq, EMEA Region 2001–02, Sr Vice-Pres. and Gen. Man. Hewlett Packard, EMEA Region 2002–04; Exec. Vice-Pres., Human Resources, Purchasing, Information Technologies, Infrastructure Services, Henkel KGaA 2005–07, Vice-Chair. Man. Bd Henkel KGaA and Exec. Vice-Pres. Human Resources and Infrastructure Services 2007–08, CEO Henkel Group AG, responsible for Human Resources, Infrastructure Services 2008–, mem. Man. Bd Henkel Group and Chair. 2005–, Exec. Vice-Pres. Human Resources and Infrastructure Services 2005–, CEO Henkel Group 2008–, Exec. Vice-Pres. Human Resources, Purchasing, Information Technologies and Infrastructure Services, Henkel KGaA (subsidiary of Henkel Group) 2005–, Vice-Chair. Man. Bd Henkel KGaA 2007–08, Chair. Henkel KGaA 2008–; mem. Bd of Dirs Cable & Wireless Plc (UK), Henkel Norden AB (Sweden), Danfoss A/S (Denmark). *Address:* Henkel AG & Co. KGaA, Henkelstrasse 67, Düsseldorf 40191, Germany (office). *Telephone:* (211) 797-0 (office). *Fax:* (211) 7982484 (office). *E-mail:* info@henkel.com (office). *Website:* www.henkel.com (office).

ROS, Enrique Jorge, LLD; Argentine lawyer and diplomatist; b. 16 July 1927; ed Univs of Buenos Aires and Paris; practised as lawyer 1949–54; joined diplomatic service 1954; served at Perm. Mission to OAS 1956–58, UN 1959–63; Chargé d'Affaires, The Hague 1965–67; served at Embassy in London 1967–71; Head of Mission, Beijing 1973–75; Amb. to Israel 1976–77; Perm. Rep. to UN, New York 1977–80; Dir-Gen. Foreign Policy Bureau, Ministry of Foreign Affairs 1980, Under-Sec. for Foreign Affairs 1980–82; Amb. to Spain 1982–84, to Japan 1984–89, to Viet Nam (non-resident) 1985–89; mem. Higher Council of Ambs of Ministry of Foreign Affairs 1990–; Chair. Bilateral Admin. Comm. of River Plate 1991; decorations from Bolivia, Brazil, Chile, Colombia, Ecuador, Paraguay, Peru, Venezuela, Japan. *Leisure interests:* reading, gardening. *Address:* c/o Ministry of Foreign Affairs, International Trade and Worship, Esmeralda 1212, C1007ABR Buenos Aires, Argentina.

ROSA BAUTISTA, Leonidas; Honduran lawyer, politician and diplomatist; *Permanent Representative, Organization of American States;* b. 4 Feb. 1947, Lepaera; s. of Leonidas Rosa and Alejandrina Vda. de Rosa; m. Abogada Irma Violeta Suazo de Rosa; three c.; ed Instituto Ramón Rosa, Gracias, Lempira, Universidad Nacional Autónoma de Honduras; fmr legal adviser to Main Directorate of Transport; Vice Minister of the Interior and of Justice 1978–1980; Deputy to Constituent Nat. Ass. 1980–82; fmr Prof., Universidad Nacional Autónoma de Honduras; Minister of Foreign Affairs 2003–05; Attorney-Gen. 2005–09; Perm. Rep., OAS, Washington, DC 2011–; Sr Pnr and Dir, Bufete Rosa y Asociados, S.A. de C.V. (law firm), Tegucigalpa; Pres. Honduran Bar Asscn 1990–92; Prof., Universidad Nacional Autónoma de Honduras. *Address:* Permanent Mission of Honduras to the Organization of American States, 3007 Tilden Street, NW, Suite 4M-400, Washington, DC 20008, USA (office); Bufete Rosa y Asociados, S.A. de C.V., Edificio Rosa y Asociados, Colonia San Rafael Retorno Kobe n. 29, Tegucigalpa, Honduras (office). *Telephone:* (202) 244-5260 (DC) (office); 239-2688 (Bufete Rosa) (office). *Fax:* 239-2718 (Bufete Rosa) (office). *E-mail:* honduras@oas.org (office); lrosab@bufeterosa.com (office). *Website:* www.oas.org (office); www.bufeterosa.com (office).

ROSADILLA, Luis; Uruguayan politician; *Minister of National Defence;* b. 21 Dec. 1953, Montevideo; m.; six c.; began working in a bakery at age 13; spent nine years in prison for guerrilla activity with Tupamaros Movimiento de Liberación Nacional 1973–82; f. own bakery business 1992; Sec. to Senator Eleuterio Fernández Huidobro 1999–2004; mem. Cámara de Representantes (Parl.) for

Montevideo constituency 2005–09, Chair. Defence Cttee; Minister of Nat. Defence 2010–; mem. Frente Amplio./Movimiento de Participación Popular. *Address:* Ministry of National Defence, Edif. General Artigas, Avda 8 de Octubre 2628, Montevideo, Uruguay (office). *Telephone:* (2) 4872828 (office). *Fax:* (2) 4809397 (office). *E-mail:* rrpp.secretaria@mdn.gub.uy (office). *Website:* www.mdn.gub.uy (office).

ROSAIAH, Konijeti, BCom; Indian politician; *Governor of Tamil Nadu;* b. 4 July 1933, Vemooru, Guntur Dist; m. Sivalaxmi Garu; three s. one d.; ed Guntur Hindu Coll., Andhra Univ.; elected as mem. Andhra Pradesh Legis. Council 1968, 1974, 1980; State Minister for Transportation, Roads and Building 1979, for Transportation and Housing 1980, for Home Affairs 1982, for Finance, Transportation and Electricity 1989, for Finance, Health and Educ. and Electricity 1990, 1992, for Finance 2004–09; MP for Narasaraopeta 1998; Chief Minister of Andhra Pradesh 2009–10 (resgnd); Gov. of Tamil Nadu 2011–; mem. Indian Nat. Congress party, Pres. Pradesh Congress Cttee 1995–97; Dr hc (Andhra Univ.) 2007. *Address:* Governor's Secretariat, Raj Bhavan, Chennai 600 022, India (office). *Telephone:* (44) 22351313 (office). *Fax:* (44) 22350570 (office). *E-mail:* governor@tn.nic.in (office). *Website:* www.tnrajbhavan.gov.in (office).

ROSALES BOLAÑOS, Antenor; Nicaraguan lawyer, banking executive and fmr central banker; b. 1955, Leon; s. of Rodolfo Rosales and Angela Bolaños; ed Central American Univ., Managua; joined Sandinista Nat. Liberation Front 1970, Pres.Nat. Asscn of Students of Eng. and Allied Careers and Coordinator Exec. Cttee Revolutionary Student Front, joined Sandinista People's Army and served as commdr during insurrection of Esteli, retd with rank of Col 1999; fmr mem. Bd of Dirs Superintendency of Banks and Other Financial Institutions; Co-founder and fmr Dir ProCredit Bank; fmr Dir Intercontinental Bank; Gov. Banco Central de Nicaragua (Cen. Bank of Nicaragua) 2007–12; Alternate Gov., Inter-American Devt Bank. *Address:* c/o Banco Central de Nicaragua, Carretera Sur, Km 7, Apdos 2252/3, Zona 5, Managua, Nicaragua (office).

ROSALES GUERRERO, Manuel; Venezuelan politician; b. 12 Dec. 1952, Santa Bárbara, Zulia; m. Eveling Trejo de Rosales; eight c.; Auditor, Colón Municipal Council 1973–74; Councillor, Santa Bárbara 1979–82; Deputy Zulia Legis. Ass. 1983–94; Mayor of Maracaibo 1996–2000; Gov. Zulia prov. 2001–08; Mayor of Maracaibo 2008–09; fled country to avoid corruption charges April 2009; unsuccessful cand. in presidential election 2006; fmr mem. Acción Democrática; f. Un Nuevo Tiempo party 2000.

ROSANVALLON, Pierre, PhD; French historian and academic; *Professor of Modern and Contemporary Political History, Collège de France;* b. 1 Jan. 1948, Blois; ed Ecole des Hautes Etudes Commerciales de Paris; econ. adviser, Confédération française démocratique du travail 1969–72, political adviser to Edmond Maire and Ed. CFDT-Aujourd'hui 1973–77; mem. staff, Univ. of Paris-Dauphine 1978, Dir of Research 1978–82; Univ. Lecturer, Ecole des hautes études en sciences sociales 1983–89, Dir of Studies 1989–92, Head of Raymond Aron Centre of Political Research 1992–2005; Prof. of Modern and Contemporary Political History, Collège de France 2001–; co-f. (with François Furet) Fondation Saint-Simon (think-tank) 1982–99 (now disbanded); mem. Scientific Counsel of French Nat. Library 2002–, Scientific Counsel of Ecole Normale Supérieure de Paris 2004–; Founder and Pres. La République des Idées 2002–. *Publications include:* L'Âge de l'autogestion 1976, La Crise de l'Etat-providence 1981 (trans. as The New Social Question: Rethinking the Welfare State 2000), Le Moment Guizot 1985, L'Etat en France de 1789 à nos jours 1990, La Monarchie impossible 1994, La Nouvelle Question sociale 1995, Le Nouvel Âge des inégalités (with Jean-Paul Fitoussi) 1996, Le Peuple introuvable: Histoire de la représentation démocratique en France 1998, La Démocratie inachevée. Histoire de la souveraineté du peuple en France 2000, Le Sacre du citoyen. Histoire du suffrage universel en France 2001, Pour une histoire conceptuelle du politique 2003, Le Modèle politique français. La société civile contre le jacobinisme de 1789 à nos jours 2004, La contre-démocratie. La politique à l'âge de la défiance 2006 (trans. as Counter-Democracy: Politics in an Age of Distrust 2008), Democracy Past and Future (ed. Samuel Moyn) (excerpts) 2006, The Demands of Liberty – Civil Society in France since the Revolution 2007, La légitimité démocratique. Impartialité, réflexivité, proximité 2008 (trans. by Arthur Goldhammer as Democratic Legitimacy: Impartiality, Reflexivity, Proximity 2011), La Société des égaux 2011. *Address:* Collège de France, 11 place Marcelin Berthelot, 75231 Paris Cedex 05, France (office). *Telephone:* 1-44-27-12-11 (office). *Fax:* 1-44-27-11-47 (office). *E-mail:* message@college-de-france.fr (office). *Website:* www.college-de-france.fr (office).

ROSATI, Dariusz Kajetan, DEcon; Polish economist and politician; b. 8 Aug. 1946, Radom; s. of Angelo Rosati and Wanda Pleszczyńska; m. Teresa Nowińska 1971; one s. one d.; ed Main School of Planning and Statistics, Warsaw; scientific researcher, Main School of Planning and Statistics (now Cen. School of Commerce), Warsaw 1969, Asst Prof. 1978, Prof. 1990–; with Citibank, New York 1978–79; Visiting Prof., Princeton Univ., NJ 1986–87; Founder and first Dir Inst. of World Economy, Warsaw School of Econs 1985; Dir Foreign Trade Research Inst., Warsaw 1988–91; Partner, TKD-Ernst & Young Poland 1989–92; Head UN Section for Cen. and E Europe, Geneva 1991–95; Minister of Foreign Affairs 1995–97; mem. Council of Monetary Policy of Nat. Bank of Poland 1998–2004; mem. Bd Dirs Int. Exchange Program (IREX), Washington, DC 1998–2001; mem. Polish United Workers' Party (PZPR) 1966–90; mem. Cttee on Econ. Reform 1987–90, team of econ. advisers to Prime Minister 1988–89, Econ. Strategy Cttee to the Cabinet 1994–97; Adviser to Pres. of EC 2001–; Rector Richard Łazarski Univ. of Commerce and Law, Warsaw 2003–; mem. European Parl. (Socialist Group) 2004–09, mem. Cttee on Econ. and Monetary Affairs, mem. Del. to ACP-EU Jt Parl. Ass.; mem. Sejm (Parl.) for Warsaw 2011–; mem. Polish Econ. Soc. 1969–, Econ. Studies Cttee Polish Acad. of Sciences 1999–, European Econ. Asscn, European Asscn of Comparative Econ. Studies; mem. Civic Platform (PO) (Platforma Obywatelska) 2011–; Silver Cross of Merit 1981, Kt's Cross Order of Poland Restituta 1989, Orders of Merit from France, Italy, Greece, Ukraine and Lithuania. *Publications:* Decision-Making 1977, Inflation 1989, Export Policies 1990, Polish Way to Market 1998, An Agenda for a Growing Europe: The Sapir Report 2004, Facing the Challenge: Lisbon Strategy for growth and employment 2004, New Europe: Report from Transformation 2005; more than 250 scientific articles. *Leisure interests:* sports, reading. *Address:* c/o Sejm, 00–902 Warsaw, ul. Wiejska 2/6, Poland (office). *Telephone:* (22) 6942500 (office). *Fax:* (22) 6941446

(office). *E-mail:* zjablon@sejm.gov.pl (office); dariusz@rosati.pl (office). *Website:* www.rosati.pl (office).

ROSATTI, Horacio; Argentine lawyer, academic and fmr government official; b. Santa Fe; elected mem. Constituent Ass. 1994; Mayor of Santa Fe 1995–99; Co-Judge, Supreme Court 2002–03; Attorney-Gen. of the Treasury 2003–04; Minister of Justice, Security and Human Rights 2004–05; fmr Dean of Faculty of Law, Catholic Univ. of Santa Fe; fmr Dean Universidad del Litoral; Corresp. mem. Instituto de Federalismo; mem. Partido Justicialista (PJ). *Address:* c/o Ministry of Justice, Security and Human Rights, Sarmiento 329, 1041 Buenos Aires, Argentina (office).

ROSBASH, Michael, PhD; American geneticist, biologist and academic; *Professor of Biology and Inaugural Peter Gruber Endowed Chair in Neuroscience, Brandeis University;* b. 7 March 1944, Kansas City, Mo.; m. Nadja Abovich; one d. one step-d.; ed California Inst. of Tech., Institut de Biologie Physico-Chimique, Paris (Fulbright Scholar), Massachusetts Inst. of Tech., Univ. of Edinburgh, UK; joined Faculty of Brandeis Univ. 1974, Dir Brandeis Nat. Center for Behavioral Genomics, Prof. of Biology and Inaugural Peter Gruber Endowed Chair in Neuroscience; Investigator, Howard Hughes Medical Inst. 1989–; Co-founder and mem. Scientific Advisory Bd, Hypnion, Inc.; mem. Nat. Center for Sleep Disorders Advisory Panel, NIH, Center for Biological Timing, NSF; mem. American Acad. of Arts and Sciences 1997, NAS 2003; Fellow, AAAS 2007; Helen Hay Whitney Fellow 1971–74, NIH Research Career Devt Award 1976–80, Guggenheim Fellow 1989–90, California Inst. of Tech. Distinguished Alumni Award 2001, Aschoff's Rule Winner, Soc. for Research on Biological Rhythms 2008, Gruber Prize in Neuroscience 2009, Louisa Gross Horwitz Prize, Columbia Univ. 2011, Gairdner Int. Award (co-recipient) 2012, Shaw Prize in Life Science and Medicine (co-recipient) 2013. *Achievements include:* cloned, with Michael Rosbash, the Period gene in *Drosophila melanogaster* controlling its biological rhythms 1984; also discovered that the mRNA and protein encoded by this gene show circadian oscillations. *Publications:* numerous papers in professional journals. *Address:* Carl J. Shapiro Science Center, Room 2-24B, Brandeis University, 415 South Street, Waltham, MA 02453, USA (office). *Telephone:* (781) 736-3160 (office). *Fax:* (781) 736-3164 (office). *E-mail:* rosbash@brandeis.edu (office). *Website:* www.bio.brandeis.edu (office).

ROŞCA, Iurie; Moldovan journalist and politician; *Deputy Chairman of Parliament;* b. 31 Oct. 1961, Telenești; m.; three c.; ed Moldova State Univ.; active in pro-democracy movement in 1980s; Ed., Teleradio-Moldova Co.; mem. Parl. 1994–, Deputy Chair. of Parl. 1998–2000, 2005–, mem. Standing Bureau of Parl.; Chair. People's Christian Democratic Party 1994–. *Publications:* Escape from the Darkness 1995, Exercises of Lucidity 2000. *Address:* Office of the Deputy Speaker, Chisinau, Stefan cel Mare 105 (office); People's Christian Democratic Party (Partidul Popular Creştin Democrat—PPCD), 2009 Chişinău, str. Nicolae Iorga 5, Moldova (office). *Telephone:* (22) 23-73-09 (Parl.) (office); (22) 23-45-47 (office). *Fax:* (22) 23-20-65 (Parl.) (office); (22) 23-86-66 (office). *E-mail:* rosca@parlament.md (office); magic@ppcd.md (office). *Website:* www.parlament.md; www.ppcd.md (office).

ROSCITT, Richard R. (Rick), BEng, MBA; American business executive; *Chairman, Sapien LLC;* ed Stevens Inst. of Tech., Sloan School of Management, MIT; joined AT&T 1973, fmr Pres. AT&T Business Services, then Pres. and CEO AT&T Solutions, fmr mem. Operations Group, AT&T; Chair. and CEO ADC Telecommunications 2001–03; Pres. and COO MCI Group 2003–04; Chair. Sapien LLC 2005–; Chair. (non-exec.) Orion Telecommunications, SMOBILE Systems; Pnr Core Value Pnrs Investments; mem. Bd of Trustees Stevens Inst. of Tech. *Address:* Sapien Corporate Headquarters, 7 Washington Street, Morristown, NJ 07960, USA (office). *Telephone:* (866) 372-7436 (office). *Fax:* (973) 944-7558 (home). *E-mail:* info@sapiensoftware.com (office). *Website:* www.sapiensoftware.com (office).

ROSE, Charles (Charlie) Peete, Jr, BA, JD; American broadcaster and journalist; b. 5 Jan. 1942, Henderson, NC; s. of Charles Peete Rose, Sr and Margaret Rose (née Frazier); m. Mary King (divorced); pnr Amanda Burden; ed Duke Univ.; began career with Bankers Trust; first broadcasts as weekend reporter for WPIX-TV, New York 1972; Man. Ed. Bill Moyers' International Report (PBS) 1974–75, Exec. Producer Bill Moyers Journal 1975–76; Political Correspondent, NBC News 1976–77; Program Man. and host, The Charlie Rose Show, KXAS-TV, Dallas-Fort Worth 1979–81; Anchor, CBS News Nightwatch 1984–90; presented Personalities (syndicated programme produced by Fox Broadcasting Co.) 1990; Exec. Producer, Exec. Ed. and host The Charlie Rose Show (interview show) PBS station Thirteen/WNET 1991–; Correspondent for 60 Minutes 1999–2005; Co-Presenter CBS This Morning 2012–; Dir Citadel Broadcasting Corpn 2003–09; Dr hc (C.W. Post Coll., Univ. of North Carolina, Pembroke); George Foster Peabody Award 1976, Emmy Award 1987, 1992, Cable ACE Award 1992, Futrell Award 2005, Lifetime Achievement Award in Entertainment Journalism, Savannah Film Festival 2007. *Address:* Charlie Rose Inc., 731 Lexington Avenue, New York, NY 10022, USA (office). *Website:* www.charlierose.com (office).

ROSE, Sir Clive (Martin), GCMG, MA, FRSA, FICDDS; British diplomatist (retd); b. 15 Sept. 1921, Banstead, Surrey; s. of Bishop Alfred Rose; m. Elisabeth MacKenzie Lewis 1946 (died 2006); two s. three d.; ed Marlborough Coll. and Christ Church, Oxford; Rifle Brigade (rank of Maj., mentioned in despatches), Europe, India, Iraq 1941–46; Commonwealth Relations Office 1948; High Comm. Madras 1948–49; Foreign Office 1950; served in Bonn, Montevideo, Paris, Washington and London 1950–73; Imperial Defence Coll. 1968; Amb. and Head of UK Del. to Mutual and Balanced Force Reduction talks, Vienna 1973–76; Deputy Sec. to Cabinet Office 1976–79; UK Perm. Rep. on N Atlantic Council 1979–82; Consultant to Control Risks Group Ltd 1983–95; Chair. Control Risks Information Services Ltd 1991–93 (Dir 1986–93); Pres. Emergency Planning Asscn 1987–93; mem. Advisory Bd Royal Coll. for Defence Studies 1985–92; Chair. Council Royal United Services Inst. 1983–86, Vice-Pres. 1986–93, Vice-Patron 1993–2001; Vice-Pres. Suffolk Preservation Soc. 1988–2007 (Chair. 1985–88), Vice-Patron 2007. *Publications:* Campaigns Against Western Defence: NATO's Adversaries and Critics 1985, The Soviet Propaganda Network: a Directory of Organisations Serving Soviet Foreign Policy 1988, The Unending Quest: A Search for Ancestors 1996, Detente, Diplomacy and MBFR (Contrib.) 2002, Alice Owen: The Life and Times and Marriages of a Tudor Lady 2006, Fanfare for Lavenham (epic poem) 2007. *Leisure interests:* genealogy, writing poetry. *Address:* Chimney House, Lavenham, Suffolk, CO10 9QT, England (home).

ROSE, Harald, PhD; German physicist and academic; *Carl Zeiss Senior Guest Professor for Electron Optics, University of Ulm;* b. 14 Feb. 1935, Bremen; ed Darmstadt Univ. of Tech.; Visiting Researcher, Enrico Fermi Inst., Univ. of Chicago, USA 1973–74; Prin. Research Scientist, New York State Dept of Health 1976–80; Prof., Dept of Physics, Darmstadt Univ. of Tech. 1980–2000, now Prof. Emer.; Visiting Researcher, Cornell Univ., Univ. of Maryland 1995–96; Research Fellow, Dept of Materials Science, Oak Ridge Nat. Lab., Tenn. 2000–01, Dept of Materials Science, Argonne Nat. Lab., Ill. 2001–02, Advanced Light Source, Lawrence Berkeley Nat. Lab., Calif. 2003–05; Carl Zeiss Sr Guest Prof. for Electron Optics, Univ. of Ulm 2010–, Guest Scientist, Sub-Angstrom Low-Voltage Electron Microscopy I-II Project (SALVE); Visiting Lecturer, Univ. of Illinois, Urbana-Champaign 2011; Hon. mem. Microscopy Soc. of America, German Soc. of Electron Microscopy, 141 Cttee of Japanese Soc. for the Promotion of Sciences; Hon. Prof., Jiaotong Univ., Xian, China 1987; Hon. FRS; Distinguished Scientist Award, Microscopy Soc. of America 2003, Karl Heinz Beckurts Prize (jtly) 2006, Honda Prize (jtly) 2008, Wolf Prize in Physics (jtly) 2011. *Achievements include:* inventor of the practical realisable aberration correction and considered leading expert in theoretical electron optics; holder of 105 patents on scientific instruments and electron optical components. *Publications:* numerous publications including Geometrical Charged-Particle Optics 2009; 105 patents of scientific instruments and electro-optical components. *Address:* Room N27/2.005, Electron Microscopy Group of Materials Science, University of Ulm, Albert-Einstein-Allee 11, 89081 Ulm, Germany (office). *Telephone:* (731) 50-22941 (office). *E-mail:* harald.rose@uni-ulm.de (office). *Website:* www.uni-ulm.de/en/einrichtungen/electron-microscopy-group-of-materials-science.html (office); www.salve-project.de (office).

ROSE, Gen. Sir (Hugh) Michael, KCB, CBE, DSO, QGM, DL; British army officer (retd); b. 5 Jan. 1940, India; s. of the late Lt-Col Hugh Rose and of the late Barbara Allcard; m. Angela Shaw 1968; two s.; ed Cheltenham Coll., St Edmund Hall, Oxford and Royal Coll. of Defence Studies; commissioned, Gloucestershire Regt Territorial Army Volunteer Reserve 1959; RAF Volunteer Reserve 1962; Coldstream Guards 1964; served Germany, Aden, Malaysia, Gulf States, Dhofar, NI, Falkland Islands; Brigade Maj., 16 Para. Brigade 1973–75; CO 22 SAS Regt 1979–82; Command, 39 Infantry Brigade 1983–85; Commdt School of Infantry 1987–88; Dir Special Forces 1988–89; GOC NE Dist and Commdr 2nd Infantry Div. 1989–91; Commdt Staff Coll. 1991–93; Commdr UK Field Army and Insp.-Gen. of Territorial Army 1993–94; Commdr (UN Forces in) Bosnia-Herzegovina 1994–95; Adjutant Gen. 1995–97; aide de Camp Gen. to the Queen 1995–97; Col Coldstream Guards 1999–2010; fmr Dir Control Risks Group; Dir Eurocontrol Technics; Hon. DLitt (Nottingham) 1999. *Television:* presenter Power House 2000. *Publications:* Fighting for Peace 1998, Washington's War 2007. *Leisure interests:* sailing, skiing. *Address:* c/o Regimental H.Q. Coldstream Guards, Wellington Barracks, Birdcage Walk, London, SW1E 6HQ, England (office).

ROSE, Irwin (Ernie), BS, PhD; American biologist and academic; *Specialist, Department of Physiology and Biophysics, College of Medicine, University of California, Irvine;* b. 16 July 1926, Brooklyn, NY; m. Zelda Budenstein Rose; ed Washington State Coll., Univ. of Chicago; Radio Technician, USN during Second World War; faculty mem., Yale Univ. Medical School Dept of Biochemistry 1954–63; Sr Mem., Fox Chase Cancer Center, Phila 1963–95 (retd); Specialist, Dept of Physiology and Biophysics, Coll. Medicine, Univ. of Calif., Irvine 1995–; mem. NAS; Nobel Prize in Chemistry (jt recipient) 2004. *Address:* Department of Physiology and Biophysics, College of Medicine, University of California, Irvine, CA 92697, USA (office). *Telephone:* (949) 824-4097 (office). *Fax:* (949) 824-8571 (office). *Website:* www.ucihs.uci.edu/pandb (office).

ROSE, Sir John E. V., Kt, MA, FRAeS; British business executive; b. 1953, Blantyre, Malawi; m. Felicity Rose; two s. one d.; ed Univ. of St Andrews, Scotland; fmrly with First Nat. Bank of Chicago and Security Pacific; joined Rolls-Royce 1994, Dir of Corp. Devt 1989–94, mem. Bd 1992–2011, Pres. and Chief Exec. Rolls-Royce plc 1993–96, Man. Dir Aerospace Group 1995–2011, Chief Exec. 1996–2011 (retd); Dir (non-exec.) Eli Lilly & Co. 2003–; mem. JP Morgan Int. Council, CBI Int. Advisory Bd, Advisory Bd of the Econ. Devt Bd of Singapore, The Englefield Advisory Bd, European Round Table of Industrialists; Trustee Eden Project; fmr Pres. European Assen of Aerospace Industries, Soc. of British Aerospace Cos; fmr Chair. The Prince's Trust; Commdr, Légion d'honneur 2008; Hon. DSc (St Andrews) 1975, Hon. DEng (Exeter) 2010; Singapore Public Service Star 2008. *Leisure interests:* scuba diving, skiing, the arts. *Address:* c/o Rolls-Royce plc, 65 Buckingham Gate, London, SW1E 6AT, England.

ROSE, Justin Peter; British (b. South African) professional golfer; b. 30 July 1980, Johannesburg, South Africa; m. Kate Rose 2006; one s. one d.; moved to UK aged five and began playing golf at Hartley Wintney Golf Club, Hants.; played in the Walker Cup 1997; turned professional 1998; PGA Tour wins include Memorial Tournament 2010, AT&T National 2010, BMW Championship 2011, WGC-Cadillac Championship 2012, US Open 2013; European Tour wins include Dunhill Championship 2002, Victor Chandler British Masters 2002, MasterCard Masters 2006/07, Volvo Masters 2007; Japan Golf Tour wins include The Crowns 2002; Sunshine Tour wins include Nashua Masters 2002; other wins include Bilt Skins (India) 2004, Turkish Airlines World Golf Final 2012, Tyco Golf Skills Challenge (USA) 2012; has played most of his golf on the PGA Tour since 2003, whilst keeping his membership on the European Tour since 1999; professional team appearances include World Cup (representing England) 2002, 2003, 2007, 2011, Seve Trophy (representing GB & Ireland) 2003 (winners), 2007 (winners), Ryder Cup (representing Europe) 2008, 2012 (winners); Order of Merit on European Tour 2007. *Address:* c/o Excel Sports Management, 1700 Broadway, 29th Floor, New York, NY 10019, USA (office). *E-mail:* info@justinrose.com. *Website:* www.justinrose.com.

ROSE, Matthew K., BS; American transport industry executive; *Chairman, President and CEO, Burlington Northern Santa Fe Corporation;* b. 1960; ed Univ. of Missouri; began career as Man. Trainee Missouri Pacific Railroad 1981; various positions Schneider National, International Utilities; Vice-Pres. Triple Crown Services –1993; joined Burlington Northern 1993, Vice-Pres. Vehicles and Machinery 1994–95, Vice-Pres. Chemicals 1995–96 (following merger with Santa Fe 1995), Sr Vice-Pres. Merchandise Business Unit 1996–97, Sr Vice-Pres. and COO 1997–99, Pres. and COO 1999–2000, Pres. and CEO 2000–, also Chair. 2002–; Chair. Assen of American Railroads; mem. Bd of Dirs AMR Corpn, Centex Building Community, Center for Energy & Econ. Devt; mem. Gov. of Tex. Business Council, Business Roundtable; mem. Bd Trustees Texas Christian Univ.; mem. NW Univ. Transportation Center Business Advisory Cttee; American Soc. Transportation and Logistics Distinguished Logistics Professional Award 2007. *Address:* Burlington Northern Santa Fe Corpn, 2650 Lou Menk Drive, Fort Worth, TX 76131-2830, USA (office). *Telephone:* (800) 795-2673 (office). *Fax:* (817) 352-7171 (office). *Website:* www.bnsf.com (office).

ROSE, Richard, BA, DPhil, FBA; American writer, professor of public policy and consultant; *Professor of Public Policy, University of Strathclyde;* b. 9 April 1933, St Louis, Mo.; s. of Charles Imse Rose and Mary C. Rose; m. Rosemary J. Kenny 1956; two s. one d.; ed Clayton High School, Mo., Johns Hopkins Univ., London School of Econs, Univ. of Oxford; worked in political public relations, Miss. Valley 1954–55; reporter, St Louis Post-Dispatch 1955–57; Lecturer in Govt, Univ. of Manchester 1961–66; Prof. of Politics, Strathclyde Univ. 1966–82, Prof. of Public Policy and Dir Centre for the Study of Public Policy 1976–2005, 2012–; Prof. of Public Policy, Univ. of Aberdeen 2005–11; Visiting Prof., European Univ. Inst., Florence 1975–77, 2011–; Specialist Adviser, House of Commons Public Admin Cttee 2002–03; Consultant Psephologist, The Times, ITV, Daily Telegraph, etc. 1964–; Sec. Cttee on Political Sociology, Int. Sociology Assen 1970–85; Founding mem. European Consortium for Political Research 1970; mem. US/UK Fulbright Comm. 1971–75; Guggenheim Fellow 1974; Visiting scholar at various insts, Europe, USA, Hong Kong; mem. Home Office Working Party on Electoral Register 1975–77; Co-founder British Politics Group 1974–; Convenor Work Group on UK Politics, Political Studies Assen 1976–88; mem. Council Int. Political Science Assen 1976–82; Tech. Consultant OECD, UNDP, World Bank, Council of Europe, Int. IDEA; Dir SSRC Research Programme, Growth of Govt 1982–86, Scotland in the World Forum 2008–11; Ed. Journal of Public Policy 1985–2011, Chair. 1981–85; Scientific Adviser, New Democracies Barometer, Paul Lazarsfeld Soc., Vienna 1991–; Fellow, British Acad.; Sr Fellow in Governance, Oxford Internet Inst. 2003–05; Hon. Vice-Pres. UK Political Studies Assen, Hon. Fellow American Acad. of Arts and Sciences, Finnish Acad. of Science and Letters, Acad. of Learned Socs in the Social Sciences 2000; Dr hc (Örebro Univ., Sweden), (European Univ. Inst., Florence); AMEX Prize in Int. Econs 1992, Lasswell Prize for Lifetime Achievement, Policy Studies Org. 1999; Lifetime Achievement Award, UK Political Studies Assen 2000, Lifetime Achievement, Int. Council on Comparative Study of Electoral Systems 2008, Prize for European Political Sociology, ECPR Dogan Foundation 2009, Sir Isaiah Berlin Award for Lifetime Achievement in Political Studies 2009. *Publications include:* numerous books on politics and public policy including Politics in England 1964, People in Politics: Observations Across the Atlantic 1970, Governing Without Consensus: An Irish Perspective 1971, International Almanack of Electoral History (co-author) 1974, The Problem of Party Government 1974, Northern Ireland: A Time of Choice 1976, Managing Presidential Objectives 1976, What is Governing? Purpose and Policy in Washington 1978, Can Government Go Bankrupt? (co-author) 1978, Do Parties Make A Difference 1984, Understanding Big Government 1984, Public Employment in Western Nations (co-author) 1985, Taxation by Political Inertia (co-author) 1987, Ministers and Ministries 1987, Presidents and Prime Ministers, The Postmodern President 1988, Ordinary People in Public Policy 1989, Training With Trainers? How Germany Avoids Britain's Supply-side Bottleneck (co-author) 1990, The Loyalties of Voters (co-author) 1990, Lesson-Drawing in Public Policy 1993 Inheritance in Public Policy (co-author) 1994, What is Europe? 1996, How Russia Votes (co-author) 1997, Democracy and Its Alternatives, Understanding Post-Communist Societies (co-author) 1998, A Society Transformed: Hungary in Time-Space Perspective, International Encyclopedia of Elections (co-author) 2000, The Prime Minister in a Shrinking World 2001, Elections without Order: Russia's Challenge to Vladimir Putin (co-author) 2002, Elections and Parties in New European Democracies 2003, Learning from Comparative Public Policy 2005, Russia Transformed (co-author) 2006, Parites and Elections in New European Democracies 2009, Understanding Post-Communist Transformation 2009, Popular Support for an Undemocratic Regime 2011, Representing Europeans: A Pragmatic Approach 2013, Learning about Politics in Time and Space 2013; hundreds of papers in academic journals. *Leisure interests:* architecture, music, writing. *Address:* Centre for the Study of Public Policy, University of Strathclyde, Glasgow, G1 1XQ (office); 1 East Abercromby Street, Helensburgh, G84 7SP, Scotland (home). *Telephone:* (1436) 672164 (office). *Fax:* (1436) 673125 (home). *E-mail:* richard.rose@strath.ac.uk (office). *Website:* www.cspp.strath.ac.uk (office).

ROSE, Sir Stuart Alan Ransom, Kt; British retail industry executive; *Non-Executive Chairman, Ocado Group Plc;* b. 17 March 1949, Gosport, Hants., England; s. of Harry Ransom Rose and the late Margaret Ransom Rose; m. Jennifer Cook 1973 (divorced 2010); one s. one d.; ed St Joseph's Convent, Dar-es-Salaam, Tanzania, Bootham School, York; various exec. positions with Marks & Spencer PLC 1972–89, Commercial Exec. (Europe), CEO Marks & Spencer Group PLC 2004–10, Exec. Chair. 2008–10, Chair. (non-exec.) 2010–11; joined Burton Group 1989, Chief Exec. Multiples Div. 1994–97; CEO Argos PLC 1998, Booker PLC 1998–2000, Iceland Group PLC (after merger with Booker) 2000, Arcadia PLC 2000–02; Ind. Dir (non-exec.) and Chair. (non-exec.) Ocado Group Plc (internet-only grocery retailer) 2013–; Dir (non-exec.) Land Securities plc, Woolworths Holdings Ltd 2011–; Chair. British Fashion Council 2003–, Business in the Community 2008–; mem. European Advisory Cttee Bridgepoint (pvt. equity firm) 2010–; Hon. LLD (Leeds) 2010; 2006 Business Leader of the Year, World Leadership Forum 2007. *Address:* Ocado Group Plc, Titan Court, 3 Bishop Square, Hatfield Business Park, Hatfield, Herts., AL10 9NE, England (office). *Telephone:* (1707) 227800 (office). *Fax:* (1707) 227999 (office). *E-mail:* company.secretary@ocado.com (office). *Website:* www.ocado.com (office).

ROSEANNE; American comedienne and actress; b. (Roseanne Cherrie Barr), 3 Nov. 1952, Salt Lake City; d. of Jerry Barr and Helen Barr; m. 1st Bill Pentland 1974 (divorced 1989); m. 2nd Tom Arnold 1990 (divorced 1994); three c. (from previous m.); m. 3rd Ben Thomas 1994; one s.; fmr window dresser, cocktail waitress; worked as comic in bars and church coffeehouse, Denver; produced forum for women performers Take Back the Mike, Univ. of Colo; performer, The Comedy

Store, LA; featured on TV special Funny and The Tonight Show; TV special, On Location: The Roseanne Barr Show 1987; star of TV series, Roseanne (ABC) 1988–97; Host Search for America's Funniest Mom 2007–; Emmy Award (Outstanding Leading Actress in a Comedy Series) 1993. *Films:* She Devil 1989, Look Who's Talking Too (voice) 1990, Freddy's Dead: The Final Nightmare 1991, Even Cowgirls Get the Blues 1993, Blue in the Face 1995, Unzipped 1995, Meet Wally Sparks 1997, Home on the Range (voice) 2004, A Dairy Tale (voice) 2004. *Television includes:* Little Rosie (series) (voice) 1990, Backfield in Motion 1991, Rosey and Buddy Show (series) (voice) 1992, The Woman Who Loved Elvis 1993, General Hospital (series) 1993, Saturday Night Special (series) 1996, The Roseanne Show (host) 1998–2000, Get Bruce 1999. *Publications:* My Life as a Woman 1989, Roseanne: My Lives 1994. *E-mail:* askroseanne@roseanneworld .com. *Website:* www.roseanneworld.com.

ROSELLE, David, PhD; American mathematician and university administrator; *Executive Director, Winterthur Museum and Country Estate;* b. 30 May 1939, Vandergrift, Pennsylvania; s. of William Roselle and Suzanne Clever; m. Louise H. Dowling 1967; one s. one d.; ed West Chester State Coll., Duke Univ.; Asst Prof., Univ. of Maryland 1965–68; Assoc. Prof. later Prof., Los Angeles State Univ. 1968–74; Prof. Virginia Polytechnic Inst. and State Univ. 1974–87; Dean, Grad. School 1979–81, Dean of Research and Grad. Studies 1981–83, Univ. Provost 1983–87; Pres. Univ. of Kentucky 1987–90, Univ. of Delaware 1990–2007, Pres. Emer. 2007–; Exec. Dir Winterthur Museum and Country Estate, Wilmington 2008–; several hon. degrees; numerous grants and honours. *Publications:* numerous mathematics articles in graph theory and combinatorics. *Leisure interests:* golf, reading, walking. *Address:* Office of the Executive Director, Winterthur Museum and Country Estate, Route 52, Wilmington, DE 19735 (office); 14 Laurel Ridge Lane, Wilmington, DE 19807, USA (home). *Telephone:* (302) 888-4770 (office); (302) 421-3603 (home). *E-mail:* roselle@udel.edu (office). *Website:* www .winterthur.org (office).

ROSEN, Hilary B.; American music industry executive and public relations consultant; *Managing Director, SKDKnickerbocker;* ed George Washington Univ.; worked for NJ Gov. Brendan Byrne and US Senator Bill Bradley; worked on transition team of US Senator Dianne Feinstein 1992; government affairs specialist with Liz Robbins Assocs and later with her own firm; joined Recording Industry Asscn of America 1987, Chair. and CEO 1998–2003; involved in establishing Secure Digital Music Initiative, passage of Digital Performance Rights Act, US ratification of World Intellectual Property Org. treaties regarding copyright laws, adoption of Digital Millennium Copyright Act; Founding Partner, Berman Rosen Global Strategies LLC (intellectual property consultant), Washington, DC 2006; Man. Dir Brunswick Group, Washington, DC 2008–10; Man. Dir SKDKnickerbocker, Washington, DC 2010–; commentator, CNN 2008–; fmr Political Dir Huffington Post; Founding Bd mem. Rock the Vote; Bd mem. Ford's Theater, Human Rights Campaign Foundation, Kaiser Family Foundation, LifeBeat, Meridian Int. Center, Nat. Cancer Foundation, Nat. Music Council, Y.E.S. to Jobs; American Civil Liberties Union Torch of Liberty.

ROSEN, Milton William, BS; American engineer and physicist; b. 25 July 1915, Philadelphia, Pa; s. of Abraham Rosen and Regina Rosen (née Weiss); m. Josephine Haar 1948; three d.; ed Univ. of Pennsylvania, Univ. of Pittsburgh and California Inst. of Tech.; engineer, Westinghouse Electric and Mfg Co. 1937–38; engineer-physicist, Naval Research Lab., Washington, DC 1940–58, Scientific Officer, Viking Rocket 1947–55, Head, Rocket Devt Branch 1953–55, Tech. Dir Project Vanguard (earth satellite) 1955–58; engineer, NASA 1958–74; Chief of Rocket Vehicle Devt Programs 1958–59, Asst Dir Launch Vehicle Programs 1960–61, Dir Launch Vehicles and Propulsion 1961–63; Sr Scientist, Office of DOD and Interagency Affairs, NASA 1963–72; Deputy Assoc. Admin. for Space Science (Eng) 1972–74; Exec. Sec. Space Science Bd 1974–78; Exec. Sec. Cttee on Impacts of Stratospheric Change, NAS 1978–80, Cttee on Underground Coal Mine Safety 1980–83; Exec. Dir Space Applications Bd 1983–85; Chair. Greater Washington Assocn of Unitarian Churches 1966–68; Study Leader, Inst. for Learning in Retirement, American Univ., Washington, DC 1987–; first James H. Wyld Award for the Application of Rocket Power 1954. *Publication:* The Viking Rocket Story 1955. *Leisure interests:* music, art collecting, rug making. *Address:* 5610 Alta Vista Road, Bethesda, MD 20817, USA (home). *Telephone:* (301) 530-1497 (home).

ROSENBERG, Pamela, BA, MA; German (b. American) music administrator and academic; *Dean of Fellows and Programs, American Academy in Berlin;* b. (Pamela Lyn Henry), 24 April 1945, Los Angeles, Calif.; m. Wolf Rosenberg (deceased); two c.; ed Univ. of California, Berkeley, Ohio State Univ., Guildhall School of Music and London Opera Centre, UK; previous positions at Netherlands Opera, Amsterdam, Deutschen Schauspielhaus, Hamburg; Scenic Supervisor, subsequently Artistic Admin. Frankfurt Opera; Co-Dir (Co-Intendant) Stuttgart Opera 1991–2000; Gen. Dir San Francisco Opera 2001–06; Intendant (Gen. Man.) Berlin Philharmonic Orchestra 2006–10; Dean of Fellows and Programs, American Acad. in Berlin 2010–; Chair. Man. Bd, Barenboim Musikkindergarten Berlin, Musiktheater im Revier Foundation; Vice-Chair. Senate of German-Brandenburgische Akad. der Wissenschaften; mem. Univ. Council (Hochschulrat) of Hochschule für Musik, Freiburg; mem. Bd of Advisors, Cogut Center for the Humanities, Brown Univ., Man. Bd, Liz Mohn Foundation; Trustee, Univ. of California, Berkeley Foundation. *Address:* American Academy in Berlin, Am Sandwerder 17–19, 14109 Berlin, Germany (office). *Telephone:* (30) 80483103 (office). *Fax:* (30) 80483111 (office). *E-mail:* pr@americanacademy.de (office). *Website:* www.americanacademy.de (office).

ROSENBERG, Pierre Max; French curator; b. 13 April 1936, Paris; s. of Charles Rosenberg and Gertrude Rosenberg; m. 2nd Béatrice de Rothschild 1981; one d.; ed Lycée Charlemagne, Faculté de droit de Paris and Ecole du Louvre; Chief Curator Dept des Peintures, Musée du Louvre 1983, Inspecteur gén. des musées 1988, Conservateur gén. du Patrimoine 1990–94, Pres. and Dir 1994–2001; Curator Musée Nat. de l'Amitié et des Relations franco-américaines de Blérancourt 1981–93; mem. Acad. Française 1995; Foreign mem. American Acad. Arts and Sciences, American Philosophical Soc., Accad. Naz. dei Lincei, Accad. Naz. di San Luca, Accad. del Disegno, Florence, Accad. Pietro Vanucci, Accad. Clementina, Ateneo Veneto, Istituto Veneto di Scienze, Lettere ed Arti; Hon. Fellow, Royal Academy, London; Chevalier Ordre des Arts et des Lettres, Ordre nat. du Mérite,

Officier Légion d'honneur, Grand officier de l'ordre du Mérite (Italy), Commdr de l'ordre du Mérite (Germany). *Publications include:* Il Seicento francese 1970, Georges de La Tour 1973, Chardin. Tout l'œuvre peint 1983, Peyron 1983, Saint-Non. Fragonard. Panopticon italiano. Un diario di viaggio ritrovato. 1759-1761 1986, Fragonard. Tout l'œuvre peint 1989, Les frères Le Nain. Tout l'œuvre peint 1993, Nicolas Poussin. 1594-1665 1994, Antoine Watteau 1996, Georges de La Tour 1998, Julien de Parme, 1736-1799 1998, La pittura in Europa 1999, From Drawing to Painting 2000, Michel-François Dandré-Bardon: 1700-1783 2001, Jacques-Louis David: 1748-1825 2002, De Raphaël à la Révolution. Les relations artistiques entre la France et l'Italie 2005, Gesamtverzeichnis Französische Gemälde des 17. und 18. Jahrhunderts in deutschen Sammlungen 2005, En Amérique seulement 2006, Dictionnaire amoureux du Louvre 2007. *Address:* 35 rue de Vaugirard, 75006 Paris (home); Institut de France, 23 quai Conti, 75006 Paris, France (office). *Telephone:* 1-45-48-78-13 (home). *E-mail:* pierre.rosenberg@ wanadoo.fr (home).

ROSENBERG, Richard Morris, BA, MBA, LLB; American banker (retd); b. 21 April 1930, Fall River, Mass; s. of Charles Rosenberg and Betty Peck; m. Barbara K. Cohen 1956; two s.; ed Suffolk and Golden Gate Univs; Publicity Asst, Crocker-Anglo Bank, San Francisco 1959–62; Banking Services Officer, Wells Fargo Bank 1962–65, Asst Vice-Pres. 1965–68, Vice-Pres. Marketing Dept 1968, Vice-Pres. Dir of Marketing 1969, Sr Vice-Pres. Marketing and Advertising Div. 1970–75, Exec. Vice-Pres. 1975, Vice-Chair. 1980–83; Vice-Chair. Crocker Nat. Corpn 1983–85; Pres. and COO Seafirst Corpn 1986–87; Dir, Pres. and COO Seattle-First Nat. Bank 1985–87; Vice-Chair. Bd Bank America Corpn San Francisco 1987–90; Chair. and CEO BankAmerica Corpn/Bank of America 1990–96 (retd); mem. Bd of Dirs Buck Inst. for Age Research, Health Care Property Investors, Inc., San Francisco Symphony, Naval War Coll. Foundation; mem. Advisory Bd Shorenstein Properties LLC; fmr mem. Bd of Dirs Airborne Express, Northrop Grumman Corpn, Pacific Mutual Life Insurance Co., United Way; Chair. Exec. Council Univ. of Calif. Medical Center; mem. State Bar of Calif.; Trustee, Calif. Inst. of Tech.; Horatio Alger Award, American Acad. of Arts and Science. *Leisure interests:* tennis, avid reader, history. *Address:* Bank of America Center, 555 California Street, Retired Executives, CA5-705-11-01, 11th Floor, PO Box 37000, San Francisco, CA 94104, USA. *Telephone:* (415) 913-4177. *Fax:* (415) 913-4188.

ROSENBERG, Steven A., BA, MD, PhD; American physician and immunologist; *Chief of Surgery, National Cancer Institute;* b. 2 Aug. 1940, New York; s. of Abraham Rosenberg and Harriet Wendroff; m. Alice R. O'Connell 1968; three d.; ed Bronx High School of Science and Johns Hopkins Univ., Harvard Univ.; Intern, Peter Bent Brigham Hosp. Boston 1963–64, Surgical Resident 1968–69, further surgical training 1972–74; Fellow in Immunology, Harvard Medical School 1969–70, NIH 1970–72; Chief of Surgery, Nat. Cancer Inst. Bethesda, Md 1974–; Prof. of Surgery, Uniformed Services Univ. of Health Sciences and George Washington Univ. School of Medicine and Health Sciences, Washington, DC; mem. American Soc. of Clinical Oncology (fmr mem. Bd of Dirs), Inst. of Medicine, NAS, Soc. of Univ. Surgeons, American Surgical Asscn, American Assocn for Cancer Research, American Assocn of Immunologists; Meritorious Service Medal, US Public Health Service 1981, 1986, Friedrich Sasse Prize, Univ. of West Berlin, Germany 1986, Nils Alwell Prize 1987, Distinguished Alumnus Award, Johns Hopkins Univ. 1987, Simon M. Shubitz Prize, Univ. of Chicago Cancer Research Center 1988, Griffuel Prize for Research, French Assocn for Research on Cancer 1988, Milken Family Foundation Cancer Award 1988, Armand Hammer Cancer Prize 1985, 1988, Karnofsky Prize 1991, Ellis Island Medal of Honor 1998, John Wayne Award for Clinical Research 1996, Heath Memorial Award 2002, Flance-Karl Award 2002, American-Italian Cancer Foundation Prize 2003, Richard V. Smalley, MD, Memorial Award 2002. *Publications:* eight books and more than 800 articles in medical journals. *Address:* Center for Cancer Research, Building 10-CRC, Room 3-3940, 10 Center Drive, MSC 1201, Bethesda, MD 20892 (office); National Cancer Institute, 9000 Rockville Pike, Building 10, Room 3-3944, Bethesda, MD 20892, USA (office). *Telephone:* (301) 496-4164 (office). *Fax:* (301) 402-1738 (office). *E-mail:* SAR@nih.gov (office). *Website:* ccr.cancer.gov (office).

ROSENFELD, Arthur H., PhD; American physicist and academic; *Professor Emeritus of Physics, University of California, Berkeley;* b. 1927; ed Univ. of Chicago; specialist in energy efficiency tech.; joined Dept of Physics, Univ. of Calif., Berkeley 1955, worked with particle physics group of Luis Alvarez, Prof. of Physics 1957–94, Prof. Emer. 1994–; Founder and Dir Energy Efficient Buildings Program (later Center for Building Science), Lawrence Berkeley Nat. Lab. 1975–94, Co-f. Heat Islands Research Project 1985; Sr Adviser to US Dept of Energy's Asst Sec. for Energy Efficiency and Renewable Energy 1994–99; Commr, Calif. Energy Comm. 2000–, Chair. Research, Devt and Demonstration Cttee, second mem. Energy Efficiency Cttee; Co-founder American Council for an Energy Efficient Economy (ACEEE), Univ. of Calif. Inst. for Energy Efficiency, Center for Energy and Climate Solutions; Szilard Award for Physics in the Public Interest 1986, Carnot Award for Energy Efficiency, US Dept of Energy 1993, Enrico Fermi Award 2006. *Publication:* The Art of Energy Efficiency. *Address:* California Energy Commission, 1516 Ninth Street, MS-35, Sacramento, CA 95814, USA (office). *Telephone:* (916) 654-4930 (office). *Fax:* (916) 653-3478 (office). *E-mail:* ahrosenfeld@lbl.gov (office). *Website:* www.energy.ca.gov/commission/ commissioners/rosenfeld.html (office).

ROSENFELD, Irene B., BA/BS, MS, PhD; American business executive; *Chairman and CEO, Mondelēz International Inc.;* m.; two c.; ed Cornell Univ.; joined Kraft Foods in 1981, worked in market research and product man., later Exec. Vice-Pres. Kraft and Gen. Man. Desserts and Snacks, Exec. Vice-Pres. Beverages and Marketing Dir Beverages 1991–96, Exec. Vice-Pres. Kraft and Pres. Kraft Canada 1996–2000, Group Vice-Pres. Kraft Foods N American Operations, Tech., Procurement and Information Systems for Canada, Puerto Rico and Mexico 2000–02, Group Vice-Pres. Kraft Foods N America 2002–03 (resgnd), CEO Kraft Foods Inc. 2006–12, Chair. 2007–12, Chair. and CEO Mondelēz International (following spin off of two ind. public cos, Kraft Foods Group and Mondelēz International (global snacks business)) Oct. 2012–; Chair. and CEO Frito-Lay Inc. (div. of PepsiCo Inc.) 2004–06; mem. Bd Dirs AutoNation Inc.; Chair. Grocery Mfrs of America Industry Affairs Council 2001; Co-Chair. Jt GMA/Food Marketers Inst. Trading Pnr Alliance, Food and Health Strategy Group; fmr Chair. Food and Consumer Products Mfrs of Canada; mem. The

Economic Club of Chicago; Trustee, Cornell Univ.; elected to YWCA Acad. of Women Achievers, ranked by Fortune magazine amongst the 50 Most Powerful Women in Business in the US (31st) 2004, (27th) 2005, (fifth) 2006–07, (second) 2008–10, (first) 2011, (fourth) 2012, Masters of Excellence Award Center for Jewish Living 2005, ranked by Forbes magazine amongst the World's 100 Most Powerful Women (11th) 2006, (ninth) 2007, (sixth) 2008–09, (second) 2010, (tenth) 2011, (13th) 2012, (20th) 2013, ranked first by the Financial Times amongst the Top 50 Women in Global Business 2011. *Leisure interests:* playing the piano, rollerblading. *Address:* Mondelēz International, Inc., Three Parkway, North Deerfield, IL 60015, USA (office). *Telephone:* (847) 943-4000 (office). *E-mail:* info@mondelezinternational.com (office). *Website:* www.mondelezinternational .com (office).

ROSENSHINE, Allen Gilbert, BA; American advertising executive (retd); *Chairman Emeritus, BBDO Worldwide;* b. 14 March 1939; s. of Aaron Rosenshine and Anna Zuckerman; m. Suzan Weston-Webb 1979; two s.; ed Columbia Coll.; copywriter, J.B. Rundle, New York 1962–65; copywriter, Batten, Barton, Durstine & Osborn, New York 1965, copy supervisor 1967, Vice-Pres. 1968, Assoc. Creative Dir 1970, Sr Vice-Pres. and Creative Dir 1975–77, Exec. Vice-Pres. 1977–80, Pres. 1980–82, CEO 1981–86, Chair. 1983–86; Pres. and CEO BBDO Int. New York 1984–86; Pres. and COO Omnicom Group, New York 1986–88, CEO BBDO Worldwide (subsidiary), New York 1989–2004, Chair. 1989–2006, now Chair. Emer.; Founding mem. Partnership for a Drug-Free America, currently Vice Chair. and Exec. Creative Dir; mem. Creative Review Cttee, Advertising Council; mem. Bd of Dirs Business for Diplomatic Action. *Address:* c/o BBDO Worldwide, 1285 Avenue of the Americas, New York, NY 10019, USA (office). *Website:* www .allenrosenshine.com.

ROSENTHAL, Gert, MA; Guatemalan economist and diplomatist; *Permanent Representative, United Nations;* b. 11 Sept. 1935, Amsterdam, Netherlands; s. of Ludwig Rosenthal and Florence Rosenthal (née Koenigsberger); m. Margit Uhlmann; four d.; ed American School of Guatemala, Univ. of California, Berkeley, USA, Universidad de San Carlos de Guatemala; worked in pvt. sector 1959–67; economist, Nat. Planning Secr. 1960–64, Head Econ. Devt Div. 1965, Sec.-Gen. (rank of Minister) 1969–70, 1973–74; Officer in charge of external financing, Ministry of Finance 1966–67; Asst to Sec.-Gen., Secr. of Cen. American Common Market (SIECA) 1968, Project Dir UNCTAD project to promote SIECA, Guatemala City 1972–73; Prof. of Econ. Devt and Public Finance, Universidad Rafael Landivar, Guatemala 1969–74; Dir Sub-regional Office UN ECLA, Mexico 1974–85, Deputy Exec. Sec. UN ECLA, Santiago, Chile 1985–87, Exec. Sec. (rank of Under-Sec.-Gen. of UN) 1988–97; mem. Oversight Comm. of Guatemalan Peace Accords 1998; Amb. and Perm. Rep. to UN, New York 1999–2004, 2008–; Pres. UN ECOSOC 2003–04; Minister of Foreign Affairs 2006–08; Dr hc (Universidad del Valle) 1996. *Publications:* more than 120 articles on various topics related to devt in Latin America, with emphasis on Cen. America. *Address:* Permanent Mission of Guatemala to United Nations, 57 Park Avenue, New York, NY 10016, USA (office); Calle de los Duelos #6, Antigua, Guatemala (home). *Telephone:* (212) 679-4760 (office); 832-3659 (home). *Fax:* (212) 685-8741 (office); 832-3666 (home). *E-mail:* grosenthal@minex.gob.gt; guatemala@un.int (office). *Website:* www.guatemalaun.org (office).

ROSENTHAL, Sir Norman Leon, Kt, BA; British art curator; b. 8 Nov. 1944; s. of Paul Rosenthal and Kate Zucker; m. Manuela Beatriz Mena Marques 1989; two d.; ed Westminster City Grammar School, Univ. of Leicester; librarian Thomas Agnew & Sons 1966–68; Exhbns Officer, Brighton Museum and Art Gallery 1970–71, Exhbn Organizer Inst. Contemporary Arts 1974–76, Exhbns. Sec. RA 1977–2008; freelance curator 2008–; organizer of many exhbns including: Art into Society, I.C.A. 1974, A New Spirit in Painting, 1981, Zeitgeist, W Berlin 1982, German Art of the Twentieth Century and Staatsgalerie, Stuttgart 1985–86, Italian Art of the Twentieth Century, Royal Acad 1989, Metropolis, Berlin 1991, American Art in the Twentieth Century and Martin-Gropius Bau, Berlin 1993, Sensation 1997, Charlotte Salomon, RA 1998, Apocalypse RA 2000, The Genius of Rome 2001, Botticelli's Dante 2001, The Aztecs 2002/03, Kirchner 2004, Illuminating the Renaissance—The Triumph of Flemish Manuscript Painting in Europe 2004, The Art of Philip Guston 2004, Turks: A Journey of a Thousand Years 600–1600 2005; TV and radio broadcasts on contemporary art; mem. Opera Bd, Royal Opera House 1994–98, Bd Palazzo Grassi, Venice 1995–; Hon. Fellow RCA 1987; Officier, Ordre des Arts et des Lettres 2003, Cavaliere Ufficiale, Order of Merit (Italy) 1992, Cross, Order of Merit (Germany) 1993; Hon. DLitt (Southampton) 2003; German/British Forum Award 2003. *Television and radio:* undertakes many television and radio broadcasts and frequently addresses international conferences. *Publications:* contributes numerous articles and essays to catalogues and journals throughout the world. *Leisure interest:* music, especially opera. *Address:* c/o The Royal Academy of Arts, Burlington House, Piccadilly, London, W1J 0BD, England (office).

ROSENTHAL, Uri; Dutch political scientist, academic and politician; b. 19 July 1945, Montreux, Switzerland; m.; two c.; ed Univ. of Amsterdam, Erasmus Univ., Rotterdam; Lecturer, Univ. of Amsterdam 1970–73; Lecturer, Erasmus Univ. 1973–79, Prof. of Political Science 1980–; Prof. of Public Admin, Leiden Univ. 1987–; Chair., Inst. for Safety, Security and Crisis Man., The Hague –2010; mem. Senate (People's Party for Freedom and Democracy—VVD) 1999–2010, Leader VVD Group in Senate 2005–10; Minister of Foreign Affairs 2010–12; Chair. Editorial Bd Liberaal Reveil 1998–2005; Deputy Chair. Netherlands Org. for Scientific Research 1997–2002; Consultant, Centre for Risk and Crisis Man., Nanjing Univ., People's Repub. of China; mem. bd Centre for Parl. History, Int. Inst. for Social History, Urban Regeneration Forum; mem. Social and Econ. Council, Dutch Transport Safety Bd; Officer, Order of Orange-Nassau. *Address:* c/o Ministry of Foreign Affairs, Bezuidenhoutseweg 67, POB 20061, 2500 EB The Hague, Netherlands.

ROSHAL, Leonid Mikhailovich, MD, DSc; Russian paediatrician; *Executive Director, Moscow Institute of Emergency Children's Surgery and Traumatology;* b. 27 April 1933, Livnya, Orel Region; s. of Mikhail Filippovich Roshal and Emilia Lazarevna Roshal; m. 1st; one s.; m. 2nd Veda Zuponcic; ed Moscow Medical Inst.; paediatrician and specialist, paediatric surgeon Moscow hosps 1957–61; jr then sr researcher, then sr research paediatric surgeon MONIKI Inst. 1961–81; Dir Emergency Surgery and Children's Trauma Dept, Moscow Pediatric Scientific

Research Inst.1981–, Exec. Dir Moscow Inst. of Emergency Children's Surgery and Traumatology 2003–; Chair. Int. Task Force Cttee on Paediatric Disaster Medicine; mem. Exec. Cttee World Asscn for Emergency and Disaster Medicine, Exec. Cttee Russian Union of Paediatrics; Pres. Int. Charitable Fund for Children in Disasters and Wars; mem. Bd of Dirs Russian Asscn of Paediatric Surgery, British Asscn of Paediatric Surgeons, Georgian Acad. of Medical Sciences; organized and carried out rescue operations and rendered medical assistance following earthquakes and wars in many countries in Europe, Asia and America; took part in negotiations with terrorists taking hostages in Moscow theatre Sept. 2002, provided medical assistance to hostages and negotiated release of some children; acted as intermediary during Beslan school siege; elected Children's Doctor of the World by Moscow Journalists Community 1995; Order of Courage 2002; awarded title of National Hero 2002, Person of the Year (chosen by several Russian periodicals) 2002; numerous other awards. *Publications:* 7 books and more than 200 scientific articles on surgery and problems of children in catastrophes and wars. *Leisure interest:* music. *Address:* Children's Hospital, B. Polyanka str. 20, 103118 Moscow, Russia. *Telephone:* (495) 238-30-00 (office); (495) 137-87-08 (home). *Fax:* (495) 230-29-98. *E-mail:* roshal@lamport.ru.

ROSHCHEVSKY, Mikhail Pavlovich; Russian physiologist; *Chairman, Presidium of Komi Scientific Centre;* b. 5 March 1933; m.; two d.; ed Ural State Univ.; jr then sr researcher, scientific sec. Ural Research Inst. of Agric. 1958–60; Sr Researcher, Inst. of Biology Komi ASSR 1960–70; Deputy Chair. Presidium Scientific Cen. Komi ASSR 1970–83, Chair. 1983–; Dir Inst. of Physiology Komi Scientific Cen. Ural br. USSR Acad. of Sciences 1983–; Corresp. mem. USSR (now Russian) Acad. of Sciences 1987, mem. 1990; studies of ecological-physiological aspects of blood circulation, electrophysiolog of heart, electrocardiology; mem. Dept of Physiology Russian Acad. of Sciences. *Publications:* books and scientific works. *Address:* Presidium of Komi Scientific Centre, Kommunisticheskaya str. 24, 167982 Syktyvkar, Komi Republic, Russia. *Telephone:* (8212) 24-16-08 (office); (8212) 42-25-11 (home). *Fax:* (8212) 24-22-64 (office). *E-mail:* roshchevsky@ presidium.komisc.ru (office). *Website:* www.komisc.ru/en (office).

ROSI, Francesco; Italian film director; b. 1922, Naples; apprenticed as asst to Antonioni and Visconti; Dir first feature, La Sfida (The Challenge) 1958. *Films:* Salvatore Giuliano, Hands Over the City, More than a Miracle, Just Another War, Lucky Luciano, The Mattei Affair, Three Brothers, Chronicle of a Death Foretold, To Forget Palermo, Diario napoletano 1992, The Truce 1997.

RÖSLER, Philipp, MD; German physician and politician; b. 24 Feb. 1973, Khanh Hung, Ba Xuyen Prov., fmr South Vietnam (now Soc Trang Prov., Viet Nam); adopted from a RC orphanage near Saigon by a German couple 1973; m. Wiebke Rösler; twin d.; ed Medizinische Hochschule, Hanover, Fed. Armed Forces Hosp., Hamburg; joined Bundeswehr (army) as medical officer cadet 1992; qualified as doctor 2001; mem. FDP 1992–, mem. Lower Saxony FDP Exec. Cttee 1996, Gen. Sec. Lower Saxony FDP 2000–04, Chair. 2006, Chair. FDP 2011–13; mem. Lower Saxony Landtag (prov. parl.) 2003–09, Chair. FDP Parl. Group 2003; Prov. Minister for Econs and Deputy Minister-Pres. of Lower Saxony Feb.–Oct. 2009; Fed. Minister of Health 2009–11, of Econs and Tech. 2011–13; Vice-Chancellor of Germany 2011–13; Chair. Bd of Supervisory Dirs KfW Bankengruppe 2012–. *Address:* Federal Ministry of Economics and Technology, 11019 Berlin (office); Federal Ministry of Economics and Technology, Scharnhorststr. 34–37, 10115 Berlin, Germany (office). *Telephone:* (30) 18615-9 (office). *Fax:* (30) 18615-7010 (office). *E-mail:* info@bmwi.de (office). *Website:* www.bmwi.de (office); www.philipp -roesler.de.

ROSNER, Robert, PhD; American physicist, astronomer and astrophysicist; *William Wrather Distinguished Service Professor in Astronomy and Astrophysics and Physics Director, Energy Policy Institute of Chicago, University of Chicago;* b. 26 June 1947, Garmisch-Partenkirchen, Germany; s. of Heinz Rosner and Faina Rosner; m. Marsha R. Rosner 1971; two d.; ed Brandeis Univ., Harvard Univ.; Asst Prof., later Assoc. Prof. of Astronomy, Harvard Univ. 1978–86; Prof. of Astronomy and Astrophysics, Univ. of Chicago, 1987, Chair. Dept of Astronomy and Astrophysics 1991–97, William E. Wrather Distinguished Service Prof. 1998–, Prof. of Physics 2000–, Co-Dir Energy Policy Inst. of Chicago 2010–, Prof., Harris School of Public Policy Studies 2011–; Assoc. Lab. Dir and Chief Scientist, Argonne Nat. Lab. 2002–05, Dir 2005–09; Rothschild Visiting Prof., Newton Inst. for Math. Sciences, Univ. of Cambridge, UK 2004; mem. American Acad. of Arts and Sciences 2001; Foreign mem. Norwegian Acad. of Science and Letters 2004; Fellow, American Physical Soc. 1988; Visiting Prof., Center for Int. Security and Conflict, Stanford Univ. 2009–10; Life mem. Clare Hall, Cambridge 2005–; Hon. PhD (Illinois Inst. of Tech.) 2007, (Northern Illinois Univ.) 2008; Woodrow Wilson Fellow 1969, Gordon Bell Prize (Supercomputing) 2000, Thompson Lecturer, Nat. Center for Atmospheric Research 2001, Rosseland Lecturer, Univ. of Oslo 1998, Parker Lecturer, American Astronomical Soc./Solar Physics Div. 1995. *Publications include:* more than 190 publs in scientific journals. *Leisure interests:* sailing, skiing, hiking, reading. *Address:* Enrico Fermi Institute, University of Chicago, 5640 South Ellis Avenue, Chicago, IL 60637, USA (office). *Telephone:* (773) 702-0560 (office). *E-mail:* r-rosner@uchicago.edu (office).

ROSS, Christopher W. S., BA, MA; American diplomatist and UN official; *Personal Envoy of Secretary-General for Western Sahara, United Nations;* b. 3 March 1943, Quito, Ecuador; one s.; ed Princeton Univ., Johns Hopkins Univ.; Editorial Asst, Middle East Journal 1965–68; teacher of Arabic, Columbia Univ. 1966, Princeton Univ. 1967; Jr Officer Trainee, US Information Agency (USIA), Washington, DC 1968–69, served in Tripoli 1969–70, Br. Public Affairs Officer and Dir American Cultural Center, Fez, Morocco 1970–73, Information Officer, Beirut 1973–76, Public Affairs Officer, Algiers 1976–79; held several positions at US Dept of State, including Deputy Chief of Mission, Embassy in Algiers 1979–81, Public Affairs Adviser to Asst Sec. for Near Eastern and S Asian Affairs 1981–82, Special Asst to Special Presidential Envoys to Lebanon and Middle East 1982–84, Dir of Regional Affairs, Bureau of Near Eastern and S Asian Affairs 1984–85, Exec. Asst to Under-Sec. for Political Affairs 1985–88, Amb. to Algeria 1988–91, to Syria 1991–98, Coordinator for Counterterrorism 1998–99, Sr Adviser to Under-Sec. of State for Public Diplomacy and Public Affairs 2001–03, Sr Adviser, Coalition Provisional Authority and Embassy in Baghdad 2004, Special Adviser (on Iraq), Bureau of Near Eastern Affairs 2004–09, Sr Adviser for Middle East and N Africa 2006–09, Exec. Dir Search for Common Ground Middle East and N Africa Program

1999–2001, Personal Envoy of UN Sec.-Gen. for Western Sahara 2009–; Dr hc (Lewis and Clark Coll.) 2002; USIA Superior Honor Awards 1976, 1984, Presidential Meritorious Service Awards 1983, 1985, 1989, 1993, Dept of State's Superior Honor Award 1988 and Distinguished Honor Award 1997, Dept of Defense's Distinguished Public Service Medal 2005. *Address:* Room 3400, UN Headquarters, 760 United Nations Plaza, New York, NY 10017, USA (office). *Telephone:* (917) 420-0701 (office). *E-mail:* rossc@un.org (office). *Website:* www.un .org (office).

ROSS, Dennis B., PhD; American academic, diplomatist and fmr government official; *Counselor, Washington Institute for Near East Policy;* b. 26 Nov. 1948, San Francisco; m. Deborah Ross; one s. two d.; ed Univ. of California, Los Angeles; Deputy Dir Office of Net Assessment, US Defense Dept, Washington, DC 1982–84, 1989–92; Exec. Dir of program on Soviet Int. Behavior sponsored by Univ. of California, Berkeley and Stanford Univ. 1984–86; Dir Near East and S Asian Affairs, Nat. Security Council (during Reagan Admin); Dir Policy Planning Office, US State Dept 1988–92, Special Middle East Co-ordinator 1992–2001, helped achieve the 1995 Interim Agreement and brokered the Hebron Accord 1997; Counsellor and Ziegler Distinguished Fellow, Washington Inst. for Near East Policy 2001–08, Counsellor (part–time) 2008–09, Counselor 2011–; Special US Envoy to Middle East, US State Dept 2009; Special Asst to the Pres. and Sr Dir for Cen. Region, Nat. Security Council 2009–10; Adjunct Lecturer, Kennedy School of Govt, Harvard Univ. 2002–04; Fred and Rita Richman Distinguished Visiting Prof., Brandeis Univ. 2003, 2005; Allis-Chalmers Distinguished Prof. of Int. Affairs, Marquette Univ. 2004–05; Adjunct Prof., Georgetown Univ. School of Foreign Service 2006–07, also Adjunct Prof. of Govt, Georgetown Univ. 2007; Bartels World Affairs Fellow, Cornell Univ. 2005; Chair. Inst. for Jewish People Policy Planning, Jerusalem; has served as Foreign Affairs Analyst for Fox News Channel; Hon. DHumLitt (Amherst Coll.) 2002, Dr hc (Jewish Theological Seminary, Syracuse Univ.); UCLA Alumnus of the Year; Presidential Medal for Distinguished Fed. Civilian Service, Truman Peace Prize from Harry S. Truman Research Inst. for the Advancement of Peace, Hebrew Univ. of Jerusalem 2008. *Publications include:* The Missing Peace: The Inside Story of the Fight for Middle East Peace 2004, Statecraft: And How to Restore America's Standing in the World 2007, Myths, Illusions and Peace: Finding a New Direction for America in the Middle East (with David Makovsky) 2009; numerous articles in learned journals and newspapers. *Address:* Washington Institute for Near East Policy, 1828 L Street, NW, Suite 1050, Washington, DC 20036, USA (office). *Telephone:* (202) 452-0650 (office). *Fax:* (202) 223-5364 (office). *Website:* www.washingtoninstitute.org (office).

ROSS, Diana; American singer and actress; b. 26 March 1944, Detroit; d. of Fred Ross and Ernestine Ross; m. 1st Robert Ellis Silberstein 1971 (divorced 1976); three d.; m. 2nd Arne Naess 1985 (died 2004); one s.; fmr lead singer the Supremes (later Diana Ross and the Supremes), solo singer 1970–; citation from US Vice-Pres. Hubert Humphrey for efforts on behalf of Pres. Lyndon Johnson's Youth Opportunity Programme, from Mrs. Martin Luther King and Rev. Abernathy for contrib. to Southern Christian Leadership Conf. cause, Billboard, Cash Box and Record World magazine awards as world's outstanding female singer, Grammy Award 1970, Female Entertainer of the Year, Nat. Assocn for the Advancement of Colored People 1970, Cue Award as Entertainer of the Year 1972, Golden Apple Award 1972, Gold Medal Award, Photoplay 1972, Antoinette Perry Award 1977, Golden Globe Award 1972, Kennedy Center Honor 2007, BET Lifetime Achievement Award 2007. *Films include:* Lady Sings the Blues 1972, Mahogany 1975, The Wiz 1978. *Recordings include:* albums: I'm Still Waiting 1971, Touch Me In The Morning 1973, Diana 1980, Why Do Fools Fall in Love? 1981, Eaten Alive 1984, Chain Reaction 1986, Workin' Overtime 1989, Surrender 1989, Ain't No Mountain High Enough 1989, The Forces Behind the Power 1991, The Remixes 1994, Take me Higher 1995, Gift of Love 1996, The Real Thing 1998, Every Day is a New Day 1999, Voice of Love 2000, Gift of Love 2000, Blue 2006, I Love You 2006. *Publications include:* Secrets of a Sparrow (autobiog.) 1993. *Address:* c/o Creative Artists Agency, 2000 Avenue of the Stars, Los Angeles, CA 90067, USA (office). *Website:* www.dianaross.de (home).

ROSS, Rt Hon. Lord Donald MacArthur, PC, MA, LLB, FRSE; British judge (retd); b. 29 March 1927, Dundee, Scotland; s. of John Ross and Jessie MacArthur Thomson; m. Dorothy M. Annand 1958 (died 2004); two d.; ed High School of Dundee, Univ. of Edinburgh; nat. service with Black Watch 1947–49; TA rank of Capt. 1949–58; Advocate 1952; QC (Scotland) 1964; Vice-Dean, Faculty of Advocates 1967–73, Dean 1973–76; Sheriff Prin. of Ayr and Bute 1972–73; Senator, Coll. of Justice, Scotland and Lord of Session 1977–97; Lord Justice Clerk of Scotland and Pres. of Second Div. of the Court of Session 1985–97; Chair. Judicial Studies Cttee for Scotland 1997–2001; mem. Parole Bd for Scotland 1997–2002; Deputy Chair. Boundary Comm. for Scotland 1977–85; mem. Scottish Cttee of Council on Tribunals 1970–76, Cttee on Privacy 1970; mem. Court of Heriot Watt Univ. 1978–90 (Chair. 1984–90); mem. Council Royal Soc. of Edin. 1997–99, Vice-Pres. 1999–2002; Lord High Commr to Gen. Ass. of Church of Scotland 1990, 1991; Hon. LLD (Edin.) 1987, (Dundee) 1991, (Abertay, Dundee) 1994, (Aberdeen) 1998; Hon. DUniv (Heriot Watt) 1988; Royal Soc. of Edinburgh Bicentenary Medal 2004. *Publication:* contrib. to Stair Memorial Encyclopaedia of Scots Law. *Leisure interests:* gardening, walking, travelling. *Address:* 7/1 Tipperlinn Road, Edinburgh, EH10 5ET, Scotland. *Telephone:* (131) 447-6771. *Fax:* (131) 446-3813. *E-mail:* rosd33@aol.com.

ROSS, Ian Gordon, AO, MSc, PhD, FAA; Australian chemist and academic; b. 5 July 1926, Sydney; s. of Gordon R. Ross and Isabella M. Jenkins; m. Viola Bartlett 1975; ed Univs of Sydney and London; Research Assoc., Fla State Univ. 1953; Lecturer, then Reader in Physical Chem., Univ. of Sydney 1954–67, Prof. of Chem. 1968–90; Pro-Vice-Chancellor ANU 1975, 1989–90, Deputy Vice-Chancellor 1977–88; Chair. Australian Research Grants Cttee 1977–79, Inquiry into Govt Labs 1982–83, Australian & New Zealand Asscn for the Advancement of Science 1984–86, Communication Research Inst. of Australia 1994–2004; Sec. for Science Policy, Australian Acad. of Science 1989–93; Dir Anutech Pty Ltd 1979–97; Hon. LLD; H. G. Smith Medal, Royal Australian Chem. Inst. 1972. *Publications:* scientific papers on theoretical chemistry and molecular spectroscopy. *Address:* 16/18 George Street, Queanbeyan, NSW 2620, Australia. *Telephone:* (2) 6297-3510. *Fax:* (2) 6299-6324.

ROSS, James Hood, OBE, BA; British business executive; b. 13 Sept. 1938, London; s. of Capt. T. D. Ross RN and Lettice Ferrier Hood; m. Sara B. V. Purcell 1964; one s. two d.; ed Sherborne School, Jesus Coll., Oxford and Manchester Business School; British Petroleum Co. PLC 1959–92, Gen. Man. BP Zaïre, Burundi and Rwanda, Gen. Man. BP Tanker Co., Gen. Man. Stolt-Nielsen (USA), Gen. Man. Corp. Planning BP, Chief Exec. BP Oil Int., Chair. and Chief Exec. BP America; Chief Exec. Cable & Wireless PLC 1992–95; Chair. Littlewoods Org. 1996–2002, Nat. Grid Group PLC (later) 1999–2002, Co-Chair. Nat. Grid Transco (after Nat. Grid merger with Lattice) 2002–04; mem. Bd of Dirs (non-exec.) McGraw Hill Inc. 1988–, Schneider Electric 1996, Datacard Inc. 1997–, Prudential PLC 2004–11; Trustee, The Cleveland Orchestra 1988–; Chair. Leadership Foundation for Higher Education 2003–10. *Leisure interests:* music, gardening, sailing.

ROSSANT, Janet, PhD, FRS, FRSC; British/Canadian geneticist; *Senior Scientist in the Developmental and Stem Cell Biology Program and Chief of Research, The Hospital for Sick Children;* b. 13 July 1950, Chatham, Kent, England; d. of Leslie Rossant and Doris Rossant; m. Alex Bain 1977; one s.; ed St Hugh's Coll., Oxford, Darwin Coll., Cambridge; Research Fellow in Zoology, Univ. of Oxford 1975–77; Asst Prof. of Biological Sciences, Brock Univ., Canada 1977–82, Assoc. Prof. 1982–85; Assoc. Prof. of Molecular and Medical Genetics, Univ. of Toronto 1985–88, Prof. 1988–, Univ. Prof. 2001–; Sr Investigator, Programme in Devt and Foetal Health, Samuel Lunenfeld Research Inst. 1985–2005; currently Sr Scientist in the Developmental and Stem Cell Biology Program and Chief of Research, Hospital for Sick Children, Toronto; Pres. Soc. for Developmental Biology; mem. American and Canadian Socs for Cell Biology; Gibb's Prize for Zoology, Oxford 1972, Beit Memorial Fellowship 1975, E.W.R. Steacie Memorial Fellowship 1983, Howard Hughes Int. Scholar 1991, MRC Distinguished Scientist 1996, McLaughlin Medal (Royal Soc. of Canada) 1998, NCIC/Eli Lilly Robert L. Noble Prize 2000, Killam Prize for Health Sciences 2004, Michael Smith Prize for Health Research 2005. *Publications include:* Experimental Approaches to Mammalian Embryonic Development (with R. A. Pedersen) 1986, Mouse Development (with P. P. L. Tam) 2001; over 200 articles in scientific journals. *Leisure interests:* running, cooking, theatre. *Address:* Rossant Lab, Room 13-305, 101 College Street, Toronto, ON M5G 1L7, Canada (office). *Telephone:* (416) 813-7929 (office). *E-mail:* janet.rossant@ sickkids.ca (office). *Website:* www.sickkids.ca/research/rossant (office).

ROSSEINSKY, Matthew (Matt) Jonathan, BSc, DPhil, FRS, FRSC; British chemist and academic; *Professor of Inorganic Chemistry, University of Liverpool;* m.; three c.; ed St John's Coll. and Merton Coll., Oxford; spent two years at Bell Labs, NJ, USA 1990–92; Univ. Lecturer, Dept of Chem., Univ. of Oxford 1992–99; Prof. of Inorganic Chem., Univ. of Liverpool 1999–; Royal Soc. Research Prof. 2013–; Wolfson Merit Award, Royal Soc. 2002, RSC Tilden Lectureship 2005, Distinguished Summer Lecturer in Inorganic Chem., Northwestern Univ., USA 2006, inaugural De Gennes Prize, RSC 2009, C.N.R. Rao Award, Chemical Research Soc. of India 2010, Hughes Medal, Royal Soc. 2011. *Publications:* numerous papers in professional journals. *Address:* Department of Chemistry, University of Liverpool, Crown Street, Liverpool, L69 7ZD, England (office). *Telephone:* (151) 794-3499 (office). *Fax:* (151) 794-3587 (office). *E-mail:* m.j .rosseinsky@liv.ac.uk (office). *Website:* www.liv.ac.uk/chemistry/research/ rosseinsky-group (office).

ROSSEL, Eduard Ergartovich, CandTechSc; Russian politician; *Governor of Sverdlovsk Region;* b. 8 Oct. 1937, Bor, Gorki region; m.; one d.; ed Sverdlovsk Ore Inst.; master construction site, head of construction trust Sreduralstroi; supervised construction of Krasnouralsk superphosphate factory, Nevyansk cement factory, Nizhny Tagil metallurgy plant; head Sverdlovsk regional exec. cttee, then Gov. Sverdlovsk Region 1991–93, tried to proclaim Ural Repub., discharged by Pres. Yeltsin, re-elected Head of Admin. and Gov. Sverdlovsk Region 1995–; mem. Russian Council of Fed. 1993–94, 1995–2001; Chair. Sverdlovsk regional Duma 1994–95; Founder and Chair. Org. Preobrazhenie Otechestva; Pres. Asscn for Econ. Co-operation of Ural Region 1995–; mem. Bd Union of Russian Govs 1996; mem. Int. Acad. of Regional Devt and Co-operation; mem. United Russia (UR) (Yedinaya Rossiya); Order 'Decoration of Honour' 1975, 1980, Order for Achievement to Fatherland Fourth Degree 1996, Third Degree 2000; Lenin Centenary Anniversary Medal 'For Valiant Labour' 1970, Honoured Constructor of Russian Soviet Federal Socialist Repub. 1983. *Address:* Governor's Office, Oktyabrskaya pl. 1, 620031 Ekaterinburg, Russia (office). *Telephone:* (343) 217-87-17 (office). *Fax:* (343) 378-18-30 (office). *E-mail:* so@midural.ru (office). *Website:* www.rossel.ru.

ROSSELLINI, Isabella; American actress and model; b. 18 June 1952, Rome; d. of Roberto Rossellini and Ingrid Bergman; m. 1st Martin Scorsese (q.v.) 1979 (divorced 1982); m. 2nd Jonathan Wiedemann (divorced); one d.; ed Acad. of Fashion and Costume, Rome and New School for Social Research, New York; worked briefly as costume designer for father's films; went to New York 1972; worked as journalist for Italian TV; cover-girl for Vogue 1980; contract to model Lancôme cosmetics 1982–95; Vice-Pres. Lancaster Cosmetics GPs Marketing Dept 1995–. *Films include:* A Matter of Time 1976, White Nights 1985, Blue Velvet 1986, Tough Guys Don't Dance 1987, Siesta 1987, Zelly and Me, Cousins 1989, Wild at Heart 1990, The Siege of Venice 1991, Death Becomes Her, The Pickle, The Innocent, Fearless 1994, Wyatt Earp 1994, Immortal Beloved 1994, The Innocent 1995, The Funeral 1996, Big Night 1996, Left Luggage 1998, The Imposters, The Real Blonde 1998, Rodger Dodger 2002, Empire 2002, The Tulse Luper Suitcases, Part 1: The Moab Story 2003, The Saddest Music in the World 2003, The Tulse Luper Suitcases, Part 2: Vaux to the Sea 2004, King of the Corner 2004, Heights 2005, La Fiesta del chivo 2005, The Architect 2006, Infamous 2006, The Accidental Husband 2008, Two Lovers 2008, Flat Love 2009, My Dog Tulip 2009, The Solitude of Prime Numbers 2010, Keyhole 2011. *Television includes:* Ivory Hunters 1990, Lies of the Twins 1991, The Gift 1994, Crime of the Century 1996, The Odyssey 1997, Don Quixote 2000, Napoleon 2002, Monte Walsh 2003, Legend of Earthsea 2004, Green Porno 2008, The Phantom 2009. *Publications:* In the Name of the Father, the Daughter and the Holy Spirits: Remembering Roberto Rossellini 2006. *Address:* c/o United Talent Agency, 9560 Wilshire Blvd., Suite 500, Beverly Hills, CA 90212, USA.

ROSSELLÓ, Hon. Pedro, BS, MD, MPH; American politician and surgeon; b. 5 April 1944, San Juan, Puerto Rico; m. Irma Margarita Nevares; three s.; ed Notre Dame Univ., Yale Univ., Harvard Univ., Univ. of Puerto Rico; fmr paediatric surgeon, Prof. of Medicine; Dir of Health, City of San Juan 1985–87; cand. elections to Congress 1988; Chair. New Progressive Party 1991–99; Gov. of Puerto Rico 1993–2001, unsuccessful cand. 2004; mem. Senate 2005–; Pres. Council of State Govts 1998; Chair. Democratic Govs' Asscn, Southern Govs' Asscn 1998–2001, Southern Int. Trade Council 1998–99, Southern Tech. Council 1998–99, Southern Growth Policies Bd 1999–2000; mem. Advisory Council Welfare to Work Partnership, USA, Democratic Nat. Cttee, Nat. Advisory Bd of Initiative and Referendum Inst., Bd of Dirs US–Spain Council and other bodies; five times men's singles tennis champion, Puerto Rico; Hon. LLD (Notre Dame) 1995, (Mass.) 1995; Pres.'s Award, US Hispanic Chamber of Commerce 1996, LULAC 1998, Rolex Achievement Award 1999. *Address:* Senado-Capitolio, POB 9023431, San Juan, 00902-3431, Puerto Rico (home). *Telephone:* (787) 724-2030, ext. 2931 (office). *E-mail:* lmuniz@senadopr.us (office). *Website:* www.senadopr.us/senadores/sen_prossello .php (office).

ROSSI, Agustín Oscar; Argentine civil engineer and politician; *Minister of Defence;* b. 18 Oct. 1959, Vera, Santa Fe Prov.; m. María Raquel Pezzelato; four c.; ed Universidad Nacional de Rosario; joined Peronist Youth movt 1980, participated in Peronist Renewal group; mem. Rosario city council 1987–91, 2002–05, Pres. 1991, 2004–05; private practice as engineer in 1990s; mem. Cámara de Diputados (lower house of parl.) for Santa Fe Prov. (Frente para la Victoria—FPV) 2005–13, also Pres. FPV parl. group; unsuccessful cand. for governorship of Santa Fe 2007; Minister of Defence 2013–. *Address:* Ministry of Defence, Azopardo 250, C1328ADB Buenos Aires, Argentina (office). *Telephone:* (11) 4346-8800 (office). *E-mail:* mindef@mindef.gov.ar (office). *Website:* www.mindef.gov.ar (office); www .agustinrossi.com.ar.

ROSSI, Derrick, BSc, MSc, PhD; Canadian biologist and academic; *Assistant Professor of Stem Cell and Regenerative Biology, Pathology Department,, Harvard Medical School and Harvard University;* b. 1965, Toronto; ed Univ. of Toronto, Univ. of Helsinki; Post-doctoral Fellow, Stanford Univ. 2003–07; Asst Prof. of Stem Cell and Regenerative Biology, Pathology Dept, Harvard Univ. 2007–, Faculty mem. Immune Disease Inst., Harvard Medical School 2007–; Researcher Children's Hosp., Boston. *Address:* Harvard University Immune Disease Institute, Warren Alpert 253, 200 Longwood Avenue, Boston, MA 02115, USA (office). *Telephone:* (617) 713-8900 (office). *Fax:* (617) 713-8910 (office). *E-mail:* rossi@idi .harvard.edu (office). *Website:* www.hsci.harvard.edu/people/derrick-j-rossi-phd (office).

ROSSI, José Lucien André, DenD; French politician and lawyer; *President, Agence de Développement Economique de la Corse;* b. 18 June 1944, Ajaccio, Corsica; s. of Pierre Rossi and Emilie Leca; m. Denise Ferri 1968; two d.; ed Ecoles Sainte-Lucie and Castelvecchio, Lycée Fesch, Ajaccio, Faculté de Droit and Inst. d'Etudes Politiques, Paris; Asst Faculté de Droit, Paris 1969–73; served in pvt. office of Minister of Labour 1972, Minister of Educ. 1972–74; Press Officer to Minister of Health 1974–75; Parl. Relations Officer to Minister of Labour 1975–78, to Minister of Educ. 1978; pvt. office of Pres. of Senate 1981–82; mem. Conseil Général, Corsica 1973–, Pres. 1985–98; Conseiller Régional, Corsica 1975–85; Deputy Mayor of Ajaccio 1983–90, 1995–; Pres. Corsica Tourism and Leisure Agency 1983–84; Pres. Regional Information Centre 1979–85; Deputy to Nat. Ass. 1988–94; Sec.-Gen. Parti Républicain 1989–91; Mayor of Grosseto-Prugna 1990–95; Vice-Pres. Union pour la Démocratie Française (UDF) group in Nat. Ass. 1993–94; Minister of Industry, Posts and Telecommunications and Foreign Trade 1994–95; Deputy to Nat. Ass. 1995–2002; Deputy Sec.-Gen. UDF 1996–97; Titular Judge Higher Court of Justice 1997–; Pres. Démocratie Liberale Group, Nat. Ass. 1998–2000, Assemblée de Corse 1998–2004, Vice-Pres. Démocratie Libérale 2000–02; currently Pres. Agence de Développement Economique de la Corse. *Publication:* Les Maires de grandes villes en France 1972. *Address:* Agence de Développement Economique de la Corse, Immeuble Le Regent, 1 Avenue Eugène Macchini, 20000 Ajaccio, France (office); 461 boulevard Rive Sud, 20166 Porticcio, France (home). *Telephone:* 4-95-50-91-00 (office). *Fax:* 4-95-50-91-60 (office). *E-mail:* adec@corse-adec.org (office). *Website:* www.corse-adec.org (office).

ROSSI, Valentino; Italian motorcycle racer; b. 16 Feb. 1979, Urbino; s. of Graziano Rossi and Stefania Rossi; began in go-karts, then minimoto before progressing to motorcycles; won first World Championship Grand Prix at Brno, Czech Repub. 1996; by 2004 68 Grand Prix victories; World Champion 125cc class 1997, 250cc class 1999, 500cc class 2001, MotoGP class 2002, 2003, 2004, 2005; currently races for Yamaha team. *Leisure interests:* football, skiing. *E-mail:* info@ yamahamotogp.com.

ROSSIER, William; Swiss economist and international organization official; b. 25 Oct. 1942; ed Univ. of Lausanne; joined Foreign Econ. Service 1970; Head Secr., Conf. on Security and Co-operation in Europe, Geneva 1972–73; Deputy Head Div. for Gen. Foreign Econ. Questions, Berne 1973–76; Counsellor, Mission to the EC, Brussels 1976–80; with Fed. Office for External Econ. Affairs 1981–88, apptd Head Div. in charge of Relations with Countries of Eastern Europe and the People's Repub. of China 1981, later Head Div. in Charge of Relations with Western Europe; fmrly involved in negotiations with GATT, OECD, UNCTAD; Plenipotentiary Amb. of Switzerland to Int. Econ. Orgs in Geneva (GATT/WTO, UNCTAD, UN-ECE, EFTA); Chair. EFTA 2000–06; fmr Chair. ECE, UNCTAD Trade and Devt Bd; Chair. World Trade Org. Gen. Council 1996; Perm. Rep. to EFTA, Sec.-Gen. 2000–06. *Address:* c/o Federal Department of Foreign Affairs (FDFA), Bundeshaus West, 3003 Berne 1, Switzerland (office). *Telephone:* 313222111 (office). *Fax:* 313234001 (office). *E-mail:* info@eda.admin.ch (office). *Website:* www .eda.admin.ch (office).

ROSSIN, Lawrence G., BA; American diplomatist and UN official; b. 3 Nov. 1952; m. Debra J. McGowan; one s. one d.; ed Claremont Men's Coll., California, NATO Defence Coll., Rome, Massachusetts Inst. of Tech.; fmr Dir, Chief of Mission Authority and Overseas Staffing State Dept; fmr Counsellor for Political Affairs, The Hague and Port-au-Prince; fmr Peru Desk Officer; fmr Staff Asst to Secs of State for Inter-American Affairs; Dir Inter-American Affairs, Nat. Security Council 1993–94; Deputy Chief of Mission, Spain 1995–98; Dir Office S Cen. European Affairs, Dept of State, led dels to Rambouillet and Paris confs on Kosovo 1999, directed govt outreach to Kosovo Liberation Army (KLA); first Chief of Mission, Kosovo, opened and headed American Office, Pristina 1999–2000, responsible for all policy initiatives and collaboration with UN Interim Admin.

in Kosovo and NATO Kosovo Force; Amb. to Croatia 2001–2003; Special Asst to Pres. and Sr Dir for Strategic Planning and Southwest Asia, Nat. Security Council 2003–04 (retd from US Sr Foreign Service); Sec.-Gen.'s Prin. Deputy Special Rep. for UN Interim Admin. in Kosovo 2004–06; Sec.-Gen.'s Prin. Deputy Special Rep. for the UN Stabilization Mission in Haiti (MINUSTAH) 2006–07; Sr Int. Coordinator, Save Darfur Coalition 2007–08; Prin. Deputy Special Rep. of the UN Sec. Gen., Interim Admin. in Kosovo 2008; Deputy Asst Sec.-Gen. for Operations, NATO 2008–11; State Dept Award for Valour, three Superior Hon. Awards, Meritorious Hon. Award.

ROSSINI MIÑÁN, Renzo Guillermo, BEcons, MSc (Econ); Peruvian central banker; *General Manager, Banco Central de Reserva del Perú;* ed Univ. of the Pacific, London School of Econs, UK, courses with CAF, FMI, BID, The British Council, JICA and Studienzentrum Gerzensee-Suiza, Univ. of Piura; joined Banco Cen. de Reserva del Perú 1982, worked in Dept of Analysis and Financial Planning, Dept of Global Analysis and Dept of Conjunctural Research 1982–91, Head of Dept of External Sector Analysis 1988–90, Deputy Man. of Research and Global Analysis 1990–91, Chief Economist, Banco Cen. de Reserva del Perú 1991–2003, Gen. Man. 2003–; Prof. of Political Economy, Univ. of the Pacific 1998–; Dir Fondo Consolidado de Reservas Previsionales; mem. American Econ. Asscn, Latin American and Caribbean Econ. Asscn, Comité Editorial de la Revista Economía Chilena; Assoc. Asociación Civil Pro Universidad del Pacífico. *Publications include:* El Sesgo Anti-Exportador de la Política Comercial en el Perú (with Adrian Armas and Luis Palacios) 1990, Liberalización del Comercio Exterior en el Perú 1991, Estabilización y Dolarización en el Perú: Comentarios 1993; numerous book chapters and articles in professional journals. *Address:* Banco Central de Reserva del Perú, Jirón Antonio Miró Quesada 441–445, Lima 1, Peru (office). *Telephone:* (1) 4278307 (office). *Fax:* (1) 4266125 (office). *E-mail:* rrossini@bcrp.gob .pe (office). *Website:* www.bcrp.gob.pe (office).

ROSSINOT, André, DenM; French politician and physician; *Mayor of Nancy;* b. 22 May 1939, Briey, Meurthe-et-Moselle; s. of Lucien Rossinot and Jeanne Fondeur; m. 3rd Françoise Cordelier 1985; one s. one d.; three c. from previous marriages; ed Lycée Poincaré and Faculty of Medicine, Nancy; early career as ear, nose and throat specialist in pvt. practice; Town Councillor, Nancy 1969–71; Mayor of Nancy 1983–; Vice-Pres. Greater Nancy Urban Council 1996–2001, Pres. 2001–; Deputy to Nat. Ass. (UDF) 1978–86, 1988–93, 1995–97, Vice-Pres. 1988–89; Pres. Parti Radical 1983–88, 1994–97, Hon. Pres. 1997–, Co-Pres. 2005–07, Nat. Vice-Pres. UDF 1983–90, 1994–; mem. Political Bureau Union pour la France 1990–, UDF 1991–2000; Minister for Relations with Parl. 1986–88, of Civil Service 1993–95; Pres. Conf. Permanente des caisses de crédit municipal 1987–93; Pres. Nouveau Contrat Social 1992–, TGV 1994–99, Fed. nat. des agences d'urbanisme 1995–, Inst. nat. du génie urbain 1996–98, Asscn Seine-Moselle-Rhône 1999–; Founder and Pres. Agence des villes 1998–; Vice-Pres. Asscn des Eco Maires 1990–; Sec-Gen. l'Association des maires des grandes villes de France (AMGVF) 2001–; Chevalier, Légion d'honneur, Commdr Order of Merit (Germany). *Publication:* Stanislas, Le Roi philosophe 1999. *Leisure interests:* walking, tennis, fishing. *Address:* Hôtel de Ville, place Stanislas, 54000 Nancy, France. *Telephone:* (3) 83-85-30-00 (office). *Fax:* (3) 83-32-90-96 (office). *E-mail:* arossinot@mairie -nancy.fr (office). *Website:* www.mairie-nancy.fr (office).

ROSSITER, Robert E., BBA; American automotive industry executive; *Chairman, President and CEO, Lear Corporation;* b. Detroit; ed Northwood Univ.; joined Lear Corpn (automotive supplier) 1973, various position in sales man. and operations, mem. Bd of Dirs 1988–, Pres. and COO 1988–2000, Pres. and COO Int. Operations, Sulzbach, Germany 1997–2000, Pres. Lear Corpn 2000–03, CEO 2000–, Chair. 2003–, also currently Pres.; Vice-Chair. Michigan Minority Business Devt Council; mem. Bd Trustees Mfg Alliance, Northwood Univ.; mem. Soc. of Automotive Engineers, Int. Supplier Advisory Council, Automotive Advisory Council. *Address:* Lear Corporation, 21557 Telegraph Road, Southfield, MI 48086-5008, USA (office). *Telephone:* (248) 447-1500 (office). *Fax:* (248) 447-1722 (office). *Website:* www.lear.com (office).

ROSSWALL, (Per) Thomas; Swedish scientist, ecologist and academic; b. 20 Dec. 1941, Stockholm; s. of Axel Rosswall and Britta Rosswall; partner Mats Edlund; Science Sec. Swedish Council fo Planning and Co-ordination of Research 1975–77; Dir SCOPE/UNEP Int. Nitrogen Unit, Royal Swedish Acad. of Sciences (RSAS) 1977–80, Exec. Dir Geosphere-Biosphere Programme: A Study of Global Change 1987–94; Asst Prof. in Microbiology and Assoc. Prof. in Soil Ecology, Univ. of Agric. Sciences, Uppsala 1980–84, Rector 1994–2000, Prof. of Water and Environmental Studies 2000–09; Prof., Dept of Water and Environmental Studies, Linköping Univ. 1984–92; Dir Int. START Secr., Washington, DC 1992–93; Prof. of Water and Environmental Studies, Univ. of Stockholm 1992–94; Sec.-Gen. SCOPE 1986–88; Chair. Int. Cttee on Microbial Ecology 1980–83; Dir Int. Foundation for Science 2000–01; Exec. Dir Int. Council for Science 2002–09; Chair. CGIAR Programme on Climate Change, Agric. and Food Security 2009–, Mistra Council for Evidence-based Environmental Man., RSAS 2011–; Mistra Urban Futures, Chalmers Univ. of Tech. 2014–; Vice-Chair Swedish InfrasTructure for Ecosystem Science (SITES) 2014–; mem. Bd for Polar Research, Ministry of Educ. 1993–96, Scientific Council Foundation for Strategic Environmental Research 1994–97, Cttee on Global Biogeochemical Cycles, Natural Science Research Council 1994–99, Environmental Advisory Council Ministry of the Environment 1995–2001, Bd of Inst. for Ecological Sustainability 1999–2001, Bd of Foundation for Int. Co-operation in Research and Higher Educ. 2000–04, Bd Beijer Inst. of Ecological Econs 2001–06, Council of Int. Cell Research Org. 1987–91, European Environmental Research Org. 1990–2004, Exec. Cttee Int. Soc. for Tropical Ecology 1995–2005, Int. Scientific Advisory Bd UNESCO 1996–2004, Bd Millennium Ecosystem Assessment 2003–05, Bd and Exec. Cttee Stockholm Resilience Centre 2008–13, Prize and Awards Cttee, Royal Swedish Acad. of Agric. and Forestry (RSAAF) 2012–, Cttee on a Green Economy, RSAAF 2013; Ed.-in-Chief Ecological Bulletins 1975–85; mem. or fmr mem. Editorial Bd Advances in Microbial Ecology, Biogeochemistry, Global Biogeochemical Cycles, Soil Biology and Biochemistry, Biology and Fertility of Soils, FEMS Microbial Ecology Journal, Landscape Ecology, MIRCEN Journal of Applied Microbiology and Biotechnology, European Journal of Soil Biology, Revista Estudos Avançados (USP), Brazil; Fellow, Academia Europaea 1989, RSAS 1989, RSAAF 1995, Swedish Royal Patriotic Soc. 1996, Royal Acad. of Arts and Sciences, Uppsala 1999, World Acad. of

Arts and Science 2006; Assoc. Fellow, Third World Acad. of Sciences (renamed TWAS, The World Acad. of Sciences in 2012) 2002; Royal Order of Merit 12th Grade with Serafim Ribbon (Sweden) 2000; Second Prof. John Roger Porter Memorial Lecturer, Univ. of Bombay, India 1981, First Industrial Memorial Lecturer, Haarlem, the Netherlands 1989, Fourth Hendrik De Waard Lecturer, Univ. of Groningen, the Netherlands 1990, Award of Excellence in Ecosystem Science, Natural Resources Ecology Lab., Colorado State Univ. 2002, Carl Gustaf Bernhard Lecturer, RSAS 2003, ISI Highly Cited Researcher 2003, Beijer Fellow, The Beijer Inst. of Ecological Econs 2007, Medal of Finnish Acad. of Science and Letters 2008. *Publications:* more than 10 edited books; more than 100 papers in scientific journals. *Address:* 57 chemin du Belvédère, 06530 Le Tignet, France (home). *Telephone:* 6-30-48-77-98 (mobile). *E-mail:* thomas.rosswall@gmail.org (home). *Website:* ccafs.cgiar.org (office).

ROST, Andrea; Hungarian operatic soprano; b. 1962, Budapest; d. of Ferenc Rost and Erzsébet Privoda; ed Ferenc Liszt Acad. of Music, Budapest; operatic debut as Juliette in Gounod's Romeo et Juliette, Budapest 1989; solo artist at Wiener Staatsoper 1991; La Scala debut as Gilda in Rigoletto 1994; debut, Metropolitan Opera, New York as Adina in L'Elisir d'amore 1996; took part in Superconcert with José Carreras and Plácido Domingo, Budapest 1996; appeared as Elisabeth in Donizetti's opera, London 1997; debut, Tokyo Opera, as Violetta 1998; took part in concert in memory of Lehár with José Carreras and Plácido Domingo, Bad Ischl, Austria 1998; has also appeared at Staatsoper, Vienna, Salzburg Festival, Opéra Bastille, Paris, Royal Opera House, Covent Garden and Chicago Opera; Lammermoori Lucia debut, Munchen, Wigmore Hall recital, London, Valencia recital 2002; Traviata debut, Deutsche Oper, Berlin, Desdemona, Otello, Tokyo, Lammermoori Lucia premier, Covent Garden, London 2003, Gilda, Rigoletto, Metropolitan, New York 2004; First Prize, Helsinki Competition 1989, Bartók Béla – Pásztory Ditta Award, Ferenc Liszt Artistic Merit of Honour 1997, Nat. Artistic Merit of Honour 1999, Medal Obersvoszky, Prima Primissima Award 2003, Kossuth Prize 2004. *Recordings include:* Mozart – Le nozze di Figaro (Susanna) 1994, Mahler – Symphony No. 8 1995, Verdi – Rigoletto (Gilda) 1995, Mendelssohn – Elias (die Witwe/ein Engel) 1996, Andrea Rost – Le delizie dell'amor 1997, Gaetano Donizetti – Lucia Di Lammermoori (Lucia) 1998, A Tribute to Operetta 1999, Amore II 2000, Escape Through Opera 2001, Erkel: Bánk bán (Melinda) 2003, …che cosa è amor… [Mozart Arias] 2004. *DVD videos include:* Johann Strauss Gala 2000, Wolfgang Amadeus Mozart: Don Giovanni (Zerlina) 2000, A Verdi Gala from Berlin 2002, Erkel: Bánk bán (Melinda) (opera film) 2003. *Address:* Theateragentur Dr Hilbert, attn z.Hd.: Christine Sienel, Maximilianstrasse 22, 80539 Munich, Germany (office); c/o Katalin Zsigo, Pf. 190, 1276 Budapest (office); Nefelejes u. 27, 2040 Budaörs, Hungary (home). *Telephone:* (89) 290747-0 (office). *Fax:* (89) 290747-90 (office); (23) 416-583 (home). *E-mail:* agentur@hilbert.de (office); info@andrearost.com (home). *Website:* www.hilbert.de (office); www.andrearost.com (home).

ROST, Yuri Mikhailovich; Russian journalist and photographer; b. 1 Feb. 1939, Kiev, Ukraine; s. of Arkadyevich Rost and Georgiyevna Rost; m. (divorced); columnist Komsomolskaya Pravda (newspaper) 1966–79; reviewer Literaturnaya Gazeta (newspaper) 1979–94; author TV programme Stables of Rost 1994–97; reviewer Obshchaya Gazeta (newspaper) 1993–; mem. Russian PEN Centre; Prizes of Acad. of Free Press 1998, 1999; Tsarskoye Selo Artistic Prize 1999; Gilyarovsky Medal 1990; Triumph Prize. *Publications include:* People 1980, 10 Short Stories about Leningrad 1976, Everest 1983, My View 1988, Armenian Tragedy 1990; Birds (jtly); numerous essays. *Leisure interest:* collecting smoking pipes. *Address:* Makarenko str. 1/19, Apt. 21, 103062 Moscow, Russia (home).

RØSTVIG, Maren-Sofie, PhD; Norwegian fmr professor of English literature; b. 27 March 1920, Melbo; d. of Olaf Røstvig and Sigrid Røstvig; ed Univ. of Oslo and Univ. of Calif., Los Angeles; imprisoned by Nazi regime 1943, subsequently released; joined Resistance Movt and published underground newspaper until end of World War II 1944–45; Reader in English Literature, Univ. of Oslo 1955–67, Prof. 1968–87, Sr Research Fellow 1988, retd 1990; mem. Norwegian Acad. of Science and Letters; Mil. Medal of Participation in World War II. *Publications:* The Happy Man. Studies in the Metamorphoses of a Classical Ideal 1600–1760 (two vols) 1954–58, The Hidden Sense and Other Essays 1963, Fair Forms 1975, Configurations. A Topomorphical Approach to Renaissance Poetry 1994; contribs to learned journals and collections of scholarly essays on English literature. *Address:* 14 Urb. Rosa de Piedras, Carretera de Coín, 29650 Mijas, Málaga, Spain. *Telephone:* (95) 2486938. *Fax:* (95) 2485125.

ROTELLA, Stephen J., BEcons, MBA; American banking executive; *President and COO, Washington Mutual, Inc.;* m.; one d.; ed State Univ. NY, Stony Brook and Albany; held various positions with JP Morgan Chase 1987–2005, including COO Chase Home Finance 1998–2001, mem. Exec. Cttee and CEO 2001–04, fmr Chair. Housing Advisory Bd, mem. Bd of Dirs –2005; mem. Exec. Cttee, Pres. and COO Washington Mutual, Inc. 2005–, Pres., Retail Banking 2008–; mem. Bd of Dirs Mortgage Bankers Asscn, St Barnabas Medical Center, NJ; mem. Exec. Cttee Financial Services Roundtable's Housing Policy Council. *Address:* Washington Mutual Inc., 1301 Second Avenue, Seattle, WA 98101, USA (office). *Telephone:* (206) 461-2000 (office). *E-mail:* info@wamu.com (office). *Website:* www.wamu.com (office).

ROTFELD, Adam Daniel, PhD; Polish academic, researcher and fmr politician; *Co-Chairman, Polish-Russian Group on Difficult Matters;* b. 4 March 1938, Przemyślany; one d.; ed Diplomatic-Consular Faculty, Main School of Foreign Service and Faculty of Journalism, Warsaw Univ., Faculty of Law and Admin, Jagiellonian Univ., Kraków; Researcher in Int. Law and Int. Relations, Polish Inst. of Int. Affairs 1961–89; Fellow, Inst. of East-West Security Studies, New York, USA 1984–85; Assoc. Prof. and Prof. in Humanities, Univ. of Warsaw 2001–; Leader, Project on Building a Co-operative Security System in and for Europe, Stockholm Int. Peace Research Inst. (SIPRI) 1989, Dir SIPRI 1991–2002, apptd Personal Rep. OSCE Chairman-in-Office to settle conflicts in Trans-Dniester region of Moldova 1992; Ed. SIPRI Yearbook: Armaments, Disarmament and International Security 1991–; mem. Nat. Security Council 2001–05; apptd Under-Sec. of State, Ministry of Foreign Affairs 2001, Sec. of State 2003–04; Minister of Foreign Affairs Jan.–Oct. 2005; Co-Chair. Polish-Russian Group on Peace and Conflict 1993–2008, Difficult Matters 2008–; Commr of Euro-Atlantic Security Initiative Comm. 2010–; mem. Royal Swedish Acad. of War Studies 1996,

Governing Bd of Hamburg Inst. for Peace Research and Security Policy at Univ. of Hamburg 1995–2007, Advisory Bd of Geneva Centre for Democratic Control of Armed Forces 2001, NATO Group of Experts for the New Strategic Concept 2009–10, Scientific Council of Inst. of Political Studies, Polish Acad. of Sciences 2006–, and many other research centres; Commandoria of the Polar Star 2001 (Sweden), Great Cross of Germany 2005, Great Cross of Polonia Restituta 2010 and many others. *Publications:* has published and edited more than 20 books, including Where is the World Headed? 2008, White Spots – Black Spots. Difficult Matters in Polish–Russian Relations 1918–2008 (co-ed. with Anatoly W. Torkunov) 2010; more than 400 articles on legal and political aspects of relations between Germany and Cen. and Eastern Europe after World War II, human rights, cooperative security, CSBMs, multilateral security structures, and political and legal aspects of security system in Europe. *Address:* Polish Institute of International Affairs, 1A Warecka Street, PO Box 1010, 00-950 Warsaw (office). *Telephone:* (22) 5568033 (office); (22) 6201706 (home). *Fax:* (22) 5568099 (office). *E-mail:* rotfeld@pism.pl (office). *Website:* www.pism.pl (office).

ROTH, Alvin E., BS, MS, PhD; American economist and academic; *George Gund Professor of Economics and Business Administration, Harvard Business School;* b. 18 Dec. 1951; m.; two c.; ed Columbia Univ., Stanford Univ.; Asst Prof., Dept of Business Admin and Dept of Econs, Univ. of Illinois 1974–77, Assoc. Prof. 1977–79, Prof. 1979–81, Beckman Assoc., Center for Advanced Study 1981–82; A.W. Mellon Prof. of Econs, Univ. of Pittsburgh 1982–98, also Fellow, Center for Philosophy of Science 1983 and Prof. of Business Admin, Graduate School of Business 1985; George Gund Prof. of Econs and Business Admin, Dept of Econs, Harvard Univ. and Harvard Business School 1998– (Prof. Emer. 2013–); Visiting Prof., Dept of Econs, Univ. of Tel-Aviv, Israel 1995; Bogen Visiting Prof., Dept of Econs, Hebrew Univ. of Jerusalem, Israel 1995; Mendes-France Visiting Prof. of Econs, Technion, Haifa, Israel 1986; Visiting Prof., Stanford Univ. 2012; Research Assoc., Nat. Bureau of Econ. Research 1998–; Founder, New England Program for Kidney Exchange; Fellow, Econometric Soc. 1983, American Acad. of Arts and Sciences 1998; Lanchester Prize, Operations Research Soc. of America 1991, T.W. Schultz Prize, Dept of Econs, Univ. of Chicago 2006, Sveriges Riksbank Prize in Econ. Sciences in Memory of Alfred Nobel (Nobel Prize) (jtly with Lloyd S. Shapley) 2012. *Publications include:* Game-Theoretic Models of Bargaining 1985, Laboratory Experimentation in Economics: Six Points of View 1987, The Shapley Value: Essays in Honor of Lloyd S. Shapley (Ed.) 1988. *Address:* Harvard Business School, 441 Baker Library, Boston, MA 02163, USA (office). *E-mail:* al_roth@harvard.edu (office). *Website:* www.hbs.edu; kuznets.fas.harvard.edu/~aroth/alroth.html (office).

ROTH, Jean-Pierre, DEcon; Swiss fmr central banker; b. 28 April 1946, Saxon, Canton of Valais; m. Floriane Tognetti; three c.; ed Univ. of Geneva, Institut Universitaire des Hautes Etudes Internationales, Geneva and MIT, USA; fmr Lecturer, Univ. of Geneva and Institut Universitaire de Hautes Etudes Internationales; Scientific Collaborator, Swiss Nat. Bank (Schweizerische Nationalbank/Banque nationale suisse) 1979, mem. Bd of Dirs, Vice-Chair. and Head of Dept II (capital market, banknotes, business relations with the Confed., admin of gold holdings), Berne 1996, Chair. of Governing Bd and Head of Dept I (Int. Affairs Div., Econ. Div., Legal and Admin. Econ.) 2006–09; Chair. BIS, Basel 2006–09; Gov. IMF for Switzerland, Washington, DC; Switzerland's Rep. in Financial Stability Forum 2007–09. *Address:* c/o Swiss National Bank, Börsenstrasse 15, PO Box, 8022 Zurich, Switzerland (office).

ROTH, Joe; American film executive and producer; b. 1948; fmrly production asst various commercials and films; fmrly lighting dir Pitched Players, also producer; co-f. Morgan Creek Productions 1987–89; Chair. Twentieth Century Fox Film Corpn 1989–92; f. Caravan Pictures 1992–94; Chair. Walt Disney Motion Pictures Group 1994–97, Walt Disney Studios, Burbank 1997–2000; f. Revolution Studios 2000–07; Producer Sony Pictures Entertainment, Inc. 2007–; mem. Bd of Dirs Pixar Studios 2000–06; majority owner Seattle Soccer Group (Major League Soccer team in Seattle) 2007–. *Films produced include:* Tunnelvision, Cracking Up, Americathon, Our Winning Season, The Final Terror, The Stone Boy, Where the River Runs Black, Bachelor Party, Off Beat, Streets of Gold (also Dir), Revenge of the Nerds (also Dir), Young Guns, Dead Ringers, Skin Deep, Major League, Renegades, Coupe de Ville (also Dir), Enemies: A Love Story; films for Caravan Pictures include Walt Disney's The Three Musketeers, Angie, Angels in the Outfield, I Love Trouble, A Low Down Dirty Shame, Houseguest, The Jerky Boys, Heavyweights, Tall Tale, While You Were Sleeping 1995, Before and After 1996, Tears of the Sun 2003, Daddy Day Care 2003, Hollywood Homicide 2003, Mona Lisa Smile 2003, The Forgotten 2004, An Unfinished Life 2005, The Great Debaters 2007, Demons 2007, Hellboy II: The Golden Army 2008. *Film directed:* Freedomland 2005. *Address:* c/o Sony Pictures Entertainment Inc., 10202 West Washington Blvd., Culver City, CA 90232, USA. *Website:* www.sonypictures.com; www.mlsinseattle.com.

ROTH, John Andrew, MEng; Canadian communications executive; b. 6 Oct. 1942, Alberta; s. of Henry Roth and Sophia Brix; m. Margaret Anne Roth 1968; ed McGill Univ., Montreal; with RCA 1964–69; joined Nortel 1969, Head Wireless Div. 1991–93, Pres. Nortel N. America 1993–95, Group COO 1995–97, Chief Exec. 1997–2001. *Leisure interest:* making stained-glass windows. *Address:* R.R. #5, Morningview, Orangeville, ON LGW 2Z2, Canada (office).

ROTH, Klaus Friedrich, PhD, FRS; British mathematician and academic; *Honorary Research Fellow, Department of Mathematics, University College London;* b. 29 Oct. 1925, Breslau, Germany; s. of the late Dr Franz Roth and Mathilde Roth; m. Dr Melek Khairy 1955 (died 2002); ed St Paul's School, London, Peterhouse, Cambridge and Univ. Coll., London; Asst Master Gordonstoun School 1945–46; postgraduate student Univ. Coll., London 1946–48; mem. Math. Dept, Univ. Coll., London 1948–66 (title of Prof. in Univ. of London conferred 1961), Fellow 1979, Hon. Research Fellow, Dept of Math. 1996–; Prof. of Pure Math. (Theory of Numbers), Imperial Coll., London 1966–88, Visiting Prof. 1988–96, Fellow 1999; Visiting Lecturer, MIT 1956–57, Visiting Prof. 1965–66; Foreign Hon. Mem. AAAS 1966; Hon. Fellow, Peterhouse, Cambridge 1989; Hon. FRSE 1993; Fields Medal, Int. Math. Union 1958, De Morgan Medal, London Math. Soc. 1983, Sylvester Medal, Royal Soc. 1991. *Publications:* papers in journals of learned socs. *Leisure interests:* chess, cinema, ballroom dancing.

ROTH, Philip Milton, MA; American writer and academic; b. 19 March 1933, Newark, NJ; s. of Herman Roth and Bess Finkel Roth; m. 1st Margaret Martinson 1959 (died 1968); m. 2nd Claire Bloom (q.v.) 1990 (divorced 1994); ed Bucknell Univ. and Univ. of Chicago; served in US Army 1955–56; Lecturer in English, Univ. of Chicago 1956–58; Visiting Lecturer, Univ. of Iowa Writers' Workshop 1960–62; Writer-in-Residence, Princeton Univ. 1962–64, Univ. of Pennsylvania 1967–80; Distinguished Prof. of Literature, Hunter Coll. 1989–92; Visiting Lecturer, State Univ. of NY, Stony Brook 1967, 1968; Houghton Mifflin Literary Fellow 1959; mem. American Acad. of Arts and Letters 1970–; Dr hc (Harvard) 2003; Guggenheim Fellowship Grant 1959–60, Daroff Award of Jewish Book Council of America 1959, Nat. Inst. of Arts and Letters Award 1959, Rockefeller Grant 1965, Ford Foundation Grant 1966, Nat. Arts Club's Medal of Honor for Literature 1991, Karel Capek Prize 1994, Nat. Medal of Arts 1998, Gold Medal in Fiction, American Acad. of Arts and Letters 2002, Nat. Book Foundation Medal for Distinguished Contribution to American Letters 2002, PEN/Nabokov Award for Lifetime Achievement 2006, PEN/Saul Bellow Award for Achievement in American Fiction 2007, Nat. Humanities Medal 2011, Man Booker Int. Prize 2011, Prince of Asturias Award for literature 2012. *Publications include:* Goodbye Columbus (novella and stories) 1959, Letting Go 1962, When She Was Good 1967, Portnoy's Complaint 1969, Our Gang 1971, The Breast 1972, The Great American Novel 1973, My Life as a Man 1974, Reading Myself and Others (essays) 1975, The Professor of Desire 1977, The Ghost Writer 1979, A Philip Roth Reader 1980, Zuckerman Unbound 1981, The Anatomy Lesson 1983, The Prague Orgy 1985, Zuckerman Bound 1985, The Counterlife (Nat. Book Critics' Circle Award 1987) 1986, The Facts: A Novelist's Autobiography 1988, Deception 1990, Patrimony (Nat. Book Critics' Circle Award 1992) 1991, Operation Shylock (PEN/Faulkner Award) 1993, Sabbath's Theater (Nat. Book Award for Fiction) 1995, American Pastoral (Pulitzer Prize in Fiction 1998) 1997, I Married a Communist (Ambassador Book Award of the English-Speaking Union) 1998, The Human Stain (PEN/Faulkner Award 2001, Prix Médicis Étranger 2002) 2000, The Dying Animal 2001, Shop Talk 2001, The Plot Against America (WHSmith Literary Award 2005, Soc. of American Historians' Award 2005, Sidewise Award for Alternate History 2005) 2004, Everyman (PEN/Faulkner Award 2007) 2006, Exit Ghost 2007, Indignation 2008, The Humbling 2009, Nemesis 2011. *Address:* c/o The Wylie Agency, 250 West 57th Street, Suite 2114, New York, NY 10107, USA (office).

ROTH, Tim; British actor; b. 14 May 1961, Dulwich, London; m. Nikki Butler; two s.; ed Dick Sheppard Comprehensive School, Brixton and Camberwell Coll. of Art; began acting career with fringe groups including Glasgow Citizens Theatre, The Oval House and the Royal Court; appeared on London stage in Metamorphosis. *Films include:* The Hit 1984, A World Apart 1988, The Cook The Thief His Wife and Her Lover 1989, Vincent & Theo 1990, Rosencrantz and Guildenstern are Dead 1990, Jumpin' at the Boneyard 1992, Reservoir Dogs 1992, Bodies Rest and Motion, Pulp Fiction 1994, Little Odessa 1994, Captives 1994, Rob Roy 1995, Four Rooms 1995, Everyone Says I Love You 1996, Hoodlum 1997, Deceiver 1997, Animals 1997, The Legend of the Pianist on the Ocean 1998, The War Zone (dir) 1999, Vatel 2000, Lucky Numbers 2000, Planet of the Apes 2001, Invincible 2001, The Musketeer 2001, The Beautiful Country 2004, Silver City 2004, Don't Come Knockin' 2005, Dark Water 2005, Jump Shot 2005, Youth Without Youth 2007, Funny Games 2008, The Incredible Hulk 2008, King Conqueror 2009, Pete Smalls Is Dead. *Television:* Made in Britain 1982, Skellig 2009, Lie to Me (series) 2009–11. *Address:* Ilene Feldman Agency, 8730 West Sunset Boulevard, Suite 490, Los Angeles, CA 90069, USA (office).

ROTH, Urs Philipp, DrIur; Swiss lawyer; b. 1947; joined UBS 1976, worked as Group Gen. Counsel –2001; CEO Swiss Bankers Asscn and Del. of Bd of Dirs 2001–10; Chair. Exec. Cttee Int. Financial Centre Switzerland (LAIF); mem. Foundation Bd Swiss Finance Inst.; teaches at Univ. of Zurich. *Publications:* contrib. of numerous papers on banking and stock exchange law. *Address:* c/o Swiss Bankers Association, Aeschenplatz 7, PO Box 4182, 4002 Basel, Switzerland.

ROTHBLATT, Martine, PhD, JD, MBA; American laywer and business executive; *Chairman and CEO, United Therapeutics;* b. (Martin Rothblatt), 1954; four c.; ed Univ. of Southern Calif., Queen Mary, Univ. of London; began career with Covington & Burlington, Washington, DC –1983; f. PanAmSat, CD Radio, WorldSpace 1980s; co-f. Sirius Satellite Radio; opened The Law Offices of Martine Rothblatt specializing in satellite communications law; Pres. Geostar 1985–89; opened a second law firm 1989; Pnr Makon & Patusky (law firm), Washington, DC 1990–; endowed the PPH (Primary Pulmonary Hypertension) Cure Foundation to find a treatment for her daughter Jenesis' condition 1994–; f. United Therapeutics (pharmaceutical co.); Founding mem. and Co-Chair. Bioethics Sub cttee, Int. Bar Asscn 1993–; Pres. William Harvey Medical Research Foundation. *Publications include:* The Apartheid of Sex: A Manifesto on the Freedom of Gender 1995, Unzipped Genes: Taking Charge of Baby-Making in the New Millennium 1997. *Address:* United Therapeutics Corporate Headquarters, 1110 Spring Street, Silver Spring, MD, 20910, USA (office). *Telephone:* (301) 608-9292 (office). *Fax:* (301) 608-9291 (office). *Website:* www.unither.com (office).

ROTHENBERG, Alan I., BA, JD; American lawyer and business executive; *Chairman and CEO, 1st Century Bank, N.A.;* b. 10 April 1939, Detroit; m. Georgina Rothenberg; three c.; ed Univ. of Michigan; admitted to Calif. Bar 1964; Assoc. O'Melveny & Myers (law firm), LA 1963–66; Founder and Man. Pnr, Manatt Phelps Rothenberg & Phillips (law firm), LA 1968–90, Pnr, Latham & Watkins, LA 1990–2000 (retd); Instructor in Sports Law, Univ. of Southern Calif. 1969, 1976, 1984, Whittier Coll. of Law 1980, 1984; Pres. and Gen. Counsel LA Lakers (professional basketball team) and LA Kings (professional ice hockey team) 1967–79, LA Clippers (professional basketball team) 1982–89; Pres. US Soccer Fed., Chicago 1990–98, now Hon. Pres. and Life Mem.; Founder and fmr Chair. Major League Soccer 1993, now mem. Bd of Dirs; Chair. Goal Media 1993–; Organizer and Bd Mem. First Los Angeles Bank 1973–84; Founder, Chair. and CEO First Century Bank NA, LA 2004–; Chair. Premier Partnerships (sports and entertainment marketing firm); mem. Bd of Dirs Arden Realty Inc., Zenith National Corpn, California Pizza Kitchen Inc. 2006–; Full Time Neutral, ADR Services (dispute resolution service) 2001–; mem. Soccer Comm. 1984 Olympic Games; mem. Equal Educ. Opportunities Comm. State of Calif. Bd of Educ. 1972–75; mem. Bd of Govs Nat. Basketball Asscn 1971–79; Pres. Constitutional Rights Foundation 1987–90; Chair. Pres. CEO 1994 World Cup Organizing Cttee 1990–94; fmr Vice Pres. Confed. of North, Cen. America and Caribbean Asscn Football (CONCACAF); inducted into US Nat. Soccer Hall of Fame 2007. *Address:* 1st Century Bank, NA, 1875 Century Park East, Suite 1400, Los Angeles, CA 90067, USA (office). *Telephone:* (310) 270-9500 (home). *E-mail:* jdinapoli@1stcenturybank.com (home). *Website:* www.1stcenturybank.com (office).

ROTHERMERE, 4th Viscount, cr. 1919, of Hemsted; **Jonathan Harold Esmond Vere Harmsworth,** BA; British newspaper publisher; *Chairman, Daily Mail and General Trust PLC;* b. 3 Dec. 1967, London, England; s. of the late 3rd Viscount Rothermere and Patricia Evelyn Beverley Brooks; m. Claudia Clemence 1993; two s. three d.; ed Gordonstoun School, Scotland, Kent School, Conn., USA, Duke Univ., USA; joined Mirror Group 1993; joined Northcliffe Newspapers Group Ltd 1995; Deputy Man. Dir, then Man. Dir Evening Standard 1997; Chair. Assoc. Newspapers Ltd 1998–; Chair. Assoc. New Media 1998, Daily Mail and Gen. Trust PLC 1998–; Pres. Newspaper Press Fund 1999–. *Leisure interests:* family, tennis, golf, polo, skiing, riding. *Address:* Daily Mail and General Trust PLC, Room 602, Northcliffe House, 2 Derry Street, London, W8 5TT, England (office). *Telephone:* (20) 7938-6613. *Fax:* (20) 7937-0043. *E-mail:* chairman@chairman.dmgt.com (office). *Website:* www.dmgt.com (office).

ROTHMAN, James Edward, PhD; American biochemist/biophysicist and academic; *Professor of Chemistry, Professor and Chairman of Cell Biology and Fergus F. Wallace Professor of Biomedical Sciences, Yale University;* b. 3 Nov. 1950, Haverhill, Mass; ed Yale Univ. and Harvard Medical School; post-doctoral work at MIT; Asst Prof., Dept of Biochemistry, Stanford Univ. 1978–81, Assoc. Prof. 1981–84, Prof. 1984–88; E. R. Squibb Prof. of Molecular Biology, Princeton Univ. 1988-91; Chairman, Cellular Biochemistry and Biophysics Program, Sloan-Kettering Inst., New York 1991–2003, Paul A. Marks Chair, Memorial Sloan-Kettering Cancer Center, Chair. Cellular Biochemistry and Biophysics Program, Rockefeller Research Lab. 1991–2004, Vice-Chair. Sloan-Kettering Inst. 1994–2003; Prof., Dept Physiology and Cellular Biophysics, Columbia Univ. 2004–05, Clyde '56 and Helen Wu Prof. of Chemical Biology 2005–08, Dir Chemical Biology Center 2004–08, Dir Columbia Genome Center 2005–08, mem. Columbia Cancer Center 2004–08; Prof. of Chem., Prof. and Chair. of Cell Biology and Fergus F. Wallace Prof. of Biomedical Sciences, Yale Univ. 2008–; fmr Chief Science Adviser, GE Healthcare; mem. Bd of Sr Eds, Journal of Clinical Investigation 2002–; Assoc. Ed., Annual Review of Biochemistry 2003–; mem. NAS, Inst. of Medicine 1995; Fellow, American Acad. of Arts and Sciences 1994, European Molecular Biology Asscn; Hon. mem. Japanese Biochemical Soc. 2005; Dr hc (Regensburg) 1995, (Geneva) 1997; Eli Lilly Award for Fundamental Research in Biological Chem. 1986, Passano Young Scientist Award 1986, Alexander Von Humboldt Award 1989, Heinrich Wieland Prize 1990, Rosenstiel Award in Biomedical Sciences (with R. Schekman) 1994, V.D. Mattia Award 1994, Fritz Lipmann Award 1995, Gairdner Foundation Int. Award 1996, King Faisal Int. Prize in Science 1996, Felix Hoppe-Seyler Lecturer 1996, Harden Medal 1997, NAS Lounsbery Award 1997, Feodor Lynen Award (with G. Blobel and G. Schatz) 1997, Jacobæus Prize 1999, Dr H.P. Heineken Prize for Biochemistry 2000, Otto-Warburg Medal 2001, Louisa Gross Horwitz Prize (with R. Schekman) 2002, Albert Lasker Basic Medical Research Award (with R. Schekman) 2002, Nobel Prize in Medicine (with Randy W. Schekman and Thomas C. Sudhof) 2013. *Publications:* more than 200 articles in scientific journals. *Address:* Rothman Laboratory, Sterling Hall of Medicine, C-207 or C-434 (lab), PO Box 208002, New Haven, CT 06520-8002, USA (office). *Telephone:* (203) 737-5293 (office). *Fax:* (203) 737-3585 (office). *E-mail:* james.rothman@yale.edu (office). *Website:* www.chem.yale.edu/faculty/rothman.html (office); medicine.yale.edu/lab/rothman/index.aspx (office).

ROTHSCHILD, Baron David René James de; French banker; *Chairman, N.M. Rothschild & Sons Ltd;* b. 15 Dec. 1942, New York; s. of the late Baron Guy de Rothschild and Baroness Alix Schey de Koromla; m. Olimpia Aldobrandini 1974; ed Lycée Carnot, Paris and Inst. d'Études Politiques, Paris; Dir Société Le Nickel 1970–73; Dir-Gen. Cie du Nord 1973–78; Chair. Man. Bd Banque Rothschild 1978–82; Pres.-Dir-Gen. Paris-Orléans Man. 1982–84, Paris-Orléans Banque 1984–86; Chair. Rothschild & Cie Banque 1986–, Rothschild NA Inc. 1986–, Rothschild Canada 2001–; Chair. Man. Bd Saint-Honoré-Matignon (investment co.) 1986–94; Pres.-Dir-Gen. Francarep; Pres. Financière Viticole SA, Rothschild Europe; Dir Cie Financière Martin-Maurel, Imetal, Asscn française des entreprises privées (Afep), Rothschilds Continuation Ltd, etc.; Vice-Pres. Incolder 1990; Deputy Chair. N. M. Rothschild & Sons Ltd, London 1992–2004, Chair. 2004–; Chair. N. M. Rothschild Corporate Finance 1996–; Pres. Fondation Rothschild. *Leisure interests:* golf, skiing, tennis. *Address:* N.M. Rothschild & Sons Limited, New Court, St. Swithin's Lane, London, EC4P 4DU, England (office); 6 rue de Tournon, 75006 Paris, France (home). *Telephone:* (20) 7280-5000 (office). *Fax:* (20) 7929-1643 (office). *Website:* www.rothschild.com (office).

ROTHSCHILD, Sir Evelyn de, Kt; British banker; b. 29 Aug. 1931, London; s. of the late Anthony Gustav de Rothschild; m. 1st Victoria Schott 1972 (divorced 2000); two s. one d.; m. 2nd Lynn Forester 2000; ed Harrow, Trinity Coll., Cambridge; Chair. Economist Newspaper 1972–89, United Racecourses Ltd 1977–94, British Merchant Banking and Securities Houses Asscn (fmrly Accepting Houses Cttee) 1985–89; fmr Chair. N. M. Rothschild & Sons Ltd 1976–2004. *Leisure interests:* art, racing. *Address:* c/o N. M. Rothschild & Sons Ltd, New Court, St Swithin's Lane, London, EC4P 4DU, England. *Telephone:* (20) 7280-5302 (office). *Fax:* (20) 7220-7108 (office). *Website:* www.rothschild.com (office).

ROTHSCHILD, 4th Baron, cr. 1885; **(Nathaniel Charles) Jacob Rothschild,** OM, GBE, BA; British banker and business executive; *Chairman, RIT Capital Partners plc;* b. 29 April 1936; eldest s. of the late Nathaniel Mayer Victor Rothschild, 3rd Baron Rothschild GBE, GM, FRS and Barbara Hutchinson, Baroness Rothschild; succeeded his father 1990; m. Serena Mary Dunn 1961; one s. three d.; ed Eton Coll. and Christ Church, Oxford; Chair. St James's Place Capital PLC (fmrly J. Rothschild Holdings) 1971–96, RIT Capital Partners plc 1980–, Five Arrows Ltd 1980–; Deputy Chair. BSkyB Group plc 2003–; Chair. Bd of Trustees, Nat. Gallery 1985–91, Bd of Trustees Nat. Heritage Memorial Fund 1992–98 (administering Heritage Lottery Fund 1995–98), Yad Hanadiv Foundation; Pres. Inst. of Jewish Affairs 1992–; mem. Council, RCA 1986–92 (Sr Fellow 1992); co-f. Butrint Foundation to record and conserve the archaeological site of Butrint in

Albania 1993; Trustee Open Russia Foundation 2001–; Hon. Fellow, City of Jerusalem 1992; Hon. FBA 1998; Hon. FRIBA 1998; Hon. FRAM 2002; Hon. Fellow, King's Coll. London 2002; Commdr, Order of Henry the Navigator (Portugal) 1985; Hon. PhD (Hebrew Univ of Jerusalem) 1992; Hon. DLitt (Newcastle) 1998, (Warwick) 2003; Hon. LLD (Exeter) 1998; Hon. DUniv (Keele) 2000; Hon. DCL (Oxon.) 2002; Hon. DSc (Econs) (London) 2004; Weizmann Award for Humanities and Sciences 1997. *Address:* The Pavilion, Eythrope, Aylesbury, Bucks., HP18 0HS, England (home). *Telephone:* (1296) 653235 (office). *E-mail:* fsinclair@ritcap.co.uk (office).

ROTHWELL, Dame Nancy, DBE, PhD, DSc, FRS, FMedSci, FIBiol; British neuroscientist, academic and university administrator; *President, Vice-Chancellor and Medical Research Council Research Professor, University of Manchester;* b. 1956, Tarleton, nr Preston, Lancs.; ed Penwortham Girls' Grammar School, Queen Elizabeth Coll. and King's Coll., Univ. of London; Prof. of Physiology, Univ. of Manchester 1994–98, Chair. Div. of Neuroscience 1998–2000, MRC Research Prof. 1998–, Deputy Pres. and Deputy Vice-Chancellor 2007–10, Pres. and Vice-Chancellor 2010–; fmr mem. MRC Council, Biotechnology and Biological Sciences Research Council, Research Chair in Physiology 1998, Chair. MRC Neuroscience Bd; mem. Council Acad. of Medical Sciences; Chair. Biosciences Fed. Animal Science group, Research Defence Soc., Wellcome Trust Public Engagement Strategy Cttee; fmr Pres. British Neuroscience Asscn 2000, Biosciences Fed.; columnist, Times Higher Educ. Supplement; currently Vice-Pres. and Council mem. Royal Soc., Chair. Royal Soc. Educ. Comm.; Dir (non-exec.) Astrazeneca; Trustee, Cancer Research UK, the Campaign for Medical Progress, NESTA 2002– (mem. Fellowship Cttee); Hon. FRCP; Royal Soc. Research Fellowship 1984, Royal Inst. Christmas Lecturer 1998, Pfizer Research Prize for Innovative Science 2003. *Television:* several TV appearances, including Superhuman. *Publications:* Cytokines in the Nervous System, Interleukin-1 in the Brain, Obesity and Cachexia: Physiological Mechanisms and New Approaches to Pharmacological Control (co-ed.), Brain Control of Responses to Trauma (co-ed.), Immune and Inflammatory Responses in the Nervous System (co-ed.), Who Wants to Be a Scientist? Choosing Science as a Career, Obesity and Leanness: Basic Aspects (co-author); more than 300 research publs. *Address:* Office of the President and Vice-Chancellor, John Owens Building, University of Manchester, Oxford Road, Manchester, M13 9PL (office); Faculty of Life Sciences, University of Manchester, Hill Building, Oxford Road, Manchester, M13 9PT, England (office). *Telephone:* (161) 306-6010 (office); (161) 275-5744 (office). *Fax:* (161) 275-5586 (office). *E-mail:* nancy.rothwell@manchester.ac.uk (office); president@manchester.ac.uk (office). *Website:* www.manchester.ac.uk/aboutus/governance (office); www.manchester.ac.uk/research/Nancy.rothwell (office).

ROTICH, Henry K., BA, MA, MPA; Kenyan economist and politician; *Secretary for the National Treasury;* b. 1969, Kerio Valley, Rift Valley Prov.; s. of Kimatui Rotich and Pauline Rotich; m.; two s.; ed Univ. of Nairobi, Harvard Univ. Kennedy School of Govt, USA; began career as economist with Central Bank of Kenya 1996, Asst Dir 2004–06; economist with IMF, Nairobi 2001–04; joined Ministry of Finance 2006, Head of Macroeconomics at Treasury 2006–13, Sec. for the Nat. Treasury (Minister of Finance) 2013–. *Address:* National Treasury, Treasury Bldg, Harambee Avenue, POB 30007, Nairobi, Kenya (office). *Telephone:* (20) 228411 (office). *Website:* www.treasury.go.ke (office).

ROTTERMUND, Andrzej; Polish curator and art historian; *Director, The Royal Castle, Warsaw;* b. 11 May 1941, Warsaw; s. of Julian Rottermund and Zofia Lenart; m. Maria Reklewska 1963; one d.; ed Warsaw Univ.; Prof. Inst. of Art, Polish Acad. of Sciences, Warsaw 1990; Dept Dir Nat. Museum, Warsaw 1975–83, The Royal Castle, Warsaw 1987–90 (Dir 1991–); Deputy Minister of Culture and Arts 1991; mem. Polish Acad. of Sciences, Polish Art Historians' Asscn 1987–91, Polish ICOM Cttee 1990–96; organized exhbns in Poland and abroad including Treasures of a Polish King, Dulwich Picture Gallery London 1992, Land of the Winged Horsemen: Art in Poland 1572–1764, USA 1999–2000, Thesauri Poloniae, Austria 2002, Treasures of Poland, Japan 2010; Ordre de la Couronne (Belgium) 2002, Officier, Légion d'honneur 2002, Commdr's Cross of Merit (Germany) 2003, Golden Gloria Artis 2009, Great Cross, Order of Polonia Restituta 2011. *Publications:* 130 books, articles and essays including Katalog rysunków architektonicznych ze zbiorów Muzeum Narodowego w Warszawie (The Catalogue of Architectural Drawings of the Nat. Museum in Warsaw) 1970, Klasycyzm w Polsce (Neoclassicism in Poland) 1984, Zamek Królewski – funkcje i treści rezydencji monarszej wieku Oświecenia (The Royal Castle in the Age of the Enlightenment – the Functions and Symbolic Meaning of the Monarch's Residence) 1988, J.N.L. Durand a polska architektura I połowy XIX wieku (J.N.L. Durand and the Polish Architecture of the First Half of the 19th Century) 1990, Warsaw 2000, The Royal Castle in Warsaw 2003. *Leisure interests:* music, cinema. *Address:* The Royal Castle, pl. Zamkowy 4, 00-277 Warsaw, Poland (office). *Telephone:* (22) 6350808 (office). *Fax:* (22) 6357260 (office). *E-mail:* a.rottermund@zamek-krolewski.pl (office). *Website:* www.zamek-krolewski.art.pl (office).

RÖTTGEN, Norbert, DrIur; German lawyer and politician; b. 2 July 1965, Meckenheim; m.; two s. one d.; ed Univ. of Bonn; mem. CDU 1982–, Chair. CDU Junge Union (youth org.), N Rhine-Westphalia 1992–96, 2009–, Vice-Chair. CDU 2009–; practiced as lawyer at regional court, Cologne 1993–99, at higher regional court 1999–; mem. Bundestag (Parl.) for Rhein-Sieg-Kreis II constituency 1994–, legal policy spokesman for CDU/CSU parl. group 2002–05, Chief Parl. Sec. (chief whip) 2005–; Chair. Christian Lawyers Asscn 2001–09; Fed. Minister of Environment, Nature Conservation and Nuclear Safety 2009–12. *Address:* c/o Federal Ministry of the Environment, Nature Conservation and Nuclear Safety, Alexanderstr. 3, 10178 Berlin, Germany (office). *Website:* www.norbert-roettgen.de (office).

ROUCO VARELA, HE Cardinal Antonio María, LicenDer, DCL; Spanish ecclesiastic; *Archbishop of Madrid;* b. 20 Aug. 1936, Villalba; s. of Vicente Rouco and María Eugenia Varela; ordained priest of Mondoñedo-Ferrol 1959; taught at Mondoñedo Seminary, Lugo 1964–66, Univ. of Munich 1966–69, Univ. Pontificia de Salamanca 1969–76 (Vice-Rector 1972–76); Titular Bishop of Gergis 1976; Auxiliary Bishop of Santiago de Compostela 1976–84, Archbishop of Santiago de Compostela 1984–94, of Madrid 1994–; cr. Cardinal (Cardinal-Priest of San Lorenzo in Damaso) 1998; participated in Papal Conclave 2005, 2013; Pres.

Spanish Bishops Conf. 1999–2005, 2008–; Gran. Canciller San Dámaso Faculty of Theology. *Publications:* Staat und Kirche im Spanien des XVI Jahrhunderts 1965, Sacramento e diritto: antinomia nella Chiesa (with E. Corecco) 1972. *Leisure interests:* music, reading. *Address:* Arzobispado de Madrid, C/ Bailen 8, 28071 Madrid, Spain (office); Conferencia Episcopal Española, Calle Añastro 1, 28033 Madrid, Spain (office). *Telephone:* (91) 4546100 (office); (91) 3439600 (office). *Fax:* (91) 5427906 (office); (91) 3439602 (office). *E-mail:* infomadrid@planalfa.es (home); conferenciaepiscopal@planalfa.es (office). *Website:* www.archimadrid.es (office); www.conferenciaepiscopal.es (office).

ROUHANI, Hassan, DJur, PhD, MPhil; Iranian cleric, lawyer, government official and head of state; *President;* b. (Hassan Feridon), 12 Nov. 1948, Sorkheh; m.; one s. three d.; ed Semnan Seminary, Qom Seminary, Glasgow Caledonian Univ., UK; mem. Majlis (Parl.) 1980–2000, Deputy Speaker 1992–2000, Chair. Defence Cttee, Foreign Policy Cttee; mem. Supreme Defence Council 1982–88; Commdr Iran Air Defence Force 1986–91, as Deputy to Second-in-Command of Iranian Jt Chiefs of Staff 1988–89; mem. and rep. of Ayatollah Khamenei, Supreme Leader of Iran on Supreme Nat. Security Council 1989–, Sec. 1989–2005; mem. Expediency Council 1991–; Dir Centre for Strategic Research 1992–; mem. Ass. of Experts 1999–; Pres. of Iran 2013–. *Publications include:* Islamic Revolution, the Roots and Challenges 1999, Rohani's Memories Vol. 1 2008, Islamic Political Thought, Vols 1–3 2009, National Security and Economic System: The Case of Iran 2010; numerous articles in Iranian journals and magazines on domestic and foreign affairs related to Iran's nat. security interests. *Leisure interests:* hiking, swimming. *Address:* Office of the President, PO Box 1423-13185, Pasteur Avenue, Tehran 13168-43311, Iran (office). *Telephone:* (21) 64451 (office). *E-mail:* webmaster@president.ir (office). *Website:* www.president.ir (office).

ROUILLY, Jean, LenD; French television executive and senior media adviser; *Chairman and CEO, International Media Partners;* b. 21 Dec. 1943, Villennes-sur-Seine; s. of Roger Rouilly and Nicole Antigna; m. Annyck Graton 1987; one s.; ed Lycées Jules Verne and Georges Clémenceau, Nantes, Faculté de Droit, Bordeaux and Inst. d'Etudes Politiques, Bordeaux; Asst to the Dir, Office de Radiodiffusion-Télévision Francaise, 1966–70, Admin. Documentary Programmes 1970–72, Gen. Man. to Del. Gen. of TV Production 1972–74; Sec.-Gen. Production, Antenne 2 1975–81, Asst Dir Finance 1981–85, Production Man. 1985–87, Dir-Gen. Programme Production 1987–90; Asst Dir-Gen. Antenne 2 1987–90; Dir Films A2 1981–87, Dir-Gen. 1987–90; Sec.-Gen. TV5 1983–85; Dir-Gen. Hachette Int. TV (now Europe Images Int.) 1990–2003, CEO 1999–2003; CEO Lagardère Images Int. and Lagardère Networks Int. 2001– (merged in 2007 to form Lagardère TV Int.); currently Chair. and CEO Int. Media Partners; Chevalier Ordre National du Mérite. *Address:* Lagardère Television International, 149-151 rue Anatole France, 92534 Levallois-Peret Cedex, France (office). *E-mail:* jean.rouilly@imcpartners.fr (office). *Website:* www.lni.tv (office).

ROULEAU, Joseph-Alfred, CC; Canadian singer (bass); *President, Jeunesses Musicales du Canada;* b. 28 Feb. 1929, Matane, Québec; s. of Joseph-Alfred Rouleau and Florence Bouchard; m. 1st Barbara Whittaker 1952; one d.; m. 2nd Renée Moreau; one s. two d.; ed Coll. Jean de Brebeuf, Montréal, Univ. of Montréal, Conservatoire of Music, Province of Québec; debut in Montréal Opera Guild in Un Ballo in Maschera 1951; Royal Opera House, Covent Garden 1957–87, singing 48 roles; guest artist at prin. opera houses all over the world; tours of Canada 1960, Australia (with Joan Sutherland) 1965, Russia 1966, 1969, Romania, S Africa 1974, 1975, 1976; Paris Opera 1975, Metropolitan Opera, New York 1984, 1985, 1986, San Francisco 1986, 1987; roles include Boris Godunov in Boris Godunov, Philip II and Inquisitore in Don Carlos, Basilio in Barber of Seville, Mephistopheles in Faust, Dosifei in Khovanshchina, Don Quixote in Don Quixote, Ramfis in Aida, Prince Gremin in Onegin, Father Lawrence in Roméo et Juliette, Colline in La Bohème, Raimondo in Lucia di Lammermoor, Titurel in Parsifal, Abimelech in Samson et Dalila, Crespel in Contes d'Hoffmann, Arkel in Pelléas et Mélisande, Sarastro, Osmin in Die Entführung, Daland in Der fliegende Holländer, Oroveso in Norma, Don Marco in The Saint of Bleecker Street, Trulove in The Rake's Progress, The Prince in Adriana Lecouvreur, Bartolo; Prof. of Voice, Univ. of Québec 1980–98, mem. Admin. Bd, Prof. Emer. 2004–; mem. Bd Corpn of Montreal Opera Co. 1980–; Pres., Jeunesses Musicales du Canada 1989– (Prix Joseph Rouleau for Vocal Art named after him 1995); Co-Founder and mem. Bd Concours Musical Int. de Montréal 2002–; Compagnon, Ordre du Canada, Ordre Nat. du Québec 2004; Dr hc (Université de Québec à Rimouski, McGill Univ.); Prix Archambault 1967, La Société St Jean Baptiste Prix Calixa-Lavallée, Montréal 1967, Royal Opera House, Covent Garden Silver Medal 1983, Felix Award for Best Classical Artist of the Year 1989, Prix du Québec pour les Arts d'interprétation 1990, Panthéon de l'art lyrique du Canada 1992, Jeunesses Musicales du Canada Médaille du mérite exceptionnel 1995, Conseil québecois de la musique Prix Opus Hommage 2003, Prix du Gov. Gen. de Canada (Performing Arts Award) 2004, Opéra Canada Prix Ruby 2004, Médaille de la Ville de Marseille 2007. *Recordings include:* scenes from Anna Bolena, Ruddigore, Roméo et Juliette (Gounod), L'Enfance du Christ (Berlioz), Semiramide, Lucia di Lammermoor, Don Carlos, Aida, Il Trovatore, Renard (Stravinsky), F. Leclerc's Songs, Les abîmes du rêve de Jacques Hêtu (song cycle), French operatic arias (with Royal Opera House Orchestra), Boris Godunov (Prix Félix 2000), Don Carlos/Lucia di Lammermoor, L'Africaine (Meyerbeer), with Domingo & Verrett, San Francisco Opera; Don Carlo, Royal Opera House Covent Garden. *Leisure interests:* tennis, golf, reading. *Address:* c/o Jeunesses Musicales, 305 avenue du Mont-Royal Est, Montréal, PQ H2T 1P8 (office); 7 Roosevelt, Suite 20, Ville Mont-Royal, PQ H3R 1Z3, Canada (home). *Telephone:* (514) 739-3238 (home); (819) 688-3676 (home); (514) 845-4108 (ext. 232) (office). *Fax:* (514) 739-9135 (home); (514) 845-8241 (office). *E-mail:* Jrouleau@jmcanada.ca (office); renee_rouleau@hotmail.com (home). *Website:* www.jmcanada.ca (office).

ROUNDS, Marion Michael (Mike), BS; American politician and business executive; *President and CEO, Fischer, Rounds & Associates Inc.;* b. 24 Oct. 1954, Huron, SDak; s. of Don Rounds; m. Jean Vedvei 1978; three s. two d.; ed South Dakota State Univ., Brookings; Pres. and CEO, Fischer, Rounds & Assocs Inc. (insurance and real estate agency), Pierre; mem. from Dist 24, SDak State Senate 1991–2000, Minority Whip 1993–94, Senate Majority Leader 1995–2002; Gov. of SDak 2003–11; Pres. Bd Oahe YMCA, Pierre-Ft. Pierre Exchange Club; Vice-Pres. St Joseph School Home & School Asscn; mem. Midwestern Govs' Asscn (Chair.),

Govs' Council, Health Project, Bipartisan Policy Center, Washington, DC 2011–, Elks, Ducks Unlimited, Kts of Columbus, Pierre Elks Lodge; Republican; Guardian of Small Business, Nat. Fed. of Ind. Business 1992, 1998, Agent of the Year, SDak Ind. Insurance Agents 1999, Special Award, SDak Horsemen 2000. *Leisure interests:* flying, hunting, racquetball, camping, boating, family. *Address:* Fischer Rounds & Assocs Inc., 125 East Dakota, PO Box 218, Pierre, SD 57501, USA (office). *Telephone:* (605) 224-9223 (office). *Fax:* (605) 224-5831 (office). *E-mail:* info@fischerrounds.com (office). *Website:* www.fischerrounds.com (office).

ROURKE, Philip Andre (Mickey); American actor and fmr boxer; b. 16 Sept. 1956, Schenectady, NY; m. 1st Debra Feuer (divorced); m. 2nd Carre Otis 1992 (divorced 1998); ed Actors' Studio, New York; film debut in Steven Spielberg's film 1941; appeared in numerous TV movies; left acting and became professional boxer 1991–95. *Film appearances include:* Fade to Black, 1941 1979, Heaven's Gate 1980, Body Heat 1981, Diner (Boston Soc. of Film Critics Best Actor Award 1983, Nat. Soc. of Film Critics Best Supporting Actor Award) 1982, Eureka 1983, Rumblefish 1983, Rusty James 1983, The Pope of Greenwich Village 1984, 9½ Weeks 1984, Year of the Dragon 1985, Angel Heart 1986, A Prayer for the Dying 1986, Barfly 1987, Johnny Handsome 1989, Homeboy 1989, Francesco 1989, The Crew 1989, The Desperate Hours 1990, Wild Orchid 1990, On the Sport 1990, Harley Davidson and the Marlboro Man 1991, White Sands 1992, F.T.W., Fall Time, Double Time, Another 9½ Weeks, The Rainmaker 1997, Love in Paris 1997, Double Team 1997, Buffalo '66 1997, Thursday 1998, Shergar 1999, Shades 1999, Out in Fifty 1999, The Animal Factory 2000, Get Carter 2000, The Pledge 2001, The Hire: Follow 2001, Picture Claire 2001, They Crawl 2001, Spun 2002, Once Upon a Time in Mexico 2003, Man on Fire 2004, Domino 2005, Sin City (Chicago Film Critics Assn Best Supporting Actor Award, Irish Film and Television Awards Best Int. Actor Award) 2005, Stormbreaker 2006, The Wrestler (Golden Globe for Best Actor 2009, BAFTA Award for Leading Actor 2009) 2008, The Informers 2008, Killshot 2008, Iron Man 2 2010. *Address:* c/o Progressive Artists Agency, 400 South Beverly Drive, Beverly Hills, CA 90212, USA (office).

ROUSE, Cecilia Elena, BA, PhD; American economist and academic; *Lawrence and Shirley Katzman and Lewis and Anna Ernst Professor in the Economics of Education and Dean, Woodrow Wilson School of Public and International Affairs, Princeton University;* m.; two d.; ed Harvard Univ.; fmrly Theodore A. Wells '29 Prof. of Econs and Public Affairs and Prof. of Econs and Public Affairs, Woodrow Wilson School of Public and Int. Affairs, Princeton Univ., Founding Dir Princeton Univ. Educ. Research Section, Dir Industrial Relations Section, currently Lawrence and Shirley Katzman and Lewis and Anna Ernst Professor in the Economics of Education and Professor of Economics and Public Affairs, Dean, Woodrow Wilson School 2012–; fmr Sr Ed. The Future of Children, Journal of Labor Economics; fmr mem. MacArthur Foundation's Research Network on the Transition to Adulthood; served in Nat. Econ. Council, The White House 1998–99, mem. Council of Econ. Advisers 2009–11; mem. Bd of Dirs MDRC, T. Rowe Price Equity Mutual Funds; mem. Advisory Bd T. Rowe Price Fixed Income Mutual Funds; Research Assoc., Nat. Bueau of Econ. Research 1992–. *Publications:* numerous articles on labour econs and the econs of educ. *Address:* 424 Robertson Hall, Woodrow Wilson School, Princeton University, Princeton, NJ 08544-1013, USA (office). *Telephone:* (609) 258-4800 (office). *Fax:* (609) 258-1418 (office). *E-mail:* rouse@princeton.edu (office). *Website:* wws.princeton.edu (office).

ROUSSEFF, Dilma Vana, BEcons, MA; Brazilian politician, fmr political activist and head of state; *President;* b. 14 Dec. 1947, Belo Horizonte, Minas Gerais; d. of Pedro Rousseff (born Pétar Rusév, Bulgarian) and Dilma Jane Silva; m. 1st Cláudio Galeno de Magalhães Linhares 1968 (divorced 1981); one d. with common-law husband Carlos Franklin Paixão de Araújo 1976 (divorced 2000); ed Fed. Univ. of Rio Grande do Sul, Univ. of Campinas, São Paulo; mem. of Política Operária (Polop) 1967; mem. Comando de Libertação Nacional (Colina) 1968–70; arrested 1970 and imprisoned 1970–73; mem. Partido Democrática Trabalhista (PDT) from 1982; Planning and Budget Sec., Porto Alegre 1986–88; Communications, Mines and Energy Sec., Rio Grande do Sul 1991–94, 1999–2002; joined Partido dos Trabalhadores (PT) 2001; Mines and Energy Minister 2003–05; Chief-of-Staff, Presidency 2005–10; PT cand. in presidential election Oct. 2010, Pres.-Elect (first woman) Oct.–Dec. 2010, Pres. 2011–; Chair. Petrobras and Petrobras Distribui-dora SA 2003–10; ranked by Forbes magazine amongst The World's 100 Most Powerful Women (95th) 2010, (third) 2011–12, (second) 2013, ranked by Forbes magazine amongst The World's Most Powerful People (16th) 2010, (22nd) 2011, (18th) 2012, (20th) 2013. *Leisure interests:* history, opera, Greek mythology, embroidery, reading. *Address:* Palácio do Planalto, 4° andar, Praça dos Três Poderes, 70150-900 Brasilia, DF, Brazil (office). *Telephone:* (61) 3411-1166. *Fax:* (61) 3411-1667. *E-mail:* casacivil@planalto.gov.br. *Website:* www.casacivil.gov.br; www.dilma13.com.br.

ROUSSELET, André Claude Lucien, LenD; French business executive; b. 1 Oct. 1922, Nancy; s. of Marcel Rousselet and Yvonne Rousselet (née Brongniart); m. Catherine Roge (divorced); two s. one d.; ed Lycée Claude Bernard, Paris, Faculté de Droit, Paris and Ecole Libre des Sciences Politiques; Chef de Cabinet, Prefects of Ariège and L'Aube 1944; Sub-Prefect of Condom 1946, Pointe-à-Pitre 1948, Issoudun 1935; Chef de Cabinet, Minister of the Interior 1954; Special Asst Office of Minister of Posts and Telecommunications 1955; Chef de Cabinet, Minister of Justice 1956; Dept of External Relations, Simca 1958; Pres.-Dir-Gen. Socs nouvelles des autoplaces G7 1962–67, 1972–; Deputé for Haute-Garonne 1967–68; Man. Galerie de France and Dir du Cabinet, Pres. of Repub. 1981–82; Pres.-Dir-Gen. Agence Havas 1982–86 (now Dir); mem. Comité stratégique de Havas 1987; Pres.-Dir-Gen. Canal Plus 1984–94; Pres. Soc. éditrice de InfoMatin (Sodepresse) 1994–; Pres. Advisory Council Tonna Electronique 1990, Sodepresse 1995; Dir Information; Pres. Editorial Soc. Sodepresse; Dir Télévision le mensuel (publ). *Leisure interests:* golf, tennis, painting, skiing. *Address:* 44 avenue Georges V, 75008 Paris; 28 rue Henri Barbusse, 92110 Clichy, France.

ROUSSELY, François, MEcon; French industrial executive; *Vice-Chairman, Crédit Suisse Europe;* b. 9 Jan. 1945, Belvès, Dordogne; ed Paris Inst. of Political Science, French Nat. School of Admin, Univ. of Paris; auditor, State Accounting Office 1978; sr civil servant, Ministry of Interior, Prin. Pvt. Sec. 1981–86; assigned to chair. of a parl. cttee, Assemblée Nat. 1986–88; Dir-Gen. Nat. Police (Ministry of Interior) 1989–91; Gen. Sec. for Admin. of Ministry of Defence 1991–97; Sec.-Gen. and mem. Exec. Cttee Soc. Nat. des Chemins de Fer (SNCF) 1997; Prin. Pvt. Sec.

Ministry of Defence 1997–98; Chair. and CEO Electricité de France (EDF) 1998–2004; Chair. Crédit Suisse France 2005–, Vice-Chair. Crédit Suisse Europe 2005–; mem. Comité de l'Energie Atomique; mem. Bd Usinor, Framatome, Aérospatiale-Matra 1998; mem. Advisory Bd of La Banque de France; Advisor, Int. Business Leaders Advisory Council of Mayor of Beijing, Int. Business Leaders Advisory Council of Gov. of Guangdong 1998; Pres. Bd of Dirs Ecole Nationale de Ponts et Chaussées; mem. Supervisory Bd DALKIA Holding 2000; Chair. EDF Foundation 2001; Admin. AFII (French Agency for Int. Investments) 2002; Officier, Légion d'honneur 1998, Commdr 2013; Officier, Ordre nat. du Mérite, des Arts et des Lettres 2003; Prix 2004 de l'Asscn France-Chine 2000. *Leisure interests:* jogging, classical music, rugby. *Address:* Crédit Suisse, 25 Avenue Kléber, 75784 Paris Cedex 16, France (office). *Telephone:* 1-70-39-01-01 (office). *Fax:* 1-70-39-00-75 (office). *Website:* www.credit-suisse.com (office).

ROUTS, Robert J.; Dutch business executive; *Chairman of the Supervisory Board, AEGON NV;* b. 1946; fmr Exec. Dir Downstream, Royal Dutch Shell; mem. Supervisory Bd AEGON NV 2008–, Chair. 2010–, Chair. Nominating Cttee and mem. Compensation Cttee; Chair. Supervisory Bd Royal DSM NV; mem. Supervisory Bd Royal KPN NV; mem. Bd of Dirs Canadian Utilities Ltd, A.P. Møller – Mærsk A/S, UPM-Kymmene Corpn, AECOM Technology Corpn. *Address:* Supervisory Board, AEGON NV, PO Box 202, 2501 The Hague, Netherlands (office). *Telephone:* (70) 344-3210 (office). *E-mail:* info@aegon.com (office). *Website:* www.aegon.com (office).

ROUVILLOIS, Philippe André Marie; French government official; *Inspector General of Finance;* b. 29 Jan. 1935, Saumur; s. of Gen. Jean Rouvillois and Suzanne Hulot; m. Madeleine Brigol 1960; four s.; ed Lycée Fustel-de-Coulanges, Strasbourg, Lycée Louis-le-Grand, Faculté de Droit, Paris and Inst. d'Etudes Politiques, Paris; Insp. of Finance 1959; Office of Revenue 1964; Adviser, Pvt. Office of Minister of Econ. and Finance 1966–68; Deputy Dir Office of Revenue, Ministry of Econ. and Finance 1967, Head of Service 1969; Deputy Dir-Gen. of Revenue 1973, Dir-Gen. 1976; Insp.-Gen. of Finance 1982–; Deputy Dir-Gen. SNCF 1983–87, Dir-Gen. 1987–88, Pres. Admin. Bd 1988; Gen. Man. and Pres. Admin. Council, Atomic Energy Comm. (CEA) 1989–95; Pres. CEA-Industrie 1989–92, 1993–99; Pres. Pasteur Inst. 1997–2003, Hon. Pres. 2003–; Commdr Légion d'honneur, Croix de Valeur militaire. *Address:* Inspection générale des finances, 139 rue de Bercy, 75572 Paris, cedex 12 France (office). *E-mail:* igf-contact@igf.finances.gouv.fr (office). *Website:* www.igf.minefi.gouv.fr (office).

ROUVOET, André; Dutch politician; *Deputy Prime Minister and Minister for Youth and Families;* b. 4 Jan. 1962, Hilversum; ed VU Univ. Amsterdam; mem. Reformed Political Fed. 1985–2001; mem. Christian Union 2001–, Leader 2002–; mem. House of Reps 1994–; Deputy Prime Minister and Minister for Youth and Families 2007–, also Acting Minister of Educ., Culture and Science 2010–; fmr Chair. Dutch Reformed Churches' Youth Welfare Asscn; mem. Bd Protestant Children's Homes Foundation, Foundation for the New South Africa. *Address:* Office of the Prime Minister, Ministry of General Affairs, Binnenhof 20, PO 20001, 2500 EA The Hague, The Netherlands (office). *Telephone:* (70) 356-41-00 (office). *Fax:* (70) 356-46-83 (office). *E-mail:* info@minaz.nl (office). *Website:* www.minaz.nl (office).

ROUX, Albert Henri, OBE; French chef and restaurateur; b. 8 Oct. 1935, Semur-en-Brionnais; s. of the late Henri Roux and of Germaine Roux (née Triger); brother of Michel André Roux (q.v.); m. 1st Monique Merle 1959; one s. one d.; m. 2nd Cheryl Deborah 2006; ed Ecole Primaire, St Mandé; mil. service, Algeria; founder (with brother Michel Roux), Le Gavroche Restaurant, London 1967 (now owned jtly with his son Michel Jr), The Waterside Inn, Bray 1972 (now owned solely by Michel Roux); opened 47 Park Street Hotel 1981; opened Le Poulbot, Le Gamin, Gavvers, Les Trois Plats and Rouxl Britannia (all as part of Roux Restaurants Ltd) 1969–87; commenced consultancy practice 1989; f. House of Albert Roux (retail catering co.) 1994; Founder-mem. Acad. Culinaire de Grande Bretagne (now renamed Acad. of Culinary Arts) 1980; Hon. Prof. of Hospitality Man., Bourne-mouth Univ. 1995–; Maître Cuisinier de France 1968, Officier du Mérite Agricole 1987, Chevalier de la Légion d'Honneur 2005; Hon. DSc (Council for Nat. Academic Awards) 1987, Hon. PhD (Bournemouth Univ.) 1987; Catey Lifetime Achievement Award (with Michel Roux) 1995, Watreford Wegdwood Hospitality Award 1999, AA Lifetime Achievement Award for Hospitality 2007. *Publications:* with Michel Roux: New Classic Cuisine 1983, The Roux Brothers on Pâtisserie 1986, The Roux Brothers on French Country Cooking 1989, Cooking for Two 1991. *Leisure interests:* fishing, racing. *Address:* Albert Roux Consultancy, 539 Wandsworth Road, London, SW8 3JX, England (office). *Telephone:* (20) 7720-6148 (office). *Fax:* (20) 7627-0267 (office). *E-mail:* albertroux@le-gavroche.com. *Website:* www.albertroux.co.uk (home).

ROUX, Michel André; French chef and restaurateur; b. 19 April 1941, Charolles, Saône-et-Loire, Burgundy; s. of the late Henri Roux and Germaine Roux (née Triger); brother of Albert Henri Roux (q.v.); m. 1st Françoise Marcelle Becquet (divorced 1979, died 2004); one s. two d.; m. 2nd Robyn Margaret Joyce 1984; ed Ecole Primaire St Mandé, Brevet de Collège; commis pâtissier and cuisinier, British Embassy, Paris 1955–57; commis cook to Cécile de Rothschild 1957–59, Chef 1962–67; mil. service 1960–62; Propr Le Gavroche 1967, The Waterside Inn 1972, Le Gavroche (Mayfair) 1981; mem. Acad. Culinaire de France (UK Br.), Asscn Relais et Desserts, Asscn Relais et Châteaux; Chevalier, Ordre nat. du Mérite 1987, Ordre des Arts et des Lettres 1990, Légion d'honneur 2004; Hon. OBE 2002; numerous other decorations; numerous culinary awards including Gold Medal Cuisiniers Français (Paris) 1972, Laureate Restaurateur of the Year 1985. *Publications:* New Classic Cuisine 1983, Roux Brothers on Pâtisserie 1986, At Home with the Roux Brothers 1987, French Country Cooking 1989, Cooking for Two 1991, Desserts, a Lifelong Passion 1994, Sauces 1996 (revised edn) 2009, Life is a Menu (autobiography) 2000, Only the Best 2002, Eggs 2005, Pastry Savoury and Sweet 2008, Desserts 2011, Michel Roux: The Collection 2012, The Essence of French Cooking 2014. *Leisure interests:* shooting, skiing, walking, golf. *Website:* www.waterside-inn.co.uk (office).

ROVE, Karl Christian; American political consultant, fmr government official, author, broadcaster and columnist; b. 25 Dec. 1950, Denver; ed Univ. of Utah, Univ. of Maryland-College Park, George Mason Univ., Univ. of Texas, Austin; Founder and Pres. Karl Rove & Co. (public affairs firm), Austin Tex. 1981–99;

political adviser to George W. Bush campaigns for Gov. of Texas and US presidency 1993–2001; Sr Advisor and Chief Policy Aide to George W. Bush 2000–07, Deputy Chief of Staff for Policy 2004–07, oversaw Offices of Strategic Initiatives, Political Affairs, Public Liaison, and Intergovernmental Affairs, became known as "The Architect" of Pres. Bush's 2000 and 2004 campaigns; Political Commentator, Fox News Channel 2008–. *Publications:* Courage and Consequence: My Life as a Conservative in the Fight 2010; articles for The Daily Beast, Financial Times, Forbes, FoxNews.com, HumanEvents.com, Newsweek, The Times, Washington Post, The Weekly Standard, amongst others. *Address:* c/o FOX News Channel, 1211 Avenue Of The Americas, New York, NY 10036, USA. *E-mail:* karl@rove.com. *Website:* www.rove.com.

ROVERATO, Jean-François; French business executive; *Chairman and Managing Director, Eiffage SA;* ed Lycée Carnot, Dijon, Ecole Polytechnique, Ecole Nationale des Ponts et Chaussées; engineer, Roads and Bridges, Directorate of Ministry of Construction Equipment 1969–72, Tech. Adviser to Cabinet of Robert Andrew Vivien (Sec. of State for Housing) 1971–72; Dir Public Office of HLM du Val-de-Marne 1972–74; Dir, Guiraudie et Auffève 1975; joined Fougerolle group (became Eiffage 1993), Dir 1975, Man. Dir Fougerolle Construction 1980, Man. Dir Fougerolle France 1982, Man. Dir Fougerolle International 1984, Man. Dir Eiffage SA 1985–2007, Chair. and Man. Dir 2007–; Chair. and Man. Dir Autoroutes Paris Rhin Rhône 2006–; Pres. AREA 2006–; Chair. Ecole Nationale des Ponts et Chaussées 2006–, Etablissement public de la porte Dorée – Cité nationale de l'histoire de l'immigration 2007–; Officier, Légion d'honneur 2003, Commdr 2009. *Address:* Eiffage SA, 163 Quai du Dr Dervaux, 92601 Asnières-sur-Seine, France (office). *Telephone:* 1-41-32-80-00 (office). *Fax:* 1-41-32-81-13 (office). *E-mail:* info@eiffage.fr (office). *Website:* www.eiffage.fr (office).

ROVERSI, Paolo; Italian photographer; b. 25 Sept. 1947, Ravenna; fashion photographer since 1973, working for numerous magazines including British and Italian Vogue, Uomo Vogue, W Magazine and others; advertising for Georgio Armani, Cerruti 1881, Comme des Garçons, Christian Dior, Alberta Ferretti, Romeo Gigli and Yohji Yamamoto; dir commercials. *Publications:* Una Donna 1989, Angeli 1993, Nudi 1999, Libretto 2000, Studio 2006, Studio (French edn) 2009. *Address:* 9 rue Paul Fort, 75014 Paris, France (office). *Telephone:* 1-45-40-40-49 (office). *Fax:* 1-45-40-72-98 (office). *E-mail:* info@paoloroversi.com (office). *Website:* www.paoloroversi.com (office).

ROWE, John W., BS, JD; American lawyer and energy industry executive; *Chairman and CEO, Exelon Corporation;* b. 1946, Wis.; m. Jeanne M. Rowe; one s.; ed Univ. of Wisconsin; joined Isham, Lincoln & Beale (law firm), Chicago 1970, Partner 1978–80, served as Gen. Counsel to Trustees of Chicago, Milwaukee, St Paul & Pacific Railroad Co. 1978–80; Sr Vice-Pres. of Law, Consolidated Rail Corpn (Conrail) 1980–84; Pres. and CEO Cen. Maine Power Co. 1984–89; Pres. and CEO New England Electric System (NEES) 1989–98; Chair., Pres. and CEO Unicom Corpn and Commonwealth Edison 1998–2000; Chair. and CEO Exelon Corpn (following merger of Unicom Corpn and PECO Energy 2000) 2000–; Commr Nat. Comm. on Energy Policy; fmr Chair. Edison Electric Inst., Mass Business Roundtable; mem. Bd of Dirs Sunoco, The Northern Trust Corpn 2002–; fmr mem. Bd of Dirs Unum Provident Corpn, Fleet Boston Financial Corp, Wisconsin Cen. Transportation Co., MidSouth Corpn; mem. Bd of Govs Argonne Nat. Lab., Chicago Urban League, Field Museum, Art Inst. of Chicago, Northwestern Univ., Edison Electric Inst., Chicago Club; mem. The Econ. Club of Chicago, The Commercial Club of Chicago; mem. Bd of Trustees, Bryant Coll. 1994–98, Chicago Council on Foreign Relations, Chicago Historical Soc., Wisconsin Alumni Research Foundation, American Enterprise Inst., The Nature Conservancy (Ill. Chapter); fmr Pres. USS Constitution Museum; Fellow, American Acad. of Arts and Sciences 2009; Hon. DHumLitt (Bryant Coll.), Hon. DBA (Univ. of Massachusetts at Dartmouth) 2002, Hon. PhD (Illinois Inst. of Tech., Drexel Univ., DePaul Univ., Thomas Coll.); Distinguished Alumni Award, Univ. of Wisconsin, World of Difference Award, Anti-Defamation League 2000, Citizen of the Year Award, City Club of Chicago 2002, Corp. Leadership Award, Spanish Coalition for Jobs 2002, City Club of Chicago's Citizen of the Year Award 2002, Civic Leadership Award, American Jewish Cttee 2004, Founder's Award for Business Leadership, Union League of Philadelphia 2005, Univ. of Arizona Executive of the Year 2007, Illinois Holocaust Museum's Humanitarian Award 2008, named by Institutional Investor magazine as Best Electric Utilities CEO in America 2008, 2009, Daniel H. Burnham Award for Business and Civic Leadership, Chicagoland Chamber of Commerce 2008, inducted into Jr Achievement's Chicago Business Hall of Fame 2008, Humanitarian Award, Illinois Holocaust Museum 2008, Lyman Gage Award for Outstanding Civic Leadership, Civic Fed. of Chicago 2008, Corp. Leadership Award, Nat. Latino Educ. Inst. 2008, Distinguished Leadership Award, Edison Electric Inst. 2009, Chicago Council on Global Affairs Global Leadership Award 2009. *Address:* Exelon Corpn, PO Box 805398, 48th Floor, 10 South Dearborn Street, Chicago, IL 60680-5398, USA (office). *Telephone:* (312) 394-7398 (office). *Fax:* (312) 394-7945 (office). *E-mail:* info@exeloncorp.com. *Website:* www.exeloncorp.com (office).

ROWE, John W., MD; American physician and business executive (retd); b. 1944; ed Univ. of Rochester; began career with residency in internal medicine, Beth Israel Hosp., Boston, later becoming Chief of Gerontology; Clinical and Research Fellow, Mass. Gen. Hosp.; Research Fellow and later Prof. of Medicine, Harvard Medical School (Founding Dir Div. on Aging); Pres. School of Medicine and Chief Exec. Mount Sinai NYU Health 1988–2000 (renamed Mount Sinai/NYU Medical Center and Health System 1999), also Prof. of Medicine and Geriatrics; Chair., Pres. and Chief Exec. Aetna Inc. 2000–06, Exec. Chair. 2006 (retd); Chair. Bd of Trustees Univ. of Conn.; mem. NAS Inst. of Medicine; Fellow, American Acad. of Arts and Sciences; fmr Dir MacArthur Foundation on Successful Aging; mem. Bd of Govs American Bd of Internal Medicine; fmr Pres. Gerontological Soc. of America; Medicare Payment Advisory Comm.; numerous honours and awards. *Publications:* over 200 scientific pubns on the aging process; Successful Aging (jt author) 1998. *Address:* 352 Mansfield Road, Storrs, CT 06269-2048, USA. *Telephone:* (860) 486-2333.

ROWE, R. Kerry, BSc, PhD, FRS, DEng, FREng, FRSC, FCAE, FEIC, FIE (Aust), FASCE, FCSCE; Canadian (b. Australian) engineer and academic; *Professor and Canada Research Chair in Geotechnical and Geoenvironmental Engineering, Queen's University;* ed Univ. of Sydney; worked as geotechnical engineer with Australian Govt Dept of Construction; emigrated to Canada 1978; served 22 years as Prof., Dept of Civil and Environmental Eng, Univ. of Western Ont.; Vice-Prin. (Research), Queen's Univ., Kingston 2000–10, Prof. and Canada Research Chair in Geotechnical and Geoenvironmental Eng 2011–; Pres. Int. Geosynthetics Soc. 1990–94, Canadian Geotechnical Soc. 2001–02; Vice-Pres. N American Geosynthetics Soc. 1987–91; Chair. Standards Council of Canada Int. Subcommittee on Geotextiles and Geomembranes 1989–2000, NSERC Civil Eng Grant Selection Cttee 1998–99; Founding Chair. London Dist Section, Canadian Soc. for Civil Eng and Canadian Geotechnical Soc. 1993–96; Tech. Chair. 6th Int. Conf. on Geosynthetics, Atlanta, Ga 1998, 6th Canadian Environmental Eng Conf. 2000; mem. Bd of Dirs High Performance Computing Virtual Lab. (Chair. 2000–10), Canadian Microelectronics Corpn 2000–08, PARTEQ Innovations Inc. (Chair.) 2000–10, CANARIE Inc. 2003–08; mem. Editorial Bd Canadian Geotechnical Journal (Assoc. Ed. 1983–), International Journal for Geotextiles & Geomembranes (Ed. 1997–), International Journal on Computers and Geotechnics, International Journal for Numerical and Analytical Methods in Geomechanics, Geosynthetics International, Journal of Japanese Geotechnical Society, Italian Geotechnical Journal, Lowland Technology International, Geotechnique, Geotechnical Engineering, Transport in Porous Media, International Journal of Geomechanics (Co-Ed. 2001–), Journal of Environmental Engineering and Science, Waste Management; Fellow, Royal Acad. of Eng, Eng Inst. of Canada, American Soc. of Civil Engineers, Canadian Soc. for Civil Eng; Hon. mem. Int. Geosynthetics Soc. 2006; Edward G. Pleva Award, Univ. of Western Ont. 1996, Ont. Confed. of Univ. Faculty Asscns Excellence in Teaching Award 1997, Professional Engineers Ont. Eng Medal 1997, Ont. Ministry of the Environment Award of Excellence 1999, Keefer Medal 2001, Legget Medal 2003, K. Y. Lo Medal 2003, Killam Prize 2004, Int. Geosynthetics Soc. Award 2004, 45th Rankine Lecturer 2005, XXIII Manuel Rocha Lecturer 2006, Thomas C. Keefer Medal 2007, Casimir Gzowski Medal 2011, 7th Authur Casagrande Lecturer 2011, Third Terzaghi-Ferroco Oration 2012, Queen's Diamond Jubilee Medal 2012, Sir John Kennedy Medal 2012. *Publications include:* Barrier Systems for Waste Disposal Facilities (co-author), Geotechnical and Geoenvironmental Engineering Handbook (ed.); more than 600 articles, papers and chapters in journals, confs and books. *Address:* Department of Civil Engineering, Ellis Hall, Queen's University, Kingston, ON K7L 3N6, Canada (office). *Telephone:* (613) 533-3113 (office). *Fax:* (613) 533-2128 (office). *E-mail:* kerry@civil.queensu.ca (office). *Website:* www.civil.queensu.ca (office).

ROWLAND, Sir (John) David, Kt, MA; British business executive (retd); b. 10 Aug. 1933, London; s. of Cyril Arthur Rowland and Eileen Mary Rowland; m. 1st Giulia Powell 1957 (divorced 1991); one s. one d.; m. 2nd Diana L. Matthews 1991; ed Trinity College, Cambridge Univ.; joined Matthews Wrightson and Co. 1956, Dir 1965; Dir Matthews Wrightson Holdings 1972; Dir Project Fullemploy 1973–88; Deputy Chair. Stewart Wrightson Holdings PLC 1978–81, Chair. 1981–87; Vice-Pres. British Insurance and Investment Brokers Asscn 1980–; Chair. Westminster Insurance Agencies 1981–88; Dir Royal London Mutual Insurance Soc. 1985–86; Deputy Chair. Willis Faber PLC 1987–88; Dir Fullemploy Group Ltd 1989–90; Chair. Sedgwick Group PLC 1989–92; Pres. Templeton Coll., Oxford 1998–2003; mem. Council, Lloyd's 1987–90, Chair. 1993–97; Trustee Somerset House Trust 1997–2003, NatWest Group 1998–2000; Chair. NatWest 1999–2000 (Jt Deputy Chair. 1998–99); mem. Templeton Coll.; Gov. Coll. of Insurance 1983–85, Chair. 1985; Gov. St Paul's Girls School, St Paul's School (also Deputy Chair.) 1991–2007; Hon. Fellow Faculty of Actuaries; Hon. Fellow (Cardiff) 1999, (Templeton Coll., Oxford); Hon. MA (Oxford) 1993; Hon. DPhil (London Guildhall) 1996; Hon. DSc (City) 1997. *Leisure interests:* golf, running slowly, admiring his wife's garden. *Address:* Giffords Hall, Wickhambrook, Newmarket, Suffolk, CB8 8PQ, England (home). *Telephone:* (1440) 820221 (home).

ROWLANDS, Christopher John, MA, FCA, FRSA; British fmr business executive; b. 29 Aug. 1951, Leeds, Yorks., England; s. of the late Wilfred John Rowlands and of Margaretta Rowlands (née Roberts); m. Alison Mary Kelly 1978; two d.; ed Roundhay School, Leeds, Gonville and Caius Coll., Cambridge; articled clerk Peat Marwick Mitchell 1973–75, Man. 1981, seconded as partner, Zambia 1981–83, Sr Man., London 1983–85; Controller Business Planning Asda Group PLC 1985–86, Div. Dir Group Finance 1986–88, Deputy Man. Dir and Finance Dir Property Devt and Investment 1988–92; Group Finance Dir HTV 1992–93, Chief Exec. 1993–97; Chief Exec. The TV Corpn 1998–2001; Dir (non-exec.), ITouch PLC 2002–05; Deputy Chair. and COO Apace Media PLC 2005–09; mem. Bd of Dirs Standard Life Equity Income Trust PLC 2003–12; mem. Council, Ind. TV Asscn Co. 1993–97. *Leisure interests:* family, theatre, church, reading, skiing, tennis, travel, cycling. *Telephone:* (7813) 919452 (mobile).

ROWLANDS, Gena; American actress; b. (Virginia Cathryn Rowlands), 19 June 1930, Madison, Wis.; m. John Cassavetes 1958 (died 1989); three c.; ed Univ. of Wis., American Acad. of Dramatic Arts; Nat. Bd of Review Career Achievement Award 1996. *Play:* Middle of the Night 1955. *Films include:* The High Cost of Loving 1958, Lonely Are the Brave 1962, The Spiral Road 1962, A Child is Waiting 1963, Tony Rome 1967, Faces 1968, Minnie and Moskowitz 1971, A Woman Under the Influence (Golden Globe Award for Best Actress in a Drama, Nat. Bd of Review Award for Best Actress) 1974, Opening Night (Silver Bear for Best Actress, Berlin Int. Film Festival) 1977, The Brink's Job 1978, Gloria 1980, Tempest 1982, Love Streams 1984, Light of Day 1987, Another Woman 1988, Once Around 1991, Night on Earth 1991, Ted and Venus 1991, Something to Talk About 1995, The Neon Bible 1995, Anything for John 1995, Unhook the Stars 1996, She's So Lovely 1997, Paulie 1998, Hope Floats 1998, The Mighty 1998, Playing by Heart 1998, Taking Lives 2004, The Notebook 2004, The Skeleton Key 2005, Paris, je t'aime 2006, Broken English 2007, Persepolis (voice) 2007, Olive 2011. *Television includes:* Peyton Place 1967, The Betty Ford Story (Emmy Award) 1987, Face of a Stranger (Emmy Award) 1991, Crazy in Love 1992, Parallel Lives 1994, Grace and Glory 1998, Hysterical Blindness 2002, Charms for the Easy Life 2002, The Incredible Mrs Ritchie 2003, What If God Were the Sun? 2007. *Address:* c/o ICM, 10250 Constellation Blvd, Los Angeles, CA 90067, USA.

ROWLING, J(oanne) K(athleen), (Robert Galbraith), OBE, BA; British writer; b. 31 July 1965, Yate, Glos., England; d. of Peter James Rowling and Anne Rowling (née Volant); m. 1st Jorge Arantes 1992 (divorced 1995); one d.; m. 2nd Neil Murray 2001; one s. one d.; ed Wyedean Comprehensive School, Univ. of Exeter,

Moray House Teacher Training Coll.; Pres. Gingerbread (single parents charity); f. Volant (charitable trust), Lumos (charity for disadvantaged children); Freedom of the City of London 2012; Chevalier, Légion d'honneur 2009; Hon. DJur (Univ. of Aberdeen) 2006; hon. degrees from Univ. of Edinburgh, Edinburgh Napier Univ., Univ. of Exeter, Univ. of St Andrews, Dartmouth Coll. and Harvard Univ., USA; Author of the Year, British Book Awards 2000, Premio Príncipe de Asturias 2003, Variety UK Entertainment Personality Award, British Ind. Film Awards 2004, British Book Award for Outstanding Achievement 2008, ranked by Forbes magazine amongst The World's 100 Most Powerful Women (85th) 2004, (40th) 2005, (61st) 2011, (78th) 2012, (93rd) 2013 and as the 48th most powerful celebrity of 2007, named by TIME magazine as a runner-up for its Person of the Year 2007, Blue Peter Badge (Gold) 2007, Lifetime Achievement, British Book Awards 2008, The Edinburgh Award 2008, James Joyce Award, Univ. Coll. Dublin 2008, Outstanding Achievement Award, South Bank Show Awards 2008, named Most Influential Woman in Britain by leading magazine editors 2010, inaugural winner, Hans Christian Andersen Literature Award 2010, Outstanding British Contrib. to Cinema for the Harry Potter film series, British Acad. Film Awards (shared with David Heyman, cast and crew) 2011. *Publications:* Harry Potter and the Philosopher's Stone (aka Harry Potter and the Sorcerer's Stone) (Smarties Book Prize 1997, British Book Awards Children's Book of the Year 1998) 1997, Harry Potter and the Chamber of Secrets (Smarties Book Prize 1998, British Book Awards Children's Book of the Year 1999) 1998, Harry Potter and the Prisoner of Azkaban (Smarties Book Prize 1999, Whitbread Children's Book of the Year 1999) 1999, Harry Potter and the Goblet of Fire (Hugo Award for Best Novel 2001) 2000, Quidditch Through the Ages by Kennilworthy Whisp 2001, Fantastic Beasts and Where to Find Them by Newt Scamander 2001, Harry Potter and the Order of the Phoenix (Bram Stoker Award for Best Work for Young Readers 2003, WH Smith People's Choice Fiction Prize 2004) 2003, Harry Potter and the Half-Blood Prince (Quill Book Award for Book of the Year, Best Children's Book, British Book Awards, WH Smith Book of the Year 2006, Royal Mail Award for Scottish Children's Books) 2005, Harry Potter and the Deathly Hallows 2007, The Tales of Beedle the Bard 2008, The Casual Vacancy 2012, The Cuckoo's Calling (as Robert Galbraith) 2013. *Address:* c/o The Blair Partnership, Fourth Floor, Middlesex House, 34–42 Cleveland Street, London, W1T 4JE, England (office). *Telephone:* (20) 7504-2520 (office). *Fax:* (20) 7504-2521 (office). *E-mail:* info@theblairpartnership.com (office). *Website:* www.theblairpartnership.com (office); www.jkrowling.com.

ROWLINSON, Sir John Shipley, Kt, FRS, BCE, FREng; British chemist and fmr academic; b. 12 May 1926, Handforth, Cheshire, England; s. of Frank Rowlinson and Winifred Rowlinson (née Jones); m. Nancy Gaskell 1952; one s. one d.; ed Trinity Coll., Oxford; Research Assoc., Univ. of Wis. 1950–51; Research Fellow, then Lecturer, then Sr Lecturer in Chem., Univ. of Manchester 1951–60; Prof. of Chemical Tech., Univ. of London 1961–73; Dr Lee's Prof. of Chem., Univ. of Oxford 1974–93; Fellow, Exeter Coll., Oxford 1974–; A.D. White Prof.-at-Large, Cornell Univ. 1990–96; Mary Upson Prof. of Eng, Cornell Univ. 1988; Physical Sec. and Vice-Pres. Royal Soc. 1994–99; Fellow, Royal Acad. of Eng; Meldola Medal, Royal Inst. of Chem. 1954, Marlow Medal, Faraday Soc. 1956, Hoffman Lecturer, Gesellschaft Deutscher Chemiker 1980, Faraday Lecturer 1983, RSC Lennard-Jones Lecturer 1985, Leverhulme Medal, Royal Soc. 1993, ACS Edelstein Award 2009. *Publications:* Liquids and Liquid Mixtures (co-author) 1982 (third edn), The Perfect Gas 1963, Thermodynamics for Chemical Engineers (co-author) 1975, Molecular Theory of Capillarity (co-author) 1982, J.D. van der Waals: On the Continuity of the Gaseous and Liquid States (ed.) 1988, Record of the Royal Society 1940–89 (co-author) 1992, Van der Waals and Molecular Science (co-author) 1996, Cohesion: A Scientific History of Intermolecular Forces 2002, Sir James Dewar (1842–1923) – A Ruthless Chemist 2012. *Leisure interest:* mountaineering. *Address:* Physical and Theoretical Chemistry Laboratory, South Parks Road, Oxford, OX1 3QZ (office); 12 Pullens Field, Headington, Oxford, OX3 0BU, England (home). *Telephone:* (1865) 275157 (office); (1865) 767507 (home). *Fax:* (1865) 275410 (office). *E-mail:* john.rowlinson@chem.ox.ac.uk (office). *Website:* www.chem.ox.ac.uk (office).

ROWNY, Lt-Gen. (retd) Edward Leon, BCE, MA, MS, PhD; American diplomatist and army officer (retd); b. 3 April 1917, Baltimore, Md; s. of Gracyan J. Rowny and Mary Ann Rowny (née Rodgers); m. Mary Rita Leyko 1941; four s. one d.; ed Johns Hopkins Univ., US Mil. Acad., Yale Univ.; commissioned Second-Lt in US Army 1941, served in WWII African campaign 1942, European and Middle Eastern campaigns 1944–45, Korea 1950–52, Viet Nam 1962–63, with Operations Div. of War Dept, Washington, DC 1945–47; Special Asst Tactical Mobility Dept of Army 1963–75; Commdg Gen. 24th Infantry Div., Europe 1965–66; Deputy Chief of Staff Logistics, Europe 1968–69; Deputy Chief of Research and Devt 1969–70; Commdg Gen. Intelligence Corps, Korea, 1970–71; Deputy Chair. Mil. Comm., NATO 1971–73; Jt Chiefs of Staff rep. to SALT del., Geneva 1973–79 (retd); Chief Arms Control Negotiator 1981–85; Special Adviser to Pres. 1985–89; Special Counsellor to US State Dept 1989–90; Pres. Nat. War Coll. Alumni Asscn 1987–88, Paderewski Living Memorial 1994; est. Paderewski Scholarship Fund 2004; mem. Advisory Bd Critical Incident Analysis Group, Univ. of Virginia Health System; DSM (twice), Silver Star with two oak leaf clusters (four times), Legion of Merit with four oak clusters (twice), Combat Infantry Badge with star; named Distinguished Mil. Grad. from West Point 1993, Truman-Reagan Medal of Freedom 2005, Walter Judd Freedom Award 2007. *Publication:* It Takes One to Tango 1992, An American Soldier's Saga of the Korean War 2013, Smokey Joe & the General 2013. *E-mail:* erowny@paderewskischolarship.org. *Website:* www.paderewskischolarship.org.

ROXAS, Manuel (Mar) II, BEcons; Philippine politician; b. 13 May 1957; grandson of Manuel Roxas, fmr Pres. of Philippines; s. of Senator Gerry Roxas; ed Ateneo de Manila Univ., Wharton Business School, Univ. of Pennsylvania, Kennedy School of Govt, Harvard Univ., USA; fmr Dir Kauswagan Devt Corpn, Myapo Prawn Farm Corpn; fmr Vice-Pres. Progressive Devt Corpn; fmr Dir/Pres. Northstar Capital Inc., Atok Big Wedge Mining Co.; fmr banker, Wall Street, New York, USA; mem. House of Reps, First Dist, Capiz 1992–2001; fmr leader admin.-aligned parties in Lower House of Legislature; Co-Chair. Philippines IT Devt; Sec. Dept Trade and Industry 2001–03; Senator 2004–; Co-founder Books for the Barangay Foundation Inc., Capiz Alliance for Ecological Devt Inc.; mem. Liberal Party, currently Exec. Vice-Pres. *Address:* Room 523, 5/F Senate of the Philippines, GSIS Bldg. Roxas Blvd., Pasay City (office); 157 P. Tuazon Street, Cubao, Quezon City, The Philippines. *Telephone:* (2) 8328280 (office). *E-mail:* mar@marroxas.com (office). *Website:* marroxas.com/new (office).

ROY, Aruna, MA; Indian social activist and fmr government official; *Head, Mazdoor Kisan Shakti Sangathana;* b. 26 May 1946, Chennai; d. of Elupai Doraiswami Jayaram and Hema Roy; m. Sanjit Roy (divorced); ed Indraprastha Coll. for Women, Univ. of Delhi; fmr Lecturer, Indraprastha Coll. for Women; worked for Admin. Services 1968–74; worked with Social Work and Research Centre –1983; Founder and Head of Mazdoor Kisan Shakti Sangathana 1990–; mem. Nat. Campaign for People's Right to Information; mem. Nat. Advisory Council, Nat. Employment Guarantee Council, People's Union for Civil Liberties, Concerned Citizens Tribunal; Ramon Magsaysay Award for Community Leadership 2000. *Publications:* Education of Out-of-School Children: Case Studies of Selected Non-formal Learning Programmes in South Asia (ed) 1984. *Address:* National Advisory Council, c/o Prime Minister's Office, Room Number 148 B, South Block, New Delhi 110 001, India (office). *E-mail:* aruna.roy@nac.nic.in (office). *Website:* www.nac.nic.in (office).

ROY, Arundhati; Indian writer, artist, actress and activist; b. 24 Nov. 1960, Shillong, Meghalaya; d. of Mary Roy; m. 1st Gerard Da Cunha (divorced); m. 2nd Pradeep Krishen; ed School of Planning and Architecture, New Delhi; fmrly with Nat. Inst. of Urban Affairs; judge, Cannes Film Festival 2000–; Lannan Prize for Cultural Freedom 2002, Sydney Peace Prize 2004, Norman Mailer Prize for Distinguished Writing 2011. *Screenplays:* In Which Annie Gives It Those Ones (TV) 1988, Electric Moon 1992, DAM/AGE 2002. *Publications:* The God of Small Things (Booker Prize 1997) 1997, The End of Imagination (essay) 1998, The Cost of Living (essays) 1998, The Great Common Good (essay) 1999, War is Peace 2000, The Algebra of Infinite Justice (essays) (2001, Power Politics 2002, The Ordinary Person's Guide to Empire (essays) 2004, Public Power in the Age of Empire Seven Stories 2004, Introduction to 13 December, a Reader: The Strange Case of the Attack on the Indian Parliament 2006, The Shape of the Beast: Conversations with Arundhati Roy 2008, Listening to Grasshoppers (essays) 2009; contribs to periodicals. *Address:* c/o India Ink Publishing Co. Pvt. Ltd, C-1, Soami Nagar, New Delhi 110 017, India.

ROY, Donkupar, PhD; Indian politician and government official; *President, United Democratic Party;* b. 10 Nov. 1954; ed North Eastern Hill Univ., Shillong; worked as prof. before entering politics; first won Shella Ass. seat in Meghalaya as ind. cand. 1987, re-elected 1993, subsequently re-elected three times; joined United Democratic Party (UDP) 1998, currently Pres.; held several portfolios under Chief Minister of Meghalaya, including Health, Educ., Finance and Planning Implementation, before becoming Deputy Chief Minister, formed alliance with other parties to form govt under banner of Meghalaya Progressive Alliance, Chief Minister of Meghalaya 2008–09, state govt was dismissed and UDP left Progressive Alliance March 2009. *Leisure interests:* reading, chess, fishing. *Address:* c/o Office of the Chief Minister, Shillong 793 001, India. *Telephone:* (364) 2226599 (home); (364) 2227121 (home).

ROY, Prannoy, CA; Indian broadcasting executive, political analyst and economist; *Executive Chairman, New Delhi Television Ltd;* b. 15 Oct. 1949, Kolkata; m. Radhika Roy 1972; ed Doon School, Dehradun, Haileybury School, Queen Mary Coll. and Univ. of London, UK, Delhi School of Econs; Chartered Accountant, PriceWaterhouse India 1979–83; Election Analyst 1980–85; Assoc. Prof., Delhi School of Econs 1985–86; Econ. Adviser, Ministry of Finance 1985–87; Anchor and Ed.-in-Chief for several TV news, budget and election programmes 1998–; Founder and Exec. Chair. New Delhi TV Ltd (NDTV) 1988–; Leverhulme Fellow; mem. Int. Advisory Bd Council On Foreign Relations; Priyadarshini Acad. Bombay Felicitations Award, Dynasty Culture Club Hall of Fame Award for Best Anchor Person 1991, TV and Video Award for Best Anchor Person 1993, B. D. Goenka Award for Excellence in Journalism 1994, 1995, Maharana Mewar Foundation Award for Contrib. to Journalism 1996, Indian Dance Theatre Best Personality of the Year Award 1998, Screen Videocon Award for Lifetime Achievement 1998, Ernst & Young Entrepreneur of the Year Award (Media). *Address:* New Delhi Television Convergence Ltd, 207, Okhla Industrial Estate, Phase 3, New Delhi 110 020, India (office). *Telephone:* (11) 26446666 (office). *Fax:* (11) 41735110 (office). *E-mail:* prannoy@ndtv.com (office). *Website:* www.ndtv.com (office).

ROY SAHARA, Subrata; Indian business executive; *Managing Worker and Chairman, Sahara India Pariwar;* b. 10 June 1946, Araria, Bihar; m. Swapna Roy 1974; two s.; f. Sahara Group 1978, currently and Man. Worker and Chair. Sahara India Pariwar, cos include Sahara India Financial Corpn Ltd, Sahara Care House, Sahara Infrastructure and Housing; Noble Citizen Award 1986, Baba-E-Rozgar 1992, Karmaveer Samman 1995, Nat. Citizen Award 2001, Businessman of the Year Award 2002, Global Leadership Award 2004, Lifetime Achievement Award 2004, Mother Teresa Millenium Award for Renowned Industrialist 2005, ITA ICON 2007. *Publications:* Shanti Sukh: Santushti, Maan-Samman: Atmasamman. *Address:* Sahara India Pariwar, Sahara Information and Contact Point, POB 2, Gomti Nagar, Lucknow 10, India (office). *Fax:* (522) 2303818 (office). *E-mail:* info@saharaindiapariwar.org (office). *Website:* www.sahara.in (office); www.sahara.in/saharasri.

ROYAL, HRH The Princess; (Princess Anne Elizabeth Alice Louise), LG, GCVO; British; b. 15 Aug. 1950; d. of Queen Elizabeth II (q.v.) and Prince Philip, Duke of Edinburgh (q.v.); m. 1st Capt. Mark Anthony Peter Phillips 1973 (divorced 1992); one s., Peter Mark Andrew, b. 15 Nov. 1977, one d., Zara Anne Elizabeth, b. 15 May 1981; m. 2nd Rear Adm. Timothy Laurence MVO, ADC 1992; ed Benenden School, Kent; Col-in-Chief, 14th/20th King's Hussars, Worcs. and Sherwood Foresters Regt (29th/45th Foot), Royal Regina Rifles, 8th Canadian Hussars (Princess Louise's), Royal Corps of Signals, The Canadian Armed Forces Communications and Electronics Br., The Royal Australian Corps of Signals, The Royal Scots, Royal NZ Corps of Signals, King's Royal Hussars, Royal Logistics Corps; Royal NZ Nursing Corps, The Grey and Simcoe Foresters Militia; Chief Commdt, WRNS; Hon. Air Commodore, RAF Lyneham; Pres. WRNS Benevolent Trust, British Acad. of Film and TV Arts, Hunters' Improvement and Light Horse Breeding Soc., Save the Children Fund, Windsor Horse Trials, The Royal School for Daughters of Officers of the RN and Royal Marines (Haslemere), British

Olympic Asscn, Council for Nat. Acad. Awards; Patron, Asscn of Wrens, Riding for the Disabled Asscn, Jersey Wildlife Preservation Fund, The Royal Corps of Signals Asscn, The Royal Corps of Signals Inst., Missions to Seamen, British Knitting and Clothing Export Council, The Army and Royal Artillery Hunter Trials, Glos. and North Avon Fed. of Young Farmers' Clubs, Royal Lymington Yacht Club, Royal Port Moresby Soc. for the Prevention of Cruelty to Animals, Horse of the Year Ball, Benenden Ball, British School of Osteopathy, Communications and Electronics Branch Inst., All England Women's Lacrosse Asscn, Home Farm Trust; Vice-Patron, British Show Jumping Asscn; Commdt-in-Chief, St John Ambulance and Nursing Cadets, Women's Transport Service; Life mem. Royal British Legion Women's Section, Royal Naval Saddle Club; mem. Island Sailing Club; Visitor, Felixstowe Coll.; official visits abroad to the 14th/20th King's Hussars in FRG 1969, 1975, to see the work of the Save the Children Fund in Kenya 1971, to the 2,500th anniversary celebrations of the Iranian monarchy 1971, to 14th/20th King's Hussars and to see the work of the Save the Children Fund, Hong Kong 1971, to SE Asia 1972, Munich 1972, Yugoslavia 1972, Ethiopia and the Sudan 1973, to visit Worcs. and Sherwood Foresters Regt in Berlin 1973, in Hereford, FRG 1974, to Canada 1974, to Australia 1975, to USA 1977, to FRG and Norway 1978, to Portugal, FRG, Thailand, Gilbert Islands, NZ, Australia and the Bahamas, Canada 1979, to Royal Corps of Signals in Cyprus, France, Belgium and Fiji 1980, Royal Corps of Signals in Berlin, Nepal, Worcs. and 14th/20th King's Hussars in FRG; USA, Canada and tour of Africa, North Yemen and Lebanon 1982, to France, Japan, Hong Kong, Singapore, Pakistan, Australia, Netherlands and BAOR 1983, USA, Africa, India, Bangladesh, FRG, UAE 1984; Chancellor, Univ. of London 1981–, Univ. of Edinburgh 2011–; has accompanied the Queen and the Duke of Edinburgh on several State Visits; has taken part in numerous equestrian competitions including Montreal Olympics 1976, Horse of the Year Show, Wembley and Badminton Horse Trials; winner of Raleigh Trophy 1971 and Silver Medal in 1975 in Individual European Three Day Event; Freeman of the City of London, of the Fishmongers' Co., Master Warden Farriers' Co., Master and Hon. Liveryman, Carmen's Co., Hon. Liveryman Farriers' Co., Yeoman, Saddlers' Co., Hon. Freeman, Farmers' Co., Loriners' Co.; Hon. mem. British Equine Veterinary Asscn, Royal Yacht Squadron, Royal Thames Yacht Club, Minchinhampton Golf Club, Lloyds of London; Hon. Life mem. RNVR Officers' Asscn; Sportswoman of the Year, Sports Writers' Asscn, Daily Express, World of Sport, BBC Sports Personality 1971, Special BAFTA Award 1993. *Publication:* Riding Through My Life 1991. *Address:* Buckingham Palace, London, SW1, England. *Website:* www.royal.gov.uk.

ROYAL, Ségolène; French politician; *Minister of Ecology, Sustainable Development and Energy;* b. 22 Sept. 1953, Dakar, Senegal; d. of Jacques Royal and Hélène Dehaye; fmr pnr Francois Hollande; two s. two d.; ed Univ. of Nancy, Institut d'Etudes Politiques, Paris, Ecole Nationale d'Admin; Conseillère Gen. La Mothe Saint Héray (Deux-Sèvres); Sec. Comm. for Production and Exchange, Nat. Ass.; mem. Nat. Cttee on Tourism; adviser on environment, town planning and social affairs to Pres. of Repub. 1982–88; Deputy to Nat. Ass. (Parti socialiste) from Deux-Sèvres 1988–; Minister of the Environment 1992–93, Deputy Minister of Educ. 1997–2000, of Family and Childhood 2000–01, of Family Childhood and Disabled Persons 2001–02, of Ecology, Sustainable Devt and Energy 2014–Pres. region Poitou-Charentes 2004–; Pres. Nat. Council of Socialist Group 1994–95; unsuccessful Parti socialiste cand. in 2007 presidential elections. *Publications:* Le Printemps des Grands Parents 1987, Le Ras-le-bol des Bébés Zappeurs 1989, Pays, Paysans, Paysages 1993, La Vérité d'une femme 1996, Désirs d'avenir 2006, Maintenant 2007, Les Droits de l'Enfant 2007, Ma plus belle histoire, c'est vous 2007. *Address:* Casier de la Poste, Palais Bourbon, 75355 Paris Cedex 07 (office); Ministry of Ecology, Sustainable Development and Energy, La Défense 92055 Paris Cedex, France (office). *Telephone:* 1-40-63-93-23 (office); 1-40-81-21-22 (office). *Fax:* 1-40-63-93-39 (office). *Website:* www.assemblee-nationale.fr (office); www.developpement-durable.gouv.fr; www.desirsdavenir.org.

ROYALL OF BLAISDON, Baroness (Life Peer), cr. 2004, of Blaisdon in the County of Gloucestershire; **Janet Anne Royall,** PC, BA (Hons); British politician; *Leader of the Opposition, House of Lords;* b. 20 Aug. 1955, Glos., England; d. of Basil Royall and Myra Royall; m. Stuart Hercock (died 2010); two s. one d.; ed Royal Forest of Dean Grammar School, Westfield Coll., London; Sec.-Gen. British Labour Group, European Parl. 1979–85; policy adviser to Neil Kinnock, Leader of Opposition 1986–92; mem. of Kinnock Cabinet, EC 1995–2001; Parl. Coordinator, Directorate Gen. of Communications, EC 2001; Head, European Comm. Office in Wales 2003–04; Govt Spokesperson for Health, for Int. Devt and for FCO 2005–08; Capt., Hon. Corps of Gentlemen at Arms (Chief Whip, House of Lords) 2007–08; mem. Select Cttees on Admin and Works, Privleges and Procedure 2008–, Leader of the House of Lords 2008–10, Lord Pres. of the Council 2008–09, Chancellor of the Duchy of Lancaster 2009–10; Govt Spokesperson for Equality 2008–10, for NI 2008–10, for the Cabinet Office 2009–10, Leader of the Opposition 2010–, Opposition Spokesperson for the Cabinet Office 2010–12, for Educ. 2010, for NI 2010–11, for Work and Pensions 2010, for Equalities Office 2010–12; Vice-Pres. European Socialist Party 2012–; mem. USDAW (trade union). *Leisure interests:* reading, travel, gardening, swimming. *Address:* House of Lords, Westminster, London, SW1A 0PW, England (office). *Telephone:* (20) 7219-6370 (office). *E-mail:* royall@parliament.uk (office). *Website:* www.parliament.uk/biographies/lords/baroness-royall-of-blaisdon/3703 (office).

ROYE, Marcia, BSc, PhD; Jamaican biotechnologist and academic; *Lecturer in Biotechnology, University of the West Indies;* b. Newforest, Manchester, Jamaica; ed Hampton High School for Girls, St Elizabeth, Univ. of the West Indies; Fulbright Fellow, Int. Lab. for Agricultural Biotechnology, Danforth Plant Science Center, St Louis, Mo., USA 2003; currently Lecturer in Biotechnology, Univ. of the West Indies, also Assoc. Dean of Grad. Studies, Faculty of Pure and Applied Sciences and Leader, Gemini Virus Research Team (research into crop-destroying insect-borne virus); co-f. research programme into detection of anti-retroviral drug resistance of HIV in Jamaican patients at Inst. of Human Virology, Univ. of Maryland School of Medicine 2008; fmr Visiting Researcher, Univ. of Wisconsin-Madison; Scientific Research Council Young Scientist Award 2000, L'Oréal Fellowship for Young Women in Science 2000, L'Oréal-UNESCO Special Fellowship 'in the footsteps of Marie Curie' 2011. *Address:* Biotechnology Centre, The University of the West Indies, Mona, Jamaica (office). *Telephone:* 977-1828 (office).

Fax: 977-3331 (office). *E-mail:* marcia.roye@uwimona.edu.jm (office). *Website:* myspot.mona.uwi.edu/biotech (office).

ROYO SÁNCHEZ, Arístides, LLB, JD; Panamanian politician, diplomatist and lawyer; *Partner, Morgan & Morgan;* b. 14 Aug. 1940, La Chorrera; s. of Roberto Royas and Gilma Sánchez; m. Adele Ruíz 1963; one s. two d.; ed Nat. Institute, Panama City, Univs of Salamanca and Bologna; Gen. Sec. of the Gen. Solicitorship of the Repub. of Panama 1965–68; Prof. of Consular, Notarial and Mercantile Law, Univ. of Panama 1968–74; mem. Law Codification Comm. 1969; mem. drafting comms for Penal Code 1970, Constitution 1972; mem. Legis. Comm. of Nat. Council of Legislation 1972–73; Gen. Sec. School of Lawyers of Panama 1973; Pnr, Morgan & Morgan (law firm) 1968–; a negotiator of Torrijos-Carter Canal Treaties between Panama and USA 1977; mem. Org. Comm. of Democratic Revolutionary Party; Minister of Educ. 1973–78; Pres. of Panama 1978–82; Amb. to Spain 1982–84, 1994–96, to France 1996–99, Perm Amb. to OAS 2004–; mem. Nat. Bar Asscn of Panama, Union Iberoamericana de Abogados, Instituto Hispano-Luso-Americano de Derecho Internacional, Instituto de Derecho Comparado de la Universidad Complutense de Madrid, Sociedad Bolivariana de Panamá, Fuji-Baru Asscn; hon. mem. Spanish Law Soc. 1979; Grand Cross, Alfonso X the Wise (Spain) 1977, Extraordinary Grand Cross, Vasco Núñez de Balboa (Panama) 1978; Grand Collar, Order of Manuel Amador Guerrero (Panama) 1978; Grand Collar, Order of Isabel la Católica (Spain) 1979; Grand Cross, Légion d'honneur 1979; Extraordinary Grand Cross, Order of Boyaca (Colombia) 1979; Dr hc (Univ. San Martín de Porres, Lima, Peru) 1979. *Publications:* Philosophy of Law in Cathrein and Del Vecchio 1963, History of Spanish Commercial Code 1964, The Responsibility of the Carrier in Sea Shipping 1965, Extraterritoriality of the Panamanian Criminal Law 1967, Draft Criminal Code of Panama, The Participation of Labourers in the Utilities of Enterprises, Revolution or De Facto Government, Manager in the Enterprise 1970, Commentaries to the Law on Retiring Funds for Journalists 1971, The Technician and the Politician in Public Administration 1973, Popular Consultation of the Law 1972. *Leisure interests:* reading, writing, skiing, jogging. *Address:* Morgan & Morgan, MMG Tower, 16th Floor, 53 E Street, Urbanizacion Marbella, PO Box 0832-00232, World Trade Center, Panama City, Panama (office). *Telephone:* (507) 265-7777 (office). *Fax:* (507) 265-7700 (office). *E-mail:* aroyo@morimor.com (office). *Website:* www.morimor.com (office).

ROZANOV, Yevgeny Grigoryevich, PhD; Russian architect; b. 8 Nov. 1925, Moscow; s. of Grigory Alexandrovich Rozanov and Anastasiya Nikolaevna Rozanova; m. Aida Ilyenkova 1952; one s.; ed Moscow Inst. of Architecture; mem. CPSU 1964–91; Dir of Mezentsev Inst. of Standard and Experimental Design of Culture and Sports Activities 1970–85; major bldgs designed in Essentuki, Vladivostok, Tashkent, Moscow (notably Dinamo Sports Centre); teacher of architecture at Moscow Architectural Inst. 1960–85, Prof. 1953–85; Chair. State Cttee on Architecture and Town Planning 1987–; Sec. USSR Union of Architects 1981–92; People's Deputy of the USSR 1989–91; mem. USSR (now Russian) Acad. of Arts 1979; Pres. Int. Acad. of Architecture (Moscow br.) 1991–; Vice-Pres. Russian Acad. of Arts 1998–; mem. Russian Acad. of Architecture and Construction Sciences 1997, Acad. of Architecture, Paris 1998; Hon. mem. Acad. of Architecture of Ukraine 1995; Dr hc (Moscow Architectural Inst.) 2001; Khamza Uzbek State Prize 1969, 1970, Navoi Uzbek State Prize 1975, USSR State Prize 1975, 1980, First Prize in Borovitskaya Square Competition, Moscow 1997, People's Architect of USSR 1983. *Publication:* The Works of E. G. Rozanov 1995. *Leisure interests:* painting, drawing, sculpture, music. *Address:* International Academy of Architecture, 6, Secodn Brestskaya Street 6, Rooms 8–9, 125047 Moscow (office); Kosygina Street 9, Apt. 74, Moscow, Russia (home). *Telephone:* (495) 972-47-85 (office); (495) 137-56-09 (home). *Fax:* (495) 972-47-85.

ROZARIO, Patricia, OBE; singer (soprano); b. 1960, Bombay, India; m. Mark Troop; one d.; ed Guildhall School of Music; concerts with Songmakers' Almanac, including tour to USA; solo recitals, South Bank, London and elsewhere; frequent performances of Bach, Handel, Mozart; Vaughan Williams' Serenade to Music, BBC Proms 1988; Schumann's Paradies und der Peri, Madrid with Gerd Albrecht; appearances at Bath and Edin. Festivals; season 1993–94 included Wexford Festival appearance, tour of Germany with BBC Nat. Orchestra of Wales/Otaka, Hong Kong Philharmonic, world premiere of Taverner's Apocalypse, BBC Proms; season 1994–95 included recital in Lebanon, Purcell Room with Nash Ensemble; sang Les illuminations at St John's Smith Square, London 1997; performed in Handel's Triumph of Time and Truth, BBC Proms 1999; British Song Prize, Barcelona, Maggie Teyte Prize, Sängerforderungspreis, Salzburg Mozarteum, Guildhall School of Music Gold Medal, Asian Women of Achievement Arts and Culture Award 2002. *Operatic roles include:* Giulietta (Jommelli's La schiava liberata) for Netherlands Opera, Gluck's Euridice for Opera North, Mozart's Bastienne and Pamina for Kent Opera, Ilia on Glyndebourne tour, Ismene in Lyon production of Mithridate and Zerlina at Aix, Statue in Rameau's Pygmalion and Purcell's Belinda for Kent Opera; Florinda in Handel's Rodrigo at Innsbruck, Nero in L'incoronazione di Poppea and Massenet's Sophie; concert performance of Il re pastore, Queen Elizabeth Hall, London, world premiere of John Casken's Golem, as Miriam, Almeida Festival, London, Ismene at Wexford Festival 1989, cr. title role in premiere of Taverner's Mary of Egypt, Aldeburgh Festival 1992, season 1992–93 in Monteverdi's Il combattimento, ENO and Haydn's L'infedeltà delusa, Garsington Opera, Romilda in Serse, Brussels 1996. *Recordings include:* Mahler Symphony No. 4, London Symphony Orchestra, Songs of the Auvergne with John Pritchard (conductor), Haydn Stabat Mater with Trevor Pinnock (conductor), Golem (Gramophone Award 1991), Taverner: We Shall See Him As He Is, Mary of Egypt, To a Child Dancing in the Wind; Spanish Songs, Britten's Rape of Lucretia. *Address:* c/o Rayfield Artists, Southbank House, Black Prince Road, London, SE1 7SJ, England (office). *Telephone:* (20) 7193-1531 (office). *E-mail:* ben@rayfieldartists.com (office). *Website:* www.rayfieldartists.com/patriciarozario.html (office).

ROZENTAL, Andrés, AM, MEconSc; Mexican diplomatist and consultant; *President, Rozental & Asociados;* b. 27 April 1945, Mexico City; s. of Leonid Rozental Wurhaft and Neoma Gutman Rudnicki; m. Vivian Holzer; two d.; ed Universidad de las Américas, Mexico, Univ. of Pennsylvania, USA, Univ. of Bordeaux, France; Amb. to OAS 1971–74; Perm. Rep. to UN, Geneva 1982–83; Amb. to Sweden 1983–88; Deputy Foreign Minister 1988–94; Amb. to UK 1995–97; Amb.-at-Large and Special Presidential Envoy for Pres. Fox 2000–02; Founder and

Pres. Rozental & Asociados (consultancy), Mexico City 1997–; Pres. Mexican Council on Foreign Relations 2002–06; Chair. Bd ArcelorMittal Mexico, Grupo Industrial Omega; mem. Bd of Dirs Ocean Wilson Holdings, ArcelorMittal Brazil, HSBC Mexico; mem. Bd of Govs Int. Devt Research Centre 2007–12; mem. Bd of Advisors, Latin America Advisor, Inter-American Dialogue 2005–, Advisory Bd EADS Mexico, Kansas City Southern de Mexico, Panel of Sr Advisors, Chatham House, Operating Bd Centre for Int. Governance Innovation, Int. Advisory Bd APCO Worldwide, Washington, DC, Advisory Bd Woodrow Wilson Center Mexico Inst., Washington, DC; fmr mem. Editorial Bd Reforma (newspaper); Sr Non-resident Fellow, The Brookings Inst., Washington, DC 2007–; Trustee, Migration Policy Inst., Washington, DC; Grand Cross of the Polar Star (Sweden), Grand Cross, Civil Merit Order (Spain), Officier, Ordre nat. du Mérite, Ordre Nat. du Québec, Eminent Amb. of Mexico 1994. *Publications:* five books on Mexican foreign policy and numerous articles on int. affairs. *Address:* Rozental & Asociados, Campos Elíseos no 345, Edif. Omega, piso 6, México DF, Mexico (office). *Telephone:* (55) 5279-6090 (office). *Fax:* (55) 5279-6089 (office). *E-mail:* mexconsult@gmail.com (office).

ROZES, Simone, LenD, DèsSc, DES; French lawyer; *Honorary President, Cour de Cassation;* b. 29 March 1920, Paris; d. of Léon Ludwig and Marcelle Cetre; m. Gabriel Rozes 1942; one s. one d.; ed Lycée de Sèvres, Lycée de St-Germain-en-Laye, Univ. of Paris, Ecole Libre des Sciences Politiques; trainee lawyer, Paris 1947–49; Surrogate Judge, Bourges 1949–50; Judge 1951–; attaché, Justice Dept 1951–58; Admin. Chief, Cabinet of the Minister of Justice 1958–62, Vice-Pres. Tribunal de Grande Instance de Paris 1969–73, Pres. 1975–81; Dir Reformatory Educ. 1973–76; mem. UN Crime Prevention and Control Cttee 1977; Advocate-Gen. European Court of Justice 1981–84; First Advocate Gen. 1982–84; Pres. Cour de Cassation (Chief Justice) 1984–88, Hon. Pres. 1989–; Int. and Nat. Arbitrator 1989–; Pres. Int. Soc. of Social Defence, fmr Pres. Soc. of Comparative Law; Hon. Vice-Pres. Int. Asscn of Penal Law; Inst. Frederik R. Bull; mem. Bd Alliance Française, Vice-Pres. 1994–; Grand Croix, Légion d'honneur; Officier, Ordre nat. du Mérite; Médaille de l'Educ. Surveillée, Médaille de Admin. Pénitentiaire, Commdr Cross, Order of Merit (FRG); Hon. LLD (Edin.). *Publication:* Le Juge et l'avocat (jtly) 1992. *Leisure interest:* travelling. *Address:* c/o Cour de Cassation, 5 quai de l'Horloge, 75055 Paris Cedex 01 (office); 34 rue Bayen, 75017 Paris, France. *Telephone:* 1-43-80-16-67 (office). *Fax:* 1-47-63-42-90 (office). *E-mail:* simone.rozes@neuf.fr (office). *Website:* www.courdecassation.fr (office).

ROZHDESTVENSKY, Gennady Nikolayevich; Russian conductor; b. 4 May 1931, Moscow; s. of Nikolai Anosov and Natalia Rozhdestvenskaya; m. Viktoria Postnikova; one s.; ed Moscow State Conservatoire; Asst Conductor, Bolshoi Theatre 1951, Conductor 1956–60, Prin. Conductor 1965–70, Artistic Dir 2000–01; Chief Conductor of USSR Radio and TV Symphony Orchestra 1961–74; Chief Conductor Stockholm Philharmonia 1974–77, 1992–95, Moscow Chamber Opera 1974–83; Founder, Artistic Dir and Chief Conductor State Symphony Orchestra of Ministry of Culture 1983–92; Prin. Conductor BBC Symphony Orchestra 1978–82, Vienna Symphony Orchestra 1980–83; has been guest conductor of numerous orchestras throughout Europe, USA and Asia; Chair. of Conducting, Moscow State Conservatoire 1965–; Prin. Guest Conductor, Iceland Symphony Orchestra 2011–; Hon. mem. Swedish Royal Acad. 1975, Royal Acad., London; Chevalier, Légion d'honneur, Order of the Rising Sun (Japan); People's Artist of the RSFSR 1966, People's Artist of the USSR 1976, Hero of Socialist Labour 1991, Lenin Prize 1970 and other awards. *Publications:* The Fingering of Conducting 1974, Thoughts about Music 1975; numerous articles. *Leisure interest:* music. *Address:* c/o Robert Slotover, Allied Artists, 42 Montpelier Square, London, SW7 1JZ, England (office). *Telephone:* (20) 7589-6243 (office). *Fax:* (20) 7581-5269 (office). *E-mail:* robert@alliedartists.co.uk (office). *Website:* www.alliedartists.co.uk (office).

ROZHKOV, Pavel Alekseyevich; Russian politician and fmr wrestler; *First Vice-President and Chairman, Executive Committee, Russian Paralympic Committee;* b. 30 June 1957, Ramenskoye, Moscow region; m. Larisa Viktorovna Rozhkova; ed Moscow Inst. of Physical Culture; metal worker Radipribor plant 1974–75; coach Urozhai classical wrestling team Moscow 1977–78; jr researcher All-Union Research Inst. of Physical Culture, Moscow 1979–82; coach State Sports Cttee 1982–87; docent Cen. State Inst. of Physical Culture, Moscow 1992; Sr coach Olympic Greek-Roman wrestling team 1992–96; Dir-Gen. Olymp-Tour co., Moscow 1997–99; Deputy Minister of Physical Culture, Sports and Tourism 1999, First Deputy Minister 1999–2000; Chair. State Cttee on Physical Culture, Sports and Tourism 2000–02, First Deputy Chair. 2002; currently First Vice-Pres. and Chair. Exec. Cttee, Russian Paralympic Cttee. *Address:* Russian Paralympic Committee, 32-40 Office, 42, Leninskiy prospect, 119119 Moscow, Russia (office). *Telephone:* (495) 930-79-21 (office). *Fax:* (495) 938-85-21 (office). *E-mail:* npcrus@paralymp.ru (office). *Website:* www.paralymp.ru (office).

ROZOVSKY, Mark Grigorievich; Russian theatre director and scriptwriter; b. 3 April 1937, Petropavlovsk; ed Moscow Univ. Higher Scriptwriters' School; f. and managed 'Our Home' (amateur studio theatre) with fellow students of Moscow Univ. 1958–70; theatre officially disbanded 1970, revived in 1987 as professional co. U Nikitskikh Vorot; wrote 3 books on theatre, dir versions of Karamzin, Kafka, Dostoevsky and others in Leningrad, Moscow and Riga 1970–87; Chief Dir Moscow State Music Hall 1974–79; Dir Orpheus and Eurydice (rock-opera) 1975 and a musical adaptation of 'Strider' jtly with Georgii Tovstonogov, by L. N. Tolstoy for Gorky Theatre, Leningrad; Theatre of Nations Prize Hamburg and Avignon 1979. *Other productions include:* Amadeus (P. Shaffer) for Moscow Arts Theatre; libretto for opera about Mayakovsky; work for TV including documentary on Meyerhold, Triumphal Square 1984; works for Gorky Theatre, Leningrad and Theatre of Russian Drama, Riga, Latvia and his own Studio Theatre, Moscow; Romances with Oblomov, Alexandrinsky Theatre, St Petersburg 1992. *Address:* Theatre U Nikitskikh Vorot, 103009 Moscow, Bolshaya Nikitskaya Str. 23/9, Russia. *Telephone:* (495) 291-84-19.

ROZWADOWSKI, Jean F., MBA; French business executive and international organization official; b. 1947, Netherlands; s. of a Polish father and French mother; m.; two c.; ed Ecole Supérieure de Commerce de Paris, Amos Tuck School of Business Admin, Dartmouth Coll., NH, USA; grew up in S Africa; spent 20 years with American Express, including Head of SE Asia, Middle East and Brazil Divs; fmr Pres. American Chamber of Commerce, Sao Paulo, Brazil; Exec. Vice-Pres. for Europe, Middle East and Africa, MasterCard –1999, Pres. Latin American and

Caribbean Div. 1999–2004; Sec.-Gen. ICC 2009–11; mem. UN Global Compact Bd 2009–11. *Address:* c/o International Chamber of Commerce, 38 cours Albert 1er, 75008 Paris, France.

RUAN, Chongwu; Chinese politician; b. 1933, Huai'an Co., Hebei Prov.; ed Moscow Auto-Eng Inst.; Deputy Dir Shanghai Materials Research Inst.; joined CCP 1952; Deputy Sec. Shanghai Municipal Scientific Workers' Asscn; Science and Tech. Counsellor, Embassy in Bonn 1978; Vice-Mayor Shanghai 1983–85; Sec. CCP, Shanghai Municipality 1983–85; Minister of Public Security 1985–87; Vice-Minister Science and Tech. Comm., State Council 1987–89, of Labour 1989–93; Sec. CCP 2nd Hainan Prov. Cttee 1993; Gov. of Hainan Prov. 1993–98; mem. 12th CCP Cen. Cttee 1982–87, 13th Cen. Cttee 1987–92, 14th Cen. Cttee 1992–97; Del., 15th CCP Nat. Congress 1997–2002; mem. 9th Standing Cttee of NPC 1998–2003. *Address:* c/o National People's Congress, Beijing, People's Republic of China (office).

RUBALCABA, Alfredo Pérez, PhD; Spanish chemist, academic and politician; b. 28 July 1951, Solares, Cantabria; ed Complutense Univ.; worked at Univ. of Constance, Germany, Univ. of Montpellier, France; Dir Technical Office, Sec. of State for Univs and Research 1982–85; Dir Gen. of Univ. Educ. 1985–86; Sec.-Gen. of Educ. 1986; Sec. of State for Educ. 1988–92; mem. Congreso de los Diputados (Congress of Deputies), Deputy for Toledo prov. 1993–96, for Madrid prov. 1996–2004, for Cantabria prov. 2004–08, Cádiz prov. 2008–; Acting Minister of Defence May–June 2008, Minister of Educ. and Science 1992–93, of the Presidency 1993–96, of Interior 2006–11 (resgnd); Deputy Prime Minister 2010–11 (resgnd), also Govt Spokesman; Prof. of Organic Chem., Complutense Univ.; fmr spokesman Parl. Group Socialists, Cttee on Science and Tech.; mem. Fed. Exec. Cttee of Socialist Party. *Address:* c/o Ministry of the Interior, Paseo de la Castellana 5, 28046 Madrid, Spain.

RUBBIA, Carlo; Italian physicist and academic; *Professor of Physics, Università degli Studi di Pavia;* b. 31 March 1934, Gorizia; s. of Silvio Rubbia and Bice Rubbia; m. Marisa Rubbia; one s., one d.; ed high school, Pisa and Rome Univs and Columbia Univ., USA; joined CERN as Sr Physicist 1961, mem. Cttee CERN 1985–89, Dir-Gen. 1989–93; Higgins Prof. of Physics, Harvard Univ. 1970–88; currently Full Prof. of Physics, Pavia Univ.; Pres. Ente per la Nuove tecnologie, l'Energia e l'Ambiente (ENEA) 1999–2005; Adviser, EC Commr for Research and Educ. Policies 2002; mem. Papal Acad. of Science 1986–; mem. American Acad. of Arts and Sciences, Accad. dei Lincei, European Acad. of Sciences, Accademia dei XL, Pontifical Acad. of Sciences, Polish Acad. of Sciences (Foreign Mem.), Croatian Acad. of Sciences and Arts, Royal Society, UK, (Foreign Mem.), NAS (Foreign Mem.), Russian Acad. of Sciences (Foreign Mem.), Third World Acad. of Sciences, European Acad. of Sciences, Société Européenne de Culture, Ateneo Veneto, Société Française de Physique, Istituto Lombardo, Austrian Acad. of Sciences; Cavaliere di Gran Croce (Knight Grand Cross) 1985, Officier de la Légion d'Honneur 1989, Polish Order of Merit 1993, Senator for Life (highest Italian honour) 2013; Dr hc (Geneva) 1983, (Carnegie Mellon) 1985, (Genoa) 1985, (Udine) 1985, (La Plata, Argentina) 1986, (Northwestern) 1986, (Camerino) 1987, (Chicago) 1987, (Loyola) 1987, (Boston) 1988, (Sofia, Bulgaria) 1990, (Moscow)1991, (Chile) 1991, (Polytechnic Univ. of Madrid) 1992, (Padova) 1992, (Tech. Univ. of Rio de Janeiro) 1993, (Trieste) 1994, (Oxford) 1994, (Catholic Univ. of Lima, Peru) 1994, (Nat. Univ. of St Antonio Abad of Cusco, Peru) 1994, (Bordeaux) 1998, (Haute Savoie) 1999, (St John's Univ.) 2003, (Università di Torino) 2004; Nobel Prize for Physics 1984, Leslie Prize for Exceptional Achievements 1985, Jesolo d'Oro 1986. *Address:* Physics Department, Università degli Studi di Pavia, Corso Strada Nuova 65, 27100 Pavia, Italy (office). *Telephone:* 0382-504217 (office). *Fax:* 0382-504529 (office). *Website:* www.unipv.it (office).

RUBENSTEIN, David M., BA, JD; American lawyer and business executive; *Managing Director, The Carlyle Group;* b. 1949, Baltimore; m. Alice Rogoff; three c.; ed Duke Univ., Univ. of Chicago; with Paul, Weiss, Rifkind, Wharton & Garrison (legal practice), New York 1973–75; Chief Counsel, US Senate Judiciary Cttee Sub-Cttee on constitutional amendments, Washington DC 1975–76; Deputy Asst to Pres. Jimmy Carter for domestic policy 1977–81; admitted to DC Bar Asscn 1981; with Shaw, Pittman, Potts & Trowbridge (now Pillsbury, Winthrop, Shaw Pittman), Washington DC 1982–87; Co-founder and Man. Dir The Carlyle Group 1987–; mem. Business Council, World Econ. Forum; mem. Nat. Advisory Cttee JPMorgan Chase; Vice-Chair. Lincoln Center for Performing Arts; mem. Bd of Trustees Hoover Inst., Duke Univ., Johns Hopkins Univ., Memorial Sloan Kettering Cancer Center, Nat. Gallery of Art; mem. Visiting Cttee Kennedy School of Govt, Harvard Univ.; mem. Advisory Bd School of Econs and Man., Tsinghua Univ., People's Repub. of China, Stanford Inst. for Econ. Policy Research; mem. council Nat. Trust for Historic Preservation. *Address:* The Carlyle Group, 1001 Pennsylvania Ave, NW, Washington, DC 20004-2505, USA (office). *Telephone:* (202) 729-5626 (office). *Fax:* (202) 347-1818 (office). *Website:* www.carlyle.com (office).

RUBENSTEIN, Edward, MD; American physician, scientist and academic; *Professor Emeritus of Medicine (Clinical), School of Medicine, Stanford University;* b. 5 Dec. 1924, Cincinnati; s. of Louis Rubenstein and Nettie Nathan; m. Nancy Ellen Millman 1954; three s.; ed Cincinnati Univ. Coll. of Medicine; Laboratory Asst, Dept of Physiology, Cincinnati Univ. 1947; Intern, then Jr Asst, then Sr Asst Resident in Medicine, Cincinnati Gen. Hosp. 1947–50, Medical Chief, Psychosomatic Service 1953–54; Research Fellow, May Inst., Cincinnati 1950; Chief of Medicine, USAF Hosp., March Airforce Base 1950–52; Sr Asst Resident in Medicine, Barnes Hosp., St Louis 1952–53; Chief, Clinical Physiology Unit, San Mateo Co. Gen. Hosp. 1955–63, Chief of Medicine 1960–70; Prof. of Medicine and Assoc. Dean of Postgraduate Medical Educ., Stanford Univ. School of Medicine 1971, now Prof. Emer.; Founding Ed.-in-Chief Scientific American Medicine 1977–93; mem. Inst. of Medicine of NAS 1981–, Soc. of Photo-Optical Engineers 1981–; Master, American Coll. of Physicians 1987; TV documentary Being Human 1979; research in synchrotron radiation; Fellow, AAAS 1992–, Royal Soc. of Medicine 1992; Henry Kaiser Award 1989, Albion Walter Hewlett Award 1995. *Publications:* Intensive Medical Care 1971, Handbook on Synchrotron Radiation Vol. 4 (ed.), Introduction to Molecular Medicine (ed.), Synchrotron Radiation in the Life Sciences (ed.); numerous scientific papers. *Address:* Stanford University School of Medicine, 300 Pasteur Drive, Stanford, CA 94305, USA (office).

Telephone: (650) 343-2992 (office). *Fax:* (650) 343-2992 (office). *E-mail:* exr@leland.stanford.edu (office). *Website:* med.stanford.edu (office).

RUBENSTEIN, Howard Joseph, LLB; American lawyer and public relations executive; *President, Rubenstein Associates Inc.;* b. 3 Feb. 1932, New York; s. of Samuel Rubenstein and Ada Sall; m. Amy Forman 1959; three s.; ed Univ. of Pa, Harvard Univ. and St John's Law School; admitted New York State Bar 1960; Pres. Rubenstein Assocs Inc. (public relations consultants), New York 1954–, also Chair. Rubenstein Communications, Inc.; Co-Chair. Holocaust Comm. 1993; mem. Exec. Cttee Real Estate Bd of New York, NYC & Co., Asscn for a Better New York; mem. Bd of Dirs Albert Einstein Coll. of Medicine 1997–; mem. Mayor's Business Advisory Council, New York 1996–, communications adviser Gov.'s Jerusalem 3000 Cttee 1996–; mem. Bd of Govs Jewish County Relations Council 1999–; Trustee Police Athletic League, Inner City Scholarship Fund of the Archdiocese of New York, Foundation for Nat. Archives; mem City Univ. of New York Business Leadership Council; Hon. LLD (St John's Law School) 1990. *Address:* Rubenstein Associates Inc., 1345 Avenue of the Americas, New York, NY 10105 (office); 993 Fifth Avenue, New York, NY 10028, USA (home). *Telephone:* (212) 843-8000 (office). *E-mail:* info@rubenstein.com (office). *Website:* www.rubenstein.com (office).

RUBIANO SÁENZ, HE Cardinal Pedro; Colombian ecclesiastic; *Archbishop of Santafé de Bogotá;* b. 13 Sept. 1932, Cartago; ordained priest 1956; Bishop of Cúcuta 1971–83; Coadjutor Archbishop of Cali 1983–85, Bishop of Cali 1985–94; Archbishop of Santafé de Bogotá 1994–; cr. Cardinal 2001, Cardinal Priest of Trasfigurazione di Nostro Signore Gesù Cristo 2001; mem. Congregation for Catholic Educ., Pontifical Council for the Pastoral Care of Migrants and Itinerant People; Apostolic Admin. of Popayán 1990–91. *Address:* Arzobispado, Carrera 7 N. 10–20, Bogotá, DC1, Colombia (office). *Telephone:* (1) 3505511 (office). *Fax:* (1) 3347867 (office). *Website:* www.arquibogota.org.co (office).

RUBIK, Ernő, BA; Hungarian inventor, architect and designer; b. 13 July 1944, Budapest; s. of Ernő Rubik, Sr and Magdolna Szántó; one s. two d.; ed Univ. of Tech. Educ., Budapest, Hungarian Acad. of Applied Arts and Design, Budapest, Budapest School of Commercial Art; consecutively Asst Prof., then Assoc. Prof., Acad. of Applied Arts, Dir of Postgraduate Studies 1983–86; Hon. Prof. Acad. of Crafts and Design, Budapest 1987; inventor of Rubik's Cube 1974, and other games and puzzles; Pres. Rubik Studio; Pres. Hungarian Acad. of Eng 1990–96; Labour Order of Merit Gold Medal of the Hungarian People's Repub.; Toy of the Year Award 1981–82 of UK, FRG, Italy, Sweden, Finland, France, USA, State Prize 1983. *Publications:* co-author and ed A büvös kocka (The Magic Cube) 1981, Rubik's Magic 1986, Rubik's Cubic Compendium 1987. *Leisure interests:* swimming, skiing, sailing. *Address:* Rubik Studio, Városmajor u. 74, 1122 Budapest, Hungary (office). *Telephone:* (1) 356-9533 (office). *Website:* www.rubiks.com (office).

RUBIKS, Alfrēds; Latvian politician; *Chairman, Latvian Socialist Party;* b. 1935, Daugavpils, Latvia; m.; two s.; ed Riga Tech. Higher School and Leningrad Higher Party School; mem. CPSU 1958–91; engineer and foreman, Riga Electrotechnical Plant 1957–61; Komsomol and party work; Sec. Latvian Komsomol Cen. Cttee; First Sec. of Leningradsky Region of Riga Regional CP Cttee 1976–82; Minister of Local Industry for Latvian SSR 1982–84; Chair. Exec. Cttee Riga City Council of People's Deputies 1984–90; First Sec. Cen. Cttee Latvian CP 1990–91; USSR People's Deputy 1989–91; mem. CPSU Cen. Cttee 1990–91; mem. CPSU Politburo July 1990–91; arrested by Latvian authorities Aug. 1991, accused of high treason; elected to Saeima (Parl.) 1993; sentenced to eight years' imprisonment 1995; released 1997; mem. Saeima 1998–; Chair. Latvian Socialist Party 1998–. *Address:* Saeima, Jecaba Str. 11, 1811 Riga; Latvian Socialist Party, Burtnieku iela 23, Riga, Latvia. *Telephone:* 6755-5535. *Fax:* 6755-5535. *Website:* www.latsocpartija.lv.

RUBIN, Hon. James P., BA, MIA; American academic, broadcast journalist and fmr government official; *Adjunct Professor of International and Public Affairs, School of International Affairs, Columbia University;* b. 1960, New York; m. Christiane Amanpour; one s.; ed Columbia Univ.; Research Dir Arms Control Asscn, Washington DC 1985–89, also consultant to US Senate Foreign Relations Cttee on nuclear arms control issues; fmr staff mem., US Senate Foreign Relations Cttee, Sr Foreign Policy Adviser to Joseph R. Biden, Jr (q.v.); Sr Adviser and spokesman for US Rep. to UN Madeleine Albright (q.v.) 1993–96; Dir of Foreign Policy and Spokesman Clinton/Gore presidential campaign Aug.–Nov. 1996; Sr Adviser to Sec. of State 1996–97; Asst Sec. of State for Public Affairs 1997–2000; Pnr, Brunswick 2001–04; Visiting Prof. of Int. Relations, LSE 2001–04; foreign policy adviser John Kerry US presidential campaign 2004; Anchor, World News Tonight, Sky News (UK) 2005–06, World Affairs Commentator 2006–07;, Vice Chair. Atlantic Partnership; mem. Bd of Dirs Columbia Univ. School of Int. Affairs, currently Adjunct Prof. of Int. and Public Affairs; mem. Bd of Dirs Int. Rescue Cttee, UK; mem. Council on Foreign Relations; John Jay Award for Distinguished Professional Achievement (Columbia Univ.) 1998, Distinguished Service Award, Sec. of State 2000. *Address:* Columbia University, International Affairs Building, 420 West 118th Street, 13th Floor, New York, NY 10027, USA (office). *Telephone:* (212) 854-3213 (office). *E-mail:* jr2818@columbia.edu (office). *Website:* www.sipa.columbia.edu (office).

RUBIN, Robert, BA, LLB; American financial services industry executive, lawyer and fmr government official; b. 29 Aug. 1938, New York; s. of Alexander Rubin and Sylvia Rubin (née Seiderman); m. Judith L. Oxenberg 1963; two s.; ed Harvard Univ., LSE, Yale Univ. Law School; lawyer, Cleary, Gottlieb, Steen & Hamilton New York 1964–66; joined Goldman, Sachs 1966, Vice-Chair. & Co-COO 1987–90, Co-Chair. 1990–92; Chair. New York Host Cttee 1992 Democratic Convention; Asst to Pres. Clinton for Econ. Policy 1993–95; Sec. of Treasury 1995–99; Chair. Exec. Cttee and mem. Office of the Chair. Citigroup Inc. 1999–2007, Chair. Nov.–Dec. 2007, Sr Advisor 2007–09 (resgnd); Advisor, Taconic Capital Advisors LP, New York Farallon Capital Management LLC, San Francisco 2009–10; Counsellor, Centerview Partners, New York 2010–; mem. Bd Trustees Mount Sinai-New York University Health; fmr mem. Advisory Bd Insight Venture Partners, General Atlantic LLC; fmr Special Advisor Tinicum Capital Partners, LP; mem. Harvard Corpn 2002–; Vice-Chair. Council on Foreign Relations 2003–07, Co-Chair. 2007–; fmr mem. Bd of Dirs Ford Motor Co., Harvard

Management Co., New York Stock Exchange, New York Futures Exchange, New York City Partnership, Center for Nat. Policy; Chair. Local Initiatives Support Corpn (LISC); launched Hamilton Project 2006; mem. Africa Progress Panel 2007–; Hon. DHumLitt (Yeshiva Univ.) 1996; Hon. LLD (Univ. of Miami) 2008; Nat. Asscn of Christians and Jews Award 1977, Columbia Business School Award 1996, Euromoney Magazine's Finance Minister of the Year Award 1996, Medal for High Civic Service, Citizens' Budget Comm. 1997, Foreign Policy Asscn Medal 1998, Jefferson Award, American Inst. for Public Service 1998, Award of Merit, Yale Univ. 1998, Paul Tsongas Award 1998, Global Leadership Award, UN Asscn 1998. *Publication:* In an Uncertain World: Tough Choices from Wall Street to Washington 2003 (with Jacob Weisberg). *Leisure interest:* fly fishing. *Address:* Centerview Partners LLC, 31 West 52nd Street, 22nd Floor, New York, NY 10019, USA (office). *Telephone:* (212) 380-2650 (office). *Fax:* (212) 380-2651 (office). *Website:* www.centerviewpartners.com (office).

RUBIN, Vera Cooper, MA, PhD; American astronomer; *Senior Fellow, Department of Terrestrial Magnetism, Carnegie Institution of Washington;* b. (Vera Florence Cooper), 23 July 1928, Philadelphia; d. of Philip Cooper and Rose Applebaum Cooper; m. Robert J. Rubin 1948 (died 2008); three s. one d.; ed Vassar Coll., Cornell Univ., Georgetown Univ.; Research Assoc. to Asst Prof., Georgetown Univ. 1955–65; mem. Staff Dept of Terrestrial Magnetism, Carnegie Inst. of Wash. 1965–, now Sr Fellow; Distinguished Visiting Astronomer, Cerro Tololo Inter-American Observatory 1978, Chancellor's Distinguished Prof. of Astronomy, Univ. of Calif., Berkeley 1981; Pres.'s Distinguished Visitor, Vassar Coll. 1987; B. Tinsley Visiting Prof., Univ. of Texas 1988; Oort Visiting Prof., Univ. of Leiden 1995; has observed at Kitt Peak Nat. Observatory, Lowell, Palomar, McDonald, Las Campanas, Chile Observatories; Chair. Nat. Comm. for Int. Astronomical Union 1998–2000; Assoc. Ed. Astronomical Journal 1972–77, Astrophysical Journal of Letters 1977–82; mem. Council American Astronomical Soc. 1977–80, Nat. Science Bd 1996–2002; mem. Editorial Bd Science Magazine 1979–87, mem. Sr Editorial Bd 1998–; mem. Council Smithsonian Inst. 1979–85, Space Telescope Science Inst. 1990–92; Pres. Galaxy Comm. Int. Astronomical Union 1982–85; mem. Bd Science Service 2003–; Judge, Intel Science Talent Search 2001–; mem. NAS, American Acad. of Arts and Sciences, American Philosophical Soc., Pres.'s Cttee to select recipients of Nat. Medal of Science, Pontifical Acad. of Sciences; Hon. DSc (Creighton Univ.) 1978, (Harvard Univ.) 1988, (Yale Univ.) 1990, (Williams Coll.) 1993, (Univ. of Michigan) 1996, (Ohio State Univ.) 1998, (Smith Coll.) 2001, (Grinnell Coll.) 2002, (Ohio Wesleyan) 2004, (Princeton Univ.) 2005; Hon. DHL (Georgetown) 1997; Nat. Medal of Science 1993, Dickson Prize for Science, Carnegie Mellon Univ. 1994, Jansky Lecturer, Nat. Radio Astronomy Observatory 1994, Russel Lecturer, American Astronomical Soc. 1995, Helen Hogg Prize, Canadian Astronomical Soc. 1997, Weizmann Women and Science Award 1996, Gold Medal Royal Astronomical Soc., London 1996, Canadian Astronomy Soc. Helen Hogg Prize 1997, Peter Gruber Foundation Cosmology Prize 2003, Astronomical Soc. of the Pacific Catherine Wolfe Bruce Medal 2003, NAS Watson Medal 2004. *Publications:* Bright Galaxies, Dark Matters 1999; over 150 scientific papers on the dynamics of galaxies in specialist journals. *Leisure interests:* family, garden, hiking, travel. *Address:* Department of Terrestrial Magnetism, Carnegie Institution of Washington, 5251 Broad Branch Road, NW, Washington, DC 20015-1305, USA (office). *Telephone:* (202) 478-8861 (office). *E-mail:* rubin@dtm.ciw.edu (office). *Website:* www.dtm.ciw.edu (office).

RUBINA, Dina Ilyinichna; Israeli writer; b. 19 Sept. 1953, Tashkent, Uzbekistan; ed Tashkent State Conservatory; music teacher, Tashkent Inst. of Culture 1977–90; literary debut in Yunost magazine 1971; emigrated to Israel 1990; edited newspaper (Pyatnitza and others); Head Dept of Public and Cultural Relations, The Jewish Agency in Russia 1999–2003; Ministry of Culture Award 1982, Arye Dulchin Award (Israel) 1991, Israel Writers' Union Award 1995, Best Book of literary season, France 1996. *Films:* Zavtra, kak obychno 1984, Na Verhney Maslovke 2004. *Publications include:* The Double-Barrelled Name (short stories) 1990, In Thy Gates 1994, An Intellectual Sat Down on the Road 1995, Here Comes the Messiah 1997, The Escort Angel 1998, The Last Wild Boar from Pontevedra Forest 1998, High Water in Venice 1999, Several Hurried Words of Love (short stories) 2003, Syndicate 2009, Platanthera 2009, Adam and Miriam 2010, Window 2012. *Leisure interest:* travelling. *Address:* Et Ha'zmir, 11/8, 98491 Maale-Adumim, Israel (home). *Telephone:* 2-5352435 (home). *Fax:* 2-5352435 (home). *E-mail:* contacts@dinarubina.com (home). *Website:* www.dinarubina.com (home).

RUBINSTEIN, Amnon, BA, LLM, PhD; Israeli author, academic and fmr politician; *Professor of Law, Radzyner School of Law, Interdisciplinary Center (IDC), Herzliya;* b. 5 Sept. 1931, Tel-Aviv; s. of Aaron Rubinstein and Rachel Rubinstein (née Vilozny); m. Ronny Havatzeleth 1959; one s. one d.; ed Hebrew Univ. of Jerusalem, London School of Econs; mil. service in Israeli Defence Forces; fmr Dean, Faculty of Law and Prof. of Law, Tel-Aviv Univ.; mem. Knesset (Parl.) 1977–2001 (resgnd), mem. Constitution and Justice Cttee (Chair. 1999–2001), State Audit Cttee; Minister of Communications 1984–87, of Energy and Infra-structure and Science and Tech. 1992–93, of Educ. and Culture 1993–96; currently Prof. of Law, Interdisciplinary Center (IDC), Herzliya, fmr Dean Radzyner School of Law; Dr hc (Bradford) 1968, (Hewbrew Union Coll., Jerusalem) 1969. *Publications:* Jurisdiction and Illegality 1965, The Zionist Dream Revisited 1985 (French trans. Le Rêve et l'histoire), The Constitutional Law of Israel (5th edn) 1997, From Herzl to Rabin 1999. *Leisure interests:* music, drama, swimming. *Address:* Radzyner School of Law, Interdisciplinary Center Herzliya, Kanfei Nesharim Street, POBox 167, Herzliya 46150, Israel. *Telephone:* 9-9527325 (office). *Fax:* 9-9513075 (office). *E-mail:* amnon_r@idc.ac.il (office). *Website:* portal.idc.ac.il/en/main/academics/law/Pages/General.aspx (office).

RUBINSTEIN, Ariel, BSc, MA, MSc, PhD; Israeli economist and academic; *Professor of Economics and Salzberg Chair, Tel-Aviv University;* b. 13 April 1951, Jerusalem; s. of Yehuda Rubinstein and Leah Rubinstein; m. Yael Rubinstein; one s. one d.; ed The Hebrew Univ.; Sr Lecturer, Dept of Econs, The Hebrew Univ. 1981–84, Assoc. Prof. 1984–86, Prof. 1986–1990; Prof. of Econs and Salzberg Chair, Tel-Aviv Univ. 1990–, Chair. Dept of Econs 1991–93; Lecturer in rank of Prof. Princeton Univ., USA 1991–2004; Prof. of Econs, New York Univ. 2004–; fmr Visiting Prof., Nuffield Coll. Oxford 1979–80, LSE 1986–89, Univ. of Chicago 1988, Univ. of Pennsylvania 1989, Columbia Univ., New York 1990, Russell-Sage

Foundation 1996–97; Assoc. Ed. Econometrica 1984–92, Journal of Econ. Theory 1986–94, Games and Economic Behavior 1988–2002, Mathematics of Social Sciences 1993–2001; mem. Editorial Bd Review of Economic Studies 1987–88 (Foreign Ed. 1988–92), Review of Economic Design 1993–, Economics and Philosophy 1994–, International Journal of Game Theory 1995–2000, NAJ Economics 2001–; mem. Advisory Cttee Journal of European Economic Association 2003–; mem. Exec. Bd Theoretical Economics 2005–; Fellow, Econometric Soc. 1985– (Pres. 2004), Israeli Acad. of Sciences 1995–, European Econ. Asscn 2004–; mem. European Acad. of Sciences and Arts; Foreign Hon. mem. American Acad. of Arts and Sciences 1994–, American Econ. Asscn 1995–, Hon. Fellow, Nuffield Coll. 2002–; Dr hc (Tilburg) 2002; Michael Bruno Memorial Award 2000, Pras Israel 2002, Nemmers Prize, Northwestern Univ. 2004, EMET Prize 2006. *Publications:* Bargaining and Markets (with M. Osborne) 1990, A Course in Game Theory (with M. Osborne) 1994, Modeling Bounded Rationality 1998, Economics and Language 2000, Lecture Notes in Microeconomic Theory: The Economic Agent 2005, Economic Tales 2009, more than 80 articles in academic journals. *Address:* School of Economics, Tel-Aviv University, Tel-Aviv 69978, Israel (office). *Telephone:* (3) 6409601 (office); (3) 6421111 (home). *Fax:* (3) 6409908 (office). *E-mail:* rariel@post.tau.ac.il (office). *Website:* arielrubinstein.tau.ac.il (office).

RUBIO, Juan Carlos; Spanish writer, director, actor and academic; *Director, SC Productions;* b. 1967, Montilla; ed School of Theatre de Alcorcón, Royal School of Drama and Dance, Madrid; Prof., Colectivo de Lesbianas, Gays, Transexuales y Bisexuales de Madrid 1999–2000; Prof., TB/IGUELDO 2000; Prof., Antena 3 TV 2000; Prof., Massart 2008; Prof., El Ejido (Almería) 2008; Prof., Leganés (Madrid) 2008; Prof., Lucena (Córdoba) 2008; currently Dir SC Productions. *Films:* writer: Fin de curso 2005, El Calentito 2005, Dolly 2007, Lola, la película 2007, Bon appétit (Best Screenplay Málaga Spanish Film Festival) 2010; film writer: El idiota 2000, Slam 2002, El calentito 2005, Fin de curso 2005, Retorno a Hansala 2008; actor: Las trampas del azar 1995, Los padres terribles 1996–97, El cerco de Numancia 1998; playwright: Esta noche no estoy para nadie (City Theatre Prize Alcorcón) 1997, Las heridas del viento (Premio Hermanos Machado 2000) 1999, Tres 2000, El bosque es mío 2001, 10 2001, ¿Dónde se esconden los sueños? (Premio teatro infantil Escuela Navarra de Teatro) 2004, Epitafio (Premio Animasur 2005) 2004, Humo (also dir) (Premio SGAE 2005, Premio telón Chivas 2008) 2005, Arizona (also dir) (Premio Raúl Moreno-Fatex, Mención Especial del Premio Lope de Vega) 2006, No quemes la vida 2007, 100 metros cuadrados 2007; dir: The Big Kahuna 2009. *Publications:* No mires a los ojos de la diosa (City of Alcorcón) 1982, Mama ¿qué es un wellspringt? (Colmenar Viejo) 1982. *Address:* SC Productions, 15 Mutis Bocaue Avenue, PO 8, 14550 Montilla, Spain. *Telephone:* (95) 7651227. *E-mail:* carlosrubio06@yahoo.es; jcrguion@hotmail.com. *Website:* www.juancarlosrubio.com; www.mutisproducciones.com.

RUBIO, Marco Antonio, BS, JD; American lawyer and politician; *Senator from Florida;* b. 28 May 1971, Miami, Fla; s. of the late Mario Rubio and of Oria Garcia (Cuban exiles); m. Jeanette Dousdebes 1997; two s. two d.; ed South Miami Sr High School, Tarkio Coll. (football scholarship), Santa Fe Coll., Univs of Florida and Miami; interned for Congresswoman Ileana Ros-Lehtinen while studying law; served as City Commr for West Miami –2000; mem. Florida House of Reps for 111th Dist 2000–08, Majority Leader 2003–06, Speaker of the House 2006–08; Senator from Fla 2011–; mem. Commerce, Science and Transportation Cttee, Select Cttee on Intelligence, Cttee on Foreign Relations; Political Analyst, Univision 2008; mem. Bd Alafit International, Latin Builders Asscn, Miami Performing Arts Center; Florida Chair. Grand Old Party Action Cttee; Visiting Prof., Florida Int. Univ. Metropolitan Center 2008; Republican; Freshman Legislator of the Year, Florida Petroleum Marketers Asscn. *Publications:* 100 Innovative Ideas for Florida's Future: A Plan of Action 2006. *Address:* 317 Hart Senate Office Building, Washington, DC 20510, USA (office). *Telephone:* (202) 224-3041 (office). *Website:* rubio.senate.gov (office).

RUCKAUF, Carlos Federico; Argentine politician; b. 10 July 1944; m.; three c.; ed Nat. Univ. of Buenos Aires; Asst Sec. Insurance Union 1969–72; Labour Judge 1973–75; Sec. Trabajo de la Nación (Labour of the Nation) 1975–76; Pres. Partido Justicialista de Capital Federal (Fed. Justice Party) 1983, Vice-Pres. 1993, Pres. 1994; Senatorial Cand. 1983; Nat. Deputy 1987–89, 1991–93; Amb. to Italy, Malta and FAO 1990–91; Pres. Foreign Affairs Comm. 1991–93; Minister of the Interior 1993; apptd Vice-Pres. of Argentina 1995; Gov. Buenos Aires Prov. 1999–; Minister of Foreign Affairs 2002–03; mem. Parl. (Partido Justicialista—PJ) 2003–07; Kt of the Grand Cross, Order of Merit (Italy) 1995, Grand Cross, Order Bernardo O'Higgins (Chile) 1996, Medal of the Congress of Deputies (Spain) 1997, Commdr, Légion d'honneur (France) 1997, Alaoui Order (Morocco) 1998, Grand Cross, Ordem Nacional do Cruzeiro do Sul (Brazil) 1998, Special Grand Cross, Nat. Order of Merit (Paraguay) 1999. *Address:* c/o Ministry of Foreign Affairs, International Trade and Worship, Esmeralda 1212, 1007 Buenos Aires, Argentina (office).

RUCKELSHAUS, William Doyle; American business executive and fmr government official; *Strategic Director, Madrona Venture Group LLC;* b. 24 July 1932, Indianapolis, Ind.; s. of John K. Ruckelshaus and Marion Covington Ruckelshaus (née Doyle); m. Jill E. Strickland 1962; one s. four d.; ed Portsmouth Priory School, RI and Princeton and Harvard Univs; served with US Army 1953–55; admitted to Ind. Bar 1960; attorney with Ruckelshaus, Bobbit & O'Connor 1960–68; Partner, Ruckelshaus, Beveridge, Fairbanks & Diamond (fmrly Ruckelshaus, Beveridge & Fairbanks), Sr Partner 1974–76; Deputy Attorney-Gen. Ind. 1960–65; Minority Attorney, Ind. State Senate 1965–67; mem. Ind. House of Reps 1967–69; Asst Attorney-Gen., US Civil Div., Dept of Justice 1969–70; Dir Environmental Protection Agency 1970–73, 1983–84; Acting Dir FBI 1973 and Deputy Attorney-Gen. 1973 (resgnd); Sr Vice-Pres. Weyerhaeuser Co. 1976–83; mem. firm Perkins Coie, Seattle 1985–88; Chair. CEO Browning-Ferris Industries Inc., Houston 1988–95; Founder and Prin. Madrona Investment Group (now Madrona Venture Group LLC) 1996–; trategic Dir; Chair. World Resources Inst., Washington, DC 1999–2006; mem. Bd of Dirs Cummins Engine Co., Inc., Vykor, Isilon Systems; fmr Dir Peabody Int. Corpn, Church and Dwight Co. Inc.; fmr Chair. Bd Geothermal Kinetics Inc., Trustees of Urban Inst.; mem. Bd American Paper Inst., Council on Foreign Relations, Twentieth Century Fund; mem. Public Interest Advisory Cttee Harvard Univ. Medical Project, Bd of Overseers, Kennedy School of Govt, Harvard Univ., Bd of Regents, Seattle Univ., World Resource Inst. (Chair. 1998–), Comm. on Ocean Policy 2001–, Science

Advisory Bd, Nat. Oceanic and Atmospheric Admin 2003–; Chair. Salmon Recovery Funding Bd for State of Washington, Puget Sound Cleanup, Univ. of Washington and Washington State Univ. Policy Consensus Center, Seattle Aquarium Soc.; Co-Chair. Puget Sound Partnership 2005–; Trustee, Pacific Science Center Foundation, Seattle Chamber of Commerce, The Conservation Foundation, Seattle Art Museum; mem. bd numerous other non-profit orgs, several US Bar asscns; numerous awards and distinctions. *Publication:* Reapportionment – A Continuing Problem 1963. *Leisure interests:* tennis, fishing, reading. *Address:* Madrona Investment Group LLC, 1000 2nd Avenue, Suite 3700, Seattle, WA 98104, USA (office). *Telephone:* (206) 674-3009 (office). *Fax:* (206) 674-3013 (office). *E-mail:* bill@madrona.com (office). *Website:* www.madrona.com (office).

RÜCKER, Joachim; German diplomatist and fmr UN official; *Inspector General, Ministry of Foreign Affairs;* b. 30 May 1951; one s.; two d.; has served in several positions within Ministry of Foreign Affairs (MFA) including Head, Budget and Finance Div. 2002–05; Mayor of Sindelfingen, Germany 1993–2001; Deputy High Rep. for Admin and Finance, Office of the UN High Rep., Sarajevo, Bosnia and Herzegovina 2001–02; Deputy Special Rep. of Sec.-Gen. in charge of EU Pillar for Econ. Reconstruction, UN Interim Admin Mission in Kosovo (UNMIK) 2005–06, Special Rep. of Sec.-Gen. and Head of UNMIK 2006–08; Amb. to Sweden 2008–11; Inspector Gen., MFA 2011–. *Address:* Federal Ministry of Foreign Affairs, Werderscher Markt 1, 10117 Berlin, Germany (office). *Telephone:* (30) 18170 (office). *Fax:* (30) 18173402 (office). *E-mail:* poststelle@auswaertiges-amt.de (office). *Website:* www.joachim-ruecker.def (home).

RÜCKL, Jiří; Czech business executive and fmr politician; *President, Rückl Crystal a.s.;* b. 20 Oct. 1940, Prague; s. of Jiří Rückl and Věra Rückl; m. Jana Hrabánková; two d.; ed Econ. Univ., Prague; specialist positions in glassware 1961–90; Pres. Rückl Crystal 1992–; Dir Ministry of Industry 1990–92; Councillor for Nibor 1994–; Senator 1996–2004. *Publications include:* specialist papers about glass production. *Address:* Rückl Crystal a.s., 26705 Nižbor 141, Czech Republic (office). *Telephone:* (3) 11696232 (office). *Fax:* (3) 11693510 (office). *E-mail:* ruckl@ruckl.cz (office). *Website:* www.ruckl.eu (office); www.ruckl.cz (office).

RUDD, Sir (Anthony) Nigel (Russell), Kt, DL, FCA; British business executive; *Chairman, Invensys plc;* b. 31 Dec. 1946; m. Lesley Elizabeth Rudd (née Hodgkinson) 1969; two s. one d.; ed Bemrose Grammar School, Derby; chartered accountant 1968; Div. Finance Dir London & Northern Group 1970–77; Chair. C. Price & Son Ltd 1977–82; Chair. Williams Holdings (later Williams PLC) 1982–2000; Deputy Chair. Raine Industries 1992–94 (Chair. (non-exec.) 1986–92); Dir Pilkington PLC 1994, Chair. 1995–2006; Deputy Chair. Boots PLC 2002, Chair. 2003–06, Chair. Alliance Boots PLC (after merger with Alliance Unichem) 2006–07; Chair. (non-exec.) Pendragon PLC 1989–2010, East Midlands Electricity 1994–97 (Dir 1990–97), Kidde 2000–03, BAA plc 2007–; Deputy Chair. Invensys plc Jan.–July 2009, Chair. July 2009–; Dir (non-exec.) Williams Man. Services 1985–96, Westminster Securities 1987–96, Gartmore Value Investment 1989–93, Gartmore 1993–96, Derby Pride 1993–98, Mithras Investment Trust 1994–98, Barclays Bank 1996–2009 (Deputy Chair. 2004–09), BAE Systems 2006–, Sappi Ltd 2006–; mem. European Round Table of Industrialists –2001, Council CBI 1999–; mem. Chartered Accountants' Co.; DL Derbyshire 1996; Freeman, City of London; Hon. DTech (Loughborough) 1998; Hon. DUniv (Derby) 1998. *Leisure interests:* golf, skiing, theatre, field sports. *Address:* Invensys plc, 3rd Floor, 40 Grosvenor Place, London, SW1X 7AW, England (office). *Telephone:* (20) 3155-1200 (office). *Fax:* (20) 3155-1201 (office). *Website:* www.invensys.com (office).

RUDD, Kevin, BA; Australian politician; b. 21 Sept. 1957, Nambour, Queensland; m. Therese Rudd; two s. one d.; ed Australian Nat. Univ.; joined Dept of Foreign Affairs and Trade 1981, worked in Embassies in Stockholm and Beijing; Chief of Staff to Queensland State Opposition Leader 1988–92; Premier, Queensland State Govt 1989–92, Dir-Gen. of Cabinet 1992–95; China Consultant, KPMG 1996–98; Adjunct Prof. of Asian Languages, Univ. of Queensland 1997–; mem. Parl. (Labor Party) for Griffith 1998–, Chair. Fed. Parl. Labor Party's Cttee on Foreign Affairs, Defence and Trade 1998–2001, Shadow Minister for Foreign Affairs 2001–04, Shadow Minister for Foreign Affairs and Int. Security 2004–05, Shadow Minister for Foreign Affairs, Trade and Int. Security 2005–07; Leader, Australian Labor Party 2006–10, June–Sept. 2013; Prime Minister 2007–10, June–Sept. 2013; Minister for Foreign Affairs and Trade 2010–12 (resgnd); mem. Australian-American Leadership Dialogue; mem. Advisory Council, Australia-Asia Centre, Korea-Australia Centre. *Publications include:* numerous articles on Chinese politics. *Address:* PO Box 6022, House of Representatives, Parliament House, Canberra, ACT 2600 (office); Griffith Electorate Office, POB 476A, Morningside, Qld 4170, Australia (office). *Telephone:* (02) 6277 7500 (Canberra) (office). *Fax:* (02) 6273 4112 (Canberra) (office). *E-mail:* Kevin.Rudd.MP@aph.gov.au (office). *Website:* www.aph.gov.au/K_Rudd_MP (office); www.kevinrudd.org.au.

RUDD, Paul; American actor; b. 6 April 1969, Passaic, New Jersey; m. Julie Yaeger; one s. one d.; ed Univ. of Kansas, American Acad. of Dramatic Arts-West, Los Angeles. *Television includes:* Sisters 1992–95, Friends 2002–04, Cheap Seats 2006, Little Britain USA 2008. *Films include:* Clueless 1995, The Locusts 1997, The Object of My Affection 1998, Wet Hot American Summer 2001, The Shape of Things 2003, Anchorman: The Legend of Ron Burgundy 2004, P.S. 2004, The 40-Year-Old Virgin 2005, Tennis, Anyone? 2005, Night at the Museum 2006, Knocked Up 2007, Forgetting Sarah Marshall 2008, I Love You, Man 2009, Monsters vs Aliens (voice) 2009, Dinner for Schmucks 2010, How Do You Know 2010, Wanderlust 2011, The Perks of Being a Wallflower 2012, This Is 40 2012, Admission 2013. *Address:* c/o Brillstein-Grey Entertainment, 9150 Wilshire Blvd, Suite 350, Beverly Hills, CA 90212, USA (office).

RUDDEN, Bernard (Anthony), LLD, DCL, FBA; British professor of law; *Professor Emeritus, University of Oxford;* b. 21 Aug. 1933, Carlisle; s. of John Rudden and Kathleen Rudden; m. Nancy Campbell 1957; three s. one d.; ed City of Norwich School and St John's Coll., Cambridge; Fellow and Tutor, Oriel Coll. Oxford 1965–79; Prof. of Comparative Law, Univ. of Oxford and Fellow, Brasenose Coll. Oxford 1979–99, Prof. Emer. 1999–; Hon. LLD (McGill) 1979. *Publications:* Soviet Insurance Law 1966, The New River 1985, Basic Community Cases 1987, Source-Book on French Law (co-author) 1991, Basic Community Law (co-author) 1996, Law of Property 2002. *Address:* 15 Redinnick Terrace, Penzance, Cornwall,

TR18 4HR, England (home). *Telephone:* (1736) 360395 (home). *E-mail:* bernard .rudden@law.ox.ac.uk (office).

RUDDOCK, Rt Hon. Dame Joan Mary, DBE, PC, BSc, ARCS; British politician; b. 28 Dec. 1943, Abergavenny; d. of Ken Anthony and Eileen Anthony; m. 1st Keith Ruddock 1963 (died 1996); m. 2nd Frank Doran 2010; ed Pontypool Grammar School for Girls, Imperial Coll., London; worked for Shelter (nat. campaign for the homeless) 1968–73; Dir Oxford Housing Aid Centre 1973–77; Special Programmes Officer with unemployed young people, Manpower Services Comm. 1977–79; Man., Reading Citizens Advice Bureau 1979–87; Chair. Campaign for Nuclear Disarmament (CND) 1981–85, Vice-Chair. 1985–86; MP for Lewisham Deptford 1987–, mem. Select Cttee on Televising House of Commons, mem. British Del., Council of Europe 1988–89, Shadow Spokesperson on Transport 1989–92, on Home Affairs 1992–94, on Environmental Protection 1994–97, Select Cttee on Modernization 2001–05, Select Cttee on Environment, Food and Rural Affairs 2003–05, Select Cttee of Int. Devt 2005–07; Parl. UnderSec. of State for Women 1997–98; Co-founder Women Say No to GMOs 1999; Founder and Co-ordinator UK Women's Link with Afghan Women 2001; Labour Party. Under-Sec. of State Dept of Environment, Food and Rural Affairs 2007–08; Parl. Under-Sec. of State, Dept of Energy and Climate Change 2008–09; Minister of State for Energy and Climate Change 2009–10; mem. Bd Trinity Laban; mem. Privy Council 2010; Hon. Assoc., Nat. Secular Soc.; Hon. Fellow, Goldsmith's Coll., Univ. of London 1996, Laban Centre, London; Frank Cousins Peace Award 1984. *Publications:* The CND Story (contrib.) 1983, CND Scrapbook 1987, Voices for One World (contrib.) 1988. *Leisure interests:* gardening, music, art. *Address:* House of Commons, Westminster, London, SW1A 0AA, England (office). *Telephone:* (20) 7219-4513 (office). *Fax:* (20) 7219-6045 (office). *E-mail:* joan.ruddock.mp@parliament.uk (office). *Website:* www.joanruddock.org.

RUDDOCK, Hon. Philip M., BA, LLB; Australian solicitor and politician; b. 12 March 1943, Canberra; s. of the Hon. Max S. Ruddock; m. Heather Ruddock 1971; two d.; ed Barker Coll., Hornsby, Sydney Univ.; Shadow Minister for ACT and Shadow Minister Assisting Opposition Leader on Public Service Matters 1983–84, Immigration and Ethnic Affairs 1984–85, 1989–93, Shadow Minister for Social Security and Sr Citizens 1993, mem. Shadow Cabinet 1996; Minister for Immigration and Multicultural Affairs 1996–2001, also Minister Assisting Prime Minister for Reconciliation 1998–2001, 2002–03, Minister for Immigration and Multicultural and Indigenous Affairs 2001–02; Attorney Gen. 2003–07; Shadow Cabinet Sec. 2009–. *Leisure interests:* jogging, bushwalking, gardening, opera, reading. *Address:* PO Box 6022, House of Representatives, Parliament House, Canberra 2600 (office); Teletech Building, Level 7, Suite 701, 423 Pennant Hills Road, Pennant Hills, NSW 2120, Australia. *Telephone:* (2) 9980-1822 (office). *Fax:* (2) 9980-1833 (office). *Website:* www.ruddockmp.com.au.

RUDENSTINE, Neil Leon, PhD; American university administrator and academic; b. 21 Jan. 1935, Ossining, NY; s. of Harry Rudenstine and Mae Rudenstine; m. Angelica Zander 1960; one s. two d.; ed Princeton Univ., Oxford Univ., Harvard Univ.; instructor, English Dept, Harvard Univ. 1964–66, Asst Prof. 1966–68, Prof. of English and Pres., Harvard Univ. 1991–2001, now Pres. Emer.; Assoc. Prof. of English, Princeton Univ. 1968–73, Dean of Students 1968–72, Prof. of English 1973–88, Dean of Coll. 1972–77, Provost 1977–88, now Provost Emer.; Exec. Vice-Pres. Andrew W. Mellon Foundation, New York 1988–91; Chair. Bd of Trustees ARTstor Inc. 2001–; Chair. Bd of Trustees Rockefeller Archive Center; mem. Council on Foreign Relations, American Philosophical Soc., Cttee for Econ. Devt, American Acad. of Arts and Sciences; Trustee, Princeton Univ. 2002–06, New York Public Library, Courtauld Inst. of Art, Barnes Foundation, Getty Trust; Hon. Fellow, New Coll., Oxford, Emmanuel Coll., Cambridge; Dr hc (Harvard, Oxford, Princeton, Yale). *Publications:* Sidney's Poetic Development 1967, English Poetic Satire: Wyatt to Byron (with George Rousseau) 1972, In Pursuit of the PhD (with William G. Bowen) 1992, Pointing Our Thoughts 2001. *Address:* 41 Armour Road, Princeton, NJ 08540 USA (home); ARTstor, 151 East 61st Street, New York NY 10021, USA (office). *Telephone:* (212) 500-2419 (office); (609) 683-7516 (home). *Fax:* (212) 500-2418 (office). *Website:* www.artstor.org (office).

RUDIN, Alexander Izraliyevich; Russian cellist, pianist and conductor; *Artistic Director and Chief Conductor, Musica Viva Moscow Chamber Orchestra;* b. 28 Nov. 1960, Moscow; m. Rudina Olga Ryurikovna; two s.; ed Gnessin Music Inst., Moscow State Conservatory; has appeared as a soloist with numerous orchestras including Royal Philharmonic, Danish Radio, St Petersburg Philharmonic, Moscow Philharmonic, Austrian Symphony, Bolshoi Theatre; has worked as conductor with orchestras in Finland, Germany, Italy, Norway, Russia; has participated in festivals in Edin., Istanbul, Kuhmo, Vaasa; Artistic Dir and Chief Conductor Musica Viva Chamber Orchestra 1987–; Artistic Dir Int. Festival Music Ensembles; Prof., Moscow State Conservatory; Visiting Prof. Sibelius Acad., Helsinki; winner of Concertino Prague 1973, J. S. Bach Competition, Leipzig 1976, Nat. Competition, Vilnius 1977, Tchaikovsky Competition, Moscow 1978, 1982, Gaspar Cassado Competition, Florence 1979. *Address:* ploshad Zhuravleva, 1-1, 107023, Moscow (office); Malaya Ostroumovskaya str. 1/10, Apt. 46, 107014 Moscow, Russia (home). *Telephone:* (495) 964-1965 (office); (499) 268-15-77 (home). *Fax:* (495) 964-1965 (office). *E-mail:* musica-viva@mail.ru (office). *Website:* musicaviva.ru/eng (office).

RUDIN, Scott; American film and theatre producer; b. 14 July 1958, New York; production asst, asst to theatre producers Kermit Bloomgarden and Robert Whitehead; Casting Dir, Producer with Edgar Scherick; Exec. Vice-Pres. Production 20th Century Fox 1984–86, Pres. Production 1986–87; f. Scott Rudin Productions 1990–. *Films produced include:* He Makes Me Feel Like Dancing 1982 (Outstanding Children's Program Emmy Award 1982, Feature Documentary Acad. Award 1982), Mrs Soffel 1984, Flatliners 1990, Pacific Heights 1990, Regarding Henry 1991, Little Man Tate 1991, The Addams Family 1991, Sister Act 1992, Jennifer Eight 1992, Life With Mikey 1993, The Firm 1993, Searching for Bobby Fischer 1993, Sister Act 2 1993, Addams Family Values 1993, I.Q. 1994, Nobody's Fool 1994, Sabrina 1995, Clueless 1995, Up Close and Personal 1996, Ransom 1996, Marvin's Room 1996, The First Wives' Club 1996, In and Out 1997, Twilight 1998, The Truman Show 1998, A Civil Action 1998, Wonder Boys 1999, Rules of Engagement 1999, Brokeback Mountain 1999, Angela's Ashes 1999, Bringing Out the Dead 1999, Sleepy Hollow 1999, Shaft 2000, Rules of Engagement 2000, Zoolander 2001, The Royal Tenenbaums 2001, Iris: A Memoir of Iris

Murdoch 2001, Orange County 2002, The Hours 2002, Changing Lanes 2002, Marci X 2003, The School of Rock 2003, The Stepford Wives 2004, The Manchurian Candidate 2004, The Village 2004, I Heart Huckabees 2004, Team America: World Police 2004, The Life Aquatic with Steve Zissou 2004, Closer 2004, Lemony Snicket's A Series of Unfortunate Events 2004, Freedomland 2005, Failure to Launch 2006, The Queen 2006, Venus 2006, Notes on a Scandal 2006, No Country for Old Men 2007, Margot at the Wedding 2007, The Darjeeling Limited 2007, Nothing Is Private 2007, There Will Be Blood 2007, The Other Boleyn Girl 2008, Stop Loss 2008, Extremely Loud & Incredibly Close 2011. *Theatre includes:* Passion 1994 (Tony Award Best Musical 1994), Indiscretions 1995, Hamlet 1995, Seven Guitars 1995, A Funny Thing Happened on the Way to the Forum 1996, Skylight 1997, On the Town (New York Shakespeare Festival) 1997, The Chairs 1998, The Judas Kiss 1998, Closer (London) 1998, Amy's View 1999, Wide Guys 1999, Copenhagen 1999 (Tony Award), The Book of Mormon 2011. *Recordings include:* as producer: The Book of Mormon (Grammy Award for Best Musical Theater Album 2012) 2011. *Address:* Scott Rudin Productions, 10th Floor, 120 West 45th Street, New York, NY 10036, USA.

RUDINI, Gen.; Indonesian army officer; b. 15 Dec. 1929, Malang, E. Java; s. of R. I. Poespohandojo and R. A. Koesbandijah; m. Oddyana Rudini 1959; one s. two d.; ed Breda Mil. Acad., Netherlands, reaching rank of Second Lt; Commdr Kostrad Infantry/Airborne Brigade 1972–73; Commdr Indonesian contingent of UN Peacekeeping Force in Middle East 1973–76; Commdr Kostrad Airborne Combat 1976–81; Commdr N. and Cen. Sulawesi Mil. Region, Manado 1981, later Commdr of Kostrad; Chief of Staff, Indonesian Army 1983–88; Minister of Home Affairs 1988–93, concurrently Chair. of the Election Cttee. *Leisure interests:* sport, music. *Address:* c/o Ministry of Home Affairs, Jalan Merdeka Utara 7, Jakarta Pusat, Indonesia.

RUDISHA, David Lekuta; Kenyan track and field athlete; b. 17 Dec. 1988, Trans Mara; s. of Daniel Rudisha and Naomi Rudisha; m. Lizzy Naanyu; one d.; ed St Patrick's, Kimuron Secondary School; initially 400m. runner; gold medal, 800m., World Junior Championships, Beijing 2006; gold medal, 800m., African Junior Championships, Ouagadougou 2007; gold medal, 800m., African Championships, Addis Ababa 2008; won Int. Asscn of Athletics Feds. (IAAF) Grand Prix, (set new African record of 1:42.01) Rieti 2009, Ostrava 2009; gold medal, 800m., World Athletics Final, Thessaloniki 2009; winner 800m., Golden League, Brussels 2009, Zurich 2009; gold medal, 800m., Continental Cup, Split 2010; gold medal, 800m., African Championships, Nairobi 2010; won 800m., Diamond League, Doha 2010, Oslo 2010, Lausanne 2010, 2011, Brussels 2010, 2011, Monaco 2011, New York 2012, Paris Saint-Denis 2012; also won 800m., World Challenge, Melbourne 2010, 2011, 2012, Ostrava 2010, Berlin 2010, Rieti 2010, 2011; gold medal, 800m., World Championships, Daegu 2011; gold medal, 800m. (1:40:91, world record), Olympic Games, London 2012; IAAF World Athlete of the Year Award 2010, Kenyan Sportsman of the Year Award 2010. *Address:* c/o National Olympic Committee, POB 46888, Olympic House, Upper Hill, Kenya Road, Nairobi 00100, Kenya.

RUELLE, David Pierre, PhD; French research mathematician and physicist; *Professor Emeritus, Institut des Hautes Etudes Scientifiques;* b. 20 Aug. 1935, Ghent, Belgium; s. of Pierre Ruelle and Marguerite de Jonge; m. Janine Lardinois 1960; one s. two d.; ed high school at Mons and Free Univ. of Brussels; Research Asst and Privatdozent, ETH, Zürich 1960–62; mem. Inst. for Advanced Study, Princeton, NJ, USA 1962–64; mem. Acad. des Sciences 1985, Academia Europaea 1993; Foreign Assoc. NAS 2002–; Foreign mem. Accad. Nazionale dei Lincei 2003–; Foreign Hon. mem. American Acad. of Arts and Sciences 1992; Hon. Prof., Institut des Hautes Etudes Scientifiques, Bures-sur-Yvette 1964–2000; Chevalier, Légion d'honneur; Dannie Heineman Prize 1985, Boltzmann Medal 1986, Matteuci Medal 2004, Henri Poincaré Prize 2006. *Publications:* Statistical Mechanics: Rigorous Results 1969, Thermodynamic Formalism 1978, Elements of Differentiable Dynamics and Bifurcation Theory 1989, Chance and Chaos 1991, The Mathematician's Brain 2007. *Address:* I.H.E.S., 91440 Bures-sur-Yvette (office); 1 avenue Charles-Comar, 91440 Bures-sur-Yvette, France (home). *Telephone:* 1-60-92-66-52 (office); 1-69-07-61-52 (home). *Website:* www.ihes.fr/~ruelle (office).

RUEMMLER, Kathryn, BA, JD; American lawyer and government official; *White House Counsel;* b. Wash.; ed Univ. of Washington, Seattle, Georgetown Univ. Law Center; fmr Ed.-in-Chief Georgetown Law Journal; clerked for the Hon. Timothy K. Lewis on the US Court of Appeals for the Third Circuit; Assoc. Counsel to Pres. Bill Clinton 2000–01; served as a Fed. Prosecutor 2001–07, Co-Lead Prosecutor in successful prosecution of fmr CEOs of Enron; Litigation Partner, Latham & Watkins, Washington, DC 2007–09; Prin. Assoc. Deputy Attorney Gen., Dept of Justice 2009–10; Prin. Deputy Counsel to the Pres. 2010–11, White House Counsel 2011–; Attorney Gen.'s Award for Exceptional Service for work on Enron investigation. *Address:* The White House, 1600 Pennsylvania Avenue, NW, Washington, DC 20500, USA (office). *Telephone:* (202) 456-1414 (switchboard) (office). *Fax:* (202) 456-2461 (office). *Website:* www.whitehouse.gov (office).

RUF, Beatrix; German/Swiss art gallery curator; *Director/Curator, Kunsthalle Zürich;* b. 1960; ed studied in Vienna, New York and Zurich; Curator Canton of Thurgau Kunstmuseum 1994–98; Curator Ringier Collection 1995–; Dir/Curator Kunsthaus Glarus 1998–2001; Dir/Curator Kunsthalle Zürich 2001–; mem. Bd Schweizerische Graphische Gesellschaft 1999–, Art Comm., Swiss Re, Cultural Advisory Bd for CERN; Assoc. Ed. JRP/Ringier (publr) 2003–; Curator Tate Triennial 2006; Player/Co-Curator Lyons Biennale 2007; Co-Curator Yokohama Triennale 2008; mem. Jury, Deutsche Börse Photography Prize 2012, Artissima Illy Present Future Prize 2012. *Publications include:* Jenny Holzer: Xenon 2001, The Tate Triennial Exhibition of Contemporary British Art 2006, The Metaphor Problem Again: A Conversation Between John Baldessari, Lawrence Weiner, and Liam Gillick 2006, Terence Koh (co-author) 2007, Blasted Allegories (ed.) 2008, Liam Gillick 2009, Mark Morrisroe 2010 and many others. *Address:* Kunsthalle Zürich, Limmatstrasse 270, 8005 Zurich, Switzerland (office). *Telephone:* (44) 2721515 (office). *Fax:* (44) 2721888 (office). *E-mail:* info@kunsthallezurich.ch (office). *Website:* www.kunsthallezurich.ch (office).

RUFFALO, Mark; American actor and director; b. 22 Nov. 1967, Kenosha, Wis.; s. of Frank Lawrence Ruffalo, Jr and Marie Rose Ruffalo (née Hebert); m. Sunrise Coigney; one s. two d.; ed Stella Adler Conservatory, Los Angeles; co-f. Orpheus Theatre Co., Los Angeles. *Television includes:* Due South 1994. *Films include:* The

Last Big Thing 1996, Ride with the Devil 1999, You Can Count on Me (Montreal World Film Festival Award for Best Actor) 2000, Windtalkers 2002, My Life Without Me 2003, Eternal Sunshine of the Spotless Mind 2004, 13 Going on 30 2004, Collateral 2004, Just Like Heaven 2005, Rumor Has It 2005, All the King's Men 2006, Reservation Road 2007, Zodiac 2007, Blindness 2008, What Doesn't Kill You 2008, The Brothers Bloom 2008, Sympathy for Delicious 2009, Where the Wild Things Are 2009, Shutter Island 2010, The Kids Are All Right (New York Film Critics Circle Award for Best Supporting Actor, Comedy Film Award for Best Supporting Actor) 2010, Date Night 2010, Avengers Assemble 2012. *Address:* Robert Stein Management, 1180 South Beverly Drive, Suite 304, Los Angeles, CA 90035, USA (office). *Telephone:* (310) 550-2176 (office). *Fax:* (310) 550-2178 (office).

RUFIN, Jean-Christophe, MD; French writer, physician and diplomatist; b. 28 June 1952, Bourges; s. of Marcel Rufin and Denise Bonneau; one s. two d.; ed Lycées Janson-de-Sailly and Claude Bernard, Paris, Pitié-Salpêtrière School of Medicine, Paris, Institut d'études politiques, Paris; Hosp. Intern, Paris 1975–81, Dir of Clinic and Asst Hôpitaux de Paris 1981–83, attaché Hôpitaux de Paris 1983–86; Chief of Mission of Sec. of State for Human Rights 1986–88; Cultural Attaché French Embassy in Brazil 1989–90; Vice-Pres. Médécins sans Frontières 1991–93; Adviser to Minister of Defence 1993–95; doctor, Nanterre Hosp. 1994–95; Practitioner, St Antoine Hosp., Paris 1995–98; Dir French Red Cross 1994–96, Inst. Pasteur, Groupe France Télévisions, Office français de protection des réfugiés et apatrides 2005–; Medical Dir, then Pres. Action contre la faim 2002–07; Amb. to Senegal (also accred to Gambia) 2007–10; mem. Acad. Française 2008–; Chevalier des Arts et des Lettres; Officier, Légion d'honneur; Dr hc (Laval Univ., Catholic Univ. of Louvain). *Publications include:* Le Piège humanitaire 1986, L'Empire et les nouveaux barbares 1992, La Dictature libérale (Prix Jean-Jacques Rousseau) 1994, L'Aventure humanitaire 1994, L'Abyssin (Prix Goncourt du Premier Roman, Prix Méditerranée) 1997, Sauver Ispahan 1998, Les Causes perdues (Prix Interallié) 1999, Rouge Brésil (Prix Goncourt) 2001, Globalia 2004, La Salamandre 2005, Le Parfum d'Adam 2006, Un léopard sur le garrot 2008, 100 Stunden 2009, Katiba 2010, Sept histoires qui reviennent de loin 2011, Le grand Coeur 2012, Immortelle randonnée 2013, Le collier rouge 2014. *Leisure interest:* mountain climbing. *Address:* c/o Les Editions Gallimard, 5 rue Gaston-Gallimard, 75328 Paris cedex 07, France.

RUGAR, Daniel, PhD; American scientist; *Manager, Nanoscale Studies, IBM Almaden Research Center;* ed Stanford Univ.; Research Assoc. in Applied Physics, Stanford Univ.; joined IBM in 1984, contributed to early devts of atomic force microscopy, especially for imaging magnetic materials and for applications to data storage; currently Man. Nanoscale Studies, IBM Almaden Research Center, San Jose, Calif.; has received IBM internal awards for contribs to scanning probe microscopy, near field optical data storage and single spin detection 1999–2000, Distinguished Lecturer, IEEE Magnetic Soc., Scientific American 50 Award for research leadership in the field of imaging 2004, World Tech. Award in Materials, The World Tech. Network (co-recipient) 2005. *Achievements include:* co-inventor thermo-mechanical recording technique that is basis of IBM 'Millipede' AFM storage device; pioneered mechanical detection of ultrasmall forces, achieving current record of 800 zeptonewtons in a 1 Hertz bandwidth; made first demonstrations of magnetic resonance force microscopy (MRFM) 1992, work reached key milestone with manipulation and detection of individual electron spin 2004. *Publications:* more than 100 scientific papers in professional journals on scanning microscopy; 20 patents. *Address:* IBM Almaden Research Center, Mailstop K13/D1, 650 Harry Road, San Jose, CA 95120-6099, USA (office). *Telephone:* (408) 927-2027 (office). *Fax:* (408) 927-2100 (office). *E-mail:* rugar@almaden.ibm.com (office). *Website:* almaden.ibm.com (office).

RUGARLI, Giampaolo; Italian writer; b. 5 Dec. 1932, Naples; s. of Mirko Rugarli and Rubina De Marco; m. Maria Pulci 1985; three c.; ed legal studies; bank dir since 1972; dir of Cariplo 1981–85; contrib. to Messaggero and Corriere della Sera and other reviews; Premio Bagutta Opera Prima 1987, Premio Capri 1990, Premio Selezione Campiello. *Publications:* Il Superlativo assoluto, La troga, Il nido di ghiaccio, Diario di un uomo a disagio, Andromeda e la notte, L'orrore che mi hai dato 1987, Una montagna australiana 1992, Per i pesci non è un problema 1992, I camini delle fate 1993, Il manuale del romanziere (The Novelist's Handbook) 1993, L'infinito, forse 1995, Una gardenia nei capelli 1997, Il brano dei crepuscoli (Leopardi) 1998, La Viaggiatrice del tram numero 4 2001, Il Cavaliere e la vendita della saggezza 2002, La mia Milano 2003, I giardini incantati 2005, La luna di Malcontenta 2006, Il buio di notte 2008, La galassie lontane 2010, La patria delle mezzecalzette 2010, Un bacio e l'oblio 2011, Il battello smarrito 2012. *Leisure interest:* gardening. *Address:* Via Colle di Giano 62, Olevano Romano 00035, Italy. *Telephone:* (06) 9564518.

RUGGIERO, Riccardo; Italian telecommunications industry executive; *Managing Director, Executive Director and Member of Strategy Committee, Telecom Italia SpA;* b. 26 Aug. 1960, Naples; s. of Renato Ruggiero; Sales Man. Fininvest SpA 1986–88; Sales and Marketing Man. AT&T Italia 1988–90; Asst to CEO, Olivetti Group 1990, Vice-Pres. Int. Customers and Communications Sales Devt 1992–94, Vice-Pres. Telemedia Sales and Marketing Devt 1994–96, CEO Infostrada (subsidiary co.) 1996–2001, also CEO Italia On Line 1996–99; joined Telecom Italia Group 2001, Head, Telecom France Business Unit 2001, CEO Telecom Italia Domestic Wireline Business Unit 2001–02, CEO Telecom Italia SpA 2002–07, CEO of Operations 2005, currently Man. Dir, Exec. Dir and Mem. of Strategy Cttee; mem. Bd of Dirs Societa Azionaria Fabbrica Italiana Lavorazione Occhiali SpA 2005–. *Address:* Telecom Italia SpA, Corso d'Italia 41, 00198 Rome, Italy (office). *Telephone:* (6) 3688-2840 (office). *Fax:* (6) 3688-2803 (office). *Website:* www.telecomitalia.com (office).

RUGOFF, Ralph; American art critic and gallery director; *Director, Hayward Gallery;* b. 1957, New York; fmr research fellow, Goldsmiths Coll., London; fmr Pew Arts Journalism Fellow, Columbia Univ., New York; started curating career after presenting lecture on "the pathetic in art", followed by Just Pathetic exhbn, Los Angeles 1991; Dir CCA Wattis Inst., San Francisco 2000–06; Curatorial Adviser to Sydney Biennale 2002; Dir Hayward Gallery, London 2006–; Ordway Prize 2005. *Publications include:* numerous monographs; Art of Susan Rios 1988, Circus Americanus 1995, Transformers 1995, Gallaccio Anya: Chasing Rainbows 1999, Great Illusions 1999, The Greenhouse Effect 2000, Baja to Vancouver: The West Coast and Contemporary Art (with Douglas Coupland) 2003, Monuments for

the USA 2005, Scene of the Crime, At the Threshold of the Visible, The Painting of Modern Life: 1960s to Now 2008, Amateurs 2008. *Address:* The Hayward Gallery, Southbank Centre, Belvedere Road, London, SE1 8XX, England (office). *Telephone:* (20) 7960-4200 (office). *Website:* www.southbankcentre.co.uk/venues/hayward-gallery (office).

RUGUNDA, Ruhakana; Ugandan physician, politician and diplomatist; *Minister of Health;* b. 7 Nov. 1947, Kabale Dist; s. of Surumani Rugunda; m. Jocelyn Rugunda; ed Kigezi High School, Busoga Coll. (Head Prefect), Makerere Univ. Medical School, Univ. of Zambia, Univ. of California, Berkeley, USA; worked as Medical Officer in Zambia, as a physician at DC Gen. Hosp., Washington, DC and at Kenyatta Nat. Hosp., Nairobi, Kenya; served as Pres. Nat. Union of Students of Uganda; mem. Uganda People's Congress; involved with Ugandan Nat. Resistance Movt (NRM) mid-1980s; fmr Minister of Internal Affairs, of Foreign Affairs, of Information, of Works, Transport and Communication; Minister of Information and Communication Technology 2011–13, of Health 2013–; fmr Commr for Animal Industry, Game and Fisheries; fmr Chair. NRM Electoral Comm.; fmr mem. of Parl. for Kabale Municipality; fmr Pres. Governing Council UNEP; led Ugandan Govt negotiating team to Juba, Sudan to hold peace talks with Lord's Resistance Army July 2006; elevated to cabinet ministerial level and apptd Amb. and Perm. Rep. to UN, New York 2009–11, Pres. UN Security Council July 2009. *Leisure interests:* reading, playing tennis, chess. *Address:* Ministry of Health, Plot 6, Lourdel Road, Nakasero, POB 7272, Kampala, Uganda (office). *Telephone:* (41) 4340874 (office). *Fax:* (41) 4231584 (office). *E-mail:* info@health.go.ug (office). *Website:* www.health.go.ug (office).

RÜHE, Volker; German politician; b. 25 Sept. 1942, Hamburg; m. Anne Rühe 1968; two s. one d.; ed Univ. of Hamburg; fmr teacher; mem. Hamburg City Council 1970–76; mem. Bundestag 1976–2005, Chair. Foreign Policy Cttee 2002; Deputy Chair. CDU/CSU Parl. Group 1982–89, 1998; Sec. Gen. CDU 1989–92, Deputy Party Leader 1998–2002; Minister of Defence 1992–98; Adviser, Cerberus Deutschland Beteiligungsberatung GmbH (private equity co.). *Address:* c/o Cerberus Deutschland Beteiligungsberatung GmbH, Bockenheimer Landstr. 2-4, 60323 Frankfurt, Germany (office).

RUHUL AMIN, M. M., LLB, MA; Bangladeshi judge; b. 23 Dec. 1942, Laxmipur; ed Dhaka Univ., Nat. Judicial Coll., USA; began career as asst judge in fmr East Pakistan, promoted to dist judge 1984, served courts in Chittagong, Cox's Bazar, Kishoreganj and Jessore, visited several US courts to learn about alternative dispute resolution and court admin 1990, apptd High Court Judge 1994, visited Sri Lanka, India and Nepal to learn about their judicial services and salary structure of judges; Judge, Sr Appellate Div., Supreme Court of Bangladesh 2003–08; Chair. Judicial Service Comm. 2004–08; Chief Justice of Bangladesh 2008–10. *Address:* c/o Supreme Court of Bangladesh, Ramna, Dhaka 1000, Bangladesh. *E-mail:* supremec@bdcom.com.

RUI, Xiaowu, BA, MA; Chinese business executive; *Chairman, China Electronics Corporation;* b. 1959; ed Nat. Univ. of Defence Tech., 710 Inst. of Ministry of Space Industry; qualified in computer-aided design as researcher from 710 Inst. of Ministry of Space Industry 1985; held several posts, including Deputy Dir and Dir 710 Inst. of China Aerospace Science and Tech. Corpn (CASC), Business Asst of Pres. and Dir of Planning and Operation Dept, mem. Party Leadership Group, Pres. Asst and Vice-Pres. of CASC, also Pres. and Sec. Party Cttee of China Satellite Communications Co. Ltd; also Chair. China Spacesat Co. Ltd, Beijing NavInfo Science and Technology Co. Ltd, China Aerospace Int. Holdings Ltd, CASIL Telecommunications Holdings Ltd, APT Satellite Holdings Ltd; Chair. China Electronics Corpn 2011–, Sec. Party Leadership Group; winner Special Govt Allowance from the State Council 1986. *Address:* China Electronics Corporation, 27 Wanshou Road, Haidian District, Beijing 100846, People's Republic of China (office). *Telephone:* (10) 68218529 (office). *Fax:* (10) 68213745 (office). *E-mail:* webmaster@cec.com.cn (office). *Website:* www.cec.com.cn (office).

RUIA, Shashi; Indian business executive; *Chairman, Essar Group;* b. 1944, Mumbai; s. of Nand Kishore Ruia; m.; two c.; Co-founder (with brother Ravi), Essar Group, currently Chair.; fmr Pres. Indian Nat. Shipowners Asscn; fmr Chair. Indo-US Jt Business Council; fmr mem. Man. Cttee, Fed. of Indian Chambers of Commerce and Industry; Business India Businessman of the Year Award 2010. *Address:* Essar Group, Essar House, 11 Keshavrao Khadye Marg, Mahalaxmi, Mumbai, 400 034, Maharashtra, India (office). *Telephone:* (22) 50011100 (office). (22) 66601100 (office). *Fax:* (22) 66601809 (office). *E-mail:* corporatecommunications@essar.com (office). *Website:* www.essar.com (office).

RUIJGH, Cornelis Jord, DPhil; Dutch academic; *Professor Emeritus of Ancient Greek Language, University of Amsterdam;* b. 28 Nov. 1930, Amsterdam; s. of Jord Ruijgh and Trijntje Swart; ed Univ. of Amsterdam and Ecole Pratique des Hautes Etudes, Paris; Asst in Greek Philology, Univ. of Amsterdam 1954–66, Lecturer in Ancient Greek Language 1966–69, Prof. of Ancient Greek Language, Dialectology and Mycenology 1969–95, Prof. Emer. 1995–; mem. Royal Netherlands Acad., Int. Perm. Cttee of Mycenaean Studies 1970–; Prix Zographos 1957, Michael Ventris Memorial Award 1968. *Publications:* L'élément achéen dans la langue épique, 1957, Etudes sur la grammaire et le vocabulaire du grec mycénien 1967, Autour de 'te épique' 1971, Scripta Minora I 1991, Scripta Minora II 1996 etc. *Leisure interest:* music. *Address:* Keizersgracht 800, 1017 ED Amsterdam, Netherlands. *Telephone:* (20) 6247995.

RUING, Puri; Papua New Guinea politician; *Minister for Civil Aviation;* fmr police officer; mem. Nat. Parl. for Dei Open electorate 1997–2002, 2007–; Vice-Minister for Treasury and Finance 1999, Minister for Justice 2000, Minister of Internal Security Dec. 2010, Minister for Civil Aviation 2011–; fmr mem. People's Democratic Movement, Papua New Guinea Party; mem. United Resource Party 2010–. *Address:* Department of Transport and Civil Aviation POB 1489, Port Moresby, Papua New Guinea (office). *Telephone:* 3222580 (office). *Fax:* 3200236 (office).

RUINI, HE Cardinal Camillo; Italian ecclesiastic; *Vicar General Emeritus of Rome;* b. 19 Feb. 1931, Sassuolo; ed Pontifical Gregorian Univ. and Almo Collegio Capranica, Rome, Italy; ordained priest 1954; returned to Reggio Emilia and taught philosophy at diocesan seminary until 1968; taught dogmatic theology at Studio Teologico Interdiocesano di Modena-Reggio-Emilia-Carpi-Guastalla

1968–86, Headmaster 1968–77; taught dogmatic theology at Studio Teologico Accademico Bolognese 1977–83; Chaplain to Catholic Univ. grads 1958–66; Del. for Catholic Action 1966–70; Pres. John XXIII Diocesan Cultural Centre 1968; Auxiliary Bishop of Reggio Emilia and Guastalla and Titular Bishop of Nepte 1983; Vice-Pres. Preparatory Cttee, Ecclesial Convention of Lorreto 1985; elected mem. Bishops' Comm. for Catholic Educ., Culture and School 1985; Sec.-Gen. Italian Episcopal Conf. 1986, Pres. 1991–2007; currently Vicar Gen. Emer. of Rome; mem. Cen. Cttee for Marian Year 1987–88; Consultor, Congregation for Bishops 1988–; elected mem. Council of Gen. Secr., 8th Gen. Ass. of Synod of Bishops 1990; Archbishop and Pro-Vicar Gen. of Pope for Diocese of Rome 1991, Vicar Gen. and Archpriest of Patriarchal Lateran Basilica, Grand Chancellor Pontifical Lateran Univ. and Pres. Emer. Peregrinatio ad Petri Sedem 1991–; Relator for Special Ass. for Europe of Synod of Bishops, Vatican City 1991; cr. Cardinal (Cardinal Priest of S. Agnese fuori le mura) 1991; mem. Cttee of the Great Jubilee of the Year 2000. *Publications:* has published many essays and research work since 1971. *Address:* Viale Vaticano 42, 00165 Roma, Italy (office). *Telephone:* (06) 6988-2509 (office). *Fax:* (06) 6988-2153 (office). *E-mail:* camillo.ruini@vicariatusurbis.org (office). *Website:* www.vatican.va (office).

RUITENBERG, Elis Joost, DVM, PhD; Dutch professor of immunology; b. 24 May 1937, Amersfoort; s. of E J. Ruitenberg and D. H. van Mechelen; m. Christiane Friederike Ambagtsheer 1963; three d.; ed Univ. of Utrecht; veterinarian, Lab. Zoonoses, Nat. Inst. of Public Health, Bilthoven 1964, Head Pathology Lab. 1970–86, Dir Div. of Immunology 1979, Vaccine Production 1980–86, Dir Div. of Microbiology and Immunology, Nat. Inst. of Public and Environmental Protection, Bilthoven 1984, Deputy Dir-Gen. –1986; Prof. of Veterinary Immunology, Univ. of Utrecht 1984, now Prof. Emer.; Gen. and Scientific Dir Sanquin Blood Supply Foundation (CLB) 1989–2001; Prof. of Int. Healthcare, Vrije Universiteit, Amsterdam 2001–; Chair. Netherlands-Vietnam Medical Cttee 1998–; mem. Non-exec. Bd AGLAIA BioMedical Ventures B.V.; Visiting Prof., Nat. School of Public Health, Madrid, Spain 1987; retd, mem. numerous advisory cttees including Advisory Council for Devt Research, Advisory Bd Royal Numico N.V.; mem. Royal Netherlands Acad. of Arts and Sciences; Schimmel Viruly Award 1976, Annual Award, Nat. Journal of Veterinary Medicine 1977, Award Medical Acad., Poznan, Poland, Kt, Order of Netherlands Lion 1988, Schornagel Award 1996. *Publications include:* Anisakiasis, Pathogenesis, Diagnosis and Prevention 1970, Preventive Screening of Adults (with D.A.T. Griffiths) 1987, Statistical Analysis and Mathematical Modelling of AIDS (with J.C. Jager) 1988, AIDS Impact Assessment Modelling and Scenario Analysis (with J.C. Jager) 1992; numerous articles on immunology, vaccinology, pathology and parasitology. *Leisure interests:* European languages, history, cycling. *Address:* c/o Non-Executive Board, AGLAIA BioMedical Ventures B.V., Professor Bronkhorstlaan 10-XI, 3723 MB Bilthoven, Netherlands. *Telephone:* (30) 2296090. *Fax:* (30) 2296099. *E-mail:* info@aglaia -biomedical.com. *Website:* www.aglaia-biomedical.com.

RUIZ, Gisel, BS; American business executive; *Executive Vice-President and Chief Operating Officer,* of Walmart US; ed Santa Clara Univ.; began career at Walmart as store man. trainee 1992, held a variety of leadership positions in store operations, labour relations and human resources, Vice-Pres. and Regional Gen. Man. in Field Operations Div. 2006–08, responsible for 150 Walmart stores in western Texas and New Mexico, Sr Vice-Pres., Walmart People 2008–10, Exec. Vice-Pres., People, Walmart US 2010–12, Exec. Vice-Pres. and COO Walmart US 2012–; recognized by the Minority Enterprise Exec. Council as one of the Top 25 Powerful Minority Women in Business 2008, Walmart Leadership Award 2008, chosen by Hispanic Business Magazine as one of the Top 25 Business Women 2009, honoured by Latina Style as 2010 Latina Exec. of the Year 2011, ranked by Fortune magazine amongst the 50 Most Powerful Women in Business in the US (21st) 2012. *Address:* Walmart, 702 SW 8th Street, Bentonville, AR 72716-8611, USA (office). *Telephone:* (479) 273-4000 (office). *Fax:* (479) 277-1830 (office). *E-mail:* info@walmartstores.com (office). *Website:* walmartstores.com (office).

RUIZ, Hector de Jesus, BEng, MEng, DEng, PhD; Mexican business executive; b. 25 Dec. 1945, Piedras Negras, Coahuila; m. 1st (deceased); one s.; m. 2nd Judy Ruiz; two step-c.; ed Univ. of Texas, Rice Univ., USA; held various positions with Texas Instruments; fmr Pres. Semiconductor Products Sector, Motorola; COO and Pres. Advanced Micro Devices (AMD), Inc. 2000–02, CEO 2002–08, Chair. 2004–08; Chair. Spansion Inc.; Chair. GlobalFoundries 2009–10; currently Chair. and CEO Advanced Nanotechnology Solutions, Inc.; Co-founder and CEO Bull Ventures (consultancy) 2011–; Board Advisor, EDCO Ventures 2010–; mem. Bd of Dirs, Eastman Kodak Co., Semiconductor Industry Asscn; mem. Bd of Trustees Rice Univ., RAND Corpn; fmr mem. Pres.'s Council of Advisors for Science and Tech.; mem. Hispanic Professional Engineers; Fellow, Int. Eng Consortium 2002–; Hispanic Engineer Nat. Awards Conference Hall of Fame 2000, CEO of the Year, Electronic Business 2005, Exec. of the Year, EE Times 2005, Semico Bellwether Award 2009. *Address:* Bull Ventures, LLC, 601 Van Ness Avenue, Suite E603, San Francisco, CA 94102, USA (office). *Telephone:* (415) 373-0197 (office). *E-mail:* info@ bullventuresllc.com (office). *Website:* bullventuresllc.com (office).

RUIZ-GALLARDÓN JÍMENEZ, Alberto; Spanish lawyer and politician; *Minister of Justice;* b. 11 Dec. 1958, Madrid; s. of José María Ruiz-Gallardón; m. María del Mar Utrera; four s.; ed Complutense Univ., Madrid, San Pablo CEU Univ.; began career in prov. courts in Málaga; elected to Madrid City Council 1983; mem. Partido Popular Exec. 1986; elected as mem. Regional Parl. for Autonomous Community of Madrid 1987, spokesperson in the Senate for Partido Popular parl. group 1987–95; Pres. Community of Madrid 1995–2003; Mayor of Madrid 2003–11; Minister of Justice 2011–; mem. Partido Popular. *Address:* Ministry of Justice, San Bernardo 45, 28015 Madrid, Spain (office). *Telephone:* (91) 3904500 (office). *Fax:* (91) 3902244 (office). *E-mail:* prensa@mjusticia.es (office). *Website:* www.mjusticia .es (office).

RUIZ GUINAZU, Magdalena; Argentine journalist; b. 13 Feb. 1935, Buenos Aires; four c.; fmr mem. Comision Nacional por la desaparicion de Personas (Nat. Comm. on the Disappearance of People); currently host Magdalena Tempranisimo, Radio Continental and La vuelta con Magdalena (Back with Magdalena) 2002–; columnist, La Nación and Pagina 12 newspapers; Co-founder and fmr Pres. Asociación para la Defensa del Periodismo Independiente (Asociación Periodistas) (press freedom org.); Officer, Legion d'Honneur, Order of Merit (Italy); Martin Fierro de Oro (Gold Martin Fierro Award) for Lifetime Achievement 1994, Int.

Women's Media Foundation Lifetime Achievement Award 2003, Diamond Konex, Communication-Journalism 2007. *Publications include:* Huésped de un verano 1994, Había una vez...la vida 1995, Qué mundo nos ha tocado! (with Father Rafael Braun) 2001, Historias de hombres, mujeres y jazmines 2002. *Address:* c/o Asociación Periodistas, Piedras 1675 Oficina B, Secretaría de Derechos, 1140 Buenos Aires, Argentina. *E-mail:* magdalena@continental.com.ar (office). *Website:* www.continental.com.ar; www.magdalenatempranisimo.blogspot.com.

RUIZ MARMOLEJO, Francisco José; Colombian anthropologist and international organization official; b. Cali; ed Nat. Univ. of Colombia, Fed. Univ. of Pará, Brazil, Univ. of Las Palmas, Gran Canaria; previous posts include Environmental Del. Comptroller, Colombia, Chair. Technological Transfer Nat. Program (Pronatta), mem. Panel of Experts on the Amazon, Co-Dir Ecofondo (org. of environmental NGOs); Exec. Dir Amazon Cooperation Treaty Org. (Organización del Tratado de Cooperación Amazónica) 2003, Acting Sec.-Gen. 2007–09. *Address:* Amazon Cooperation Treaty Organization, SHIS–QI 05, Conjunto 16, casa 21, Lago Sul, Brasília, DF 71615-160, Brazil (office). *Telephone:* (61) 3248-4119 (office). *Fax:* (61) 3248-4238 (office). *E-mail:* fjruiz@otca.org.br (office). *Website:* www.otca.org.br (office).

RUIZ MATEOS, Gerardo; Mexican business executive and politician; ed Instituto Tecnológico de Estudios Superiores de Monterrey; Dir Gen. Automotive Moulding Mexico (now Linde Pullman Mexico) 1989–; Pres. Mexican Foundation for Rural Devt 1995; mem. Nat. Action Party 1995–, Exec. Sec. Nat. Exec. Cttee 1996–98, mem. Cttee 2002–05; Pres. Surveillance Comm., Nat. Council 2001–02; Admin and Finance Coordinator, Felipe Calderón's Presidential Campaign 2005–06; Coordinator of Cabinets and Special Projects of the Pres.'s Office 2006–08; Sec. of the Economy 2008–10; mem. Council of the Social Union of Mexican Businessmen 1996–2000, Pres. 2000. *Address:* c/o Secretariat of State for the Economy, Alfonso Reyes 30, Col. Hipódromo Condesa, 06170 Mexico City, Mexico (office).

RUKAVISHNIKOV, Aleksander Yulianovich; Russian sculptor; b. 2 July 1950, Moscow; s. of Yulian Rukavishnikov and of Anagelina Filippova; m. Olga Mikhailovna Rukavishnikova; one s.; ed Surikov Moscow State Inst. of Arts; freelance artist; Prof., Surikov Inst.; mem. Presidium, Russian Acad. of Fine Arts; mem. Union of Artists; People's Artist of the Russian Fed. *Major works include:* portraits: Feofan Grek 1977, Sergey of Radonezh 1981, Dmitry Donskoy 1982, Aleksander Peresvet 1983, John Lennon 1982, Tamara Bykova 1983; Vladimir Vysotsky memorial; installation Intrusion 1988; Tatishchev monument, Togliatti 1997; Dostoyevsky statue 1997, Nikulin monument 2000. *Address:* Bolshaya Molchanovka str. 10, Moscow (office); Granatny per. 11, Apt 30, 103001 Moscow, Russia (home). *Telephone:* (495) 290-67-60 (office); (495) 291-05-52 (home). *Fax:* (495) 291-01-52 (home).

RUKINGAMA, Luc, PhD; Burundian academic, UNESCO official and fmr politician; *Regional Director to Southern Africa Region and to South African Development Community (SADC) Secretariat, United Nations Educational, Scientific and Cultural Organization (UNESCO);* b. 23 Dec. 1952, Kiremba; m. Thérèse Niyonzima; two s. two d.; ed Univ. of the Sorbonne, Paris; mem. Parl.; fmr Minister for Higher Educ., for Cooperation, for Foreign Affairs and Cooperation; Minister of Communication and Govt Spokesman 2000–01; stakeholder in Burundian peace process 1994–2004; fmr Co-Pres. Union pour le Progrès National (UPRONA); Sr Programme Specialist and Chief of Higher Educ. Unit, UNESCO/ BREDA (Regional Bureau for Educ. in Africa) –2008; UNESCO Dir and Rep. to Ethiopia 2008–10, UNESCO Rep. to Zimbabwe, Malawi, Botswana, Zambia and to SADC 2010–13, Regional Dir to Southern Africa Region and to SADC Secr. 2013–; Chevalier, Ordre des Palmes académiques, Medaille de l'Unité Nationale; UNESCO Medal. *Publications:* Voyage au Congo d'André Gide ou la stéréotype au cœur de l'image 1995, Intahe et la gestion de la cité, Société colonisée et écriture romanesque, Migration et diversité: le cas de l'Afrique (conf., Univ. of Sherbrooke 2011); numerous articles. *Leisure interests:* reading, sport, music. *Address:* UNESCO Cluster Office, 8 Kenilworth Road, PO Box HG 435, Newlands, Harare, Zimbabwe (office); Avenue de Juillet 4, Kiriri, PO Box 704, Bujumbura, Burundi (home). *Telephone:* (4) 788312 (office); 77-2232779 (Zimbabwe, mobile). *Fax:* (4) 776055 (office); 226561 (home). *E-mail:* l.rukingama@unesco.org (office). *Website:* www.hahare.unesco.org.

RULI, Genc, DEcon; Albanian economist, academic and politician; *Minister of Agriculture, Food and Consumer Protection;* b. 4 Nov. 1958; m.; ed Univ. of Tirana; Lecturer in Econs, Univ. of Tirana 1982–90, Prof. of Finance and Accounting 1996–; Minister of Finance June-Dec. 1991, of Finance and the Economy 1992–93, of Economy, Trade and Energy 2007–09, of Agriculture, Food and Consumer Protection 2009–; Deputy, People's Ass. for Tirana 1991, for Gjirokaster 1992–96, Chair. Perm. Parl. Comm. for Finance and Economy 1994–96; Chair. Bd of Govs Albanian Inst. of Insurance 1992–; Chair. Inst. for Contemporary Science 1996–2005; mem. Democratic Party of Albania. *Address:* Ministry of Agriculture, Food and Consumer Protection, Bulevardi Dëshmorët e Kombit 2, Tirana, Albania (office). *Telephone:* (4) 2230851 (office). *Fax:* (4) 2230851 (office). *E-mail:* altin.telo@ mbu.gov.al (office). *Website:* www.mbumk.gov.al (office).

RUMHI, Muhammad bin Hamad bin Saif al-; Omani petroleum engineer and government official; *Minister of Oil and Gas;* fmr Prof. of Petroleum Eng., Sultan Qaboos Univ.; Minister of Oil and Gas 1997; Chair. Petroleum Devt Oman 2003–. *Address:* Ministry of Oil and Gas, POB 551, Muscat 113 (office); Petroleum Development Oman (PDO), Bait Saih Maleh Building, Mina Al Sahel Street, PO Box 81, 113 Muscat, Oman (office). *Telephone:* 24603333 (Ministry) (office); 24678111 (PDO) (office). *Fax:* 2469672 (Ministry) (office); 24677106 (PDO) (office). *E-mail:* external-affairs@pdo.co.om (office). *Website:* www.mog.gov.om (office); www.pdo.co.om (home).

RUML, Jan; Czech journalist and fmr politician; b. 5 March 1953, Prague; s. of Jiří Ruml; m. Marie Ruml; two s.; ed grammar school, Prague, Faculty of Law, Univ. of Plzeň; stoker, woodcutter, hosp. technician, mechanic, bookseller, cattle-minder; signed Charter 77, Feb. 1977; freelance journalist 1977–79; mem. Cttee for Protection of the Unjustly Persecuted 1979–89; in custody, indicted for subversive activities 1981–82; co-founder Lidové noviny (monthly samizdat) 1988–90; spokesman of Charter 77 1990; First Deputy Minister of Interior of CSFR 1990–91; Deputy Minister of Interior 1991–92; mem. Civic Democratic Party

(ODS) 1992–97; Deputy to House of Nations, Fed. Ass. June–Dec. 1992; Minister of Interior of Czech Repub. 1992–97; mem. Interdepartmental Anti-drug Comm. 1993–97, Comm. for Prevention of Crime 1994–97; mem. of Parl. 1996–98, Senator 1998–2004, Vice-Pres. of Senate (Parl.) 2000–04; Gen Man Secar Bohemia 2010–; Founder Freedom Union (US), Chair. 1998–99; Chair. Olympic Watch; Hon. Medal of the French Nat. Police 1992. *Films:* Hledání Pevného Bodu (Looking for a Stable Point). *Publication:* (with Jana Klusáková) What Was, Is and Will Be (in Czech). *Address:* Secar Bohemia, Londýnská 48, 12000 Prague 2, Czech Republic (office). *Telephone:* 513- 111 (office). *Website:* www.janruml.cz.

RUMMEL, Reinhard Franz, DrIng; German scientist and academic; *Carl von Linde Senior Fellow, Institute for Advanced Study, Technical University of Munich;* b. 3 Dec. 1945, Landshut; m. Renate Schophaus 1970; one s. one d.; ed Hans Leinberger Gymnasium, Technical Univ. of Munich, Technische Hochschule, Darmstadt; Research Assoc. Dept of Geodetic Science, Ohio State Univ., Columbus, Ohio 1974–76; scientist, German Geodetic Research Inst. and Bavarian Acad. of Science, Munich 1976–80; Prof. of Physical Geodesy, Faculty of Geodetic Eng, Delft Univ. of Tech. 1980–93; Prof., Institut für Astronomische and Physikalische Geodäsie, Technical Univ. of Munich 1993–2011, Carl von Linde Sr Fellow, Inst. for Advanced Study 2011–; mem. Netherlands Acad. of Science, Bavarian Acad. of Sciences and Humanities, German Acad. of Sciences Leopoldina; Fellow, American Geophysical Union; Bavarian Order of Merit; Dr hc (Bonn), (Tech. Univ. of Graz); Speuerwerkpreis, KIVI, Netherlands 1987, Vening Meinesz Medal, European Geophysical Union. *Publications:* Zur Behandlung von Zufallsfunktionen and -folgen in der physikalischen Geodäsie 1975, Geodesy's Contribution to Geophysics 1984, Satellite Gradiometry 1986, Encyclopedia of Earth System Science, Vol. II (on geodesy) 1992; articles in professional journals. *Address:* Institut für Astronomische and Physikalische Geodäsie, Room 3610, Technische Universität München, Arcisstrasse 21, 80290 Munich, Germany (office). *Telephone:* (89) 28923189 (office). *Fax:* (89) 28923178 (office). *E-mail:* rummel@bv.tum.de (office). *Website:* www.iapg.bv.tum.de/iapg.html (office).

RUMSFELD, Donald H., BA; American business executive, fmr politician and fmr government official; b. 9 July 1932, Chicago; s. of George Rumsfield and Jeannette Rumsfeld (née Husted); m. Joyce Pierson 1954; one s. two d.; ed New Trier High School, Ill., Princeton Univ.; aviator, USN 1954–57; Admin. Asst, House of Reps 1957–59; investment broker, A. G. Becker & Co., Chicago 1960–62; mem. 88th–91st Congresses; Republican; Asst to Pres. and Dir Office of Econ. Opportunity 1969–70; Dir Econ. Stabilization Program, Counsellor to Pres. 1971–72; Amb. to NATO, Brussels 1973–74; White House Chief of Staff 1974–75; Sec. of Defense 1975–77, 2001–06; Pres., CEO then Chair. G. D. Searle and Co., Skokie, Ill. 1977–85; Sr Advisor, William Blair and Co. 1985–90; Chair. and CEO General Instrument Corpn 1990–93; Chair. Gilead Sciences, Inc. 1997–2000; Pres.'s Special Middle East Envoy 1983–84; Chair. Eisenhower Exchange Fellowships 1986–93; US Ballistic Missile Threat Comm. 1998–99; mem. Presidential Advisory Cttee on Arms Control 1982–86, Nat. Econ. Comm. 1988–89, Trade Deficit Review Cttee, US Comm. to Assess Nat. Security, Space Man. and Org. 2000–01; Distinguished Visiting Fellow, Hoover Inst., Stanford Univ. 2007–08; f. Rumsfeld Foundation 2007; 11 hon. degrees; Presidential Medal of Freedom 1977, Woodrow Wilson Award 1985, Outstanding Pharmaceutical CEO 1980, Eisenhower Medal 1993, Statesmanship Award, Claremont Inst. 2007 and many other awards. *Publication:* Known and Unknown (memoirs) 2011. *Leisure interests:* skiing, squash, ranching, reading. *Address:* c/o Hall & Hall, 924 Stoneridge Drive, Suite 2, Bozeman, MT 59718, USA (office).

RUMYANTSEV, Aleksandr Yu., Dr Phys., Math., Sciences; Russian physicist and diplomatist; *Ambassador to Finland;* b. 26 July 1945, Kushka, Turkmenistan; m.; one d.; ed Moscow Inst. of Physics and Eng; trained as engineer; Jr, then Sr Researcher, Head of Div., Dir of Scientific Devt, Russian Scientific Centre, Kurchatov Inst. of Atomic Energy 1969–94, Dir 1994–2001; Minister of Atomic Energy of the Russian Fed. 2001–04; Head of Fed. Agency for Atomic Energy 2004–05; Amb. to Finland 2006–; Prof., Moscow Inst. of Physics and Eng; Chair. Bd of Trustees, Global Energy Int. Prize 2005–; mem. Bd of Dirs Nuclear Soc. of the Russian Fed.; mem. Russian Acad. of Sciences (Corresp. mem. 1997–2000); Order of Honour 2001; USSR State Prize 1986. *Publications:* more than 100 scientific papers in professional journals on new methods of solid-state physics studies by means of stationary nuclear reactors. *Address:* Embassy of Russia, Tehtaankatu 1B, 00140 Helsinki, Finland (office). *Telephone:* (9) 661876 (office). *Fax:* (9) 661006 (office). *E-mail:* rusembassy@co.inet.fi (office). *Website:* www.rusembassy.fi (office).

RUNDGREN, Todd; American singer, songwriter, musician (guitar) and record producer; b. 22 June 1948, Philadelphia, Pa; mem. Woody's Truck Stop; Founder-mem. The Nazz 1967–70; solo recording artist 1970–; formed progressive rock group Utopia 1974–. *Recordings include:* albums: with The Nazz: Nazz 1968, Nazz Nazz 1969, Nazz III 1970; with Utopia: Todd Rundgren's Utopia 1974, Another Live 1975, Ra 1977, Oops! Wrong Planet 1977, Adventures In Utopia 1980, Deface The Music 1980, Swing To The Right 1982, Utopia 1982, Oblivion 1984; solo: Runt 1970, The Ballad of Todd Rundgren 1971, Something / Anything? 1972, A Wizard, A True Star 1973, Todd 1974, Initiation 1975, Faithful 1976, Hermit of Mink Hollow 1978, Back To The Bars 1978, Healing 1981, The Ever Popular Tortured Artist Effect 1983, A Cappella 1985, POV 1985, Anthology – Todd Rundgren 1988, Nearly Human 1989, Second Wind 1991, No World Order 1993, No World Order Lite 1994, The Individualist 1995, With a Twist 1997, Up Against It 1998, Live in Chicago 1991 1999, One Long Year 2000, Liars 2004, Arena 2008, (re)Production 2011, State 2013; record producer, Bat Out of Hell, Meat Loaf 1977; also producer/engineer, recordings by New York Dolls, Grand Funk Railroad, Hall and Oates, XTC, The Band. *Website:* www.tr-i.com.

RUNDQUIST, Dmitri Vasilyevich; Russian geologist and mineralogist; b. 10 Aug. 1930; m.; two d.; ed Leningrad Inst. of Mines; jr, then sr researcher, Deputy Dir All-Union Research Inst. of Geology 1954–84; Dir Inst. of Geology and Geochronology Russian Acad. of Sciences 1984–90, Head of Lab. 1990–; Corresp. mem. USSR (now Russian) Acad. of Sciences 1984, mem. 1990, Acad.-Sec. Dept of Geology, Geophysics, Geochemistry and Mining Sciences 1996–2002; research in mineralogy, petrography, developed theory on laws of mineral deposit location; USSR State Prize, Merited Geologist of Russian Fed., Demidov's Prize 2010. *Publications include:* Greisen Deposits 1971, Zones of Endogenic Mineral Deposits

1975, Precambrian Geology 1988, Largest Mineral Deposits of the World 2006. *Address:* Vernadsky State Geological Museum, Morkhovaya 11, 103009 Moscow, Russia. *Telephone:* (495) 629-77-03.

RUOSLAHTI, Erkki, MD, PhD; Finnish medical scientist and academic; *Distinguished Professor, The Sanford Burnham Medical Research Institute;* b. 16 Feb. 1940, Puumala; ed Univ. of Helsinki, California Inst. of Tech.; various appts Univ. of Helsinki, Univ. of Turku, City of Hope Nat. Medical Center, Duarte, Calif., USA; joined The Burnham Inst. for Medical Research (now The Sanford Burnham Medical Research Inst.) 1979, Pres. and CEO 1989–2002, Distinguished Prof. 2002–; Adjunct Distinguished Prof., Dept of Molecular, Cellular and Developmental Biology, Univ. of California, San Diego 2006– (after establishment of programme affiliation with Burnham); mem. NAS, Inst. of Medicine, American Acad. of Arts and Sciences, European Molecular Biology Org., Finnish Acad. of Sciences; Nobel Fellow, Karolinska Inst., Stockholm; title of Academician granted by the Pres. of Finland 2009; Kt, Order of the White Rose of Finland; Commdr, Order of the Lion of Finland 2010; Hon. MD (Lund, Sweden); Gairdner Foundation Int. Award, G.H.A. Clowes Award, American Asscn for Cancer Research, Robert J. and Claire Pasarow Foundation Award, Jacobaeus Int. Prize, Jubilee Award British Biochemical Soc., Japan Prize in Cell Biology (jtly), Science and Tech. Foundation of Japan 2005, Thomson Reuters Citation Laureate 2012. *Publications:* numerous articles and essays in professional journals. *Address:* The Sanford Burnham Medical Research Institute, 10901 North Torrey Pines Road, La Jolla, CA 92037, USA (office). *Telephone:* (805) 646-3101 (office). *Fax:* (805) 795-5323 (home). *E-mail:* ruoslahti@burnham.org (office). *Website:* www.sanfordburnham .org (office).

RUOZI, Roberto; Italian economist, academic and business executive; *Chairman, Gruppo Mediolanum SpA;* Dean of L. Bocconi Univ. 1995–2000, Prof. of Econs of Financial Intermediaries –2002, now Prof. Emer.; Prof. at Univs of Ancona, Siena, Parma, Paris (Sorbonne) and Milan Politecnico; Chair. Gruppo Mediolanum SpA, Palladio Finanziaria SpA, Touring Club Italiano, Retelit SpA; Chair. Bd of Statutory Auditors, Borsa Italiana SpA; mem. Bd of Dirs Gewiss SpA, Cerruti Tessile SpA. *Publications:* numerous publs on banking and finance. *Address:* Mediolanum SpA, Palazzo Meucci, Via Francesco Sforza 15, 20080 Basiglio Milan 3, Italy (office). *Telephone:* (02) 90491 (office). *Fax:* (02) 90493434 (office). *E-mail:* info@mediolanum.it (office). *Website:* www.mediolanum.it (office).

RUPARELIA, Sudhir; Ugandan business executive; *Chairman, Ruparelia Group of Companies;* b. 1 Jan. 1956, Mengo, Kampala; m. Jyostna Ruparelia; three c.; ed Jinja Secondary School, Kololo Secondary School; moved to UK 1972; initially worked in a factory making test tubes, also drove taxis; returned to Uganda 1985; began importing commodities such as salt, sugar, cigarettes, alcoholic beverages to Kampala; started Uganda's first foreign exchange bureau; Founder-Chair. Ruparelia Group of Cos; owns Crane Bank, Goldstar Insurance, Speke Resort, Conference Centre Ltd, Premier Finance Ltd, Kabira Leisure Centre, Crane Man. Services Ltd, Crane Financial Services Ltd, Munyonyo Commonwealth Resort Ltd, Speke Hotel, Kabira Country Club, Tourist Hotel, Speke Apartments, Equator Rafts, Speke Resort, Bujagali, Sanyu FM, Sunrise Radio, Kampala Parents School (acquired in 2004), Kampala International School, Kabira Forex Bureau Ltd; Dr hc (Uganda Pentecostal Univ.) 2007. *Address:* Ruparelia Group of Companies, PO Box 3673, Kampala, Uganda (office). *Telephone:* (41) 4343500 (office). *Fax:* (41) 4231578 (office). *E-mail:* info@ rupareliagroup.com (office). *Website:* www.rupareliagroup.com (office).

RUPEL, Dimitrij, PhD; Slovenian politician, diplomatist and writer; b. 7 April 1946, Ljubljana; m. Marjetica-Ana Rudolf-Rupel; ed Univ. of Ljubljana, Brandeis Univ., Mass, USA; worked as journalist in Yugoslav newspapers and magazines; was considered as dissident for criticism of Yugoslav Communist regime; Asst Prof., Ljubljana Univ. 1980–89, Prof. 1989–; Lecturer, Queen's Univ. (Canada) 1977–78, New School for Social Research, NY (USA) 1985, Cleveland State Univ. (USA) 1989; Co-founder Cultural-Political journal Nova Revija 1984–87; Founder and first Pres. Opposition Slovenian Democratic Alliance Party 1989–90; Minister of Foreign Affairs 1990–93, mem. first elected Govt of Slovenia 1990, Chair. Cttee for Culture, Educ. and Sports; mem. State Ass. 1992–95; Mayor of Ljubljana 1994–97; Amb. to USA 1997–2000; Minister of Foreign Affairs 2000–08; Pres. Council of the EU 2008; Prime Ministerial Special Envoy for Foreign Affairs 2008; Boris Kidrič Prize 1986, Golden Medal of Honour of the Repub. of Slovenia 1992. *Publications include:* novels: Half Way to the Horizon 1968, White Rooms 1970, Secretary of the Sixth International 1971, Tea and Guns at Four 1972, Fifth Floor of the Three-Floor House 1972, Time in It the Cruel Hangman 1974, Chi Square 1975, The Family Connection 1977, Cold Storms, Mad Homes 1978, Pleasant Life 1979, Max 1983, Follow the Addressee, Job 1984, Forgotten Invited 1985, Why is the World Upside Down? 1987, Lion's Share 1989, Story About Time 1989; non-fiction: Reading 1973, Free Words 1976, Words and Acts 1981, Reality Tests 1982, Sociology of Literature 1982, Sociology of Culture and Art 1986, Words of God and Words Divine 1987, Slovenian Intellectuals 1989, Slovenian Holidays and Everydays 1990, Slovenian Faith 1992, Slovenian Path to Independence and Recognition 1992, Secret of the State (memoirs) 1992, Disenchanted Slovenia 1993, Time of Politics 1994, Unity, Happiness, Reconciliation 1996, Freedom Against State 1998, Meetings and Partings 2001, Taking Over the Success Story 2004; plays: Less Terrible Night 1981, Job 1982, PDFS (Follow the Addressee) 1984; film screenplay: Oxygen 1971. *Address:* c/o Office of the Prime Minister, 1000 Ljubljana, Gregorčičeva 20, Slovenia.

RUPÉREZ, Francisco Javier, LLB; Spanish diplomatist, politician and author; *Consul-General, Chicago;* b. 24 April 1941, Madrid; m. Rakela Cerovic; two d.; ed El Pilar Coll., Univ. of Madrid; joined Diplomatic Service 1965, posts in Addis Ababa 1967–69, Warsaw 1969–72, Helsinki 1972–73; mem. Del. to CSCE, Helsinki 1972–73, to Int. Orgs, Geneva 1973–75; Chief of Staff of Under-Sec. of Foreign Affairs 1976; Chief of Staff of Ministry of Foreign Affairs 1976–77; mem. Exec. Cttee, Union of Democratic Centre (UCD) 1977–82; mem. Parl. for Cuenca 1979–82, 1986–89, for Madrid 1989–93, for Ciudad Real 1993–2000; Amb. and Head of Del. to Madrid Session of CSCE 1980–82; First Spanish Amb. to NATO 1982–83; Senator and mem. Regional Parl. of Castilla La Mancha 1983–86; Vice-Pres. Democratic People's Party (PDP) 1983–87; Pres. Christian Democratic Party 1987–89; Vice-Pres. People's Party (PP) 1989–90, Spokesman in Parl. Defence Cttee 1989–91, Spokesman in Parl. Foreign Affairs Cttee 1991–96; Vice-Pres.

NATO Parl. Ass. 1994–96, Pres. Parl. Ass. 1998–2000; Pres. Parl. Ass. of OSCE 1996–98, Spanish Atlantic Assen (AAE) 1996–2000; Pres. Foreign Affairs Cttee, House of Deputies 1996–2000, Cttee on Defence 2000; Pres. Christian-Democratic Int. (CDI) 1998–2000; Amb. to USA 2000–04; Asst Sec.-Gen. and Exec. Dir UN Counter-Terrorism Exec. Directorate 2004–07; Consul-Gen. to Chicago 2007–; Pres. Foundation for Humanism and Democracy 1989–2000; Co-founder Cuadernos para el Diálogo (monthly political magazine) 1963–77; lectures regularly and directs courses at Int. Univ. Menéndez Pelayo, Univ. of Madrid and the Diplomatic School; Gran Cruz de la Orden de Isabel la Católica, Comendador de la Orden de Carlos III, Oficial de Isabel la Católica, Oficial de la Orden del Mérito Civil, Orden Bernardo O'Higgins (Chile), Gran Cruz de Vasco Núñez de Balboa (Panama), Grand Ordre de Léopold II (Belgium), Comendador con Placa de la Orden del Infante Don Enrique (Portugal), Kt Commdr of the Order of Alistical (Jordan), Kt Commdr, Order of the Arab Repub. of Egypt, Officier, Légion d'honneur (France). *Publications include:* Confessional State and Religious Liberty 1970, Europe Between Fear and Hope 1976, Spain in NATO 1986, First Book of Short Stories 1987, Kidnapped by ETA: Memoirs 1990, The Price of a Shadow (novel) 2005, El espejismo multilateral 2009; contribs to co-authored books and numerous articles in the Spanish press and specialized publs. *Leisure interests:* music, cinema, theatre, literature. *Address:* Consulate-General of Spain, 180 North Michigan Avenue, Suite 1500, Chicago, IL 60601, USA (office). *Telephone:* (312) 782-4589 (office). *Fax:* (312) 782-1635 (office). *E-mail:* conspainchicago@sbcglobal.net (office); javieruperez@hotmail.com (home). *Website:* www.mae.es/Consulados/Chicago (office).

RUPERT, Johann; South African business executive; *Chairman, Compagnie Financiere Richemont SA;* b. 6 Jan. 1950, Stellenboch; s. of the late Anton Rupert and of Huberte Rupert; m. Gaynor Rupert; three c.; ed Paul Roos Gymnasium, Univ. of Stellenbosch; worked at Chase Manhattan Bank 1975–79; Business Apprentice, Lazard Freres, New York, USA 1976–79; Founder and CEO Rand Merchant Bank 1979–84; apptd Gen. Man. Rembrandt Group Ltd 1985, Vice-Chair. 1989–92, Chair. 1992–; Chair. (non-exec.) Gold Fields Ltd 1997–; f. VenFin Ltd 2000, Chair. (non-exec.) 2006–; Founder-Chair. (non-exec.) Remgro Ltd 2000–; CEO Compagnie Financiere Richemont SA (luxury goods) 2000–04, 2010–13, Chair. 2002–, mem. Group Man. Cttee 1988–; Chair. (non-exec.) Access Freight International (Pty) Ltd; Chair. Peace Parks Foundation, South African PGA Tour, Rembrandt Controlling Investments Ltd, South African Golf Devt Bd; Founder Small Business Devt Corpn 1979–, Laureus Sport for Good Foundation 1990–; Vendôme Luxury Group 1990–; owner Rupert & Rothschild and L'Ormarins wine estates; Developer, Leopard Creek Golf Club, Mpumalanga; Dir (non-exec.) Rothmans International Plc 1988–; Chancellor, Stellenbosch Univ. 2009–; f. Franschhoek Motor Museum; fmr Trustee, Southern African Nature Foundation; Hon. Vice-Pres., European Golf Tour 2010–; Officier, Ordre national de la Légion d'honneur; Dr hc (Stellenbosch Univ.) 2004, (Nelson Mandela Metropolitan Univ.) 2008, (Univ. of St Andrews, Scotland); Businessman of the Year, Sunday Times 1988, 1996, Business Leader of the Year, Die Burger newspaper, Cape Town Chamber of Commerce 1990, M.S. Louw Award, Afrikaanse Handelsinstituut 1993, Free Market Award, Free Market Foundation of South Africa 1999, Man. Excellence Award, Wits Business School 2009, Int. Wine Entrepreneur of the Year 2009, Voted South Africa's Most Admired Business Leader 2010. *Address:* Compagnie Financiere Richemont SA, 50, Chemin De La Chênaie, Geneva, Switzerland (office); Office of the Chancellor, Stellenbosch University, Private Bag X1, Matieland 7602, South Africa (office). *Telephone:* 227153500 (Switzerland) (office); (21) 808 4896 (South Africa) (office). *E-mail:* mvdl@sun.ac.za (office). *Website:* www.richemont.com (office).

RUPNIK, Jacques, MA PhD; French political scientist and academic; *Director of Research, National Foundation for Political Science, Centre for International Studies and Research (CERI);* b. 21 Nov. 1950, Prague, Czech Republic; s. of Anton Rupnik and Micheline Bauvillain-Rupnik; m.; ed Harvard Univ., USA, Univ. of Paris (Sorbonne), Institut d'Etudes Politiques de Paris; Research Assoc., Russian Research Center, Harvard Univ. 1974–75; Eastern Europe specialist BBC World Service 1977–82; Prof., Institut d'Etudes Politiques de Paris 1982–96; adviser to Czech Pres. Vaclav Havel 1990–92; Exec. Dir Int. Comm. for Balkans, Carnegie Endowment for Int. Peace 1995–96; mem. Ind. Int. Comm. on Kosovo 1999–2000; Visiting Prof., Coll. of Europe 1999–, Harvard Univ. 2006; currently Research Dir Nat. Foundation for Political Science, Centre for Int. Studies and Research (CERI); adviser to EC 2007–; mem. Research Council of Int. Forum for Democracy Studies, Washington, DC 2013–; Sr Fellow, Davis Center 2008, Center for European Studies, Harvard Univ. 2011; Ordre Nat. du Mérite 1995, Order of T.G. Maseryk, Czech Repub. 2002. *Television includes:* writer and presenter, The Other Europe (6-part documentary series) (Channel 4 TV, UK) 1988. *Publications include:* The Other Europe 1988, Unfinished Peace 1996, Le Europe en face à l'élargissement 2004, Les Banlieues de l'Europe, les politiques de voisinage de l'UE 2007, The Western Balkans and the EU: The Hour of Europe 2011, Europe and the New International System 2013; numerous articles focused on central and Eastern Europe, and the Balkans. *Address:* Centre for International Studies and Research (CERI), 56 rue Jacob, 75006 Paris, France (office). *Telephone:* 1-58-71-70-51 (office); 1-49-57-08-54 (home). *Fax:* 1-58-71-70-90 (office). *E-mail:* rupnik@ceri-sciences-po.org (office); jacquesrupnik@hotmail.com (home). *Website:* www.ceri-sciencespo.com/cherlist/rupnik.htm (office).

RUPP, George, AB, BD, PhD; American professor of religion, university president and international organization official; *President and CEO, International Rescue Committee;* b. 22 Sept. 1942, Summit, NJ; m. Nancy Katherine Farrar 1964; two d.; ed Univ. of Munich, Germany, Princeton Univ., Yale Divinity School, Univ. of Sri Lanka, Harvard Univ.; Faculty Fellow in Religion, Johnston Coll., Univ. of Redlands, Calif., 1971–73, Vice-Chancellor 1973–74; Asst Prof. of Theology, Divinity School, Harvard Univ. 1974–76, Assoc. Prof. of Theology and Chair. Dept of Theology 1976–77, Dean and John Lord O'Brian Prof. of Divinity 1979–85; Dean for Acad. Affairs and Prof. of Humanistic Studies, Univ. of Wisconsin-Green Bay 1977–79; Pres. and Prof. of Religious Studies, Rice Univ. 1985–93; Pres. and Prof. of Religion, Columbia Univ., New York 1993–2002; Pres. and CEO Int. Rescue Cttee 2002–13; mem. Bd Inst. of Int. Educ., Council on Foreign Relations, Interaction, Henry Luce Foundation, Josiah Macy Foundation and other orgs; Hon. DD (Austin Coll.) 1992, (Gen. Theological Seminary) 2011; Hon. DLit (Columbia) 1993; Hon. DHumLitt (Univ. of Redlands) 1994, (George-

town Univ.) 2001; Hon. LLD (Hamilton Coll.) 1995; Danforth Grad. Fellowship, Yale and Harvard Univs 1964–71; Honors Scholarship, Yale Univ. 1964–65, Dwight Fellowship, Yale Univ. 1966–67, Center for the Study of World Religions travel grant, Harvard Univ. 1969–70, Ford Foundation summer research grant, Univ. of Redlands 1972, Association of Theological Schools research grant for leave in Tübingen, Germany, Harvard Univ. 1976, Alexander Hamilton Medal, Columbia Univ. 2002, Centennial Medal for Contrib. to Society, Harvard Univ. Grad. School of Arts and Sciences 2004, Gold Medal, Nat. Inst. of Social Sciences 2005, Woodrow Wilson Award, Princeton Univ. 2006. *Publications:* Christologies and Cultures: Toward a Typology of Religious Worldviews 1974, Culture-Protestantism: German Liberal Theology at the Turn of the Twentieth Century 1977, Beyond Existentialism and Zen: Religion in a Pluralistic World 1979, Commitment and Community 1989, Globalization Challenged 2006; numerous book chapters and articles. *Address:* International Rescue Committee, 122 East 42nd Street, 12th Floor, New York, NY 10168-1289, USA (office). *Telephone:* (212) 551-3002 (office). *Fax:* (212) 551-3179 (office). *Website:* www.rescue.org (office).

RUPPRECHT, Rudolf, DipEng; German business executive; *Member of the Supervisory Board, MAN Aktiengesellschaft;* b. 12 Jan. 1940, Berlin; ed Munich Tech. Univ.; began career as sales engineer, MAN Group 1966, various positions including Tech. Dir MAN subsidiary in Argentina, Exec. Dir Diesel Engines Div. 1981–84, apptd mem. Exec. Bd MAN B&W Diesel AG, Augsburg 1984, Chair. Exec. Bd 1989–93, Chair. Exec. Bd MAN Nutzfahrzeuge AG, Munich 1993–96, Chair. Exec. Bd MAN Aktiengesellschaft, Munich 1996–2004, now mem. Supervisory Bd; mem. Supervisory Bd Bayerische Staatsforsten AöR, KME AG, Salzgitter AG, SMS GmbH (Chair.). *Address:* MAN Aktiengesellschaft, Ungererstrasse 69, 80805 Munich, Germany (office). *Telephone:* (89) 360980 (office). *Fax:* (89) 36098250 (office). *E-mail:* public.relations@ag.man.de (office). *Website:* www.man.de (office).

RUPRECHT, William F.; American auctioneer and business executive; *President, CEO and Director, Sotheby's Holdings, Inc.;* b. St Louis; ed Univ. of Colorado, Univ. of Vermont; began career as apprentice to furniture maker, Vermont; joined Sotheby's 1980, Dir of Marketing Sotheby's Inc., New York 1986–92, Dir of Marketing Sotheby's worldwide 1992–94, Man. Dir Sotheby's N and S America 1994–2000, Pres., CEO and Dir Sotheby's Holdings, Inc. 2000–. *Address:* Sotheby's, 1334 York Avenue at 72nd Street, New York, NY 10021, USA (office). *Telephone:* (212) 606-7000 (office). *Fax:* (212) 606-7107 (office). *Website:* www.sothebys.com (office).

RUS, Ioan, PhD; Romanian engineer, academic and politician; b. 21 Feb. 1955, Urisor, Cluj Co.; m.; two c.; ed Faculty of Mechanical Eng, Technical Univ. of Cluj-Napoca; mil. service 1976–77, attained rank of Lt Col; engineer at TSMA, Cluj 1982–84; Research Engineer, Polytechnic Inst. of Cluj 1984–85; Asst Prof., Tech. Univ. of Cluj-Napoca 1985–90, Lecturer 1990–94, Assoc. Prof. 1995–2000, Prof. and Dept Co-ordinator of Computation and Construction Vehicles 2002, PhD supervisor 2003; Gen. Dir SC RMB Inter-Auto SRL (Representation of Mercedes-Benz Transilvania) 1993–2000, Man. 2004–12; mem. Party of Social Democracy of Romania (Partidul Democrației Sociale din România—PDSR) 1994–98; Prefect of Cluj Co. Aug.–Dec. 1996, Chair. Cluj Co. Council June–Dec. 2000; mem. Exec. Cabinet of Adrian Nastase 2000–03; Minister of the Interior 2000–03; Deputy Prime Minister 2003–04; Pres. Cluj Co. Org. of Social Democratic Party (Partidul Social Democrat—PSD) 2001–02, Vice-Pres. of the party 2002–04; campaigned for election as Mayor of Cluj; resigned as Pres. of PSD Cluj 2007; Minister of Admin and the Interior May–Aug. 2012; mem. of several professional asscns in Romania and abroad, including Gen. Assen of Engineers in Romania, Soc. of Automotive Engineers of Romania, Romania Assen of Agricultural Mechanical Engineers, Soc. of Automotive Engineers (USA), Romanian Assen for the Club of Rome, Societé des Ingenieurs de l'Automobile (France); Kt, Order of the Romanian Star 2002. *Publications include:* author or co-author of 14 books and numerous papers and scientific articles. *Address:* c/o Ministry of Administration and the Interior, 010086 Bucharest 1, Piața Revoluției 1A, Romania.

RUSBRIDGER, Alan, BA, MA; British journalist and publishing executive; *Editor, The Guardian and Executive Editor, The Observer;* b. 29 Dec. 1953, Lusaka, Zambia; s. of G. H. Rusbridger and B. E. Rusbridger (née Wickham); m. Lindsay Mackie 1982; two d.; ed Cranleigh School, Magdalene Coll., Cambridge; reporter, Cambridge Evening News 1976–79; reporter, The Guardian 1979–82, diary ed. and feature writer 1982–86, special writer 1987–88, launch ed. Weekend Guardian 1988–89, Features Ed. 1989–93, Deputy Ed. 1993–95, Ed. 1995–; TV critic and feature writer, The Observer 1986–, Exec. Ed. 1996–; Washington Corresp., London Daily News 1987; Chair. Photographer's Gallery 2001–; mem. Bd Guardian Newspapers Ltd 1994–, Guardian Media Group 1999–; mem. Scott Trust 1997–; Ed. of the Year, What the Papers Say Awards (Granada TV) 1996, 2001, Nat. Newspaper Ed., Newspaper Industry Awards 1996, Editor's Ed., Press Gazette 1997, Judges' Award, What the Papers Say 2006, Goldsmith Career Award for Excellence in Journalism, Kennedy School of Govt, Harvard Univ. 2012. *Television:* presenter of What the Papers Say (Granada TV) 1983–94, co-writer (with Ronan Bennett) of Fields of Gold (BBC TV) 2001. *Publications include:* New World Order (ed.) 1991, Altered State (ed.) 1992, Guardian Year 1994, The Coldest Day in the Zoo 2004, The Wildest Day at the Zoo 2005, The Smelliest Day at the Zoo 2007, Play it Again 2013. *Leisure interests:* golf, music, painting. *Address:* The Guardian, Kings Place, 90 York Way, London, N1 9GU, England (office). *Telephone:* (20) 3353-2000 (office). *Fax:* (20) 7239-9997 (office). *E-mail:* alan.rusbridger@guardian.co.uk (office). *Website:* www.guardian.co.uk (office).

RUSCHA, Edward (Ed) Joseph; American artist; b. 16 Dec. 1937, Omaha, Neb.; s. of Edward Joseph Ruscha and Dorothy Driscoll; m. Danna Knego 1967; one s.; ed Chouinard Art Inst., Los Angeles; first solo exhbn Los Angeles 1963; produced films Premium 1970, Miracle 1975; maj. exhbns include San Francisco Museum of Modern Art 1982, Musée St Pierre, Lyons, France 1985, Museum of Contemporary Art, Chicago 1988, Centre Georges Pompidou, Paris 1989, Serpentine Gallery, London 1990, Museum of Contemporary Art, Los Angeles 1990, Robert Miller Gallery, New York 1992, Thaddaeus Ropac, Salzburg, Austria 1992, Hayward Gallery, London 2009, Museum of Contemporary Art, Florida 2012; first public comm., for Miami Dade Cultural Center's Main Library, Miami, Fla 1985; other comms. include Great Hall, Denver Cen. Library 1994–95, Auditorium Getty Center, Los Angeles 1997; represented in numerous perm. collections; Guggenheim Foundation Fellowship 1971; mem. American Acad. of Arts and Letters 2001; Artistic Excellence Award, Americans for the Arts 2009. *Publications include:* 12 books, including Twenty-six Gasoline Stations 1963, The Sunset Strip 1966. *Website:* www.edruscha.com.

RUSH, Geoffrey Roy; Australian actor; b. 6 July 1951, Toowoomba, Queensland; s. of Roy Baden Rush and Merle Kiehne; m. Jane Menelaus 1988; one s. one d.; studied at Jacques Lecoq School of Mime, Paris, began professional career with Queensland Theatre Co.; Hans Christian Andersen Amb. 2005–; became the 19th actor to win the 'Triple Crown of Acting': Academy, Tony and Emmy Awards; Pres. Australian Acad. of Cinema and Television Arts 2011–; Patron, Melbourne International Film Festival, Toowoomba's Empire Theatre Foundation, Spina Bifida Foundation Victoria; Australian Centenary Medal 2001; Hon. DLitt (Univ. of Queensland); Sidney Myer Performing Arts Awards 1994, Supporting Actor of the Year, Hollywood Film Festival 2003, Global Achievement Award, Australian Film Inst. 2003, Chauvel Award, Brisbane Int. Film Festival 2004, Longford Life Achievement Award, Australian Film Inst. 2009, Montecito Award, Santa Barbara Int. Film Festival 2011, Helpmann Award 2011, Australian of the Year 2012. *Theatre includes:* Hamlet 1994, The Alchemist 1996, The Marriage of Figaro 1998, The Small Poppies 1999, Exit the King (Tony Award for Best Actor 2009) 2009; also dir of numerous productions. *Films include:* The Wedding 1980, Starstruck 1981, Twelfth Night 1985, Midday Crisis 1994, Dad and Dave on our Selection 1995, Shine (Academy Award for Best Actor 1997, BAFTA Award, Australian Film Inst. Award, Golden Globe Award, numerous other awards) 1996, Children of the Revolution 1996, Les Miserables 1997, Elizabeth 1998, Shakespeare in Love (BAFTA Award for Best Supporting Actor) 1998, Mystery Men 1999, House on Haunted Hill 1999, Quills 1999, The Magic Pudding (voice) 2000, Tailor of Panama 2001, Lantana 2001, Frida 2002, The Banger Sisters 2002, Swimming Upstream 2003, Ned Kelly 2003, Finding Nemo (voice) 2003, Pirates of the Caribbean: The Curse of the Black Pearl 2003, Intolerable Cruelty 2003, Harvie Krumpet (voice) 2003, The Life and Death of Peter Sellers (Best Actor in a Miniseries or TV Movie, Golden Globe Awards 2005, Screen Actors Guild Awards 2005, Emmy Award for Best Actor in a Mini-Series or Movie 2005) 2004, Swimming Upstream 2005, Munich 2005, Candy 2006, Pirates of the Caribbean: Dead Man's Chest 2006, Pirates of the Caribbean: At World's End 2007, Elizabeth: The Golden Age 2007, $9.99 2008, Bran Nue Dae 2009, The King's Speech (British Independent Film Award for Best Supporting Actor, Central Ohio Film Critics Asscn Award for Best Supporting Actor, Nat. Soc. of Film Critics Award for Best Supporting Actor, BAFTA Award for Best Supporting Actor 2011) 2010, Legend of the Guardians: The Owls of Ga'Hoole 2010, The Warrior's Way 2010, The Eye of the Storm 2011, Pirates of the Caribbean: On Stranger Tides 2011, Green Lantern (voice) 2011, The Eye of the Storm 2011. *Television includes:* Menotti 1980–81, The Burning Piano 1992, Mercury 1996, Bonus Mileage 1996, Twisted (series) 1996, Frontier (mini-series) 1997, Kath & Kim (series) 2004, Lowdown (series) 2010. *Address:* c/o Shanahan Management, PO Box 478, King's Cross, NSW 2011, Australia.

RUSHAYLO, Col-Gen. Vladimir Borisovich; Russian politician and inter-national organization official; b. 28 July 1953, Tambov; m.; three c.; ed Omsk Higher School of Militia, USSR Ministry of Internal Affairs; militiaman 1972–76; investigator Moscow Dept of Internal Affairs 1976–88, later Head Moscow Dept of Internal Affairs; Head Dept for Struggle against Organized Crime 1988–93, 1998–99, Head Regional Dept for Struggle against Organized Crime 1993–96; Counsellor Council of Fed. 1996–98; Deputy Minister of Internal Affairs 1998–99, Minister of Internal Affairs 1999–2001; Sec. Security Council of Russia 2001–04; Exec. Sec. and Chair. Exec. Cttee CIS 2004–07; Head, CIS mission to observe presidential election in Belarus 2006; mem. Presidium of Russian Govt, Security Council; Order of Sign of Honour; Order for Personal Courage and numerous other decorations. *Address:* c/o Office of the Executive Secretary, Commonwealth of Independent States, 220000 Minsk, Kirava 17, Belarus (office).

RUSHDIE, Sir (Ahmed) Salman, Kt, MA, FRSL; British writer and academic; *University Distinguished Professor, Emory University;* b. 19 June 1947, Bombay (now Mumbai), India; s. of Anis Ahmed and Negin (née Butt) Rushdie; m. 1st Clarissa Luard 1976 (divorced 1987, died 1999); one s.; m. 2nd Marianne Wiggins 1988 (divorced 1993); one step-d.; m. 3rd Elizabeth West 1997 (divorced); one s.; m. 4th Padma Lakshmi 2004 (divorced); ed Cathedral and John Connon Boys' High School, Bombay, Rugby School, England, King's Coll., Cambridge; mem. Footlights revue, Univ. of Cambridge 1965–68; actor, fringe theatre, London 1968–69; advertising copywriter 1969–73; wrote first published novel Grimus 1973–74; part-time advertising copywriter while writing second novel 1976–80; mem. Int. PEN 1981–, Soc. of Authors 1983–, Exec. Cttee Nat. Book League 1983–, Council Inst. of Contemporary Arts 1985–, British Film Inst. Production Bd 1986–, PEN American Center (Pres. 2004–06); Distinguished Writer-in-Residence, then Univ. Distin-guished Prof., Emory Univ., Atlanta 2007–; Exec. mem. Camden Cttee for Community Relations 1977–83; Distinguished Fellow in Literature, Univ. of East Anglia 1995; Foreign Hon. mem. American Acad. of Arts and Letters 2008–; Hon. Prof. MIT 1993; Hon. Spokesman Charter 88 1989; Hon. DLitt (Bard Coll.) 1995; Booker McConnell Prize for Fiction 1981, Arts Council Literature Bursary 1981, English Speaking Union Literary Award 1981, James Tait Black Memorial Book Prize 1981, Kurt Tucholsky Prize Sweden 1992, Prix Colette Switzerland 1993, Austrian State Prize for European Literature 1994, Whitbread Fiction Award 1996, British Book Awards Author of the Year 1996, London Int. Writers Award 2002, Booker of Bookers Prize 2008, James Joyce Award 2008, Kitty Carlisle Hart Award for Outstanding Contrib. to the Arts, Americans for the Arts 2009; Commdr., Ordre des Arts et des Lettres 1999. *Television film screenplays:* The Painter and the Pest 1985, The Riddle of Midnight 1988. *Film appearance:* Then She Found Me 2007. *Publications include::* Grimus 1975, Midnight's Children 1981, Shame (Prix du Meilleur Livre Etranger 1984) 1983, The Jaguar Smile: A Nicaraguan Journey 1987, The Satanic Verses 1988, Is Nothing Sacred (lecture) 1990, Haroun and the Sea of Stories (novel) 1990, Imaginary Homelands: Essays and Criticism 1981–91 1991, The Wizard of Oz 1992, East, West (short stories) 1994, The Moor's Last Sigh (novel) 1995, The Vintage Book of Indian Writing 1947–97 (ed. with Elizabeth West) 1997, The Ground Beneath Her Feet 1999, Fury 2001, Step Across the Line: Collected Non-Fiction 1992–2002 2002, Telling Tales (contrib. to charity anthology) 2004, Shalimar the Clown 2005, The Enchantress of Florence 2008, Luka and the Fire of Life 2010, Joseph Anton (memoir) 2012; articles for New York Times, Washington Post, The Times and Sunday Times.

Leisure interests: films, chess, table tennis, involvement in politics, especially race relations. *Address:* Wylie Agency (UK) Ltd, 4–8 Rodney Street, London, N1 9JH, England (office). *Website:* www.salman-rushdie.com (office).

RUŠKO, Pavol; Slovak politician; b. 20 Aug. 1963, Liptovský Hrádok; m.; two c.; ed Comenius Univ.; Sports Ed. Slovak TV 1985, Head Dept of Program Research, Head of Transmitting Centre and Deputy of Gen. Dir 1989–94; with Lottop Co. 1994–96; Gen. Dir and Co-Owner TV Markiza 1995–2000, Chair. STS Markiza Bd of Owners 2000–; Dir-Gen. Slovenska Televizna Spolocnost; Chair. New Citizens' Alliance (NCA) (Aliancia nového občana—ANO) 2001–07; Vice-Chair. Nat. Council of Slovak Repub. 2002–03; Deputy Prime Minister and Minister of the Economy, and Admin and Privatization of Nat. Property 2003–05. *Address:* c/o New Citizens' Alliance (NCA) (Aliancia nového občana—ANO), Drobného 27, 841 01 Bratislava, Slovakia. *Telephone:* (2) 6920-2918. *Fax:* (2) 6920-2920. *E-mail:* ano@ano-aliancia .sk. *Website:* www.ano-aliancia.sk.

RUSMAJLI, Ilir; Albanian lawyer and politician; b. 24 April 1965, Elbasan; ed Univ. of Tirana; fmrly Minister of Foreign Affairs; Deputy Prime Minister 2005–07; Minister of Justice 2007 (resgnd); currently Deputy, Kuvendi Popullor (People's Assembly); mem. Parl. Ass., Council of Europe 2009–. *Address:* Kuvendi Popullor (People's Assembly), Bulevardi Dëshmorët e Kombit 4, Tirana, Albania (office). *Telephone:* (4) 2264887 (office). *Fax:* (4) 2221764 (office). *E-mail:* marlind@ parlament.al (office). *Website:* www.parlament.al (office).

RUSNOK, Jiří, MEcon; Czech politician and economist; b. 16 Oct. 1960, Ostrava-Vítkovice; m.; three c.; ed Univ. of Economics, Prague; various positions in state admin.; Econ. Adviser, Czech-Moravian Confed. of Trade Unions 1992–98; mem. Czech Social Democratic Party (CSDP) 1998–2010; Deputy Minister for Labour and Social Affairs 1998–2001; Minister of Finance 2001–02, of Industry and Trade 2002–03; Chief Economist, Exec. Adviser to the Man. Cttee and Dir of Pensions, ING Insurance Czech Repub./Slovak Repub. 2003–13; Pres. Czech Pension Funds Asscn 2005–12, Audit Public Oversight Council of Czech Repub. 2009–13; mem. Nat. Econ. Council of Govt; Prime Minister 2013–14. *Leisure interests:* gardening, nature, history, sport. *Address:* c/o Office of the Government, náb. Edvarda Beneše 4, 118 01 Prague 1, Czech Republic. *E-mail:* posta@vlada.cz.

RUSSELL, David Owen; American film director and screenwriter; b. 20 Aug. 1958, New York; s. of Bernard Russell and Maria Russell (née Muzio); m. Janet Grillo 1992–2007; ed Amherst Coll., Mass; mem. Bd of Dirs Ghetto Film School, South Bronx, New York; Career Tribute, Gotham Independent Film Awards 2012, Indie Impact Award, Variety 2012, Screenwriters Tribute Award, Nantucket Film Festival 2013. *Films directed:* Bingo Inferno (also writer and producer) 1987, Hairway to the Stars 1990, Spanking the Monkey (also writer and exec. producer) (Independent Spirit Award for Best First Screenplay) 1994, Flirting with Disaster (also writer) 1996, Three Kings (Boston Soc. of Film Critics Award for Best Dir) 1999, I Heart Huckabees (also writer and producer) 2004, Soldiers Pay (documen-tary short) 2004, Nailed (also writer) (shot in 2008, unfinished), The Fighter 2010, Silver Linings Playbook (also writer) (BAFTA Award for Best Adapted Screenplay 2013) 2012, American Hustle (BAFTA Award for Best Original Screenplay 2014) 2013. *Television:* Outer Space Astronauts (series) (executive producer) 2009. *Address:* c/o WME Entertainment, 9601 Wilshire Boulevard, Beverley Hills, CA 90210-5213, USA (office). *Website:* www.davidorussell.com (office).

RUSSELL, Sir George, Kt, CBE, BA, FRSA, CBIM, FID; British business executive; b. 25 Oct. 1935; s. of William H. Russell and Frances A. Russell; m. Dorothy Brown 1959; three d.; ed Gateshead Grammar School, Univ. of Durham; Vice-Pres. and Gen. Man. Welland Chemical Co. of Canada Ltd 1968, St Clair Chemical Co. 1968; Man. Dir Alcan UK Ltd 1976; Asst Man. Dir Alcan Aluminium (UK) Ltd 1977–81, Man. Dir 1981–82; Man. Dir and CEO British Alcan Aluminium 1982–86; Dir Alcan Aluminiumwerke GmbH, Frankfurt 1982–86, Alcan Aluminium Ltd 1987–2000; Group Chief Exec. Marley PLC 1986–89, Chair. and CEO 1989–93, Chair. (non-exec.) 1993–97; Deputy Chair. Channel Four TV 1987–88; Chair. Ind. TV News (ITN) 1988; Chair. Ind. Broadcasting Authority (IBA) 1989–90, Ind. Television Comm. (ITC) 1991–96; Chair. Camelot Group PLC 1995–2002; Chair. Luxfer Holdings Ltd 1976; mem. Bd of Dirs Northern Rock Building Soc. (now Northern Rock PLC) 1985–2006, 3i Group PLC 1992–2001 (Chair. non-exec. 1993–2001), Taylor Woodrow PLC 1992–2004 (Deputy Chair. 2000–03); Chair. Northern Devt Co. 1994–99; Deputy Chair. Granada PLC 2002–04, ITV PLC 2003–09; Chair. Comm. on Public Service Reform in the North East 2007–09; Dir Wildfowl & Wetlands Trust 2002–08, Vice-Pres. 2008–; Visiting Prof., Univ. of Newcastle-upon-Tyne 1978; mem. Northern Industrial Devt Bd 1977–80, Washington Devt Corpn 1978–80, IBA 1979–86, Megaw Cttee of Enquiry into Civil Service Pay 1981–82, Council CBI 1984–85, Widdicombe Cttee of Inquiry into Conduct of Local Authority Business 1985; mem. of Court, Univ. of Newcastle 2004–10; Fellow, Inst. of Industrial Mans; Trustee Beamish Devt Trust 1985–90, Thomas Bewick Birthplace Trust; Hon. FRIBA 1993; Hon. FRTS 1994; Hon. FRAM 2001; Hon. DEng (Newcastle upon Tyne) 1985; Hon. DBA (Northumbria) 1992; Hon. LLD (Sunderland) 1995, (Durham) 1997. *Leisure interests:* tennis, badminton, bird watching. *Address:* 46 Downshore Hill, London NW3 INX, England.

RUSSELL, Ian, CBE, BCom; British chartered accountant and business execu-tive; *Chairman, Advanced Power AG Advisory Board;* b. 16 Jan. 1953, Edinburgh; s. of James Russell and Christine Clark; m. Fiona Russell 1975; one s. one d.; ed Univ. of Edinburgh; Finance Dir HSBC Asset Man., Hong Kong 1987–90; Dir Finance Control, Tomkins, London 1991–94; Finance Dir Scottish Power plc 1994, Deputy CEO 1998–2001, CEO 2001–06; Industrialist in Residence, 3i Group (pvt. equity firm) 2007–, Chair. Advanced Power AG Advisory Bd (after 3i investment in Advanced Power) 2007–; mem. Bd of Dirs Johnston Press plc, JPMorgan Fleming Mercantile Investment Trust plc; Head Govt Comm. on Nat. Youth Volunteering Strategy 2004–05; mem. Edinburgh Int. Festival Council, Scottish Council of the Prince's Trust. *Leisure interests:* golf, rugby. *Address:* Advanced Power AG, Baarer Str. 12, 6300 Zug, Switzerland (office); 3i Group, 16 Palace Street, London SW1E 5JD, England (office). *Telephone:* 417297297 (office); (20) 7928-3131 (3i) (office). *Fax:* 417297299 (office); (20) 7928-0058 (3i) (office). *E-mail:* info@advancedpower .ch (office). *Website:* www.advancedpower.ch (office); www.3i.com (office).

RUSSELL, Kurt von Vogel; American actor; b. 17 March 1951, Springfield, Mass; s. of Bing Oliver Russell and Louise Julia Russell (née Crone); m. Season

Hubley 1979 (divorced); one s.; pnr Goldie Hawn; one s.; lead role in TV series The Travels of Jamie McPheeters 1963–64; child actor in many Disney shows and films; professional minor league baseball player 1971–73; numerous TV guest appearances; mem. Professional Baseball Players' Asscn, Stuntman's Asscn; Co-founder Cosmic Entertainment (production co.) 2003; recipient five acting awards, ten baseball awards, one golf championship. *Films include:* Follow Me, Boys! 1966, Mosby's Marauders 1967, Guns in the Heather 1968, The One and Only, Genuine, Original Family Band 1968, The Horse in the Gray Flannel Suit 1968, The Computer Wore Tennis Shoes 1969, The Barefoot Executive 1971, Fools' Parade 1971, Now You See Him, Now You Don't 1972, Charley and the Angel 1973, Superdad 1973, The Strongest Man in the World 1975, The Captive: The Longest Drive 2 1976, Used Cars 1980, Escape from New York 1981, The Thing 1982, Silkwood 1983, Swing Shift 1984, Mean Season 1985, Best of Times 1986, Big Trouble in Little China 1986, Overboard 1987, Tequila Sunrise 1988, Winter People 1989, Tango & Cash 1989, Backdraft 1991, Unlawful Entry 1992, Captain Ron 1992, Tombstone 1993, Stargate 1994, Executive Decision 1996, Escape from LA 1996, Breakdown 1997, Soldier 1998, 3000 Miles to Graceland 2001, Vanilla Sky 2001, Interstate 60 2002, Dark Blue 2002, Miracle 2004, Jiminy Glick in La La Wood 2004, Dreamer 2005, Sky High 2005, Poseidon 2006, Grindhouse 2007, Death Proof 2007, Cutlass 2007, Touchback 2011. *Television series include:* Sugarfoot 1957, Travels with Jamie McPheeters 1963–64, The New Land 1974, The Quest 1976. *Television films include:* Search for the Gods 1975, The Deadly Tower 1975, Christmas Miracle in Caulfield USA 1977, Elvis 1979, Amber Waves 1988. *Address:* Cosmic Entertainment, 9255 Sunset Boulevard, Suite 1010, West Hollywood, CA 90069; Creative Artists' Agency, 9830 Wilshire Boulevard, Beverly Hills, CA 90212-1825, USA. *Telephone:* (310) 275-8080 (Cosmic Entertainment).

RUSSELL, Paul; British lawyer and music industry executive; *Founding Partner, R2M Music LPP & LLC;* b. 3 July 1944, London; m. Elizabeth Russell; three s. two d.; ed Coll. of Law; fmrly band mem. Red Diamond; fmrly with law firm Balin & Co.; joined CBS 1973, fmrly Man. Dir, Pres. Sony Music Europe 1993–; Chair. Sony Music Europe 1997–2000; Sr Vice-Pres. Sony Music Entertainment Inc. 2000–; Chair. Sony ATV Music Publishing 2000–, Chair. Sony ATV Music Publishing 2000–; Founding Pnr R2M Music LPP & LLC; co-f. Brit Awards; f. Platinum Europe Awards. *Leisure interests:* music, films, theatre, golf, swimming, all sports. *Telephone:* (1344) 841768 (office). *E-mail:* pr44@btopenworld.com (office).

RUSSELL, Stuart, BA, PhD; British computer scientist and academic; *Professor of Computer Science, University of California, Berkeley;* b. 1962, Portsmouth; ed St Paul's School, London, Wadham Coll., Univ. of Oxford, Stanford Univ.; Programmer, IBM Systems Eng Centre, Warwick 1978–80; Programmer, graphics research project, IBM Scientific Center, Los Angeles 1981; Teaching Asst, Computer Science Dept, Stanford Univ. 1983, Research Asst 1985–86; Asst Prof., Computer Science Div., Univ. of California, Berkeley 1986–91, Assoc. Prof. 1991–96, Prof. 1996–, Michael H. Smith and Lotfi A. Zadeh Chair in Eng 2001, Chair. Computer Science Div. 2006–, also Chair. Dept of Electrical Eng and Computer Sciences 2008–; Fellow, American Asscn for Artificial Intelligence 1997– (mem. Exec. Council 1997–2000); Fellow, Asscn for Computing Machinery 2003–; mem. British Scientists Abroad (Chair. 1993–96); numerous awards including NSF Presidential Young Investigator Award 1990, IJCAI Computers and Thought Award (co-winner) 1995. *Publications:* over 150 papers on artificial intelligence; The Use of Knowledge in Analogy and Induction 1989, Do the Right Thing: Studies in Limited Rationality (with Eric Wefald) 1991, Artificial Intelligence: A Modern Approach (with Peter Norvig) 1995. *Address:* Computer Science Division, 387 Soda Hall, University of California, Berkeley, CA 94720-1776, USA (office). *Telephone:* (510) 642-8736 (office). *E-mail:* russell@cs.berkeley.edu (office). *Website:* www.cs .berkeley.edu/~russell (office).

RUSSELL, William (Willy) Martin; British writer; b. 23 Aug. 1947; s. of William Russell and Margery Russell; m. Ann Seagroatt 1969; one s. two d.; ed St Katharine's Coll. of Educ., Liverpool; hairdresser 1963–69; teacher 1973–74; Fellow in Creative Writing, Manchester Polytechnic 1977–78; Founder-mem. and Dir Quintet Films; Hon. Dir Liverpool, Playhouse; TV and radio plays; Hon. MA (Open Univ.) 1983; Hon. DLit (Liverpool Univ.) 1990. *Plays:* Blind Scouse (three short plays) 1971, When the Reds (adaptation) 1972, John, Paul, George, Ringo and Bert (musical) 1974, Breezeblock Park 1975, One for the Road 1976, Stags and Hens 1978, Educating Rita 1979, Blood Brothers (musical) 1983, Our Day Out (musical) 1983, Shirley Valentine 1986. *Screenplays include:* Educating Rita 1981, Shirley Valentine 1988, Dancing Through the Dark 1989. *Publications:* Breezeblock Park 1978, One for the Road 1980, Educating Rita 1981, Our Day Out 1984, Stags and Hens 1985, Blood Brothers 1985, Shirley Valentine 1989, The Wrong Boy (novel) 2000; songs and poetry. *Leisure interests:* playing the guitar, composing songs, gardening, cooking. *Address:* c/o Casarotto Company Ltd, National House, 60–66 Wardour Street, London, W1V 3HP, England. *Telephone:* (20) 7287-4450. *Website:* www.willyrussell.com.

RUSSELL BEALE, Simon, CBE, BA; British actor; b. 12 Jan. 1961, Penang, Malaya; s. of Lt-Gen. Sir Peter Beale and Lady Beale; ed Gonville and Caius Coll., Cambridge; Assoc. Artist of RSC 1986; Pres. Anthony Powell Soc.; Patron, English Touring Theatre, South London Theatre, London Symphony Chorus, For Short. Theatre co.; Hon. Bencher, Middle Temple 2010; Freedom of the City of London 2011; Dr hc (Open Univ.) 2010. *Theatre includes:* (Traverse Theatre, Edin.): Die House, Sandra/Manon, Points of Departure, The Death of Elias Sawney; (Lyceum, Edin.): Hamlet (Royal Court, London): Women Beware Women, The Duchess of Malfi, Volpone, Rosencrantz and Guildenstern are Dead, Candide (Olivier Award for Best Actor in a Musical 2000), Money 1999, Sommerfolk, Hamlet (Royal Nat. Theatre) 2000, Uncle Vanya (Olivier Award for Best Actor 2003; Donmar Warehouse, London) 2002, Macbeth (Almeida, London) 2005, The Philanthropist (Evening Standard Award for Best Actor 2005) (Donmar Warehouse, London) 2005, Monty Python's Spamalot (Palace Theatre, London) 2005–06, London Assurance (Royal Nat. Theatre) 2010, Timon of Athens (Royal Nat. Theatre) 2012, Privates on Parade (part of Michael Grandage's new West End season at the Noël Coward Theatre) 2012–13, The Hothouse (Trafalgar Studios) 2013, King Lear (Royal Nat. Theatre) 2014. *RSC productions include:* The Winter's Tale, The Art of Success, Everyman in his Humour, The Fair Maid of the West, The Storm, Speculators, The Constant Couple, The Man of Mode, Restoration, Mary and

Lizzie, Some Americans Abroad, Playing with Trains, Troilus and Cressida, Edward II (title role), Love's Labours Lost, The Seagull, Richard III (title role), The Tempest, King Lear, Ghosts, Othello. *Films include:* Orlando 1992, Persuasion 1995, Hamlet 1996, An Ideal Husband 1999, Blackadder Back & Forth (short) 1999, The Gathering 2003, Deep Water (voice) 2006, 1320 2011, The Deep Blue Sea 2011, My Week with Marilyn 2011. *Radio includes:* played George Smiley in BBC Radio 4 adaptation of all the John Le Carré novels in which Smiley featured 2009–10, Discovering Music (presenter) 2011, Collaborators 2012, Copenhagen 2013. *Television includes:* Time and the Conways (film) 1985, A Very Peculiar Practice (series) 1988, Downtown Lagos (mini-series) 1992, The Mushroom Picker (mini-series) 1993, A Dance to the Music of Time (mini-series) (Royal TV Soc. Award for Best Actor 1997, BAFTA Award for Best Actor 1998) 1997, The Temptation of Franz Schubert (film) 1997, Alice in Wonderland (film) 1999, The Young Visiters (film) 2003, Dunkirk (documentary) 2004, The American Experience (series documentary) 2006, Sacred Music (series presenter) 2007, Sacred Music 2 (series presenter) 2009, Spooks 2010, Alice's Adventures in Wonderland (film) 2011, Symphony (series) 2011, God's Composer (presenter) 2011, The Hollow Crown (BAFTA Award for Supporting Actor for his performance as Falstaff in BBC series of TV films about Shakespeare's historical dramas Richard II; Henry IV, Part 1; Henry IV, Part 2 and Henry V 2013) 2012, Parkinson – Masterclass 2013. *Leisure interests:* medieval history, music, history of religion. *Address:* c/o The Richard Stone Partnership, Suite 3, De Walden Court, 85 New Cavendish Street, London, W1W 6XD, England (office). *Telephone:* (20) 7497-0849 (office). *Fax:* (20) 7497-0869 (office). *E-mail:* mpoole@thersp.com (office). *Website:* www .therichardstonepartnership.co.uk/artist-details/simon_russell_beale (office).

RUSSO, Patricia F., BA; American communications industry executive; b. 1953, Trenton, NJ; m.; two step-c.; ed Lawrence High School, Georgetown Univ., Harvard Business School; Sales and Marketing Man. Exec., IBM 1973–81; joined AT&T, Murray Hill, NJ 1981, Pres. business unit, Business Communications Systems 1992–96, Exec. Vice-Pres. Strategy Business Devt and Corp. Operations 1997–99, Exec. Vice-Pres. and CEO Service Provider Networks Group 1999–2000, Pres. and CEO Lucent Technologies Inc. (spin-off of AT&T) 2002–03, Chair. and CEO 2003–06, CEO jt Alcatel-Lucent co. (following Alcatel acquisition of Lucent) 2006–08; Chair. Avaya, Inc. (fmr Business Communications Systems unit of Lucent Technologies) –2001; Pres. and COO Eastman Kodak 2001–02; mem. Bd of Dirs Xerox Corpn, Schering-Plough Corpn (Chair. Governance Cttee), New Jersey Manufacturers Insurance Co., Georgetown Univ.; Vice-Chair. Nat. Security Telecommunications Advisory Cttee 2003–06; mem. Network Reliability Interoperability Council; Trustee, Georgetown Univ.; Hon. DEng (Stevens Inst. of Tech.); Dr hc (Columbia Coll., SC); ranked by Fortune magazine amongst 50 Most Powerful Women in Business in the US 1998–2000, (26th) 2001, (15th) 2002, (21st) 2003, (14th) 2004, (14th) 2005, and amongst 50 Most Powerful Women in Business outside the US (first) 2006, (fourth) 2007, ranked by Forbes magazine amongst 100 Most Powerful Women (56th) 2004, (13th) 2005, (25th) 2006, (10th) 2007, ranked by the Financial Times amongst Top 25 Businesswomen in Europe (seventh) 2007. *Address:* c/o Alcatel–Lucent, 54, rue de la Boétie, 75008 Paris, France. *Telephone:* 1-40-76-10-10. *E-mail:* execoffice@alcatel-lucent.com.

RUSSO, Rene; American actress; b. 17 Feb. 1954, Burbank, Calif.; d. of Shirley Russo; one d.; fmrly model Eileen Ford Agency. *Film appearances include:* Meanwhile in Santa Monica 1988, Major League 1989, Mr Destiny 1990, One Good Cop 1991, Freejack 1992, Lethal Weapon 3 1992, In the Line of Fire 1993, Major League II 1994, Outbreak 1995, Get Shorty 1995, Tin Cup 1996, Ransom 1996, Buddy 1997, Lethal Weapon 4 1998, The Thomas Crown Affair 1999, The Adventures of Rocky and Bullwinkle 2000, Showtime 2002, Big Trouble 2002, 2 for the Money 2005, Yours, Mine & Ours 2005, Thor 2011. *Television appearance:* Sable (series) 1987. *Address:* c/o Progressive Artists Agency, 400 South Beverly Drive, Suite 216, Beverly Hills, CA 90212, USA.

RUST, Edward B., Jr, BA, MBA, JD; American insurance industry executive; *Chairman and CEO, State Farm Insurance Companies;* b. Ill.; m. Sally Rust; one s.; ed Illinois Wesleyan Univ., Southern Methodist Univ.; joined Tex. Regional Office, State Farm 1975, Pres. and CEO State Farm Insurance Cos 1985–87, Chair. and CEO 1987–, also Chair. and CEO State Farm Mutual Automobile Insurance Co., Pres. and CEO State Farm Fire and Casualty Co.; mem. Bd of Dirs Caterpillar Inc., Peoria, Helmerich and Payne Inc., McGraw-Hill Cos Inc.; Vice-Chair. US Chamber of Commerce; mem. Bd America's Promise Alliance, James B. Hunt, Jr Inst. for Educational Leadership, Achieve, Inc.; Co-Chair. The Business Roundtable for seven years (currently mem. Exec. Cttee); Chair. Emer. Illinois Business Roundtable, Business Higher Educ. Forum, The Business Roundtable's Educ. Initiative; fmr Chair. American Enterprise Inst., Financial Services Roundtable, Nat. Alliance for Business, Insurance Inst. for Highway Safety; Dir Achieve, Nat. Center for Educational Accountability; mem. Business Advisory Council, Illinois Coll. of Commerce and Business Admin; fmr mem. Advisory Council Stanford Univ. Grad. School of Business, Bd of Overseers Inst. for Civil Justice, Nat. (Glenn) Comm. on Math. and Science Teaching for the 21st Century, No Child Left Behind Comm.; Trustee, The Conference Bd, Cttee for Econ. Devt, Illinois Wesleyan Univ.; fmr Trustee, American Inst. for Property and Liability Underwriters; mem. Tex. and Ill. Bar Asscns. *Address:* State Farm Insurance Cos, 1 State Farm Plaza, Bloomington, IL 61710-0001, USA (office). *Telephone:* (309) 766-2311 (office). *Fax:* (309) 766-3621 (office). *E-mail:* info@statefarm.com (office). *Website:* www.statefarm.com (office).

RUSTAMOV, Elman Siraj oglu, CandEconSci, DEconSci; Azerbaijani economist and central banker; *Chairman, National Bank of Azerbaijan;* b. 29 June 1952, Jabrail dist; m.; three c.; ed Azerbaijan Nat. Economy Inst. (named after D. Bunyadzade); economist, Scientific Research Inst. of Economy, USSR State Planning Cttee July–Dec. 1973, Head Economist 1980–90, Doctorantura 1990–92; with Azerbaijan Nat. Economy Inst. 1973–78; mil. service, Smolensk, USSR 1974–75; Chief of Dept of Economy, Baku Fine Broadcloth Union of Azerbaijan SSR, Ministry of Light Industry 1978–80; Chief Adviser, Presidential Apparatus of Azerbaijan Repub. 1991–92; First Deputy Chair. Man. Bd Nat. Bank of Azerbaijan 1992–93, Deputy Chair. Man. Bd Agrarian – Industrial Union Jt Stock Bank 1993–94, First Deputy Chair. Man. Bd Nat. Bank of Azerbaijan 1994–95, Admin. for Azerbaijan at World Bank Group, MIGA and EBRD 1995, Chair. Man. Bd Nat. Bank of Azerbaijan 1995–. *Address:* National Bank of

Azerbaijan, 32 Rashid Beybutov Avenue, Baku 370014, Azerbaijan (office). *Telephone:* (12) 931122 (office). *Fax:* (12) 935541 (office). *E-mail:* rustamov@nba .az (office). *Website:* www.nba.az (office).

RUTAN, Elbert L. (Burt), BS; American aerospace engineer; *Owner, Scaled Composites, LLC;* b. 17 June 1943, Portland, Ore.; m. 4th Tonya Rutan; ed Calif. Polytechnic Univ.; first solo flight in Aeronca Champ aeroplane aged 16 1959; flight test project engineer, USAF, Edwards Air Force Base 1965–72; Dir Bede Test Center for Bede Aircraft, Newton, Kan. 1972–74; f. Rutan Aircraft Factory to develop light aircraft for homebuilt aircraft market 1974; f. Scaled Composites, LLC 1982, designed several aircraft including Voyager aircraft that his brother Dick and Jeana Yeager flew in first nonstop, un-refuelled flight around the world 1986, SpaceShipOne (first pvt. vehicle to achieve suborbital, 62.5 miles/100 km, spaceflight), Raytheon Beechcraft Starship, Proteus, VariEze, Long-EZ, Quickie, Quickie 2, Defiant, and Boomerang; won $10 million Ansari X Prize for making two flights in SpaceShipOne within two weeks 29 Sept. and 4 Oct. 2004. *Address:* Scaled Composites, LLC, 1624 Flight Line, Mojave, CA 93501, USA (office). *Telephone:* (661) 824-4541 (office). *Fax:* (661) 824-4174 (office). *Website:* www .scaled.com (office).

RUTELLI, Francesco; Italian politician; *Leader, Alleanza per l'Italia;* b. 14 June 1954, Rome; m. Barbara Palombelli; four c.; mem. Camera dei Deputati (Parl.) (Radicals) 1983–93, then mem. Green Party, then Founder-mem. Democrats party; Minister for Environment (resgnd after one day) 1993; Mayor of Rome 1993–2001; mem. European Parl. 1999–2004; Pres. Democrazia è Libertà—La Margherita (Democracy is Liberty—The Daisy) 2001–07; Deputy Prime Minister and Minister of Cultural Assets and Activities 2006–08; Chair. Parl. Cttee for the Security of the Repub. (COPASIR) 2008–09; Leader Alleanza per l'Italia 2009–. *Address:* Alleanza per l'Italia, Largo Fontanella Borghese 84, 00186 Rome, Italy (office). *Telephone:* (06) 91712000 (office). *Fax:* (06) 68802560 (office). *E-mail:* info@ alleanzaperlitalia.it (office). *Website:* www.alleanzaperlitalia.it (office).

RUTHVEN, Kenneth Knowles, PhD; British academic; *Visiting Professor of English, University of Adelaide;* b. 26 May 1936; ed Univ. of Manchester; Asst Lecturer, Lecturer, Sr Lecturer, Univ. of Canterbury, Christchurch, NZ 1961–72, Prof. of English 1972–79; Prof. of English, Univ. of Adelaide, Australia 1980–85, Univ. of Melbourne, Vic., Australia 1985–99, Prof. Emer. 2000–; Visiting Prof. of English, Univ. of Adelaide 2002–. *Publications:* A Guide to Ezra Pound's Personae 1969, The Conceit 1969, Myth 1976, Critical Assumptions 1979, Feminist Literary Studies: An Introduction 1984, Ezra Pound as Literary Critic 1990, Beyond the Disciplines: The New Humanities (ed.) 1992, Nuclear Criticism 1993, Faking Literature 2001, The Complete Poems of William Barnes, Vol. 1 (co-ed.) 2013; editor: Southern Review (Adelaide) 1981–85, Interpretations series (gen.) 1993–96 (19 vols). *Address:* 27 Fairleys Road, Rostrevor 5073, SA, Australia (home). *Telephone:* (8) 8336-6348 (home). *E-mail:* kenruthven@bigpond.com (home). *Website:* www.hss.adelaide.edu.au/english (office).

RUTSKOY, Maj.-Gen. Aleksandr Vladimirovich, CandEconSc; Russian politician and military officer; b. 16 Sept. 1947, Proskurov, Kamenets Podolsk Region (now Khmelnitsky, Ukraine); s. of Vladimir Alexandrovich Rutskoy and Zinaida Iosifovna Rutskaya; m. 3rd Irina Rutskaya; three s. one d.; ed Higher Air Force Coll., Barnaul, Y. Gagarin Higher Air Force Acad., Acad. of Gen. Staff; fmr mem. CPSU (expelled 1991); Regimental Commdr, Afghan War 1985–86; Deputy Commdr Army Air Force 1988; RSFSR People's Deputy, mem. Supreme Soviet, mem. Presidium of Supreme Soviet 1990–91; Leader Communists for Democracy (renamed People's Party of Free Russia 1991, renamed Russian Social Democratic Party 1994); Vice-Pres. RSFSR (now Russian Fed.) 1991–93; Head Centre for the Operational Supervision of the Progress of Reforms 1991–93; Leader Civic Union coalition 1992–93; declared Acting Pres. of Russia by Parl. Sept. 1993; arrested as one of organizers of failed coup d'état Oct. 1993; freed on amnesty Feb. 1994; Chair. Social-Patriotic Movt Derzhava 1994; Gov. of Kursk Region 1996–2000; mem. Council Europe Parl. 1996–2000; Pro-Rector Moscow State Sociological Univ. 2001; Hero of Soviet Union 1988, Order of Lenin, seven Russian and Afghan orders; 15 medals. *Publications include:* Agrarian Reform in Russia 1992, Unknown Rutskoy 1994, About Us and Myself 1995, Finding Faith 1995, Lefortovo Protocols 1995, March Records 1995, Bloody Autumn 1996, Liberal Reforms – Strong Power 1996. *Leisure interests:* painting, gardening, designing, fishing. *Telephone:* (495) 292-66-98.

RUTTE, Mark, MA; Dutch business executive and politician; *Prime Minister;* b. 14 Feb. 1967, The Hague; ed Univ. of Leiden; joined Unilever 1992, various positions within group including Human Resources Man., Personnel Man., Van den Bergh Nederland (Calvé) 1997–2000, Dir of Human Resources, IGLOMora Group BV 2002; mem. Tweede Kamer (House of Reps) Jan.–May 2003, 2006–10; mem. People's Party for Freedom and Democracy (VVD), Parl. Leader 2006–10; Sec. of State for Social Affairs and Employment 2002–04, for Educ., Culture and Science 2004–06; Prime Minister 2010–2012 (resgnd), re-elected 2012–; Minister of Gen. Affairs 2010–2012, 2012– (after re-elections). *Address:* Office of the Prime Minister, Ministry of General Affairs, Binnenhof 20, POB 20001, 2500 EA The Hague, Netherlands (office). *Telephone:* (70) 3564100 (office). *Fax:* (70) 3564683 (office). *Website:* www.government.nl (office); www.vvd.nl (office).

RUTTENSTORFER, Wolfgang, DEcon; Austrian business executive; *Chairman of the Executive Board and CEO, OMV AG;* b. 1950, Vienna; m.; three c.; ed Univ. of Econs and Business Admin, Vienna; joined OMV AG 1976, with Planning and Control Dept 1985, Head of Strategic Devt 1989–90, Head of Marketing 1990, mem. Exec. Bd 1992–97, 2000–, CEO and Chair., Exec. Bd 2002–; Deputy Minister of Finance 1997–2000. *Address:* OMV AG, Trabrennstrasse 6–8, 1020 Vienna, Austria (office). *Telephone:* (1) 40440-21401 (office). *Fax:* (1) 40440-29496 (office). *E-mail:* wolfgang.ruttenstorfer@omv.com (office). *Website:* www.omv.com (office).

RUTTER, John Milford, CBE, MA, BMus; British composer and conductor; *Director, The Cambridge Singers;* b. 24 Sept. 1945, London; m. JoAnne Redden 1980; two s. (one deceased) one step-d.; ed Highgate School and Clare Coll., Cambridge; Dir of Music Clare Coll., Cambridge 1975–79; part-time Lecturer in Music, Open Univ. 1975–87; Founder and Dir The Cambridge Singers 1981–; Hon. FGCM 1988, Hon. Fellow, Westminster Choir Coll., Princeton, Clare Coll., Cambridge 2001, Hon. Freeman Worshipful Co. of Barbers 2008, Hon. Bencher Middle Temple 2008; Hon. DMus (Lambeth) 1996, Dr hc (Anglia Ruskin Univ.)

2004, (Leicester) 2005, (Hull) 2008; Ivor Novello Classical Music Award 2007. *Compositions include:* The Falcon 1969, Gloria 1974, Bang! (opera for young people) 1975, The Piper of Hamelin (opera for young people) 1980, Requiem 1985, Magnificat 1990, I my best beloved's am (unaccompanied choral work for BBC Sounding the Millennium series) 1999, Mass of the Children 2003; numerous carols, anthems and songs; orchestral works and music for TV. *Recordings include:* original version of Fauré Requiem 1984. *Publications:* Opera Choruses (ed.) 1995, European Sacred Music (ed.) 1996, Christmas Motets (ed.) 1999. *Address:* Old Laceys, St John's Street, Duxford, Cambridge, CB22 4RA, England (home).

RUTTER, Sir Michael Llewellyn, Kt, CBE, MD, FRS, FRCP, FRCPsych; British physician and academic; *Research Professor, Institute of Psychiatry, King's College London;* b. 15 Aug. 1933; s. of Llewellyn Charles Rutter and Winifred Olive Rutter; m. Marjorie Heys 1958; one s. two d.; ed Univ. of Birmingham Medical School; practised at Maudsley Hosp. 1958–61; Nuffield Medical Travelling Fellow, Albert Einstein Coll. of Medicine, New York 1961–62; scientist with MRC Social Psychology Research Unit 1962–65; Sr Lecturer, then Reader, King's Coll. London Inst. of Psychiatry 1966–73, Prof. of Child Psychiatry 1973–98, Research Prof. 1998, now Prof. of Developmental Psychopathology, Dir MRC Research Centre for Social, Genetic and Developmental Psychiatry 1994–98, consultant psychiatrist, Maudsley Hospital 1966–; est. Medical Research Council Child Psychiatry Research Unit, Hon. Dir 1984–98, the Social, Genetic and Developmental Psychiatry Research Centre, Hon. Dir 1994–98; Deputy Chair. Wellcome Trust 1999–2004; Fellow, Center for Advanced Study in Behavioral Sciences, Stanford Univ. 1979–80; Pres. Soc. for Research in Child Devt 1999–2001 (Pres. 1997–99); Clinical Vice-Pres. Acad. of Medical Sciences 2004–07; Hon. Fellow, British Psychological Soc. 1978, American Acad. of Pediatrics 1981, Royal Soc. of Medicine 1996; Dr hc (Leiden) 1985, (Catholic Univ. of Leuven) 1990, (Birmingham) 1990, (Edinburgh) 1990, (Chicago) 1991, (Minnesota) 1993, (Jyväskylä) 1996, (Warwick) 1999, (East Anglia) 2000. *Publications include:* Children of Sick Parents 1966: A Neuropsychiatric Study in Childhood (jtly) 1970, Education, Health and Behaviour (ed. jtly) 1970, Infantile Autism (ed.) 1971, Maternal Deprivation Reassessed (ed.) 1981, The Child with Delayed Speech (jtly) 1972, Helping Troubled Children (jtly) 1975, Cycles of Disadvantage (jtly) 1976; Child Psychiatry (ed. jtly) 1976, (2nd edn as Child and Adolescent Psychiatry 1985), Autism (ed. jtly) 1978, Changing Youth in a Changing Society (jtly) 1979, Fifteen Thousand Hours: Secondary Schools and Their Effect on Children 1979, Scientific Foundations of Developmental Psychiatry (ed.)1981, A Measure of Our Values: Goals and Dilemmas in the Upbringing of Children (jtly) 1983, Lead versus Health (jtly) 1983, Juvenile Delinquency 1983, Developmental Neuropsychiatry (ed.) 1983, Stress, Coping and Development (ed. jtly) 1983, Depression and Young People (ed. jtly) 1986, Studies of Psychosocial Risk: The Power of Longitudinal Data (ed.) 1988, Parenting Breakdown: The Making and Breaking of Inter-generational Links (jtly) 1988, Straight and Devious Pathways from Childhood to Adulthood (ed. jtly) 1990, Biological Risk Factors for Psychosocial Disorders (ed. jtly) 1991, Developing Minds (jtly) 1993, Development Through Life: A Handbook for Clinicians (ed. jtly) 1994, Stress, Risk and Resilience in Children and Adolescents (ed. jtly) 1994, Psychological Disorders in Young People 1995, Antisocial Behaviour by Young People (jtly) 1998, Genes and Behaviour: Nature-Nurture Interplay Explained 2006. *Leisure interests:* fell walking, tennis, wine tasting, theatre. *Address:* Institute of Psychiatry, King's College London, Box P, De Crespigny Park, London SE5 8AF (office); 190 Court Lane, Dulwich, London, SE21 7ED, England (home). *Telephone:* (20) 7848-0882 (office). *Fax:* j.wickham@iop.kcl.ac.uk (office). *Website:* www.kcl.ac.uk/iop/index.aspx (office).

RÜÜTEL, Arnold, PhD, DrAgrSc; Estonian politician, agronomist and fmr head of state; *Honorary Chairman, Estonian People's Union;* b. 10 May 1928, Laimjala, Saaremaa Island; s. of Feodor Rüütel and Juulia Rüütel; m. Ingrid Rüütel (née Ruus) 1935; two d.; ed Jäneda Agric. Coll., Estonian Agricultural Acad.; Sr Agronomist, Saaremaa Dist, Estonian SSR 1949–50; mil. service 1950–55; teacher, Tartu School of Mechanization of Agric. 1955–57; Deputy Dir Estonian Inst. of Livestock-breeding and Veterinary Sciences 1957–63; mem. CPSU 1964–90; Dir Tartu Model State Farm 1963–69; Rector Estonian Agric. Acad. 1969–77; Agricultural Sec. of Cen. Cttee of Estonian CP 1977–79; First Deputy Chair. Council of Ministers of Estonia 1979–83; Chair. Presidium of Supreme Soviet of Estonian SSR 1983–90, of Supreme Council of Repub. of Estonia 1990–92; Deputy Pres. of USSR Presidium of Supreme Soviet 1984–91; mem. Constitutional Ass. 1991–92; Founder, Dir Inst. for Nat. Devt and Cooperation 1993–2001; Founder and Chair. Estonian Rural People's Party (Maarahva) 1994–99, Chair. Estonian People's Union 1999–2000, Hon. Chair. 2006–; mem. Riigikogu (Parl.) 1995–2001, Vice-Chair. 1995–97, Chair. ruling coalition's council 1995–99; Head Del. of Riigikogu to Baltic Ass. 1995–99, mem., alternately Chair. Presidium 1995–99; presidential cand. 1996; Pres. of Estonia 2001–06; Chair. Estonian Soc. for Nature Protection 1981–88, Keep Estonian Sea Clean, Forselius (educational org.); Pres. Estonian Green Cross 1993–2001; mem. Tallinn City Council 1993–2001; Chair. Estonian Soc. for Nature Conservation 1981–88 (Hon. mem. 1989–), B.G. Forselius Soc. 1989–2002, Hon. Chair. 2002–, Movt 'Protect the Estonian Sea' 1993–2002 (Hon. Chair. 2002–); Pres. Estonian Nat. Org. of the Green Cross Int. 1993–2001, 2006–; Foreign mem. Ukranian Acad. of Agrarian Sciences 2002; Hon. mem. Estonian Academic Agricultural Soc. 2002–, Int. Raoul Wallenberg Foundation 2002–; Collar of Order of Grand Cross of Terra Mariana (Estonia) 2001, Grand Cross Order of the White Rose with Collar (Finland) 2001, Grand Cross Order of the White Eagle (Poland) 2002, Grand Cross Royal Order of St Olaf (Norway) 2002, Grand Cross Order of Merit (Hungary) 2002, Grand Cross Order of Adolph de Nassau (Luxembourg) 2003, Grand Collar Nat. Order of Merit (Malta) 2003, Grand Collar Nat. Order of Merit (Romania) 2003, Grand Collar Order of Makarios III (Cyprus) 2004, Grand Cross with Collar, Order of Merit (Italy) 2004, Order of Falcon (Iceland) 2004, Order of 1st Class of Vytautas the Great (Lithuania) 2004, Order of 1st Class White Double Cross (Slovak Repub.) 2005; Dr hc (Bentley Coll.) 1991, (Estonian Agricultural Univ.) 1991, (Univ. of Helsinki) 2002, (Nat. Agricultural Univ. of Ukraine) 2002, (Univ. of Naples II) 2002, (Szent Istvan Univ., Hungary) 2004, (L.N. Gumilyov Eurasian Nat. Univ. of Kazakhstan) 2004, (Yerevan, Armenia) 2004; Rotary Foundation Distinguished Service Award 2002, Andres Bello Commemorative Medal 2002. *Publications:* Tuleviku taassünd (The Rebirth of the Future) (memoirs) 2003. *Leisure interests:* nature protection, sports. *Address:*

Kaare Street 10, 11618 Tallinn, Estonia (home). *Telephone:* 6316291 (office). *E-mail:* ryytel.office@vpk.ee (office).

RUVKUN, Gary Bruce, BS, PhD; American molecular biologist, geneticist and academic; *Professor, Department of Genetics, Harvard Medical School;* b. 26 March 1952, Berkeley, Calif.; ed Univ. of California, Berkeley, Harvard Univ., Massachusetts Inst. of Tech.; currently Prof., Dept of Genetics, Harvard Medical School; mem. NAS 2008, American Acad. of Arts and Sciences 2009, Inst. of Medicine 2009; Lewis S. Rosenstiel Award for Distinguished Work in Medical Research, Brandeis Univ. (co-recipient) 2005, Warren Triennial Prize, Massachusetts Gen. Hosp. (co-recipient) 2007, Albert Lasker Award for Basic Medical Research (co-recipient) 2008, Benjamin Franklin Medal in Life Science (co-recipient) 2008, Gairdner Foundation Int. Award (co-recipient) 2008, Louisa Gross Horwitz Prize, Columbia Univ. (co-recipient) 2009, Massry Prize, Keck School of Medicine, Univ. of Southern California (co-recipient) 2009, Dan David Prize 2011, 2012 Dr Paul Janssen Award for Biomedical Research (co-recipient) 2012. *Publications:* more than 150 papers in professional journals. *Address:* Department of Molecular Biology, Massachusetts General Hospital, Simches CPZN7806, 185 Cambridge Street, Boston, MA 02114, USA (office). *Telephone:* (617) 726-5959 (office). *Fax:* (617) 726-5949 (office); (617) 726-5973 (office). *E-mail:* ruvkun@molbio.mgh.harvard.edu (office). *Website:* www.hms.harvard.edu/dms/bbs (office); ccib.mgh.harvard.edu/ruvkun (office); molbio.mgh.harvard.edu/laboratories/ruvkun (office).

RUYS, Anthony; Dutch business executive; b. 20 July 1947, Antwerp, Belgium; m. Melanie E. van Haaften; two s.; ed Univ. of Utrecht, Harvard Business School; marketing trainee Van den Bergh & Jurgens 1974–80; Marketing Dir Cogra Lever S.A. 1980–84, Chair. 1984–87; Chair. Van den Bergh Italy; mem. Bd Italian Unilever Cos 1987–89; Chair. Van den Bergh Netherlands; mem. Bd Dutch Unilever Cos 1989–92; Sr Regional Man. Food Exec., North European Region, Unilever NV 1992–93; mem. Exec. Bd Heineken NV 1993–96, Vice-Chair. 1996–2002, Chair. 2002–05; Dir TRN, BAT Europe (Netherlands) BV, Rembrandt Foundation, Gtech Corpn, NH Hotels SA 1994–2003; Pres. Supervisory Bd Rijksmuseum, Amsterdam, Stop Aids Now Foundation, ECR Europe 2004–06; mem. Supervisory Bd Gtech Holdings Corpn (now Lottomatica Italy), USA, ABN Ambro Bank, Sara Lee Int. B.V., Rijksmuseum, Amsterdam, Tourism Recreation Netherlands, Aiesec Netherlands 1996–2004, Veerstichting 1997–2007; mem. Bd of Dirs Netherlands Asscn for Int. Affairs, Int. Chamber of Commerce Netherlands, Nationaal Fonds Kunstbehoud, British American Tobacco PLC 2006–, Luchthaven Schipol NV, Rothmans Europe 1997–2001, Robeco Group NV 2001–04, Trilateral Comm. 2003–06, European Round Table of Industrialists 2004–05; mem. European Advisory Bd Harvard Business School 2003–07; mem. Int. Council INSEAD. *Address:* c/o Heineken NV, Tweede Weteringsplantsoen 21, Postbus 28, 1000 Amsterdam AA, Netherlands (office).

RUZICKA, Karel Zdenek; Czech musician and composer; b. 2 June 1940, Prague; s. of Zdenek Ruzicka and Vlasta Ruzicka; m. Marie-José; one s.; ed Conservatory of Prague; pianist, Semafor Theatre, Prague 1960–66; mem. Prague Radio Big Band 1966–90; teacher Conservatory of Jaroslav Jezek, Prague 1969; imprisoned for political activities 1969; pianist, composer, arranger, conductor 1970–2000; f. Karel Ruzicka Jazz Quartet; has toured and performed in Canada, Poland, Cuba, France and Czech Repub.; has collaborated with Laco Deczi's Jazz Cellula septet, Czech–Polish Big Band, Veleband All-Stars and with numerous musicians including Rudolf Dasek (guitarist), Jarmo Sermila (trumpeter), Jiri Stivin(flutist), Wilson de Oliveira (saxophonist); Celebration Jazz Mass and Te Deum compositions performed during The Prague Spring Music Festival and also in Europe and USA; Monte Carlo Int. Jazz Festival composition awards (Interlude) 1977, (Echoes) 1978, (Triste) 1979; numerous awards from the Czech Composers Soc. and Musical Acad. of Monaco; Ministry of Culture Prize 1989. *Recordings:* 10 albums, 100 compositions, including Fata Morgana, Going Home, Flight, Celebration Jazz Mass, Te Deum. *Publications:* Jazz Echoes, Best of Arta, In the Garden of Time. *Leisure interest:* literature. *Address:* c/o Conservatory of Jaroslav Jezek, Roskotova 4/1692, 14000 Prague 4 (office); Devonska 1, 15200 Prague 5, Czech Republic (home). *E-mail:* karuz@barr.cz (home); karuzjazz@gmail.com (home).

RUZIMATOV, Farukh Sadilloyevich; Tajikistani ballet dancer and ballet director; *Artistic Director, Mikhailovsky Theater Ballet Company;* b. 26 June 1963, Tashkent; ed Vaganova Acad. of Russian Ballet; soloist State Academic Mariinsky Theatre 1981–86, Prin. Dancer 1986–2007; guest dancer Bolshoi Theatre, Moscow; Prin. Guest Dancer, American Ballet Theater 1990–91; Artistic Dir Mikhailovsky Theater Ballet Company, St Petersburg 2007–; Pres. Farukh Ruzimatov The Renaissance of the Dance Art Foundation 2006–; chevalier, Order For the Spiritual Renaissance of Russia; Silver Medallist, Sixth Varna Int. Competition 1983, awarded special diploma by Paris Acad. of Dance, Honoured Artist of Russia 1995, Golden Sofit Award 1995, Baltika Prize 1998, Peoplés Artist of Russia 2000. *Principal roles include:* Albert in Giselle, Siegfried in Swan Lake, Basil in Don Quixote, The Prince in The Nutcracker, José in Carmen, Golden Slave in Sheherazade, Désiré Prince in Sleeping Beauty, James in La Sylphide, Solor in Bayadere, Ali in Corsair, Abderahman in Raymonda, Ferhad in Fokin's The Legend about love, Tariel in Vinogradov's The Knight in Tiger Skin. *Address:* Mikhailovsky Theatre, Arts Square, 1, St Petersburg, Russia (office). *Telephone:* (812) 595-43-05 (office). *E-mail:* pr@mikhailovsky.ru (office). *Website:* www.mikhailovsky.ru (office).

RUZOWITZKY, Stefan; Austrian film director and screenwriter; b. 25 Dec. 1961, Vienna; m.; two d.; ed Univ. of Vienna; began career by directing documentaries and commercials and also music videos for N'Sync, Scorpions and Die Prinzen. *Films:* Tempo (Max Ophüls Preis) 1996, Die Siebtelbauern (The Inheritors; aka The One-Seventh Farmers) (Best Picture, Rotterdam Film Festival, Flanders Film Festival, prize at Int. Film Festival, Valladolid) 1998, Anatomie (Anatomy) 2000, All the Queen's Men (Die Männer Ihrer Majestät) 2001, Anatomie 2 2003, Die Fälscher (The Counterfeiters) (Academy Award for Best Foreign Language Film 2008) 2007. *Address:* c/o Miriam Rönn, Corporate Communications, Studio Babelsberg AG, August-Bebelstr. 26–53, 14482 Potsdam, Germany. *Telephone:* (331) 721-21-32. *Fax:* (331) 721-21-35. *E-mail:* mroenn@studiobabelsberg.com. *Website:* www.studiobabelsberg.com.

RWANGOMBWA, John; Rwandan politician and government official; *Governor, National Bank of Rwanda;* fmr Chair. School of Finance and Banking, Kigali; Perm. Sec., Ministry of Finance and Econ. Planning and Sec. to Treasury 2006–09, Minister of Finance and Econ. Planning 2009–13; Gov. Nat. Bank of Rwanda 2013–. *Address:* National Bank of Rwanda, ave Paul VI, BP 531, Kigali, Rwanda (office). *Telephone:* 250575282 (office). *Fax:* 250572551 (office). *E-mail:* info@bnr.rw (office). *Website:* www.bnr.rw (office).

RYABOV, Nikolai Timofeyevich; Russian politician, lawyer and diplomatist; b. 9 Dec. 1946, Salsk, Rostov Region; ed Rostov Univ.; mem. CPSU 1968–91; worked as tractor driver, engineer Salsk Agricultural Machine Factory 1966–72; taught in higher educ. school of Rostov Region 1973–90; People's Deputy of Russia 1990–93; mem. Supreme Soviet 1990–92, Chair. Sub-Cttee for legis. 1990–91; Chair. Council of Repubs 1991–92, Deputy Chair. Supreme Soviet 1992–93; Deputy Chair. Constitutional Comm. 1991–93, Chair. Cen. Election Comm. of Russian Fed. 1993–96; Amb. to Czech Repub. 1996–2000, to Azerbaijan 2000–04, to Moldova 2004–06. *Address:* c/o Ministry of Foreign Affairs, 119200 Moscow, Smolenskaya-Sennaya pl. 32/34, Russia.

RYABOV, Vladimir Vladimirovich, PhD; Russian composer and pianist; *Composer in Residence, Moscow Symphony Orchestra;* b. 15 Sept. 1950, Chelyabinsk; m. 1st; one d.; m. 4th Ellen Levine; ed Moscow State Conservatory (expelled twice for non-conformist attitudes), Gnessin Pedagogical Inst. of Music (under Aram Khachaturyan), Leningrad State Conservatory; taught composition in Leningrad and Sverdlovsk conservatories 1977–81; Artistic and Repertoire Consultant, Moscow Symphony Orchestra 1993–; toured as pianist in Russia, Finland, USA, Germany, Austria, Hungary, Italy and Spain, performing standard repertoire and own compositions; mem. Int. Informatization Acad.; winner First S. Prokofiev Int. Composers' Competition 1991, Merited Artist of Russia 1995, Pushkin Gold Medal 1999. *Film:* The Life of Frederic Chopin (pianist) 1992. *Compositions include:* over 30, including 4 symphonies (Nine Northern Tunes 1977, Pushkin 1980, Listen! 1981, In Memoriam of J. Brahms 1983), 5 string quartets, works for full and chamber orchestras, sonatas and other compositions for piano, violin, viola, organ, choir, song cycles on Russian poetry and English, American, Spanish and German poetry in Russian trans., transcriptions of classical music and folk songs, 6 cycles of sacred music, European Cathedrals (7 cycles for different chamber ensembles), Norwegian Suite for symphony orchestra. *Leisure interests:* reading Russian poetry on stage, collecting illustrations of owls. *Address:* Novoyasenevsky pr. 14, kor. 2 Apt. 48, Moscow 117574, Russia (home); Orisaarentie 6E, 00840 Helsinki, Finland (home). *Telephone:* (495) 143-97-13 (Moscow) (home); (9) 6984059 (Helsinki) (home). *E-mail:* moscowsymphonyorchestra@mtu-net.ru (office). *Website:* www.moscowsymphony.ru (office).

RYAN, Alan James, BA, MA, DLitt, FBA; British political scientist, academic and writer; *Professor Emeritus of Political Theory, Princeton University;* b. 9 May 1940, London, England; s. of James W. Ryan and Ivy Ryan; m. Kathleen Alyson Lane 1971; one d.; ed Christ's Hosp., Horsham, Balliol Coll. Oxford, Univ. Coll., London; Asst Lecturer/Lecturer, Keele Univ. 1963–66; Lecturer, Univ. of Essex 1966–; Fellow and Tutor in Politics, New Coll. Oxford 1969, Univ. Lecturer in Politics 1969–78, Reader *ad honinem* 1978–88; Prof. of Politics, Princeton Univ., USA 1988–96, now Prof. Emer.; Mellon Fellow, Inst. for Advanced Study, Princeton, NJ 1991–92; Warden, New Coll., Oxford 1996–2009; Visiting Prof., CUNY 1967–, Univ. of Texas 1972, Univ. of California, Santa Cruz 1977, Univ. of Witwatersrand, SA 1973, 1978, ANU 1974–75, Univ. of Cape Town, SA 1982–84; Visiting Fellow, ANU 1979; de Carle Lecturer, Univ. of Otago, NZ 1983; Fellow, Center for Advanced Studies in the Behavioral Sciences, Stanford Univ., USA 2002–03; Official mem. CNAA 1975–83; Del., Oxford Univ. Press 1982–87; Sr Consulting Ed., Bertrand Russell Project 1987–; mem. Exec. Cttee Conf. for the Study of Political Thought 1988–; Assoc. Ed. 1991–; Chair. Conf. for the Study of Political Thought 1992–96; Almoner, Christ's Hosp. 1998–2004; Coll. prizes in philosophy and politics, Powell English Essay Prize, Convocation Lecturer, Lawrence Univ. 1993 Whidden Lecturer, McMaster Univ. 1993. *Publications:* The Philosophy of John Stuart Mill 1970, The Philosophy of the Social Sciences 1970, J. S. Mill 1974, Property and Political Theory 1984, Property 1987, Russell: A Political Life 1988, John Dewey and the High Tide of American Liberalism 1995, Liberal Anxieties and Liberal Education 1998. *Leisure interests:* dinghy sailing, long train journeys. *Address:* Department of Politics, 249 Corwin Hall, Princeton University, Princeton, NJ 08544, USA (office). *Telephone:* (609) 258-2874 (office). *E-mail:* alan.ryan@new.ox.ac.uk (office); ajryan@princeton.edu (office). *Website:* users.ox.ac.uk/~ajryan (office); www.princeton.edu (office).

RYAN, Arthur (Art) Frederick; American insurance industry executive; b. 14 Sept. 1942, Brooklyn, NY; s. of Arthur Ryan and Gertrude Wingert; m. Patricia Kelly; two s. two d.; ed Providence Coll.; Area Man. Data Corpn Washington, DC 1965–72; Project Man. Chase Manhattan Corpn and Bank, New York 1972–73, Second Vice-Pres. 1973–74, Vice-Pres. 1974–75, Operations Exec. 1978, Exec. Vice-Pres. 1982, later Vice-Chair., Pres. 1990–94; CEO Prudential Insurance Co. of America (now Prudential Financial Inc.) 1994–2007, Chair. 1994–2008; mem. American Bankers Asscn. *Address:* c/o Prudential Financial Inc., 751 Broad Street, 24th Floor, Newark, NJ 07102, USA (office).

RYAN, Meg; American actress; b. 19 Nov. 1961, Fairfield, Conn.; m. Dennis Quaid 1991 (divorced); one s.; ed Bethel High School and New York Univ.; fmrly appeared in TV commercials; TV appearances in As the World Turns, One of the Boys, Amy and the Angel, The Wild Side, Charles in Charge; f. Prufrock Pictures (production co., fmrly Fandango Films) 1994. *Films:* Rich and Famous 1981, Amityville III-D, Top Gun, Armed and Dangerous, Innerspace, D.O.A., Promised Land, The Presidio, When Harry Met Sally, Joe Versus the Volcano, The Doors, Prelude to a Kiss, Sleepless in Seattle, Flesh and Bone, Significant Other, When a Man Loves a Woman, I.Q., Paris Match, Restoration, French Kiss 1995, Two for the Road 1996, Courage Under Fire 1996, Addicted to Love 1997, City of Angels 1998, You've Got Mail 1998, Hanging Up 1999, Lost Souls 1999, Proof of Life 2000, Kate & Leopold 2001, In the Cut 2003, Against the Ropes 2004, In the Land of Women 2007, The Deal 2008, My Mom's New Boyfriend 2008, The Women 2008, Serious Moonlight 2009,. *Television includes:* Web Therapy (series) 2013. *Address:* c/o Steve Dontanville, ICM, 8942 Wilshire Boulevard, Beverly Hills, CA 90211, USA.

RYAN, Thomas M. (Tom), BS; American pharmacist and retail executive; b. 15 Aug. 1952, NJ; m. Cathy Ryan; four c.; ed Univ. of Rhode Island; began career as pharmacist, CVS Pharmacy Inc. 1975, various man. and professional positions including Pres. and CEO CVS Pharmacy Inc. 1994–2007, Vice-Chair. and COO CVS Corpn 1996–98, Chair. 1999–2007, CEO CVS Caremark Corpn (following merger of Caremark Rx Inc. and CVS Corpn 2007) 1998–2011, Pres. CVS Caremark Corpn 1998–2010, Chair. 2007–11; Dir Bank of America Corpn, Yum! Brands Inc.; Co-Chair. Blue Ribbon Steering Cttee, Univ. of RI, Chair. Leadership Gifts Cttee, URI Convocation Center; Hon. DHumLitt (Univ. of Rhode Island) 1999. *Address:* The Board of Directors, Yum! Brands Inc., 1441 Gardiner Lane, Louisville, KY 40213, USA (office). *Telephone:* (502) 874-8300 (office). *Fax:* (502) 874-8790 (office). *E-mail:* info@yum.com (office). *Website:* www.yum.com (office).

RYAZANOV, Eldar Aleksandrovich; Russian film director, writer and television broadcaster; b. 18 Nov. 1927, Samara; studied at VGIK under Pyriev, Kozintsev and Eisenstein; writes most of his own scripts (often together with playwright Emil Braginsky); Chevalier, Légion d'honneur; State Prize of USSR, State Prize of Russia, People's Artist of the USSR 1984, People's Artist of Russia. *Films include:* Voices of Spring 1955, Carnival Night 1956, The Girl without an Address 1957, How Robinson was Created 1961, The Hussar Ballad 1962, Let Me Make a Complaint 1964, Look out for the Cars 1966, The Zigzag of Success 1968, The Old Rascals 1971, The Amazing Adventures of Italians in Russia 1973, The Irony of Fate 1975, An Official Romance 1978, Garage 1979, Put in a Word for the Poor Hussar 1981, Railway Station for Two 1983, A Cruel Romance 1984, Forgotten Melody for Flute 1988, Dear Elena Sergeevna 1988, The Promised Heaven 1991 (Nika Prize 1992), The Prediction 1993, Hey, Fools! 1996, The Old Horses 2000, The Quiet Streams 2000, The Key of the Bedroom 2003, Andersen. Life Without Love 2006; numerous TV productions, including interviews with Boris Yeltsin and Naina Yeltsin 1993. *Television:* The Paris Secrets (series), The Conversations on Fresh Air (series), The Woman's Summer (series). *Publication:* Not Summarizing (memoirs), Nostalgia (poems), The Prediction (novel), Irony of Fate, The Quiet Streams, Eldar TV or My Portrait's Gallery (memoirs) 2002. *Address:* Bolshoi Tishinski per. 12, Apt 70, 123557 Moscow, Russia. *Telephone:* (495) 721-83-70; (495) 546-94-15. *Fax:* (495) 546-94-15 (office).

RYBAK, Volodymyr Vasylovych, DEconSci; Ukrainian politician; b. 3 Oct. 1946, Stalino (now Donetsk); ed Donetsk State Univ.; Chair. Donetsk City Council, Exec. Cttee and Mayor of Donetsk 1993–2002; first Leader, Party of Regional Revival of Ukraine (predecessor of Party of Regions); Co-organizer and first Chair. Party of Regions 1997–2001; mem. Verkhovna Rada (Parl.) 1998–2006, 2007–, Chair. (Speaker) 2012–14 (resgnd); First Deputy Prime Minister and Minister of Construction, Architecture and Housing and Utility 2006–07; Deputy Prime Minister March–Dec. 2007; Merited Builder of Ukraine 1995, Order of Prince Yaroslav the Wise 2011. *Address:* Verkhovna Rada, 01008 Kyiv, vul. M. Hrushevskoho 5, Ukraine. *E-mail:* umz@rada.gov.ua. *Website:* www.rada.gov.ua; partyofregions.ua.

RYBKIN, Ivan Petrovich, DrPolitSch, CandTechSc; Russian politician; b. 20 Oct. 1946, Semigorovka, Voronezh Region; m.; two d.; ed Volgograd Inst. of Agric. Acad. of Social Sciences at Cen. Cttee CPSU; Sr Engineer Kolkhoz Zavety Ilyicha Volgograd Region 1968–69; Lecturer, Prof., Head of Chair, Deputy Dean, Volgograd Inst. of Agric. 1970–87; Sec. Party Cttee 1983–87, First Sec. CPSU Dist Cttee in Volgograd, Second Sec. Volgograd Regional Cttee CPSU 1987–91; Head of Div. Cen. Cttee CP of RSFSR 1991; People's Deputy of Russia 1990–93; co-founder and Co-Chair. Communists of Russia faction 1990–91; mem. Agrarian Party, concurrently co-founder Socialist Party of Workers 1991–93; Deputy in State Duma (Parl.) 1993–96, Chair. 1994–95; mem. Council on Personnel Policy of Pres. Yeltsin 1994–95, mem. Security Council 1994–96, Sec. 1996–98; head of group negotiating with Chechen leaders 1996–98; Deputy Prime Minister 1998; Plenipotentiary Rep. of Russian Pres. to CIS states 1998; Chair. Political Union Regions of Russia, concurrently of Election Bloc 1995–96; Chair. Political Consultative Council of Pres. of Russia 1999–2000; cand. in 2004 presidential elections; Prize for Contribution to Peace with Chechnya (Ichkeria) 1996. *Publications:* State Duma, Fifth Attempt, We are Doomed to Consensus, Russia and the World: The Way to Security; numerous articles. *Address:* c/o Socialist Party, Novo-Basmannaya str. 14, Building 1, 107078 Moscow, Russia (office).

RYCHETSKÝ, Pavel, JuDr; Czech politician and judge; *Chairman, Constitutional Court;* b. 17 Aug. 1943, Prague; m.; three c.; ed Charles Univ.; Sr Lecturer and Asst Prof., Dept of Civil Law, Charles Univ. Law School, Prague 1966–70, compelled to leave for political reasons; worked as co. lawyer for Fortuna commercial agency, Mladá fronta publrs and for housing devt co-operative; mem. CP 1966–69; Co-founder and signatory Charter 77; Co-founder Civic Forum, Rep. Civic Forum Liberal Club and later of Civic Movt; Public Prosecutor-Gen. of Czech Repub. 1990; Deputy Prime Minister and Chair. Legis. Council of the then Czech and Slovak Fed. Repub. 1990; f. solicitor's practice 1992; Lecturer in Political Sciences, Prague School of Econs Faculty of Int. Relations 1992; joined Czech Social Democrat Party 1995; elected Senator for Strakonice Constituency No. 12, later Chair. Constitutional Law Cttee of the Senate; Deputy Prime Minister of Czech Repub. and Chair. Govt Legis. Council 1998–2003; Chair. Govt Council for Research and Devt 1998–2002, Govt Council for Roma Community Affairs 1998–2002, Govt Council for Ethnic Minorities 1998–2002; Minister of Justice 2000–01, 2002–03; Chair. Constitutional Court, Brno 2003–; Chair. Czech Lawyers' Asscn 1990–92; Pres. Bd Trustees Pro-Bohemia Foundation 1992–98; Founder Práchensko Region Citizens' Endowment Fund; Officier, Légion d'honneur 2005. *Address:* The Constitutional Court of the Czech Republic, Jostova 8, 660 83 Brno 2, Czech Republic (office). *Telephone:* (54) 2214360 (office). *Fax:* (54) 2218326 (office). *E-mail:* pavel.rychetsky@usoud.cz (office). *Website:* www.usoud .cz (office).

RYCKMANS, Pierre, (Simon Leys), PhD; Belgian/Australian academic and writer; b. 28 Sept. 1935, Brussels; m. Chang Han-fang; three s. one d.; ed Univ. of Louvain; taught Chinese Literature, ANU 1970–86; Prof. of Chinese Studies, Univ. of Sydney 1987–93; Fellow, Australian Acad. of Humanities; mem. Acad. Royale de Littérature Française (Brussels) 1991–; Officer Ordre de Léopold, Commdr Ordre des Arts et Lettres 1999; Prix Stanislas-Julien (Institut de France), Prix Jean Walter (Acad. Française); The Independent (UK) Foreign Fiction Award 1992, Christina Stead Prize for Fiction (NSW) 1992, Prix Bernheim 1999, Prix

Renaudot 2001, Prix Henri Gal (Acad. Française) 2001, Prix Guizot 2004, Prix Fémina (100th anniversary) 2004, Prix del Duca (Acad. Française) 2005. *Film:* The Emperor's New Clothes (Dir Alan Taylor, Producer U. Pasolini) 2001, adapted from Simon Leys' The Death of Napoleon. *Publications:* (under pen-name Simon Leys) The Chairman's New Clothes: Mao and the Cultural Revolution 1977, Chinese Shadows 1977, The Burning Forest 1985, La Mort de Napoléon 1986 (English trans. 1991), Les Entretiens de Confucius 1989, L'humeur, l'honneur, l'horreur 1991, The Analects of Confucius 1996, Essais sur la Chine 1998, The View from the Bridge 1996, The Angel and the Octopus 1999, Protée et autres essais 2001, Les Naufragés du Batavia 2003, La Mer dans la littérature française 2003, Les idées des autres 2005 (trans. as Other People's Thoughts 2007), The Wreck of the Batavia 2005, Le Bonheur des petits poissons 2008, With Stendhal 2010, The Hall of Uselessness 2011; (under own name Pierre Ryckmans) Les Propos sur la peinture de Shitao 1969, La Vie et l'oeuvre de Su Renshan, rebelle, peintre et fou 1970. *Address:* 6 Bonwick Place, Garran, ACT 2605, Australia. *Fax:* (2) 6281-4887.

RYDBERG-DUMONT, Josephine, MBA; Swedish business executive; b. 1955; ed Gothenburg School of Econs, Univ. of San Francisco, USA; served as Man. IKEA Catalogue Production to Gen. Man. IKEA of Sweden, responsible for purchasing and product devt of IKEA Group, Man. Dir IKEA of Sweden 2000–07, Head of IKEA Communication and Global Positioning –2008, mem. IKEA's Group Man. 2000–08; mem. Bd of Dirs Cederoth Intressenter AB, Skanska AB 2010–; ranked 30th by Fortune magazine amongst 50 Most Powerful Women in Business outside the US 2006.

RYDER, Guy, CBE; British trade union official and international organization official; *Director-General, International Labour Organization;* b. 3 Jan. 1956, Liverpool; m. Carine Verstichel; ed Univ. of Cambridge; Asst, Int. Dept, TUC, London 1981–85; Sec., Industry Trade Section, Int. Fed. of Commercial, Clerical, Professional and Tech. Employees (FIET), Geneva, Switzerland 1985–88; Asst Dir, then Dir ICFTU, Geneva 1988–98, Gen. Sec. 2002–06, Gen. Sec. Int. Trade Union Confed. (formed after merger of ICFTU with World Confed. of Labour and eight nat. trade union orgs) 2006–10; Sec., Workers' Group, ILO 1993–96, 1996–98, Int. Labour Conf. 1994–98, Dir of Bureau for Workers' Activities 1998–99, Chief of Cabinet 1999–2001, Special Adviser to Dir-Gen. –2001, Exec. Dir Standards and Fundamental Principles and Rights at Work Sector 2010–12, Dir-Gen. ILO 2012–. *Address:* International Labour Organization, 4 route des Morillons, 1211 Genève 22, Switzerland (office). *Telephone:* (22) 7996019 (office). *Fax:* (22) 7998533 (office). *E-mail:* cabinet@ilo.org (office). *Website:* www.ilo.org (office).

RYDER, Winona; American actress; b. (Winona Horowitz), 29 Oct. 1971, Winona, Minn.; d. of Michael Horowitz and Cynthia Istas; ed Petaluma Jr High School, San Francisco and acting classes at American Conservatory Theatre, San Francisco. *Films include:* Lucas 1986, Square Dance 1987, Beetlejuice 1988, '1969' 1988, Heathers 1989, Great Balls of Fire! 1989, Welcome Home, Roxy Carmichael 1990, Edward Scissorhands 1990, Mermaids 1990, Night on Earth 1991, Bram Stoker's Dracula 1992, The Age of Innocence 1993, The House of the Spirits 1993, Reality Bites 1994, Little Women 1994, How to Make an American Quilt 1995, Boys 1996, The Crucible 1996, Looking for Richard 1996, Alien Resurrection 1997, Celebrity 1998, Girl, Interrupted 1999, Autumn in New York 2000, Lost Souls 2000, Mr Deeds 2002, S1m0ne 2002, The Day My God Died (voice) 2003, The Heart is Deceitful Above All Things 2004, The Darwin Awards 2006, A Scanner Darkly 2006, The Ten 2007, Sex and Death 101 2007, Welcome 2007, Water Pills 2008, The Last Word 2008, The Informers 2009, The Private Lives of Pippa Lee 2009, Star Trek 2009, Stay Cool 2009, Black Swan 2010, The Dilemma 2011, Frankenweenie 2012. *Television includes:* The Simpsons (episode: Lisa's Rival, voice) 1994, Dr Katz, Professional Therapist (episode: Monte Carlo, voice) 1996, From the Earth to the Moon (mini-series) 1998, Strangers with Candy (episode: The Last Temptation of Blank) 2000, Friends (episode: The One with Rachel's Big Kiss) 2001, When Love Is Not Enough: The Lois Wilson Story 2010. *Address:* c/o Thruline Entertainment, 9250 Wilshire Blvd, Beverly Hills, CA 90212, USA (office). *Telephone:* (310) 595-1500 (office). *E-mail:* info@thrulinela.com (office). *Website:* www.thruline.com (office).

RYDER OF WENSUM, Baron (Life Peer), cr. 1997, of Wensum in the County of Norfolk; **Richard Andrew Ryder,** OBE, PC, BA; British politician and company director; b. 4 Feb. 1949; s. of Richard Stephen Ryder, DL, JP and Margaret MacKenzie; m. Caroline Mary Stephens, CVO, MBE 1981; one s. (deceased) one d.; ed Radley Coll., Magdalene Coll., Cambridge; journalist 1972–75; Political Sec. to Margaret Thatcher, Leader of the Opposition and Prime Minister 1975–81; MP for Mid-Norfolk 1983–97; Parl. Pvt. Sec. to Financial Sec. to the Treasury 1984, Parl. Pvt. Sec. to Foreign Sec. 1984–86; Govt Whip 1986–88; Parl. Sec. Ministry of Agric. 1988–89; Econ. Sec. to Treasury 1989–90; Paymaster Gen. 1990; Parl. Sec. to Treasury and Govt Chief Whip 1990–95; Chair. Conservative Foreign and Commonwealth Council 1984–89; Chair. Eastern Counties Radio 1997–2001, Inst. of Cancer Research 2005–13, UNCANDOIT 2011–14, Child Bereavement UK 2013–; Vice-Chair. BBC Govs 2002–04; Chair. (Acting) 2004; Dir Great Bradley Farms, also dir of other businesses. *Address:* House of Lords, Westminster, London, SW1A 0PW, England (office).

RYDIN, Bo, BSc; Swedish business executive; *Honorary Chairman, Svenska Cellulosa Aktiebolaget SCA;* b. 7 May 1932; s. of Gunnar Rydin and Signe Rydin (née Höög); m. 1st Monika Avréus 1955 (died 1992); m. 2nd Françoise Yon 1997; with Stockholms Enskilda Bank 1956–57; Marma-Långrör AB 1957–60; AB Gullhögens Bruk 1960, Pres. 1965–71; Pres. and CEO Svenska Cellulosa AB SCA 1972–88, Chair. and CEO 1988–90, Chair. 1990, Hon. Chair. 2002–; Chair. AB Industrivärden, Graningeverken, Skanska AB –2002, Vice-Chair. Svenska Handelsbanken, mem. Bd SAS Assn of Reps; Vice-Chair. Volvo 1988–93; Chair. Fed. of Swedish Industries 1993–94; mem. Skandia 1983–93; mem. Royal Swedish Acad. of Eng Sciences, Royal Swedish Acad. of Agric. and Forestry; King's Medal 12th Dimension of Order of the Seraphim, Chevalier, Légion d'Honneur; Hon. DEcon; Hon. DTech. *Leisure interests:* golf, hunting, opera. *Address:* AB Industrivärden, Storgatan 10, Box 5403, 114 84 Stockholm (office); Karlavägen 3, 114 24 Stockholm, Sweden (home).

RYKIEL, Sonia; French fashion designer; b. 25 May 1930, Paris; d. of Alfred Flis and Fanny Tesler; m.; one s. one d.; began designing rabbit-hair sweaters which est. her reputation 1963; opened own boutique, Paris 1968; opened further boutiques specializing in men's knitwear and household linens 1976, 1981; launched first perfume 7e Sens 1979; supervised renovation of Hotel Crillon, Paris 1982; first boutique opened New York 1983; launched first children's collection 1984; Vice-Pres. Chambre Syndicale du Prêt-à-Porter des Couturiers et des Créateurs de Mode, Paris 1982; launched Sonia Rykiel perfume 1997; Hon. Prof., China Textile Univ., Shanghai 1998; Officier, Ordre des Arts et Lettres 1993, Légion d'honneur 1996; Award for Design Excellence (Costume Cttee, Chicago Historical Soc. *Publications:* Et je la voudrais nue 1979, Célébration 1988, La collection 1989, Colette et la mode 1991, Collection terminée, collection interminable 1993, Tatiana Acacia (jtly) 1993, Les lèvres rouges 1996, Sonia Rykiel (memoirs) 1997. *Address:* Sonia Rykiel C.D.M. S.A, 175 boulevard Saint Germain, 75006 Paris, France. *Telephone:* 1-49-54-60-00. *Fax:* 1-49-54-60-96. *E-mail:* info@soniarykiel.fr. *Website:* www.soniarykiel.com.

RYLANCE, Mark; British actor and director; b. 1960, Ashford, Kent; ed Royal Acad. of Dramatic Art and Chrysalis Theatre School, Balham; joined The Citizen's Theatre, Glasgow 1980; has since worked with RSC, Royal Nat. Theatre, Royal Opera House, Scottish Ballet, Shared Experience, Bush Theatre, Tricycle Theatre, London Theatre of Imagination, Contact Theatre, Oxford Playhouse, Project Theatre, Dublin, Mermaid Theatre, Royal Court, American Repertory Theatre, Boston, Theatre for a New Audience, New York, Pittsburgh Playhouse, Thelma Holte; now assoc. actor, RSC; Artistic Dir Shakespeare's Globe 1996–2005; Artistic Dir Phoebus Cart. *Theatre includes:* Much Ado About Nothing (Olivier Award for Best Actor 1994) 1993, title role in Phoebus Cart's production of Macbeth (also Dir) 1995, Proteus in The Two Gentlemen of Verona, Shakespeare's Globe's Prologue Season 1996, title role in Henry V in Shakespeare's Globe's opening season 1997, Bassanio in The Merchant of Venice and Hippolito in The Honest Whore, Shakespeare's Globe 1998, Cleopatra in Antony and Cleopatra, Shakespeare's Globe 1999, Life x3 2000, Twelfth Night, Shakespeare's Globe 2002, Vincentio in Measure for Measure, Shakespeare's Globe 2004, Peer Gynt (Minneapolis) 2008, Boeing Boeing (Tony Award for Best Performance by a Leading Actor in a Play) 2008, Jerusalem (Critics' Circle Theatre Award for Best Actor 2009) (Royal Court Theatre) 2009, 2010, La Bete (Comedy Theatre, London) 2010, (Broadway) 2010. *Television appearances include:* The Grass Arena, Love Lies Bleeding 1993, In Lambeth, Incident in Judea, Leonardo 2003, Richard II 2003, The Government Inspector (British Academy TV Award for Best Actor) 2005. *Films:* Prospero's Books 1991, Angels and Insects 1995, Institute Benjamenta 1995, Hearts of Fire 1987, Intimacy 2001, The Other Boleyn Girl 2008, Anonymous 2011, Sinister 2012. *Address:* Markham and Froggatt Ltd, 4 Windmill Street, London, W1T 2HZ, England (office). *Telephone:* (20) 7636-4412 (office).

RYLKO, HE Cardinal Stanisław; Polish ecclesiastic; *President of the Pontifical Council for the Laity;* b. 4 July 1945, Andrychów; ordained priest of Kraków 1969; fmr Prof. of Pastoral Theology, Kraków Theological Acad.; apptd Head of Youth Section of Pontifical Council for the Laity 1988, responsible for planning celebrations for World Youth Day; later served as official of Vatican Secr. of State; apptd Titular Archbishop of Novica and Sec. Pontifical Council for the Laity 1995, Pres. Pontifical Council for the Laity 2003–05, 2005–13, 2013–; cr. Cardinal (Cardinal-Deacon of Sacro Cuore di Cristo Re) 2007; participated in Papal Conclave 2013. *Address:* Pontifical Council for the Laity, Piazza S. Calisto 16, 00153 Rome, Italy (office); 00120 Città del Vaticano, Italy. *Telephone:* (06) 6988-7322 (office); (06) 6988-7141 (office). *Fax:* (06) 6988-7214 (office).

RYMAN, Robert; American painter; b. 30 May 1930, Nashville, Tenn.; m. 1st Lucy Lippard (divorced); m. 2nd Merrill Wagner; ed George Peabody Coll. for Teachers, Nashville; in US Army Reserve band during Korean War 1950–52; moved to New York to try and make it as jazz saxophonist; first exhibited in staff show at Museum of Modern Art when working as a guard there 1958; began painting full-time 1961; mem. American Acad. of Arts and Letters. *Address:* c/o Pace Wildenstein, 32 East 57th Street, 2nd floor, New York, NY 10022, USA. *Telephone:* (212) 421-3292. *Fax:* (212) 421-0835. *Website:* www.pacewildenstein.com.

RYMBAI, J. Dringwel, BA, BEd; Indian politician; *Chairman, Meghalaya Economic Development Council;* b. 26 Oct. 1934; m. Peggymon Pathaw; two s. three d.; high school teacher –1988; entered Meghalaya Legis. Ass. representing Jirang constituency in Ri-Bhoi 1988, later Deputy Speaker, re-elected 1993, Speaker 1993; Minister of Food and Civil Supply 1993; held portfolios of Consumer Affairs, Taxation, Information Tech. and Tourism and Fisheries 2003–06; Minister for Parl. Affairs –2006; elected Leader Congress Legislature Party 2006; Chief Minister of Meghalaya with responsibility for Cabinet Affairs, Industries, Personnel, Planning, Political Programme Implementation and Taxation 2006–07; Chair. Meghalaya Econ. Devt Council 2007–. *Address:* Meghalaya Economic Development Council, Planning Department, Government of Meghalaya, Shillong 793 001 India (office). *Telephone:* (364) 2225470 (office); (364) 2224388 (home). *E-mail:* planning-shil-meg@nic.in. *Website:* megplanning.gov.in/medc.htm (office).

RYNNE, Etienne Andrew, MA, MRIA, FSA; Irish archaeologist and academic; *Professor Emeritus of Archaeology, National University of Ireland, Galway;* b. 11 Sept. 1932, Dublin; s. of Dr Michael Rynne and Nathalie Fournier; m. Aideen Lucas 1967; four s. one d.; ed Terenure Coll., Dublin, Ecole des Roches, Verneuil-sur-Avre, France, Clongowes Wood Coll., Clane, Co. Kildare and Univ. Coll. Dublin; part-time Archaeological Asst, Nat. Museum of Ireland 1954–56, Asst, Irish Antiquities Div. 1957–66, Asst-Keeper 1966–67; Lecturer in Celtic Archaeology, Univ. Coll., Galway (now Nat. Univ. of Ireland, Galway) 1967–78, Prof. of Archaeology 1978, now Prof. Emer.; Hon. Curator Galway City Museum 1972–86; Pres. Royal Soc. of Antiquaries of Ireland 1985–89, Galway Archaeological & Historical Soc. 1989–95; Ed. North Munster Antiquarian Journal 1964; mem. Royal Irish Acad.; Travelling Studentship Prize, Nat. Univ. of Ireland 1956. *Publications:* Ed. North Munster Studies 1967, Figures from the Past 1987; about 200 articles in learned journals. *Leisure interests:* archaeology (visiting ancient sites, museums etc.), art history, sport (boxing, athletics). *Address:* c/o Department of Archaeology, National University of Ireland, Galway, University Road, Galway, Ireland. *Website:* www.nuigalway.ie/archaeology.

RYSALIYEV, Maj.-Gen. Zarylbek; Kyrgyzstani police official and politician; *Chairman, State Service for Punishment Execution;* b. 19 Dec. 1960, Urmaral village, Talas Oblast, Kyrgyz SSR, USSR; ed Kyrgyz State Inst. of Physical Culture, Kyrgyz State Nat. Univ.; engineer, Admin of Corrective Labour Insts, Ministry of Internal Affairs 1985–95; Commdr 'Berkut' unit, Internal Affairs Unit, Alamadun Dist 1995–96; Sr Official, Criminal Investigation Dept, Ministry of Internal Affairs 1996–99, Sr Official for Serious Affairs 1999–2000, Dir Main Criminal Investigation Dept 2000–01, Sr Official for Serious Affairs, Main Inspectorate for the Combating Organized Crime 2001, Sr Official for Serious Affairs, Main Criminal Investigation Dept 2001–02, Dir Dept for Combating Organized Crime Groups 2002–04, Deputy Dir Ministry of Internal Affairs, Jalal-Abad Oblast 2004–05, Deputy Dir Main Criminal Investigation Dept, Ministry of Internal Affairs 2005–08, Dir Dept for Combating Narcotics 2008, Head of Section for Combating Organized Crime, Chief Criminal Investigation Dept 2008–09, Head of 9th Section, Ministry of Internal Affairs 2009, Head of Internal Affairs Section, Sverdlovsk Dist, Bishkek 2009–10, Head of Main Internal Affairs Section, Bishkek May–Sept. 2010, Minister of Internal Affairs Sept. 2010–12 (resgnd); Chair. State Service for Punishment Execution 2012–. *Address:* Ministry of Internal Affairs, 720040 Bishkek, Frunze 469, Kyrgyzstan (office). *Telephone:* (312) 66-24-50 (office). *Fax:* (312) 68-20-44 (office). *E-mail:* pressa@mail.mvd.kg (office). *Website:* www.mvd.kg (office).

RYU, Seung-min; South Korean table tennis player; b. 5 Aug. 1982; began playing table tennis age nine; plays for Sichuan team club; won Gold Medal at Athens Olympics 2004, Men's Singles, ITTF Pro Tour Killerspin US Open 2004; Bronze Medal, Men's Team Event, Beijing Olympics 2008; ranked No. 8 in the world (ITTF) as of 5 Dec. 2007. *Address:* c/o Korea Table Tennis Association, Room 411, 88 Olympic Center, Oryun-Dong, Songpa-ku, Seoul, Republic of Korea. *Telephone:* (2) 4204240. *Fax:* (2) 4205913. *E-mail:* tabletennis@sports.or.kr. *Website:* www.koreatta.or.kr.

RYWIN, Lew; Polish film producer and business executive; b. 10 Nov. 1945, Niżne Alkiejewo; m. Eżbieta Sitek; one s.; ed Warsaw Univ.; Asst Inst. of Applied Linguistics, Warsaw Univ. 1969–70; Head Dept Orgmasz, Warsaw 1970–78; fmr interpreter and Sec. Main Bureau of Co-operation with Foreign Countries, Polish Interpress Agency; Man. Poltel Commerce Bureau of Polish Radio and TV Cttee 1983–88, 1st Deputy Chair. 1988–91; Chair. Heritage Films 1991–97, Canal+ Polska 1997–; Co-Founder and mem. Polish Interpreters' Asscn 1981–; convicted of soliciting a bribe, sentenced to two and a half years in prison and a fine of 100,000 Polish Złoty April 2004, released 2006. *Films produced include:* Korczak 1990, Europa, Europa 1991, Pierścionek z orłem w koronie (The Crowned-Eagle Ring) 1992, Schindler's List (Humanitas Prize, jt recipient with co-producer 1994) 1993, Pułkownik Kwiatkowski (Colonel Kwiatkowski) 1994, Les Milles 1995, Tato (Dad) 1995, Erotic Tales II 1995, Der Unhold 1996, Wielki Tydzień (Holy Week) 1996, Matka swojej matki (Mother of Her Own Mother) 1996, Sara 1996, Ostatni rozdział (Last Chapter) 1997, 13 Posterunek (13 Police Station) 1997, Un Air Si Pur (exec. producer) 1997, Jakub kłamca (Jacob the Liar) 1998, Podróże (Travels) 1998, Złoto dezerterów (Deserter's Gold) 1998, Brute 1998, Pan Tadeusz (Last Foray in Lithuania) 1999, Wiedzmin 2002, The Pianist (exec. producer) 2002, Pornografia 2003. *Leisure interests:* tennis, fishing. *Address:* c/o Heritage Films, ul. Marszałkowska 2/65, 00-581 Warsaw, Poland (office). *Telephone:* (22) 6252553 (office). *Fax:* (22) 6252601 (office). *E-mail:* heritage@heritage.com.pl (office).

RYZHKOV, Nikolai Ivanovich; Russian politician; b. 28 Sept. 1929, Donetsk; m. Lyudmila Sergeyevna Ryzhkova; one d.; ed S. M. Kirov Ural Polytechnic Inst.; mem. CPSU 1956–91; Chief Engineer 1965–70, Deputy Dir, later Dir S. Orzhonikidze Ural Factory of Heavy Machine Bldg 1970; Gen. Dir of Production Uralmash Factory 1971–75; First Deputy Minister of Heavy and Transport Machine Bldg 1975–79; mem. Cen. Cttee CPSU in charge of Heavy Industry 1981–90; mem. Politburo 1985–90; Chair. Council of Ministers 1985–90; First Deputy Chair. of Gosplan 1979–82; Head Econ. Affairs 1982–85; Deputy of the USSR Supreme Soviet 1974–89; People's Deputy of the USSR 1989–91; cand. for Pres. of Russia 1991; Chair. Bd Tverunivsalbank; 1993–95, Pres. Int. Public Union; leader pre-election bloc 'Power to People'; mem. State Duma 1995–99, Chair. deputies bloc Narodovlastiye 1996–; mem. Fed. Council 2002–, Chair. Comm. for Natural Monopolies, mem. Cttee of Local Govt; mem. Acad. of Social Sciences, Acad. of Tech. Sciences, Int. Eng Acad., Int. Acad. of Man.; Order of Lenin (twice), Order of Red Banner of Labour (twice) and other decorations; USSR State Prizes 1969, 1979. *Publication:* Perestroika: a series of betrayals. *Address:* Sovet Federatsii (Federation Council), 103426 Moscow, ul. B. Dmitrovka 26, Russia (office). *Telephone:* (495) 203-90-74 (office). *Fax:* (495) 203-46-17 (office). *E-mail:* post_sf@gov.ru (office). *Website:* www.council.gov.ru (office).

RYZHKOV, Vladimir Aleksandrovich, DHist; Russian politician; b. 3 Sept. 1966, Altai Territory; ed Altai State Univ.; Deputy Head, Altai Territory Soc. of Encouraging Perestroika 1988–90; Deputy Chair. Altai Territory Movt Democratic Russia 1990–91; Vice-Gov. Altai Territory; mem. State Duma (Parl.) 1993–2007, mem. Cttee on Fed. and Regional Policy 1994–95, First Deputy Chair. State Duma 1997–99, ind. mem. 2000–05; Deputy Chair. faction Russia Our Home 1996–97, Chair. 1999–2000; founding mem. Democratic Alternative 2004, Co-Chair. Republican Party of Russia 2006, now associated with The Other Russia coalition. *Publications:* Chetvertaya respublika (The Fourth Republic in Russia) 1999; more than 80 articles on contemporary policy. *E-mail:* press-centre@theotherrussia.ru (office). *Website:* www.ryzkov.ru (office).

RYZHOV, Yuri Alexeevich, DTech; Russian politician, scientist, diplomatist and university administrator; *President, International Engineering University;* b. 28 Oct. 1930, Moscow; m.; two d.; ed Moscow Physical Tech. Inst.; mem. CPSU 1961–90; engineer 1954–60; Sr Researcher, Moscow Inst. of Aviation 1960–92, Prof. 1970, Pro-Rector 1972–86, Rector 1986–92; mem. Presidium of the Supreme Soviet of USSR 1989–91; Chair. Scientific Cttee of the Soviet Parl. 1989–91; mem. Presidential Council of the Russian Fed. 1991–2000; mem. USSR (now Russian) Acad. of Sciences 1987; mem. Interregional Group of Deputies 1989; Amb. to France 1992–98; Pres. Int. Eng Univ. 1999–; Chair. Russian Pugwash Group. *Leisure interest:* music. *Address:* International Engineering University, 119991 Moscow, Leninsky prosp. 6, Russia (office). *Telephone:* (495) 236-50-66 (office); (495) 135-12-44 (home). *Fax:* (495) 236-14-69 (office). *E-mail:* info@miu.ru (office). *Website:* www.miu.ru (office).

S

SAÁ, Adolfo Rodríguez; Argentine lawyer and politician; b. 25 July 1947, San Luis; s. of Juan Rodríguez Saá and Lilia Ester Paez Montero; m.; six c.; ed Nat. Univ. of Cuyo, Univ. of Buenos Aires; lawyer 1971–; Rep. of Partido Justicialista (PJ—Justice Party) 1971–83; Prov. Deputy and Pres. Justicialista Block 1973–76; Prov. Congressman 1976–85; Nat. Congressman (PJ) 1983–91; Nat. Councillor 1987–94; Pres. Partido Justicialista (San Luis Dist) 1985–95, Third Vice-Pres. Nat. Partido Justicialista 1996–2000; Gov. of San Luis Prov. 1983–2001; Interim Pres. of Argentina 23 Dec.–30 Dec. 2001; unsuccessful cand. for Pres. 2003. *Address:* c/o Partido Justicialista (PJ), Buenos Aires, Argentina.

SAAB, Elie; Lebanese fashion designer; b. 4 July 1964, Beirut; m. Claudine Saab; three s.; began sewing as a child aged nine; moved to Paris to study fashion 1981, returned and launched Beirut-based fashion label 1982; first non-Italian designer to become mem. Italian Camera Nazionale della Moda 1997; showed first collection outside Lebanon in Rome 1997; started ready-to-wear in Milan 1998; showed first haute couture collection in Paris 2000; showed first ready-to-wear Spring-Summer collection in Paris 2006; launched first fragrance 'Le Parfum' 2011; Corresp. mem. Chambre Syndicale de la Haute Couture 2006; Chevalier, Ordre Nat. du Cèdre 2003; ranked by Arabian Business amongst the Power 500: The World's Most Influential Arabs (22nd) 2012, (19th) 2013. *Address:* Elie Saab Building, 2021-4516 Beirut Central District, Lebanon (office). *Telephone:* (1) 981982 (office). *Fax:* (1) 981983 (office). *E-mail:* hautecouture-lb@eliesaab.com (office). *Website:* www .eliesaab.com (office).

SAAB, Najib; Lebanese architect, publisher and international organization official; *Secretary General, Arab Forum for Environment and Development;* b. 1953; ed American Univ. of Beirut; work experience ranges from designing for multinationals including General Motors and lecturing on corporate architecture at American Univ. of Beirut, to advising various govts and agencies on environment and writing on sustainable devt and tech.; Ed.-in-Chief Al-Bia Wal-Tanmia (Environment and Development); Sec. Gen. Arab Forum for Environment and Devt; UNEP Global 500 Award for environmental achievement 2003, Zayed Int. Prize for Environment (co-recipient) 2011. *Publications include:* Environment: From One Catastrophe to Another (in Arabic) 1999, Arab Environmentalists, Unite! (in Arabic) 2001, Arab Environment: Climate Change Impact of Climate Change on Arab Countries (co-ed.), Nature Book (Book of the Year Award, Beirut Arab Book Fair) 2002, Environmental Agenda (in Arabic) 2006, Arab Environment: Future Challenges (co-ed.) 2008, Environment in Arab Media (in Arabic) 2008, Impact of Climate Change on Arab Countries (co-ed.) 2009, Arab Environment: Water Sustainable Management of a Scarce Resource (co-ed.) 2010, Green Economy: Sustainable Transition in a Changing Arab World (co-ed.) 2010, Water: Sustainable Management of a Scarce Resource 2010. *Address:* Arab Forum for Environment and Development, Eshmoun Building, Rue de Damas, PO Box 113-5474, Downtown Beirut, Lebanon (office). *Telephone:* (1) 321800 (office). *Fax:* (1) 321900 (office). *E-mail:* nsaab@mectat.com.lb; info@afedonline.org (office). *Website:* www.afedonline.org (office); www.najibsaab.com.

SAAD, Stephen, BComm, CA; South African business executive; *Group CEO, Aspen Pharmacare Holdings Ltd;* b. 23 June 1964, Durban; m.; four d.; ed South Africa Inst. of Chartered Accountants, Univ. of Natal (now Univ. of KwaZulu-Natal); fmr Articled Clerk, Cooper and Lybrand, Durban; Co-owner of Quickmed 1990s; Co-founded Aspen Pharmacare Holdings Ltd 1997, then Jt Chief Exec., Group CEO 1999–, mem. Bd of Dirs 1999–; Owner, Covan Zurich; inducted into Ernst & Young Entrepreneur of the Year Hall of Fame 2005, Business Leader of the Year 2012. *Address:* Aspen Pharmacare Holdings Ltd, PO Box 25125, Gateway 4321, Umhlanga, South Africa (office). *Fax:* (31) 5808647 (office). *Website:* www .aspenpharma.com (office).

SAADAT, Air Chief Marshal (retd) Kaleem; Pakistani air force officer; b. 12 Dec. 1951, Faisalabad; joined Pakistan Air Force 1971, fmr Dir of Plans, Air HQ, fmr Deputy Chief of Air Staff (operational), Chief of Air Staff 2003–06; fmr Asst Commdt, Coll. of Flying Training, Risalpur; mem. Nat. Security Council; fmr Pres. Pakistan Squash Fed.; Chevlier, Légion d'honneur 2005; Hilal-e-Imtiaz, Sitar-e-Imtiaz, Sitar-e-Basalat, Nishan-e-Imtiaz, Tamgha-e-Imtiaz. *Address:* c/o Pakistan Squash Federation, Mushaf Squash Complex, Jinnah Stadium, Aabpara, Islamabad, Pakistan.

SAADAWI, Nawal el-, MA, MD; Egyptian physician and writer; b. 27 Oct. 1931, Kafr Tahla; m. 1st Ahmed Helmi (divorced); m. 2nd (divorced); m. 3rd Sherif Hetata 1964; one s. one d.; ed Cairo Univ., Columbia Univ., New York, USA; physician at University Hospital and Ministry of Health 1955–65; Dir-Gen. of Health Educ. Dept, Ministry of Health 1966–72; Researcher, Faculty of Medicine, Ain Shams Univ., Cairo 1973–78, also writer, High Inst. of Literature and Science; Head of Women's programme, UN Econ. Comm. for Africa, Addis Ababa 1978–79, UN Econ. Comm. for Africa, Beirut 1978–80; arrested and detained in Egypt for three months 1981; Founder, Arab Women's Solidarity Asscn 1982, Pres. 1982–91 (prohibited by Egyptian govt); fled to USA 1991, returned to Egypt 1996; Distinguished Visiting Prof., Duke Univ. 1993–96, taught at Univ. of Washington 1995, Univ. of Illinois, Chicago 1998, Florida Atlantic Univ. 1999 Montclair Univ. 2001–02, Univ. of Southern Maine 2003 Univ. of Autonoma, Barcelona 2004 Smith Coll., 2004 Claremont Univ. 2005, Spelman Coll. (Cosby Chair) 2007–09; formally charged with apostasy 2007, court dismissed all charges; fmr Ed.-in-Chief, Health magazine; fmr Asst Gen.-Sec. Medical Asscn; First Degree Decoration of the Republic of Libya 1989; Hon. DUniv (York) 1994, (Univ. of Illinois, Chicago) 1996, (Univ. of St Andrews, Scotland) 1997, (Univ. of Tromso, Norway) 2003, Dr hc (Université libre de Bruxelles) 2007, (Flemish Univ.) 2007, (French Univ.) 2007, (Mexico Univ.) 2010; High Council of Literature Award 1974, Short Story Award 1974, Franco-Arab Literary Award 1982, Literary Award of Gubran 1988, XV Premi Int. Catalunia Award 2003, North South Prize, Council of Europe 2004, Inana Int. Prize 2005, African Literature Asscn Award, Univ. of West Virginia 2007, Pan African Writers Asscn Literary Award 2009. *Publications include:* Memoirs of a Woman Doctor 1958, Two Women in One 1968, Women and Sex 1971, She Has No Place in Paradise (short story) 1972, Woman at Point Zero 1975, God Dies by the Nile 1976, The Hidden Face of Eve: Women in the Arab World (non-

fiction) 1977, The Circling Song 1977, The Veil (short story) 1978, Death of an Ex-Minister 1979, Memoirs from the Women's Prison 1983, My Travels Around the World 1986, The Fall of the Imam 1987, The Innocence of the Devil 1992, Nawal el-Saadawi in the Dock 1993, The Well of Life and The Thread: Two Short Novels 1993, The Nawal el-Saadawi Reader 1997, A Daughter of Isis: The Autobiography of Nawal el-Saadawi 1999, Love in the Kingdom of Oil 2001, Walking Through Fire: A Life of Nawal el-Saadawi 2002, The Novel 2005, God Resigns in the Summit Meeting 2007, Zeina 2009; contrib. to newspapers and magazines. *Leisure interests:* swimming, walking. *Address:* 19 Maahad Nasser Street, Bldg 1, Shoubra Gardens, 11241, Cairo, Egypt. *Telephone:* 2022279. *Fax:* 2035001. *E-mail:* shns@ tedata.net.eg; nawalalsaadawi@yahoo.com. *Website:* www.nawalsaadawi.net.

SAAKASHVILI, Mikheil, LLM, SJD; Georgian politician, lawyer and fmr head of state; b. 21 Dec. 1967, Tbilisi; s. of Nikoloz Saakashvili and Giuli Alasania; m. Sandra Roelofs; two s.; ed Faculty of Int. Relations, Kyiv State Univ., Ukraine, Columbia Univ. Law School, New York, USA, George Washington Univ., Washington, DC, USA, Int. Inst. of Human Rights, Strasbourg, France, Norwegian Inst. of Human Rights; worked for Patterson, Belknap, Webb & Tyler (law firm), New York 1994; returned to Ukraine 1995; mem. Parl. (Union of Citizens of Georgia) 1995, Chair. Parl. Cttee responsible for creating new electoral system, ind. judiciary and non-political police force 1995–2000; Vice-Pres. Parl. Ass. of Council of Europe 2000; Minister for Justice 2000–01 (resgnd); resgnd from Union of Citizens of Georgia Party 2001; f. Nat. Movt opposition party 2001; elected Head, City Council of Tbilisi 2002–03; Pres. of Georgia 2004–13. *Address:* c/o Office of the President, 0103 Tbilisi, M. Abdushelishvili 1, Georgia. *E-mail:* secretariat@admin .gov.ge.

SAAKIAN, Suren Mushegovich; Armenian politician and diplomatist; b. 1 Jan. 1958; m.; three c.; ed Yerevan State Univ.; Chair. of Nuclear Physics, Yerevan State Univ. 1979–81; Researcher, Inst. of Physical Studies, Armenian SSR Acad. of Sciences 1981–88; Head, Lazernaya Tekhnika Div. 1988–90; Head, Armenian Ministry of Higher Educ. Dept 1990–91; Deputy Minister of Internal Affairs 1991; Minister of Armenian State Tax Service 1991–94; envoy to Russian Fed. 1994–96, Amb. to Russian Fed. 1999–2002; Rep. to Bd of Int. Econs Cttee 1996–99. *Address:* Ministry of Foreign Affairs, 0010 Yerevan, Republic Square, Government House 2, Armenia. *Telephone:* (10) 54-40-41. *Fax:* (10) 54-39-25. *E-mail:* info@ armeniaforeignministry.com. *Website:* www.mfa.am.

SAATCHI, Charles; British advertising executive and art collector; *Partner, M&C Saatchi;* b. 9 June 1943, Baghdad, Iraq; s. of Nathan Saatchi and Daisy Saatchi (née Ezer); brother of Maurice Saatchi (q.v.); m. 1st Doris Lockhart Dibley 1973 (divorced 1990); m. 2nd Kay Hartenstein 1990 (divorced 2001); one d.; m. 3rd Nigella Lawson 2003 (divorced 2013); one step-s. and one step-d.; ed Christ's Coll. Finchley, London Coll. of Communication; fmr jr copywriter, Benton & Bowles (US advertising agency), London; Assoc. Dir Collett Dickenson Pearce 1966–68; with Ross Cramer formed freelance consultancy, Cramer Saatchi, Dir 1968–70; Co-founder (with Maurice Saatchi), of Saatchi & Saatchi (advertising agency) 1970, (Saatchi & Saatchi PLC 1984), Dir 1970–93, Pres. 1993–95; Co-founder and Partner, M&C Saatchi Agency 1995–; f. Saatchi Gallery 2003, donated gallery and more than 200 works of art to the British public 2010; Co-founder with his brother, Saatchi Shul (ind. Orthodox Jewish synagogue), Maida Vale, London 1998. *Television:* School of Saatchi (BBC) 2009. *Publication:* My Name is Charles Saatchi and I Am an Artoholic 2009. *Address:* M&C Saatchi, 36 Golden Square, Soho, London, W1F 9EE (office); Saatchi Gallery, Duke of York's Square, King's Road, London, SW3 4SQ, England (office). *Telephone:* (20) 7543-4500 (M&C Saatchi); (20) 7730-8135 (Saatchi Gallery). *Website:* www.mcsaatchi.com (office); www .saatchi-gallery.co.uk (office).

SAATCHI, Baron (Life Peer), cr. 1996, of Staplefield in the County of West Sussex; **Maurice Saatchi,** BSc; British advertising executive and politician; *Partner, M&C Saatchi;* b. 21 June 1946, Baghdad, Iraq; s. of Nathan Saatchi and Daisy Saatchi; brother of Charles Saatchi (q.v.); m. 1st Gillian Osband 1972 (divorced 1984); m. 2nd Josephine Hart (deceased 2011) 1984; one s.; one step-s.; ed London School of Econs; started career with Haymarket Publications; Co-Founder Saatchi & Saatchi Co. 1970; Chair. Saatchi & Saatchi Co. PLC 1984–94, Dir –1994; Co-Founder and Partner, M&C Saatchi Agency 1995–; Chair. Megalomedia PLC 1995–; Dir (non-exec.) Loot 1998–; Shadow Treasury Minister in House of Lords 1999–2003, Cabinet Office Minister 2001–03; Co-Chair. Conservative Party 2003–05; Chair., Centre for Policy Studies 2009–, Finsbury Foods PLC; Dir Centre for Policy Studies; mem. Council RCA 1997–2000; Gov. LSE 1996–; Trustee, Victoria and Albert Museum 1988–96, Museum of Garden History; MacMillan Prize for Sociology 1967, St George's Soc. Medal of Honour. *Publication:* The War of Independence 1999, Happiness Can't Buy Money 1999, The Bad Samaritan 2000, Poor People! Stop Paying Tax! 2001, The Science of Politics 2001, If This is Conservatism, I Am a Conservative 2005, In Praise of Ideology 2006, The Sleeping Beauty of America 2007, The Myth of Inflation Targeting 2009. *Address:* M&C Saatchi, 36 Golden Square, Soho, London, W1F 9EE, England (office). *Telephone:* (20) 7543-4500 (office). *Fax:* (20) 7543-4501 (office). *E-mail:* maurices@ mcsaatchi.com (office). *Website:* www.mcsaatchi.com (office).

SAAVEDRA-ALESSANDRI, Pablo, LLM, JSD; Chilean lawyer and international organization executive; *Secretary, Inter-American Court of Human Rights (Corte Interamericana de Derechos Humanos);* ed Univ. of Notre Dame Law School, USA; Deputy Sec. Inter-American Court of Human Rights (Corte Interamericana de Derechos Humanos) –2003, Sec. 2003–. *Address:* Corte Interamericana de Derechos Humanos, Apdo Postal 6906-1000, San José, Costa Rica (office). *Telephone:* 2527-1600 (office). *Fax:* 2234-0584 (office). *E-mail:* corteidh@corteidh.or.cr (office). *Website:* www.corteidh.or.cr (office).

SAAVEDRA SOTO, Rubén; Bolivian lawyer and politician; worked at Contraloría General (nat. audit office); Exec. Dir Unidad de Investigaciones Financieras (financial intelligence office) –2010; Minister of Nat. Defence 2010–11. *Address:* c/o Ministry of National Defence, Plaza Avaroa, esq. Pedro Salazar y 20 de Octubre 2502, La Paz, Bolivia (office).

SABA, Elias, BLitt; Lebanese economist and politician; b. 1932; s. of Shukri Saba and Guilnar Abou Haidar; m. Hind Sabri Shurbagi 1960; five d.; ed American Univ. of Beirut and Univ. of Oxford, UK; Econ. Adviser to Ministry of Finance and Petroleum, Kuwait and Kuwait Fund for Arab Econ. Devt 1961–62; Chair. Dept of Econs, American Univ. of Beirut 1963–67, Assoc. Prof. of Econs 1967–69; Deputy Prime Minister of Lebanon, Minister of Finance and of Defence 1970–72; Econ. and Financial Adviser to the Pres. 1972–73; Chair., Gen. Man. St Charles City Centre SARL 1974–; Vice-Chair. Banque du Crédit Populaire, Chair. Allied Bank, Beirut 1983; Chair., CEO The Associates, SARL 1981–; Minister of Finance 2004–05; mem. Nat. Dialogue Cttee 1975. *Publication:* Postwar Developments in the Foreign Exchange Systems of Lebanon and Syria 1962. *Leisure interests:* hunting, vintage and classic cars. *Address:* c/o Ministry of Finance, 4e étage, Immeuble MOF, place Riad es-Solh, Beirut, Lebanon.

SABAH, Sheikh Ahmad Fahad al-Ahmad al-, BSc; Kuwaiti politician; *Director, National Security Agency;* b. 1963; ed Univ. of Kuwait, Kuwait Military Acad.; officer Kuwaiti Army 1985–90, reaching rank of Maj.; Deputy Chair. Public Authority for Youth and Sports 1992–2000, Chair. (rank of cabinet minister) 2000; Minister of Information 2000; Minister of Energy 2002; fmr Chair. Kuwait Petroleum Corpn; Sec.-Gen., OPEC Jan.–Dec. 2005; Pres. Kuwait Olympic Cttee 1990–2001; Dir Nat. Security Agency 2006–; fmr Pres. Olympic Council of Asia; mem. IOC 2001–; fmr Chair. Nat. Council for Culture, Arts and Literature; Hon. degrees from Dong-A Univ., Repub. of Korea, Taipei Univ., Taiwan, American Acad. Kingdom of Saudi Arabia Sports Medal. *Leisure interest:* sport. *Address:* National Security Agency, Kuwait City, Kuwait (office).

SABAH, Ahmad Homoud al-Jaber al-; Kuwaiti politician; Minister of the Interior 1991–92, of Defence 1994, First Deputy Prime Minister and Minister of the Interior 2011–13. *Address:* c/o Ministry of the Interior, POB 11, 13001 Safat, Kuwait.

SABAH, Lt-Gen. Ahmad Khaled al-Hamad al-; Kuwaiti army officer and government official; Chief of Staff of Kuwait Army –2012; Deputy Prime Minister and Minister of Defence 2012–13. *Address:* c/o Ministry of Defence, POB 1170, 13012 Safat, Kuwait City, Kuwait.

SABAH, Sheikh Jaber Mubarek al-Hamad as-; Kuwaiti politician; *Prime Minister;* b. 1948; Head of Admin. Affairs, Ministry of Amiri Diwan 1971–75; Gov. Hawally prov. 1979–85, Al-Ahmadi prov. 1985–86; Minister of Social Affairs 1986–88, of Information 1988–90; Deputy Prime Minister and Minister of Defence 2001–06; First Deputy Prime Minister and Minister of Defence 2006–11, Prime Minister 2011–12 (resgnd), Feb. 2012–; Medal of King Issa First Class 2007, Grand Cordon, Order of the Rising Sun, Japan 2009. *Address:* Diwan of the Prime Minister, POB 1397, 13014 Kuwait City, Kuwait (office). *Telephone:* 22000000 (office). *Fax:* 22223150 (office). *E-mail:* contact@pm.gov.kw (office). *Website:* www.pm.gov.kw (office).

SABAH, Lt-Gen. (retd) Khaled Al-Jarrah as-; Kuwaiti politician and fmr army officer; *Deputy Prime Minister and Minister of Defence;* Army Chief of Staff 2012–13; Deputy Prime Minister and Minister of Defence 2013–. *Address:* Ministry of Defence, POB 1170, 13012 Safat, Kuwait City, Kuwait (office). *Telephone:* 24848300 (office). *Fax:* 24846059 (office). *E-mail:* mod_info@mod.gov .kw (office). *Website:* www.mod.gov.kw (office).

SABAH, Muhammad Sabah as-Salim as-, PhD; Kuwaiti politician and diplomatist; b. 1955; ed Univ. of California and Harvard Univ., USA; Lecturer in Econs, Faculty of Commerce, Economy and Political Sciences, Kuwait Univ. 1979–85, Kuwaiti Inst. of Scientific Research 1987–88; Amb. to USA 1993–2001; Minister of State for Foreign Affairs 2001–03; Minister of Foreign Affairs 2003–12; Deputy Prime Minister 2006–12. *Address:* c/o Ministry of Foreign Affairs, POB 3, Gulf Street, Kuwait City, Kuwait (office).

SABAH, Sheikh Nasser al-Muhammad al-Ahmad as-; Kuwaiti government official and diplomatist; b. 1940; ed secondary education in Britain; Univ. of Geneva; began career at Ministry of Foreign Affairs 1964; Perm. Rep. to UN, Geneva 1965–68; Consul-Gen., Kuwaiti Embassy, Switzerland 1967–68; Amb. to Iran 1968–79; Under-Sec., Ministry of Information 1979–85; Minister of Information 1985–88, of Social Affairs and Labour 1988–90, of State for Foreign Affairs 1990–98, of Amiri Diwan Affairs 1998–2006; Prime Minister of Kuwait 2006–11 (resgnd). *Address:* c/o Office of the Prime Minister, Council of Ministers, General Secretariat, Kuwait City, Kuwait.

SABAH, HH Sheikh Nawaf al-Ahmad al-Jaber as-; Kuwaiti government official; b. 25 June 1937; s. of the late Amir Sheikh Ahmed al-Jaber as-Sabah; four s. one d.; ed univ in UK; Gov. of Hawalli 1962–78; Minister of the Interior 1978–88, of Defence 1988–92; Deputy Prime Minister and Minister of the Interior from 2003, First Deputy Prime Minister 2003–06; proclaimed Crown Prince 20 Feb. 2006–. *Address:* Diwan of HH The Crown Prince, PO Box 4, 13001 Safat, Kuwait (office).

SABAH, Sheikh Sabah al-Ahmad al-Jaber as-, (Amir of Kuwait); b. 1928; ed Mubarakiyyah Nat. School, Kuwait and privately; mem. Supreme Cttee 1955–62; Minister of Public Information and Guidance and of Social Affairs 1962–63, of Foreign Affairs 1963–91, acting Minister of Finance and Oil 1965, Minister of the Interior 1978; Deputy Prime Minister 1978–91; acting Minister of Information 1981–84; fmrly First Deputy Prime Minister and Minister of Foreign Affairs; Prime Minister 2003–06; Amir of Kuwait 2006–. *Address:* Bayan Palace, Amiry Diwan, Kuwait.

SABAH, Sabah al-Khaled al-Hamad al-, BA; Kuwaiti diplomatist and politician; *Deputy Prime Minister and Minister of Foreign Affairs;* b. 3 March 1953; m. Ayda Salim al-Ali al-Sabah; one s. one d.; ed Univ. of Kuwait; joined Ministry of Foreign Affairs as Diplomatic Attaché 1978, with Arab Affairs Desk, Political Dept 1978–83, posted to Perm. Mission to UN, New York 1983–89, Deputy Dir, Arab World Dept 1989–92, Dir, Under-Sec.'s Office 1992–95 Amb. to Saudi Arabia 1995–98, Chief of Nat. Security Apparatus 1998–2006; Minister of Labour and Social Affairs 2006–07, of Information 2007–09, also Minister of Justice and Awqaf and Islamic Affairs April–May 2009, Deputy Prime Minister and Minister of Foreign Affairs 2011–; Chair. Kuwait Fund for Arab Econ. Devt; mem. Nat. Security Council, Supreme Council of Petroleum, Supreme Council for Planning

and Devt, Supreme Council of the Environment Public Authority. *Address:* Ministry of Foreign Affairs, POB 3, 13001 Safat, Gulf Street, Kuwait (office). *Telephone:* 22425141 (office). *Fax:* 22420429 (office). *E-mail:* mofa.site@mofa.gov .kw (office). *Website:* www.mofa.gov.kw (office).

SABAH, Sheikh Salem Abd al-Aziz Sa'ud as-, BA (Econs); Kuwaiti government official and fmr central banker; b. 1 Nov. 1951; ed American Univ. of Beirut, Lebanon; worked in Econ. Analyst Studies Section, Foreign Operations Dept, Cen. Bank of Kuwait 1977–78, Head of Dept 1978–80, Deputy Man. and Head of Investment and Studies Section 1980–84, Deputy Man. and Head of Inspection Section, Banking Supervision Dept March–Aug. 1984, Man. Banking Supervision Dept 1984–85, Exec. Dir for Banking Supervision and Monetary Policy 1985–86, Deputy Gov. Feb.–Sept. 1986, Gov. and Chair. Bd of Dirs 1986–2012; Deputy Prime Minister and Minister of Finance Aug.–Dec. 2013; Chair. Inst. of Banking Studies; Alternate Gov. of the State of Kuwait, IMF and Arab Monetary Fund; mem. Higher Planning Council, Higher Petroleum Council; mem. Bd of Dirs Kuwait Investment Authority, Higher Cttee for Econ. Devt and Reform; Gov. of the Year Award, Euromoney magazine 1988, Personality in Banking Management Award, Arab Research Center 1997. *Publications include:* Casting Light on the Monetary Policy and the Kuwaiti Economy 1988, Recent Issues of Central Bank Policy in Kuwait 1989, Prominent Landmarks in the Operation of the Central Bank of Kuwait 1995, Monetary Policy and the Role of the Central Bank of Kuwait: Current Concerns and Future Prospects 1997. *Address:* c/o Ministry of Finance, POB 9, 13001 Safat, al-Morkab Street, Ministries Complex, Kuwait City, Kuwait.

SABAN, Haim; American/Israeli media executive; *CEO, Saban Capital Group, Inc.;* b. Alexandria, Egypt; m. Cheryl Saban; four c.; ed agricultural school, Israel; fled to Tel-Aviv with his parents aged 12 after Suez War 1956; served in Israeli Defense Force; est. leading tour business; relocated to France 1975, est. ind. record co. that sold over 18 million records in eight years; moved to Los Angeles, USA 1983, launched chain of recording studios that became leading suppliers of music for TV; f. Saban Entertainment 1988, merged with Fox Kids Network 1995, acquired Fox Family Channel (restructured as Fox Family Worldwide) 1997, sold to Walt Disney Co. 2001; Founder and CEO Saban Capital Group, Inc. (SCQ) 2002–; acquired ProSiebenSat.1 Media AG, Chair. Supervisory Bd –2007 (co. sold); with group of investors acquired Bezeq The Israel Telecommunication Corp., Ltd 2005, Univision Communications Inc. 2007; apptd to California Bd of Regents 2002–(13); Founder Saban Inst. for the Study of the American Political System, Univ. of Tel-Aviv; f. Saban Family Foundation 1999; f. Saban Center for Middle East Policy, Brookings Inst. 2002, currently Chair. Int. Advisory Bd; mem. Bd of Trustees, Brookings Inst. *Address:* Saban Capital Group, Inc., 10100 Santa Monica Blvd, Los Angeles, CA 90067, USA (office). *Telephone:* (310) 557-5100 (office). *Website:* www.saban.com (office).

SABANCI, Güler; Turkish business executive; *Chairman and Managing Director, Hacı Ömer Sabancı Holding A.Ş.;* b. 1955, Istanbul; d. of İhsan Sabancı and Yüksel Sabancı; ed TED Ankara Coll. and Bosphorus Univ.; worked for LASSA Tyre Manufacturing and Trading Co., Kocaeli Prov. 1978; Gen. Man. and mem. Bd KORDSA Tyre Cord Manufacturing and Trading Co. 1985–99, led teams that set up several jt ventures for Sabancı Group such as Brisa, Beksa and Dusa International LLC, Pres. Tire and Reinforcement Materials Group –2004, Chair. Hacı Ömer Sabancı Holding A.Ş. (also Head of Human Resources Cttee) 2004–; Founder and Chair. Bd of Trustees Sabancı Univ. 2002–; Chair.-Elect Sabancı Foundation, VAKSA; Order of Civil Merit, Encomienda de Numero (Spain) 2009; ranked by The Wall Street Journal amongst the 30 Most Powerful Women in Europe 2004, ranked by Fortune magazine amongst the 50 Most Powerful Women in Business outside the US (20th) 2004, (17th) 2005, (11th) 2006, (eighth) 2007, (ninth) 2008, (eighth) 2009, (seventh) 2010, (sixth) 2011–12, ranked by Forbes magazine amongst The World's 100 Most Powerful Women (65th) 2006, (65th) 2007, (75th) 2008, (27th) 2009, (52nd) 2010, (78th) 2011, (93rd) 2012, (94th) 2013, ranked by the Financial Times amongst the Top 25 Businesswomen in Europe (eighth) 2005, (ninth) 2006, (eighth) 2007, Woman of Distinction Award, Daughters of Atatürk 2006. *Leisure interest:* running vineyard producing wine under her own brand name. *Address:* Hacı Ömer Sabancı Holding A.Ş., Sabancı Center 4.Levent, 34330 Istanbul, Turkey (office). *Telephone:* (212) 2816600 (office); (212) 2816611 (office). *Fax:* (212) 2810272 (office). *E-mail:* info@sabanci.com (office). *Website:* www.sabanci.com (office).

SABBAGH, Nemeh Elias, MA, MBA; Jordanian banking executive; *CEO, Arab Bank Plc;* ed Institut d'Études Politiques, France, Austin Coll., Johns Hopkins Univ. and Univ. of Chicago, USA; worked for First National Bank, Chicago, USA 1974–76; joined Industrial Bank in Kuwait 1976; worked with National Bank of Kuwait 1979–98, Gen. Man. Int. Banking Group in charge of bank's int. activities, branches and subsidiaries world-wide; also worked with World Bank, Washington, DC; Man. Dir and CEO Arab National Bank, Riyadh, Saudi Arabia 1998–2006; Exec. Gen. Man. BankMed Sal 2006–09; mem. Bd of Dirs Arab Bank Plc 2010–, CEO 2012–; Dir (non-exec.) Europe Arab Bank plc 2010–, Oger Telecom Ltd; Dir, Arab National Bank –2005, BankMed Sal 2006–09, Jordan Mortgage Refinance Co. PLC 2011–. *Address:* Arab Bank Plc, PO Box 950545, Amman 11195, Jordan (office). *Telephone:* (6) 560-0000 (office). *Fax:* (6) 560-6793 (office). *E-mail:* info@ arabbank.com (office). *Website:* www.arabbank.com (office).

SABBAGH, Rachid; Tunisian judge and politician; *Minister of National Defence;* ed Ez-Zitouna Univ., Tunis; fmr judge (specialist in Islamic law); fmr Pres. Cour de Cassation (Supreme Court); Head of Cabinet of Ministers of Justice Mohamed Bellalouna 1971–73, Slaheddine Baly 1973–80; joined transitional govt of Beji Caid Essebsi as Pres. Higher Islamic Council 2011; Minister of Nat. Defence 2013–. *Address:* Ministry of National Defence, blvd Bab Menara, 1008 Tunis, Tunisia (office). *Telephone:* (71) 560-240 (office). *Fax:* (71) 561-804 (office). *E-mail:* defnat@defense.tn (office). *Website:* www.defense.tn (office).

SABBAH, Michel, PhD; ecclesiastic; *Emeritus Latin (Roman Catholic) Patriarch of Jerusalem;* b. 19 March 1933, Nazareth; ed Patriarchate Seminary of Beit-Jala and in Beirut and Paris; ordained priest for Latin Patriarchate, Jerusalem 1955; fmr Dir Gen. of Schools, Patriarchate of Jerusalem –1967; taught Arabic and Islamic studies in Djibouti –1973; priest, Misdar, nr Amman; apptd Pres. Frères Univ. Bethlehem 1980; Latin (Roman Catholic) Patriarch of Jerusalem 1988–2008, Emer. Patriarch 2008–; Pres. Bishops' Conf. for Arab Countries; Int. Pres. Pax

Christi 1999–; Grand Prior, Equestrian Order of the Holy Sepulchre of Jerusalem. *Publication:* Lire et Vivre la Bible au Pays de la Bible 2003; eight pastoral letters. *Address:* Office of the Latin Patriarch, POB 14152, 91141 Jerusalem, Israel (office). *Telephone:* 2-6282323 (office). *Fax:* 2-6271652 (office). *E-mail:* chancellery@latinpat.org (office). *Website:* www.lpj.org (office).

SABBIONI, Enrico; Italian biochemist; *Researcher, Institute for Health and Consumer Protection, European Commission Joint Research Center;* currently Researcher, Inst. for Health and Consumer Protection, EC Jt Research Center, Ispra, Italy; Chief Adviser, European Center for the Sustainable Impact of Nanotechnology 2010–; Task Leader, Inst. for Health and Consumer Protection; Pres., Società Italiana di Nanotossicologia 2010–; mem. European Centre for Validation of Alternative Methods; mem. Int. Soc. for Trace Element Research in Humans; Fellow, Int. Union of Pure and Applied Chem.; mem. Editorial Bd Science of the Total Environment, Alternatives to Laboratory Animals; mem. Bd of Dirs Università Carlo Cattaneo (LIUC); Commemorative Medal of Charles Univ. of Prague 1993, Hevesy Medal 2002. *Address:* Institute for Health and Consumer Protection, European Commission Joint Research Center, Ispra, 21 020 (office); Via Gramsci 25, Biandronno, 21 024 Italy (home). *Telephone:* (332) 789070 (office); (338) 3754492 (mobile). *Fax:* (332) 785994 (office). *E-mail:* enrico.sabbioni@jrc.it (office); enrico.sabbioni@alice.it. *Website:* ihcp.jrc.ec.europa.eu (office).

SABHARWAL, Sharat, MA; Indian diplomatist (retd); b. 1952; joined Indian Foreign Service 1975, served in various positions including Perm. Mission to UN, Geneva and Indian missions in Madagascar, France and Mauritius, Dir/Jt Sec., Ministry of External Affairs 1990–95, Deputy High Commr to Pakistan 1995–99, Deputy Perm. Rep. to UN, Geneva 1999–2002, Amb. to Uzbekistan 2002–05, Special Sec. in charge of Admin, Consular, Passport and Visa Affairs, Ministry of External Affairs 2005–09, High Commr to Pakistan 2009–13 (retd).

SABHARWAL, Yogesh Kumar; Indian judge; b. 14 Jan. 1942; two s.; enrolled as Advocate, Delhi 1964, represented Delhi in Bar Council of India 1969–73; Advocate Indian Railway 1969–81; Advocate Delhi Admin 1973–76, Additional Standing Counsel 1980–81, later Standing Counsel; Cen. Govt Counsel 1980–86; Additional Judge High Court of Delhi 1986–87, Perm. Judge 1987, Acting Chief Justice –1999; Chief Justice High Court of Bombay 1999–2000; Judge Supreme Court of India 2000–05, Chief Justice 2005–07 (retd); fmr Chair. Bd COFEPOSA; fmr Sec., Pres. Delhi High Court Bar Asscn; fmr Hon. Sec. Int. Law Asscn. *Address:* c/o Supreme Court, Tilak Marg, New Delhi 110 001, India. *Telephone:* (11) 23794976 (home).

SABIA, Michael J., BA, MA, MPh; Canadian telecommunications industry executive; b. 1954, St Catharines, Ont.; m. Hilary M. Pearson; one d.; ed Trinity Coll., Univ. of Toronto, Yale Univ., USA; began career with Canadian Fed. Public Service, held various sr positions including Dir-Gen., Tax Policy, Dept of Finance, Deputy Sec. of the Cabinet (Plans), Privy Council Office –1993; Vice-Pres. Corp. Devt, Canadian Nat. Railway Authority (CN) 1993, Exec. Vice-Pres. and Chief Financial Officer 1995–99; Vice-Chair. and CEO Bell Canada Int. Inc. 1999–2000, Exec. Vice-Pres. Bell Canada Enterprises (BCE) Inc. and Vice-Chair. Bell Canada 2000, Pres. and COO BCE Inc. March–April 2002, COO Bell Canada March–May 2002, Pres. and CEO BCE Inc. 2003–08, also CEO Bell Canada; CEO Caisse de dépôt et placement du Québec 2009–. *Address:* Edifice Price 65, rue Sainte-Anne 14e étage Québec, Québec, PQ G1R 3X5, Canada (office). *Telephone:* (418) 684-2334 (office). *Fax:* (418) 684-2335 (office). *Website:* www.lacaisse.com (office).

SABIT, Abdul Jabar; Afghan lawyer and government official; b. 1945, Nangarhar Prov.; legal adviser, Ministry of the Interior –2006; Attorney-Gen. 2006–08; fmr Asst Dir of Afghan Islamic Univ.; fmr Legal Adviser to Attorney Gen.; also worked as Reporter for Voice of America; mem. official del. that visited Afghan prisoners held by US Govt in Guantánamo Bay detainment camp, Cuba 2006. *Address:* c/o Office of the Attorney-General, Ministry of Justice, Pashtunistan Wat, Kabul, Afghanistan. *Telephone:* (20) 2101322.

SABORÍO CHAVERRI, Lineth; Costa Rican politician; b. 4 Nov. 1960; d. of Germain Saborío Chaverri and Haydee Segura Saborío Chaverri; m. Roger Carvajal Bonilla; three c.; started career as Asst Internal Affairs, Judicial Investigation Org., Head 1997–2001; First Vice-Pres. and Minister of Justice 2002, First Vice-Pres. 2002–06, also Coordinator of Ministries of Justice, Security, Interior, External Relations and Inst. of Devt; Minister of Nat. Planning and Econ. Policies 2002–03; Pres. Council of Security and Citizens' Participation 2002–04. *Address:* c/o Ministry of the Presidency and Planning, Avdas 3 y 5, Calle 4, Apdo 10.127, 1000 San José, Costa Rica.

SABOURET, Yves Marie Georges; French civil servant; b. 15 April 1936, Paris; s. of Henri Sabouret and Colette Sabouret (née Anthoine); m. 1st Anne de Caumont la Force 1965 (divorced); one s. two d.; m. 2nd Laurence Vilaine 1991; one d.; ed Ecole Nat. d'Admin; Inspecteur des finances 1964–81; tech. counsellor, Office of Minister of Supply and Housing 1968–69; Dir Office of Minister of Labour, Employment and Population 1969–72; Counsellor for Social and Cultural Affairs to Prime Minister Pierre Messmer 1972–74; Conseiller général, Côtes du Nord (Canton de Matignon) 1973–92; Pres. Soc. de développement régional de la Bretagne 1977–2000; Vice-Pres., Soc. Matra 1979; Dir-Gen. Hachette 1981–90, Vice-Pres. 1981–90; Pres. Atlas Copco France 1984–; Co-Dir-Gen. La Cinq 1990; Dir-Gen. NMPP 1994–2003; Pres. Fondation de France 2007; Chevalier Légion d'honneur, Officier Ordre nat. du Mérite, Croix de la Valeur militaire. *Address:* c/o NMPP, 52 rue Jacques Hillairet, 75012 Paris; 5 rue Mignard, 75116 Paris, France.

SABOURIN, Louis, LLL, PhD, FRSC; Canadian academic; *Professor of International Economic Organizations and Director, Groupe d'Etude de Recherche et de Formation Internationales, Ecole Nationale d'Administration Publique, University of Québec;* b. 1 Dec. 1935, Québec City; s. of Rolland Sabourin and Valeda Caza; m. Agathe Lacerte 1959; one s. two d.; ed Univ. of Ottawa, Univ. of Paris, France, Institut d'Etudes Politiques de Paris, France, Columbia Univ., USA; Prof., Dir Dept of Political Science, Univ. of Ottawa, Dean of Faculty of Social Science; Founder and Dir Inst. of Int. Co-operation and Devt, Visiting Sr Research Fellow, Jesus Coll., Oxford and Queen Elizabeth House, England 1974–75; Pres. OECD Devt Centre, Paris 1977–82; Prof. of Int. Econ. Orgs, Ecole Nationale d'Admin Publique, Univ. of Québec 1983–, Dir Groupe d'Etude, de Recherche et de Formation Internationales 1983–; Visiting Prof., Univ. of Paris (Sorbonne) 1982, Univ. of Notre Dame and Stanford Univ. 1992, Hanoi, Viet Nam 2000; Founding

mem. Asia-Pacific Foundation, Montreal Council of Foreign Relations; mem. Pontifical Comm. on Justice and Peace; Pres. Soc. de Droit Int. Economique 1988; Legal Counselor Hudon, Gendron, Harris, Thomas 1989–; Ford Int. Fellow 1962, Canada Council Scholar 1963; mem. Pontifical Acad. of Social Sciences, Rome 1994; Chevalier Pléiade de la Francophonie 1988; Chevalier Légion d'honneur; Dr hc (Sorbonne, Paris) 1998. *Publications:* Le système politique du Canada 1969, Dualité culturelle dans les activités internationales du Canada 1970, Canadian Federalism and International Organizations 1971, Le Canada et le développement international 1972, Allier la théorie à la pratique: le développement de la Chine nouvelle 1973, International Economic Development: Theories, Methods and Prospects 1973, The Challenge of the Less Developed Countries 1981, La crise économique: contraintes et effets de l'interdépendance pour le Canada 1984, Passion d'être, désir d'avoir, le dilemme Québec-Canada dans un univers en mutation 1992, Les organisations économiques internationales 1994, The Social Dimensions of Globalization 2000, Globalization and Inequalities 2002, The Governance of Globalization 2004; numerous articles. *Leisure interests:* music, travel, wine-tasting (Grand officier du Tastevin), skiing, tennis, cycling. *Address:* GERFI-ENAP, 4750 avenue Henri-Julien, Montreal, PQ H2T 3E5, Canada (office). *Telephone:* (514) 849-3989 (office); (514) 735-4541 (home). *Fax:* (514) 849-3369 (office). *E-mail:* louis.sabourin@enap.ca (office). *Website:* www.enap.ca (office).

SABRI, Naji, MA, PhD; Iraqi journalist, diplomatist and government official; b. 1951; Foreign Ed. and Man. Ed. al-Thawra Daily 1968–75; Lecturer in English, Coll. of Arts, Univ. of Baghdad 1969–75; Councillor at Iraqi Embassy, London 1975–80; Founder and Dir Iraqi Cultural Centre, London 1977–80; Founder and Ed.-in-Chief UR (journal of modern Arab arts) 1977–80; Dir-Gen. Dar al-Mamun House (trans. and publishing) 1980–90; Ed.-in-Chief Baghdad Observer 1980–98; Founder and Ed.-in-Chief Gilgamesh (journal of modern Iraqi arts) 1986–95; Vice-Pres. Iraqi Nat. Cttee of Educ., Science and Culture 1986–95; Dir-Gen. of Foreign Information, Ministry of Information and Culture 1990–91, Deputy Minister of Information and Culture 1991–95, Adviser to Minister of Information and Culture 1997–98; Lecturer, Coll. of Arts, Univ. of Mustansiriya 1995–99; Adviser, Presidential Office 1995–98; at Ministry of Foreign Affairs, Baghdad 1998, Amb. to Austria and Perm. Rep. to IAEA, UNIDO and UN Office, Vienna 1999–2001, Amb. (non-resident) to Slovakia 2000–01, Minister of State for Foreign Affairs April–Aug. 2001, Minister of Foreign Affairs 2001–03; currently teaches journalism in Qatar. *Publications include:* trans. into Arabic: The Genius of Show (Michael Holroyd), Aspects of Biography (André Maurois), Lectures on Literature (Vladimir Nabokov); several Iraqi political books into English; Iraq's Year Book (Ed.-in-Chief) 1988, 1990, 1995, 1998, 1999. *Address:* c/o Ministry of Foreign Affairs, opp. State Organization for Roads and Bridges, Karradat Mariam, Baghdad, Iraq.

SACA GONZÁLEZ, Elías Antonio (Tony); Salvadorean politician, business executive and fmr head of state; b. 9 March 1965, Usulután; m. Ana Ligia Mixco Sol de Saca; three c.; ed Instituto San Agustín de Usulatán, Colegio Cristóbal Colón; fmr sports commentator and journalist; launched TV channel and several radio programmes 1990s including Radio América (with Alfonso Rivas) 1987, Radio Astral 1993; Pres. Asociación Salvadoreña de Radiodifusores (ASDER) 1997–2001, currently Vice-Pres.; Pres. Asociación Nacional de Empresa Privada (ANEP; National Private Enterprise Asscn) 2001–04; fmr Pres. Círculo de Informadores Deportivos (CID); currently Pres. FEDEPRICAP (Fed. of Cen. American and Dominican Repub. Business Execs); Pres. of El Salvador 2004–09; cand. in presidential election Feb. 2014; mem. Alianza Republicana Nacionalista (ARENA) –2010, Gran Alianza por la Unidad Nacional (GANA) 2010–; Micrófono de Oro 1991, Distinguished Broadcaster Award 2003. *Address:* c/o Alianza Republicana Nacionalista (ARENA), Prolongación Calle Arce 2423, entre 45 y 47 Avda Norte, San Salvador, El Salvador (office).

SACCO, Desmond, BSc; South African geologist and business executive; *Chairman and Managing Director, Assore Ltd;* b. 22 Sept. 1942, Johannesburg; s. of Guido Sacco; ed Univ. of the Witwatersrand; joined Assore Ltd 1968, mem. Bd of Dirs 1974, Chair. and Man. Dir 1992–; Dir African Mining and Trust Co. Ltd 1975, Chair. 1992–; Chair. Ore and Metal Co. Ltd 1992–; Deputy Chair. Assmang Ltd 1992–99, Chair. 1999–; Fellow, Geological Soc. of South Africa, Inst. of Dirs; Italian Business Man of the Year, Italian Chamber. *Publication:* The Desmond Sacco Collection. *Address:* Assore Ltd, Private Bag X03, Northlands 2116, South Africa (office). *Telephone:* (11) 770 6800 (office). *Website:* www.assore.com (office).

SACCOMANI, Fabrizio; Italian banking executive and government official; b. 22 Nov. 1942, Rome; m.; ed Bocconi Univ. (degree in econs), Princeton Univ., USA; joined Bank of Italy 1967, with Supervision Office 1967–70, with Int. Econ. Corpn Dept, then Econ. Research Dept 1975–84, Head of Foreign Dept 1984–97, Cen. Man. for Int. Affairs 1997–2003, Dir-Gen. 2006–13; Minister of Economy and Finance 2013–14; Rep. at Int. Relations Cttee, European Cen. Bank, Cttee on the Global Financial System, BIS, Econ. and Finance Cttee, EU; with Economist, Exchange and Trade Relations Dept, then Asst to Exec. Dir for Italy, IMF 1970–75; Chair. Foreign Exchange Policy Sub-Cttee, European Monetary Inst. 1991–97; Vice-Pres. EBRD 2003–06; mem. Bd of Dirs Einaudi Inst. for Econs and Finance, Istituto Italiano di Tecnologia; mem. Istituto Affari Internazionali, Società Italiana degli Economisti. *Address:* c/o Ministry of the Economy and Finance, Via XX Settembre 97, 00187 Rome, Italy.

SACHINIDIS, Philippos, MEconSc, PhD; Greek economist, academic and politician; b. 27 March 1963, Vancouver, BC, Canada; m. Ourania Karageorgou 1990; one s.; ed Univ. of Piraeus Grad. School of Industrial Studies, Queens Coll., City Univ. of New York, USA, Univ. of Manchester, UK; Lecturer in Econs, Manchester School of Man. 1991–94; fmr Researcher, Foundation of Econ. and Industrial Research (IOBE), Athens 1996; Sr Economist, Strategic Planning Div., Nat. Bank of Greece 1997–2000, 2004–07; fmr Special Adviser, Econ. Office of Prime Minister Konstantinos Simitis 2000–04; mem. (Panhellenic Socialist Movt—PASOK) of the Vouli (Parl.) for Larissa 2007–, mem. Parl. Standing Cttee of Production and Trade 2007–09; Deputy, then Alt. Minister of Finance 2009–12, Minister of Finance March–May 2012; mem. Nat. Council and Sec. PASOK Cttee 2007–09. *Publications:* several articles in academic journals and newspapers. *Address:* 1 Defkalionos str., 41222 Larisa, Greece (office). *Telephone:* (241) 0530848 (office). *Fax:* (241) 0252810 (office). *E-mail:* philippos@sachinidis.gr (office).

SACHS, Jeffrey David, BA, MA, PhD; American economist, writer and academic; *Special Adviser to the Secretary-General on Millennium Development Goals, United Nations;* b. 5 Nov. 1954, Detroit, Mich.; s. of Theodore Sachs and Joan Sachs; m. Sonia Ehrlich; one s. two d.; ed Harvard Univ.; Research Assoc. Nat. Bureau of Econ. Research, Cambridge, Mass. 1980–85; Asst Prof. of Econs, Harvard Univ. 1980–82, Assoc. Prof. 1982–83, Galen L. Stone Prof. of International Trade 1984–2001, Dir Harvard Inst. for International Devt 1995–2002, Center for International Devt –2002; Quetelet Prof. of Sustainable Devt and Prof. of Health Policy and Man. and Dir The Earth Inst., Columbia Univ. 2002–; Adviser, Brookings Inst., Washington, DC 1982–; Special Adviser to UN Sec.-Gen. on Millennium Devt Goals 2002–, Dir Millennium Project 2002–06; Founder Millennium Villages Project; Founder and Co-Pres. Millennium Promise Alliance; Founder and Chair. Exec. Cttee Inst. of Econ. Analysis, Moscow 1993–; Chair. Comm. on Macroeconomics and Health, WHO 2000–01; Co-Chair. Advisory Bd The Global Competitiveness Report; mem. International Financial Insts Advisory Comm., US Congress 1999–2000; econ. adviser to various govts in Latin America, Eastern Europe, the fmr Soviet Union, Asia and Africa, Jubilee 2000 movt; fmr consultant to IMF, World Bank, OECD and UNDP; Adviser to Pres. of Bolivia 1986–90; Fellow, World Econometric Soc.; Research Assoc. Nat. Bureau of Econ. Research; syndicated newspaper column appears in more than 50 countries; mem. American Acad. of Arts and Sciences, Harvard Soc. of Fellows, Brookings Panel of Economists, Bd of Advisers, Inst. of Medicine, Fellows of the World Econometric Soc., Nat. Bureau of Econ. Research, Bd of Advisors Chinese Economists Soc., among other international orgs; Distinguished Visiting Lecturer, LSE, Univ. of Oxford, Tel-Aviv, Jakarta, Yale Univs; Hon. Prof., Universidad del Pacífico, Peru; Commdr's Cross, Order of Merit (Poland) 1999; Hon. PhD (St Gallen, Switzerland) 1990, (Universidad del Pacífico, Peru) 1997, (Lingnan Coll., Hong Kong) 1998, (Varna Econs Univ., Bulgaria) 2000, (Iona Coll., New York) 2000; hon. degrees from Pace Univ., State Univ. of New York, Kraków Univ. of Econs, Ursinus Coll., Whitman Coll., Mount Sinai School of Medicine, Ohio Wesleyan Univ., Coll. of the Atlantic, Southern Methodist Univ., Simon Fraser Univ., McGill Univ., Southern New Hampshire Univ., St John's Univ.; Frank E. Seidman Award in Political Econ. 1991, cited in New York Times Magazine as "probably the most important economist in the world" 1993, named by TIME magazine as "the world's best-known economist", cited by Le Nouvel Observateur magazine as "one of the world's 50 most important leaders on globalization" 1997, Berhard Harms Prize (Germany) 2000, Distinguished Public Service Award, Sec. of State's Open Forum 2002, named by TIME magazine as one of the 100 Most Influential People in the World 2004, 2005, Sargent Shriver Award for Equal Justice 2005, named by the World Affairs Councils of America as one of the "500 Most Influential People in the Field of Foreign Policy" 2007, Padma Bhushan, Govt of India 2007, Cardozo Journal of Conflict Resolution International Advocate for Peace Award 2007, Centennial Medal, Harvard Grad. School of Arts and Sciences for his contribs to society 2007, BBC Reith Lecturer 2007, first holder of Royal Prof. Ungku Aziz Chair in Poverty Studies, Centre for Poverty and Devt Studies, Univ. of Malaya, Kuala Lumpur, Malaysia 2007–09, ranked 98th by Vanity Fair magazine on its list of 100 members of the New Establishment 2008, gave commencement address to Lehigh Univ.'s Class of 2009. *Publications include:* Economics of Worldwide Stagflation (with Michael Bruno) 1985, Developing Country Debt and the Economic Performance (ed.) 1989, Global Linkages: Macroeconomic Interdependence and Cooperation in the World Economy (with Warwick McKibbin) 1991, Peru's Path to Recovery (with Carlos Paredes) 1991, Macroeconomics in the Global Economy (with Felipe Larrain) 1993, Poland's Jump to the Market Economy 1993, The Transition in Eastern Europe (with Olivier Blanchard and Kenneth Froot) 1994, Russia and the Market Economy (in Russian) 1995, Economic Reform and the Process of Global Integration (with A. Warner) 1995, The Collapse of the Mexican Peso: What Have We Learned? (co-author) 1995, Natural Resource Abundance and Economic Growth (with A. Warner) 1996, The Rule of Law and Economic Reform in Russia (co-ed.) 1997, Economies in Transition (co-ed.) 1997, The End of Poverty 2005, Common Wealth: Economics for a Crowded Planet 2008, The Price of Civilization 2011; more than 200 scholarly articles. *Leisure interests:* skiing, biking, watching ballet. *Address:* The Earth Institute at Columbia University, 405 Low Library, 535 West 116th Street, MC 4335, New York, NY 10027, USA (office). *Telephone:* (212) 854-8704 (office). *Fax:* (212) 854-8702 (office). *Website:* www.earth.columbia.edu/about/director (office); www.un.org/millenniumgoals (office).

SACHS, Leo, PhD, FRS; British/Israeli biologist and academic; *Otto Meyerhof Professor of Molecular Biology, Department of Molecular Genetics, Weizmann Institute of Science;* b. 14 Oct. 1924, Leipzig, Germany; s. of Elias Sachs and Louise Sachs; m. Pnina Salkind; one s. three d.; ed City of London School, Univ. of Wales, Bangor, Trinity Coll., Cambridge; research scientist in genetics, John Innes Inst. 1951–52; Research Scientist, Weizmann Inst. of Science, Rehovot, Israel 1952–, Assoc. Prof. 1960, est. Dept of Genetics and Virology 1960, Prof. 1962, Head, Dept of Genetics 1962–89, Dean Faculty of Biology 1974–79, now Otto Meyerhof Prof. of Biology; mem. European Molecular Biology Org. 1965, Israel Acad. of Sciences and Humanities 1975; Foreign Assoc. NAS 1995–; Foreign mem. European Acad. 1998; Samuel Rudin Visiting Prof., Coll. of Physicians and Surgeons, Columbia Univ., USA 1980; Charles B. Smith Visiting Research Prof., Memorial Sloan-Kettering Cancer Center, USA 1981; Hon. Fellow, Univ. of Wales 1999, Hon. Life mem. Int. Cytokine Soc. 2001–; Dr hc (Bordeaux) 1985, Hon. DMed (Lund) 1997; Israel Prize for Natural Sciences 1972, Harvey Lecturer, Rockefeller Univ., USA 1972, Rothschild Prize in Biological Sciences 1977, Wolf Prize in Medicine 1980, Bristol-Myers Award for Distinguished Achievement in Cancer Research 1983, Royal Soc. Wellcome Foundation Prize 1986, R. E. Bob Smith Lecturer, Univ. of Texas Cancer Center, USA 1986, General Motors Cancer Research Foundation Lecturer, Walter and Elisa Hall Inst., Australia 1986, Karl Bayer Lecturer, Univ. of Wisconsin, USA 1987, Jan Waldenstrom Lecturer, Swedish Soc. of Medicine 1987, Sloan Prize, General Motors Cancer Research Foundation 1989, Warren Alpert Foundation Prize, Harvard Medical School, Mass 1997, Donald Van Slyke Distinguished Lecturer, Brookhaven Nat. Lab., USA 1997, Ham-Wasserman Lecturer, American Soc. of Hematology 2000, Emet Prize for Life Sciences 2002. *Publications:* papers in various scientific journals on stem cells, blood cells, devt and cancer research. *Leisure interests:* music, museums. *Address:* Department of Molecular Genetics, Weizmann Institute of Science, Belfer 226, Rehovot 76100, Israel (office). *Telephone:* (8) 9344068 (office). *Fax:* (8) 9344108 (office). *E-mail:* leo

.sachs@weizmann.ac.il (office). *Website:* www.weizmann.ac.il/molgen/members/sachs.html (office).

SACKER, Ulrich, PhD; German cultural administrator; b. 16 March 1951, Luenen; s. of Erich Sacker and Dorothea Sacker; m. Christina Sacker; one s.; ed Univ. of Münster, Munich, Aix-en-Provence, France; mem. Bureau Int. de Documentation et de Liaison Franco-Allemandes, Paris; Prof. of French and Russian, Univ. of Bonn, Cologne; Commr Promotion of Germany Worldwide, Goethe-Institut HQ, Munich, Dir Goethe-Institut San Franciso, USA, Hong Kong, London, Berlin, currently in Lyon, France. *Address:* Goethe-Institut Lyon, 18 rue François Dauphin, 69002 Lyon, France (office). *Telephone:* (4) 72-77-08-88 (office). *Fax:* (4) 72-40-91-55 (office). *E-mail:* info@lyon.goethe.org (office). *Website:* www.goethe.de/lyon (office).

SACKETT, Penny Diane, PhD; Australian (b. American) physicist, astronomer, strategic analyst and academic; *Adjunct Professor, Australian National University;* b. 28 Feb. 1956, Lincoln, Neb.; ed Univ. of Nebraska, Univ. of Pittsburgh; fmr reporter for Science News; fmr J. Seward Johnson Fellow, Inst. of Advanced Study, Princeton; fmr Program Dir Nat. Science Foundation; fmr Prof., Univ. of Groningen, Netherlands; fmr Researcher and Prof. of Astronomy, Kapteyn Astronomical Inst., Netherlands; Dir ANU Research School of Astronomy and Astrophysics 2002–07, also Dir Mount Stromlo and Siding Spring Observatories 2002–07, Adjunct Prof. 2011–; Chief Scientist of Australia 2008–11; mem. Bd of Dirs Assen of Univs for Research in Astronomy, Giant Magellan Telescope –2008; mem. Australian Astronomical Soc., American Astronomical Soc., Int. Astronomical Union, Assen for Women in Science; Int. Fellow, Royal Astronomical Soc.. *E-mail:* Penny.Sackett@anu.edu.au (office).

SACKS, Baron Jonathan Henry Sacks, PhD; British rabbi; b. 8 March 1948, London, England; s. of Louis Sacks and Louisa Sacks (née Frumkin); m. Elaine Taylor 1970; one s. two d.; ed Christ's Coll. Finchley, Gonville & Caius Coll., Cambridge, New Coll., Oxford, Univ. of London, Jews' Coll., London and Yeshivat Etz Hayyim, London; Lecturer in Moral Philosophy, Middlesex Polytechnic 1971–73; Lecturer in Jewish Philosophy, Jews' Coll., London 1973–76, in Talmud and Jewish Philosophy 1976–82, Chief Rabbi Lord Jakobovits Prof. (first incumbent) in Modern Jewish Thought 1982–, Dir Rabbinic Faculty 1983–90, Prin. 1984–90; Chief Rabbi, United Hebrew Congregations of British Commonwealth of Nations 1991–2013 (retd); Assoc. Pres. Conf. of European Rabbis 2000; Visiting Prof., King's Coll. London 1998–, Birkbeck Coll. 2008–; Visiting Prof. of Philosophy, Univ. of Essex 1989–90; fmr Visiting Prof. of Philosophy, Hebrew Univ., Jerusalem; Rabbi, Golders Green Synagogue, London 1978–82, Marble Arch Synagogue, London 1983–90; Ed. Le'ela (journal) 1985–90; mem. CRAC; Presentation Fellow, King's Coll. London 1993; mem. (Crossbench) House of Lords 2009–; Trustee, Tuck Trust, Aria Trust; Hon. Fellow, Gonville and Caius Coll., Cambridge 1993; Hon. DD (Cantab.) 1993, (Archbishop of Canterbury) 2001; Dr hc (Middx Univ.) 1993, (Haifa Univ., Israel) 1996, (Yeshiva Univ., NY) 1997, (St Andrews Univ.) 1998; Hon. LLD (Univ. of Liverpool) 1997; Sherman Lecturer, Manchester Univ. 1989, Reith Lecturer 1990, Jerusalem Prize 1995, Cook Lecturer 1997. *Publications include:* Torah Studies 1986, Tradition and Transition (essays) 1986, Traditional Alternatives 1989, Tradition in an Untraditional Age 1990, The Persistence of Faith (Reith Lecture) 1991, Orthodoxy Confronts Modernity (Ed.) 1991, Crisis and Covenant 1992, One People?: Tradition, Modernity and Jewish Unity 1993, Will We Have Jewish Grandchildren? 1994, Faith in the Future 1995, Community of Faith 1995, The Politics of Hope 1997, Morals and Markets 1999, Celebrating Life 2000, Radical Then Radical Now 2001, The Dignity of Difference: How To Avoid the Clash of Civilizations 2002, The Chief Rabbi's Hagadah 2003, To Heal a Fractured World 2005, The Home We Build Together – Recreating Society 2007, Koren Sacks Siddur 2009, Covenant & Conversation: A Weekly Reading of the Jewish Bible 2009, Future Tense: Jews, Judaism, and Israel in the Twenty-first Century 2009, The Great Partnership: God, Science and the Search For Meaning 2011, The Koren Sacks Rosh HaShana Mahzor 2011, The Koren Sacks Pesah Mahzor 2013. *Leisure interests:* walking, music. *Address:* House of Lords, Westminster, London, SW1A 0PW, England. *Telephone:* (20) 7286-6391. *Fax:* (20) 7219-5979. *E-mail:* sacksj@parliament.uk. *Website:* www.parliament.uk/biographies/lords/lord-sacks/3901.

SACKS, Oliver Wolf, CBE, MD, FRCP; British neurologist, writer and academic; *Professor of Neurology, School of Medicine, New York University;* b. 9 July 1933, London; s. of Dr Samuel Sacks and Dr Muriel Elsie Sacks (née Landau); ed St Paul's School, London and Queen's Coll., Oxford; Research Asst, Parkinsonism Unit, Mt Zion Hospital, San Francisco 1960–61; Resident, UCLA 1962–65; Consultant Neurologist, Headache Unit, Montefiore Hosp., Bronx, New York 1966–68, Beth Abraham Hosp., Bronx 1966–2007, Bronx Psychiatric Center 1966–91, Little Sisters of the Poor, NY 1972–, Bronx Developmental Services 1974–76; Consultant Neurologist and mem. Medical Advisory Bd, Gilles de la Tourette Syndrome Assen, New York 1974–; Asst Prof. of Neurology, Albert Einstein Coll. of Medicine, Bronx 1975–78, Assoc. Clinical Prof. 1978–85, Clinical Prof. 1985–2007; Adjunct Prof. of Psychiatry, New York Univ. (NYU) School of Medicine 1992–2007, Prof. of Neurology 2012–, Consulting Neurologist, NYU Comprehensive Epilepsy Center 1999–2007, 2012–; Prof. of Neurology and Psychiatry, Medical Center, Columbia Univ. 2007–12, Columbia Univ. Artist 2007–12; mem. American Acad. of Neurology, American Fern Soc., Authors Guild, British Pteridological Soc., Bronx Co. and NY State Medical Socs, New York Mineralogical Club, New York Stereoscopic Soc., PEN, Soc. for Neuroscience; Hon. Fellow, American Acad. of Arts and Letters 1996, American Acad. of Arts and Sciences, American Neurological Assen, Assen of British Neurologists, Jonathan Edwards Coll., Yale Univ., New York Acad. of Sciences, New York Inst. for the Humanities, NYU, Queen's Coll., Oxford, Royal Coll. of Physicians. Univ. of California, Santa Cruz, Cowell Coll.; Hon. DHumLitt (Georgetown Univ.) 1990, (Staten Island Coll., CUNY) 1991; Hon. DSc (Tufts Univ.) 1991, (New York Medical Coll.) 1991, (Bard Coll.) 1992; Hon. DMedSc (Medical Coll. of Pennsylvania), (Karolinska Institutet, Stockholm) 2003; Hon. LLD (Gallaudet Univ.) 2005; Hon. DCL (Oxford Univ.) 2005, (Pontificia Universidad Católica del Perú) 2006; Dr hc (Cold Spring Harbor Laboratory, Watson School of Biological Sciences) 2008; Oskar Pfister Award, American Psychiatric Assen 1988, Harold D. Vursell Memorial Award, American Acad. and Inst. of Arts and Letters 1989, Prix Psyche' 1991, Nat. Headache Foundation Professional Support Award 1991, Presidential

Citation, American Acad. of Neurology 1991, Special Presidential Award, American Neurological Asscn 1991, Communicator of the Year Award, Royal Nat. Inst. for the Deaf 1991, Award for Educ. in Neuroscience, Asscn of Neuroscience Depts and Programs 1991, Lewis Thomas Prize for the Scientist as Poet, Rockefeller Univ. 2002, Public Communication Award, NSF 2004, Mental Health Award, Coalition of Voluntary Mental Health Asscns 2004, E.A. Wood Scientific Writing Award, American Crystallographic Asscn 2004. *Publications:* Migraine 1970, Awakenings (Hawthornden Prize 1974, Book of the Year, The Observer 1973, The Scriptor Award, Univ. of Southern California 1991) 1973, A Leg to Stand On 1984, The Man Who Mistook His Wife For A Hat 1985, Seeing Voices: A Journey Into The World of the Deaf (Odd Fellows Social Concern Book Award 1991, Mainichi Publishing Culture Award, Tokyo, Best Natural Science Book 1996) 1989, An Anthropologist on Mars (Esquire/Apple/Waterstones Book of the Year) 1995, The Island of the Colourblind 1996, Uncle Tungsten (New York Times Editors' Choice, Jewish Quarterly Wingate Prize, Literature Award of the German Chemical Industry Fund 2004) 2001, Oaxaca Journal 2002, Musicophilia: Tales of Music and the Brain 2007, The Mind's Eye 2010, Hallucinations 2012. *Address:* 2 Horatio Street, 3G, New York, NY 10014 (home); School of Medicine, New York University, 550 1st Avenue, New York, NY 10016, USA (office). *Telephone:* (212) 633-8373 (home). *Fax:* (212) 633-8928 (home). *E-mail:* mail@oliversacks.com (home). *Website:* school.med.nyu.edu (office); www.oliversacks.com.

SADAN, Rahbeh; Algerian football coach; b. 3 May 1946, Batna; ed Lycée Ahmed Reda Houhou; fmr professional football player (defender) with teams MSP Batna 1964–68, MO Constantine 1968–69, JS El-Biar 1969–71, Stade Rennais 1971–72, USM Blida 1972–73; injury in car accident forced move to managing; man. of several teams including Algerian Under-20s 1979–81, Algerian Nat. Team 1981–82, 1985–86, 1999, 2003–04, 2007–10. *Address:* c/o Algerian Football Federation, Chemin Ahmed Ouaked, BP 39, Dely Brahim, Algiers, Algeria (office). *Website:* www.faf.dz (office).

SADANG, Elbuchel, BS; Palauan politician; b. 6 March 1955; s. of Sadang Etibek and Dirrabang Delmau Sadang; m. Shangrang Wenty; four c.; ed Grand Valley State Univ., Mich., USA; legislator for Ngaraard State 1990–2001; Dir Bureau of Nat. Treasury, Ministry of Finance 1994–2001; Minister of Finance 2001–08, also Gov. for Asian Devt Bank and IMF on behalf of Palau; mem. Asian Pacific Asscn for Fiduciary Studies, Island Govt Finance Officers Asscn; fmr mem. Bd of Trustees Civil Service Pension Plan, charged with pension fraud 2008 along with other bd mems; Chief of Staff to Pres. 2013–. *Address:* Office of the President, PO Box 6051, Koror, PW 96940, Palau (office). *Telephone:* 488-2403 (office). *Fax:* 488-1662 (office). *E-mail:* esadang@palaugov.net (office). *Website:* www.palaugov.net/minfinance/mofinance.html (office).

SADER CASTELLANOS, Eugenia; Venezuelan paediatrician, politician and fmr military officer; *Minister of Health;* d. of Rubén Sader Pérez; Pres. Mission Barrio Adentro (social welfare porgramme) 2009; fmr Col, Bn 51 (army medical group); Deputy Minister of Community Health Network 2010, Minister of Health 2010–; Pres. Fundación de Edificaciones y Equipamiento Hospitalario; mem. Partido Socialista Unido de Venezuela. *Address:* Ministry of Health, Edif. Sur, 8°, Avda Baralt, Centro Simón Bolívar, El Silencio, Caracas 1010, Venezuela (office). *Telephone:* (212) 408-0033 (office). *Fax:* (212) 483-2560 (office). *E-mail:* mpps@mpps.gob.ve (office). *Website:* www.msds.gov.ve (office).

SADIK, Nafis, MD; Pakistani physician and UN official; b. 18 Aug. 1929, Jaunpur, India; d. of Mohammad Shoaib and Iffat Ara; m. Azhar Sadik 1954; one s. two d. and two adopted d.; ed Loretto Coll. Calcutta, Calcutta Medical Coll., Dow Medical Coll. Karachi and Johns Hopkins Univ., Intern, Gynaecology and Obstetrics, City Hosp., Baltimore, Md 1952–54; civilian medical officer in charge of women's and children's wards in various Pakistani armed forces hosps. 1954–63; Resident, Physiology, Queen's Univ., Kingston, Ont. 1958; Head, Health Section, Planning Comm., on Health and Family Planning, Pakistan 1964; Dir of Planning and Training, Pakistan Cen. Family Planning Council 1966–68, Deputy Dir-Gen. 1968–70, Dir-Gen. 1970–71; Tech. Adviser, UN Population Fund (UNFPA) 1971–72, Chief, Programme Div. 1973–77, Asst Exec. Dir 1977–87, Exec. Dir UNFPA 1987–2000; fmrly UN Under-Sec.-Gen.; Sec.-Gen. Int. Conf. on Population and Devt 1994; UN Special Envoy for HIV/AIDS in Asia 2002–12; Pres. Soc. for Int. Devt 1994–97; Fellow ad eundem, Royal Coll. of Obstetricians and Gynaecologists; Order of Merit, First Class (Egypt) 1994, Hilal-I-Imtiaz (Pakistan); Hon. DHumLitt (Johns Hopkins) 1989, (Brown) 1993, (Duke) 1995; Hon. LLD (Wilfrid Laurier) 1995; Hon. DSc (Mich.) 1996, (Claremont) 1996, (Long Island) 1997, (Tulane) 1999, (Univ. of the West Indies) 2000; Hon. DLitt (Nepal Tribhuvan) 1998; Hon. DEcon (Nihon) 1999; Dr hc (Al-Ahfad) 2000; Bruno H. Schubert-Stiftung Prize 1995, Hugh Moore Award 1976, Women's Global Leadership Award 1994, Peace Award (UNA) 1994, Prince Mahidol Award 1995, Population Award, UN 2001, Defender of Democracy, Peoples Global Action 2006. *Publications:* Population: National Family Planning Programme in Pakistan 1968, Population: The UNFPA Experience (ed.) 1984, Population Policies and Programmes: Lessons Learned from Two Decades of Experience 1991, Making a Difference: Twenty-five Years of UNFPA Experience 1994; articles in professional journals. *Leisure interests:* bridge, reading, theatre, travel. *Address:* c/o Special Envoy of the UN Secretary-General for HIV/AIDS in Asia, 300 East 56th Street, 9J New York, NY 10022, USA (office).

SADIQ, Mohammad, MA, MIA, MS; Pakistani diplomatist; *Ambassador to Afghanistan;* m.; two d.; ed Peshawar Univ., Columbia Univ., New York; Nat. Defence Univ., Islamabad; Dir CIS Dept, Ministry of Foreign Affairs 1993–94; First Sec./Counsellor, Embassy in Brussels 1994–98; Counsellor, Embassy in Beijing 1998–2000; Dir Kashmir Affairs Dept 2001–02; Minister/Deputy Chief of Mission, Embassy in Washington, DC 2002–05; Dir Gen. (Personnel) Jan.–July 2006, June-Dec. 2007; Spokesman, Ministry of Foreign Affairs 2007–09; Amb. to Afghanistan 2009–; mem. UN Election Observer Team that oversaw elections in South Africa 1994. *Address:* Embassy of Pakistan, Karte Parwan, Kabul, Afghanistan (office). *Telephone:* (20) 2202745 (office). *Fax:* (20) 2202871 (office). *E-mail:* parepkabul@yahoo.com (office). *Website:* (office); www.mohammadsadiq.com.

SADIQ, Sardar Ayaz, BCom; Pakistani politician; *Speaker, National Assembly;* b. 17 Oct. 1954, Lahore; m.; two s. one d.; ed Aitchison Coll., Hailey Coll. of Punjab

Univ.; began political career from Pakistan Tehreek-e-Insaf 1996, left the party after differences with its leader Imran Khan 1998, joined Pakistan Muslim League (N) (PML-N) 2001; mem. Nat. Ass. (Parl.) 2002–, Speaker 2013–; Chair. Sardar Trust Eye Hosp. 1994–. *Address:* Office of the Speaker, National Assembly of Pakistan, Parliament House, Islamabad, Pakistan (office). *Telephone:* (51) 9221082 (office). *Fax:* (51) 9221106 (office). *Website:* www.na.gov.pk (office).

SADOVNICHIY, Victor Antonovich, D.Phys-MathSc; Russian mathematician and university administrator; *Rector, Moscow State University 'M. V. Lomonsov';* b. 3 April 1939, Krasnopavlovka, Kharkov Region; m.; three c.; ed Moscow State Univ. 'M. V. Lomonsov'; Asst. Docent, Deputy Dean Chair of Mechanics and Math., Moscow State Univ. 'M. V. Lomonsov' 1972–78, Prof., Prorector 1982–84, First Pro-Rector 1982–92, Rector 1992–, also Chair. Dept of Math. Analysis; Pres. Russian Union of Rectors (mem. Perm. Cttee), Eurasia Univ. Asscn; Corresp. mem. Russian Acad. of Sciences 1994, mem. 1997, mem. Presidium, Vice-Pres. 2008; Dir Inst. of Math. Problems of Complex Systems 1995–; Prof., Int. Acad. of Marketing; mem. Russian Acad. of Tech. Sciences; Sec.-Gen. Asscn of USSR Univs. 1987–91; Vice-Pres. Int. Acad. of Higher School 1992–; mem. Yedinaya Rossia (United Russia) party; Hon. Citizen of Moscow City; Hon. mem. Russian Acad. of Educ.; Order of Merit for the Country, Class II, III, IV, two Orders of the Red Banner of Labour, Order St Prince Daniil Moskovsky II, Order of Venerable Sergius of Radonezh I, Commdr, Legion d'honneur, Order For Merit (Ukraine), Order Dostyk, Order of Francysk Skaryna (Belarus), Order Danaker (Kyrgyzstan), Order Dostyk (Kazakhstan), Order of the Rising Sun (Japan), Order of Honour (South Ossetia); Lomonosov Prize 1973, USSR State Prize laureate 1989, Russian Fed. State Prize for Science and Tech. 2002, Medal for Distinguished Labour, Medal for the 850th Anniversary of Moscow, Kazakhstan State Prize. *Address:* Moscow State University 'M. V. Lomonsov', Leninskie Gory, 119992 Moscow, Russia (office). *Telephone:* (495) 939-27-29 (office). *Fax:* (495) 939-01-26 (office). *E-mail:* rector@rector.msu.ru (office). *Website:* www.msu.ru (office).

SADR, Moqtada as-; Iraqi religious leader; b. 12 Aug. 1973, Baghdad; s. of Grand Ayatollah Muhammad al-Sadr; f. al-Hawzah weekly newspaper; est. Mahdi Army (Shiite resistance group) and Sadr Bureau in Sadr City, suburb of Baghdad 2003; went on self-imposed exile 2007, returned from exile 2011; strongly opposes presence of US coalition forces in Iraq.

ŠADŽIUS, Rimantas, LLM; Lithuanian physicist, lawyer and politician; *Minister of Finance;* b. 8 Oct. 1960, Vilnius; m. Dalia Šadžiuvienė; one s. one d.; ed Lomonosov Moscow State Univ., Russia and Vilnius Univ.; began career as scientific researcher specialising in quantum chem. and solid-state physics; Deputy Minister of Social Security and Labour 2003–04, of Health 2004–06, of Finance 2006–07; Minister of Finance 2007–08, 2012–; Lecturer, Vilnius Pedagogical Univ. 2009–12; mem. Lithuanian Social Democratic Party (LSDP). *Address:* Ministry of Finance, Lukiškių g. 2, Vilnius 01512 (office); c/o Lithuanian Social Democratic Party (Lietuvos Socialdemokratų Partija), Barboros Radvilaites g. 1, Vilnius 01124, Lithuania. *Telephone:* (5) 239-0005 (office); (5) 261-3907. *Fax:* (5) 212-6387 (office); (5) 261-5420. *E-mail:* finmin@finmin.lt (office); info@lsdp.lt. *Website:* www.finmin.lt (office); www.lsdp.lt; www.sadzius.lt.

SÆBØ, Magne, DTheol; Norwegian fmr professor of Old Testament theology; *Professor Emeritus of Old Testament Theology, Free Faculty of Theology;* b. 23 Jan. 1929, Fjelberg; s. of Samson Sæbø and Malla Ølfaernes; m. Mona Uni Bjørnstad 1953; three s.; ed Free Faculty of Theology, Oslo and Univ. of Oslo; studied Old Testament and Semitic languages in Jerusalem, Kiel and Heidelberg; teacher of Biblical Hebrew, Univ. of Oslo 1961–70; Lecturer in Old Testament, Free Faculty of Theology (now Norwegian School of Theology) 1969–70, Prof. 1970–99, Dean 1975–77, 1988–90, currently Prof. Emer.; Ed.-in-Chief Int. project on Hebrew Bible/Old Testament: The History of Its Interpretation I–III; Ed.-in-Chief Tidsskrift for Teologi og Kirke (Univ. Press), Oslo 1977–94; mem. Bd Norwegian Bible Soc. 1965–91, Chair. O.T. Trans. Cttee 1968–78, Gen. Trans. Cttee 1978–91; Chair. Norwegian Israel Mission 1978–87; mem. WCC Consultation on the Church and the Jewish People 1976–81; Chair. Lutheran European Comm. on the Church and the Jewish People, Hanover 1979–82; Pres. Int. Org. for the Study of Old Testament 1995–98; mem. Royal Soc. of Science and Letters, Trondheim, Norwegian Acad. of Science and Letters, Oslo, Nathan Söderblom Soc., Uppsala; received on 65th birthday Festschrift Text and Theology 1994; Kt 1st Class of Royal Norwegian Order of St Olav 1994; Fridtjof Nansen Award for Eminent Research 1995. *Publications include:* Sacharja 9-14. Untersuchungen von Text und Form 1969, Gjennom alle tider 1978, Ordene og Ordet. Gammeltestamentlige studier 1979, Salomos ordsprak, Forkynneren, Høysangen, Klagesangene (Commentary) 1986, On the Way to Canon: Creative Tradition History in the Old Testament 1998, The Book of Esther, (Ed.), Megilloth, Edn Biblia Hebraica Quinta Editione 2004; articles in int. journals and theology books. *Leisure interests:* biographies, stamp collecting, mountain walking. *Address:* The Free Faculty of Theology, POB 5144, Majorstua, N-0302 Oslo (office); Lars Muhles vei 34, N-1338 Sandvika, Norway (home). *Telephone:* 22-59-05-00 (office); 67-54-38-06 (home). *Fax:* 22-69-18-90 (office); 67-54-38-06 (home). *E-mail:* msabo@mf.no (office); m-saebo@online.no (home).

SAEED, Abdullah, BA (Hons), LLM; Maldivian lawyer and judge; b. 25 Sept. 1964, Meedhoo, Seenu Atoll; s. of Mohamed Saeed and Maumoona Mohammed Didi; descendant of Dhiyamigili dynasty of the Maldives; comes from a family of scholars, jurists and educators, eight of whom have filled the office of Chief Justice of the Maldives since 16th century; m. Moomina Nafiz; one s. one d.; ed early educ. in India, English Preparatory and Secondary School, Malé, higher secondary educ. in Cairo, Egypt, Faculty of Sharia and Law, Al-Azhar Univ., Cairo, IMO Int. Maritime Law Inst., Malta, legal drafting course at Lok Sabha, India; admitted as advocate 1995; began legal career with Attorney Gen.'s Office, apptd State Attorney 1995, represented the State in lower courts and High Court and advised govt depts on legal matters, later Asst Dir Gen., Public Prosecutions; apptd first Dean of Faculty of Sharia and Law, Maldives Coll. of Higher Educ.; Chief Justice of the Maldives 2008–10, mem. Supreme Court 2010–. *Address:* Supreme Court of the Maldives, Theemuge, Orchid Magu, Malé, Maldives (office). *Telephone:* 3009990 (office). *Fax:* 3008554 (office). *E-mail:* info@supremecourt.gov.mv (office). *Website:* www.supremecourt.gov.mv (office).

SAEED, Fathimath Dhiyana, LLB, LLM; Maldivian lawyer, politician and international organization official; b. 22 Nov. 1974, S. Hulhudhoo (now Addu City), Southern Prov.; m. Abdullah Jabir; two s.; ed Univ. of Tasmania, Australia, Grad. School of Law and Politics, Osaka Univ., Japan; began legal career as State Attorney in Attorney Gen.'s Office, responsible for providing legal opinions to Govt and for reviewing draft laws and regulations, Exec. Dir 2005–08; Attorney Gen. of first multi-party Govt 2008–11; apptd to People's Majlis (Parl.) and mem. People's Special Majlis (Constitutional Ass.) 2005–11; served as Maldivian Govt Envoy for South Asia 2010–11; Sec.-Gen. SAARC (youngest and first woman) 2011–12; Founding mem. Dhivehi Rajyithunge Party, served as mem. Exec. Council; later joined Jumhooree Party, elected Leader of Women's Wing. *Leisure interests:* jogging, reading contemporary Asian writing. *Address:* c/o Jumhooree Party (Republican Party), M. Chan'beyleege, 4th Floor, Malé, The Maldives.

SAEED, Hassan, PhD; Maldivian politician and lawyer; *President, Dhivehi Qaumee Party;* b. 14 Jan. 1970, Seenu Feydhoo; s. of Mohmed Saeed and Khadeeja Hussein; m. Fatin Yusof; ed Int. Islamic Univ. Malaysia, Univ. of Queensland, Australia; Chief Judge, Criminal and Juvenile Courts 2003; Attorney-Gen. of Maldives 2003–07 (resgnd); Pres. Maldives Alumni Asscn of Int. Islamic Univ. Malaysia; mem. and Deputy Leader Dhivehi Rayyithunge Party (DRP—Maldivian People's Party) –2007; mem. New Maldives Movt 2007–; Special Adviser to the Pres. 2009; Pres. Dhivehi Qaumee Party (DQP—Maldivian Nat. Party) 2009–; Partner, Raajje Chambers (law firm); unsuccessful cand. in presidential elections 2008. *Address:* Dhivehi Qaumee Party (Maldivian Nationa Party), M. Maahi, Third Floor, Malé, Maldives (office). *Telephone:* 3343842 (office); 3304548 (office). *Fax:* 3343844 (office). *E-mail:* saeed@raajjechambers.com.mv (office); sitee@qaumee.org.mv (office). *Website:* www.qaumee.org.mv (office); raajjechambers.com.mv (office).

SÁENZ ABAD, Alfredo; Spanish banker; b. Nov. 1942, Getxo, Vizcaya; ed Univ. of Valladolid, Deusto Univ., Bilbao; mem. Bd of Dirs and Exec. Vice-Pres. Tubacex (Basque steel pipe producer) 1965–80; Dir of Planning, Banco de Vizcaya 1981; Man. Dir Banca Catalana 1983, Chair. –1993; Man. Dir Banco Bilbao Vizcaya 1988, First Vice-Pres. 1990–93; Chair. Banco Español de Crédito (Banesto) 1994–2002; Second Vice-Chair. and CEO Santander Central Hispano SA (subsequently Banco Santander SA) 2002–13 (resgnd); Vice-Chair. Compañía Española de Petróleos (CEPSA) 2002–; mem. Bd Dirs San Paolo IMI SpA, Auna Operadores de Telecomunicaciones SA; Dir (non-exec.) France Telecom España SA; chosen as second best CEO of the European banking sector, Institutional Investor magazine 2013. *Address:* c/o Ciudad Grupo Santander, Edificio Pereda, 1st Floor, Avenida de Cantabria s/n, 28660 Boadilla del Monte, Madrid, Spain. *E-mail:* info@gruposantander.com.

SÁENZ DE SANTAMARÍA ANTÓN, (María) Soraya, LLB; Spanish lawyer and politician; *Deputy Prime Minister;* b. 10 June 1971, Valladolid; m. Iván Rosa; one s.; ed Univ. of Valladolid; Chief State Lawyer, León Prov. 1999–2000; State Lawyer before the High Court of Justice, Madrid 2004; Adviser to Cabinet of First Vice-Pres. of the Govt, Ministry of the Presidency and Ministry of Home Affairs 2000–03; Assoc. Prof. of Admin. Law, Carlos III Univ., Madrid 2002–03; mem. Congreso de los Diputados (Parl.) for Madrid 2004–, Deputy Spokesperson of Constitutional Comm. 2004–08; Exec. Sec. for Regional and Local Policy 2004–08; Deputy Prime Minister 2011–; mem. Partido Popular, Parl. Spokeswoman 2008–11. *Address:* c/o Office of the President of the Government, Complejo de la Moncloa, Avda de Puerta de Hierro s/n, 28071 Madrid, Spain (office). *Fax:* (91) 3900217 (office). *E-mail:* jlrzapatero@presidencia.gob.es (office). *Website:* www.la-moncloa.es (office).

SAEZ, Emmanuel, BA, MD, PhD; French academic; *E. Morris Cox Professor of Economics,, University of California, Berkeley;* b. 26 Nov. 1972; ed Ecole Normale Superieure, Massachusetts Inst. of Tech.; Asst Prof. of Econs, Harvard Univ. 1999–2002; Visiting Asst Prof., Univ. of California, Berkeley 2001–02, Asst Prof. of Econs 2002–03, Assoc. Prof. 2003–05, Prof. 2005–10, E. Morris Cox Prof. of Econs 2010–, Dir Center for Equitable Growth 2010–; Visiting Prof., Dept of Econs, MIT 2009; Nat. Fellow, Hoover Inst., Stanford Univ. 2004–05, Fellow, Center for Advanced Study in Behavioral Sciences 2007–08; Fellow, American Acad. of Arts and Sciences 2010–; MacArthur Foundation 2010–; Faculty Research Fellow, Public Econs Group, Nat. Bureau of Econ. Research 1999–2003, Research Assoc. Public Econs Program 2003–; Research Affiliate, Public Policy Group, Centre for Econ. Policy Research 2001–04, Research Fellow, Public Policy Program 2004–, Co-Dir 2009–; Research Affiliate, CESifo 2002–05, Research Fellow 2005–; Research Fellow, Inst. for Study of Labor 2009–; Alfred P. Sloan Doctoral Dissertation Fellowship 1998, Alfred P. Sloan Research Fellowship 2003; Dissertation Prize, Nat. Tax Asscn 1999, CESifo prize in Public Econs 2002, Best Grad. Teacher Award, Econ. Grad. Students Asscn, Univ. of California, Berkeley 2002, Purvis Memorial Prize, Canadian Econ. Asscn 2006, John Bates Clark Medal, American Econ. Asscn 2009. *Publications include:* contrib. to several journals. *Address:* University of California, Department of Economics, 549 Evans Hall 3880, Berkeley, CA 94720, USA (office). *Telephone:* (510) 642-4631 (office). *Fax:* (510) 642-6615 (office). *E-mail:* saez@econ.berkeley.edu (office). *Website:* elsa.berkeley.edu/~saez (office).

SAFADI, Mohammad A., BBA; Lebanese business executive and politician; b. 28 March 1944, Tripoli; m. Mona Sidaoui; five c.; ed American Univ. of Beirut; Chair. Safadi Group Holding SAL; mem. Majlis al-Nuab (Nat. Ass.) 2000–; Minister of Public Works and Transport 2005–08, Acting Minister of Water and Energy 2007–08, Minister of Economy and Trade 2008–11, of Finance 2011–14; f. Safadi Foundation (non-profit NGO) 2001, currently Hon. Pres.; mem. Bd of Trustees Al Jinan Univ., Tripoli, Entrepreneurial Training Foundation, American Community School at Beirut; mem. Dean's Council, John F. Kennedy School of Govt, Harvard Univ.; Bundesverdienstkreuz (Germany). *Address:* c/o Ministry of Finance, MOF Bldg, place Riad el-Solh, Beirut, Lebanon (office). *Website:* www.mohammad-safadi.com.

SAFAR, Adel Ahmad, PhD; Syrian politician, biotechnologist and academic; *Prime Minister;* b. 1953, Damascus; m.; four c.; ed Damascus Univ., Ecole Nationale Supérieur de l'Agric. et des Industries Alimentaires (ENSAIA), Nancy, France, Int. Centre for Agricultural Research in the Dry Areas; agricultural engineer, Arab Centre for the Studies of Arid Zones and Dry Lands (ACSAD)

1978–81; Deputy Lecturer, ENSAIA 1981–87; Deputy Dean for Admin. Affairs, Faculty of Agric., Damascus Univ. 1992–97, mem. Perm. Cttee for Agricultural Research 1996–2001, Dean of Faculty of Agric. 1997–2000; Deputy Rapporteur, Comm. for Scientific Agricultural Research and Veterinary Medicine, Supreme Council of Sciences 1997–2001; mem. Advisory Cttee Agricultural Productivity Admin, Productive Projects Admin 1999–2003; Sec., Damascus Univ. Br. of al-Baath Arab Socialist Party 2000–02; Head of Nat. Cttee for Man and the Biosphere Program in Syria 2000–04, Arab Network of Man and Biosphere Program in the Arab World 2001–04; Dir-Gen. ACSAD 2002–03; Minister of Agric. and Agrarian Reform 2003–11 (resgnd with rest of cabinet at Pres.'s request following popular protests); Prime Minister of Syria 3 April 2011–; mem. Econ. Cttee, High Council for Investment; mem. Baath Party 1990–. *Address:* Office of the Prime Minister, rue Chahbandar, Damascus, Syria (office). *Telephone:* (11) 2226000 (office). *Fax:* (11) 2237842 (office).

SAFAYEV, Sodyk Solihovich; Uzbekistani politician and diplomatist; b. 3 Feb. 1954; ed Harvard Univ.; Lecturer, later Sr Lecturer, Tashkent State Univ. 1976–87; Head, Communist Party of Uzbekistan 1987–90; Sr Research Fellow, Inst. for Productive Forces, Acad. of Sciences of Uzbekistan 1990–91; Sr Consultant and Head, Dept of Int. Econ. Relations of Pres. of Uzbekistan 1991–92; First Deputy Minister of External Econ. Relations –1993; Minister of Foreign Affairs 1993–94, 2003–05, First Deputy Minister 2001–03; Amb. to Germany 1994–96, to USA 1996–2001; Rep. to Afghanistan 2001–03; Minister of Foreign Affairs 2003–05; Chair. Senat (Senate) Foreign Affairs Cttee 2005–09. *Address:* Senat, 100029 Tashkent, Mustaqillik maydoni 6, Uzbekistan (office). *Telephone:* (71) 138-26-66 (office). *Fax:* (71) 138-29-01 (office). *Website:* www.senat.uz (office).

SAFIN, Marat Mikhailovic; Russian professional tennis player (retd) and politician; b. 27 Jan. 1980, Moscow; s. of Mikhail Alexeivich Safin and Rausa Islanova; started playing aged six; moved to train in Valencia, Spain aged 14; turned professional 1997; winner ATP Tennis Masters Series, Toronto 2000, Paris 2000, 2002, 2004, Madrid 2004, Beijing 2004; winner US Open 2000, Australian Open 2005; retd 2009; Official, Russian Tennis Fed. 2009–; mem. Russian Olympic Cttee 2009–; mem. State Duma (Parl. (United Russia Party) for Nyzhny Novgorod region 2011–; ATP Newcomer of the Year 1998, ATP Most Improved Player 2000, Newcomer of the Year Laureus World Sports Awards, Monte Carlo 2000. *Address:* State Duma (Gosudarstvennaya Duma), 103265 Moscow, Okhotnyi ryad 1 (office); Tennis Federation of Russia, 101000 Moscow, st. Myasnitskaya 22/2/5, Russia. *Telephone:* (495) 692-80-00 (Duma) (office); (495) 232-13-81 (Tennis Fed.). *Fax:* (495) 203-42-58 (Duma) (office); (495) 624-64-27 (Tennis Fed.). *E-mail:* stateduma@duma.ru (office). *Website:* www.duma.gov.ru (office); www.tennis-russia.ru.

SAFONOV, Col-Gen. Anatoly Yefimovich; Russian politician; *Special Representative to the President of the Russian Federation in International Co-operation for Combating Terrorism and Transitional Organized Crime;* b. 5 Oct. 1945, Krasnoyarsk; m. Galina Nikolayevna Safonova; one s. one d.; ed Krasnoyarsk Polytechnic Inst., Higher KGB School, Minsk; engineer-topographer, expeditions to regions of Chukotka, Magadan, Yakutia, Krasnoyarsk –1969; KGB service –1970, Head Counter-Espionage Dept 1983–87, Head, Territorial KGB 1988–92; Deputy Minister of Security 1992–93; First Deputy Dir Fed. Service of Security, Russian Fed. 1994–97, Chair. Cttee on Security Problems of Union State of Russia and Belarus 1997; People's Deputy of Russian Fed. 1990–93; Deputy Minister of Foreign Affairs 2002–; Special Rep. to the Pres. of the Russian Fed. for int. co-operation in combating terrorism and transitional organized crime 2004–; Corresp. mem. Int. Acad. of Information Tech.; Amb. Extraordinary and Plenipotentiary; Hon. Worker of Counterespionage; Hon. Worker MFA of Russia; governmental and departmental awards. *Address:* Ministry of Foreign Affairs, 121200 Moscow, Smolenskaya-Sennaya pl. 32–34, Russia (office). *Telephone:* (495) 244-95-20 (office). *Fax:* (495) 244-16-57 (office). *E-mail:* safonov@mid.ru (office).

SAFONOVA, Yelena Vsevolodovna; Russian actress; b. 14 June 1956, Leningrad; d. of Vsevolod Safonov; m. 1st C. Labartona; m. 2nd Samuel Labarthe 1992; two c.; ed All-Union Inst. of Cinematography, Leningrad Inst. of Theatre, Music and Cinema; actress Mosfilm Studio 1986–; mem. of jury, Cannes Film Festival 1988. *Films include:* Looking For My Destiny 1974, Return of Butterfly 1982, Winter Cherries 1985, Dark Eyes (David di Donatello Prize 1988) 1987, Winter Cherries 2 1990, Winter Cherries 3 1995, Music for December 1995, The President and His Woman 1996, Princess on a Bean 1997, Sofia Kovalevskaya, Secret of the Earth, Strange Call, Confrontation, Sleuth, Continuation of the Clan, Taxi Blues, Butterflies, All Red, Alissa 1998, Woman's Own 1999, The Sky Will Fall 2000, Poklonnik 2001, Zayats nad bezdnoy 2006, La Traductrice 2006, Vy ne ostavite menya 2006, Kakraki 2009. *Plays:* Pay forward (The Seagull-99 Award), Rumors, Dangerous Liaisons, Hen Party. *Television:* Next II (series) 2003, Atlantida 2007. *Address:* Taganskaya pl. 31/22, Apt. 167, 109004 Moscow, Russia. *Telephone:* (495) 278-07-36.

SAFRA, Joseph; Brazilian banker; *Chairman, Grupo Safra SA;* b. 1934, Beirut, Lebanon; s. of Jacob Safra and Esther Safra; m. Vicky Safra; (neé Sarfatty); two s.; currently Chair. Grupo Safra SA, family business group that includes Banco Safra SA (f. 1967), Banco JS de Investimento (f. 1998), Bank Jacob Safra, Switzerland (f. 2000), Safra Nat. Bank of New York, Safra Asset Man. Corpn, Banque Safra-Luxembourg SA, Banque Safra-France SA, Banco Safra (Cayman Islands) Ltd, Safra Int. Bank and Trust Ltd, Aracruz Celulose SA; Pres. Safra Cultural Inst.; Perm. mem. Advisory Council, Albert Einstein Soc. *Address:* Safra National Bank of New York, 546 5th Avenue, New York, NY 10036, USA (office). *Telephone:* (212) 704-5500 (office). *Fax:* (212) 704-5527 (office). *Website:* www.safra.com.br (office).

SAGALAYEV, Eduard Mikhailovich; Russian journalist; b. 3 Oct. 1946, Samarkand; m.; one s. one d.; ed Samarkand Univ., Acad. of Social Sciences Cen. Cttee CPSU; Dir, Sr Ed. Cttee on TV and Radio Samarkand; on staff, Deputy Exec. Sec. Leninsky Put 1969–72; Exec. Sec. Komsomolets Uzbekistana Tashkent 1972–73; instructor Propaganda Div. Cen. Comsomol Cttee Moscow 1973–75; Deputy Ed.-in-Chief programmes for youth, USSR Cen. TV 1975–80, Ed.-in-Chief 1980–88; Ed.-in-Chief Information section of Cen. TV 1988–90; Dir Gen. Studio Channel IY 1990; First Deputy Chair. All-Union State Radio and TV Corpn 1991–92; Dir-Gen. TV Ostankino Jan.–July 1992; Founder and Pres. TV-6,

Moscow's first ind. broadcasting co. 1992–96, 1997–; Chair. Russian TV and Broadcasting Co. (RTR) 1996–97; now Chair. Bd of Dirs and Pres. Moscow Ind. Broadcasting Corpn, Deputy Chair. Bd of Dirs ORT (Channel 1); Co-Chair. Int. TV and Radio Broadcasting Policies Comm. 1990–97; Dir-Gen. RTR Signal Co.; Chair. Bd of USSR Journalists' Union 1990–91; Chair. Confed. of Journalists' Unions of CIS 1992–97, Pres. Nat. Asscn of TV and Radio Producers of Russia 1995–; mem. Acad. of Russian TV 1995–, Fed. Tenders Comm. 2004–; Order of Friendship (twice); USSR State Prize 1978. *Address:* National Association of TV and Radio Producers, 101000 Moscow, Myasnitskaya str. 13/11, Russia. *Telephone:* (495) 924-24-38. *Fax:* (495) 923-23-18.

SAGARRA, Eda, MA, DPhil, LittD, MRIA; Irish professor of German and university administrator; *Professor Emerita, Trinity College, Dublin;* b. 15 Aug. 1933, Dublin; d. of Kevin O'Shiel and Cecil Smiddy; m. Albert Sagarra i Zacarini 1961; one d.; ed Loreto Convent, Foxrock, Farnborough Hill Convent, Hants., England, Univ. Coll. Dublin and Univs of Freiburg, Zürich and Vienna; jr lecturer, lecturer, Univ. of Manchester 1958–68; Special Lecturer in German History 1968–75; Prof. of German, Trinity Coll. Dublin 1975–98, Dean of Visiting Students 1979–86, Registrar 1981–86, Pro-Chancellor 1999–2008, currently Prof. Emerita; Chair. Irish Research Council for Humanities and Social Sciences 2000–, Salzburg Univ. Arts Faculty 2002–; Founder-Chair. Irish Research Council for Humanities and Social Sciences 2000–05; mem. Germanistische Kommission of German Research Council 1982–90; mem. Council, Royal Irish Acad. (Sec. 1993–2000), Nat. Council for Educational Awards 1991–96; mem. Standing Cttee for Humanities, European Science Foundation 1996–2002; Corresponding mem. Austrian Acad. of Sciences 1996; mem. Bd Inst. of Germanic Studies of Univ. of London 1983–87; mem. Academia Europaea 1991–, Quality Review Group 1998–, Max Planck Inst., Quality Review Group, Swiss Research Council 2001–, Bd Giessen Univ., Germany; Bundesverdienstkreuz (Austria), Bundesverdienstkreuz (FRG); Goethe Medal 1990, Jacob and Wilhelm Grimm Prize 1995. *Publications include:* Tradition and Revolution 1971, A Social History of Germany 1648–1914 1977, Theodor Fontane: Der Stechlin 1986, Literatur and Anthropologie um 1800 (Ed. with Jürgen Barkhoff) 1992, Companion to German Literature 1494 to the Present (with Peter Skrine) 1997, Germany in the 19th Century: History and Literature 2001, A Social History of Germany 1648-1914 2002; scientific bibliographies/ review essays on German women writers; articles on legal, social and literary history of servants in Germany. *Leisure interests:* golf (county golfer 1969–75), ornithology, cooking, European politics. *Address:* Trinity College, College Green, Dublin 2 (office); 30 Garville Avenue, Rathgar, Dublin 6, Ireland (home). *Telephone:* (1) 8961000 (office); (1) 4975967 (home). *Fax:* (1) 6772694 (office). *E-mail:* esagarra@irchss.ie (office); esagarra@tcd.ie (home). *Website:* www.tcd.ie (office).

SAGAWA, Masato, BA, MA, DrEng; Japanese electrical engineer and business executive; *President, Intermetallics Company Ltd;* b. 3 Aug. 1943; ed Kobe and Tohoku Univs; worked for Fujitsu Co. 1972–82; with Sumitomo Special Metals (SSM) 1982–88; Founder and Pres. Intermetallics Co. Ltd 1988–; consultant for several cos, including Ugimag SA (France), Showa Denko (Japan); Osaka Prize 1984, Agency Award, Minister of Science and Tech. 1985, Int. Prize for New Materials, American Physical Soc. 1986, Asahi Prize 1990, Japan Magnetics Soc. Award 1991, J. Herbert Hollomon Award, Acta Matellurgica 1999, Honda-kinen Prize 2003, Kato-kinen Prize 2006, Japan Prize (co-recipient) 2012. *Address:* Intermetallics Company Ltd, Kyodaikatsura #2211, 1-39 Goryo Ohara, Nishikyo-Ku, Kyoto, 615-8245, Japan (office). *Telephone:* (75) 392-8637 (office). *Fax:* (75) 392-8634 (office). *E-mail:* info@intermetallics.co.jp (office). *Website:* www .intermetallics.co.jp (office).

SAGDEEV, Roald Zinnurovich, DSc; Russian physicist and academic; *Distinguished University Professor and Director, East-West Space Science Center, University of Maryland;* b. 26 Dec. 1932, Moscow; m. Susan Eisenhower (grand-d. of the late US Pres. Dwight Eisenhower) 1990; ed Moscow State Univ.; Research Worker, Inst. of Atomic Energy, USSR Acad. of Sciences 1956–61; Head of Lab., Inst. of Nuclear Physics, Siberian Dept, Acad. of Sciences 1961–70, Inst. of High Temperature Physics of USSR Acad. of Sciences 1970–73; Prof., Novosibirsk State Univ. 1964–73; Dir Inst. of Space Research 1973–88, Sr Researcher 1988; Distinguished Univ. Prof., Univ. of Maryland, USA 1990–, Founder and Dir East-West Space Science Center 1992–; Corresp. mem. USSR (now Russian) Acad. of Sciences 1964, mem. 1968–; mem. Council of Dirs Int. Fund for Survival and Devt of Mankind 1988–; Head of Scientific-Methodical Centre for Analytical Research, Inst. of Space Research 1988; mem. NAS Swedish Royal Acad., Max Planck Soc.; USSR People's Deputy 1989–91; Order of October Revolution, Order of Red Banner and other decorations; Dr hc (Tech. Univ., Graz, Austria) 1984; Hero of Socialist Labour 1986; Lenin Prize 1984. *Address:* 2309A Computer and Space Sciences Building, University of Maryland, College Park, MD 20742, USA (office). *Telephone:* (301) 405-8051 (office). *E-mail:* rzs@umd.edu (office). *Website:* www .physics.umd.edu/people/faculty/sagdeev.html (office).

SAĞINTAEV, Bakıtjan Äbdiruli; Kazakhstani politician; *First Deputy Prime Minister;* b. 13 Oct. 1963, Üşaral village, Talas dist, Jambıl Oblast; m.; two d.; ed Kazakh S.M. Kirov State Univ.; taught at Almatı Inst. of Nat. Economy 1985–88; Deputy Akim of Jambıl Oblast 1998–99 Deputy Chair. Republican Agency for Support of Small Businesses June–Oct. 1999; Chair. 'Fund for Devt of Small Enterprises' 1999–2001; Chair. Republican Agency for the Regulation of Natural Monopolies 2004–07; Head of the Chancellery of the Prime Minister 2007–08; Akim of Pavlodar Oblast 2008–12; Minister of Econ. Devt and Trade 2012–13; First Deputy Prime Minister 2013–, also Minister of Regional Devt Jan.–Nov. 2013; First Deputy Chair. Light of the Fatherland Nat. Democratic Party (Nur Otan) 2012–. *Address:* Office of the Prime Minister, 010000 Astana, Beibitshilik kosh. 11, Kazakhstan (office). *Telephone:* (7172) 74-54-00 (office). *Fax:* (7172) 32-40-89 (office). *Website:* www.government.kz (office).

SAGLIO, Jean-François; French mining engineer; b. 29 July 1936, Toulon; s. of Georges Saglio; m. Odile Bertrand 1968; two s. one d.; ed Ecole Polytechnique and Ecole Supérieure des Mines, Paris; engineer, govt del., Algiers 1960–61; mining engineer, Mines de Metz 1961–66; Founder Dir Agence de Bassin Rhin-Meuse, Metz 1966–69; Adviser, Cabinet of Pres. of France 1969–73; Head, Perm. Secr. for Study of Water Problems of Paris 1971–73; Dir in charge of Pollution and Nuisance, Ministry of Environment 1973–78; Pres. Dir-Gen. Agence Foncière et

Technique de la Région Parisienne 1979–81; Dir of Innovation and Valorization of Research, Elf Aquitaine, also Dir of New Projects 1981–84; Pres. Dir-Gen. INOVELF 1981–84; Asst Dir-Gen. Soc. Elf-France 1984; Asst Dir-Gen. Refineries and Distribution, Soc. Nat. Elf Aquitaine 1984; Dir-Gen. of Industry, Ministry of Industry, Posts & Telecommunications and Tourism 1987–88; Dir Soc. Roussel-Uclaf 1989–91; Vice-Pres. SCH Consultants; Pres. Admin. Council Rhin-Meuse 1992–97, ERSO 1993; Dir-Gen. CEA Industrie 1992–94; Pres. Dexter SA 1992–99, Inst. français de l'environnement 1995–98; Pres. BNFL SA 1996; mem. Conseil Général des Mines 1991–99; mem. Bd Dirs and Strategy Cttee Gascogne SA; Officier, Légion d'honneur, Ordre nat. du Mérite, Croix de la Valeur militaire. *Address:* 143 rue de la Pompe, 75116 Paris, France (home). *Telephone:* 1-45-53-05-44 (home).

SAHABDEEN, Desamanya Abdul Majeed Mohamed, BA, PhD; Sri Lankan foundation president, entrepreneur, scholar and fmr civil servant; *Chairman, Sifani Group of Companies;* b. 19 May 1926, Gampola; s. of Abdul Majeed and Shaharwan Majeed; m. Ruchia Halida 1959; one s. one d.; ed Univ. of Ceylon; joined Ceylon Civil Service 1950, served as Sec., Dir, Commr, Chair. several maj. govt orgs –1973; Visiting Head, Dept of Western Philosophy, Univ. of Sri Lanka, Vidyodaya (now Sri Jayawardanapura) 1957–59; Chair. Majeedsons Group of Cos 1973–, Sifani Group of Cos; Chair. Muslim Law (Amendments) Cttee 1990; Founder and Chair. A.M.M. Sahabdeen Trust Foundation 1991; Mohamed Sahabdeen Int. Awards for Science, Literature and Human Devt est. by Act of Parl. 1991; f. Mohamed Sahabdeen Inst. for Advanced Studies and Research in Pahamune 1997; Pres. Ceylon Muslim Scholarship Fund 1999; Chair. Pahamune House (Narammala, Sri Lanka) Rehabilitation Centre for Children –2005; mem. Presidential Comms on Delimitation of Electoral Dists 1988, Taxation 1989, Finance and Banking 1990, Industrialization 1990, Public Service Comm. 1989; mem. Press Council 1998; Vice-Patron Sri Lanka-India Friendship Soc. 1998; Life mem. Sri Lanka Cancer Soc.; mem. Royal Asiatic Soc. of Sri Lanka; received Desamanya (highest civilian honour) 1992. *Publications include:* several articles and books on philosophy and allied subjects, including Sufi Doctrine in Tamil Literature 1986, God and the Universe 1995, The Circle of Lives. *Leisure interests:* philosophy, classical music. *Address:* A.M.M. Sahabdeen Trust Foundation, No. 86, 4th Floor, Galle Road, Colombo 03 (office); 30/12 Bagatalle Road, Colombo 03, Sri Lanka (home). *Telephone:* (11) 2399601 (office); (11) 2399602 (office); (11) 2502447 (home); (11) 2586327 (home); (11) 2399605 (office). *Fax:* (11) 2399603 (office); (11) 2399604 (office). *E-mail:* sifanicare@eureka.lk (office); ammstrust@ gmail.com. *Website:* www.ammstrustfoundation.org (office).

SAHAKIAN, Bako S.; Azerbaijani government official; *President of the 'Republic of Nagornyi Karabakh';* b. 30 Aug. 1960, Stepanakert (Xankändi), Nagornyi Karabakh Autonomous Oblast, Azerbaijan SSR, USSR; m.; two c.; ed Stepanakert High School, Artsakh State Univ.; served in Soviet Army 1978–80; metalworker and mechanical engineer, Stepanakert Mechanical Works 1981–83; worked on restoration of historical monuments 1983–87; worked for Stepanakert dist council 1987–90; various roles within 'Repub. of Nagornyi Karabakh' Self Defence Forces including Deputy Commdr of External Relations and Commdr of HQ 1990–97; Asst to Minister for Home Affairs and Nat. Security 1997–99; Minister for Home Affairs 1999–2001; Head, State Dept for Nat. Security 2001–07; Pres. of 'Repub. of Nagornyi Karabakh' 2007–; Fighting Cross Order, Sparapet Vazgen Sargsian, Order of Peter the Great (Russia). *Address:* Office of the President of the 'Republic of Nagornyi Karabakh', 374430 Stepanakert, Petrvari 20 poghots 3, Nagornyi Karabakh, Azerbaijan (office). *Telephone:* (47) 94-52-22 (office). *Fax:* (47) 94-52-22 (office). *E-mail:* ps@president.nkr.am (office). *Website:* www.president.nkr.am (office).

SAHAYA, Dinesh Nandan, MA; Indian police officer and politician; b. 2 Feb. 1936, Madhepur, Madhubani Dist, Bihar; s. of the late Deva Nandan Sahaya and Kishori Devi; m. Manju Sahaya; one s. two d.; ed Patna Coll.; began career as Lecturer, H. D. Jain Coll., Ara (Composite Bihar Univ.); selected for Indian Police Service as R.R. and allotted to Bihar Cadre 1960, held various sr positions in the field and Secr., also with CBI, retd as Dir-Gen. of Police 1994; entered public life and joined Samata Party 1995, Sr Vice-Pres. Bihar Pradesh Samata Party and mem. Nat. Exec. 1995–2000; Gov. of Chhattisgarh (first) 2000–03, of Tripura 2003–09; Chair. Bihar State Br. of UN Students Asscn, Deputy Leader of del. on Goodwill Mission to Ceylon 1959; Patna Coll. Blue, Pres.'s Police Medal for Distinguished Services (highest award in Police Service). *Publications:* contrib. of articles to journals and magazines. *Leisure interests:* avid reader of books, particularly on political and social science, NGOs and voluntary orgs. *Address:* c/o Raj Bhavan, Kunjaban, Tripura (office); 'Sai Niwas' 123, Patliputra Colony, Patna, Bihar, India (home).

SAHEL, Mostafa, LenD; Moroccan politician and diplomatist; *Ambassador to France;* b. 5 May 1946, Ouled Frej, El Jadida; s. of Maati Sahel and Hajja Ghita; m. Farida Benmansour Nejjai 1972; two s.; ed Lycée Mohamed V, Casablanca, Univ. Mohamed V, Rabat and Univ. de Sorbonne, Paris; Insp. des Finances 1968–70; Financial Controller 1970–74; Head of Service of Working Budget 1974–81, Equipment Budget 1981–86; Dir of Budget 1986–91; Sec.-Gen. Ministry of Finance 1992–93; Dir-Gen. of Communal Equipment Funds 1993–; Minister for Maritime Fisheries and Merchant Marine 1993–97, of Admin. Affairs and Relations with Parl. 1997–98; Chair. SOMED Investment Group (devt co.) 1998–2001; Prefect of Rabat region 2001–02; Minister of Interior 2002–06; Perm. Rep. to UN, New York 2006–08; Amb. to France (also accred to Andorra) 2009–; Ordre de Mérite, Ordre du Trône. *Leisure interest:* golf. *Address:* Embassy of Morocco, 5 rue Le Tasse, 75016 Paris, France (office). *Telephone:* 1-45-20-69-35 (office). *Fax:* 1-45-20-22-58 (office). *E-mail:* info@amb-maroc.fr (office). *Website:* www.amb-maroc.fr (office).

SAHGAL, Nayantara, BA; Indian journalist and novelist; b. 10 May 1927, Allahabad; d. of Ranjit Sitaram Pandit and Vijaya Lakshmi Pandit; m. 1st Gautam Sahgal 1949 (divorced 1967); one s. two d.; m. 2nd E. N. Mangat Rai 1979 (died 2003); ed Wellesley Coll., USA; Adviser English Language Bd, Sahitya Akademi (Nat. Acad. of Letters), New Delhi 1972–75; Scholar-in-Residence, holding creative writing seminar, Southern Methodist Univ., Dallas, Texas 1973, 1977; mem. Indian Del. to UN Gen. Ass. 1978; Vice-Pres. Nat. Exec., People's Union for Civil Liberties 1980–85; Fellow, Radcliffe Inst. (Harvard Univ.) 1976, Wilson Int. Center for Scholars, Washington, DC 1981–82, Nat. Humanities Center, NC 1983–84; mem. jury Commonwealth Writers' Prize 1990, Chair. Eurasia Region 1991; Annie

Besant Memorial Lecture (Banaras Hindu Univ.) 1992; Arthur Ravenscroft Memorial Lecture (Univ. of Leeds) 1993; mem. American Acad. of Arts and Sciences 1990; Foreign Hon. mem. American Acad. Arts and Sciences 1990; Hon. DLitt (Univ. of Leeds) 1997; Diploma of Honour, Int. Order of Volunteers for Peace, Salsomaggiore, Italy 1982, Sinclair Prize 1985, Doon Ratna Citizens' Council Prize 1992, Wellesley Coll. Alumni Achievement Award 2002, Pride of Doon Award 2002, Woodstock School Alumni Achievement Award 2004, Nanjanagudu Thirumalamba Award 2008, Zee TV Awadh Samman 2009. *Publications:* Prison and Chocolate Cake 1954, A Time to Be Happy 1958, From Fear Set Free 1962, This Time of Morning 1965, Storm in Chandigarh 1969, History of the Freedom Movement 1970, The Day in Shadow 1972, A Situation in New Delhi 1977, A Voice for Freedom 1977, Indira Gandhi's Emergence and Style 1978, Indira Gandhi: Her Road to Power 1982, Rich Like Us (Sinclair Prize 1985, Sahitya Akad. Award 1987) 1985, Plans for Departure 1985 (Commonwealth Writers' Prize 1987), Mistaken Identity 1988, Relationship: Extracts from a Correspondence 1994 (co-author), Point of View 1997, Before Freedom: Nehru's Letters to His Sister 1909–47 (ed.) 2000, Lesser Breeds 2003, Jawaharlal Nehru: Civilizing a Savage World 2010, Indira Gandhi: Tryst with Power 2012, The Story of India's Freedom Movement 2013; contribs to newspapers and magazines including India Today. *Leisure interests:* walking, reading, music. *Address:* 181B Rajpur Road, Dehra Dun 248 009 India (home). *Telephone:* (135) 2734278 (home).

ŞAHIN, Fatma; Turkish engineer and politician; *Minister of Family and Social Policies;* b. 20 June 1966, Gaziantep; m. İzzet Şahin; two c.; ed Istanbul Tech. Univ.; trained as an engineer; worked as operations man. in textiles industry; Co-f. Justice and Devt Party; mem. Grand Nat. Ass. (Büyük Millet Meclisi) for Gaziantep 2002–; Minister of Family and Social Policies 2011–. *Address:* Grand National Assembly (Büyük Millet Meclisi), 06543, Bakanlıklar, Ankara, Turkey (office). *Telephone:* (312) 4205784 (office). *Fax:* (312) 4206973 (office). *E-mail:* fsahintbmm@gmail (home); fsahin@fatmasahin.net. *Website:* www.fatmasahin .net.

ŞAHIN, Mehmet Ali; Turkish politician; b. 16 Sept. 1950, Karabük; m.; four c.; ed Faculty of Law, Istanbul Univ.; early career as lawyer; fmr Mayor Fatih Municipality; Founding mem. AK Party; Deputy Prime Minister and Minister of State responsible for Sport and Youth Affairs 2002–07, Minister of Justice 2007–09; Speaker, Büyük Millet Meclisi (Grand Nat. Ass.) 2009–11. *Address:* c/o Büyük Millet Meclisi, Ankara, Turkey (office). *E-mail:* mehmetsahin44@tbmm.gov .tr (office). *Website:* www.tbmm.gov.tr (office).

SAHINGUVU, Yves, MD, MSc (Tech.); Burundian ophthalmologist and politician; b. 20 Dec. 1949, Bukeye, Muramvya Prov.; m.; two s., one d.; ed Univ. of Kinshasa, Catholic Univ. of Leuwen, Belgium; physician in pvt. practice in Kinshasa 1984–97; fmr Asst Prof., Faculty of Medicine, Univ. of Kinshasa; mem. Parl. (Union for Nat. Progress) for Muramvya 1998–2000, 2005–07, 2010–(15), mem. Cttee on Good Governance; Senator 2000–05, First Vice-Pres. of Burundi 2007–10, also Chair. Cttee on the Strategic Framework for Peacebuilding for Burundi; currently Chair. SOCAR Insurance Co.; currently Pres. Asscn for Friendship Chine-Burundi; currently mem. Bd of Dirs Parl. Network on the World Bank, IMF; currently District Gov., Lions Club District 2007–08; Lions Club Int. Melvin Jones Fellow Award 2009. *Leisure interests:* tennis, swimming. *Address:* Assemblée Nationale, Bujumbura (office); 63 Avenue de la Révolution, Bujumbura, Burundi (home). *Telephone:* 76644645 (office); 79350350 (home). *E-mail:* yvesahi@ yahoo.fr. *Website:* .

SAHL, Morton (Mort) Lyon, BS; American comedian; b. 11 May 1927, Montreal, Canada; s. of Harry Sahl; m. 1st Sue Babior 1955 (divorced 1957); m. 2nd China Lee; one c.; ed Compton Jr Coll., Univ. of Southern California; Ed. Poop from the Group; magazine writing; many night club engagements; radio and TV performances, including Comedy News TV show, Steve Allen Show, Jack Paar Show, Eddie Fisher Show, Nightline, Wide Wide World; monologues on long-playing records; in Broadway revue, The Next President 1958; one-man show Broadway 1987; Mort Sahl: The Loyal Opposition (TV) 1989; Visiting Lecturer, Claremont McKenna Coll. 2007–. *Films include:* In Love and War 1958, All the Young Men 1960, Johnny Cool 1963, Doctor, You've Got to be Kidding 1967, (TV) Inside the Third Reich 1982, Nothing Lasts Forever 1984. *Publication:* Heartland 1976. *Address:* c/o Gould Center for Humanistic Studies, Claremont McKenna College, 850 Colombia Avenue, Claremont, CA 91711-6420; 2325 San Ysidro Drive, Beverly Hills, CA 90210, USA. *Website:* www.mortsahl.com.

SAHLIN, Mona; Swedish politician; b. 9 March 1957, Sollefteå; d. of Hans Andersson; m. Bo Sahlin 1982; three c.; ed Correspondence School, Swedish Cooperative Movt 1978–80; Vice-Chair. Swedish Pupils' Asscn 1976–77; Sec. State Employees' Union 1980–82; Mem. Parl. (Riksdag) 1982–90; Minister of Employment 1990–91; Gen. Sec. Sveriges Socialdemokratiska Arbetareparti (SAP—Social Democratic Party of Sweden) 1992–94, Chair. 2007–11; Govt Rep. Bd of Swedish Sports Confed. 1983–90; Chair. Cttee on Working Hours 1982–90; mem. Bd Centre for Working Life 1982–90; Deputy Prime Minister and Minister with Special Responsibility for Equality Issues 1994–95; self-employed 1995–98; Minister, Ministry of Industry, Employment and Communications 1998–2002; Minister (Democracy and Integration Issues), Ministry of Justice 2002–04, Minister for Sustainable Devt 2004–06. *Address:* Sveriges Socialdemokratiska Arbetareparti (SAP), Sveavägen 68, 105 60 Stockholm, Sweden (office). *Telephone:* (8) 700-26-00 (office). *Fax:* (8) 20-42-57 (office). *E-mail:* info@socialdemokraterna.se (office). *Website:* www.socialdemokraterna.se (office).

SAHNOUN, Mohamed, BA, MA; Algerian diplomatist, international organization official and fmr UN official; *Founder and Chairman, Caux Forum for Human Security, University for Peace;* b. 8 April 1931, Chlef; ed Univ. of the Sorbonne, Paris, France, New York Univ., USA; Deputy Sec.-Gen. OAU (in charge of Political Affairs) 1964–73; League of Arab States (for Arab-African dialogue) 1973–75; Amb. to FRG 1975–79, to France 1979–82, Perm. Rep. to the UN, New York 1982–84, Amb. to USA 1984–89, to Morocco 1989–1990; Sec. Maghreb Union 1989–90; Counsellor to Pres. of Algeria for Foreign Affairs 1990–92; UN Special Rep. in Somalia 1992; OAU Special Rep. in the Congo 1993; UN/OAU Special Envoy in Great Lakes Region of Africa, later Special Adviser to UN Sec.-Gen. on the Horn of Africa region 1997–2006 (resgnd); Pres. Initiatives for Change International 2006–08; Founder and Chair. Caux Forum for Human Security 2008–; fmr Special

Adviser to Sec.-Gen.'s UN Conf. on Environment and Devt (UNCED); fmr Special Adviser to Culture of Peace Progress, UNESCO, Paris, War-Torn Societies Project, UN Research Inst. for Social Devt, Geneva; fmr Exec. Dir Earth Charter Project; Hon. Bd Int. Inst. for Sustainable Devt, Winnipeg 1990–96, Int. Council for Human Rights; Distinguished Fellow, US Inst. of Peace, Washington, DC 1992–93; Pearson Fellow, Int. Devt Research Centre, Ottawa, Canada 1993–94; mem. Univ. for Peace Council, Costa Rica and consultant on Africa Programme; Dr hc (Addis Ababa). *Publications:* Somalia: The Missed Opportunities 1994, Managing Conflicts in the Post-Cold War Era 1996, Mémoire blessée, Algérie 1957, Presses de la Renaissance 2007. *Address:* Caux Forum for Human Security (CFHS) Secretariat, c/o Initiatives of Change International, PO Box 3, 1211 Geneva 20, Switzerland (office). *Telephone:* (22) 749-16-20 (office). *Fax:* (22) 733-02-67 (office). *E-mail:* sahnoun@iofc.org (office); sahnoun@upeace.ch (office). *Website:* www.iofc.org (office); cauxforum.net (office).

SAID, HH Sayyid Fahd bin Mahmoud al-; Omani government official; *Deputy Prime Minister for the Council of Ministers;* m. Sayyidah Berthe Fahad Al-Said; fmr Deputy Prime Minister for Legal Affairs; Deputy Prime Minister for the Council of Ministers 2011–. *Address:* Diwan of the Royal Court, POB 632, Muscat 113, Oman. *Telephone:* 24738711. *Fax:* 24739427.

SAÏD, Wafic Rida; Canadian (b. Syrian) financier and business executive; *Chairman, Investment Committee, Said Holdings Ltd;* b. 21 Dec. 1939, Damascus; s. of Dr Rida Said; m. Rosemary Thompson; one s. one d. (and one s. deceased); ed Collège de Notre Dame de Jamhour, Lebanon and at Inst. of Banking, London, UK; began banking career at UBS, Geneva 1962; f. TAG System Construction for design and construction projects in Saudi Arabia 1969; became Saudi Arabian citizen 1981; f. Said Holdings Ltd 1987 and Sagitta Asset Man. (Bermuda) Ltd 1995; mem. Bd Banque Libano-Française, Oxford Univ. Court of Benefactors; Trustee, Said Business School Foundation;; Amb. and Perm. Del. of Saint Vincent and the Grenadines to UNESCO 1996–; Amb. to the Holy See 2012–; f. Saïd Foundation 1982; Hon. Fellow, Trinity Coll., Oxford; Grand Commdr, Ordre de Mérite du Cèdre (Lebanon), Ordre Chérifien (Morocco); Sheldon Medal, Univ. of Oxford 2003. *Leisure interests:* music, architecture and art. *Address:* Said Holdings Ltd, 5B Waterloo Lane, Hamilton HM 08, Bermuda (office); Said Foundation, 24 Queen Anne's Gate, London, SW1H 9AA, England. *Telephone:* (20) 7691-2772. *Fax:* (20) 7691-2780. *E-mail:* heather.gray@saidholdings.com (office); admin@ saidfoundation.org. *Website:* www.saidfoundation.org; www.waficsaid.com; www .shl.bm (office).

SAID ABU EL-NOUR, Mumtaz; Egyptian fmr central banker and government official; fmr Dir Central Bank of Egypt (as Ministry of Finance Rep.); long career with Ministry of Finance, returned from retirement July 2011 to serve as deputy to Finance Minister Hazem al-Beblawi; Minister of Finance 2011–13. *Address:* c/o Ministry of Finance, Ministry of Finance Towers, Cairo (Nasr City), Egypt (office).

SAÏD HASSANE, El-Anrif, PhD; Comoran diplomatist and politician; *Minister of External Relations and Co-operation;* b. Fassi, Mitsamiouli; ed univ. in Jordan, Univ. Paris-IV (Sorbonne), France; Political Counsellor, Embassy in Paris 2007–13; Minister of External Relations and Co-operation, with responsibility for the Diaspora, and for Francophone and Arab Relations 2013–; mem. Bd of Dirs Rassemblement des Mitsamiouliens, Paris. *Address:* Ministry of External Relations and Co-operation, BP 428, Moroni, Comoros (office). *Telephone:* 7732306 (office). *Fax:* 7732108 (office). *E-mail:* mirex@snpt.km (office).

SAIDENOV, Anvar Galimullaevich, MS; Kazakhstani economist and banker; *Chairman, Board of Directors, BTA Bank;* b. 19 Sept. 1960; ed Moscow State Univ. M. G. Lomonsov, Univ. of London; early career as Lecturer and Head of Sector Social and Economic Disciplines, Dzhambul Irrigation and Construction Inst.; Consultant, EBRD London 1994–96; Deputy Gov. Nat. Bank of Kazakhstan 1996–98, First Deputy Chair. 2002–04, Gov. 2004–09; Vice-Minister of Finance 1999–2000, also Exec. Dir State Cttee of Kazakhstan for Investment; Chair. Man. Bd BTA Bank 2009–11, Chair. Bd of Dirs 2011–; Acting Chair. then Chair. Halyk People's Savings Bank of Kazakhstan 2000–02; mem. Bd of Dirs Sekerbank Turk AS 2010–. *Address:* BTA Bank, 97, Dzholdasbekov str., md Samal-2, 050051 Almaty, Kazakhstan (office). *Telephone:* (727) 250-51-00 (office). *Fax:* (727) 250-02-24 (office). *Website:* www.bta.kz/en (office).

SAIDOV, Davlatali; Tajikistani politician; *First Deputy Prime Minister;* Gov. Islamic Devt Bank; Chair. State Cttee on Investments and State Property Man. –2013; First Deputy Prime Minister 2013–. *Address:* Secretariat of the Prime Minister, 734023 Dushanbe, Xiyoboni Rudaki 80, Tajikistan (office). *Telephone:* (372) 21-18-71 (office). *Fax:* (372) 21-51-10 (office).

SAIF, HE Abdulla Hassan; Bahraini banker and government official; *Chairman, Islamic Bank of Asia;* b. 10 March 1945, Muharraq; ed Inst. of Cost and Man. Accountants, UK, IMF Inst.; joined Bahrain Petroleum Co. as apprentice, 1957, served in various depts –1971; Head of Finance and Admin., Civil Aviation Directorate 1971–74; Deputy Dir-Gen. Bahrain Monetary Agency 1974–77, Dir-Gen. 1977, fmr Gov.; Chair. Gulf Int. Bank BSC; Minister of Finance and Nat. Economy 1999–2005; Econ. Affairs Adviser to Prime Minister 2005–; Chair. Islamic Bank of Asia 2005–; mem. Bd of Dirs Gulf Air Co., Org. for Social Insurance, Civil Service Pension Bd; Alt. Gov. IMF; Fellow, Chartered Inst. of Man. Accountants, UK; Dr hc (DePaul Univ., USA) 2002. *Address:* Office of the Chairman, Islamic Bank of Asia, 45th Floor, West Tower, Bahrain Financial Harbour, PO Box 1317, Manama, Bahrain (office). *Telephone:* 1710 2050 (office). *Fax:* 1710 4990 (office). *Website:* www.islamicbankasia.com (office).

SAIFULLAH KHAN, Javed, BA, MBA; Pakistani business executive; *Chairman, Saif Holdings;* ed Carnegie Mellon Univ., Univ. of Pittsburgh, USA; joined Saif Group of Cos 1973, Chair. Saif Holdings 1990–, holding co. of Saif Group consisting of interests in telecommunications, information tech., cement and textiles, including Pakistan Mobile Communications Pvt. Ltd, Saif Telecom Ltd, Transworld Assocs Pvt. Ltd, Saif Textile Mills; Sr Adviser Galen Capital Group LLC, USA; mem. Bd of Dirs Pakistan Mobile Communications Ltd (Mobilink); mem. Exec. Cttee Pakistan Petroleum Exploration and Production Cos; fmr mem. Bd of Investment, Govt of Pakistan; fmr Chair. Cen. Man. Cttee, All Pakistan Textile Mills Asscn; fmr mem. Task Force, Information Tech. and Telecommunication

Advisory Bd, Ministry of Science and Tech.; Sitara I Imtiaz 2007. *Address:* Saif Group, Kulsum Plaza, 42 West, Jinnah Aveneu, Blue Area, Islamabad 44000, Pakistan (office). *Telephone:* (51) 2874670 (office). *Fax:* (51) 2873606 (office). *E-mail:* info@saifgroup.com (office). *Website:* www.saifgroup.com (office).

SAIGOL, Mian Naseem; Pakistani business executive; *Chairman, Saigol Group of Companies;* Chair. Saigol Group of Cos, conglomerate with interests in automobiles, eng, power, information tech., including Kohinoor Textile Mills; Chair. Pak Elektron Ltd (PEL); Chair. and CEO Kohinoor Power Co. Ltd; est. Union Bank 1991; mem. Commonwealth Business Council, mem. Bd of Dirs 2006–08. *Address:* Pak Electron Ltd, 17 Aziz Ave, Canal Bank, Lahore, Pakistan (office). *Telephone:* (42) 5717364-5 (office). *Fax:* (42) 5715105 (office). *Website:* www.pel.com.pk (office).

SAINSBURY, Keith J., BS, PhD; New Zealand marine research scientist; *Director, SainSolutions Pty Ltd;* b. 22 Feb. 1951, Christchurch; ed Univ. of Canterbury; research scientist, NZ Ministry of Agric. and Fisheries 1975–76; research scientist, CSIRO, Australia 1977–78; project leader and Man. Australian Tropical Fisheries Resources 1978–79, Man. Pelagic Fisheries Resources Program and Multi-Div. Program for Design and Evaluation of Marine Man. Strategies 1990–97, Man. Multiple Use Man. of Exclusive Econ. Zone program 1997–2002, Sr Prin. Research Scientist and Program Leader, Div. of Marine Research 2002–06; Prof. of Marine Systems Management, Univ. of Tasmania 2006–; mem. Bd of Commrs Australian Fisheries Man. Authority 2004–, Bd Fisheries Research and Devt Corpn 2008–12; Pres. SainSolutions, Tasmania, Dir SainSolutions Pty Ltd 2006–; Vice-Chair. Marine Stewardship Council, mem. Tech. Advisory Bd; Award for Outstanding Design and Production of an Australian Book, Australian Book Publrs' Asscn 1985, Japan Prize for contrib. to understanding of shelf ecosystems and their sustainable utilization 2004, Swedish Seafood Award in the Sustainable Fisheries for contrbiution to the Ecosystem Approach to Fishery Management 2011. *Publications:* Continental Shelf Fishes of Northern and Northwestern Australia (co-author) 1985; contrib. numerous chapters in books and articles in journals including Science and Journal of Marine Science. *Address:* SainSolutions Pty Ltd, 41 Powell Road, Blackmans Bay, Tasmania, Australia (office). *Telephone:* (3) 6229-1767 (home). *E-mail:* ksainsbury@netspace.net.au (home). *Website:* www.sainsolutions.net (office).

SAINSBURY, (Richard) Mark, DPhil, FBA; British academic; *Professor of Philosophy, University of Texas at Austin;* b. 2 July 1943, London, England; s. of Richard Eric Sainsbury and Freda Margaret Horne; m. 1st Gillian McNeill Rind 1969 (divorced); one s. one d.; m. 2nd Victoria Goodman 2000; ed Sherborne School, Corpus Christi Coll., Oxford; Radcliffe Lecturer in Philosophy, Magdalen Coll., Oxford 1968–70; Lecturer in Philosophy, St Hilda's Coll., Oxford 1970–73, Radcliffe Lecturer in Philosophy, Brasenose Coll., Oxford 1973–75; Lecturer in Philosophy, Univ. of Essex 1975–78, Bedford Coll., Univ. of London 1978–84; King's Coll., London 1984–87, Reader 1987–89, Stebbing Prof. of Philosophy 1991–2003; Prof. of Philosophy, Univ. of Texas at Austin 2002–; Ed. Mind 1990–2000; Radcliffe Fellow 1987–88; Fellow, King's Coll., London 1994, British Acad. 1998; Leverhulme Sr Research Fellow 2000–02; Hon. Fellow, Corpus Christi Coll., Oxford 2013. *Publications:* Russell 1979, Paradoxes 1988 (3rd edn 2009), Logical Forms 1991 (2nd edn 2001), Departing From Frege 2002, Reference Without Referents 2005, Fiction and Fictionalism 2009, Seven Puzzles of Thought (with Michael Tye) 2012. *Leisure interest:* baking bread. *Address:* Department of Philosophy, WAG 403A, 1 University Station, University of Texas, Austin, TX 78712, USA (office). *Telephone:* (512) 417-5433 (office). *E-mail:* marksainsbury@austin.utexas.edu (office). *Website:* webspace.utexas.edu/rms9/www (office).

SAINSBURY OF PRESTON CANDOVER, Baron (Life Peer), cr. 1989, of Preston Candover in the County of Hampshire; **John Davan Sainsbury,** KG, MA; British business executive; b. 2 Nov. 1927, London; s. of A. J. (later Baron) Sainsbury; m. Anya Linden 1963; two s. one d.; ed Stowe School and Worcester Coll., Oxford; Dir J Sainsbury Ltd 1958–92, Vice-Chair. 1967–69, Chair., CEO 1969–92, Pres. 1992–; Chair. Anglo-Israel Asscn 2001–; Dir Royal Opera House, Covent Garden 1969–85 (Chair. 1987–91), The Economist 1972–80, Royal Opera House Trust 1974–84, 1987–97; Chair. Friends of Covent Garden 1969–81, Benesh Inst. of Chorology 1986–87, Dulwich Picture Gallery 1994–; Vice-Pres. Contemporary Arts Soc. 1984–; mem. Council, Retail Consortium 1975–79, Pres. 1993–97; mem. Nat. Cttee for Electoral Reform 1976–85; Jt Hon. Treas. European Mov. 1972–75; Fellow, Inst. of Grocery Distribution 1973; Hon. Fellow Worcester Coll., Oxford 1982; Gov. Royal Ballet School 1965–76, 1987–91, Royal Ballet 1987– (Chair. 1995–); Trustee Nat. Gallery 1976–83, Westminster Abbey Trust 1977–83, Tate Gallery 1982–83, Rhodes Trust 1984–98, Prince of Wales Inst. of Architecture 1992–96; Hon. Bencher, Inner Temple 1985; Hon. DSc (London) 1985; Hon. DLitt (South Bank) 1992; Albert Medal (RSA) 1989. *Address:* House of Lords, London, SW1A 0PW, England. *Telephone:* (20) 7219-5353.

SAINSBURY OF TURVILLE, Baron (Life Peer), cr. 1997, in the County of Buckinghamshire; **David John Sainsbury,** BA, MBA, FRS; British business executive and fmr government official; *Chancellor, University of Cambridge;* b. 24 Oct. 1940; s. of Sir Robert Sainsbury and Lisa Ingeborg (née Van den Bergh); m. Susan Carroll Reid 1973; three d.; ed King's Coll., Cambridge and Columbia Univ., New York, USA; joined J Sainsbury 1963, Finance Dir 1973–90, Deputy Chair. J Sainsbury PLC 1988–92, Chair. and CEO 1992–98; Parl. Under-Sec. of State for Science and Innovation 1998–2006; mem. Cttee of Review of Post Office (Carter Cttee) 1975–77; Trustee, Social Democratic Party (SDP) 1982–90; mem. Gov. Body, London Business School 1985–98 (Chair. 1990–98); Visiting Fellow, Nuffield Coll., Oxford 1987–95; Chancellor Univ. of Cambridge 2011–; mem. IPPR Comm. 1995–97; Chair. Transition Bd, Univ. for Industry 1998–99; Chair., Inst. for Govt 2009–; f. Gatsby Charitable Foundation 1967 (one of Sainsbury Family Charitable Trusts); mem. (Labour) House of Lords 1997–; Hon. FREng 1994; Hon. LLD (Cambridge) 1997; Dr hc (Oxford), (Manchester), (Imperial Coll., London), (Rockefeller Univ.); Andrew Carnegie Medal of Philanthropy (on behalf of Sainsbury family), Carnegie Inst. 2003. *Publications:* Government and Industry: A New Partnership 1981, Wealth Creation and Jobs (with C. Smallwood) 1987, A Race to the Top: a Review of Government's Science and Innovation Policies 2007, Progressive Capitalism: How to Achieve Economic Growth, Liberty and Social Justice 2013. *Address:* House of Lords, London, SW1A 0PW, England. *Telephone:*

(20) 7072-4405. *E-mail:* tracy.mattinson@gayfere.org.uk. *Website:* www.parliament.uk/biographies/lords/lord-sainsbury-of-turville/2161.

ST ARNAUD, Bill, BEng, MEng, PEng; Canadian computer engineer; *Chief Research Officer and Director of Network Projects, CANARIE Inc.;* b. 1951; ed Carleton Univ. School of Eng; Consultant and Chief Engineer, Switzer Engineering 1975–79; Project Man., Motorola, Inc. 1979–81; Founder and Pres. TSA Proforma 1981–88; consultant for several high-tech start-ups 1988–92; Project Dir, Vision 2000 1992–93; Sr Dir of Network Projects, CANARIE Inc. 1993–, led devt, coordination and implementation of world's first nat. optical R&D Internet network, CA*net3, Chair. CA*net 3 Tech Applications Cttee 1994–, currently, Chief Architect of CA*net4; mem. various cttees and bds, including Bd of Trustees for The Internet Society (ISOC), NomComm Cttee for Internet Corpn for Assigned Names and Numbers (ICANN), UKlight Steering Cttee, GLORIAD Policy Cttee, Neptune Canada Oversight Cttee, Global Lambda Integrated Facility Policy Cttee, Steering Cttee SPIE Tech. Group on Optical Networks 2000–, amongst others; NSF Reviewer; Ed. CAnet-3-NEWS@canarie.ca; mem. Editorial Bd Optical Networking Magazine; Globecomm Fellow, Center for Global Communications 2000; World Tech. Award in Communication Tech., The World Tech. Network 2005. *Publications:* numerous scientific papers in professional journals. *Address:* CANARIE Inc., 4th Floor, 110 O'Connor Street, Ottawa, ON K1P 5M9, Canada (office). *Telephone:* (613) 785-0426 (office). *Fax:* (613) 943-5443 (office). *E-mail:* bill.st.arnaud@canarie.ca (office); bill.st.arnaud@gmail.com (home). *Website:* www.canarie.ca/~bstarn (office); billstarnaud.blogspot.com.

ST AUBIN de TERÁN, Lisa Gioconda, (Lisa Duff-Scott), FRSL; British author; *Director, Teran Foundation;* b. (Lisa Gioconda Carew), 2 Oct. 1953, London; d. of Jan Rynveld Carew and Joan Mary St Aubin; m. 1st Jaime Terán 1970 (divorced 1981); one d.; m. 2nd George Macbeth 1981 (divorced 1989, deceased); one s.; m. 3rd Robbie Duff-Scott (divorced) 1989; one d.; pnr Mees van Deth; ed James Allen's Girls' School, Dulwich; travelled widely in France and Italy 1969–71; managed sugar plantation in Venezuelan Andes 1971–78; moved to Italy 1983; fmr Vice-Pres. Umbria Film Festival, now Hon. Pres.; CEO Radiant Pictures 2002 (film production co.); f. Teran Foundation and Makua Coll. of Tourism and Agriculture, Mozambique 2004; Somerset Maugham Award 1983, John Llewelyn Rhys Award 1983, Eric Gregory Award for Poetry 1983. *Screenplays:* The Slow Train to Milan (co-writer with Michael Radford), The Hacienda, The Blessing, A Woman Called Solitude, The Orange Sicilian (co-writer with Alex Macbeth, animated feature film). *Television:* wrote and presented documentaries Santos to Santa Cruz in Great Railway Journeys series (BBC) 1994, Great Railway Journeys of the World (BBC and PBS). *Radio:* adapted and read (for BBC) Off the Rails 1995, The Bay of Silence 1996. *Publications:* fiction: Keepers of the House 1982, The Slow Train to Milan 1983, The Tiger 1984, The Bay of Silence 1986, Black Idol 1987, The Marble Mountain (short stories) 1989, Joanna 1990, Nocturne 1993, Distant Landscapes (novella) 1995, The Palace 1998, The Virago Book of Wanderlust and Dreams (ed.) 1998, Southpaw (short stories) 1999, Otto: A Novel 2004, Sapa's Blessing and Other Stories 2005, Swallowing Stones 2006; poetry: The Streak 1980, The High Place 1985; memoirs: Off the Rails 1989, Venice: The Four Seasons 1992, A Valley in Italy 1994, The Hacienda 1997, My Venezuelan Years 1997, Memory Maps 2001, Mozambique Mysteries 2007. *Leisure interests:* travelling, medicinal plants, gardening, architecture, falconry, antiques, reading, Mozambique. *Address:* Caixa Postal 81, Ilha de Moçambique, Provincia de Nampula (home); c/o Teran Foundation, Sunset Boulevard Guest House, Mossuril Sede, Distrito Mossuril, Provincia de Nampula, Mozambique (office). *E-mail:* info@teranfoundation.org (office). *Website:* www.teranfoundation.org (office); www.staubindeteran.com.

SAINT-GEOURS, Frédéric; French civil servant and business executive; *Chairman, Union des Industries et Métiers de la Métallurgie;* b. 20 April 1950, Clamart (Hauts-de-Seine); s. of Jean Saint-Geours, fmr Pres. Comm. des opérations de bourse; m. Eva Bettan; three c.; ed Institut d'Etudes Politiques and Ecole Nationale d'Admin, Paris; joined Ministry of Finance 1975, worked as forecaster for Finance Minister Jacques Delors, held series of govt posts in finance, including adviser to Pres. of Nat. Ass., finally Chief Tech. Adviser to Sec. of State for the Budget, Henri Emmanuelli 1984–86; Deputy Chief Financial Dir PSA Peugeot-Citroën 1986–88, Financial Dir 1988–90, Deputy Dir-Gen. Automobiles Peugeot 1990, oversaw Jean Todt's successful Peugeot 905 sports car campaigns 1991, 1992, 1993, Dir-Gen. Automobiles Peugeot 1998–2007; Chair. Union des Industries et Métiers de la Métallurgie 2007–; mem. Bd of Dirs Casino Guichard Perrachon and Cie SA 2006–, Faurecia SA 2009–. *Address:* Union des Industries et Métiers de la Métallurgie, 56 avenue de Wagram, 75017 Paris, France (office). *Telephone:* 1-40-54-20-20 (office). *Fax:* 1-47-66-22-74 (office). *E-mail:* uimm@uimm.fr (office). *Website:* www.uimm.fr (office).

SAITO, Akihiko, PhD; Japanese engineer and business executive; m.; three s.; ed Nagoya Univ.; joined Toyota Motor Corpn 1968, responsible for several tech. assignments, including work in vibration testing, chassis design, product planning and production eng, mem. team that handled product planning work for Toyota's best-selling car, the Corolla 1980, served as Chief Engineer in devt of sixth and seventh generation Corollas, Gen. Man. Product Planning Div. 1987–91, mem. Bd of Dirs 1991–, Man. Dir 1996–98, Sr Man. Dir 1998–2001, Exec. Vice-Pres. 2001–05; Pres. Int. Fed. of Automotive Eng Socs 2006–08; Vice-Chair. DENSO Corpn 2005–07, Chair. 2007–09. *Leisure interests:* skiing, golf, music and art. *Address:* c/o DENSO Corpn, 1-1 Showa-cho, Kariya, Aichi 448-8661, Japan.

SAITO, Atsushi; Japanese business executive; *President and CEO, Tokyo Stock Exchange Group;* ed Keio Univ.; joined Nomura Securities Co. Ltd 1963, apptd Dir 1986, Vice-Pres. 1995–98 (retd); Pres. Sumitomo Life Investment Co. Ltd 1998–2002, Chair. 2002–03; Pres. and CEO Industrial Revitalization Corpn of Japan 2003–07; Pres. and CEO Tokyo Stock Exchange Group 2007–. *Address:* Tokyo Stock Exchange Group, 2-1 Nihombashi Kabutocho, Chuo-ku, Tokyo 103-0026, Japan (office). *Telephone:* (3) 3666-0141 (office). *Website:* www.tse.or.jp (office).

SAITO, Gunzi, PhD; Japanese scientist and academic; *Professor Emeritus, Department of Chemistry, Graduate School of Science, Kyoto University;* b. 10 March 1945, Otaru, Hokkaido; s. of Nenosuke Saito and Toyo Saito; m. Atsuko Nishikawa 1971; three s.; ed Otaru Choryo High School, Hokkaido Univ.; Postdoctoral Fellow, Emory Univ., Atlanta, Georgia, USA 1973–74, Guelph

Univ., Ont., Canada 1975–76; Welch Fellow Univ. of Tex., Dallas, USA 1977–78; Research Assoc., Inst. for Molecular Science, Okazaki 1979–84; Assoc. Prof., Inst. for Solid State Physics, Tokyo Univ. 1984–89; Prof., Dept of Chem., Graduate School of Science, Kyoto Univ. 1989–2008, currently Prof. Emer.; mem. Science Council, Ministry of Educ., Sport and Culture 1996–2003; Inoue Award 1988, Nishina Award 1988, Japan Surface Science Award 1991, The Chemical Soc. of Japan Award 2003, Medal with Purple Ribbon Award 2009. *Publications include:* Organic Superconductors (co-author) 1998; more than 500 scientific articles on organic superconductors, organic metals and other organic functional materials. *Address:* 35-1-504 Kakinoki-cho, Nishigamo, Kita-ku, Kyoto 603-8821, Japan (home). *Telephone:* (75) 493 1046 (home). *Fax:* (75) 493 1046 (home).

SAITO, Jiro; Japanese business executive, government official and fmr diplomatist; ed Univ. of Tokyo; joined Ministry of Finance 1959, worked in budget and tax bureaus, Vice-Minister of Finance 1993–95 (resgnd); also worked as diplomat in Germany; Pres. and CEO Tokyo Financial Exchange Inc. –2010; Pres. and CEO Japan Post Holdings Co. Ltd 2010–13, Outside Dir, Japan Post Network Co. Ltd. *Address:* c/o Japan Post Holdings Co. Ltd, 1-3-2 Kasumigaseki, Chiyoda-ku, Tokyo 100-8798, Japan.

SAITO, Katsutoshi; Japanese insurance industry executive; *Chairman and Representative Director, Dai-ichi Life Insurance Company Limited;* ed Hitotsubashi Univ., Harvard Business School Advanced Man. Program, USA; joined Dai-ichi Life Insurance Co. 1967, Gen. Man., Int. Planning Dept 1989–91, Gen. Man., Research Dept 1991–94, Dir and Gen. Man. 1994–95, Dir, Chief Gen. Man. (Corp. Planning, Public Relations) and Gen. Man., Research Dept 1995–97, Man. Dir 1997–2001, Sr Man. Dir 2001–03, Sr Man. Dir (Rep. Dir) 2003–04, Pres. 2004–10, Vice-Chair. 2010–11, Chair. 2011–; Chair. Life Insurance Asscn of Japan; mem. Bd of Dirs Japan Cancer Soc. *Address:* Dai-ichi Life Insurance Co. Ltd, 13-1, Yurakucho 1-chome, Chiyoda-ku, Tokyo 100-8411, Japan (office). *Telephone:* (3) 3216-1211 (office). *E-mail:* info@dai-ichi-life.co.jp (office). *Website:* www.dai-ichi-life.co.jp (office).

SAITO, Tetsuo, BSc, MSc, DEng; Japanese engineer, academic and politician; b. 5 Feb. 1952, Ōchi Dist, Shimane Pref.; ed Tokyo Inst. of Tech.; joined Shimizu Corpn 1976; Visiting Fellow, Princeton Univ., USA 1986–89; mem. House of Reps for Chugoku Dist 1993–; Parl. Sec., Vice-Minister for Science and Tech. 1999–2004; Chair. Cttee on Educ., Culture, Sports, Science and Tech., House of Reps; Chair. Policy Research Council of New Komeito Party 2006–08; Minister of the Environment 2008–11. *Leisure interest:* swimming. *Address:* c/o Ministry of the Environment, 1-2-2, Kasumigaseki, Chiyoda-ku, Tokyo 100-8975, Japan.

SAITO, Toshitsugu, BA, MBA; Japanese politician; b. 27 Dec. 1944; m.; two c.; ed Sophia Univ., Univ. of Washington; Pres. Japan Jr Chamber 1984; mem. House of Reps for Shizuoka Prefecture, 5th Electoral Dist 1986–; Dir Youth Div., Party Org. HQ, Liberal Democratic Party 1991, Dir Communications Div., Policy Research Council 1995, Dir-Gen. Information Research Bureau 1996, Deputy Chair. Diet Affairs Cttee 1996, Acting Chair. Public Relations HQ 1999, Dir-Gen. Int. Bureau 2001; Parl. Vice-Minister, Ministry of Posts and Telecommunications 1992; Chair. Standing Cttee on Commerce and Industry, House of Reps 1997, Standing Cttee on Local Admin 1999; fmr Minister of State and Dir-Gen. of Defence Agency. *Address:* Liberal Democratic Party (Jiyu-Minshuto), 1-11-23, Nagata-cho, Chiyoda-ku, Tokyo 100-8910, Japan (office). *Telephone:* (3) 3581-6211 (office). *E-mail:* koho@ldp.jimin.or.jp (office). *Website:* www.jimin.jp (office).

SAITO, Yasuo; Japanese fmr diplomatist; b. 5 Jan. 1948, Okayama; m. Chieko Saito; two c.; joined Ministry of Foreign Affairs 1971, positions included Dir-Gen. European Affairs Bureau; served as Amb. to UNESCO, Consul-Gen. in Atlanta, USA, Amb. to Saudi Arabia 2003, Amb. to Russia 2006–09, to France 2009–11; Ind. Dir Ajinomoto Inc. 2012–; Grand officier, Ordre nat. du Mérite 2012. *Address:* c/o Ajinomoto Inc, 15-1, Kyobashi 1-chome, Chuo-ku, Tokyo 104-8315, Japan (office). *Website:* www.ajinomoto.co.jp.

SAITOV, Oleg; Russian boxer; b. 26 May 1974, Jigalevsk, Samara Region; gold medal, Summer Olympics, Atlanta 1996, Summer Olympics, Sydney 2000, gold medal European Amateur Boxing Championships 2004, bronze medal Summer Olympics, Athens 2004; named Best Boxer of Sydney Olympic Games 2000, honored Master of Sports of Russia 1995, Fair Play Award, Russian Olympic Cttee 1998. *Address:* c/o Russian Olympic Committee, Luzhnetskaya Nab. 8, 119992 Moscow, Russia.

SAJI, Nobutada, MBA; Japanese business executive; *Chairman, President and CEO, Suntory Ltd;* b. 25 Nov. 1945; s. of the late Keizo Saji; m.; ed Keio Univ., Univ. of California, Los Angeles, USA; began career at Sony Trading Co.; joined Suntory Ltd (family business) 1974, becoming Pres. and CEO 2001–, also Chair. 2002–, fmr Pres. Suntory Int. Corpn, USA; Chair. Advertising Council of Japan. *Leisure interest:* swimming. *Address:* Office of the Chairman, Suntory Holdings Limited, Dojimahama 2-1-40, Kita-ku, Osaka City, Osaka 530-8203, Japan (office). *Telephone:* (6) 6346-1131 (office). *Fax:* (6) 6345-1169 (office). *Website:* www.suntory.com (office).

SAJJADPOUR, Seyed Mohammad Kazem, PhD; Iranian diplomatist and academic; ed George Washington Univ., USA; Post-doctoral Fellow, Harvard Univ.; taught at Coll. of Int. Relations, Tehran Univ., Azad Univ., Nat. Defence Univ. of Iran; fmr Dir Inst. for Political and Int. Studies, Ministry of Foreign Affairs, currently Sr Faculty Member, School of International Relations (think-tank); fmr Amb. and Deputy Perm. Rep. to UN and other int. orgs, Geneva; mem. Bd of Advisers, Dialogues: Islamic World-US-The West program, New York Univ.; fmr Dir-Gen. Inst. for Political and Int. Studies (IPIS), Tehran, later Sr Fellow; currently Ed.-in-Chief Inst. for Strategic Research Journals; mem. Bd of Advisors Center for Dialogues, New York Univ. *Address:* Center for Dialogues, New York University, 194 Mercer Street, 4th Floor, New York, NY 10012, USA (office). *Telephone:* (212) 998-8693 (office). *Website:* islamuswest.org/about_Dialogues_Islam_US_West (office).

SAKAGUCHI, Chikara; Japanese politician; b. 1 April 1934, Mie Prefecture; ed Mie Univ.; mem. House of Reps for Tokai Dist 1976–, fmr Dir Finance Cttee; Minister of Labour 1993–94, of Health, Labour and Welfare 2000–04; fmr Chair. Komeito Policy Bd, currently Rep. of New Komeito, House of Reps. *Address:* New Komeito, 17, Minami-Motomachi, Shinjuku-ku, Tokyo 160-0012, Japan (office).

Telephone: (3) 3353-0111 (office). *Website:* www.komei.or.jp (office); www.chikara.serio.jp.

SAKAIYA, Taichi; Japanese economist, politician, author and fmr civil servant; b. (Kotaro Ikeguchi), 13 July 1935, Osaka; ed Tokyo Univ.; Ministry of Int. Trade and Industry 1960–78, directed 1970 World Exposition in Osaka and Okinawa Int. Ocean Exposition 1975; became full-time writer 1978; Chair. Event and Project Cttee Osaka 21st Century Plan 1982; Pres. Asian Club Foundation 1985; mem. Cttee for Ten Year Support for Regions Stricken by the Hanshin Awaji, Kobe Earthquake 1995; Co-Chair. US-Japan 21st Century Cttee 1996; Minister of State for Econ. Planning 1998–2000; Special Adviser to the Prime Minister 2000; fmr Pres. Asia Crime Foundation Asscn; apptd mem. Advisory Bd for Japan, Lehman Brothers Holdings Inc. 2005; mem. Bd of Dirs Osaka Securities Exchange Co. Ltd, Chair. Sakaiya Advisory Cttee 2002; Special Assignment Prof. Waseda Univ. *Publications include:* Yudan 1975, Dankai no sedai (Baby Boom Generation), Oinaru Kuwadate (The Grand Plan), Hidenaga Toyotomi, Toge no Gunzo, Chika Kakumei (The Knowledge-Value Revolution) 1991, Nihon to wa Nanika (What is Japan?) 1995, Soshiki no seisui (The Rise and Fall of Organizations).

SAKAKI, Hiroyuki, BS, MS, PhD; Japanese scientist and academic; *Professor, Institute of Industrial Science, University of Tokyo;* b. 6 Oct. 1944, Aichi; s. of Yoneichiro Sakaki and Fumiko Sakaki; m. Mutsuko Sakaki 1973; one s. four d.; ed Univ. of Tokyo; Assoc. Prof., Inst. of Industrial Science, Univ. of Tokyo 1973–87, Prof. 1987–, Prof., Research Center for Advanced Science and Tech. 1988–98; Visiting Scientist, IBM T. J. Watson Research Center (group of Dr Leo Esaki) 1976–77; Dir Quantum Wave Project (Japan's government project for Exploratory Research for Advanced Tech.) 1988–93; Dir Japan–US Jt Research Project on Quantum Transition 1994–98; Outstanding Achievement Award (jtly) 1974, Applied Physics Soc. Award 1983, Japan Applied Physics Soc. Prize 1983, 1990, Japan IBM Science Prize 1989, Hattori-Hokokai Prize 1990, Shimazu Science Prize, Outstanding Achievement Award, Inst. of Electronic Communications Engineers of Japan 1991, David Sarnoff Award, IEEE 1996, Fujiwara Prize 2000, Medal with Purple Ribbon (Japan) 2001, Esaki Award (jtly) 2004, Japan Acad. Prize (jtly) 2005. *Leisure interests:* listening to classical music, looking at paintings. *Address:* Sakaki Laboratory, Ee-403, Institute of Industrial Science, University of Tokyo, 4-6-1 Komaba, Meguro-ku, Tokyo 153-8505 (office); 1-41-5 Kagahara, Tsuzukiku, Yokohama 224, Japan (home). *Telephone:* (3) 5452-6235 (office); (45) 943-1539 (home). *E-mail:* sakaki@iis.u-tokyo.ac.jp (office). *Website:* quanta.iis.u-tokyo.ac.jp (office).

SAKAMOTO, Ryûichi, MA; Japanese composer, musician and actor; b. 17 Jan. 1952, Tokyo; m. Akiko Yano 1979; ed Shinjuku High School, Composition Dept, Tokyo Fine Arts Univ.; began composing at age of ten; mem. group Yellow Magic Orchestra 1978–83; worked with David Sylvian 1982–83; solo recording artist, composer 1982–; conductor, arranger, music for Olympic Games opening ceremony, Barcelona, Spain 1992; UN Environment Programme's Echo Award, Order of the Cavaleiro Admissão (Govt of Brazil), Ordre des Arts et des Lettres 2009. *Film appearances:* Merry Christmas Mr Lawrence 1982, The Last Emperor 1987, New Rose Hotel 1998. *Film soundtracks:* Merry Christmas Mr Lawrence (BAFTA Award 1983) 1982, Daijôbu, mai furendo 1983, Koneko monogatari 1986, The Last Emperor (with David Byrne and Cong Su, Academy Award, Golden Globe Award, Grammy Award) 1987, Ôritsu uchûgun Oneamisu no tsubasa 1987, The Laser Man (title song) 1988, The Handmaid's Tale 1990, The Sheltering Sky (Golden Globe Award) 1990, Tacones lejanos 1991, Topâzu 1992, Wuthering Heights 1992, Wild Palms (TV series) 1993, Little Buddha 1993, Rabbit Ears: Peachboy 1993, Wild Side 1995, Snake Eyes 1998, Love is the Devil 1998, Gohatto 1999, Poppoya (theme) 1999, Femme Fatale 2002, Alexei to izumi 2003, Derrida 2003, Los Rubios 2003, Life Is Journey 2003, Appurushîdo 2004, Original Child Bomb 2004, Hoshi ni natta shonen 2005, Zarin 2005, Tony Takitani 2007, Silk 2007. *Recordings include:* albums: Thousand Knives 1978, B-2 Unit 1980, Hidariudeno (A Dream Of The Left Arm) 1981, Coda 1983, Ongaku Zukan (A Picture Book Of Music) 1984, Illustrated Musical Encyclopedia 1984, Esperanto 1985, Miraiha Yarô (A Futurist Chap) 1986, Media Bahn Live 1986, Oneamisno Tsubasa (The Wings Of Oneamis) 1986, Neo Geo 1987, Playing The Orchestra 1988, Tokyo Joe 1988, Sakamoto Plays Sakamoto 1989, Grupo Musicale 1989, Beauty 1989, Heartbeat 1991, Neo Geo (with Iggy Pop) 1992, Sweet Revenge 1994, Soundbites 1994, Hard To Get 1995, 1996 1996, Music For Yohji Yamamoto 1997, Smoochy 1997, Discord 1998, Love Is The Devil 1998, Raw Life 1999, Intimate 1999, Space 1999, BTTB 1999, Gohatto 1999, Complete Index of Gut 1999, Cinemage 2000, Casa 2002; singles: Bamboo Houses (with David Sylvian) 1982, Forbidden Colours (with David Sylvian) 1983, Field Work (with Thomas Dolby) 1986, Risky 1988, We Love You 1991, Moving On 1994, Prayer/Salvation 1998, Anger 1998, O Grande Amor 2001, World Citizen 2003, Sala Santa Cecillia 2005, Revep 2006, Koko 2008, Nord 2009. *Address:* David Rubinson Management, PO Box 411197, San Francisco, CA 94141, USA (office). *Website:* www.sitesakamoto.com.

SAKANE, Masahiro; Japanese business executive; *Chairman, Komatsu Ltd;* b. 7 Jan. 1941, Shimane Pref.; ed Osaka City Univ.; joined Komatsu Ltd 1963, COO Komatsu Dresser Co. 1990–94, Man. Dir 1994–97, Exec. Man. Dir 1997–99, Exec. Vice-Pres. 1999–2001, Pres. 2001–07, CEO 2003–07, Chair. 2007–; Vice-Chair. Japan Construction Equipment Mfrs Asscn 2001–04, Chair. 2004–; mem. Bd of Exec. Dirs Japan Business Fed., Chair. Sub-Saharan Africa Cttee 2003–, Deputy Chair. Japan-Russia (NIS) Business Cooperation Cttee 2003–; mem. Bd of Dirs Tokyo Electron Ltd 2008–, Nomura Holdings, Inc. 2008–; Japan Inst. of Invention and Innovation Nat. Commendation for Invention 2003. *Address:* Komatsu Ltd, 2-3-6 Akasaka, Minato-ku, Tokyo 107-8414, Japan (office). *Telephone:* (3) 5561-2687 (office); (3) 5561-2616 (office). *Fax:* (3) 3505-9662 (office). *E-mail:* info@komatsu.com (office). *Website:* www.komatsu.com (office).

SAKINE, Ahmat Awad; Chadian politician and diplomatist; m. Mariam Sakine; Dir-Gen. of the Treasury –2004; Minister of the Economy and Finance 2004–05; Amb. to Belgium (also accred to UK) 2011–13. *Address:* Ministry of External Relations and African Integration, BP 746, N'Djamena, Chad (office). *Telephone:* 22-51-80-50 (office). *Fax:* 22-51-45-85 (office). *E-mail:* tchaddiplomatie@gmail.com (office). *Website:* www.tchad-diplomatie.org (office).

SAKMANN, Bert, BA, MD; German physician; *Scientific Director and Research Group Leader, Max Planck Florida Institute;* b. 12 June 1942, Stuttgart; s. of

Berthold Sakmann and Annemarie Schaeffer Sakmann; m. Dr Christiane Wulfert 1970; two s. one d.; ed Univ. of Tübingen, Univ. of Munich, Univ. Hosp., Munich, Univ. of Göttingen; Research Asst, Max-Planck-Institut für Psychiatrie, Munich 1969–70; British Council Fellow, Dept of Biophysics, Univ. Coll., London 1971–73; Research Asst, Max-Planck-Institut für biophysikalische Chemie, Univ. of Göttingen 1974–79, Research Assoc., Membrane Biology Group 1979–82, Head, Membrane Physiology Unit 1983–85, Dir 1985–87, Prof. Dept of Cell Physiology 1987–89; Dir Dept of Cell Physiology Max-Planck-Institut für medizinische Forschung, Heidelberg 1989–2008, Research Group Leader 2008–; currently Scientific Dir and Research Group Leader, Max Planck Florida Inst.; Prof. of Physiology, Univ. of Heidelberg 1990–; Foreign mem. NAS 1993, Royal Soc. (UK) 1994; Hon. DSc (London) 1999; Nobel Prize for Medicine (jtly) 1991 (for discoveries about single-ion channels in cells), Bunsen Prize, Feldberg Prize, Spencer Prize, Leibniz Prize, Gross-Horwitz Prize, Louis Jeantet Prize, Gairdner Prize, Magnes Award (Hebrew University) 1982, Harvey Prize of the Technion 1991. *Publications include:* The Visual System: Neurophysiology, Biophysics and Their Clinical Applications 1972 (contrib.), Advances in Pharmacology and Therapeutics 1978 (contrib.), Single Channel Recording 1983 (co-author), Membrane Control of Cellular Activity 1986 (contrib.), Calcium and Ion Channel Modulation 1988 (contrib.), Neuromuscular Junction 1989 (contrib.). *Leisure interests:* music, reading, tennis, skiing. *Address:* Max Planck Florida Institute, 5353 Parkside Drive, MC19-RE, 33458-2906 Jupiter, FL, USA (office). *Telephone:* (561) 972-9400 (office). *Fax:* (561) 972-9001 (office). *E-mail:* bert.sakmann@maxplanckflorida.org (office), bsakmann@neuro.mpg.de (office). *Website:* www.maxplanckflorida.org (office).

SAKO, Soumana, PhD, MPA; Malian politician, civil servant and international civil servant; b. 23 Dec. 1950, Nyamina; s. of Sayan Sako and Djeneba Traore; m. Cisse Toure; two s. two d.; ed Univ. of Pittsburgh, Pa, USA, Ecole Nationale d'Admin du Mali; Staff mem. Gen. Inspectorate, Office of the Pres. of Repub. of Mali 1974; Admin. and Finance Man., Operation Puits Project 1975–76; Staff mem. Ministry of Industrial Devt and Tourism 1981; Adviser Ministry of Foreign Affairs and Int. Co-operation 1981–82; Sr Adviser Ministry of Planning and Econ. Man. 1982–84; Dir of Sr Staff, Ministry of State-Owned Enterprises 1985–87; Minister of Finance and Commerce Feb.–Aug. 1987; Deputy Controller-Gen. Office of the Pres. 1988–89; UNDP official serving in Cen. African Repub. 1989–91, Sr Economist for Madagascar and Comoros Islands 1993–97; Prime Minister of Mali 1991–92; Prof. of Devt Econs and Public Finance, Univ. of Mali 1997–2000; int. consultant 1998–; Exec. Sec. African Capacity Bldg Foundation, Harare 2000–08; Commdr, Nat. Order of Mali 2000, Grand-Officer 2005; AFGRAD Distinguished Alumnus 1992, Sennen Andriamirado Prize of Excellence 2000. *Publication:* Determinants of Public Policy—A Comparative Analysis of Public Expenditure Patterns in African States Trade Related Capacity Building. *Leisure interests:* soccer, chess, gardening. *Address:* Villa f4 bis 48, Sema Gexco Bamako, Mali (home); BP 433, Bamako, Mali. *Telephone:* 236196 (home). *Fax:* 229748.

SAKS, Gene; American actor and director; b. 8 Nov. 1921, New York; m. the late Beatrice Arthur (divorced); two s. one d.; ed Cornell Univ.; began acting career off-Broadway at Provincetown Playhouse and the Cherry Lane Theatre; appeared in Dog Beneath the Skin (Auden), Him (e. e. cummings), The Bourgeois Gentilhomme (Molière); Broadway appearances in Mr Roberts, South Pacific, Middle of the Night, The Tenth Man, A Shot in the Dark, Love and Libel, A Thousand Clowns; debut as dir on Broadway with Enter Laughing 1963. *Plays directed:* Nobody Loves an Albatross, Half a Sixpence, Generation, Mame, Same Time, Next Year, California Suite, I Love My Wife (Tony Award), Brighton Beach (Tony Award), Biloxi Blues 1985 (Tony Award), Broadway Bound 1986, A Month of Sundays 1987, Rumours 1988, Jake's Woman 1992, Lost in Yonkers (original Broadway stage production), Barrymore 1997. *Films directed:* Barefoot in the Park 1967, The Odd Couple 1968, Cactus Flower 1969, Last of the Red Hot Lovers 1972, Brighton Beach Memoirs 1986, Cin cin 1991, Bye Bye Birdie (TV) 1995. *Film appearances:* A Thousand Clowns 1965, Prisoner of Second Avenue 1965, The One and Only 1978, Lovesick 1983, The Goodbye People 1984, The Good Policeman 1991, Nobody's Fool 1994, IQ 1994, Deconstructing Harry 1997. *Address:* c/o ICM, 40 West 80th Street, New York, NY 10024, USA.

SAKSKOBURGGOTSKI, Simeon; Bulgarian politician and fmr King of Bulgaria; b. 16 June 1937, Sofia; s. of the late King Boris III and of Queen Joanna; m. Margarita Gómez y Acebo 1962; four s. one d.; ed in England, Victoria Coll., Alexandria, Egypt, Lycée Français, Spain and Valley Forge Mil. Acad., USA; proclaimed King of Bulgaria 1943, deposed 1946; sought refuge in Egypt in 1947; has since lived mainly in Spain; Constitutional Court ruled in 1998 that confiscation of royal property by communist regime had been illegal; returned to Bulgaria 1996; Founder and Leader, Nat. Movt for King Simeon II (renamed Nat. Movt for Stability and Progress 2007) 2001–09 (resgnd); Prime Minister of Bulgaria 2001–05. *Address:* National Movement for Stability and Progress (Natsionalno dvizhenie za stabilnost i vazhod), 1000 Sofia, ul. Vrabcha 23, Bulgaria (office). *Telephone:* (2) 980-38-09 (office). *Fax:* (2) 980-38-07 (office). *E-mail:* ndsv@ndsv.bg (office). *Website:* www.ndsv.bg (office).

SAKURADA, Kengo; Japanese business executive; *Representative Director, President and Executive Officer, NKSJ Holdings, Inc.;* b. 11 Feb. 1956; joined Yasuda Fire & Marine Insurance Co. Ltd (Sompo Japan Insurance Inc.) 1978, Gen. Man. Consolidated Planning Dept 2000–01, Gen. Man. Consolidated Planning Dept and Dai-Ichi Life Office Integration Planning Dept 2001–02, Gen. Man. Business Strategy Planning Dept April–June 2002, Gen. Man. Corporate Planning Dept 2002, Exec. Officer and Gen. Man. Financial Insts Dept 2005–07, Man. Exec. Officer April–June 2007, Dir and Man. Exec. Officer 2007–10, Dir and Exec. Officer, NKSJ Holdings, Inc. (following establishment of jt holding co. by Sompo Japan Insurance Inc. and Nipponkoa Insurance Co. Ltd 2010) 2010–12, Rep. Dir, Pres. and Exec. Officer 2012–. *Address:* NKSJ Holdings, Inc., 26-1, Nishi-Shinjuku 1-chome, Shinjuku-ku, Tokyo 160-8338, Japan (office). *Telephone:* (3) 3349-3000 (operator) (office); (3) 3349-3111 (office). *Fax:* (3) 3349-4697 (office). *E-mail:* info@nksj-hd.com (office). *Website:* www.nksj-hd.com (office).

SAKURAI, Masamitsu, CBE, BSc; Japanese business executive; *Representative Director and Chairman, Ricoh Company Ltd;* b. 8 Jan. 1942, Tokyo; m. Yokohama Sakurai; ed Faculty of Science and Tech., Waseda Univ.; joined Ricoh Co. Ltd 1966, Gen. Man. of Eng Admin Office 1980–84, Pres. Ricoh UK Products Ltd 1984–92,

apptd Dir 1992, Gen. Man. of Purchasing Div. 1992–93, Pres. Ricoh Europe BV 1993–94, Man.-Dir Ricoh Co. Ltd 1994–95, Gen. Man. Research and Devt Group 1995–96, Pres., COO and CEO 1996–2007, Rep. Dir and Chair. 2007–13. *Leisure interests:* travel, golf, reading. *Address:* c/o Ricoh Co. Ltd, 8-13-1 Ginza, Chuo-ku, Tokyo 104-8222, Japan. *E-mail:* www-admin@ricoh.co.jp.

SAKURAI, Takahide; Japanese insurance industry executive; *Adviser, Dai-ichi Mutual Life Insurance Company;* Chair. Dai-ichi Mutual Life Insurance Co. –2004, Adviser 2004–; Vice-Chair. Bd of Councillors, Japan Business Fed. 2002, Chair. Fed. of Econ. Orgs (Keidanren) 2004; Corp. Auditor, JFE Holdings Inc. 1999, The Tokyo Group 2001, Asahi Breweries Ltd 2004; Acting Chair. Keizai Koho Center; mem. Bd of Dirs Imperial Hotel Ltd 1999–, IY Bank Co. Ltd 2001; Vice-Chair. Keizai Koho Centre, Japan Inst. for Social and Econ. Affairs 2000; mem. Advisory Cttee, Ritsumeikan Asia Pacific Univ., Steering Cttee, The 21st Century Public Policy Inst. 2004. *Address:* Dai-ichi Mutual Life Insurance Company, 13-1 Yurakucho 1-chome, Chiyoda-ku, Tokyo 100-8411, Japan (office). *Telephone:* (3) 3216-1211 (office). *Fax:* (3) 5221-4360 (office). *Website:* www.dai-ichi-life.co.jp (office).

SALA, Marius, PhD; Romanian linguist and academic; *Director, Institutul de Lingvistică 'Iorgu Iordan – Al Rosetti', Bucharest;* b. 8 Sept. 1932, Vașcău, Bihor Co.; s. of Sabin Sala and Eleonora Tocoianu; m. Marina Sala 2003; one d.; ed Coll. of Philology, Bucharest Univ.; researcher, Inst. of Linguistics 'Iorgu Iordan – Al Rosetti', Bucharest 1955–90, Deputy Dir 1990–94, Dir 1994–; Prof. Faculty of Foreign Languages, Bucharest; Visiting Prof., Heidelberg 1971, Málaga 1968, 1970, 1973, 1979, Madrid 1978, 1981, 1987, Mexico City 1981, Cologne 1984, Frankfurt 1992, Oviedo 1994, Nancy 1999; Corresp. mem. Royal Acad. Spain 1978, Mexican Inst. of Culture 1981, Romanian Acad. 1993, Full mem. 2001, Acad. Nacional de Letras, Montevideo 1994–, Academia Peruana de la Lengua, Lima 2004–, Int. Cttee of Onomastic Studies 1969; mem. Int. Cttee of the Mediterranean Linguistic Atlas 1960; mem. Man. Junta of the Int. Asscn of Hispanists 1974–80; mem. Cttee Soc. of Romance Linguistics 1974–80, 1989–1995, hon. mem. 2003; mem. Perm. Int. Cttee of Linguists 1987–92; Prize of Romanian Acad. 1970, Prize of Mexican Acad. Centennial 1976. *Publications include:* Contribuții la fonetica istorică a limbii române (Contributions to the Historical Phonetics of the Romanian Language) 1970, Phonétique et Phonologie du Judéo-Espagnol de Bucarest 1971, Le judéo-espagnol 1976, Contributions à la phonétique historique du roumain 1976, El léxico indígena del español americano, Apreciaciones sobre su vitalidad (co-author) 1977, El español de América, (Vol. 1), Léxico (co-author) 1982, Limbile lumii. Mică enciclopedie (The Languages of the World: A Concise Encyclopaedia) (co-author), 1981, Les langues du monde (Petite Encyclopédie) (co-author) 1984, Etimologia și Limba Română (Etymology and the Romanian Language) (co-author) 1987, Vocabularul Reprezentativ Al Limbilor Romanice (The Representative Vocabulary of the Romance Languages) (co-author) 1988, Enciclopedia Limbilor Romanice (Encyclopaedia of the Romance languages) (co-author) 1989, Unité des langues romanes 1996, Limba română, limbă romanică (Romanian Language, Romance Language) 1997, Limbi în contact (Languages in Contact) 1997, Introducere în etimologia limbii române (Introduction to the Etymology of Romanian) 1999, May We Introduce the Romanian Language to You? (co-author) 1999, Du latin au roumain 2000, Limbile Europei (The Language of Europe) (jtly) 2001, Ratengo kara rumaniago he – rumania goshi 2001, Made in Spain 1 – Logos, Made in Spain 2 – Packaging 2002, Made in Spain 3 – Editorial 2002, Made in Spain 4 2003, Made in Spain 5 2003, From Latin to Romanian: The Historical Development of Romanian in a Comparative Romance Context 2005. *Leisure interests:* philately, cooking. *Address:* Institutul de Lingvistică, Calea 13 Septembrie 13, 79515 Bucharest, B.O. 42-37 (office); Aleea Bistra 1, E1, 39, Bucharest, Romania (home). *Telephone:* 3182452 (office); 3182416 (office); 7457564 (home). *Fax:* 3182417 (office). *E-mail:* inst@lingv.ro (office).

SALA-I-MARTÍN, Xavier, MA, PhD; Spanish economist and academic; *Professor of Economics, Columbia University;* b. 17 June 1963, Barcelona; ed Univ. Autònoma, Barcelona, Harvard Univ., USA; Assoc. Prof., Yale Univ., USA 1990–95; Visiting Prof., Univ. Pompeu Fabra, Barcelona 1994–2006; Prof. of Econs, Columbia Univ., USA 1996–; Visiting Prof., Harvard Univ. 2003–04; Research Assoc., Nat. Bureau of Econ. Research, Cambridge, Mass 1991–; Sr Econ. Advisor, World Econ. Forum 2002–; consultant, IMF 1993–2001, World Bank 1996–2001; Assoc. Ed. Journal of Economic Growth 1995–; Pres. Barcelona Football Club 2006, CEOs Without Borders 2006–; NSF Award 1998, King Juan Carlos I Prize for Social Sciences 1998, Kenneth Arrow Prize 1999, King Juan Carlos I Prize for Econs 2004. *Publications include:* Apuntes de Crecimiento Económico 1994, Economic Growth 1995, Economia Liberal para No Economistas y No Liberales, Converses amb Xavier Sala-i-Martin 2007; numerous articles in learned journals. *Address:* Columbia University, Department of Economics, International Affairs Building, MC 3308, 420 West 118th Street #1005, New York, NY 10027, USA (office). *Telephone:* (212) 854-7055 (office). *Fax:* (212) 854-8059 (office). *E-mail:* xs23@columbia.edu (office). *Website:* www.columbia.edu/~xs23 (office).

SALADÍN SELIN, Roberto B.; Dominican Republic diplomatist and politician; b. 23 July 1936, Santo Domingo; ed Universidad de Santo Domingo; public sector experience includes postings as Commercial Attaché, Embassy in Bonn (also Chargé d'affaires a.i.), Admin. Sec. of Perm. Del. to UNESCO, Paris, and rep. at various int. forums; has been involved in academic programmes in Germany, France, Japan and USA; Co-founder Dominican Export Promotion Center (CEDOPEX), Exec. Dir early 1980s; Sec. of State for Finance 1986–87; Gov. Cen. Bank and Pres. Monetary Bd 1987–89; presidential cand. with support of the Christian Popular Party 1990; journal columnist and frequent guest speaker on TV; fmr Producer daily programme Diario Económico 1991–96; CEO Banco de Reservas 1996–99; Amb. to USA 1999–2002, 2009–11; Alt. Exec. Dir representing the Dominican Repub. and Mexico on Bd of Dirs at IDB Bank 2004–09. *Publications include:* two books on Banco de Reservas. *Address:* c/o Secretariat of State for Foreign Affairs, Avenida Independencia 752, Estancia San Gerónimo, Santo Domingo, DN, Dominican Republic (office). *Telephone:* 987-7001 (office). *Fax:* 987-7002 (office). *E-mail:* relexteriores@serex.gob.do (office). *Website:* www.serex.gov.do (office).

SALADINO ARANDA, Irving Jahir; Panamanian athlete; b. 23 Jan. 1983, Colón; World and Olympic men's long jump Champion; Silver Medal, World Indoor

Championships, Moscow 2006 (set South American indoor record of 8.29m); won five (Oslo, Rome, Zurich, Brussel, Berlin) out of six Golden League events in same season 2006; jumped 8.56m May 2006 (South American record); jumped 8.53m (–0.2m/s wind) to win Grande Prêmio Rio Caixa de Atletismo, Rio de Janeiro 13 May 2007; Gold Medal, World Championships, Osaka 2007 (jump of 8.57m); set new personal record of 8.73m (+1.2m/s wind) during FBK-Games, Hengelo May 2008; Gold Medal, Olympic Games, Beijing 2008 (jump of 8.34m); Panama's first Olympic gold medallist. *Address:* c/o Federacion Panamena de Atletismo, Avenida Jose Agustin Arango, Estadio Rommel Fernandez, Planta Baja, Panama City, Panama.

SALAKHITDINOV, Makhmud, DSc; Uzbekistani mathematician; b. 23 Nov. 1933, Namangan, Uzbek SSR; s. of Salahiddin Shamsuddinov and Zuhra Shamsuddinova; m. Muharram Rasulova 1955; three s. one d.; ed Cen. Asian State Univ.; Asst Tashkent State Univ. 1958–59; Scientific Fellow, Chief of Section, Deputy Dir then Dir Inst. of Math. Uzbek SSR Acad. of Sciences 1959–85, Chief, Differential Equation Section 1974–, Vice-Pres. Uzbek SSR Acad. of Sciences 1984–85, Pres. 1988–94, Chair. Dept of Physical and Math. Sciences 1994–; Chief of Chair. (Jt), Tashkent State Univ. 1980–85; Minister of Higher and Secondary Specialized Educ. of Uzbek SSR 1985–88; Uzbekistan People's Deputy 1990–; Ed. papers of Uzbekistan Acad. of Sciences; Fellow, Islamic World Acad. of Sciences (IAS) 1993–; Al-Bairuni Prize1974; Honoured Scientist of Uzbek SSR; Badge of Honour 1974, Uzbek State Prize. *Publications:* more than 150 scientific papers; Mixed-Complex Type Equation 1974, Ordinary Differential Equation 1982; contribs to professional publs. *Leisure interests:* walking, reading fiction. *Address:* Uzbekistan Academy of Sciences, st. Acad. Gulyamova Yaya, 70, 700047 Tashkent, Uzbekistan (office). *Telephone:* (71) 133-14-45 (office). *Fax:* (71) 133-49-01 (office). *E-mail:* academy@uzsci.net (office). *Website:* www.academy.uz (office).

SALAKHOV, Tair Teimur ogly; Azerbaijani/Russian painter; *Vice-President, Russian Academy of Arts;* b. 29 Nov. 1928, Baku, Azerbaijan; s. of Teimur and Sona Salakhov; m. Varvara Salakhova; three d.; ed Azerbaijan Azim-zade Higher School of Fine Arts, Moscow State Inst. of Fine Arts; Docent, Prof. Azerbaijan State Inst. of Arts 1963–74, also teacher Baku Aliyev Art School; Chair. Exec. Bd Azerbaijan Union of Artists 1972–74; Head of Studio Moscow State Inst. of Fine Arts 1974–92; First Sec. Exec. Bd USSR Union of Artists 1973–91; mem. Exec. Bd USSR Acad. of Fine Arts, Sec. 1986–; author of numerous portraits, landscapes, theatre decorations; Sec. Academician for painting section Russian Acad. of Arts 1979–, Vice-Pres. Russian Acad. of Arts 1996–; mem. Acad. of Arts of Kyrghyz Repub., Azerbaijan Acad. of Arts; Corresp. mem. French Acad. of Fine Arts 1986–, San Fernando Royal Academy of Fine Arts (Spain), Real Academia San Fernando, Madrid –1998; Hon. Pres. Int. Asscn of Art, Paris, Int. Asscn of Art attached to UNESCO; Hon. mem. Austrian Soc. of Fine Arts 1975, Acad. of Fine Arts, Kazakhstan, Acad. of Fine Arts, Kyrgyzstan, Union of Artist, Germany, Montana Arts, USA; Hon. citizen Trenton, NJ, Santa Fe, NM and Billings, Mont.; Order of Istiglal of Azerbaijan 1998, Order of Za Zaslugi pered Otechestvom (3rd class) (Russia) 1998, Orders of Poland, Bulgaria, Mongolia, France; Prize of Cen. Komsomol Cttee 1959, Akhundov Prize of Azerbaijan SSR 1964, USSR State Prize 1968, State Prize of Azerbaijan 1970 (for picture New Sea), Grekov's Gold Medal 1977, Hero of Socialist Labour 1989, People's Painter of Russia 1996, Plastov Prize (Global Names category), Russia 2012. *Address:* 3 Mamedyarov lane, h.1 'Icheri Sheher', Baku, Azerbaijan (home); Russian Academy of Arts, Prechistenka str. 21, 119034 Moscow (office); Kutizovskiy pr. 18, ap.29, 121151 Moscow, Russia (home). *Telephone:* (495) 637-39-71 (home). *Fax:* (495) 637-39-71 (home). *E-mail:* adv@rah.ru (office). *Website:* www.rah.ru (office).

SALAKHOVA, Aidan; Russian artist; b. 1964, Moscow; ed Surikov Art Inst.; curator and co-dir First Gallery, Moscow 1989–92; f. Aidan Gallery, Moscow 1992; collections at Rudolf Budja Gallery, Vienna, Orel Art, Paris, XL Gallery, Moscow, D137 – The Gallery of Contemporary Art, St Petersburg. *Address:* Aidan Gallery, Winzavod, 4th Syromyatnicheskiy lane 1/6, Moscow 150120, Russian Federation (office). *Telephone:* (495) 228-1158 (office). *Fax:* (495) 228-1158 (office). *E-mail:* info@aidan-gallery.ru (office). *Website:* www.aidan-gallery.ru (office).

SALAM, Tamman Saeb, BEcons, BBA; Lebanese politician; *Prime Minister;* b. 13 May 1945, Beirut; s. of the late Saeb Salam (fmr Prime Minister of Lebanon) and Tamima Mardam Beik; m. Lama Badreddine; three c.; ed Broummana High School, Haigazian Univ., Beirut, American Univ. of Beirut, univ. in UK; f. reformist Ruwwad Al Islah movt 1974 (disbanded at outbreak of Civil War 1975); Dir Makassed Philanthropic Islamic Asscn of Beirut (non-profit educational, healthcare and social org.) 1978–, Chair. 1982–2000, now Hon. Chair.; mem. Majlis al-Nuab (Nat. Assembly) (list of Rafik Hariri) 1996–2000, (list of Saad Hariri) for Beirut Third Dist 2009–, currently ind. mem.; Minister of Culture 2008–09; apptd Pres. Council of Ministers (Prime Minister) Desig. April 2013, Pres. Council of Ministers 2014–; Chair. Saeb Salam Foundation for Culture and Higher Educ.; Légion d'honneur 1998. *Address:* Office of the President of the Council of Ministers, Grand Sérail, place Riad el-Solh, Beirut, Lebanon (office). *Telephone:* (1) 746800 (office). *Fax:* (1) 983065 (office). *E-mail:* Conseilm@pcm.gov.lb (office). *Website:* www.pcm.gov.lb (office); www.tammamsalam.net

SALAMA, Hussein Samir Abdul-Rahman, BSc, MSc, PhD, DSc; Egyptian entomologist and academic; *Research Professor Emeritus, National Research Centre;* b. 26 Jan. 1936, Gharbia; m.; two c.; ed Ain Shams Univ., Cairo Univ.; Research Asst, Entomology Research Unit, Nat. Research Centre (NRC) 1956–62, Researcher 1962–67, Assoc. Research Prof. 1967–73, Research Prof. of Entomology, NRC 1973, Vice-Pres. NRC, Pres. 1988–92, Research Prof. Emer. 1996–; fmr Vice-Pres. Research Council for Basic Sciences, Egyptian Acad. of Scientific Research and Tech., Nat. Cttee for Biological Sciences; Vice-Pres. Egyptian Inst. for Scientific Culture 1991; fmr Pres. Int. Union of Biological Sciences, now mem. Exec. Cttee; Vice-Pres. Entomological Soc. of Egypt; mem. Bd Egyptian Acad. of Sciences, African Acad. of Sciences; Post-Doctoral Fellow, Dept of Entomology, Univ. of Alberta 1963–65, Fellow, Alexander Von Humboldt Foundation, Univ. of Munich 1974–76, Islamic Acad. of Sciences 1987, African Acad. of Sciences 1990, TWAS 1991; State Prize for Biological Sciences 1973, Golden Medal of NRC 1981, Golden Medal of the Entomological Soc. of Egypt 1982, State Prize for Sciences Prize for Agricultural Sciences 1983, African Acad. of Sciences Prize for Agric. 1991, Recognition State Prize for Basic Sciences 1994 and numerous other awards. *Publications include:* 230 scientific publs and review articles. *Address:* 76 Mohyee

Abonlezz str., Dokki, Cairo, Egypt (home). *Telephone:* (2) 3377399 (home). *E-mail:* hsarsalama@hotmail.com.

SALAMATIN, Dmytro; Ukrainian/Russian politician; b. 26 April 1965, Karaganda, Kazakh SSR, USSR; ed Karaganda Polytechnic Inst., Moscow Mining Inst.; worked in Russia 1991–99; moved to Ukraine 1999; Deputy (Party of Regions) to Verkhovna Rada (Parl.) 2006–; Dir-Gen. Ukrspetsexport (state arms exporter) 2010–11; Dir-Gen. of newly created Ukroboronprom state concern 2011–12; Minister of Defence Feb.–Dec. 2012. *Address:* Party of the Regions (PR), 01021 Kyiv, vul. Lypska 10, Ukraine (office). *Telephone:* (44) 594-95-31 (office). *Fax:* (44) 594-74-30 (office). *E-mail:* webmaster@mil.gov.ua (office). *Website:* www.partyofregions.org.ua (office).

SALAMÉ, Ghassan, MPhil, PhD; Lebanese/French politician, academic and fmr UN official; *Dean, Paris School for International Affairs;* b. 18 May 1951, Kfarzebian, Mount Lebanon; m.; two d.; ed Lyons Univ. in Beirut, Saint-Joseph Univ., Beirut, Paris III Univ., Paris I Univ.; taught Political Science at Saint-Joseph Univ., Beirut, American Univ. of Beirut and Paris I Univ.; Rockefeller Fellow in Int. Relations, Brookings Inst., Washington, DC 1981, Visiting Fellow 1985–86; mem. Social Science Research Council, New York 1985–90, Co-Dir 'State, Nation and Integration in the Arab World' study program 1986–91; Minister of Culture 2000–03; Prof. of Int. Relations, Institut d'Etudes Politiques (Sciences Po), Paris 1988–; Dean, Paris School for Int. Affairs; Visiting Prof., Columbia Univ., New York, USA; Co-founder and Chair. Euro-Mediterranean Studies, European Univ. Inst., Florence, Italy; Sr Adviser to UN Sec.-Gen. 2003–06; Vice-Chair. Int. Crisis Group 2004–, Humanitarian Dialogue Center 2011–; Chevalier, Légion d'honneur 2003. *Publications:* author of ed. 12 books, including Al-mujtama' wa al-dawla fi al-mashriq al-arabi (State and Society in the Arab Levant) 1987, The Foundations of the Arab State 1987, The Politics of Arab Integration 1988, Democracy without Democrats: Politics of Liberalization in the Arab and Muslim World (ed.) 1994, Appels d'empire: ingérences et résistances à l'âge de la mondialisation (Phoenix Award, APELF Award) 1996, Quand L'Amerique refait le monde 2005, and others; articles published in several periodicals, including La Revue Française de Science Politique, Foreign Policy, The Middle East Journal, Security Dialogue. *Address:* Sciences Po, 27 rue Saint-Guillaume, 75337 Paris Cedex 07, France (office). *Telephone:* 1-45-49-72-40 (office). *Fax:* 1-42-22-40-26 (office). *E-mail:* ghassan.salame@sciences-po.fr (office). *Website:* www.sciences-po.fr (office).

SALAMEH, Riad T., BA (Econs); Lebanese central banker; *Governor, Banque du Liban;* b. 17 July 1950, Beirut; s. of Toufic Salameh and Renée Salameh; ed Jesuits' Coll. Notre Dame de Jamhour, American Univ. of Beirut; with Merrill Lynch, Beirut 1973–76, 1978–85, Paris 1976–78, Sr Vice-Pres. and Financial Counsellor, Paris 1985–93; Gov. Banque du Liban 1993–; Kt, Légion d'honneur 1997, Chevalier, Légion d'honneur 2009; Dr hc (Lebanese American Univ. of Beirut) 2009, Hon. DHumLitt (Lebanese Univ.) 2010; Arab Creativity Award in Economics, Best Arab Banker Award, Euromoney 1996, Man of the Year, Best Cen. Bank Gov., Euromoney 2003, World's Best Cen. Bank Gov., Euromoney 2006, Hon. Sash and Shield Award (Hariri Canadian Univ.) 2011, Banker Magazine Best Central Bank Governor in the Middle East 2012; ranked by Arabian Business amongst the Power 500: The World's Most Influential Arabs (40th) 2013. *Address:* Banque du Liban, Hamra, rue Masraf Loubnan, PO Box 11-5544, Beirut, Lebanon (office). *Telephone:* (1) 750000 (office). *Fax:* (1) 747600 (office). *E-mail:* bdlfx@bdl.gov.lb (office). *Website:* www.bdl.gov.lb (office).

SALAMI, Alawi Salih as-, BA; Yemeni politician; b. 21 Dec. 1945, Radaa; ed Univ. of Baghdad, Iraq; Gen. Man. Financial and Admin. Affairs, Ministry of Educ. 1970–73; fmr Chair. Ministerial Cttee for Crude Oil Marketing; Gen. Man. Budget Gen. Office 1973–75; Deputy, Budget Div. 1975–86, with rank of Vice-Minister 1986; Minister of Finance 1986–94, 1997–2001; Gov. Yemen Cen. Bank 1994–97; Deputy Prime Minister and Minister of Finance 2001–06. *Address:* c/o Ministry of Finance, POB 190 San'a, Yemen.

ŠALAMUN, Tomaž Franjo Rudolf, MA; Slovenian poet, writer and academic; b. 4 July 1941, Zagreb, Yugoslavia; m. 1st Marusa Krese 1969 (divorced 1975); m. 2nd Metka Krašovec 1979; one s. one d.; ed Univ. of Ljubljana, Univ. of Iowa, USA, Scuola Normale Superiore, Pisa, Italy, Universidad National Autónoma de México; Asst Curator Modern Gallery, Ljubljana 1968–70; Asst Prof., Acad. of Fine Arts, Ljubljana 1970–73; workshops Univ. of Tennessee at Chattanooga 1987–88, 1996; Visiting Writer, Vermont Coll. 1988, Berlin 2003–04, Bogliasco Foundation 2004; Consul, Slovenian Cultural Attaché, New York 1996–99; currently Distinguished Writer-in-Residence and Visiting Prof., Univ. of Richmond, USA 2007–09; mem. PEN, Slovenian Writers' Asscn, Slovenian Acad. of Science and Art; Mladost Prize 1969, residencies at Yaddo 1973–74, 1979, 1986, 1989, MacDowell Colony 1986, Karoly Foundation, Vence, France 1987, Maisons des écrivains étrangers, Saint-Nazaire, France 1996, Civitella Ranieri, Umbertide, Italy 1997, Bogliasco Foundation 2002, Fulbright Fellowship 1987, Jenko Prize 1988, Pushcart Prize 1994, Civitella Ranieri Fellowship 1997, Prešeren Prize 1999, Alta Marea Prize 2002, Festival Prize, Constanţa 2004, Europäische Preis für Poesie, Münster (Germany) 2007, Jenko Prize 2007, Laurel Wreath, Struga Poetry Evenings, Macedonia 2009. *Publications include:* Turbines: Twenty-One Poems 1973, Snow 1973, Pesmi (Poems) 1980, Maske (Masks) 1980, Balada za Metka Krašovec (trans. as A Ballad for Metka Krašovec) 1981, Analogije svetlobe 1982, Glas 1983, Sonet o mleku 1984, Soy realidad 1985, Ljubljanska pomlad 1986, Mera casa 1987, Ziva rana, zivi sok 1988, The Selected Poems of Tomaz Salamun 1988, Otrok in jelen 1990, Painted Desert: Poems 1991, The Shepherd, The Hunter 1992, Ambra 1994, The Four Questions of Melancholy: New and Selected Poems 1997, Crni labod 1997, Knjiga za mojega brata 1997, Homage to Hat and Uncle Guido and Eliot 1998, Morje 1999, Gozd in kelihi 2000, Feast 2000, Ballad for Metka Krašovec 2001, Table 2002, Poker 2003, Od tam 2003, Blackboards 2004, Z Arhilohom po Kikladih 2004, The Book For My Brother 2006, Woods and Chalices 2008, There's the Hand and There's the Arid Chair 2009, Levu sem zribal glavo potem sem nehal 2009, Mrzle pravljice 2010; contrib. to anthologies and periodicals. *Address:* Dalmatinova 11, 1000 Ljubljana, Slovenia (home). *Telephone:* (1) 2314522 (home). *E-mail:* metka.krasovec@siol.net (home); salamun.tomaz@gmail.com (home).

SALAS COLLANTES, Javier; Spanish association executive; *President, European Federation of Cleaning Industries (FENI/EFCI);* b. 1949; ed Faculty of Econs

Univ. of Madrid; joined Instituto Nacional de Industria 1973, apptd Chair. 1990; Chair. Iberia 1993–95; mem. Bd of Dirs Telvent; fmr Pres. Fundación Entorno; Pres. Asociación Profesional de Empresas de Limpieza (ASPEL) 2005–, European Fed. of Industrial Cleaning (FENI/EFCI) 2007–. *Leisure interest:* hill-trekking. *Address:* ASPEL, General Alvarez de Castro, 41, 1° Madrid 28010, Spain (office); European Federation of Cleaning Companies, Rue de l'Association 27, 1000 Brussels, Belgium (office). *Telephone:* (2) 225-83-30 (Brussels) (office). *Fax:* (2) 225-83-39 (Brussels) (office). *E-mail:* office@feni.be (office). *Website:* www.feni.be (office); asociados.aspel.es (office).

SALAS FALGUERAS, Margarita, PhD; Spanish biologist and academic; *Professor ad honorem, Severo Ochoa Centre for Molecular Biology, Universidad Autónoma de Madrid;* b. 30 Nov. 1938, Canero, Oviedo (Asturias); m. Dr Eladio Viñuela (died 1999); one d.; ed Univ. Complutense of Madrid; Post-doctoral work, Dept of Biochemistry, New York Univ. 1964–67; Prof. of Molecular Genetics, Complutense Univ. of Madrid 1968–92; Prof. in Research, Severo Ochoa Centre for Molecular Biology, Consejo Superior de Investigaciones Científicas-Universidad Autónoma de Madrid (CSIC-UAM), Madrid 1974–, Dir 1992–93; Pres. Spanish Inst. 1995–2003, Social Council of Oviedo Univ. 1999–2003, Fundación Severo Ochoa, Royal Bd of Nat. Library of Spain; mem. Bd Cervantes Inst. 1996–; mem. External Advisory Bd of Oviedo Univ., Inst. of Predictive and Personalized Medicine of Cancer, Barcelona, Nat. Centre of Cardiovascular Research, Madrid; mem. Spanish Acad. of Sciences 1988, Spanish Acad. of Language 2003, European Molecular Biology Org. (EMBO), Academia Europaea, Academia Scientiarum et Artium Europaea, American Acad. of Microbiology, American Acad. of Arts and Sciences; Foreign mem. NAS; Hon. Pres. Royal Acad. of Medicine of Asturias and Leon 1996–, Hon. mem. Spanish Soc. of Biochemistry and Molecular Biology 1998–; Great Cross of the Civil Order of Alfonso X el Sabio 2003; Dr ad honorem, Spanish Nat. Research Council; Dr hc (Oviedo) 1996, (Tech. Univ. of Madrid) 2000, (Extremadura) 2002, (Murcia) 2003, (Cádiz) 2004, (Univ. of Malaga) 2009, (Universidad Nacional de Educación a Distancia) 2011, (Universidad Internacional Menendez Pelayo—UIMP) 2011, (Jaén) 2012; numerous prizes and distinctions, including Severo Ochoa Prize of Research, Carlos J. Finlay of UNESCO, Rey Jaime I of Research, Mexico Prize of Science and Tech., L'Oréal-UNESCO Prize 'Women in Science', Nat. Prize of Research, Santiago Ramón y Cajal, Gold Medal of Madrid Community, Honour Medal, UIMP and Complutense Univ., Madrid, Human Values Prize, Correo Group. *Publications:* more than 400 articles in scientific journals on DNA replication and control of gene expression using the bacterial virus ø29 as a model system. *Address:* Severo Ochoa Centre for Molecular Biology, Universidad Autónoma de Madrid, Nicolás Cabrera 1, Cantoblanco, 28049 Madrid, Spain (office). *Telephone:* (91) 1964675 (office); (91) 1964402 (office). *Fax:* (91) 1964420 (office). *E-mail:* msalas@cbm.uam.es (office). *Website:* www.cbm.uam.es (office).

SALAYEV, Eldar Unis ogly, D.Phys-Math.Sc; Azerbaijani physicist and politician; b. 31 Dec. 1933, Nakhichevan City; s. of Yunis Sala oglu Salayev and Telly Tahir kizi Salayeva; m. Dilara Ashraf Guseynova; two s.; ed Azerbaijan Univ., mem. CPSU 1963–91; Jr Researcher then Deputy Dir Inst. of Physics, Azerbaijan Acad. of Sciences 1956–73, Dir 1973–83, currently Chief Scientific Worker; Corresp. mem. Acad. of Sciences of Azerbaijan 1980, mem. 1983, Pres. 1983–97, fmr Chair. Repub. Council, Presidium of Acad. of Sciences of Azerbaijan; mem. Council on co-ordination of scientific activities of Acads of Sciences, Presidium of USSR Acad. of Sciences 1985–91; Ed.-in-Chief Doklady Akademii Nauk Azerbaijana; Deputy to USSR Supreme Soviet 1985–89; USSR People's Deputy 1989–91; accused of preparing the return of Rasul Quliyev to Azerbaijan and imprisoned 2005 but released; Merited Worker of Arts of Azerbaijan. *Publications include:* Dynamics and Statistics, Non-linear Effects on Layer Crystals, Type of Selenite Gallium 1993; more than 200 scientific publs in numerous journals. *Leisure interest:* sport. *Address:* Institute of Physics, 33, H.Javid Avenue, 1143 Baku, Azerbaijan (office). *Telephone:* (12) 4326143 (office); (12) 4959310 (home). *Fax:* (12) 4325229 (office). *E-mail:* azhep@physics.ab.az (office). *Website:* www.elm.az/en/physic (office).

SALAZAR, Ken Lee, BA, JD; American lawyer, politician and government official; b. 2 March 1955, Alamosa, Colo; s. of Henry Salazar and Emma Salazar; m. Hope Salazar; two d.; ed Centauri High School, Conejos Co., St Francis Seminary, Colorado Coll., Univ. of Michigan Law School; worked as a farmer for more than 30 years, helped establish El Rancho Salazar partnership 1981; Assoc. Sherman & Howard (law firm), Denver Colo 1981–86; Chief Legal Counsel to Gov. of Colo 1986–90, apptd Exec. Dir Colo Dept of Natural Resources 1990–94; returned to pvt. law practice 1994–98; elected Colo Attorney Gen. 1999–2005; Dir Parcel, Mauro, Hultin & Spaanstra 1994–98; Senator from Colo 2005–08; US Sec. of the Interior, Washington, DC 2009–13; mem. ABA, American Judicature Soc., Hispanic Bar Asscn, Denver Bar Asscn, Colorado Bar Asscn, American Farmland Trust, Pres.'s Council; mem. Bd of Trustees Colorado Coll.; Democrat; Hon. LLD (Colorado Coll.) 1993, (Univ. of Denver) 1999; Distinguished Alumni Award, Univ. of Michigan Law School. *Address:* c/o Department of the Interior, 1849 C Street, NW, Washington, DC 20240, USA (office).

SALAZAR GÓMEZ, HE Cardinal Rubén, LicDogTheol, LicSacrTheol; Colombian ecclesiastic; *Archbishop of Bogotá;* b. 22 Sept. 1942, Bogotá; ed seminary of Ibague, Pontifical Gregorian Univ. and Pontifical Biblical Inst., Rome; ordained priest, Archdiocese of Ibagué 1967; held various positions, including pastor, seminary prof., Dir Dept of Social Pastoral of Colombian Episcopal Conf., Vicar for Pastoral Care; Bishop of Cúcuta 1992–99; Archbishop of Barranquilla 1999–2010; Archbishop of Bogotá 2010–; cr. Cardinal (Cardinal-Priest of San Gerardo Maiella) 2012; Pres. Colombian Episcopal Conf.; mem. Pontifical Comm. for Latin America 2013–, Pontifical Council for Justice and Peace 2013–. *Address:* Arzobispado, Carrera 7a N. 10-20, Bogota DC, Colombia (office). *Telephone:* (1) 350-5511 (office). *Fax:* (1) 350-7290 (office). *E-mail:* sistemas@arquidiocesisbogota.org.co (office). *Website:* www.arquidiocesisbogota.org.co (office).

SALDIVAR, John Birchman, BSc, MSc; Belizean politician; *Minister of National Security, Police and Defence;* ed Minnesota State Univ., Florida State Univ., USA; mem. House of Reps (Parl.) for Belmopan constituency 2003–; Minister of the Public Service, Governance Improvement and Elections and Boundaries 2008–12, of Nat. Security, Police and Defence 2012–; mem. United Democratic Party. *Address:* Ministry of National Security, Police and Defence,

Curl Thompson Bldg, Belmopan, Belize (office). *Telephone:* 822-2817 (office). *Fax:* 822-2195 (office). *E-mail:* minofnatsec@mns.gov.bz (office).

SALEEM, Ahmed; Maldivian diplomatist and international organization official; *Secretary-General, South Asian Association for Regional Cooperation;* b. 26 May 1949, Malé; m. Ayesha Saleem; four c.; ed in the Maldives and India; joined Foreign Service 1968, held several positions including Chief of Protocol and Head of Multilateral Div., served at High Comm. in Sri Lanka and Perm. Mission to UN, New York; with Ministry of Finance 1977, served as Alt. Gov. to World Bank, IDA, Asian Devt Bank; apptd Dir SAARC Secr. 1990, Sec.-Gen. SAARC 2012–; mem. Human Rights Comm. of the Maldives 2003–10 (Pres. 2006–10); fmr mem. Maldivian Democratic Party. *Publications:* numerous articles on human rights, int. affairs and regionalism. *Address:* South Asian Association for Regional Cooperation, PO Box 4222, Tridevi Marg, Kathmandu, Nepal (office). *Telephone:* (1) 4221785 (office). *Fax:* (1) 4227033 (office). *E-mail:* saarc@saarc-sec.org (office). *Website:* www.saarc-sec.org (office).

SALEH, Field Marshall Ali Abdullah; Yemeni army officer and fmr head of state; b. 21 March 1942, Beit al-Ahmer, Sanhan Dist; m.; several c.; entered mil. service 1958; participated in 1974 coup; Mil. Gov., Taiz Prov. until June 1978; mem. Provisional Presidential Council, Deputy C-in-C of Armed Forces June–July 1978; Pres. of Yemen Arab Repub. 1978–90, Pres. Presidential Council of Repub. of Yemen 1990–94, of Repub. of Yemen 1994–2012; C-in-C of Armed Forces 1978–90; Sec.-Gen. People's Gen. Congress 1982; rank of Marshal 1997; Hon. M.Mil.Sc.; Nat. Republican Award. *Address:* c/o Office of the President, San'a, Republic of Yemen (office). *Fax:* (1) 274147 (office). *Website:* www.presidentsaleh.ye.

SALEH, Ali Bin Saleh al-, BCom; Bahraini business executive and government official; *Chairman, Shura Consultative Council;* b. 28 Dec. 1942; s. of Saleh Al Saleh; m. Afaf Radhi Salman Almousawi 1970; one s. two d.; ed Ain Shams Univ., Egypt; mem. Founding Council 1973, Nat. Ass. 1973–75; Deputy Chair. Bahrain Chamber of Commerce and Industry 1975–93; Deputy Chair. Shura (Consultative Council) 1993–95, Chair. 2006–; Minister of Commerce 1995–2006; Chair. Bahrain Promotions and Marketing Bd 1995–2000, Bahrain Convention and Exhbn Bureau, Bahrain Stock Exchange; mem. Bd of Trustees Univ. of Bahrain 1985–95, Bahrain Centre for Studies and Research, Econ. Devt Bd. *Leisure interests:* reading, music, travel. *Address:* Office of the Chairman, Shura Council, PO Box 2991, Manama, Bahrain (office). *Telephone:* 17748888 (office). *E-mail:* info@shura.bh (office). *Website:* www.shura.bh (office).

SALEH, Amrullah; Afghan government official; b. 1972, Panjshir Prov.; ed high school educ., Afghanistan; served as trans. between CIA officers and Northern Alliance leader Ahmad Shah Massoud 2001, helped remove Taliban from power with support of US-led coalition late 2001; fmr Chief Liaison Officer with foreign mil. and diplomatic corps, Kabul; fmr political officer, spokesman and relief co-ordinator; fmr Deputy Chief of Afghanistan Intelligence, focused on foreign relations; Sr mem. Nat. Security Directorate, Head of Directorate 2004–10; Hon. DSc (Cleary Univ., Mich.) 2005. *Address:* c/o National Security Directorate, Kabul, Afghanistan. *E-mail:* ahmad.afg@gmail.com.

SALEH, Maj.-Gen. Bakri Hassan; Sudanese military officer and government official; *First Vice- President;* Mil. Officer, Revolutionary Command Council for Nat. Salvation (RCC–NS) 1989–; Chief of Security Forces 1997; Minister of Presidential Affairs 2001; fmr Minister of Nat. Defence; fmr Minister of the Presidency; First Vice-Pres. 2013–; mem. Nat. Congress. *Address:* c/o National Congress, Khartoum, Sudan (office).

SALEH, Bushra Hussein; Iraqi politician; *Minister without Portfolio;* Deputy from Fadhila (small Shiite fundamentalist party belonging to Nat. Alliance grouping of Shiite parties); Minister without Portfolio 2010–; participant in Iraq Foundation's Post Election Democracy Project. *Address:* Office of the Prime Minister, Baghdad, Iraq (office).

SALEH, Jaime Mercelino; Dutch government official, chief justice and university professor; *Minister of State, Netherlands Antilles;* b. 20 April 1941, Bonaire; m. Marguerite Marie Halabi; two s. two d.; ed State Univ. of Utrecht; Deputy Public Prosecutor, Netherlands 1967–68, Curaçao 1968–74; attorney-at-law, Curaçao 1971–74; Deputy mem. High Court of the Netherlands Antilles 1974–76; Justice 1976–79; Chief Justice High Court of Justice of the Netherlands Antilles and Aruba 1979–90, Vice-Pres. Dutch Navy Mil. Court for the Netherlands Antilles 1978–79, Pres. Dutch Navy Mil. Court for the Netherlands Antilles and Aruba 1979–90; Gov.-Gen. of Netherlands Antilles 1990–2002; Minister of State 2004–; Prof., Univ. of Utrecht 2005–; Order of Merit of Corps Consulaire 1989; Order of Libertador en el grado de Gran Cordón, Venezuela 1996; Order of Knighthood of the Dutch Lion; Commdr, Order of Orange Nassau 2002; Royal Medal 1980, Almirate Luis Brion Naval Medal 1994, Dutch ICN Dales Award for Integrity 2004, Dutch Lawyers Asscn Award 2008. *Publications:* various works on law and politics, with particular reference to the Netherlands Antilles. *Address:* B7 Villapark Zuurzak, Willemstad, Curaçao, Netherlands Antilles (home). *Telephone:* (9) 7382800 (home). *Fax:* (9) 7382801 (home). *E-mail:* jaime.saleh@gmail.com (home).

SALEH ABBAS, Youssouf, LLM; Chadian politician; b. 1953, Abéché, Ouaddai Region; Head, Multilateral Co-operation Div. and Dir of Int. Co-operation, Ministry of Foreign Affairs 1979–81; Diplomatic Adviser to Pres. 1981; Dir Cabinet of Head of State 1981–82; Adviser to Dir-Gen., Ministry of Foreign Affairs 1992–96; Vice-Pres. Sovereign Nat. Conf. Jan.–April 1993; Dir-Gen. Ministry of Planning and Co-operation 1996–97; mem. Movt for Democracy and Justice in Chad 1998–2001; Special Rep. to UN and EUFOR (peacekeepng force) 2007–08; Adviser to Pres. on Int. Relations and Co-operation 2006–08; Prime Minister 2008–10 (resgnd). *Address:* c/o Office of the Prime Minister, BP 463, N'Djamena, Chad (office).

SALEHI, Ali Akbar, BSc, PhD; Iranian physicist, international organization official and government official; *Head, Atomic Energy Organization of Iran;* b. 24 March 1949, Karbala, Iraq; m. Zahra Rad; ed American Univ. of Beirut, Lebanon, Massachusetts Inst. of Tech., USA; fmr Full Prof., Sharif Univ. of Tech., Tehran, Chancellor 1982–85, 1989–93; Iranian Rep. to IAEA 1998–2003; Scientific Adviser to Ministry of Foreign Affairs 2004; Deputy Sec.-Gen. Org. of the Islamic Conf. 2007–09; Head, Atomic Energy Org. of Iran 2009–10, 2013–; Minister of Foreign

Affairs 2011–13; mem. Acad. of Sciences of Iran, Int. Centre for Theoretical Physics, Italy. *Publications:* more than 20 scientific publs. *Address:* Atomic Energy Organization, Amir Abad, Tehran, Iran (office). *Telephone:* 88221203 (office). *Fax:* 88221209 (office). *E-mail:* head_office@aeoi.org.ir (office). *Website:* www.aeoi.org.ir (office).

SALEM, Elie Adib, PhD; Lebanese politician, academic and university administrator; *President, University of Balamand;* b. 5 March 1930, Bterram Kurah; s. of Adib Salem and Lamia Salem (née Malik); m. Phyllis Sell (died 2001); two s. two d.; ed American Univ. of Beirut, Univ. of Cincinnati, USA, Johns Hopkins Univ., USA; Instructor in Public Admin, American Univ. of Beirut 1954–56, Assoc. Prof. of Political Studies and Public Admin 1962–68, Asst Dean of Arts and Sciences 1966–68, Chair. Middle East Area Program and Prof. of Political Studies and Public Admin 1969–74, Chair. Dept of Political Studies and Public Admin 1972–74, Dean of Arts and Sciences 1974–82; Asst Prof. of Middle East Politics, School of Advanced Int. Studies, Johns Hopkins Univ. 1956–62; Visiting Prof., Dept of Govt and Research Scholar Int. Devt Research Centre, Int. Univ. 1968–69; Deputy Prime Minister and Minister of Foreign Affairs 1982–84; Adviser to Pres. on Foreign Affairs 1984–88; Founder and fmr Pres. Lebanese Centre of Policy Studies; Pres. Univ. of Balamand 1993–. *Publications include:* The Arab Public Administrative Conference 1954, Political Theory and Institutions of the Khawarij 1956, Modernization without Revolution: Lebanon's Experience 1973, 'Rusum Dar al-Khilafah al Abbasiyah' manuscript by Hlal al Sab' (trans.) 1977, Violence and Diplomacy in Lebanon 1982–88 1994, My American Bride: A Tale of Love and War 2008; articles in professional journals. *Leisure interests:* tennis, swimming, table tennis. *Address:* Université de Balamand, PO Box 100, Tripoli, Lebanon (office). *Telephone:* (6) 930250, ext. 103 (office). *Fax:* (6) 930278 (office). *E-mail:* president@balamand.edu.lb (office). *Website:* www.balamand.edu.lb (office).

SALERNO, F. Robert; American car rental industry executive; *Vice-Chairman, Avis Budget Group, Inc.;* b. Springfield, Mass; m.; one d.; ed Marquette Univ.; Vice-Pres., Eastern Region and Zone Devt, Avis Rent-a-Car 1982–87, Vice-Pres. Field Operations 1987–90, Sr Vice-Pres. and Gen. Man. 1990–95, Exec. Vice-Pres. of Operations 1995–96, Pres. and COO 1996–2002, Pres. and COO Cendant Car Rental 2002–03, CEO Cendant Vehicle Rental Services Div. 2003–05, Pres. and COO Avis Budget Group Inc. (cr. after Cendant separated into four units) 2005–10, Vice-Chair. 2010–, currently also mem. Bd of Dirs. *Address:* Avis Budget Group Inc., 6 Sylvan Way, Parsippany, NJ 07054, USA (office). *Telephone:* (973) 496-3500 (office). *Fax:* (888) 304-2315 (office). *Website:* www.avisbudgetgroup.com (office).

SALES, Wayne C.; American business executive; b. 28 Dec. 1949; served in several sr marketing, merchandising and store operations leadership positions with US div. of Kmart Corpn until 1991; joined Canadian Tire Corpn Ltd 1991, Pres. and CEO 2000–06, Vice-Chair. 2006–10; Dir (non-exec.) Supervalu Inc. 2006–12, Exec. Dir 2012–, Chair. (non-exec.) 2010–12, Exec. Chair., Pres. and CEO 2012–13; Dir and Chair. Compensation Cttee Tim Hortons Inc.; Dir, Axiall Corpn (fmrly Georgia Gulf Corpn) 2007–12, Discovery Air Inc. 2008–12; Chair, Communications and Media, for the United Way of Greater Toronto's 2002 campaign; several awards, including Distinguished Retailer of the Year, Retail Council of Canada 2004, CEO of the Year, Canadian Business Magazine 2005, also inducted into Canadian Marketing Hall of Legends 2009. *Address:* Supervalu Inc., East View Innovation Center, 7075 Flying Cloud Drive, Eden Prairie, MN 55344, USA (office). *Telephone:* (952) 828-4000 (office). *Fax:* (952) 828-8998 (office). *E-mail:* info@supervalu.com (office). *Website:* www.supervalu.com (office).

SALGADO, Sebastião Ribeiro, Jr, PhD; Brazilian photographer; b. 8 Feb. 1944, Aimorés, Minas Gerais; m. Lélia Deluiz Wanick 1967; two s.; ed São Paulo Univ., Vanderbilt Univ., USA, Univ. of Paris; with Brazilian Ministry of Finance 1968–69; with Investment Dept, Int. Coffee Org., London 1971–73; photo-reporter, working in Europe, Africa (particularly covering drought in Sahel) and Latin America 1973–, with Sygma News Agency of Paris 1974, with Gamma Agency 1975–79, mem. Magnum Photos 1979–; UNICEF Goodwill Amb. 2001; collections at Musée de l'Elysée, Lausanne, Switzerland, Nat. Museum of Modern Art, Japan, Tokyo Metropolitan Museum of Photography, Japan, Ville du Port, Ile de la Réunion, France, Glasgow Arts Centre, Scotland, Fundação Cultural de Curitiba, Brazil, Bibliothèque Nationale de France, France, Maison Européenne de la Photographie, France, Museum für Moderne Kunst, Germany, Australian Nat. Gallery, Australia, San Francisco Museum of Modern Art, USA, New York Museum of Modern Art, USA, Chicago Art Inst., USA, Minneapolis Museum of Art, USA Museum of Photographic Arts, USA, Smithsonian Inst., Washington, DC, USA, Los Angeles County Museum of Art, USA, Deutsche Börse, Germany, Museu Historico Abilio Barreto, Belo Horizonte, Brazil, J. Paul Getty Museum, USA, Centre Pompidou, France; Hon. mem. American Acad. of Arts and Sciences, Hon. Fellow, Royal Photographic Soc. of Great Britain, England; Commdr, Order of Rio Branco 2004; Dr hc (Univ. of Evora, Portugal) 2001, Univ. of Nottingham) 2002, Hon. DFA (New School Univ., New York) 2001, (Lesley Univ., Boston) 2001; Eugene Smith Award 1982, Oskar Barnack Prize, World Press Photo Award 1985, Photojournalist of the Year Award, Int. Centre of Photography, New York 1986, 1988, Photographer of the Year Award, American Soc. of Magazine Photographers 1987, Olivier Rebbot Award, Overseas Press Club, New York 1987, King of Spain Award 1988, Erich Salomon Award, Germany 1988, Erna and Victor Hasselblad Award, Sweden 1989, Centenary MedalAward, Royal Photographic Soc. of Great Britain, England 1994, Award of Excellence, Soc. of Newspaper Design, USA, Silver Medal, Art Directors Club, USA 1995, Germany 1995, 1998, Prêmio Nacional de Fotografia, Brazil 1997, Principe de Asturias Award for Arts, Spain 1998, UNESCO Prize for Culture in Brazil 1999, Presidenza della Repubblica Italiana Medal, Int. Research Centre, Italy 2000, Int. Award, Photographic Soc. of Japan 2003, Gold Medal Award for Photography, Nat. Arts Club, New York 2005, Faz Diferença Prize, Rio de Janeiro, Brazil 2008, Excellence in Reporting of Social Issues Award, American Sociological Asscn, USA 2010, NANPA Lifetime Achievement Award, North American Nature Photography Asscn, USA, Save the Children Int. Prize, Spain 2010, Gold Medal of Honour 2010, Al-Thani Award for Photography, Qatar 2010. *Publications include:* several books of photographs and exhbn catalogues, including Autres Amériques (Prix de la Ville de Paris et Kodak) 1986, Sahel: L'Homme en Détresse (Prix du Livre) 1986, Les Cheminots 1988, Sahel: El Fin del Camino 1988, Workers: An Archaeology of the Industrial Age (World Hunger Year Harry Chapin Media Award) 1993, Terra: Luta dos Sem-

Terra (Prêmio Jabuti) 1997, Exodus 2000, O Fím do Pálio 2003, Um Incerto Estado de Graça 2004, O Berço da Desigualdade 2005, Africa 2007. *Address:* c/o Amazonas Images, 93 Quai de Valmy, 75010 Paris, France (office). *Telephone:* 1-42-09-90-68 (office). *Fax:* 1-42-09-76-64 (office). *E-mail:* amazonas@amazonasimages.fr (office). *Website:* www.amazonasimages.com (office).

SALGADO MÉNDEZ, Elena, MA; Spanish politician, industrial engineer, economist and telecommunications executive; b. 12 May 1949, Ourense; ed Universidad Politécnica de Madrid, Escuela Organización Industrial, Universidad Complutense de Madrid; industrial engineer, Universidad Politécnica de Madrid 1972; with Econs Dept, School of Industrial Org. 1976–82; Dir Dept of Studies, Inst. for Small and Medium-sized Businesses, Ministry of Industry 1982–84; Dir-Gen. for Personnel Expenditure and Public Pensions, Ministry of Economy and Finance 1985–91; Sec.-Gen. for Communications, Supervision of Postal and Telecommunication Policy, Ministry of Public Works 1991–96; Dir of Strategic Consulting Services, Lenci Consulting SL 1997–2002; Exec. Dir Vallehermoso Telecom 2002–03; apptd Pres. Nueva Información Telefónica 2003; Minister of Health and Consumer Affairs 2004–07, of Public Admin 2007–09; Second Vice-Pres. and Minister of Economy and Finance 2009–11; mem. Congreso de los Diputados for Cantabria Prov. 2008–; Pres. Bd of Dirs Hispasat SA, Correos y Telégrafos; mem. Bd of Dirs Abertis Telecom 2004, Telefónica SA, Caja Postal, Hunosa, RENFE, Trasmediterranea, Nat. Mint; mem. Advisory Council, Arthur Andersen 1999–2000, Social Council, Universidad Politécnica de Madrid 1999–2002; Gran Cruz de la Orden del Mérito Civil 1987, Gran Cruz de la Orden de Mérito Militar con distintivo blanco 1996. *Leisure interest:* cinema. *Address:* c/o Ministry of the Economy and Finance, Alcalá 9, 28014 Madrid, Spain.

SALGADO TAMAYO, Wilma, PhD; Ecuadorean economist and government official; b. 20 Oct. 1952, Pifo; ed Liceo Municipal Fernández Madrid, Univ. Católica del Ecuador, Univ. of Paris, Sorbonne, Univ. Nacional Autónoma, Mexico; Researcher, Univ. Católica del Ecuador 1973–74; Researcher and Dir Econ. Forecasting, Banco Central del Ecuador 1986–91; Econ. Adviser to Pres. 1991; Researcher, Centro Andino de Acción Popular 1993; Prof., Univ. Andina Simón Bolívar 1994–2002; Consultant to WFP 1999–2001; Gen. Man. Agencia de Garantía de Depósitos 2003–04; mem. Andean Parl. 2007–; Minister of Economy and Finance July–Sept. 2008 (resgnd). *Address:* General Secretariat, Andean Parliament, Avenida Caracas No. 70A–61, Bogotá, Colombia (office). *Telephone:* (1) 326-6000 (office). *Fax:* (1) 348-2805 (office). *E-mail:* correo@parlamentoandino.org (office). *Website:* www.parlamentoandino.org (office).

SALGUERO CARRILLO, Elizabeth Cristina; Bolivian politician; *Minister of Culture;* b. 1964, Argentina; co-f. RED ADA (women's political group) 1994; fmr Coordinator, Nat. Women's Network for Equity and Equality (Amupei); Dir Crónica Azul (magazine) 1996–2000; fmr columnist, La Razón (newspaper), La Paz, Bolpress (news agency), Alternative Women's Communication Network (Fempress); mem. Cámara de Diputados (Parl.) 2005–, mem. Int. Relations Cttee, Vice-Pres. Social Policy and Human Rights Comm. 2009; mem. Asamblea Legislativa Plurinacional 2010–; unsuccessful cand. for Mayor of La Paz 2010; Minister of Culture 2011–; fmr Pres. Unión Interparlamentaria-Bolivia; mem. Movimiento al Socialismo-Instrumento Político por la Soberanía de los Pueblos. *Address:* Ministry of Culture, Palacio Chico, Calle Ayacucho, esq. Potosí, Casilla 7846, La Paz, Bolivia (office). *Telephone:* (2) 220-0910 (office). *Fax:* (2) 220-2628 (office). *E-mail:* despacho@minculturas.gob.bo (office). *Website:* www.minculturas.gob.bo (office).

SALIH, Barham, BE; Iraqi politician; *Prime Minister, Kurdistan Regional Government;* b. 12 Sept. 1960, Kurdistan; m. Sarbagh Salih; one s. one d.; ed Univ. of Cardiff, Univ. of Liverpool, UK; joined Patriotic Union Kurdistan (PUK) 1976, served as spokesman in London, UK; Rep. to US, Patriotic Union Kurdistan and Kurdistan Regional Govt 1991–2001; Regional Admin. Sulaimaniya; Deputy Prime Minister for Nat. Security Affairs 2004–05, 2006–09; Minister of Planning and Devt Co-operation 2005–06; Prime Minister, Kurdistan Regional Govt 2009–. *Address:* Office of the Prime Minister, Kurdistan Regional Government, Council of Ministers Building, Erbil, Iraq (office). *Website:* www.krg.org (office).

SALIH, Khaled, BA, MA, PhD; Iraqi academic and government official; *Senior Adviser to Prime Minister, Kurdistan Regional Government;* b. 16 Feb. 1957, Sulaimania, Kurdistan; ed Gothenburg Univ., Sweden; fmr Lecturer in Int. and Middle E Politics, Dept of Political Science, Gothenburg Univ. 1989–97; Sr Lecturer, Univ. of Linköping, Sweden 1997–98; Assoc. Prof. in Middle E Politics, Centre for Contemporary Middle E Studies, Univ. of Southern Denmark, Odense 1998–; mem. Kurdistan Int. Constitutional Advisory Team 2003, also served as political adviser to Kurdistan Regional Govt and Kurdistan Nat. Ass.; apptd Official Spokesperson for Kurdistan Regional Govt 2006; currently Sr Adviser to Prime Minister and Minister of Natural Resources, Kurdistan Regional Govt; fmr Advisory Ed. Democratiya (journal). *Publications include:* State-Making, Nation-Building and the Military: Iraq, 1941-1958 1996, The Future of Kurdistan in Iraq (co-ed.) 2005. *Address:* Kurdistan Regional Government, Council of Ministers Building, Erbil, Iraq (office). *Website:* www.krg.org (office).

SALIH, Muhammad; Uzbekistani writer, poet and politician; *Chairman, Freedom Democratic Party of Uzbekistan (O'zbekiston Erk Demokratik Partiyasi);* b. 20 Dec. 1949, Xorazm; m.; five c.; ed Tashkent State Univ., Moscow High Literary Inst., Russian SFSR; mil. service in army 1968–70; worked as screenwriter in 1980s; wrote letter to Politburo protesting at political situation in Uzbekistan 1984; work published in Soviet newspapers 1985–86; elected Chair. Union of Writers of Uzbekistan 1988; co-f. Birlik (Unity People's Movt) 1988; f. Freedom Democratic Party of Uzbekistan (ERK) 1990, currently Chair.; Deputy, Oliy Majlis (Supreme Ass.—Parl.) 1990–92 (resgnd); presidential cand. 1991; f. Democratic Forum 1992; refused offer of Deputy Prime Minister role in return for dissolution of Democratic Forum 1992, arrested and jailed for three days, and subsequently put under house arrest, left Uzbekistan to continue political activity abroad 1992; received sentence in absentia of $15\frac{1}{2}$ years 1999; flew to Prague by from Amsterdam at invitation of Radio Free Europe Nov. 2001, arrested by Czech police and Interpol at Ruzyně Airport under int. arrest warrant issued by Uzbekistan Interpol bureau alleging his participation in terrorist activities; currently living in exile in Norway with political asylum status; f. Nat. Salvation Cttee 2005; arrested and detained by the Swedish police at Stockholm-Arlanda

Airport under same int. arrest warrant May 2006, released the next day after Norwegian Govt confirmed his asylum status. *Publications:* The Golden Head of the Avenger (screenplay), more than 20 books, including: Oydinlik sari 1993, E'tikodning chorrahasi bolmaydi 1994, Ikror 1995, Devlet sirlari (in Turkish) 1997, Turkistan suuru (in Turkish) 1997, Agaclar sair olsa (in Turkish) 1997, Yolnoma (in Uzbek) 1999, Yo'lnoma (in Turkish) 2002, The Articles 2003, Valfajr, Ko'men nashriyoti, Konya 2005, Publisistika, Izdatelstvo Bilgeoguz 2005. *Address:* c/o Freedom Democratic Party of Uzbekistan (O'zbekiston Erk Demokratik Partiyasi), 100055 Tashkent, Ipakchi ko'ch. 38, Uzbekistan (office). *Telephone:* (216) 4152887 (Turkey, mobile). *E-mail:* m.salih@uzbekistanerk.com (office). *Website:* www.uzbekistanerk.com (office); muhammadsalih.com.

SALIH MUHAMMAD, Osman, BSc; Eritrean politician; *Minister of Foreign Affairs;* b. 1948; ed Haile Selassie I Univ. (Addis Ababa Univ.), Ethiopia; Head, Eritrean People's Liberation Front refugee schools, Sudan 1983–87; Head, Educ. Dept 1987; Commr for Eritrean Refugees' Affairs 1987–92; mem. Nat. Ass. 1993–; Minister of Educ. 1993–2007, of Foreign Affairs 2007–; mem. People's Front for Democracy and Justice (PFDJ), mem. Exec. Bd 1993–, mem. Cen. Ass. 1993–. *Address:* Ministry of Foreign Affairs, PO Box 190, Asmara, Eritrea (office). *Telephone:* (1) 127838 (office). *Fax:* (1) 123788 (office). *E-mail:* tesfai@wg.eol (office).

SALIJ, Rev. Jacek, MA, PhD; Polish ecclesiastic and professor of theology; *Director, Chair of Dogmatic Theology, Cardinal Stefan Wyszyński University;* b. 19 Aug. 1942, Budy; ed Acad. of Catholic Theology, Warsaw; ordained priest 1966; Asst Acad. of Catholic Theology (now Cardinal Stefan Wyszyński Univ.), Warsaw 1970–71, Asst Prof. 1971–90, Extraordinary Prof. 1990–99, Ordinary Prof. 2000–, currently Dir of the Chair of Dogmatic Theology; Co-Founder Gaudium Vitae Movt 1979–; mem. Council of Educ. attached to the Pres. of Poland 1992–95, Main Council of Higher Educ. 1993–96; consultant to Educ. of Faith Comm. of Episcopate of Poland 1997–; mem. Polish Soc. of Philosophy 1982–, PEN Club 1989–, Cttee for Theological Studies, Polska Akademia Nauk; Order of Polonia Restituta 2007; FENIKS Award 2004. *Publications include:* Modlitwa za świętych w liturgii rzymskiej 1974, Królestwo Boże w was jest 1980, Legendy dominikańskie (composition and translation) 1982, Rozpacz pokonana 1983, Rozmowy ze św. Augustynem 1985, Pytania nieobojętne 1986, Dekalog 1989, Wiara na co dzień 1994, Nadzieja poddawana próbom 1995, Nasze czasy są OK. 1997, Praca nad wiarą 1999, Divinations, Astrology, Reincarnation (in Russian). *Leisure interest:* cycling. *Address:* Cardinal Stefan Wyszyński University, ul. Dewajtis 5, 01-815 Warsaw, Poland (office). *Telephone:* (22) 5618 00 (office). *Website:* www.uksw.edu.pl (office).

SALIKHOV, Shavkat Ismailovich; Uzbekistani biochemist; *President, Uzbek Academy of Sciences;* fmr Dir Sadykov Inst. of Bioorganic Chemistry; fmr CHAP/Uzbekistan Program Man.; Pres. Uzbek Acad. of Sciences 2006–. *Address:* Uzbek Academy of Sciences, 70 Acad. Gulyamov street, 100047 Tashkent, Uzbekistan (office). *Telephone:* (71) 136-76-29 (office). *Fax:* (71) 133-49-01 (office). *Website:* www.uzsci.net/academy (office).

SALIM, Anthoni; Indonesian business executive; *President and CEO, Salim Group;* m.; three c.; ed Ewell County Technical Coll., UK; currently Pres. and CEO Salim Group (family business conglomerate); Propr, Universal Integrated Corpn Consumer Products Pte Ltd; CEO PT Indofood Sukses Makmur Tbk PT 2004–; Dir First Pacific Co. Ltd 1981–, Chair. (non-exec.); Pres. Commr and Commr Fastfood Indonesia PT; Dir (non-exec.) Futuris Corpn Ltd 2003–; Dir Elders Australia Ltd; fmr Pres. Commr and Commr PT Indomobil Sukses Internasional TBK; mem. Int. Advisory Bd and Jt Advisory Council Allianz AG; mem. Advisory Bd Rabobank (Netherlands); fmr mem. Int. Advisory Bd GE International; mem. Asia Business Council 2004–. *Address:* Office of the President, Salim Group, Sudirman Plaza, Indofood Tower, Jawa Barat, Jakarta 12910, Indonesia (office). *Telephone:* (21) 57958822 (office). *Fax:* (21) 57935960 (office).

SALIM, Salim Ahmed; Tanzanian journalist and diplomatist; *Chairman, Board of Trustees, Mwalimu Nyerere Foundation;* b. 23 Jan. 1942, Pemba Island, Zanzibar; m. Amne Salim; two s. one d.; ed Lumumba Coll., Zanzibar, Univ. of Delhi, India, and Columbia Univ., USA; Publicity Sec., UMMA Party and Chief Ed. of Sauti ya UMMA 1963; Exec. Sec., United Front of Opposition Parties and Chief Ed. of its newspaper; Sec. Gen. All-Zanzibar Journalists Union 1963; Amb. to UAR 1964–65, High Commr to India 1965–68, Dir African and Middle East Affairs Div., Ministry of Foreign Affairs 1968–69, Amb. to China and Democratic People's Repub. of Korea June–Dec. 1969, Perm. Rep. to UN, New York 1970–80 (Pres. of Gen. Ass. 1979, Chair. UN Security Council Cttee on Sanctions against Rhodesia Jan.–Dec. 1975, Chair. UN Special Cttee on Decolonization 1972–80), also High Commr to Jamaica, accred to Guyana, Trinidad and Tobago, Barbados and Amb. to Cuba 1971–80, Minister of Foreign Affairs 1980–84; Prime Minister of Tanzania 1984–85, Deputy Prime Minister, Minister of Defence and Nat. Service 1986–89; Sec.-Gen. OAU 1989–2001; mem. Bd of Dirs South Centre (inter-governmental body) 2002–05; Chair. Bd of Trustees, Mwalimu Nyerere Foundation 2002–; African Union Special Envoy for Darfur Talks and Chief Mediator for the Inter-Sudanese Peace Talks on the Darfur Conflict 2004–08; Hon. LLD (Univ. of Philippines) 1980, Hon. DH (Univ. of Maiduguri, Nigeria) 1983, Hon. DCL (Univ. of Mauritius) 1991, Hon. Dr of Arts (Univ. of Khartoum, Sudan) 1995, Hon. PhD (Univ. of Bologna, Italy) 1996, Hon. DJur (Univ. of Cape Town) 1998; Order of the United Republic of Tanzania 1985, Order of Mille Collines, Rwanda 1993, Grande Croix de l'Ordre Congolais du Dévouement, Republic of Congo 1994, Grand Officier de l'Ordre du Mérite, Central African Republic 1994, Grand Officier de l'Ordre National du Lion, Senegal 2000, Order of the Two Niles, Sudan 2001, Ordre El-Athir, Algeria 2001, Ordre du Mono, Togo 2001, Commandant de l'Ordre Nat., Mali 2001; Star of Africa, Liberia 1980, Medal of Africa, Libya 1999. *Address:* Mwalimu Nyerere Foundation, 6 Sokoine Drive, POB 71000, Dar es Salaam, Tanzania (office). *Telephone:* (22) 2118354 (office). *Fax:* (22) 2119216 (office). *E-mail:* mnf-tanzania@raha.com (office). *Website:* www.nyererefoundation.org (office).

SALINAS DE GORTARI, Carlos, PhD; Mexican economist, academic, government official and fmr head of state; b. 1948, Mexico City; m.; six c.; ed Nat. Univ. of Mexico and Harvard Univ., USA; Asst Prof. of Statistics, Nat. Univ. of Mexico 1970; Research Asst, Harvard Univ. 1974; taught Public Finance and Fiscal Policy

in Mexico 1976, 1978; Asst Dir of Public Finance, Ministry of Finance 1971–74, Head of Econ. Studies 1974–76, Asst Dir of Financial Planning 1978, Dir-Gen. 1978–79; Dir-Gen. of Econ. and Social Policy, Ministry of Programming and Budget 1979–81; Dir-Gen. Inst. of Political, Social and Econ. Studies 1981–82; Minister of Planning and Fed. Budget 1982–87; named as pres. cand. by Partido Revolucionario Institucional 1987, Pres. of Mexico 1988–94. *Publications include:* Mexico: The Policy and the Politics of Modernization 2002; numerous articles and essays. *Address:* c/o Partido Revolucionario Institucional (PRI), Edif. 2, Insurgentes Norte 59, Col. Buenavista, Del. Cuauhtémoc, 06359 México, DF, Mexico.

SALINAS PLIEGO, Ricardo B., BA, MBA; Mexican business executive; *Chairman and President, Grupo Elektra SA de CV;* b. 1955; m. María Laura Medina; three c.; ed Instituto Tecnológico y de Estudios Superiores de Monterrey, Tulane Univ., USA; fmrly with Arthur Andersen, Brinkman Co.; joined Grupo Elektra Sa de CV 1981, Pres. 1989–, Chair. 1993–, business interests in retail, broadcasting, telecommunications and financial services, including TV Azteca, Banco Azteca, Elektra, Iusacell, Unefon; Chair. Exec. Cttee Grupo Salinas 1999–; est. Empresario Azteca Program, Empresario Azteca Asscn; f. Fundación Azteca 1997; mem. Business Advisory Bd International Organization for Migration. *Address:* Grupo Elektra, SA de CV, Avenida Insurgentes Sur 3579, Colonia, Tlalpán La Joya, 14400 México DF, Mexico (office). *Telephone:* (55) 1720-7000 (office). *Fax:* (55) 1720-7822 (office). *Website:* www.grupoelektra.com.mx (office); www.ricardosalinas.com.

SALISBURY, David Murray, MA; British financial services industry executive; *Chairman, Dimensional Fund Advisors Ltd;* b. 18 Feb. 1952; s. of Norman Salisbury and Isobel Sutherland Murray; m. Lynneth Mary Jones 1977; two d.; ed Harrow School, Trinity Coll., Oxford; joined J. Henry Schroder Wagg & Co. Ltd 1974, Chief Exec. Schroder Capital Man. Int. Inc. 1986–2001, Jt Chief Exec. Schroder Investment Man. Ltd 1995–97, Chair. 1997–2001, CEO Schroders PLC 2000–01; mem. Bd of Dirs Dimensional Fund Advisors Inc. 1988–96, CEO Dimensional Fund Advisors Ltd 2002–09, Chair. 2002–; Gov. Harrow School 1996–99, 2001–06. *Leisure interests:* tennis, skiing. *Address:* Dimensional Fund Advisors Ltd, 20 Triton Street, London, NW1 3BF (office); The Dutch House, West Green, Wintney, Hants., RG27 8JN, England (home). *Telephone:* (20) 3033-3300 (office). *Fax:* (20) 3033-3324 (office). *Website:* www.dfaus.com (office).

SALISBURY, 7th Marquess of; **Most Hon. Robert Michael James Gascoyne-Cecil,** PC, DL; British politician and university chancellor; *Chancellor, University of Hertfordshire;* b. 30 Sept. 1946; s. of the late 6th Marquess of Salisbury; m. Hannah Ann Stirling 1970; two s. three d.; ed Eton Coll., Univ. of Oxford; MP for Dorset S 1979–87; mem. House of Lords (Conservative) 1992–, sits in House of Lords as Lord Gascoyne-Cecil 1999–, on leave of absence 2002–; Parl. Under-Sec. of State for Defence 1992–94; Lord Privy Seal 1994–97; Shadow Leader of House of Lords 1997–98; Chair. Council of Royal Veterinary Coll. 1999–2007, Combined Clinical Science Foundation 2004–, Court of Patrons, Thrombosis Research Inst. 2010–; Chancellor Univ. of Hertfordshire 2005–; Gov. The Charterhouse 2009–; fmr Pres. Royal Agricultural Soc. of England; DL Herts. 2007. *Address:* Hatfield House, Hatfield, Herts., AL9 5NF, England (home). *Telephone:* (20) 7351-7458 (office). *Fax:* (20) 7351-7450 (office).

SALJE, Ekhard Karl Hermann, MA, PhD, FRS, FGS, FInstP, FRSA; British/German professor of mineralogy and petrology; *Professor of Mineralogy and Petrology and Head, Department of Earth Sciences, University of Cambridge;* b. 26 Oct. 1946, Hanover; s. of Gerhard Salje and Hildegard Salje (née Drechsler); m. Elisabeth Démaret; one s. four d.; ed Univ. of Hanover, Univ. of Cambridge, UK; Prof. of Crystallography, Univ. of Hanover 1983–86; Lecturer in Mineral Physics, Univ. of Cambridge 1986–92, Prof. 1992–94, Prof. of Mineralogy and Petrology 1994–, Head, Dept of Earth Sciences 1998–; Pres. Clare Hall, Cambridge 2002–08; Visiting Prof. in Paris, Grenoble, Le Mans (France), Nagoya (Japan), Bilbao (Spain), Max Planck Institute for Mathematics, Leipzig 2008–09, Univ. of Paris VII 2009; Pres. Alexander von Humboldt Asscn (UK) 2004–, European Trust UK; Programme Dir Cambridge-MIT Inst. CMI 2001–03; mem. Bd Univ. of Hamburg, Germany 2004–; mem. Working Party, Royal Soc. on Nuclear Waster, British Pugwash Group, Wissenschaftsrat Germany; Bd mem. EIT Poland 2008, Parl. Office for Science and Tech.; Fellow, Akad. Leopoldina (Germany); Hon. Fellow, Darwin Coll., Cambridge 2001, Clare Hall 2008; Chevalier des Palmes académiques; Abraham-Gottlieb-Werner Medal 1997, Schlumberger Medal 1997, Humboldt Research Prize 1999, Ernst Ising Prize 2000, Gold Medal, Univ. of Hamburg 2002, Agricola Medal for Mineralogy 2006. *Publications:* over 400 scientific publs including book on phase transitions in ferroelastic and co-elastic crystals. *Leisure interests:* music, painting. *Address:* Department of Earth Sciences, University of Cambridge, Downing Street, Cambridge, CB2 3EQ, England (office). *Telephone:* (1223) 333478 (office). *E-mail:* es10002@esc.cam.ac.uk (office). *Website:* www.esc.cam.ac.uk/new/v10/index_mineralogy.html (office).

SALKIND, Ilya; film producer; b. 27 July 1947, Mexico City; s. of Alexander Salkind; ed Univ. of London; Assoc. Producer, Cervantes, The Light at the Edge of the World, Spain, 1974; f. Illya Salkind Co., Los Angeles (film production co.), currently CEO and Pres. *Films produced include:* Bluebeard 1972, The Three Musketeers 1973, The Four Musketeers 1974, The Twist 1976, The Prince and the Pauper 1977, Superman 1978, Superman II 1980, Superman III 1983, Supergirl 1984, Santa Claus: The Movie 1985, Christopher Columbus: The Discovery 1992, Heads N TailZ 2005, Young Alexander the Great 2007. *Television includes:* Superboy (series) 1988–92. *Website:* www.ilyasalkindcompany.net.

SALL, Macky; Senegalese geologist, politician and head of state; *President;* b. 11 Dec. 1961, Fatick; m.; three c.; ed Université Cheikh Anta Diop, Institut Français du Pétrole, Paris; Head of Div., Société des Pétroles du Sénégal 1993–2002, Dir-Gen. 2000–01; fmr Special Adviser to the Pres. on Energy and Mining; Minister of Energy, Mining and Hydraulics 2001–03, concurrently Minister for Equipment and Transport Oct.–Nov. 2002; Minister of State, Minister of the Interior and Local Communities, Govt Spokesperson 2003–04; Prime Minister of Senegal 2004–07; Pres. Nat. Ass. 2007–08; Mayor of Fatick 2002–08, 2009–; Pres. of Senegal 2012–; fmr mem. Parti démocratique sénégalais; Grand Croix de l'Ordre nat. du Lion, Grand Officier, Ordre de la Pléade, Ordre de la Francophonie, Légion d'honneur. *Address:* Office of the President, ave Léopold Sédar Senghor, BP 168, Dakar,

Senegal (office). *Telephone:* 33-880-8080 (office). *Website:* www.presidence.sn (office).

SALLAH, Halifa; Gambian politician, sociologist and editor; *Leader, People's Democratic Organization for Independence and Socialism;* currently Leader, People's Democratic Org. for Independence and Socialism and Coordinator (Nat. Alliance for Democracy and Devt), represents constituency of Serrekunda Central; expelled from Nat. Ass. for membership of two political parties 2005, re-elected later same year; unsuccessful cand. in presidential election 2006; mem. Pan-African Parl.; Co-Ed. Foroyaa (newspaper). *Publications include:* The Sene-Gambia Confederation 1985, Where We Differ in Principle 1986, Are We For or Against Unity Among Opposition Forces? (with Sam Sarr) 1987, Hope Never Dies Where the Just are Alive 2006; numerous other books and articles. *Address:* People's Democratic Organization for Independence and Socialism (PDOIS), POB 2306, 1 Sambou Street, Churchill, Serrekunda, The Gambia (office). *Telephone:* 4393177 (office). *Fax:* 4393177 (office). *E-mail:* foroyaa@qanet.gm (office). *Website:* www.foroyaa.gm.

SALLAH, Ousman Ahmadou, BA; Gambian diplomatist and business executive; *Managing Director, Dandimayo Enterprise;* b. 26 July 1938, Kudang; s. of Ahmadou Jabel Sallah and Haddy Sallah; m. Ramou Sallah 1966; two s. two d.; ed Trinity Coll., Hartford, Conn., School of Int. Affairs, Columbia Univ., New York, London School of Econs; Asst Sec., Prime Minister's Office 1967; Asst Sec. Ministry of External Affairs 1967–68, Deputy Perm. Sec. 1973–74; First Sec., Head of Chancery and Acting High Commr, London 1971; Amb. to Saudi Arabia (also accred to Egypt, Iran, Kuwait, Qatar and UAE) 1974–79, to USA 1979–83; Perm. Rep. to UN 1979–83; Perm. Sec., Ministry of External Affairs and Head of Gambian Diplomatic Service 1982–87, Amb. to USA and Perm. Rep. to UN, New York 1987–94; Consultant, World Bank 1996–99; Man. Dir Dandimayo Enterprise 1999–; Hon. LLD (Trinity Coll., Hartford); Diploma in Int. Relations and Diplomacy from UNITAR. *Leisure interest:* tennis. *Address:* PO Box 667, Banjul, The Gambia. *Telephone:* 820-39-12 (office); 820-39-13 (home); 653-82-64. *Fax:* 820-39-06 (office). *E-mail:* torodo@sentoo.sn (office); sallahlamtoro@yahoo.com.

SALLE, David, BFA, MFA; American artist; b. 1952, Norman, Okla; s. of Alvin S. Salle and Tillie D. Salle (née Brown); ed California Inst. of Arts; retrospective exhbn Museum of Contemporary Art, Chicago 1987; Guggenheim Fellow 1986; public collections at Dallas Museum of Art, Dallas, Guggenheim Museum, New York, Metropolitan Museum of Art, New York, Museum of Modern Art, New York, Nat. Gallery of Australia, Australia, Indianapolis Museum of Art, Indianapolis, Museo di Arte Moderna e Contemporanea, Italy, Museum of Contemporary Art, Chicago, Museum of Contemporary Art, Los Angeles, North Carolina Museum of Art, Raleigh, Tate Gallery, England, Tel Aviv Museum of Art, Israel, Virginia Museum of Fine Arts, Richmond. *Films:* Search and Destroy (directed) 1995. *Address:* c/o Gagosian Gallery, 980 Madison Avenue, New York, NY 10021, USA.

SALLEH, Dato' Seri Mohd Nor, BSc, MSc, PhD; Malaysian scientist and academic; b. 20 Oct. 1940, Negeri Sembilan; s. of Mohammed Nor and Nyonya Nor; m. Habiba Alias 1966; two s. one d.; ed Univ. of Adelaide, Australia, Australian Forestry School, Canberra, ITC Delft, Netherlands, Michigan State Univ., USA; Deputy Conservator of Forests, Forest Dept Peninsular Malaysia 1965, Dir Forest Inventory 1971; Dir Forestry Research Inst., Kepong 1977–85; Dir Gen. Forest Research Inst. of Malaysia 1985–95 (retd); Adjunct Prof., Univ. Putra Malaysia 1994–96, Univ. Malaysia Sabah 2001–; Vice-Pres. Int. Union of Forest Research Orgs 1986–90, Pres. 1991–95; Pres. Malaysian Nature Soc. 1978–; mem. Nat. Environment Quality Council 1995–; fmr Vice-Pres. then Sec. Gen. Malaysian Acad. of Sciences; mem. Advisory Cttee Nat. Science Center, Nat. Planetarium and Nat. Park; mem. Malaysian Human Rights Comm. 2000–02; mem. Bd of Dirs Forest Trends, CIFOR, Inter Acad. Council; mem. Panel of Eminent Experts on Ethics in Food and Agricultural of FAO 2000, Scientific and Tech. Advisory Panel of Global Environmental Facility, FAO High-Level Panel of External Experts on Forestry (Chair. 2003), Ind. Panel to Review the Tropical Forestry Action Plan; Chair. International Union for Conservation of Nature East Asia Group on Sustainable Use Initiative; fmr Chair. Asia Pacific Asscn of Forest Research Insts; Trustee, Int. Network on Bamboo and Rattan; Dr hc (Nat. Univ. of Malaysia) 1992, (Aberdeen) 1993; KMN 1981, DSNS 1989, Award of Third World Network of Scientific Orgs for Public Understanding of Science 1991, Langkawi Environmental Award 1991, Nat. Science Award 1993. *Publications include:* The Tropical Garden City 1990, The Malaysian Marine Heritage 1991, over 100 articles and contribs. to seminars, books and journals. *Leisure interests:* squash, badminton, reading, nature-oriented activities. *Address:* c/o Malaysian Academy of Sciences (Akademi Sains Malaysia), 902-4 Jalan Tun Ismail, 50480 Kuala Lumpur, Malaysia.

SALLENAVE, Danièle; French novelist, journalist and academic; b. 28 Oct. 1940, Angers; worked for Le Monde, Le Messager européen (review), Temps modernes; taught literature and film history at Univ. of Paris-X Nanterre 1968–2001; weekly columnist, France Culture 2009–; seventh woman since 1635 to become mem. of Acad. française (Seat 30 of Maurice Druon) April 2011; Grand prix de littérature de l'Acad. française 2005. *Publications:* novels: Paysages de ruines avec personnages 1975, Le voyage d'Amsterdam ou les règles de la conversation 1977, Les Portes de Gubbio (Prix Renaudot 1980) 1980, Un printemps froid 1983, La vie fantôme 1986, Rome 1986, Conversations conjugales 1987, Adieu 1988, Le don des morts 1991, Le théâtre des idées 1991, Passages de l'Est 1991, Villes et villes 1991, Le principe de ruine 1991, Lettres mortes 1995, Les trois minutes du diable 1994, Viol 1997, A quoi sert la littérature? 1997, L'Amazone du grand Dieu 1997, Carnets de route en Palestine occupée: Gaza-Cisjordanie 1997, Stock 1998, D'amour 2002, Nos amours de la France – République, identités, régions (with Perico Legasse) 2002, dieu.com 2003, La Fraga (Grand Prix Jean Giono 2005) 2004, Quand même (Prix Marguerite Duras 2006) 2006, Castor de guerre (Prix Jean Monnet de littérature européenne du département de Charente 2008) 2008, Nous, on n'aime pas lire 2009, La vie éclaircie: Réponses à Madeleine Gobeil 2010; trans. of Italian, including The Divine Mimesis by Pier Paolo Pasolini. *Address:* c/o Editions Gallimard, 5 rue Gaston-Gallimard, 75328 Paris Cedex 07, France. *Telephone:* 1-49-54-42-00. *Fax:* 1-45-44-94-03. *E-mail:* info@gallimard.fr. *Website:* www.gallimard.fr.

SALLES, Walter; Brazilian film director and screenwriter; b. 12 April 1956, Rio de Janeiro; s. of the late Walther Moreira Salles and Elisa Margarida Gonçalves; m.; one s.; mem. jury, Cannes Film Festival 1999, 2002;. *Films include:* Socorro Nobre (Fipa d'Or 1996) 1995, Foreign Lane (Grand Prix du Public Rencontres de Cinéma de Paris 1995), Central do Brasil (co-directed) (Golden Bear Berlin Int. Film Festival, Best Screenplay Sundance Inst.-NHK, Best Foreign Film British Acad. Awards, Best Foreign Film Golden Globes) 1998, O Primeiro Dia (co-directed) (Best Latin-American Film Mexican Acad. Awards) 1998, Abril Despedaçado (Little Golden Lion Award Venice Film Festival) 2001, Diarios de Motocicleta (The Motorcycle Diaries) 2004, Dark Water 2005, Paris, Je T'aime 2006, Linha de Passe 2008, On the Road 2011. *Achievements include:* competed as a kart driver winning Rio de Janeiro's championship twice. *Address:* c/o The Endeavour Agency, 9601 Wilshire Boulevard, 10th Floor, Beverly Hills, CA 90212, USA. *Telephone:* (310) 248-2000. *Fax:* (310) 248-2020.

SALLINEN, Aulis Heikki; Finnish composer and academic; b. 9 April 1935, Salmi; s. of Armas Rudolf Sallinen and Anna Malanen; m. 1st Pirkko Holvisola 1955 (died 1997); four s.; m. 2nd Maija Lokka 1999; ed Sibelius Acad.; primary school teacher 1958–60; Man. Finnish Radio Orchestra 1960–70; Prof. of Arts, Sibelius Acad. 1965–76; mem. Bd of Dirs TEOSTO (Finnish Composers' Copyright Soc.) 1970–84, Chair. 1988–90; mem. Swedish Royal Music Acad. 1979–; mem. Finnish Composers' Soc., Sec. 1958–73, Chair. 1971–73; fmr mem. Bd Finnish Nat. Opera; Hon. DPhil (Turku) 1991, (Helsinki) 1994; Nordic Council Music Prize 1978, Prof. of Arts for Life (by the Finnish Govt) 1981, Wihuri Int. Sibelius Prize 1983. *Compositions include:* eight symphonies, violin concerto, cello concerto, flute concerto, horn concerto and other orchestral music, five string quartets and other chamber music; film score for The Iron Age 1983. *Operas include:* The Horseman 1975, The Red Line 1978, The King Goes Forth to France 1982, Kullervo 1988, The Palace 1993, King Lear 1999. *Address:* c/o TEOSTO, Lauttasaarentie 1, 00 200 Helsinki 20, Finland (office).

SALLING, Augusta; Greenlandic politician; b. 1954; m. Jens Salling; two c.; ed Greenland Coll. of Educ.; teacher, deputy head then man. head of school, Qeqertarsuaq 1980–86; Gen. Man. Disko Havfiskeri SpA 1986–93; mem. Qeqertarsuaq Local Council 1993–2001; Mayor of Qeqertarsuaq 1993–97; mem. Landtag (Atassut) 1999–, Chair. 2002–05; Minister of Economy 2001–02; Vice-Premier and Minister of Finance 2003; Vice-Chair., Landsting and Deputy, Nordic Council, Del. from Greenland 2005–, also Deputy Centre Group. *Address:* Nordic Council, Delegation from Greenland, Grønlands Landstings Bureau, POB 1060, 3900 Nuuk, Greenland (office). *Telephone:* 345000 (office). *Fax:* 324606 (office). *E-mail:* aus@gh.gl (office). *Website:* www.nanoq.gl (office).

SALLOUKH, Fawzi; Lebanese government official and diplomatist; b. 1931, Qammatieh; m. Hind Basma; three c.; ed American Univ. Beirut; Prof. 1955–57; Dir of Public Relations, Franklin Publishing 1957–60; Amb. to Sierra Leone 1964–71; Cen. Dept, Ministry of Foreign Affairs 1971–78; Amb. to Nigeria 1978–85, to Algeria 1985–87; Dir of Econ. Affairs 1987–90; Amb. to Austria 1990–94, to Belgium 1994–95; Sec.-Gen. Islamic Univ. 1998–; Minister of Foreign Affairs and Emigrants 2005–06 (resgnd, resignation not accepted), 2008–09. *Address:* c/o Ministry of Foreign Affairs and Emigrants, rue Sursock, Achratieh, Beirut, Lebanon (office).

SALMAN, Sheikh Ali; Bahraini politician; *President, Al-Wefaq (Islamic National Accord Association—INAA);* b. 30 Oct. 1965, Bilad Al Qadeem; ed in Qom; Shia cleric; exiled to Dubai 1995, then sought asylum in London, returned to Bahrain 2001; currently Pres. Al-Wefaq (Islamic Nat. Accord Asscn—INAA); mem. Parl. for Jid Hafas 2006–. *E-mail:* webmaster@alwefaq.org. *Website:* www.alwefaq.org; www.toqa.net.

SALMON, Peter Andrew, BA; British broadcasting executive; *Director, BBC North;* b. 15 May 1956, Burnley; m. Sarah Lancashire; four s.; ed Univ. of Warwick; fmr Dir of Programmes, Granada TV and Controller of Factual Programmes, Channel 4; fmr producer and Series Ed. BBC TV, later Head of Features, BBC Bristol, Controller, BBC One 1997–2000, Dir BBC Sport 2000–05; CEO The Television Corpn 2005–06; Chief Creative Officer, BBC Vision 2006–08, Dir BBC North, Salford 2008–; mem. Bd Liverpool Culture Co. 2005–. *Leisure interests:* cycling, football, tennis. *Address:* BBC North, The Greenhouse, MediaCityUK, Salford, M50 2EQ, England (office). *Telephone:* (1618) 865300 (office). *Website:* www.bbc.co.uk/jobs/north (office).

SALMOND, Alexander (Alex) Elliot Anderson, MA; British politician; *First Minister of Scotland;* b. 31 Dec. 1954, Linlithgow, Scotland; s. of Robert F. Salmond and Mary S. Milne; m. Moira McGlashan; ed Linlithgow Acad., St Andrews Univ.; Vice-Pres. Fed. of Student Nationalists 1974–77, St Andrews Univ. Students' Rep. Council 1977–78, Founder-mem. Scottish Nat. Party (SNP) 79 Group 1979, mem. SNP Nat. Exec. Cttee 1981–82, 1983–, SNP Exec. Vice Convener for Publicity 1985–87, SNP Nat. Convener (Leader) 1990–2000, 2004–; Asst Economist, Dept of Agric. and Fisheries 1978–80; Economist, Bank of Scotland 1980–87; MP for Banff and Buchan 1987–2010, SNP Parl. Spokesperson on Constitution and Fishing 1997–99; MSP for Banff and Buchan 1999–2001, for Gordon 2007–; First Minister of Scotland 2007–; Visiting Prof. of Econs, Univ. of Strathclyde. *Leisure interests:* golf, reading. *Address:* Office of the First Minister, 5th Floor, St Andrew's House, Regent Road, Edinburgh, EH1 3DG (office); Constituency Office, 84 North Street, Inverurie, Aberdeenshire, AB51 4QX, Scotland (office). *Telephone:* (1467) 670070 (Constituency Office) (office); (845) 7741741 (Edinburgh) (office). *Fax:* (131) 244-6915 (Edinburgh) (office). *E-mail:* firstminister@scotland.gsi.gov.uk (office); alex .salmond.msp@scottish.parliament.uk (office). *Website:* www.scottish.gov.uk (office); www.snp.org (office).

SALOLAINEN, Pertti Edvard, MSc(Econ); Finnish diplomatist and politician; *Chairman, Foreign Affairs Committee, Eduskunta (Parliament of Finland);* b. 19 Oct. 1940, Helsinki; s. of Edvard Paavali Salolainen and Ella Elisabeth Salolainen; m. Anja Sonninen 1964 (died 2005); one s. one d.; ed Helsinki School of Econs; TV journalist, Finnish Broadcasting Co. 1962–65, producer 1965–66, corresp. in London 1966–69, mem. Working Cttee, Supervisory Bd 1970–87; journalist, BBC, London 1966; Head of Dept, Finnish Employers' Confed. 1969–89; mem. Parl. (Eduskunta) 1970–96, 2007–, Chair. Foreign Affairs Cttee 2007–; Minister for Foreign Trade 1987–95; Deputy Prime Minister 1991–95; Head, negotiating team for entry of Finland into EU 1993–95, negotiating team of GATT (Uruguay Round);

Amb. to UK 1996–2004; Chair. Finance Cttee IPU 1982–87; Hon. Founder Worldwide Fund for Nature (WWF) Finland 1972, Chair. WWF Finland; mem. Supervisory Bd's Working Cttee Outokumpu Mining Co. 1979–91; mem. Supervisory Bd Suomi-Salama Insurance Co. 1980–91, Finnair 1995–2002; mem. Legal Cttee Nordic Council 1982–87, Finnish Defence Forces Evaluation Team 2011–; holds mil. rank of Maj.; Nat. Coalition Party (Leader 1991–94); several solo exhbns of nature photographs in Finland, Germany and UK; Freeman of the City of London 1998; Grand Cross of the Lion of Finland 1994, Grand Cross of the Nordstjerna Order (Sweden) 1996, Grand Cross of FRG, of Hungary, of Austria, of Estonia (Maaria Maa); Medal of Merit, Finnish Defence Force 1997; Int. Conservation Award, Worldwide Fund for Nature, Gold Medal of Merit, Finnish Asscn for Nature Conservation, Jaakko Honko Medal, School of Econs, Helsinki. *Leisure interests:* nature conservation, nature photography, sports, tennis, swimming, foreign and security policy. *Address:* Parliament of Finland, 00100 Helsinki, Finland (office). *Telephone:* (50) 5122270 (office). *E-mail:* pertti.salolainen@eduskunta.fi (office). *Website:* web.eduskunta.fi (office).

SALOMÃO, Tomaz Augusto, BA MA; Mozambican international organization official; *Executive Secretary, Southern African Development Community;* b. 16 Oct. 1954, Inhambane Prov.; m.; ed Commercial and Industrial School Vasca da Gama-Inhambane, Commercial Inst. of Lurenco Marques, Eduardo Mondlane Univ.; expert for study unit of Montepio Savings Bank of Mozambique 1974–76; expert at Ministry of Industry and Trade 1976–78; head of production unit at CIFEL 1978–81; Sec. of State for Nat. Defence 1983–89; Lecturer, Eduardo Mondlane Univ. 1990–93; Deputy Minister of Planning and Finance 1990–94, Minister of Planning and Finance, Gov. for Mozambique at African Devt Bank, IMF, World Bank 1994–99; Chair. SADC Transport and Communications Ministers' Cttee 2000–02, Chair. SADC Ministers' Cttee on ICTs 2002–03; Chair. African Union Ministers' Cttee on ICTs 2003–04; Minister of Transport and Communications of Mozambique 2000–04; Exec. Sec. SADC 2005–; mem. Ass. of the Repub. (Parl.) 2005–. *Leisure interests:* music, swimming, soccer, jogging, tennis, reading, gardening. *Address:* SADC HQ, CBD 54385, Square, Private Bag 0095, Gaborone, Botswana (office). *Telephone:* 3951863 (office); 3951866 (office). *Fax:* 3972848 (office); 3910038 (office). *E-mail:* registry@sadc.int (office). *Website:* www.sadc.int (office).

SALONEN, Esa-Pekka, FRCM; Finnish conductor and composer; *Principal Conductor and Artistic Adviser, Philharmonia Orchestra;* b. 30 June 1958, Helsinki; ed Sibelius Acad., Helsinki, studied composition with Rautavaara and conducting with Panula, studied composition with Niccolò Castiglioni and Franco Donatoni in Italy; conducting debut with Finnish Radio Symphony Orchestra 1979; London conducting debut with the Philharmonia Orchestra 1983, Prin. Guest Conductor 1984–94, Prin. Conductor and Artistic Adviser 2008–; Prin. Guest Conductor, Oslo Philharmonic Orchestra 1985–; Music Dir and The Walt and Lilly Disney Chair, Los Angeles Philharmonic Orchestra 1992–2009; Prin. Conductor, Swedish Radio Symphony Orchestra 1985–95; Artistic Adviser, New Stockholm Chamber Orchestra 1986; Artistic Dir, Helsinki Festival 1995–96; Co-founder and Artistic Dir, Baltic Sea Festival 2003–; Hon. mem. American Acad. of Arts and Sciences 2010; Dr hc (Sibelius Acad.) 2003, (Hong Kong Acad. of Performing Arts) 2009, (Univ. of Southern California) 2010, (Royal Coll. of Music, London) 2011; Officier, Ordre des Arts et des Lettres 1998; Siena Prize, Accad. Chigiana 1993, Royal Philharmonic Soc. Opera Award 1995, Litteris et Artibus Medal (Sweden) 1996, Royal Philharmonic Soc. Conductor Award 1997, Helsinki Medal 2005, Musical Americana Musician of the Year 2006, Artist of the Year, Int. Classical Music Awards 2011. *Compositions include:* orchestral: Concerto for alto saxophone and orchestra 1980–81, Giro 1982–97; chamber music: YTA I for alto flute 1985, YTA II for piano 1985, YTA III for cello 1986, Floof for soprano and chamber ensemble (UNESCO Rostrum Prize) 1990, Mimo II 1992, LA Variations 1996, Gambit 1998, Five Images after Sappho 1999, Mania 2000, Foreign Bodies 2001, Violin Concerto (Univ. of Louisville Grawemeyer Award for Musical Composition 2012) 2009. *Film appearance:* Sketches of Frank Gehry 2006. *Address:* c/o Fidelio Arts Ltd, 103 Whitecross Street, No 5, London, EC1Y 8JD, England (office); Philharmonia Orchestra, 6th Floor, The Tower Building, 11 York Road, London, SE1 7NX, England (office). *Telephone:* (07733) 011145 (office); (20) 7921-3900 (office). *E-mail:* jessica@fidelioarts.com (office); mark@fidelioarts.com (office); orchestra@philharmonia.co.uk (office). *Website:* www.fidelioarts.com (office); www.philharmonia.co.uk (office); www.esapekkasalonen.com. *Fax:* (20) 7921-3950 (office).

SALOUM, Nasir ibn Muhammad as-, PhD; Saudi Arabian engineer; b. 4 Nov. 1936, Medina; resident engineer, Ministry of Communications 1965; Head of Study Dept, Ministry of Communications 1965–68; Deputy Minister of Communications 1976–96, Minister 2000; Minister of Transport 1991–2000; mem. Bd of Saudi Arabian Railways Authority. *Leisure interests:* reading, travel. *Address:* c/o Ministry of Communications, Intercontinental Road, Riyadh 11112, Saudi Arabia.

SALOVEY, Peter, AB, AM, MS, MPhil, PhD; American psychologist, academic and university administrator; *President, Yale University;* m. Marta Elisa Moret; ed Stanford Univ., Yale Univ.; mem. Faculty, Yale Univ. 1986–, Chair. Dept of Psychology 2000–03, Dean Grad. School of Arts and Sciences 2003–04, Dean of Yale Coll. 2004–08, currently Chris Argyris Prof. of Psychology, holds secondary faculty appointments in Schools of Man. and Public Health, Inst. for Social and Policy Studies, and Sociology Dept, Provost of Yale Univ. 2008–13, Pres. 2013–; co-developed, with John D. Mayer, framework called Emotional Intelligence; mem. American Acad. of Arts and Sciences 2013; Dr hc (Univ. of Pretoria, South Africa) 2009; William Clyde DeVane Medal for Distinguished Scholarship and Teaching, Yale Coll., Lex Hixon '63 Prize for Teaching Excellence in the Social Sciences. *Publications include:* has written or edited more than a dozen books; hundreds of journal articles and essays, focused primarily on human emotion and health behaviour. *Address:* President's Office, Yale University, PO Box 208229, New Haven, CT 06520-8229, USA (office). *Telephone:* (203) 432-2550 (office). *Fax:* (203) 432-7105 (office). *E-mail:* presidents.office@yale.edu (office). *Website:* president .yale.edu (office).

SALTER, John Rotherham, MA, FRGS, FRSA, FCMI, FCIWM, ACIArb; British international business lawyer, solicitor and academic; *Visiting Professor of Law, Cranfield University;* b. 2 May 1932, London, England; s. of Herbert Salter and Nora Salter; m. Cynthia Brewer 1961; one s. two d.; ed Queen Elizabeth's School,

Ashridge Coll., Lincoln Coll., Oxford and King's Coll. London; Lt RA 1951–53; partner, Denton Hall 1961–94, consultant 1994–99; Chair. Environmental Law Group 1994–98, Chair. Maj. Projects Group 1994–98; Vice-Chair. IBA Cttee of Energy and Natural Resources Law 1976–79, IBA Cttee on International Environmental Law 1979–82; Chair. North Sea Gas Gathering Consortium 1979–80; Chair. Section on Business Law, International Bar Asscn 1986–88; Chair. ABA Cttee on International Law 1993–95, Legal Issues Group of ISWA 1994–2000; Treas. Anglo-American Real Property Inst. 1985–86; Trustee, Petroleum Law Educ. Trust 1980–98, IBA Educ. Trust 1983–95; consultant, UNIDO 1983–84; Vice-Chair. ABA Cttee on Comparative Govt Law 1988–91; Chair. IBA Cttee on Oil and Gas Construction Law 1989–93; Bd mem. International Capital Markets Group 1987–89; mem. Planning Panel, Law Soc. 1991–97; Legal Assoc., Royal Town Planning Inst. 1992–98; Chair. Silver Soc. 1986–87, Care Foundation 1994–2001, Hospice in the Weald 1994–2001, IBA Standing Cttee on UN and World Orgs (UNWOC) 1995–2000, Murray Soc. 1996–98; Pres. The Wine Label Circle 1986–87; Dir John Ray Initiative 1997–2004; mem. Soc. of Chemical Industry, London Chapter of Lamda Alpha International, Advisory Cttee on Integrated Environmental Man. by Distance Learning, Bath Univ., Scientific and Tech. Cttee, ISWA 1994–2000; Visiting Fellow Cranfield Univ. 1993–97, mem. of Court 1995–, Visiting Prof. of Law 1997–, Chair. Legislation and Policy Unit 2000–08; mem. Sr Common Room, Lincoln Coll., Oxford 1991–; mem. of Court Worshipful Co. of Fan-Makers 1997–, Tercentenary Master Fan Maker 2009, Court of City of London Solicitors' Co. 2010–12; Partner, John Salter & Assocs 1999–; mem. Advisory Panel, US Inst. of Peace 2001–08; Assoc., Chartered Inst. of Arbitrators; Fellow, Chartered Man. Inst., Chartered Inst. of Wastes Man.; Freeman of London and of Glasgow, Hon. mem. Bar of Madrid 1987–, Ind. Social Work Assocs 2000–, ICC (UK) 2000–, IBA 2001–, Hon. Fellow, Centre for Petroleum and Mineral Law and Policy, Univ. of Dundee. *Television appearances:* The Law is Yours series. *Publications include:* Planning Law for Industry (co-author) 1981, UK Onshore Oil and Gas Law 1986, Corporate Environmental Responsibility – Law and Practice 1992; contrib. to UK Oil and Gas Law 1984, Halsbury's Laws of England (Vol. 58) 1986, Law of the European Communities 1986, Vaughan's Law of the European Communities Service 1990, Environment and Planning Law 1991, Frontiers of Environmental Law 1991, Directors' Guide to Environmental Issues 1992, European Community Energy Law 1994 (95th edn 2012), European Environmental Law 1994, How to Understand an Act of Parliament (with D. J. Gifford) 1996, Understanding the English Legal System (with D. J. Gifford) 1997, Sauce Labels (1750–1950) 2002, Wine Labels (1730–2003) 2004, Boudoir Labels (1753–1965) 2012; numerous articles in professional journals. *Leisure interests:* the arts, archaeology, sailing, tennis, bowls. *Address:* John Salter & Associates, 120 Oak Hill Road, Sevenoaks, TN13 1NU (office); Jumpers Hatch, Oak Hill Road, Sevenoaks, TN13 1NU, England (home). *Telephone:* (1732) 458338 (office); (1732) 458388 (home). *Fax:* (870) 052-2008 (office); (1732) 458388 (home). *E-mail:* john_salter@sky.com (home). *Website:* fanmakers.com (office).

SALTYKOV, Boris Georgievich; Russian politician and economist; *Director, Polytechnical Museum;* b. 27 Dec. 1940, Moscow; s. of Georgy Saltykov and Evdokia M. Saltykova (née Pukaleva); m. Lubov N. Klochkova 1972; two d.; ed Moscow Inst. of Physics and Tech.; researcher, Head of lab., Head of Div. Cen. Inst. of Econ. and Math. USSR (now Russian) Acad. of Sciences 1967–86; Head of Div. Inst. of Econ. and Forecasting of Progress in Science and Tech. (now Forecasting of Econ.) USSR Acad. of Sciences 1986–91; Deputy Dir Analytical Centre USSR Acad. of Sciences 1991; Minister of Science, Higher School and Tech. Policy of Russian Fed. 1991–92; Deputy Prime Minister of Russian Fed. 1992–93; Minister of Science and Tech. Policy 1993–96; apptd Pres. Russian House of Int. Science and Tech. Cooperation 1996; currently Dir Polytechnical Museum; Chair. Russian Comm. for UNESCO 1992–97; Dir-Gen. Fed. State Unitary Co. Russian Technologies 1998–2000; mem. State Duma (Parl.) 1993–95; mem. Supervisory Council, RUSNANO Fund for Infrastructure and Educational Programs; Hon. Foreign mem. American Acad. of Arts and Letters 1999–. *Leisure interest:* cars. *Address:* Polytechnical Museum, d/4, Entrance 1, Novaya Ploshad, 101000 Moscow (office); Protochny per. 11, ap. 99, 121099 Moscow, Russia (home). *Telephone:* (495) 923-07-56 (office); (495) 241-44-03 (home). *Fax:* (495) 923-42-87 (office).

SALTZ, Jerry; American art critic; *Senior Art Critic, New York Magazine;* m. Roberta Smith; fmr sr art critic, The Village Voice; sr art critic, New York Magazine 2006–; fmr visiting critic, Columbia Univ., Yale Univ.; contributing ed. Art in America. *Publications include:* Seeing Out Loud: The Village Voice Art Columns 1998–2003 2003. *Address:* New York Media, 75 Varick Street, New York, NY 10013, USA (office). *Telephone:* (212) 508-0700 (office). *E-mail:* jerry_saltz@newyorkmag.com (office). *Website:* nymag.com (office).

SALVADOR CRESPO, María Isabel; Ecuadorean politician; *Permanent Representative, Organization of American States (OAS);* b. 1962; Minister of Tourism 2005–07, of External Relations, Trade and Integration 2007–08 (resgnd); currently Perm. Rep. to OAS, also Chair Perm. Council. *Address:* Organization of American States (OAS), 17th Street, Constitution Avenue, NW, Washington, DC 20006, USA (office). *Telephone:* (202) 458-3000 (office). *Website:* www.oas.org (office).

SALVATORI, Carlo; Italian business executive; *Chairman, Lazard S.r.l.;* b. 7 July 1941, Sora, Frosinone; m.; three c.; ed Univs of Bologna and Siena; began career with Banca Naz. del Lavoro (BNL); Deputy Gen. Man. Cassa di Risparmio di Parma 1980–87; Gen. Man. in charge of Business Devt Div., BNL 1987–90; Gen. Man., then Man.-Dir, Banco Ambrosiano Veneto 1990–96; Gen. Man. and Dir Cariplo 1996–98; Man.-Dir Banca Intesa 1998–2000; Chair. UniCredito Italiano SpA 2002–06; CEO Unipol Gruppo Finanziario 2006–10; Chair. SeaChange International 2009–, Lazard Italy 2010–; Deputy Chair. Mediobanca SpA –2006, Inst. for Int. Political Studies; mem. Bd of Dirs Riunione Adriatica di Sicurtà, Abi, Ras; mem. Man. Bd and Gen. Council, Assonime; Grand Officer of the Order of Merit of the Italian Republic 1993. *Address:* Lazard S.r.l., Via Dell'Orso 2, 20121 Milan, Italy (office). *Website:* www.lazard.com (office).

SALWAI, Charlot; Ni-Vanuatu accountant and politician; accountant, Union Electrique du Vanuatu Ltd (electricity and water co.) 1987–88; accountant, Development Bank of Vanuatu 1988–90; accountant, Melanesia Shell Products Ltd 1990–91; Private Sec. to Prime Minister Carlot Korman 1991–95; Second Sec., Ministry of Finance 1996, First Sec., Ministry of Educ. 1997–98, First Political

Adviser, Ministry of Trade 1998–99, First Political Adviser, Ministry of Youth 2000–02; mem. Parl. for Pentecost constituency, Deputy Leader of Opposition 2004–05, Opposition Whip 2005–07; Minister of Lands Aug.–Dec. 2004, of Educ. 2007, of Justice and Community Services Jan.–Oct. 2012, of Finance and Econ. Man. 2012–13; fmr mem. Union of Moderate Parties, fmr Vice-Pres. (expelled 2012); mem. Reunification Movement for Change 2012–. *Address:* c/o Ministry of Finance and Economic Management, PMB 9058, Port Vila, Vanuatu (office).

SALYANOVA, Aida Jenishbekovna, LLB; Kyrgyzstani lawyer and government official; *Prosecutor-General;* b. 6 Aug. 1972, Naryn; m.; one s. one d.; ed Frunze Coll. of Soviet Trade, Bishkek, Kyrgyz State Nat. Univ.; Teacher, Bishkek Commercial Coll. 1992–96; Prof., Chui Univ., Bishkek 1996–97; Adviser, Jogorku Kenesh (Supreme Council, Parl.) 1997–2005, Head of Legal Dept (responsible for constitutional law, govt, rule of law and judicial reform) 2005–08; Sec. of State, Ministry of Justice 2008–10; Minister of Justice April–Dec. 2010; Plenipotentiary Rep. of Pres. in Jogorku Kenesh 2010–12; Acting Prosecutor-Gen. March–April 2011, Prosecutor-Gen. April 2011–; State Counsellor of Justice, Third Class. *Address:* Office of the Prosecutor-General, 720040 Bishkek, Avenue Erkindik 39, Kyrgystan (office). *Telephone:* 66-33-73 (office). *Website:* www.prokuror.kg (office).

SALZ, Sir Anthony Michael Vaughan, Kt, LLB, FRSA; British lawyer; *Executive Vice-Chairman, N M Rothschild & Sons Limited;* b. 30 June 1950, Tavistock, Devon, England; s. of Michael H. Salz and Veronica Edith Dorothea Elizabeth Salz (née Hall); m. Sally Ruth Hagger 1975; one s. two d.; ed Summerfields School, Oxford, Radley Coll. and Univ. of Exeter; articled clerk, Kenneth Brown Baker Baker 1972–74, Asst Solicitor 1974–75; Asst Solicitor, Freshfields 1975–77, seconded to Davis Polk & Wardwell, New York, USA 1977–78, solicitor, Freshfields 1978–80, Partner 1980–96, Sr Partner 1996–2000, Co-Sr Partner, Freshfields Bruckhaus Deringer 2000–06; Vice-Chair. Bd of Govs, BBC 2004–06, Acting Chair. 2006; Exec. Vice-Chair. N M Rothschild & Sons (investment bank) 2006–; Chair. Bloomsbury Publishing Plc 2013–; currently Chair. Eden Trust; Chair. Ind. Comm. on Youth Crime and Anti-Social Behaviour; Dir, Scott Trust 2009–; mem. Tate Gallery Corp. Advisory Group 1997– (Chair. 1997–2002); mem. Business Action on Homelessness Exec. Forum –2006, Business in the Community Nat. Educ. Leadership Team –2010; apptd to lead review of business practices at Barclays following Libor rigging scandal 2012; Lead Ind. mem. (non-exec.) Bd, Dept for Educ.; Gov. of Wellington Acad.; Trustee, Tate Foundation 2000–, Paul Hamlyn Foundation 2005–, Media Standards Trust 2007–, Royal Opera House Covent Garden Ltd 2008–, Reprieve 2011–, The High Street Fund 2011–13; mem. Advisory Bd, Univ. of Exeter School of Business and Econs 2003–, Financial Services Knowledge Transfer Network 2010–. *Publications include:* contribs to various legal books and journals. *Leisure interests:* fishing, soccer, sports, theatre, arts. *Address:* N M Rothschild & Sons Ltd, New Court, St Swithin's Lane, London, EC4N 8AL, England (office). *Telephone:* (20) 7280-5186 (office). *Fax:* (20) 7280-3505 (office). *Website:* www.rothschild.com (office).

SALZA, Enrico; Italian banking executive; *Chairman, Tecno Holding SpA;* b. 1937, Turin; Deputy Chair. and CEO Il Sole 24 Ore 1971–89; Deputy Chair. Sanpaolo 1984–95; Dir and mem. Exec. Cttee Sanpaolo IMI SpA (now Intesa Sanpaolo SpA) 1998–2001, Deputy Chair. Man. Bd 2001–04, Chair. Sanpaolo IMI Group 2004–07, Chair. Man. Bd Intesa Sanpaolo SpA 2007–10; CEO Cerved SpA –2002; Chair. Tecno Holding SpA, Italconsult SpA, Techno Investments Ltd; Founder and first Chair. Confindustria Young Entrepreneurs; fmr Chair. Turin Chamber of Commerce, Unioncamere Piemontese, Chairman ASP (Asscn for Scientific and Technological Devt of Piedmont); Dir Centro Congressi Torino Incontra, Nomisma; fmr Dir Union Bank of Switzerland, Compagnia di San Paolo; mem. Exec. Council ICC; Hon. Chair. Associazione Sviluppo Scientifico e Tecnologico di Piedmont; Cavaliere del Lavoro, Cavaliere di Gran Croce dell'Ordine al Merito della Repubblica 2007; hon. degree in Man. Eng (Politecnico di Torino). *Address:* Tecno Holding SpA, Piazza Sallustio 9, 00187 Rome, Italy (office). *Telephone:* (06) 42020125 (office). *Fax:* (06) 42814495 (office). *E-mail:* enrico.salza@tecnoholding.it (office). *Website:* www.tecnoholding.it (office).

SAM-SUMANA, Samuel, BSc; Sierra Leonean business executive and politician; *Vice-President;* b. 17 April 1962, Koidu Town, Kono Dist; s. of the late Chief Sam-Sumana and Haja Sia Hawa Sam-Sumana; m.; three c.; ed Metropolitan State Univ., Minn., USA, America Inst. of Diamond Cutting and Polishing, Deerfield Beach, Fla, USA, Knollwood Computer and Business School, St Louis Park, Minn.; fmr System Officer of network support for Prudential Financial Group, USA; fmr Vice-Pres. Network Support System, Allina Health Services and Seagate Technologies, USA; served as Regional Man. for C-12 International, Tex., USA (co. engaged in diamond buying in Sierra Leone, Guinea and Liberia); fmr Man. Dir United Diamond Mining Co., Kodu Town, Kono Dist; CEO Aries Rehabilitation Construction and Supplies (ARCS) SL Ltd –2007; mem. All People's Congress party, mem. 'Five-Man Committee'; Vice-Pres. of Sierra Leone 2007–; Vice-Chair. Kono-Union Chapter USA, Minn. *Address:* c/o Office of the President, Tower Hill, Freetown, Sierra Leone (office). *Telephone:* (22) 22467 (office). *E-mail:* vicepresident@statehouse.gov.sl (office). *Website:* www.statehouse.gov.sl (office).

SAMA, Koffi, DMV; Togolese lawyer and politician; b. 1944, Amoutchou, Ogou Prefecture; m.; ed Lycée Bonnecarrère, Lomé and Ecole Nat. Vétérinaire de Toulouse, France; qualified as a vet 1972; Minister of Youth, Sport and Culture 1981–84; Dir-Gen. SOTOCO (Société Togolaise de Coton) 1990–96; Minister of Health 1996–99, of Nat. Educ. and Research 1999–2002; Prime Minister of Togo 2002–05; Special Adviser to Pres. 2005; mem. Rassemblement du peuple togolais— RPT (fmr Sec.-Gen.); Officier, Ordre de Mono, Grand Officier, Ordre du Mérite agricole. *Address:* c/o Rassemblement du peuple togolais (RPT), pl. de l'Indépendance, BP 1208, Lomé, Togo (office).

SAMAAN, Alice Thomas; Bahraini diplomatist and politician; *Ambassador to UK;* b. 1 Jan. 1939, Manama; single; ed British Lebanese Training Coll., Beirut, Univ. of Southern California, USA; fmr teacher, American Mission School, Bahrain; fmr producer, presenter and dir of radio programmes for a religious radio station in Beirut, Lebanon; fmr Head of Overseas and Local Training, Ministry of Health; fmr Int. Program Officer for UNICEF in Bahrain and Oman; fmr Ed., Producer and Presenter of News, Bahrain Radio and TV Station; mem. Shura Council (Advisory Council) 2000–02, presided over as most sr mem. in absence of Chair. and two Deputy Chairs (first non-Muslim to act as Chair.) 2005,

later Second Deputy Chair. Majlis ash-Shoura, mem. Services Cttee for initial term, Vice-Chair. for second and fourth sessions of first legis. term; mem. Ad-hoc Cttee for Women and Children for first term; Amb. to UK (also accred to Ireland) 2011–; mem. Exec. Bd, American Mission Hosp., Bd of Dirs Al-Raja School for one term, Supreme Council for Vocational Training in Bahrain for one term, Bd of the Coll. of Health Sciences, Ministry of Health, Exec. Cttee, Nat. Program for Mother and Child Care, Oman. *Address:* Embassy of Bahrain, 30 Belgrave Square, London, SW1X 8QB, England (office). *Telephone:* (20) 7201-9170 (office). *Fax:* (20) 7201-9183 (office). *E-mail:* information@bahrainembassy.co.uk (office). *Website:* www.bahrainembassy.co.uk (office).

SAMAKUVA, Isaías; Angolan politician; *President, União Nacional para a Independência Total de Angola (UNITA);* b. 8 July 1946, Cunje; fmr Treas., União Nacional para a Independência Total de Angola (UNITA), Chief of Logistics mid-1980s, Rep. in Paris 1998–2002, fmr Interim Leader, Pres. 2003–. *Address:* União Nacional para a Independência Total de Angola (UNITA), Rua 28 de Maio, 1ª Travessa 2, Maianga, Luanda, Angola (office). *Telephone:* 222331215 (office). *Website:* www.unitaangola.com (office); www.kwacha.net (office); www.samakuva .com (office).

SAMANDOV, Lt-Gen. Atanas Nikolov; Bulgarian military officer; *Commander of the Joint Operational Command;* b. 17 Sept. 1955, Gotse Delchev, Blagoevgrad Region; divorced; two c.; ed Yane Sandanski Polytechnic School, Gotse Delchev, Vasil Levski Nat. Mil. Univ., Veliko Tarnovo, G.S. Rakovski Nat. Defence Acad., Gen. Staff Acad., Russia; promoted to rank of Second Lt 1977; Platoon Commdr 1977–79; rank of Lt 1979; Co. Commdr 1979–83; rank of First Lt 1983; Bn Commdr 1985–87; rank of Capt. 1986; Deputy Regt Commdr 1987–91; rank of Maj. 1991; Regt Commdr 1991–94; rank of Lt-Col 1993; Deputy Div. Commdr 1994–95; rank of Col 1996; Brigade Commdr 1996–98; Div. Commdr 1998–2001; Commdr of Special Operations Forces Command 2001–04; rank of Brig.-Gen. 2002; Commdr of Operational Forces Command 2004–06; rank of Maj.-Gen. 2006; Land Forces Chief of Staff 2006–08; Deputy Land Forces Commdr 2008–09; rank of Lt-Gen. 2009; Commdr of Jt Operational Command 2009–; Order of Honours of Bulgarian Armed Forces, Order of Merit of Bulgarian Armed Forces, Commendation Medal 'For Meritorious Service under the Colours' – II Class, Commendation Medal 'For Meritorious Service under the Colours' – I Class, inscribed personal weapon and other decorations. *Address:* Ministry of Defence, 3 Dyakon Ignatiy ul, 1000 Sofia, Bulgaria (office). *Telephone:* (2) 922-09-66 (office). *Fax:* (2) 922-09-68 (office). *E-mail:* presscntr@mod.bg (office). *Website:* www.mod.bg (office).

SAMAR, Sima, OC, DMed; Afghan politician, physician and human rights activist; *Chairperson, Afghanistan Independent Human Rights Commission;* b. 3 Feb. 1957, Jaghori, Ghazni; m. Abdul Raoof; one s. one d.; ed Kabul Univ.; exiled in Pakistan following Soviet invasion; Founder and Dir Shuhada Org., f. Shuhada hosp. for Afghan women and children, Quetta, Pakistan 1989, founder of three medical clinics, four hosps and girls' schools in rural Afghanistan (also providing medical training, literacy programmes and food aid), f. school for refugee girls in Quetta, f. Shuhada Org.; mem. Women Living Under Muslim Law; political activist and opponent of women's subjugation under Taliban regime; Vice-Chair. and Minister of Women's Affairs, Afghan Interim Admin 2001–02; currently Chair. Afghanistan Ind. Human Rights Comm.; UN Special Rapporteur for Human Rights in Sudan 2005–09; mem. Truth and Justice Party 2011; Hon. LLD (Univ. of Alberta) 2004, (Univ. of Carleton) 2010; Hon. DHumLitt (Brown Univ.) 2005, (Salem State Univ., USA) 2013; numerous awards, including Community Leadership Award, Ramon Magsaysay Award Foundation 1994, Global Leader for Tomorrow, World Econ. Forum 1995, 100 Heroines Award 1998, Paul Gruniger Human Rights Award 2001, Voice of Courage Award, Women's Comm. for Refugee Women and Children 2001, Best Social Worker, Mailo Trust Foundation, Pakistan 2001, Int. Human Rights Award, Int. Human Rights Law Group 2002, Freedom Award, Women's Asscn for Freedom and Democracy, Spain 2002, Lawyers Cttee for Human Rights Award 2002, Silver Banner Award, Italy 2002, Women for Peace, Together for Peace Foundation, Rome 2002, Silver Rose Award, Brussels 2003, Perdita Huston Human Rights Award 2003, UN Asscn of the Nat. Capital Area 2003, Paul Schiller Stiftung Award 2004, Global Women's Rights Award 2007, Ypres Peace Prize 2008, Asia Democracy and Human Rights Award 2008, ranked by Forbes magazine amongst the 100 Most Powerful Women (74th) 2004, (28th) 2006, (92nd) 2007, Don and Arvonne Fraser Human Rights Award, Advocates for Human Rights 2009, Politikens Freedom Prize (Denmark) 2009, Geuzen Medal (Netherlands) 2011, Tipperary Peace Prize (Ireland) 2011, Stephen J. Solarz Award for Commitment to Peace, Justice and Security, Int. Crisis Group, New York 2011, Right Livelihood Award 2012, Allard Prize for Int. Integrity (Canada) 2013. *Address:* Afghanistan Independent Human Rights Commission, Pul-i-Surkh, Karti 3, Kabul (office); Darulaman Road, Street No. 9, House No. 566, 6th District, Kabul, Afghanistan (home). *Telephone:* (20) 2500676 (office); 700-276283 (mobile). *Fax:* (20) 2500677 (office). *E-mail:* aihrc@aihrc.org.af (office); sima_samar@yahoo.com (home). *Website:* www.aihrc.org.af (office).

SAMARAS, Antonis C., BA, MBA; Greek economist and politician; *Prime Minister;* b. 23 May 1951, Athens; son of the late Prof. Constantine Samaras and Lena Samaras (née Zannas); m. Georgia Kretikos; one s. one d.; ed Athens Coll., Amherst Coll. and Harvard Business School, USA; mem. New Democracy –1993, Sec. 1989–92, rejoined party 2004, Pres. New Democracy 2009–; mem. Vouli (Parl.) for Pref. of Messenia 1977–93, 2007–, Leader of the Opposition 2009–11 (then supported Govt of Lucas Papademos), mem. Econ. Affairs and European Affairs Cttees 2007–; Minister of Finance July–Oct. 1989, of Foreign Affairs 1989–90, of Culture Jan.–Oct. 2009; Prime Minister of Greece following formation of coalition govt with Panhellenic Socialist Movt (PASOK) and Democratic Left (Dimokratiki Aristera) 20 June 2012–; mem. Messinian Political Spring 1993–, Pres. –2004; mem. European Parl. 2004–09, mem. Budget Cttee, Cttee on Econ. and Monetary Policy, Comm. for the Lisbon Strategy, Cttee on Parl. Co-operation EU-Russia. *Address:* Office of the Prime Minister, Maximos Mansion, Herodou Atticou 19, 106 74 Athens (office); New Democracy (Nea Demokratia), Odos Rhigillis 18, 106 74 Athens, Greece (office). *Telephone:* (210) 3385491 (PM) (office); (210) 7418131 (New Democracy) (office). *Fax:* (210) 3238129 (PM) (office); (210) 7251491 (New Democracy) (office). *E-mail:* primeminister@primeminister.gr (office); indpress@ nd.gr (office). *Website:* www.primeminister.gov.gr (office); www.nd.gr (office); www .antonis-samaras.gr.

SAMARASEKERA, Indira V., OC, BSc, MS, PhD, DSc, FRSC, FCAE; Canadian (b. Sri Lankan) professor of metals and materials engineering and university administrator; *President and Vice-Chancellor, University of Alberta;* b. 11 April 1952, Colombo; m.; two c.; ed Univ. of Ceylon, Univ. of California, USA, Univ. of British Columbia, Canada; fmr mechanical engineer, Refinery of Ceylon Petroleum Corpn; emigrated to Canada 1977; fmr Hays-Fulbright Scholar; fmr Dir of Student Affairs, Minerals, Metals and Materials Soc. of AIME; apptd Prof. Dept of Metals and Materials Eng and Centre for Metallurgical Process Eng, Univ. of British Columbia 1980, first Dofasco Chair in Advanced Steel Processing 1996, Vice-Pres. Research 2000–05; Pres. and Vice-Chancellor Univ. of Alberta 2005–; mem. Bd of Dirs Scotiabank 2008–, Discovery Parks Inc., Genome British Columbia, Canadian Microelectronics Corpn, Michael Smith Foundation for Health Research, The Stem Cell Network, Canadian Genetics Diseases Network, Provincial Health Services Authority; E.W.R. Steacie Fellow 1991; advisor to Canadian Minister of Environment at Copenhagen Summit 2009; moderator and speaker at World Econ. Forum in Davos 2010, 2011, 'Summer' Davos in China; mem. Science and Eng Advisory Cttee, Alberta Ingenuity Fund, Presidential Advisory Cttee, MIT, Carnegie Mellon Univ.; Vice-Chair. UNESCO Forum Scientific Cttee for Europe and N America; fmr Pres. Metallurgical Soc. of CIM; fmr mem. Nat. Research Council of Canada, Nat. Advisory Bd on Minerals and Metals, British Columbia Research Inst. for Children and Women's Health, Killam Selection Cttee for Canada Council for the Arts, Int. Review Cttee for Ontario Challenge Fund, Aquanet-NCE; fmr mem. Bd Children and Women's Health Centre of BC, TRIUMF; Fellow, Canadian Inst. of Mining, Metallurgy and Petroleum; Dr hc (Univ. of British Columbia, Univ. of Waterloo, Univ. of Montreal, Western Univ., Queen's Univ., Belfast, NI); Iron and Steel Soc. of AIME Robert W. Hunt and Charles H. Herty Best Paper Awards (jtly), UK Materials Soc. Williams Prize and Ablett Prize, TMS Extraction and Processing Technology Award, Univ. of British Columbia, Killam Prize and McDowell Medal for research excellence, British Columbia Science Council Award for New Frontiers in Research, Canadian Learning Partnership Award 2008, named by the Globe and Mail as one of five runners up for the Nation Builder of the Year 2010, named by the Women Executive Network as one of the top 100 women 2010, Peter Lougheed Leadership Award, Public Policy Forum (Canada) 2012, Leadership Award, CASE Dist VII (USA) 2012. *Address:* Office of the President, 2-24 South Academic Building, University of Alberta, Edmonton, Alberta, T6G 2G7, Canada (office). *Telephone:* (780) 492-3212 (office). *Fax:* (780) 492-9265 (office). *E-mail:* uofapres@ualberta.ca (office). *Website:* www.president.ualberta.ca (office).

SAMARASINGHE, Hudson; Sri Lankan journalist, broadcasting executive and fmr politician; *Chairman, Sri Lanka Broadcasting Corporation;* b. Peradeniya; ed Arethusa Coll., Howard Univ., USA; has worked in various positions for Sri Lanka Broadcasting Corpn for 40 years, including broadcaster, Chair. (for fourth time) 2010–; mem. Parl. (UNP) for Colombo East constituency 1992–94. *Address:* Office of the Chairman, Sri Lanka Broadcasting Corporation, Independence Square, POB 574, Colombo 7, Sri Lanka (office). *Telephone:* (11) 2696417 (office). *Fax:* (11) 2695488 (office). *E-mail:* chairman@slbc.lk (office). *Website:* www.slbc.lk (office).

SAMARASINGHE, Maj.-Gen. M. C. Mendaka P., MSc, MPh; Sri Lankan army officer; b. 1 April 1958, Colombo; ed St Thomas' Coll., Mount Lavinia, Coll. of Mil. Eng, India, Royal Mil. Coll. of Science, Cranfield, UK, Fort Leonardswood, USA, Madras Univ., India; joined Sri Lanka Mil. Acad. as Officer Cadet 1978, passed out 1980, rank of 2nd Lt 1980, joined 1st Field Engineer Regt, becoming Commdr Combat Engineers, later Col-Gen. Staff, 55 Infantry Div., Gen. Officer Commanding, 22 Div., Trincomalee, Chief Instructor, Army Command and Staff Coll., Brig.-Gen. Staff Security Forces, Commdr Security Forces, Jaffna –2009, Army Chief of Staff 2009–10, transferred to Jt Operations Command 2010; mem. Advisory Group to Govt of Sri Lanka Del. during peace talks with Liberation Tigers of Tamil Eelam (LTTE), Geneva, Switzerland Feb. 2006; Rana Wickrama Padakkama, Rana Sura Padakkama for gallantry during operations, Utthama Seva Padakkama for meritorious service; Sri Lanka Mil. Acad. Sword of Honour for Best All Round Cadet 1980. *Address:* c/o Army Headquarters, Baladaksha Mawatha, Colombo 03, Sri Lanka.

SAMARASINGHE, Adm. Thisara Sugeeshwara Gunasekara; Sri Lankan naval officer (retd) and diplomatist; *High Commissioner to Australia;* b. 16 July 1954, Colombo; s. of Francis Samarasinghe and Umawathie Samarasinghe; m. Malathie Samarasinghe; one s. one d.; ed Royal Coll., Colombo (Sr Prefect and Regimental Sergeant Maj. of the Cadet Corps), Naval and Maritime Acad., Britannia Royal Naval Coll., UK, Navigation and Direction School, INS Venduruthy, India, Naval Staff Coll. (Class 38), Naval War Coll., Newport, RI, USA, Nat. Defence Coll., New Delhi; joined Sri Lanka Navy as an Officer Cadet 1974; served on board Short Patrol Craft, Long Patrol Craft and in command of one of first two Dvora-Mk I Fast Attack Crafts 1985; later served on board Fast Gun Boats of 3rd Fast Gun Boats Squadron and Surveillance Command Tender and Surveillance Command Ship (then the Flagship) of 7th Surveillance Command Squadron; shore commands included a naval base in northern naval area and of two training establishments; also served in several Staff and Deputy Dir/Dir appointments at Naval HQ; ADC to HRH The Prince of Wales during his state visit to Sri Lanka for 50th Anniversary Indep Day Celebrations 1998; as a Cdre, posted as Deputy Area Commdr of Northern Naval Area, Eastern Naval Area and Southern Naval Area, before being apptd Commdr of Southern Naval Area 2002–04; first Dir, Gen. Services, and concurrently Dir Naval Projects and Plans, Naval Asst to Commdr of the Navy and Prin. Staff Officer of Jt Operations HQ under the Chief of Defence Staff 2004–05; led Naval dels to India, Russia, Israel and USA on bilateral issues 1995–2006; rank of Rear Adm. 2005; Acting Commdr Northern Naval Area 2005–06; Dir Gen. Naval Operations 2006–07; Commdr Eastern Naval Area during Eastern operations and in 2008, Commdr Northern Naval Area during Northern offensive 2007–09; apptd Chief of Staff of the Navy 2009, Commdr of the Navy 2009–11; rank of Rear Adm. 2005, Vice-Adm. 2009, Adm. 2011 (retd); High Commr to Australia 2011–; mem. Prime Ministerial del. on state visit to Indonesia 2006, of Presidential del. on state visit to Libya 2009; Rana Sura Padakkama (RSP) for gallantry in combat, Vishista Seva Vibhushanaya (VSV) and Uttama Seva Padakkama (USP) service medals, Sri Lanka Armed Services Long Service Medal, Purna Bhumi Padakkama Medal, North and East Operations Medal, and others; won Sword of Honour of 4th intake at Naval and Maritime Acad., Best Int. Midshipman Award, Britannia Royal Naval Coll. 1976,

five commendation letters from four Commdrs of the Navy 1977–2006. *Address:* Sri Lanka High Commission, 35 Empire Circuit, Forrest, ACT 2603, Australia (office). *Telephone:* (2) 6239-7041 (office). *Fax:* (2) 6239-6166 (office). *E-mail:* admin@slhcaust.org (office). *Website:* www.slhcaust.org (office).

SAMARAWEERA, Mangala; Sri Lankan politician; *Leader, Sri Lanka Freedom Party—Mahajana Wing;* b. 21 April 1956; s. of Mahanama Samaraweera and Khema Samaraweera; ed St Martin's School of Art, London, UK; fmr Design Consultant Nat. Design Centre of Sri Lanka; Organizer for Matara, Sri Lanka Freedom Party (SLFP) 1983–, Chief Opposition Whip and Treas. SLFP 2002–04, currently Asst Sec.; mem. Parl. 1989–; fmr Minister of Post and Telecommunications, of Urban Devt, Construction and Public Utilities; fmr Deputy Minister of Finance; Minister of Ports, Aviation, Information and Media and Deputy Minister of Educ. –2005; Minister of Foreign Affairs 2005–07, of Ports and Aviation 2005–07; Founder and Leader, Sri Lanka Freedom Party—Mahajana Wing 2007–. *Address:* Sri Lanka Freedom Party—Mahajana Wing, Colombo 1, Sri Lanka (office).

SAMARDŽIC, Vice-Adm. Dragan; Montenegrin naval officer and government official; *Chief of the General Staff, Army of Montenegro;* b. 14 May 1963, Kotor; m. Branka Samardžic; one s. one d.; ed Naval Acad., Gen. Staff School, War Coll., Belgrade; commissioned as Ensign in Montenegrin Navy, served aboard 401-type missile gun boats as Weapons Officer, XO, CO and Commdr of Squadron 1985–95; various positions in 18th Flotilla HQ including Chief of Staff and Deputy Flotilla Commdr 1995–2001, Flotilla Commdr 2001–03; Deputy of Mil. Cabinet to Pres. of State Union of Serbia and Montenegro, Belgrade 2003; Chief of Staff Naval Corps and promoted to Flag Officer 2003–05; C-in-C Serbia and Montenegro Navy 2005–06; Deputy Chief of Gen. Staff, Army of Montenegro 2006–07, Chief of Gen. Staff 2008–; Asst Minister for Material Resources, Ministry of Defence 2007–08; Cavaliere dell'Ordine 'Al Merito della Repubblica Italiana', numerous decorations from Montenegrin Govt. *Address:* Ministry of Defence, 81000 Podgorica, Jovana Tomaševića 29, Montenegro (office). *Telephone:* (81) 483561 (home). *Fax:* (81) 224702 (office). *E-mail:* dragan.samardzic@vojska.me (office). *Website:* www .odbrana.gov.me/ministarstvo (office); www.vojska.me/me (office).

SAMAWI, Khalid al-; Syrian banker and gallery owner; *Founder, Ayyam Gallery;* fmr banker based in London and Switzerland –2006; Founder Ayyam Gallery, Damascus 2006, also of sister galleries in Dubai, Beirut, Jeddah, London and Cairo; Entrepreneur of the Year, Arabian Business Achievement Awards 2009, ranked by Arabian Business amongst its Power 500: The World's Most Influential Arabs (21st) 2010, (32nd) 2012, (30th) 2013. *Address:* Ayyam Gallery, Mezzeh West Villas 30, Chile Street, Samawi Building, Damascus, Syria (office). *Telephone:* (11) 6131088 (office). *Fax:* (11) 6131087 (office). *E-mail:* info@ayyamgallery.com (office). *Website:* www.ayyamgallery.com (office).

SAMBA-PANZA, Catherine, DESS; Central African Republic lawyer and politician; *Interim President;* b. 26 June 1954, Fort Lamy, French Equatorial Africa (now N'Djamena, Chad); m. Cyriaque Samba-Panza; three c.; ed Panthéon-Assas Univ., France; early career as lawyer with Central African Repub. br. of Allianz.Group; Mayor of Bangui 2013–14; apptd Interim Pres. of Central African Repub. 23 Jan. 2014–; mem. Asscn des femmes juristes de Centrafrique, Asscn des maires francophones. *Address:* Office of the President, Palais de la Renaissance, Bangui, Central African Republic (office). *Telephone:* 21-61-46-63 (office). *Website:* presidencerca.com (office).

SAMBI, Ahmed Abdallah; Comoran politician, business executive and fmr head of state; b. 5 June 1958, Mutsamudu, Anjouan; m. Hadjira Djoudi 1988; two s. five d.; ed in Saudi Arabia, Sudan and Hawzat Al Qaaim Coll., Iran; f. madras for girls 1986, imprisoned for 21 days following riot after closure of school by authorities in 1987; co-f. Ulézi Radio and TV Ulézi 1990; co-f. National Front for Justice Party 1990, soon left politics to concentrate on business activities; owner of factories producing mattresses, bottled water, and perfume; Pres. of Comoros 2006–11. *Leisure interests:* basketball, football, tennis. *Address:* c/o Office of the Head of State, BP 521, Moroni, The Comoros (office). *Telephone:* (74) 4808 (office). *Fax:* (74) 4829 (office). *Website:* www.beit-salam.km (office).

SAMBLES, J(ohn) Roy, BSc, PhD, FRS, FInstP; British physicist and academic; *Professor of Experimental Physics, University of Exeter;* b. Callington, Cornwall; ed Imperial Coll., London; Postdoctoral Research Assoc. in Surface Physics, Imperial Coll., London 1970–72; Lecturer in Physics, Univ. of Exeter 1972–91, Prof. of Experimental Physics 1991–, currently Academic Lead of Electromagnetic and Acoustic Materials Research Group; Council mem. Eng and Physical Sciences Research Council 2008–, Chair. Resource Audit Cttee; Pres.-elect, Inst. of Physics 2013–; consultant, Defence Scientific Advisory Council 2005–11, DSAC Independent (ISTA mem.) 2011, Atlas Electronics 2012; Academic Bd mem. 2006; George William Gray Medal, British Liquid Crystal Soc. 1998, Thomas Young Medal and Prize, Inst. of Physics 2003, Faraday Medal and Prize, Inst. of Physics 2012. *Publications:* The Optics of Thermotropic Liquid Crystals (co-ed.) 1998; more than 400 papers in professional journals. *Address:* School of Physics, University of Exeter, Stocker Road, Exeter, EX4 4QL, England (office). *Telephone:* (1392) 724103 (office). *Fax:* (1392) 724111 (office). *E-mail:* j.r.sambles@exeter.ac.uk (office). *Website:* emps.exeter.ac.uk/physics-astronomy (office); newton.ex.ac.uk/staff/JRS (office).

SAMBO, Namadi, BSc, MArch; Nigerian architect and politician; *Vice-President;* b. 2 Aug. 1954, Kaduna; m. Amina Sambo; six c.; ed Govt Secondary School (now Alhuda-Huda Coll.), Zaria, Ahmadu Bello Univ., Zaria; with Ministry of Works and Housing Nat. Youth Service Corps, Oyo State 1978–79; Commr for Works, Transport and Housing, Kaduna State 1988–90; pvt practice as architect in 1990s with Coplan Assocs, Nalado Nigeria Ltd, Manyatta Engineering Services Ltd; mem. People's Democratic Party; Gov. Kaduna State 2007–10; Vice-Pres. of Nigeria 2010–. *Address:* Office of the Vice-President, New Federal Secretariat Complex, Shehu Shagari Way, Central Area District, Abuja, Nigeria (office). *Telephone:* (9) 5233536 (office).

SAMBROOK, Richard, BA, MSc; British media executive; *Global Vice-Chairman and Chief Content Officer, Edelman;* b. 24 April 1956, Canterbury; m.; two c.; ed Oakwood Grammar School, Maidstone, Reading Univ., Birkbeck Coll. London Univ.; trainee journalist Thomson Regional Newspapers 1977; spent three years with Celtic Press in Welsh Valleys and South Wales Echo; joined BBC as sub-ed. in radio newsroom 1980, later producer and programme ed. on nat. TV news, sr producer and deputy ed. Nine O'Clock News, News Ed. BBC Newsgathering 1992–96, Head of Newsgathering 1996–99, Deputy Dir News Div. 1999–2001, Dir BBC News 2001–04, Dir World Service and Global News Div. 2004–10; Global Vice-Chair. and Chief Content Officer, Edelman (public relations co.) 2010–. *Address:* Edelman, Southside, 105 Victoria Street, London, SW1E 6QT, England (office). *Telephone:* (20) 3047-2000 (office). *Fax:* (20) 3047-2507 (office). *E-mail:* contactus@edelman.co.uk (office). *Website:* www.edelman.co.uk (office).

SAMBÚ, Soares; Guinea-Bissau politician; *Minister of the Economy and Regional Integration;* Pres. Cttee on Agric., Fisheries, Natural Resources, Environment and Tourism 1997–98; mem. Cen. Cttee Partido Africano da Independência da Guiné e Cabo Verde (PAIGC), Dir election campaign 2004; mem. Nat. Ass., Deputy Speaker –2003, PAIGC MP for Bafata e Cosse constituency 2009–; Minister of Foreign Affairs, Int. Co-operation and Communities 2004–05, of Natural Resources 2007–09, Minister of the Economy and Regional Integration 2013–. *Address:* Ministry of the Economy and Regional Integration, Av. dos Combatentes da Liberdade da Pátria, CP 67, Bissau (office); Partido Africano da Independência da Guiné e Cabo Verde, CP 106, Bissau, Guinea-Bissau (office). *Website:* www.paigc .org (office).

SAMIOS, Nicholas Peter, AB, PhD; American physicist and academic; *Director, RIKEN BNL Research Center, Brookhaven National Laboratory;* b. 15 March 1932, New York, NY; s. of Peter Samios and Niki Samios; m. Mary Linakis 1958; two s. one d.; ed Columbia Coll., Columbia Univ., New York; Instructor, Dept of Physics, Columbia Univ. 1956–59, Adjunct Prof. 1970–; Asst Physicist Brookhaven Nat. Lab. Dept of Physics 1959–62, Assoc. Physicist 1962–64, Physicist 1964–68, Group Leader 1965–75, Sr Physicist 1968–, Chair. Div. of Particles and Fields 1975–76, Chair. PEP Experimental Program Cttee (of SLAC & LBL) 1976–78, Chair. Dept of Physics 1975–81, Deputy Dir 1981, Acting Dir 1982, Dir 1982–97, Deputy Dir RIKEN BNL Research Center 1998–, now Dir; Adjunct Prof., Stevens Inst. of Tech. 1969–75; mem. Bd of Dirs Stony Brook Foundation 1989–2004, Adelphi 1989–97, Long Island Asscn 1990–97; mem., fmr mem. or fmr chair. numerous specialist cttees and bds; Corresp. mem. Akademia Athenon 1994–; mem. NAS; Fellow, American Physical Soc. 1964 (mem. Exec. Cttee 1976–77), American Acad. of Arts and Sciences; E.O. Lawrence Memorial Award 1980, New York Acad. of Sciences Award in Physical and Math. Sciences 1980, AUI Distinguished Scientist 1992, W.K.H. Panofsky Prize 1993, Bruno Pontecorvo Prize, Jt Inst. for Nuclear Research, Moscow 2001, G.C. Wick Gold Medal 2009. *Address:* RIKEN BNL Research Center, Building 510A, Room 1-70, Physics Department, Brookhaven National Laboratory, Upton, NY 11973-5000, USA (office). *Telephone:* (631) 344-6281 (office). *Fax:* (631) 344-4906 (office). *E-mail:* samios@bnl.gov (office). *Website:* www.bnl.gov/riken (office).

SAMMONS, Mary F., BA; American retail executive; b. 1947, Portland, Ore.; ed Maryhurst Coll.; began career with Fred Meyer Inc. 1973, sr positions, including as Exec. Vice-Pres., in all areas of operations and merchandising 1985–97, Pres. and COO Fred Meyer Stores (food, drug and gen. merchandise retailer and subsidiary of The Kroger Co.) 1998–99, Pres. and CEO April–Dec. 1999; mem. Bd of Dirs, Pres. and COO Rite Aid Corpn 1999–2003, Pres. and CEO 2003–08, Chair. 2007–12, CEO 2008–10, Dir 2012–, Pres. The Rite Aid Foundation; mem. Bd of Dirs StanCorp Financial Group, Inc.; fmr mem. Bd of Dirs First Horizon National Corpn; mem. Exec. Cttee Nat. Asscn of Chain Drug Stores (fmr Chair.); ranked by Fortune magazine amongst 50 Most Powerful Women in Business in the US (37th) 2003, (33rd) 2004, (39th) 2005, (34th) 2006, (35th) 2007, ranked by Forbes magazine amongst 100 Most Powerful Women (40th) 2004, (27th) 2005, (16th) 2006, (15th) 2007, (18th) 2008, (21st) 2009. *Address:* Rite Aid Corpn, PO Box 3165, Harrisburg, PA 17105 (office); Rite Aid Corpn, 30 Hunter Lane, Camp Hill, PA 17011, USA (office). *Telephone:* (717) 761-2633 (office). *Fax:* (717) 975-5871 (office). *E-mail:* contacttheboard@riteaid.com (office). *Website:* www.riteaid.com (office).

SAMMOUR, Gen. Saeed Muhammad; Syrian army officer and government official; b. 1950, Jable; m.; four c.; Chair. regional br. in mil. intelligence dept –2005, Deputy Chair. mil. intelligence br. 2005–09; Minister of the Interior 2009–11 (resgnd with rest of cabinet at Pres.'s request following popular protests). *Address:* c/o Ministry of the Interior, rue al-Bahsah, al-Marjeh, Damascus, Syria.

SAMMUT, Salv; Maltese trade union official (retd); b. (Saviour Lawrence), 4 March 1947, Lija; m. Doris Sammut; two s. one d.; ed Diploma in Social Studies and Industrial Relations, Univ. of Malta; mem. Nat. Comm. for Health and Safety 1994, Bd Health and Safety Authority 2001–09; Vice-Pres. General Workers' Union (GWU) 1999–2001, Pres. 2001–09, represented GWU at int. congresses and confs relating to EU issues on matters of health and safety dealing with trade unions; fmr mem. EU Advisory Cttee on Health and Safety; Substitute mem. Bilbao Agency on Health and Safety; Sec. Maltese Poets Soc. *Plays:* eight short plays. *Radio:* readings of three novels and several short stories and poems have been broadcast. *Publications:* four novels, book of poetry (Second Place, Prize of the Year nat. award) 2000, book of verse 2008, novels 2010, 2011; essays and articles for journals. *Leisure interests:* reading, writing literature. *Address:* 'The Quest', Maisonette 2, Block R, Trejqet il-Gilju, Mtarfa, MTF 1430, Malta (home). *Telephone:* (2145) 4903 (home); 79-64550 (mobile). *E-mail:* dorsal@maltanet.net (home).

SAMPAIO, Jorge Fernando Branco de; Portuguese politician, fmr head of state and UN official; b. 18 Sept. 1939; m. Maria José Ritta; one s. one d.; ed Univ. of Lisbon; leader of students' union and led protests against govt as student in Lisbon 1960–61; following graduation as lawyer defended several political prisoners; fmr mem. Socialist Left Movt then joined Socialist Party (PS), elected Deputy to Nat. Parl. 1979, Pres. Parl. Bench 1986–87, Sec.-Gen. 1989–91; mem. European Comm. for Human Rights 1979–84; Mayor of Lisbon 1989–95; Pres. of Portugal 1996–2006; Special Envoy of the Sec.-Gen. to Stop Tuberculosis, UN 2006–13, High Rep. of the Sec.-Gen. for the Alliance of Civilizations, UN 2006–12; Order of the Three Stars (Latvia), Order of the White Eagle (Poland) 1997, Order of the White Double Cross, First Class (Slovakia) 2003, Grand Cordon of the Order of Leopold (Belgium) 2005, Grand Master, Order of the Tower and Sword (Portugal), Kt Grand Cross with Grand Cordon of the Order of Merit (Italy), Collar of the Order of the Cross of Terra Mariana (Estonia), Kt Grand Cross of the Order of St

Olav (Norway), Kt Grand Cross of the Order of St Michael and St George (UK), Grand Cross of the Order of Vytautas the Great (Lithuania); Council of Europe North–South Prize 2008. *Leisure interests:* music, golf. *Address:* Socialist Party (PS), Largo do Rato 2, 1269-143 Lisbon (office); Tapada das Necessidades, 1350-213 Lisbon, Portugal. *Telephone:* (21) 3822000 (office); (21) 3931440. *Fax:* (21) 3822022 (office); (21) 3965079. *E-mail:* portal@ps.pt (office); tp.olagerodasac@lareg. *Website:* www.ps.pt (office); jorgesampaio.pt.

SAMPATH, Veeravalli Sundaram; Indian civil servant and government official; b. 16 Jan. 1950; joined the Admin. Service 1973, Dist Collector 1975–86; apptd, Food and Public Distribution Dept, Industries Dept, Finance Dept 1989, apptd Sec., Agriculture Dept 1990; fmr Prin. Sec., Energy Dept, Finance Dept, served in Ministry of Rural Devt; Man. Dir Godavari Fertilizers and Chemicals Ltd –2004; apptd Dir-Gen. Nat. Inst. of Rural Devt 2005; fmr Sec. Chemicals and Petrochemicals, Ministry of Power; Election Commr 2009–12, Chief Election Commr 2012–13; fmr Man. Dir Apex Co-operative Bank, Handloom Marketing Soc., Oil Seeds Fed. *Address:* c/o Election Commission of India, Nirvachan Sadan, Ashoka Road, New Delhi 110 001, India.

SAMPERMANS, Françoise, MA, LèsL; French business executive; *Publishing Consultant and Director, UPM-Kymmene;* b. 10 July 1947, Paris; d. of Jacques Durand and Jeannine Behot; one s. one d.; joined CIT-TRANSAC 1974; est. public relations service, Chapelle Darblay 1978; Head of Public Relations, Entreprise et Crédit 1981; Dir of Communications, Transmission, Group Thomson 1982; subsequently Deputy Dir, Dir of Communications, Alcatel CIT; Dir of Communications, Alcatel NV 1987, Alcatel Alsthom 1987; Dir-Gen. Générale Occidentale 1991–95; Pres. Dir-Gen. Groupe Express 1992–95; Vice-Pres. Québecor-Europe 1996–2000; apptd Pres., Dir-Gen. Nouvel Economiste 1999; apptd Dir-Gen. Marianne and L'Evènement du Jeudi 1999; Vice-Pres. Nouvelles Messageries de la Presse Parisienne 2000–04; apptd Pres. Asscn for radiation of Chateau de Vincennes 2008; mem. Bd UPM-Kymmene (Finland) 2004–, currently Publishing Consultant, Dir; mem. Bd DATEM (France); Chevalier, Ordre des Arts et des Lettres. *Address:* 18 rue Charles Silvestri, 94300 Vincennes, France.

SAMPHAN, Khieu (see KHIEU Samphan).

SAMPLE, Steven Browning, BS, MS, PhD; American electrical engineer and university administrator; *President, University of Southern California;* b. 29 Nov. 1940, St Louis, Mo.; m. Kathryn Sample (née Brunkow); two d.; ed Univ. of Illinois, Urbana-Champaign; Sr Scientist, Melpar Inc., Falls Church, Va 1965–66; Assoc. Prof. of Electrical Eng, Purdue Univ. 1966–73; Deputy Dir Ill. Bd of Higher Educ., Springfield 1971–74; Exec. Vice Pres. of Academic Affairs, Dean Grad. Coll. and Prof. of Electrical Eng, Univ. of Neb. 1974–82; Prof. of Electrical and Computer Eng and Pres. State Univ. of New York (SUNY), Buffalo 1982–91; Pres. Univ. of Southern California 1991–, holder, Robert C. Packard Pres.'s Chair; Co-founder Asscn of Pacific Rim Univs; fmr Chair. Asscn of American Univs; Fellow, Nat. Acad. of Eng 1998–, American Acad. of Arts and Sciences 2003–; Dr hc (Canisius Coll., Buffalo) 1989, (Sheffield, UK) 1991, (Hebrew Union Coll.) 1994, (Purdue) 1994, (Neb.) 1995, (Northeastern) 2004, (Notre Dame) 2005, (SUNY, Buffalo) 2006; Los Angeles Area Chamber of Commerce Distinguished Business Leader Award, Central City Asscn of Los Angeles Heart of the City Award, Chancellor Charles P. Norton Medal, State Univ. of NY, Buffalo, Nat. Conference of Christians and Jews Humanitarian Award, Jewish Fed. Council of Greater Los Angeles Hollzer Memorial Award, Los Angeles Co. Econ. Devt Corpn Eddy Award, Alumni Achievement Award, Univ. of Illinois, Chancellor Charles P. Norton Medal, SUNY, Buffalo 2004, IEEE Founders Award 2008. *Achievements include:* has licensed numerous patents in field of digital appliance controls to major mfrs. *Publications:* The Contrarian's Guide to Leadership 2001; numerous journal articles and published papers in science, eng and higher educ. *Address:* Office of the President, University of Southern California, University Park Campus, ADM 110, MC 0012, Los Angeles, CA 90089, USA (office). *Telephone:* (213) 740-2111 (office). *Fax:* (213) 821-1342 (office). *Website:* www.usc.edu/president (office).

SAMPOERNA, Putera; Indonesian business executive; *Founder, Sampoerna Foundation;* b. 13 Oct. 1947, The Netherlands; m.; four c.; ed Univ. of Houston, Tex., USA; began career with family-owned palm oil and rubber plantations in Malaysia 1970–80; took over family tobacco business PT Hanjaya Mandala Sampoerna Tbk 1986 (sold to Philip Morris International 2005); currently Dir PT Sampoerna Strategic (holding co.), business interests include Sampoerna Agro (palm plantation); Founder Putera Sampoerna Foundation (educational charity) 2001; Peace Through Commerce Medal Award, US Int. Trade Admin 2011. *Leisure interest:* football. *Address:* Putera Sampoerna Foundation, Sampoerna Strategic Square, North Tower, 27th Floor, Jl. Jendral Sudirman, Kav. 45, Jakarta 12930, Indonesia (office). *Telephone:* (21) 5772340 (office). *Fax:* (21) 5772341 (office). *Website:* www.sampoernafoundation.org (office).

SAMPRAS, Pete; American fmr professional tennis player; b. 12 Aug. 1971, Washington, DC; s. of Sam Sampras and Georgia Sampras; m. Brigette Wilson 2000; two s.; turned professional 1988; holds US men's record for most Grand Slam singles titles (14); US Open Champion 1990, 1993, 1995, 1996, 2002; Grand Slam Cup Winner 1990; IBM/ATP (Asscn of Tennis Professionals) Tour World Championship—Frankfurt Winner 1991; US Pro-Indoor Winner 1992; Wimbledon Singles Champion 1993, 1994, 1995, 1997, 1998, 1999, 2000; European Community Championships Winner 1993, 1994; ranked No. 1 1993–98 (record); Winner Australian Open 1994; RCA Championships 1996, ATP Tour World Championships, 1996, Australian Open 1997; Winner San José Open 1997, Philadelphia Open 1997, Cincinnatti Open 1997; Munich Open 1997, Paris Open 1997, Hanover Open 1997, Advanta Championship 1998; mem. US Davis Cup Team 1991, 1995; won 64 US Tour singles titles, two doubles titles and US $43,280,489; Chair. ATP Tour Charities Programme 1992; investor, partner and special consultant, Tennis Magazine 2003–; Co-founder Pure Sports Management, LLC 2007; f. Acres for Charity Fund; Jim Thorpe Tennis Player of the Year 1993, ATP Tour Player of the Year 1993–97, US Olympic Cttee Sportsman of the Year 1997, inducted into Int. Tennis Hall of Fame 2007. *Leisure interests:* golf, basketball, Formula 1 racing. *Address:* c/o Pure Sports Management, LLC, 904 Silver Spur Road, #350, Rolling Hills, CA 90274, USA (office). *Telephone:* (424) 241-3151 (office). *Fax:* (310) 807-9255 (office). *E-mail:* info@puresportsmgmt.com (office). *Website:* www .puresportsmanagement.com (office); www.petesampras.com (office).

SAMS, Jeremy Charles; British director, writer, composer and translator; b. 12 Jan. 1957, Croydon, Surrey, England; s. of Eric Charles Sydney Sams and Enid Sams (née Tidmarsh); one c.; ed Whitgift School, Magdalene Coll., Cambridge, Guildhall School of Music. *Plays:* directed: The Wind in the Willows (Tokyo) 1993, 1995, (Old Vic) 1995, Neville's Island (Nottingham Playhouse and West End), Forty Years On (West Yorks. Playhouse), Maria Friedman by Special Arrangement (Donmar Warehouse and West End), Enjoy (Nottingham Playhouse), Wild Oats (Royal Nat. Theatre) 1995, Passion (West End) 1996, Marat/Sade (Royal Nat. Theatre) 1997, 2 Pianos 4 Hands (Birmingham Repertory and West End) 1999, Spend Spend Spend (Plymouth and West End) 1999–2000, (tour) 2001, Noises Off (Royal Nat. Theatre) 2000, (West End, Broadway and tour) 2001, What The Butler Saw (Theatre Royal Bath and tour) 2001, Benefactors (West End) 2002, Water Babies (Chichester Festival Theatre) 2003, Little Britain Live (tour) 2005, Donkey's Years (West End) 2006, The Sound of Music (West End, Toronto and UK tours) 2006, 13 (Broadway) 2008, The King and I (Royal Albert Hall) 2009, Educating Rita (Menier Chocolate Factory) 2010, The Wizard of Oz (Palladium) 2011, (Toronto) 2012. *Music:* composed for stage: Ring Round The Moon, The Country Wife, Jumpers, Don Carlos, Edward II, As You Like It, Some Americans Abroad, Ghetto, The Wind in the Willows, The Scarlet Pimpernel, Talking Heads, Kean, The Rehearsal, Arcadia, Merry Wives of Windsor; composed for BBC: Nativity Blues, Welcome Home Comrades, Uncle Vanya, Old Times, Down Town Lagos, Persuasion (BAFTA for Best Original Television Music), Have Your Cake. *Films:* composed: Enduring Love (Ivor Novello Award for Best Film Score), The Mother, Hyde Park on Hudson. *Address:* c/o The Agency (London) Ltd, 24 Pottery Lane, Holland Park, London, W11 4LZ, England (office). *Telephone:* (20) 7727-1346 (office). *Fax:* (20) 7727-9037 (office). *E-mail:* info@theagency.co.uk (office). *Website:* www.theagency.co.uk (office).

SAMSONOWICZ, Henryk, PhD; Polish politician, historian and academic; *Professor, Instytut Historyczny, University of Warsaw;* b. 23 Jan. 1930, Warsaw; m. Agnieszka Lechowska; one s. one d.; ed Univ. of Warsaw; joined staff, Univ. of Warsaw 1950, Asst Lecturer then Sr Asst Lecturer 1950–60, Asst Prof. 1960–69, Prof., History Inst. 1969–, Vice-Dean 1967–69, Dean Dept of History 1969–74, Dir 1975–80, Rector 1980–82; mem. Civic Cttee attached to Lech Wałęsa (q.v.), Chair. Science and Educ. Comm., Solidarity Trade Union 1988–89; Head of Dept of Social Sciences, Polish Acad. of Sciences 2001–; participant, Round Table plenary debates, mem. group for political reforms and team for science, educ. and tech. progress Feb.–April 1989; Minister of Nat. Educ. 1989–90; Deputy Head of Scientific Research Cttee 1994–97; mem. Polish Historical Soc. (Chair. Gen. Bd 1977–82), Soc. for Advancement and Propagation of Sciences 1980–, Academia Europaea 1992–94, Acad. des Belles Lettres, Polish Acad. of Sciences 1994–; Hon. citizen Pułtusk and Ostrowiec Świętokrzyski; Gold Cross (Hungary), Commdr's Cross, Order of Polonia Restituta, Gold Cross of Merit, Officier, Légion d'honneur 1984, Order of White Eagle 2010; Dr hc (Duquesne Univ., USA, High School of Educ., Kraków, Nicolaus Copernicus Univ., Toruń, Marie Curie-Skłodowska Univ., Lublin); Nat. Educ. Comm. Medal. *Publications include:* Bürgerkapital in Danzig des XV Jh 1970, Złota jesień polskiego Średniowiecza (Golden Autumn of the Polish Middle Ages) 1971, Dzieje miast i Polscę (History of the Towns of Poland) 1984, Republic of Nobles 1990, Dziedzictwo Średniowiecza (Heritages of the Middle Ages) 1994, Miejsce Polski w Europie (Poland's Place in Europe) 1996, Europe – North-South 1999; numerous articles in professional journals. *Address:* Instytut Historyczny Uniwersytetu Warszawskiego, ul. Krakowskie Przedmieście 26/28, 00-927 Warsaw (office); ul. Wilcza 22 m. 5, 00-544 Warsaw, Poland (home). *Telephone:* (22) 8261988 (office); (22) 6214061 (home). *Fax:* (22) 8261988 (office). *E-mail:* wydzial1@pan.pl (office); h.samsonowicz@gmail.com (home). *Website:* www.ihuw.pl (office).

SAMUELI, Henry, BS, MS, PhD; American electrical engineer, computer scientist, academic and business executive; *Chief Technical Officer and Chairman, Broadcom Corporation;* b. 20 Sept. 1954, Buffalo, NY; s. of Aron Samueli and Sala Samueli; m. Susan Samueli; three c.; ed Fairfax High School, Univ. of California, Los Angeles; Prof. of Electrical Eng, UCLA 1985–; Co-founder and Chief Tech. Officer, Broadcom Corpn 1991–, Chair. 1991–2008, 2011–; mem. Nat. Acad. of Eng 2003; Distinguished Adjunct Prof., Dept of Electrical Eng and Computer Science, Univ. of California, Irvine 2003–; Co-owner (with his wife) Anaheim Ducks professional ice hockey team 2005–; IEEE Circuits and Systems Soc. Industrial Pioneer Award 2000, Presidential Medal, Univ. of California 2000, University of California, Irvine Medal 2000, Alumnus of the Year Award, UCLA School of Eng and Applied Science 2000, UCLA Medal 2010, Dr Morris Chang Exemplary Leadership Award, Global Semiconductor Alliance 2011, Marconi Prize and Fellowship 2012. *Publications:* more than 100 technical papers in professional journals on digital signal processing and communications systems engineering; 70 US patents. *Address:* Broadcom Corporation, 5300 California Avenue, Irvine, CA 92617, USA (office). *Telephone:* (949) 926-5000 (office). *Fax:* (949) 926-5203 (office). *E-mail:* czegarel@broadcom.com (office). *Website:* www.broadcom.com (office).

SAMUELSSON, Bengt Ingemar, DMS, MD; Swedish medical chemist and academic; *Professor of Physiological Chemistry, Karolinska Institutet;* b. 21 May 1934, Halmstad; s. of Anders Samuelsson and Stina Nilsson; m. Inga Bergstein 1958; two c.; ed Karolinska Inst., Stockholm; Asst Prof., Karolinska Inst. 1961–66, Prof. of Physiological Chemistry 1972–, Chair. Dept of Physiological Chem. 1973–83, Dean, Faculty of Medicine 1978–83, Rector 1983–95; Research Fellow, Harvard Univ., USA 1961–62; Prof. of Medical Chem., Royal Veterinary Coll., Stockholm 1967–72; mem. Nobel Cttee of Physiology or Medicine 1984–89, Chair. 1987–89; Chair. Nobel Foundation 1993–2005; mem. Bd of Dirs Svenska Handelsbanken AB, Pharmacia & Upjohn, The Liposome Co., NicOx; mem. Advisory Bd Odlander Fredrikson & Co. AB; mem. Research Advisory Bd Swedish Govt 1985–88, Nat. Comm. on Health Policy 1987–90, European Science and Tech. Ass. 1994; Special Advisor to Commr for Research and Educ., EC 1995; mem. Royal Swedish Acad. of Sciences 1981–; Foreign Assoc. NAS; Foreign mem. Royal Soc. (London), Mediterranean Acad. of Sciences, Acad. Europaea, French Acad. of Sciences, Spanish Soc. of Allergology and Clinical Immunology, Royal Nat. Acad. of Medicine (Spain), Int. Acad. of Sciences; Hon. Prof., Bethune Univ. of Medical Sciences, Changchun, China 1986; Hon. mem. Asscn of American Physicians 1982, AAAS 1982, Swedish Medical Asscn 1982, American Soc. of Biological Chemists, Italian Pharmacology Soc., Acad. Nat. Medicina de Buenos Aires, Int. Soc. of Haematology; Hon. DSc (Chicago) 1978, (Illinois) 1983, (Louisiana State Univ.)

1993; Dr hc (Rio de Janeiro) 1986, (Complutense Univ., Madrid) 1991, (Milan) 1993; Hon. DUniv (Buenos Aires) 1986; Jubilee Award, Swedish Medical Asscn 1968, 1981, Anders Jahres Award, Oslo Univ. 1970, Louisa Gross Horwitz Award, Columbia Univ. 1975, Intrascience Medalist 1976, Albert Lasker Basic Medical Research Award 1977, Ciba Geigy Drew Award 1980, Lewis S. Rosenstiel Award 1981, Gairdner Foundation Award 1981, Heinrich Wieland Prize 1981, Bror Holmberg Medal, Swedish Chemical Soc. 1982, Medical Chemistry Award, ACS 1982, Waterford Bio-Medical Science Award 1982, Int. Asscn of Allergology and Clinical Immunology Award 1982, Nobel Prize in Physiology or Medicine 1982, Abraham White Science Achievement Award 1991, City of Medicine Award 1992, Maria Theresa Medal 1996. *Publications include:* numerous articles in professional journals. *Address:* Karolinska Institutet, Department of Medical Biochemistry and Biophysics, C2, Departments, Physiological Chemistry II, Scheeles Väg 2, 171 77 Stockholm, Sweden (office). *Telephone:* (8) 524-87-60 (office). *Fax:* (8) 736-04-39 (office). *E-mail:* Bengt.Samuelsson@ki.se (office). *Website:* kikatalogen.ki.se (office).

SAMUKAI, Brownie J.; Liberian government official; *Minister of Defence;* ed Univ. of Liberia, American Univ.; Commdr, Black Berets (paramilitary police force) 1993–94; Dir Liberian Nat. Police 1994–95; Deputy Minister of State for Admin 1995–97; fmr Deputy Minister of Defence, Deputy Minister of State for Presidential Affairs; fled Liberia and worked with UN and UNHCR in East Timor and Tanzania 1999–2004; Minister of Defence 2006–. *Address:* Ministry of Defence, Benson Street, POB 10-9007, 1000 Monrovia, Liberia (office). *Telephone:* 226077 (office). *Website:* www.mod.gov.lr (office).

SAMURA, Sorious; Sierra Leonean journalist and documentary filmmaker; b. 1964; mem. Bd Insight News Television, London; arrested along with mems of Channel 4 (UK) TV crew in Liberia on alleged espionage charges 2000, imprisoned for one week; now lives in UK; Dr hc (Univ. of East Anglia) 2003; CNN African Journalist of the Year 1999, Rory Peck Award 1999, Mohamed Amin Award 1999, Amnesty International Media Award for TV Documentary 2000, George Foster Peabody Award 2000, ICRC Dignity in Conflict Award 2000, Columbia-DuPont Award 2001, BAFTA Award for News and Current Affairs Journalism 2001, TV Documentary Award, One World Media Awards 2000, 2001, two Emmy Awards, two further Amnesty International Media Awards, Prix Europa, Japan Prize, Harry Chapin Media Award, three Overseas Press Club of America Awards, Golden Nymph, Monte Carlo Television Festival, Bronze World Medal, New York Festivals. *Films documentaries:* Cry Freetown 1999, Return to Freetown 2000, Exodus from Africa 2001, 21st Century War 2002, Living with Hunger 2003, Living with Illegals 2006, Africa's Last Taboo 2010.

SAMYN, Gilles; French/Belgian banking executive; *CEO, Compagnie Nationale à Portefeuille (CNP);* b. 2 Jan. 1950, Cannes; m. Myriam Goethals; five c.; ed Solvay Business School, Université Libre de Bruxelles; Asst Solvay Business School 1969–75, Lecturer 1975; Adviser Mouvement Co-operatif Belge 1972–74; with Groupe Bruxelles Lambert 1974–82; Ind. Adviser 1982–83; joined Groupe Frère-Bourgeois 1983, becoming Man. Dir Erbe SA 1986–, Dir Cie Nationale à Portefeuille 1988–, currently CEO and mem. Exec. Cttee; mem. Bd of Dirs Groupe Bruxelles Lambert 1987–, Pargesa Holding 1992–, Transcor, Astra Group, Groupe Flo, Entremont Alliance, Gruppo Banca Leonardo, M6, Affichage Holding, Imetal, CLT-UFA, Grand Hôpital de Charleroi, Acide Carbonique Pur. *Address:* Compagnie Nationale à Portefeuille, Rue de la Blanche Borne 12, 6280 Loverval, Gerpinnes, Belgium (office). *Telephone:* (71) 60-60-60 (office). *Fax:* (71) 60-60-70 (office). *E-mail:* cnp@cnp.be (office). *Website:* www.cnp.be (office); www.npm-cnp .be (office).

SAN GIACOMO, Laura; American actress; b. 14 Nov. 1962, West Orange, NJ; d. of John San Giacomo and MaryJo San Giacomo; m. 1st Cameron Dye 1990 (divorced 1998); one s.; m. 2nd Matt Adler 2000; ed Morris Knolls High School, NJ, Carnegie Mellon Univ., Pa; started career in regional theatre productions; co-f. CHIME Charter Elementary School 2001. *Theatre includes:* North Shore Fish, Beirut, The Love Talker, Italian American Reconciliation. *Films include:* Sex, Lies and Videotape (New Generation Award, LA Film Critics' Asscn) 1989, Pretty Woman 1990, Vital Signs 1990, Quigley Down Under 1990, Once Around 1991, Under Suspicion 1991, Where the Day Takes You 1992, Nina Takes a Lover 1994, Stuart Saves His Family 1995, Eat Your Heart Out 1997, Suicide Kings 1997, Apocalypse 1997, With Friends Like These . . . 1998, Mom's on the Roof, House on a Hill 2003, Havoc 2005, Checking Out 2005, Saving Grace 2007. *Television includes:* The Stand (miniseries) 1994, Just Shoot Me (series) 1997–2003, Sister Mary Explains It All 2001, Jenifer 2001, Saving Grace (series) 2007. *Leisure interests:* horse riding, playing piano, gymnastics, ballet. *Address:* More Medavoy Management, 7920 West Sunset Boulevard, Suite 401, Los Angeles, CA 90046, USA.

SAN MIGUEL RODRIGUEZ, Walker, BA; Bolivian lawyer and government official; b. 6 Aug. 1963, Ciudad de La Paz; m. Tatiana Núñez Ormachea; ed Universidad Mayor de San Andrés, Univ. of Salamanca, Spain, Univ. of Nancy, France; fmr Dir Lloyd Bolivian Airlines; fmr Exec. Chair. Colegio de Abogados de La Paz; Vice-Chair. Colegio Nacional de Abogados de Bolivia; Minister of Nat. Defence 2006–10; mem. Nat. Acad. of Judicial Sciences of Bolivia, Inter-American Fed. of Lawyers. *Address:* c/o Ministry of National Defence, Plaza Avaroa, esq. Pedro Salazar y 20 de Octubre 2502, La Paz, Bolivia (office).

SANADER, Ivo, PhD; Croatian politician; b. 8 June 1953, Split; m. Mirjana Sanader 1978; two d.; ed Univ. of Innsbruck, Austria; Programme Ed., later Ed.-in-Chief Logos publishing house, Split 1983–88; mem. Editorial Bd Mogućnosti (Possibilities) magazine 1987–90; man. own cos, Innsbruck 1988–91; Gen. Man. Croatian Nat. Theatre, Split 1991–92; mem. Parl. (House of Reps of Croatian Parl.) 1992–, Minister of Science and Tech. 1992–93; Deputy Minister of Foreign Affairs 1993–95; Chief of Staff to Pres. of Repub. of Croatia and Sec.-Gen. Defence and Nat. Security Council 1995–96; Deputy Minister of Foreign Affairs 1996–2000; Prime Minister of Croatia 2003–09 (resgnd); Pres. Croatian Democratic Union (HDZ) 2000–09; Deputy Chair. Foreign Affairs Cttee 2000; mem. Croatian Writers' Asscn, Croatian-PEN; attempted a political comeback inside HDZ but was ejected from party membership Jan. 2010; charged by Croatian authorities with two corruption indictments Dec. 2010, arrested, held in custody and questioned in Austria. *Publications:* author of several books on literary history and contemporary politics. *Leisure interests:* golf, reading, music. *Address:* Parliament of Croatia, 10000 Zagreb, Trg sv. Marka 6, Croatia (office). *Telephone:* (1) 4569222 (office). *Fax:* (1) 1 6303018 (office). *E-mail:* sabor@sabor.hr (office). *Website:* www.sabor.hr (office).

SANAKOYEV, Dimitri; Georgian government official; *Head of Administration of South Ossetia;* b. 10 May 1969, Tskhinvali, S Ossetian Autonomous Oblast, Georgian SSR, USSR; ed A. Tibilov South Ossetian State Univ.; fought on Ossetian side during Georgian–Ossetian conflict 1991–92; Minister of Defence in break-away region of S Ossetia 2000; Prime Minister 2001–03; apptd Pres. of the Provisional Admin of S Ossetia by Georgian Pres. Mikheil Saakashvili 2007–; mem. The Salvation Union of S Ossetia (political party). *Address:* 14/16 Gagarin str., Tbilisi, Georgia (home). *Telephone:* 95-958119 (mobile) (office); (32) 2998990 (office). *E-mail:* so_frede@yahoo.com (office). *Website:* www.soa.gov.ge (office).

SANBAR, Samir H., BBA; Lebanese international civil servant and consultant; b. 9 March 1934, Haifa; s. of Habib Sanbar and Georgette Khoury; ed American Univ. of Beirut; Deputy Ed. Al Howadeth, Al-Sayyad (Arab weeklies) and journalist with various Lebanese, Arab and int. media; Political Ed. Al-Usbu Al Araby (pan-Arab weekly), Beirut 1954–65; Information Officer of Special Rep. of Sec.-Gen. for UNYOM 1964; Special Asst to Personal Rep. of Sec.-Gen. of UNITAR 1965–70; Special Asst to Exec. Dir UNITAR 1970–73; accompanied UN Sec.-Gen. on all visits to Middle East 1973–87; Dir UN Information Centre, Beirut, Chief, Information Services of ECWA and Co-ordinator of UN public information activities in Gulf countries 1975–82; special assignment to assist Office of Sec.-Gen. in liaison and media functions during establishment of UNIFIL 1978–82; Chief UN Centres Services 1982–87; mem. and Chair. UN Appointment and Promotions Bd 1986–96; Dir UN Information Centres, Dept of Public Information 1987–93; Special Rep. of UN Sec.-Gen. to head UN mission to verify Referendum in Eritrea 1993; Asst Sec.-Gen. UN Dept of Public Information 1994–98; int. communications consultant; mem. Bd of Dirs UN International School 1994–96; Chair. Joint UN Information Committee 1996–98, UN Staff Recreation Council 1996–98; mem. Bd of Dirs Dag Hammarskjold Tower, The International Council of the Nat. Acad. of TV Arts and Sciences; currently Exec. Ed. UNforum. *Publication:* Hold on to Your Dreams; (short stories in Arabic): Characters From Ras Beirut, Aleikum Salam (Greetings). *Website:* www.unforum.com.

SÁNCHEZ CERÉN, Salvador; Salvadorean politician and head of state; *President;* b. 18 June 1944, Quezaltepeque; s. of Antonio Alfonso Sánchez and Dolores Rodas; m. Margarita Villalta; ed Univ. Salvadoreña Alberto Masferrer; began career as teacher; mem. Frente Farabundo Martí para la Liberación Nacional (FMLN), guerrilla leader in civil war 1980–92, Commanding Gen. of FMLN 1984; mem. Legis. Ass. (FMLN) 2000, re-elected 2003 and 2006; Vice-Pres. of El Salvador 2009–14, Pres. 2014–. *Address:* Ministry for the Presidency, Alameda Dr Manuel Enrique Araujo 5500, San Salvador, El Salvador (office). *Telephone:* 2248-9000 (office). *Fax:* 2248-9370 (office). *Website:* www.presidencia .gob.sv (office); sanchezceren.com.

SANCHEZ, Felix; Dominican Republic athlete; b. 30 Aug. 1977, New York; ed Univ. City High School, San Diego, Calif., Mesa Community Coll., San Diego, Univ. of Southern Calif.; sprinter and 400m hurdler; represents Dominican Republic (birthplace of his parents); 400m hurdles personal best 47.25 seconds (Paris, France Aug. 2003), 400m 44.90 seconds (Gateshead, UK Aug. 2001), 200m 20.87 seconds (Irvine, California May 2001); gold medal, 400m hurdles (1st Dominican Republic World Championship medal), World Championships 2001, 2003, 400m hurdles, Pan-American Games 2003; gold medal, 400m hurdles, Olympic Games, Athens 2004; silver medal, 400m hurdles, World Championships 2007, 4x400m relay, Pan American Games 2011; bronze medal, 4x400m relay, Pan American Games 2003, 4x400m relay, Pan American Games 2007; gold medal, 400m hurdles, Olympic Games, London 2012; ranked 1st in 2004 at 400m hurdles; won 43 consecutive 400m hurdles races; hurdles coach Harvard-Westlake School, Calif.; Central American and Caribbean Confed.'s Male Athlete of the Year 2002, 2003; Latin American Sportsman of the Year 2003. *Address:* c/o Harvard-Westlake School Athletics Department, 3700 Coldwater Canyon, Studio City, North Hollywood, CA 91604, USA.

SÁNCHEZ DE LOZADA, Gonzalo; Bolivian politician; b. 1 July 1930; m. Ximena Iturralde Monje; one s. one d.; ed Univ. of Chicago; Founder and Man. Telecine Ltda (documentary and commercial film production co.) 1953–57; Founder and Gen. Man. Andean Geo-Services Ltd 1957–62; Founder and Pres. Compañía Minera del Sur (COMSUR) 1962–79, Pres. 1980–82; mem. Parl. 1979–80, 1982–85; Senator for Cochabamba and Pres. Senate 1985–86; Minister for Planning and Coordination 1986–88; Presidential cand. 1989; Leader, Movimiento Nacionalista Revolucionario (Histórico) (MNR) 1988–2006; Pres. of Bolivia 1993–97, 2002–03; currently in exile in USA; mem. Club de Madrid. *Address:* c/o Movimiento Nacionalista Revolucionario, Avda Hernando Siles 21, Curva Sur del Estado Hernando Siles, La Paz, Bolivia.

SÁNCHEZ GALÁN, (José) Ignacio; Spanish industrial engineer and business executive; *Chairman and CEO, Iberdrola SA;* b. Sept. 1950, Salamanca; m.; four c.; ed Eng Tech. School (ICAI), Universidad Pontificia de Comillas, Madrid; Commercial Dir SE Acumulador Tudor SA, Operations Man., Man. Dir Industrial Batteries Div., Pres. and CEO several cos in Grupo Tudor 1972–91; Gen. Man. and CEO ITP 1991–95; CEO Airtel Movil 1995–2001; Vice-Chair. and CEO Iberdrola SA 2001, Chair. and CEO 2001–, Chair. Iberdrola Renovables SA –2011, Iberdrola Immobiliaria SA, El Desafío Español 2007 SA (co. that manages participation of Spanish boat in America's Cup), Chair. Scottish Power Ltd (part of Iberdrola Group) 2007–; Dir Page Ibérica, Bodegas Matarromera; mem. Bd Nutreco Holding BV, Page Iberica, GALP, Red Electrica de España, Bodegas Matarromera, Corporación IBV, Puleva Biotech and other cos; mem. Advisory Bd Accenture Energy; mem. Advisory Cttee Prince of Asturias Endowed Chair in Information Tech., Univ. of New Mexico; mem. Círculo de Empresarios Vascos, Círculo de Empresarios (Madrid), Círculo de Economía, Asociación para el Progreso de la Dirección, American Man. Asscn; Trustee, Fundación Universitaria Pontificia de Salamanca, Fundación Atapuerca, Fundación Consejo España-Estados Unidos, Fundación de Estudios Financieros, Fundación Premysa, Fundación Iberdrola; fmr Prof., School of Industrial Engineers, ICAI; Best CEO in European Utilities sector, Institutional Investor magazine 2007, Top Exec. of the Year, Platts Global

Energy Awards 2006, three Best CEO awards, Investor Relations magazine, Business Leader of the Year, Spain-US Chamber of Commerce 2008, Premio Internacional de Economía, Fundación Cristóbal Gabarrón 2008. *Leisure interests:* hunting, horse riding. *Address:* Iberdrola SA, Plaza Euskadi 5, 48009 Bilbao, Spain (office). *Telephone:* (94) 4151411 (office). *Fax:* (94) 4663194 (office). *E-mail:* informacion@iberdrola.com (office). *Website:* www.iberdrola.com (office); www .iberdrola.es (office).

SÁNCHEZ-VICARIO, Arantxa; Spanish fmr professional tennis player; b. 18 Dec. 1971, Barcelona; d. of Emilio Sánchez and Marisa Vicario; m. 1st Juan Vehils (divorced 2001); m. 2nd Jose Santacana 2008; one d.; most successful Spanish tennis player ever; turned professional in 1984 and won first professional title at Brussels 1988; winner French Open Women's title 1989, 1994, 1998, Int. Championships of Spain 1989, 1990, Virginia Slims Tournaments Newport 1991, Washington 1991, Canadian Open 1992, Australian Open Women's Doubles 1992, Mixed Doubles 1993, US Open 1994; named Int. Tennis Fed. World Champion 1994; silver medal (doubles), bronze medal (singles) 1992 Olympics; silver medal (singles), bronze medal (doubles) 1996 Olympics; Spanish Fed. Cup team 1986–98, 2000–01; winner of 14 Grand Slam titles, 96 WTA Tour titles and over US $16 million in prize money at retirement Nov. 2002; mem. Spanish Olympic Cttee 2001; Infiniti Commitment to Excellence Award 1992, Tennis Magazine Comeback Player of the Year 1998, Principe de Asturiasi Award (Spain) 1998, Int. Tennis Fed. Award of Excellence 2001. *Publication:* The Young Tennis Player: A Young Enthusiast's Guide to Tennis 1996. *Leisure interests:* soccer, water skiing, reading, horse riding, languages. *Address:* IMG, 1360 East 9th Street, Suite 100, Cleveland, OH 44114, USA (office).

SANCHO-ROF, Juan, DChemEng; Spanish business executive; *Vice-President, Board of Directors, Técnicas Reunidas Internacional SA;* b. 9 Feb. 1940, Madrid; m. Paloma Suils; two s. three d.; ed Universidad Complutense de Madrid and Instituto de Estudios Superiores de la Empresa, Barcelona; Technical–Commercial post Petronor SA (Petróleos del Norte) 1970–76, Deputy Gen. Man. 1976–85; Chair. and CEO Repsol Petróleo SA 1985, Pres. 1995, then Pres. Petronor and Exec. Vice-Pres. of Downstream, Repsol YPF –2003; mem. Bd of Dirs Gas Natural SDG 2003; currently Vice-Pres. Bd of Dirs Técnicas Reunidas Internacional, SA; Pres. Gen. Council of the Colls of Chemists of Spain. *Publications include:* several technical works. *Address:* Técnicas Reunidas Internacional SA, Arapiles 13, Madrid, Spain, (office). *Telephone:* (91) 5920300 (office). *Fax:* (91) 5920397 (office). *Website:* www.tecnicasreunidas.es (office).

SANDAGIRI, Adm. Daya, MSc; Sri Lankan naval officer; *Chairman, Phosphate Corporation;* b. Veyangoda; ed St Mary's Coll. Veyangoda, Kegalu Maha Vidyalaya; joined Royal Ceylon Navy (now Sri Lanka Navy) 1966, Sub-Lt 1973, Commdr of the Navy 2001–05, promoted to rank of Adm. 2005; Chief of Defence Staff 2004–06; apptd Deputy Sec., Ministry of Defence 2006, suspended June 2006 accused of engaging in malpractice in arms purchases; Chair. Phosphate Corpn 2011–. *Address:* c/o Ministry of Defence, 15/5 Baladaksha Mawatha, POB 572, Colombo 3, Sri Lanka.

SANDBERG, Baron (Life Peer), cr. 1997, of Passfield in the County of Hampshire; **Michael Graham Ruddock Sandberg,** Kt, CBE, FCIB, FRSA; British banker (retd); b. 31 May 1927, Thames Ditton, Surrey; s. of the late Gerald Arthur Clifford Sandberg and Ethel Marion (née Ruddock) Sandberg; m. Carmel Mary Roseleen Donnelly 1954; two s. two d.; ed St Edward's School, Oxford; mil. service 1945–48, commissioned into 6th Duke of Conaught's Own Lancers, Indian Army, later 1st King's Dragoon Guards; joined Hongkong and Shanghai Banking Corpn 1949, Deputy Chair. 1973–77, Chair. 1977–86; Chair. British Bank of the Middle East 1980–86; Pres. Surrey County Cricket Club 1987–88; Vice-Pres. Chartered Inst. of Bankers 1984–87; JP Hong Kong 1972–86; Dir New World Devt Ltd, Winsor Ind. Corpn; mem. of Exec. Council of Hong Kong 1978–86; Treasurer Univ. of Hong Kong 1977–86; Chair. of Stewards, Royal Hong Kong Jockey Club 1981–86, Hon. Steward 1986; Freeman City of London; Liveryman Worshipful Co. of Clock-makers; Hon. LLD (Hong Kong) 1984, (Pepperdine) 1986. *Publication:* The Sandberg Watch Collection 1998. *Leisure interests:* horse racing, cricket, bridge, horology. *Address:* House of Lords, London, SW1A 0PW (office); 11 St James's Square, London, SW1Y 4LB (office); Waterside, Passfield, Liphook, Hants., GU30 7RT, England (home). *Telephone:* (20) 7219-5353 (House of Lords) (office); (20) 7930-9924 (office); (1428) 751225 (home). *Fax:* (20) 7930-7028 (office); (1428) 751636 (home). *E-mail:* patriciawhetnall@btconnect.com (office).

SANDBERG, Sheryl Kara, AB, MBA; American business executive; *Chief Operating Officer, Facebook Inc.;* b. 28 Aug. 1969, Washington, DC; d. of Joel Sandberg and Adele Sandberg; m. 1st Brian Kraff (divorced 2004); m. 2nd David Goldberg 2004; two c.; ed Harvard Coll., Harvard Business School; grew up in North Miami Beach, Fla; taught aerobics while at high school 1980s; economist, World Bank 1991–93; Man. Consultant, McKinsey & Co. 1995–96; Chief of Staff to Sec., US Dept of Treasury, Washington, DC 1996–2001; Vice-Pres. Global Online Sales and Operations, Google Inc. 2001–08; COO Facebook Inc. 2008–, mem. Bd of Dirs 2012–; mem. Bd of Dirs eHealth Inc. 2006–08, Walt Disney Co. 2009–, Starbucks 2009–; mem. Bd Brookings Inst., Women for Women International, V-Day, Ad Council; John H. Williams Prize for top graduating student in econs, Harvard Coll. 1991, ranked by Fortune magazine amongst the 50 Most Powerful Women in Business in the US (29th) 2007, (34th) 2008, (22nd) 2009, (16th) 2010, (12th) 2011, (eighth) 2012, ranked by The Wall Street Journal on its list of 50 Women to Watch (19th) 2007, (21st) 2008, named as one of the 25 Most Influential People on the Web 2010, ranked by Forbes magazine amongst The World's 100 Most Powerful Women (66th) 2010, (fifth) 2011, (tenth) 2012, (sixth) 2013. *Publication:* Lean In: Women, Work, and the Will to Lead 2013. *Address:* Facebook Inc., 156 University Avenue, Suite 300, Palo Alto, CA 94301, USA (office). *Telephone:* (650) 543-4800 (office). *Fax:* (650) 543-4801 (office). *Website:* www .facebook.com (office).

SANDER, Jean-Marie; French business executive and politician; *Chairman, Crédit Agricole SA;* b. 23 Dec. 1949, Ohlungen, Alsace; engaged in industrial action with Jeunes Agriculteurs, Canton of Haguenau 1971; Pres. Jeunes Agriculteurs du Bas-Rhin 1972; elected City Councillor and Deputy Mayor of Ohlungen 1983, Mayor 1995; mem. Bd of Dirs Crédit Agricole SA 2003–, Chair. 2010–, Chair. Strategic Cttee and mem. Appointments and Governance Cttee; Chair. CRCAM d'Alsace-Vosges 1993–, CICA, Grameen Crédit Agricole Foundation, Caisse d'Assurance Accidents du Bas Rhin; Deputy Chair. SAS Sacam Développement; mem. Bd Fédération nationale du Crédit agricole, Chair. 2003–10, Deputy Chair. 2010–; Dir, SAS Rue La Boétie, SAS SACAM Participations, SCICAM, 'Pays de France' Crédit Agricole Foundation, 'Un Avenir Ensemble' Foundation, Société Electricité de Strasbourg; mem. Man. Cttee Gecam (GIE); Pres. Chambre d'agric. d'Alsace 1989–. *Address:* Crédit Agricole SA, 91–93 boulevard Pasteur, 75015 Paris, France (office). *Telephone:* 1-43-23-52-02 (office). *Fax:* 1-43-23-34-48 (office). *E-mail:* info@credit-agricole-sa.fr (office). *Website:* www.credit-agricole-sa.fr (office).

SANDER, Heidemarie Jiline (Jil); German fashion designer; b. 1944, Wesselburen; stylist on fashion magazine; designs clothes for working women; owns own co. Jil Sander, fmr Chair.; opened flagship store Hamburg 1968, Paris 1993, Tokyo 1999, New York 2008; launched first women's collection 1973; launched first fragrances Woman Pure and Man. Pure 1979; f. Jil Sander Italia SpA, Milan 1994, Jil Sander America, Inc. 1995; launched first men's collection 1997; introduced menswear range Jan. 1997; left Jil Sander AG 2000 after co. sold to Prada, returned as Chief Designer 2003. *Leisure interests:* modern art, gardening. *Address:* Jil Sander, Via Beltrami 5, 20121 Milan, Italy (office). *Telephone:* (80) 69131 (office). *E-mail:* info@JilSander.de (office). *Website:* www.jilsander.com (office).

SANDERS, Bernard (Bernie), BS; American politician; *Senator from Vermont;* b. 8 Sept. 1941, Brooklyn, NY; m. Dr Jane O'Meara Sanders; two s. two d.; ed James Madison High School, Brooklyn, Brooklyn Coll., Univ. of Chicago; moved to Vt 1964; worked as carpenter and journalist; political career began when he joined anti-Viet Nam War Liberty Union Party 1971, resgnd 1977; unsuccessful ind. cand. for election to Senate 1972, 1974, and for Gov. of Vt 1972, 1976, 1986; worked as writer and Dir American People's Historical Soc.; Mayor of Burlington 1981–86; cand. in elections for US House of Reps 1988, mem. House of Reps for Vermont-At Large Dist 1991–2006 (first ind. mem. of House since 1950, longest-serving ind. mem. of the House), mem. Cttee on Financial Services, Cttee on Govt Reform; Co-founder House Progressive Caucus, chaired group for its first eight years; Senator from Vermont 2007–; mem. Faculty, Harvard Univ. 1989, Hamilton Coll. 1991, Ind. (caucuses with Democrats and is counted as Democrat for purposes of cttee assignments). *Radio:* regular guest appearances on the Thom Hartmann radio programme for Friday segment Brunch with Bernie. *Publication:* Outsider in the House (autobiography) 1997. *Address:* 332 Dirksen Senate Office Building, Washington, DC 20510, USA (office). *Telephone:* (202) 224-5141 (office). *Fax:* (202) 228-0776 (office). *E-mail:* bernie@bernie.org. *Website:* sanders.senate.gov (office); bernie.org (office).

SANDERS, Donald Neil, AO, CB, BEcons; Australian banker; b. 21 June 1927, Sydney; s. of L. G. Sanders and R. M. Sanders; m. Betty Elaine Constance 1952; four s. one d.; ed Wollongong High School, Univ. of Sydney; with Commonwealth Bank of Australia 1943–60; with Australian Treasury 1956; with Bank of England 1960–61; with Reserve Bank of Australia 1961–87, Supt, Credit Policy Div. of Banking Dept 1964–66, Deputy Man. of Banking Dept 1966–67, of Research Dept 1967–70, Chief Man. of Securities Markets Dept 1970–72, of Banking and Finance Dept 1972–74, Adviser and Chief Man. 1974–75, Deputy Gov. and Deputy Chair. of Bd 1975–87; with Australian Embassy, Washington, DC 1968; Man. Dir Commonwealth Banking Corpn 1987–91; Man. Dir CEO Commonwealth Bank of Australia 1991–92; Chair. H-G Ventures Ltd 1995–2000; Dir Lend Lease Corpn Ltd, MLC Ltd 1992–99, Queensland Investment Corpn 1992–98, Australian Chamber Orchestra Pty Ltd 1992–99. *Publications:* Collected Speeches 1969–92. *Leisure interests:* golf, music. *Address:* 106 Blaxland Road, Wentworth Falls, NSW 2782, Australia (home). *Telephone:* (2) 4757-3900 (home).

SANDERS, Jeremy Keith Morris, BSc, PhD, ScD, FRS; British chemist, academic and university administrator; *Professor of Chemistry and Pro-Vice-Chancellor (Institutional Affairs), University of Cambridge;* b. 3 May 1948, London, England; s. of Sidney Sanders and Sylvia Sanders (née Rutman); m. Louise Elliott 1972; one s. one d.; ed Wandsworth School, Imperial Coll. London, Univ. of Cambridge; Research Assoc. in Pharmacology, Stanford Univ., USA 1972–73; Demonstrator in Chem., Univ. of Cambridge 1973–78, Lecturer 1978–92, Reader 1992–96, Prof. of Chem. 1996–, Head of Dept of Chem. 2000–06, Deputy Vice-Chancellor, Univ. of Cambridge 2006–10, Head of School of Physical Sciences 2009–11, Pro-Vice-Chancellor (Institutional Affairs) 2011–, Chair. Chem. Sub-panel, 2008 Research Assessment Exercise 2004–08, Fellow, Selwyn Coll. Cambridge 1976–; Visiting Fellow, Japan Soc. for the Promotion of Science 2002; Visiting Prof., Pole Balard Chimie, Montpellier, France 2013; mem. Editorial Bd Magnetic Resonance in Chemistry 1984–92, Journal of the Chemical Society Perkin Transactions 1988–93; mem. Editorial Advisory Bd Chemical Society Reviews 1996–2002, Chair. 2000–02; Assoc. Ed. New Journal of Chemistry 1998–2000; mem. Int. Supervisory Bd Nat. Research Consortium on Catalysis (Netherlands) 1999–2009; mem. Scientific Bd Inst. of Chemical Research of Catalonia 2002–; mem. Scientific Advisory Bd Cresset BioMolecular Discovery Ltd 2002–07; mem. Editorial Advisory Bd Journal of American Chemical Society 2009–; mem. Int. Advisory Bd Israel Journal of Chemistry 2010–, Chemistry sub-panel, 2014 Research Excellence Framework 2011–; Meldola Medal, Royal Inst. of Chem. 1975, RSC Hickinbottom Award 1981, Pfizer Award 1984, 1988, RSC Josef Loschmidt Prize 1994, RSC Pedler Lecturer 1996, Izaat Christensen Award, USA 2003, AstraZeneca Lecturer, Univ. of Alberta, Canada 2003, Merck-Frosst Lecturer, Simon Fraser Univ. 2003, IAP Lecturer, Columbia Univ. 2003, J. Clarence Karcher Lecturer, Univ. of Oklahoma 2005, Barré Lecturer, Univ. of Montreal 2007, Davy Medal, Royal Soc. 2009, Diamond Jubilee Anniversary Day Lecturer, Nat. Chemical Lab., India 2010, Pres. 'Burgenstock' Stereochemistry Conf., Switzerland 2011, Novartis Lecturer, Scripps Inst. 2011, Bender Distinguished Lecturer, Northwestern Univ., USA 2013. *Publications:* Modern NMR Spectroscopy (with B. K. Hunter, second edn) 1993; numerous papers in scientific journals. *Address:* Chemical Laboratory, University of Cambridge, Lensfield Road, Cambridge, CB2 1EW, England (office). *Telephone:* (1223) 336411 (office). *Fax:* (1223) 336017 (office). *E-mail:* jkms@cam.ac.uk (office). *Website:* www.ch.cam.ac.uk/person/jkms (office).

SANDERS, Sir Ronald Michael, Kt, KCMG, KCN, MA; Antigua and Barbuda diplomatist, international relations consultant, business executive and writer; b.

26 Jan. 1948, Guyana; m. Susan Ramphal 1975; ed Sacred Heart RC School, Guyana, Boston Univ., USA, Univ. of Sussex, UK; Man. Dir Guyana Broadcasting Service, Public Affairs Adviser to Prime Minister of Guyana 1973–76; Lecturer in Communications, Univ. of Guyana 1975–76; Consultant to Pres. of Caribbean Devt Bank, Barbados 1977–78; Special Adviser to the Minister of Foreign Affairs of Antigua and Barbuda 1978–82; Deputy Perm. Rep. of Antigua and Barbuda to the UN, New York 1982–83; Antigua and Barbuda Amb. Extraordinary and Plenipotentiary accred to UNESCO 1983–87; Antigua and Barbuda High Commr in UK 1984–87, 1995–2004 (also accred to FRG 1986–87, 1996–2004, to France 1996–2004), Chief Foreign Affairs Rep. with Ministerial Rank 1999–2004; Deputy Chair. Caribbean Financial Action Task Force 2002–; Pres. Caribbean Broadcasting Union 1975–76; Chair. Caribbean Sub-Group at UNESCO 1983–85; mem. Bd Dirs of Caribbean News Agency 1976–77; mem. Inter-Governmental Council of the Int. Programme for the Devt of Communications at UNESCO 1983–87; mem. Exec. Bd UNESCO 1985–87; Visiting Fellow, Univ. of Oxford 1987–89; freelance broadcaster with BBC World Service 1987–89; Consultant (Int. Relations) Atlantic Tele-Network, US Virgin Islands 1989–97; mem. Bd of Dirs Swiss American Nat. Bank of Antigua 1990–97, Guyana Telephone and Telegraph Co. 1991–97, Innovative Communication Corpn, US Virgin Islands 1998 (Exec. Dir for Int. Relations 2004); mem. Advisory Council Commonwealth Broadcasting Asscn 2005–; mem. Eminent Persons Group 2010–; currently columnist, Antigua Sun newspaper. *Publications include:* Broadcasting in Guyana 1978, Antigua and Barbuda: Transition, Trial, Triumph 1984, Inseparable Humanity: Anthology of Reflections of the Commonwealth Secretary-General (ed.) 1988, Antigua Vision: Caribbean Reality, Perspectives of Prime Minister Lester Bird (ed.) 2002, Crumbled Small: The Commonwealth Caribbean in World Politics 2005; numerous articles on media ownership and control, communication and development and Antarctica. *Leisure interests:* reading, West Indian history, cinema. *E-mail:* ronaldsanders29@hotmail.com. *Website:* www.sirronaldsanders.com.

SANDERSON, Bryan Kaye, CBE, BSc; British business executive; b. 14 Oct. 1940, Co. Durham; s. of Eric Sanderson and Anne Sanderson; m. Sirkka Kärki 1966; one s. one d.; ed Dame Allan's School, London School of Econs, UK, International Man. Inst. Lausanne, Switzerland; VSO Peru 1962–64; joined British Petroleum (BP) 1964, Sr Rep. for SE Asia and China 1984–87, CEO BP Nutrition 1987–90, CEO BP Chemicals, then BP Amoco Chemicals 1990–97, mem. Bd BP 1992–2000; Dir (non-exec.) Corus (fmrly British Steel) 1994–2000, Six Continents hotel group 2001–03; Chair. (non-exec.) BUPA 2001–06; Dir (non-exec.) Standard Chartered PLC 2002–03, Exec. Chair. 2003–06; Chair. QGS Synergy (now Business Impact UK Ltd) 2007–08; Chair. Northern Rock PLC 2007–08; mem. Advisory Group to the Labour Party on Industrial Competition Policy 1997–98, Dept for Trade and Industry (DTI) Advisory Group on Competitiveness 1998, King's Fund Man. Cttee 1999, DTI Co. Law Steering Group 1998, DTI Industrial Devt Advisory Bd 2000–04; Pres. European Chemical Industry Council 1998–2000; Chair. Learning and Skills Council 2000–04, Sunderland Urban Regeneration Co. 2001–08; mem. Bd of Dirs Glodyne Technoserve Ltd 2011–, Sunderland Football Club PLC 1998– (Chair. 1998–2004), Durham Co. Cricket Club 2005–; Gov. LSE 1997– (Vice-Chair. 1998–2004); mem. Commonwealth Business Council; Hon. FIChemE 2002; Hon. DBA (Sunderland) 1998, (York) 1999. *Leisure interests:* reading, golf, walking, gardening. *Address:* c/o Board of Directors, Sunderland Football Club, The Sunderland Stadium of Light, Sunderland, SR5 1SU, England.

SANDERSON, Theresa Ione (Tessa), CBE, OBE, MBE; British sports administrator and fmr athlete; b. 14 March 1956, St Elizabeth, Jamaica; ed Bilston Coll. of Further Educ.; Silver Medal for javelin, Euro Championships 1978; Gold Medal, Commonwealth Championships 1978, 1986, 1990; Gold Medal (Olympic record), Olympic Games, LA 1984; Gold Medal, World Cup, Cuba 1990; competed at six Olympic Games, Montreal 1976, Moscow 1980, Los Angeles 1984, Seoul 1988, Barcelona 1992, Atlanta 1996; retd from sport 1997; sports presenter, Sky News 1989–92; Vice-Chair. Sport England 1999–; mem. Bd English Sports Council 1998–, Olympic Park Legacy Co. 2009–11; Patron, Disabled Olympics; apptd to work with Newham Council to head Newham 2012 Sports Acad. 2006; f. Tessa Sanderson Foundation and Acad. 2009–; Hon. Fellow, South Bank Univ., Wolverhampton Polytechnic; Hon. MSc (Birmingham); Sunday Times Life Times Achievement Award 2004. *Publication:* My Life in Athletics (autobiog.) 1985. *Leisure interest:* cardiofunk (low impact aerobic exercise workout). *Address:* c/o Abingdon Management, Mortlake Business Centre, 20 Mortlake High Street, London, SW14 8JN, England (office); The Newham Unit for the 2012 Games, The Old Dispensary, Romford Road, London, E15 4BZ, England (office). *Telephone:* (20) 8430-3693 (office). *Website:* www.tessa.co.uk.

SANDIFORD, Rt Hon. Sir Lloyd Erskine, PC, JP, MA (Econs); Barbadian politician and diplomatist; b. 24 March 1937; s. of the late Cyril G. Sandiford and of Eunice Sandiford; m. Angelita P. Ricketts 1963; one s. two d.; ed Coleridge-Parry Secondary School, Harrison Coll., Barbados, Univ. Coll. of the West Indies, Jamaica and Univ. of Manchester, UK; Asst Master, Modern High School, Barbados 1956–57, Kingston Coll., Jamaica 1960–61; part-time Tutor and Lecturer, Univ. of the West Indies, Barbados 1963–65; Sr Grad. Master, Harrison Coll. 1964–66; Asst Tutor, Barbados Community Coll. 1976–86; mem. Barbados Senate 1967–71, MP for St Michael S 1971–99; Personal Asst to Prime Minister 1966–67; Minister of Educ. 1967–71, of Educ., Youth Affairs, Community Devt and Sport 1971–75, of Health and Welfare 1975–76; Deputy Prime Minister and Minister of Educ. and Culture 1986–87; Prime Minister of Barbados and Minister of Finance 1987–93, Prime Minister and Minister of Econ. Affairs and the Civil Service 1987–94, also of Defence; Amb. to People's Repub. of China 2010–14; Pres. Sandiford Centre for Public Affairs; Visiting Scholar, Pennsylvania State Univ., Harrisburg, Pa, USA; Founder, Acad. of Politics; mem. Democratic Labour Party, also Asst Sec., Gen. Sec., Pres. 1974–75; mem. Council of Freely Elected Presidents and Prime Ministers, Carter Center, Atlanta; mem. Global Peace Council, Universal Peace Fed.; Life mem. Barbados Cricket Asscn; tutor, Barbados Community Coll.; Order of the Liberator (Venezuela), Kt of St Andrew 2000; Hon. LLD (Univ. of the West Indies) 2009; Barbados Scholar 1956, Distinguished Fellow, Sir Arthur Lewis Inst. of Social and Econ. Studies, Univ. of the West Indies 1999, Pres.'s Medal of Excellence, Bowie State Univ., Maryland. *Poetry:* Ode to the Environment, When She Leaves You. *Publications include:* The Essence of Economics 1997, Caribbean Politics and Society 2000, Speeches (six vols). *Leisure* *interests:* choral singing, reading, gardening, swimming, cricket. *Address:* c/o Ministry of Foreign Affairs, 1 Culloden Road, St Michael, Barbados; Hillvista, Porters, St James, Barbados (home). *Telephone:* 422-3458 (home). *Fax:* 422-0281 (home). *E-mail:* lesandiford@carbsurf.com.

SANDILA, Adm. Mohammad Asif, BBA, MSc; Pakistani army officer; *Chief of Naval Staff;* b. 1954, Shaikhupura; ed Cadet Coll., Pakistan Naval Acad., Britannia Royal Naval Coll., UK, Nat. Defence Univ., Naval Command and Staff Coll., Indonesia; joined Navy as Non-commissioned Officer 1972, Sub-Lt Naval Operations Branch 1975, Air Defence Command, Fleet Operations Officer to Commdr Fleet 2001, Flag Lt to Chief of Staff, Dir Project (Plans), Asst Chief of Naval Staff (Plans), Prin. Sec. to Chief of Naval Staff, Chief of Staff, Coast Guard 2002–05, Commdr of Naval Logistics 2006–07, Commdr Naval Fleet 2008, Commdr of Naval Combatant Fleet and Naval Combatant Operations 2008–09, Chief of Staff, Naval Staff 2011–; Chevalier de II order mil. due merit 2004; Hilal-e-Imtiaz. *Address:* Pakistan Navy Headquarters, Mushaf Road, E-9, Islamabad, Pakistan (office). *E-mail:* webmaster@paknavy.gov.pk (office). *Website:* www.paknavy.gov.pk (office).

SANDLE, Michael Leonard, FRBS, DFA, ARA; British artist and fmr professor of art; b. 18 May 1936, Weymouth, Dorset; s. of Charles E. Sandle and Dorothy G. Sandle (née Vernon); m. 1st Cynthia D. Koppel 1971 (divorced 1974); m. 2nd Demelza Spargo 1988 (divorced 2004); one s. one d.; ed Douglas High School, Isle of Man, Douglas School of Art and Tech. and Slade School of Fine Art; studied lithography, Atelier Patris, Paris 1960; began sculpture 1962; held various teaching posts in UK 1961–70; Lecturer Coventry Coll of Art 1964–68; resident in Canada 1970–73; Visiting Prof., Univ. of Calgary 1970–71; Visiting Assoc. Prof., Univ. of Victoria, British Columbia 1972–73; Lecturer in Sculpture, Fachhochschule für Gestaltung, Pforzheim, FRG 1973–77, Prof. 1977–80; Prof., Akad. Für Bildenden Künste, Germany 1980–99 (retd); mem. RA 1990–97 (resgnd), re-elected 2004; Fellow, Kenneth Armitage Foundation 2004–06; designed architecture and executed sculpture for the Malta Siege Memorial, Grand Harbour, Valletta 1999–92; designed Int. Memorial for Seafarers at International Maritime Org's HQ, London 2001; works in many public collections in UK, Germany, Australia, USA; Nobutaka Shikanai Prize, 1st Rodin Grand Prize Exhbn, Japan 1986, Henry Hering Memorial Medal, Nat. Sculpture Soc. of America 1995.

SANDLER, Adam, BFA; American actor and screenwriter; b. 9 Sept. 1966, Brooklyn, New York; s. of Stanley Sandler and Judy Sandler; m. Jacqueline Samantha Titone; two d.; ed New York Univ.; People's Choice Award 2000. *Albums:* They're All Gonna Laugh at You! 1993, What the Hell Happened to Me? 1996, What's Your Name? 1997, Stan and Judy's Kid 2000, Shhh..Don't Tell 2004. *Films include:* Going Overboard (1989, Shakes the Clown 1992, Coneheads 1993, Airheads (1994), Mixed Nuts 1994, Billy Madison 1995, Happy Gilmore 1996, Bulletproof 1996, The Wedding Singer 1998, The Water Boy 1998, Big Daddy 1999, Little Nicky 2000, Punch-Drunk Love 2002, Mr Deeds 2002, Anger Management 2003, 50 First Dates 2004, Spanglish 2004, The Longest Yard 2005, Click 2006, Reign Over Me 2007, I Now Pronounce You Chuck and Larry 2007, You Don't Mess with the Zohan 2008, Funny People 2009, Grown Ups 2010, Just Go with It 2011, That's My Boy 2012, Hotel Transylvania 2012. *Television appearances include:* actor, writer Saturday Night Live 1991–95, Saturday Night Live Mother's Day Special 1992, MTV Music Video Awards 1994, Saturday Night Live Presents Pres. Bill Clinton's All-Time Favorites 1994, 37th Annual Grammy Awards 1995, ESPY Awards 1996. *Screenplays:* (co-writer) Billy Madison, Happy Gilmore, The Water Boy, You Don't Mess with the Zohan. *Publications:* Little Nicky 2000. *Address:* c/o The Endeavor Agency, 9601 Wilshire Blvd., 10th Floor, Beverly Hills, CA 90212; Agency for Performing Arts, 888 7th Avenue, Suite 602, New York, NY 10106, USA (office). *Website:* www.adamsandler.com.

SANDLER, Joanne; American international organization official; *Deputy Director for Programmes, UN Women;* ran consulting business that provided organizational devt support to women's orgs, New York; joined UNIFEM 1997, fmr Chief of Organisational Learning and Resource Devt and Deputy Dir for Programmes, Ad-Interim Exec. Dir –2008; currently Deputy Dir for Programmes, UN Women; mem. bd of dirs of several orgs including Asscn for Women's Rights in Devt, Gender at Work, Women Make Movies. *Address:* UN Women, 304 East 45th Street, 15th Floor, New York, NY 10017, USA (office). *Telephone:* (212) 906-6400 (office). *Fax:* (212) 906-6705 (office). *Website:* www.unwomen.org (office).

SANDLER, Ron, CBE, MA, MBA; South African business executive; *Executive Chairman, Towry Holdings Ltd;* b. 5 March 1952, Durban, South Africa; s. of Bernard M. Sandler and Carla Sandler; m. Susan Lee 1977; two s.; ed Queens' Coll. Cambridge, Stanford Univ., USA; worked at Boston Consulting, Los Angeles, USA, then Booz Allen, London, England; f. own man. consultancy firm 1988; apptd. Chair. Quadrex Holdings 1990; joined Lloyd's of London 1994, Chief Exec. 1995–99; COO Nat. Westminster Bank PLC 1999–2000; apptd Chair. Kyte Group 2000; Chair. Computacenter 2001–08; Chair. (non-exec.) Northern Rock PLC 2008–10, Exec. Chair. Feb.–Oct. 2008, 2010–11; Chair. Paternoster Ltd, Phoenix Group Holdings, Ironshore Inc.; Exec. Chair. Towry Holdings Ltd 2014–; Advisor, Palamon Capital Partners, LP; Deputy Chair. KiFin Ltd; Trustee, Royal Opera House 1999–; Head, Inquiry into Long-term Savings 2001; led Govt-sponsored review of UK Long Term Savings Industry 2002; fmr Pres. Chartered Inst. of Bankers. *Leisure interests:* poker, opera, golf, skiing. *Address:* Towry House, Western Road, Bracknell, RG12 1TL (office); 5 Southside, Wimbledon, London, SW19 4TG, England (home). *Telephone:* (20) 8946-1179 (home). *E-mail:* info@towry.com (office). *Website:* www.towry.com (office).

SANDMO, Agnar, DrOecon; Norwegian economist and academic; *Professor of Economics Emeritus, Norwegian School of Economics and Business Administration;* b. 9 Jan. 1938, Tønsberg; m. Tone Sverdrup 1959; two s. one d.; ed Tønsberg Gymnasium, Norwegian School of Econs and Business Admin. (NHH); Grad. Fellow, NHH 1963–66, Asst Prof. of Econs 1966–71, Prof. of Econs 1971–2007, Prof. Emer. 2007–, Vice-Rector 1985–87; Visiting Fellow, Catholic Univ. of Louvain 1969–70; Visiting Prof., Univ. of Essex 1975–76; mem. Petroleum Price Bd 1976–80, several govt bds and cttees on social science and gen. research policy; Pres. European Econ. Asscn 1990; mem. Norwegian and Swedish Acads of Science; Fellow, Econometric Soc.; Order of St Olav 1997; Dr hc (Oslo) 1997, (Uppsala)

2008; Research Council of Norway Prize for Outstanding Research 2002. *Publications:* articles and books on econs and econ. policy. *Address:* Norwegian School of Economics and Business Administration, Helleveien 30, 5045 Bergen (office); Måseskjærveien 8, 5035 Bergen, Norway (home). *Telephone:* 55-95-92-76 (office); 55-25-65-86 (home). *E-mail:* agnar.sandmo@nhh.no (office). *Website:* www.nhh.no (office).

SANDOVAL, Arturo; American musician (trumpet); b. 6 Nov. 1949, Artemisa, Cuba; m. Marianela Sandoval; one s.; ed Nat. School of Art; began trumpet playing aged 12 and made first public appearances in Cuba aged 13; played in group with Chucho Váldez until 1981; formed own group, Irakere, in 1981 and now undertakes annual maj. world tour; granted political asylum in USA 1990; currently Prof. of Music, Florida Int. Univ.; opened Arturo Sandoval Jazz Club, Miami Beach 2006; festival appearances at Tokyo, Newport, Montreux, Antibes, Chicago, The Hague and the Hollywood Bowl; several record albums; numerous Grammy and Billboard Awards. *Recordings include:* albums: Havana (with David Amram) 1976, New York (with David Amram) 1977, Irakere 1979, To a Finland Station (with Dizzy Gillespie) 1982, Breaking the Sound Barrier 1983, No Problem 1986, Tumbaito 1987, Straight Ahead 1988, Classics 1989, Arturo Sandoval 1989, Flight to Freedom 1991, I Remember Clifford 1992, Danzón 1993, Dream Come True 1993, Passion 1993, Cubano 1994, Arturo Sandoval y el Tren Latino 1995, Double Talk (with Ed Calle) 1996, Swingin' 1996, Just Music 1997, Hot House 1998, Americana 1999, Sunset Harbour (with Ed Calle) 1999, Los Elefantes (with Wynton Marsalis) 1999, For Love or Country 2000, Piedras y Flores (with Amaury Gutiérrez) 2001, L.A. Meetings 2001, My Passion for the Piano 2002, From Havana With Love 2003, Trumpet Evolution 2003, Rumba Palace (Latin Grammy Award for Best Latin Jazz Album 2007) 2007, Arturo Sandoval & the Latin Jazz Orchestra 2007, A Time for Love (Latin Grammy Award for Best Instrumental Album) 2010, Dear Diz (Grammy Award for Best Large Jazz Ensemble Album 2013) 2012. *Address:* Turi's Music Enterprises Inc., 6701 Collins Avenue, Regency No. 1, Miami Beach, FL 33141, USA (office). *Telephone:* (305) 866-6511 (office). *Fax:* (305) 866-6516 (office). *E-mail:* fanmail@arturosandoval.com. *Website:* www.arturosandoval.com.

SANDOVAL, Brian Edward, BA, JD; American lawyer, politician and state governor; *Governor of Nevada;* b. 5 Aug. 1963, Redding, Calif.; s. of Ronald L. Sandoval and Gloria Sandoval; m. Kathleen Teipner; one s. two d.; ed Bishop Manogue High School, Reno, Nev., Univ. of Nevada, Ohio State Univ. Moritz Coll. of Law; entered pvt. practice with several Reno law firms: McDonald, Carano, Wilson, McCune Bergin, Frankovich & Hicks 1989–91, Robinson, Belaustegui, Robb & Sharp 1991–95, Gamboa, Sandoval & Stovall 1995–99; est. Sandoval Law Office, Reno 1999–2003; mem. Nevada State Ass. representing 25th Legis. Dist 1995–97, served on Judiciary, Taxation and Natural Resources Cttees, also served on Nev. Legis. Comm., Advisory Comm. on Sentencing, Juvenile Justice Comm., Advisory Council on Community Notification of Sex Offenders, Tahoe Regional Planning Agency Oversight Cttee; mem. Nevada Gaming Comm. 1998–2001, Chair. 1999–2001 (youngest ever chair.); Attorney Gen. of Nev. 2003–05; Judge, US Dist Court for Dist of Nevada 2005–09; Gov. of Nevada 2011–; mem. Bd of Trustees, Children's Cabinet, Reno, St Jude's Ranch for Children, Washoe Co. Law Library; Republican; several awards and certificates, including Hispanics in Politics Broche de Oro Award 1996, Torch of Liberty Award, Anti-Defamation League 2003, Access to Justice Public Lawyer Award, Nevada State Bar 2004, Most Influential Hispanic in the US Award, The Latino Coalition 2004, Alumnus of the Year Award, Univ. of Nevada 2004, Against the Hip-Hop Ban Award, WEB: www.myspace.com/LVH702, Excellence in Leadership Award, Latino Coalition 2010. *Achievements include:* first Hispanic cand. elected to statewide office in Nev. *Leisure interests:* running, travelling, spending time with his family. *Address:* Office of the Governor, State Capitol, 101 N Carson Street, Carson City, NV 89701, USA (office). *Telephone:* (775) 684-5670 (office). *Fax:* (775) 684-5683 (office). *Website:* gov.nv.gov (office); www.briansandoval.com

SANDOVAL CÓRDOVA, Wellington, MD, PhD; Ecuadorean physician and government official; *Ambassador to Argentina;* ed Universidad Central del Ecuador, Univ. of Michigan, USA, Univ. of Toronto, Canada; dir of mobile hosp. during Paquisha war 1981; cardiovascular and thoracic surgeon, Armed Forces Hosp., Quito 1977–91; Dir Hospital Metropolitano, Quito 1992–2005, currently cardiothoracic surgeon; Prof. and Head of Surgery, Faculty of Medical Sciences, Universidad Internacional del Ecuador 2004–; Minister of Public Health April–Dec. 2005; Pres. Inst. for Social Security 2006–07; Minister of Nat. Defence 2007–08 (resgnd); Amb. to Argentina 2008–. *Address:* Embassy of Ecuador, Quintana 585, 9°, C1129ABB Buenos Aires, Argentina (office); Universidad Internacional del Ecuador, Avenida Jorge Fernández y Simón Bolívar, Quito, Ecuador (office). *Telephone:* (11) 4804-0073 (office); (2) 298-5600 (office). *Fax:* (11) 4804-0074 (office); (2) 298-5666 (office). *E-mail:* embecuador@embecuador.com.ar (office); wsancor39@hotmail.com. *Website:* www.internacional.edu.ec (office).

SANDOVAL IÑIGUEZ, HE Cardinal Juan; Mexican ecclesiastic; *Archbishop Emeritus of Guadalajara;* b. 28 March 1933, Yahualica, Jalisco; s. of Esteban Sandoval and María Guadalupe Iñiguez; ed Seminario Diocesano de Guadalajara, Pontifica Universidad Gregoriana; ordained as a Catholic priest 1957; teacher Seminario de Guadalajara 1961, Prof. of Philosophy, Vice-Rector 1971, Rector 1980; Bishop's Coadjutor, Juárez 1988, Bishop of Juárez 1992; Archbishop of Guadalajara 1994–2011, Archbishop Emer. 2011–; cr. Cardinal (Cardinal-Priest of Nostra Signora di Guadalupe e San Filippo Martire in Via Aurelia) 1994; participated in Papal Conclave 2005, 2013; mem. IV Latin American Archbishop's Conf., Santo Domingo 1992, Congregation for Insts of Consecrated life and Societies of Apostolic Life, Congregation for Catholic Educ., Pontifical Council for Culture, Pontifical Comm. for Latin America, Prefecture for Econ. Affairs of the Holy See, Cardinal Comm. for the Supervision, Inst. for Works of Religion, Special Council for America, Gen. Secr. of the Synod of Bishops. *Address:* Arzobispado, Calle Liceo 17, Apdo. 1-331, 44100 Guadalajara, Mexico (office). *Telephone:* (3) 614-5504 (office). *Fax:* (3) 658-2300 (office). *Website:* www.arquidiocesisgdl.org.mx (office).

SANDRE, Didier (Didier de Maffre); French actor; b. 17 Aug. 1946, Paris; s. of Pierre Maffre and Geneviève Gevril; m. 2nd Nada Strancar 1990; one d.; ed Lycée Gustave Monod, Enghien-les-Bains, Collège Estienne, Paris; internship roles include: Don Juan, The Tempest, The Winter's Tale, Phaedra, L'Ecole des

Femmes, The Misanthrope, Tartuffe, The Screens, Fake Next, Foreign Land, Martyrdom of Saint Sebastian, Madame de Sade, The Marriage Figaro, Le Soulier de Satin, Ivanov, The Way Solitaire, Sharing Midi, An Ideal Husband, Dinner with Friends, Thomas Becket, Berenice, Histoire du Soldat, My Life with Mozart, Mr. Hunting, Dance of Death, The Cherry Orchard, RER, Collaboration; mem. Comédie Française Co.; Chevalier des Arts et des Lettres, Ordre nat. du Mérite; Prix Syndicat de la Critique, Molière Prize for Best Actor 1996, Prix du Brigadier 2013, Notes d'automne Prize 2013. Plays by: Molière, Racine, Shakespeare, J. Ford, H. Ibsen, T. Mann, M. Yourcenar, J. Lenz, W. Witkiewicz, Marivaux, Beaumarchais, Y. Mishima, J. Genet, J. Anouilh, A. Gatti, D. Margulies, G. Feydeau, A. Strndberg, A. Schnitzler, P. Claudel, E. Bond, O. Wilde, A. Moravia, R. Schimmelpfennig, EA Schmitt, JM Besset, Chekhov, R. Harwood. Films include: La java des ombres 1983 Train d'enfer 1985, Code Name: Emerald 1985, Woman of My Life 1986, Vent de galerne 1989, Les mannequins d'osier 1989, Boulevard des hirondelles 1992, The Lie 1993, 3000 Scenarios Against a Virus 1994, Mazeppa (voice) 1993, I Can't Sleep (voice) 1994, Petits arrangements avec les morts 1994, An Autumn Tale 1998, The Mystery Paul 2000, La légende de Parva (voice) 2003, Hell 2006, Montparnasse 2009, Memory Lane 2009, One Night 2012, A.L.F. 2012, Foto 2012, Au bout du conte 2013. Television includes: Médecins de nuit (series) 1978, Le misanthrope (film) 1980, Peer Gynt (film) 1981, Saint Louis ou La royauté bienfaisante (film) 1982, Conrad Killian, le fou du désert (series) 1982, Deux amies d'enfance (mini-series) 1983, Capitaine X (mini-series) 1983, Two Childhood Friends 1983, Richelieu ou La journée des dupes (film) 1983, La fausse suivante (film) 1985, L'année terrible (film) 1985, Manon Roland (film) 1989, Eurocops (series) 1989, Liberté, Libertés (film) 1989, Jeanne d'Arc, le pouvoir de l'innocence (film) 1989, Les grandes familles (mini-series) 1989, Le chemin solitaire (film) 1990, Ivanov (film) 1990, Turbulences (film) 1992, Flash – Der Fotoreporter (series) 1993, L'amour assassin (film) 1993, Turbulence 1992, 3000 scénarios contre un virus (series) 1994, Une famille formidable (series) 1992–96, Sandra princesse rebelle (mini-series) 1995, L'allée du roi (mini-series) 1996, L'uomo che ho ucciso (film) 1996, La femme d'un seul homme (film) 1998, Passion interdite (film) 1998, Intime conviction (film) 1998, Deux frères (film) 2000, L'enfant éternel (film) 2002, Saint-Germain ou La négociation (film) 2003, Les amants du Flore (film) 2006, Le sang noir (film) 2007, Moi, Louis, enfant de la mine (film) 2007, Sous un autre jour (film) 2009, À la recherche du temps perdu (film) 2011, Nicolas Le Floch (series) 2012. Leisure interests: music, gardening, reading. Address: c/o Laurence Bagoe, 10 rue Louvois, 75002 Paris, France (office). Telephone: 6-70-70-18-37 (mobile) (office). E-mail: laurencebagoe@gmail.com (office). Website: www.didiersandre.info.

SANDRI, HE Cardinal Leonardo, BCL; Argentine ecclesiastic; *Prefect of the Congregation for the Oriental Churches;* b. 18 Nov. 1943, Buenos Aires; born to parents of Italian descent; ordained priest in Buenos Aires 1967; entered Vatican diplomatic corps 1974, served at Vatican Embassy in Madagascar, worked at Secr. of State 1977–89, assigned to Nunciature in USA 1989–91, returned to the Vatican 1991–97; apptd Titular Archbishop of Aemona 1997; Apostolic Nuncio to Venezuela 1997–2000, to Mexico 2000; Substitute (Sostituto) Sec. for Gen. Affairs, Secr. of State 2000–07; Prefect of the Congregation for the Oriental Churches 2007–; cr. Cardinal (Cardinal-Deacon of Santi Biagio e Carlo ai Catinari) 2007; participated in Papal Conclave 2013; mem. Congregation for the Doctrine of the Faith, Congregation for the Evangelization of Peoples, Pontifical Council for Promoting Christian Unity, Pontifical Council for Interreligious Dialogue, Pontifical Council for Legis. Texts, Pontifical Comm. for Latin America, Pontifical Comm. for Vatican City State, Congregation for Bishops 2010–, Apostolic Signatura 2011–, Congregation for Catholic Educ. 2012–; named by Pope Benedict XVI as Co-Pres. of special Synod of Bishops for the Middle East, The Vatican Oct. 2010. Address: Congregation for the Oriental Churches, Via della Conciliazione 34, Palazzo del Bramante, 00193 Rome, Italy (office). Telephone: (06) 6988-4281 (office). Fax: (06) 6988-4300 (office). E-mail: cco@orientchurch.va (office). Website: www.vatican.va/roman_curia/congregations/orientchurch (office).

SANDS, Peter A., MPA; British banking executive; *Group Chief Executive, Standard Chartered PLC;* b. 8 Jan. 1962; m.; four c.; ed Univ. of Oxford, Harvard Univ., USA (Harkness Fellow); grew up in Asia; worked for FCO –1988; joined McKinsey & Co. 1988, worked extensively in banking and tech. sectors, Pnr 1996–2002, mem. Bd of Dirs 2000–02; Group Finance Dir and Group Exec. Dir Standard Chartered PLC 2002–06, Group Chief Exec. 2006–; Lead Dir (non-exec.) Dept of Health. Address: Standard Chartered PLC, 1 Basinghall Avenue, London, EC2V 5DD, England (office). Telephone: (20) 7885-8888 (office). Fax: (20) 7885-9999 (office). E-mail: info@standardchartered.com (office). Website: www.standardchartered.com (office).

SANDS, Sarah; British editor and writer; *Editor, London Evening Standard;* b. (Sarah Harvey), 3 May 1961, Cambridge; m. 1st Julian Sands; one s.; m. 2nd Kim Fletcher; two c.; ed Goldsmiths Coll., London; worked at Kent and Sussex Courier 1983–86; worked at Evening Standard, London, as diary reporter, Ed. of the Londoner's Diary, later Features Ed., then Assoc. Ed. 1986–95; Deputy Ed. The Daily Telegraph 1996–2005, responsible for The Daily Telegraph Saturday edn, Ed. The Sunday Telegraph 2005–06; Consulting Ed. The Daily Mail 2006–08; Ed.-in-Chief Reader's Digest UK 2008–09; Deputy Ed., London Evening Standard 2009–12, Editor 2012–. Publications include: novels: Playing the Game 2003, Hothouse 2005, Chiswick Wives 2006. Address: London Evening Standard, Northcliffe House, 2 Derry Street, London, W8 5TT, England (office). Telephone: (20) 7938-6000 (office). Fax: (20) 7937-2648 (office). E-mail: editor@standard.co.uk (office). Website: www.standard.co.uk (office).

SANDSTRÖM, Sven, BA, MBA, PhD; Swedish banker and international finance official; *CEO, Hand in Hand International, UK;* ed Univ. of Stockholm, Stockholm School of Econs, Royal Inst. of Tech.; consultancy work 1966–68; Research Assoc., MIT and Harvard Business School, USA 1969–72; joined IBRD (World Bank) 1972, Project Analyst, Urban Projects Dept 1973, Deputy Div. Chief 1977, Div. Chief 1979, Div. Chief Urban Devt and Water Supply, S Asia Projects 1986, Dir Southern Africa Dept 1987–90, Dir Office of the Pres. 1990–91, Man. Dir 1991–2001, Chair. Operation Cttee, Chair. Information and Knowledge Man. Council; Secr. Dir International Task Force on Global Public Goods, Stockholm 2003–06; Vice-Chair. Voluntary Replenishment Mechanism, Global Fund to Fight AIDS, Tuberculosis and Malaria; fmr Treas. World Conservation Union, also mem. Governing Council;

Coordinator and Chair. for the replenishment of African Devt Fund, African Devt Bank; fmr Special Adviser to EU, also fmr Adviser to World Bank; mem. Bd of Dirs AES Corpn 2002–, Hifabgruppen AB, Sweden; Adviser to Hand in Hand, India, currently CEO Hand in Hand International, UK; also served as Consultant and Adviser to several European govt ministries and pvt. cos. Address: Hand in Hand International, 20 York Street, London, W1U 6PU, England (office). Telephone: (20) 7514-5091 (office). Fax: (20) 7514-5099 (office). Website: www.hihinternational.org (office).

SANDURA, Wilson Runyararo, BA, LLB; Zimbabwean judge; *Judge of Appeal, Supreme Court;* b. 29 July 1941, Shamva; s. of the late Fore Sandura and Gilliet Sandura; m. 1st Joyce Alexis Sandura 1972 (divorced 1976); m. 2nd Caroline Elizabeth Sandura 1985; two s. one d.; ed Mavuradonha Mission, Goromonzhi High School, Morehouse Coll., USA, Univ. of London, UK; called to the Bar, Lincoln's Inn, London; pvt. practice as barrister 1973–80; Regional Magistrate 1980–82; Perm. Sec., Ministry of Justice 1982–83; Judge, High Court 1983–84, Judge Pres. 1984–97, 2000, Supreme Court 1998–, currently Judge of Appeal; Chair. delimitation comms 1985, 1989, 1990, 1991, 1995, 2000; Walter Kamba Rule of Law Award, Law Soc. of Zimbabwe 2009. Leisure interest: gardening. Address: Supreme Court, POB 870, Causeway, Harare, Zimbabwe (office). Telephone: (4) 736951 (office). E-mail: supreme_court@gta.gov.zw (office).

SANDVED, Arthur Olav, DPhil; Norwegian professor of English; b. 2 Feb. 1931, New York; s. of Ole Sandved and Ane Aarsland; m. Ruth Øgaard 1953; three d.; ed Univ. of Oslo; Lecturer in English Language, Univ. of Trondheim 1959–63, Univ. of Oslo 1963–71; Reader in English Philology, Univ. of Oslo 1971–74, Prof. of English Language 1974–96; mem. Norwegian Acad., Royal Norwegian Acad. Trondheim; . Publications include: Studies in the Language of Caxton's Malory and that of the Winchester Manuscript 1968, An Advanced English Grammar (with P. Christophersen) 1969, Introduction to Chaucerian English 1985, Vers fra Vest (anthology of Old English verse translated into Norwegian) 1987, Peter Plogmann (extracts from Piers Plowman translated into Norwegian) 1990, Paradise Lost (translated into Norwegian) 1993, trans. King Lear into Norwegian 1995, trans. the three parts of King Henry VI into Norwegian 1996, trans. Henry VIII into Norwegian 1997, Fra 'Kremmersprog' til Verdensspråk (history of English studies in Norway 1850–1943) 1998, trans. A History of Reading into Norwegian 1999, trans. Joseph Andrews into Norwegian 1999, trans. Revelation of Divine Love into Norwegian 2000, Fra 'Kremmersprog' til Verdensspråk, Vol. II (1945–57) 2002, trans. Canterbury Tales (extracts) into Norwegian 2002, Engelsk språkguide (a handbook of English usage), Norwegian adaptation of J. Svartvik and R. Svartvik, Handbok i Engelska, 2003, Paradise Regained (translated into Norwegian) 2005, King Arthur and His Knights: Selected Tales by Sir Thomas Malory (ed. E. Vinaver) (translated into Norwegian) 2007. Address: I. F. Gjerdrums vei 74, 1396 Billingstad, Norway. Telephone: 66-84-57-77.

SANDY, Brig. (retd) John, BSc, MSc; Trinidad and Tobago politician and fmr army officer; m. Jacqueline Sandy 1971; one s. three d.; ed Univ. of the West Indies, Springfield Coll., Mass, USA; joined Trinidad and Tobago Defence Force 1966, served 36 years in various positions including Contingent Commdr, CARICOM peacekeeping forces in Haiti 1994–95, Defence and Mil. Attaché, Embassy in Washington, DC 1997–2000, Chief of Defence Staff 2000–02, Exec. Chair. Exercise Tradewinds 2002; fmr Security Consultant, CL Financial Group, Colonial Life Insurance Co. (Trinidad) Ltd; Man. Dir and CEO Premium Security Services Ltd; Chief Security Liaison Officer with Trinidad and Tobago Nat. Football Team at FIFA World Cup Finals 2006; Minister of Nat. Security 2010–12; mem. People's Partnership coalition; US Meritorious Service Medal. Leisure interests: cricket, basketball. Address: c/o Ministry of National Security, Temple Court, 31–33 Abercromby St, Port of Spain, Trinidad and Tobago (office).

SANÉ, Pierre Gabriel Michel, MSc, MBA; Senegalese administrator and UN official; *President, Imagine Africa Institute;* b. 7 May 1948, Dakar; s. of Nicolas Sané and Thérèse Carvalho; m. Ndeye Coumba Sow 1981; two s. one d.; ed Lycée Van Vollenhoven, Dakar, Ecole Supérieure de Commerce de Bordeaux, France, Ecole Nouvelle d'Organisation Economique et Sociale, Paris, London School of Econs, UK, Carleton Univ., Ottawa, Canada; Vice-Pres. Fédération des Etudiants d'Afrique Noire en France 1971–72; auditor with audit firms in France 1973–77; Deputy Gen. Man. Société Sénégalaise Pharmaceutique (Senepharma) 1977–78; joined Int. Devt Research Centre (IDRC) 1977, various positions Ottawa, Nairobi and Dakar, to Regional Dir W and Cen. Africa, Dakar 1988–92; mem. Amnesty Int. 1988–, Sec.-Gen. 1992–2001; Asst Dir-Gen. UNESCO, Paris 2001–10; Founder and Exec. Pres. Imagine Africa Inst., Paris; winner, Concours Nat. de Commercialisation, France 1972. Publications: books on poverty and regional integration; papers and reports on African devt, science and tech. and human rights research man. for IDRC. Leisure interests: reading, travelling, music, museums, arts. Address: Imagine Africa Institute, 24 rue Tronchet, 75008 Paris, France (office). Telephone: 1-44-94-05-13 (office). Fax: 1-44-94-05-26 (office). E-mail: p.sane@imagineafricainstitute.org (office). Website: www.imagineafricainstitute.org (office).

SANEJOUAND, Jean Michel, DenL; French painter; b. 18 July 1934, Lyon; s. of Henri Felix Sanejouand and Angèle Fardel; m. Michelle Bourgeois 1957; two s.; ed Institut d'études politiques, Faculté de Droit, Lyon; self-taught in art; worked as artist, Lyon 1955–59, Paris 1959–93, Vaulandry 1993–; 'charges-objets' (assemblage works) 1963–67, 'organisations d'espaces' (environmental works) 1967–75, 'calligraphies d'humeurs' (calligraphic works on canvas) 1968–77, 'espaces-peintures' (painted and drawn works) 1978–86, black and white paintings 1987–93, sculptures 1988–, colour paintings 1993–96; 'sculptures-peintures' (paintings of sculptures) 1997–2002; retrospective exhbn Centre Georges Pompidou, Paris 1995; Espaces critiques (imaginary landscapes organised with earlier works) 2002–. Address: Belle-Ville, 49150 Vaulandry, France. Telephone: (2) 41-82-88-71. E-mail: web-site@sanejouand.com (office). Website: www.sanejouand.com.

SANFORD, Marshall Clement (Mark), Jr, BBA, MBA; American politician, business executive and fmr state governor; b. 28 May 1960, Fort Lauderdale, Fla; s. of Marshall Clement Sanford, Sr and Peggy Sanford (née Pitts); m. Jennifer Sullivan 1989 (divorced 2010); four s.; ed Furman Univ., Greenville, SC, Univ. of Virginia Darden Grad. School of Business Admin; attained rank of Eagle Scout in

Boy Scouts of America; assoc. for Coldwell Banker 1983; worked as project supervisor for Beachside Real Estate, Isle of Palms 1984–86; training positions with Goldman Sachs 1987–88; Financial Analyst, Chemical Realty Corpn 1988–90; Prin. Southeastern Partners 1989–93; real estate broker Brumley Co., Charleston, SC 1990–91; Propr Norton & Sanford Real Estate Investment 1992, Prin. 1993–95, 2001–02; mem. from 1st S Carolina Dist, US House of Reps, Washington, DC 1995–2001; Gov. of SC 2003–11; Chair. Republican Govs Asscn 2008–09 (resgnd); medical admin officer, USAF Reserve; mem. Preservation Soc., Charleston; Republican; Taxpayers' Best Friend Award, Nat. Taxpayers Union, Deficit Hawk Award, Concord Coalition Citizens Council, Taxpayer Hall of Fame, Taxpayers for Common Sense, Golden Bulldog Award, Watchdogs of the Treasury Inc., Spirit of Enterprise Award, US Chamber of Commerce, Congressional Youth Leadership Council Award. *Publication:* The Trust Committed to Me 2000. *Leisure interests:* windsurfing, running. *Address:* 1725 Avenue, Sullivans Island, Columbia, SC 29482-9794, USA (office).

SANGAJAVYN, Bayartsogt, MSc; Mongolian economist and politician; b. 28 March 1967, Selenge; m.; two c.; ed Lomonosov Moscow State Univ., Baden-Wuerttemberg Acad. for Foreign Trade, Nat. Univ. of Mongolia, Columbia Univ.; Sec. Youth Comm., Nat. Central Hospital 1980–82; Vice-Chair. Mongolian Youth Comm. Cttee 1990–91; mem. State Baga Hural (Parl.) 1990–92; Pres. Mongolian Youth Union 1991–97; mem. Great Hural (Parl.) 1996–2000, 2004–06, 2008–; Cabinet mem. and Minister of Nature and Environment 1998; adviser to Tovhon Khan Ltd 2002–04; Chief, Cabinet Secr. of Govt 2004–06; Minister of Finance 2008–12. *Address:* c/o Ministry of Finance, Government Building 2, United Nation's street - 5/1, Chingeltei District, Ulan Bator, Mongolia.

SANGAKKARA, Kumar Chokshanada; Sri Lankan professional cricketer; b. 27 Oct. 1977, Matale; s. of Kshema Sangakkara and Kumari Sangakkara; m. Yehali Sangakkara 2003; one s. one d. (twins); ed Trinity Coll., Kandy, law student at Sri Lanka Law Coll.; wicketkeeper; left-handed batsman; right-arm off-break bowler; ambidextrous; plays for Nondescripts Cricket Club 1997–, Sri Lanka 2000– (Vice-Capt. 2006, Capt. 2009–11), World XI One-Day Team 2005, Warwicks. 2007, Kings XI Punjab 2008–10, Deccan Chargers 2011–12, Kandurata Warriors 2012–, Asia XI, Cen. Prov., Colombo Dist Cricket Asscn, ICC (Int. Cricket Council), Kandurata, MCC, Lancs. 2010–; First-class debut: 1997/98; Test debut: Sri Lanka v S Africa, Galle 20–23 July 2000; One-Day Int. (ODI) debut: Sri Lanka v Pakistan, Galle 5 July 2000; T20I debut: England v Sri Lanka, Southampton 15 June 2006; captained Sri Lanka to reach final of ICC Cricket World Cup, losing to India, Mumbai 2 April 2011, stepped down as Capt. of Sri Lanka in one-day formats 5 April 2011; Trinity Lion Award, Trinity Coll., Kandy 1996, Ryde Medallist, Trinity Coll. 1996, Test Batsman of the Year, Sri Lanka Cricket Awards 2006, Test Batting Prize, Cricinfo Awards 2007, Outstanding Young Persons of Sri Lanka Award (Personal Improvement and Accomplishment category) 2008, ICC ODI Player of the Year 2011, LG People's Choice Award, ICC Awards 2011, honoured as one of the top-five Wisden Cricketers of the Year 2012, ICC Outstanding One-Day Player in the World 2013. *Achievements include:* shared record-breaking partnership of 624 with Mahela Jayawardene (world record in both Test and First-class cricket, first case of partnership of 600 or more in First-class or Test match innings) July 2006; became one of only a few Test batsmen who have scored five or more double centuries 2007; became sixth man in history to score back-to-back double centuries with consecutive unbeaten innings of 200 and 222 in second and third Tests against Bangladesh; named as new No. 1 batsman in LG ICC Test player rankings with a rating of 938 Dec. 2007; first batsman ever to score in excess of 150 in four consecutive tests Dec. 2007; ranked first on Test batting rankings Sept. 2009. *Address:* c/o Sri Lanka Cricket, Sinhalese Sports Club, Colombo, Sri Lanka. *E-mail:* info@srilankacricket.lk; *Website:* www.srilankacricket.lk; www.kumarsangakkara.lk.

SANGALA, Aaron; Malawi politician; *Minister of National Defence;* b. 1958; worked for Lever Brothers 1974–81; mem. Parl. for Blantyre Ndirande Malabada 2004–; Deputy Minister of Health 2006–07; Deputy Minister of Women and Child Devt 2007–08; Minister of Nat. Defence 2008–09, 2011–, of Home Affairs and Internal Security 2009–11. *Address:* Ministry of National Defence, Private Bag 331, Lilongwe 31, Malawi (office). *Telephone:* 1789177 (office). *Fax:* 1789509 (office). *E-mail:* defence@malawi.gov.mw (office).

SANGARE, Oumou; Malian singer and songwriter; b. 25 Feb. 1968, Bamako; m. Ousmane Haidara; one c.; began singing aged five; first performance at Stade des Omnisports aged six; mem. Nat. Ensemble of Mali; mem. Djoliba percussion 1986–89; solo artiste with own backing group 1989–; regular concert tours in W Africa and Europe; first US concert 1994; campaigner for women's rights; apptd Amb. to FAO 2003; Performance of the Year 1993; numerous African Music Awards. *Recordings include:* Moussolou (Women) (Best Selling Album of the Year 1990) 1990, Ko Sira (Marriage Today) (European World Music Album of the Year 1993) 1993, Worotan 1996, Moussolou 1999, Ko Sira 2000, Oumou (compilation) 2003, Seya 2009, Kounadia 2012; appears on African Blues 1998, Belowed 1998; also recordings with Ali Farka Touré, Trilok Gurtu. *Address:* c/o World Circuit Records, First Floor, Shoreditch Stables, 138 Kingsland Road, London, E2 8DY, England (office). *E-mail:* post@worldcircuit.co.uk (office). *Website:* www.worldcircuit.co.uk (office).

SANGAY, Lobsang, LLB, BA (Hons), LLM, SJD; Tibetan legal scholar and politician; *Prime Minister of the Central Tibetan Administration (Tibetan Government-in-Exile);* b. 1968, village in Darjeeling, India; s. of Kelsang Choden; m. Kesang Yangdon Shakchang 1998; one d.; ed Tibetan Refugee High School, Darjeeling, Univ. of Delhi, India, Harvard Univ.; expert on Tibet and int. human rights law; fmr mem. of radical Tibetan Youth Congress, took part in protests against Chinese rule in Tibet; organized five confs between Chinese and Tibetan scholars, including a meeting between the Dalai Lama and 35 Chinese scholars at Harvard Univ. 2003; became the first Tibetan (among six million) to earn a doctorate degree from Harvard Law School; Visiting Research Fellow, East Asian Legal Studies Program, Harvard Law School; elected as the next Kalon Tripa, or Prime Minister, of the Cen. Tibetan Admin (Tibetan Govt-in-Exile) 26 April 2011, succeeding the 5th Samdhong Rinpoche, took oath of office 8 Aug. 2011–; Tibetan Fulbright Fellowship for study at Harvard Law School 2004, Yong K. Kim' 95 Prize of Excellence for his dissertation, Democracy in Distress: Is Exile Polity a Remedy? A Case Study of Tibet's Government-in-Exile 2004, selected as

one of the 24 Young Leaders of Asia by the Asia Soc. 2006. *Publications:* We Sing a Song of Sadness – Tibetan Political Prisoners Speak Out (co-ed.) 2006; several articles in scholarly journals. *Address:* Office of the Kalon Tripa, Kashag Secretariat, Central Tibetan Administration, Dharamshala 176215, Himachal Pradesh, India (office). *Telephone:* (1892) 222218 (office); (1892) 222713 (office); (1892) 223546 (office). *Fax:* (1892) 224914 (office). *E-mail:* katri-pa@gov.tibet.net (office); katri-pa@tibet.net (office); kadrung@gov.tibet.net (office). *Website:* www.tibet.net (office).

SANGHELI, Andrei; Moldovan business executive and fmr politician; *Director-General, Limagrain Moldova SRL;* b. 20 July 1944, Grinautsy; m.; one s.; ed Kishinev Agric. Inst., Kishinev Higher CP School; mem. CPSU 1967–91; agronomist, Deputy Dir, then Dir of collective farms, Moldova 1971–75, Sec., Kamenka Regional CP Cttee 1975–79, Vice-Chair. Council of Collective Farms of Moldova 1979–80; Chair. Dondushansk Regional Exec. Cttee; First Sec., Regional CP Cttee 1980–86; First Deputy-Chair. Council of Ministers, Chair. State Agric.-Industrial Cttee 1986–89, First Deputy Prime Minister of Moldova; Minister of Agric. and Food 1990–92; Prime Minister of Moldova 1992–96; currently Dir-Gen. Limagrain Moldova SRL (agricultural co.); Chair. Union of Agrarians 1997–. *Address:* Limagrain Moldova SRL, 2004 Chisinau, blvd Stefan cel Mare, 162, Moldova (office). *Telephone:* (22) 21-00-49 (office). *Fax:* (22) 21-00-67 (office). *E-mail:* limagrain@moldovacc.md (office).

SANGMA, Mukul M., MB BS; Indian physician and politician; *Chief Minister of Meghalaya;* b. 20 April 1965, Chengkompara, Ampati, West Garo Hills Dist; s. of Binoy Bhushan M. Marak and the late Roshanara M. Sangma; ed Govt High School, Ampati, West Garo Hills, St Anthony's Coll., Shillong, Regional Inst. of Medical Sciences (RIMS), Imphal, North Eastern Regional Medical Coll., Imphal; mem. Youth Congress as a student; held different positions in Governing Body of Students Council of RIMS; practised as pvt. medical practitioner at pvt. clinic at Tura 1990–91; joined and served as Medical and Health Officer, Zikzak PHC, West Garo Hills under Govt of Meghalaya 1991; left Govt Service to enter into politics 1993, elected as Ind. MLA from 58-Ampatigre L.A. Constituency 1993; Chair. Meghalaya Transport Corpn Feb.–Sept. 1993; posts held have included Parl. Sec., Govt of Meghalaya 1996–98, Cabinet Minister in charge of depts including Co-operation, Fisheries, Taxation and others, Govt of Meghalaya 1998–99, Cabinet Minister in charge of portfolios including Taxation, IPR and others, Govt of Meghalaya 2001–03, Cabinet Minister, Govt of Meghalaya and looked after Taxation, PWD, Home (P), Educ. (both Higher and Tech. Educ. and Elementary and Mass Educ.), Forest and Environment, Information Tech., Election, IPR and other Depts 2003–05; Deputy Chief Minister, Govt of Meghalaya April–Oct. 2005; Deputy Chief Minister in charge of Planning, IPR, Election, PID, Power, including Non-Conventional Energy, Reorganization Depts 2007–08; Deputy Chief Minister in charge of Finance, Power and Non-Conventional Energy, Health and & Family Welfare, IPR, Labour, Horticulture, Home (Passport) Admin. Reforms 2009–10; Chief Minister of Meghalaya 2010–; held various posts as Party functionary of Indian Nat. Congress in State of Meghalaya; Sec., Dist Congress Cttee, West Garo Hills 1998–99; Pres. Dist Congress Cttee, West Garo Hills 1999–2000; Gen. Sec. Meghalaya Pradesh Congress Cttee, in charge of Frontal Wings 2000–, involved in mobilization of Frontal Wings of Indian Nat. Congress in State of Meghalaya; Chief Patron Ampati Youth Welfare Club; Founder-mem. Mirachel Foundation; contested parl. elections 2004, Gen. Election, by-election for Tura Lok Sabha seat 2006. *Address:* Office of the Chief Minister, Government of Meghalaya, Jaiaw Main Road, Shillong 793 001, Meghalaya, India (office). *Telephone:* 2224282 (ext. 2200) (office). *E-mail:* cmoffice@shillong.meg.nic.in (office). *Website:* www.meghalaya.nic.in (office).

SANGMA, Purno Agitok, MA, LLB; Indian lawyer and politician; b. 1 Sept. 1947, Chapahati Village, West Garo Hills Dist; s. of Dipchon Ch. Marak and Chimri A. Sangma; m. Soradini K. Sangma 1973; two s. two d.; ed Dalu High School, St Anthony's Coll. Shillong and Dibrugarh Univ.; mem. Lok Sabha 1977–79, 1980–84, 1985–89, 1991–2009, Speaker 1996–98; Deputy Minister, Ministry of Industry 1980–82, Ministry of Commerce 1982–85; Minister of State for Commerce 1985–86, for Home Affairs 1986; Minister of State (Independent Charge) for Labour 1986–88; Chief Minister of Meghalaya State 1988–90; Minister of State (Independent Charge) for Coal 1991–95, also for Labour 1993–95; Minister of Information and Broadcasting 1995–96; unsuccessful cand. in presidential election 2012; del. to various int. confs; Founder mem. Nationalist Congress Party; left party to join All India Trinamool Congress 2004; Founder, Nationalist Trinamool Congress; Tata Workers' Union Michael John Roll of Honour for Distinguished Contrib. to the Cause of Labour and to the Parl. System 1997, Golden Jubilee Award of the Indian Nat. Trade Union Congress 1997, Saraswati Nat. Eminence Award for Public Leadership, South Indian Educ. Soc. 2003. *Leisure interests:* reading, discussion, music, indoor games. *Address:* All India Trinamool Congress, 30B Harish Chatterjee Street, Kolkata 700 026 (office); 34, Aurangzeb Road, New Delhi 110 011 (home); Walbakgre, Tura PO, West Garo Hills, India (home). *Telephone:* (33) 24540881 (office); (11) 23018396. *Fax:* (33) 24540880 (office). *Website:* www.trinamoolcongress.com (office).

SANGUINETTI CAIROLO, Julio María; Uruguayan lawyer, politician and international organization official; *President, Círculo de Montevideo;* b. 1936; m. Marta Canessa; one s. one d.; mem. Gen. Ass. 1962–73; Minister of Industry and Labour 1969–72, of Educ. and Culture 1972–73; then Pres. Comisión Nacional de Artes Plásticas and Pres. of UNESCO Comm. for promotion of books in Latin America; Pres. of Uruguay 1985–89, 1995–2000; Leader (Foro Batllista) Colorado Party 1989–94; Pres. Círculo de Montevideo, Nat. Fine Arts Council; mem. InterAcción Council, Club of Madrid; Lifetime Achievement Award, Cristóbal Gabarrón Foundation 2007. *Address:* Círculo de Montevideo, José Luis Zorrilla de San Martín 248, Montevideo, Uruguay. *E-mail:* secretaria@circulodemontevideo.com. *Website:* www.circulodemontevideo.com.

SANHÁ, Issufo; Guinea-Bissau politician; Minister of the Economy 1998–2007, of Finance 2007–09; mem. Partido Africano da Independência da Guiné e Cabo Verde (PAIGC). *Address:* Partido Africano da Independência da Guiné e Cabo Verde, CP 106, Bissau, Guinea-Bissau (office). *Website:* www.paigc.org (office).

SANKARANARAYANAN, Kateekal; Indian politician; *Governor of Maharashtra and Goa;* b. 15 Oct. 1932, Kerala; s. of the late A. Sankaran Nair and K.

Lekshmi Amma; m. Radha Sankaranarayanan; one d.; active mem. students' org. from 1946; elected to 5th Kerala Legis. Ass. (KLA) from Thrithala, 6th KLA from Sreekrishnapuram, 8th KLA from Ottappalam, 11th KLA from Palghat Constituency, as Indian Nat. Congress mem.; Convenor United Democratic Front 1985–2001; Minister for Agric., Animal Husbandry and Dairy Devt and Community Devt 11–25 April 1977, 27 April–Oct. 1978; Chair. Cttee on Govt Assurances 1980–82, Cttee on Public Accounts 1989–91; Minister for Finance and Excise 2001–04, continued as MLA –2006; served as minister in state govt of Kerala; Gov. of Nagaland 2007–09, of Arunachal Pradesh (Additional Charge) during absence on leave of S. K. Singh 2007–08, of Assam June–July 2009, Gov. of Jharkand 2009–10, of Maharashtra 2010–, of Goa 2011–. *Address:* Office of the Governor, The Raj Bhavan, Malabar Hills, Mumbai 400 035, India (office). *Telephone:* (22) 23632660 (office). *Fax:* (22) 23633272 (office). *E-mail:* rajbhavan@maharashtra.gov .in (office). *Website:* www.maharashtra.gov.in (office).

SANKEY, John Anthony, CMG, PhD; British fmr diplomatist; *Legacies Officer, Saint Francis Leprosy Guild;* b. 8 June 1930, London, England; m. Gwendoline Putman 1958; two s. two d.; ed Cardinal Vaughan School, Kensington, Peterhouse, Cambridge, NATO Defence Coll., Rome, Univ. of Leeds; served in Colonial Office 1953, UK Mission to UN, New York, USA 1961, FCO 1964, Guyana 1968, Singapore 1971, Malta 1973, The Hague 1975, Special Counsellor for African Affairs, FCO 1980–82; High Commr in Tanzania 1982–85; Perm. Rep. to the UN in Geneva 1985–90; Sec.-Gen. Soc. of London Art Dealers 1991–96; Dir Int. Art and Antiques Loss Register 1993–96; Chair. Tanzania Devt Trust 1999–2004; Legacies Officer, St Francis Leprosy Guild 2005–. *Publication:* Thomas Brock, Forgotten Sculptor of the Victoria Memorial (ed.). *Leisure interest:* Victorian sculpture. *Address:* 108 Lancaster Gate, London, W2 3NW, England (home). *Telephone:* (20) 7723-2256 (home).

SANNIKAU, Andrey Alegavich; Belarusian politician; b. 8 March 1954, Minsk; m. Iryna Khalip; two s.; ed Minsk State Linguistic Univ., Diplomatic Acad. of Ministry of Foreign Affairs of Russian Fed., Moscow; worked for a Soviet oil co. in Pakistan and worked on construction of an aluminium plant in Egypt; worked at Union of Soviet Socs for Friendship and Cultural Relations with Foreign Countries; served at UN Secr., New York, USA 1982–87; worked in Ministry of Foreign Affairs of Belorussian SSR; headed del. on Nuclear and Conventional Weapons Armament Negotiations 1992, retained authority of signature on behalf of Belarus until 1995; also served as adviser to Belarusian diplomatic mission in Switzerland; Deputy Minister of Foreign Affairs with rank of Amb. 1995–96 (resgnd); Co-founder of civil initiative Khartiya-97 (Charter '97), becoming its int. coordinator, opposition group to Lukashenko party in Belarus; cr., with Hienadz Karpienka, The Coordinating Council (Rada) of the Congress of Democratic Forces of Belarus 1999; initiated, with other politicians, civil campaign European Belarus advocating joining country with EU 2008; unsuccessful presidential cand. 2010; imprisoned in a Minsk KGB facility for protesting at a demonstration after the elections, named a prisoner of conscience by Amnesty International, sentenced to five years' imprisonment on charges of organizing mass disturbances May 2011, pardoned and released by Pres. Lukashenka 14 April 2012; Bruno Kreisky Prize 2005. *E-mail:* charter97@gmail.com. *Website:* www.charter97.org.

SANO, Seiichiro; Japanese business executive; *Executive Director and President, SANYO Electric Co. Ltd;* b. 20 Nov. 1952, Osaka; ed Kwansei Gakuin Univ.; joined SANYO Electric Co. Ltd 1977, Human Resources Div., Audio Business 1977–89, Labour Admin Div., Human Resources HQ 1989–92, Man. Labour Admin Div. 1992–97, Man. Human Resouces Dept 1997–2000, Gen. Man., Gen. Affairs/Human Resources 2000–07, Gen. Man. Human Resources Group 2001–03, Gen. Man. Corp. Admin Dept 2003–05, Vice-Pres. 2005–07, Exec. Dir and Pres. 2007–. *Address:* SANYO Electric Co. Ltd, 5-5 Keihan-Hondori, 2-chome, Moriguchi, Osaka 570-8677, Japan (office). *Telephone:* (6) 6991-1181 (office). *Fax:* (6) 6991-5411 (office). *E-mail:* info@sanyo.com (office). *Website:* sanyo.com (office).

SANOGO, Capt. Amadou Haya; Malian army officer; b. 1972, Ségou; ed mil. training in USA including Lackland Air Force Base, Tex., Fort Huachuca, Ariz., Fort Benning, Ga, Quantico Marine Corps Base, Va; fmr English teacher; instructor, Koulikoro Mil. Coll. –2012; led coup d'état which displaced Pres. Amadou Toumani Touré 22 March 2012; Chair. Nat. Cttee for the Restoration of Democracy and State (head of state) March–April 2012 (stood down 6 April under agreement brokered by ECOWAS). *Address:* Comité national pour le redressement de la démocratie et la restauration de l'Etat, Bamako, Mali (office).

SANT, Alfred, MSc, MBA, DBA; Maltese politician, consultant and author; b. 28 Feb. 1948; one d.; ed Univ. of Malta, Inst. Int. d'Admin Publique, France, Boston Univ. and Harvard Business School, USA; Second Sec., First Sec., Malta Mission to European Communities, Brussels 1970–75; Adviser on gen. and financial man., Ministry of Parastatal and People's Industries, Valletta 1977–78; Man. Dir Medina Consulting Group 1978–80; Exec. Deputy Chair. Malta Devt Corpn 1980–82; consultant to pvt. and public sectors 1982–; Chair. Metal Fond Ltd, Bottex Clothing 1982–84, First Clothing Cooperative 1983–87; Lecturer, Man. Faculty, Univ. of Malta 1984–87; Adviser to Prime Minister on econ. and diplomatic affairs 1985–87; Chair. Dept of Information, Malta Labour Party 1982–92; Pres. Malta Labour Party 1984–88, Leader 1992–2008; MP 1987–2013; Prime Minister of Malta 1996–98; Leader of the Opposition 1998–2008. *Plays:* Fid-Dell Tal-Katidral 1994, Qabel Tiftah L-Inkjesa 1999. *Publications include:* Min Hu Evelyn Costa? (plays) 1979, L-Ewwel Weraq tal-Bajtar (novel), Silg fuq Kemmuna (novel) 1985, Malta's European Challenge (essay) 1995, Bejgh u Xiri (novel) 1999, La Bidu, La Tmiem (novel) 2001, Confessions of a Maltese European 2003, L-Ghalqa tal-Iskarjota (novel) 2009 (English trans., The Iscariot Field 2011), Pupu bil-Bahar (short stories) 2009, Bhal f'Dizzjunarju 2011, Malta and the Euro 2012, George Bush f'Malta 2013, Cpar 2013; contrib. articles in the press and professional publs. *Leisure interests:* travel, reading, writing, listening to music. *Address:* 18A, Victory Street, B'Kara, Malta (home). *Telephone:* (2149) 5742 (office). *E-mail:* alfred.sant@ gov.mt (office). *Website:* alfredsant.org.

SANTANA, Carlos; Mexican musician; b. 20 July 1947, Autlán de Navarro; s. of José Santana; played Tijuana night clubs; debut with the Santana Blues Band 1966, played at Woodstock Festival Aug. 1969; guitarist, Santana Man. 1987–; Prin. Guts and Grace Records 1993; performed with Mike Bloomfield, Al Kooper, Buddy Miles, McCoy Turner, Jose Feliciano, Herbie Hancock, Wayne Shorter,

Alice Coltrane, Aretha Franklin, Mahavishnu, John McLaughlin; co-founder Milagro Foundation supporting young people in the arts, health and education 1998; Santana Band first to earn CBS Records' Crystal Globe Award, multiple Best Pop-Rock Guitarist in Playboy Magazine's Readers' Poll, Grammy for Best Rock Instrumental Performance 1988, Nosotros Golden Eagle Legend Award 1992, Recording Acad. (NARAS) tribute concert and induction into Hollywood Rock Walk, Billboard Magazine Century Award 1996, ten Bay Area Music Awards, BAMMY Hall of Fame, Chicano Music Awards Latino Music Legend of the Year 1997, Rock 'n' Roll Hall of Fame, Hollywood Walk of Fame 1998, also won nine Grammys Feb. 2000, Latin Recording Acad. Person of the Year 2004; numerous civic and humanitarian commendations. *Films:* Viva Santana 1988, Sacred Fire 1993, A History of Santana: The River Of Color And Sound 1997, A Supernatural Evening With Santana 2000. *Recordings include:* albums: Santana 1969, Abraxas 1970, Santana III 1971, Greatest Hits 1974, Moonflower 1977, Inner Secrets 1978, Zebop! 1981, Shango 1982, Freedom 1987, Freedom 1987, Viva Santana 1988, Milagro 1992, Sacred Fire 1993, Dance Of The Rainbow Serpent 1995, Live At The Fillmore 1997, Best of Santana 1998, Supernatural 1999, All That I Am 2005, Guitar Heaven: The Greatest Guitar Classics of All Time 2010. *Address:* Santana Management, PO Box 10348, San Rafael, CA 94912, USA (office). *E-mail:* info@ jensencom.com. *Website:* www.santana.com (office).

SANTANA LOPES, Pedro; Portuguese lawyer and politician; b. 29 June 1956, Lisbon; five c.; ed Univ. of Lisbon; joined Social Democratic Party 1976, Vice-Pres., Pres. 2004–05; Deputy Prime Minister, IV Constitutional Govt 1978, 1979; Legal Adviser to the Prime Minister 1980–81; mem. European Parl. 1987, 1989; Chair. Congress, General Council of the Nat. Asscn of Portuguese Municipalities, Central Region 1998, 2001; fmr Sec. of State for Culture; fmr Mayor of Figueira da Foz, then Lisbon 2002–July 2004, Feb. 2005–Oct. 2005; Vice-Chair. Cttee of the Regions 2002, 2004; Prime Minister of Portugal July 2004–Feb. 2005 (resgnd); Alderman, City of Lisbon 2009–; currently mem. Parl. *Address:* Office of Alderman PPD/PSD Lisbon, Rua do Ouro, No. 49–5°, 1100-060, Lisbon, Portugal (office). *Telephone:* (21) 3227225 (office). *Fax:* (21) 8171361 (office). *E-mail:* gvppdpsd@cm-lisboa.pt (office). *Website:* lisboa-ppdpsd.com (office).

SANTER, Jacques, DenD; Luxembourg politician and banker; *Chairman, Unicredit International Bank;* b. 18 May 1937, Wasserbillig; s. of Josef Santer and Marguerite Santer; m. Danièle Binot; two s.; ed Athénée de Luxembourg, Univs of Paris and Strasbourg and Inst. d'Etudes Politiques, Paris; advocate, Luxembourg Court of Appeal 1961–65; attaché, Office of Minister of Labour and Social Security 1963–65; Govt attaché 1965–66; Parl. Sec. Parti Chrétien-Social 1966–72, Sec.-Gen. 1972–74, Pres. 1974–82; Sec. of State for Cultural and Social Affairs 1972–74; mem. Chamber of Deputies 1974–79; Municipal Magistrate, City of Luxembourg 1976–79; Minister of Finance, of Labour and of Social Security 1979–84; Prime Minister, Minister of State and Minister of Finance 1984–89, Prime Minister, Minister of State, of Cultural Affairs and of the Treasury and Financial Affairs 1989–94, now Hon. Minister of State; MEP 1975–79, 1999–2004, Vice-Pres. 1975–77; Pres. European Comm. 1994–99; Pres. Robert Schuman Foundation 1998–; currently Pres. Fondation Mérite Européen; Chair. Bd CLT-UFA 2004–; Chair. Bd Unicredit International Bank 2005–, mem. Bd RTL Group 2005–, mem. Bd Unicredit Luxembourg 2009–, mem. Bd European Sovereign Bond Protection Facility; Hon. LLD (Wales) 1998, (Miami Univ.), (Sacred Heart Univ., Ohio), (Univ. of Urbino, Italy), (Kyoto Univ., Japan) and others; Prince of Asturias Prize (Spain) 1998, Robert Schumann Prize, Jean Monnet Medal (Lausanne, Switzerland) and others. *Leisure interests:* walking, swimming. *Address:* 33 boulevard F.D. Roosevelt, 2450 Luxemburg (office); 69 rue J.-P. Huberty, 1742 Luxemburg (home). *Telephone:* 24-78-81-55 (office); 42-00-40 (home). *Fax:* 26-27-08-37 (office); 26-43-09-99 (home). *E-mail:* jacques.santer@me.etat.lu (office).

SANTER, Rt Rev. Mark, MA, DD; British ecclesiastic (retd); b. 29 Dec. 1936, Bristol; s. of Rev. Canon E. A. R. Santer and Phyllis C. Barlow; m. 1st Henriette Cornelia Weststrate 1964 (died 1994); m. 2nd Sabine Böhmig Bird 1997; one s. two d.; ed Marlborough Coll., Queens' Coll. and Westcott House, Cambridge; curate, All Saints Cuddesdon 1963–67; tutor, Cuddesdon Coll. Oxford 1963–67; Dean and Fellow, Clare Coll. Cambridge 1967–72; Asst Lecturer in Divinity, Univ. of Cambridge 1968–72; Prin. Westcott House 1973–81; Area Bishop of Kensington, London 1981–87; Bishop of Birmingham 1987–2002; Co-Chair. Anglican/RC Int. Comm. 1983–99; Hon. Fellow, Clare Coll. Cambridge 1987, Queens' Coll. Cambridge 1991; Hon. DD (Birmingham) 1998, (Lambeth) 1999, Hon. DUniv (Univ. of Cen. England) 2003. *Publications include:* Documents in Early Christian Thought (with M. F. Wiles) 1975, Their Lord and Ours (ed.) 1982. *Address:* 81 Clarence Road, Birmingham, B13 9UH, England (home). *Telephone:* (121) 441-2194 (home). *E-mail:* msanter@btinternet.com (home).

SANTO CARVALHO, Evaristo do Spirito; São Tomé and Príncipe politician; b. 1942; Prime Minister of São Tomé e Príncipe July–Oct. 1994, Sept. 2001– March 2002; mem. Partido de Convergência Democrática-Grupo de Reflexão (PCD-GR) (expelled from party July 1994); currently mem. Acção Democrática Independente; unsuccessful cand. in presidential elections July–Aug. 2011. *Address:* c/o Office of the Prime Minister, Rua do Município, CP 302, São Tomé, São Tomé e Príncipe.

SANTORUM, Richard (Rick) John, BA, MBA, JD; American lawyer and politician; b. 10 May 1958, Winchester, Va; s. of Aldo Santorum and Catherine Santorum (née Dughi); m. Karen Garver 1990; six c. and one s. (deceased); ed Carmel High School, Mundelein, Ill., Pennsylvania State Univ., Univ. of Pittsburgh and Dickinson Law School; called to the Bar of Pa 1986; Admin. Asst to Pa State Senator Doyle Corman, Harrisburg, Pa 1981–86, Exec. Dir Local Govt Cttee, Pa State Senate 1981–84, Transport Cttee 1984–86; Assoc. Attorney, Kirkpatrick and Lockhart, Pittsburgh 1986–90; mem. US House of Reps from 18th Pa Dist, Washington, DC 1991–95; Senator from Pennsylvania 1995–2007, Chair. Senate Republican Conf. 2001–07; joined Eckert Seamans Cherin & Mellott, LLC law firm 2007; Sr Fellow, Ethics and Public Policy Center, Washington, DC 2007–11, est. and directed America's Enemies programme; unsuccessful cand. for Republican US presidential nomination 2012; contrib. to Fox News 2007–11; Co-f. Patriot Voices (nonprofit org.); columnist, Word Net Daily website 2013–; CEO EchoLight Studios (film production co.) 2013–; Republican. *Publications include:* It Takes a Family: Conservatism and the Common Good 2005, Rick Santorum 2005, Darwin's Nemesis: Phillip Johnson and the Intelligent Design Movement (foreword) 2006, American Patriots 2012. *Leisure interests:* golf, cross-country skiing, racquet sports. *Address:* Patriot Voices, PO Box 247, Verona, PA 15147, USA (office). *E-mail:* info@patriotvoices.com (office). *Website:* www.patriotvoices.com (office); www.ricksantorum.com (office); www.echolight.com (office).

SANTOS CALDERÓN, Francisco; Colombian journalist and politician; b. 14 Oct. 1961, Bogotá; ed Univ. of Kansas, Univ. of Texas at Austin, USA; in late 1980s taught journalism and US–Latin American relations at several Colombian univs including Universidad Central, Universidad Javeriana, Universidad Jorge Tadeo Lozano; fmr Ed. El Tiempo (daily newspaper); kidnapped with other journalists by Pablo Escobar, leader of Medellín drug cartel 1990, held for eight months; Nieman Fellow, Harvard Univ. 1992; moved to Madrid, Spain and worked as journalist for daily newspaper El País 2000–02; Vice-Pres. of Colombia 2002–10; co-f. Fundación Pais Libre (Free Country Foundation); Paul Harris Medal, Rotary Int. *Address:* c/o Office of the President, Palacio de Nariño, Carrera 8a, No. 7–26, Bogotá, Colombia (office).

SANTOS CALDERÓN, Juan Manuel; Colombian politician and head of state; *President;* b. 10 Aug. 1951, Bogotá; m. María Clemencia Rodríguez; two s. one d.; ed Cartagena Naval Acad. of Colombia, Univ. of Kansas, USA, London School of Econs, UK, Harvard Univ., USA; fmr leader Colombian Del. to int. Coffee Org. negotiations, London; fmr journalist, Deputy Dir and Pres. Editorial Bd El Tiempo (daily); apptd Minister of Foreign Trade 1991; Vice-Pres. 1993; apptd Minister of Finance and Public Credit 2000; managed Pres. Alvaro Uribe's re-election campaign 2006; Minister of Nat. Defence 2006–09 (resgnd); Pres. of Colombia 2010–; Pres. UNCTAD 1992–96, UN ECLA 1997–99; fmr Vice-Pres. Press Freedom Comm. of Inter-American Press Soc.; Founder and Chair. Fundación Buengobierno; Bernardo O'Higgins en el Grado de Comendador 1996, Gran Oficial de la Orden Nacional Francesca del Mérito 2001; Fulbright and Neiman Fellowships, King of Spain Prize for journalism. *Publications:* several books including The Third Way, An Alternative for Colombia. *Address:* Office of the President, Palacio de Nariño, Carrera 8, No 7-26, Bogotá, DC, Colombia (office). *Telephone:* (1) 562-9300 (office). *Fax:* (1) 286-8063 (office). *Website:* www .presidencia.gov.co (office).

SANTOS LÓPEZ, Samuel; Nicaraguan politician; *Minister of Foreign Affairs;* b. 13 Dec. 1938, Managua; s. of Samuel Santos Fernández and Lucila López Bermúdez; m. Annelly Molina de Santos; early business career with several managerial roles including roles at Publicidad Noble y Asociados, Honduras, Hotel Best Western Las Mercedes, Inversiones Inmobiliaras Acuario S.A., Inmobiliarios Penta S.A., Inmobiliarios Alpha S.A., Inmobiliarios Beta S.A; Founder and fmr Dir Stock Market of Nicaragua; mem. Nat. Govt for Reconstruction 1979–85; Vice-Pres. Nat. Devt Bank 1979–80; Minister in charge of Reconstruction of Managua 1980–85; Mayor of Managua 1984–85; Chair. ADYSA and Editorial El Amanecer 1986–92; Finance Sec. Frente Sandinista de Liberación Nacional 1992, Exec. Sec. –2001, Int. Relations Spokesperson 2001–06; Minister of Foreign Affairs 2007–; Founding mem. Nicaragua Wall Street; mem. Chamber of Commerce, Chamber of Tourism, Union of Latin American Capital Cities, Exec. Cttee of the Bolivian Congress for Town Devt, Works Comm. for the Inter-Oceanic Canal of Nicaragua; Order of Friendship (South Ossetia) 2010. *Address:* Ministry of Foreign Affairs, Del Cine González al Sur sobre Avenida Bolivar, Managua, Nicaragua (office). *Telephone:* (2) 244-8000 (office). *Fax:* (2) 228-5102 (office). *E-mail:* samuel.santos@ cancilleria.gob.ni (office). *Website:* www.cancilleria.gob.ni (office).

SANTOS ORDÓÑEZ, Elvin Ernesto, BSc; Honduran engineer, business executive and politician; b. 18 Jan. 1963, Tegucigalpa; s. of Elvin Santos Lozano and Sonia Ordóñez de Santos; m. Becky Manzanares de Santos; four c.; ed Lamar Univ., USA; CEO Santos y Compañía Construction Co.; fmr Consul in Austin, Tex; fmr Chair. Honduras Chamber of Industry and Construction, Dir Honduras Pvt. Enterprise Council, Nat. Asscn of Industrialists; mem. Partido Liberal de Honduras; Vice-Pres. of Honduras 2006–08 (resgnd); Partido Liberal candidate for 2009 presidential election; mem. Colegio de Ingenieros Civiles de Honduras, American Soc. of Civil Engineers. *Address:* Partido Liberal, Col. Miramonte, Tegucigalpa, Honduras (office). *Telephone:* 232-0520 (office). *Fax:* 232-0797 (office). *E-mail:* multimedia@partidoliberal.net (office). *Website:* www.partidoliberal.net (office).

SANTOS PAIS, Marta, BA, MA; Portuguese diplomatist and UN official; *Special Representative of the Secretary-General on Violence against Children, United Nations;* b. 1952; m.; two c.; ed Univ. of Lisbon; more than 25 years' experience on human rights issues and engagement in intergovernmental processes; Rapporteur, UN Cttee on the Rights of the Child 1991–97, served as Vice-Chair. Coordinating Cttee on Childhood Policies, Council of Europe; Dir of Evaluation, Policy and Planning, UNICEF 1997–2001, served as Co-Chair. UN Devt Group Working Group on Human Rights, Dir UNICEF Innocenti Research Centre, Florence, Italy 2001–09; Special Rep. on Violence against Children at level of Asst Sec.-Gen. 2009–; held several advisory positions on human rights and legal issues in Portugal; served as Special Adviser to Machel Study on children affected by armed conflict and to UN Study on Violence against Children. *Publications:* numerous studies and publs. *Address:* 633 Third Avenue, Room 6053, New York, NY 10017, USA (office). *Telephone:* (212) 824-6322 (office). *Website:* srsg .violenceagainstchildren.org (office).

SANTOS PEREIRA, Álvaro, BA, MSc, PhD; Portuguese economist, academic and politician; b. 1972, Viseu; ed Univ. de Coimbra, Simon Fraser Univ., Vancouver, Canada; Lecturer, Simon Fraser Univ., Vancouver 2000–04, concurrently Visiting Prof., Dept of Econs, Univ. of British Columbia 2000–04; Prof. of Econs and European Econ. Devt, Dept of Econs, Univ. of York, UK 2004–07; Minister of the Economy and Employment 2011–13; columnist for several newspapers including o Diário de Notícias, Jornal Público, Diário Económico, Expresso, Exame, Jornal de Notícias; author of Desmitos blog; Ind. *Publications include:* Portugal na Hora da Verdade, Os Mitos da Economia Portuguesa 2007, Diário de um Deus Criacionista, O Medo do Insucesso Naciona 2009. *Address:* c/o Ministry of the Economy, Rua da Horta Seca 15, 1200-221 Lisbon, Portugal.

SANTOS SILVA, Augusto, PhD; Portuguese academic and politician; b. 1956, Porto; m.; three c.; ed Inst. for Labour and Business Sciences, Univ. of Porto; Lecturer in Econs, Univ. of Porto 1981, currently Sr Prof., also Head, Academic Council, Faculty of Econs 1998–99, Deputy Vice-Rector, Univ. of Porto 1998–99; mem. Partido Socialista (PS) 1990–, mem. Nat. Cttee 1998–, Nat. Political Cttee

2002–05, 2006–, Nat. Secr. 2006–, Dir Acção Socialista (official PS journal) 2002–05; mem. Assembléia da República (Parl.) for Porto constituency 2002–, Coordinator, PS Parl. Group for Culture, Science and Higher Educ. 2002–05; Sec. of State for Educ. Admin 1999–2000, Minister of Educ. 2000–01, of Culture 2003–06, Minister for Parl. Affairs 2005–06, Minister of Nat. Defence 2009–11; columnist, Jornal de Notícias 1978–86, Público (newspaper) 1992–99, 2002–05, TSF-Rádio Jornal 1997–98; mem. Nat. Educ. Council 1996–99; mem. Bd Fundação José Fontana 2002–05, Fundação Res Publica 2008–. *Publications include:* Entre a Razão e o Sentido: Durkheim, Weber e a Teoria das Ciências Sociais 1988, Educação de Adultos, Educação para o Desenvolvimento 1990, Tempos Cruzados: um Estudo Interpretativo da Cultura Popular 1994, De que Vale Ter Poder? Crónicas no Público 1995–97 1997, Cultura e Desenvolvimento: Estudos sobre a Relação entre Ser e Agir 2000, A Sociologia e o Debate Público: Estudos sobre a Relação entre Conhecer e Agir 2006. *Address:* c/o Ministry of National Defence, Av. Ilha da Madeira 1, 1400-204, Lisbon, Portugal (office).

SANTOS SIMÃO, Leonardo, LicMed, MSc; Mozambican politician and medical practitioner; *Executive Director, Joaquim Chissano Foundation;* b. 6 June 1953, Mandlakaze; s. of Antonio Santos Simão Sitoi and Amélia Muchanga; m. Josephine P. Simão; two d.; ed Liceu Salazar, Maputo, Eduardo Mondlane Univ., Univ. of London, UK, Boston Univ., USA; Dir Centre of Dist Formation of Chicumbane, Gaza 1981–1982; Prov. Health Dir Zambezia Prov. 1982–84; Dir Prov. Hosp. of Quelimane, Zambezia Prov. 1984–88; Minister of Health 1988; apptd Prof. of Medicine, Eduardo Mondlane Univ. 1988; Minister of Foreign Affairs and Co-operation 1994–95; currently Exec. Dir Joaquim Chissano Foundation; Chair. Nat. Mine Clearance Comm., Muyake SA; mem. Cen. Cttee Frelimo Party; mem. Medical Asscn of Mozambique, Mozambique Asscn of Public Health; Great Cross, Order of Rio Branco (Brazil) 1996, Order of Good Hope, II Grade (South Africa) 1997, Great Cross, Order of Merit (Portugal) 1998, Order of Eduardo Mondlane (Mozambique) 2005, Diploma of Honour (Mozambique) 2005. *Leisure interests:* music, reading, swimming. *Address:* The Joaquim Chissano Foundation, 954, Av. Zimbabwe, Maputo, Mozambique (office). *Telephone:* (21) 484000 (office). *Fax:* (21) 484001 (office). *E-mail:* l.simao@fjchissano.org.mz (office). *Website:* www .fjchissano.org.mz (office).

SANUSI, Sanusi Lamido, BSc, MSc, CON; Nigerian central banker; *Governor, Central Bank of Nigeria;* b. 31 July 1961, Kano; s. of Muhammad Lamido Sanusi; m.; c.; ed King's Coll., Lagos, Ahmadu Bello Univ., Zaria, Int. Univ. of Africa, Khartoum; Lecturer in Econs, Ahmadu Bello Univ. 1983–85; started banking career with Icon Ltd (merchant banker) 1985; joined Credit and Risk Man. Div., United Bank for Africa PLC 1997, becoming Gen. Man.; Exec. Dir in charge of Risk and Man. Control, First Bank of Nigeria PLC 2005, Group Man. Dir (CEO) 2009; Gov. Cen. Bank of Nigeria 2009–; fmr Chief Risk Officer with UBA PLC; fmr Chair. Kakawa Discount House; fmr Dir FBN Bank (UK) Ltd; Fellow, Chartered Inst. of Bankers of Nigeria; Cen. Bank Gov. of the Year, Banker magazine 2010. *Publications include:* author of numerous papers published in academic journals, books and newspapers. *Address:* Central Bank of Nigeria, Plot 33, Abubakar Tafawa Balewa Way, Central Business District, Cadestral Zone, PMB 0187, Garki, Abuja, Nigeria (office). *Telephone:* (9) 46239701 (office). *Fax:* (9) 46236012 (office). *E-mail:* info@cenbank.org (office). *Website:* www.cenbank.org (office).

SANYAL, Meera H., BCom, MBA, FCIB; Indian investment banker; *Chairperson and Country Executive, Royal Bank of Scotland, India;* b. 15 March 1961, Cochin; d. of G. Hiranandani; m. Ashish Sanyal; ed Univ. of Mumbai, Institut Européen d'Administration des Affaires, Harvard Business School, USA; Planning Officer for East India, ANZ Grindlays Bank PLC 1984–87; Head of Advisory Services, Lazard Creditcapital (now Lazard) 1987–90; Founder and Man. Dir MIRA (think tank) 1990–92; Head of Corp. Finance, ABN AMRO Bank NV (now Royal Bank of Scotland (RBS), India) 1992–97, Head of Corp. Finance Advisory for Asia 1997–99, COO and Chief Financial Officer 1999–2001, Head of Services Asia 2006–07, Chair. and Country Exec. 2007–, Chair. and Man. Dir ABN AMRO Cen. Enterprise Services (ACES) 2001–05, currently Chair. RBS India Foundation, RBS Financial Services Co. Ltd, RBS Equities India Ltd; Pres. Indian Liberal Group; Assoc., Chartered Inst. of Bankers, UK 1989, Fellow 1996; unsuccessful cand. in nat. parl. elections 2009; mem. Nat. Advisory Bd Asscn Internationale des Étudiants en Sciences Économiques et Commerciales; Woman Banker of the Year, Indian Merchants Chamber 2006, Karmaveer Puraskaar 2008, iCONGO Confed. of NGOs, AIESEC Hall of Fame Award. *Address:* Royal Bank of Scotland India, Sakhar Bhavan, Nariman Point, Mumbai 400 021, India (office). *Fax:* (22) 22818252 (office). *Website:* www.rbs.in (office); www.meerahsanyal.in.

SAPIN, Michel, BA, MPhil; French politician; *Minister of Finance and National Accounts;* b. 9 April 1952, Boulogne-Billancourt (Hauts-de-Seine); m. Yolande Millan 1982; three c.; ed Lycée Henri IV, Paris-Sorbonne Univ., Ecole Normale Supérieure, Institut d'études politiques de Paris, École nationale d'admin, Strasbourg; joined Parti Socialiste 1975; elected Deputy Nat. Ass. for Indre 1981–86, 2007–12, for Hauts-de-Seine 1986–91, Sec. 1983–84, Vice-Pres. 1984, Chair. of the Cttee for Law 1988–91, currently mem. Finance Cttee; town councillor, Nanterre 1989–94; Minister Del. for Justice 1991–92; Minister of Economy and Finance 1992–93, of Civil Service, of Admin. Reform 2000–02; Regional Councillor, Île de France 1992–94; mem. Council for Monetary Policy of Banque de France 1994–95; Mayor of Argenton-sur-Creuse 1995–2004, Deputy Mayor 2004–08; Gen. Councillor of Indre 1998–; Pres. Centre Regional Council 1998–2000, 2004–07, Vice-Pres. 2000–01; First Vice-Pres. Asscn of the Regions of France 1998–2000; Nat. Sec. on Economy, Parti Socialiste 2007–; Minister of Labour, Employment, Professional Training and Social Dialogue 2012–14, of Finance and Nat. Accounts 2014–. *Address:* Ministry of Finances, 139 rue de Bercy, 75572 Paris Cedex 12 (office). *Telephone:* 1-40-04-04-04 (office). *Fax:* 1-43-43-75-97 (office). *E-mail:* mediateur@economie.gouv.fr (office). *Website:* www .economie.gouv.fr (office).

SAPUTO, Emanuele (Lino), CM; Canadian business executive; *Chairman, Saputo Inc.;* b. 10 June 1937, Sicily, Italy; s. of Giuseppe Saputo and Maria Saputo; m. Mirella Saputo; two s. one d.; family emigrated to Canada 1952; with parents f. dairy processor Saputo Inc. 1954, Chair. 1969–, Pres. 1969–2004, CEO 1998–2004; mem. Bd of Dirs Arbec Forest Products Inc. 1996–, Tembec Inc. 2006–07; mem. Bd of Trustees TransForce Income Fund 2008–; f. Jolina Capital (investment co.). *Address:* Saputo Inc., 6869 Metropolitain Boulevard East, Montreal, PQ H1P 1X8,

Canada (office). *Telephone:* (514) 328-6662 (office). *Fax:* (514) 328-3364 (office). *Website:* www.saputo.com (office).

SAR, Kheng; Cambodian politician; *Deputy Prime Minister and Minister of the Interior;* b. 15 Jan. 1951, Prey Veng; m. Nhem Sakhan; mem. Cen. Cttee Cambodian People's Party 1984–, Pres. Org. Comm. 1990–; Deputy Prime Minister 1992–, Co-minister of the Interior 1998–2006, Minister of the Interior 2006–; fmr Acting Prime Minister; fmr Chair. Nat. Census Cttee; fmr Co-Chair. Nat. Cttee to Support Commune/Sangkat; Membership Award, Natural Sciences Acad. of the Russian Fed. 2002. *Address:* Ministry of the Interior, 275 Blvd Norodom, Khan Chamkarmon, Phnom-Penh, Cambodia (office). *Telephone:* (23) 721190 (office). *Fax:* (23) 726052 (office). *E-mail:* info@interior.gov.kh (office). *Website:* www .interior.gov.kh (office).

SARABI, Habiba; Afghan politician, haematologist, pharmacist and women's rights activist; *Governor of Bamiyan Province;* b. 5 Dec. 1957, Mazar-e Sharif; m.; three c.; ed Aisha Durani High School, Kabul Univ.; licensed pharmacist; with Nat. Inst. of Medicine, Kabul 1983–87; teacher, Intermediate Medical Inst., Kabul 1988–96; exile in Pakistan 1996–2001; Prof. and Gen. Man. Afghanistan Inst. of Learning 1997–2001; medical aid to women and children in refugee camps on Afghanistan-Pakistan border 2001; Dir of Humanitarian Assistance for the Women and Children of Afghanistan, Peshawar 2002; Minister of Women's Affairs 2002–04; Gov. of Bamiyan Prov. (first female gov. in Afghanistan) 2005–; est. Band-e Amir Nat. Park; WHO Fellowship Training Programme, All India Inst. of Medical Science 1998; Jason Award, USA 2005, Malalai Maiwand Medal from Pres. Karzai 2005, named by Time magazine a Hero of the Environment 2008, Medal of Commdr from Pres. of France. *Address:* Governor's Office, Chawney, Bamyan, Bamyan Province, Afghanistan (office). *Telephone:* (79) 9300120 (mobile) (office); (70) 0286585 (mobile) (home). *E-mail:* bamyangovernor@yahoo.com (office).

SARACENO, Chiara, PhD; Italian sociologist and academic; *Honorary Fellow, Collegio Carlo Alberto;* b. 20 Oct. 1941, Milan; m.; two d.; Assoc. Prof. then Full Prof., Faculty of Sociology, Univ. of Trento 1971–90, Vice-Rector Univ. of Trento 1989–90; Prof. of Sociology of the Family, Faculty of Political Sciences, Univ. of Turin 1990–2008, Chair. Dept of Social Sciences 1991–97, Chair. Univ. Gender and Women Studies Centre (CIRSDe) 1997–2006, Chair. PhD Programme in Comparative Social Research 1996–2005; Chair. Italian Comm. on Social Exclusion 1999–2001; Research Prof., Wissenschaftszentrum Berlin fuer Sozialforschung 2006–11, Prof. Emer. 2011–; Corresp. Fellow, British Acad. 2011; Hon. Fellow, Collegio Carlo Alberto, Turin, 2011–; Grandufficiale/Great Kt of the Italian Repub. *Publications:* Genere. La costruzione sociale del femminile e del maschile (co-ed) 1996, Separarsi in Italia (with Marzio Barbagli) 1998, Sociologia della famiglia (co-author) 2001, Età e corso della vita 2001, Commissione d'indagine sull'esclusione sociale, Rapporto sulle politiche contro la povertà e l'esclusione sociale. 1997–2001 2002, Social Assistance Dynamics in European Welfare States (ed.) 2002, Diversi da chi? Gay, lesbiche, transessuali in un'area metropolitana (ed.) 2003, Mutamenti della famiglia e politiche sociali in Italia 2003, Dinamiche assistenziali in Europa (ed.) 2004, Quality of Life in the Enlarged European Union (co-ed.) 2007, Povertà e benessere (co-ed.) 2007, Childhood – Changing Contexts (co-ed.) 2008, Families, Aging and Social Policy (ed.) 2008, Dimensioni della disuguaglianza in Italia: povertà, salute, abitazione (co-ed.) 2009; numerous scientific papers in academic journals on comparative family changes, gender patterns, family and social policies, poverty and anti-poverty policies in comparative perspective; writes regularly for major Italian newspapers. *Leisure interests:* reading, theatre and movie going, walking and swimming, spending time with my grandson. *Address:* Collegio Carlo Alberto, Via Real Collegio 30, 10024 Moncalieri (TO), Italy (office). *Telephone:* (011) 6705234. *E-mail:* chiara.saraceno@unito.it (office). *Website:* www .carloalberto.org/people/faculty/honorary/chiara-saraceno (office).

SARAGA, Peter, CBE, OBE, FIEE, FREng; British engineer and academic; *Vice-President, Royal Academy of Engineering;* m. Anne Coffey MP (Stockport); one s. one d.; ed Univ. of Cambridge, Imperial Coll. London; early career as research scientist specializing in robotics and image processing; Man. Dir Philips Research Laboratories UK 1992–2002; currently consultant; Visiting Prof. and mem. Strategic Advisory Group, Dept of Electric and Electronic Eng, Imperial Coll. London, Adviser to Inst. of Biomedical Eng; Chair. School of Electronics and Physical Sciences Advisory Bd, Univ. of Surrey; mem. Council and Dir of Sussex Intellectual Property Ltd, Univ. of Sussex 2003–, Vice-Chair. Council 2007–09; mem. of Court, Brunel Univ.; Vice-Pres. and Hon. Sec. for Int. Activities, Royal Acad. of Eng; Pres.-elect Inst. of Physics 2005–06, Pres. 2006–08, Past Pres. 2008–09; mem. Bd Higher Educ. Funding Council for England 2002–, Chair. Business and the Community Cttee; has also served on UK Govt Govt cttees relating to tech. issues and acted as adviser to UK research councils. *Publications:* numerous papers in professional journals. *Address:* Room 1108, Control and Power Group, Electrical and Electronic Engineering, Imperial College, South Kensington Campus, London, SW7 2AZ (office); Royal Academy of Engineering, 3 Carlton House Terrace, London, SW1Y 5DG, England (office). *Telephone:* (20) 7594-6272 (Imperial Coll.) (office); (20) 7766-0600 (RAEng) (office). *Fax:* (20) 7594-6282 (Imperial Coll.) (office); (20) 7930-1549 (RAEng) (office). *E-mail:* peter.saraga@ imperial.ac.uk (office). *Website:* www.imperial.ac.uk/controlandpower (office); www.raeng.org.uk (office).

SARAH, HE Cardinal Robert; Guinean ecclesiastic; *President of the Pontifical Council 'Cor Unum';* b. 15 June 1945, Ourous; ed Seminary of Bingerville, Ivory Coast, Seminary of Dixinn, Seminary Jean XXIII, Grand Seminary of Nancy, France, Sébikotane, Senegal, Pontifical Gregorian Univ., Rome, Studium Biblicum Franciscanum of Jerusalem, Israel; returned to Guinea 1974; ordained priest, Diocese of Conakry 1969; Archbishop of Conakry 1979–2001; Sec. Congregation for the Evangelization of Peoples 2001–10; Pres. Pontifical Council 'Cor Unum' 2010–13, 2013–; cr. Cardinal (Cardinal-Deacon of San Giovanni Bosco in via Tuscolana) 2010; participated in Papal Conclave 2013. *Address:* Pontifical Council 'Cor Unum', Palazzo San Pio X, Via della Conciliazione 5, 00120 Città del Vaticano, Rome, Italy (office). *Telephone:* (06) 69889411 (office). *Fax:* (06) 69887301 (office). (06) 69887311 (office). *E-mail:* corunum@corunum.va (office). *Website:* www .vatican.va/roman_curia/pontifical_councils/corunum/corunum_en/index_en.htm (office).

SARAIVA MARTINS, HE Cardinal José; Portuguese ecclesiastic; *Cardinal-Bishop of Palestrina;* b. 6 Feb. 1932, Gagos de Jarmelo, Guarda; ed Pontifical Gregorian Univ., Pontifical Univ. of St Thomas Aquinas, Rome; ordained priest 1957, Bishop 1988; fmr teacher Claretianum, Rome; fmr teacher Pontifical Urbanian Univ., Rector 1977–80, 1980–83, 1986–88; Titular Archbishop of Thuburnica 1988; Prefect of the Congregation for the Causes of Saints 1998–2008, Prefect Emer. 2008–; cr. Cardinal 2001, apptd Cardinal-Deacon of Nostra Signora del Sacro Cuore 2001; Cardinal-Bishop of Palestrina 2009–. *Address:* c/o Congregation for the Causes of Saints, Palazzo delle Congregazioni, Piazza Pio XII 10, 00193 Rome, Italy.

SARANDON, Susan Abigail; American actress; b. 4 Oct. 1946, New York; d. of Philip Tomalin and Lenora Criscione; m. Chris Sarandon 1967 (divorced 1979); one d. with Franco Amurri; fmr pnr Tim Robbins (q.v.); two s.; ed Catholic Univ. of America; numerous TV appearances; UNICEF Goodwill Amb. *Films include:* Joe 1970, Lady Liberty 1971, The Rocky Horror Picture Show 1974, Lovin' Molly 1974, The Great Waldo Pepper 1975, The Front Page 1976, Dragon Fly 1976, Walk Away Madden, The Other Side of Midnight 1977, The Last of the Cowboys 1977, Pretty Baby 1978, King of the Gypsies 1978, Loving Couples 1980, Atlantic City 1981, Tempest 1982, The Hunger 1983, Buddy System 1984, Compromising Positions 1985, The Witches of Eastwick 1987, Bull Durham 1988, Sweet Hearts Dance 1988, Married to the Mob, A Dry White Season 1989, The January Man 1989, White Palace, Thelma and Louise 1991, Light Sleeper 1991, Lorenzo's Oil, The Client, Little Women 1995, Safe Passage 1995, Dead Man Walking (Acad. Award for Best Actress 1996) 1996, James and the Giant Peach 1996, Illuminata 1998, Twilight 1998, Stepmom 1999, Anywhere But Here 1999, The Cradle Will Rock 1999, Rugrats in Paris 2000, Joe Gould's Secret 2000, Cats and Dogs 2001, Igby Goes Down 2002, The Banger Sisters 2003, The Nazi Officer's Wife 2003, Last Party 2000 2003, Noel 2004, Shall We Dance? 2004, Alfie 2004, Elizabethstown 2005, Romance & Cigarettes 2005, Irresistible 2006, In the Valley of Elah 2007, Mr. Woodcock 2007, Emotional Arithmetic 2007, Bernard and Doris 2007, Enchanted 2007, Speed Racer 2008, The Lovely Bones 2009, Wall Street: Money Never Sleeps 2010, Jeff, Who Lives At Home 2011, That's My Boy 2012, Cloud Atlas 2012. *Stage appearances include:* A Coupla White Chicks Sittin' Around Talkin', An Evening with Richard Nixon, A Stroll in the Air, Albert's Bridge, Private Ear, Public Eye, Extremities, Exit the King. *Address:* c/o Samuel Cohen, ICM, 40 West 57th Street, New York, NY 10019, USA (office).

SARANDOS, Theodore (Ted) Anthony; American business executive; *Chief Content Officer, Netflix, Inc.;* b. 30 July 1964, Phoenix, Ariz.; m. Nicole Alexandra Avant; one s. one d.; Vice-Pres., Product & Merchandising, Video City 1983–88; Western Regional Dir, Sales & Operations and Gen. Man., ETD (video distributor) 1988–2000; Vice-Pres., Content and Chief Content Officer, Netflix, Inc. 2000–; mem. Film Advisory Bd Tribeca and Los Angeles Film Festivals; mem. Retail Advisory Bd Digital Entertainment Group; Henry Crown Fellow, Aspen Inst. *Address:* Netflix, Inc, 100 Winchester Circle, Los Gatos, CA 95032, USA (office). *Telephone:* (408) 540-3700 (office). *E-mail:* tsarandos@netflix.com (office). *Website:* www.netflix.com (office).

SARASSORO, Fidele, BEcons, MEcons, PhD; Côte d'Ivoirian UN official; *Deputy Special Representative of the Secretary-General for the Democratic Republic of the Congo and Head, United Nations Organization Stabilization Mission in the Democratic Republic of the Congo (MONUSCO);* b. 1960; m.; three d.; ed Université de Côte d'Ivoire, Univ. of Illinois, USA; served as UN Capital Devt Fund Program Specialist, USAID Regional Office, Abidjan 1988–91, Sr Portfolio Man., UN Office for Project Services (UNOPS) Regional Office, Abidjan 1997–2001, Acting Chief 2001–02, UN Resident Coordinator and UNDP Resident Rep., Togo 2002–06, UN Resident and Humanitarian Coordinator and UNDP Resident Rep., Ethiopia 2006–09, Deputy Special Rep. of Sec.-Gen. for Democratic Repub. of the Congo and Head, UN Org. Stabilization Mission in the Democratic Repub. of the Congo (MONUSCO) 2010–. *Address:* United Nations Organization Stabilization Mission in the Democratic Republic of the Congo (MONUSCO), 12 Av. Des Aviateurs, Kinshasa-Gombe, Democratic Republic of the Congo (office). *Telephone:* (81) 890-6000 (office). *Fax:* (81) 890-56208 (office). *Website:* monusco .unmissions.org (office); www.un.org (office).

SARASTE, Jukka-Pekka; Finnish conductor; *Chief Conductor and Music Director, Oslo Philharmonic Orchestra;* b. 22 April 1956, Heinola; m. Marja-Lisa Ollila; three s. one d.; ed Sibelius Acad., Helsinki; debut with Helsinki Philharmonic 1980; Prin. Conductor and Music Dir Finnish Radio Symphony Orchestra 1987–2001, now Conductor Laureate; Music Dir Toronto Symphony Orchestra 1994–2001; Prin. Guest Conductor BBC Symphony Orchestra 2002–05; Chief Conductor and Music Dir Oslo Philharmonic Orchestra 2006–(12); Artistic Advisor Lahti Symphony Orchestra 2008–(11), Artistic Dir Lahti Sibelius Festival 2008–(11); has been guest conductor with Boston Symphony Orchestra, Cleveland Orchestra, San Francisco Orchestra, Frankfurt Radio Orchestra, NY Philharmonic Orchestra, London Philharmonic Orchestra, Orchestre Philharmonique de Radio France, BBC Symphony Orchestra, Munich Philharmonic Orchestra); has toured Japan, Hong Kong, Taiwan, Germany, USA, Canary Islands Festival; Artistic Adviser, Finnish Chamber Orchestra; Dr hc (Univ. of York, UK). *Recordings include:* complete Sibelius symphonies 1995 (with Finnish Radio Symphony Orchestra) Mussorgsky (with Toronto Symphony Orchestra) Nielsen Symphonies 4, 5 (with Finnish Radio Symphony Orchestra), Romeo and Juliet Suite (Prokofiev). *Address:* c/o Till Janczukowicz, Columbia Artists Management GmbH, Reinhardtstrasse 47, 10117 Berlin, Germany (office); Oslo Philharmonic Orchestra, Postboks 1607, Vika, 0119 Oslo, Norway (office). *Telephone:* (30) 20648078 (office); 22-01-49-00 (office). *Fax:* (30) 20453480 (office); 22-01-49-01 (office). *Website:* www.cami.com (office); www.oslofilharmonien.no (office). *E-mail:* administrasjon@oslofilharmonien.no (office).

SARAYA, Osama, BA; Egyptian journalist and editor; *Editor-in-Chief, Al Ahram (The Pyramids);* b. 24 March 1952; ed Cairo Univ.; has held various positions at Al-Ahram (state-owned daily newspaper) since 1975, including Econs Ed., Supervisor of the Econ. Page (weekly edn), Dir of Arab Econs Dept, Man. of Al-Ahram Regional Press Inst., Dir of Al-Ahram office in Saudi Arabia, Ed.-in-Chief 2005–, supervised training programmes for Egyptian, Arab and African journalists of Al-Ahram Regional Press Inst., represented Al-Ahram in Arab and int. conventions, est. The Devt and Environment Media Unit in Al-Ahram Regional Press Inst.;

mem. Egyptian Journalists Syndicate, fmr Sec.-Gen. and Treas.; helped establish Nat. Democratic Party—NDP (ruling party), mem. sub-cttee of NDP's policy secr.; Gen. Union for Egyptians Abroad Unity Prize 2005. *Address:* Al Ahram, Sharia al-Galaa, Cairo 11511, Egypt (office). *Telephone:* (2) 5801600 (office). *Fax:* (2) 5786023 (office). *E-mail:* Osaraya@ahram.org.eg (office). *Website:* www.ahram.org.eg (office).

SARBANES, Paul Spyros, BA, LLB; American lawyer and fmr politician; b. 3 Feb. 1933, Salisbury, Md; s. of the late Spyros P. Sarbanes and Matina (née Tsigounis) Sarbanes; m. Christine Dunbar 1960 (deceased 2009); two s. one d.; ed Princeton Univ., Balliol Coll., Oxford, UK, Harvard Law School; Rhodes Scholar, Balliol Coll., Oxford 1954–57; admitted to Maryland Bar 1960; law clerk to circuit judge 1960–61; Assoc., Piper and Marbury, Baltimore 1961–62; Admin. Asst to Chair. Council of Econ. Advisers 1962–63; Exec. Dir Charter Revision Comm., Baltimore 1963–64; Assoc., Venable, Baetjer & Howard, Baltimore 1965–70; mem. Maryland House of Dels 1967–71, House of Reps 1971–76, Senator from Maryland 1977–2007 (retd), Chair. Cttee on Banking, Housing and Urban Affairs 2001–07, fmr ranking mem. Senate Sub-Cttee on Int. Econ. Policy, Export and Trade Promotion, co-author Sarbanes-Oxley Act; Democrat; Paul H. Douglas Ethics in Govt Award, Univ. of Illinois 2003, Woodrow Wilson Award, Princeton Univ. 2007. *Address:* Tower 1, Suite 1710, 100 South Charles Street, Baltimore, MD 21201, USA.

SARCINELLI, Mario; Italian banker, economist and academic; *Chairman, Dexia Crediop;* b. 9 March 1934, Foggia; m. Giovanna Longardi; two s.; ed Univ. of Pavia, Univ. of Cambridge; joined Bank of Italy 1957, fmr Head Data Processing and Information Systems Dept, Cen. Man. for Banking Supervision 1976, Deputy Dir-Gen. 1976; Econ. Adviser to Italian Del. to UN 1960; Dir-Gen. Treasury 1982–91; Minister of Foreign Trade April–July 1987; Vice-Pres. EBRD 1991–94; Chair. Monetary Cttee 1989–90, Banca Nazionale del Lavoro SpA 1994–98; Chair. Diners Club Sim p.a. 1999–2001; Prof. of Int. Monetary Econs, Università degli Studi di Roma 'la Sapienza' 1998–2002; Lecturer in Global Banking, LUISS Guido Carli 2001–04, Pres. Centro di Ricerca per il Diritto d'Impresa (CERADI) 1999–2004; Chair. Dexia Crediop, Rome 2007–; alt. mem. EEC Cttee of Govs of Cen. Banks 1978–81, Bd of Dirs BIS 1978–81; Officier Légion d'honneur, Cavaliere del Lavoro 1996; Dr hc Univ. of Bari. *Address:* Dexia Crediop, Via Venti Settembre 30, 00187 Rome, Italy (office). *Telephone:* (06) 47711 (office). *Fax:* (06) 47715961 (office). *E-mail:* mario.sarcinelli@dexia-crediop.it (office). *Website:* www.dexia-crediop.it (office).

SARDESAI, Rajdeep, BA, MA, BCL; Indian journalist and television presenter; *Editor-in-Chief, CNN-IBN;* b. 24 May 1965, Gujarat; s. of Dilip Sardesai and Nandini Sardesai; m. Sagarika Ghose; two c.; ed St Xavier's Coll., Mumbai, Univ. of Oxford; Asst Ed. then City Ed. and Chief of News Service, Times of India, Mumbai 1988–94; Special Corresp. and Political Ed., New Delhi TV (NDTV) 1994–2002, Man. Ed. NDTV 24x7 and NDTV India 2002–05; Co-Founder IBN18 Network 2005, Ed.-in-Chief CNN-IBN 2005–; Pres. Eds Guild of India 2008–; mem. Population Council; columnist for leading Indian English–language dailies; Padma Shri 2008, Int. Broadcasters Award, Ramnath Goenka Excellence in Journalism Award 2007, Asian TV Award, News Anchor of the year, Indian TV Acad. Academy (last six years). *Address:* CNN-IBN Network, Express Trade Tower, Plot No. 15-16, Sector-16A, Noida 201 301, India (office). *Telephone:* (12) 04341818 (office); (12) 03987777 (office). *Fax:* (12) 04324106 (office). *E-mail:* editor@ibnlive.com (office). *Website:* www.ibnlive.in.com (office).

SARDI, HE Cardinal Paolo, STL; Italian ecclesiastic; b. 1 Sept. 1934, Ricaldone, Prov. of Alessandria; ed Università Cattolica del Sacro Cuore, Milan; ordained priest 1958; taught moral theology in Turin –1976; called to the Vatican to work in Secr. of State 1976; Vice-Councillor for Gen. Affairs 1992–96; Apostolic Nuncio with special responsibilities 1996–2004; Titular Archbishop of Sutrium 1996–; Vice-Chamberlain of the Apostolic Chamber 2004–11; Pro-Patron of the Sovereign Mil. Order of Malta 2009–; cr. Cardinal (Cardinal-Deacon of Santa Maria Auxiliatrice in via Tuscolana) 2010; participated in Papal Conclave 2013. *Address:* c/o Apostolic Chamber, Palazzo Apostolico, 00120 Città del Vaticano, Rome, Italy (office). *Telephone:* (06) 69883554 (office). *Website:* www.vatican.va (office).

SARDJOE, Ramdien; Suriname politician; b. 10 Oct. 1935, Dist Suriname; mem. Parl. 1964–80, 1987–; Chair. Vooruitstrevende Hervormings Partij (VHP); Speaker, Nat. Ass. –2005; Perm. Rep. of Suriname Nat. Ass. to Jt Parl. ACP-EU Meeting, Co-Pres. –2004; Vice-Pres. of Suriname 2005–10; Officer, Order of the Netherlands Lion, Officer, Order of the Yellow Star, Grand Officer, Order of the Yellow Star. *Address:* c/o Office of the Vice-President, Paramaribo, Suriname (office).

SARDO, Gabriele, LLB; Italian diplomatist; b. 9 Jan. 1944, Trieste; m. Enrica Sardo; ed Univ. of Trieste; Seasonal Lecturer in Int. Law, Univ. of Trieste 1966–68; entered Foreign Service 1968; assigned to Directorate General for Political Affairs 1968–70; Vice-Consul, Munich 1970–973; posted to Buenos Aires, Argentina 1973–1975; served in Foreign Ministry Cabinet 1975–77; posted to Mexico City 1977–82; First Counsellor in Washington, DC 1984–91; with Middle East Dept, Ministry of Foreign Affairs 1991–1993, Co-ordinator for the Schengen Convention Implementation 1995–1996; Deputy Head, Minister's Cabinet 1996–98; Head, Perm. Representation to UNESCO, Paris 1998–2002; Diplomatic Counsellor for Minister for Environment and Protection of Natural Resources, Rome 2002–05; Amb. to Canada 2006–09; Diplomatic Adviser to Minister of Infrastructure and Transport 2009–; currently Lecturer, LUISS School of Govt, Rome. *Address:* LUISS School of Government, Via di Villa Emiliani 14, 00197 Rome, Italy (office). *Telephone:* (06) 85225053 (office). *E-mail:* schoolofgovernment@luiss.it (office). *Website:* http://sog.luiss.it/ (office).

SARFATI, Alain; French architect and town planner; b. 23 March 1937, Meknès, Morocco; s. of Maurice Sarfati and Sarah Levy de Valencia; two d.; ed Lycée Poeymirau, Meknès, Lycée Laknal, Sceaux, Ecole des Beaux Arts, Paris and Inst. d'Urbanisme, Univ. de Paris; town planner, Inst. d'Urbanisme, Paris region 1966; Founder of review A.M.C. and Atelier de Recherche et d'Etudes d'Amènagement (AREA) (now Sarea Alain Sarfati Architecture) 1967, currently Head; Prof. of Architecture, Nancy 1969; Prof. and Head of Dept, Ecole des Beaux Arts, Paris-Conflans 1979; architectural adviser, Ministry of Public Works, Urban Devt, Housing and Transport 1985–; Vice-Pres. of Construction Planning, Ministry of

Public Works, Housing, Transport and the Sea 1988–; mem. Consultative Cttee, Centre Scientifique et Technique du Bâtiment 1990–; Vice-Pres. Ordre Nat. des Architectes 1992–96; work includes housing, schools, hosps, leisure centres and Centre des Archives du Monde du Travail, Roubaix 1993; also designed French Embassy in China 2011; Chevalier, Ordre du Mérite, Officier, Ordre des Arts et Lettres. *Leisure interests:* opera, cinema, art, golf, skiing. *Address:* Atelier de Recherche et d'Etudes d'Amènagement, 43 rue Maurice Ripoche, 75014 Paris (office); 79 rue du Cherche-Midi, 75006 Paris, France (home). *Telephone:* 1-58-14-24-00 (office). *Fax:* 1-58-14-24-13 (office). *E-mail:* sarea@sarea.fr (office). *Website:* www.sarea.fr (office).

SARGENT, Ronald (Ron) L., BA, MBA; American retail executive; *Chairman and CEO, Staples Inc.;* b. 1956; ed Harvard Univ., Harvard Business School; began retail career with The Kroger Co., man. positions in operations, human resources, strategy, sales and marketing –1989; Regional Vice-Pres. of Operations, Staples Inc. 1989–91, Head of Staples Direct 1991, Vice-Pres. Staples 1991–94, Pres. Staples Contract & Commercial 1997, Pres. N American Div. 1997–98, Pres. and COO Staples Inc. 1998–2002, Pres. and CEO 2002–05, Chair. and CEO 2005–; fmr mem. Bd of Dirs Literacy Volunteers of America; mem. Bd of Dirs The Kroger Co., Mattel, Inc., Yankee Candle Co., Bd of Advisers Boston Coll. Carroll School of Man. *Address:* Staples Inc., 500 Staples Drive, Framingham, MA 01702, USA (office). *Telephone:* (508) 253-5000 (office). *Fax:* (508) 253-8989 (office). *E-mail:* info@staples.com (office). *Website:* www.staples.com (office).

SARGENT, Thomas (Tom) John, BA, PhD; American economist and academic; *William R. Berkley Professor of Economics, New York University;* b. 19 July 1943, Pasadena, Calif.; ed Univ. of California, Berkeley, Harvard Univ.; Research Assoc., Carnegie Inst. of Tech. 1967–68; First Lt and Capt., US Army 1968–69, served as Staff mem. and Acting Dir, Econs Div., Office of Asst Sec. of Defense (Systems Analysis) 1968–69; Assoc. Prof. of Econs, Univ. of Pennsylvania 1970–71; Assoc. Prof. of Econs, Univ. of Minnesota 1971–75, Prof. of Econs 1975–87; Research Assoc., Nat. Bureau of Econ. Research 1970–73, 1979–; mem. Brookings Panel on Econ. Activity 1973; Ford Foundation Visiting Research Prof. of Econs, Univ. of Chicago 1976–77, David Rockefeller Prof. of Econs 1991–98; Advisor, Fed. Reserve Bank of Minneapolis 1971–87; Visiting Prof. of Econs, Harvard Univ. and Research Assoc., Nat. Bureau of Econ. Research 1981–82; Visiting Scholar, Hoover Inst., Stanford Univ., Calif. 1985–87, Sr Fellow, Hoover Inst. 1987–, Donald Lucas Prof. of Econs, Stanford Univ. 1998–2002, Prof. Emer. 2002–; first William R. Berkley Prof. of Econs and Business, New York Univ. 2002–; mem. American Econ. Asscn (mem. Exec. Cttee 1986–88, Vice-Pres. 2000–01, Pres.-elect 2006, Pres. 2007), Econometric Soc. (mem. Council 1987–92, 1995–99, Second Vice-Pres. 2003, First Vice-Pres. 2004, Pres. 2005); Pres. Soc. for Econ. Dynamics and Control 1989–92; Fellow, Econometric Soc. 1976, NAS 1983, American Acad. of Arts and Sciences 1983; Corresp. Fellow, British Acad. 2011; Dr hc (Stockholm School of Econs) 2003; Hon. DEcon (European Univ. Inst.) 2008; Univ. Medallist as Most Distinguished Scholar in Class of 1964, Univ. of California, Berkeley, Mary Elizabeth Morgan Prize for Excellence in Econs, Univ. of Chicago 1979, Erwin Plein Nemmers Prize in Econs, Northwestern Univ. 1996–97, NAS Award for Scientific Reviewing 2011, Nobel Prize in Econs 2011. *Publications:* Macroeconomic Theory 1979 (second edn 1987), Rational Expectations and Econometric Practice (co-ed. with Robert E. Lucas, Jr) 1981, Energy, Foresight and Strategy (ed.) 1985, Dynamic Macroeconomic Theory 1987, Exercises in Dynamic Macroeconomic Theory (with Rodolfo Manuelli) 1987, Rational Expectations Econometrics (with Lars Hansen) 1991, Rational Expectations and Inflation (reprinted articles, second edn) 1992, Bounded Rationality in Macroeconomics 1993, The Conquest of American Inflation 1999, The Big Problem of Small Change (with François Velde) 2002, Recursive Macroeconomic Theory (second edn, with Lars Ljungqvist) 2004, Robustness (with Lars Peter Hansen) 2008; numerous papers in professional journals. *Address:* Department of Economics, New York University, 19 West Fourth Street, Sixth Floor, New York, NY 10012-1119 (office); Leonard N. Stern School of Business, Kaufman Management Center, 44 West Fourth Street 7-75, New York, NY 10012 (office); Hoover Institution, 434 Galvez Mall, Stanford University, Stanford, CA 94305-6010, USA (office). *Telephone:* (212) 998-3548 (New York) (office); (650) 723-0965 (Stanford) (office). *Fax:* (212) 998-4186 (New York) (office). *E-mail:* thomas.sargent@nyu.edu (office); tsargent@stern.nyu.edu (office). *Website:* econ.as.nyu.edu (office); files.nyu.edu/ts43/public (office); www.hoover.org (office); www.stern.nyu.edu (office).

SARID, Yossi, MA; Israeli journalist and fmr politician; b. 24 Oct. 1940, Rehovot; m. Dorit Sarid; three c.; ed New School for Social Research, New York, USA; served in artillery corps and as mil. corresp., Israel Defense Forces; mem. Knesset 1974–2006, served on Educ. and Culture Cttee 1974–77, House Cttee 1974–92, Immigration and Absorption Cttee 1996–99 and Foreign Affairs and Security Cttee 1972–92, 1996–99; Minister of Environment 1993–96, of Educ. 1999–2000; Chair. Meretz–Yahad Party 1996–2006, Leader of the Opposition –2006; currently Lecturer, Interdisciplinary Centre, Herzliya; currently also political columnist Ha'aretz (The Land) (daily newspaper). *Address:* Ha'aretz (The Land), 21 Schocken Street, Tel-Aviv 61001, Israel (office). *Telephone:* 3-5121212 (office). *Fax:* 3-6810012 (office). *E-mail:* contact@haaretz.co.il (office). *Website:* www.haaretz.co.il (office).

SARIN, Arun, MS, MBA; American/Indian telecommunications industry executive; b. 21 Oct. 1954, Pachmarhi, MP; s. of Krishan Sarin and Ramilla Sarin; m. Rummi Anand; two c.; ed Indian Inst. of Tech., Univ. of California, Berkeley; fmr corp. developer, Natomas Co., Pacific Telesis Group, San Francisco, Chief Financial Officer, Chief Strategy Officer, Pacific Bell, Vice-Pres., Gen. Man. San Francisco Bay Area Telephone Co. (div. of Pacific Bell); Sr Vice-Pres. of Corp. Strategy and Devt, AirTouch Communications (on demerger from Pacific Telesis), Pres. and CEO AirTouch Int., Pres. AirTouch Communications, CEO USA and Asia Pacific region 1999–2000, Vodafone Airtouch PLC; CEO Infospace 2000–01, Accel-KKR Telecom, San Francisco 2001–03; Group CEO Vodafone Group plc 2003–08; Dir (non-exec.) Vodafone 2000–08, Charles Schwab Corpn –2009, Court of the Bank of England 2005–09, Cisco Systems 2009–, Safeway Inc. 2009–, Aricent Inc. 2010–; Sr Advisor, Kohlberg Kravis Roberts & Co. 2009–; Hon. KBE 2010; B.C. Roy Gold Medal 1975, Haas School Business Leader of Year 2000, Univ. of California Trust (UK) Award 2003. *Leisure interests:* golf, travel. *Address:* c/o

Kohlberg Kravis Roberts & Co., 9 West 57th Street, Suite 4200, New York, NY 10019, USA (office). *Telephone:* (212) 750-8300. *Website:* www.kkr.com (office).

SARIYEV, Temir, BA; Kyrgyzstani business executive and politician; *Minister of Economics and Anti-monopoly Policy;* b. 17 June 1963, Tosh Bulak, Sokuluk Dist.; m.; two c.; ed Kyrgyz State Nat. Univ.; began career with freight forwarder Alamedin fur factory 1983, becoming Sr Economist 1987; Instructor with Komsomol (Soviet youth org.), later Head, Youth Work Dept 1987–89; Party work, becoming Deputy Chair., Alamedin Exec. Cttee 1989–91; Founder and Pres. Kyrgyzstan Commodity and Raw Materials Exchange 1991–95; CEO Totoni financial and industrial firms 1995; mem. Jogorku Kenesh (Supreme Council, Parl.) 2000–07, mem. Budget and Finance Cttee; mem. Constitutional Council 2005; acting Deputy Chair. Provisional Govt 2010 (resgnd); Minister of Finance 2010 (resgnd), of Econs and Anti-monopoly Policy 2011–; Co-Chair. For Reforms! Movement 2007; Co-Chair. Al Shumkar Union of Democratic Forces Party 2007; Chair. White Falcon Political Party (Ak Shumkar) 2008–; Order of Manas, third degree. *Address:* Ministry of Economics and Anti-monopoly Policy, 7200002 Bishkek, pr. Chui 106, Kyrgyzstan (office). *Telephone:* (312) 62-52-41 (office). *Fax:* (312) 66-18-37 (office). *E-mail:* t.sariev@mineconom.kg (office). *Website:* www.mert.kg (office).

SARKAR, Manik, BCom; Indian politician; *Chief Minister of Tripura;* b. 22 Jan. 1949, Radhakishorepur; m. Panchali Bhattacharya; ed Maharaja Bir Bakram Coll., Calcutta Univ.; mem. Communist Party of India—Marxist 1968–, mem. State Cttee 1972, State Secr. 1978, mem. Central Cttee 1985, State Sec. 1993, State Left Front Convenor, mem. Politburo 1998; mem. Tripura Legis. Ass. 1980–; Chief Minister of Tripura 1998–. *Address:* Chief Minister's Secretariat, Agartala, India (office). *Telephone:* (381) 2324000 (office); (381) 2324001 (home). *Fax:* (381) 2223201 (office). *E-mail:* cmo-trp@hub.nic.in (office). *Website:* tripura.nic.in (office).

ŠARKINAS, Reinoldijus; Lithuanian economist and fmr central banker; b. 16 July 1946, Toliūnų Village, Ukmergės Dist; m.; two d.; ed Vilnius Univ.; Chief Engineer Spindulys factory and Head Div. of Labour and Earnings Lithuanian Chemicals Co. 1968–72; Deputy Head Dept of Planning and Finance, Head Financial Accounting Dept, Ministry of Educ. 1972–80; Finance Adviser, Ministry of Educ., Repub. of Cuba 1980–82; Deputy Head, Head of Culture and Health Care Financing Dept, Dir Budget Dept, Ministry of Finance 1983–90; Deputy Minister and Sec., Ministry of Finance 1991–95, Minister of Finance 1995–96; mem. Bd Bank of Lithuania 1992–95, Chair. Bd of Govs 1996–2011; Commdr's Cross, Order of Lithuanian Grand Duke Gediminas 2003. *Address:* c/o Lietuvos Bankas, Gedimino pr. 6, Vilnius 01103, Lithuania.

SARKISOV, Ashot Arakelovich; Russian nuclear energy specialist; *Adviser, Nuclear Safety Institute, Russian Academy of Sciences;* b. 30 Jan. 1924, Tashkent, USSR; s. of Arakel A. Sarkisov and Evgeniya B. Grigoryan; m. Nelli G. Sarkisov 1951; two s.; ed F. Dzerzhinsky Higher Marine Eng School, Leningrad Univ.; worked as engineer Baltic fleet; Chair. Higher Marine School, Sevastopol; Deputy Dir Naval Acad.; Chair. Scientific-Tech. Council of the Navy; Head of Dept, Inst. for Nuclear Safety; currently Chair. Expert Council on Naval and Shipbuilding Problems of Higher Certification Comm., Int. Russian-American Scientific-Technical Program of International Science and Technology Center; Chair. Panel of Experts, Int. Scientific and Engineering Program on Radioactive Waste; apptd Academician, Russian Acad. of Sciences (RAS) 1994, mem. and Adviser, Nuclear Safety Inst. 1990–, currently also Deputy Chair Scientific Council on Atomic Energy; research in theory of dynamic processes and automatic protection of nuclear plants, problems of safety and security in nuclear energy; currently Chief-Ed. Arctic: Economics & Ecology (professional magazine); ten Orders of the USSR and of Russia; more than 30 state medals, including Aleksandrov Gold Medal, Russian Acad. of Sciences 2007. *Publications include:* Dynamics of Nuclear Power Plants of Submarines 1964, Nuclear Propulsion Power Plants 1968, Dynamic Regimes in the Operation of Nuclear Propulsion Power Plants 1971, Physics of Transitional Processes in Nuclear Reactors 1983, Nuclear Propulsion Power Plants and Steam Generators 1985, Thermo-Electric Generators with Nuclear Sources of Heat 1987, Physical Principles of Nuclear Steam-Productive Plants 1989, Nuclear Submarine Decommissioning and Related Problems 1996, Analysis of Risks Associated with Nuclear Submarine Decommissioning, Dismantling and Disposal 1999, Remaining Issues in the Decommissioning of Nuclear Powered Vessels 2003, Overcoming Impediments to US–Russian Cooperation on Nuclear Nonproliferation 2004, Status, Problems and Priorities of NS Complex Decommissioning in the North-West Russia (Basic Provisions of Strategic Master Plan Initial Phase) 2004, Strategic Approaches in Solving Decommissioning Problems of Retired Russian Nuclear Fleet in the Northwest Region: Executive Summary of Strategic Master Plan, Phase 1 2004, Strengthening US–Russian Cooperation on Nuclear Nonproliferation Recommendations for Action 2005, Scientific and Technical Issues in the Management of Spent Nuclear Fuel of Decommissioned Nuclear Submarines 2006, Atomic Legacy of the Cold War at the Artic Seabed. Radioecological Consequences and Technical and Economic Problems of Radiation Remediation at the Arctic Seas 2006, Strategic Master Plan for Decommissioning of the Retired Russian Nuclear Fleet and Environmental Rehabilitation of Its Supporting Infrastructure in Northwest Russia. Priority Project Programme 2006, Strategic Master Plan for Decommissioning of the Retired Russian Nuclear Fleet and Environmental Rehabilitation of Its Supporting Infrastructure in Northwest Russia. Executive Summary 2007, The Nuclear Legacy of the "Cold War" at the Bottom of the Arctic 2008, Expected Radiation and Radioecological Consequences from Floating NPPs' Use 2008, The Salient Need to Develop New Approaches to Address Nuclear Weapons Proliferation Issues, Future of the Nuclear Security Environment in 2015 2009, Nuclear and Radiation Safety Challenges at the Disposal Sites of the Nuclear Fleet in the Far East of Russia 2010,. International Cooperation in Cold War Legacy Elimination in the Arctic Region of Russia 2011, Low-power NPPs - a New Development Trend of Nuclear Energy 2011, Risk Assessment and Safeguard of Industry and Energy Facilities. Integrative approach 2011. *Leisure interests:* tennis, history of the navy. *Address:* Nuclear Safety Institute, Russian Academy of Sciences, 115191 Moscow, B. Tulskaya str. 52, Russia (office). *Telephone:* (495) 952-24-21 (office); (495) 955-22-80 (office). *Fax:* (495) 958-00-40 (office). *E-mail:* sarkisov@ibrae.ac.ru (office). *Website:* www.ibrae.ac.ru (office).

SARKISSIAN, Aram; Armenian politician; *Chairman, Republic (Hanrapetutiun);* b. 2 Jan. 1961, Ararat; m.; three c.; ed Yerevan School of Arts, Yerevan Polytechnical Inst.; army service 1981–83; various positions with Araratstroytrust 1989–93; Asst Dir-Gen., then Deputy Dir-Gen. Araratcement 1993–98, Exec. Dir 1998–99; mem. Republican Party of Armenia, Yerkrapah Union of Volunteers; Prime Minister of Armenia 1999–2000; in pvt. business; Chair. Republic (Hanrapetutiun); Chair. Armenian Democratic Party. *Address:* Republic, 0002 Yerevan, Mashtotsi Avenue 37/30, Armenia (office). *Telephone:* (10) 53-86-34 (office). *E-mail:* republic@arminco.com (office).

SARKISSIAN, Serge Azati; Armenian philologist, politician and head of state; *President;* b. 30 June 1954, Stepanakert (Xankändi), Nagornyi Karabakh Autonomous Oblast, Azerbaijan SSR, USSR; m. Rita Sarkissian; two d.; ed Yerevan State Univ.; served in USSR army 1972–74; metal turner, Electrical Devices Factory, Yerevan 1975–79; Komsomol Sec., Head of Propaganda section City Cttee, Stepanakert 1979–88; Head of Self-Defence Cttee, 'Repub. of Nagornyi Karabakh' 1989–93; Deputy Supreme Council (Parl.) 1990–93, Minister of Defence 1993–95, 2000–07, of Nat. Security 1995–96, 1999, of Internal Affairs and Nat. Security 1996–99; Chief of Staff to Pres. 1999–2000; Sec. Council of Nat. Security 1999–2007; mem. Republican Party of Armenia (RPA) 2006–, Chair. Party Council 2006–07, Chair. RPA 2007–; Prime Minister 2007–08; Pres. of Armenia 2008–; Chair. Bd of Trustees, Yerevan State Univ.; Chair. Chess Federation of Armenia; Order of Martakan Khach (First Degree), Kt of Voske Artsiv (Golden Eagle) Order, Hero of Artsakh, Armenian Battle Cross 'Tigran Mets', First Class of the Order of Prince Yaroslav the Wise (Ukraine) 2011. *Address:* Office of the President, 0077 Yerevan, Marshal Baghramian Avenue, Armenia (office). *Telephone:* (10) 58-87-12 (office). *Fax:* (10) 58-87-12 (office). *E-mail:* frd@gov.am (office). *Website:* www.president.am (office); www.serzhsargsyan.am.

SARKISSIAN, Tigran, PhD; Armenian politician and fmr central banker; b. 29 Jan. 1960, Kirovakan (now Vanadzor), Armenian SSR, USSR; m.; two s. one d.; ed Tech. Coll. No. 14, Yerevan, Inst. of Nat. Economy, Planning and Economy Dept, Yerevan, Voznesenskii Financial and Econ. Inst., Leningrad (now St Petersburg), USSR, Int. Inst. of Law, Washington, DC, USA; Chief of Dept for Foreign Econ. Relations, Scientific Research Inst. of Econ. Planning 1987–90; Chair. Republican Council of Young Specialists and Scientists 1988–93; mem. Supreme Council of the Repub. of Armenia and Chair. of Standing Comm. for Financial, Credit and Budget Affairs 1990–95; Reader in Banking Man., Yerevan State Univ. 1993–94; Dir of Scientific Research, Inst. of Social Reforms 1995–98; Chair. Armenian Banks Asscn 1995–98; Chair. Cen. Bank of Armenia 1998–2008, Interstate Bank Council 2005–07; Dir Transition Soc. Inst. 1995–2008; Prime Minister 2008–14 (resgnd); holds mil. rank of Reserve Officer; Anania Shirakatsi Medal, First Degree Medal 'For Services to Motherland' 2012; Dr hc (State Econs Univ.). *Publications:* more than 20 scientific articles. *Address:* c/o Office of the Prime Minister, 0010 Yerevan, Republic Square, Government House 1, Armenia (office). *Website:* tigransargsyan.am/en.

SARKISYAN, Armen, CandPhys-MathSc; Armenian physicist, academic and diplomatist; *Ambassador to UK;* b. 23 June 1953, Yerevan; m.; two s.; ed Yerevan State Univ.; Prof. of Physics, Yerevan State Univ., Founder Dept of Computer Modelling of Complex Systems at Univ.'s Dept of Theoretical Physics 1976–84; Visiting Research Fellow, Univ. of Cambridge, UK 1984–85; Lecturer, Yerevan State Univ. 1985–90;; Prof., Inst. of Math., Univ. of London 1989–91; apptd. Chargé d'affaires a.i., then Amb. to UK 1991–95, 1998–99, 2013–; Amb., Doyen of Armenian Diplomatic Corps to Europe, Amb. and Perm. Rep. to the EU (also accred to Belgium, the Netherlands, Luxembourg and the Holy See (Vatican City)) 1991–99, Head of Mission to the EU 1995–96; Prime Minister of Armenia 1996–97; Special Advisor to Pres. of EBRD and Dir of EBRD 1993–2000; Founding Pres. Eurasia House International 2000; Founder and Dir Eurasia Centre, Univ. of Cambridge's Judge Business School 2001–11; Initiator of Eurasian Media Forum (Astana) 2002; Founder High Power Annual Conf., Univ. of Cambridge 2003; Sr Advisor, British Petroleum, Alcatel, Telefonica, Bank of America Merrill Lynch and other multinational corpns 2001–13; Chair. Global Council on Energy Security (WEFForum); Vice-Chair. East West Inst. (EWI); Comm. mem. Euro-Atlantic Security Initiative (Chair. of Energy Security); Founding Pres. British-Armenian All Party Parl. Group; mem. Bd Global Leadership Foundation; mem. Dean's Advisory Council, Kennedy School of Govt, Harvard Univ., Dean's Advisory Council, Harris School of Public Policy Studies, Univ. of Chicago; mem. John Smith Trust, London, Int. Econ. Alliance, Global Leadership Foundation; Hon. mem. Royal Soc. of Int. Relations and Cen. of Strategic Studies, Univ. of Oxford; Hon. Sr Research Fellow, School of Math. Sciences, Queen Mary and Westfield Coll., London; Dr hc (Nat. Acad. of Sciences of Armenia); St Gregory the Great Award from His Holiness Pope John Paul II 1997, St Gregory the Illuminator Medal from His Holiness Karekin II, Catholicos Patriarch of All Armenians 2008. *Publications include:* numerous articles on politology, theoretical physics, astronomy and math. modelling. *Address:* Embassy of Armenia, 25A Cheniston Gardens, London, W8 6TG, England (office). *Telephone:* (20) 7938-5435 (office); (20) 7376-0542 (Amb.'s office) (office). *Fax:* (20) 7938-2595 (office). *E-mail:* armembassyuk@mfa.am (office). *Website:* www.armenianembassyuk.com (office); uk.mfa.am (office).

SARKÖZY DE NAGY BOCSA, Nicolas Paul Stéphane, LLM; French politician, barrister, civil servant and fmr head of state; b. 28 Jan. 1955, Paris; s. of Paul Sarközy de Nagy Bocsa and Andrée Mallah; m. 1st Marie-Dominique Culioli 1982 (divorced 1996); two s.; m. 2nd Cecilia Ciganer-Albeniz 1996 (divorced 2007); one s.; m. 3rd Carla Bruni 2008; one d.; ed Inst. of Political Studies, Paris, Paris Univ.; barrister, Paris 1981–87; Assoc., Leibovici Claude Sarközy 1987; mem. Neuilly-sur-Seine Municipal Council 1977–83, Mayor of Neuilly-sur-Seine 1983–2002; Vice-Chair. Hauts-de-Seine Gen. Council, responsible for Educ. and Culture 1986–88, Chair. 2004; RPR Deputy to Nat. Ass. from Hauts-de-Seine 1988–2002; Govt Spokesman 1993–95; Minister of the Budget 1993–95, of Communications 1994–95, of the Interior, Internal Security and Local Freedoms 2002–04, of the Economy, Finance and Industry 2004, of the Interior and Town and Country Planning 2005–07 (resgnd); Pres. of France 2007–12, Co-Prince of Andorra 2007–12; Nat. Sec. RPR responsible for Youth and Training 1988, for Activities, Youth and Training 1989, Deputy Gen.-Sec. responsible for local brs 1992–93, mem. Political Bureau 1993, Gen. Sec. RPR 1998, Interim Pres. April–Oct. 1999, Pres. RPR Regional Cttee of Hauts-de-Seine 2000; Leader RPR-DL List, European

Elections 1999; Pres. Union pour un Mouvement Populaire (UMP) 2004–07; Chevalier, Légion d'honneur 2004, Grand'Croix, Légion d'honneur 2007, Grand'Croix, Ordre nat. du Mérite 2007, Stara Planina (Bulgaria) 2007, Commdr, Ordre de Léopold (Belgium); ranked by Forbes magazine amongst The World's Most Powerful People (56th) 2009, (19th) 2010, (13th) 2011. *Publications include:* Georges Mandel, moine de la politique 1994, Au bout de la passion, l'équilibre (co-author) 1995, Libre 2001, La République, les Religions, l'Espérance 2004, Témoignage 2006. *Leisure interests:* tennis, cycling. *Address:* c/o Union pour un Mouvement Populaire, 55 rue La Boétie, 75384 Paris Cedex 8, France.

SARMADI, Morteza, BSc, MA; Iranian politician and diplomatist; *Executive Director, Indian Ocean Rim Association for Regional Cooperation (IOR-ARC);* b. July 1954, Tehran; m. Fatima Hosseini 1982; four d.; ed Sharif Univ., Tehran; joined Ministry of Foreign Affairs 1981, Dir-Gen. of Press and Information 1982–89, Deputy Foreign Minister for Communication 1989–97, Deputy Foreign Minister for Europe and America 1997, Amb. to UK 2000–05, Deputy Foreign Minister for Euro-American Affairs 2005; Sr Del. Iran-Iraq peace talks; currently Exec. Dir, Indian Ocean Rim Asscn for Regional Cooperation (IOR-ARC); Trustee, Islamic Thought Foundation, Islamic Repub. News Agency, Islamic High Council of Propagation Policy, Inst. for Political and Int. Studies. *Publications:* numerous political articles. *Leisure interests:* reading, writing, watching TV, spending time with family. *Address:* Indian Ocean Rim Association for Regional Cooperation (IOR-ARC), Soreze House, 14, Angus Road, Vacoas, Mauritius (office). *E-mail:* iorarchq@intnet.mu (office).

SARMI, Massimo, BEng; Italian postal service executive; *CEO and Managing Director, Poste Italiane SpA;* b. 4 Aug. 1948, Malcesine; ed Univ. of Rome; began career in Italian Air Force; then joined SIP as Head Buyer and Head of Operations –1995; Gen. Man. TIM 1995–98, Telecom India 1998–2001; CEO Siemens, Italy 2001–02; CEO and Man. Dir Poste Italiane SpA 2002–; Prof., Univ. 'La Sapienza' and Univ. 'Luiss', Rome; mem. Admin. Bd Univ. Bocconi, Milan 2006–; Bd mem. of several Italian and int. cos including Int. Post Corpn; fmr Vice-Pres. Federcomin; fmr mem. Exec. of Confindustria; Cavaliere del Lavoro 2009; American Chamber of Commerce Business and Culture Award 2006, Business and Culture Award 2006, GEI Award 2007. *Address:* Poste Italiane SpA, Viale Europa 190, Rome 00144, Italy (office). *Telephone:* (06) 59587162 (office). *Fax:* (06) 59589100 (office). *E-mail:* sarmim@posteitaliane.it (office). *Website:* www.poste.it (office).

SARNE, Tanya, OBE, BA (Hons); British fashion designer; b. 15 Jan. 1945, West London, England; d. of Jean-Claude Gordon and Daphne Tucar; m. Michael Sarne 1969 (divorced); one s. one d.; ed Univ. of Sussex; worked as model, teacher, also involved in film production; travelled extensively throughout S America and Europe; returned to England and set up co. importing Alpaca wool knitted garments influenced by traditional Inca designs which launched career in 1970s; introduced Scandinavian labels In Wear and Laize Adzer to UK; est. successful labels Miz 1978–83; Founder and Creative Dir Ghost Ltd 1984–2006; launched clothing line Handwritten 2008; British Apparel Export Award for Womenswear 1993, 1995, 2009. *Leisure interests:* cooking, tennis. *Address:* Handwritten, 1–3 Middle Row, London, W10 5AT, England (office). *Telephone:* (20) 8962-9600 (office). *Fax:* (20) 8964-8524 (office). *E-mail:* anton@handwrittenuk.com (office); tanyasarne@me.com (home). *Website:* www.handwrittenuk.com (office).

SARNEY, José; Brazilian politician and author; *President, Federal Senate;* b. 24 April 1930, Pinheiro, Maranhão; s. of Sarney de Araújo Costa and Kyola Ferreira de Araújo Costa; m. Marli Macieira Sarney; two s. one d.; Asst to Maranhão State Gov. 1950; Maranhão State Rep. 1956, re-elected 1958, 1962; elected Gov. of Maranhão 1965; State Senator (Arena Party, now Partido Democrático Social—PDS) 1970; Nat. Pres. Arena 1970; fmr Chair. PDS; mem. Partido Frente Liberal 1984, PMDD; Acting Pres. of Brazil March–April 1985, Pres. 1985–90; Senator 1971–85, 1991–, Pres. of the Fed. Senate 2003–05, 2009–; fmr Pres. Nat. Congress; mem. Brazilian Acad. of Letters; Brazilian Union of Writers Aluízio de Azevedo Award 2003. *Publications:* A canção inicial 1952, Norte das Águas (Tales of Rain and Sunlight) 1970, Os maribondos de fogo 1978, O Dono do Mar (The Master of the Sea) 1995, Saraminda 2003, Saudades Mortas 2004, Tempo de Pacotilha 2004. *Leisure interests:* literature, painting. *Address:* Senado Federal, Praça dos Três Poderes, Anexo 1, 6 andar, Brasília DF, 70165-900, Brazil (office). *Telephone:* (61) 3311-4141 (office). *Fax:* (61) 3303-1776 (office). *E-mail:* sarney@senado.gov.br (office); jose-sarney@uol.com.br (home). *Website:* www.senado.gov.br (office).

SAROIAN, Konstantin R., PhD; Armenian economist and business executive; *CEO, NASDAQ OMX Armenia;* b. 14 June 1978; m. Viktorya Avetisyan; ed Yerevan State Univ.; started career 1999, heading marketing and strategic planning depts in several Armenian banks, as well as in clearing and settlement dept of Central Depository of Armenia; exec. positions with Armswissbank 2004–11, including Head of Internal Audit –2006, mem. Bd of Man. 2006–11, man. several depts including marketing, PR, human resources, strategic planning and business devt 2006–11; CEO NASDAQ OMX Armenia (stock exchange) 2011–; Lecturer, French Univ. of Armenia, Yerevan. *Address:* NASDAQ OMX Armenia, 0010 Yerevan, Mher Mkrtchyan Street 5b, Armenia (office). *Telephone:* (10) 543-321 (office). *Fax:* (10) 543-321 (office). *E-mail:* info@nasdaqomx.am (office). *Website:* www.nasdaqomx.am (office).

SAROTA, Angelina, DrIur; Polish civil servant and business executive; *Chairman of the Supervisory Board, PKN Orlen;* ed Faculty of Law and Admin of Jagiellonian Univ., Nat. School of Public Admin, Leon Koźmiński Admin; employed in Court Representation Dept and Restructuring and Public Help Dept, Ministry of State Treasury 2001–03; adviser to Minister of Science and Information Tech. 2003, Deputy Dir Dept of Strategy and Science Devt 2003–05, acted as Law Dir 2005; Dir of Law Dept, Chancellery of Prime Minister 2005–08; Sec. Supervisory Bd, PKN Orlen 2008–13, Chair. 2013–; mem. Man. Bd Coll. of Europe, Warsaw; fmr Vice-Chair. Supervisory Bd, Warsaw Tech. Park; fmr mem. Supervisory Bd, Cerg Ltd, Gliwice, Chemar Ltd, Kielce. *Address:* PKN Orlen, 09-411 Plock, ul. Chemikow 7, Poland (office). *Telephone:* (24) 3650000 (office). *Fax:* (24) 3654040 (office). *E-mail:* info@orlen.pl (office). *Website:* www.orlen.pl (office).

SARR, HE Cardinal Théodore-Adrien; Senegalese ecclesiastic; *Archbishop of Dakar;* b. 28 Nov. 1936, Fadiouth; ordained priest of Dakar 1964; Bishop of Kaolack 1974–2000; Archbishop of Dakar 2000–; cr. Cardinal (Cardinal-Priest of Santa Lucia a Piazza d'Armi) 2007; participated in Papal Conclave 2013; first Vice-

Pres. Symposium of Episcopal Confs of Africa and Madagascar; also served as Pres. Bishops' Conf. of Senegal, Mauritania, Cape Verde and Guinea-Bissau. *Address:* Archeveche, BP 1908, Avenue Jean XXIII, Dakar, Senegal (office). *Telephone:* 8890600 (office). *Fax:* 8234875 (office).

SARRIS, Michalis, BSc (Econs), DEcon; Cypriot banker and government minister; b. 14 April 1946, Nicosia; ed London School of Econs, UK, Wayne State Univ., USA; joined research dept of Central Bank of Cyprus 1972; moved to Bank of Cyprus 1974; Dir World Bank 1975–2004; Minister of Finance 2005–08, Feb.–April 2013, of Defence (acting) 2007–08; apptd Dir (non-exec.) FxPro Financial Services Ltd 2010; mem. Bd of Dirs Marfin CLR Public Co. Ltd –2005, Logicom Public Ltd, Laiki Group; fmr mem. Bd of Govs European Investment Bank. *Address:* c/o Ministry of Finance, Cnr Michalakis Karaolis Street and Gregoriou Afxentiou Street, 1439 Nicosia, Cyprus (office).

SARTORIUS, Norman H., MD, PhD; German/Croatian psychiatrist and psychologist; *President, International Association for the Improvement of Mental Health Programmes;* b. 28 Jan. 1935, Münster, Germany; s. of Prof. F. Sartorius and Doz Dr F. Fischer-Sartorius; m. Vera Pecikozić 1963; one d.; ed Univ. of Zagreb, Univ. of London; Consultant, Dept of Psychiatry, Univ. of Zagreb 1959–64; Research Fellow, Inst. of Psychiatry, Univ. of London, UK 1964–65; WHO medical officer in psychiatric epidemiology 1967–68; Medical Officer in charge of Epidemiological and Social Psychiatry and Standardization of Psychiatric Diagnosis, Classification and Statistics, WHO 1969–73, Chief, Office of Mental Health 1974–76, Dir Div. of Mental Health 1976–93; Pres. World Psychiatric Asscn (WPA) 1993–99, Scientific Dir WPA Global Programme Against Stigma and Discrimination because of Schizophrenia 1999–2006; currently Pres. Int. Asscn for Improvement of Mental Health Programmes; Pres. AEP 1999–2001; Prof., Univ. of Zagreb; Visiting Prof., Univ. of Prague, St Louis Univ., Univ. of Beijing, Univ. of London; mem. Council of WPA, WHO Expert Advisory Panel on Mental Health; Corresp. mem. Royal Spanish Acad. of Medicine, Croatian Acad. of Arts and Science; Hon. Fellow, Royal Coll. of Psychiatrists (UK), Royal Australian and NZ Coll. of Psychiatrists, Amercan Coll. of Psychiatry; Distinguished Fellow, American Psychiatric Asscn; Hon. mem. Peruvian Acad. of Medicine, Croatian Medical Acad. and of numerous professional and scientific orgs; Hon. DrMed (Umeå), (Prague); Hon. DSc (Bath), (Copenhagen); Rema Lapouse Medal, Prince Mahidol Prize for Medicine 2005, Harvard Prize in Psychiatric Epidemiology, Burgholzli Prize. *Publications:* more than 400 articles, numerous books (author or ed.) on schizophrenia, transcultural psychiatry, mental health policy, scientific methodology, ethics, human rights and stigma. *Leisure interests:* chess, reading, history. *Address:* 14 Chemin Colladon, 1209 Geneva, Switzerland (office). *Telephone:* (22) 7882331 (office). *Fax:* (22) 7882334 (office). *E-mail:* sartorius@normansartorius.com (office).

SARTZETAKIS, Christos A., LLD; Greek fmr head of state and lawyer; b. 6 April 1929, Salonika; m. Efi Argyriou; one d.; ed Salonika Univ. and Law Faculty, Paris (Sorbonne); joined Faculty of Law, Univ. of Thessaloniki 1946; called to Bar 1954; apptd JP 1955, Judge of 1st Instance 1956; Investigating Magistrate in Lambrakis affair (which inspired Vasilis Vasilikos' novel Z, later made into film) 1963–64; postgraduate studies Paris 1965–67; mem. Société de Législation Comparée, Paris 1966–; fmr mem. Admin. Council Hellenic Humanistic Soc.; arrested and detained on unspecified charges 1969; reinstated as Appeal Judge 1974; Sr Appeal Judge, Nauplion 1981, Justice of Supreme Court 1982–85; Pres. of Greece 1985–90; mem. Société de Législation Comparée, Paris 1966–; fmr mem. Admin. Council Hellenic Humanistic Soc.; Hon. mem. High Court of Portugal, Literary Soc. of Thessalonica, Hon. Prof., Dimokrition Univ. of Thrace. *Address:* Aghias Sophias street 6, 152 36 Nea Penteli, Greece (home). *Website:* www.sartzetakis.gr.

SARUNGI, Philemon, MD, MCh; Tanzanian surgeon and politician; ed Bugema Coll., Medical Univ. of Szeged, Hungary, Univ. of Vienna, Austria, Univ. of Shanghai, China; Medical Officer, Muhimbili Hosp. 1971–72; Lecturer in Surgery, Univ. of Dar es Salaam 1972–76; Prof. and Head of Dept of Orthopaedics/Trauma, Muhimbili Medical Centre 1977–84, Dir Gen. 1984–90; Minister for Health 1990–95; Regional Commr, Coast Region 1996–97, Kilimanjaro Region 1998–2000; mem. Parl. for Tarime Constituency 2000–, Minister for Defence and Nat. Service 2000–06. *Address:* c/o Ministry of Defence and National Service, POB 9544, Dar es Salaam, Tanzania.

SARWAN, Ramnaresh Ronnie; Guyanese professional cricketer; b. 23 June 1980, Wakenaam Island, Essequibo; right-handed batsman; right-arm leg-break bowler; plays for West Indies (Capt. 2007–08, Vice-Capt. 2008–), Glos. 2005, Guyana (domestic) 1996–, Kings XI Punjab 2008–, Leicestershire 2012–, Stanford Superstars, Georgetown Cricket Club; First-class debut: 1995/96; Test debut: West Indies v Pakistan, Bridgetown 18–22 May 2000; One-Day Int. (ODI) debut: England v West Indies, Nottingham 20 July 2000; T20I debut: S Africa v West Indies, Johannesburg 11 Sept. 2007. *Achievements include:* youngest West Indian to score 5,000 runs 2008; equalled record for most centuries (13) in fourth innings 2009. *Address:* c/o Guyana Cricket Board, Bourda, Georgetown, Guyana. *Telephone:* (227) 7130. *Fax:* (225) 4814. *E-mail:* gcb@solutions2000.net. *Website:* www.windiescricket.com.

SASAE, Kenichiro, LLB; Japanese diplomatist; *Ambassador to USA;* b. 25 Sept. 1951; ed Hiroshima Univ., Tokyo Univ.; joined Ministry of Foreign Affairs 1974, postings overseas include Embassies in Washington, DC and London, Perm. Mission to Int. Orgs, Geneva, Deputy Dir-Gen. Asian Affairs Bureau 1999, Exec. Asst to Prime Minister for Foreign Affairs 2000, Deputy Dir-Gen. Foreign Policy Bureau 2001, Dir-Gen., Econ. Affairs Bureau 2002–05, Dir-Gen., Asian and Oceania Affairs Bureau 2005–08, Deputy Minister for Foreign Affairs 2008–10, Vice-Minister for Foreign Affairs 2010–12, Amb. to USA 2012–. *Address:* Embassy of Japan, 2520 Massachusetts Avenue NW, Washington, DC 20008-2869, USA (office). *Telephone:* (202) 238-6700 (office). *Fax:* (202) 328-2187 (office). *E-mail:* press@embjapan.org (office). *Website:* www.us.emb-japan.go.jp/english/html/index .html (office).

SASAKAWA, Yohei; Japanese foundation executive; *Chairman, The Nippon Foundation;* b. 1939, Tokyo; s. of Ryoichi Sasakawa; ed Meiji Univ.; Trustee, Nippon Foundation 1981–88, Pres. 1988–89, Pres. 1989–2005, Chair. 2005–; Founder and Trustee, Sasakawa Memorial Health Foundation 1974, US-Japan Foundation 1980, Scandinavia-Japan Sasakawa Foundation 1984, GB Sasakawa Foundation 1985, Sasakawa Peace Foundation 1986, Sasakawa Africa

Asscn 1986, Sasakawa Young Leaders Fellowship Fund 1987, Sasakawa Pacific Island Nations Fund 1989, Sasakawa Cen. Europe Fund 1990, Foundation Franco-Japonaise Sasakawa 1990, Sasakawa Pan Asia Fund 1992; Vice-Chair. Sasakawa Japan-China Friendship Fund 1990; adviser, Tokyo Foundation, AsiaResearch Fund; WHO Global Alliance for Elimination of Leprosy (GAEL) 2001, WHO Goodwill Amb. for Leprosy Elimination 2004; Goodwill Amb. for the Human Rights of People Affected by Leprosy, Ministry of Foreign Affairs 2007; Hon. Prof., Yanbian Univ. 2000, China Medical Univ. 2003, Harbin Medical Univ. 2004, Heilongjiang Univ. 2004, Shanghai Maritime Univ. 2004; Grand Officier, Ordre du Mono (Togo) 1989, La Grande Etoile de Djibouti 1995, Order of Merit for Distinguished Service, Third Grade (Peru) 1996, Order of Friendship (Russian Fed.) 1996, Al Hussein Bin Ali Decoration for Accomplishment, First Degree (Jordan) 1998, Order of Merit in the Rank of Grand Officer (Romania) 2000, Officier, Ordre Nat. (Madagascar) 2003, Commdr, Ordre Royal du Monisaraphon (Cambodia) 2003, Commdr, Ordre Nat. du Mali 2006, Coast Guard Legion of Honour (Degree of Maginoo) 2007, Polestar Order (Mongolia) 2007, Commdr, Order of the White Rose of Finland 2010, The Patriarch's Chart of the Patriarch of Moscow and All Russia Kirill 2010, Dr Norman E. Borlaug Medallion of the World Food Prize 2010, Kt, Order of the Dannebrog (Denmark) 2010, Grand Cross, Order of the Falcon with Star (Iceland) 2010, Ordem de Timor-Leste 2010, Commdr, Order of the Defender of the Realm (Panglima Mangku Negara) Tan Sri (Malaysia) 2010, Commdr, First Class, Royal Order of the Polar Star (Sweden) 2010, Ethiopian Millenium Gold Medal 2010, Commdr, Royal Norwegian Order of Merit 2010, Commdr, Medal of Gratitude Central Africa 2010, Royal Order of Sahametrei Class Maha Sirivudha (Grand Cross) (Cambodia) 2011; Dr hc (Univ. of Bucharest) 2000, (Univ. of Cape Coast) 2000, (Acad. of Man., Mongolia) 2003, (World Maritime Univ.) 2004, Diploma of an Academician of the Russian Academy of Natural Sciences 2010; Medal for Merits, Third Degree (Ukraine) 1996, Frantsiska Scarina Medal (Belarus) 1996, China Health Medal 1997, WHO Health-for-All Gold Medal 1998, Decerne la Medaille d'Honneur de Menerbes (France) 2000, Int. Leprosy Union Millennium Gandhi Award 2001, Vaclav Havel Memorial Medal 2001, Nat. Construction Medal (Cambodia) 2003, Yomiuri Int. Cooperation Prize (Japan) 2004, Int. Gandhi Award (India) 2006, Science for Society Award, Hungarian Acad. of Sciences 2009. *Publications (in English):* Those with Wisdom Fail for Wisdom 1996, Real Faces of the World Unknown to the Ministry of Foreign Affairs 1998, This Country and That Country 2004, The Day Leprosy is Eradicated from the World 2004. *Address:* The Nippon Foundation, 1-2-2 Akasaka, Minato-ku, Tokyo 107-8404, Japan (office). *Telephone:* (3) 6229-5121 (office). *Fax:* (3) 6229-5120 (office). *Website:* www.nippon-foundation.or.jp (office).

SASAKI, Hajime, MSc; Japanese computer industry executive; *Executive Adviser, NEC Corporation;* b. 6 April 1936; ed Univ. of Tokyo; joined NEC Corpn 1961, designed integrated circuits for communications applications 1961–82, Gen. Man. VLSI Devt Div. 1982–84, Gen. Man. Microcomputer Products Div. 1984–86, Vice-Pres. 1986–88, Assoc. Sr Vice-Pres. 1988–91, Exec. Vice-Pres. 1994–96, Sr Exec. Vice-Pres. 1996–99, Chair. and Rep. Dir 1999–2008, Chair. 2008–10, currently Exec. Adviser; Exec. Dir Semiconductor Industry Research Inst. Japan 1994–96; Pres. Semiconductor Leading Edge Technologies Inc. 1996–98; Chair. Communications Industry Asscn of Japan (CIAJ) 1999–2000, Japan Electronics and Information Technology Industries Asscn 2003–04, Cttee on Global Environment and Energy Policy, Japan Asscn of Corporate Execs 2003–06; apptd Chair. Nanotechnology Business Creation Initiative 2005; currently Pres. NEC C&C Foundation; mem. Bd of Dirs Komatsu Ltd, Asunaro Aoki Construction Co. Ltd, Bull SA; Sheffield Fellowship, Yale Univ. 2006; IEEE Fellow 1996; Foreign Assoc. Nat. Acad. of Eng 2000; Inst. of Electronics Information and Communications Engineers (IEICE) Fellow 2000; IEEE Life Fellow 2001; Chevalier, Légion d'honneur 2006; Science and Tech. Agency Award, Govt of Japan 1997, IEICE Third Millennium Medal 2000, IEICE Achievement Award 2001, IEEE Robert N. Noyce Medal 2001, Deming Prize for Individuals 2005. *Address:* NEC Corporation, 7-1 Shiba 5-chome, Minato-ku, Tokyo 108-8001, Japan (office). *Telephone:* (3) 3457-7711 (office). *Fax:* (3) 3798-7818 (office). *E-mail:* a-shikimori@ay.jp.nec.com (office). Lwojtecji@necusa.com (office). *Website:* www.nec.com (office).

SASAKI, Mikio, DEng; Japanese business executive; b. 8 Oct. 1937; m.; c.; ed Waseda Univ.; joined Mitsubishi Corpn 1960, various sr and man. positions including assignments in Chile 1973, Iran 1979–83, USA 1980s, Germany and UK 1990s, apptd Dir Mitsubishi Corpn and Mitsubishi Heavy Industries Ltd 1992, Man. Dir 1994–98, Pres. and CEO 1998–2004, Chair. 2004–10, Dir, Mitsubishi External Motors Corpn, fmr Dir (non-exec.) Mitsubishi Motors Corpn, Outside Dir, Mitsubishi Electric Corpn; Vice-Chair. Nippon Keidanren; Chair. Japan Foreign Trade Council Inc. 2004–; Dir (non-exec.) Nissin Foods Holdings Co. Ltd (Nissin Food Products Co. Ltd); fmr Dir Aeon Co. Ltd; fmr Ind. Dir Nikko Cordial Corpn; mem. Advisory Council of Japan Finance Corpn (aka Japan Bank for Int. Co-operation); mem. Bd of Dirs ICC 2008–. *Address:* Mitsubishi Corporation, Mitsubishi Shoji Building, 3-1, Marunouchi 2-chome, Chiyoda-ku, Tokyo 100-8086, Japan (office). *Telephone:* (3) 3210-2121 (office). *Fax:* (3) 3210-8583 (office). *E-mail:* info@mitsubishicorp.com (office). *Website:* www.mitsubishicorp.com (office).

SASAKI, Norio; Japanese business executive; *Vice-Chairman, Toshiba Corporation;* b. 1 June 1949; ed Waseda Univ.; joined Toshiba Corpn 1972, Tech. Exec., Nuclear Energy Systems, Power Systems and Services Co. 2001–03, Vice-Pres., Nuclear Energy Systems and Services Div., Industrial and Power Systems and Services Co. 2003–05, Corp. Vice-Pres., Exec. Vice-Pres., Industrial and Power Systems and Services Co. 2005–06, Corp. Vice-Pres., Pres. and CEO Power Systems Co. 2006–07, Corp. Exec. Vice-Pres. and CEO Infrastructure Systems Group 2007–08, Rep. Exec. Officer, Corp. Sr Exec. Vice-Pres. and Dir 2008–09, Rep. Exec. Officer, Pres., CEO and Dir 2009–13, Vice-Chair. 2013–. *Address:* Toshiba Corpn, 1-1, Shibaura 1-chome, Minato-ku, Tokyo 105-8001, Japan (office). *Telephone:* (3) 3457-4511 (office). *Fax:* (3) 3455-1631 (office). *E-mail:* info@toshiba .co.jp (office). *Website:* www.toshiba.co.jp (office).

SASSEN, Saskia, MA, PhD; American (b. Dutch) sociologist and academic; *Robert S. Lynd Professor of Sociology and Co-Chair, Committee on Global Thought, Columbia University;* b. (Saskia Sassen Van Elsloo), 5 Jan. 1947, The Hague, Netherlands; d. of Willem Sassen Van Elsoo and Mara Van de Voort; m. Richard Sennett; one s.; ed Univ. of Notre Dame, Université de Poitiers, France, Harvard

Univ.; Prof. of Sociology, Queens Coll., CUNY, New York 1976–85; Prof. of Urban Planning, Columbia Univ., New York 1985–98, Robert S. Lynd Prof. of Sociology 2007–, mem. Cttee on Global Thought 2007– (Co-Chair. 2010–); Ralph Lewis Prof. of Sociology, Univ. of Chicago 1998–2007; Visiting Centennial Prof., LSE, UK 1998–2006; Helen McCahn Fellow, Girton Coll., Cambridge; Chair. Information Tech. and Int. Cooperation Cttee of the Social Science Research Council; Dir Transnationalism Project, Univ. of Chicago; mem. Global Chicago Project, Bd Urban Age of LSE, Panel on Urban Population Dynamics, Cttee on Population, NAS; participant, expert for MasterCard Worldwide Centers of Commerce Index; mem. Council on Foreign Relations, Sociological Research Asscn, European Acad. of Sciences; Hon. Geographer 2012; Hon. Global Devt Scholar, ISA 2012; Dr hc (Delft Univ., Netherlands), (De Paul Univ., Chicago), (Université de Poitiers, France), (Royal Swedish Tech. Inst.), (Univ. of Ghent, Belgium), (Univ. of Warwick, UK), (Univ. of Murcia, Spain); First Most Distinguished Alumnus (Arts and Sciences), Univ. of Notre Dame; Best Book awards in several categories, recipient of awards from the Ford Foundation, Mellon Foundation, Tinker Foundation, Revson Foundation, Chicago Inst. for Architecture and Urbanism, Twentieth Century Fund, Nat. Prize of the American Inst. of Certified Planners, Distinguished Lecturer, Inst. for Advanced Studies, Vienna, Henry Luce Lecturer, Clark Univ., Georg Simmel Lectures, Humboldt Univ., Eilert Sundt Lecture, Univ. of Oslo, Sheril Lecturer and Storrs Lecturer, Yale Univ. Law School, Luhman Lecturer, Bielefeld Univ., Germany, Zygmund Baumann Inst. Fellow, named by Foreign Policy Magazine as one of the Top 100 Global Thinkers of 2011, numerous other awards and honours. *Publications include:* author: The Mobility of Labor and Capital 1988, The Global City 1991, Cities in a World Economy 1994 (fourth revised edn 2011), Losing Control? Sovereignty in an Age of Globalization 1996, Migranten, Siedler, Flüchtlinge 1996, Globalization and its Discontents – Selected Essays 1984–98 1998, Guests and Aliens 1999, Territory, Authority, and Rights: From Medieval to Global Assemblages (Distinguished Book Award, American Sociological Asscn 2007, Robert Jervis and Paul Schroeder Best Book Award, American Political Science Asscn 2007) 2006, A Sociology of Globalization 2007, Expulsions, Brutality and Complexity in the Global Economy 2014; editor: Global Networks/Linked Cities 2002, Deciphering the Global: Its Spaces, Scales and Subjects 2007; co-editor: Digital Formations 2005; books translated into 21 languages. *Address:* Department of Sociology, Columbia University, 713 Knox Hall, 606 West 122nd Street, New York, NY 10027, USA (office). *Telephone:* (212) 854-0790 (office). *Fax:* (212) 854-2963 (office). *E-mail:* sjs2@columbia.edu (office). *Website:* www.sociology.columbia.edu (office); www.columbia.edu/~sjs2 (office); www.saskiasassen.com; cgt.columbia.edu (office).

SASSER, Hon. James (Jim) Ralph, JD; American lawyer, fmr diplomatist and fmr politician; *Senior Counselor, APCO Worldwide;* b. 30 Sept. 1936, Memphis, Tenn.; s. of Joseph Ralph Sasser and Mary Nell Sasser (née Gray); m. Mary Ballantine Gorman 1962; one s. one d.; ed Vanderbilt Univ.; served in US Marine Corps Reserve 1958–65; Partner, Goodpasture, Carpenter, Woods & Sasser, Nashville, Tenn. 1961–76; Chair. Tennessee Democratic State Cttee 1973–76; Senator from Tennessee 1977–95; Amb. to People's Repub. of China 1996–99; Foreign Policy Adviser to Vice-Pres. Al Gore 2000; J.B. and Maurice C. Shapiro Prof., Elliott School of Int. Affairs, George Washington Univ. 2000–02; currently Sr Advisor to FedEx Corpn and Sr Counselor to APCO Worldwide, Washington, DC; mem. Bd of Dirs GreenHunter Energy, Inc. 2008–; mem. Council on Foreign Relations, ABA, UN Asscn; Trustee, Nat. Geographic Soc. *Address:* c/o APCO Worldwide, 700 12th Street NW, Suite 800, Washington, DC 20005, USA (office). *Telephone:* (202) 778-1010 (office). *Website:* www.apcoworldwide.com (office).

SASSOON, David; British fashion designer; *Director, Bellville Sassoon;* b. 5 Oct. 1932, London; s. of George Sassoon and Victoria Gurgi; ed Chelsea Coll. of Art and Royal Coll. of Art; designer, Belinda Bellville 1958; first ready-to-wear collection 1963; Dir Belinda Bellville 1964; Licensee Vogue Butterick USA 1966 (became Bellville Sassoon 1970); Dir Bellville Sassoon 1983–; Trustee Fashion and Textile Museum; UK Fashion Export Award in Women's Fashion 2005, Lifetime Achievement Award, Asscn of Design Professionals, Chicago 2008. *Publication:* The Glamour of Bellville Sassoon. *Leisure interests:* theatre, ballet.

SASSOU-NGUESSO, Gen. Denis; Republic of the Congo army officer and head of state; *President;* b. 1943, Edou; joined Congolese Armed Forces 1960, mil. training in Cen. Africa, Algeria and France 1961–68; mem. Parti Congolais du Travail (PCT) 1970–, First Vice-Pres., Mil. Cttee, co-ordinator of PCT activities 1977–79, Pres. 1979–, Leader, Forces Démocratiques Unies (alliance of six parties including PCT) 1994–95; apptd Minister of Defence 1975; Pres. of the Republic of the Congo 1979–92, 1997–; Chair. African Union 2006–07. *Address:* Palais du Peuple, Brazzaville, Republic of the Congo (office). *Telephone:* 22-281-17-11 (office). *Website:* www.presidence.cg (office).

SASSU, Alexandru; Romanian politician and television executive; b. 26 Oct. 1955; ed Faculty of Electronics and Telecommunications, Tech. Inst., Bucharest; fmr Vice-Pres. Partidul Democrat (PD—Democratic Party); Interim Dir-Gen. Televiziunea Română (TVR—state broadcaster) May–Sept. 2007, apptd Pres. and Dir-Gen. 2007; mem. Bd of Dirs Truth TV 2010–; fmr mem. Chamber of Deputies 1992–2004; fmr mem., Sec. and Vice-Pres. Comm. of Culture, Art and Mass Media. *Address:* c/o Televiziunea Română, PO Box 63-1200, Calea Dorobanților 191, 015089 Bucharest, Romania.

SASTRY, Sosale Shankar, B.Tech, MS, MA, PhD; Indian electrical engineer, computer scientist and academic; *Dean, College of Engineering, University of California, Berkeley;* ed Indian Inst. of Tech., Univ. of Calif., Berkeley; Asst Prof., MIT 1980–82; Gordon McKay Prof., Harvard Univ. 1994; Dir, Electronics Research Lab., Berkeley 1996–99; Chair., Dept of Electrical Eng, Univ. of Calif., Berkeley 2001–04, Dean, Coll. of Eng 2007–, Nippon Electronics Corpn (NEC) Distinguished Prof. of Electrical Eng and of Computer Science and Prof. of Bioengineering, College of Engineering and the Walter A. Haas School of Business, Faculty Dir Richard C. Blum Center for Developing Economies; Dir Center for Information Tech. in the Interest of Soc. 2005–07, Dir Emer. 2007–; fmr Visiting Prof., Australian Nat. Univ., Univ. of Rome, Univ. of Pisa, Inst. Nat. Polytechnique de Grenoble, Center for Intelligent Control Systems, MIT; Chair., Int. Computer Science Inst. 2004–; mem. Nat. Acad. of Eng 2001–; fmr Assoc. Ed., IEEE Transactions on Automatic Control, IMA Journal of Control and Information, Journal of Biomimetic Systems and Materials, International Journal of Adaptive

Control and Signal Processing; Fellow, IEEE 1994–; Hon. MA (Harvard) 1994; Hon. PhD (Royal Inst. of Tech., Stockholm) 2007; numerous awards including Pres. of India Gold Medal 1977, Eckman Award, American Automatic Control Council 1990, Ragazzini Award 2005. *Publications include:* over 250 technical papers; books include Essays in Mathematical Robotics (jt author), Adaptive Control: Stability, Convergence and Robustness (jt author) 1989, A Mathematical Introduction to Robotic Manipulation (jt author) 1994, Nonlinear Systems: Analysis, Stability and Control 1999, An Invitation to 3D Vision: From Images to Models (jt author) 2003. *Address:* Dean's Office, 320 McLaughlin Hall # 1700, UC Berkeley, Berkeley, CA 94720-1700, USA (office). *Telephone:* (510) 642-5771 (office). *E-mail:* sastry@eecs.berkeley.edu (office); sastry@coe.berkeley.edu (office). *Website:* www.eecs.berkeley.edu/Faculty/Homepages/sastry (office); robotics.eecs .berkeley.edu/~sastry (office).

SATA, Michael Chilufya; Zambian politician and head of state; *President;* b. 1937, Mpika, Northern Rhodesia (now Zambia); s. of Sata Langford Mubanga and Bukali Kabuswe; m.; eight c.; spent time in London during Northern Rhodesia colonial admin, including period as porter at London Victoria railway station; fmr police officer, Northern Rhodesia Police Force; also worked as railwayman and trade unionist during colonial rule; became political activist during run-up to independence 1963; City Councillor and later Gov. of Lusaka 1981–88; fmr MP for Kabwata constituency; fmr Minister for Local Govt, Labour and Health, Minister without Portfolio 1995; fmr mem. United Nat. Independence Party; joined Movt for Multiparty Democracy 1991; f. Patriotic Front 2001, currently Pres.; unsuccessful cand. in presidential elections 2001, 2006, 2008; Pres. of Zambia 2011–. *Address:* Office of the President, POB 30135, Lusaka 10101, Zambia (office). *Telephone:* (21) 1260317 (office). *Fax:* (21) 1254545 (office). *Website:* www.statehouse.gov.zm (office).

SATCHELL, Keith, BSc, FIA; British insurance industry executive; *Chairman, Rothesay Life Ltd;* b. 3 June 1951; worked for UK Provident then joined Friends Provident 1986, Divisional Gen. Man. 1987–95, apptd Man. Dir Business Operations 1995, Exec. Dir Friends Provident Life Office 1992–2001, CEO 1997–2001, Group CEO and mem. Bd of Dirs Friends Provident plc 2001–07; mem. Bd of Dirs F & C Asset Man. plc 1995–2007; Chair. Barnett Waddingham LLP 2007–; Chair. Rothesay Life Ltd (insurance co. est. in UK as wholly-owned subsidiary of Goldman Sachs Group, Inc.) 2007–; Chair. Whiteford LLP 2009–; fmr mem. Supervisory Bd of European Alliance Pnrs B.V., Swiss Mobiliar Cooperative Co.; mem. Sr Bd Banco Comercial Português SA; Chair. Asscn of British Insurers 2005–07. *Address:* Rothesay Life Ltd, PO Box 545, Redhill, Surrey, RH1 1YX (office); Barnett Waddingham LLP, Cheapside House, 138 Cheapside, London, EC2V 6BW, England (office). *Telephone:* (20) 7776-2200 (Barnett Waddingham) (office). *Fax:* (20) 7776-3800 (office). *Website:* www.rothesaylife.co.uk (office); www .barnett-waddingham.co.uk (office).

SATCHIDANANDAN, Koyamparambath, BA, MA, PhD; Indian poet and writer; b. 28 May 1946, Pullut, Thrissur Dist, Kerala; m.; two d.; ed Univ. of Kerala, Univ. of Calicut; writer in Malayalam and English; Lecturer, then Prof. of English, Christ Coll., Kerala 1977–92; Ed. Indian Literature journal 1992–96; Pres. Sahitya Akademi 1996–2003; fmr consultant, India Dept of Higher Educ., Nat. Trans. Mission; Cavaliere, Ordine al Merito della Repubblica Italiana; Kerala Sahitya Akademi Award 1984, 1989, 1999, 2001, Oman Cultural Centre Award, UAE 1993, Mahakavi Ulloor Award 1996, Mahakavi P.Kunhiraman Nair Award 1997, Bharatiya Bhasha Parishad Samvatsar Award 1998, Kumaran Asan Award 2000, Odakkuzhal Award 2001, Baharain Kerala Samaj Award, UAE 2002, Gangadhar Meher Nat. Award, Sambalpur Univ., Orissa 2002, Pandalam Kerala Verma Award 2005, Bappureddy Nat. Award 2005, Vayalar Award 2005, India-Poland Friendship Medal, Govt of Poland 2005, K.Kuttikrishnan Memorial Award 2007, Subrahmanya Shenoi Memorial Award 2008, NTR Nat. Literary Award 2009. *Plays:* Saktan Thampuran 1983, Gandhi 1995. *Publications include:* poetry: Anchu Sooryan 1971, Atmagita 1974, Kavita 1977, Indian Sketchukal 1978, Ezhuthachan Ezhutumbol 1979, Peedana Kalam 1981, Venal Mazha 1982, Randu Deergha Kavyangal 1983, Satchidandante Kavithakal 1962–82 1983, Socratee-sum Kozhiyum 1984, Ivanekkoodi 1987, Veedumattam 1988, Kayattam 1990, Kavibuddhan 1992, Ente Satchidanandan Kavitakal 1993, Desatanam 1994, Malayalam 1996, Apoornam 1998, Theranjedutha 1999, Sambhashanathinu Oru Sramam 2000, Vikku 2002, Sakshyangal 2004, Satchidanandante Kavitakal 1965–2005 2006, Onaam Padham 2006, Anantam 2007, Ente Kavita 2008; non-fiction: Kurukshetram 1970, Janatayun Kavitayum 1982, Marxian Soundarya Sadtram 1983, Thiranjedutha Lekhanangal 1985, Samvadangal 1986, Sameepa-nangal 1986, Samskarathinte Rashtreeyam 1989, Sambhashanangal 1989, Brechtinte Kala 1989, Padavukal 1990, Kazhchakal, Kazhachappadukal 1991, Anveshanangal 1991, Veenduvicharangal 1992, Soundaryavum Adhikaravum 1993, Muhurtangal 1996, Pala Lokam, Pala Kalam 1998, Kalayum Nishedhavum 1999, Moonnu Yatra 2004, Kizhakkum Padinjarum 2005, Adithattukal 2006, Mukjamukham 2006; prose: Kurukshetram 1970, Janatayum Kavitayum 1982, Marxian Soundarya Sastram 1983, Thiranjedutha Lekhanangal 1985, Pablo Neruda 1985, Samvadangal 1986, Sameepanangal 1986, Samskarathinte Rash-treeyam 1989, Sambhashanangal 1989, Brechtinte Kala 1989, Padavukal 1990, Kazhchakal, Kazhachappadukal 1991, Anveshanangal 1991, Veenduvicharangal 1992, Soundaryavum Adhikaravum 1993, Muhurtangal 1996, Pala Lokam, Pala Kalam 1998, Kalayum Nishedhavum 1999, Bharateeya Kavitayile Pratirodha Paramparyam 2002, Moonnu Yatra 2004, Kizhakkum Padinjarum 2005, Adithat-tukal 2006, Mukhamukham 2006, Indian Literature: Positions and Propositions 1999, Indian Literature: Paradigms and Praxis 2008, Indian Literature and Beyond 2009. *E-mail:* satchida@gmail.com (home). *Website:* satchidanandan .blogspot.com.

SATHASIVAM, Palanisamy, BA; Indian lawyer and fmr judge; b. 27 April 1949, Kadappanallur, Erode Dist, Tamil Nadu; s. of Palanisamy Sathasivam and Natchiamma Sathasivam; m. Saraswathi Sathasivam; ed Govt Law Coll., Chennai; enrolled as an advocate at Madras 1973, apptd as Additional Govt Pleader and further as Special Govt Pleader in Madras High Court, also worked as legal adviser for several state-owned transport corpns, municipalities, nationa-lized banks etc., apptd as a perm. Judge of the Madras High Court 1996, transferred to the Punjab and Haryana High Court 2007, Judge of Supreme Court

2007–14, Chief Justice of India 2013–14 (retd). *Address:* c/o Supreme Court of India, Tilak Marg, New Delhi 110 001, India.

SATHIRATHAI, Surakiart, LLM, MALD, SJD; Thai economist and politician; b. 7 June 1958, Bangkok; m. Thanpuying Dr Suthawan Sathirathai; one s.; ed Chulalongkorn Univ., Tufts Univ., Harvard Univ., USA; policy adviser to Prime Minister 1988–92, to Nat. Ass. 1989–91, to Prime Minister on econ. affairs 1991–92; Co-founder Siam Premier Int. Law Office Ltd 1990, Chair. Exec. Bd 1990–2001; Dean and Assoc. Prof., Chulalongkorn Univ. 1992–95; Chair. Crown Property Bureau, Securities Exchange Comm., House Select Cttee on Budget Review 1995–96, PTTEP Co. Ltd 1998–2000, Laem Thong Bank Co. Ltd 1998–99, Petroleum Authority of Thailand, Thai Oil Co. Ltd 1999–2000; Minister of Finance 1995–96; Vice-Chair. of Prime Minister's Advisory Council on Econ. and Foreign Affairs 1996–97; Councillor of State 1997–2001; Pres. Inst. of Social and Econ. Policy (ISEP) 1997–2001, Chair. ISEP Foundation 1999–2001; Minister of Foreign Affairs 2001–05; Deputy Prime Minister 2005–06; Kt Grand Cordon (Special Class) of the Most Noble Order of the Crown of Thailand, Kt Grand Cross (First Class) of the Most Exalted Order of the White Elephant, Genesis Decoration; Red Cross Medal, Psalm Scout Medal, Tertiary Military Academy Magic. *Address:* c/o Siam Premier International Law Office Limited, 26th Floor, The Offices at Central World, 999/9 Rama 1 Road, Pathumwan, Bangkok 10330, Thailand (office). *Website:* www.siamlaw.co.th.

SATO, Hiroshi; Japanese engineer and business executive; *President, CEO and Representative Director, Kobe Steel Ltd (KOBELCO);* ed Kyusyu Univ.; joined Kobe Steel Ltd in 1970, acted as Head of Tech. Devt Div. and Material Research Centre, served as Exec. Vice-Pres., Tech. Devt Group, Pres., CEO and Rep. Dir, Kobe Steel Ltd (KOBELCO) 2009–. *Address:* Kobe Steel Ltd, Shinko Building, 10-26 Wakinohamacho 2-chome, Kobe 651-8585, Japan (office). *Telephone:* (78) 261-5111 (office). *Fax:* (78) 261-4123 (office). *E-mail:* info@kobelco.co.jp (office). *Website:* www.kobelco.co.jp (office).

SATO, Humitaka, PhD; Japanese astrophysicist and academic; *Professor of Physics, Konan University;* b. 23 March 1938, Yamagata; s. of Mokichi Sato and Kane Sato; m. Keiko Okazaki 1965; one s. one d.; ed Kyoto Univ.; Prof. of Astrophysics and Relativity, Kyoto Univ. 1974–2006, Dean Faculty of Sciences 1993, Prof. Emer. 2001–, Dir Yukawa Inst. for Theoretical Physics 1976–80; Pres. Physical Soc. of Japan 1998–2000, Yukawa Memorial Foundation; Prof. of Physics, Konan Univ. 2001–; fmr Visiting Physicist, Univ. of California, Berkeley; fmr Ed. Progress of Theoretical Physics and other journals; fmr Chair. Physics Cttee, Science Council of Japan, C19 of IUPAP; Nishina Prize 1973, Matsunaga Prize 1975, Asahi Scientific Subsidy 1983, First Award for Essay on Gravitation 1985, Purple Medal of Honour 1999. *Publications include:* Black Holes 1976, Discovery of Big Bang 1983, Invitation to Cosmology 1988, Dark Matter in the Universe 1990; 140 papers on astrophysics, Theory of General Relativity, Theory of Expanding Universe. *Address:* Yukawa Memorial Foundation, Yukawa Institute of Theoretical Physics, Kyoto University, Kitasirakawa, Sakyo-ku, Kyoto 606-8502, Japan (office). *E-mail:* sato@tap.scphys.kyoto-u.ac.jp (office). *Website:* www .kyoto-u.ac.jp (office).

SATO, Masatoshi, BEcons; Japanese insurance industry executive; b. 2 March 1949, Toshima-ku; ed Keio Univ.; joined Yasude Fire & Marine Insurance Co. Ltd 1972, Man. Yamanashi Br. 1994–96, Gen. Man. System Planning Dept 1996, Gen. Man. Information System Dept 1997–99, Gen. Man. Presidential Staff Office 1999–2000, Dir and Gen. Man. Presidential Staff Office 2000–02, Dir and Man. Exec. Officer 2002–05, Pres. and CEO Sompo Japan Insurance Inc. 2006–10, Rep. Dir, Pres. and Co-CEO NKSJ Holdings, Inc. (following establishment of jt holding co. by Sompo Japan Insurance Inc. and Nipponkoa Insurance Co. Ltd) 2010–12, Dir 2012–; Pres. and Rep. Dir Sompo Japan Reseach Inst.; Dir Nippon Keidanren Cttee on Nature Conservation. *Address:* NKSJ Holdings, Inc., 26-1, Nishi-Shinjuku 1-chome, Shinjuku-ku, Tokyo 160-8338, Japan (office). *Telephone:* (3) 3349-3000 (operator) (office); (3) 3349-3111 (office). *Fax:* (3) 3349-4697 (office). *E-mail:* info@nksj-hd.com (office). *Website:* www.nksj-hd.com (office).

SATO, Mikio, BSc, PhD; Japanese mathematician and academic; *Professor Emeritus, Research Institute for Mathematical Sciences, Kyoto University;* b. 1928; ed Tokyo Univ.; Lecturer, Tokyo Univ. 1960–63, Prof. 1968–70;; Prof., Osaka Univ. 1963–68; Prof., Research Inst. for Math. Sciences (RIMS), Kyoto Univ. 1970–92, Prof. Emer. 1992–, Dir RIMS 1987–91; mem. NAS 1993–; Asahi Prize of Science 1969, Japan Acad. Prize 1976, Fujiwara Prize 1987, Rolf Schock Prize in Math., Royal Swedish Acad. of Sciences 1997, Wolf Prize 2003. *Publications:* numerous articles in math. journals on algebraic analysis and theory of hyperfunctions. *Address:* Research Institute for Mathematical Sciences, Kyoto University, Kyoto 606-8502, Japan (office). *Fax:* (75) 7537276 (office). *E-mail:* sato@kurims.kyoto-u .ac.jp (office). *Website:* www.kurims.kyoto-u.ac.jp (office).

SATO, Ryuzo, PhD, DEcon; Japanese economist and academic; b. 5 July 1931, Akita-ken; m. Kishie Hayashi 1959; one s. one d.; ed Hitotsubashi Univ., Tokyo, Johns Hopkins University, Baltimore, Md, USA; Fulbright Scholar, Johns Hopkins Univ. 1957–62; Prof. of Econs, Brown Univ. 1967–85; C. V. Starr Prof. of Econs, New York Univ. 1985–2006 (retd), Dir Center for Japan–US Business and Econ. Studies, Stern School of Business –2006; Adjunct Prof. of Public Policy, John F. Kennedy School of Govt, Harvard Univ. 1983; Visiting Prof. of Econs, Univ. of Tokyo 2003–; Guggenheim Fellow; Ford Foundation Fellow; Rondan Prize, Yomiuri (newspaper), Economics Award (Nikkei Prize), Nihon-Keizai (newspaper). *Publications include:* Theory of Technical Change and Economic Invariance 1981, Research and Productivity (with G. Suzawa) 1983, The Chrys-anthemum and the Eagle (Rondansho Prize) 1991, Growth Theory and Technical Change 1996, Global Competition and Integration (with R. V. Ramachandran and Kazuo Mino) 1998, Symmetry and Economic Invariance (with R. V. Ramachan-dran) 1998, Production, Stability and Dynamic Symmetry 1999, Biased Technical Change and Economic Conservation Laws 2010. *Leisure interests:* skiing, music, gardening. *Address:* c/o Center for Japan–US Business and Economic Studies, Stern School of Business, 44 West Fourth Street, KMC 7-91, New York, NY 10012, USA.

SATO, Tsutomu, BEng; Japanese politician; *Minister of Internal Affairs and Communications and Minister of State for Decentralization Reform;* b. 20 June 1952, Tochigi; ed Univ. of Nihon; Deputy, Tochigi Prefectural Ass. 1987–99; mem.

House of Reps 1996–, Chair. House of Reps Gen. Affairs Cttee 2006; mem. LDP, Vice-Chair. LDP Diet Policy Cttee 2002–05, Chair. LDP Gen. Affairs Div. 2005; Vice-Minister of Health, Labour and Welfare 2001, Vice-Minister of Internal Affairs and Communications 2007, Minister of State, Chair. Nat. Public Safety Comm. 2008–09, Minister of State in charge of Okinawa and N Territories and Disaster Man. 2008–09, Minister of Internal Affairs and Communications 2009–, also Minister of State for Decentralization Reform. *Address:* Ministry of Internal Affairs and Communications, 2-1-2, Kasumigaseki, Chiyoda-ku 8, Tokyo 100-8926, Japan (office). *Telephone:* (3) 5253-5111 (office). *Fax:* (3) 3504-0265 (office). *Website:* www.soumu.go.jp (office).

SATO, Yasuhiro; Japanese business executive; *Representative Director, President and CEO, Mizuho Financial Group, Inc.;* b. 15 April 1952; ed Univ. of Tokyo; joined Mizuho Financial Group 1976, worked in New York late 1980s, Exec. Officer/Sr Corp. Officer, Int. Banking Unit, Mizuho Corp. Bank Ltd 2003–04, Man. Exec. Officer 2004–06, Man. Dir/Head of Corp. Banking Unit 2006–07, Deputy Pres./Chief Auditor 2007–09, Pres. and CEO 2009–, Dir of Mizuho Financial Group, Inc. 2009–, Dir of Mizuho Bank Ltd 2011–, Rep. Dir, Pres. and CEO Mizuho Financial Group, Inc. (Group CEO) 2011–. *Address:* Mizuho Financial Group, Inc., Marunouchi 2-chome Building, 2-1-1, Marunouchi, Chiyoda-ku, Tokyo 100-8333, Japan (office). *Telephone:* (3) 5224-1111 (office). *Fax:* (3) 3215-4616 (office). *E-mail:* info@mizuho-fg.co.jp (office). *Website:* www.mizuho-fg.co.jp (office).

SATO, Yoshio; Japanese insurance industry executive; *President, CEO and Representative Director, Sumitomo Life Insurance Company;* Man. Dir Sumitomo Life Insurance Co. –2007, Pres., CEO and Rep. Dir 2007–; mem. Bd of Dirs Life Insurance Assen of Japan; Trustee Japan Inst. of Life Insurance. *Address:* Sumitomo Life Insurance Co., 1-4-35 Shiromi, Chuo-ku, Osaka 540-8512, Japan (office). *Telephone:* (6) 6937-1435 (office). *E-mail:* info@sumitomolife.co.jp (office). *Website:* www.sumitomolife.co.jp (office).

SATOH, Yukio, BA; Japanese diplomatist; *Vice-Chairman, Japan Institute of International Affairs;* b. 6 Oct. 1939; m.; two c.; ed Tokyo Univ., Univ. of Edinburgh; entered Foreign Service 1961, with Ministry of Foreign Affairs, Tokyo, then Embassy, Washington, DC –1976, Dir Div. of Security Affairs, American Affairs Bureau, Ministry of Foreign Affairs 1976–77, Pvt. Sec. to the Foreign Minister 1977–79, Counsellor, London 1981–84, also Consul-Gen., Dir Policy Coordination Div. 1985–87, Asst Vice-Minister for Parl. Affairs, Ministry of Foreign Affairs 1987–88; Chief of Prefectural Police, Miyazaki 1984–85; Consul-Gen., Hong Kong 1988–90; Dir-Gen. North American Affairs Bureau and Dir-Gen. Information Analysis, Research and Planning Bureau, Ministry of Foreign Affairs 1990–94, Amb. to the Netherlands 1994–96, to Australia 1996–98; Perm. Rep. to the UN 1998–2002; Pres. The Japan Inst. of Int. Affairs 2002–09, Vice-Chair. 2009–. *Publications:* numerous articles on Japanese foreign and security policy. *Address:* The Japan Institute of International Affairs, Kasumigaseki Building 11 Floor, 3-2-5 Kasumigaseki, Chiyoda-ku, Tokyo, 100-6011, Japan (office). *Telephone:* (3) 3503-7295 (office). *Fax:* (3) 3503-7411 (office). *E-mail:* satoh@jiia.or.jp (office). *Website:* www.jiia.or.jp (office).

SATOMI, Susumu, MD; Japanese surgeon, academic and university administrator; *President, Tohoku University;* b. June 1948, Kagoshima Pref.; ed School of Medicine, Tohoku Univ.; Lecturer, Second Dept of Surgery, Tohoku Univ., then Prof. 1995–, Prof., Div. of Advanced Surgical Science and Tech., Grad. School of Medicine, Dir Tohoku Univ. Hosp. 2004–05, Vice-Pres. Tohoku Univ. 2005–08, Dir Innovation of New Biomedical Eng Centre 2008–12, Pres. Tohoku Univ. 2012–; Pres. Japan Surgical Soc. 2008. *Address:* Office of the President, Tohoku University, 1-1 Katahira, 2-chome, Aoba-ku, Sendai 980-8577, Japan (office). *Telephone:* (22) 217-4807 (office). *E-mail:* ssatomi@bureau.tohoku.ac.jp (office). *Website:* www.tohoku.ac.jp (office).

SATRAPI, Marjane, MA; Iranian writer, illustrator and film director; b. (Marjan Ebrahimi-Ripa), 22 Sept. 1969, Rasht; ed Visual Communication School of Fine Arts, Tehran, Ecole des Arts Decoratifs de Strasbourg, France; Dr hc (Katholieke Universiteit Leuven, Université catholique de Louvain) 2009; Gat Perich Award. *Films:* Persepolis (dir and writer with Vincent Paronnaud) (Sutherland Trophy, British Film Inst. Awards 2007, Jury Prize, Cannes Film Festival 2007, Special Jury Prize, Cinemanila Int. Film Festival 2007, César Award for Best First Work 2007, Audience Award, Rotterdam Int. Film Festival 2008, Audience Award, São Paulo Int. Film Festival 2007, Most Popular Film, Vancouver Int. Film Festival 2007) 2007, Poulet aux prunes 2011. *Publications include:* Persepolis: The Story of a Childhood (four vols) (Angoulême Coup de Coeur Award 2001, Angoulême Prize 2002) 1999–2002, Persepolis 2: The Story of a Return (adapted as screenplay 2007) 2005, Embroideries 2005, Chicken with Plums (Angoulême Best Comic Book Award) 2006; several children's books; contrib. illustrations to French magazines and periodicals. *Address:* 13 rue de Thorigny, 75003 Paris, France (home). *Telephone:* 6-64-99-04-52 (home). *Fax:* 1-42-72-65-15 (home). *E-mail:* marjanesatrapi@yahoo.fr (home).

SATTAR, Abdul, MA; Pakistani diplomatist; b. 10 July 1931, Narowal; m. Yasmine Sattar 1955; one s. two d.; ed Forman Christian Coll., Lahore, Punjab Univ. and Fletcher School, USA; served in Pakistan Missions in Australia, Sudan and the USA; Rep. of Pakistan to IAEA and Amb. to Austria 1975–78; Amb. to India 1978–82, 1990–92, to USSR 1988–90; Dir, then Dir-Gen. and Additional Sec. at Foreign Office, for Asia 1982–86; Foreign Sec., Islamabad 1986–88; Sr Del. to Geneva Talks on Afghanistan 1988; Minister of Foreign Affairs 1999–2002; mem. Nat. Security Council. *Publications:* Pakistan's Foreign Policy: A Concise History 1947–2007 2007; articles in learned journals on nuclear non-proliferation and regional studies; columns in Pakistani newspapers. *Address:* House 7, College Road, F-7/3, Islamabad, Pakistan (home). *Telephone:* (51) 2611144 (home). *E-mail:* sattara@comsats.net.pk (home).

SATYANAND, Rt Hon Sir Anand, GNZM, QSO, KStJ, LLB; New Zealand lawyer, judge and ombudsman; *Chairman, Commonwealth Foundation;* b. 22 July 1944, Auckland; m. Susan Satyanand 1970; three c.; ed Univ. of Auckland Law School; admitted to the Bar 1970; practised law with Crown Solicitors' Office and Pnr, pvt. law practice; Dist Court Judge, Palmerston N and Auckland, with specialist warrant for criminal jury trials 1982–94; Parl. Ombudsman 1995–2005; Gov.-Gen. of New Zealand 2006–11; Chair. Confidential Forum for Fmr In-Patients of Psychiatric Hosps –2006; Registrar of Pecuniary Interests of Mems of

Parl. –2006; Chair. Commonwealth Foundation 2013–; fmr mem. Bd of Dirs New Zealand Inst. of International Affairs, Transparency International; fmr exec. New Zealand Rugby League; Hon. mem. Royal Order of the Crown by the King of Tonga 2011; Distinguished Companion, New Zealand Order of Merit 2005, Principal Companion, New Zealand Order of Merit (redesignated Grand Commdr, New Zealand Order of Merit 2009) 2006; Hon. LLD (Auckland Univ.) 2006; New Zealand Commemoration Medal 1990, Pravasi Bharatiya Samman Award 2011. *Leisure interests:* sport, reading, int. affairs. *Address:* c/o PO Box 9062, Marion Square, Wellington 6141, New Zealand (office).

SATYBALDIYEV, Jantoro Joldoshevich; Kyrgyzstani politician; b. 6 Jan. 1956, Mirza-Aki village, Uzgen dist, Osh Oblast; m.; four c.; fmr First Deputy Minister of Transport, later Minister of Transport; headed town admin of Osh; Pres.'s Special Rep. on Electroenergy Security for southern Kyrgyzstan 2003–05; removed as Gov. of Osh dist due to deficiencies in his work and legal case launched against him accusing him of misusing an official position 2007; later apptd Regional Dir of TRACECA (project to develop Europe-Caucasus-Asia transport corridor); fmr Head of Directorate to rebuild and develop Osh and Jalal-Abad; Head of Pres.'s Office 2011–12; Prime Minister 2012–14; Medal in honour of 300th anniversary of the foundation of St Petersburg (Russia) 2004. *Address:* c/o Office of the Government, 720003 Bishkek, Dom Pravitelstva, Kyrgyzstan (office).

SA'UD, HM The King of Saudi Arabia; Abdullah ibn Abd al-Aziz as-; *Head of State and Prime Minister;* b. 1924, Riyadh; s. of the late King Abdul Aziz ibn Sa'ud and Fahda bint Asi ash-Shuraim; brother of HRH Crown Prince Sultan ibn Abd al-Aziz as-Sa'ud; Commdr Nat. Guard 1962–2005; Second Deputy Prime Minister 1975–82, First Deputy Prime Minister and Commdr Nat. Guard 1982–2005; became Crown Prince June 1982; succeeded to throne upon death of half-brother HM King Fahd 1 Aug. 2005; Patron Nat. Heritage and Cultural Festival, Jenadriyah 1985–; ranked by Forbes magazine amongst The World's Most Powerful People (ninth) 2009, (third) 2010, (sixth) 2011, (seventh) 2012, (eighth) 2013. *Leisure interests:* hunting, horse racing. *Address:* Royal Diwan, Riyadh, Saudi Arabia.

SA'UD, Prince Ahmed ibn Abd al-Aziz as-; Saudi Arabian government official; *Minister of the Interior;* b. 1940; s. of the late King Abd al-Aziz and Hassa as-Sudairi; ed Redlands Coll., USA; Deputy Gov. Makkah Prov. 1971–75; Deputy Minister of the Interior 1978–2012, Minister of the Interior 2012–. *Address:* Ministry of the Interior, POB 2933, Airport Road, Riyadh 11134, Saudi Arabia (office). *Telephone:* (1) 401-1111 (office). *Fax:* (1) 403-3125 (office). *Website:* www .moi.gov.sa (office).

SA'UD, HRH Prince Bandar ibn Sultan ibn Abd al-Aziz as-, MA; Saudi Arabian diplomatist and army officer; *Secretary-General, National Security Council;* b. 2 March 1949, Taif; s. of HRH Crown Prince Sultan ibn Abd al-Aziz as-Sa'ud; m. HRH Princess Haifa bint Faisal ibn Abd al-Aziz as-Sa'ud; four s. four d.; ed RAF Coll., Cranwell, USAF Advanced Program and Johns Hopkins Univ.; fighter pilot, Royal Saudi Air Force 1969–82; in charge of special Saudi Arabian liaison mission to USA for purchase of AWACS and other defence equipment 1981; Defence and Mil. Attaché, Saudi Arabian Mil. Mission to USA 1982–83; Amb. to USA 1983–2005; promoted to rank of Minister 1995; Sec.-Gen. Nat. Security Council 2005–; numerous medals and decorations, including Hawk Flying Medal of Aviation, King Faisal Medal, King Abdul Aziz Sash, as well as honours from other nations. *Leisure interests:* flying, racquetball, reading. *Address:* c/o Ministry of Foreign Affairs, PO Box 55937, Riyadh 11544, Saudi Arabia.

SA'UD, HRH Prince Muhammad ibn Nawaf ibn Abd al-Aziz as-; Saudi Arabian diplomatist; *Ambassador to UK;* b. 22 May 1953, Riyadh; m. HH Princess Fadwa bint Khaled bin Abdallah bin Abdulrahman; five c.; ed The Capital Inst. High School, Riyadh, School of Foreign Service, Georgetown Univ. and John F Kennedy School of Govt, Harvard Univ., USA; worked for Royal Comm. for Jubail and Yanbu for two years; transferred to Ministry of Foreign Affairs where he held several positions, including the Minister's Cabinet before being promoted to Insp. Gen.; Amb. to Italy and Malta 1995–2005, to UK (also accred to Ireland) 2005–; Pres. Council of Admin for the Islamic Cultural Centre of Italy 1998; fmr Dean of Arab Ambs' Corps. *Address:* Embassy of Saudi Arabia, 30 Charles Street, Mayfair, London, W1J 5DZ, England (office). *Telephone:* (20) 7917-3000 (office). *Fax:* (20) 7917-3330 (office). *E-mail:* ukemb@mofa.gov.sa (office). *Website:* www .saudiembassy.org.uk (office).

SA'UD, Muhammad ibn Nayef ibn Abd al-Aziz al-, BA; Saudi Arabian government official; *Minister of the Interior;* b. 30 Aug. 1959, Jeddah; s. of the late Nayef ibn Abd al-Aziz al-Saud (Crown Prince of Saudi Arabia) and Al Jawhara bint Abdulaziz ibn Musaed al-Jiluwi; brother of Prince Saud ibn Nayef; ed Al-Asemah Inst., Riyadh; worked in the private sector –1999; Asst Minister of Interior for Security Affairs 1999–2004, Minister 2004–12, Deputy Minister of the Interior July–Nov. 2012, Minister Nov. 2012–; mem. Supreme Information Council 1999–, Nat. Anti-Narcotics Cttee, Perm. Cttee of the Econ. Council, High Comm. of Prince Nayef ibn Abd al-Aziz Al-Saud Award for Prophet's Sunnah and Contemporary Islamic Studies; King Abd al-Aziz Sash, first class 2008. *Leisure interests:* shooting, equestrianism, swimming. *Address:* Ministry of the Interior, POB 2933, Airport Road, Riyadh 11134, Saudi Arabia (office). *Telephone:* (1) 401-1111 (office). *Fax:* (1) 403-3125 (office). *Website:* www.moi.gov.sa (office).

SA'UD, HRH Crown Prince Salman ibn Abd al-Aziz as-; Saudi Arabian politician; *Crown Prince, Deputy Prime Minister, and Minister of Defence and Civil Aviation;* b. 13 Dec. 1935; s. of the late King Abd al-Aziz as-Sa'ud and Hussah bint Ahmad as-Sudairi; half brother of HRH King Abdullah ibn Abd al-Aziz as-Sa'ud; m. Princess Sultana bint Turki as-Sudairi (deceased); thirteen c.; Gov. of Riyadh 1962–2011; Minister of Defence and Civil Aviation 2011–, also Deputy Prime Minister 2012–; named Crown Prince (following death of brother Nayef ibn Abd al-Aziz as-Sa'ud) 18 June 2012; Chair. Bd Riyadh Water and Sanitary Drainage Authority and numerous other orgs; est. Prince Salman Centre for Disability Research, Prince Fahd bin Salman Charitable Soc. for Care of Kidney Patients; also active in Abdul Aziz Foundation. *Leisure interest:* reading. *Address:* Ministry of Defence and Civil Aviation, PO Box 26731, Airport Road, Riyadh 11165, Saudi Arabia (office). *Telephone:* (1) 478-9000 (office). *Website:* www.moda.gov.sa (office).

SA'UD, HRH Sattam ibn Abd al-Aziz as-, BBA; Saudi Arabian politician and royal; *Governor of Riyadh*; b. 21 Jan. 1941, Riyadh; s. of the late King Abd al-Aziz of Saudi Arabi; brother to King Abdullah ibn Abd al-Aziz as-Sa'ud; full brother to deceased Prince Majid, Prince Nasr, Princess Sultana and Princess Haya; ed The Princes' School, Riyadh, Alangal Inst., Univ. of San Diego, USA, Univ. of Cambridge, UK; sr member of Saudi royal family; Deputy Gov. of Riyadh with rank of Minister 1968–2011, Gov. 2011–; chaired numerous cttees and entities, including as Chair. Cttee on the Release of Insolvent Prisoners, Vice-Chair. Supreme Saudization Cttee, Deputy Head of Supreme Mission of Developing Riyadh City, Deputy Chair. Water and Sanitation in Riyadh, Deputy Prime Gen. Riyadh Charity Soc., Vice-Chair. Prince Salman Charity Housing Project, Deputy Prime of Orphanage Soc. of Ibn Baz, Vice-Pres. Soc. of Care for Orphans in Riyadh, Chair. local fund-raising for Muslims of Kosovo and Chechnya in Riyadh, Deputy Chair. Civil Defence, Deputy Prime of Care Asscn of Renal Disease in Riyadh; Hon. Vice-Pres. Cttee of Patients' Friends; Highness Scarf of King Abd al-Aziz (First Class); Dr hc (Univ. of San Diego) 1975. *Address:* Office of the Governor, Riyadh, Saudi Arabia (office).

SA'UD, HRH Prince Sa'ud al-Faisal as-, BA (Econs); Saudi Arabian politician and diplomatist; *Minister of Foreign Affairs*; b. 2 Jan. 1941, Riyadh; s. of the late King Faisal ibn Abd al-Aziz as-Sa'ud; m.; three s., three d.; ed Princeton Univ., USA; Deputy Minister of Petroleum and Mineral Resources 1971–74; Minister of State for Foreign Affairs March–Oct. 1975, Minister of Foreign Affairs Oct. 1975–; Leader del. to UN Gen. Ass. 1976; Special Envoy of HM King Khalid ibn Abd al-Aziz as-Sa'ud in diplomatic efforts to resolve Algerian–Moroccan conflict over Western Sahara and the civil war in Lebanon; mem. Saudi Arabian del. to Arab restricted Summit, Riyadh 1976; mem. Summit Conf. of Arab League 1976; led del. at G-20 Summit 2010; Founding mem. King Faisal's International Charity Soc.; Trustee, King Faisal Foundation. *Leisure interest:* reading. *Address:* Ministry of Foreign Affairs, POB 55937, Riyadh 11544, Saudi Arabia (office). *Telephone:* (1) 405-5000 (office). *Fax:* (1) 403-0645 (office). *E-mail:* info@mofa.gov.sa (office). *Website:* www.mofa.gov.sa (office).

SA'UD, HRH Prince Sa'ud bin Abdullah bin Thunayan as-, BSc; Saudi Arabian business executive; *Chairman, Saudi Basic Industries Corporation (SABIC);* ed King Sa'ud Univ.; early career as engineer, Riyadh Municipality, becoming Dir-Gen. for Survey and Drawings and Dir-Gen. for Operations and Maintenance; Under-Sec. for Planning and Programmes, Ministry of Municipality and Rural Affairs 1989; Chair. Admin. Bd Saudi Basic Industries Corpn (SABIC) 2003–; Chair. Royal Comm. for Jubail and Yanbu, Utility and Water Co. of Jubail and Yanbu; Deputy Chair. Prince Salman Social Centre; mem Bd Royal Family Bd; mem several cttees formed by Royal Decree to regulate needs of Al-Jouf, Jizan, northern border and Hail areas in Saudi Arabia, in addition to villages and areas in western coast and needs of people of Yanbu Governorates; mem jt cttee that supervises co-ordination and follows work between Ministry of Municipality and Rural Affairs, Ministry of Transportation, Ministry of Agric. and Higher Cttee for Childhood. *Address:* Saudi Basic Industries Corporation, PO Box 5101, Riyadh 11422, Saudi Arabia (office). *Telephone:* (1) 225-8000 (office). *Fax:* (1) 225-9000 (office). *E-mail:* info@sabic.ocm (office). *Website:* www.sabic.com (office); www .thunayan-al-saud.com.

SA'UD, HRH Prince Talal ibn Abd al-Aziz as-; Saudi Arabian politician and international official; *President, Arab Gulf Programme, United Nations Development Organizations (AGFUND);* b. 1934; s. of the late King Abd al-Aziz as-Sa'ud; brother of King Abdullah ibn Abd al-Aziz as-Sa'ud; m. 1st Umm Faisal; m. 2nd Muana As-Solh (divorced 1968); m. 3rd Moudie bint Abdul-Mohsen Alangary; m. 4th Magdah bint Turki Al-Sudairi; nine s. six d.; ed Prince's School, Royal Palace, Riyadh; positions held in his early 20s include responsibility for the Royal Palaces, Minister of Communications; fmr Minister of Economy and Finance; fmr Amb. to France; f. Riyadh's first girls' school 1957, first pvt. hosp. 1957 and Mecca's first coll. for boys 1957; passport cancelled 1962; exile in Egypt (for activities promoting human rights and democracy); returned to Saudi Arabia 1964; fmr Special Envoy, UNICEF; Pres. Arab Gulf Programme for UN Devt Orgs 'AGFUND'; Pres. Arab Council for Childhood and Devt. *Leisure interests:* history, amateur radio, swimming. *Address:* AGFUND, PO Box 18371, Riyadh 11415, Saudi Arabia (office); 7 rue Beaujon, 75008 Paris, France. *Telephone:* 1-43-80-22-97 (office). *E-mail:* HRH.Office@agfund.org (office). *Website:* www.princetalal.net.

SA'UD, HRH Prince Turki al-Faisal ibn Abd al-Aziz as-, LLB, MA; Saudi Arabian diplomatist; *Chairman, King Faisal Center for Research and Islamic Studies;* b. 15 Feb. 1945; s. of the late King Faisal ibn Abd al-Aziz as-Sa'ud; m. HRH Princess Nouf bint Fahad; three s. three d.; ed Lawrenceville School, NJ, Princeton and Georgetown Univs, USA, Univs of Cambridge and London, UK; adviser to Royal Court 1973–77; Dir-Gen. Saudi Arabian Intelligence Dept 1977–2001; Del. to Afghanistan 1997–98; Amb. to Court of St James (UK), London 2003–05, to USA 2005–06; Co-founder King Faisal Foundation; Chair. Bd of Dirs King Faisal Center for Research and Islamic Studies; Trustee Effat Coll., Jeddah. *Address:* King Faisal Center for Research and Islamic Studies, PO Box 51049, Riyadh 115434, Saudi Arabia (office). *Telephone:* (1) 465-2255 (office). *Fax:* (1) 465-9993 (office). *E-mail:* sjameel@kff.com (office). *Website:* www.kfcris.com (office); www.kff.com (office).

SAUDARGAS, Algirdas; Lithuanian politician, biophysicist and diplomatist; b. 17 April 1948, Kaunas; m. Laima Saudargenè; one s. one d.; ed Kaunas Inst. of Medicine; Research Asst Inst. of Math. and Information Tech., Lithuanian Acad. of Sciences 1972–77; Sr Lecturer, Lithuanian Acad. of Agriculture 1977–82; Researcher Kaunas Inst. of Medicine (now Acad.) 1982–90; Founder-mem. Sajūdis Movt, Chair. Sajūdis Seimas (Parl.) Political Cttee 1988–90; elected to Supreme Soviet Repub. of Lithuania 1990; Minister of Foreign Affairs 1990–92, 1996–99; mem. official del. to negotiations with Soviet Union; mem. Seimas, Cttee on Foreign Affairs, mem. Seimas del. to European Parl. 1992–2004, Chair. Sub-cttee on European Affairs 1995–2004; Chair. Lithuanian Christian Democratic Party 1995– (mem. 1989–); mem. Seimas Del. to OSCE 2003–04; Amb. to the Holy See, Vatican City 2004–08; mem. European Parl. 2009–. *Leisure interest:* reading. *Address:* Street Theatre, 8-17A, 03107 Vilnius, Lithuania (office). *Telephone:* (85) 261-0480 (office). *E-mail:* algirdas.saudargas@europarl.europa.eu (office); info@asaudargas.lt. *Website:* www.algirdassaudargas.lt.

SAUDEK, Jan; Czech photographer; b. 13 May 1935, Prague; s. of Gustav Saudek and Pavla Saudková; m. 1st Marie Geislerová 1958 (divorced 1973); m. 2nd Marie Šrámková 1974 (died 1993); two s. three d.; studied reproduction photography at graphic school; factory worker 1953–83; over 500 solo exhbns world-wide, over 500 jt exhbns; works include Hey Joe! 1956, Life (Man Holding New Born Child) 1966, Destiny 1969, Artist's Father on the Jewish Cemetery 1972, Marie nr. 1 1974, Hungry for Your Touch 1975, 120 km/hr. 1975, Mothers and Daughters 1979, Walkman 1984, Desire 1985, Playcards 1986, The Death of an Soldier 1987, F. Sisters 1987, Hommage to Great Vincent 1989, The Wedding 1990, Black Sheep & White Crow 1993, The Deep Devotion 1994, Pretty Girl I Loved 1995, Joan of Arc 1998, Pimp & Hooker 2000; Chevalier, Ordre des Arts et des Lettres 1990; Award for album cover 'Soul Asylum' 1999, Int. Award of Photography 2012 (Photo Festival, Spillimbergo, Italy). *Television:* Jan Saudek (Czech TV project GEN) 1993, Brothers Saudek (Czech TV) 2001. *Films include:* Jerôme du Missolz, France 1991, Jan Saudek – Czech Photographer (documentary), Telewizia Wroslaw, Poland 1997, V pekle svých vášní 2008. *Publications include:* Il Teatro de la Vita 1980, The World of Jan Saudek 1983, Jan Saudek – 200 Photographs 1953–1986 1987, Life, Love, Death and Such Other Trifles 1992, Theatre of the Life 1992, The Letter 1995, Jubilations and Obsessions 1995, Album 1997, Jan Saudek... 1998, Love is a 4 Letter Word 1999, Single, Married, Divorced, Widower 1999, Realities 2002, Saudek 2005, Best of Jan Saudek 2005, Chains of Love 2007, Le allegorie dell Umanita (co-author) 2012. *Leisure interests:* women, running long distances, painting, drinking. *Address:* Ke hrbitovu 11, 152 00 Prague 5, Czech Republic (home). *Telephone:* 737960682 (office). *E-mail:* jan@saudek.com; sarah@saudek .com. *Website:* www.saudek.com.

SAUER, Fernand Edmond; French international official, pharmacist and lawyer; *Honorary Director for Public Health, European Commission;* b. 14 Dec. 1947, St Avold, Moselle; m. Pamela Sheppard; one s. two d.; ed Univs of Strasbourg and Paris II; fmr hosp. pharmacist and pharmaceutical insp. French Ministry of Health; joined European Comm., Brussels, Head of Pharmaceuticals 1986; Exec. Dir European Agency for Evaluation of Medicinal Products (EMEA), London 1994–2000; Dir for Public Health, EC, Luxembourg 2001–06, Hon. Dir 2006–; Hon. Fellow, School of Pharmacy, Univ. of London, Hon. mem. Royal Pharmaceutical Soc.; Chevalier, Légion d'honneur, Ordre national du Mérite. *Address:* DG Sanco C – Public Health and Risk Assessment, Jean Monnet Building, Office C5/120, European Commission, rue Alcide de Gasperi, 2920 Luxembourg (office). *Telephone:* 43-01-32-71-9 (office). *Fax:* 43-01-34-51-1 (office). *E-mail:* Fernand.Sauer@cec.eu.int (office). *Website:* www.ec.europa.eu.

SAUER, Louis, FAIA; American/Canadian fmr architect, urban planner and professor of architecture; *Visiting Professor, School of Architecture and Design, Royal Melbourne Institute of Technology;* b. 15 June 1928, Forest Park, Ill.; s. of Frank J. Sauer and Jeanne LaFazia; m. 1st Elizabeth Mason 1956; two c.; m. 2nd Perla Serfaty 1990; ed Univ. of Pennsylvania, Int. School of City Planning, Venice, Italy, Illinois Inst. of Tech.; Prin. Louis Sauer Assoc. Architects, Phila, Pennsylvania 1961–79; Prof. of Architecture, Univ. of Pennsylvania 1974–79, Carnegie-Mellon Univ., Pittsburgh, Pennsylvania 1979–85, Univ. of Colorado 1985–89; Commr, Ville de Montreal Jacques Viger Comm. 1991–; Pnr, Archiris Inc., Pittsburgh 1981–84; Prin. Louis Sauer Architect, Boulder,Colorado 1985–89; Dir of Urban Design, Daniel Arbour and Assocs, Montreal, Canada 1989–2000; currently Visiting Prof., School of Architecture and Design, Royal Melbourne Inst. of Technology, Australia; currently also Chair Design Advisory Panel, Mornington Peninsula Shire; fmr consultant to USAID to advise govts of Lebanon, Egypt and Portugal on low-income housing devt; works include: Water Plaza and high-rise housing, Cincinnati, renewal plan for Fells Point waterfront, public open-space landscape, pvt. housing and housing for the elderly, Baltimore, new town devt for Golf Course Island, Reston, Virginia, Oaklands Mills Village Centre, Columbia, Maryland, housing at Society Hill, Philadelphia; work in Canada includes master-plans for Verdun Nuns Island 1991, Bois-Franc St-Laurent New Town 1992, Ville de Laval 1993, Angus C. P. Rail Rosemont Community 1993, Gatineu City Town Centre 1993, Ile Bizard Town Centre 1993; Nat. Endowment for the Arts Design Fellowship 1978, over 50 design and public service awards. *Leisure interests:* gardening, fishing. *Address:* School of Architecture and Design, Royal Melbourne Institute of Technology, PO Box 2476V, Melbourne, Vic. 3001, Australia (office). *Telephone:* (3) 9925-3555 (office). *Fax:* (3) 9925-3507 (office). *E-mail:* archdes@rmit .edu.au (office). *Website:* www.rmit.edu.au (office).

SAUERLÄNDER, Willibald, DPhil; German art historian; *Director Emeritus, Zentralinstitut für Kunstgeschichte;* b. 29 Feb. 1924, Waldsee; s. of Wilhelm Sauerländer and Anita Sauerländer-Busch; m. Brigitte Rückoldt 1957; one s.; ed Univ. of Munich; Visiting mem. Inst. for Advanced Study, Princeton 1961–62, 1973; Prof. of History of Art, Univ. of Freiburg Br. 1962–70; Dir Zentralinstitut für Kunstgeschichte, Munich 1970–89, Dir Emer. 1989–; Visiting Prof., Inst. of Fine Arts, New York Univ. 1964–65, Collège de France, Paris 1981, Univ. of Wisconsin 1982, Harvard Univ. 1984–85, Univ. of California, Berkeley 1989; Mellon Lectures, Washington 1991, New York Univ. 1992; mem. Bayerische Akad. der Wissenschaften, Medieval Acad. of America, British Acad., Soc. Nat. des Antiquaires de France, Royal Soc. of Antiquaries, London, Kon. Acad. Voor Wetenschappen, Letteren en Schone Kunsten van Belgie, Acad. Europaea, Acad. des Inscriptions et Belles-Lettres, American Acad. of Arts and Sciences; Bavarian Maximilian Order for Arts and Sciences (1995); Dr hc (Strasbourg) 1982, (Pertezionto Scuola Normale, Pisa, Italy); Grand Prix de la Societé française d'archéologie 2007. *Publications include:* Die Kathedrale von Chartres 1954, Jean-Antoine Houdon: Voltaire 1963, Von Sens bis Strassburg 1966, Gotische Skulptur in Frankreich 1140-1270 1970, Das Königsportal in Chartres 1984, Das Jahrhundert der grossen Kathedralen 1990, Initialen 1996, Gegenwart der Kritik 1999, Cathedrals and their Sculptures 2000, An Essay on the Faces of Houdon's 2002, The Air at the Tip of the Brush 2002, Witness to History: The Face in Medieval Sculpture 2006, Von Bildern Und Menschen 2010, Der Katholische Rubens 2011, Ein Sommer in Argenteuil: Manet malt Monet 2012. *Leisure interests:* reading, travelling. *Address:* Zentralinstitut für Kunstgeschichte, Meiserstrasse 10, 80333 Munich (office); Victoriastrasse II, 80803 Munich, Germany (home). *Telephone:* (89) 5591546 (office); (89) 390988 (home).

SAUL, Hon. David John, JP, BA, BSc, MEd, PhD; British/Bermudian politician (retd) and business consultant; b. 27 Nov. 1939, Bermuda; s. of John A. Saul and

Sarah Elizabeth Saul; m. Christine Hall 1963; one s. one d.; ed Mount St Agnes Acad., Saltus Grammar School, Loughborough Coll., UK, Queen's and Toronto Univs, Canada; teacher 1962–67; consultant to Ont. Educ. Communications Authority 1970–72, to Bermuda Dept of Educ. 1972–73; Visiting Prof., Univ. of Toronto 1972; Perm. Sec. Ministry of Educ. 1972–76; Financial Sec. Ministry of Finance 1976–81; Chief Admin. Officer, Gibbons Co. 1981–84; Pres. Fidelity Int. Bermuda Ltd 1984–95, Bermuda Audubon Soc. 1998, Bermuda Debating Soc. 1998; Chair. Bermuda Council on Int. Affairs 1983–85; Dir Bermuda Monetary Authority 1986–88, 1997–99, London Bermuda Reins Co. Ltd 1987–2009, Bermuda Track and Field Asscn 1987–99, Fidelity Investments 1984–, Lombard Odier (Bermuda) Ltd 1989–2009, Odyssey Marine Exploration, Inc. 2001–; Trustee, Bermuda Underwater Exploration Inst. 1992–99 (Life Trustee 1999); MP 1989–97; Minister of Finance 1989–95; Prime Minister of Bermuda 1995–97; mem. Bermuda Defence Bd 1997–2001; Fellow, Explorers' Club, New York 1999; Hon. BSc (Loughborough Univ.) 2009. *Leisure interests:* scuba diving, fly-fishing, ocean kayaking, oil painting, carving, arctic exploration. *Address:* Rocky Ledge, 18 Devonshire Bay Road, DV 07, Bermuda. *Telephone:* 236-7338. *Fax:* 236-5087. *E-mail:* davidjsaul@aol.com.

SAUL, John Ralston, CC, PhD; Canadian essayist, writer and philosopher; *President, International PEN;* b. 19 June 1947, Ottawa; m. Adrienne Clarkson 1999; ed McGill Univ., King's Coll., London; Gen. Ed., Penguin Extraordinary Canadians project; Pres. Canadian PEN 1990–92, co-creator, Canadian PEN Writers In Exile Network 2004, Pres. Int. PEN 2009–; Co-Chair Inst. for Canadian Citizenship; Founder and Hon. Chair. Le français pour l'avenir/French for the Future, LaFontaine-Baldwin symposium; Patron, PLAN; mem. Centre québécois du PEN international; mem. Council of Writers and Experts, Int. Cities of Refuge Network (ICORN), Norway; Chevalier, Ordre des Arts et des Lettres; 17 hon. degrees including McGill Univ., Herzen State Pedagogical Univ., St Petersburg (Russia); Pablo Neruda Medal, Chile, Manhae Grand Prize for Literature, South Korea 2010. *Publications include:* non-fiction: Voltaire's Bastards: The Dictatorship of Reason in the West 1992, The Doubter's Companion: A Dictionary of Aggressive Common Sense 1994, The Unconscious Civilization (Gov. Gen.'s Literary Award for Non-Fiction 1996, Gordon Montador Award for Best Canadian Book on Social Issues 1996) 1995, Le citoyen dans un cul-de-sac?: Anatomie d'une société en crise 1995, Reflections of a Siamese Twin 1997, On Equilibrium: Six Qualities of the New Humanism 2001, The Collapse of Globalism and the Reinvention of the World 2005, Joseph Howe and the Battle for the Freedom of Speech 2006, A Fair Country: Telling Truths about Canada 2008, Louis-Hippolyte LaFontaine and Robert Baldwin 2010; fiction: The Paradise Eater (Premio Lettarario Internazionale, Italy), The Birds of Prey 1977, Baraka or The Lives, Fortunes and Sacred Honor of Anthony Smith 1983, The Next Best Thing 1986, The Paradise Eater 1988, De Si Bons Americains 1994, Dark Diversions 2012; contrib. articles and essays to magazines and anthologies. *Address:* c/o Andrea Damiani, Westwood Creative Artists, 94 Harbord Street, Toronto, ON M5B 1G6, Canada (office). *Telephone:* (416) 964-3302 (office). *Fax:* (416) 975-9209 (office). *E-mail:* wca_office@wcaltd.com (office); jrs.ahouse12@rogers.com. *Website:* www .wcaltd.com (office); www.johnralstonsaul.com.

SAUL, Ralph Southey, BA, LLB; American lawyer, business executive and fmr stock exchange official; *Chairman, Executive Committee, Knox & Company;* b. 21 May 1922, Brooklyn, NY; s. of Walter Emerson and Helen Douglas; m. Bette Jane Bertschinger 1956; one s. one d.; ed Univ. of Chicago and Yale Law School; war service, USNR 1943–46; attached to American Embassy, Prague 1947–48; admitted to District of Columbia Bar 1951, to New York Bar 1952; Assoc., firm of Lyeth and Voorhees, New York 1951–52; Asst Counsel to Gov. of New York State 1952–54; Staff Attorney, Radio Corpn of America 1954–58; with Securities and Exchange Comm. 1958–65, Dir Div. of Trading and Markets 1963–65; Vice-Pres. for Corporate Devt, Investors Diversified Services, Inc. 1965–66; Pres. American Stock Exchange 1966–71; Vice-Chair. First Boston Corpn 1971–74; Chair. and CEO INA Corpn, Phila 1975–81; Chair. CIGNA Corpn (fmrly Connecticut Gen. and INA Corpn) 1982–84; Co-founder Peers and Co. 1985; currently Chair. Exec. Cttee Knox & Co. (investment banking and corp. advisory firm); mem. Bd of Dirs American Buildings Corpn, Horace Mann Educators Corpn, PH II Inc., Commonwealth Ventures, Brookings Inst. Cttee for Econ. Devt, Regulatory Advisory Cttee, New York Stock Exchange; mem. Advisory Bd to Grad. School of Educ., Univ. of Pennsylvania; fmr mem. Bd of Dirs Sun Co. 1976, Certain Teed Corpn 1983, Drexel Burnham (fmr Chair.) 1989; mem. ABA, Council on Foreign Relations; Dr hc (Alfred Univ., Mercer Univ.). *Leisure interest:* golf. *Address:* Knox & Co., 830 Post Road East, Suite 205, Westport, CT 06880, USA (office). *Telephone:* (203) 226-6288 (office). *Fax:* (203) 226-8022 (office). *Website:* www.knoxandco.com (office).

SAUMAREZ SMITH, Charles Robert, CBE, PhD, FSA; British gallery administrator; *Secretary and CEO, Royal Academy of Arts;* b. 28 May 1954, Redlynch, Wilts., England; s. of the late William Hanbury Saumarez Smith and of Alice Elizabeth Harness Saumarez Smith (née Raven); m. Romilly Le Quesne Savage 1979; two s.; ed King's Coll., Cambridge, Harvard Univ., USA, Univ. of London, Warburg Inst.; Christie's Research Fellow in Applied Arts, Christ's Coll. Cambridge 1979–82; apptd Asst Keeper Victoria & Albert (V&A) Museum 1982, with special responsibility for V&A/RCA MA course in History of Design, Head of Research 1990–94; Dir Nat. Portrait Gallery 1994–2002, Nat. Gallery 2002–07; Sec. and CEO Royal Academy of Arts 2007–; Slade Prof., Univ. of Oxford 2002; Chair. English Art Museum Dir's Conf. 1999–2003; Pres. Museum Asscn 2004–06; mem. Advisory Council, Warburg Inst. 1997–2003, Inst. of Historical Research 1999–2004, Expert Panel for Museums, Libraries and Archives of the Heritage Lottery Fund 1998–2002; Gov. Univ. of the Arts 2005–13; Prof. of Cultural History, Queen Mary, Univ. of London 2007–; Chair. Advisory Bd, Fondazione Palazzo Strozzi 2008–13; Hon. Fellow, RCA 1991; Hon. FRIBA 2000; Hon. DLitt (Univ. of E Anglia) 2001, (Westminster) 2002, (London) 2003, (Sussex) 2003, (Essex) 2005. *Publications:* The Building of Castle Howard (Alice Davis Hitchcock Medallion) 1990, Eighteenth Century Decoration 1993, The National Portrait Gallery 1997, The National Gallery 2009, The Company of Artists: The Origins of the Royal Academy of Arts 2012. *Address:* Royal Academy of Arts, Burlington House, Piccadilly, London, W1J 0BD, England (office). *Telephone:* (20) 7300-8020 (office). *E-mail:* chiefexecutive@royalacademy.org.uk (office). *Website:* www.royalacademy .org.uk (office).

SAUNDERS, Jennifer; British actress and writer; b. 6 July 1958, Sleaford, Lincs., England; m. Adrian Edmondson; three d.; ed Cen. School of Speech and Drama, London; Hon. Rose, Montreux 2002, Acad. Fellowship, BAFTA 2009. *Theatre:* An Evening with French and Saunders (nat. tour) 1989, Me and Mamie O'Rourke 1993, French and Saunders Live in 2000 (nat. tour) 2000. *Films include:* The Supergrass 1985, Dangerous Brothers Present: World of Danger (video) 1986, Eat the Rich 1987, Prince Cinders (voice) 1993, In the Bleak Midwinter 1995, Muppet Treasure Island 1996, Spice World: the Movie 1997, Fanny and Elvis 1999, Maybe Baby 2000, Absolutely Fabulous 2001, Shrek 2 (voice) 2004, L'Entente cordiale 2006, Coraline (voice) 2009. *Television includes:* The Comic Strip (short) 1981, The Young Ones (series) 1982–84, The Comic Strip Presents… 1982–2011, The Lenny Henry Show (series) 1984, Happy Families (series) 1985, Girls on Top 1985–86, Saturday Live (series) 1986, French and Saunders 1987–2005, The Storyteller (series) 1988, The Jim Henson Hour (series) 1989, Rita Rudner (series) 1990, The Tale of Little Pig Robinson (film) 1990, Absolutely Fabulous (Emmy Award 1993, BAFTA Award for Best Comedy 1993, Writers' Guild of Great Britain Award TV for Situation Comedy 1993, BAFTA Award for Best Female Performance in a Comedy Programme 2012) 1992–2012, French and Saunders Live (video) 1993, Queen of the East (film) 1995, Roseanne (series) 1996, Absolutely Fabulous: Absolutely Not! (video) 1998, Friends (series) 1998, Let Them Eat Cake (series) 1999, The Magician's House (series short) 1999, The Nearly Complete and Utter History of Everything (film) 1999, French & Saunders Live (video) 2000, Mirrorball (short) 2000, Pongwiffy (series) 2002, Comic Relief 2003: The Big Hair Do (film) 2003, Comic Relief: Red Nose Night Live 05 (film) 2005, Jam and Jerusalem 2006–09, The Life and Times of Vivienne Vyle (series) 2007, A Bucket o' French and Saunders (series) 2007, The Vivienne Vyle Show (film) 2007, French & Saunders Still Alive (video) 2008, Comic Relief 2009 (film) 2009, Comic Relief: Uptown Downstairs Abbey (film) 2011, This is Jinsy (series) 2011, Blandings (series) 2012. *Publications:* A Feast of French and Saunders (with Dawn French) 1992, Absolutely Fabulous: The Scripts 1993, Absolutely Fabulous 'Continuity' 2001. *Address:* c/o Maureen Vincent, United Agents, 12–26 Lexington Street, London, W1F 0LE, England (office). *Telephone:* (20) 3214-0800 (office). *Fax:* (20) 3214-0801 (office). *E-mail:* info@unitedagents.co.uk (office). *Website:* unitedagents .co.uk (office).

SAUNDERS, Stuart John, MD, FRCP; South African physician, professor of medicine and university administrator; *Senior Advisor, South Africa Program, Andrew W. Mellon Foundation;* b. 28 Aug. 1931, Cape Town; s. of Albert Frederick Saunders and Lilian Emily; m. 1st Noreen Merle Harrison 1956 (died 1983); one s. one d.; m. 2nd Anita Louw 1984; ed Christian Brothers Coll. and Univ. of Cape Town; Registrar in Pathology and Medicine, Groote Schuur Hosp. and Univ. of Cape Town 1955–58, Lecturer and Sr Lecturer 1961–70, Prof. and Head of Medicine Dept 1971–80, Deputy Principal for Planning, Univ. of Cape Town 1978–80, Vice-Chancellor and Prin. Univ. of Cape Town 1981–96, Vice-Chancellor Emer. 1996–, Co-founder Liver Clinic and Liver Research Unit; Research Asst Royal Postgraduate Medical School, London 1959–60; Fellow in Medicine, Harvard Medical School and Massachusetts Gen. Hosp. 1963–64; currently Sr Advisor for South Africa program, Andrew W. Mellon Foundation; Past Pres. South Africa Inst. of Race Relations; Fellow, Royal Soc. of South Africa 1995, Coll. of Medicine of South Africa 1996; Life Fellow, Univ. of Cape Town; mem. Faculty of Consulting Physicians of South Africa; Grand Counsellor, Order of the Baobab; Hon. LLD (Aberdeen), (Sheffield), (Princeton), (Rhodes), Hon. DSc (Toronto), (Cape Town). *Publications include:* Access to and Quality in Higher Education: A Comparative Study 1992, Vice-Chancellor on a Tightrope 2000; numerous scientific publications particularly in the field of liver diseases. *Leisure interests:* reading, fishing. *Address:* Andrew W. Mellon Foundation, 140 East, 62nd Street, New York, NY 10065, USA (office); 45 Belvedere Avenue, Oranjezicht, 8001 Cape Town, South Africa (home). *Telephone:* (212) 838-8400 (office); 453035 (home). *Fax:* (212) 888-4172 (office); 4620047 (home). *Website:* www.mellon.org (office).

SAUPER, Hubert, BA; Austrian film director, producer and writer; b. Kitzbühel, Tyrol; ed Univ. of Performing Arts, Vienna, Univ. of Paris VIII. *Films as writer / director include:* On the Road with Emil (documentary) (Int. Festival, Würzburg Best Short Film 1994, Prix Max Ophülz for Best Documentary Nexon, France 1995) 1993, So I Sleepwalk in Broad Daylight (also producer) (Premio da casa de Figueira da Foz, Portugal 1995, Best First Film, Best Film School Production) 1994, Lomographer's Moscow 1995, Kisangani Diary (documentary, also producer) (seven int. awards) 1998, Alone With Our Stories (documentary) 2000, Darwin's Nightmare (documentary, also producer) (six int. awards, including European Film Awards Best Documentary and Vienna Film Prize) 2004. *Films as director include:* Wer fürchtet sich vorm schwarzen Mann 1988, Era Max 1989, Piraten in Österreich 1990, Blasi, Der 1990, Ich habe die angenehme Aufgabe 1993. *Films as actor:* In the Circle of the Iris, Blue Distance. *E-mail:* hubert.sauper@free.fr.

SAURA, Carlos; Spanish film director; b. 4 Jan. 1932, Huesca; s. Antonio Saura Pacheco and Fermina Torrente; m. 1st Adela Medrano 1957; two s.; m. 2nd Mercedes Pérez 1982; three s.; ed Inst. of Cinema Research and Studies; professional photographer 1949–; teacher, Instituto de Investigaciones y Experiencias Cinematograficas, Madrid 1957–64, dismissed for political reasons; Lifetime Achievement Award, European Film Awards 2004. *Films include:* Cuenca 1958, Los golfos 1959, Llanto por un bandido 1964, La Caza (Silver Bear, Berlin Film Festival) 1966, Peppermint Frappé (Silver Bear, Berlin Film Festival 1968) 1967, Stress-es tres-tres 1968, La madriguera 1969, El jardín de las delicias 1970, Ana y los lobos 1972, La Prima Angelica (Jury Prize, Cannes Film Festival 1974) 1973, Cría cuervos (Grand Prix of the Jury, Cannes Film Festival 1976) 1975, Elisa, vida mía 1977, Los ojos vendados 1978, Mamá cumple cien años 1979, Deprisa, Deprisa (Silver Bear, Berlin Film Festival 1981) 1980, Bodas de Sangre 1981, Sweet Hours 1982, Carmen (Technical Grand Prize and Award for Best Artistic Contribution, Cannes Film Festival, BAFTA Award) 1983, El Dorado 1987, The Dark Night 1989, Ay Carmela! 1990, Sevillanas 1992, Dispara! 1993, Flamenco 1995, Taxi 1996, Pajarico 1997, Tango 1998, Esa Luz! 1998, Goya en Burdeos 1999, Buñuel y la mesa del rey Salomón 2001, Salome 2002, El Séptimo día 2004, Iberia 2005, Fados 2007, Sinfonía de Aragón 2008, Io, Don Giovanni 2009, Flamenco, Flamenco 2010. *Website:* www.carlos-saura.com.

SAUVAGE, Jean-Pierre, BEng, PhD; French chemist and academic; *Director of Research, Organo-Mineral Chemistry Laboratory, University of Strasbourg;* b. 21

Oct. 1944, Paris; s. of Camille Sauvage and Lydie Angèle Arcelin; m. Simone Carmen Boni; one s.; ed Ecole Nationale Supérieure de Chimie, Strasbourg, Université Louis Pasteur; Post-doctoral Researcher, Univ. of Oxford, UK 1973–74; Research Asst, CNRS, Strasbourg 1971–75, Research Assoc. 1975–79, Master of Research 1979, Sr Researcher 1979–81, Prof. 1981–, Dir of Research, Organo-Mineral Chem. Lab., Univ. Louis Pasteur, Strasbourg 1988–, CNRS Dir of Research Prof., Univ. of Strasbourg; Distinguished Visiting Scholar, Northwestern Univ., Evanston, USA 2010–12; Ed.-in-Chief Chemical Society Reviews 1997–2000; mem. Editorial Bd Bioorganic Chemistry Frontiers, Act Chimica Scandinavia, Bulletin of the Chemical Society of Japan, New Journal of Chemistry, Compte Rendu de l'Academie des Sciences, Bulletin de la Société Française de Chimie, Inorganic Chem. 1997–99, Structure and Bonding 1997–; Chair. 21st Solvay Conf. in Chem., From Non-covalent Assemblies to Molecular Machines, Brussels, 28 Nov.– 1st Dec. 2007; mem. Acad. des sciences 1997, Japanese Soc. for the Promotion of Science 1994; Fellow, European Acad. of Sciences; Chevalier, Légion d'honneur 2000; Dr hc (Zurich) 2010; Bronze Medal, CNRS 1978, Award in Coordination Chemistry, Société Française de Chimie 1979, Jean-Baptiste Dumas Award, Acad. des sciences 1980, Award in Organic Chem., Société Française de Chimie 1987 Silver Medal, CNRS 1988, Izatt-Christensen Award in Macrocyclic Chem. 1991, Prelog Gold Medal, ETH-Zurich (Switzerland) 1994, World Nessim Habif Award, Univ. of Geneva 1995, Centenary Lecturer and Medal, RSC (UK) 2000, Pierre Süe Prize, Société Française de Chimie 2005, Catalan Sabatier Prize, Royal Spanish Soc. of Chem. 2005, R.B. Woodward Award in Porphyrin Chem. 2008, Japan Coordination Chem. Award 2009, 'Luigi Tartufari' Int. Prize, Accad. Nazionale dei Lincei (Italy) 2012, Blaise Pascal Medal in Chem., European Acad. of Sciences 2012; named lectures: Albright and Wilson Lecturer, Univ. of Warwick, UK 1988, Donders Lectureship, Univ. of Utrecht, Netherlands 1992, Univ. of Pavia, Italy 1992, Univ. of Bern, Switzerland 1992, Univ. of Bologna, Italy 1993, The Pfizer Lecturer, Univ. of Sheffield, UK 1993, Univ. of Louvain la Neuve, Belgium 1994, Andrews Lecturer, Univ. of Sydney, Australia 1994, Earl Muetterties Memorial Lecturer, Univ. of Berkeley, USA 1995, H.H. King Lecturer, Kansas State Univ., USA 1995, Reilly Lecturer, Notre Dame Univ., USA 1996, Frontiers in Chemical Research Lecturer, Texas A&M Univ., USA 1996, Morris S. Kharasch Lecturer, Univ. of Chicago, USA 1998, Taft Lecturer, Univ. of California, Irvine, USA 1999, Barré Lecturer, Univ. of Montréal 1999, Centenary Lecturer, RSC (UK) 2000, Descartes Lecturer, Royal Netherlands Acad. of Arts and Sciences 2000, Univ. of La Laguna, Spain 2001, Univ. of Santiago de Compostela, Spain 2001, Musher Lecturer, The Hebrew Univ. of Jerusalem, Israel 2001, Les Power Lecturer, James Cook Univ., Townsville, Australia 2004, Steinhofer Lecturer 2006, Tech. Univ. of Kaiserslautern, Germany 2007, Univ. of Hokkaido, Sapporo, Japan 2010, Inst. for Molecular Science, Okazaki, Japan 2010, The Heinlen Hall Lectures, Bowling Green State Univ., USA 2012, Univ. of Geneva, Switzerland 2012. *Address:* Laboratoire de Chimie Organo-Minérale, Institut de Science et Ingénierie Supramoléculaires, 8 Allée Gaspard Monge, Université de Strasbourg, 67000 Strasbourg, France (office). *Telephone:* (3) 68-85-51-43 (office). *E-mail:* jpsauvage@unistra.fr (office). *Website:* www-chimie.u-strasbg.fr/~lcom (office).

SAVAGE, Francis (Frank) Joseph, CMG, LVO, OBE; British administrator, diplomatist and consultant; *Adviser, Foreign and Commonwealth Office;* b. 8 Feb. 1943, Preston, Lancs., England; s. of Francis Fitzgerald Savage and Mona May Savage (née Parsons); m. Veronica Mary McAleenan 1966; two s.; ed St Stephen's RC School, Welling, N Kent Coll., Dartford; joined Foreign Office 1961, Embassy, Cairo 1967–70, Washington, DC 1971–73, Vice-Consul, Aden 1973–74, Foreign Office 1974–78, Consul, Düsseldorf 1978–82, Consul, Peking (now Beijing) 1982–86, First Sec., Lagos and Consul, Benin 1987–90; First Sec./Counsellor, Foreign Office 1990–93; Gov. of Montserrat 1993–97, of the British Virgin Islands 1998–2002; Chair. Friends of British Virgin Islands 2005–; adviser to FCO 2003–; freelance consultant 2003–; mem. Bd Visar Trust 2002–; adviser on overseas territories to FCO; Pres. Soc. of London Ragamuffins 2008–09; Trustee, Montserrat Foundation 2008–; Kt Commdr, Pontifical Order of St Gregory the Great 2002; Montserrat Badge of Honour 2000. *Leisure interests:* cricket, travel, volcano watching. *Address:* Foreign and Commonwealth Office, King Charles Street, London, SW1A 2AH (office); 19 Cleeve Park Gardens, Sidcup, Kent, DA14 4JL, England (home). *Telephone:* (20) 8309-5061 (home). *E-mail:* frank.savage@fco.gov.uk (office); fjsavage@savagef.fsnet.co.uk (home).

SAVAGE-RUMBAUGH, (Emily) Sue, MS, PhD; American primatologist, academic and writer; *Associate Program Director, Great Ape Trust;* b. 1946; m. Duane Rumbaugh; ed Southern Methodist Univ., Univ. of Oklahoma; fmr Asst Research Prof., Yerkes Regional Primate Research Center, Emory Univ., Assoc. Research Prof. 1984–92; associated with Language Research Center, Georgia State Univ. 1981–2005, also Adjunct Assoc. Prof. of Biology 1983–92, Prof. of Biology and Psychology 1992–2005; Dir Bonobo Research, Great Ape Trust 2005–08, Assoc. Program Dir and Scientist with Special Standing 2008–; Dr hc (Chicago) 1997, (Missouri State) 2008; Leighton A. Wilkie Award in Anthropology, Indiana Univ. 2000. *Publications include:* Ape Language: From Conditioned Response to Symbol 1986, Kanzi: The Ape at the Brink of the Human Mind (co-author) 1995, Apes, Language and the Human Mind (co-author) 1996; numerous articles in professional journals. *Address:* Great Ape Trust, 1515 Linden Street, Suite 220, Des Moines, IA 50320, USA (office). *Telephone:* (515) 243-9367 (office). *Fax:* (515) 243-9367 (office). *E-mail:* info@greatapetrust.org (office). *Website:* www.greatapetrust.org (office).

SAVARIN, Charles Angelo; Dominican politician and diplomatist; *President;* b. 2 Oct. 1943, Portsmouth; m. Clara Etienne; one s. two d.; ed Dominica Grammar School, Roseau, Ruskin Coll., Oxford, UK; Asst Master, Dominica Grammar School 1963–70; Gen. Sec., Dominica Civil Services Asscn 1966–83; Senator, House of Ass. 1979–85; Minister without Portfolio, Prime Minister's Office 1983–85; Minister Counsellor, Dominica High Comm., London 1985–86; Perm. Rep. of Dominica to EU, Brussels 1986–93, concurrently Amb. to Belgium, Luxembourg and Switzerland and Perm. Rep. to UN, Geneva 1986–93; Gen. Man. Nat. Devt Corpn 1993–95; mem. Parl. for Roseau Cen. Constituency 1995–2005; Leader, Freedom Party 1996–2006; Minister of Tourism 2000–05, of Foreign Affairs, Trade and Labour 2005–07, Minister for the Public Service 2005–, Minister of Public Utilities, Energy and Ports 2007–09, of Nat. Security, Immigration and Labour 2009–13; Pres. 2013–; Dominica Award of Honour 2013. *Address:* Office of the President, Morne Bruce, Roseau, Dominica (office). *Telephone:* 4482054 (office). *Fax:* 4498366

(office). *E-mail:* presidentsoffice@dominica.gov.dm (office). *Website:* presidentoffice.gov.dm (office).

SAVART, Michel; French business executive; *President and CEO, Foncière Euris SA;* ed Ecole Polytechnique, École Nationale Supérieure des Mines de Paris; began career at Havas 1986; successively in charge of missions at Bank Louis Dreyfus 1987; managed projects then adviser to Man. Bd/Exec. Bd Banque Arjil (Lagardère Group) 1988–94; Man. Dir Mergers & Acquisitions, Dresdner Kleinwort Benson (DKB) 1995–99; joined Euris-Rally as a Dir-Adviser to the Pres. 1999, within Euris Group, served as Adviser to Chair. of Rallye SA, Perm. Rep. of Rallye on Board of Groupe Go Sport (listed co.), Rep. of Foncière Euris: Chair. Marigny Belfort SAS, Marigny Elysées SAS, Marigny Foncière SAS, Matignon Abbeville SAS, Matignon Bail SAS, Matignon Corbeil Centre SAS, Man. of SCI Sofaret and SCI Les Herbiers, Rep. of Marigny Foncière, Chair. Mat-Bel 2 SAS, Co-Man. SNC Centre Commercial Porte de Châtillon, SCI Les Deux Lions, SCI Palais des Marchands, SCI Ruban Bleu Saint-Nazaire and Man. SCI Pont de Grenelle, Rep. of Matignon Abbeville and Man. of Centrum K Sarl, Centrum J Sarl, and Centrum Z Sarl, Rep. of Centrum NS Luxembourg Sarl and Man. of Manufaktura Luxembourg Sarl, Co-Man. of Alexa Holding GmbH, Alexa Shopping Centre GmbH, Alexanderplatz Voltairestrasse GmbH, Einkaufszentrum am Alex GmbH, Guttenbergstrasse BAB5 GmbH, HBF Königswall GmbH, Loop 5 Shopping Centre GmbH, Man. (category A) of Centrum NS Luxembourg Sarl, Rep. of Foncière Euris, Chair. Marigny Expansion, and Man. of SNC Alta Marigny Carré de Soie, Rep. of Matignon Abbeville and Chair. of Mat-Bel 2 SAS, Rep. of Marigny Elysées and Co-Man. of SCCV des Jardins de Seine 1, SCCV des Jardins de Seine 2, SNC Centre Commercial du Grand Argenteuil, Pres. and CEO Foncière Euris SA 2010–; outside Euris Group, served as mem. Bd Groupe Go Sport; Perm. Rep. of Parande SAS on Bd of Matussière et Forest SA; Co-Man. SNC Centre Commercial Porte de Chatillon, SCI Les Deux Lions, SCI Palais des Marchand, amongst others; Man. EURL Montmorency, EURL Aubriot Investissements; mem. Bd of Dirs Casino Guichard Perrachon & Cie SA 2005–, C Discount SA 2005–, Mercialys SA 2010–. *Address:* Foncière Euris SA, 83 rue du Faubourg Saint-Honoré, 75008 Paris, France (office). *Telephone:* 1-44-71-14-00 (office). *Fax:* 1-44-71-14-50 (office). *E-mail:* info@fonciere-euris.fr (office). *Website:* www.fonciere-euris.fr (office); www.rallye.fr.

SAVÉANT, Jean-Michel, DèsSc; French chemist and professor of electrochemistry; *Emeritus Research Director, Centre National de la Recherche Scientifique, Université Paris 7 – Denis Diderot;* b. 19 Sept. 1933, Rennes; ed Ecole Normale Supérieure, Paris, Instituto di Chimica Fisica dell'Universita de Padova, Italy; Asst Dir, Chem. Lab., Ecole Normale Supérieure, Paris 1968–70; Prof., Univ. Paris 7 – Denis Diderot 1971–85, CNRS Research Dir 1985–2000, Emer. 2000–, currently also Sr Scientist; Prof., California Inst. of Technology, Pasadena, USA 1988–89; apptd Oscar K. Rice Distinguished Lecturer, Univ. of North Carolina, Chapel Hill 1995, Nelson Leonard Distinguished Lecturer, Univ. of Illinois, Urbana-Champaing 1999, Baker Lecturer, Cornell Univ. 2002; mem. Editorial Bd Journal of the American Chemical Society, Inorganic Chem., Journal of Physical Organic Chem., ChemPhysChem, Journal of Electroanalytical Chem.; mem. Acad. des Sciences 2000–; Foreign Assoc. mem. NAS 2001–; French Chemical Soc. Prix Louis Ancel 1966, CNRS Silver Medal 1976, Royal Soc. of Chem. Faraday Medal 1983, Medaglia Luigi Riccoboni 1983, Prix Emile Jungfleisch, Acad. des sciences 1989, Electrochemical Soc. Palladium Medal 1993, Societa Chimica Italiana Luigi Galvani Medal 1997, Manuel Baizer Award, Electrochemical Soc. 2002, Bruno Breyer Medal, Royal Australian Chemical Inst. 2005. *Publication:* Elements of Molecular and Biomolecular Electrochemistry 2006. *Address:* Laboratoire d'Electrochimie Moléculaire UMR CNRS - P7 7591, Université Paris Diderot - Paris 7, 15 rue Jean-Antoine de Baïf, 7e Etage - case 7107, 75205 Paris, Cedex 13, France (office). *Telephone:* 1-57-27-87-95 (office). *Fax:* 1-57-27-87-88 (office). *E-mail:* saveant@univ-paris-diderot.fr (office). *Website:* www.lemp7.cnrs.fr (office).

SAVELYEVA, Lyudmila Mikhailovna; Russian actress; b. 24 Jan. 1942, Leningrad (now St Petersburg); m. Aleksandr Zbruyev 1965 (divorced); one c.; ed Vaganova Ballet School, Leningrad; soloist, Kirorskiy (Mariinskiy) Theatre 1961–65; People's Artist of the RSFSR 1985. *Films include:* Sleeping Beauty 1964, War and Peace 1967, The Sunflowers (de Sica) 1971, Flight 1971, The Headless Horseman 1973, The Seagull 1973, Yulia Vrevskaya 1978, The Hat 1982, The Fourth Year of War 1983, Success 1985, Another's Belaya and Ryaboy 1986, White Rose–Emblem of Grief, Red Rose–Emblem of Love 1989, The Mystery of Nardo 1999, The Tender Age 2000. *Television:* Anna Karenina (mini-series) 2009. *Theatre productions include:* The Price (Miller), M. Rozovsky theatre. *Address:* Tverskaya Str. 19, Apt. 76, 103050 Moscow, Russia. *Telephone:* (495) 299-99-34.

SAVI, Toomas, PhD; Estonian physician and politician; b. 30 Dec. 1942, Tartu; m. Kirsi Savi; two d.; ed Tartu State Univ.; Chief Physician, USSR light athletics team, concurrently Sr Researcher Tartu State Univ. 1970–80; nat. team physician, Olympic Games, Munich 1972, Montreal 1976, Moscow 1980, Lillehammer 1994; Chief Physician, Tartu Medical Centre of Physical Educ. 1979–93; Asst Medical Officer, Kuopio Univ. Hosp. and Kajaani Hosp., Finland 1991–92; mem. Tartu Town Council 1989–93, 1996–97, 1999–2000; Deputy Mayor of Tartu 1993–95; mem. Eesti Reformierakond (Estonian Reform Party) 1994–; Speaker of Riigikogu (State Ass.) 1995–2003, Deputy Speaker 2003–04; Observer, European Parl. 2003–04; mem. European Parl. (Group of the Alliance of Liberals and Democrats for Europe) 2004–09, Del. for Relations with Canada, mem. Cttee on Devt, Substitute mem. Cttee on Regional Devt, Del. to the ACP-EU Jt Parl. Ass.; Founder-mem. Estonian Olympic Cttee 1989–, Vice-Pres. 2008–; Pres. Estonian Skiing Assen 1999–; mem., Tartu Rotary Club 1993–, Bd Eluterve Eesti exercise assen 1994–, Bd Estonian Assen 2001–, Supervisory Bd of Tartu St Mary's Church Foundation 2003–; Grand Cross, Royal Norwegian Order of Merit 1998, Nat. Order of Merit (Malta) 2001, Grand Cross, Ordre nat. du Mérite (France) 2001, Commdr Grand Cross, Order of the Lion (Finland) 2002, Badge of the Order of the Nat. Coat of Arms (Second Class) (Estonia) 2003, Grand Officier, Order of Infante Dom Henrique (Portugal) 2003. *Address:* Näituse 22-8, 50 407 Tartu, Estonia.

SAVILL, Dame Rosalind Joy, DBE, CBE, FBA, FSA; British museum director; *President, French Porcelain Society;* b. 12 May 1951, Hants.; d. of Guy Savill and Lorna Williams; one d.; ed Wycombe Abbey School, Chatelard School, Montreux and Univ. of Leeds; Museum Asst, Ceramics Dept, Victoria & Albert Museum 1973–74; Museum Asst and Sr Asst, The Wallace Collection 1974–78, Asst to Dir

1978–92, Dir 1992–2011; Pres. French Porcelain Soc. 1999–; mem. Arts Panel, Nat. Trust 1995–, Art Advisory Cttee, Nat. Museums & Galleries of Wales 1998–2003, Museums and Collections Advisory Cttee English Heritage 1998–2002, Royal Mint Advisory Cttee 1999–; Visiting Prof., Univ. of Arts in London 2008–; Gov. Camden School for Girls 1996–; Trustee, Somerset House 1997–2004, Campaign for Museums 1999–2009, Holburne Museum of Art, Bath 2004–08, Samuel Courtauld Trust 2008–, Living Landscape Trust 2009–; Dr hc (Buckinghamshire and Chiltern Univ. Coll.); Leverhulme Scholar 1975, Getty Scholar 1985, Nat. Art Collections Fund Prize 1990, European Women of Achievement Award 2005. *Publications include:* The Wallace Collection Catalogue of Sèvres Porcelain (three vols) 1988; articles, reviews, contrib. to exhbn catalogues etc. *Leisure interests:* music, birds, wildlife, gardening. *Address:* The French Porcelain Society, 66C Kensington Church Street, London, W8 4BY, England (office). *Website:* www .thefrenchporcelainsociety.com (office).

SAVIN, Anatoliy Ivanovich, DTechSc; Russian specialist in radio analysis and systems analysis; b. 6 April 1920; ed Bauman Tech. Inst., Moscow; mem. CPSU 1944–91; fmrly employed as engineer and constructor; constructor with machine-bldg plant 1944–51; positions of responsibility on eng side of radio-tech. industry 1951–; Gen. Dir Scientific and Production Asscn Kometa 1973–98, Scientific Dir 1999–; Corresp. mem. Acad. of Sciences 1979, mem. 1984–, Prof. 1984; Academician Russian Acad. of Sciences; Acad. of Sciences Raspletin Prize 1972, Lenin Prize 1972, Hero of Socialist Labour 1976, State Prizes 1946, 1949, 1951, 1981. *Achievements include:* inventor of cosmic radio-telescope KRT-10. *Address:* Kometa Association, 109280 Moscow, Velozavodskaya Str. 5, Russia. *Telephone:* (495) 275-15-33.

SAVISAAR, Edgar; Estonian politician; *Mayor of Tallinn;* b. 31 May 1950, Harjumaa, Harju Co.; m. 1st Kaire Savisaar; one s.; m. 2nd Liis Savisaar; one s. one d.; m. 3rd Vilja Savisaar (divorced 2009); one d.; ed Tartu Secondary School, Tartu State Univ.; worked in governmental insts dealing with planning of economy 1980–88; Academic Dir Mainor consultancy co. 1988–89; mem. CP –1990; Leader Estonian Popular Front; Vice-Chair. Council of Ministers of Estonian SSR and Head of State Plan Cttee 1989 (resgnd), Chair. Council of Ministers 1990–91, then Prime Minister of Repub. of Estonia following independence 1991–92; Minister of Economy 1990; Deputy Speaker of Riigikogu 1992–95; Chair. Estonian Centre Party –1995 (resgnd), re-appointed Chair. following split in party 1996–; Deputy Prime Minister and Minister of the Interior April–Nov. 1995, dismissed from posts following scandal over taped conversations; Chair. Tallinn City Council 1996–99; Mayor of Tallinn 2001–04, 2007–; briefly Prime Minister of Estonia following legis. election 2003; Minister of Econ. Affairs and Communications 2005–07; Order of State Coat of Arms 2001. *Publications include:* four books. *Address:* Estonian Centre Party (Eesti Keskerakond), Toom-Rüütli 3/5, Tallinn 10130 (office); Office of the Mayor, Tallinn City Government, Vabaduse väljak 7, Tallinn 15199, Estonia (office). *Telephone:* 627-3460 (office); 640-4141 (Mayor's office) (office). *Fax:* 627-3461 (office); 640-4327 (Mayor's office) (office). *E-mail:* keskerakond@keskerakond.ee (office); foreign@tallinnlv.ee (office). *Website:* www .keskerakond.ee/savisaar (office); www.tallinn.ee (office).

SAVOLA, Kai Kari; Finnish theatre director, actor and translator; b. 30 Sept. 1931, Helsinki; s. of Tauno Savola and Hilppa Korpinen; m. Terttu Byckling 1958; two s. one d.; ed Helsinki Univ.; Admin. Dir Helsinki Student Theatre 1959–62; Man. Dir Finnish Drama Agency 1962–65; Literary Man. Helsinki City Theatre 1965–68; Dir-Gen. Tampere Workers' Theatre 1968–73; Dir Finnish Nat. Theatre 1973, Dir-Gen. 1974–92; stage direction of Finnish, English, Russian and Japanese drama; designed the two experimental stages of the Finnish Nat. Theatre (with Prof. Heikki Siren) 1976, 1987; Hon. Prof. 1983; Commdr, Order of White Rose of Finland 1991, Golden Medal of Honour of Tampere 1973, Golden Medal, Helsinki 1992. *Publications:* translations of English and German plays into Finnish. *Leisure interest:* farming. *Address:* Laivurinkatu 39 A 12, 00150 Helsinki, Finland (home). *Telephone:* (9) 636939 (home). *E-mail:* t.savola@kolumbus.fi (office).

SAVOSTYANOV, Maj.-Gen. Yevgeny Vadimovich; Russian politician; b. 28 Feb. 1952, Moscow; m. Julia Savostyanova; two s.; ed Moscow Mining Inst.; Jr researcher Inst. of Physics of the Earth USSR Acad. of Sciences 1975–77; researcher Inst. for Problems of Complex Use of Mineral Wealth USSR Acad. of Sciences 1975–90; Founder and Co-Chair. Club of Voters of Acad. of Sciences for election of Andrey Sakharov and other scientists as people's deputies from Acad. of Sciences; Asst to Chair. Moscow City Soviet, then Dir-Gen. Dept Moscow Mayor's Office 1990–91; mem. Co-ordination Council Movt Democratic Russia; mem. Org. Cttee of Democratic Reforms 1991; Deputy Dir Russian Fed. Service of Counter-espionage, Head of Dept Moscow and Moscow Region 1991–94; Adviser to Chair. Russian Fed. of Independent Trade Unions 1995–96; Deputy Head Admin. of Russian Presidency 1996–98; Vice-Pres. Moscow Oil and Gas Co. 1999–2005; currently Pres. Metro-Navtika; currently also Deputy Chief Exec. Centre for Assisting Rapprochement Between Russia and USA; Chair. Supervisory Bd Kemerovo Mining Co. 2000; mem. Bd of Dirs Sibir Energy PLC 2004; unsuccessful cand. for Pres. of Russian Fed. 2000.

SAVOVA, Olga B.; Russian actress and singer (mezzo-soprano); b. 14 Nov. 1964, Leningrad; m. Yefimov Dmitri; two s.; ed Leningrad State Inst. of Music Theatre and Cinematography, Leningrad State Conservatory; actress at Leningrad Tovstonogov Drama Theatre –1995; singer at Mariinsky Opera Theatre (Kirov Opera) 1996–; repertoire includes Verdi's Requiem, Emilia in Othello, Eboli in Don Carlos, Flora in La Traviata, Carmen, Amneris and Preziosilla, Olga in Eugene Onegin, Prokofiev's Semyon Kotko, Azucena in Il Trovatore, Marfa in Tsar's Bride, Bobilikha in Rimsky-Korsakov's The Snow Maiden, Blanche in The Gambler by Prokofiev, Lyubov in Mazeppa, Marina Mnishek in Boris Godunov, Hélène in War and Peace, Paulina in The Queen of Spades and Teresa in La Sonnambula, The Nurse in Die Frau ohne Schatten; performances in France, Belgium, Holland, Italy, Japan, China and Israel; Voci Verdiani Int. Competition prizewinner, Italy 1992. *Leisure interests:* diving, skiing. *Address:* St Petersburg State Academic Mariinsky Opera Theatre, Teatralnaya pl.1, St Petersburg 130000, Russia (office).

SAVOY, Guy; French chef and restaurateur; *Proprietor, Restaurant Guy Savoy;* b. 24 July 1953, Nevers; m. Marie Danielle Amann 1975; one s. one d.; for three years Chef at La Barrière de Clichy, Paris; Propr Restaurant Guy Savoy, Paris 1980–, Restaurant Le Bistrot de l'Etoile Troyon 1989–, Restaurant Le Bistro de l'Etoile-

Niel 1989–, Restaurant Le Bistrot l'Etoile-Lauriston 1991, Restaurant La Butte Chaillot 1992, Les Bookinistes 1994, Le Cap Vernet, Paris 1995; Légion d'honneur. *Publications include:* Les Légumes gourmands 1985, La Gourmandise apprivoisée 1987, Vegetable Magic 1989, La Cuisine de mes bistrots 1998, 120 recettes comme à la maison 2000, Guy Savoy: Simple French Recipes for the Home Cook 2004. *Leisure interest:* modern painting. *Address:* Restaurant Guy Savoy, 18 rue Troyon, 75017 Paris (office); 101 boulevard Pereire, 75017 Paris, France (home). *Telephone:* 1-43-80-40-61 (office); 1-42-67-25-95 (Bistrot de l'Etoile). *Fax:* 1-46-22-43-09 (office). *Website:* www.guysavoy.com (office).

SAWA, Metropolitan Michał Hrycuniak, MA, ThD; Polish ecclesiastic; *Metropolitan of Warsaw and All Poland; Primate of the Polish Autocephalous Orthodox Church;* b. 15 April 1938, Śniatycze; ed Christian Acad. of Theology, Warsaw, Univ. of Belgrade; teacher Orthodox Seminary, Warsaw 1962–, Rector Int. Section 1964–65; Rector Orthodox Theological Seminary, Jabłeczna 1970–79; Assoc. Prof. and Prof. Christian Acad. of Theology, Warsaw 1966–, Prof. of Theological Sciences 1990–; ordained deacon 1964; ordained priest 1966; Dir Chancellery of Metropolitan of Warsaw and All Poland 1966–70; Superior Monastery of St Onufrey at Jabłeczna 1970–79; ordained Bishop 1979, Bishop of Łódź and Poznań 1979–81, of Białystok and Gdańsk 1981–99; Archbishop 1987; Metropolitan of Warsaw and All Poland, Primate of the Polish Autocephalous Orthodox Church 1998–; Orthodox Ordinary of the Polish Armed Forces 1994–98, rank of Brig.-Gen. 1996; f. quarterly publs of Diocese of Białystok and Gdańsk and of Orthodox Ordinate of Polish Armed Forces; Dean and Prof. of Chair of Orthodox Theology, Univ. in Białystok 1999–; Ed.-in-Chief Kalendarz Polskiego Autokefa-licznego Kościoła Prawosławnego, Elpis, Rocznik Teologiczny (annual), Cerkiewny Wiestnik (quarterly), Wiadomości Polskiego Autokefalicznego Kościoła Prawo-sławnego (monthly); Hon. Prof. of Theological Sciences; Dr hc (St Vladimir's Orthodox Seminary, New York) 2000, (Univ. in Białystok, Poland) 2001, (Univ. of Thessaloniki, Greece) 2002, (Theological Acad., Minsk, Belarus) 2003. *Publications include:* Prawosławne pojmowanie małżeństwa (The Orthodox Understanding of Marriage) 1994, Chrystus najwierniejszy przyjaciel człowieka (Christ the Only Beloved Friend) 2003, Slova (Speeches) 2004. *Address:* Al. Solidarności 52, 03-402 Warsaw, Poland (office). *Telephone:* (22) 6190886 (office). *Fax:* (22) 6190886 (office). *Website:* www.orthodox.pl (office).

SAWAD, Ahmed Ali, PhD; Maldivian politician; s. of Ali Hussein Sawad; worked as sub-ed. and reporter at Times of India and Indian Express while studying in Bangalore; was involved in family business Alysen as Dir of Legal Affairs; vice-presidential running mate of Qasim Ibrahim in presidential elections 2008; Minister of Tourism, Arts and Culture 2008–10 (resgnd); Gold Medal, Nat. Law School of India Univ. 2000. *Address:* c/o Ministry of Tourism, Arts and Culture, Ghazee Building, First Floor, Ameer Ahmed Magu, Malé 20-05, Maldives.

SAWCHUK, Arthur R., BSc; Canadian fmr business executive; m. Mary Sawchuk; one s. one d.; ed Univ. of Manitoba; joined DuPont Eng group, Kingston, Ont. 1958; transferred to Montreal, holding managerial positions in Fibres Marketing 1967; Div. Man. Home Furnishings, Toronto 1974; Man. Corp. Planning and Devt 1981; Div. Man. Packaging 1984; Vice-Pres. and Gen. Man. Fibres and Intermediate Chemicals 1985; Sr Vice-Pres. and mem. Corp. Policy Advisory Council 1988; Pres., CEO and Dir DuPont Canada Inc. 1992–97, Chair. 1995–97; Chair. Manulife Financial Corpn 1998–2008 (retd); mem. Bd of Dirs Manitoba Telecom Services Inc., Bowater Inc. Canadian Inst. for Advanced Research; fmr Dir Canadian Chemical Producers' Asscn, Avenor Inc., Mfrs Life Insurance Co., Ontario Hydro.

SAWERS, Sir John, KCMG, BSc; British diplomatist and crown servant; *Chief, Secret Intelligence Service (MI6);* b. 26 July 1955; m.; three c.; ed Univ. of Nottingham; Prin. Pvt. Sec. to Foreign Sec. 1992–95; Int. Fellow, Harvard Univ. 1995; served at Embassy in Washington, DC 1996–98; Foreign Affairs Adviser to Prime Minister 1999–2001; Amb. to Egypt 2001–03; Political Dir Foreign and Commonwealth Office 2003–07; Perm. Rep. to UN, New York 2007–09; Chief, Secret Intelligence Service (MI6) 2009–. *Address:* Secret Intelligence Service, PO Box 1300, London, SE1 1BD, England (office). *Website:* www.sis.gov.uk (office).

SAWIRIS, Naguib Onsi; Egyptian business executive and politician; b. 15 June 1954; s. of Onsi Sawiris; m.; four c.; ed German Evangelical School, Cairo, Swiss Inst. of Tech. (ETH), Zurich; joined Orascom 1979, Chair. and CEO Orascom Telecom Holding S.A.E. (after Orascom split into separate operating cos) 1997–2011; f. Weather Investments (now Wind Telecom SpA) 2005; Founder Free Egyptians Party 2011; Jt Chair. Italian-Egyptian Business Council 2006–07; Chair. Egyptian Co. for Mobile Services (MobiNil); Pres. German-Arab Chamber of Industry and Commerce 2008–09; mem. Bd of Dirs Arab Thought Foundation, Egyptian Council for Foreign Affairs, Consumer Rights Protection Asscn, Cancer Soc. of Egypt; mem. Int. Advisory Cttee New York Stock Exchange 2005–, Int. Advisory Bd, Nat. Bank of Kuwait; Trustee and Head of Financial Cttee, French Univ. in Cairo; Légion d'honneur; Sitara-e-Quaid-e-Azam Award 2006, CIC Globalist of the Year 2011. *Address:* c/o Orascom Telecom, 2005A Nile City Towers, South Tower, Cornish El Nile Ramlet Beaulac, Cairo 11221, Egypt. *Website:* www.fep.org.eg.

SAWIRIS, Nassef, BA; Egyptian business executive; *Chairman and CEO, Orascom Construction Industries;* b. 1961; s. of Onsi Sawiris; m.; four c.; ed Univ. of Chicago, USA; CEO Orascom Construction Industries 1998–, Chair. 2010–, mem. Bd of Dirs 1998–; Chair. Building Materials and Refractory Council, Fed. of Egyptian Industries; mem. Bd of Dirs Cairo Stock Exchange 2004–07, Alexandria Stock Exchanges 2004–07, Lafarge SA, Dubai International Financial Exchange, NNS Holding, Luxembourg, Besix, Belgium; mem. American Chamber of Commerce, German-Arab Chamber of Industry and Commerce, Business Secr. of Egyptian Nat. Democratic Party. *Address:* Orascom Construction Industries, Nile City Towers, Corniche El Nil, Cairo 11221, Egypt (office). *Telephone:* (2) 24611111 (office). *Website:* www.orascomci.com (office).

SAWIRIS, Onsi, BSc; Egyptian business executive; *Chairman Emeritus, Orascom Construction Industries;* b. 1930; m. Youssreya Loza Sawiris; three s.; ed Cairo Univ.; est. Orascom Construction Industries (fmrly Orascom Onsi Sawiris & Co.) 1976, currently Chair. Emer. and Dir (non-exec.); currently also Hon. Chair. and mem. Bd of Dirs MobiNil; fmr Chair. for AIG Insurance Co., Egypt, YMCA, Cairo, Egyptian-Scandinavian Business Asscn in Egypt; Advisor to Bd, Swiss

Foundation for Social Development; Commdr in the Order of the Crown (Belgium), L'Order de Leopold 1998–, Royal Order of the Polar Star (Sweden) 2008. *Address:* Orascom Construction Industries, Nile City Towers, Corniche El Nil, Cairo 11221, Egypt (office). *Telephone:* (2) 24611111 (office). *Website:* www.orascomci.com (office).

SAWIRIS, Samih; Egyptian/Montenegrin business executive; *Chairman, Orascom Development Holding;* b. 28 Jan. 1957, Cairo; s. of Onsi Sawiris; m.; one s. three d.; ed German School, Cairo, Technical Univ. of Berlin, Germany; f. Nat. Marine Boat Factory, Orascom Projects for Touristic Devt 1996, Orascom Hotel Holdings 1997, El Gouna Beverages Co. (sold in 2001) 1997; CEO Orascom Devt Holding –2011, now Chair.; mem. Bd of Dirs Beltone Financial, Guggenheim Museum, Jordan Projects for Tourism Devt Co.; Founder-mem. Sawiris Foundation for Social Devt 2001–. *Address:* Orascom Development Holding, Gotthardstrasse 12, 6460 Altdorf, Switzerland (office). *Telephone:* (41) 8741717 (office). *Fax:* (41) 8741707 (office). *Website:* www.orascomdh.com (office).

SAWYER, Amos, BA, MA, PhD; Liberian academic and political activist; *Chairman, Governance Commission of Liberia;* b. 1945; s. of Abel Sawyer and Sarah Sawyer; ed Univ. of Liberia, Northwestern Univ., USA; Chair. Constitution Drafting Comm. 1980s; fmrly installed as Leader of Interim Govt of Nat. Unity (by nat. conf. of Liberian leaders that included leaders of political parties, civil soc. orgs and of combined guerrilla forces which overthrew regime of fmr Pres. Samuel Doe 1990) Aug. 1990, inaugurated Nov. 1990; fmr Leader Liberian People's Party; fmr Dir Inst. of Research and Dean Coll. of Social Science and Humanities, Univ. of Liberia; Co-Dir and Research Scholar, Workshop in Political Theory and Policy Analysis, Indiana Univ. 2000–09; currently Chair. Governance Comm. of Liberia; mem. Panel of Eminent Persons, African Peer Review Mechanism. *Publications include:* The Emergence of Autocracy in Liberia: Tragedy and Challenge 1992, Beyond Plunder: Toward Democratic Governance in Liberia 2005. *Address:* Governance Commission, S.D. Cooper Road, Paynesville, Liberia (office). *E-mail:* acsawyer45@aol.com (office). *Website:* www.goodgovernanceliberia.org (office).

SAWYER, Diane, BA; American broadcast journalist; *Anchor, ABC World News with Diane Sawyer;* b. 22 Dec. 1945, Glasgow, Ky; d. of Erbon Powers 'Tom' Sawyer and Jean W. Sawyer (née Dunagan); m. Mike Nichols 1988; ed Seneca High School, Louisville, Ky, Wellesley Coll., Mass, Univ. of Louisville (one semester); toured country as America's Junior Miss to promote Coca-Cola Pavilion at 1964–65 New York World's Fair 1962–65; reporter, WLKY-TV, Louisville, Ky 1967–70; Admin. White House Press Office 1970–74; mem. Nixon-Ford transition team 1974–75; Asst to Richard Nixon (fmr US Pres.) 1974, 1975; Gen. Reporter, later State Dept Corresp., CBS News 1978–81, apptd Co-Anchor Morning News 1981, Co-Anchor Early Morning News 1982–84, Corresp. and Co-Ed. 60 Minutes 1984–89; Co-Anchor PrimeTime Live (now Primetime Thursday), ABC News 1989–99, Good Morning America 1999–2009, Anchor, ABC World News with Diane Sawyer 2009–; won America's Junior Miss scholarship pageant as rep. from State of Kentucky, nine Emmy awards, Nat. Headliner Awards, George Foster Peabody Award for Public Service, Robert F. Kennedy Journalism Award, Special Dupont Award, Ohio State Award, IRTS Lifetime Achievement Award, inducted TV Acad. of Fame 1997, named by the Ladies' Home Journal as one of the 30 most powerful women in America 2001, ranked by Forbes magazine amongst The World's 100 Most Powerful Women (26th) 2004, (55th) 2005, (60th) 2006, (62nd) 2007, (65th) 2008, (46th) 2010, (47th) 2011, (23rd) 2012, (73rd) 2013, Peabody Award for work on A Hidden America: Children of the Mountains 2009. *Address:* ABC World News with Diane Sawyer, ABC News, 47 West 66th Street, New York, NY 10023, USA (office). *Website:* abcnews.go.com/wn (office).

SAWYERS, Charles Lazelle, BA, MD; American physician, oncologist and academic; *Marie-Josée and Henry R. Kravis Chair in Human Oncology and Pathogenesis, Memorial Sloan-Kettering Cancer Center;* b. 1959, Nashville, Tenn.; m.; two c.; ed Princeton Univ., Johns Hopkins Medical School; Residency, Univ. of California, San Francisco; worked at Jonsson Cancer Center, UCLA for nearly 18 years; currently Marie-Josée and Henry R. Kravis Chair in Human Oncology and Pathogenesis, Memorial Sloan-Kettering Cancer Center, New York; a Howard Hughes Medical Inst. Investigator; Past Pres. American Soc. of Clinical Investigation; mem. Bd of Scientific Councilors, Nat. Cancer Inst.; mem. Inst. of Medicine, NAS; Fellow, UCLA; numerous honours and awards, including the Doris Duke Distinguished Clinical Scientist Award, Richard & Hinda Rosenthal Foundation Award, American Asscn of Cancer Research, David A. Karnofsky Award, American Soc. of Clinical Oncology, Dorothy P. Landon-AACR Prize for Translational Cancer Research, Lasker-DeBakey Award for Clinical Medical Research (co-recipient) 2009, Breakthrough Prize in Life Sciences (co-recipient) 2013. *Achievements include:* developed, with Brian J. Druker and Nicholas B. Lydon, imatinib (or Gleevac) and dasatinib – targeted treatments for chronic myeloid leukemia. *Publications:* numerous papers in professional journals. *Address:* Memorial Sloan-Kettering Cancer Center, 1275 York Avenue, New York, NY 10065, USA (office). *Telephone:* (646) 888-2594 (office); (646) 888-2163 (Lab.) *Fax:* (646) 888-2595 (office). *E-mail:* martinb@mskcc.org (office). *Website:* www.mskcc.org/research/lab/charles-sawyers (office).

SAYARI, Sheikh Hamad Sa'ud al-, MA; Saudi Arabian economist and fmr central banker; b. 1941; ed Univ. of Maryland, USA; taught econs at Inst. of Public Administration, Riyadh; Dir-Gen. Saudi Industrial Devt Fund 1979–80; Controller Gen. Saudi Arabian Monetary Agency (SAMA) 1979–80, Vice-Gov. 1980–83, Acting Gov. 1983–85, Gov. 1985–2009, also Chair. Bd of Dirs; mem. Supreme Econ. Council; mem. Bd of Dirs Public Investment Fund (Sec.-Gen. 1973–74), Gulf Investment Corpn; mem. Regional Advisory Group (Middle East), IMF. *Address:* c/o Saudi Arabian Monetary Agency, Al-Ma'ather Street, POB 2992, Riyadh 11169, Saudi Arabia.

SAYAVONG, Khammy; Laotian government official; b. 9 April 1944, Khai Village; m. Boun Ngiem; ed Inst. of Party, Moscow, Russia; Head of Propaganda and Training Div., Vientiane Prov. 1992–95; Vice-Chair. Propaganda and Training Cen. Cttee 1996–98; Vice-Chair. Cen. Control Cttee 1999–2000; Pres. People's Supreme Court 2001–11. *Address:* Sisavat Village, Chanthabouly District, Vientiane Municipality, Laos (home). *Telephone:* (21) 212355 (home).

SAYED, Ahmad Mohamed al-, LLB, MBA; Qatari lawyer and business executive; *Managing Director and CEO, Qatar Holding LLC;* b. 1976; ed Boston

Univ., New York Univ., USA; legal counsel, Qatar Holding LLC –2009, Man. Dir and CEO 2009–; Vice-Chair. Qatar Exchange 2009–; CEO Qatar Investment Authority (sovereign wealth fund) 2013–; mem. Int. Advisory Bd Russian Direct Investment Fund; Dir (non-exec.) Canary Wharf Group PLC 2009–; fmr Dir Qatar Oman Investment Co. *Address:* Qatar Holding LLC, Q-Tel Tower, Diplomatic Area Street, West Bay, POB 23224, Doha, Qatar (office). *E-mail:* qhinfo@qatarholding .qa (office). *Website:* www.qatarholding.qa (office).

SAYED, Karimat El, PhD; Egyptian academic and physicist; *Professor Emeritus of Solid State Physics, Ain Shams University;* m.; two s. one d.; ed Ain Shams Univ., Cairo, Univ. Coll. London; currently Prof. Emer. of Solid State Physics, Ain Shams Univ., Cairo; UNESCO-L'Oréal Award for Women in Science 2003. *Address:* Physics Department, Faculty of Science, Ain Shams University, Elkhalifa Elmaamoon Street, Abbassia, Cairo, Egypt (office). *Telephone:* (2) 282-2189 (office). *Fax:* (2) 284-2123 (office). *E-mail:* karima@frcu.eun.eg (office). *Website:* sci.shams.edu.eg (office).

SAYED, Mostafa Amr el-, BSc, PhD, FAAS; American chemical physicist and academic; *Julius Brown Chair and Regents Professor and Director, Laser Dynamics Laboratory, School of Chemistry and Biochemistry, Georgia Institute of Technology;* b. 8 May 1933, Zifta, Egypt; s. of Amr el-Sayed and Zakia Ahmed; m. Janice Jones 1957; two s. two d.; ed Ain Shams Univ., Cairo, Egypt, Florida State, Yale and Harvard Univs, Calif. Inst. of Tech.; Prof., Univ. of Calif., LA 1961–94; Ed.-in-Chief Journal of Physical Chem. 1980–2004; Julius Brown Prof. and Dir Laser Dynamics Lab., Ga Inst. of Tech. 1994–, Regents Prof. 2000–; Visiting Prof., American Univ. of Beirut 1968, Univ. of Paris 1976, 1991; Mem.-at-Large US Nat. Research Council Cttee for IUPAC 1987–91 (Chair. 1990–92); mem. American Acad. of Sciences 1980, Third World Acad. of Arts and Sciences 1984, NSF 2000; mem. NAS; Alexander von Humboldt Sr Fellow, Tech. Univ. of Munich 1982; Fellow American Acad. of Arts and Sciences 1986, AAAS, American Physical Soc. 2000; mem. Bd of Trustees Assoc. Univs Inc. 1988–91; mem. Advisory Bd NSF Chem. Div. 1990–93; mem. Dept of Energy Basic Energy Sciences Advisory Cttee; Hon. Fellow Indian and Chinese Chem. Socs; Dr hc (Hebrew Univ., American Univ. of Beirut, Alexandria Univ. Medical School, Ain Shams Univ., Mansoura Univ., Beni-Suef Univ.); Medal of the Egyptian Repub., First Class 2008; Fresenius Nat. Award in Pure and Applied Chem. 1967, Alexander von Humboldt Sr US Scientist Award, 1982, King Faisal Int. Prize in Sciences (Chem.) 1990, Harris Award, Univ. of Nebraska 1995, Nat. Medal of Science 2007, and many other honours and awards. *Publications:* over 630 articles in scientific and medical journals. *Leisure interest:* travelling. *Address:* Department of Chemistry and Biochemistry, Office 104-B (LDL), Georgia Institute of Technology, 901 Atlantic Drive, Atlanta, GA 30332 (office); 579 Westover Drive, Atlanta, GA 30305, USA (home). *Telephone:* (404) 894-0292 (office); (404) 352-0453 (home). *Fax:* (404) 894-7452 (office). *E-mail:* mostafa.el-sayed@chemistry.gatech.edu (office). *Website:* www.chemistry.gatech.edu/faculty/El-Sayed (office).

SAYEED, Hafiz Mohammad; Pakistani military leader; fmr Prof. of Eng., Univ. of Tech. and Eng, Lahore; Co-Founder and Leader, Lashkar-e-Taiba (banned militant group), Founder and Leader Jamaat-ud-Dawa; detained, then placed under house arrest 2002, released Nov. 2002. *Address:* Jamaat-ud-Dawa, Bdehai Rd, Peshawar, Pakistan. *Telephone:* (521) 2262189. *Fax:* (521) 2260800. *E-mail:* Jdawa@hotmail.com. *Website:* www.jamaatuddawa.org.

SAYEED, Mufti Mohammed; Indian politician; b. 12 Jan. 1936, Bijbehara; ed S.P. Coll., Aligarh Muslim Univ.; joined Nat. Conf. party 1950, left to join Congress Party, then left to join Janata Dal, rejoined Congress Party, left and f. Jammu and Kashmir People's Democratic Party 1999, fmr Chair., now Patron; fmr Minister of Home Affairs (India's first Muslim Home Minister); daughter kidnapped by Kashmiri militants 1989, released in exchange for militants; Chief Minister of Jammu and Kashmir 2002–05 (resgnd). *Address:* Jammu and Kashmir People's Democratic Party, A-2, Government Quarter, Gandhinagar, Jammu 180 004 India (office). *Website:* www.jkpdp.org (office).

SAYEF, Abdul Rasul; Afghan politician and academic; *Leader, Tanzim-i Dawat-i Islami (Organization for Invitation to Islam);* ed Kabul Univ., Al-Azhar Univ., Cairo, Egypt; fmr Prof. of Islamic Law, Shariat in Kabul –1973, tenure ended when he plotted with Burhanuddin Rabbani, Ahmed Shah Massoud and Gulbuddin Hekmatyar to overthrow Pres. Daoud Khan from Panjshir Valley; fmr mem. Akhwan-ul-Muslimeen (Muslim Brotherhood); fought against Soviet occupying forces Afghanistan during 1980s, chair. first rebel alliance 1980, one of the most important resistance leaders during Soviet invasion that ended in 1992; Leader Islamic Union for the Liberation of Afghanistan (Ittihad-i Islami Bara-yi Azadi— only anti-Taliban Pashtun leader to be part of Northern Alliance), now called Tanzim-i Dawat-i Islami (Organization for Invitation to Islam) 2005–; mem. constitutional Loya Jirga 2003–04; elected to Wolasi Jirga (House of People, Nat. Ass.); cand. in presidential election 2014. *Address:* Tanzim-i Dawat-i Islami (Organization for Invitation to Islam), Ansari Square, Road 1, District 4, Kabul; Wolasi Jirga, Darul Aman Road, Kabul, Afghanistan. *Telephone:* (70) 277007. *Website:* www.nationalassembly.af.

SAYEGH, Bishop Selim Wahban, PhD; Jordanian ecclesiastic; *Titular Bishop of Aquae in Proconsulari and Vicar General for Transjordan;* b. 15 Jan. 1935, Jordan; s. of Wahban Sayigh; ed Lateran Univ., Rome; Pres. of the Latin Patriarchal Court, Jerusalem 1967–79; Rector of the Latin Patriarchal Seminary 1976–81; apptd Auxiliary Bishop of Jerusalem 1981; Titular Bishop of Aquae in Proconsulari, Vicar Gen. for Transjordan 1982–; Commdr of the Equestrian Order of the Holy Sepulchre of Jerusalem. *Publications:* Le Statu Quo des Lieux-Saints 1971, The Christian Family's Guidebook. *Leisure interests:* chess, table tennis, volleyball, history, ecclesiastical law. *Address:* Latin Vicariate, PO Box 851379, Amman 11185, Jordan. *Telephone:* (6) 5929546. *Fax:* (6) 5920548.

SAYEH, Antoinette Monsio, PhD; Liberian economist, government official and international organization official; *Director, African Department, International Monetary Fund;* b. 12 July 1958, Monrovia; one s.; ed Swarthmore Coll., Fletcher School, Tufts Univ., USA; fmrly with Ministry of Planning, Ministry of Finance; worked for 17 years at World Bank, positions included Country Dir for Benin, Niger and Togo 2000–03 and working on public finance man. and civil service reform in Pakistan; Minister of Finance 2006–08; Dir African Dept, IMF 2008–; Lucretia Mott Award, Swarthmore Coll., Service to Country Award, Govt of Niger.

Address: International Monetary Fund, 700 19th Street, NW, Washington, DC 20431, USA (office). *Telephone:* (202) 623-6220 (office). *E-mail:* publicaffairs@imf .org (office). *Website:* www.imf.org (office).

SAYLES, John Thomas, BS; American writer, film director, actor and script-writer; b. 28 Sept. 1950, Schenectady, NY; s. of Donald John Sayles and Mary Sayles (née Rausch); pnr, Maggie Renzi; ed Williams Coll.; John D. MacArthur Award, Eugene V. Debs Award, John Steinbeck Award, John Cassavetes Award, Ian McLellan Hunter Award. *Films include:* Return of the Secaucus Seven (dir, screenwriter, actor, ed.) (Los Angeles Film Critics Award) 1980, Baby It's You (dir, screenwriter) 1983, Lianna (dir, screenwriter, actor, ed.) 1983, The Brother from Another Planet (dir, screenwriter, actor, ed.) 1984, Matewan (dir, screenwriter, actor) 1987, Eight Men Out (dir, screenwriter, actor) 1989, Bruce Springsteen: Video Anthology 1978–1988 (dir videos Born in the USA, Glory Days, I'm on Fire), City of Hope (dir, screenwriter, actor, ed.) 1991, Passion Fish (dir, screenwriter, actor, ed.), The Secret of Roan Inish (dir, screenwriter, ed.) 1994, Lone Star (dir, screenwriter, ed.) 1996, Men With Guns (dir, screenwriter, ed.) 1997, Limbo (dir, screenwriter, ed.) 1999, Sunshine State (dir, screenwriter, ed.) 2002, Casa de los babys (dir, screenwriter, ed.) 2003, Silver City (dir, screenwriter, ed.) 2004, Honeydripper (dir, screenwriter, actor, ed.) (Jury Prize for Best Screenplay, San Sebastian Film Festival 2007, NAACP Image Award for Outstanding Ind. or Foreign Film 2008) 2007; writer: Piranha 1978, The Lady in Red 1979, Battle Beyond the Stars 1980, The Howling 1981, Alligator 1981, The Challenge 1982, Enormous Changes at the Last Minute 1983, The Clan of the Cave Bear 1986, Something Wild 1986, Wild Thing 1987, Breaking In 1989, Men of War 1994, The Spiderwick Chronicles 2008; actor: Malcolm X 1992, Straight Talk 1992, Matinee 1993, My Life's in Turnaround 1993, Gridlock'd 1997, Girlfight (also producer) 2000. *Television:* writer: A Perfect Match 1980, Unnatural Causes 1986, Shannon's Deal (also dir) 1989, Piranha 1995. *Publications:* Pride of the Bimbos 1975, Union Dues 1979, Thinking in Pictures 1987, I-80 Nebraska, M.490-M.205 (O. Henry Award) 1975, Breed, Golden State (O. Henry Award) 1977, Hoop, The Anarchists' Convention 1979, New Hope for the Dead (play) 1981, Turnbuckle (play), Los Gusanos 1991, Dillinger in Hollywood 2004. *Address:* c/o Lucy Stille, Paradigm, 360 N Crescent Drive, North Building, Los Angeles, CA 90210, USA (office). *Website:* www.johnsayles.com.

SBEIH, Nouria (see SUBEEH, Nouriya Subeeh Barrak as-).

SCACCHI, Greta; Italian/Australian actress; b. 18 Feb. 1960, Milan, Italy; d. of Luca Scacchi Gracco and Pamela Carsaniga; m. 1st Vincent D'Onofrio 1991 (divorced 1993); one d.; one s. by Carlo Mantegazza; ed Bristol Old Victoria Drama School. *Films:* Das Zweite Gesicht, Heat and Dust, Defence of the Realm, The Coca-Cola Kid, A Man in Love, Good Morning Babylon, White Mischief, Paura e Amore (Three Sisters), La Donna della Luna, Presumed Innocent, Shattered, Fires Within, Turtle Beach, The Player, Salt on Our Skin, The Browning Version, Jefferson in Paris 1994, Country Life 1995, Emma 1996, The Serpent's Kiss 1997, The Red Violin 1998, Ladies Room 1999, The Manor 1999, Tom's Midnight Garden 2000, Looking for Alibrandi 2000, One of the Hollywood Ten 2000, Cotton Mary 2000, Festival in Cannes 2002, Baltic Storm 2003, Sotto falso nome 2004, Beyond the Sea 2004, Flightplan 2005, The Book of Revelation 2006, The Handyman 2006, Icicle Melt 2006, L'Amour caché 2007, Hidden Love 2007, Brideshead Revisited 2008, Shoot on Sight 2008, Miss Austen Regrets 2008, Ways to Live Forever 2010, Un altro mondo 2010. *Television:* The Ebony Tower, Dr Fischer of Geneva, Waterfront (Australia), Rasputin (Emmy Award 1996), The Odyssey (series) 1996, Macbeth 1998, The Farm (Australia) 2000, Daniel Deronda, Jeffrey Archer – The Truth 2002, Maigret: Lombra cinese 2004, Marple: By the Pricking of My Thumbs 2006, Broken Trail 2006, Nightmares and Dreamscapes: From the Stories of Stephen King (miniseries) 2006, The Trojan Horse (miniseries) 2008, Hindenburg (film) 2011, Agatha Christie: Poirot (series) 2013. *Theatre:* Cider with Rosie, In Times Like These, Airbase, Uncle Vanya 1988, A Doll's House, Miss Julie, Simpatico, A Midsummer Night's Dream, Easy Virtue, The Guardsman 2000, Old Times 2000, The True-Life Fiction of Mata Hari 2002, The Deep Blue Sea 2008. *Address:* c/o Nicola van Gelder, Conway van Gelder, Third Floor, 8/12 Broadwick Street, London, W1F 8HW, England (office). *Telephone:* (20) 7287-0077 (office). *E-mail:* info@conwayvg.co.uk (office). *Website:* www.conwayvangeldergrant.com (office).

SCACE, Arthur Richard Andrew, CM, QC, MA, LLB; Canadian lawyer, banking industry executive and company director; b. 22 July 1938, Toronto, Ont.; m. Susan Margaret Kernohan; one s. one d.; ed Univ. of Toronto, Univ. of Oxford, UK, Harvard Univ., Osgoode Hall; called to the Bar, Ont. 1967; began career at McCarthy Tétrault (law firm) 1967, became Partner 1972, Man. Partner, Toronto 1989–96, Nat. Chair. 1997–99, currently Counsel; mem. Bd of Dirs Scotiabank (Nat. Bank of Nova Scotia) 1997–2009, Chair. 2004–09; Dir The Canada Life Assurance Co., Canada Life Financial Corpn 2000–04; fmr Chair. Canadian Opera Co.; fmr Treas. Law Soc. of Upper Canada; mem. Bd of Dirs Garbell Holdings Ltd, Gardiner Group Capital Ltd, Gerdau Ameristeel Corpn, Lallemand Inc., N.M. Davis Corpn Ltd, Sceptre Investment Counsel Ltd, WestJet Airlines Inc.; fmr mem. Bd of Dirs The Canada Life Assurance Co., Canada Life Financial Corpn, Brompton Equity Split Corpn, Brompton Split Banc Corpn; Sec., Rhodes Scholarships in Canada; Hon. DIur (Law Soc. of Upper Canada, York Univ.); Robinette Medal, Osgoode Hall Law School 2003. *Publication:* The Income Tax Law of Canada (co-author). *Address:* The Henry White Kinnear Foundation, Suite 3910, PO Box 142, 66 Wellington Street West, Toronto, ON M5K 1H1, Canada (office). *Telephone:* (416) 361-3117 (office). *Fax:* (416) 944-5718 (office). *E-mail:* ascace@ mccarthy.ca (office).

SCAGLIA, Silvio; Italian telecommunications industry executive; *Founder and Chairman, Babelgum;* b. 1958, Lucerne, Switzerland; m.; three c.; ed Polytechnic Univ. of Turin; began career at Aeritalia Spazio, then worked for Arthur Andersen Management Consulting; later Consultant with McKinsey & Co. and Bain & Co.; apptd Gen. Man. Motovespa 1991, then Sr Vice-Pres.; fmr CEO Omnitel (now Vodafone Italy); f. Fastweb (fibre-to-the-home (FTTH) broadband co.) 1999, CEO 1999–2003, Chair. 2003–07; Founder and Chair. Babelgum (on-demand TV over the internet service) 2007–; arrested over money laundering and tax fraud scam 2010, currently on trial. *Address:* Babelgum, 24-26, City Quay, Dublin 2, Ireland (office). *E-mail:* info@babelgum.com (office). *Website:* www.babelgum.com (office).

SCAIFE, Brendan Kevin Patrick, PhD, DSc (Eng), MRIA, CEng, FIET, CPhys, FInstP; Irish electrical engineer and academic; b. 19 May 1928, London, England; s. of James Scaife and Mary Kavanagh; m. Mary Manahan 1961; three s. one d.; ed Cardinal Vaughan Memorial School, London, Chelsea Polytechnic and Queen Mary Coll. London; GEC Research Labs, Wembley 1953–54; Scholar, School of Theoretical Physics, Dublin Inst. for Advanced Studies 1954–55; Inst. for Industrial Research and Standards, Dublin 1955–56; Electricity Supply Bd Dublin 1956; Coll. of Tech., Dublin 1956–61; Lecturer in Electronic Eng, Trinity Coll. Dublin 1961–66, Fellow 1964, Reader 1966, Assoc. Prof. 1967–72, Prof. of Eng Science 1972–86, Prof. of Electromagnetics 1986–88, Sr Fellow 1987–88, Fellow Emer. 1988–; Visiting Prof., Univ. of Salford 1969–82; Fellow, Inst. of Engineers of Ireland, Inst. of Eng and Tech.; Boyle Medal, Royal Dublin Soc. 1992. *Publications:* Complex Permittivity (compiler) 1971, Studies in Numerical Analysis (ed.) 1974, Principles of Dielectrics (revised edn) 1998, The Mathematical Papers of Sir William Rowan Hamilton Vol. IV (ed.) 2000. *Address:* Department of Electronic and Electrical Engineering, Trinity College, Dublin 2 (office); 6 Trimleston Avenue, Booterstown, Blackrock, Co. Dublin, Ireland (home). *Telephone:* (1) 8961580 (office); (1) 2693867 (home). *Fax:* (1) 6772442 (office). *E-mail:* bscaife@ eircom.net (home).

SCAJOLA, Claudio; Italian lawyer and politician; b. 15 Jan. 1948, Imperia, Liguria; m.; two c.; mem. staff Inpdap; Chair. Unità Sanitaria Locale of Imperia 1980–83; Mayor of Imperia 1990–95; mem. Camera dei Deputati (Forza Italia) for Liguria 1996–; Minister of the Interior 2001–02, for Implementation of Govt Programs 2003–04, of Productive Activities 2005–06, of Econ. Devt 2008–10 (resgnd); Pres. Parl. Cttee for the Information and Security Services and for the Secrets of the State 2007–08; Chair. ANCI Liguria, Rivera Trasporti. *Publication includes:* Ai Confini d'Italia: Storia e Immagini del Ponente Ligure.

SCALES, Prunella Margaret Rumney, CBE; British actress; b. (P. M. R. Illingworth), 22 June 1932, Sutton Abinger, Surrey, England; d. of John Richardson Illingworth and Catherine Scales; m. Timothy West (q.v.) 1963; two s.; ed Moira House, Eastbourne, Old Vic Theatre School, London, Herbert Berghof Studio, New York; in repertory, Huddersfield, Salisbury, Oxford, Bristol Old Vic etc.; seasons at Stratford and Chichester 1967–68; numerous radio broadcasts, readings, poetry recitals, fringe productions; has directed plays at numerous theatres including Bristol Old Vic, Arts Theatre, Cambridge, Nottingham Playhouse, W Yorkshire Playhouse (Getting On); Pres. Council for the Protection of Rural England 1997–2002; Amb. Howard League for Penal Reform 2007–; Freeman of the City of London 1990; Hon. DLitt (Bradford) 1995, (East Anglia) 1996. *Plays include:* The Promise 1967, Hay Fever 1968, The Wolf 1975, Make and Break 1980, An Evening with Queen Victoria 1980, The Merchant of Venice 1981, Quartermaine's Terms 1981, When We Are Married 1986, Single Spies (double bill) 1988, School for Scandal, Long Day's Journey into Night (Nat. Theatre), Happy Days 1993, Staying On 1996, Some Singing Blood (Royal Court), The Mother Tongue, The Editing Process 1994, The Birthday Party 1999, The Cherry Orchard 2000, The External 2001, Too Far to Walk (King's Head) 2002, A Woman of No Importance 2004, Gertrude's Secret, New End Theatre 2007. *Films include:* Laxdale Hall 1953, Waltz of the Toreadors 1962, What Every Woman Wants 1954, Hobson's Choice 1954, The Crowded Day 1954, The Hound of the Baskervilles 1978, The Boys from Brazil 1978, The Wicked Lady 1983, The Lonely Passion of Judith Hearne 1987, Consuming Passions 1988, A Chorus of Disapproval 1988, Howards End 1992, Freddie as F.R.O.7 (voice) 1992, Sherwood's Travels 1994, Second Best 1994, Wolf 1994, An Awfully Big Adventure 1994, Phoenix 1997, An Ideal Husband 1998, Stiff Upper Lips 1998, Mad Cows 1999, The Ghost of Greville Lodge 2000, Brand Spanking (short) 2004, Helix (short) 2006, Think. What Does it Take to Change a Habit?. (short) 2007, Horrid Henry: The Movie 2011. *Radio includes:* After Henry 1985–89, Smelling of Roses 2000, Ladies of Letters 2001, 2004, 2010, Rumpole 2007. *Television includes:* Pride and Prejudice (mini-series) 1952, What Every Woman Wants 1954, The Crowded Day 1954, French for Love 1955, Room at the Top (uncredited) 1959, The New Man 1960, The Secret Garden (series) 1960, The Seven Faces of Jim – The Face of Genius 1961, Coronation Street 1961, Marriage Lines (series) 1961–66, On the Margin (series) 1966, Blues in the Morning 1971, Seven of One – One Man's Meat 1973, Comedy Playhouse – The Big Job 1974, Decisions, Decisions 1975, The Apple Cart 1975, Fawlty Towers (series) 1975, 1979, Escape from the Dark 1976, Mr Big (series) 1977, Pickersgill People (series) 1978, Target 1978, Doris and Doreen 1978, Bergerac 1981, Grand Duo 1982, S.W.A.L.K. (series) 1982, Never the Twain 1982, Outside Edge 1982, The Merry Wives of Windsor 1982, Wagner (mini-series) 1983, Mapp and Lucia (series) 1985–86, Absurd Person Singular 1985, Unnatural Causes 1986, What the Butler Saw 1987, When We Are Married 1987, After Henry (series) 1988–92, Beyond the Pale 1989, A Question of Attribution 1991, My Friend Walter 1992, The Rector's Wife (series) 1994, Fair Game 1994, Look at the State We're In! (mini-series) 1995, Signs and Wonders 1995, Searching (series) 1995, Lord of Misrule 1996, Emma 1996, Dalziel & Pascoe 1996, Breaking the Code 1996, The Tale of Mrs Tiggy-Winkle and Mr Jeremy Fish (voice) 1998, Midsomer Murders – Beyond the Grave 2000, Silent Witness – Faith 2001, Station Jim 2001, Dickens (series) 2002, Looking for Victoria (film) 2003, Essential Poems for Christmas 2004, Casualty (series) 2004, Where the Heart Is (series) 2005, Mr. Loveday's Little Outing (film) 2006, The Shell Seekers 2006, Marple: A Pocket Full of Rye (film) 2008, The Royal (series) 2008. *Publication:* So You Want To Be An Actor?. *Leisure interests:* gardening, crosswords, canal boat. *Address:* c/o Jeremy Conway, 18–21 Jermyn Street, London, SW1Y 6HP, England (office). *Telephone:* (20) 7287-0077 (office). *Fax:* (20) 7287-1940 (office). *E-mail:* vena@conwayvg.co.uk (office). *Website:* www .conwayvg.co.uk (office).

SCALFARI, Eugenio, DIur; Italian editor and journalist; b. 6 April 1924, Civitavecchia; m. Simonetta de Benedetti 1959; two d.; Dir L'Europeo (news magazine) 1945–54, Ed.-in-Chief –1963; Promoter, Partito Radicale 1958, L'Espresso 1955–, Ed.-in-Chief 1963–68, Man. Dir 1970–75; Promoter, La Repubblica 1976–, Ed.-in-Chief 1976–96, Dir 1988–; Deputy to Parl. 1968–72; currently columnist, La Repubblica and L'Espresso; Siena Award 1985, Journalist of the Year Award 1986, Premio Ischia alla Carriera 1996, Premio St Vincent alla Carriera. *Publications include:* Incontro con Io 1994, Alla ricerca della morale perduta 1995, Il Labirinto 1998, La ruga sulla fronte 2001, La Ruga Sulla Fronte 2001, Le Prince inconstant (co-author) 2003, L'uomo che non credeva in Dio 2008, La Sera Andavamo in Via Veneto 2009, Per l'alto mare aperto 2010, Scuote l'anima mia Eros 2011, Rapporto sul Neocapitalismo Italiano, Il Potere Economico in URSS, L'Autunno della Repubblica, Razza Padrona, Interviste ai Potenti, L'Anno di Craxi. *Address:* c/o La Repubblica, Via Cristoforo Colombo 90, 00147 Rome, Italy. *Telephone:* (06) 49821.

SCALIA, Antonin, AB, LLB; American lawyer and judge; *Associate Justice, Supreme Court;* b. 11 March 1936, Trenton, NJ; s. of Salvatore Eugene Scalia and Catherine L. Scalia (née Panaro); m. Maureen McCarthy 1960; five s. four d.; ed Georgetown Univ., Univ. of Fribourg, Switzerland and Harvard Univ. Law School; called to Bar, Ohio 1962, Virginia 1970; Assoc., Jones, Day, Cockley & Reavis, Cleveland 1961–67; Assoc. Prof., Univ. of Va Law School 1967–70, Prof. 1970–74; Gen. Counsel, Office of Telecommunications Policy, Exec. Office of President 1971–72; Chair. Admin. Conf. US, Washington 1972–74; Asst Attorney Gen., Office of Legal Counsel, US Justice Dept 1974–77; Prof., Univ. of Chicago Law School 1977–82; Visiting Prof., Georgetown Law Center 1977, Stanford Law School 1980–81; Judge, US Court of Appeals (DC Circuit) 1982–86; Assoc. Justice, US Supreme Court 1986–; Hon. Master of the Bench, Inner Temple, London 1986. *Publication:* A Matter of Interpretation 1998, Making Your Case: The Art of Persuading Judges (with Bryan A. Garner) 2008. *Address:* United States Supreme Court, One First Street, NE, Washington, DC 20543, USA (office). *Telephone:* (202) 479-3211 (home). *Website:* www.supremecourtus.gov (office).

SCANLAN, John Oliver, MEng, PhD, DSc, MRIA, FIEE, FIEEE; Irish electronic engineer and professor of electronic engineering; *Professor Emeritus of Electronic Engineering, University College Dublin;* b. 20 Sept. 1937, Dublin; s. of John Scanlan and Hannah Scanlan; m. Ann Weadock 1961; ed St Mary's Coll., Dundalk, Univ. Coll. Dublin; Research Engineer, Mullard Research Laboratories, Surrey, UK 1959–63; Lecturer, Univ. of Leeds, UK 1963–68, Prof. of Electronic Eng 1968–73; Prof. of Electronic Eng, Univ. Coll. Dublin 1973–2002, Prof. Emer. 2002–; Sec. Royal Irish Acad. 1981–89, Pres. 1993–96; Dir Bord Telecom Eireann 1984–97; f. International Journal of Circuit Theory and Applications 1973, Ed. 1973–2006, currently Hon. Ed.; Golden Jubilee Medal, IEEE Circuits and Systems Soc. 1999, Royal Irish Acad. Gold Medal in Engineering Sciences 2011. *Publications:* Analysis and Synthesis of Tunnel Diode Circuits 1966, Circuit Theory (Vols 1 and 2) 1970. *Leisure interests:* music, golf. *Address:* School of Electrical, Electronic and Communications Engineering, Engineering and Materials Science Centre, University College Dublin, Belfield, Dublin 4, Ireland (office). *Telephone:* (1) 7161884 (office); (1) 7161787 (office). *Website:* www.ucd.ie/eacollege/eece (office).

SCARAMUZZI, Franco; Italian agricultural scientist; *President, Accademia dei Georgofili;* b. 26 Dec. 1926, Ferrara; s. of Donato Scaramuzzi and Alberta Rovida; m. Maria Bianca Cancellieri 1955; one s. one d.; Prof. of Pomology, Univ. of Pisa 1959, Univ. of Florence 1969, now Prof. Emer.; Rector Magnificus, Univ. of Florence 1979–91; Pres. Int. Soc. of Horticultural Science 1986–90, Accad. dei Georgofili 1986–, Società di San Giovanni Battista 2001–05; mem. Soviet (now Russian) Acad. of Agricultural Sciences 1982–; Hon. Pres. Italian Horticultural Soc. 1976–, Italian Acad. of Vine and Wine; Hon. mem. Rotary International; Cavaliere di Gran Croce 1998; Dr hc (Bucharest); Gold Medal of the Minister of Educ. 1983, Gold Medal, Univ. of Florence. *Publication:* Fruit Pomology. *Address:* Accademia dei Georgofili, Logge Uffizi Corti, 50122 Florence (office); Viale Amendola 38, 50121 Florence, Italy (home). *Telephone:* (55) 213360 (office); (55) 2342825 (home). *Fax:* (55) 2302754 (office). *E-mail:* accademia@georgofili.it (office). *Website:* www.georgofili.it (office).

SCARDINO, Dame Marjorie Morris, DBE, BA, JD, FRSA; American/British journalist, lawyer and business executive; b. 25 Jan. 1947, Flagstaff, Ariz.; d. of Robert Weldon Morris and Beth Lamb Morris; m. Albert James Scardino 1974; two s. one d.; ed Baylor Univ., Univ. of San Francisco; started career as reporter, Associated Press; Partner, Brannen, Wessels & Searcy law firm, Savannah, Ga 1975–85; Co-founder (with husband) and Publr The Georgia Gazette Co. (won Pulitzer Prize) 1978–85; Pres. The Economist Newspaper Group Inc., New York 1985–93, Chief Exec. The Economist Group, London 1993–97, mem. Bd of Dirs and CEO Pearson PLC 1997–2012; Dir (non-exec.) Nokia Corpn 2001–, Vice-Chair. 2007–, Chair. Corp. Governance and Nomination Cttee, mem. Personnel Cttee; mem. Bd of Dirs Twitter 2013–; mem. Bd of Trustees The MacArthur Foundation, Carter Center, Victoria & Albert Museum; Hon. Fellow, London Business School, City and Guilds of London Inst., RSA; Hon. LLD (Univ. of Exeter); Hon. DHumLitt (New School Univ.); Dr hc (Heriot-Watt Univ., Brunel Univ.); Veuve Clicquot Businesswoman of the Year Award 1998, Benjamin Franklin Medal, RSA 2001, ranked by Fortune magazine amongst the 50 Most Powerful Women in Business outside the US (first) 2001–03, (third) 2004–05, (fifth) 2006, (third) 2007, (fifth) 2008, (third) 2009–11, (tenth) 2012, ranked by Forbes magazine amongst The World's 100 Most Powerful Women (59th) 2004, (18th) 2005, (31st) 2006, (17th) 2007, (20th) 2008, (19th) 2009, (63rd) 2010, (94th) 2011, (86th) 2012. *Leisure interests:* horse riding, playing golf, watching Manchester United football team. *Address:* c/o Pearson PLC, 80 Strand, London, WC2R 0RL, England.

SCARF, Herbert Eli, AB, MA, PhD; American economist and professor of economics; *Sterling Professor Emeritus of Economics, Yale University;* b. 25 July 1930, Philadelphia, Pa; s. of Louis H. Scarf and Lena Elkman; m. Maggie Scarf 1953; three d.; ed Temple Univ., Princeton Univ.; worked at RAND Corpn, Santa Monica, Calif. 1954–57; Asst and Assoc. Prof., Dept of Statistics, Stanford Univ., Calif. 1957–63; Fellow, Centre for Advanced Study in the Behavioral Sciences, Stanford, Calif. 1962–63; Prof. of Econs, Yale Univ. 1963–70, Stanley Resor Prof. of Econs 1970–78, apptd Sterling Prof. of Econs 1979, currently Sterling Prof. Emer. of Econs; Dir Cowles Foundation for Research in Econs 1967–71, 1981–84, Dir Div. of Social Sciences 1971–72, 1973–74; Visiting Prof., Stanford Univ., Calif. 1977–78, Mathematical Sciences Research Inst. Spring 1986; Ford Foundation Sr Faculty Fellowship 1969–70; Fellow, Econometric Soc., Pres. 1983; Fellow, American Acad. of Arts and Sciences; mem. NAS 1979–, American Philosophical Soc.; Distinguished Fellow, American Econ. Asscn 1991, INFORMS 2002; Hon. LHD (Chicago) 1978; Lanchester Prize, (Operations Research Soc. of America) 1974, Von Neumann Medal 1983. *Publications include:* Studies in the Mathematical Theory of Inventory and Production (with K. Arrow and S. Karlin) 1958, The Optimality of (S, s) Policies in the Dynamic Inventory Problem 1960, The Computation of Economic Equilibria (with Terje Hansen) 1973, Applied General Equilibrium Analysis (ed with John Shoven) 1984; articles in learned journals. *Leisure interests:* music, reading, hiking. *Address:* Cowles Foundation, Yale University,

PO Box 208281, New Haven, CT 06520-8281 (office); 88 Blake Road, Hamden, CT 06517, USA (home). *Telephone:* (203) 432-3693 (office); (203) 776-9197 (home). *Fax:* (203) 432-6167 (office). *E-mail:* herbert.scarf@yale.edu (office). *Website:* cowles .econ.yale.edu/faculty/scarf.htm (office); cowles.econ.yale.edu/~hes/index.htm (office).

SCARFE, Gerald A., CBE; British cartoonist; b. 1 June 1936, London; m. Jane Asher; two s. one d.; joined Daily Mail as political cartoonist 1966; political cartoonist London Sunday Times 1967–; contributed cartoons to Punch 1960–, Private Eye 1961–, Time 1967–; animation and film directing BBC 1969–; designer and dir of animation for Pink Floyd The Wall concerts and film 1975–78; consultant designer and character design for film Hercules 1997; Hon. Fellow, London Inst. 2001; Hon. LLD (Liverpool) 2001, (Dundee) 2007; Zagreb Prize for BBC film Long Drawn Out Trip 1973, BAFTA Award for Scarfe on Scarfe 1987, Olivier Award for Absolute Turkey 1993, Cartoonist of the Year, British Press Awards 2006. *Television includes:* dir and presenter Scarfe on Art 1991, Scarfe on Sex 1991, Scarfe on Class 1992, Scarfe in Paradise 1992; subject of Scarfe and His Work with Disney (South Bank Special). *Theatre design:* Ubu Roi (Traverse Theatre) 1957, What the Butler Saw (Oxford Playhouse) 1980, No End of Blame (Royal Court, London) 1981, Orpheus in the Underworld (English ENO, Coliseum) 1985, Who's a Lucky Boy (Royal Exchange, Manchester) 1985, Born Again 1990, The Magic Flute (Los Angeles Opera) 1992, An Absolute Turkey 1993, Mind Millie for Me (Haymarket, London) 1996, Fantastic Mr. Fox (Los Angeles Opera) 1998, Peter and the Wolf (Holiday on Ice, Paris and world tour) 2000, The Nutcracker 2002. *Publications include:* Gerald Scarfe's People 1966, Indecent Exposure 1973, Expletive Deleted: The Life and Times of Richard Nixon 1974, Gerald Scarfe 1982, Father Kissmass and Mother Claus 1985, Scarfe by Scarfe (autobiog.) 1986, Gerald Scarfe's Seven Deadly Sins 1987, Line of Attack 1988, Scarfeland 1989, Scarfe on Stage 1992, Scarfe Face 1993, Hades: The Truth at Last 1997, Heroes & Villains 2003, Drawing Blood: Forty-five Years of Scarfe Uncensored 2005, Monsters: How George Bush Saved The World & Other Tall Stories 2008, The Making of Pink Floyd's The Wall 2010. *Leisure interests:* drawing, painting, sculpting. *Address:* 24 Cale Street, London, SW3 3QU (office); c/o Simpson Fox Associates, Shaftesbury Mansions, 52 Shaftsbury Avenue, London, W1D 6LP, England (office). *Website:* www.geraldscarfe.com (office).

SCARGILL, Arthur; British trade union official and fmr coal miner; *General-Secretary, Socialist Labour Party;* b. 11 Jan. 1938, Worsborough, Yorks.; s. of Harold Scargill and Alice Scargill; m. Anne Harper 1961; one d.; ed White Cross Secondary School; worked first in a factory, then Woolley Colliery 1955; mem. Barnsley Young Communist League 1955–62; mem. Nat. Union of Mineworkers (NUM) 1955–, NUM Br. Cttee 1960, Br. del. to NUM Yorks. Area Council 1964, mem. NUM Nat. Exec. 1972–, Pres. Yorks. NUM 1973–82, Pres. NUM 1981–2002, Hon. Pres. and Consultant 2002–, involved in litigation over membership of NUM 2010–; Chair. NUM Int. Cttee; Pres. Int. Miners Org. 1985–; mem. Labour Party 1966–95; mem. TUC Gen. Council 1986–88; f. Socialist Labour Party 1996, Gen.-Sec. 1996–; contested Newport East 1997, Hartlepool 2001. *Address:* Socialist Labour Party, PO Box 706, Barnsley, S70 9LE, England (office). *Telephone:* (1226) 212951 (office). *E-mail:* slpscot@btinternet.com (office); info@socialist-labour-party .org.uk (office). *Website:* www.socialist-labour-party.org.uk (office).

SCARLETT, Sir John McLeod, Kt, KCMG, OBE, MA; British crown servant; b. 18 Aug. 1948, London; s. of James Henri Stuart Scarlett and of Clara Dunlop Scarlett (née Morton); m. Gwenda Mary Rachel Stilliard 1970; one s. three d. (and one s. deceased); ed Epsom Coll., Magdalen Coll., Oxford; with Secret Intelligence Service 1971–2001, FCO London 1971–73, 1977–84, 1988–91, 1994–2001 (Dir of Security and Public Affairs 1999–2001), Third Sec., Nairobi 1973–74; language student 1974–75; Second, later First Sec., Moscow 1976–77; First Sec., Paris 1984–88, Political Counsellor, Moscow 1991–94; Chair. Jt Intelligence Cttee and Intelligence and Security Dir, Cabinet Office 2001–04; Chief, Secret Intelligence Service (MI6) 2004–09; Strategic Adviser, Statoil ASA 2011–. *Leisure interests:* history, family. *Address:* c/o Statoil ASA, Forusbeen 50, Stavanger 4035, Norway (office). *Website:* www.statoil.com (office).

SCARONI, Paolo, MBA; Italian business executive; *CEO, Eni SpA;* b. 28 Nov. 1946, Vicenza; m.; three c.; ed Univ. of Bocconi, Milan, Columbia Univ., New York, USA; staff mem. Chevron 1969–71; consultant, McKinsey & Co. 1972–73; joined Saint Gobain Group 1973, various exec. positions including Financial Man. St German Italia, Gen. Man. Balzaretti & Modigliani SpA, Chair. Borma SpA and Air Industrie SpA –1978; Gen. Del. St Gobain Venezuela, Colombia, Ecuador and Peru, Caracas 1978–81; Gen. Del. St Gobain Italia 1981–84; Chair. St Gobain Flat Glass Div., Paris 1984; Chair. and Man. Dir St Gobain Vitrage SA; CEO St Gobain Group –2002; Chair. Fabbrica Pisana SpA, Vegla GmbH, Cristaleria Espanola SA, Saint Roch SA; Vice-Chair. and Man. Dir Techint 1985; Vice-Chair. Falck SpA 1986–88; Man. Dir SIV SpA 1993–95; Group CEO Pilkington PLC 1996–2002; CEO and COO Enel SpA 2002–05; CEO Eni SpA 2005–; Chair. Alliance Unichem (UK) 2005–06; Vice-Chair. Sadi SpA; Dir (non-exec.) Assicurazioni Generali, Veolia Environnement; Deputy Chair. (non-exec.) London Stock Exchange Group; mem. Bd of Overseers of Columbia Business School and Fondazione Teatro alla Scala; Cavaliere del Lavoro della Repubblica Italiana 2004; Officier, Légion d'honneur 2007, Commdr 2013. *Publication:* Professione manager 1985. *Leisure interests:* reading, skiing, golf, football. *Address:* Eni SpA, Piazzale Enrico Mattei 1, 00144 Rome, Italy (office). *Telephone:* (06) 59821 (office). *Fax:* (06) 59822141 (office). *E-mail:* segreteriasocietaria.azionisti@eni.it (office); ufficio.stampa@eni.it (office). *Website:* www.eni.com (office).

SCAZZIERI, Roberto, MLitt, DPhil, DrScPol; Italian economist and academic; *Professor of Economics, University of Bologna;* b. 1 May 1950, Bologna; s. of Guerrino Scazzieri and Fosca Lambertini; m. Maria Cristina Bacchi 1983; one s.; ed Liceo Minghetti, Bologna, Univ. of Bologna, Univ. of Oxford, UK; Asst Lecturer, Univ. of Bologna 1974–79, Lecturer in Theory and Policy of Econ. Growth 1980–83, in Econ. Principles 1983–86, in Advanced Econ. Analysis 1985–87, Assoc. Prof. of Econs, Faculty of Political Sciences 1986–87, Full Prof. of Econs, Faculty of Econs and Commerce and Dept of Econs 1990–, mem. Teaching Bd, PhD Programme in Science, Tech. and Humanities 2007–10, PhD Programme in Science, Cognition and Tech. 2011–; Prof. of Econs, Faculty of Statistics, Univ. of Padua 1987–90; Sr Research Assoc., Centre for Financial History, Newnham Coll., Cambridge 2012–; Visiting Scholar, Dept of Applied Econs, Univ. of Cambridge 1987, 1989, Research

Assoc. 1992–93; Visiting Fellow, Clare Hall 1992, Life mem. 1992–; Visiting Fellow, Gonville and Caius Coll. 1999, Sr mem. 1999–, Centre for Research in the Arts, Social Sciences and Humanities, Univ. of Cambridge 2004; Visiting Prof., Interdisciplinary Research Centre 'Beniamino Segre', Accad. Nazionale dei Lincei 2012–(15); Resident Fellow, Bologna Inst. of Advanced Study 1997, Founding Scientific Dir 2000–03, Deputy Scientific Dir 2003–06; Visiting Prof., Univ. of Lugano, Switzerland 1997; Visiting Research Fellow, Centre for History and Econs, King's Coll., Cambridge 2005, Visiting Scholar, Gonville and Caius College and Clare Hall 2007–08; Faculty Advisor, Market Square-The Polity, Economy and Society, Cambridge Research Group, Centre for Research in the Arts, Social Sciences and Humanities, Univ. of Cambridge 2011–; Man. Ed. Structural Change and Economic Dynamics 1990–; Assoc. Ed. Journal of Economic Methodology 2003–05, Economia Politica, Journal of Analytical and Institutional Economics 2006–; mem. Steering Cttee Bologna-Cambridge-Harvard Sr Seminars Network, Bologna Inst. for Advanced Study, European Consortium of Humanities Centres and Insts, Cambridge Seminar in the History of Econ. Analysis (CAMHIST), Clare Hall 2008–, Cambridge Research Seminar in Political Economy, Emmanuel Coll. 2013–; mem. Man. Bd European Summer School in Structural Change and Econ. Dynamics, Selwyn Coll., Cambridge 1995–97; mem. Scientific Cttee Int. Centre for the History of Univs and Science 1994–, Scientific Cttee Research Centre in Econ. Analysis and Int. Econ. Devt (CRANEC), Catholic Univ. of Milan, Scientific Cttee Centre for Research on Complex Automated Systems (CASY), Univ. of Bologna 2002–; mem. Man. Bd 'Federigo Enriques' Centre for Epistemology and History of Sciences, Univ. of Bologna, Int. Microfinance Observatory, Univ. of Bologna; Foundation Fellow, Kyoto Univ.; Rector's Del., Bologna-Clare Hall Fellowship 1993–; mem. Bologna Acad. of Sciences 1994, Istituto Lombardo Accad. di Scienze e Lettere 2010, Accad. Nazionale dei Lincei 2013; Bonaldo Stringher Prize Scholarship (Bank of Italy) 1974, St Vincent Prize for Econs 1985, Linceo Prize for Econs, Nat. Lincei Acad. 2004. *Publications:* Efficienza produttiva e livelli di attività 1981, Protagonisti del pensiero economico (co-author) 1977–82, Sui momenti costitutivi dell'economia politica 1983 (co-author), Foundations of Economics: Structures of Inquiry and Economic Theory 1986, The Economic Theory of Structure and Change 1990, A Theory of Production: Tasks, Processes and Technical Practices 1993, Production and Economic Dynamics 1996, Incommensurability and Translation. Kuhnian Perspectives on Scientific Communication and Theory Change 1999, Knowledge, Social Institutions and the Division of Labour 2001, Economics of Structural Change (co-author) 2003, Reasoning, Rationality, and Probability (co-author) 2008, Markets, Money and Capital – Hicksian Economics for the Twenty First Century (co-author) 2008, Migration of Ideas (co-author) 2008, Capital, Time and Transitional Dynamics (co-author) 2009, Fundamental Uncertainty – Rationality and Plausible Reasoning (co-author) 2011, Resources, Production and Structural Dynamics (co-author) 2014, The Political Economy of the Eurozone (co-author) 2014, Periodic Overproduction Crises (first English edn of Aftalion, 1913) (co-ed.) 2014, Palgrave Handbook of Political Economy (co-ed.) 2015; numerous articles. *Leisure interests:* reading and conversation, art and classical music, walking and travelling. *Address:* Università degli Studi di Bologna, Piazza Scaravilli 2, 40126 Bologna (office); Via Garibaldi 5, 40124 Bologna, Italy (home). *Telephone:* (051) 2098146 (office); (051) 2098132 (Sec.) (office). *Fax:* (051) 2098040 (office). *Website:* www.dse.unibo.it (office); www .lincei.it/modules.php?name=Centro_Linceo (office); www.clarehall.cam.ac.uk (office); www.crassh.cam.ac.uk (office); www.accademiascienzebologna.it (office).

SCHAAL, Barbara A., BS, MPh, PhD; American/German plant biologist and academic; *Mary-Dell Chilton Distinguished Professor, Department of Biology, Washington University in St Louis;* b. 1947, Berlin, Germany; ed Univ. of Illinois, Chicago, Yale Univ.; became US citizen in 1956; grew up in Chicago; mem. Faculty, Univ. of Houston, Ohio State Univ. –1980; joined Faculty, Washington Univ. in St Louis 1980, later Spencer T. Olin Prof. in Arts & Sciences, currently Mary-Dell Chilton Distinguished Prof., Dept of Biology; Assoc. Ed. Molecular Biology and Evolution, The American Journal of Botany, Molecular Ecology, Conservation Genetics; Pres. Botanical Soc. of America 1995–96; fmr Pres. Soc. for the Study of Evolution; mem. Bd of Trustees St Louis Acad. of Sciences, Missouri Chapter of the Nature Conservancy; mem. Advisory Bd, Science and Entertainment Exchange; Fellow, AAAS; mem. NAS 1999, Vice-Pres. (first woman) NAS 2005–. *Achievements include:* recognized for her work on the genetics of plant species, particularly for her studies using DNA sequences to understand evolutionary processes such as gene flow, geographical differentiation, and the domestication of crop species. *Publications:* numerous scientific papers in professional journals. *Address:* 304 McDonnell Hall, Department of Biology, Washington University in St Louis, Campus Box 1137, One Brookings Drive, St Louis, MO 63130-4899, USA (office). *Telephone:* (314) 935-6822 (office). *E-mail:* schaal@biology.wustl.edu (office). *Website:* www.biology.wustl.edu/faculty/schaal (office).

SCHABRAM, Hans, DPhil; German professor of english; *Professor Emeritus, Abteilung für Englische Sprache und Literatur des Mittelalters, University of Göttingen;* b. 27 Sept. 1928, Berlin; s. of Paul Schabram and Lucia Schabram; m. Candida Larisch 1956; two s. one d.; ed Univs of Berlin and Cologne; Asst. English Dept, Univ. of Heidelberg 1957–63; Prof. of Medieval English Language and Literature, Univ. of Giessen 1964–67; apptd Prof., Abteilung für Englische Sprache und Literatur des Mittelalters, Univ. of Göttingen 1968, currently Prof. Emer.; mem. Akad. der Wissenschaften, Göttingen. *Publications:* 55 publs on English Philology since 1956. *Address:* Seminar für Englische Philologie, Abteilung für Englische Sprache und Literatur des Mittelalters, Georg-August-Universität, Käte-Hamburger Weg 3, 37073 Göttingen (office); Heinz-Hilpert-Str. 6, 37085 Göttingen, Germany (home). *Telephone:* (551) 55444 (home). *Website:* www.uni-goettingen.de (office).

SCHACHMAN, Howard Kapnek, PhD; American biochemist and academic; *Professor of the Graduate School, Division of Biochemistry and Molecular Biology, University of California, Berkeley;* b. 5 Dec. 1918, Philadelphia, Pa; s. of Morris H. Schachman and Rose Kapnek Schachman; m. Ethel H. Lazarus 1945; two s.; ed Mass. Inst. of Technology and Princeton Univ.; Fellow, Rockefeller Inst. for Medical Research, Princeton, NJ, 1947–48; Instructor (Biochemistry), Univ. of California, Berkeley 1948–50, Asst Prof. 1950–54, Assoc. Prof. 1955–59, Prof. of Biochemistry and Molecular Biology 1959–91, Prof. Emer. 1991–94, Faculty Research Lecturer 1994, Prof. of Grad. School 1994–, Chair. Dept of Molecular Biology, Dir Virus Lab. 1969–76; Scholar-in-Residence, Fogarty Int. Center, NIH

1977–78; Carl and Gerty Cori Lecturer, Washington Univ. School of Medicine, St Louis 1993; Pres. American Soc. for Biochemistry and Molecular Biology 1987–88, Chair. Public Affairs Cttee 1989–2000; Pres. Fed. of American Socs for Experimental Biology 1988–89; mem. Scientific Council and Scientific Advisory Bd of Stazione Zoologica Naples, Italy 1988–, Bd of Scientific Consultants of Memorial Sloan-Kettering Cancer Center 1988–97, Bd of Scientific Counselors Nat. Cancer Inst., Div. of Cancer Biology and Diagnosis 1989–92, Cttee on Scientific Freedom and Responsibility 1998–; apptd Special Adviser to Dir of NIH and Ombudsman in the Basic Sciences 1994; mem. NAS 1968 (Chair. Biochemistry Section 1990–93), AAAS, American Acad. of Arts and Sciences 1966; Foreign mem. Accad. Nazionale dei Lincei, Rome 1996; Hon. DSc (Northwestern Univ.) 1974, Hon. MD (Naples) 1990; ACS (Calif. Section) Award 1958, ACS E.H. Sargent & Co. Award for Chemical Instrumentation 1962, John Scott Award, City of Philadelphia 1964, Warren Triennial Prize, Mass Gen. Hosp. 1965, Merck Award, American Soc. of Biological Chemists 1986, Alexander von Humboldt Award 1990, NAS Panel on Scientific Responsibility and the Conduct of Research 1990–92, Alberta Heritage Foundation for Medical Research Visiting Professorship, Univ. of Alberta 1996, Herbert A. Sober Award, American Soc. for Biochemistry and Molecular Biology 1994, Public Service Award, FASEB 1994, Theodor Sredberg Award 1998, Burroughs Wellcome Fund Lecturer 1999, AAAS Scientific Freedom and Responsibility Award 2001. *Publications:* Ultracentrifugation in Biochemistry 1959; numerous articles in scientific journals. *Leisure interest:* sports. *Address:* 508A Stanley Hall, University of California, Berkeley, CA 94720, USA (office). *Telephone:* (510) 642-7046 (office). *Fax:* (510) 642-8699 (office). *E-mail:* howardschachman@berkeley.edu (office). *Website:* mcb.berkeley.edu/faculty/BMB/schachmanh.html (office).

SCHACHT, Henry Brewer, MBA; American business executive; *Managing Director and Senior Advisor, Warburg Pincus LLC;* b. 16 Oct. 1934, Erie, Pa; s. of Henry Schacht and Virginia Schacht; m. Nancy Godfrey 1960; one s. three d.; ed Yale and Harvard Univs; Investment Man. Irwin Man. Co. 1962–64; Vice-Pres. Finance, Subsidiaries and Int. Areas, Cummins Engine Co., Inc. 1964–69; Pres. Cummins Engine Co., Inc. 1969–77, Chair. 1977–95, CEO 1977–94; Man. Dir Warburg Pincus LLC, New York 1995, Man. Dir and Sr Advisor 2004–; Chair. and CEO Lucent Techs, Murray Hill, NJ 1995–98, 2000–03; fmr mem. Bd of Dirs CBS, AT&T, Chase Manhattan Corpn, Chase Manhattan Bank NA, Johnson & Johnson, New York Times Co., Avaya, Aluminum Company of America (Alcoa); fmr mem. Business Council; Trustee, Metropolitan Museum of Art; fmr Chair. Bd of Trustees Ford Foundation; fmr Trustee Yale Univ., Brookings Inst., Business Enterprise Trust, Calver Educ. Foundation; fmr Sr mem. The Conference Board. *Address:* Warburg Pincus LLC, 450 Lexington Avenue, New York, NY 10017, USA (office). *Telephone:* (212) 878-0600 (office). *Fax:* (212) 878-9351 (office). *Website:* www .warburgpincus.com (office).

SCHACK, Bo, BL, MBA; Danish lawyer and UN official; *Deputy Special Representative of the Secretary-General in the Central African Republic and UN Resident Coordinator, Humanitarian Coordinator and Resident Representative, United Nations Integrated Peacebuilding Office in the Central African Republic (BINUCA);* b. 1955; m.; three c.; ed Univ. of Copenhagen, European Coll., Bruges, Belgium, Open Univ., UK; Assoc. Attorney, Ministry of Industry –1985; worked for UNHCR in Senegal 1985–88, in Hong Kong 1988–91, at Asia Bureau HQ 1991–94, Special Operation in fmr Yugoslavia 1994–97, in Sri Lanka 1997–2000, Deputy Rep. in Tehran, Iran 2000–03, Head of Policy Unit, Europe Bureau, UNHCR HQ, Geneva 2003–07, Rep. in Burundi 2007–09; Deputy Special Rep. of the Sec.-Gen. in Cen. African Repub. and UN Resident Coordinator, Humanitarian Coordinator and Resident Rep., UN Integrated Peacebuilding Office in Cen. African Repub. (BINUCA) 2010–. *Address:* Office of the Secretary-General, United Nations, New York, NY 10017, USA (office). *Telephone:* (212) 963-1234 (office). *Fax:* (212) 963-4879 (office). *E-mail:* balepe@un.org (office). *Website:* binuca.unmissions.org (office).

SCHAEFER, George A., Jr, BS, MBA; American business executive; *Chairman, WellPoint, Inc.;* ed US Mil. Acad. at West Point, Xavier Univ.; mem. Bd of Dirs Fifth Third BanCorp 1988, now Dir Emer., Pres. Fifth Third BanCorp 1990–2006, CEO 1990–2007, Chair. Fifth Third BanCorp 2006–08, Pres. and CEO Fifth Third Bank, Cincinnati, Ohio (subsidiary of Fifth Third BanCorp) from 1990, Pres. Fifth Third Leasing Co., Pres. and CEO Fifth Third Bank of Northeastern Ohio; mem. Bd of Dirs WellPoint Inc. (fmrly Anthem Inc.) 2001–, Chair. 2013–; Chair. Bd of Univ. of Cincinnati; mem. Bd of Dirs Anthem Insurance (subsidiary of WellPoint, Inc.) 1995–2003, Ashland Inc. 2003–, Kenton Co. Airport; mem. Advisory Bd Federal Reserve Bank of Cleveland; mem. Bd of Trustees, Univ. of Cincinnati, Children's Hosp., Cincinnati. *Address:* WellPoint, Inc., 120 Monument Circle, Indianapolis, IN 46204, USA (office). *Telephone:* (317) 532-6000 (office). *Fax:* (317) 488-6028 (office). *E-mail:* boardofdirectors@wellpoint.com (office). *Website:* www .wellpoint.com (office).

SCHAEFER, Henry Frederick, III, BS, PhD; American chemist, researcher and academic; *Graham-Perdue Professor of Chemistry and Director, Center for Computational Chemistry, University of Georgia;* b. 8 June 1944, Grand Rapids, Mich.; s. of Henry Frederick Schaefer, Jr and Janice Christine Trost Schaefer; m. Karen Regine Rasmussen; three s. two d.; ed Massachusetts Inst. of Tech., Stanford Univ.; Prof. of Chem., Univ. of Calif., Berkeley 1969–87; Wilfred T. Doherty Prof. and Dir Inst. for Theoretical Chem., Univ. of Tex. 1979–80; Graham-Perdue Prof. of Chem. and Dir Center for Computational Chem., Univ. of Ga 1987–; Ed. Molecular Physics 1991–2005, Encyclopedia of Computational Chem. 1995–2004; Pres. World Asscn of Theoretical and Computational Chemists 1996–2005; Alfred P. Sloan Research Fellow 1972–74; John Simon Guggenheim Fellow 1976–77; Fellow, American Physical Soc. 1977–, AAAS, American Acad. of Arts and Sciences 2004–, Royal Soc. of Chemistry 2005–, American Chemical Soc. 2009, Int. Union of Pure and Applied Chemistry 2013; mem. Int. Acad. of Quantum Molecular Sciences; numerous lectureships including Guelph-Waterloo Distinguished Lecturer, Univ. of Guelph and Univ. of Waterloo, Ont., Canada 1991, John M. Templeton Lecturer, Case Western Reserve Univ. 1992, Herbert H. King Lecturer, Kansas State Univ. 1993, Francis A. Schaeffer Lectures, Washington Univ., St Louis 1994, Mary E. Kapp Lecture, Va Commonwealth Univ. 1996, Abbott Lectures, Univ. of ND 1997, C.S. Lewis Lecture, Univ. of Tenn. 1997, Joseph Frank McGregory Lecture, Colgate Univ. 1997, Kenneth S. Pitzer Lecture,

Univ. of Calif. at Berkeley 1998, Donald F. Othmer Lectures in Chem., Tokyo 2000, Israel Pollak Lectures, Technion-Israel Inst. of Tech., Haifa 2001, Coochbehar Lectures, Indian Asscn for the Cultivation of Science, Kolkata 2001, Lise Meitner Lecture, Hebrew Univ., Jerusalem 2001, Oakley Vail Lecture, Wake Forest Univ. 2002, Lawrence J. Schaad Lecture, Vanderbilt Univ. 2002, Annual Lecture of the Croatian Chemical Soc., Zagreb 2002, The Pres.'s Lecture, Univ. of Texas at Arlington 2002, Distinguished Theory Lecturer, Max Planck Inst., Mülheim, Germany 2003, John Marks Templeton Lecture, Princeton Univ. 2004, The New Coll. Lectures, Univ. of New South Wales 2004, Nanqiang Lecture, Xiamen Univ. 2005, C. V. Raman Memorial Lecture, Calcutta 2007, Per-Olov Löwdin, Univ. of Uppsala 2007, Herman Hotz Trust Lecture, Univ. of Arkansas 2008, Steven Adelman Lectures, Purdue Univ. 2009, Russel Pitzer Lecture, Ohio State Univ. 2009, Coll. of Sciences Distinguished Lecturer, Univ. of Cen. Florida, Orlando 2011, Distinguished Lecturer, Texas A&M Univ. 2011, William E. Palke Lecture, Univ. of Calif., Santa Barbara 2013, Science at the Edge Lecture Series, Michigan State Univ., East Lansing 2013, Jan Almlöf – Odd Gropen Lectures, Univ. of Tromsø and Univ. of Oslo 2013, Australian Asscn of Theoretical and Computational Chemists Lecture, Australian Nat. Univ. and Univ. of Sydney 2014, James William McBain Lecture, Nat. Chemical Lab., Pune, India 2014, Inst. Lecture, Indian Inst. of Tech. Bombay, Mumbai 2014; 27 hon. degrees; ACS Award in Pure Chem. 1979, Leo Hendrik Baekeland Award (ACS) 1983; Schroedinger Medal, World Asscn of Theoretical Organic Chemists 1990, Centenary Medal, RSC, London 1992, ACS Award in Theoretical Chem. 2003, ACS Ira Remson Award 2003, Joseph O. Hirschfelder Prize 2006, Chemical Pioneer Award 2013, ACS Peter Debye Award in Physical Chemistry 2014. *Publications:* The Electronic Structure of Atoms and Molecules 1972, Modern Theoretical Chemistry 1977, Quantum Chemistry 1984, A New Dimension to Quantum Chemistry 1994, Science and Christianity: Conflict or Coherence? 2013; more than 1450 publs in scientific journals. *Leisure interests:* Bible study, hiking. *Address:* Center for Computational Chemistry, University of Georgia, 1004 Cedar Street, Athens, GA 30602-2525, USA (office). *Telephone:* (706) 542-0364 (office); (706) 542-2067 (office). *Fax:* (706) 542-0406 (office). *E-mail:* qc@uga.edu (office). *Website:* ccqc.uga.edu (office).

SCHAEFER, Michael, PhD; German diplomatist; *Ambassador to the People's Republic of China;* b. 6 March 1949, Paderborn; m.; three c.; ed Ludwig-Maximilian Univ., Munich, Max Planck Inst., Heidelberg/Univ. of Mannheim; Second State Exam Law, Heidelberg 1978; joined Foreign Service 1978, postings include UN Missions in New York and Geneva, Singapore; Head, Western Balkans Task Force, Fed. Foreign Office, Berlin 1999–2001, Special Envoy for S Eastern Europe and Deputy Political Dir 2001–02, Head, Legal Dept 2002, Political Dir 2002–07; rank of Amb. 2002–; Amb. to People's Repub. of China 2007–; Hon. Prof., China Univ. of Political Science and Law; Officier, Légion d'honneur 2007. *Publications:* Der Sicherheitsmechanismus der Vereinten Nationen 1980, Berufsbild Diplomat: Auswahl und Ausbildung im Auswärtigen Dienst 1995; contrib. to Südosteuropa Mitteilungen, Zeitschrift Vereinte Nationen. *Address:* Embassy of Germany, 17 Dongzhimenwai Dajie, San Li Tun, Chaoyang District, Beijing 100600, People's Republic of China (office). *Telephone:* (10) 85329000 (office). *Fax:* (10) 65325336 (office). *E-mail:* embassy@peki.diplo.de (office). *Website:* (office).

SCHAEFFER, Bogusław, DPhil; Polish/Austrian composer, music critic, playwright and pianist; b. 6 June 1929, Lwów (now Lviv, Ukraine); s. of Władysław Schaeffer and Julia Schaeffer; m. Mieczysława Hanuszewska 1953; one s.; ed State Higher School of Music (student of A. Malawski), Jagiellonian Univ., Kraków (student of Zdzisław Jachimecki); wrote first dodecaphonic music for orchestra in Eastern Europe, Music for Strings: Nocturne 1953; Assoc. Prof. State Higher School of Music, Kraków 1963–98, Ordinary Prof. of Composition, Higher School of Music, Mozarteum, Salzburg 1986–89, Prof. 1989–; Chief Ed. Forum Musicum 1967–; leads int. summer courses for new composition in Salzburg and Schwaz (Austria) 1976–; Hon. mem. Int. Soc. for Contemporary Music 1998, Pro Sinfonica 2003; Gold Cross of Merit 1969; Kt's Cross of Polonia Restituta Order 1972; numerous prizes include G. Fitelberg Prize 1959, 1960, 1964, A. Malawski Prize 1962, Minister of Culture and Arts Prize 1971, 1980, Union of Polish Composers Prize 1977, Alfred Jurzykowski Award 1999. *Main compositions:* Extrema, Tertium datur, Scultura, S'alto for alto saxophone, Collage and Form, Electronic Music, Visual Music, Heraclitiana, Missa Electronica, Jangwa, Missa Sinfonica, eight Piano Concertos, Maah, Sinfonia, Hommage à Guillaume for two cellos and piano 1995, Sinfonietta for 16 instruments 1996, Symphony in One Movement 1997, Enigma for Orchestra 1997, Four Psalms for choir and orchestra 1999, Musica Omogènea for 32 violins 1999, Si Quaeris Miracula for soprano and orchestra 2000, Model XXI (Wendepunkt) for piano 2000, De Profundis for soprano and chamber orchestra 2000, Monophonie VIII for 24 violins 2000, Ave Maria for soprano and orchestra 2000, opera Liebesblicke 2000, five violin concertos, three cello concertos, Concerto for vibraphone and orchestra 2001, Concerto for harp, Celtic harp and orchestra 2002, Concerto for saxophone, piano and orchestra 2002, 9th Symphony 2003, Concert for piano and choir 2004, For violin and electronics 2004, Blues VII for piano and orchestra 2004, Quartet for four cellos 2005, Panorama for orchestra 2005, Fragment III for two actors, clarinet, cello, piano and electronic media 2005, Second Symphony in One Movement 2005, OCSENOT for soprano and ensemble of seven instruments, Impresiónes Liricas for piano and electro-acoustic medias 2005, Model XXXIII for piano 2005, Contemporaneamente o Alternatamente for violin and piano 2005, Model XXXIV for piano 2006, Concerto for viola and 12 various instruments 2007, Quartet for four violins and chamber orchestra 2009, 10th Symphony 2010, SaVi for saxophone and violin 2011, Mini opera, also film and theatre music, Miserere, Organ Concerto, 17 string quartets, Orchestral and Electronic Changes, Concerto for Violin, Piano and Orchestra, Symphony/Concerto for 15 solo instrumentalists and orchestra, Heideggeriana, Winter Musik for horn and piano, Concerto for percussion, electronic media and orchestra. *Plays:* 46 stage plays including: Three Actors 1970, Darknesses 1980, Screenplay for Sins of Old Age 1985, The Actor 1990, Rehearsals 1990, Séance 1990, Tutam 1991, Rondo 1991, Together 1992, Toast 1991, Harvest 1993, Promotion 1993, Gloss 1993, Daybreak 1994, Multi 1994, Largo 1996, Blockheads 1997, Stage Demon 1998, Alles 1998, Advertisement 1998, Walks Through Parc 1998, InOut 1998, Farniente 1998, Chance 1999, Dwa Te (Two Te) 2000, Skala 2000, Scale 2008, Something Multimedial 2009, Case; plays trans. into 17 languages. *Publications:* Nowa Muzyka. Problemy współczesnej techniki kompo-

zytorskiej (New music. Problems of Contemporary Technique in Composing) 1958, Klasycy dodekafonii (Classics of Dodecaphonic Music) 1964, Leksykon kompozytorów XX wieku (Lexicon of 20th Century Composers) 1965, W kręgu nowej muzyki (In the Sphere of New Music) 1967, Mały informator muzyki XX wieku 1975, Introduction to Composition (in English) 1975, Historia muzyki (Story of Music) 1980, Kompozytorzy XX wieku (20th Century Composers) 1990, Trzy rozmowy (kompozytor, dramaturg, filozof) (Three Conversations: Composer, Playwright and Philosopher) 1992. *Leisure interests:* literature, theatre. *Address:* Osiedle Kolorowe 4, m.6, 31-938 Kraków, Poland; St. Julienstrasse 7A, Apartment 27, 5020 Salzburg, Austria. *Telephone:* (12) 6441960 (Poland) (home). *E-mail:* bsch@ceti.pl (office). *Website:* www.usc.edu/dept/polish_music/composer/schaeffer.html#intro.

SCHAEFFER, Leonard D., BA; American business executive; *Senior Advisor, Texas Pacific Group;* b. 28 July 1945, Chicago; m. Pamela Schaeffer (née Sidford); two c.; ed Princeton Univ.; Man. Consultant, Arthur Andersen & Co. 1969–73; Deputy Dir of Man. Illinois Mental Health and Developmental Disabilities, Springfield, Ill. 1973–75; Dir Ill. State Bureau of Budget 1975–76; Vice-Pres. Citibank NA, New York 1976–78; Asst Sec., Man and Budget, US Dept of Health and Human Services, Washington, DC 1978, Admin. Health Care Financing Admin 1978–80; Exec. Vice-Pres. and COO Student Loan Marketing Asscn 1980–82; Pres. and CEO Group Health Inc., Minneapolis, Minn. 1983–86; Chair. and CEO Blue Cross of Calif. 1986–96, managed transition to WellPoint, Chair. and CEO WellPoint Health Networks Inc. (now WellPoint Inc.) 1993–2004, Chair. 2004–05; Dir Allergan, Inc. 1993–; est. Calif. Endowment and Calif. HealthCare Foundation 1996; Sr Advisor Texas Pacific Group (Pvt. investment firm) 2006–; mem. Bd of Dirs Allergan, Inc., Amgen Inc. 2004–; Chair. Nat. Inst. for Health Care Man.; fmr Chair. Health Insurance Asscn of America, Nat. Health Foundation; Founding Chair. Coalition for Affordable and Quality Healthcare; Chair. WellPoint Foundation; mem. Inst. of Medicine, Nat. Acad. of Science; mem. Bd Trustees, The Brookings Inst.; mem. Bd of Fellows and Co-Chair., Advisory Council, Dept of Healthcare Policy, Harvard Medical School; mem. Advisory Council Dept of Economics, Princeton Univ.; mem. Bd of Councilors, School of Policy, Planning, and Development, Univ. of Southern Calif.; Citation for Outstanding Service, American Acad. of Paediatrics, Distinguished Public Service Award, US Dept of Health, Educ. and Welfare, Exec. Leadership Award, UCLA Anderson School of Man. 2003. *Address:* Texas Pacific Group, 301 Commerce Street, Suite 3300, Fort Worth, TX 76102, USA (office). *Telephone:* (817) 871-4000 (office). *Fax:* (817) 871-4010 (office). *Website:* www.texaspacificgroup.com (office).

SCHAFER, Edward (Ed) Thomas, BA, MBA; American business executive, government official and fmr state governor; b. 8 Aug. 1946, Bismarck, ND; s. of Harold Schafer and Marian Schafer; m. Nancy Jones 1992; four c.; ed Univ. of North Dakota and Univ. of Denver; quality control insp., Gold Seal 1971–73, Vice-Pres. 1974, Chair. Man. Cttee 1975–78, Pres. 1978–85; Owner/Dir H & S Distribution 1976; Pres. Dakota Classics 1986, TRIESCO Properties 1986, Fish 'N Dakota 1990–94; Gov. of N Dakota 1993–2000; Civilian Aide to US Sec. of the Army 2002; Co-founder and CEO Extend America (wireless communications co.) 2000–08; advisor, Americans for Prosperity 2006–08; US Sec. of Agric., Washington, DC 2008–09; Republican. *Address:* c/o Department of Agriculture, 1400 Independence Avenue, SW, Washington, DC 20250, USA.

SCHÄFERKORDT, Anke; German television executive; *CEO, RTL Mediengruppe Deutschland GmbH;* b. 1962; began career at Bertelsmann AG in 1988; Exec. Asst for Sales Controlling and Strategic Planning, RTL Television GmbH, Cologne 1991–92, Head, Controlling Dept 1992–93, Dir in charge of Corp. Planning and Controlling Div. 1993–95, Head of Business Affairs, VOX Television 1995–97, Program Dir 1997–99, CEO VOX Television 1999–, COO and Deputy CEO of RTL Television Feb.–Sept. 2005, CEO Sept. 2005–, Co-CEO RTL Group 2012–, currently CEO Mediengruppe RTL Deutschland GmbH; mem. Supervisory Bd BASF SE 2010–, Software AG 2010–; ranked by the Financial Times amongst the Top 25 Businesswomen in Europe (24th) 2006, (24th) 2007. *Address:* RTL Television GmbH, Picassoplatz 1, 50679 Cologne, Germany (office). *Telephone:* (221) 456-0 (office). *Fax:* (221) 456-1690 (office). *Website:* www.rtl-television.de (office).

SCHÄFERS, Reinhard; German diplomatist; *Ambassador to Italy;* b. 27 May 1950; m.; two c.; joined Fed. Ministry of Foreign Affairs 1977, Second Sec. 1979; Consul, Embassy in Prague 1979–82; Deputy Head of Mission, Embassy in Mogadishu; First Sec. and Counsellor, Ministry of Foreign Affairs 1985–88; Counsellor, Embassy in Moscow 1988–91; Counsellor USSR Div., Ministry of Foreign Affairs 1991–92, Head of Cen., E and SE Europe Div. 1992–98; Minister, Embassy in Paris 1998–2000; Perm. Rep. to WEU 2000, to EU Political and Security Cttee 2001; Amb. to Ukraine 2006–08, to France 2008–12, to Italy 2012–. *Address:* Embassy of Germany, Via San Martino della Battaglia 4, 00185 Roma, Italy (office). *Telephone:* (06) 492131 (office). *Fax:* (06) 49213319 (office). *E-mail:* info@rom.diplo.de (office). *Website:* www.rom.diplo.de (office).

SCHALLER, George Beals, PhD; American zoologist, academic and author; *Vice-President, Panthera Inc.;* b. 26 May 1933, Berlin, Germany; s. of George Ludwig Schaller and Bettina Iwersen (née Byrd); m. Kay Suzanne Morgan 1957; two s.; ed Univ. of Alaska, Univ. of Wisconsin-Madison; moved to USA in his teens; Fellow, Dept of Behavioral Sciences, Stanford Univ. 1962–63; Research Assoc., Johns Hopkins Univ., Baltimore 1963–66; Adjunct Assoc. Prof., Rockefeller Univ., New York 1966–72; Research Zoologist, Wildlife Conservation Soc. 1966–, Dir Int. Conservation Program, New York Zoological Soc. 1979–88, then Vice-Pres. Science and Exploration Program and Ella Millbank Foshay Chair in Wildlife Conservation, now Sr Conservationist; Vice-Pres. Panthera Inc.; Adjunct Prof., Peking Univ.; Research Assoc., American Museum of Natural History; Fellow, Guggenheim Foundation 1971; Hon. Dir Explorers' Club 1991; Order of Golden Ark (Netherlands) 1978; Int. Cosmos Prize (Japan) 1996, Tyler Prize for Environmental Achievement 1997, Gold Medal, World Wildlife Fund 1980, Beebe Fellowship, Wildlife Conservation Soc. 2006, Lifetime Achievement Award, Nat. Geographic Soc. 2007, Indianapolis Prize 2008. *Achievements include:* recognized as one of the world's leading field biologists, studying wildlife throughout Africa, Asia and S America. *Publications:* The Mountain Gorilla 1963, The Year of the Gorilla 1964, The Deer and the Tiger 1967, The Serengeti Lion (Nat. Book Award 1973) 1972, Mountain Monarchs 1977, Stones of Silence 1980, The Giant Pandas of Wolong (co-author) 1985, The Last Panda 1993, Tibet's Hidden Wilderness 1997, Wildlife of the Tibetan Steppe 1998, Antelopes, Deer and Relatives (co-ed.) 2000, Giant Pandas in the Wild: Saving an Endangered Species (jtly) 2005, A Naturalist and Other Beasts: Tales from a Life in the Field 2007, Tibet Wild: A Naturalist's Journey on the Roof of the World 2012. *Leisure interests:* photography, reading. *Address:* Panthera, Inc., 8 West 40th Street, 18th Floor, New York, NY 10018 (office); Wildlife Conservation Society, 2300 Southern Boulevard, Bronx, New York, NY 10460, USA (office). *Telephone:* (646) 786-0400 (Panthera) (office). *E-mail:* info@panthera.org; asiaprogram@wcs.org (office). *Website:* www.panthera .org (office); www.wcs.org (office).

SCHALLY, Andrew Victor, PhD; American medical researcher and academic; *Distinguished Medical Research Scientist, Department of Veterans' Affairs;* b. 30 Nov. 1926, Wilno, Poland (now Vilnius, Lithuania); s. of Casimir Peter Schally and Maria Schally (née Lacka); m. 1st Margaret Rachel White; one s. one d.; m. 2nd Ana Maria de Medeiros-Comaru 1976 (died 2004); m. 3rd Maria Rasmussen 2011; ed Bridge of Allan, Scotland and Univ. of London, UK, McGill Univ., Montreal, Canada; Asst Prof. of Physiology and Asst Prof. of Biochemistry, Baylor Univ. Coll. of Medicine, Houston, Tex. 1957–62; Chief, Endocrine and Polypeptide Labs, Veterans' Admin. Hosp., New Orleans, La 1962–2005; Sr Medical Investigator, Veterans' Admin. 1973–99, Distinguished Medical Research Scientist, Dept of Veterans' Affairs 1999–; Assoc. Prof. of Medicine, Tulane Univ. School of Medicine, New Orleans, La 1962–67, Prof. of Medicine 1967–2005; Distinguished Leonard Miller Prof. of Pathology, Prof., Div. of Hematology/Oncology and Div. of Endocrinology, Dept of Medicine, Miller School of Medicine, Univ. of Miami; mem. NAS, AAAS and numerous other socs and nat. acads; Chevalier, Légion d'honneur 2004; decorations from USA, Spain, France, Ecuador and Venezuela; more than 30 hon. degrees, including Hon. MD and Hon. DSc; Charles Mickle Award 1974, Gairdner Foundation Award 1974, Edward T. Tyler Award 1975, Borden Award in the Medical Sciences (Asscn of American Medical Colls) 1975, Lasker Award 1975, shared Nobel Prize for Physiology or Medicine with Roger Guillemin (q.v.) for discoveries concerning peptide hormones 1977, US Govt Distinguished Service Award 1978. *Publications:* more than 2,300 scientific papers, particularly concerning hormones and cancer. *Leisure interests:* swimming, soccer. *Address:* Veterans' Administration Hospital Research Service, 1201 NW 16th Street, Miami, FL 33125 (office); 3801 Collins Avenue, Apt 1506, Miami Beach, FL 33140, USA (home). *Telephone:* (305) 575-3477 (office); (305) 575-7000 (ext. 3810) (Maria Gajardo) (office). *Fax:* (305) 575-3126 (office). *E-mail:* andrew .schally@va.gov (office); maria.gajardo@va.gov (office).

SCHAMA, Simon Michael, CBE, MA; British historian, academic, writer and art critic; *University Professor of Art History and History, Columbia University;* b. 13 Feb. 1945, London; s. of the late Arthur Schama and of Gertrude Steinberg; m. Virginia Papaioannou 1983; one s. one d.; ed Christ's Coll., Cambridge; Fellow and Dir of Studies in History, Christ's Coll., Cambridge 1966–76; Fellow and Tutor in Modern History, Brasenose Coll., Oxford 1976–80; Prof. of History (Mellon Prof. of the Social Sciences), Harvard Univ. 1980; Univ. Prof. of Art History and History, Columbia Univ. 1997–; art critic, New Yorker 1995–; Contributing Ed., Financial Times 2009–; Vice-Pres. Poetry Soc.; Wolfson Prize 1977, Leo Gershoy Prize, American Historical Asscn 1978, Nat. Cash Register Book Prize for Non-Fiction (for Citizens) 1990. *Television:* Rembrandt: The Public Eye and the Private Gaze (film for BBC) 1992, A History of Britain (series) 2000–01, The Power of Art (series) 2006, The American Future: A History (series) 2008, Story of the Jews 2013. *Publications:* Patriots and Liberators: Revolution in the Netherlands 1780–1813 1977, Two Rothschilds and the Land of Israel 1979, The Embarrassment of Riches: An Interpretation of Dutch Culture in the Golden Age 1987, Citizens: A Chronicle of the French Revolution 1989, Dead Certainties (Unwarranted Speculations) 1991, Landscape and Memory 1995, Rembrandt's Eyes 1999, A History of Britain Vol. 1: At the Edge of the World? 3000 BC–AD 1603 2000, Vol. 2: The British Wars 1603–1776 2001, Vol. 3: The Fate of Empire 1776–2001 2002, Hang-Ups: Essays on Painting 2004, Rough Crossings: Britain, the Slaves and the American Revolution 2005, Power of Art 2006, The American Future: A History 2008, Scribble, Scribble, Scribble 2010, Story of the Jews 2013. *Leisure interests:* wine, Dutch bulbs, children's fiction. *Address:* Department of History, 522 Fayerweather Hall, Columbia University, New York, NY 10027, USA (office). *Telephone:* (212) 854-4593 (office). *E-mail:* sms53@columbia.edu (office). *Website:* www.columbia.edu/cu/arthistory (office).

SCHANBERG, Sydney H., BA; American journalist, author and academic; b. 17 Jan. 1934, Clinton, Mass; s. of L. Schanberg and F. Schanberg; m. Jane Freiman Schanberg; two d.; ed Harvard Univ.; joined New York Times 1959, reporter 1960, Bureau Chief, Albany, New York 1967–69, New Delhi, India 1969–73, SE Asia Corresp., Singapore 1973–75, City Ed. 1977–80, Columnist 1981–85; Assoc. Ed., Columnist Newsday newspaper, New York 1986–95; Chief of Investigative Unit, APBnews.com 2000–01; columnist for Village Voice, New York 2002–06; Adjunct Prof., Dept of Communication and Media, State Univ. of New York, New Paltz, first Fellow apptd to the James H. Ottaway Sr Visiting Professorship 2002; numerous awards, including Page One Award for Reporting 1972, George Polk Memorial Award 1972, Overseas Press Club Award 1972, Bob Considine Memorial Award 1975, Pulitzer Prize 1975, Elijah Parish Lovejoy Award, Colby Coll. 1992, Bart Richards Award for Outstanding Media Criticism 2005. *Film:* Academy Award-winning film 'The Killing Fields' based on his experiences covering the war in Cambodia for The New York Times. *Publications include:* The Death and Life of Dith Pran 1985, Beyond the Killing Fields – War Writings 2010, The Death and Life of Dith Pran (e-book) 2013. *Address:* Box 236, Rifton, NY 12471, USA. *Telephone:* (917) 846-1946. *E-mail:* sydneyschanberg@yahoo.com. *Website:* www .beyondthekillingfields.com.

SCHAPIRO, Morton, BEcons, PhD; American economist, academic and university administrator; *President, Northwestern University;* m. Mimi Schapiro; one s. two d.; ed Hofstra Univ., Univ. of Pennsylvania; Prof. of Econs and Asst Provost, Williams Coll. 1980–91, Pres. Williams Coll. 2000–09; Chair. Dept of Econs, Univ. of Southern California 1991–94, Dean Coll. of Letters, Arts and Sciences 1994–2000, Vice-Pres. for Planning 1998–2000; Prof. of Econs, Judd A. and Marjorie Weinberg Coll. of Arts and Sciences, Northwestern Univ. 2009–, also holds appointments in Kellogg School of Man. and School of Educ. and Social Policy, Pres. Northwestern Univ. 2009–; Fellow, American Acad. of Arts and Sciences 2010. *Publications include:* Keeping College Affordable: Government and Educational Opportunity 1991, Paying the Piper: Productivity, Incentives and Financing in Higher Education (co-author) 1993, The Student Aid Game: Meeting Need and Rewarding Talent in American Higher Education 1998; College Success: What It Means and How to Make It Happen (ed.) 2008, College Access: Opportunity or Privilege? (ed.) 2006; more than 100 articles. *Address:* Office of the President, Northwestern University, 2-130 Rebecca Crown Center, 633 Clark Street, Evanston, IL 60208, USA (office). *Telephone:* (847) 491-7456 (office). *Fax:* (847) 467-3104 (office). *E-mail:* nu-president@northwestern.edu (office). *Website:* www.northwestern.edu/president (office).

SCHARIOTH, Klaus, MA, MALD, PhD; German diplomatist; b. 8 Oct. 1946, Essen, North Rhine-Westphalia; m.; three c.; ed studies in Caldwell, Ida, USA, in Bonn and Freiburg, Germany, and in Geneva, Switzerland, Fletcher School of Law and Diplomacy, Harvard Law School, John F. Kennedy School of Govt; mil. service 1966–67; entered Foreign Service 1976, Asia Div., Press Div. and State Sec.'s Office, Fed. Foreign Office 1977–79, Embassy in Quito, Ecuador 1979–82, Policy Planning Staff, Fed. Foreign Office 1982–86, Perm. Mission to UN, New York, Vice-Chair. UN Legal and Charter Cttees 1986–90, Int. Law Div., Fed. Foreign Office 1990–93, Chef de Cabinet (Dir pvt. office) to NATO Sec.-Gen., Brussels 1993–96, Head of Defence and Security Policy Div., Fed. Foreign Office 1996–97, Office of the Foreign Minister 1997–98, Head of Office April 1998, Head of Int. Security and N America Directorate 1998–99, Political Dir and Head of Political Directorate-Gen. 1999–2002, State Sec. of the Foreign Office 2002–06, Amb. to USA 2006–11. *Address:* Federal Ministry of Foreign Affairs, 11013 Berlin, Germany (office). *Telephone:* (30) 5000-0 (office). *Fax:* (30) 18173402 (office). *E-mail:* poststelle@auswaertiges-amt.de (office). *Website:* www.auswaertiges-amt .de (office).

SCHARP, Anders, MSc; Swedish business executive; b. 8 June 1934; s. of the late John Henry Scharp and Esther Scharp; m. Maud Hermansson 1957; ed Royal Inst. of Tech., Stockholm; joined AB Electrohelios 1960 (merged with AB Electrolux 1963), Exec. Vice-Pres. (Production and Research & Devt) 1974; apptd Pres. AB Electrolux 1981, CEO 1986; Chair. Saab-Scania 1990–95; Chair. Saab AB 1995–2006, AB Nederman; Chair., CEO AB SKF 1992–2008; Chair. Incentive AB 1992–98; Chair. White Consolidated Industries 1993–98, fmrly CEO; mem. Bd of Dirs Investor AB 1988–, Vice Chair. 2005–; fmr Chair. AB Nederman & Co.; fmr mem. Bd of Dirs Swedish Asscn of Metalworking Industries, Swedish Metal Trades Employers' Asscn, Swedish Employers' Confed.; Bd mem. Fed. of Swedish Industries, Asscn of Swedish Engineering Industries; mem. Royal Swedish Acad. of Engineering Sciences. *Address:* c/o AB Nederman & Co., Sydhamnsgatan 2, 252 28 Helsingborg, Sweden.

SCHARPING, Rudolf; German politician; *CEO, Rudolf Scharping Strategie Beratung Kommunikation GmbH;* b. 2 Dec. 1947, Niederelbert, Westerwald; m. 1st Jutta Scharping (divorced 2000); three c.; m. 2nd Countess Kristina Pilati Borggreve 2000; ed Univ. of Bonn; joined Social Democratic Party (SPD) 1966; State Chair. and Nat. Deputy Chair. Jusos (Young Socialists) 1966; mem. State Parl. of Rhineland-Palatinate 1975–94; Party Leader of SPD in Rhineland-Palatinate 1985; Leader of Opposition in Rhineland-Palatinate 1987; Minister-Pres. of Rhineland-Palatinate 1991–94; mem. Bundestag (German Parl.) 1994–2005; Leader, SPD 1993–95, Deputy Chair. 1995–2003, Chair. SPD Parl. Group, Leader of the Opposition 1994; Chair. Social Democratic Party of Europe –2003; Minister of Defence 1998–2002; Deputy Chair. Party of European Socialists 1995–2001; currently CEO Rudolf Scharping Strategie Beratung Kommunikation GmbH; Research Asst to mems of Bundestag and European Parl. Deutsch 1969–75; Visiting Prof., Fletcher School for Law and Diplomacy, Tufts Univ. 2004–06; Pres. Bundes Deutscher Radfahrer (Fed. of German Cyclists) 2005–. *Publications include:* Was Jetzt Butun Ist 1994, Wir Dürfen Nicht Wegsehen – Der Kosovo-Krieg und Europa 1999; numerous articles on German and European politics. *Address:* Rudolf Scharping Strategie Beratung Kommunikation GmbH, Schweizer strasse 1, 60594 Frankfurt, Germany (office). *Telephone:* (69) 6612770 (office). *Fax:* (69) 66127712 (office). *Website:* www.rsbk.de (office).

SCHATZ, Brian Emanuel, BA; American politician and organization executive; *Senator from Hawaii;* b. 20 Oct. 1972, Ann Arbor, Mich.; s. of Irwin Schatz; m. Linda Kwok Kai Yun; one s. one d.; ed Punahou School, Pomona Coll., Claremont, Calif., spent a term studying in Kenya as part of the Int. Training Program; family moved to Hawaii 1974; taught at Punahou before taking other positions in the non-profit sector; active in Youth for Environmental Services 1980s; CEO Helping Hands Hawaii 2002–10; fmr Dir Makiki Community Library and of the Center for a Sustainable Future; mem. Hawaii House of Reps from the 24th Dist 1998–2002, from the 25th Dist 2002–06; Chair. Democratic Party of Hawaii 2008–10; Lt-Gov. of Hawaii 2010–12; Senator from Hawaii (to fill the vacancy caused by the death of Daniel Inouye) 2012–, mem. Cttee on Commerce, Science and Transportation, Cttee on Energy and Natural Resources, Cttee on Indian Affairs; Democrat. *Address:* G11 Dirksen Senate Office Building, Washington, DC 20510, USA (office). *Telephone:* (202) 224-3934 (office). *Website:* schatz.senate.gov (office).

SCHATZ, Gottfried (Jeff), PhD; Austrian biochemist and academic; *Professor Emeritus of Biochemistry, University of Basel;* b. 18 Aug. 1936, Strem; s. of Andreas Schatz and Anna Schatz; m. Merete Bjorn Petersen; three c.; ed Univ. of Graz, Univ. of Vienna; Asst Prof., Univ. of Vienna 1961–64; Postdoctoral Fellow, Public Health Research Inst., City of New York 1964–66; Assoc. Prof., then Prof. Cornell Univ. 1968–74; Prof. of Biochemistry, Univ. of Basel 1974, now Prof. Emer.; Pres. Swiss Science and Tech. Council 2000–03; Chair. Science Council of the Inst. Curie; Scientific Councilor, Inst. Pasteur; mem. Scientific Advisory Bd ORIDIS Biomed GmbH; Fellow, AAAS 2007–; mem. NAS, Royal Swedish Acad., Netherlands Acad. Sciences; Dr hc (Bratislava) 1996, (Stockholm) 2000; Innitzer Prize 1967, Hansen Gold Medal 1983, Sir Hans Krebs Medal 1985, Otto Warburg Medal 1988, Louis Jeantet Prize 1990, Prix Benoist 1993, Gairdner Award 1998, E. B. Wilson Medal 2000, Antonio Feltrinelli International Prize 2004, European Award for Science and Culture 2009. *Publications include:* Jeff's View: on Science and Scientists 2005; about 200 scientific publns in biochemical journals. *Leisure interests:* music, jogging. *Address:* Unterer Rebbergweg 33, 4153 Reinach, Switzerland (home). *Telephone:* (61) 7112795 (office). *Fax:* (61) 7112448 (office). *E-mail:* gottfried.schatz@unibas.ch (office). *Website:* www.chemie.unibas.ch (office).

SCHAUB, Alexander, DJ; German lawyer and civil servant; *Of Counsel, Freshfields Bruckhaus Deringer;* b. 14 June 1941, Duisburg; s. of Franz Schaub and Gertrud Stockert; m. Nicole Van der Meulen 1974; one s. two d.; ed Univs of Freiburg, Lausanne, Cologne and Bonn and Coll. of Europe, Bruges; with Fed. Ministry of Econ. Affairs 1971; mem. Secr. of Ralf Dahrendorf 1973; mem. Secr. and Deputy Chef de Cabinet of Guido Brunner 1974–78; Deputy Chef de Cabinet Messrs Davignon and Burke 1980, of Pres. Gaston Thorn 1981; Chef de Cabinet of Willy de Clercq 1985–89; Dir DG External Relations and Trade Policy, EC 1989–90, Deputy Dir-Gen. DG Internal Market and Industrial Affairs 1990–93, Deputy Dir-Gen. DG Industry 1993–95, Dir-Gen. for Competition 1995–2002; Dir-Gen. DG Internal Market and Services 2002–06 (retd); Of Counsel, Freshfields Bruckhaus Deringer, Brussels 2007–; mem. Schindler Group 2007–10; Grosses Silbernes Ehrenzeichen mit Stern (Austria), Verdienstkrent 1 klasse des Verdinstordens der Bundesrepublik Deutschland. *Publications include:* the Anhörung des Europäischen Parlaments in Rechtsetzungsverfahren der EWG 1971, Food Quality in the Internal Market 1993, Gentechnik im Lebensmittelbereich – Die Politik der EG-Kommission 1994 and numerous contribs to legal and professional journals, articles in newspapers etc. *Leisure interests:* tennis, skiing. *Address:* Freshfields Bruckhaus Deringer, Bastion Tower, Place du Champ de Mars/Marsveldplein 5, 1050 Brussels, Belgium (office). *Telephone:* (2) 504-76-57 (office). *Fax:* (2) 404-76-57 (office). *E-mail:* alexander.schaub@freshfields.com (office). *Website:* www.freshfields.com (office).

SCHÄUBLE, Wolfgang, DrIur; German politician and lawyer; *Federal Minister of Finance;* b. 18 Sept. 1942, Freiburg; s. of Karl Schäuble and Gertrud Schäuble (née Göhring); m. Ingeborg Hensle 1969; one s. three d.; ed Univs of Freiburg and Hamburg; Regional Pres., Junge Union, S Baden 1969–72; worked in admin. of taxes, Baden-Württemberg 1971–72; mem. Bundestag 1972–, Exec. Sec. CDU/CSU Parl. Group 1981–84, Vice-Chair. in charge of Foreign Security and European Policies 2002–; mem. parl., European Council 1975–84; Chair. CDU Cttee on Sport 1976–84; Regional Vice-Pres. S Baden CDU 1982–95, mem. Federal Exec. Cttee CDU, mem. Presidium CDU 2000–; Federal Minister with special responsibility and Head of Chancellery 1984–89, of Interior 1989–91, 2005–09, of Finance 2009–; Deputy Chair. Bd of Supervisory Dirs KfW Bankengruppe 2011–; CDU Parl. Leader 1991–2000, Leader 1998–2000; legal practice in Offenburg 1978–84; Chair. Arbeitsgemeinschaft Europäischer Grenzregionen (AGEG) 1979–82; Ordine al Merito della Repubblica Italiana 1986, Grosses Bundesverdienstkreuz 1991, Ordre de la couronne de chêne (Luxembourg) 2011. *Publications:* Der Vertrag 1991, Und der Zukunft zugewandt 1994, Und sie bewegt sich doch 1998, Mitten im Leben 2000, Scheitert der Westen? 2003. *Leisure interests:* chess, music. *Address:* Federal Ministry of Finance, Wilhelmstr. 97, 10117 Berlin, Germany (office). *Telephone:* (30) 186820 (office). *Fax:* (30) 186823260 (office). *E-mail:* poststelle@bmf.bund.de (office). *Website:* www.bundesfinanzministerium.de (office).

SCHAVAN, Annette, DPhil; German politician and theologian; b. 10 June 1955, Neuss am Rhein; Scientific Adviser, Religious Studies Dept, Cusanuswerk Inst., Bonn 1980–84, Dir 1988–95; Lecturer, Univ. of Düsseldorf 1988–93; Dept Leader for Further Educ., Parish of Aachen 1984–87; Leader, CDU Women's Union 1987–88, Vice-Chair. CDU 1998–; Baden-Württemberg Regional Minister for Culture, Youth and Sport 1995–2005; mem. Bundestag 2005–; Fed. Minister of Educ. and Research 2005–13; Officier de la Légion d'honneur 2002. *Leisure interests:* rambling. *Address:* Bundestag, Platz der Republik 1, 11011 Berlin, Germany (office). *Telephone:* (30) 22779253 (office). *Fax:* (30) 22776794 (office). *E-mail:* annette.schavan@bundestag.de (office). *Website:* www.annette-schavan .de.

SCHECK, Adolf; German business executive; *Chairman of the Supervisory Board, Edeka Zentrale AG & Co. KG;* joined Edeka AG Sparkasse Offenburg 1965, completed training as retail trade buyer 1969, various posts as dept man. within regional co., took over parent's Edeka business 1979, Man. Dir Scheck-, In-Einkaufscenter GmbH, Edeka Handelsgesellschaft Südwest mbH (Chair.), Bau & Grün AG (Chair.), Edeka AG Sparkasse Offenburg/Ortenau –2010, mem. Supervisory Bd Edeka AG 2002–, Chair. Supervisory Bd Edeka AG and Edeka Zentrale AG & Co. KG 2010–; mem. Supervisory Bd Ava Allgemeine Handelsgesellschaft Der Verbraucher AG (fmrly Ava AG) 2004–. *Address:* Edeka Zentrale AG & Co. KG, New-York-Ring 6, 22297 Hamburg, Germany (office). *Telephone:* (40) 63-77-0 (office). *Fax:* (40) 63-77-22-31 (office). *E-mail:* info@edeka.de (office). *Website:* www .edeka.de (office).

SCHECKTER, Jody David; South African business executive and fmr racing driver; b. 29 Jan. 1950, East London, nr Durban; m. Pam Bailey; two s.; raced karts from age of 11, graduated to motorcycles and racing cars; won SA Formula Ford Sunshine Series in 1970, competed in Britain from 1971; Formula One World Champion 1979, runner-up 1977, third place 1974 and 1976; Grand Prix wins: 1974 Swedish (Tyrrell-Ford), 1974 British (Tyrrell-Ford), 1975 South African (Tyrrell-Ford), 1976 Swedish (Tyrrell-Ford), 1977 Argentine (Wolf-Ford), 1977 Monaco (Wolf-Ford), 1977 Canadian (Wolf-Ford), 1979 Belgian (Ferrari), 1979 Monaco (Ferrari), 1979 Italian (Ferrari); retd from motor racing 1980; est. business in Atlanta, Ga, designing and building simulation equipment for firearms training, later retd; currently Owner, Laverstoke Park Farm (organic farm), UK; International Jewish Sports Hall of Fame 1983. *Leisure interest:* keeping fit. *Address:* Laverstoke Park Offices, Overton, Hants., RG25 3DR, England. *Telephone:* (1256) 772800. *Fax:* (1256) 772809. *E-mail:* info@laverstokepark.co.uk. *Website:* www .laverstokepark.co.uk.

SCHEEL, Walter; German politician; b. 8 July 1919, Solingen; m. 1st Eva Kronenberg 1942 (died 1966); one s.; m. 2nd Dr Mildred Wirtz 1969 (died 1985); one s. two d.; m. 3rd Barbara Wiese 1988; ed Reform-Gymnasium, Solingen; served with German Air Force during World War II; fmr head of market research org.; mem. Landtag North Rhine-Westphalia 1950–53; mem. Bundestag 1953–74, Vice-Pres. 1967–69; Fed. Minister for Econ. Co-operation 1961–66; Chair. of Free Democrats 1968–74 (Hon. Chair. 1979); Vice-Chancellor, Minister of Foreign Affairs 1969–74; Pres. FRG 1974–79; mem. European Parl. 1958–61; Pres. Bilderberg Conf. –1985; Chair. German Council of European Movt 1980–85; Chair. Bd of Trustees, Friedrich Naumann Foundation 1979–90; Chair. Admin. Council, Germanic Nat. Museum, Nuremberg 1978, Cttee European Music Year 1983–86; apptd Chair. Supervisory Bd, DEG-German Investment and Devt Co. 1980, Directory for Thoroughbreds and Races 1981; Pres. Europa-Union Deutsch-

land 1980–89; mem. Supervisory Bd ROBECO Group 1982–89, Supervisory Bd Thyssen AG, Supervisory Bd Thyssen Stahl AG; Hon. Pres. German Fed. of Artists; Hon. Pres. 4th Choir Olympics, Xiamen, People's Repub. of China 2006; Grosses Bundesverdienstkreuz (special class); numerous hon. degrees and awards from Germany and abroad; Theodor Heuss Prize 1971, Peace Prize (Kajima Inst., Tokyo) 1973, Gold Medal, Fondation du Mérite Européen 1984. *Publications include:* Konturen einer neuen Welt 1965, Schwierigkeiten, Ernüchterung und Chancen der Industrieländer 1965, Formeln deutscher Politik 1968, Warum Mitbestimmung und wie 1970, Die Freiburger Thesen der Liberalen (with K.-H. Flach and W. Maihofer) 1972, Bundestagreden 1972, Reden und Interviews 1974–79, Vom Recht des anderen – Gedanken zur Freiheit 1977, Die Zukunft der Freiheit 1979, Nach 30 Jahren, Die Bundesrepublik Deutschland, Vergangenheit, Gegenwart, Zukunft 1979, Die andere deutsche Frage 1981, Wen Schmerzt noch Deutschlands Teilung? 1986. *Leisure interest:* modern art. *Address:* Flemingstrasse 107, 81925 Munich, Germany.

SCHEELE, Sir Nicholas Vernon, Kt, KCMG, BA; British business executive; *Chairman, Key Safety Systems Inc.;* b. 3 Jan. 1944, Essex, England; s. of Werner James Scheele and Norah Edith Scheele (née Gough); m. Rosamund Ann Jacobs 1967; two s. one d.; ed Durham Univ.; with Purchasing, Supply, Procurement, Ford of Britain 1966–78; Purchasing, Supply, Procurement Man., Ford of USA 1978–83, Dir Supply Policy and Planning 1983–85, Dir Body and Chassis Parts Purchasing 1985–88; Pres. Ford of Mexico 1988–91; mem. Supervisory Bd Ford Werke AG 1999–2001, Vice-Chair. Jaguar Cars Jan.–April 1992, Chair. and CEO 1992–99, Chair. Ford of Europe –2001, Vice-Pres. for N America, Ford Motor Co. Dearborn, Mich. 2001, COO and Pres. 2001–04, Pres. and Dir responsible for product planning, information tech. and global purchasing 2004; Chair. Prince of Wales Business and Environment Cttee 1999–2006, Mfg Theme Group, Foresight 2020 1999–2002; Chancellor Univ. of Warwick 2002–08; Chair. Key Safety Systems Inc. 2007–, Metalsa 2010–, Stackpole International; Dir Grupo Proeza, Mexico 2005–, Pegasus Group, USA 2006–09; Chair. CMI 2005–08; mem. of Council Midlands Region Inst. of Dirs 1994–99, Exec. Cttee Soc. of Motor Mfrs and Traders, Bd of Dirs British American Tobacco plc 2005–, Advisory Bd British American Chamber of Commerce 1995–99, Fulbright Comm., Univ. of Coventry 1995–, Univ. of Durham 1996–; six hon. doctorates. *Leisure interests:* reading, classical music, tennis, squash.

SCHEEPBOUWER, Adrianus (Ad) Johannes; Dutch telecommunications industry executive; b. 22 July 1944, Dordrecht; Pres. Air Freight Div. Pakhoed Holding NV (later Pandair Group) 1976–88; Man. Dir PTT Post 1988–98; mem. Bd of Man. Royal KPN NV (fmr holding co. of PTT Post and PTT Telecom) 1992–98, Chair. and CEO TPG 1998–2001, Chair. Bd of Man. and CEO Royal KPN 2001–11, CEO Getronics 2010–; Chair. Supervisory Bd Havenbedrijf Rotterdam NV, Supervisory Council of Maasstad Hosp.; mem. Supervisory Bd RFS Holland Holding BV (Wehkamp), Supervisory Bd Bank Oyens & van Eeghen, Advisory Bd ECP. NL; Chair. Audit Cttee 'Sleutelgebieden' of the Innovationplatform; mem. Supervisory Council of Foundation for Nat. Art Collection; Amb. 'Randstad Urgent' (Project International City The Hague). *Address:* c/o Royal KPN, Maanplein 55, 2516 CK The Hague, Netherlands.

SCHEER, François, DèsSc; French diplomatist (retd); b. 13 March 1934, Strasbourg; s. of Alfred Scheer and Edmée Lechten; m. 2nd Nicole Roubaud 1985; one s. one d.; one s. three d. from 1st m.; ed Faculty of Law, Univ. of Paris, Inst. d'Etudes Politiques de Paris, Ecole Nat. d'Admin.; Second Sec. Embassy, Algiers 1962–64; Direction des Affaires Economiques et Financières, Admin Cen. 1964–67; Cultural Attaché Embassy, Tokyo 1967–71; Deputy Dir for Budget 1971, also for Financial Affairs 1972–76; Amb. to Mozambique and Swaziland 1976–77; Deputy Perm. Rep. to European Community 1977–79, Dir of Cabinet to Pres. of European Parl. 1979–81; Dir of Cabinet of Minister of Foreign Affairs 1981–84; Amb. to Algeria 1984–86; Amb. Perm. Rep. for France to EC (now EU) 1986–88, 1992–93; Sec.-Gen. Ministry of Foreign Affairs 1988–92; Amb. to FRG 1993–99; mem. Cttee for Atomic Energy 1988–92; Admin. Cie générale des matières nucléaires (Cogema) 1989–93; mem. Conseil d'Admin. Ecole Nat. d'Admin. 1991–95; adviser, Pres. of Cogema 1999–2001, Pres. Exec. Bd Areva 2001–11; Commdr, Légion d'honneur, Ordre nat. du Mérite. *Address:* 10 square Adanson, 75005 Paris, France (home). *Telephone:* 1-45-81-35-84 (home). *E-mail:* francoischeer@orange.fr (home).

SCHEFFER, Ingrid, MB BS, PhD, FRACP; Australian paediatrician, medical scientist and academic; *Chair of Paediatric Neurology Research, University of Melbourne;* Chair of Paediatric Neurology Research, Univ. of Melbourne, Prof., Depts of Medicine and Paediatrics, Sr Prin. Research Fellow, Florey Neuroscience Insts; Dir of Paediatrics, Austin Health, Heidelberg, Vic., Dir Children's Epilepsy Program; Paediatric Neurologist and Epileptologist, Neurosciences, Monash Medical Centre, Clayton, Vic., Dept of Neurology, Royal Children's Hosp., Parkville, Vic.; Hon. Fellow of Genetic Health Services, Vic.; Hon. Research Fellow, Murdoch Children's Research Inst.; Nat. Health and Medical Research Council (NHMRC) Medical Postgraduate Scholar 1992–94, Jr Investigator Award, American Epilepsy Soc. 1993, Commendation for Premier of Vic.'s Award for Medical Research 1998, Harbison-Higinbotham Research Scholarship, Univ. of Melbourne 1998, Chancellor's Prize, Univ. of Melbourne 1999, Nat. Asscn of Research Fellows of NHMRC Post-Doctoral Investigator Award 2003, Henry Dunn Lecturer, Vancouver Gen. Hosp., Canada 2008, MacKeith Lecturer, British Paediatric Neurology Asscn 2009, Prof. R. Gulati Oration, Postgraduate Inst. of Medical Educ. and Research, Chandigarh, India 2009, Tibbles Lecturer, Annual 46th Congress of the Canadian Neurological Sciences Fed. 2011, Jacobsen Lecturer, Royal Victoria Infirmary, Newcastle, UK 2011, NHMRC Program Grant Chief Investigator 2002–(15), NHMRC Practitioner Fellowship 2001–05, 2011–(15), Research Recognition Award for Clinical Research, American Epilepsy Society 2007, Eric Susman Prize, Royal Australasian Coll. of Physicians 2009, L'Oréal-UNESCO For Women in Science Award (Asia-Pacific) for identifying genes involved in some forms of epilepsy) 2012. *Publications:* numerous papers in professional journals. *Address:* Epilepsy Research Centre, Level 2, Melbourne Brain Centre, 245 Burgundy Street, Austin Health, Heidelberg, Vic. 3084, Australia (office). *Telephone:* (3) 9035-7344 (office). *Fax:* (3) 9496-2291 (office). *E-mail:* scheffer@unimelb.edu.au (office). *Website:* www.brain.org.au/epilepsyresearch/staff/profiles/i_scheffer.htm (office). www.ingridscheffer.com.

SCHEFFLER, Israel, PhD; American philosopher and academic; *Professor Emeritus, Harvard University;* b. 25 Nov. 1923, New York, NY; s. of Leon Scheffler and Ethel Grünberg Scheffler; m. Rosalind Zuckerbrod 1949; one s. one d.; ed Brooklyn Coll., Jewish Theological Seminary and Univ. of Pennsylvania; mem. faculty, Harvard Univ. 1952–, Prof. of Educ. 1961–62, Prof. of Educ. and Philosophy 1962–64, Victor S. Thomas Prof. of Educ. and Philosophy 1964–92, Prof. Emer. 1992–, Hon. Research Fellow in Cognitive Studies 1965–66, Co-Dir Philosophy of Educ. Research Center 1983–, Dir 1999–; Mead-Swing Lecturer, Oberlin Coll. 1965; Patten Foundation Lecturer, Indiana Univ. 1981; Scholar-in-Residence, Mandel Center, Brandeis Univ., Mass 2003–09; Founding mem. Nat. Acad. of Educ. 1965; Fellow, Center for Advanced Study in Behavioral Sciences, Palo Alto, Calif. 1972–73; fmr Pres. Philosophy of Science Asscn, Charles S. Peirce Soc.; Fellow, American Acad. of Arts and Sciences; Hon. AM (Harvard Univ.) 1959, Hon. DHL (Jewish Theological Seminary) 1993; Guggenheim Fellow 1958–59, 1972–73, Alumni Award of Merit, Brooklyn Coll. 1967, Distinguished Service Medal, Teachers' Coll., Columbia 1980. *Publications:* Philosophy and Education 1958, The Language of Education 1960, The Anatomy of Inquiry 1963, Conditions of Knowledge 1965, Science and Subjectivity 1967, Logic and Art (co-ed.) 1972, Reason and Teaching 1973, Four Pragmatists 1974, Beyond the Letter 1979, Of Human Potential 1985, Inquiries 1986, In Praise of the Cognitive Emotions 1991, Work, Education and Leadership (co-author) 1995, Teachers of My Youth 1995, Symbolic Worlds 1997, Visions of Jewish Education (co-ed.) 2003, Gallery of Scholars 2004, Worlds of Truth 2009. *Leisure interests:* reading, crosswords, research. *E-mail:* israel_scheffler@harvard.edu (office).

SCHEFFLER, Matthias Robert, Dr rer. nat; German physicist and academic; *Director, Theory Department, Fritz Haber Institute;* b. 1951, Berlin; ed Technische Universität Berlin; Scientific Staff mem., Physikalisch-Technische Bundesanstalt, Braunschweig 1978–88; Researcher, IBM T.J. Watson Research Center, Yorktown Heights, NY, USA 1979–80; Researcher, Max-Planck-Inst., Stuttgart 1982; Dir, Theory Dept, Fritz Haber Inst., Berlin 1988–; Visiting Scientist, Instituto de Fisica, Universidade de Sao Paulo, Brazil 1995; Visiting Scientist, Kavli Inst. for Theoretical Physics, Univ. of Calif., Santa Barbara, USA 2002; Hon. Prof., Technische Universität Berlin 1989–, Freie Universitat Berlin 2001–, Visiting Prof., Dalian Inst. of Chem. Physics, Chinese Acad. of Sciences 2004–, Distinguished Visiting Prof., Univ. of California, Santa Barbara 2004–; Dr hc; Max-Planck Research Award for Int. Co-operation 2001, Medard W. Welch Medal and Prize, American Vacuum Soc. 2003, Max Born Medal and Prize 2004, Ernst Mach Hon. Medal, Acad. of Sciences of the Czech Repub. 2008, Rudolf Jaeckel Prize, German Vacuum Soc. 2010. *Publications:* Walter Kohn: Personal Stories and Anecdotes Told by Friends and Collaborators (co-ed.) 2003; 409 articles in scientific journals. *Address:* Fritz-Haber-Institut der Max-Planck-Gesellschaft, Faradayweg 4–6, 14195 Berlin-Dahlem, Germany (office). *Telephone:* (30) 8413-4711 (office). *Fax:* (30) 8413-4701 (office). *E-mail:* scheffler@FHI-Berlin.MPG.de (office). *Website:* (office).

SCHEIBER, Harry N., AB, MA, PhD; American academic, writer and editor; *Stefan A. Riesenfeld Professor of Law and History and Director, Institute for Legal Research, University of California, Berkeley;* b. 1935, New York, NY; ed Columbia Univ., Cornell Univ.; Instructor to Assoc. Prof., Dartmouth Coll. 1960–68, Prof. of History 1968–71; Fellow, Centre for Advanced Study in the Behavioural Sciences, Stanford 1967, 1971; Prof. of American History, Univ. of California, San Diego 1971–80, Prof. of Law, Univ. of California, Berkeley 1980–, Assoc. Dean 1990–93, 1996–99, Stefan A. Riesenfeld Prof. of Law and History 1991–, Dir Center for the Study of Law and Society 2000–01, Earl Warren Legal Inst. 2002–05, Inst. for Legal Research 2005–, Sho Sato Program in Japanese and US Law, Law of the Sea Inst. 2004–; Fulbright Distinguished Sr Lecturer, Australia 1983; Ed. Yearbook of the California Supreme Court Historical Society 1994–2008; Visiting Research Prof., Univ. of Uppsala, Sweden 1995; mem. American Historical Asscn, California Supreme Court Historical Soc., Economic History Asscn, Law and Society Asscn, Org. of American Historians, American Acad. of Arts and Sciences 2003–, American Soc. for Legal History (Pres. 2003–05); mem. Bd of Advisors, National Sea Grant Legal Center 2004–; mem. Scientific Advisory Bd, Joint Ocean Commission Initiative 2007–; Fellow, Japan Soc. for the Promotion of Science 2001; Hon. MA (Dartmouth Coll.) 1965; Hon. DJur (Uppsala) 1998; Guggenheim Fellowships 1971, 1988, Rockefeller Foundation Fellowship 1979, Nat. Endowment for the Humanities Fellowship 1985–86, Riesenfeld Award in Int. Law 2012, Univ. of California, Berkeley Citation 2012. *Publications:* The Wilson Administration and Civil Liberties 1960, United States Economic History 1964, America: Purpose and Power (co-author) 1965, The Condition of American Federalism 1966, The Frontier in American Development (co-ed.) 1969, The Old Northwest 1969, The Ohio Canal Era 1820–1861 1969 (revised edns 1987, 2012), Black Labor in American History 1972, Agriculture in the Development of the Far West 1975, American Economic History (co-author) 1976, American Law and the Constitutional Order 1978, Perspectives on Federalism (ed.) 1987, Power Divided (co-ed.) 1989, Federalism and the Judicial Mind (ed.) 1993, Legal Culture and the Legal Profession (co-author) 1995, The State and Freedom of Contract 1998, Law of the Sea: The Common Heritage and Emerging Challenges 2000, Inter-Allied Conflicts and Ocean Law, 1945–1952 2001, Bringing New Law To Ocean Waters (co-ed.) 2004, Earl Warren and the Warren Court (ed.) 2007, Japanese Family Law (co-ed.) 2009, Oceans in the Nuclear Age (co-ed.) 2010, Japanese Legal System (co-ed.) 2012; contribs to professional journals. *Address:* School of Law, 442 Boalt Hall (North Addition), University of California, Berkeley, CA 94720, USA (office). *Telephone:* (510) 643-9788 (office). *Fax:* (510) 643-2698 (office). *E-mail:* scheiber@berkeley.edu (office); hscheiber@law.berkeley.edu (office). *Website:* www.law.berkeley.edu (office).

SCHEID, HE Cardinal Eusébio Oscar, SCI, DTheol; Brazilian ecclesiastic; *Archbishop of São Sebastião do Rio de Janeiro;* b. 8 Dec. 1932, Bom Retiro, Joaçaba; s. of Alberto Reinaldo Scheid and Rosalia Joana Scheid; ed Congregation of Priests of Sacred Heart of Jesus (Dehonian Fathers') Seminary, Seminary of Priests of Heart of Jesus, Corupa, Pontifical Gregorian Univ., Rome, Italy; ordained priest 1960; Prof. of Theology, Christ the King Seminary and Northeast Regional Seminary, Recife 1964–65 Prof. of Dogma and Liturgy, Theological Inst. of Taubate 1965–81; Prof. of Religious Culture, Pontifical Catholic Univ. of São Paulo 1966–68; Coordinator of Catechesis, Taubate 1970–74; Dir Faculty of Theology, Taubate; Bishop of São José dos Campos 1981–91; Archbishop of

Florianópolis 1991–2001; attended Fourth Gen. Conf. of Latin American Episcopate, Santo Domingo, Dominican Repub. 1992, Ninth Ordinary Ass. of World Synod of Bishops, Vatican City 1994, Tenth Ordinary Ass. 2001; Archbishop of São Sebastião do Rio de Janeiro and Bishop of Brazil, Faithful of the Oriental Rites 2001–; cr. Cardinal (Cardinal Priest of SS Bonifacio ed Alessio) 2003; Pres. South Region IV of Brazilian Bishops' Conf., currently Counsellor, Pontifical Comm. for Latin America; mem. Pontifical Council for Social communications, Pontifical Comm. for Latin America, Council of Cardinals. *Address:* Archdiocese of São Sebastião do Rio de Janeiro, Rua Benjamin Constant 23/502, Gloria, C.P. 1362, 20241-150 Rio de Janeiro, RJ, Brazil (office). *Telephone:* (21) 292-3132 (office). *Fax:* (21) 242-9295 (office). *Website:* www.arquidiocese.org.br (office).

SCHEIFELE, Bernd, LLM; German business executive; *Chairman of the Managing Board, HeidelbergCement;* b. 5 May 1958, Freiburg; m.; four c.; ed Univ. of Freiburg, Univ. of Dijon, France; worked with Gleiss Lutz Hootz Hirsch law firm, Stuttgart 1988–94; as attorney, prepared incorporation of Phoenix Pharmahandel AG & Co. KG, Mannheim, Chair. Phoenix 1994–2005, currently Chair. Advisory Bd; Chair. Man. Bd HeidelbergCement 2005–; Chair. Supervisory Bd Tamro Group, Vantaa (Finland); Deputy Chair. Supervisory Bd Georg von Holtzbrinck publishing group; mem. Bd of Dirs Helaba (Landesbank Hessen-Thüringen); Fulbright Scholarship 1984. *Address:* HeidelbergCement, Berliner Strasse 6, 69120 Heidelberg, Baden-Württemberg, Germany (office). *Telephone:* (6221) 481-0 (office). *Fax:* (6221) 481-554 (office). *E-mail:* info@heidelbergcement.com (office). *Website:* www.heidelbergcement.com (office).

SCHEIFF, Dieter Christian, BA, MBA; German business executive; b. 8 June 1952, Koblenz; m.; three c.; ed Univ. of Applied Sciences (Fachhochschule) Aachen; held various sales and marketing roles at 3M 1987–98; joined Johnson and Johnson Cordis 1998, becoming Vice-Pres. for Europe 2001; Head of Sales and Marketing, DIS Deutscher Industrie Service AG 2001–02, CEO 2002–06, CEO Adecco Management & Consulting SA (following acquisition of DIS by Adecco) 2006–09. *Address:* c/o Adecco Management & Consulting SA, Sägereistrasse 10, PO Box, 8152 Glattbrugg, Switzerland. *Telephone:* (44) 878-88-88. *Fax:* (44) 829-88-88. *E-mail:* info@adecco.com. *Website:* www.adecco.com.

SCHEKMAN, Randy Wayne, PhD; American biologist and academic; *Professor of Cell and Developmental Biology, University of California, Berkeley;* b. 30 Dec. 1948, St Paul, Minn.; ed Univ. of California, Los Angeles and Stanford Univ. School of Medicine; Cystic Fibrosis Postdoctoral Fellow, Biology Dept, Univ. of California, San Diego, La Jolla 1974–76; Asst Prof., then Assoc. Prof., then Prof., Dept of Biochemistry, Univ. of California, Berkeley 1976–89, Prof. of Cell and Developmental Biology, Dept of Molecular and Cell Biology 1989–, Head, Div. of Biochemistry and Molecular Biology 1990–94, Investigator, Howard Hughes Medical Inst. 1990–, Co-Chair. Dept of Molecular and Cell Biology 1997–2000; Chair. FASEB Conf. on Protein Folding in the Cell 1992, Gordon Conf. on Molecular Membrane Biology 1997; mem. Bd of Scientific Advisors, Jane Coffin Childs Memorial Fund for Medical Research 1992–2000, Scientific Dir 2002–; mem. Eli Lilly Award Cttee 1988–90, Chair. 1990; mem. Advisory Cttee, Pew Scholars Program 1996–2002; Ed. eLife 2012–; Assoc. Ed. Molecular Cell Biology 1988–91, Molecular Biology of the Cell 1992–99 (Ed. 1999–), Annual Reviews of Cell and Developmental Biology 1993–98, Journal of Cell Biology (later Ed.) 1993–; mem. Editorial Bd Journal of Cell Biology 1985–92, Journal of Membrane Biology 1986, Biochemistry 1986–93, Cell 2001–; mem. NAS 1992 (Chair. Biochemistry Section 2002–, Ed.-in-Chief Proceedings of the National Academy of Sciences 2007–11), NIH Cell Biology (Study Section), American Soc. for Microbiology, American Acad. for Microbiology, American Soc. for Biochemistry and Molecular Biology, American Soc. for Cell Biology (Council mem. 1991–94); Foreign Assoc., European Molecular Biology Org. 2001; Foreign mem. Royal Soc. 2013; Hon. mem. Japanese Biochemical Soc. 1993; Dr hc (Geneva) 1997; Undergraduate Research Award, UCLA Zoology Dept 1970, Woodrow Wilson Fellow 1970, Guggenheim Fellowship 1982–83, Lewis S. Rosenstiel Award in Basic Biomedical Science 1994, Gairdner Foundation International Award 1996, Amgen Award Lecturer Protein Society 1999, Berkeley Faculty Research 1999, Albert Lasker Award for Basic Medical Research 2002, Louisa Gross Horwitz Prize, Columbia Univ. 2002, Massry Prize 2010, Nobel Prize in Medicine (with James E. Rothman and Thomas C. Sudhof) 2013. *Publications include:* more than 200 articles in scientific journals on mechanism and control of intracellular protein transport. *Address:* Schekman Lab, Department of Molecular and Cell Biology, University of California, Berkeley, 475D Li Ka Shing Center #3370, Berkeley, CA 94720-3370, USA (office). *Telephone:* (510) 642-5686 (office). *Fax:* (510) 642-7846 (office). *E-mail:* schekman@berkeley.edu (office). *Website:* mcb.berkeley.edu/labs/schekman (office).

SCHELL, Orville Hickok, BA, MA, PhD; American journalist, writer and academic; *Senior Fellow, Center on Communication Leadership, Annenberg School for Communication, University of Southern California;* b. 20 May 1940, New York, NY; m.; three s.; ed Stanford Univ., National Taiwan Univ., Harvard Univ., Univ. of California, Berkeley; Overseas Development Training Associate Fellowship, Ford Foundation, Jakarta, Indonesia 1964–66; Foreign Area Training Fellowship, Center for Chinese Studies, Univ. of California 1967–68; Co-Dir Bay Area Institute 1968–71; Founder and Ed.-in-Chief, Pacific News Service 1970–71; China Correspondent, New Yorker Magazine 1975; Research Assoc. Univ. of California, Berkeley 1986, Regents' Lecturer 1990, Dean, Graduate School of Journalism 1996–2007; Sr Fellow, Center on Communication Leadership, Annenberg School for Communication, Univ. of Southern California 2007–; Arthur Ross Director, Center on US-China Relations, Asia Soc. 2007–; Visiting Distinguished Prof., Chico State Univ. 1987; Moderator, Issues and Perspectives on China, Voice of America 1995–97; Editor, Project Syndicate China column 2000–; Sr Fellow, Freedom Forum Media Studies Center, Columbia Univ. 1995; mem. Bd of Dirs World Affairs Council of San Francisco 1999–, Current Media 2005–, Homelands Productions; mem. Media Council, Davos World Economic Forum 1998–; mem. Authors' Guild, Council on Foreign Relations 1992–, Global Business Network, Human Rights Watch Board, Pacific Council, PEN, National Committee on US-China Relations 1984–; Dr hc (Dominican Univ.) 2001; Alicia Patterson Foundation Journalism Fellowship 1981, MacDowell Colony Fellowship 1983, 1986, Guggenheim Fellowship 1989–90, Emmy Award (for 60 Minutes report Made In China) 1992, Overseas Press Club of American Award 1993, George Foster

Peabody Award (as producer of WGBH-Frontline documentary The Gate of Heavenly Peace) 1997, Shorenstein Journalism Award for Covering Asia, Shorenstein Center on the Press, Politics and Public Policy and Stanford Univ. Asia-Pacific Research Center 2003, Fred Cody Lifetime Achievement Award, Northern California Book Awards 2005. *Publications include:* The China Reader (with Frederick Crews) 1970, Modern China: The Story of a Revolution 1972, The Town That Fought to Save Itself 1976, In the People's Republic 1976, Brown 1978, Watch Out for the Foreign Guests: China Encounters the West 1981, Modern Meat: Antibiotics, Hormones and the Pharmaceutical Farm 1983, To Get Rich is Glorious: China in the 1980s 1984, Discos and Democracy: China in the Throes of Reform 1988, Mandate of Heaven: A New Generation of Entrepreneurs, Dissidents, Technocrats, and Bohemians Grasp for Power in China 1994, The China Reader: The Reform Years (ed. with David Shambaugh) 1999, Virtual Tibet: The West's Fascination with the Roof of the World 1999; contributions: numerous books, reviews, and journals. *Address:* Center on Communication Leadership and Policy, 350 South Grand Avenue, Suite 3350, Los Angeles, CA 90071, USA (office). *Telephone:* (213) 337-3100 (office). *E-mail:* commlead@usc.edu (office). *Website:* communicationleadership.usc.edu (office); orvilleschell.com.

SCHELLER, Richard H., BS, PhD; American medical scientist, academic and business executive; *Executive Vice-President of Research and Early Development, Genentech, Inc.;* b. 30 Oct. 1953, Milwaukee, Wis.; m. Prof. Susan McConnell; ed Univ. of Wisconsin, California Inst. of Tech.; Postdoctoral Fellow in Molecular Neurobiology, Coll. of Physicians and Surgeons, Columbia Univ. 1981–82; Asst Prof., Dept of Biological Sciences, Stanford Univ. 1982–87, Assoc. Prof. 1987–90, Assoc. Prof., Dept of Molecular and Cellular Physiology 1990–93, Prof. 1993–2002, Assoc. Investigator, Howard Hughes Medical Inst., Stanford Univ. Medical Center 1990–94, Investigator 1994–2001; Adjunct Prof., Dept of Biochemistry and Biophysics, Univ. of California, San Francisco 2004–10; Sr Vice-Pres., Genentech, Inc. 2001–03, Exec. Vice-Pres. of Research 2003–09, Chief Scientific Officer and Exec. Vice-Pres. of Research 2008–09, Exec. Vice-Pres., Genentech Research and Early Development and mem. Enlarged Roche Corp. Exec. Cttee 2009–; mem. NAS 2000; Foreign mem. Norwegian Acad. of Science and Letters 2010; Fellow, American Acad. of Arts and Sciences 1998; Alan T. Waterman Award 1989, W. Alden Spencer Award 1993, NAS Award in Molecular Biology 1997, Kavli Prize in Neuroscience (co-recipient) 2010, Life Sciences Distinguished Alumni Award, Univ. of Wisconsin 2013, Albert Lasker Award for Basic Medical Research (co-recipient) 2013. *Publications:* more than 280 papers in professional journals. *Address:* Genentech, Inc., 1 DNA Way, South San Francisco, CA 94080, USA (office). *Telephone:* (650) 225-1000 (office). *Fax:* (650) 225-6000 (office). *Website:* www.gene.com (office).

SCHELLNHUBER, Hans Joachim, PhD (Habil.); German physicist and academic; *Director, Potsdam Institute for Climate Impact Research;* b. 7 June 1950, Ortenburg, Passau; m. Margret Boysen; one c.; ed Vilshofen Secondary School, Univs of Regensburg and Oldenburg; Student Asst, Physics Dept, Univ. of Regensburg 1971–76, Scientific Asst 1976–81; Postdoctoral Fellow, Inst. for Theoretical Physics, Univ. of California, Santa Barbara, USA 1981–82; Asst Prof., Physics Dept, Univ. of Oldenburg 1982–87, Prof. of Theoretical Physics 1988–93, Man. Dir Interdisciplinary Inst. for Coastal Environment Studies 1992; Founder and Dir Potsdam Inst. for Climate Impact Research, in conjunction with a Chair of Theoretical Physics at Univ. of Potsdam 1993–; Research Dir, Tyndall Centre for Climate Change Research (Distinguished Science Adviser 2005–09) and Prof., Environmental Sciences School, Univ. of East Anglia, Norwich, UK 2001–09; External Prof., Santa Fe Inst., USA 2010–; Visiting Prof., Inst. of Nonlinear Sciences, Univ. of California, Santa Cruz, USA 1987–88; Visiting Prof. in Physics and Visiting Fellow of Christ Church Coll., Oxford 2005–09; Co-Chair. German Advisory Council on Global Change (WBGU); mem. Intergovernmental Panel on Climate Change; Amb. of Int. Geosphere-Biosphere Programme 2003; Amb. of Science, State of Brandenburg 2009; mem. Max Planck Soc., German Nat. Acad. (Leopoldina), NAS, Leibniz Science Asscn, Geological Soc. of London, Int. Research Soc. Sigma Xi, Academia Europaea; Fellow, Heisenberg Programme of the German Science Foundation 1987–89; Hon. CBE 2004; Order of Merit (Roter-Adler-Orden), State of Brandenburg 2008; Order of Merit of FRG 2011; Dr hc (Copenhagen) 2011, (Technische Universität Berlin) 2012; Bavarian Scholarship for Exceptionally Gifted 1970, Heisenberg Fellow, German Science Foundation 1987, Wolfson Research Merit Award and Research Fellow, Royal Soc. 2002, German Environment Prize 2007, Environment Prize of Bundesdeutscher Arbeitskreis für Umweltbewusstes Management e.V. 2008, Times Higher Education Award: Research Project of the Year, Univ. of East Anglia 2008, Volvo Environment Prize 2011, Pioneer of German Energy Transformation (Wirtschaftswoche) 2011, Wilhelm Foerster Prize, URANIA Potsdam 2013. *Publications:* numerous papers in professional journals. *Address:* Potsdam Institute for Climate Impact Research, PO Box 601203, 14412 Potsdam, Germany (office). *Telephone:* (331) 2882502 (office). *Fax:* (331) 2882600 (office). *E-mail:* director@pik-potsdam.de (office). *Website:* www.pik-potsdam.de/members/john (office).

SCHENKER, Joseph G., MD; Israeli physician; b. 20 Nov. 1933, Kraków, Poland; s. of Itzhak Schenker; m. Ekaterina Idels 1959; two s.; ed Herzlia High School, Tel-Aviv and the Hebrew Univ. of Jerusalem; Exec. Chief of Teaching Obstetrics and Gynaecology, Hebrew Univ. Medical School 1977–84; Chair. Dept of Obstetrics and Gynaecology, Hadassah Univ. Hosp., Jerusalem 1978; Prof. of Obstetrics and Gynaecology, Hebrew Univ. Jerusalem 1979–; Pres. Israel Soc. of Obstetrics and Gynaecology 1984–92, Deputy Pres. and Sec. 1993–; Pres. Israel Medical Asscn, Jerusalem br. 1984–; Chair. of Directory, Bd Examination in Obstetrics and Gynaecology, State of Israel 1979–83, of Advisory Cttee 1979–86; Acting Chair. of Hadassah Org. of Heads of Depts. 1983–; Chair. Residency Programme, Medical Council 1987, of Cttee Licensing Physicians, Ministry of Health 1987; Pres. of Int. Soc. for Study of Pathophysiology 1983; Chair. European Residency Exchange Programme, Extended European Bd of Gynaecology and Obstetrics 1993– (Pres. of Bd 1994–), Cttee for European Examination for Excellence in Gynaecology and Obstetrics 1993–, FIGO (Int. Fed. of Gynaecology and Obstetrics) Cttee for Study of Ethical Aspects of Human Reproduction 1994–2004 (mem. Exec. Bd FIGO 1991–); Pres. Int. Acad. of Human Reproduction 1996–; Deputy Pres. and Sec. Israel Medical Council 1985–, European Asscn of Gynaecology and Obstetrics 1996–2000; Founder mem. European Soc. of Human Reproduction, Int. Soc. of Gynaecological Endocrinology, Int. Soc. of Study of

Pathophysiology of Pregnancy and other orgs; mem. exec. bds and cttees, hon. mem. or mem. numerous int. professional orgs; mem. Editorial Bd Human Reproduction (Oxford), Int. Journal of Gynaecology and Obstetrics (USA), Int. Journal of Foeto-Maternal Medicine (Germany), European Journal of Obstetrics, Gynaecology and Reproductive Biology and several other journals; Hon. Fellow, American Coll. of Obstetricians and Gynaecologists, Royal Coll. of Obstetricians and Gynaecologists and other int. orgs, Hon. Citizen of City of Jerusalem; Award for Outstanding Contribution to the Field of Human Reproduction 1999. *Publications include:* Recent Advances in Pathophysiological Conditions in Pregnancy (ed.)1984, The Intrauterine Life-Management and Therapy 1986, Female and Male Infertility 1997, Pregnancy and Delivery 1998, Textbook of Gynecology 2000; more than 550 articles in medical journals on obstetrics and gynaecology, new tech. in reproduction, ethical and legal aspects of IVF etc. *Leisure interests:* history, chess. *Address:* Department of Orbital Gynaecology, Hadassah Medical Center, PO Box 12000, Jerusalem 91120 (office); 5 Mendele Street, Jerusalem 91147, Israel (home). *Telephone:* 2-6777779 (office); 2-637775 (home). *Fax:* 2-6432445. *E-mail:* schenker@cc.huji.ac.il (office).

SCHEPISI, Frederic Alan, AO; Australian film writer, director and producer; b. 26 Dec. 1939, Melbourne; s. of Frederic Thomas Schepisi and Loretto Ellen Schepisi (née Hare); m. 1st Joan Mary Ford 1960; two s. two d.; m. 2nd Rhonda Elizabeth Finlayson 1973 (divorced 1983); two d.; m. 3rd Mary Rubin 1984; one s.; ed Assumption Coll., Kilmore, Victoria, Marist Brothers' Juniorate, Macedon, Victoria, Marcellin Coll., Melbourne; Carden Advertising, Melbourne, Press TV Production; Patron Advisory Service, Melbourne 1961–64; Victorian Man. Cinesound Productions, Melbourne 1964–66; Man. Dir, The Film House, Melbourne 1966–79, Chair. 1979–92; Dr hc (Griffith Univ., Australia) 1995; Raymond Longford Award 1991, Chauvel Award 1994, Outstanding Achievement Award 2003. *Television:* Empire Falls (Golden Globe Award 2005, Emmy Award 2005) 2003. *Films include:* A Devil's Playground (Australian Film Inst. Award for Best Direction) 1975, The Chant of Jimmie Blacksmith (Writers Guild Award) 1978, Barbarosa 1981, Iceman 1983, Plenty 1985, Roxanne (Writers Guild Award 1988) 1986, Evil Angels (Australian Film Inst. Award for Best Film 1989) (also known as A Cry in the Dark (Longford Award 1991) 1990, The Russia House 1990, Mr. Baseball 1991, Six Degrees of Separation 1993, IQ 1994, Fierce Creatures 1997, That Eye the Sky (exec. producer), Last Orders 2001, It Runs in the Family 2002, The Eye of the Storm 2011. *Television includes:* Empire Falls 2005. *Leisure interests:* tennis, swimming. *Address:* PO Box 743, South Yarra, Vic. 3141, Australia.

SCHERAGA, Harold A., PhD; American scientist and academic; *George W. and Grace L. Todd Professor Emeritus, Department of Chemistry and Chemical Biology, Cornell University;* b. (Abraham Harold Scheraga), 18 Oct. 1921, Brooklyn, NY; s. of Samuel Scheraga and Etta Scheraga; m. Miriam Kurnow 1943; one s. two d.; ed City Coll. of New York and Duke Univ.; ACS Postdoctoral Fellow, Harvard Medical School 1946–47; Instructor of Chem., Cornell Univ. 1947–50, Asst Prof. 1950–53, Assoc. Prof. 1953–58, Prof. 1958–92, Todd Prof. 1965–92, Todd Prof. Emer. 1992–; Chair. Chem. Dept 1960–67; Guggenheim Fellow and Fulbright Research Scholar, Carlsberg Lab., Copenhagen 1956–57, Weizmann Inst., Rehovoth, Israel 1963; NIH Special Fellow, Weizman Inst., Rehovoth, Israel 1970; Visiting Lecturer, Wool Research Labs, CSIRO, Australia 1959; Visiting Prof., Weizmann Inst., Rehovoth, Israel 1972–78, Japan Soc. for the Promotion of Science 1977; Regional Dir Nat. Foundation for Cancer Research 1982–; mem. NAS, American Acad. of Arts and Sciences; Vice-Chair. Cornell Section ACS 1954–55, Chair. 1955–56, Councillor 1959–62; mem. Advisory Panel in Molecular Biology NSF 1960–62; mem. editorial bd of numerous scientific journals; mem. Biochemical Training Cttee, NIH 1963–65, Fogarty Scholar 1984, 1986, 1988, 1989, 1990, 1991; mem. Comm. on Molecular Biophysics Int. Union for Pure and Applied Biophysics 1967–69; mem. Comm. on Macromolecular Biophysics, Int. Union for Pure and Applied Biophysics 1969–75, Pres. 1972–75; mem. Comm. on Subcellular and Macromolecular Biophysics, Int. Union for Pure and Applied Biophysics 1975–81; mem. Exec. Comm. Div. of Biological Chem. ACS 1966–69; Vice-Chair. Div. of Biological Chem. ACS 1970, Chair. 1971; mem. Council Biophysical Soc. 1967–70; mem. Research Career Award Cttee NIH 1967–71; mem. Bd Govs Weizmann Inst., Rehovoth, Israel 1970–97; Fellow, Biophysical Soc. 1999; Hon. Life Mem. New York Acad. of Sciences 1985; Hon. Mem. Hungarian Biophysical Soc. 1989; Hon. ScD (Duke Univ.) 1961, (Univ. of Rochester) 1988, (Univ. of San Luis) 1992, (Technion) 1993, (Univ. of Gdansk) 2006; ACS Eli Lilly Award in Bio chem. 1957, Welch Foundation Lecturer 1962, Harvey Lecturer 1968, Gallagher Lecturer 1968–69, Townsend Harris Medal, CCNY 1970, Lemieux Lecturer 1973, Nichols Medal, NY Section, ACS 1974, Hill Lecturer 1976, City Coll. Chem. Alumni Scientific Achievement Award Medal 1977, ACS Kendall Award in Colloid Chem. 1978, Venable Lecturer 1981, Linderstrøm-Lang Medal 1983, Kowalski Medal 1983, Pauling Medal, ACS 1985, Mobil Award, ACS 1990, Repligen Award, ACS 1990, Stein and Moore Award, Protein Soc. 1995, ACS Award for Computers in Chemical and Pharmaceutical Research 1997, Hirschmann Award in Peptide Chem., ACS 1999, Ramachandran Lecturer 2002. *Publications:* Protein Structure 1961, Theory of Helix-Coil Transitions in Biopolymers 1970; more than 1,200 articles in profession journals on the physical chem. of proteins and other macromolecules, structure of water, and the chem. of blood clotting and growth factors. *Leisure interest:* golf. *Address:* 212 Homestead Terrace, Ithaca, NY 14850 (home); Department of Chemistry and Chemical Biology, 136A Baker Laboratory, Ithaca, NY 14853-1301, (office). *Telephone:* (607) 272-5155 (home); (607) 255-4034 (office). *Fax:* (607) 254-4700 (office). *E-mail:* has5@cornell.edu (office). *Website:* www.chem.cornell.edu (office).

SCHERBAK, Yuri, MD, PhD, DSc; Ukrainian diplomatist, politician, environmentalist and academic; b. 12 Oct. 1934, Kiev; m. Maria Scherbak; two c.; ed Kyev Medical Inst.; worked as social and political publicist in Ukrainian and Soviet media 1988–91; began active political career 1989, won seat in USSR Supreme Soviet, Chair. Sub-cttee on Energy and Nuclear Safety; f. Ukrainian Green Movt, Leader Zeleny Svit (Green World) 1988, Leader Green Party of Ukraine 1990; apptd Minister of Environmental Protection 1991; Amb. to Israel 1992–94, to USA 1994–98 (also accred to Mexico 1997), to Canada 2000–03; Foreign Policy Adviser to Pres. of Ukraine 1998–2000; Int. Affairs Adviser to Volodymyr Lytvyn, Speaker of the Verkhovna Rada (Parl.) –2006; currently Prof., Vernadsky Inst. for

Sustainable Devt; mem. Nat. Security and Defence Council 1991; mem. Acad. of Ecological Sciences of Ukraine, Writers' Union of Ukraine (mem. Bd 1987–89), Cinematographers' Union of Ukraine; Hon. mem. Scientific Studies Inst., Harvard Univ., USA; Yuri Yanovski Literary Prize 1984, Olexander Dovzhenko Prize in Cinematography 1985. *Publications include:* Chornobyl (eye-witness account) 1986, The Strategic Role of Ukraine 1998, Ukarine: Challenge and Choice 2004; 20 books of poetry, prose, plays and essays; over 200 publs on epidemiology, theoretical issues in medicine and ecology. *Address:* c/o Vernadsky Foundation, 119019 Moscow, Gogolevsky blvd 17, office 517, Russia (office). *Telephone:* (495) 697-1662 (office). *Fax:* (495) 690-4792 (office). *E-mail:* info@vernadsky.ru (home). *Website:* www.vernadsky.ru (office).

SCHERER, Frederic M. (Mike), AB, MBA, PhD; American economist and academic; *Aetna Professor Emeritus of Public Policy and Corporate Management, John F. Kennedy School of Government, Harvard University;* b. (Frederic Walter Scherer), 1 Aug. 1932, Ottawa, Ill.; s. of Walter K. Scherer and Margaret Lucey Scherer; m. Barbara Silbermann 1957; one s. two d.; ed Univ. of Michigan, Harvard Univ., Hohenheim Univ., Germany; served in US Army Counter-Intelligence Corps 1954–56; research asst then assoc. Harvard Business School 1958–63; professorial appointments, Princeton Univ. 1963–66, Univ. of Michigan 1966–72, Int. Inst. of Man. 1972–74, Northwestern Univ. 1976–82, Swarthmore Coll. 1982–89; Chief Economist, US Fed. Trade Comm. 1974–76; Aetna Prof. of Public Policy and Corp. Man., John F. Kennedy School of Govt, Harvard Univ. 1989–2000, Prof. Emer. 2000–; Ludwig Erhard Visiting Prof., Univ. of Bayreuth 2000; Lecturer, Woodrow Wilson School of Public and International Affairs, Princeton Univ. 2000–05; Visiting Prof., Haverford Coll., Pa 2004–06; Co-founder European Asscn for Research in Industrial Econs; pioneering work on theory of research and devt strategy and timing; Lanchester Prize, Operations Research Soc. of America 1964, O'Melveny & Myers Centennial Research Prize 1989, Distinguished Fellow, Industrial Org. Soc. 1999, Lifetime Achievement Award, American Antitrust Inst. 2002, Baker Scholar, Copeland Award, Harvard Business School. *Publications include:* The Weapons Acquisition Process: Economic Incentives 1964, Industrial Market Structure and Economic Performance 1970, The Economics of Multi-Plant Operation 1975, Mergers, Sell-offs, and Economic Efficiency 1987, Innovation and Growth: Schumpeterian Perspectives 1984, Industry Structure, Strategy and Public Policy 1996, Quarter Notes and Bank Notes: The Economics of Music Composition in the 18th and 19th Centuries 2004. *Leisure interest:* 17th–19th century music. *Address:* John F. Kennedy School of Government, Harvard University, Mailbox 82, 79 JFK Street, Cambridge, MA 02138 (office); 53 Tolman Street, Unit 2, Cambridge, MA 02138 USA (home). *Telephone:* (610) 495-1154 (office); (610) 872-2557 (home). *Fax:* (610) 496-0063 (office). *E-mail:* mike_scherer@ harvard.edu (office). *Website:* www.hks.harvard.edu/fs/fmscherer (office).

SCHERER, HE Cardinal Odilo Pedro, PhD; Brazilian ecclesiastic; *Archbishop of São Paulo;* b. 21 Sept. 1949, São Francisco; s. of Edwin Scherer and Francisca Wilma Scherer; ed Pontifical Brazilian Coll., Pontifical Gregorian Univ.; ordained priest in Toledo, Paraná 1976; served as pastor in Diocese of Toledo, taught at and served as rector of several seminaries and religious insts in southern Brazil; worked as official of Vatican's Congregation for Bishops 1994–2001; Auxiliary Bishop of São Paulo and Titular Bishop of Novi 2001–02; Sec.-Gen. Brazilian Bishops' Conf. 2003–; Archbishop of São Paulo 2007–; cr. Cardinal (Cardinal-Priest of San Andrea al Quirinale) 2008; participated in Papal Conclave 2013; named one of two Secs Fifth Gen. Conf. of Bishops of Latin America and the Caribbean, Brazil 2007. *Address:* Archdiocese of São Paulo, Avenida Higienopolis 890, 01238-908 São Paulo (office); CP 1670, 01064-970 São Paulo, Brazil. *Telephone:* (11) 3826-0133 (office). *Fax:* (11) 3825-4414 (office). *E-mail:* imprensa@arquidiocesedesaopaulo .org.br (office). *Website:* www.arquidiocesedesaopaulo.org.br (office).

SCHERER, Peter Julian; New Zealand journalist; b. 15 Aug. 1937, Stratford; s. of Arnold F. Scherer and Constance M. White; m. Gaelyn P. Morgan 1964; one s. one d.; ed Browns Bay School and Takapuna Grammar School; joined New Zealand Herald 1955; mem. later Chief, Wellington Bureau 1960–71; Chair. Parl. Press Gallery 1965; leader writer, Duty Ed., Business News Ed. 1973–76, Editorial Man. 1977–83, Asst Ed. 1977–85; Ed. New Zealand Herald 1985–96; Dir Community Newspapers Ltd 1972–73, Wilson & Horton Group 1989–96, New Zealand Press Asscn 1991–96; Chair. New Zealand Associated Press 1985–90, New Zealand section, Commonwealth Press Union (CPU) 1989–94; Chair. Planning Cttee, North Health Medical Workforce 1996–97; Councillor, CPU, London 1989–94; mem. New Zealand Press Council 1988–97, Communications and Media Law Asscn 1990–97; mem. Communications Advisory Council New Zealand Comm. for UNESCO 1989–94; mem. Bd of Control, Newspaper Publishers Asscn of New Zealand 1991–96; mem. New Zealand Nat. Cttee for Security Co-operation in Asia-Pacific 1994–96, New Zealand Div., Inst. of Dirs 1989–96; other professional appointments; CPU Fellowship 1963; Cowan Prize 1959. *Leisure interests:* reading, tennis, gardening, fishing, golf. *Address:* Apartment C, 25 Ring Terrace, St Mary's Bay, Auckland 1001 (home); 267 School Road, Tomarata, RD4 Wellsford 1242, New Zealand (home). *Telephone:* (9) 378-9184 (Auckland) (home); (9) 431-5244 (Wellsford) (home). *Fax:* (9) 431-5244 (Wellsford) (home); (9) 378-9184 (Auckland) (home). *E-mail:* gandpscherer@xtra.co.nz (home).

SCHERPENHUIJSEN ROM, Willem; Dutch business executive; b. 1933, Utrecht; ed Univ. of Amsterdam; Chair. NMB Postbank 1976–92; Chair. Int. Nederlande (formed by merger of NMB Postbank and Internationale Nederlande Groep in 1991) 1992; mem. and Treas. (for Europe) Trilateral Comm.; Founding mem. and Deputy Chair. Institut für Sozialforschung MAITRI e.V; mem. Anthroposophical Soc. 1992–; mem. Advisory Bd Arleen Auger Memorial Fund. *Address:* Arleen Auger Memorial Fund, 14 Townsend Avenue, Hartsdale, NY 10530, USA (office). *Telephone:* (914) 948-4581 (office). *Fax:* (914) 761-3382 (office). *E-mail:* aaugerfund@aol.com (office). *Website:* www.arleen-auger-memorial-fund .org (office).

SCHERRER, Anton, BSc, Dr Sci.Techn.; Swiss business executive; b. 1942; ed Swiss Inst. of Tech. (ETH-Zurich); headed biological research lab. and experimental brewery at Swiss brewing industry trial facility 1970–73; Plant Man. and Deputy Man. Eglisau (mineral spring) and Deputy Head Tech. Dept Unifontes Group 1973–76; held several man. positions at Brauerei Hürlimann 1977–91, including Deputy Man. and Master Brewer 1977–82, apptd Chief Tech. Officer 1983, Chair. Exec. Bd 1984–89; apptd Chair. Retail Trade Cttee Migros

Cooperative Asscn 2001, Chair. Admin. Del. 2001–03; Chair. Exec. Bd Migrosbank 2003–05; Vice-Chair. Swisscom AG 2005–06, Chair. 2006–11; mem. Bd of Dirs Hürlimann Holding AG 1984–91, Orior AG 2007–13; mem. Exec. Bd economie-suisse 2006–11; mem. Advisory Bd Capvis Equity Partners AG, Theo Müller Gmbh & Co., Germany –2008; mem. Bd of Trustees, Agrovision Foundation Muri, Swiss Inst. of Technology Zurich Foundation –2011; mem. Managerial Cttee Inst. for Marketing and Trade, Univ. of St Gallen –2011; mem. Nat. Comm. for Tech. and Innovation 2012–;*Telephone:* (44) 7150660 (home). *E-mail:* anton@scherrer.com (home).

SCHETYNA, Grzegorz; Polish politician; *Chairman, Foreign Affairs Committee, Sejm (Parliament);* b. 18 Feb. 1963, Opole; ed Wrocław Univ.; fmr mem. Solidarność Walcząca (Fighting Solidarity); Chair. Ind. Students' Union (Nieza-leżne Zrzeszenie Studentów, NZS), Wrocław Univ. 1986–89, later mem. Presidium NZS Nat. Co-ordinating Cttee; Dir Voivodship Office, Wrocław 1990, Deputy Voivod 1991–92; Chair. Liberal and Democratic Congress (Kongres Liberalno-Demokratyczny), Wrocław 1991, later becoming Sec.-Gen.; mem. Freedom Union (Unia Wolności) 1994–2001; Co-founder Civic Platform (Platforma Obywatelska) 2001; mem. Sejm (Parl.) for Legnica 1997–, Marshall of the Sejm 2010–11, Chair. Foreign Affairs Cttee 2011–; Deputy Prime Minister and Minister of the Interior and Admin 2007–09; launched Radio Eska, Wrocław 1993. *Leisure interests:* basketball, football, travelling, American literature. *Address:* Civic Platform (Platforma Obywatelska), 00-159 Warsaw, ul. Andersa 21, Poland (office); Wiejska 4/6/8, 00-902 Warsaw, Poland. *Telephone:* (22) 6357879 (office); (22) 6941820. *Fax:* (22) 6357641 (office); (22) 6941900. *E-mail:* poczta@platforma.org (office); biuro@ schetyna.pl (office). *Website:* www.platforma.org (office).

SCHICKEL, Richard, BS; American writer, film critic and film producer; *President, Lorac Productions Inc.;* b. 10 Feb. 1933, Milwaukee; s. of Edward J. Schickel and Helen Schickel (née Hendricks); two d.; ed Univ. of Wisconsin; Ed. Look Magazine 1957–60, Show Magazine 1960–63; self-employed 1963–; Film Critic, Life Magazine 1965–72, Time Magazine 1972–2009; Pres. Lorac Productions Inc. 1986–; Consultant, Rockefeller Foundation 1965; Lecturer in History of Art, Yale Univ. 1972, 1976; apptd Adjunct Prof., Dept of Film and Television, Univ. of Southern California 1989; Guggenheim Fellow 1964; mem. Nat. Soc. of Film Critics, New York Film Critics; Dr hc (American Film Inst.) 2003; Maurice Bessy Award 2001, William K. Everson Award, Nat. Bd of Review 2005, Silver Medal, Telluride Film Festival 2008. *Television:* Producer, Dir, Writer: The Man Who Made the Movies 1973, Life Goes to the Movies 1976, Funny Business 1978, Into the Morning: Willa Cather's America 1978, The Horror Show 1979, SPFX 1980, James Cagney: That Yankee Doodle Dandy 1981, From Star Wars to Jedi: The Making of a Saga 1983, Minnelli on Minnelli: Liza Remembers Vincent 1987, Cary Grant, A Celebration 1988, Gary Cooper: American Life, American Legend 1989, Myrna Loy: So Nice to Come Home To 1990, Barbara Stanwyck: Fire and Desire 1991, Eastwood & Co: Making Unforgiven 1992, Hollywood on Hollywood 1993, Elia Kazan: A Director's Journey 1995, The Moviemakers 1996, Eastwood on Eastwood 1997, The Harryhausen Chronicles 1998, Shooting War: World War II Combat Cameramen 2000, Woody Allen: A Life in Film 2002, Charlie: The Life and Art of Charles Chaplin 2003, The Big Red One: The Reconstruction 2004, Scorsese on Scorsese 2004, Watch the Skies! 2005, Spielberg on Spielberg 2007, Bienvenue à Cannes 2007, You Must Remember This: The Warner Bros. Story (with George Perry) 2008, The Eastwood Factor 2010. *Publications include:* The World of Carnegie Hall 1960, The Stars 1962, The Disney Version 1968, The World of Goya 1968, Second Sight: Notes on Some Movies 1972, His Pictures in the Papers 1974, The Men Who Made the Movies 1975, Another I, Another You 1978, Cary Grant: A Celebration 1984, D.W. Griffith: An American Life (British Film Institute Book Prize 1985) 1984, Intimate Strangers: The Culture of Celebrity 1985, James Cagney, A Celebration 1985, Striking Poses 1987, Schickel on Film 1989, Brando: A Life in Our Times 1991, Double Indemnity 1992, Clint Eastwood: A Biography 1996, Matinee Idylls: Reflections on the Movies 1999, Good Morning, Mr. Zip Zip Zip 2003, Woody Allen: A Life in Film 2004, Elia Kazan: A Biography 2005, Film On Paper 2008, You Must Remember This: The Warner Bros. Story (co-author) 2008, Bette Davis: Larger than Life (co-author) 2009, Clint: A Retrospective 2010, Conversations with Scorsese 2011. *Address:* Lorac Productions Inc, 170 S. Beverly Drive, Suite 310, Beverly Hills, CA 90212, USA (office). *Telephone:* (310) 550-5820 (office). *Fax:* (310) 550-5870 (office). *E-mail:* info@lorac.tv (office). *Website:* www .lorac.tv (office); www.richardschickel.com.

SCHIEFFER, Robert (Bob), BA; American broadcast journalist; b. 25 Feb. 1937, Austin, Tex.; m. Patricia Penrose; two d.; ed Texas Christian Univ.; reporter, Fort Worth Star-Telegram; news anchor, WBAP-TV, Dallas; began work at CBS News 1969, Pentagon Corresp. 1970–74, White House Corresp. 1974–79, Chief Washington Corresp. 1982–, anchor, CBS Sunday Nightly News 1973–74, Sunday ed. CBS Evening News, then Sun. Ed. 1976, anchor Saturday ed. CBS Evening News 1976–96, co-anchor, CBS Morning News 1985, anchor and moderator Face the Nation, CBS News 1991–, interim anchor CBS Evening News 2005–06, currently weekly commentator and political analyst; participant numerous CBS special reports including Peace and the Pentagon 1974, Watergate: The White House Transcripts 1974, Mysterious Alert 1974, Ground Zero 1981; six Emmy Awards and two Sigma Delta Chi Awards, Broadcaster of the Year, Nat. Press Foundation 2002, Paul White Award from Radio-TV News Dirs Asscn 2003, Int. Radio and TV Soc. Foundation Award 2004, American News Women's Club Helen Thomas Award for Excellence in Journalism 2004, and numerous other awards. *Publications include:* The Acting President (with Gary P. Gates) 1989, This Just In: What I Couldn't Tell You on TV 2003, Face the Nation: My Favorite Stories from the First 50 Years of the Award-Winning News Broadcast, Bob Schieffer's America. *Address:* Face the Nation with Bob Schieffer, CBS News, 2020 M Street, NW, Washington, DC 20036, USA (office). *Telephone:* (202) 457-4481 (office). *E-mail:* ftn@cbsnews.com (office). *Website:* www.cbsnews.com (office).

SCHIEFFER, J(ohn) Thomas (Tom), BA, MA; American lawyer, politician, diplomatist and business executive; *Senior Counsel, Akin Gump Strauss Hauer & Feld LLP;* b. 4 Oct. 1947, Fort Worth, Tex.; m. Susanne Silber 1979; one s.; ed Arlington Heights High School and Univ. of Texas; worked in offices of Tex. State Senator Don Kennard and Tex. Gov. John Connally; elected to Tex. House of Reps 1972, served three terms; admitted to Tex. Bar 1979; Pnr with George W. Bush and Edward W. (Rusty) Rose in ownership of Texas Rangers (professional baseball club) 1989–99, Pnr-in-Charge of Ballpark Devt 1990, Pres. 1991–99; Pres. J. Thomas Schieffer Man. Co., Pablo Operating Co. –2001; Amb. to Australia 2001–05, to Japan 2005–09; Sr Counsel, Akin Gump Strauss Hauer & Feld LLP, Dallas 2010–; mem. Bd Dirs Maureen and Mike Mansfield Foundation; mem. Bd Councilors US-Japan Council; mem. Advisory Bd US Studies Centre, Univ. of Sydney, Japan-America Soc. of Dallas/Fort Worth; fmr mem. Bd Dirs Drew Industries, White Plains, NY; fmr mem. Advisory Bd JP Morgan Chase Bank, Fort Worth; fmr Tarrant Co. Coordinator for Gov. Mark White; has served on numerous charitable and civic bds, including The Penrose Foundation, Dallas Co. Community Coll. Foundation, Dallas 2012 Olympic Cttee, Tarrant Co. Coll. Foundation, Winston School; fmr mem. Exec. Cttee Dallas Chamber of Commerce, Co-Chair. Legis. Affairs Cttee; Trustee, Tarrant Co. Jr Coll. 1987; Hon. Order of Australia; honoured by FBI for efforts to combat int. scourge of child pornography, Nat. Intelligence Reform Medal, Dir of Nat. Intelligence, CIA Donovan Award, Defense Intelligence Agency Director's Award Medal, Nat. Security Agency Director's Distinguished Service Medal, Nat. Geospatial-Intelligence Agency Medallion for Excellence, Dept of Defense Medal for Distinguished Public Service 2009. *Address:* Akin Gump Strauss Hauer & Feld LLP, 1700 Pacific Avenue, Suite 4100, Dallas, TX 75201-4675 (office); 1000 Ballpark Way, Arlington, TX 76011-5168, USA. *Telephone:* (817) 886-5072 (office). *Fax:* (214) 969-4343 (office). *E-mail:* tschieffer@akingump.com (office). *Website:* www.akingump.com (office).

SCHIEFFER, Rudolf; German historian and academic; *President, Monumenta Germaniae Historica;* b. 31 Jan. 1947, Mainz; s. of Theodor Schieffer and Annelise Schreibmayr; Research Assoc. DFG project, Spätantike Reichskonzilien 1971–75; Research Assoc. Monumenta Germaniae Historica, Munich 1975–80; Prof. of Medieval and Modern History, Univ. of Bonn 1980–94; Prof. of Medieval History, Univ. of Munich; Pres. Monumenta Germaniae Historica, Munich 1994–; Corresp. mem. Nordrhein-Westfäl. Acad. of Sciences, Austrian Acad., Goettingen Acad.; Corresp. Fellow, Royal Historical Soc., Medieval Acad. of America, Socio straniero Accad. dei Lincei, Rome. *Publications:* Die Entstehung von Domkapiteln in Deutschland 1976, Hinkmar v. Reims, De ordine palatii (with T. Gross) 1980, Die Entstehung des päpstlichen Investiturverbots für den deutschen König 1981, Die Karolinger 1992, Die Streitschriften Hinkmars v. Reims und Hinkmars v. Laon 2003, Die Zeit des karolingischen Grossreichs 2005, Gregor VII 2010. *Address:* Monumenta Germaniae Historica, Postfach 340223, 80099 Munich, Germany (office). *Telephone:* (89) 286382383 (office). *Fax:* (89) 281419 (office). *E-mail:* rudolf.schieffer@mgh.de (office). *Website:* www.mgh.de (office).

SCHIFANI, Renato Giuseppe, LLB; Italian lawyer and politician; *President, Senato della Repubblica;* b. 11 May 1950, Palermo; m. Franca Schifani; two s.; lawyer, Court of Appeal; f. Siculabrokers 1979, becoming Dir; f. GMS (credit agency) 1992; fmr mem. Partito della Democrazia Cristiana; mem. Forza Italia 1995–, Pres. 2001–06; mem. Popolo della Libertà (People of Freedom) 2007–; mem. Senato (Upper House) for Sicily constituency 1996–, Pres. 2008–. *Address:* Senato della Repubblica, Piazza Madama, 00186 Rome, Italy (office). *Telephone:* (6) 67061 (office). *E-mail:* schifani_r@posta.senato.it (office). *Website:* www.senato.it (office).

SCHIFF, András; Hungarian pianist; b. 21 Dec. 1953, Budapest; s. of Odon Schiff and Klara Schiff (née Csengeri); ed Franz Liszt Acad. of Music, Budapest with Pal Kadosa, Gyorgy Kurtag and Ferenc Rados, pvt lessons with George Malcolm, England; recitals in London, New York, Paris, Vienna, Munich, Florence; concerts with New York Philharmonic, Chicago Symphony, Vienna Philharmonic, Concertgebouw, Orchestre de Paris, London Philharmonic, London Symphony, Philharmonia, Royal Philharmonic, Israel Philharmonic, Berlin Philharmonic, Cleveland, Philadelphia, Washington Nat. Symphony; played at Salzburg, Edinburgh, Aldeburgh, Feldkirch Schubertiade, Lucerne and Tanglewood Festivals; f. Musiktage Mondsee Festival 1989 (Artistic Dir 1989–98); f. own orchestra Cappella Andrea Barca 1999; Special Supernumerary Fellow, Balliol Coll., Oxford, UK 2011–; Hon. Prof., Music Schools in Budapest, Detmold and Munich 2011–; Mem. of Honour, Vienna Konzerthaus 2012; Ordre pour le Mérite for Sciences and Arts 2012; Prizewinner at Tchaikovsky Competition, Moscow 1974 and Leeds Piano Competition 1975, Liszt Prize 1977, Premio dell' Accad. Chigiana, Siena 1987, RPS/Charles Heidsieck Award for best concert series of 1988–89, Wiener Flötenuhr 1989, Bartók Prize 1991, Instrumentalist of the Year, Royal Philharmonic Soc. 1994, Claudio Arrau Memorial Medal 1994, Kossuth Prize 1996, Sonning Prize, Copenhagen 1997, Palladio d'Oro della Città di Vicenza 2003, Musikfest Prize, Bremen 2003, Abbiati Prize 2007, RAM Bach Prize 2007, Wigmore Medal 2008, Klavier-Festival Ruhr Prize for outstanding achievements and to honour a lifetime's work as a pianist 2009, Schumann Prize, City of Zwickau 2011, Gold Medal, Royal Philharmonic Soc. 2013. *Recordings include:* Bach Goldberg Variations, Bach Partitas, Bach Piano Concertos, Mendelssohn Concertos 1 and 2, all the Schubert Sonatas, Schubert Trout Quintet, Schumann and Chopin 2, all the Mozart Concertos, Bach Two- and Three-part Inventions, Bach Well-Tempered Klavier, Beethoven Violin and Piano Sonatas with Sandor Vegh, Beethoven Piano Concertos, Bartók Piano Concertos, Tchaikovsky Piano Concerto, Bach English Suites (Grammy Award 1990), Bach French Suites, Lieder with Peter Schreier, Robert Holl and Cecilia Bartoli, etc., Beethoven Piano Sonatas Op. 2 Nos 1–3 and Op. 7 No. 4 2005, Beethoven Piano Sonatas Op. Nos 6–8 2008, Schumann Geistervariationen (Int. Classical Music Award for Recording of the Year and Best Solo Instrument Recording 2012) 2011. *Television:* The Wanderer – A Film About Schubert with Andras Schiff (BBC Omnibus, narrator), Chopin with Andras Schiff (BBC Omnibus, narrator). *Leisure interests:* literature, languages, soccer, theatre, cinema, art. *Address:* c/o Harrison Turner Artists Management, 53 Ticknell Piece Road, Charlbury, Oxon., OX7 3TN, England (office). *Telephone:* (1608) 810330 (office). *Fax:* (1608) 811331 (office). *E-mail:* artists@harrisonturner.co.uk (office). *Website:* www.harrisonturner.co.uk (office).

SCHIFF, Heinrich; Austrian cellist and conductor; b. 18 Nov. 1951, Gruunden; London and Vienna debuts 1973; subsequently undertook extensive concert tours in Europe, Japan and USA appearing with maj. orchestras; interpreter of contemporary music including work of Lutosławski, Henze, Krenek and Penderecki and has given first performances of many new works; Artistic Dir Northern Sinfonia 1990–96; prin. guest conductor, Deutsche Kammerphilharmonie 1990–92; apptd Prin. Conductor, Musikkollegium, Winterthur and Copenhagen Philharmonic Orchestra 1995; Chief Conductor, Vienna Chamber Orchestra 2005–08, continues to lead the orchestra in concerts. *Address:* Vienna Chamber

Orchestra, Schachnerstrasse 27, 1220 Vienna, Austria (office). *Telephone:* (1) 203-63-57 (office). *Fax:* (1) 204-37-50 (office). *E-mail:* wiener@kammerorchester.com (office). *Website:* www.kammerorchester.com (office).

SCHIFFER, Claudia; German actress and fmr fashion model; b. 25 Aug. 1970, Düsseldorf; m. Matthew Vaughn 2002; one s. two d.; fashion model for Karl Lagerfeld 1990, model for Revlon 1992–96, Chanel –1997; has appeared on numerous covers for magazines and journals; designs calendars; appears on TV specials; has share in Fashion Café, New York 1995–; announced retirement from modelling 1998; mem. US Cttee UNICEF 1995–98. *Films include:* Richie Rich 1994, Pret-a-Porter 1994, The Blackout 1997, And She Was 1999, Friends and Lovers 1999, Black and White 2000, Chain of Fools 2000, Reckless + Wild 2001, Life Without Dick 2001, Love Actually 2003. *Publication:* Memories 1995. *Address:* c/o Heidi Gross GmbH, Hartungstrasse 5, 20146 Hamburg, Germany. *E-mail:* info@model-management.de. *Website:* claudiaschiffer.com.

SCHIFRES, Michel Maurice Réné; French journalist; *Vice-President, Editorial Committee, Le Figaro;* b. 1 May 1946, Orléans; s. of Jacques Schifres and Paulette Mauduit; m. Josiane Gasnier (divorced); two c.; ed Lycée du Mans, Lycée de Caen, Faculté des Lettres de Caen, Centre de Formation des Journalistes; journalist with Combat 1970–72, with Monde 1972–74; Head of Political Affairs Quotidien de Paris 1974–76; Asst Head of Political Affairs France-Soir 1976; Head of Political Affairs Journal du Dimanche 1977, Deputy Ed. 1979–82, Ed. 1982–86, Deputy Editorial Dir 1985–89; mem. Comm. on quality of radio and TV broadcasts 1977–79; Editorial Dir France-Soir 1989–92, Asst Dir-Gen. 1992; Asst Editorial Dir Le Figaro (newspaper) 1992–98, Man. Dir 1998–2000, Man. Ed. Le Figaro magazine 2005–07, Vice-Pres. Editorial Cttee 2000–; mem. Editorial Cttee La Revue de l'Intelligent 2003–; Chevalier, Ordre nat. du Mérite. *Television:* L'Elysée 1988, Ville de Chiens 1989, Un Siecle d'Ecrivain: Jules Romains 1998. *Publications include:* La CFDT des militants 1972, D'une France à l'autre 1974, L'enaklatura 1987, L'Elysée de Mitterrand 1987, La désertion des énarques 1999. *Leisure interest:* antiques. *Address:* Le Figaro, 14 blvd Haussmann, 75009 Paris (office); 150 avenue Emile Zola, 75015 Paris, France (home). *Telephone:* 1-42-21-29-73 (office); 1-40-58-16-64 (home); 6-07-59-40-91 (mobile). *Fax:* 1-42-21-63-82 (office). *E-mail:* mschifres@lefigaro.fr (office); mschifres@noos.fr (home).

SCHIFTER, Richard, BA, LLB; American lawyer, diplomatist and politician; *Chairman, American Jewish International Relations Institute;* b. 31 July 1923, Vienna, Austria; m.; five c.; ed Coll. of the City of New York, Yale Law School; served in US Army 1943–46; practising attorney, Washington, DC 1951–84; Rep. to UN Human Rights Comm. 1983–86; Deputy Rep. to UN Security Council (with rank of Amb.) 1984–85; Asst Sec. of State for Human Rights and Humanitarian Affairs 1985–92, Counsellor, Nat. Security Council (organized SE Europe Cooperative Initiative 1996), Dept of State Rep. to CSCE, Special Adviser to Sec. of State 1993–2001; Chair. Centre for Democracy and Reconciliation in SE Europe 2001–08; currently Chair. American Jewish International Relations Inst.; Grand Decoration of Honour in Gold (Austria) 1998, Order Stara Planina (Bulgaria), Commander, Order of the Star of Romania; Distinguished Service Award of the Sec. of State. *Publication:* Human Rights, Perestroika and The End of the Cold War (co-author) 2009. *Address:* American Jewish International Relations Institute, PO Box 42732, Washington, DC 20015, USA (office). *Telephone:* (301) 229-0357. *E-mail:* rschifter@aol.com (office). *Website:* www.ajiri.us (office).

SCHILLER, Vivian, MA; American media executive; *Chief Digital Officer, NBC News;* b. 13 Sept. 1961; ed Cornell Univ., Middlebury Coll.; Russian interpreter and tour guide, Moscow 1984–88; Production Co-ordinator, Turner Broadcasting System Inc., Moscow 1988, Supervising Producer, Sr Producer, then Vice-Pres. and Gen. Man., Turner Original Productions, Turner Entertainment Networks 1994–2002; fmr Exec. Vice-Pres. CNN Productions, Turner Broadcasting System Inc.; Sr Vice-Pres. and Gen. Man. Discovery Times Channel, The New York Times Co. 2002–05, Sr Vice-Pres. TV and Video 2005–06, Exec. Vice-Pres. and Gen. Man. Discovery Times Channel 2005–06; Sr Vice-Pres. and Gen. Man. NYTimes.com 2006–08; Pres. and CEO, National Public Radio, Washington, DC 2009–11 (resgnd); Chief Digital Officer, NBC News 2011–; mem. Council on Foreign Relations; five Emmy Awards, two Peabody Awards, two Alfred I. DuPont-Columbia Univ. Award, CableACE Award, Int. Documentary Asscn Award. *Television:* as supervising producer: A Century of Women 1994, Moon Shot 1994; as sr producer: Hank Aaron: Chasing the Dream 1995, Hollywood's Amazing Animal Actors 1996, Biker Women 1996, Survivors of the Holocaust 1996, Animal ER 1996, Pirate Tales 1997, Twin Stories 1997, Warner Bros. 75th Anniversary: No Guts, No Glory 1998, Dying to Tell the Story 1998; as exec. producer: Word Wars 2004, Off to War 2005. *Address:* NBC News, 30 Rockefeller Plaza, New York, NY 10112, USA (office). *Telephone:* (212) 664-3720 (office). *Fax:* (212) 664-4426 (office). *Website:* www.nbc-news-sports (office).

SCHILTZ, Jean-Louis; Luxembourg lawyer and politician; b. 14 Aug. 1964, Luxembourg; ; m.; three c.; ed Université Paris I Panthéon Sorbonne; worked for Schiltz & Schiltz (law firm), Luxembourg 1989–2004; Academic Asst, Law Faculty Université Paris I Panthéon Sorbonne 1989–90; mem. Cttee Young Bar Asscn 1990, Chair. 1997–98, then mem. Bar Council; mem. Parl. 2004–; Minister for Devt Cooperation and Humanitarian Action, Minister for Communications and Minister of Defence 2004–09; apptd Gov. Asian Development Bank for Luxembourg 2004; Sec.-Gen. Parti Chrétien Social (Chrëschtlech Sozial Volekspartei) (PCS/CSV) (Christian Social Party), Pres. 2009–11; First Asst, then Chargé de Cours, Centre universitaire de Luxembourg 1991–2004; Co-ed. Assurances et Responsabilité 1994–2004; mem. Editorial Bd European Lawyer, Int. Bar Asscn; fmr mem. Legal Comm., Nat. Olympic Cttee. *Sport achievements:* Luxembourg team fencing champion 1983. *Leisure interests:* running, biking. *Address:* c/o Parti Chrétien Social (Christian Social Party), 4 rue de l'Eau, BP 826, 2018, Luxembourg.

SCHILY, Otto; German lawyer and politician; b. 20 July 1932, Bochum; s. of Franz Schily; m. (divorced); two d.; ed Munich, Hamburg and Berlin Univs; mem. Bundestag 1983–86, 1987–89, 1990–; mem. SPD 1990–, Deputy Chair. 1994–; Minister of the Interior 1998–2005; mem. Presidium Neue Gesellschaft für bildende Kunst; Adviser, Humanist Union; Bavarian Order of Merit 2001; Leo Baeck Medal 2005. *Address:* Platz der Republik 1, 11011 Berlin (office); Oberanger 38, 80331 Munich, Germany (office). *Telephone:* (30) 22777971 (office). *Fax:* (30)

22776971 (office). *E-mail:* otto.schily@bundestag.de (office). *Website:* www.otto
-schily.de (office).

SCHIMMEL, Paul Gordon; American museum curator; *Chief Curator, Museum of Contemporary Art, Los Angeles;* m. Yvonne Schimmel; ed Syracuse Univ., New York Univ.; internship, Contemporary Arts Museum, Houston, Tex. 1975–78, then mem. curatorial staff; Curator, Newport Harbor Art Museum 1981–89; Chief Curator, Museum of Contemporary Art, Los Angeles 1990–; has lectured at Kanazawa Museum of Modern Art, Japan, RCA, London, Centre Georges Pompidou, Paris, Whitney Museum of American Art, J. Paul Getty Museum, Los Angeles Co. Museum of Art, and others; panelist, Nat. Endowment for the Arts; Bard Coll. Center for Curatorial Studies Award for Curatorial Excellence. *Publications include:* Ecstasy: In and About Altered States (co-ed with Lisa Gabrielle Mark); contrib.: articles in journals and magazines including The Art Book. *Address:* The Museum of Contemporary Art, 250 South Grand Avenue, Los Angeles, CA 90012, USA (office). *Telephone:* (213) 621-2766 (office). *E-mail:* pschimmel@moca.org (office). *Website:* www.moca.org (office).

SCHINDLER, David W., OC, BSc, DPhil, FRS, FRSC; Canadian biologist, ecologist and academic; *Killam Memorial Professor Emeritus of Ecology, University of Alberta;* b. 3 Aug. 1940, Fargo, ND, USA; ed North Dakota State Univ., Univ. of Oxford, UK; Asst Prof. of Biology, Trent Univ., Canada 1966–68; Founder and Dir Experimental Lakes Project, Canadian Dept of Fisheries and Oceans 1968–89; Killam Memorial Prof. of Ecology, Univ. of Alberta 1989–2013, Prof. Emer. 2013–, Chair. Limnology Lab. 1993–2012; Chair. Alberta Br., Safe Drinking Water Foundation; mem. Bd of Dirs Canadian Arctic Resources Cttee (Chair. Cumulative Effects Sub-Cttee); mem. Scientific Advisory Cttee and Aquatic Sciences Cttee, Yukon to Yellowstone; mem. NAS 2002–; Foreign mem. Royal Swedish Acad. of Eng Science 2003–; Assoc. Ed. Canadian Journal of Fisheries and Aquatic Sciences; mem. Editorial Bd Aquatic Sciences, Proceedings of the National Academy of Sciences; mem. Advisory Bd Ecosytems (journal); Queen's Golden Jubilee Medal 2002, Alberta Order of Excellence 2008; Hon. DSc (N Dakota State Univ., Acadia Univ., Brock Univ., Queen's Univ. and Univs of Victoria, Alberta, Winnipeg and Lethbridge); Hon. DLaws (Univ. of Windsor, Trent Univ.); Outstanding Achievement Award, American Inst. of Fisheries Research Biologists 1984, Frank Rigler Award, Canadian Soc. of Limnologists 1984, Hutchinson Medal, American Soc. of Limnology and Oceanography 1985, Naumann-Thieneman Medal, Int. Limnology Soc. 1989, First Stockholm Water Prize, Stockholm Water Foundation 1991, Manning Distinguished Achievement Award 1993, First Romanowski Medal, RSC 1994, Walter Bean–Canada Trust Award for Environmental Science 1996, Volvo Environment Prize 1998, J. Gordin Kaplan Award for Excellence in Research, Univ. of Alberta 1999, Distinguished mem., Int. Water Acad., Norway 1999, Alberta Science and Tech. Award for Outstanding Leadership in Alberta Science 1999, Natural Sciences and Eng Research Council (NESRC) Award of Excellence 2000, 2001, Douglas H. Pimlott Award for Conservation, Canadian Nature Fed. 2001, NESRC Gerhard Herzberg Canada Gold Medal for Science and Eng 2001, Environment Canada, EcoLogo/Natural Marine Environmental Award 2002, Award of Distinction, City of Edmonton 2002, Killam Prize 2003, Tyler Prize for Environmental Achievement (co-recipient) 2006, David Schindler Endowed Professorship in Aquatic Sciences est. at Trent Univ. 2008, Sandford Fleming Medal, Royal Canadian Inst. 2009. *Publications:* more than 280 articles and reports, more than 20 of them in Science and Nature magazine. *Address:* University of Alberta, Room Z 811, Biological Sciences Building, Edmonton, AB T6G 2R3, Canada (office). *Telephone:* (780) 492-1291 (office). *Fax:* (780) 492-9234 (office). *E-mail:* d.schindler@ualberta.ca (office). *Website:* www.biology.ualberta.ca (office).

SCHINZLER, Hans-Jürgen, DJur; German insurance industry executive; *Honorary Chairman of the Supervisory Board, Münchener Rückversicherungsgesellschaft AG (Munich Re);* b. 12 Oct. 1940, Madrid, Spain; m. Monika Somya; three c.; ed Univs of Munich and Würzburg; training at Bayerische Vereinsbank 1968–69; joined Münchener Rückversicherungsgesellschaft AG (Munich Re) 1968, mem. Bd of Man. 1981–93, Chair. Bd of Man. 1993–2003, Chair. Supervisory Bd 2004–12, Hon. Chair. 2013–, Chair. Munich Reinsurance America, Inc. 1997–2003, Chair. Bd of Trustees Munich Re Foundation; Chair. Wittelsbacher Ausgleichsfonds; Deputy Chair. Allgemeine Kreditversicherung AG, Mainz, Allianzversicherung AG, Munich; Chair. Supervisory Bd ERGO Versicherungsgruppe AG –2003, MR Beteiligungen AG, Grafelfing, Bonn Metro AG, MRE Beteiligungen AG, Munich; Deputy Chair. Supervisory Bd Stuttgart, Metro AG, Dusseldorf Aventis SA, Schiltigheim, France –2004, Bayerische Hypo- und Vereinsbank 2004–05; Deputy Chair. and mem. Supervisory Bd HVB Group (holding co. of Bayerische Hypo-und Vereinsbank AG); mem. Supervisory Bd Man AG –2003, Sanofi-Aventis AG 1999–2004, METRO AG 2002–, Bayerische Hypo- und Vereinsbank AG 2003–05, Deutsche Telekom AG 2003–; mem. Bd of Man. Freundeskreis des Bayerischen Nationalmuseums e.V.; fmr Deputy Chair. Supervisory Bd Man AG; Vice-Chair. Statutory Supervisory Bd Allianz Lebensversicherungs AG –2002, Dresdner Bank AG –2002; Ind. Dir, UniCredit SpA 2005–; Dir, Munich Reinsurance America, Inc. (fmrly American Re Corpn) 1996–; mem. Bd Deutscher Verein für Versicherungswissenschaft e.V.; mem. Bd of Dirs Munich-American Holding Corpn, Del.; mem. Bd of Trustees Gemeinnützige Hertie-Stiftung, Hypo-Kulturstiftung, State of Bavaria of Stifterverband für die Deutsche Wissenschaft, Stiftung Demoskopie Allensbach, Stiftung Pinakothek der Moderne; mem. Comparable German and Foreign Corp. Bd of Business Enterprises of Aventis SA; mem. Insurance Advisory Council Bundesanstalt fur Finanzdienstleistungsaufsicht; Treas. and mem. Senate of Max-Planck-Gesellschaft zur Förderung der Wissenschaften e.V. *Address:* Munich Re Group, Königinstrasse 107, 80802 Munich, Germany (office). *Telephone:* (89) 38913534 (office). *Fax:* (89) 399056 (office). *Website:* www.munichre.com (office).

SCHIRO, James J., BBA; American business executive; b. 2 Jan. 1946; m. Tomasina Schiro; two. c.; ed St John's Univ., Dartmouth Coll.; joined Price Waterhouse 1967, Chair. Mining Special Services Group 1979–88, Nat. Dir Mergers and Acquisitions Services 1988–91, Vice-Chair. and Man. Partner for New York Metropolitan Region 1991, apptd to Council of Partners 1990, to Gen. Council 1992, Deputy Chair. World Exec. Group and World Bd 1995, Chair. and Sr Partner, Price Waterhouse 1995, CEO 1997, CEO PricewaterhouseCoopers 1998–2001; COO Group Finance, Zurich Financial Services March–May 2002,

CEO May 2002–09; mem. Bd Dirs PepsiCo 2002–; Ind. Dir The Goldman Sachs Group 2009–; Vice-Chair. Swiss-American Chamber of Commerce, American Friends of Lucerne Festival (also mem. Bd Trustees); mem. Foundation Bd IMD (business school), Bd Inst. for Advanced Study, Bd Trustees St John's Univ.; mem. Advisory Bd Tsinghua Univ. School of Econs and Man.; Trustee, Inst. for Advanced Study, Lucerne Festival; Hon. DCS (St John's Univ.) 1994; Ellis Island Medal of Honor 1994, St John's Univ. Alumni Pietas Medal 1992, Avenue of the Americas Asscn's Gold Key Award 1992. *Address:* Goldman, Sachs & Co., 200 West Street, 29th Floor, New York, NY 10282, USA (office). *Telephone:* (212) 902-0300 (office). *E-mail:* info@goldmansachs.com (office). *Website:* www2.goldmansachs.com (office).

SCHIZER, David M., BA, MA, JD; American professor of law; *Lucy G. Moses Professor of Law and Dean of the Faculty of Law, Columbia University;* ed Yale Univ.; Exec. Ed. Yale Law Journal; clerk for Judge Alex Kozinski of US Court of Appeals for the Ninth Circuit 1993–94, for US Supreme Court Assoc. Justice Ruth Bader Ginsburg 1994–95; worked at Davis Polk & Wardwell –1998; Wilbur H. Friedman Prof. of Tax Law, Columbia Law School –2004, Lucy G. Moses Prof. of Law and Dean of Columbia Law School (youngest ever dean) 2004–; mem. Bd of Dirs Tax Club, Tax Forum; mem. Exec. Cttee and Co-Chair. Cttee on Financial Insts, NY State Bar Asscn Tax Section; Willis L.M. Reese Prize for Excellence in Teaching, Columbia Law School. *Publications:* more than 25 books and numerous articles on taxation, financial instruments and regulation. *Address:* Dean's Office, Columbia Law School, 8th Floor, Jerome L. Greene Hall, Box B12, 435 West 116th Street, New York, NY 10027, USA (office). *Telephone:* (212) 854-2675 (office). *Fax:* (212) 854-9740 (office). *E-mail:* dschiz@law.columbia.edu (office). *Website:* www .law.columbia.edu (office).

SCHJELDAHL, Peter; American art critic and poet; *Senior Art Critic, The New Yorker;* b. 1942, Fargo, ND; m. Brooke Alderson; ed Carleton Coll., The New School, Manhattan; fmr Lecturer, Dept of Visual and Environmental Studies, Harvard Univ.; fmr columnist, The Village Voice; Contributing Ed. Art in America; Sr Art Critic, The New Yorker magazine 1998–; regular art critic for The New York Sunday Times, Vanity Fair, Seven Days; Guggenheim Fellowship for poetry, Cooper Union Frank Jewett Mather Award for art criticism, Clark Prize for Excellence in Arts Writing 2008. *Publications:* White Country 1968, An Adventure of the Thought Police 1971, Dreams 1973, Since 1964: New and Selected Poems 1978, The Seven Days Art Columns 1991, Hydrogen Jukebox: Selected Writings of Peter Schjeldahl 1978-1990 1991, De Kooning and Dubuffet: The Late Works 1993, Columns & Catalogues 1994, Let's See: Writings on Art from The New Yorker 2008. *Address:* The New Yorker, 4 Times Square, New York, NY 10036-7448, USA (office). *Telephone:* (212) 286-5400 (office). *Website:* www.newyorker.com (office).

SCHLAGMAN, Richard Edward, FRSA; British publisher; b. 11 Nov. 1953, London, England; s. of Jack Schlagman and the late Shirley Schlagman (née Goldston); m. Mia Hagg; two s.; ed Univ. Coll. School, Hampstead, Brunel Univ.; Co-Founder, Jt Chair., Man. Dir Interstate Electronics Ltd 1973–86; purchased Bush from Rank Org., renamed IEL Bush Radio Ltd 1981, floated on London Stock Exchange 1984, sold as Bush Radio PLC 1986; acquired Phaidon Press Ltd 1990, Chair. and Publr 1990–2012; mem. Exec. Cttee Patrons of New Art, Tate Gallery 1994–97, Glyndebourne Festival Soc.; Patron Bayreuther Festspiele, Salzburger Festspiele, Schubertiades; Pres. Judd Foundation, MARFA, Tex. 1999–2001, mem. Bd 2001–; Acquired Cahiers du Cinema 2009. *Leisure interests:* music, art, architecture. *Address:* Piazza Grande 26, 6600 Locarno, Switzerland (office). *Telephone:* 917596000 (office). *Fax:* 917596006 (office). *E-mail:* rsoffice@quoig.com (office).

SCHLANGER, Marvin O.; Dutch business executive; *Chairman and CEO, Ceva Logistics BV;* joined Lyondell Chemical Worldwide Inc. (fmrly ARCO Chemical Co.) as an Officer 1987, Vice-Pres., Worldwide Business Man. 1988–89, Sr Vice-Pres. and Chief Financial Officer 1989–92, Sr Vice-Pres. and Pres. ARCO Chemical Americas Co. 1992–94, Exec. Vice-Pres. and COO Lyondell Chemical Worldwide Inc. 1994–98, Pres. and CEO May–Oct. 1998, Chair. Supervisory Bd LyondellBasell Industries 2010–13; Prin., Cherry Hill Chemical Investments, LLC 1998–; CEO Resolution Performance Products Inc. (holding co. of Resolution Performance Products LLC) 2000–05, Pres. RPP LLC and RPP Capital Corpn –2001, CEO 2001–; Interim Pres. OneChem Ltd 1999–2000; Chair. CEVA Group Plc 2009–, CEO Ceva Logistics BV 2012–; Chair. Berry Plastics Corpn (fmrly Covalence Specialty Materials Corpn) 2006–07, Resolution Specialty Materials Co. 2004–05, Resolution Performance Products LLC and its subsidiary RPP Capital Corpn 2000–; Vice-Chair. Hexion Specialty Chemicals Inc. (now Momentive Specialty Chemicals Inc.) 2005–10; mem. Bd of Dirs UGI Utilities Inc 1998–, UGI Corpn 1998–, Wellman Inc. 1999–, OneChem Ltd 2002–, Momentive Specialty Chemicals Inc. 2005–10, Momentive Performance Materials Holdings Inc. 2006–10, AmeriGas Propane Inc. (Gen. Partner of AmeriGas Partners, LP) 2009–, Taminco Global Chemical Corporation 2012–, RPP Capital. *Address:* Ceva Logistics BV, Siriusdreef 20, PO Box 483, 2132 WT Hoofddorp, Netherlands (office). *Telephone:* (23) 568-3300 (office). *Fax:* (23) 568-3301 (office). *E-mail:* info@cevalogistics.com (office). *Website:* www.cevalogistics.com (office).

SCHLECKER, Anton; German retail executive; *CEO, Fa. Anton Schlecker;* b. 1944; m.; two c.; began career as apprentice butcher in father's co. 1965, built first self-service dept store in Ehingen 1967, opened first drugstore in Kirchheim 1975, began expanding into other European countries 1987, currently CEO Fa. Anton Schlecker. *Address:* Fa. Anton Schlecker, Talstrasse 12, 89579 Ehingen, Germany (office). *Telephone:* (73) 91 584-0 (office). *Fax:* (73) 91 584-300 (office). *Website:* www .schlecker.com (office).

SCHLESSINGER, Joseph, PhD; American molecular biologist, biochemist and academic; *William H. Prusoff Professor and Chairman, Department of Pharmacology, School of Medicine, Yale University;* b. 26 March 1945, Topusko, Croatia; s. of Ehud Schlessinger and Avner Schlessinger; m. Dr Irit Lax; ed The Hebrew Univ., Jerusalem and The Weizmann Inst. of Science, Rehovot, Israel; Postdoctoral Assoc., Dept of Chem., School of Applied and Eng Physics, Cornell Univ., Ithaca, NY 1974–76; Visiting Scientist, Immunology Br., Nat. Cancer Inst., NIH, Bethesda, Md 1977–78; Sr Scientist, Dept of Chemical Immunology, The Weizmann Inst. of Science 1978–80, Assoc. Prof. 1980–85, Prof. 1985–91, The Ruth and Leonard Simon Prof. of Cancer Research, The Weizmann Inst. of Science

1985–91; Research Dir Rorer Biotechology, Inc., Rockville, Md and King of Prussia, Pa 1985–90; The Milton and Helen Kimmelman Prof. and Chair. Dept of Pharmacology, New York Univ. Medical Center 1990–2001; William H. Prusoff Prof. and Chair. Dept of Pharmacology, Yale Univ. School of Medicine, New Haven, Conn. 2001–; Founder SUGEN, Inc. 1991, Plexxikon 2000; mem. Editorial Bd European Molecular Biology Organization (EMBO) Journal, Cell, Molecular Cell, Genes and Development, Molecular Biology of the Cell, Journal of Biological Chemistry, Cancer Research, Journal of Cell Biology, Growth Factors, Protein Engineering, Cell Growth and Differentiation, Structure; mem. EMBO 1982, NAS 2000, American Acad. of Arts and Sciences 2001, Inst. of Medicine 2006, Russian Acad. of Sciences 2006, Croatian Acad. of Sciences 2008; Hon. mem. Japanese Biochemical Soc. 1999; Michael Landau Prize for PhD Thesis 1973, Sara Leedy Prize 1980, Hestrin Prize 1983, Levinson Prize 1984, Keynote Presidential Lecturer, The Endocrine Soc. 1986, Lamport Lecturer, Univ. of Seattle 1993, E. Fisher Lecturer, Univ. of Geneva 1993, E.J. Cohn Lecturer, Harvard Univ. Medical School 1993, Randall Lecturer, Univ. of Pennsylvania 1994, Feigen Lecturer, Stanford Univ. Medical School 1994, Opening Keynote Lecturer, American Soc. for Biochemistry and Molecular Biology 1994, Deans Lecturer, Mount Sinai Medical School 1994, Harvey Lecturer, Rockefeller Univ. 1994, Antoine Lacassagne Prize 1995, Drew-Ciba Prize 1995, Opening Keynote Lecturer, Whitehead Inst. Symposium 1995, Howard Hughes Medical Inst. Symposium on Signal Transduction 1995, Sigma-Tau Lecturer 1995, Lindner Lecturer, The Weizmann Inst. of Science 1996, Burroughs Wellcome Lecturer, Indiana Univ. 1997, Juan March Lecturer 1998, 6th Ray A. and Robert L. Kroc Lecturer, Univ. of Massachusetts Medical School 1999, Bayer Lecturer, Univ. of California, Berkeley 1999, Distinguished Service Award, Miami Nature Biotechnology 1999, 16th Annual Kenneth F. Naidorf Memorial Lecturer, Columbia Univ. 2000, Distinguished Speakers Program, Univ. of Texas Health Science Center 2000, NIH Director's Lecturer 2000, The Taylor Prize 2000, Dan David Prize 2006, Inaugural Pfizer Lecture Michigan 2006, Keith Porter Lecture, ASCB San Diego 2006, NIH-WALS Lecture, Bethesda 2008, Helen Coley-Nauts Lecture, Moscow 2008, 24th Medical Scientist Lecture Series, UC Irvine 2008. *Publications:* more than 450 articles in scientific journals. *Address:* Department of Pharmacology, Yale University School of Medicine, Sterling Hall of Medicine, PO Box 208066, 333 Cedar Street, B-204, New Haven, CT 06520-8066, USA (office). *Telephone:* (203) 785-7395 (office). *Fax:* (203) 785-3879 (office). *E-mail:* joseph.schlessinger@yale.edu (office); Laura.copela@yale.edu (office). *Website:* info.med.yale.edu/pharm (office).

SCHLIFSKE, John E., BA, MA; American business executive; *Chairman, President and CEO, Northwestern Mutual;* b. Milwaukee, Wis.; m.; six c.; ed Carleton Coll., Kellogg Grad. School of Man., Northwestern Univ.; joined Northwestern Mutual as an investment specialist 1987, held positions of increasing authority in Securities and Real Estate Depts, later Exec. Vice-Pres. Northwestern Mutual and mem. Man. Cttee, Exec. Vice-Pres.– Investment Products and Services 2004–08, Interim Pres. and CEO Russell Investment Co. (subsidiary) 2008–09, Interim Pres. Feb.–March 2009, Pres. Northwestern Mutual 2009–10, Chair. Pres., and CEO 2010–, mem. Bd of Trustees; Dir Russell Investment Co.; mem. Bd Children's Hosp. of Wisconsin, Froedtert and Community Health; mem. Greater Milwaukee Cttee. *Address:* Northwestern Mutual, 720 East Wisconsin Avenue, Milwaukee, WI 53202-4797, USA (office). *Telephone:* (414) 271-1444 (office). *Fax:* (414) 299-7022 (office). *E-mail:* info@northwesternmutual.com (office). *Website:* www.northwesternmutual.com (office).

SCHLINK, Bernhard; German judge, academic and writer; *Professor Emeritus of Public Law and Legal Philosophy, Humboldt University of Berlin;* b. 1944, Grossdornberg, North Rhine-Westphalia; s. of the late Prof. Dr Edmund Schlink; ed Heidelberg, Berlin, Darmstadt, Bielefeld and Freiburg Univs; Prof., Bonn Univ. 1981–91; Judge, Constitutional Law Court of North Rhine-Westphalia, Münster 1987–2005; Prof., Frankfurt Univ. 1991–92; Prof., Humboldt Univ. of Berlin 1992–; Visiting Prof. of Law, Benjamin Cardozo School of Law, Yeshiva Univ., New York 1994–; qualified as masseur in Calif.; began writing fiction in 1980s. *Publications:* fiction: Selbs Justiz (with Walter Popp, trans. as Self's Punishment) 1987, Die Gordische Schleife 1988, Selbs Betrug (trans. as Self's Betrayal) 1992, Der Vorleser (trans. as The Reader) 1995, Liebesfluchten (short stories; trans. as Flights of Love) 2001, Selbs Mord (trans. as Self's Murder) 2005, Die Heimkehr (trans. as Homecoming) 2006, Das Wochenende (trans. as The Weekend) 2008, Guilt About the Past 2009, Summer Lies 2012; non-fiction: Weimar: A Jurisprudence of Crisis (with Arthur Jacobson), several books on constitutional law, fundamental separation of powers and admin. law. *E-mail:* schlink@rewi.hu-berlin.de (office). *Website:* schlink.rewi.hu-berlin.de (office).

SCHLISSEL, Mark S., BA, MD, PhD; American medical scientist, academic and university administrator; *President, University of Michigan;* b. 24 Nov. 1957, Brooklyn, NY; m. Monica Schwebs; four c.; ed Princeton Univ., Johns Hopkins Univ. School of Medicine; residency training in internal medicine at Hopkins Hosp.; postdoctoral research as Bristol-Myers Cancer Research Fellow, Whitehead Inst., MIT; began ind. research career at Johns Hopkins Univ. School of Medicine 1991, earned several awards and fellowships; Assoc. Prof., Dept of Molecular and Cell Biology, Univ. of California, Berkeley 1999–2002, Prof. 2002–11, Chair. Grad. Admission Cttee 2001, Vice-Chair. Dept of Molecular and Cell Biology 2002–07, Dean of Biological Sciences 2008–11; Provost, Brown Univ. 2011–14, Chair. Academic Priorities Cttee, Univ. Resource Council; Pres. Univ. of Michigan 2014–; mem. Immunobiology Study Section, NIH 2002–04, Chair. 2004–06; mem. Scientific Review Bd, Howard Hughes Medical Inst.; mem. American Asscn of Immunologists 1992, American Soc. of Clinical Investigators 1998. *Publications:* about 100 papers in professional journals on developmental biology of B lymphocytes. *Address:* Office of the President, University of Michigan, 2074 Fleming Administration Building, 503 Thompson Street, Ann Arbor, MI 41809-1340, USA (office). *Telephone:* (734) 764-6270 (office). *Fax:* (734) 936-3529 (office). *E-mail:* presoff@umich.edu (office). *Website:* president.umich.edu (office).

SCHLÖGL, Herwig, PhD; German fmr international organization official; b. 17 Aug. 1942; ed Univ. of Marburg; mem. German Perm. Representation to European Econ. Union, Brussels 1969–72; mem. staff Industrial Policy Div., Ministry of Econs 1972–76, Head of Foreign Econ. Affairs Div. of Industry Dept 1980–84, Head Div. for Foreign Econ. Policy, Export Promotion 1984–96; Head Econs Dept,

German-American Chamber of Commerce, New York 1976–80; Deputy Dir-Gen. for Trade Policy, Bonn 1996–98; Deputy Sec.-Gen. OECD, Paris 1998–2006. *Publications include:* books and articles on competition policy and trade issues.

SCHLÖNDORFF, Volker; German film director; b. 1939, Wiesbaden; m. Margarethe von Trotta (q.v.) 1971 (divorced 1991); m. 2nd Angelika Schlöndorff; one d.; has directed numerous cinema and TV films; mem. German PEN Centre; Officier, Ordre Nat. de la Légion d'Honneur 2002 Prize of the Int. Film Critics, Cannes 1966, Konrad-Wolf-Prize 1997, Blue Angel Award for Best European Film 2000. *Films include:* Der junge Törless, Mord und Totschlag, Michael Kohlhaas, Der plötzliche Reichtum der armen Leute von Kombach, Baal, Die Moral der Ruth Halbfass, Strohfeuer, Die Ehegattin, Übernachtung in Tirol, Die verlorene Ehre der Katharina Blum, Die Blechtrommel (The Tin Drum) (Golden Palm of Cannes, Acad. Award for Best Foreign Film) 1979, Die Fälschung 1981, Circle of Deceit 1982, Eine Liebe von Swann (Swann in Love) 1984, Death of a Salesman 1985, The Handmaid's Tale 1989, Voyager 1991, The Ogre 1996, Palmetto 1997, Die Stille nach dem Schuss 2000, Ten Minutes Older: The Cello (segment) 2002, Der Neunte Tag (The Ninth Day) 2004, Strike 2006, Ulzhan 2007. *Television includes:* Death of a Salesman 1985, Enigma: Eine uneingestandene Liebe 2005, Billy Wilder Speaks 2006.

SCHLÜTER, Poul Holmskov, LLB; Danish lawyer and fmr politician; b. 3 April 1929, Tønder; s. of Johannes Schlüter; m. 1st Lisbeth Schlüter 1979 (died 1988); two s. one d.; m. 2nd Anne Marie Vessel Schlüter 1989; ed Univs of Århus and Copenhagen; barrister and Supreme Court Attorney; Leader of Conservative Youth Movt (KU) 1944, Nat. Leader 1951; Del. to Int. Congress of World Asscn of Youth 1951, 1954; Chair. Young Conservatives, mem. Exec. Cttee Conservative Party 1952–55, 1971, Nat. Chair. Jr Chamber 1961, Vice-Pres. Jr Chamber Int. 1962; mem. Folketing (Parl.) 1964–94, Prime Minister of Denmark 1982–93; Chair. Jt Danish Consultative Council on UN 1966–68; MP Foreign Affairs Cttee 1968, Chair. 1982; mem. Council of Europe 1971–74; fmr Chair. Conservative People's Party 1974–77, 1981–93; Chair. Danish Del. to Nordic Council and mem. Presiding Cttee 1978–79; Dir Nat. Cleaning Group 1993, Int. Service System (ISS); Co-founder Danish Centre for Political Studies 2004. *Address:* c/o Danish Centre for Political Studies, Landgreven 3, 3. sal, 1301 Copenhagen, Denmark.

SCHMID, Hans Heinrich, DTheol; Swiss university rector (retd); b. 22 Oct. 1937, Zürich; s. of Gotthard Schmid and Erika Hug; m. Christa Nievergelt 1962; two s. two d.; ed Zürich and Göttingen Univs; Asst Prof. Univ. of Zürich 1967–69; Prof. for Old Testament, Kirchliche Hochschule Bethel/Bielefeld 1969–76, Univ. of Zürich 1976–88; Rector Univ. of Zürich 1988–2000; mem. Constitutional Council of Zurich 2002–05; Goldenes Ehrenkreuz der Republik Österreich 1996; Hon. DTheol (Leipzig) 1991. *Publications include:* Altorientalische Welt in der alttestamentlichen Theologie (essays) 1974, Der sogennante Jahwist. Beobachtungen und Fragen zur Pentateuchforschung 1976. *Leisure interest:* conducting a chamber orchestra. *Address:* In der Halden 11, 8603 Schwerzenbach, Switzerland (home). *Telephone:* 448252533 (home). *Fax:* 448252517 (home). *E-mail:* hans-heinrich.schmid@bluewin.ch (home).

SCHMID, Samuel; Swiss lawyer and politician; b. 8 Jan. 1947; m.; three s.; ed Univ. of Bern; with Swiss Fed. Finance Admin 1973; joined legal practice, Bern 1973; independent advocate and notary, Lyss 1978–; solicitor with Kellerhals & Pnrs LLC, Bern 1998–; adviser to econ. and trade asscns; local councillor 1972–74, Pres. Municipality of Rueti 1974–82; mem. Berni Greater Council 1982–93, Chair. Cttee for new Berni State Canton Constitution, mem. Finance Cttee; mem. Nat. Council 1994–98, mem. Standing Cttee for Econ. Affairs and Taxation, Cttee for Econs and Deliveries, Nat. Policy Cttee, Constitutional Affairs Cttee, Comm. for Strategic Questions, Comm. for Reorganization of the Intelligence Service; Pres. Swiss People's Party (Schweizerische Volkspartei) Parl. Group of the Presidential Election Council 1998–99, currently mem. Conservative Democratic Party (Bürgerlich-Demokratische Partei); mem. Comm. for Foreign Policy 1999– (also Vice-Pres.), Comm. for Econs and Deliveries, Comm. for Social Security and Health, Nat. Political Comm.; mem. Upper House of Parl. 2001–; Head of Fed. Dept of Defence, Civil Protection and Sport 2001–08; Vice-Pres. Swiss Confed. 2004, Pres. 2005; Pres. Berni Trade Asscn 1990–; mem. Exec. Cttee Swiss Trade Asscn 1991–; Col, Commdt of infantry regiment 1993–96, Commdt Stv F Div. 3 1998–99. *Address:* c/o Federal Department of Defence, Civil Protection and Sport, Bundeshaus-Ost, 3003 Bern, Switzerland (office).

SCHMID, Walter Jürgen, DrIur; German lawyer and diplomatist; *Ambassador to the Holy See;* b. 1946; ed Univ. of Tübingen, studied law at Munich and Aix-en-Provence; served in mil. 1966–67; jr court lawyer 1973–75; Attaché, Minister of Foreign Affairs 1976–78, Adviser to Minister of State 1978–79; served in embassies in Montevideo 1979–82, Ankara 1982–85; Senate Dir, Senatskanzlei Freie and Hamburg 1986–91; Amb. to Guinea 1992–94; served at Royal Coll. of Defence Studies, London, UK 1995; Disarmament Dept, Ministry of Foreign Affairs 1996–2000, Deputy Rep. for Disarmament and Arms Control 2000–03, Commr for Disarmament and Arms Control 2003–05; Amb. to Russia 2005–10, to the Holy See (Vatican City) 2010–. *Address:* Embassy of Germany, Via di Villa Sacchetti 4–6, 00197 Rome, Italy (office). *Telephone:* (06) 809511 (office). *Fax:* (06) 80951227 (office). *Website:* www.vatikan.diplo.de (office).

SCHMIDBAUR, Hubert, Dr rer. nat; German chemist, academic and consultant; *Professor Emeritus, Technische Universität München;* b. 31 Dec. 1934, Landsberg; s. of Johann B. Schmidbaur and Katharina S. Ehelechner; m. Rose-Marie Fukas; one s. one d.; ed Univ. of Munich; Asst Prof., Univ. of Munich 1960–64; Assoc. Prof., Univ. of Marburg 1964–69; Prof., Univ. of Würzburg 1969–73; Prof. of Chem. and Head of Dept, Tech. Univ. of Munich 1973–2002, Dean Faculty of Science 1983–86, Prof. Emer. 2002–; Assoc. Prof., Univ. of Stellenbosch, SA 2002–06, Nat. Univ. of Singapore 2008, King Abdulaziz Univ., Jeddah, Saudi Arabia 2012–; mem. Göttingen, Leopoldina, Bavarian and Finnish Acads, Acatech, Senate, German Science Foundation; Bundesverdienstkreuz, Maximiliansorden für Wissenschaft & Kunst; Dr hc (Westfälische Wilhelms-Universität Münster) 2005; A. Stock Prize, German Chemical Soc., Wacker Silikon Preis, Bonner Chemie-preis, ACS F. Kipping Award, Leibniz Award, German Science Foundation, Dwyer Medal, Bailar Medal, Ludwig Mond Medal, Birch Medal, RSC Centenary Medal. *Publications:* about 850, including books, monographs and scientific papers on inorganic, metalorganic and analytical chem. *Address:* Technische Universität

München, Department Chemie, Lichtenbergstrasse 4, 85747 Garching (office); Königsbergerstr. 36, 85748 Garching, Germany (home). *Telephone:* (89) 28913130 (office). *Fax:* (89) 28913125 (office). *E-mail:* h.schmidbaur@lrz.tum.de (office). *Website:* aac.anorg.chemie.tu-muenchen.de (office).

SCHMIDT, Andreas; German singer (baritone); *Kammersänger Professor, Hochschule für Musik und Theater, Munich;* b. 30 June 1960, Düsseldorf; m. Jeanne Pascale 2003; two s. three d.; ed studied piano, organ, conducting in Düsseldorf, singing in Düsseldorf and Berlin; youngest mem. Deutsche Oper Berlin 1983; debut Hamburg State Opera 1985, Munich State Opera 1985, Covent Garden London 1986, Vienna State Opera 1988, Geneva Opera 1989, Salzburg Festival 1989, Aix-en-Provence Festival 1991, Metropolitan New York 1991, Edin. Festival 1991, Paris Bastille 1992, Paris Garnier 1993, Glyndebourne Festival 1994, State Opera Berlin 1995, Amsterdam Opera 1995, Bayreuth Festival 1996; has sung with major orchestras, including Berlin, Geneva, Vienna, Munich, Hamburg, London, Paris, Rome, Amsterdam, Copenhagen, Stockholm, Helsinki, New York, Israel Philharmonic orchestras, Cincinnati, Cleveland, Chicago, San Franciso and Philadelphia Symphony orchestras, La Scala, Milan, and with conductors including Bernstein, Solti, Levine, Barenboim, Sinopoli, Thielemann, Conlon, Eschenbach, Masur, Nagano and others; currently Prof., Hochschule für Musik und Theater, Munich; Hon. mem., Richard-Wagner-Verband; first prize Deutscher Musikwettbewerb, several German and int. awards and prizes. *Recordings:* more than 130 CDs. *Leisure interests:* fly-fishing, golf, literature, art. *Address:* c/o Hartmut Haase, Artists Management, Aalgrund 8, 31275 Lehrte, Germany (office). *Telephone:* (5175) 953232 (office). *Fax:* (5175) 953233 (office). *E-mail:* artists@t-online.de (office). *Website:* www.artists-haase.de (office).

SCHMIDT, Benno C., Jr; American academic and university administrator; *Chairman, Avenues: The World School;* b. 20 March 1942, Washington; s. of the late Benno Charles Schmidt, Sr and Martha Chastain; m. 2nd Helen Cutting Whitney 1980; one d. (one s. one d. by previous marriage); ed Yale Coll. and Yale Law School; clerk to US Supreme Court Chief Justice Earl Warren 1966–67; with US Dept of Justice 1967–69; mem. Faculty, Columbia Univ. Law School 1969–86, Dean 1984–86; Pres. and Prof. of Law, Yale Univ. 1986–92; Pres. and CEO The Edison Project (now Edison Schools) 1992–98, also Chair.; Chair. Avenues: The World School, New York 2011–; Chair. Nations Acad. 2007–, Council on Aid to Educ.; Chair. Bd of Trustees, CUNY; Dir Nat. Humanities Center, Chapel Hill, NC 1985–; mem. Council on Foreign Relations, The American Acad. of Arts and Sciences; Trustee, Ewing Marion Kauffman Foundation 2007–; Hon. Master of Bench, Gray's Inn 1988, Hon. AO 1991. *Publications include:* Freedom of the Press versus Public Access 1976, The Judiciary and Responsible Government 1910–1921 (with A. M. Bickel) 1984; papers on constitutional law, freedom of the press and first amendment issues. *Address:* Avenues: The World School, 11 East 26th Street, 17th Floor, New York, NY 10010-1420, USA (office). *Telephone:* (212) 935-5000 (office). *Fax:* (646) 625-7600 (office). *Website:* www.avenues.org (office).

SCHMIDT, Brian P., AC, BS, AM, PhD, FRS, FAA; American/Australian astronomer and academic; *Australian Research Council Laureate Fellow and Distinguished Professor, Australian National University;* b. 24 Feb. 1967, Missoula, Mont.; s. of Dana Charles Schmidt and Donna Pentz Schmidt; m. Jennifer Margaret Gordon; two s.; ed Univ. of Arizona, Harvard Univ.; Postdoctoral Fellow, ANU 1993–94, Post-doctoral Fellow, ANU Mount Stromlo and Siding Spring Observatories 1995–96, Research Fellow 1997–99, Fellow, Research School of Astronomy and Astrophysics 1999–2002, Australian Research Council Professorial Fellow 2003–05, Australian Research Council Fed. Fellow 2005–09, Australian Research Council Laureate Fellow and Distinguished Prof. 2009–, Scientific Leader, SkyMapper Telescope and Southern Sky Survey; Chair. LOC and SOC of Astronomical Soc. of Australia's AGM 2002, Australian Time Allocation Cttee (Gemini/AAT/UK-Schmidt) 2002–03, Australia Telesope Nat. Facility Time Allocation Cttee 2002–04, Australian Nat. Acad. LOFAR Working Group 2003, Australian Decade Plan Working Group on Int. Facilities 2004; mem. Major Nat. Research Facility Selection Panel 2001, Council of Astronomical Soc. of Australia 2001–03, Australian Square Kilometre Array Steering Cttee 2001–, Anglo Australian Telescope Bd 2004–; Dir (non-exec.) Astronomy Australia Ltd 2007–; mem. Australian Decadal Working Group on Int. Facilities, Mid Term Review of the Australian Astronomy Decadal Plan; Fellow, Japanese Soc. for the Promotion of Science 1999, NAS 2008; Glenn C. Purviance Scholarship, Univ. of Arizona 1988, Vesto Slipher Scholarship, Univ. of Arizona 1988–89, Most Outstanding Student in Physics, Univ. of Arizona 1989, Danforth Award for Excellence in Teaching, Harvard Univ. 1991, NASA Grad. Student Researchers Program Fellowship Recipient 1992–93, Science Magazine's 'Breakthrough of the Year' 1998, Bok Prize for Outstanding Astronomical Thesis, Harvard Univ. 2000, Inaugural Malcolm McIntosh Prize, Australian Govt 2000, Pawsey Medal, Australian Acad. of Sciences 2001, Harley Wood Lecturer, Astronomical Soc. of Australia 2001, Burbidge Lecturer, Auckland Astronomical Soc. 2001, Inaugural Oliphant Lecturer, Australian Acad. of Science 2001, Vainu Bappu Medal, Astronomical Soc. of India 2002, Dean's Lecturer, Univ. of Western Australia 2004, Australian Academy of Science 50th Anniversary Lecture 2004, Bulletin Magazine's Scientist of the Year 2004, Marc Aaronson Memorial Lecturer 2005, Shaw Prize in Astronomy (co-recipient) 2006, Gurevitch Lecture, Portland State Univ. 2007, Niels Bohr Lecturer, Copenhagen 2007, Gruber Prize for Cosmology (co-recipient) 2007, Sackler Lecturer, Princeton Univ. 2008, ISI Most Cited Australian in Space Sciences 1997–2007 2008, Oxford Univ. Halley Lecturer 2010, Nobel Prize in Physics (jtly) 2011. *Publications include:* more than 110 scientific papers in professional journals on observational cosmology, studies of supernovae, gamma ray bursts, large surveys, photometry and calibration. *Leisure interest:* winemaker and vigneron. *Address:* The Research School of Astronomy and Astrophysics, ANU Mount Stromlo Observatory, via Cotter Road, Weston Creek, ACT 2611, Australia (office). *Telephone:* (2) 6125-8042 (office). *E-mail:* brian .schmidt@mso.anu.edu.au (office). *Website:* msowww.anu.edu.au/~brian (office).

SCHMIDT, Chauncey Everett, BS, MBA; American banker and business executive; b. 7 June 1931, Oxford, Ia; s. of Walter F. Schmidt and Vilda Saxton; m. Anne Garrett McWilliams 1954 (deceased); one s. two d.; ed US Naval Acad., Harvard Graduate School of Business Admin.; with First Nat. Bank of Chicago 1959–75, Vice-Pres. 1965, Gen. Man., London 1966, Gen. Man. for Europe, Middle East and Africa 1968, Sr Vice-Pres. 1969–72, Exec. Vice-Pres. 1972, Vice-Chair.

1973, Pres. 1974–75; Chair. and CEO Bank of Calif. 1976–84; Chair., Pres. and CEO BanCal Tri-State Corpn 1976–84; apptd Chair. Cybernet Software Systems 2004; Founder and Chair. C. E.Schmidt and Assocs Inc.; mem. Bd of Dirs Docuton, Barry Financial, UBS Asset Man., Amfac Ltd, Calif. Bankers Clearing House Asscn, Calif. Roundtable, Bay Area Council; mem. Exec. Bd San Francisco Bay Area Council of Boy Scouts of America; mem. Bd of Govs San Francisco Symphony; mem. Fed. Advisory Council of Fed. Reserve System, Advisory Council of Japan– US Econ. Relations, SRI International, Council, Int. Monetary Conf., American Bankers Asscn. *Address:* 40 Why Worry Farm, Woodside, CA 94062, USA (home).

SCHMIDT, Christian, PhD, DSc (Econ), PhD; French economist and academic; *President, European Neuroeconomics Association;* b. 20 July 1938, Neuilly-sur-Seine; s. of Paul Schmidt and Jeanne Loriot; m. Marie-Pierre de Cossè Brissac 1988; ed Facultés de lettres, droit, sciences, Institut d'etudes politiques, Paris, Institut des hautes études de défense nationale, École des hautes études en sciences sociales, Acad. of Int. Law, The Hague; Research Asst Inst. of Applied Econ. Sciences Laboratoire Coll. de France 1964–67; Asst La Sorbonne 1967–70; Chargé de Mission Forecasting Admin. Ministry of Finances 1970–72; f. Dir Econ. Perspectives 1969–86; Asst Dir French Inst. of War Studies 1980–82; Pres. Charles Gide Asscn for the Study of Econ. Thought 1981–90; Consultant on Econ. Aspects of Disarmament UN 1980; Prof. of Econs, Univ. of Paris IX (Paris Dauphine) 1983–2012, Prof. Emer. 2012–, Dir Lab. of Econs and Sociology of Defence Orgs (LESOD) 1984–2005; Founder and Pres. Asscn française des économistes de défense 1981–2001, Int. Defence Econ. Asscn 1985–; Co-Dir (Research Group) CNRS 1990–; Chair. Scientific Council of European Soc. of Econ. Thought; Pres. European Neuroeconomics Asscn 2011–; mem. Council French Econs Asscn 2000–04, Soc. d'Economie Politique 2000–; mem. various editorial bds; Officier, Légion d'honneur; Prix de L'institut (Acad. des Sciences Morales et Politiques) 1986, 1993, Prix Risques 2010. *Publications include:* Conséquences Economiques et Sociales de la Course aux Armaments 1983, Essai sur l'Economie Ricardienne 1984, La Semantique Economique en Question 1985, Peace, Defence and Economic Analysis 1987, The Economics of Military Expenditures 1989, Penser la Guerre, Penser l'Economie 1991, Game Theory and International Relations 1994, Uncertainty and Economic Thought 1996, Game Theory and International Relations (co-ed.) 1996, The Rational Foundations of Economic Behaviour (co-ed.) 1996, La Theorie des Jeux: Essai d'Interpretation 2001, Game Theory and Economic Analysis 2002, Neuroeconomie: Comment les neurosciences transforment l'analyse economique 2010; numerous articles in learned journals. *Leisure interests:* theatre, opera. *Address:* Université de Paris-IX Dauphine, Place du Maréchal de Lattre de Tassigny, 75775 Paris Cedex 16 (office); 109 rue de Grenelle, 75007 Paris, France (home). *Telephone:* 1-44-05-49-39 (office); 1-45-51-01-78 (home); 6-07-62-89-51 (mobile). *Fax:* 1-44-05-48-04 (office); 1-45-51-22-70 (home). *E-mail:* christian .schmidt@dauphine.fr (office); schmidtchristian.f@orange.fr (home).

SCHMIDT, Eric E., BS, MS, PhD; American computer industry executive; *Executive Chairman, Google Inc.;* b. 27 April 1955, Washington, DC; m. Wendy Schmidt; two c.; ed Princeton Univ., Univ. of California, Berkeley; began career with Bell Labs and Zilog; mem. Research Staff Computer Science Lab., Xerox Palo Alto Research Center (PARC) 1979–83; Software Man. Sun Microsystems 1983–84, Software Dir 1984–85, Vice-Pres. Software Products 1985–88, Vice-Pres. Gen. Systems Group 1988–91, Chief Tech. Officer 1994–97, Pres. Sun Tech. Enterprises 1991–94; Chair. and CEO Novell Inc. 1997–2001; CEO Google Inc. 2001–11, Exec. Chair. 2001–04, 2007–; mem. Bd of Dirs Siebel Systems Inc., Integrated Archive Systems, Tilion, Apple Computer Inc. 2006–09 (resgnd); Chair. New America Foundation 2008–; mem. Pres. Obama's Council of Advisors on Science and Tech., Prime Minister's Advisory Council (UK); Trustee, Inst. for Advanced Study, Princeton, NJ 2008–; mem. IEEE, Asscn of Computing Machinery, Nat. Acad. of Eng 2006; Fellow, American Acad. of Arts and Sciences 2007. *Publication:* The New Digital Age 2013. *Address:* Google Inc., 1600 Amphitheatre Parkway, Mountain View, CA 94043, USA (office). *Telephone:* (650) 330-0100 (office). *Fax:* (650) 618-1499 (office). *Website:* www.google.com (office).

SCHMIDT, Helmut; German politician, economist and publisher; *Co-Publisher, Die Zeit;* b. 23 Dec. 1918, Hamburg; s. of Gustav Schmidt and Ludovica Schmidt; m. Hannelore Glaser 1942 (died 2010); one d.; ed Lichtwarkschule and Univ. Hamburg; Man. Transport Admin. of State of Hamburg 1949–53; mem. Social Democrat Party 1946–; mem. Bundestag 1953–61, 1965–87; Chair. Social Democrat (SPD) Parl. Party in Bundestag 1967–69; Vice-Chair. SPD 1968–84; Senator (Minister) for Domestic Affairs in Hamburg 1961–65; Minister of Defence 1969–72, for Econ. and Finance July–Dec. 1972, of Finance 1972–74; Fed. Chancellor 1974–82; Co-Publr Die Zeit (weekly newspaper), Hamburg 1983–; Co-founder Inter Action Councils 1983; Hon. DCL (Oxford) 1979; Dr hc (Newberry Coll.) 1973, (Johns Hopkins) 1976, (Cambridge) 1976, (Harvard) 1979, (Sorbonne) 1981, (Louvain) 1984, (Georgetown) 1986, (Bergamo) 1989, (Tokyo) 1991, (Haifa) 2000, (Potsdam) 2000 and others; European Prize for Statesmanship (FUS Foundation) 1979, Nahum Goldmann Silver Medal 1980, Athinai Prize 1986. *Publications:* Defence or Retaliation 1962, Beiträge 1967, Strategie des Gleichgewichts (trans. as Balance of Power) 1969, Kontinuität und Konzentration 1976, Als Christ in der politischen Entscheidung 1976, Der Kurs heisst Frieden 1979, Pflicht zur Menschlichkeit 1981, Kunst im Kanzleramt 1982, Freiheit verantworten 1983, Die Weltwirtschaft ist unser Schicksal 1983, Eine Strategie für den Westen (trans. as A Grand Strategy for the West) (Adolphe Bentinck Prize) 1986, Vom deutschen Stolz: Bekenntnisse zur Erfahrung von Kunst 1986, Menschen und Mächte (trans. as Men and Powers) 1987, Die Deutschen und ihre Nachbarn 1990, Mit Augenmass und Weitblick 1990, Einfügen in die Gemeinschaft der Völker 1990, Kindheit und Jugend unter Hitler 1992, Ein Manifest – Weil das Land sich ändern muss (co-author) 1992, Handeln für Deutschland 1993, Jahr der Entscheidung 1994, Was wird aus Deutschland? 1994, Weggefährten 1996, Jahrhundertwende 1998, Allgemeine Erklärung der Menschenpflichten 1998, Globalisierung 1998, Auf der Suche nach einer öffentlichen Moral 1998, Die Selbstbehauptung Europas 2000, Hand aufs Herz 2002, Die Mächte der Zukunft 2005. *Address:* Die Zeit, Speersort 1, Pressehaus, 20095 Hamburg, Germany (office). *Telephone:* (40) 32800 (office). *Fax:* (40) 327111 (office). *Website:* www.zeit.de (office).

SCHMIDT, Klaus, PhD; German economist and academic; *Professor, Faculty of Economics, Ludwig-Maximilians-Universität München;* b. 16 June 1961, Koblenz; m. Monika Schnitzer; three d.; ed Univs of Marburg, Hamburg and Bonn and

London School of Econs; Visiting Asst Prof., MIT, USA 1992; Asst Prof., Univ. of Bonn 1993–95; Full Prof. of Econs, Ludwig-Maximilians-Universität München 1995–; Visiting Prof., Stanford Univ. 2000, Yale Univ. 2004. *Address:* Department of Economics, Ludwig-Maximilians-Universität München, Room 08, Ludwigstr. 28, 80539 Munich, Germany (office). *Telephone:* (89) 21802250 (office). *Fax:* (89) 21803510 (office). *E-mail:* klaus.schmidt@lrz.uni-muenchen.de (office). *Website:* www.vwl.uni-muenchen.de (office).

SCHMIDT, Maarten, PhD, ScD; Dutch astronomer and academic; *Professor Emeritus of Astronomy, California Institute of Technology;* b. 28 Dec. 1929, Groningen; s. of W. Schmidt and A. W. Haringhuizen; m. Cornelia J. Tom 1955; three d.; ed Univs of Groningen and Leiden; Scientific Officer, Univ. of Leiden Observatory 1949–59; Carnegie Fellow, Mount Wilson Observatory, Pasadena 1956–58; Assoc. Prof., Calif. Inst. of Tech. 1959–64, Prof. of Astronomy 1964–96, Prof. Emer. 1996–; Pres. American Astronomical Soc. 1984–86; mem. Norwegian Acad. of Science and Letters; Helen B. Warner Prize 1964, Rumford Award, American Acad. of Arts and Sciences 1968, Karl Schwarzschild Medal 1968, Jansky Prize, Nat. Radio Astronomy Observatory 1979, Royal Astronomy Soc. Gold Medal 1980, James Craig Watson Medal, NAS 1991, Bruce Medal 1992, Kavli Prize 2008. *Achievements include:* discovered large red shifts in spectra of quasi-stellar radio sources (quasars). *Leisure interest:* classical music. *Address:* California Institute of Technology, 204 Robinson Laboratory, 1200 East California Boulevard, Pasadena, CA 91125, USA (office). *Telephone:* (626) 395-4671 (office). *E-mail:* mxs@astro.caltech.edu (office). *Website:* www.astro.caltech.edu (office).

SCHMIDT, Renate; German fmr politician; b. 12 Dec. 1943, Hanau/Main; m. 2nd Hasso von Henninges 1998; three c.; worked as programmer, systems analyst and mem. of works cttee of mail-order co.; mem. SPD 1972–, Chair. SPD Bavaria 1991–2000, Deputy Chair. SPD 1997; mem. Bundestag (Parl.) 1980–94, 2005–09; Deputy Chair. SPD Parl. Party in Bundestag (Chair. of Equal Rights for Woman and Man working group) 1987–90, Vice-Pres. Bundestag 1990–94; directly elected mem. of Parl. for Nuremberg North in Bavarian Landtag; Chair. SPD Parl. Party in Bavarian Landtag 1994–2002; Federal Minister for Family Affairs, Senior Citizens, Women and Youth 2002–05; currently Ombudsman for Data Protection and Anti-Corruption, Vodafone D2; Pres. Bavarian Red Cross 1993–2002, Deutscher Familienverband May–Oct. 2002, Zentralstelle für Recht und Schutz der Kriegsdienstverweigerer aus Gewissensgründen e.V. 2002; mem. HBV, AWO, Socialist Youth Germany 'Die Falken', Bund Naturschutz, AIDS-Hilfe, Bd of Trustees of the Deutscher Kinderschutzbund; Chair. Nestle Future Forum on Nutrition; Consultant for Roche on Rheumatoid Arthritis. *Address:* Rohrmattenstr. 18, 90480 Nurenburg, Germany. *Fax:* (911) 407641. *E-mail:* renate .schmidt@vodafone.com. *Website:* www.renateschmidt.de.

SCHMIDT, Werner; German banking executive; b. 13 July 1943, Sindelfingen; m.; two c.; Man. Landesbank Stuttgart 1971–74, mem. Bd of Man. Dirs 1974–86, Deputy Chair. 1986–89; Chair. Südwestdeutsche Landesbank 1989–99; Chair. Landesbank Baden-Württemberg 1999–2001; Chair. Bd of Man BayernLB (Bayerische Landesbank Girozentrale) 2001–08 (resgnd), Chair. Supervisory Bd Hypo Group Alpe Adria (after acquisition by BayernLB) 2007–08; fmr Deputy Chair. BAWAG (Bank für Arbeit und Wirtschaft AG). *Address:* c/o Bayerische Landesbank Girozentrale, Briennerstrasse 18, 80333 Munich, Germany.

SCHMIDT-HOLTZ, Rolf; German lawyer and music company executive; b. 31 Aug. 1948, Martinsreuth; ed Univs of Erlangen and Kiel, Germany; journalist, television correspondent, Ed.-in-Chief and Publisher, magazines, newspapers; television exec.; Ed.-in-Chief WDR (German public broadcaster) 1986–88; Publr Gruner + Jahr's Stern news magazine 1988, Ed.-in-Chief 1990, mem. Exec. Bd Gruner + Jahr 1989–94; CEO UFA (Bertelsmann TV c.) 1994, CEO CLT-UFA (after merger with CLT) 1997, then merger with Pearson Television to form RTL Group 2000; Chair. and CEO BMG 2001–04, Non-Exec. Chair. Sony BMG (following merger with Sony Music Entertainment) 2004–06, Chair. Man. Bd and CEO 2006–11; mem. Bertelsmann Stiftung Bd of Trustees 2005–; Co-Chair. Advisory Bd Art Dirs Club Inst., Berlin 2004–; mem. Supervisory Bd Gruner & Jahr AG, Druck-und Verlagshaus; mem. Bd of Dirs RTL Group SA 2002–. *Address:* c/o Board of Directors, RTL Group, 45, Bd Pierre Frieden, 1543 Luxembourg, Luxembourg.

SCHMIDT-JORTZIG, Edzard, DrIur; German academic, politician and lawyer; *Of Counsel, Schmidt-Jortzig Petersen Penzlin;* b. 8 Oct. 1941, Berlin; s. of Rear-Adm. Friedrich-Traugott Schmidt and Carla Freiin von Frydag; m. Marion von Arnim 1968; two d. two s.; ed Univs of Bonn, Lausanne and Kiel; early career as municipal lawyer; Asst Lecturer, then Prof., Univ. of Göttingen 1977; Prof. of Public Law, Univs of Münster and Kiel 1977–2007, Head of Law Dept, Univ. of Kiel 1992; judge, Higher Admin. Courts of Lüneburg and Schleswig and at Constitutional Court of Saxony 1989–94; mem. Bundestag (FDP) 1994–2002; Fed. Minister of Justice 1996–98; Chair. German Ethical Council (Deutscher Ethikrat) 2008–12; currently Of Counsel, Schmidt-Jortzig Petersen Penzlin, Hamburg; Bundesverdienstkreuz 2002. *Publications include:* Zur Verfassungsmässigkeit von Kreisumlagesätzen 1977, Kommunale Organisationshoheit 1979, Die Einrichtungsgarantien der Verfassung 1979, Kommunalrecht 1982, Gemeindliches Eigentum an Meereshäfen 1985, Reformüberlegungen für die Landessatzung Schleswig-Holstein 1988, Handbuch des Kommunalen Finanz und Haushaltsrechts (with J. Makswit) 1991, Staatsangehörigkeit im Wandel 1997, Wann ist der Mensch tot? 1999, Rechtsfragen der Biomedizin 2003. *Address:* Schmidt-Jortzig Petersen Penzlin, Rechtsanwälte Partnerschaftsgesellschaft, Alstertor 9, 20095 Hamburg, Germany (office). *Telephone:* (40) 3095496 (office). *Fax:* (40) 309549650 (office). *E-mail:* info@sjpp.de (office). *Website:* www.sjpp.de (office); www.uni-kiel.de/oeffrecht/schmidt-jortzig (office).

SCHMIED, Wieland; Austrian art historian and academic; b. 5 Feb. 1929, Frankfurt am Main; m. Erika Schmied 1966; two d.; ed Univ. of Vienna; reader, Insel Verlag, Frankfurt 1960–62; Art Critic, Frankfurter Allgemeinen Zeitung 1960–62; Dir Kestner-Gesellschaft, Hannover 1963–74; Dir Berliner Künstlerprogramm DAAD (Artists-in-Residence Programme) 1978–86; Prof. of Art History, Acad. of Fine Arts, Munich 1986–94, Rector 1988–93; Pres. Int. Summer Acad. of Fine Arts, Salzburg 1981–99; mem. Bayerische Akad. der Schönen Künste 1988–, Dir Abteilung Bildenden Kunst 1992–95, Pres. 1995–2004; Dr hc (Athens Art Acad.); Vienna City Prize for Essays 1984, Staatspreis for Essays, Vienna 1992,

Friedrich Märker Award for Essays, Munich 1994, Theo Wormland Award, Munich 1997. *Publications:* Schach mit Marcel Duchamp 1980, De Chirico und sein Schatten 1989, Berührungen (essays) 1991, Caspar David Friedrich (also in English) 1992, 2002, De Chiricos beunruhigende Musen 1993, Ezra Pound. Ein Leben zwischen Kunst und Politik 1994, Edward Hoppers Amerika (also in English) 1995, Thomas Bernhards Häuser 1995, Francis Bacon (also in English) 1996, Max Weiler – Ein anderes Bild der Natur. Der Weg zum Spätwerk 1998, Thomas Bernhards Welt. Schauplätze seiner Jugend 1999, Caspar David Friedrich – Zyklus, Zeit und Ewigkeit 1999, Museum der Malerei 1999, Thomas Bernhards Österreich. Schauplätze seiner Romane 2000, Ezra Pound Studien 2000, Giorgio de Chirico – Reise ohne Ende (also in English) 2001, Der kühle Blick – Kunst der 20er Jahre 2001, H. C. Artmann: Erinnerungen und Essays 2001, Die andere Moderne – De Chirico und Savinio (with Paolo Baldacci) 2001, Geschichte der Bildenden Künste in Österreich Das 20. Jhdt. 2002, Wohin geht die Reise der bildenden Kunst? 2003, Die schwierige Schönheit. Ezra Pound und die bildende Kunst 2003, Hundertwassers Paradiese 2003, Leidenschaft und kühler Blick (essays) 2004, Begegnung mit Samuel Beckett in Berlin 2006, Lust am Widerspruch (autobiography) 2008, Guten Abend, Maestro, Nächtliche Gespräche im Museum 2010, Paul Celan 2011; major catalogues on modern art. *Address:* Bayerische Akademie der Schönen Künste, Max Joseph Platz 3, 80539 Munich, Germany (office). *Telephone:* (89) 2900770 (office). *Fax:* (89) 29007723 (office). *E-mail:* bayerische-akademie@gmx.de (office). *Website:* www.badsk.de/home (office).

SCHMITT, Allison Rodgers; American swimmer; b. 7 June 1990, Pittsburgh, Pa; d. of Ralph Schmitt and Gail Schmitt; started swimming at the age of nine, four-time champion in 200 and 500-yard freestyle swimming events, Nat. Collegiate Athletic Asscn (NCAA); trained at North Baltimore Aquatic Club with Michael Phelps; bronze medal, 4x200m freestyle relay, qualified to semifinals in 200m freestyle, Beijing Olympics 2008; silver medal, 200m freestyle, 4x200m freestyle relay, World Aquatics Championships 2009; gold medal, 200m and 400m freestyle, Duel in the Pool, Manchester 2009; gold medal, 200m freestyle, 4x200m freestyle relay, finished fourth in 400m freestyle, Pan Pacific Championships 2010; gold medal, 200m freestyle, USA Nat. Championships 2010; gold medal, 4x200m freestyle relay, World Aquatics Championships 2011; gold medal, 200m and 400m freestyle, Santa Clara Int. Grand Prix 2011; gold medal, 200m freestyle (Olympic Record), 4x100m medley relay, 4x200m freestyle relay, silver medal, 400m freestyle, bronze medal, 4x100m freestyle relay, London Olympics 2012; attends Univ. of Georgia; mem. Club Wolverine. *Address:* c/o Club Wolverine, PO Box 130229, Ann Arbor, MI 48113, USA. *Website:* swimallison.com

SCHMITT, Harrison H., BS, PhD; American geologist, business executive, fmr politician and fmr astronaut; *Chairman Emeritus, The Annapolis Center for Science-Based Public Policy;* b. 3 July 1935, Santa Rita, NM; s. of Harrison A. Schmitt and Ethel Hagan Schmitt; m. Teresa Fitzgibbons 1985; ed California Inst. of Tech., Univ. of Oslo, Norway and Harvard Univ.; Fulbright Fellowship 1957–58, Kennecott Fellowship in Geology 1958–59, Harvard Fellowship 1959–60, Harvard Travelling Fellowship 1960, Parker Travelling Fellowship 1961–62, NSF Post-doctoral Fellowship, Dept of Geological Sciences, Harvard 1963–64; has done geological work for Norwegian Geological Survey, Oslo, for US Geological Survey, New Mexico and Montana and in Alaska 1955–56; with US Geological Survey Astrogeology Dept –1965; Project Chief on photo and telescopic mapping of moon and planets; selected as scientist-astronaut by NASA 1965; completed flight training 1966; Lunar Module pilot Apollo XVII 1972; Chief, Astronaut Office, Science and Applications, Johnson Space Center 1974; Asst Admin., Energy Programs, NASA, Washington, DC 1974–76; Senator from New Mexico 1977–83; Consultant 1983–; mem. Pres.'s Foreign Intelligence Advisory Bd 1984–85, Army Sciences Bd 1985–89, Army Research Lab. Tech. Review Bd 1993–; co-leader group to monitor Romanian elections 1990; Chair., Pres. Annapolis Center for Science-Based Public Policy 1994–98, currently Chair. Emer. and mem. Bd of Dirs; Adjunct Prof., Univ. of Wisconsin 1995–; Republican; Hon. Fellow, Geological Soc. of America 1984; Lovelace Award, NASA 1989, Gilbert Award, GSA 1989. *Publications include:* Return to the Moon: Exploration, Enterprise, and Energy in the Human Settlement of Space 2006. *Address:* c/o Board of Directors, The Annapolis Center for Science-Based Public Policy, 111 Forbes Street, Suite 200, Annapolis, MD 21401, USA.

SCHMITT, Pál, PhD; Hungarian diplomatist, international organization official, sportsman, politician and fmr head of state; b. 13 May 1942, Budapest; m. Katalin Makray; ed Univ. of Econs; hotel manager 1965–80; won Team Épée Gold Medal at Olympic Games, Mexico City 1968, Munich 1972; Deputy Under-Sec. of State for Sport 1981–90; mem. IOC 1983–, First Sec., Hungarian Olympic Cttee 1983–89, Chair. 1989–2010, Vice-Chair. Athletes Comm. of IOC 1984–88, mem. IOC Exec. Bd 1991–99, Chair. Sport and Environment Comm. of IOC 1995–, Vice-Pres. IOC 1995–99; Pres. World Olympians Asscn 1999–2007; Amb. to Spain 1993–97, to Switzerland 1998–2002; mem. Fidesz–Hungarian Civic Union, Vice-Chair. 2003–07; mem. European Parl. (Group of the European People's Party) 2004–10, Vice-Chair. Cttee on Culture and Educ. 2004–09, Chair. Del. to EU-Croatia Jt Parl. Cttee 2004–09, Vice-Pres. European Parl. 2009–10; Speaker of the Nat. Ass. (Országgyülés) May–Aug. 2010; Pres. of Hungary 2010–12 (resgnd). *Address:* c/o Office of the President, 1014 Budapest, Szent György tér 1–2, Hungary.

SCHMITTER, Philippe, BA, PhD; American academic; *Emeritus Professor, European University Institute;* b. 19 Nov. 1936, Washington, DC; m. (divorced); one d. one s.; ed Dartmouth Coll., Univ. Nacional Autónoma de México, Mexico, Univ. of Geneva, Switzerland, Univ. of Calif. at Berkeley; Research Asst, Univ. of Calif., Berkeley 1961–62, Fellowship Coordinator, Inst. of Int. Studies 1964, Research Political Scientist 1966–67; Lecturer, Sacramento State Coll. 1967; Asst Prof., Dept of Political Sciences, Univ. of Chicago 1967–71, Chair. Cttee on Latin American Studies 1970–73, 1974–76, Assoc. Prof. 1971–75, Founding Chair. Cttee on Western Europe 1974–77, Prof. 1975–84; Dir European Univ. Inst. (EUI) Summer School, Florence, Italy 1983, Prof. Dept of Social and Political Sciences 1982–86, Prof. of Political Science –2004, Emerit. Prof. 2004–; Prof., Stanford Program-in-Paris 1993; Prof., Dept of Political Science, Stanford Univ. 1985–98, Prof. Emer. 1999–; Visiting Prof., Univ. of Brazil 1965–66, INTAL, Buenos Aires 1969, Harvard Univ. 1970, Univs of Geneva 1973–74, Paris I 1976, Mannheim 1977–78, Zurich 1978, Barcelona 1984, Univ. Autónoma de Madrid 1990, Univ.

Menendez Pelayo, Valencia 1993, Inst. of Political Studies, Paris 1994, Bilkent Univ., Ankara 1995, Univ. of Siena 1999–2002; Recurrent Visiting Prof. Central European Univ. 2005–; mem. Editorial Bd Comparative Political Studies 1974–77, Armed Forces and Society 1976–82, Historical Social Research 1976–83, Papers: Revista de Sociologia 1979–85, Politics and Soc. 1982–86, Stato e mercato 1983–86, 1997–, Journal of Democracy 1992–, The Encyclopedia of Democracy 1992–, Review Int. de Politique Comparée 1993–, Swiss Political Science Review 1995–, Politique et Sociétés 1995–; mem. numerous academic advisory bds; mem. Société Tocqueville 1977–, Asscn Française de Science Politique 1981–, Schweizerische Vereinigung für Politische Wissenschaft 1981–, Società italiana di scienza politica 1982–, Deutsche Vereinigung für Politische Wissenschaft 1982–; mem. Research Cttee on European Unification, Int. Political Science Asscn 1993–; Int. Fellow, Council on Foreign Relations, New York 1972–73, Fellow, Alexander von Humboldt Stiftung 1977, J.S. Guggenheim Foundation 1978, Center for Advanced Studies in the Behavioural Sciences 1991–92, Collegium Budapest 2005–06; Recurring Visiting Prof., Central European Univ. 2004–; numerous fellowships and research grants; Hon. Prof. Konstanz Univ. 1999–2002; Dissertation Prize, Univ. of Calif., Berkeley 1968, ECPR Lifetime Acheivement Prize 2008, EUSA Contrib. to European Integration Prize 2009, IPSA Mattei Doggan Award 2009, Johan Skytte Prize, Univ. of Uppsala 2009. *Publications*: Corporatism and Public Policy in Authoritarian Portugal 1975, Trends Toward Corporatist Intermediation (co-author) 1984, Patterns of Corporatist Policy-Making (co-author) 1982, La politica degli interessi nei paesi industrializzati (co-author) 1984, Private Interest Government and Public Policy (co-ed.) 1985, Transitions from Authoritarian Rule: Tentative Conclusions about Uncertain Democracies (co-author) 1986, Transitions from Authoritarian Rule: Prospects for Democracy, Vols I–IV (co-author) 1986, Neocorporativismo (co-author) 1992, Sustainable Democracy (co-author) 1995, Governance in the European Union (co-author) 1996, El fin del siglo del corporativismo (co-author) 1998, Portugal: do autoritarismo à democracia 1999, Come democratizzare l'Unione Europea...e perché 2000; numerous articles in professional journals and chapters in books. *Address*: Department of Social and Political Sciences, European University Institute, Badia Fiesolana, Via dei Roccettini, 9, 50016 San Domenico di Fiesole (FI), (office); Via di Monteloro 31/A, 50069 Le Sieci (FI), Italy (home). *Telephone*: 055 4685274 (office); 055 8300613 (home). *Fax*: 055 4685201 (office). *E-mail*: philippe.schmitter@iue.it (office). *Website*: www.iue.it (office).

SCHMÖGNEROVÁ, Brigita, PhD; Slovak international organization official and politician; *Vice-President, European Bank for Reconstruction and Development*; b. 17 Nov. 1947, Bratislava; m.; one s.; ed School of Econs, Bratislava; teacher, Univ. of Athens, Greece, Georgetown Univ., USA; Researcher, Inst. of Econs, Slovak Acad. of Sciences; Lecturer, Univ. of Econs, Bratislava; Econ. Adviser to Pres. of Slovak Repub. 1993; Deputy Prime Minister 1994; mem. Parl. 1995–98; Minister of Finance 1998–2002; Exec. Sec., UN Econ. ECE 2002–05; adviser to IMF, IBRD and EBRD; Vice-Pres. EBRD 2005–; World Finance Minister of the Year Award, Euromoney Inst. Investor 2000. *Address*: European Bank for Reconstruction and Development, One Exchange Square, London, EC2A 2JN, England (office). *Telephone*: (20) 7338-6000 (office). *Fax*: (20) 7338-6910 (office). *Website*: www.ebrd.com (office).

SCHNABEL, Julian, BFA; American painter and film director; b. 26 Oct. 1951, Brooklyn, New York; ed Univ. of Houston, Whitney Museum Ind. Study Program, New York. *Films*: Basquiat 1996, Before Night Falls 2000, Sketches of Frank Gehry 2006, Le Scaphandre et le Papillon (Best Dir, Cannes Film Festival 2007, Best European Film, San Sebastian Film Festival 2007, Best Foreign Film, Nat. Bd of Review 2007, Golden Globe for Best Foreign Language Film, Golden Globe for Best Director 2008) 2007, Berlin 2007, Miral 2011. *Publication*: Nicknames of Maître D's and Other Excerpts From Life 1988. *Address*: c/o PaceWildenstein Gallery New York, 32 East 57th Street, New York, NY 10022, USA.

SCHNACKENBERG, Gjertrud, BA; American poet and writer; b. 27 Aug. 1953, Tacoma, Wash.; d. of Walter Charles Schnackenberg and Doris Ione Schnackenberg (née Strom); m. Robert Nozick 1987 (died 2002); ed Mount Holyoke Coll.; Fellow in Poetry, The Radcliffe Inst. 1979–80; Christensen Fellow, Saint Catherine's Coll., Oxford 1997; Visiting Scholar, Getty Research Inst., J. Paul Getty Museum 2000; Fellow, American Acad. of Arts and Sciences 1996, Civitella Ranieri 2012, William B. Hart Poet in Residence, The American Acad. in Rome 2014; Dr hc (Mount Holyoke Coll.) 1985; Glascock Award for Poetry 1973, 1974, Acad. of American Poets Lavan Younger Poets Award 1983, American Acad. and Inst. of Arts and Letters Rome Prize 1983–84, Amy Lowell Traveling Prize 1984–85, Nat. Endowment for the Arts grant 1986–87, Guggenheim Fellowship 1987–88, American Acad. of Arts and Letters Award in Literature 1998, Los Angeles Times Book Prize in Poetry 2001, Daimler Chrysler Berlin Prize Fellow, American Acad., Berlin 2004, Griffin Int. Poetry Prize 2011. *Publications*: Portraits and Elegies 1982, The Lamplit Answer 1985, A Gilded Lapse of Time 1992, The Throne of Labdacus 2000, Supernatural Love: Poems 1976–1992 2000, Heavenly Questions 2010; contrib. to books and journals. *Address*: c/o Farrar, Straus & Giroux Inc., 18 West 18th Street, New York, NY 10011, USA. *Telephone*: (212) 741-6900 (office). *Website*: us.macmillan.com/FSG.aspx (office).

SCHNAPPER, Dominique, PhD; French sociologist, academic and writer; *Professor, École des Hautes Études en Sciences Sociales*; b. (Dominique Aron), 9 Nov. 1934, Paris; d. of Raymond Aron and Suzanne Gauchon; m. Antoine Schnapper 1958; three c; ed Institut d'Études Politiques de Paris, Sorbonne, Université Paris V; Prof. and Dir of Studies, École des Hautes Études en Sciences Sociales, Paris 1980–; mem. Comm. Marceau Long on the reform of the nation 1987, Comm. 2000 1989, Comm. on Drugs Henrion 1994, Comm. on Educ. Fauroux 1995–96; mem. Steering Cttee of French Soc. of Sociology 1991–95, Pres. 1995–99; mem. Conseil Constitutionnel (Supreme Court) 2001–10; Hon. mem. Conseil Constitutionnel; Officier, Légion d'honneur, des Arts et des Lettres, Ordre nat. du Mérite; Prix de l'Assemblée Nat. 1994, Balzan Prize for Sociology 2002. *Publications include*: La Communauté des citoyens 1994, La Rélation à l'autre 1998, Qu'est ce que la citoyénneté? 2000, La Démocratie providentielle 2002, Diasporas et nations 2006, Qu'est ce que l'intégration? 2007, La condition juive en France 2009, Une sociologue au Conseil constitutionnel 2010, Travailler et aimer 2913, L'esprit démocratique des lois 2014. *Address*: Maison des Sciences de l'Homme,

105 boulevard Raspail, 75007 Paris, France. *Telephone*: 1-53-63-51-51. *E-mail*: schnappe@ehess.fr (office).

SCHNEIDER-AMMANN, Johann Niklaus, BEng, MBA; Swiss business executive and politician; *Head, Federal Department of Economic Affairs*; b. 18 Feb. 1952, Sumiswald; m. Katharina Schneider-Ammann; one s. one d.; ed Swiss Federal Inst. of Tech., Zurich, European Inst. of Business Admin (INSEAD), France; Project Leader, Oerlikon Bührle 1978–81; Asst, Ammann-Unternehmungen 1981–84, Dir U. Ammann Maschinenfabrik AG 1984–89, Pres. and Del., Ammann Group Holding AG (mechanical eng co.), Langenthal 1990–; mem. Nationalrat (Nat. Council) 1999–2010; mem. Federal Council 2010–, Head, Federal Dept of Econ. Affairs 2010–; mem. Free Democratic Party. *Address*: Federal Department of Economic Affairs, Bundeshaus Ost, 3003 Bern, Switzerland (office). *Telephone*: 313222007 (office). *Fax*: 313222194 (office). *E-mail*: info@gs-evd.admin.ch (office). *Website*: www.evd.admin.ch (office); www.johann-schneider-ammann.ch.

SCHNEIDER, Cynthia Perrin, BA, PhD; American professor of art history and fmr diplomatist; *Distinguished Professor in Practice of Diplomacy, School of Foreign Service, Georgetown University*; b. 16 Aug. 1953, Pennsylvania; m. Thomas J. Schneider; two c.; ed Harvard Univ., Oxford Univ.; Asst Curator of European Paintings, Museum of Fine Arts, Boston 1980–84; Asst Prof. of Art History, Georgetown Univ. 1984–90, apptd Assoc. Prof. 1990, Distinguished Prof. in Practice of Diplomacy, School of Foreign Service 2004–, Pfizer Medical Humanities Scholar in Residence, Public Policy Inst. and Dir Life Sciences and Society Initiative 2004–06; Vice-Chair. Pres.'s Cttee on the Arts and Humanities 1994–98; Amb. to Netherlands 1998–2001; mem. Bd of Advisors, Inst. for Cultural Diplomacy, Sustainable Preservation Initiative, Center on Policy for Emerging Technologies, Singapore Technologies Telemedia (ST Telelemedia) Eircom 2010–; mem. Supervisory Bd, Royal Ahold, Zaandam, Netherlands 2001–05; Non-resident Sr Fellow, Saban Center for Middle East Policy, Brookings Inst. 2006–, Coordinator, Arts and Culture Initiative 2006–; fmr mem. Bd of Dirs Nat. Museum of Women in the Arts, Australian-American Leadership Dialogue; Honor Award, Dept of Treasury, US Secret Service 2001, Flevo Award 2001, Exceptional Public Service Award, Office of the Sec. of Defense 2001, Rockefeller Foundation Grant 2003. *Publications*: Rembrandt's Landscapes 1990, Rembrandt's Landscapes: Drawing and Prints 1990. *Address*: Georgetown University, 3700 O Street, NW, Washington, DC 20057, USA (office). *Telephone*: (202) 687-0100 (office). *E-mail*: schneidc@georgetown.edu (office). *Website*: www.georgetown.edu (office).

SCHNEIDER, Etienne; Luxembourg economist and politician; *Deputy Prime Minister and Minister of the Economy, of Internal Security and of Defence*; b. 29 Jan. 1971, Dudelange; ed Inst. catholique des hautes études commerciales, Brussels, Belgium, Greenwich Univ., London, UK; Research Asst, European Parl., Brussels 1995–96; Municipal Councillor, Kayl 1995–2005, First Alderman 2005–10; economist for LSAP parl. group 1996–97, Sec.-Gen. 1997–2004; Project Leader with NATO, Brussels 1997; Govt Adviser to Ministry of the Economy and Foreign Trade, responsible for Directorates of Energy, E-Commerce and Internet Security 2004, Sr Govt Adviser responsible for Directorates of Econ. Devt, Infrastructures and Energy 2009, for Directorate-Gen. of Econ. Devt, Industry and Businesses 2011; Minister of Economy and Foreign Trade 2012–13, Deputy Prime Minister and Minister of the Economy, of Internal Security and of Defence 2013–; Chair. and Man. Dir Société électrique de l'Our 2005; Chair. Exec. Bd Cegedel SA 2004; Chair. Enovos International SA, Enovos Deutschland AG 2010–12; Chair. and Man. Dir Creos (grid co.) 2010–12; Vice-Chair. Société nationale de crédit et d'investissement (SNCI) 2010–12; mem. Lëtzebuerger Sozialistesch Arbechterpartei (LSAP). *Address*: Ministry of the Economy, 19–21 blvd Royal, 2449 Luxembourg, Luxembourg (office). *Telephone*: 247-82478 (office). *Fax*: 46-04-48 (office). *E-mail*: info@eco.public.lu (office). *Website*: www.eco.public.lu (office).

SCHNEIDER, Manfred, Dr rer. pol; German business executive; *Chairman of the Supervisory Board, RWE AG*; b. 21 Dec. 1938, Bremerhaven; m.; one d.; ed Univs of Freiburg, Hamburg and Cologne; fmr Asst to Prof. of Business Man., Aachen Tech. Univ.; joined Bayer AG, Leverkusen 1966, Head Finance and Accounting Dept of subsidiary co. Duisburger Kupferhütte, later Chair. of Bd, returned to Bayer AG 1981, apptd. Head of Regional Co-ordination, Corp. Auditing and Control 1984, mem. Bd of Man. 1987–2002, Chair. 1992–2002, Chair. Supervisory Bd 2002–12; Chair. Supervisory Bd RWE AG 2009–, Linde AG; mem. Supervisory Bd Daimler AG, Stuttgart (mem. Chair.'s Council 2001–), TUI AG Hanover; Pres. German Chemical Industry Asscn (VCI) 1999–2001. *Address*: RWE AG, Opernplatz 1, 45128 Essen, Germany (office). *Telephone*: (201) 1215025 (office). *Fax*: (201) 1215265 (office). *E-mail*: info@rwe.com (office). *Website*: www.rwe.com (office).

SCHNEIDER, Peter; German politician and business executive; *President, Sparkassenverband Baden-Württemberg*; b. 27 July 1958, Riedlingen; m. Rose Marie Schneider 1978; two s.; mem. CDU 1976–; with Co. Dept Sigmaringen 1986–88; Pvt. Sec. to Ministry of Interior Dietmar Schlee 1988–92; worked for Biberach Dist 1992–2006; mem. State Parl. of Baden-Württemberg 2001–; Pres. Sparkassenverband Baden-Württemberg (Savings Bank Asscn of Baden-Württemberg), Stuttgart 2006–; mem. Supervisory Bd Landesbank Baden-Württemberg, Chair. -2010; Dist Chair. German Red Cross Biberach. *Address*: Sparkassenverband Baden-Württemberg, Am Hauptbahnhof 2, 70173 Stuttgart (office); Landesbank Baden-Württemberg, Am Hauptbahnhof 2, 70173 Stuttgart, Germany (office). *Telephone*: (711) 127-0 (office). *Fax*: (711) 12743544 (office). *E-mail*: Peter.Schneider@sv-bw.de (office); Peter.Schneider@CDU.landtag-bw.de (office). *Website*: www.peter-schneider-bc.de.

SCHNEIDER, Ulf Mark, Lic. oec., PhD, MBA; German business executive; *Chairman of the Management Board, Fresenius SE*; ed Univ. of St Gallen, Switzerland, Harvard Univ., USA; held several exec. positions with Franz Haniel & Cie. GmbH from 1989; Group Finance Dir Gehe UK plc (pharmaceutical wholesale and retail distributor), Coventry, UK; joined Fresenius 2001, Chief Financial Officer Fresenius Medical Care 2001–03, Chair. Man. Bd Fresenius SE 2003–. *Address*: Management Board, Fresenius SE, 61346 Bad Homburg (office); Fresenius SE, Else-Kröner-Straße 1, 61352 Bad Homburg, Germany (office). *Telephone*: (6172) 608-0 (office). *E-mail*: pr-fre@fresenius.com (office). *Website*: www.fresenius.com (office); www.fresenius.se (office).

SCHNEIDERHAN, Gen. Wolfgang; German army officer; b. 26 July 1946, Riedlingen, Donau; m. Elke Schneiderhan (née Speckhardt); three s. two d.; ed Bundeswehr Command and Staff Coll., Hamburg; began career with Bundeswehr (German Armed Forces) 1966; Youth Information Officer, 10th Armoured Div., Sigmaringen 1972–74; Co. Commdr Armoured Battalion 293, Stetten am Kalten Markt 1974–77; Asst Br. Chief, Mil. Intelligence, Armed Forces Staff 1979–81; Asst Chief of Staff, G-3 Operations, Home Defence Brigade 55, Böblingen 1981–83; Sr Officer, G-3, Operations, NATO Cen. Europe HQ, Brunssum, The Netherlands 1983–86; CO Armoured Battalion 553, Stetten am Kalten Markt 1986–88; Chief of Staff, 4th Mechanized Div., Regensburg 1988–90; Sr Officer, Arms Control, NATO HQ, Brussels 1990–92; Dir Faculty of Army Doctrine, Bundeswehr Command and Staff Coll. 1992–94; CO Armoured 39 Brigade Thüringen, Erfurt 1994–97; Asst Chief of Staff, Planning, Fed. Ministry of Defence 1997–99; Chief of Policy and Advisory Staff 2000–02; apptd Chief of Defence 2002; Inspector Gen. of the Bundeswehr 2002–09; apptd Brig.-Gen. 1996, Maj.-Gen. 1999, Lt-Gen. 2000, Gen. 2002; Gold Cross of Honour of the Bundeswehr. *Leisure interests:* contemporary history, music. *Address:* c/o Ministry of Defence, Stauffenbergstr. 18, 10785 Berlin, Germany (office).

SCHNIEDERS, Richard J., BA; American food distribution executive; b. 6 March 1948, Remsen, Ia; s. of the late Bob Schnieders and of Helen Schnieders; m. Beth Schnieders; two d.; ed Univ. of Iowa; began career at Randall's Super Valu Stores, Iowa City; with John Morrell & Co., Des Moines, Bettesdorf and Memphis; joined Exec. Devt Program, Hardin's-Sysco, Memphis 1982, Pres. and CEO 1989–90, Chair., Pres. and CEO 1990–92; apptd Sr Vice-Pres. Merchandising Sysco Corpn, Houston, Tex. 1992, mem. Bd Dirs and Sr Vice-Pres., Merchandising and Multi-unit Sales 1997–2009, Exec. Vice-Pres., Foodservice Operations 1999–2000, COO Jan.–July 2000, Pres. and COO July 2000–03, Chair. and CEO 2003–March 2009, Pres. 2005–07, Chair. March–June 2009 (retd), fmr Chair. Exec. Cttee, Employee Benefits Cttee; fmr mem. Finance Cttee; mem. Bd of Dirs Aviall, Inc. 1997–. *Address:* c/o Sysco Corpn, 1390 Enclave Parkway, Houston, TX 77077-2099, USA. *Telephone:* (281) 584-1390. *Fax:* (281) 584-2721. *E-mail:* info@sysco.com. *Website:* www.sysco.com.

SCHOCKEMÖHLE, Alwin; German fmr show jumper and horse breeder; b. 29 May 1937, Osterbrock, Kreis Meppen; s. of Aloys Schockemöhle and Josefa Schockemöhle (née Borgerding); m. 2nd Rita Wiltfang; two s. one d.; two d. from previous m.; began riding 1946, in public events 1948; trained in mil. riding 1954–55; reserve for Mil. and Showjumping, Melbourne Olympics 1956; specialized in showjumping 1956–77; first Derby win, riding 'Bachus', Hamburg 1957; continually in int. showjumping events 1960–77; Showjumping Champion FRG (four times); second in European Championship (three times); European Champion riding 'Warwick' 1975, 1976; gold medal (Team Award) Rome Olympics 1960; gold medal (Individual Award) and silver medal (Team Award) riding 'Warwick' Montreal Olympics 1976; currently owner Gestüt und Rennstall Alwin Schockemöhle (stud and racing stables). *Publication:* Sportkamerad Pferd (A Horse for Sports Companions). *Address:* Münsterlandstraße 53, 49453 Mühlen, Germany (office). *Telephone:* (54) 923823 (office). *Fax:* (54) 923794 (office). *E-mail:* info@alwin-schockemoehle.de (office). *Website:* www.alwinschockemoehle.de (office).

SCHOESSLER, Don H.; American engineer; worked as engineer on Corona programme for Lockheed Corpn, collaborated with Eastman Kodak Co. to engineer, supply and process film used in system; later worked at Eastman Kodak Co. and continued to support Corona, U-2 the Nat. Reconnaissance Office reconnaissance projects –1986 (retd); Corona Pioneer Award 1995, Charles Stark Draper Prize, Nat. Acad. of Eng (co-recipient) 2005. *Address:* c/o National Academy of Engineering, 500 Fifth Street, NW, Washington, DC 20001, USA.

SCHOLAR, Sir Michael Charles, Kt, KCB, BA, MA, PhD, ARCO; British civil servant, academic and college principal; *President, St John's College, Oxford;* b. 3 Jan. 1942, Merthyr Tydfil, Wales; s. of Richard Scholar and Blodwen Scholar (née Jones); m. Angela Sweet 1964; three s. one d. (deceased); ed St Olave's and St Saviour's Grammar School, St John's Coll., Cambridge, Univ. of California, Berkeley, Harvard Univ., USA; worked at HM Treasury 1969–93; Sr Int. Man. Barclay's Bank 1979–81; Pvt. Sec. to Prime Minister 1981–83; Perm. Sec., Welsh Office 1993–96; Perm. Sec. Dept of Trade and Industry 1996–2001; Pres. St John's Coll., Oxford 2001–; Dir (non-exec.) Council of Man., Nat. Inst. of Econ. and Social Research 2001–05, Legal and General Investment Man. 2002–07; Chair. Benton Fletcher Advisory Cttee 2004–; Chair. Statistics Authority 2007–; Hon. Fellow, Univ. of Wales (Aberystwyth), St John's Coll., Cambridge, Cardiff Univ.; Dr hc (Univ. of Glamorgan). *Leisure interests:* playing the organ and piano, opera, long-distance walks. *Address:* St John's College, Oxford, OX1 3JP, England (office). *Telephone:* (1865) 277419 (office). *Fax:* (1865) 277482 (office). *E-mail:* president@sjc.ox.ac.uk (office). *Website:* www.sjc.ox.ac.uk (office).

SCHOLES, Myron S., BA, MBA, PhD; American/Canadian professor of finance and business executive; b. 1 July 1941, Timmons, Ont., Canada; two d.; ed McMaster Univ., Canada, Univ. of Chicago; instructor at Business School, Univ. of Chicago 1967–68; Asst Prof., MIT Man. School 1968–72, Assoc. Prof. 1972–73; Assoc. Prof. Univ. of Chicago 1973–75, Prof. 1975–79, Edward Eagle Brown Prof. of Finance 1979–82; Prof., Business School and the Law School, Stanford Univ. 1983–96, Frank E. Buck Prof. Emer. of Finance 1996–; Man. Dir Salomon Bros 1991–93; Dir Center for Research in Security Prices, Univ. of Chicago 1975–81; Sr Research Fellow, Hoover Inst., Stanford Univ. 1988–; Co-founder and Prin. Long-Term Capital Man. (hedge fund) 1994–99; f. Platinum Grove Asset Man. 1999, Chair. –2009 (retd); Dir Capital Preservation Fund, Capital Preservation Fund II; Research Assoc. NBER; fmr Dir The Chicago Mercantile Exchange; mem. American Econ. Asscn American Finance Assoc; Dr hc (Univ. of Paris-Dauphine) 1989, (McMaster Univ.) 1990, (Katholieke Universiteit Leuven) 1998; shared Nobel Prize for Econs 1997 for devising Black-Scholes Model for determining value of derivatives. *Leisure interests:* skiing, golf. *Address:* Stanford Graduate School of Business, Knight Management Center, Stanford University, 655 Knight Way, Stanford, CA 94305-7298, USA (office). *Telephone:* (650)723-2146 (office). *E-mail:* mscholes@pgamlp.com (office). *Website:* www.gsb.stanford.edu (office).

SCHOLEY, Sir David (Gerald), Kt, CBE, FRSA; British banker; *Senior Adviser, UBS Investment Bank;* b. 28 June 1935, Chipstead, Surrey, England; s. of Dudley Scholey and Lois Scholey; m. Alexandra Beatrix Drew 1960; one s. one d.; ed Wellington Coll., Berks. and Christ Church, Oxford; served in RAC, 9th Queen's Royal Lancers (Nat. Service) 1953–55, TA Yorks Dragoons 1955–57, 3/4 CLY (Sharpshooters) 1957–61, Metropolitan Special Constabulary (Thames Div.) 1961–65; with Thompson Graham & Co. (Lloyd's Brokers) 1956–58; Dale & Co. (Insurance Brokers), Canada 1958–59; Guinness Mahon & Co. Ltd 1959–64; joined S.G. Warburg & Co. Ltd 1965, Dir 1967–95, Deputy Chair. 1977–80, Jt Chair. 1980–84, Chair. 1985–95; Chair. S.G. Warburg Group plc (now UBS Investment Bank) 1985–95, SBC Warburg July–Nov. 1995, Sr Adviser 1995–; mem. Bd of Dirs Mercury Securities plc 1969–86, Chair. 1984–86; mem. Bd of Dirs Orion Insurance Co. Ltd 1963–87, Stewart Wrightson Holdings Ltd 1972–81, Union Discount Co. of London Ltd 1976–81, Bank of England 1981–98, British Telecom plc 1986–94, Chubb Corpn, USA 1991–2008, Gen. Electric Co. 1992–95, J Sainsbury plc 1996–2000, Vodafone Group plc 1998–2005, Anglo American plc 1999–2005; Sr Adviser, International Finance Corpn 1996–2005, Financial Services Authority 2010–; mem. Export Guarantees Advisory Council 1970–75, Deputy Chair. 1974–75; Chair. Construction Exports Advisory Bd 1975–78; mem. Institut International d'Etudes Bancaires 1976–94 (Pres. 1988), Cttee on Finance for Industry, Nat. Econ. Devt Office 1980–87, IISS Studies Council 1984–93, (Hon. Treas. 1984–90), Business in the Community, Pres.'s Cttee 1988–91, General Motors European Advisory Council 1988–97, Save the Children Fund, Industry and Commerce Group 1989–95 (Lord Mayor's Appeal Cttee 2002–03), London First 1993–96, London Symphony Orchestra Advisory Council 1998–2004, Fitch Int. Services Advisory Cttee 2001–, Mitsubishi Int. Advisory Cttee 2001–07, Sultanate of Oman Financial Advisory Group 2002–06; Gov. Wellington Coll. 1978–88, 1996–2004 (Vice-Pres. 1998–2004); Dir, BBC 1994–2000, Nat. Inst. for Econ. and Social Research 1984–; Trustee, Glyndebourne Arts Trust 1989–2002, Nat. Portrait Gallery (Chair.) 1992–2005; Hon. DLitt (Guildhall) 1993; Hon. DSc (UMIST) 1999. *Address:* UBS Investment Bank, 1 Finsbury Avenue, London, EC2M 2PP (office); Heath End House, Spaniards Road, London, NW3 7JE, England (home). *Telephone:* (20) 7568-2400 (office). *Fax:* (20) 7568-4225 (office). *E-mail:* david.scholey@ubs.com (office). *Website:* www.ubs.com (office).

SCHOLL, Andreas; German singer (countertenor); b. 1967, Eltville; ed Schola Cantorum Basiliensis, Basel, Switzerland; mem. Kiedricher Chorbuben choir as child; soloist, Pueri Cantors Gathering, St Peter's Basilica, Rome 1981; debut int. recital at Théâtre de Grévin, Paris 1993; opera debut in Handel's Rodelinda, Glyndebourne Festival Opera, England 1998; title role in Handel's Giulio Cesare in Egitto 2002 and Partenope 2008, Royal Danish Opera; debut at Metropolitan Opera, New York in Rodelinda 2006; performed at Belgian Royal Wedding Dec. 1999; teacher, Schola Cantorum Basiliensis, Basel 2000–; numerous int. tours and recitals, working with the world's leading Baroque conductors and ensembles, including London Proms 2005, Liceu Barcelona 2011, Adelaide Opera 2011; title role in Giulio Cesare in Egitto at Salle Pleyel, Paris 2010, Salzburg Festival 2012; Bertarido in Rodelinda, Met Opera 2011; Conseil de l'Europe Award 1992, Fondation Claude Nicolas Ledoux Award 1992, Cannes Classical Award 1998, Artist of the Year, German Kultur Radio 1998, Belgian Musical Press Union Prize 1999. *Recordings include:* Handel's Messiah, Solomon, Italian Cantatas and Opera Arias, Bach's Christmas Oratorio, St Matthew Passion, St John Passion, Solo Cantatas for Alto and B Minor Mass, Vivaldi's Stabat Mater (Gramophone Award) 1996, Nisi Dominus (Edison Award) 2001, Monteverdi's L'Orfeo and 1610 Vespers, works by Pergolesi and Caldara; Heroes (Echo Classic Award) 1999, Wayfaring Stranger 2001, Arcadia 2003, Arias for Senesino (Classical BRIT Award for Singer of the Year 2006) 2005, Crystal Tears (with Julian Behr) 2008, Bach Cantatas 2011, O Solitude, Songs & Arias by Purcell (BBC Music Magazine Vocal Award 2012). *Address:* Harrison Parrott Ltd, 5–6 Albion Court, London, W6 0QT, England (office). *Telephone:* (20) 7229-9166 (office). *E-mail:* info@harrisonparrott .co.uk (office). *Website:* www.harrisonparrott.com (office).

SCHOLL, Hermann, DrIng; German business executive; *Honorary Chairman, Bosch Group;* b. 21 June 1935, Stuttgart; m.; one d.; ed Univ. of Stuttgart; joined Robert Bosch GmbH, Advanced Eng Dept, Automotive Tech. 1962, Chief Engineer Electronic Fuel Injection 1968–71, Dir of Eng, Electrical and Electronic Engine Equipment 1971–73, Assoc. mem. Bd of Man. 1973–75, Deputy mem. 1975–78, mem. 1978–2003, Chair. 1993–2003, Man. Partner Robert Bosch Industrietreuhand KG (holding co.) 1995–, Chair. Supervisory Council Robert Bosch GmbH 2003–12, Hon. Chair. Bosch Group 2012–; mem. Supervisory Bd BASF AG; conferred with title of Prof. by Gov. of Baden-Württemberg 2005; Hon. DrIng (Kettering Univ., Mich., USA) 1988, (Tech. Univ. of Munich) 1993. *Address:* Robert Bosch GmbH, Postfach 106050, 70049 Stuttgart, Germany (office). *Telephone:* (711) 811-0 (office). *Fax:* (711) 8116630 (office). *E-mail:* info@bosch.com (office). *Website:* www.bosch.com (office).

SCHOLZ, Olaf; German politician and lawyer; *Vice-Chairman, Sozialdemokratische Partei Deutschlands (Social Democratic Party of Germany);* b. 14 June 1958, Osnabrück; m. Britta Ernst; joined SPD youth wing 1975; Deputy Chair. Socialist Youth Org. 1982–88; Vice-Pres. Int. Union of Socialist Youth 1987–89; Partner, Zimmermann, Scholz & Partners (law firm), Hamburg 1985–; mem. Bundestag (parl.) 1998–, Vice-Chair. SPD Parl. Group 2009–; Minister of the Interior, City of Hamburg May–Oct. 2001; Gen. Sec. SPD 2002–04, Vice-Chair. 2009–; Minister of Labour and Social Affairs 2007–09; legal adviser to Cen. Assen of German Consumer Cooperatives 1990–98. *Address:* Büro Olaf Scholz, Deutscher Bundestag, 11011 Berlin, Germany (office). *Telephone:* (30) 22773435 (office). *Fax:* (30) 22770435 (office). *E-mail:* olaf.scholz@bundestag.de (office). *Website:* www .bundestag.de (office); www.spd.de; www.olafscholz.de.

SCHOLZ, Rupert, DJur; German lawyer, professor of public law and politician; *Of Counsel, Gleiss Lutz;* b. 23 May 1937, Berlin; m.; ed Free Univ. of Berlin, Univ. of Heidelberg; Prof. of Public Law, Free Univ. of Berlin 1972–78; Chair of Public Law, Univ. of Munich 1978–2005, Prof. Emer. 2005–; Senator for Justice, W Berlin 1981–88, for Fed. Affairs 1983–88; Minister of Defence 1988–90; mem. Bundestag 1990–2002, Chair. legal affairs cttee 1998–2002; Of Counsel, Gleiss Lutz (law firm), Berlin 2005–; mem. CDU 1983–. *Address:* Gleiss Lutz, Friedrichstrasse 71, 10117 Berlin, Germany (office). *Telephone:* (30) 800979171 (office). *Fax:* (30) 800979979 (office). *E-mail:* rupert.scholz@gleisslutz.com (office). *Website:* www .gleisslutz.com (office).

SCHÖNBERG, Claude-Michel; French composer; b. 6 July 1944; s. of Adolphe Schönberg and Julie Nadás; one s. two d.; m. Charlotte Talbot 2003; started as producer for EMI France and as pop song writer 1967–72; recording his own songs in France 1974–77; recipient of Tony, Grammy, Evening Standard and Laurence Olivier Awards, French 'Molière' and 'Victoires de la musique' for musicals; Grammy Award for Outstanding Contrib,. *Ballet:* Wuthering Heights with the Northern Ballet Theatre 2002, cr. Cleopatra 2011. *Films:* Les Misérables (screenplay) 2012. *Compositions:* musicals: La Révolution Française 1973, Les Misérables 1980–85, Miss Saigon 1989, Martin Guerre 1996–, Pirate Queen 2006–, Marguerite 2008; for cinema: Les Misérables 2012. *Address:* c/o Cameron Mackintosh Limited, 1 Bedford Square, London, WC1B 3RA, England (office). *Telephone:* (20) 7637-8866 (office).

SCHÖNBORN, HE Cardinal Christoph, OP; Austrian ecclesiastic; *Archbishop of Vienna;* b. 22 Jan. 1945, Skalsko (now in Czech Repub.); ordained priest 1970; student pastor, Univ. of Graz 1973–75; Assoc. Prof. of Dogma, Univ. of Fribourg 1975–76, Prof. of Theology 1976–81, Prof. of Dogmatic Theology 1981–91; apptd Auxiliary Bishop of Vienna 1991, Coadjutor 1995, Archbishop of Vienna 1995–; cr. Cardinal (Cardinal-Priest of Gesù Divin Lavoratore) 1998; Pres. Austrian Bishop's Conf. 1998–; participated in Papal Conclave 2005, 2013; curial mem. Congregations for the Doctrine of the Faith, Oriental Churches, and Catholic Educ.; mem. Pontifical Council on Culture, Comm. on the Cultural Heritage of the Church, Special Council for Europe of the Gen. Secr. of the Synod of Bishops; mem. Pontifical Council for Promoting the New Evangelization 2011–; Ordinary for the faithful of Byzantine Rite in Austria. *Address:* Archdiocese of Vienna, Wollzeile 2, 1010 Vienna, Austria (office). *Telephone:* (1) 515-52-0 (office). *Fax:* (1) 515-52-3760 (office). *Website:* stephanscom.at; www.cardinalschonborn.com.

SCHÖNE, Albrecht, DPhil; German philologist and professor of German philology; *Professor Emeritus, University of Göttingen;* b. 17 July 1925, Barby; s. of Friedrich Schöne and Agnes Moeller Schöne; m. Dagmar Haver 1952; one s. one d.; ed Univs of Freiburg, Basle, Göttingen and Münster; Extraordinary Prof. of German Literature, Univ. of Münster 1958–60; Prof. of German Philology, Univ. of Göttingen 1960–90, Prof. Emer. 1990–; Pres. Int. Asscn for Germanic Studies 1980–85; mem. Akad. der Wissenschaften, Göttingen, Deutsche Akad. für Sprache und Dichtung, Bayerische, Nordrhein-Westfäl. Akad. der Wissenschaften, Austrian and Netherlands Acads; Hon. mem. Modern Language Asscn of America, Foreign Hon. mem. American Acad. of Arts and Sciences; Officier, Ordre nat. du Mérite, Grand Cross with Star of Merit (Germany), Order Pour le mérite for Sciences and Arts; Hon. DPhil, Hon. DTheol; several prizes. *Publications:* numerous books and articles on German literature and philology. *Leisure interests:* riding, hunting, painting. *Address:* Grotefendstrasse 26, 37075 Göttingen, Germany (home). *Telephone:* (551) 56449 (home).

SCHÖNFELDER, Wilhelm Heinrich, PhD; German fmr lobbyist and fmr diplomatist; b. 12 Nov. 1940, Marburg; Dir for European Affairs, Federal Foreign Ministry –1999; Perm. Rep. to EU, Brussels 1999–2007; Head of Govt Affairs, Siemens AG, Brussels 2007–10 (retd); Grand Federal Cross of Merit (Germany) 2008. *Address:* c/o Siemens AG, Wittelsbacherplatz 2, 80333 Munich, Germany.

SCHÖNHOLZER, Annette, MA; Swiss/American arts administrator; *Director of Operations and Finance, Art Basel;* b. 1964; ed Univ. of Zürich, Int. Centre for Culture and Man. (ICCM), Salzburg, Austria; mem. Program Cttee and Curator, VIPER Int. Film, Video and Multimedia Festival, Basel 1994–98; worked for various public and private orgs promoting the arts; Co-Head of Cultural Competence Center, Aargau Canton 1997–2001; Project Man. BIOPOLIS show, Expo 02 (Swiss nat. exhbn) 2000–02; Show Man. Art Basel Miami Beach Int. Art Show, USA 2002–, currently Co-Dir, also Dir Operations and Finance, Art Basel. *Address:* MCH Swiss Exhibition (Basel) Ltd, Art Basel, 4005 Basel, Switzerland (office); Art Basel Miami Beach, 300 West 41st Street, Miami Beach, FL 33140-3627, USA (office). *Telephone:* 582002020 (Switzerland) (office); (305) 674-1292 (office). *Fax:* 582063130 (Switzerland) (office); (305) 673-1242 (office). *E-mail:* miamibeach@artbasel.com (office). *Website:* www.artbasel.com (office); www .artbaselmiamibeach.com (office).

SCHOTTE, Gerrit Fransisco; Curaçao business executive and politician; b. 9 Sept. 1974; s. of Hendrik Schotte and Maria Kruz; ed Peter Stuyvesant Coll.; f. The Shoppers (purchasing office) 1995–2000; Founding Dir Bad Boyz Toyz NV; mem. Nat. Professional Paintball League 1997–99; Founding Dir Food4U Delivery Service 2000–02; Gen. Man. Lido Hotel Resort & Casino NV 2001–05; fmr mem. Frente Obrero; co-f. Movementu Patriotiko Kòrsou (MPK), fmr Pres.; mem. Curaçao Parl. 2007–10, 2010–; fmr Commr in charge of Tourism, Econ. Affairs, Agric., Husbandry and Fishery, Curaçao Exec. Council; mem. Netherlands Antilles Parl. Jan.–Aug. 2010 (parl. dissolved); f. Movementu Futuro Korsou 2010; Prime Minister of Curaçao Oct. 2010–12 (first Prime Minister following dissolution of Netherlands Antilles). *Address:* c/o Office of the Prime Minister, Fort Amsterdam 17, Willemstad, Curaçao. *Website:* www.gerritschotte.com (office).

SCHRADER, Hans Otto; German business executive; *Chairman of the Executive Board and CEO, Otto Group;* b. 8 Dec. 1956, Bevensen; joined Otto Group 1977, becoming Deputy Head, Hong Kong Office, Vice-Pres. for Import, Vice-Pres. for Merchandising 1993–99, mem. Exec. Bd Otto GmbH & Co. KG 1999–, Otto Group 2005–, Chair. Exec. Bd and CEO 2007–. *Address:* Otto Group, Wandsbeker Strasse 3–7, 22172 Hamburg, Germany (office). *Telephone:* (40) 6461401 (office). *Fax:* (40) 64618571 (office). *E-mail:* info@ottogroup.com (office). *Website:* www.ottogroup .com (office).

SCHRADER, Paul Joseph, MA; American screenwriter and director; b. 22 July 1946, Grand Rapids, Mich.; m. 1st Jeannine Oppewall (divorced); m. 2nd Mary Beth Hurt 1983; ed Calvin Coll. and Univ. of California, Los Angeles; film critic for Los Angeles Free Press magazine 1970–72; Ed. Cinema magazine 1970; fmr Prof., Columbia Univ. *Films include:* screenplays/written by: The Yazuka 1974, Taxi Driver 1976, Obsession 1976, Rolling Thunder 1977, Old Boyfriends 1979, Raging Bull 1981, The Mosquito Coast 1986, Light of Day 1987, The Last Temptation of Christ 1988, City Hall 1996, Affliction 1997, Bringing Out the Dead 1999, The Walker (also dir) 2007; directed: Bluecollar (also co-writer) 1978, Hardcore 1978, American Gigolo (also co-writer) 1979, Cat People 1982, Mishima (also co-writer) 1985, Patty Hearst 1989, The Comfort of Strangers 1990, Light Sleeper 1991 (also writer), Witch-hunt 1994, Touch 1997, Forever Mine 1999 (also writer), Auto Focus

2002, Paul Schrader's Exorcist: The Beginning 2005, Adam Resurrected 2008. *Publications include:* Transcendental Style in Film: Ozu, Bresson, Dreyer 1972, Schrader on Schrader (with Kevin Jackson) 1990, A Hundred Years of Japanese Film (with Donald Richie) 2005. *Address:* c/o Johnnie Planco, Parseghian Planco 322, 8th Avenue, Suite 601, New York NY, 10001, USA. *Telephone:* (212) 777-7786. *Fax:* (212) 777-8642. *E-mail:* schraderproductions@gmail.com. *Website:* paulschrader.org.

SCHRAMECK, Olivier Claude Martin; French politician and civil servant; *President, Section du rapport et des études, Conseil d'État;* b. 27 Feb. 1951, Paris; s. of Jean Schrameck and Stéphanie Schrameck (née Epstein); m. Hélene Rioust de Largentaye 1980; one s. one d.; ed Lycées Carnot, Paris and Pasteur, Neuilly-sur-Seine, Univ. of Paris II (Université Panthéon Assas), Ecole Nat. d'Admin., Inst. d'Etudes Politiques, Paris; Auditeur, Conseil d'État 1977–83; Governing Commr, Ass. du contentieux et les autres formations de jugement du Conseil d'État 1981–82, 1987–88; Tech. Adviser 1982–84; Chargé de mission, Ministry of the Interior and of Decentralization 1984; Chief of Staff, Sec. of State of Ministry of Nat. Educ., with responsibility for Univs 1984–85, Dir of Higher Educ. 1985–86; Maître des requêtes, Conseil d'État 1983; Chief of Staff, Minister of State, Ministry of Nat. Educ., Youth and Sports 1988–91; Assoc. Prof., Univ. of Paris I (Panthéon-Sorbonne) 1991–97, 2005–; Assoc. Prof.,_Sciences-Po Paris; currently Pres. Section du rapport et des études, Conseil d'État; Gen. Reporter to High Council for Integration 1991–93; Sec.-Gen. Constitutional Council 1993–97; Vice-Pres. Comité d'appel de la Banque mondiale 2010–12; mem. Ass. and Perm. Comm., Conseil d'État 1995, 2005–; Chief of Staff to Prime Minister 1997–2001; mem. Admin. Council, Nat. Caisse of Historic Monuments 1992–97, Comité de réflexion et de proposition sur la modernisation et le rééquilibrage des institutions (Cttee for Institutional Reform) 2007–; Amb. to Spain 2002–05; mem. Commision de rénovation et de déontolgie de la vie publique 2012; Pres. Commission de suivi de la procédure d'affectation des élèves de l'ENA 2012; Officier, Légion d'honneur, Chevalier, Ordre nat. du Mérite. *Publications include:* Les Cabinets ministériels 1995, La Fonction publique territoriale 1995, Matignon, Rive Gauche 1997–2001, Mémoire d'Alternance: L'Espagne de Zapatero 2005, Dans l'Ombre de la République: Les Cabinets Ministériels 2007; numerous articles on decentralization law, immigration and constitutional law. *Address:* Conseil d'État, 1 place du Palais Royal, 75001 Paris, France (office). *Telephone:* 1-40-20-83-90 (office). *E-mail:* olivier.schrameck@conseil-etat.fr (office). *Website:* www.conseil-etat.fr (office).

SCHREIBER, Stuart L., BA, PhD; American chemist and academic; *Scientific Co-Director, Harvard Center for Genomics Research;* b. 6 Feb. 1956; ed Univ. of Virginia, Harvard Univ.; Asst Prof., Yale Univ. 1981–84, Assoc. Prof. 1984–86, Prof. 1986–88; Morris Loeb Prof., Harvard Univ. 1988–, Co-Dir, Harvard Inst. of Chem. and Cell Biology 1997–, Scientific Co-Dir, Harvard Center for Genomics Research 1998–, Assoc. mem. Harvard Univ. Medical School, Molecular and Cell Biology Div. 1988–; Investigator, Howard Hughes Medical Inst., Chevy Chase, Md 1994–, Assoc. mem., Dept of Molecular and Cellular Biology 1994–; Founder and Co-Chair. Scientific Advisory Bd Infinity Pharmaceuticals 2002–06; Founder and Chair. Bd of Scientific and Medical Advisors ARIAD Pharmaceuticals 1991–, Founder ARIAD Gene Therapeutics 1994–; Founder and mem. Scientific Advisory Bd Vertex Pharmaceuticals 1988–90; Advisor, Theravance 2000–04; consultant to Pfizer 1983–91; Founder and Co-Ed. Chemistry and Biology 1993–2004, Founding Ed. 2005–; mem. Bd of Consulting Eds Tetrahedron Publications 1983–; mem. Editorial Bd or Advisory Ed. The Scientist 2005–, Proceedings of NAS 1995–98, Current Biology, Topics in Stereochemistry, Comprehensive Organic Synthesis, Current Opinion in Chemical Biology, Nature Chemical Biology, ACS Chemical Biology, ChemBioChem, Synthesis Letters, Journal of Organic Chemistry, Journal of Medicinal Chemistry, Bioorganic and Medicinal Chemistry Letters, Bioorganic and Medicinal Chemistry; mem. NAS 1995–, American Acad. of Arts and Sciences 1995–; Trustee Rockefeller Univ. 1999–2004; Founding mem. Broad Inst., Dir Chemical Biology Program; numerous awards including ICI Pharmaceuticals Award for Excellence in Chem. 1986, Arthur C. Cope Scholar Award, ACS 1986, Award in Pure Chem., ACS 1989, Arun Guthikonda Memorial Award, Columbia Univ. 1990, Ciba-Geigy Drew Award for Biomedical Research 1992, Thieme-IUPAC Award in Synthetic Organic Chem. 1992, NIH Merit Award 1992, Rhone-Poulenc Silver Medal, Royal Soc. of Chem. 1992, Eli Lilly Award in Biological Chem., ACS 1993, Leo Hendrik Baekeland Award, ACS 1993, Nat. Cancer Inst. Derek Barton Medal 1999, William H. Nichols Medal 2001, Chiron Corpn Biotechnology Research Award, American Acad. of Microbiology 2001 Soc. for Biomolecular Screening Achievement Award 2004, Asscn of American Cancer Insts Distinguished Scientist Award 2004, Academic Scientist of the Year, Finalist for the 2005 Pharmaceutical Achievement Awards 2005, Thomson Laureate Award in Chem. (with Gerald R. Crabtree) 2006. *Address:* Schreiber Research Laboratory, 7 Cambridge Center, Cambridge, MA 02142 (office); Department of Chemistry and Chemical Biology, Harvard University, 12 Oxford Street, Cambridge, MA 02138-2902, USA (office). *Telephone:* (617) 324-4380 (Lab.) (office); (617) 495-5318 (office). *Fax:* (617) 324-9601 (Lab.) (office); (617) 495-0751 (office). *E-mail:* stuart_schreiber@harvard.edu (office). *Website:* www.fas.harvard.edu/ ~biophys/Stuart_L_Schreiber.htm (office).

SCHREIER, Ethan J., BSc, PhD; American astronomer; *President, Associated Universities Inc.;* b. New York, NY; ed Bronx High School of Science, City Coll. of New York, Massachusetts Inst. of Tech.; Researcher, American Science and Eng Inc. 1970–73; Sr Scientist, Harvard-Smithsonian Center for Astrophysics 1973; Co-founder, Space Telescope Science Inst., Baltimore, Md 1981, becoming Chief Data and Operations Scientist, Assoc. Dir for Next Generation Space Telescope, and Head of Strategic Planning and Devt; Adjunct Prof., Dept of Physics and Astronomy, Johns Hopkins Univ.; Exec. Vice-Pres., Associated Universities Inc. 2001–04, Pres. 2004–; mem. numerous NASA advisory cttees, including Nat. Virtual Observatory Exec. Cttee, Int. Virtual Observatory Alliance Exec. *Address:* Associated Universities Inc., 1400 16th Street NW, Washington, DC 20036, USA (office). *Telephone:* (202) 462-1676 (office). *Fax:* (202) 232-7161 (office). *E-mail:* ejs@ aui.edu (office). *Website:* www.aui.edu (office).

SCHREIER, Peter; German singer (tenor) and conductor; b. 29 July 1935, Meissen; ed Dresden Hochschule für Musik; sang with Dresden State Opera 1959–63; joined Berlin Staatsoper 1963; has appeared at Vienna State Opera, Salzburg Festival, La Scala, Milan, Sadler's Wells, London, Metropolitan Opera,

New York and Teatro Colón, Buenos Aires; recital debut London 1978; debut as conductor 1969; has conducted recordings of several choral works by J. S. Bach, Mozart and Schubert; retd as opera singer 1999, continues to conduct; mem. Musical Academies of Munich and Berlin 1989–; Royal Swedish Arts Acad. 1989–; Hon. mem. Musical Soc. of Vienna 1986–; Order of Federal Republic of Germany (Bundesverdienstkreuz); Sonning Award 1988, Ernst von Siemens Music Prize 1988, Georg Philipp Telemann Prize 1994, Wartburg Prize 1994, European Church Music Prize, Royal Acad. of Music/Kohn Foundation Bach Prize 2009. *Address:* Calberlastr. 13, 01326 Dresden, Germany.

SCHREYER, Rt Hon. Edward Richard, PC, CC, C.M.M., OM, CD, MA, LLD; Canadian politician and diplomatist; b. 21 Dec. 1935, Beausejour, Manitoba; s. of John J. Schreyer and Elizabeth Gottfried; m. Lily Schulz 1960; two s. two d.; ed Cromwell Public School, Beausejour Collegiate, United Coll., St John's Coll. and Univ. of Manitoba; mem. for Brokenhead, Manitoba Legislature 1958, re-elected 1959, 1962; Prof. of Political Science and Int. Relations, Univ. of Manitoba 1962–65; mem. Manitoba prov. legis. ass. for Springfield Constituency 1965–68, for Selkirk 1968; Leader, Manitoba New Democratic Party 1969–78; Premier of Manitoba, Minister of Dominion-Provincial Relations 1969–77, Minister of Hydro 1971–77, of Finance 1972–74; Leader of the Opposition 1977–78; Gov.-Gen. of Canada 1979–84; High Commr to Australia, also accred to Papua New Guinea and Solomon Islands 1984–88; Amb. to Vanuatu 1984–88; Distinguished Visiting Prof., Univ. of Winnipeg 1989–90, Simon Fraser Univ. 1991; Distinguished Fellow, Inst. of Integrated Energy Systems, Univ. of Victoria 1992–94, Dept of Geography, Univ. of BC 1995–96; Chair. Canadian Shield Foundation 1984–; Dir Perfect Pacific Investments 1989–, China Int. Trust and Investment Corpn (Canada) Ltd 1991–, Swan-E-Set Bay Resort and Country Club 1991–, Habitat for Humanity Canada 1992–, Sask. Energy Conservation and Devt Authority 1993–96, Alt. Fuel Systems Inc. (Calgary) 1994–, Cephalon Oil and Gas Resource Corp. (Calgary) 1994–95; mem. Int. Asscn of Energy Econs, Churchill Econ. Advisory Cttee, Pacific Inst. of Deep Sea Tech.; Counsellor Canada West Foundation 1989–; Sr Adviser Summit Council for World Peace (World Peace Fed.), Washington DC 1991–; Chancellor, Brandon Univ. 2002–08; Hon. Dir Sierra Legal Defence Fund 1991–, Hon. Patron, John Diefenbaker Soc. 1991–, Hon. Adviser, Canadian Foundation for the Preservation of Chinese Cultural and Historical Treasures 1994–; Hon. LLD (Manitoba) 1979, (Mount Allison) 1983, (McGill) 1984, (Simon Fraser) 1984, (Lakehead) 1985; Gov.-Gen. Vanier Award 1975. *Leisure interests:* reading, golf, sculpting, woodworking. *Address:* 250 Wellington Center, Unit 401, Winnipeg, Man. R3M 0B3, Canada.

SCHREYER, Michaele, PhD; German organization official and fmr politician; *Vice-President, Netzwerks Europäische Bewegung Deutschland;* b. 9 Aug. 1951, Cologne; ed Univ. of Cologne, Free Univ. of Berlin; Research Asst, Inst. for Public Finances and Social Policy, Free Univ. of Berlin 1977–82, Lecturer 1996–99, Lecturer, Otto-Suhr-Institut 2004–; research asst and adviser for Green Caucus, Bundestag 1983–87; Researcher, Inst. for Econ. Research (IFO), Munich 1987–88; Minister for Urban Devt and Environmental Protection in Senate of Berlin 1989–90; mem. State Parl., Berlin 1991–99, mem. Budget and Public Finance Cttee, Chair. Sub-Cttee on Funds for Public Housing 1995–97; Chair. Green Caucus, Berlin Parl. 1998–99; EU Commr for Budget, Financial Control and Fraud Prevention 1999–2004; currently Vice-Pres. Netzwerks Europäische Bewegung Deutschland (non-partisan union of European political orgs); Vice-Pres. European Movement Germany 2006–; mem. Advisory Bd for Transatlantic Relations and European Affairs, Heinrich Böll Foundation; mem. Advisory Bd Transparency International Germany; fmr mem. numerous co. bds; fmr mem. Bd Berlin br. of German Soc. for UN. *Address:* Netzwerk Europäische Bewegung Deutschland, Sophienstr. 28/29, 10178 Berlin, Germany (office). *Telephone:* (30) 3036201 (office). *Fax:* (30) 3036201 (office). *E-mail:* netzwerk@europaeische-bewegung.de (office). *Website:* www.europaeische-bewegung.de (office).

SCHRIEFFER, John Robert, BS, MS, PhD; American physicist and fmr professor of physics; b. 31 May 1931, Oak Park, Ill.; s. of John Henry Schrieffer and Louise Anderson; m. Anne Grete Thomson 1960; one s. two d.; ed Massachusetts Inst. of Technology, Univ. of Illinois; NSF Fellow, Univ. of Birmingham, UK and Univ. Inst. for Theoretical Physics, Copenhagen 1957–58; Asst Prof., Univ. of Chicago 1957–60, Univ. of Illinois 1959–60; Assoc. Prof., Univ. of Illinois 1960–62; Prof., Univ. of Pennsylvania 1962, Mary Amanda Wood Prof. of Physics 1962–79, Mary Amada Wood Prof. of Physics 1964–79; Andrew D. White Prof., Cornell Univ. 1969–75; Prof. of Physics, Univ. of California, Santa Barbara 1980–91, Essan Khashoggi Prof. of Physics 1985, Dir Inst. for Theoretical Physics 1984–89, Chancellor's Prof. 1984–91; Prof., Florida State Univ., Tallahassee 1992–2006, Chief Scientist Nat. High Magnetic Field Lab. 1992–2006, Univ. Eminent Scholar, Florida State Univ. System 1996–2006 (retd); Vice-Pres. American Physical Soc. 1994–96, apptd Pres. 1996; mem. NAS, American Acad. Arts and Sciences, American Philosophical Soc. 1974, Royal Danish Acad. of Science and Letters, Nat. Medal of Science Cttee 1996–; Guggenheim Fellow 1967–68; Fellow, American Physical Soc. (Pres. 1997); Dr hc (Technische Hochschule, Munich, Univs of Geneva, Pennsylvania, Illinois, Cincinatti, Tel-Aviv, Alabama); Oliver E. Buckley Solid State Physics Prize 1968, Comstock Prize, NAS 1968, Nobel Prize for Physics (with J. Bardeen and L.N. Cooper) 1972, John Ericsson Medal, American Soc. of Swedish Engineers 1976, Alumni Achievement Award, Univ. of Ill. 1979, Nat. Medal of Science 1985, Superconductivity Award of Excellence, World Congress of Superconductivity 1996, Robert A. Holton Medal for Distinguished Research Service, Florida State Univ. 2004. *Publication:* Theory of Superconductivity 1964. *Address:* c/o National High Magnetic Field Laboratory, Florida State University, 1800 E Paul Dirac Drive, Tallahassee, FL 32310-3706, USA.

SCHROCK, Richard R., AB, PhD; American chemist and academic; *Frederick G. Keyes Professor of Chemistry, Massachusetts Institute of Technology;* b. 4 Jan. 1945, Berne, Ind.; m. Nancy F. Carlson 1971; two s.; ed Univ. of California, Riverside, Harvard Univ., Univ. of Cambridge, UK; Research Chemist, Cen. Research and Devt Dept, E.I. du Pont de Nemours & Co. 1972–75; Asst Prof. of Chem., MIT 1975–78, Assoc. Prof. 1978–80, Prof. 1980–89, Frederick G. Keyes Prof. of Chem. 1989–; Sherman T. Fairchild Scholar, Calif. Inst. of Tech. 1986, Science and Eng Research Council Visiting Fellow, Univ. of Cambridge 1991; ACS Award in Organometallic Chem. 1985 and Harrison Howe Award 1990, Inorganic Chem. Award 1996, Bailar Medal, Univ. of Ill. 1998, ACS Cope Scholar Award

2001, RSC Sir Geoffrey Wilkinson Medal 2002, Nobel Prize in Chem. (co-recipient) 2005. *Publications:* numerous papers in scientific journals. *Address:* Department of Chemistry, 6-331, Massachusetts Institute of Technology, 77 Massachusetts Avenue, Cambridge, MA 02139, USA (office). *Telephone:* (617) 253-1596 (office). *Fax:* (617) 253-7670 (office). *E-mail:* rrs@mit.edu (office). *Website:* web.mit.edu/rrs/www/home.html (office); web.mit.edu/chemistry/www/faculty/schrock.html (office).

SCHRODER, Baron Bruno Lionel, MBA; British business executive; b. 17 Jan. 1933; s. of Baron Bruno Schroder and Margaret Eleanor Phyllis Schroder (née Darell); m. Patricia Leonie Mary Holt 1969; one d.; ed Eton Coll., Univ. Coll., Oxford, Harvard Business School, USA; Second Lt, Life Guards 1951–53; joined Schroders PLC 1960, mem. Bd of Dirs 1963–, J. Henry Schroder & Co. Ltd 1966–, Schroders Inc. 1984–; Gov. English Nat. Ballet; mem. Exec. Cttee Air Squadron, Court of Assts Worshipful Co. of Goldsmiths, Liveryman Guild of Air Pilots and Air Navigators; Cross of the Order of Merit (Germany) 2006; Queen Beatrix of Netherlands Wedding Medal. *Leisure interests:* flying, stalking, shooting. *Address:* Schroders PLC, 31 Gresham Street, London, EC2V 7QA, England (office). *Telephone:* (20) 7658-6000 (office). *Fax:* (20) 7658-6965 (office). *Website:* www.schroders.com (office).

SCHRÖDER, Gerhard, LL.B.; German business executive and fmr politician; *Chairman, Nord Stream AG;* b. 7 April 1944, Mossenburg, Lippe; s. of the late Fritz Schröder and of Erika Schröder; m. 1st Eva Schubach; m. 2nd Anna Taschenmacher; m. 3rd Hiltrud Hensen 1984; m. 4th Doris Köpf 1997; one adopted d. one adopted s.; ed Univ. of Göttingen; apprentice as shop asst 1961; joined SPD 1963, Chair. 1999–2004; lawyer, Hanover 1976; Nat. Chair. of Young Socialists 1978–80; mem. Bundestag 1980–86; Leader of Opposition in State Parl. of Lower Saxony 1986; Minister-Pres. of Lower Saxony 1990–98; Chancellor of Germany 1998–2005; consultant to Ringier Group (publr) 2005; Adviser, Rothschild Group 2006–; Chair. Nord Stream AG (consortium owned by OAO Gazprom, BASF AG, E.On AG for construction and operation of planned Nord Stream submarine pipeline) 2006–; mem. Bd of Dirs TNK BP Ltd 2009–; mem. InterActionCouncil, 21st Century Council, Council for the Future of Europe; Patron Aladdin Project, Gesicht Zeigen! Für ein weltoffenes Deutschland, Hilfe für ALS-kranke Menschen; Hon. Chair. Nah- und Mittelostvereins (NuMOV); Mittelstandspreis 1997, Quadriga Award 2007. *Address:* Nord Stream AG, Grafenauweg 2, 6304 Zug, Switzerland (office). *Telephone:* (41) 7669191 (office). *Fax:* (41) 7669192 (office). *E-mail:* info@nord-stream.com (office). *Website:* www.nord-stream.com (office).

SCHRODER, Soren, BA (Econ); American business executive; *CEO, Bunge Limited;* ed Connecticut Coll.; worked for more than 15 years at Continental Grain and Cargill; joined Bunge 2000, served in a variety of agribusiness leadership roles in USA and Europe, CEO Bunge North America 2010–13, mem. Bd of Dirs and CEO Bunge Ltd 2013–. *Address:* Bunge Ltd, 50 Main Street, 6th Floor, White Plains, NY 10606, USA (office). *Telephone:* (914) 684-2800 (office). *Fax:* (914) 684-3499 (office). *E-mail:* info@bunge.com (office). *Website:* www.bunge.com (office).

SCHRÖDER, Ulrich, MCL, DrIur; German banking executive; *Chairman of the Executive Board and CEO, KfW Bankengruppe;* b. 19 March 1952, Melle; m.; three c.; ed Univ. of Münster, Univ. of Illinois, USA; Research Asst, Univ. of Münster 1980–82; with Westdeutsche Landesbank Girozentrale (WestLB), Düsseldorf/Münster 1983–, mem. Bd of Dirs 1983–87, Head of Exec. Secr. 1985–87, Account Man., WestLB Br., London, UK 1987–92, Head of Dept 1991, Head of Münster and Bielefeld Brs 1992–97, Bank Man. 1995, mem. Man. Bd WestLB France 1997–2002, Man. of WestLB Paris Br. and Head of Chemicals/Life Sciences Unit 2001–02, mem. Man. Bd WestLB April–July 2002; mem. Man. Bd NRW.BANK, Düsseldorf/Münster 2002–, Chair. Man. Bd 2006–08; Chair. Exec. Bd and CEO KfW Bankengruppe 2008–; mem. Supervisory Bd Deutsche Post AG, Deutsche Telekom AG. *Address:* KfW Bankengruppe, Palmengartenstrasse 5–9, 60325 Frankfurt am Main, Germany (office). *Telephone:* (69) 7431-0 (office). *Fax:* (69) 7431-2944 (office). *E-mail:* presse@kfw.de (office). *Website:* www.kfw.de (office).

SCHROEDER, Barbet; French film producer, director and actor; b. 26 Aug. 1941, Tehran, Iran; s. of Jean-William Schroeder and Ursula Schroeder; m. Bulle Ogier; ed Sorbonne, Paris; worked as jazz tour operator Europe, photo journalist India, critic for Cahiers du Cinéma and L'Air de Paris 1958–63; Asst to Jean-Luc Godard on Les Carabiniers 1963; f. own production co. Les Films du Losange 1964; worked as actor and producer. *Films produced:* Méditerranée 1963, La Carrière de Suzanne 1963, La Boulangère de Monceau 1963, Nadja à Paris 1964, Paris vu par... 1965, Fermière à Montfaucon 1967, La Collectionneuse 1967, More 1969, Ma nuit chez Maud 1969, Le Genou de Claire 1970, Sing-Sing 1971, Maquillages 1971, Le Cochon aux patates douces 1971, L'Amour l'après-midi 1972, Céline et Julie vont en bateau 1974, Marquise von O..., Die 1976, Chinesisches Roulette 1976, Perceval le Gallois 1978, Le Pont du Nord 1981, Flügel und Fesseln 1985, Barfly 1987, Single White Female 1992, Kiss of Death 1995, Never Talk to Strangers 1995, Before and After 1996, Desperate Measures 1998, Shattered Image 1998, La Virgen de los sicarios 2000, Murder by Numbers 2002. *Films directed:* More 1969, Sing-Song (documentary) 1971, Le Cochon aux patates douces 1971, La Vallée 1972, General Idi Amin Dada (documentary) 1974, Maîtresse 1976, Koko, the Talking Gorilla (documentary) 1978, Tricheurs 1984, Charles Bukowski (50 four-minute videos) 1985, Barfly 1987, Reversal of Fortune 1990, Single White Female 1992, Kiss of Death 1995, Before and After (also producer) 1996, Desperate Measures 1998, La Virgen de los Sicarios 2000, Murder by Numbers 2002, L'Avocat de la terreur (French César, Best Documentary) 2007, Inju: The Beast in the Shadow 2008. *Films as actor:* La Boulangère de Monceau 1963, Les Carabiniers 1963, Paris vu par... 1965, Out 1, noli me tangere 1971, Out 1: Spectre 1972, Céline et Julie vont en bateau 1974, Roberte 1979, L'Amour par terre 1984, The Golden Boat 1990, La Reine Margot 1994, Beverly Hills Cop III 1994, Mars Attacks! 1996, La Virgen de los sicarios 2000, Ne fais pas ça 2004, Une aventure 2005, Paris, je t'aime (segment) 2006, Ne touchez pas la hache 2007, The Darjeeling Limited 2007, The Counsel 2010.

SCHROEDER, Patricia Nell Scott, JD; American organization executive and fmr politician; b. (Patricia Nell Scott), July 1940, Portland, Ore.; m. James W. Schroeder; one s. one d.; ed Univ. of Minn., Harvard Law School; mem. US House of Reps 1972–96, served on House Armed Services and Judiciary Cttees and several other cttees, Chair. House Select Cttee on Children, Youth and Families 1991–93;

Prof., Woodrow Wilson School of Public and Int. Affairs, Princeton Univ. Jan.–June 1997; Pres. and CEO Asscn of American Publrs 1997–2009; mem. Bd Marguerite Casey Foundation (currently Vice-Chair.), ABA Center for Human Rights; Chair. Peace PAC, Council for a Livable World; elected to Nat. Women's Hall of Fame, Seneca Falls, New York 1995. *Publications:* Champion of the Great American Family 1989, 24 Years of House Work and the Place is Still a Mess 1998. *Address:* 621 Nadina Place, Orlando, FL 34747, USA (home).

SCHROEDER, Steven Alfred, MD; American physician and academic; *Distinguished Professor of Health and Health Care, Department of Medicine, University of California, San Francisco;* b. 26 July 1939, New York, NY; s. of Arthur E. Schroeder; m. Sally Ross Schroeder 1967; two s.; ed El Cerrito High School, Stanford Univ., Harvard Univ.; Fellow, Harvard Community Health and Medical Care and Instructor Harvard Medical School 1970–71; Asst Prof. of Medicine and Health Care Sciences, later Assoc. Prof., The George Washington Univ. Medical Center 1971–76, Medical Dir The George Washington Univ. Health Plan 1971–76; Assoc. Prof. of Medicine, Univ. of Calif., San Francisco 1976–80, Prof. 1980–90, Chief, Div. of Gen. Internal Medicine 1980–90, Distinguished Prof. of Health and Health Care, Dept of Medicine 2003–, Dir Smoking Cessation Leadership Center 2003–; Clinical Prof., Univ. of Medicine and Dentistry of NJ, Robert Wood Johnson Medical School 1991–2002; Pres. Robert Wood Johnson Foundation 1990–99, Pres. and CEO 1999–2003; Founding Chair. Int. Advisory Cttee of The Health Services, Ben-Gurion Univ. of the Negev, Israel 1996–2009; mem. Bd of Dirs American Legacy Foundation 2000–05 (Vice-Chair. 2001–03, Chair. 2003–05), James Irvine Foundation 2004–, Charles R. Drew Univ. of Medicine and Science 2005–09, Marin Gen. Hosp. 2009–, Mathematica Policy Research 2011–, Marin Community Foundation 2013–; mem. Bd of Overseers, Harvard Coll. 2000–06; mem. Editorial Bd New England Journal of Medicine 1994–2013; Visiting Prof., Dept of Community Medicine, St Thomas's Hosp. Medical School, London 1982–83; Pres. Harvard Medical Alumni Asscn 2005–06; numerous hon. degrees; numerous awards. *Publications include:* more than 300 articles. *Leisure interests:* climbing, hiking, tennis, gardening, literature, history. *Address:* Smoking Cessation Leadership Center, University of California, 3333 California Street, Suite 430, San Francisco, CA 94143 (office); Box 1211, University of California, San Francisco, San Francisco, CA 94143-1211 (office); 10 Paseo Mirasol, Belvedere Tiburon, CA 94920, USA (home). *Telephone:* (415) 502-1881 (office); (415) 435-3872 (home). *Fax:* (415) 502-5739 (office). *E-mail:* schroeder@medicine.ucsf.edu (office). *Website:* smokingcessationleadership.ucsf.edu (office).

SCHUBARTH, Martin, DrIur; Swiss judge and professor of law; *Avocat-Conseil, Rusconi & Associés;* b. 9 June 1942, Basel; m. Musa Retschmedin 1944; one d.; ed Univ. of Basel; began practising as lawyer, Basel 1969; mem. Bar of Basel 1969–83; Lecturer, Univ. of Basel 1973; Prof. Univ. of Bonn 1976–80, Univ. of Hanover 1980–83; Fed. Judge 1983–2004, Pres. Fed. Supreme Court 1999–2000, Pres. Criminal Court 1999–2002; Judge, Court of Cassation 1987–2004; Avocat-Conseil, Rusconi & Associés, Lausanne 2004–. *Publication:* Kommentar zum Schweizerischen Strafrecht 1982 ff. *Address:* Rusconi & Associés, 4 rue de la Paix, CP 7268, 1002 Lausanne (office); Ch. du Levant 44, 1005 Lausanne, Switzerland (home). *Telephone:* (21) 321-50-80 (office); (21) 728-83-82 (home). *Fax:* (21) 320-29-60 (office). *E-mail:* info@rusconi-avocats.ch (office); m.schubarth@bluewin.ch (home). *Website:* www.rusconi-avocats.ch; www.martinschubarth.ch.

SCHUBERT, John Michael, AO, PhD; Australian business executive; *Chairman, Great Barrier Reef Foundation;* b. 11 Dec. 1942, Adelaide, South Australia; m. Prudence Schubert; two c.; began career at ESSO in Australia 1969, held numerous positions at ESSO in Australia and internationally, fmr Chair. and Man. Dir Esso Australia Ltd; fmr Man. Dir and CEO Pioneer International Ltd, led business to merger at Hanson Plc 2000; mem. Bd of Dirs Commonwealth Bank of Australia 1991–2010, Deputy Chair. 2000–04, Chair. 2004–10; Chair. G2 Therapies Pty Ltd 2000–; joined Worley Parsons Ltd (fmrly Worley Group Ltd) as Chair. Advisory Bd 2000, Chair. (non-exec.) 2002–05; Dir BHP Ltd 2000–, Ind. Dir, BHP Billiton plc 2001–, Dir (non-exec.) BHP Billiton Ltd 2001–, Dir BHP Billiton Group; Ind. Dir (non-exec.) Qantas Airways Ltd 2000–12; mem. Bd of Dirs, Hanson Ltd 2000–03; fmr Pres. Business Council of Australia; Dir, Australian Grad. School of Man., Great Barrier Reef Research Foundation (Chair.), Salvation Army Advisory Bd; Fellow, Acad. of Technological Science and Eng, Inst. of Engineers; Hon. mem. Business Council of Australia. *Address:* Great Barrier Reef Foundation, PO Box 2725, Fortitude Valley, Queensland 4006, Australia (office). *Telephone:* (7) 3252-7555 (office). *Fax:* (7) 3252-7666 (office). *E-mail:* johnmschubert@bigpond.com; frances.grant2@bigpond.com. *Website:* www.barrierreef.org (office).

SCHULLER, Gunther Alexander; American composer, conductor, music educator and record producer; b. 22 Nov. 1925, New York, NY; s. of Arthur E. Schuller and Elsise Schuller (née Bernartz); m. Marjorie Black 1948 (died 1992); two s.; ed St Thomas Choir School, New York, Manhattan School of Music; Principal French horn, Cincinnati Symphony Orchestra 1943–45, Metropolitan Opera Orchestra 1945–59; teacher, Manhattan School of Music 1950–63, Yale Univ. 1964–67; Head Composition Dept, Tanglewood 1963–84; Music Dir First Int. Jazz Festival, Washington, DC 1962; active as conductor since mid-1960s with maj. orchestras in Europe and USA; reconstructed and orchestrated Der Gelbe Klang by De Hartmann/Kandinsky; Pres. New England Conservatory of Music 1967–77; Pres. Nat. Music Council 1979–81; Artistic Co-Dir, then Artistic Dir Summer Activities, Boston Symphony Orchestra, Berkshire Music Center, Tanglewood 1969–84, Festival at Sandpoint 1985–98; Founder and Pres. Margun Music Inc. 1975–2000, GM Recordings 1981–; mem. American Acad. of Arts and Sciences, American Acad. of Arts and Letters; Order of Merit (Germany) 1997; Hon. DMus (Northeastern Univ.) 1967, (Colby Coll.) 1969, (Univ. of Illinois) 1970, (Williams Coll.) 1975, (Rutgers Univ.) 1980, (Oberlin Coll.) 1989, (Florida State Univ.) 1991; Creative Arts Award, Brandeis Univ. 1960, Nat. Inst. Arts and Letters Award 1960, Guggenheim Grant 1962, 1963, ASCAP Deems Taylor Award 1970, Rogers and Hammerstein Award 1971, William Schuman Award, Columbia Univ. 1989, McArthur Foundation Fellowship 1991, McArthur Genius Award 1994, Gold Medal, American Acad. of Arts and Letters 1996, Max Rudolf Award 1998, Pulitzer Prize in Music 1999. *Compositions include:* Horn Concerto No. 1 1945, Vertige d'Eros 1946, Concerto for cello and orchestra 1946, Jumpin' in the Future 1946, Quartet for Four Brasses 1947, Oboe Sonata 1947, Duo Concertante

for cello and piano 1947, Symphonic Study (Meditation) 1948, Trio for Oboe, Horn, Viola 1948, Symphony for brass and percussion 1950, Fantasy for Unaccompanied Cello 1951, Recitative and Rondo for violin and piano 1953, Dramatic Overture 1951, Five Pieces for Five Horns 1952, Adagio for flute, string trio 1952, Music for Violin, Piano and Percussion 1957, Symbiosis for violin, piano, percussion 1957, String Quartet No. 1 1957, Contours 1958, Woodwind Quintet 1958, Spectra 1958, Concertino for jazz quartet and orchestra 1959, Seven Studies on Themes of Paul Klee 1959, Conversations 1960, Lines and Contrasts for 16 horns 1960, Abstraction for jazz ensemble 1960, Variants on a Theme of Thelonious Monk 1960, Music for Brass Quintet 1960, Contrasts for woodwind quintet and orchestra 1961, Variants (ballet with choreography by Balanchine) 1961, Double Quintet for woodwind and brass quintets 1961, Meditation for concert band 1961, Concerto for piano and orchestra 1962, Journey into Jazz 1962, Fantasy Quartet for four cellos 1963, Threnos for oboe and orchestra 1963, Composition in Three Parts 1963, Five Bagatelles for Orchestra 1964, Five Etudes for orchestra 1964, The Power Within Us 1964, Five Shakespearean Songs for baritone and orchestra 1964, String Quartet No. 2 1965, Symphony 1965, American Triptych (on paintings of Pollock, Davis and Calder) 1965, Sacred Cantata 1966, Gala Music concerto for orchestra 1966, The Visitation (opera) 1966, Movements for flute and strings, Six Renaissance Lyrics, Triplum I 1967, Study in Textures for concert band 1967, Diptych for brass quintet and orchestra 1967, Shapes and Designs 1968, Concerto for double bass and orchestra 1968, Consequents for orchestra 1969, Fisherman and his Wife (opera) 1970, Concerto da Camera No. 1 1971, Capriccio Stravagante 1972, Tre Invenzioni 1972, Three Nocturnes 1973, Five Moods for tuba quartet 1973, Four Soundscapes 1974, Triplum II 1975, Violin Concerto 1976, Concerto No. 2 for horn and orchestra 1976, Diptych for organ 1976, Concerto No. 2 for orchestra 1977, Concerto for contrabassoon and orchestra 1978, Deaï for three orchestras 1978, Sonata Serenata 1978, Octet 1979, Concerto for trumpet and orchestra 1979, Eine Kleine Posaunenmusik 1980, In Praise of Winds symphony for large wind orchestra 1981, Concerto No. 2 for piano and orchestra 1981, Symphony for organ 1981, Concerto Quaternio 1984, Concerto for alto saxophone 1983, Duologue for violin and piano 1983, On Light Wings piano quartet 1984, Piano Trio 1984, Concerto for viola and orchestra 1985, Concerto for bassoon and orchestra 1985, Farbenspiel Concerto No. 3 for orchestra 1985, String Quartet No. 3 1986, Chimeric Images 1988, Concerto for string quartet and orchestra 1988, Concerto for flute and orchestra 1988, Horn Sonata 1988, On Winged Flight: A Divertimento for Band 1989, Chamber Symphony 1989, Five Impromptus for English horn and string quartet 1989, Impromptus and Cadenzas for chamber sextet 1990, Song and Dance for violin and concert band 1990, Concerto for piano three hands 1990, Violin Concerto No. 2 1991, Brass Quintet No. 2 1993, Reminiscences and Reflections 1993, The Past is the Present for orchestra 1994, Sextet for left-hand piano and woodwind quintet 1994, Concerto for organ and orchestra 1994, Mondrian's Vision 1994, Lament for M 1994, Blue Dawn into White Heat concert band 1995, An Arc Ascending 1996, Ohio River Reflections 1998, A Bouquet for Collage 1998, Fantasia Impromptu for flute and harpsichord 2000, Quod Libet for violin, cello, oboe, horn and harp 2001, String Quartet No. 4 2002, Concerto da Camera No. 2 2002, String Trio 2003, Encounters for jazz orchestra and symphony orchestra 2003, Where the World Ends 2008. *Publications:* Horn Technique 1962, Early Jazz: Its Roots and Musical Development, Vol. I 1968, Musings: The Musical Worlds of Gunther Schuller 1985, The Swing Era: The Development of Jazz 1930–45 1989, The Compleat Conductor 1997. *Address:* GM Recordings, 167 Dudley Road, Newton Center, MA 02459, USA. *Telephone:* (617) 332-6328. *Fax:* (617) 969-1079. *E-mail:* contact@gmrecordings.com. *Website:* www.gmrecordings.com.

SCHULMAN, Amy Weinfeld, BA, JD; American lawyer and business executive; *Executive Vice-President and General Counsel, Pfizer Inc.;* b. 16 Oct. 1960, New York; d. of Alvin Harold Schulman and Ann Schulman; m. David Eli Nachman; three s.; ed Wesleyan Univ., Yale Law School; law clerk to Judge Harold Ackerman 1989; Assoc., Cleary Gottlieb 1990–97; Of Counsel, Piper & Marbury 1997, Pnr, Piper Rudnick 1998–2004, Pnr, DLA Piper Rudnick Gray Cary (litigation practice) 2005–08; joined Pfizer Inc. as Gen. Counsel 2008, now Exec. Vice-Pres. and Gen. Counsel, also Business Unit Lead, Consumer Healthcare div.; mem. Bd of Dirs Brooklyn Acad. of Music 2002–, Wesleyan Univ.; Visiting Prof., Harvard Law School; mem. Fed. Bar Council, ABA, Int. Asscn of Defense Counsel, Defense Research Inst.; ranked by Forbes magazine amongst 100 Most Powerful Women (81st) 2009, ranked by National Law Journal amongst 20 Most Influential General Counsels 2009, Margaret Brent Women Lawyers of Achievement Award, ABA 2012. *Address:* Pfizer Inc., 235 East 42nd Street, New York, NY 10017, USA (office). *Telephone:* (212) 733-2323 (office). *Website:* www.pfizer.com (office).

SCHULMAN, Joshua G.; American business executive; *CEO, Jimmy Choo;* b. Beverly Hills, Calif.; at Perry Ellis International from 1991 to 1993.; Vice President/Director of Sales and Marketing at Richard Tyler from 1993 to 1997; Worldwide Dir Women's Ready to Wear for Gucci brand 1997–2000, Exec. Vice-Pres. Worldwide Merchandising and Wholesale for Yves Saint Laurent brand, Paris 2000–05; Man. Dir of Int. Strategic Alliances for Gap, Inc. and Sr Vice-Pres. Int. Product Devt and Merchandising for Gap Brand 2006; Pres. Kenneth Cole Productions, Inc. New York brand 2006–07; CEO Jimmy Choo (shoe label) 2007–. *Address:* J. Choo Ltd, Ixworth House, 37 Ixworth Place, London, SW3 3QH, England (office). *Telephone:* (20) 7591-7000 (office). *Fax:* (20) 7591-7077 (office). *E-mail:* info@jimmychoo.com (office). *Website:* www.jimmychoo.com (office).

SCHULTE-NOELLE, Henning, MBA, DrJur; German insurance executive; b. 26 Aug. 1942, Essen; m.; one s. one d.; ed Univs of Tübingen, Bonn, Cologne, Edinburgh, UK and Pennsylvania, USA; attorney, Eckholt, Westrick & Partners, Frankfurt 1974; joined Allianz Group 1975, Head of Chair.'s Office, Munich 1979–83, Head of Regional Office for North Rhine-Westphalia, Cologne 1984–87, mem. Man. Bd Allianz Versicherung 1988–90, Allianz Leben 1988–90 (Chair. 1991), Chair. Allianz AG (renamed Allianz SE 2006) 1991–2003, Chair. Supervisory Bd 2003–12; mem. Supervisory Bd E.ON AG; fmr mem. Supervisory Bd Thyssen Krupp AG, Siemens AG, BASF AG, Linde AG, Vodafone AG and others; Bavarian Order of Merit 2001; Manager of the Year, Manager Magazine 1996. *Address:* c/o Allianz SE, Königinstrasse 28, 80802 Munich, Germany. *E-mail:* info@allianz.com.

SCHULTZ, Howard, BS; American business executive; *Chairman, CEO and Chief Global Strategist, Starbucks Corporation;* b. 19 July 1953, Brooklyn, New York; m. Sheri Kersch Schultz; one s. one d.; ed Canarsie High School and Northern Michigan Univ.; began career as sales trainee for Xerox; Vice-Pres. of US Sales, Hammerplast (subsidiary of Swedish-based Perstorp); joined Starbucks Coffee Co. (now Starbucks Corpn) in Sales and Marketing Dept 1982, Chair. 1987– (after buying out original owners), CEO 1987–2000, 2008–, now also Chief Global Strategist; Co-founder Maveron (venture capital firm) 1998, mem. Bd of Dirs Pinkberry Inc.; fmr Owner, Seattle SuperSonics professional basketball team (Nat. Basketball Asscn) and Seattle Storm professional basketball team (Women's Nat. Basketball Asscn); Israel 50th Anniversary Tribute Award 1998, National Leadership Award 1999, International Distinguished Entrepreneur Award 2004, FIRST Responsible Capitalism Award 2007, Rev. Theodore M. Hesburgh, C.S.C., Award for Ethics in Business 2007. *Publications:* Pour Your Heart Into It: How Starbucks Built a Company One Cup at a Time (with Dori Jones Yang) 1997, Onward: How Starbucks Fought for Its Life Without Losing Its Soul (with Joanne Gordon) 2011. *Address:* Starbucks Corporation, 2401 Utah Avenue South, Seattle, WA 98134, USA (office). *Telephone:* (206) 447-1575 (office). *Fax:* (206) 447-0828 (office). *Website:* www.starbucks.com (office).

SCHULTZ, Peter G., BS, PhD; American chemist and academic; *Scripps Professor of Chemistry, The Scripps Research Institute;* b. 23 June 1956, Cincinnati, OH; ed California Inst. of Tech., Pasadena, Massachusetts Inst. of Tech.; Asst Prof., Dept of Chem., Calif. Inst. of Tech. 1985–87, Assoc. Prof. 1987–89, Prof. 1989–99; Prin. Investigator, Lawrence Berkeley Lab. 1985–; Founding Scientist and Chair., Scientific Advisory Bd, Affymax Research Inst., Palo Alto, Calif. 1988–; Investigator, Howard Hughes Medical Inst. 1994–98; Founder and Dir Symyx Technologies, Palo Alto 1995–; Scripps Prof. of Chem., Scripps Research Inst., La Jolla, Calif. 1999–; Inst. Dir Genomics Inst., Novartis Research Foundation, La Jolla 1999–2010; mem. Bd of Dirs Nanosphere 2005–; Founder and Dir Syrrx Inc. 2000–, Kalypsys 2001–, Phenomix 2002–, Ambrx 2003–, Ilypsa 2004–; mem. American Acad. of Arts and Sciences 1990–, NAS 1993–, Caltech Chem. Advisory Cttee 1998–, Searle Advisory Cttee 1995–, Welch Foundation Scientific Advisory Bd 2002–, Daman Runyon Advisory Bd 1999–2004, Princeton Chem. Advisory Cttee 1994–96; Dr hc (Uppsala Univ., Sweden) 1994; numerous awards including NSF Presidential Young Investigator Award 1985, Alan T. Waterman Award 1988, ACS Award in Pure Chem. 1990, Eli Lilly Award in Biological Chem. 1991, Humboldt Research Award 1992, Wolf Prize in Chem. 1994, Calif. Scientist of the Year 1995, Alfred Bader Award in Bioorganic and Bioinorganic Chem. 2000, Ludwig Darmstaedter Prize 2002, Paul Ehrlich Prize 2003, Arthur C. Cope Award, ACS 2005. *Address:* The Scripps Research Institute, Attn: Peter Schultz, SR207, 10550 North Torrey Pines Road, SR202, La jolla, CA 92037, USA (office). *Website:* schultz.scripps.edu (office).

SCHULTZE, Charles Louis, BA, MA, PhD; American economist and fmr government official; *Senior Fellow Emeritus in Economic Studies, Brookings Institution;* b. 12 Dec. 1924, Alexandria, Va; s. of Richard Lee Schultze and Nora Woolls Schultze (née Baggett); m. Rita Irene Hertzog 1947; one s. five d.; ed Georgetown Univ. and Univ. of Maryland; Economist, US Office of Price Stabilization, Washington, DC 1951–52, Council of Econ. Advisers 1952–53, 1955–59; Assoc. Prof. of Econs, Indiana Univ. 1959–61; Assoc. Prof., Adjunct Prof. of Econs, Univ. of Md 1961–87; Asst Dir US Bureau of the Budget, Washington, DC 1962–65, Dir 1965–68; Sr Fellow, Brookings Inst., Washington, DC 1968–76, 1981–87, 1991–96, Sr Fellow Emer. 1997–, Dir Econ. Studies 1987–90, John C. and Nancy D. Whitehead Chair 1997; Chair. Council of Econ. Advisers, The White House 1977–81; mem. Econ. Advisory Bd, Warburg Pincus; Hon. Pres. American Econ. Asscn 1984. *Publications include:* National Income Analysis 1964, The Politics and Economics of Public Spending 1969 (co-author), Setting National Priorities: The 1974 Budget, The Public Use of Private Interest 1977, Other Times, Other Places 1986, American Living Standards (co-ed. and co-author) 1988, Barriers to European Growth (co-ed. and co-author) 1989, An American Trade Strategy: Options for the 1990s (co-ed.) 1990, Memos to the President 1992. *Address:* Brookings Institution, 1775 Massachusetts Avenue, NW, Washington, DC 20036 (office); 5520 33rd Street, NW, Washington, DC 20015, USA (home). *Telephone:* (202) 797-6163 (office). *Fax:* (202) 797-6181 (office). *E-mail:* escomment@brookings.edu (office). *Website:* www.brookings.org/scholars/cschultze.htm (office).

SCHULZ, Ekkehard D., Dr-Ing; German business executive; *Chairman of the Executive Board, ThyssenKrupp AG;* b. 24 July 1941, Bromberg, Westpreussen; m.; two c.; ed Clausthal Mining Acad., Clausthal Univ.; mem. scientific staff and Chief Engineer, Inst. for Gen. Metallurgy and Casting, Clausthal Univ. 1967–72; joined Thyssen Group 1972, Deputy Mem. (Production) Exec. Bd, Thyssen Stahl AG 1985, mem. (Production) 1986, (Tech.) 1988, Chair. 1991; mem. Exec. Bd, Thyssen AG 1991, Chair. 1998, Chair. Exec. Bd, ThyssenKrupp Stahl AG 1997, ThyssenKrupp AG 1999–, Thyssen Krupp Steel AG 1999–2001; Pres. EUROFER, Brussels; mem. supervisory bds/advisory councils, AXA Konzern AG, Commerzbank AG, Hapag Lloyd AG, MAN AG, RAG AG, RWE Plus AG, STRABAG AG; mem. int. advisory Bd, Salomon Smith Barney, New York; mem. Exec. Cttee and Bd, Wirtschaftsvereinigung Stahl und VDEh; mem. Advisory Council of BDI (Vice-Pres.); Hon. Prof. (Clausthal Univ.) 1999; Hon. Dr rer. pol (Berlin) 2004; Hon. Dr-Ing. (Aachen) 2005. *Address:* ThyssenKrupp AG, August-Thyssen-Strasse 1, 40211 Dusseldorf, Germany (office). *Telephone:* (211) 8240 (office). *Fax:* (211) 82436000 (office). *E-mail:* info@thyssenkrupp.com (office). *Website:* www.thyssenkrupp.com (office).

SCHULZ, Martin; German politician and fmr bookseller; *President, European Parliament;* b. 20 Dec. 1955, Hehlrath; m.; two c.; began career as apprentice in publishing trade 1975–77, worked in various bookshops 1977–82, bookshop propr, Würselen 1982–94; mem. SPD 1974–, Chair. Aachen Dist SPD 1996–, mem. SPD Fed. Exec. 1999–; mem. Würselen town council 1984–99, Mayor of Würselen 1987–98; mem. European Parl. 1999–, Leader, SPD Group in European Parl. 2000–04, Leader, Progressive Alliance of Socialists and Democrats 2004–12, Pres. European Parl. 2012–. *Leisure interests:* reading, football. *Address:* Office of the President, European Parliament, Bâtiment Altiero Spinelli, 05F243, 60 rue Wiertz, 1047 Brussels, Belgium (office). *Telephone:* (2) 284-56-31 (office). *Fax:* (2) 284-97-69 (office). *E-mail:* mschulz@europarl.eu.int (office); europabuero.schulz@spd.de (office). *Website:* www.martin-schulz.info (office).

SCHULZE, Ingo; German writer; *Director, Literary Section, Akademie der Künste, Berlin;* b. 15 Dec. 1962, Dresden; s. of Christa Schulze; m. Natalia Schulze; two d.; ed Univ. of Jena; Dramatic Producer, Theatre of Altenburg 1988–90; Founder of weekly newspaper in Altenburg 1990–92, weekly newspaper in St Petersburg 1993; writer in Berlin 1993–; mem. Akad. der Künste, Berlin (Dir Literary Section), Akad. für Deutsche Sprache und Dichtung, Darmstadt, Sächsische Akad., Dresden; Ernst Willner Prize 1995, Aspekte Literature Prize 1995, Berlin Literature Prize 1998, Johannes Bobrowski Medal 1998, Joseph Breitbach Prize 2001, Peter Weiss Prize 2006, Thuringia Literature Prize 2007, Leipzig Book Fair Prize 2007, Premio Grinzane Cavour 2008, Stadtschreiber Mainz 2011, Bertolt-Brecht Prize 2013, Int. Manhae Prize for Culture (S Korea) 2013. *Television:* Rettung aus dem Regenwald? – Die Wiederentdeckung der Terra Preta (documentary, with Christine Traber) (ZDF/3SAT) 2011. *Publications:* 33 Augenblicke des Glücks (Aspekte-Literatur Prize for best debut) 1995, Simple Storys: Ein Roman aus der ostdeutschen Provinz 1998, Von Nasen, Faxen und Ariadnefäden, Fax-Briefe (with Zeichnungen von Helmar Penndorf) 2000, Telling Tales (contrib. to charity anthology) 2004, Neue Leben (novel) 2005, Handy – 13 Geschichten in alter Manier (stories) 2007, Adam und Evelyn (novel) 2008, Der Herr Augustin (with Julia Penndorf), Tausend Geschichten sind nicht genug (essays), Was Wollen Wir? (essays) 2009, Orangen und Engel (with photos by Matthias Hoch) (stories) 2010, Unsere schönen neuen Kleider (essay) 2012, Henkerslos. Ein Märchenbrevier (stories/fairy tails written together with Christine Traber) 2013; contrib. to Granta 100 (anthology) 2010. *Address:* c/o Carl Hanser Verlag, Hanser Berlin, Friedrichstrasse 210, 10969 Berlin, Germany. *Telephone:* (30) 2529480-15. *Fax:* (30) 2529480-29. *E-mail:* thomas.rohde@hanser.de. *Website:* www.hanser-literaturverlage.de; www.ingoschulze.com.

SCHULZE, Richard (Dick) M.; American retail executive; b. St Paul, Minn.; m.; one d.; ed St Paul Cen. High School; tech. electronics training with USAF and Minn. Air Nat. Guard; began career as ind. mfrs rep. for consumer electronics brands 1960s; f. Sound of Music (stereo component retail stores chain) 1966, Chair. and Dir 1966–83; f. Best Buy Co. Inc. (consumer electronics retailer) 1983, mem. Bd Dirs, Chair. and CEO 1983–2002, Chair. 2002–12 (resgnd); mem. Minn. Business Partnership; mem. Bd Dirs Pentair Inc., The Nat. Entrepreneur of the Year Inst., Bd Overseers Carlson School of Man., Advisory Bd Science and Tech. Center; Trustee, Univ. of St Thomas, Chair. Exec. and Institutional Advancement Cttee; Chair. Bd of Govs Univ. of St Thomas Business School, Best Buy Children's Foundation 1994–; Hon. PhD (Univ. of St Thomas) 1998; Dealer's Pride Award, Dealerscope Merchandising 1997, Corp. Leader of the Year, Juvenile Diabetes Foundation 1999, America's Promise Red Wagon Award for Community Service 1999, Lifetime Achievement Award, Ernst & Young 1999, Outstanding Marketing Exec. of the Year, Minn. DECA 2000. *Address:* c/o Best Buy Company Inc., 7601 Penn Avenue South, Richfield, MN 55423, USA.

SCHUMACHER, Joel, BA; American film director and producer; b. 29 Aug. 1939, New York City; s. of Francis Schumacher and Marian Kantor; ed Parsons School of Design, New York; began to work in fashion industry aged 15; later opened own boutique Paraphenalia; costume designer for Revlon in 1970s; also set and production designer; wrote screenplays Sparkle, Car Wash, The Wiz; also wrote and directed for TV. *Films include:* The Incredible Shrinking Woman 1981, DC Cab (also screenplay) 1983 St Elmo's Fire (also screenplay) 1985, The Lost Boys 1987, Cousins 1989, Flatliners 1990, Dying Young 1991, Falling Down 1993, The Client 1994, Batman Forever 1995, A Time to Kill 1996, Batman and Robin 1997, Eight Millimeter 1999, Flawless (also screenplay and producer) 1999, Gossip (producer) 2000, Tigerland 2000 Phone Booth 2002, Bad Company 2002, Veronica Guerin 2003, The Phantom of the Opera 2004, The Number 23 2007, Town Creek 2009, Twelve 2010. *Address:* Joel Schumacher Productions, 400 Warner Boulevard, Burbank, CA 91522, USA (office).

SCHUMACHER, Michael; German motor racing driver; b. 3 Jan. 1969, Hürth-Hermülheim; s. of Rolf Schumacher and the late Elisabeth Schumacher; m. Corinna Betsch 1995; one d. one s.; began professional career 1983; 2nd place, Int. German Formula 3 Championship 1989; driver for Mercedes 1990; Int. German Champion, Formula 3 Championship 1990; European Formula 3 Champion 1990; World Champion, Formula 3, Macau and Fiji 1990; Formula 1 racing driver for the Jordan team 1991, Benetton team 1992–95, Ferrari team 1996–2006 (retd); ended retirement to sign for Mercedes GP team 2010–12 (retd); Grand Prix wins: Argentina 1998, Australia 2000, 2001, 2002, 2004, Austria 2002, 2003, Bahrain 2004, Belgium 1992, 1995, 1996, 1997, 2001, 2002, 2004, Brazil 1994, 1995, 2000, 2002, Britain 1998, 2002, 2004, Canada 1994, 1997, 1998, 2000, 2002, 2003, 2004, China 2006, Europe 1994, 1995, 2000, 2001, 2004, 2006, France 1994, 1995, 1997, 1998, 2001, 2002, 2004, 2006, Germany 1995, 2002, 2004, 2006, Hungary 1994, 1998, 2001, 2004, Italy 1996, 1998, 2000, 2003, 2006, Japan 1995, 1997, 2000, 2001, 2002, 2004, Malaysia 2000, 2001, 2004, Monaco 1994, 1995, 1997, 1999, 2001, Pacific 1994, 1995, Portugal 1993, San Marino 1994, 1999, 2000, 2002, 2003, 2004, 2006, Spain 1995, 1996, 2001, 2002, 2003, 2004, USA 2000, 2003, 2004, 2005, 2006; Formula One World Champion 1994, 1995, 2000, 2001, 2002, 2003, 2004 (record seven times). *Publications:* Schumacher: Driving Force 2003, Schumacher 2006, 7 91 2009. *Leisure interests:* football, skiing, motorbiking, climbing. *Address:* c/o Sabine Kehm, The MS Office, Avenue du Mont-Blanc 14B, 1196 Gland, Switzerland (office). *Telephone:* (22) 999-68-00 (office). *Fax:* (22) 999-68-09 (office). *Website:* www.michael-schumacher.de.

SCHUMANN, William H., III, BS, MS; American business executive; *Chairman, Avnet, Inc.;* ed Univ. of California, Los Angeles, Marshall School of Business, Univ. of Southern California; with Sunkist Growers, Inc. and Hughes Helicopter –1981; Dir of Pension Investments, FMC Corpn 1981, served in various man. positions throughout 1980s, including as Treas. 1987, Dir of North American Operations, Agricultural Products Group and Exec. Dir of Corp. Devt 1991–93, Vice-Pres. and Gen. Man. Agricultural Products Group 1995–98, Vice-Pres. of Corp. Devt 1998–99, Sr Vice-Pres. and Chief Financial Officer (CFO) 1999–2001 (until creation and spin-off of FMC Technologies), Exec. Vice-Pres. and CFO, FMC Technologies, Inc. 2001–11; mem. Bd of Dirs, Avnet, Inc. 2010–, Chair. 2012–; mem. Bd of Dirs AMCOL International, McDermott International; voted one of the top CFOs in oilfield service and equipment by sell side analysts 2010. *Address:*

Avnet, Inc., 2211 South 47th Street, Phoenix, AZ 85034, USA (office). *Telephone:* (480) 643-2000 (office). *E-mail:* info@avnet.com (office). *Website:* www.avnet.com (office).

SCHUMER, Charles (Chuck) Ellis, BA, JD; American politician; *Senator from New York;* b. 23 Nov. 1950, Brooklyn, NY; s. of Abraham Schumer and Selma Schumer (née Rosen); m. Iris Weinshall 1980; two d.; ed Madison High School, Harvard Coll. and Harvard Law School; called to the NY Bar 1975; mem. staff, US Senator Claiborne Pell 1973; Assoc. Paul, Weiss, Rifking, Wharton & Garrison (law firm) 1974; mem. New York State Ass. 1975–80, Chair. Sub-cttee on City Man. and Governance 1977, Cttee on Oversight and Investigation 1979; elected to US Senate 1998, Sr Senator from New York 2000–, Chair. Democratic Senatorial Campaign Cttee 2005–09, Cttee on Rules and Admin 2009–, mem. Banking, Housing, and Urban Affairs Cttee, Judiciary Cttee (Chair. Subcommittee on Immigration, Refugees, and Border Security), Finance Cttee, Jt Cttee on the Library; Chair. Democratic Policy and Communications Center 2010–; Vice-Chair. Democratic Conf. 2006–; Democrat. *Publication:* Positively American: Winning Back the Middle-Class Majority One Family at a Time (with Daniel Squadron) 2007. *Address:* 322 Hart Senate Office Building, Washington, DC 20510, USA (office). *Telephone:* (202) 224-6542 (office). *Fax:* (202) 228-3027 (office). *Website:* www.schumer.senate.gov (office).

SCHÜSSEL, Wolfgang, DJur; Austrian politician; b. 7 June 1945, Vienna; m.; two c.; ed Univ. of Vienna; Sec. Parl. Group, Austrian People's Party (ÖVP) 1968–75, Sec. Gen. Austrian Business Fed. 1975–91, Chair. ÖVP 1995–2007, Chair. Parl. Group 2006–08, Group Leader in Parl. 2007–11; mem. Parl. 1979–2011 (retd); Minister of Econ. Affairs 1989–95; Vice-Chancellor of Austria and Minister of Foreign Affairs 1995–2000; Pres. EU Council of Gen. and Foreign Affairs July-Dec. 1998; Chancellor of Austria 2000–07; Pres. EU July–Dec. 2006; Minister of the Interior Jan. 2007; mem. Bd of Trustees, Bartelsmann Foundation 2007–; Hon. Citizen, Tirana, Albania; Grand Cross of the Royal Order of Merit (Norway) 1996, Grand Cross with Diamonds of the Order of Merit (Liechtenstein) 2001, Grand Cross of the Order of the Star (Romania) 2004, Grand Cross of Order of Merit (Poland) 2006, Grand Cross of Merit (Hungary) 2006, Bavarian Order of Merit 2007; Medal of Baden-Württemberg 2007. *Publications:* several books on issues relating to democracy and economics. *Address:* Austrian People's Party (ÖVP), Lichtenfelsgasse 7, 1010 Vienna, Austria (office). *Telephone:* (1) 401-26-0 (office). *Fax:* (1) 401-26-109 (office). *E-mail:* mail@oevp.at (office). *Website:* www.oevp.at (office).

SCHUSTER, Rudolf, PhD; Slovak politician, diplomatist, writer and engineer; b. 4 Jan. 1934, Košice; s. of Alojz Schuster and Mária Benediková; m. Irene Trojáková (deceased 2008); one s. one d.; ed Slovak Tech. Univ., Bratislava, Tech. Univ. Košice; designer, Regional Agric. Inst., Bratislava 1960; Asst Hydrology and Hydraulic Inst., Slovak Acad. of Sciences 1960–62; Dir Energy Investment Dept and Tech. Dir E Slovak Steelworks 1963–74; Vice-Mayor of Košice 1975–83, Mayor 1983–86, 1994–99, Chair. E Slovak Region Nat. Cttee 1986–89; Chair. Nat. Council 1989–90; Amb. of Czech Repub. and Slovakia to Canada 1990–92; with Ministry of Foreign Affairs 1993–94; Mayor of Košice 1994–99; Pres. of Slovakia 1999–2004; Hon. Citizen, Miskolc 1999; Order of Labour 1988, Pribina Cross, First Class 1998, Grand Cross of Merit with Collar (Malta) 1999, Grand Gross (Greece) 2000, Grand Star (Romania) 2000, Pour le Merite, First Class (Lebanon) 2001, Decoration Jose San Martin (Argentine) 2001, Cross Kenedy (Argentine) 2001, Decoration of Merit with Chain (Chile) 2001, Grand Chain of the Southern Cross (Brasil) 2001, Grand Decoration of the King Tomislav with Ribbon and Star (Croatia) 2001, Grand Cross of Merit (Germany) 2001, Decoration Seraphine (Sweden) 2002, White Eagle, First Class (Poland) 2002, Decoration Isabel La Catolica (Spain) 2002, Knight of the Grand Cross with Grand Gibbon (Italy) 2002, Knight Decoration with Chain (The Holy See) 2002, Golden Lion (Luxembourg) 2002, Golden Lion (Netherlands) 2002, Grand Chain, Prince Don Henrique (Portugal), Golden Honest Insignia of Freedom (Slovenia) 2003, Grand Cross of Merit with Chain (Hungary) 2003, Grand Honest Star Decoration of Merit (Austria) 2004, Decoration Prince Jaroslav the Sage First Class (Ukraine) 2004; Dr hc (Tech. Univ. Košice) 1998, (Wuppertal) 1999, (Moscow) 2001, (Kraków) 2002, (Bratislava) 2002, (St Petersburg) 2002, (Sofia) 2002, (Kiev) 2002, (Ottawa) 2002, (Ostrava) 2003, and four others; Merit Award for Peace and Democratic Achievement 2000 and numerous other decorations. *Achievements:* open-air performance of Bocatius, eight broadcast performances and 21 literary sessions. *Publications:* Ultimatum (memoirs, translated into eight languages) 1997, more than 40 books (travel, crime fiction and detective novels, memoirs); numerous screenplays. *Leisure interests:* documentaries, literature, collecting historical photocameras, film-cameras and cine-projectors.

SCHÜTZEICHEL, Rudolf, DPhil; German professor of philology; b. 20 May 1927, Rahms; s. of Matthias Schützeichel and Gertrud Schützeichel; m. Margrit Britten 1955; two d.; ed Univ. of Mainz; Docent Univ. of Cologne 1960–63; Prof. of German Philology, Univ. of Groningen 1963–64, Univ. of Bonn 1964–69, Univ. of Münster 1969–; mem. Akad. Wissenschaften, Göttingen, Kgl. Akad., Göteborg; Hon. DPhil (Leipzig) 1992; Festschrift 1987 (Althochdeutsch 2 Bände Heidelberg); Officer Order of Orange-Nassau. *Publications:* Mundart, Urkundensprache und Schriftsprache 1974, Grundlagen d.w. Mitteldeutsch 1976, Das alem. Memento Mori 1967, Codex. Pal. lat. 52 1982, Mittelrh. Passionsspiel 1978, Gottschald Namenkunde 1982, Addenda und Corrigenda (I) 1982, (II) 1985, (III) 1991, Textgebundenheit 1981, Althochdeutsch. Wörterb. (7th Edn) 2012; Ed. various publs including BNF.NF. 1966–, Sprachwissenschaft 1976–, NOWELE 1983–, Die älteste Überlieferung von Williams Kommentar des Hohen Liedes 2001, Bahuvrihi und Derivation im Althochdeutschen 2001, Althochdeutsche und Altsächsischer Glossenwortschatz I–XII 2004. *Address:* Potstiege 16, 48161 Münster, Germany. *Telephone:* (251) 861345.

SCHUWIRTH, Lt.-Gen. Klaus; German army officer; Commdr of German army's 4th Corps in Potsdam; apptd Dir of Mil. Staff, EU Rapid Reaction Force 2001. *Address:* c/o Ministry of Defence, Stauffenbergstr. 18, 10785 Berlin, Germany.

SCHUWIRTH, Gen. (retd) Rainer; German army officer; b. 12 July 1945, Regensburg, Bavaria; m. Barbara Hackbarth; one s., one d.; enlisted into Fed. Armed Forces 1964; trained as Artillery Officer 1964–66; assignments as Artillery Officer and Honest John Battery Commdr 1966–76; Fed. Armed Forces Command

and Staff Coll., Hamburg 1976–78; G2 Staff Officer (Intelligence Estimates), HQ Centag, Heidelberg 1978–81; G3 Staff Officer (Operations) at III Corps, Koblenz 1981–83; Commdr Missile Artillery Bn 150 (Lance), Wesel 1983–85; Asst Br. Chief, Mil. Leadership and Civic Educ., Armed Forces Staff, Fed. Ministry of Defence, Bonn 1985–88, Br. Chief of Mil. Policy 1990–91; Mil. Asst to Fed. Minister of Defence 1988–90; Commdr Armoured Brigade 8, Luneberg 1991–93; Head of Mil. Policy Div., Perm. Mission to NATO 1994–96; Asst Chief of Staff, Armed Forces Staff Politico-Mil. Affairs and Operations, Ministry of Defence 1996–99; Commdg Gen. IV Corps, Potsdam 1999–2001; Dir-Gen., EU Mil. Staff 2001–04; Chief of Staff, SHAPE 2004–07 (retd); contracted by European Defence Agency to produce draft concept for EU to exploit Network Enabled Capabilities (NEC) in support of crisis-man. operations 2007; work with Stiftung Wissenschaft und Politik, Berlin 2008–; Silver Cross of Honour, Fed. Armed Forces, Gold Cross of Honour, Fed. Armed Forces, Cross of Order of Merit, Cross of Order of Merit (First Class), Commdr de l'Ordre nat. de Mérite, Gold Medal, Polish Armed Forces. *Address:* Stiftung Wissenschaft und Politik, German Institute for International and Security Affairs, Ludwigkirchplatz 3-4, 10719 Berlin, Germany (office). *Telephone:* (30) 880070 (office). *Fax:* (30) 88007100 (office). *E-mail:* swp@swp-berlin.org (office). *Website:* www.swp-berlin.org (office).

SCHWAB, Charles R., BA (Econs), MBA; American business executive; *Chairman, Charles Schwab Corporation;* b. 29 July 1937, Sacramento, Calif.; m. Helen O'Neill; five c.; ed Stanford Univ., Stanford Grad. School of Business; f. Charles Schwab Corpn, San Francisco 1971, Chair. 1986–, CEO 1986–97, 2004–08, Co-CEO 1998–2003; Chair. Parent's Educational Resource Center, San Mateo; currently Chair. San Francisco Museum of Modern Art; Chair. President's Advisory Council on Financial Literacy 2008–; mem. Bd The Gap Inc., Transamerica Corpn, AirTouch Communications, Siebel Systems, Inc.; mem. World Business Forum, CEO Org., San Francisco CEO Cttee on Jobs; mem. Bd and Treas. Nat. Park Foundation; mem. Bd of Trustees, Stanford Univ.; co-founder Charles and Helen Schwab Foundation 1987, currently Chair.; mem. San Francisco Golf Club. *Publication:* How To Be Your Own Stockbroker 1984, Charles Schwab's Guide to Financial Independence 1998, It Pays To Talk (co-author), You're Fifty — Now What?. *Leisure interests:* golf. *Address:* Charles Schwab Corporation, 211 Main Street, San Francisco, CA 94105 (office); Charles and Helen Schwab Foundation, 530 Lytton Avenue, Suite 200, Palo Alto, CA 94301, USA (office). *Telephone:* (415) 667-7000 (office). *Website:* www.schwab.com (office).

SCHWAB, Klaus, DEcon, DrIng, MPA; German foundation director and academic; *Executive Chairman, World Economic Forum;* b. 30 March 1938, Ravensburg; m. Hilde Schwab; one s. one d.; ed Swiss Federal Inst. of Tech., Univ. of Fribourg, Harvard Univ.; Founder and Exec. Chair. World Econ. Forum 1971–; Prof. of Business Policy, Univ. of Geneva 1972–2002; fmr mem. UN High-Level Advisory Bd on Sustainable Devt; fmr Vice-Chair. UN Cttee for Devt Planning; fmr mem. Earth Council; co-f. The Schwab Foundation for Social Entrepreneurship 1998; f. The Forum of Young Global Leaders 2004; Trustee, Peres Center for Peace, Israel; Hon. Prof., Ben Gurion Univ., Israel; Hon. KCMG, Grosses Goldenes Ehrenzeichen für Verdienste um die Republik Österreich 1997, Grosses Verdienstkreuz mit Stern 2012; 11 hon. doctorates, including from Bishops Univ., Quebec, Canada, Univ. Autonoma de Guadalajara, Mexico, LSE, UK, Nankai Univ., Tianjin, People's Repub. of China, Vietnam Nat. Univ.; The Candlelight Award Foundation for Prevention and Early Resolution of Conflict 2001, ranked 66th by Forbes magazine amongst The World's Most Powerful People 2009. *Publications:* several books and The Global Competitiveness Report (annually 1979–). *Leisure interests:* cross-country ski marathons, mountain climbing. *Address:* World Economic Forum, 91–93 route de la Capite, 1223 Cologny/Geneva, Switzerland (office). *Telephone:* (22) 869-1212 (office). *Fax:* (22) 786-2744 (office). *E-mail:* chairman@weforum.org (office). *Website:* www.weforum.org (office).

SCHWAB, Susan Carroll, PhD; American academic administrator and fmr government official; *Strategic Advisor, Mayer Brown LLP;* m. Curtis Carroll (died 2006); ed Williams Coll., Stanford Univ., George Washington Univ.; agricultural trade negotiator, Office of US Trade Rep. 1977–79; Trade Policy Officer, US Foreign Service, Embassy in Tokyo 1979–81; Chief Econ. and Legis. Asst, Office of US Senator John C. Danforth 1981–86, Legis. Dir 1986–89; Asst US Sec. of Commerce and Dir Gen., US and Foreign Commercial Service, US Dept of Commerce, Washington, DC 1989–93; Dir of Corp. Business Devt, Motorola Inc. 1993–95; Dean, School of Public Affairs, Univ. of Md 1995–2003, Pres. and CEO Univ. of Md Foundation 2004–05, Prof., School of Public Policy 2009–; Deputy US Trade Rep., Washington, DC 2005–06, US Trade Rep. 2006–09; Strategic Advisor, Mayer Brown LLP (global law firm) 2010–; mem. Bd of Dirs Caterpillar Inc. 2009–, FedEx Corpn 2009–, Boeing 2010–, Signature Theatre; mem. Bd of Advisors, Miller Buckfire; mem. Council on Foreign Relations, Aspen Strategy Group; Fellow, Nat. Acad. of Public Admin; Trustee, The Conference Board. *Publications:* Trade-Offs: Negotiating the Omnibus Trade Act 1994; numerous articles in magazines and journals. *Address:* Mayer Brown LLP, 1999 K Street, NW, Washington, DC 20006-1101 (office); School of Public Policy, University of Maryland, 4105 Van Munching Hall, College Park, MD 20742, USA. *Telephone:* (202) 2630-3331 (Mayer Brown) (office); (301) 405-6347. *Fax:* (202) 263-3300 (Mayer Brown) (office). *E-mail:* sschwab@mayerbrown.com (office); sschwab@umd .edu. *Website:* www.mayerbrown.com (office); www.publicpolicy.umd.edu.

SCHWAN, Gesine Marianne, Dr rer. pol; German political scientist, professor of political science and university administrator; *President, Humboldt-Viadrina School of Governance;* b. 22 May 1943, Berlin; d. of Hildegard Schneider (née Olejak) and Hans R. Schneider; m. 1st Alexander Schwan 1969 (died 1989); m. 2nd Peter Eigen 2004; one s. one d.; ed Lycée Français de Berlin, Free Univ. of Berlin; Asst Prof., Dept of Political Sciences, Free Univ. of Berlin 1971–77, Prof. 1977–; Fellow, Woodrow Wilson Int. Center for Scholars 1980–81; apptd By-Fellow, Robinson Coll., Cambridge, UK 1984; Chair. German Asscn for Political Science 1985–87, Bd mem. 1994–2000; Dean, Otto-Suhr Inst. 1992–95; Pres. Europa-Univ. Viadrina 1999–2008; unsuccessful candidate for Pres. of Germany 2004, 2008; Chair. Scientific Advisory Bd, Centre Marc Bloch in Berlin 2001–; Co-Chair. German-Polish Forum 2002–09; Co-ordinator for civil social cooperation near to Repub. of Poland 2005–09; co-founder, Pres. Humboldt-Viadrina School of Governance 2010–; mem. of Senate, Max Planck Soc. 2005–; mem. Scientific

Advisory Bd, Centre d'études et de recherche Interdisciplinary sur l'Allemagne 2006–; mem. Académie de Berlin 2006–; mem. Bd of Trustees, German Inst. of Poland, Theodor-Heuss-Stiftung 1994–, Haniel Foundation 2006–, Stone Award, Alfred Töpfer Foundation 2007–, Science Center Berlin 2008–; Fed. Cross of Merits 1993, Verdienstkreuz (1st class) 2002; Dr hc (European Univ. Inst., Florence) 2006, Golden Badge of Honour, Bridge Foundation Award 2010; Urania Medal 1999, Marion Dönhoff Award 2004, Asscn of Berlin Foreign Press Award 2004, Pauline Staegemann Award 2004, Women in Europe Award, Network European Movt Germany 2005, Tolerance Award, Tolerance Ecumenical Foundation 2005. *Publications include:* Leszek Kolakowski, Eine Philosophie der Freiheit nach Marx 1971, Die Gesellschaftskritik von Karl Marx 1974, Sozialdemokratie u. Marxismus (with Alexander Schwan) 1974, Sozialismus in der Demokratie; Eine Theorie Konsequent sozialdemokratischen Politik 1982, Der normative Horizont moderner Politik I und II (with Alexander Schwan) 1985, Politik und Schuld: Die zerstörerische Macht des Schweigens 1997; Jahrbuch für Politik (co-ed.) 1991–. *Leisure interests:* music, theatre, travelling. *Address:* Humboldt-Viadrina School of Governance, Wilhelmstraße 67, 10117 Berlin (office); Teutonenstrasse 6, 14129 Berlin, Germany (home). *Telephone:* (30) 200597123 (office); (30) 8038366 (home). *Fax:* (30) 200597111 (office). *Website:* www.humboldt-viadrina.org (office).

SCHWAN, Severin, Mag.rer.soc.oec., MagIur, DrIur; Austrian pharmaceuticals industry executive; *CEO, Roche Group;* b. 1967; m.; three c.; ed Univ. of Innsbruck, Univs of York and Oxford, UK, Univ. of Louvain, Belgium; trainee, Corp. Finance, Roche, Basel 1993–95, Head of Finance and Admin, Roche, Brussels 1995–98, Head of Finance and Informatics, Roche, Grenzach, Germany and mem. Exec. Bd Roche Deutschland Holding GmbH 1998–2000, Head of Global Finance and Services, Roche Diagnostics, Basel 2000–04, Head of Asia Pacific Region, Roche Diagnostics, Singapore 2004–06, CEO Roche Diagnostics Div. 2006–08, CEO Roche Group 2008–, mem. Bd of Dirs Roche Holding Ltd 2013–; mem. Int. Business Leaders Advisory Council for the Mayor of Shanghai 2009–, European Round Table of Industrialists 2013–. *Address:* Roche Holding Ltd, Grenzacherstrasse 124, 4070 Basel, Switzerland (office). *Telephone:* (61) 688-11-11 (office). *Fax:* (61) 691-93-91 (office). *E-mail:* info@roche.com (office). *Website:* www.roche.com (office).

SCHWARTZ, Gerald W., OC, BCom, LLB, MBA; Canadian financial services industry executive; *Chairman, President and CEO, Onex Corporation;* b. Toronto, Ont.; ed Univ. of Manitoba, Harvard Univ. Grad. School of Business Admin; fmr specialist in mergers and acquisitions, investment banking firm, New York; Co-founder and Pres. CanWest Capital (renamed CanWest Global Communications) –1983; f. Onex Corpn 1983, Chair., Pres. and CEO 1983–; mem. Bd of Dirs Indigo Books and Music Inc., Canadian Council of Christians and Jews; mem. Cttee of Univ. Resources, Harvard Univ. Bd of Overseers, Business School, Canadian Council of Christians and Jews; Vice-Chair. and mem. Exec. Cttee, Mount Sinai Hosp.; Gov. Jr Achievement of Metro Toronto; Trustee, The Simon Wiesenthal Center; Hon. Dir Bank of Nova Scotia; Hon. LLD (St Francis Xavier Univ.), Hon. DPhil (Tel-Aviv Univ.); inducted into Canadian Business Hall of Fame. *Address:* Onex Corpn, 161 Bay Street, PO Box 700, Toronto, ON M5J 2S1, Canada (office). *Telephone:* (416) 362-7711 (office). *Fax:* (416) 362-5765 (office). *E-mail:* info@onex .com (office). *Website:* www.onex.com (office).

SCHWARTZ, Jonathan Ian; American computer industry executive; *CEO, Picture of Health;* b. 20 Oct. 1965; ed Wesleyan Univ.; early career at McKinsey & Co., New York 1987–89; Co-founder and CEO Lighthouse Design –1996, joined Sun Microsystems Inc. 1996 after Sun's acquisition of Lighthouse, held several sr positions including Vice-Pres., Venture Fund, Vice-Pres., Developer Products, Vice-Pres., Enterprise Software, Dir of Product Marketing, Javasoft, Sr Vice-Pres. of Corp. Strategy and Planning –2002, Exec. Vice-Pres. for Software 2002–04, Pres. and COO 2004–06, Pres. and CEO 2006–10; f. Picture of Health 2010, currently CEO; mem. Bd of Dirs Taleo Corpn 2010–. *leisure interests:* golf, ice hockey. *Address:* c/o Board of Directors, Taleo Corporation, 4140 Dublin Boulevard, Suite 400, Dublin, CA 94568, USA. *E-mail:* jis@pictureofhealth.com (office). *Website:* www.pictureofhealth.com (office).

SCHWARTZ, Maxime; French writer and scientist (retd); b. 1 June 1940, Blois; ed Ecole Polytechnique; entered Inst. Pasteur 1963, Head of Lab. 1973–84, mem. Scientific Council 1973–85, Head of Dept of Molecular Biology 1984–85, Deputy Dir 1985–87, Dir-Gen. 1988–99; Dir Dept Lab. Programming, l'Agence Française de Sécurité Sanitaire des aliments (AFSSA) –2007. *Publications include:* How the Cows Turned Mad 2001, Microbes or Man, Who Will Win? (in French) 2008. *Address:* L'Institut Pasteur, 25–28 rue du Dr. Roux, 75015 Paris, France (office).

SCHWARTZENBERG, Roger-Gérard, DenD; French politician and professor of law; b. 17 April 1943, Pau, Pyrénées-Atlantiques; s. of André Schwartzenberg and Simone Gutelman; ed Inst. d'Etudes Politiques, Paris; Prof., Univ. de Droit, d'Economie et de Sciences Sociales de Paris II 1969–, Inst. d'Etudes Politiques 1972–83; Pres., Mouvement des Radicaux de Gauche 1981–83, Hon. Pres. 1983–; mem. European Parl. 1979–83; Sec. of State, Ministry of Educ. 1983–84; Sec. of State responsible for univs, Ministry of Educ. 1984–86; Deputy to Nat. Ass. for Val de Marne 1986–2000, 2002–07; Sec. to Nat. Ass. 1988–92, 1993–97, Vice-Pres. Foreign Affairs Comm. 1992–2000; Mayor of Villeneuve-Saint-Georges 1989–95, 2001–08; Deputy Judge, High Court of Justice and Court of Justice of the Repub. 1993–97; Pres., Groupe parlementaire radical, citoyen et vert 1999–2000; Minister of Research 2000–02; Chevalier, Légion d'honneur 2009, Grand Officer, Order of Merit (Germany), Grand Decoration of Honour (Austria). *Publications:* books on political and legal topics including La Campagne présidentielle de 1965 1967, L'Autorité de la chose décidée ou la Force juridique des décisions administratives 1969, La Guerre de succession ou les élections présidentielles de 1969 1969, Traité de sociologie politique 1971, L'Etat spectacle, Essai sur et contre le star-system en politique 1977, La Droite absolue 1981, La Politique mensonge 1998, 1788: Essai sur la maldémocratie 2006, L'Etat spectacle 2 2009. *Leisure interest:* tennis. *Address:* Université de Droit de Paris, 12 Place du Panthéon, 75005 Paris, France (office).

SCHWARZ, Antoine, LenD; French administrator and business executive; b. 9 Aug. 1943, Paris; s. of Willy Schwarz and Elisabeth du Brusle de Rouvroy; m. Christine Coudreau 1974; two s. one d.; ed Inst. d'Etudes Politiques de Paris, Ecole Nat. d'Admin; Admin. to the Treasury, Ministry of the Economy and Finance 1971–74; Prin. Inst. d'Etudes Politiques 1972–74; Head Service Juridique et

Technique de l'Information 1974; Head of Cabinet André Rossi 1975–76, Raymond Barre 1977; Dir Radio Monte-Carlo 1978–81, Editions Mondiales 1982–83; Counsellor Centre Nat. de la Cinématographie 1984–85; Pres. and Dir-Gen. Soc. Financière de Radiodiffusion (SOFIRAD) 1986–89; Pres. Sofica-valor 1988–89, Consultant 1990; Founder-Pres. Radiofina 1993; Pres. SFP-Productions 1994–99, Sportotal 2000–; CEO Radio France Internationale 2004–08; Chevalier, Ordre nat. du Mérite, Chevalier, Ordre de la Légion d'honneur. *Address:* Sportotal, 51 rue d'Amsterdam, 75008 Paris (office); 20 place de la Motte-Piquet, 75015 Paris, France (home).

SCHWARZ, Gerard; American conductor; *Music Director, Seattle Symphony Orchestra;* b. 19 Aug. 1947, Weehawken, NJ; m. Jody Greitzer 1984; two s. two d.; ed Professional Children's School, Juilliard School; joined American Brass Quintet 1965; Music Dir Erick Hawkins Dance Co. 1966, Eliot Feld Dance Co. 1972; Co-Prin. Trumpet, New York Philharmonic 1973–74; Founding Music Dir Waterloo Festival 1975; Music Dir New York Chamber Symphony 1977–2002, LA Chamber Orchestra 1978–86; est. Music Today series, Merkin Concert Hall, New York 1981 (Music Dir 1988–89); Music Adviser Mostly Mozart Festival, Lincoln Center, New York 1982–84, Music Dir 1984–, Music Adviser Seattle Symphony 1983–84, Prin. Conductor 1984–85, Music Dir 1985–(2011); Artistic Adviser Tokyu Bunkamura's Orchard Hall, Japan 1994–; Music Dir Royal Liverpool Philharmonic Orchestra 2001–06; Guest Conductor, Cosmopolitan Symphony, Aspen Festival Chamber, Tokyo Philharmonic, Residentie, The Hague, St Louis Symphony, Kirov, St Petersburg, Royal Liverpool Philharmonic and Vancouver Symphony Orchestras, City of London Symphonia and London Mozart Players; has conducted many US orchestras and Hong Kong Philharmonic, Jerusalem Symphony, Israeli Chamber and English Chamber Orchestras, London Symphony, Helsinki Philharmonic and Monte Carlo Philharmonic Orchestras, Ensemble Contemporain, Paris and Nat. Orchestra of Spain; operatic conducting debut, Washington Opera 1982; has also conducted Seattle Opera 1986, San Francisco Opera 1991 and New Japan Philharmonic 1998; numerous recordings for Delos, Nonesuch, Angel and RCA labels; numerous TV appearances; Hon. Fellow (John Moores Univ., Liverpool) 2001; Hon. DFA (Fairleigh Dickinson Univ., Seattle Univ.); Hon. DMus (Univ. of Puget Sound); named Conductor of the Year by Musical America Int. Directory of the Performing Arts 1994, Ditson Conductor's Award, Columbia Univ. 1989, two Record of the Year Awards, one Mumms Ovation Award. *Address:* Columbia Artists Management Inc., 1790 Broadway, New York, NY 10019-1412, USA (office); Seattle Symphony Orchestra, PO Box 21906, Seattle, WA 98111-3669, USA (office). *Telephone:* (212) 841-9500 (office). (206) 215-4700 (office). *Fax:* (212) 841-9744 (office). (206) 215-4701 (office). *E-mail:* info@cami.com (office); info@ seattlesymphony.org (office). *Website:* www.cami.com (office); www .seattlesymphony.org (office).

SCHWARZ-SCHILLING, Christian, DPhil; German politician, consultant and fmr UN official; *President, Dr. Schwarz-Schilling and Partner GmbH;* b. 19 Nov. 1930, Innsbruck, Austria; s. of Rheinhard Schwarz-Schilling and Duzsa Schwarz-Schilling; m. Marie Luise Jonen 1957; two d.; ed Univs of Berlin and Munich; mem. Landtag, Hesse, FRG 1966–76; Sec.-Gen. Hesse CDU 1966–80, Deputy Chair. 1967–96; Chair. Coordinating Cttee for Media Policy CDU/CSU 1975–83; mem. Bundestag 1976–2002; Minister of Posts and Telecommunications 1982–92; Deputy Chair. CDU/CSU Fed. Medium and Small Business Asscn 1977–97; Pres. Exec. Cttee European Medium and Small Business Union 1979–82; Chair. Inquiries Cttee Bundestag New Information and Communication Technologies 1981–82; Chair. Bundestag Subcttee on Human Rights and Humanitarian Aid 1995–98, Deputy Chair. 1998; Int. Mediator-Arbitrator for Fed. of Bosnia and Herzegovina 1996–98, also for Repub. Srpska 1997; Pres. Dr. Schwarz-Schilling and Pnr GmbH 1993–; Chair. Bd Prima Com AG, Mainz, 1999–, Mox Telecom AG Ratingen 1999–; High Rep. UN Mission in Bosnia and Herzegovina 2006–07; Hon. Citizen of Büdingen 2004; Grosses Bundesverdienstkreuz mit Stern; Hon. DUniv (Bryant Coll., USA) 1997; Achievement Cross with Star of the Order of Achievement (Germany) 1992, Manfred Wörner Medal 2005, Hessian Peace Prize 2007. *Publication:* Unsere Geschichte Schicksal oder Zufall, Lansfristig Sichere Rente. *Leisure interests:* swimming, skiing, piano. *Address:* Dr. Schwarz-Schilling and Partner GmbH, Industriestrasse 35, 63654 Büdingen (office); Am Dohlberg 10, 63654 Büdingen, Germany (home). *Telephone:* (6042) 96440 (office). *Fax:* (6042) 964432 (office). *E-mail:* css@schwarz-schilling.de (office). *Website:* www.schwarz -schilling.de (office).

SCHWARZENBERG, Prince of Schwarzenberg, Count of Sulz, Princely Land-grave in Klettgau, and Duke of Krumlov; **Karel;** Czech/Swiss politician; *Chairman, Tradition Responsibility Prosperity 09 (TOP 09) party;* b. (Karl Johannes Nepomuk Josef Norbert Friedrich Antonius Wratislaw Menas von Schwarzen-berg), 10 Dec. 1937, Prague, Czechoslovakia; s. of Prince Karl VI of Schwarzenberg of the minor line and Princess Antonie von Fürstenberg; m. Therese von Hardegg 1967 (divorced 1988, re-married 2008); two s. one d.; ed Univs of Vienna and Graz, Austria, Univ. of Munich, Germany; family exiled to Austria after Communist takeover of Czechoslovakia 1948; Pres. Int. Helsinki Cttee for Human Rights (concerned with human rights issues in fmr USSR, Bulgaria, fmr Yugoslavia (Kosovo) and Czechoslovakia) 1984–91; est. Czechoslovak Documentation Centre (archive of prohibited literature) with Dr Vilém Prečan in Bavaria, Germany 1985; returned to Czechoslovakia 1990; Chancellor, Office of the Pres. 1990–92; Head of first OSCE del. to Nagorno Karabakh, Azerbaijan 1992; mem. Senate (Civic Democratic Alliance, ODA) 2004–08; mem. Poslanecká sněmovna (TOP 09) 2010; Chair. Foreign Affairs, Defence and Security Cttee 2005–07, Alt. mem. Perm. Del. of Parl. to Parl. Ass. of Council of Europe 2005; mem. Perm. Czech del. to Parl. Ass., NATO 2006; mem. Caucus of Open Democracy 2006–07; Minister of Foreign Affairs 2007–09, 2010–13; Deputy Prime Minister 2010–13; Chair. Tradition Responsibility Prosperity 09 (Tradice Odpovědnost Prosperita 09, TOP 09) party 2009–, mem. Poslanecká sněmovna (TOP 09) 2013, Chair. Foreign Affairs Cttee 2013–; unsuccessful cand. in presidential election 2013; mem. Bd of Dirs Forum 2000 2005–07; Kt, Order of the Golden Fleece (Austrian br.) 1991, Order of Tomáš garrigue Masaryk (Third Class) 2002, Decoration for Services to the Repub. of Austria in Silver with Sash 2005, Grand Cross of the Fed. Cross of Merit (Germany) 2008; Prize for Human Rights, Council of Europe (with Lech Wałęsa) 1989. *Address:* Tradition Responsibility Prosperity 09 (TOP 09), Michnův palác, budova č. 2, Ujezd 450/40, Malá Strana, 118 00 Prague 1, Czech Republic (office).

Telephone: 255790999 (office). *Fax:* 255790899 (office). *E-mail:* info@top09.cz (office). *Website:* www.top09.cz (office); www.karelschwarzenberg.cz.

SCHWARZENEGGER, Arnold Alois, BA; American (b. Austrian) actor, business executive, fmr politician and fmr bodybuilder; b. 30 July 1947, Thal, nr Graz, Austria; s. of Gustav Schwarzenegger and Aurelia Schwarzenegger (née Jadrny); m. Maria Owings Shriver 1985 (divorced 2011); two s. two d. and one s. with Mildred Baena; ed Santa Monica Coll., Univ. of Wisconsin-Superior; went to USA 1968, naturalized 1983; Nat. Weight Training Coach Special Olympics, later Global Amb.; Bodybuilding Champion 1965–80; volunteer, prison rehabilitation programmes; Chair. Pres.'s Council on Physical Fitness and Sport 1990; Nat. Chair. Nat. Inner-City Games Foundation; elected Gov. of Calif. (after recall of Gov. Gray Davis) 2003–11; Governor Downey Prof. of State and Global Policy, Schwarzenegger Inst. for State and Global Policy, Univ. of Southern California 2012–; Republican; First Prize, Styrian Jr Weightlifting Championships 1964, First Prize, German Austrian Weightlifting Championships 1965, Jr Mr Europe 1965, Best Built Man of Europe 1966, Mr Europe 1966, First Prize, Int. Powerlifting Championships 1966, Mr International 1968, Mr Universe (amateur) 1967, Mr Universe (professional) 1968, 1969, 1970, First Prize, German Power-lifting Championships 1968, Mr Olympia 1970–75, 1980, Nat. Theater Owners' Int. Star of the Decade, 1993, Simon Wiesenthal Center Nat. Leadership Award, ShoWest Humanitarian of the Year Award 1997, Boys and Girls Town Father Flanagan Service to Youth Award 2000, American Film Marketing Association (AFMA) World Wide Box Office Champ 2002, Muhammad Ali Humanitarian Award 2002, and numerous other prizes. *Film appearances include:* Stay Hungry 1976 (Golden Globe Award), Pumping Iron 1977, The Jayne Mansfield Story 1980, Conan the Barbarian 1982, Conan The Destroyer 1984, The Terminator 1984, Commando 1985, Raw Deal 1986, Predator 1987, Running Man 1987, Red Heat 1988, Twins 1989, Total Recall 1990, Kindergarten Cop 1990, Terminator II: Judgment Day 1991, Last Action Hero 1993, Dave (cameo) 1993, True Lies 1994, Junior 1994, Eraser 1996, Jingle All the Way 1996, Batman and Robin 1997, End of Days 1999, The Sixth Day 2000, Collateral Damage 2002, Terminator 3: Rise of the Machines 2003, Around the World in 80 Days 2004, The Expendables (uncredited) 2010, The Expendables 2 2012. *Publications:* Arnold: The Education of a Bodybuilder 1977, Arnold's Bodyshaping for Women 1979, Arnold's Bodybuilding for Men 1981, Arnold's Encyclopedia of Modern Bodybuilding 1985, Arnold's Fitness for Kids (co-author) 1993, Total Recall: My Unbelievably True Life Story (autobiog.) 2012. *Address:* Sol Price School of Public Policy, University of Southern California, Lewis Hall 312, Los Angeles, CA 90089-0626, USA.

SCHWARZMAN, Stephen A., BA, MBA; American investment banker; *Chairman and CEO, The Blackstone Group;* b. 14 Feb. 1947, Philadelphia; m. Christine Hearst; three c. from previous marriages; ed Yale Univ., Harvard Business School; began career in Mergers and Acquisitions (M&A) at Lehman Brothers 1977–84, at age 31, elected Man. Dir 1978–84, Chair. M&A Cttee 1981–84; Co-founder, Chair. CEO The Blackstone Group 1985–; Chair. Bd John F. Kennedy Center for the Performing Arts, Washington, DC 2004–10; mem. Council on Foreign Relations; mem. Bd New York City Ballet, New York Public Library, Film Soc. of Lincoln Center, Harvard Business School Visiting Cttee, JPMorgan Chase Nat. Advisory Bd, New York City Partnership Bd of Dirs; Trustee Frick Collection. *Address:* The Blackstone Group, 345 Park Avenue, New York, NY 10154, USA (office). *Telephone:* (212) 583-5000 (office). *Fax:* (212) 583-5712 (office). *Website:* www .blackstone.com (office).

SCHWEBEL, Stephen Myron, BA, LLB; American judge, lawyer, arbitrator and mediator; *President of the Administrative Tribunal, World Bank;* b. 10 March 1929, New York, NY; s. of Victor Schwebel and Pauline Pfeffer Schwebel; m. Louise I. N. Killander 1972; two d.; ed Harvard Coll., Univ. of Cambridge, UK, Yale Law School; attorney 1954–57; Asst Prof. of Law, Harvard Univ. 1959–61; Asst Legal Adviser, then Special Asst to Asst Sec. of State for Int. Org. Affairs 1961–67; Exec. Vice-Pres. and Exec. Dir American Soc. of Int. Law 1967–73; Consultant, then Counsellor on Int. Law, Dept of State 1967–74, Deputy Legal Adviser 1974–81; Prof. of Int. Law, then Edward B. Burling Prof. of Int. Law and Org., Johns Hopkins Univ., Washington, DC 1967–81; Legal Adviser to US Del. and Alt. Rep. in 6th Cttee, UN Gen. Ass. 1961–65; Visiting Lecturer or Prof., Univ. of Cambridge 1957, 1983, ANU 1969, Hague Acad. of Int. Law 1972, Inst. Univ. de hautes études int., Geneva 1980 and various American univs 1987–; rep. in various cttees UN 1962–74; Assoc. Rep., Rep., Counsel or Deputy Agent in cases before Int. Court of Justice 1962–80; Judge, Int. Court of Justice 1981–2000, Vice-Pres. 1994–97, Pres. 1997–2000; mem. Int. Law Comm. 1977–81, Perm. Court of Arbitration, The Hague 2006–; arbitrator or chair. in int. commercial arbitrations 1982–; mem. Tribunal in Eritrea-Yemen Arbitration 1997–99, Ethiopia-Eritrea Boundary Comm. 2000–; Pres. Barbados-Trinidad and Tobago Arbitration Tribunal 2004–; Pres. Admin. Tribunal, IMF 1994–, World Bank 2011–; Pres. Southern Blue Fin Tuna Arbitration 2000, Pakistan-India Indus Waters Arbitration 2011–; mem. Panels of Arbitrators and of Conciliators of the Int. Centre for the Settlement of Investment Disputes of the World Bank 2000–; mem. Bd of Eds, American Journal of Int. Law 1967–81, 1994–; mem. Council on Foreign Relations, Inst. of Int. Law; mem. Bars of State of New York, Dist of Columbia, Supreme Court of the USA; Hon. Bencher, Gray's Inn 1998–, Hon. Fellow, Lauterpacht Centre for Int. Law, Univ. of Cambridge; Hon. Fellow, Trinity Coll. Cambridge 2005; Hon. LL (Bhopal Univ.) 1983, (Hofstra Univ.) 1997, (Univ. of Miami) 2002; Gherini Prize, Yale Law School 1954, Medal of Merit, Yale Law School 1997, Manley O. Hudson Medal, American Soc. of Int. Law 2000. *Publications:* The Secretary-General of the United Nations 1952, The Effectiveness of International Decisions (ed.) 1971, International Arbitration: Three Salient Problems 1987, Justice in International Law 1994; author of some 175 articles in legal periodicals and the press on problems of international law and relations. *Leisure interests:* music, cycling. *Address:* 1501 K Street NW, Washington, DC 20005 (office); 1917 23rd Street NW, Washington, DC 20008, USA (home). *Telephone:* (202) 736-8328 (office); (202) 232-3114 (home). *Fax:* (202) 736-8709 (office); (202) 797-9286 (home). *E-mail:* judgeschwebel@aol.com (office).

SCHWEIGER, Til; German actor, producer and director; b. 19 Dec. 1963, Freiburg, Germany; m. Dana Schweiger; four c.; ed acting acad., Cologne; Best Actor Award, Moscow Film Festival 1997. *Films include:* Manta Manta 1991, Ebbie's Bluff (Max Ophuls Prize for Best Actor) 1992, Der Bewegte Mann 1994,

Maennerpension, Das Superweib, Brute 1996, Knocking on Heaven's Door 1996 (also producer and co-writer), Replacement Killers, Judas Kiss 1997, Der Eisbär (also producer), Der grosse Bagarozy 1998, Magicians 1999, Investigating Sex, Driven 2000, Was tun wenn's brennt 2000, Jetzt oder Nie (producer) 2000, Auf Herz und Nieren (producer) 2000, Joe and Max 2001, Tomb Raider 2 2002, King Arthur 2003, A Surprise Period 2003, The Daltons vs. Lucky Luke 2004, Barfuss 2005, Deuce Bigalow: European Gigolo 2005, Bye Bye Harry! 2006, Wo ist Fred? 2006), Video Kings 2007, Body Armour 2007, Keinohrhasen 2007, Already Dead 2007, Der Rote Baron 2008, Far Cry 2008, 1 1/2 Ritter 2008, Inglourious Basterds 2009, This Means War 2012. *Address:* c/o Players Agentur Management GmbH, Sophienstr. 21, 10178 Berlin, Germany (office). *Telephone:* (30) 2851680 (office). *Fax:* (30) 2851686 (office). *E-mail:* mai@players.de (office). *Website:* www.players .de (office).

SCHWEIKER, Mark, BSc, MA; American fmr politician; b. 31 Jan. 1953, Bucks Co., Pa; s. of John Schweiker and Mary Schweiker; m. Katherine Schweiker; two s. one d.; ed Bloomsburg Univ., Rider Univ.; began career with Merrill Lynch, then McGraw-Hill; first elected to public office as Middletown Township Supervisor 1979; Bucks Co. Commr 1987–94; Lt-Gov. of Pennsylvania 1994–2001, Gov. 2001–2003; Pres. and CEO Greater Philadelphia Chamber of Commerce 2003–09 (resgnd); currently Chair. PRWT Business Process Solutions; currently also Sr Advisor Stradley Ronon (law firm); mem. Bd of Dirs minSEC Holdings Inc., Network of Victim Assistance; Dr hc (Rider Univ.); Bloomsburg Univ. Alumnus of the Year 1990, Pennsylvania Nature Conservancy Award for Outstanding Service to Conservation 1993, Tech. Council of Pennsylvania Advocate of the Year 1996, Pennsylvania Econ. League Commitment to Excellence in Local Govt Award 1998, Pennsylvania League of Cities Outstanding Public Service Award 1999, Life Sciences Public Official of the Year, Speaker of the Year for Communications Excellence, Tech. Advocate of the Year. *Address:* Stradley Ronon, 2005 Market Street, Suite 2600, Philadelphia, PA 19103, USA (office). *Telephone:* (215) 564-8003 (office). *Fax:* (215) 564-8120 (office). *E-mail:* mschweiker@stradley.com (office). *Website:* www.stradley.com (office).

SCHWEIKER, Richard Schultz, BA; American business executive and fmr politician; b. 1 June 1926, Norristown, Pa; s. of Malcolm A. Schweiker and Blanche Schultz; m. Claire Joan Coleman 1955 (died 2013); two s. three d.; ed Pennsylvania State Univ.; business exec. 1950–60; mem. House of Reps. 1960–68; Senator from Pennsylvania 1969–80; Sec. of Health and Human Services 1981–83; Pres. American Council of Life Insurance 1983–94; Chair. Partnership for Prevention 1991–97; mem. Bd of Dirs Tenet Healthcare Corpn 1984, LabOne Inc. 1994–2002; Republican; ten hon. degrees and numerous awards. *Address:* 904 Lynton Place, McLean, VA 22102-2113, USA (office).

SCHWEIKERT, Emile Alfred, PhD; American (b. Swiss) chemist and academic; *Director, Center for Chemical Characterization, Department of Chemistry, Texas A&M University;* b. 10 Sept. 1939, Flawil, Switzerland; s. of Emil Martin Schweikert and Olga Elisa Schweikert-Niederer; m. Marta Teresa Guzman de Schweikert; one s. two d.; ed Univ. of Paris; fmr Head, Dept of Chem. Texas A&M Univ., currently Prof., also Dir Center for Chemical Characterization; mem. Program Advisory Cttee, Nat. Inst. of Standards and Tech. (NIST) Center for Neutron Research, Gaithersburg, Md 1997–98; George Hevesy Medal 1986. *Address:* Department of Chemistry, Texas A&M University, College Station, TX 77843-3255, USA (office). *Telephone:* (979) 845-2341 (office). *Fax:* (979) 845-1655 (office). *E-mail:* schweikert@mail.chem.tamu.edu (office). *Website:* www.chem .tamu.edu/faculty/schweikert (office); www.chem.tamu.edu/rgroup/schweikert (office).

SCHWEITZER, Brian David, BS, MS; American politician, fmr state governor and rancher; b. 4 Sept. 1955, Havre, Mont.; s. of Adam Schweitzer and Kathleen (Kay) Schweiter (née McKernan); m. Nancy Hupp 1981; two s. one d.; ed The Abbey School, Holy Cross Abbey, Canon City, Colo, Colorado State Univ., Montana State Univ.; began career in irrigation devt working in Africa, Asia, Europe and S America 1981–86; returned to Montana to raise family and build ranching and irrigation business 1986; apptd by Sec. of Agric. to serve on Montana State Dept of Agric. Farm Service Agency Cttee 1993–99; apptd to Montana Rural Devt Partnership Bd 1996, Nat. Drought Task Force 1999; cand. in US Senate elections 2000; Gov. of Montana 2005–13; fmr Chair. Western Govs Asscn, Democratic Govs Asscn; fmr Pres. Council of State Govts; Democrat; Sec. of Agric. Award for outreach efforts to Native Americans 1995. *Address:* c/o Office of the Governor, PO Box 200801, State Capitol, Helena, MT 59620-0801, USA. *E-mail:* governor@mt .gov.

SCHWEITZER, Louis, LenD; French business executive; *Chairman, High Authority against Discrimination and for Equality (HALDE);* b. 8 July 1942, Geneva, Switzerland; s. of Pierre-Paul Schweitzer and Catherine Hatt; m. Agnes Schmitz 1972; two d.; ed Inst. d'Etudes Politiques, Paris, Faculté de Droit, Paris and Ecole Nat. d'Admin; Insp. of Finance 1970–; special assignment, later Deputy Dir, Ministry of the Budget 1974–81; Dir du Cabinet to Minister of Budget 1981–83, of Industry and Research 1983, to Prime Minister 1984–86; Prof. Inst. d'Etudes Politiques de Paris 1982–86; Vice-Pres. for Finance and Planning Régie Renault SA 1986–90, Chief Finance Officer 1988–90, Exec. Vice-Pres. 1989–90, Pres. and COO 1990, Chair. and CEO 1992–2005, Chair. 2005–08; mem. Bd of Dirs Volvo Group 2001–12, Chair. 2010–12; mem. Bd of Dirs AstraZeneca PLC 2004–12, Chair. (non-exec.) 2005–12; Chair. Haute autorité de lutte contre les discriminations et pour l'égalité (HALDE) 2005–; Admin., Société Générale 1989–93, UAP 1988–94, Inst. Pasteur 1998–94, Péchiney 1989–92, IFRI 1989–, Réunion des Musées Nat. 1990–96, Renault Véhicules Industriels 1992–2001, BNP Paribas SA 1993–, Roussel UCLAF 1994–97, Crédit Nat. (now Natexis) 1995–99, Philips 1997–, Electricite de France SA 1999–2008, Véolia Environnement SA 2003–, L'Oréal SA 2005–; Chair. Ecole des mines de Nancy 1999–; Chair. Supervisory Bd Groupe Le Monde 2008–; Pres. Festival d'Avignon 2005–; Officier, Légion d'honneur, Commdr 2005, Officier, Ordre nat. du Mérite. *Address:* 1 rue Dauphine, 75006 Paris (home); La Halde, 11 rue Saint Georges, 75009 Paris, France (office). *Website:* defenseurdesdroits.fr (office).

SCHWERY, HE Cardinal Henri; Swiss ecclesiastic; *Bishop Emeritus of Sion;* b. 14 June 1932, St Léonard, Valais; s. of the late Camille Schwery and Marguerite Terroux; ed Lycée-Coll. de Sion, Valais, Faculty of Sciences, Univ. de Fribourg,

Grand Séminaire de Sion and Pontificia Università Gregoriana, Rome; ordained priest 1957; teacher of science, math. and religious studies, Lycée-Coll. de Sion 1961–, Rector 1972–77; Dir Pensionnat de la Sitterie (Petit Séminaire) de Sion 1968–72; Diocesan Chaplain, Action Catholique de Jeunesse Etudiante 1958–66; Mil. Chaplain 1958–77; Bishop of Sion 1977–95, Bishop Emer. 1995–; cr. Cardinal 1991; Cardinal-Priest of Ss. Protomartiri a Via Aurelia Antica 1991–; Kt of the Grand Cross, Order of the Holy Sepulchre of Jerusalem. *Publications:* Un Synode extraordinaire 1986, Chemin de Croix, chemin de lumière, L'Année Mariale dans le diocèse de Sion 1987, Sentiers Pastoraux 1988, Sentiers épiscopaux – Regards sur nos familles (two vols) 1992, Magnificat (in collaboration) 1992, Chrétien au quotidien 1996. *Leisure interest:* spirituality. *Address:* Diocèse de Sion, 12 rue de la Tour, PO Box 2124, 1950 Sion 2, Switzerland (office). *Telephone:* (27) 3291818 (office). *Fax:* (27) 3291836 (office). *E-mail:* diocese.sion@cath-vs.ch (office). *Website:* www.cath-vs.ch (office).

SCHWIMMER, David, BS; American actor, writer and director; b. 12 Nov. 1966, New York; s. of Arthur Schwimmer and Arlene Schwimmer; m. Zoe Buckman 2010; ed Beverly Hills High School and Northwestern Univ., Chicago; Co-founder Lookingglass Theater Co., Chicago 1988; mem. Bd of Dirs Rape Foundation for Rape Treatment Center of Santa Monica. *Theatre includes:* West, The Odyssey, Of One Blood, In the Eye of the Beholder all with Lookingglass Theater Co.), The Master and Margarita (all with Lookingglass Theater Co.), Some Girl(s) (Gielgud Theatre, London) 2005, The Caine Mutiny Court-Martial (Broadway) 2006. *Theatre directed includes:* The Jungle (six Joseph Jefferson Awards), The Serpent, Alice in Wonderland (Edin. Festival, Scotland). *Films include:* Flight of the Intruder 1990, Crossing the Bridge 1992, Twenty Bucks 1993, The Waiter 1993, Wolf 1994, The Pallbearer 1996, Shooting the Moon (exec. producer) 1996, Apt Pupil 1998, Kissing a Fool (exec. producer) 1998, Six Days Seven Nights 1998, The Thin Pink Line 1998, All the Rage 1999, Picking Up the Pieces 2000, Hotel 2001, Dogwater (also Dir), Duane Hopwood 2005, Madagascar (voice) 2005, Big Nothing 2006, Run, Fat Boy, Run (dir) 2007, Nothing But the Truth 2008, Madagascar 2 (voice) 2008, Trust (dir) 2011, Madagascar 3: Europe's Most Wanted (voice) 2012. *Television includes:* The Wonder Years 1988, Monty 1993, NYPD Blue 1993, Friends 1994–2004, L.A. Law, The Single Guy (NBC), Happy Birthday Elizabeth: A Celebration of Life 1997, Breast Men 1997, Since You've Been Gone (dir) 1998, Band of Brothers (mini series) 2001, Uprising 2001, Curb Your Enthusiasm (series) 2004; hosted Montreal's 13th Annual Just for Laughs Festival. *Leisure interests:* writing, playing softball and basketball. *Address:* c/o The Gersh Agency, PO Box 5617, Beverly Hills, CA 90210 (office); Lookingglass Theatre Company, 2936 North Southport Avenue, Chicago, IL 60657, USA. *Website:* www .lookingglasstheatre.org.

SCHWIMMER, Walter, LLD; Austrian politician, international organization official and lawyer; *Chairman, International Coordination Committee, World Public Forum – Dialogue of Civilizations;* b. 16 June 1942, Vienna; s. of Walter Schwimmer and Johanna Schwimmer; m. Martina Pucher-Schwimmer; two s.; ed Univ. of Vienna; mem. Nationalrat (Austrian Parl.) 1971–99, Chair. Parl. Cttee on Health 1989–94, on Justice 1995–96; Vice-Chair. Parl. Group, Austrian People's Party (ÖVP) 1986–94; mem. Council of Europe Parl. Ass. 1991–, Vice-Pres. Council of Europe 1996, Jan.–Sept. 1999, Sec.-Gen. 1999–2004; Chair. European People's Party Group–Christian Democrats 1996–99; Dir and Exec. Vice-Pres. Vienna Health Insurance Fund 1979–99; Chair. Int. Coordination, World Public Forum – Dialogue of Civilizations 2005–; Pres. European Democracy Forum, Strasbourg 2006–, Megatrend Univ., Belgrade 2010–12; mem. Bd Crans Montana Forum 2004–09; consultant on int. relations and European affairs 2004–; Hon. Sec.-Gen. Maison de la Méditerranée 2004–; Grosses Goldenes Ehrenzeichen am Bande (Austria) 2004; Grosses Silbernes Ehrenzeichen mit dem Stern (Austria), Grosses Silbernes Ehrenzeichen der Stadt Wien, Grand Cross, Order of the Star of Romania 2001, Commdr's Cross, Order of Grand Duke Gaudemes (Lithuania), Chevalier, Légion d'honneur 2003, Grand Cross of the Equestrian Order of St Agatha (San Marino) 2003, Order of the Aztec Eagle (Mexico), Grande Ufficiale dell'Ordine al Merito (Italy) 2004; Leopold-Kunschak Award 1975, Peter the Great Int. Prize of the Russian Fed., European Pro Humanitate European Foundation for Culture Prize, Germany, Medal of the European Inst. of Moscow, Person of the Year Award (Ukraine) 2002. *Publications:* Christian Trade Unions in Austria 1975, Social Consequences of Inflation 1988, A Union Goes Down in History 1993, Der Traum Europa 2003, The European Dream 2004, Sognare l'Europa 2004, San Evropa 2004. *Leisure interests:* books, history, stamps, art. *Address:* World Public Forum – Dialogue of Civilizations, Vienna Headquarters, Stubenring 4, 1010 Vienna (office); Consultancy Office, Dietschen 2, 3400 Klosterneuburg, Austria (office). *Telephone:* (1) 513-01-38-2 (Vienna) (office); (2243) 87694 (Klosterneuburg) (office). *Fax:* (1) 513-01-38-4 (Vienna) (office); (2243) 87649 (Klosterneuburg) (office). *E-mail:* schwimmer@wpfdc.at (office); schwimmer.consult@aon.at (office). *Website:* www.wpfdc.org (office); www.socialstudies.at (office).

SCHWYZER, Robert, DPhil; Swiss molecular biologist and academic (retd); b. 8 Dec. 1920, Zürich; s. of Robert Schwyzer and Rose Schätzle; m. Rose Nägeli 1948; two s. one d.; ed primary school, Nathan Hale, Minneapolis, USA, Canton High School (A), Zürich and Dept of Chem., Univ. of Zürich; Privatdozent, Univ. of Zürich 1951–59, Asst Prof. 1960–63; initiation of Polypeptide Research, Head of Polypeptide Research Group, Ciba Ltd, Basel 1952–63, Asst Man. 1960–63; apptd Prof. and Head of Dept of Molecular Biology, Swiss Fed. Inst. of Tech., Zürich 1963; apptd Prof.-in-Residence, Clinical Research Inst. of Montréal 1991; Werner Award, Swiss Chemical Soc. 1957, Ruzicka Prize, Swiss Fed. Inst. of Tech. 1959, Otto Nägeli Award, Switzerland 1964, Vernon Stouffer Award, American Heart Asscn, Cleveland 1968, Ernesto Scoffone Award 1982, Alan E. Pierce Award, American Peptide Symposia 1985, Rudinger Gold Medal, European Peptide Symposia 1988. *Publications:* scientific papers on syntheses of biologically active polypeptides; structure activity relationships; relationships between structure and biophysical interactions with lipid-bilayer membranes; molecular mechanisms of opioid receptor selection by peptides, new principles governing receptor specificity. *Leisure interests:* mountain climbing, skiing, literature. *Address:* Institut für Molekularbiologie und Biophysik, Eidgenössische Technische Hochschule, Hartriegelstrasse 12, 8180 Bülach, Switzerland (office). *Telephone:* (44) 8607111 (home).

SCHYGULLA, Hanna; German actress; b. 1943, Bundesverdienstkreuz Erster Klasse; Hon. Award, Antalya Golden Orange Film Festival 2007, Berlin Film Festival Hon. Golden Bear 2010. *Stage appearances include:* Mother Courage 1979. *Films include:* Die Ehe der Maria Braun (Silberner Bär Berlinale) 1979, Die Dritte Generation 1979, Lili Marleen 1980, Die Fälschung 1981, La Nuit de Varennes 1982, Eine Liebe in Deutschland 1983, The Story of Piera 1983, Miss Arizona 1987, The Summer of Mr. Forbes, Dead Again 1991, Beware of a Holy Whore 1993, The Merchant of Four Seasons 1998, Werckmeister Harmonies 2001, Die Blauwe Grenze 2005, Vendredi ou un autre jour 2005, Winterreise 2006, The Edge of Heaven 2007, Faust 2011, Avanti 2012, Pandemia 2012. *Television appearances include:* 8 Stunden sind kein Tag (series) 1972, Absolute 2001, Das unreine Mal 2006, Clara, une passion française 2009. *Leisure interests:* travel, painting.

SCICLUNA, Edward, BA, MEconSc, DEcon; Maltese economist and politician; *Minister of Finance;* b. 12 Oct. 1946, Naxxar; m. Astrid Bartoli; one s. one d.; ed Univ. of Malta, Univ. of Oxford, UK, Univ. of Toronto, Canada; Prof. and Head, Dept of Econs, Univ. of Malta 1981–90; Electoral Commr 1987–93; Dir Central Bank of Malta 1996–2003; Chair. Malta Financial Services Authority 1997–99; mem. Council of Europe's Devt Bank Auditing Cttee 1997–2000; Chair. Malta Council of Econ. and Social Devt 1999–2003; mem. Nat. Euro Change-over Cttee 2005–08; mem. European Parl. 2009–13; mem. House of Reps (Parl.) for 5th and 8th Dists 2013–; Minister of Finance 2013–; fmr Chair. CWG PLC, HSBC's Malta Funds Sicav PLC, Structured Funds Sicav PLC; fmr Dir San Antonio Hotel and Spa; mem. Partit Laburista (PL, Labour Party) 2009–. *Address:* Ministry of Finance, the Economy and Investment, Maison Demandols, South Street, Valletta VLT 1102, Malta (office). *Telephone:* 25998244 (office). *Fax:* 21233605 (office). *E-mail:* info.mfin@gov.mt (office). *Website:* www.finance.gov.mt (office).

SCICLUNA, Martin, BCom; British accountant and business executive; *Chairman, RSA Insurance Group;* b. 1952, Malta; s. of William Scicluna and Miriam Scicluna; two s. one d.; ed Berkhamsted School, Univ. of Leeds; joined Deloitte (fmrly Touche Ross) 1973, Articled Clerk 1973–76, Audit Partner Deloitte & Touche LLP (formerly Touche Ross & Co.) 1982–2008, Group Partner 1985–90, Head of London Audit Div. 1990–95, Partner, Chair. Deloitte UK 1995–2007; Dir (non-exec.), Worldpay 2013–; Chair. Great Portland Estates 2009–; Chair. Royal and Sun Alliance (RSA) Insurance Group PLC 2013–; mem. Bd of Dirs Deloitte Touche Tohmatsu 1998–2007, Lloyds Banking Group PLC 2008–13; Gov. Berkhamsted School 2008–; Freeman of the City of London; Hon. LLD (Leeds) 2008. *Leisure interests:* Arsenal FC, wine, gardening. *Address:* RSA Insurance Group plc, 9th Floor, One Plantation Place, 30 Fenchurch Street, London EC3M 3BD, England (office). *Telephone:* (20) 7111-7000 (office). *Website:* www.rsagroup .com (office).

SCINDIA, Jyotiraditya Madhavrao, MBA; Indian politician; *Minister of State for Power;* b. 1 Jan. 1971, Mumbai; s. of Madhavrao Scindia and Madhavi Raje Scindia; m. Priyadarshini Raje Scindia 1994; one s. one d.; ed Campion School, Mumbai, The Doon School, Dehradun, Harvard Univ., USA, Stanford Graduate School of Business; fmr Financial Analyst, Morgan Stanley Asia Ltd, Hong Kong and Mumbai; fmr Summer Intern with UN, New York and Merrill Lynch, Los Angeles; elected to 13th Lok Sabha (lower house of Parl.) for Guna Dist constituency 2002, re-elected to 14th Lok Sabha 2004, 15th Lok Sabha 2009–; mem. Cttee on Finance 2002–04, Cttee on External Affairs 2002–04, Cttee on Defence 2004; Union Cabinet Minister of State for Communications and Information Tech. 2008, for Commerce and Industry 2009–12, for Power 2012–; Pres. Madhya Pradesh Cricket Asscn; Gov. Madhav Inst. of Tech. & Science, Gwalior; mem. Indian Nat. Congress (Congress). *Leisure interests:* cricket, swimming, reading, wild life conservation. *Address:* Ministry of Power, Shram Shakti Bhavan, Rafi Marg, New Delhi 110 001, India (office). *Telephone:* (11) 23710271 (office). *E-mail:* harisankar@nic.in (office). *Website:* powermin.nic.in (office).

SCLATER, John G., BS, PhD, FRS; British geophysicist and professor of geophysics; *Professor of Geophysics, Scripps Institution of Oceanography, University of California, San Diego;* b. 17 June 1940, Edinburgh, Scotland; s. of John G. Sclater and Margaret Bennett Glen; m. 1st Fredrica R. Sclater 1968 (divorced 1985); two s.; m. 2nd Paula Ann Edwards 1985 (divorced 1991); m. 3rd Naila G. Burchett 1992; ed Stonyhurst Coll., Univs of Edinburgh and Cambridge; Postdoctoral Research Geophysicist, Scripps Inst. of Oceanography, Univ. of California, San Diego 1965–67, Asst Research Geophysicist 1967–72, Prof. of Geophysics 1991–; Assoc. Prof., MIT 1972–77, Prof. 1977–83; MIT Dir, Jt Program in Oceanography with the Woods Hole Oceanographic Inst. 1981–83; Assoc. Dir Inst. for Geophysics, Univ. of Texas at Austin, Prof., Dept of Geological Sciences and Shell Distinguished Chair. in Geophysics 1983–91; mem. NAS 1989; Fellow, Geological Soc. of America 1975, American Geophysical Union 1977; Swiney Lecturer, Edin. Univ. 1976; Guggenheim Fellow 1998–99; Rosenstiel Award 1978, Bucher Medal, American Geophysical Union 1985. *Leisure interests:* running, swimming, golf. *Address:* Scripps Institution of Oceanography, Geosciences Research Division, University of California, San Diego, 9500 Gilman Drive, La Jolla, CA 92093-0220, USA (office). *Telephone:* (619) 534-3051. *E-mail:* jsclater@ ucsd.edu (office). *Website:* grd.ucsd.edu (office).

SCLATER, John Richard, CVO, MA, MBA; British company chairman and farmer; *Managing Partner, Sutton Hall Farms;* b. 14 July 1940, Camborne, Cornwall, England; s. of Arthur William Sclater and Alice Sclater (née Collett); m. 1st Nicola Mary Gloria Cropper 1967 (divorced); one s. one d. (deceased); m. 2nd Grizel Elizabeth Catherine Dawson MBE 1985; ed Charterhouse, Gonville and Caius Coll., Cambridge and Yale and Harvard Univs, USA; Commonwealth Fellow 1962–64; Glyn, Mills & Co. 1964–70; Dir Williams, Glyn & Co. 1970–76; Man. Dir Nordic Bank 1976–85, Chair. 1985–87; Dir and Deputy Chair. Guinness Peat Group PLC 1985–87, Jt Deputy Chair. 1987; Dir and Deputy Chair. Guinness Mahon & Co. Ltd 1987, Chair. 1987; Dir Foreign & Colonial Investment Trust PLC 1981–2002, Chair. 1983–2002; Chair. Foreign & Colonial (now Graphite) Enterprise Trust PLC 1986–2009, Foreign & Colonial Ventures Ltd 1990–98, Berisford PLC 1990–2000 (Dir 1986–2000), Hill Samuel Bank Ltd 1992–96, Dir 1990–96, Vice-Chair. 1990–92), Foreign & Colonial (now Graphite) Pvt. Equity Trust PLC 1994–2002, Finsbury Life Sciences Investment Trust PLC (renamed Finsbury Emerging Biotechnology Trust PLC 2005, then The Biotech Growth Trust PLC 2007) 1997–2012, Argent Group Europe Ltd 1998–2012; Man. Partner, Sutton

Hall Farms 2012–; Pres. Equitable Life Assurance Soc. 1994–2001 (Dir 1985–2001); Deputy Chair. Yamaichi Int. (Europe) Ltd 1985–97, Union (fmrly Union Discount Co. of London) PLC 1986–96 (Dir 1981–96, Chair. 1996), Grosvenor Group Ltd (fmrly Grosvenor Group Holdings Ltd) 2000–05 (Dir 1999), Grosvenor Estate Holdings 1989–2002; Dir Berner Nicol & Co. Ltd 1968 (Chair. 2002–04, 2005–), James Cropper PLC 1972–2008, Holker Estates Co. Ltd 1974–, Angerstein Underwriting Trust PLC 1985–96, Foreign & Colonial Group (Holdings) Ltd 1989–2001, Fuel Tech (Europe) 1990–98, Millennium & Copthorne Hotels PLC 1996–2007, Wates Group Ltd 1999–2004; Chair. Asscn of Consortium Banks 1980–82; Consultant RP&C Int. 1997–2003; First Church Estates Commr 1999–2001 (mem. Archbishops' Council and Gen. Synod, Church of England 1999–2001); Dir and Gov. Brambletye School 1976–2006; mem. City Taxation Cttee 1973–76, London Bd of Halifax Building Soc. 1983–90, Council of Duchy of Lancaster 1987–2000, CBI City Advisory Group 1988–99; Gov. Int. Students House 1976–99; Trustee, The Grosvenor Estate 1973–2005, The Coll. of Arms 1994–; Freeman of the City of London 1993–; Liveryman Goldsmiths' Co. 1993–. *Leisure interest:* country pursuits. *Address:* Sutton Hall, Barcombe, nr Lewes, East Sussex, BN8 5EB, England. *Telephone:* (1273) 400450. *Fax:* (1273) 401086. *E-mail:* john.sclater@newickandsuttonhall.com.

SCOFIDIO, Ricardo; American artist, architect and academic; *Professor Emeritus of Architecture, Cooper Union for the Advancement of Science and Art;* co-f. (with Elizabeth Diller q.v.), Diller & Scofidio (now Diller Scofidio + Renfro), New York 1979, cr. installations and electronic media projects; Prof. of Architecture, The Cooper Union 1965, now Prof. Emer.; Fellow, American Acad. of Arts and Sciences 2009–; Jt recipient (with Elizabeth Diller) fellowships from Graham Foundation for Advanced Study in the Fine Arts 1986, New York Foundation for the Arts 1986, 1987, 1989, Chicago Inst. for Architecture and Urbanism 1989, Tiffany Foundation Award for Emerging Artists 1990, Progressive Architecture Award (for Slow House) 1991, Chrysler Award for Achievement and Design 1997. *Publications:* (with Elizabeth Diller) Flesh 1995, Back to the Front: Tourisms of War. *Address:* Diller Scofidio + Renfro, 601 West 26th Street, Suite 1815, New York, NY 10001, USA (office). *Telephone:* (212) 260-7971 (office). *E-mail:* disco@dsrny.com (office). *Website:* www.dillerscofidio.com (office).

SCOGNAMIGLIO PASINI, Carlo Luigi, DEcon; Italian politician, economist and professor of economics; *Professor of Economics, Libera Università Internazionale degli Studi Sociali Guido Carli;* b. 27 Nov. 1944, Varese; s. of Luigi Scognamiglio and Esther Scognamiglio (née Pasini); m. Cecilia Pirelli; one s. one d.; ed L. Bocconi Univ., Milan, London School of Econs; Asst Lecturer, L. Bocconi Univ., Asst Prof. of Industrial Econs 1968–73, Prof. 1973; Asst Prof. of Finance, Univ. of Padua 1973–79; Prof. of Econs and Industrial Policy, Libera Università Internazionale degli Studi Sociali Guido Carli, Rome 1979–, Dean and Rector 1984–92; Liberal Party cand. in Milan constituency, elected to Senate 1992, Chair. European Affairs Cttee, mem. Budget Cttee, re-elected to Senate 1994; Pres. of Senate 1994–96; Acting Pres. of Italy 1994–96; Pres. Rizzoli-Corriere della Sera 1983–84, later Vice-Pres.; Minister of Defence 1998–99; Co-Founder, Bocconi School of Business Admin 1979; Pres. Italian Liberal Party 2009–; fmr Pres. Aspen Inst. Italia, currently Hon. Chair. and life-time Trustee; Acad. of France Award for Econs 1988. *Publications include:* The Stock Exchange 1973, Industrial Crises 1976, The White Book on PPSS 1981, The White Book on the Italian Financial Market 1982, Theory and Policy of Finance 1987, Industrial Economics 1987, Report to Minister of Treasury of Commission for Privatization of Industry 1990, The Liberal Project 1996. *Leisure interests:* economics, history. *Address:* Department of Economics, Libera Università Internazionale degli Studi Sociali Guido Carli, Viale Romania 32, 00197 Rome, Italy (office). *Website:* www.luiss.edu (office).

SCOLA, HE Cardinal Angelo, PhD, DTheol; Italian ecclesiastic; *Archbishop of Milan;* b. 7 Nov. 1941, Malgrate; s. of Carlo Scola and Regina Colombo; ed Catholic Univ. of Sacred Heart, Milan, Seminary of Saronno, Milan, Seminary of Venegono, Milan, Univ. of Fribourg, Switzerland; ordained priest 1970; successively, until 1991, active collaborator of Comunione e Liberazione, Dir Inst. of Studies for Transition, Milan, collaborator in establishment and mem. Exec. Cttee Italian edn of Rivista Internazionale Communio, pastoral work in Italy and abroad; Research Asst to Chair of Political Philosophy 1979, later Asst to Chair of Fundamental Moral Theology, Univ. of Fribourg; Prof. of Theological Anthropology, Pontifical John Paul II Inst. for Studies on Marriage and Family, Pontifical Lateran Univ., Rome 1982, later Prof. of Contemporary Christology, Faculty of Theology, Rector Magnifico Pontifical Lateran Univ. and Pres. Pontifical John Paul II Inst. for Studies on Marriage and the Family 1995; attended Seventh Ordinary Ass. of World Synod of Bishops as an asst to Special Sec., Vatican City 1987; Bishop of Grosseto 1991–95 (resgnd); Patriarch of Venice 2002–11; Archbishop of Milan 2011–; cr. Cardinal (Cardinal Priest of Santi XII Apostoli) 2003; participated in Papal Conclave 2005, 2013; Relator Gen. 11th Gen. Ordinary Ass. of World Synod of Bishops 2005. *Address:* Archdiocese of Milan, Palazzo Arcivescovile, Piazza Fontana 2, 20122 Milan, Italy (office). *Telephone:* (02) 85561 (office). *Fax:* (02) 861396 (office). *E-mail:* direzioneportale@chiesadimilano.it (office). *Website:* www.chiesadimilano.it (office).

SCOLA, Ettore; Italian fmr film director; b. 10 May 1931, Trevico (Avellino); m. Gigliola Fantoni 1956; two d.; ed Univ. of Rome; studied law, then worked in journalism and radio; directed films 1952–2011 (retd); Nastro d'Argento Award 1966, 1978, 1980, 1981, 1987, Cannes Film Festival Award 1980, César Award 1977, 1978, 1984, Golden Globe Award 1978, Silver Bear, Berlin Film Festival 1984, Pietro Bianchi Award, Venice Film Festival 1990, Flaiano Film Festival Award 1995, Moscow Film Festival Award 2001, Taormina Arte Award, Taormina Film Fest 2001. *Films:* Se permettete parliamo di donne 1964, La Congiuntura 1965, Thrilling 1965, L'arcidiavolo 1966, Riusciranno i nostri eroi a ritrovare l'amico misteriosamente scomparso in Africa? 1968, Il commissario Pepe 1969, Dramma della gelosia (tutti i particolari in cronaca) (Jealousy, Italian Style) 1970, Permette? Rocco Papaleo 1971, La più bella serata della mia vita 1972, Trevico—Torino. . . viaggio nel Fiat-nam 1973, C'eravamo tanto amati 1974, Brutti, sporchi e cattivi 1976 (Best Dir, Cannes Film Festival), Signore e signori buonanotte 1976, Una giornata particolare (A Special Day) 1977 (Special Jury Prizes, Cannes Film Festival), I nuovi mostri 1977, La terrazza 1979, Passione d'amore 1980, Il mondo nuovo 1982, Le bal 1983, Maccheroni 1985, La Famiglia (The Family) 1987,

Splendor 1988, Che Orà È? 1989, Il Viaggio di Capitan Fracassa 1990, Mario, Maria e Mario 1992, Romanzo di un giovane povero 1995, I Corti italiani (segment) 1997, La Cena 1998, Concorrenza sleale 2001, Un Altro mondo è possibile (Another World Is Possible) 2001, Lettere dalla Palestina (Letters from Palestine) 2002, Gente di Roma 2003. *Television:* Live from Lincoln Center 2005.

SCOLARI, Luiz Felipe; Brazilian professional football manager and fmr professional footballer; *Manager, Football Club Bunyodkor;* b. 9 Nov. 1948, Passo Fundo, Rio Grande do Sul; defender; pyouth player, Aymoré de São Leopoldo-RS 1966–73; sr player for Caxias 1973–79, Juventude 1980, Novo Hamburgo 1980–81, Centro Sportivo Alagoano (CSA) 1981; Man. CSA 1982 (won Campeonato Alagoano 1982), Juventude 1982–83, Brasil de Pelotas 1983, Al-Shabab 1984–85, Brasil de Pelotas 1986, Juventude 1986–87, Grêmio 1987, 1993–96 (won Campeonato Gaúcho 1987, 1995, 1996, Copa do Brasil 1994, Copa Libertadores 1995, Campeonato Brasileiro Série A 1996, Recopa Sudamericana 1996), Goiás 1988, Al Qadisiya 1988–90 (won Kuwait Emir Cup 1989), Kuwait 1990 (won Gulf Cup of Nations 1990), Criciúma 1991 (won Copa do Brasil 1991), Al-Ahli 1991, Al Qadisiya 1992, Júbilo Iwata 1996–97, Palmeiras 1997–2000 (won Copa do Brasil 1998, Copa Mercosur 1998, Copa Libertadores 1999, Torneio Rio-São Paulo 2000), Cruzeiro 2000–01 (won Copa Sul-Minas 2001); Man. Brazilian nat. team 2001–02, led Brazil to record fifth World Cup June 2002, resgnd July 2002; Man. Portuguese nat. team 2002–08; Man. Chelsea FC, London 2008–09, FC Bunyodkor, Tashkent, Uzbekistan 2009–; South American Coach of the Year 1999, 2002. *Address:* FC Bunyodkor, Jar Sport Complex, 3 Beruniy Street, Shaykhontohur District, Tashkent, Uzbekistan (office). *Telephone:* (71) 1508351 (office). *Fax:* (71) 1508355 (office). *E-mail:* info@fcbunyodkor.com (office). *Website:* www.fcbunyodkor.com (office).

SCOLES, Giacinto, MSc, FRS; Italian physicist and professor of science; *Donner Professor Emeritus of Science, Princeton University;* b. 2 April 1935, Turin; ed Univ. of Genoa, Univ. of Leiden, Netherlands; began career in Physics Dept, Univ. of Genoa –1961; mem. staff, Univ. of Leiden 1961–64; Prof. of Chem. and Physics, Univ. of Waterloo, Canada –1986, Acting Dir Guelph-Waterloo Centre for Grad. Work in Chem. 1974–75, Dir Centre for Molecular Beams and Laser Chem. 1982–85; Prof. of Solid State Physics, Univ. of Trento 1975–82; Donner Prof. of Science, Princeton Univ. Chem. Dept and Princeton Materials Inst. 1987–2008, Donner Prof. Emer. of Science 2008–; Prof., Depts of Biophysics and Condensed Matter Physics, Int. School for Advanced Studies, Trieste 2003–; Elettra Synchrotron Lab., Trieste 2003–09; Distinguished Visiting Prof., Univ. of Florida, Gainesville 2003; Moscowitz Lecturer, Univ. of Minnesota 2004; Distinguished Adjunct Prof. of Biology, Temple Univ., Phila 2008–; apptd Sr Consultant to International Center for Science and High Technology, UNIDO 2009; Foreign mem. Royal Acad. of Arts and Sciences, Netherlands 2000, American Chemical Soc.; Fellow, Optical Soc. of America, American Physical Soc., Chemical Inst. of Canada; Dr hc (Univ. of Genova) 1996, (Univ. of Waterloo, Canada) 2000; Lippincott Award, Optical Soc. of America, Coblentz Soc., Soc. for Applied Spectroscopy 1995, Peter Debye Award, American Chemical Soc. 2002, E.K. Plyler Prize 2003, Creativity Award 2005, Benjamin Franklin Medal in Physics (co-recipient) 2006. *Publications:* numerous scientific papers in professional journals on the devt of helium droplet spectroscopy. *Address:* Department of Chemistry, Princeton University, Washington Road, Princeton, NJ 08544-1009, USA (office). *Telephone:* (609) 258-5570 (office). *E-mail:* gscoles@princeton.edu (office). *Website:* www.princeton.edu/~gscoles (office); prism.princeton.edu (office).

SCORSESE, Martin Charles, BA, MA; American film director, producer, actor and screenwriter; b. 17 Nov. 1942, Queens, NY; s. of Charles Scorsese and Catherine Scorsese (née Cappa); m. 1st Laraine Marie Brennan 1965 (divorced 1971); one d.; m. 2nd Julia Cameron 1976 (divorced 1977); one d.; m. 3rd Isabella Rossellini (q.v.) 1979 (divorced 1982); m. 4th Barbara DeFina 1985 (divorced 1991); m. 5th Helen Morris 1999; ed Cardinal Hayes High School, New York Univ.; Faculty Asst and Instructor, Film Dept, New York Univ. 1963–66, instructor 1968–70; dir and writer of films: What's a Nice Girl Like You Doing in a Place Like This? 1963, It's Not Just You, Murray 1964, Who's That Knocking At My Door? 1968, The Big Shave 1968; dir play The Act 1977–78; dir and writer of documentaries; Supervising Ed. and Asst Dir Woodstock 1970; Assoc. Producer and Post-Production Supervisor Medicine Ball Caravan 1971; Order of Merit (Italy) 2001, Légion d'honneur 2005; Dr hc (Nat. Film School, Łódź) 2011; Edward J. Kingsley Foundation Award 1963, 1964, First Prize, Rosenthal Foundation Awards of Soc. of Cinematologists 1964, named Best Dir, Cannes Film Festival 1986, First Prize, Screen Producer's Guild 1965, Brown Univ. Film Festival 1965, shared Rosellini Prize 1990, Award American Museum of Moving Image 1996, American Film Inst. Lifetime Achievement Award 1997, Int. Fed. of Film Award for Preservation 2001, Kennedy Center Honor 2007, listed amongst TIME magazine's 100 Most Influential People in The World 2007, named second greatest director of all time in a poll by Total Film magazine, ahead of Steven Spielberg and behind Alfred Hitchcock 2007, honoured by Nat. Italian American Foundation 2007, Cecil B. DeMille Award for Lifetime Achievement 2010, BAFTA Fellowship 2012. *Films include:* Street Scenes 1970, Boxcar Bertha 1972, Mean Streets 1973, Italianamerican 1974, Alice Doesn't Live Here Any More 1974, Taxi Driver 1976, New York, New York 1977, The Last Waltz 1978, Raging Bull 1980, King of Comedy 1981, After Hours 1985, The Color of Money 1986, The Last Temptation of Christ (Courage in Filmmaking Award, LA Film Teachers Asscn 1989) 1988, Good Fellas 1990, Made in Milan 1990, Cape Fear 1991, The Age of Innocence 1993, Casino 1995, Kundun 1997, Bringing Out the Dead 1999, Gangs of New York (Golden Globe for Best Dir 2003) 2002, The Aviator 2004, The Departed (Nat. Bd of Review Award for Best Dir 2006, Golden Globe for Best Dir 2007, Dirs' Guild of America Award 2007, Acad. Award for Best Picture, Best Dir 2007) 2006, Shine a Light 2007, Shutter Island 2010, Public Speaking (documentary) 2010, George Harrison: Living in the Material World (documentary) 2011, Hugo (Golden Globe Award for Best Dir 2012) 2011, The Wolf of Wall Street 2013; exec. producer: The Crew 1989, Naked in New York 1994, Grace of My Heart 1996, Kicked in the Head 1996, You Can Count on Me 2000, Deuces Wild 2002, Soul of a Man 2003, Something to Believe In 2004, Brides 2004, The Aviator 2004, Life Itself (documentary) 2014, Revenge of the Green Dragons 2014, The Third Side of the River 2014, The Wannabe 2014; producer: The Grifters 1989, Naked in New York 1994, Casino 1996, Kundun 1998, Bringing Out the Dead 1999, Gangs of New York 2002; co-producer Mad Dog and Glory 1993; acted in Cannonball 1976, Triple Play

1981, Dreams 1990, The Muse 1999. *Television includes:* Lady by the Sea: The Statue of Liberty 2004, No Direction Home: Bob Dylan 2005, American Masters (series documentary) 2005, 2010, A Letter to Elia 2010; exec. producer The Blues (mini-series) 2003, Boardwalk Empire (Emmy Award for Outstanding Directing for a Drama Series 2011) 2010–13. *Publications include:* Scorsese on Scorsese 1989, The Age of Innocence: The Shooting Script (with Jay Cocks) 1996, Casino (with Nicholas Pileggi) 1996. *Address:* c/o Artists Management Group, 9465 Wilshire Boulevard, Suite 519, Los Angeles, CA 90212 (office); Jeff Doolly Starr & Co., 350 Park Avenue, 9th Floor, New York, NY 10022, USA (office).

SCOTLAND OF ASTHAL, Baroness (Life Peer), cr. 1997, of Asthal in the County of Oxfordshire; **Patricia Janet Scotland**, PC, QC, LLB; British barrister and politician; b. 19 Aug. 1955, Dominica; d. of the late Arthur Leonard Scotland and of Dellie Marie Genevieve; m. Richard Mawhinney 1985; two s.; ed Mid Essex Tech. Coll., Chelmsford (pursued external Univ. of London law degree); called to the Bar, Middle Temple 1977, QC 1991 (first black woman), Bencher 1997; mem. the Bar, Antigua, Recorder 2000; mem. Privy Council 2001; Parl. Under-Sec. of State, Foreign and Commonwealth Office 1999–2001; Parl. Sec., Lord Chancellor's Dept 2001–03; Alt. UK Govt Rep. of the European Convention 2002–03; Minister of State, Home Office 2003–07; Attorney Gen. for England and Wales (first woman) 2007–10, Attorney Gen. for NI 2007–10, Advocate Gen. for NI 2010; Shadow Attorney Gen. 2010–11; fmr mem. Comm. for Racial Equality, Gen. Council Bar Race Relations Cttee, Professional Conduct Cttee, Judicial Studies Bd Ethnic Minority Advisory Cttee, House of Commons Working Party on Child Abduction, Legal Advisory Panel on the Nat. Consumer Council, Ind. Cttee for the Supervision of Standards of Telephone Information Services, Nat. Advisory Cttee on Mentally Disordered Offenders; Commr Millennium Comm. 1994–; Chair. HMG Caribbean Advisory Group; Dominican Rep. of Council of The British Commonwealth Ex-Service League; Founder-mem. and fmr Head of Chambers, 1 Gray's Inn Square; fmr Chair. Inner London Educ. Authority Disciplinary Tribunal; fmr mem. BBC World Service Consultative Group; Hon. Pres. Trinity Hall Law Soc.; Hon. Fellow, Cardiff Univ., Soc. for Advanced Legal Studies, Wolfson Coll. Cambridge; Dame, Sacred Mil. Constantinian Order of St George; Dr hc (Westminster, Buckingham, Leicester, East London 2005, Newman Univ. Coll., Birmingham); Black Woman of the Year (Law) 1992, Peer of the Year, House Magazine Awards 2004, Peer of the Year, C4 Political Awards 2004, Parliamentarian of the Year, Political Studies Association Awards 2004, The Spectator Parliamentarian of the Year Awards 2005. *Leisure interests:* church, sport, dancing, theatre. *Address:* House of Lords, Westminster, London, SW1A 0AP, England (office). *Telephone:* (20) 7219-5700 (office); (20) 7219-3000 (office). *Website:* www.parliament.uk/biographies/lords/patricia-scotland/26608 (office).

SCOTT, Charles Thomas, CA; British business executive; *Director of Sales and Marketing, AddressVision Inc.;* b. 22 Feb. 1949; with Binder Hamlyn 1967–72; Chief Accountant, ITEL Int. Corpn 1972–77; Controller, IMS Int. Inc. 1978–84, Chief Financial Officer 1985–89; Chief Financial Officer, Saatchi & Saatchi Co. (later Cordiant PLC, now Cordiant Communications Group PLC) 1990–91, COO 1991–92, CEO 1993–95, Chair. 1995–2003; Chair. Bates Worldwide 1997; Sr Exec. Dir William Hill PLC 2002–04, Chair. (non-exec.) 2004–07, Chair. 2007–10; Dir (non-exec.) InTechnology PLC 2001–, TBI Ltd (fmrly TBI PLC) 1998–2005; Dir of Sales and Marketing, AddressVision Inc. 2010–; mem. Bd of Dirs, Emcore Corpn 1998–, Flybe Group PLC, Kircal Ltd; fmr Chair. Robert Walters PLC. *Leisure interests:* golf, tennis. *Address:* Addressvision Inc, 200 Main St, La Crosse, WI 54601-9301, USA (office). *Telephone:* (608) 796-2876 (office). *E-mail:* chuck.scott@bull.com (office). *Website:* www.addressvisioninc.com (office).

SCOTT, Guy Lindsay, BA (Econs), PhD; Zambian politician; *Vice-President;* b. 1 June 1944, Livingstone; s. of Alexander Scott; m. 1st (divorced), three c.; m. 2nd Charlotte Scott, one d.; ed Trinity Hall, Cambridge, Univ. of Sussex; joined Ministry of Finance as planner 1965; f. Walkover Estates (agribusiness venture) 1970; co-f. Mpongwe Devt Co. 1978; mem. Movement for Multi-Party Democracy 1990–96; co-f. Lima Party 1996; elected mem. Nat. Ass. for Mpika constituency 1991, for Lusaka Central constituency 2006–; Minister of Agric., Food and Fisheries in 1990s; Vice-Pres. of Zambia 2011–; mem. Patriotic Front 2001–, currently Sec.-Gen. *Address:* Office of the Vice-President, Lusaka, Zambia (office).

SCOTT, James, MSc, FRS, FRCP, FMedSci; British physician and professor of cardiovascular medicine; *Professor of Cardiovascular Medicine, National Heart and Lung Institute, Imperial College, London;* b. 13 Sept. 1946, Ashby-de-la-Zouch; s. of Robert B. Scott and Iris O. Scott (née Hill); m. Diane M. Lowe 1976; two s. one d.; ed Univ. of London, London Hosp. Medical Coll.; house surgeon London Hosp. 1971–72; House Physician Hereford Co. Hosp. July–Dec. 1972; Sr House Officer Queen Elizabeth Hosp., Midland Centre for Neurosurgery and Neurology, Birmingham Jan.–Dec. 1973; Registrar Gen. Hosp., Birmingham Jan.–Dec. 1974, Royal Free Hosp., Academic Dept of Medicine 1975–76; Hon. Sr Registrar, MRC Research Fellow Hammersmith Hosp., Dept of Medicine 1976–80; Post-doctoral Fellow Univ. of California, Dept of Biochemistry and Biophysics 1980–83; Clinical Scientist, Head Div. of Molecular Medicine, MRC Research Centre 1983–91; Hon. Consultant Physician Northwick Park Hosp., Harrow 1983–91, Hammersmith Hosp. 1992–97; Prof., Chair. of Medicine Royal Postgraduate Medical School 1992–97; Hon. Dir MRC Molecular Medicine Group 1992–; Dir of Medicine Hammersmith Hosps NHS Trust, Dir Div. of Medical Cardiology 1994–97; Prof. of Medicine, Imperial Coll. School of Medicine 1997–, Deputy Vice-Prin. for Research 1997–, Founder-Dir Genetics and Genomics Research Inst., Imperial Coll. 2000, currently Prof. of Cardiovascular Medicine, Nat. Heart and Lung Inst.; Founder-mem. Acad. of Medical Sciences; mem. European Molecular Biology Org.; Fellow, Inst. of Biology; European Ed. Arteriosclerosis, Thrombosis and Vascular Biology (Journal of American Heart Asscn); several prizes and awards include Graham Bull Prize (Royal Coll. of Physicians) 1989, Squibb Bristol Myers Award for Cardiovascular Research 1993, etc. *Publications:* numerous articles on molecular medicine, molecular genetics, atherosclerosis, RNA modification, RNA editing and gene expression. *Leisure interests:* family and friends, the twentieth-century novel, British impressionist and modern painting, long distance running, swimming. *Address:* Genetics and Genomics Research Institute, The Flowers Building, Imperial College, London, SW7 2AZ, England (office). *Telephone:* (20) 7594-3614 (office). *Fax:* (20) 7594-3653 (office). *E-mail:* j.scott@imperial.ac.uk (office). *Website:* www3.imperial.ac.uk (office).

SCOTT, (Harold) Lee, Jr, BBA; American retail executive; *Operating Partner, Solamere Capital LLC;* b. 14 March 1949, Joplin, Mo.; s. of Harold Lee Scott and Avis Viola Scott (née Parsons); m. Linda Gale Aldridge 1969; two s.; ed Pittsburg State Univ., Pittsburg, Kan.; Br. Man. Yellow Freight System, Springdale 1972–78; Man. Queen City Warehouse, Springfield 1978–79; joined Wal-Mart Stores, Inc., Bentonville 1979, Dir of Transportation 1979–83, Vice-Pres. of Distribution, Sr Vice-Pres. of Logistics, Exec. Vice-Pres. of Logistics, Pres. and CEO Wal-Mart Stores Div. 1996, COO and Vice-Chair. 1999–2000, Pres. 2000–09, CEO 2000–09, Chair. Exec. Cttee 2009–11 (retd); Operating pnr Solamere Capital LLC 2009–, also mem. Investment Cttee; mem. Bd of Dirs Pvt. Truck Council, Washington, DC 1985–86, Goldman Sachs Group 2010–11, Cooper Industries Inc., United Negro Coll. Fund; Bd mem. Tsinghua Univ., China 1999–, currently also mem. Advisory Bd, School of Economics and Man.; mem. Republican party. *Leisure interests:* reading, quail hunting. *Address:* Solamere Group LLC, 137 Newbury Street, Seventh Floor, Boston, MA 02116 (office); 611 Prairie Creek Road, Rogers, AR 72756-3019, USA (home). *Telephone:* (857) 362-9205 (office). *Website:* investorrelations@solameregroup.com (office); www.solameregroup.com (office).

SCOTT, Mark, AO, BA, MA; Australian editor, media executive and academic; *Managing Director, Australian Broadcasting Corporation (ABC);* s. of Brian Scott; grand-s. of Sir Walter Scott (govt adviser); ed Univ. of Sydney, Harvard Univ.; Editorial Dir John Fairfax Publs –2006, Ed.-in-Chief Metropolitan Newspapers 2003–05, Regional and Community Newspapers 2005–; also worked for Sydney Morning Herald, Sun Herald, Age and Sunday Age; Man. Dir Australian Broadcasting Corpn (ABC) 2006–. *Address:* Australian Broadcasting Corporation (ABC), 14th floor, 700 Harris Street, Ultimo, Sydney, NSW 2007, Australia (office). *Telephone:* (2) 8333-5342 (office). *E-mail:* comments@your.abc.net.au (office). *Website:* www.abc.net.au (office).

SCOTT, Peter Denys John, CBE, MA, QC; British lawyer and arbitrator; b. 19 April 1935; s. of John Ernest Dudley Scott and Joan G. Steinberg; ed Monroe High School, Rochester, New York, USA, Balliol Coll., Oxford; called to Bar 1960, QC 1978; Chair. of Bar 1987 (Vice-Chair. 1985–86); Standing Counsel to Dir-Gen. of Fair Trading 1974–78, to Dept of Employment 1973–78; mem. Interception of Communications Tribunal 1986–2000, Lord Chancellor's Advisory Cttee on Legal Educ. and Conduct 1991–94; Chair. Inst. of Actuaries Appeal Bd 1995–2000; Judicial Chair. City Disputes Panel 1997–; Chair. Panel on Takeovers and Mergers 2000–10; Harmsworth Scholar of Middle Temple; Bencher of Middle Temple; Chair. Kensington Housing Trust 1999–2002; Chair. Bd of Trustees, Nat. Gallery 2000–08, Scott Review (NI) 2007–; mem. Investigatory Powers Tribunal 2000–10. *Leisure interests:* art, gardening, theatre. *Address:* 4 Eldon Road, London, W8 5PU, England (home). *Telephone:* (20) 7937-3301 (home). *Fax:* (20) 7376-1169 (home).

SCOTT, Richard Lynn (Rick), BBA, LLB; American lawyer, business executive, politician and state governor; *Governor of Florida;* b. 1 Dec. 1952, Bloomington, Ill.; m. Ann Scott (née Frances Annette Holland) 1972; two d.; ed Univ. of Missouri-Kansas City, Southern Methodist Univ.; raised in Kansas City, Mo.; served in USN on USS Glover as radar technician 1971–74; while a student, bought two Kansas City doughnut shops; practised law in Dallas, Tex.; Pnr, Johnson & Swanson (law firm), Dallas; Partner, HM Capital Partners, Dallas; helped found Columbia Hospital Corpn 1987 (merged with Hospital Corpn of America to form Columbia/HCA 1989, later became largest pvt. for-profit health care co. in USA), forced to resign as Chair. and CEO of Columbia/HCA amid questions over co.'s business and Medicare billing practices 1997; Partner of George W. Bush in ownership of Texas Rangers professional baseball team 1990s; Founder and CEO Richard L. Scott Investments, LLC, Naples, Fla (originally in Stamford, Conn.) 1997–; Co-founder and Chair. Solantic Corpn, Jacksonville 2001–; mem. Bd of Dirs Associated Industries of Florida, CyberGuard 2001–03, Secure Computing Corpn 2006–, Envestnet Asset Management, Continental Structural Plastics, Inc.; f. Conservatives for Patients Rights 2009; Founder Conservatives for Patients' Rights 2009–; Gov. of Florida 2011–; mem. Nat. Bd of The United Way 1997–2003, Business Council, Business Roundtable, Healthcare Leadership Council; Republican; Second Century Award for Excellence in Health Care, Columbia Univ. School of Nursing 1995, Silver Award for the CEO of the Year, Financial World magazine 1995, cited by U.S. News and World Report magazine as one of the Top 25 Performers of 1995, named by TIME magazine amongst America's 25 Most Influential People June 1996, Entrepreneurship Award, George Washington Univ. 2007. *Address:* Office of the Governor, PL 05 The Capitol, 400 South Monroe Street, Tallahassee, FL 32399-0001 (office); Richard L. Scott Investments, LLC, 1400 Gulfshore Blvd North, Suite 148, Naples, FL 34102, USA. *Telephone:* (850) 488-7146 (office); (239) 263-9030 (Naples). *Fax:* (850) 487-0801 (office); (239) 263-9031 (Naples). *Website:* www.flgov.com (office); www.rlsi.net.

SCOTT, Sir Ridley, Kt; British film director; b. 30 Nov. 1937, South Shields; ed Royal Coll. of Art; Dir of numerous award-winning TV commercials since 1970; Hon. DLitt (Sunderland) 1998. *Films:* Boy and Bicycle (dir, prod.) 1965, The Duellists (dir) 1977, Alien (dir) 1979, Blade Runner (dir, co-prod.) 1982, Legend (dir) 1985, Someone to Watch Over Me (dir, exec. prod.) 1987, Black Rain (dir) 1989, Thelma and Louise (dir, prod.) 1991, 1492: Conquest of Paradise (dir, prod.) 1992, Monkey Trouble (exec. prod.) 1994, The Browning Version (prod.) 1994, White Squall (dir, exec. prod.) 1996, G.I. Jane (dir, prod.) 1997, Clay Pigeons (prod.) 1998, Where the Money Is (prod.) 2000, Gladiator (dir, exec. prod.) (Acad. Award for Best Picture) 2000, Hannibal (dir, prod.) 2001, Black Hawk Down (dir, prod.) 2001, Six Bullets from Now (prod.) 2002, The Hire: Hostage (exec. prod.) 2002, The Hire: Beat the Devil (exec. prod.) 2002, The Hire: Ticker (exec. prod.) 2002, Matchstick Men (dir, prod.) 2003, Kingdom of Heaven (dir, prod.) 2005, In Her Shoes (prod.) 2005, Domino (prod.) 2005, Tristan & Isolde (exec. prod.) 2006, A Good Year (dir, prod.) 2006, American Gangster (dir, producer) 2007, Body of Lies (dir, producer) 2008, Tell-Tale 2009, Robin Hood 2010, Prometheus 2012. *Television:* Z Cars (dir, series) 1962, The Troubleshooters (dir, series) 1965, Adam Adamant Lives! (dir, series) 1966, The Informer (dir, series) 1966, Robert (dir, film) 1967, The Hunger (exec. prod., series) 1997, RKO 281 (exec. prod., series) 1999, The Last Debate (exec. prod., film) 2000, AFP: American Fighter Pilot (exec. prod., series) 2002, The Gathering Storm (exec. prod., film) (Emmy Award for Best Made-for-TV Film) 2002, Numb3rs (exec. prod., series) 2005. *Address:* William Morris Agency, One William Morris Place, Beverly Hills, CA 90212, USA (office);

Scott Free, 42/44 Beak Street, London, W1R 3DA, England. *Telephone:* (310) 859-4000 (office); (20) 7437-3163. *Fax:* (310) 859-4462 (office); (20) 7734-4978. *Website:* www.wma.com (office).

SCOTT, Robert G., BA, MBA; American fmr financial services executive; *Chairman (non-executive), Genpact Ltd;* b. 1946, Montclair, NJ; m. Karen Scott; ed Williams Coll., Stanford Graduate School of Business; investment banker, Morgan Stanley 1970–79, Man. Dir 1979–97, Dir Capital Market Services 1985–92, Corp. Finance 1992–94, Investment Banking 1994–96, Chief Financial Officer and Exec. Vice-Pres. Morgan Stanley Dean Witter (now Morgan Stanley) 1997–2001, Pres. and COO 2001–03, currently Advisory Dir; Chair. (non-exec.) Genpact Ltd 2011–, mem. Bd of Dirs 2006–; Exec. Vice-Pres. Greater New York Council of Boy Scouts of America 1992–2004; Ind. mem. Bd of Dirs NYSE Euronet; mem. Advisory Council, Stanford Graduate School of Business; Trustee, The Seeing Eye Inc. 1984–2004, New York-Presbyterian Hospital, Williams Coll., Naples Children and Education Foundation; fmr Trustee, Japan Soc.; fmr Chair. American Museum of Fly Fishing; Excellence in Leadership Award, Stanford Business School 2004. *Leisure interests:* flu fishing, golf, downhill skiing. *Address:* Genpact Ltd, 105 Madison Avenue, 2nd Floor, New York, NY 10016-7418, USA (office). *Website:* www.genpact.com (office).

SCOTT, Timothy (Tim), AADipl; British sculptor; b. 18 April 1937, Richmond, Surrey, England; s. of A. C. Scott and Dorothea Scott; m. Yvonne Jeanne Malkanthi Wirekoon 1958; two s. three d.; ed Lycée Jaccard, Lausanne, Architectural Asscn and St Martin's School of Art, London; worked at Atelier Le Corbusier-Wogensky and others, Paris 1959–61; Sr Lecturer Canterbury Coll. of Art 1975–76; Head of Fine Art Dept, Birmingham Polytechnic 1976–78; Head Dept of Sculpture, St Martin's School of Art 1980–86; Prof. of Sculpture, Akad. der Bildenden Künste Nürnberg 1993–2002; numerous visiting lectureships in USA, Canada, Australia, Germany, UK, Chile. *Leisure interests:* music, architecture, travel, Sri Lanka, Indian culture, food. *Address:* 'High House', 71 Gangawata Para Anniewatte, Kandy, Sri Lanka (office); Keeper's Cottage, Troutsdale, N Yorks., YO13 9PS (home); 50 Clare Court, Judd Street, London, WC1H 9QW, England (home). *Telephone:* (81) 2226913 (Sri Lanka) (office); (1723) 859087 (UK) (home). *E-mail:* timscottsculptor@yahoo.com (office).

SCOTT, Timothy (Tim) Eugene, BS; American politician and business executive; *Senator from South Carolina;* b. 19 Sept. 1965, Charleston, South Carolina; s. of Ben Scott, Sr and Frances Scott; ed Presbyterian Coll., Charleston Southern Univ.; owns an insurance agency and works as a financial adviser; Partner, Pathway Real Estate Group, LLC; mem. Charleston Co. Council from the 3rd Dist 1995–2009; mem. S Carolina House of Reps from the 117th Dist 2009–11; mem. US House of Reps for the 1st Congressional Dist of S Carolina 2011–13, mem. Cttee on Transportation, Cttee on Small Business, Cttee on Rules; Senator from S Carolina 2013–; Republican. *Address:* 113 Hart Senate Office Building, Washington, DC 20510, USA (office). *Telephone:* (202) 224-6121 (office). *Website:* scott.senate.gov (office).

SCOTT, Hon. W(illiam) Alexander, CBE, JP, BFA; Bermudian politician; b. 1940; s. of the late Willard Scott and Edith Lucille Scott; m. Olga Scott 1969; one s. one d.; ed Temple Univ., USA; Owner public relations agency; Founder-mem. and fmr Chair. Big Brothers; mem. Pitt Comm. investigating causes of riots 1977; apptd to Senate 1985, Opposition Leader in the Senate 1989; elected to Parl. 1993, Deputy Leader of the Opposition Progressive Labour Party 1996, currently MP for Warwick South East Constituency, Minister of Works and Eng 1998–2003, Premier of Bermuda and Govt Leader 2003–06. *Leisure interest:* photography. *Address:* Progressive Labour Party, Alaska Hall, 16 Court Street, Hamilton, HM 17, Bermuda (office). *Telephone:* 236-8633 (office). *E-mail:* ascott@plp.bm (office). *Website:* www.plp.bm (office).

SCOTT, Walter, Jr, BS; American business executive; *Independent Chairman, Level 3 Communications Inc.;* b. 21 May 1931; m. Suzanne Scott; three s. three d.; ed Colorado State Univ.; began career with Peter Kiewit Sons Inc., Omaha 1953, Man. Cleveland Dist 1962–64, Vice-Pres. 1964–65, Exec. Vice-Pres. 1965–79, Pres. 1979–97, Chair. Emer. 1998–, Ind. Chair. Level 3 Communications (cr. after spinoff from Peter Kiewit Sons) 1979–, mem. Bd of Dirs 1964–; Chair. MidAmerican Energy Holdings 1992–93, currently mem. Bd of Dirs; Pres. Joslyn Art Museum, Omaha 1987–97, currently Dir; mem. Bd of Dirs George Industries Inc. 1981–, Valmont Industries 1981–, Berkshire Hathaway 1988–, Burlington Resources 1988–, Commonwealth Telephone Enterprises Inc. 1993–, WorldCom 1996–97, RCN Corpn 1997–, Peter Kiewit Sons Inc., ConAgra Inc., Kiewit Materials Co.; currently Chair. Bd of Trustees, Open World Leadership Center; Chair. Bd of Policy Advisors, Peter Kiewit Inst. for Information Science, Tech. and Eng, Heritage Services, Omaha Zoological Soc.; Dir Neb. Game and Parks Foundation, Horatio Alger Asscn, Nat. Forest Asscn; f. Suzanne and Walter Scott Foundation; Hon. member, Chi Epsilon Soc. 1986; Hon. DLitt (Univ. of Nebraska) 1983, Hon. DHumLitt (Coll. of Saint Mary) 1988, Hon. DComm (Bellevue Univ.) 1996; Nebraska Builder Award, Univ. of Nebraska 1983, Outstanding Achievement in Construction Award 1986, Brotherhood Award, Nat. Conf. of Christians and Jews 1986, Philanthropist of the Year, Nat. Soc. of Fund-Raising Executives 1987, Man of the Year, Mid-America Council Boy Scouts of America 1988, Spirit of Youth Award 1988, Perry W. Branch Distinguished Service Award, Univ. of Nebraska Foundation 1989, Golden Plate Award, American Acad. of Achievement 1991, Golden Apple Award, Metropolitan Community Coll. Foundation 1993, Headliner Award, Greater Omaha Chamber of Commerce 1996, Horatio Alger Award 1997, Distinguished Eagle Scout Award 1991, Nebraskalander Award, Nebraskaland Foundation 1998, Manresa Award, Creighton Univ. 1998, Community Builder Award, Greater Omaha Chamber of Commerce 1999, Midlander of the Year, Omaha World-Herald 2000. *Address:* Level 3 Communications, Inc., 1025 Eldorado Boulevard Broomfield, CO 80021, USA (office). *Telephone:* (720) 888-1000 (office). *Website:* www.level3.com (office).

SCOTT, W(illiam) Richard, PhD; American sociologist and academic; *Professor Emeritus and Senior Scholar, Global Research Projects Center and John Gardner Center, Stanford University;* b. 18 Dec. 1932, Parsons, Kan.; s. of Charles H. Scott and Hildegarde Hewit; m. Joy Lee Whitney 1955; three c.; ed Parsons Jr Coll., Kan., Univ. of Kansas, Univ. of Chicago; Asst Prof., Dept of Sociology, Stanford Univ. 1960–65, Assoc. Prof. 1965–69, Prof. 1969–99, Prof. Emer. 1999–, Chair.

Dept of Sociology 1972–75, Dir Orgs. Research Training Program 1972–89; Dir Stanford Center for Orgs. Research 1988–96; Prof. by courtesy, Dept of Health Research and Policy, School of Medicine 1972– and of Educ., School of Educ. and of Organizational Behaviour, Graduate School of Business, Stanford Univ. 1977–, Sr Scholar, John W. Gardner Center for Youth and Their Communities 2002–08, 2013–, Collaboratory for Global Research; Sr Researcher, Nat. Center for Health Services Research, Dept of Health, Educ. and Welfare, Washington, DC 1975–76; Visiting Prof., Kellogg Grad. School of Man., Northwestern Univ. 1997, Hong Kong Univ. of Science and Tech. 2000; Visiting Distinguished Scholar, Singapore Management Univ. 2006; Visiting Prof., Said Business School and Green Coll., Univ. of Oxford 2008; Ed. Annual Review of Sociology 1986–91; mem. Gov. Bd, Comm. on Social and Behavioral Sciences and Educ., NAS 1990–96; Woodrow Wilson Fellow 1954–55; Social Science Research Council Fellow 1958–59, Fellow, Center for Advanced Study in the Behavioral Sciences 1989–90; Resident Fellow, Bellagio Center 2002; mem. Inst. of Medicine; Dr hc (Copenhagen Business School) 2000; Hon. DEcon (Helsinki School of Econs) 2001; Dr Scientiarum Socialium (Arhus Univ., Denmark) 2010; Distinguished Scholar Award, OMT Div. of Acad. of Man. 1988, Richard D. Irwin Award for Distinguished Scholarly Career, Acad. of Man. 1996, Distinguished Educator Award, OMT Div. of Acad. of Man. 2013. *Publications:* Metropolis and Region (co-author) 1960, Formal Organizations (co-author) 1962, Social Processes and Social Structures 1970, Evaluation and the Exercise of Authority (co-author) 1975, Organizations: Rational, Natural and Open Systems 1981 (fifth edn 2003), Organizational Environments (co-author) 1983, Hospital Structure and Performance (co-author) 1987, Institutional Environments and Organizations: Structural Complexity and Individualism (co-author) 1994, Institutions and Organizations 1995 (third edn 2008), Institutional Change and Healthcare Organizations: From Professional Dominance to Managed Care (co-author) 2000, Organizations and Organizing (co-author) 2007, Organizations and Organizing: Rational, Natural and Open System Perspectives 2007, Between Movement and Establishment (co-author) 2009, Global Projects: Institutional and Political Challenges (co-author) 2011. *Leisure interests:* reading, gardening, hiking. *Address:* Stanford University Department of Sociology, Building 120, Stanford, CA 94305 (office); 940 Lathrop Place, Stanford, CA 94305, USA (home). *Telephone:* (650) 723-3416 (office); (650) 857-1834 (home). *Fax:* (650) 725-6471 (office). *E-mail:* scottwr@stanford.edu (office). *Website:* www.stanford.edu/dept/soc (office).

SCOTT BROWN, Denise, MArch, MCP, RIBA, Int. FRIBA; American architect, planner, urban designer, writer and academic; *Principal, Venturi, Scott Brown and Associates;* b. (Denise Valda Lakofski), 3 Oct. 1931, Nkana, Zambia; d. of Simon Lakofski and Phyllis Hepker; m. 1st Robert Scott Brown 1955 (died 1959); m. 2nd Robert Venturi (q.v.) 1967; one s.; ed Kingsmead Coll. Johannesburg, Univ. of Witwatersrand, Architectural Asscn London and Univ. of Pennsylvania; Asst Prof., Univ. of Pennsylvania School of Fine Arts 1961–65; Assoc. Prof., UCLA 1965–68; mem. Venturi, Scott Brown & Assocs, Inc., Philadelphia 1967–, Pnr 1969–89, Prin. 1989–; Visiting Prof., Univ. of California, Berkeley 1965, Yale Univ. 1967–71, Univ. of Pennsylvania 1982–83; mem. MIT School of Architecture and Urban Planning Visiting Cttee 1973–83; Fellow, Butler Coll., Princeton Univ. 1983–; Eliot Noyes Visiting Critic, Harvard Univ. 1990; Kassler Lecturer and Whitney J. Oates Fellow, Humanities Council, School of Architecture 2006; Jury mem., Prince of Wales Prize in Urban Design 1993; mem. Advisory Bd, Carnegie Mellon Univ. Dept of Architecture 1992–, Bd of Overseers for Univ. Libraries, Univ. of Pennsylvania 1995–2004; Adviser to Bd of Visitors, Tyler School of Art and Architecture, Temple Univ. 2008–; numerous other academic and professional appointments; Hon. DEng (Tech. Univ. of Nova Scotia) 1991, Hon. DHumLitt (Pratt Inst.) 1992, (Lehigh Univ.) 2002, Hon. DFA (Univ. of Pennsylvania) 1994, Hon. DLit (Univ. of Nev.) 1998; Dr hc (Univ. of the Witwatersrand) 2011; President's Medal, Architectural League of NY 1986; Chicago Architecture Award 1987; Commendatore, Repub. of Italy 1987; Nat. Medal of Arts 1992, Philadelphia Award 1992, Benjamin Franklin Medal Award (RSA) 1993, ACSA–AIA Jt Award for Excellence in Architecture Educ., Topaz Medallion 1996, Giants of Design Award, House Beautiful Magazine 2000, Joseph Pennell Medal, Philadelphia Sketch Club 2000, Edith Wharton Women of Achievement Prize for Urban Planning 2002, Harvard Radcliffe Inst. Medal 2005, Vileck Prize 2007, Athena Award 2007, Nat. Design Mind Award, Cooper Hewitt Nat. Design Museum 2007, Int. Award, Soc. of American Registered Architects, Philadelphia 2010, Edmund N. Bacon Prize, Ed Bacon Foundation 2010. *Publications:* Learning from Las Vegas (with R. Venturi and S. Izenour) 1977, A View from the Campidoglio: Selected Essays, 1953–84 (with R. Venturi) 1984, Urban Concepts 1990, Architecture and Decorative Arts: Two Naifs in Japan (with R. Venturi) 1991, Architecture as Signs and Systems for a Mannerist Time (with R. Venturi) 2004, Supercrit 2 2007, AA Words 4: Having Words 2009; articles in professional journals. *Leisure interests:* travelling, writing, teaching, lecturing. *Address:* Venturi, Scott Brown & Associates, Inc., 4236 Main Street, Philadelphia, PA 19127-1696, USA (office). *Telephone:* (215) 487-0400 (office). *Fax:* (215) 487-2520 (office). *E-mail:* info@vsba.com (office). *Website:* www.vsba.com (office).

SCOTT-JOYNT, Rt Rev. Michael, MA; British ecclesiastic; *Bishop of Winchester;* b. 15 March 1943, Bromley, Kent; m. Louise White 1965; two s. one d.; ed King's Coll. Cambridge and Cuddesdon Theological Coll.; ordained deacon 1967, priest 1968; Curate, Cuddesdon 1967–70; Tutor, Cuddesdon Coll. 1967–71, Chaplain 1971–72; Team Vicar, Newbury 1972–75; Priest-in-Charge, Caversfield 1975–79, Bicester 1975–79, Bucknell 1976–79; Rector, Bicester Area Team Ministry 1979–81; Rural Dean of Bicester and Islip 1976–81; Canon Residentiary of St Albans 1982–87; Dir of Ordinands and In-Service Training, Diocese of St Albans 1982–87; Bishop Suffragan of Stafford 1987–95; Bishop of Winchester 1995–. *Address:* Wolvesey, Winchester, Hants., SO23 9ND, England (office). *Telephone:* (1962) 854050 (office). *Fax:* (1962) 897088 (office). *Website:* www .winchester.anglican.org (office).

SCOTT OF FOSCOTE, Baron (Life Peer), cr. 2000, of Foscote in the County of Buckinghamshire; **Richard Rashleigh Folliott Scott,** BA, LLB; British lawyer; b. 2 Oct. 1934, Dehra Dun, India; s. of the late Lt Col C. W. F. Scott and Katharine Scott (née Rashleigh); m. Rima E. Ripoll 1959; two s. two d.; ed Michaelhouse Coll. Natal, Univ. of Cape Town and Trinity Coll. Cambridge; called to Bar, Inner Temple 1959; practising barrister, Chancery Bar 1960–83; QC 1975; Attorney-Gen. to Duchy of Lancaster 1980–83; Bencher, Inner Temple 1981; Chair. of the

Bar 1982–83 (Vice-Chair. 1981–82); High Court Judge, Chancery Div. 1983–91; Vice-Chancellor, County Palatine of Lancaster 1987–91; a Lord Justice of Appeal 1991–94; Vice-Chancellor of the Supreme Court of Justice 1994–2000; Head of Civil Justice 1995–2000; Lord of Appeal in Ordinary 2000–09; non-Perm. Judge, Hong Kong Court of Final Appeal 2004–12; currently Judge, Civil and Commercial Court of Qatar; conducted inquiry into the sale of arms to Iraq 1992–96; Ed.-in-Chief Supreme Court Practice 1996–2001; Hon. mem. American Bar Assoc., Canadian Bar Assoc; Hon. LLD. (Birmingham) 1996, (Buckingham) 1999. *Publications:* Report of the Inquiry into the Export of Defence Equipment and Dual-Use Goods to Iraq and the Related Prosecutions; articles in legal journals. *Leisure interests:* equestrian activities, tennis, bridge. *Address:* House of Lords, London, SW1A 0PW (office); The Old Rectory, Foscote, Buckingham, MK18 6AE, England (home). *Telephone:* (20) 7219-6373 (office); (1280) 813142 (home). *E-mail:* rrfscott.foscote@gmail.com (home).

SCOTT OF NEEDHAM MARKET, Baroness (Life Peer), cr. 2000, of Needham Market in the County of Suffolk; **Rosalind Carol (Ros) Scott,** BA; British politician; b. (Rosalind Carol Leadbeater); 10 Aug. 1957, Bath, Somerset, England; d. of Kenneth Vincent Leadbeater and Carol Leadbeater; m. 1st (divorced); one s. one d.; m. 2nd Mark Valladares 2008; ed Whitby Grammar School, Kent School, Univ. of East Anglia; Councillor, Mid-Suffolk Dist Council 1991–94, Suffolk Co. Council 1993–2005 (Vice-Chair. 1996–97); Chair. Local Govt Asscn Transport Exec. 2002–05; mem. (Liberal Democrat) House of Lords 2000–, mem. Appointments Comm. 2010–; Liberal Democrat Whip 2001–02, Deputy Chief Whip 2002, Spokesperson for Transport, Local Govt and the Regions 2001–02, for Transport 2002–04, for Office of the Deputy Prime Minister/Communities and Local Govt 2004–09, currently Chair. House of Lords EU Scrutiny Cttee D; Pres. Liberal Democrat Party 2009–10; mem. North Sea Comm. 1997–2005, Council of European Municipalities and Regions 1997–2003, Congress of Local and Regional Authorities in Europe 1997–2003, EU Cttee of the Regions 1998–2002, Inter-Parl. Union 2000–, Commonwealth Parl. Asscn 2000–; Bd mem. Audit Comm. 2004–06; Dir (non-exec.) Lloyd's Register, ITV Anglia, Entrust, the Landfill Tax regulator; mem. Comm. for Integrated Transport (think-tank); Lecturer for Dod's 'Westminster Explained'; mem. Bd Harwich Haven Authority 2013–; Hon. Pres. East Coast Sailing Trust. *Address:* House of Lords, Westminster, London, SW1A 0PW, England (office). *Telephone:* (20) 7219-8660 (office). *Fax:* (20) 7219-5979 (office). *E-mail:* scottr@parliament.uk (office). *Website:* www.parliament.uk/biographies/lords/baroness-scott-of-needham-market/2542 (office).

SCOTT-THOMAS, Kristin, OBE; British actress; b. 24 May 1960, Redruth, Cornwall; m. François Olivienne s (divorced); two s. one d.; ed Cen. School of Speech and Drama and Ecole Nat. des Arts et Technique de Théâtre, Paris; stage debut in Schnitzler's La Lune Déclinante Sur 4 ou 5 Personnes Qui Danse while student in Paris; has lived in France since age of 18; Chevalier, Légion d'honneur 2005. *Plays include:* La Terre Etrangère, Naive Hirondelles, Yes Peut-Etre, Bérénice, Three Sisters 2003, The Seagull (Olivier Award for Best Actress 2008) 2007. *Television includes:* L'Ami d'Enfance de Maigret, Blockhaus, Chameleon La Tricheuse, Sentimental Journey, The Tenth Man, Endless Game, Framed, Titmuss Regained, Look At It This Way, Body and Soul. *Films include:* Djamel et Juliette, L'Agent Troublé, La Méridienne, Under the Cherry Moon, A Handful of Dust, Force Majeure, Bille en Tête, The Bachelor, Bitter Moon, Four Weddings and a Funeral (BAFTA Award), Angels and Insects (Evening Standard Film Award), Richard III, The English Patient, Amour et Confusions, The Horse Whisperer 1998, Random Hearts, Up at the Villa, Gosford Park, Life As a House 2001, Petites Coupures 2003, Résistantes 2004, The Three Ages of the Crime 2004, Arsène Lupin 2004, Man to Man 2005, Keeping Mum 2005, La Doublure 2006, Ne le dis à personne 2006, The Walker 2007, The Golden Compass (voice) 2007, I've Loved You So Long 2008, The Other Boleyn Girl 2008, Seuls two 2008, Easy Virtue 2008, Largo Winch 2008, Confessions of a Shopaholic 2009, Partir (Leaving) 2009, Nowhere Boy 2010, Contre Toi 2010, Salmon Fishing in the Yemen 2011, The Woman in the Fifth 2011, Bel Ami 2012, In the House 2012. *Address:* c/o TESS Management, 4th Floor, 9-10 Market Place, London W1W 8AQ, England (office). *Telephone:* (20) 7557-7100 (office). *Fax:* (20) 7557-7101 (office). *E-mail:* info@tessmanagement.com (office). *Website:* www.tessmanagement.com (office).

SCOTTO, Renata; Italian singer (soprano); b. 24 Feb. 1935, Savona; m. Lorenzo Anselmi; one s. one d.; ed Giuseppe Verdi Conservatory, Milan with Emilio Ghiriardini; debut as Violetta, Teatro Nuovo, Milan 1953; joined La Scala opera co. from 1954; London debut at the Stoll Theatre 1957; US debut in Chicago 1960; Covent Garden debut 1962, as Madama Butterfly; roles at the Metropolitan Opera from 1965, directed Butterfly at the Metropolitan 1986 and sang there for the last time in 1987; numerous festival appearances; sang roles in Adriana Lecouvreur, Andrea Chénier, Anna Bolena, Cavalleria Rusticana, Der Rosenkavalier (Marschallin), Elektra (Klytämnestra), Edgar, Falstaff, Gilda, I Capuleti e i Montecchi, I Lombardi, I Puritani, I Vespri Siciliani (Helena), L'Elisir d'amore, La Bohème, La Sonnambula (Amina), La Straniera, La Traviata, La Voix Humaine, Lucia di Lammermoor, Madama Butterfly, Manon Lescaut, Otello, Pagliacci, Pirata, Robert le Diable, The Medium, Tosca, Trittico, Turandot; as stage dir: Il Pirata, Bellini Festival, Catania, Madama Butterfly, Arena di Verona, Genoa, Thessaloniki, Ancona, Dallas Opera, Lucia di Lammermoor, Thessaloniki, Tosca, Traviata, Sonnambula, Florida Grand Opera, Sonnambula, Detroit, Commendatore della Reppublica (Italy); Dr hc (Saint John's Univ.); Metropolitan Opera Guild Opera News Award 2006. *Publication:* More than a Diva (autobiog.) 1984. *Address:* c/o Robert Lombardo Associates, 61 West 62nd Street, Suite 6F, New York, NY 10023, USA (office). *Telephone:* (212) 586-4453 (office). *Fax:* (212) 581-5771 (office). *E-mail:* lewis@rlombardo.com (office). *Website:* www.rlombardo.com (office).

SCOTTY, Ludwig Derangadage; Nauruan politician and fmr head of state; b. 20 June 1948, Anabar; ed Univ. of South Pacific, Fiji; mem. Parl. for Anabar Dist 1983–, Speaker –2000, 2003–13; Pres. and Minister of Foreign Affairs May–Aug. 2003 (removed in a no-confidence vote), mem. of Opposition 2003–04, re-elected Pres. 2004–07 (removed in a no-confidence vote), also fmr Minister of Civil Aviation, of Customs and Immigration and of Public Service. *Address:* Parliament of Nauru, Parliament House, Yaren, Nauru (office). *Telephone:* 557-3133 (office). *E-mail:* parliament.info@naurugov.nr (office). *Website:* www.naurugov.nr/parliament/index.html (office).

SCOWCROFT, Lt-Gen. Brent, PhD; American consultant, fmr government official and air force officer (retd) *President, Scowcroft Group;* b. 19 March 1925, Ogden, Utah; s. of James Scowcroft and Lucile Balantyne Scowcroft; m. Marian Horner 1951 (died 1995); one d.; ed US Mil. Acad., West Point and Columbia Univ.; Operational and Admin. positions in USAF 1948–53; taught Russian history as Asst Prof., Dept of Social Sciences, US Mil. Acad., W Point 1953–57; Asst Air Attaché, US Embassy, Belgrade 1959–61; Assoc. Prof., Political Science Dept, USAF Acad., Colorado 1962–63, Prof., Head of Dept 1963–64; Plans and Operations Section, Air Force HQ, Washington 1964–66; various Nat. Security posts with Dept of Defense 1968–72; Mil. Asst to Pres., The White House 1972, Deputy Asst to Pres. for Nat. Security Affairs 1973–75, Asst to Pres. for Nat. Security Affairs 1975–77, 1989–93; Pres. Forum for Int. Policy 1993–; Pres. The Scowcroft Group 1994–; mem. Pres.'s Gen. Advisory Cttee on Arms Control 1977–81; Dir Atlantic Council, US Bd of Visitors USAF Acad. 1977–79, Council on Foreign Relations, Rand Corpn, Mitre Corpn; Vice-Chair. UNA/USA; Chair. Presidential Comm. on Strategic Forces 1983–89; mem. Cttee to Advise Dir of CIA 1995–; Chair. Pres.'s Foreign Intelligence Advisory Bd 2001–04, Eisenhower Inst. 2004–; mem. Cttee of Enquiry into Nat. Security Council 1986–87; Defense DSM, Air Force DSM (with two oak leaf clusters), Legion of Merit (with oak leaf cluster), Air Force Commendation Medal, Nat. Security Medal; Hon. KBE 1993. *Publication:* A World Transformed (with George Bush) 1998, America and the World: Conversations on the Future of American Foreign Policy (with Zbigniew Brzezinski) 2008. *Address:* The Scowcroft Group, Suite 900, 900 17th Street, NW, Washington, DC 20006, USA (office). *Telephone:* (202) 296-9312 (office). *Fax:* (202) 296-9395 (office). *Website:* www.scowcroft.com (office).

SCREECH, Rev. Michael Andrew, MA, DLitt, FBA, FRS; British clergyman and Renaissance scholar; *Fellow Emeritus, All Souls College, Oxford;* b. 2 May 1926, Plymouth, Devon, England; s. of Richard John Screech MM and Nellie Screech (née Maunder); m. Anne Reeve 1956; three s.; ed Sutton High School, Plymouth and Univ. Coll., London; in mil. service, mainly Far East 1944–48; Lecturer then Sr Lecturer, Univ. of Birmingham 1951–61; Reader, Univ. Coll. London –1966, Prof. of French 1961–71, Fielden Prof. of French Language and Literature 1971–84; Sr Research Fellow, All Souls Coll., Oxford 1984–93, Fellow Emer. 1993–, Fellow and Chaplain 2001–03; Extraordinary Fellow, Wolfson Coll., Oxford 1993–2001, Hon. Fellow 2001–; ordained deacon 1993, priest 1994; Non-Stipendiary Minister, St Giles' Church, St Margaret's Church, Oxford 1993–; Visiting Prof., London, Ont. 1964, Albany 1969; Johnson Prof., Madison 1979; Edmund Campion Lecturer, Regina, Sask. 1985, Dorothy Ford Wiley Prof. of Renaissance Culture, Chapel Hill 1986; Prof., Collège de France 1989; Visiting Prof., Sorbonne 1990; Comité de Publ d'Humanisme et Renaissance 1965–; Corresp. mem. Soc. Historique et Archéologique de Geneva 1988, Institut de France: Acad. des Inscriptions et Belles Lettres, Paris 1999; Fellow, Univ. Coll. London 1980; Ordre National du Mérite 1983, Chevalier, Légion d'honneur 1992; Hon. DLitt (Exeter) 1993, Dr hc (Geneva) 1998, (Neuchâtel) 2010; Médaille de la Ville de Tours. *Publications:* The Rabelaisian Marriage 1958, L'Evangélisme de Rabelais 1959, Le Tiers Livre de Pantagruel 1964, Les 52 Semaines de Lefèvre d'Etaples 1965, Les Regrets et Antiquités de Du Bellay 1966, Gargantua 1967, Marot Evangélique 1967, La Pantagruel ine Prognostication 1975, Rabelais 1979, Ecstasy and the Praise of Folly 1981, 1988, Montaigne and Melancholy 1983, A New Rabelais Bibliography (with Stephen Rawles) 1987, Montaigne: An Apology for Raymond Sebond 1987, Montaigne: The Complete Essays 1991, Some Renaissance Studies 1992, Rabelais and the Challenge of the Gospel 1992, Clément Marot: A Renaissance Poet Discovers the Gospel 1993, The Doctrina et Politia Ecclesiae Anglicanae of Warden Mocket (ed.) 1995, Monumental Inscriptions in All Souls College, Oxford 1997, Laughter at the Foot of the Cross 1998, Montaigne's Copy of Lucretius 1998, 'Isaiah Berlin' in Armchair Athenians 2001. *Leisure interest:* walking. *Address:* 5 Swanston-field, Whitchurch-on-Thames, Reading, Berks., RG8 7HP, England. *Telephone:* (118) 984-2513. *E-mail:* michael .screech@btinternet.com.

SCRIVENER, Christiane; French public official and mediator; *President Ombudsman, Société Générale;* b. 1 Sept. 1925, Mulhouse; d. of Pierre Fries and Louise Fries; m. Pierre Scrivener 1944; one s. (deceased); ed Harvard Business School and Univ. of Paris; businesswoman involved since 1958 in org. of French tech. co-operation with more than 100 countries, devt of int. tech. and industrial exchanges and promotion of French tech. abroad; State Sec. for Consumer Affairs 1976–78; MEP 1979–89; mem. Union pour la Démocratie (UDF); EEC Commr for Taxation and Customs Union and Consumers' Interests 1989–95; Pres. Ombudsman Société Générale 1996–, Plan Int. France 1997–; mem. Bd Alliance Française 1995–97; Grand Officier, Légion d'honneur; Grand-croix Ordre de Leopold (Belgium); Grand-croix de Mérite (Luxembourg); Officier de Polonia Restituta (Poland). *Publications:* Le rôle et la responsabilité à l'égard du public 1978, L'Europe, une bataille pour l'avenir 1984, Histoires du petit Troll 1986. *Leisure interests:* skiing, music. *Address:* 21 avenue Robert-Schuman, 92100 Boulogne-Billancourt, France. *Telephone:* 1-48-25-44-11 (home). *E-mail:* ch.scrivener@wanadoo.fr (home).

SCRIVER, Charles Robert, OC, CC, MD, CM, FRS, FRSC, FAAS; Canadian paediatrician and geneticist; *Alva Professor Emeritus of Human Genetics, McGill University;* b. 7 Nov. 1930, Montreal; s. of Walter DeMoulpied and Jessie Marion Boyd; m. Esther Peirce 1956; two s. two d.; intern Royal Victoria Hosp. Montreal 1955–56, Resident 1956–57, Resident Montreal Children's Hosp. 1956–57, Chief Resident (Pediatrics) 1960–61, physician 1961–; Children's Medical Center, Boston, USA 1957–58; McLaughlin Travelling Fellow, Univ. Coll., London, UK 1958–60; Asst Prof. of Pediatrics, McGill Univ. 1961, Markle Scholar 1961–66, Assoc. Prof. 1965–69, Prof. of Pediatrics, Genetics and Biology 1969–, Co-Dir MRC Genetics Group 1972–95, Alva Prof. of Human Genetics 1994, Alva Prof. Emer. of Human Genetics 2002–; Assoc. Dir Canadian Genetic Diseases Network 1989–98; Pres. Canadian Soc. for Clinical Investigation 1974–75, Soc. for Pediatric Research 1975–76, American Soc. Human Genetics 1986, American Pediatric Soc. 1994–95; mem. Medical Advisory Bd/Scientific Advisory Bd Howard Hughes Medical Inst. 1981–88; Hon. DSc (Manitoba) 1992, (Glasgow, Montreal) 1993, (Utrecht) 1999, (British Columbia) 2002, (Montreal); Allen Award, American Soc. of Human Genetics 1978, Gairdner Foundation Int. Award 1979, McLaughlin Medal, Royal Soc. of Canada 1981, Canadian Rutherford Lectureship, Royal Soc., London 1983, Ross Award, Canadian Pediatric Soc. 1990, Award of Excellence, Genetic Soc. of

Canada 1992, Prix du Québec 1995, Friesen Award 2001, Querci Prize (Italy) 2001, ASHG Award for Excellence in Human Genetics Educ. 2001, John Howland Award, American Pediatric Soc. 2010. *Publications:* Amino Acid Metabolism and its Disorders (co-author) 1973, Garrod's Inborn Factors in Disease (co-author) 1989, Metabolic Basis of Inherited Disease (6th, 7th, 8th edns, online, Sr Ed.) (co-author) 1989–; author or co-author of more than 500 scientific articles. *Leisure interests:* literature, music, photography. *Address:* Department of Human Genetics, McGill University, Room N5-13, Stewart Biology Building, 1205 Dr Penfield Avenue, Montreal, PQ H3A 1B1 (office); 232 Strathearn Avenue, Montreal, PQ H4X 1Y2, Canada (home). *Telephone:* (514) 412-4417 (office). *E-mail:* charles .scriver@mcgill.ca (office); thomas.leslie@mcgill.ca (office). *Website:* www.mcgill.ca (office).

SCRUTON, Roger, BA, PhD, FRSL, FBA; British philosopher and writer; b. 27 Feb. 1944, Buslingthorpe; s. of John Scruton and Beryl C. Haines; m. 1st Danielle Laffitte 1975 (divorced 1983); m. 2nd Sophie Jeffreys 1996; ed High Wycombe Royal Grammar School, Jesus Coll. Cambridge and Inner Temple, London; Fellow, Peterhouse, Cambridge 1969–71; Lecturer in Philosophy, Birkbeck Coll. London 1971–79, Reader 1979–86, Prof. of Aesthetics 1986–92; Prof. of Philosophy, Boston Univ. 1992–95; Founder and Dir The Claridge Press 1987–2004; Ed. The Salisbury Review 1982–2000, now on Editorial Bd; currently Visiting Prof. of Philosophy, Univ. of Oxford; Sr Fellow, Ethics & Public Policy Center, Washington DC; mem. Editorial Bd British Journal of Aesthetics, Arka (Kraków); Dr hc (Adelphi Univ.) 1995, (Masaryk Univ., Brno, Czech Repub.) 1998, (Hillsdale Coll., Michigan, USA) 2012; Medal of Merit, First Class (Czech Repub.) 1998. *Compositions:* The Minister (opera in one act) 1994, Violet (opera in two acts) 2006. *Publications:* Art and Imagination 1974, The Aesthetics of Architecture 1979, The Meaning of Conservatism 1980, The Politics of Culture and Other Essays 1981, Fortnight's Anger (novel) 1981, A Short History of Modern Philosophy 1982, A Dictionary of Political Thought 1982, The Aesthetic Understanding 1983, Kant 1983, Untimely Tracts 1985, Thinkers of the New Left 1986, Sexual Desire 1986, Spinoza 1987, A Land Held Hostage: Lebanon and the West 1987, The Philosopher on Dover Beach (essays) 1989, Francesca (novel) 1991, A Dove Descending (stories) 1991, Conservative Texts: An Anthology 1991, The Xanthippic Dialogues 1993, Modern Philosophy 1993, The Classical Vernacular 1994, Modern Philosophy 1996, Animal Rights and Wrongs 1996, An Intelligent Person's Guide to Philosophy 1997, The Aesthetics of Music 1997, On Hunting 1998, Town and Country (co-ed.) 1998, An Intelligent Person's Guide To Modern Culture 1998, On Hunting 1999, Perictione in Colophon 2000, England: An Elegy 2000, The West and the Rest: Globalization and the Terrorist Threat 2002, Death-Devoted Heart: Sex and the Sacred in Wagner's Tristan and Isolde 2004, News from Somewhere: On Settling 2004, Gentle Regrets (autobiog.) 2005, A Political Philosophy 2006, Culture Counts: Faith and Feeling in a World Besieged 2007, Beauty 2009, Understanding Music: Philosophy and Interpretation 2009, I Drink Therefore I Am 2009, The Uses of Pessimism and the Danger of False Hope 2010, Green Philosophy 2012, The Face of God 2012, Notes from Underground 2014. *Leisure interests:* music, literature, hunting. *Address:* Sunday Hill Farm, Brinkworth, Wilts., SN15 5AS, England. *Website:* www.roger-scruton.com.

SCULLY, Marlan Orvil, BS, MS, PhD; American physicist and academic; *Burgess Distinguished Professor, Physics and Astronomy, Texas A&M University;* b. 3 Aug. 1939, Casper, Wyoming; ed Casper Coll., Univ. of Wyoming, Rensselaer Polytechnic Inst., Yale Univ.; Instructor, Yale Univ. 1961–62; Asst Prof., Massachusetts Inst. of Tech. 1967–69, Assoc. Prof. 1969–71; Prof., Univ. of Arizona 1969–80; Distinguished Prof., Univ. of New Mexico 1980–92; External Scientist, Max Planck Inst. for Quantum Optics 1980–; Univ. Prof., Texas A&M Univ. 1992–96, Burgess Distinguished Prof. 1996–; Visiting Burgess Prof. (Chem.), Princeton Univ. 2003–05, Lecturer with rank of Prof. 2005–; mem. NAS, Academia Europaea, Max Planck Soc.; Fellow, American Acad. of Arts and Sciences, AAAS, American Physical Soc., Optical Soc. of America; Dr hc (Ulm); numerous awards, including Schawlow Prize, American Physical Soc., Townes Award, Optical Soc. of America, IEEE Quantum Electronics Award, Elliott Cresson Medal, Franklin Inst., Lomb Medal, Optical Soc. of America, Humboldt Sr Faculty Prize, named Harvard Loeb Lecturer, Hebert Walther Award, Optical Soc. of America/Deutsche Physikalische Gesellschaft, Guggenheim Fellowship, Alexander von Humboldt Distinguished Faculty Prize. *Publications:* Laser Physics (co-author), Quantum Optics (co-author); more than 700 papers in professional journals. *Address:* Department of Physics and Astronomy, Texas A&M University, 4242 TAMU, College Station, TX 77843-4242 (office); Department of Mechanical and Aerospace Engineering, Princeton University, Room D416, Engineering Quadrangle, Princeton, NJ 08544, USA. *Telephone:* (979) 862-2333 (College Station) (office); (609) 258-3962 (Princeton) (office). *Fax:* (979) 845-2590 (Princeton) (office). *E-mail:* scully@tamu.edu (office); mscully@princeton.edu (office). *Website:* physics.tamu.edu (office); iqse.tamu.edu (office); www.princeton.edu/mae/people/faculty/scully (office).

SCULLY, Sean Paul, BA; Irish/American artist; b. 30 June 1945, Dublin, Ireland; s. of John Anthony Scully and Holly Scully; m. Catherine Lee; ed Croydon Coll. of Art, Newcastle Univ., Harvard Univ.; with Fine Art Dept, Newcastle Univ. 1967–71; Lecturer, Harvard Univ. 1972–73; Lecturer, Chelsea School of Art and Goldsmiths' School of Art, London 1973–75; Lecturer, Princeton Univ. 1978–83; Lecturer in Painting, Parsons School of Design, New York 1983–; works in public collections in UK, USA, Australia, Germany, Ireland;; Hon. mem., London Inst. 1994; Hon. DFA (Massachusetts Coll. of Art) 2003, (Nat. Univ. of Ireland) 2003; Stuyvesant Foundation Prize 1970, 1972 Prize John Moores Liverpool Exhbn 8, 1974 Prize John Moores Liverpool Exhbn 9, Guggenheim Fellowship 1983, Artist's Fellowship, Nat. Endowment for the Arts. *Address:* Galerie Lelong, 528 West 26th Street, New York, NY 10001, USA (office); Waddington Galleries, 11 Cork Street, London, W1S 3LT, England (office). *Telephone:* (212) 315-0470 (office); (20) 7851-2200 (office). *Fax:* (212) 262-0624 (office); (20) 7734-4146 (office). *E-mail:* mail@waddington-galleries.com (office). *Website:* www.galerielelong.com (office); www.waddingtoncustot.com (office).

SCULTHORPE, Peter Joshua, AO, OBE; Australian composer; b. 29 April 1929, Launceston, Tasmania; s. of Joshua Sculthorpe and Edna Moorhouse; ed Launceston Grammar School, Univ. of Melbourne and Wadham Coll., Oxford; Lecturer, Sr Lecturer in Music, Univ. of Sydney 1963–68; Visiting Fellow, Yale

Univ. 1965–67; Reader in Music, Univ. of Sydney 1968–91, Prof. in Musical Composition and Sydney Moss Lecturer in Music 1992–; Visiting Prof. of Music, Univ. of Sussex 1971–72; commissions from bodies including Australian Broadcasting Comm., Birmingham Chamber Music Soc., Australian Elizabethan Theatre Trust, Australian Ballet, Musica Viva Australia, Australian Chamber Orchestra; Order of Isabella the Catholic (Spain); Hon. DLitt (Tasmania, Sussex), Hon. DMus (Melbourne), Australian Council Composers' Award 1975–77, Australian Film Inst. Award 1980, Ted Albert Award 1993, Sir Bernard Heinze Award 1994, ABC Classic FM Listeners' Choice Award 1998 and numerous other awards; Casa Asia Award 2009. *Compositions include:* The Loneliness of Bunjil 1954, Sonatina 1954, Irkanda I 1955, II 1959, III 1960, IV 1961, Ulterior Motifs, a musical farce and music for various revues 1957–59, Sonata for Viola and Percussion 1960, Theme and Journey's End (from film They Found a Cave) 1962, The Fifth Continent 1963, String Quartet No. 6 1965, No. 7 1966, No. 8 1969, No. 9 1975, No. 10 1983, No. 11 1990, Sun Music I 1965, Sun Music for Voices and Percussion 1966, Sun Music III 1967, IV 1967, Morning Song for the Christ Child 1966, Red Landscape 1966, Tabuh Tabuhan 1968, Autumn Song 1968, Sea Chant 1968, Sun Music II 1969, Orchestral Suite (from film The Age of Consent) 1968, Sun Music Ballet 1968, Love 200 for pop group and orchestra 1970, The Stars Turn 1970, Music for Japan 1970, Dream 1970, Night Pieces 1971, Landscape 1971, How The Stars Were Made 1971, Ketjak 1972, Koto Music I 1973, II 1976, Rites of Passage 1973, The Song of Tailitnama 1974, Postcard from Nourlangie to Clapham Common 1993, From Saibai 1993, Memento Mori for orchestra 1993, From Ubirr for string quartet and didgeridoo 1994, From Oceania 2003, Beethoven Variations 2006, Songs of Sea and Sky, Mangrove, for orchestra, My Country Childhood, Shining Island 2011; various works for radio, TV, theatre and film. *Leisure interests:* gardening, collecting Sung ceramics. *Address:* Faber Music Limited, Bloomsbury House, 74-77 Great Russell Street, London, WC1B 3DA, England; 91 Holdsworth Street, Woollahra, NSW 2025, Australia (home). *Telephone:* (20) 7908-5311. *Fax:* (20) 7908-5339. *E-mail:* promotion@fabermusic.com. *Website:* www .fabermusic.com.

SEABRA, Antônio Luíz; Brazilian business executive; *Chairman, Natura Cosméticos;* b. 1943, São Paulo; began career as trainee in Human Resources Dept, Remington Brazil, Man. 1964–66; f. Natura Cosméticos 1969, mem. Bd of Dirs 1998–, co-Chair. 2001–; Most Valuable Exec. Award, Valor Econômico 2003. *Address:* Natura Cosméticos S.A, Rodavia Régis Bittencourt, km 293, Building 1, Potuverá, 06882-700 Itapecerica da Serra, São Paulo, Brazil (office). *Telephone:* (11) 5694-7655 (office). *Website:* www.natura.net (office).

SEACREST, Ryan John; American radio personality, television host and producer; b. 24 Dec. 1974, Atlanta, Ga; s. of Gary Lee Seacrest and Constance Marie Seacrest (née Zullinger); ed Univ. of Georgia; hosted first season of ESPN's Radical Outdoor Challenge 1993; host of talent competition American Idol since 2002; won Emmy Award for producing ABC TV show Jamie Oliver's Food Revolution; host of On Air with Ryan Seacrest Los Angeles morning drive-time radio show for Clear Channel's 102.7 KIIS-FM, also of American Top 40 radio show; hosted the 59th Primetime Emmy Awards 2007; f. The Ryan Seacrest Foundation; Daytime Emmy Award for co-hosting the Walt Disney World Christmas Day Parade with Regis Philbin and Kelly Ripa 2005. *Address:* Ryan Seacrest Productions, 5750 Wilshire Boulevard, 4th Floor, Los Angeles, CA 90036, USA (office). *Telephone:* (323) 954-2400 (office). *Website:* ryanseacrest.com (office).

SEAGA, The Most Hon. Edward Philip George, BA, PC, ON; Jamaican academic and fmr politician; *Chancellor, University of Technology;* b. 28 May 1930, Boston, USA; s. of Philip Seaga and Erna Seaga (née Maxwell); m. 1st Marie Elizabeth Constantine 1965 (divorced 1995); two s. two d.; m. 2nd Carla Frances Vendryes 1996; one d.; ed Wolmers Boys' School, Kingston and Harvard Univ.; Field Researcher with Inst. of Social and Econ. Research (Univ. of West Indies) on devt of child and revival spirit cults; nominated to Upper House, Legis. Council 1959; Asst Sec. to Jamaican Labour Party 1960, Sec. 1962; MP for Western Kingston 1962–2005; Minister of Devt and Social Welfare 1962–67, of Finance and Planning 1967–72; Leader of Jamaican Labour Party 1974–2005; Leader of Opposition 1974–80, 1989–2005; Prime Minister 1980–89; Minister of Finance and Planning, Information and Culture 1980–89, of Defence 1987–89; Chair. Premium Group 1989; Hon. Distinguished Fellow, Univ. of the West Indies at Mona 2005–; Chancellor Univ. of Technology 2010–; Grand Cross, Order of Merit (FRG) 1982, The Order of the Nation 2002 (Jamaica); five Hon. LLD degrees from US univs; Gold Mercury Int. Award (Venezuela) 1981, Dr Martin Luther King Humanitarian Award 1984, Enviromental Leadership Award, UNEP 1987 and other awards. *Publications:* Development of the Child, Revival Spirit Cults, Faith Healing in Jamaica, My Life and Leadership- Volume 1: Clash of Ideologies 1930–1960 2010. *Leisure interests:* classical music, reading, hunting, sports, futurology. *Address:* University of Technology, 237 Old Hope Road, Kingston 6 (office); 24–26 Grenada Crescent, New Kingston, Kingston 5, Jamaica (home). *Telephone:* (876) 927-1680 (office). *Fax:* (876) 977-4388 (office). *E-mail:* websupport@utech.edu.jm (office); edward.seaga@uwimona.edu.jm (office). *Website:* www.utech.edu.jm (office).

SEAGAL, Steven; American film actor and martial arts expert; b. 10 April 1951, Lansing, Mich.; s. of Samuel Steven Seagal and Patricia Seagal; m. 1st Miyako Fujitoni 1974 (divorced 1987); one s. one d.; m. 2nd Kelly Le Brock 1987 (divorced 1996); one s. two d.; moved to Japan aged 17 remaining there for 15 years; established martial arts acads (dojo) in Japan and LA; CEO Steamroller Productions; PETA Humanitarian Award 1999. *Television:* Steven Seagal: Lawman 2009–. *Films:* Above the Law 1988, Hard to Kill 1990, Marked for Death 1990, Out for Justice 1991, Under Siege 1992, On Deadly Ground (dir) 1994, Under Siege 2 1995, The Glimmer Man 1996, Executive Decision 1996, Fire Down Below 1997, The Patriot 1998, Get Bruce 1999, Ticker 2001, Exit Wounds 2001, Ticker 2001, Half Past Dead 2002, The Foreigner 2003, Out for a Kill 2003, Belly of the Beast 2003, Clementine 2004, Out of Reach 2004, Into the Sun 2005, Mercenary for Justice 2006, Attack Force 2006, Flight of Fury 2007, Urban Justice 2007, Pistol Whipped 2008, Kill Switch 2008, Against the Dark 2009, The Keeper 2009, A Dangerous Man 2010, Born to Raise Hell 2010, True Justice 2011, Skin Trade 2011. *Recording:* Songs from The Crystal Cave 2004, Mojo Priest (album) 2007. *Address:* c/o ICM, 8942 Wilshire Blvd, Beverly Hills, CA 90211-1934, USA. *Website:* www.stevenseagal.com.

SEAL, Basil (see BARNES, Julian Patrick).

SEAMAN, Christopher, MA, ARCM; British conductor; b. 7 March 1942, Faversham, Kent, England; s. of Albert Edward Seaman and Ethel Margery Seaman (née Chambers); ed Canterbury Cathedral Choir School, The King's School, Canterbury, King's Coll., Cambridge; Prin. Timpanist, London Philharmonic Orchestra 1964–68; Asst Conductor BBC Scottish Symphony Orchestra 1968–70, Chief Conductor 1971–77; Chief Conductor Northern Sinfonia Orchestra 1973–79; Prin. Conductor BBC Robert Mayer Concerts 1978–87; Conductor-in-Residence, Baltimore Symphony Orchestra 1987–98; Chief Guest Conductor Utrecht Symphony Orchestra 1979–83; Music Dir Naples Philharmonic Orchestra, Fla 1993–, Rochester Philharmonic Orchestra, NY 1998–2011; Artistic Adviser, San Antonio Symphony; Dir Symphony Australia Conductor Programme; appears as guest conductor world-wide and has appeared in USA, Germany, France, the Netherlands, Belgium, Italy, Portugal, Spain, Australia and throughout UK; Hon. FGSM 1972. *Publication:* Inside Conducting 2013. *Leisure interests:* people, reading, shopping, theology. *Address:* c/o Harrison Parrott, 5–6 Albion Court, Albion Place, London, W6 0QT, England (office). *Telephone:* (20) 7229-9166 (office). *Fax:* (20) 7221-5042 (office). *E-mail:* info@harrisonparrott.co.uk (office). *Website:* www.harrisonparrott.com (office).

SEARLE, John R., BA, MA, DPhil; American academic; *Willis S. and Marion Slusser Professor of Philosophy of the Mind and Language, University of California, Berkeley;* b. 1932, Denver, Colo; s. of George W. Searle and Hester Beck Searle; m. Dagmar Carboch 1958; two s.; ed Univ. of Wisconsin, Univ. of Oxford, UK; Asst Prof. of Philosophy, Univ. of California, Berkeley 1959–64, Assoc. Prof. 1964–67, Prof. 1967–, later Slusser Prof. of Philosophy, Chair. Dept of Philosophy 1973–75, Special Asst to Chancellor for Student Affairs 1965–67; mem. Scholar Council, Library of Congress 2000–; mem. Editorial Bd Journal of Psycholinguistic Research, Linguistics and Philosophy, Philosophy and Artificial Intelligence, Journal of Consciousness Studies, Cognitive Science Series, Harvard Univ.Press; mem. American Acad. of Arts and Sciences 1976–, Cognitive Science Group, Univ. of California, Berkeley 1981–, European Acad. of Science and Art 1993–, Scientific Bd, Vilem Mathesius Centre, Charles Univ., Prague 1994–, Nat. Council of Nat. Endowment of Humanities 1992–96; mem. Bd of Dirs American Council of Learned Socs 1979–87; mem. Bd of Trustees Nat. Humanities Center 1976–90; Fellow and Lecturer, World Econ. Forum, Davos 1991, 1995, 1998, 2001; Educ. TV series in Calif. 1960–74; Advisor to Pres.'s Comm. on Student Unrest (Scranton Comm.) 1970; Hon. Prof., Tsinghua Univ., Beijing 2007, East China Normal Univ., Shanghai 2007; Dr hc (Adelphi) 1993, (Wisconsin) 1994, (Bucharest) 2000, (Torino) 2000, (Lucano) 2003; Rhodes Scholar 1952, Reith Lecturer 1984, Tasan Award, South Korean 2000, Jean Nicod Prize 2000, Jovellanos Prize 2000, Nat. Humanities Medal 2005, Mind and Brain Prize, Torino, Italy 2006, Puffendorf Medal, Sweden 2006. *Publications include:* Speech Acts 1969, The Campus War 1972, Expression and Meaning 1979, Intentionality 1983, Minds, Brains and Science 1984, The Foundations of Illocutionary Logic (with D. Vanderveken) 1985, The Rediscovery of the Mind 1992, (On) Searle on Conversation 1992, The Construction of Social Reality 1995, Mystery of Consciousness 1997, Mind, Language and Society 1998, Conversations with John Searle 2001, La Universidad Desafiada 2002, Consciousness and Language 2002, Liberté et Neurobiologie (trans. as Freedom and Neurology) 2004, Mind, A Brief Introduction 2004, Making the Social World 2010, Thinking About the Real World 2011. *Leisure interests:* literature, opera, skiing, travel. *Address:* Department of Philosophy, 314 Moses Hall 2390, University of California, Berkeley, CA 94720-2390, USA (office). *Telephone:* (510) 642-3173 (office). *Fax:* (510) 642-5160 (office). *Website:* philosophy.berkeley.edu (office).

SEARS, Hon. Alfred M., BA, JD; Bahamian politician and lawyer; b. 13 Jan. 1953, Fort Charlotte; s. of Winifred Sears; m. Marion Bethel 1987; three c.; ed Boys' Industrial School, St Augustine Coll., Columbia Univ., USA, New York Law School, USA, Univ. of the West Indies, Jamaica; f. Interdenominational Christian Youth Asscn (ICYA); Lecturer in Caribbean Politics, Hunter Coll., Univ. of New York 1977–87; fmr Attorney, Civil Court of Manhattan, USA, Berthan Macaulay, Jamaica, Gibson & Co., The Bahamas; Founder and Pnr, Sears & Co. (law firm) 1992–; Attorney-Gen. and Minister of Educ. 2002–07; Head of Caribbean Financial Action Task Force (CFTAF) 2002. *Address:* Sears & Co., POB N-3645, Nassau, The Bahamas (office). *Telephone:* 326-3481 (office). *Fax:* 326-3483 (office). *E-mail:* info@searschambers.com (office). *Website:* www.searschambers.com (office); alfredsears .org.

SEATON, David T.; American business executive; *Chairman and CEO, Fluor Corporation;* ed Univ. of South Carolina, Advanced Man. Program, Wharton School of Business, Int. Man. Program, Thunderbird Univ.; joined Fluor Corpn (eng, procurement, construction and maintenance services co.) 1984, held numerous exec. positions in both operations and sales globally, including Sr Group Pres., Energy and Chemicals, Govt and Power Groups, was responsible for Fluor's activities in China and the Middle East, led co.'s global business activities, including ICA Fluor (jt venture in Mexico) also served as Sr Vice-Pres. and Group Exec. for global corp. sales, COO Fluor Corpn 2009–11, mem. Bd of Dirs and CEO 2011–, Chair. 2012–; mem. Bd of Dirs Mosaic Co.; mem. Business Roundtable, Bd American Petroleum Inst., US-Saudi Arabian Business Council, World Econ. Forum's Partnering Against Corruption Initiative (Co-Chair. Forum's Global Agenda Council on Corruption). *Address:* Fluor Corporation, 6700 Las Colinas Blvd, Irving, TX 75039, USA (office). *Telephone:* (469) 398-7000 (office). *Fax:* (469) 398-7255 (office). *E-mail:* info@fluor.com (office). *Website:* www.fluor.com (office).

SEBAN, Alain; French arts organization executive; *President, Centre Georges Pompidou;* b. 15 July 1964, Toulouse; ed École Polytechnique, ENSAE ParisTech (École nationale de la statistique et de l'admin économique), Inst. d'Études Politiques de Paris; auditor, Conseil d'État 1991, Maître de requêtes 1994, Govt Commr 1997; adviser to the Minister of Culture 1995–97, Media Devt Dir 2002–05; Chargé de mission, Ministry of Foreign Affairs 2002–05; adviser on culture and education to Pres. Jacques Chirac 2005–07; Pres. Centre Georges Pompidou, Paris 2007–; Conseiller juridique, Musée du quai Branly 1997–2002; Vice-Pres. Exec. Cttee, Opéra de Paris pension fund 1997; Lecturer, École nationale d'admin 1996–99; Commdr, Ordre des Arts et des Lettres 2002, Chevalier, Légion d'honneur 2011. *Address:* Office of the President, Centre Georges Pompidou, 19 rue Beaubourg, 75191 Paris Cedex 04, France (office). *Telephone:* 1-44-78-12-33 (office). *Fax:* 1-44-78-12-07 (office). *Website:* www.centrepompidou.fr (office).

SEBASTIAN, Sir Cuthbert (Montraville), GCMG, OBE, FRCS, BSc, MD, CM; Saint Christopher and Nevis government official and surgeon; b. 22 Oct. 1921; ed Mount Allison Univ., Dalhousie Univ., Canada; pharmacist and lab. technician, Cunningham Hosp., St Kitts 1942–43; served in RAF 1944–45; Capt. St Kitts Nevis Defence Force 1958–80; Medical Supt, Cunningham Hosp. 1966, Joseph N. France Gen. Hosp. 1967–80; Chief Medical Officer Saint Christopher and Nevis 1980–83; pvt. medical practitioner 1983–95; Gov.-Gen. of Saint Christopher and Nevis 1996–2012; Dr hc (Dalhousie Univ.) 1998, (Mount Allison Univ.) 2005. *Leisure interests:* farming, reading, dancing. *Address:* c/o Government House, Basseterre; 6 Cayon Street, Basseterre, Saint Christopher and Nevis (home). *Telephone:* 465-2344 (home).

SEBASTIANI, HE Cardinal Sergio; Italian ecclesiastic; *President Emeritus, Prefecture for Economic Affairs of The Holy See;* b. 11 April 1931, Montemonaco (Ascoli-Piceno); s. of Angelo Sebastiani and Lucia Valeri; ed Pontifical Gregorian Univ., Pontifical Lateran Univ., Pontifical Ecclesiastical Acad.; ordained priest 1956; Sec. of Apostolic Nunciature, Peru 1960; Sec. of Apostolic Nunciature, Brazil 1962; Uditore, Apostolic Nunciature, Chile 1966, Office Chief, Vatican Secr. of State, Counsellor Apostolic Nunciature in Paris, with special assignment to Council of Europe 1974; ordained Titular Archbishop of Cesarea in Mauritania; Apostolic Pro-Nuncio to Madagascar and Apostolic Del. to Réunion and Comoros 1976, Apostolic Nuncio to Turkey 1985; Sec.-Gen. Cen. Cttee of Great Jubilee Year 2000 1994; Pres. Pref. for Econ. Affairs of The Holy See 1997–2008 (resgnd), Pres. Emer. 2008–; apptd Cardinal-Deacon of St Eustachio 2001, Cardinal-Priest of St Eustachio 2011–; Commendadore Order of Merit, Italy, Nat. Order of Madagascar, Grand Cross Order O'Higgins, Chile. *Publications:* La Chiesa all'uomo del XX secolo, La Sapienza nell'Antico Testamento. *Address:* Prefecture for the Economic Affairs of the Holy See, Palazzo delle Congregazioni, Largo del Colonnato 3, 00193 Rome (office); Via Rusticucci 13, 00193 Rome, Italy (home). *Telephone:* (06) 69884263 (office). *Fax:* (06) 69885011 (office).

SEBBAN, Guy; French business executive and fmr international organization official; b. 1944, Mostaganem, Algeria; m. Michelle Sebban; ed Ecole de Physique et Chimie de Paris, Univ. of Paris (Sorbonne), Université de Paris Dauphine; fmr Man. at Rhône-Poulenc, later at Aventis, Brussels, in charge of relations with EU insts; Sr Adviser to CEO of Vivendi Universal –2005; Sec.-Gen. ICC 2005–09. *Address:* c/o International Chamber of Commerce, 38 cours Albert 1er, 75008 Paris, France. *Telephone:* 1-49-53-28-18. *E-mail:* sg@iccwbo.org.

SEBELIUS, Kathleen, MPA; American government official and fmr politician; b. 15 May 1948, Ohio; d. of fmr Ohio Gov. John Gilligan; m. Gary Sebelius; two s.; ed Trinity Coll., Conn., Univ. of Kansas, Trinity Washington Univ.; first woman employee in Kan. Dept of Corrections 1975–87; mem. Kan. State House of Reps 1987–94, mem. Ethics Comm.; Insurance Commr, Kan. 1994–2002; Gov. of Kan. 2003–09; Sec. of Health and Human Services, Washington, DC 2009–14; Democrat; named amongst Top Ten Public Officials in America, Governing Magazine 2001, named by TIME magazine as one of the Five Best Governors in America 2005, named by the White House Project as one of its "8 in '08" (group of eight female politicians who could possibly have run and/or have been elected president in 2008) 2006, ranked by Forbes magazine amongst The World's 100 Most Powerful Women (57th) 2009, (23rd) 2010, (13th) 2011, (31st) 2012, (25th) 2013, ranked by Forbes magazine amongst The World's Most Powerful People (68th) 2012. *Leisure interest:* avid fan of jazz music (unbroken run of annually attending Jazz Fest in New Orleans since 1979). *Address:* c/o Department of Health and Human Services, 200 Independence Avenue, SW, Washington, DC 20201, USA.

ŠEBRLE, Roman; Czech fmr decathlete; b. 26 Nov. 1974, Lanškroun, Czechoslovakia; m. Eva Kasalová 2000; one s. one d.; ed Gymnázium Františka Martina Pelcla, Rychnov nad Kněžnou, Gymnázium Pardubice, extension course of Information Science and Computer Tech.; competed in first decathlon competition in Týniště nad Orlicí, reaching 5,187 points 1991; met coach Jiří Čechák; compulsory military service in Czech Armed Forces 1995–97; joined army sports club TJ Dukla Praha of which he is still a mem.; achieved a score of more than 8,000 points for the first time, reaching 8,210 points at a meeting in Prague 1996; won World Univ. Games in Sicily 1997; came ninth at World Championships, Athens 1997; mem. Czech Olympic athletics team, Sydney 2000 (silver medal for decathlon); set world record for decathlon (9,026 points, lasted until 2012), World Championships, Götziz, Austria May 2001; gold medals in decathlon, Universiade, Catania 1997, heptathlon, World Indoor Championships, Lisbon 2001, heptathlon, European Indoor Championships, Vienna 2002, Madrid 2005, Birmingham 2007, decathlon, European Championships Munich 2002, Gothenburg 2006, heptathlon, World Indoor Championships, Budapest 2004, decathlon, Olympic Games, Athens 2004 (set Olympic record with 8,893 points), World Championships, Osaka 2007; silver medal in heptathlon, European Indoor Championships, Ghent 2000, decathlon, World Championships, Paris 2003, Helsinki 2005; bronze medal, heptathlon, World Indoor Championships, Maebashi 1999, Birmingham 2003, Moscow 2006, heptathlon, European Indoor Championships, Turin 2009, Paris 2011; Men's Decathlon European record holder 2001–; Men's Heptathlon European record holder 2004–; retd June 2013; Czech Athlete of the Year 2002, 2003, 2004, World's Greatest Athlete 2004, No. 8 on TIME's list of 100 Olympic Athletes To Watch 2008. *Leisure interests:* computers, the Internet, football, sci-fi, music, spaghetti. *Address:* c/o Czech Olympic Committee, Benesovská 6, 10100 Prague 10; Česká sportovní a.s., Na Příkopě 9/11, 110 00, Prague 1, Czech Republic. *Telephone:* (2) 71734734 (Czech Olympic Committee); (2) 24233725 (Česká sportovní). *E-mail:* info@olympic.cz; sekretariat@ceskasportovni.cz. *Website:* www.ceskasportovni.cz; www.iaaf.org/athletes/czech-republic/roman-sebrle -130083.

SECHIN, Igor Ivanovich, PhD; Russian politician and business executive; *President, Chairman of the Management Board and Deputy Chairman of the Board of Directors, Rosneft;* b. 7 Sept. 1960, Leningrad (now St Petersburg); m.; one d.; ed Leningrad State Univ.; army service 1984–86; leading instructor, Exec. Cttee, Dept of Foreign Econ. Relations, Leningrad City Soviet 1988–91; Chief Expert, Asst to Head of Admin to First Vice-Mayor, Chair. Cttee on Foreign Relations, Office of Mayor of Leningrad 1991–96; Expert, Deputy Head of Div., Public Relations Dept, Dept of Foreign Affairs 1996–97; Head, Gen. Admin Dept, Adviser to Deputy Head then Head Chief Control Dept, Admin of the Russian Pres. 1998–99; Head, Secr. of First Deputy Chair., later Chair., Govt of Russian Fed.

1999–2000; Deputy Chief of Staff, Presidential Exec. Office 2002–08, Aide to the Pres. 2004–08; Deputy Chair. of the Govt (Deputy Prime Minister), in charge of industry devt, nuclear power and environment 2008–12; Dir (non-exec.) Rosneft Oil Co. 2004–11, Chair. 2004–11, Chair. Man. Bd, Pres. and Deputy Chair. 2012–; Chair. OJSC Rosneftegaz, OJSC Consolidated Shipbuilding Corpn, OJSC Inter RAO UES; ranked by Forbes magazine amongst The World's Most Powerful People (42nd) 2009, (52nd) 2010, (60th) 2013. *Address:* Rosneft, 117997 Moscow, Sofiyskaya Embankment 26/1, Russia (office). *Telephone:* (499) 517-88-99 (office). *Fax:* (499) 517-72-35 (office). *E-mail:* postman@rosneft.ru (office). *Website:* www .rosneft.com (office).

SECK, Idrissa; Senegalese politician; b. 9 Aug. 1959, Thies; m.; three c.; ed Institut d'Etude Politique, Paris, Princeton Univ., USA; consultant with Price Waterhouse 1986–92; mem. Parti démocratique sénégalais—PDS (Democratic Party), Deputy Sec.-Gen.; fmr Minister Without Portfolio; Sec. of State, Dir Office of the Pres. 2000–02; Prime Minister of Senegal 2002–04; Mayor of Thies 2002; unsuccessful cand. for Pres. 2007. *Address:* c/o Parti démocratique sénégalais (PDS), Blvd Dial Diop, Immeuble Serigne Mourtada Mbacké, Dakar, Senegal.

SEDAKA, Neil; American singer, pianist, songwriter and record producer; b. 13 March 1939, Brooklyn, New York; s. of Mac Sedaka and Eleanor Appel; m. Leba M. Strassberg 1962; one s. one d.; ed Juilliard School of Music, New York; recipient of numerous gold records and recording industry awards, Ivor Novello Special Int. Award 2010. *Composed numerous popular songs including:* Breaking Up Is Hard to Do, Stupid Cupid, Calendar Girl, Oh! Carol, Stairway to Heaven, Happy Birthday Sweet Sixteen, Laughter in the Rain, Bad Blood, Love Will Keep Us Together, Lonely Night (Angel Face). *Recordings include:* Rock with Sedaka 1959, Circulate 1961, Neil Sedaka Sings His Greatest Hits 1963, Smile 1965, Sounds of Sedaka 1969, Workin' on a Groovy Thing 1969, Emergence 1971, Solitaire 1972, The Tra-La Days Are Over (UK) 1973, Sedaka's Back 1974, In the Pocket 1980, The Hungry Years 1975, Steppin' Out 1976, A Song 1977, All You Need Is The Music 1978, Neil Sedaka Canta en Espanol 1983, Come See About Me 1984, All Time Greatest Hits 1988, Oh! Carol and Other Hits 1990, Timeless – The Very Best of Neil Sedaka 1991, Tales of Love (and Other Passions) 1998, The Show Goes On 2003, Neil Sedaka in Italiano 1999, The Singer and His Songs 2000, RCA 100th Anniversary Series: The Very Best of Neil Sedaka 2001, Brighton Beach Memories – Neil Sedaka Sings Yiddish 2003, Oh! Carol: The Complete Recordings, 1955–66 2003, Stairway to Heaven: The Best of Neil Sedaka 2004, Love Songs 2005, The Very Best of Neil Sedaka: The Show Goes On 2006, Neil Sedaka: Live at the Royal Albert Hall – The Show Goes On (2 DVD set filmed in London) 2006, The Definitive Collection 2007, Oh! Carol (LT Series album, compilation of 1970s hits recorded live in concert) 2007, The Miracle of Christmas 2008, Waking Up Is Hard to Do 2009, Flashback (compilation of Italian recordings) 2009, The Music of My Life (UK) 2009, The Miracle of Christmas: The Deluxe Edition 2009, The Music of My Life 2010, Neil Sedaka Sings Little Devil and His Other Hits/The Many Sides of Neil Sedaka 2010. *Address:* Neil Sedaka Music, 641 Lexington Avenue, 14th Floor, New York, NY 10022, USA (office). *Fax:* (212) 593-0526 (office). *E-mail:* rob@ neilsedaka.com. *Website:* www.neilsedaka.com.

SEDGWICK, (Ian) Peter; British business executive; b. 13 Oct. 1935; m. Verna Mary Sedgwick 1956; one s. one d.; with Nat. Provincial Bank 1952–59, Ottoman Bank Africa and Middle East 1959–69, J. Henry Schroder Wagg & Co. Ltd 1969–90; Dir Schroders Nominees Ltd 1981–95, CEO Schroder Investment Man. Ltd 1985–94, Dir Schroder Unit Trusts Ltd 1987–95, Group Man. Dir Investment Man. Schroders PLC 1987–95, Deputy Chair. (Chair. Desig.) 1995–2000, Chair. 2000–03, CEO (interim) 2001, Dir (non-exec.) Schroder & Co. Inc. 1991–99, Chair. 1996–2002, Pres. and CEO Schroders Inc., New York 1996–2000, Chair. Schroder All-Asia Fund 1991–99, Schroder UK Growth Fund 1994, Pres. CEO Schroder US Holdings Inc. 1996; Dir (non-exec.) Equitable Life Assurance Soc. 1991–2001, INVESCO City & Commercial Investment Trust PLC (fmrly New City & Commercial Trust PLC) 1992–2001; Chair. Queen Elizabeth Foundation 2007–10 (Trustee 2002–10); mem. European Advisory Bd JER Pnrs. *Leisure interests:* golf, grandchildren, theatre.

ŠEDIVÝ, Jaroslav, CSc, DPhil; Czech politician and diplomatist (retd); b. 12 Nov. 1929, Prague; s. of Jaroslav Šedivý and Marie Šedivý; m. Marie Poslušná 1962; one s. one d.; ed Charles Univ., Prague; with Czech Acad. of Sciences 1954–57; scientist, Inst. of Int. Policy and Econ. 1957–70; imprisoned on charges of subversion of the state 1970–71; worker, driver, window cleaner 1972–88; researcher, Prognostic Inst., Prague 1989; adviser to Minister for Foreign Affairs 1989–90; Amb. to France 1990–95, to Belgium, Luxembourg and NATO 1995–97; Perm. Rep. to UNESCO 1993–95; Minister for Foreign Affairs 1997, Jan.–July 1998; Amb. to Switzerland 1998–2002; Adviser, Analysis Section, Ministry of Foreign Affairs 2002–03; Grand Officier, Ordre nat. du Mérite 1994, Chevalier, Ordre de la Légion d'honneur 2005, Ordre of Merit (Czech Repub.) 2005; Dr hc (J.F. Kennedy Univ., Buenos Aires) 1998. *Publications:* Policy and Relations 1969, Humiliated Revolution (published under pseudonym Y. Hertová) 1978, Metternich contra Napoleon 1998, Palace Cernín in the Year Zero 1997, Mystery and Sins of the Templars 1999, Decembrists: Anatomy of an Unsuccessful Coup 2000. *Telephone:* (2) 41431707 (home). *E-mail:* sedivay@seznam.cz (home).

SEDLEY, Rt Hon. Sir Stephen John, Kt, PC, BA; British judge and writer; b. 9 Oct. 1939; s. of William Sedley and Rachel Sedley; m. 1st Ann Tate 1968 (divorced 1995); one s. two d.; m. 2nd Teresa Chaddock 1996; ed Mill Hill School, Queens' Coll., Cambridge; writer, musician, trans. 1961–64; called to Bar, Inner Temple 1964, Bencher 1989, QC 1983, Lord Justice of Appeal 1999–2011; mem. Int. Comm. on Mercenaries, Angola 1976; Visiting Professorial Fellow, Univ. of Warwick 1981; Pres. Nat. Reference Tribunals for the Coalmining Industry 1983–88; Visiting Fellow, Osgoode Hall Law School, Canada 1987; Visiting Prof. 1997; Dir Public Law Project 1989–93; Chair. Sex Discrimination Cttee, Bar Council 1992–95; Judge of the High Court of Justice, Queen's Bench Div. 1992–99; Distinguished Visitor, Hong Kong Univ. 1992; Hon. Prof., Univ. of Wales, Cardiff 1993–, Univ. of Warwick 1994–; Visiting Fellow, Victoria Univ. of Wellington, NZ 1998; Judicial Visitor, Univ. Coll. London 1999–; Pres. British Inst. of Human Rights 2000–, British Tinnitus Asscn 2006–; Chair. British Council Advisory Cttee on Governance 2002–05; mem. Admin. Law Bar Asscn (Hon. Vice-Pres. 1992–), Haldane Soc. (Sec. 1964–69); Hon. Fellow, Inst. for Advanced Legal Studies 1997; Dr hc (North London) 1996; Hon. LLD (Nottingham Trent) 1997, (Bristol) 1999, (Warwick)

1999, (Durham) 2001, (Hull) 2002, (Southampton) 2003, (Exeter) 2004, (Essex) 2007. *Publications include:* Whose Child? 1987, The Making and Remaking of the British Constitution (with Lord Nolan) 1997, Freedom, Law and Justice 1999, Human Rights: A New World or Business as Usual 2000; editor: Seeds of Love (anthology) 1967, A Spark in the Ashes 1992; translator: From Burgos Jail, by Marcos Ana and Vidal de Nicolas 1964; contrib. essays to numerous books, including Freedom of Expression and Freedom of Information 2000, Judicial Review in International Perspective 2000, Discriminating Lawyers 2000; contrib. to periodicals and journals, including Civil Justice Quarterly, Industrial Law Journal, Journal of Law and Society, Journal of Legal Ethics, Law Quarterly Review, London Review of Books, Modern Law Review, Public Law. *Address:* Cloisters, Temple, London, EC4Y 7AA, England (office).

SEDNEY, Jules; Suriname academic and politician; b. 28 Sept. 1922, Paramaribo; s. of Eugene Edwin Leonard Sedney and Marie Julia Linger; m. Ina Francis Waaldyk 1951 (divorced 1985); two s. two d.; one d. by A. Calor; ed Graaf van Zinzendorfschool, Mulo and Univ. of Amsterdam; fmr teacher; held sr post with Cen. Bank of Suriname 1956–58, Pres. 1980; Minister of Finance 1958–63; Dir Industrial Devt Corpn of Suriname and Nat. Devt Bank 1963; left Nationale Partij Suriname (NPS) and joined Progressieve Nationale Partij (PNP) 1967; Prime Minister and Minister of Gen. Affairs 1970–73; Prof. of Econs, Univ. of Suriname 1976–80; Chair. Nat. Planning Council 1980; fmr Dir Suriname Trade and Industry Asscn 1990–92; Chair. Monitoring Group Suriname Structural Adjustment Programme 1992–96, Tripartite Advisory Bd to Govt of Suriname 1994–98, Seniority Bd of Econ. Advisers to Pres. of the Repub. 1998–2000, Center for the Promotion and Protection of Democracy and Civil Soc. 1999; Gran Cordón Simón Bolívar (Venezuela), Groot-Officier Oranje Nassau (Netherlands), Kt, Nederlandse Leeuw (Netherlands). *Publications:* Growth Without Development 1978, To Choose and To Divide 1980, The Future of Our Past 1998. *Leisure interests:* bridge, golf. *Address:* Maystreet 34, Paramaribo, Suriname. *Telephone:* (597) 439114. *Fax:* (597) 421029.

SEDWILL, Mark Philip, CMG, BSc (Hons), MPhil, FRGS, FIoD; British diplomatist, government official and international organization official; *Permanent Secretary, Home Office;* b. 21 Oct. 1964, Ealing, London, England; m.; one d.; ed Bourne Grammar School, St Andrews Univ., St Edmund Hall, Oxford; joined FCO 1989, with Security Co-ordination Dept and Gulf War Emergency Unit 1989–91, Second Sec., Egypt 1991–94, Resource Man. Group, FCO 1994–96, First Sec. and UN Weapons Inspector, Iraq 1996–97, First Sec., Political-Mil. and Counter-Terrorism, Cyprus 1997–99, Europe and Middle East Press Officer, FCO 1999–2000, Pvt. Sec. to Foreign Sec. Robin Cook and Foreign Sec. Jack Straw 2000–02, British Govt Spokesman on Middle East 2002, Deputy High Commr in Pakistan 2003–04, Deputy Dir Middle East and North Africa, FCO 2005, Int. Dir UK Border Agency 2006–08, Amb. to Afghanistan 2009–10, NATO Sr Civilian Rep. in Afghanistan 2010–11, Prime Minister's Special Rep. for Afghanistan and Pakistan, FCO 2011–, Dir Gen. (Political) 2012–13; Perm. Sec., Home Office 2013–; NATO Meritorious Service Medal, US Distinguished Service Medal, NATO Afghanistan Medal, UK Afghanistan Civilian Service Medal. *Address:* Direct Communications Unit, 2 Marsham Street, London, SW1P 4DF, England (office). *Telephone:* (20) 7035-4848 (office). *Fax:* (20) 7035-4745 (office). *E-mail:* public .enquiries@homeoffice.gsi.gov.uk (office). *Website:* www.gov.uk/government/ people/mark-sedwill (office).

SEEBACH, Dieter, BS, PhD, FRSC; German chemist and academic (retd); *Professor Emeritus, Eidgenössische Technische Hochschule Zürich;* b. 31 Oct. 1937, Karlsruhe; m. Ingeborg Reichling (deceased); three c.; ed Univ. of Karlsruhe; Post-doctoral Fellow and Lecturer in Chem., Harvard Univ., USA 1965–66; Prof., Justus Liebig Universität, Giessen 1971–77; Prof., ETH, Zürich 1977–2003, Prof. Emer. 2003–; Visiting Prof. at numerous int. univs including Harvard Univ. 2007; mem. Advisory Bd Synthesis 1984–, Angewandte Chemie 1985–94, Chimia 1985–, Helvetica Chimica Acta 1986–91; mem. Schweizerischer Chemiker Verband 1981–92, Chemische Gesellschaft, European Chemical Soc., ACS, Gesellschaft Deutscher Chemiker, Chemical Soc. of Japan, ACS, Deutsche Akad. der Naturforscher Leopoldina 1984, Neue Schweizerische Chemische Gesellschaft 1992–95 (Hon. mem.) 2004, Einzelmitglied der Schweizerischen Akad. der Technischen Wissenschaften 1998; Corresp. mem. Akad. der Wissenschaften und Literatur, Mainz 1990, Academia Mexicana de Ciencias 2001; Fellow, Japan Soc. for the Promotion of Science 1985–; Foreign Assoc. NAS (USA) 2007–; Dr hc (Montpellier) 1989; hon. lecturer at numerous int. univs; numerous awards, including Univ. of Karlsruhe Wolf Prize 1964, Stichting Havinga Fonds Havinga Medal 1985, Gesellschaft Deutscher Chemiker Karl Ziegler Prize 1987, Harvard Univ. Tischler Prize 1990, King Faisal Int. Prize in Science (Saudi Arabia) 1999, Marcel Benoist Prize (Switzerland) 2000, Yamada Prize (Japan) 2000, Nagoya Medal (Japan) 2002, A.W. von Hofmann Medal 2003, Tetrahedron Prize 2003, American Peptide Soc. Vincent du Vigneaud Award 2004, Ryoji Noyori Prize 2004, Max Bergmann Medal 2005, EuCheMS Award 2006. *Publications:* more than 800 research papers and more than 1,000 lectures world-wide. *Address:* Laboratorium für Organische Chemie, Eidgenössische Technische Hochschule, Hönggerberg HCI H 331, Wolfgang-Pauli-Strasse 10, 8093 Zürich, Switzerland (office). *Telephone:* (44) 632-2990 (office). *Fax:* 44) 632-1144 (office). *E-mail:* seebach@org .chem.ethz.ch (office). *Website:* infosee.ethz.ch/seebach/seebach.html (office).

SEEHOFER, Horst Lorenz; German politician; *Minister-President of Bavaria;* b. 4 July 1949, Ingolstadt; m. Karin Seehofer 1985; one s. three d.; ed Verwaltungs- und Wirtschaftsakademie, Munich; began career in local govt, Ingolstadt and Eichstätt; joined Christlich-Soziale Union (CSU) 1971; mem. Parl. for Ingolstadt 1980–2008, CSU Speaker on Social Affairs 1983–89; Parl. Sec. of State, Ministry of Employment 1989–92; Minister of Health 1992–98; Vice-Chair. CSU 1994–2008, Chair. 2008–; Vice-Chair. CDU/CSU Parl. Group 1998–2004, Regional Chair., Christlich Soziale Arbeitnehmerschaft 2000–08; Minister of Food, Agric. and Consumer Protection 2005–08; Minister-Pres. of Bavaria 2008–; Pres. Bundesrat 2011–12; Acting Pres. of Germany following resignation of Pres. Christian Wulff 17 Feb.–18 March 2012. *Address:* Franz Josef Strauß-Haus, Nymphenburger Strasse 64, 80335 Munich, Germany (office). *Telephone:* (89) 12430 (office). *Fax:* (89) 1243299 (office). *E-mail:* info@csu-bayern.de (office). *Website:* www.bayern.de/ Ministerpraesident-.257.9248860/index.htm (office); www.csu.de/seehofer/aktuell (office).

SEELERT, Robert (Bob) Louis; American business executive; *Chairman, Saatchi & Saatchi Worldwide;* b. 1 Sept. 1942, Manchester, Conn.; m. Sarah Seelert; ed Harvard Univ.; Gen. Man. Gen. Foods 1966–86, Pres. Coffee and Int. Foods Div. 1986–89; Pres. and CEO Kayser-Roth (hosiery group) 1991–94; Pres. and CEO Topco American (grocery co.) 1989–91; Chief Exec. Cordiant Communications Group PLC (fmrly Saatchi & Saatchi, later Cordiant PLC) 1995–97; CEO Saatchi & Saatchi Worldwide 1997–, currently Chair. (non-exec.). *Publication:* Start With the Answer 2009. *Address:* Saatchi & Saatchi Worldwide, 375 Hudson Street, New York, NY 10014-3620, USA (office). *Telephone:* (212) 463-2000 (office). *Fax:* (212) 462-2267 (office). *Website:* www.saatchi.com (office); www .startwiththeanswer.com.

SEEMAN, Nadrian (Ned) Charles, BS, PhD, FRSC; American chemist, crystallographer and academic; *Margaret and Herman Sokol Professor of Chemistry, New York University;* b. 16 Dec. 1945, Chicago, Ill.; s. of Herman Seeman and Emma Seeman; m. Nora Lapin; ed Univs of Chicago and Pittsburgh; Postdoctoral researcher, Columbia Univ., New York 1970–72, MIT, Cambridge, Mass 1972–77; Asst Prof., Dept of Biology, State Univ. of NY, Albany 1977–83, Assoc. Prof. 1983–88; Prof., Dept of Chem., New York Univ. 1988–, Margaret and Herman Sokol Chair in Chem. 2001–; Founding Pres. Int. Soc. for Nanoscale Science, Computation and Eng; Einstein Prof., Chinese Acad. of Science 2012; Fellow, AAAS 1998; Hon. Prof., Universidad Peruana Cayetano Heredia 1998; NATO Advanced Study Fellow 1970, Damon Runyon Fellow 1972–73, NIH Postdoctoral Fellow 1973–76, Sidhu Award 1974, Basil O'Connor Fellow 1978–81, NIH Research Career Devt Award 1982–87, Popular Science Magazine Science and Tech. Award 1993, Feynman Prize in Nanotechnology 1995, Discover Magazine Emerging Tech. Award 1997, Margaret and Herman Sokol Faculty Award in the Sciences 1999, Rozenberg Tulip Award in DNA-Based Computation 2004, MERIT Award, Nat. Inst. of Gen. Medical Sciences 2005, Nano50 Award, Nanotech Briefs 2005, World Tech. Award in Biotechnology, The World Tech. Network 2005, Nichols Medal, New York Section of ACS 2008, Frontiers of Science Award 2009, Alexander Rich Medal 2010, Kavli Prize 2010, Guggenheim Fellow 2010–11, ISNSCE Award 2011, Distinguished Alumnus, Univ. of Pittsburgh 2012. *Publications:* numerous scientific papers in professional journals on DNA nanotechnology, macromolecular design and topology, biophysical chem. of recombinational intermediates, DNA-based computation, and crystallography. *Address:* Room 1066, Department of Chemistry, New York University, New York, NY 10003-6688, USA (office). *Telephone:* (212) 998-8395 (office). *Fax:* (212) 995-4475 (office). *E-mail:* ned.seeman@nyu.edu (office). *Website:* seemanlab4.chem.nyu.edu (office).

SEEPERSAD-BACHAN, Carolyn, BSc, MSc; Trinidad and Tobago engineer and politician; *Minister of Public Administration;* b. San Fernando; m. Suresh Bachan; one s. one d.; ed Univ. of the West Indies; began career as Lecturer in Eng, Univ. of the West Indies, also mem. Bd of Eng Inst.; Opposition Senator 2002–06; mem. House of Reps for San Fernando West 2010–; Minister of Energy and Energy Affairs 2010–11, of Public Admin 2011–; fmr Chair. Nat. Petroleum Co. Ltd; fmr dir of several private cos; mem. Congress of the People (fmr Deputy Leader). *Address:* Ministry of Public Administration, National Library Bldg, Level 7, cnr Hart and Abercromby Streets, Port of Spain, Trinidad and Tobago (office). *Telephone:* 625-6724 (office). *Fax:* 623-6027 (office). *E-mail:* communicationsdivision@mpa.gov.tt (office). *Website:* www.mpa.gov.tt (office).

ŠEFČOVIČ, Maroš, JUDr, PhD; Slovak lawyer, diplomatist, politician and international organization official; *Commissioner for Inter-Institutional Relations and Administration and Vice-President, European Commission;* b. 24 July 1966, Bratislava; m. Helena Šefčovič; three c.; ed Univ. of Econs, Bratislava, Moscow State Inst. of Int. Relations, USSR, Comenius Univ., Bratislava, Université d'Eté de Perpignan, Paris, France, Hoover Inst., Stanford Univ., USA, Alliance française, Harare, Zimbabwe, Salzburg Global Seminar, Austria, Ulpan Akiva, Netanya and Dale Carnegie Assocs, Tel-Aviv, Israel; Adviser to First Deputy Foreign Minister, Ministry of Foreign Affairs, Prague, Czechoslovakia 1990; Desk Officer, Dept of EU and NATO countries, Ministry of Foreign Affairs, Slovak Repub., Bratislava 1995, Deputy Dir 1996, Deputy Dir, Office of the Foreign Minister 1997, Dir 1998, Dir-Gen., Bilateral Cooperation Section 2002, Dir-Gen., European Affairs Section 2003–04; overseas postings include Third Sec. and Consul, Embassy of the Czech and Slovak Fed. Repub., Zimbabwe 1991–92; Deputy Chief of Mission and Second Sec., Embassy of the Slovak Repub., Ottawa, Canada 1992, Deputy Head of Mission, Mission to the EC, Brussels 1998; Amb. to Israel 1999; Perm. Rep. to the EU 2004–09; Commr for Educ., Training, Culture and Youth 2009–10, Vice-Pres. EC responsible for Inter-Institutional Relations and Admin 2010–; Interim Vice-Pres. EC responsible for Inter-Institutional Relations and Admin and Health and Consumer Policy Oct.–Nov. 2012; Chatam Sofer Medal for promotion of Slovak-Israeli relations. *Publications:* various articles on issues related to European integration. *Leisure interests:* sport (tennis, jogging, skiing), biographies. *Address:* Office of the Vice-President, European Commission, Rue de la Loi 200, 1049 Brussels, Brussels (office). *Telephone:* (2) 297-59-90 (office); (2) 299-11-11 (switchboard) (office). *Fax:* (2) 295-01-38 (office). *E-mail:* cab-sefcovic@ec.europa.eu (office). *Website:* ec.europa.eu/commission_2010 -2014/sefcovic (office).

SEFRIOUI, Anas; Moroccan business executive; *President and Director-General, Douja Promotion Groupe Addoha SA;* b. 16 May 1957, Fes; s. of Haj Abdeslam Sefrioui; m.; three c.; left school to work with father in Gassoul (Moroccan clay) business; est Douja Promotion Groupe Addoha SA 1988, currently Pres. and Dir-Gen., also Chair. Ciments de l'Atlas; Vice-Chair. Supervisory Bd, Banque Populaire de Casablanca; mem. Bd of Dirs Lasry Maroc; mem. Supervisory Bd, Maroc Assistance; mem. Gen. Confed. of Moroccan Enterprises Foundation. *Address:* Douja Promotion Groupe Addoha SA, Km 7 Route De Rabat, Casablanca, Morocco (office). *Telephone:* (52) 2679900 (office). *Website:* www.groupeaddoha.com (office).

SEGAL, Anthony (Tony) Walter, MD, PhD, DSc, FRS, FRCP, FMedSci; British medical scientist and consultant physician; *Charles Dent Professor of Medicine and Director, Centre for Molecular Medicine, Department of Medicine, University College London;* b. 24 Feb. 1944, Johannesburg, S Africa; s. of Cyril Segal and Doreen Segal (née Hayden); m. Barbara Miller 1966; three d.; ed Univ. of Cape Town, S Africa and Univ. of London; Sr Clinical Fellow, Wellcome Trust 1975–86; Charles Dent Prof. of Medicine, Univ. Coll., London 1986–, also Dir Centre for

Molecular Medicine. *Leisure interests:* golf, sculpture, theatre, art. *Address:* Department of Medicine, University College London, 2nd Floor, Rayne Institute, 5 University Street, London, WC1E 6JJ (office); 48B Regents Park Road, London, NW1 7SX, England (home). *Telephone:* (20) 7679-6175 (office); (20) 7586-8745 (home). *Fax:* (20) 7679-6175 (office). *E-mail:* t.segal@ucl.ac.uk (office). *Website:* www.ucl.ac.uk/CMM (office).

SEGAL, George, BA; American film actor and producer; b. 13 Feb. 1934, New York, NY; s. of George Segal and Fanny Segal (née Bodkin); m. 1st Marion Sobol 1956 (divorced 1983); two d.; m. 2nd Linda Rogoff 1983 (deceased); m. 3rd Sonia Schulz; ed Manhasset Bay School, Great Neck Junior High School, George School, Haverford Coll., Columbia Coll. *Films include:* The Young Doctors 1961, Act One 1962, The Longest Day 1962, Invitation to a Gunfighter 1964, The New Interns 1964, Ship of Fools 1965, King Rat 1965, Who's Afraid of Virginia Woolf? 1966, The Quiller Memorandum 1966, Bye Bye Braverman 1968, No Way to Treat a Lady 1968, The Bridge at Remagen 1969, She Couldn't Say No 1969, The Southern Star 1969, Loving 1970, Where's Poppa? 1970, The Owl and the Pussy Cat 1970, Born to Win 1972, The Hot Rock 1972, A Touch of Class (Golden Globe Award 1972) 1972, Blume in Love 1972, The Terminal Man 1973, California Split 1973, Blackbird 1974, Russian Roulette 1975, The Duchess and the Dirtwater Fox 1976, Fun with Dick and Jane 1976, Rollercoaster 1977, Who is Killing the Great Chefs of Europe? 1978, Lost and Found 1979, The Last Married Couple in America 1980, Stick 1983, The Endless Game (TV) 1989, Look Who's Talking 1990, The Clearing, For The Boys 1991, The Mirror has Two Faces 1996, Flirting with Disaster 1996, The Cable Guy 1996, The November Conspiracy 1997, Heights 2004, 2012 2009. *Play:* Art, New York 1999, West End, London 2001. *Television includes:* Just Shoot Me (NBC sitcom) 1996–2003, Houdini 1998, The Linda McCartney Story 2000, Boston Legal 2008, Entourage 2009. *Leisure interest:* banjo playing. *Address:* c/o Starr & Co., 350 Park Avenue, New York, NY 10022, USA.

SEGAL, Graeme Bryce, BSc, MA, DPhil, FRS; British mathematician and academic; *Emeritus Fellow, All Souls College, Oxford;* b. 21 Dec. 1941; ed Univ. of Sydney, Australia, Balliol Coll., Oxford, St John's Coll., Cambridge; Jr Research Fellow, Worcester Coll., Oxford 1964–66, Jr Lecturer in Math., Univ. of Oxford 1965–66, CUF Lecturer 1966–70, Science Research Council Research Assoc. 1971–75. Univ. Lecturer 1975–78, Reader 1978–89, Prof. of Math. (ad hominem) 1989–90, Fellow, St Catherine's Coll., Oxford 1966–90, Sr Research Fellow, All Souls Coll., Oxford 1999–2009, Emer. Fellow 2009–; Lowndean Prof. of Astronomy and Geometry and Fellow of St John's Coll., Cambridge 1990–99; Pres. London Math. Soc. 2011–; mem. Inst. for Advanced Study 1969–70; Ed. Topology 1970–90; Sylvester Medal, Royal Soc. 2010. *Publications:* Loop Groups (co-author) 1986; numerous papers in professional journals. *Address:* Room 3.07, Mathematical Institute, University of Oxford, Andrew Wiles Building, Radcliffe Observatory Quarter, Woodstock Road, Oxford, OX2 6GG, England (office). *Telephone:* (1865) 279379 (office); (1865) 273525 (office). *Fax:* (1865) 279299 (office). *E-mail:* graeme .segal@maths.ox.ac.uk (office). *Website:* www.maths.ox.ac.uk (office); www.all -souls.ox.ac.uk (office).

SEGAL, Julian, BSc (ChemEng), MBA; Australian business executive; *Managing Director and CEO, Caltex Australia Limited;* ed Israel Inst. of Tech., Macquarie Grad. School of Man.; held several sr man. positions at Orica, including Man. of Strategic Market Planning, Gen. Man.– Australia/Asia Mining Services, and Sr Vice-Pres.– Marketing for Orica Mining Services 1999–2005; Man. Dir and CEO Incitec Pivot Ltd (global chemicals co.) 2005–09; Man. Dir and CEO Caltex Australia Ltd 2009–; Dir Australian Inst. of Petroleum Ltd 2009–. *Address:* Caltex Australia Ltd, GPO Box 3916, Sydney, NSW 2001 (office); Caltex Australia Ltd, Level 24, Market Street, Sydney, NSW 2000, Australia (office). *Telephone:* (2) 9250-5000 (office). *Fax:* (2) 9250-5742 (office). *E-mail:* info@caltex.com.au (office). *Website:* www.caltex.com.au (office).

SEGAL, Uriel (Uri); Israeli orchestral conductor; *Principal Guest Conductor, Jacobs School of Music, Indiana University;* b. 7 March 1944, Jerusalem; s. of Alexander Segal and Nehama Segal; m. Ilana Finkelstein 1966; one s. three d.; ed Rubin Acad., Jerusalem and Guildhall School of Music, London; debut with Tivoli Orchestra, Copenhagen 1969; Prin. Conductor Bournemouth Symphony Orchestra 1980–82, Philharmonia Hungarica 1981–85; Music Dir Israeli Chamber Orchestra, Chautauqua Festival, NY 1990–2007, Louisville Orchestra, KY 1998–2004; founder/Chief Conductor Century Orchestra, Osaka 1990–98, Laureate Conductor 1998–; currently Prin. Guest Conductor Jacobs School of Music, Ind. Univ.; fmr Prin. Guest Conductor Stuttgart Radio Symphony; orchestras conducted include Berlin Philharmonic, Stockholm Philharmonic, Concertgebouw, Orchestre de Paris, Vienna Symphony, Israel Philharmonic, London Symphony, London Philharmonic, Philharmonia, Orchestre de la Suisse Romande, Warsaw Philharmonic, Spanish Nat. Orchestra, Pittsburgh Symphony, Chicago Symphony, Detroit Symphony, Dallas Symphony, Houston Symphony, Montréal Symphony and Rochester Symphony; tours have included Austria, Switzerland, Spain, Italy, France, UK, Scandinavia and the Far East; operatic debut conducting The Flying Dutchman at Sante Fe Opera 1973, has since conducted opera in Italy, France, Germany, Japan, Israel and USA; recent guest appearances include with Hamburg Symphony, Düsseldorf Symphony, Polish Nat. Orchestra, Orchestre Nat. de Lille, Rochester Philharmonic, Detroit Symphony Orchestra, Jerusalem Symphony, London Philharmonia, Tokyo Chamber Opera Theater; First Prize, Int. Mitropoulos Conducting Competition, New York 1969. *Recordings:* Mahler Symphony No. 4 (with NZ Symphony Orchestra), music by Britten (Bournemouth Symphony), Stravinsky's Firebird Suite and Symphony in C with the Suisse Romande Orchestra), Mozart Piano Concertos with Radu Lupu and the English Chamber Orchestra, Schumann's Piano Concerto with Ashkenazy and the London Symphony, Beethoven Piano Concertos with Rudolf Firkusny and the Philharmonia, Mozart Piano Concertos with Alicia de Larocha and Wiener Symphoniker. *Leisure interests:* reading, photography, cooking. *Address:* c/o Michal Schmidt Artists Management, 59E 54th Street, Suite 83, New York, NY 10022, USA (office). *Telephone:* (212) 421-8500 (office); (54) 801-9086 (Israel) (home). *Fax:* (212) 421-8583 (office); (77) 332-5508 (office). *E-mail:* mws@schmidtart.com (office); usegal@ attglobal.net (home). *Website:* www.schmidtart.com (office); www.urisegal.com.

SEGLIŅŠ, Mareks; Latvian lawyer and politician; b. 4 July 1970, Aizpute; ed Aizputes Secondary School, Univ. of Latvia; worked in prosecutor's office and court of Liepāja City; worked in law office Pomerancis un Kreicis 1994–98; elected to 7th

Saeima (Parl.) 1998; mem. Parl. (People's Party Parl. Group), Chair. Legal Affairs Cttee, Sub-cttee on Drafting Criminal Procedure Law of the Legal Affairs Cttee, Deputy Chair. Nat. Security Cttee, mem. Baltic Affairs Sub-cttee of Foreign Affairs Cttee, Sports Sub-cttee of Educ., Culture and Science Cttee, Latvian del. to Baltic Ass., Latvia Interparliamentary Co-operation Groups with Australia and NZ, Azerbaijan, Canada, Chile, China, Ecuador, Germany, Italy, Kuwait, Taiwan, Turkey, UK and USA; Minister of Interior 1999–2002, 2007–09; Chair. People's Party 2008–; Minister of Justice 2009–10. *Address:* People's Party (Tautas partija), Dzirnavu iela 68, Rīga, Latvia (office). *Telephone:* 6728-6441 (office). *Fax:* 6728-6405 (office). *E-mail:* priekssedatajs@tautaspartija.lv (office). *Website:* www.tautaspartija.lv (office).

SEGUELA, Jacques Louis, PhD; French advertising executive; *Vice-President and Chief Creative Officer, Havas Advertising;* b. 23 Feb. 1934, Paris; s. of Louis Seguela and Simone Le Forestier; m. Sophie Vinson 1978; one s. four d.; ed Lycée de Perpignan, Faculté de Pharmacie de Montpellier; reporter, Paris Match 1960; with France Soir group's leisure magazines 1962; produced several TV programmes; joined Delpire 1964, then Axe; f. Roux Seguela Agency; co-f. Roux Seguela Cayzac & Goudard (RSGC) 1978; Vice-Pres. (Euro-RSCG) 1991–96; Chief Creative Officer Havas Advertising 1996–, currently also Vice-Pres.; est. Bleu comme bleu (restaurant), Paris 1995; co-founder Havas Tunisia 2010; Chevalier, Légion d'honneur 2008, Chevalier des Arts et des Lettres; César winner. *Publications:* Terre en rond 1961 (Prix littérature sportive), Ne dites pas à ma mère que je suis dans la publicité, elle me croit pianiste dans un bordel 1979, Hollywood lave plus blanc 1982, Fils de pub 1984, Cache Cache Pub, Demain il sera tros star 1989, C'est gai la pub 1990, Vote au-dessus d'un nid de cocos 1992, Pub Story 1994, La parole de Dieu 1995, le Futur a de l'avenir 1996, 80 ans de publicité Citroën et toujours 20 ans 1999, La Vertige des urnes 2000, Job Guide des métiers de demain 2001, Tous ego: Havas, moi et les autres 2005, Soeur Courage 2006, La prise de l'Elysée: Les campagnes présidentielles de la Ve République 2007, Autobiographie non autorisée 2009, Génération QE 2009, Le pouvoir dans la peau 2011. *Address:* Havas Advertising, 2 allée de Longchamp, 92281 Suresnes Cedex, France (office). *Telephone:* 1-58-47-90-00 (office). *Fax:* 1-58-47-99-99 (office). *Website:* www.havas.com (office).

SEGUY, Georges; French trade union official; *Honorary President, Institut CGT d'Histoire Sociale;* b. 16 March 1927, Toulouse; s. of André Seguy and Gabrielle Monfouga; m. Cécile Sédeillan 1949; two s. one d.; ed Armand-Leygues School, Toulouse; apprentice typographer 1942; mem. French CP 1942–, mem. Cen. Cttee 1954–, Political Bureau 1956–82; arrested by Gestapo and deported to Mauthausen Concentration Camp 1944; electrician, SNCF (French Railways) 1946; mem. Railway Workers' Union, Toulouse 1946–49; Sec. Fédération des cheminots Confédération Générale du Travail (CGT) 1949, Sec.-Gen. 1961–65; Sec. CGT 1965–67, Sec.-Gen. 1967–82; Hon. Pres. Institut CGT d'Histoire Sociale 1982–; mem. Exec. Cttee Fédération syndicale mondiale 1970–83; Officier, Légion d'honneur, Order of the October Revolution 1982. *Publications:* Le mai du la CGT 1972, Lutter (autobiography) 1975, Le 1er Mai les 100 printemps 1989, La Grève 1993, Résister: de Mauthausen à Mai 68 2008. *Leisure interests:* shooting, fishing. *Address:* Institut CGT d'histoire sociale, 263 rue de Paris, 93510 Montreuil Cedex, France (office). *Telephone:* 1-48-18-84-90 (office). *Fax:* 1-48-18-84-52 (office). *E-mail:* ihs@cgt.fr (office). *Website:* www.ihs.cgt.fr (office).

SEHGAL, Tino; British/German artist; b. 1976, London, England; ed studied political economy and dance in Berlin and Essen with Xavier Le Roy and Jerome Bel; grew up mostly in Düsseldorf and Paris; began to work as an artist in 2000; works ('constructed situations') involve one or more people carrying out instructions conceived by the artist; has exhibited at several venues, including Inst. of Contemporary Arts (ICA), London, Tate Gallery, Manifesta 4 and Venice Biennale 2005; first major exhbn in Italy presented by Nicola Trussardi Foundation at Galleria d'Arte Moderna, Villa Reale, Milan 2008; Bâloise Prize, Art Basel, Switzerland 2004, Golden Lion for the Best Artist in the Int. Exhibition Il Palazzo Enciclopedico, Venice Biennale 2013.

SEHWAG, Virender; Indian professional cricketer; b. 20 Oct. 1978, Delhi; s. of Krishan Sehwag and Krishna Sehwag; m. Aarti Ahlawat 2004; two s.; ed Arora Vidya School; right-handed opening batsman; occasional right-arm off-break bowler; plays for Delhi 1997–, India 1999–2013 (Vice-Capt. 2005–06, 2008–09), Leics. 2003, Int. Cricket Council (ICC) World XI 2005, Asian Cricket Council XI 2005, Delhi Daredevils 2008–, India Blue, Rajasthan Cricket Asscn Pres.'s XI; First-class debut: 1997/98; Test debut: South Africa v India, Bloemfontein 3–6 Nov. 2001; One-Day Int. (ODI) debut: India v Pakistan, Mohali 1 April 1999; T20I debut: S Africa v India, Johannesburg 1 Dec. 2006; mem. winning Indian cricket team in ICC Cricket World Cup against Sri Lanka 2011; highest score made by an Indian in Test cricket (319), which was also fastest triple century in history of int. cricket (reached 300 off only 278 balls); holds record for highest individual score in ODI matches (219 off 149 balls, v West Indies at Indore) 2011; one of three batsmen in the world to have surpassed 300 runs twice in Test cricket, only cricketer to score two triple centuries and take a five-wicket innings haul; scored fastest century ever by an Indian in ODI cricket, from 60 balls; opened vegetarian restaurant, Sehwag Favourites, Delhi 2005; Padma Shri 2010; Arjuna Award 2002, Wisden Leading Cricketer of the World 2008, 2009, ICC Test Player of the Year 2010. *Address:* Delhi & District Cricket Association, Ferozeshah Kotla Grounds, Bahadur Shah Zafar Marg, New Delhi 110 002, India (office). *Telephone:* (11) 23319323 (office). *Fax:* (11) 23722097 (office). *Website:* www.ddca.in (office); www.delhidaredevils.com (office).

SEIDELMAN, Susan, MFA; American film director; b. 11 Dec. 1952, nr Philadelphia, Pa; ed Drexel Univ. and New York Univ. Film School; directing debut with And You Act Like One Too (Student Acad. Award, Acad. of Motion Picture Arts and Sciences); then Dir Deficit (short film funded by American Film Inst.) and Yours Truly, Andrea G. Stern, The Dutch Master; Hon. PhD (Drexel); Mary Pickford Award for Best Female Dir 2002. *Films:* Smithereens (dir, producer, co-scriptwriter) 1982, Desperately Seeking Susan 1985, Making Mr Right 1987, Cookie 1989, She-Devil 1989, Confessions of a Suburban Girl 1992, Dutch Master 1994, Tales of Erotica 1996, Gaudi Afternoon 2001, The Boynton Beach Club 2005, Musical Chairs 2011. *Television:* The Barefoot Executive 1995, Sex and The City (pilot episode) 1998, A Cooler Climate 1999, Now and Again (series) 1999, Power and Beauty 2002, The Ranch 2004, The Electric Company 2009. *Leisure interest:*

travel. *Address:* c/o Michael Shedler, 350 Fifth Avenue, New York, NY 10118; c/o Gary Pearl Pictures, 10956 Weyburn Avenue, Suite 200, Los Angeles, CA 90024, USA. *E-mail:* stonehedge185@aol.com.

SEIDENBERG, Ivan G., BA, MBA; American telecommunications industry executive; *Advisory Partner, Perella Weinberg Partners LP;* b. 1946; m. Phyllis Seidenberg; two c.; ed Lehman Coll., City Univ. of New York, Pace Univ.; began career in communications as cable splicer's asst 1965; sr exec. positions at AT&T; fmr govt affairs dir Bell Atlantic; mem. Bd of Dirs NYNEX Inc. 1991–97, CEO (oversaw merger between NYNEX and Bell Atlantic 1997) –1997; CEO Bell Atlantic (oversaw merger between Bell Atlantic and GTE 1999) 1997–99; co-f. Verizon Wireless (cr. from merger of wireless assets of Bell Atlantic, GTE and Vodafone Airtouch) 1999, Co-CEO 1999–2002, Pres. and CEO Verizon Communications Inc. 2002–03, Chair. and CEO 2004–11, Chair. Aug.–Dec. 2011; Advisory Partner, Perella Weinberg Partners LP (investment banking firm) 2012–; mem. or fmr mem. Bd of Dirs Honeywell, Museum of TV and Radio, Viacom Inc., Verizon Foundation, Wyeth (pharmaceuticals co.), BlackRock Inc.; named by Pres. George W. Bush to Nat. Security Telecommunications Advisory Cttee 2007; Chair. Business Roundtable 2009–11; apptd by Pres. Obama to Pres.'s Export Council 2010; fmr Chair. US Telecom Assen; mem. New York Acad. of Sciences' Pres.'s Council; Trustee, New York Presbyterian Hosp., The New York Hall of Science, Pace Univ., Paley Center for Media. *Address:* Perella Weinberg Partners LP, 767 Fifth Avenue, New York, NY 10153, USA (office). *Telephone:* (212) 287-3200 (office); (212) 287-3197 (Kara Findlay, media inquiries) (office). *Fax:* (212) 287-3201 (office). *E-mail:* kfindlay@pwpartners.com (office). *Website:* www.pwpartners.com (office).

SEIERSTAD, Åsne; Norwegian journalist and writer; b. 10 Feb. 1970, Oslo; ed Univ. of Oslo; mem. of staff, ITAR-TASS news agency, Moscow; covered wars in Chechnya, Kosovo, Afghanistan, Iraq for several Scandinavian newspapers 1994–2004; correspondent, Norwegian television news 1998–2000; award for television reporting from Kosovo, Chechnya and Afghanistan, Gullruten Award 1999, Fritt Ord Honorary Award 2001, Årets Frilanser Award 2002, Journalist of the Year, Norway 2003, EMMA Award, London 2004, Bookseller's Prize, France 2004. *Publications:* non-fiction: With Their Backs to the World 2000, The Bookseller of Kabul 2002, A Hundred and One Days: A Baghdad Journal 2004, Angel of Grozny: Inside Chechnya 2008. *Leisure interests:* skiing, nature. *Address:* Tidemands gt. 20, 0260 Oslo, Norway (home). *E-mail:* aaseie@frisurf.no.

SEIKE, Tomio; Japanese artist and photographer; b. 13 July 1943, Tokyo; m. Junko Seike; ed Sapporo Jr Coll., Japan Photographic Acad.; asst photographer, Japan 1970–74; moved to England 1974; freelance photographer, Tokyo 1975–; public collections at Bibliothèque Nationale Paris, Maison Européenne de la Photographie, Jane Voorhees Zimmerli Art Museum, Rutgers Univ., Museum of Fine Arts, Houston. *Publications include:* Portrait of Zoe, Paris, Waterscape 2003. *Address:* Hamiltons Gallery, 13 Carlos Place, London, W1 2EU, England. *Telephone:* (20) 7499-9494. *Fax:* (20) 7629-9919. *E-mail:* art@hamiltonsgallery.com. *Website:* www.hamiltonsgallery.com.

SEILLIÈRE de LABORDE, Ernest-Antoine; French business executive and fmr civil servant; b. 20 Dec. 1937, Neuilly-sur-Seine; s. of Jean Seillière de Laborde and Renée de Wendel; m. Antoinette Barbey 1971; two s. three d.; ed Ladycross Coll., Lycée Janson-de-Sailly, Faculty of Law, Paris, Nat. School of Admin.; attaché, High Comm. of Algeria 1962; with Ministry of Information 1963, Sec. for Foreign Affairs 1966, mem. French del. at negotiations for EEC, Brussels and Gen. Agreement on Tariffs and Trade, Geneva 1966–69; Adviser on Foreign Affairs 1969, Adviser to the Prime Minister 1969–72, Tech. Adviser to Minister for Foreign Affairs 1972–73; Minister of Armed Forces 1973–74; Lecturer, Centre for Int. Affairs, Harvard Univ. 1975; Jt Dir-Gen. of Industrial Politics, Marine-Wendel 1976, Pres. 1992–2002, Pres. Wendel Investissement 2012–13 (following merger of CGIP and Marine Wendel, now Wendel Group); Gen. Dir, Admin. CGIP 1978–87, Pres., Dir-Gen. 1987–2002; Vice-Pres. Carnaud SA (later CMB Packaging) 1984–91; Vice-Chair. Cap Gemini 2000–; Vice-Pres. Fed. of Mechanical Industries 1985; Vice-Pres. Nat. Council of French Employers (CNPF) 1988–97, Pres. 1997, Pres. MEDEF (newly named CNPF) 1997–2005; Pres. Business Europe (European business lobby group fmrly known as UNICE) 2005–09; currently Chair. Legrand Holding, Supervisory Bd Oranje-Nassau Groep BV; mem. Supervisory Bd Editis Holding, Peugeot SA, Hermès Int; Commdr, Légion d'honneur, Officier, Ordre nat. du Mérite. *Address:* Wendel Group, 89 rue Taitbout, 75009 Paris, France. *Telephone:* 1-42-85-30-00 (office). *Fax:* 1-42-80-68-67 (office). *Website:* www.wendelgroup.com (office).

SEINFELD, Jerome (Jerry) Allen; American comedian; b. 29 April 1954, Brooklyn, New York; s. of Kalmen Seinfeld and Betty Seinfeld; m. Jessica Sklar 1999; three c.; ed Queens Coll., New York; fmrly salesman; stand-up comedian 1976–; joke-writer Benson (TV series) 1980; cr. (with Larry David) The Seinfeld Chronicles (later Seinfeld) 1989, actor Seinfeld (TV series) 1990–98, also co-writer, producer; Emmy Award Outstanding Comedy Series (for Seinfeld) 1993, American Comedy Award 1988, 1992, ranked by Comedy Central as one of the 12 greatest stand-up comedians of all time in its four-part special The 100 Greatest Standups Of All Time 2005. *Films include:* Pros & Cons 1999, A Uniform Used to Mean Something 2004, Hindsight Is 20/20 (short, writer) 2004, The Thing About My Folks 2005, Bee Movie (voice, writer and producer) 2007, New Family (video short) 2008. *Television includes:* Benson (series) 1980–81, The Ratings Game (film) 1984, The Seinfeld Chronicles 1989, One Night Stand (series) 1990, Seinfeld (series) 1990–98, Carol Leifer: Gaudy, Bawdy & Blue (film) 1992, The Larry Sanders Show (series) 1993, I'm Telling You for the Last Time 1998, Larry David: Curb Your Enthusiasm (film) 1999, Dilbert (series) 2000, Curb Your Enthusiasm (series) 2004–09, Sincerely, Ted L. Nancy (film, creator) 2008, The Marriage Ref (series writer and exec. producer) 2010–11, Colin Quinn Long Story Short (film) (exec. producer) 2011. *Publications:* Seinlanguage 1993, Halloween (juvenile) 2002. *Leisure interests:* Zen, yoga. *Address:* c/o Creative Artists Agency, 2000 Avenue of the Stars, Los Angeles, CA 90067, USA. *Website:* www.caa.com; www.jerryseinfeld.com.

SEINO, Satoshi; Japanese transport industry executive; *Chairman, East Japan Railway Company;* b. 1947; ed Tohoku Univ.; joined Japanese Nat. Railways (predecessor of East Japan Railway Co.) 1970, served as Head of Human Resources

Div. and as Man. Dir East Japan Railway Co., Exec. Vice-Pres., Corp. Planning HQ and IT Business Devt HQ, East Japan Railway Co. 2002–06, Pres. and CEO 2006–12. *Address:* East Japan Railway Co., 2-2-2 Yoyogi, Shibuya-ku, Tokyo 151-8578, Japan (office). *Telephone:* (3) 5334-1150 (office); (3) 5334-1310 (office). *Fax:* (3) 5334-1110 (office); (3) 5334-1297 (office). *E-mail:* ir@jreast.co.jp (office); bond@jreast.co.jp (office); info@jreast.co.jp (office). *Website:* www.jreast.co.jp (office).

SEIP, Anne-Lise, DPhil; Norwegian historian and academic; *Professor of Modern History, University of Oslo;* b. 6 Nov. 1933, Bergen; d. of Edvin Thomassen and Birgit Thomassen; m. Jens Arup Seip 1960 (died 1992); one s. one d.; ed Univ. of Oslo; Sr Lecturer Inst. of Criminology and Penal Law, Univ. of Oslo 1974–75, Dept of History 1975–85, Prof. of Modern History 1985–; mem. Norwegian Acad. of Science, Det kongelige danske videnskabernes selskab. *Publications include:* Videnskap og virkelighet T.H. Asehehoug 1974, Eilert Sundt. 1983, Sosialhjelp-staten blir til 1984, Veier til velferdsstaten 1994, Norges historie, Vol. 8 1830–70 1997, Demringstid. Johan Sebastian Welhaven og nasjonen 2007; numerous articles. *Leisure interests:* books, music, gardening. *Address:* Gamle Drammensvei 144, 1363 Høvik (home); Department of History, University of Oslo, PO Box 1008, Blindern, 0315 Oslo, Norway (office). *Telephone:* 22-85-68-78 (office); 67-53-40-39 (home). *E-mail:* a.l.seip@hi.uio.no (office). *Website:* www.hf.uio.no/hi/english (office).

SEIPP, Walter, DJur; German banker and business executive; b. 13 Dec. 1925, Langen; m. 1954; two s.; ed Univ. of Frankfurt am Main; jr barrister 1950–53; with Deutsche Bank AG 1951–74 (Exec. Vice-Pres. 1970–74); mem. Man. Bd Westdeutsche Landesbank Girozentrale 1974–77, Vice-Chair. 1978–81; Chair. Man. Bd Commerzbank AG 1981–91, fmr Chair. Supervisory Bd, now Hon. Chair.; Chair. Supervisory Bd Berliner Commerzbank AG, Rheinische Hypothekenbank AG, Frankfurt, Essen; Chair. Admin. Bd Commerzbank Int. SA, Luxembourg, Commerzbank (Schweiz) AG, Zürich; Chair. Supervisory Bd Commerz Int. Capital Man. GmbH, Frankfurt; Chair. Commerzbank Capital Markets Corpn, New York, Commerz-Securities (Japan) Co. Ltd, Commerzbank, SE Asia Ltd, Singapore; mem. Bd of Dirs Int. Monetary Conf., Washington, DC (Pres. 1987–88); mem. Supervisory Bd Bayer AG, Leverkusen, Daimler Benz AG, Stuttgart, Deutsche Shell AG, Hamburg, Vereinigte Industrie-Unternehmungen AG, Bonn, Linde AG Wiesbaden, Allianz Versicherungs AG, Munich, MAN AG, Munich, Thyssen AG, Duisburg; mem. Bd of Man. Dirs Bundesverband deutscher Banken eV, Cologne.

SEITERS, Rudolf; German politician; *President, German Red Cross;* b. 13 Oct. 1937, Osnabrück; s. of Adolf Seiters and Josefine Gördel; m. Brigitte Kolata; three c.; ed Univ. of Münster; qualified as lawyer; joined Junge Union and CDU 1958, Regional Chair. Junge Union, Osnabrück-Emsland 1963–65, Chair. CDU Land Asscn Hanover 1965–68, mem. Junge Union Fed. Exec. Cttee 1967–71, Sr Chair. CDU Land Asscn Lower Saxony 1968–70; Head Econ. and Housing Dept, Office of Regierungspräsident (Regional Gov.), Osnabrück 1967–69; mem. Deutscher Bundestag 1969–; mem. CDU Fed. Exec. Cttee 1971–73; Parl. Party Man. CDU/Christian Social Union (CSU) Parl. Party in Bundestag 1971–76, Sr Parl. Man. 1984–89; Parl. Party Man. 1982–84; Fed. Minister for Special Tasks and Head of Fed. Chancellery 1989–91, of the Interior 1991–93; Deputy Chair. CDU/CSU in Bundestag 1994–; Vice-Pres. Bundestag 1998–2002; Pres. German Red Cross 2003–; Hon. Dr rer. pol; Grosses Bundesverdienstkreuz mit Stern 1995, Grosses Silbernes Ehrenzeichen (Austria) 1995, Officier, Légion d'honneur 1996. *Publications:* Aussenpolitik im 21. Jahrhundert 1996, In der Spur Bleiben 2005. *Address:* Deutschen Roten Kreuzes Generalsekretariat, Carstenstr. 58, 12205 Berlin, Germany (office). *Telephone:* (30) 85404277 (office). *E-mail:* praesident@drk.de (office). *Website:* www.drk.de (office).

SEITZ, John N., BSc, MSc; American geologist and petroleum industry executive; *Vice-Chairman, Endeavour International Corporation;* ed Univ. of Pittsburgh, Rensselaer Polytechnic Inst., Univ. of Pennsylvania; Sr Exploration Geologist, Anadarko Petroleum Corpn 1977–82, Chief Geologist 1982–83, Gen. Man. 1983–89, Vice-Pres. of Exploration and Production 1989–95, Sr Vice-Pres. of Exploration 1995–97, Exec. Vice-Pres. of Exploration and Production 1997–99, mem. Bd of Dirs 1997–2003, Pres. and COO 1999–, then CEO –2003; f. North Sea Oil Ventures 2003; Co-founder Endeavour International (cr. after merger of North Sea Oil Ventures and Continental Southern Resources), Houston, Tex 2003, Co-CEO 2003–06, currently Vice-Chair.; mem. Bd of Dirs ION Geophysical Corpn 2003–, Constellation Energy Partners LLC 2004–, Gulf United Energy 2011–, Input/Output Inc., Elk Resources Inc.; mem. Advisory Bd Spindletop; mem. American Asscn of Petroleum Geologists, Geological Soc. of America, American Inst. of Professional Geologists, Houston Geological Soc., Soc. of Petroleum Engineers; Trustee, American Geological Inst. Foundation. *Address:* Endeavour International Corporation, 1001 Fannis, Suite 1600, Houston, TX 77002, USA (office). *Telephone:* (713) 307-8700 (office). *Website:* www.endeavourcorp.com (office).

SEITZ, Konrad, MA, DrPhil; German diplomatist (retd) and writer; b. 18 Jan. 1934, Munich; m. Eva Kautz 1965; ed Univ. of Marburg, The Fletcher School of Law and Diplomacy, Tufts Univ., USA; Prof. of Classics, Univs of Marburg and Munich 1956–64; entered Foreign Office 1965; served in New Delhi 1968–72, UN Mission, New York 1972–75; main speech writer for Minister of Foreign Affairs 1975; Head, Policy Planning Staff, Foreign Office 1980–87; Amb. to India 1987–90; Co-Chair. Comm. Economy 2000, Baden-Württemberg 1992–93; Amb. to Italy 1992–95, to China 1995–99; Grosses Bundesverdienstkreuz 1996, Baden-Württemberg Medal of Honour 1998. *Publications include:* The Japanese-American Challenge: Germany's Hi-tech Industries Fight for Survival 1990, The Aimless Elites – Are the Germans Losing the Future? (with others), Europa – Una Colonia Tecnológica? 1995, Race into the 21st Century – The Future of Europe Between America and Africa 1998, China – A World Power Comes Back 2000; contribs to foreign and econ. journals and newspapers. *Leisure interests:* history of ideas, literature, art, collecting Indian miniature paintings. *Address:* Dahlienweg 4, 53343 Wachtberg-Pech, Germany. *Telephone:* (228) 327811. *Fax:* (228) 9325154. *E-mail:* k.seitz@freenet.de.

SEITZ, Hon. Raymond George Hardenbergh; American fmr diplomatist and business executive; b. 8 Dec. 1940, Honolulu, Hawaii; m. Caroline Gordon Richardson; two s. one d.; ed Yale Univ.; joined Foreign Service 1966, served as Political Officer in Montreal, Political Officer, Embassy in Nairobi, also Vice-

Consul, Seychelles 1968–70; Prin. Officer, Bukavu, Zaire 1970–72; served on Secretariat Staff, Washington, DC 1972 then Dir of Staff; Special Asst to Dir-Gen. Foreign Service 1974; Political Officer, London 1975–79; Deputy Exec. Sec., Dept of State 1979–81, Sr Deputy Asst Sec. for Public Affairs 1981–82, Exec. Asst to Sec. Shultz 1982–84; Minister, Embassy in London 1984–89; Asst Sec. of State for European and Canadian Affairs 1989–91; Amb. to UK 1991–94 (retd); Vice-Chair. Lehman Bros. Int. (Europe) (now Lehman Bros.) Europe Ltd) 1995–2003; Chair. (non-exec.) Sun-Times Media Group Inc., Chicago 2003–08; mem. Bd of Dirs Chubb Corpn 1994–2007, British Airways PLC 1995–2002, Cable and Wireless 1995–, Rio Tinto 1996–2003, Authorizor Inc. 1999–, PCCW Ltd 2005–, Marconi PLC, Hollinger Int.; Contributing Ed. Conde Nast Traveller magazine (UK) 2004–; Trustee, Nat. Gallery 1996–2001; fmr Trustee, Royal Acad. of Arts and the World Monuments Fund; Gov. Ditchley Foundation; Hon. DUniv (Herriot-Watt) 1994, Dr hc (Open Univ.) 1997, received several hon. degrees from Univs of Durham, Newcastle upon Tyne, Bath, Buckingham, Royal Holloway, Leeds, Reading Univ., Leicester Univ.; Presidential Award 1986, 1988, Benjamin Franklin Medal 1995, Churchill Medal of Honour 1999, Freedom of the City of London 1999. *Publication:* Over Here 2001. *Address:* c/o Sun-Times Media Group Inc., 350 North Orleans, Chicago, IL 60654-1975, USA.

SEJDIU, Fatmir, PhD; Kosovo politician, academic and fmr head of state; b. 23 Oct. 1951, Pakashticë/Pakaštica, nr Podujevë/Podujevo; m. Nezafete Sejdiu; three c.; ed Univ. of Prishtina; Prof. of Law, Univ. of Prishtina; mem. Ass. of Kosovo –2006, fmr mem. Cttee for Rules and Procedures of Ass., Cttee for Int. Cooperation and EU Integration; Pres. of Kosovo 2006–10 (resgnd); mem. Democratic League of Kosovo, Chair. –2010; Dr hc (Tirana). *Publication:* Constitutional Framework of Kosovo (co-author) 2001, The History of State and Law (co-author) 2000, 2005, Agrarian Politics as an Instrument of National Repression (monograph) 2000, Glossary of Parliamentary and Legal Terms (co-author) 2005. *Address:* Democratic League of Kosovo (Lidhja Demokratike e Kosovës), 10000 Prishtina, Kompleksi Qafa, Kosovo (office). *Telephone:* (38) 245305 (office). *E-mail:* ldk@ldk-ks.eu (office). *Website:* www.ldk-ks.eu

SEJIMA, Kazuyo, MArch; Japanese architect; *Principal, SANAA/Kazuyo Sejima & Ryue Nishizawa Associates;* b. 1956, Ibaraki Pref.; ed Japan Women's Univ.; worked for Toyo Ito Architect & Assocs 1981–87; f. Kazuyo Sejima & Assocs 1987; Founder and Prin. (with Ryue Nishizawa), SANAA Ltd/Kazuyo Sejima & Ryue Nishizawa Assocs 1995–; teacher, Dept of Architecture, Univ. of Illinois, USA; Winner, Competition for MCH House 1990, Second Prize, Nasunogahara Harmony Hall Design Competition 1991, Second Prize, GID Competition 1992, Second Prize, Commercial Space Design Award 1992, Young Architect of the Year, Japan Inst. of Architects 1992, Grand Prize, Commercial Space Design 1994, Architect of the Year 1994, Vincenzo Scamozzi Architecture Award 2003, Rolf Schock Prize in Visual Arts (with Ryue Nishizawa) 2005, Pritzker Prize (with Ryue Nishizawa) 2010. *Works include:* MCH House (Kajima Prize, SD Review) 1990, Platform One Katsuura, Platform Two Yamanashi, Saishunkan Seiyaku Women's Dormitory, Pachinko Parlors I, II & III, Y-House Katsuura, Chino Villa in the Forest, Police Box at Chofu Station, N-House Kumamoto, Yokohama Int. Port Terminal, Apartment Bldg in Gifu, Expo Tokyo 96, Oogaki Multi Media Studio. *Exhibitions include:* Nat. Panasonic Gallery, Tokyo 1989, Artpolis, Kumamoto 1992, Sezon Museum 1993, MA Gallery, Tokyo 1993, Nat. Museum of Modern Art, Seoul, Korea 1994. *Address:* SANAA Ltd/Kazuyo Sejima, Ryue Nishizawa & Associates, 7-A Shinagawa-Soko, 2-2-35 Higashi-Shinagawa, Shinagawa-ku, 140 Tokyo, Japan. *Telephone:* (3) 34501757. *E-mail:* sanaa@sanaa.co.jp.

SEKERAMAYI, Sydney Tigere, MB, ChB, DTM; Zimbabwean politician; *Minister of Defence;* b. 30 March 1944; m.; fmr govt positions include Minister for Lands and Resettlement, Minister of State Security, Energy Minister, Intelligence Dir; Minister of Defence 2001–09, 2013–; mem. Parl. (Zanu-PF) for Marondera E 2005–08; Senator from Marondera-Hwedza 2008–09; Minister of State for Nat. Security 2009–13. *Address:* Ministry of Defence, Defence House, cnr Kwame Nkuruma and 3rd Streets, Harare, Zimbabwe (office). *Telephone:* (4) 700155 (office). *Fax:* (4) 727501 (office). *Website:* www.mod.gov.zw (office).

SEKERINSKA, Radmilla, BSc, MA; Macedonian politician; *Chairperson, National Council for European Integration;* b. 10 June 1972, Skopje; s. of Aleksandar Sekerinski and Jelena Sekerinska; m. Bozidar Jankovski; ed Skopje Univ., Fletcher School of Law and Diplomacy, Tufts Univ., USA; fmr Public Relations Asst, Open Soc. Inst., Asst at Faculty of Electrical Eng, Skopje Univ.; started political career with Social Democratic Youth of Macedonia 1992, Pres. 1995; mem. Skopje City Council 1996–98; Deputy Coordinator, Spokesperson and mem. Cen. Bd Social Democratic Alliance of Macedonia 1999–, Vice-Chair., Chair. 2006–08; mem. Parl. 1998–2002, 2006–, Ass. Del. to Inter-Parl. Union, Ass. Group for Cooperation with the European Parl. 1998–2002; Deputy Prime Minister, with responsibility for European Integration 2002–06; Pres. Nat. Council for European Integration 2007–; Young Global Leader, World Econ. Forum 2004. *Publications include:* scientific articles. *Address:* Social Democratic Alliance of Macedonia (Socijaldemokratski Sojuz na Makedonija, SDSM), 1000 Skopje, Bihačka 8, Republic of Macedonia (office). *Telephone:* (2) 3293101 (office). *Fax:* (2) 3293111 (office). *E-mail:* president@sdsm.org.mk (office). *Website:* www.sdsm.org.mk (office).

SEKIGUCHI, Ken-ichi; Japanese insurance industry executive; *Senior Advisor, Meiji Yasuda Life Insurance Company;* Gen. Man. Aomori Br. Meiji Yasuda Life Insurance Co. 1994–96, Gen. Man. Int. Investment Dept, Meiji Yasuda Life Insurance Co. 1996–97, Gen. Man. Global Investment Dept 1997–2000, Gen. Man. Financial Planning Dept 2000–03, later Man. Dir, mem. Bd of Dirs 1999–, Chair. and Rep. Exec. Officer 2005–13, Sr Advisor 2013–; mem. Nominating Cttee, Compensation Cttee, Chief Exec. New Market Devt; mem. Bd Dirs UBS Wealth Man., USA (fmrly Paine Webber Group Inc.) 1999–. *Address:* Meiji Yasuda Life Insurance Co., 1-1, Marunouchi 2-chome, Chiyoda-ku, Tokyo 100-0005, Japan (office). *Telephone:* (3) 3283-8293 (office). *Fax:* (3) 3215-8123 (office). *E-mail:* info@meijiyasuda.co.jp (office). *Website:* www.meijiyasuda.co.jp (office).

SEKIMIZU, Koji, BS, MS; Japanese engineer and international organization official; *Secretary-General, International Maritime Organization;* b. 3 Dec. 1952, Yokohama; m.; one s. one d.; ed Osaka Univ.; joined Ministry of Transport 1977, Ship Inspector 1977–79, Tech. Official 1979–80, Special Tech. Researcher,

Shipbuilding Research Assen 1981–82, Deputy Dir Environment Div. 1982–84; Deputy Dir, Second Int. Orgs Div., Econ. Affairs Bureau, Ministry of Foreign Affairs 1984–86; Deputy Dir Safety Standards Div., Maritime Tech. and Safety Bureau, Ministry of Transport 1986–89; Tech. Official, Maritime Safety Div., IMO 1989–97, Sr Deputy Dir Marine Environment Div. 1997–2000, Dir Marine Environment Div. 2000–04, Dir Maritime Safety Div. 2004–12, Sec.-Gen. IMO 2012–; mem. Japan Soc. of Naval Architects and Ocean Engineers. *Leisure interests:* golf, playing guitar, composing songs. *Address:* International Maritime Organization, 4 Albert Embankment, London, SE1 7SR, England (office). *Telephone:* (20) 7735-7611 (office). *Fax:* (20) 7587-3210 (home). *E-mail:* info@imo .org (office). *Website:* www.imo.org (office).

SEKIYA, Katsutsugu; Japanese politician; ed Chuo Univ., Univ. of British Columbia, Canada; joined Japan Airlines 1963; sec. to a mem. of House of Reps 1966; mem. LDP; mem. for Ehime, House of Reps 1976–2007, Chair. House of Reps Transport Cttee; fmr Minister of Posts and Telecommunications; Minister of Construction 1998–99; Dir-Gen. Nat. Land Agency 1999. *Address:* c/o Liberal-Democratic Party—LDP (Jiyu-Minshuto) 1-11-23, Nagata-cho, Chiyoda-ku, Tokyo 100-8910, Japan.

SEKIZAWA, Tadashi, BEng; Japanese business executive; *Senior Executive Adviser, Fujitsu Ltd;* b. 6 Nov. 1931, Tokyo; m. Misako Sekizawa; two s.; ed Tokyo Univ.; joined Fujitsu Ltd 1954, Gen. Man. Switching Systems Group 1982–84, Bd Dir 1984, Man. Dir 1986–88, Exec. Dir 1988–90, apptd Pres. and Rep. Dir 1990, later Chair., currently Sr Exec. Adviser; Vice-Chair. Communication Industry Assen of Japan 1990–98, apptd Chair. 1998, Japan Electronic Industry Devt Assen 1990. *Leisure interests:* literature, travel, motoring. *Address:* Fujitsu Ltd, Shiodome City Center, 1-5-2, Higashi-Shimbashi, Minato-ku, Tokyo 105-7123, Japan (office). *Telephone:* (3) 6252-2220 (office). *Fax:* (3) 6252-2783 (office). *Website:* www.fujitsu.com (office).

ŠEKS, Vladimir, LLB; Croatian politician; b. 1 Jan. 1943, Osijek; m. Anica Resler-Šeks; one s. one d.; ed Univ. of Zagreb; trainee, Municipal Public Prosecutors Office, Vinkovci 1967–69; Deputy Municipal Public Prosecutor, Vinkovci 1970; Municipal Court Judge, Osijek 1970–71; Deputy Regional Public Prosecutor, Osijek 1971; barrister in prt. law firm 1972–81; sentenced to seven-month prison term for conspiracy against the state 1981; mem. Croatian Democratic Union (Hrvatska demokratska zajednica—HDZ), Vice-Chair. 1989–91, 1995–99, Chair. Rep. Group 1995, Acting Chair. Jan.–April 2000, Chair. Parl. Group 2000, Deputy Chair. Cen. Cttee 2002–03; mem. Sabor (Parl.) 1990–, Deputy Pres. 1992–2000, Pres. 2003–08; Public Prosecutor of Croatia 1992; Chair. State Amnesty Comm. 1996–2000; Chair. Cttee on Constitutional Affairs 1990–92, Deputy Chair. 1995–99; mem. Defence and Nat. Security Council 1995–99, Council for Strategic Decisions of the Pres. 1995–99; Founder and Co-chair. Yugoslav Helsinki Cttee 1987–; mem. Amnesty Int.; Grand Order of King Dmitar Zvonimir, Order of Ante Starčević, Order of Stjepan Radić, Order of the Croatian Trefoil, Vukovar Medal. *Publications:* Expression of Opinion Treated as Offence, Contemplations on the Freedom of Conscience, Dangerous Times, Reminiscences from Prison; over 20 professional papers on law and politics. *Address:* Hrvatska demokratska zajednica, trg Žrtava fašizma 4, 10000 Zagreb, Croatia (office). *Telephone:* (1) 4553000 (office). *Fax:* (1) 4552600 (office). *E-mail:* hdz@hdz.hr (office). *Website:* www.hdz.hr (office).

SELA, Michael, PhD; Israeli immunologist, chemist and academic; *W. Garfield Weston Chair of Immunology, Weizmann Institute of Science;* b. (Mieczysław Salomonowicz), 6 March 1924, Tomaszow, Poland; s. of Jakob Salomonowicz and Roza Salomonowicz; m. 1st Margalit Liebman 1948 (died 1975); two d.; m. 2nd Sara Kika 1976; one d.; ed Hebrew Univ., Jerusalem and Univ. of Geneva, Switzerland; joined Weizmann Inst. of Science 1950, Head Dept of Chemical Immunology 1963–75, Vice-Pres. 1970–71, Dean Faculty of Biology 1970–73, mem. Bd of Govs 1970–, Pres. 1975–85, Deputy Chair. 1985–, W. Garfield Weston Prof. of Immunology 1966–, currently also W. Garfield Weston Chair of Immunology; Visiting Scientist, NIH, Bethesda 1956–57, 1960–61; Visiting Prof. of Molecular Biology, Univ. of Calif., Berkeley 1967–68; Visiting Prof., Dept of Medicine, Tufts Univ. School of Medicine, Boston 1986–87; Inst. Prof. 1985; Fogarty Scholar-in-Residence, Fogarty Int. Center, Bethesda, Maryland 1973–74; mem. WHO Expert Advisory Panel of Immunology 1962–; Chair. Council, European Molecular Biology Org. 1975–79; Pres. Int. Union Immunological Socs 1977–80; Chair. Scientific Advisory Cttee European Molecular Biology Lab., Heidelberg 1978–81; WHO Advisory Cttee on Medical Research 1979–82, WHO Special Programme for Research and Training in Tropical Diseases 1979–81; mem. Council Paul Ehrlich Foundation (Frankfurt) 1980–97; mem. Advisory Bd UCLAF, France 1980–92; Founding mem. Bd of Dir Int. Foundation for Survival and Devt of Humanity, Moscow and Washington, DC 1988–92; Nat. mem. Gen. Cttee Int. Council of Scientific Unions 1984–93; mem. Scientific Advisory Group of Experts, Programme for Vaccine Devt, WHO 1987–92; mem. Int. Guidance Panel, Israel Arts and Science Acad. 1987–; Vice-Pres. Assen Franco-Israélienne pour Recherche Scientifique et Technologique 1992–98; mem. Exec. Bd Int. Council of Human Duties, Trieste 1995–; mem. other int. bodies; serves on many editorial bds, including Exec. Advisory Bd of Dictionary for Science and Tech. 1989–, Ed. Acad. of the Int. Journal of Molecular Medicine 1997, Int. Advisory Bd of Russian Journal of Immunology 2000, Int. Ed. Bd Reviews in Auto-immunity 2001, Cambridge Encyclopedia of the Life Sciences, Handbook of Biochemistry and Molecular Biology, Experimental and Clinical Immunogenetics, Receptor Biology Reviews, Encyclopedia of Human Biology, Encyclopedia of the Life Sciences; mem. Israel Acad. of Sciences and Humanities 1971, Pontifical Acad. of Sciences 1975, Deutsche Akad. der Naturforscher Leopoldina 1989; Foreign mem. Max-Planck Soc., Freiburg 1967, French Acad. of Sciences 1995, French Acad. of Medicine 2008; Active mem. European Acad. of Sciences and Arts 2004; Foreign Assoc. NAS 1976, Russian Acad. of Sciences 1994, Italian Acad. of Sciences 1995, American Philosophical Soc. 1995; Fellow, Polish Acad. of Arts and Sciences 1998; Hon. mem. American Soc. Biological Chemists 1968, American Assen of Immunologists 1973, Scandinavian Soc. for Immunology 1971, Harvey Soc. 1972, French Soc. for Immunology 1979, Chilean Soc. for Immunology 1981, Romanian Acad. 1991, Romanian Acad. of Medical Sciences 1991, Romanian Soc. for Immunology; Foreign Hon. mem. American Acad. Arts and Sciences 1971; Hon. Fellow, The Open Univ. of Israel 2004; Commdr's Cross of Order of Merit Award (FRG) 1986,

Officier, Légion d'honneur 1987, Commdr 2011, Caballero, Order of San Carlos (Colombia) 1997, Gran Ufficiale of Italian Solidarity Star 2007; Dr hc (Bordeaux II) 1985, (Nat. Autonomous Univ. of Mexico) 1985, (Tufts Univ.) 1989, Colby Coll. 1989, (Univ. Louis Pasteur) 1990, (Hebrew Univ. of Jerusalem) 1995, (Tel-Aviv) 1999, (Ben Gurion Univ. of the Negev) 2001; awarded NIH Lectureship 1973; Israel Prize Natural Sciences 1959, Rothschild Prize for Chem. 1968, Otto Warburg Medal, German Soc. of Biological Chem. 1968, Emil von Behring Prize, Phillipps Univ. 1972, Gairdner Int. Award, Toronto 1980, Prize, Inst. de la Vie Fondation Electricité de France, Lille 1984, Prix Jaubert, Faculty of Science, Univ. of Geneva 1986, Interbrew-Baillet Latour Health Prize 1997, Karl Landsteiner Medal, Toronto 1986, Albert Einstein Gold Medal 1995, Harnak Medal, Max-Planck-Soc. 1996, Wolf Prize in Medicine 1998. *Publications:* more than 800 in immunology, biochemistry and molecular biology; Ed. The Antigens (seven vols published). *Address:* Weizmann Institute of Science, Wolfson Building for Biological Research, Room no 708, Rehovot, 76100, Israel (office). *Telephone:* (8) 9344021 (office), (8) 9344022 (office); (8) 9471132 (home). *Fax:* (8) 9469713 (office). *E-mail:* michael.sela@weizmann.ac.il (office). *Website:* www.weizmann.ac.il/ immunology/SelaPub.html (office).

SELANGOR, HRH The Sultan of; Tuanku Sharafuddin Idris Shah Salahuddin Abdul Aziz Shah, DK; Malaysian; b. 24 Dec. 1945, Klang; s. of the late Sultan Salahuddin Abdul Aziz Shah and Raja Shaidatul Ihsan binti Tengku Badar Shah; m. 1st Raja Zarina binti Raja Zainul 1968 (divorced 1986); m. 2nd Lisa Davis (Puan Nur Lisa Abdullah) 1988 (divorced 1997); two d. one s.; ed Hale School, Perth, Australia and Langhurst Coll., Surrey, England; fmr Regent of Selangor, proclaimed ninth Sultan of Selangor on the death of his father Nov. 2001; held various admin. posts in state and fed. govt services, including Selangor State Secr., Dist Office and Royal Malaysian Police Dept, Kuala Lumpur 1968–; mem. The Conf. of Rulers, Malaysia; Pro-Chancellor Universiti Teknologi MARA 2000; Chancellor Universiti Putra Malaysia 2002; Chair. Semi-Professional Football Assen; Chair. Bd of Trustees Yayasan Seni Selangor (Selangor Art Foundation), Galeri Shah Alam; Patron Malaysian branch of the Royal Asiatic Soc., Royal Selangor Club; circumnavigated the world on his yacht, S. Y. Jugra 1995–96; participated in Peking to Paris Challenge vintage car race 1997; Dr hc (Universiti Teknologi MARA) 2001; Hon. Life Pres. Selangor Football Assen. *Website:* www.selangor.gov.my.

SELBORNE, 4th Earl, cr. 1882; John Roundell Palmer, GBE, BA, MA, FRS, FIBiol, FLS; British peer, farmer and business executive; b. 24 March 1940; s. of the late Capt. William Palmer, Viscount Wolmer and Priscilla Egerton-Warburton; m. Joanna van Antwerp James 1969; three s. one d.; ed Eton Coll., Christ Church, Oxford; Man. Dir Blackmoor Estate Ltd 1962–; Treas. King Edward's School, Witley 1972–83; Chair. Hops Marketing Bd 1978–82, Agricultural and Food Research Council 1983–89; Pres. Royal Agricultural Soc. of England 1987–88; Chair. Jt Nature Conservation Cttee 1991–97; Chair. House of Lords Select Cttee on Science and Tech. 1993–97; mem. Govt Panel on Sustainable Devt 1994–97; Chair. AMC 1994–2002, UK Chemical Stakeholder Forum 2000–09; Dir Lloyds TSB Group 1995–2006; Chancellor Univ. of Southampton 1996–2006; Pres. Royal Agricultural Soc. of England 1987–88, Royal Inst. of Public Health and Hygiene 1991–97, Royal Geographical Soc. (with Inst. of British Geographers) 1997–2000; Vice-Pres. Royal Soc. for the Protection of Birds 1996–2007; elected Hereditary mem. House of Lords 1999–, Chair. Sub-cttee D (Agric. and Environment), House of Lords EU Select Cttee 1999–2003; Chair. Bd of Trustees, Royal Botanic Gardens, Kew 2003–09; Chair. Council of the Foundation for Science and Tech. 2006–, Rank Prize Funds; mem. World Comm. on the Ethics of Science and Tech., UNESCO 1999–2003; Patron Inst. of Ecology and Environmental Man.; Fellow, Inst. of Biology; Conservative; Master of the Worshipful Co. of Mercers 1989; Hon. LLD (Bristol) 1988; Hon. DSc (Cranfield) 1991, (East Anglia) 1996, (Southampton) 1996, (Birmingham) 2000; Massey-Ferguson Nat. Award for Services to UK Agric. 1990. *Address:* House of Lords, Westminster, London, SW1A 0PW, England (office); Temple Manor, Selborne, Alton, Hants., GU34 3LR, England (home). *Telephone:* (20) 7219-6171 (office); (1420) 473646 (home). *E-mail:* selbornejr@ parliament.uk (office).

SELBY, Philip; British composer; b. 6 Feb. 1948; s. of the late George Selby and Sarah Selby (née Knott); m. Rosanna Burrai 1974; one s.; ed Manor Park Grammar School, Nuneaton, Royal Northern Coll. of Music; composition studies with G. Petrassi, C. Camilleri and Karlheinz Stockhausen; appeared as guitar soloist, Birmingham Town Hall 1966, Royal Albert Hall, London 1970, All-India Radio and TV, Pakistani TV, Youth Palace, Tehran, Istanbul Univ.; debut as composer with first performance of From the Fountain of Youth (for guitar and chamber orchestra), Leamington 1975; mem. British Acad. of Composers and Songwriters, Inc. Soc. of Musicians, Performing Right Soc.; Chevalier, Ordre Souverain et Militaire de la Milice du Saint Sépulcre 1988. *Compositions include:* Suite for guitar 1965–67, Two Meditations for Piano 1972–74, Symphonic Dance for orchestra 1973, Ten Little Studies for Guitar Solo 1973–76, Fantasia for guitar 1974, Rhapsody for piano and orchestra 1975, Three Scottish Songs for voice and violin 1975, A Nature Meditation for violin and small orchestra, Guitar Concerto 1976–77, Suite for String Quartet 1977–78, Sonatina for piano 1978, Spirit of the Earth for flute 1978, Branch Touches Branch, pastorale 1978, Isa Upanishad (cantata sacra for double chorus and orchestra) 1979–87, Sonata for timpani 1980, Greek Suite for Oboe Solo 1981, Siddhartha (dance symphony) 1981–84, Logos for trumpet 1982, Ring Out Ye Bells (carol) 1988, Symphony of Sacred Images (for soprano and bass soli, double chorus and orchestra) 1986–92, Anthem for Gibraltar (unison voices and organ) 1994, Beatus Vir (motet) 1995, String Quartet No. 1 (Non Potho Reposare, Amore Coro) 1996–97, Autoritratto Vittorio Alfieri (for soprano, violin and guitar) 1998, Sonata Atma Brahma for Piano 1998–99, Fear No More the Heat of the Sun, madrigal 2001, Agape for solo violin 2001–02, Agape II for solo viola 2002, Eight Poems of J. G. Brown, song cycle 2005, Four American Portraits for speaking choir 2006, Ode to Earth and Sky (for double string orchestra) 2007–08. *Leisure interests:* reading, travel, the arts. *Address:* Hill Cottage, Via I Maggio 93, 00068 Rignano Flaminio, Rome, Italy. *Telephone:* (0761) 507945.

SELEBI, Jackie; South African police commissioner and international organization official; b. 7 March 1950, Johannesburg; elected Head African Nat. Congress (ANC) Youth League whilst in exile 1987, mem. ANC Exec. Cttee 1987–91, apptd Head, Dept of Welfare 1993; elected to Parl. 1994; Perm. Rep. to UN, Geneva

1995–98; Dir-Gen. Ministry of Foreign Affairs, Pretoria 1998–99; Nat. Commr South African Police Service 2000–08; Vice-Pres. (African Region) Interpol, Pres. 2004–08 (resgnd); fmr Chair. UN Human Rights Comm. 54th Session, Anti-Landmine Conf., Oslo; fmr Chair. Justice, Crime Prevention and Security Cluster; charged with corruption 2008, found guilty and sentenced to 15 years imprisonment 2010; Int. Human Rights Award 1997.

SELEŠ, Monica; American/Hungarian (born Yugoslav) fmr professional tennis player; b. 2 Dec. 1973, Novi Sad, Yugoslavia (now Serbia and Montenegro); d. of the late Karolj Seleš and of Ester Seleš; moved to USA 1986; became US citizen 1994; semi-finalist, French Open 1989; won French Open 1990, 1991, 1992; Virginia Slims Championships 1990, 1991, 1992; US Open 1991, 1992; Australian Open 1991, 1992, 1993, 1996; Canadian Open 1995, 1996; winner LA Open 1997, Canadian Open 1997, Tokyo Open 1997; bronze medal Olympic Games, Sydney 2000; quarter-finalist, Wimbledon Championships 1990; off court for over two years after being stabbed by spectator during Hamburg quarter-final 1993; 59 WTA Tour titles, nine Grand Slam titles and US $14,891,762 in prize money; mem. winning US Fed. Cup team 1996, 1999, 2000; retd 2008; partner, the All-Star Café; played exhibition match Australia 2005; currently Goodwill Amb. of Laureus Sports Foundation, Intergovernmental Inst. for the use of Microalgae Spirulina Against Malnutrition; Ted Tinling Diamond Award 1990, Associated Press Athlete of the Year 1990–91, Tennis Magazine Comeback Player of the Year 1995, Flo Hyman Award 2000, Sanex Hero of the Year award 2002, elected to Int. Tennis Hall of Fame 2009. *Publication:* Monica: From Fear to Victory 1996, Getting A Grip: On My Body, My Mind, My Self 2009. *Leisure interests:* ice skating, horse riding, basketball, guitar, swimming, reading autobiographies. *Address:* c/o International Management Group, 1360 E, 9th Street, Suite 100, Cleveland, OH 44114, USA.

SELEZNEV, Gennadiy Nikolaevich; Russian politician and journalist; b. 6 Nov. 1947, Serov, Sverdlovsk Region; m. Irina Borisovna Selezneva 1978; one c.; ed Leningrad Univ. (by correspondence); mem. CPSU 1970–91, CP of Russian Fed. 1992–; work in komsomol 1968–74; Ed.-in-Chief Smena 1974–80, Komsomolskaya Pravda 1980–88, Uchitelskaya Gazeta (newspaper for teachers) 1988–91; Ed.-in-Chief, Pravda 1991–93; Ed.-in-Chief Pravda Rossii 1995–96; mem. State Duma (Parl.) 1993–95, Chair. State Duma II and III Convocation 2004–08, Deputy of State Duma IV Convocation 2004–08; Co-Chair. Interparliamentary Ass. of CIS; Chair. Parl. Union of Russia and Belarus 1997–2003; Founder Russia Social Org. 2000; expelled from CP 2002; Deputy Chair. Parl. Ass. of OSCE 1999–; Chair. a commercial bank 2009–; Pres. Russian Equestrian Fed. 2005–09; Hon. Prof. Inst. of Youth, Heilongjiang Univ.; Order of Friendship of Peoples 1984, Order for Service to the Fatherland, Class II, 2000 and other state awards. *Publications:* All Power to Law 1997, Law, Power and Politics: National and Local Levels 1998; numerous articles on the state. *Leisure interests:* reading, swimming, riding. *Address:* 3/2 str. Solyanka, 109028 Moscow, Russia (office). *Telephone:* (495) 626-21-01 (office). *Fax:* (495) 626-21-05 (office). *E-mail:* seleznev555@mail.ru (office). *Website:* mosoblbank.ru (office).

SELF, Colin Ernest, DFA; British artist; b. 17 July 1941, Rackheath; s. of Ernest Walter Self and Kathleen Augustine Self (née Bellamy); m. 1st Margaret Ann Murrell 1963; m. 2nd Jessica Prendergast 1978; one s. two d.; ed Norwich Art School, Slade School of Fine Art, London Univ.; Drawing Prize Biennale de Paris 1967, Giles Bequest Prize Bradford Biennale 1969, Tolly Cobbold Prize 1979. *Leisure interests:* nature study, music. *Address:* 31 St Andrew's Avenue, Thorpe, Norwich, NR7 0RG, England.

SELF, William (Will) Woodward, MA; British writer, cartoonist and academic; b. 26 Sept. 1961, London, England; s. of Peter John Otter Self and Elaine Rosenbloom; m. 1st Katharine Sylvia Anthony Chancellor 1989 (divorced 1996); one s. one d.; m. 2nd Deborah Jane Orr 1997; two s.; ed Christ's Coll., Exeter Coll., Oxford; cartoon illustrations appeared in New Statesman and City Limits 1982–88; Publishing Dir Cathedral Publishing 1988–90; Contributing Ed. London Evening Standard magazine 1993–95; columnist, The Observer 1995–97, The Times 1997–99, Ind. on Sunday 2000–, Evening Standard 2002–, The Independent 2003–; Prof. of Contemporary Thought, Brunel Univ. 2012–; Geoffrey Faber Memorial Prize 1992. *Publications:* short stories: Quantity Theory of Insanity 1991, Grey Area 1994, A Story for Europe 1996, Tough Tough Toys for Tough Tough Boys 1998, Dr Mukti and Other Tales of Woe 2003, Liver 2008; novellas: Cock and Bull 1992, The Sweet Smell of Psychosis 1996; novels: My Idea of Fun 1993, Great Apes 1997, How the Dead Live 2000, Perfidious Man 2000, Feeding Frenzy 2001, Dorian 2002, Dr Mukti 2004, The Book of Dave 2006, Umbrella 2012; non-fiction: Junk Mail (selected journalism) 1995, Sore Sites (collected journalism) 2000, Psychogeography (collected journalism) 2007, The Butt 2008, Psycho Too (with Ralph Steadman) 2009, Walking to Hollywood 2010, Umbrella 2012; collected cartoons 1985. *Leisure interest:* walking. *Address:* c/o The Wylie Agency, 17 Bedford Square, London, WC1B 3BA, England (office). Gaskell Building, 134 Brunel University, Uxbridge, UB8 3PH. *E-mail:* will.self@brunel.ac.uk; info@will-self.com. *Website:* will-self.com.

SELIGMAN, Joel, AB, JD; American lawyer, academic and university administrator; *President, University of Rochester;* b. 11 Jan. 1950, New York, NY; m. 2nd Delores Conway 2012; one s. two d.; ed Univ. of California, Los Angeles, Harvard Law School; attorney, Accountability Research Group, Washington, DC 1974–77; Prof., Northeastern Univ. School of Law 1977–83; Prof., George Washington Univ. Law School 1983–86; Prof., Univ. of Michigan Law School 1987–95; Dean and Samuel M. Fegtly Prof. of Law, Univ. of Arizona Coll. of Law 1995–99; Dean and Ethan A.H. Shepley Univ. Prof., School of Law, Washington Univ., St Louis 1999–2005; Pres. Univ. of Rochester 2005–; mem. Bd of Govs Financial Industry Regulatory Authority; reporter, Nat. Conf. of Commrs on Uniform State Laws, Revision of Uniform Securities Act 1998–2002; Chair. SEC Advisory Cttee on Market Information 2000–01; consultant to US Fed. Trade Comm., Washington, DC 1979–82, US Dept of Transportation 1983, Office of Tech. Assessment 1988–89; Dir Nat. Asscn of Securities Dealers 2004–07; mem. American Law Inst., State Bar of Calif., American Inst. of Certified Public Accountants (fmr mem. Professional Ethics Exec. Cttee. *Publications:* author or co-author of 20 books, including (co-author with the late Louis Loss) Securities Regulation (11 vols) and The Transformation of Wall Street: A History of the Securities and Exchange Commission and Modern Corporation Finance; over 40 articles. *Address:* Office

of the President, 240 Wallis Hall, University of Rochester, Rochester, NY 14627, USA (office). *Telephone:* (585) 275-8356 (office). *Fax:* (585) 256-2473 (office). *E-mail:* seligman@rochester.edu (office). *Website:* www.rochester.edu/president (office).

SELIGMAN, Nicole Kay, BA, JD; American lawyer and electronics industry executive; *Executive Vice-President, General Counsel and Corporate Executive Officer, Sony Corporation;* b. 1956; m. Joel I. Klein 2000; ed Radcliffe Coll., Harvard Law School; edited the Harvard Law Review; Assoc. Editorial Page Ed. Asian Wall Street Journal, Hong Kong 1978–80; law clerk for Judge Harry T. Edwards, US Court of Appeals, DC Circuit, Washington, DC 1983–84; law clerk to Justice Thurgood Marshall, US Supreme Court, Washington, DC 1984–85; Pnr, Williams & Connolly LLP (law firm), Washington, DC –2001; Exec. Vice-Pres. and Gen. Counsel, Sony Corpn of America, New York 2001–12, Pres. 2012–, Corp. Exec. Officer, Sony Corpn 2003–, Group Deputy Gen. Counsel 2003–05, Exec. Vice-Pres. and Gen. Counsel, Sony Corpn 2005–. *Address:* Sony Corporation of America, 550 Madison Avenue, New York, NY 10022-3211, USA (office). *Telephone:* (212) 833-6800 (office). *Fax:* (212) 833-6938 (office). *Website:* www.sony.com (office).

SELINGER, Benjamin Klaas (Ben), AM, Dr rer. nat, DSc; Australian chemist, environmental consultant and academic; *Professor Emeritus of Chemistry, Australian National University;* b. 23 Jan. 1939, Sydney, NSW; s. of Herbert Selinger and Hilde Wittner; m. Veronica Hollander 1967; two s.; ed Sydney Boys High School, Univ. of Sydney, Tech. Univ. Stuttgart and Australian Nat. Univ.; Lecturer in Physical Chem., ANU 1966–71, Sr Lecturer 1971–78, Head, Dept of Chem. 1988–91, Prof. of Chem. 1992–98, Prof. Emer. 1999–; Chair. Bd of Nat. Registration Authority for Agric. and Veterinary Chemicals 1993–97; mem. numerous Govt bodies, advisory cttees, etc.; various academic posts overseas; Deputy Chair. ANZAAS 1994–96; Chair. Australian Science Festival Ltd 2001–; Fellow, Royal Australian Chem. Inst., Royal Inst. of GB, Australian Acad. of Tech. Sciences and Eng, Australian Acad. of Forensic Sciences; mem. CHOICE (Council Australian Consumers Asscn) 2000–, Life mem. 2007; consultant, Versel Scientific Consulting; columnist, Canberra Times 1972–2005, Burke's Backyard magazine 2000–05; Alexander von Humboldt Fellow; Archibald Olle Prize 1979, Special Eureka Prize for Science Communication (ABC/Australian Museum) 1991, ANZAAS Medallist 1993, Centenary of Fed. Medal 2003; many other awards and distinctions. *Film:* appeared as a forensic expert in An Act of Necessity, Film Australia 1991. *Radio:* Dial-a-Scientist, ABC, also on talk back radio. *Television:* has appeared in ABC World Series Debates on Science Is a Health Hazard, compered Home and Away (BBC) 1991, many interviews on environmental questions. *Publications:* Chemistry in the Market Place 1975–98 (5th edn), Thinking with Fourier 1992, Expert Evidence 1992, Why the Watermelon Won't Ripen in Your Armpit 2000. *Leisure interests:* bushwalking, science museums, forensic chem. *Address:* 2005/71–73 Spring Street, Bondi Junction, NSW 2022, Australia. *Telephone:* (2) 9389-8595; 407-460339 (mobile). *E-mail:* benselinger39@gmail.com.

SELINGER, Greg, BA, MPA, PhD; Canadian politician; *Premier of Manitoba;* m. Claudette Toupin; two s.; ed Univ. of Manitoba, Queen's Univ., Kingston, Ont., London School of Econs, UK; fmr Assoc. Prof., Faculty of Social Work, Univ. of Manitoba; elected to Winnipeg City Council 1989, becoming mem. Exec. Policy Cttee and Chair. Finance Cttee; unsuccessful cand. for Mayor of Winnipeg 1992; mem. Manitoba Legis. Ass. as MP for St Boniface 1999–; Manitoba Prov. Minister of Finance 1999–2001, also Minister responsible for French Language Services and for Crown Corpns Public Review and Accountability Act 1999–2001, Minister of Civil Service Comm. 2001–06, Minister responsible for Manitoba Hydro 2006–09, also responsible for Liquor Control Comm. and Manitoba Lotteries Corpn 2007–09, Premier of Manitoba 2009–, also Pres., Exec. Council and Minister of Fed.-Prov. Relations; mem. New Democratic Party of Manitoba, Leader 2009–. *Address:* Office of the Premier, 204 Legislative Building, 450 Broadway, Winnipeg, MB R3C 0V8, Canada (office). *Telephone:* (204) 945-3714 (office). *Fax:* (204) 949-1484 (office). *E-mail:* premier@leg.gov.mb.ca (office). *Website:* www.gov.mb.ca/minister/premier (office).

SELIVON, Mykola Jedosovych, PhD; Ukrainian lawyer, judge and diplomatist; b. 30 Oct. 1946, Shestovytsya, Chernigiv Region; one s. one d.; ed Faculty of Law, Kyiv Taras Shevchenko State Univ.; Research Fellow, Inst. of State and Law, Acad. of Sciences of Ukraine 1973; apptd Sr Asst Govt Legal Group 1979, later Chief of Legal Dept; fmr Deputy Minister of Cabinet of Ministers, later First Deputy Minister –1996; Judge, Constitutional Court of Ukraine 1996–99, Deputy Chair. 1999–2002, Chair. 2002–06; Amb. to Kazakhstan 2006–10; Academician, Ukrainian Acad. of Law Sciences; mem. Perm. Court of Arbitration, The Hague; Order for Service, Third Class; Distinguished Lawyer of Ukraine. *Leisure interests:* classical music, theatre, sport.

SELKOE, Dennis J., BA, MD; American neurologist and professor of neurology; *Vincent and Stella Coates Professor of Neurologic Diseases, Harvard Medical School;* b. 25 Sept. 1943, New York; ed Columbia Univ., New York and Univ. of Virginia School of Medicine; US Public Health Service Summer Research Fellow in Pediatrics, Michael Reese Medical Research Inst., Chicago 1966, US Public Health Service Summer Research Fellow in Neurochemistry, McLean Hosp., Belmont, Mass 1968; Intern in Medicine, Hosp. of the Univ. of Pennsylvania, Phidelphia 1969–70; Research Assoc., Nat. Inst. of Neurological Disorders and Stroke, NIH, Bethesda, Maryland 1970–72; Resident in Neurology, Peter Bent Brigham, Children's and Beth Israel Hosps Boston, Mass 1972–74, Chief Resident in Neurology, Peter Bent Brigham and Children's Hosps 1974–75, United Cerebral Palsy Fellow, Children's Hosp. 1974–75; NIH Postdoctoral Fellow in Neuroscience, Children's Hosp., Harvard Medical School, Boston 1975–78, Research Assoc. in Neuroscience, Children's Hosp. Medical Center 1975–78, Instructor in Neurology, Harvard Medical School 1975–78, Asst Neurologist Children's Hosp. and Brigham and Women's Hosp. 1975–82, Asst Prof. of Neurology, Harvard Medical School 1978–82 (Faculty mem. Div. on Aging 1979–, Program in Neuroscience 1985–), Assoc. Physician (Neurology), Children's Hosp. and Brigham and Women's Hosp. 1982–85, Assoc. Prof. of Neurology 1982–85, Assoc. Prof. of Neurology (Neuroscience) 1985–90, Physician (Neurology), Brigham and Women's Hosp. 1985–92, Dir Center for Neurologic Diseases, Brigham and Women's Hosp. 1985–, Prof. of Neurology (Neuroscience), Harvard Medical School 1990–, Sr Physician (Neurology), Brigham and Women's Hosp. 1992–99, Clinical Assoc. in Neurology, Massachusetts Gen. Hosp. 1997–, Sr Neurologist, Brigham and Women's Hosp.

1999–, Vincent and Stella Coates Prof. of Neurologic Diseases, Harvard Medical School 2001–, currently also Co-Dir Center for Neurologic Diseases; Assoc. Neuropathologist, McLean Hosp., Belmont 1978–85; Investigator, Huntington's Disease Research Center Without Walls, Boston 1980–83; Andrew Floud Memorial Lecturer, Neurological Inst. 1984; Arling Lecturer, Univ. of Cincinnati Medical Center 1991; Distinguished Alumnus/Keynote Speaker, Univ. of Virginia Medical Alumni Symposium 1994; Wellcome Visiting Professorship in the Basic Medical Sciences, Louisiana State Univ. Medical School 1995; Royston C. Clowes Annual Memorial Lecturer, Univ. of Texas, Dallas 1996; Lowell O. Randall Lecturer in Pharmacology, Univ. of Pennsylvania School of Medicine 1996; Frank A. Elliott Lecturer, Penn Neurological Inst., Univ. of Pennsylvania Health System 1999; Rotary Chair for Alzheimer's Disease, Univ. of Leiden (Netherlands) 2000; Co-Chair. Governance Cttee and Chair. Harvard Center for Translational Neurology Research, Harvard Center for Neurodegeneration and Repair, Harvard Medical School 2000–; mem. Medical and Scientific Advisory Bd Alzheimer's Asscn (USA) 1983–90; mem. Exec. Cttee Massachusetts Alzheimer's Disease Research Center 1984–; Founding mem. Dana Alliance for Brain Initiatives 1992–; mem. Scientific Review Bd (Neuroscience) Howard Hughes Medical Inst. 1995–; mem. NIH Nat. Advisory Council on Aging 1998–; Consulting Ed. Journal of Clinical Investigation 1998–; mem. Editorial Bd Neurobiology of Aging 1983–93, Alzheimer's Disease 1986–, Neurodegeneration 1990–93, Neuron 1993–99, Neurobiology of Disease 1993–, Amyloid 1994–, American Journal of Alzheimer's Disease 1997–; mem. Editorial Advisory Bd Synapse 1994–; mem. Editorial Cttee Annual Review of Neuroscience 1996–2001; Editorial Advisor, Neurology, BioMed Central 2000–; mem. American Soc. for Neurology 1973, Soc. for Neuroscience 1980, Massachusetts Neurologic Assn 1980, AAAS 1982, American Soc. for Neurochemistry 1983, American Assn for Neuropathologists 1983, American Neurological Assn 1983, World Fed. of Neurology 1985, American Soc. for Investigative Pathology 1992, American Soc. for Cell Biology 1998; Fellow, American Acad. of Neurology 1996 (Chair. Potamkin Prize Cttee 1998–); Matthew and Marcia Simons Lecturer, Alzheimer's Asscn; Hon. MA (Harvard) 1991; Neuropathology Award, Univ. of Virginia School of Medicine 1966, Medical Student Research Award in Experimental Neurology (First Prize), American Acad. of Neurology 1968, Nat. Foundation Merit Award 1968, Univ. Research and Devt Prize, Univ. of Virginia 1969, Teacher Investigator Devt Award, NIH (NINDS) 1978–83, Wood Kalb Foundation Prize for Research on Alzheimer's Disease 1984, Metropolitan Life Foundation Award for Medical Research 1986, McKnight Foundation Award for Neuroscience Research 1988–91, Leadership and Excellence in Alzheimer's Disease (LEAD) Award, NIH Nat. Inst. on Aging 1988–95, Potamkin Prize, American Acad. of Neurology 1989, NIH MERIT Award, Nat. Inst. on Aging 1991, Commonwealth of Massachusetts 1992, Lifetime Science Award, Inst. for Advanced Studies in Immunology and Aging, Washington, DC 1992, Rita Hayworth Award, Alzheimer's Assn 1995, Arthur Cherkin Memorial Award, UCLA 1996, Leonard Berg Hon. Symposium on Alzheimer's Disease, Washington Univ. School of Medicine 1997, Mathilde Solowey Award in the Neurosciences, NIH Foundation for Advanced Education in the Sciences 1998, Boerhaave Medal, Univ. of Leiden 1998, Robert J. Huebner Memorial Symposium, Kimmel Cancer Center, Jefferson Univ. 1999, Pioneer Award, Alzheimer's Assn 1999. Publications: more than 630 articles in medical journals. Address: Brigham and Women's Hospital, Center for Neurologic Diseases, HIM 730, 77 Avenue Louis Pasteur, Boston, MA 02115-5817, USA (office). Telephone: (617) 525-5200 (office). Fax: (617)525-5252 (office). E-mail: dselkoe@rics.bwh.harvard.edu (office). Website: www.hms.harvard.edu/dms/neuroscience/fac/selkoe.html (office); selkoelab.bwh.harvard.edu (office).

SELLA, Phillippe; French fmr rugby union player; *Co-Director, Sella Communication;* b. 14 Feb. 1962, Tonneins; centre/wing; 111 appearances with French nat. team 1982–1995, fmr world record number of caps, scored 30 tries including one in every game of the 1986 Five Nations Championship; appeared in three World Cups, retd from nat. team 1995; with English club Saracens 1995–97; still involved in rugby, fmrly co-coach of Barbarians; currently involved in business ventures; co-Dir Sella Communication 2003–. *Address:* Sella Communication, 1 rue du Parc des Princes, 47300 Villeneuve-sur-Lot, France (office). *Telephone:* 5-53-40-15-22 (office). *Fax:* 5-53-36-70-10 (office). *E-mail:* contact@sellacommunication.com (office). *Website:* www.sellacommunication.com (office).

SELLAL, Abdelmalek; Algerian politician and fmr diplomatist; *Prime Minister;* b. 1 Aug. 1948, Constantine; ed Ecole Nat. d'Admin, Algiers; Admin. and Chief of Staff, Guelma Wilaya (Dist) 1975; Tech. Adviser, Ministry of Nat. Educ. 1976; Chief, Daïra Tamanrasset and Arzew Dists 1977–84, Boumerdes, Adrar, Sidi Bel, Abbes, Oran and Laghouat Dists 1984–89; Adviser to Minister of the Interior 1989–94; Chief of Staff to Minister of Foreign Affairs 1994–95, Dir-Gen. of Resources, Ministry of Foreign Affairs 1995–96, Amb. to Hungary 1996–97; Minister of the Interior, Local Govt and Environment 1998–99, of Youth and Sports 1999–2001, of Public Works 2001–02, of Transport 2002–04, of Water Resources 2004–12; Prime Minister 2012–14, 2014–. *Address:* Office of the Prime Minister, rue Docteur Saâdane, Algiers, Algeria (office). *Telephone:* (21) 73-12-00 (office). *Fax:* (21) 71-79-29 (office). *Website:* www.cg.gov.dz (office).

SELLARS, Peter, BA; American theatre and opera director and professor of theatre and arts; *Professor, Department of World Arts and Cultures, University of California, Los Angeles;* b. 27 Sept. 1957, Pittsburgh, Pa; ed Harvard Univ.; Dir, Boston Shakespeare Co. 1983–84; Dir and Man., American Nat. Theater at J.F. Kennedy Center, Washington, DC 1984–86; Artistic Advisor, Boston Opera Theatre 1990; currently Dept of World Arts and Culture, UCLA; Fellow, MacArthur Foundation, Chicago 1983; fmr Visiting Prof., Center for Theatre Arts, Univ. of California, Berkeley; Artistic Dir, New Crowned Hope Festival 2006–; Erasmus Prize 1998, The Dorothy and Lillian Gish Prize 2005, Opera News Award for invaluable contrib. to opera 2011, Polar Music Prize 2014. *Libretto:* Doctor Atomic (Adams). *Productions include:* Ajax, Armida, Così fan tutte, The Death of Klinghoffer, Die Zauberflöte, Don Giovanni, The Electrification of the Soviet Union, Le Grand Macabre, Idomeneo, The Lighthouse, The Marriage of Figaro, Mathis der Maler, Merchant of Venice, The Mikado, El Niño, Nixon in China, Orlando, The Rake's Progress, Saul and Orlando, St François d'Assise, Tannhäuser, Theodora, Zangezi, Mozart's Zaide (Mostly Mozart Festival at Lincoln Center, New York 2006), Saariaho's La Passion de Simone 2006, Adams' A Flowering Tree 2006, Othello (New York City's Public Theater) 2009, Adams' Nixon in China (Metropolitan Opera) 2011, Vivaldi's Griselda (Santa Fe Opera) 2011, Tristan and

Isolde (Helsinki Festival) 2012, (Toronto) 2013, (Real Opera Madrid) 2014, (Paris Opera) 2014, Johannes-Passion (Baden-Baden) 2014. *Address:* Department of World Arts and Cultures, UCLA, Glorya Kaufman Hall 114, 120 Westwood Plaza, Suite 150, PO Box 951608, Los Angeles, CA 90095-1608, USA (office). *Telephone:* (310) 825-3951 (office). *E-mail:* djmalecki@aol.com. *Website:* www.wac.ucla.edu (office).

SELLECK, Tom; American actor and producer; b. 29 Jan. 1945, Detroit, Mich.; s. of Robert D. Selleck and Martha Selleck; m. 1st Jackie Ray (divorced 1982); one step-s.; m. 2nd Jillie Mack 1987; one d.; ed Univ. of Southern California; mem. Bd Michael Josephson Inst. of Ethics, Advisory Bd Character Counts Coalition (fmr Nat. Spokesperson), Student/Sponsor Partnership Program, New York, Cttee of John F. Kennedy Center for the Performing Arts; fmr Hon. Chair. Skin Cancer Foundation; Spokesman for Nat. Fatherhood Initiative; fmr spokesperson for Los Angeles Mission to Help the Homeless; Hon. LLD (Pepperdine Univ.) 2004; Distinguished American Award, Horatio Alger Assn 2004. *Films include:* Myra Breckenridge, Midway, Coma, Seven Minutes, High Road to China, Runaway, Lassiter, Three Men and a Baby, Her Alibi 1988, Quigley Down Under, An Innocent Man 1989, Three Men and a Little Lady 1991, Folks 1991, Mr Baseball 1991, Christopher Columbus: The Discovery 1992, In & Out, The Love Letter 1999, Running Mates 2000, Meet the Robinsons (voice) 2007, Killers 2010. *Television includes:* Returning Home, Bracken's World, The Young and the Restless, The Rockford Files, The Sacketts, played Thomas Magnum in Magnum PI 1980–88, Divorce Wars, Countdown at the Super Bowl, Gypsy Warriors, Boston and Kilbride, The Concrete Cowboys, Murder She Wrote, The Silver Fox, The Closer (series) 1998, Last Stand at Saber River, Friends, 1996, 2000, Ruby, Jean and Joe, Broken Trust 1995, Washington Slept Here 2000, Louis l'Amour's Crossfire Trail 2000, Monte Walsh 2003, 12 Mile Road 2003, Reversible Errors 2004, Ike, Countdown to D Day 2004, Stone Cold 2005, Jesse Stone: Night Passage 2006, Jesse Stone: Death in Paradise 2006, Jesse Stone: Sea Change 2007, Las Vegas (series) 2007–08, Blue Bloods (series) 2010. *Leisure interests:* volleyball (Hon. Capt. US Men's Volleyball Team for 1984 Olympic Games), outrigger canoe specialist, baseball, horseback riding. *Address:* c/o Esme Chandlee, 2967 Hollyridge Drive, Los Angeles, CA 90068, USA. *Telephone:* (323) 962-5704 (office). *Fax:* (323) 962-5705 (office).

SELLERT, Wolfgang, DJur; German legal scholar and professor of history; *Professor Emeritus and Chairman, Abteilung für Deutsche Rechtsgeschichte, University of Göttingen;* b. 3 Nov. 1935, Berlin; s. of Horst-Günther Sellert and Else Kaiser; m. Dr Urte Wenger 1962; two d.; Asst in Dept for History of German Law, Univ. of Frankfurt 1965–72, Prof. 1972–77; Prof. of History of German Law and Civil Law, Georg-August Univ., Göttingen 1977–, currently Prof. Emer. and Chair. Dept for German Historical Jurisprudence; Dir German-Chinese Inst. of Econ. Law, Univ. of Nanjing 1995–; mem. Akad. der Wissenschaften, Göttingen 1984–. *Publications:* Über die Zuständigkeitsabgrenzung von Reichshofrat und Reichskammergericht 1965, Prozessgrundsätze über Stilus Curiae am Reichshofrat 1973, Die Ordnungen des Reichshofrats 1980, Studien- u. Quellenbuch zur Geschichte der dt. Strafrechtspflege 1989, Recht u. Gerechtigkeit in der Kunst 1991. *Leisure interests:* collecting old manuscripts and baroque literature. *Address:* Konrad-Adenauer-Strasse 25, 37075 Göttingen; Juridicum, Räume 131-133, Platz der Göttinger, Sieben 6, 37073 Göttingen, Germany (office). *Telephone:* (551) 397444 (office); (551) 23771. *Fax:* (551) 394872 (office); (551) 23771. *E-mail:* eszepst@gwdg.de (office).

SELTEN, Reinhard, DrPhilNat; German economist and academic; *Research Co-ordinator, Experimental Economics Laboratory, University of Bonn;* b. 5 Oct. 1930, Breslau; s. of Adolf Selten and Käthe Luther; m. Elisabeth Langreiner 1959; ed Univ. of Frankfurt am Main; Prof., Freie Univ. Berlin 1969; Prof., Univ. of Bielefeld; Prof. of Econ. Theory, Univ. of Bonn 1984–96, Prof. Emer. 1996–, currently Research Co-ordinator Experimental Econ. Lab. (BonnEconLab); mem. Rheinisch-Westfalen Akad. der Wissenschaften; Fellow, Econometric Soc.; Order of Merit, Arts and Sciences 2006;Foreign Hon. mem. American Acad. of Arts and Sciences, Hon. Senator, Univ. of Bonn 2007; Dr hc (Bielefeld) 1989, (Frankfurt) 1991, (Graz) 1996, (E Anglia) 1996, (Norwich) 1997, (Cachan) 1998, (Innsbruck) 2000, (Hong Kong) 2003, (Osnabrück) 2006; Nobel Memorial Prize in Econ. Sciences (Nobel Prize in Econs) (jt recipient with John C. Harsanyi and John F. Nash Jr) 1994, Nordrhein-Westfalen State Prize 2000. *Publications:* Preispolitik der Mehrproduktenunternehmung in der stat. Theorie 1970, General Equilibrium with Price Making Firms (with T. Marschak) 1974, Models of Strategic Rationality 1988, A General Theory of Equilibrium Selection in Games (with J. Harsanyi) 1988. *Address:* Laboratorium für Experimentelle Wirtschaftsforschung, Universität Bonn, Adenauerallee 24-42, 53113 Bonn, Germany (office). *Telephone:* (228) 739192 (office). *Fax:* (228) 739193 (office). *E-mail:* rselten@uni-bonn.de (office). *Website:* www.bonneconlab.uni-bonn.de/econlab (office).

SEMAGO, Vladimir Vladimirovich; Russian politician; *Leading Expert, Accounts Chamber of the Russian Federation;* b. 10 Jan. 1947; m. Olga Valentinovna Myasnikova; one s. one d.; ed Moscow Inst. of Construction Eng, All-Union Acad. of Foreign Trade; with Mosoblstroi 1973–77; joined Goskominturist 1977; Deputy CEO Solnechny 1979–81; accountant, tourist co., commerce Dept, State Cttee of Tourism 1981–83; Deputy Chair., Domodedovo Dist Consumers' Union 1983–86; Chief Engineer, State Cttee of Science and Tech. of USSR Council of Ministers 1986–87; Founder Jt Venture Moscow Commercial Club 1990; co-f. Ecology and Energy Resources 1992; mem. CP of Russian Fed. 1993–2004; apptd Chair. Rosebusinesbank 1995; Founder and leader New Left (political movt) 1999; mem. State Duma Cttee on Int. Affairs 1999; mem. Presidium, Co-ordination Council Round Table of Russian Business; elected mem. United Russia (UR) (Yedinaya Rossiya) 2006; Leading expert Accounts Chamber of the Russian Fed. 2007–. *Films include:* as actor: Vstretimsya na Taiti 1991, The Rifleman of the Voroshilov Regiment 1999, V avguste 44-go 2001, Tycoon 2002; as producer: V avguste 44-go 2001. *Leisure interests:* travelling, collecting modern paintings. *Address:* Accounts Chamber of the Russian Federation, 119991 Moscow, Zubovskaya street 2, Russia (office). *Telephone:* (495) 986-05-09 (office). *Fax:* (495) 986-09-52 (office). *E-mail:* info@ach.gov.ru (office). *Website:* www.ach.gov.ru (office).

SEMAKULA KIWANUKA, Matia Mulumba, PhD; Ugandan government official and diplomatist; m.; several c.; ed Makerere Univ. and Univ. of London,

UK; fmr univ. lecturer, researcher and admin.; Sr Presidential Adviser 1979–81; worked with UNEP 1985–87; Counterpart Chief Tech. Adviser and Dir of Planning and Project Co-ordination for a UNDP project on capacity-building and institutional strengthening 1988–90; Dean, Makerere Univ. School of Post grad. Studies and Research 1991–94; Exec. Dir Man. Training and Advisory Centre, Uganda 1994–96; Amb. and Perm. Rep. to UN, New York 1996–2003, Chair. Gen. Ass.'s Fourth Cttee (Special Political and Decolonization) 2000; Minister of State in Charge of Luwero 2003–05, of Investment 2005; fmr Minister of Culture, Royal Kingdom of Buganda; mem. Royal Council. *Address:* c/o Office of the Minister of Investment, Ministry of Finance, Appollo Kaggwa Road, Plot 2/4, POB 8147, Kampala, Uganda (office).

SEMASHKA, Uladzimir I.; Belarusian politician; *First Deputy Prime Minister;* b. 20 Nov. 1949, Kalinkovichi, Gomel Oblast; m.; two d.; ed Belarusian Polytechnic Inst.; mil. service 1972–74; Design Engineer, then Head of Design Bureau No. 44, then Chief Engineer of Special Mechanical Eng Design Bureau, then Chief Engineer of Mechanical Eng Dept, Dzerzhinsky Plant, Research and Production Asscn Integral 1974–96; Gen. Man. Minsk Production Asscn Horizont, Dir, Minsk Plant Horizont 1996–2001; Minister of Energy 2001–03; Acting Deputy Prime Minister July–Dec. 2003; First Deputy Prime Minister Dec. 2003–; Chair. Supervisory Bd Beltransgaz 2007–10; Order of Honour 2008. *Address:* Office of the Council of Ministers, 220010 Minsk, vul. Savetskaya 11, Belarus (office). *Telephone:* (17) 222-41-73 (office). *Fax:* (17) 222-66-65 (office). *E-mail:* contact@ government.by (office). *Website:* government.by (office).

SEMEL, Terry, BS; American media executive; b. 24 Feb. 1943, New York; s. of Ben Semel and Mildred Semel (née Wenig); m. 1st Maryann Semel (divorced); m. 2nd Jane Bovingdon 1977; one s. two d.; ed Long Island Univ., City Coll. of New York; Domestic Sales Man. CBS Cinema Center Films, Studio City, Calif. 1970–72; Vice-Pres., Gen. Man. Walt Disney's Buena Vista, Burbank, Calif. 1972–75; Pres. W.B. Distribution Corpn, Burbank 1975–78; Exec. Vice-Pres., COO Warner Bros. Inc., Burbank 1979–80, Pres., COO 1980–96, Chair., CEO 1994–99; Chair., Co-CEO Warner Music Group Inc. 1995–99; Chair., CEO and Dir Yahoo! Inc. 2001–07, Chair. (non-exec.) 2007–08; Vice-Chair. San Diego Host Cttee for Republican Nat. Convention 1996; mem. Bd of Dirs Polo Ralph Lauren Corpn, Paley Center for Media, Guggenheim Museum, Emerson Coll., Los Angeles County Museum of Art; Vanguard Award from Producers Guild of America 2005, UCLA Medal 2005, Legend in Leadership Award, Yale School of Man. 2005. *Address:* c/o Board of Directors, Polo Ralph Lauren Corporation, 650 Madison Avenue, New York, NY 10022, USA.

SEMENOV, Victor Aleksandrovich; Russian politician and business executive; *Chairman of the Supervisory Board, Belaya Dacha Group;* b. 14 Jan. 1958, Novokuryanovo, Moscow Region; m.; one s. one d.; ed Moscow K. Timiryazev Acad. of Agric.; on state farm, later Agric. Co. Belaya Dacha 1980–85; instructor Agric. Dept, Lyubertsy Town CP Cttee 1987–88; f. Belaya Dacha Group, Pres. and Dir-Gen. Belaya Dacha 1989–98, currently Chair. Supervisory Bd; Minister of Agric. and Food of Russian Fed. 1998–99; mem. State Duma (Otechestvo faction) 1999–; Chair. Union of Agricultural Scientific Complex Asscns of the Russian Fed. (ASSAGROS); Pres. Russian Interregional Asscn for Assistance of Field Experiments (AAFEI); Chair. Agricultural Cttee, Chamber of Commerce; founder-mem. Agricultural Asscn; mem. Russian Acad. of Agricultural Sciences. *Leisure interests:* travelling, fishing, horse-riding. *Address:* Belaya Dacha Group, 2, Yanichkin Proezd, Kotelniki, Lubertsy District, Moscow 140053, Russia (office). *Telephone:* (495) 995-90-00 (office). *Fax:* (495) 554-10-90 (office). *E-mail:* info@ belaya-dacha.ru (office). *Website:* www.belaya-dacha.ru (office).

SEMENOV, Yuri Pavlovich; Russian fmr mechanical engineer; b. 20 April 1935, Toropets, Kalinin region; m.; two d.; ed Dnepropetrovsk State Univ.; worked in rocket and space industry as engineer, head of group, Leading Designer 1967–72, Chief Designer 1972–78, Deputy Gen. Designer, Chief Designer 1978–81; First Deputy Gen. Designer, Chief Designer of BURAN Orbiter, Manned Spacecrafts and Stations 1981–89, Gen. Designer of ENERGIA Scientific and Production Asscn (NPO ENERGIA) 1989–91, Dir Gen., Gen. Designer 1991–94; Gen. Designer and Pres. S. P. Korolev RSC ENERGIA 1994–2005 (responsible for devt and operation of Buran reusable vehicle, devt, manufacture and operation of Soyuz, Progress-type vehicles, Salyut and Mir in-orbit complexes, rocket segment of the Sea Launch rocket and space complex-RSC, satellite systems based on YAMAL spacecraft of new generation communication satellites and devt of Russian segment of Int. Space Station and its main modules, devt and construction of the AURORA/ONEGA RSC); retd 2005; mem. Int. Acad. of Astronautics 1986; Corresp. mem. USSR (now Russian) Acad. of Sciences 1987, mem. 2000–; Hero of Socialist Labour 1976, Lenin Prize 1978, USSR State Prize 1985, USSR Acad. of Sciences K. Tsyolkovsky Gold Medal 1987, Alan De Emil IAF State Prize 1991, State Prize of Russian Fed. 1999, François-Xavier Bagnoud Aeropace Prize 1999, RAS S.P. Korolev Gold Medal 2001 and others. *Publications:* more than 360 publs including S.P. Korolev Rocket and Space Corporation Energia 1946–96 1996, S.P. Korolev Rocket and Space Corporation ENERGIA at the Turn of Two Centuries 1996–2001 2001. *Leisure interests:* sports. *Address:* c/o S.P. Korolev RSC Energia, Lenina str. 4A, 141070 Korolev, Moscow Region, Russia.

SEMENYAKA, Lyudmila Ivanovna; Russian ballerina; b. 16 Jan. 1952, Leningrad (St Petersburg); m. (divorced); one s.; ed Vaganova Ballet Acad., Leningrad (now St Petersburg); danced with Kirov Ballet 1970–72; Prima Ballerina Bolshoi Theatre Co., Moscow 1972–96; has worked with English Nat. Ballet 1990–91 and Scottish Nat. Ballet; ballet teacher 1994–, with Moscow State Acad. of Choreography 1999–, coach at Bolshoi Theatre 2000–, works with Svetlana Zakharova, Elena Andrienko, Anastasia Meskova, Anastasia Goryacheva, Anna Nikulina, Eugenia Obraztsova, Viktorya Osipova, Darya Hochlova and others; trained as actress, Studio Theatre of Modern Dramaturgy 2001–03; mem. jury several int. ballet competitions; performed in Europe, USA and Argentina; winner Moscow Int. Ballet competition 1969, 1972, Varna 1972, Tokyo (First Prize and Gold Medal) 1976, Anna Pavlova Prize, Paris 1976, USSR State Prize 1977, USSR People's Artist 1986, Evening Standard Prize 1986. *Films:* Ludmila Semenyaka Danse, The Bolshoi Ballerina, Spartacus, The Stone Flower, Raymonda, The Nutcracker, Fantasy on the Theme of Casanova and others. *Plays:* An Excellent Medicine for Anguish, The Seagull. *Roles include:* all of classical repertoire, debut in Odette/Odile, Swan Lake, Moscow; all of Y. Grigorovitch

ballets: Phrygia (Spartak), Anastasia (Ivan the Terrible), Katerina (Stony Flower) etc; roles in ballets by Balanchin, Petit, Lavrovsky, Vassilyev, Boccadoro, Ben Stivenson, May Murdmaa; has partnered Mikhail Baryshnikov, Vladimir Vassilyev, Irek Mukhamedov, Farukh Ruzimatov etc; as balletmaster has staged performances of Fountain of Bakhchisarai, Astrakhan 2008, Giselle, Ekaterinburg 2009, Swan Lake, Ekaterinburg 2010. *Address:* Bolshoi Theatre, Teatralnaya ploshchad 1, Moscow, Russia. *Telephone:* (499) 151-26-75 (home). *Fax:* (499) 151-26-75 (home). *Website:* www.bolshoi.ru (office).

SEMENZA, Giorgio, MD; Swiss biochemist and academic; *Professor Emeritus of Biochemistry, Swiss Federal Institute of Technology, Zurich;* b. 23 June 1928, Milan, Italy; s. of Prof. Carlo Semenza and Clementina Gerli; m. Berit Andersson 1958 (died 2005); three c.; ed Univ. of Milan; post-doctoral studies, Univ. of Uppsala 1955–56; Asst Lecturer, Lecturer, Dept of Biochem. Univ. of Zürich 1956–64, Asst Prof. 1964–69; Prof. of Gen. Physiology, Univ. of Milan 1967–69; Prof. of Biochemistry, Swiss Fed. Inst. of Tech., Zürich 1969–95, Chair. or Co.-Chair., Dean of School of Natural Sciences 1980–82, currently Prof. Emer. of Biochemistry; Prof. of Biochemistry, Univ. of Milan 1995–2003; Visiting Prof. at numerous foreign univs; Man. Ed. FEBS (Fed. of European Biochemical Socs) Letters 1985–99; mem. editorial advisory bds of a number of scientific journals; mem. Academia Europaea 1989–2006, Istituto Lombardo di Scienze e Lettere, Milan 2000–; Foreign mem. Accad. Nazionale dei Lincei 2006–; Hon. mem. Italian Soc. of Experimental Biology 1978, Spanish Soc. of Biochemistry and Molecular Biology 1997; Hon. PhD (Univ. Autónoma de Madrid) 1985, Hon. MD (Nice Sophia Antipolis, France, Copenhagen, Denmark) 1999; Int. Prize of Modern Nutrition 1975, Iorio-Rustichelli Prize 1985, European Pharmaceutical Industry Research Award 1988, Purkine Gold Medal, Prague 1988. *Publications:* 19 books ed or co-ed; more than 250 publs in peer-reviewed journals. *Leisure interests:* literature, films, theatre. *Address:* Swiss Institute of Technology, ETH-Zentrum, PO Box 35, 8092 Zurich, Switzerland (office); Dipartimento di Chimica, Biochimica e Tecnologie per la Medicina, Università di Milano, Via Saldini 50, 20133 Milan, Italy (office). *Telephone:* (44) 391-75-06 (Zurich). *E-mail:* semenza@bc.biol.ethz.ch (office).

ŠEMETA, Algirdas Gediminas; Lithuanian economist, international organization official and fmr government official; *Commissioner for Taxation and Customs Union, Audit and Anti-Fraud, European Commission;* b. 23 April 1962; m.; three c.; ed Univ. of Vilnius; Economist (Younger Fellowship), Lithuanian Economy Inst. 1985–90; Head of Subdivision of the Economy Devt Strategy Div., Ministry of the Economy 1990–91, Adviser on Privatization 1991–92; Chair. Securities Comm., Ministry of Finance 1992–96, Chair. Securities Comm. of Lithuania 1996–97; Minister of Finance 1997–99, 2008–09; Vice-Pres. AB Nalšia June–Nov. 1999; Govt Sec. Office of the Govt 1999–2001; Dir Gen. Dept of Statistics 2001–08; Commr for Financial Programming and Budget, EC, Brussels 2009–10, Commr for Taxation and Customs Union, Audit and Anti-Fraud 2010–; mem. Knowledge Economy Forum. *Address:* European Commissioner for Taxation and Customs Union, Audit and Anti-Fraud, European Commission, 1049 Brussels, Belgium (office). *Fax:* (2) 298-84-90 (office). *E-mail:* cab-semeta-commissaire@ec.europa.eu (office). *Website:* ec.europa.eu/commission_2010-2014/semeta (office).

SEMIGIN, Gennady Yuryevich, Dr rer. pol; Russian business executive and politician; *Leader, Patriots of Russia (Patrioty Rossii);* b. 23 March 1964; m.; three c.; ed Riga Higher Mil. Political School, Moscow Juridical Inst., Acad. of Finance; army service 1985–90; f. Centre of Econs and Russian AKROS 1990; f. Russian Group of Finance and Industry 1991; mem. Council on Business, Russian Presidency 1992–; mem. Exec. Bd Russian Union of Businessmen, Pres. Russian Group of Finance and Industry 1991–; f. Nat. Public Scientific Fund 1996; Founder and Head, Inst. of Comparative Politology, Russian Acad. of Sciences; Pres. Congress of Russian Business Circles; mem. CP 1998; mem. State Duma (Agrarian faction, then CP faction) 1999–, Deputy Chair. 2000–03; Founder and Leader Patriots of Russia (Patrioty Rossii) 2002–, Head Rodina faction 2007–; mem. Comm. on Regulation of Labour and Social Relations, Russian Acad. of Social Sciences, Acad. of Political Sciences; corresp. mem. Acad. of Natural Sciences. *Publications:* Social Partnership in the Contemporary World, Political Stability of Society, ed. New Philosophical Encyclopedia (4 Vols). *Leisure interests:* swimming, tennis, running, classical music, boxing, history, philosophy, art, economics. *Address:* Patriots of Russia (Patrioty Rossii), 119121 Moscow, Smolensky Blvd 11/2 (office); State Duma, Okhotny Ryad 1, 103205 Moscow, Russia (office). *Telephone:* (495) 692-15-50 (Patrioty Rossii) (office); (495) 292-76-75 (office). *Fax:* (495) 692-15-50 (Patrioty Rossii) (office). *E-mail:* partia-korn@rambler.ru (office). *Website:* www .patriot-rus.ru (office); www.duma.ru (office).

SEMIKHATOV, Mikhail Alexandrovich; Russian geologist; *Editor-in-Chief, Stratigrafiya. Geologicheskaya korrelyatsiya;* b. 21 Feb. 1932; m.; one s.; ed Moscow State Univ.; jr, sr researcher, head of lab. Inst. of Geology, USSR (now Russian) Acad. of Sciences 1954, Corresp. mem. 1990, mem. 1994–; currently Ed.-in-Chief Stratigrafiya. Geologicheskaya korrelyatsiya (journal); N. Shatsky Prize. *Publications include:* General Problems of the Proterozoic Stratigraphy in the USSR. *Leisure interest:* expeditions to Siberia. *Address:* Institute of Geology, Russian Academy of Sciences, Pyzhevsky per. 7, 109017 Moscow, Russia (office). *Telephone:* (495) 230-81-32 (office). *E-mail:* semikhatov@ginran.ru (office); semikhatov@geo.tv-sign.ru. *Website:* www.ras.ru (office).

SEMIZOROVA, Nina Lvovna; Russian ballerina; b. 15 Oct. 1956, Krivoi Rog, Ukraine; d. of Lev Alexandrovich Semizorov and Larisa Dmitrievna Semizorova; m. 1st Maris Liepa 1980; m. 2nd Mark Peretokin 1988; one d.; ed Kiev Choreographic School; danced with Shevchenko Theatre of Opera and Ballet, Kiev 1975–78, with Bolshoi Ballet, Moscow 1978–; many appearances abroad; First Prize, Int. Ballet Competition, Moscow 1977, Artist of Merit of Ukrainian SSR 1977, Honoured Artist of Russia 1987, Laureate of Moscow Komsomol 1987. *Roles include:* Odette/Odile (Swan Lake), Giselle, Aurora (Sleeping Beauty), Kitri (Don Quixote), Raymonda, Mistress of the Copper Mountain (The Stone Flower), Lady Macbeth (Macbeth), Aegina and Phrygia (Spartacus), Luska (The Golden Age). *Leisure interest:* reading. *Address:* 2 Zhukovskaya Street, Apt. 8, Moscow, Russia (home). *Telephone:* (495) 923-40-84 (home). *Fax:* (495) 923-40-84 (home).

SEMJÉN, Zsolt, DTheol; Hungarian theologian, sociologist and politician; *Deputy Prime Minister and Minister without Portfolio;* b. 8 Aug. 1962, Budapest;

s. of Dr Miklós Semjén and Erzsébet Niklász; m.; two s. one d.; ed High School Szilágyi Erzsébet, Budapest, Pázmány Péter Catholic Theological Acad., Sociology Faculty, Eötvös Loránd Univ.; worked for Termeltető Craft Co., Budapest 1981–84; Co-founder Christian Democratic People's Party (KDNP) 1989, Pres. 1990, mem. Exec. Cttee 1990–91, Chair. Disciplinary and Ethics Cttee 1993–94, Vice-Pres. KDNP 1997, left party to join Hungarian Democratic Forum (MDF) 1997, rejoined 2002, Pres. KDNP 2003–, Leader Parl. Group 2006, 2010; Dist Municipal Councillor, Budapest II 1990–94; mem. Parl. 1994–98, 2002–; State Sec. for Church Affairs and Vice-Chair. Cttee on Human Rights, Ministry of Nat. Cultural Heritage 1998–2002; Deputy Prime Minister and Minister without Portfolio 2010–; mem. Pontifical Acad. of Tiberina 1999; Hon. Assoc. Prof. 1996; Winner, Pro Caritate and Pro Ecclesia Hungariae. *Address:* c/o Office of the Prime Minister, 1055 Budapest, Kossuth Lajos tér 4 (office); c/o Office of the Prime Minister, 1357 Budapest, Budapest, Pf. 6, Hungary (office); Christian Democratic People's Party (Kereszténydemokrata Néppárt), 1078 Budapest, István u. 44, Hungary. *Telephone:* (1) 795-6978 (office); (1) 489-0878. *Fax:* (1) 795-0381 (office). *E-mail:* titkarsag@me.gov.hu (office); elnok@kdnp.hu. *Website:* www.kormany.hu (office); www.kdnp.hu; semjenzsolt.hu.

SEMKOW, Jerzy, MMus; Polish/ French conductor; b. 12 Oct. 1928, Radomsko; s. of Aleksander Semkow and Waleria Sienczak Semkow; ed Jagiellonian Univ., Kraków, State Higher School of Music (student of A. Malawski), Kraków and Leningrad Music Conservatoire; Asst Conductor, Leningrad Philharmonic Orch. 1954–56; Conductor, Bolshoi Opera and Ballet Theatre, Moscow 1956–58; Artistic Dir and Prin. Conductor, Warsaw Nat. Opera 1960–62; Perm. Conductor, Danish Royal Opera, Copenhagen 1965–68; Prin. Conductor Italian Radio and TV (RAI) Orchestra, Rome 1969–73; Musical Dir and Prin. Conductor Saint Louis Symphony Orchestra 1975–; Artistic Dir and Prin. Conductor, Rochester Philharmonic Orchestra, New York 1986–; Guest Conductor Berlin Philharmonic, London Philharmonic, Nat. Orchestra of Madrid, Orchestre de la Suisse Romande, Cleveland Symphony Orchestra, Orchestre Nat. de France and the orchestras of Paris, Strasbourg, Lyon, Bordeaux, Monte Carlo, Jerusalem, Stockholm, Frankfurt, St Petersburg, Toronto, New York, Cleveland, Chicago, Boston, Detroit, Washington, Cincinatti, Houston, Dallas, Pittsburgh, Rochester, Utah and Minneapolis; engagements at Covent Garden, La Scala, Milan, Staatsoper, Berlin, Staatsoper, Vienna, Teatro Real, Madrid, Paris Opera, Teatro del Opera, Rome, Maggio Musicale, Florence, La Fenice, Venice, Grand Theatre, Geneva, etc.; master classes at Yale Univ., Manhattan School of Music, New York; Dr hc (Acad. Chopin, Warsaw) 2005; Commdr Cross Order of Polonia Restituta, Gold Cross Gloria Artis, Commdr Ordre des Arts et des Lettres. *Recordings include:* Boris Godunov (Musorgski) with Polish Nat. Radio Symphony Orchestra, Kniaź (Borodin) with Group from Opera of Sofia, Symphony No. 3 and Symphonic Concerto No. 4 (Szymanowski), Symphony Nos 2 and 3 (Scriabin) with Nat. Philharmonic Symphony Orchestra, Warsaw, Beethoven and Schumann works with Saint Louis Orchestra, Brahms' works with Warsaw Philarmonic Orchestra, Mozart Symphonies (Disque d'Or). *Leisure interests:* reading, yachting. *Address:* Opus 3 Artists, 470 Park Avenue South, 9th Floor, New York, NY 10016, USA (office). *Telephone:* (212) 584-7569 (office). *Fax:* (616) 300-8200 (office). *E-mail:* icma_publicity@icmtalent.com (office). *Website:* www.opus3artists.com (office).

SEMPÉ, Jean-Jacques; French cartoonist; b. 17 Aug. 1932, Bordeaux; s. of Ulysse Sempé and Juliette Marson; one s. one d.; ed Ecole Communale à Bordeaux; started career as toothpaste salesman, then apprentice in wine trade; published first drawings 1950; work has appeared in various publications including: L'Express magazine, Paris-Match, Punch (now defunct), New Yorker, New York Times; has produced an album annually for 30 years for Editions Denoël; Officier des Arts et des Lettres. *Publications include:* Le Petit Nicolas series from 1960, Rien n'est simple 1962, Tout se complique 1963, Sauve qui peut 1964, Monsieur Lambert 1965, La grande panique 1966, St Tropez 1968, Information-Consommation 1968, Des Hauts et des Bas 1970, Face à Face 1972, Bonjour Bonsoir 1974, L'Ascension Sociale de Mr Lambert 1975, Simple question d'equilibre 1977, Un léger décalage 1977, Les Musiciens 1979, Comme par hasard 1981, De bon matin 1983, Vaguement compétitif 1985, Luxe, calme et volupté 1987, Par Avion 1989, L'Histoire de Monsieur Sommer (with Patrick Süsskind) 1991, Ames Soeurs 1991, Insondables Mystères 1993, Raoul Taburin 1995, Les Musiciens 1996, Grands rêves 1997, Beau Temps 1999, Multiples intentions 2003, Sentiments distingués 2007. *Address:* Galerie Bartsch & Chariau GmbH, Galeriestrasse 6, 80539 Munich, Germany. *Telephone:* (89) 29555. *Fax:* (89) 2904789. *E-mail:* galerie@bartsch-chariau.de. *Website:* www.bartsch-chariau.de.

SEMPLE, Sir John Laughlin, KCB, BSc (Econ), MA (Cantab.); British fmr civil servant; b. 10 Aug. 1940, Belfast, NI; s. of J. E. Semple and Violet E. G. Semple; m. Maureen Anne Kerr 1970; two s. one d.; ed Campbell Coll., Belfast and Corpus Christi Coll., Cambridge; joined Home Civil Service, Ministry of Aviation 1961, transferred to NI Civil Service 1962, succession of posts relating to industrial training, financial planning, community relations, physical planning, Belfast Devt and housing policy, Perm. Sec., NI Dept of Finance and Personnel 1988–97, Head, NI Civil Service 1997–2000, (also Second Perm. Sec., NI Office 1998–99), Sec. to NI Exec. Cttee 1999–2000; mem. Consumer Council for Postal Services 2000, Regional Chair. for NI 2000–01; Dir of NI Affairs, Royal Mail Group plc 2001–06; Chair. Bd of Trustees, Northern Ireland Police Fund 2001–05; Head, Independent Affordability Review, Dept for Social Devt 2006–07. *Leisure interests:* golf, tennis, skiing, history. *Address:* 24 Ailsa Road, Cultra, Holywood, Co. Down, BT18 0AS, Northern Ireland. *Telephone:* (28) 9042-1078. *E-mail:* johnsemple1@btinternet.com.

SEN, Amartya Kumar, BA, PhD, FBA; Indian economist and academic; *Thomas W. Lamont University Professor Emeritus and Professor of Economics and Philosophy, Harvard University;* b. 3 Nov. 1933, Santiniketan, Bengal; s. of the late Ashutosh Sen and of Amita Sen; m. 1st Nabaneeta Dev 1958 (divorced 1975); two d.; m. 2nd Eva Colorni 1978 (died 1985); one s. one d.; m. 3rd Emma Rothschild 1991; ed Presidency Coll., Calcutta and Trinity Coll., Cambridge; Prof. of Econs, Jadavpur Univ., Calcutta 1956–58; Fellow, Trinity Coll., Cambridge 1957–63; Prof. of Econs, Univ. of Delhi 1963–71, Chair. Dept of Econs 1966–68; Hon. Dir Agricultural Econs Research Centre, Delhi 1966–68, 1969–71; Prof. of Econs, LSE 1971–77, Univ. of Oxford 1977–80, Drummond Prof. of Political Economy 1980–88; Thomas W. Lamont Univ. Prof., Harvard Univ. 1987–98, 2004–, Prof. Emer.

1998–2004, Prof. of Econs and Philosophy 2004–; Master Trinity Coll., Cambridge 1998–2003; Visiting Prof., Univ. of Calif., Berkeley 1964–65, Harvard Univ. 1968–69; Andrew D. White Prof.-at-Large, Cornell Univ. 1978–84; Pres. Int. Econ. Asscn 1986–89; Fellow, Econometric Soc., Pres. 1984; Hon. Prof., Delhi Univ.; Foreign Hon. mem. American Acad. of Arts and Sciences; Hon. Fellow, Inst. of Social Studies, The Hague, Hon. Fellow LSE, Inst. of Devt Studies; Hon. CH 2000, Grand Cross, Order of Scientific Merit (Brazil) 2000, Commdr, Légion d'honneur 2013; Hon. DLitt (Univ. of Saskatchewan, Canada) 1979, (Visva-Bharati Univ., India) 1983, (Oxford) 1996; Hon. DUniv (Essex) 1984, (Caen) 1987; Hon. DSc (Bath) 1984, (Bologna) 1988; Dr hc (Univ. Catholique de Louvain) 1989, (Padua) 1998, numerous others; Senator Giovanni Agnelli Inst. Prize for Ethics 1989, Nobel Memorial Prize in Econ. Sciences 1998, UN Econ. and Social Comm. for Asia and the Pacific (UNESCAP) Lifetime Achievement Award 2007. *Publications include:* Choice of Techniques: An Aspect of Planned Economic Development 1960, Growth Economics 1970, Collective Choice and Social Welfare 1970, On Economic Inequality 1973, Employment, Technology and Development 1975, Poverty and Famines 1981, Utilitarianism and Beyond (jtly with Bernard Williams) 1982, Choice, Welfare and Measurement 1982, Resources, Values and Development 1984, Commodities and Capabilities 1985, On Ethics and Economics 1987, The Standard of Living 1988, Hunger and Public Action (with Jean Drèze) 1989, Social Security in Developing Countries (jtly) 1991, Inequality Re-examined 1992, The Quality of Life (jtly) 1993, Development as Freedom 1999, The Argumentative Indian: Writings on Indian History, Culture and Identity 2005, Identity and Violence: The Illusion of Destiny 2006, The Idea of Justice 2009; articles in various journals in econs, philosophy and political science. *Address:* Department of Economics, 1805 Cambridge Street, Littauer 205, Harvard University, Cambridge, MA 02138, USA (office). *Telephone:* (617) 495-1871 (office). *Fax:* (617) 496-5942 (office). *E-mail:* asen@fas.harvard.edu (office). *Website:* www.economics.harvard.edu/faculty/sen (office).

SEN, Laura J.; American retail executive; *President and CEO, BJ's Wholesale Club, Inc.;* ed Boston Coll.; several positions in mass retailing, including service with Zayre Corpn and Jordan Marsh Co.; Vice-Pres. of Logistics, BJ's Wholesale Club, Inc. 1989–93, Sr Vice-Pres. of Gen. Merchandise 1993–97, Exec. Vice-Pres. of Merchandising and Logistics 1997–2003, 2007–08, COO BJ's Wholesale Club, Inc. 2008–09, mem. Bd of Dirs and Pres. 2008–, CEO 2009–; Prin. of Sen Retail Consulting 2003–06; mem. Bd Saint Coletta and Cardinal Cushing Schools of Massachusetts, Inc.; mem. Bd of Dirs Abington Bancorp Inc. (and its subsidiary Abington Savings Bank) 2001–; provides support to non-profit orgs, including the Women's Inn at Pine Street, the Neely House and the Cardinal Cushing Centers Springtime Event; ranked by Forbes magazine amongst The World's 100 Most Powerful Women (82nd) 2010, ranked by Fortune magazine amongst the 50 Most Powerful Women in Business in the US (44th) 2011, (42nd) 2012. *Address:* BJ's Wholesale Club, Inc., One Mercer Road, Natick, MA 01760, USA (office). *Telephone:* (508) 651-7400 (office). *Fax:* (508) 651-6114 (office). *E-mail:* info@bjs.com (office). *Website:* www.bjs.com (office).

SEN, Mrinal; Indian film director; b. 14 May 1923, Faridpur (now Bangladesh); s. of the late Dinesh Chandra Sen and Saraju Sen; m. Gita Shome 1953; one s.; ed Scottish Church Coll., Univ. of Calcutta; started making films 1956, directed 27 feature films; mem. jury numerous int. film festivals; Chair. Gov. Council Film & TV Inst. of India 1983–85; Chair. Indian People's Human Rights Comm. 1987–90; Vice-Chair. Fed. of Film Socs of India 1980–92, Cinéma et Liberté (Paris) 1992; fmr Pres. Int. Fed. of Film Socs; Hon. mem. Rajya Sabha (Parl.) 1998–2003; Commdr, Ordre des Arts et Lettres 1985, Order of Friendship (Russia) 2001; Hon. DLitt (Burdwan Univ.) 1981; Padma Bhushan 1981, Dadasaheb Phalke Award 2005, Lifetime Achievement Awards, Osian's-Cinefan Festival, Int. Film Festival, India, Int. Film Festival of Kerala, Taj Enlighten Tareef Award 2008. *Films include:* The Dawn 1956, Wedding Day 1960, Up in the Clouds 1965, Two Brothers 1966, Bhuvan Shome (Nat. Film Award 1969) 1968, Calcutta Trilogy—The Interview, Calcutta 71 and Guerrilla Fighter (Calcutta Trilogy 1971–73), Chorus (Silver Prize, Moscow Int. Film Festival 1975), Royal Hunt 1976, The Outsiders (Special Jury Prize, Karlovy Vary Int. Film Festival) 1977, Man With an Axe (Silver Prize, Moscow Int. Film Festival 1979, Interfilm Award, Berlin Int. Film Festival 1979) 1978, And Quiet Rolls the Dawn (Nat. Film Award 1980) 1979, In Search of Famine (Nat. Film Award, Interfilm Award, Grand Jury Prize, Berlin Int. Film Festival 1979) 1980, The Kaleidoscope 1982, The Case is Closed (Nat. Film Award, Jury Prize, Cannes Film Festival 1983, Golden Spike Award, Valladolid Int. Film Festival) 1983, The Ruins (Special Jury Prize, Montreal World Film Festival) 1984, Genesis 1986, Suddenly One Day 1989, World Within, World Without 1992, Antareen 1993, This, My Land (Silver Pyramid for Best Dir, Cairo Int. Film Festival) 2002. *Publications include:* Cheat 1943, Charlie Chaplin 1961, Views on Cinema 1977, Cinema Adhunikata 1995, Montage 2002, Always Being Born 2004. *Leisure interests:* reading, travelling, loafing about. *Address:* C-501, Talkatora Road, New Delhi 110 001 (office); 4E, Motilal Nehru Road, Kolkata 700029, India (home). *Telephone:* (11) 3351866 (office); (22) 4754799 (home). *Website:* www.mrinalsen.org.

SENANI, Mawlawi Abdol Ghafur; Afghan ecclesiastic; fmr Chair. High Council of Ulema and Clergy of Afghanistan. *Address:* c/o High Council of Ulema and Clergy of Afghanistan, Kabul, Afghanistan.

SENARD, Jean-Dominique, MA; French business executive; *Managing General Partner and CEO, Michelin;* b. 7 March 1953; m.; three c.; ed HEC (Hautes Études Commerciales) business school, Paris; early career serving in various financial and operational positions with Total 1979–87, then with Saint Gobain 1987–96; mem. Group Exec. Council and Chief Financial Officer Pechiney 1996–2001, also head of Pechiney's Primary Metal section –2004, mem. Exec. Cttee Alcan, in charge of integrating Pechiney and served as Chair. Pechiney SA; joined Michelin as Chief Financial Officer and mem. Michelin Group Exec. Council 2005, Man. Partner, Michelin Group 2007–11, Man. Gen. Partner alongside Michel Rollier 2011–12, Man. Gen. and CEO 2012–. *Address:* Compagnie Générale des Etablissements Michelin, 12 cours Sablon, 63000 Clermont-Ferrand, France (office). *Telephone:* (4) 73-98-59-00 (office). *Fax:* (4) 73-98-59-04 (office). *E-mail:* info@michelin.com (office). *Website:* www.michelin.com (office).

SENDANYOYE RUGWABIZA, Valentine, BSc, MSc; Rwandan diplomatist, business executive and international organization executive; *Deputy Director-*

General, World Trade Organization; ed Nat. Univ. of Zaïre (now Democratic Repub. of the Congo); sr man. with major Swiss multinational co., first as head of its commercial devt and marketing operations for Cen. Africa, based in Yaoundé, Cameroon, and then as its regional man. for Cen. and West Africa, based in Abidjan, Côte d'Ivoire 1989–97; managed her own co. 1997–2000; joined govt 2000, served simultaneously as Perm. Rep. to UN in Geneva, Head of Del. to WTO and Amb. to Switzerland 2002–05; Deputy Head of Del. for Rwanda's first Trade Policy Review 2004; adviser, Council of Econ. and Social Affairs, Office of Pres. of Rwanda, Kigali –2005; Deputy Dir-Gen. WTO 2005–, Coordinator of African Group in WTO; Founding mem. Rwandese Pvt. Sector Fed., Rwanda Women Entrepreneurs' Org., Rwandese Women Leaders' Caucus; one of two Ambs representing Least Developed Countries in Integrated Framework Working Group. *Address:* World Trade Organization, Centre William Rappard, rue de Lausanne 154, 1211 Geneva 21, Switzerland (office). *Telephone:* (22) 739-51-11 (office). *Fax:* (22) 731-42-06 (office). *E-mail:* enquiries@wto.org (office). *Website:* www.wto.org (office).

SENDERENS, Alain; French restaurateur; *Manager, Senderens Restaurant;* b. 2 Dec. 1939, Hyères; s. of René Senderens and Lucette Senderens (née Azan); m. Eventhia Senderens (née Pappadinas) 1974; one s.; ed Lycée de Vic-en Bigorre; apprentice chef, Hôtel des Ambassadeurs, Lourdes 1957–59, La Tour d'Argent, Paris 1963; Sauce Cook Lucas Carton Restaurant 1964–65, Man. 1985–2005; Chief Sauce Cook and Fish Cook, Berkeley, Paris 1965–66, Chief Sauce Cook, Orly Hilton Hotel, Paris 1966–68; Proprietor and Chef, l'Archestrate, Paris 1968–85; Man. Senderens Restaurant 2005–; Chair. Bd of Dirs, Auberge Franc Comtoise, Lucas Carton; Pres. Chambre Syndicale de la Haute Cuisine Française 1990–92, Conseil Nat. des Arts Culinaires 1990–98; Chevalier, Légion d'honneur 1993, Officier des Arts et des Lettres 1985, Ordre nat. du Mérite 1978; Chevalier du Mérite Agricole 1978, Ordre nat. du Mérite en titre de l'Industrie 1986, Ordre des Palmes Académiques 1993; Officier dans l'Ordre Nat. de la Légion d'honneur 2004; Médaille Vermeil de la Ville de Paris 1988. *Publications:* La Cuisine Réussie 1981, La Grande Cuisine à Petits Prix 1984, Figues sans barbarie 1991, Proust, la Cuisine retrouvée (jtly) 1991, Manger, c'est la santé (jtly) 1992, L'Atelier d'Alain Senderens 1997, Les Festins de Balthazar (jtly) 1997, Le vin et la table d'Alain Senderens 1999. *Leisure interests:* classical music, contemporary art, reading. *Address:* Restaurant Senderens, 9 place de la Madeleine, 75008 Paris (office); 11 place de la Madeleine, 75008 Paris, France (home). *Telephone:* 1-42-65-22-90 (office). *Fax:* 1-42-65-06-23 (office). *E-mail:* restaurant@senderens.fr (office). *Website:* www.senderens.fr (office).

SENDOV, Blagovest Hristov, PhD, DSc; Bulgarian mathematician, academic, politician and diplomatist; *Researcher, Bulgarian Academy of Sciences;* b. 8 Feb. 1932, Assenovgrad; s. of Christo Sendov and Marushka Sendov; m. 1st Lilia Georgieva 1958 (divorced 1982); two d.; m. 2nd Anna Marinova 1982; one s.; ed gymnasium in Assenovgrad, Sofia Univ., Moscow State Univ. and Imperial Coll., London, UK; cleaner in Sofia 1949–52; teacher in Boboshevo and Elin Pelin 1956–58; Asst, Dept of Algebra, Univ. of Sofia 1958–60, Asst in Numerical Analysis and Computer Science 1960-63, Asst Prof. of Computer Sciences 1963–67, Prof. of Computer Science 1967, Dean, Faculty of Math. 1970–73, Rector 1973–79; mem. Parl. 1976–90, 1994–, Pres. of Parl. 1995–97, Vice-Pres. 1997–2003; Amb. to Japan 2003–09; Vice-Pres. Bulgarian Acad. of Sciences 1980–82, Vice-Pres. and Scientific Sec.-Gen. 1982–88, Dir Centre for Informatics and Computer Tech. 1985–90, Pres. 1988–91; Pres. Comm. of Science 1986–88; Vice-Pres. Int. Fed. for Information Processing 1985–88, Pres. 1989–91; Vice-Pres. World Peace Council 1983–86, IIP—UNESCO 1986–90; Extraordinary Vice-Pres. ICSU 1990–93; mem. Exec. Cttee and Bd of Dirs Int. Foundation for Survival and Devt of Humanity 1988–2003; Hon. Pres. Int. Asscn of Univs 1985–; two Orders of People's Repub. of Bulgaria and many others; Dr hc 1969, 1977, 2005, 2010, 2012; Dimitrov Prize for Science, Honoured Scientist 1984. *Publications:* Numerical Analysis, Old and New 1973, Hausdorff Approximation 1979, Averaged Moduli of Smoothness (monograph); textbooks and more than 200 articles in learned journals. *Leisure interests:* tennis, gardening, travelling. *Address:* 5 Plachkoviza Str., 1126 Sofia, Bulgaria (home). *Telephone:* (2) 862-6083 (home). *Fax:* (2) 870-8494 (office). *E-mail:* sendov2003@yahoo.com (home); acad@sendov.com (office). *Website:* www.sendov .com.

SENEQUIER, Dominique, DEA; French investment manager and business executive; *Chairman and CEO, AXA Private Equity;* b. 1953, Toulon; m.; one s. one d.; ed Ecole Polytechnique, Univ. of Paris (Sorbonne); worked for French Insurance Comm. 1975–80; Group Acquisitions Man., Groupe GAN (insurance co.) 1980–87, Founder and Dir GAN Participations 1987–95; joined AXA Investment Managers 1996, Founder of subsidiary AXA Private Equity, Chair. and CEO 1997–; mem. Bd of Dirs Hewlett-Packard 2011–12, Cytheris, Alitheia Capital; non-voting mem. Bd Bourbon 2009–; mem. Institut des Actuaries Français, Int. Actuarial Asscn; acquired Chateau Kirwan and Chateau Clinet wineries in Bordeaux; Chevalier, Légion d'honneur 2012; ranked by Forbes magazine amongst The World's 100 Most Powerful Women (53rd) 2008, (50th) 2009, (100th) 2010, (98th) 2011, ranked by Fortune magazine amongst the 50 Most Powerful Women in Business outside the US (32nd) 2008, (18th) 2009, (19th) 2010, (16th) 2011, (25th) 2012, named by European Dow Jones (Awards for Excellence in Private Equity) "the most influential woman of capital investment" 2010, named one of Financial News' 100 most influential women. *Leisure interests:* playing the piano, opera. *Address:* AXA Private Equity, 20 place Vendôme, 75001 Paris, France (office). *Telephone:* 1-44-45-92-52 (office). *Fax:* 1-44-45-93-31 (office). *E-mail:* mylan.gaillard@axa-im .com (office). *Website:* www.axaprivateequity.com (office).

ŞENER, Abdüllatif, DEcon; Turkish politician; ed Ankara Univ.; served in several academic posts; entered Parl. 1991 as RP Deputy; Minister of Finance 1996–97; founding mem., Justice and Progress Party (AKP), becoming Deputy Chair.; Deputy Prime Minister and Minister of State 2002–07; Pres., Exec. Cttee, e-Transformation Turkey. *Address:* c/o Office of the Deputy Prime Minister, Başbakan yard. ve Devlet Bakanı, Bakanlıklar, Ankara, Turkey (office). *E-mail:* abdullatif.sener@basbakanlik.gov.tr (office).

SENEVIRATNE, Hon. Athauda; Sri Lankan teacher and politician; *Senior Minister of Rural Affairs;* b. 19 Sept. 1931, Kegalle; m.; mem. Parl. (United Peoples Freedom Alliance) for Kegalle; Minister of Labour Relations and Foreign Employment –2010, of Justice and Law Reforms 2010, Senior Minister of Rural

Affairs 2010–. *Address:* C 78, Gregories Avenue, Colombo 07, Sri Lanka (home). *Telephone:* (112) 301592 (office).

SENEVIRATNE, (Welathanthirige Don) John; Sri Lankan lawyer and politician; *Minister of Public Administration and Home Affairs;* b. 15 Jan. 1941, Kahawatta, Ratnapura; s. of the late Welathanthirige Podi Appuhami and Soma Wijesundara; ed Sri Lanka Law Coll., Palmadulla Gangkanda Vidyalaya, Horana Thakshilawa, Aquinas Coll.; entered politics 1977; MP (United People's Freedom Alliance) for Ratnapura 1989–, Chair. Parl. Cttee on Public Expenditure (COPE) 2008; Deputy Minister of Educ. 1995–97, Minister of Labour 1997–2000, of Health 2000–04, of Justice and Judicial Reforms 2004–05, of Power and Energy 2005–10, of Public Admin and Home Affairs 2010–. *Address:* Ministry of Public Administration and Home Affairs, Independence Square, Colombo 7, Sri Lanka (office). *Telephone:* (11) 2662340 (office). *Fax:* (11) 2693304 (office). *E-mail:* minister@ pubad.gov.lk (office). *Website:* www.pubad.gov.lk (office); johnseneviratne.net.

SENGHAAS, Dieter, DPhil; German professor of social science; *Professor of Peace, Conflict and Development Research, University of Bremen;* b. 27 Aug. 1940, Geislingen; m. Eva Knobloch 1968; one d.; ed Univs of Tübingen, Michigan and Frankfurt and Amherst Coll.; Research Fellow, Center for Int. Affairs, Harvard Univ. 1968–70; Research Dir, Peace Research Inst., Frankfurt 1971–78; Prof. of Int. Relations, Univ. of Frankfurt 1972–78; Prof. of Peace, Conflict and Devt Research, Univ. of Bremen 1978–; mem. several nat. and int. scientific orgs; Dr hc (Tübingen) 2000; Lentz Int. Peace Research Award 1987, Göttingen Peace Award 1999, Villa Ichon Culture and Peace Prize 2006, Leopold Kohr Prize 2010. *Publications include:* Aggressivität und kollektive Gewalt 1972, Aufrüstung durch Rüstungskontrolle 1972, Gewalt-Konflikt-Frieden 1974, Abschreckung und Frieden (3rd edn) 1981, Rüstung und Militarismus (2nd edn) 1982, Von Europa lernen 1982, The European Experience 1985, Die Zukunft Europas 1986, Europas Entwicklung und die Dritte Welt 1986, Weltwirtschaftsordnung und Entwicklungspolitik (5th edn) 1987, Konfliktformationen im internationalen System 1988, Europa 2000: Ein Friedensplan 1990, Friedensprojekt Europa 1992, Wohin driftet die Welt 1994, Zivilisierung wider Willen 1998, Klaenge des Friedens 2001, The Clash Within Civilizations 2001, Zum irdischen Frieden 2004, On Perpetual Peace 2007, Weltordnung in einer zerklüfteten Welt 2012, Dieter Senghaas Pioneer of Peace and Development Research 2013; ed. or co-ed. of 33 books related to political science, int. affairs, music, etc. *Leisure interest:* music. *Address:* University of Bremen, Fachbereich 8/ InIIS, Postfach 330440, 28334 Bremen (office); Freiligrathstrasse 6, 28211 Bremen, Germany (home). *Telephone:* (421) 21867489 (office); (421) 230436 (home). *Fax:* (421) 21867491 (office); (421) 249169 (home). *E-mail:* tmenge@iniis.uni-bremen.de (office). *Website:* www.iniis.uni-bremen.de/ homepages/senghaas (office).

SENGOKU, Yoshito; Japanese lawyer and politician; *Chief Cabinet Secretary;* b. 15 Jan. 1946, Tokushima; ed Tokyo Univ.; pvt. practice as lawyer 1971–; mem. House of Reps for Tokushima Pref. 1990–93, 1996–, fmr Chair. Parl. Cttee on Audit and Oversight of Admin; fmr mem. Social Democratic Party of Japan; currently mem. Democratic Party of Japan; fmr Next (Shadow) Minister of State for Econ. and Fiscal Policy, fmr Shadow Chair. Econ. Strategy Meeting; Minister of State for Admin. Innovation and for Civil Service Reform 2009–10; Chief Cabinet Sec. 2010–. *Address:* Cabinet Office, 1-6-1, Nagata-cho, Chiyoda-ku, Tokyo 100-8914, Japan (office). *Telephone:* (3) 5253-2111 (office). *Website:* www.cao.go.jp (office).

SENN, Martin; Swiss banking executive; *CEO, Zurich Insurance Group (Zurich) Limited;* b. 1957; ed Business School in Basel, Int. Exec. Program, Institut Européen d'Admin des Affaires (INSEAD), Fontainebleau, France, Advanced Man. Program, Harvard Business School, USA; worked at fmr Swiss Bank Corpn 1976–94, posts included Treas. in Hong Kong and Regional Treas. for Asia and the Pacific region in Singapore, later managed co.'s Tokyo office; joined Credit Suisse 1994, exec. roles included that of Treas. for Head Office and Europe, Chair. and Turnaround Man. Credit Suisse Group Japan, mem. Credit Suisse Banking Exec. Bd and Head of Trading and Investment Services Div. 2001–03, mem. Corp. Exec. Bd and Chief Investment Officer Swiss Life Group 2003–06; mem. Group Exec. Cttee and Chief Investment Officer, Zurich Financial Services Ltd (renamed Zurich Insurance Group Ltd 2012) 2006–09, CEO 2010–; mem. Bd of Dirs Castle Alternative Invest AG 2003–, Maerki Baumann & Co. AG, Zurich 2002–, Nomura Bank (Switzerland) Ltd, Zurich 2002–, Banca Del Gottardo 2005–06; mem. Foundation Bd Avenir Suisse; Treas. Zurich Asscn of Econs; mem. Bd of Dirs Swiss-American Chamber of Commerce; mem. Bd Geneva Asscn, Inst. of Int. Finance; Rep. of the Property and Casualty CEO Roundtable; mem. Pan European Insurance Forum, European Financial Services Roundtable, Advisory Bd of Tsinghua School of Econs and Man., Bd of Trustees, Lucerne Festival; Hon. Consul of Repub. of Korea in Zurich. *Address:* Zurich Insurance Group Ltd, 2 Mythenquai, PO Box 8022, Zurich, Switzerland (office). *Telephone:* (44) 625-25-25 (office); (44) 625-02-99 (office). *E-mail:* info@zurich.com (office). *Website:* www.zurich.com (office).

SENTAMU, Most Rev. Rt Hon John Tucker Mugabi, LLB, MA, PhD, FRSA, PC; Ugandan/British ecclesiastic; *Archbishop of York;* b. 1949; m. Margaret Sentamu; two c.; ed Makerere Univ., Univ. of Cambridge, UK; trained barrister and Advocate of the High Court of Uganda; Asst Chaplain Selwyn Coll. Cambridge; ordained 1979; Chaplain, Latchmere Remand Centre 1979–82; curate, St Andrew's Ham in Southwark 1979–82; curate, St Paul's, Herne Hill 1982–83; Priest-in-Charge, Holy Trinity, Tulse Hill 1983–84; Parish Priest St Matthias, Upper Tulse Hill 1983–84; Vicar Holy Trinity and St Matthias, Tulse Hill 1985–96; mem. Gen. Synod 1985–96, 2005–, mem. Standing, Policy and Appointments Cttees; mem. Archbishop's Comm. for Urban Priority Areas 1988–92; mem. Revision Cttee for the Ordination of Women to the Priesthood; Priest-in-Charge, St Saviour, Brixton Hill 1987–89; mem. Family Welfare Asscn 1989–; mem. Decade of Evangelism Steering Group; mem. Exec. Springboard; Prolocutor Convocation of Canterbury 1990–96; Chair. Cttee for Minority Ethnic Anglican Concerns 1990–99; Area Bishop of Stepney 1996–2002; Bishop of Birmingham 2002–05, Archbishop of York 2005–; Adviser to the Stephen Lawrence Judicial Inquiry 1997–99; Gov. Univ. of North London 1998–2002; Pres. and Chair. London Marriage Guidance Council 2000–04; Chair. Review into the murder investigation of Damilola Taylor 2001–02; Chancellor, York St John Univ. 2006–, Univ. of Cumbria 2007–; Pres. Youth for Christ, YMCA England; Chair. NHS Haeomoglobinopathy Screening Programme, EC1 New Deal Devt Programme; mem. Health

Advisory Cttee HM Prisons, CTE Forum, Birmingham Hosp. NHS Trust, Yorkshire Soc. 2009–; Custodian Trustee Birmingham Diocesan Fund; Trustee, Tower Hamlets Summer Univ.; Deputy Chair. Comm. on Urban Life and Faith 2003–; Tourism Amb. Visit York 2010; Fellow, Univ. Coll., Christ Church, Canterbury, Queen Mary, Univ. of London; Hon. Fellow Selwyn Coll. Cambridge, Hon. Canon Southwark Cathedral 1993–96; Hon. Master Bencher, Grays Inn 2007; Freeman of the City of London 2000, Freeman of the City of Montego Bay 2007; Dr hc (Open Univ.), (Birmingham City Univ.), (York) 2010; Hon. DPhil (Gloucestershire); Hon. DD (Birmingham), (Hull), (Cambridge), (Nottingham), (Wycliffe Coll., Toronto), (Univ. of the South, Sewanee, TN) 2010, (London) 2010; Hon. LLD (Leicester), (Teeside), (Leeds) 2010; Hon. DL (Sheffield), (Univ. of the West Indies); Hon. DCL (Northumbria); Hon. DTheol (Univ. of Chester) 2009; Midlander of the Year 2003, Yorkshire Man of the Year 2007, Speaker of the Year 2007. *Leisure interests:* music, cooking, reading, athletics, rugby, football. *Address:* Bishopthorpe Palace, Bishopthorpe, York, YO23 2GE, England (office). *Telephone:* (1904) 707021 (office). *Fax:* (1904) 709020 (office). *E-mail:* office@archbishopofyork .org (office). *Website:* www.archbishopofyork.org (office).

SEPE, HE Cardinal Crescenzio; Italian ecclesiastic; *Archbishop of Naples;* b. 2 June 1943, Carinaro, Aversa; ed Pontifical Lateran Univ., Univ. of Rome La Sapienza.; taught theology at Lateran and Urbanian Pontifical Univs; ordained priest 1967; apptd Assessor for Gen. Affairs, Secr. of State 1987; consecrated Bishop 1992; apptd Titular Archbishop of Grado 1992; apptd Sec. Congregation for the Clergy 1992; Chair. Peregrinatio ad Petri Sedem 1997–2001; cr. Cardinal (Cardinal-Priest of Dio Padre misericordioso) 2001; Prefect of Congregation for the Evangelization of Peoples, Roman Curia 2001–05, 2005–06; Archbishop of Naples 2006–; participated in Papal Conclave 2005, 2013; currently also Grand Chancellor, Pontifical Urban Univ. *Address:* Curia of Naples, Largo Donnaregina 22, 80138 Naples (office); Villa Betania, Via Urbans VIII 16, 00165 Rome, Italy (home). *Telephone:* (081) 5574111 (office). *Fax:* (081) 451797 (office). *E-mail:* ucs.na@iol.it (office). *Website:* www.chiesadinapoli.it (office).

SEPÚLVEDA-AMOR, Bernardo, LLB; Mexican lawyer, judge and politician; *Judge and Vice-President, International Court of Justice;* b. 14 Dec. 1941, Mexico City; s. of Bernardo Sepúlveda and Margarita Sepúlveda; m. Ana Yturbe 1970; three s.; ed Nat. Univ. of Mexico and Queen's Coll., Cambridge; fmrly taught int. law, El Colegio de México and Faculty of Political Science, Univ. of Mexico; Asst Dir of Juridical Affairs, Ministry of Presidency 1968–70; Dir-Gen. of Int. Financial Affairs, Ministry of Finance 1976–81; Int. Adviser, Minister of Programming and Budget 1981; Amb. to USA March–Dec. 1982; Sec. of Foreign Affairs 1982–88; Amb. to UK 1989–93; Foreign Affairs Adviser to Pres. of Mexico 1993–; mem. UN Int. Law Comm. 1996–2005; fmr Judge ad hoc, Int. Court of Justice, Judge 2006–, Vice-Pres. 2012–; Sec. Int. Affairs Institutional Revolutionary Party (PRI) 1981–82; Pres. to UN Sixth Comm. on Transnational Corpns 1977–80; Hon. Fellow Queens' Coll., Cambridge 1991; Hon. GCMG; Dr hc (Univ. of San Diego), (Univ. of Leningrad); Premio Príncipe de Asturias, Premio Simón Bolivar; Kt Grand Cross, Most Distinguished Order of St Michael and St George (UK), Grand Cross, Order of Isabel The Catholic (Spain), Grand Cross, Order of Civil Merit (Spain), Grand Cross, Order of Cruzeiro do Sul (Brazil), Grand Cross, Order of Rio Branco (Brazil), Grand Cross, Order of Boyacá (Columbia), Ribbon, Order of Kwang-Wha (S Korea), Grand Cross, Order of Gen. San Martin (Argentina), Gran Cordón, Order of the Libertador (Venezuela), Grand Cross, Orden de la Bandera Yugoslava (Yugoslavia), Grand Cross Orden de Cristo (Portugal), Grand Cross, Order Infante Don Henrique (Portugal), Grand Cross, Ordre de la Couronne (Belgium), Grand Officier, Ordre d la Légion d'honneur (France), Commdr Insignia of the Order of Merit, with the Star (Poland), Superior Commdr, Grand Order of the Saviour (Greece), Grand Cross, Order of Vasco Núñez de Balboa (Panama), Grand Cross, Order of the Quetzal (Guatemala), Grand Cordon, Order of the Rising Sun (Japan), Grand Cross, Order of El Sol de Peru (Peru), Order of the Repub., First Class (Egypt), Commdr, Order of Distinction (Jamaica). *Publications:* Foreign Investment in Mexico 1973, Transnational Corporations in Mexico 1974, A View of Contemporary Mexico 1979, Planning for Development 1981. *Address:* International Court of Justice, Peace Palace, 2517 KJ, The Hague, Netherlands (office); Rocas 185, México, DF 01900, Mexico. *Telephone:* (70) 302-2323 (office); (5) 652-0641. *Fax:* (70) 364-9928 (office); (5) 652-9739. *E-mail:* info@icj -cij.org (office). *Website:* www.icj-cij.org (office).

SEQUEIRA, Luis, BA, MA, PhD; American plant biologist and professor of plant biology; *Professor Emeritus, Department of Plant Pathology, University of Wisconsin, Madison;* b. 1 Sept. 1927, San José, Costa Rica; s. of Raul Sequeira and the late Dora Jenkins; m. Elisabeth Steinvorth 1954; one s. three d.; ed Harvard Univ.; Teaching Fellow, Harvard Univ. 1949–52; Parker Fellow, Harvard and Instituto Biológico, São Paulo, Brazil 1952–53; Plant Pathologist, Asst Dir, then Dir Coto Research Station, United Fruit Co., Costa Rica 1953–60; Research Assoc., North Carolina State Univ., Raleigh, North Carolina 1960–61; Assoc. Prof., then Prof., Dept of Plant Pathology, Univ. of Wis., Madison 1961–78, Prof., Depts of Bacteriology and Plant Pathology 1978–82, apptd J.C. Walker Prof. 1982, currently Prof. Emer.; Consultant Agracetus, Madison 1982–93; Chief Scientist, Competitive Grants Office, USDA, Washington, DC 1987–88; research interests include physiology and biochemistry of plant–parasite interactions, identification of genes for virulence in pathogens, particularly bacteria and breeding plants for disease resistance; Fellow, American Phytopathological Soc. (Pres. 1985–86), American Acad. of Microbiology; mem. NAS, Linnean Soc. of London, Nat. Science Bd 1991–; Hon. Prof. (Univ. of Queensland) 1997; Award of Distinction, American Phytopathological Soc. 1994, E.M. Stakman Award. *Publications:* approximately 260 publs in journals and covering plant pathology, bacteriology, biochem. and genetics. *Leisure interests:* classical music, cross-country skiing. *Address:* 10 Appomattox Court, Madison, WI 53705, USA (home). *Telephone:* (608) 833-3440 (home).

SERAGELDIN, Ismail, BSc, MRP, PhD; Egyptian international organization official; *Director, Bibliotheca Alexandrina;* b. 1944, Guiza; m.; one s.; ed Cairo Univ., Harvard Univ.; fmr lecturer Cairo and Harvard Univs; fmr consultant in city and regional planning; joined World Bank 1972, held numerous positions including Economist in Educ. and Human Resources 1972–76, Div. Chief for Tech. Assistance and Special Studies 1977–80, for Urban Projects in Europe, the Middle E and N Africa 1980–83, Dir for Programs in W Africa 1984–87, Co-Dir for Cen.

and Occidental Africa 1987–89, Tech. Dir for Sub-Saharan Africa 1990–92, Vice-Pres. for Environmentally and Socially Sustainable Devt 1992–98, Co-Chair. Non Governmental Org.-Bank Cttee 1997–99, Vice-Pres. for Special Programs 1998–2000; Chair. Global Water Partnership 1996–2000, World Comm. for Water in the 21st Century 1998–2000; currently Dir Bibliotheca Alexandrina (Library of Alexandria); Amb. Alliance of Civilizations; also Chair. Exec. Council, World Digital Library; Prof., Int. Chair Savoirs contre pauvreté (Knowledge Against Poverty), Collège de France; Chair. and mem. of numerous advisory cttees including Egyptian Acad. of Science, Acad. of Sciences for the Developing World, Indian Nat. Acad. of Agricultural Sciences, European Acad. of Sciences and Arts; Foreign Fellow, Bangladesh Acad. of Sciences; fmr Distinguished Univ. Prof. Univ. of Wageningen, Netherlands; Officier, Ordre des Arts et des Lettres 2003, Order of the Rising Sun (Gold and Silver Star), Japan 2008, Ordre national de la Légion d'honneur 2008, Commandeur, Ordre des Arts et des Lettres 2011; Grameen Foundation Award, USA 1999, Pablo Neruda Medal of Honor, Chile 2004, Jamnalal Bajaj Award 2006, Champion of Youth Award, World Youth Congress, Quebec 2008, M. S. Swaminathan Award for Environmental Protection 2010, Millennium Excellence Award, Excellence Awards Foundation, Ghana 2010, Public Welfare Medal, NAS 2011; Hon. DSc (Indian Agricultural Research Inst.) 1997, (Punjab Agricultural Univ.) 1998, (Tamil Nadu Veterinary and Animal Sciences Univ.) 1998, (Tamil Nadu Agricultural Univ.) 1999, (Egerton Univ., Kenya) 1999, (SNHU, Manchester, NH) 2002, (McGill Univ., Montreal) 2003, (Azerbaijan State Economic Univ., Baku) 2007, numerous other hon. degrees. *Publications:* Nurturing Development 1995, Sustainability and the Wealth of Nations 1996, Architecture of Empowerment 1997, Rural Well-Being: From Vision to Action (jtly) 1997, The Modernity of Shakespeare 1998, Biotechnology and Biosafety (jtly) 1999, Very Special Places 1999, Promethean Science (jtly) 2000 and numerous other books and articles. *Address:* Bibliotheca Alexandrina, POB 138, El Shatby, Alexandria, 21526, Egypt (office). *Telephone:* (203) 4839999 (office). *Website:* www.bibalex.org (office); www.serageldin.com.

ŞERBAN, Andrei; Romanian theatre and opera director; *Director, Oscar Hammerstein II Center for Theatre Studies, Columbia University;* b. 21 June 1943, Bucharest; s. of Gheorghe Şerban and Elpis Şerban; m.; two c.; ed Bucharest Theatrical and Cinematographic Art Inst.; int. scholarships Ford 1970, Guggenheim 1976, Rockefeller 1980; associated with Robert Brustein's American Repertory Theatre Company for more than 20 years 1970–; worked also with LaMama Theatre, Public Theater, Lincoln Center, Circle in the Square, Yale Repertory Theatre, Guthrie Theatre, ACT, New York City, Seattle and Los Angeles Operas; in Europe: at Paris, Geneva, Vienna, and Bologna Opera Houses, Welsh Nat. Opera, Covent Garden, Théâtre de la Ville, Helsinki Lilla Teatern, Comédie Française, among others; worked with Shiki Co. of Tokyo, Japan; has delivered numerous lectures; Gen. Man. Nat. Theatre of Romania 1990–93; Dir, Oscar Hammerstein II Center for Theatre Studies, Columbia Univ., New York 1992–; Order of the Star of Romania (Steaua României); Prize for the Best Performance, World Students' Theatre Festival, Zagreb 1965, Obie Awards, Tony Award, George Abbott Award, Soc. of Stage Dirs and Choreographers, prizes at Avignon, Belgrade and Shiraz Festivals. *Productions include:* (in Romania) Ubu Roi 1966, Julius Caesar 1968, Jonah 1969, An Ancient Trilogy (Medea, The Trojan Women, Elektra) 1990; (in USA) Medea (Euripides) 1972, Fragments of a Trilogy (Medea, Elektra, The Trojan Women) 1974, As You Like It 1976, The Cherry Orchard 1977, Uncle Vanya 1979, The Umbrellas of Cherbourg 1980, The Seagull 1981, Three Sisters 1983, The King Stag 1985, The Miser 1988, Twelfth Night 1989, Sweet Table at the Richelieu 1989, Hamlet 1999 (in France, at the Comédie Française), L'Avare 2000, Le Marchand de Venise 2001, Lysystrata 2002 Pericles 2003, Cleansed 2006, Uncle Vanya 2005, King Lear 2006, Cries and Whispers (in Romania, three UNITER awards including Best Dir 2011) 2011, Hedda Gabler 2012, Angels in America (in Hungary, Best Dir, Hungarian Theatre Critics Asscn 2013) 2013, Chung Young 2014. *Opera productions include:* Eugene Onegin 1980, Turandot 1984, Norma 1985, Fidelio (Covent Garden) 1986; Paris Opera: L'Ange de feu 1991, Lucia Di Lammermoor 1995, The Puritans 1997, L'Italienne à Alger 1998, Les Indes Galantes 1999, La Khovantchina 2001, Les Vêpres Siciliennes 2003, Otello 2004; Wiener Staatsoper: Les Contes d'Hoffman 1993, Die Lustige Witwe 1999, Werther 2005, Manon 2007, etc. *Address:* School of the Arts, Columbia University, 601 Dodge Hall, Mail Code 1807, 2960 Broadway, New York, NY 10027, USA (office). *Telephone:* (212) 854-3408 (office). *Fax:* (212) 854-3344 (office). *E-mail:* as160@columbia.edu (office).

SERDENGEÇTİ, Süreyya, BS, MA; Turkish economist, academic and fmr central banker; *Director, Stability Institute, Economic Policy Research Foundation of Turkey (TEPAV);* b. Istanbul; m. Çiğdem Son Deniz; ed Middle East Tech. Univ., Ankara, Vanderbilt Univ., USA; with Central Bank of Turkey 1980–2006, positions included Foreign Exchange, Markets, External Relations, Communication Depts, Vice-Gov. 1998–2001, Gov. 2001–06; Sr Lecturer, Dept of Econs, TOBB University of Econs and Tech., Ankara 2006–; Dir Stability Inst., Econ. Policy Research Foundation of Turkey. *Address:* TEPAV Söğütözü Cd 43, Söğütözü, Ankara 06560, Turkey (office). *Telephone:* (312) 2925547 (office). *Fax:* (312) 2871946 (office). *E-mail:* serdengecti@tepav.org.tr (office); serdengecti@etu.edu.tr (office). *Website:* www.tepav.org.tr/en (office).

SERDYUKOV, Anatolii Eduardovich; Russian business executive and politician; b. 8 Jan. 1962, Kholmskii village, Abin Dist, Krasnodar Krai; m. Yuliya Zubkova; ed Leningrad (now St Petersburg) Inst. of Soviet Trade and St Petersburg State Univ.; mil. service 1984–85; worked in furniture shop 1985–95, then Marketing Dir and Dir-Gen. St Petersburg furniture market 1995–2000; Deputy Head, Dist Inspectorate of Taxes, Ministry of Taxes and Dues 2000–01; Deputy Head then Head, St Petersburg Tax Authority 2001–04; Deputy Minister of Taxes and Dues Feb.–July 2004, Head of Fed. Tax Service 2004–07; Minister of Defence 2007–12. *Address:* c/o Ministry of Defence, 119169 Moscow, ul. Znamenka 19, Russia.

SEREBREAN, Oleg, PhD; Moldovan politician; *First Deputy Chairman, Democratic Party;* b. 1969; ed Universitatea Pedagogică de Stat Ion Creangă, European Inst. of High Int. Studies, Nice, France; Spokesperson, Ministry of Foreign Affairs 1998–99; Deputy Rector Free Univ. of Moldova 1999–2002; Chair. Social Liberal Party 2001, now First Deputy Chair, Democratic Party; currently mem. Parl., Democratic Moldova electoral bloc, mem. Cttee for Foreign Policy and European

Integration, two Special Cttees, Standing Bureau of Parl. *Publications:* Geopolitics of the Black Sea Region 1998, Politosphere 2001, Politics and Geopolitics 2004, Dictionary of Geopolitics 2006. *Address:* Parlamentul, 2073 Chişinău, bd. Ştefan cel Mare 105, Moldova (office).

SEREBRIER, José, MA; American conductor and composer; b. 3 Dec. 1938, Montevideo, Uruguay; s. of David Serebrier and Frida Serebrier (née Wasser); m. Carole Farley 1969; one d.; ed Univ. of Minn., Curtis Inst. of Music, Phila; started conducting at age of 12; went to USA 1956; studied composition with Aaron Copland and Vittorio Giannini, Curtis Inst., Phila 1956–58 and conducting with Antal Dorati and Pierre Monteux; guest conductor in USA, S America, Australia and Europe; Assoc. Conductor American Symphony Orchestra, with Leopold Stokowski 1962–68; conducted alongside Leopold Stokowski world première of Charles Ives' Fourth Symphony, Carnegie Hall, New York 1964; conducted first performance in Poland of Charles Ives' Fourth Symphony 1971 and premieres of over 500 works; Rockefeller Foundation Composer-in-Residence with Cleveland Orchestra 1968–70; Music Dir Cleveland Philharmonic Orchestra 1968–71; Artistic Dir Int. Festival of the Americas, Miami 1984–, Miami Festival 1985– (also Founder), Festival Miami; toured frequently with Russian Nat. Orchestra in S America and China; two Guggenheim Fellowships, Ford Foundation Conducting Award, Nat. Endowment for the Arts Comm. Award 1969, Ditson Award for Promotion of New Music, Columbia Univ. 1980, Deutsche Schallplatten Critics' Award 1991, UK Music Retailers' Asscn Award for Best Symphony Recording (Mendelssohn symphonies) 1991, Diapason d'Or Recording Award, France, Best Audiophile Recording (Scheherazade), Soundstage 2000, BMI Award, Koussevitzky Foundation Award, Latin Grammy for Best Classical Album of 2004. *Compositions:* Solo Violin Sonata 1954, Quartet for Saxophones 1955, Pequeña música (wind quintet) 1955, Symphony No. 1 1956, Momento psicológico (string orchestra) 1957, Solo Piano Sonata 1957, Suite canina (wind trio) 1957, Symphony for Percussion 1960, The Star Wagon (chamber orchestra) 1967, Nueve (double bass and orchestra) 1970, Colores mágicos (variations for harp and chamber orchestra) 1971, At Dusk, in Shadows (solo flute), Andante Cantabile (strings), Night Cry (brass), Dorothy and Carmine (flute and strings), George and Muriel (contrabass), Winter (violin concerto) 1995, Winterreise (for orchestra) 1999; composed music for several films; all compositions published and recorded; over 350 recordings to date. *Television includes:* int. TV broadcast of Grammys Ceremony, LA 2002, conducting suite from Bernstein's West Side Story. *Recordings:* more than 300 recordings with major orchestras. *Publications:* orchestration of 14 songs by Edvard Grieg 2000, orchestration of Gershwin's works 2002, Suite from Janacek's Makropulos Case 2004; more than 100 works published. *Leisure interests:* reading, swimming, football. *Address:* 20 Queensgate Gardens, London, SW7 5LZ, England (office). *Fax:* (212) 662-8073 (New York) (office). *E-mail:* caspi123@aol.com (office). *Website:* www.joseserebrier.com.

SERETSE, Brig. Ramadeluka; Botswana lawyer, politician and fmr army officer; served as Brig. in Botswana Defence Force, mem. Parl. for Serowe North East (Botswana Democratic Party) 2004–, Minister for Lands and Housing –2008, for Defence, Justice and Security 2008–10 (resgnd). *Address:* c/o Ministry for the Administration of Justice, Gaborone, Botswana.

SERGEANT, Carol, CBE, BA, MBA; British financial officer; b. 1952, Berlin, Germany; d. of Frank Hawksworth and Norah MacCauley; m. Philip Sergeant; one s. one d.; ed Newnham Coll. Cambridge, City Univ. Business School; joined Bank of England 1970s, various positions in research, negotiations with IMF, EEC issues, foreign exchange –1998; joined Financial Services Authority 1998, various positions including Dir Strategic Change, Man. Dir responsible for Regulatory Processes and Risk Directorate, Deputy Chair. Building Societies Comm., Dir Banks and Building Societies, mem. Bd 2001–03 (resgnd); Chief Risk Dir and mem. Group Exec. Cttee, Lloyds TSB 2004–10; mem. Bd of Dirs Secure Trust Bank 2011–; mem. Advisory Bd and Strategy Cttee, Cass Business School; mem. Trustee and Audit Cttee, Court of Int. Guild of Bankers. *Leisure interest:* fencing. *Address:* Secure Trust Bank, One Arleston Way, Shirley, Solihull, B90 4LH, England (office). *Telephone:* (12) 1693-9100 (office). *Website:* www.securetrustbank.com (office).

SERGEYEV, Ivan Ivanovich; Russian civil servant and diplomatist; *Director General, GlavUpDK, Ministry of Foreign Affairs;* b. 7 Sept. 1941, Electrostal, Moscow Region; Deputy, First Deputy Chair., Exec. Cttee Moscow Regional Soviet 1976–83; Deputy, First Deputy Head, Dept on Problems of Diplomatic Corps USSR (now Russian) Ministry of Foreign Affairs 1983–97; Deputy Minister of Foreign Affairs 1997–2003; Deputy Chair. Bd Black Sea Bank for Trade and Devt 1998–2003; currently Dir Gen. GlavUpDK (Main Admin. for Service to Diplomatic Corps), Ministry of Foreign Affairs; State Prize of Russia 2002. *Address:* GlavUpDK, 119034 Moscow, Prechistenka, 20, Russia (office). *Telephone:* (495) 230-2329 (office). *Fax:* (495) 230-2329 (home). *E-mail:* info@updk.ru (office). *Website:* updk.ru (home).

SERGEYEV, Victor Mikhailovich, DHist; Russian mathematician, political scientist and professor of political studies; *Professor of Comparative Politics and Director, Centre for International Research, Moscow State Institute of International Relations;* b. 22 April 1944, Moscow; m. Marina Alekseyevna Sergeyeva; one s.; ed Moscow Inst. of Energy, Moscow State Univ.; Sr Researcher All-Union Research Inst. of Meteorological Service, USSR State Cttee of Standards 1975–78, Problem Lab. of System Analysis, Moscow State Inst. of Int. Relations 1978–86, Prof. of Comparative Politics and Dir Centre for Int. Research 1998–; Head of Lab. Inst. of USA and Canada, USSR (now Russian) Acad. of Sciences 1986–90; Deputy Dir Analytical Centre on Scientific and Industrial Policy, Ministry of Science and Tech. 1998–; Visiting Prof. and Fellow, Leiden Univ., Santa Fe Inst., Netherlands Inst. for Advanced Studies, Svedish Collegium for Advanced Studies in Social Science, Uppsala Univ., Leeds Univ.; mem. Russian Acad. of Nat. Sciences, Asscn of Political Studies, Kant Soc., Russian Asscn of Artificial Intellect, Exec. Bd Centre of Philosophy, Psychology and Sociology of Religion; Hon. mem. Leeds Univ., UK. *Publications:* numerous scientific works published in Russia and abroad on political and religious culture, cognitive studies etc., including The Wild East 1998, Limits of Rationality 1998. *Leisure interest:* foreign languages. *Address:* Centre for International Research, Moscow State Institute of International Relations, prospekt Vernadskogo 76, 119454 Moscow, Russia (office). *Telephone:*

(495) 434-20-44 (office). *Fax:* (495) 434-20-44 (office). *E-mail:* tsmi@mgimo.ru (office); av205@comtv.ru.

SERGIENKO, Valentin I., MS, PhD, DSc; Russian chemist; *Chairman, Far East Branch, Russian Academy of Sciences;* b. 18 Aug. 1944, Novosysoyevka, Primorsky territory; m.; two c.; ed Far East State Univ., Vladivostok; has held numerous positions at Inst. of Chemistry, Far East Br., Russian Acad. of Sciences 1970–92, including Jr Researcher, Sr Researcher, Head of Group, Head of Lab., Head of Div., Deputy Dir, Acting Dir, Deputy Chair. Far East Br. of Russian Acad. of Sciences 1992, currently Chair., concurrently Head of Div., Inst. of Chem., Far East Br. of Russian Acad. of Sciences; Scientific Head, Inst. of Engineering and Social Ecology, Far East State Technical Univ.; Dir Far East Br. of Agency for Man. of Property, Russian Acad. of Sciences; mem. Russian Acad. of Sciences (Corresp. mem. 1997–2000); Bd mem. Russian Foundation for Basic Research; Prize of Russian Fed. Govt in the field of science and technology; Order of Labour Red Banner, various medals. *Achievements include:* owner of six patents. *Publications include:* over 160 scientific papers, monographs on theoretical chemistry, spectrochemistry, structure of fluorides, technology of purification and utilization of waste. *Address:* Presidium of Far Eastern Branch, Russian Academy of Sciences, Svetlanskaya street. 50, Vladivostok 690950, Russia (office). *Telephone:* 4232-22 86 30 (office). *E-mail:* sergienko@hg.febras.ru (office). *Website:* www.febras.ru (office).

SERJEANT, Graham Roger, CMG, MD, FRCP; British medical research scientist and academic; *Chairman, Sickle Cell Trust (Jamaica);* b. 26 Oct. 1938, Bristol; s. of Ewart E. Serjeant and Violet E. Serjeant; m. Beryl E. King 1965; ed Sibford School, Banbury, Bootham School, York, Clare Coll., Cambridge, London Hosp. Medical School and Makerere Coll. Kampala; House Physician, London Hosp. 1963–64, Royal United Hosp. Bath 1965–66, Hammersmith Hosp., London 1966; Registrar, Univ. Hosp. of the West Indies 1966–67; Wellcome Research Fellow, Dept of Medicine, Univ. Hosp. of the West Indies 1967–71; Visiting Prof., Dept of Biochemistry, Univ. of Tennessee, USA 1971; mem. scientific staff, MRC Abnormal Haemoglobin Unit, Cambridge 1971–72, Epidemiology Research Unit, Jamaica 1972–74; Dir MRC Labs, Jamaica 1974–99; Prof. of Epidemiology, Faculty of Medicine, Univ. of the West Indies 1981–99, Prof. Emer. 1999–; Visiting Prof., London School of Hygiene and Tropical Medicine 1999, Guy's, King's and St Thomas' Combined Medical School, London 1999; Chair. Sickle Cell Trust (Jamaica); Hon. FRCPE 1998; Hon. Prof. Dept of Public Health, Guy's Hosp., London 1999; Hon. CD (Jamaica), Ordre du Mérite Congolais; Vice-Chancellor's Award for Excellence 1999, Pan American Health Org. Jamaican Hero of Health 2002. *Publications:* The Clinical Features of Sickle Cell Disease 1974, Sickle Cell Disease (3rd edn) 2001; more than 400 papers on sickle cell disease in medical journals. *Leisure interests* squash, music. *Address:* 14 Milverton Crescent, Kingston 6, Jamaica (home). *Telephone:* 970-0077 (office); 927-2300 (home). *Fax:* 970-0074 (office). *E-mail:* grserjeant@cwjamaica.com (home). *Website:* www .sicklecelltrustjamaica.com (office).

SERKIN, Peter Adolf; American concert pianist; b. 24 July 1947, New York; s. of Rudolf Serkin and Irene Busch; m. Regina Serkin; five c.; ed Curtis Inst. of Music; debut, New York 1959; taught at Juilliard School, Curtis Inst. of Music; currently teaches at Bard Coll. Conservatory of Music, Longy School of Music; co-founder TASHI; concert appearances in recital and with orchestras worldwide including Philadelphia, Cleveland, New York, Chicago, Berlin, London, Zürich, Paris, Japan, Vienna; has premiered works composed for him by Knussen, Takemitsu, Lieberson, Berio; has given benefit performances to aid hunger and war victims; Dr hc (New England Conservatory) 2001; Grammy Award 1966, Premio Accademia Musicale Chigian Siena 1983. *Address:* CM Artists, 127 West, 96th Street, #13B, New York, NY 10025, USA (office). *Telephone:* (212) 864-1005 (office). *Fax:* (212) 864-1066 (office). *Website:* www.cmartists.com (office).

SEROTA, Sir Nicholas Andrew, Kt, CH, MA; British art gallery director; *Director, The Tate Gallery;* b. 27 April 1946, Hampstead, London, England; s. of Stanley Serota and Baroness Serota; m. 1st Angela M. Beveridge 1973 (divorced 1995); two d.; m. 2nd Teresa Gleadowe 1997; ed Haberdashers' Aske's School, Hampstead and Elstree, Christ's Coll., Cambridge and Courtauld Inst. of Art; Regional Art Officer and Exhbn Organizer, Arts Council of GB 1970–73; Dir Museum of Modern Art, Oxford 1973–76; Dir Whitechapel Art Gallery 1976–88; Dir The Tate Gallery, London 1988–; Chair. British Council Visual Arts Advisory Cttee 1992–98 (mem. 1976–98); Sr Fellow Royal Coll. of Art 1996; Trustee Public Art Devt Trust 1983–87, Architecture Foundation 1991–99, The Little Sparta Trust 1995–2007; Commr Comm. for Architecture and the Built Environment 1999–2006; mem. Olympic Delivery Authority 2006–12; Hon. Fellow, Queen Mary and Westfield Coll., Univ. of London 1988, RIBA 1992, Goldsmiths Coll., Univ. of London 1994; Hon. DArts (City of London Polytechnic) 1990; Hon. DLitt (Plymouth) 1993, (Keele) 1994, (South Bank) 1996, (Exeter) 2000; Hon. DUniv (Surrey) 1997. *Publication:* Experience or Interpretation: The Dilemma of Museums of Modern Art 1997. *Address:* Tate Britain, Millbank, London, SW1P 4RG, England (office). *Telephone:* (20) 7887-8000 (office). *Fax:* (20) 7887-8007 (office). *Website:* www.tate.org.uk (office).

SERRA, José; Brazilian politician, economist and academic; b. 19 March 1942, São Paulo; m. Monica Serra; two c.; ed Univ. of São Paulo, CEPAL-ILPES, Santiago, Chile, Univ. of Chile, Cornell Univ., USA; Leader of Nat. Students' Union 1963–64; forced to flee to Chile for opposing Brazil's mil. regime in early 1970s, in exile for 14 years; Prof. of Econs, Univ. of Chile 1968–73; mem. Inst. for Advanced Study, Princeton Univ., USA 1976–78; Prof., Univ. of Campinas; Sec. for Economy and Planning, São Paulo 1983–86; Co-founder and mem. Brazilian Social Democratic Party (PSDB) 1988–; elected mem. Nat. Congress of Brazil (Chamber of Deputies) 1986–94; elected Senator 1994–; Minister of Planning 1995–96; Minister of Health 1998–2002; unsuccessful presidential cand. 2002, 2010; Mayor of São Paulo 2004–06; Gov. State of São Paulo 2007–10. *Address:* Partido da Social Democracia Brasileira (PSDB), SGAS, Quadra 607, Edif. Metrópolis, Asa Sul, 70200–670 Brasília, DF Brazil (office). *Telephone:* (61) 3424-0500 (office). *Fax:* (61) 3424-0515 (office). *E-mail:* tucano@psdb.org.br (office). *Website:* www.psdb.org.br (office).

SERRA, Maj. Gen. Paolo, BSc, MSc; Italian army officer and UN official; *Head of Mission and Force Commander, United Nations Interim Force in Lebanon (UNIFIL);* b. 7 April 1956, Turin; s. of Carlo Serra and Maria Serra; m. Antonella

Filippi; one d.; ed Italian Mil. Acad., Modena, Univ. of Turin, Army War Coll., Carlisle, Pa, USA, patrol and paratrooper courses in Pisa, Long Range Patrol Course in Weingarten, Germany, skiing and climbing courses for instructors in Aosta, 114th Jr and Sr Staff Courses in Civitavecchia, Rome; Cadet, Italian Mil. Acad., Modena 1975–77, Cadet, Italian Army Jr Officers Advanced School, Turin 1977–79, commissioned as 'Alpini' Lt 1979; Platoon Leader, Alpini Bn 'Saluzzo', Cuneo 1979–80; Anti-Tank Co. Commdr, Alpini Brigade 'Taurinense', Turin 1980–90; rank of Capt. 1990; Staff Officer, Alpini Brigade 'Orobica', Merano 1990–91; apptd Anti-Tank Co. Commdr in Italian Contingent of ACE Mobile Force – AMF(L); Staff Officer, Alpini Brigade 'Tridentina', Bressanone 1991–93; Jr Asst to Chief of Cabinet, Gen. Staff, Rome 1993–94; rank of Lt Col 1994; Commdr of 'Susa' Alpini Bn 1994, led relief efforts in aftermath of the flood that hit Northern Italy and commanded a Task Force to support law and order against organized crime in Southern Italy; Bn Commdr, Alpini Bn 'Susa', Pinerolo 1994–96; Asst to the Defence Chief of Staff, Defence Gen. Staff, Rome 1996–99; rank of Col 1999; commanded 9th Alpini Regt, deployed in Kosovo 1999, in charge of Prov. of Dakovica/Djacova in southern part of the region, took control of the borders and provided defence of religious sites and ensured security of ethnic enclaves; Regt Commdr 9th Alpini Regt, L'Aquila 1999–2000; Int. Fellow, US Army War Coll. 2000–01; became first ACoS Plans of the future Italian, NATO Rapid Deployment Corps (NRDC-IT) 2001–03, successfully planning and conducting the Exercises' assessments (IOC and FOC) required by NATO; Exec. to Army Chief of Staff, Rome 2003–4; rank of Brig. Gen. 2005; Army Attaché, Embassy in Washington, DC 2004–07; Brigade Commdr 'Julia' Alpini Brigade and Multinational Land Force, Udine 2007–08; Regional Command West Commdr within ISAF mission, Herat, Afghanistan 2008–09, directed and coordinated the efforts of 5,000 men and women from 12 different countries; rank of Maj. Gen. 2009; Chief of Staff of NATO Rapid Deployable Corps – Italy, Solbiate Olona (Varese) 2009–10; Chief of 4th Logistic Div. and Chief of Land Transformation Dept, Army Gen. Staff, Rome 2010–12; Commdr UN Interim Force in Lebanon (UNIFIL) and Force Commdr in South Lebanon 2012–; participated in second Italian expedition to Antarctica 1987–88; Kt, Mil. Order of Italy; Silver Cross for Meritorious Service (Army); Officer, Order of Merit of the Italian Repub.; 'Mauriziana' Medal for Meritorious Service; Silver Medal for Long Command (Army); Gold Cross (Long Service); Meritorious Medal for the Mission in Afghanistan; Meritorious Cross for Peace Operations in Kosovo; Meritorious Cross for Peace Operations in Lebanon; Meritorious Medal for Public Order Operation 'Riace'; UN Medal for the Mission in Lebanon (UNIFIL); NATO Medal for the Mission in Afghanistan; NATO Medal for the Mission in Kosovo; Nat. Humanitarian Award for Relief Operations (flooding in Piemonte, Italy); Antarctica Scientific Expedition Medal; Legion of Merit, degree of Officer (USA); Multinational Cooperation Medal (1st Degree) (Slovenia); Alliance Service Medal (Hungary); Bronze Sport Medal (German Army). *Address:* United Nations Interim Force in Lebanon (UNIFIL), Department of Peace-keeping Operations, United Nations, New York, NY 10017, USA (office). *Telephone:* (212) 963-1234 (office). *Fax:* (212) 963-4879 (office). *Website:* www.un.org/en/peacekeeping/missions/unifil (office).

SERRA, Richard, MFA; American sculptor; b. 2 Nov. 1939, San Francisco, Calif.; m. Clara Weyergraf-Serra; ed Univ. of California, Berkeley, Univ. of California, Santa Barbara, Yale Univ.; works in many perm. collections including Whitney Museum of Modern Art, Guggenheim Museum, Museum of Modern Art, New York, Art Gallery of Ontario, Stedelijk Museum, Amsterdam, Dia Center for the Arts, New York, Colby Coll.; Hon. DFA (Calif. Coll. of Arts and Crafts, Oakland) 1994, (Williams Coll.) 2008, (Harvard Univ.) 2010; Skohegan School Medal 1975, Japan Art Asscn Praemium Imperiale 1994. *Publications:* Weight and Measure 1992, Writings/Interviews 1994. *Address:* c/o Gagosian Gallery, 980 Madison Avenue, New York, NY 10075, USA.

SERRA RAMONEDA, Antoni, PhD; Spanish economist, academic and fmr university rector; *Professor Emeritus, Department d'Economia de l'Empresa, Universitat Autònoma of Barcelona;* b. 20 July 1933, Barcelona; s. of Antoni Serra Riera and Enriqueta Ramoneda Ruis; m. Margarita de la Figuera Buñuel 1958; one s. two d.; ed Lycée Français, Barcelona and Univ. Complutense of Madrid; Sec. Faculty of Econ. Sciences, Univ. of Barcelona 1960–64; Founding mem. Universitat Autònoma de Barcelona and Dept d'Economia de l'Empresa, Univ. Autónoma de Barcelona, Sec.-Gen. 1960–72, Dir Inst. of Educ. Sciences 1977–78, Rector 1980–85, Full Prof. of Managerial Econs and mem. Business Efficiency and Competitiveness Group –2003, Prof. Emer. 2003–; currently Pres. Generalitat de Catalunya's Managing Council for University-System Quality; Treas. Institut d'Estudis Catalans (IEC) 1992–98, Vice-Pres. 1998–2001; Pres. Caixa Catalunya 1984–2005; Pres. Comisión de Control Caja de Pensiones para la Vejez y de Ahorros 1979–82, Sec.-Gen. 1982–84; Pres. Caja de Ahorros de Cataluña 1984; Officier et Chevalier de l'Ordre du Mérite Nat., Cross of St George 2005; Medalla al Mèrit Científic, Medalla Narcís Monturiol al Mèrit Científic i Tecnològic. *Publications:* Libro Blanco sobre los efectos para Cataluña del ingreso de España en la CEE, La industria textil algodonera y el Mercado Común Europeo, Sistema Económico y Empresa. *Address:* Department d'Economia de l'Empresa, Universitat Autònoma of Barcelona, Edifici B, 08193 Cerdanyola (office); Pl. Bonanova 5, Barcelona 08022, Spain (home). *Telephone:* (93) 5811209 (office); (93) 2478101 (home). *Fax:* (93) 5812555 (office). *E-mail:* d.econ.empresa@uab.es (office). *Website:* www.uab.es (office).

SERRA REXACH, Eduardo, LLB; Spanish business executive and fmr politician; *President, Eduardo Serra y Asociados SL;* b. 19 Dec. 1946, Madrid; m. 1st; one s.; m. 2nd Luz del Carmen Municio; ed Complutense Univ., Madrid; began career as state lawyer; mem. staff Ministry of Educ. and Industry –1982; Under-Sec. of Defence 1982–84, Sec. of State for Defence 1984–87, Minister of Defence 1996–2000; Chair. Telettra 1986; Vice-Chair. Cubiertas y MZOV 1989–91, Chair. 1991; Chair. Peugeot Spain 1992, Airtel 1994–96; Chair. UBS Warburg Spain 2000–06; currently Founder and Pres. Eduardo Serra y Asociados (ESYA) SL; Vice-Pres. Everis, Pres. Everis Foundation; mem. Bd of Dirs Zeltia, ONO, Everis, Deutsche Bank, Instituto de Empresa, European Advisory Group; Chair. Bd of Trustees, Prado Museum, Madrid 2000–; Chair. Elcano Royal Inst., Madrid 2001–05; Patron, Real Instituto Elcano for Int. and Strategic Studies. *Address:* Eduardo Serra y Asociados SL, Ayala, 7, 28001 Madrid, Spain (office). *Telephone:* (91) 7817700 (office). *Fax:* (91) 5766057 (office). *E-mail:* ndemiguel@esya.es (office).

SERRA SERRA, Narcís, DEcon; Spanish politician; *President, Barcelona Centre of International Affairs;* b. 30 May 1943, Barcelona; ed Barcelona Univ. and London School of Econs; Prof. of Econ. Theory, Autonomous Univ. of Barcelona 1976–77; Minister of Public Works in Catalan Autonomous Govt 1977–79; Mayor of Barcelona 1979; Minister of Defence in Spanish Govt 1982–91, Deputy Prime Minister 1991–95; Gen. Sec. Catalan Socialist Party 1996–2000; currently Pres. Center for Int. Relations and Devt Studies (CIDOB), Institut Barcelona d'Estudis Internacionals (IBEI), Caixa Catalunya; Hon. Fellow, LSE 1991. *Publications:* Guerra y paz en el siglo XXI – una perspectiva Europea 2003, Europa en construcción – integración, identidades y seguridad 2004, Visiones sobre el Desarrollo en América Latina 2007, Hacia un nuevo pacto social. Políticas económicas para un desarrollo integral en América Latina 2008, The Washington Consensus Reconsidered: Towards a New Global Governance 2008, La transición militar. Reflexiones en torno a la reforma democrática de las fuerzas armadas 2008, The Military Transition – Democratic Reform of the Armed Forces 2010. *Address:* CIDOB, Elisabets 12, 08001 Barcelona, Spain (office). *Telephone:* (93) 3180807 (office). *Fax:* (93) 3427550 (office). *E-mail:* lmoya@cidob.org (office). *Website:* www.cidob.org (office).

SERRANO AGUILAR, Nicanor Alejandro; Ecuadorean politician; b. 14 Jan. 1933; m.; four c.; ed Colegio de los Padres Jesuitas, Universidad de Cuenca; fmr engineer and business exec.; fmr Councillor Prov. Council of Azuay; also served as Mayor of Cuenca; Pres. Instituto de Estudios de Régimen Seccional del Ecuador (IERSE); Vice-Pres. of Ecuador 2005–07; lecturer at Coegio Rafael Borja, Colegio Benigno Malo, Garaicoa Colegio, Colegio Rosa de Jesús Cordero, Colegio Fray Vicente Solano, fmr dean Faculty of Philosophy and Literature, Univ. of Cuenca; Prof., Faculty of Law, Univ. del Azuay in society; Bd mem. Canton Cuenca, later mem. House of Reps, Province of Azuay; Sport and Promotion of Olympism Trophy, Int. Olympic Cttee 2007. *Address:* c/o Office of the Vice-President, Calle Benalcázar N4-40, entre Calles Espejo y Chile, Quito, Ecuador.

SERRANO ELIAS, Jorge, PhD; Guatemalan fmr head of state and business executive; b. 26 April 1945; s. of Jorge Adán Serrano and Rosa Elías; m. Magda Bianchi de Serrano; three s. two d.; ed Univ. of San Carlos, Stanford Univ., USA; Pres. Advisory Council of State 1982–83; Pres. of Guatemala 1991–93 (resgnd).

SERRE, Jean-Pierre, BSc, PhD, DèsSc; French mathematician and academic; *Honorary Professor, Collège de France;* b. 15 Sept. 1926, Bages; s. of Jean Serre and Adèle Serre (née Diet); m. Josiane Heulot 1948; one d.; ed Lycée de Nîmes, Ecole Normale Supérieure, Université de Paris; worked at Centre National de la Recherche Scientifique, Paris 1948–54, Université de Nancy 1954–56; Prof. of Algebra and Geometry, Coll. de France 1956–94 (retd), Hon. Prof. 1994–; mem. Acad. des Sciences 1977, acads in the Netherlands 1978, USA 1979, Sweden 1987, Russia 2003, Norway 2009, Taiwan 2010, Turin 2010; Foreign mem. Royal Soc., London 1974; Fellow, American Math. Soc. 2012; Hon. mem. London Math. Soc. 1973; Grand Croix, Légion d'honneur, Ordre nat. du Mérite; Dr hc (Cambridge) 1978, (Stockholm) 1980, (Glasgow) 1983, (Athens) 1996, (Harvard) 1998, (Durham) 2000, (London) 2001, (Oslo) 2002, (Oxford) 2003, (Bucharest, Barcelona) 2004, (Madrid) 2006; Fields Medal 1954, Prix Peccot-Vimont, Collège de France 1955, Prix Francoeur, Académie des Sciences 1957, Prix Gaston Julia 1970, Médaille Émile Picard, Académie des Sciences 1971, Balzan Prize 1985, Médaille d'or du CNRS 1987, American Math. Soc. Steele Prize 1995, Wolf Prize 2000, Abel Prize 2003. *Publications:* Homologie singulière des espaces fibrés 1951, Faisceaux algébriques cohérents 1955, Groupes algébriques et corps de classes 1959, Corps Locaux 1962, Cohomologie galoisienne 1964, Abelian l-adic representations 1968, Cours d'arithmétique 1970, Représentations linéaires des groupes finis 1971, Arbres, amalgames, SL2 1977, Lectures on the Mordell-Weil Theorem 1989, Topics in Galois Theory 1992, Collected Papers (four vols) 1949–1998, Local Algebra 2000, Correspondence Grothendieck-Serre 2004, Lectures on NX 2012. *Address:* Collège de France, 11, place Marcelin Berthelot, 75231 Paris Cedex 05, France (office); 6 avenue de Montespan, 75116 Paris (home). *Telephone:* 1-44-27-11-11 (office); 1-45-53-35-63 (home). *E-mail:* serre@noos.fr (office). *Website:* www.college-de-france.fr (office).

SERREAU, Coline; French film director, film writer and actress; b. 29 Oct. 1947, Paris; d. of Jean-Marie Serreau and Geneviève Serreau; m. Benno Besson (deceased 2006); one c.; has acted in several stage plays including Lapin, lapin in Paris; wrote and acted in Bertuccelli's On s'est trompé d'histoire d'amour 1973; directed Oedipus the King for Italian TV; f. trapeze school in Canada. *Television:* Pont dormant 1972, La folie des bêtes 1974. *Films include:* A Little, a Lot, Passionately 1971, The Lion's Share 1971, We Were Mistaken About a Love Story 1974, Mais qu'est-ce qu'elles veulent? (documentary) 1975, Sept morts sur ordonnance 1975, Pourquoi pas! 1976, Le fou de mai 1980, Qu'est-ce qu'on attend pour être heureux! 1982, Trois hommes et un couffin (Three Men and a Cradle – also screenwriter) 1985, Romuald et Juliette 1989, Mama, There's a Man in Your Bed 1990, La crise 1992, La belle Verte 1996, Chaos (also screenwriter) 2003, 18 ans après (also screenwriter) 2003, Saint-Jacques... La Mecque (also screenwriter) 2005, Solutions locales pour un désordre global (documentary) 2010.

SERRY, Robert H.; Dutch diplomatist and UN official; *Special Coordinator for the Middle East Peace Process, Secretary-General's Personal Representative to the Palestine Liberation Organization and the Palestinian Authority, and Secretary-General's Envoy to the Quartet, United Nations;* b. 1950, Calcutta, India; m.; three c.; ed Univ. of Amsterdam; led Middle Eastern Affairs Div., Ministry of Foreign Affairs, The Hague, participated in events leading to Middle East Peace Conf., Madrid during Netherlands EC presidency 1991, diplomatic postings in Bangkok, Moscow, New York (UN) and Kyiv, also held position of Deputy Asst Sec.-Gen. for Crisis Man. and Operations, NATO, fmr Amb. to Ireland; UN Special Coordinator for Middle East Peace Process, Sec.-Gen.'s Personal Rep. to Palestine Liberation Org. and Palestinian Authority, and Sec.-Gen.'s Envoy to Quartet 2007–. *Publications:* Standplaats Kiev 1997; several articles on political and peacekeeping topics, ranging from the Middle East to Eastern Europe. *Address:* Office of the Secretary-General, UN Headquarters, First Avenue at 46th Street, New York, NY 10017, USA (office). *E-mail:* info@un.org (office). *Website:* www.un.org (office).

SERVAN-SCHREIBER, Jean-Claude, LenD; French media executive and journalist; b. 11 April 1918, Paris; s. of the late Robert Servan-Schreiber and Suzanne Crémieux; m. 1st Christiane Laroche 1947 (divorced); m. 2nd Jacqueline

Guix de Pinos 1955 (divorced); two s. three d.; m. 3rd Paule Guinet 1983 (divorced); ed Exeter Coll., Oxford and Univ. of Paris (Sorbonne); served World War II in Flanders 1940, in Resistance 1941–42, in N Africa 1943, France 1944, Germany 1945; with Les Echos 1946–65, Gen. Man. 1957, Dir 1963–65; Deputy for Paris, Nat. Ass. 1965–67; Asst Sec.-Gen. UNR-UDT 1965; Pres. Rassemblement français pour Israël 1967; Dir-Gen. Régie française de publicité 1968–78; mem. Haut Conseil de l'audiovisuel 1973–81; Pres. Groupe Européen des Régisseurs de Publicité Télévisée 1975–78; mem. Conseil politique, RPR 1977–81; Conseiller du Groupe de Presse L'Expansion 1980–93; Special Adviser Mitsubishi Electric (Europe) 1992–2000; Pres. Inst. Arthur Vernes (Medical and Surgical Center) 1993–; Commdr, Légion d'honneur; Médaille mil.; Commdr Ordre nat. du Mérite; Croix de guerre; Croix du Combattant volontaire de la Résistance; Legion of Merit (USA), etc. *Address:* 147 bis rue d'Alésia, 75014 Paris, France. *Telephone:* 1-45-39-96-11. *E-mail:* jcss@orange.fr.

SERVATIUS, Bernhard, DJur; German lawyer; *Partner, Servatius Jenckel Noelle;* b. 14 April 1932, Magdeburg; s. of Rudolf Servatius and Maria Servatius; m. Ingeborg Servatius 1985; ed Univs of Fribourg, Hamburg and other univs; lawyer 1959–; Sr Pnr Dr Servatius & Pnr (legal firm), currently Pnr Servatius Jenckel Noelle; Man. Pnr Treubesitz GmbH, Hamburg (trust co.); legal adviser to Axel Springer and Springer Publishing Group 1970; Chair. Axel Springer Verlag AG, Berlin 1985–2002; Chair. Supervisory Bd Rheinische Merkur GmbH; Chief Rep. of Axel Springer and Acting Chair. of Man. Admin. Verlagshaus Axel Springer 1984; Prof. Hochschule für Musik und Theater, Hamburg; Deputy Chair. Supervisory Bd AWD Holding AG –2008; Chair. German Foundation for Monument Protection 2002–10; mem. Supervisory Bd equitrust Aktiengesellschaft; mem. Advisory Bd EnBW Energie Baden-Württemberg AG, Hapag-Lloyd AG; Hon. Prof., Univ. of Music and Theatre, Hamburg 1984; Federal Cross of Merit (Germany), Bavarian Order of Merit; Hon. DPhil (Weizmann Inst. of Science, Israel) 2000; Austrian Medal for Science and Art. *Address:* Servatius Rechtsanwälte Partnerschaftsgesellschaft, Gänsemarkt 50, 20354 Hamburg, Germany (office). *Telephone:* (40) 35016145 (office). *Fax:* (40) 35016100 (office). *E-mail:* bernhard.servatius@servatius-law.de (office). *Website:* www.servatius -rechtsanwaelte.de (office).

SESAY, Sheku Sambadeen, BA, MA; Sierra Leonean economist and central banker; *Governor, Bank of Sierra Leone;* b. 20 Aug. 1949, Kambia; ed Howard Univ., USA; Econ. Devt and Planning Officer, Ministry of Planning and Econ. Devt Aug.–Dec. 1978; Part-time Lecturer, History of Econ. Thought and Money and Banking, Fourah Bay Coll., Univ. of Sierra Leone 1978–84; Sr Project Officer, Nat. Devt Bank 1979–84; joined ADB as Loans Officer 1984, becoming Sr Country Economist, Prin. Country Economist, Chief Country Economist, North Region 1984–2000, Acting Div. Man., Country Operations Div. 2000–01, Div. Man. 2001–04, Resident Rep., ADB Tanzania Country Office 2004–07; Financial Sec., Ministry of Finance 2007–09; Gov., Bank of Sierra Leone (central bank) 2009–. *Address:* Office of the Governor, Bank of Sierra Leone, Siaka Stevens Street, POB 30, Freetown, Sierra Leone (office). *Telephone:* (22) 226501 (office). *Fax:* (22) 224764 (office). *E-mail:* info@bankofsierraleone.com (office). *Website:* www.bsl.gov.sl (office).

ŠEŠELJ, Vojislav, DJur; Serbian politician, writer and lawyer; *President, Serbian Radical Party;* b. 11 Oct. 1954, Sarajevo; s. of Nikola Šešelj and Danica Šešelj (née Misita); m. Jadranka Pavlović; four s.; ed Sarajevo Univ.; Docent, Sarajevo Univ. 1981–84; Prof., Prishtina Univ. 1991–, was persecuted by authorities for nationalistic activities, arrested and sentenced to eight years' imprisonment 1984, released after 22 months; later arrested twice 1990, 1994–95; Head of Četnik (royalist) Movt 1989; Founder and Pres. Serbian Radical Party 1990–; supported war against Croatia 1991; cand. for presidency of Serbia 1997; Deputy Prime Minister 1998–2001; worked and lectured in European countries, USA, Canada; indicted by Int. Criminal Tribunal for the fmr Yugoslavia (ICTY) for crimes against humanity and war crimes Feb. 2003, trial began Nov. 2007, trial suspended because of alleged witness intimidation 2009, trial resumed Jan. 2009, sentenced to a further 15 months in custody for not respecting the court 24 July 2009, trial resumed Jan.–March 2010, trial still under way and still in custody as of Jan. 2013. *Publications:* more than 100 books including Political Essence of Militarism and Fascism 1979, Dusk of Illusions 1986, Democracy and Dogma 1987, Debrozovisation of Public Mentality 1990, Destruction of Serbian National Being 1992, Actual Political Challenges 1993, Are We Threatened with Slobotomia 1994, Selected Works 1994. *Address:* c/o Serbian Radical Party (Srpska Radikalna Stranka), 11080 Belgrade, Zemun, Magistratski trg 3, Serbia (office); UN Detention, Pompstationsweg 32, Scheveningen (The Hague), The Netherlands. *E-mail:* info@srpskaradikalnastranka.rs (office); info@vseselj.com. *Website:* www .srpskaradikalnastranka.org.rs (office); www.vseselj.com.

SESHADRI, Conjeevaram Srirangachari, BA, PhD, FRS; Indian mathematician and academic; *Professor and Director, Chennai Mathematical Institute;* b. 29 Feb. 1932; m. Sundari 1962; two s.; ed Loyola Coll., Madras Univ., Tata Inst. of Fundamental Research, Bombay Univ.; Research Scholar, Tata Inst. of Fundamental Research, Bombay 1953, Prof., 1965–75, Sr Prof., 1975–84; Sr Prof., Inst. of Math. Sciences, Madras 1984–89; Prof. and Founding Dir Chennai Math. Inst. 1989–; Visiting Prof., Univ. of Paris 1957–60, Harvard Univ. 1974–75, Inst. for Advanced Study, Princeton 1975–76, UCLA, Brandeis Univ., Univ. of Bonn, Kyoto Univ.; Fellow, Indian Nat. Science Acad.; Hon. DSc (Banaras Hindu Univ.); Shanti Swarup Bhatnagar Award 1972, Srinivasa Ramanujan Medal, Indian Acad. of Sciences, Third World Acad. of Sciences Science Award, Trieste Science Prize in Math. (co-recipient) 2006, Padma Bhushan 2009. *Publications:* numerous papers in professional journals on algebraic geometry. *Leisure interest:* Carnatic music. *Address:* Chennai Mathematical Institute, Plot H1, SIPCOT IT Park, Padur PO, Siruseri 603 103, India (office). *Telephone:* (44) 32983441 (office); (44) 27470226 (office). *Fax:* (44) 27470225 (office). *E-mail:* css@cmi.ac.in (office). *Website:* www .cmi.ac.in (office).

SESSIONS, Jefferson Beauregard, III, BA, JD; American lawyer and politician; *Senator from Alabama;* b. 24 Dec. 1946, Selma, Ala; s. of Jefferson Beauregard Sessions and Abbie Sessions (née Powe); m. Mary Montgomery Blackshear 1969; one s. two d.; ed Huntingdon Coll., Montgomery and Univ. of Alabama; grew up in Hybart; admitted to the Ala Bar 1973; Assoc., Guin, Bouldin & Porch, Russellville, Ala 1973–75; Asst US Attorney, US Dept of Justice, Mobile,

Ala 1975–77, US Attorney 1981–93; Assoc. Pnr, Stockman & Bedsole Attorneys, Mobile 1977–81; mem. US Attorney-Gen.'s Advisory Cttee 1987–89, Vice-Chair. 1989; Pnr, Stockman, Bedsole & Sessions 1993–94; Attorney-Gen. for Ala 1996; Senator from Alabama 1997–, mem. Environment and Public Works Cttee, Judiciary Cttee; mem. Bd of Trustees, Exec. Cttee Mobile Bay Area Partnership for Youth 1981–; Chair. Advisory Bd, Ashland Place United Methodist Church, Mobile 1982; First Vice-Pres. Mobile Lions Club 1993–94; Capt. US Army Reserves 1975–85; mem. ABA, Ala Bar Assen, Mobile Bar Assen; US Attorney-Gen.'s Award 1992. *Address:* 326 Russell Senate Office Building, Washington, DC 20510-0104 USA (office). *Telephone:* (202) 224-4124 (office). *Fax:* (202) 224-3149 (office). *Website:* sessions.senate.gov (office).

SESSIONS, William S., JD; American lawyer, government official and judge; *Partner, Holland & Knight LLP;* b. 27 May 1930, Fort Smith, Ark.; s. of William A. Sessions and Edith A. Steele; m. Alice June Lewis 1952; three s. one d.; ed Baylor Univ.; called to Texas Bar 1959; Pnr, McGregor & Sessions, Waco, Tex. 1959–61; Assoc. Tirey, McLaughlin, Gorin & Tirey, Waco 1961–63; Pnr, Haley, Fulbright, Winniford, Sessions & Bice, Waco 1963–69; Chief, Govt Operations Section, Criminal Div. Dept of Justice 1969–71; US Attorney, US Dist Court (Western Dist) Texas, San Antonio 1971–74, US Dist Judge 1974–80, Chief US Dist Judge 1980–87; Dir Fed. Bureau of Investigation (FBI) 1987–93; Pnr, Sessions & Sessions 1995–2000, Holland & Knight LLP 2000–; apptd Vice-Chair. Gov.'s Task Force on Homeland Security for the State of Texas 2002; mem. Gov.'s Anti- Crime Comm. 2002, Judiciary Relations Cttee for the State Bar of Texas; fmr Pres. Waco-McLennan Co. Bar Assen, Fed. Bar Assen of San Antonio, Dist Judges' Assen of the Fifth Circuit; fmr mem. Bd of Dirs Fed. Judicial Center, Washington, DC; mem. Steering Cttee of Coastal Texas 2020, Innocence Project of Nat. Capital Region, Innocence Comm. for Virginia, Texas Comm. on Judicial Efficiency 1995–97, Texas Comm. on a Rep. Student Body 1997–98; serves as arbitrator and mediator for American Arbitration Assen, Int. Center for Dispute Resolution, CPR Inst. of Dispute Resolution (Dist Panelist), Nat. Panel of Distinguished Neutrals, Arbitration Appeal Panel; mem. DC Bar, State Bar of Texas, San Antonio Bar Assen, Fed. Bar Assen, ABA (Initial Chair. Cttee on Independence of the Judiciary 1997, Hon. Co-Chair. Comm. on the 21st Century Judiciary 2002, mem. Advisory Comm. to Standing Cttee on the Law Library of Congress), American Bar Foundation, Judicature Soc., William S. Sessions American Inn of Court, Nat. Assen of Fmr United States Attorneys; mem. Bd of Trustees, Nat. Environmental Educ. and Training Foundation Inc. 2001–; Hon. Dir Martin Luther King Jr Fed. Holiday Comm. 1991–93, 1994–; several hon. degrees; Baylor Univ. Law School Lawyer of the Year 1988, Price Daniel Distinguished Public Service Award 2002, listed in The Best Lawyers In America for Alternative Dispute Resolution 2005–06, Chesterfield Smith Award, Holland & Knight 2008, Constitution Project's Inaugural Constitutional Champion Award 2008. *Publications:* articles in professional journals. *Leisure interests:* climbing, hiking, canoeing. *Address:* Holland & Knight LLP, 2099 Pennsylvania Avenue, NW, Suite 100, Washington, DC 20006, USA (office). *Telephone:* (202) 419-2410 (office). *Fax:* (202) 955-5564 (office). *E-mail:* william.sessions@hklaw.com (office). *Website:* www.hklaw.com (office).

SETCH, Terry, RA, RWA; British artist; b. 11 March 1936, Lewisham, London, England; s. of Frank Setch and Florence Skeggs; m. Dianne Shaw 1967; one d.; ed Sutton and Cheam School of Art and Slade School of Fine Art; Sr Lecturer in Painting, School of Art, Univ. of Wales Inst. 1964–2001; Visiting Lecturer, Emily Carr Coll. of Art, Vancouver, Canada 1981; Artist in Residence, Victorian Coll. of Art, Melbourne, Australia 1983; elected to the Faculty of Painting, British School at Rome 1984; Examiner BA, Slade School of Art, Univ. Coll., London 1985–87; Examiner in Painting MA, Chelsea School of Art, London 1986–89; elected to Faculty of Fine Arts, British School at Rome 1987; External Examiner BA, Faculty of Art, Univ. of Reading 1989–92; mem. Derek Williams Cttee, Nat. Museum and Galleries of Wales 1996–2005; elected to Royal West of England Acad. 2002; elected to RA 2009; Welsh Arts Council comm. for large-scale hoarding poster print 1968, Royal Nat. Eisteddfod Main Prizewinner 1968, Welsh Arts Council Painting Award 1971, John Moores 8 Prizewinner 1972, Welsh Arts Council Comm. Award for Coleg Harlech 1972, Welsh Arts Council Major Artist Award 1978, Print Comm., Royal Nat. Eisteddfod 1978, Third Prize, John Moores Exhbn 1985, shortlist prizewinner, Athena Awards 1988, comm. for a painting for restaurant in Nat. Museum of Wales, Cardiff 1993, Bryan Robertson Trust Award 2009. *Radio:* Art Work: Terry Setch (BBC Radio 3) 2000, Terry Setch – How I Spend My Sundays (Radio Wales) 2001, Inspired – Sisley and his Work in Penarth (BBC Radio Wales) 2007, Pitch (Cardiff Radio) 2011. *Television:* Statements (BBC 2 Wales) 1990, A Word in Your Eye (HTV Wales) 1997, Catalyst (BBC 1 Wales) 1997, Painting the Dragon (BBC Wales) 2000, Jamie Owen Welsh Journeys (BBC 1) 2006, Picturing the Century (BBC Wales), Inspired, Sisley and his Work in Penarth, Framing Wales (presented by Kim Howells, BBC 2 Wales) 2011. *Publications:* New Work by Terry Setch 1992, Terry Setch: A Retrospective 2001, Terry Setch 2009. *Address:* 111 Plymouth Road, Penarth, Vale of Glamorgan, CF64 5DF, Wales. *Telephone:* (29) 2071-2113. *E-mail:* setch@terrysetch.co.uk. *Website:* www.terrysetch.co.uk.

SETCHELL, David Lloyd, MA, FCA; British chartered accountant; b. 16 April 1937, Anston, Yorks., England; s. of Raymond Setchell and Phyllis Jane Lloyd; m. Muriel Mary Davies 1962 (deceased); one s. one d.; ed Woodhouse Grammar School and Jesus Coll., Cambridge; Peat Marwick 1960–64; Shawinigan Ltd 1964–71; Vice-Pres. Gulf Oil Chemicals (Europe) 1971–82; Man. Dir Gulf Oil (GB) Ltd 1982–98; Pres. Inst. of Petroleum 1996–98, Oil Industries Club 1993–95; Council mem. Univ. of Gloucestershire 1994–2007, Chair. 2002–07; Gov. Cheltenham Coll. 1998–2004; Dir Cheltenham Arts Festivals 1994–2005, RAF Personnel and Training Command Bd 2000–06; Fellow Energy Inst.; Dr hc (Univ. of Gloucestershire). *Leisure interests:* golf, music, theatre. *Address:* South Hayes, Sandy Lane Road, Cheltenham, Glos., GL53 9DE, England. *Telephone:* (1242) 571390.

SETH, Vikram, CBE, MA, PhD; Indian author and poet; b. 20 June 1952, Calcutta (now Kolkata); s. of Premnath Seth and Leila Seth; ed Doon School, India, Tonbridge School, UK, Corpus Christi Coll., Oxford, Stanford Univ., USA, Nanjing Univ., People's Repub. of China; Hon. Fellow, Corpus Christi Coll., Oxford 1994; Chevalier des Arts et des Lettres 2001; Pravasi Bharatiya Samman 2005, Padma Shri 2007. *Publications:* Mappings 1980, From Heaven Lake: Travels Through

Sinkiang and Tibet (non-fiction) (Thomas Cook Travel Book Award) 1983, The Humble Administrator's Garden (Commonwealth Poetry Prize) 1985, All You Who Sleep Tonight (trans.) 1985, The Golden Gate: A Novel in Verse 1986, Three Chinese Poets (trans.) 1992, A Suitable Boy (novel) (W. H. Smith Literary Prize 1994, Commonwealth Writers Prize 1994) 1993, Arion and the Dolphin (libretto) 1994, Beastly Tales (animal fables) 1994, An Equal Music (novel) (EMMA BT Ethnic and Multicultural Media Award 2001) 1999, Two Lives (biog.) 2005; several vols of poetry. *Leisure interests:* Chinese calligraphy, music, swimming. *Address:* c/o Jonny Geller, Curtis Brown, Haymarket House, 28–29 Haymarket, London, SW1Y 4SP, England (office). *Telephone:* (20) 7393-4400 (office). *Fax:* (20) 7393-4401 (office). *E-mail:* cb@curtisbrown.co.uk (office). *Website:* www.vikramseth.co.uk.

SETHI, Geet, BA, MBA; Indian billiards player; b. 17 April 1961, Delhi; m. Kiran Sethi; two c.; ed St Xavier's Coll., Ahmedabad, K.K. School of Business Man.; Nat. Billiards Champion 1982, 1985, 1986, 1987, 1988, 1997, 2007; Nat. Snooker Champion 1985' 1986' 1987, 1988; Int. Pontins Snooker Champion 1984, World Amateur Billiards Champion 1985, 1987, 2001, Asian Billiards Champion 1986, World Professional Billiards Champion 1992, 1993, 1995, 1998, 2006, Asian Games (gold medal), Bangkok 1998, Asian Billiards Champion 1987, World Team Snooker Masters Champion 2006, Asian Indoor Games (silver medal), Macau 2007; Co-Founder and mem. Bd of Dirs Olympic Gold Quest program, Foundation for Promotion of Sports and Games; Padma Shri 1986, Arjuna Award 1986, Rajiv Gandhi Khel Ratna 1992–93, K.K. Birla Award 1993, Billiards Player of the Year, World Professional Billiards and Snooker Asscn 1999. *Publication:* Success is Joy 2005. *Address:* Foundation for Promotion of Sports and Games, 3 Neel Kamal, Gandhi Baug Society, Law Garden, Ahmedabad 380 006 (office); 307, Next to Army CSD Depot, Airport Road, Ahmedabad 380 003, India (home). *Telephone:* (79) 26564396 (office); (79) 26564396 (office). *E-mail:* geetsethi@olympicgoldquest.in (office). *Website:* www.olympicgoldquest.in (office).

SETHNESS, Charles Olin, AB, MBA; American government official, financial executive, university administrator and investment banker; *Resident Country Director, Vanuatu, Millennium Challenge Corporation;* b. 24 Feb. 1941, Evanston, Ill.; s. of C. Olin Sethness and Alison Louise Burge; four c. and step-c.; ed New Trier High School, Princeton Univ. and Harvard Business School; Sr Credit Analyst, American Nat. Bank and Trust Co. of Chicago 1963–64; Research Asst, Harvard Business School 1966–67; with Morgan Stanley & Co. 1967–73, 1975–81, Vice-Pres. 1972–73, Man. Morgan & Cie Int. SA, Paris 1971–73, Man. Dir 1975–81; Exec. Dir World Bank Group and Special Asst to Sec. of Treasury 1973–75; Assoc. Dean for External Relations, Harvard Business School, Boston 1981–85; Asst Sec. of the Treasury for Domestic Finance 1985–88; Dir Capital Markets Dept, Int. Finance Corpn 1988–89; Chief Financial Officer IDB 1990–2004; Vice-Pres., Monitoring and Evaluation, interim CEO, Vice-Pres., Accountability, Sr Investment Counsellor and Resident Country Dir, Millennium Challenge Corpn 2004–; Alexander Hamilton Medal, US Treasury Dept 1988. *Leisure interests:* Washington Inst. of Foreign Affairs, Washington Recorder Soc., Nat. Cathedral Choral Soc. *Address:* Millennium Challenge Corporation, P.O. Box 3231, Port Vila, Vanuatu (office); 14525 SW Millikan #80479, Beaverton, OR 97005-2343, USA (home). *Telephone:* (678) 24824 (office); (678) 7756740 (home). *Fax:* (678) 25016 (office). *E-mail:* sethnessc@mcc.gov (office); charlessethness@aol.com (home). *Website:* www.mcc.gov (office).

SETIAWAN, Boenjamin, MD, PhD; Indonesian pharmacologist and business executive; *Founder, Kalbe Farma Tbk;* b. 1933; m.; two c.; ed Univ. of Indonesia, Univ. of California, San Francisco, USA; co-f. Kalbe Farma Tbk with five siblings 1966, becoming Pres. Commr –2008; Adviser, Faculty of Pharmacology, Univ. of Indonesia, Stem Cell Inst. of Indonesia; mem. Bd of Dirs KOMNAS Lansi; mem. Advisory Bd GP Farmasi, KOMNAS Perempuan; Co-founder and Treas., Yayasan Pengembangan Kreativitas Indonesia; mem. Supervisory Bd Kehati (Indonesian Biodiversity Foundation); Lifetime Achievement Entrepreneur of the Year 2005. *Address:* Kalbe Farma Tbk, Kawasan Industri Delta Sillicon, Jl. MH Thamrin Blok A3-I, Lippo-Cikarang, Bekasi 17550, Indonesia (office). *Telephone:* (21) 89907333-37 (office). *Fax:* (21) 89907360 (office). *Website:* www.kalbe.co.id (office).

ŞEULEANU, Dragoş, BA, MBA; Romanian radio journalist, public relations consultant and organization executive; ed Acad. of Econ. Studies, Bucharest, Romanian-American Business School, Univ. of Washington at Seattle; apptd Pres. Trade-Tourism Dept, Romanian Chamber of Commerce and Industry 2001, Vice-Pres. Romanian Chamber of Commerce and Industry –2007, Interim Pres. 2007; fmr Pres. Gen. Man. Romania's Radio Broadcasting Corpn (ROR) where he served as Deputy Dir for Programming, later Human Resources Dir, later Sec.-Gen., later CEO during a 15-year career, active radio journalist at ROR, covered Democratic and Republican conventions 2000, 2004; est. Effective Management Solutions (public relations co.); Pres. Foundation for Democracy, Culture and Liberty; Adjunct Fellow (non-resident), New European Democracies Project, Center for Strategic and Int. Studies, Washington, DC; mem. Int. Press Inst., Vienna; Founding mem. Romanian Chapter of Transparency International, Romanian Asscn of Public Relations Professionals; mem. Bd European Broadcasting Union; fmr Vice-Chair. Forum of the Information Society (Romanian Acad.); expert on ethnic politics, governance, business, information tech. and communications, and regional security; Hon. Adviser, Ministry of the Interior 2000; Hon. mem. Romanian Acad. of Scientists, Foundation of the Romanian Gendarmerie Magazine; Young European for 1994 Prize, Del. of EC in Romania 1994, Medal for 'Faithful Service' in the rank of Cavalier, Pres. of Romania. *Address:* c/o Romanian Chamber of Commerce and Industry, Blvd Octavian Goga nr 2, Sector 3, Bucharest 030982, Romania.

SEVAN, Benon V., MA; Cypriot fmr UN official; b. 18 Dec. 1937; m.; one d.; ed Melkonian Educational Inst. and Columbia Coll. and School of Int. and Public Affairs, Columbia Univ., New York, USA; joined UN 1965; with Dept of Public Information 1965–66; with Secr. of Special Cttee on Decolonization 1966–68; served UN in W Irian (Irian Jaya), Indonesia 1968–72; with Secr. of UN Econ. and Social Council 1973–88; Dir and Sr Political Adviser to Rep. of Sec.-Gen. on Settlement of Situation relating to Afghanistan 1988–89; Personal Rep. of Sec.-Gen. in Afghanistan and Pakistan 1989–92; Rep. of Sec.-Gen. on Implementation of Geneva Accords on Afghanistan 1990–92; Dir Office for Co-ordination of UN Humanitarian and Econ. Assistance Programmes in Afghanistan 1991–92; Asst

Sec.-Gen. Dept of Political Affairs 1992–94; Asst Sec.-Gen. for Conf. and Support Services 1994–97; Asst Sec.-Gen. Office of Security Co-ordination 1994–2002; apptd Exec. Dir Office of Iraq Programme 1997–2004, Head Oil-for-Food Program 1996–2003, resgnd from UN 2005, indicted in 2007 by US Govt on charges of bribery and conspiracy to commit wire fraud, in connection with the UN Oil-for-Food Program.

SEVELE, Hon. Feleti (Fred), BSc, BA, MA, PhD; Tongan politician, business executive and academic; b. 7 July 1944, Ma'ufanga, Nuku'alofa; s. of Viliami Vaka'uta Sevele and Mele Yarnton; m. Ainise Manu; three c.; ed Univ. of Cambridge, UK; mem. Legis. Ass. 1999–, Minister of Labour, Commerce, Industries 2005–08; Interim Prime Minister Feb.–March 2006, Prime Minister (first non-noble) 2006–10, Minister of Finance and Defence 2009–10. *Address:* c/o Office of the Prime Minister, POB 62, Taufa'ahau Road, Kolofo'ou, Nuku'alofa, Tonga.

SEVERIANO TEIXEIRA, Nuno, PhD; Portuguese academic and politician; *Pro-Rector and Full Professor of International Relations, New University of Lisbon;* b. 5 Nov. 1957, Bissau; ed Univ. of Lisbon, European Univ. Inst., Florence, Italy, New Univ. of Lisbon; Researcher, European Univ. Inst., Florence 1989–92; Visiting Prof., Dept of Govt, Georgetown Univ., USA 2000; Visiting Fellow, Center for European Studies, Univ. of Calif., Berkeley, USA 2003; Prof., Dept of Political Sciences and Int. Relations, Faculty of Social and Human Sciences, New Univ. of Lisbon, currently Pro-Rector and Dir Portuguese Inst. of Int. Relations, currently Full Prof. of Int. Relations; Dir Inst. of Nat. Defence 1996–2000; Minister of Internal Admin 2000–02, of Nat. Defence 2006–09; Ordem do Infante D. Henrique Comendados 2000, Grande Oficial 2006. *Publications include:* O Ultimatum Inglês. Política Externa e Política Interna no Portugal de 1890 1990, O Poder e a Guerra. Objectvos nacionais e estratégias políticas na entrada de Portugal na Grande Guerra 1914–1918 1996, The International Politics of Democratization (ed.) 2011, The Europeanization of Portuguese Democracy (co-ed.) 2012; numerous articles in professional journals. *Address:* Universidade Nova de Lisboa, Avenida de Berna, 26-C, 1069-061, Lisbon, Portugal (office). *Telephone:* 213845133. *Fax:* 213845134. *E-mail:* nst@unl.pt (office). *Website:* www.unl.pt (office).

SEVERIN, (Giles) Tim, MA, BLitt; British traveller and writer; b. 25 Sept. 1940, Jorhat, Assam, India; s. of Maurice Watkins and Inge Severin; m. Dorothy Virginia Sherman 1966 (divorced 1979); one d.; ed Tonbridge School, Keble Coll., Oxford; Commonwealth Fellow, USA 1964–66; expeditions: led motorcycle team along Marco Polo's route 1961, canoe and launch down River Mississippi 1965, Brendan Voyage from W Ireland to N America 1977, Sindbad Voyage from Oman to China 1980–81, Jason Voyage from Greece to Soviet Georgia 1984, Ulysses Voyage, Troy to Ithaca 1985, Crusade: on horseback from Belgium to Jerusalem 1987–88, Travels on horseback in Mongolia 1990, China Voyage: bamboo sailing raft Hong Kong-Japan-Pacific 1993, Spice Islands Voyage in Moluccas, E Indonesia 1996, Pacific travels in search of Moby Dick 1998, Latin America travels seeking Robinson Crusoe sources 2000; historical novelist 2005–; Hon. DLitt (Trinity Coll., Dublin) 1996, (Nat. Univ. of Ireland) 2003; Royal Geographical Soc. Gold Medal, Royal Scottish Geographical Soc. Livingstone Medal. *Publications:* Tracking Marco Polo 1964, Explorers of the Mississippi 1967, The Golden Antilles 1970, The African Adventure 1973, Vanishing Primitive Man 1973, The Oriental Adventure 1976, The Brendan Voyage 1978, The Sindbad Voyage 1982, The Jason Voyage 1984, The Ulysses Voyage 1987, Crusader 1989, In Search of Genghis Khan 1991, The China Voyage 1994, The Spice Islands Voyage 1997, In Search of Moby Dick 1999, Seeking Robinson Crusoe 2002, Viking: Odinn's Child (novel) 2004, Viking: Sworn Brother 2005, Viking: King's Man 2005, Corsair 2007, Buccaneer 2008, Sea Robber 2009. *Address:* Inchy Bridge, Timoleague, Co. Cork, Ireland. *Telephone:* (23) 88446127. *E-mail:* severin.tim@gmail.com. *Website:* www.timseverin.net.

SEVERINO, Rodolfo, MA; Philippine diplomatist; *Head, ASEAN Studies Centre, Institute of Southeast Asian Studies;* b. 22 March 1936, Manila; m. Rowena V. Romero; two s. one d.; ed Ateneo de Manila Univ., Johns Hopkins Univ. School of Advanced Int. Studies, Washington, DC; Assoc. Ed. Manor Press Inc. 1956–59, Philippine Int. 1957–59, Marketing Horizons 1961–64; with Operation Brotherhood, Laos 1959–61; Special Asst to Senator Raul S. Manglapus, Philippine Senate 1961–64; information asst, UN Information Centre, Manila 1964–65; Third, then Second and First Sec., Embassy in Washington, DC 1967–74; Special Asst to Under-Sec. of Foreign Affairs 1974–76, Under-Sec. 1992–97; Chargé d'Affaires, Embassy in Beijing 1976–78; Consul-Gen., Houston, Texas 1979–86; Asst Sec. for Asian and Pacific Affairs 1986–88; Amb. to Malaysia 1988–92; Under-Sec. of Foreign Affairs 1992–97; Sec.-Gen. ASEAN 1998–2003; adviser to Cambodian Govt Jan.–June 2002; Prof., Asian Inst. of Man., Manila 2003–04; Visiting Sr Research Fellow, Inst. of Southeast Asian Studies, Singapore 2004–, currently also Head, ASEAN Studies Centre; Order of Sikatuna, rank of Datu (Philippines) 1997, rank of Rajah; Royal Award (Cambodia) 2002. *Publications include:* ASEAN Faces the Future 2001, ASEAN Today and Tomorrow 2002, Framing the ASEAN Charter 2005, Southeast Asia in Search of an ASEAN Community 2006, ASEAN 2008, ASEAN Regional Forum 2009, Where in the World is the Philippines? 2010. *Address:* ASEAN Studies Centre, Institute of Southeast Asian Studies, 30 Heng Mui Keng Terrace, Pasir Panjang, Singapore 119614 (office); 2D Hong San Walk, Palm Gardens #16-06, Singapore 689050, Singapore (home). *Telephone:* 67780955 (office); 63101794 (home). *Fax:* 67756264 (office). *E-mail:* severino@iseas.edu.sg (office); roseverino@hotmail.com. *Website:* www.aseanstudiescentre.org (office); www.iseas.edu.sg (office).

SEVERINO DI BENEDETTO, Paola; Italian lawyer, academic and politician; *Professor of Criminal Law, LUISS Guido Carli University;* b. 22 Oct. 1948, Naples; ed La Sapienza Univ., Rome; fmr Assoc. Prof. of Criminal Law, Faculty of Economy and Trade, Univ. of Perugia, later Chair. of Criminal and Commercial Law 1987, Full Prof., Faculty of Econs 1995–; Lecturer and Chair. of Criminal Law, LUISS Guido Carli Univ., Rome 1987–90, Asst Prof. 1990–95, Prof. 1998–, Dean, Faculty of Law 2003–06, Deputy Vice-Chancellor 2006–; Vice-Pres. Military Council of the Magistracy 1997–2001; Minister of Justice (in Mario Monti's 'govt of technocrats') 2011–13; fmr Lecturer in Criminal Law, Scuola Ufficiali Carabinieri, Rome; mem. Editorial Bd Enciclopedia giuridica Treccani; legal adviser to numerous cos, banks and trade asscns; mem. Avvocati di Roma (bar asscn) 1975–; fmr mem. several ministerial cttees on reform of criminal law and criminal procedure. *Address:* Department of Law, LUISS Guido Carli University, Viale Porec, 11, 00198 Rome,

Italy (office). *Telephone:* (06) 85225294 (office). *Fax:* (06) 85225852 (office). *E-mail:* pseverino@luiss.it (office). *Website:* didattica.giurisprudenza.luiss.it (office).

SEVIGNY, Chloë Stevens; American actress; b. 18 Nov. 1974, Darien, Conn.; d. of H. David Sevigny and Janine Sevigny (née Malinowski); early career as fashion model, New York; film debut in Kids 1995; has also designed several vintage-style clothing collections 2006–. *Films include:* Kids 1995, The Last Days of Disco 1998, Boys Don't Cry (Satellite Award for Best Supporting Actress in a Drama, Sierra Award for Best Supporting Actress, Independent Spirit Award for Best Supporting Actress) 1999, A Map of the World 1999, American Psycho 2000, Demonlover 2002, Dogville 2003, The Brown Bunny 2003, Shattered Glass 2003, Melinda and Melinda 2004, Broken Flowers 2005, Sisters 2006, The Killing Room 2009, Barry Munday 2010, Mr Nice 2010, The Wait 2011, Lovelace 2013. *Television:* Will & Grace 2004, Big Love (Golden Globe Award for Best Supporting Actress 2010) 2006–11, Louie 2012, Hit and Miss 2012, American Horror Story: Asylum 2012–13, Portlandia 2013, The Mindy Project 2013. *Address:* Endeavor, 9601 Wilshire Blvd, Beverly Hills, CA 90210, USA (office). *Telephone:* (310) 248-2000 (office).

SEVILLA, Adolfo Leonel; Honduran politician; mem. Partido Liberal (PL), Financial Sec., PL Cen. Exec. Council 2001–; Deputy Minister of Defence –2009, Minister of Defence 2009–10. *Address:* c/o Ministry of National Defence, 5a Avda, 4a Calle, Tegucigalpa, Honduras (office).

SEVÓN, Leif, LLM; Finnish judge; b. 31 Oct. 1941, Helsingfors; s. of Enzio Sevón and Ulla Sevón; m. (divorced); one s. one d.; ed Univ. of Helsinki; Asst Univ. of Helsinki 1966–71, asst Prof. 1971–74; Counsellor of Legislation, Ministry of Justice 1973–78; Sr Judge, Chamber Pres. City Court of Helsinki 1979–80; Dir of Legislation, Ministry of Justice 1980–86, Dir-Gen. Dept of Legislation 1986–91; Judge, Supreme Court of Justice 1991; Counsellor, Dept of Trade, Ministry of Foreign Affairs 1991–92; Pres. EFTA Court 1994; Judge, Court of Justice of European Communities 1995–2002; Pres. Supreme Court of Finland 2002–05 (retd); Commdr, Grand Cross Order of White Rose of Finland 2003, Nordstjärn-corden (Sweden) 2003; Hon. LLD (Stockholm) 1999, (Helsinki) 2000. *Publications:* books, articles and translations. *Address:* c/o The Supreme Court of Finland, Pohjoisesplanadi 3, 00170 Helsinki, Finland.

SEWELL, Brian; British art historian and art critic; *Art Critic, Evening Standard;* art critic for Evening Standard newspaper; British Press Awards Critic of the Year 1988, Arts Journalist of the Year 1994, Hawthornden Prize for Art Criticism 1995, Foreign Press Asscn Arts Writer of the Year 2000, The Orwell Prize 2003, Critic of the Year, British Press Awards 2004. *Television includes:* The Works: Minette Walters and the Missing Masterpiece 1996, The Naked Pilgrim 2003, The Road to Santiago 2003, Grand Tour 2006, Dirty Dalì: A Private View 2007. *Publications:* South from Ephesus 1988, The Reviews that Caused the Rumpus 1994, An Alphabet of Villains 1995, Outsider (autobiog.) 2011, Naked Emperors 2012. *Leisure interests:* dogs, old motor cars. *Address:* Vasari Press, 74 Leopold Road, London, SW19 7JQ, England (office). *Telephone:* (20) 8946-9300 (office).

SEWELL, Rufus Frederick; British actor; b. 29 Oct. 1967; s. of Bill Sewell; London Critics' Circle Best Newcomer 1992, Broadway Theatre World Award 1995, London Evening Standard Award for Best Actor 2006. *Stage appearances include:* Royal Hunt of the Sun, Comedians, The Lost Domain, Peter and the Captain, Pride and Prejudice, The Government Inspector, The Seagull, As You Like It, Making it Better, Arcadia, Translations, Rat in the Skull, Macbeth, Luther, Rock 'N' Roll (London Critics' Circle Best Actor 2006, Best Actor, Laurence Olivier Awards 2007). *Television appearances include:* The Last Romantics, Gone to Seed, Middlemarch, Dirty Something, Citizen Locke, Cold Comfort Farm, Henry IV, Charles II: The Power and the Passion 2003, Taming of the Shrew 2005, Eleventh Hour (series) 2008–09, The Pillars of the Earth (series) 2010. *Film appearances include:* Twenty-One 1991, Dirty Weekend 1993, A Man of No Importance 1994, Victory 1995, Carrington 1995, Hamlet 1996, The Woodlanders 1997, Dangerous Beauty 1998, Dark City 1998, Martha, Meet Frank, Daniel and Laurence 1998, Illuminata 1998, At Sachem Farm 1998, In a Savage Land 1999, Bless the Child 2000, A Knight's Tale 2001, Extreme Ops 2002, Victoria Station 2003, The Legend of Zorro 2005, Tristan + Isolde 2006, The Illusionist 2006, Paris, je t'aime 2006, Amazing Grace 2006, The Holiday 2006, The Ushers 2010, Abraham Lincoln: Vampire Hunter 2012. *Address:* c/o Julian Belfrage Associates, 3rd Floor, 9 Argyll Street, London, W1F 7TG, England (office). *E-mail:* renata@rufussewell.net (office). *Website:* www.rufussewell.net (office).

SEWERYN, Andrzej; Polish actor and theatre director; b. 25 April 1946, Heilbronn, Germany; s. of Zdzisław Seweryn and Zofia Seweryn; m. 1st Krystyna Janda (divorced 1979); m. 2nd Laurence Swweryn (divorced); m. Mireille Maalouf 1988; two s. one d.; ed State Higher School of Drama, Warsaw; actor Athenaeum Theatre, Warsaw 1968–82, Peter Brook's Group 1984–88, perm. mem. Comédie Française, Paris 1993–; co-operation with film, TV and radio; mem. SPATiF (Asscn of Polish Theatre and Film Actors) 1969–82; Prof. School of Theatre National de Chaillot, Nat. School of Arts and Technical Theatre, Lyon; Prof. of Drama, Nat. Conservatory of Dramatic Art, Paris 2001–; Chevalier des Arts et des Lettres 1995, Kt's Cross, Order of Polonia Restituta 1997, Ordre Nat. du Mérite 1999; Prize Berlin Int. Film Festival for Conductor 1979, Best Actor, French Film Awards for Unpleasant Man 1996, Prize of Le Syndicat professionnel de la Critique dramatique et musicale de France 1996, Polish TV Award, Polish Film Festival, Gdansk 2000. *Films:* Zenon in The Border 1977, Rościszewski in Without Anaesthetic 1978, Ksiądz in The Brute 1979, Kung-fu 1979, Conductor 1979, Mahabharata 1988, French Revolution 1989, Schindler's List 1994, Journey to the East 1994, Total Eclipse 1995, Unpleasant Man 1996, With Fire and Sword 1998, Billboard 1998, Pan Tadeusz (The Last Foray in Lithuania) 1999, The Primate 2000, The Revenge 2002, Par amour (TV) 2003, A ton image 2004, Who Never Lived (dir) 2006, Nightwatching 2007, Possibility of an Island 2008. *Theatre:* (actor) leading roles in Don Carlos, Peer Gynt, Don Juan; (dir) Le Mariage forcé by Molière, Comédie Française 1999, Le Mal court by Jacques Audiberti, Comédie Française 2000, Tartuffe 2002. *Television includes:* Kliefhorn in Polish Roads 1977, Marek in On the Silver Globe 1976–79, Bukacki in Połaniecki's Family 1977, Roman in Roman and Magda 1979, Ekipa 2007, 39 i pół 2009, Little Rose 2010, Uwiklanie 2011, Vous n'avez encore rien vu 2012; numerous other roles on TV.

Address: Comédie Française, Place Colette, 75001 Paris, France (office). *E-mail:* informations@comedie-francaise.org (office); www.comedie-francaise.fr (office).

SEXTON, John Edward, BA, MA, PhD, JD; American professor of law, university administrator and lawyer; *President, New York University;* b. 1944, Brooklyn, NY; m. Lisa E. Goldberg (died 2007); one s. one d.; ed Fordham Coll., Fordham Univ., Harvard Law School; Prof. of Religion, St Francis Coll., Brooklyn 1966–73, Dept Chair. 1970–75; Law Clerk, Judges David Bazelon and Harold Leventhal Court of Appeals 1979–80, to Chief Justice Warren Burger, Supreme Court 1980–81; joined Law Faculty, New York Univ. (NYU) 1981, apptd Dean 1988, currently Dean Emer., Benjamin Butler Prof. of Law and Pres. NYU 2002–; served as Special Master Supervising Pretrial Proceedings in Love Canal Litigation 1983–93; Founding Chair. NASD Dispute Resolution 2000–02; Chair. New York Acad. of Sciences, Comm. of Ind. Colls and Univs of New York, Fed. Reserve Bank of New York 2003–06, Fed. Reserve Systems Council of Chairs 2006; mem. Bd of Dirs Nat. Asscn of Securities Dealers 1996–98, New York State Comm. on Higher Educ., American Council on Educ., Inst. of Int. Educ., Asscn for a Better New York; fmr Pres. American Asscn of Law Schools; mem. Asscn of American Univ. Presidents, Council on Foreign Relations; Fellow, American Acad. of Arts and Sciences, Foreign Policy Asscn, New York; Chevalier, Légion d'honneur 2008; Dr hc (Fordham Univ., St Francis Coll., St John's Univ., Syracuse Univ., Katholieke Universiteit Leuven, St Joseph's Coll., Univ. of Rochester, Univ. of Surrey, Univ. of Warwick); Vol. 60 of NYU's Annual Survey of American Law dedicated in his honour, named by Emory University as "Outstanding High School Debate Coach of the Last 50 Years" for work he did from 1960–75, honoured at Harvard Law Review Annual Banquet, named Alumnus of the Year, Fordham Univ. and Brooklyn Prep, NASPA President's Award 2012. *Publications:* Redefining the Supreme Court's Role: A Theory of Managing the Federal Court System, Civil Procedure: Cases and Materials (co-author), Baseball as a Road to God: Seeing Beyond the Game 2013; numerous book chapters and articles. *Address:* Office of the President, New York University, 70 Washington Square South, New York, NY 10012, USA (office). *Telephone:* (212) 998-2345 (office). *Fax:* (212) 995-4790 (office). *E-mail:* john.sexton@nyu.edu (office). *Website:* www.nyu .edu/about/leadership-university-administration/office-of-the-president.html (office).

SEXWALE, (Gabriel) Tokyo; South African business executive and politician; b. 5 March 1953, Orlando West, Soweto; s. of Frank Sexwale; m. Judy Moon; one s. one d.; ed Univs of Botswana, Lesotho, Swaziland; joined African Nat. Congress (ANC) in 1970s; went into exile and underwent officers' mil. training in Soviet Union 1975; returned to South Africa as underground fighter in ANC's Spear of the Nation armed wing 1976, imprisoned for 13 years on Robben Island for guerrilla activities; returned to Johannesburg, served as Head Public Liaison Dept of ANC HQ, then apptd Head Special Projects under Mil. HQ 1989; elected mem. Exec. Cttee ANC, Pretoria-Witwatersrand-Vereeniging (now Gauteng) Prov. 1990, Chair. 1994–97, Premier 1994–97; Minister of Human Settlements 2009–13; mem. ANC Nat. Exec. Cttee 1991–97; left politics for business sector and co-f. Mvelaphanda Mining, expanded into Mvelaphanda Holdings Pty Ltd (now Mvelaphanda Group Ltd), Chair. 2002–07, Chair. (non-exec.) 2007, currently Exec. Chair., also Chair. of related cos Trans Hex Group Ltd, Mvelaphanda Resources Ltd, Northam Platinum Ltd; Owner, Jonga Entabeni; CEO Batho Bonke; mem. Bd of Dirs GFI-SA, Gold Fields Ltd, ASBA Group, Allied Electronics Corpn Ltd, Desta Power Matla, Voltex, De Montfort Univ., UK; Pres. South African/Russian Business, Technological and Cultural Asscn; Vice-Pres. South African/Japanese Business Forum; Chancellor Vaal Univ. of Technology; Trustee, Nelson Mandela Foundation, Business Trust, Robben Island Ex-Prisoners Trust, Global Philanthropists Circle, Synergos Inst.; Patron Johannesburg Child and Family Welfare Soc., Streetwise South Africa, Save the Family Fund, The Sky is No Limit; Hon. Consul General of Finland in South Africa; Légion d'honneur, Cross-of-Valour (Ruby Class) (South Africa), Order of the Freedom of Havana (Cuba); Dr hc (Univ. of Nottingham, UK, De Montfort Univ.); Reach and Teach Leadership Award, USA. *Address:* Mvelaphanda Group Ltd., POB 1639, Rivonia 2128, South Africa (office). *Telephone:* (11) 2904200 (office). *Website:* www .mvelagroup.co.za (office).

SEYDOUX FORNIER DE CLAUSONNE, Jérôme; French business executive; *Co-President, Pathé;* b. 21 Sept. 1934, Paris; s. of René Seydoux Fornier de Clausonne and Geneviève Schlumberger; m. 1st (divorced); three s. one d.; m. 2nd Sophie Desserteaux-Bessis 1988; one s.; ed Lycées Montaigne, Louis-le-Grand and Buffon; financial analyst Istel, Lepercq and Co. Inc. NY 1962–63; sleeping pnr Bank of Neuflize, Schlumberger, Mallet 1964, Pnr 1966, mem. Bd of Dirs 1969–70; Admin. Schlumberger Ltd 1969, Exec. Vice-Pres. 1970, Dir Gen. 1975–76; Admin. Compagnie Deutsch 1964–; mem. Bd of Dirs Danone (fmrly BSN) 1970–2005, fmr Admin.; Pres. Pricel 1976; Pres. Chargeurs 1980–96, later Vice-Pres., Dir-Gen., currently Vice-Chair., CEO and Dir; Pres. Admin. Council of France 5 1986; Pres., Dir-Gen. Pathé Palace (fmrly Pathé Cinema) 1991–2000, Chair. Supervisory Cttee 2000–02, Co-Pres. 2002–; Vice-Pres. Advisory Bd, Mont-Blanc Co. 2000–; Chair. BSkyB 1998–99; owner Libération newspaper; Officier, Légion d'honneur. *Leisure interests:* skiing, golf. *Address:* Pathé, 2 rue Lamennais, 75008 Paris, France (office). *Website:* www.pathe.com (office).

SEYDOUX FORNIER DE CLAUSONNE, Michel; French business executive and film producer; *Chairman and President, Lille OSC Football Club;* b. 11 Sept. 1947, Paris; grand-s. of Marcel Schlumberger; brother of Jerome and Nicolas Seydoux Fornier de Clausonne; ed École Alsacienne; began career as Asst to Pres. of Org. centrale des camps et activités de jeunesse 1968–71; Founder and Pres. Caméra One (production co.); Pres. Air Littoral 1992–98; Admin., Gaumont; mem. Bd of Trustees, Pathé; co-owns, with Pierre Gagnaire, Le Gaya rive gauche (seafood restaurant), Paris; Chair. and Pres. Lille OSC football club 2002–; mem. Council of Admin, Ligue de football professionelle (LFP) 2005–, Bureau of LFP 2007–, Pres. Marketing Comm. 2008–; Chevalier des Arts et des Lettres. *Films produced:* Lily aime-moi 1974, F . . . comme Fairbanks 1976, Don Giovanni 1979, Hôtel de France 1987, Cyrano de Bergerac 1990, Urga 1991, Prospero's Books 1991, Anna 1992, Toxic Affair 1993, Smoking/No Smoking 1993, Soleil trompeur 1994, On connaît la chanson 1997, Le Barbier de Sibérie 1999, René 2002, Le Filmeur 2005, Les Ambitieux 2006. *Address:* LOSC Lille Métropole, Domaine de Luchin, Grand Rue BP 79, 59780 Camphin-en-Pévèle, France (office). *Telephone:*

(8) 92-68-56-72 (office). *Fax:* (3) 20-17-71-78 (office). *E-mail:* info@losc.fr (office). *Website:* www.losc.fr (office).

SEYDOUX FORNIER DE CLAUSONNE, Nicolas Pierre, LenD; French business executive; *President-Director-General, Gaumont;* b. 16 July 1939, Paris; s. of René Seydoux Fornier de Clausonne and Geneviève Schlumberger; m. Anne-Marie Cahen-Salvador 1964; two c.; ed Lycée Buffon, Faculté de Droit, Paris, New York Business School and Inst. d'Etudes Politiques, Paris; Head of Legal Service, Cie Int. pour l'Informatique, Paris 1967–70; financial analyst Morgan, Stanley & Co. Inc. New York 1970–71, Morgan & Cie Int. SA Paris 1971–74; Vice-Pres.-Dir-Gen. Gaumont 1974, Pres.-Dir-Gen. 1975–; Pres. Fédération Nat. des Distributeurs de Films 1988–2001, Bureau de liaison des industries cinématographiques (BLIC) 2000, Asscn de Lutte contre la Piraterie Audiovisuelle (ALPA), Asscn des Producteurs Indépendants (API); Chair. Forum d'Avignon - Culture, Economy, Media 2008–; Vice-Chair. Supervisory Bd Arte France; mem. Bd of Dirs Schlumberger 1982–; Officier Légion d'honneur. *Leisure interests:* vintage cars, skiing. *Address:* Gaumont, 30 Avenue Charles de Gaulle, 92200 Neuilly-sur-Seine (office); 5 place du Palais-Bourbon, 75007 Paris, France (home). *Telephone:* 1-46-43-24-24 (office). *Fax:* 1-46-43-21-25 (office). *Website:* www.gaumont.com (office).

SEYMOUR, Lynn, CBE; Canadian fmr ballet dancer and choreographer; b. 8 March 1939, Wainwright, Alberta; d. of E.V. Springett; m. 1st Colin Jones 1963 (divorced 1974); three s.; m. 2nd Philip Pace 1974; m. 3rd Vanya Hackel 1983 (divorced 1988); ed Sadler's Wells School, Royal Ballet School; graduated into Royal Ballet 1957; promoted to Soloist rank 1958, to Prin. 1958; prima ballerina Berlin Opera Ballet 1966–69; Principal Guest Ballerina Artist, Royal Ballet 1971–78; Artistic Dir Munich State Opera Ballet 1978–80, Ballet Bayerische Staatsoper 1979–80, Greek Nat. Opera Ballet 2006–07 (resgnd); Guest Artist with other cos including Alvin Ailey; Evening Standard Drama Award 1977. *Ballets:* The Burrow 1958, Swan Lake 1958, Giselle 1958, The Invitation 1960, The Two Pigeons 1961, Symphony 1963, Romeo and Juliet 1965, Anastasia 1967, Dances at a Gathering, The Concert, The Seven Deadly Sins, Flowers 1972, Shukumei, The Four Seasons 1975, Side Show, Rituals 1975, Manon Lescaut 1976, A Month in the Country 1976, Mayerling 1978, Manon 1978, Choreography for Rashomon 1976, The Court of Love 1977, Intimate Letters 1978, Mae and Polly, Boreas, Tattooed Lady, Wolfy, the Ballet Rambert 1987. *Films:* as actress: Dancers 1987, Wittgenstein 1993, Relative Values 2000. *Television:* Tempo 1965, The Little Vampire 1986–87, Dance for the Camera 1998. *Publication:* Lynn: Leaps and Boundaries (autobiography with Paul Gardner) 1984.

SEZER, Ahmet Necdet, BA, LLM, PhD; Turkish judge and fmr head of state; b. 13 Sept. 1941, Afyon; m.; three c.; ed Univ. of Ankara; served in mil. service at Land Forces Acad.; Judge in Ankara, then Dicle and Yerköy; Supervisory Judge High Court of Appeal, Ankara; mem. High Court of Appeal 1983, Constitutional Court 1988–2000, Chief Justice 1998–2000; Pres. of Turkey 2000–07. *Address:* c/o Office of the President, Cumhurbaşkanlığı, Köşku, Çankaya, Ankara, Turkey.

SGOUROS, Dimitris; Greek pianist; b. 30 Aug. 1969, Athens; s. of Sotirios Sgouros and Marianthi Sgouros; ed Univ. of Athens, Athens Conservatory of Music, Univ. of Maryland, USA, St Peter's Coll., Oxford and Royal Acad. of Music, London, UK; debut in Piraeus aged seven; numerous concerts in Europe from 1980; solo piano recital aged 11, to audience of 4,000 at Herodes Atticus Theatre of Athens 1981; first US appearance aged 12, with Nat. Symphony Orchestra of Washington, Carnegie Hall, New York 1982; appeared at Prague Spring Festival with Sir Charles Mackeras and the Czech Philharmonic Orchestra playing Beethoven's Piano Concerto No. 4 1986; played 12 different piano concertos over six nights with Singapore Symphony Orchestra, Sgouros Festival, Singapore 1990; has played in all the major cities and concert houses and on all the major radio and TV stations world-wide; repertoire of 45 piano concertos and large number of solo piano and chamber music works; took part in cultural events at Los Angeles Olympics 1984, Athens Olympics 2004, Beijing Olympics 2008; opening recital, Newport Music Festival, RI 2011; Italian tour with Budapest Festival Orchestra 2013; Rotary Club of Athens Award 1981, Acad. of Athens Award 1982, Los Angeles 1984, Athens Conservatory Gold Medal 1984, Tom Brandley Award, Los Angeles 1984, Leonardo da Vinci Int. Prize, The Lions: Melvin Jones Fellow 2000, Chopin Diploma (Poland) 2010, and many other awards. *Television:* Chopin's Piano Concerto No. 1 with Simon Bolivar Youth Orchestra, Conservatory of Music, Caracas (televised nationally on American A&E Network) 1982; Tonight Show Starring Johnny Carson (NBC). *Recordings include:* works by Schumann, Brahms, Rachmaninov, Tchaikovsky, Liszt, Mozart and Chopin with the Berlin Philharmonic, London Philharmonic and Sofia Philharmonic Orchestras and the Radio Orchestra of Slovenia, Capriccio's Elysium Recordings (USA), Grieg Piano Concerto with Borusan Istanbul Philharmonic Orchestra 2000, Rachmaninov Piano Concertos Nos 2 and 3 with Cyprus State Orchestra (for Steinway Club 150th anniversary, recorded live). *Leisure interests:* mathematics, conducting opera, languages. *Address:* Tompazi 28, 18537 Piraeus (home); Sahturi 25, 18535 Piraeus, Greece (office). *Telephone:* 693-2265110 (mobile); (210) 8959778 (office). *Fax:* (210) 8956477 (home); (210) 4538737 (office). *E-mail:* info@sgouros-pianist .com (office). *Website:* www.sgouros-pianist.com (office).

SGRECCIA, HE Cardinal Elio; Italian ecclesiastic; *President Emeritus of the Roman Curia;* b. 6 June 1928, Arcevia, Prov. of Ancona, Marche region; ordained priest 1952; Titular Bishop of Zama Minor 1992–; Sec. Pontifical Council for the Family 1992–96; Pres. Pontifical Acad. for Life 2005–08, Pres. Emer. of the Roman Curia 2008–; apptd Cardinal-Deacon of S. Angelo in Pescheria, cr. Cardinal (non-voting) 20 Nov. 2010. *Address:* c/o Pontifical Academy for Life, Via della Conciliazione 1, 00193 Rome, Italy. *Telephone:* (06) 69882423. *E-mail:* pav@ acdlife.va. *Website:* www.vatican.va/roman_curia/pontifical_academies/acdlife; www.academiavita.org.

SHA, Ming; Chinese business executive; Gen. Man. Xinxing Cathay International Group Co. Ltd (fmrly Xinxing Ductile Iron Pipes Co. Ltd). *Address:* Xinxing Cathay International Group, 27F Office Tower, Beijing Fortune Plaza, 7 Dongsanhuan Zhong Road, Beijing 100020, People's Republic of China (office). *Telephone:* (10) 59290000 (office). *Fax:* (10) 59290029 (office). *E-mail:* service@xxpgroup.com (office). *Website:* english.xxcig.com (office).

SHA, Zukang; Chinese diplomatist and UN official; b. Sept. 1947, Jiangsu prov.; m.; one s.; ed Nanjing Univ.; staff mem., Embassy in London 1971–74, in Sri Lanka

1974–80, Attaché and Third Sec., Embassy in Delhi 1980–85, Deputy Div. Dir and First Sec. Dept of Int. Orgs and Confs 1985–88, Adviser and Deputy Dir-Gen. 1992–95, First Sec. and Adviser, Perm. Mission to UN, New York 1988–92, Amb. for Disarmament Affairs and Deputy Perm. Rep. to UN Office and Other Int. Orgs, Geneva, Switzerland 1995–97, Dir-Gen. Dept of Arms Control 1997–2001, Perm. Rep. to UN, Geneva 2001–07; Under-Sec.-Gen. for Econ. and Social Affairs, UN, New York 2007–12, Sec.-Gen. Rio+20 (UN Conf. on Sustainable Devt 2012) 2010–12. *Address:* c/o Office of the Under-Secretary-General for Economic and Social Affairs, United Nations, Room DC2-2320, New York, NY 10017, USA.

SHAABAN, Shaaban, PhD; Egyptian diplomatist and UN official; *Under-Secretary-General, United Nations Department for General Assembly and Conference Management;* b. 13 June 1942, Port Said; m.; three c.; ed Brussels Univ.; rep. to ECOSOC, UNDP and various other cttees 1984–88; Amb. to Belgium and Luxembourg 1993–97, to Denmark and Lithuania 1998–2000; Head of Perm. Mission to EU, Brussels 1993–97; Deputy Minister of Foreign Affairs responsible for Africa 1997–98; Deputy Minister for Information, Research and Assessment 2000–01; Deputy Minister for Foreign Affairs responsible for Europe 2001–04; Co-ordinator of First Session of Euro-Mediterranean Parl. Ass. 2005; Adviser to Minister of Foreign Affairs 2004–07; Nat. Co-ordinator for Reform Initiatives in Middle East 2004–07; Diplomatic Adviser to Speaker of the House, Egyptian Parl. 2004–07; Under-Sec.-Gen., Dept for Gen. Ass. and Conf. Man., UN, New York 2007–; Order of Merit (Egypt) 1977, Chevalier, Ordre nat. du Mérite 1978, Grand Croix de l'Ordre de la Couronne (Belgium) 1997. *Publications:* The United Nations Secretary-General: The Man and the Post 1971, The Analysis of International Relations (in Arabic) 1984. *Leisure interests:* tennis, swimming, reading. *Address:* Department for General Assembly and Conference Management, United Nations, New York, NY 10017, USA (office). *Telephone:* (212) 963-8363 (office). *Fax:* (212) 963-4879 (office). *E-mail:* shaabans@un.org (office). *Website:* www.un.org/Depts/ DGACM (office).

SHAATH, Nabeel A., BA, MBA, PhD, DJur; Palestinian politician, diplomatist, consultant and academic; *Senior Adviser to President of Palestinian National Authority;* b. 1938, Safad; m.; two s. two d.; ed Univ. of Alexandria, Egypt, Univ. of Pennsylvania, Wharton School of Business, USA; fmr Business School Prof., taught Finance and Econs, Univ. of Pennsylvania, USA 1961–65, academic positions at Univs of Cairo and Alexandria 1965–69; Dean, School of Business Admin, American Univ. in Beirut 1969–75; consultant to several govts, in Org. of Shuaiab industrial zone, Kuwait, power sector in Saudi Arabia, public transportation in Gulf Area; est. Engineering and Management Inst. and Arab Centre for Admin. Devt in Beirut, Cairo and 14 brs in other Arab countries; mem. Fatah Cen. Cttee, del. to Middle E Peace Conf., Madrid 1991; mem. PLO–Israel peace negotiations, Oslo, Norway and Washington, DC; First Head of PLO Del. to UN, Adviser to Yasser Arafat, wrote his speech to UN Gen. Ass. 1974; Palestinian Authority Minister of Planning and Int. Co-operation 1994–2003, Minister of Foreign Affairs 2003–05; Deputy Prime Minister 2005–06; elected to Palestinian Legis. Council, Rep. of Khan Younis, Gaza Strip 1996–; Rep. of Palestine to world media confs, including World Econ. Forum; Acting Prime Minister of Palestinian Authority 2005, currently Sr Adviser to Pres. of Palestinian Nat. Authority. *Address:* c/o Fatah, Ramallah, Palestinian Autonomous Areas.

SHABDURASULOV, Igor Vladimirovich; Russian civil servant; *President, Triumph Fund;* b. 3 Oct. 1957, Tashkent; m.; three c.; ed Moscow State Univ.; Head, UNESCO Project Great Silk Way, Russian Acad. of Sciences 1983–86; on staff Div. of Science, Culture and Educ., Russian Govt; mem., Admin. of Russian Presidency, then Head, Dept of Culture, Russian Govt 1993–94; Head, Dept of Culture and Information, Russian Govt 1994–98; Deputy Head, Admin. of Russian Presidency, Head Group of Speech Writers April–Sept. 1998; Dir-Gen. Russian Public TV 1998–99; Deputy Head Admin. of Russian Presidency 1999–2000; Pres. Triumph Fund 2000–; Chair. Bd of Dirs TV-6 Co. March–May 2001; mem. Bd of Trustees, Virtual Radio and TV Museum. *Address:* Triumph Fund, Povarskaya str. 8/1, 102069 Moscow, Russia (office). *Telephone:* (495) 916-54-96 (office).

SHACKLETON OF BELGRAVIA, Baroness (Life Peer), cr. 2010, of Belgravia in the City of Westminster; **Fiona Shackleton,** LVO, LLD; British solicitor; *Partner, Payne Hicks Beach;* b. (Fiona S. Charkham), 26 May 1956, London; d. of Jonathan Charkham and Moira Elizabeth Frances Charkham (née Salmon); Salmon family co-owners of J. Lyons & Co. cornerhouse empire, cousin to Nigella and Dominic Lawson and George Monbiot; m. Ian Shackleton (relative of Antarctic explorer Sir Ernest Shackleton); two d.; ed Benenden School, Kent, Univ. of Exeter; qualified as a solicitor 1980; Partner, Brecher & Co. 1981–84; Partner, Farrer & Co. 1986–2001; Partner, Payne Hicks Beach 2001–, Solicitor for Prince William and Prince Harry; Gov., Benenden School 1986–2007; Hon. Bencher, Inner Temple 2011; Hon. LLD (Exeter) 2010. *Publications:* The Divorce Handbook 1992. *Leisure interests:* travel, opera, fashion. *Address:* Payne Hicks Beach, 10 New Square, Lincoln's Inn, London, WC2A 3QG (office); House of Lords, Westminster, London, SW1A 0PW, England. *Telephone:* (20) 7465-4300 (office); (20) 7219-5353 (House of Lords). *Fax:* (20) 7465-4329 (office); (20) 7219-5979 (House of Lords). *E-mail:* fshackleton@phb.co.uk (office). *Website:* www.paynehicksbeach.co.uk (office).

SHAFAI, Lotfollah, PhD, FRSC; Canadian electronics engineer and academic; *Distinguished Professor and Canada Research Chair in Applied Electromagnetics, University of Manitoba;* ed Univ. of Tehran, Univ. of Toronto; moved to Canada from Iran 1964; Lecturer, Dept of Electrical and Computer Eng, Univ. of Manitoba 1969, currently Distinguished Prof. and Canada Research Chair in Applied Electromagnetics; Fellow, IEEE, Canadian Acad. of Engineers, Eng Inst. of Canada; Killam Prize in Eng, Canada Council for the Arts 2011. *Achievements include:* early work led to development of first generation picoterminals for the Canadian Hermes satellite – ultra-small fully portable satellite ground stations with antennas now in use around the globe, making direct satellite broadcasting accessible to the public; recent work has focused on electromagnetic mapping of Arctic sea ice to provide data for understanding effects of climate-warming trends. *Publications:* numerous papers in professional journals. *Address:* Room E3-404C, Engineering and Information Technology Complex, University of Manitoba, 75 Chancellor's Circle, Winnipeg, MB R3T 5V6, Canada (office). *Telephone:* (204) 474-9615 (office). *E-mail:* shafai@umanitoba.ca; shafai@cc.umanitoba.ca (office). *Website:* umanitoba.ca/ece (office).

SHAFAREVICH, Igor Rostislavovich, DSc; Russian mathematician; b. 3 June 1923, Zhitomir; s. of Rostislav Stepanovich and Yulia Yacovlevna; m.; two c.; ed Moscow Univ.; Research Officer Moscow Math. Inst. 1943–44; staff mem. Faculty of Mechanics and Math., Moscow Univ. 1944–52; Prof., Moscow Univ. 1953–75 (dismissed for dissident activities); Lecturer and Head of Dept, V. Steklov Math. Inst. 1960–; Corresp. mem. USSR (now Russian) Acad. of Sciences 1958, mem. 1991; mem. Bd Moscow Math. Soc. 1964, Pres. 1970–74; mem. USSR Human Rights Cttee; mem. Political Council, Nat. Salvation Front 1992; Hon. mem. US Acad. of Sciences, Acad. Leopoldina, American Acad. of Arts and Sciences, Royal Soc., London; Dr hc (Paris); Lenin Prize 1959, Heinemann Prize, Göttingen Acad. of Sciences 1975. *Publications include:* Has Russia a Future? and 'Socialism' in Solzhenitsyn's From Under the Rubble, Socialism as a Phenomenon in Global History 1977, The Socialist Phenomenon 1980, Russophobia 1990, Three Thousand Year Old Mystery 2002. *Address:* V. Steklov Mathematical Institute, Ul. Gubkina 8, 117966 Moscow, Russia. *Telephone:* (495) 135-25-49 (office), (495) 135-13-47 (home).

SHAFEEU, Ismail; Maldivian politician; fmr Minister of Planning, Human Resources and Environment; Minister of Educ. 2002–03, of Home Affairs and Environment 2003–04, of Defence and Nat. Security 2004–08; Chair. Dhiraagu Ltd. *Address:* c/o Ministry of Defence and National Security, Bandaara Koshi, Ameer Ahmed Magu, Malé 20-126, Maldives. *Telephone:* 3322607. *E-mail:* admin@defence.gov.mv.

SHAFFER, Sir Peter Levin, Kt, CBE, FRSL; British playwright; b. 15 May 1926, Liverpool, England; s. of Jack Shaffer and Reka Shaffer (née Fredman); ed St Paul's School, London, Trinity Coll., Cambridge; with Acquisitions Dept, New York Public Library 1951; returned to UK 1954; with Symphonic Music Dept, Boosey and Hawkes 1954; Literary Critic, Truth 1956–57, Music Critic, Time and Tide 1957; playwright 1957–; Cameron Mackintosh Prof. of Contemporary Theatre, St Catherine's Coll., Oxford 1994–95; mem. European Acad., Yuste 1998–; Hon. DLitt (Bath) 1992, (St Andrews) 1999; London Drama Critics' Award, Hamburg Shakespeare Prize 1987, William Inge Award for Distinguished Achievement in the American Theater 1992. *Plays include:* The Salt Land (BBC) 1954, Five Finger Exercise, London (Evening Standard Drama Award 1957, New York Drama Critics' Circle Award 1959–60) 1958, New York 1959 (New York Drama Critics Circle Award), The Private Ear and The Public Eye, London 1962, USA 1963, The Royal Hunt of the Sun, London 1964, New York 1964, Black Comedy, London 1965, New York 1967, White Lies, New York 1967 (revised as The White Liars, London 1968 and as White Liars, London 1976), The Battle of Shrivings 1970, Equus, London (Tony Award for Best Play 1975, New York Drama Critics Circle Award 1975) 1973, New York 1974, Amadeus, London (Evening Standard Drama Award 1980, Tony Award for Best Play 1981, Theatre Critics Award, New York Drama Critics' Circle Award 1981) 1979, New York 1980, Yonadab 1985, Lettice and Lovage, London (Best Comedy, Evening Standard Awards 1988, Tony Award for Best Play 1990) 1987, New York 1990, The Gift of the Gorgon 1992; also performed on stage, Chichester, Guildford, Malvern 1996. *Film screenplays:* Five Finger Exercise 1962, The Public Eye 1962, The Royal Hunt of the Sun 1965, Equus 1977, Amadeus (Golden Globe Award for Best Screenplay, Academy Award for Best Adapted Screenplay) 1984. *Radio play:* Whom Do I Have the Honour of Addressing? 1989. *Television:* several TV plays, including The Salt Land 1955, Balance of Terror. *Leisure interests:* architecture, walking, music. *Address:* Macnaughton Lord, 44 South Molton Street, London, W1K 5RT, England (office). *Telephone:* (20) 7499-1411 (office). *Fax:* (20) 7493-2444 (office).

SHAFIK, Nemat, (Minouche), BA, MSc, DPhil; economist and international official; *Deputy Managing Director, International Monetary Fund;* ed Univ. of Massachusetts, Amherst, USA, London School of Econs, Univ. of Oxford, UK; Economist, Int. Econs Dept 1990, Economist, World Devt Report 1992, Country Economist, Cen. European Dept 1992–94, Sr Economist, Office of the Chief Economist 1994–95, Middle East and N Africa (MENA) Region 1996–97, Dir Pvt. Sector and Finance, MENA 1997–99, Vice-Pres. Pvt Sector Devt and Infrastructure 1999–2003, Vice-Pres. Infrastructure 2003–04; Dir-Gen. Country Programmes, Dept for Int. Devt, UK 2004–08, Perm. Sec. 2008–11; Deputy Man. Dir IMF 2011–; Adjunct Prof., Econs Dept, Georgetown Univ. 1989–94; Chair. Consultive Group to Assist the Poorest 1999–2004, InfoDev 1999–2004, Global Water and Sanitation Program 1999–2004, Pvt. Participation in Infrastructure Advisory Facility 1999–2004, Energy Sector Man. and Advisory Program 1999–2004; Visiting Assoc. Prof., Wharton School, Univ. of Pennsylvania 1996; mem. Bd of Advisory Eds The Middle East Journal 1996–2002; mem. Bd Operating Council, Global Alliance for Workers and Communities, Int. Youth Fed. 1999–2003; Hon. DJur (Warwick Univ) 2012; Woman of the Year in Global Leadership and Global Diversity 2009. *Publications:* numerous books and articles in academic journals on int. econs, development, the Middle East, and environment; various blogs and newspaper columns. *Address:* International Monetary Fund, 700 19th Street, NW, Washington, DC 20431, USA. *Telephone:* (202) 623-7000. *Fax:* (202) 623-4661. *Website:* www.imf.org.

SHAGARI, Alhaji Shehu Usman Aliu; Nigerian teacher and fmr head of state; b. 25 Feb. 1925, Shagari; m.; eight s. ten d.; ed Middle School, Sokoto, Barewa Coll., Kaduna, Teacher Training Coll., Zaria; Science Teacher Sokoto Middle School 1945–50; Headmaster Argungu Sr Primary School 1951–52; Sr Visiting Teacher Sokoto Prov. 1953–58; mem. Fed. Parl. 1954–58; Parl. Sec. to the Prime Minister 1958–59; Fed. Minister of Econ. Devt 1959–60, of Establishments 1960–62, of Internal Affairs 1962–65, of Works 1965–66; Sec. Sokoto Prov. Educ. Devt Fund 1966–68; State Commr for Educ., Sokoto Prov. 1968–70; Fed. Commr for Econ. Devt and Reconstruction 1970–71, for Finance 1971–75; fmr Chair. Peugeot Automobile Nigeria Ltd; mem. Constituent Ass. 1977–83; Presidential candidate for the Nat. Party of Nigeria (NPN) 1979; Pres. of Nigeria and C-in-C of the Armed Forces 1979–83 (deposed by mil. coup), also Minister of Defence 1982–83; under house arrest 1983–86, banned from holding public office and from political activity Aug. 1986; confined to Shagari Village 1986–88; granted unrestricted freedom 1988; Grand Commdr Order of the Niger 1993; Hon. LLD (Ahmadu Bello Univ.) 1976. *Publications include:* Wakar Nigeria (poem), Shehu Usman Dan-Fodio: Ideas and Ideals of his Leadership.

SHAH, Pir Karam Ali; Pakistani politician; *Governor of Gilgit-Baltistan;* first elected unopposed as mem. Northern Areas Advisory Council 1970, three decades

as mem. Northern Areas Legis. Council (now Gilgit-Baltistan Legis. Ass.), fmr Deputy Chief Exec.; Gov. Gilgit-Baltistan 2011–; mem. Pakistan People's Party. *Address:* Office of the Governor, Gilgit, Gilgit-Baltistan, Pakistan (office). *Telephone:* 5811-920573 (office). *E-mail:* info@gilgitbaltistan.gov.pk (office). *Website:* www.gilgitbaltistan.gov.pk (office).

SHAH, Prakash, BA, LLB, MCom; Indian diplomatist; *Chairman, PRS International Consultants;* b. 4 July 1939, Bombay; s. of H. Shah; m. Radhika; two d.; joined Indian Foreign Service 1961; Third Sec. EEC 1962–64; Second Sec. Washington, DC 1964–67; Ministry of External Affairs 1967–69; Ministry of Finance 1969–71; First Sec., Petroleum Counsellor, Embassies, Iran and Gulf States 1971–75; Dir Ministry of Petroleum 1975–77; Dir Indian Petrochemicals Ltd, Petrofils Co-operatives Ltd 1976–77; Dir/Jt Sec. Ministry of External Affairs 1977–78; Jt Sec. to Prime Minister 1978–80; High Commr in Malaysia and Brunei 1980–83; Amb. to Venezuela and Consul-Gen. to Netherlands Antilles 1983–85; Jt Sec. Ministry of External Affairs 1985–88, Additional Sec. 1989–90; Dir Kudremakh Iron Ore Ltd 1986; Amb. and Perm. Rep. to UN, Geneva 1991–92; Amb. to Japan 1992–95; Perm. Rep. to UN, New York 1995–97; Special Rep. of UN Sec.-Gen. to Iraq 1998; Dir Pathfinder Int.; Adviser Dodsal Group, UPS, Washington, USA, Sloan Global Consultants, Washington, DC; mem. Bd Khandwala Securities Bombay, Global Educ. Man., Indo-American Arts Council, Hinduja Group, Falcon Corp. Advisors, Symbiosis Int. Educ. Soc.; mem. Indo-Japan Eminent Persons Group; Chair. PRS Int. Consultants; del. to numerous int. confs. *Publications:* articles in professional journals. *Leisure interests:* cricket, tennis, golf, bridge. *Address:* G-20, Athashree, Magarpatta Road, Hadapsar, Pune 411 028, India (home). *Telephone:* (22) 23676714 (office); (22) 23676717 (home). *Fax:* (22) 24974208 (office). *E-mail:* prakashun@yahoo.com (office); prakash4739@gmail.com (office).

SHAH, Saira; British/Afghan journalist, writer and documentary film producer; b. 5 Oct. 1964, London; d. of the late Idries Shah and of Cynthia Kabraji; m. (divorced); ed School of Oriental and African Studies, Univ. of London,; freelance journalist in Afghanistan, covering guerrilla war against Soviet invasion 1986–89, in Baghdad, Iraq, covering Gulf War 1990–91; journalist with Channel Four News (UK) –2001. *Television:* documentary films: Beneath the Veil (Int. Documentary Asscn Courage under Fire Award) 2001, Unholy War 2001, Zarmina: Lifting the Veil 2002, Death in Gaza (with James Miller, for Frostbite Films/HBO/Channel 4) (BAFTA Award for Current Affairs 2005) 2004, The 50 Greatest Documentaries 2005; Breakfast with Frost (TV series). *Publication:* Storyteller's Daughter 2003. *Address:* Conville and Walsh Literary Agency, 2 Ganton Street, London, W1F 7QL, England (office). *Telephone:* (20) 7287-3030 (office). *Website:* www .convilleandwalsh.com (office).

SHAH, Syed Mehdi; Pakistani politician; *Chief Minister of Gilgit-Baltistan;* b. Skardu; mem. Pakistan Peoples Party (PPP), Acting Pres. PPP Gilgit-Baltistan; Chief Minister of Gilgit-Baltistan (first chief minister of Gilgit-Baltistan following its new constitutional position) 2009–. *Address:* Office of the Chief Minister, Government of Gilgit-Baltistan, Gilgit, Gilgit-Baltistan (office); Peoples Secretariat, Pakistan Peoples Party, Skardu, Gilgit-Baltistan, Pakistan. *Telephone:* (58831) 58111 (office). *E-mail:* smshah_ppp@hotmail.com (office). *Website:* www .ppp.org.pk (office).

SHAH, Syed Qaim Ali, BA, LLB; Pakistani lawyer and politician; *Chief Minister of Sindh;* b. 1935, Khairpur dist; s. of Syed Ramzan Ali Shah; m. 1st (deceased); m. 2nd (deceased); m. 3rd; four s. seven d. from three marriages; ed Univ. of Karachi, SM Law Coll., Karachi; elected Chair. Dist Council, Khairpur in Ayub Khan's era; pioneer mem. Pakistan People's Party (PPP) 1967; elected mem. Nat. Ass. 1970; Fed. Minister for Industries and Kashmir Affairs during Zulfikar Ali Bhutto's premiership; Pres. PPP Sindh 1973–77, 1987–97, 2004–; elected mem. Prov. Ass. 1990, later Leader of Sindh Ass., re-elected five times; elected Senator 1997; Chief Minister of Sindh 1988–90, 2008–13, 2013–. *Address:* Jilani House, Khairpur, Pakistan (office). *Website:* www.sindh.gov.pk (office); www.cmsindh.gov.pk (office).

SHAHABUDDEEN, Mohamed, LLB, LLM, BSc, PhD, LLD; Guyanese international judge; b. 7 Oct. 1931, Vreed-en-Hoop; s. of Sheikh Abdul and Jamillah Hamid; m. Bebe Sairah 1955; two s. one d.; ed Univ. of London and Middle Temple London, UK; called to the Bar, Middle Temple, London 1954; pvt. legal practice 1954–59; magistrate 1959; Crown Counsel 1959–62; Solicitor-Gen. (with rank of Justice of Appeal from 1971) 1962–73; Attorney-Gen. 1973–87; Minister of Justice and sometimes Acting Foreign Minister 1978–87; Vice-Pres. of Guyana 1983–87; Judge Int. Court of Justice 1988–97; Judge, Appeals Chamber, UN Int. Criminal Tribunal for Fmr Yugoslavia and for Rwanda 1997–2009, Vice-Pres. Int. Tribunal for Fmr Yugoslavia 1997–99, 2001–03; Judge, Int. Criminal Court Jan.–Feb. 2009 (resgnd); Chair. Legal Practitioners' Disciplinary Cttee, Advisory Council on the Prerogative of Mercy; mem. Guyana del. to numerous int. confs; Hon. Bencher of the Middle Temple; HQ mem. Int. Law Asscn; mem. Soc. Française pour le droit int., Advisory Bd European Journal of International Law, Bd of Editors of Whewell Professorship of Int. Law of Cambridge Univ., Inst. de Droit int. (first Vice-Pres. 1999–2001), Int. Acad. of Comparative Law; Hon. mem. American Soc. of Int. Law; Order of Excellence, Order of Roraima, Cacique's Crown of Honour (Guyana). *Publications:* several books and articles. *Address:* c/o International Criminal Tribunal for the Former Yugoslavia, Churchillplein 1, 2517 JW The Hague, The Netherlands (office).

SHAHEED, Ahmed, PhD; Maldivian diplomatist, politician, government official and UN official; *Special Rapporteur for Human Rights in Iran, United Nations;* b. 1964; m.; one s. two d.; ed Univ. of Wales, Aberystwyth, UK, Univ. of Queensland, Australia; joined Ministry of Foreign Affairs 1982, Attaché, Perm. Mission to UN, New York 1982–84, est. Research and Analysis section, Ministry of Foreign Affairs 1989–91, Officer, Bilateral Relations Dept 1995–96, Head of SAARC Div. 1996–98, Head of Multilateral Affairs Dept 1998–99, Perm. Sec. 1999–2004; speech writer for Pres. 1996; Chief Govt Spokesman 2004–05; Minister of Foreign Affairs 2005–07 (resgnd), 2008–10, 2010–11; UN Special Rapporteur for Human Rights in Iran 2011–; mem. Dhivehi Rayyithunge Party (DRP—Maldivian People's Party), Co-founder and Leader New Maldives faction; Co-founder and Patron Open Soc. Asscn 2006–; Muslim Democrat of the Year Award, Centre for the Study of Islam and Democracy, Washington, DC 2009. *Address:* Office of the United Nations High Commissioner for Human Rights, Palais des Nations 1211, Geneva 10, Switzerland (office). *Telephone:* 229179220 (office). *E-mail:* InfoDesk@ohchr.org (office). *Website:* www.ohchr.org (office).

SHAHEEN, C. Jeanne, BA, MSc; American politician and fmr state governor; *Senator from New Hampshire;* b. 28 Jan. 1947, St Charles, Mo.; d. of Ivan Bowers and Belle Bowers; m. William H. Shaheen; three d.; ed Shippensburg Univ. and Univ. of Mississippi; taught high school in Miss. and NH; fmr small business owner; directed several New Hampshire statewide political campaigns; mem. NH Senate 1990–96; Gov. of NH (first woman) 1997–2003; mem. Democratic Nat. Cttee Comm. on Presidential Nomination Timing and Scheduling 2004; Nat. Chair Kerry-Edwards Campaign for Pres. 2004; Sr Fellow, Inst. of Politics, Kennedy School of Govt, Harvard Univ., Dir 2005–07; Senator from New Hampshire 2009–, mem. Cttee on Foreign Relations, Cttee on Energy and Natural Resources, Cttee on Armed Services, Cttee on Small Business and Entrepreneurship; mem. Bd of Dirs Nellie Mae Educ. Foundation; fmr Sr Fellow, Coll. of Citizenship and Public Service, Tufts Univ.; Democrat. *Address:* 520 Hart Senate Office Building, Washington, DC 20510, USA (office). *Telephone:* (202) 224-2841 (office). *Fax:* (202) 228-3194 (office). *Website:* shaheen.senate.gov (office); www.jeanneshaheen .org.

SHAHI, Manarup, BA; Nepalese business executive; b. (Motirup Shahi), 31 July 1966, Shipkhana VDC-6, Kalikot dist; s. of the late Birkha Bahadur Shahi and Kalika Shahi; m. Usha Shah; two s.; apptd Treas., Social Welfare Council 2007; Exec. Chair. Nepal Airlines Corpn 2011–12; Dir, Civil Aviation Authority of Nepal 2011–12; Council mem. Nepal Devt Council, Nat. Planning Comm.) 2006–. *Publications:* four books of poetry and six other training and development related books. *Address:* c/o Nepal Airlines Corporation Building, Kantipath, Kathmandu, Nepal.

SHAHID, Abdulla, BA, MA; Maldivian civil servant and politician; *Speaker of People's Majlis;* b. 26 May 1962, Malé; m.; three c.; ed Canberra Coll. of Advanced Educ., Australia, Fletcher School of Law and Diplomacy, Tufts Univ., USA; began civil service career in Foreign Ministry 1983; mem. Constitutional Ass. 1994; mem. People's Majlis (Parl.) 1995–, Speaker 2009–; Exec. Sec. to the Pres. 1995–2005; Minister of State for Foreign Affairs 2005–07, Minister of Foreign Affairs 2007–08. *Leisure interests:* soccer, badminton, writing Dhivehi poetry. *Address:* People's Majlis Secretariat, Medhuziyaaraiy Magu, Malé 20-080, The Maldives (office). *Telephone:* 3313214 (office). *Fax:* 3315258 (office). *E-mail:* speaker@majlis.gov.mv (office). *Website:* www.majlis.gov.mv (office).

SHAHRANI, Nematullah, PhD; Afghan politician and scholar; b. Jorm Dist, Badakhshan; ed Abu Hanifa School, Kabul Univ., Al-Azhar Univ., Egypt, The George Washington Univ., USA; fmr Prof. of Sharia, Kabul Univ.; fmr Ed.-in-Chief, Sharayat magazine; Vice-Pres. Transitional Authority 2002–04; Dir Constitutional Drafting Cttee 2002; Minister of Hajj and Religious Affairs 2004–08; known as "the teacher of teachers", one of the most prominent Afghan scholars. *Publications include:* more than 30 books, including Quran Shenaasy (Knowing the Holy Quran), Feqeh Islami Wa Qanoon e Gharb (Islamic Fiqh and Western Law); several hundred articles on Sharia law. *Address:* c/o Ministry of Hajj and Religious Affairs, nr District 10, Shir Pur, Shar-i-Nau, Kabul, Afghanistan.

SHAHRUDI, Ayatollah Sayed Mahmoud Hashemi; Iranian jurist; b. Aug. 1948, Najaf, Iraq; s. of the late Ayatollah Seyed Ali Housseini Shahrudi; ed Alavi School, Iraq; jailed under Baathist regime of Iraq 1974; returned to Iran 1979; teacher of Islamic jurisprudence and methodology, Qum School of Theology 1979–, mem. Supreme Man. Council, Vice-Chair. Asscn of Instructors; est. Inst. of Encyclopedia of Islamic Jurisprudence; Head of the Judiciary 1999–2009; jurist mem. Council of Guardians; mem. Ass. of Experts. *Publications include:* Islamic Criminal Law (discretionary punishments), The Book of Khoms (religious tax) I, II, Hire, Sale, Dormant Partnership, Co-Partnership, Agricultural and Cultivation Partnership etc, Discourses in Islamic Methodology. *Address:* c/o Ministry of Justice, Panzdah-e-Khordad Square, Tehran, Iran.

SHAHUMI, Suleiman Sasi ash-; Libyan politician; Sec. for Foreign Affairs, Gen. People's Congress –2011. *Address:* Secretariat of the General People's Congress, Tripoli, Libya (office).

SHAIBANI, Mohammed al-, BA; United Arab Emirates government official and business executive; *Director-General, Ruler's Court, Dubai;* started professional career with Dubai Ports Authority and Jebel Ali Free Zone; four years as Man. Dir, Al Khaleej Investments, Singapore; Pres. Dubai Office (pvt. man. office for Dubai royal family) 1998–; currently Dir-Gen., Ruler's Court, Dubai; Vice-Chair. Supreme Fiscal Cttee of Dubai; Chair. Dubai Islamic Bank; CEO and Exec. Dir Investment Corpn of Dubai (govt investment holding co.); Dir Dubai World 2010–; Dubai Aerospace Enterprise Ltd, The Knowledge Fund, International Humanitarian City. *Address:* HH Ruler's Court, POB 90300, Dubai, United Arab Emirates (office). *Website:* www.dubai.ae (office).

SHAIKH, Abdul Hafeez, PhD; Pakistani economist and politician; b. 26 Dec. 1954, Jacobabad, Sindh; s. of Abdul Nabi Shaikh and Afroz Nabi Shaikh; m. Nadene Nichols Shaikh; ed Boston Univ., USA; worked at Harvard Univ., USA; served as country head of World Bank's operations in Saudi Arabia 1990s, led assignments and advised more than 18 countries of Europe, Latin America, Asia and Africa as a Sr World Bank official, also led teams for successful privatization in many countries in fields of telecommunication, electricity, transport, aviation, banking and manufacturing; Pnr, New Silk Route (pvt. equity firm); Minister for Finance, Planning and Devt, Sindh govt 2000–02; Fed. Minister for Privatization and Investment; elected mem. of the Senate 2010; Adviser to the Prime Minister on Finance, Revenue, Econ. Affairs, Statistics and Planning and Devt on March–June 2010; Minister of Finance, Planning and Devt, Econ. Affairs, Revenue and Statistics 2010–13; fmr Chair. Senate Cttee on World Trade Org.; Man of the Year 2004. *Publications include:* numerous publs, including book Argentina's Privatisation. *Address:* c/o Ministry of Finance, Revenue and Planning and Development, Block Q, Pakistan Secretariat, Islamabad, Pakistan.

SHAIMIYEV, Mintimer Sharipovich; Russian engineer and politician; b. 20 Jan. 1937, Anyakovo, Aktanyshski Dist, Tatar ASSR; s. of Sharip Shaimiev and Naghima Safioullina; m. Sakina Shaimiyeva; two s.; ed Kazan Inst. of Agric.; Engineer, Chief Engineer Service and Repair Station, Mouslyumovski Dist, Tatar ASSR 1959–62; Man. Selkhoztekhnika Regional Asscn, Tatar ASSR 1962–67;

Instructor, Deputy Chief of Agricultural Dept, Tatar Regional Cttee of CPSU, Tatar ASSR 1967–69; Minister of Land Improvement and Water Man., Tatar ASSR 1969–83; First Deputy Chair. Council of Ministers, Tatar ASSR 1983, Chair. 1985–89; Sec. Tatar Regional Cttee of CPSU 1983–85, First Sec. 1989–90; Chair. Supreme Soviet, Tatar ASSR 1990–91; Pres. of Tatarstan 1991–2010; Tatarstan State Counsellor; Chair. Bd of Trustees, The Republican Foundation for the Revival of Historical and Cultural Monuments of the Repub. of Tatarstan 2010–; f. All Russia political movt 1999, now part of United Russia (Yedinaya Rossiya); mem. Acad. of Tech. Sciences; Co-Chair., Higher Council, United Russia Party; Hon. mem. Presidium, Int. Parl. of World Confed. of Kts (under auspices of UN), Int. Acad. of Informatization; Hon. Prof., Moscow State Inst. of Int. Relations; Order of Lenin 1966, Order of Red Banner of Labour 1971, Order of Oct. Revolution 1976, Order of Friendship of Peoples 1987, Order for Services to the Fatherland, Grade II 1997, Kazakhstan Order of Friendship, First Class 2010; Silver Avitsenna Medal, UNESCO 2001. *Leisure interests:* chess, gardening, skiing. *Address:* c/o Office of the President, 420014 Tatarstan, Kazan, Kreml, Russia.

SHAKAR, Karim Ebrahim ash-, BA; Bahraini diplomatist; *Under-Secretary for International Affairs;* b. 23 Dec. 1945, Manama; m. Fatima Al-Mansouri 1979; three d.; ed Univ. of New Delhi; joined Ministry of Foreign Affairs 1970; mem. Perm. Mission to the UN, rising to rank of Second Sec. 1972–76; Chief of Int. Relations and Orgs Section, Bahrain 1977–82; apptd First Sec., Ministry of Foreign Affairs 1978, Counsellor 1981; Perm. Rep. to the UN Office, Geneva and Consul-Gen., Switzerland 1982–87; Perm. Rep. to the UN Office, Vienna 1984–87; Perm. Rep. to the UN Office 1987–90; Amb. to UK (also accred to Ireland, Netherlands, Denmark) 1990–95; Dir Int. Directorate, Ministry of Foreign Affairs, Bahrain 1995–2001; Amb. to People's Repub. of China (also accred to Malaysia, Philippines, Thailand) 2001–07; Amb.-at-Large, Ministry of Foreign Affairs 2007–09; Under-Sec. for Int. Affairs, Ministry of Foreign Affairs 2009–; Shaikh Isa Bin Salman Al-Khalifa Medal of Merit 2001. *Leisure interests:* reading, travelling. *Address:* Ministry of Foreign Affairs, PO Box 547, Government House, Government Road, Manama, Kingdom of Bahrain. *Telephone:* 17227555 (office). *Fax:* 17212603 (office). *E-mail:* kalshakar@mofa.gov.bh (office). *Website:* www .mofa.gov.bh (office).

SHAKED, Shaul, PhD; Israeli professor of Iranian studies and comparative religion; *Schwarzmann University Professor Emeritus, Hebrew University of Jerusalem;* b. 5 March 1933, Debrecen, Hungary; s. of Joshua Scharf and Irma Scharf; m. Miriam Schächter 1960; one s. two d.; ed Hebrew Univ. Jerusalem and School of Oriental and African Studies, Univ. of London; Asst Lecturer, SOAS 1964–65, Lecturer 1964–65; Lecturer, Assoc. Prof., Prof., Hebrew Univ., Jerusalem 1965–2001, Chair. Dept of Indian, Iranian and Armenian Studies 1971–72, 1974–75, Chair. Dept of Comparative Religion 1972–74, 1977–79, Chair. Ben Zvi Inst. for Study of Jewish Communities in the East 1975–79, Inst. of Asian and African Studies 1981–85, Chair. Academic Bd, Centre for the Study of Christianity 1999–2001, currently Schwarzmann Univ. Prof. Emer.; Visiting Prof., Univ. of California, Berkeley 1969–70, Columbia and New York Univs 1980–81, Univ. of Heidelberg 1987–88; Visiting Fellow, Wolfson Coll., Cambridge, Netherlands Inst. for Advanced Study; Vice-Pres. Societas Iranologica Europaea 1995–99, Int. Academic Union 1998–2001, Pres. 2001–04, Hon. Pres. 2004–; mem. Israel Acad. of Sciences and Humanities 1986 (Chair. Section of Humanities and Social Sciences 1995–2001), Magyar Tudományos Akadémia 2013; Hon. Fellow, Univ. Coll. London 1995–; Yoram Ben-Porat Prize for Distinguished Research 1993, Israel Prize in Linguistics 2000. *Publications include:* A tentative bibliography of Geniza documents 1964, Amulets and Magic Bowls (with J. Naveh) 1985, Dualism in Transformation 1994, From Zoroastrian Iran to Islam 1995, Magische Texte aus der Kairoer Geniza (with P. Schäfer) (three vols) 1994–99, Aramaic Documents from Ancient Bactria (with J. Naveh) 2012, Aramaic Bowl Spells 1 (with J. N. Ford and S. Bhayro) 2013; articles and book chapters. *Address:* Institute of Asian and African Studies, The Hebrew University, Mount Scopus, Jerusalem 91905, Israel (office). *Telephone:* (2) 6416005 (home). *Fax:* (2) 6446273 (home). *E-mail:* shaul .shaked@huji.ac.il (office). *Website:* religions.huji.ac.il (office).

SHAKER, Mohamed Ibrahim, LLB, DèsScPol; Egyptian diplomatist; b. 16 Oct. 1933, Cairo; m. Mona El Kony 1960; one s. one d.; ed Cairo Univ., Inst. of Int. Studies, Univ. of Geneva, Switzerland; Rep. of Dir-Gen. of IAEA to UN, New York 1982–83; Deputy Perm. Rep. of Egypt to UN, New York 1984–86; Amb. to Austria, Perm. Rep. to UN in Vienna, Gov. on IAEA Bd of Govs, Perm. Rep. to UNIDO 1986–88; Amb. to UK 1988–97, Dean of Diplomatic Corps; fmr mem. Core Group, Programme for Promoting Nuclear Non-proliferation (PPNN) 1987–97, UN Sec.-Gen.'s Advisory Bd on Disarmament Matters 1993–98 (Chair. 1995); Vice-Chair. Egyptian Council for Foreign Affairs 1999–; Sawires Foundation for Social Devt 2001–, Regional Information Tech. Inst. 2002–; Order of the Republic (Second Grade) 1976; Order of Merit (First Grade) 1983. *Publications:* The Nuclear Non-Proliferation Treaty: Origin and Implementation, 1959–1979 1980; several articles and contribs to books on nuclear energy and nuclear non-proliferation. *Leisure interests:* tennis, music. *Address:* 9 Aziz Osman Street, Zamalek, Cairo, Egypt (home). *Telephone:* (2) 27359593 (home). *Fax:* (2) 27359593 (home).

SHAKESPEARE, Frank; American fmr diplomatist and fmr radio and television executive; b. 9 April 1925, New York; s. of Frank J. Shakespeare, Sr and Frances Hughes Shakespeare; m. Deborah Ann Spaeth Shakespeare 1954; one s. two d.; ed Holy Cross Coll., Worcester, Mass.; Liberty Mutual Insurance Co., Washington, DC 1947–49; Procter and Gamble Co. 1949–50; Radio Station WOR, New York 1950, CBS 1950; Gen. Man. WXIX-TV, Milwaukee, Wis. 1957–59; Vice-Pres. and Gen. Man. WCBS-TV, New York 1959–63; Vice-Pres. and Asst to Pres. CBS-TV Network 1963–65; Exec. Vice-Pres. CBS-TV Stations 1965–67; Pres. CBS Television Service Div. 1967–69; Dir US Information Agency 1969–73; Exec. Vice-Pres. Westinghouse Electric Co. 1973–75; Pres. RKO Gen. 1975–83, Vice-Chair. 1983–85; Chair. Bd Radio Free Europe/Radio Liberty Inc. 1982–85; Amb. to Portugal 1985–86, to the Holy See 1986–89; Trustee, Heritage Foundation 1979–, Chair. Bd 1981–85; currently also Trustee, Lynde and Harry Bradley Foundation of Milwaukee, Wis.; Kt Grand Cross with Palm, Order of the Holy Sepulchre and other honours; nine hon. degrees. *Address:* The Heritage Foundation, 214 Massachusetts Ave, Washingtona, DC 20002-4999, USA (office). *Telephone:* (202) 546-4400 (office). *E-mail:* info@heritage.org (office). *Website:* www.heritage.org (office).

SHAKHANBEH, Abed Ali, LLM, PhD; Jordanian lawyer, judge and politician; *Head, Anti-Corruption Commission;* b. 1950, Jdaideh-Madba; ed Damascus Univ., Syria, Jordan Univ., Cairo Univ., Egypt; civil servant, lawyer, then judge 1973–93; Sec.-Gen. Court of Control and Admin. Audit 1993–95, Pres. of Court 1995–2001; Pres. Court of Audit 2003; Minister of State for Judiciary Affairs 2001–03, 2003–05; Minister of Justice 2005–07; currently Head of Anti-Corruption Comm., Amman. *Address:* Anti-Corruption Commission, PO Box 5000, 11953 Amman, Jordan (office). *Telephone:* (6) 5503162 (office). *Fax:* (6) 5503171 (office). *E-mail:* bayan109@jacc.gov.jo (office). *Website:* www.jacc.gov.jo (office).

SHAKHNAZAROV, Karen Georgyevich; Russian film director; *Chairman and Director-General, Mosfilm Cinema Concern;* b. 8 July 1952, Krasnodar; s. of Georgy Shakhnazarov and Anna Shakhnazarova; m. Darya Igorevna Mayorova 1972; two s. one d.; ed All-Union Inst. of Cinematography; Asst Film Dir Mosfilm Studio 1973–75; on staff Mosfilm 1976–; Artistic Dir VI Creative Union 1987; Chair. Bd of Dirs Courier Studio at Mosfilm 1991–, Dir-Gen. Mosfilm Cinema Concern 1998–, currently also Chair.; mem. Public Chamber of Russia 2005–; Boris Polevoy Prize 1982, Special Prize of the Jury (Grenoble) 1984, Silver Medal of Int. Film Festival, Lodz 1984, Prize of Int. Film Festival in Moscow for Courier 1986, Comsomol Prize 1986, Brothers Vassilyev State Prize 1988, Special Prize of Karlovy Vary Film Festival for Day of Full Moon 1998, Merited Worker of Arts of Russia, People's Artist of the Russian Fed. 2002. *Film scripts:* debut as scriptwriter Ladies Invite Partners 1981. *Films include:* God Souls 1980, Jazzmen (Diplomas of Int. Film Festivals in London, Chicago, Belgrade 1984) 1983, Winter Night in Gagra 1985, Courier 1986, Town Zero 1989, Assassin of the Tsar (Grand Prix of Int. Film Festival in Belgrade 1991) 1991, Dreams 1993, American Daughter 1995, Day of Full Moon 1998, Poisons or the World History of Poisoning 2001, Rider Named Death 2004, The Vanished Empire 2008, Ward Number 6 (Crystal Simorgh Awards, Int. Film Festival, Tehran) 2009. *Leisure interests:* swimming, driving. *Address:* Mosfilmovskaya str. 1, 119991 Moscow, Russia (office). *Telephone:* (499) 143-91-18 (office). *Fax:* (495) 705-93-00 (office). *E-mail:* referent@mosfilm.ru (office). *Website:* www.mosfilm.ru (office).

SHAKHRAY, Sergey Mikhailovich, LLD; Russian politician; *Head, Parliamentary Accounts Chamber;* b. 30 April 1956, Simferopol; s. of Mikhail A. Shakray and Zoya A. Shakray; m. Tatyana Shakhray 1985; two s. one d.; ed Rostov State Univ.; Head of Law, Moscow State Univ.; People's Deputy of Russia 1990–92; Chair. of the Legis. Cttee of Russian Supreme Soviet 1990; State Councillor on legal issues of Russian Fed. 1991–92; Vice-Prime Minister of Russia 1991–92, 1993, 1994–95; Chair. State Cttee for nat. problems; Founder and Chair. Party of Russian Unity and Consent (PRES) 1993–; Head interim admin in zone of emergency situation in N Ossetia and Ingushetia 1992–93; mem. State Duma (Parl.) 1993; Minister for Nationalities and Nat. Problems 1994–95; Deputy Head of Pres. Yeltsin's Admin, Pres.'s Rep. at Constitutional Court 1996–98; Deputy Chair. Political Consultative Council of Pres. Yeltsin; adviser to Prime Minister 1998–; Prof., Moscow State Inst. of Int. Relations 1999–; Deputy Head, Parl. Accounts Chamber Admin 2001–04, Head 2004–; Honoured Jurist of the Russian Fed. *Publications:* Constitution of the Russian Federation. Encylopaedic Dictionary (co-author) 1995, Constitutional Justice in the System of Russian Federalism 2002, Constitutional Law of the Russian Federation 2003, Globalization in the Contemporary World – Political-Legal Aspects 2003, Globalization State Law 2003. *Leisure interests:* fishing, bicycling, badminton, Russian baths. *Address:* Accounts Chamber of the Russian Federation, Zubovskaya str. 2, 119992 Moscow, Russia (office). *Telephone:* (495) 986-00-14 (office). *Fax:* (495) 986-01-53 (office). *E-mail:* zemochka@mail.ru (office); shahray@ach.gov.ru (office). *Website:* www.ach .gov.ru (office).

SHAKIRA; Colombian singer, songwriter, dancer, record producer and choreographer and model; b. (Shakira Isabel Mebarak Ripoll), 2 Feb. 1977, Barranquilla; d. of William Mebarak Chadid and Nidia Ripoll; wrote first song aged eight, signed recording contract with Sony Music Colombia aged 13; f. Fundación Pies Descalzos (Barefoot Foundation) 1997; Founding mem. Fundación América Latina en Acción Solidaria; apptd UNICEF Goodwill Amb. 2003; helped organize Live Aid Latino series of concerts 2008–; began own beauty line, S by Shakira, with parent co. Puig 2010, released two perfumes, S by Shakira and S by Shakira Eau Florale, new fragrance Elixir by Shakira 2012; Hon. Chair. for Educ. Action Week, Global Campaign for Educ. April 2008; mem. White House Initiative on Educational Excellence for Hispanics 2011; Latin Grammy Awards for Best Female Vocal Performance 2000, for Best Music Video (for Suerte) 2002, five MTV Video Awards 2002, MTV Europe Music Award for Best Female 2005, American Music Award for Favorite Latin Music Artist 2005, 2006, Billboard Music Awards for Latin Song of the Year (for La Tortura), for Latin Pop Album Artist of the Year 2005, MTV Video Award for Best Choreography 2006, MTV Latin America Music Award for Song of the Year (for Hips Don't Lie) 2006, Latin Grammy Award for Best Song (for La Totura), for Record of the Year (for La Totura) 2006, MTV Video Music Award for Best Collaboration (for Beautiful Liar with Beyoncé) 2007, Latin Recording Academy Person of the Year 2011, Premios Lo Nuestro Award for Artist of the Year 2012, Premios Lo Nuestro Award for Female Artist of the Year 2012, Premios Lo Nuestro Award for Song of the Year (for Rabiosa) 2012, ranked by Forbes magazine amongst The World's 100 Most Powerful Women (40th) 2012, (52nd) 2013. *Recordings include:* albums: Magia 1991, Peligro 1993, Pies Descalzos 1996, ¿Dónde Están Los Ladrones? 1998, Laundry Service 2002, Washed And Dried: Laundry Service Limited Edition 2002, Fijación Oral Vol. 1 (Billboard Music Award for Latin Pop Album of the Year 2005, Grammy Award for Best Latin Rock/ Alternative Album 2006, Latin Grammy Awards for Best Album and Best Female Pop Vocal Album 2006) 2005, Fijación Oral Vol. 2 2005, She Wolf 2009, Sale el Sol (Premios Lo Nuestro Award for Album of the Year 2012) 2010. *Television includes:* El oasis (Colombian TV drama series) 1994, Tania (series) 2002, coach and judge on The Voice (NBC) 2013. *Address:* c/o Sony BMG Entertainment, 550 Madison Avenue, New York, NY 10022-3211, USA (office). *Website:* www.shakira.com.

SHAKOOR, Aishath Azima; Maldivian lawyer, politician and government official; *Attorney-General;* Deputy Minister of Home Affairs 2005–07; Attorney-Gen. 2007–08, 2012–; mem. Parl. apptd by Pres. Maumoon Abdul Gayoom; Pres. Women's Wing, Dhivehi Rayyithunge Party (Maldivian People's Party). *Address:* Attorney-General's Office, Huravee Bldg, 3rd Floor, Ameer Ahmed Magu, Malé

20–05, Maldives (office). *Telephone:* 3323809 (office). *Fax:* 3314109 (office). *E-mail:* it@agoffice.gov.mv (office). *Website:* www.agoffice.gov.mv (office).

SHAKOORU, Uza Aishath Azima; Maldivian lawyer and government official; *Attorney-General;* served as Attorney-Gen. under Pres. Maumoon Abdul Gayoom, then Attorney-Gen. 2012–. *Address:* Attorney-General's Office, Velaanaage, 6th Floor, Ameer Ahmed Magu, Malé 20-096, Maldives (office). *Telephone:* 3323809 (office). *Fax:* 3314109 (office). *E-mail:* info@agoffice.gov.mv (office). *Website:* agoffice.gov.mv (office).

SHAKUROV, Sergey Kayumovich; Russian actor; b. 1 Jan. 1942, Moscow; ed Theatre School of Cen. Children's Theatre; with K. Stanislavsky Drama Theatre 1978–88; acted in several other theatres; USSR State Prize 1980, prizes of All-Union Film Festivals for Best Actor 1988, 1991, People's Actor of Russia 1991. *Stage roles include:* Ivanov (Chekhov), Hamlet and others. *Films include:* Svoy sredi chuzhikh, chuzhoy sredi svoikh (At Home among Strangers) 1974, Sto dney posle detstva (100 Days after Childhood) 1975, The Taste of Bread 1979, Portret zheny khudozhnika (Portrait of the Artist's Wife) 1982, Retsept yeyo molodosti (Recipe of Her Youthfulness) 1984, Dogs' Feast 1991, Szwadron (Squadron) 1992, Hagy-Trager 1993, Declaration of Love 1995, Cranberries in Sugar 1995, Armaviz 1998, Pan Tadeusz 1999, Rozhdestvenskaya mysterya 2000, Dikarka 2001, Antikiller 2002, Dnevnik kamikadze (Diary of a Kamikaze) 2003, Antikiller 2: Antiterror 2003, Sdvig 2006, Junk 2006, Konservy 2007, Paragraph 78 2007, O, Luckyman! 2009, Zvorykin-Muromets 2010. *Television includes:* Vizit k Minotavru (Visit to Minotaurus) (mini-series) 1987, Chyornaya komnata 2000, Brezhnev 2005, Master i Margarita (mini-series) 2005, Na puti k serdtsu 2007, Petr Perviy. Zaveshanie 2011. *Address:* Bibliotechnaya str. 27, Apt. 94, 109544 Moscow, Russia (home). *Telephone:* (495) 270-15-32 (home).

SHALA, Ahmet, BA, MBA, PhD; Kosovo politician; m. Hatixhe Shala; four c.; ed Univ. of Prishtina, Univ. Autonoma de Barcelona, Spain, Vaxjo Univ., Sweden; fmr Policy Advisor for Econ. Devt, EU Mission in Kosovo; Deputy Head Dept for Trade and Industry 2000–02; Deputy Man. Dir Kosovo Trust Agency 2002–08; Minister of the Economy and Finance 2008–11; fmr Lecturer in Math., Statistics and Econ. Modelling, Univ. of Prishtina, currently Prof. of Marketing Modelling and Statistics; f. Cambridge School (English language teaching inst.). *Address:* c/o Ministry of Finance, 10000 Prishtina, Sheshi Nënë Terezë, Kosovo.

SHALALA, Donna Edna, PhD; American professor of political science, university president and fmr government official; *President, University of Miami;* b. 14 Feb. 1941, Cleveland, Ohio; d. of James A. Shalala and Edna Smith; ed Western Coll. and Syracuse Univ.; volunteer, Peace Corps, Iran 1962–64; Asst to Dir Metropolitan Studies Program, Syracuse Univ. 1965–69; Instructor and Asst to Dean, Maxwell Grad. School, Syracuse Univ. 1969–70; Asst Prof. of Political Science, Bernard Baruch Coll., CUNY 1970–72, Prof. of Political Science and Pres. Hunter Coll. 1980–88; Assoc. Prof. of Politics and Educ., Teachers' Coll., Columbia Univ. 1972–79; Asst Sec. for Policy Devt and Research, US Dept of Housing and Urban Devt Washington, DC 1977–80; Chancellor and Prof. of Political Science, Univ. of Wis., Madison 1988–92; Sec. of Health and Human Services 1993–2001; Pres. Univ. of Miami 2001–; Dir Inst. of Int. Econs 1981–93, Ditchley Foundation 1981–93; mem. Bd of Dirs Gannett Co. 2001–11, Lennar Corpn, Mednax Inc.; mem. Nat. Acad. of Arts and Sciences, American Soc. for Public Admin.; 24 hon. degrees; Presidential Medal of Freedom 2008. *Publications:* Neighborhood Governance 1971, The City and the Constitution 1972, The Property Tax and the Voters 1973, The Decentralization Approach 1974. *Leisure interests:* tennis, mountain-climbing, reading, spectator sports. *Address:* Office of the President, University of Miami, 230J Ashe Administration Building, Coral Gables, FL 33146, USA (office). *Telephone:* (305) 284-5155 (office). *E-mail:* dshalala@miami.edu (office). *Website:* www.miami.edu (office).

SHALGAM, Abd ar-Rahman Muhammad, BA; Libyan government official, diplomatist and fmr newspaper editor; *Permanent Representative, United Nations;* b. 22 Nov. 1949, Al-Ghrefa; s. of Mohamed Shalgam and Rahma Shalgam; m. Mabrouk el-Araby; three s.; ed Cairo Univ., Egypt; Ed. Al-Fajr Al-Jadid newspaper 1973–75, Ed.-in-Chief 1975–77; Ed.-in-Chief Al-Usbu Al-Thaqafi (cultural weekly) and Al-Usbu Al-Siaysi (political weekly) newspapers 1977–79; Dir Gen. Jamahiriya News Agency (JANA) 1979–89; Sec. (Minister) of Information 1981–83; Sec. (Amb.), Libyan People's Bureau, Rome (Libyan Embassy) 1984–95; Sec. of Foreign Affairs, Secr. of the Gen. People's Congress 1998–2000, Sec. of the Gen. People's Cttee for Foreign Liaison and Int. Co-operation 2000–09; Amb. and Perm. Rep. to UN, New York 2009–, Pres. of the Security Council March 2009; Chair. Jt Libyan Italian Co.; mem. Cultural Innovation Cttee, Libyan Arabic Language Acad.; El-Fatah Medal. *Publications include:* Al-Huruf (Words) – Articles in Literature and Politics, The Future Africa – Studies in African Literature, Art, and History, Asrar (Secrets) (poetry anthology), Revelations from the Conscience to the Destiny, Articles and Quotations 2009, I Decided to be Happy, Poems 2009; several articles published in Libyan papers and magazines on political and cultural issues. *Leisure interests:* music, playing the lute and piano. *Address:* Permanent Mission of Libya to the United Nations, 309–315 East 48th Street, New York, NY 10017, USA (office). *Telephone:* (212) 752-5775 (office). *Fax:* (212) 319-3866 (office); (212) 593-4787 (office). *E-mail:* libya_mis_us@foreign.gov.ly (office). *Website:* www .libyanmission-un.org (office).

SHALHOUB, Anthony (Tony) Marcus, MA; American actor; b. 9 Oct. 1953, Green Bay, Wis.; m. Brooke Adams 1992; two d.; ed Univ. of Southern Maine, Yale School of Drama; spent four seasons with American Repertory Theatre, Cambridge, Mass 1980–84. *Films include:* Longtime Companion 1990, Big Night (Best Supporting Actor Nat. Soc. of Film Critics) 1996, Men in Black 1997, Primary Colors 1998, A Civil Action 1998, The Siege 1998, Galaxy Quest 1999, Impostor 2001, Spy Kids 2001, Spy Kids 2 2002, Men in Black II 2002, Spy Kids 3-D 2003, Against the Ropes 2004, The Great New Wonderful 2005, Careless 2007, American East 2007. *Television includes:* Wings (series) 1991–97, Stark Raving Mad (series) 1999, Monk (also exec. producer) (Best Actor in a Comedy Acad. of Television Arts and Sciences 2003, 2005, Golden Globe Award, SAG Award 2004, 2005) 2002–10, Men in Black: The Series. *Plays:* The Scene 2007, Golden Boy 2012. *Address:* Creative Artists Agency, Inc, 9830 Wilshire Blvd., Beverly Hills, CA 90212-1825, USA. *Telephone:* (310) 288-4545. *Fax:* (310) 288-4800. *Website:* www.caa.com.

SHALOM, Silvan, BA, MA, LLB, CPA; Israeli politician and journalist; *Minister for Regional Co-operation and the Development of the Negev and Galilee;* b. 1958, Tunisia; m. Judy Shalom Nir-Mozes; five c.; ed Tel-Aviv Univ., Ben Gurion Univ.; attained rank of Sergeant during mil. service; mem. Knesset 1992–; Deputy Minister of Defence 1997, Minister of Science and Tech. 1998, Deputy Prime Minister and Minister of Finance 2001–03, Deputy Prime Minister and Minister of Foreign Affairs 2003–06 (resgnd), Vice-Prime Minister 2009–13, Minister for Regional Co-operation and the Devt of the Negev and Galilee 2009–, Minister of Energy and Water Resources 2013–; Chair. Bd of Dirs Israel Electric Co., Dir-Gen. Ministry of Energy and Infrastructure; Deputy Chair. Public Council for Youth Exchange; mem. Exec. of the Broadcasting Authority; Adviser to Ministers of Finance, Econ., Planning and Justice; Israel Airport Authority, Dir Sun d'Or Int. Airlines; mem. Likud. *Publications:* numerous articles on the Israeli press. *Address:* Ministry for the Development of the Negev and Galilee, 8 Shaul Hamelech Blvd, Tel-Aviv 64733 (office); Knesset, HaKiryah, Jerusalem 91950, Israel (office). *Telephone:* 3-6060700 (office); 2-6408377 (office). *Fax:* 3-6958414 (office). *E-mail:* lilach.nb@gmail.com (office); sshalom@knesset.gov.il (office). *Website:* www.vpmo.gov.il (office); www.knesset.gov.il (office).

SHAMANOV, Lt-Gen. Vladimir Anatolyevich; Russian army officer and politician; *Commander, Russian Airborne Troops;* b. 15 Feb. 1957, Barnaul, Altai territory; m.; one s. one d.; ed Ryazan Higher Military School of Paratroopers, M. Frunze Military Acad. of General Army, Military Acad. of General Staff; Commdr of artillery platoon, Pskov region 1978–85, Bn Commdr 1985–87; Deputy Regt Commdr Kishinev, Moldova 1990–91; Regt Commdr Kirovabad, Azerbaijan 1991–93, Regt moved to Ulyanovsk 1994; Head of Staff Novorossiysk div. 1994–95, transferred to Chechnya as Commdr operation group; Deputy Commdr army group, Ministry of Defence 1995–96; Head of Staff 20th Gen. Troops Army, Voronezh 1998–99; Commdr 58th Army N Caucasus Mil. Command 1999, W Direction of United Group of Fed. Forces 1999; participated in devt and realization of Operation Hunting for Wolves, Grozny, Chechnya 2000; Commdr 58th Army 2000; Gov. Ulyanovsk Region 2000–04; fmr Counselor to Minister of Defence Sergei Ivanov; Co-Chair. US-Russia Jt Comm. on POW/MIAs –2007; Head, Armed Forces Combat Training Directorate 2007–; Commdr Russian Airborne Troops 2009–; Hon. Citizen of Makhachkala, Dagestan; Hero of Russia 1999, Order of Courage, Order of Saint George 2008, Order for Service to the Homeland in the Armed Forces of the USSR. *Address:* Ministry of Defence, 119160 Moscow, ul. Znamenka 19, Russia (office). *Telephone:* (495) 696-84-37 (office). *Fax:* (495) 696-84-37 (office). *Website:* www.mil.ru (office).

SHAMASK, Ronaldus; Dutch fashion designer; b. 24 Nov. 1945, Amsterdam; self-educated in design; window-dresser for dept store in Melbourne, Australia 1959; fashion illustrator, The Times and The Observer newspapers, London 1967–68; set and costume designer, Company of Man (multi-media artists' org.) Buffalo, New York 1968–71; subsequently undertook design and clothing commissions for pvt. clients in New York; Founder-pnr with Murray Moss, Moss Shamask Fashion Co., New York 1978–89; opened Moss boutique, Madison Avenue, New York, presented first collection 1979; costume designer, Lucinda Childs Dance Co. premiere of Available Light, Next Wave Fall Festival, Brooklyn Acad. of Music 1983; launched own co. Shamask 1996; work in perm. collection of Smithsonian Inst.; American Fashion Critics Coty Award 1981, Conf. Internationale du Lin Fil d'Or Award 1985, 1987, 1989, Council of Fashion Designers of America Award 1987, Woolmark Award 1989.

SHAMBA, Sergei Miron-ipa, PhD; Georgian (Abkhaz) politician; b. 15 March 1951, Gudauta, Abkhazian ASSR, Georgian SSR, USSR; ed Yerevan Inst. of Archeology; Head of Aidgylara (played leading role in Abkhazia's struggle for independence) –1992; First Deputy Minister of Defence during war in Abkhazia 1992–93; Minister of Foreign Affairs of Abkhazia 1997–June 2004 (resgnd), Dec. 2004–10; attained rank of Amb. 2001; unsuccessful presidential cand. 2004; co-f. Social-Democratic Party of Abkhazia 2004; Prime Minister of the 'Republic of Abkhazia' Feb. 2010–Sept. 2011. *Address:* c/o Office of the Prime Minister of the 'Republic of Abkhazia', 384900 Abkhazia, Sukhumi, nab. Makhajirov 32, Georgia.

SHAMGAR, Meir; Israeli lawyer, fmr government official and fmr judge; b. 13 Aug. 1925, Danzig (now Gdańsk, Poland); s. of Eliezer Sterenberg and Dina Sterenberg; m. Geula Shamgar 1955 (deceased); two s. one d.; ed Balfour Coll. Tel-Aviv, Hebrew Univ. and Govt Law School, Jerusalem and Univ. of London; served in Israeli army attaining rank of Brig.-Gen. 1948–68; Mil. Advocate-Gen. 1961–68; Legal Adviser, Ministry of Defence April–Aug. 1968; Attorney-Gen. of Israel 1968–75; Justice, Supreme Court 1975, Deputy Chief Justice 1982, Pres. of Supreme Court (Chief Justice of Israel) 1983–95, Pres. Emer. 1995–; Chair. Comm. of Inquiry into Judiciary in Mil. Justice 1977, into Hebron Massacre 1994, into Murder of Prime Minister Yitzhak Rabin 1995, into Appointment and Powers and Duties of Attorney-Gen. of Israel 1999, into Pollution on Kishon River 2001; Head, govt cttee drafting code for ministers' ethics 2007; mem. Perm. Court of Arbitration, The Hague; mem. Council Open Univ. of Israel, World Jurist Asscn (Peace Through Law); Hon. Fellow, Open Univ. of Israel, Hon. Chair. Council for Ethiopian Jewry; Dr hc (Weizman Inst.) 1987, (Hebrew Univ. Jerusalem) 1990, (Ben Gurion Univ., Beer-Sheva) 1996, (Tel Aviv Univ.) 1997, (Bar Ilan Univ.) 1998; Israel Prize for Special Service to Society and State 1996, Ben Gurion Prize 1998, Democracy Award, Israel Democracy Inst. 2008. *Publications:* The Military Government of the Territories Administered by Israel 1967–80: The Legal Aspects 1982; numerous articles and essays in legal publs. *Address:* Kiriat Ben Gurion, Rehov Shaare Mishpat 1, Jerusalem 91909, Israel (office).

SHAMI, Ali Hussein al-; Lebanese academic (retd) and politician; fmr univ. prof.; mem. Amal (Hope—Afwaj al-Muqawamah al-Lubnaniyyah—Lebanese Resistance Detachments); Minister of Foreign Affairs and Emigrants 2009–11 (resgnd). *Address:* c/o Ministry of Foreign Affairs and Emigrants, As-Sultana Bldg, Al Jnah, Sultan Ibrahim, Beirut, Lebanon.

SHAMI, Misbah-Ud-Din, BSc, MSc, PhD; Pakistani chemist, academic and university administrator; b. 1 Oct. 1930, Jalandhar, India; m.; four c.; ed Punjab Univ., Washington State Univ., USA; Prof., Punjab Univ. 1970, Dean, Faculty of Natural Sciences, Eng and Pharmacy 1973, Pro-Vice-Chancellor 1974–76; mem. Univs' Grants Comm. 1976–80; Chair. Pakistan Science Foundation 1980–90; Ed. Pakistan Journal of Science 1972–79; Adviser to Chancellor, Hamdard Univ.,

Karachi 1998–; Postdoctoral Fellowship, Royal Soc. 1969; mem. and fmr Pres. Pakistan Asscn for the Advancement of Science, Pakistan Asscn of Scientists and Scientific Professions, Past-Pres. Scientific Soc. of Pakistan; Founding Fellow, Islamic Acad. of Sciences, mem. Council 1994–99; Fellow, Pakistan Acad. of Sciences, Treas. 2005–; Fellow and Past-Pres. Pakistan Inst. of Chemical Engineers; Allama Iqbal Centenary Commemorative Medal, 1979, Nat. Award of the Pakistan Talent Forum 1987, UNESCO Kalinga Prize 1990, Sitara-Imtiaz 1990, UNESCO Niels Bohr Medal 1990, Pakistan Acad. of Sciences Golden Jubilee Medal 2002. *Address:* c/o Pakistan Academy of Sciences, 3-Constitution Avenue, G-5/2, Islamabad, Pakistan. *Telephone:* (51) 9204657. *Fax:* (51) 9206770. *E-mail:* pasisb@yahoo.com.

SHAMIR, Shimon, PhD; Israeli historian, professor of history and fmr diplomatist; *Professor Emeritus, Department of Middle Eastern and African History, Tel-Aviv University;* b. 15 Dec. 1933, Romania; m. Daniela (née Levin) Shamir 1958; one s. two d.; ed Hebrew Univ. of Jerusalem and Princeton Univ.; Instructor, Lecturer in Modern History of the Middle East, Hebrew Univ. of Jerusalem 1960–66, Fellow, Inst. for Advanced Studies 1978–79; Sr Lecturer, Modern History of the Middle East, Tel-Aviv Univ. 1966, Head of Dept of Middle Eastern and African History 1966–71, Head of Shiloah Center for Middle Eastern and African Studies 1966–73, Assoc. Prof. of Modern History of the Middle East 1970, Head of Grad. School of History 1973–76, mem. Bd of Govs 1974–77, Head of Dept of Middle Eastern and African History 1978–79, Full Prof. 1979, Kaplan Chair in the History of Egypt and Israel 1980, currently Prof. Emer., mem. Steering Cttee 1990–91, Head of Tami Steinmetz Center for Peace Research 1992–95; Dir Israeli Academic Center, Cairo 1982–84, mem. Bd of Dirs 1985–93; Amb. to Egypt 1988–90, to Jordan 1995–97; Fellow, Center for Middle Eastern Studies, Harvard Univ. 1968–69; Visiting Assoc. Prof. of Oriental Studies and Political Science, Univ. of Pennsylvania 1976–77, Dept of Near Eastern Studies, Cornell Univ. 1982; Distinguished Fellow, US Inst. of Peace 1991–92; mem. Council for Higher Educ. 1971–76. *Publications:* A Modern History of the Arabs in the Middle East, 1798–1918 1965, Egypt Under Sadat: The Search for a New Orientation 1978, Self-Views in Historial Perspective in Egypt and Israel 1981, The Jews of Egypt: A Mediterranean Society in Modern Times 1987, Egypt from Monarchy to Republic (ed.) 1995. *Address:* Department of Middle Eastern History, Gilman Building, Room 405, Tel-Aviv University, Ramat-Aviv, 69 978 Tel-Aviv, Israel (office). *Telephone:* (3) 6409313 (office). *Fax:* (3) 6415802 (office). *E-mail:* shimons@post.tau.ac.il (office).

SHAMKHANI, Rear-Adm. Ali, BSc, MSc, MA; Iranian military officer; *Director, Centre for Strategic Defense Research;* b. 29 Sept. 1955, Ahvaz, Khuzestan; ed Univ. of Ahvaz, Univ. of State Man. Org.; held various military posts in Iran-Iraq War including Commdr Islamic Revolution's Guards Corps (IRGC) of Khuzestan province 1981–82, Deputy Commdr of IRGC 1982–89, Chief Commdr of ground force 1984–89, Deputy chiefs of staff of the armed forces in charge of intelligence and operations 1987–89, IRGC Minister 1988–89, Head of implementation cttee of UN Resolution 598 on ending Iran-Iraq War 1988–89; Commdr of IRGC Naval Forces 1989–97; Minister of Defence and Armed Forces Logistics 1997–2005; currently Head, Centre for Strategic Defense Research, Tehran. *Address:* c/o Ministry of Defence, Shadid Yousuf Kaboli Street, Sayed Khandan Area, Tehran, Iran.

SHAMLAN, Ali Abdullah ash-, BSc, MSc, PhD; Kuwaiti geologist, professor of geology and administrator; *Professor of Geology, Kuwait University;* b. 8 March 1945, Kuwait; m.; ed Kuwait Univ.; apptd Demonstrator, Kuwait Univ. 1967, Asst Prof. of Geology 1973, Assoc. Prof. 1978, Prof. 1985–; Chair. Geology Dept, Kuwait Univ. 1975–78, Asst Dean 1978–82, fmr Dean Faculty of Science; fmr Dir-Gen. Kuwait Foundation for the Advancement of Sciences; Chair. Science Coll. Council of Kuwait; fmr Minister of Higher Educ.; mem. Higher Cttee for the Evaluation of the Educational System; mem. Arabian Gulf Univ., Bahrain, Gulf Univ. for Science and Tech., Kuwait, Oxford Center for Islamic Studies, Oxford Univ., UK, Prince Charles School of Traditional Arts, American Soc. of Petroleum Geologists, Soc. of Econ. Palaeontologists and Mineralogists; Founding Fellow, Islamic Acad. of Sciences 1986–; Trustee, American Univ. of Sharjah; Dr hc (Univ. of Massachusetts, USA). *Address:* Kuwait University, PO Box 5969, 13060 Safat, Kuwait City, Kuwait (office); Islamic World Academy of Sciences, PO Box 830036, Zahran, Amman 11183, Jordan (office). *Telephone:* 4811188 (office). *E-mail:* ias@go.com.jo (office). *Website:* www.kuniv.edu/ku (office); www.iasworld.org (office).

SHAMOLIN, Mikhail; Russian business executive; *President and CEO, AFK Sistema;* b. 1970; ed Russian Acad. of Public Admin, Wharton Business School, Univ. of Pennsylvania, USA; worked at McKinsey & Co. 1998–2004; Man. Ferroalloys Div., Interpipe Corpn (Ukraine) 2004–05; joined MTS as Vice-Pres. for Sales and Customer Service 2005–06, Vice-Pres. and Head of MTS Russia business unit 2006–08, Pres. and CEO MTS Group 2008–11; Pres. and CEO, Exec. Bd, Dir and Chair. Man. Bd AFK Sistema 2011–. *Address:* AFK Sistema, 125009 Moscow, 13 Mokhovaya Street, Russia (office). *Telephone:* (495) 228-15-01 (office). *Fax:* (495) 629-12-52 (office). *E-mail:* chairman@sistema.ru (office). *Website:* www.sistema.ru (office); www.sistema.com (office).

SHAMS, Mohammad Jalil, PhD; Afghan economist, academic and politician; ed Sultan Ghias-ud-din Ghoori High School, Herat, Cairo Univ., Egypt, Bochum Univ., Germany; Asst Prof., School of Econs, Kabul Univ. 1964–66; Vice-Pres. Banke Milli-e-Afghan, Hamburg, Germany 1969–71; Man. Dir Afghan Nat. Bank, London, UK 1971–74; Lecturer in Econs, Essen Polytechnic Germany 1973–74; Deputy Minister of Foreign Affairs 1992–94 (resgnd in protest against internal conflict in Afghanistan); Deputy Minister of Energy and Water 2005–06; Minister of Economy 2006–09. *Address:* c/o Ministry of Economy, 5th Floor, Malik Asghar Square, Kabul, Afghanistan. *Telephone:* (20) 2100394. *E-mail:* info@moec.gov.af.

SHAMSIE, Kamila, BA, MFA, FRSL; Pakistani writer; b. 1973, Karachi; d. of Muneeza Shamsie; ed Hamilton Coll., New York, Univ. of Massachusetts, Amherst, USA; columnist and reviewer, The Guardian; Trustee, English PEN, Free Word. *Publications include:* In the City by the Sea (Prime Minister's Award for Literature, Pakistan 1999) 1998, Salt and Saffron (Orange's list of 21 Writers for the 21st century) 2000, Kartography 2002, Broken Verses 2005, Burnt Shadows 2009. *Address:* c/o AM Heath & Co. Ltd, 6 Warwick Court, London, WC1R 5DJ, England (office).

SHAMUZAFAROV, Anvar Shamukhamedovich; Russian politician and architect; *Vice-President, Russian Union of Builders;* b. 10 Nov. 1952; m.; one s.; ed Tashkent Polytech. Inst.; architect, then sr architect, Tashkent Research Inst. of USSR State Cttee on Construction 1974–85; worked in Armenia after earthquake in town restoration projects 1985–88; Chief Expert, Deputy Head of Dept, then Head of Dept Russian State Cttee on Construction (Gosstroi Rossii), Ministry of Construction 1991–96, Chair. 1999–2002; Statistics-Sec., Deputy Minister 1996–98; First Deputy Minister of Land Construction 1998–; consultant to World Bank on problems of financing and reform 1992–98; Chair. Observation Bd Agency of Ipotech Credits (jt stock co.) 1998–99; currently Vice-Pres. Russian Union of Builders; Friendship of Peoples Order. *Address:* c/o Gosstroi Rossii, Stroitelei str. 8, korp. 2, 117987 Moscow, Russia.

SHANDAL, Abd al-Husayn; Iraqi lawyer and politician; b. 1945, Baghdad; trained and worked as criminal lawyer; Minister of Justice in Transitional Govt 2005; mem. Iraqi Nat. Congress 2005–. *E-mail:* info@inciraq.com (office). *Website:* inciraq.com (office).

SHANG, Fulin, PhD; Chinese banker; *Chairman, China Banking Regulatory Commission;* b. Nov. 1951, Jinan, Shandong Province; ed Beijing Finance and Trade Coll., Southwestern Univ. of Finance and Economics, Chengdu; soldier, PLA 1969–73; worker, Municipal Br., Agricultural Bank of China, Beijing, Yingtaoyuan 1973–78, Deputy Div. Dir Financial Planning Dept, Agricultural Bank of China 1982, then Div. Dir, then Deputy Dept Dir, then Dept Dir; Asst Gov. People's Bank of China 1994–96, Deputy Gov. 1996–2001, Head of Monetary Policy Cttee 1997, Del. to Bank for Int. Settlements (BIS) 1998; Gov. Agricultural Bank of China 2001–03; Chair. China Securities Regulatory Comm. 2002–11; Vice-Chair. Exec. Cttee, Int. Securities Regulatory Comm. 2008–; Chair. China Banking Regulatory Comm. 2011–; Alt. mem. 16th CCP Cen. Cttee 2002–07; mem. 17th CCP Cen. Cttee 2007–12, 18th CCP Cen. Cttee 2012–. *Publications:* China's Monetary Policy and Credit System of China 1995, The Operation, Efficiency and Development of Central Banks 1996, China's Success in Controlling Inflation and Its Future Policy Orientation 1997, Encyclopedia of Financial Guarantees 1999, A Study on the Transmission Mechanism of Monetary Policy 2000, The Situational Analysis on State-Owned Commercial Banks 2002. *Address:* Office of the Chairman, China Banking Regulatory Commission, No. 26 Building of Jinyang, Financial Street, West City District, Beijing 100032, People's Republic of China (office). *Telephone:* (10) 58391816 (office). *Fax:* (10) 58391602 (office). *Website:* www.cbrc.gov.cn (office).

SHANGE, Ntozake, MA; American playwright and poet; b. (Paulette Williams), 18 Oct. 1948, Trenton, NJ; d. of Paul Williams and Eloise Williams; m. David Murray 1977 (divorced); one d.; ed Barnard Coll. and Univ. of Southern California; mem. Faculty, Sonoma State Univ. 1973–75, Mills Coll. 1975, City Coll. of New York 1975, Douglass Coll. 1978; fmr Artist-in-Residence, Univ. of Florida; performing mem. Sounds in Motion Dance Co.; author, An Evening with Diana Ross: The Big Event 1977; Guggenheim Fellow 1981; mem. Nat. Acad. of TV Arts and Sciences, Acad. of American Poets, PEN America; recipient of numerous drama and poetry awards. *Publications include:* plays: For Colored Girls Who Have Considered Suicide/When the Rainbow is Enuf 1975, A Photograph: Lovers-in-Motion 1977, Boogie Woogie Landscapes 1979, Spell #7 1979, Black and White Two Dimensional Planes 1979, Mother Courage and Her Children 1980, Three for a Full Moon 1982, Bocas 1982, Educating Rita 1982, From Okra to Greens/A Different Kinda Love Story 1983, Three Views of Mt. Fuji 1987, Daddy Says 1989; novels: Sassafrass, Cypress and Indigo 1976, Betsey Brown 1985, The Love Space Demands 1991, I Live in Music 1994, Liliane: Resurrection of the Daughter 1995, Some Sing, Some Cry (with Ifa Bayeza) 2010; poetry: Melissa and Smith 1976, Natural Disasters and Other Festive Occasions 1977, Nappy Edges 1978, Three Pieces 1981, A Daughter's Geography 1983, From Okra to Greens 1984; essays, short stories, non-fiction, adaptations; contribs to magazines and anthologies. *Address:* c/o St Martin's Press, 175 Fifth Avenue, New York, NY 10010, USA (office).

SHANGHVI, Dilip S., BCom; Indian pharmaceutical industry executive; *Chairman and Managing Director, Sun Pharmaceutical Industries Ltd;* b. Amreli, Gujarat; m.; two c.; ed Univ. of Calcutta; Founder and Man. Dir Sun Pharmaceutical Industries Ltd 1983–, Chair. 1999–; Chair. Bd of Dirs Caraco Pharmaceutical Labs Ltd 1997–; Dir Sun Speciality Chemicals Pvt. Ltd, Sun Resins & Polymers Pvt. Ltd, Sun Fastfin Services Pvt. Ltd, Sun Petrochemicals Pvt. Ltd, SPARC Bio-Research Pvt. Ltd, Sun Pharma Global Inc., British Virgin Island, Sun Pharma De Mexico SA DE CV, SPIL De Mexico SA DE CV, Shantilal Shanghvi Foundation; mem. Advisory Cttee Global Bio Pharma Conf. Group; Ernst & Young Entrepreneur of the Year in Health Care and Life Sciences 2005, Entrepreneur of the Year Award, The Economic Times 2008, CEO of the Year, The Business Standard, First Generation Entrepreneur of the Year, CNBC- TV 18 India Business Leader Awards 2007, Lifetime Honour, Indian Merchants Chamber 2008. *Leisure interests* reading, travelling, listening to music. *Address:* Acme Plaza, Andheri–Kurla Rd, Andheri East, Mumbai 400 059, India (office). *Telephone:* (22) 56455645 (office). *Fax:* (22) 56455685 (office). *E-mail:* piedadedsouya@sunpharma.com (office). *Website:* www.sunpharma.com (office).

SHANKAR, Ramamurti, BTech, PhD; Indian physicist and academic; *John Randolph Huffman Professor of Physics, Yale University;* b. 28 April 1947, New Delhi; ed Indian Inst. of Tech., Madras, Univ. of California, Berkeley, USA; Jr Fellow, Harvard Soc. of Fellows 1974–77; J.W. Gibbs Instructor of Physics, Yale Univ. 1977–79, Asst Prof. 1979–83, Assoc. Prof. 1983–88, Prof. 1988, Chair., Dept of Physics 2001, John Randolph Huffman Prof. of Physics 2004–; Visiting Assoc. Prof., Ecole Normale Supérieure, Paris, France 1982; A.P. Sloan Fellow 1982–86; Visiting Prof., Inst. for Theoretical Physics, Santa Barbara, Calif. 1989; mem. Editorial Bd Journal of Statistical Physics 1988–90; mem. Aspen Center for Physics 1998–2003, Trustee 2004–; mem. numerous cttees at Yale and elsewhere including Cttee of Visitors, NSF 1999, Dannie Heineman Prize Cttee 1997–98; Fellow, American Physical Soc. 2001–; Byrnes and Sewel Teaching Prize, Yale Univ. 2005, Julius Edgar Lilienfeld Prize, American Physical Soc. 2008. *Publications:* Principles of Quantum Mechanics 1980, Basic Training in Mathematics 1995; numerous journal articles. *Address:* 554 Sloane Physics Laboratory, Department of Physics, Yale University, POB 208120, New Haven, CT 06520, USA (office). *Telephone:* (203) 432-6917 (office). *Fax:* (203) 432-6175 (office).

E-mail: r.shankar@yale.edu (office). *Website:* pantheon.yale.edu/~rshankar (office).

SHANKAR, Uday, MPhil; Indian journalist and media executive; *CEO, Star India;* b. 16 Sept. 1962; m.; ed Jawaharlal Nehru Univ., New Delhi, Times School of Journalism; worked at The Times of India, Sunday Mail, India Today and Sahara (launched news div. of Sahara TV); fmr Ed. and News Dir Aaj Tak, launched Aaj Tak Headlines Today; joined Star News as CEO Media Content and Communications Services, Star Group 2004–07, COO Star India May–Oct. 2007, CEO Oct. 2007–; Industry Leadership Award, 8th Annual Indian Film Festival Los Angeles 2010. *Address:* Star India, 1st Floor, Central Wing, Thapar House, 124 Janpath, New Delhi 110 001, India (office). *Telephone:* (11) 42494900 (office). *Fax:* (11) 41049490 (office). *E-mail:* info@star.co.in (office). *Website:* www.star.co.in (office); www.indya.com (office).

SHANKARDASS, Raghuvansh Kumar Prithvinath, MA, LLM; Indian lawyer; b. 9 June 1930, Nairobi, Kenya; s. of P. N. Shankardass and Pushpavati Shankardass; m. Ramma Handoo 1955; ed Trinity Coll., Cambridge and Lincoln's Inn, London, UK; Gen. Sec. Bar Asscn of India 1975–85, Vice-Pres. 1985–; Asst Sec.-Gen. Int. Bar Asscn 1980–82, Vice-Pres. 1984–86, Pres. 1986–88; Gen. Sec. Indian Law Foundation 1975–1991, Pres. 1991–; Chair. Panel of Commrs UN Compensation Comm. 1996–2005; Fellow, American Bar Foundation 1997; Ed. The Indian Advocate 1990–; Pres. Cambridge Univ. Majlis 1953; Vice-Pres. Indian Soc. of Int. Law 2003–06; fmr Advisor, Govt of Qatar; currently Int. Law Advisor to Ministry of Water Resources, Ministry of External Affairs; Trustee India Foundation for the Arts 1994–2000, Talwar Research Foundation 1996, Nurul Hasan Educational and Research Foundation 1998–, Pratichi (India) Trust 2003–; mem. governing council, Centre for Policy Research, India 2008–; Hon. OBE; Hon. LLD (North Orissa Univ.) 2012. *Leisure interests:* golf, music, reading, travel. *Address:* 87 Lawyer's Chambers, Supreme Court of India, New Delhi 110 001 (office); B-12 Maharani Bagh, New Delhi 110 065, India (home). *Telephone:* (11) 23381041 (office); (11) 26830636 (home). *Fax:* (11) 26848104 (home). *E-mail:* rkpslaw@hotmail.com (office).

SHANKS, Ian Alexander, OBE, PhD, FRS, FIEE, FRSA, FRSE; British scientist; *Honorary Professor, University of Glasgow;* b. 22 June 1948, Glasgow; s. of Alexander Shanks and Isabella A. Beaton; m. Janice Coulter 1971; one d.; ed Dumbarton Acad., Univ. of Glasgow and Portsmouth Polytechnic; Projects Man. Scottish Colorfoto Labs Ltd, Alexandria 1970–72; Jr Research Fellow, Royal Signals and Radar Establishment, Malvern, later Sr Scientific Officer, Prin. Scientific Officer 1973–82; Sr Scientist, later Prin. Scientist/Sr Man. Unilever Research Lab., Sharnbrook, Beds. 1982–86, Divisional Science Adviser 1994–2000, Vice-Pres. Physical and Eng Sciences 2001–03, Vice-Pres. Physical and Eng Sciences 2001–; Chief Scientist, Thorn EMI PLC 1986–94; Visiting Prof. of Electrical and Electronic Eng, Univ. of Glasgow 1985–, now Hon. Prof.; Founder Optoelectronics Coll.; Vice-Pres. The Royal Soc. 1989–91; Chair. Inter-Agency Cttee for Marine Science and Tech. 1991–93; Pres. Asscn for Science Educ., Scotland 2007–08; mem. Optoelectronics Cttee, Rank Prize Fund 1985–, Steering Group for Science and Eng Policy Studies Unit 1988–90, Science Consultative Group, BBC 1989–91; mem. Advisory Bd for Research Councils 1990–93, Science Advisory Group for Nat. Physical Lab. (currently Chair.), Royal Acad. of Eng Science 1998–2007, Advisory Bd for Inst. of Nanotechnology 2001–06; Fellow, Royal Acad. of Eng; Hon. Fellow, Inst. of Nanotechnology 2005; Hon. DEng (Univ. of Glasgow) 2002; Clifford Paterson Medal and Prize, Inst. of Physics 1984. *Achievements include:* over 75 patents mainly on liquid crystals, displays and biosensors. *Leisure interests:* music, collecting antique pocket watches, scientific instruments and art deco figures. *Address:* Electronics and Electrical Engineering Department, Rankine Building, University of Glasgow, Glasgow G12 8LT, Scotland (office); Kings Close, 11 Main Road, Biddenham, Bedford, MK40 4BB, England (home). *Telephone:* (1234) 328773 (home). *Website:* www.gla.ac.uk (office).

SHANMUGAM, K(asiviswanathan), LLD; Singaporean lawyer and politician; *Minister for Foreign Affairs and Law;* b. 1959, Singapore; ed Raffles Inst., Nat. Univ. of Singapore; admitted to Singapore Bar as advocate and solicitor 1985; several years' private legal practice, becoming Sr Pnr and Head of Litigation and Dispute Resolution, Allen & Gledhill LLP (law firm); apptd Sr Counsel, Supreme Court of Singapore 1998; MP for Nee Soon Group Representation Constituency 1988–; Minister for Law 2008–, Second Minister for Home Affairs 2008–11, also Minister for Foreign Affairs 2011–; mem. Singapore Indian Devt Asscn (Pres. 2002–09); mem. People's Action Party. *Address:* Ministry of Foreign Affairs, MFA Bldg, Tanglin, off Napier Road, Singapore 248163, Singapore (office). *Telephone:* 63798000 (office). *Fax:* 64747885 (office). *E-mail:* mfa@mfa.gov.sg (office). *Website:* www.mfa.gov.sg (office).

SHANMUGARATNAM, Tharman, MPA; Singaporean politician and economist; *Deputy Prime Minister and Minister of Finance;* b. 1957, London, England; m. Jane Yumiko Ittogi; three s. one d.; ed London School of Econs, Univ. of Cambridge, UK, Harvard Univ., USA; early professional career as Man. Dir Monetary Authority of Singapore (MAS), Chair. 2011–; mem. Parl. for Jurong GRC (Taman Jurong) 2001–; Sr Minister of State, Ministry of Trade and Industry and Ministry of Educ. 2001–03, Minister for Educ. 2003–08, Second Minister of Finance 2006–07, Minister of Finance 2007–, Minister for Manpower 2011–12, Deputy Prime Minister 2011–; became first Asian apptd Chair. of Int. Monetary and Financial Cttee (policy steering cttee of IMF) 2011–; Chair. Ong Teng Cheong Labour Leadership Inst.; Chair. Bd of Trustees, Singapore Indian Devt Asscn (SINDA); Lucius N. Littauer Fellow Award, Harvard Univ., Singapore Public Admin Gold Medal 1999. *Address:* Ministry of Finance, The Treasury 100 High Street, #10-01, Singapore 179434 (office). *Telephone:* 63322717 (office). *Fax:* 63367001 (office). *E-mail:* tharman_s@mof.gov.sg (office). *Website:* www.mof.gov.sg (office).

SHANNON, M. Frances, BSc, PhD; Irish biochemist and academic; *Vice-Chancellor, Research, University of Canberra;* ed Univ. Coll. Dublin; Postdoctoral Fellow, Univ. of Adelaide, then Founding mem. Hanson Centre for Cancer Research, Inst. of Medical and Veterinary Science, Adelaide; joined faculty as Prof., ANU, Interim Dir John Curtin School of Medical Research (JCSMR) 2008–09, Deputy Dir 2007–08, also served as head of Div. of Molecular Bioscience and Group Leader, Gene Expression and Epigenomics Lab., now Prof. (hon.);

currently Deputy Vice-Chancellor, Research, Univ. of Canberra; mem. Editorial Bd FEBS Letts (journal of Fed. of European Biochemical Socs); Australian Soc. for Biochemistry and Molecular Biology Boehringer Medal, Lorne Genome Meeting Julian Wells Medal. *Address:* Office of the Vice-Chancellor, Research, 1D129, University of Canberra, Canberra, ACT 2601, Australia (office). *Telephone:* (2) 6201-5914 (office). *Fax:* (2) 6201-5466 (office). *E-mail:* Frances.Shannon@canberra .edu.au (office). *Website:* www.canberra.edu.au (office).

SHANNON, Richard Thomas, PhD; New Zealand/British historian and professor of modern history; *Professor Emeritus, University of Wales, Swansea;* b. 10 June 1931, Suva, Fiji; s. of Edward Arthur Shannon and Grace Shannon (née McLeod); ed Mount Albert Grammar School, Auckland, New Zealand, Auckland Univ. Coll., Gonville and Caius Coll., Cambridge; Lecturer and Sr Lecturer in History, Univ. Coll. Auckland 1955–57, 1961–62; Lecturer in English History, Univ. of E Anglia, Norwich, UK 1963–65, Sr Lecturer 1965–71, Reader 1971–79; Prof. of Modern History, Univ. of Wales, Swansea 1979–97, Head, History Dept 1982–88, Dean Faculty of Arts 1985–88, Prof. Emer. 1997–; Visiting Fellow, Peterhouse, Cambridge 1988–89; Leverhulme Sr Research Fellowship 1988–90; Fellow, St Deiniol's (Gladstone Foundation) 2000. *Publications:* Gladstone and the Bulgarian Agitation, 1876 1963, The Crisis of Imperialism, 1865–1915 1974, Gladstone, Vol. I 1809–1865 1982, The Age of Disraeli 1868–1881 1992, The Age of Salisbury, 1881–1902 1996, Gladstone Vol. II 1865–1898 1999, A Press Free and Responsible. Self-regulation and the Press Complaints Commission, 1991–2001 2001. *Leisure interest:* mid-Wales borders. *Address:* Flat A, 86 Portland Place, London, W1B 1NU, England (home). *Telephone:* (20) 7436-0214 (London) (home). *E-mail:* dickshannon86@hotmail.com (home).

SHANTSEV, Valery Pavlinovich; Russian politician; *Governor, Nizhny Novgorod Region;* b. 1947, Susanino Kostroma Region; m.; one s. one d.; ed Moscow Aviation School, Moscow Inst. of Radiotech., Electronics and Automation, Acad. of Nat. Econs; asst to master factory Salut 1968–75; instructor Perov Dist CP Cttee, Deputy Head Machine Construction Dept Moscow City CP Cttee 1975–85; Chair. Exec. Cttee Perov Dist Soviet, First Sec. Perov Dist CP Cttee, Chair. Perov Dist Soviet of People's Deputies 1985–90; Sec. Moscow City CP Cttee 1990–91; Deputy of Perovo District Council of People's Deputies 1983–93; Deputy of Moscow Soviet 1987–93; Commercial Dir Hockey Club Dynamo 1991–94; Prefect of S Admin. Dist of Moscow 1994–96; Vice-Mayor of Moscow, First Deputy Prime Minister, Moscow Govt and Head of Social Complex 1996–99; Vice-Mayor of Moscow, First Deputy Prime Minister, Moscow Govt and Head of Econ. Policy and Devt Complex 1999–2001; Vice-Mayor of Moscow and Head of Econ. Policy and Devt Complex 2001–05; Gov. Nizhny Novgorod Region 2005–. *Address:* Office of the Governor, Kremlin, Corpus 1 and 2, Nizhny Novgorod 603082, Russia (office). *Telephone:* (8314) 33-52-51 (office). *Fax:* (8314) 33-49-03. *E-mail:* official@mvs .kreml.nnov.ru. *Website:* www.government.nnov.ru (office).

SHAO, Lt-Gen. Huaze; Chinese journalist, army officer and government official; *Dean, School of Journalism and Mass Communication, Peking University;* b. June 1933, Chun'an Co., Zhejiang Prov.; ed PLA Political Cadres' School No. 2, Chinese People's Univ.; joined PLA 1950, CCP 1957; Ed. Jiefangjun Ribao (PLA Daily) 1964; Vice-Dir Jiefangjun Ribao 1981; Dir Propaganda Dept PLA Gen. Political Dept 1985; rank of Maj.-Gen. 1988, Lt-Gen. 1992; Ed.-in-Chief Renmin Ribao (People's Daily) 1989–92, Dir 1992–2000; Chair. All-China Journalists' Asscn 1996–2006; currently Dean, School of Journalism and Mass Communication, Peking Univ.; Vice-Chair. China Great Wall Soc.; mem. 14th CCP Cen. Cttee 1992–97, 15th CCP Cen. Cttee 1997–2002; mem. Standing Cttee 9th CPPCC Nat. Cttee 1998–2003; fmr Hon. Pres. Chinese Soc. of News Photography, Chinese Newspapers Asscn. *Address:* School of Journalism and Mass Communication, Peking University, Beijing 100871, People's Republic of China (office). *Telephone:* (10) 62754683 (office). *Fax:* (10) 62754485 (office). *E-mail:* sjc18@pku.edu.cn (office). *Website:* sjc.pku.edu.cn (office).

SHAO, Qihui; Chinese administrator and engineer; b. 1934, Yixing, Jiangsu Prov.; ed Harbin Inst. of Tech.; joined CCP 1953; Vice-Gov. Heilongjiang Prov. 1988–89, Gov. 1989–94; mem. 14th CCP Cen. Cttee 1992–97; Vice-Minister, Ministry of Machine-Building Industry 1994–98; Dir State Admin of Machine-Building Industry 1998–99; Vice-Chair. Econ. Cttee and Standing mem. CPPCC; mem. 9th CCP Cen. Cttee Nat. Cttee 2003–08; currently Dir (non-exec.) Sinotruk (Hong Kong) Ltd; Adviser, Nat. Cttee for Science and Tech. Award; Hon. Chair. Soc. of Automotive Engineers of China, Fed. of Machinery Industry of China; People's Friendship Medal of Russia 1991. *Leisure interest:* photography. *Address:* Sinotruk (Hong Kong) Limited, Room 2102-2103, 21/F Shun Tak Ctr China, Merchants Tower, 168-200 Connaught Road C, Sheung Wan, Hong Kong Special Administrative Region, People's Republic of China (office).

SHAPIRO, Bernard, OC, BA, PhD; Canadian (b. American) academic administrator and fmr government official; *Principal Emeritus, McGill University;* b. 8 June 1935, Montreal; s. of Maxwell Shapiro and Mary Tafler; twin brother of Harold T. Shapiro (q.v.); m. Phyllis Schwartz 1957 (died 2005); one s. one d.; ed McGill Univ., Harvard Univ., USA; started career as Assoc. Dean, School of Educ., Boston Univ.; Dean, Faculty of Educ., Univ. of Western Ontario 1976, Vice-Pres. (Academic) and Provost 1978; Dir Ontario Inst. for Studies in Educ. 1980–86; Deputy Minister of Educ., Ont. Prov. 1986–89, of Skills Devt 1988–89; Deputy Sec. of Prov. Cabinet, Ont. 1989–90, Deputy Minister and Sec., Man. Bd 1990–91, of Colls and Univs 1991–93; Prof. of Educ. and Public Policy, Univ. of Toronto 1992–94; Prin. and Vice-Chancellor McGill Univ. 1994–2003, currently Prin. Emer.; Ethics Commr of Canada 2004–07 (resgnd); Officer, Order of Canada 1999, Grand Officer, Nat. Order of Quebec 2004; Hon. LLD (McGill) 1988, (Toronto) 1994, (Ottawa) 1995, (Yeshiva) 1996, (Montreal) 1998, (Edin.) 2000, (Glasgow) 2001, (Bishop's) 2001, Dr hc (McMaster), (Nipissing), (Melbourne). *Address:* c/o McGill University, James Administration Building, Room 506, 845 Sherbrooke Street West, Montreal, PQ H3A 2T5, Canada.

SHAPIRO, Ehud (Udi), BA, BSc, PhD; Israeli computer scientist and academic; *Harry Weinrebe Professorial Chair of Computer Science and Biology, Weizmann Institute of Science;* b. 28 Feb. 1955, Jerusalem; ed Tel-Aviv Univ., Yale Univ., USA; Postdoctoral Fellow, Dept of Computer Science and Applied Math., Weizmann Inst. 1982–93, co-operated closely with Japanese Fifth Generation Computer Systems project to invent high-level programming language for parallel

and distributed computer systems, named Concurrent Prolog, on leave of absence 1993–98, Assoc. Prof., Depts of Computer Science and Applied Math., and Biological Chem., holds Harry Weinrebe Professorial Chair of Computer Science and Biology 1998–; Founder and CEO Ubique Ltd (Israeli software co., sold to AOL 1995, sold again to IBM in 1988 following man. buy-out in 1997); World Tech. Award in Biotechnology, The World Tech. Network 2004, Research Leader in Nanotechnology, Scientific American 50 2004. *Achievements include:* studied molecular biology in attempt to build biomolecular computer to operate inside the living body ('Doctor in a Cell'); has also developed method for tracing 'genealogy' of cells in the human body. *Publications:* Algorithmic Program Debugging 1983, Inductive Inference of Theories from Facts 1986, The Art of Prolog: Advanced Programming Techniques (with L. Sterling) 1986 (translated into Japanese, Dutch, French, German and Russian, second edn 1994), Concurrent Prolog: Collected Papers, Vols 1 and 2 (ed.) 1987, Hebrew Prolog for Beginners (with Z. Scherz and O. Maler; in Hebrew) 1988; several scientific papers in professional journals; five US patents. *Address:* Department of Computer Science and Applied Mathematics, Weizmann Institute of Science, Rehovot 76100, Israel (office). *Telephone:* (8) 934-4506 (office). *Fax:* (8) 947-1746 (office). *E-mail:* ehud.shapiro@ weizmann.ac.il (office). *Website:* www.wisdom.weizmann.ac.il/~udi (office).

SHAPIRO, Harold Tafler, MA, PhD; American university president and professor of economics; *Professor of Economics and Public Affairs, Department of Economics and Woodrow Wilson School of Public and International Affairs, Princeton University;* b. 8 June 1935, Montreal, Canada; s. of Maxwell Shapiro and Mary Tafler; twin brother of Bernard Shapiro (q.v.); m. Vivian Shapiro; four d.; ed McGill Univ. and Princeton Univ. Grad. School; Asst Prof. of Econs Univ. of Mich. 1964, Assoc. Prof. 1967, Prof. 1970, Vice-Pres. for Academic Affairs 1977, Pres. 1980–88; Pres. Princeton Univ. 1988–2001, Pres. Emer. 2001–, Prof. of Econs and Public Affairs, Dept of Econs and Woodrow Wilson School of Public and Int. Affairs 1988–; currently Chair. Cttee on Organizational Structure of NIH; mem. Conf. Bd Inc., Bretton Woods Cttee; mem. Pres.'s Council of Advisors on Science and Tech. 1990–92; Chair. Nat. Bioethics Advisory Comm. 1996–; Dir Dow Chemical Co., Nat. Bureau of Econ. Research; mem. Bd of Dirs, Inst. for Advanced Study 2009–; Chair, InterAcademy Council Cttee on the Review of International Panel on Climate Change 2010–; mem. Inst. of Medicine of NAS, American Philosophical Soc.; mem. Bd of Overseers, Robert Wood Johnson Medical Center, Bd of Trustees Educational Testing Service 1994–2000, Univ. Corpn for Advanced Internet Devt 2000–; Fellow, American Acad. of Arts and Sciences 1990, Coll. of Physicians of Philadelphia 2000, American Asscn for the Advancement of Science 2006; Trustee, Alfred P. Sloan Foundation, Univ. of Pennsylvania Medical Center, Univs Research Asscn, Educational Testing Service; Harold Helm Fellow 1961–64, Harold Dodds Sr Fellow 1963–64; Hon. DSc (Michigan Technological Univ., Michigan) 1980, Hon. LLD (Wayne State Univ., Michigan) 1980, (Grand Valley State Colleges, Michigan) 1983, (Albion College, Michigan) 1985, (Michigan State Univ., Michigan) 1987, (Univ. of Michigan, Michigan) 1987, (Rutgers Univ., New Jersey) 1988, (Yale Univ., Connecticut 1988), (McGill Univ., Quebec, Canada) 1988, (Centenary Coll., New Jersey 1992, (Univ. of Toronto, Ontario, Canada) 1994, Hon. DHL (Yeshiva Univ., New York) 1996, Dr hc (Univ. of Edinburgh) 2000, Carnegie Mellon Univ., Pennsylvania 2009, Thomas Edison State Coll., New Jersey 2009; Lieutenant Gov.'s Medal in Commerce 1956, William D. Carey Lectureship Award 2006, Clark Kerr Award, Univ. of California 2009. *Address:* Department of Economics and The Woodrow Wilson School of Public and International Affairs, 359 Wallace Hall, Princeton University, Princeton, NJ 08544-0015 (office); 10 Campbelton Circle, Princeton, NJ 08540, USA (home). *Telephone:* (609) 258-6184 (home). *Fax:* (609) 258-7120 (office). *E-mail:* hts@ princeton.edu (office). *Website:* www.princeton.edu/~hts (office).

SHAPIRO, Irwin I., PhD, FAAS; American physicist and academic; *Timken University Professor, Department of Astronomy, Harvard University;* b. 29 Oct. 1929, New York; s. of Esther Feinberg and Samuel Shapiro; m. Marian Helen Kaplan 1959; one s. one d.; ed Cornell and Harvard Univs; mem. staff, MIT Lincoln Lab. 1954–70, Prof. of Geophysics and Physics 1967–80; Redman Lecturer, McMaster Univ. 1969; Sherman Fairchild Distinguished Scholar, Calif. Inst. of Tech. 1974; Schlumberger Prof., MIT 1980–85, Prof. Emer. 1985–; Sr Scientist, Smithsonian Astrophysical Observatory 1982–; Paine Prof. of Practical Astronomy and Prof. of Physics, Harvard Univ. 1982–97, Timken Univ. Prof., Dept of Astronomy 1997–, Dir Harvard-Smithsonian Center for Astrophysics 1983–2004 (Chair. Bd 1980–81); John C. Lindsay Lecturer, NASA Goddard Space Flight Center 1986; mem. Editorial Bd Celestial Mechanics 1969–75, Annals of Physics 1977–82; Assoc. Ed. Icarus 1969–75; Fellow, American Geophysical Union, American Physical Soc.; mem. Int. Astronomical Union, NAS 1974, American Acad. of Arts and Sciences 1969, American Astronomical Soc., American Philosophical Soc. 1998; mem. Radio Science Teams, Mariner Venus–Mercury, Viking and Pioneer–Venus Missions 1970–79, Space Science Bd (NAS) 1977–80, NSF Astronomy Advisory Cttee 1983–86, Task Group on Astronomy and Astrophysics of Nat. Research Council Space Science Bd Study 'Major Directions for Space Science: 1995–2015' 1984–86, Tech. Oversight Cttee of Nat. Earth Orientation Service 1986–, NASA Advisory Council 1987–90; Chair. NASA Astrophysics Sub-cttee 1988–92, mem. 1992–96; Albert A. Michelson Medal of Franklin Inst. 1975, Benjamin Apthorp Gould Prize of NAS 1979, John Simon Guggenheim Fellowship 1982, New York Acad. of Sciences Award in Physical and Math. Sciences 1982, Dannie Heineman Award of American Astronomical Soc. 1983, Whitten Medal (American Geophysical Union) 1991, Bowie Medal (American Geophysical Union) 1993, Einstein Medal 1994, Gerard Kuiper Award 1997, Sec.'s Gold Medal for Exceptional Service, Smithsonian Inst. 1999. *Publications:* over 350 including Prediction of Ballistic Missile Trajectories from Radar Observations 1958; Ed. of trans. of Mathematical Foundations of Quantum Statistics (Khinchin) 1960; numerous scientific articles, tech. reports and text books for students. *Address:* Harvard-Smithsonian Center for Astrophysics, 60 Garden Street, MS 51, Cambridge, MA 02138 (office); 17 Lantern Lane, Lexington, MA 02421, USA (home). *Telephone:* (617) 495-7100 (office). *Fax:* (617) 495-7105 (office). *E-mail:* ishapiro@cfa.harvard.edu (office). *Website:* cfa-www.harvard.edu (office); cfa-www .harvard.edu/ast (office).

SHAPIRO, Joel, BA, MA; American sculptor; b. 27 Sept. 1941, New York, NY; s. of Dr Joseph Shapiro and Dr Anna Shapiro; m. Ellen Phelan; one d.; ed New York Univ., Peace Corps in India; teacher, Princeton Univ. 1974–75, 1975–76, School of

Visual Arts 1977–82; group exhbns in UK, USA, Australia, France, Germany, Spain, the Netherlands, Switzerland, China, Singapore 1969–2012; Nat. Endowment for the Arts 1975; mem. Swedish Royal Acad. of Art 1994, American Acad. of Arts and Letters 1998; Chevalier des Arts et des Lettres 2005; Visual Arts Fellowship, Visual Arts Program, Nat. Endowment for the Arts 1975, Brandeis Univ. Creative Arts Award 1984, Skowhegan Medal for Sculpture 1986, Award of Merit Medal for Sculpture, American Acad. and Inst. of Arts and Letters, New York 1990, Resident in the Visual Arts, American Acad. in Rome 1998–99, Smithsonian Archives of American Art Award 2008, Distinguished Alumni, New York Univ. 2010, Gabarron Int. Award for Visual Art 2012, Nat. Art Award, Americans for the Arts 2013. *Film:* 20 Elements 2005, Michael Blackwood. *Radio:* Giornale radio (interview with Peter Boswell, Radio RAI, Italy) 1999, New York and Company (interview with Leonard Lopate, WNYC-AM, New York) 2001, Leonard Lopate Remote, Whitney Museum of American Art (WNYC-AM) 2002, Art Talk (interview with Edward Goldman, KCRW-FM, Los Angeles) 2004. *Television:* Julião Sarmento/Joel Shapiro 1997, L'Exposition Impossible, Musée d'Orsay, Paris 2005, Joel Shapiro: Twenty Elements (Michael Blackwood Productions, Inc., New York) (DVD) 2006, Getty Museum Audio Tour Interview on Matisse, Nasher Museum 2006. *Publications:* numerous exhbn catalogues with text by others. *Address:* c/o The Pace Gallery, 32 East 57th Street, New York, NY 10022, USA. *Telephone:* (212) 421-3292 (office). *E-mail:* studio@jeshapiro.com (office). *Website:* www.thepacegallery.com (office).

SHAPIRO, Larry J., AB, MD; American geneticist, paediatrician and academic; *Dean, School of Medicine, Washington University in St Louis;* b. 6 July 1946, Chicago; m. Carol-Ann Uetake; one s. two d.; ed Washington Univ. in St Louis; intern, St Louis Children's Hosp. 1971–72, resident 1971–73; Research Assoc., Nat. Inst. of Arthritis, Metabolism and Digestive Diseases, Bethesda, Md 1973–75; Asst Prof. of Pediatrics, UCLA 1975–79, Assoc. Prof. 1979–83, Prof. of Pediatrics and Biological Chemistry 1983–91; Investigator, Howard Hughes Medical Inst. 1987–91, also W.H. and Marie Wattis Distinguished Prof.; Prof. and Chair. Dept of Pediatrics, Univ. of California, San Francisco School of Medicine 1991–2003, also Chief of Pediatric Services, Univ. of California, San Francisco Children's Hosp.; Spencer T. and Ann W. Olin Distinguished Prof., Exec. Vice Chancellor for Medical Affairs and Dean, School of Medicine, Washington Univ. in St Louis 2003–; Fellow, AAAS, American Acad. of Pediatrics; mem. NAS Inst. of Medicine, American Acad. of Arts and Sciences, American Pediatric Soc. (Pres. 2003–04), American Soc. for Clinical Investigation, American Soc. for Human Genetics (Pres. 1997), Asscn of American Physicians, Soc. for Inherited Metabolic Disease (Pres. 1986–87), Western Soc. for Pediatric Research (Pres. 1989–90), Soc. for Pediatric Research (Pres. 1991–92); numerous awards including Ross Award, Western Soc. for Pediatric Research 1981. *Address:* Office of the Dean, School of Medicine, Washington University in St Louis, 660 South Euclid Avenue, St Louis, MO 63110, USA (office). *Telephone:* (314) 362-6827 (office). *Website:* medschool.wustl .edu (office).

SHAPIRO, Robert Leslie, BS, JD; American lawyer; b. 2 Sept. 1942, Plainfield, NJ; m. Linell Shapiro; two s. (one deceased); ed Univ. of California, Los Angeles, Loyola Univ. Law School; called to the Bar, Calif. 1969, US Court of Appeals 1972, US Dist Court, Calif. 1982; Deputy Dist Attorney, LA 1969–72; sole practice 1972–87; Counsel, Bushkin, Gaims, Gaines, Jonas 1987–88; with Christensen, White, Miller, Fink & Jacobs 1988–95, currently Pnr, Glaser Weil Fink Jacobs Howard Avchen & Shapiro LLP and Head, White-Collar Criminal Defense Section; f. Trial Lawyers for Public Justice 1982; mem. Nat. Asscn of Criminal Defence Lawyers, Calif. Attorneys for Criminal Justice, Bar Asscn; Founder and Chair. Brent Shapiro Foundation for Drug Awareness; American Jurisprudence Award, Bancroft Whitney 1969; Best Criminal Defence Lawyer, Bar Asscn 1993, Lawyer of the Year 1995, Bruce K. Gould Award, Touro Law Center 1997, Author of One of the Ten Best Legal Articles of the Decade, Calif. State Bar Journal, Pro-Bono Lawyer of the Year, Nevada, 100 Most Influential Lawyers in America, National Law Journal. *Publications:* Search for Justice 1996, Misconception (novel) 2001. *Address:* Glaser Weil Fink Jacobs Howard Avchen & Shapiro LLP, 10250 Constellation Boulevard, 19th Floor, Los Angeles, CA 90067, USA (office). *Telephone:* (310) 556-7886 (office). *Fax:* (310) 556-2920 (office). *E-mail:* rs@ glaserweil.com (office). *Website:* www.robertshapiro.com (office); www .brentshapiro.org.

SHAPLEY, Lloyd Stowell, PhD; American professor of mathematics and economics; *Professor Emeritus, Department of Mathematics, University of California, Los Angeles;* b. 2 June 1923, Cambridge, Mass.; s. of Harlow Shapley and Martha Betz; m. Marian Ludolph 1955 (died 1997); two s.; ed Belmont Hill School, Phillips Exeter Acad., Harvard and Princeton Univs; served in Army Air Corps in meteorology and cryptanalysis 1943–45; research mathematician, RAND Corpn 1948–54, 1954–81; visiting appointments at California Inst. of Tech. 1955–56, Indian Statistical Inst. 1979, Hebrew Univ. of Jerusalem 1979–80, Catholic Univ. of Louvain, Belgium 1982, Nat. Univ. of Defence Tech., China 1987; intermittent teaching, RAND Grad. Inst. 1970; apptd Prof. of Math. and Econs, UCLA 1981, currently Prof. Emer.; Procter Fellow, Princeton Univ. 1951–52; Fellow, Econometric Soc. 1967, American Acad. of Arts and Sciences 1974, Inst. for Operations Research and Management Sciences 2002; Distinguished Fellow, American Econ. Asscn 2007; mem. NAS 1979; Hon. PhD (Hebrew Univ. of Jerusalem) 1986; Bronze Star, US Army 1943; Von Neumann Theory Prize, ORSA/ TIMS 1981, Nobel Prize in Econ. Sciences 2012. *Publications include:* Geometry of Moment Spaces (with S. Karlin) 1953, Values of Non-Atomic Games (with R. Aumann) 1974. *Leisure interest:* Kriegsspiel. *Address:* Department of Mathematics and Department of Economics, UCLA, PO Box 951555, Los Angeles, CA 90095-1555, USA (office). *Telephone:* (310) 825-3233 (office). *Fax:* (310) 206-6673 (office). *E-mail:* shapley@math.ucla.edu (office). *Website:* www.math.ucla.edu/people/ pages/shapley.shtml (office).

SHAPOSHNIKOV, Air Marshal Yevgeny Ivanovich; Russian air force officer and politician; b. 3 Feb. 1942, Bolshoy Log, Rostov region; s. of Ivan Sevastinovich Shaposhnikov and Klavdia Stepanova Shaposhnikova; m. Zemfira Nikolayevna Shaposhnikova 1980; one s. two d.; ed Kharkov Higher Aviation School, Y. Gagarin Aviation Acad., Gen. Staff Acad.; served Soviet Army 1959–; Head, Soviet Air Force in Germany 1987–88; First Deputy Commdr All-Union Soviet Air Force 1988–, Commdr 1990–91; Minister of Defence and Head Soviet Armed Forces

Aug.–Dec. 1991; C-in-C of the Armed Forces of the CIS 1991–93; Sec. of Security Council, resgnd 1993; rep. of Pres. Yeltsin in Rosvooruzhenie (state-owned armaments exports co.); Gen. Dir Aeroflot 1995–97; Asst to Pres. Russian Fed. 1997–2004; mem. Bd Democratic Reforms Movt 1993–98. *Leisure interests:* literature, theatre, tennis. *Address:* c/o Office of the President, Staraya pl. 4, 103132, Moscow, Russia.

SHAPOVALYANTS, Andrei Georgiyevich; Russian economist; b. 23 Feb. 1952, Moscow; m.; two d.; ed Moscow Plekhanov Inst. of Nat. Econs; researcher, Inst. Elektronika, Main Computation Centre, USSR State Planning Cttee, Head of Div., USSR State Planning Cttee 1969–90; Head, Div. of Financial-Credit Policy, USSR Ministry of Econs and Prognosis 1991; Deputy, First Deputy Minister of Econs and Finance of Russian Fed. 1991–93; Acting Minister of Econs and Finance, First Deputy Minister 1993–98, Minister of Econs 1998–99; mem. Presidium, Russian Govt 1998; Man. Black Sea Bank of Trade and Devt 1999; apptd Pres. Bd of Dirs KAMAZ co. 1999; Dir-Gen. Centre of Reconstruction and Devt of Enterprises 2001; currently mem. Bd of Dirs Murmansk Commercial Seaport. *Address:* Murmansk Commercial Seaport, Murmansk 183024, Russia (office). *Telephone:* (8152) 48-06-44 (office). *Fax:* (8152) 42-31-27 (office). *E-mail:* mmtp@portmurmansk.ru (office). *Website:* www.portmurmansk.ru (office).

SHAPPS, Rt Hon. Grant, PC; British politician and business executive; *Co-Chairman, Conservative Party;* b. 14 Sept. 1968, Watford, Herts., England; m. Belinda Goldstone 1997; three c.; ed Watford Grammar School for Boys, Cassio Coll., Manchester Polytechnic (now Manchester Metropolitan Univ.); f. Print-House Corpn, London 1990; contested North Southwark and Bermondsey constituency in Gen. Election 1997, Welwyn Hatfield 2001; MP for Welwyn Hatfield 2005–, mem. Public Admin Select Cttee 2005–07; Shadow Minister for Housing (attending Shadow Cabinet) 2007–10; Minister of State for Housing and Local Govt, Dept for Communities and Local Govt 2010–12; mem. Speaker's Cttee on Electoral Comm. 2010–; Minister without Portfolio, Cabinet Office 2012–; Br. Chair. Barnhill, Brent North 1995–99; mem. Conservative Friends of Israel 1995; Selsdon Group 1996, Conservative Foreign Affairs Forum 1996; Vice-Pres. North Southwark and Bermondsey Asscn 1997; Vice-Chair. (Campaigning) Conservative Party 2005–09, Co-Chair. Conservative Party 2012–. *Address:* Conservative and Unionist Party, 30 Millbank, London, SW1P 4DP (office); House of Commons, Westminster, London, SW1A 0AA, England (office). *Telephone:* (20) 7219-8497 (London) (office). *E-mail:* shappsg@parliament.uk (office). *Website:* www .conservatives.com (office); www.shapps.com (office).

SHARA', Farouk al-, BA; Syrian politician and diplomatist; *Vice-President, responsible for Foreign Affairs and Information;* b. 10 Dec. 1938; m.; one s. one d.; ed Damascus Univ.; several sr positions in Syrian Air 1963–76; Amb. to Italy 1976–80; Minister of State for External Affairs 1980–84, Minister of Foreign Affairs 1984–2006; Vice-Pres., responsible for Foreign Affairs and Information 2006–; several times Acting Minister of Information; Deputy Prime Minister 2001–03; mem. Regional Leadership of Al-Baath Socialist Party 2000–; involved in two attempts to negotiate a reconciliation with Israel 1991, 2000. *Address:* Office of the Vice-President, Abu Rummaneh, Almadfaa Square, Damascus, Syria (office).

SHARAF, Essam, MSc, PhD; Egyptian engineer, professor of civil engineering and politician; b. 1952, Giza; ed Cairo Univ., Purdue Univ., USA; Visiting Asst Prof., School of Civil Eng, Purdue Univ. 1984–85; Asst Prof. of Highway and Traffic Eng, Cairo Univ. 1985–90; Asst Prof. of Civil Eng, King Saud Univ., Saudi Arabia 1990–96; Minister of Transport 2004–05; Prime Minister of Egypt March–Nov. 2011 (resgnd); fmr Adviser to Roads and Transport Authority of Dubai; co-f. Egypt Scientific Soc.; Fellow, Chartered Inst. of Logistics and Transport (UK) 2007; Acad. of Scientific Research and Tech. State Prize in Eng Sciences 1987, 1997, First Class State Medal of Excellence 1995, Purdue Univ. Excellence Award in Eng 2005. *Address:* c/o Office of the Prime Minister, 2 Sharia Majlis al-Sha'ab, Cairo, Egypt.

SHARANSKY, Natan; Israeli (b. Soviet) politician and human rights activist; *Chairman of the Executive, Jewish Agency for Israel;* b. 20 Jan. 1948, Donetsk, USSR (now Ukraine); s. of the late Ida Milgrom; m. Natalya (now Avital) Stiglitz 1974; two d.; ed Physical Tech. Inst., Moscow; leading spokesman for Jewish emigration movt in USSR; arrested by Soviet authorities for dissident activities 1977; received 13-year prison sentence on charges of treason 1978, released him in exchange for spies held in West, took up residence in Israel Feb. 1986; Assoc. Ed. The Jerusalem Report 1990–96; co-f. Peace Watch 1994; mem. Knesset 1996–2006 (resgnd); Minister of Trade and Industry 1996–99, of the Interior 1999–2000; Minister without Portfolio responsible for Jerusalem, Social and Diaspora Affairs 2003–05; Inst. Chair. and Distinguished Fellow, Adelson Inst. for Strategic Studies, Shalem Center 2006–; Chair. of the Exec., Jewish Agency for Israel 2009–; Chair. One Jerusalem, Beit Hatefutsot (Jewish diaspora museum), Tel-Aviv; fmr Visiting Prof., Brandeis Univ., Waltham, Mass.; Founder and fmr Leader, Yisrael B'Aliya Party 1996 (merged with Likud 2003); US Congressional Medal of Honor, US Presidential Medal of Freedom. *Publications include:* Fear No Evil 1988, The Case for Democracy: The Power of Freedom to Overcome Tyranny and Terror (with Ron Dermer) 2005, Defending Identity: It's Indispensable Role in Protecting Democracy 2008. *Address:* Jewish Agency for Israel, POB 92, 48 King George Street, Jerusalem 91000, Israel (office). *Telephone:* (2) 620-2080 (office). *E-mail:* inquiries@shalem.org.il (office). *Website:* www.jafi.org.il (office).

SHARAPOVA, Maria Yuryevna; Russian professional tennis player; b. 19 April 1987, Nyagan, Siberia, USSR; d. of Youri Sharapov and Yelena Sharapova; turned professional 19 April 2001; Women's Tennis Asscn (WTA) singles titles include Tokyo 2003, 2004, 2005, Quebec City 2003, Birmingham 2004, 2005, Seoul 2004, WTA Championships, Los Angeles 2004, Doha 2005, Italian Open 2011, 2012, BNP Paribas Open, Indian Wells 2013, Porsche Tennis Grand Prix, Stuttgart 2013, Mutua Madrid Open 2014; WTA Championships, Istanbul 2012; Grand Slam results: winner, Wimbledon 2004 (second-youngest Wimbledon Champion in Open era, fourth-youngest winner of any Grand Slam title), US Open 2006, Australian Open 2008, French Open 2012, finalist, Australian Open 2007, 2012, Wimbledon 2011, semi-finalist, French Open 2007, 2011; silver medal, Olympic Games, London 2012; WTA doubles titles, Luxembourg 2003 (with Tamarine Tanasugarn), Japan Open 2003 (with Tanasugarn), Birmingham 2004 (with Maria Kirilenko); highest ranking: World No. 1 22 Aug. 2005; coached by father and by Robert Landsdorp; signed with IMG Models 2003; apptd UNDP Goodwill Amb. 2007; WTA

Newcomer of the Year 2003, WTA Player of the Year 2004, WTA Most Improved Player of the Year 2004, ESPY Best Female Tennis Player 2005, 2007, 2008, named the country's best female player for the year by Russia's tennis fed. 2005, 2006, Master of Sports of Russia 2005, Prix de Citron Roland Garros 2005, Whirlpool 6th Sense Player of the Year 2006, ESPY Best Int. Female Athlete 2007, ESPN Hottest Female Athlete 2007, named the January 2008 female Athlete of the Month by the US Sports Acad. for her performance at the Australian Open 2008, named the world's highest-paid female athlete 2008, 2010, WTA Fan Favorite Singles Player 2010, WTA Humanitarian of the Year 2010, WTA Most Fashionable Player (On Court) 2010, WTA Most Fashionable Player (Off Court) 2010, WTA Most Dramatic Expression 2010, named by TIME magazine as one of the 30 Legends of Women's Tennis: Past, Present and Future 2011. *Leisure interests:* fashion, singing, dancing, movies. *Address:* IMG, 200 5th Avenue, 7th Floor, New York, NY 10010, USA. *Website:* www.mariasharapova.com.

SHARAR, Muhammad Dhaifallah, LLB; Kuwaiti lawyer and politician; *Adviser to Amir Sheikh Sabah al-Ahmad al-Jaber al-Sabah;* b. 1948; ed Kuwait Univ.; pvt. law practice 1985–90; elected to Nat. Ass. 1996, Minister of Justice, Awqaf and Islamic Affairs –1998, State Minister for Nat. Ass. Affairs 1998, State Minister for Cabinet and Nat. Ass. Affairs 2001–06; currently Adviser to Amir Sheikh Sabah al-Ahmad al-Jaber al-Sabah (Amir of Kuwait). *Address:* Al Diwan Al Amiri, Sief Palace, Building 100, Safat, 13001, Kuwait (office). *Website:* www.da .gov.kw (office).

SHAREEF, Mohammed Hussain; Maldivian government official; *Minister of Human Resources, Youth and Sports;* fmr Chair. State Trading Org. plc; fmr Dir-Gen. Post and Telecommunications Section, Ministry of Communication, Science and Tech.; fmr Chief Govt Spokesman; Minister of Human Resources, Youth and Sports 2012–. *Address:* Ministry of Human Resources, Youth and Sports, Haveeree Hingun, Malé 20-125, Maldives (office). *Telephone:* 3347300 (office). *Fax:* 3347490 (office). *E-mail:* admin@employment.gov.mv (office). *Website:* www.employment .gov.mv (office).

SHARER, Kevin W., BS, MS, MBA; American business executive and academic; b. 2 March 1948; s. of Keith Sharer and Heather Sharer; m. Carol Sharer; five c.; ed US Naval Acad., Univ. of Pittsburgh; fmr Consultant, McKinsey & Co.; fmr Exec., Gen. Electric Corpn; Exec. Vice-Pres. and Pres. of Business Markets Div., MCI Communications Corpn –1992; COO and mem. Bd of Dirs Amgen 1992–2000, Pres. 1992–2010, CEO 2000–12, Chair. 2001–12; Exec. Partner, Foundation Medical Partners (venture capital firm) 2013–; Sr Lecturer of Business Administration, Harvard Business School 2013–; mem. Bd of Dirs Chevron, Northrop Grumman Corpn, US Naval Acad. Foundation; Chair. Bd of Trustees, LA Co. Museum of Natural History; mem. The Business Council. *Address:* Foundation Medical Partners, 105 Rowayton Avenue, Rowayton, CT 06853 (office); Division of Faculty and Research, Harvard Business School, Soldiers Field, Boston, MA 02163, USA (office). *Telephone:* (617) 495-6353 (Harvard) (office). *E-mail:* ksharer @ foundmed .com (office). *Website:* www.foundmed.com (office); www.hbs.edu (office).

SHARIATMADARI, Hossein; Iranian newspaper industry executive; *Managing Director and Editor-in-Chief, Kayhan;* imprisoned in Tehran before Islamic Revolution of 1979; served as Revolutionary Guards Commdr during war with Iraq; currently Man. Dir and Ed.-in-Chief Kayhan (daily newspaper); Pres. Kayhan Inst. and Rep. of the Supreme Leader of the Islamic Revolution. *Address:* Kayhan, POB 11365-3631, Shahid Shahcheraghi Alley, Ferdowsi Avenue, Tehran 11444, Iran (office). *Telephone:* (21) 33110251 (office). *Fax:* (21) 33111120 (office). *E-mail:* kayhan@kayhannews.ir (office). *Website:* www.kayhannews.ir (office).

SHARIF, Mian Mohammed Nawaz; Pakistani politician and industrialist; *Prime Minister and Minister of Defence;* b. 25 Dec. 1949, Lahore; s. of Mian Muhammad Sharif; m. 1971; two s. two d.; ed Govt Coll. and Punjab Univ. Law Coll., Lahore; started work in Ittefaq faction industrial group 1969; Finance Minister, Govt of the Punjab 1981–85, Chief Minister of Punjab 1985–90; Prime Minister 1990–93 (dismissal ruled unconstitutional), resgnd July 1993, Prime Minister 1997–99, concurrently Minister of Defence and Finance (removed in coup by Gen. Pervez Musharraf), Prime Minister and Minister of Defence 2013–; sentenced to life imprisonment for terrorism and hijacking April 2000; released from imprisonment, went into exile in Jeddah, Saudi Arabia Dec. 2000, allowed to return to Pakistan Aug. 2007; Pres. Pakistan Muslim League, Punjab 1985, Islami Jamhoori Ittehad 1988; Leader, Pakistan Muslim League—Nawaz (PML—N) 2002–; best known internationally for ordering Pakistan's nuclear tests in response to those of India May 1998; barred by Supreme Court from contesting elections or holding public office early 2009, defied house arrest to lead anti-govt protests March 2009. *Leisure interests:* social work, photography, hunting, playing cricket. *Address:* Prime Minister's Secretariat, Cabinet Secretariat, Cabinet Division, Islamabad (office); Pakistan Muslim League—Nawaz, House 20-H, Street 10, Sector F-8/3, Islamabad (office); 180–181-H, Ittefaq Colony, Model Town, Lahore, Pakistan (home). *Telephone:* (51) 925190512 (Prime Minister's Secretariat) (office); (51) 2852662 (Pakistan Muslim League) (office). *Fax:* (51) 2852662 (Pakistan Muslim League) (office). *E-mail:* contact@cabinet.gov.pk (office); pmlisb@hotmail.com (office). *Website:* www.cabinet.gov.pk (office); www.pmln.org .pk (office).

SHARIF, Mian Muhammad Shahbaz; Pakistani politician; *Chief Minister of Punjab;* b. 23 Sept. 1951, Lahore, Punjab Prov.; brother of Nawaz Sharif, Prime Minister of Pakistan; m. 1st Nusrat Shahbaz 1973 (died 1993); two s. three d.; m. 2nd Aaliya Honey 1993 (divorced); m. 3rd Tehmina Durrani 2003; Chief Minister of Punjab 1997–99 (ousted in mil. coup of Gen. Pervez Musharraf 1999), 2008–March 2013, June 2013–; Pres. Pakistan Muslim League—Nawaz 2002–11; lived in exile in Saudi Arabia and London before being allowed to return to Pakistan 2007. *Address:* Chief Minister Secretariat, 7-Club Road GOR-I, Lahore, Pakistan (office). *Telephone:* (42) 99204906 (office). *Fax:* (42) 99204915 (office). *E-mail:* cmshehbaz@pmln.org (office). *Website:* www.cm.punjab.gov.pk (office).

SHARIF, Muhammad Safwat esh-; Egyptian politician; b. 1933, Cairo; ed Mil. Acad., Inst. of Strategic Studies; with Presidency of the Repub. 1957–74; Dir Gen. Local Information, State Information Dept 1975, Dir Foreign Information Service, State Information Dept; mem. Arab Information Cttee 1975; Sec. Ministry of Information 1977; Chair. Information Authority 1978; mem. Media Cttee 1979; mem. Constituent Cttee Nat. Democratic Party; Chief, Council of TV and Radio

Trustees 1980; Minister of Information 1982–2004. *Address:* Ministry of Information, Radio and TV Bldg, Corniche en Nil, Cairo, Egypt.

SHARIF, Omar; Egyptian actor; b. (Michael Dimitri Shalhoub), 10 April 1932, Cairo; s. of Joseph Chalhoub and Claire Saada; m. 1st Faten Hamama 1955 (divorced 1967); one s.; m. 2nd 1973; ed Victoria Coll., Cairo Univ.; fmr salesman in lumber-import firm; made first film The Blazing Sun 1953; starred in 24 Egyptian films and two French co-production films during following five years; commenced int. film career with Lawrence of Arabia; UNESCO Medal 2005. *Films include:* Shaytan al-Sahra 1954, Ayyamna al-Holwa 1955, Siraa Fil-Mina 1956, Ard al-Salam 1957, Goha 1958, Fadiha fil-zamalek 1959, Bidaya wa nihaya 1960, A Man in Our House 1961, Lawrence of Arabia 1962, The Fall of the Roman Empire 1964, Behold a Pale Horse 1964, Genghis Khan 1965, The Yellow Rolls-Royce 1965, Doctor Zhivago 1965, Night of the Generals 1967, Funny Girl 1968, Mackenna's Gold 1969, Mayerling 1968, The Appointment 1969, Che! 1969, The Last Valley 1970, The Horsemen 1971, The Burglars 1971, The Mysterious Island 1973, The Tamarind Seed 1974, Juggernaut 1974, Funny Lady 1975, Crime and Passion 1975, Bloodline 1979, Green Ice 1981, Top Secret 1984, The Possessed 1988, The Opium Connection 1990, Memories of Midnight 1991, Beyond Justice 1992, Grand Larceny 1992, Mayrig 1992, 588 rue paradis 1992, Lie Down With Lions 1994, Catherine the Great 1995, Gulliver's Travels 1996, Heaven Before I Die 1997, Mysteries of Egypt 1998, The 13th Warrior 1999, The Parole Officer 2001, Hidalgo 2004, Imperium: St Peter 2005, One Night with the King 2006, Hassan & Marcus 2008, The Traveller 2009. *Television:* Peter the Great 1986, Hanan W Haneen 2007, The Ten Commandments 2007, The Last Templar 2008. *Publication:* The Eternal Male (autobiography) 1978. *Leisure interests:* bridge, horse racing. *Address:* WME, 9601 Wilshire Blvd, Beverly Hills, CA 90210, USA.

SHARIF, Osama Al, BA; Jordanian/Canadian publisher, journalist, columnist and media consultant; *Chairman, Media-Arabia;* b. 14 June 1960, Jerusalem, Jordan; s. of Mahmoud Al Sharif and Aida Al Sharif; m. Ghada Yasser Amr 1984; one s. one d.; ed Univ. of Missouri, Columbia, USA; Chief Ed. The Jerusalem Star 1985–88; Pres. Info-Media, Jordan 1989–; Publr, Chief Ed. and weekly columnist, The Star, Jordan 1990–; Publr Arabian Communications & Publishing (ACP) 1994–97, BYTE Middle East 1994–97, Al Tiqaniyyah Wal 'Amal 1995–97; Chief Ed. and Dir General Arabia.com 1999–2002; Chief Ed. Addustour Newspaper 2003–06; Ed. Al-Ittihad daily newspaper, Abu Dhabi, UAE Jan.–June 2009; Chair. Media-Arabia 2006–; mem. Royal Cttee for the Nat. Agenda, Amman, Jordan 2005. *Leisure interests:* novel and short-story writing, travel, photography, horse riding. *Address:* PO Box 9313, Amman 11191, Jordan (office). *Telephone:* (6) 5922161 (office). *Fax:* (6) 5922161 (office). *E-mail:* osama@mediaarabia.com (office). *Website:* www.mediaarabia.com (office).

SHARIFOV, Samir Rauf oğlu, MA; Azerbaijani economist and government official; *Minister of Finance;* b. 7 Sept. 1961; m.; two c.; ed Kiev State Univ.; foreign econ. relations specialist in USSR 1983–91; Deputy Chief, Dept of Int. Econ. Relations, Ministry of Foreign Affairs 1991–95; Chief of Dept, then Exec. Dir Nat. Bank of Azerbaijan 1995–2001; Exec. Dir State Oil Fund of Repub. of Azerbaijan (SOFAZ) 2001–06, also Azerbaijan Rep. and Dir Black Sea Trade and Devt Bank 2001–06; Chair. Govt Comm. on Extractive Industries Transparency Initiative 2003–06; Minister of Finance 2006–. *Address:* Ministry of Finance, 1022 Baku, Samed Vurghun küç. 83, Azerbaijan (office). *Telephone:* (12) 493-30-12 (office). *Fax:* (12) 493-05-62 (office). *E-mail:* office@maliyye.gov.az (office). *Website:* maliyye .gov.az (office).

SHARKEY, Baron (Life Peer), cr. 2010, of Niton Undercliff in the County of Isle of Wight; **John Sharkey;** British/Irish management consultant and advertising executive; *Chairman, Sharkey Associates Ltd;* Co-founder and fmr Chair. Bainsfair Sharkey Trott advertising agency; fmr Jt Man. Dir Saatchi & Saatchi UK; fmr Deputy Chair. Saatchi International; fmr Chair. BDDP Holdings Ltd, Highland Partners Europe; fmr COO Blue Arrow Plc; Adviser to Nick Clegg, Leader of Liberal Democratic Party, on Strategic Communications 2008–10, Chair. Liberal Democrat Gen. Election campaign 2010; Chair. Sharkey Assocs Ltd (man. consultancy) 1998–; mem. Council of Hansard Soc. 2004–, Hon. Treas. 2007–10; mem. (Liberal Democrat) House of Lords 2010–. *Address:* Sharkey Associates Ltd, Carmelite, 50 Victoria Embankment, Blackfriars, London, EC4Y 0LS (office); House of Lords, Westminster, London, SW1A 0PW, England (office). *Telephone:* (20) 7219-5353 (House of Lords) (office). *Fax:* (20) 7219-5979 (House of Lords) (office). *Website:* www.parliament.uk/biographies/lords/john-sharkey/73136 (office).

SHARMA, Arun Kumar, DSc, FNA, FASc., FNASc, F.TWAS; Indian botanist, cytogeneticist and academic; *Chairman, West Bengal Biodiversity Board;* b. 31 Dec. 1924, Calcutta (now Kolkata); s. of the late Charu Chandra Sharma and of Shovamoyee Sharma; m. Archana Mookerjea Sharma 1955 (died 2008); ed Univ. of Calcutta; Research Scholar, Botanical Survey of India 1946–48; Asst Lecturer, Univ. of Calcutta 1948–52, Lecturer, 1952–62, Reader, 1962–69, Prof. and Head, Dept of Botany 1969–80, Programme Coordinator, Centre of Advanced Study, Dept of Botany 1980–90; Pres. Indian Nat. Science Acad. 1983–84, Golden Jubilee Prof., 1985–90; Chair. Steering Cttee Nat. Biosource Devt Bd, Govt of India 2000–; Chair. West Bengal Biodiversity Bd 2004–; Gen. Pres. Indian Science Congress Asscn 1981; Founding Pres. Fed. of Asian Scientific Acads and Socs 1986–; Fellow, Third World Acad. of Sciences; Hon. Prof., Indian Nat. Science Acad. 1990–; S.S. Bhatnagar Award in Biology, CSIR 1967, Padma Bhushan 1983, Om Prakash Bhasin Foundation Award 1993, First J. C. Bose Memorial Prize 1994, G. M. Modi Research Award 1994, Centenary Award in Biology 1999, M. N. Saha Memorial Award (Indian Nat. Science Acad.) 1999, Centenary Award (Sataboli Award), Indian Science Congress Asscn 1999, Vasvik Award 2001, and numerous other awards. *Publications:* Chromosome Techniques: Theory and Practice (with Archana Sharma) 1980, Chromosome in Evolution of Eukaryotic Groups, Vols I and II (with Archana Sharma) 3rd edn 1983, Chromosome Techniques—A Manual (with Archana Sharma) 1994, Plant Chromosomes: Analysis, Manipulation and Engineering (with Archana Sharma) 1999, Chromosome Painting (with A. Sharma) 2002; book chapters, more than 300 articles in professional journals. *Leisure interests:* photography, bird-watching. *Address:* West Bengal Biodiversity Board, Department of Environment, Government of West Bengal, Paribesh Bhawan, Salt Lake City, Kolkata 700 098 (office); Flat No. 2F2, 18/3 Gariahat Road, Kolkata 700 019, India (home). *Telephone:* (33) 24405802 (home). *E-mail:*

chairman.wbbb@nic.in (office); nuclaks@cal2.vsnl.net.in (home). *Website:* wbbb .gov.in (office).

SHARMA, Kamalesh; Indian diplomatist and international organization official; *Secretary-General, The Commonwealth;* b. 30 Sept. 1941; m. Babli Sharma; one s. one d.; ed St Stephen's Coll., Delhi Univ., King's Coll. Cambridge, UK; joined Indian Foreign Service 1965, Head of Divs of Econ. Relations, Int. Orgs and Policy Planning, Head of Div. Ministry of Finance, postings in Bonn, Hong Kong, Saudi Arabia and Turkey, Amb. to fmr GDR, Kazakhstan, Kyrgyzstan, Amb. to UN, Geneva, also Amb. for Disarmament and Spokesman for developing countries in UNCTAD, Perm. Rep. to UN, New York 1997–2002; Special Rep. of UN Sec.-Gen. for East Timor (now Timor-Leste) and Head of UN Mission of Support in East Timor (UNMISET) 2002–04; Dir Int. Peace Acad., New York; High Commr to UK 2004–08; Sec.-Gen. The Commonwealth 2008–; Chancellor, Queen's Univ. Belfast 2009–; Fellow, Weatherhead Center for Int. Affairs, Harvard Univ.; mem. US Foreign Policy Asscn; fmr mem. Bd of Dirs Peace Acad., New York, Education Consultants India Ltd; Gov. Ditchley Foundation; Hon. LLD (De Montfort Univ., UK); Medal of US Foreign Policy Asscn. *Publications include:* Mille Fleurs: Poetry from Around the World (compilation of poems by diplomats and officials) (ed.), Imagining Tomorrow: Rethinking the Global Challenge. *Leisure interests:* literature, cosmology, cricket, Indian and western classical music and jazz. *Address:* Commonwealth Secretariat, Marlborough House, Pall Mall, London, SW1Y 5HX, England (office). *Telephone:* (20) 7747-6500 (office). *Fax:* (20) 7930-0827 (office). *E-mail:* info@commonwealth.int (office). *Website:* www.thecommonwealth.org (office).

SHARMA, Konkona Sen, BA; Indian actress; b. 3 Dec. 1979, New Delhi; d. of Mukul Sharma and Aparna Sen Sharma; m. Ranvir Shorey 2010; ed St Stephen's Coll., Univ. of Delhi; film debut 1983; hosted TV show My Brilliant Brain 2007. *Films include:* Indira 1983, Picnic 1989, The Girl Ria 2000, Mr and Mrs Iyer (Nat. Film Award 2003) 2002, Chai Pani Etc. 2004, Amu Kaju 2005, Page 3 (Kalakar Award 2005) 2005, Karkat Rashi 2005, 15 Park Avenue 2005, Dosar (Mahindra Indo-American Arts Council Film Festival Award 2007) 2005, Mixed Doubles 2005, The Companion 2006, Yun Hota Toh Kya Hota 2006, Omkara (Nat. Film Award 2007) 2006, Deadline: Sirf 24 Ghante 2006, Meridian Lines 2007, Life in a Metro (Filmfare Award 2008, Popular Award 2008) 2007, Traffic Signal 2007, Aaja Nachle 2007, Laaga Chunari Mein Daag (Filmfare Best Supporting Actress Award 2007) 2007, Zeinab 2008, Dil Kabaddi 2008, The President Is Coming 2009, Wake Up Sid 2009, Atithi Tum Kab Jaoge 2010, Right Ya Wrong 2010, Mirch 2010. *Play:* The Blue Mug 2009. *Telephone:* 98300507589 (mobile).

SHARMA, Lt-Gen. (retd) Nirbhay, MSc, MPhil; Indian state official and fmr army officer; *Governor of Arunachal Pradesh;* b. 1946; m. Jyotsna Sharma; one s. one d.; ed Nat. Defence Acad., Univ. of Madras; commissioned into Indian Army 1966, service included combat in Indo-Pakistani War 1971 as part of Airborne Assault Group, later roles include Dir Gen. (Perspective Planning) at Army HQ, Master Gen. of Ordnance, Corps Commdr and Security Adviser to Govt of Jammu and Kashmir, retd from army 2008; mem. Union Public Service Comm. of India 2008–13; Gov. of Arunachal Pradesh 2013–; Distinguished Fellow, Observer Research Foundation, New Delhi; mem. Indian Nat. Congress; numerous mil. awards including Param Vishisht Seva Medal, Uttam Yudh Seva Medal, Ati Vishisht Seva Medal, Vishisht Seva Medal. *Address:* Office of the Governor, Raj Bhavan, Itanagar 791 111, Arunachal Pradesh, India (office). *Telephone:* (360) 2212432 (office). *Fax:* (360) 2212442 (office). *E-mail:* ps-gov-arn@nic.in (office). *Website:* www.arunachalgovernor.gov.in (office).

SHARMA, R. S.; Indian energy industry executive; *Managing Director, Jindal Power Ltd;* ed Govt Eng Coll., Rewa, MP; Dir (Finance) Oil and Natural Gas Corpn (ONGC) Ltd 2002, Acting Chair. and Man. Dir May–Aug. 2006, Chair. and Man. Dir 2006–11; joined Nat. Thermal Power Corpn (NTPC) 1980, Gen. Man. of Singrauli (Northern Region), Exec. Dir Corporate Planning –2008, Chair. and Man. Dir Ltd 2008–10; Dir (non-exec.) PTC India Ltd 2004–08; Man. Dir Jindal Power Ltd 2010–; mem. Bd of Dirs ONGC Videsh Ltd 2002–, Mangalore Refinery and Petrochemicals Ltd –2011, ONGC Mittal Energy Services Ltd, NTPC Vidyut Vyapar Nigam Ltd, Indian Oil Corpn Ltd –2007; Fellow and mem. Inst. of Cost and Works Accountants of India; Assoc. mem. Indian Inst. of Bankers; Hon. Fellow, All India Man. Asscn 2010; India Chief Financial Officer Award 2005 – Excellence in Finance in a PSU, CNBC-TV18 CFO Award 2006 for Excellence in Finance in Oil and Allied Services, Amity Leadership Award for Corp. Excellence in Oil & Gas Industry, Amity Business School 2009. *Address:* Jindal Power Limited Jindal Centre 12, Bhikaiji Cama Place, India New Delhi 110 066, India (office). *Telephone:* (11) 2618 8340 (office). *Fax:* (11) 2616 1271 (office). *E-mail:* info@jindalpower.com (office). *Website:* www.jindalpower.com (office).

SHARMA, Sheel Kant, MS, PhD; Indian diplomatist and international organization executive; b. 10 Jan. 1950; m. Meenu Sharma; ed Indian Inst. of Tech., Mumbai; joined Indian Foreign Service 1973, served as Third Sec., Embassy in Kuwait and Second Sec., Embassy in Riyadh 1976–77, Under-Sec., Middle East Desk, Ministry of External Affairs 1978–81; Fellow, Inst. of Defence Studies and Analysis, New Delhi 1981–82, Deputy Sec. (North), Ministry of External Affairs 1982–83; First Sec. (Disarmament), Perm. Mission to UN, Geneva and Alt. Rep. to UN Conf. on Disarmament 1983–86; Counsellor and Deputy Chief of Mission, Embassy in Algiers 1986–89; Dir (UN Div.) and Disarmament Head, Ministry of External Affairs, New Delhi 1989–91; Jt Sec. (South and Disarmament) in charge of India's relations with ASEAN, Indo-China and South Pacific 1991–94; seconded to IAEA, Vienna; served as sr professional in External Relations and Policy Coordination Div. 1994–2000; Jt Sec. (Disarmament and Int. Security Affairs) 2000–03; Additional Sec. (Int. Orgs), Ministry of External Affairs 2003–04, Amb. to Austria and Perm. Rep. to all Int. Orgs, Vienna 2004–08; Sec.-Gen. SAARC 2008–11; Chair. G-77 Vienna Chapter 2005; Rep. of India/Del., Non-Aligned Summit, New Delhi 1983, Kuala Lumpur 2003, Annual Six Nation Summits on Nuclear Disarmament 1985–89, Conf. on Disarmament 1983–86, UN Gen. Ass. 1983–86, 2000–03, UN Disarmament Comm. 1984–86, 2001, UN Conf. Rio+5 1997, IAEA Gen. Conf. 1994–99, Int. Confs on Nuclear and Energy Issues 1994–99, ARF Ministerial Meetings 2000–04; mem. India Int. Centre, India Habitat Centre; Distinguished Aluminus Award, Indian Inst. of Tech. Mumbai 2007. *Publications include:* UN Report on Verification (co-author) 1991, UN Report on Defensive Security Concepts (co-author) 1992, UNIDIR Monograph on Verification of Fissile

Materials Cut-Off and Non-use of Nuclear Weapons 1992, article in IAEA Bulletin 1995, paper presented at Pugwash Conf. on Energy in Malta 1995, UN panel's report on missile in all their aspects (co-author) 2002; articles in scientific journals and in newspapers and periodicals. *Leisure interests:* literature, readings on science and tech., basketball, tennis, swimming, yoga, chess.

SHARMA, Shika; Indian financial executive; *Managing Director and CEO, Axis Bank Ltd;* began career with Industrial Credit and Investment Corpn India Ltd in 1980, was instrumental in setting up group's investment banking business, Head of ICICI Prudential Life Insurance Co. Ltd –2009; Man. Dir and CEO Axis Bank Ltd (India's third-largest pvt. bank) 2009–; ranked by Forbes magazine amongst The World's 100 Most Powerful Women (89th) 2010, ranked by Fortune magazine amongst the 50 Most Powerful Women in Business outside the US (33rd) 2011, (37th) 2012. *Address:* Axis Bank Ltd, 131 Maker Tower – F, Cuffe Parade, Colaba, Mumbai 400 005, India (office). *Telephone:* (22) 6707-4407 (office). *Fax:* (22) 2218-1429 (office). *E-mail:* info@axisbank.com (office). *Website:* www.axisbank.com (office).

SHARMAN, Baron (Life Peer), cr. 1999, of Redlynch in the County of Wiltshire; **Colin Morven Sharman,** OBE, FCA, CIMgt; British chartered accountant and business executive; b. 19 Feb. 1943; s. of Col Terence John Sharman and Audrey Emmiline Newman; m. Angela M. Timmins 1966; one s. one d.; ed Bishops Wordsworth School, Salisbury; qualified as accountant with Woolgar Hennel & Co. 1965; joined Peat Marwick Mitchell 1966 (later KPMG Peat Marwick, now KPMG), Man. Frankfurt Office 1970–72, The Hague Office 1972–81 (Partner 1973, Partner-in-Charge 1975), London Office 1981–, Sr Partner, Nat. Marketing and Industry Groups 1987–90, Sr Man. Consultancy Partner 1989–91, Sr Regional Partner, London and SE 1990–93, Sr Partner 1994–98, Chair. KPMG Int. 1997–99; Deputy Chair. Aegis Group plc 1999, Chair. 1999–2008; Deputy Chair. (non-exec.) Group 4 Securicor (now G4S) plc 2003, 2004–05, Chair. (non-exec.) Nov. 2003–04; mem. Bd of Dirs Aviva plc 2005–12, Chair. (non-exec.) 2006–12; Pres. GamCare 2011–; Dir (non-exec.) AEA Technology plc 1996–2002, Young & Co.'s Brewery plc 1999–2002, BG Group PLC 2000–11, Reed Elsevier plc 2002–11; mem. Supervisory Bd ABN AMRO Holding NV 2003–07; mem. Industrial Soc.; completed a study of Cen. Govt Audit and Accountability commissioned by Chief Sec. to The Treasury 2002; Hon. mem. Securities Inst.; Dr hc (Cranfield Univ.) 1998. *Publication:* Living Culture 2001. *Leisure interests:* food and wine, sailing, opera. *Address:* House of Lords, Westminster, London, SW1A 2PW, England (office). *Telephone:* (20) 7219-8622 (office). *Website:* www.parliament.uk/biographies/lords/colin-sharman/26706 (office).

SHARMAN, Helen Patricia, OBE, BSc, MA, CChem, FRAeS, FRGS, FBIS; British manager and fmr astronaut; *Faculty Technical Manager, Kingston University;* b. 30 May 1963, Sheffield; ed Univ. of Sheffield, Birkbeck Coll., London and Univ. Coll., London; Engineer and Section Head, Marconi Osram Valve 1984–87; Research Technologist, Mars Confectionery Ltd 1987–89; selected to be first Briton in space as part of Juno Space Mission of fmr USSR 1989, travelled to Mir space station 1991; science communicator and broadcaster 1991–99; Group Leader, Surface and Nanoanalysis Group, Nat. Physical Lab. 2010–13; Faculty Tech. Man., Kingston Univ. 2013–; Fellow, British Interplanetary Soc.; Hon. FRSC;Freedom of the City of Sheffield 1991. *Publications:* Seize the Moment 1993, The Space Place 1997.

SHARP, Hon. John Randall; Australian politician (retd) and company director; *Chairman, EADS Australia Pacific;* b. 15 Dec. 1954, Sydney; s. of J.K. Sharp; m. Victoria Sharp 1986; two s. one d.; ed The King's School, NSW, Orange Agricultural Coll.; fmr farmer; mem. House of Reps for Gilmore, NSW 1984–93; MP (Nat. Party of Australia) for Hume, NSW 1993–98, Shadow Minister for Tourism and Sport 1988, for Tourism, Sport and Youth Affairs 1988–89, for Land Transport and Shipping 1989–90, for Shipping and Waterfront Reform 1990–93, for Transport 1993–96; Minister for Transport and Regional Devt 1996–97, Deputy Man. of Opposition Business in the House 1990–94; Exec. Dir Linfox (now ADI–Fox) 1999–2001, Corp. adviser 1999–2001; Chair. Thenford Consulting transport consulting co.) 1998–; Chair. Aviation Safety Foundation Australia 2001–; Chair. Power and Data Corpn 2003–; mem. Bd of Dirs EADS Australia Pacific, Australian Aerospace 2002–, French-Australian Chamber of Commerce and Industry, Sky Traders 2005–; Deputy Chair. Regional Express Airlines 2005–; Chair. Pel Air 2006–; mem. Advisory Council Parsons Brinckerhoff 2007–; mem. Univ. of Wollongong Vice-Chancellor's Advisory Bd; mem. Nat. Party of Australia, Hon. Fed. Treas. 2000–05; Chair. Winifred West Foundation 2001–; Co-Chair. Cancer Council of NSW, Southern Highlands Br.; Fellow, Chartered Inst. of Transport; Trustee John McKeown House; Hon. Sec. Nat. Party of Australia. *Leisure interests:* rugby union, scuba diving, skiing, tennis, aviation. *Address:* EADS Australia Pacific, Se 1002, L 10 Gateway 1 Macquarie Pl, Sydney, NSW 2000 (office); Ashby Park, Nowra Road, Moss Vale, NSW 2577, Australia. *Telephone:* (2) 8864-0500 (office). *Fax:* (2) 8864-0501 (office). *E-mail:* info.syd@aerospatiale.com .au (office); sharp@hinet.net.au (office).

SHARP, Phillip Allen, PhD; American biologist, academic and academic administrator; *Institute Professor, Massachusetts Institute of Technology;* b. 6 June 1944, Falmouth, Ky; s. of Joseph W. Sharp and Katherin A. Sharp; m. Ann H. Holcombe 1964; three d.; ed Union Coll., Ky, Univ. of Illinois, California Inst. of Tech. and Cold Spring Harbor, New York; Research Asst, Dept of Chem., Univ. of Ill. 1966–69; Postdoctoral Fellow, Lab. of Prof. Norman Davidson, Calif. Inst. of Tech. 1969–71, Cold Spring Harbor Lab. 1971–72, Sr Research Investigator 1972–74; Assoc. Prof., Center for Cancer Research and Dept of Biology, MIT 1974–79, Prof. 1979–99, Inst. Prof. 1999–; Assoc. Dir Center for Cancer Research 1982–85, Dir 1985–91, Head of Dept of Biology 1991–99; Founding Dir The McGovern Inst. for Brain Research 2000–04; Co-founder and Chair. Scientific Bd Biogen Idec, Inc. –2002, mem. Bd of Dirs –2009; mem. Bd of Dirs Almylam Pharmaceuticals, Whitehead Inst., MIT 2005–; mem. Scientific Advisory Bd, Fidelity Biosciences Group 2004–; Chair. Gen. Motors Cancer Research Foundation Awards Ass. 1994–2006, Scientific Advisory Cttee Dana-Farber Cancer Inst. 1996, Scientific Review Council Cancer Prevention and Research Inst. of Texas 2009–12, Scientific Advisory Cttee, SU2C Project, AACR 2008–; Co-Chair. NRC Cttee on A New Biology for the 21st Century: Ensuring the United States Leads the Coming Biology Revolution, NAS 2008–10, MIT's Production in an Innovation Economy (PIE) Comm. 2010–; mem. Cttee on Science, Eng and Public Policy

1992–95, Pres.'s Advisory Council on Science and Tech. 1991–97, Nat. Cancer Advisory Bd, NIH (Presidential appointment) 1996, Scientific Bd of Advisors, Van Andel Inst. 1996–, Scientific Cttee Ludwig Inst. for Cancer Research 1998–2008, Bd of Scientific Govs, Scripps Research Inst. 1999–, Bd FDA's Reagan-Udall Foundation 2008–, Howard Hughes Medical Inst. Medical Advisory Bd and Review Cttee 2011–; mem. and Trustee Alfred P. Sloan Foundation 1995–2004; mem. Bd Trustees Massachusetts Gen. Hosp. 2002–10, Cttee Research and Educ., Partners HealthCare Systems Inc. 2003–, Bd Advisors Polaris Ventures; mem. NAS, NAS Inst. of Medicine, American Acad. of Arts and Sciences, American Philosophical Soc.; Pres.-Elect, AAAS 2012–; Foreign Fellow, Royal Soc. (UK); Hon. mem. Nat. Acad. of Sciences, Repub. of Korea; Hon. Academician, Academia Sinica, Repub. of China (Taiwan); Hon. DSc (Univ. of Kentucky), (Univ. of Tel-Aviv), (Thomas More Coll., Ky), (Univ. of Glasgow), (Albright Coll., Pa) (Rippon Coll., Wis.), (Univ. of Minnesota); Hon. MD (Uppsala Univ.); Dr hc (Union Coll., Ky), (Univ. of Buenos Aires), (McGill Univ.); Howard Ricketts Award, Eli Lilly Award, NAS US Steel Foundation Award, Gen. Motors Research Foundation Alfred P. Sloan, Jr Prize for Cancer Research, Gairdner Foundation Int. Award, New York Acad. of Sciences Award in Biological and Medical Sciences, Louisa Gross Horwitz Prize, Albert Lasker Basic Medical Research Award, Dickson Prize (Univ. of Pittsburgh), shared Nobel Prize for Medicine 1993, Benjamin Franklin Medal, American Philosophical Soc. 1999, Walter Prize, Museum of Science, Boston, Nat. Medal of Science 2004, Inaugural Double Helix Medal for Scientific Research, Cold Spring Harbor Lab., AACR Irving Weinstein Distinguished Lectureship Award 2006, Karl Friedrich Bonhoeffer Lecture, Max Planck Inst., Göttingen, Germany, Winthrop-Sears Award, Chemists' Club of New York 2007. *Publications:* numerous papers in scientific journals. *Leisure interests:* family, reading, sports. *Address:* Room 76-461, Koch Institute for Integrative Cancer Research, Massachusetts Institute of Technology, 500 Main Street, Cambridge, MA 02139, USA (office). *Telephone:* (617) 253-6421 (office). *Fax:* (617) 253-3867 (office). *E-mail:* sharppa@mit.edu (office). *Website:* web.mit.edu/sharplab (office).

SHARP, Richard L.; American computer programmer and business executive; *Managing Director, V-Ten Capital Partners;* b. 12 April 1947; m. Sherry Sharp; two d.; ed Univ. of Virginia, Coll. of William and Mary; f. Applied Systems Corpn 1975, CEO 1975–81; joined consumer electronics and personal computer retailer Circuit City Stores Inc. 1982, Pres. 1984–97, CEO 1986–2000, Chair. 1994–2002; Co-founder Carmax Inc., Chair. and CEO 2002–07; Founding investor, Flextronics Int. Ltd 1993–2008; Founding investor, Crocs Inc., Chair. 2005–10; Founder and Man. Dir V-Ten Capital Partners 2007–; mem. Bd of Dirs Star Scientific Inc. 2011, Johns Hopkins Univ., Univ. of Virginia Schools of Medicine, Boys and Girls Clubs of Metro Richmond, Virginia Commonwealth Univ. School of Engineering Foundation; Chair. Emer. Health Foundation Bd, Univ. of Virginia; fmr Chair. Nat. Retail Fed., Virginia Business Council, Children First America; Trustee, Virginia Commonwealth Univ., Univ. of Richmond; Dr hc (Univ. of Richmond) 1999. *Address:* V-Ten Capital Partners, 9020 Stony Point Parkway, Suite 180, Richmond, VA 23235, USA (office). *Telephone:* (804) 327-0710 (office). *Fax:* (804) 327-0739 (office). *E-mail:* info@vtencp.com (office). *Website:* www.vtencp.com (office).

SHARPE, William Forsyth, PhD; American economist and academic; *STANCO 25 Professor Emeritus of Finance, Graduate School of Business, Stanford University;* b. 16 June 1934, Cambridge, Mass; s. of Russell Thornley Sharpe and Evelyn Forsyth Maloy Sharpe (née Jillson); m. 1st Roberta Ruth Branton 1954 (divorced 1986); one s. one d.; m. 2nd Kathryn Dorothy Peck 1986; one step-s. one step-d.; ed Univ. of California, Los Angeles; Economist, RAND Corpn 1957–61; Asst Prof. of Econs, Univ. of Washington 1961–63, Assoc. Prof. 1963–67, Prof. 1967–68; Prof., Univ. of Calif., Irvine 1968–70; Timken Prof. of Finance, Stanford Univ. 1970–89, Prof. Emer. 1989–92, Prof. of Finance 1993–95, STANCO 25 Prof. of Finance 1995–99, Prof. Emer. 1999–; Pres. William F. Sharpe Assocs 1986–92; Founder and Chair. Financial Engines Inc. 1996–2003; Hon. DHumLitt (De Paul Univ.) 1997; Dr hc (Alicante Univ.) 2003, (Univ. of Vienna) 2004; Hon. DSc (Econs) (London Business School) 2008; Graham and Dodd Award 1972, 1973, 1986, 1988, Nicholas Molodovsky Award 1989, Nobel Prize for Econ. Sciences 1990, UCLA Medal 1998. *Publications:* Economics of Computers 1969, Portfolio Theory and Capital Markets 1970, Asset Allocation Tools 1987, Investments 1999, Fundamentals of Investments (second edn) 2000, Investors and Markets 2007. *Leisure interests:* sailing, all kinds of music. *Address:* Graduate School of Business, Stanford University, Stanford, CA 94305, USA (office). *E-mail:* wfsharpe@stanford .edu (office). *Website:* www.stanford.edu/~wfsharpe (office).

SHARPLESS, K(arl) Barry, BA, PhD; American chemist and academic; *W.M. Keck Professor of Chemistry, Scripps Research Institute;* b. 28 April 1941, Philadelphia, Pa; s. of Dr E. Dallett Sharpless and Evelyn Anderson Sharpless; m. Jan Sharpless; two s. one d.; ed Dartmouth Coll., New Hampshire, Stanford Univ., Harvard Univ.; mem. Chem. Faculty, MIT 1970–77, 1980–90, Arthur C. Cope Prof. 1987–90; mem. Chem. Faculty, Stanford Univ. 1977–80; W.M. Keck Prof. of Chem., The Scripps Research Inst. (TSRI), La Jolla, Calif. 1990–, Skaggs Inst. for Chemical Biology, TSRI 1996–; mem. AAAS 1984, American Acad. of Arts and Sciences 1984, NAS 1985; Hon. mem. RSC 1998; numerous hon. degrees, including Dr hc (Dartmouth Coll.) 1995, (Royal Inst. of Tech., Stockholm) 1995, (Tech. Univ., Munich) 1995, (Catholic Univ. of Louvain) 1996, (Wesleyan Univ.) 1999; numerous fellowships, including A.P. Sloan Foundation Fellow 1973, Camille and Henry Dreyfus Foundation Fellow 1987, Simon Guggenheim Foundation Fellow 1987, ten prizes from the ACS including Arthur C. Cope Scholar 1986, and Award 1992, San Diego Scientist of the Year 1992, Roger Adams Award in Organic Chem. 1997; Janssen Prize 1986, Prelog Medal, ETH, Zürich 1988, Sammet Award, Goethe Univ., Frankfurt 1988, Chemical Pioneer Award (American Inst. of Chemists) 1988, Scheele Medal (Swedish Acad. of Pharma Sciences) 1991, Tetrahedron Prize 1993, King Faisal Prize for Science (Saudi Arabia) 1995, Microbial Chem. Award, Kitasato Inst., Tokyo 1997, Harvey Science and Tech. Prize, Israel Inst. of Tech. 1998, Organic Reactions Catalysis Soc. Richard Rylander Award 2000, NAS Chemical Sciences Award 2000, Chirality Medal, Italian Chemical Soc. 2000, Nobel Prize in Chem. 2001 (jt recipient), Benjamin Franklin Medal Medal, Philadelphia 2001, Wolf Prize in Science (jtly) 2001, Rhône-Poulenc Medal (UK) 2001, John Scott Prize and Medal, Philadelphia 2001. *Publications:* more than 300 publns in learned journals and 20 patents. *Address:* Scripps Research Institute, 10550 North Torrey Pines Road, BCC-315, La

Jolla, CA 92037, USA (office). *Telephone:* (858) 784-7505 (office). *Fax:* (858) 784-7562 (office). *E-mail:* sharples@scripps.edu (office). *Website:* www.scripps.edu/chem/sharpless (office).

SHARQI, HH Sheikh Hamad bin Muhammad ash-, (Ruler of Fujairah); United Arab Emirates; b. 25 Sept. 1948; m. Fatima bint Thani Al Maktoum; three s. three d.; ed Mons Mil. Acad., Hendon Police Coll.; Minister of Agric. and Fisheries, UAE Fed. Cabinet 1971–74; Ruler of Fujairah 1974–; mem. Supreme Council 1974–. *Address:* Emiri Court, PO Box 1, Fujairah, United Arab Emirates.

SHASHKIN, Dimitri; Georgian politician; *Minister of Defence;* b. 8 Aug. 1975, Tbilisi; m.; two c.; ed Tbilisi State Univ.; Inspector, Weapons Office, Ministry of Internal Affairs 1992–93; Lt, Akhaltsikhe Military Base, Georgian Armed Forces –1996; Program Asst, ABA, Tbilisi 1997–98; Asst Program Officer, Int. Republican Inst., Tbilisi 1998–2001, Resident Program Officer 2001–07, Resident Country Dir 2007–09; Minister of Corrections and Legal Assistance Feb.–Dec. 2009, Minister of Educ. and Science 2009–12, of Defence 2012–. *Address:* Ministry of Defence, 0112 Tbilisi, Gen. Kvinitadze 20, Georgia (office). *Telephone:* (32) 291-04-21 (office). *Fax:* (32) 291-06-45 (office). *E-mail:* pr@mod.gov.ge (office). *Website:* ww.mod.gov.ge (office).

SHATIGADUD, Col Hassan Mohamed Nur; Somali politician; *Chairman, Rahanwin Resistance Army;* fmr mem. Nat. Security Service; Chair. Rahanwin Resistance Army 1995–; Pres. of self-proclaimed state of Southwestern Somalia (SWS) 2002; elected mem. Transitional Fed. Govt 2004; Minister of Finance 2005–07. *Address:* Rahanwin Resistance Army, Baidoa, Somalia.

SHATNER, William, BA; American (b. Canadian) actor and film director; b. 22 March 1931, Montreal, PQ; s. of Joseph Shatner and Anne Shatner; m. 1st Gloria Rand 1956 (divorced 1969); m. 2nd Marcy Lafferty 1973 (divorced 1996); m. 3rd Nerine Kidd 1997 (died 1999); three d.; m. 4th Elizabeth Martin 2001; ed McGill Univ.; appeared Montreal Playhouse 1952, 1953; juvenile roles, Canadian Repertory Theatre, Ottawa 1952–53, 1953–54; appeared Shakespeare Festival, Stratford, Ont. 1954–56; Broadway appearances include: Tamburlaine the Great 1956, The World of Suzie Wong 1958, A Shot in the Dark 1961, Shatner's World: We Just Live In It (one-man show) 2012; Founder and Presenter Hollywood Charity Horse Show, Los Angeles 1991–; CEO C.O.R.E. Digital Pictures, Inc., Toronto 1994–; . *Films include:* The Brothers Karamazov 1957, The Explosive Generation 1961, Judgment at Nuremberg 1961, The Intruder 1962, The Outrage 1964, Dead of Night 1974, The Devil's Rain 1975, Star Trek 1979, The Kidnapping of the President 1979, Star Trek: The Wrath of Khan 1982, Star Trek III: The Search for Spock 1984, Star Trek IV: The Voyage Home 1986, Star Trek V: The Final Frontier (also dir) 1989, Star Trek VI: The Undiscovered Country 1991, National Lampoon's Loaded Weapon 1993, Star Trek: Generations 1994, Ashes of Eden 1995, Star Trek: Avenger 1997, Tek Net 1997, Free Enterprise 1999, Miss Congeniality 2000, Groom Lake (also dir and co-writer) 2002, Dodgeball 2004, Miss Congeniality 2: Armed & Fabulous 2005, Stalking Santa (voice) 2006, The Wild (voice) 2006, Over the Hedge (voice) 2006, Fanboys 2009, Quantum Quest: A Cassini Space Odyssey (voice) 2009. *Albums:* The Transformed Man 1968, Has Been 2004. *TV appearances include:* Star Trek 1966–69, TekWar (also exec. producer and dir. of two episodes), T.J. Hooker 1982–86, Land of the Free, The Fresh Prince of Bel-Air 1992, Cosby, Third Rock from the Sun 1999–2000, Boston Legal (Best Supporting Actor in a Series, Miniseries or TV Movie, Golden Globe Awards 2005, Emmy Award for Best Supporting Actor in a Drama 2005) 2004–08, The Practice (Emmy Award for Outstanding Guest Actor in a Drama Series 2004) 2004, Everest (miniseries) 2007, Shatner's Raw Nerve 2009, William Shatner's Weird or What? 2010. *Publications include:* TekWar 1989, Star Trek Memories (jtly) 1993, Star Trek Movie Memories 1994, Ashes of Eden (jtly) 1995, Man O' War 1996, Tek Kill 1996, The Return 1996, Avenger 1997, Delta Search: Quest For Tomorrow 1997, Delta Search: In Alien Hands 1998, Step into Chaos 1999, Dark Victory 1999, Step Into Chaos 1999, Get a Life (jtly) 1999, The Preserver 2000, Spectre 2000, Up Till Now: The Autobiography (with David Fisher) 2008. *Leisure interests:* tennis, yoga, skiing, riding, horse breeding, scuba diving, parasailing. *Address:* c/o Melis Productions Inc., 12750 Ventura Blvd, # 101, Studio City, CA 91604, USA. *Website:* www.williamshatner.com.

SHATTER, Alan Joseph, LLB; Irish lawyer and politician; b. 14 Feb. 1951, Dublin; m. Carol Shatter; two c.; ed Trinity Coll., Dublin, Europa Instituut, Univ. of Amsterdam; mem. Dáil Éireann (Fine Gael, FG) for Dublin South 1981–2002, 2007–, FG Front Bench Spokesperson on Law Reform 1982, 1987–88, on the Environment 1989–91, on Labour 1991, Justice 1992–93, Equality and Law Reform 1993–94, Health and Children 1997–2000, Justice, Law Reform and Defence 2000–02, on Children 2007–10; mem. Dublin County Council 1991–99; Minister for Justice, Equality and Defence 2011–14; Partner, Gallagher Shatter (legal practice) 1977–; fmr Consultant on Family Law to Law Soc. of Ireland; Fellow, Int. Acad. of Matrimonial Lawyers. *Publications include:* Family Law in the Republic of Ireland 1977, Family Planning Irish Style 1979, Laura (novel) 1989. *Address:* c/o Gallagher Shatter, 4 Upper Ely Place, Dublin 2, Ireland.

SHATTUCK, Mayo A., III, BA, MBA; American energy industry executive; *Chairman, Exelon Corporation;* b. 7 Oct. 1954, Boston, Mass; s. of Mayo Adams Shattuck Jr and Jane Bergwall; m. Molly George Shattuck; five c.; ed Williams Coll., Stanford Univ. (Arjay Miller Scholar); analyst, Morgan Guaranty Trust Co. 1976–78; Man. Bain & Co. 1980–83; Pres., COO and Dir Alex Brown Inc. 1991–97; Vice-Chair. Bankers Trust Corpn 1997–99; Co-Chair. and Co-CEO Deutsche Banc Alex Brown Inc. 1999–2001; Pres. and CEO Constellation Energy Group Inc. 2001–12, Chair. 2002–12 (acquired by Exelon Corpn 2012), Chair. Exelon Corpn 2012–, mem. Exec. Cttee 2007–; Chair. Baltimore Gas and Electric Co. 2002–; mem. Bd of Dirs Constellation Holdings Inc. 1994–98, Gap Inc. (Chair. Audit and Finance Cttee) 2002–, Capital One Financial Corpn (Chair. Compensation Cttee) 2003–, Edison Electric Inst. (Chair. Finance Cttee), Nuclear Energy Inst., Inst. of Nuclear Power Operations, Walters Art Museum; Chair. Bd of Visitors Univ. of Maryland, Baltimore Co.; mem. Advisory Council Grad. School of Business, Stanford Univ.; mem. Bd of Trustees, Seagram Co. Ltd 1997, Johns Hopkins Medicine; Vice-Chair. and Dir Bankers Trust Corpn 1997–99; Dr hc (Univ. of Maryland, Baltimore Co.). *Leisure interests:* tennis, golf. *Address:* Exelon Corporation, PO Box 805398, Chicago, IL 60680-5398, USA (office). *Telephone:* (800) 483-

3220 (office). *E-mail:* info@exeloncorp.com (office). *Website:* www.exeloncorp.com (office).

SHAW, Audley, BA, MA; Jamaican politician; b. 13 June 1952, Christiana, Manchester; m. Susan Duhaney; four d.; ed Northern Illinois Univ., USA; began career as Lab. Technician, Jamaica Milk Products; worked for Jamaica Promotions Ltd; fmr Area Literacy Officer, JAMAL Movt; MP for Manchester N E 1993–, served as Shadow Minister of Information and Culture, of Public Utilities and Transport, of Industry and Commerce, fmr Chair. Public Accounts Cttee, Shadow Minister of Finance and Public Service 1997–2007, Minister of Finance and Public Service 2007–12; Deputy Leader, Labour Party 1999– (fmr Gen. Sec.). *Address:* The Jamaica Labour Party, 20 Belmont Road, Kingston 5, Jamaica (office). *Telephone:* 964-3300 (office). *E-mail:* fitzalbert_2@yahoo.com (office); nemanchester@hotmail.com (office). *Website:* www.audleyshawjamaica.com (office).

SHAW, Bernard Leslie, PhD, FRS; British scientist and academic; *Professor Emeritus and Honorary Research Professor, School of Chemistry, University of Leeds;* b. 28 March 1930, Springhead, Yorks., England; s. of Tom Shaw and Vera Shaw; m. Mary Elizabeth Neild 1951 (died 2003); two s.; ed Hulme Grammar School, Oldham and Manchester Univ.; Sr DSIR Fellow, Torry Research Station, Aberdeen 1953–55; Research Scientist, Ministry of Defence 1955–56; Research Scientist, ICI Ltd 1956–61; Lecturer, School of Chem., Univ. of Leeds 1962–65, Reader 1965–71, Prof. 1971–94, Research Prof. 1995, now Prof. Emer. and Hon. Research Prof.; Visiting Prof., Univ. of Western Ont., Carnegie Mellon Univ. 1969, ANU 1983, Univ. of Auckland 1986, Univ. of Strasbourg 1993; mem. Science and Eng Research Council Chem. Cttee 1975–78, 1981–84; research consultant, Union Carbide Corpn, USA for 31 years; Chemical Soc. Award in Transition Metal Chem. 1975, Tilden Lecturer, Chemical Soc. 1975, Liversidge Lecturer, Royal Soc. of Chem. (RSC) 1987–88, RSC Ludwig Mond Lecturer and Prizewinner 1992–93, Sir Edward Frankland Lecturer and Prizewinner 1995, Calabria Prize for Science 2001. *Publications:* Inorganic Hydrides, Organo-Transition Metal Compounds and Related Aspects of Homogeneous Catalysis and over 400 research papers; several patents. *Leisure interests:* walking, pottery, gardening, tennis, classical music, opera. *Address:* School of Chemistry, University of Leeds, Leeds, LS2 9JT (office); 14 Monkbridge Road, Leeds, West Yorks., LS6 4DX, England (home). *Telephone:* (113) 343-6454 (office); (113) 275-5895 (home). *Fax:* (113) 343-6565 (office). *E-mail:* B.L.Shaw@Leeds.ac.uk (office). *Website:* www.chem.leeds.ac.uk (office).

SHAW, Caroline Adelaide, BMus, MMus; American violinist, singer, composer and academic; *Doctoral Fellow in Composition, Princeton University;* b. 1973, North Carolina; ed Rice Univ., Yale Univ.; musician since early childhood; fmr Thomas J. Watson Fellow; Doctoral Fellow in Composition, Princeton Univ. 2010–; mem. Roomful of Teeth (vocal quartet); also performs as violinist with American Contemporary Music Ensemble; has worked with Trinity Wall Street Choir, Alarm Will Sound, Wordless Music, Signal, The Yehudim, Victoire, Mark Morris Dance Group Ensemble, Opera Cabal, Yale Baroque Ensemble; work has been performed by So Percussion, Brentano String Quartet, Edward T. Cone Performers-in-Residence (Princeton); regular collaboration with artist Jane Philbrick as part of permanent landscape installation 'The Expanded Field' at Massachusetts Museum of Contemporary Art; Pulitzer Prize for Music (for composition Partita for 8 Voices) 2013. *Recording:* Roomful of Teeth 2012. *Address:* Department of Music, Princeton University, Princeton, NJ 08544, USA (office). *Telephone:* (609) 258-4241 (office). *E-mail:* hello@carolineshaw.com (office). *Website:* carolineshaw.com (office).

SHAW, Colin Don, CBE, MA, FRTS; British fmr broadcasting executive, writer and lecturer; b. 2 Nov. 1928, Liverpool; s. of Rupert M. Shaw and Enid F. Shaw (née Smith); m. Elizabeth A. Bowker 1955; one s. two d.; ed Liverpool Coll., St Peter's Hall, Oxford, Inner Temple; served with RAF 1947–49; joined BBC as radio drama producer 1953–57, variety of posts 1957–69, Sec. to Bd 1969–71, Chief Sec. 1972–77; Dir of TV IBA 1977–83; Dir Programme Planning Secr. Ind. Cos TV Asscn 1983–87; Dir Broadcasting Standards Council 1988–96; mem. Arts Council of GB 1978–80; Gov. English Speaking Union of GB 1976–83; Trustee, Int. Inst. of Communications 1983–89; Hon. Visiting Prof., Univ. of Manchester 1996–99. *Publications includes:* Deciding What We Watch 1999, Acccountability and the Public Interest in Broadcasting (with Andrea Millwood Hargrave); several radio plays and a stage play for children. *Leisure interests:* travel, reading, theatre. *Address:* Lesters, Little Ickford, Aylesbury, Bucks., HP18 9HS, England. *Telephone:* (1844) 339225.

SHAW, Fiona, BA, FRSA; Irish actress; b. 10 July 1958, Cork; d. of Dr Denis Joseph Wilson and Mary Teresa Flynn; ed Univ. Coll. Cork, Royal Acad. of Dramatic Art (RADA); joined RSC 1985; Hon. Prof. of Drama, Trinity Coll. Dublin; Officier des Arts et des Lettres 2001; Hon. CBE 2002; Hon. DUniv (Open Univ.) 1999; Hon. LLD (Nat. Univ. of Ireland) 2000; Hon. DLitt (Trinity Coll. Dublin) 2002, (Ulster) 2004; RADA Tree Prize 1982, RADA Ronson Award 1982, Olivier Award, Evening Standard Award for Machinal 1995, Evening Standard Award for Best Actress 2001, RADA Bancroft Gold Medal, OBIE Award, New York 2002, William Shakespeare Award, Washington, DC 2003. *Plays include:* debut in Love's Labours Lost, Julia in The Rivals, Nat. Theatre, Mary Shelley in Howard Brenton's Bloody Poetry (Hampstead), appeared with RSC as Celia in As You Like It, Tatyana in Gorky's Philistines, Madame des Volonges in Les Liaisons Dangereuses, Beatrice in Much Ado About Nothing, Portia in The Merchant of Venice, Kate in The Taming of the Shrew, Mistress Carol in James Shirley's Hyde Park and as Sophocles's Electra; appeared as Rosalind in As You Like It, Old Vic 1990, as Shen Te/Shui Ta in Brecht's The Good Person of Sichuan (Nat. Theatre) 1990 (Olivier Award for Best Actress 1990, London Critics' Award for Best Actress 1990), in Hedda Gabler (Abbey Theatre, Dublin and West End) 1991 (London Critics' Award 1992), in Beckett's Footfalls 1994, as Richard II in Richard II and in The Waste Land 1996, The Prime of Miss Jean Brodie, Royal Nat. Theatre 1998, Widower's Houses 1999, Medea (Abbey Theatre, Dublin) 2000, (West End) 2001, The Power Book (Nat. Theatre) 2002, The Seagull (Edinburgh Festival) 2003, Julius Caesar (Barbican) 2005, My Life is a Fairy Tale (Lincoln Centre) 2005, Readings (Nat. Theatre of Challot, Paris) 2005, Woman and Scarecrow (Royal Court Theatre) 2006, Happy Days (Royal Nat. Theatre) 2007, Mother Courage and Her Children 2009, London Assurance 2010, John Gabriel Borkman (Abbey Theatre, Dublin) 2010. *Films include:* The Man Who Shot Christmas 1984, Sacred

Hearts 1985, My Left Foot 1989, Mountains of the Moon 1990, 3 Men and a Little Lady 1990, London Kills Me 1991, Super Mario Brothers 1992, Undercover Blues 1993, The Waste Land 1995, Persuasion 1995, Jane Eyre 1996, The Avengers 1997, The Butcher's Boy 1997, Anna Karenina 1997, The Last September 1999, The Triumph of Love 2000, Harry Potter and The Philosopher's Stone 2001, Doctor Sleep 2001, The Triumph of Love 2001, Harry Potter and The Chamber of Secrets 2002, Harry Potter and the Prisoner of Azkaban 2004, El sueño de una noche de San Juan (A Midsummer Night's Dream) (voice; English version) 2005, The Black Dahlia 2006, Catch and Release 2006, Fracture 2007, Harry Potter and the Order of the Phoenix 2007, Dorian Gray 2009, Harry Potter and the Deathly Hallows: Part 1 2010, The Tree of Life 2011, The English Teacher (narrator) 2013. *Radio includes:* Transfiguration 2000, Aiding and Abetting 2000. *Television includes:* The Adventures of Sherlock Holmes – The Crooked Man 1984, Love Song 1985, Iphigenia at Aulis 1990, For the Greater Good 1991, Maria's Child 1992, Shakespeare: The Animated Tales – Twelfth Night 1992, Hedda Gabler 1993, Seascape 1994, Richard II 1997, RKO 281 1999, Gormenghast (BBC) (mini-series) 1999, Mind Games 2001, The Sweetest Thing 2002, Empire (mini-series) 2005, The British Face 2006, Trial and Retribution XIV: Mirror Image 2007, 2011 True Blood (series) 2011. *Leisure interests:* opera, running, snorkling. *Address:* Eglantine, Montenotte, Cork, Ireland (home). *E-mail:* shawassist@aol.com (home).

SHAW, Sir Neil McGowan, Kt; Canadian business executive; b. 31 May 1929, Montreal; s. of Harold LeRoy Shaw and Fabiola Shaw (née McGowan); m. 1st Frances Audrey Robinson 1952 (divorced 1980); two s. three d.; m. 2nd Elizabeth Fern Mudge 1985; ed Knowlton High School, Lower Canada Coll.; Trust Officer, Crown Trust Co. 1947–54; with Canada Dominion Sugar (now Redpath Industries) 1954–98, Merchandising Man. 1954–66, Vice-Pres. 1967–72, Pres. 1972–80, Vice-Chair. 1981–98; Group Man. Dir Tate and Lyle PLC, England 1980–86, Chair. 1986–93, CEO 1986–92, Exec. Chair. 1992–98 (retd); fmrly Chair. Tate and Lyle Holdings Ltd, England, Tate and Lyle Industries Ltd, England, Tate and Lyle Inc., New York; Chair. World Sugar Research Org. 1994–96 (Dir 1982–97), Foundation and Friends of Royal Botanic Gardens, Kew 1994 (Trustee 1990), Anglo-Canadian Support Group CARE 1989; mem. Canadian Memorial Foundation 1989, Council of Advisers to Premier of Québec 1987, Advisory Council Prince's Youth Business Trust 1990, London Enterprise Agency 1986, Food Asscn 1989, Listed Cos Advisory Cttee 1991–, British N American Cttee 1991; Trustee, Rogers Sugar Income Fund 2004; Gov. Montreal Gen. Hosp., Reddy Memorial Hosp., World Food and Agro Forum 1988–96; Hon. LLD (East London) 1997. *Leisure interests:* sailing, skiing, golf.

SHAW, Yu-Ming, PhD; Taiwanese public servant and professor of history; *Chairman, Coordination Council for North American Affairs;* b. 3 Nov. 1938, Harbin; m. Shirley Shiow-jyu Lu; one s. one d.; ed Nat. Chengchi Univ., Tufts Univ. and Univ. of Chicago, USA; Asst Prof. of History, Newberry Coll., SC 1967–68, 1972–73; Assoc. Prof. of History, Univ. of Notre Dame, Ind. 1973–82; held various research posts in Asian studies in USA; Dir Asia and World Inst., Taiwan 1983–84; Dean, Grad. School of Int. Law and Diplomacy, Nat. Chengchi Univ. 1984, Dir Inst. of Int. Relations 1984–87, 1994, Prof. of History 1991; Dir-Gen. Govt Information Office and Govt spokesman 1987–91; currently Prof., Chinese Culture Univ., Pres. Cultural Foundation of the United Daily News Group 1992–; Chair. Coordination Council for North American Affairs 2009–; awards from American Council of Learned Socs, Asia Foundation, Inst. of Chinese Culture, USA and others. *Publications include:* China and Christianity 1979, Problems in Twentieth Century Chinese Christianity 1980, Twentieth Century Sino-American Relations 1980, History and Politics in Modern China 1982, International Politics and China's Future 1987, Beyond the Economic Miracle 1988, An American Missionary in China: John Leighton Stuart and Chinese-American Relations 1993. *Address:* Coordination Council for North American Affairs, 4201 Wisconsin Avenue, NW, Washington, DC 20016, USA (office); Chinese Culture University, 55, Hwa-Kang Road, Yang-Ming-Shan, Taipei 111, Taiwan (office). *Telephone:* (202) 895-1800 (office); (2) 2861-0511 (office). *Website:* www.pccu.edu.tw (office).

SHAWAYS, Rowsch Nouri, DEng; Iraqi engineer and politician; *Deputy Prime Minister;* b. 1947; Head, Kurdish Student Union, Germany; returned to Iraq 1979 joining Kurdish rebellion; Deputy Prime Minister, Jt Kurdistan Regional Govt 1996; Prime Minister, Kurdistan Regional Govt Arbil 1996–99; Pres. Iraqi Kurdistan Nat. Ass. 1999–2004; Interim Vice-Pres. 2004–05; Deputy Prime Minister 2005–06, 2009–; mem. Political Bureau, Kurdistan Democratic Party. *Address:* Kurdistan Democratic Party, c/o KDP Europe, PO Box 301 516, 10749 Berlin, Germany (office). *Telephone:* (30) 79743741. *Fax:* (30) 79743746. *E-mail:* KDPEurope@t-online.de; party@kdp.se. *Website:* www.kdp.se.

SHAWCROSS, William; British journalist, writer and broadcaster; *Chairman, Charity Commission;* b. 28 May 1946, Sussex; s. of Baron Shawcross; m. 1st Marina Warner 1972 (divorced 1980); one s.; m. 2nd Michal Levin 1981 (divorced); one d.; m. 3rd Olga Forte 1993; ed Eton, Univ. Coll., Oxford; freelance journalist in Czechoslovakia 1968–69; corresp. for The Sunday Times, London 1969–72; Chair. Article 19, Int. Centre on Censorship 1986–96, Charity Comm. 2012–; mem. Bd Int. Crisis Group 1995–, mem. Exec. Cttee 2000–; mem. Council of Disasters Emergency Cttee 1997–; mem Informal Advisory Bd UNHCR 1995–2000. *Publications:* Dubček 1970, Crime and Compromise: Janos Kadar and the Politics of Hungary Since Revolution 1974, Sideshow: Kissinger, Nixon and the Destruction of Cambodia 1979, Quality of Mercy: Cambodia, the Holocaust and Modern Conscience 1984, The Shah's Last Ride 1989, Kowtow: A Plea on Behalf of Hong Kong 1989, Murdoch 1992, Cambodia's New Deal 1994, Deliver Us from Evil: Warlords & Peacekeepers in a World of Endless Conflict 2000, Queen and Country 2002, Allies: The United States, Britain, Europe and the War in Iraq (aka Allies: The US, Britain and Europe in the Aftermath of the Iraq War) 2003, Queen Elizabeth The Queen Mother 2009, Justice for the Enemy 2011; contrib. to newspapers and journals. *Leisure interests:* sailing, walking. *Address:* c/o Janklow and Nesbit Ltd, 13a Hillgate Street, London, W8 7SP, England (office). *Telephone:* (20) 7243-2975 (office). *Fax:* (20) 7243-4339 (office). *E-mail:* queries@janklow.co.uk (office). *Website:* www.williamshawcross.com; www.charity-commission.gov.uk.

SHAWN, Wallace, BA; American actor and playwright; b. 12 Nov. 1943, New York; s. of William Shawn and Cecille Lyon; brother-in-law of Jamaica Kincaid (q.v.); pnr Deborah Eisenberg; ed Harvard Univ., Magdalen Coll., Oxford Univ. *Films include:* My Dinner with André (also writer) 1981, Manhattan 1979, The

Princess Bride 1987, The Moderns 1988, Scenes from the Class Struggle in Beverly Hills 1989, We're No Angels 1989, Shadows and Fog 1992, Mom and Dad Save the World 1992, Nickel and Dime 1992, The Cemetery Club 1993, Vanya on 42nd Street 1994, Mrs Parker and the Vicious Circle 1994, Clueless 1995, Canadian Bacon 1995, Toy Story (voice) 1995, The Wife 1995, House Arrest 1996, All Dogs Go To Heaven II (voice), Critical Care 1997, My Favorite Martian 1999, Toy Story 2 (voice) 1999, The Prime Gig 2000, Blonde 2001, The Curse of the Jade Scorpion 2002, Love Thy Neighbor 2002, Personal Velocity: Three Portraits 2002, Duplex 2003, The Haunted Mansion 2003, Teacher's Pet (voice) 2004, Melinda and Melinda 2004, The Incredibles (voice) 2004, Chicken Little (voice) 2005, Southland Tales 2006, Tom and Jerry: Shiver Me Whiskers (voice) 2006, Happily N'Ever After (voice) 2007, New York City Serenade 2007, Kit Kittredge: An American Girl 2008, Mia and the Migoo (voice) 2008, Jack and the Beanstalk 2010, Furry Vengeance 2010, Toy Story 3 (voice) 2010, Cats & Dogs: The Revenge of Kitty Galore (voice) 2010, The Speed of Thought 2011, Vamps 2012. *Television includes:* Clueless (series) 1996–1997, Blonde 2001, Crossing Jordan 2001–06, Mr. St. Nick 2002, Monte Walsh 2003, Karroll's Christmas 2004, Crossing Jordan (series) 2001–06, Gossip Girl 2008, The L Word 2008–09, Gossip Girl (series) 2008–12. *Plays:* as writer: A Thought in Three Parts 1976, Marie and Bruce 1979, Aunt Dan and Lemon 1985, The Fever 1990, The Designated Mourner 1996, Grasses of a Thousand Colours 2009. *Stage appearances include:* My Dinner with André, A Thought in Three Parts, Marie and Bruce 1979, Aunt Dan and Lemon 1985, The Fever 1991. *Address:* c/o Casarotto Ramsay & Associates Ltd, Waverley House, 7-12 Noel Street, London, W1F 8GQ, England (office); c/o William Morris Endeavor Entertainment, 1325 Avenue of the Americas, New York, NY 10019, USA (office).

SHAYE, Robert Kenneth, JD; American lawyer, actor, film producer and film director; *Co-Chairman and Co-CEO, New Line Cinema Corporation;* b. 3 March 1939, Detroit, Mich.; s. of Max Shaye and Dorothy Shaye; m. Éva G. Lindsten 1970; two c.; ed Univ. of Michigan, Columbia Univ. Law School; won First Prize in Soc. of Cinematologists' Rosenthal Competition for Best Film Directed by American Under 25; wrote, produced, directed and edited short films and TV commercials, including award-winning shorts, Image and On Fighting Witches; f. New Line Cinema Corpn 1967, Co-Chair. and Co-CEO; mem. Bd of Trustees, Neuroscience Inst., Motion Picture Pioneers, American Film Inst., Legal Aid Soc.; mem. New York State Bar. *Films:* as producer: Stunts (also writer) 1977, Polyester 1981, Alone in the Dark (also writer) 1982, XTRO 1983, The First Time 1983, Critters 1986, Quiet Cool 1986, My Demon Lover 1987, A Nightmare on Elm Street (Parts 1–6) 1984–2010, The Hidden 1987, Stranded 1987, Critters 2 1988, Hairspray 1988, Heart Condition 1990, Blink 1994, Frequency 2000, Lord of the Rings trilogy 2001–03, Freddy Vs. Jason (also actor) 2003, The Last Mimzy (also dir) 2007, The Golden Compass 2007, The Mortal Instruments 2012, Shiver 2012; as dir: Image 1963, On Fighting Witches 1965, Book of Love 1990; as actor: Quiet Cool 1986, A Nightmare on Elm Street 4: The Dream Master 1988, Freddy's Dead: The Final Nightmare 1991, Man's Best Friend 1993, Festival in Cannes 2001, Cellular 2004. *Television:* Freddy's Nightmare: The Series (exec. producer) 1988–90. *Leisure interest:* cooking. *Address:* New Line Cinema Corporation, 110 Leroy Street, New York, NY 10014-3911, USA (office). *Telephone:* (212) 924-4044 (office). *Website:* www.newline.com (office).

SHCHAPOV, Yaroslav Nikolayevich; Russian historian; *Councillor, Institute of Russian History, Russian Academy of Sciences;* b. 6 May 1928, Moscow; s. of Nikolai Mikhailovich Shchapov and Eugenia Nikolayevna Shchapova (née Dobrobozhenko); m. Yulia Leonidovna Shchapova (née Sinelnikova) 1954; one s.; ed Moscow State Univ.; Sr, Chief Librarian V. Lenin State Library 1952–57; Jr, Sr, Leading, Chief Researcher, Inst. of History of USSR, USSR Acad. of Sciences 1957–90; Head of Centre of Church and Religious History, Inst. of Russian History, Russian Acad. of Sciences 1990–99, Councillor 1999–; Corresp. mem. USSR (now Russian) Acad. of Sciences 1987; Pres. Russian Soc. of Historians and Archivists 1990–96; Dir County Estate Schapovo Municipal Museum, Podolsk 1998–2008; Chair. Scientific Council Role of Religion in History 1998–2001; mem. Russian Ass. of the Nobility; Pres. Imperial Orthodox Palestine Soc. 2003–07, Hon. mem. 1993; research in history of old Russia, law, social relations, religion, culture, old Russian manuscripts, Russian-Byzantine relations, Russian Orthodox Church, cultural and charitable activity of Russian pre-revolutionary business owners; Hon. Citizen of Podolsk Dist 2004; Order of Friendship of the Peoples 1988, Church Order St Sergius of Radonezh (Second Class) 1997, Order of Honour 1998, Church Order St Prince Daniil of Moscow 2003, Church Order of St Metropolitan Macarios 2008, Russian Imperian Dynasty Order of St Anna (Second Class) 2008; B. Grekov Prize 1992, Restoration of Russian Country Estate Fund 2007, Metropolitan Macarios Fund 2009. *Publications:* Byzantine and South Slavic Legal Heritage in Russia of 11th–13th Centuries 1978, State and Church in Early Russia 10th–13th Centuries 1989 (published in USA 1993), Russian Orthodox Church and the Communist State (Documents from Secret Archives) 1996, Historical Country Estates in South Moscow District 2000, Shchapov's Agricultural School 1903–2003: Call Over the Centuries 2003, Small Museum and Small Country Estate in Moscow District 2007, Rostov Age-Old Lace-Patterns from the Collection of the Shchapov Family 2009; more than 360 articles. *Leisure interests:* family history. *Address:* Institute of Russian History, Russian Academy of Sciences, D. Ulyanov str. 19, 117036 Moscow, Russia (office). *Telephone:* (495) 126-26-65 (office); (495) 438-22-89 (home). *Fax:* (495) 126-39-55 (office); (495) 438-22-89 (home). *E-mail:* y_schapov@mail.ru (home). *Website:* www.museum.ru/museum/schapovo (office); www.shchapovo.ru.

SHCHEDRIN, Rodion Konstantinovich; Russian composer and pianist; b. 16 Dec. 1932, Moscow; s. of Konstantin Mikhailovich Shchedrin and Konkordia Ivanovna Shchedrin; m. Maya Plisetskaya 1958; ed Moscow Conservatoire; Chair. RSFSR (now Russian) Union of Composers 1973–90; USSR People's Deputy 1989–91; f. International Maya Plisetskaya and Rodion Shchedrin Foundation 2000; mem. Acad. of Fine Arts, Berlin 1989–, Bavarian Acad. of Fine Arts; Hon. mem. American Liszt Soc., Rachmaninov Soc., Int. Music Council, Hon. Prof., Moscow Conservatoire, St Petersburg Conservatoire; Lenin Prize, USSR and Russian State Prizes, Russian Union of Composers Prize, Shostakovich Prize, Beethoven Soc. Prize. *Compositions include:* operas: Not Only Love 1961, Lenin Oratory 1972, Dead Souls 1976, Lolita 1994, The Enchanted Wanderer 2002, Boyarinya Morozova 2006; ballets: Little Humpbacked Horse 1960, Carmen Suite 1967, Anna Karenina 1972, The Seagull 1980, Lady with a Lapdog 1985; for

orchestra: three symphonies 1958, 1965, 2000, 5 concertos for orchestra 1963, 1968, 1988, 1989, 1998; Self-Portrait 1984, Stykhira 1988, Old Russian Circus Music 1989; 6 concertos for piano and orchestra 1954, 1966, 1973, 1992, 1999, 2003, Concerto for cello and orchestra 1994, Concerto for trumpet and orchestra 1995, Two Tangos by Albéniz for orchestra 1996, Concerto dolce for viola and string orchestra 1997; other: Poetoria 1974, Musical Offering for organ and nine soloists 1983, The Sealed Angel (Russian Liturgy) 1988, Nina and the Twelve Months (musical) 1988, Piano Terzetto 1996, Concerto Cantabile (for violin and strings) 1997, Preludium for 9th Symphony by Beethoven 1999, Lolita-serenade 2001, Parabola concertante (for cello and strings) 2001, Dialogue with Shostakovich 2001, The Enchanted Wanderer (concert opera) 2002, Tanja-Katya 2002, My Age, My Wild Beast 2003; works for chamber orchestra, piano, violin, organ and cello and song cycles, music for theatre and cinema. *Leisure interests:* jogging, fishing, water-skiing, wind surfing. *Address:* International Maya Plisetskaya and Rodion Shchedrin Foundation, Weihergarten 9, 55116 Mainz (office); Theresienstrasse 23, 80333 Munich, Germany (home); 25/9, Tverskaya St, apt. 31, 103050 Moscow, Russia (home). *Telephone:* (89) 285834 (home); (495) 299-72-39 (home). *Fax:* (89) 282057 (home). *E-mail:* infoplisetskaya.de (office); infoshchedrin.de (office); rshchedrin@yahoo.com. *Website:* www.shchedrin.de (office).

SHCHEGOLEV, Igor Olegovich; Russian politician; *Minister of Communications and the Mass Media;* ed Moscow State Inst. of Foreign Languages, Germanic Studies Faculty, Leipzig Univ., Germany; ITAR-TASS Corresp., Paris, France 1993–97, Ed. of European News, ITAR-TASS, Moscow 1997–98, later Deputy Head of ITAR-TASS; Deputy Head of Dept of State Information, Russian Govt 1998; Press Sec. to the Prime Minister, later Head of Dept of State Information 1998–2002; Head of Presidential Press Service 2000–02; Head of Protocol Office of Pres. of Russian Fed. 2002–08; Minister of Communications and the Mass Media 2008–. *Address:* Ministry of Communications and the Mass Media, 125375 Moscow, Ulitsa Tverskaya 7, Russia (office). *Telephone:* (495) 771-81-00 (office); (495) 771-87-10 (office). *Fax:* (495) 771-8718 (office). *E-mail:* office@minsvyaz.ru (office). *Website:* www.minsvyaz.ru (office).

SHCHERBAKOV, Vladimir Ivanovich, DEconSc; Russian business executive; *Head, Avtotor Investment Group;* b. 5 Dec. 1949, Novo-Sysoyevka, Primorsky territory; s. of Ivan Shcherbakov and Elena Shcherbakova; m. Natalia Shcherbakova; one s.; ed Togliatti Polytech. Inst., Higher Comsomol School; engineer-mechanic; mem. CPSU 1970–91; party work in Togliatti 1971–74; engineer, controller, Chief Planning and Econ. Dept, Volga Motor Car Plant 1970–82; Deputy Dir-Gen., Dir Econ. and Planning Dept, Kama Big Lorries Plant 1982–85; Chief Machine Bldg and Metal Trade Plant Dept, USSR State Cttee for Labour and Social Affairs 1985–88; First Deputy Chief Nat. Economy Man. Dept, USSR Council of Ministers 1988–89; Minister of Labour and Social Affairs 1989–91; Deputy Prime Minister, later First Deputy Prime Minister, Minister of Economy and Planning of the USSR March–Aug. 1991; Pres. Interprivatization Fund 1991–; Head, Avtotor Investment Group 1995–; Chair. Russian United Industrial Party 1995–97; Vice-Pres. Russian Union of Mfrs and Entrepreneurs 1996–; Vice-Pres. Free Econ. Soc. of Russia 1997–; mem. Russian Acad. of Natural Sciences; Hon. Consul of Greece in Kaliningrad. *Publications include:* about 50 monographs and articles, concerning Big Economic Complexes: Mechanism of Management, Industrial Labour and its Remuneration, New Mechanisms of Labour Remuneration etc. *Leisure interests:* hunting, sports. *Address:* Avtotor Holding, 3/3 Solyanka Street, 109028 Moscow, Russia (office). *Telephone:* (495) 624-60-61 (office). *E-mail:* scherbakov@avtotor.ru (office). *Website:* www.avtotor.ru (office).

SHE, Lulin, BSc (Pharm), MBA; Chinese business executive; *Non-Executive Chairman, China National Pharmaceutical Group Corporation (Sinopharm);* ed Nanjing Pharmaceutical Inst. (now China Pharmaceutical Univ.), Tsinghua Univ.; served successively as Deputy Head of Gen. Man.'s Office, Asst to Gen. Man., Deputy Gen. Man. and Gen. Man. China Nat. Pharmaceutical Group Guangzhou Corpn 1982–96, Vice-Chair. and Gen. Man. China Nat. Pharmaceutical Group Corpn (Sinopharm) 1998–2004, Dir, Gen. Man. and Sec. of Party Cttee 2004–09, Vice-Chair., Gen. Man. and Sec. of Party Cttee 2009–, Pres. and Legal Rep. of Sinopharm Industrial Investment Co. Ltd 2008–, Chair. Sinopharm Group Holdings Co. Ltd 1998–2001, Dir (non-exec.) 2003–, Chair. (non-exec.) Sinopharm Group Co. Ltd 2007–. *Address:* Sinopharm, 20 Zhichun Road, Beijing 100088, People's Republic of China (office). *Telephone:* (10) 82287727 (office). *E-mail:* webmaster@sinopharm.com (office). *Website:* www.sinopharm.com (office).

SHEA, The Hon. Gail; Canadian politician; *Minister of Fisheries and Oceans;* mem. Legis. Ass., PEI 2000–07; Minister of Community and Cultural Affairs 2000–03, of Transportation and Public Works 2003–07, of Fisheries and Oceans 2008–11, 2013–, of Nat. Revenue 2011–13; MP for Egmont 2008–; mem. Conservative Party of Canada. *Address:* Department of Fisheries and Oceans, Centennial Towers, 13th Floor, 200 Kent Street, Station 13E228, Ottawa, ON K1A 0E6, Canada (office). *Telephone:* (613) 993-0999 (office). *Fax:* (613) 990-1866 (office). *E-mail:* info@dfo-mpo.gc.ca (office). *Website:* www.dfo-mpo.gc.ca (office); gailshea.ca.

SHEA, Jamie Patrick, BA, DPhil; British international organization official and university professor; *Deputy Assistant Secretary General for Emerging Security Challenges, NATO;* b. 11 Sept. 1953, London, England; m.; two c.; ed Univ. of Sussex, Lincoln Coll., Oxford; joined NATO 1980, Administrator in Council Operations Section, Exec. Secr. 1980–82, Head of Youth Programmes 1982–85, Head of External Relations Confs and Seminars 1985–88, Asst to Sec.-Gen. for Special Projects (speechwriting, press releases, official communiqués), also adviser to Sec. Gen. on political and mil. issues 1988–91, Deputy Head and Sr Planning Officer, Policy Planning Unit and Multilateral Affairs Section, Political Directorate, also Speechwriter to Sec. Gen. 1991–93, Spokesman and Deputy Dir of Information and Press 1993–2001, Dir 2000–03, Temporary Spokesman 2003–04, Deputy Asst Sec.-Gen. for External Relations 2003–05, Dir Policy Planning, Pvt. Office of the Sec.-Gen. 2005–10, Deputy Asst Sec.-Gen. for Emerging Security Challenges 2010–; currently Visiting Prof., European Political and Administrative Studies Dept, Coll. of Europe; Visiting Lecturer, Sussex Univ.; Prof. of Int. Relations, Assoc. Prof. of Int. Relations, American Univ., Washington, DC; Lecturer, Brussels School of Int. Studies, Univ. of Kent; Adjunct Assoc. Prof. of Int. Relations, James Madison Coll., Michigan State Univ. also Dir MSU Summer School in Brussels; Chair of Transatlantic Programme, Royal Holloway Coll.,

Univ. of London; Bd mem., Geneva Centre for Security Policy; mem. Advisory Council Int. Relations Studies and Programme, Université Libre de Bruxelles and Jean Monnet Visiting Prof.; Visiting Prof., LSE; Sr Transatlantic Fellow, German Marshall Fund of USA; mem. Academic Advisory Council, Vesalius Coll., Brussels; mem. Advisory Council European Policy Centre, Brussels; Founder and mem. Security and Defence Agenda, Brussels; mem. Centre for European Policy Studies, European-Atlantic Movt, Int. Studies Asscn; mem. Advisory Bd, Centre for Defence Studies, Estonia; Assoc. mem. Institut Royal des Relations Internationales, Brussels; 30th Anniversary Fellow, Univ. of Sussex; Hon. Fellow, Security and Strategy Inst., Univ. of Exeter; Golden Eagle (Albania), Gold Londen Medal (Czech Repub.), NATO Medal for Meritorious Service; Hon. PhD (Nat. School of Political and Admin. Studies, Bucharest) 2012; European Communicator of the Year 1999. *Address:* NATO, Boulevard Leopold III, 1110 Brussels, Belgium (office). *Telephone:* (2) 707-44-13 (office). *E-mail:* shea.jamie@hq.nato.int (office). *Website:* www.nato.int (office).

SHEARER, Alan, OBE, DL; British fmr professional football manager and fmr professional footballer; b. 13 Aug. 1970, Gosforth, Newcastle upon Tyne; s. of Alan Shearer and Anne Shearer; m. Lainya Shearer 1991; one s. two d.; striker; coached as a child at Wallsend Boys' Club –1986; yout player for Southampton 1986–88; sr player for Southampton 1988–92, Blackburn Rovers 1992–96 (won Premier League 1994–95), becoming the only player in English football ever to score 30 or more goals in three consecutive seasons; signed by Newcastle United for then world record transfer fee of £15 million 1996, Capt. 1999–2006, player-Coach 2005–06 (retd); played for England U-21 team 1990–92, England B team 1992, England nat. team 1992–2000 (63 caps, 30 goals), Capt. 1996–2000, won Tournoi de France 1997; first player to score 200 Premiership goals and first to score 100 League goals for two different clubs; Premiership all-time leading scorer with 260 goals in 441 games; record for most Premier League goals (34) in a 42-game season 1992–95; Sporting Amb. for Newcastle United 2006–07; football commentator, Match of the Day and other BBC broadcasts 2006–; Man. Newcastle United Football Club April–May 2009 (retd); Patron, Sir Bobby Robson Foundation 2009–; Freeman of Newcastle upon Tyne 2000; Hon. DCL (Northumbria Univ.) 2006, (Newcastle Univ.) 2009; Southampton FC Player of the Season 1990–91, Euro 96 Golden Boot Winner (five goals) 1996, UEFA Cup top scorer 2003/04, 2004/05, Professional Footballers Asscn Players' Player of the Year 1995, 1997, Football Writers' Asscn Footballer of the Year 1994, (Football Asscn) Hall of Fame 1998, inducted into English Football Hall of Fame 2004, Newcastle United FC Player of The Year 2005, named by Pelé as one of the 125 greatest living footballers, Premier League 10 Seasons Awards (1992/93–2001/02): Domestic and Overall Player of the Decade, Domestic and Overall Team of the Decade, Outstanding Contribution to the FA Premier League, Top Goalscorer (204). *Leisure interest:* golf. *Address:* Match of the Day, BBC Sport, Quay House, BBC MediaCity UK, Salford, M50 2QH (office); The Alan Shearer Foundation, St Cuthberts House, West Road, Newcastle upon Tyne, NE15 7PY, England. *Website:* www.alanshearerfoundation.org.uk.

SHEBBEARE, Sir Thomas (Tom) Andrew, Kt, KCVO, BA; British charity administrator; *Director, The Prince's Charities;* b. 25 Jan. 1952; s. of the late Robert Austin Shebbeare and Frances Dare Graham; m. Cynthia Jane Cottrell 1976; one s. one d.; ed Malvern Coll., Univ. of Exeter; with World Univ. Service 1973–75; Gen. Sec. British Youth Council 1975–80; Admin. Council of Europe 1980–85; Exec. Dir European Youth Foundation 1985–88; Exec. Dir Prince's Trust 1988–99, CEO 1999–2003; apptd Dir Royal Jubilee Trusts 1988; Dir The Prince's Charities 2004–; Dir Inst. for Citizenship Studies 1991–2000, Gifts in Kind 1996; Trustee, InKind Direct, School Food Trust, Turquoise Mountain Foundation; Dir (non-exec.) Virgin Money Giving, CIM Investments; mem. Council Queen's Coll. 1999–; Hon. LLD (Univ. of Exeter) 2005. *Leisure interests:* family, cooking, food and drink. *Address:* The Prince's Charities, Office of The Prince of Wales and The Duchess of Cornwall, Clarence House, London, SW1 1BA, England (office). *Telephone:* (20) 7024-5832 (office). *Fax:* (20) 7024-5783 (office). *E-mail:* tom .shebbeare@royal.gsx.gov.uk (home). *Website:* www.princescharities.org (office).

SHECHTMAN, Daniel, BSc, MSc, PhD; Israeli/American physicist and academic; *Philip Tobias Professor of Materials Science, Technion Israel Institute of Technology;* b. Tel-Aviv; m. Zipora Shechtman; four c.; ed Technion Israel Inst. of Tech., Haifa; Nat. Research Council Fellow, Wright Patterson Air Force Base, OH, USA 1973–75; Dept of Materials Eng, Technion Israel Inst. of Tech., Haifa 1975–, becoming Philip Tobias Prof. of Materials Science; Prof., Dept of Materials Science and Eng, Iowa State Univ., USA 2004–; Research Fellow, Johns Hopkins Univ., Baltimore 1981–83; Researcher, Nat. Inst. of Standards and Tech. (NIST), Gaithersburg, Md 1992–94; mem. Israel Acad. of Sciences 1996, Nat. Acad. of Eng (USA) 2000, European Acad. of Sciences 2004; Hon. mem. Materials Research Soc. of India 1997, ISIS-Symmetry (Int. Soc. for Interdisciplinary Sciences 1998, Israel Soc. for Microscopy 1998, Israel Crystallographic Asscn 1999, French Physical Soc. 2000, Japan Inst. of Metals 2005; Friedenberg Fund for the Advancement of Science and Educ. Physics Award 1986, American Physical Soc. Int. Award for New Materials 1987, Technion England Academic Award for Academic Excellence 1987/88, Rothchild Prize in Eng 1990, Weizmann Prize in Science 1993, Israel Prize in Physics 1998, Wolf Prize for Physics 1999, Swedish Royal Acad. of Sciences Gregori Aminoff Prize 2000, EMET Prize in Chem. 2002, Nobel Prize in Chem. 2011. *Address:* Technion Israel Institute of Technology, Room 617, Technion City, Haifa 32000, Israel (office). *Telephone:* (4) 8294299 (office). *Fax:* (4) 8295677 (office). *E-mail:* dannys@tx.technion.ac.il (office). *Website:* materials.technion.ac.il/dan-shechtman-quasi-crystals-nobel (office).

SHECTMAN, Stephen A., BS, PhD; American astronomer; *Staff Member, Carnegie Observatories;* b. 25 Sept. 1949, New York; s. of Arthur Shectman and Dorothy Shectman; divorced; one s. one d.; ed Yale Univ., California Inst. of Tech. (Caltech); Post-Doctoral Scholar in Astronomy and Lecturer in Physics, Univ. of Michigan 1973–75; Alfred P. Sloan Research Fellow 1984–88; staff mem. Carnegie Observatories, Pasadena, California 1975–; Project Scientist, Magellan Telescope Project 1986–2004; mem. American Acad. of Arts and Sciences 1997–; Weber Award for Astronomical Instrumentation, American Astronomical Soc. 2005, Jackson-Gwilt Medal, Royal Astronomical Soc. 2008. *Publications include:* numerous articles in astronomical journals. *Leisure interests:* opera, cycling. *Address:* Carnegie Observatories, 813 Santa Barbara Street, Pasadena, CA 91101, USA (office). *Telephone:* (626) 577-1122 (office). *Fax:* (626) 795-8136 (office).

E-mail: shec@obs.carnegiescience.edu (office). *Website:* obs.carnegiescience.edu/users/shec (office).

SHEEHAN, (Cornelius Mahoney) Neil, AB; American journalist and author; b. (Cornelius Mahoney Sheehan), 27 Oct. 1936, Holyoke, Mass; s. of Cornelius Sheehan and Mary O'Shea; m. Susan Margulies 1965; two d.; ed Harvard Univ.; Viet Nam Bureau Chief, UPI, Saigon 1962–64; reporter, New York Times, New York, Jakarta, Saigon, Washington, DC 1964–72, obtained classified Pentagon Papers from Daniel Ellsberg 1971, subsequently published in New York Times winning newspaper Pulitzer Prize; Guggenheim Fellow 1973–74; Adlai Stevenson Fellow 1973–75; Fellow, Lehrman Inst. 1975–76; Rockefeller Foundation Fellow 1976–77; Fellow, Woodrow Wilson Center for Int. Scholars 1979–80; mem. Soc. of American Historians, Acad. of Achievement; Hon. LittD (Columbia Coll., Chicago) 1972; Hon. LHD (American Int. Coll.) 1990, (Lowell Univ.) 1991; recipient of numerous awards for journalism. *Publications:* The Arnheiter Affair 1972, A Bright Shining Lie: John Paul Vann and America in Viet Nam (Nat. Book Award 1988, Pulitzer Prize for non-fiction 1989, J.F. Kennedy Award 1989, chosen by The Modern Library as one of 100 Best Works of Non-Fiction in 20th Century 1999) 1988, After the War Was Over: Hanoi and Saigon 1992, A Fiery Peace in a Cold War: Bernard Schriever and the Ultimate Weapon 2009; contrib. to The Pentagon Papers 1971; articles and book reviews for popular magazines. *Address:* 4505 Klingle Street, NW, Washington, DC 20016, USA (home).

SHEEHY, Sir Patrick, Kt; British business executive (retd); b. 2 Sept. 1930; s. of Sir John Francis Sheehy and Jean Sheehy (née Newton); m. Jill Patricia Tindall 1964; one s. one d.; ed Ampleforth Coll., Yorks.; served in Irish Guards 1948–50; joined British-American Tobacco Co. 1950, first appointment, Nigeria, Ghana 1951, Regional Sales Man. Nigeria 1953, Ethiopian Tobacco Monopoly 1954, Marketing Dir Jamaica 1957, Gen. Man. Barbados 1961, Netherlands 1967; Dir British-American Tobacco 1970–82, mem. Chair.'s Policy Cttee and Chair. Tobacco Div. Bd 1975; Deputy Chair. BAT Industries 1976–81, Vice-Chair. 1981–82, Chair. 1982–95; Chair. BAT Financial Services 1985–90, Barder Marsh (now Marlborough) 1995–96, Perpetual Income Investment Trust Ltd 1996–2007; Dir Eagle Star Holdings 1984–87, British Petroleum 1984–98, The Spectator Ltd 1988–, Cluff Resources 1992–96, Celtic Football Club 1996–; Dir (non-exec.) British Petroleum Co. Plc 1984–98, Asda Property Holdings Plc 1994–, Abdela Holdings UK Ltd 1996, Sherritt Int. Corpn 1996–, Celtic Plc 1996, EFG Private Bank Ltd 1996, Cluff Mining 1997–; Pvt. Bank and Trust Co. 1996–; Chair. Council of Int. Advisors Swiss Bank Corpn 1985–97, UK Home Office Inquiry into Police Responsibilities and Rewards 1992–93; CEO Rainbow 1993–; fmr mem. Pres.'s Cttee, CBI, European Roundtable of Industrialists, Action Cttee for Europe; mem. Trade Policy Research Centre 1984–89, Task Force on Urban Regeneration; Chevalier, Légion d'honneur 1995. *Leisure interests:* golf, reading, skiing. *Address:* 11 Eldon Road, London, W8 5PU, England. *Telephone:* (20) 7937-6250.

SHEEN, Charlie; American actor; b. (Carlos Irwin Estevez), 3 Sept. 1965, New York, NY; s. of Martin Sheen (q.v.) and Janet Sheen (née Templeton); brother of Emilio Estevez; m. 1st Donna Peele 1995 (divorced 1996); m. 2nd Denise Richards 2002 (divorced 2006); two d.; m. 3rd Brooke Mueller 2008 (divorced 2011); two s.; one c. with Paula Profit; ed Santa Monica High School; first film appearance aged nine in father's film The Execution of Private Slovik 1974; launched Sheen Kidz children's clothing line 2006; nationwide tour, My Violent Torpedo of Truth/Defeat is Not An Option 2011; partner in business venture of electronic cigarettes, NicoSheen 2011. *Films include:* Red Dawn 1984, The Boys Next Door 1986, Lucas 1986, Ferris Bueller's Day Off 1986, Platoon 1986, The Wraith 1986, Wisdom 1986, A Life in the Day 1986, No Man's Land 1987, Three for the Road 1987, Grizzly II: The Predator 1987, Young Guns 1988, Wall Street 1987, Eight Men Out 1988, Major League 1989, Comicitis 1989, Catchfire 1989, Cadence 1990, Men at Work 1990, Courage Mountain 1990, Navy SEALS 1990, The Rookie 1990, Stockade (dir), Secret Society, Hot Shots! 1991, Beyond the Law 1992, Hot Shots! Part Deux 1993, Deadfall 1993, The Three Musketeers 1993, The Chase 1994, Major League II 1994, Terminal Velocity 1994, All Dogs Go To Heaven II (voice) 1996, The Arrival (aka Shockwave) 1996, Shadow Conspiracy 1997, Loose Women 1997, Money Talks 1997, The Fireman 1997, Bad Day on the Block 1997, Postmortem 1998, No Code of Conduct 1998, Free Money 1998, A Letter From Death Row 1998, Five Aces 1999, Being John Malkovich 1999, Rated X 2000, Good Advice 2001, Scary Movie 3 2003, Deeper Than Deep 2003, Scary Movie 3 2003, The Big Bounce 2004, Scary Movie 4 (uncredited) 2006, Foodfight! (voice) 2009, Wall Street: Money Never Sleeps (uncredited) 2010, Due Date 2010, Winning Recipes (short) 2011, She Wants Me 2012, A Glimpse Inside the Mind of Charles Swan III 2012, Scary Movie 5 2013. *Television includes:* The Execution of Private Slovik (film) 1974, Silence of the Heart (film), The Boys Next Door (film), Sugar Hill 1999, Spin City (Golden Globe for Best Actor 2002) 2000–02, Two and a Half Men (series) 2003–11, Anger Management (series) 2012–. *Leisure interests:* baseball, music, film-making. *Address:* c/o Jeffrey Ballard Public Relations, 4814 Lemara Avenue, Sherman Oaks, CA 91403, USA (office). *Website:* www.charliesheen.com.

SHEEN, Ching-Jing; Taiwanese business executive and property developer; *Chairman, Core Pacific Group;* b. 1947, Nanjing, China; moved with family to Taiwan 1947; joined Sea Snake Gang (triads) 1962; in prison 1966–69; mil. service 1969–71; worked on cargo ships 1971–73; govt clerk 1974; est. co. to buy and sell textile quotas; f. Core Pacific property co. 1985, Core Pacific Securities 1988, negotiated merger between Core Pacific Securities and Yuanta 2000, currently Chair. Core Pacific Group; Chair. Sheen Chuen-Chi Cultural and Educational Foundation. *Address:* Core Pacific - Yamaichi International (HK) Limited, 36th Floor, Cosco Tower, Grand Millennium Plaza, 183 Queen's Road Central, Hong Kong, People's Republic of China (office). *Telephone:* (852) 2166-3888 (office). *Fax:* (852) 2918-0409 (office). *Website:* www.cpy.com.hk (office).

SHEEN, Martin; American actor; b. (Ramon Estevez), 3 Aug. 1940, Dayton, Ohio; s. of Francisco Estevez and Mary Ann Phelan; m. Janet Templeton 1961; three s. one d.; worked as shipping clerk, American Express Co., New York; Hon. Mayor of Malibu 1989–; Laetare Medal, Univ. of Notre Dame, Indiana 2008. *Stage appearances:* The Connection (début, New York and European tour), New Live Over A Pretzel Factory, The Subject Was Roses, The Crucible. *Films:* The Incident, Catch-22, Rage, Badlands, Apocalypse Now, Enigma, Gandhi, The King of Prussia, That Championship Season, Man, Woman and Child, The Dead Zone, Final Countdown, Loophole, Wall Street, Nightbreaker, Da 1988, Personal Choice 1989,

Cadence (also Dir) 1990, Judgement in Berlin 1990, Limited Time, The Maid 1990, Cadence (also Dir), Hear No Evil, Hot Shots Part Deux (cameo), Gettysburg 1993, Trigger Fast, Hits!, Fortunes of War, Sacred Cargo, The Break, Dillinger & Capone, Captain Nuke and the Bomber Boys, Ghost Brigade, The Cradle Will Rock, Dead Presidents, Dorothy Day, Gospa, The American President, The War At Home, Spawn, Storm 1999, Monument Avenue, Free Money, Lost & Found 1999, Apocalypse New Redux 2001, Catch Me If You Can 2003, Milost mora 2003, The Commission 2003, Jerusalemski sindrom 2004, The Departed 2006, Bobby 2006, Bordertown 2007, Flatland: The Movie 2007, Talk to Me 2007, Love Happens 2009, The Way 2010, The Amazing Spider-Man 2012. *Television appearances include:* The Defenders, East Side/West Side, My Three Sons, Mod Squad, Cannon, That Certain Summer, The Execution of Private Slovik, Missiles of October, The Last Survivors, Blind Ambition, Shattered Spirits, Nightbreaker, The Last P.O.W.?, Roswell, The West Wing (Golden Satellite Award 2000, Golden Globe Award 2000) 1999–2006. *Address:* c/o Jeff Ballard, 4814 Lemara Avenue, Sherman Oaks, CA 91403, USA.

SHEEN, Michael, OBE; British actor; b. 5 Feb. 1959, Newport, Gwent, Wales; s. of Meyrick Sheen and Irene Sheen; ed Royal Acad. of Dramatic Art. *Films include:* Othello 1995, Mary Reilly 1996, Wilde 1997, Heartlands 2002, The Four Feathers 2002, Bright Young Things 2003, Underworld 2003, Timeline 2003, Laws of Attraction 2004, The Banker 2004, Dead Long Enough 2005, Kingdom of Heaven 2005, The League of Gentlemen's Apocalypse 2005, Underworld: Evolution 2006, The Queen 2006, Blood Diamond 2006, Music Within 2007, Airlock, or How to Say Goodbye in Space 2007, Frost/Nixon 2008, Underworld: Rise of the Lycans 2009, The Damned United 2009, My Last Five Girlfriends 2009, New Moon 2009, Unthinkable 2010, Alice in Wonderland (voice) 2010, Beautiful Boy 2010, The Special Relationship 2010, Tron Legacy 2010, Jesus Henry Christ 2012. *Television includes:* Gallowglass 1993, Lost in France 1998, The Deal 2003, Dirty Filthy Love 2004, Kenneth Williams: Fantabulosa! 2006, Ancient Rome: The Rise and Fall of an Empire 2006, HG Wells: War with the World 2006, The Battle for Rome 2006, A Child's Christmases in Wales (voice) 2009, 30 Rock (two episodes) 2010. *Address:* c/o Roxanne Vacca Management, 73 Beak Street, London, W1F 9SR, England (office). *Telephone:* (20) 7734-8085 (office). *Fax:* (20) 7734-8086 (office).

SHEERAN, Josette, BA; American newspaper editor, diplomatist and international organization official; *Vice-Chairman, World Economic Forum;* b. Orange, NJ; ed Univ. of Colorado; Deputy Man. Ed., Washington Times newspaper 1985–92, Man. Ed. 1992–97; Man. Dir Starpoint Solutions, NY; fmr Pres. and CEO Empower America; Deputy US Trade Rep., Office of US Trade Rep. –2005; Under-Sec. of State for Econ., Business and Agricultural Affairs, US State Dept 2005–07; apptd to UN High-Level Panel on System-wide Coherence in Devt, Humanitarian Assistance and the Environment, Exec. Dir UN WFP 2007–12, Chair. UN High-Level Cttee on Man., mem. UN Devt Group, UN High-Level Task Force on the Global Food Crisis; mem. World Econ. Forum, fmr Chair. Global Agenda Council on Food Security, Vice-Chair. World Econ. Forum 2012–; mem. Council on Foreign Relations; mem. Bd of Dirs Overseas Pvt. Investment Corpn; mem. Council on Foreign Relations, served on its Washington Advisory Bd; fmr mem. Washington Bd, Urban League, United Negro Coll. Fund; Grand Official, Order of Rio Branco (Brazil); Press Award for Journalistic Achievement, Nat. Order of Women Legislators, nat. award for developing and promoting African-American journalists, ranked by Forbes magazine amongst The World's 100 Most Powerful Women (30th) 2011. *Address:* World Economic Forum, 91-93 route de la Capite, 1223, Cologny/Geneva, Switzerland (office). *Telephone:* 228691212 (office). *Fax:* 227862744 (office). *E-mail:* contact@weforum.org (office). *Website:* www.weforum .org (office).

SHEETZ, Michael Patrick, BS, PhD; American cell biologist and academic; *William R. Kenan, Jr Professor of Cell Biology and Chair of Biological Sciences, Columbia University;* ed Albion Coll., California Inst. of Tech.; Postdoctoral Fellow, Univ. of California, San Diego; began career at Univ. of Connecticut Health Center; Washington Univ. in St Louis Medical School 1985–90; Chair of Cell Biology, Duke Medical Center 1990–2000; William R. Kenan, Jr Professor of Cell Biology and Chair of Biological Sciences, Columbia Univ. 2000–, Prin. Investigator for Nanomedicine Center for Mechanical Biology; Distinguished Prof. and Founding Exec. Dir Mechanobiology Inst., Nat. Univ. of Singapore; Ed.-in-Chief MBInfo; L.L.M. van Deenen Prize in Membrane Biology 2004, Wiley Prize in Biomedical Sciences 2012, Albert Lasker Award for Basic Medical Research 2012. *Publications:* numerous papers in professional journals. *Address:* Department of Biological Sciences, Columbia University, 713 Fairchild Center, MC 2408, 1212 Amsterdam Avenue, New York, NY 10027, USA (office); Mechanobiology Institute, Singapore National University of Singapore, T-Lab, #05-01, 5A Engineering Drive 1, Singapore 117411 (office). *Telephone:* (212) 854-4857 (New York) (office); (212) 854-8002 (lab.) (office). *Fax:* (212) 865-8246 (New York) (office). *E-mail:* ms2001@ columbia.edu (office). *Website:* www.columbia.edu/cu/biology (office); www .mechanicalbiology.org (office); www.mechanobio.info/Home/mbinfoteam/michael -sheetz (office).

SHEHATA, Hassan; Egyptian fmr footballer and football coach; *Coach, Egyptian National Football Team;* b. 19 June 1949, Kafr El-Dawwar; footballer (forward), Zamalek SC 1967–68, 1971–83; mem. Egyptian Nat. Football Team 1972–80; man. of several teams including Zamalek SC 1983–85, Al Wasl 1986–88, Shourta 1990–92, 1993–94, Menia 1996–97, Egypt U20 2001–03; Coach, Egyptian Nat. Team 2004–; several awards including Best Footballer in African Cup 1974, Best Footballer in Egypt 1976, Egyptian Merit of Sport 1980. *Address:* Egyptian Football Association, 5 Gabalaya Street, Gezira El Borg Post Office, Cairo, Egypt (office). *Telephone:* (2) 27351793 (office). *E-mail:* efa_football@hotmail.com (office). *Website:* www.efa.com.eg (office).

SHEIKH AHMED MOHAMED, Abdiweli, MA, PhD; Somali/Canadian economist and politician; *Prime Minister;* b. 1959, Bardera; m.; c.; ed Somali Nat. Univ., Univ. of Ottawa, Canada; Dir-Gen., Livestock Marketing and Health Agency, Mogadishu 1984–90; CEO, MISK Enterprises (livestock exporting firm) 1991–98; Programme Man., African Union Red Sea Livestock Trade Comm., Nairobi 2003–06; Sr Livestock and Pastoralism Adviser, COMESA (Common Market for Eastern and Southern Africa), Lusaka 2007–09; Sr Agric. and Rural Devt Officer, Islamic Devt Bank 2010–13; Prime Minister 2013–; over 20 years' experience with regional and int. devt orgs including Islamic Devt Bank, World Bank, USAID,

African Union/IBAR, COMESA, European Union; mem. Canadian Econs Soc., Int. Livestock and Pastoralism Devt Network, Arab-African Int. Devt Professionals. *Address:* Office of the Prime Minister, 1 Villa Somalia, 2525 Mogadishu, Somalia (office). *Telephone:* (5) 543050 (office). *Fax:* (5) 974242 (office). *E-mail:* primeminister@opm.somaligov.net (office). *Website:* www.opm.somaligov.net (office).

SHEIKH HUSSEIN, Hussein Mahmud; Somali politician; Minister of Finance 2002–04, of Higher Education and Culture 2004–07. *Address:* c/o Ministry of Higher Education and Culture, Mogadishu, Somalia.

SHEIKH MOHAMUD, Hassan; Somali politician and head of state; *President;* b. 29 Nov. 1955, Jalalaqsi, Central Hiran Region; ed Somali Nat. Univ., Bhopal Univ. (now Barkatullah Univ.), India; began career as teacher, Lafole Technical Secondary School; Prof., Somali Nat. Univ. 1981; consultant with various NGOs, UN agencies and devt projects during civil war; Educ. Officer, UNICEF, Cen. and S Somalia 1993–95; co-f. Somali Inst. of Man. and Admin (SIMAD), Mogadishu 1999, Dean –2010; Consultant, Ministry of Planning and Int. Cooperation, Transitional Fed. Govt 2009–10; Founder and Chair. Peace and Devt Party 2011; mem. newly-formed Fed. Parl. 2012–; Pres. of Somalia 2012–. *Address:* Office of the President, 1 Villa Baidao, 2525 Baydhabo, Somalia (office). *E-mail:* president@president .somaligov.net (office). *Website:* www.president.somaligov.net (office).

SHEIN, Ali Mohammed, MSc, PhD; Tanzanian physician and politician; *President of Zanzibar;* b. 1948, Chokocho, Pemba Island; m. Mwanamwema Shein; ed Odessa State Univ., USSR, Univ. of Newcastle Medical School, UK; Clerk, Ministry of Educ. and Asst to Deputy Prin. Sec. May–Sept 1969; Head, Dept of Diagnosis and Dept of Pathology, Ministry of Health 1976–84, Specialist in Diagnosis and Head, Dept of Pathology 1989–91, Programme Man., AIDS Prevention Project 1991–95; mem. Zanzibar House of Reps 1995; Deputy Minister of Health 1995–2000, Minister of State, Pres.'s Office, Constitution and Good Governance, Zanzibar 2000–01; Vice-Pres. of Tanzania 2001–10; Pres. of Zanzibar 2010–; mem. Chama Cha Mapinduzi (CCM). *Address:* Office of the President, State House, PO Box 9120, Zanzibar, Tanzania (office). *Telephone:* (22) 2116538 (office). *Fax:* (22) 2113425 (office). *Website:* www.tanzania.go.tz/poffice.htm (office).

SHEINWALD, Sir Nigel Elton, Kt, GCMG, KCMG; British diplomatist; b. 26 June 1953, London, England; s. of Leonard Sheinwald and Joyce Sheinwald; m. Dr Julia Dunne; three s.; ed Harrow Co. Grammar School, Balliol Coll., Oxford; joined Diplomatic Service 1976, Japanese Desk, FCO 1976–77, Embassy in Moscow 1978–79, mem. Lancaster House Conf. team on Zimbabwe 1979–80, Head of Anglo-Soviet Section, FCO 1981–83, Embassy in Washington, DC 1983–87, Deputy Head of Policy Planning Staff, FCO 1987–89, Deputy Head of EC Dept 1989–92, Perm. Rep. to EU, Brussels 1993–95, Head of News Dept, FCO 1995–98, Dir EU Div. 1998–2000, Amb. and Perm. Rep. to EU, Brussels 2000–03; Foreign Policy and Defence Adviser to the Prime Minister and Head, Cabinet Office Defence and Overseas Secr. 2003–07; Amb. to USA 2007–12; Dir (non-exec.), Royal Dutch Shell 2012–. *Address:* Foreign and Commonwealth Office, King Charles Street, London, SW1A 2AH, England (office).

SHELAH, Saharon, PhD; Israeli mathematician and academic; *A. Robinson Chair for Mathematical Logic, Hebrew University of Jerusalem;* b. 3 July 1945, Jerusalem; ed Tel-Aviv Univ. and Hebrew Univ. of Jerusalem; mil. service, Israel Defence Forces Army 1964–67; Teaching Asst, Inst. of Math., Hebrew Univ. of Jerusalem 1967–69, Instructor 1969, Asst Prof. 1971–72, Assoc. Prof. 1972–74, Prof. 1974–, A. Robinson Chair for Math. Logic 1978–; Head, Model Theory Group, Inst. for Advanced Studies, Princeton NJ 1980–81; Lecturer, Dept of Math., Princeton Univ., 1969–70; Asst Prof., UCLA 1970–71; Visiting Prof., Univ. of Wis. 1977–78, Univ. of California, Berkeley 1978, 1982, Dept of Electrical Eng and Computer Science, Univ. of Mich 1984–85, Simon Fraser Univ., Burnaby, BC, Canada 1985, Rutgers Univ., New Brunswick, NJ 1985–86; Distinguished Visiting Prof., Rutgers Univ. 1986–; Chair. European Research Confs: Infinite Combinatorics and its Impact to Algebra, Hattingen, Germany 1999; Vice-Chair. European Science Foundation Meeting, Barcelona, Spain 1997; Head, Israeli Del., US-Israel Conf. in Classification Theory, Chicago, Ill. 1984; Ed. Proceedings American Math. Soc. Summer Conf. on Set Theory, Boulder, Colo 1983, Fundamenta Mathematicae 1994–, Journal of Applied Analysis 1996–, Asian Journal of Mathematics 1998–; mem. Gen. Editorial Bd Journal D'Analyse Mathématique 1992–, Israel Journal of Mathematics 1992; mem. Asscn of Symbolic Logic, Israel Math. Soc., American Math. Soc., Israeli Acad. of Science and Humanities 1988–; Foreign hon. mem. American Acad. of Arts and Sciences 1991; Hon. Ed. Mathematica Japonica 1994–; Erdös Prize 1977, Rothschild Prize in Math. 1982, C. Karp Prize, Asscn for Symbolic Logic 1983, Conf. in Honour of S. Shelah, Tulane Univ., New Orleans 1987, George Polya Prize in Applications of Combinatorical Math., Soc. for Industrial and Applied Math. 1991, Plenary Lecturer, Canadian Math. Soc. Annual Meeting 1992, Plenary Lecturer, European Logic Colloquium, Haifa, Israel 1995, Gödel Lecturer, Asscn for Symbolic Logic Annual Meeting, Madison, WI 1996, Israel Prize in Math. 1998, Japanese Asscn of Math. Sciences Prize 1999, Janos Bolyai Prize, Hungarian Acad. of Sciences 2000, Wolf Foundation Prize in Math. 2001. *Publications:* more than 840 articles in math. journals. *Address:* Einstein Institute of Mathematics, Hebrew University of Jerusalem, Edmond Safra Campus, Givat Ram, Kaplun 205, 91904 Jerusalem, Israel (office). *Telephone:* (2) 658-41-22 (office). *Fax:* (2) 563-07-02 (office). *E-mail:* shelah@math .huji.ac.il (office). *Website:* shelah.logic.at (office).

SHELBY, Richard Craig, BA, LLB; American politician; *Senator from Alabama;* b. 6 May 1934, Birmingham, Ala; s. of Ozie Houston Shelby and Alice L. Shelby (née Skinner); m. Annette Nevin 1960; two s.; ed Univ. of Alabama; law clerk, Supreme Court of Ala 1961–62; law practice, Tuscaloosa, Ala 1963–78; Tuscaloosa City Prosecutor 1963–71; US Magistrate, Northern Dist of Ala 1966–70; Special Asst Attorney-Gen., State of Ala 1969–71; Pres. Tuscaloosa Co. Mental Health Asscn 1969–70; mem. Ala State Senate 1970–78; mem. 96th–99th US Congresses, 7th Ala Dist 1979–87; Senator from Alabama 1987–, Chair. Senate Banking Cttee 2003–07, mem. Appropriations Cttee; fmr mem. Exec. Cttee Ala State Democratic Party; joined Republican Party 1994; mem. ABA; Republican. *Address:* 304 Russell Senate Office Building, Washington, DC 20510 (office); 1414 High Forest Drive, North Tuscaloosa, AL 35406, USA (home). *Telephone:* (202) 224-5744 (office). *Fax:* (202) 224-3416 (office). *Website:* shelby.senate.gov (office).

SHELDRICK, George Michael, MA, PhD, FRS; British scientist and academic; *Professor of Structural Chemistry, University of Göttingen;* b. 17 Nov. 1942, Huddersfield, England; s. of George Sheldrick and Elizabeth Sheldrick; m. Katherine E. Herford 1968; two s. two d.; ed Huddersfield New Coll. and Jesus Coll., Cambridge; Fellow, Jesus Coll. Cambridge and Univ. Demonstrator/ Lecturer, Univ. of Cambridge 1966–78; Prof. of Structural Chem., Univ. of Göttingen 1978–; mem. Akad. der Wissenschaften zu Göttingen 1989; RSC Meldola Medal 1970, RSC Corday-Morgan Medal 1978, RSC Award for Structural Chem. 1981, Leibniz Prize, Deutsche Forschungsgemeinschaft 1987, Patterson Prize, American Crystallographic Asscn 1993, mineral Sheldrickite named after him 1996, Carl-Hermann Medal, Deutsche Gesellschaft für Kristallographie 1999, Dorothy Hodgkin Prize, British Crystallographic Asscn 2004, Max Perutz Prize, European Crystallographic Asscn 2004, Gregori Aminoff Prize, Royal Swedish Acad. of Science 2009. *Achievements include:* author of widely used computer programme for crystal structure determination (SHELX); author of most-cited scientific paper in all subjects of period 2006–10 (http://info.scopus.com/topcited). *Publications:* more than 750 scientific papers. *Leisure interests:* chess, tennis. *Address:* Department of Inorganic Chemistry, University of Göttingen, Tammannstr. 4, 37077 Göttingen, Germany. *Telephone:* (551) 393021 (office). *Fax:* (551) 3922582 (office). *E-mail:* gsheldr@shelx.uni-ac.gwdg.de (office). *Website:* shelx.uni-ac.gwdg.de (office).

SHELLEY, Howard Gordon, OBE; British concert pianist and conductor; b. 9 March 1950, London, England; s. of Frederick Gordon Shelley and Anne Taylor; m. Hilary MacNamara 1975; one s. one step-s.; professional debut at Wigmore Hall, London 1971; soloist with all London and prov. British orchestras; regular tours to USA and Canada, Australia, Hong Kong and Europe; three piano concertos written for him (Cowie, Chapple, Dickinson); conducting debut with London Symphony Orchestra 1985; Assoc. Conductor, London Mozart Players 1990–92, Prin. Guest Conductor 1992–98; Music Dir, Prin. Conductor Uppsala Chamber Orchestra, Sweden 2001–03; opera conducting debut 2002; current engagements as conductor or soloist or combined role of conductor/soloist; Hon. FRCM 1993; Dannreuther Concerto Prize 1971. *Repertoire:* from Mozart through Liszt to Gershwin; first pianist to perform in concert complete solo piano works of Rachmaninov 1983. *Recordings include:* more than 140 recordings, including complete solo piano music of Rachmaninov (nine vols) and complete Rachmaninov song-cycle (three vols), vols of solo piano music by Chopin and Schumann, Hummel solo piano works, the complete Clementi sonatas (six double CDs) and currently a survey of Mendelssohn's music for piano solo, piano concertos of many British composers including Alwyn, Lennox Berkeley, Carwithen, Dickinson, Ferguson, Leighton, Rubbra, Tippett, Vaughan Williams and Britten, the symphonies of Alice Mary Smith, Gershwin's piano concerto and rhapsodies, piano concertos of Balakirev, Korngold (Left Hand), Liapounov, Hindemith's Four Temperaments, Szymanowski's Symphony No. 4 and Messiaen's Turangalila; conducting from the keyboard, has recorded Mendelssohn's piano concertos and Mozart piano concertos (six vols); Hummel piano concertos (eight vols), Cramer piano concertos with London Mozart Players; with Tasmanian Symphony Orchestra, piano concertos by Moscheles, Herz, Hiller, Kalkbrenner, Pixis, Döhler & Dreyschock, Rosenhain & Taubert; with Orchestra of Opera North has recorded Schumann, Grieg and Saint-Saëns piano concertos and the complete works for piano and orchestra of Beethoven (two-CD set); conducting the Royal Philharmonic Orchestra has recorded Mozart symphonies 35 and 38 and Schubert symphonies 3 and 5; with Tasmanian Symphony Orchestra Reinecke symphonies 2 and 3; and with Orchestra Svizzera Italiana in Lugano Haydn's London symphonies and symphonies of Spohr. *Television:* documentary on Ravel with Tasmanian Symphony Orchestra (Australian Broadcasting Co.) featured Shelley as presenter, conductor and pianist (Gold Medal for Best Arts Biog., 40th New York Festival Awards); documentary on Rachmaninov by Hessische Rundfunk (Channel 4). *Address:* c/o Caroline Baird Artists, Pinkhill House, Oxford Road, Eynsham, Oxon., OX29 4DA, England (office); 38 Cholmeley Park, London, N6 5ER, England. *Telephone:* (1865) 882771 (office). *Fax:* (1865) 882771 (office). *E-mail:* caroline@cbartists.sol.co.uk (office). *Website:* www.carolinebairdartists.co.uk (office).

SHELOV-KOVEDYAYEV, Fedor Vadimovich, PhD; Russian politician; *Head, Russian Public Policy Centre;* b. 15 June 1956, Moscow; m.; two c.; ed Moscow State Univ.; researcher, Inst. of History of USSR (now Russian) Acad. of Sciences; mem. Club of Moscow Intellectuals Moskovskaya Tribuna 1989–91; RSFSR People's Deputy; mem. Cttee on Human Rights, Supreme Soviet 1990–93; First Deputy Minister of Foreign Affairs 1991–92; mem. State Duma 1993–95; mem. Political Council, Democratic Choice of Russia Party 1993–96; Dir Inst. of Contemporary Policy and Economics 1995–98; Prof. Moscow School of Econs, M.V. Lomonosov Moscow State Univ. 2005–07; Co-Chair., Int. Russian Club; Vice-Pres. Expert Fund of Social Research (ELF); currently Head, Russian Public Policy Centre; mem. Constitutional Comm. on Regional Policy and Co-operation; mem. Parl. Block Coalition of Reforms. *Publications:* History of the Bosphorus from 6th to 14th Century BC and over 90 scientific works. *Address:* c/o Moscow School of Economics, M.V. Lomonosov Moscow State University, 119992, Moscow, GSP-1, 1-61 Leninskiye Gory, Russia.

SHELTON, Gen. H(enry) Hugh, MSc; American fmr army officer; *Chairman, Red Hat Corporation;* b. 2 Jan. 1942, Tarboro, NC; s. of the late Hugh Shelton and of Sarah Shelton (née Laughlin); m. Carolyn L. Johnson; three s.; ed North Carolina State Univ., Auburn Univ., Harvard Univ., Air Command and Staff Coll., Nat. War Coll.; commissioned into Infantry 1963; served in mainland USA, Hawaii, 2 tours of Vietnam; fmrly Commdr 3rd Bn 60th Infantry Div., Fort Lewis, Wash., Asst Chief of Staff for Operations 9th Infantry Div., Commdr 1st Brigade 82nd Airborne Div., Fort Bragg, NC, Chief of Staff 10th Mountain Div., Fort Drum, NY; rank of Brig.-Gen. 1987; Deputy Dir for Operations, Nat. Mil. Command CTR, Jt Staff Operations Directorate 1987–89; Asst Div. Commdr for Operations 101st Airborne Div. (Air Assault) (including during Operations Desert Shield and Desert Storm 1990–91) 1989–91; rank of Maj.-Gen. 1991; Commdr 82nd Airborne Div., Fort Bragg, NC 1991–93; rank of Lt-Gen. 1993; Commdr XVIIIth and Fort Bragg Airborne Corps. 1993, Commdr Jt Task Force for Operation Restore Democracy, Haiti 1994; attained rank of Gen. 1996; C-in-C US Special Operations Command 1996–97; Chair. Jt Chiefs of Staff 1997–2001 (retd); Pres. International Operations, M.I.C. Corpn 2002–05; Chair. Red Hat Corpn 2010– (mem. Bd of Dirs 2003–); mem. Bd of Dirs Anheuser-Busch Cos, CACI Int. Inc., Ceramic Protection Corpn, Anteon Int., Protective Products of America; recipient Defense DSM (with 2 oak leaf clusters) 1989, 1994, 1997, DSM 1994, Legion of Merit (with oak leaf cluster) 1985, 1991, Bronze Star Medal (with V device, 3 oak leaf clusters) 1968, 1969, 1991, Purple Heart 1967, Congressional Gold Medal and numerous other decorations. *Publication:* Without Hesitation: The Odyssey of an American Warrior (autobiography) 2010. *Leisure interests:* jogging, woodworking, reading, playing guitar. *Address:* Red Hat Corporation, 1801 Varsity Drive, Raleigh, NC 27606, USA (office). *Telephone:* (919) 754-3700 (office). *Fax:* (919) 754-3701 (office).

SHELTON, Robert Neal, BS, MS, PhD; American physicist, academic and university administrator; *President, University of Arizona;* b. 5 Oct. 1948, Phoenix; m. Adrian Shelton (née Millar) 1969; two s. one d.; ed Stanford Univ., Univ. of California, San Diego; Asst Research Physicist, Univ. of California, San Diego 1975–78; Asst Prof. of Physics, Iowa State Univ. 1978–81, Assoc. Prof. 1981–84, Prof. 1984–87; Prof. of Physics, Univ. California, Davis 1987–2001, Chair. Dept of Physics 1987–90, Vice Chancellor for Research 1990–96, Vice Provost for Research, 1996–2001; Prof. of Physics, Univ. of North Carolina, Chapel Hill 2001–06, Exec. Vice Chancellor and Provost 2001–06; Pres. Univ. of Arizona 2006–, also Prof. of Physics; Fellow, American Physical Soc., AAAS; Ed. Journal of Physics and Chemistry of Solids. *Publications:* over 240 publs. *Address:* Office of the President, University of Arizona, Administration Building, Room 712, PO Box 210066, Tucson, AZ 85721-0066, USA (office). *Telephone:* (520) 621-5511 (office). *Fax:* (520) 621-9323 (office). *E-mail:* robert.shelton@arizona.edu (office). *Website:* www.president.arizona.edu (office).

SHELTON-COLBY, Sally, BA, MA; American fmr diplomatist and international organization official; *Treasurer, Pan American Health and Education Foundation;* b. 29 Aug. 1944, San Antonio; m. William Colby 1984 (deceased 1996); ed Univ. of Missouri, Johns Hopkins School of Advanced Int. Studies, Institut des Sciences Politiques, Paris; fmr Deputy Asst Sec. of State for Inter-American Affairs; fmr mem. Perm. Mission to UN, New York; Amb. to Grenada, Barbados and other Caribbean nations 1979–81; Sr Fellow and Adjunct Prof., Center for Latin American Studies, Georgetown Univ.; Asst Admin. for Global Problems, US Agency for Int. Devt 1994–99; Deputy Sec.-Gen. OECD 1999–2002; fmr Vice-Pres. Bankers Trust Co., New York; fmr Dir Valero Energy Corpn, Baring Brother & Co. Ltd's Puma Fund; Pres. Helen Keller International/Europe 2002, then Chair.; Bd mem. Pan American Health and Education Foundation 2008–, currently Treasurer; Fulbright scholar, Institut d'Études Politiques de Paris; Founder and fmr Chair. Joint UN Programme on HIV/AIDS (UNAIDS); mem. American Acad. of Diplomacy 2002–; adviser to several multi-nat. corpns on int. trade and investment strategies; fmr Co-Ed. Global Assessment (econ. journal); Dr hc (Univ. of Missouri), (St Mary's Coll.). *Address:* Pan American Health and Education Foundation, PO Box 27733, Washington, DC, 20038-7733, USA (office). *E-mail:* education@pahef.org (office). *Website:* www.pahef.org (office).

SHEMYAKIN, Mikhail Mikhailovich; Russian sculptor and painter; b. (Kardanov), 4 May 1943, Moscow; ed Il'ya Repin Inst. of Painting, Sculpture and Architecture, Leningrad (now St Petersburg); started career at Hermitage Museum; one-man exhbn Leningrad 1962; arrested for dissident activities, interned in lunatic asylums; emigrated in 1971; lived in Paris 1971–81; living in USA 1981–; f. Foundation for Helping Soviet Veterans of the War in Afghanistan 1989; visited Russia frequently after citizenship was restored 1990; Chief Designer on Gofmaniada film project, Soyuzmultfilm 2006–; mem. European Acad. of Arts, Paris, New York Acad. of Sciences and Arts; private collections at Metropolitan Museum, New York, State Russian Museum, St Petersburg, Tretyakov Gallery, Moscow; public works include: double-faced Sphinxes on Robespierre Embankment, St Petersburg, Architects-Founders of Petersburg (at the graveyard of Sampsonievsky Monastery), St Petersburg, Peter the First, Peter and Paul Cathedral, St Petersburg, Children as the Victims of Vices of Adults, Bolotnaya square, Moscow, Cybele: the Goddess of Fertility, New York, The Carnival of St Petersburg, Paris, In memory of the 200th anniversary of the death of Casanova, Venice; Ordre des Arts et des Lettres, Order of Friendship (Russia); Dr hc (San Francisco); State Prize 1993, Pres. of Russia Prize 1995. *Publication:* Two Destinies. *Address:* c/o Soyuzmultfilm, 127006, Moscow, ul.Dolgorukovskaya, d.25, Russia. *Website:* www.kck.ru/shemyakin/shemyakin.nsf/index.html.

SHEMYAKIN, Yevgeniy Ivanovich, DTech; Russian mining specialist and academic; *Professor, Moscow State University;* b. 9 Dec. 1929, Novosibirsk; s. of I. Shemyakin and Ella Shemyakina; m. L. T. Petrova 1952; one s. one d.; ed Leningrad Univ.; Sr Research Asst at USSR Acad. of Sciences Inst. of Chemico-Physics 1955–60; head of lab. of USSR Acad. of Sciences Inst. of Theoretical and Applied Mechanics 1960–70; Prof. Novosibirsk State Univ. 1963–87, Chair. of Elasticity 1967–87; Acting Dir of USSR Acad. of Sciences Inst. of Mining (Siberian Div.) 1970–72, Dir 1972–87; Chair. Supreme State Cttee of Attestation, Moscow 1987–92; Prin. Consultant, Russian Acad. of Sciences Inst. of Dynamics of Geospheres 1987–92; Prof. Moscow State Univ. 1987–, Chair. of Wave and Gas Dynamics 1988–; Vice-Pres. of Presidium, Siberian Div., Acad. of Sciences 1980–85; Chair. Russian Acad. of Sciences Scientific Council on Underground Space and Underground Construction 1994–; mem. of USSR (now Russian) Acad. of Sciences 1984, Royal Swedish Soc. of Engineers 1987, Czech Acad. of Science, Slovak Acad. of Science, Int. Soc. for Rock Mechanics (Vice-Pres. 1988–92), Int. Mining Congress; mem. CPSU 1963–91; mem. several scientific editorial bds; USSR State Prize 1984. *Publications:* author and co-author of more than 200 scientific and technical papers. *Leisure interests:* ancient history, old underground constructions. *Address:* Department of Mechanics and Mathematics, Moscow Lomonosov State University, 119991 Moscow, GSP-1, 1 Leninskiye Gory, Main Building, Russia (office). *Telephone:* (495) 939-12-44 (office); (495) 332-62-63 (home). *Fax:* (495) 939-20-90 (office). *E-mail:* mmmf@mech.math.msu.su (office). *Website:* mech.math.msu.su (office).

SHEN, Beizhang; Chinese business executive; b. Jan. 1929, Cixi Co., Zhejiang Prov.; ed Jiaotong Univ., Shanghai; apptd Chair. Shanghai Overseas Corpn; Chair. and Gen. Man., Shanghai Int. Group Corpn 1991; fmr Chair. Shanghai Int. Holding Corpn America 1996, then Hon. Chair.; Chair. Chinese Chamber of Commerce in USA 1996; fmr Pres. Shanghai Int. Trust and Investment Corpn; fmr Dir Shanghai Foreign Econ. and Trade Comm.; mem. 8th CPPCC 1993–98.

SHEN, Dali; Chinese historian and translator; b. 4 Sept. 1938, Yan'an, Shanbei region, Shaanxi Prov.; s. of the late Shen Xu and Song Ying; m. Dong Chun 1993; one s. one d.; ed Beijing Foreign Languages Univ.; Prof. titulaire and Dir Doctoral Theses, French Dept, Beijing Foreign Languages Univ. 1960–2010; trans. at UNESCO, Paris 1979–81, réviseur 1985; Chinese del. WIPO 1984; visiting scholar in France 1990–91; Prof., Univ. of Montreal, Canada 1994, 2005; Prof., INALCO, Paris 1995, Univ. of Aix and Marseille 2003, 2007; Président du Jury 'Grands Reportages', FIPA 1996; del. to Cultural Comm. CIO, Lausanne, Switzerland 1997; mem. Chinese Writers' Asscn 1982–, Editorial Cttee Revue des Deux Mondes (France) 1999–2009; Chevalier, Ordre des Arts et des Lettres 1991, Croix de vermeil du Mérite et Dévouement français 1996; awarded title 'Membre d'honneur' by L'Asscn des Amis de la Commune de Paris 1981. *Translations include:* Le temps des cerises, Montserrat, Selected Poems of Eugene Pottier (additional trans): Les fleurs jumelles (play) 1982, L'epreuve (novel) 1985, Les trésors de la cité interdite 1986, Poésies choisies de la Commune de Paris 1986, l'Internationale, la Marseillaise, Le Chant du départ, N'a qu'un oeil, La paix du ménage, Le Vésuve, Les couteaux, Les yeux de demain, La vraie Dame aux camélias, Byron et les femmes 2002, Bruges la morte 2002, Biographie de Victor Hugo 2003. *Publications:* The Humble Violet (novel) 1980, The Meteor (novel) 1981, The Children of Yenan (novel, also in French and Italian) 1985, Les fleurs du rêve (poetry) 1986, Les lys rouges (novel) 1987, La flûte des Titans (play) 1987, Le rêve dans le pavillon d'azur, Le temps des cigales, Le tableau de Paris (prose) 1989, L'etoile filante (novel) 1993, (augmented edn) 1995, Voyage en Europe et en Amérique du Nord 1996, La rose de Jéricho (film) 1999; painting and poetry (in Italian, French and English): Matisse/Frasnedi 2001, Chagall/Vangeli 2001, Renoir/Zejtlin 2005, Rublev/Ambrosino 2006, Michelangelo/Günter Roth 2006, Les lettres et arts en France (essay) 2003, Les Amoureux du lac (novel) 2004, Biographie de Berlioz 2005, Lega/Vacca 2008, Roberto Panichi 2009, Su Manshu et Paul Verlaine (comparative study), Biographie de Frida Kahlo 2010, Le Jardin latin (essay) 2010. *Leisure interest:* music. *Address:* Building No. 49-1-4, Dongdaqiaolu, Beijing 100020, People's Republic of China (home). *Telephone:* (10) 65007458 (home). *Fax:* (10) 65007458 (home). *E-mail:* chun.shen@free.fr (home).

SHEN, Guofang; Chinese forestry engineer and university professor; b. 15 Nov. 1933, Jiashan, Zhejiang Prov.; ed Leningrad Forestry Inst.; currently Prof., Beijing Forestry Univ. (Pres. 1986–93); fmr Pres. Chinese Soc. of Forestry; Fellow, Chinese Acad. of Eng 1995–, Vice-Pres. 1998–2006. *Publication:* Silviculture. *Address:* Beijing Forestry University, Xiaozhaang, Haidan District, Beijing 100083, People's Republic of China (office). *Telephone:* (10) 62338279 (office). *Fax:* (10) 62335071 (office). *E-mail:* shengf@public.bta.net.cn (office).

SHEN, Hao; Chinese engineer and business executive; *Chairman, Shaanxi Yanchang Petroleum (Group) Company Limited;* has been leader of several govt depts and state-owned enterprises that engage in oil and natural gas exploration and exploitation and coal and chemical production and operation; fmr Pres. Tongchuan Mining Bureau of Shaanxi, Vice-Gen. Man. Shaanxi Coal Transportation of Marketing (Group) Ltd, Chair. Shaanxi Binchang Mining Development and Construction Co., Chair. Shaanxi Coal Industrial Group, Chair. Shaanxi Coal Chemical and Industrial Group Ltd; Dir-Gen. and Sec. Yanchang Oil Mine Admin. Bureau; Exec. Dir Shaanxi Yanchang Petroleum (Group) Co. Ltd 2010–, Chair. and Sec. of Party Cttee 2011–; Exec. Vice-Pres. China Petroleum Enterprise Asscn 2009; Rep. of 17th Nat. Congress of CCP, of 11th Prov. Party Congress and Alt. mem. Comm. of CP of Shaanxi Prov.; Rep. of 9th and 11th People's Congress of Shaanxi Prov.; mem. Cttee, 9th CPPCC. *Address:* Shaanxi Yanchang Petroleum (Group) Co. Ltd, 75 Keji Road, Xi'an 710075, Shaanxi, People's Republic of China (office). *Telephone:* (29) 88899666 (office). *Fax:* (29) 88899669 (office). *E-mail:* webmaster@sxycpc.com (office). *Website:* www.sxycpc.com (office).

SHEN, Heting; Chinese engineer and business executive; b. Aug. 1954; ed Tianjin Commercial Coll., Postgraduate School of Party School of CCP; fmr Asst Man., Deputy Man. and Man. Furnace Construction Co. of 22nd China Metallurgical Construction Corpn, Gen. Man. 1997–2004, Dir, Deputy Sec. of Party Cttee and Legal Rep., China Metallurgical Group Corpn 2004–, Pres. 2008–13; Nat. Labour Day Prize 2004. *Address:* China Metallurgical Group Corpn, 11 Gaoliangqiao Xiejie, Haidian, Beijing 100081, People's Republic of China (office). *Telephone:* (10) 82169999 (office). *Fax:* (10) 82169988 (office). *E-mail:* mcc@mcc.com.cn (office). *Website:* www.mcc.com.cn (office).

SHEN, Jerry, MEng; Taiwanese computer industry executive; *CEO, ASUSTeK Computer;* ed Nat. Taiwan Univ.; spent 10 years holding several sr R&D positions at computer cos and IT research insts; Pres. AOOP (ASUS Open Optimal Platform) Group for Motherboard (MB), Graphics Card (VGA), Desktop, Chassis, Digital Home, EMS and Server businesses 1994–2007, CEO ASUSTeK Computer 2008–. *Address:* ASUSTeK Computer Inc., 15 Li-Te Road, Peitou, Taipei 112, Taiwan (office). *Telephone:* (2) 2894-3447 (office). *Fax:* (2) 2892-6140 (office). *E-mail:* info@asus.com (office). *Website:* www.asus.com (office).

SHEN, Jianhua, PhD; Chinese automotive industry executive; *President, SAIC Motor Corporation Limited;* b. March 1953; ed Tongji Univ.; served as Office Dean of Shanghai Motorcycle Plant, Section Head and Deputy Dean of Gen. Man. Office, Shanghai Automotive and Tractor Industry Jt Business Co., Gen. Man. Shenzhen Zhongrui Automotive Machinery Industry Co. Ltd, Dean of Pres.'s Office, Vice-Chief Economist, Pres.'s Asst, Vice-Pres. Shanghai Automotive Industry Corpn (Group), Vice-Pres. SAIC Motor Corpn Ltd, Chair. auto parts business –2007, mem. Bd of Dirs, Pres. and Vice-Sec. Party Cttee 2007–, also Vice-Chair. HUAYU Automotive Systems Co. Ltd. *Address:* SAIC Motor Corporation Ltd, 5/F Building A, 563 Songtao Road, Zhangjiang, High Technology Park, Pu Dong, Shanghai 201203 (office); SAIC Motor Corporation Ltd, 489 Weihai Road, Shanghai 200041, People's Republic of China (office). *Telephone:* (21) 50803757 (office); (21) 22011688 (office). *Fax:* (21) 50803780 (office); (21) 22011188 (office). *E-mail:* info@saicgroup.com (office). *Website:* www.saicgroup.com (office); www.saicmotor.com (office).

SHEN, Lyushun, LLB, MA, PhD; Taiwanese diplomatist and academic; *Representative to UK;* ed Nat. Chung-Hsing Univ., Univ. of Pennsylvania, USA; Research Assoc., School of Law, Univ. of Maryland, USA 1981–82; Staff Consultant, Congressional Liaison Coordination Council for North American Affairs (CCNAA), USA 1982–88; Sr Specialist and Chief of First Section, Dept of N American Affairs, Ministry of Foreign Affairs (MFA), Taipei 1988–91; Dir-Gen., CCNAA Office in Kansas City 1991–93, Dir Political Affairs Div., CCNAA 1993–94, Dir Public Affairs (Congressional Liaison) Div., Taipei Econ. and Cultural Rep. Office in USA (TECRO, fmrly CCNAA) 1994–96; Dir-Gen., Dept of N American Affairs, MFA 1996–99; Deputy Rep., TECRO 1999–2003; Dir-Gen. (rank of Amb.), Taiwan Cultural and Econ. Del., Geneva 2003–08; Rep., Taipei Rep. Office in EU and Belgium, Brussels 2008–09; Deputy Minister of Foreign Affairs 2009–11; Rep., Taipei Rep. Office in UK 2011–; Visiting Adjunct Prof. of Int. Studies, Univ. of Kansas, USA 1992–93; Hon. PhD (Park Univ., Missouri) 1993. *Address:* Taipei Representative Office in the UK, 50 Grosvenor Gardens, London, SW1W 0EB, England (office). *Telephone:* (20) 7881-2650 (office). *Fax:* (20) 7730-7379 (office). *E-mail:* tro@taiwan-tro.uk.net (office). *Website:* www.roc-taiwan.org/UK (office).

SHEN, Peng; Chinese calligrapher, poet and editor; *Honorary Chairman, Chinese Calligraphers Association;* b. Sept. 1931, Jiangyin, Jiangsu Prov.; began to learn poetry, calligraphy and art from an early age; majored in Chinese literature in coll., later studied journalism; Assoc. Ed.-in-Chief People's Fine Arts Press; fmr Vice-Chair. Chinese Calligraphers Asscn, currently Hon. Chair.; Sr Ed. and Art Counsellor, China Fine Arts Publishing Group; Adjunct Prof., Peking Univ., China Ren Min Univ.; Vice-Pres. and Deputy Chair. Nat. Book Reward Evaluation Cttee; est. Art Museum of ShenPeng Calligraphy in Jiangyin, Jiansu Prov. and Mengjin, Henan Prov.; attended China Art Museum Contemporary Famous Calligraphers Exhbn 2005; organized draft Chinese Calligraphy Devt Compendium 2001–2002; Chief Ed. numerous nat. art magazines, including Art China, Chinese Art, Friends of Chinese Fine Art, and Art Guide; Ed. The laws of the People's Republic of China, Carvings Review, Calligraphy, and 500 other magazines; visits to USA, France, Japan, Sweden, USSR, Singapore, Italy, Korea, Malaysia, Canada, Peru, Venezuela, Hong Kong, Macao and Taiwan; mem. Nat. Cttee CPPCC; Hon. Commr China Fed. of Literary and Art Circles; among first group of experts honoured by State Council of China for Special Contribs, Modeling Art Creation Study Award, China Fed. of Literary and Art Circles 2006, China Calligraphy Lan Ting Lifelong Accomplishment Award, China Fed. of Literary and Art Circles and China Calligraphy Asscn 2006, World Peace and Art Authority Prize, UN Acad. *Publications:* academic thesis 'Tradition and Criticism' (First Prize, Fourth Art Review Reward, China Fed. of Literary and Art Circles), Origins and Branches (Special Award, Fifth Art Review Reward) Criticism on Calligraphy and Art, Shen Peng's Talks on Calligraphy and Art, San Yu Lyrics on Grass, San Yu Lyrics Continues, Collections of San Yu Poems, Anthology of Contemporary Calligraphers – Shen Peng, Selections of Shen Peng's Calligraphy Works, Collections of Shen Peng's Calligraphy (published in Japan), Shen Peng's Calligraphy of BaiJuyi's Works, Shen Peng's Calligraphy of DuFu's Works, Shen Peng's Running Script of 'Front and Back Chibi', Collections of Running Script, Collections of Regular Script, Script of Words about Yue Yang Pavilion, Shen Peng's Script of Nineteen Ancient Poems, Collections of China Art Museum Contemporary Famous Calligraphers Exhibition. *Address:* People's Fine Arts Press, Beijing, People's Republic of China. *Telephone:* (10) 65245237.

SHEN, Rong; Chinese writer; b. (Shen Derong), Oct. 1936, Hubei Prov.; Perm. mem. Chinese Writers' Asscn 1985–, China PEN 1986–; mem. Chinese Int. Exchange Asscn 1990–. *Publications:* Forever Green (novel), No Way Out, Light and Dark, A Middle-aged Woman 1980, True and False, The Secret of Taizi Village, Wrong, Wrong, Wrong!. *Address:* Chinese Writers' Association, 15 Nongzhanguan Nanli, Chaoyang District, Beijing, People's Republic of China (office).

SHEN, Wenrong; Chinese engineer, economist and business executive; *Chairman and President, Jiangsu Shagang Group Inc.;* fmr steelworker; built Jiangsu Shagang into one of China's largest steel-makers, currently Chair., Pres. and Party Chief, Jiangsu Shagang Group Inc., took 45% stake in Australian iron ore prospector Grange Resources, merged it with its Australian iron ore unit, Australian Bulk Minerals; Exec. Vice-Chair. Promotion Asscn for Pvt. Enterprises in Jiangsu Prov.; Chair. Metallurgical Industry Asscn of All-China Fed. of Industry and Commerce; Vice-Chair. China Iron and Steel Asscn; mem. 17th CCP Cen. Cttee 2007–12; Nat. Model Worker of China. *Address:* Jiangsu Shagang Group Inc., Jin feng, Zhang, Jiagang City 215625, Jiangsu Province, People's Republic of China (office). *Telephone:* (512) 58568800 (office). *Fax:* (512) 58551627 (office). *E-mail:* info@sha-steel.com (office). *Website:* www.sha-steel.com (office).

SHENG, Datuk Seri Panglima Andrew Len Tao, LLD, FCA; Malaysian/Chinese economist and financial regulator; *President, Fung Global Institute;* b. 26 Aug. 1946; m. Lim Suan Poh; ed Sabah Coll., Kota Kinabalu, Sabah, Univ. of Bristol, UK; began career as trainee accountant with Arthur Andersen, London; Chief Economist and Asst Gov., Bank and Insurance Regulations, Bank Negara Malaysia 1976–89; Sr Man., Dept of Financial Sector Devt, World Bank, Washington, DC 1989–93; Deputy Chief Exec., Dept of Reserves Man. and External Affairs, Hong Kong Monetary Authority 1993–98; Chair. Hong Kong Securities and Futures Comm. 1998–2005; Chief Adviser, China Bank Regulatory Comm.; Pres. Fung Global Inst., Hong Kong 2011–; Pro-Chancellor, Universiti Tun Abdul Razak 2009–; Hon. Fellow, Hong Kong Securities and Investment Inst. 2013; Silver Bauhinia Star, Yang di-Pertua Negeri Sabah 2005. *Publication:* From Asian to Global Financial Crisis: An Asian Regulator's View of Unfettered Finance in the 1990s and 2000s 2009. *Address:* Fung Global Institute, Cyberport 1, Level 12, 100 Cyberport Road, Hong Kong Special Administrative Region, People's Republic of China (office). *Telephone:* 23002728 (office). *Fax:* 23002729 (office). *E-mail:* as@andrewsheng.net (office). *Website:* www.fungglobalinstitute.org (office).

SHENG, Huaren; Chinese politician; b. 1935, Xieyang Co., Jiangsu Prov.; joined CCP 1954; Office Sec. CCP Party Cttee, Nanjing Chemical Industry Corpn, Jiangsu Prov.; mem. Exec. Council China Council for the Promotion of Peaceful Reunification; Deputy Office Dir CCP Party Cttee, Chemical Fertilizer Industry Corpn, Ministry of Chemical Industry 1965; Deputy Head, Long-Term Planning Group, Ministry of Fuel and Chemical Industries 1970; Deputy Dir, later Dir Planning Dept, Ministry of Chemical Industry; Deputy Gen. Man., later Exec. Deputy Gen. Man. Sinopec Corpn 1983 (Deputy Sec. CCP Leading Party Group), Gen. Man. 1990–98; Vice-Pres. China-ROK Non-Governmental Econ. Asscn; Minister of State Econ. and Trade Comm. 1998–2001; Del., 14th CCP Nat. Congress 1992–97, 15th CCP Nat. Congress 1997–2002; Vice-Chair. and Sec.-Gen. 10th Standing Cttee of NPC 2003–08; mem. State Leading Group for Science and

Tech. 1998; mem. 9th Standing Cttee of NPC 1998–2003. *Address:* c/o National People's Congress, No. 23, Xijiaominxiang, Xicheng Dist, Beijing 100805, People's Republic of China.

SHENG, Zhongguo; Chinese violinist; b. 1941, Chongqing, Sichuan Prov.; s. of Sheng Xue and Zhu Bing; m. Seta Hiroko; ed Moscow Acad. of Music, USSR, studied with Leonid Kogan; fmr Instructor, Cen. Acad. of Music; solo performer (First Class), Nat. Symphony Orchestra; performed Bach's concerto for two violins with Yehudi Menuhin 1979; performed 15 concerts in five Australian cities 1980; mem. 7th, 8th, 9th, 10th sessions CPPCC; Founder Sheng Zhongguo Foundation; Chair. Chinese Violin Soc.; Hon. Prof., Central Conservatory of Music and over 20 other music colls; prize at Int. Tchaikovsky Violin Competition 1962, 1st Prize for Musical Instruments at Competitive Performance by Troupes and Insts (Ministry of Culture) 1981. *Recordings:* many albums, including Butterfly Lovers Violin Concerto, Tchaikovsky Concerto, with Louis Frémaux. *Leisure interests:* Chinese and European fine arts, antiques, good food. *Address:* National Symphony Orchestra, Beijing, People's Republic of China (office). *Telephone:* (10) 64917519 (home). *Fax:* (10) 64917519 (home). *E-mail:* ich23248@nifty.com (home).

SHENGELAIA, Eldar; Georgian film director and politician; b. 26 Jan. 1933, Georgia; s. of Nikolai Shengelaia and Nato Vachnadze; brother of Georgiy Nikolayevich Shengelaia (q.v.); m. 1st Ariadna Shengelaia (Shprink) 1957 (divorced 1980); two d.; m. 2nd Nelly Davlianidze 1981; one d.; ed Moscow Inst. of Cinematography; Dir at Mosfilm 1958–59, at Kartuli Pilmi film studio, Georgia 1960–; mem. CPSU 1966–90; Chair. Georgian Film-makers' Union 1976–; fmr sec. USSR Film-makers' Union; teacher, Tbilisi Theatre Inst., Tbilisi State Univ., Head of Film and TV Dept; Deputy, Supreme Soviet of Georgian SSR 1980–85, 1986–90, mem. Presidium 1989–90; elected to Supreme Soviet of Georgian Repub. (representing Democratic Centre) 1990–91; People's Deputy of USSR, USSR Supreme Soviet 1989–91; mem. State Council, Georgia, Parl. Repub. of Georgia 1992–; mem. Georgian Parl. 1995–, Deputy Chair.; Chair. Cultural Comm.; People's Artist of Georgia 1979, People's Artist of USSR 1987; USSR Prize 1985, numerous other prizes. *Films include:* The Legend of the Ice Heart 1957, The Snow Fairy Tale 1958, White Caravan 1963, Mikela 1965, An Extraordinary Exhibition 1968, The Screwballs 1974, Stepmother of Samanishvili 1978, Blue Mountains or an Improbable Event 1984, Tbilisi 9 April Chronicles 1989, Express Information 1994, Dog Rose 1996. *Address:* c/o Georgian Film-makers' Union, Kakabadze Street 2, 380008 Tbilisi (office); Ioseliani Street 37, Flat 58, 380091 Tbilisi, Georgia (home). *Telephone:* (32) 99-75-18 (office); (32) 93-14-05 (Parl.) (office); (32) 99-80-80 (home).

SHENGELAIA, Georgiy Nikolayevich; Georgian film director and actor; b. 11 May 1937, Tbilisi; s. of Nicolai Shengelaia and Nato Vachnadze; brother of Eldar Shengelaia (q.v.); m. 1st Sofiko Chiaureli 1957 (divorced); m. 2nd Ketevan Ninya 1985; three s.; ed Moscow Inst. of Cinematography; freelance artist; mem. Parl., Deputy Chair. 2000; Georgian State Prize 1980. *Films include:* as dir: Alaverdoba 1960, Matsi Khvitia 1966, Pirosmani 1969, Veris Ubnis Melodiebi 1973, Kvishani Darchebian 1976, Sikvaruli Kvelas Unda 1980, Akhalgazrda Kompozitoris Mogzauroba (also writer) 1986, Khareba Da Gogia (also writer) 1987, Orpeosis Sikvdili (also writer) 1996, Kahdzhi Murat (also writer) 1996, Midioda Matarebeli (also writer) 2005; as actor: In Our Courtyard 1956, Otaraant Qvrivi 1958, Rats Ginakhavs, Vegar Nakhav 1965, Ambavi Erti Kalishvilisa 1960, Kvishani Darchebian 1976; as producer: Tsre 1992, Aslani da Elza 1992, Gilotsavt Akhal Tsels 1995. *Address:* Kekelidze Street 16, Apartment 12, 380009 Tbilisi, Georgia. *Telephone:* (32) 22-64-11. *Fax:* (32) 99-07-54; (32) 93-50-97.

SHENNAN, Joseph Hugh, PhD, FRHistS, FRSA; British historian and academic; b. 13 March 1933, Liverpool, England; s. of Hugh Cringle Shennan and Mary Catherine Jones; m. Margaret King Price 1958; three s.; ed St Edward's Coll. Liverpool, Univ. of Liverpool and Corpus Christi Coll. Cambridge; Asst Lecturer, Lecturer in History, Univ. of Liverpool 1960–65; Lecturer, Sr Lecturer, Reader in History, Lancaster Univ. 1965–74, Prof. of European Studies 1974–79, Prof. of European History 1979–98, Pro-Vice-Chancellor (Academic) 1985–93, Deputy Vice-Chancellor 1993–98, Prof. Emer. of History 1998–; Sr Research Scholar (Visiting Fellow), Corpus Christi Coll. Cambridge 1984–85; Founding Ed. European Studies Review (now European History Quarterly) 1970–79. *Publications:* The Parlement of Paris 1968 (second edn 1998), Government and Society in France 1461–1661 1969, The Origins of the Modern European State 1450–1725 1974, Philippe, Duke of Orleans: Regent of France, 1715–1723 1979, France Before the Revolution 1983, Liberty and Order in Early Modern Europe: The Subject and the State, 1650–1800 1986, Louis XIV 1986, International Relations in Europe, 1689–1789 1995, A History of Lancaster Golf Club 2001, The Bourbons: History of a Dynasty. *Leisure interests:* golf, the 18th century, supporting Liverpool Football Club. *Address:* Bull Beck House, Brookhouse, Lancaster, LA2 9JW, England (home). *Telephone:* (1524) 770517. *E-mail:* j.shennan@lancaster.ac.uk (home).

SHEPARD, Donald J., MBA; American insurance industry executive; b. 1946; ed Univ. of Chicago; began career with Life Investors Inc., Ia 1970, served in various man. and exec. positions including Exec. Vice-Pres. and COO 1985–89, Pres. and CEO AEGON USA (following acquisition of Life Investors by AEGON USA 1989) 1989–2002, Chair. Exec. Bd and CEO AEGON, The Hague 2002–08; mem. Bd of Dirs Mercantile Bankshares Corpn, European Financial Services Roundtable, US Chamber of Commerce, CSX Corpn, Financial Services Roundtable; Trustee, Johns Hopkins Medicine, Johns Hopkins Univ.; mem. Bd of Visitors, Univ. of Maryland Univ. Coll. *Address:* c/o Board of Visitors, University of Maryland University College, Office of the President, 3501 University Boulevard East, Adelphi, MD 20783, USA.

SHEPARD, Sam; American playwright, actor, director and screenwriter; b. (Samuel Shepard Rogers) 5 Nov. 1943, Fort Sheridan, Ill.; s. of Samuel Shepard Rogers and Jane Schook Rogers; m. O-Lan Johnson Dark 1969 (divorced); one s.; one s. one d. with Jessica Lange (q.v.); ed Duarte High School, Mount San Antonio Jr Coll. *Television appearances include:* Lily Dale 1996, Purgatory 1999, Hamlet 2000. *Plays include:* Cowboys and Rock Garden (double bill), Chicago, Icarus's Mother and Red Cross (triple bill; Obie Award) 1966, Melodrama Play 1966, The 4-H Club, La Turista (Obie Award) 1967, Forensic and the Navigators (Obie Award) 1968, The Unseen Hand (rock opera) 1969, Cowboy Mouth (with Patti Smith) 1971, The Mad Dog Blues 1971, The Tooth of Crime (Obie Award) 1973, Geography of a

Horse Dreamer 1974, Black Dog Beast Bait, Operation Sidewinder, Shaved Splits, Rock Garden (included in Oh! Calcutta!), Curse of the Starving Class (Obie Award) 1978, Buried Child (Pulitzer Prize) 1979, True West 1980, Fool for Love 1982, A Lie of the Mind 1985 (New York Drama Critics Circle Award for Best Play 1986), States of Shock 1991, Simpatico 1994, Eyes for Consuela 1998, The Late Henry Moss 2000, The God of Hell 2004, Kicking a Dead Horse 2007, Ages of the Moon 2010. *Film appearances include:* Days of Heaven 1978, Resurrection 1980, Francis 1982, The Right Stuff 1983, Paris, Texas 1984, Country, Crimes of the Heart, Baby Boom, Defenceless 1989, Voyager 1991, Thunderheart 1992, The Pelican Brief 1994, Safe Passage 1995, The Good Old Boys 1995, Curtain Call 1997, The Only Thrill 1997, Snow Falling on Cedars 1999, One Kill 2000, All the Pretty Horses 2001, Shot in the Heart 2001, Swordfish 2001, Black Hawk Down 2001, The Pledge 2001, The Notebook 2004, Don't Come Knockin' 2005, Stealth 2005, Walker Payne 2006, Bandidas 2006, The Return 2006, Charlotte's Web (narrator) 2006, The Assassination of Jesse James by the Coward Robert Ford 2007, The Accidental Husband 2008, Brothers 2009, Inhale 2010, Blackthorn 2011, Darling Companion 2012, Safe House 2012, Killing Them Softly 2012, Mud 2012. *Screenplays:* Zabriskie Point 1970, Paris, Texas (Palme d'Or, Cannes Film Festival 1984), Fool for Love 1985, Far North (also Dir) 1989, Silent Tongue (also Dir) 1994, Don't Come Knockin' 2005. *Publications:* Hawk Moon 1972, Motel Chronicles 1982, A Murder of Crows (novel) 1996, Cruising Paradise (autobiog.) 1996, Great Dream of Heaven (short stories) 2002, The Rolling Thunder Logbook 2005, Day Out of Days (short stories) 2010. *Address:* c/o ICM, 10250 Constellation Boulevard, Los Angeles, CA 90067, USA (office).

SHEPARD, Stephen Benjamin, BS, MS; American journalist, editor and professor of journalism; *Founding Dean, Graduate School of Journalism, City University of New York;* b. 20 July 1939, New York; s. of William Shepard and Ruth Shepard (née Tanner); m. Lynn Povich 1979; one s. one d.; ed City Coll., Columbia Univ.; reporter and writer, Business Week 1966–75, Exec. Ed. 1982–84, Ed.-in-Chief 1984–2005; Adjunct Prof., Grad. School of Journalism, Columbia Univ. 1971–76, also co-founder and Dir Walter Bagehot Fellowship Program in Econs and Business Journalism, mem. Bd of Visitors, Grad. School of Journalism 1998–2004; Sr Ed. Newsweek 1976–81; Ed. Saturday Review 1981–82; Founding Dean, Grad. School of Journalism, CUNY 2005–; mem. American Soc. of Magazine Eds (Vice-Pres. 1990–92, Pres. 1992–94), Council on Foreign Relations, Overseas Press Club, Century Asscn; Gov. Soc. of American Business Eds and Writers; Gerald Coeb Foudation Lifetime Achievement Award 1999, Henry Johnson Fisher Award for Magazine Publisher of America 2000, Pres.'s Award, Overseas Press Club 2003, Soc. of American Business Eds and Writers Distinguished Achievement Award 2005. *Publication:* Deadlines and Disruption: The Turbulent Path From Print to Digital (memoir) 2012. *Address:* Graduate School of Journalism, City University of New York, 219 West 40th Street, New York, NY 10018 (office); 322 Central Park West, New York, NY 10025, USA (home). *Telephone:* (646) 758-7800 (office). *Website:* www.journalism.cuny.edu/faculty/stephen-shepard (office).

SHEPHARD OF NORTHWOLD, Baroness (Life Peer), cr. 2005, of Northwold in the County of Norfolk; **Gillian Patricia Shephard,** PC, JP, MA, DL; British politician; b. 22 Jan. 1940; d. of Reginald Watts and Bertha Watts; m. Thomas Shephard 1975; two step-s.; ed North Walsham High School for Girls, St Hilda's Coll., Oxford; Educ. Officer and Schools Inspector 1963–75; Lecturer, Univ. of Cambridge Extra-Mural Bd 1965–87; Councillor Norfolk Co. Council 1977–89 (Chair. Social Services Cttee 1978–83, Educ. Cttee 1983–85); Chair. W Norfolk and Wisbech Health Authority 1981–85, Norwich Health Authority 1985–87; MP for SW Norfolk 1987–97, for Norfolk SW 1997–2005; Co-Chair. Women's Nat. Comm. 1990–91; Parl. Pvt. Sec. to Econ. Sec. to the Treasury 1988–89; Parl. Under-Sec. of State Dept of Social Security 1989–90; Minister of State (Treasury) 1990–92; Sec. of State for Employment 1992–93, for Agric., Fisheries and Food 1993–94, for Educ. 1994–95, for Educ. and Employment 1995–97; Shadow Leader of House of Commons and Shadow Chancellor of Duchy of Lancaster 1997–99; Opposition Spokesman on Environment, Transport and the Regions 1998–99; Deputy Chair. Conservative Party 1991–92, 2002–03; Vice-Pres. Hansard Soc. 1997–2003; mem. Council Univ. of Oxford 2000–06, Bd mem. Dept for Continuing Educ., Univ. of Oxford; Hon. Fellow, St Hilda's Coll. 1991, Queen Mary, Univ. of London; Chevalier, Légion d'honneur 2009. *Publications:* The Future of Local Government 1991, Shephard's Watch 2000, Knapton Remembered (ed.) 2007. *Leisure interests:* music, gardening, France. *Address:* House of Lords, Westminster, London, SW1A 0PW, England (office). *Telephone:* (20) 7219-4457 (office). *E-mail:* westm@parliament.uk (office).

SHEPHERD, Cybill; American actress; b. 18 Feb. 1950, Memphis, Tenn.; d. of William Jennings Shepherd and Patty Shobe Micci; m. 1st David Ford 1978 (divorced); one d.; m. 2nd Bruce Oppenheim 1987 (divorced 1990); one s. one d.; fmr magazine cover girl; eight years of commercials for L'Oréal Préférence. *Films include:* The Last Picture Show 1971, The Heartbreak Kid 1973, Daisy Miller 1974, At Long Last Love 1975, Taxi Driver 1976, Special Delivery 1976, Silver Bears 1977, The Lady Vanishes 1978, Earthright 1980, The Return 1986, Chances Are 1988, Texasville 1990, Alice 1990, Once Upon A Crime 1992, Married to It 1993, The Last Word 1995, Open Window 2005, Another Harvest Moon 2009, Expecting Mary 2010, Family Jewels 2010, Listen to Your Heart 2010, Another Harvest Moon 2010, Annie and the Gypsy 2012. *Plays include:* A Shot in the Dark 1977, Vanities 1981, The Muse 1999, Marine Life 2000. *Television includes:* The Yellow Rose 1983–84, Moonlighting (Emmy Award 1985) 1985–89, Cybill 1994–98, Due East 2002, Martha Inc.: The Story of Martha Stewart (film) 2003, The Detective 2004, Martha Behind Bars (film) 2005, Psych (series) 2008–13, Eastwick (series) 2009–10, The Client List (film) 2010, My Freakin' Family (film) 2011, The Client List (series) 2012–13. *Albums include:* Cybill Getz Better 1978, Vanilla 1979, Moonlighting 1984, Somewhere Down the Road 1990, Songs from the Cybill Show 2003, At Home with Cybill 2004. *Publication:* Cybill Disobedience 2000. *Website:* www.cybill.com.

SHEPPARD OF DIDGEMERE, Baron (Life Peer), cr. 1994, of Roydon in the County of Essex; **Allen John George Sheppard,** KB, KCVO, BSc; British company director; *Chairman, Namibian Resources;* b. 25 Dec. 1932, London; s. of John Baggott Sheppard and Lily Sheppard (née Palmer); m. 1st Peggy Damaris (née Jones) 1959 (divorced 1980); m. 2nd Mary Stewart 1980; ed Ilford Co. School, London School of Econs; with Ford 1958–68, Chrysler 1968–71, British Leyland

1971–75; with Grand Metropolitan 1975–96, CEO 1986–93, Chair. 1987–96; Pres. London First 1992–, Group Trust PLC 1994–2001, McBride PLC 1995, GB Railways PLC 1996–2004, Unipart 1996–, OneClickHR, Unipart Group of Cos; Vice-Pres. Brewers' Soc. 1987–; Chair. Bd of Trustees, Prince's Youth Business Trust 1990–94, Advisory Bd, British American Chamber of Commerce 1991–94, Business in the Community 1994–97, Namibian Resources 2004–; Gov. LSE 1989–; Dir High Point Rendel 1997–2003, One Click HP PLC, Wyne PLC 2000–, Transware PLC 2001–03; Chancellor Middlesex Univ. 2000–; Hon. Fellow and Gov. LSE;; Hon. LLD (South Bank Univ.) 1994; Dr hc (Westminster) 1998, (Middx) 1999, (LSE) 2001; Gold Medal, British Inst. of Man. 1993. *Publications:* Your Business Matters 1958, Maximum Leadership 1995, various articles in professional journals. *Leisure interests:* reading, gardens, red setter dogs. *Address:* House of Lords, Westminster, London, SW1A 0PW (office); Namibian Resources plc, 302 High Street, Croydon, Surrey, CR0 1NG, England. *Telephone:* (20) 7219-5353 (House of Lords) (office). *E-mail:* namibianplc@btconnect.com. *Website:* www .namibianresources.com.

SHER, Sir Antony, Kt, KBE; British actor, artist and author; b. 14 June 1949, Cape Town, South Africa; civil partnership with Gregory Doran 2005; ed Webber Douglas Acad. of Dramatic Art; numerous appearances at Nat. Theatre, RSC (RSC Assoc. Artist 1982–) and in West End; directorial debut with Fraser Grace's play Breakfast with Mugabe at The Other Place, Stratford-upon-Avon; Hon. DLitt (Liverpool) 1998 (Exeter) 2003, (Warwick) 2007, (Cape Town) 2010; Best Actor Awards from The Evening Standard Awards, for performance as Richard III (RSC) 1985, Olivier Award for Best Actor, Soc. of West End Theatres, for performances as Richard III, as Arnold in Torch Song Trilogy 1985, for Stanley 1997, Best Actor Award, Martini TMA Awards, for performance as Titus Andronicus 1996, Peter Sellers Evening Standard Film Award for performance as Disraeli in Mrs. Brown 1998. *Plays include:* John, Paul, Ringo and Bert (Lyric Theatre), Teeth 'n' Smiles, Cloud Nine, A Prayer for My Daughter (Royal Court Theatre), Goosepimples (Hampstead and Garrick Theatres), King Lear, Tartuffe, Richard III, Merchant of Venice, The Revenger's Tragedy, Hello and Goodbye, Singer, Tamburlaine the Great, Travesties, Cyrano de Bergerac, The Winter's Tale, Macbeth, The Roman Actor, The Malcontent, Othello, The Tempest (RSC), Torch Song Trilogy (Albery Theatre), True West, Arturo Ui, Uncle Vanya, Titus Andronicus, Travelling Light, The Captain of Köpenick (Nat. Theatre), Stanley (Nat. Theatre, Circle in the Square Theater, New York), Mahler's Conversion (Aldwych Theatre), ID (Almeida Theatre) 2003, Primo (Nat. Theatre, London) 2005, (Music Box Theater, New York), (New York Drama Desk and Outer Critics' Circle Awards for Best Solo Performance 2005–06, S. Africa Fleur du Cap Award for Best Solo Performance 2005) 2005, Kean (Apollo Theatre) 2007, The Tempest (on tour) 2008, An Enemy of the People (Sheffield Crucible) 2010, Broken Glass (Kilburn Tricycle) 2010. *Films include:* Mark Gertler: Fragments of a Biography 1981, Shadey 1985, The Young Poisoner's Handbook 1995, Alive and Kicking (aka Indian Summer) 1996, Mrs. Brown 1997, Shakespeare in Love 1998, Churchill: The Hollywood Years 2004, Three and Out 2008, The Wolfman 2010. *Television includes:* ITV Playhouse – Cold Harbour, Pickersgill People – The Sheik of Pickersgill 1978, Collision Course 1979, The History Man 1981, Tartuffe 1983, Changing Step 1990, The Land of Dreams 1990, The Comic Strip Presents... – The Crying Game 1992, Genghis Cohn 1993, Moonstone 1996, Hornblower: The Frogs and the Lobsters 1999, Macbeth 2001, The Jury (mini-series) 2002, Home 2003, Murphy's Law – Jack's Back 2004, Primo 2007, God on Trial 2008, The Shadow Line 2011. *Publications:* Year of the King (theatre journal) 1986, Middlepost (novel) 1988, Characters (paintings and drawings) 1989, Changing Step (screenplay) 1989, The Indoor Boy (novel) 1991, Cheap Lives (novel) 1995, Woza Shakespeare! (theatre journal, co-written with Gregory Doran) 1996, The Feast (novel) 1998, Beside Myself (auto-biog.) 2001, I.D. (play) 2003, Primo (play) 2005, Primo Time (theatre journal) 2005, The Giant (play) 2007. *Address:* c/o Mic Cheetham Literary Agency, 50 Albemarle Street, London, W1S 4BD, England (office). *Telephone:* (20) 7495-2002 (office). *E-mail:* simon@miccheetham.com (office). *Website:* www.miccheetham.com (office).

SHERCHAN, Amik; Nepalese politician; Chair. People's Front Nepal (Jana-morcha Nepal) –2008 (deposed); Deputy Prime Minister and Minister of Health and Population 2006–07; joined Unified Communist Party of Nepal (Maoist) 2009, mem. Standing Cttee. *Address:* c/o Ministry of Health and Population, Singh Durbar Plaza, Ramshah Path, Kathmandu, Nepal.

SHERIMKULOV, Megetkan; Kyrgyzstani politician and diplomatist; b. 17 Nov. 1939, Tchapaevo (Kyrgyzia); m.; three d.; ed Kyrgyz Univ., Moscow Univ.; mem. CPSU 1962–91; Lecturer, Kyrgyz Univ., Prof. 1995–; Prof., Centre of Strategic Studies and Political Sciences, Kyrgyz Nat. Univ. 1998–; Instructor, Div. of Science, Cen. Cttee CP of Kyrgyzia 1971–73; Sec., Party Cttee, Kyrgyz Univ. 1973–76; Sec., Issyk-Kul Regional CP Cttee 1976–80; Head, Div. of Propaganda, Cen. Cttee CP, Kyrgyz SSR 1986–90; Chair. Supreme Soviet (now Uluk Kenesh) of Repub. of Kyrgyzstan 1990–94; cand. for presidency of Kyrgyzstan 1995; Amb. to Turkey 1996–2002. *Address:* c/o Ministry of Foreign Affairs, 720050 Bishkek, Razzakova, 59, Kyrgyzstan (office).

SHERMAN, Bernard (Barry), BSc, MS, PhD; Canadian pharmaceuticals industry executive; *Chairman and CEO, Apotex Incorporated;* b. 1942; m. Honey Sherman; four c.; ed Univ. of Toronto, Massachusetts Inst. of Tech., USA; major shareholder of Barr Laboratories, New York; f. Apotex Inc. 1974, currently Chair. and CEO; Hon. PhD (Technion Univ., Israel) 2004. *Address:* Apotex Inc., 150 Signet Drive, Toronto, Ont. M9L 1T9, Canada (office). *Telephone:* (800) 268-4623 (office). *Fax:* (800) 609-9444 (office). *Website:* www.apotex.com (office).

SHERMAN, Cindy, BA; American artist and photographer; b. 19 Jan. 1954, Glen Ridge, NJ; m. Michel Auder 1984 (divorced 1999); ed State Univ. Coll., Buffalo; perm. collections at Museum of Contemporary Art, Los Angeles, Museum of Modern Art, New York, Philadelphia Museum of Art, Philadelphia, San Francisco Museum of Modern Art, San Francisco, Solomon R. Guggenheim Museum, New York, Whitney Museum of American Art, New York, Albright-Knox Art Gallery, Buffalo, Corcoran Gallery of Art, Washington, DC, Metropolitan Museum of Art, New York, Museum Ludwig, Cologne, Germany, Tate Gallery, London, UK, Victoria and Albert Museum, London, UK, Art Gallery of Ontario, Toronto, Canada, Centre Georges Pompidou, Paris, France, Centro de Arte Reina Sofia, Madrid, Spain, Louisiana Museum, Humlebaek, Denmark, Musée d'art Con-

temporain, Montréal, Canada, Museum Boymans-van Beuningen, Rotterdam, The Netherlands; Nat. Arts Award 2001, American Acad. of Arts and Sciences Award 2003, Lifetime Achievement Award for Visual Arts, Guild Hall Acad. of the Arts 2005, Jewish Museum's Man Ray Award 2009. *Film:* Office Killer. *Address:* c/o Metro Pictures, 519 West 24th Street, New York, NY 10011, USA. *Telephone:* (212) 206-7100. *Fax:* (212) 337-0070. *E-mail:* gallery@metropictures.com. *Website:* www .metropicturesgallery.com/artists/cindy-sherman/.

SHERMAN, Martin; American playwright; b. 1938, New Jersey; ed Boston Univ. *Plays include:* A Solitary Thing 1963, Fat Tuesday 1966, Next Year in Jerusalem 1968, Night Before Paris 1969, Things Went Badly In Westphalia 1971, Passing By 1974, Soaps 1975, Cracks 1975, Rio Grande 1976, Blackout 1978, Bent 1978, Messiah 1982, When She Danced 1985, Madhouse In Goa 1989, Some Sunny Day 1996, Rose 1999, Chain Play 2001, Passage To India 2002, Absolutely! (Perhaps) 2003, Aristo 2008, Onassis 2010. *Films include:* The Clothes in the Wardrobe 1992, Indian Summer 1996, Mrs Henderson Presents 2005. *Address:* c/o Casarotto Ramsay and Associates Ltd, Waverley House, 7–12 Noel Street, London, W1F 8GQ, England (office). *Telephone:* (20) 7287-4450 (office). *Website:* www.casarotto .co.uk (office).

SHERMAN, Wendy, BA, MA; American diplomatist and government official; *Under-Secretary for Political Affairs, Department of State;* ed Smith Coll., Boston Univ., Univ. of Maryland; Asst Sec. for Legis. Affairs, US State Dept 1993–96, Counselor and Special Advisor to Pres. Clinton and Policy Coordinator on N Korea 1997–2001; Vice-Chair. Albright Stonebridge Group (global strategy firm) 2001–11, mem. Investment Cttee of Albright Capital Management (affiliated investment advisory firm); served on US Dept of Defense's Defense Policy Bd; apptd by Congressional Leadership to serve on Comm. on the Prevention of Weapons of Mass Destruction, Proliferation and Terrorism 2008; Under-Sec. of State for Political Affairs 2011–; fmr Chair. Oxfam America. *Address:* Department of State, 2201 C Street, NW, Washington, DC 20520, USA (office). *Telephone:* (202) 647-4000 (office). *Fax:* (202) 647-6738 (office). *Website:* www.state.gov/p (office).

SHERPAO, Aftab Ahmad Khan; Pakistani politician; b. 20 Aug. 1944; f. Pakistan People's Party—PPP (Sherpao Group), breakaway faction, faction rejoined PPP 2002; fmr Chief Minister of North-West Frontier Prov.; fmr Minister of Water and Power, of Inter-Prov. Co-ordination of and Kashmir Affairs, Northern Areas and State and Frontier Regions; Minister of the Interior 2004–07. *Address:* Pakistan People's Party, House 8, St 19, F-8/2, Islamabad, Pakistan (office). *Telephone:* (51) 2255264 (office). *Fax:* (51) 2282741 (office). *E-mail:* ppp@comsats .net.pk (office). *Website:* www.ppp.org.pk (office).

SHERRINGTON, David, MA, PhD, FRS, FInstP; British physicist and academic; *Wykeham Professor Emeritus of Physics, University of Oxford;* b. 29 Oct. 1941, Blackpool, Lancs., England; s. of James A. Sherrington and Elfreda Cameron; m. Margaret Gee-Clough 1966; one s. one d.; ed St Mary's Coll. Middlesbrough and Univ. of Manchester; Asst Lecturer in Theoretical Physics, Univ. of Manchester 1964–67, Lecturer (on leave) 1967–69; Asst Research Physicist, Univ. of Calif., San Diego 1967–69; Lecturer in Solid State Physics, Imperial Coll. London 1969–74, Reader 1974–83, Prof. of Physics 1983–89; Cadre Supérieur, Inst. Laue Langevin, Grenoble 1977–79; Wykeham Prof. of Physics, Univ. of Oxford 1989–2008, Prof. Emer. 2008–; Ulam Scholar, Los Alamos Nat. Lab., USA 1995–96; Fellow, New Coll. Oxford 1989–; Visiting Prof., Hong Kong Univ. of Science and Tech. 1994, Ecole Normale Supérieure, Paris 2003; External Prof., Santa Fe Inst. 2004–; Visiting Scientist, IBM 1975, Schlumberger-Doll Research 1984, Inst. for Advanced Study, Princeton 2003, Univ. of California, Santa Barbara 2003, Univ. of California, San Diego 2008, Los Alamos Nat. Lab.; Ed. Communications in Physics 1975–76, Advances in Physics 1984–, Journal of Physics A 1989–93; mem. Editorial Bd Journal of Physics C 1981–85, Oxford Monographs in Physics 1995–, Quantitative Finance 2001–; Del., Oxford University Press 2001; Fellow, American Physical Soc., European Acad. of Sciences (Pres. 2014–); Bakerian Lecture, Royal Soc. 2001, Dirac Medal and Prize, Inst. of Physics 2007, Scott Lectureship, Cambridge 2009, Blaise Pascal Medal, European Acad. of Sciences 2010. *Publications:* articles in scientific journals, co-ed. of seven books. *Leisure interests:* travel, wine, theatre, walking, skiing, science, history. *Address:* Rudolf Peierls Centre for Theoretical Physics, 1 Keble Road, Oxford, OX1 3NP, England (office). *Telephone:* (1865) 273999 (office). *Fax:* (1865) 273947 (office). *Website:* www2.physics.ox.ac.uk/contacts/people/sherr (office).

SHERSTYUK, Col-Gen. Vladislav Petrovich; Russian security official and academic; *Director, Institute of Information Security Issues, Lomonosov Moscow State University;* b. 16 Oct. 1940, Novoplastunovskaya, Krasnodar Region; m.; one s.; ed Moscow State Univ., Higher KGB School; with KGB 1966–; Head Dept of Radioelectronic Espionage Telecommunications, Fed. Agency of Govt Telecommunications and Information 1995–98, Deputy Dir-Gen. 1998, Dir-Gen. 1998–99; First Deputy Sec., Security Council 1999; Dir Fed. Agency of Govt Communications and Information (FAPSI) 2001–02; currently Dir Inst. of Information Security Issues, Lomonosov Moscow State Univ.; Order of Labour Red Banner 1975, Order for Service to Motherland 1996 and numerous other decorations USSR State Prize 1978, State Prize of Russian Fed. 1996, Red Star 1988. *Address:* Institute of Information Security Issues, Lomonosov Moscow State University, 19234 Moscow, Michurinsky pr. 1, Russia (office). *Telephone:* (495) 932-89-58 (office). *Fax:* (495) 939-20-96 (office).

SHERWIN, Susan, BA, PhD, FRSC, FCAHS; Canadian academic; *Research Professor Emerita, Department of Philosophy and Department of Gender and Women's Studies, Dalhousie University;* b. 6 June 1947, Toronto; ed York Univ., Stanford and Case Western Reserve Univs, USA; Asst Prof., Dept of Philosophy, Dalhousie Univ. 1974–80, Assoc. Prof. 1980–90, Prof. Dept of Philosophy 1982–87, Prof. 1990, Univ. Research Professor 2002–08, now Prof. Emer., Co-ordinator Women's Studies 1987–88, 1996–2000, also taught in Gender and Women's Studies Program, Faculty of Health Professions; mem. Canadian Comm. for UNESCO (Ethics Cttee 2001–03, Sectoral Comm. on Natural and Social Sciences 2001–03), Canadian Soc. for Women in Philosophy (Co-ordinator 1985–86, 1994–95), Canadian Philosophical Asscn (Exec. Cttee 1983–85), Canadian Research Inst. for Advancement of Women, Nova Scotia Women's Health Educ. Network, Canadian Soc. of Bioethics, Int. Asscn of Bioethics (Bd mem. 1995–2000), Int. Feminist Approaches to Bioethics (Jt Coordinator

2001–03); mem. Ethics and Equity Cttee, Royal Coll. of Physicians and Surgeons of Canada, Research Council, Canadian Inst. of Advanced Research 2002–05, CIHR Standing Cttee on Ethics 2000–06; CAUT Sarah Shorten Award 2000, American Soc. for Women and Philosophy Distinguished Woman Philosopher 2004, Killam Prize in Humanities 2006, Canadian Bioethics Soc. Lifetime Achievement Award 2007. *Publications:* Moral Problems in Medicine (co-ed.) 1983, No Longer Patient: Feminist Ethics and Health Care 1992, Health Care Ethics in Canada (co-ed.) 1995, The Politics of Women's Health: Exploring Agency and Autonomy (ed.), Women 1992, Medicine, Ethics, and the Law (co-ed.) 2002; Engaged Philosophy (co-ed.) 2007, Agency and Embodiment (co-ed.) 2009; contribs: numerous articles in journals including Journal of Medicine and Philosophy, Humane Medicine, Bioethics, Politeia. *Address:* Department of Philosophy, Dalhousie University, Halifax, NS B3H 4P9, Canada (office). *Telephone:* (902) 494-3393 (office). *Fax:* (902) 494-3518 (office). *E-mail:* susan.sherwin@dal.ca (office). *Website:* philosophy .dal.ca (office).

SHERWOOD, James Blair, BEcons; American shipping industry executive; b. 8 Aug. 1933; s. of William Earl Sherwood and Florence Balph Sherwood; m. Shirley Angela Masser Cross 1977; two step s.; ed Yale Univ.; Lt USNR 1955–58; Man. French Ports, later Asst Gen. Freight Traffic Man., US Lines Co. 1959–62; Gen. Man. Container Transport Int. Inc. 1963–64; Founder and Pres. Sea Containers Ltd 1965–2006 (resgnd). Chair. Orient-Express Hotels Ltd 1987–2006, GE Senco SRL 1998–2006, Silja Oy 1999–2006; with Mark Birley est. Harry's Bar Club, London 1979; restored and brought into service Venice Simplon-Orient-Express 1982; Trustee, Solomon R. Guggenheim Foundation 1989; Hon. Citizen of Venice, Italy 1990; Order of the Southern Cross (Brazil) 2004. *Publication:* James Sherwood's Discriminating Guide to London 1975. *Leisure interests:* skiing, tennis, sailing. *Address:* Hinton Manor, Hinton Waldrist, Oxon., SN7 8SA, England (home). *Telephone:* (1865) 820260 (home).

SHERZAI, Gul Agha; Afghan politician; b. (Mohammad Shafiq), Gov. of Kandahar prior to Taliban takeover, in exile in Quetta, Pakistan 1994–2001, reinstated as Gov. of Kandahar 2002–04, Gov. of Nangarhar 2004–13; Minister of Urban Affairs 2003; fmr Minister of Urban Devt and Housing; Minister of Public Works –2004; fmr ministerial adviser to Pres. Hamid Karzai; cand. in presidential election 2014. *Address:* c/o Office of the Governor, Jalalabad, Nangarhar Province, Afghanistan (office).

SHESHINSKI, Eytan, PhD; Israeli economist and academic; *Sir Isaac Wolfson Professor of Public Finance, Department of Economics, Hebrew University of Jerusalem;* b. 29 June 1937, Haifa; s. of Alice Sheshinski and Baruch Sheshinski; m. Ruth H. Sheshinski 1960; four d.; ed Hebrew Univ. Jerusalem, Mass Inst. of Tech., USA; Asst Prof., Harvard Univ. 1966–67; Lecturer, then Assoc. Prof. 1971–74, Prof. of Econs 1974–, now Sir Isaac Wolfson Prof. of Public Finance, Hebrew Univ. of Jerusalem; Visiting Prof., Harvard Univ., Stanford Univ., MIT, Columbia Univ.; Chair. Bd Koor Industries 1990–, Khevrat Ha'Ovdim 1989–92, Cttee appointed by Govt on iscal policy regarding offshore gas and oil drills; Fellow, Econometric Soc.; mem. Royal Swedish Acad. of Sciences, American Acad. of Arts and Sciences; Dr hc (Stockholm School of Econs); American Acad. of Arts and Sciences Award. *Publications:* The Optimal Linear Income Tax (Review of Economic Studies 1972), Inflation and Costs of Price Adjustment (Review of Economic Studies 1977), Optimum Pricing, Inflation and the Costs of Price Adjustments (ed.) 1993. *Leisure interests:* hiking, sailing. *Address:* Hebrew University of Jerusalem, Mount Scopus, 91905 Jerusalem, Israel (office). *Telephone:* (2) 5883144 (office); (2) 6242442 (home). *Fax:* (2) 5883357 (office); (2) 6255571 (home). *E-mail:* mseytan@mscc.huji.ac.il (office). *Website:* economics.huji .ac.il/sheshinski (office).

SHESTAKOV, Sergey Vasilyevich; Russian biologist; *Chief Scientific Officer, Moscow State University;* b. 23 Nov. 1934, Leningrad; s. of Vasily Ivanovich Shestakov and Ludmila Shestakova; m. Galina A. Grigorieva 1964; one s.; ed Moscow State Univ.; on staff, Moscow State Univ. 1957–, Chair. Dept of Genetics 1980–2009, now Chief Scientific Officer; Dir Int. Biotechnology Centre 1991–2003; Dir N. Vavilov Inst. of Genetics, USSR (now Russian) Acad. of Sciences 1988–91; Corresp. mem. USSR (now Russian) Acad. of Sciences 1987, mem. 2000; Chair. Scientific Council on Genetics 1988–2004, Scientific Council on Life Sciences, Moscow State Univ. 1998–; mem. Int. Acad. of Science; Visiting Prof., Michigan State Univ., USA 1992; Visiting Researcher, Chicago Univ., USA 1994, Univ. of Wales, UK 1998; Ed.-in-Chief Russian Journal of Genetics 2011; Hon. Distinguished Scientist of Russian Fed. 1995; Hon. Prof. (Univ. of Wales) 2000; Hon. Distinguished Worker of Higher School of Russian Fed. 2011; Fulbright-Hays Fellowship 1975 UNESCO Fellowship Award 1985, USSR State Prize 1988, Lomonosov Prize 1995, N. Vavilov Gold Medal 1997, P. Ehrlich Medal (Germany) 2006. *Publications:* papers and articles on microbial and plant molecular genetics of DNA repair and recombination, photosynthesis, nitrogen-fixation, resistance to stresses, functional genomics, photobiotechnology. *Leisure interest:* sports. *Address:* Department of Genetics, Moscow State University, 119899 Moscow, Russia (office). *Telephone:* (495) 939-09-75 (office). *Fax:* (495) 939-43-09 (office). *E-mail:* shestakovgen@mail.ru (office).

SHESTAKOVA, Tatyana Borisovna; Russian actress; b. 23 Oct. 1948, Leningrad; d. of Boris Shestakov and Aleksandra Shestakova; m. Lev Dodin 1972; ed Leningrad Theatre Inst.; Leningrad Theatre for Children 1972–75; Leningrad Comedy Theatre 1975–80; Bolshoi Drama Theatre 1980–83; Maly Drama Theatre 1983–; also played for Moscow Art's Theatre; toured abroad 1983, 1987–2001; apptd Dir Stars In the Morning Sky 2005; USSR State Prize 1986, RSFSR Merited Artist 1987, Nat. 'Triumph' Prize 1992. *Films include:* Tsarevich Prosha 1974, Solyonyy Pyos 1975, Chelovek, Kotoromu Vezlo 1978, Idi i Smotri 1985, Podsudimyy 1986. *Theatre roles include:* Liza (The House) 1980, Sonya (Uncle Vanya) 1982, She (The Meek One) 1985, Anfisa (Brothers and Sisters) 1986, Anna (Stars of the Morning Sky) 1987, Lebyadkina (The Possessed), Lubov Andreevna (The Cherry Orchard) 1994, Dame Elegant (Roberto Zucco) 1994, Katya and Ivanova (Claustrophobia) 1994, Anna Petrovna (Play Without a Name) 1997, Sonya (Chevengur) 2000, Arcadina (The Seagull) 2001. *Television:* Na vsyu ostavshuyusya zhizn... (mini-series). *Leisure interests:* travelling, books, music. *Address:* Maly Drama Theatre, 18 Rubinstein Street, St Petersburg (office). Michurinskaya St 1-140, St Petersburg, Russia (home). *Telephone:* (812) 713-20-78 (office). *E-mail:* mdt@sp.wplus.net (office).

SHETREET, Shimon, LLB, LLM, LLD; Israeli politician, legal scholar and academic; *Professor of Law, Hebrew University of Jerusalem;* b. 1 March 1946, Erfoud, Morocco; m.; four c.; ed Hebrew Univ., Chicago Univ.; Sec., Council for Public Justice; Chair. Cttee on Broadcasting Authority Law; Chair. Int. Conf. on Legal Matters; Prof. of Law, Hebrew Univ. 1973–, Chair., Asscn of Lecturers 1974–77, currently also Greenblatt Chair of Public and International Law, fmr Pres. Sacher Inst. of Legislative Research and Comparative Law; Chair. Mishan, Old Age Home Enterprise 1986–88, Int. Inst. for Devt, Cooperation and Labour Studies, Afro-Asian Inst. 1988–92; mem. Bd of Dirs Bank Leumi 1987–89; Visiting Prof. of Law, Univ. of Manitoba 1977–78, Wuerzburg Univ., Germany 1980, Univ. of San Diego School of Law 1983, New York Univ. Law School 1983–84, School of Law, Case Western Reserve Univ. 1999; Minister of Economy and Planning 1992–95, Science and Tech. 1992–93, in charge of Second Television and Radio Authority 1993–95, of Religious Affairs 1995–96; Sr Deputy Mayor of Jerusalem 1998–2003; Visiting Sr Fellow, Inst. of Advanced Legal Studies, Univ. of London 1999; mem. Knesset 1988–96; served on numerous cttees 1988–92, including Landau Comm. on Israeli Court System, Council for Admin. Courts, plenum of Israel Broadcasting Authority 1984–87; Dir Leumi Bank; mem. Labour Party; Ethics Prize 1994, Int. Jurists Award 2010. *Publications include:* The Good Land Between Power and Religion, Judges on Trial 1976, Justice in Israel 1994, Women in Law 1998; and articles on legal matters. *leisure interests* Bible study. *Address:* Hebrew University of Jerusalem, Mount Scopus, Jerusalem 91905 (office); 6 Hahavtacha Street, Jerusalem, Israel (home). *Telephone:* 2-5882534 (office); 2-5866444 (home). *Fax:* 2-5883042 (office); 2-5864503 (home). *E-mail:* mshetree@ mscc.huji.ac.il (office); shetreet@gmail.com (home). *Website:* mishpatim.mscc.huji .ac.il (office); law.mscc.huji.ac.il/law1/newsite/english.html (office).

SHETTAR, Jagadish, BCom, LLB; Indian lawyer and politician; b. 17 Dec. 1955, Badami Taluk, Bagalkot District; s. of Shivappa Shivamurthappa Shettar; m. Shilpa Shettar 1984; two s.; ed Jagadguru Gangadhar Coll. of Commerce, Hubli, Karnatak Univ., Dharwad; practised for 20 years as lawyer, Hubli Bar; mem. Karnataka Legis. Ass. from Hubli rural segment 1994–, Leader of the Opposition 1999, Speaker 2008–09; Revenue Minister, Karnataka State Govt 2006, Minister of Rural Devt and Panchayat Raj 2009; Chief Minister of Karnataka 2012–13; mem. Bharatiya Janata Party (BJP), Pres. Hubli Rural Constituency BJP 1990–94, Head of Dharwad BJP District Unit 1994–96, BJP State Sec. 1996–99, BJP State Pres. 2005. *Address:* c/o Office of the Chief Minister, Vidhana Soudha, 3rd Floor (Room 323), Bangalore 560 001, India. *Website:* jagadishshettar.com.

SHETTY, Devi Prasad, MB BS, MS, FRCS; Indian cardiologist, philanthropist and entrepreneur; *Chairman, Narayana Hrudayalaya Hospitals;* b. 8 May 1953, Mangalore; m.; four c.; ed Kasturba Medical Coll., Manipal, Univ. of Mysore; sr house officer in cardiothoracic surgery, Killing Beck Hosp., Leeds, UK 1983–84, Brompton Hosp., London, July–Sept. 1984; Registrar in Cardiothoracic Surgery, West Midlands Cardiothoracic Rotation programme between Walsgrave Hosp., Coventry and East Birmingham Hosp. 1984–86; Registrar in Cardiothoracic Surgery, Guy's Hosp., London 1986–89; Chief Cardiac Surgeon and Clinical Dir, B.M. Birla Heart Research Centre, Kolkata 1989–97; Chief Cardiac Surgeon and Vice-Chair. Manipal Heart Foundation, Bangalore 1997–2001; Founder, Chair. and Sr Consultant Cardiac Surgeon, Narayana Hrudayalaya Group of Hosps 2001–; Rajyotsava Award 2002, Sir M. Visvesvaraya Memorial Award 2003, Ernst & Young Entrepreneur of the Year 2003, Padmashree 2003, Dr B.C. Roy Award 2004, Citizen Extraordinaire, Rotary International 2004, Social Entrepreneurship Award, World Econ. Forum 2005, Commendation for driving affordable and quality healthcare for all, Healthcare Awards Program presented by ICICI Lombard & CNBC TV18 2010, Indian of the Year 2010 from NDTV 2011, Business Process Award Winner, The Economist's Innovation Awards 2011, Padma Bhusan 2012, Economic Times Entrepreneur of the Year Award 2012, FICCI Healthcare Excellence Lifetime Achievement Award 2012, Indian of the Year (Public Service category), CNN-IBN 2012. *Address:* Narayana Hrudayalaya, No. 258/A, Bommasandra Industrial Area, Anekal Taluk, Bangalore 560 099, India (office). *Telephone:* (80) 27835000 (office); (80) 27835018 (office). *Fax:* (80) 27832648 (office). *E-mail:* devishetty@hrudayalaya.com (office). *Website:* www.nhhospitals .in (office).

SHETTY, Salil, MSc, MBA; Indian international organization official; *Secretary-General, Amnesty International;* b. 3 Feb. 1961, Mumbai; s. of V. T. Rajashekhar; m. Bina Rani Shetty; one s. one d.; ed Bangalore Univ., Indian Inst. of Man., Ahmedabad, LSE, UK; joined ActionAid 1985, postings to Africa and India, CEO 1998–2003; Dir UN Millennium Campaign 2003–10; Sec.-Gen. Amnesty International 2010–; mem. Bd The Overseas Devt Inst., London, Agence France-Presse Foundation, Paris, Inst. of Devt Studies, Sussex; mem. Advisory Council, American India Foundation, New York, Strategic Planning Group of Amnesty International, Global Leadership Council of the Tech. Museum of Innovation, San Jose, Calif. *Address:* Amnesty International, 1 Easton Street, London, WC1X 0DW, England (office). *Telephone:* (20) 7413-5500 (office). *Fax:* (20) 7956-1157 (office). *Website:* www.amnesty.org (office).

SHEVARDNADZE, Eduard; Georgian politician and fmr head of state; b. 25 Jan. 1928, Mamati, Larchkhuti, Transcaucasian SFSR (now in Georgia); s. of Ambrosi Shevardnadze and Sophio Pateishvili; m. Nanuli Tsagareishvili 1950 (died 2004); one s. one d.; ed Party School of the Cen. Cttee, CP of Georgia and Kutaisi Pedagogical Inst.; mem. CPSU 1948–91; Komsomol and party work 1946–56; Second Sec. 1956–57, First Sec., Komsomol in Georgia 1957–61; First Sec., Mtskheti raion 1961–63, Pervomaisky raion, Tbilisi, CP of Georgia 1963–64; First Deputy Minister 1964–65, Minister of Public Order (renamed Ministry of Internal Affairs 1968) 1965–72; First Sec., Tbilisi City Cttee of Cen. Cttee, CP of Georgia 1972; mem. Cen. Cttee, CP of Georgia 1958–64, 1966–91, mem. Politburo 1972–91, First Sec. 1972–85; mem. Cen. Cttee of CPSU 1976–91, Cand. mem. Politburo 1978–85, mem. 1985–90; Deputy to USSR Supreme Soviet 1978; mem. Political Consultative Council 1991; Minister of Foreign Affairs 1985–90, Nov.–Dec. 1991; Head of Soviet Foreign Policy Asscn 1991–92; mem. Presidential Council 1990–91; Founder mem. Bd Democratic Reform Movt 1991; Chair. Georgian State Council March–Oct. 1992; Chair. Parl. of Georgia and Head of State 1992–95, Pres. of Georgia 1995–2003 (resgnd). Hon. GCMG 2000; various other decorations; Dr hc from numerous univs. *Publications:* My Choice 1991, The Future Belongs to

Freedom 1991, The Great Silk Road 1999, Thoughts About The Past and Future 2006. *Address:* c/o Office of the President, 0134 Tbilisi, P. Ingorovka 7, Georgia.

SHEVCHENKO, Andrei Mikolayovich; Ukrainian professional footballer; b. 29 Sept. 1976, Dvrkivshchyna, Yahotynskyi Raion, Kiev Oblast, USSR; m. Kristen Pazik; two s.; striker; family forced to abandon home and relocate to coast to escape Chernobyl disaster 1986; competitive boxer in LLWI Ukrainian jr league for a time; youth player, Dynamo Kiev 1986–94; sr player for Dynamo Kiev 1994–99, 2009– (128 league appearances, 64 goals, won Ukrainian Premier League 1994/95, 1995/96, 1996/97, 1997/98, 1998/99, Ukrainian Cup 1996, 1998, 1999, CIS Cup 1996, 1997, 1998), AC Milan, Italy 1999–2006, 2008–09 (208 appearances, 127 goals, won Serie A 2003/04, Coppa Italia 2002/03, Supercoppa Italiana 2004, UEFA Champions League 2003, UEFA Super Cup 2003, Dubai Challenge Cup 2009), Chelsea 2006–09 (won League Cup 2007, FA Cup 2007, World Football Challenge 2009, FA Community Shield 2009); played for Ukraine U-18 1994–95, Ukraine U-21 1994–95, Ukraine 1995– (92 caps, 43 goals); Ukrainian Footballer of the Year 1997, 1999–2001, 2004–05, CIS Cup Top Scorer 1997, Ukrainian Premier League Top Scorer 1998–99, UEFA Champions League Top Scorer 1998–99, 2000–01, 2005–06, UEFA Champions League Best Forward 1998–99, Serie A Top Scorer 1999–2000, 2003–04, Serie A Foreign Footballer of the Year 2000, Ballon d'Or (European Footballer of the Year) 2004, named in FIFA 100 2004, FIFPro World XI 2004–05, Ukraine nat. team all-time top scorer, AC Milan second all-time scorer. *Leisure interests:* pool, tennis, cars. *Address:* c/o Gary Dixon, Wasserman Media Group LLC, 5th Floor, 33 Soho Square, London, W1D 3QU, England (office). *Telephone:* (20) 7009-6000 (office). *Fax:* (20) 3230-1053 (office). *E-mail:* gdixon@wmgllc.com (office). *Website:* www.sheva7.com.

SHEVCHENKO, Col-Gen. Yuri Leonidovich, DMed; Russian politician and physician; *President, National Medical-Surgical Centre;* b. 7 April 1947, Yakutsk; m.; two c.; ed Leningrad Acad. of Mil. Medicine; teacher, then Prof., then Head of Chair., Leningrad Mil. Acad. of Medicine 1980–92, Head of Acad. 1992–99; Chief Cardiosurgeon St Petersburg and Leningrad Region, Head, Regional Centre of Cardiac Surgery 1992–99; Minister of Public Health 1999–2004; Rep. of Russian Fed. to WHO Exec. Cttee –2004; Pres. Nat. Medical-Surgical Centre 2004–; Vice-Pres. Russian Acad. of Natural Sciences; Vice-Pres. Peter's Acad. of Sciences and Arts; mem. Bd F. Lang Scientific Soc. of Cardiologists; Corresp. mem. Russian Acad. of Medical Sciences. *Publications:* over 300 articles. *Address:* c/o Ministry of Health and Social Development, 127994 Moscow, Rakhmanovskii per. 3, Russia.

SHEVCHUK, Yevgenii Vasilyevich; Moldovan (ethnic Ukrainian) lawyer and politician; *President of the 'Transnistrian Moldovan Republic';* b. 19 June 1968, Ribniţa, Moldavian SSR, USSR; Deputy to Supreme Soviet of Transnistria 2000–11; Speaker of Transnistria Supreme Soviet 2005–09 (resgnd); Leader of opposition party Renewal –2010, spearheaded a reform drive by his party to introduce changes to Transnistria's electoral code prior to 2005; has worked both in government and in pvt. business; banned by European Parl. from entering EU countries; Pres. of the 'Transnistrian Moldovan Republic' 2011–. *Address:* Office of the President of the 'Transnistrian Moldovan Republic', 3300 Tiraspol, ul. 25 Oktyabrya 45, Moldova (office). *Telephone:* (533) 62720 (office); (533) 73218. *Fax:* (533) 80502 (office). *E-mail:* psp.pmr@mail.ru (office). *Website:* www.pmr-gov.org (office).

SHEYNIS, Viktor Leonidovich, DrSc; Russian historian, politician and economist; *Chief Research Fellow, Institute of World Economy and International Relations;* b. 16 Feb. 1931, Kiev; s. of Leonid M. Sheynis and Liah O. Kimelfeld; m. Alla K. Nazimova 1953; ed Leningrad Univ.; history teacher in secondary school 1953–56; manual worker, Kirov factory, Leningrad 1958–64; teacher, Leningrad Univ. 1966–75; on staff as researcher at Inst. of World Economy and Int. Relations (IMEMO) 1975–92, Chief Research Fellow 2000–; co-author of Russian Constitution and electoral laws 1993–99; People's Deputy 1990–93, mem. State Duma (Parl.) 1993–99; mem. Supreme Soviet of Russia 1991–93; Co-Founder Consent in Name of Progress faction 1992–93; mem. Council of Reps of 'Democratic Russia' Movt 1990–93, Yabloko Movt 1993–95, Yabloko Party 1995–, Political Bureau and Fed. Council; mem. Cttee on Legislation and Reform of the Judicial System; Imre Nagy Medal (Hungary) 1993. *Publications include:* Developing Nations at the Turn of the Millennium 1987, Capitalism, Socialism and Economic Mechanism of Present-day Production 1989, Die Präsidentenwahlen in Russland: Ergebnisse und Perspektiven, Osteuropa 1996, O caminho histórico da Revolução de Outubro visto sob a prisma de 1997 1997, Il tormentato cammino della Constituzione russa 1998, Wie Russland gewaklt hat: Osteuropa 2000, The Constitution: In Between Dictatorship and Democracy 2004, The Rise and Fall of Parliament: Watershed Years in Russian Politics 1985–93 (two vols) 2005. *Leisure interests:* tourism, cinematography, reading. *Address:* Institute of World Economy and International Relations, Profsoyuznaya str. 23, 117859 Moscow (office); Vavilova str. 91, corp. 1, Apartment 41, 117335 Moscow, Russia (home). *Telephone:* (495) 120-52-36 (office); (495) 132-73-15 (home). *Fax:* (495) 120-65-75 (office). *E-mail:* imemoran@imemo.ru (office); nazimova@mtu-net.ru (home). *Website:* www.imemo.ru (office).

SHI, Dahua; Chinese railway industry executive; ed Southwest Jiaotong Univ., Cen. Communist Party School; joined China Railway Group Ltd 1997, Deputy Sec. to CCP Cttee, China Railway Construction Corpn 1995–97, Deputy Sec. to CCP Cttee, China Railway Eng Corpn (CRECG) 1997–98, Sec. 1998–2007, Deputy Gen. Man. CRECG 2002–06, Chair. 2006–10, Chair. and Exec. Dir China Railway Group Ltd 2007–10; Alt. mem. 16th CCP Cen. Cttee 2002–07, 17th CCP Cen. Cttee 2007–; Dir of Transportation Professionals Co-operation Cttee of Consultant Council for the Promotion of Econ. and Tech. Cooperation of China-Spain Forum; Deputy Dir Steering Cttee of Nat. Construction Enterprise Career Man. Certification and Construction Enterprises Qualifications Admin and Research; recognized as a sr economist by Ministry of Personnel 2007. *Address:* c/o China Railway Group Ltd, 26 Lianhuachi Nanli, Beijing 100055, People's Republic of China.

SHI, Dazhen; Chinese electrical engineer and government official; b. 1932, Wuxi City, Jiangsu Prov.; ed Shandong Inst. of Tech. 1955; joined CCP 1978; Vice-Minister of Energy and Resources 1988–93, Minister of Electric Power Industry 1993–98; Gen. Man. State Electric Power Corpn 1997–98; mem. Standing Cttee 9th CPPCC Nat. Cttee 1998–2003, Vice-Chair. Econ. Sub-cttee 1998–2003; Alt. mem. 13th Cen. Cttee CCP 1988–92, 14th Cen. Cttee CCP 1992–97. *Address:* c/o

National Committee of Chinese People's Political Consultative Conference, 23 Taipingqiao Street, Beijing, People's Republic of China.

SHI, Guangsheng; Chinese politician; b. Sept. 1939, Changli, Hebei Prov.; ed Beijing Inst. of Foreign Trade; joined CCP 1965; clerk, Deputy Section Dir, later Deputy Gen. Man. China Metals and Minerals Import and Export Corpn 1974–86; Special Commr Ministry of Foreign Econ. Relations and Trade, Shanghai 1986–88; Dir Import and Export Dept, Ministry of Foreign Trade 1988–91, Asst Minister of Foreign Econ. Relations and Trade 1991–93; Vice-Minister of Foreign Trade and Econ. Co-operation 1993–98, Minister 1998–2003; fmr Pres. China Asscn of Enterprises with Foreign Investment; fmr Exec. Vice-Chair. World Econ. Devt Declaration Conf. *Address:* c/o China Association of Enterprises with Foreign Investment, 21 F, Ruoy Chai International Building, No. 8 Yongandongli Jianguomenwai Avenue, Beijing 100022, People's Republic of China.

SHI, Jiliang; Chinese economist and banker; b. Feb. 1945; ed Cen. Inst. of Banking and Finance; Vice-Pres. Heilongjiang br., Agricultural Bank of China 1983–88, Vice-Pres. Tianjing br. 1988–91, Pres. Tianjing br. 1991–94, Pres. Agricultural Bank of China 1994–97; Vice-Pres. People's Bank of China 1997–2003; Vice-Chair. China Banking Regulatory Comm. 2003–05; Chair. Bd of Supervisors China Merchants Bank Co. Ltd –2010; mem. 10th Nat. Cttee CPPCC. *Address:* c/o China Merchants Bank Co., Ltd, China Merchants Bank Tower, 7088 Shennan Blvd, Shenzhen 518040, People's Republic of China.

SHI, Jiuyong, MA; Chinese lawyer, professor of international law and judge (retd); b. 9 Oct. 1926, Zhejiang; m. Zhang Guoying 1956; one s.; ed St John's Univ., Shanghai and Columbia Univ., New York, USA; Asst Research Fellow, Inst. of Int. Relations, Beijing 1956–58; Sr Lecturer, Assoc. Prof. of Int. Law, Foreign Affairs Coll. Beijing 1958–64; Research Fellow in Int. Law, Inst. of Int. Law, Beijing 1964–73, Inst. of Int. Studies, Beijing 1973–80; Prof. of Int. Law, Foreign Affairs Coll. Beijing 1984–93, Foreign Econ. Law Training Centre of Ministry of Justice; Legal Adviser, Ministry of Foreign Affairs 1980–93, Chinese Centre of Legal Consultancy, Office of Chinese Sr Rep. Sino-British Jt Liaison Group (on question of Hong Kong) 1985–93; Adviser to Chinese Soc. of Int. Law –2003; mem. American Soc. of Int. Law; mem. Standing Cttee Beijing Cttee of CPPCC 1988–93, mem. 8th Nat. Cttee 1993–98; mem. Int. Law Comm. 1987–93, Chair. 1990; Judge, Int. Court of Justice, The Hague 1994–2010, Vice-Pres. 2000–03, Pres. 2003–06; mem. Advisory Bd, The Global Community Yearbook of Int. Law and Jurisprudence; Pres. Curatorium Xiamen Acad. of Int. Law 2005–; Hon. Prof. Eastern China Univ. of Political Science and Law 2001–, Hon. Pres. Chinese Soc. of Int. Law 2004–. *Publications:* numerous publs on int. law. *Leisure interest:* classical music. *Address:* c/o International Court of Justice, Peace Palace, Carnegieplein 2, 2517 KJ The Hague, Netherlands (office).

SHI, Xiushi; Chinese politician; b. July 1942, Shangqiu, Henan Prov.; ed Beijing Civil Eng Inst.; joined CCP 1978; technician and engineer, later Deputy Dir Building Materials Research Inst. 1964–80; Engineer and Deputy Chief, Building Materials Industry Div., Heavy Industry Bureau, State Econ. Comm. 1980–86; Deputy Div. Chief, later Div. Chief, Office of Tourist Industry Coordination 1986–88; Deputy Dir, later Dir Bureau of the State Council 1988–96; Deputy Sec.-Gen. State Council 1996–2000; Vice-Gov. of Guizhou 2001, Gov. 2001–06; Deputy Sec. Guizhou Prov. Cttee 2000–06; mem. 16th CCP Cen. Cttee 2002–07; Deputy Dir 10th Financial and Econ. Cttee of NPC 2006–08; Chair. 11th Financial and Econ. Cttee of NPC 2008–. *Address:* National People's Congress, No. 23, Xijiaominxiang Xicheng District, Beijing 100805, People's Republic of China (office). *E-mail:* english@npc.gov.cn (office). *Website:* www.npc.gov.cn (office).

SHI, Adm. Yunsheng; Chinese fmr naval officer; b. Jan. 1940, Fushun City, Liaoning Prov.; ed PLA Air Force Aviation School and PLA Navy Acad.; joined PLA 1956, CCP 1960; pilot, Squadron Leader, Deputy Group Commdr and Deputy Regt Commdr Naval Aviation 1962–70; Deputy Commdr Naval Fleet Aviation 1976–81; Div. Commdr Naval Aviation 1981–83; Commdr Naval Fleet Aviation 1983–90; Deputy Commdr PLA Naval Aviation Dept 1990–92; Deputy Commdr PLA Navy 1992–96, Commdr 1996–2003; rank of Adm. 2000; Del. 13th CCP Nat. Congress 1987–92; mem. 15th CCP Cen. Cttee 1997–2002, 16th CCP Cen. Cttee 2002–07. *Address:* c/o Ministry of National Defence, 20 Jingshanqian Jie, Beijing 100009, People's Republic of China.

SHI, Zhengrong, BSc, MSc, PhD; Chinese/Australian electrical engineer, research scientist and business executive; *Executive Chairman and Chief Strategy Officer, Suntech Power Holdings Company Ltd;* b. 1963, Yangzhong, Jiangsu Prov.; m.; two c.; ed Changchun Univ. of Science and Tech., Shanghai Inst. of Optics and Fine Mechanics, Chinese Acad. of Sciences, Univ. of New South Wales, Australia; Sr Research Scientist and Leader, Thin Film Solar Cells Research Group, Centre of Excellence for Photovoltaic Eng, Univ. of NSW, Australia 1992–95; Research Dir and Exec. Pacific Solar Pty, Australia 1995–2001 acquired Australian citizenship 2001; Founder, Chair. and CEO Suntech Power Holdings Co., Ltd (manufacturer of photovoltaic cells for use in solar panels), Wuxi, China 2001–13, Exec. Chair. and Chief Strategy Officer 2013–; Wuxi Prize for Excellence in Innovation and Pioneering, Nat. Prize for Excellent Achievements by Home-coming Chinese, named by TIME magazine one of its Heroes of the Environment, World Tech. Award (co-recipient) 2009. *Publications:* numerous scientific papers. *Address:* Suntech Power Holdings Company Ltd, 9 Xinhua Road, New District, Wuxi 214028, Jiangsu Province, People's Republic of China (office). *Telephone:* (86510) 85318888 (office). *Fax:* (86510) 85343321 (office). *E-mail:* ir@suntech -power.com (office). *Website:* www.suntech-power.com (office).

SHI, Zhong-ci; Chinese computer scientist and professor of mathematics; *Chairman, Academic Committee, Institute of Computational Mathematics and Scientific/Engineering Computing, Chinese Academy of Sciences;* b. 5 Dec. 1933, Ningpo Co., Zhejiang Prov.; ed Fudan Univ., Steklov Inst. of Math., Moscow; Asst Research Fellow, Inst. of Computing Tech., Chinese Acad. of Sciences 1961–64; Lecturer, Univ. of Science and Tech. 1965–77, Assoc. Prof. 1978–79, Prof. 1980–86, Chair. Dept of Math. and Dir of Computer Center 1984–88, Dir Inst. of Computational Math. and Scientific/Engineering Computing (fmrly Computer Center), Chinese Acad. of Sciences 1987–91, Sr Research Fellow 1987–94; currently Vice-Dean Coll. of Sciences, Zhejiang Univ., also Researcher Center of Mathematical Sciences; currently Chair. Academic Cttee, Lab. of Scientific and Eng Computing (LSEC), Chair. Academic Cttee, Inst. of Computational Mathematics and Scientific/Engineering Computing (ICMSEC); Vice-Pres. Chinese Math. Soc. 1988-1995; Vice-Pres. Chinese Soc. of Computational Math. 1985–89, Pres. 1994–; Chief Scientist Nat. Key Project for Fundamental Research; mem. Chinese Sciences Acad. 1992–; also served as Visiting Prof. to numerous univs; 2nd Prize Award, Chinese Acad. of Sciences 1980, 1st Prize Award, Chinese Acad. of Sciences 1986, Nat. Natural Science Award 1987. *Leisure interests:* travel, classical music. *Address:* Institute of Computational Mathematics and Scientific/Engineering Computing, Chinese Academy of Sciences, No.55, ZhongGuanCun DongLu, POB 2719, Beijing 100090, People's Republic of China (office). *Telephone:* 62587583 (office). *Fax:* 62542285 (office). *E-mail:* shi@lsec.cc.ac.cn (office). *Website:* www.cc.ac.cn (office); lsec.cc.ac.cn/~shi/homepage.html.

SHI, Zongyuan; Chinese politician; *Chairman, Guizhou Provincial People's Congress Standing Committee;* b. July 1946, Baoding, Hebei Prov.; ed Northwest Ethnic Inst.; worker, People's Govt, Hezheng Co., Gansu Prov. 1968–80, CCP Co. Cttee 1978–80; joined CCP 1978; fmrly clerk in various govt offices in Hezheng Co., Gansu Prov.; Deputy Magistrate Hezheng Co. (Dist) People's Court 1981–82, Magistrate 1981–84; Deputy Chief Magistrate Linxia Hui Autonomous Pref., Gansu Prov., Deputy Sec. and then Sec. CCP Linxia Hui Autonomous Pref. Cttee 1984–93; Dir Propaganda Dept of CCP Gansu Prov. Cttee 1993–98; Dir Propaganda Dept of CCP Jilin Prov. Cttee, also Vice-Sec. CCP 1998–2000; Dir Press and Publications Admin and Dir State Bureau of Copyrights 2000–05; Sec. Guizhou Provincial CCP Cttee 2005–10; Chair. Provincial People's Congress Standing Cttee, Guizhou Prov. 2006–; Vice-Chair. 11th Internal and Judicial Affairs Cttee NPC 2010–; Alt. mem. 14th CCP Cen. Cttee 1992–97, 15th CCP Cen. Cttee 1997–2002, mem. 16th CCP Cen. Cttee 2002–07; mem. 17th CCP Cen. Cttee 2007–. *Address:* Guizhou Provincial People's Congress, Guizhou, People's Republic of China (office).

SHIARLY, Vassos; Cypriot banker and government official; b. 1948, London, UK; worked for 19 years in various accounting firms in London, becoming Sr Man., Coopers & Lybrand –1985; joined Bank of Cyprus Group 1985, becoming Sr Man., Customer Man. Services Unit, Group Gen. Man., Branch Banking 1998–2003, Group Gen. Man., Domestic Banking 2003–09, Sr Group Gen. Man. 2009–10, Group Chief Gen. Man. 2010–11, also Head, Domestic Corporate Banking and Int. Corporate Lending; Minister of Finance 2012–13; Chair. Asscn of Cyprus Banks 2009–10; fmr Group Adviser and Chair. Cypriot Health Insurance Org.; mem. Bd of Dirs Nicosia Junior School 1986–92. *Address:* c/o Ministry of Finance, Cnr Michalakis Karaolis Street and Gregoriou Afxentiou Street, 1439 Nicosia, Cyprus.

SHIBATA, Ai; Japanese swimmer; b. 14 May 1982, Fukuoka Pref.; ed Nat. Inst. of Fitness and Sports, School of Physical Educ. Univ.; gold medal, 800m freestyle, Athens Olympics 2004; silver medal, 400m freestyle, bronze medal, 800m freestyle, World Championships, Montreal 2005; bronze medal, 400m freestyle, bronze medal, 1500m freestyle, World Championships, Melbourne 2007; gold medal, 400m freestyle, silver medal, 800m freestyle, bronze medal, 1500m freestyle, Pan Pacific Championships, Victoria 2006; swims for Team Arena Club. *Address:* Japan Amateur Swimming Federation, Kishi Memorial Hall, 1-1-1 Jinnan, 1-chome, Shibuyo-Ku, Tokyo 150-8050, Japan. *Telephone:* (3) 3481-2306. *Fax:* (3) 3481-0942. *Website:* www.descente.co.jp/arena-jp/fan/ai.html.

SHIBIBI, Sinan Muhammad Rida ash-, MA, PhD; *Governor, Central Bank of Iraq;* ed Univs of Manchester and Bristol, UK; consultant on trade, debt and finance; Head, importation and marketing section, Ministry of Oil 1975–77; served in Iraqi Ministry of Planning 1977–80; taught at Baghdad Univ. and Mustansiryah Univ., Iraq; Sr Economist, UNCTAD –2001, consultant 2001–03; Gov. Cen. Bank of Iraq 2003–; spoke at Senate hearings on Iraq Aug. 2002, on disappearance of Iraqi middle class under sanctions, and reconstruction of Iraq, and at AEI Conf. on post-Saddam Iraq Oct. 2002 (mem. follow-up cttee Dec. 2002). *Publications:* OPEC Aid: Issues and Performance 1987, The Arab Share in OPEC Aid: Some Related Facts 1988, Prospects for the Iraqi Economy: Facing the New Reality 1997, Globalisation of Finance: Implications for Macroeconomic Policies and Debt Management 2001. *Address:* Central Bank of Iraq, PO Box 64, Rashid Street, Baghdad, Iraq. *Telephone:* (1) 816-5170 (office). *Fax:* (1) 816-6802 (office). *E-mail:* cbi@cbiraq.org (office). *Website:* www.cbiraq.org (office).

SHIEH, Samuel C.; Taiwanese banker and academic; ed Univ. of Minnesota; fmr Prof.; Gov. Cen. Bank of China 1989–94; Nat. Policy Adviser to Pres. 1994–2000; Chair. Industrial Bank of Taiwan 1999–2002; Sec.-Gen. Vice-Chair. Straits Exchange Foundation 1997–2002, fmr Sec.-Gen.; mem. Advisory Cttee Research Center for Taiwan Econ. Devt, Nat. Cen. Univ. *Address:* Research Center for Taiwan Economic Development, National Central University, Chung-li 320, Taiwan (office). *Telephone:* (3) 4227151 (office). *Fax:* (3) 4263067 (office). *E-mail:* rcted@cc.ncu.edu.tw (office). *Website:* rcted.ncu.edu.tw (office).

SHIELDS, Brooke Christa Camille, BA; American actress and model; b. 31 May 1965, New York; d. of Francis Shields and Teri Schmon; m. Andre Agassi 1997 (divorced 1999); m. Chris Henchy 2001; two d.; ed Princeton Univ.; began modelling in Ivory Soap commercials 1966, later for Calvin Klein jeans and Colgate toothpaste. *Theatre includes:* Grease (Broadway) 1994–95, Wonderful Town (Broadway) 2004, Chicago (Adelphi Theatre, London) 2005. *Films:* Communion (aka Alice, Sweet Alice) 1976, Pretty Baby 1977, King of the Gypsies 1978, Wanda Nevada 1978, Just You and Me, Kid 1978, Tilt 1979, The Blue Lagoon 1979, Endless Love 1980, Sahara 1983, The Muppets Take Manhattan 1984, Brenda Starr 1986, Speed Zone! 1988, Backstreet Dreams (aka Backstreet Strays) 1989, Running Wild 1992, Freaked 1993, The Seventh Floor 1993, Freeway 1996, The Misadventures of Margaret 1998, The Weekend 1999, Black and White 1999, The Bachelor 1999, After Sex 2000, Mariti in affitto 2004, The Easter Egg Adventure 2005, Bob the Butler 2005, The Midnight Meat Train 2008, Furry Vengeance 2010, Chalet Girl 2011, The Greening of Whitney Brown 2011, The Hot Flashes 2013. *Television:* After the Fall (film) 1974, The Prince of Central Park (film) 1977, Wet Gold (film) 1984, The Diamond Trap (film) 1988, I Can Make You Love Me (film) 1993, Un Amore americano (film) 1994, Nothing Lasts Forever (mini series) 1995, Suddenly Susan (series) 1996, The Almost Perfect Bank Robbery (film) 1998, What Makes a Family (film) 2001, Widows (mini series) 2002, Miss Spider's Sunny Patch Kids (film, voice) 2003, Gone But Not Forgotten (mini series) 2004, Hannah Montana (series) 2007–09, Lipstick Jungle (series) 2008–09, The Middle 2010,

Army Wives (series) 2013. *Publication:* Down Came the Rain: A Mother's Story of Depression and Recovery 2005.

SHIELDS, Hon. Margaret Kerslake, QSO, BA; New Zealand fmr politician; b. 18 Dec. 1941, Wellington; d. of Ernest Blake Porter and Dorothy Bessie Porter (née Levy); m. Patrick John Shields 1960; two d.; ed Victoria Univ., Wellington; researcher, Consumers' Inst. and Dept of Statistics; MP for Kapiti 1981–90; Minister of Customs and of Consumer Affairs 1984–87, of Women's Affairs, Consumer Affairs and Statistics 1987–88, 1989–90, of Customs 1988–89, Assoc. Minister of Educ. 1989–90; mem. Wellington Regional Council 1995–, Deputy Chair. 1998–2001, apptd Chair. 2001; Vice-Pres. Local Govt; Co-founder, Pres. and Nat. Sec., Soc. for Research on Women; Dir UN Int. Research and Training Inst. for the Advancement of Women (INSTRAW) 1991–94; Co-convenor of Second UN Women's Convention 1975; mem. Wellington Hosp. Bd 1977–80, Complaints Review Tribunal of New Zealand Human Rights Comm. 1994–2000, Council of Victoria Univ. of Wellington 1996–99; Deputy Chair. Hutt Valley Dist Health Bd 2000–01; Chair. Plenary Session, Int. Conf. of Women Mayors and Elected Councillors, Phitsanulok, Thailand 2001; Govt Del. to UN Int. Women's Year Conf. Mexico 1975, participated in IPU Conf., Seoul 1983, speaker, IPU Conf., Geneva 1989. *Leisure interests:* hiking, gardening, music, drama. *Address:* Greater Wellington Regional Council, 142 Wakefield Street, PO Box 11646, Wellington 6142 (office); 23 Haunui Road, Pukerua Bay, Porirua, New Zealand (home). *Telephone:* (4) 384-5708 (office); (4) 239-9949 (home). *Fax:* (4) 385-6960 (office); (4) 239-9084 (home). *E-mail:* margaret.shields@gw.govt.nz (office); marg.shields@xtra .co.nz. *Website:* www.gw.govt.nz (office).

SHIGA, Toshiyuki; Japanese automotive industry executive; *Co-Chairman, Chief Operating Officer and Senior Vice-President, Nissan Motor Co. Ltd;* Head of China operations, Nissan Motor Co. Ltd –2007, COO Nissan Motor Co. Ltd 2005–, also Co-Chair. and Sr Vice-Pres. *Address:* Nissan Motor Co. Ltd, 1-1, Takashima 1-chome, Nishi-ku, Yokohama-shi, Kanagawa 220-8686, Japan (office). *Telephone:* (45) 523-5523 (office). *Website:* www.nissan-global.com (office).

SHIGEHARA, Kumiharu, BL; Japanese economist; *President, International Economic Policy Studies Association;* b. 5 Feb. 1939, Maebashi; s. of Seizaburo Shigehara and Rutsu Tanabe; m. Akiko Yoshizawa 1965; one s. one d.; ed Maebashi High School, Univ. of Tokyo and Univ. of Poitiers; economist, Bank of Japan 1962–70; economist OECD 1970–71, Sr Economist 1971–72, Head, Monetary Div. 1972–74; Councillor for Policy Planning, Bank of Japan 1974–76, Man. Int. Affairs 1976–80; Deputy Dir Gen. Econs Branch, OECD 1980–82; Gen. Man. Bank of Japan 1983–87; Dir Gen. Econs Branch, OECD 1987–89; Dir-Gen. Inst. for Monetary and Econ. Studies and Chief Economist, Bank of Japan 1989–92; Head, Econs Dept and Chief Economist, OECD 1992–97, Deputy Sec.-Gen. OECD 1997–99; Special Adviser Int. Friendship Exchange Council 2001; Head, Int. Econ. Policy Studies Group 2002–08; Pres. Int. Econ. Policy Studies Asscn 2008–; Hon. PhD; Dr hc (Liège) 1998; Hozumi Special Award, Univ. of Tokyo 1960. *Publications:* The Role of Monetary Policy in Demand Management (co-author) 1975, Europe After 1992 1991, The Problems of Inflation in the 1990s (ed.) 1992, Evolving International Trade and Monetary Regimes 1992, Causes of Declining Growth in Industrialised Countries 1992, Price Stabilization in the 1990s 1993, Long-term Tendencies in Budget Deficits and Debt 1995, The Options regarding the Concept of a Monetary Policy Strategy 1996, Monetary and Economic Policy: Then and Now 1998, Causes and Implications of East Asian Financial Crises 1998, International Aspects of Competition Policy 1999, Monetary Policy and Economic Performance 2001, Looking for Models in Pursuit of Economic Prosperity 2002, Managing the International Economic Crisis 2008, Surveillance by International Institutions: Lessons from the Global Financial and Economic Crisis (with Paul Atkinson) 2011. *Leisure interests:* golf, tennis, hiking. *E-mail:* office.shigehara@ online.fr (office). *Website:* office.shigehara.online.fr (office).

SHIGEMOTO, Hiroshi (Hiro), BA, BSc; Dutch politician; b. 22 June 1970, Sint Maarten, Netherlands Antilles; s. of Jesiman Veronica Lake; m. Zetsia Robin Shigemoto-Duncan; one s.; ed Christelijke Hogeschool, Netherlands, Univ. of Tampa, USA; Head of Finance, Island Govt of Sint Maarten 2003–06, Dir of Resources 2006–10; Minister of Finance (first holder after dissolution of Netherlands Antilles) 2010–12 (resgnd); mem. United People's Party; numerous awards for participation in lectures and seminars. *Leisure interests:* gardening, music appreciation.

SHIH, Chi-Yang, LLM, DJur; Taiwanese politician; b. 5 May 1935, Taichung City; m. Jeanne Tchong-Koei Li 1968; ed Nat. Taiwan Univ. and Univ. of Heidelberg; Asst Dept of Law, Nat. Taiwan Univ. 1959–62, Assoc. Prof. 1967–71, Prof. (part-time) 1971–84; Research Asst Inst. of Int. Relations, Nat. Chengchi Univ. 1967–69, Research Fellow 1969–71; Deputy Dir 5th Section, Cen. Cttee, Kuomintang 1969–72, Deputy Dir Dept of Youth Activities 1972–76; Admin. Vice-Minister, Ministry of Educ. 1976–79; Political Vice-Minister, Ministry of Educ. 1979–80, Ministry of Justice 1980–84; Minister of Justice 1984–88; Vice-Premier 1988–93; Sec.-Gen. Nat. Security Council 1993–94; Pres. Judicial Yuan 1994–99. *Address:* c/o Judicial Yuan, 124 Chungching S Road, Sec. 1, Taipei, Taiwan.

SHIH, Choon Fong, MSc, PhD; Singaporean scientist, fmr university administrator and professor of mechanical engineering; b. 23 Oct. 1945; ed Singapore Polytechnic, Harvard Univ., USA; Research Fellow, Harvard Univ. 1973–74; Leader, Fracture Research Group, Corp. Research Lab., General Electric, NY 1974–81; Visiting Assoc. Prof., Brown Univ. 1981–83, Assoc. Prof. 1983–86, Prof. 1986–97; Visiting Prof., Japan Soc. for Promotion of Science, Tokyo Univ. 1989; Fellow, Applied Mechanics Div., ASME 1999; Founding Dir Inst. of Materials Research and Eng, Singapore 1996–99; Founding Pres. Materials Research Soc. of Singapore; Deputy Vice-Chancellor Nat. Univ. of Singapore 1997–2000, Vice-Chancellor and Pres. 2000–08; Founding Pres. King Abdullah Univ. of Science and Tech. (KAUST) 2008–13; Chair. Emer. Asscn of Pacific Rim Univs (APRU), fmr Chair. Governing Bd, APRU World Inst.; Dir Agency for Science, Tech. and Research, Biomedical Research Council, Science and Eng Research Council, Inst. of Policy Studies, Singapore Int. Fed.; Foreign Assoc., Nat. Acad. of Eng (USA) 2004; fmr Founding Pres. Materials Research Soc. of Singapore; fmr consultant to NASA, Oak Ridge Nat. Lab., Nuclear Regulatory Comm.; fmr mem. Singapore Int. Foundation; Foreign Hon. mem. American Acad. of Arts and Sciences 2006, Hon. mem. Medical Alumni Asscn, Singapore 2007; Chevalier, Légion d'honneur 2005;

Dr hc (Loughborough Univ.) 2005, (Waseda Univ.) 2007, (Brown Univ.) 2008; George Rankin Irwin Medal, American Soc. for Testing and Materials 1986, Swedlow Award, American Soc. for Testing and Materials 1998, Chief Exec. Leadership Award, Council for Advancement and Support for Educ. 2007, Ted Belytschko Applied Mechanics Award, American Soc. for Mechanical Engineers 2008. *Publications:* more than 200 papers in academic journals. *Address:* c/o King Abdullah University of Science & Technology, Thuwal 23955-6900, Saudi Arabia.

SHIH, Jonney, BSc, MBA; Taiwanese business executive; *Chairman, ASUSTeK Computer Inc.;* b. 1951; ed Nat. Taiwan Univ., Nat. Chao-Tung Univ.; fmr research and devt engineer at Acer Inc.; Chair. and CEO ASUSTeK Computer Inc. 1993–2008, Chair. 2008–; named as one of the nation's Ten Most Outstanding Managers 1986, named as one of the Top Ten Scholars of Applied Science 1986, selected by Nat. Chamber of Commerce as one of the Ten Outstanding Youths for outstanding success and contribs to society 1990, recognized by BusinessWeek Magazine as one of the 50 Stars of Asia 1998, 1999, Outstanding Tech. Man. Award, Chinese Soc. for Man. of Tech. 2006, Outstanding Entrepreneur Award, Chinatimes and Taiwan DHL 2006, Pan Wen Yuan Prize 2012. *Address:* ASUSTeK Computer Inc., 15 Li-Te Road, Peitou, Taipei 112, Taiwan (office). *Telephone:* (2) 2894-3447 (office). *Fax:* (2) 2892-6140 (office). *E-mail:* info@asus.com (office). *Website:* www.asus.com (office).

SHIH, Ming-Teh; Taiwanese politician; b. 15 Jan. 1941, Kaohsiung; s. of Shih Kuo-tsui; m. 1st Chen Li-chu (divorced); m. 2nd Linda Gail Arrigo; ed Kaohsiung Jr High-School, Kaohsiung's Chung-Cheng Sr High School; fmr political prisoner in Taiwan, spent 25 years in prison, 13 years in solitary confinement and over 4 years on hunger strike; reporter Liberty Times; Chair. Democratic Progressive Party 1994–96; mem. Taiwan Legis. Council; initiated Million Voices Against Corruption-Chen Must Go campaign 2006. *Address:* Room 601, 10 Tsingtao E Road, Taipei, Taiwan.

SHIH, Stan, PhD; Taiwanese fmr business executive; *Chairman, iD SoftCapital;* b. 18 Dec. 1944, Taiwan; m. Carolyn Yeh; two s. one d.; ed Nat. Chiao Tung Univ.; with Unitron Industrial Corpn 1971–72, Qualitron Industrial Corpn 1972–76; f. Acer Inc. (electronics co. previously known as Multitech) 1976, Chair. and CEO 1976–2004 (retd), currently Chair. Emer.; Founder-Chair. iD SoftCapital 2004–; apptd Special Rep. of Pres. to APEC Meeting, Australia 2007; currently Hon. Chair. Brand Int. Promotion Asscn; fmr Chair. Asia Business Council; mem. Bd of Dirs Taiwan Semiconductor Manufacturing Co. Ltd; mem. Int. Advisory Panel, Malaysia's Multimedia Super Corridor; Gov. Asian Inst. of Man.; Hon. Fellow, Univ. of Wales; title of Dato (Malaysia) 1994; Dr hc (Hong Kong Polytechnic Univ.), (American Grad. School of Int. Man.), (Thunderbird School of Global Man.); named among Taiwan's Ten Most Outstanding Young Persons 1976, Int. Business Exec. of the Year, Acad. of Int. Business 1999, Outstanding Contribution to Brand Building Award 2003, Asian Star of the Year, Businessweek magazine 2004, named as one of Asian Heroes, Time magazine 2006. *Publications:* more than 100 articles on man., marketing etc. *Address:* Acer Inc., 8f, 88, Sec. 1, Hsin Tai Wu Road, Hsichih, Taipei 221, Taiwan (office). *Telephone:* (2) 26961234 (office). *Fax:* (2) 26963535 (office). *Website:* www.acer.com (office).

SHIH, Yen-Shiang, PhD; Taiwanese politician and business executive; *Minister of Economic Affairs;* b. 1950; m. Ei-Wang Chang; ed Nat. Taiwan Univ., Massachusetts Inst. of Tech., USA; Assoc. Prof. and Prof. of Chemical Eng and Tech., Nat. Taiwan Inst. of Tech. (now Nat. Taiwan Univ. of Science and Tech.) 1979–89, Head of Dept of Chemical Eng and Tech. 1981–86; Prof., Grad. Inst. of Tech. and Innovation Man., Nat. Cheng-Chih Univ. 1996–2002; Deputy Dir Office of Science and Tech. Advisors (now Dept of Industrial Tech.), Ministry of Econ. Affairs 1986–87, later Dir, Dir-Gen. Small and Medium Enterprises Admin 1992–95, Dir-Gen. Industrial Devt, Bureau 2001–02; Dir-Gen. Taiwan Tobacco and Wine Bureau (now Taiwan Tobacco and Liquor Co.) 1995–2000; Chair. CPC Corpn March–Sept. 2009; Deputy Minister of Econ. Affairs 2002–09, Minister of Econ. Affairs 2009–. *Address:* Ministry of Economic Affairs, 15 Foo Chou Street, Taipei 10015, Taiwan (office). *Telephone:* (2) 23212200 (office). *Fax:* (2) 23919398 (office). *E-mail:* service@moea.gov.tw (office). *Website:* www.moea.gov.tw (office).

SHIHAB, Hussain, MSc; Maldivian politician and diplomatist; *High Commissioner to Sri Lanka;* b. 1949; m.; six c.; ed Kuban Agric. Inst., Russia; Under-Sec., Ministry of Home Affairs and Social Services 1975, Ministry of Agric. 1976–78; Man. TV Maldives 1978–81, Deputy Dir, then Dir 1985; Dir of Environmental Affairs, Ministry of Home Affairs and Social Services 1986–88, Dir of Environmental Affairs, Ministry of Planning and the Environment 1988–93, Deputy Minister 1993–95, July–Sept. 1998; Dir South Asia Co-operative Environment Programme 1995–98; Perm. Rep. to the UN 1998–2002; del. to numerous UN meetings on the environment, including Conf. on Environment and Devt 1992 and Global Conf. on the Sustainable Devt of Small Island Developing States 1994; fmr Deputy Minister of Foreign Affairs; fmr Minister of State for the Arts; Amb. to Saudi Arabia 2007–08; High Commr to Sri Lanka 2008–; formulated Maldives' first nat. environment action plan; Silver Pen Award 1987. *Films:* Fidhaa 1985, Hadmiya 1993, Rihun 2002, Vissaradmuni 2005. *Publications:* Ochid Eyanarse Maa (short stories) 1983; papers on the environment and sustainable devt presented at int. confs. *Leisure interests:* film, reading, writing. *Address:* Maldives High Commission, 25 Melbourne Ave, Colombo 4, Sri Lanka (office). *Telephone:* (11) 2587827 (office). *Fax:* (11) 2581200 (office). *E-mail:* info@maldiveshighcom.lk (office). *Website:* www.maldiveshighcom.lk (office).

SHIHAB, Mohamed, BEcons; Maldivian economist and politician; b. 2 Oct. 1957, Malé; s. of Ibrahim Shihab and Jameela Ibrahim; ed James Cook Univ. of N Queensland, Australia; Project Officer, Nat. Planning Agency, Malé 1980–81, Asst Dir 1981–82; Under-Sec., Ministry of Planning and Devt 1982–85, Sr Under-Sec. 1985–89, Dir of External Resources 1989–94; Dir Maldives Transport and Contracting Co. Ltd 1994–99; fmr sr mem. Maldivian Democratic Party, MP (Jumhooree Party) for Dhaal Atoll 1985–2005, for Malé 2005–, Speaker of People's Majlis 2008–09; Minister of Home Affairs 2009–10 (resgnd), of Finance Jan.–Mar. 2012; Man. Dir Maldives Post Ltd 2006; mem. Bd of Dirs Maldives Transport and Contracting Co. Ltd 1991–99, Bank of Maldives 1994–96, Maldives Tourism Devt Corpn PLC 2007–08. *Address:* c/o Ministry of Finance and Treasury, Ameenee Magu, Malé 20-379, Maldives.

SHIHAB-ELDIN, Adnan, BSc, MSc, PhD; Kuwaiti engineer and international organization official; *Senior Research Advisor, Oxford Institute for Energy Studies;* b. 1943; ed Univ. of California, Berkeley, USA; trained as nuclear engineer; Asst Prof. of Physics, then Vice-Rector of Academic Affairs, Kuwait Univ. 1970–80; Dir-Gen. Kuwait Inst. for Scientific Research 1976–86; Dir of UNESCO Regional Office for Science and Tech. and UNESCO Rep. in Egypt, Sudan and Yemen 1991–99; Dir Africa, E Asia and Pacific Div., Dept of Tech. Cooperation, Int. Atomic Energy Agency (IAEA) 1999–2001; Dir Research Div., OPEC 2001–06, Acting Sec.-Gen. 2005; currently Sr Research Advisor, Oxford Inst. for Energy Studies, UK; serves as consultant to numerous public and pvt. orgs; mem. UN Advisory Cttee on Science and Tech. for Devt, NY, Arab Thought Forum, Amman, Jordan, Int. Scientific Council for Science and Tech. Policy Devt, UNESCO; mem. numerous professional socs. *Address:* Oxford Institute for Energy Studies, 57 Woodstock Road, Oxford, OX2 6FA, England (office). *Telephone:* (1865) 311377. *Fax:* (1865) 310527 (office). *E-mail:* information@oxfordenergy.org (office). *Website:* www .oxfordenergy.org (office).

SHIIMI, Ipumbu Wendelinus, BCom, MSc; Namibian economist and central banker; *Governor, Bank of Namibia;* ed Univ. of Western Cape, Univ. of Stellenbosch, Wits Business School, South Africa, Univ. of London, UK, Maastricht School of Man., Netherlands; several years with Bank of Namibia (central bank), including as Head of Research and Sr Man., Banking Supervisor, Dir, Financial Intelligence Centre, becoming Asst Gov., responsible for overseeing Reserve Man., Banking Supervision, Financial Stability and Financial Intelligence 2006–10, Gov. 2010–. *Address:* Office of the Governor, Bank of Namibia, 71 Robert Mugabe Avenue, POB 2882, Windhoek, Namibia (office). *Telephone:* (61) 2835111 (office). *Fax:* (61) 2835067 (office). *E-mail:* jerome.mutumba@bon.com.na (office). *Website:* www.bon.com.na (office).

SHIKAPWASHA, Lt-Gen. Ronnie; Zambian politician and fmr air force officer; b. 25 Dec. 1948; fmr Amb. to UN; MP for Keembe constituency; Minister of Home Affairs 2003–05, 2006–08, of Foreign Affairs 2005–06, of Information and Broadcasting Services 2008–11, Acting Health Minister 2006. *Address:* c/o Ministry of Information and Broadcasting Services, Independence Avenue, POB 51025, Lusaka, Zambia.

SHILLER, Robert James, BA, SM, PhD; American economist and academic; *Sterling Professor of Economics, Yale University;* b. 29 March 1946, Detroit, MI; ed Univ. of Michigan, Massachusetts Inst. of Tech.; Asst Prof. of Econs, Univ. of Minnesota 1972–74; Assoc. Prof. of Econs, Univ. of Pennsylvania 1974–80; Research Fellow, Nat. Bureau of Econs Research, Cambridge, Mass 1980–81; Visiting Prof., MIT 1981–82; apptd Stanley B. Resor Prof. of Econs, Yale Univ. 1982, currently Sterling Prof. of Econs, also Prof., School of Man.; Co-founder Case Shiller Weiss Inc., Cambridge, Mass 1991, Macro Securities Research LLC 1999; research in behavioural finance and behavioural macroecons at Nat. Bureau of Econ. Research; Guggenheim Fellowship 1991, Paul Samuelson Award 1996, Commonfund Prize 2000, Nobel Prize in Econs (with Eugene Fama and Lars Peter Hansen) 2013. *Publications:* Market Volatility 1989, Macro Markets: Creating Institutions for Managing Society's Largest Economic Risks 1993, Irrational Exuberance 2000, The New Financial Order 2003, Animal Spirits: How Human Psychology Drives the Economy, and Why It Matters for Global Capitalism 2009, Finance and the Good Society 2012. *Address:* 30 Hillhouse Avenue, New Haven, CT 06520 (office); Cowles Foundation, Box 208281, New Haven, CT 06511-8281, USA (office). *Telephone:* (203) 432-3708 (office). *Fax:* (203) 432-6167 (office). *E-mail:* robert.shiller@yale.edu (office). *Website:* aida.wss.yale.edu/~shiller (office).

SHILOV, Aleksandr Maksovich; Russian artist; b. 6 Oct. 1943, Moscow; s. of Ludmila Sergeevna Pazhenova; ed V.I. Surikov Inst. of Fine Arts, Moscow; painted series of portraits of contemporary village people, social and political leaders, astronauts, intellectuals and clergy, also present-day social phenomena, genre paintings, landscapes and still lifes; f. Moscow State A. Shilov Picture Gallery 1997, currently Art Dir; mem. Acad. of Social Sciences 1997–, Council for Culture and Art 1999–; Corresp. mem. Russian Acad. of Arts 1997–2001, mem. 2001–; Order for Services to the Motherland (Fourth Degree) 1997, (Third Degree) 2004, Order of Francisk Skorina (Belarus) 2003; Lenin Komsomol Prize 1977, People's Artist of RSFSR 1981, People's Artist of USSR 1985. *Achievements include:* asteroid named after him 1992. *Address:* Romanov per. 3, Apartment 71, 103009 Moscow, Russia. *Telephone:* (495) 203-42-08. *Fax:* (495) 203-69-75 (office). *E-mail:* shilov_gallery@mail.ru (office). *Website:* www.shilov.su (office).

SHILTON, Peter Leslie, MBE, OBE; British fmr professional footballer; b. 18 Sept. 1949, Leicester, England; s. of Les Shilton and May Shilton; m. Sue Shilton 1970; two s.; ed King Richard III School, Leicester; goalkeeper; youth player, Leicester CIty 1963–66; sr player, Leicester City 1966–74 (won Football League Second Div. 1970/71, FA Charity Shield 1971), Stoke City 1974–77, Nottingham Forest 1977–82 (won First Div. League Championship 1977/78, FA Charity Shield 1978, League Cup 1979, European Cup 1979, 1980, European Super Cup 1979), Southampton 1982–87 (won Trofeo Ciudad de Vigo 1983), Derby County 1987–92, Plymouth Argyle 1992–95, Wimbledon 1995, Bolton Wanderers 1995, Coventry City 1995–96, West Ham United 1996, Leyton Orient 1996–97 (retd); Man. Plymouth Argyle FC 1992–95; mem. England U-23 team 1968–72, England 1970–90 (125 caps—record), won Rous Cup 1986, 1988, 1989; first England goalkeeper to win more than 100 caps at European Championships 1988; record English league appearances (1,005); conceded only 80 int. goals; holds all-time record for most competitive appearances in world football; Southampton FC Player of the Season 1984/85, 1985/86, Professional Footballers' Asscn (PFA) Players' Player of the Year 1978, PFA Order of Merit 1990, Football Writers' Tribute Award 1991, Inaugural Inductee into English Football Hall of Fame 2002. *Address:* c/o Champions PR Ltd, Meadow End, Leake Road, Costock, Loughborough, Leics., LE12 6XA, England (office). *Telephone:* (845) 3313031 (office). *E-mail:* mail@ championspr.com (office). *Website:* www.championspr.com (office), www .petershilton.com.

SHIMALI, Mustafa Jassem ash-; Kuwaiti civil servant and politician; *Deputy Prime Minister and Minister of Oil;* served in several sr govt posts, including Under-Sec. for Econ. Affairs 1986–2006 and Under-Sec. for Finance 2006–07; Minister of Health 2011–12, of Finance 2012–13, Deputy Prime Minister and

Minister of Oil 2013–; Chair. Kuwait Investment Authority. *Address:* Ministry of Oil, PO Box 5077, 13051 Safat, Kuwait City, Kuwait (office). *Telephone:* 22406990 (office). *E-mail:* alnaft@moo.gov.kw (office). *Website:* www.moo.gov.kw (office).

SHIMAMURA, Yoshinobu; Japanese politician; b. 27 March 1934, Edogawa; ed Gakushuin Univ.; with Nippon Oil Corpn 1956–71; fmr Parl. Vice-Minister of Agric., Forestry and Fisheries; mem. House of Reps (LDP) for Tokyo 16th Dist, fmr Chair. Cttee on Transport; Minister of Agric., Forestry and Fisheries 1997–98, 2004–05; fmr Chair. LDP Diet Affairs Cttee. *Address:* c/o Liberal-Democratic Party—LDP, 1-11-23, Nagata-cho, Chiyoda-ku, Tokyo 100-8910, Japan.

SHIMELL, William; British singer (baritone) and actor; b. 23 Sept. 1952, Ilford, Essex, England; s. of W. Shimell and F.E. Shimell; m. Olga Slavka 1996; ed Westminster Abbey Choir School, St Edward's School, Oxford, Guildhall School of Music and Drama, Nat. Opera Studio, London; debut with Kent Opera in Rigoletto 1980; best known for interpretations of Don Giovanni, Count Almaviva (Marriage of Figaro) and Don Alfonso (Così fan Tutte), has sung in opera houses world-wide including La Scala, Milan, Metropolitan Opera House, New York, Paris Opéra, Rome Opera, Vienna Staatsoper, Covent Garden, London; Assoc. Guildhall School of Music and Drama; numerous recordings. *Films:* Certified Copy 2010, Amour 2012. *Television:* as himself: Mozart – His Life with Music (series) 1985, The Fabulous Picture Show (series) 2010, Cinema 3 (series) 2010; actor: L'enfance du Christ (film) 1986, Hercules (film) 2005, The Rake's Progress (film) 2008. *Leisure interests:* sailing, cooking. *Address:* c/o Celebrity Talent International, 33 Gateview, Fallbrook, CA 92028, USA (office). *Telephone:* (760) 729-2000 (office). *E-mail:* info@celebritytalent.net (office). *Website:* www.celebritytalent.net (office).

SHIMIZU, Kayoko; Japanese nurse and politician; b. 1936; ed Faculty of Medicine, Univ. of Tokyo; fmr Dir Nursing Div., Health and Welfare Ministry; elected mem. House of Councillors (LDP) 1989, Chair. House of Councillors Cttee on Educ.; Parl. Vice-Minister for Labour; Dir-Gen. Environment Agency 1999–2000; Sec.-Gen. Secr. of Japan Parliamentarians Fed. for Population; fmr Vice-Chair. Asian Population and Devt Assen. *Address:* c/o Asian Population and Development Association, 2-19-5-8F Nishi-Shinbashi, Minato-ku, Tokyo 105-0003, Japan.

SHIMIZU, Masataka; Japanese business executive; ed Keio Univ.; joined Tokyo Electric Power Co., Inc. (TEPCO) 1968, served as Head of Supplies Div., Man. Dir 2004–06, Vice-Pres. 2006–08, Pres. 2008–11 (resgnd following $15bn loss as a result of the Japan earthquake and tsunami); Vice-Chair. Nippon Keidanren. *Address:* c/o Tokyo Electric Power Co., Inc., 1-1-3 Uchisaiwai-cho, Chiyoda-ku, Tokyo 100-8560, Japan.

SHIMIZU, Shinobu; Japanese transport industry executive; *Executive Corporate Adviser, Tokyu Corporation;* m.; ed Dept of Econs, Hitotsubashi Univ.; joined Tokyu Corpn 1953, Pres. Tokyo Express Electric Railway 2001, Chair. and Rep. Dir –2005, currently Exec. Corp. Adviser; Sr Vice-Pres. Japan Airline System Corpn 2002; Chair. Assen of Japanese Pvt. Railways 2001–; mem. Man. Council, Devt Bank of Japan 2004–, Registers of Council. *Address:* Tokyu Corporation, 5-6 Nanpeidai-cho, Shibuya-ku, Tokyo 150-8511, Japan (office). *Telephone:* (3) 3477-6111 (office). *Fax:* (3) 3462-1690 (office). *Website:* www.tokyu.co.jp (office).

SHIMIZU, Yasuyuki; Japanese mining executive; Exec. Vice-Pres. Nippon Mining and Metals Co. 1999; Exec. Vice-Pres. Toho Titanium Co. 1999–2000, Pres. 2000–01; Sr Man. Dir and Chief Div. Officer, Corp. Support Div., Nippon Mining Holdings, Inc. (fmrly Japan Energy Co.) 1998–2001, Chair. and Rep. Dir 2001–03, CEO 2003, Pres. and Rep. Dir 2003–06, Chair. and Rep. Dir 2006–10 (following merger with Nippon Oil Corpn to form JX Holdings 2010); Chair. Japan Titanium Soc. *Address:* c/o JX Holdings, Inc., 2-6-3, Ote-machi, Chiyoda-ku, Tokyo 100-0004, Japan. *Telephone:* (3) 3502-1131. *Website:* www.hd.jx-group.co.jp.

SHIMOGAICHI, Yoichi; Japanese business executive; *Adviser, JFE Holdings Inc.;* b. 26 Aug. 1934; two s.; ed Univ. of Tokyo; joined NKK Corpn 1958, Gen. Man. Sales Co-ordination, Export and Corp. Planning Depts 1981–86, mem. Bd of Dirs, Gen. Man. Corp. Planning Dept 1987, Man. Dir 1989, Sr Man. Dir, Deputy Dir Steel Div. 1991, apptd Exec. Vice-Pres., Exec. Dir Steel Div. 1994, Exec. Vice-Pres. 1997, apptd Pres. 1997, Pres., CEO 2000–02, Chair. of Bd 2002, Pres., Co-CEO and Rep. Dir JFE Holdings Inc. (jt holding co. of NKK Corpn and Kawasaki Steel) 2002–05, Adviser 2005–; exec. mem. Bd of Dirs Japan Fed. of Econ. Orgs 1997; mem. Export and Import Transaction Council 1996–98, Coal Mining Council 1997; Dir Japan Iron and Steel Fed. 1997. *Address:* JFE Holdings, Inc., 1- 5-1 Marunouchi, Chiyoda-ku, Tokyo, 100-6527, Japan (office).

SHIMOKOBE, Kazuhiko, LLB; Japanese lawyer and business executive; *Chairman, Tokyo Electric Power Company (TEPCO), Inc.;* ed Kyoto Univ.; worked for Japan Post Holdings Co. Ltd and Chori Co. Ltd; fmr bankruptcy lawyer in charge of Nuclear Damage Liability Facilitation Fund state bailout facility; Ind. Chair. Tokyo Electric Power Co. (TEPCO), Inc. 2012–, Chair. Audit Cttee, mem. Nominating Cttee, Compensation Cttee. *Address:* Tokyo Electric Power Co., Inc., 1-1-3 Uchisaiwai-cho, Chiyoda-ku, Tokyo 100-8560, Japan (office). *Telephone:* (3) 4216-1111 (office). *Fax:* (3) 4216-2539 (office). *E-mail:* info@tepco.co.jp (office). *Website:* www.tepco.co.jp (office).

SHIMOMURA, Hakubun; Japanese politician; *Minister of Education;* b. 23 May 1954, Takasaki, Gunma Pref.; ed Waseda Univ.; mem. Tokyo Metropolitan Ass. 1989–97; mem. House of Reps (lower house of Parl.) for Tokyo No. 11 constituency (LDP) 1996–, mem. Council Foreign Affairs Cttee, Exec. Cttee on Legal Affairs, Cttee on Rules and Admin; Deputy Chief Cabinet Sec. 2006; Minister of Educ., Culture, Sports, Science and Tech. and for Rebuilding Educ. 2012–; mem. Japanese Nat. Comm. for UNESCO; Vice-Chair. Ashinaga (non-profit org.); mem. Liberal Democratic Party (LDP), Deputy Chair. LDP Policy Research Council. *Address:* Ministry of Education, Culture, Sports, Science and Technology, 3-2-2, Kasumigaseki, Chiyoda-ku, Tokyo 100-8959, Japan (office). *Telephone:* (3) 5253-4111 (office). *Fax:* (3) 3595-2017 (office). *Website:* www.mext.go.jp (office).

SHIMOMURA, Osamu, BS, MS, PhD; Japanese organic chemist and marine biologist; *Senior Scientist Emeritus, Woods Hole Marine Biological Laboratory;* b. 27 Aug. 1928, Kyoto; m. Akemi Shimomura; two c.; ed Nagasaki Univ., Nagoya Univ.; Asst, Faculty of Pharmaceutical Sciences, Nagasaki Univ. 1958–60;

Research Biochemist, Dept of Biology, Princeton Univ. 1960–82; Adjunct Assoc. Prof., Boston Univ. Medical School 1982–84, Adjunct Prof. of Physiology and Biophysics 1984, now Prof. Emer.; Sr Scientist, Woods Hole Marine Biological Lab. 1982–2001, Sr Scientist Emer. 2001–; mem. NAS 2013; Order of Culture 2008; Pearse Prize, Royal Soc. for Microscopy 2004, Emile Chamot Award, Microscopy Soc. of Ill. 2005, Asahi Prize 2006, Nobel Prize in Chem. (co-recipient with Martin Chalfie and Roger Tsien) 2008. *Address:* c/o Marine Biological Laboratory, 7 MBL Street, Woods Hole, MA 02543, USA (office). *Telephone:* (508) 548-3705 (office). *Fax:* (508) 289-7423 (office). *E-mail:* oshimomura@mbl.edu (office). *Website:* www .mbl.edu (office).

SHIMOMURA, Setsuhiro; Japanese business executive; *Chairman, Mitsubishi Electric Corporation;* b. 1945, Tottori Pref.; joined Mitsubishi Electric Corpn in 1969, first served as an engineer in Himeji Works, named to Mitsubishi Electric's Bd of Dirs 2001–, Exec. Vice-Pres. and Group Pres. of Building Systems 2004–06, Rep. Exec. Officer, Pres. and CEO Mitsubishi Electric Corpn 2006–10, Chair. 2010–. *Address:* Mitsubishi Electric Corpn, Tokyo Bldg, 2-7-3, Marunouchi, Chiyoda-ku, Tokyo 100-8310, Japan (office). *Telephone:* (3) 3218-2111 (office). *E-mail:* info@mitsubishi.com (office). *Website:* www.mitsubishi.com (office).

SHIN, Chang-jae, MD, PhD; South Korean physician and business executive; *Chairman and CEO, Kyobo Life Insurance Co. Ltd;* b. 1953, Seoul; s. of Shin Yong-ho; m.; two c.; ed Seoul Nat. Univ.; began career as obstetrician; fmr Prof. of Medicine, Seoul Nat. Univ.; Chair. Daesan Foundation 1993–, Vice-Pres. Kyobo Life Insurance Co. Ltd 1996–98, Pres. 1998–99, Chair. 1999–2000, CEO and Chair. 2000–; Vice-Chair. Korea Mecenat Asscn; several awards including Best CEO Award, Korea Man. Asscn 2001, Presidential Citation for Service Quality Innovation 2006, Korean Montblanc de la Culture Arts Patronage Award 2010. *Address:* Kyobo Life Insurance Co. Ltd, Jongno-1ga, Jongno-gu, Seoul 110-714, South Korea (office). *Telephone:* (2) 721-2121 (office). *Fax:* (2) 737-9970 (office). *Website:* www.kyobo.co.kr (office).

SHIN, Dong-bin, BEcons, MBA; South Korean retail executive; *CEO, Lotte Shopping Co. Ltd;* b. 1955, Japan; s. of Shin Kyuk-ho and Shigemitsu Hatsuko; m.; three c.; ed Aoyama Gakuin Univ., Japan, Columbia Univ., USA; Asst Man. Dir Honam Petrochemical Corpn –2006; Vice-Chair. Lotte Group, Dir and CEO, Lotte Shopping Co. Ltd 2006–; Chair. Visit Korea Year Cttee; Co-Chair. Asia Soc. Korea Center. *Address:* Lotte Shopping Co. Ltd (Chul Woo Lee), Sogongdong 1, Jung-gu, Seoul, South Korea (office). *Telephone:* (2) 2118-2021 (office). *Fax:* (2) 2118-2028 (office). *Website:* www.lotte.co.kr (office).

SHIN, Heon-cheol, BA, MBA; South Korean business executive; ed Busan Nat. Univ., Yonsei Univ.; joined SK Corpn as Head Man. of Business Team, Pres.'s Office 1985–89, Sr Man. in charge of developing man. skills 1989–91, Dir 1991, Head, Metropolitan Marketing Br. SK Telecom Co. Ltd 1995–98, Sr Man. Dir 1998, Sr Vice-Pres. and Man. Dir SK Telink Co. Ltd 1998–2002, Man. Dir SK Gas Co. Ltd 2002–05, Pres. and CEO SK Corpn 2004–, apptd Vice-Chair. and Co-CEO 2006, mem. Bd of Dirs 2004–, mem. Bd of Dirs SK Energy Co. Ltd 2007, currently CEO and Pres.; Vice-Chair. Korea Listed Companies Asscn; mem. Bd of Dirs Korea YMCA. *Address:* SK Corporation, 99 Seorin-dong, Jongno-gu, Seoul 110-110, Republic of Korea (office). *Telephone:* (2) 2121-5114 (office). *Fax:* (2) 2121-7001 (office). *Website:* www.skcorp.com (office).

SHIN, In-ryung, PhD, LLM; South Korean professor of law and fmr university president; *Professor Emeritus, Ewha Women's University;* ed Coll. of Law, Ewha Women's Univ.; Exec. Sec. in charge of Educ., Korea Dialogue Acad. 1971–80, Dir 2003–; part-time Lecturer in Labor Law, Coll. of Law, Lecturer in Women's Studies, Dept of Women's Studies, Ewha Women's Univ. 1974–84, Asst Prof. Coll. of Law 1985–87, Assoc. Prof. 1987–92, apptd Prof. 1992, Dean 2000–02, Dir Law Div. 1992–94, Pres. Ewha Women's Univ. 2002–06, currently Prof. Emer.; Visiting Research Prof., Hitotsubasi Univ., Japan 1994–95; Visiting Scholar, Univ. of Wash. School of Law, USA 1998–99; Exec. Dir Korean Soc. of Labor Law 1990–97, Deputy Pres. 1998–2001, Pres. 2001–02; Dir Korean Public Law Asscn 1991–96, Korea Law Profs Asscn 1995–, Korea Asscn of Labor Studies 1995–, Korea Labour and Soc. Inst. 1995–, Korean Inst. for Labor Studies and Policies 1996–, Korean Constitutional Law Asscn 1997–98, Korea Democracy Foundation 2001–03, Korea Advanced Inst. of Science and Tech. 2003–, Sungkok Acad. and Cultural Foundation 2004–; Deputy Pres. Korean Industrial Relations Research Asscn 1995–96; mem. Deliberation Cttee of Employment Policy, Ministry of Labor 1994–2000, Examination Cttee of Industrial Accident Insurance 2000–02; Co-Pres. Korean Fed. for Environmental Movement 2003–; rep. Korean Legal Center 1995–97; Chair. Cttee of Women's Affairs, Advisory Council on Democratic and Peaceful Unification 2003–; mem. Comm. for the Prevention of Corruption, Bd of Audit and Inspection of Korea 1999, Lawyers Disciplinary Cttee, Ministry of Justice 2000–02, Comm. for the Evaluation of Unification Policy, Ministry of Unification 2001–02; non-exec. mem. Nat. Labor Relations Comm. 1997–98, 1999–2002; Adviser Constitutional Court of Korea 2003–, Presidential Advisory Council on Korea Unification 2003–05; mem. Bd of Dirs Samsung Dream Scholarship Foundation; mem. Bd Korea Dialogue Acad. 2003–, Korea Advanced Inst. of Science and Tech. 2003–, Sungkok Acad. and Cultural Foundation 2004–, Korea Inst. of Science and Tech. 2004–, I-Sang Yoon Peace Foundation 2005–, Korea Research Foundation 2005–; mem. Commrs Bd Korea Independent Comm. against Corruption 2004–; mem. Presidential Cttee on Judicial Reform 2005–, Prosecutor's Office Policy Advisory Bd 2005–. *Publications:* Women Labor Law 1985, A Research on Fundamental Rights of Labor 1985, Labor Law and Labor Campaigns 1987, The Overcoming of the Division of the Korean Peninsula, and Korean Women Emancipation Campaigns 1989, Law and Women Studies 1989, Law and Modern Society 1992, Law and Social Justice 1992, A Research on Labor Law Cases – Cases on Labor Union Campaigns 1995, Human Rights of Labor and the Law of Labor 1996, An Introduction to Korean Law 1998, The Historical Development of Korean Labor Legislations 1999, The Globalization and Workers' Rights of Labor 2002. *Address:* Ewha Woman's University, 52, Ewhayeodae-gil, Seodaemun-gu, Seoul 120-750, Republic of Korea (office). *Telephone:* (2) 3277-2114 (office). *Fax:* (2) 393-5903 (office). *E-mail:* irshin@ewha.ac.kr (office). *Website:* www .ewha.ac.kr (office).

SHIN, Kyuk-ho; South Korean business executive; *Chairman, Lotte Group;* b. 4 Oct. 1922, Ulsan, S Kyungsang Prov.; m.; three c.; ed Waseda Univ.; went to Japan

1941 to study while working as paper boy and milk boy; est. factory to manufacture cutting oil 1944, factory destroyed in World War II; f. Lotte Group (maker of bubble gum), Japan 1948, Chair. –2010, Pres. –2011, currently mem. Bd of Dirs; f. Lotte Confectionery Co. Ltd 1967, now a leading food and leisure group spanning hotels, confectionary and an amusement park; Standing Dir Lotte Shopping Co. Ltd 2009–; currently also Chair. Lotte Chilsung Beverage Co. Ltd, Canon Korea Business Solutions Inc. *Address:* Lotte Confectionery Co. Ltd, 23, 4-ga, Yangpyeong-dong, Yeongdeungpo-gu, Seoul, Republic of Korea (office). *Telephone:* (2) 670-6114 (office). *Fax:* (2) 6672-6600 (office). *Website:* www.lotte.com (office); www.lottetown.com (office).

SHIN, Kyung-sook; South Korean writer; b. 1963, Jeong-eup, Jeolla Prov.; m.; ed Seoul Inst. of the Arts; Today's Young Artist Award from Ministry of Culture and Sports, Dong-in Literary Award (for When Will He Come) 1997, 21st Century Literary Prize (for The Place Where He Doesn't Know) 2000, Yi Sang Literature Prize (for Buseok Temple) 2001, Oh Young-soo Literary Prize (for Linden Tree in Front of the Castle Gate) 2006. *Publications include:* novels: Deep Sorrow 1994, A Lone Room (Manhae Literature Prize 1996, Prix de l'Inapercu 2009) 1995, The Train Departs at 7 1999, Violet 2001, Yi Jin 2007, Please Look After Mom (Man Asian Literary Prize 2012) 2009, Somewhere A Phone Is Ringing For Me, 2010; novella: Winter Fables (Munye Joongang New Author Prize) 1985; short story collections: Until It Turns into River 1990, Where the Harmonium Once Stood 1992, Potato Eaters 1997, Strawberry Fields 2000, The Sound of Bells 2003; non-fiction: Beautiful Shade 1995, Sleep, Sorrow 2003. *Address:* Barbara J. Zitwer Agency, 525 West End Avenue, Suite 11H, New York, NY 10024, USA (office). *E-mail:* bjzitwerag@aol.com (office). *Website:* www.barbarajzitweragency.com (office).

SHIN, Yoshiaki; Japanese business executive; *Chairman, Mitsui Sumitomo Insurance Group Holdings, Inc.;* Sr Man. Dir and Sr Exec. Officer, Mitsui Sumitomo Insurance Group Holdings, Inc. –2006, Rep. Dir, Pres. and Co-CEO 2006–08, Chair. 2008–. *Address:* Mitsui Sumitomo Insurance Group Holdings, Inc., 27-2 Shinkawa 2-chome, Chuo-ku, Tokyo 104-8252, Japan (office). *Telephone:* (3) 3297-1111 (office). *Fax:* (3) 3297-6888 (office). *E-mail:* info@msig.com (office). *Website:* www.msig.com (office); www.ms-ins.com (office).

SHIN, Young-soo, MD; South Korean health official and international organization official; *Regional Director for the Western Pacific, World Health Organization;* b. 15 Oct. 1943, Seoul; m.; one s. two d.; ed Coll. of Medicine, Seoul Nat. Univ., School of Public Health, Yale Univ., USA; began career as Research Asst in Preventive Medicine, Coll. of Medicine, Seoul Nat. Univ., becoming Prof. of Health Policy and Man. 1978–; three years as medical officer in Korean Navy; several positions with Ministry of Health and Welfare in 1990s, including Pres., Korea Inst. of Health Services Man. 1999–2002, Dir Nat. Health Insurance Review and Assessment Service 2002–03; mem. WHO Exec. Bd as rep. from Repub. of Korea 1995–98, Dir Regional Office for W Pacific, WHO 2009–; Pres. Korean Soc. of Preventive Medicine 2005–06, Korean Soc. of Quality Assurance in Health Care 2006–08; Nat. Order of Merit, Moran Medal 2003. *Address:* World Health Organization Regional Office for the Western Pacific, PO Box 2932, Manila 1000, Philippines (office). *Telephone:* (2) 528-8001 (office). *Fax:* (2) 521-1036 (office); (2) 526-0279 (office). *E-mail:* pio@wpro.who.int (office). *Website:* www.wpro.who.int (office).

SHINDE, Sushilkumar Sambhaji Rao, BA, LLB; Indian politician and lawyer; *Minister of Home Affairs;* b. 4 Sept. 1941, Solapur, Maharashtra; s. of Sambhaji Rao Shinde and Sakhubai Shinde; m. Ujwala Shinde; three d.; ed Law Coll., Pune, Sangameshwar and Dayanand Coll., Solapur, Shivaji Univ., Kolhapur, New Law Coll., Univ. of Mumbai; Boy Peon, then Court Peon and then Court Clerk, Sessions Court Solapur 1956–65; officer Mumbai Police Crime Investigation Dept 1965–71; mem. Rajya Sabha 1992–98, 2006–; elected to Lok Sabha 1998, re-elected 1999, 2009; fmr Minister of Finance and Planning, of Industry, of Urban Devt and of Youth and Social Welfare, Maharashtra; Chief Minister of Maharashtra 2003–04; Gov. of Andhra Pradesh 2004–06 (resgnd); Minister of Power 2006–12, of Home Affairs 2012–; mem. Congress Party; Nat. Citizens Award 1993, 1994. *Leisure interests:* reading, travelling. *Address:* Ministry of Home Affairs, North Block, Central Secretariat, New Delhi 110 001 (office); 19, Ashok Nagar, Jai-Jui, Vijapur Road, Solapur, 413 001, India (home). *Telephone:* (11) 23092011 (office). *Fax:* (11) 23093750 (office). *E-mail:* skshinde@sansad.nic.in (office). *Website:* www.mha.nic .in (office).

SHINDO, Yoshitaka, BA; Japanese politician; *Minister of Internal Affairs;* b. 20 Jan. 1958, Kawaguchi, Saitama Pref.; ed Meiji Univ.; worked in city planning, Kawaguchi Municipal Office 1980–90; mem. Kawaguchi Municipal Ass. 1991–95; mem. House of Reps (lower house of Parl.) for 2nd District, Saitama Pref. (LDP) 1996–2003, 2005–, Chair. Cttee on Audit and Oversight of Admin 2011; Vice-Minister for Internal Affairs and Communications 2001–02, for Foreign Affairs 2002, Minister of Economy, Trade and Industry 2007, Minister for Internal Affairs and Communications, for Regional Revitalization and for Regional Govt (Doshu-Sei), and Minister of State for Decentralization Reform 2012–; Dir LDP Nat. Defence Div. 2005, Chair. Cttee on Orgs Involved with Land Devt and Construction 2006. *Address:* Ministry of Internal Affairs and Communications, 2-1-2, Kasumigaseki, Chiyoda-ku, Tokyo 100-8926, Japan (office). *Telephone:* (3) 5253-5111 (office). *Fax:* (3) 3504-0265 (office). *Website:* www.soumu.go.jp (office).

SHINEFIELD, Henry Robert, BA, MD; American pediatrician and vaccine researcher; *Clinical Professor of Pediatrics and of Dermatology, University of California, San Francisco;* b. 11 Oct. 1925, Paterson, NJ; s. of Louis Shinefield and Sarah Shinefield (née Kaplan); m. Jacquelline Walker 1983; one s. three d.; ed Columbia Univ.; Asst Resident Pediatrician, New York Hosp. (Cornell) 1950–51, Pediatrician Outpatients 1953–59, Instructor in Pediatrics 1959–60, Asst Prof. 1960–64, Assoc. Prof. 1964–65; Chief of Pediatrics, Kaiser-Permanente Medical Center, San Francisco 1965–89, Chief Emer. 1989–; Co-Dir Kaiser Permanente Pediatric Vaccine Study Center, Calif.; currently Adjunct Investigator, Div. of Research, Kaiser Permanente N Calif.; Assoc. Clinical Prof. of Pediatrics, Univ. of Calif., San Francisco 1966–68, Clinical Prof. of Pediatrics 1968–, Clinical Prof. of Dermatology 1970–; mem. Inst. of Medicine, NAS 1980, American Bd of Pediatrics; Fellow, American Acad. of Pediatrics. *Leisure interests:* skiing, tennis, travel. *Address:* Kaiser Permanente, 4131 Geary Boulevard, San Francisco, CA 94118

(office); 2705 Larkin Street, San Francisco, CA 94109, USA (home). *Telephone:* (415) 202-3597 (office); (415) 771-5372 (home). *E-mail:* henry.shinefield@kp.org (office). *Website:* www.dermatology.ucsf.edu (office).

SHINKAI, Seiji, BS, PhD; Japanese chemist and professor of chemistry; *Professor, Sojo University;* b. 5 July 1944, Fukuoka; ed Kyushu Univ.; Lecturer, Kyushu Univ., Fukuoka City 1972, Asst Prof. 1975–87, Prof. 1988–2008, Prof. Emer. 2008–, Leader, Kyushu Univ. Centre of Excellence (COE) Project 'Design and Control of Advanced Molecular Assembly Systems' 1998–2002, 21st Century COE Project 'Functional Innovation of Molecular Informatics' 2002–06; Asst Prof., Nagasaki Univ. 1976; currently Prof. Sojo Univ.; Project Leader, Research Devt Corpn of Japan/Exploratory Research for Advanced Tech. Project (ERATO) 'Shinkai Chemirecognics Project', Kawaguchi City 1990–95; Research Dir Japan Science and Tech. Corpn/Int. Collaboration Project (ICORP) 'Chemotransfiguration' 1997–2001, Japan Science and Tech. Corpn/Solution Oriented Research for Science and Tech. (SORST) 'Gene Manipulators Based on the Polysaccharide-Polynucleotide Interactions' 2002–04; Pres. Inst. of Systems, Information Technologies and Nanotechnologies; mem. Editorial Bd Bioorganic Chemistry 1986–, Journal of the Chemical Society, Perkin Transactions 1992–2001, Supramolecular Chemistry 1992–, Nanotechnology 1993–, Current Opinion in Chemical Biology 1997–, Angewandte Chemie 1999–, European Journal of Organic Chemistry 2000–; Postdoctoral Fellow, Dept of Chem., Univ. of California, Santa Barbara, USA 1972–74; Chemical Soc. of Japan Award for Advanced Research 1978, Soc. of Polymer Science Award 1985, Izatt-Christensen Int. Award, ISMC Cttee 1998, Backer Lecture Award, Univ. of Groningen 1999, Vielberth Lectureship Award, Univ. of Regensburg 2002, named Thomson Reuters Citation Laureate in Chemistry 2003. *Publications:* more than 750 articles in scientific journals and more than 131 book chapters and reviews on host/guest chem., molecular recognition, liquid crystals/organic gelators, sugar sensing/sugar-based combinatorial chem., polysaccharide-polynucleotide interactions, sol-gel transcription and inorganic combinatorial chem. *Address:* Sojo University, 4-22-1 Ikeda, Kumamoto 860 (office); Department of Chemistry and Biochemistry, Kyushu University, Graduate School of Engineering, 6-10-1 Hakozaki, Higashi-ku, Fukuoka-shi, Fukuoka 819-0395, Japan (office). *Telephone:* (96) 326 3111 (Kumamoto) (office); (92) 642-3583 (Fukuoka) (office). *Fax:* (96) 326 3000 (Kumamoto) (office); (92) 642-3611 (Fukuoka) (office). *E-mail:* seijitcm@mbox.nc.kyushu-u.ac.jp (office). *Website:* www.sojo-u.ac.jp (office); www.kyushu-u.ac.jp (office).

SHINMACHI, Toshiyuki; Japanese airline executive; *Resident Adviser, Japan Airlines (JAL) International Co. Ltd;* b. 20 Jan. 1943; ed Gakushuin Univ.; joined Japan Airlines Corpn 1965, Deputy Dir Cargo Export, Tokyo Regional Cargo Sales Office 1987–88, Dir 1988–89, Regional Man. Cargo Sales, New York Regional Cargo Sales Office 1989–91, Gen. Man., Admin, JAL Cargo 1991–93, Vice-Pres. JAL Cargo, Tokyo Regional Cargo Sales Office 1993–95, Vice-Pres. JAL Cargo Sales, Japan Region 1995–97, Sr Vice-Pres. Japan Airlines 1997–2000, mem. Bd of Dirs 1997–, Man. Dir 2000–01, Sr Man. Dir 2001–03, Sr Man. Dir Japan Airlines System Corpn 2002–03, Exec. Vice-Pres. Japan Airlines and Japan Airlines System Corpn 2003–04, Pres. Japan Airlines and Japan Airlines Corpn 2004–05, CEO JAL Group 2005–06, Chair. JAL Group 2006–08 (retd), Resident Adviser, JAL International Co. Ltd 2008–. *Address:* Japan Airlines International Co. Ltd, 4-11, Higashi-shinagawa 2-chome, Shinagawa-ku, Tokyo 140-8637, Japan (office). *Telephone:* (3) 5460-6600 (office). *E-mail:* info@jal.com (office). *Website:* www.jal .com/en/corporate/gaiyo/gaiyo_i.html (office).

SHINODA, Masahiro; Japanese fmr film director and fmr screenwriter; b. 9 March 1931, Gifu Pref.; m. Shima Iwashita 1967; ed Waseda Univ., Tokyo; started career as Asst Dir, Ofuna Studio, Shochiku 1953; worked as asst to Ozu 1957; directing career 1960–2003 (retd); Izumi Kyōka Prize 2010. *Films:* as dir: Koi no katamichi kippu (One-Way Ticket for Love) 1960, Kawaita mizummi (Dry Lake) 1960, Yuhi ni akai ore no kao (My Face Red in the Sunset) 1961, Waga koi no tabiji (Epitaph to My Love) 1961, Watakushi-tachi no kekkon (Our Marriage) 1961, Shamisen to otobai (Love Old and New or Shamisen and Motorcycle) 1961, Namida o shishi no tategami ni (Tears on the Lion's Mane) 1962, Yama no sanka: moyuru wakamono tachi (Glory on the Summit: Burning Youth) 1962, Kawaita hana (Pale Flower) 1964, Ansatsu (The Assassin) 1964, Utsukushisa to kanashimi to (With Beauty and Sorrow, UK) 1965, Ibun sarutobi sasuke (Samurai Spy) 1965, Shokei no shima (Punishment Island) 1966, Akane-gumo (Clouds at Sunset, USA) 1967, Shinjû: Ten no amijima (Double Suicide) 1969, Buraikan (The Scandalous Adventures of Buraikan) 1970, Chinmoku (Silence) 1971, Sapporo Orinpikku (Sapporo Winter Olympics) 1972, Kaseki no mori (The Petrified Forest) 1973, Himiko 1974, Sakura no mori no mankai no shita (Under the Cherry Blossoms) 1975, Hanre Goze Orin (Ballad of Orin, USA, Melody in Gray) 1977, Yashagaike (Demon Pond) 1979, Akuryo-To (Akuryo Island) 1981, Setouchi shonen yakyu dan (MacArthur's Children) 1984, Yari no gonza (Gonza the Spearman) (Silver Bear Award, Berlin) 1986, Maihime (The Dancer) 1989, Shonen jidai (Childhood Days) (several prizes at Japanese Acad. Awards) 1990, Sharaku 1995, Setouchi munraito serenade (Setouchi Moonlight Serenade) 1997, Fukuro no shiro (Owls' Castle, USA) 1999, Spy Sorge 2003; screenplays: Waga koi no tabiji (Epitaph to My Love) 1961, Watakushi-tachi no kekkon (Our Marriage) 1961, Namida o shishi no tategami ni (Tears on the Lion's Mane) 1962, Kawaita hana (Pale Flower) 1964, Shinjû: Ten no amijima (Double Suicide) 1969, Himiko 1974, Hanre Goze Orin (Ballad of Orin, USA or Melody in Gray) 1977, Maihime (The Dancer) 1989, Sharaku 1995, Spy Sorge 2003; Music for the Movies: Tom Takemitsu (as himself) 1994.

SHINOHARA, Yoshiko; Japanese business executive; *President, Tempstaff Co. Ltd;* b. Kanagawa Pref.; ed Takagi High School of Commerce, studied languages and secretarial skills in Switzerland and UK; with Mitsubishi Heavy Industries Ltd 1953–57; spent time in Japan before moving to Australia in 1971; joined P.R.S.A. Inc. (marketing co.) as asst to Pres. 1971–73; Founder, Rep. Dir and Pres. Tempstaff Co. Ltd 1973–; mem. Exec. Council Japan Staffing Business Asscn 1986–; Dir Health Insurance Soc. for Temporary Workers; Flower Award, 14th Econ. Awards 1989, Veuve Clicquot Business Woman of the Year 1992, Venture of The Year in Female Entrepreneurs 1993, one of 50 World-Class Executives 1996, selected by Nat. Foundation for Women Business Owners as one of Leading Women Entrepreneurs of the World 1997, Harvard Business School's Business Stateswoman of the Year 2001, ranked by Fortune magazine amongst the 50 Most

Powerful Women in Business outside the US (30th) 2001, (28th) 2002, (39th) 2003, (34th) 2004, (38th) 2005, (36th) 2006, (39th) 2007, (45th) 2008, (35th) 2009, (37th) 2010, (36th) 2011, ranked by Financial Times amongst Women at the Top (8th) 2009, (7th) 2010. *Address:* Tempstaff Co. Ltd, Shinjuku Maynds Tower, 2-1-1, Yoyogi, Shibuya-ku, Tokyo 151-0053, Japan (office). *Telephone:* (3) 5350-1212 (office). *Fax:* (3) 5350-1219 (office). *Website:* www.tempstaff.co.jp (office).

SHINSEKI, Gen. (retd) Eric Ken, BS, MA; American army officer (retd) and government official; *Secretary of Veterans Affairs;* b. 28 Nov. 1942, Lihue, Kauai, Hawaii; m. Patricia Shinseki; two c.; ed US Mil. Acad., Duke Univ., Nat. War Coll., Fort Lesley J. McNair, Washington, DC; commissioned 2nd Lt in US Army 1965, Forward Observer B battery 2nd Battalion, 9th Artillery, 3rd Brigade, 25th Infantry Div., Viet Nam 1965–66; Asst S1 Base Defense Command, XXIV Corps, Viet Nam 1969–70, Commdr A Troop, 3rd Squadron, 5th Cavalry, 9th Infantry Div., Viet Nam 1970 Personnel Staff Officer US Army Pacific, Fort Shafter, Hawaii 1971–74, Instructor, Dept of English, US Mil. Acad., West Point 1976–78, Commdr 3rd Squadron, 7th Cavalry, 3rd Infantry Div. then Asst Chief of Staff, G-3, US Army Europe and 7th Army, Germany 1982–85, Commdr 2nd Brigade, 3rd Infantry Div. then Asst Chief of Staff G3 VII Corps, US Army Europe and 7th Army 1987–90, Deputy Chief of Staff, Admin/Logistics, Allied Land Forces, Southern Europe, Germany 1990–92, Asst Div. Commdr, 3rd Infantry Div., US Army and 7th Army Europe, Germany 1992–93, Commanding Gen. 1st Cavalry Div., Fort Hood, Tex. 1994–95, Asst Deputy Chief of Staff for operations and plans then Deputy Chief of Staff, US Army, Washington, DC 1995–97, Commdr in Chief and Commdr Stabilization Force, US Army Europe and 7th Army in Bosnia-Herzegovina 1997–98, Vice Chief of Staff, Washington, DC 1998–99, Chief of Staff 1999–2003 (retd); Sec. of Veterans Affairs, Washington, DC 2009–; Defense Distinguished Service Medal, Distinguished Service Medal, Legion of Merit with oak leaf cluster, Bronze Star with V device with three oak leaf clusters, Purple Heart with oak leaf cluster, Meritorious Service Medal with two oak leaf clusters, Air Medal, Army Commendation Medal with oak leaf cluster, Army Achievement Medal. *Address:* Department of Veterans Affairs, 810 Vermont Ave, NW, Washington, DC 20420, USA (office). *Telephone:* (202) 273-6000 (office). *Website:* www.va.gov (office).

SHINYO, Takahiro, PhD; Japanese political scientist, academic and diplomatist; b. 11 Jan. 1950, Kagawa; ed Faculty of Law, Osaka Univ., Univ. of Göttingen, Germany; joined Ministry of Foreign Affairs 1972, int. law studies 1973–75, served at Embassies in Berne, Beijing and Bonn 1975–89, Head of Div. for Disarmament and later for UN Policy, Ministry of Foreign Affairs 1989–93, Minister, Embassy in Berlin 1996–99, Deputy Dir-Gen., European and Oceanian Affairs Bureau, Ministry of Foreign Affairs 1999–2001, Deputy Dir-Gen., European Affairs Bureau 2001–02, Consul-Gen. in Düsseldorf, Germany Jan. 2002, Amb. and Dir-Gen., Global Issues Dept, Ministry of Foreign Affairs Jan. 2005, Amb. and Deputy Perm. Rep. to UN 2006–09, Amb. to Germany 2009–12; Visiting Prof., Ritsumeikan Univ., Kyoto 1992–95, Grad. School, Tokyo Univ. 2000–01; Prof., Osaka School of Int. Public Policy, Osaka Univ. 1993–96. *Publications:* Shin Kokuren Ron (New UN Theory) 1995, Kokusai Heiwa Kyoryoku Nyumon (Introduction to International Peace Co-operation) (ed.) 1995, Atarashii Kokusai Chitsujo wo Motomete (Looking for a New World Order) (co-author) 1994, Yobou Gaikou (Preventive Diplomacy) (co-author) 1996, Kokusai Kiki to Nihongaikou (International Crisis and Japanese Diplomacy) 2005. *Address:* c/o Embassy of Japan, Hiroshimastraße 6, 10785 Berlin, Germany.

SHIOKAWA, Masajuro; Japanese politician; *Chancellor, Toyo University;* b. 13 Oct. 1921, Fuse City (now Higashi-Osaka City), Osaka Pref.; ed Keio Univ.; f. Mitsuaki Corpn 1946; public official, Fuse City Govt 1964–66, directed the merger to form Higashi-Osaka 1966; mem. House of Reps for Osaka 4th Dist 1967–96, 2000–03; Parl. Vice-Minister of Int. Trade and Industry 1972–73; Deputy Chief Cabinet Sec. 1976–77, Chair. Commerce and Industry Cttee 1979–80; Minister of Transport 1980–81, of Educ. 1986–87; Chief Cabinet Sec. 1989; Minister of Home Affairs 1991–92, of Finance 2001–03 (resgnd); mem. LDP, Sec.-Gen. 1995, fmr Deputy Chair. Gen. Council; fmr Pres. Toyo Univ., currently Chancellor; Dir Kansai Shogi Hall; active within the Japan Sumo Asscn. *Address:* c/o Office of the President, Toyo University, 28-20 Hakusan 5-chome, Bunkyo-ku, Tokyo 112-8606, Japan (office).

SHIOZAKI, Yasuhisa, MPA; Japanese politician; *Chairman, Press Bureau, Liberal Democratic Party;* b. 7 Nov. 1950; m.; two s.; ed Univ. of Tokyo, John F. Kennedy School of Govt, Harvard Univ.; with Bank of Japan 1975–86; Political Asst to Minister of State for Econ. Planning Agency 1982–83, to Minister of State for Man. and Coordination Agency 1990; mem. House of Reps (Ehime 1st Dist) 1993–95, 2000–, apptd Dir Standing Cttee on Judicial Affairs 2001, Chair. Standing Cttee on Judicial Affairs 2004–05, apptd Dir Cttee on Budget 2010; mem. House of Councillors (Ehime Dist) 1995–2000, apptd Dir Standing Cttee on the Budget 1996, Standing Cttee on Audit 1996–97, Chief Dir Standing Cttee on Justice 1999–2000; Parl. Vice-Minister of Finance 1997–98; Sr Vice-Minister for Foreign Affairs 2005–06; Chief Cabinet Sec. and Minister of State for the Abduction Issue 2006–07; Chair. LDP Judicial Affairs Div., Policy Research Council (PRC) 1999–2000, Foreign Affairs Div. 2000–01, Treasury and Finance Div. 2002–03, apptd Deputy Chair. LDP PRC 2003, LDP Party Reform and Task Force HQ, Man. Admin. Reform HQ, Vice-Chair. Research Cttee on the Financial Issues, Chair. Sub-cttee on Int. NGOs, Sub-cttee on Corp. Accounting, Sub-cttee on Commercial Law, Man. Research Cttee on the Tax System, PRC, Chair. Press Bureau 2011–; Sec.-Gen. Japan-Thailand Parliamentarians' Friendship League, Japan-Singapore Parliamentarians' Friendship League, Japan-US Parliamentarians' Friendship League; Pres. KSG Club of Japan. *Address:* Liberal-Democratic Party (Jiyu-Minshuto), 1-11-23, Nagata-cho, Chiyoda-ku, Tokyo 100-8910, Japan (office). *Telephone:* (3) 3581-6211 (office). *E-mail:* koho@ldp.jimin.or.jp (office); shiozaki@y-shiozaki.or.jp (home). *Website:* www.jimin.jp (office); www.y-shiozaki.or.jp.

SHIPLEY, Rt Hon. Dame Jennifer Mary (Jenny), DNZM, FNZIM; New Zealand politician, company director, consultant and fmr prime minister; *Managing Director, Jenny Shipley NZ Ltd;* b. (Jennifer Mary Robson), 4 Feb. 1952, Gore; d. of Leanord Cameron Robson and Adele Doreen Goodall; m. Burton Shipley 1973; one s. one d.; fmr primary school teacher; farming partnership 1973–88; joined Nat. Party 1975; fmr Malvern Co. Councillor; MP for Ashburton (now

Rakaia) 1987–; Minister of Social Welfare 1990–93 and of Women's Affairs 1990–98, of Health 1993–96, of State Services 1996–97, also of State Owned Enterprises, of Transport, of Accident Rehabilitation and Compensation Insurance, Minister Responsible for Radio New Zealand; Minister in Charge of NZ Security Intelligence Service 1997–99; Prime Minister of NZ 1997–99; Leader of the Opposition 1999–2001; Man. Dir Jenny Shipley NZ Ltd; Chair. Genesis Energy, SMI; mem. Bd of Dirs China Construction Bank, ISI, Momentum, Mainzeal Group Ltd –2013; Vice-Pres. Club of Madrid; mem. World Women's Leaders' Council; Fellow, NZ Inst. of Man.; Dame Companion, NZ Order of Merit. *Leisure interests:* family, int. affairs, gardening, sailing. *Address:* PO Box 6636, Auckland, New Zealand (home). *Telephone:* (9) 358-5360 (office). *E-mail:* jenny@jsnz.com (office). *Website:* www.national.org.nz (office).

SHIPLEY, Walter Vincent, BS; American business executive (retd); b. 2 Nov. 1935, Newark, NJ; s. of Linwood Parks Shipley and Emily Shipley (née Herzog); m. Judith Ann Lyman 1957; one s. four d.; ed Williams Coll., New York Univ.; with Chemical Bank 1956–96, Exec. Vice-Pres. Int. Div., New York 1978–79, Sr Exec. Vice-Pres. –1981, Pres. 1982–83, Chair. Bd 1983–92, Pres., COO 1992–93, Chair., CEO 1994–96; Chair. Chase Manhattan Banking Co. 1996–99, CEO 1996–99 (after merger of Chomzal Banking Corpn with Chase Manhattan Corpn); retd 2000; mem. Bd of Dirs Wallace Foundation 1991–2007, Chair. 2002–07; fmr Dir Lincoln Center for the Performing Arts Inc., now Dir Emer.; mem. Bd of Dirs Japan Soc. New York City Partnership Inc., New York Chamber of Commerce and Industry, Goodwill Industries of Greater New York Inc., United Way of Tri-State, Verizon New York Inc. (fmrly New York Telephone Co.), Wallace-Reader's Digest Funds (also mem. Advisory Bd), Bell Atlantic Corpn; mem. Business Council, Business Roundtable, Council for Foreign Relations, Pilgrims of US, English-Speaking Union; fmr Trustee, American Museum of Natural History.

SHIRAISHI, Takashi, PhD; Japanese economist and academic; *Professor Emeritus, Keio University;* b. 1921, Tokyo; m. Toshiko Shiraishi; one d.; ed Keio Univ., Harvard Business School; Lecturer, Keio Univ. 1947–49, Asst Prof. 1949–58, Prof. 1958–86, Vice-Pres. 1965–77, Dean, Faculty of Business and Commerce 1975–77, Prof. Emer. 1986–; Prin. Keio High School 1964–65; Dean Faculty of Social Sciences, Kyorin Univ. 1984–92; Dir Japan Soc. of Int. Econs 1974–; Dir and Pres. Union of Nat. Econ. Asscns in Japan 1975–90; mem. Int. Exchange Program Cttee of Japan Soc. for the Promotion of Science 1982–84; mem. Exec. Cttee, Int. Econ. Asscn 1984–89. *Publications:* Economic Development and Direct Investment 1978, History of Economic Growth and Policy of Japan since the Second World War 1983, Japan's Trade Policies 1989, Reformation of World Economy and Japan 1991, History of Japan's Machine Export 1992, New Age of Asia and Japan 1993, Foreign Exchange Rates and the Japanese Economy 1996. *Address:* 1-19-10, Jiyugaoka, Meguroku, Tokyo, Japan. *Telephone:* (3) 3717-7118.

SHIRAKAWA, Hideki, BS, PhD; Japanese scientist and professor of chemistry; *Professor Emeritus, Institute of Materials Science, University of Tsukuba;* b. 20 Aug. 1936, Tokyo; s. of Hatsutaroo Shirakawa and Fuyuno Shirakawa; m. Chiyoko Shibuya 1966; two s.; ed Tokyo Inst. of Tech.; Asst Chemical Resources Laboratory, Tokyo Inst. of Tech. 1966; pioneered work on conductive polymers; Assoc. Prof., Inst. of Materials Science, Univ. of Tsukuba 1979–82, Prof. 1982–2000, Prof. Emer. 2000–, Chair Master's School in Sciences and Eng, Grad. School 1991–93; Provost 3rd Cluster of Colls 1994–97; elected mem. Council for Science and Tech. Policy, Japanese Cabinet Office 2001; Soc. of Polymer Science Award, Japan 1983, Award for Distinguished Service in Advancement of Polymer Science, Soc. of Polymer Science 2000, Nobel Prize for Chem. (jt recipient) 2000, Person of Cultural Merits 2000, Special Award, Chemical Soc. of Japan 2001. *Address:* Institute of Materials Science, University of Tsukuba, 1-1-1 Ten-nodai, Tsukuba, Ibaraki 305-8573, Japan (office). *Telephone:* (298) 53-2111 (office). *Fax:* (298) 53-6012 (office). *E-mail:* hideki@ims.tsukuba.ac.jp (office). *Website:* www.ims.tsukuba.ac.jp/Eng/Eims .html (office).

SHIRAKAWA, Masaaki, BA, MA; Japanese fmr central banker; b. 27 Sept. 1949, Kitakyushu; ed Univ. of Tokyo, Univ. of Chicago, USA; joined Nippon Ginko (Bank of Japan) 1972, held various positions including Dir and Head of Financial System 1990–93, Head of Planning Div., Policy Planning Dept 1993–94, Gen. Man. Oita Br. 1994–95, Gen. Man. for Americas, New York 1995–96, Deputy Dir-Gen. Inst. for Monetary and Econ. Studies 1996–97, Deputy Dir-Gen. Int. Dept 1997, Adviser to Gov. Credit and Market Man. Dept 1997, Adviser to Gov. Financial Markets Dept 1998, Adviser to Gov. Policy Planning Dept 2000–02, Exec. Dir 2002–06, Deputy Gov. 2008, Gov. 2008–13 (resgnd); Prof., Kyoto Univ. School of Govt 2006–08; Chevalier, Legion d'honneur 2012; ranked by Forbes magazine amongst The World's Most Powerful People (26th) 2009, (38th) 2010, (36th) 2011, (40th) 2012, included in the 50 Most Influential ranking of Bloomberg Markets Magazine 2011. *Publications include:* numerous papers on Japanese monetary policy. *Address:* c/o Nippon Ginko (Bank of Japan), 2-1-1, Hongoku-cho, Nihonbashi, Chuo-ku, Tokyo 103-8660, Japan.

SHIRDON, Abdi Farah, BEcons; Somali politician, economist and business executive; b. 1958, Dhusamareb, central Galguduud region; m. Asha Haji Elmi; four c.; ed Somali Nat. Univ.; briefly worked as economist at Ministry of Finance and Ministry of Agric. during Siad Barre admin 1983–85; left govt to pursue business career; est. Shirdon International and served as CEO; moved to Nairobi, Kenya following outbreak of civil war in Somalia 1991 and est. import-export business; Co-founder Rajo Forum (Somali civil society inst.), Chair. 2012–; Prime Minister of Somalia 2012–13; Ind. *Address:* c/o Office of the Prime Minister, 1 Villa Somalia, 2525 Mogadishu, Somalia.

SHIRE, Bare Adan; Somali politician; commdr Marehan Somali National Front during civil war; fmr Minister of Reconstruction and Resettlement and fmr Minister of Defence in Transitional Fed. Govt 2004; Chair. Juba Valley Alliance (JVA) 1998–2006. *Address:* c/o Ministry of Defence, Mogadishu, Somalia.

SHIRINOV, Abdujabbor; Tajikistani mathematician, banker and diplomatist; *Chairman, National Bank of Tajikistan;* b. 20 June 1953, Khatlon region; m.; five c.; ed Tajik State Nat. Univ.; computer programmer, later Head of Dept for Designing Automatic Control Systems, Data-Processing Centre, Tajik State Univ. 1974–92; Chief Engineer, later Dir Settlement Dept, Nat. Bank of Tajikistan 1992–98; Deputy Chair., later First Deputy Chair. Exec. Bd Jt Stock Commerce

Agro-Industrial Investment Bank 1998–2000; Deputy Chair., later First Deputy Chair. Nat. Bank of Tajikistan 2000–06, Chair. 2012–; Chair. State Financial Control Cttee 2006–07; First Deputy Dir Agency for State Finance Control and Struggle Against Corruption 2007; Amb. to USA 2007–12; Honoured Worker of Tajikistan. *Address:* National Bank of Tajikistan (Bonki Millii Tochikiston), 734003 Dushanbe, Xiyoboni Rudaki 107A, Tajikistan (office). *Telephone:* (44) 600-32-01 (office); (44) 600-32-09 (office). *Fax:* (44) 600-32-35 (office). *E-mail:* info@nbt .tj (office). *Website:* www.nbt.tj (office).

SHIRKOV, Dmitrii Vasilevich, PhD, DrSci; Russian physicist; *Honorary Director, Bogoliubov Laboratory of Theoretical Physics, Joint Institute for Nuclear Research;* b. (Dmitry Vasilevich Shirkov), 3 March 1928, Moscow; s. of Vasili Shirkov and Elizaveta Makushina; m. Svetlana Rastopchina 1950; two s. one d.; ed Moscow State Univ., Steklov Math. Inst., Moscow; attached to Inst. of Chemical Physics, Acad. of Sciences, Moscow 1948–50, Sarov (Arzamas-16) Nuclear Weapon Centre 1950–54, Steklov Math. Inst. of Acad. of Sciences, Moscow 1954–58 and Jt Inst. for Nuclear Research, Dubna 1958–60, 1971–; worked at Inst. of Math., Siberian Div. of Acad. of Sciences, Novosibirsk 1960–70; Prof., Univ. of Novosibirsk 1963–69; Nobel Guest Prof., Lund Univ., Sweden 1970–71; Prof., Moscow State Univ. 1972–2001, Prof. Emer. 2001–; Corresp. mem. USSR (now Russian) Acad. of Sciences 1960, mem. 1994; Foreign mem. Saxonian Acad. of Sciences; Hon. Dir Bogoliubov Lab. at Jt Inst. for Nuclear Research; Orders of USSR, Bulgaria and Russian Fed.; USSR Lenin Prize 1958, USSR State Prize 1984, Bogoliubov Gold Medal, Russian Acad. of Sciences 2005. *Publications:* co-author: Introduction to the Theory of Quantized Fields 1957, A New Method in the Theory of Superconductivity 1958, Dispersion Theories of Strong Interactions at Low Energies 1967, Quantum Fields 1980, Theory of Particle Interactions 1986; more than 200 published papers mainly on the theory of fundamental interactions and particles. *Leisure interests:* tourism, skiing, photography. *Address:* Bogoliubov Laboratory of Theoretical Physics, Joint Institute for Nuclear Research, Joliot Curie str. 6, 141980 Dubna, Moscow Region, Russia (office). *Telephone:* (49621) 65088 (office). *Fax:* (49621) 65084 (office). *E-mail:* shirkovd@theor.jinr.ru (office). *Website:* theor .jinr.ru (office).

SHIRLEY, Donna Lee, BA, BS, MS; American aeronautical engineer, academic and consultant; *President, Managing Creativity;* b. 1941, Wynnewood, Okla; m. (divorced); one d.; ed Univ. of Oklahoma, Univ. of Southern California; specifications writer, McDonnell Aircraft, St Louis, Mo. 1963; joined NASA Jet Propulsion Lab. 1966, mission analyst for Mariner 10 mission to Venus and Mercury 1970–74, Energy and Environmental System Man. 1974–79, Task Man. 1979–81, Man. Mission Design Section 1981–82, Man. Space Station Program Office 1982–85, Man. Automation and Robotics Office 1985–87, Man. Rover Concept Team 1987–90, Leader, Surface Transportation Vehicle Systems Eng 1989–91, Man. Exploration Initiative Studies 1990–91, project engineer, Cassini Mission 1991–92; Man. Mars Pathfinder Microrover Flight Experiment 1992–94, Man. Mars Exploration Program 1994–98; Asst Dean of Eng for Advanced Program Devt, Coll. of Eng, Univ. of Oklahoma 1999–2002, now mem. Bd of Visitors; Pres. Managing Creativity (consulting firm) 1997–; Sr Fellow, School of Public Policy, UCLA 1997; NASA Group Achievement Awards, including for Telerobotics Tech. Team 1991 and Pathfinder Mars Rover Devt Team 1997, NASA Outstanding Leadership Medal 1997, Holley Medal for Lifetime Achievement, ASME 1998, Judith Resnick Award, Soc. of Women Engineers 1998, Wernher Von Braun Memorial Award, Nat. Space Soc. 2000, Washington Award for Eng Achievement, Western Engineer Soc. 2000, inducted into Women in Tech. Int. Hall of Fame 1997. *Publication:* Managing Martians – The Extraordinary Story of a Woman's Lifelong Quest to Get to Mars and of the Team Behind the Space Robot That Has Captured the Imagination of the World (memoir) 1998. *Leisure interests:* acting, painting, playing the guitar, sailing. *Address:* Managing Creativity, 1517 Oklahoma Avenue, Norman, OK 73071-0466, USA (office). *Telephone:* (405) 307-0313 (office). *Fax:* (405) 307-0331 (office). *E-mail:* dshirley@earthlink.net (office). *Website:* www.managingcreativity .com (office).

SHIRLEY, George Irving, BEd; American singer (tenor) and academic; *Joseph Edgar Maddy Distinguished University Professor Emeritus of Music (Voice), School of Music, Theatre and Dance, University of Michigan;* b. 18 April 1934, Indianapolis, Ind.; s. of Irving E. Shirley and Daisy Shirley (née Bell); m. Gladys Lee Ishop 1956; one s. one d.; ed Wayne State Univ.; New York City premiere with Amato Opera in Verdi's Aroldo 1961; debuts with Metropolitan Opera, New York Opera, Festival of Two Worlds (Spoleto, Italy), Santa Fé Opera 1961, Teatro Colón, Buenos Aires 1965, La Scala, Milan 1965, Glyndebourne Festival 1966, Royal Opera, Covent Garden, Scottish Opera 1967, Vienna Festival 1972, San Francisco Opera 1977, Chicago Lyric Opera 1977, Théâtre Municipal d'Angers 1979, Edin. Festival 1979, Nat. Opera Ebony, Philadelphia 1980, Spoleto Festival, Charleston, SC 1980, Tulsa Opera, Okla 1980, Ottawa Festival 1981, Deutsche Oper 1983, Guelph Spring Festival 1983, Bregenz Festival, Austria 1998; Glimmerglass Opera, Cooperstown, NY 1999, Eugene Opera, Ore. 2009; Prof. of Voice, Univ. of Maryland 1980–87; Prof. of Music, Univ. of Michigan School of Music, Theatre & Dance 1987–2007, Joseph Edgar Maddy Distinguished Univ. Prof. of Music (Voice) 1992–2007, Prof. Emer. 2007–, also Dir Emer., Vocal Arts Div.; mem. Bd Santa Fe Opera, Sullivan Foundation, Voice Foundation; mem. Univ. of Michigan Soc. of Fellows 1989, American Acad. of Teachers of Singing 1990; Hon. HDH (Wilberforce Univ.) 1967, Hon. LLD (Montclair State Coll.) 1984, Hon. DFA (Lake Forest Coll.) 1988, Hon. DHumLitt (Northern Iowa) 1997; numerous awards including Nat. Arts Club Award 1960, Concorso di Musica e Danza (Vercelli, Italy) 1960, Grammy Award for recording of Mozart's Così fan tutte 1968, Distinguished Scholar-Teacher Award, Univ. of Md 1985–86, Univ. of Mich. School of Music Alumni Asscn Distinguished Achievement Award 2005, Opera Noire Grazioso Award, New York 2005, Dr. Charles H. Wright Legacy Award for Excellence in Fine Arts, Detroit 2006, Nat. Asscn for the Study and Performance of African American Music Trail Blazer Award 2007; various citations from the City of Detroit and State of Mich. *Leisure interests:* golf, sketching and cartoons, photography, writing. *Address:* University of Michigan School of Music, Ann Arbor, MI 48109-2085, USA (office). *Telephone:* (734) 665-7821 (office). *Fax:* (734) 763-5097 (office). *E-mail:* gis@umich .edu (office). *Website:* www.music.umich.edu (office).

SHIRO, Hiruta; Japanese business executive; b. 1942; joined Asahi Kasei Corpn 1964, held several sr positions including Man. Dir, Sr Man. Dir, Exec. Vice-Pres. 2002–03, Pres. 2003–10, also Presidential Exec. Officer of Research and Devt and mem. Group Advisory Cttee, Adviser 2010–, apptd Dir Asahi Chemical Industry Co. Ltd 1998; Special Adviser at Iwato Partners Co., Ltd; mem. Bd of Dirs Olympus Corpn 2012–; fmr Pres. Petrochemical Industry Asscn. *Address:* Asahi Kasei Corporation, Jinbocho-Mitsui Building, 1-105 Kanda Jinbocho, Chiyoda-Ku, Tokyo 101-8101, Japan (office).

SHIRVINDT, Alexander Anatolyevich; Russian actor and screenwriter; *Artistic Director, Moscow Academic Theatre of Satire;* b. 19 July 1934, Moscow; ; m. Natalya Belousova; one s.; ed Shchukin School of Theatre Art; actor, Moscow Theatre of Lenin's Comsomol 1957–70, actor Moscow Academic Theatre of Satire 1957–, Artistic Dir 2000–; teacher, Shchukin School of Theatre Art; mem. Union of Cinematographers; People's Artist of Russia 1989, Order of Merit for the Fatherland, Order of Friendship of Peoples. *Films include:* Grandads-Robbers 1971, Irony of the Fate 1975, Twelve Chairs 1976, Three in a Boat Not to Mention a Dog 1979, A Station for Two 1982, Irony of the Fate 2 2007, Cossack Chieftain Kodr, Come Tomorrow, Major Vikhr, Facts of the Passed Day, Winter Evening in Gagry, Blackmailer, Once Again About Love, Crankies, Imaginary Invalid. *Stage appearances include:* Trigorin (The Seagull), Dobchinsky (The Government Inspector), King Louis (Bondage of Hypocrites), Akhmed Ryza (Crank), Count Almaviva (The Marriage of Figaro), Press Secretary (Burden of Decisions), Molchalin (Misfortune from Intellect), Nehrish (Red Horse with Small Bells), President of the Reportage (Bug). *Plays produced include:* Small Comedies of a Big House, Melancholy, Shut Up, Wake Up and Sing; two-man variety shows with M. Derzhavin. *Leisure interest:* fishing. *Address:* Moscow Academic Theatre of Satire, Triumfalnaya pl. 2, 103050 Moscow (office); Kotelnicheskaya nab. 1/15, korp. A, Apartment 50, 109240 Moscow, Russia (home). *Telephone:* (495) 699-63-05 (office); (495) 916-49-82 (home). *Fax:* (495) 699-36-42 (office). *Website:* www.satire.ru (office).

SHISHKIN, Mikhail Pavlovich; Russian author; b. 18 Jan. 1961, Moscow; ed Moscow State Pedagogical Inst.; journalist for Rovesni 1982–85; teacher of English and German 1985–95; debut as writer with short story Calligraphy Lesson 1993; contrib., Znamya magazine. *Publications:* novels: One Night Befalls Us All 1993, The Taking of Izmail (Russian Booker Prize 2000) 1999, Maidenhair (Big Book Award 2006, Nat. Best-Seller Prize 2006, Int. Literature Award 2011) 2005, Pismovnik 2010, The Light and the Dark 2013; novella: Blind Musician 1994; short stories: Saved Language 2001; non-fiction: Russian Switzerland 2000, Montreux-Missolunghi-Astapovo, in the Steps of Byron and Tolstoy (Prix du Meilleur Livre Étranger 2005) 2002. *Address:* c/o Quercus Books, 55 Baker Street, 7th Floor, South Block, London, W1U 8EW, England (office). *Telephone:* (20) 7291-7200 (office). *E-mail:* enquiries@quercusbooks.co.uk (office). *Website:* www .quercusbooks.co.uk (office).

SHISLER, Arden L.; American insurance industry executive; b. 1941, Massillon, Ohio; ed Dalton High School, Ohio State Univ.; served in US Army; COO K&B Transport Inc. 1986–92, Pres. and CEO 1992–2003, Consultant 2003–04; mem. Bd of Dirs Nationwide Mutual Insurance Co. 1984–2008, Chair. 1992–2008, mem. Bd of Dirs Nationwide Financial Services Inc., Chair. 2003–09, later also Chair. Nationwide Mutual Fire Insurance Co., Nationwide Life Insurance Co.; fmr Pres. Ohio Agricultural Marketing Asscn; mem. Bd of Dirs Ohio 4-H Foundation; mem. Advisory Cttee, Ohio State Univ. Agric. Tech. Inst.; mem. Wayne Co. Farm Bureau, Cornerstone Community Church; Trustee, Aberdeen Select Equity Fund 2000–, Nationwide Variable Insurance Trust 2000–, Nationwide Mutual Funds 2000–, Gartmore Variable Insurance Trust 2000–, Dreyfus Gvit International Value Fund 2000–; fmr Trustee, Aberdeen Funds, Natiowide NVIT Mid Cap Growth Fund, Aberdeen Health Sciences Fund, Gartmore Convertible Fund. *Address:* c/o Nationwide Mutual Insurance Company, 1 Nationwide Plaza, Columbus, OH 43215-2220, USA.

SHIYAM, Maj.-Gen. Ahmed; Maldivian army officer; *Chief of National Defence Force;* m.; one s. three d.; ed Royal Mil. Acad., UK, Nat. Defence Coll., India, Command and Staff Coll., Pakistan; started career as Instructor, Girifushi Training Center, CO of the Unit, Commdt; CO, Defence Inst. for Training and Educ.; joined Nat. Defence Force 1986, CO, Northern Regional HQ, CO, Southern Regional HQ, CO, Regional HQ, Exec. Officer for Chief of Defence Force and Minister of Defence, CO, Electrical and Mechanical Engineers, CO, Support Battalion II, Commdr Rapid Reaction Forces, First Commdt Marine Corps, Nat. Defence Force 2009, Commdr Cen. Area, Second Commdt, Coast Guard 2011–12, Chief of Nat. Defence Force 2012–; Distinguished Service Medal, Presidential Medal, Defence Force Service Medal, Dedicated Service Medal, Good Conduct Medal, Nov. 3rd Medal, Centenary Medal. *Address:* Maldives National Defence Force Headquarters, Bandaarakoshi, Ameer Ahmed Magu, Malé, Maldives (office). *Telephone:* 3322607 (office). *Fax:* 3322496 (office). *E-mail:* media@mndf .gov.mv (office). *Website:* www.mndf.gov.mv (office).

SHKOLNIK, Vladimir Sergeyevich; Kazakhstani mining engineer and politician; *President, Kazatomprom;* b. 17 Feb. 1949, Serpukhov, Moscow Region; m.; two c.; ed Moscow Inst. of Physics and Math.; mem. Kazakhstan Acad. of Sciences; various posts from engineer to Deputy Dir Mangistauz Energy Complex 1973–92; Dir-Gen. Agency of Atomic Energy Repub. of Kazakhstan 1992–94; Minister of Science and New Tech. 1994–96; Minister of Science 1996–99; Pres. Kazakhstan Acad. of Sciences 1996–; Minister of Energy and Mineral Resources 1999–2001, 2005, of Industry and Trade –2007; Vice-Chair. Pres.'s Admin. 2007; Pres. JSC Kazatomprom NAC 2009–. *Address:* Kazatomprom, 480012 Almaty, ul Bogenbai Batyr 168, Kazakhstan (office). *Telephone:* (3272) 67-53-06 (office). *Fax:* (3272) 50-35-41 (office). *E-mail:* nac@kazatomprom.com (office). *Website:* www.kazatomprom .kz (office).

SHMAKOV, Mikhail Viktorovich; Russian trade union official; *Chairman, Federation of Independent Trade Unions of Russia;* b. 12 Aug. 1949, Moscow; m.; one s.; ed Bauman Moscow State Tech. Univ.; engineer in defence industry factories 1972–75, 1977–86; army service 1975–77; Chair. Moscow City Trade Union of Workers in Defence Industry 1986–90; Chair. Moscow City Council of Trade Unions (later transformed into Moscow Fed. of Trade Unions) 1990–93; Chair. Fed. of Ind. Trade Unions of Russia 1993–; Pres. Gen. Confed. of Trade

Unions 2004–; mem. Exec. Bureau and Gen. Council, International Trade Union Confed. 2006–, Pres. Pan-European Regional Council 2007–; Titular mem. Governing Body, ILO 2010–; mem. Organizational Cttee Otechestvo Movt; Order of Honour 1998, Order of Merit for the Fatherland, IV degree 1999, Order of Merit for the Fatherland, III degree 2006; Person of the Year 2009. *Leisure interest:* sports. *Address:* Federation of Independent Trade Unions of Russia, Leninsky Prospekt 42, 119119 Moscow, Russia (office). *Telephone:* (495) 938-73-12 (office). *Fax:* (495) 137-06-94 (office). *E-mail:* shmakov@fnpr.ru (office). *Website:* www.fnpr .ru (office).

SHMAROV, Valery Nikolayevich, PhD; Ukrainian politician; b. 14 Aug. 1945, Zholobi, Vinnitsa; m. Olga Viktorivna Shmarova; one s. one d.; ed Kiev Coll. of Radioelectronics, Kiev State Univ.; radio equipment mechanic, Head of lab., Kiev Radiozavod 1966–72; head of lab., chief of div., chief of workshop, chief of Dept 1973–87, Dir Zhulyany Machine Construction Factory 1987–92; First Deputy Dir-Gen. Nat. Space Agency of Ukraine 1992–93; Deputy Prime Minister on problems of mil.-industrial complex 1993–94; Deputy Prime Minister and Minister of Defence 1994–96; Pres. Asscn of State Aviation Industry Ukraviaprom (Asscn of Aviation Enterprises of Ukraine) 1996–2001; mem. Verhovna Rada (Parl.) 1998–; Dir-Gen. Ukrspetsexport (state co. for export and import of mil. equipment and arms), Kiev 2002–04; Prof., Kiev Int. Univ. of Civil Aviation; mem. Cttee for Nat. Security and Defence 1998; mem. Ukrainian Tech. Acad. *Leisure interests:* history, literature, swimming. *Address:* Bastionna str. 9, 01014 Kiev, Ukraine (office). *Telephone:* (44) 294-81-00 (office); (44) 294-88-49 (home). *Fax:* (44) 294-81-47 (office). *E-mail:* avia@iptelecom.net.ua (office).

SHMATKO, Sergei Ivanovich; Russian politician; *Minister of Energy;* b. 26 Sept. 1966, Stavropol; ed Faculty of Political Economy, Ural State Univ., Mil. Acad., Jt Staff VS of Russia; worked as auditor in BDO Binder 1992–94; Dir RFI GmbH (official rep. of Russian Fed. Property Fund in EU) 1994–95; scientific employee, Inst. of Problems of Investment 1995–97, supervised man. of external relations of All-Russia devt bank of regions; Head of Analytical Centre of Econ. Strategy, Rosenergoatom 1997–99; adviser on econ. strategy to Gen. Dir All-Russian Scientific Research Inst. for Nuclear Power Plant Operation (VNIIAES) 1999–2001; Chair. State fund of conversion 2002–05; adviser to Chair. Gazprom-bank Feb.–June 2005; adviser to Vice-Pres. Atomstroyexport (jt stock co.) Feb.–June 2005, Pres. Atomstroyexport 2005–08; Minister of Energy 2008–. *Address:* Ministry of Energy, 107996 Moscow, ul. Shchepkin 42, Russia (office). *Telephone:* (495) 631-98-58 (office). *Fax:* (495) 631-83-64 (office). *E-mail:* minenergo@ minenergo.gov.ru (office). *Website:* minenergo.gov.ru (office).

SHMELYEV, Nikolai Petrovich, DEcon; Russian economist and author; *Director, Institute of Europe, Russian Academy of Sciences;* b. 18 June 1936, Moscow; s. of Petr Shmelyev and Maria Shmelyeva; m. Gulia Shmelyeva 1965; one d.; ed Moscow Univ.; mem. CPSU 1962–91; researcher, Inst. Econ., USSR Acad. of Sciences 1958–61; Prof., Head of Dept, Inst. of Econ. of World Socialist System (IEMSS), USSR Acad. of Sciences 1961–68, 1970–82; Sr scientific researcher, Inst. of USA and Canada 1982–92; Sr Researcher, Head CIS-Europe Dept, Russian Acad. of Sciences Inst. of Europe 1992–, Dir 2000–; researcher, Slavic Research Centre, Hokkaido Univ., Japan 1995; USSR People's Deputy 1989–91; Corresp. mem. Russian Acad. of Sciences 1994–, mem. 2000–; Lecturer, Stockholm Inst. of Econ. of East European Countries 1992; Lecturer, Middlebury Coll. Vermont, USA 1993. *Publications:* books and articles on econ. problems, World Economic Tendencies, Progress and Contradictions 1987, Advances and Debts 1989, The Turning Point 1990; novels and stories include Pashkov House 1987, Performance for Mr. Prime Minister 1988, Pirosmani 1988, Silvestr 1991, V Puti Ya Zanemog 1995, Bezumnaya Greta 1995, Curriculum Vitae (o sebe) 2001. *Leisure interests:* books, travelling. *Address:* Institute of Europe, 11-3B, Mokhovaya street, 125993 Moscow (office); 3-d Frunzenskaya 7, Apt 61, 119270 Moscow, Russia (home). *Telephone:* (495) 629-45-07 (office); (495) 242-13-06 (home). *Fax:* (495) 629-92-96 (office). *E-mail:* europe@ieras.ru (office); europe_ins@mail.ru (office). *Website:* www.ieras.ru (office).

SHNAIDER, Alexander, BA; Canadian (b. Russian) business executive; *Co-Founder and Director, Midland Group;* b. 1969, Leningrad (now St Petersburg), USSR; m.; three c.; ed York Univ., Toronto; est. steel-trading business in Belgium, expanded business by trading with steel mills in Soviet Union; Co-f. (with Eduard Shifrin) Midland Resources (later Midland Group) 1994, bought large stakes in Zaporizhstal steel mill, Ukraine, nat. electricity grid, Armenia and now has interests in steel, shipping, construction, real estate in Russia, Ukraine and worldwide; Chair. Royal Laser Corpn 2006–; bought Jordan Grand Prix racing team 2005, renamed Midland Racing, sold team 2006; fmr mem. Bd of Dirs Magellan Energy Ltd. *Address:* Midlands Metal International Inc, 259 Yorkland Road, Toronto, ON M2J 5B2, Canada (office). *Telephone:* (416) 733-9500 (office). *Fax:* (416) 733-8306 (office). *E-mail:* info@mrh.gg (office). *Website:* www.midland .gg (office).

SHOCHAT, Avraham, BSc; Israeli construction engineer, company director and fmr politician; b. 14 June 1936, Tel-Aviv; ed Haifa Technion; fmr paratrooper in Israel Defence Forces; Br. Dir Solel Boneh (Histadrut construction co.); Co-f. City of Arad, Mayor of Arad 1967–89, Chair. Citizens' Cttee Arad, Devt Towns Council, Econ. Cttee, Finance Cttee, Deputy Chair. Union of Local Authorities; mem. Knesset (Parl.) 1988–2003; Minister of Finance 1992–96, 1999–2001, of Nat. Infrastructure 2000–01; Chair. Investment Cttee, Israel Infrastructure Fund, IDI Technologies Ltd; mem. Bd of Dirs Alon USA Energy Inc. 2005–, Israel Chemicals Ltd 2006–, Kali Capital Markets Insurance Agency Ltd, Mizrahi Tefahot Bank Ltd 2006–, Direct Insurance Financial Investments Ltd, ICL Fertilizers Ltd, ICL Industrial Products; fmr mem. Bd of Dirs Israel Aircraft Industries, Desalination Engineering; headed Govt Cttee on higher educ. reforms 2007; mem. Labour Party. *Address:* c/o Board of Directors, Mizrahi Tefahot Bank Ltd, 7 Jabotinsky Street, Ramat Gan, 52136, Israel.

SHOCK, Sir Maurice, Kt, MA; British academic; *Honorary Fellow, University College, Oxford;* b. 15 April 1926; s. of Alfred Shock and Ellen Shock; m. Dorothy Donald 1947 (died 1998); one s. three d.; ed King Edward's School, Birmingham and Balliol and St Antony's Colls, Oxford; served in Intelligence Corps 1945–48; Lecturer in Politics, Christ Church and Trinity Coll. Oxford 1955–56; Fellow and Praelector in Politics, Univ. Coll. Oxford 1956–77, currently Hon. Fellow; Estates

Bursar 1959–74; Vice-Chancellor, Univ. of Leicester 1977–87; Rector, Lincoln Coll. Oxford 1987–94, Hon. Fellow 1995; Chair. Nuffield Trust 1988–2003; mem. Franks Comm. of Inquiry into Univ. of Oxford 1964–66; mem. Hebdomadal Council, Univ. of Oxford 1969–75; Chair. Cttee of Vice-Chancellors and Prins 1985–87, Rand Health Bd of Advisors 1999–; mem. Gen. Medical Council 1989–95; Hon. Vice-Pres. Political Studies Asscn 1989, Hon. FRCP 1989; Hon. LLD (Leicester) 1987. *Publications:* The Liberal Tradition; articles on politics and recent history. *Leisure interests:* gardening, theatre. *Address:* University College, Oxford OX1 4BH, England (office). *Telephone:* (1865) 276601 (office). *Fax:* (1865) 276790 (office). *E-mail:* academic.office@univ.ox.ac.uk (office). *Website:* www.univ.ox.ac.uk (office).

SHOEMAKER, Sydney S., BA, PhD, FBA; American academic; *Susan Linn Sage Professor Emeritus of Philosophy, Cornell University;* b. 29 Sept. 1931, Boise, Idaho; s. of Roy Hopkins Shoemaker and Sarah Anderson Shoemaker; m. Molly McDonald 1960; one s.; ed Reed Coll., Edinburgh Univ., Cornell Univ.; instructor, Ohio State Univ. 1957–60; Santayana Fellow, Harvard Univ. 1960–61; Asst then Assoc. Prof., Cornell Univ. 1961–67, apptd Prof. 1970, Susan Linn Sage Prof. 1978, currently Prof. Emer.; Assoc. Prof., Rockefeller Univ. 1967–70; ed. The Philosophical Review, many terms 1964–; Gen. Ed. Cambridge Studies in Philosophy 1982–90; Vice-Pres. Eastern Div. American Philosophical Asscn 1992–93, Pres. 1993–94; John Locke Lecturer, Univ. of Oxford 1972; Josiah Royce Lecturer, Brown Univ. 1993; Fulbright Scholar 1953–54, mem. American Philosophical Asscn; Fellow, Center for Advanced Study in Behavioral Sciences 1973–74, Nat. Endowment for the Humanities Fellowship 1980–81, Nat. Humanities Center 1987–88, American Acad. of Arts and Sciences. *Publications include:* Self-Knowledge and Self-Identity 1963, Identity, Cause and Mind 1984, Personal Identity (with Richard Swinburne) 1984, The First Person Perspective 1996, Physical Realization 2007. *Leisure interests:* music, reading, gardening. *Address:* Sage School of Philosophy, 218 Goldwin Smith Hall, Cornell University, Ithaca, NY 14853-3201 (office); 104 Northway Road, Ithaca, NY 14850, USA (home). *Telephone:* (607) 255-3687 (office); (607) 257-7382 (home). *Fax:* (609) 255-8177 (office). *E-mail:* ss56@cornell.edu (office); philosophy@cornell.edu (office). *Website:* www.arts.cornell.edu/phil/faculty/shoemaker (office).

SHOEMATE, Charles Richard (Dick), MBA; American business executive; b. 10 Dec. 1939, LaHarpe, Ill.; s. of Richard Osborne Shoemate and Mary Jane Shoemate (née Gillette); m. Nancy Lee Gordon 1962; three s.; ed Western Illinois Univ., Univ. of Chicago; Comptroller, Corn Products Unit, CPC Int. 1972–74, Plant Man. 1974–76, Vice-Pres. of Operations 1976–81, Corpn Vice-Pres. 1983–88, Pres. 1988–98, Chair. and CEO 1990–98, Chair., Pres., CEO Bestfoods (fmrly CPC Int.) 1998–2000; Pres. Canada Starch Co. 1981–83, mem. Bd of Dirs 1981–88; mem. Bd of Dirs Corn Refiners Asscn 1985–88, CIGNA Corpn 1991–2005, Chevron-Texaco, Inc. (now Chevron Corpn) 1998–2012; Ind. Dir Int. Paper Co. 1994–2005; Advisory Dir Unilever 2001–03; fmr Chair. Conference Board; mem. Business Roundtable, Cttee for Econ. Devt; mem. Advisory Council Indian River Medical Center Foundation.

SHOIGU, Col-Gen. Sergei Kuzhugetovich; Russian engineer and politician; *Minister of Defence;* b. 21 May 1955, Chadan, Tuva ASSR (now Repub. of Tyva); m. Irina Shoigu; two d.; ed Krasnoyarsk Polytech. Inst.; engineer, Sr master construction trust in Krasnoyarsk 1977–78; man. construction trusts Achinska-mulinstroi, Cayantyazhstroi, Abakanvagonstroi 1979–88; Second Sec. Abakan City CP Cttee, insp. CP Cttee KrasnoyarskKrai 1989–90; Deputy Chair. State Cttee on Architecture and Construction RSFSR 1990–91; Chair. State Cttee of Russian Fed. on Civil Defence, Emergencies and Natural Disasters 1991–94; Minister of Civil Defence, Emergencies and Clean-up Operations 1994–2012; Deputy Prime Minister Jan.–May 2000; Gov. Moscow Oblast May–Nov. 2012; Minister of Defence Nov. 2012–; Pres. Russian Geographic Soc. 2009–; mem. Security Council of Russia; Co-founder and leader pre-election bloc (then party) Yedinstvo (Unity) 1999–; Co-Chair. of Unity and Fatherland-United Russia (later United Russia) 2001–05; mem. State Duma 1999; Hon. Citizen of Kemerovo Region 2005; Order for Personal Courage (Russia) 1994, Danaker Order (Kyrgyzstan) 2002, Order of St Sava (1st class) (Serbia) 2003, Order of Merit for the Fatherland (3rd class) (Russia) 2005, Order of Honour (Russia) 2009, Order of Merit for the Fatherland (2nd class) (Russia) 2010; Medal "Dank" (Kyrgyzstan) 1997, Hero of Russian Fed. 1999, Nat. Public Prize of Peter the Great 1999, Moscow Medal. *Leisure interests:* singing, playing guitar. *Address:* Ministry of Defence, 119169 Moscow, ul. Znamenka 19, Russia (office). *Telephone:* (495) 696-71-71 (office); (495) 696-86-73 (office). *Website:* mil.ru (office).

SHOISMATOV, Ergash Rahmatullayevich; Uzbekistani politician; *Deputy Prime Minister, responsible for Geology, the Fuel-Energy Complex, and the Chemical and Petroleum Industries and Metallurgy;* apptd Minister of Power Eng and Electrification 2000; Chair. Uzbekenergo (state energy co.) –2006; Deputy Prime Minister (various changing energy responsibilities) 2006–, currently Deputy Prime Minister, responsible for Geology, the Fuel-Energy Complex, and the Chemical and Petroleum Industries and Metallurgy. *Address:* Office of the Cabinet of Ministers, 100078 Tashkent, Mustaqillik maydoni 5, Uzbekistan (office). *Telephone:* (71) 139-82-95 (office). *Fax:* (71) 139-84-63 (office). *Website:* www.gov.uz (office).

SHOKHIN, Aleksandr Nikolayevich; Russian politician; *President, Russian Union of Industrialists and Entrepreneurs;* b. 25 Nov. 1951, Savinskoye, Arkhangelsk Region; m. Tatyana Valentinovna Shokhina; one s. one d.; ed Moscow Univ.; on staff, Inst. of Econ., State Planning Cttee, Inst. of Labour, State Cttee of Labour 1974–82; researcher, Cen. Econ.-Math. Inst. and Inst. for Industrial Prognostics, USSR Acad. of Sciences 1982–87; adviser, Head of Dept of Int. Econ. Relations, Ministry of Foreign Affairs 1987–91; Dir Inst. of Employment Problems May–Aug. 1991; Russian Minister of Labour Aug.–Nov. 1991; Deputy Chair. of Russian Govt 1991–94; Minister of Labour and Employment 1991–92, of Foreign Econ. Relations 1992–93, of Econs 1994; Man. for Russia, IMF and IBRD 1992–94; mem. Bd State Specialized Export-Import Bank 1995–; Pres. Higher School of Econs 1995–; mem. Bd Russian Party of Unity and Consent 1993–95; Co-ordinator pre-election Union 'Our Home Russia' 1995, Chair. 1997–98; mem. State Duma (Parl.) 1993–97, First Deputy Chair. 1996–97; Deputy Prime Minister Sept. 1998 (resgnd); Chair. Interdepartmental Comm. of Security Council for Econ. Security 1998–99; Pres. Bureau of Russian Union of Industrialists and Entrepreneurs 2003–, Pres. RSPP International Council for Cooperation and Investment 2008–, Russia-US Council on Business Cooperation 2009–; Chair. Coordinating Council of Employers' Unions of Russia 2008–; currently Ind. Dir LUKoil, TNK-BP Management, TMK and Russian Railways; Chair. Supervisory Bd, Renessans Capital (investment group) 2002–06, Expert Council, Fed. Comm. on Securities Market 2003–; Ind. mem. Cttee of Credit Org. and Financial Markets 1999–, currently Chair.; mem. Nat. Council of Corp. Governance 2003–; apptd Perm. mem. Russian part of Russian-French Council on Economic, Financial, Industrial and Trade Matters 2007; Order of Distinguished Service (4th degree) (Russia), Medal of Honor. *Publications:* several books including *Social Problems of Perestroika* 1989, *Consumer's Market* 1989, *Interactive of Powers in the Legislative Process* 1997; over 200 scientific articles. *Address:* Russian Union of Industrialists and Entrepreneurs, 17 Kotel'nicheskaya naberezhnaya, 109240 Moscow, Russia (office). *Telephone:* (495) 663-04-04 (office). *Fax:* (495) 663-04-32 (office). *E-mail:* rspp@rspp.ru (office). *Website:* www.rspp.ru (office).

SHOKIN, Yurii Ivanovich; Russian mathematician and academic; *Director, Institute of Computational Technologies, Russian Academy of Sciences;* b. 9 July 1943, Kansk; m. 1968; two d.; ed Novosibirsk State Univ.; Sr Researcher, Head of Lab. Computers, Cen. Siberian br., USSR Acad. of Sciences 1969–76, Head of Lab., Inst. Theoretical and Applied Mechanics (Siberian br.) 1976–83, Dir Computers, Cen. Siberian br. in Krasnoyarsk 1983–90; Dir Inst. of Computational Technologies (Siberian br.), Russian Acad. of Sciences 1990–, Gen. Scientific Sec. (Siberian br.) 1992–97, Gen. Dir United Inst. of Informatics 1997–2003, Chair. Scientific Council on Nano- and Information Technologies 2008–; Dir Technopark, Novosibirsk 1998–; Corresp. mem. USSR (now Russian) Acad. of Sciences 1984, mem. 1994; research in computational math., numerical methods of mechanics, applied math., informatics, telecommunication, math. simulation; Order of Merit 1982, Order of Friendship 1999, Badge of Repub. of Kazakhstan for services in Devt of Science 2002, Order of Honour 2004, Medal For Belief and Good 2006. *Publications: Interval Analysis* 1981, *Numerical Modelling of Tsunami Waves* 1983, *Method of Differential Approximation: Application in Gas Dynamics* 1985, *Methods of Interval Analysis* 1986, *Fortran 90 for the Fortran Programmer* 1995, *Numerical Simulation of Environmental Problems* 1997, *Modelling of Jet Flows in Steel Converters* 2000, *Numerical Modelling of Fluid Flows with Surface Waves* 2001, *Methods of Riemann's Geometry in Construction Problems of Computational Meshes* 2005, *Modeling and Optimization of Systems with Distributed Parameters* 2006, *Construction of Differential Meshes by Means of Beltrami Equations Diffusion* 2007, *Differential Meshes and Coordinate Transformations for Computational Solution of Singular Perturbed Problems* 2008; numerous scientific articles. *Address:* Lavrentyev av. 6, 630090 Novosibirsk 90 (office); Voevodskogo 10, 630090 Novosibirsk 90, Russia (home). *Telephone:* (383) 330-61-50 (office). *Fax:* (383) 330-63-42 (office). *E-mail:* shokin@ict.nsc.ru (office). *Website:* www.ict.nsc.ru/eng/shokin (office).

SHOMAN, Abdel Hamid Abdul Majeed, BSc; Palestinian banking executive; b. 1 Jan. 1947; s. of Abdul Majeed Shoman; m.; three c.; ed American Univ. of Beirut; first joined Arab Bank 1970, Asst Gen. Man. Arab Bank plc, later Deputy Chair. and CEO 2001–05, Chair. and CEO 2005–10, Exec. Chair. 2010–12, also Chair. Islamic International Arab Bank (Amman), Arab Bank (Switzerland) Zurich 2002–12, Europe Arab Bank 2005–12, Al Arabi Investment Group Co. 2004, AB Capital 2005, Arab National Leasing Co. LLC 2004, Commercial Buildings Co., Lebanon 2005, Abdul Hamid Shoman Foundation 2007; Deputy Chair. Oman Arab Bank 2001; mem. Senate (Upper House of Parl.) of Jordan 2005–11; Dir Arab Nat. Bank (Saudi Arabia) 2001–, Central Bank of Jordan; mem. Bd of Trustees, King Hussein Cancer & Biotechnology Inst.; Arabian Business Magazine Banker of the Year Award 2008, ranked by Arabian Business amongst the Power 500: The Worlds's Most Influential Arabs (44th) 2012. *Address:* c/o Arab Bank plc, PO Box 950545, Shmeisani, Amman 11195, Jordan.

SHONEKAN, Chief Ernest Adegunle Oladeinde, LLB, CBE; Nigerian lawyer, business executive, politician and fmr head of state; *Founder and Non-Executive Partner, African Capital Alliance;* b. 9 May 1936, Lagos; m. Beatrice Oyelayo Oyebola 1965; two s. three d.; ed Church Missionary Soc. (CMS) Boys' School, Lagos, CMS Grammar School, Lagos and Univ. of London, UK; legal asst, UAC of Nigeria Ltd 1964–67, Asst Legal Adviser 1967–73, Deputy Legal Adviser 1974–75, Legal Adviser 1975–78, Dir 1976, Chair. 1980; Gen. Man. Bordpak Premier Packaging Co. 1978–79; Chair. Transitional Council of Nigeria Jan.–Aug. 1993; Pres. of Nigeria and Head of Interim Govt Aug.–Nov. 1993; currently Founder and Non-Exec. Pnr African Capital Alliance; Bd mem. Nigerian-German Chemicals plc, MAERSK Line Nigeria Ltd; Grand Officier, Ordre national de la Légion d'honneur. *Address:* African Capital Alliance, 8th Floor, C & C Towers, Plot 1684, Sanusi Fafunwa Street, Victoria Island, Lagos (office); 12 Alexander Avenue, Ikoyi, Lagos, Nigeria (home). *Telephone:* (1) 2706909 (office); 681437 (home). *Fax:* (1) 2706908 (office). *E-mail:* info@aca-web.com (office). *Website:* www.aca-web.com (office).

SHOOMBE, Pashukeni; Namibian fmr politician; b. 12 Dec. 1936, Okadiva, Oshana Region; m.; five c.; ed Okahao Training Coll., UN Inst. for Namibia, Lusaka, Zambia; teacher 1958–74; Prin. Oshigambo Girls' School 1960–63; mem. South-West Africa People's Org. (SWAPO) 1963–, joined mil. arm abroad 1974, elected mem. SWAPO Women's Council Cen. Cttee and Exec. Cttee 1980, SWAPO Cen. Cttee 1982, 1991; rep. SWAPO as Exec. Sec. for Information and Publicity, Pan-African Women's Org., Algeria and Angola 1985–89; apptd Election Deputy Commr for Northern Region, Oshakati 1989; mem. Constitutional Ass. 1989, Nat. Ass. 1990, Chair. Nat. Ass. Select Cttee on Human Resources, mem. Cttee on Standing Rules and Orders, Public Accounts Cttee; SWAPO Sec. for Finance 1991; mem. nat. group of IPU; UNESCO Int. Award for work in SWAPO refugee camps 1980–85. *Leisure interests:* fighting against the oppression of women, reading, cooking, baking. *Address:* PO Box 1971, Windhoek, Namibia. *Telephone:* 258994. *Fax:* 232368.

SHOR, Peter Williston, BS, PhD; American mathematician and academic; *Morss Professor of Applied Mathematics, Department of Mathematics, Massachusetts Institute of Technology;* b. 14 Aug. 1959, New York; m. Jennifer S. Collins Shor; two d.; ed California Inst. of Tech., Massachusetts Inst. of Tech.; Postdoctoral Fellow, Math. Sciences Research Inst., Berkeley, Calif. 1985; mathematician, AT&T Bell Labs 1986, with Information Sciences Research Lab., AT&T Fellow 1998; Morss Prof. of Applied Mathematics, Dept of Math., MIT 2003–; specialises in algorithms, quantum computing and quantum information theory; mem. NAS; Fellow, American Acad. of Arts and Sciences 2011–; Nevanlinna Award 1998, Int. Quantum Communications Award 1998, Goedel Prize (shared) 1999, Dickson Prize in Science 1999, MacArthur Fellowship 1999, King Faisal Int. Prize in Science (shared) 2002, Distinguished Alumni Award, Caltech 2007. *Publications:* frequent contribs to professional journals. *Address:* Room 2-369, Massachusetts Institute of Technology, 77 Massachusetts Avenue, Cambridge, MA 02139, USA (office). *Telephone:* (617) 253-4362 (office). *E-mail:* shor@math.mit.edu (office). *Website:* math.mit.edu/~shor (office).

SHORE, Howard; Canadian film score composer; b. 18 Oct. 1946, Toronto, Ont.; ed Berklee Coll. of Music, Boston; f. band Lighthouse; Musical Dir Saturday Night Live TV comedy show 1970s; began composing film music 1978; has collaborated on films by David Cronenberg, Peter Jackson; composed title music for Late Night with Conan O'Brien TV show 1993; mem. ASCAP; Officier, Ordre des Arts et des Lettres; Dr hc (Berklee Coll. of Music), Hon. DLitt (York Univ., Toronto) 2007; Career Achievement for Music Composition Award, Nat. Bd of Review of Motion Pictures, ASCAP Lifetime Achievement Award 2004, Max Steiner Film Music Achievement Award, City of Vienna 2010, Frederick Loewe Award. *Film scores include:* I Miss You, Hugs and Kisses 1978, The Brood 1979, Scanners 1980, Videodrome 1983, Nothing Lasts Forever 1984, After Hours 1985, Fire with Fire 1986, The Fly 1986, Heaven 1987, Nadine 1987, Dead Ringers 1988, Big 1988, Signs of Life 1989, She-Devil 1989, The Local Stigmatic 1989, An Innocent Man 1989, Made in Milan 1990, The Lemon Sisters 1990, Naked Lunch 1991, The Silence of the Lambs 1991, A Kiss Before Dying 1991, Prelude to a Kiss 1992, Single White Female 1992, Philadelphia 1993, Mrs Doubtfire 1993, Guilty As Sin 1993, Sliver 1993, M. Butterfly 1993, Nobody's Fool 1994, The Client 1994, Ed Wood (Los Angeles Film Critics' Asscn Award) 1994, Se7en 1995, Moonlight and Valentino 1995, White Man's Burden 1995, Before and After 1996, The Truth About Cats and Dogs 1996, Striptease 1996, Looking For Richard 1996, Crash 1996, That Thing You Do! 1996, The Game 1997, Cop Land 1997, Gloria 1999, Existenz 1999, Dogma 1999, Analyze This 1999, The Yards 2000, High Fidelity 2000, Esther Kahn 2000, The Cell 2000, Camera 2000, The Score 2001, The Lord of the Rings: The Fellowship of the Ring (Acad. Award for Best Original Score 2002, Grammy Award for Best Soundtrack) 2001, Spider 2002, Panic Room 2002, The Lord of the Rings: The Two Towers 2002, Gangs of New York 2002, The Lord of the Rings: The Return of the King (Golden Globe Award for Best Original Score 2004, Acad. Award for Best Song, for 'Into the West' 2004) 2003, The Aviator (Golden Globe Award for Best Original Score 2005) 2004, The Departed 2006, The Last Mimzy 2007, Eastern Promises 2007, Doubt 2008, The Betrayal 2008, The Twilight Saga: Eclipse 2010, Edge of Darkness 2010, A Dangerous Method 2011, Hugo (Golden Globe Nominee) 2011, The Spider 2011, The Rise of Theodore Roosevelt 2011, The Hobbit: An Unexpected Journey 2012, Cosmopolis 2012. *Opera:* The Fly. *Address:* Gorfaine/Schwartz Agency Inc, 4111 W. Alameda Avenue, Suite 509, Burbank, CA 91505-4161, USA (office). *Telephone:* (818) 260-8500 (office). *Website:* www.gsamusic.com (office); www.howardshore.com.

SHORT, Rt Hon. Clare, PC, BA; British politician and international organization official; *Chair, Extractive Industries Transparency Initiative;* b. 15 Feb. 1946, Birmingham, England; d. of Frank Short and Joan Short; m. 1st 1964 (divorced 1974); one s.; m. 2nd Alex Lyon 1981 (died 1993); ed Univs of Keele and Leeds; with Home Office 1970–75; Dir All Faith for One Race 1976–78, Youthaid and Unemployment Unit 1979–83; MP for Birmingham Ladywood 1983–2010, mem. Select Cttee on Home Affairs 1983–95; Shadow Employment Spokesperson 1985–89, Social Security Spokesperson 1989–91, Environment Protection Spokesperson 1992–93, Spokesperson for Women 1993–95; Shadow Sec. of State for Transport 1995–96, for Overseas Devt 1996–97; Sec. of State for Int. Devt 1997–2003; resgnd from the Govt 2003, resgnd Labour whip; Vice-Chair. All-Party Parl. Group on Trafficking of Women and Children; Chair. All Party Group on Race Relations 1985–86, Int. Advisory Bd of Cranfield Masters in Security Sector Man. Programme; mem. Nat. Exec. Cttee Labour Party 1988–98, Chair. Women's Cttee 1993–97; Vice-Pres. Socialist International Women 1992–97; mem. Advisory Cttee of Int. Lawyers for Africa, Advocacy Panel of Cities Alliance 2006–; Chair. Extractive Industries Transparency Initiative 2011–; mem. UNISON; Trustee, Africa Humanitarian Action; hon. degree (Bradford Peace Studies, Cardinal Wiseman Coll., Coventry Univ.); Wilberforce Medal 2004, Order of Volta Companion 2008; Spectator Campaigning MP of the Year 1992, Channel 4 Politician's Politician Award 2002. *Publication:* An Honourable Deception? New Labour, Iraq and the Misuse of Power (Channel 4 Political Book of the Year 2005) 2004. *Leisure interests:* books, family, swimming. *Address:* 23 Larkhall Rise, London, SW4 6JB, England (home). *Telephone:* (20) 7720-1525 (office). *E-mail:* shortclare@gmail.com (office).

SHORT, Nigel David; British chess player, writer, coach and commentator; b. 1 June 1965, Leigh, Lancs.; s. of David Short and Jean Gaskell; m. Rea Karageorgiou 1987; one s. one d.; ed Bolton School, Leigh Coll.; at age of 12 beat Jonathan Penrose in British championship; Int. Master 1980, Grandmaster 1984; British Champion 1984, 1987, 1998, English Champion 1991; Pres. Grandmasters' Asscn 1992; defeated Anatoly Karpov 1992; defeated by Kasparov 1993; chess columnist, The Daily Telegraph 1991, The Sunday Telegraph 1996–2006; stripped of int. ratings by World Chess Fed. June 1993, reinstated 1994; resgnd from Fédération Internationale des Echecs (FIDE) and est. Professional Chess Asscn (PCA) with Garry Kasparov 1993, left PCA 1995; Commonwealth Champion 2004, 2006, 2008; EU Champion 2006; Pres. Commonwealth Chess Asscn 2006–08; Hon. Fellow, Univ. of Bolton 1993–; Hon. MBE 1999. *Publication:* Learn Chess with Nigel Short 1993. *Leisure interests:* guitar playing, cricket, history, olive farming, swimming. *E-mail:* nigelshort@gmail.com (office).

SHORT, Roger Valentine, AM, ScD, FAA, FRS, FRCPE, FRANZCOG, FRSE, FRCVS, FRCOG, FAAS; Australian/British professor of reproductive biology and academic; *Honorary Professorial Fellow, Faculty of Medicine, University of Melbourne;* b. 31 July 1930, Weybridge, Surrey, England; s. of F. A. Short and M. C. Short; m. 1st Dr Mary Bowen Wilson 1958 (divorced 1981); one s. three d.; m. 2nd Prof. Marilyn Bernice Renfree 1982; two d.; ed Sherborne School, Univs of Bristol and Cambridge, Univ. of Wisconsin, USA; mem. ARC Unit of Reproductive Physiology and Biochemistry, Cambridge 1956–72; Lecturer, then Reader, Dept of

Veterinary Clinical Studies, Univ. of Cambridge 1961–72, Fellow, Magdalene Coll. 1961–72; Dir MRC Unit of Reproductive Biology, Edinburgh, Scotland 1972–82; Prof. of Reproductive Biology, Monash Univ., Australia 1982–95; currently Hon. Professorial Fellow, Faculty of Medicine, Univ. of Melbourne; J. D. White Visiting Prof., Cornell Univ., USA 2002, Regent's Prof., Univ. of California 2001; Chair. Family Health Int., NC 1985–95 (Bd mem. 1983–97); Fellow, American Acad. of Arts and Sciences, Royal Coll. of Veterinary Surgeons, Royal Australian and NZ Coll. of Obstetricians and Gynaecologists; Hon. Prof., Univ. of Edin. 1976–82; Hon. DSc (Guelph, Bristol, Edin.). *Achievements include:* holder of patents for use of melatonin to control jet lag 1983, 1986, 1987, and of topical oestriol administration to the foreskin to prevent HIV infection 2009. *Publications include:* Reproduction in Mammals, Vols 1–8 (with C. R. Austin) 1972–86, Contraceptives of the Future 1976, Ever Since Adam and Eve: The Evolution of Human Sexuality (with M. Potts) 1999; contrib. to numerous scientific journals. *Leisure interests:* gardening, wildlife, history of biology. *Address:* Level 4, 766 Elizabeth Street, University of Melbourne, Melbourne, Vic. 3010 (office); 18 Gwingana Crescent, Glen Waverley, Vic. 3150, Australia (home). *Telephone:* (3) 8344-3370 (office); (3) 9561-8873 (home). *Fax:* (3) 9347-8939 (office). *E-mail:* r.short@unimelb.edu.au (office). *Website:* www.unimelb.edu.au (office).

SHORTEN, Bill, BA, LLB, MBA; Australian lawyer and politician; b. 12 May 1967, Melbourne; s. of William Robert Shorten and Ann Shorten (née McGrath); m. Chloe Shorten; three c.; ed Monash Univ., Melbourne Business School; mil. service, Australian Army Reserve 1985–86; 18 months as lawyer with Maurice Blackburn Cashman; Organiser, Australian Workers' Union 1994, State Sec. (Vic.) 1998, Nat. Sec. 2001–07; Dir, Australian Super (formerly Superannuation Trust Australia) 1998–2007; Dir Victorian Funds Man. Corpn 2005–07; mem. House of Reps (Parl.) for Maribyrnong 2007–; Parl. Sec. for Disabilities and Children's Services 2007–10, for Victorian Bushfire Reconstruction 2009–10, Asst Treas. 2010–11, Minister for Financial Services and Superannuation 2010–13, for Employment and Workplace Relations 2011–13, for Educ. and for Workplace Relations July–Sept. 2013; Leader of the Opposition 2013–; mem. Australian Labor Party (ALP), ALP State Pres. (Vic.) 2005–08, mem. ALP Nat. Exec. 2004–, Leader, Federal Parl. Labor Party 2013–; Centenary Medal 2003. *Address:* Australian Labor Party, POB 6222, Kingston, ACT 2604, Australia (office). *Telephone:* (2) 6120-0800 (office). *Fax:* (2) 6120-0801 (office). *E-mail:* info@cbr.alp .org.au (office). *Website:* www.alp.org.au (office).

SHORTER, Wayne, BA; American jazz musician (saxophone); b. 25 Aug. 1933, Newark, New Jersey; ed New York Univ.; served in US Army 1956–58; played saxophone with Art Blakey 1959–63, Miles Davis 1964–70, Weather Report 1970–86, Miles Davis Tribute Band 1992; solo artist 1962–, and with Wayne Shorter Quartet; Hon. DMus (Berklee Coll. of Music) 1999; winner of numerous Down Beat Magazine Awards, Best Soprano Sax 1984, 1985, Grammy Awards for Best Jazz Instrumental Performance (for A Tribute to Miles) 1994, for Best Jazz Instrumental Solo (for In Walked Wayne) 1999, for Best Instrumental Composition (for Sacajawea) 2003, for Best Improvised Jazz Solo (for Orbits) 2014, Jazz Journalists' Asscn Awards for Lifetime Achievement in Jazz 2013, for Soprano Saxophonist of the Year 2013, for Small Ensemble 2013. *Recordings include:* albums: solo: Blues á la Carte 1959, Introducing Wayne Shorter 1959, Second Genesis 1960, Free Form 1961, Wayning Moments 1962, Search for a New Land 1964, Night Dreamer 1964, Some Other Stuff 1964, JuJu 1964, Speak No Evil 1964, The Soothsayer 1965, Et Cetera 1965, The Collector 1965, The All Seeing Eye 1965, Adam's Apple 1966, Schizophrenia 1967, Super Nova 1969, Moto Grosso Felo 1970, Odyssey of Iska 1970, Shorter Moments 1972, Wayne Shorter 1974, Native Dancer 1974, Atlantis 1985, Phantom Navigator 1986, Joy Ryder 1988, High Life (Grammy Award for Best Contemporary Jazz Album 1996) 1994, Portrait 2000, All or Nothing at All 2002, Footprints Live! 2002, Alegría (Grammy Award for Best Jazz Instrumental Album by an Individual or Group) 2003, Footprints 2005, Beyond the Sound Barrier (Grammy Award for Best Jazz Instrumental Album by an Individual or Group 2006) 2005, Without a Net 2013; with Weather Report: Weather Report 1971, I Sing the Body Electric 1972, Sweetnighter 1973, Mysterious Traveler 1974, Tail Spinnin' 1975, Black Market 1976, Black Market/Heavy Weather 1978, Mr Gone 1978, 8.30 (Grammy Awards for Best Jazz Fusion Performance) 1979, Night Passage 1980, Procession 1983, Domino Theory 1984, Sportin' Life 1985, This is This! 1986. *Address:* c/o International Music Network, 278 Main Street, Gloucester, MA 01930, USA (office). *Telephone:* (978) 283-2883 (office). *Fax:* (978) 283-2330 (office). *E-mail:* info@imnworld.com (office). *Website:* www.imnworld.com (office); www.wayneshorter.com (office).

SHOSTAKOVICH, Maksim Dmitriyevich; American (b. Russian) conductor and pianist; b. 10 May 1938, Leningrad (now St Petersburg); s. of the late Dmitriy Shostakovich and of Nina Varzar; m. 1st; one s.; m. 2nd Marina Tisie 1989; one s. one d.; ed Cen. Music School, Moscow Conservatory; studied conducting under Rabinovich, Gauk, Rozhdestvensky (q.v.); Asst Conductor, Moscow Symphony Orchestra; Conductor, State Academic Symphony Orchestra; piano debut age 19 in father's Second Piano Concerto; Prin. Conductor and Artistic Dir USSR Radio and TV Symphony Orchestra; requested and granted political asylum in USA while on tour with USSR Radio and TV Symphony Orchestra, Nuremberg April 1981; conducted Nat. Symphony Orchestra, Capitol steps, Washington, DC, USA 1981; Prin. Guest Conductor Hong Kong Philharmonic 1982–; Music Dir New Orleans Symphony Orchestra 1986–91; Hon. Music Dir Louisiana Philharmonic Orchestra 1993–94. *Performances:* Touring Western Europe with USSR Radio and TV Symphony Orchestra, Japan, USA 1971–81; has conducted all maj. N American orchestras and many in Europe, Asia, S America; conducted premiere of father's 15th Symphony and recorded virtually all father's symphonies in USSR; has performed with leading soloists, including Emil Gilels, Oistrakh, Rostropovich. *Address:* PO Box 273, Jordanville, NY 13361, USA.

SHOTWELL, Gwynne, BS, MS; American business executive; *President and Chief Operating Officer, SpaceX (Space Explorations Technologies Corporation);* ed Northwestern Univ.; originally enrolled in Chrysler Corpn's man. training programme; began work at El Segundo, Calif. research centre of Aerospace Corpn 1988, did tech. work on mil. space research and devt contracts 1988–98; Dir Space Systems Div., Microcosm Inc. 1998–2002; joined SpaceX 2002, now Pres. and COO, World Technology Prize (Space) 2011. *Address:* Space Exploration Technologies Corporation (SpaceX), 1 Rocket Road, Hawthorne, CA 90250, USA (office).

Telephone: (310) 363-6000 (office). *E-mail:* media@spacex.com (office). *Website:* www.spacex.com (office).

SHOWALTER, Elaine, MA, PhD, FRSL; American academic, literary critic and writer; *Professor Emerita of English, Princeton University;* b. 14 Jan. 1941, Cambridge, Mass.; d. of Paul Cottler and Violet Cottler (née Rottenberg); m. English Showalter 1963; one s. one d.; ed Bryn Mawr Coll., Brandeis Univ.; Teaching Asst, Dept of English, Univ. of Calif. 1964–66, Assoc. Prof. 1967–78; Prof. of English, Rutgers Univ. 1978–84; Avalon Foundation Prof. of Humanities, Princeton Univ. 1984–2003, Prof. Emer. 2003–; columnist and writer, The Guardian newspaper, UK 2003–; R. Stanton Avery Distinguished Fellow, Huntington Library 2004–05; Visiting Prof. of English and Women's Studies, Univ. of Del. 1976–77; Visiting Prof., School of Criticism and Theory, Dartmouth Coll. 1986; Guggenheim Fellow 1977–78; Rockefeller Humanities Fellow 1981–83; Chair. Man Booker Int. Prize jury 2007 mem. Modern Language Assocn; Dr hc (Univ. of St Andrews) 2012; Howard Behrman Humanities Award, Princeton Univ. 1989. *Publications:* A Literature of Their Own 1977, The Female Malady 1985, Sexual Anarchy 1990, Sister's Choice 1991, Hysteria Beyond Freud (jt author) 1993, Hystories 1997, Faculty Towers: The Academic Novel and Its Discontents 2005, A Jury of Her Peers (Truman Capote Award for Literary Criticism) 2009; also ed. of several feminist publs and writer of numerous articles and reviews. *Address:* c/o Department of English, Princeton University, 22 McCosh Hall, Princeton, NJ 08544, USA.

SHOYAMA, Etsuhiko, BS; Japanese electronics industry executive; *CEO, Hitachi China Ltd;* b. 9 March 1936, Niigata Pref.; ed Tokyo Inst. of Tech.; began career as power plant engineer, Hitachi Works 1959–82, Deputy Gen. Man. Hitachi Works 1982–85, Gen. Man. Kokubu Works 1985–87, Gen. Man. Tochigi Works 1987–90, Gen. Man. Household Appliances Div. 1990–1991, elected to Bd of Dirs Hitachi Ltd 1991, Gen. Man. Consumer Electronics Div. 1991–93, Exec. Man. Dir 1993–95, Sr Exec. Man. Dir 1995–97, Exec. Vice-Pres. and Rep. Dir 1997–99, Pres. and Rep. Dir 1999–2003, Pres. and CEO 2003–06, Chair. and Dir 2006–07, Chair. and Advisor 2007–09, mem. Bd of Dirs and CEO Hitachi China Ltd 2006–, Chair. Hitachi Europe Ltd, Chair. Hitachi America Ltd 2006–07; Chair. Babcock-Hitachi K.K.; mem. Bd of Dirs Nippon Mining Holdings Inc.; fmr Vice-Chair. Nippon Keidanren; Chair. Information and Communications Council, Ministry of Internal Affairs and Communications 2005–; fmr Chair. Exec. Bd Japan Electronics and Information Tech. Industries Asscn; mem. Council for Science and Tech., Policy Cabinet Office 2006–; Officier, Légion d'honneur 2007. *Address:* Hitachi China Ltd, 4/F, North Tower, World Finance Centre, Harbour City, Tsimshatsui, Kowloon, Hong Kong Special Administrative Region, People's Republic of China (office). *Telephone:* 2735-9218 (office). *Fax:* 2375-3192 (office). *E-mail:* service@cm.hbi.co.jp (office). *Website:* www.hitachi.com.cn (office).

SHPAK, Col-Gen. Georgy Ivanovich; Russian army officer and politician; b. 6 Sept. 1943, Osipovichi, Mogilev Region, Ukraine; m.; one s. (deceased) one d.; ed M. Frunze Mil. Acad., Mil. Acad. of Gen. Staff; commdr paratroopers' regt, head of staff, deputy commdr paratroopers' div., commdr of div. 1978–88; Deputy Commdr of Army Odessa Mil. Command 1988–89; Army Commdr, First Deputy Commdr Turkestan Mil. Command 1989–92; First Deputy Commdr Volga Mil. Command; Commdr Airborne Troops 1996–2003; Gov. Ryazan Oblast 2004–08; mem. State Duma 2004; three orders, ten medals. *Leisure interests:* countryside, fishing. *Address:* c/o Office of the Head of the Regional Administration (Governor), ul. Lenina 30, 39000 Ryazan, Russia.

SHPEK, Roman Vasilyevich; Ukrainian economist and diplomatist; b. 10 Nov. 1954, Broshniv, Ivano-Frankivsk Region; m. Maria Romanivna Shpek; one s. one d.; ed Forestry Eng Inst., Lviv, Int. Inst. of Wood Man., Kiev, Dalover Univ.; processing engineer and head of woodworking manufacturing plant, Ivano-Frankivsk Region 1976–78, Chief Engineer, wood and woodworking plant 1978–81, Dir 1981–89; Deputy Minister of Forestry, Woodworking and Furniture Industry, Ukrainian SSR 1989–92; Minister of Privatization, Ukraine April–Oct. 1992; First Deputy Minister of the Economy of Ukraine 1992–93, Minister 1993–95, Deputy Prime Minister on Econ. Policy 1995–96; Head Nat. Agency for Devt and European Integration 1996–2000; Co-Chair. Ukrainian-German Council on Econ. Co-operation, Ukrainian-Italian Council on Econ. Co-operation, Comm Kuchma-Gor on Econ. Devt Cttee; Acting Gov., then Gov. for Ukraine, World Bank Group; Chair. Currency and Finance Council to Cabinet of Ministers of Ukraine; Nat. Co-ordinator of Tech. Assistance Programme for Ukraine 1993–2000; Ukrainian Rep. to UNDP 1996–; apptd Amb. and Head of Mission of Ukraine to EU 2000; Order for Merits, 3rd Degree (Ukraine). *Leisure:* oil painting, classical music, travelling, sport (football, boxing). *Address:* 29 Avenue de Saturne, 1180 Brussels, Belgium (home). *Telephone:* (2) 379-09-87 (home). *E-mail:* roman.shpek@ gmail.com.

SHRESTHA, Ambica, BA; Nepalese business executive; *Managing Director, Kathmandu Travels and Tours Limited;* b. 12 Feb. 1933, Kathmandu; two d.; ed in India; Man. Dir Kathmandu Travels and Tours Ltd, Nepal Trek and Natural History Expeditions; Dir Davs Enterprises Pvt. Ltd; Pres. Dwarika's Hotel; mem. Transparency Int. Nepal anti-corruption organisation (Pres. Exec. Cttee 1996–); Pres. Int. Fed. of Business and Professional Women; Hon. Consul of Spain; Order of the Gorkha Dakshina Bahu, Prakhyat Trisakti Patta, Birendra-Aishwarya Sewa Padak, Cross of Order of Civil Merit (Spain), Cross, Orden de Isabel La Catolica (Spain); Pata Heritage Award, Business and Professional Women's Club 1980, Rotary Int. Service Above Self Award 2012–13, Golden Mike Award, Radio and TV Asscn of Spain, Badge of Honour, BPW Int., Public Admin Asscn of Nepal Bahadur Malla Award. *Address:* Kathmandu Travels and Tours Ltd, PO Box 459, Battisputali, Kathmandu, Nepal (office). *Telephone:* (1) 471577 (office). *Fax:* (1) 471379 (office). *E-mail:* info@dwarikas.com (office); ktt@mail.com.np (office). *Website:* dwarikas.com (office).

SHRESTHA, Indra Bahadur; Nepalese business executive; *Chairman, Hetauda Cement Industries Ltd;* fmr Pres. CCI Makawanpur; Chair. Hetauda Cement Industries Ltd; Pres. Lalitpur Chamber of Commerce and Industry; mem. Nat. Exec. Cttee, Amnesty Int. Nepal 2004. *Address:* Hetauda Cement Industries Ltd, POB 24, Hetauda, Makawanpur (office); Lalitpur Chamber of Commerce and Industry, Mangal Bazar, POB 26, Lalitpur, Nepal (office). *Telephone:* (1) 5521740 (office). *Fax:* (1) 5530661 (office). *E-mail:* lcci@mos.com.np (office).

SHRESTHA, Narayan Kaji; Nepalese politician; b. Jaubari village, Gorkha; s. of Megh Narayan Shrestha and Jyoti Maya Shrestha; Lecturer in math., Siddhartha Vanasthali Inst. in 1980s; imprisoned as political leader in 1980, 1986; mem. Constituent Ass. (Janamorcha Nepal) 2008–; Deputy Prime Minister and Minister of Home Affairs 1 Aug.–29 Aug. 2011; Deputy Prime Minister and Minister of Foreign Affairs 2011–13; currently Sr Leader, Unified Maoists Party. *Address:* c/o Ministry of Foreign Affairs, Narayanhiti, Kathmandu, Nepal.

SHRESTHA, Rt Hon Ram Prasad, LLB, MA; Nepalese judge; b. 5 May 1956, Palpa; ed Tribhuvan Univ.; joined judicial service, Asar 1971; Judge, Dist Courts of Sangjya, Parsa, Kaski 1975–84; Judge, Zonal Courts of Mahakali, Koshi and Veri 1984–91; Judge, Appellate Courts of Patan, Nepalgunj 1991–96; Chief Judge, Appellate Courts of Nepalgunj, Pokhara 1996–2003; Justice Supreme Court 2003–10, Chief Justice 2010–11. *Address:* c/o Supreme Court, Ram Shaha Path, Kathmandu, Nepal.

SHREVE, Susan Richards, MA; American writer and academic; *Professor of English Literature, George Mason University;* b. 2 May 1939, Toledo, OH; d. of Robert Richards and Helen Richards; m. 1st Porter Shreve (divorced 1987); m. 2nd Timothy Seldes 1987; two s. two d.; ed Univs of Pennsylvania and Virginia; Prof. of English Literature, George Mason Univ., Fairfax, Va 1976–; Visiting Prof., Columbia Univ., New York 1982–, Princeton Univ. 1991, 1992, 1993; fmr Pres. PEN/Faulkner Foundation; producer, The American Voice for TV 1986–; Essayist, MacNeil/Lehrer Newshour; George Washington Univ. Jenny Moore Award 1978, Guggenheim Fellowship 1980, Nat. Endowment for the Arts Fellowship 1982. *Publications include:* A Fortunate Madness 1974, A Woman Like That 1977, Children of Power 1979, Miracle Play 1981, Dreaming of Heroes 1984, Queen of Hearts 1986, A Country of Strangers 1989, Daughters of the New World 1992, The Train Home 1993, Skin Deep: Women and Race 1995, The Visiting Physician 1995, The Goalie 1996, Narratives on Justice (co-ed.) 1996, Outside the Law 1997, How We Want to Live (co-ed.) 1998, Plum and Jaggers 2000, A Student of Living Things 2006, Warm Springs: Traces of a Childhood at FDR's Polio Haven 2007, Kiss Me Tomorrow 2007, Trout and Me 2009, Under the Watsons' Porch 2009, The Lovely Shoes 2011, You Are the Love of My Life 2012; juvenile: The Flunking of Joshua T. Bates 1993, Jonah, The Whale 1997, Ghost Cats 1999, The End of Amanda, The Good 2000. *Address:* Graduate Creative Writing Program, Department of English, George Mason University, 4400 University Drive, Fairfax, VA 22030 (office); 3319 Newark Street, NW, Washington, DC 20008, USA (home). *E-mail:* writing@gmu.edu (office). *Website:* creativewriting.gmu.edu (office); www.susanshreve.com.

SHRIVER, Duward F., BS, PhD; American scientist and academic; *Morrison Professor Emeritus of Chemistry, Northwestern University;* b. 20 Nov. 1934, Glendale, Calif.; s. of D.L. Shriver and J.S. Shriver; m. Shirley A. Clark 1957; two s.; ed Univ. of California, Berkeley, Univ. of Michigan; instructor, Northwestern Univ., Evanston, Ill. 1961–62, Asst Prof. 1962–67, Assoc. Prof. 1967–71, Prof. 1971–78, Morrison Prof. of Chem. 1988–, now Prof. Emer., Chair. Chem. Dept 1992–95; Alfred P. Sloan Research Fellow 1967–69; Guggenheim Fellow 1983–84, mem. Inorganic Syntheses Inc. 1974–, Pres. 1982–85; ACS Award for Distinguished Service in Inorganic Chem. 1987, Materials Research Soc. Medal 1990. *Publications include:* Inorganic Chemistry (jtly) 1990, Manipulation of Air-Sensitive Materials; 295 scientific papers. *Address:* Department of Chemistry, Tech K124, Northwestern University, 2145 Sheridan Road, Evanston, IL 60208-3113 (office); 1100 Colfax Street, Evanston, IL 60201, USA (home). *Telephone:* (847) 491-5371 (office). *Fax:* (847) 491-7713 (office). *E-mail:* sashriver@sbcglobal.net (office). *Website:* www.chem.northwestern.edu (office).

SHRIVER, Maria Owings, BA; American broadcaster and journalist; b. 6 Nov. 1955, Chicago, Ill.; d. of Robert Sargent Shriver and Eunice Mary Shriver (née Kennedy); m. Arnold Schwarzenegger 1986; two s. two d.; ed Stone Ridge School of the Sacred Heart, Bethesda, Md, Georgetown Univ., Washington, DC; began career as writer and producer on TV news at KYW-TV, Philadelphia 1977; journalist on Evening Magazine, WJZ-TV, Baltimore 1978–80; Nat. Corresp. on PM Magazine 1981–83; W Coast Reporter for CBS Morning News, then Co-Presenter, New York 1985–86; joined NBC News 1986, Co-Presenter Sunday Today 1987–90, Main Street 1987, Yesterday, Today and Tomorrow 1989, Presenter NBC Nightly News Weekend Edition 1989–90, Cutting Edge with Maria Shriver 1990, First Person with Maria Shriver 1991–2003; writer and presenter of many news programmes, documentaries and TV specials including The Baby Business, Men, Women, Sex and AIDS, Wall Street: Money, Greed and Power, and Fatal Addictions (Christopher Award 1990); exclusive interviews with King Hussein of Jordan, Fidel Castro, US Vice-Pres. J. Danforth Quayle and Pres. Corazón Aquino of the Philippines (Exceptional Merit Media Award, Nat. Women's Political Caucus); First Lady of Calif. 2003–11; ranked by Forbes magazine amongst The World's 100 Most Powerful Women (53rd) 2010. *Publications:* Ten Things I Wish I'd Known Before I Went Out into the Real World 2000, What's Wrong With Timmy? 2001, What's Happening to Grandpa? (juvenile) 2004, And One More Thing Before You Go. . . 2005, What's Heaven? 2007, Just Who Will You Be?: Big Question, Little Book, Answer Within 2008. *E-mail:* info@mariashriver.com. *Website:* www.mariashriver.com.

SHTAUBER, Zvi Meir, PhD; Israeli diplomatist, academic and fmr military officer; b. 15 July 1947; s. of Yisrael Shtauber and Jaffa Shtauber; m. Nitza Rousso; two s. one d.; ed Harvard Business School, Fletcher School of Law and Diplomacy, Tufts Univ., USA; with Israel Defence Forces 1970–95, Head of Strategic Planning Div. 1995, retd with rank of Brig.-Gen. 1995; Vice-Pres. Ben-Gurion Univ. of the Negev 1996–99; Foreign Policy Adviser to Prime Minister Ehud Barak (q.v.) 1999–2000; Amb. to UK 2001–04; Head, Jaffee Center for Strategic Studies, Tel-Aviv Univ. 2005, Dir Inst. for Nat. Security Studies (incorporated Jaffee Center) –2008. *Address:* c/o Institute for National Security Studies, 40 Haim Levanon Street, Tel-Aviv 61398, Israel.

SHU, Frank H., BS, PhD; American (b. Chinese) astrophysicist, astronomer and academic; *Professor Emeritus of Astronomy, University of California, San Diego;* b. (Shu Hsia-Sae), 2 June 1943, China; s. of Shien-Siu Shu; ed Massachusetts Inst. of Tech., Harvard Univ.; has held faculty appointments at State Univ. of NY, Stony Brook and Univ. of California, Berkeley, now Emer., Chair. Astronomy Dept, Univ. of California, Berkeley 1984–88; Pres. Nat. Tsing Hua Univ. 2002–06; apptd Distinguished Prof. of Physics, Univ. of California, San Diego 2006, now Prof.

Emer., also Univ. Prof.; Pres. American Astronomical Soc. 1994–96; mem. NAS 1987, Academia Sinica 1990, American Acad. of Arts and Sciences 1992, American Philosophical Soc. 2003, TWAS, Acad. of Sciences for Developing World 2006; Foreign Assoc., Royal Astronomical Soc. 2005; Warner Prize, American Astronomical Soc. 1977, Oort Prof., Leiden Univ. 1996, Brouwer Award, Div. of Dynamical Astronomy 1997, Bruno Rossi Lecturer, Arcetri Observatory, Italy 1999, Heineman Prize, American Inst. of Physics and American Astronomical Soc. 2000, Faculty Research Lecturer, Univ. of California, Berkeley 2001, Outstanding Scholar Award, Taiwan 2002–06, Ta-You Wu Lecturer, Univ. of Michigan 2007, Caroline Herschel Lecturer, Space Telescope Science Inst. 2007, Centennial Medal, Harvard Univ. 2008, Shaw Prize in Astronomy (co-recipient) 2009, main-belt asteroid 18238 Frankshu named in his honour. *Publications:* numerous papers in professional journals on the origin of meteorites, the birth and early evolution of stars and the structure of spiral galaxies. *Address:* Department of Physics, University of California, San Diego, SERF 427, 9500 Gilman Drive, La Jolla, CA 92093, USA (office). *Telephone:* (858) 822-1214 (office). *E-mail:* fhshu@ucsd.edu (office). *Website:* www-physics.ucsd.edu (office).

SHU, Huiguo; Chinese politician and agronomist; b. July 1938, Jing'an Co., Jiangxi Prov.; ed Zhejiang Agricultural Coll.; joined CCP 1980; Dir Dept of Agric., Animal Husbandry and Fishery, Jiangxi Prov.; Vice-Gov. Jiangxi Prov. 1991–2001; Vice-Sec. CCP Jiangxi Prov. Cttee 1995, Sec. 1997–2001; Chair. Standing Cttee Jiangxi Prov. People's Congress 1998–2001; apptd Vice-Minister of Personnel 2001; mem. 15th CCP Cen. Cttee 1997–2002. *Address:* c/o Ministry of Personnel, 12 Hepingli Central Street, Beijing 100716, People's Republic of China.

SHU, Qi; Taiwanese actress and fmr model; b. (Lin Li-Hui), 16 April 1976, Xindian, Taipei Co. (now New Taipei City); moved to Hong Kong aged 17; appeared on cover of Penthouse Hong Kong and Chinese edn of Playboy magazine; came under management of Hong Kong producer Manfred Wong; selected by Kenzo for third advertising campaign for its successful fragrance, Flower by Kenzo 2006–09; also worked as a spokesperson for Shiatzy Chen; represents Frederique Constant in Asia as brand amb. 2008–; Jury mem. Berlinale (Berlin Int. Film Festival) 2008, Cannes Film Festival 2009. *Films include:* Sex & Zen II 1996, Viva Erotica (Best New Performer and Best Supporting Actress, Hong Kong Film Awards, Best Supporting Actress, Golden Bauhinia Awards 1996) 1996, Growing Up 1996, Street Angels 1996, Till Death Do Us Laugh 1996, A Queer Story 1996, The Fruit is Swelling (cameo) 1997, Love: Amoeba Style 1997, Those Were the Days 1997, Love Is Not a Game, But a Joke 1997, My Dad Is a Jerk 1997, L-O-V-E. . . Love 1997, The Lucky Guy 1998, Young and Dangerous 5 1998, The Storm Riders 1998, Love Generation Hong Kong 1998, Bishonen 1998, City of Glass 1998, Young & Dangerous: The Prequel 1998, Portland Street Blues (Best Supporting Actress, Hong Kong Film Awards 1998) 1998, Another Meltdown 1998, Extreme Crisis 1998, Your Place or Mine (Best Supporting Actress, Golden Horse Awards 1998) 1998, Gorgeous 1999, True Woman 1999, A Man Called Hero 1999, Iron Sister 1999, The Island Tales 1999, When I Look Upon the Stars 1999, Metade Fumaca 1999, My Loving Trouble 7 1999, Unexpected Challenges 2000, Hidden Whisper 2000, Born to Be King 2000, Flyin' Dance 2000, Skyline Cruisers 2000, Dragon Heat 2000, My Name is Nobody 2000, For Bad Boys Only 2000, Martial Angels 2001, Millennium Mambo 2001, Visible Secret 2001, Love Me, Love My Money 2001, Beijing Rocks 2001, The Wesley's Mysterious File 2002, Women From Mars 2002, So Close 2002, Just One Look (cameo) 2002, The Transporter 2002, Haunted Office 2002, Looking for Mr. Perfect 2003, The Foliage 2003, The Eye 2 2004, Seoul Raiders 2005, Three Times (Best Actress, Golden Horse Awards 2005) 2005, Home Sweet Home 2005, Hong Fu Nu 2006, Confession of Pain 2006, My Wife is a Gangster 3 2006, Forest of Death 2007, Blood Brothers 2007, If You Are the One 2008, Look for a Star 2009, New York, I Love You 2009, City Under Siege 2010, Legend of the Fist: The Return of Chen Zhen 2010, If You Are the One 2 2010, A Beautiful Life 2011, The Assassin 2011. *Other:* Hong Kong (audio walking tour by Louis Vuitton and Soundwalk) 2008.

SHU, Shengyou; Chinese politician; b. Dec. 1936, Yushan Co., Jiangxi Prov.; joined CCP 1959; Mayor of Jingdezhen City; Vice-Gov. Jiangxi Prov. 1991, Gov. 1996–2001; Vice-Sec. CCP Jiangxi Prov. Cttee 1995–2001; mem. 15th CCP Cen. Cttee 1997–2002; mem. Standing Cttee 9th CPPCC Nat. Cttee 1998–2003. *Address:* c/o Jiangxi Provincial Government, Nanchang, Jiangxi Province, People's Republic of China.

SHU, Ting; Chinese poet and writer; b. (Gong Peiyu), 1952, Shima, Zhangzhou City, Fujian Prov.; d. of Shi Mo Gang and Xiu Zhen Yong; m. Chen Zhongyi 1981; one s.; sent to work in countryside during Cultural Revolution –1973, then worked on construction sites and in factories; published poems in Today (underground literary magazine); mem. Writers' Asscn, Fujian 1983– (Vice-Chair. 1985), Council of Writers' Asscn of China 1985–; Dir Chinese Writers' Union; Nat. Poetry Award 1981, 1983. *Publications:* Shuangweichuan 1982, Shu Ting Shuqing Shixuan 1984, Poesiealbum Shu Ting 1989, Hui Changge de Yiweihua, Shizuniao, Selected Poems of Seven Chinese Poets 1993, Selected Poems: An Authoritative Collection 1994, Mist of my Heart: Selected Poems of Shu Ting 1995. *Address:* 13 Zhonghua Road, Gulangyu, Xiamen City, Fujian Province, 361002, People's Republic of China.

SHUE, Elisabeth; American actress; b. 6 Oct. 1963, Wilmington, Del.; d. of James Shue and Anne Wells; m. Davis Guggenheim 1994; one s. two d.; ed Wellesley Coll., Harvard Univ.; studied with Sylvie Leigh, Showcase Theater; appeared in Broadway plays including Some Americans Abroad, Birth and After Birth. *Films include:* The Karate Kid 1984, Link 1986, Adventures in Babysitting 1987, Cocktail 1988, Body Wars 1989, Back to the Future Part II 1989, Part III 1990, Soapdish 1991, The Marrying Man 1991, Twenty Bucks 1993, Heart and Souls 1993, Radio Inside 1994, Blind Justice 1994, The Underneath 1995, Leaving Las Vegas (Chicago Film Critics Asscn Award for Best Actress, Dallas-Fort Worth Film Critics Asscn Award for Best Actress, Independent Spirit Award for Best Lead Female, Los Angeles Film Critics Asscn Award for Best Actress, Nat. Soc. of Film Critics Award for Best Actress) 1995, The Trigger Effect 1996, The Saint 1996, Palmetto 1997, Deconstructing Harry 1997, Cousin Bette 1997, Molly 1998, Hollow Man 2000, Amy and Isabelle 2001, Leo 2004, Mysterious Skin 2004, Hide and Seek 2005, Gracie 2007, Don McKay 2009, Waking Madison 2010, House at the End of the Street 2012, Chasing Mavericks 2012. *Television films include:* The Royal Romance of Charles and Diana 1982, Double Switch 1987, Hale the Hero

1992, Blind Justice 1994, Dreamer: Inspired by a True Story 2005. *Television series:* Call to Glory 1984. *Address:* c/o Creative Arts Agency, 9830 Wilshire Boulevard, Beverly Hills, CA 90212, USA.

SHUGAIRI, Ahmad al-, MBA; Saudi Arabian religious TV presenter; b. 1973; m. 1995 (divorced); two s.; ed California State Univ., Northridge, USA; began studying with cleric Adnan al-Zahrani; TV debut 2002, presenter of own show Khawater 2004–; opened Andalucia Café, Jeddah. *Television:* Yallah Shabab (Hey, Young People) 2002, Khawater (Thoughts) 2004–. *Address:* c/o Middle East Broadcasting Center (MBC), POB 76267, Dubai, United Arab Emirates (office). *Website:* www.mbc.net (office).

SHULEVA, Lidiya Santova, BE, MA; Bulgarian economist, business executive and politician; b. 23 Dec. 1956, Velingrad; m. (widowed); two c.; ed Tech. Univ., Sofia, Univ. of Nat. and World Economy, Sofia; specialised in marketing and finance, Man. Acad., Munich, Germany; worked in man. and finance, Japan; fmr man. consultant, EEC, Greece; Owner and Man. Business Intellect EOOD 1992–96; Exec. Man. Albena Invest Holding AD 1996–2000; Chair. Asscn of Industrial Capital 2000–; Minister of Labour and Social Policy 2001; Deputy Prime Minister and Minister of the Economy 2001–05; mem. Governing Bd Assistance to Charity Foundation 2000–; mem. Nat. Ass. 2005–, mem. Econ. Policy Cttee 2005–, Budget and Finance Cttee 2005–; mem. Bulgarian New Democracy Parl. Group 2007–; Observer in European Parl. 2005–06, mem. European Parl. Jan.–May 2007. *Address:* National Assembly, 2 Narodno sabranie Square, 1169 Sofia, Bulgaria (office). *Telephone:* (2) 939-39 (office). *Fax:* (2) 981-31-31 (office). *E-mail:* infocenter@parliament.bg (office). *Website:* www.parliament.bg (office).

SHULMAN, Alexandra, OBE, BA; British journalist and editor; *Editor, British Vogue;* b. 13 Nov. 1957, London; d. of Milton Shulman and Drusilla Beyfus; one s.; ed St Paul's Girls' School and Univ. of Sussex; Sec. Over-21 magazine; joined Condé Nast 1982, Writer and Commissioning Ed., later Features Ed. Tatler 1982–87; Ed. Women's Page, Sunday Telegraph 1987, later Deputy Ed. 7 Days current affairs photo/reportage; Features Ed. Vogue 1988; Ed. GQ 1990; Ed. British Vogue 1992–; Trustee, Nat. Portrait Gallery, London 1999–2008, Arts Foundation 2001–10, Royal Marsden Hospital cancer campaign 2009–. *Publication:* Can We Still Be Friends 2012. *Address:* Condé Nast Publications, Vogue House, Hanover Square, London, W1S 1JU, England (office). *Telephone:* (20) 7152-3635 (office). *Website:* www.vogue.co.uk/person/alexandra-shulman.

SHULMAN, Robert Gerson, MA, PhD; American biophysicist; *Sterling Professor Emeritus of Molecular Biophysics and Biochemistry, Yale University;* b. 3 March 1924, New York; s. of Joshua S. Shulman and Freda Shulman (née Lipshay); m. 1st Saralee Deutsch 1952 (died 1983); three s.; m. 2nd Stephanie S. Spangler 1986; ed Columbia Univ.; Research Assoc., Columbia Univ. Radiation Lab., New York 1949; AEC Fellow in Chem., Calif. Inst. of Tech. 1949–50; Head, Semiconductor Research Section, Hughes Aircraft Co. Culver City, Calif. 1950–53; mem. tech. staff, Bell Labs, Murray Hill, NJ 1953–66, Head, Biophysics Research Dept 1966–79; Prof. of Molecular Biophysics and Biochemistry, Yale Univ. 1979–94, Dir Div. of Biological Sciences 1979–94, apptd Sterling Prof. of Biophysics and Biochemistry 1994, currently Sterling Prof. Emer. and Sr Research Scientist, Diagnostic Radiology, fmr Emissary for Clinical Research; mem. NAS, Inst. of Medicine; Guggenheim Fellow, Cambridge 1961–62. *Address:* Department of Molecular Biophysics and Biochemistry, Yale University, 300 Cedar Street, PO Box 208024, New Haven, CT 06520-8024, USA (office); (203) 432-1333 (home). *Telephone:* (203) 785-6201 (office). *Fax:* (203) 785-7979 (office). *E-mail:* robert .shulman@yale.edu (office). *Website:* www.mbb.yale.edu (office).

SHULTZ, George Pratt, BA, PhD; American economist, academic and fmr government official; *Thomas W. and Susan B. Ford Distinguished Fellow, Hoover Institution, Stanford University;* b. New York, NY; s. of Birl E. Shultz and Margaret Lennox Pratt Shultz; m. 1st Helena M. O'Brien 1946; two s. three d.; m. 2nd Charlotte Mailliard Swig 1997; ed Princeton Univ. and Massachusetts Inst. of Tech.; Assoc. Prof. of Industrial Relations, MIT 1955–57; Sr Staff Economist, Pres.'s Council of Econ. Advisors 1955–56; Prof. of Industrial Relations, Grad. School of Business, Univ. of Chicago 1957–68, Dean, Grad. School of Business 1962–68; Pres. Industrial Research Asscn 1968; US Sec. of Labor 1969–70; Dir Office of Man. and Budget, Exec. Office of the Pres. 1970–72; US Sec. of Treasury, Washington, DC 1972–74; Chair. Council on Econ. Policy 1973–74; Sec. of State 1982–89; Exec. Vice-Pres. Bechtel Corpn 1974–75, Pres. 1975–77, Vice-Chair. 1977–81, Pres. Bechtel Group Inc. 1981–82; Prof. of Man. and Public Policy, Grad. School of Business, Stanford Univ. 1974–82, of Int. Economy 1989–91, Prof. Emer. 1991–; Chair. JP Morgan Chase Int. Council, Accenture Energy Advisory Bd 2003–07, Advisory Council Inst. of Int. Studies, Stanford, Govs' Econ. Policy Advisory Bd, Calif., Gov.'s Council of Econ. Advisors 2004–11; mem. Bd Bechtel Group Inc. 1989–2007; Chair. Pres. Reagan's Econ. Policy Advisory Bd 1981–82; Chair. Advisory Bd Precourt Inst. for Energy Efficiency; Chair. External Advisory Bd MIT Energy Initiative; mem. Bd of Trustees, Center for Advanced Study in the Behavioral Sciences, Stanford, Calif.; Distinguished Fellow, Hoover Inst., Stanford Univ. 1989–, Thomas W. and Susan B. Ford Distinguished Fellow, Hoover Inst. 2001–, Distinguished Fellow, American Econ. Asscn 2005; Grand Cordon, Order of the Rising Sun 1989; Jefferson Award 1989, Presidential Medal of Freedom 1989, Seoul Peace Prize 1992, Eisenhower Medal 2001, Reagan Distinguished American Award 2002, Ralph J. Bunche Award for Diplomatic Excellence 2002, Nat. World War II Museum American Spirit Award 2006, George Marshall Award 2007, Truman Medal for Econ. Policy 2007, American Acad. of Arts and Sciences Rumford Prize 2008, Commdt's Leadership Award, Marine Corps-Law Enforcement Foundation 2009, Congressional Medal of Honor Soc.'s Distinguished Citizen Award 2011, Nat. Endowment for Democracy Service Medal 2012. *Publications include:* Pressures on Wage Decisions, Labor Problems, The Dynamics of a Labor Market, Management Organization and the Computer, Strategies for the Displaced Worker, Guidelines, Informal Controls and the Market Place, Workers and Wages in the Urban Labor Market, Leaders and Followers in an Age of Ambiguity, Economic Policy beyond the Headlines, Turmoil and Triumph: My Years as Secretary of State 1993, Putting Our House in Order: A Guide to Social Security and Health Care Reform (with John Shoven) 2008, Ideas & Action, Featuring 10 Commandments of Negotiations 2010, Issues on My Mind: Strategies for the Future 2013. *Leisure interest:* golf. *Address:* Hoover Institution, Stanford,

CA 94305-6010, USA (office). *Telephone:* (650) 725-3492 (office). *Fax:* (650) 723-5441 (office). *Website:* www-hoover.stanford.edu (office).

SHUMEIKO, Vladimir Filippovich, DEcon; Russian economist and politician; *Founder and Chairman, Reforms-New Course Movement;* b. 10 Feb. 1945, Rostov Don; m.; two d.; ed Krasnodar Polytech. Inst.; worked in factories as foreman, engineer, chief engineer, Dir-Gen. Concern Krasnodar Factory of Measuring Instruments –1991; People's Deputy of Russia 1990–92; Vice-Chair. Supreme Soviet of Russia 1991–92, First Deputy Prime Minister of Russia 1992–93; Pres. Confed. of Entrepreneurs' Unions of Russia 1992–93; mem. Council of Fed. (Upper House of Parl.) 1993–96, Chair. 1994–96; Founder and Chair. Reforms-New Course Movt 1996–; Lecturer, Acad. of Border Service; apptd Chair. Interregional Auction and Stock Corpn 1998, Moskva Bank 2002. *Publication:* Russian Reforms and Federalism 1995, Pelmeny po Protocoly 2001. *Leisure interests:* fishing, woodworking, collecting small bells. *Address:* Reforms-New Course Movement, Novi Arbat 19, Moscow, Russia (office). *Telephone:* (495) 203-33-47 (office).

SHUMLIN, Peter Elliott; American business executive, politician and state governor; *Governor of Vermont;* b. 24 March 1956, Brattleboro, Vt; s. of George J. Shumlin and Kitty Shumlin (née Weber); m. Deborah Holway 1989; two d.; ed Buxton School, Wesleyan Univ.; mem. Windham Co. Democratic Cttee 1980–90; mem. Comm., Windham Regional Community 1983–85; Chair. Putney Bd Selectmen 1983–89; helped found Landmark Coll., Putney, Vt; apptd to fill vacancy in Vt House of Reps from Putney Dist 1990–92; mem. Vt Senate for Windham Dist 1992–2002, 2007–11, Senate Minority Leader 1992–94, Pres. Pro Tempore 1994–2002, 2006–11; unsuccessful cand. for Lt Gov. 2002; returned to family business, Putney Student Travel 2003–06; Gov. of Vermont 2011–; Chair. Nat. Democratic Govs Asscn 2013; mem. River Valley Arts Center, River Valley Playhouse (Founder); Democrat. *Address:* Office of the Governor, Pavilion Office Building, 109 State Street, Montpelier, VT 05609, USA (office). *Telephone:* (802) 828-3333 (office). *Fax:* (802) 828-3339 (office). *E-mail:* info@shumlinforgovernor .com. *Website:* governor.vermont.gov (office); shumlinforgovernor.com.

SHUSHKEVICH, Stanislaw, DSc; Belarusian physicist, politician and fmr university rector; *Chairman, Belorusian Social Democratic Party (Hramada);* b. 15 Dec. 1934, Minsk, Byelorussian SSR, USSR; s. of Stanislaw Shushkevich and Helena Romaouskaya; m. Irina Kuzminichna Shushkevich; one s. one d.; ed Belarus State Univ.; CPSU 1967–91; researcher, Inst. of Physics, Belarus Acad. of Sciences 1959–60; engineer Minsk Radio Plant 1960–61; Chief Engineer, Head of Section Belarus Univ. 1961–67; Prof. and Pro-Rector Minsk Radiotechnical Inst. 1966–69; Head of Chair., Belarus Univ. 1969–86, Pro-Rector 1986–90; began involvement in politics 1989 as critic of Govt negligence in aftermath of Chernobyl accident; mem. Supreme Soviet 1990–91; Chair. Supreme Soviet 1991–94, mem. –1996; Dir Centre of Political and Econ. Studies, European Humanitarian Inst. 1994–; mem. Civil Action faction; cand. in presidential elections 1994; Chair. Belarusian Social Democratic Party (Hramada) 1997–; Corresp. mem. Belarus Acad. of Sciences 1991–; Highest Order of Lithuanian Repub. for contrib. to democratic transformation of Lithuania 1989–94; hon. doctorates from four univs; State Prize of Byelorussian SSR 1986, Govt of USSR Prize 1988, Ukrainian Int. Pylyp Orlyk Award, Jan Nowak-Jezioranski Award, Medal of Truman-Reagan Freedom Award 2012. *Publications:* Belarus – Self-Identification and Statehood, Belorussian Newcommunism, My Life, Collapse Revival USSR; more than 100 articles and papers on problems of nuclear electronics and political problems. *Leisure interest:* building with his own hands. *Address:* c/o Belaruskaya Satsyaldemakratychnaya Partya (Hramada), 220013 Minsk, vul. Kulman 4; Masherova avenue 78-14, 220035 Minsk, Belarus (home). *Telephone:* (17) 226-70-71 (home); (29) 339-66-86 (office). *Fax:* (17) 226-70-71 (home). *E-mail:* stastashu@mail.ru (home).

SHUVALOV, Igor Ivanovich; Russian politician and lawyer; *First Deputy Chairman of the Government;* b. 4 Jan. 1967, Bilibino, Chukot Autonomous Okrug; m. Olga Viktorovna Shuvalova; two s. two d.; ed Moscow State Univ.; lab. worker, EKOS Research Inst., Moscow 1984–85; army service 1985–87; attaché, Ministry of Foreign Affairs, Russian Fed. 1993; Sr Legal Adviser, Stock Co. (ALM) Consulting Moscow 1993–95; Dir Advocates' Bureau (ALM) 1995–97; Head, Dept of State Cttee on Man. of State Property 1997–98; Deputy Minister of State Property 1998; Chair., Russian Foundation of Fed. Property 1998–2000; Head of Govt Admin and Minister Without Portfolio 2000–02, Deputy Head of Presidential Admin 2003–08; First Deputy Chair. of the Govt, in charge of external econ. relations and foreign trade, WTO negotiations and small business 2008–; Head of Organizing Cttee for the 27th World Summer Universiade 2009–13; Head of Russia's bid cttee to host the 2018 FIFA World Cup 2009–10, now co-ordinates the organization, preparation and holding of the World Cup in 2018; Hon. Citizen of the City of Kazan 2013; Hon. Diploma, Govt of the Russian Fed. 2003; Order for Service to the Repub. of Tatarstan 2013, Order of Alexander Nevsky 2013. *Address:* Office of the Government, 103274 Moscow, Krasnopresnenskaya nab. 2, Russia (office). *Telephone:* (495) 605-53-29 (office). *Fax:* (495) 605-52-43 (office). *E-mail:* duty_press@aprf.gov.ru (office). *Website:* www.government.ru (office).

SHUVALOV, Vladimir A.; Russian biologist; *Director, Russian Academy of Sciences Institute of Basic Biological Problems;* b. 13 Oct. 1943, Omsk; m.; two c.; ed Moscow State Univ.; Sr Lab Worker, then Jr Researcher, Bach Inst. of Biochemistry 1968–72; Sr Researcher, Inst. of Soil Science and Photosynthesis, USSR (now Russian Acad. of Sciences) 1972–79, Head of Lab. 1979, now Dir, Inst. of Basic Biological Problems; State Prize 1991. *Publications include:* author of more than 150 scientific papers on primary light energy transformation at photosynthesis, including The Primary Photoreactions in the Complex P-890-bacteriophophylin 760 1976, Burning of a Narrow Spectral Note at 1.7 K in the Absorption Band of the Primary Electron of Rhodosendomous Vividis Reaction Centres with Blocked Electron Transfer 1988. *Address:* Institute of Basic Biological Problems, Russian Academy of Sciences, Pushchino 142290, Moscow region, Russia (office). *Telephone:* (967) 73-36-01 (office); (495) 939-10-92 (office). *Fax:* (967) 33-05-32 (office). *E-mail:* shuvalov@issp.serpukhov.su (office).

SHVYDKOI, Mikhail Yefimovich, PhD, DFA; Russian theatre scholar and politician; *Head, Federal Agency of Culture and Cinematography;* b. 5 Sept. 1948, Kyrgyzia; m. Marina Shvydkaya; two c.; ed Moscow Lunacharsky Inst. of Theatre Art; reviewer, Radio Co., Deputy Ed.-in-Chief Theatr magazine 1973–90; Ed.-in-

Chief Publrs Co. Kultura, Russian Fed. Ministry of Culture 1990–93; Deputy Minister of Culture 1993–97; Prof. of Foreign Theatre, Acad. of Humanitarian Sciences; commentator on cultural problems on Russian TV; Deputy Chair. Russian TV and Radio Co., Ed.-in-Chief Cultura TV Channel 1997–98; Chair. All-Russian State Radio and TV Holding 1998–2000; Minister of Culture 2000–04; Head, Fed. Agency of Culture and Cinematography 2004–; Chair. Nat. Comm. World Decade of Culture at UNESCO, mem. Bd of Dirs Pervyi Kanal 2004–; Govt Award of the Russian Fed. for Literature and Art 1999; numerous awards, prizes and decorations from France, Poland, Ukraine, Kazakhstan and Russian Fed. *Television:* broadcaster on Cultural Revolution (Cultura TV channel) 2002–, Life is Wonderful (STS TV channel) 2004–. *Publications:* Dramatic Composition: Theatre and Life, Secrets of Lonely Comedians, Sketches on Foreign Theatre of the Late 20th Century; numerous articles on history and contemporary state of theatre in Russian and foreign periodicals. *Address:* c/o 7/6 Maliy Gnezdnikovskiy per., Moscow 125009, Russia (office). *Telephone:* (495) 629-23-11 (office). *Fax:* (495) 629-22-48 (office). *Website:* www.rosculture.ru/en (office).

SHWAYRI, Ramzi; Lebanese chef; *General Director, Al-Kafaàt Catering School;* b. 1971, Beirut; m. Tanya Jamous; ed Univ. of Lyon, France, Univ. of London, England; studied econs and law in France; Received training in France with Int. French Chef, Jean Masson; Lebanon's first TV chef, live programmes three times weekly on Future Television; joined Al-Kafaàt Foundation (f. by his father) 1992, mem. Bd of Trustees, Gen. Dir Hotel Management Inst. (now Al-Kafaàt Catering School) 1995–, also gives training in vocational skills to disabled or troubled young people; est. 'Chef Ramzi' (co. for production of Chef Ramzi ready-to-eat meal dishes for int. export and distribution) 2001; est. 'Chef Ramzi' magazine 2003; Hon. mem. French Syndicate of Baking and Dessert Making Arts. *Television:* Alam Al Sabbah (Future Television Network) 1994. *Publication:* Chef Ramzi 1998, Chef Ramzi from the Lebanese Heritage 2001. *Address:* Al-Kafaàt Foundation, PO Box 47, Hadath, Lebanon (office). *Telephone:* (961) 1879301 (office). *Fax:* (961) 1879307 (office). *E-mail:* foundation@al-kafaat.org (office); chefRamzi@chefRamzi.com.lb. *Website:* www.al-kafaat.org (office).

SHYAMALAN, M. Night, BA; Indian film director, screenwriter, actor and producer; b. (Manoj Nelliyattu Shyamalan), 6 Aug. 1970, Pondicherry, Tamil Nadu Prov.; s. of Nelliyattu C. Shyamalan and Jayalakshmi Shyamalan; m. Bhavna Vaswani 1993; two d.; ed New York Univ.; Co-founder M. Night Shyamalan Foundation; Distinguished Alumni Award, Episcopal Academy 2001, Padma Shri Award 2008. *Films:* Praying with Anger (writer, dir, actor, producer) 1992, Wide Awake (writer, dir) 1998, The Sixth Sense (writer, dir, actor) 1999, Stuart Little (screenplay writer) 1999, Unbreakable (writer, dir, actor, producer) 2000, Signs (writer, dir, producer) 2002, The Village (writer, dir, producer) 2004, Lady in the Water (writer, dir, producer) 2006, The Happening 2008, The Last Airbender 2010. *Publications:* juvenile: Stuart Finds His Way Home (with Kitty Richards) 1999, Stuart and the Stouts (with Greg Brooker) 2001, Stuart and Snowbell (with Greg Brooker) 2001. *Leisure interest:* comic books. *Address:* Creative Artists Agency, 2000 Avenue of the Stars, Los Angeles, CA 90057, USA (office). *Telephone:* (424) 288-2000 (office). *Fax:* (424) 288-2900 (office). *Website:* www.caa.com (office); www .mnightshyamalan.com.

SIALE BILEKA, Silvestre; Equatorial Guinean lawyer and politician; fmr Minister of Justice and Religion; Prime Minister and Head of Govt of Equatorial Guinea 1991–93, 1993–95; Minister of Foreign Affairs and Francophone Affairs 1991–92; Pres. Supreme Tribunal 2000–04; later Presidential Councillor on Human Rights; mem. Partido Democrático de Guinea Ecuatorial. *Address:* Siale Bileka Law Firm, Malabo, Equatorial Guinea (office). *Telephone:* (09) 35-34 (office).

SIAZON, Domingo L., Jr, BA, BSc, MPA; Philippine diplomatist and international civil servant; b. 1939, Aparri, Cagayan; m.; ed Ateneo de Manila Univ., Tokyo Univ., Japan, Harvard Univ., USA; interpreter and trans., then Attaché and Third Sec. and Vice-Consul, Embassy in Tokyo 1964–68; Acting Resident Rep. to IAEA, Alt. Perm. Rep. to UNIDO, Third, Second, then First Sec., Embassy in Berne 1968–73; First Sec. and Consul-Gen., Embassy in Vienna, then Amb. to Austria, also Perm. Rep. to IAEA, UNIDO and UN at Vienna 1973–85; Dir-Gen. UNIDO 1985–93; Minister of Foreign Affairs 1995–2000; Amb. to Japan 2002–10. *Address:* Department of Foreign Affairs, DFA Bldg, 2330 Roxas Blvd, Pasay City, 1330 Manila, Philippines (office). *Telephone:* (2) 8344000 (office). *Fax:* (2) 8321597 (office). *E-mail:* webmaster@dfa.gov.ph (office). *Website:* www.dfa.gov.ph (office).

SIBAL, Kanwal, MA, LLB; Indian fmr diplomatist; *Chair, EADS India;* b. 18 Nov. 1943, Baddomalhi, British India; m. Elisabeth Sibal; one s. one d.; joined Foreign Service 1966, Third Sec., then Second Sec., Embassy in Paris 1968–73, Under-Sec. Ministry of External Affairs 1973–75, Jt Sec. 1986–89, Deputy High Commr, High Comm. in Dar-es-Salaam 1976–79, Counsellor, Embassy in Lisbon 1980–82, Deputy Chief of Mission, Embassy in Kathmandu 1982–85, Amb. to Turkey 1989–92, Deputy Chief of Mission, Embassy in Washington, DC 1992–95, Amb. to Egypt 1995–98, to France 1998–2002, Foreign Sec. 2002–04, Amb. to Russia 2004–07; mem. Nat. Security Advisory Bd 2008–10; Pres. Asscn of Indian Diplomats; Chair. EADS India; mem. Advisory Bd Vivekananda Int. Foundation, Bd of Dirs East-West Inst., New York; Dir JSC Sitronics 2010–12; Grand Officier, Ordre nat. du Mérite. *Address:* 171 Jor Bagh, New Delhi 110 003, India. *Telephone:* (11) 24644755. *E-mail:* kanwalsibal@gmail.com.

SIBAL, Kapil, LLB, MA, LLM; Indian lawyer and politician; *Minister of Communications and Information Technology;* b. 8 Aug. 1948, Jalandhar, Punjab; s. of H.L. Sibal; m. 1st Nina Sibal (died 2000); two s.; m. 2nd Promila Sibal 2005; ed St John's High School, Chandigarh, Univ. of Delhi, Harvard Law School, USA; joined Bar Asscn 1970, set up own law practice, designated Sr Lawyer 1983; Additional Solicitor Gen. of India 1989–90; MP Rajya Sabha 1998–2004, MP Lok Sabha (Congress Party) for Chandni Chowk constituency 2004–; Union Minister for Science, Tech. and Earth Sciences 2004–10, Minister of Human Resource Devt 2009–12, Minister of Communications and Information Tech. 2010–; Pres. Supreme Court Bar Asscn 1995–96, 1997–98, 2001–02; mem. Bd of Man., Indira Gandhi Nat. Open Univ. 1993; mem. Exec. Council, Inst. of Constitutional and Parl. Studies 2001; mem. Business Advisory Cttee 2001, Cttee on Home Affairs 2002, Bd of International AIDS Vaccine Initiative 2002, Programme Bd of Bill and Melinda Gates Foundation of Indian AIDS Initiative 2003, Human Rights Comm. Working Group on Arbitrary Detention, Geneva; Living Legend of the Law,

International Bar Asscn 1994, Padma Bhushan Award 2006. *Publications include:* poems: I Witness: Partial Observation 2008; numerous articles on issues including security, terrorism and nuclear proliferation. *Address:* Ministry of Communications and Information Technology, Electronic Niketan, CGO Complex, Lodhi Road, New Delhi 110 003, India (office). *Telephone:* (11) 24369191 (office). *Fax:* (11) 24362333 (office). *E-mail:* webmaster@mit.gov.in (office). *Website:* www.mit.gov.in (office); kapilsibalmp.com.

SIBBETT, Wilson, CBE, BSc, PhD, FRS, FRSE; British physicist and academic; *Professor of Natural Philosophy, University of St Andrews;* b. 15 March 1948, Portglenone, Co. Antrim, Northern Ireland; s. of John Sibbett and Margaret Sibbett (née McLeister); m. Barbara Anne Brown 1979; three d.; ed Ballymena Tech. Coll., Queen's Univ. Belfast, Imperial Coll.; Post-doctoral Research Fellow, Imperial Coll., London, later Lecturer and Reader in Physics; Prof. of Natural Philosophy, Univ. of St Andrews 1985–; Chair. Scottish Science Advisory Cttee 2002–06; Fellow, Optical Soc. of America 1998, European Optical Soc. 2007; Hon. DSc (Dundee), (Glasgow), Hon. ScD (Trinity Coll. Dublin), Hon. DUniv (Strathclyde); Schardin Gold Medal 1978, Inst. of Physics Boys Medal and Prize 1993, Rank Prize for Optoelectronics 1997, Royal Soc. Rumford Medal 2000, European Physical Soc. Quantum Electronics Prize 2002, Royal Medal, Royal Soc. of Edinburgh 2009, Charles Hard Townes Award 2011. *Publications:* 385 papers published in scientific journals. *Leisure interests:* golf, DIY, gardening. *Address:* School of Physics and Astronomy, University of St Andrews, North Haugh, St Andrews, KY16 9SS (office); 1 Lawhead Road East, St Andrews, KY16 9ND, Scotland (home). *Telephone:* (1334) 463100 (office); (1334) 472778 (home). *Fax:* (1334) 463104 (office). *E-mail:* ws@st-andrews.ac.uk (office). *Website:* www.st -andrews.ac.uk/physics (office).

SIBER, Sibel; Turkish-Cypriot politician and fmr physician; *Speaker, Legislative Assembly;* b. 13 Dec. 1960, Nicosia; m.; two c.; ed Istanbul Univ., Univ. of Virginia, Rush Univ. Medical Center, USA; early career as physician; resident in internal medicine, Şişli Etfal Hosp., Istanbul 1987; est. private medical practice; mem. Legis. Ass. (Parl.) 2009–, Pres. (Speaker) 2013–; Prime Minister (first female) June–Aug. 2013; mem. Cumhuriyetçi Türk Partisi (Republican Turkish Party). *Address:* Assembly of the TNRC, Badr Demirel Avenue, Lefkoşa, Mersin 10, Turkey (office). *E-mail:* info@cm.gov.nc.tr (office). *Website:* www.cm.gov.nc.tr (office).

SIBLEY, Dame Antoinette, CBE, DBE; British ballerina; *President, Royal Academy of Dance;* b. 27 Feb. 1939, Bromley, Kent; d. of Edward G. Sibley and Winifred Smith; m. 1st Michael Somes 1964 (divorced 1973, died 1994); m. 2nd Panton Corbett 1974; one s. one d.; joined the Royal Ballet 1956, Soloist 1959, Prin. Ballerina 1960–; Vice-Pres. Royal Acad. of Dance 1989–91, Pres. 1991–. *Ballets:* leading roles in: Swan Lake, Sleeping Beauty, Coppelia, The Nutcracker, La Fille Mal Gardée, Romeo and Juliet, Jabez and the Devil (cr. role of Mary), The Dream (cr. Titania), Jazz Calendar (cr. Friday's Child), Enigma Variations (cr. Dorabella), Thais (cr. Thais), Triad (cr. the Girl), Manon (cr. Manon), Soupirs (cr. pas de deux), Symphonic Variations, Daphnis and Chloë, Varii Capricci (cr. La Capricciosa), The Good-Humoured Ladies, A Month in the Country, L'Invitation au Voyage (cr. a lead role), Anastasia (cr. Kschessinska pas-de-deux), Pavane (cr. pas-de-deux). *Television:* Cinderella (TV movie), The Rosalina Neri Show 1959, The London Palladium Show 1967. *Films:* The Turning Point 1978, Mime Matters (video). *Publications:* Sibley and Dowell 1976, Antoinette Sibley 1981, Reflections of a Ballerina 1985. *Leisure interests:* doing nothing, opera, cinema, reading. *Address:* Royal Academy of Dance, 36 Battersea Square, London, SW11 3RA, England (office). *Telephone:* (20) 7326-8000 (office). *E-mail:* info@rad.org.uk (office). *Website:* www.rad.org.uk (office).

SIDDARAMAIAH, K., BSc, LLB; Indian lawyer, politician and government official; *Chief Minister of Karnataka;* b. 12 Aug. 1948, Siddaramanahundi, Varuna Hobli, Mysore Dist; s. of Siddarame Gowda and Boramma; m. Parvathi Siddaramaiah; two s.; ed Univ. of Mysore; a leader of the Kuruba Gowda community in Karnataka; was a junior under a lawyer in Mysore and later taught law; began political career when elected to Mysore Taluka 1978; contested on a Bharatiya Lok Dal ticket from Chamundeshwari constituency and entered 7th Karnataka Legis. Ass. 1983; joined ruling Janata Party and became first Pres. Kannada Watchdog Cttee (Kannada Kavalu Samiti) set up to supervise the implementation of Kannada as an official language; re-elected from same constituency 1985; Minister for Animal Husbandry and Veterinary Services from 1985, handled portfolios including Sericulture, Animal Husbandry and Transport at different times, defeated in Ass. elections 1989; apptd Sec. Gen. of Janata Dal 1992; elected again in state elections 1994; Minister for Finance in Janata Dal Govt 1994–96; Deputy Chief Minister of Karnataka 1996–99; joined Janata Dal (Secular) faction of Deve Gowda following split in the Janata Dal and became Pres. of its state unit, defeated in state elections 1999; Deputy Chief Minister of Karnataka 2004–06; expelled from JD (S) 2006; joined the Nat. Congress; re-elected for Varuna constituency in state ass. elections 2008, re-elected 2013; elected Leader of the Congress Legis. party in Karnataka Ass. 2013; Chief Minister of Karnataka 2013–. *Address:* Office of the Chief Minister, Vidhana Soudha, 3rd Floor (Room 323), Bangalore 560 001, India (office). *Telephone:* (80) 22253414 (office). *Fax:* (80) 22281021 (office). *E-mail:* chiefminister@karnataka .gov.in (office); cm@kar.nic.in (office). *Website:* www.karnataka.gov.in (office).

SIDDIQI, Nazim Hussain, BA, LLM; Pakistani fmr judge; b. 30 June 1940; s. of the late Mukarram Hussain Siddiqi; ed Univs of Hyderabad and Karachi; lawyer, Hyderabad 1961–67; fmr Civil Judge, Sr Civil Judge, Customs Judge, Special Judge; apptd Judge, High Court of Sindh 1992, Chief Justice 1999–2000; Judge, Supreme Court 2000–05, Chief Justice 2004–05 (retd); Chair. Cen. Zakat Council of Pakistan; mem. Selection Bd, Quaid-i-Azam Univ. *Address:* c/o Supreme Court, Constitution Avenue, Islamabad, Pakistan.

SIDDIQI, Suhaila, MD, PhD; Afghan surgeon and politician; b. 1931, Kabul; ed Kabul Medical Univ.; studied in Afghanistan and Russia; practising surgeon 1970s–; joined mil. during Soviet occupation of Afghanistan, first and only woman to attain rank of Gen. during communist Najibullah regime; worked two decades in Kabul's 400-bed mil. hosp. then Chief of Surgery, Wazir Akbar Khan Hosp., Kabul; Minister of Public Health, Interim Govt of Afghanistan 2001–08. *Address:* c/o Ministry of Public Health, Wazir Akbar Khan, Sub-district 9, Kabul, Afghanistan.

SIDDIQUI, Brig. Rashid; Pakistani army officer (retd) and business executive; ed Command and Staff Coll., Nat. Defence Coll., Islamabad; army service 1971–2002, becoming Dir of Military Intelligence and Faculty mem., Nat. Defence Coll., Islamabad; Exec. Dir (Admin) Pakistan Nat. Shipping Corpn 2002–, Chair. 2009–11. *Leisure interests:* golf, jogging. *Address:* Pakistan National Shipping Corporation, PNSC Building, M.T. Khan Road, PO Box No. 5350, Karachi 74000, Pakistan (office). *Telephone:* (21) 99203975 (office); (21) 5636660 (office); (21) 99210296 (office). *Fax:* (21) 99203974 (office). *E-mail:* communication@pnsc.com.pk (office). *Website:* www.pnsc.com.pk (office).

SIDEROV, Volen Nikolov; Bulgarian politician; *Leader, Attack Party;* b. 19 April 1956, Yambol; ed degree in Applied Photography in Sofia; worked as photographer at Nat. Literature Museum –1989; mem. Movt for Human Rights 1990; Ed.-in-Chief Democracy (official newspaper of Democratic Party) 1990–92; journalist, 168 Hours (weekly newspaper); press attaché for Sasho Donchev (Serbian Radical Party) Topenergy and Overgas mid-1990s; journalist, Monitor (newspaper) –2003; hosted talk show on cable TV channel SKAT 2003–05; Founder and Leader, Attack Nat. Union (later Attack Party) 2005–, mem. Parl. 2005–; unsuccessful presidential cand. 2006; known for hardline attitude towards minorities in Bulgaria; Union of Bulgarian Journalists Award 2000. *Address:* Attack Party (Partiya Ataka), 1000 Sofia, ul. Vrabcha 1, Bulgaria (office). *Telephone:* (2) 980-55-70 (office). *Fax:* (2) 980-55-70 (office). *E-mail:* volenataka@abv.bg (office); atakacentrala@abv.bg (office). *Website:* www.ataka.bg (office).

SIDHU, Shivinder Singh, MA (Econ.), PhD; Indian civil servant and government official; b. 13 Oct. 1929, Punjab; ed Delhi School of Econs, Univ. of Kanpur, Ecole Nationale d'Administration, Paris; joined Indian Admin. Service 1952; Sec. to three Chief Ministers of UP 1964–67; Dist Magistrate, Kanpur 1967–70; Div. Commr, Agra 1978–80; Sec. to Govt of India, Ministry of Health and Family Welfare 1981–83; Adviser to the Gov. of Punjab 1983–84; Sec. to Ministry of Industrial Devt 1984–85, to Ministry of Tourism and Civil Aviation Feb. 1985–Oct. 1987; Additional charge Chair. Air India and Indian Airlines 1985–86; Adviser to the Gov., Tamil Nadu Feb.–July 1988; Dir Civil Aviation Admin 1985–87; Sec. Gen. Int. Civil Aviation Org., Montreal, Canada 1988–91; Special Assignment, Commonwealth Secr.: Evaluation of Commonwealth Fund for Tech. Devt in Islands of South Pacific Ocean June–Aug. 1994; Pres. Foundation for Aviation and Sustainable Tourism 1992–2004; Gov. of Manipur 2004–08, of Meghalaya 2007–08, of Goa 2008–11. *Publications include:* Steel Industry in India: Problems & Perspective, Aviation & Sustainable Tourism: Emerging Trends, New Horizons in Travel & Tourism Symbiosis, Tourism & Aviation: Airborne for Progress, Aviation and Tourism: Synergy for Success. *Address:* 804 Asha Deep, 9 Hailey Road, New Delhi 110001, India.

SIDHWA, Bapsi; American/Pakistani writer and academic; b. 11 Aug. 1939, Karachi; d. of Peshotan Bhandara and of Tehmina Bhandara; m. 1st (divorced); m. 2nd Nosher Rustam Sidhwa; two d. one s.; ed Kinnaird Coll. for Women, Lahore; self-published first novel The Crow Eaters 1978; Asst Prof., Creative Writing Program, Univ. of Houston, Tex., USA 1985; Bunting Fellowship, Radcliffe Coll., Harvard Univ. 1986–87; Asst Prof., Writing Div., Columbia Univ., New York 1989; Visiting Scholar, Rockefeller Foundation Centre, Bellagio, Italy 1991; Prof. of English and Writer-in-Residence, Mount Holyoake Coll., South Hadley, Mass 1997; Fannie Hurst Writer-in-Residence, Brandeis Univ., Mass 1998–99; Post-colonial Teaching Fellowship, Univ. of Southampton, UK 2001; Chair. Commonwealth Writers' Prize 1993; mem. Advisory Cttee to Prime Minister Benazir Bhutto on Women's Devt –1996, Punjab Rep., Asian Women's Conf., Alma Ata; Sec. Destitute Women's and Children's Home, Lahore; Sitara-I-Imtiaz 1991, Nat. Award for English Literature, Pakistan Acad. of Letters 1991, Patras Bokhari Award for Literature 1992, Lila Wallace Reader's Digest Award 1993, Excellence in Literature Award, Zoroastrian Congress 2002, South Asian Excellence Awards for Literature 2008, HCC Asian-American Legacy Award 2008. *Play:* Sock 'em With Honey 1993. *Film:* Earth (film of Ice-Candy-Man aka Cracking India) 1999. *Publications include:* The Crow Eaters (David Higham Award) 1978 (commercially published 1980), The Bride 1982, Ice-Candy-Man (aka Cracking India) (Notable Book of the Year, New York Times) 1991, An American Brat 1993, Bapsi Sidhwa Omnibus 2001, Water: A Novel (Premio Mondello for Foreign Authors 2007) 2006, City of Sin and Splendour: Writings on Lahore 2006, The Pakistani Bride 2008, Their Language of Love: Collection of Short Stories 2013; numerous short stories and reviews. *Leisure interests:* reading, theatre, cinema, cooking, bridge. *Address:* Milkweed Editions, 1011 Washington Avenue, South Suite 300, Open Book, Minneapolis, MN 55415 (office); 5442 Cheena Drive, Houston, TX 77096, USA (home). *Telephone:* (612) 332-3192 (office); (713) 283-0811 (home). *Website:* hometown.aol.com/bsidhwa; bapsisidhwa.com.

SIDI, Baba Ould; Mauritanian politician; b. 1946, Méderdra; fmr Man. Soc. Mauritanienne de Commercialization de Produits Petroliers; fmr Dir Banque Int. pour la Mauritanie; Minister for Fisheries and Maritime Economy 1996, for Public Works, Employment, Youth and Sports 2000–02, for Nat. Defence 2003–07; mem. Al Jamiya al-Wataniyah (Nat. Ass.) for Méderdra. *Address:* c/o Ministry of National Defence, BP 184, Nouakchott, Mauritania.

SIDI, Ibrahima Houmadi; Comoran politician; Minister of Defence, the Interior and Information 2010–11. *Address:* c/o Ministry of Defence, the Interior and Information, Moroni, Comoros (office).

SIDIBA, Cisse Mariam Kaidama; Malian civil servant and politician; b. 4 Jan. 1948, Tombouctou; m.; four c.; ed École nat. d'admin, Bamako, École int. de Bordeaux, France, École nat. d'admin publique, Québec, Canada; civil servant in Ministère de Tutelle des Sociétés et Entreprises d'Etat (Ministry of Oversight for State Cos and Socs) 1974–89, becoming Asst to Minister 1987–89; Special Adviser to Pres. 1991, 2001; Minister of Planning and Int. Cooperation 1991–92, also Minister of Agric. May–June 1992; Exec. Sec., Interstate Cttee on the Fight Against Desertification in the Sahel (Cilss), Ouagadougou 1993–2000; Minister of Rural Devt March–June 2002; Pres. Admin Council, Société nat. des tabacs et allumettes du Mali (govt-owned tobacco corpn) 2003–11; Prime Minister of Mali (first woman) 2011–12 (deposed in coup d'état 22 March); mem. Réseau des femmes ministres et parlementaires du Mali, Alliance contre la faim, Asscn pour la sauvegarde de Tombouctou. *Address:* c/o Office of the Prime Minister, Quartier du Fleuve, BP 790, Bamako, Mali (office).

SIDIBÉ, Malick; Malian photographer; b. 1935, Soloba (then French Sudan); ed Ecole des Artisans Soudanais, Bamako; trained to be designer and goldsmith; switched to photography apprenticeship 1955–58; f. Studio Malick 1958; Hasselblad Foundation Int. Prize for Photography, Sweden 2003, Golden Lion Lifetime Achievement Award, Venice Biennale 2007, ICP Infinity Award for Lifetime Achievement 2008, Baume & Mercier Award (PhotoEspana) 2009. *Publications:* Malick Sidibé Monograph 1998, The 1960's in Bamako: Malick Sidibé and James Brown 2001, You are looking beautiful like that 2001, Chemises de Malick Sidibé 2008, Malick Sidibé Bagadadji 2008. *Address:* FIFTY ONE Fine Art Photography, Zirkstraat 20, 2000 Antwerp, Belgium. *Telephone:* (3) 289-84-58. *Fax:* (3) 289-84-59. *E-mail:* info@gallery51.com. *Website:* www.gallery51.com.

SIDIBÉ, Michel, MA; Malian UN official; *Executive Director, UNAIDS;* b. 1952; m.; four c.; ed Blaise Pascal Univ.; joined UNICEF, Zaire (now Democratic Repub. of the Congo) 1987, served as UNICEF country rep. in several African countries, including Burundi, Swaziland and Uganda; apptd Dir Country and Regional Support Dept, UNAIDS 2001, Deputy Exec. Dir of Programmes, UNAIDS and UN Asst Sec.-Gen. 2007–09, Exec. Dir UNAIDS and UN Under-Sec.-Gen. 2009–; mem. Bd of Dirs Grassroot Soccer 2011; Hon. Prof., Stellenbosch Univ. of South Africa 2007; Order of St Charles (Monaco) 2009, Chevalier, Légion d'honneur 2010; Emerging Leader Award 2010. *Address:* UNAIDS, 20, Avenue Appia, 1211 Geneva 27, Switzerland (office). *Telephone:* 227913666 (office). *Fax:* 227914187 (office). *Website:* www.unaids.org (office).

SIDIBÉ, Modibo, LLM; Malian politician; b. 4 Nov. 1952, Bamako; brother of Mandé Sidibé; m.; five c.; ed Univ. of Reims, Univ. of Aix-en-Provence, France; fmr police commr; Chef de Cabinet for Minister Del. of Nat. Defence 1989–91; Cabinet Dir for Minister Del. of Internal Security 1991; Cabinet Dir for Pres. of Transitional Cttee for Health 1991–92; Minister of Health, Solidarity and the Elderly 1992–97, of Foreign Affairs and Malians Abroad 1997–2002; Sec.-Gen., Office of the Pres. 2002–07; Prime Minister 2007–11 (resgnd); Pres. Foreign Affairs Council, Econ. Community of West African States (ECOWAS) 1999–2001, Pres. Mediation and Peace Council 1999–2001; Commandeur, Ordre National du Mali, Commandeur, Légion d'Honneur. *Address:* c/o Office of the Prime Minister, Quartier du Fleuve, BP 790, Bamako, Mali.

SIDIMÉ, Lamine; Guinean lawyer, politician and judge; b. 1944; ed studied law in Paris; lecturer, Univ. of Dakar 1980, Senegal, Univ. of Conakry 1984, Prof. of Law 1985–; mem. Constitutional Council 1990; Pres. Supreme Court 1992–99, 2004; Prime Minister of Guinea, Co-ordinator of Govt Affairs 1999–2004; mem Parti de l'Unité et du Progrès (PUP). *Address:* c/o Supreme Court, Corniche-Sud, Camayenne, Conakry, Guinea (office). *Telephone:* 30-41-29-28 (office).

SIDLIN, Murry, MM; American conductor and professor of conducting; *Professor of Conducting, Benjamin T. Rome School of Music, Catholic University of America;* b. 6 May 1940, Baltimore, Md; ed Academia Chigiana, Siena, Cornell Univ.; Asst Conductor, Baltimore Symphony Orchestra 1971–73; Dir of Maryland Ballet Co. 1971–73; Prin. Conductor Baltimore Chamber Players 1971–73; Resident Conductor Nat. Symphony Orchestra under Dorati 1973–77, Wolf Trap American Univ. Music Acad. 1974; Host and Conductor Children's TV series Music is... 1977; Music Dir Tulsa Philharmonic Orchestra 1978–80; Music Dir New Haven Symphony 1977–88, Long Beach Symphony 1980–88, Resident Conductor Aspen Music Festival 1978–93; Resident Conductor Oregon Symphony Orchestra 1994–2002; Dean, Benjamin T. Rome School of Music, Catholic Univ., Washington, DC 2002–10, currently Prof. of Conducting; currently Founder-Pres. Defiant Requiem Foundation; Co-founder, Assoc. Dir and Program Coordinator, American Acad. of Conducting, Aspen; Artistic Dir Cascade Festival of Music; guest conductor: St Louis Symphony, major orchestras of San Francisco, Pittsburgh, Minnesota, Atlanta, Colorado, Utah, Florida, Jerusalem, major orchestras of Madrid, I Solisti Veneti, Honolulu, Seattle, Monte Carlo, Vancouver, Victoria, and Edmonton and Quebec, George Enescu Philharmonic of Bucharest, Czech Nat. Symphony, MVD Orchestra of Budapest, Iceland Symphony, Boston Pops, San Antonio Symphony and Opera, Houston Symphony; repeated performances with Lindberg Orchestra of Holland; Winner, Baltimore Symphony Orchestra Young Conductor's Competition 1962, Educator of the Year, Nat. Asscn of Ind. Schools of Music in America 1997, Distinguished Alumnus Award, Peabody Conservatory of Music, Johns Hopkins Univ. 2011, Excellence in Arts Award, City Choir of Washington 2011. *Television:* Music Is... *Address:* Benjamin T. Rome School of Music, 111 Ward Hall, Catholic University of America, 620 Michigan Avenue, Washington, DC 20064 (office); Defiant Requiem Foundation, PO Box 6242, Washington, DC 20015, USA (office). *Telephone:* (202) 319-5414 (Benjamin T. Rome School of Music) (office); (202) 244-0220 (Defiant Requiem Foundation) (office). *Fax:* (202) 319-6280 (Benjamin T. Rome School of Music) (office). *E-mail:* sidlin@cua.edu (office); cua-music@cua.edu (office). *Website:* music.cua.edu (office); defiantrequiem.org (office).

SIDOROV, Vasily Sergeyevich; Russian diplomatist; b. 2 Jan. 1945, Moscow; m.; three c.; ed Moscow Inst. of Int. Relations; on staff, Ministry of Foreign Affairs 1967–; fmr Amb. to Greece; Deputy Head, Dept of Int. Orgs 1990–91; Deputy, First Deputy Perm. Rep. to UN, New York 1991–95, Deputy Minister of Foreign Affairs 1995–98; Perm. Rep. to UN, Geneva 1998–2001; Head, Russian del. to UN Comm. on Human Rights 1999–2001; Russian Rep. to Conf. on Disarmament, Geneva 2001–03. *Address:* Ministry of Foreign Affairs, Smolenskaya-Sennaya pl. 32/34, 119200 Moscow, Russia (office). *Telephone:* (495) 244-41-19 (office). *Fax:* (495) 244-41-12 (office). *E-mail:* dip@mid.ru (office). *Website:* www.mid.ru (office).

SIDOROV, Yevgeniy Yurievich, DSc; Russian politician and literary critic; b. 11 Feb. 1938, Sverdlovsk (now Ekaterinburg); s. of Yuri Sidorov and Natalia Sidorova; m. Vera Indurskaya 1972; two s.; ed Moscow State Univ., Acad. of Social Sciences of Cen. Cttee of CPSU; mem. CPSU 1962–92; Head, Dept Moskovski Komsomolets 1962–65, Literaturnaya Gazeta 1965–67, Yunost 1967–72; maj. works devoted to analysis of Russian contemporary literature; Prof., Pro-rector, Moscow Gorky Literary Inst. 1978, Rector 1987–92; Minister of Culture 1994–97; mem. State Duma (Parl.) 1993–95; Perm. Rep. to UNESCO 1998–2003; Vice-Pres. European Union of Writers, Scientists, Artists; several nat. and int. literary prizes including Mediterranium Golden Oliva (Palermo, Italy) 1991. *Publications:* On the Stylistic Variety of Soviet Prose, Time to Write, On the Way to Synthesis, Yevgeniy

Yevtushenko, The Flow of Poetry Days, Pages and Fates; articles on cinema and theatre. *Leisure interests:* friends, chess, travelling.

SIDORSKY, Syarhey Syarheyovich, DEngSci; Belarusian politician; b. 13 March 1954, Gomel; m.; two d.; ed Belarus Inst. of Railway Transport Engineers; worked as electrical fitter and electrician; foreman of assembly shop, head of lab., head of dept, Deputy Dir Gomel Radio Equipment Plant 1976–91, Dir 1991–92; Gen. Man. Gomel Scientific Production Asscn RATON 1992–98; Deputy Chair. and First Deputy Chair. Gomel Oblast Admin 1998–2001; Deputy Prime Minister 2001–02, First Deputy Prime Minister 2002–03, Acting Prime Minister July–Dec. 2003, Prime Minister 2003–10; Academician, Int. Eng Acad.; Honoured Workman of Industry (Belarus). *Publications include:* more than 40 scientific publs and monographs. *Address:* c/o Office of the Prime Minister, 220010 Minsk, vul. Savetskaya 11, Belarus.

SIEGEL, François; French editor, newspaper executive and publisher; Co-founder, *We Demain;* b. of Maurice Siegel; Ed. VSD (Vendredi Samedi Dimanche) group 1981–96; Ed. Le Monde2 –2004; Co-founder with Jean-Dominique Siegel of GS Presse, We Demain 2012–. *Address:* Rédaction We Demain – GS Editions, 92 avenue Victor Cresson, 92130 Issy-les-Moulineaux, France (office). *Telephone:* 1-40-95-57-00 (office). *E-mail:* infos@cherche-midi.com (office). *Website:* www .wedemain.fr (office).

SIEGEL, Ned L., JD; American lawyer, business executive and fmr diplomatist; m. Stephanie Moak Siegel; two s. one d.; ed Univ. of Connecticut, Dickinson School of Law; served as law clerk to Chief Justice Mitchell H. Cohen in Fed. Dist Court, Camden, NJ; joined Kimmelman, Wolff & Samson law firm, NJ; joined Howard Siegel Companies 1977, Pres. and Man. Pnr, Weingarten-Siegel Group, Inc. 1980; currently Pnr, Paramount Residential, LLC; fmr Chair. The Siegel Group; apptd by Gov. Jeb Bush to Enterprise Fla's Bd of Dirs and to Space Research and Commerce Park Planning and Devt Cttee, John F. Kennedy Space Center; fmr Trustee Gov.'s Mansion Foundation, Greater Boca Raton Chamber of Commerce; apptd by Pres. George W. Bush to Bd of Dirs Overseas Pvt. Investment Corpn 2003; US Rep. to UN 2006; Amb. to the Bahamas 2007–09; fmr Chair. Republican Jewish Coalition of Fla; fmr mem. Nat. Bd of Dirs Republican Jewish Coalition, Washington, DC, Bd American Jewish Cttee, S Cen. Fla Chapter; fmr Co-Pres. Bd Jewish Nat. Fund's S Palm Beach Co. Region; active in Israeli Bonds program, Temple B'nai Torah, Boca Raton, Chabad Lubavitch of Greater Boynton (served as Exec. Chair. Exec. Cttee). *Address:* 3835 NW Boca Raton Blvd, Suite 300, Boca Raton, FL 33431-5861, USA.

SIEGERT, Theo, MBA, PhD; German business executive; *Member, Supervisory Board, E.ON AG;* b. 8 April 1947, Düsseldorf; m.; two c.; ed Univ. of Munich; joined Franz Haniel & Cie. GmbH 1975, held several sr positions including in Controlling Dept, then Head of Strategic Planning Dept, Dir of Finance and Mergers & Acquisitions, Deputy Mem. Managing Bd 1994–96, mem. 1996–2005, Chair. 2005; Chair. Supervisory Bd Metro AG 2004–06; mem. Supervisory Bd Commercial Pharmaceutique S.A., Saint-Ouen/France –2002, Merck KGaA 2006–, Deutsche Bank AG 2006–, Henkel AG & Co. 2009–, E.ON AG 2009–, Ergo Versicherungs-gruppe AG –2010; mem. Bd of Pnrs E. Merck OHG 2006–; mem. Bd of Dirs DKSH, ERGO Insurance Group AG 2009–; Chair. Foundation Council, Stiftung Marktwirtschaft; Hon. Prof. of Financial Analysis and Co. Man., Ludwig-Maximilians Univ. of Munich; Hon. Prof., Univ. of Munich. *Address:* E.ON AG, E.On-Platz 1, 40479 Düsseldorf, Germany (office). *Telephone:* (49) 21145790 (office). *Fax:* (49) 2114579 501 (office). *E-mail:* info@eon.com (office). *Website:* www .eon.com (office).

SIELICKI, Tomasz, BEcons; Polish business executive; *Vice-Chairman, Super-visory Board, Sygnity Group;* ed Warsaw Univ. of Tech.; joined ComputerLand 1991, Pres., Man. Bd 1992–2005, Pres. ComputerLand Group (now Sygnity Group after merger with Emax 2007) 2005–07, Vice-Chair. Supervisory Bd 2007–, also mem. Man. Bd; Pres. Polish Chess Fed. 2009–; mem. Man. Bd Polish Confed. of Pvt. Employers LEWIATAN; mem. Man. Bd Stock Exchange Court, Warsaw Stock Exchange, Council of Junior Achievement Foundation, Program Council, Acad. of Capital Market Leaders operating at Foundation of Leslaw Paga, Polish Private Employees Confed., Trilateral Comm.; mem. Supervisory Bd Agora SA, Budimex SA, Sygnity SA; INFO-STAR prize, listed among Cen. Europe's Top 10 Executives by The Wall Street Journal 1999, Global Leader for Tomorrow Prize 1999. *Leisure interests:* chess. *Address:* Sygnity Group, Al. Jerozolimskie 180, 02-486 Warsaw, Poland (office). *Telephone:* (22) 5711000 (office). *Fax:* (22) 5711001 (office). *E-mail:* bdrzewicz@sygnity.pl (office). *Website:* www.sygnity.pl (office).

SIEMIĄTKOWSKI, Zbigniew, DH; Polish politician; b. 8 Oct. 1957, Ciechanów; m.; one d.; ed Warsaw Univ.; Sr Asst, Warsaw Univ. 1981–; Deputy to Sejm (Parl.) 1991–2005, mem. Comm. for Nat. and Ethnic Minorities, Comm. of Justice; mem. Polish United Workers' Party (PZPR) 1978–90; mem. Social Democracy of Polish Repub. (SDRP) 1990–99; Minister of Internal Affairs 1996; mem. Council of Ministers 1997; mem. Democratic Left Alliance (SLD) 1999–; Sec. of State in Chancellery of Prime Minister 2001–; Acting Head, Office of State Protection (Urzad Ochrony Panstwa—UOP) 2001–02, Head, Foreign Intelligence Agency (Agencji Wywiadu—AW) (following absorption of UOP into AW and Interior Security Agency (Agencja Bezpieczenstwa Wewnetrznego—AWB)) 2002–04 (resgnd); Ordre National du Mérite, France 1996, Legion of Merit (Commdr), USA 2004. *Publications:* Intelligence and Power: The Role of the Civil Intelligence in the PRZ Government Political System. *Leisure interest:* family, tourism. *Address:* c/o Democratic Left Alliance (SLD), 00-419 Warsaw, ul. Rozbrat 44a, Poland. *E-mail:* malsiemiat@onet.eu (home).

SIEMONIAK, Tomasz; Polish communications industry executive and politician; *Minister of National Defence;* b. 2 July 1967; m.; one s., one d.; ed Warsaw School of Econs; fmrly with Ind. Student Asscn; Chair. in Main School of Planning and Statistics; fmr Sec., Nat. Coordination Cttee; Dir Office for Field Branches, Telewizja Polska SA (Polish public television) and Gen. Dir Channel 1 1994–96; Coordinator, Media and Democracy Programme, Inst. of Public Affairs 1997; Dir Press and Information Office, Ministry of Nat. Defence 1998–2000; Deputy Chair. Supervisory Bd of Polish News Agency 1998–2002; mem. Warsaw-City Centre District Council 1998–2000; Deputy Chair. of Culture Cttee 1998–2000; Deputy Mayor of Warsaw 2000–02; mem. Man. Bd Polskie Radio SA (Polish public radio) 2002–06; Deputy Marshal, Marshal's Office of Mazowieckie Voivodeship 2006–07;

Sec. of State, Ministry of Interior and Admin 2007–11; Minister of Nat. Defence 2011–. *Address:* Ministry of National Defence, 00-909 Warsaw, ul. Klonowa 1, Poland (office). *Telephone:* (22) 6840213 (office). *Fax:* (22) 6840213 (office). *E-mail:* newsroom.dpimon@mon.gov.pl (office). *Website:* www.mon.gov.pl (office).

SIENKIEWICZ, Bartłomiej Henryk; Polish politician; *Minister of the Interior;* b. 29 July 1961, great-grandson of novelist and journalist Henryk Sienkiewicz; m.; three s. one d.; ed Faculty of Philosophy and History, Jagiellonian Univ.; participated in Kraków opposition movt early 1980s; co-f. Office for State Protection 1990; co-f. Centre for Eastern studies (think-tank) 1990, Vice-Pres. for Programme Affairs 1991–93, 1996–2001, currently Chair. Centre for Eastern Studies; worked in pvt. sector in early 2000s; f. Sienkiewicz i Wspólnicy (now ASBS Othago); adviser to Speaker of the Sejm (Parl.) 2003–05; fmr Lecturer, Nat. Defence Univ.; mem. Programme Bd, Polish Inst. of Int. Affairs; mem. Bd Internal Security Agency Central Training Centre; Minister of the Interior 2013–. *Address:* Ministry of the Interior, 02-591 Warsaw, ul. Stefana Batorego 5, Poland (office). *Telephone:* (22) 6212020 (office). *Fax:* (22) 6013988 (office). *E-mail:* kancelaria .glowna@mswia.gov.pl (office). *Website:* www.msw.gov.pl (office).

SIEVERT, Frederick J., BA, MA; American fmr insurance industry executive; m.; five c.; ed Amherst Coll., Wayne State Univ.; fmr secondary school teacher; Sr Vice-Pres. Royal Maccabees Life Insurance Co.; joined New York Life Insurance Co. as Sr Vice-Pres. and Chief Financial Officer with responsibility for Financial Man. Dept of Individual Operations 1992–95, also responsible for Individual Life, Individual Annuity and Disability Income Depts 1994, Exec. Vice-Pres. 1995–97, Vice-Chair. 1997–2004, Pres. 2002–07 (retd); Dir Max New York Life Insurance Co. Ltd –2007, Siam Commercial New York Life Insurance Public Co. Ltd –2007, Reinsurance Group of America Inc. 2010–, CNO Financial Group Inc. 2011–; fmr Chair. Bd of Trustees, The American Coll., currently Trustee; mem. American Acad. of Actuaries; Fellow, Soc. of Actuaries. *Address:* c/o Board of Directors, CNO Financial Group Inc, 11825 North Pennsylvania Street, Carmel, IN 46032, USA (office).

SIEVERTS, Thomas C. W., DiplIng; German architect and town planner; b. 8 June 1934, Hamburg; s. of Rudolf Sieverts and Elisabeth Sieverts (née Ronnefeldt); m. Heide Pawelzick 1966; one s. two d.; ed in Stuttgart, Liverpool and Berlin; with Kossak and Zimmermann f. Freie Plannungsgruppe Berlin 1965; Prof. of Town Planning Dept of Architecture, Hochschule der Künste, Berlin 1967–70; Guest Prof., Grad. School of Design, Harvard Univ., USA 1970–71; Prof. of Town Planning, Dept of Architecture, Tech. Hochschule, Darmstadt 1971–99, now Prof. Emer.; Special Prof. of Urban Design, Inst. of Planning Studies, Univ. of Nottingham, UK 1978–83; in practice as architect and town planner, Bonn 1978–; Fellow, Inst. for Advanced Study, Berlin 1995–96; Regent's Prof., Univ. of Berkeley 2005; mem. Scientific Advisory Council World Exhbn, 'Expo 2000', Hanover 1989–99, Sächsischea Akad. der Künste; Deubau Prize (Essen) 1969, Verdienstzei-chen in Gold (Vienna) 1988, Bauherren Prize 1992, Deutsche Städtebau Prize 1993. *Buildings:* town planning consultant to the City of Vienna, planning Danubia area 1973–78, the Gürtel area 1984–88; Dir of Int. Bldg Exhbn Emscher Park (Ruhr) 1989–94. *Publications:* Zwischenstadt (3rd edn) 1999 (English edn: Cities Without Cities – An Interpretation of the Zwischenstadt 2004), Fünfzig Jahre Städtebau – Reflektion und Praxis 2001; many contribs to periodicals and books. *Leisure interest:* drawing. *Address:* skt umbaukultur, Thomas-Mann-Strasse 41, 53111 Bonn, Germany. *Telephone:* (228) 22723620 (office). *Fax:* (228) 22723629 (office). *E-mail:* info@umbaukultur.eu (office). *Website:* www.skt -umbaukultur.eu (office).

SIEW, Vincent C., LLM; Taiwanese diplomatist, fmr government official and research institute administrator; b. 3 Jan. 1939, Chiayi City, Taiwan; m.; three d.; ed Nat. Chengchi Univ., Georgetown Univ.; Vice-Consul, Kuala Lumpur, Malaysia 1966–69, Consul 1969–72; Section Chief, Asia Pacific Affairs Dept, Ministry of Foreign Affairs 1972; Deputy Dir 4th Dept Bd of Foreign Trade, Ministry of Econ. Affairs 1972–74, Dir 1974–77, Deputy Dir-Gen. Bd of Foreign Trade 1977–82, Dir-Gen. 1982–88; Vice-Chair. Council for Econ. Planning and Devt, Exec. Yuan 1988–89; Dir-Gen. Dept of Organizational Affairs, Kuomintang Cen. Cttee 1989–90, Vice-Chair. Kuomintang 2000–05; Minister of Econ. Affairs 1990–93; Minister of State, Chair. Council for Econ. Planning and Devt, Exec. Yuan 1993–94; Minister of State, Chair. Mainland Affairs Council, Exec. Yuan 1994–95; legislator 1996–97; Premier of Taiwan 1997–2000; Vice. Pres. of Taiwan 2008–12; Eisenhower Fellow, USA 1985; Chair. Chung-Hua Inst. for Econ. Research, Convenor Presidential Econ. Advisory Panel 2003–04; fmr Chair. Cross-Straits Common Market Foundation; Prof. Nat. Chengchi Univ.; Hon. D.Man (Nat. Chia-Yi Univ.), Hon. DEcon (Sung Kyun Kwan Univ., Seoul), Hon. PhD (Rangsit Univ., Thailand), Hon. Dr Public Service (Ohio State Univ., USA). *Publications:* One Plus One is Greater than Two: The Road to the Cross-Straits Common Market, To Govern the Nation with Expertise. *Address:* c/o Office of the President, 122 Chungking South Rd, Sec. 1, Taipei 10048, Taiwan (office).

SIFAKIS, Joseph, PhD; Greek/French computer scientist, institute director and consultant; *Founder, Verimag Laboratory and Research Director, Centre National de la Recherche Scientifique;* b. 26 Dec. 1946, Heraklion, Crete; ed Nat. Technical Univ. of Athens, Univ. of Grenoble, France; Research Dir, CNRS, Founder Verimag Lab., Grenoble, Dir 1993–2006; Prof., Ecole Polytechnique Fédérale de Lausanne, Switzerland 2011–; Scientific Coordinator ArtistDesign Network of Excellence on Embedded Systems Design; Chair. Chamber B (Public Research Orgs) of ARTEMISIA (industrial asscn within the ARTEMIS European Tech. Platform on Embedded Systems); mem. Bd of Dirs CARNOT Inst. 'Intelligent Software and Systems', Grenoble; Co-founder Int. Conf. on Computer Aided Verification (CAV); mem. Steering Cttee EMSOFT (Embedded Software) Conf.; mem. editorial bds of several journals; mem. Academia Europea, French Nat. Acad. of Engineering, French Acad. of Sciences; Hon. Prof., Univ. of Patras; Grand Officier, Ordre national du Mérite; Dr hc (Ecole Polytechnique Fédérale de Lausanne), (Univ. of Athens), (Int. Hellenic Univ.); CNRS Silver Medal 2001, Turing Award (co-recipient) 2007. *Achievements include:* developed theory and tech. for the SCADE tool used for design and validation of critical real-time systems, de facto standard for aeronautics; recognized for pioneering work on both theoretical and practical aspects of Concurrent Systems Specification and Verification. *Publications:* numerous scientific papers in professional journals on component-based design, modelling, and analysis of real-time systems with focus on correct-by-construction techniques. *Address:* Verimag Laboratory, Centre Equation, 2 avenue de Vignate, 38610 Gieres, France (office). *Telephone:* (4) 56-52-03-51 (office). *Fax:* (4) 56-52-04-46 (office). *E-mail:* joseph.sifakis@imag.fr (office). *Website:* www-verimag.imag.fr/~sifakis (office).

SIGALOVA, Alla Mikhailovna; Russian choreographer, ballet dancer and academic; *Professor, Chekhov Moscow Art Theatre (MKhAT);* b. 28 Feb. 1958, Volgograd; d. of Stalov Mikhail Petrovich and Viogina Tamara Aleksandrovna; m. Kozak Roman Yefimovich; one s. one d.; ed Leningrad Vaganova School of Choreography, Russian Acad. of Theatre Arts; teacher Russian Acad. of Theatre Arts 1982–2004; choreographer Theatre Satirikon 1987–89; Artistic Dir Theatre Ind. Troupe of Alla Sigalova 1989–97, Choreography Theatre of Alla Sigalova 2001–; Prof. and Head, Faculty of Eurhythmics, Studio School of Chekhov Moscow Art Theatre (MKhAT) 2004–; choreographer of New Year TV shows for ORT and NTV channels 1996–99; Honoured Artist of Russia, Golden Mask Nat. Theatre Award 2008. *Dance:* Othello 1990, Queen of Spades 1991, Salomea 1991. *Productions choreographed include:* Moscow Mayakovsky Theatre: Diary of an Ordinary Girl 1984, Bed-Bug 1986; Moscow Satirikon Theatre: Serving Girls 1988; Moscow Mossoviet Theatre: Banana 1994; Theatre of Lower Saxony: Yvonne, the Princess of Burgundy; Nuremberg Theatre: Money-bank; Ekaterinburg City Ballet: Nutcracker; Latvian Nat. Opera: Duets, Yellow Tango, Bolero; Samara Theatre of Opera and Ballet: Visions of Ivan the Terrible; New Opera Theatre: Traviata; Lithuanian Opera and Ballet Theatre: Seven Deadly Sins; Theatre of Popular Genre: Dreams of Love; Pushkin Theatre: Romeo and Juliet, Djan; Pushkin Theatre: Nights of Cabiria, Madame Bovary; Moscow Chekhov Theatre: Carmen. Etudes. *Address:* Chekhov Moscow Art Theatre (MKhAT), 3 Kamergerskiy Pereulok, Moscow 103 (office); Prechistenka str. 25/13, Apartment 10, Moscow, Russia (home). *Telephone:* (495) 629-87-60 (office); (495) 201-44-36 (home). *Fax:* (495) 201-44-36 (home). *E-mail:* mhat@theatre.ru (office); asigalova@mail.ru (home). *Website:* art.theatre.ru (office).

SIGFÚSSON, Steingrímur J., BSc; Icelandic politician; b. 4 Aug. 1955, Thistilfjordur; ed Univ. of Iceland; mem. Althingi (Parl.) 1983–, Chair. People's Alliance Parl. Group 1987–88, mem. Cttee on Fisheries 1991–98 (Chair. 1995–98), on Economy and Trade 1991–99, on Social Affairs 1999–2003, on Foreign Affairs 1999–2009, Special Cttee on Constitutional Affairs 2004–05, mem. Del. to W Nordic Council 1991–95, to Nordic Council 1996–2005, 2006–07, to Parl. Ass. of the Council of Europe 2007–13, Chair. PACE Cttee on Equal Opportunities 2008–13; Founding Chair. Left-Green Movement 1999–2013; Minister of Agric. and Communications 1988–91, of Fisheries and Agric. Feb.–May 2009, of Finance 2009–11, of Econ. Affairs Jan.–Sept. 2012, of Fisheries and Agric. Jan.–Sept. 2012, of Industries and Innovation Sept. 2012–13. *Address:* c/o Vinstrihreyfingin–grænt frambod (Left-Green Movement), Sudurgötu 3, POB 175, 101 Reykjavík, Iceland.

SIGUA, Tengiz Ippolitovich, DTechS; Georgian politician; b. 9 Nov. 1934, Lentekhi; s. of Ipolite Sigua and Lidia Schavdia; m. Nina Iwania 1975; one d.; ed Georgian Polytechnical Inst.; engineer and Dir Metallurgy Inst. Georgian Acad. of Sciences 1962–90, now mem. Georgian Acad. of Sciences; fmr leading mem. Round Table—Free Georgia Alliance, Chair. All-Georgia Rustaveli Soc.; apptd Head of Govt by Zviad Gamsakhurdia, Nov. 1990, resigned Aug. 1991 and joined the opposition; mem. State Council March–Oct. 1992; mem. Supreme Soviet 1992–95; apptd Prime Minister by Mil. Council 1992–93 (resgnd), now in Parl. Opposition; Vice-Pres. Georgian Rustaveli Soc. 1989, Pres. 1992–93; arrested with Tengiz Kitovani after an attempted march of armed Georgian refugees on Abkhazia to retake breakaway region 1995, later released. *Leisure interests:* sport, art. *Address:* Phanaskerteli str. 16, Apt 31, 380094 Tbilisi, Georgia (home).

SIGURÐARDÓTTIR, Jóhanna; Icelandic politician; b. 4 Oct. 1942, Reykjavík; m. 1st Þorvaldur Steinar Jóhannesson 1970 (divorced); two s.; civil partner Jónína Leósdóttir 2002, m. 2010; ed Commercial Coll. of Iceland; fmr flight attendant, Loftleiðir; fmr office worker; elected Social Democratic Party mem. of Althing (Parl.) (Social Democratic Party) 1978, Deputy Speaker 1979, 1983–84, 2003–07; Vice-Chair. Social Democratic Party 1984–93; Minister of Social Affairs and Social Security 1987–94, 2007–09; f. Þjóðvaki party 1994–2000; mem. Social Democratic Alliance 2000–13; Prime Minister 2009–13; Bd mem. Commercial Workers' Union 1976–83; ranked by Forbes magazine amongst The World's 100 Most Powerful Women (75th) 2009, (80th) 2010. *Address:* c/o Social Democratic Alliance, Hallveigarstíg 1, 101 Reykjavík, Iceland.

SIGURDSSON, Jón, MSc(Econ); Icelandic politician and economist; b. 17 April 1941, Ísafjörður; s. of Sigurdur Gudmundsson and Kristin Gudjona; m. Laufey Thorbjarnardóttir; four c.; ed Akureyri Coll., Univ. of Stockholm, Sweden and London School of Econs, UK; Econ. Inst. of Iceland 1964–71 (Dir Econ. Research 1970–71); Chief Econ. Research Div. Econ. Devt Inst. 1972–74; Man. Dir Nat. Econ. Inst. and Econ. Adviser to Govt 1974–80, 1983–86; Exec. Dir for Nordic Countries IMF 1980–83, Alt. Gov. IMF for Iceland 1974–87; Assoc. Jt IBRD/IMF Devt Cttee 1974–80; IBRD Gov. for Iceland 1987–; EBRD Gov. for Iceland 1991–; mem. Althing (SDP) 1987–; Minister of Justice and Ecclesiastical Affairs 1987–88, of Commerce 1987–93, of Industry 1988–93, of Nordic Co-operation 1988–89; Chair. OECD Council of Ministers 1989, Nordic Council of Ministers 1989; mem. Salaries Arbitration Court 1970–80; Rep. for Iceland Econ. and Devt Review Cttee OECD 1970–80, 1983–86; Gov. and Chair. Bd of Dirs, Cen. Bank of Iceland 1993–94; Pres. and CEO Nordic Investment Bank 1994–2005, mem. Bd of Dirs 1976–87, Chair. 1984–86; currently financial and econ. consultant. *Address:* c/o Nordic Investment Bank, Fabianinkatu 34, PO Box 249, 00171 Helsinki, Finland.

SIILASMAA, Risto, MSc (Eng); Finnish business executive; *Chairman, Nokia Corporation;* b. 1966; ed Helsinki Univ. of Tech.; Founder, Pres. and CEO F-Secure Corpn 1988–2006, Chair. 2006–; mem. Bd of Dirs Nokia Corpn 2008–, Chair. 2012–, Chair. Corp. Governance and Nomination Cttee; Chair. Fruugo Inc.; mem. Bd of Dirs Blyk Ltd, Mendor Ltd, Fed. of Finnish Tech. Industries, Elisa Corpn 2007–12 (Chair. 2008–12), Efecte Oy 2008–12 (Chair. 2007–08), Ekahau Oy 2008–11 (Chair. 2007–08), Ekahau, Inc. 2008–11 (Chair. 2006–08), Nexit Ventures Oy 1999–2009; several awards, including The Leader of the Decade 2003, Most Influential IT Leader of the Year 2007, Nordic Chairman of the Year 2009. *Address:* Nokia Corporation, Keilalahdentie 4, 00045 Espoo (office); F-Secure Corporation, Tammasaarenkatu 7, PL 24, 00181 Helsinki, Finland. *Telephone:* (7180) 08000 (Espoo) (office); (9) 2520-0700 (Helsinki) (office). *Fax:* (7180) 38226 (Espoo) (office);

(9) 2520-5001 (Helsinki) (office). *E-mail:* info@nokia.com (office); info@f-secure.com (office). *Website:* www.nokia.com (office); www.f-secure.com (office).

SIIMANN, Mart; Estonian fmr politician; b. 21 Sept. 1946, Kilingi-Nõmme; m.; two c.; ed Tartu State Univ.; psychologist, Deputy Head Lab. of Scientific Org. of Work and Man. 1971–75; Sr research Asst Tartu State Univ. 1975–82; broadcaster, Deputy Dir-Gen., Ed.-in-Chief Estonian TV 1982–87, Dir-Gen. 1989–92; Dir-Gen. Estonian Radio 1987–89; Man. Dir commercial TV station ReklamTV 1992–95; mem. Riigikugu (Parl.) 1995–97, 1999–2003; Chair. Coalition Party 1997–99; Prime Minister of Estonia 1997–99; fmr Counsellor to Pres. of Estonia on Domestic Policy; Pres. Estonian Olympic Cttee 2001–12. *Leisure interests:* sport, literature, fishing, philosophy.

SIKHARULIDZE, Vasil; Georgian physician, psychiatrist and diplomatist; b. 30 May 1968, Tbilisi; m. Anna Tsagareli; one d.; ed Tbilisi State Medical Univ.; physician and psychiatrist, Inst. of Psychiatry 1993–95; Exec. Dir Atlantic Council of Georgia 1995–96; worked in Georgian Parl. as specialist on Cttee of Defence and Security 1996–2000; Head of NATO Div., Ministry of Foreign Affairs and Deputy Head of Georgian Mission to NATO, Brussels 2000–02; NATO Fellow 2001–03; Under-Sec. Nat. Security Council of Georgia March–July 2004; Deputy Minister of Defence 2004–05, First Deputy Minister of Defence, responsible for Policy and Planning, Int. Relations and Legal Affairs 2005–06; Amb. to USA (also accred to Canada and Mexico) 2006–08; Minister of Defence 2008–09; Foreign Policy Adviser to Pres. 2009–. *Address:* c/o Office of the President, 0105 Tbilisi, P. Ingorovka 7, Georgia (office).

SIKORSKI, Radosław (Radek) Tomasz, BA, MA; Polish journalist and politician; *Minister of Foreign Affairs;* b. 23 Feb. 1963, Bydgoszcz; m. Anne Applebaum; two s.; ed Univ. of Oxford, UK; involved in Solidarity social movt early 1980s; Chair. student strike cttee Bydgoszcz 1981; political refugee in UK 1981–89; journalist reporting on wars in Afghanistan and Angola 1986–89; Deputy Minister of Nat. Defence 1992; Under-Sec. of State in Ministry of Foreign Affairs 1998–2002; Fellow, American Enterprise Inst. and Exec. Dir New Atlantic Initiative, Washington, DC 2002–05; elected to Senate for Bydgoszcz (Law and Justice Party), Minister of Nat. Defence 2005–07, of Foreign Affairs 2007–; elected to Sejm (Parl.) for Bydgoszcz 2007 (re-elected 2011); Vice-Chair. Civic Platform party 2010–; 'Millennium Star' Medal (Lithuania) 2008, Nat. Order of Merit, Grade of Companion (Malta) 2009, Order of Merit, First Class (No. 407) (Ukraine) 2009, Royal Order of the Polar Star (Sweden) 2011, Order of Prince Jaroslaw the Wise, Third Class (Ukraine) 2011, Commdr's Grand Cross, Royal Order of the Polar Star (Sweden) 2011, Grand Officier, Légion d'honneur 2012; World Press Photo Prize 1987, The Spectator and The Sunday Telegraph Young Writers' Awards 1988, Odznaka Zasłużony Działacz Kultury (Polish award for the promotion of culture), Wiktor Award for "most popular politician" 2006, Lithuanian Millennium Star Medal 2008, Gold Badge, Asscn of Poles in Lithuania 2010, named by the Foreign Policy magazine as one of the Top 100 Global Thinkers 2012. *Television:* cr. TV programme Wywiad Miesiąca (interview of the month). *Publications:* Prochy Świętych – podróż do Heratu w czas wojny (Dust of the Saints – A Journey to Herat in Time of War) 1989, The Polish House: An Intimate History of Poland 1998, Strefa Zdekomunizowana 2007; ed. of series of analytical publs entitled European Outlook. *Address:* Ministry of Foreign Affairs, 00-580 Warsaw, Al. Szucha 23, Poland (office). *Telephone:* (22) 5239201 (office). *Fax:* (22) 6257652 (office). *E-mail:* sm.sekretariat@msz.gov.pl (office). *Website:* www.msz.gov.pl (office); www.radeksikorski.pl.

SIKUA, David Derek, DipEd, BEd, MEPA, PhD; Solomon Islands educator and politician; b. 10 Sept. 1959; ed Univ. of the South Pacific, Suva, Fiji, Univ. of Southern Queensland, Australia, Monash Univ., Univ. of Waikato, New Zealand; teacher and Deputy Headmaster Pawa Secondary School 1982–84; teacher and Deputy Prin. Waimapuru, Nat. Secondary School 1984–86; Prin. Educ. Officer, Implementation and Planning Unit, Ministry of Educ. and Human Resources Devt 1986–87, Dir Implementation and Planning Unit 1988–90, Dir Secondary School Div. Jan.–Feb. 1993, Under Sec. Minister of Educ. and Human Resources Devt 1993–94, Perm. Sec. 1994–97; Perm. Sec., Ministry of Forests, Environment and Conservation 1997–98; Perm. Sec. (Special Duties), Ministry of Educ. and Human Resources Dev May–Sept. 2003, Perm. Sec. 2003–05; mem. Parl. for North East Guadalcanal 2006–; Minister for Educ. and Human Resources Devt 2006–07; Prime Minister 2007–10; Chair. Solomon Islands Nat. Comm. for UNESCO 2006–; Chair. Nat. Educ. Planning Cttee 1989–90, Nat. Library Bd 1993–94; Deputy Chair. Solomon Islands Coll. of Higher Educ. (SICHE) Council 1994–97; mem. USP Council Exec. Cttee 2007–. *Leisure interests:* reading, writing, soccer, cricket, rugby, bushwalking, bird watching. *Address:* c/o Office of the Prime Minister, PO Box G1, Honiara, Solomon Islands (office).

SILAJDŽIĆ, Haris, PhD; Bosnia and Herzegovina academic and politician; b. 1 Oct. 1945, Sarajevo; m.; one s.; ed Garyounis Univ., Libya; has held several academic positions including Arabic Language Prof., Univ. of Prishtina, Prof., Faculty of Philosophy and Dept of History, Univ. of Sarajevo, Andrew D. White Prof. at Large, Cornell Univ., New York, Guest Lecturer, Harvard Univ. and Univ. of Maryland, Chatham House (Royal Inst. for Int. Affairs), London, Carnegie Foundation, Woodrow Wilson Center, and other univs; Minister of Foreign Affairs, Repub. of Bosnia and Herzegovina 1990–93, Prime Minister 1993–96, Co-Chair. Council of Ministers of Bosnia and Herzegovina 1997–2000; Bosniak mem. Tripartite State Presidency 2006–10, Chair. (Pres. of Bosnia and Herzegovina) March–Nov. 2008, March–Nov. 2010; fmr mem. and Vice-Pres. Party of Democratic Action; Founder Party for Bosnia and Herzegovina (Stranka za Bosnu i Hercegovinu), Pres. 1996–2012; Dr hc (Geneva School of Diplomacy and Int. Relations) 2005; Rabbi Marc H. Tanenbaum Memoral Lecturer 1997. *Publications:* several books and papers on int. relations, including relations between USA and Albania. *Address:* Party for Bosnia and Herzegovina, 71000 Sarajevo, Fra Grge Martića 2/II, Bosnia and Herzegovina (office). *Telephone:* (33) 573470 (office). *Fax:* (33) 475597 (office). *E-mail:* zabih@zabih.ba (office). *Website:* www.zabih.ba (office).

SILANYO, Ahmed Mohamed, BEcons, MEcons; Somali politician; *President, 'Republic of Somaliland';* b. 1936, Burao; ed Univ. of Manchester, UK; Jr Official, Ministry of Planning and Co-ordination, Mogadishu 1965–69, Minister of Planning and Co-ordination 1969–73, of Commerce 1973–78, 1980–82; Chair. Nat.

Econ. Bd 1978–80; in exile in UK 1982 until Somaliland's declaration of independence from Somalia 1991; Chair. Somali Nat. Movt 1982–90; mem. House of Reps, Somaliland 1993–97, Somaliland Minister of Finance 1997–99, of Planning and Coordination 1999–2001; currently Chair. Peace, Unity and Devt Party (Kulmiye); unsuccessful cand. in presidential election 2003; Pres. of self-proclaimed ' Repub. of Somaliland' (NW Somalia) 2010–. *Address:* Office of the President, Hargeisa, Somaliland (office). *Website:* www.somalilandgov.com (office).

SILAPA-ARCHA, Banharn, LLM; Thai politician; b. 20 July 1932; s. of Sengkim and Sai-eng sae Ba; ed Ramkhamhaeng Univ.; elected to Suphan Buri Municipal Council 1973; Co-Founder Chart Thai party 1975, Sec.-Gen. 1976, Party Leader 1994–2008; mem. Legis. Ass. 1973–; Deputy Minister of Industry 1976; Minister of Agric. 1980; Senator 1986; Minister of Communications 1986, of Industry 1989, of Finance 1990, of Interior 1990–91, of Communications 1992; Leader of Opposition 1992–95; Prime Minister 1995–96, also Minister of the Interior. *Address:* c/o House of Representatives, U-Thong Road, Dusit, Bangkok 10300, Thailand.

SILAS, Cecil Jesse, BS; American business executive; b. 15 April 1932, Miami; s. of David Edward Silas and Hilda Videll Silas (née Carver); m. Theodosea Hejda 1965; three s. one d.; ed Miami Sr High School, Georgia Inst. of Tech.; joined Phillips Petroleum Co. 1953; Pres. Phillips Petroleum Co. Europe-Africa, Brussels and London 1968–74, Pres. and COO (also Dir and Chair. Exec. Cttee) Phillips Petroleum Co. 1982–85, Chair. and CEO 1985–94; Man. Dir NRG Europe-Africa, London 1974–76; Vice-Pres. Gas and Gas Liquids, NRG, Bartlesville, Okla 1976–78; Sr Vice-Pres. Natural Resources Group, Bartlesville 1978–80, Exec. Vice-Pres. 1980–82; Chair. Bd American Petroleum Inst. –1993, Bd US Chamber of Commerce; mem. Bd of Dirs Ethics Resource Centre, Reader's Digest Asscn Inc., Halliburton Co.; mem. Council on Foreign Relations, The Business Council; Trustee, Emer. Georgia Tech Foundation; fmr Chair. Bd of Nat. Junior Achievement; fmr Chair. Nat. Boys & Girls Clubs of America, currently Bd mem.; Dr hc (Phillips Univ. in Enid, Oklahoma); Commdr, Royal Order of St Olav, Norway 1976; Gold Medal Award, American Petroleum Inst. 1995. *Leisure interests:* golf, fishing, hunting. *Address:* 2400 Terrace Drive, Bartlesville, OK 74004, USA (home). *Telephone:* (918) 333-8577 (home).

SILAYEV, Ivan Stepanovich; Russian politician; b. 21 Oct. 1930; m.; two c.; ed Kazan Aviation Inst.; mem. CPSU 1959–91; foreman, shop supt, deputy chief engineer, chief engineer, plant dir in Gorky 1954–74; Deputy Minister of Aircraft Industry of USSR 1974–77, First Deputy Minister 1977–80, Minister 1981–85; Minister of Machine Tool and Instrument-Making Industry of USSR 1980–81; Deputy to USSR Supreme Soviet 1981–89; Deputy Pres. Council of Ministers of USSR 1985–89; Pres. Council of Ministers of RSFSR 1989–91; Pres. Inter-Republican Econ. Cttee of USSR 1991; Russian Perm. Rep. to EC (now EU) 1992–94; Pres. Bd of Dirs Ecology of Russia Consortium 1995–; Chair. Bd Moscow Interregional Commercial Bank 1996–, Int. Union of Mechanical Engineers 1997–; Pres. Industrial Union of Russia 2002–; mem. Bd of Dirs Yukos Corp. 2005–, Int. Business Club; mem. CPSU Cen. Cttee 1981–91; Order of Lenin 1971, 1975, Hero of Socialist Labour 1975, Order of the October Revolution 1981, Nat. Prize of Peter the Great 2002,; Lenin Prize 1972. *Address:* c/o Board of Directors, Yukos Corp, 31A Dubininskaya Street, 115054 Moscow, Russia.

SILBERMAN, Laurence Hirsch, LLB; American judge, banker, diplomatist and academic; *Senior Judge, United States Court of Appeals for the DC Circuit;* b. 12 Oct. 1935, York, Pa; s. of William Silberman and Anna Hirsch; m. Rosalie Gaull 1957; one s. two d.; ed Dartmouth Coll., Harvard Law School; with Moore, Torkildson & Rice, Quinn & Moore (law firm) 1961–64; Pnr, Moore, Silberman & Schulze 1964–67; lawyer, Nat. Labor Relations Bd 1967–69; solicitor, Labor Dept 1969–70, Under-Sec. for Labor Affairs 1970–73; Pnr, Steptoe & Johnson 1973–74; Deputy Attorney-Gen., Dept of Justice 1974–75; Amb. to Yugoslavia 1975–77 (withdrawn); Man. Pnr, Morrison and Foerster, Washington, DC 1978–79, 1983–85; Exec. Vice-Pres. Legal and Govt Affairs Div., Crocker Nat. Bank 1979–83; Sr Fellow, American Enterprise Inst. for Public Policy Research, Washington, DC 1977–78, Visiting Fellow 1978–85; Vice-Chair. Advisory Council on Gen. Govt, Republican Nat. Comm. 1977–80; mem. US Gen. Advisory Cttee on Arms Control and Disarmament 1981–85; Assoc. Prof. of Admin. Law, Georgetown Univ., Washington, DC 1987–94, 1999–2001, currently Adjunct Prof. and Distinguished Visitor from the Judiciary; Assoc. Prof., New York Univ. 1995–96, Harvard Univ. 1998; Judge, US Court of Appeals, DC Circuit 1985–2000, Sr Judge 2000–; Co-Chair. Pres.'s Comm. on Intelligence Capabilities of the US Regarding Weapons of Mass Destruction 2004–05; Presidential Medal of Freedom 2008. *Address:* US Court of Appeals, DC Circuit, 333 Constitution Avenue, NW, Washington, DC 20001, USA. *Website:* www.cadc.uscourts.gov (office).

SILBERSTON, (Zangwill) Aubrey, CBE, MA; British economist and academic; *Professor Emeritus and Senior Research Fellow, Tanaka Business School, Imperial College London;* b. 26 Jan. 1922, London; s. of Louis Silberston and Polly Silberston (née Kern); m. 1st Dorothy Marion Nicholls 1945 (divorced); one s. and one d. deceased; m. 2nd Michèle Ledić 1985; ed Hackney Downs School, London, Jesus Coll., Cambridge; Economist, Courtaulds Ltd 1946–50; Research Fellow, St Catharine's Coll. Cambridge 1950–53, Univ. Lecturer in Econs, Cambridge 1951–71, Fellow, St John's Coll. 1958–71, Chair. Faculty Bd of Econs and Politics 1966–70; Official Fellow in Econs, Nuffield Coll. Oxford 1971–78, Dean 1972–78; Prof. of Econs, Imperial Coll. London 1978–87, now Prof. Emer. and Sr Research Fellow, Business School 1987–; mem. Monopolies Comm. 1965–68, Bd British Steel Corpn 1967–76, Royal Comm. on the Press 1974–77, Restrictive Practices Court 1986–92, Royal Comm. on Environmental Pollution 1986–96; Sec.-Gen. Royal Econ. Soc. 1979–92, Vice-Pres. 1992–; Pres. Confed. of European Econ. Asscns 1988–90, Vice-Pres. 1990–92. *Publications:* Education and Training for Industrial Management 1955, The Motor Industry 1959, Economic Impact of the Patent System 1973, The Multi-Fibre Arrangement and the UK Economy 1984, The Future of the Multi-Fibre Arrangement 1989, Technology and Economic Progress (ed.) 1989, Environmental Economics (ed.) 1995, Beyond the Multi-Fibre Arrangement 1995, The Changing Industrial Map of Europe 1996; articles in Economic Journal, Oxford Economic Papers etc. *Leisure interests:* opera, ballet. *Address:* Tanaka Business School, Imperial College, London, SW7 2AZ, England.

SILES DEL VALLE, Juan Ignacio; Bolivian politician, diplomatist and academic; ed Univ. of Chile, Univ. of Georgia, USA; Univ. Prof. of Literature,

Greater Univ. of San Andrés; Head of Educative Reform 1994–95; Alternating Perm. Rep. to UN, Vienna, Austria and Rome, Italy; Vice-Pres. UN Comm. for Drug Control, representing Latin American and Caribbean Countries, Vienna 2001; Dir Summit Coordination in charge of Cooperation of Latin American Summits 2002; Nat. Coordinator of XIIIth Latin American Summit of Heads of State and Govt 2003; fmr Dir Diplomatic Acad.; fmr Dir Cultural Subjects, Minister of Foreign Affairs and Culture 2003–05. *Publications include:* Canción de Cuna para la Muerte de mi madre (poetry) 1995, La guerrilla de Che y la narrative boliviana (monograph) 1997, Que el sueño era tan grande (novel) 2001, 2003. *Address:* c/o Ministry of Foreign Affairs, Calle Ingavi, esq. Junin, La Paz, Bolivia (office).

SILIÉ VALDEZ, Rubén Arturo; Dominican Republic international organization official, sociologist and diplomatist; *Ambassador to Haiti;* fmr prof. at several univs and insts; fmr Vice-Rector Nat. Univ. of Santo Domingo; Dir Latin American Faculty for Social Sciences (FLACSO), Dominican Repub. 1996–; Adviser to Vice-Pres. and Sec. of State on Educ. 2001–; apptd Amb., Ministry of Foreign Affairs 2001; Sec.-Gen. Asscn of Caribbean States 2004–08; currently Amb. to Haiti; mem. Bd Batey Relief Alliance. *Address:* Embassy of the Dominican Republic, rue Panaméricaine 121, BP 56, Pétionville, Port-au-Prince, Haiti. *Telephone:* 3257-9215 (office). *Fax:* 3257-0383 (office). *E-mail:* embrepdomhai@yahoo.com (office).

SILJA, Anja; German singer (soprano) and producer; b. 17 April 1940, Berlin; m. Christoph von Dohnányi (divorced); one s. two d.; ed studied with Egon van Rijn; began concert career aged ten at Berlin Titania Palace; stage debut Brunswick 1956, as Rosina; mem., Stuttgart and Frankfurt operas 1958–59; sang the Queen of Night at Aix 1959; sang at Bayreuth Festival 1960–67, as Senta, Elsa, Eva, Elisabeth and Venus; London debut at Sadler's Wells Theatre as Leonore/Fidelio 1963; Covent Garden debut as Leonore 1969, returned as Cassandre in Les Troyens, Senta, Marie in Wozzeck, Kostelnicka in Jenůfa; Metropolitan Opera debut 1972, returned as Salome, Marie and Kostelnicka; Vienna Staatsoper 1959–, in roles including Queen of Night, Salome, Elektra, Lulu; Paris Opéra 1964–, as Salome and Brünnhilde; Glyndebourne Opera debut as Kostelnicka 1989; sang the Nurse in Die Frau ohne Schatten at San Francisco 1989; debut as opera producer at Brussels with Lohengrin 1990; sang Emilia Marty at Glyndebourne 1995; season 1997 in The Makropulos Case at Glyndebourne and as Herodias at Covent Garden; Geschwitz in Lulu at Düsseldorf 2000; Clytemnestra at Madrid, Geschwitz and Herodias at Amsterdam, The Makropulos Case at Aix and The Bassarids in Amsterdam, Pierrot Lunaire by Schoenberg at Aix 2003; season 2004 as Madame de Croissy in Milan and Mère Marie in Hamburg and Paris (both in Dialogues des Carmélites), Emilia Marty in Berlin, Clytemnestra (Elektra) in Oviedo, Gräfin Geschwitz (Lulu) in Munich; season 2005 as Kostelnicka in Lyon and Barcelona, Emilia Marty in Lyon and Berlin, Janáček's Osud in Vienna, and Gräfin Geschwitz in Munich; Kammersängerin; Bundesverdienstkreuz 1988; Janacek Medal, Opera News Award for invaluable contrib. to opera 2011. *Recordings include:* Der fliegende Holländer, Tannhäuser, Lohengrin and Parsifal from Bayreuth, Lulu, Wozzeck, Jenůfa (Grammy Award) 2001, Pierrot Lunaire, Salome, Erwartung, The Makropulos Case. *Publication:* Die Sehnsucht nach dem Unerreichbaren (autobiog.) 1999. *Address:* Artists Management Zürich, Rütistrasse 52, 8044 Zürich-Gockhausen, Switzerland (office). *Telephone:* (1) 8218957 (office). *Fax:* (1) 8210127 (office). *E-mail:* schuetz@artistsman.com (office). *Website:* www.artistsman.com

SILK, John M.; Marshall Islands lawyer and politician; b. 15 Sept. 1956, Kwajalein; m. Mary Silk; five c.; ed Regis Univ., Denver, Colo, USA; Ed. Marshall Islands Journal 1979–81; Legal Adviser, Micronesian Legal Services Corpn 1981–90; with Stege and Assocs (law firm) 1990–93; Minister of Resources and Devt 2000–07, of Foreign Affairs 2009–12; Senator, Ebon Atol 2007–; Del. to Marshall Islands Constitutional Convention 1991; mem. Marshall Islands Bar Asscn, Marshall Islands Law Soc. *Leisure interests:* tennis, baseball, fishing. *Address:* c/o Ministry of Foreign Affairs, POB 1349, Majuro, MH 96960, Marshall Islands.

SILLARD, Yves; French aerospace engineer; b. 5 Jan. 1936, Coutances, Manche; s. of Roger Sillard and Madeleine Sillard (née Guerrand); m. 1st Annick Legrand 1966 (divorced); m. 2nd Hélène Benech-Badiou 1982 (divorced); m. 3rd Martine Gautry 1999; ed Ecole Massillon, Ecole Polytechnique, Ecole nat. Supérieure de l'Aéronautique; Test Eng and then Head of Colomb-Béchard unit of Centre d'Essais en Vol 1960–62, Tech. Dir of Cazeaux annex 1963–64; Head of Concorde Programme at Secrétariat général à l'Aviation civile 1965; Head of Div. setting up French Guiana Space Centre, Kourou 1966–68; Tech. Dir and then Dir Space Centre, Kourou 1968–72; Dir of Launchers, Centre Nat. des Etudes Spatiales 1973–76, Man. Dir 1976–82; Chair. and Man. Dir Centre nat. pour l'exploitation des océans 1982–85; Chair. Conseil d'administration de l'institut français de recherche pour l'exploitation de la mer 1985–89; French Nat. Co-ordinator for EUREKA Programme 1986–89; Gen. Del., Armaments 1989–93; mem. Atomic Energy Cttee 1989–93; Chair., Man. Dir Défence conseil international 1993–97; Asst Sec. Gen. for Scientific Affairs and Environment, NATO 1998–2001; mem. Nat. Acad. for Aeronautics and Space; Commdr, Légion d'honneur; Chevalier, Ordre nat. du Mérite; Médaille de l'Aéronautique; Commdr Merit (FRG). *Address:* 8 rue de la Forge, 17800 Brives sur Charente, France. *Telephone:* (5) 46-95-01-56. *E-mail:* ysillard@club-internet.fr.

SILNOV, Andrey Alexandrovich; Russian athlete; b. 9 Sept. 1984, Shakhty, Rostov Oblast; men's high jumper; Gold Medal, European Championships, Gothenburg 2006 (jump of 2.36m); jumped 2.37m in Monaco a week later (world leading jump in 2006); Silver Medal, World Athletics Final, Stuttgart 2006, World Cup, Athens 2006; jumped new personal best of 2.38m in London Grand Prix July 2008; Gold Medal, Olympic Games, Beijing 2008 (jump of 2.36m); coached by Sergey Starykh and Yevgeniy Zagorulko. *Address:* c/o All-Russia Athletic Federation, Moscow 119992, 8 Luzhnetskaya nab., Russia.

SILUANOV, Anton Germanovich; Russian economist and politician; *Minister of Finance;* b. 12 April 1963, Moscow; ed Moscow Finance Inst.; Economist, later Sr Economist, Ministry of Finance 1985–87, Leading Economist and Subdivision Deputy Dir 1989–92, Deputy Dir Budget Dept 1992–97, Dir Macroeconomic Policy and Banking Dept 1997–2003, mem. Finance Ministry Bd 2001–, Deputy Minister of Finance 2003–04, 2005–11, Dir Inter-budget Relations Dept 2004–05, Acting

Minister of Finance Sept.–Dec. 2011, Minister of Finance Dec. 2011–; Decree of the Pres. of the Russian Fed. 2002, Minister of Finance's Decree 2002, Order 'For Merit to the Fatherland' (IVth Degree) 2011; Hon. Diploma, Ministry of Finance 2001. *Address:* Ministry of Finance, 109097 Moscow, ul. Ilinka 9, Russia (office). *Telephone:* (495) 987-91-01 (office). *Fax:* (495) 625-08-89 (office). *Website:* www .minfin.ru (office).

SILUNGWE, Hon. Mr Justice Annel Musenga, LLM; Zambian judge and barrister; b. 10 Jan. 1936, Mbala; s. of Solo Musenga Silungwe and Janet Nakafunda Silungwe; m. Abigail Nanyangwe Silungwe 1960; one s. four d.; ed Univs of Zambia and London, Inner Temple, London; Resident Magistrate 1967, Sr Resident Magistrate (Class II) 1968, (Class I) 1970; Judge of the High Court 1971; nominated MP and apptd Minister of Legal Affairs and Attorney-Gen. 1973; State Counsel 1974; Chief Justice 1975–92; Judge, Court of Appeal, Seychelles 1992–2003; Judge of High Court and Acting Judge of Supreme Court, Namibia 1999; Dir Justice Training Centre, Namibia 1994–99; Chair. Judicial Services Comm. 1975–92, Council of Legal Educ. 1975–92, Council of Law Reporting 1975–92, Technical Cttee on Drafting the Zambian Constitution 2011–; Regional Chair. Southern African Region of Nat. Cheshire Int. Homes and Foundations 1998–; Dist Gov. Rotary Int. 1982–83; mem. Council World Jurist Asscn of World Peace Through Law Center 1985–; mem. Bd Dirs The Commonwealth Judicial Educ. Inst., Halifax, Canada 1997–; Rotary Int. Award for Community Service 1989. *Leisure interests:* music, golf, photography. *Address:* Technical Committee on Drafting the Zambian Constitution, Government Complex Conference Centre, PO Box 50106, Lusaka 10101, Zambia. *Website:* zambianconstitution.org.

SILVA, Artur; Guinea-Bissau politician; Sec. of State for Int. Co-operation 2008–09; Minister of Defence –Oct. 2009, of Culture, Educ., Science, Youth and Sports 2009–12; mem. Partido Africano da Independência da Guiné e Cabo Verde (PAIGC). *Address:* Ministry of Culture, Education, Science, Youth and Sports, Rua Areolino Cruz, Bissau, Guinea-Bissau (office). *Telephone:* 3202244 (office).

SILVA, Hon. Sarath Nanda, LLM; Sri Lankan judge; ed Univ. of Brussels, Belgium; Advocate of the Supreme Court of Sri Lanka 1967; Crown Counsel, Attorney Gen.'s Dept 1968, Sr State Counsel 1975, Deputy Solicitor Gen. 1979; Lecturer, Sri Lanka Law Coll. 1981–87; Judge, Court of Appeal 1987–1994, Pres. 1994; Judge of the Supreme Court 1995–99, Chief Justice of Sri Lanka 1999–2009; Lecturer in Civil Law, Sri Lanka Law Coll. 1981–87; Attorney Gen. 1996; Pres.'s Counsel 1996. *Address:* c/o Supreme Court of Sri Lanka, Superior Courts Complex, Colombo 12, Sri Lanka. *Telephone:* (1) 328651.

SILVA, Tilwin; Sri Lankan politician; b. 26 Feb. 1956; Gen. Sec. Janatha Vimukthi Peramuna (People's Liberation Front) 1995–. *Address:* Janatha Vimukthi Peramuna, 198/19 Panchikawattha Road, Colombo 10, Sri Lanka (office). *Telephone:* (11) 4400511 (office). *Fax:* (11) 2786050 (office). *E-mail:* contact@jvpsrilanka.com (office). *Website:* www.jvpsrilanka.com (office).

SILVA BARBEIRO, Marciano; Guinea-Bissau politician; Minister of Educ. 2004–05, Minister of Nat. Defence 2007–09; mem. Partido Africano da Independência da Guiné e Cabo Verde (PAIGC). *Address:* Partido Africano da Independência da Guiné e Cabo Verde, CP 106, Bissau, Guinea-Bissau (office). *Website:* www.paigc.org (office).

SILVA LUJÁN, Gabriel; Colombian politician and diplomatist; m. Mariana Espinosa de Silva; four c.; ed Univ. of the Andes, Bogotá, Paul H. Nitze School of Advanced Int. Studies, Johns Hopkins Univ., USA; Adviser on Political Affairs to fmr Pres. Virgilio Barco 1986–90; Adviser on Int. Politics to fmr Pres. Cesar Gaviria 1990–93; Amb. to USA 1993–94, 2010–12; pursued several entrepreneurial projects, including co-founding Newbridge Andean Partners investment fund; Founding Partner and mem. Bd of Dirs PetroColombia SA; Founding Pres. Global Tuition and Education Insurance Corpn and Global Life Insurance SA 1995–2002; Gen. Man. Federación Nacional de Cafeteros de Colombia (FEDERACAFÉ—nat. coffee growers fed.) 2002–09; Minister of Defence 2009–10; fmr columnist, El Tiempo newspaper; mem. bd several non-governmental orgs dedicated to environmental conservation and protection, including Fundacion Natura and Pro-Sierrra Foundation; Hon. Fellow, Ford Foundation. *Publications:* has authored several books on Colombia. *Address:* Ministry of Foreign Affairs, Palacio de San Carlos, Calle 10, No 5-51, Bogotá, DC, Colombia (office). *Telephone:* (1) 381-4000 (office). *Fax:* (1) 381-4747 (office). *E-mail:* cancilleria@cancilleria.gov.co (office). *Website:* www.cancilleria.gov.co (office).

SILVA ROSA, Sérgio Ricardo; Brazilian banker and mining industry executive; *President and CEO, Caixa de Previdência dos Funcionários do Banco do Brasil (PREVI);* b. 1959; ed Universidade de São Paulo; joined Caixa de Previdência dos Funcionários do Banco do Brasil (PREVI) (investment fund) as Exec. Dir 2000, Pres. and CEO 2003–; mem. Bd of Dirs Companhia Vale do Rio Doce (CVRD, now called Vale) 2003–11, Chair. 2003–11; Exec. Officer, Litel Participações SA (Litel); Legislator at Municipality of São Paulo 1995–96; Dir, Brasil Telecom 2000–03, Sauípe SA 2001–, Valepar SA, Associação Brasileira das Entidades de Previdência Privada (ABRAPP); Pres. Confederação Nacional dos Bancários (CNB/CUT) 1994–97, 1997–2000; mem. Exec. Cttee UN's 'Principles for Responsible Investment' programme. *Address:* Caixa de Previdência dos Funcionários do Banco do Brasil, Praia de Botafogo 501, 3 e 4 andar, 22250-040 Rio de Janeiro, Brazil (office). *Telephone:* (21) 3870-1564 (office). *E-mail:* info@previ.com.br (office). *Website:* www.previ.com.br (office).

SILVEIRA GODINHO, José António da; Portuguese fmr politician, economist and business executive; b. 16 Oct. 1943, Lisbon; s. of Raul Catarino Godinho and Angela da Silveira Godinho; m. Isabel Maria Canhoto Segura de Faria 1972; three s.; ed Lisbon Tech. Univ.; Asst Prof. Lisbon School of Econs 1967–77; Sr Vice-Pres. Banco de Portugal 1975–79, mem. Bd of Dirs 2004–; mem. Man. Bd Banco Pinto & Sotto Mayor 1979–82; Sec. of State for Finance 1980–81; mem. Exec. Bd Banco Espírito Santo 1982–93; Sec. of State for Nat. Defence 1986–87; Minister of Internal Affairs 1987–90; Amb. to OECD 1993–96; mem. Bd of Dirs Espírito Santo, Ca. de Seguros SA 1996–, AdvanceCare, SA 1999–; mem. Gen. Council Asscn of Portuguese Economists 1999–. *Leisure interests:* reading, travelling, music, sport. *Address:* c/o Board of Directors, Banco de Portugal, R. do Ouro, 27, 1100-150 Lisbon, Portugal (office).

SILVER, Joan Micklin, BA; American film and theatre director and screenwriter; b. 24 May 1935, Omaha, Neb.; d. of Maurice Micklin and Doris Shoshone; m. Raphael Silver 1956; three d.; ed Sarah Lawrence Coll.; began career as writer for educational films; original screenplay for Limbo purchased by Universal Pictures; commissioned by Learning Corpn of America to write and direct short narrative film The Immigrant Experience 1972 and wrote and dir two children's films for same co.; Dir plays: Album and Maybe I'm Doing it Wrong; also Dir for TV. *Films include:* Hester Street (dir and screenplay), Between the Lines (dir), On the Yard (producer), Head Over Heels (dir and screenplay, retitled Chilly Scenes of Winter), Crossing Delancey (dir), Loverboy (dir), Big Girls Don't Cry, They Get Even (dir), Fish in the Bathtub 1997. *Television includes:* Bernice Bobs Her Hair (dir and screenplay), A Private Matter (dir) 1992, In the Presence of Mine Enemies (dir) 1996, Invisible Child (dir) 1998, Charms for the Easy Life (dir) 2002, Hunger Point (dir) 2003. *Radio:* Great Jewish Short Stories from Eastern Europe and Beyond (dir) 1995. *Address:* Silverfilm Productions Inc., 510 Park Avenue, Suite 9B, New York, NY 10022-1105, USA (home). *Fax:* (212) 421-8254 (home). *E-mail:* jmicksil@aol.com (office).

SILVER, Joel; American film producer; b. 14 July 1952, South Orange, NJ; ed New York Univ.; fmrly Asst to Lawrence Gordon, Pres. Lawrence Gordon Productions; producer, Vice-Pres. Universal Pictures; currently runs Silver Pictures 1985– and (with Robert Zemeckis) Dark Castle Entertainment 1999–. *Films:* The Warrior 1979, Xanadu 1980, 48 Hours 1982, Jekyll & Hyde. . . Together Again 1982, Streets of Fire 1984, Brewster's Millions 1985, Weird Science 1985, Commando 1985, Jumpin' Jack Flash 1986, Lethal Weapon 1986, Predator 1987, Action Jackson 1988, Die Hard 1988, Lethal Weapon 2 1989, Roadhouse 1989, Ford Fairlane 1990, Die Hard 2 1990, Predator 2 1990, Hudson Hawk 1991, Ricochet 1991, The Last Boy Scout 1991, Lethal Weapon 3 1992, Demolition Man 1993, The Hudsucker Proxy, Richie Rich 1994, Demon Knight 1994, Assassins 1995, Fair Game 1995, Executive Decision 1996, Conspiracy Theory, Father's Day, Lethal Weapon 4 1998, Romeo Must Die 1999, Made Men 1999, The Matrix 1999, The House on Haunted Hill 1999, Romeo Must Die 2000, Dungeons & Dragons 2000, Ritual 2001, Exit Wounds 2001, Proximity 2001, Swordfish 2001, Thir13en Ghosts 2001, Ghost Ship 2002, Cradle 2 the Grave 2003, The Animatrix: Final Flight of the Osiris 2003, The Matrix Reloaded 2003, The Matrix Revolutions 2003, Gothika 2003, Kiss, Kiss, Bang, Bang 2005, V for Vendetta 2005, The Reaping 2007, The Invasion 2007, The Brave One 2007, Fred Claus 2007, Speed Racer 2008. *Television:* Tales from the Crypt, Two Fisted Tales, Parker Can, W.E.I.R.D. World, Freedom, Next Action Star, Veronica Mars 2004–07, Moonlight 2007–08. *Address:* Silver Pictures, c/o Warner Bros Pictures, 4000 Warner Boulevard, Building 90, Burbank, CA 91522-0001, USA.

SILVERMAN, Benjamin (Ben) Noah, BA; American television executive; b. 15 Aug. 1970, Pittsfield, Mass; s. of Stanley Silverman and Mary Silverman; ed Tufts Univ.; began career as Asst, CBS and Warner Bros; Devt Exec. New World/Marvel Entertainment 1993–95; Head of Packaging Div., William Morris Agency 1995–2002; Founder and CEO Reveille Productions (ind. production and distribution co.) 2002–07; Co-Chair. NBC Entertainment and NBC Universal TV Studio (later Universal Media Studios) 2007–09; Founder Electus 2009–. *Television:* Exec. Producer: The Office, Ugly Betty, The Tudors, The Biggest Loser. *Address:* Electus, c/o IAC, 555 West 18th Street, New York, NY 10011, USA (office). *Telephone:* (212) 314-7300 (office). *E-mail:* info@iac.com (office). *Website:* www.iac .com (office).

SILVERMAN, Bernard Walter, BTh, MA, PhD, DPhil, DSc, ScD, FRS; British professor of statistics and college president; *Chief Scientific Adviser, Home Office;* b. 22 Feb. 1952, London, England; s. of Elias Silverman and Helen Silverman; m. Rowena Fowler 1985; one s.; ed City of London School, Jesus Coll., Cambridge; Research Fellow, Jesus Coll., Cambridge 1975–77; Calculator Devt Man., Sinclair Radionics 1976–77; Weir Fellow, Univ. Coll., Oxford 1977–78, also Jr Lecturer, Univ. of Oxford; Lecturer, then Reader, then Prof. of Statistics, Univ. of Bath 1978–93, Head of School of Math. Sciences 1988–91; Prof. of Statistics, Univ. of Bristol 1993–99, Head of Statistics Group 1993–97, 1998–99, Henry Overton Wills Prof. of Math. 1999–2003, Provost Inst. for Advanced Studies 2000–03; Master, St Peter's Coll. Oxford and Prof. of Statistics, Univ. of Oxford 2003–09; Chief Scientific Adviser to the Home Office 2010–; visiting appointments, Dept of Statistics, Princeton Univ., USA 1978, 1979, Univ. of Paris VI 1979, Sonderforschungsbereich 123, Univ. of Heidelberg 1980, Math. Research Center, Univ. of Wisconsin-Madison 1981, Dept of Statistics, Johns Hopkins Univ. 1981, Depts of Statistics and Biostatistics, Univ. of Washington 1984, Univ. of Frankfurt 1984, Univ. of California, San Diego 1985, CSIRO Div. of Math. and Statistics, Canberra, Sydney, Melbourne and Perth, Australia 1985, Math. Sciences Research Inst., Berkeley, Calif. 1991; Fellow, Center for Advanced Study in the Behavioral Sciences, Stanford, Calif. 1997–98; Chartered Statistician, Royal Statistical Soc., mem. Research Section Cttee 1979–82, mem. Council 1982–90, Hon. Sec. 1984–90, mem. Working Party on Official Statistics, Chair. Research Section 1991–93, Pres. 2010; Fellow, Inst. of Math. Statistics 1987, mem. Council 1991–94, 1997–2000, Pres. 2000–01; Fellow, Int. Statistical Inst./Bernoulli Soc. 1986, mem. Bernoulli Soc. European Regional Cttee 1986–92 Chair. 1988–90, mem. Bernoulli Soc. Council 1999–2003; Fellow, Royal Soc. 1997, mem. Council 2009–10, mem. several cttees, including Research Grants Cttee A 1997–2000 (Chair. 1999–2000), Sectional Cttee 1 1998–2001 (Chair. 2001), Conf. Grants Cttee 1998–2001, Dorothy Hodgkin Fellowships Cttee A 1999–2004 (Chair. 2003), Wolfson Merit Awards Cttee 2006–09; Ed. Oxford University Press Statistical Science Series 1983–87, International Statistical Review 1991–96, Chapman & Hall Monographs on Statistics and Applied Probability 1985–97, Interdisciplinary Statistics Series 1993–97, Wiley Statistics Series 1997–2001, IMS Bulletin 2002–06, Cambridge University Press Statistics Series 2003–10, Annals of Statistics 2007–09; Assoc. Ed. Annals of Statistics 1982–85, Journal of the Royal Statistical Society, Series B 1980–84; Sr Ed. Statistics and Computing 1990–2005; mem. Editorial Bd Inverse Problems 1998–2000; external examiner for numerous BA, BSc and MSc degree examinations and PhD and research MSc theses world-wide; mem. Science and Eng Research Council Statistics Panel 1990–94; frequent reviewer for US NSF, Natural Sciences and Eng Research Council of Canada, Australian Research Council, etc. Eng and Physical Sciences Research Council Math. Coll. 1994–97, 2000–03; mem. Scientific Cttee, EURANDOM, Netherlands 1997–2003, Statistics Research Assessment Panel for Higher Educ. Funding Council for England

(HEFCE) Research Assessment Exercise 2001, Scientific Steering Cttee, Isaac Newton Inst. 2003–06, Steering Group, Int. Review of UK Math. 2003–04 (Chair. Subpanel 22 (Statistics) and mem. Panel F (Math.)), HEFCE Research Assessment Exercise 2008; Patron Royal Inst. Wessex Math. Master Classes; Chair. Jt Math. Council of the UK 2003–06, UK Math. Trust 2004–08; consultant to UK Govt Inquiry (the 'Lessons Learned' Inquiry) into the Foot and Mouth Epidemic 2002, Statistics Commission 2003; consultancies with Nuclear Electric, Nat. Audit Office, Ministry of Defence, Agilent Technologies, Mass Spec Analytical Ltd; consultancy on statistical aspects of legal cases (especially financial and forensic), statistical advice to the press and advice to police in criminal cases; radio and TV programmes on statistics; mem. Advisory Bd Statistics Dept, Carnegie-Mellon Univ. 2002, Academic Chair. 2006; mem. GM Science Review Panel 2002–03, Owner's Advisory Bd (non-exec. dir) Defence Analytical Services Agency 1998–2009; Chair. Peer Review Panel on the Project for the Sustainable Devt of Heathrow 2005–06; mem. Academia Europaea 2001; ordained deacon (Church of England) 1999–, priest 2000–; Hon. Fellow, Jesus College Cambridge 2003; First Prize, Int. Math. Olympiad 1970, Mayhew Prize for Math. Tripos Part III, Univ. of Cambridge 1974, Smith's Prize, Univ. of Cambridge 1976, Guy Medal in Bronze, Royal Statistical Soc. 1984, Guy Medal in Silver 1995, Special Invited Paper, Inst. of Math. Statistics 1985, Technometrics Special Discussion Paper, American Statistical Asscn 1988, Pres.' Award, American Statistical Asscn, Inst. of Math. Statistics, Biometric Soc. (ENAR and WNAR) and Statistical Soc. of Canada for "the outstanding statistician under forty" (COPSS Award) 1991, Fulkerson Lecturer, Cornell Univ. 1993, Special Invited Paper, Inst. of Math. Statistics 1999, Henri Willem Methorst Medal, Int. Statistical Inst. 1999, Corcoran Lecturer, Univ. of Oxford 2000, Original Mem. Highly Cited Researchers database, Information Sciences Inst. 2002. *Publications include:* Density Estimation for Statistics and Data Analysis 1986, Industrial Quality and Productivity with Statistical Methods: A Joint Symposium of the Royal Society and the Royal Statistical Society (co-ed.) 1989, Nonparametric Regression and Generalized Linear Models: A Roughness Penalty Approach (with P. J. Green) 1994, Functional Data Analysis (with J. O. Ramsay) 1997, (revised and expanded second edn 2005), Wavelets: The Key to Intermittent Information? (co-ed.) 2000, Applied Functional Data Analysis (with J. O. Ramsay) 2002; more than 80 papers in peer-reviewed journals and numerous research contribs and govt reports. *Website:* www .bernardsilverman.com (office).

SILVERMAN, Fred, MA; American producer and broadcasting executive; *President, Fred Silverman Company;* b. 13 Sept. 1937, New York; m. Cathy Kihn; one s. one d.; ed Syracuse Univ., Ohio State Univ.; with WGN-TV Chicago; exec. position WPIX-TV New York; Dir Daytime Programmes CBS-TV New York, Vice-Pres. Programmes 1970–75; Pres. ABC Entertainment 1975–78; Pres. NBC 1978–81; ind. film producer 1981–; Pres. The Fred Silverman Co. 1986–. *Address:* Fred Silverman Company, 1648 Mandeville Canyon Road, Los Angeles, CA 90025, USA (office). *Telephone:* (310) 471-4676 (office). *Fax:* (310) 471-3295 (office).

SILVERMAN, Henry Richard, BA, JD; American lawyer and business executive; *Chairman, Realogy Corporation;* b. 2 Aug. 1940, New York; s. of Herbert Silverman and Roslyn Silverman (née Moskowitz); m. 1st Susan H. Herson 1965 (divorced 1977); two d.; m. 2nd Nancy Ann Kraner 1978; one d.; ed Hackley School, Tarrytown, NY, Williams Coll., Univ. of Pennsylvania Law School; with USNR 1965–73; called to Bar NY 1965; with US Tax Court 1965; with US Court of Appeals 1965; law practice 1965–66; with White, Weld & Co. 1966; Gen. Pnr, Oppenheimer & Co. 1966–70; Pres., CEO ITI Corpn 1970–72; f., Pres. Trans-York Securities Corpn 1972; CEO Vavasseur America Ltd 1974–75; Gen. Pnr,Brisbane Pnrs 1976–77; prin. in various investment groups 1977–, Silverman Energy Co. 1977, NBC Channel 20 1977–83, ABC Channel 9 1977–81, Delta Queen Steamboat 1977–86, also Dir; apptd Pres., CEO Reliance Capital Corpn (subsidiary Reliance Group Holdings Inc.) 1982, Sr Vice-Pres. Business Devt Reliance Group Holdings Inc. 1982–90; Gen. Pnr, Blackstone Group 1990–91; Founder, Chair., CEO HFS Inc. 1990–97; CEO Cendant Corpn 1997–2005, Pres. 1997–2004, Chair. 1998–2005 (co. split into four separate cos including Realogy); Chair. and CEO Realogy Corpn, Parsippany, NJ 2004–07, Chair. (non-exec.) 2007–; Chair. Business Roundtable's Fiscal Policy Task Force; Dir NY Univ. Hosp. 1987–, New York Univ. Child Study Center; Commr Port Authority of New York and New Jersey, Chair. Finance Cttee; Trustee, New York Univ. (NYU) and NYU School of Medicine and Medical Center; Univ. of Pennsylvania; mem. JP Morgan's Nat. Advisory Bd, G-100; American Heritage Award, Anti-Defamation League 1998, Jackie Robinson Foundation award 2001, US Hispanic Chamber of Commerce award 2003. *Leisure interest:* tennis. *Address:* Realogy, 1 Campus Drive, Parsippany, NJ 07054, USA (office). *Telephone:* (973) 407-2000 (office). *Website:* www.realogy.com (office).

SILVERMAN, Marcia, MEconSc; American business executive; *CEO, Ogilvy PR;* one s.; ed Univ. of Pennsylvania; fmr employee Nat. Labour Relations Bd; worked in Public Relations Div., J. Walter Thompson 1978–81; joined Washington office, Ogilvy & Mather Public Affairs 1981, Head of Washington Office 1990–2000; Pres. of the Americas, Ogilvy Public Relations Worldwide 2000–02, CEO 2002–10, CEO Ogilvy PR 2010–; mem. Faculty, Georgetown Univ. School of Continuing Studies. *Address:* Ogilvy Public Relations Worldwide, 909 Third Avenue, New York, NY 10022, USA (office). *E-mail:* silverman.marcia@ogilvypr.com (office). *Website:* www.ogilvypr.com (office).

SILVERS, Robert Benjamin, AB; American literary editor; *Editor, The New York Review of Books;* b. 31 Dec. 1929, Mineola, NY; ed Univ. of Chicago, Sorbonne, Ecole Polytechnique, Paris, France; Press Sec. to Gov. of Connecticut 1950; served in US Army 1950–53; Man. Ed. Paris Review 1954–58; Assoc. Ed. Harper's Magazine 1958–63; Co-founder and Co-Ed. New York Review of Books 1963–2006, Ed. 2006–; mem. Council of Foreign Relations, Century Asscn; Chevalier, Légion d'honneur, mem. Ordre National du Mérite; Hon. DLit (Harvard) 2007; Award for Distinguished Service to the Arts from the American Academy of Arts and Letters 2006, National Book Foundation Literarian Award 2006; Robert B. Silvers annual lectures at New York Public Library established 2002, Ivan Sandrof Lifetime Achievement Award, National Book Critics Circle 2012, Nat. Humanities Medal 2012. *Address:* New York Review of Books, 1755 Broadway, 5th Floor, New York, NY 10019-3743, USA (office). *Telephone:* (212) 757-8070 (office). *Fax:* (212) 333-5374 (office). *E-mail:* nyrev@nybooks.com (office). *Website:* www.nybooks.com (office).

SILVERSTONE, Alicia; American actress; b. 4 Oct. 1976, San Francisco, Calif.; d. of Monty Silverstone and Didi Silverstone; m. Christopher Jarecki 2005; stage debut in play Carol's Eve at Met Theatre, LA; starred in three Aerosmith videos including Cryin'; f. First Kiss Productions (production co.). *Films:* The Crush 1993, The Babysitter 1995, True Crime 1995, Le Nouveau Monde 1995, Hideaway 1995, Clueless 1995, Batman and Robin 1997, Excess Baggage (also producer) 1997, Free Money 1998, Love's Labour's Lost 1999, Blast from the Past 1999, Rock My World 2002, Scorched 2003, Scooby Doo 2: Monsters Unleashed 2004, Beauty Shop 2005, Silence Becomes You 2005, Alex Rider: Stormbreaker 2006, The Art of Getting By 2011, Butter 2011, Vamps 2012, Ass Backwards 2013. *Television includes:* Torch Song 1993, Shattered Dreams 1993, The Cool and the Crazy 1994, The Wonder Years 1997, Miss Match (series) 2003, Pink Collar 2006, Bad Mother's Handbook 2008, Suburgatory (series) 2012.

SILVESTRINI, HE Cardinal Achille; Italian ecclesiastic; *Prefect Emeritus, Congregation for Oriental Churches, Roman Curia;* b. 25 Oct. 1923, Brisighella; ordained priest 1946, consecrated Bishop 1979, elected Archbishop of Novaliciana, Mauritania 1979; Sec. Council for Public Affairs of the Church 1979; cr. Cardinal-Deacon of S. Benedetto fuori Porta S. Paolo 1988–99, Cardinal-Priest of S. Benedetto fuori Porta S. Paolo 1999–; Prefect of the Supreme Tribunal of the Apostolic Signatura 1988–91; Prefect of the Congregation for Oriental Churches, 1991–2000, Prefect Emer. and Grand Chancellor of the Pontifical Eastern Inst. 2000–; mem. Congregation for the Doctrine of the Faith, for the Oriental Churches, for the Causes of the Saints, for the Bishops, for the Evangelization of Peoples, for Catholic Educ.; mem. Pontifical Council for the Interpretation of Legislative Texts, for Inter-Religious Dialogue. *Address:* Palazzina della Zecca, 00120 Vatican City, Italy (home). *Telephone:* (06) 69884838 (home). *Fax:* (06) 69881311. *E-mail:* asilvestrini@org.va (office).

SILVESTROV, Valentin Vasilyevich; Ukrainian composer; b. 30 Sept. 1937, Kiev; ed Kiev State Conservatory (pupil of B. Lyatoshinsky); author of compositions performed in USSR and many countries of Europe and in USA; S. Koussevitsky Prize (USA) 1967, Prize of Gaudeamus Soc. (Netherlands) 1970. *Compositions include:* 5 symphonies for large symphony orchestra 1963–82, Symphony for baritone with orchestra Echo Momentum on verses of A. Pushkin 1987, string quartets 1978, 1988, Dedication – symphony for violin and orchestra 1991, Mertamusica for piano and orchestra 1992, numerous chamber ensembles, piano pieces, vocal cycles, choruses. *Address:* Entuziastov str. 35/1, Apt. 49, 252147 Kiev, Ukraine (home). *Telephone:* (44) 517-04-47 (home).

SILVIA, HM The Queen of Sweden; b. (Silvia Renate Sommerlath), 23 Dec. 1943, Heidelberg, Germany; d. of the late Walther Sommerlath and Alice Toledo; m. King Carl XVI Gustaf 1976; two d., Crown Princess Victoria Ingrid Alice Désirée b. 14 July 1977, Princess Madeleine Thérèse Amelie Josephine b. 10 June 1982; one s., Prince Carl Philip Edmund Bertil b. 13 May 1979; ed Munich School of Interpreting; lived in Sao Paulo, Brazil 1947–57, returned to FRG 1957; fmr mem. staff Argentine Consulate, Munich; mem. Organizing Cttee, Munich Olympics 1971–73, Deputy Head of Protocol, Organizing Cttee, Winter Olympics, Innsbruck, Austria 1973; Chair. Royal Wedding Fund, Jubilee Fund; est. Silvia Home, Drottningholm; Patron First World Congress Against Commercial Sexual Exploitation of Children, Stockholm 1996; f. World Childhood Foundation; Hon. mem. Menton Foundation, Swedish Amateur Athletic Asscn, Children's Cancer Foundation of Sweden, Swedish Save the Children Fed.; Dr hc (Åbo Univ.) 1990, (Karolinska Institutet) 1993, (Univ. of Linköping) 1994, (Göteborg Univ.) 1999; Deutsche Kulturpreis 1990, Chancellor's Medal, Univ. of Mass, ranked by Forbes magazine amongst 100 Most Powerful Women (68th) 2004. *Leisure interests:* theatre, opera, concerts, skiing. *Address:* Royal Court of Sweden, Royal Palace, Stockholm 111 30, Sweden. *Telephone:* (8) 4026000. *Fax:* (8) 4026062. *E-mail:* info@royalcourt.se. *Website:* www.royalcourt.se.

SIM, Wong Hoo; Singaporean business executive; *Chairman and CEO, Creative Technology Ltd;* ed Ngee Ann Polytechnic; f. Creative Technology Ltd, Singapore 1981, currently Chair. and CEO; f. Creative Labs, USA; launched Sound Blaster PC card 1989, Sound Blaster Pro 1991; Chair. Technopreneurship 21 Pvt. Sector Cttee. *Publication:* Chaotic Thoughts from the Old Millennium. *Address:* Creative Technology Ltd, 31 International Business Park, Creative Resource, 609921, Singapore (office). *Telephone:* 6895-4000 (office). *Fax:* 6895-4999 (office). *Website:* www.creative.com (office).

SIMAI, Mihály; Hungarian economist; *Professor of International Economics, Corvinus University;* b. 4 April 1930, Budapest; s. of Mátyás Simai and Jolán Rosenberg; m. Vera Bence 1953; one d.; ed Univ. of Econs, Budapest; postgraduate studies in Geneva and Paris; Fellow, UN Econ. Comm. for Europe 1959–60, Staff mem. UN Center for Devt Econs, Projections and Policies, New York 1964–68; Prof. of Int. Econs and Nat. Business, Univ. of Econs, Budapest 1971–, Dir of Grad. Studies in Int. Business and Strategy 1987–, in Int. Relations 1991–; mem. Hungarian Acad. of Sciences, Budapest 1979–, Deputy Dir of Research, Inst. for World Econs 1973–87, Dir 1987–91, now Research Prof. Emer.; Pres. Hungarian UN Ass.; Chair. Council UN Univ. 1990–92; Vice-Pres. Int. Studies Asscn 1988–90; fmr Pres. Ed. Cttee Acta Oeconomica; Dir UN Univ. World Inst. for Devt Econs Research 1993–96; mem. Governing Council, Nat. Studies Asscn 1984–90, Advisory Bd for UN TNCs 1990–, Editorial Bd Environmental Econs 1991–; Randolf Jenkins Fellow, US Inst. for Peace 1991–92; Hon. Pres. World Fed. of UN Asscns 1982–; Labour Order of Merit (Golden Degree), Order of the Star of Hungary (Golden Degree), Order of the Flag of the Hungarian Repub. 1990; UN Meritorious Service Award, Szechenyi Award. *Publications include:* Capital Export in the Contemporary Capitalist System 1962, The World Economic System of Capitalism, 1965, View from the 26th Floor 1969, The United States before the 200th Anniversary 1974, The United Nations and the Global Problems 1977, Interdependence and Conflicts in the World Economy 1981, Economic Decolonization and the Developing Countries 1981, The United Nations Today and Tomorrow 1985, Power, Technology and the World Economy of the 1990s 1990, Foreign Direct Investments in Hungary 1991, The Future of Global Governance: Managing Risk and Change in the International System 1994, International Business Policy 1996, The Democratic Process and the Market (ed.) 1999, The Reintegration of the Former Socialist Countries in Europe, China and Vietnam into the Global Economy 2000, The Ages of Global Transformations 2001, United States in the Global Economy 2005, The World Economy in the Age of Turbulence 2008, Russia between Two Worlds 2011; more than 250 articles on int. econ. and political issues. *Leisure interests:* hiking, skiing. *Address:* Institute for World Economics, Hungarian Academy of Sciences, Budapest 1112, Budaörsi ut 45 (office); Department of World Economy, Corvinus University, 1093 Budapest, Fővám tér 8, Hungary (office). *Telephone:* 30-8487069 (mobile) (office); 20-9179768 (mobile) (office). *Fax:* (1) 309-2624 (office). *E-mail:* mihalysimai@gmail.com (office). *Website:* www.vki.hu (office).

SIMÉON, Jean-Pierre; French poet, playwright, novelist and artistic director; *Artistic Director, Printemps des poètes;* b. 6 May 1950, Paris (13th arrondissement); taught at Institut universitaire de formation des maîtres, Clermont-Ferrand; contrib. to numerous literary journals (Commune, Jungle, Faites entrer l'infini, Les Cahiers de l'Archipel, etc.); co-directs, with Jean-Marie Barnaud, the collection Grands Fonds at Cheyne éditeur; literary critic and dramatic for l'Humanité; Assoc. Poet, Nat. Drama Centre, Reims for six years; currently at Théâtre Nat. Populaire, Villeurbanne; Artistic Dir Printemps des poètes; Prix Theophile Briant 1978, Prix Maurice-Scève 1981, Grand Prix du Mont-Saint-Michel 1999. *Publications include:* Traquer la louve 1978, Hypnose du silence 1981, Fuite de l'immobile (Prix Artaud 1984) 1984, Un Essaim amoureux 1986, Passage du Désir 1988, Les Douze louanges 1990, Eva R 1992, Le sentiment du monde (Prix Apollinaire 1994) 1993, Traité de la juste merveille (illustrated by Martine Mellinette) 1996, L'homme clos 1996, Les petits jardins 1996, Poèmes du corps traversé 1998, Matière nuit 1998, Ouvrant le pas 1998, Le sourire du chien 1999, D'entre les morts 2000, Stabat Mater Furiosa (suivi de) Soliloques 2000, La Lune des pauvres, 2001, Quoique. Chroniques citoyennes 2002, Fresque peinte sur un mur obscur 2002, Charles Juliet, la conquête dans l'obscur 2003, Sermons joyeux (De la lente corruption des âmes dans la nuit tombante) 2004, Lettre à la femme aimée au sujet de la mort (Prix Max-Jacob 2006) 2005, Le bois de hêtres, précédé de Le sentiment du monde, suivi de La question et la preuve 2005, Algues, sable, coquillages et crevettes: Lettre d'un poète a des comédiens et a quelques autres passeurs 2006, Le Petit Ordinaire (Cabaret macabre) 2006, Odyssée, dernier chant 2006, Témoins à charge: Ou La comparution d'Eros et Thanatos devant les hommes 2007, Quel théâtre pour aujourd'hui? 2007, Usages du poème 2008, Philoctète 2009, Le Testament de Vanda 2009, Traité des sentiments contraires 2011; for children: À l'aube du buisson 1985, La nuit respire 1987, L'étrange, curieuse, bizzare, étonnante, stupéfiante, inquiétante, fabuleuse et véridique histoire de Népomucène, d'Iphigénie et du poivron flottant (with Anne Siméon, Stéphane Queyriaux and Frédéric Siméon) 1995, Contes et légendes d'Auvergne 1996, La Mouche qui lit (illustrated by Isabelle Simon) 1998, Un homme sans manteau 2000, Sans frontières fixes 2001, Aïe! Un poète (illustrated by Nicole Claveloux, Henri Galeron and Tina Mercié) 2003, Ceci est un poème qui guérit les poissons (illustrated by Olivier Tallec) 2005, Ici 2009. *Address:* c/o Jean-François Manier and Martine Mellinette, Cheyne éditeur, 43400 Le Chambon-sur-Lignon, France. *Telephone:* (4) 71-59-76-46. *Fax:* (4) 71-65-89-00. *E-mail:* cheyne-editeur@wanadoo.fr. *Website:* www.cheyne-editeur.com.

SIMEON, Yvon; Haitian economist, politician and diplomatist; ed France; fmr consultant; fmr Chargé d'Affaires in France and Belgium; Democratic Convergence rep., Paris; Minister of Foreign Affairs 2004–05; Amb. to Italy 2005, Perm.Rep. to FAO 2006. *Address:* c/o Embassy of Haiti, Via di Villa Patrizi 7/7a, 00161 Rome, Italy (office).

SIMHON, Shalom, BA; Israeli politician and social worker; *Minister of Industry, Trade and Labour and Minister of Minority Affairs;* b. 1956; m.; two c.; ed Univ. of Haifa; Sergeant Maj. in Israel Defence Forces; Exec. Dir Youth Section, Moshav Movt 1985–91, Chair. Social Dept 1991–93, Pension Fund 1993–2001, Sec.-Gen. 1993–2001; mem. Knesset (Labour Party) 1996–2011, (Ha'atzmaut) 2011–; Chair. Agric. Cttee 1996; mem. Econ. Cttee and Finance Cttee 1996–2002 (Chair. 2003–04); Chair. Finance Cttee 1999; Minister of Agric. and Rural Devt 2001–03, 2006–11, of the Environment 2005–06, of Industry, Trade and Labour 2011–, also Minister of Minority Affairs 2011–; Sec.-Gen. Agricultural Centre 1997–2001; fmr Chair. Bd of Tnuva (food conglomerate); mem. Ha'atzmaut (Independence) party 2011–. *Address:* Ministry of Industry, Trade and Labour, 5 Bank of Israel St, Jerusalem, 91009 (office); The Knesset, HaKiryah, Jerusalem, 91950, Israel. *Telephone:* 2-6662252 (office). *Fax:* 2-6662908 (office). *E-mail:* dover@moit.gov.il (office); ssimhon@knesset.gov.il (office). *Website:* www.moit.gov.il (office).

SIMIC, Charles, BA; American poet, writer and academic; *Professor of English, University of New Hampshire;* b. 9 May 1938, Belgrade, Yugoslavia (now Serbia); s. of George Simic and Helen Matijevich; m. Helen Dubin 1965; one s. one d.; ed Oak Park High School, Chicago, Univ. of Chicago and New York Univ.; arrived in USA 1954; army service 1961–64; worked for Chicago Sun-Times as proofreader; later business Man. Aperture Magazine 1966–69; Lecturer, Calif. State Univ., Hayward 1970–73; Assoc. Prof., later Prof. of English, Univ. of New Hampshire 1973–; first vol. of poems published 1967; elected a Chancellor of The Acad. of American Poets 2000; Poet Laureate of USA 2007–08; PEN Int. Award for Translation 1970, 1980, Guggenheim Fellowship 1972, Nat. Endowment for the Arts Fellowships 1974, 1979, Edgar Allan Poe Award 1975, American Acad. of Arts and Letters Award 1976, Harriet Monroe Poetry Award 1980, Fulbright Fellowship 1982, Ingram Merrill Foundation Fellowship 1983, John D. and Catherine T. MacArthur Foundation Fellowship 1984, Acad. of American Poets Fellowship 1998, Wallace Stevens Award 2007, Frost Medal 2011. *Publications include:* poetry: What the Grass Says 1967, Somewhere Among Us A Stone Is Taking Notes 1969, Dismantling the Silence 1971, White 1972, Return to a Place Lit by a Glass of Milk 1974, Biography and a Lament 1976, Charon's Cosmology 1977, Brooms: Selected Poems 1978, School for Dark Thoughts 1978, Classic Ballroom Dances 1980, Shaving at Night 1982, Austerities 1982, Weather Forecast for Utopia and Vicinity: Poems 1967–82 1983, The Chicken Without a Head 1983, Selected Poems 1985, Unending Blues 1986, The World Doesn't End (prose poems) (Pulitzer Prize for Poetry 1990) 1989, In the Room We Share 1990, The Book of Gods and Devils 1990, Selected Poems: 1963–83 1990, Hotel Insomnia 1992, A Wedding in Hell 1994, Walking the Black Cat 1996, Jackstraws 1999, Night Picnic 2001, The Voice at 3:00AM 2003, Selected Poems 1963–2003 (Griffin Int. Poetry Prize) 2005, That Little Something 2008, Sixty Poems 2008, Monster Loves His Labyrinth 2008, The Renegade: Writings on Poetry and a Few Other Things 2009, Master of Disguises 2010, The Horse Has Six Legs: An Anthology of Serbian Poetry 2010, Confessions of a Poet Laureate 2010, New and Selected Poems 1962–2012 2013; prose: The

Uncertain Certainty 1985, Wonderful Words, Silent Truth 1990, Dimestore Alchemy 1992, The Unemployed Fortune Teller 1994, Orphan Factory (essays) 1997, A Fly in the Soup 2000, The Renegade: Writings on Poetry and a Few Other Things 2009, Dime-Store Alchemy: The Art of Joseph Cornell 2011; ed.: Another Republic: 17 European and South American Writers (with Mark Strand) 1976, The Essential Campion 1988, The Best American Poetry 1992; many trans of French, Serbian, Croatian, Macedonian and Slovenian poetry. *Address:* Department of English, University of New Hampshire, 229 Hamilton Smith Hall, PO Box 192, Durham, NH 03824, USA (office). *Telephone:* (603) 862-3991 (office). *Fax:* (603) 862-3563 (office). *E-mail:* csimic@cisunix.unh.edu (office). *Website:* www.unh.edu/english (office).

SIMION, Eugen Ioan, PhD; Romanian literary critic; *President, Department of Literature and Philology, Romanian Academy;* b. 25 May 1933, Chiojdeanca, Prahova Co.; s. of Dragomir Simion and Sultana Simion; m. Adriana Manea 1957; one d.; ed I. L.Caragiale High School, Ploiesti, Faculty of Philology, Bucharest Univ.; Researcher, Romanian Acad. 1957–62, Corresp. mem. 1991, mem. 1992, Vice-Pres. 1994–98, Pres. 1998–2006, Pres. Dept of Literature and Philology 2006–; Ed. Gazeta literară 1962–68; Asst Lecturer, Bucharest Univ. 1964, Assoc. Prof. 1971, Prof. of Romanian Literature 1990–; Visiting Prof., Sorbonne, Paris 1970–73; Dir Caiete critice (cultural review) 1991–; mem. Bd Romanian Writers' Union; Vice-Pres. Intergovernmental Cttee for the World Decade for Cultural Devt—UNESCO 1992, currently Pres.; Pres. Nat. Council for the Certification of Diplomas and Univ. Certificates; mem. Academia Europaea 1992–, Acad. of Sciences of Moldavia 1999, Int. Union of Literary Critics; Dr hc (Jassy, Galati, Târgoviste, Arad); prizes of Romanian Writers' Union (five times), Prize of Romanian Acad. 1977. *Publications include:* Eminescu's Fiction 1964, Trends in Today's Literature 1965, E Lovinescu the Sceptic Saved 1971, The Romanian Writers Today Vol. I 1974, Vol. II 1976, Vol. III 1983, Vol. IV 1989; A Time to Live, a Time to Confess (Paris Diary), The Morning of Poets 1980, Defying Rhetoric 1985, Mercutio's Death 1993, Talking to Petru Dumitriu 1994, Mircea Eliade, A Spirit Amplitude 1995, The Return of the Author 1996, Critical Fragments I–IV 1998–2000; more than 3000 articles. *Address:* Romanian Academy, Calea Victoriei 725, Bucharest (office); Dr Lister 8, Bucharest, Romania (home). *Telephone:* (1) 3122760 (office); (1) 4109748 (home). *Fax:* (1) 3120209 (office); (1) 3365855 (home). *E-mail:* esimion@acad.ro (office); mdc@rnc.ro (home).

SIMITIS, Constantine (Costas), DJur; Greek lawyer and politician; b. 23 June 1936, Athens; s. of George Simitis and Fani Cristopoulou; m. Daphne Arkadiou; two c.; ed Univ. of Marburg and London School of Econs; lawyer at Supreme Court 1961–; taught in W German univs 1971–75; Prof. of Commercial Law, Univ. of Athens 1977; mem. Nat. Council of Panhellenic Liberation Movt (PAK) during colonels' dictatorship, mem. Pasok 1974–, mem. Cen. Cttee of Pasok, Pres. 1996–2004; mem. Parl. 1985–2004; Minister of Agric. 1981–85, of Nat. Economy 1985–87, of Educ. and Religious Affairs 1989–90, of Industry, Energy, Tech. and Trade 1993–95; Prime Minister of Greece 1996–2004. *Publications include:* Politics is a Creative Greece 1996-2004 2005, Objectives, Strategies and Prospects 2007, Democracy in Crisis? 2007, The Crisis 2008, The Derailment 2012; numerous articles on legal and econ. topics. *Address:* Akademias 35, Athens 10672, Greece. *Telephone:* (210) 3708213. *Fax:* (210) 3708220. *E-mail:* contact@costas-simitis.gr. *Website:* www.costas-simitis.gr.

ŠIMKO, Ivan, IngEcon, DIur; Slovak politician; *Founder, Free Forum Party;* b. 1 Jan. 1955, Bratislava; m.; four c.; ed Univ. of Econs, Bratislava, Comenius Univ., Bratislava; mem. staff Inst. for Planning, Bratislava 1978–79; mem. staff Dept of Chief Architect, Bratislava 1979–89; Adviser to Deputy Prime Minister 1990; mem. Parl. 1990–; Vice-Chair. Legis. Council 1992; Minister of Justice 1992; Deputy Prime Minister 1994; mem. Nat. Council for the Slovak Repub. 1994–; Minister of the Interior 2001–02, of Defence 2002–03; Founder Free Forum Party (Slobodné fórum—SF) 2003–; mem. Nat. Council Cttee for Constitutional Law. *Leisure interests:* sport, literature. *Address:* Slobodné fórum, Bazová 9, 821 08 Bratislava, Czech Republic (office). *Telephone:* (2) 55642494 (office). *Fax:* (2) 55642487 (office). *E-mail:* sf@slobodneforum.sk (office). *Website:* www.slobodneforum.sk (office).

SIMMA, Bruno, DJur; German professor of law and judge; *Judge, International Court of Justice;* b. 29 March 1941, Quierschied, Saar; ed Univ. of Innsbruck; called to the Bar, Innsbruck 1967; Asst. Faculty of Law, Univ. of Innsbruck 1967–72; Expert, Directorate of Legal Affairs, Council of Europe 1972; Prof. of Int. Law and EC Law, Univ. of Munich 1973–2003, Dir Inst. of Int. Law 1973–2003, Dean Faculty of Law 1995–97; Dir of Studies, Hague Acad. of Int. Law 1976, 1982, Lecturer 1995, 2009; Lecturer in Int. Law, Training Centre for Jr Diplomats, Ministry of Foreign Affairs 1981–89; Visiting Prof., Univ. of Siena, Italy 1984–85; Visiting Prof., Univ. of Michigan Law School, USA 1986, 1995, Prof. of Law 1987–92, mem. Affiliate Overseas Faculty 1997–; mem. UN Cttee on Econ., Social and Cultural Rights 1987–96, UN Int. Law Comm. 1996–2003; Judge, Int. Court of Justice, The Hague 2003–; Co-founder and Ed. European Journal of Int. Law; Founding Pres. European Soc. of Int. Law; Assoc. Institut de Droit international; Counsel for Germany in various legal cases 1994–2003; int. arbitrator, consultant, mem. numerous legal advisory bds and professional asscns; Certificate of Merit, American Soc. of Int. Law 1996; Dr hc (Univ. of Macerata, Italy) 2006, (Univ. of Glasgow). *Publications:* articles in professional journals, books. *Address:* International Court of Justice, Peace Palace, 2517 KJ The Hague, The Netherlands (office). *Telephone:* (70) 302-23-23 (office). *Fax:* (70) 302-24-09 (office). *E-mail:* information@icj-cij.org (office). *Website:* www.icj-cij.org (office).

SIMMEL, Peter; German business executive; heads regional Edeka store chain with 32 stores in Saxony, Thuringia and Bavaria; Chair. Supervisory Bd Edeka Zentrale AG & Co. KG, Hamburg 2005–10, mem. Supervisory Bd 2010–. *Address:* Edeka Zentrale AG & Co. KG, New-York-Ring 6, 22297 Hamburg, Germany (office). *Telephone:* (40) 63-77-0 (office). *Fax:* (40) 63-77-22-31 (office). *E-mail:* info@edeka.de (office). *Website:* www.edeka.de (office).

SIMMEN, Jeannot, Dr habil.; Swiss art critic and curator; *Director, Club Bel Etage, Berlin;* b. 14 Sept. 1956, Zürich; s. of Georges Simmen and Clara Brügger; m. Dr Brigit Blass 1988; two d.; ed Univ. of Zürich, Free Univ. of Berlin; Prof. Univs of Wuppertal, Kassel, Essen 1990–2000; exhbn projects include: Licht: Objekt/Medium, Telematic, Net-Modern-Navigation; Curator Schwerelos (exhbn),

Grosse Orangerie, Charlottenburg Palace, Berlin 1991–92, Die Macht des Alters – Strategien der Meisterschaft (exhbn), Kronprinzen-Palais, Berlin 1998; Dir media future project Ars Digitalis, Acad. of Fine Arts, Berlin 1996, Club Bel Etage, Berlin 2005–; Design-Preis Schweiz 01 für 'Interaction Design', Design Center Langenthal, Switzerland. *Publications:* Kunst – Ideal oder Augenschein 1980, Der Fahrstuhl 1983, Vertigo 1990, Schwerelos 1991, Vertikal 1994, Kasimir Malewitsch 1998, 1999, Kidai Shôran (CD) 2000, Telematik 2002, TotalSchaden 2006, Berlin-2010.eu/Von WestBerlin zur Kultur-Metropole Eurplas 2010. *Leisure interests:* art and the media. *Address:* Pariser-Strasse 44, 10707 Berlin, Germany (office). *Telephone:* (30) 88550136 (office). *E-mail:* simmen@snafu.de. *Website:* www.jeannot-simmen.eu; www.club-bel-etage.de.

SIMMONDS, Rt Hon. Kennedy Alphonse, PC; Saint Christopher and Nevis physician and politician; b. 12 April 1936; s. of the late Arthur Simmonds and of Bronte Clarke; m. Mary Camella Matthew 1976; three s. two d.; ed Basse-Terre Boys' School, St Kitts-Nevis Grammar School and Univ. of the West Indies; Intern, Kingston Public Hosp., Jamaica 1963; Registrar in Internal Medicine, Princess Margaret Hosp., Bahamas 1966–68; Resident in Anaesthesiology, Pittsburgh 1968–69; medical practice in St Kitts and Anguilla 1964–66, in St Kitts 1969–80; Founder mem. People's Action Movt 1965, Pres. 1976, unsuccessfully contested elections 1966, 1971, 1975; elected to Parl. 1979; Premier 1980–83; Minister of Home and External Affairs, Trade, Devt and Industry 1980–84, of Finance, Home and Foreign Affairs 1984–95; Prime Minister 1983–95; currently Dir of Medical Services, Anguilla; Fellow, American Coll. of Anaesthesiologists. *Leisure interests:* cricket, tennis, football. *Address:* Ministry of Social Development, 3rd Floor, D3 Building, Caribbean Commercial Complex, PO Box 60, The Valley, Anguilla.

SIMMONS, David, BA, MEd; Australian organization executive and fmr politician; *Chairman, Western NSW Medicare Local Ltd;* b. 7 Nov. 1947, Broken Hill, NSW; m. Kaye Simmons; one s. one d.; ed Univ. of New England, Australia; Head of Social Science Dept, Bathurst High School, NSW; Alderman, Bathurst City Council 1978–83; MP for Calare, NSW 1983–96, mem. House of Reps Cttee on Finance and Public Admin. 1985–89; Minister for Defence, Science and Personnel 1989–90, for Arts, Tourism and Territories 1990–91, for Local Govt and Family Support 1991–93; Chair. House of Reps. Cttee on Banking, Finance and Public Admin. 1994; Exec. Dir Hunter Regional Tourism Org. 1996–97; Gen. Man. Newcastle Regional Chamber of Commerce 1997–98; CEO Newcastle & Hunter Business Chamber 1998–2001; Chair. Western NSW Medicare Local Ltd 2012–; Dir Daskay Pty Ltd 2001–, GP Training Valley to Coast Pty Ltd 2010–, Pacific Link Housing Ltd 2010–; Pres. Heart Foundation (NSW), also Dir Nat. Bd. *Leisure interests:* golf, stamp collecting, arts, travel. *Address:* Western NSW Medicare Local Ltd, Level 2/258-260 Macquarie Street, Dubbo, NSW 2830, Australia (office). *Telephone:* (2) 6884-0197 (office). *Fax:* (2) 6884-0198 (office). *E-mail:* admin@wml .org.au (office). *Website:* www.wml.org.au (office).

SIMMONS, Hardwick (Wick), AB, MBA; American business executive; b. 1940; m. Sloan T. Miller; five c.; ed Harvard Univ., Harvard Business School; with US Marine Corps Reserve 1960–66; Financial Adviser, Hayden Stone 1966–69, Vice-Pres. Data Processing and Communications Div. 1969–70, Man. Boston office 1970–73, Exec. Vice-Pres. for Shearson Hayden Stone Retail Sales and Admin. 1973–77, Sr Exec. Vice-Pres. for Marketing and Sales, Shearson/American Express 1977, Pres. Pvt. Client Group, Shearson Lehman Brothers, Inc. –1991; Pres. and CEO Prudential Securities, Inc. 1991–2001; CEO, Chair. Nasdaq Stock Market Inc. 2001–03; Dir New York City Partnership and Chamber of Commerce, Inc.; mem. Bd Nat. Acad. Foundation; mem. Bd of Dirs Raymond James Financial Inc. 2003– (Lead Dir 2006), Geneva Acquisition Corpn 2006–, Lions Gate Entertainment Corpn 2005–; Co-founder Longwing, mem. Bd of Advisors 2003–06; fmr Dir Chicago Bd Options Exchange; mem. and fmr Chair. Securities Industry Asscn; mem. and fmr Pres. Bond Club of New York, Inc.; mem. NY City Public/Pvt. Initiatives (PPI) Bd; mem. Harvard Univ. John King Fairbank Center for E Asian Research; Trustee South Street Seaport Museum; Pres. Bd of Trustees Groton School; Trustee Woods Hole Oceanographic Inst., Rippowan Cisqua School.

SIMMONS, Richard D., AB, LLB; American newspaper publisher; b. 30 Dec. 1934, Cambridge, Mass.; m. Mary DeWitt Bleecker 1961 (died 2004); two s.; ed Harvard and Columbia Univs; admitted to New York Bar; Assoc., Satterlee, Warfield & Stephens 1958–62; Gen. Counsel, Giannini Science Corpn 1962–64; Vice-Pres. and Gen. Counsel, Southeastern Publishing Service Corpn 1964–69; Counsel, Dun & Bradstreet Inc., New York 1969–70, Vice-Pres. and Gen. Counsel 1970–72; Pres. Moody's Investors Service 1973–74, Dun & Bradstreet Inc. 1975–76; Exec. Vice-Pres. Dun & Bradstreet Corpn, New York 1976–78, Dir and Vice-Chair. Bd 1979–81; Pres. and COO The Washington Post Co. 1981–91, Dir 1981, Pres. Int. Herald Tribune 1989–96; mem. Bd of Dirs Inspire. *Address:* c/o Board of Directors, Inspire, 66 Witherspoon Street, Suite 402, Princeton, NJ 08540, USA.

SIMMONS, Robert Malcolm, PhD, FRS; British biophysicist and academic; *Professor Emeritus, Randall Division of Cell and Molecular Biophysics, King's College, London;* b. 23 Jan. 1938, London, England; s. of Stanley Laurence Simmons and Marjorie Simmons (née Amys); m. Mary Ann (Anna) Ross 1967; one s. one d.; ed King's Coll., London, Royal Inst., Univ. Coll., London; Lecturer, Univ. Coll. London 1967–81; MRC Staff Scientist, King's Coll. London 1981–83, Prof. of Biophysics 1983–2002, Dir Randall Inst. 1995–99, Randall Div. of Cell and Molecular Biophysics 1999–2001, Prof. Emer. 2002–. *Publication:* Muscular Contraction 1992. *Leisure interests:* music, fishing. *Address:* 1 Woodborough Road, Pewsey, Wilts., SN9 5NH, England. *Telephone:* (1672) 562281. *E-mail:* simmons.bob@btinternet.com.

SIMMONS, Ruth J., PhD; American academic and university administrator; *Professor of Comparative Literature and Africana Studies, Brown University;* b. 3 July 1945, Grapeland, Tex.; two c.; ed Dillard Univ., Harvard Univ.; fmr Asst Prof. of French, Univ. of New Orleans, Asst Dean Coll. of Liberal Arts –1977; Visiting Assoc. Prof. of Pan-African Studies, Calif. State Univ., Northridge 1977–79, also Acting Dir Int. Programmes; Asst. then Assoc. Dean of Grad. Studies, Univ. of Southern Calif. 1979–83; Dir Afro-American Studies, Princeton Univ., Assoc. Dean 1983, Vice-Provost 1992–95; Provost, Spelman Coll., Atlanta 1990–91; Pres. Smith Coll. 1995–2001; Pres. Brown Univ. 2001–12, Prof. of Comparative Literature and Africana Studies 2013–; Chevalier, Légion dHonneur 2013; 25 hon. doctorates;

numerous awards including President's Award, United Negro College Fund 2001, Fulbright Lifetime Achievement Medal 2002, Eleanor Roosevelt Val-Kill Medal 2004, Ellis Island Medal of Honor 2010, Foreign Policy Asscn Award 2010. *Address:* Department of Africana Studies, Brown University, Box 1904, 155 Angell Street, Providence, RI 02912, USA (office). *Telephone:* (401) 863-3137 (office). *Website:* brown.edu/Departments/Africana_Studies (office).

SIMMS, David John, PhD, MRIA; Irish mathematician and academic; *Fellow Emeritus, Trinity College Dublin;* b. 13 Jan. 1933, Sankeshwar, British India; s. of John Gerald Simms and Eileen Mary Simms (née Goold-Verschoyle); m. Anngret Erichson 1965; three s.; ed Berkhamstead School, Trinity Coll., Dublin and Peterhouse, Cambridge, England; Asst in Math., Univ. of Glasgow 1958–60, Lecturer in Math. 1960–64; Instructor in Math., Princeton Univ., NJ 1962–63; Lecturer in Math., Univ. of Dublin 1964–73, Assoc. Prof. 1973–, Fellow, Trinity Coll., Dublin 1972–2002, Sr Fellow 2002–03, Fellow Emer. 2003–; Visiting Prof., Univ. of Bonn 1966–67, 1972–73, 1978–80; mem. Royal Irish Acad. 1978–, Vice-Pres. 1983–84, 1987–88, 1995–96; Gold Medal in Math., Univ. of Dublin 1955. *Publications include:* Lie Groups and Quantum Mechanics 1968, Lectures on Geometric Quantization (with N. M. Woodhouse) 1974. *Address:* School of Mathematics, Trinity College, Dublin 2, Ireland (office). *Telephone:* (1) 8961944 (office). *Fax:* (1) 6082282 (office). *E-mail:* simms@maths.tcd.ie (office). *Website:* www.maths.tcd.ie/~simms (office).

SIMMS, Sir Neville Ian, Kt, BSc, MEng, FREng, FRSA, FICE; British business executive and chartered civil engineer; *Deputy Chairman, GDF Suez Energy International;* b. 11 Sept. 1944, Glasgow, Scotland; s. of the late Arthur Neville Simms and of Anne Davidson Simms (née McCulloch); ed Queen Elizabeth Grammar School, Crediton, Newcastle Univ and Univ of Glasgow; Structural Engineer, Ove Arup and Partners 1966–69; joined Tarmac PLC 1970, Chief Exec. Tarmac Construction Ltd 1988–92, Group Chief Exec. Tarmac PLC 1992–99, (Deputy Chair. 1994–99); Group Chair. Carillion PLC 1999–2004; mem. Bd of Dirs International Power PLC 1998–2011, Chair. 2000–11 (co. acquired by GDF Suez 2012), Deputy Chair. GDF Suez Energy International 2011–; Dir Bank of England 1995–2002; Chair. BITC West Midlands 1998–2001, Chair BITC Solent Region 2005–07; Dir (non-exec.) Courtaulds 1994–98, Pvt. Finance Panel Ltd 1994–99, Nat. Power 1998–2000, Sustainable Procurement Task Force 2006; Chair BRE Trust 2006–; mem. New Deal Task Force 1999–2001; Gov. Stafford Grammar School 1997–2004, Ashridge Man. Coll. 2000–11; Hon. DTech (Wolverhampton) 1997; Dr hc (Edin.) 2000; Hon. DEng (Glasgow) 2001; Pres.'s Medal, Chartered Inst. of Bldg 1995; Prince of Wales Amb. Award 2001. *Publications:* Building Towards 2001; numerous speeches and articles on industry-related topics. *Address:* GDF Suez Energy International, Senator House, 85 Queen Victoria Street, London, EC4V 4DP, England (office). *Telephone:* (20) 7320-8600 (office). *Fax:* (20) 7320-8700 (office). *E-mail:* neville.simms@gdfsuez.com (office). *Website:* www.gdfsuez.com (office).

SIMON, Carly; American singer, songwriter and musician (piano, guitar); b. 25 June 1945, New York; d. of Richard Simon; m. 1st James Taylor 1972 (divorced 1983); one d. one s.; m. 2nd James Hart 1987; ed Sarah Lawrence Coll.; solo artist and composer 1971–; Grammy Award for Best New Artist 1971, Acad. Award (for Let The River Run) 1989, Golden Globe Award. *Film appearance:* No Nukes 1980. *Compositions include:* Romulus Hunt (opera) 1993; film scores for Heartburn 1986, Working Girl 1988, Postcards From the Edge 1990, This Is My Life 1992; theme tunes for Torchlight 1985, Phenom (TV) 1993; contrib. songs to other films. *Recordings include:* albums: Carly Simon 1971, Anticipation 1972, No Secrets 1973, Hotcakes 1974, Playing Possum 1975, Another Passenger 1976, Boys In The Trees 1978, Spy 1979, Come Upstairs 1980, Torch 1981, Hello Big Man 1983, Spoiled Girl 1985, Coming Around Again 1987, My Romance 1990, Have You Seen Me Lately? 1991, This Is My Life 1992, Letters Never Sent 1994, Clouds In My Coffee 1965–95 1996, Film Noir 1997, The Bedroom Tapes 2000, This Kind of Love 2008, Never Been Gone 2009. *Publications include:* juvenile: Amy the Dancing Bear 1989, The Boy of the Bells 1990, The Fisherman's Song 1990, The Nighttime Chauffeur 1993, Midnight Farm 1997, Basket Full of Rhymes 2000. *Address:* c/o Lee Phillips, Manatt Phelps and Phillips, 11355 West Olympic Blvd, Los Angeles, CA 90064, USA (office). *E-mail:* cesmanager1@gmail.com (office). *Website:* www .carlysimon.com.

SIMON, David, BA; American screenwriter, TV producer and fmr journalist; b. 1960, Washington, DC; m. Laura Lippman; ed Bethesda-Chevy Chase High School, Univ. of Maryland; police reporter at Baltimore Sun newspaper 1982–95; f. Blown Deadline Productions; Fellow, John D. and Catherine T. MacArthur Foundation 2010. *Television includes:* NYPD Blue (writer) 1996, Homicide: Life on the Street (producer, writer) (Writers Guild of America Award) 1993–99, The Corner (producer, writer) (three Emmy Awards) 2000, The Wire (producer, writer) 2002–08, Generation Kill (producer, writer) 2008, Treme 2010. *Publications include:* Homicide: A Year on the Killing Streets (Edgar Award 1992) 1991, The Corner: A Year in the Life of an Inner-City Neighborhood (co-author) (Notable Book of the Year, New York Times) 1997. *Website:* www.davidsimon.com.

SIMON, Josette, OBE; British actress; d. of Charles Simon and Eileen Petty; m. Mark Padmore 1996; ed Cen. School of Speech Training and Dramatic Art; appeared in TV series Blake's 7; joined RSC; Hon. MA (Leicester) 1995; appeared as Isabella in Measure for Measure 1988, as Maggie in Arthur Miller's After the Fall, Nat. Theatre, in The White Devil, Nat. Theatre 1991, as Ellida Wangel in Ibsen's The Lady from the Sea, Lyric Theatre, Hammersmith 1994, The Taming of the Shrew, Leicester 1995, The Maids, Donmar Warehouse 1997, Titania in A Midsummer Night's Dream 1999, several concert performances. *Films include:* Cry Freedom 1987, Milk and Honey (Best Actress Atlantic Film Festival 1988, Paris Film Festival 1990) 1988. *Television includes:* Henry IV, Parts 1 and 2, Bodyguards, Kavanagh QC, Bridge of Time 1997, Dalziel and Pascoe: Bones and Silence 1998, Poltergeists (series) 1999, Poirot: The Mystery of the Blue Train 2005. *Leisure interests:* cinema, gardening, travel, learning languages. *Address:* 31 Landrock Road, London, N8 9HR, England.

SIMON, Lou Anna Kimsey, PhD; American university president; *President, Michigan State University;* ed Indiana State Univ., Michigan State Univ.; joined faculty of Mich. State Univ. (MSU) 1974, Asst Dir Office of Institutional Research, then Asst Provost for Gen. Academic Admin, Assoc. Provost, Provost (also for MSU

Coll. of Law), Vice-Pres. for Academic Affairs 1993, Interim Pres. MSU May–Sept. 2003, Pres. 2005–, has taught seminars at Coll. of Educ.; mem. Exec. Cttee, Cttee on Institutional Cooperation 1999– (Chair. 2000–05); Chair. Exec. Cttee Nat. Collegiate Athletic Asscn 2012–. *Publications include:* Serving Children and Families through Community-University Partnerships, Universities and Communities: Remaking Professional and Interprofessional Education for the Next Century, Learning to Serve: Promoting Civil Society through Service Learning (coed.) 2002. *Address:* Office of the President, Michigan State University, 450 Administration Building, East Lansing, MI 48824-1046, USA (office). *Telephone:* (517) 355-6560 (office). *Fax:* (517) 355-4670 (office). *E-mail:* presmail@msu.edu (office). *Website:* president.msu.edu (office).

SIMON, Neil; American playwright; b. 4 July 1927, New York; s. of Irving Simon and Mamie Simon; m. 1st. Joan Baim 1953 (deceased); two d.; m. 2nd Marsha Mason 1973 (divorced); m. 3rd Diane Lander 1987; one d.; ed New York Univ.; wrote for various TV programmes including The Tallulah Bankhead Show 1951, The Phil Silvers Show 1958–59, NBC Special, The Trouble with People 1972; Hon. DHumLitt (Hofstra Univ.) 1981, (Williams Coll.) 1984; Evening Standard Award 1967, Writers' Guild Screen Award for The Odd Couple 1969, Writers' Guild Laurel Award 1979, American Comedy Award for Lifetime Achievement 1989, Pulitzer Prize (for Lost in Yonkers) 1991, Kennedy Center Mark Twain Prize for American Humor 2006E. *Plays:* Come Blow Your Horn 1961, Little Me (musical) 1962, Barefoot in the Park 1963, The Odd Couple 1965, Sweet Charity (musical) 1966, The Star-Spangled Girl 1966, Plaza Suite 1968, Promises, Promises (musical) 1968, Last of the Red Hot Lovers 1969, The Gingerbread Lady 1970, The Prisoner of Second Avenue 1971, The Sunshine Boys 1972, The Good Doctor 1973, God's Favorite 1974, California Suite 1976, Chapter Two 1977, They're Playing Our Song 1979, I Ought to be in Pictures 1980, Fools 1981, Little Me (revised version) 1982, Brighton Beach Memoirs 1983, Biloxi Blues 1985, The Odd Couple Female Version 1985, Broadway Bound 1986, Rumors 1988, Lost in Yonkers 1991, Jake's Women 1992, The Goodbye Girl (musical) 1993, Laughter on the 23rd Floor 1993, London Suite 1995. *Screenplays:* After the Fox 1966, Barefoot in the Park 1967, The Odd Couple 1968, The Out-of-Towners 1970, Plaza Suite 1971, The Last of the Red Hot Lovers 1972, The Heartbreak Kid 1973, The Prisoner of Second Avenue 1975, The Sunshine Boys 1975, Murder By Death 1976, The Goodbye Girl 1977, The Cheap Detective 1978, California Suite 1978, Chapter Two 1979, Seems Like Old Times 1980, Only When I Laugh 1981, I Ought to Be in Pictures 1982, Max Dugan Returns 1983, Lonely Guy (adaptation) 1984, The Slugger's Wife 1984, Brighton Beach Memoirs 1986, Biloxi Blues 1988, The Marrying Man 1991, Broadway Bound (TV film) 1992, Lost in Yonkers 1993, Jake's Women (TV film) 1996, London Suite (TV film) 1996; other motion pictures adapted from stage plays: Come Blow Your Horn 1963, Sweet Charity 1969, The Star-Spangled Girl 1971; mem. Dramatists Guild, Writers' Guild of America; many awards including Emmy Award 1957, 1959; Antoinette Perry (Tony) Awards for The Odd Couple 1965, Biloxi Blues 1985 (Best Play), Lost in Yonkers 1991 (Best Play). *Publication:* Rewrites: A Memoir 1996. *Address:* c/o Albert DaSilva, 502 Park Avenue, New York, NY 10022, USA.

SIMON, Paul F., BA; American singer and composer; b. 13 Oct. 1941, Newark, NJ; s. of Louis Simon and Belle Simon; m. 1st Peggy Harper (divorced); one s.; m. 2nd Carrie Fisher 1983 (divorced 1984); m. 3rd Edie Brickell 1992; two s. one d.; ed Queens Coll., Brooklyn Law School; mem. singing duo Simon & Garfunkel (with Art Garfunkel) 1964–71; solo artist 1972–; Hon. DMus (Berklee Coll.) 1986, (Yale) 1996, (Queens Coll.) 1997; Emmy Award (for Paul Simon Special, NBC) 1977, inducted into Songwriters Hall of Fame 1982, Simon & Garfunkel inducted into Rock and Roll Hall of Fame 1990, inducted as solo artist 2001, Kennedy Center Honor 2002, Grammy Lifetime Achievement Award 2003, Gershwin Prize for Popular Song, US Library of Congress 2007, Polar Music Prize (Sweden) 2012. *Compositions:* The Capeman (musical) (Antoinette Perry Award for Best Original Score Written for the Theatre 1998) 1997. *Film appearances:* Annie Hall 1977, The Rutles (TV) 1978, All You Need Is Cash 1978, One-Trick Pony 1980. *Recordings include:* albums: as Simon & Garfunkel: Wednesday Morning 3AM 1964, Sounds Of Silence 1966, Parsley, Sage, Rosemary And Thyme 1966, The Graduate (film soundtrack) (two Grammy Awards) 1968, Bookends 1968, Bridge Over Troubled Water (six Grammy Awards 1971) 1970, Concert In Central Park (live) 1982, Early Simon & Garfunkel 1993, Old Friends 1997; solo: The Paul Simon Songbook 1965, Paul Simon 1972, There Goes Rhymin' Simon 1973, Live Rhymin': Paul Simon In Concert 1974, Still Crazy After All These Years (two Grammy Awards) 1975, One-Trick Pony 1980, Hearts And Bones 1983, Graceland (Grammy Award 1987) 1986, Negotiations And Love Songs 1988, Rhythm Of The Saints 1990, Paul Simon's Concert In The Park 1991, Songs From The Capeman 1997, You're The One 2000, Surprise 2006. *Publications:* The Songs of Paul Simon 1972, New Songs 1975, One-Trick Pony (screenplay) 1980, At The Zoo (juvenile) 1991. *Address:* c/o C. Vaughn Hazell, Paul Simon Music, Suite 500, 1619 Broadway, New York, NY 10019, USA (office). *Website:* www.paulsimon.com.

SIMON MUNARO, Yehude; Peruvian politician and fmr teacher; b. 18 July 1947, Lima; ed Univ. Nacional Pedro Ruiz Gallo; teacher, Colegio San Vicente de Paul 1966–72; Pres. Fed. of Teachers, Univ. Nacional Pedro Ruiz Gallo 1981–85; Sec.–Gen. United Left, Lambayeque 1984; Pres. Lambayeque Defence Front 1984–90; Deputy for Lambayeque 1985–90; Pres. Movimiento Humanista Peruano 2000; Regional Pres. for Lambayeque 2003–06; Prime Minister of Peru 2008–09. *Address:* c/o Office of the President of the Council of Ministers, Avda 28 de Julio 878, Miraflores, Lima, Peru (office).

SIMON OF HIGHBURY, Baron (Life Peer), cr. 1997, of Canonbury in the London Borough of Islington; **David Alec Gwyn Simon,** Kt, CBE, MA, MBA; British business executive; b. 24 July 1939, London, England; s. of the late Roger Simon and of Barbara Hudd; m. 1st Jane Mohn 1964; two s.; m. 2nd Sarah Smith 1992; ed Gonville and Caius Coll., Cambridge; joined BP 1961, Marketing Dir, Holland 1972–75, Marketing Co-ordinator, European Region 1975–80, Marketing Dir, Oil UK 1980–82, Man. Dir, Oil Int. Ltd 1982–85, Man. Dir BP Co. PLC 1986–95, Deputy Chair. 1990–95, Group Chief Exec. 1992–95, Chair. 1995–97; Dir Bank of England 1995–97; Minister of State Responsible for Trade and Competitiveness in Europe (attached to Dept of Trade and Industry and Treasury) 1997–99; Dir (non-exec.) and Deputy Chair. Unilever 2000–04, 2005–09; Dir Centre for European Policy Studies 2002–; Sr Adviser, GDF SUEZ 2001– (also Non-exec. Dir); Lay mem.

and Deputy Chair., Univ. Council, Univ. of Cambridge 2005–10; mem. Int. Advisory Bd Dana Gas Corpn 2006–, Advisory Bd Montrose Assocs 2008–; Trustee, Hertie Foundation, Germany, Cicely Saunders International 2001–10; mem. Inst. of Dirs, Centre for European Policy Studies, Brussels, Inst. for Strategic Dialogue; Grand Commdr, Order of Leopold II (Belgium); Hon. DEcon (Hull) 1993, (Birmingham) 2003; Dr hc (Univ. of N London) 1995; Hon. LLD (Bath) 1998. *Leisure interests:* golf, books, music. *Address:* 1 St James's Square, London, SW1Y 4PD, England (office). *Telephone:* (20) 7496-5821 (office). *Fax:* (20) 7496-4436 (office). *E-mail:* sjs1@bp.com (office).

SIMONDS-GOODING, Anthony James Joseph, CBE; British business executive; *Chairman, OMG plc;* b. 10 Sept. 1937, Dublin, Ireland; s. of Maj. and Mrs Hamilton Simonds-Gooding; m. 1st Fiona Menzies 1961 (divorced 1982); three s. two d. (one s. deceased); m. 2nd Marjorie A. Pennock 1982; one step-s.; ed Ampleforth Coll. and Britannia Royal Naval Coll., Dartmouth; served in RN 1953–59; with Unilever 1960–73; Marketing Dir Whitbread & Co., PLC 1973, subsequently Man. Dir (UK), latterly Group Man. Dir until 1985; Chair. and Chief Exec. Saatchi PLC 1985–87; Chief Exec. British Satellite Broadcasting 1987–90; Chair. S.P. Lintas 1994–95, Ammirati Puris Lintas 1994–96; Chair. Designers and Art Dirs Asscn (now D&AD) 1992–; Dir ICA Devt Cttee 1992–94, Cancer Relief Macmillan Fund 1992–, Robinsons PLC 1993–, Brixton Prison 1994–97, Community Hosps Group PLC 1995–2000, Interbrand Newell & Sorrell 1996–98, Clark & Taylor 1996–99, Blick PLC 1997–, Kunick PLC 1997–, CLK MPL 1999–, Rainbow Children's Trust 2001–, Sea Cadets Asscn 2001, OMG plc 2002– (Chair. (non-exec.) 2002–). *Leisure interests:* oil painting, walking, opera, travel, tennis. *Address:* c/o Board of Directors, OMG plc, 14 Minns Business Park, West Way, Oxford, OX2 0JB; Burchetts Brook, Holmbury St Mary, Surrey, RH5 6NA, England. *Telephone:* (1306) 621266 (Surrey). *Fax:* (1865) 240527 (Oxford). *E-mail:* anthony@simonds-gooding.net. *Website:* www.simonds-gooding.net.

SIMONETI, Marko, BA, MA, PhD; Slovenian economist, financial executive and academic; *Professor of Money and Finance, Law School, University of Ljubljana;* b. 8 July 1958; m.; ed Univ. of Ljubljana, Cornell Univ., USA; Sr Research Fellow, Inst. for Econ. Research 1982–90; Under-Sec. of State in Fed. Govt 1989; Man. Dir Agency for Privatization, Ljubljana 1990–93; Co-founder CEEPN (Cen. and Eastern European Privatization Network) 1993, Chair. Steering Cttee 1991–92, Exec. Dir 1993–2004; served as Vice-Chair. Board of the Securities and Exchange Comm., mem. Supervisory Bd of Ljubljana Stock Exchange and Chair. Govt Comm. for privatization of largest bank in Slovenia; served as pvt. sector devt adviser to various int. orgs (IBRD, EBRD, OECD, UNDP, UN-ECE); Pres. and CEO Ljubljanska Borza d.d. (Ljubljana Stock Exchange) 2005–09; Chair. Supervisory Bd Nova Ljubljanska banka 2009–12; Prof. of Money and Finance, Law School, Univ. of Ljubljana 1997–; mem. Econ. Asscn of Slovenia, European Asscn for Comparative Econ. Studies. *Publications include:* Investment Funds as Intermediaries of Privatization (CEEPN Workshop Series, Vol. 5) (co-ed.) 1994, Bank Rehabilitation and Enterprise Restructuring (CEEPN Workshop series, Vol. 6) (co-ed.) 1995, The Governance of Privatization Funds: Experiences of the Czech Republic, Poland and Slovenia (co-ed.) 1999; numerous book chapters, reports and articles in professional journals. *Address:* Law School, University of Ljubljana, Poljanski nasip 2, 1000 Ljubljana, Slovenia (office). *E-mail:* marko.simoneti@pf.uni-lj.si (office). *Website:* www.pf.uni-lj.si (office).

SIMONIA, Nodari Aleksandrovich, CandEconSc, DHist; Russian political economist; *Professor, Moscow State Institute of International Relations (MGIMO);* b. 30 Jan. 1932, Tbilisi, Georgia; m.; one d.; ed Moscow Inst. of Int. Relations; Corresp. mem. Russian Acad. of Sciences 1990, mem. 1997–; Acad. Sec., Dept of Int. Relations, Jr Researcher, Sr Researcher, Prof. and Head of Sector, Head of Div., Deputy Dir, Inst. of Oriental Studies 1955–86; Deputy Dir of World Econ. and Int. Relations (IMEMO), Russian Acad. of Sciences 1986–2000, Dir 2000, currently Adviser; Prof., Moscow State Inst. of Int. Relations (MGIMO); Prof., Centre of Slavic Studies, Hokkaido Univ., Japan; main research in comparative studies: Russia and developing countries; mem. Presidium, Russian Acad. of Sciences, Scientific Council Ministry of Foreign Affairs, European Acad. of Sciences, Arts and Literature; Special Rep. of Pres. of Russian Fed. for Relations with African States' Leaders in the G-8 framework 2002–06. *Publications:* over 260 scientific works, including 16 books, articles and papers on the devt of capitalism including within modern Russia. *Address:* IMEMO, Profsoyuznaya str. 23, 117997 Moscow, GSP-7, Russia (office). *Telephone:* (499) 120-84-50 (office); (495) 434-15-68 (home). *Fax:* (499) 120-65-75 (office). *E-mail:* imemoran@imemo.ru (office). *Website:* www.imemo.ru/eng (office).

SIMONIS, HE Cardinal Adrianus Johannes; Dutch ecclesiastic; *Archbishop-Emeritus of Utrecht;* b. 26 Nov. 1931, Lisse; ed Hageveld (high school) and Warmond seminaries, Haarlem, Biblicum (Papal Inst. for the Bible), Rome and Jerusalem; ordained priest, Rotterdam 1957; consecrated Bishop of Rotterdam 1971; apptd Coadjutor Archbishop of Utrecht 1983, Archbishop of Utrecht 1983–2007, currently Archbishop-Emer.; cr. Cardinal (Cardinal-Priest of S. Clemente) 1985; mem. Congregation for the Catholic Educ., Congregation for the Insts of the Consecrated Life and the Societies of Apostolic Life, Pontifical Council for the Promotion of the Unity Among Christians, Conf. of European Bishops; Orde van de Nederlandse Leeuw 1976, Grootkruis Oranje-Nassau. *Publications:* Op de adem van het leven 1997, Een hart om te denken 2007. *Telephone:* 2334244 (office); (73) 5115976 (office); (30) 2338030. *Fax:* 2332103 (office); (30) 2311962. *Website:* www.rkkerk.nl (office).

SIMONIS, Heide, MA; German politician; b. 4 July 1943, Bonn; d. of Dr Horst Steinhardt and Sophia Brück; m. Prof. Udo E. Simonis 1967; tutor in German, Univ. of Zambia 1967–69, Goethe Inst. and Nat. TV and Radio Service, Tokyo 1970–72; mem. Bundestag 1976–88; Minister of Finance, Schleswig-Holstein 1988–93, Minister-Pres. 1993–2005; Head of UNICEF Deutschland 2005–08; mem. Social Democratic Party (SPD); Orden wider den tierischen Ernst, Aachen 1998, Order of the Cross of Terra Mariana (Estonia) 2006, Order of the Rising Sun (Japan) 2010; Bambi Award 1993, Schlitzohr Prize 1997. *Publications:* Kein Blatt vorm Mund 1998, Unter Männern (autobiog.) 2003, Ausgeteilt, eingesteckt 2007, Drei Rheintöchter (co-author) 2008, Verzockt! Warum die Karten von Markt und Staat neu gemischt werden müssen 2010. *Leisure interests:* music, literature. *Address:* Büro Heide Simonis, Kleiner Kuhberg 28-30, 24103 Kiel; Düsternbrooker Weg 70, 24105 Kiel, Germany. *Telephone:* (431) 9882000. *Fax:* (431) 9881960.

E-mail: heide.simonis@stk.landsh.de (office); tokio70@web.de (home). *Website:* www.heide-simonis.de.

SIMONITI, Vasko, PhD; Slovenian historian, academic and politician; b. 23 March 1951, Ljubljana; ed Univ. of Ljubljana; Lecturer in History, Ljubljana Univ. 1989–2000, now Prof.; mem. Slovenian Democratic Party 2000–; Minister of Culture 2004–08. *Publications:* Vojaška organizacija 1991, Slovenska zgodovina do razsvetljenstva 1995, Turki so v deželi že, Turški vpadi na slovensko ozemlje 1996, Fanfare nasilja 2003, Slovenska povjest do prosvetiteljstva 2004 (co-author), Slowenische Geschichte: Gesellschaft, Politik, Kultur (co-author) 2008. *Address:* c/o Ministry of Culture, 1000 Ljubljana, Maistrova 10, Slovenia (office).

SIMONOV, Aleksey Kirillovich; Russian film director, interpreter and human rights activist; *President, Glasnost Defence Foundation;* b. 8 Aug. 1939, Moscow; s. of Konstantin Simonov (writer and poet); m.; two s.; ed Inst. of Oriental Languages at Moscow State Univ., courses for film dirs; worked in lab. at Inst. of Permafrost Studies 1956–58; translator, USSR State Cttee for Int. Econ. Relations in Indonesia 1963–64; Ed., Khudozhestennaya Literatura 1964–67; film Dir EKRAN TV Studio 1970–91; Lecturer, All-Russian Inst. of Cinematography 1991–93; Sec., USSR Union of Cinematographists 1991; f. Konf 1991; Co.-Chair. Licence Cttee of Russian Fed. 1992–93; mem. Movt of Democratic Reforms 1991–93; mem. Public Chamber of Russian Presidency; Co-founder Movt for Mil. Reform 1995; Pres. Glasnost Defence Foundation 1991–; Vice-Pres. Russian PEN Centre 2009–; Chair. jury for Sakharov prize for Journalism, Stalker Film Festival; mem. Editorial Bd, Sovyetsky Ekran (magazine) 1988–92, Rossia (weekly) 1992–96; mem. Moscow Helsinki Group 1998–; Founder Dossier on Censorship (quarterly) 1997–, Law and Practice (monthly) 1995–2003; Moscow Int. Press Club 1997, Femida Prize (for Glasnost Defence Foundation) 1999, Nat. Endowment for Democracy 2005. *Films:* directed over 25 feature films and documentaries including Detachment 1985. *Publications:* Private Collection 1999 (prose), End of the Holyday of Disobedience 2004, Guy from Sivtsev-Vrajek (prose) 2009; edited numerous book; numerous articles in newspapers and magazines Yunost, Ogonyok, Moskva; currently columnist, Russkaya Misl, Paris, Izvestia, Moscow; translator of English plays, Indonesian and African poetry. *Leisure interest:* collecting turtles. *Address:* 119121 Moscow, Zubovski blvd. 4, apt. 438 (office); Moscow, Leningradski prosp. 60-A, apt. 2, Russia (home). *Telephone:* (495) 637-44-20 (office); (499) 155-38-39 (home). *Fax:* (495) 637-49-47 (office). *E-mail:* fond@gdf.ru (office); simonov@gdf.ru (home). *Website:* www.gdf.ru (office).

ŠIMONOVIĆ, Ivan, DJur; Croatian diplomatist, civil servant, academic, politician and UN official; *Assistant Secretary-General for Human Rights, United Nations;* b. 2 May 1959, Zagreb; m.; two c.; ed Univ. of Zagreb; staff mem. Social Research Inst., Zagreb; mem. Faculty of Law, Univ. of Zagreb 1986–93, Asst Prof., then Assoc. Prof. in Dept for Theory of Law and State 2004–05, Prof. and Vice-Dean of Law Faculty 2005–08, Head of Dept of Gen. Theory of Law and State 2006–08, Vice-Rector Univ. of Zagreb 2006–08; Guest Lecturer at univs in Graz, Austria, Kraków, Poland and Yale Univ., Pittsburg, Montana and N Dakota, USA; Fulbright Scholar, Yale Univ. Law School 1993–94; with Ministry of Foreign Affairs, serving as Asst Minister of Foreign Affairs in charge of Consular and Int. Legal Affairs 1992–93, Multilateral Affairs 1994–95, First Asst Minister and Deputy Minister of Foreign Affairs 1995–96, mem. Croatian Del. at Dayton Peace Talks 1995, Deputy Minister of Foreign Affairs 2003–04; Minister of Justice 2008–10; UN Asst Sec.-Gen. for Human Rights 2010–; mem. numerous Govt comms including Jt Comm. on Search for Missing Persons and Mortal Remains under auspices of ICRC, Comm. for Detained and Missing Persons, State Comm. for UN Protection Force (UNPROFOR); Perm. Rep. to UN, New York 1997–2003; Co-Chair. Hungarian-Croatian Jt Cttee 2003–; apptd Agent of Govt of Croatia to Int. Court of Justice in its case against Fed. Repub. of Yugoslavia for alleged genocide 2000; Sr Vice-Pres. ECOSOC 2001–02, Pres. 2002–03; Vice-Pres. Bureau of Preparatory Cttee of Int. Conf. on Financing for Devt 2002; Officier, Légion d'honneur 2004. *Publications include:* author and ed. of more than 50 publs including books, book chapters and articles in scholarly journals, in Croatian and English. *Address:* New York Office of the UN High Commissioner for Human Rights, United Nations, New York, NY 10017, USA (office). *Telephone:* (212) 963-5931 (office). *E-mail:* InfoDesk@ohchr.org (office). *Website:* www.ohchr.org (office).

SIMONS, Elwyn LaVerne, BS, MA, PhD, DPhil, DSc; American anthropologist, anatomist and academic; *James B. Duke Professor Emeritus of Biological Anthropology and Senior Primate Biologist, Duke University Primate Center, Duke University;* b. 14 July 1930, Lawrence, Kan.; s. of Verne Franklin Simons and Verna Irene Simons (née Cuddeback); m. 1st Mary Hoyt Fitch 1964; one s.; m. 2nd Friderun Annursel Ankel 1972; one s. one d.; ed Rice and Princeton Univs, Univ. of Oxford, UK; Lecturer in Geology, Princeton Univ. 1958–59; Asst Prof. of Zoology, Univ. of Pennsylvania 1959–61; Visiting Assoc. Prof. of Geology and Curator of Vertebrate Paleontology, Yale Univ. 1960–61, Assoc. Prof. and Head Curator 1961–65; Prof. of Geology 1967–77, Curator in Charge, Div. of Vertebrate Paleontology, Peabody Museum 1965–77; Prof. of Anthropology and Anatomy, Duke Univ., 1977–82, Prof. of Zoology and Dir Duke Primate Center 1977–91, James B. Duke Prof. of Biological Anthropology 1982–2009, Prof. Emer. 2009–, Scientific Dir 1991–2001, Head of Div. of Fossil Primates 2001–11, Sr Primate Biologist 2001–04, Dir Div. of Fossil Primates, Duke Lemur Center 2004–11; mem. Exec. Cttee, Center for Tropical Conservation 1991–2011, Steering Cttee, Madagascar Fauna Group 1990–2011, Bd of Lemur Conservation Foundation, Myakka, Fla 2001–; mem. NAS, American Philosophical Soc.; Hon. Citizen of Fayum Prov., Egypt 1984; Chevalier, Ordre Nat., Madagascar; Hon. MA (Yale) 1967; Hon. DSc (Oxford) 1996; public school scholarship, Houston Art Museum 1938–46, numerous awards including Annandale Medal, Asiatic Soc. of Calcutta, Charles R. Darwin Award, Asscn of Physical Anthropology 2000. *Achievements include:* has directed over 85 expeditions to Wyoming, Iran, India and Madagascar and 38 to the Egyptian Fayum in search of fossil primates and associated fauna; discovered Gigantopithecus in India, discovered and named Aegyptopithecus, Afrotarsius, Karanisia, Catopithecus, Arsinoea and Proteopithecus and others in Egypt. *Television:* appearances on Canadian TV and Dick Cavett Show 1960s. *Publications:* A Simons Family History: in England and America 1975, Caudebec in England and France 2005; more than 345 scientific articles. *Leisure interests:* drawing and painting, folk singing, genealogy. *Address:* 8232 West Adam Avenue, Peoria, AZ 85382, USA (home). *Telephone:* (623) 322-3234 (office). *E-mail:*

esimons@duke.edu (office). *Website:* www.fossils.duke.edu (office); evolutionaryanthropology.duke.edu (office).

SIMONS, John Philip, PhD, ScD, FRS; British chemist and academic; *Dr Lee's Professor Emeritus of Chemistry, University of Oxford;* b. 20 April 1934, London, England; s. of Mark Simons and Rose Simons; m. 1st Althea Screaton (died 1989); m. 2nd Elizabeth Corps; three s.; ed Sidney Sussex Coll., Cambridge; fmr Prof. of Photochemistry, Univ. of Birmingham; fmr Prof. of Physical Chem., Univ. of Nottingham; fmr Prof. of Chem., Univ. of Oxford, now Dr Lee's Prof. Emer., Emer. Professorial Fellow, Exeter Coll., Oxford; Hon. DSc (Birmingham); Davy Medal, Royal Soc., Humphry Davy Lecturer, Royal Soc., RSC Liversidge, Tilden, Polanyi and Spiers Medals, Chemical Dynamics Award, Pimentel Lecturer, Univ. of California, Berkeley. *Publications:* numerous scientific papers in professional journals on photochemistry, molecular reaction dynamics, spectroscopy and structures of biologically important molecules in the gas phase. *Address:* Physical and Theoretical Chemistry Laboratory, University of Oxford, South Parks Road, Oxford, OX1 3QZ, England (office). *Telephone:* (1865) 275400 (office). *Fax:* (1865) 275410 (office). *E-mail:* john.simons@chem.ox.ac.uk (office).

SIMONYI, András, PhD; Hungarian economist, consultant and fmr diplomatist; *Managing Director, Center for Transatlantic Relations, Paul Nitze School of Advanced International Studies, Johns Hopkins University;* b. 16 May 1952, Budapest; s. of Denes Simonyi and Maria Balazs; m. Nada Pejak; one s. one d.; ed Karl Marx Univ. of Econs (now Budapest Univ.); worked in 1980s with different orgs in field of youth exchange, particularly promoting East–West contacts, including programmes with American Council of Young Political Leaders; mem. staff Foreign Relations Dept, Socialist Workers Party 1984–89; Head of Nordic Dept, Ministry of Foreign Affairs 1989–91; Deputy Chief of Mission Embassy of Hungary, The Hague 1991–92, Hungarian Mission to EC and NATO, Brussels 1992–95; Head, Hungarian NATO Liaison Office, Brussels 1995–99; Perm. Rep. to NATO Council (first Hungarian Perm. Rep.) 1999–2001; ran own consulting co. Danison Ltd 2001–02; Man. Dir, Center for Transatlantic Relations, Paul Nitze School of Advanced Int. Studies, Johns Hopkins Univ. 2012–; Imre Nagy Award, Hungary–Ohio Partnership for Educ. *Publications include:* numerous articles on the accession process to NATO, trans-Atlantic relations and European security and the war on terror. *Leisure interest:* blues music (plays electric guitar). *Address:* SAIS Center for Transatlantic Relations, Nitze Building, 1740 Massachusetts Ave., NW, Washington, DC, 200036, USA. *Website:* www.sais-jhu.edu (office).

ŠIMONYTĖ, Ingrida, BBA, MA; Lithuanian economist and politician; b. 15 Nov. 1974, Vilnius; m.; ed Vilnius Secondary School No. 7, Vilnius Univ.; Chief Economist of Tax Div., Fiscal Policy Dept, Ministry of Finance 1997–98, Head of Indirect Taxes Div. 1998–2001, Dir Tax Dept 2002–04, Under-Sec., Ministry of Finance 2004–09, Minister of Finance 2009–12. *Address:* c/o Ministry of Finance, Lukiškių 2, Vilnius 01512, Lithuania. *E-mail:* finmin@finmin.lt.

SIMOR, András; Hungarian financial consultant and fmr central banker; b. 17 May 1954, Budapest; s. of János Simor and Zsuzsanna Beretvás; divorced; three c.; ed Budapest Univ. of Econs; Exec. Foreign Exchange Man. Dept, Hungarian Nat. Bank (Magyar Nemzeti Bank) 1976–79, with Hungarian Int. Bank Ltd, London (subsidiary) 1979–85, Gov. MNB 2007–13; CEO Creditanstalt Értékpapír Rt, Budapest 1989–97; Exec. Chair. CA IB Investmentbank AG, Vienna 1997–98; Chair. Budapest Stock Exchange 1998–2002; Chair. Deloitte Hungary 1999–2007, Chair. and Office Man. Partner Deloitte & Touche Rt, Budapest 2000–07, also mem. Bd of Dirs Deloitte & Touche Cen. Europe 2002–06; mentioned by Global Finance Magazine was one of the best bank presidents 2009, named by Euromoney as Banker of the Year in the emerging Europe region 2010. *Address:* c/o Hungarian National Bank (Magyar Nemzeti Bank), Szabadság tér 8–9, 1850 Budapest, Hungary. *E-mail:* info@mnb.hu.

SIMPSON, Alan Kooi, BS, JD; American lawyer and fmr politician; *Attorney and Shareholder, Burg Simpson Eldredge Hersh & Jardine, P.C;* b. 2 Sept. 1931, Cody, Wyo.; s. of Milward Lee Simpson and Lorna Simpson (née Kooi); m. Ann Schroll 1954; two s. one d.; ed Univ. of Wyoming; called to Wyo. Bar 1958, US Supreme Court 1964; Asst Attorney Gen. Wyo. State 1959; Attorney for Cody 1959–69; mem. Wyo. House of Reps 1964–77; Senator from Wyoming 1978–97; Asst Majority Leader 1985–87, Asst Minority Leader 1987–97; Pnr, Simpson, Kepler, Simpson & Cozzens, Cody; Attorney and Shareholder Burg, Simpson, Eldredge, Hersh & Jardine; consultant, Tongour, Simpson, Holsclaw Group, Washington, DC; Visiting Lecturer, Lambard Chair., Shorenstein Center, Harvard Univ. 1997–2000; Visiting Lecturer, Univ. of Wyo. 2000–; mem. Iraq Study Group, US Inst. of Peace 2006; Co-Chair. Nat. Comm. on Fiscal Responsibility and Reform 2010–; Trustee, Buffalo Bill Historical Center (now Chair.), Cody, Gottsche Foundation Rehabilitation Center; mem. Wyo. Bar Asscn, ABA, Asscn of Trial Lawyers of America; Hon. LLD (Calif. Western School of Law) 1983, (Colo Coll.) 1986, (Notre Dame Univ.) 1987; Hon. JD (Rocky Mountain Coll.) 1996, (Wyo.) 1999; Centennial Alum Award (Wyo. Univ.) 1987, Thomas Jefferson Award in Law, Univ. of Va 1998. *Publication:* Right in the Old Gazoo: A Lifetime of Scrapping with the Press 1997. *Address:* Burg, Simpson, Eldredge, Hersh & Jardine, 1135 14th Street, PO Box 490, Cody, WY 82414, USA (office). *Telephone:* (307) 527-7891 (office). *E-mail:* asimpson@burgsimpson.com (office). *Website:* www.burgsimpson.com (office).

SIMPSON, John Cody Fidler-, CBE, MA, FRGS; British broadcaster and writer; *World Affairs Editor, BBC;* b. 9 Aug. 1944, Cleveleys; s. of Roy Fidler-Simpson and Joyce Leila Vivien Cody; m. 1st Diane Petteys 1965 (divorced 1996); two d.; m. 2nd Adèle Krüger 1996; one s.; ed St Paul's School, London, Magdalene Coll. Cambridge; joined BBC 1966, Foreign Corresp. in Dublin, Brussels, Johannesburg 1972–78, Diplomatic Corresp., BBC TV 1978–80, Political Ed. 1980–81, Diplomatic Ed. 1982–88, Foreign Affairs Ed. (now World Affairs Ed.) 1988–; Contributing Ed. The Spectator 1991–95; columnist, Sunday Telegraph 1995–; Chancellor, Roehampton Univ. 2005–; Hon. Fellow, Magdalene Coll., Cambridge 2000; Hon. DLitt (De Montfort) 1995, (Univ. of E Anglia) 1998; Dr hc (Nottingham) 2000; Golden Nymph Award Cannes 1979, BAFTA Reporter of the Year 1991, 2001, Royal TV Soc. Dimbleby Award 1991, Peabody Award 1998, Emmy Award (for coverage of the fall of Kabul) 2002, Bayeux War Correspondents' Prize 2002, Int. Emmy Award, New York 2002. *Publications:* The Best of Granta

1966, The Disappeared 1985, Behind Iranian Lines 1988, Despatches from the Barricades 1990, From the House of War 1991, The Darkness Crumbles 1992, In the Forests of the Night 1993, Lifting the Veil: Life in Revolutionary Iran 1995, The Oxford Book of Exile 1995, Strange Places, Questionable People (autobiog.) 1998, A Mad World, My Masters 2000, News from No Man's Land: Reporting the World 2002, Days from a Different World: A Memoir of Childhood (autobiog.) 2005, Twenty Tales from the War Zone 2007, Not Quite World's End 2007, Unreliable Sources: How the 20th Century was Reported 2010. *Leisure interests:* travel, scuba diving, book collecting. *Address:* c/o BBC World Affairs Unit, Television Centre, Wood Lane, London, W12 7RJ, England. *Telephone:* (20) 8743-8000. *Fax:* (20) 8743-7591.

SIMPSON, Patricia Ann, BSc (Hons), PhD, FRS; British research scientist; *Professor Emeritus, Department of Zoology, University of Cambridge;* b. 9 Dec. 1945, Poona, India; d. of James Simpson and Peggy Simpson; ed Univ. of Southampton, Univ. Pierre et Marie Curie, Paris; ind. researcher, CGM, Gif sur Yvette 1975–80; Research Dir CNRS Strasbourg 1981–2000; Wellcome Trust Prin. Fellow, Dept of Zoology, Univ. of Cambridge 2000–11, Prof. of Comparative Embryology 2002–11, Prof. Emer. 2012–; mem. European Molecular Biology Org. 1990; Fellow, AAAS 2012; Silver Medal, CNRS, France 1993, Waddington Medal, British Soc. for Developmental Biology 2008. *Publication:* The Notch Receptors 1994. *Leisure interests:* woodwork, boating, hiking, travel, gardening. *Address:* Department of Zoology, Downing Street, Cambridge, CB2 3EJ (office); 25 Temple End, Great Wilbraham, Cambs., CB21 5JF, England (home). *Telephone:* (1223) 336669 (office); (1223) 880664 (home). *Fax:* (1223) 336676 (office). *E-mail:* pas49@cam.ac.uk (office). *Website:* www.zoo.cam.ac.uk/zoostaff/simpson.htm (office).

SIMPSON-MILLER, Most Hon. Portia Lucretia, BPA; Jamaican politician; *Prime Minister and Minister of Defence, Development, Information and Sports;* b. 12 Dec. 1945, Wood Hall, St Catherine; m. Errald Miller; ed St Martin's High School, Union Inst., Miami, Fla; Councillor in Kingston, People's Nat. Party (PNP) 1974, 1976; Vice-Pres. PNP 1978–2006, Pres. 2006–, mem. Exec. Council and Nat. Exec. Council PNP; PNP Spokesperson on Women's Affairs, Pensions, Social Security, Consumer Affairs 1983–89; MP for SW St Andrew 1989–; fmr Parl. Sec., Ministry of Local Govt, later in Office of the Prime Minister; Minister of Labour, Welfare and Sports 1989–93, of Labour and Welfare 1993–95, of Labour, Social Security and Sports 1995–2000, of Tourism and Sports 2000–02, of Local Govt and Sport 2002–06; Prime Minister (first woman) 2006–07, Prime Minister and Minister of Defence, Devt, Information and Sports 2012–; Jamaican Order of the Nation 2006; Dr hc (Union Inst.); World Women and Sport Trophy, IOC 2007, ranked by Forbes magazine amongst 100 Most Powerful Women (81st) 2007. *Address:* Office of the Prime Minister, Jamaica House, 1 Devon Rd, POB 272, 101 Kingston 6, Jamaica (office). *Telephone:* 927-9941 (office). *Fax:* 968-8229 (office). *E-mail:* pmo@opm.gov.jm (office). *Website:* www.opm.gov.jm (office).

SIMPSON OF DUNKELD, Baron (Life Peer), cr. 1997, of Dunkeld in Perth and Kinross; **Rt Hon. George Simpson,** FCIS, FCCA, FRSA; British business executive and company director; b. 2 July 1942, Scotland; s. of William Simpson and Eliza Jane Simpson (née Wilkie); m. Eva Chalmers 1963; one s. one d.; ed Morgan Acad., Dundee, Dundee Inst. of Technology; Sr Accountant Scottish Gas 1964–68; Cen. Audit Man. British Leyland 1969–73, Financial Controller, Leyland Truck and Bus Div. 1973–76, Dir of Accounting, Leyland Cars 1976–78, Finance and Systems Dir, Leyland Trucks 1978–80; Man. Dir Coventry Climax Ltd 1980–83, Freight Rover Ltd 1983–86; CEO Leyland DAF 1986–88; Man. Dir Rover Group 1989–91, Chair. 1991–94, CEO 1991–92; Dir BAe 1990–94, Deputy CEO 1992–94; Chair. Ballast Nedam Construction Ltd 1992–94, Arlington Securities 1993–94; CEO Lucas Industries PLC 1994–96; Man. Dir Marconi PLC (fmrly GEC PLC) 1996–99, CEO 1999–2001; mem. Supervisory Bd and Dir (non-exec.) Pilkington PLC 1992–99, Northern Venture Capital 1992–2000, Pro Share 1992–4, ICI PLC 1995–2001, Nestlé SA 1999–2003; mem. Bd of Dirs Triumph Group Inc. 2003–; Dir (non-exec.) Alstom SA 1997–2004, Bank of Scotland 2000–02; mem. Exec. Cttee SMMT 1986– (Vice-Pres. 1986–95, Pres. 1995–96); Industrial Prof., Univ. of Warwick 1991–; Gov. Nat. Inst. of Econ. and Social Research 1997–; Fellow, Univ. of Abertay; mem. European Round Table of Businessmen 1997–2001, Mayor of Shanghai's Business Advisory Council 1998–2000; Hon. Fellow, London Business School; hon. degrees from Univs of Warwick and Aston. *Leisure interest:* golf. *Address:* House of Lords, London, SW1A 0PW, England (office). *E-mail:* lordsimps@aol.com (home).

SIMS, Christopher A., BA, PhD; American economist and academic; *Harold H. Helm '20 Professor of Economics and Banking, Princeton University;* b. 21 Oct. 1942; ed Harvard Coll., Univ. of California, Berkeley, Harvard Univ.; Instructor in Econs, Harvard Univ. 1967–68, Asst Prof. of Econs 1968–70; Assoc. Prof. of Econs, Univ. of Minnesota 1970–74, Prof. of Econs 1974–90, mem. Grad. Faculty in Statistics 1973–90; Henry Ford II Prof. of Econs, Yale Univ. 1990–99, Dir of Grad. Studies, Dept of Econs 1992–94; Prof. of Econs, Princeton Univ. 1999–, Harold H. Helm '20 Prof. of Econs and Banking 2004–, Dir of Grad. Studies, Dept of Econs 2003–08; Research Fellow, Nat. Bureau of Econ. Research 1970–71; Visiting Prof., Yale Univ. 1974, MIT 1979–80; part-time consultant, Control Data Business Advisors 1981–83; consultant, Fed. Reserve Bank of Minneapolis 1983, 1986–87, Fed. Nat. Mortgage Asscn 1999–2002; Dir Inst. for Empirical Macroeconomics, Minneapolis 1987–91; Visiting Scholar, Fed. Reserve Bank of Atlanta most years since 1995, Fed. Reserve Bank of New York 1994–97, 2004–, Fed. Reserve Bank of Philadelphia 2000–03, IMF 2003–; Chair. Section 54, Econ. Sciences, NAS 2006–09; Co-Chair. Program Cttee, World Congress of Econometric Soc. 1990; mem. NSF Econs Advisory Panel 1973–75, Nominating Cttee of American Econ. Asscn 1974–75, American Statistical Asscn Advisory Cttee to Census 1976–81, Fellows Nominating Cttee of Econometric Soc. 1980, 1985, Program Cttee for World Congress of Econometric Soc. 1980, Brookings Panel of Econ. Activity 1975–76, 2001–02 (Sr Advisor 1977–), Cttee on Nat. Statistics of Nat. Research Council, NAS 1982–85, Panel on Natural Gas Statistics of Cttee on Nat. Statistics 1982–85, Program Cttee, Summer Meetings of the Econometric Soc. 1971, 1984, 1998, NSF Program Advisory Cttee for Advanced Scientific Computing 1984–86, SIAM FCCSET Workshop on Research in Large Scale Computational Science and Eng 1987, Search Cttee for Dir of Minnesota Supercomputer Inst. 1987–88, Comm. for Behavioral and Social Sciences and Educ., Nat. Research Council 1992–98, Nat. Acad. of Sciences Report Review Cttee 2000–03; mem. Bd Barcelona Grad. School

of Econs 2007–; American Econometrics Ed. Review of Economic Studies 1973–75; Co-Ed. Econometrica 1977–81; Assoc. Ed. Journal of Applied Econometrics 1986–89, Journal of Business and Economic Statistics 1986–93; mem. Editorial Bd Annals of Economic and Social Measurement 1975, Journal of Economics and Philosophy 1985–94, International Journal of Supercomputer Applications 1987–89, Proceedings of the National Academy of Sciences 1996–2000; mem. Council of the Econometric Soc. 1979–80, 1990–92, Exec. Cttee of Econometric Soc. 1992, Second Vice-Pres. Econometric Soc. 1993, First Vice-Pres. 1994, Pres. 1995; mem. American Acad. of Arts and Sciences 1988, NAS 1989; Fellow, Econometric Soc. 1975, Minnesota Supercomputer Inst. 1987–91; Fisher-Schultz Lecturer, European Meetings of the Econometric Soc. 1977, Nobel Prize in Econs (with Thomas Sargent) 2011. *Publications:* numerous papers in professional journals on econometric theory for dynamic models and macroeconomic theory and policy. *Address:* Department of Economics, 104 Fisher Hall, Princeton University, Princeton, NJ 08544-1021 (office); 276 Dodds Lane, Princeton, NJ 08540, USA (home). *Telephone:* (609) 258-4033 (office); (609) 688-1001 (home). *Fax:* (609) 258-6419 (office). *E-mail:* sims@princeton.edu (office). *Website:* www.princeton.edu/~sims (office).

SIMS, Geoffrey Donald, OBE, MSc, PhD, ARCS, DIC, FCGI; British fmr university vice-chancellor; b. 13 Dec. 1926, London; s. of Albert Sims and Jessie Sims; m. Pamela Richings 1949; one s. two d.; ed Wembley Co. Grammar School and Imperial Coll. London; Research Physicist, GEC, Wembley 1948–54; Sr Scientific Officer, UKAEA, Harwell 1954–56; Lecturer, then Sr Lecturer, Dept of Electrical Eng, Univ. Coll. London 1956–63; Prof. and Head of Dept of Electronics, Univ. of Southampton 1963–74, Dean of Faculty 1967–70, Sr Deputy Vice-Chancellor 1970–72; Vice-Chancellor, Univ. of Sheffield 1974–90; Chair. Council for Educ. in the Commonwealth 1991–96, Sheffield Church Burgess Educ. Foundation 1990– (Chair. 1992–), Sheffield Church Burgesses Trust 1984– (Chair. 1987, 1999); Fellow, Royal Acad. of Engineering; Hon. Fellow, Sheffield City Polytechnic 1989; Hon. DSc (Southampton) 1979, (Huddersfield) 2001, Hon. ScD (Allegheny) 1989, Hon. LLD (Dundee) 1990, (Sheffield) 1991, Dr hc (Belfast) 1990; Symons Medal (Asscn of Commonwealth Univs) 1991. *Publications include:* Microwave Tubes and Semiconductor Devices (with I. M. Stephenson) 1963, Variational Techniques in Electromagnetism (trans.) 1965; numerous papers on microwaves, electronics and education. *Leisure interests:* golf, music, travel. *Address:* Ingleside, 70 Whirlow Lane, Sheffield, S11 9QF, England (home). *Telephone:* (114) 2366196 (home). *Fax:* (114) 2366196 (home). *E-mail:* geoffreydsims@blueyonder.co.uk.

ŞIMŞEK, Mehmet; Turkish economist and politician; *Minister of Finance;* b. 1967, Batman; worked for UBS Bank, New York 1997, for Bender Securities, Istanbul 1998–2000; joined Merrill Lynch, London, UK 2000, Head, Europe, Middle East and Africa region, Econ. and Strategic Research Div. 2005–07; Minister of State and Head of Treasury 2007–09, Minister of Finance 2009–; mem. AKP (Adalet ve Kalkinma Partisi/Justice and Devt Party). *Address:* Ministry of Finance, Maliye Bakanlığı, Dikmen Cad., Ankara, Turkey (office). *Telephone:* (312) 4250018 (office). *Fax:* (312) 4250058 (office). *E-mail:* bshalk@maliye.gov.tr (office). *Website:* www.maliye.gov.tr (office).

SIMUKANGA, Stephen, BMinSc, MMinSc, PhD, CEng, FIMMM, FSAIMM, FEIZ; Zambian metallurgist, academic and university administrator; *Vice-Chancellor, University of Zambia;* b. 20 May 1957, Mufulira; ed Univ. of Zambia, Univ. of Strathclyde, UK; began career in Luanshya mine of Zambia Consolidated Copper Mines Ltd 1982; Visiting Prof., Univ. of Cape Town for ten years; Prof. of Metallurgy and Mineral Processing, Univ. of Zambia, also Vice-Chancellor; consultant and researcher in areas of mine and quarry evaluation, mineral processing and the environment; Chair. Nat. Inst. for Scientific and Industrial Research, Examinations Council of Zambia; Fellow, Inst. of Materials, Minerals and Mining, Southern African Inst. of Mining and Metallurgy, Eng Inst. of Zambia; mem. Royal Acad. of Eng. *Address:* Office of The Vice-Chancellor, University of Zambia, Central Administration Block, Great East Road Campus, PO Box 32379, Lusaka, Zambia (office). *Telephone:* (21) 1250871 (office). *Fax:* (21) 1253952 (office). *E-mail:* vc@unza.zm (office). *Website:* www.unza.zm (office).

SIMUUSA, Wylbur C., MSc, MBA; Zambian mining engineer and politician; *Minister of Foreign Affairs;* b. 9 Sept. 1962; m. Beatrice Simuusa; mem. Nat. Ass. (Parl.) for Nchanga constituency 2007–; Minister of Mines 2011, of Lands, Natural Resources and Environmental Protection –2013, of Foreign Affairs 2013–; Chair. Regional Center for Mapping of Resources for Devt Conf. of Ministers 2013; mem. Patriotic Front. *Address:* Ministry of Foreign Affairs, POB RW50069, Lusaka, Zambia (office). *Telephone:* (21) 1252718 (office). *Fax:* (21) 1222440 (office).

SINAI, Yakov G., PhD; Russian mathematician and academic; *Professor of Mathematics, Princeton University;* b. 21 Sept. 1935, Moscow; s. of Gregory Sinai and Nadezda Kagan; m. Elena Vul; one s.; ed Moscow State Univ.; Scientific Researcher, Lab. of Probabilistic and Statistical Methods, Moscow State Univ. 1960–71, Prof. of Math. 1971–93; Prof. of Math., Princeton Univ., NJ, USA 1993–, Thomas Jones Prof. 1997–98; Sr Researcher, Landau Inst. of Theoretical Physics, Russian Acad. of Sciences 1971–; Chair. Fields Medal Cttee, Int. Math. Union 2001; Foreign mem. Hungarian Acad. of Sciences 1993, Brazilian Acad. of Sciences 2000; Foreign Assoc. NAS 1999, Academia Europaea 2008; Foreign Hon. mem. American Acad. of Arts and Sciences 1983; Hon. mem. London Math. Soc. 1992; Dr hc (Warsaw) 1993, (Budapest Univ. of Tech. and Econs) 2002, (Hebrew Univ. of Jerusalem) 2005; Loeb Lecturer, Harvard Univ. 1978, Plenary Speaker, Int. Congress on Math. Physics, Berlin 1981, Marseilles 1986, Boltzman Gold Medal 1986, Distinguished Lecturer, Israel 1989, Heineman Prize 1989, Markov Prize 1990, S. Lefshetz Lecturer, Mexico 1990, Plenary Speaker, Int. Congress of Mathematicians, Kyoto 1990, Dirac Medal, Int. Centre for Theoretical Physics, Trieste 1992, Landau Lecturer, Hebrew Univ. of Jerusalem 1993, Wolf Foundation Prize in Math. 1997, Plenary Speaker, First Latin American Congress in Math. 2000, Brazilian Award of Merits in Sciences 2000, Andreewski Lecturer, Berlin 2001, Jürgen Moser Lecture Prize, Soc. for Industrial and Applied Math. 2001, Bowen Lecturer, Univ. of Calif., Berkeley 2001, Alaoglu Lecturer, Calif. Inst. of Tech. 2002, Frederic Esser Nemmers Prize in Math. 2002, Lagrange Prize 2008. *Publications:* Probability Theory: An Introductory Course 1992, Classical Nonintegrability, Quantum Chaos (jtly) 1997, Selected Works of Eberhard Hopf with Commentaries (co-ed.) 2003; more than 140 articles in math. journals on dynamical systems (Kolmogorov-Sinai entropy). *Address:* Department of Mathematics, Princeton University, 708 Fine Hall, Washington Road, Princeton, NJ 08544-1000, USA (office). *Telephone:* (609) 258-4200 (office); (609) 258-4199 (office). *Fax:* (609) 258-1367 (office). *E-mail:* sinai@math.princeton.edu (office). *Website:* www.math.princeton.edu (office).

SINAISKY, Vassily Serafimovich; Russian conductor; *Music Director, Bolshoi Theatre;* b. 20 April 1947, Abez, Komi Autonomous Repub., Russia; m. Tamara Grigoryevna Sinayskaya; one s.; ed Leningrad State Conservatory; Artistic Dir and Chief Conductor Novosibirsk State Symphony 1971–73; Latvian State Symphony 1975–89; Moscow State Philharmonic Orchestra 1991–96; State Symphony Orchestra of Russia 2000–02; Prin. Guest Conductor BBC Philharmonic 1996–2011, Conductor Emer. 2012–; worked with Orchestre Nat. de France, Berlin Philharmonic Orchestra, Orchestre Philharmonic du Luxembourg, Royal Scottish Nat. Orchestra and Finnish Radio Symphony; Principal Conductor, Malmö Symphony Orchestra 2007–; Conductor-in-Residence, Bolshoi Theatre 2009–10, Music Dir 2010–; Gold Medal and First Prize, Karajan Competition, Berlin 1973, People's Artist of Latvia 1981. *Address:* Bolshoi Theatre, 103009 Moscow, Teatralnaya pl. 1, Russia (office). *Telephone:* (495) 292-08-18 (office). *Fax:* (495) 292-33-67 (office). *E-mail:* pr@bolshoi.ru (office). *Website:* www.bolshoi.ru (office).

SINAMENYE, Mathias; Burundian politician and fmr central banker; Second Vice-Pres. of Burundi for Econ. and Social Affairs 1998–2002; Head of Del. to UN Gen. Ass. Special Session on HIV/AIDS, New York June 2001; fmr Gov. Banque de la République du Burundi. *Address:* c/o Banque de la Republique du Burundi, Avenue du Gouvernement, BP 705, Bujumbura, Burundi (office).

SINCKLER, Christopher Peter, BA, MA; Barbadian civil servant, politician and academic; *Minister of Finance and Economic Affairs;* m. Arlyn Mayers; two s. one d.; ed Univ. of the West Indies; worked on econ. policy issues with IBRD (World Bank), IMF, IDB, WTO, CARICOM, African, Caribbean and Pacific Group of States, EU, among others; Lecturer in Govt and Political Science, Univ. of the West Indies 1990–94, 2006; Exec. Dir Caribbean Policy Devt Centre (coalition of Caribbean non-governmental orgs) 1999–2008, also Principal Liaison for global NGOs to Exec. Bd of World Bank 1999–2003; mem. Democratic Labour Party, currently Gen. Sec.; MP for St Michael NW; Minister of Foreign Affairs, Foreign Trade and Int. Business 2008, of Social Care, Constituency Empowerment and Urban Devt 2008–10, of Finance and Econ. Affairs 2010–. *Leisure interests:* reading, cycling and tennis. *Address:* Ministry of Finance and Economic Affairs, Government HQ, Bay St, St Michael, Bardados, BB 14018, West Indies (office). *Telephone:* 426-3179 (office). *Fax:* 436-9280 (office). *E-mail:* csinckler@sunbeach.net.

SINCLAIR, Charles James Francis, CBE, BA, FCA; British business executive; *Chief Executive, Daily Mail and General Trust plc;* b. 4 April 1948; s. of Sir George Sinclair and the late Lady Sinclair; m. Nicola Bayliss 1974; two s.; ed Winchester Coll. and Magdalen Coll., Oxford; Voluntary Service Overseas, Zambia 1966–67; with Deardon Farrow, chartered accountants 1970–75; with Associated Newspapers Holdings Ltd 1975, Man. Dir 1988, Group Chief Exec. Daily Mail and Gen. Trust plc (after merger with Associated Newspapers) 1989–; mem. Bd of Dirs (non-exec.) Euromoney Institutional Investor PLC 1985–, SVG Capital 2005–, Schroders PLC 1990–2005, Reuters Group PLC 1994–2005; Chair. Bd of Trustees Minack Theatre Trust, Porthcuno, Cornwall. *Leisure interests:* opera, fishing, skiing. *Address:* Daily Mail and General Trust plc, Northcliffe House, 2 Derry Street, London, W8 5TT, England (office). *Telephone:* (20) 7938-6000 (office). *Fax:* (20) 7938-3909 (office). *Website:* www.dmgt.co.uk (office).

SINCLAIR, Sir Clive Marles, Kt; British inventor; *Chairman, Sinclair Research Ltd;* b. 30 July 1940, London; s. of the late George William Carter Sinclair and of Thora Edith Ella Sinclair (née Marles); m. Ann Trevor-Briscoe 1962 (divorced 1985, died 2004); two s. one d.; ed St George's Coll., Weybridge; Ed. Bernards Publrs Ltd 1958–61; Chair. Sinclair Radionics Ltd 1962–79, Sinclair Research Ltd 1979–, Sinclair Browne Ltd 1981–85, Cambridge Computer 1986–90; Chair. British Mensa 1980–98, Hon. Pres. 2001–; Visiting Fellow, Robinson Coll., Cambridge 1982–85; Visiting Prof., Imperial Coll., London 1984–92; Dir Shaye Communications Ltd 1986–91, Anamartic Ltd; Hon. Fellow, Imperial Coll., London 1984; Hon. DSc (Bath) 1983, (Warwick, Heriot Watt) 1983, (UMIST) 1984; Royal Soc. Mullard Award 1984. *Publications:* Practical Transistor Receivers 1959, British Semiconductor Survey 1963. *Leisure interests:* music, poetry, mathematics, science, poker. *Address:* Sinclair Research Ltd, 1A Spring Gardens, Trafalgar Square, London, SW1A 2BB, England (office). *Telephone:* (20) 7839-6868 (office); (20) 7839-7744 (home). *Fax:* (20) 7839-6622 (office). *E-mail:* clivesinclair@sinclair-research.co.uk (office). *Website:* (office).

SINCLAIR, Rt Hon. Ian McCahon, AC, PC, BA, LLB; Australian consultant, lawyer, farmer, company director and fmr politician; *Chairman, Foundation for Rural and Regional Renewal;* b. 10 June 1929, Sydney, NSW; s. of George Sinclair and Hazel Sinclair; m. 1st Margaret Tarrant 1956 (died 1967); one s. two d.; m. 2nd Rosemary Edna Fenton 1970; one s.; ed Knox Grammar School, Wahroonga and Sydney Univ.; barrister 1952–; mem. Legis. Council in NSW Parl. 1961–63, House of Reps 1963–98; Minister for Social Services 1965–68; Minister Assisting Minister for Trade and Industry 1966–71; Minister for Shipping and Transport 1968–71, for Primary Industry 1971–72; Deputy Leader Country Party (now Nat. Party) 1971–84, Fed. Parl. Leader 1984–89, Party Spokesman on Defence, Foreign Affairs, Law and Agric. 1973–75, Opposition Spokesman on Agric., Leader of Opposition in House of Reps 1974–75; Minister for Agric. and Northern Australia Nov.–Dec. 1975, for Primary Industry 1975–79, for Communications 1980–82, for Defence 1982–83; Leader of Govt in House of Reps 1975–82; Leader of Opposition in House of Reps 1983–87, Opposition Spokesman for Defence 1983–87, for Trade and Resources 1987–89; Shadow Special Minister of State 1994; mem. Jt Cttee of Foreign Affairs, Defence and Trade 1991–98, Chair. 1996–98; Chair. Australian Constitutional Convention 1998; Speaker, House of Reps, Fed. Parl. 1998; Adjunct Prof. of Political Science, Univ. of New England 2000–; Man. Dir Sinclair Pastoral Co. 1953–, Grazier 1953–; Dir Farmers' and Graziers' Co-operative Co. Ltd 1962–65; Chair. Australian Rural Summit 1999, Australia Taiwan Business Council 2000–10, Foundation for Rural and Regional Renewal 2000–, CRC for Sheep 2001–08, Good Beginnings Australia 2001–10; Pres. Austcare 2000–09;

Pres. Scouts Australia (NSW) 2001–, Murray-Darling Basin Comm. 2003–08; Chair. NSW Native Vegetation Reform Implementation Group 2003–06; Co-Chair. NSW Health Care Advisory Council 2005–11; Dir Regional Australia Inst. 2011–; Patron Sir Roden Cutler Charities 2004–; Hon. DUniv (Univ. of New England); Hon. DLitt (Southern Cross Univ.). *Leisure interests:* surfing, walking, farming. *Address:* PO Box 27, Cundletown, NSW 2430 (home); 'Mulberry Farm', Dumaresq Island, NSW 2430 (home); PO Box 41, Bendigo Vic. 3552, Australia (office). *Telephone:* (2) 6553-8276 (home); (3) 5430-2303 (office). *Fax:* (2) 6553-8358 (home). *E-mail:* iansinclair@ozemail.com.au (home). *Website:* www.frrr.org.au (office).

SINDAYIGAYA, Gaspard; Burundian politician and banker; *Governor, Banque Commerciale du Burundi;* fmr mem. Nat. Assembly for Rutana constituency (Front pour la Démocratie au Burundi); various posts with Burundi banking insts including CEO Banque Nationale pour le Developpement Economique SARL; Gov. Banque de la République du Burundi (central bank) 2007–12; Dir and CEO Banque Commerciale du Burundi 2012–. *Address:* Banque Commerciale du Burundi SM, 84 chaussée Prince Louis Rwagasore, BP 990, Bujumbura, Burundi (office). *Telephone:* 22222317 (office). *Fax:* 22221018 (office). *E-mail:* info@bancobu.com (office). *Website:* www.bancobu.com (office).

SINDEN, Sir Donald Alfred, Kt, CBE, DLitt, DArts, FRSA; British actor and author; b. 9 Oct. 1923, Plymouth; s. of Alfred E. Sinden and Mabel A. Sinden (née Fuller); m. Diana Mahony 1948 (died 2004); two s.; entered theatrical profession with Charles F. Smith's Co., Mobile Entertainments Southern Area 1942; with Leicester Repertory Co. 1945; with Memorial Theatre Co., Stratford-upon-Avon 1946–47; with Old Vic and Bristol Old Vic 1948–50; film actor 1952–60; Chair. British Theatre Museum Asscn 1971–77, Theatre Museum Advisory Council 1973–80; Pres. Fed. of Playgoers Socs 1968–93, Royal Theatrical Fund 1983–; Vice-Pres. London Appreciation Soc. 1960–; Assoc. Artist, RSC 1967–; mem. Council, British Actors Equity Asscn 1966–77 (Trustee 1988–2004), Council, RSA 1972, Advisory Council, V&A Museum 1973–80, Arts Council Drama Panel 1973–77, Leicestershire Educ. Arts Cttee 1974–2004, BBC Archives Advisory Cttee 1975–78, Council, London Acad. of Music and Dramatic Art 1976–, Kent and E Sussex Regional Cttee, Nat. Trust 1978–82, Arts Council 1982–86; Drama Desk Award (for London Assurance) 1974, Variety Club of GB Stage Actor of 1976 (for King Lear), Evening Standard Drama Award Best Actor (for King Lear) 1977. *Stage appearances include:* The Heiress 1949–50, Red Letter Day 1951, Odd Man In 1957, Peter Pan 1960, Guilty Party 1961, as Richard Plantagenet in Henry VI (The Wars of the Roses), as Price in Eh!, etc. (RSC) 1963–64, British Council tour of S. America in Dear Liar and Happy Days 1965, There's a Girl in My Soup 1966, as Lord Foppington in The Relapse (RSC) 1967, Not Now Darling 1968, as Malvolio, Henry VIII 1969, as Sir Harcourt Courtly in London Assurance 1972 RSC, (toured USA 1974), In Praise of Love 1973, as Stockmann in An Enemy of the People 1975, Habeas Corpus (USA) 1975, as Benedick in Much Ado About Nothing, King Lear (RSC) 1976–77, Shut Your Eyes and Think of England 1977, Othello (RSC) 1979–80, Present Laughter 1981, Uncle Vanya 1982, The School for Scandal 1983 (European tour 1984), Ariadne auf Naxos (ENO) 1983, Two into One 1984, The Scarlet Pimpernel 1985, Major Barbara 1988, Over My Dead Body 1989, Oscar Wilde 1990, Out of Order 1990 (Australian tour 1992), Venus Observed 1991, She Stoops to Conquer 1993, Hamlet 1994, That Good Night 1996, Quartet 1999, The Hollow Crown (tour to Australia and NZ 2002–03, Canada 2004); Dir The Importance of Being Earnest 1987. *Films:* appeared in 23 films including The Cruel Sea, Doctor in the House 1952–60. *Radio includes:* Doctor Gideon Fell (series). *Television series include:* Our Man from St Marks, Two's Company, Discovering English Churches, Never the Twain, Judge John Deed. *Publications:* A Touch of the Memoirs 1982, Laughter in the Second Act 1985, The Everyman Book of Theatrical Anecdotes (ed.) 1987, The English Country Church 1988, Famous Last Words (ed.) 1994. *Leisure interests:* theatrical history, architecture, ecclesiology, genealogy, serendipity. *Address:* Rats Castle, Tenterden, TN30 7HX, England (home). *Telephone:* (1797) 270340 (home).

SINDI, Hayat, PhD; Saudi Arabian biotechnologist and academic; *Founder and Head, Institute for Imagination and Ingenuity;* b. Makkah; ed King's Coll., London and Univ. of Cambridge, UK, Massachusetts Inst. of Tech. and Harvard Univ., USA; left Saudi Arabia in her teens to become first Saudi and Muslim woman from Gulf region to earn PhD in biotechnology; currently Visiting Scholar, Harvard Univ.; Co-founder and Dir of Diagnostics For All; fmr PopTech Fellow in both Science and Social Innovation; launched Inst. for Imagination and Ingenuity (helps local scientists create business plans and find investors for their ideas) 2011; announced by National Geographic as National Geographic Emerging Explorer, ranked by Arabian Business amongst the Power 500: The Worlds's Most Influential Arabs (19th) 2012. *Address:* Diagnostics For All, 840 Memorial Drive, Cambridge, MA 02139, USA (office). *Telephone:* (617) 494-0700 (office). *E-mail:* info@dfa.org (office). *Website:* www.dfa.org (office). www.i2institute.org (office).

SINEGAL, James (Jim) D.; American retail executive; b. 1 Jan. 1936; m. Janet Sinegal; two s. one d.; ed Helix High School, La Mesa, Calif., San Diego City Coll., San Diego State Univ.; joined FedMart 1954, held several exec. positions including Exec. Vice-Pres. Merchandising and Operations; fmr Exec. Vice-Pres. The Price Club; Pres. Sinegal, Chamberlain & Assocs –1983; Co-founder (with Jeff Brotman), Pres. and COO Costco 1983–93, CEO 1988–93, merged with The Price Club 1993, mem. Bd Dirs 1993–, Pres. and CEO Costco Wholesale Corpn 1993–2011 (retd); mem. Educ. Cttee, Washhington Business Roundtable; Trustee, Seattle Univ.; LCB Visionary Award – Trendsetter of the Year, Lundquist School of Business, Univ. of Oregon 2000, Business Achievement Award, Seattle Univ. 2002. *Address:* Costco Wholesale Corporation, 999 Lake Drive, Issaquah, WA 98027, USA (office). *Telephone:* (425) 313-8100 (office). *Fax:* (425) 313-8103 (office). *E-mail:* info@costco.com (office). *Website:* www.costco.com (office).

SINGAY, Lyonpo Jigme, MBBS, MPH; Bhutanese politician; b. 5 May 1954, Themnangbi, Mongar Dist; ed Delhi Univ., India, San Diego State Univ., USA; Deputy Dir Public Health Div., Dept of Health Services 1987–89, Jt Dir, Dept of Health Services 1989–1993, Dir Div. of Health Services 1994–98; Sec. Royal Civil Service Comm. 1998–2003; Minister of Health 2003–07 (resgnd); mem. People's Democratic Party; Red Scarf (Dasho) 1997, Orange Scarf (Lyonpo) 2003. *Address:* c/o People's Democratic Party, Drizang Lam, Lower Motithang, Thimphu; Tshogdu Chenmo, Secretariat, Gyelyong Tshokhang, POB 139, Thimphu (office); Themnangbi, Mongar Dzongkhag, Bhutan. *Telephone:* (2) 322729 (office); (2) 322136 (home). *Fax:* (2) 324210 (office). *Website:* www.nab.gov.bt (office).

SINGER, Isadore Manuel, PhD; American mathematician and academic; *Institute Professor, Department of Mathematics, Massachusetts Institute of Technology;* b. 3 May 1924, Detroit, Mich.; s. of Simon Singer and Freda Rose; m. Sheila Ruff 1961; five c.; ed Univs of Michigan and Chicago; C.L.E. Moore Instructor at MIT 1950–52; Asst Prof., UCLA 1952–54; Visiting Asst Prof., Columbia Univ. 1954–55; Visiting mem. Inst. for Advanced Study, Princeton 1955–56; Asst Prof., MIT 1956, Assoc. Prof. 1958, Prof. of Math. 1959, Norbert Wiener Prof. of Math. 1970–79, John D. MacArthur Prof. of Math. 1983–, Inst. Prof. 1987–; Visiting Prof. of Math., Univ. of Calif., Berkeley 1977–79, Prof. 1979–83, Miller Prof. 1982–83; mem. NAS, American Math. Soc., Math. Asscn of America, American Acad. of Arts and Sciences, American Philosophical Soc., American Physical Soc.; Sloan Fellow 1959–62, Guggenheim Fellow 1968–69, 1975–76; Bôcher Memorial Prize 1969, 1975–76, Nat. Medal of Science 1985, Wigner Prize, Int. Congress of Mathematicians 1989, Abel Prize (jtly with Sir Michael Atiyah) 2004. *Publications:* Lecture Notes on Elementary Topology and Geometry; author of research articles in functional analysis, differential geometry and topology. *Leisure interests:* literature, hiking, tennis. *Address:* Department of Mathematics, Massachusetts Institute of Technology, Room 2-387, 77 Massachusetts Avenue, Cambridge, MA 02139, USA (office). *Telephone:* (617) 253-5601 (office). *Fax:* (617) 253-8000 (office). *E-mail:* ims@math.mit.edu (office). *Website:* www-math.mit.edu (office).

SINGER, Maxine, PhD; American biochemist; *President Emerita, Carnegie Institution of Washington;* b. 15 Feb. 1931, New York; d. of Hyman Frank and Henrietta Perlowitz Frank; m. Daniel M. Singer 1952; one s. three d.; ed Swarthmore Coll. and Yale Univ.; Research Chemist, Enzymes and Cellular Biochemistry Section, Nat. Inst. of Arthritis and Metabolic Diseases, NIH, Bethesda, Md 1958–74, Chief, Nucleic Acid Enzymology Section, Lab. of Biochemistry, Div. of Cancer Biology and Diagnosis, Nat. Cancer Inst. 1974–79, Chief, Lab. of Biochem. 1979–87, research chemist 1987–88, Scientist Emer. 1988–; Pres. Carnegie Inst., Wash. 1988–2002, now Pres. Emer., Sr Scientific Advisor and mem. Bd of Trustees; Visiting Scientist, Dept of Genetics, Weizmann Inst. of Science, Rehovot, Israel 1971–72; Dir Foundation for Advanced Educ. in Sciences 1972–78, 1985–86; mem. Yale Corpn 1975–90; Chair. Smithsonian Council 1992–94 (mem. 1990–94); Chair. Comm. on the Future of the Smithsonian 1994–96; mem. Editorial Bd Journal of Biological Chem. 1968–74, Science 1972–82; Chair. Editorial Bd Proceedings of NAS 1985–88; Scientific Council Int. Inst. of Genetics and Biophysics, Naples 1982–86, Bd of Govs of Weizmann Inst., Human Genome Org. 1989–, Cttee on Science, Eng and Public Policy, NAS 1989–91, Int. Advisory Bd, Chulabhorn Research Inst. 1990–; mem. Bd Dirs Johnson & Johnson; mem. NAS, American Soc. of Biological Chemists, American Soc. of Microbiologists, ACS, American Acad. of Arts and Sciences, Inst. of Medicine of NAS, American Philosophical Soc., New York Acad. of Sciences; Trustee Wesleyan Univ., Middletown, Conn. 1972–75, Whitehead Inst. 1985–94; Hon. DSc (Wesleyan Univ.) 1977, (Swarthmore Coll.) 1978, (Univ. of Md) 1985, (Brandeis Univ.) 1988, (Radcliffe Coll.) 1990, (Williams Coll.) 1990, (Franklin and Marshall Coll.) 1991, (George Washington Univ.) 1992, (New York Univ.) 1992, (Lehigh Univ.) 1992, (Dartmouth) 1993, (Yale) 1994, (Harvard) 1994; Dir's Award, NIH 1977, Nat. Medal of Science 1992, NAS Public Welfare Medal 2007. *Publications:* molecular biology textbooks (with Paul Berg), Why Aren't Black Holes Black? (with Robert Hazen), George Beadle: An Uncommon Farmer (with Paul Berg) 2005, and numerous articles in major scientific journals. *Leisure interests:* scuba diving, cooking, literature. *Address:* 5410 39th Street, NW, Washington, DC 20015, USA (home). *Telephone:* (202) 939-1119.

SINGER, Miroslav, PhD; Czech economist and central banker; *Governor, Czech National Bank;* b. 14 May 1968, Prague; m.; two c.; ed Univ. of Econs, Prague, Univ. of Pittsburgh, USA; Researcher and Lecturer, later Deputy Dir for Research, Econs Inst. of Czech Acad. of Sciences and Centre for Econ. Research and Graduate Educ., Charles Univ. 1993–95; Chief Economist, Expandia Finance 1995, Man. Dir Expandia Investment Co. 1998–99, Man. Dir Expandia Holding 2000–01; Dir of Business Services Group, PricewaterhouseCoopers Czech Repub. 2001; mem. Bd Czech Nat. Bank (central bank) 2005–, Vice-Gov. 2005–10, Gov. 2010–; Lecturer, Centre for Econ. Research and Graduate Educ., Charles Univ., Univ. of Econs, Prague; mem. Supervisory Bd/Bd of Dirs Česká pojišťovna, Expandia Finance, Expandia Banka, Expandia Holding, Chemofond, Jitona, Vigona, Vlnap; mem. Editorial Bd Finance a úvěr (Journal of Economics and Finance), Business Central Europe; Central Banker of the Year Award for Central and Eastern Europe 2013, Central Banker of the Year Award for Europe 2014. *Address:* Office of the Governor, Czech National Bank, Na Příkopě 28, 115 03 Prague 1, Czech Republic (office). *Telephone:* 224411111 (office). *Fax:* 224412404 (office). *E-mail:* monestat@cnb.cz (office). *Website:* www.cnb.cz (office).

SINGER, Peter Albert David, AC, BPhil, MA; Australian philosopher, writer and academic; *DeCamp Professor of Bioethics, Princeton University;* b. 6 July 1946, Melbourne, Vic.; s. of Ernest Singer and Cora Oppenheim; m. Renata Diamond 1968; three d.; ed Scotch Coll., Univ. of Melbourne and Univ. Coll., Oxford, UK; Radcliffe Lecturer, Univ. Coll., Oxford 1971–73; Visiting Asst Prof., Dept of Philosophy, New York Univ. 1973–74; Sr Lecturer, Dept of Philosophy, La Trobe Univ., Bundoora, Vic., Australia 1974–76; Prof., Dept of Philosophy, Monash Univ., Clayton, Vic. 1977–99, Dir Centre for Human Bioethics 1981–91, Deputy Dir 1992–99; DeCamp Prof. of Bioethics, Princeton Univ., NJ, USA 1999–; Laureate Prof., Centre for Applied Philosophy and Public Ethics, Univ. of Melbourne 2005–; Prof., New Coll. of the Humanities, London 2011–; various visiting positions in USA, Canada, Italy and NZ. *Publications:* Democracy and Disobedience 1973, Animal Rights and Human Obligations (ed. with Thomas Regan) 1975, Animal Liberation: A New Ethics for Our Treatment of Animals 1975, Practical Ethics 1979, Marx 1980, The Expanding Circle: Ethics and Sociobiology 1981, Test-Tube Babies (co-ed.) 1982, Hegel 1983, The Reproduction Revolution: New Ways of Making Babies (with Deane Wells, aka Making Babies: The New Science and Ethics of Conception) 1984, In Defence of Animals (ed.) 1985, Should the Baby Live?: The Problem of Handicapped Infants (with Helga Kuhse) 1985, Applied Ethics (ed.) 1986, Animal Liberation: A Graphic Guide (with Lori Gruen) 1987, Animal Factories (with Jim Mason) 1990, Embryo Experimentation

(ed.) 1990, Companion to Ethics (ed.) 1991, How Are We to Live? 1993, The Great Ape Project: Equality Beyond Humanity (ed. with Paola Cavalieri) 1993, Rethinking Life and Death 1994, Ethics (ed.) 1994, The Greens 1996, Ethics into Action 1998, A Companion to Bioethics (with Helga Kuhse) 1998, A Darwinian Left 1999, Writings on an Ethical Life 2000, One World 2002, Pushing Time Away: My Grandfather and the Tragedy of Jewish Vienna 2003, The President of Good and Evil: Taking George W. Bush Seriously 2004, The Moral of the Story (co-ed.) 2005, Eating: What We Eat and Why it Matters (with Jim Mason) 2006, The Life You Can Save 2009, The Point of View of the Universe: Sidgwick and Contemporary Ethics (co-author) 2014. *Leisure interests:* bushwalking, reading, surfing. *Address:* University Center for Human Values, 5 Ivy Lane, Princeton, NJ, 08544-1013, USA (office). *Telephone:* (609) 258-2202 (office). *Fax:* (609) 258-1285 (office). *Website:* www.princeton.edu/~psinger (office); www.thelifeyoucansave.org.

SINGH SINGHA, Maj.-Gen. Iqbal; Indian army officer and UN official; *Head of Mission and Force Commander, United Nations Disengagement Observer Force (UNDOF);* b. 1956; m.; two s.; ed Nat. Defence Acad., Army War Coll., Madras Univ.; Chief Logistics Officer, UN Mission in Eritrea and Ethiopia (UNMEE) 2003–05; Col-Gen. Staff Sub-Conventional Operations, Army Training Command 2005–06, Pres. Army Standing Establishment Cttee 2007–09, Brig.-Gen. Staff Operations 2009–10, Gen. Officer, Commanding Infantry Div. 2010–12; Head of Mission and Force Commdr UN Disengagement Observer Force (UNDOF) 2012–. *Address:* United Nations Disengagement Observer Force (UNDOF), Department of Peacekeeping Operations, United Nations, New York, NY 10017, USA (office). *Telephone:* (212) 963-1234 (office). *Fax:* (212) 963-4879 (office). *Website:* www.un.org/en/peacekeeping/missions/undof/index.shtml (office).

SINGH, Lt-Gen. (retd) Ajai, MSc; Indian army officer (retd) and government official; b. 20 Nov. 1935, Rajasthan; s. of the late Raj Dalpat Singh; ed Mayo Coll., Ajmer, Madras Univ.; joined Indian Army, Tank Commdrs Course, Czechoslovakia 1966, Defence Services Staff Course, Wellington 1972, Higher Command Course, Coll. of Combat, Mhow 1979–80, Royal Coll. of Defence Studies, London, UK 1983, Discussions at RAND Co-operation, USA 1983, 1989, saw action in Indo-Pak wars 1965, 1971; Commdr Ind. Armed Brigade, Ambala 1980–82, BGS I-Corps, Mathura 1982–84, Dir-Gen. WE, Army HQ, New Delhi 1985–87, GOC 31 Armoured Div., Jhansi 1987–89, Dir-Gen. Mechanised Forces, Army HQ, New Delhi 1989–90, GOC 4 Corps, Tezpur, Assam 1990–92, Dir-Gen. Combat Vehicles, Army HQ, New Delhi 1992–93, CCR&D, Defence Research & Devt Org., Ministry of Defence 1993–95; Gov. of Assam 2003–08; Chair. North Eastern Council; Indian Mil. Acad. Sword of Honour and Silver Medal, (Best All Round Gentleman Cadet of June 1956 Batch), Mentioned in Despatches for Gallantry, Indo-Pak War 1965, Ati Vishist Seva Medal for Gallantry 1986, Param Vishist Seva Medal for Gallantry (Highest Distinguished Service Award of India) 1992. *Leisure interests:* tennis, squash, hockey, football, cricket, polo, golf, oil and crayon painting, landscaping, music, wildlife and Environment, time and personnel management techniques and resource optimization. *Address:* c/o Raj Bhawan, Kharguli, Guwahati 781 004, India (office). *Telephone:* (361) 2540250 (home).

SINGH, Capt. Amarinder; Indian politician and fmr army officer; b. 11 March 1942, Patiala, Punjab; s. of HH Late Maharaja Yadavindra Singh of Patiala and HH Rajmata Mohinder Kaur; m. Maharani Preneet Kaur; one s. one d.; ed Doon School, Dehradun, Nat. Defence Acad., Kharakvasla, Indian Mil. Acad., Dehradun; officer in Indian army 1963–66; mem. Lok Sabha (Parl.) 1980–84; mem. Legis. Ass. 1985; f. and Pres. Shiromani Akali Dal (Panthik) 1991–98; Pres. Punjab Pradesh Congress Cttee 1999–2002; Chief Minister of Punjab 2002–07; mem. Legis. Ass. (Parl.) 2002–; mem. Marylebone Cricket Club, UK, Naval and Mil. Club, London, Golf Club, Delhi, Gymkhana Club, Patiala, Officers Inst., Patiala. *Publications include:* A Ridge Too Far: War In The Kargil Heights 1999, Lest We Forget 1999, The Last Sunset: Rise and Fall of the Lahore Durbar 2010. *Leisure interests:* gardening, shooting, sports. *Address:* New Moti Bagh Palace, Patiala, 147 001, India.

SINGH, Ashni Kumar, PhD; Guyanese government official; *Minister of Finance;* ed Queens Coll., Lancaster Univ., UK; fmr Deputy Auditor Gen., Office of the Auditor General; fmr Commr Gen. Guyana Revenue Authority; Dir Budget, Ministry of Finance –2006; Minister of Finance 2006–; fmr mem. Governing Council Univ. of Guyana. *Address:* Ministry of Finance, Main Street, Kingston, Georgetown, Guyana (office). *Telephone:* 225-6088 (office). *Fax:* (office). *E-mail:* asingh@inetguyana.net (office). *Website:* www.finance.gov.gy (office).

SINGH, Bhishma Narain, BA; Indian politician; b. 13 July 1933, Palamau, Jharkhand; m. Ram Kumari Devi 1950; two s. two d.; ed Takiya High School, Sasaram, Bihar and Banaras Hindu Univ.; active Congress worker 1953–; mem. All Indian Congress Cttee; mem. Bihar Legis. Ass. 1967–69, 1969–72, 1972–76; Minister, State Gov. of Bihar 1971, 1972–73, 1973–74; mem. Rajya Sabha (Parl.) 1976, 1982, Deputy Chief Whip, Congress Parl. Party 1977, later Chief Whip; Minister of Parl. Affairs 1980–83, of Communications Jan.–March 1980, of Works and Housing, Labour, Supply and Food and Civil Supplies 1980–83; Gov. of Assam and Meghalaya 1984–89, of Sikkim 1985–86, of Arunachal Pradesh 1987, of Tamil Nadu 1991–93; Deputy Chair. Cen. Cooperative Bank, Daltonganj 1964; Pres. All India Conf. of Intellectuals; Dir Bihar State Co-operative Mktg. Union 1967; Chair. Bihar State Co-operative Housing Construction Finance Soc. 1974–75, Bihar State Credit and Investment Corpn 1974, Unity Int. Foundation; fmr Chair. North Eastern Council; mem. Inter Parl. Union, Commonwealth Parl. Asscn, India Int. Friendship Soc.; Chancellor of two dozen univs in India during tenure as Gov. of several states; Order of Friendship (Russia) 2009; Dr hc (Gandhigram Rural Inst. Deemed Univ.) 1992; Medal of Merit and Certificate of Honour, Govt of Algeria 2005. *Leisure interests:* horse riding, marksmanship, music, dance and drama, especially tribal folk dances, travel (widely travelled throughout Asia, Europe, some African countries and USA). *Address:* C-83, Upkar Apartment, Mayur Vihar Phase-I, Delhi 110 091 (home); Hamid Ganj, PO Daltonganj, Palamau Dist, Jharkhand, India (home). *Telephone:* (11) 22712322 (home). *Fax:* (11) 22714422 (home). *E-mail:* abhivns1976@yahoo.co.in (office).

SINGH, Lt-Gen. (retd) Bhopinder; Indian government official and fmr army officer; b. 20 March 1946, Allahabad, UP; s. of the late Brig. Rajmohan Singh; m. Bhawanee Singh; ed Nat. Defence Acad.; commissioned into Rajput Regt 1965, held several command, staff and instructional appointments, commanded troops in Indo-Pak wars 1965, 1971, led counter-insurgency operations in Jammu and Kashmir, Mizoram and Assam, has been an Instructor at Indian Mil. Acad., held Gen. Staff tenures at Kargil and Kashmir Valley, commanded 17 Rajput Bn, commanded Rajput Regimental Centre, Fategarh, UP; fmr Mil., Naval and Air Attaché in Addis Ababa; as Maj.-Gen. was Additional Dir-Gen. of Org. (AG's Br.), Army HQ; Mil. Sec. to Pres. of India and Col of Pres.'s Bodyguard 1997–; Col, Rajput Regt 2002; Lt-Gov. of Andaman and Nicobar Islands 2006–13, of Puducherry 2008; Param Vishisht Seva Medal (PVSM), Ati Vishisht Seva Medal (AVSM); Army Commdr's Commendation, Ethiopian Govt Commendation Certificate. *Leisure interests:* sports, outdoor adventure activities. *Address:* House No 593, Sector 16-D, Chandigarh 160 015, India (home). *E-mail:* lgandaman@hotmail .com; lgandaman@yahoo.com.

SINGH, Gen. Bikram, M.Phil; Indian army officer; *Chief of Army Staff;* m. Surjeet Kaur; two c.; ed Nat. Defence Acad., Indian Mil. Acad., Defence Services Staff Coll., Indore Univ., Army War Coll., USA; commissioned into Sikh Light Infantry regiment 1972, served as GOC Eastern Command, 15 Corps, Rashtriya Rifles, UN Peacekeeping Mission in Congo, UN Observer in Nicaragua and El Salvador, Deputy Dir-Gen. Perspective Planning (Strategy), Additional Dir-Gen. Army's Think Tank, Dir-Gen. Staff Duties, Directorate Gen. of Mil. Operations, Chief of Army Staff 2012–; Hon. ADC to Pres.; Jammu and Kashmir Rifles Gold Medal, Param Vishisht Seva Medal, Uttam Yudh Seva Medal, Ati Vishsht Seva Medal, Sena Medal, Vishisht Seva Medal; Shrinagesh Trophy, Commando Dagger, Gold Medal for 'Tactics and Leadership'. *Leisure interests:* cricket, athletics, hockey. *Address:* Indian Army, Room No B-30, ADG PI, South Block, Integrated Headquarters of Ministry of Defence, New Delhi 110 011, India (office). *Website:* www.indianarmy.nic.in (office).

SINGH, Buta, BA, MA, PhD; Indian politician; *Chairman, National Commission for Scheduled Castes;* b. 21 March 1934, Jalandhar Punjab; s. of the late Sardar Bir Singh and Sardarni Beant Singh; m. Manjit Kaur 1964; two s. one d.; ed Lyallpur Khalsa Coll., Jalandhar, Guru Nanak Khalsa Coll., Bombay and Bundelkhand Univ., Jhansi; elected to Lok Sabha 1962, 1967, 1971, 1980, 1984, 1999; Union Deputy Minister for Railways 1974–76, for Commerce 1976–77; Minister of State in Ministry of Shipping and Transport 1980–81; Minister of Supply and Rehabilitation 1981–82, of Sport 1982–83, Cabinet Minister in charge of several ministries 1983–84, Minister of Agric. 1984–86, of Home Affairs 1986–89, of Civil Supplies, Consumer Affairs and Public Distribution 1995–96, of Communications 1998; Gov. of Bihar 2004–06; mem. Nat. Small Savings Cttee 1973–74, Senate, Punjab Univ. 1974–80, Planning Comm. 1985; Gen. Sec. Indian Nat. Congress 1978–80; Pres. All India Confed. of Farmers Asscns 1969–70, Amateur Athletic Fed. of India 1976–84, Bharat Ekta Andolan 1991; fmr Pres. Dr B. R. Ambedkar All India Inst. of Social Sciences; currently Chair. Nat. Comm. for Scheduled Castes; Vice-Pres. Asian Amateur Athletics Asscn 1979. *Publications include:* Punjabi Speaking State: A Critical Analysis. *Leisure interests:* reading, writing, swimming, shooting, hiking. *Address:* Jallowal, Jalandhar, 144 001, India (home). *Telephone:* (11) 24625378 (office). *Fax:* (11) 24634743 (office).

SINGH, Chaudhary Randhir, MA, LLB; Indian politician; b. 1 July 1924, Bayanpur, Haryana; s. of the late Chaudhary Chandgi Ram and Chhoti Devi; m. Vijay Lakshmi Chaudhary 1939; four s. three d.; ed St Stephen's Coll., Delhi, Univ. of Delhi; fmr mem. Parl. (Lok Sabha), All India Congress Cttee, several parl. cttees, Exec. Congress Party in Parl.; mem. (Cabinet Rank) Nat. Comm. on Agric. 1970–76; mem. Agric. Prices Comm., Govt of India 1976–79, 1980–83, 1987–89; Gov. Sikkim 1996–2001; Chair. or mem. numerous Govt working groups on land reform and agricultural devt issues; fmrly Chair. Punjab Praja Socialist Party, mem. Nat. Exec. of Praja Socialist Party of India, Sec.-Gen. United Front of Opposition Parties Punjab, Chair. AICC Land Reforms Panel, Sr Vice-Chair. and Sec.-Gen. Farmers' Parl. Forum of India; Chair. AICC Kisan Congress 1969–86; Chair. AICC Socio-Economic Advisory Cttee to Congress Pres. and Prime Minister 1986–91; Founding mem. and Perm. Invitee, Congress Working Cttee; leader and mem., various Govt and Party delegations to different countries; associated with different educational insts; active in social work in Haryana; recipient of numerous awards for work on behalf of peasant families and minority groups; Int Man of the Year 2003, Son of India Award, Eminent Personality of India Award, Man of the Year Award, several other nat. and int. awards and honours. *Publications:* 18 books on agricultural devt and problems of rural peoples: Agriculture Development in India after Independence, Agriculture Development in Hilly Areas of India, Rural Electrification in India, Consolidation of Agricultural Holdings in India, Farmers' Organisation in India, Land Reclamation and Development in India, Glimpses of Agriculture in India, Glimpses of World Agriculture, Farmers Champion Indira Gandhi, Our Backward Areas, Farming Imperatives, Our Rural Poor, Sikkim and Himalayas, Man and God, Perception Galore, Sikkim (Socio-Cultural Peep), Baychara Kisan (Hapless Peasant), Our Tribals, Our Governors, Our Holy Gurus, Bhagwad Geeta, Threshing Floor to Raj Bhawan, Kargil Operations, Nectar of Life, Values Galore, Code of Living, The Spark Within, Our Uniqueness, Lead Kindly Light. *Leisure interests:* listening to and reading Urdu poetry, especially by Md Iqbal and Ghalib, folk songs and dances. *Address:* G-11 Tara Apartments, Alaknanda, New Delhi 110 019, India. *Telephone:* (11) 26020048 (also fax) (home).

SINGH, Dharam, LLB, MA; Indian politician; b. 25 Dec. 1936, Nelogi, Jewargi; ed Osmania Univ.; fmr advocate; Councillor, Gulbarga City Municipal Council 1968; mem. Karnataka Legis. Ass. 1972–; fmr Karnataka State Minister of Urban Devt, of Home Affairs, of Social Welfare, of Revenue, of Public Works; Chief Minister of Karnataka 2004–06 (resgnd). *Address:* c/o Office of the Chief Minister, Room 323, 3rd Floor, Vidhana Soudha, Bangalore 560 001, India (office).

SINGH, Digvijay, BEng; Indian politician; b. 28 Feb. 1947, Indore; s. of Balbhadra Singh; elected to Ass. 1977, 1980; Gen. Sec. Madhya Pradesh Youth Congress 1978–79; fmr Minister of State for Agric., Arjun Singh Ministry, later Cabinet Minister for Irrigation; elected to Lok Sabha 1991; Pres. Madhya Pradesh Congress Cttee 1980, Council 1984, 1992; Chief Minister of Madhya Pradesh 1993–98, 1998–2003. *Address:* c/o Chief Minister's Secretariat, Ballabh Bhavan, Bhopal (office); 1 Shamla Hill, Bhopal, India (home). *Telephone:* (755) 2540500 (home).

SINGH, Harpal, BA, BS, MPA; Indian business executive; ed The Doon School, St Stephen's Coll., New Delhi, CSCH, Calif., USA; has held sr positions in Tata Admin. Service, Hindustan Motors, Telco, and Bd-level responsibility at Shaw Wallace; Sr Advisor (Corp. Projects), Mahindra and Mahindra; fmr Chair. Fortis Healthcare Ltd, Fortis Financial Services Ltd, Fortis Securities Ltd; Chair. (non-exec.) Ranbaxy Labs Ltd 2007–08; mem. Bd of Dirs Religare Technologies. *Address:* c/o Board of Directors, Religare Technologies, A-3/4/5, Plot Number 11, GYS Global, Sector 125, Gurgaon 201 301, India.

SINGH, Harsha Vardhana, MA, MPhil, PhD; Indian economist and international organization executive; *Deputy Director-General, World Trade Organization;* b. 30 Aug. 1956, Delhi; m. Veena Jha; two c.; ed Delhi Univ., Univ. of Oxford, UK (Rhodes Scholar); worked as consultant with Bureau of Industrial Costs and Prices, New Delhi and with ILO and UNCTAD, Geneva; worked in GATT/WTO Secr. in various capacities, including Econ. Research and Analysis Unit 1985–89, Trade Policy Review Div. 1989–91, Rules Div. 1991–95, Trade and Environment and Tech. Barriers to Trade Div. 1995–96, Office of WTO Dir-Gen. 1996–97, served as Chair. of dispute settlement panels, Deputy Dir-Gen. WTO 2005–; Econ. Advisor, Telecom Regulatory Authority of India (TRAI) 1997–2001, Sec. cum Prin. Advisor and Head of TRAI Secr. 2001–05; fmr mem. various trade advisory cttees of Indian Govt; mem. Visiting Faculty, TERI School of Advanced Studies for their Masters programme in Regulatory Studies; Hon. Prof., Indian Council for Research on Int. Econ. Relations. *Publications:* several papers on trade policy and regulatory issues. *Address:* World Trade Organization, Centre William Rappard, rue de Lausanne 154, 1211 Geneva 21, Switzerland (office). *Telephone:* (22) 739-51-11 (office). *Fax:* (22) 731-42-06 (office). *E-mail:* enquiries@wto.org (office). *Website:* www.wto.org (office).

SINGH, Iqbal, BA; Indian business executive and politician; s. of the late Shri Lal Singh and of Santokh Kaur; m. Gurinder Bir Kaur; two s.; ed Punjab Univ.; represented Indian Nat. Youth Congress at Int. Youth Festival, Cuba 1978; fmr Gen. Sec. Punjab Youth Congress; has held several positions in Indian Nat. Congress, including Sec. All India Congress Cttee for 12 years, Perm. mem. Congress Working Cttee; mem. Parl. (Rajya Sabha) 1992–98, mem. Tourism, Steel, Scout and Raj Bhasha Cttees, Chair. Cttee constituted by Ministry of Shipping, Chair.-cum-Sec. Transport Cttee; Lt Gov. of Puducherry 2009–13; delivered address at World Hindi Conf., UN, New York; has delivered lectures in India and world-wide to promote Hindi as 'Raj Basha' (official language); attended and delivered lectures at Int. Punjabi Soc. confs in UK, USA and Canada; adviser for several trusts and educational insts; Trustee, Bhai Vir Singh Sadhan, K.L. Sehgal Memorial, B.D. Arya Educational Inst.; fmr Chief Patron Harballabh Sangeeth Maha Sabha; Founder All India Surjit Hockey Tournament; Chair. Punjab Sports Welfare Soc.; Hon. DLitt (Andhra Univ.) 2009. *Publications include:* Bhartiye Sanskriti Aur Kurukshetra (in Hindi; several awards), a book and several articles on the 10th Guru, Shri Guru Gobind Singh; several articles in leading dailies and magazines on social reforms and empowerment. *Leisure interests:* reading, writing, listening to music (especially that by Shri Sehgal, collector of his compositions), sports. *Address:* c/o Office of the Lieutenant Governor, Puducherry, India.

SINGH, Jaswant, BA, BSc; Indian politician, fmr army officer and writer; b. 3 Jan. 1938, Jasol, Rajasthan; s. of the late Thakur Sardar Singhji and Kunwar Baisa; m. Sheetal Kumari 1963; two s.; ed Mayo Coll., Ajmer, Jt Services Wing, Clement Town, Dehradun, Indian Mil. Acad., Dehradun; commissioned Gen. in India Horse 1957; resgnd his comm. and elected to Rajya Sabha 1980; Minister of Finance and Company Affairs 1996, 2002–04; Deputy Chair., Planning Comm. 1998–99; Minister of External Affairs 1999, 2001–02, of Electronics Feb.–Oct. 1999, of Surface Transport Aug.–Oct. 1999, of Defence 2000–01; Chair. Consultative Cttee for the Ministry of External Affairs 2000–01; Leader of the House, Rajya Sabha 1999–2004, Leader of the Opposition 2004; mem. Lok Sabha from Darjeeling 2009–; Outstanding Parliamentarian Award 2001. *Publications:* 23 books, including National Security: An Outline of Our Concerns 1996, Shauryo Tejo 1997, Defending India 1999, District Diary 2001, Khankhananama (Hindi) 2001, A Call to Honour: In Service of Emergent India 2006, Travels in Transoxiana 2006, Till Memory Serves 2007, Conflict & Diplomacy 2008, Our Republic – Post 6 December 1992 2008, Jinnah: India, Partition, Independence 2009, Audacity of Opinion 2012, India at Risk: Mistakes, Misconceptions and Misadventures 2013; contrib. of numerous articles on int. affairs, security and devt issues to Indian and foreign magazines, newspapers and journals. *Leisure interests:* horses, equestrian sports, reading, music, golf, chess. *Address:* Lok Sabha, Parliament House, New Delhi 110 001, India (office). *E-mail:* jaswant@sansad.nic.in (office). *Website:* www .jaswantsingh.com (office).

SINGH, Gen. (retd) Joginder Jaswant, MSc, PVSM, AVSM, VSM, ADC; Indian army officer and government official; b. 17 Sept. 1945, Bahawalpur (now in Pakistan); s. of Jaswant Singh Marwah; m. Anupama Singh; one s. one d.; ed Nat. Defence Acad., Khadakwasla, Pune Defence Services Staff Coll., Wellington; joined Ninth Maratha Light Infantry (LI) 1964, served in Jammu and Kashmir, Nagaland, Arunachal Pradesh, Uttaranchal Pradesh, Col, Fifth Maratha LI, Defence Attaché to Algeria 1987–90, Commdr 79th (Ind.) Mountain Brigade, Baramula Sector, Jammu and Kashmir 1991–92, Deputy Dir-Gen. Operational Logistics, Army HQ 1993, Commdr Ninth Infantry Div. 1996–98, Additional Dir-Gen. Mil. Operations, Mil. Operations Directorate, Army HQ 1998, Commdr One 'Strike' Corps, Mathura, GOC-in-C, Army Training Command 2003, Western Command 2004, Chief of Army Staff 2005–07; fmr Chair. Jt Chiefs of Staff Cttee; Gov. of Arunachal Pradesh 2008–13; Hon. Col, Maratha Light Infantry; Hon. DLit (Shri Jagdishprasad Jhabarmal Tibrewala Univ.); Vishisht Seva Medal, War Wound Medal, Chief of Army Staff's Commendation, Param Vishisht Seva Medal 2004, Sikh of the Year Award, Sikh Forum UK 2007, Lifetime Achievement Award, Mother Teresa's Int. and Millennium Awards Cttee 2008, Punjabi Ratan Award, World Punjabi Org. 2009, GPS Achievers Lifetime Achievement Award, Global Punjabi Soc. 2010. *Publication:* A Soldier's General (autobiog.) 2012. *Leisure interests:* basketball, squash, golf, mountaineering. *E-mail:* genjjsingh@gmail.com (office).

SINGH, Karan, MA, PhD; Indian politician; b. 9 March 1931, Cannes, France; s. of Lt-Gen. HH Maharaja Sir Hari Singh, GCSI, GCIE, GCVO and Maharani Tara Devi; m. Princess Yasho Rajya Lakshmi of Nepal 1950; two s. one d.; ed Doon

School, Univ. of Jammu and Kashmir and Delhi Univ.; appointed Regent of Jammu and Kashmir 1949; elected Sadar-i-Riyasat (Head of State) by Jammu and Kashmir Legis. Ass. Nov. 1952, recognized by Pres. of India and assumed office 17 Nov. 1952, re-elected 1957 and 1962, Gov. 1965–67; Union Minister for Tourism and Civil Aviation 1967–73, for Health and Family Planning 1973–75, 1976–77, for Educ. 1979–80; re-elected mem. of Parl. 1977, 1980; Amb. to USA 1989–91; mem. Rajya Sabha Upper House of Parl. 2005–, Deputy Leader Congress Parl. Party, Chair. Ethics Cttee; Pres. Indian Council for Cultural Relations, Delhi Music Soc.; led Indian Del. to World Population Conf., Bucharest; Vice-Pres. World Health Ass. 1975–76; fmr Chancellor Jammu and Kashmir Univ., Banaras Hindu Univ.; currently Chancellor Jawaharlal Nehru Univ.; Chair. Auroville Foundation; Vice-Chair. Jawaharlal Nehru Memorial Fund; fmr Chair. Indian Bd for Wild Life, Life Trustee of the India Int. Centre; Hon. Maj.-Gen. Indian Army; Hon. Col Jammu and Kashmir Regt 1962; Dr hc (Aligarh Muslim Univ.) 1963, (Banaras Hindu Univ., Soka Univ., Tokyo); Padma Vibhushan 2005. *Publications include:* Varied Rhythms (essays and poems) 1960, Shadow and Sunlight (folk songs) 1962, Prophet of Indian Nationalism: The Political Thought of Sri Aurobindo Ghosh 1893–1910 1963, Welcome the Moonrise (poems) 1965, Population, Poverty and the Future of India 1975, In Defence of Religion 1978, Religions of India 1983, One Man's World 1986, Bridge to Immortality 1987, Humanity at the Crossroads 1988, Autobiography 1989, Essays on Hinduism 1990, Brief Sojourn 1991, Hymn to Shiva and Other Poems 1991, The Mountain of Shiva (novel) 1994, India and the World 1995, Hinduism: the Eternal Religion 1999, The Earth has No Corners 2001; and several books on political science, philosophical essays, travelogues, trans. of Dogra-Pahari folksongs and poems in English. *Leisure interests:* reading, writing, music. *Address:* 3 Nyaya Marg, Chanakyapuri, New Delhi 110 021, India. *Telephone:* (11) 6115291; (11) 6111744. *Fax:* (11) 6873171. *E-mail:* karansingh@ karansingh.com (home); karansi@sansad.nic.in (home). *Website:* www.karansingh .com.

SINGH, Kunwar Natwar, BA; Indian diplomatist, politician and writer; b. 6 May 1931; s. of Shri Govind Singhji and Shrimati Prayag Kaur; m. Shrimati Heminder Kumari 1967; one s. one d.; ed Univ. of Delhi, Univ. of Cambridge, UK, Peking Univ., People's Repub. of China; joined Foreign Service 1953; served in Peking 1956–58; Perm. Mission to UN 1961–66; mem. Bd UNICEF 1962–66, rapporteur 1963–65; mem. Prime Minister's Secr. 1966–71; Amb. to Poland 1971–73; Deputy High Commr to UK 1973–77; High Commr to Zambia 1977–80; Amb. to Pakistan 1980–82; mem. Lok Sabha 1984–89; Union Minister of State Dept of Steel, Dept of Fertilizers 1985–86; with Ministry of External Affairs 1986–89; mem. Cttee on External Affairs, on Public Accounts 1998–99; elected to Rajya Sabha 2002; mem. Cttee on External Affairs 2002–04; Minister of External Affairs 2004–05, Minister without Portfolio 2005 (resgnd); mem. Bd Dirs Air India 1982–84; Pres. UN Conf. on Disarmament and Devt, New York 1987; Padma Bhushan 1984, E. M. Forster's Literary Award 1989. *Publications:* E. M. Forster: A Tribute 1964, The Legacy of Nehru 1965, Tales from Modern India 1966, Stories from India 1971, Maharaja Suraj Mal: 1707–63 1981, Curtain Raisers 1984, Profiles and Letters 1997, The Magnificent Maharaja Bhupinder Singh of Patiala: 1891–1938 1997, Heart to Heart 2003, My China Diary 1956-88 2009, Yours Sincerely 2009; contribs to numerous newspapers and journals. *Address:* 'Govind Niwas', Bharatpur 321 001, India (home). *Telephone:* (11) 23013855 (home). *Fax:* (11) 23793704 (home).

SINGH, Lalji, MSc, PhD; Indian molecular biologist and academic; *Director, Centre for Cellular and Molecular Biology;* b. 5 July 1947, Jaunpur Dist, Uttar Predesh; ed Banaras Hindu Univ.; Research Assoc. Dept of Zoology, Banaras Hindu Univ. 1970–72; Commonwealth Fellowship to carry out research Univ. of Edinburgh 1974–76, Research Assoc. 1977–79, 1979–87; Sr scientist Centre for Cellular and Molecular Biology 1987–, Dir 1998–; Officer on Special Duty f. Centre for DNA Fingerprinting and Diagnostics 1995; mem. Scientific Advisory Cttee Inst. of Cytology & Preventive Oncology, New Delhi, Nat. Inst. of Virology, New Delhi, Inst. of Immunohaemotology, Mumbai; Fellow Nat. Acad. of Sciences, Nat. Science Acad.; mem. Soc. of Cell Biology, Soc. of Biological Chemists of India, Soc. of Human Genetics; Junior Research Fellowship, Univ. Grants Comm. 1966; Sr Research Fellowship, Council of Scientific and Industrial Research 1972; Pres. P M Bhargava Foundation; Founder mem. and Sec., Asscn for the Promotion of DNA Fingerprinting and Oother DNA Technologies; mem. editorial Bd Journal of Biosciences, Journal of Basic & Applied Biomedicine, Journal of Genetics, Journal of Forensic Medicine and Toxicology; Hon. Prof., School of Animal Sciences, Univ. of Hyderabad 1998; Hon. DSc (Purvanchal Univ.) 2000; Dr S. P. Basu Memorial Medal Calcutta Zoological Soc. 1973, Nat. Science Acad. Medal for Young Scientists 1974, Council of Scientific and Industrial Research Technology Award 1992, Jagdish Chandra Bose Award for research in Life Sciences Hari Om Ashram Trust, Delhi 1995, VASVIK Research Award 1995, Prof. Vishwanath Memorial Lecture Award Nat. Science Acad., New Delhi 1995, Sri Om Prakash Bhasin Award for Science & Technology 1996, Padmabhushan Dr P. S. Siva Reddy Endowment Award 1997, Joy Govind Law Memorial Medal The Asiatic Soc., Kolkata 1997, Scroll of Honour – Outstanding Forensic Expert Award 1998, Padma Shri 2004, Great Son of the Soil Award, All India Conference of Intellectuals 2008, Visesha Puraskaram, Ramineni Foundation 2000, Goyal Prize in Life Sciences 2000, New Millennium Plaques of Honour Award, Indian Science Congress 2002. *Publications:* co-authored and co-ed several books, more than 80 research papers in nat. and inter nat. journals. *Address:* Centre for Cellular and Molecular Biology, Uppal Road, Hyderabad 500 007, India (office). *Telephone:* (40) 27160222 (office). *Fax:* (40) 27160591 (office). *E-mail:* lalji@ccmb.res.in (office). *Website:* www.ccmb.res.in (office).

SINGH, Manmohan, BA, MA, DPhil; Indian politician and economist; *Prime Minister and Minister-in-charge of Personnel, Public Grievances and Pensions, of Planning, of Atomic Energy, and of Space;* b. 26 Sept. 1932, Gah, Punjab (now Pakistan); s. of Gurumukh Singh and Amrit Kaur; m. Smt. Gursharan Kaur 1958; three d.; ed Panjab Univ., Chandigarh, Univs of Cambridge and Oxford, UK; Sr Lecturer in Econs, Panjab Univ. 1957–59, Reader in Econs 1959–63, Prof. of Econs 1963–65; Econ. Affairs Officer, UNCTAD, UN Secr., New York, USA 1966, Chief, Financing for Trade Section 1966–69; Prof. of Int. Trade, Delhi School of Econs, Delhi Univ. 1969–71; Econ. Adviser, Ministry of Foreign Trade 1971–72; Chief Econ. Adviser, Ministry of Finance 1972–76; Dir Reserve Bank of India 1976–80, Gov. 1982–85; mem. Econ. Advisory Council to the Prime Minister 1983–84; Mem.-Sec. Planning Comm. 1980–82, Deputy Chair. 1985–87; Sec.-Gen., Commr South

Comm. 1987–90; econ. adviser to Prime Minister 1990–91; Chair. Univ. Grants Comm. March–June 1991; Minister of Finance 1991–96, Gov. of India on Bd of Govs of IMF and IBRD (World Bank) 1991–95; mem. Rajya Sabha (Parl.) 1991–, Chair. Parl. Standing Cttee on Commerce 1996–97, Leader of Opposition 1998–2004; Prime Minister of India and Minister-in-charge of Personnel, Public Grievances and Pensions, of Planning, of Atomic Energy, of Space 2004–, also Minister of External Affairs 2005–06, Minister of Coal and of the Environment and Forests 2007–09, Minister of Finance 2008–09, June–July 2012, Minister of Culture 2009–11; Chair. India Cttee of Indo-Japan Jt Study Cttee 1980–83; Pres. Indian Econ. Asscn 1985; apptd by UN Sec.-Gen. mem. Group of Eminent Persons to advise him on Financing for Devt 2000; Leader of Indian del. to Aid India Consortium Meetings 1977–79, to Indo-Soviet Monitoring Group Meeting 1982, to Indo-Soviet Jt Planning Group Meeting 1980–82, to Commonwealth Heads of Govt Meeting, Cyprus 1993, to Human Rights World Conf., Vienna 1993, and mem. numerous other dels; Distinguished Fellow, LSE Centre for Asia Economy, Politics and Society 1994; Fellow, Nat. Acad. of Agricultural Sciences, New Delhi 1999; Hon. Prof., Jawaharlal Nehru Univ., New Delhi 1976, Delhi School of Econs, Univ. of Delhi 1996; Hon. Fellow, Indian Inst. of Bankers 1982, St John's Coll., Cambridge 1982, All India Man. Asscn 1994, Nuffield Coll., Oxford 1994; Padma Vibhushan Award, Pres. of India 1987; Hon. DLitt (Panjab Univ., Chandigarh, Guru Nanak Univ., Amritsar, Delhi Univ., Sri Venkateswara Univ., Tirupathi, Univ. of Bologna, Italy, Univ. of Mysore, Chaudhary charan Singh Haryana, Kurukshetra Univ., Nagarjuna Univ., Nagarjunanagar, Osmania Univ., Hyderabad, Dr Bhimrao Ambedkar Univ. (fmrly Agra Univ.), Pt Ravishankar Shukla Univ., Raipur); Hon. DScS (Univ. of Roorkee); Hon. LLD (Univ. of Alberta, Edmonton); Hon. DSc (Agricultural Univ., Hisar), Thapar Inst. of Eng and Tech., Patiala, Indian School of Mines, Dhanbad (Deemed Univ.); Dr hc (Univ. of Cambridge) 2006; Univ. Medal, Panjab Univ. 1952, Uttar Chand Kapur Medal, Panjab Univ. 1954, Wright's Prize for distinguished performance, St John's Coll., Cambridge 1955, Adam Smith Prize, Univ. of Cambridge 1956, Wrenbury Scholar, Univ. of Cambridge 1957, Nat. Fellow, Nat. Inst. of Educ. (NCERT) 1986, Finance Minister of the Year, Asiamoney Awards 1993, 1994, Finance Minister of the Year, Euromoney Awards 1993, Jawaharlal Nehru Birth Centenary Award, Indian Science Congress Asscn for 1994–95 1995, Nikkei Asia Prize for Regional Growth, Nihon Keizai Shimbun Inc. (NIKKEI) 1997, Justice K. S. Hegde Foundation Award for the Year 1996 1997, Lokmanya Tilak Award, Tilak Smarak Trust, Pune 1997, H.H. Kanchi Sri Paramacharya Award for Excellence from Shri R. Venkataraman (fmr Pres. of India) 1999, Annasaheb Chirmule Award, W.L.G. alias Annasaheb Chirmule Trust 2000, ranked by Forbes magazine amongst The World's Most Powerful People (36th) 2009, (18th) 2010, (19th) 2011–12, 28th (2013). *Publication:* India's Export Trends and Prospects for Self-Sustained Growth 1964; numerous articles in econ. journals. *Address:* Prime Minister's Office, South Block, Raisina Hill, New Delhi 110 011 (office); 7 Race Course Road, New Delhi 110 011, India. *Telephone:* (11) 23012312 (office); (11) 23018939 (home). *Fax:* (11) 23019545 (office). *E-mail:* manmohan@sansad.nic.in (home). *Website:* www.pmindia.nic.in (office).

SINGH, Raj Kishore, BTech (MechEng); Indian mechanical engineer and oil industry executive; *Chairman and Managing Director, Bharat Petroleum Corporation Ltd;* ed Banaras Hindu Univ., Indian Inst. of Man., Ahmedabad, Admin. Staff Coll. of India, Hyderabad, Univ. of Tennessee, USA; joined Bharat Petroleum Corpn Ltd (BPCL) 1978, held various assignments at BPCL, both in Refinery and Marketing divs, Exec. Dir of LPG –2006, also headed a group constituted for transfer of technology of LPG equipment from Denmark/Italy, Dir of Refineries, BPCL 2006–10, Chair. and Man. Dir Bharat Petroleum Corpn Ltd 2010–, Dir of Bharat Oman Refineries Ltd 2006–, Petronet LNG Ltd 2011–, Bharat PetroResources Ltd, Premier Oil Cachar BV, Bharat Petro Resources Ltd, Numaligarh Refinery Ltd 2006–. *Address:* Bharat Petroleum Corpn Ltd, 4–6 Currimbhoy Road, Ballard Estate, Mumbai 400 001, India (office). *Telephone:* (22) 2271-3000 (office). *E-mail:* info@bharatpetroleum.com (office). *Website:* www.bharatpetroleum.com (office).

SINGH, Rajnath, MSc; Indian politician and farmer; *President, Bharatiya Janata Party;* b. 10 July 1951, Bhabhora village, Tehsil Chakia of Varanasi dist, UP; s. of the late Ram Badan Singh and Gujarati Devi; m. Savitri Singh; two s. one d.; ed Gorakhpur Univ.; Lecturer in Physics, K. B. Postgraduate Coll., Mirzapur, UP; served in various capacities with Rashtriya Swayamsevak Sangh (Nat. Volunteers' Union—Hindu nationalist org.) since 1964; Org. Sec. Akhil Bharthiya Vidyarthi Parishad (Gorakhpur Div.) 1969–71; apptd Sec. Bharatiya Jana Sangh's Mirzapur Unit 1974; joined JP Movt and was apptd its Dist Convenor; apptd Dist Pres. Jana Sangh 1975; jailed during Emergency 1975, remained in jail until elections 1977; elected as mem. Legis. Ass. from Mirzapur constituency 1977; held several positions in Bharatiya Janata Yuva Morcha (BJYM), UP State Unit as well as in Nat. Exec., BJP Sec. in UP 1983–84, State Pres. BJYM 1984–86, Nat. Gen. Sec. BJYM 1986–88, Nat. Pres. BJYM 1988, Vice-Pres. BJP, UP 1990, Pres. 1997–99, mem. Nat. Exec. BJP, Gen. Sec. Cen. BJP org. 2002–05, Pres. BJP 2005–09, 2013–; mem. UP Legis. Council 1988–94; Minister of Educ. 1991–94; elected to Rajya Sabha 1994–99, 2003–08; elected to Lok Sabha 2009–; mem. BJP, Advisory Cttee on Industry 1994–96, Consultative Cttee for Ministry of Agric., Business Advisory Cttee, House Cttee, Cttee on Human Resource Devt, Cttee on Ethics 2009–, Chief Whip of BJP in Rajya Sabha; Union Minister for Surface Transport 1999–2000; Chief Minister of UP 2000–02; Union Minister of Agric. 2002. *Publication:* book on the causes of and solutions to unemployment problems. *Leisure interests:* reading books on history, culture and science and tech. *Address:* Bharatiya Janata Party (BJP), 11 Ashoka Road, New Delhi 110 001 (office); 04, Kalidas Marg, Lucknow 226 001, India (home). *Telephone:* (11) 23005700 (office); (522) 2236338 (home). *Fax:* (11) 23005787 (office). *E-mail:* webmaster@bjp.org (office). *Website:* www.bjp.org (office).

SINGH, Raman, BSc, BAMS; Indian medical practitioner and politician; *Chief Minister of Chhattisgarh;* b. 15 Oct. 1952, Thathapur, Kawardha Dist; s. of Vighnaharan Singh; m. Smt. Beena Singh; one s. one d.; ed Univ. of Ravishankar, Raipur; Ayurvedic medical practitioner; MLA 1990–92, 1993–98; mem. Bharatiya Janata Party (BJP) (Pradesh Mantri) 1996–; Pres. BJP Legislature Party 2003–; mem. Lok Lekha Samitti Public Accounts Samitti, Legis. Cttee; mem. Lok Sabha for Rajnandgaon 1990–, Chhattisgarh Legis. Ass. 2004–, later BJP Chief Whip; Union Minister of State for Commerce and Industry 1999–2003; Chief Minister of

Chhattisgarh 2003–. *Leisure interests:* sports, tourism, public welfare. *Address:* Government of Chhattisgarh, New Mantralaya, Raipur 492 002, India (office). *Telephone:* (771) 2221000 (office). *Fax:* (771) 2221306 (office). *E-mail:* cmcg@nic.in (office). *Website:* chhattisgarh.nic.in (office).

SINGH, Sujatha, MA; Indian diplomatist; *Foreign Secretary;* b. 1954; m. Sanjay Singh; two d.; ed Lady Shri Ram Coll., Delhi School of Econs; joined Foreign Service 1976, served as Second Sec., Embassy in Bonn 1978–82, Under-Sec., Nepal, Ministry of External Affairs 1982–85, First Sec., High Comm. in Ghana 1985–89, Counsellor, Embassy in Paris 1989–92, Dir Econ. Co-ordination Unit, Ministry of External Affairs 1992–95, Jt Sec., Foreign Service Inst., New Delhi 1996–97, Consul-Gen. in Milan 2000–04, Jt Sec. (West Europe), Ministry of External Affairs –2007, High Commr to Australia 2007–12, Amb. to Germany 2012–13, Foreign Sec. 2013–. *Address:* Ministry of External Affairs, South Block, 110 011 New Delhi, India (office). *Telephone:* (11) 23011127 (office). *Fax:* (11) 23013254 (office). *E-mail:* eam@mea.gov.in (office). *Website:* www.mea.gov.in (office).

SINGH, Sukhmander, MS, PhD; American (b. Indian) civil engineer and academic; *Nicholson Family Professor of Civil Engineering, Santa Clara University;* b. 15 Sept. 1939, Lambi, Punjab, India; s. of Mahla Singh and Jangir Kaur; m. Charanjit Kaur 1967; one s. one d.; ed Punjabi Univ., Patiala, Punjab, Indian Inst. of Tech. (IIT), Delhi, Univ. of Ottawa and Carleton Univ., Ottawa, Canada, Rice Univ., Houston, Tex. and Univ. of Calif., Berkeley, USA; Assoc. Lecturer, IIT, Delhi 1966–67; Teaching Asst, Univ. of Ottawa 1967–68; Visiting Lecturer, Univ. of Alaska, Anchorage 1975, San Jose State Univ., Calif. 1978; Assoc. Prof. of Civil Eng, Calif. State Univ., LA 1983–86; Assoc. Prof. of Civil Eng, Santa Clara Univ., Calif. 1986–90, Chair. Dept of Civil Eng and Chair. Eng Mechanics 1990–, Nicholson Family Prof. of Civil Eng 1994–; professional work as engineer with John V. Lowney & Assocs, Palo Alto, Calif. 1969, Dames & Moore, San Francisco, London, Houston, Anchorage and Seattle offices 1969–83, as Consultant 1983–; Consultant with Purcell, Rhoades and Assocs, Hayward, Calif. 1987–, with Calpine/Kaiser 1989–; mem. numerous cttees on soil dynamics and geotechnical eng; research on liquefaction of silts and geotechnology of cold regions; Outstanding Immigrant Award, Researcher of the Year Award, Pres.'s Special Recognition Award for scholarship, teaching and service. *Publications:* numerous scientific papers. *Leisure interests:* reading, hiking, volleyball playing. *Address:* Department of Civil Engineering, EC 238, Santa Clara University, Santa Clara, CA 95053, USA (office). *Telephone:* (408) 554-6869 (office). *Fax:* (408) 554-5474 (office). *E-mail:* ssingh@scu.edu (office). *Website:* www.scu.edu/engineering/ce/people/singh.cfm (office).

SINGH, Urmila, BA, LLB; Indian government official; *Governor of Himachal Pradesh;* b. 6 Aug. 1946, Fingeshwar, Raipur Chhattisgarh; m. Virendra Bahadur Singh (deceased); two s. one d.; mem. MP state Legis. Ass. from Ghansaur (Seoni) constituency 1985–90, 1990–98, 1998–2003; Minister of State for Finance and Dairy Devt 1993–95, for Social Welfare and Tribal Welfare Depts 1998–2003; Chair. Nat. Comm. for Scheduled Tribes 2007–10; Gov. of Himachal Pradesh 2010–; mem. Indian Nat. Congress party; Pres. MP Congress Cttee 1996–98; mem. Cen. Social Welfare Bd 1978–90 (Chair. 1988–89); mem. MP Scheduled Castes Welfare Advisory Cttee 1978–80, Nat. Food and Nutrition Bd 1986–88; Founder Pres. Ujjain Citizen Forum 1988–; Pres. MP Org. for Tribal Women 1993–; Chancellor, Himachal Pradesh Univ., Dr Y. S. Parmar Univ. of Horticulture & Forestry, Jaypee Univ. of Information Tech.; Pres. Indian Red Cross Soc., Himachal Pradesh State Branch, Himachal Pradesh State Council for Child Welfare, Rajya Sainik Welfare Bd, Himachal Pradesh. *Address:* Governor's Secretariat, Raj Bhavan, Shimla 171 002 (office); Ghurwada, Tehsil-Lakhnadaun, Seoni 480 661, India (home). *Telephone:* (177) 2624152 (office). *Fax:* (177) 2624814 (office). *Website:* www.himachalrajbhavan.nic.in (office).

SINGH, Vijay; Fijian professional golfer; b. 22 Feb. 1963, Lautoka; m. Ardena Seth; one c.; ed Univ. of N Carolina; turned professional 1982, joined PGA Tour 1983; PGA Tour victories: Buick Classic 1993, 1995, 2004, Phoenix Open 1993, Memorial Tournament 1997, Buick Open 1997, 2004, PGA Championship 1998, 2004, Sprint Int. 1998, 2004, Honda Classic 1999, Masters Tournament 2000, Shell Houston Open 2002, Phoenix Open 2003, Byron Nelson Championship 2003, John Deere Classic 2003, 2004, FUNAI Classic 2003, Pebble Beach Nat. Pro-Am 2004, New Orleans Classic 2004, Deutsche Bank Championship 2004, Canadian Open 2004, 84 Lumber Classic 2004, Chrysler Championship 2004, Sony Open 2005; int. victories: Malaysian PGA Championship 1984, Nigerian Open 1988, Swedish PGA 1988, Volvo Open di Firenze 1989, Ivory Coast Open 1989, Nigerian Open 1989, Zimbabwe Open 1989, El Bosque Open 1990, King Hassan Trophy, Morocco 1991, Turespaña Masters Open de Andalucía 1992, Malaysian Open 1992, Volvo German Open 1992, Bells Cup 1993, Scandinavian Masters 1994, Trophée Lancôme 1994, Passport Open 1995, South African Open 1997, Toyota World Match Play Championship 1997, Johnnie Walker Taiwan Open 2000, Malaysian Masters 2001, Malaysian Open 2001; ranked number one in world; first player to win US$10 million in one year 2004; PGA Arnold Palmer Award 2003, PGA Tour Player of the Year 2004. *Leisure interests:* snooker, cricket, rugby, soccer, James Bond movies. *Address:* c/o International Management Group (IMG), 420 West 45th Street, New York, NY 10036, USA (office). *Telephone:* (212) 541-5640 (office). *Fax:* (212) 265-5483 (office). *Website:* www.imgworld.com (office).

SINGH, Gen. (retd) Vijay Kumar, PVSM, AVSM, YSM, ADC, MSc, MA; Indian fmr army officer; b. 10 May 1951, Pune, Maharashtra; s. of Col Jagat Singh and Krishna Kumari; m. Bharti Singh; two d.; ed Birla Public School, Pilani, Madras Univ., Nat. Defence Acad., Defence Services Staff Coll., Wellington, US Army Rangers Course, USA, US Army War Coll., USA; third generation officer of Rajput Regt; commissioned in 2 Rajput (Kali Chindi) 1970; commanded same bn with distinction 1991–94; saw action in Liberation War of Bangladesh 1971 and Operation Pawan, Sri Lanka 1987; experience of various high profile command, staff and instructional appointments; GOC Counter Insurgency Force in Jammu and Kashmir; served in Mil. Operations Directorate, Army HQ, Col GS of Infantry Div. and was Brig. Gen. Staff of a Corps during Operation Parakram when Indian troops were mobilized on the border in the wake of attack on Parl. 2001; fmr Instructor at Infantry School, Mhow and Chief Instructor at JLW (Commando Wing), Belgaum; served as Instructor at Indian Mil. Training Team (IMTRAT) HQ, Bhutan; commanded Strike Corps Ambala-based 2 Corps in Punjab plains in

Western Sector before taking over command of Eastern Army March 2008, Chief of the Army Staff 2010–12; social and civil society activist, formed Jantantra Morcha to Reclaim India; Yudh Seva Medal 1989, Ati Vishisht Seva Medal 2006, Param Vishisht Seva Medal 2009. *Leisure interests:* trekking, photography, sports. *Address:* Maitri Bhawan, Silokra Road, Gurgaon 122 001, Haryana, India (home). *E-mail:* singhvijay3940@gmail.com (office). *Website:* jantantramorcha.org (office).

SINGH, Virbhadra, BA, MA; Indian agriculturist, horticulturist and politician; *Chief Minister of Himachal Pradesh;* b. 23 June 1934, Sarahan, Shimla Dist; s. of the late Padam Singh and of Shanti Devi; m. Pratibha Singh; ed St Stephen's Coll., Delhi; mem. Indian del. to Gen. Ass. of UN, New York 1976; elected to Lok Sabha 1962, 1967, 1972, 1980, 2009; Deputy Minister of Tourism and Civil Aviation 1976–77; Minister of State for Industries 1982–83; mem. Himachal Pradesh Legis. Ass. 1983–, Leader of Opposition 1998–2003, Chief Minister of Himachal Pradesh 1983–1990, 1993–98, 2003–07, 2012–; Minister of Steel 2009–11, of Micro, Small and Medium Enterprises 2011–12; Pres. State Congress Cttee 1992–94; Pres. Sanskrit Sahitya Sammelan, Friends of Soviet Union Soc. (Himachal State Br.); Hon. Capt., Indian Army. *Leisure interests:* reading, meeting people. *Address:* Office of the Chief Minister, Himachal Pradesh Government Secretariat, Shimla 171 002, India (office). *Telephone:* (177) 2625400 (office). *Fax:* (177) 2625011 (office). *E-mail:* cm@hp.nic.in (office); cm-hp@nic.in (office). *Website:* www .himachal.gov.in (office).

SINGH BENIWAL, Vijender, BA; Indian boxer; b. 29 Oct. 1985, Kalwas, Bhiwani Dist, Haryana; s. of Mahipal Singh Beniwal and Krishna Singh Beniwal; ed Vaish Coll., Bhiwani; middleweight boxer; all-India youth boxing champion 2003; wins include Afro-Asian Games, Hyderabad 2003 (silver medal), Summer Olympic Games, Athens 2004, Beijing 2008 (bronze medal), Commonwealth Games, Melbourne 2006 (silver medal), Asian Games, Doha 2006 (bronze medal), World Amateur Boxing Championships, Milan 2009 (bronze medal), Commonwealth Boxing Championship, India 2010 (gold medal); ranked by Int. Boxing Asscn as top-ranked boxer in middleweight category 2009; Rajiv Gandhi Khel Ratna 2009, Padma Shri 2010. *Address:* c/o Sports Authority of India, Netaji Subhas National Institute of Sports, Old Moti Bagh, Patiala 147 001 India. *Telephone:* (175) 2215289. *Fax:* (175) 2212070. *E-mail:* mail@nsnis.org.

SINGH CASSIDY, Sukhinder; American internet industry executive; *Chairman, Joyus;* ed Richard Ivey School of Business, Univ. of Western Ontario, Canada; began internet career in strategy and business devt, working for Amazon.com and interactive TV provider OpenTV; Co-founder and Sr Vice-Pres. of Business Devt, Yodlee.com Inc. 1999–2003; joined Google as first Gen. Man. for Google Local & Maps 2003, later responsible for Google Books, Scholar, and Video, Pres. Asia-Pacific and Latin American Operations –2009; CEO-in-Residence Accel Partners (global venture and growth equity firm) 2009–11; CEO and Chair. Polyvore, Inc. 2010–11; Founder and Chair. Joyus (internet shopping site) 2011–; mem. Bd of Dirs TripAdvisor, Formspring, Inc.; Advisor, Twitter; mem. Advisory Council, Dept of Computer Science, Princeton Univ. *Address:* Joyus, 375 Alabama Street, Suite 325, San Francisco, CA 94110, USA (office). *Telephone:* (866) 856-9878 (office). *E-mail:* support@joyus.com (office). *Website:* www.joyus.com (office).

SINGLETON, William Dean; American newspaper executive; *Chairman, MediaNews Group Inc.;* b. 1 Aug. 1951, Tex.; s. of the late William Hyde Singleton and of Florence E. Myrick Singleton; m. Adrienne Casale 1983; two s. one d.; Pres. Gloucester Co. Times, NJ; Vice-Chair. and CEO MediaNews Group, Inc. 1988–; Pres., Chair. The Houston Post 1984–95, The Denver Post; mem. Bd of Dirs Associated Press (news agency) 1999–2012 (Chair. 2007–12). *Leisure interest:* skiing. *Address:* MediaNews Group Inc., 101 West Colfax Avenue, Suite 1100, Denver, CO 80202, USA (office). *Telephone:* (303) 563-6360 (office). *Fax:* (303) 954-6320 (office). *E-mail:* contact@medianewsgroup.com (office). *Website:* www .medianewsgroup.com (office).

SINGSON, Gabriel C., LLM; Philippine lawyer, fmr central banker and business executive; *Director and Senior Adviser, JG Summit Holdings Inc.;* b. 18 March 1929, Lingayen, Pangasinan; m. Moonyeen Retizos; two s. one d.; ed Pangasinan Prov. High School, Ateneo de Manila and Univ. of Michigan Law School, USA; Assoc. Attorney, Law Office of Justice Jose Bengzon 1952–55; Prof. of Commercial Law and Civil Law, Ateneo de Manila Law School 1956–72; Legal and Evaluation Officer, Cen. Bank 1955–60, Tech. Asst Monetary Bd 1960–62, Asst to Deputy Gov. 1963–66, 1968–70; Legal Officer, Asian Devt Bank 1967–68; Asst to Gov. (with rank of Dir), Cen. Bank 1970–73, Special Asst to Gov. 1973–74, Gen. Counsel 1974–75, Deputy Gov. and Gen. Counsel 1975–80, Sr Deputy Gov. 1980–92; Pres. Philippine Nat. Bank 1992–93; Chair. Monetary Bd and Gov. Bangko Sentral ng Pilipinas 1993–98; Chair. PR Holdings Inc. (holding co. of Philippine Airlines); Vice-Chair., then Chair. Philippine Airlines; Chair. Great Pacific Life Insurance; Dir and Sr Adviser JG Summit Holdings Inc. 1999–, Chair. and Pres. JG Summit Capital Markets Corpn; mem. Bd of Dirs United Industrial Corpn 1999–, Multinational Finance Group Ltd., Summit Forex Brokers Corpn, Summit Point Corpn; mem. Advisory Bd Consultative Constitutional Comm.; Trustee Gokongwei Brothers Foundation Inc., Tan Yan Kee Foundation. *Publications:* articles on Asian Devt Bank, foreign loans, foreign investments and foreign exchange regulations. *Leisure interest:* golf. *Address:* JG Summit Holdings Inc., 42/F Robinsons Equitable Tower, ADB Avenue, cor. Poveda Road, Ortigas Center, Pasig City (office); 28 Polk Street, Greenhills, San Juan, Metro Manila, Philippines (home). *Website:* www.jgsummit.com.ph (office).

SINGTO, Lamnao; Laotian professional footballer; b. 15 April 1988, Vientiane; s. of Ton Singto and Khampheng Singto; ed Kasetsart Univ., Thailand; began career working for Ministry of Public Works and Transport, Vientiane; joined Raj Pracha (semi-professional second div. football team), Nonthaburi, Thailand; debut for Laos nat. team 2008; signed as striker for Buriram PEA Football Club, Thailand 2009 (first Laotian player ever to be signed by foreign club). *Address:* c/o Buriram PEA Football Club, Buriram 31150, Thailand.

SINHA, Ashok, BTech, MBA; Indian petroleum industry executive; *Non-Executive Chairman, Kochi Refineries Ltd;* ed Indian Inst. of Tech., Kanpur, Indian Inst. of Man., Bangalore; with International Computers Pvt. Ltd 1973–75; joined Bharat Petroleum Corpn Ltd 1977, Finance Dir 1995–2005, Chair. and Man. Dir 2005–10; Chair. Indraprastha Gas Ltd 2005–07; mem. Bd of Dirs Bharat Oman Refineries Ltd 1995– (Chair.), Kochi Refineries Ltd (part-time Chair. (non-exec.) 2005–), Numaligarh Refinery 2001– (Chair.), Bharat Shell Ltd; Dir (non-exec.) Petronet LNG Ltd; Econ. Intelligence Unit India/American Express India Chief Financial Officer Award for Information and Knowledge Management 2001, Alumnus of the Year Award, Indian Inst. of Man., Bangalore, Award for Customer Man., Technology Media Group. *Address:* Kochi Refineries Ltd, Post Bag 2, Maradu, Kochi 682304, India (office). *Telephone:* (48) 4270-6100 (office). *Fax:* (48) 4270-5556 (office). *E-mail:* info@kochirefineries.com (office). *Website:* www .kochirefineries.com (office).

SINHA, Shantha, MA, PhD; Indian social activist and government official; *Chairperson, National Commission for Protection of Child Rights;* b. (Mamidipudi Shantha), 7 Jan. 1950, Nellore Dist, Andhra Pradesh; d. of Mamidipudi Anandam and Sita Anandam; ed St Anns High School, Osmania Univ., Jawaharlal Nehru Univ.; fmr faculty mem., Dept of Political Science, Hyderabad Cen. Univ., currently Prof.; Chair. Nat. Comm. for Protection of Child Rights 2007–; Founder, Sec., Trustee, Mamidipudi Venkatarangaiya Foundation (M.V. Foundation) 1981–; fmr Dir Shramik Vidya Peeth; mem. Nat. Cttee, Ministry of Labour, Ministry of Human Resource Devt, Planning Comm. on Issues relating to Child Labour, Universalisation of Elementary Educ. and Rural Devt; Padma Shri 1999, Albert Shanker Int. Award, Educ. Int. 1999, Ramon Magsaysay Award 2003. *Address:* M.V. Foundation, 201 Narayan Apartments, West Marredpally, Secunderabad 500 026, India (office). *Telephone:* (40) 27801320 (office); (40) 27700290 (office). *Fax:* (40) 27808808 (office); (40) 27701656 (office). *E-mail:* mvfindia@gmail.com (office). *Website:* www.mvfindia.in (office).

SINHA, Lt-Gen. (retd) Shreenivas Kumar, BA; Indian army officer (retd) and politician; b. 7 Jan. 1926, Gaya; s. of M. K. Sinha and Radha Sinha; m. Premini Sinha; one s. three d.; ed Patna Univ., Officers' Training School; commissioned 1944, saw combat service during Second World War in Burma and Indonesia and after Independence in Kashmir, served two tenures in Nagaland and Manipur taking part in counter-insurgency operations, transferred to 5 Gorkha Rifles after Independence, fmr Col of Regt (5GR); fmr instructor, Infantry School, Mhow and Defence Services Staff Coll., Wellington; fmr Dir of Mil. Intelligence and Deputy Adjutant-Gen.; fmr Adjutant-Gen., Army HQ; Sec. Del. to UN Comm. for India and Pakistan for Kashmir 1949; Leader Del. UN Conf. on Application of Human Rights to Warfare 1972; Gen. Officer C-in-C, W Command 1981–82; Vice-Chief of Army Staff 1983 (retd); Amb. to Nepal 1990; Gov. of Assam 1997–2003, of Jammu and Kashmir 2003–08; Hon. ADC to Pres. of India 1979; fmr Pres. Gorkha Brigade; Param Vishist Sewa Medal 1973. *Publications include:* books: Operation Rescue (on the Jammu and Kashmir operation of 1947–48), A Soldier Recalls (autobiography), Of Matters Military, Pataliputra, Past to Present, Veer Kuer Singh, A Governor's Musings and Changing India, Guarding India's Integrity: A Pro-Active Governor Speaks; about 300 articles in nat. newspapers. *Leisure interest:* golf. *Address:* c/o Raj Bhawan, Jammu and Kashmir, India.

SINHA, Yashwant, MA; Indian politician, teacher and civil servant; b. 6 Nov. 1937, Patna, Bihar; s. of Bipin Bihari Saran and Dhana Devi; m. Nilima Sinha 1961; two s. one d.; ed Patna Univ.; Lecturer in Political Science, Patna Univ. 1958–60; joined Admin. Service 1960; Deputy Comm. Santhal Paraganas; Chair. Drafting Cttee of the UNCTAD Conf. on Shipping, Geneva; Consul-Gen. of India, Frankfurt; Prin. Sec. to Chief Minister, Bihar; Jt Sec. to Govt of India, Ministry of Shipping and Transport; retd from Admin. Service and joined Janata Party 1984, Gen. Sec. 1986–88; mem. Rajya Sabha (Parl.) 1988, mem. Cttee on Petitions 1989; joined Janata Dal (Samajwadi) after split in Janata Dal 1990; Minister of Finance 1998–99, 2001–02, of External Affairs 2002–04; Pres. All India Tennis Asscn; mem. Lok Sabha (Parl.) 1998–; mem. Parl. Pay Cttee 1998–99, Chair. Standing Cttee on External Affairs 2009, mem. Press Council of India 2006–, Cttee on Public Accounts 2009, Delhi Gymkhana Club; Golden Peacock Award. *Publications include:* Confessions of a Swadeshi Reformer: My Years as Finance Minister. *Leisure interests:* reading, travelling, listening to music, watching films. *Address:* Jasol House, Paotabarea, Jodhpur (home); Rishabh Vatika via College More, Village Rajgoda, Morangi, Thana -Mufassil, Demotand, Dist Hazaribagh, Jharkhand, India. *Telephone:* (6546) 233418. *E-mail:* ysinha2005@hotmail.com.

SINIORA, Fouad, MBA; Lebanese banking executive, government official and politician; b. 19 July 1943, Sidon; m.; three c.; ed Nat. Evangelical Inst., American Univ. of Beirut; various positions at First Nat. City Bank, including clerk 1967, Head Credit Dept 1970–71, Credit Account Officer, Marketing Officer, mem. Credit Cttee 1970–72; Lecturer, Lebanese Univ., American Univ. Beirut 1971–77; concurrently several positions at Finance Bank including Man. Industry and Tourism loans, mem. Credit Cttee, Sec. Bd of Dirs 1972–75; Financial Adviser, Intra Investment 1975–77; Asst Gen. Man. Middle East Cement Co. 1975–77; Banking Control Commr, Central Bank 1977–82; Dir Arab Universal Insurance 1982–92; exec. positions at several cos including Al Mal, IRAD, Méditerranée Investors Group, Méditerranée Group Sevices, Banque de la Méditerranée, Saudi Lebanese Bank 1982–92; Minister of State for Financial Affairs, Acting Minister of Finance 1992–98; Minister of Finance –2004; Prime Minister 2005–09; mem. Majlis al-Nuab (Parl.) from Saida, Leader, Future Movt parl. group. *Address:* c/o Majlis al-Nuab, Place de l'Etoile, Beirut, Lebanon (office). *Website:* www.lp.gov.lb; www.fuadsiniora.com.

SINISCALCO, Domenico Giovanni, LLB, PhD; Italian economist, business executive, writer and fmr government official; *Vice-Chairman, Country Head (Italy) and Head of Government Coverage, Europe, Middle East and Africa, Morgan Stanley (Italy);* b. 15 July 1954, Turin; m.; two c.; ed Univ. of Turin, Univ. of Cambridge, UK; Prof. of Econs, Univ. of Turin 1990–2006 (on leave of absence); Dir-Gen. Treasury, Rome Oct. 2001–04, Minister of Economy and Finance 2004–05; Man. Dir and Vice-Chair. Morgan Stanley International, London 2006–07, Country Head and Chief Exec. Morgan Stanley (Italy) 2007–11, Vice-Chair., Country Head (Italy) and Head of Govt Coverage, Europe, Middle East and Africa (EMEA) 2011–; fmr teaching posts at LUISS, Rome, Univ. of Cagliari, Johns Hopkins Univ., USA, Univ. of Cambridge, UK, Univ. Catholique de Louvain, Belgium; Chair. Collegio Carlo Alberto, Turin 2006–; mem. Steering Cttee journals Equilibri, Mercato, Concorrenza and Regole; mem. Royal Swedish Acad. of Sciences, Beijer Inst. *Publications include:* New Directions in Economic Theory of the Environment (co-ed.), The Challenges of Privatization: An International Analysis 2004; more than 90 publs on privatization, environmental and industrial econs. *Address:* Morgan Stanley Investment Banking Division, Palazzo Serbelloni,

Corso Venezia 16, 20121 Milan, Italy (office). *Telephone:* (02) 7633-5672 (office). *Fax:* (02) 7633-6174 (office). *E-mail:* domenico.siniscalco@morganstanley.com (office). *Website:* www.morganstanley.com (office).

SINN, Hans-Werner, Dr rer. pol; German economist and academic; *Director, Centre for Economic Studies, University of Munich;* b. 7 March 1948, Brake, Lower Saxony; m. Gerlinde Sinn (née Zoubek) 1971; two s. one d.; ed Helmholtz-Gymnasium, Bielefeld, Univ. of Münster, Univ. of Mannheim; Lecturer, Univ. of Münster 1972–74, Univ. of Mannheim 1974–78, Sr Lecturer 1979–83, Assoc. Prof. 1983–84; Visiting Asst Prof., Univ. of Western Ont. 1978–79; Prof. of Econs and Insurance, Univ. of Munich 1984–94, Dir Centre for Econ. Studies 1991–, Prof. of Econs and Public Finance 1994–; mem. Council of Econ. Advisers, Fed. Ministry of Econs 1989–; Chair. Verein für Socialpolitik (German Econ. Asscn) 1997–2000; Pres. Ifo Inst. for Econ. Research 1999–; Pres. Int. Inst. of Public Finance 2006–09; Order of Merit 1999, 2005; Venia Legendi 1983; Hon. Dr rer. pol (Univ. of Magdeburg) 1999; Dr hc (Helsinki) 2011; Yrjö Jahnsson Lecturer, Univ. of Helsinki 1999, Stevenson Lecturer on Citizenship, Univ. of Glasgow 2000, Prize of Advisory Council of the Union 2003, Econ. Book Prize, Financial Times Deutschland 2003, Int. Book Prize CORINE 2004, The World Economy Annual Lecturer, Univ. of Nottingham 2005, Jelle Zijlstra Lecturer, Univ. of Amsterdam 2006, Europe Award, Univ. of Maastricht 2008, D.B. Doran Lecturer on Population, Resources and Development, Hebrew Univ. of Jerusalem 2010, 10th European Economy Lecturer, College of Europe, Bruges 2011. *Publications:* Economic Decisions under Uncertainty 1980, Capital Income Taxation and Resource Allocation 1985, Jumpstart: The Economic Unification of Germany 1991, The German State Banks – Global Players in the International Financial Markets 1999, The New Systems Competition 2002, Ist Deutschland noch zu retten? 2003–05 (English version: Can Germany be Saved? 2007), Kasino-Kapitalismus 2009 (English version: Casino Capitalism 2010), Das grüne Paradoxon 2008 (English version: The Green Paradox 2012), Die Target-Falle 2012; numerous articles on public finance and other subjects; editor of several journals, including Economic Policy. *Address:* Ifo Institute-Leibniz Institute for Economic Research, Poschingerstr. 5, 81679 Munich (office); Centre for Economic Studies, University of Munich, Schackstr. 4, 80539 Munich, Germany (office). *Telephone:* (89) 92241279 (office). *Fax:* (89) 92241901 (office). *E-mail:* sinn@ifo.de (office). *Website:* www .cesifo-group.de/hws (office).

SINNOTT, Kevin, MA; British artist; b. 4 Dec. 1947, Bridgend, Wales; s. of Myles Vincent Sinnott and Honora Burke; m. Susan Forward 1969; three s. one d.; ed St Robert's School, Royal Coll. of Art; teacher Canterbury Coll. of Art 1981–88, St Martin's School of Art, London 1981–93; solo exhbns at Bernard Jacobson Gallery 1986, 1988, 1990, Bernard Jacobson, New York 1987, 1989, Flowers East 1992, 1994, 1996, 1998, Flowers West, Los Angeles 1999, Caldwell/Snyder, New York 2000; work in numerous public collections (including Arts Council of GB, British Museum, British Council, Nat. Museum of Wales, Metropolitan Museum of Art, New York). *Publications:* Behind the Canvas (autobiog.) 2008. *Leisure interests:* cinema, books, walks, opera. *Address:* Tyr Santes Fair, Pont-y-Rhyl, Bridgend, CF32 8LJ, Wales (home). *Telephone:* (1656) 871854 (home). *Fax:* (1656) 871854 (home). *E-mail:* mail@kevinsinnott.co.uk (home). *Website:* www.kevinsinnott.co .uk (home).

SINSHEIMER, Robert Louis, SB, SM, PhD; American biologist and academic; *Professor Emeritus, Department of Molecular, Cellular and Developmental Biology, University of California, Santa Barbara;* b. 5 Feb. 1920, Washington, DC; s. of Allen Sinsheimer and Rose Davidson Sinsheimer; m. 1st Flora Joan Hirsch 1943 (divorced 1972); one s. two d.; m. 2nd Kathleen Mae Reynolds 1972 (divorced 1980); m. 3rd Karen B. Keeton 1981; ed Massachusetts Inst. of Tech.; Research Assoc., Biology, MIT 1948–49; Assoc. Prof. of Biophysics, Iowa State Coll. 1949–55, Prof. 1955–57; Prof. of Biophysics, Calif. Inst. of Tech. 1957–77, Chair. Div. of Biology 1968–77, Visiting Prof. of Biology 1987–88; Prof. Dept of Biological Sciences, Univ. of Calif., Santa Barbara 1988–90, Prof. Emer. 1990–; Chancellor, Univ. of Calif., Santa Cruz 1977–87; mem. NAS, mem. Council 1970–73; Pres. Biophysical Soc. 1970–71; Chair. Bd of Ed., NAS Proceedings 1972–80; Calif. Scientist of the Year Award 1968, Beijerinck Medal of the Royal Netherlands Acad. of Sciences 1969, Univ. of Calif. Presidential Medal 2001. *Publications:* The Strands of Life (memoirs) 1994; more than 250 scientific papers 1946–. *Leisure interests:* travel, hiking and photography. *Address:* MCD Biology, University of California, Santa Barbara, CA 93106 (office); 4606 Via Cavente, Santa Barbara, CA 93110, USA (home). *Telephone:* (805) 683-2247 (home). *Fax:* (805) 893-4724 (office). *E-mail:* sinsheim@lifesci.ucsb.edu (office). *Website:* www.lifesci.ucsb.edu/ mcdb (office).

SINYAVSKAYA, Tamara Ilyinichna; Russian singer (mezzo-soprano); b. 6 July 1943, Moscow; m. Muslim Magovaev 1974; ed Moscow Music Coll. and State Theatre Art Inst.; soloist with Bolshoi Theatre 1964–; studied at La Scala, Milan 1973–74; Order of Merit 2001, Order of Lomonosov First Degree 2004; First Prize Int. Singing Competition, Sofia 1968, Grand Prix Int. Singing Competition, Belgium 1969, First Prize at Int. Tchaikovsky Competition, Moscow 1970, People's Artist of RSFSR 1976, People's Artist of USSR 1982, Irina Arkhipova Prize 2004. *Opera roles include:* Olga in Tchaikovsky's Eugene Onegin, Carmen, Blanche and Frosya in Prokofiev's Gambler and Semyon Kotko, Vanya in Glinka's A Life for the Tsar, Ratmir in Glinka's Ruslan and Lyudmila, Lyubasha in Rimsky-Korsakov's The Tsar's Bride, Varvara in Not Love Alone. *Address:* c/o Bolshoi Theatre, 103009 Moscow, 1, Teatralnaya Ploshad, Russia.

SIOUFAS, Dimitris; Greek lawyer and politician; b. 15 Aug. 1944, Ellinopyrgos, Karditsa; m. Kaity Anagnostaki; two s. one d.; ed Panteion Univ. of Athens, Univ. of Thessaloníki; attorney-at-law; mem. Nea Demokratia (New Democracy—ND), mem. Cen. Cttee 1979–85, 1994–97, 1997–, mem. Exec. Cttee 1997–2001, mem. Political Council 2001–04; mem. Parl. for Karditsa 1981–, Parl. Spokesman for ND 1990–91, 1993–96, first Parl. Spokesman 1997–2000, Chair. Parl. Cttee on Public Enterprises, Banks and Public Utilities, Cttee on Parl. Procedure, Sec.-Gen. ND Parl. Group 2000–04,; Pres. (Speaker) of Vouli (Parl.) 2007–09; Deputy Minister of Social Security 1991–92, Minister of Health, Welfare and Social Services 1992–93, of Devt 2004–07; Co-founder Konstantinos Karamanlis Inst. of Democracy 1997; Gen. Dir Hellenic Org. of Small-Medium Sized Enterprises & Handicrafts (EOMMEX) 1977–81; Deputy Chair. Consignment, Deposits & Loans Fund 1980–81. *Address:* Vouli (Parliament), Parliament Building, Leoforos Vassilissis

Sofias 2, 100 21 Athens (office); Vas. Konstantinou 25, 106 74 Athens, Greece (office). *Telephone:* (210) 3707000 (Parl.) (office); (210) 3614562 (office); (24410) 25591 (office). *Fax:* (210) 7230977 (Parl.) (office). *E-mail:* dimgsioufas@parliament .gr (office). *Website:* www.sioufas.gr.

SIPINEN, Arto Kalevi; Finnish architect; b. 20 April 1936, Helsinki; s. of Veikko Emil Sipinen and Tuovi Maria Heino; m. 2nd Sinikka Rossi 1986; one s. one d.; ed Helsinki Univ. of Tech.; worked with Alvar Aalto 1959–61, Viljo Revell 1961–63; f. architectural practice, Espoo 1963–; Lecturer, Helsinki Univ. of Tech. 1964–67, Acting Prof. of Architecture 1991–92; mem. Finnish Architects' Asscn (SAFA) Community Planning Dept Bd 1964–66; Chair. SAFA Competition Cttee 1964–66; SAFA competition judge 1965–; Dr hc (Jyväskylä) 2009; more than 45 prizes in architectural competitions, including 19 first prizes; other awards include SL Pro Finlandia Medal 1990, Concrete Structure of the Year Prize 1990, Prof. 1995, State Award for Architecture 1999, Building Project of the Year Award 1999. *Projects include:* work includes Imatra City Hall 1970, Jyväskylä Univ. Library and Admin Bldg 1974, Music and Art Bldg 1976, Raisio City Hall 1981, Imatra Cultural Centre 1986, projects in Helsinki city centre 1986–89, Mikkeli Concert Hall 1988, Espoo Cultural Centre 1989, Lahti Main Library 1990, Tammela Town Hall 1991, Mäntsälä Town Hall 1992, Kuusamo Cultural Centre 1995, Jyväskylä Univ. Agora Bldg 2000, Jyväskylä Innova Bldg 2002, Seinäjoki Frami Bldg 2003. *Address:* Arkkitehtitoimisto Arto Sipinen Oy Museokatu 3 A3, 00100 Helsinki (office); Museokatu 3 A3, 00100 Helsinki, Finland (home). *Telephone:* 9481048 (office). *Fax:* 9481048 (office). *E-mail:* arto.sipinen@arksipinen.fi (office). *Website:* www .arksipinen.fi (office).

SIRAT, René-Samuel, Grand Rabbin, Dr de Recherches; French/Israeli rabbi; *Vice-President, Conference of European Rabbis;* b. 13 Nov. 1930, Bône (now Annaba), Algeria; s. of Ichoua Sirat and Oureida Atlan; m. 1st Colette Salamon 1952; one s. two d.; m. 2nd Nicole Holzman 1978; ed Lycée St Augustin, Bône, Univs of Strasbourg and Paris (Sorbonne), Hebrew Univ. of Jerusalem, Ecole Nat. des Langues Orientales (ENLOV); Rabbi, Toulouse 1952–55; Chaplain, Jeunesse juive 1955–63; Prof. Emer., Institut Nat. des Langues et Civilisations Orientales (INALCO, fmrly ENLOV), Dir of Hebrew Studies 1965–96; Prof., Ecole Rabbinique de France 1965–70, 1977–80; Insp.-Gen. of Hebrew, Ministry of Educ. 1972–80; Pres. Hebrew Examining Bd, Certificate of Professional Aptitude and Higher Studies 1973–78; Dir Centre de Documentation et Recherches des Etudes Juives modernes et contemporaines 1974–; Pres. Hebrew Examining Bd, Agrégation 1978–80; Dir Ecole Hautes Etudes de Judaïsme 1985–; Pres. Centre Universitaire Rachi, Troyes 1989; Chief Rabbi of France 1981–87; Chief Rabbi, Consistoire Central 1988; Vice-Pres. Conférence des Rabbins européens 1989–; Pres. Acad. Hillel 1989–, Inst. des connaissances des religions du livre 1996–; Officier, Légion d'honneur, Grand Officier, Ordre nat. du Mérite, Commdr des Palmes Académiques, Commdr des Arts et des Lettres; Dr hc (Yeshiva Univ., USA) 1985, (Université Laval, Canada) 1992, (Université Cluj-Nepoca); Prix de Jérusalem. *Publications:* Omer Hasikha (co-ed.) 1973, Mélanges A. Neher (co-ed.) 1974, Mélanges Vajda 1974–80 (co-ed.), La joie austère 1990, La tendresse de Dieu 1996, Héritages de Rachi (proceedings of the int. scientific colloquium organized in Troyes in June 2005 on the occasion of the 900th anniversary of the disappearance of Rabbi Shelomo Itshaqie (Rachi) 2006, Chrétiens, Juifs, Musulmans: Lectures qui rassemblent lectures qui séparent (co-author) 2007. *Address:* 51 rue de Rochechouart, 75009 Paris, France (home).

SIRCAR, Muhammad Jamiruddin, LLB, MA; Bangladeshi barrister and politician; b. 1 Dec. 1931, Nayabari, Bhajanpur, PS: Tetulia, Dist: Panchagarh; m. Nur Akhter Sircar; two s. one d.; ed Univ. of Dhaka; Vice-Pres. Iqbal Hall (now Sergeant Johirul Hoque Hall), Univ. of Dhaka 1958–59; called to the Bar by East Pakistan High Court of Judicature 1960, Bar of England and Wales (including Commonwealth countries) 1967; Pres. Inns of Court Pakistan Soc., London 1963; Co-founder East Pakistan Soc. House, London; barrister, Supreme Court of Bangladesh in constitutional, civil and criminal law; contested Panchogarh constituency as ind. cand. in prov. parl. election 1970, as ind. cand. in Bangladesh Nat. Ass. Election 1973; Founding mem. Bangladesh Jatiyatabadi Dal (Bangladesh Nationalist Party) and mem. Standing Cttee; MP for Panchagarh-1, Seat-1 1979– (re-elected 1991, 1996, 2001, 2009), Speaker of Jatiyo Shongshod (Parl.) 2001–09; served as Minister of State of Public Works and Urban Devt (Habitat), as Minister of State for Foreign Affairs, as Minister of State for Land Admin and Law Reforms, as Minister for Science and Tech., as Minister for Educ., as Minister for Law, Justice and Parl.; Acting Pres. of Bangladesh 21 June–6 Sept. 2002; mem. Bangladesh del. to UN Gen. Ass. Session 1977, responsible for Legal Cttee 1977–80. *Publications:* Glimpses of International Law 1997, Stronger United Nations for Peaceful Welfare World 2003, The Law of the Sea 2003, London-e Chatro andolon 2005, London-e Bondhu bandhob 2006, Oshtom shongshoder Speaker 2006, Pal Raj theke Plolashi ebong British Raj theke Bongo bhobon 2006, Law of the International Rivers and Other Water Courses 2007, Pakistan-er Gonotontrer Biporjoy ebong Shadhin Bangladesh-er Obbhuddoy 2008. *Address:* Jatiyo Sangshad Bhaban, Dhaka (office); 21 Baily Rd, Ramna, Dhaka 1000, Bangladesh (home). *Telephone:* (2) 8111499 (office); (2) 933480 (home). *E-mail:* info@parliament.gov.bd (office). *Website:* www.parliament.gov.bd (office); www .parliamentofbangladesh.org (office); public.jamiruddin.com.

SIRIVADHANABHAKDI, Charoen; Thai business executive; *Chairman, Thai Beverage Public Co. Ltd;* m.; five c.; Owner, Thai Beverage Public Co. Ltd (ThaiBev), Chair 2003–; Chair. TCC Holding Co. Ltd 1987–, Beer Thai Public Co. Ltd 1991–, South East Group Co. Ltd 1997–, Berli Jucker Public Co. Ltd 2001–, TCC Land Co. Ltd 2002–, Red Bull Distillery Group of Cos 2004–, Fraser & Neave Ltd 2013–; other cos owned include Sang Som Group, Thai Charoen Corpn Group, Charoen Life (insurance co.), Sirivana Co. Ltd; Dr hc (Maejo Inst. of Agricultural Tech., Chandrakasem Rajabhat Univ., Huachiew Chalermprakiet Univ., Eastern Asia Univ., Mae Fah Luang Univ.); Kt Grand Cordon (Special Class), Most Exalted Order of the White Elephant, Kt Grand Cordon (Special Class), Most Noble Order of the Crown of Thailand, Kt Grand Cross (First Class), Most Admirable Order of the Diredgunabhorn, Kt Grand Commdr (Second Class, Higher Grade), Most Illustrious Order of Chula Chom Klao. *Address:* Thai Beverage Public Co. Ltd, 14 SangSom Building, Vibhavadee Rangsit Road, Chomphon, Chatuchak, Bangkok 10900, Thailand (office). *Telephone:* (2) 127-5555 (office). *Fax:* (2) 272-2328 (office). *Website:* www.thaibev.com (office).

SIRIWIT, Cherdpong, MA; Thai business executive and fmr government official; *Chairman of the Executive Board, The Thai Cane and Sugar Corporation;* b. 1 Sept. 1946; ed Thammasat Univ., Nat. Defence Coll., Georgetown Univ., USA; held positions in govt successively as Sec.-Gen. Office of the Cane and Sugar Bd, Deputy Dir-Gen., then Dir-Gen. Office of Industrial Econs, Dir-Gen. Dept of Mineral Resources, Sec.-Gen. Thai Industrial Standards Inst., Deputy Perm. Sec. Ministry of Industry, then Perm. Sec., Ministry of Energy; fmr Chair. PTT Public Co. Ltd, Ratchaburi Electricity Generating Holding Public Co. Ltd; mem. Bd of Dirs Thai Oil Public Co. Ltd, Chair. 2005–08; Chair. Exec. Bd The Thai Cane and Sugar Corpn; Chair. Solartron Public Co. Ltd; mem. or fmr mem. Bd of Dirs Thaioil Power Co. Ltd, PTT Exploration and Production Public Co. Ltd; mem. Council of Trustees, Petroleum Inst. of Thailand (PTIT). *Address:* The Thai Cane and Sugar Corporation, 128/345-6, Payatai Plaza Building 32nd Floor, Phyathai Road, Rajthavee, Bangkok 10400, Thailand (office). *Telephone:* (2) 216-5155 (office). *Fax:* (2) 216-5161 (office). *E-mail:* tcsc@mweb.co.th (office).

SIRRINGHAUS, Henning, PhD; Swiss physicist, business executive and academic; *Hitachi Professor of Electron Device Physics, Optoelectronics Group, Cavendish Laboratory, University of Cambridge;* ed Inst. of Solid State Physics, ETH Zurich; Postdoctoral Research Fellow, Dept of Electrical Eng, Princeton Univ., USA 1995–97; postdoctoral research at Cavendish Lab., Univ. of Cambridge, UK 1998, Royal Soc. Univ. Research Fellowship 1998, Lecturer, Cavendish Lab. 2000–02, Reader 2002–04, Hitachi Prof. of Electron Device Physics, Optoelectronics Group and Head of Microelectronics Research Centre 2004–; Co-founder and Chief Scientist, Plastic Logic Ltd (tech. start-up co. commercializing printed organic transistor tech.) 2000–; Balzers Prize, Swiss Physical Soc. 1995, Silver Medal, ETH, Zurich 1996, Descartes Prize, EC 2000, Mullard Award, Royal Soc. 2003, Hughes Medal, Royal Soc. 2013. *Publications:* more than 70 publs and 20 patents/patent applications. *Address:* Optoelectronics Group, Cavendish Laborabory, University of Cambridge, JJ Thomson Avenue, Cambridge, CB3 0HE (office); Plastic Logic Limited, 34 Cambridge Science Park, Milton Road, Cambridge, CB4 0FX, England (office). *Telephone:* (1223) 337557 (office); (1223) 706000 (Plastic Logic) (office). *Fax:* (1223) 337706 (office); (1223) 706006 (Plastic Logic) (office). *E-mail:* hs220@cam.ac.uk (office); info@plasticlogic.com (office). *Website:* www.phy.cam.ac.uk/people/sirringhaush.php (office); www-oe.phy.cam .ac.uk (office); www.plasticlogic.com (office).

SISI, Field Marshal Abd al-Fatah al-; Egyptian army officer and politician; b. 19 Nov. 1954, Cairo; ed Egyptian Mil. Acad., US Army War Coll., Carlisle, Pa, USA; long career in Egyptian Army, beginning as infantry officer, later becoming Commdr, Northern Mil. Region-Alexandria 2008, Deputy Dir, Mil. Intelligence and Reconnaissance Dept, Chief of Staff, Northern Mil. Zone; Minister of Defence and Commdr-in-Chief, Egyptian Armed Forces 2012–14 (resgnd), also First Deputy Prime Minister 2013–14; announced intention to run as cand. for Pres. of Egypt 2014; mem. Supreme Council of the Armed Forces; rank of Gen. 2012, Field Marshal 2014; numerous mil. awards including 25 April Decoration, Liberation of Sinai Medal, Mil. Duty Decoration, First and Second Class, Liberation of Kuwait Medal, 25 January Revolution Medal. *Address:* c/o Ministry of Defence, Sharia 23 July, Kobri el-Kobba, Cairo, Egypt.

SISOWATH, Prince Sirirath, BSc; Cambodian politician; b. 21 June 1946, Kampong Siem; s. of Sisowath Sirik-Matak and Norodom Kethneary; ed Univ. of Phnom Penh; fmr officer, Airborne Div., Cambodian Army; fmr Jt Minister of Defence; fmr Perm. Rep. to UN, New York; mem. FUNCINPEC Party (United National Front for an Independent, Neutral, Peaceful and Co-operative Cambodia Party), Second Vice-Pres. 2006–; mem. Privy Council; Grand Cross, Kingdom of Cambodia, Commdr, Order of Sena Cheyisith, Commdr, Order of Queen Kossamak. *Leisure interests:* reading, swimming, jogging. *Address:* FUNCINPEC Party (United Nat. Front for an Ind., Neutral, Peaceful and Co-operative Cambodia Party), 11 blvd Monivong (93), Sangkat Sras Chak, Khan Daun Penh, BP 1444, Phnom-Penh (office); 37 Vithei Preah Suramarit, Sangkat Chaktomuk, Phnom-Penh, Cambodia (home). *Telephone:* (23) 428864 (office); (12) 845126 (home). *Fax:* (23) 218547 (office); (23) 211936 (home). *E-mail:* newyorknann@yahoo .com (home); funcinpec@funcinpec.org (office). *Website:* www.funcinpec.org (office).

SISSOKO, Bouaré Fily; Malian economist and politician; *Minister of the Economy and Finance;* b. 22 Aug. 1955, Dakar, Senegal; d. of Samba Sissoko; m.; two c.; ed Lycée technique de Bamako; Minister of State Property and Land Affairs 2000–02, of Communication 2002; several sr positions within Ministry of Finance, including State Comptroller-Gen., Deputy Dir-Gen. of Customs; economist with World Bank, Bamako –2013; Minister of the Economy and Finance 2013–. *Address:* Ministry of the Economy, Finance and the Budget, Bamako, Mali (office). *Website:* www.finances.gov.ml (office).

SISSOKO, Cheick Oumar, BA; Malian politician and filmmaker; *Leader, Parti de la solidarité africaine pour la démocratie et l'indépenance;* b. 1945, San Dist, Bamako; ed Ecole nat. de cinématographie Louis Lumière, Ecole des hautes études en sciences sociales; began career in Mali Civil Service; Minister of Culture 2002–07, of Minister of Nat. Educ. 2007; Asst Dir-Gen., later Dir-Gen. Centre nat. de la production cinématographique; f. Kora Films (producers asscn); Pres. Kayira (ind. radio station); Leader, Parti de la solidarité africaine pour la démocratie et l'indépenance. *Films include:* Nyamanton ou la leçon des ordures 1987, Finzan 1991, Guimba le tyran, une époque (Grand Prize, Fespaco Festival, Ouagadougou 1995) 1993, La Genèse 1999, Battu 2000. *Documentaries include:* Africa is Moving 1992, Etre jeune à Bamako (Youth in Mali) 1992, Building a Nation – Eritrea 1996, Malnutrition in the Sahel Region 1997. *Radio includes:* L'Afrique en question (producer, weekly programme for Kayira). *Address:* Parti de la solidarité africaine pour la démocratie et l'indépendance, Djélibougou, rue 246, porte 559, BP 3140, Bamako, Mali. *Telephone:* 224-10-04 (office).

SISSONS, Peter George, MA; British journalist, broadcaster and television news presenter; b. 17 July 1942, Liverpool, England; s. of the late George Sissons and Elsie Evans; m. Sylvia Bennett 1965; two s. one d.; ed Liverpool Inst. High School for Boys and Univ. Coll., Oxford; grad. trainee, Independent TV News 1964, gen. reporter 1967, industrial corresp. 1970, industrial ed. 1972–78; presenter, News at One 1978–82, Channel Four News 1982–89; presenter, BBC TV news 1989–2009 (6 O'Clock News 1989–94, 9 O'Clock News 1994–2000, 10 O'Clock News 2000–03, BBC News 24 2003–09), Chair. BBC TV Question Time 1989–93; Hon.

Fellow, Liverpool John Moores Univ. 1997; Hon. LLD (Liverpool); Queen's Silver Jubilee Medal 1977, Broadcasting Press Guild Award 1984, Royal Television Soc. Judges' Award 1988, Television and Radio Industries Club Newscaster of the Year 2000. *Publication:* When One Door Closes (autobiog.) 2011. *Address:* c/o Knight Ayton Management, 35 Great James Street, London, WC1N 3HB, England. *Telephone:* (20) 7831-4400. *Fax:* (20) 7831-4455. *E-mail:* info@knightayton.co.uk. *Website:* www.knightayton.co.uk.

SISSOUMA, Mamadou Clazié; Malian politician; b. 6 Nov. 1950; Dir of Cabinet, Ministry of Justice 1994–95, Gen. Sec., 1995–98; Admin. Décennal Project for Judicial Reform 1998–99; Adviser, Supreme Court 1999–2003; Minister of Defence and Veterans 2004–07. *Address:* c/o Ministry of Defence and Veterans, route de Koulouba, BP 2083, Bamako, Mali (office).

SISTANI, Grand Ayatollah Sayyid Ali Husaini; Iraqi (b. Iranian) religious leader; b. 4 Aug. 1930, Mashhad, Iran; s. of Sayyid Mohammad Baqir; joined Islamic seminary, Qom 1949; fmr lecturer in jurisprudence, Najaf Ashraf; after religious training in Iran moved to Iraq to become most sr Shia cleric; apptd head of network of schools, Najaf 1992. *Publications:* numerous religious works and treatises. *Address:* Office of Grand Ayatollah Sistani, Muallim Street, POB 3514\37185, Qom, Iran. *Telephone:* 251-7741415. *Fax:* 251-7741421. *E-mail:* sistani@sistani.org. *Website:* www.sistani.org.

SISULU, Lindiwe Nonceba, BA, MA, MPhil; South African politician; *Minister for the Public Service and Administration;* b. 10 May 1954, Johannesburg; m.; ed St Michael's School, Swaziland, Waterford Kamhlaba, Swaziland, Univ. of Swaziland, Centre for Southern African Studies, Univ. of York, UK; African Nat. Congress (ANC) activist since 1970s, detained for political activities 1975–76, joined Umkhonto we Sizwe (MK) and worked for underground structures of ANC in exile 1977–78, obtained mil. training specializing in Intelligence 1977–79; teacher, Manzini Cen. High School 1981; Lecturer, Dept of History, Univ. of Swaziland 1982; sub-ed., The Times of Swaziland, Mbabane 1983; Lecturer, Manzini Teachers' Training Coll. 1985–87; Chief Examiner, History for Jr Certificate Examinations for Botswana, Lesotho and Swaziland 1985–87; returned to SA 1990; Personal Asst to Jacob Zuma, ANC Head of Intelligence 1990, Chief Admin. for ANC at Convention for Democratic South Africa (CODESA) 1991, Admin. of Intelligence, ANC Dept of Intelligence and Security 1992, mem. ANC Nat. Exec. Cttee, ANC Nat. Working Cttee; Dir Govan Mbeki Research Fellowship, Univ. of Fort Hare 1993; mem. Man. of Sub-Council on Intelligence, Transitional Exec. Council 1994; MP 1994–, Chair. Parl. Jt Standing Cttee on Intelligence 1995–96; consultant, Nat. Children's Rights Cttee, UNESCO 1992; mem. Man. Cttee, Policing Org. and Man. course, PDM, Univ. of the Witwatersrand 1993; Deputy Minister of Home Affairs 1996–2001; Minister of Intelligence 2001–04; Head of Command Centre for Emergency Reconstruction 2000–02; Minister of Housing 2004–09, of Defence and Mil. Veterans 2009–12, for the Public Service and Admin 2012–; inaugural Chair. African Ministerial Conf. on Housing and Urban Devt 2005; mem. Bd of Dirs Nelson Mandela Foundation; Trustee, South African Democracy Educ. Trust, Albertina and Walter Sisulu Trust; Human Rights Centre Fellowship in Geneva 1992, The Presidential Award, Inst. for Housing of South Africa 2004, Science Award, Int. Asscn for Housing 2005. *Publications include:* South African Women in Agricultural Sector (pamphlet) 1990; book chapter and several articles. *Address:* Ministry of Public Service and Administration, Batho Pele House, 116 Proes Street, Pretoria 0001 (office); Private Bag X916, Pretoria 0001, South Africa. *Telephone:* (12) 3361701 (office). *Fax:* (12) 3267802 (office). *E-mail:* natasha@dpsa.gov.za (office). *Website:* www .dpsa.gov.za (office).

SISULU, Sheila Violet Makate, BA; South African diplomatist and UN official; *Deputy Executive Director for Hunger Solutions, United Nations World Food Programme;* d.-in-law of Walter Max Ulyate Sisulu and Albertina Nontsikelelo Sisulu; m. Mlungisi Sisulu; one s. two d.; ed Univ. of Witwatersrand; various sr positions, South African Comm. for Higher Educ. 1978–88; Educ. Co-ordinator, African Bursary Fund, South African Council of Churches 1988–91; Dir Jt Enrichment Project 1991–94; Special Adviser, Ministry of Educ. 1994–97; Consul-Gen., South African Consulate-Gen., New York 1997–99; Amb. to USA 1999–2002; Deputy Exec. Dir UN World Food Programme 2003–08, Deputy Exec. Dir for Hunger Solutions 2008–; mem. ANC Nat. Educ. Cttee, USA–South Africa Leadership Training Program, Community Bank Foundation; Council mem. Univ. of Witwatersrand; Trustee, Equal Opportunity Foundation, Women's Devt Foundation, Women's Devt Bank, South African Broadcasting Corpn; Dr hc (Maryland, CUNY). *Address:* UN World Food Programme, Via C.G. Viola 68, Parco dei Medici, 00148 Rome, Italy (office). *Telephone:* (06) 65131 (office). *Fax:* (06) 65132840 (office). *E-mail:* wfpinfo@wfp.org (office). *Website:* www.wfp.org (office).

SITAULA, Krishna Prasad; Nepalese politician; Spokesperson for Nepali Congress, arrested several times and ordered to be released by Supreme Court Feb. 2006; Minister of Home Affairs 2006–07, Interim Minister of Home Affairs 2007; chief govt negotiator at peace talks with Maoist rebels 2006. *Address:* c/o Ministry of Home Affairs, Singha Durbar, Kathmandu, Nepal (office).

SITHANEN, Ramakrishna, BSc, MSc, PhD; Mauritian politician and economist; b. 21 April 1954, Port Louis; ed London School of Econs, Brunel Univ.; fmr Research Officer, Centre for Labour Econs, LSE; fmr Research Officer, OECD, Paris; Educ. Officer 1979–80; Econ. Consultant, De Chazal Du Mee & Co. 1980–82; Transport Economist, Air Mauritius 1982–87, Dir of Planning 1987–90; Gen. Man., Planning and Devt, Rogers & Co. Ltd 1990–91; MP for Belle Rose/Quatre Bornes Constituency 1991–; Minister of Finance 1991–95, Vice Prime Minister and Minister of Finance and Econ. Empowerment 2005–10; Grand Commdr of the Star and Key; Academic Achievement Prize, LSE, named one of 100 Global Leaders for Tomorrow, World Econ. Forum 1994. *Leisure interests:* reading, football. *Address:* c/o Government House, Ground Floor, Port Louis, Mauritius (office). *E-mail:* rsithanen@mail.gov.mu (office).

SITHOLE, Majozi Vincent; Swazi politician and central banker; *Governor, Central Bank of Swaziland;* Minister, Econ. Planning and Devt 1999–2001, Minister of Finance 2001–13; Gov. Central Bank of Swaziland 2013–; mem. House of Ass. *Address:* Central Bank of Swaziland, Mahlokohla Street, POB 546, Mbabane, Swaziland (office). *Telephone:* 24082000 (office). *Fax:* 24040013 (office). *E-mail:* info@centralbank.org.sz (office). *Website:* www.centralbank.org.sz.

SITKOVETSKY, Dmitry; American/British violinist, conductor, arranger and television presenter; *Music Director, Greensboro Symphony Orchestra;* b. 27 Sept. 1954, Baku, USSR (now Azerbaijan); s. of Julian Sitkovetsky and Bella Davidovich; m. Susan Roberts; one d.; ed Moscow Conservatory, Juilliard School of Music, New York (Artistic Diploma); debut with Berlin Philharmonic 1980; appearances with Vienna Symphony Orchestra, Orchestre de Paris and the Amsterdam, Rotterdam, Munich and Royal Philharmonic Orchestras in Europe and the Chicago, Cincinnati, Detroit, Montréal and Toronto Symphony Orchestras in N America, Carnegie Hall debut 1986; Artistic Dir Korsholm Festival, Finland 1983–93, Seattle Int. Music Festival 1992–97; Music Dir and Prin. Conductor Ulster Orchestra, NI 1996–2001; Music Dir Tuscan Sun Festival, Cortona, Italy 2003–06; Artist-in-Residence, Orchestra de Castilla & Leon, Valladolid, Spain 2006–09; currently Music Dir Greensboro Symphony Orchestra, Greensboro, N Carolina; First Prize, Fritz Kreisler Competition, Vienna 1979, Avery Fisher Career grant 1983. *Television:* role of Arkady Greenberg in film Heavy Sand (Russian Moscow TV) 2007, presenter of series Visiting with Dmitry Sitkovetsky for the Kultura channel (Russia). *Recordings:* Stravinsky: A Soldier's Tale 2012, Chopin: 12 Preludes 2013; more than 50 transcriptions. *Publications:* transcriptions: Bach – Goldberg Variations for String Trio 1985, 2012, Dohnányi – Serenade for string orchestra 1990, Shostakovich – String Symphony Op. 73 1991, Bach Sinfonias for string trio, Bach Dance Suite Nos 1 and 2 for string orchestra 2014. *Leisure interests:* movies, football. *Address:* c/o Tanja Dorn, IMG Artists GmbH, Theaterstrasse 2, 30159 Hannover, Germany (office). *Telephone:* (511) 4378134 (office). *E-mail:* tdorn@imgartists.com (office). *Website:* www.imgartists.com (office); www.greensborosymphony.org.

SITORUS, Martua, BEcons; Indonesian business executive; *Executive Deputy Chairman, Wilmar International;* b. 1960; m.; four c.; ed HKBP Nommensen Univ., Medan; began trading shrimp and other marine products 1978; bought first palm oil plantation 1994; co-f. Wilmar International (agribusiness) 1991, Exec. Deputy Chair. 2006–. *Address:* Wilmar International Ltd, 56 Neil Road, Singapore 088830, Singapore (office). *Telephone:* 62160244 (office). *Fax:* 68361709 (office). *E-mail:* info@wilmar.com.sg (office). *Website:* www.wilmar-international.com (office).

SITRUK, Joseph; French rabbi; b. 16 Oct. 1944, Tunis; m. Danielle Azoulay 1965; nine c.; ed Seminary rue Vauquelin, Paris; Asst to Rabbi Max Warsharski, Lower Rhine region 1970–75; Rabbi, Marseilles 1975–87; Chief Rabbi of France 1987–2008; mem. Nat. Cttee of Human Rights; Pres. Conf. of European Rabbis 2000–; Chevalier, Ordre Nat. du Mérite, Officier, Légion d'honneur 2001, Commdr Ordre Nat. du Mérite 2003, Légion d'honneur 2007. *Publications:* Chemin faisant 1999, Dix Commandements 2000, Rien ne vaut la vie 2006. *Address:* Consistoire Central Union des Communautés Juives de France, 19 rue Saint Georges, 75009 Paris, France. *Telephone:* 1-49-70-88-00. *Fax:* 1-40-16-06-11. *E-mail:* spgrf@free.fr.

SITTHIPHONG, Norkun, BEng (Mech), MS (MechEng), PhD; Thai business executive; *Chairman, Thai Oil Public Company Limited;* m. Bularat Sitthiphong; two d.; ed Chulalongkorn Univ., Oregon State Univ., USA, Nat. Defense Coll., Capital Market Acad., Thai Inst. of Dirs; Dean, Faculty of Eng, Chiang Mai Univ. 1985–97, Vice-Pres. for Research and Property Affairs 1989–2001, for Academic Affairs 2001–03, Sec. Chiang Mai Univ. Council; Advisor to the Bd of Dirs and Sec., The Eng Inst. of Thailand (Northern) 1986–95; Deputy Perm. Sec., Ministry of Energy 2003–10, Perm. Sec. 2010–; Chair. Electricity Generating Public Co. Ltd June–Oct. 2006; Chair. PTT Public Co. Ltd 2008–10, –2013, Chair. PTT Aromatics and Refining Public Co. Ltd 2010–11, IRPC Public Co. Ltd, PTT Exploration and Production Public Co. Ltd 2011–; Chair. Thai Oil Public Co. Ltd 2013–; fmr Dir, Electricity Generating Authority of Thailand; elected to Acad. of Distinguished Engineers, Oregon State Univ. 2005. *Address:* Thai Oil Public Co. Ltd, 555/1 Energy Complex Building A, 11th Floor, Vibhavadi Rangsit Road, Chatuchak, Bangkok 10900, Thailand (office). *Telephone:* (2) 797-2999 (office). *Fax:* (2) 797-2970 (office). *E-mail:* info@thaioilgroup.com (office). *Website:* www.thaioilgroup .com (office).

SIU, Hera K., BS, MBA; Chinese business executive; *President, SAP China;* m.; two c.; ed Univ. of Hong Kong, Penn State Univ. and Univ. of Nevada, Reno, USA; appointments have included Marketing Man., RealNetworks, Marketing Specialist, Honeywell, Vice-Pres. and Regional Man., Computer Associates China, Sr Vice-Pres., Application Service Provider, Pacific Century Cyberworks (PCCW), Hong Kong; Corp. Vice-Pres. and Gen. Man. Nokia Telecommunications Ltd (mfg jt venture based in mainland China) –2010, also managed corp. affairs, govt relations, environmental sustainability and corp. social responsibility; Pres. SAP China (business software co.) 2010–; ranked by Fortune magazine amongst the 50 Most Powerful Women in Business outside the US (45th) 2011. *Address:* SAP China, 12th Floor, Tower 2, China Central Place, 79 Jianguo Road, Chaoyang District, Beijing 100025, People's Republic of China (office). *Telephone:* (10) 65898888 (office). *Fax:* (10) 65898999 (office). *E-mail:* info@sap.com (office). *Website:* www.sap.com (office).

SIWIEC, Marek Maciej; Polish politician and journalist; b. 13 March 1955, Piekary Śląskie; m.; one s. one d.; ed Akademia Górniczo-Hutnicza Univ. of Science and Tech., Kraków, postgraduate journalist studies at Acad. of Social Sciences – Centre for Educ., Foreign Service, Warsaw; Asst, Electronics Inst. of Akademia Górniczo-Hutnicza 1980–82; trainee, Gas & Fuel Corpn of Victoria, Australia 1981–82; Ed.-in-Chief 'Student' bi-monthly 1985–87, weekly ITD weekly 1987–90, Trybuna (daily) 1990-91; mem. Democratic Left Alliance in Poland (SLD) –2012, Vice-Chair. 2011–12; Deputy to Sejm (Parl.) 1991–97, Spokesman for SLD Parl. Party 1993; mem. Nat. Council for Radio and Television 1993–96; mem. Parl. Ass. of the Council of Europe 1993–96; Sec. of State, Chancellery of the Pres. of Poland 1996–2004; Chief of Nat. Security Office 1997–2004; Sec. of Nat. Security Council 2000–04; Vice-Chair. Consultative Cttee of the Presidents of Poland and Ukraine 1997–2004; mem. European Parl. 2004–, Head of nat. del. to the PSE in European Parl. 2004–06, Vice-Pres. European Parl. 2007–09, mem. Parl. Cttee for Foreign Affairs, Substitute mem. Cttee on Internal Market and Consumer Protection, Coordinator of the S&D (Group of the Progressive Alliance of Socialists & Democrats) in Del. to Euronest Parl. Ass., mem. del. to EU-Ukraine Parl. Cooperation Cttee, Substitute mem. Del. to EU-Kazakhstan, EU-Kyrgyzstan and EU-Uzbekistan Parl. Cooperation Cttees, and for relations with Tajikistan, Turkmenistan and Mongolia; Pres. European Friends of Israel; Chair. Supervisory Bd Foundation to Counter Terrorism and Biological Threats; mem. Bd Yalta

European Strategy Foundation (YES), Global Leadership Council Colorado; Head of Polish Assen of Friends of the Peres Centre for Peace. *Leisure interests:* jogging, cycling, snow-boarding, skiing, triathlon, travelling. *Address:* ASP 15G142, 60 rue Wiertz, 1097 Brussels, Belgium (office). *Telephone:* (2) 284-76-53 (office). *Fax:* (2) 284-36-53 (office). *E-mail:* marek.siwiec-office@europarl.europa.eu (office). *Website:* www.mareksiwiec.pl (office).

SIZA VIEIRA, Álvaro (Joaquim Melo); Portuguese architect; b. 25 June 1933, Matosinhos; m. Maria Antonia Marinho Leite 1962 (died 1973); two c.; ed Univ. of Porto; in pvt. practice 1954–; Lecturer, Univ. of Porto 1966–69, Prof. of Construction 1976–; Gold Medal, Alvar Aalto Foundation 1988, Gold Medal, Colegios de Arquitectos (Spain) 1988, Pritzker Architecture Prize 1992, Berlage Prize 1994, Gubbio Prize 1994, Nara World Architecture Exhbn Gold Medal 1995, Imperial Prize, Japan Arts Assen 1998, Wolf Foundation Prize in Arts 2001, Royal Gold Medal, RIBA 2008, Int. Union of Architects Gold Medal 2011, Venice Architecture Biennale Golden Lion for lifetime achievement 2012. *Address:* Rua do Aleixo 53 2° Andar, 4150-043 Porto, Portugal (office). *Telephone:* (22) 616-72-70 (office). *Fax:* (22) 616-72-79 (office). *E-mail:* geral@sizavieira.pt (office). *Website:* www.sizavieira.pt (office).

SIZOVA, Alla Ivanovna; Russian ballet dancer; b. 22 Sept. 1939, Moscow; d. of Ivan Sizov and Ekaterina Sizova; m. Mikhail Serebrennikov 1965; one s.; ed Leningrad School of Ballet; joined Leningrad Kirov Theatre of Opera and Ballet 1958–; a frequent partner of Mikhail Baryshnikov (q.v.); teacher, A. Vagnova Choreography School 1987–91; apptd Ballet Mistress Universal Ballet School 1991; Gold Medals Youth Festival, Vienna 1959, 1st Int. Ballet Contest, Varna; Anna Pavlova Diploma, Paris 1964, People's Artist of the RSFSR 1983. *Major roles include:* Masha (Nutcracker), Mirta (Giselle), Pas de trois (Le Corsaire), Katerina (Stone Flower), Waltz and Mazurka (Chopiniana), Pas de trois (Swan Lake), Aurora (Sleeping Beauty), Maria (Fountain of Bakhchisarai), Juliet (Romeo and Juliet), Cinderella (Cinderella), Kitri (Don Quixote), Girl (Leningrad Symphony).

SJAASTAD, Anders Christian, PhD; Norwegian politician; *Senior Adviser, Norwegian Institute of International Affairs;* b. 21 Feb. 1942, Oslo; s. of Andreas Sjaastad and Ingrid Sjaastad; m. Torill Oftedal Sjaastad 1969 (died 2000); one d.; ed Univ. of Oslo; Pres. Norwegian Students' Assen, Univ. of Oslo 1967; Research Asst, Inst. of Political Science, Univ. of Oslo 1968–70; Research Assoc., Norwegian Inst. of Int. Affairs (NUPI) 1970–81, Dir of Information 1973–81, Dir European Studies 1998–2004, Sr Adviser 2004–12; mem. Høyre (Conservative Party), Vice-Chair. Oslo Høyre 1977–88, Chair. 1996–2000; mem. Storting (Parl.) 1981–2001; Minister of Defence 1981–86; Pres. European Movt in Norway 1989–92; Chair. Defence and Security Cttee (North Atlantic Ass.) 1994–97; Vice-Chair. Standing Cttee on Justice (Stortinget) 1993–97; mem. Norwegian Nat. Defence Comm. 1974–78, Norwegian Cttee on Arms Control and Disarmament 1976–81, 2002–06, N Atlantic Ass. 1989–97; proxy mem. Nobel Peace Prize Cttee 2004–06. *Publications:* Departmental Decision Making (co-author) 1972, Politikk og Sikkerhet i Norskehavsområdet (with J. K. Skogan) 1975, Norsk Utenrikspolitisk Arbok (ed.) 1975, Deterrence and Defence in the North (co-ed. and contrib.) 1985, Arms Control in a Multipolar World (contrib.) 1996, Maritime Security in Southeast Asia (contrib.) 2007. *Address:* NUPI – Norwegian Institute of International Affairs, C.J. Hambros plass 2D, PO Box 8159, Dep 0033 Oslo, Norway (office). *Telephone:* 22-99-40-00 (office). *Fax:* 22-36-21-82 (office). *E-mail:* internet@nupi.no (office). *Website:* www.nupi.no (office).

SKALICKÝ, Jiří; Czech politician; b. 26 April 1956, Kolín; m.; three s. one d.; ed Coll. of Advanced Chemical Tech., Prague; research worker with Astrid (state enterprise), Prague 1981–90; mem. Civic Democratic Alliance (ČDA) 1990–98, Deputy Chair. 1990–92; Deputy to House of Nations, Fed. Ass. of ČSFR 1990–92; mem. Plan and Budget Cttee, House of Nations, Fed. Ass. 1990–92; Minister for Nat. Property Admin. and Privatization 1992–96, for the Environment 1996–98; Chair. Presidium of Nat. Property Fund 1992–96; Deputy Chair. Civic Democratic Alliance 1995–97, Chair. 1997–98; Deputy Prime Minister 1997; Senator 1998–2004. *Address:* Zahradnickova 1220, 150 00 Prague 5, Czech Republic (home). *E-mail:* jiriskalicky@volny.cz (home).

SKÁRMETA, Antonio, BA, MA; Chilean writer and diplomatist; b. 7 Nov. 1940, Antofagasta; m. Cecilia Boisier; two s.; ed Universidad de Chile, Columbia Univ., New York; Prof. of Philosophy, Instituto Nacional 1966–68, Universidad de Chile 1968–75; escaped military dictatorship in Chile, lived in Argentina, Portugal, West Germany, Nicaragua; Distinguished Prof. of Literature and Romance Languages, Washington Univ. of St Louis, Missouri, USA 1988; Amb. to Germany 2000–03; Chevalier, Order des Arts et des Lettres (France) 1986, Commendatore dell'Ordine (Italy) 1996, Goethe Medal (Germany) 2002, Grand Cross of Merit (Germany) 2003; Fulbright Scholarship, Guggenheim Fellowship, Premio Excelencia, Universidad de Artes y Ciencias de la Comunicación 1998, Premio Neruda 2004. *Radio:* Voy y Vuelo 2000. *Publications:* El entusiasmo 1967, Desnudo en el Tejado (Premio Casa de Las Americas) 1969, Tiro Libre 1973, Soné que la nieve ardía 1975, No Pasó Nada (Boccaccio Europa Prize 1986) 1980, La Insurreción 1982, Ardiente paciencia (made into film Il Postino) 1985, Match Ball 1989, La Composición (Jane Adams Prize 2001, Premio Las Américas 2001, Gustav-Heinemann Peace Prize 2004) 1998, La Boda del Poeta (Premio Altazor 2000, Grinzane Cavour Prize 2000, Prix Médicis 2001) 1999, La Chica del Trombón (Premio Elsa Morante 2002, Premio de Narrativa José María Arguedas 2003) 2001, El Baile de la Victoria (Premio Planeta 2003, Premio Municipal de Literatura de la ciudad de Santiago 2004) 2003; trans.: An American Dream, Norman Mailer 1968, The Pyramid, William Golding 1968, Typee, Herman Melville 1968, Visions of Gerard, Jack Kerouac 1969, Love, Roger, Charles Webb 1969, The Last Tycoon, F. Scott Fitzgerald 1969. *E-mail:* cordillero@gmail.com (office). *Website:* www.antonio-skarmeta.com

SKARPHÉÐINSSON, Össur, BS, PhD; Icelandic journalist and politician; b. 19 June 1953, Reykjavik; ed Univ. of Iceland, Univ. of East Anglia, UK; ed., Pjóðviljinn newspaper 1984–87, Alþýðublaðið newspaper 1996–97, DV newspaper 1997–98; Asst Prof., Univ. of Iceland 1987–88; Deputy Dir Reykjavík Reinsurance 1989–91; mem. Althingi (Parl.) 1991–, Chair. Social Democratic Party Parl. Group 1991–93, Vice-Chair. 1995–96, Chair. Social Democratic Alliance Parl. Group 2006–07, mem. Cttee on Fisheries 1991–93, on Gen. Affairs 1991–93, on Industry 1991–93, on Agric. 1992–93, on Health and Social Security 1995–99 (Chair.)

1995–99, on Foreign Affairs 1995–99 (Vice-Chair. 1998–99), 2005–07, on the Environment 1999–2000, on the Budget 1999–2001, on Credentials 1999–2003, on Economy and Trade 2001–05, Chair. Del. to NATO Parl. Ass. 2005–07, Vice-Chair. Del. to WEU Ass. 1995–99, mem. Del. to EFTA and EEA Parl. Cttees 1991–93, 1999–2004, Parl. Ass. of the Council of Europe 2003–05; Minister for the Environment 1993–95, for Nordic Co-operation 2007–08, of Industry 2007–09, for Foreign Affairs and External Trade 2009–13. *Address:* c/o Samfylkingin (Social Democratic Alliance), Hallveigarstíg 1, 101 Reykjavík, Iceland.

SKARSGÅRD, J. Stellan; Swedish actor; b. 13 June 1951, Göteborg; s. of J. Skarsgård and Gudrun Skarsgård; m. My Günther 1976; five s. one d.; with Royal Dramatic Theatre, Stockholm 1972–87; Best Actor, Berlin Film Festival 1982; twice Best Film Actor in Sweden; Best Actor, Rouen Film Festival 1988, 1992, Best Actor, Chicago Film Festival 1991, Jury's Special Prize, San Sebastián Film Festival 1995, European Film Award. *Films include:* Simple Minded Murderer 1982, Serpent's Way 1986, Hip Hip Hurrah 1987, The Unbearable Lightness of Being 1988, Good Evening Mr Wallenberg 1990, The Ox 1992, Wind 1992, The Slingshot 1993, Zero Kelvin 1994, Breaking the Waves 1995, Insomnia 1997, Amistad 1997, Good Will Hunting 1997, Ronin 1998, Deep Blue Sea 1998, Passion of Mind 1999, Kiss Kiss (Bang Bang) 2000, Signs & Wonders 2000, Timecode 2000, Dancer in the Dark 2000, Aberdeen (also assoc. producer) 2000, The Hire: Powder Keg 2001, Taking Sides 2001, The House on Turk Street 2002, City of Ghosts 2002, Dogville 2003, King Arthur 2004, Eiffeltornet 2004, Exorcist: The Beginning 2004, Pirates of the Caribbean: Dead Man's Chest 2006, Goya's Ghosts 2006, Pirates of the Caribbean: At World's End 2007, W Delta Z 2007, Arn-Tempelriddaren 2007, Mamma Mia! 2008, Arn-Riket vid vägens slut 2008, Angels and Demons 2009, Boogie Woogie 2009, Thor 2011, Melancholia 2011, The Girl with the Dragon Tattoo 2011, Avengers Assemble 2012. *Television includes:* Hamlet 1984, Harlan County War 2000, Helen of Troy 2003, God on Trial 2008, Rouge Brésil (series) 2012. *Address:* Hogbergsgatan 40, 118 26 Stockholm, Sweden.

SKARŻYŃSKI, Henryk, DMedHab, PhD, DSc; Polish medical scientist; *Director, Institute of Physiology and Pathology of Hearing;* b. 3 Jan. 1954, Rosochate Koscielne; s. of Józef Skarzynski and Janina Skarzynska; m. Bozena Bruska; two s.; ed Warsaw Medical Univ.; researcher, Oto-rhino-laryngology Clinic, Warsaw Medical Univ. 1979–2000, Head Ward 1986–96, Asst Prof. 1991–93, Assoc. Prof. 1993–95, Full Prof. 1995–; Dir Diagnostic Treatment Rehabilitation Centre for the Deaf and Hearing-Impaired 1993–95; Dir Inst. of Physiology and Pathology of Hearing 1996–; Head, Otology Clinic, Warsaw 1999–2003, Int. Centre of Hearing and Speech 2003–; Chair of Audiology and Phoniatrics Dept, F. Chopin Acad. of Music, Warsaw 2002–; mem. American Acad. of Audiology 1994–, Collegium of Oto-Rhino-Laryngologicum Amicitiae Sacrum 1994–, New York Acad. of Sciences 1995–, American Tinnitus Assen 1995–, Int. Evoked Response Audiometry Study Group 1997–, European Acad. of Otology and Neuro-Otology 1998–; Hon. mem. Slovak Assen of Otolaryngology and Head and Neck Surgery 1998–; Hon. Prof. Audiology and Speech Therapy Dept, Brigham Young Univ., USA 1998–99; Prize of the Prime Minister 2000, Prize of the Minister of Health and Social Welfare 2000, 2001, Prof. Jan Miodonski Award 1983, Stockholm Challenge Award 2000, Gold Medal of the Acad. of Polish Success 2001, Gold Medal, Brussels Eureka 2002, Award of Chair. of State Cttee for Scientific Research 2003, Golden Medal awarded during Lepine Competition, Paris 2003, Special Prize on behalf of Warsaw City Council 2003, Irlandia Award, High-Level Conf. on eHealth, Cork (Ireland) 2004. *Achievements:* pioneer work in developing first Polish Programme for the Treatment of Hearing Disorders, Cochlear and Brainstem Implants Programme. *Publications include:* co-author: Urazy kosci skroniowej (Damages of the Temporal Bone) 1999, Anatomia topograficzna kosci skroniowej dla potrzeb otochirurgii (Topographical Anatomy of the Temporal Bone for Otosurgery) 2000, Technika komputerowa w audiologii, foniatrii i logopedii (Informatic Techniques in Audiology Phoniatrics and Speech and Language Therapy) 2002, Objawy laryngologiczne w rzadkich zespolach chorobowych (Laryngological Symptoms in Rare Diseases) 2002; monographs: Kryteria kwalifikacji do zabiegów wszczepiania implantów slimakowych (z punktu rehabilitacji calkowitej utraty sluchu u dzieci 1994, Implant nadziei. Nowe szanse dla osób nieslyszacych. Pytania i odpowiedzi (Implant of Hope. New Chances for the Hearing Impaired. Questions and Answers) 1994. *Leisure interests:* football, breeding doves. *Address:* Institute of Physiology and Pathology of Hearing, ul. Pstrowskiego 1, 01-943 Warsaw, Poland (office). *Telephone:* (22) 8356670 (office). *Fax:* (22) 8355214 (office). *E-mail:* sekretariat@ifps.org.pl (office). *Website:* www.ifps.org.pl; www.ifps.org.pl/O_nas/profesor_e.html (office).

SKATOV, Nikolai Nikolayevich, DLit; Russian linguist; b. 2 May 1931; m.; one d.; ed Kostroma State Pedagogical Inst.; Sr Teacher, Acting Head, Chair of Literature, Kostroma State Pedagogical Inst. 1956–62; Sr Teacher, Sr Researcher, Docent, Prof., Head of Dept of Literature, Leningrad State Pedagogical Inst. 1962–; Dir Inst. of Russian Literature (Pushkin House) 1987–; Chair., Comm. on Literature and Educ., Russian Acad. of Sciences, Deputy Chair., Comm. on Russian Literature, Presidium Russian Acad. of Sciences, corresp. mem. Russian Acad. of Sciences 1997–; Ed.-in-Chief Russkaya Literature (magazine). *Publications:* 12 books and over 200 scientific works. *Address:* Institute of Russian Literature, Makarova nab. 4, 199034 St Petersburg, Russia (office). *Telephone:* (812) 218-19-01 (office); (812) 311-49-58 (home). *Fax:* (812) 328-11-40 (office). *E-mail:* irli@mail.ru (office). *Website:* spbrc.nw.ru/!english/org/irli.htm (office).

SKEGG, David C. G., OBE, DCNZM, BMedSc, MB, ChB, DPhil, FRSNZ; New Zealand medical researcher, academic and university administrator; *Vice-Chancellor, University of Otago;* b. 16 Dec. 1947, Auckland; m. Dr Keren Skegg; two d.; ed King's Coll., Auckland, Univ. of Otago, Balliol Coll., Univ. of Oxford, UK; Rhodes Scholar, Univ. of Oxford 1973, 1975–76, Lecturer in Epidemiology 1976–79; Chair of Preventive and Social Medicine, Univ. of Otago 1980–2004, Vice-Chancellor 2004–; known for his work on cancer and reproductive health; Adviser to WHO's Special Programme of Research, Devt and Research Training in Human Reproduction; fmr Chair. NZ Public Health Comm.; Health Research Council of NZ; NZ Commemoration Medal 1990, Sir Charles Hercus Medal, Royal Soc. of NZ 1999, Distinguished Research Medal, Otago Univ. 2003. *Publications:* over 150 papers in academic journals. *Leisure interests:* books, art history, walking. *Address:* University of Otago, POB 56, Dunedin 9015, New Zealand (office). *Telephone:* (3) 479-8253 (office). *Fax:* (3) 479-8544 (office). *E-mail:* vice-chancellor@otago.ac.nz (office). *Website:* www.otago.ac.nz (office).

SKEHEL, Sir John James, Kt, PhD, FRS, FMedSci; British research scientist; *Visiting Worker, MRC National Institute for Medical Research;* b. 27 Feb. 1941, Blackburn, Lancs., England; s. of Joseph Skehel and Annie Skehel; m. Anita Varley 1962; two s.; ed St Mary's Coll., Blackburn, Univ. Coll. of Wales, Aberystwyth and UMIST; Postdoctoral Fellow, Marischal Coll. Aberdeen 1965–68; Fellow, Helen Hay Whitney Foundation 1968–71; mem. Scientific Staff and Head, Infection and Immunity, MRC Nat. Inst. for Medical Research 1971–84, 1984–2006, Dir 1987–2006, currently Visiting Worker; Dir World Influenza Centre 1975–94; mem. Academia Europaea 1992; Fellow, Acad. of Medical Science 1998, Vice-Pres. 2002–07; Fellow, Univ. of Aberystwyth 2007; Hon. Prof. of Virology, Univ. of Glasgow 1997–, Hon. Prof., University Coll., London 2002–, Liverpool John Moore's Univ. 2007–; Hon. DSc (University Coll., London) 2004, (Liverpool John Moore's Univ.) 2007, Laurea hc in Medicina e Chirurgia (Univ. of Padua) 2010; Feldberg Prize 1986, Robert Koch Prize 1987, Prix Louis Jeantet de Médecine 1988, ICN Int. Prize in Virology 1993, Royal Soc.'s Royal Medal 2003, Imperial Coll. Ernst Chain Prize 2004, Int. Union of Microbiological Socs Stuart Mudd Award for Basic Microbiology 2005, Int. Louis D, Institut de France Grand Prize (co-recipient) 2007. *Publications:* numerous articles in scientific journals. *Address:* National Institute for Medical Research, The Ridgeway, Mill Hill, London, NW7 1AA, England (office); 49 Homewood Road, St Albans, Herts., AL1 4BG, England (home). *Telephone:* (20) 8816-2256 (office); (1727) 860603 (home). *E-mail:* skeheljj@nimr.mrc.ac.uk (office).

ŠĶĒLE, Andris; Latvian politician; *Chairman, Tautas Partija (People's Party);* b. 16 Jan. 1958, Aluksne District; m. Dzintra Skele; two c.; ed Latvian Acad. of Agric.; Head of Sector, Sr research Asst, Deputy Dir Research Assoc. Inst. of Latvian Agricultural Mechanization and Electrification 1981–90; First Deputy Minister of Agric. 1990–93; Prime Minister of Latvia 1995–97, 1999–2000; Founder and Chair. Tautas Partija (People's Party) 1998–; mem. Saeima (Parl.) 1998–; mem. several Parl. Comms; Chair. several bds of holding cos. *Address:* Tautas Partija, Dzir navu iela 68, Rīga, Latvia (office). *Telephone:* 6728-6441 (office). *Fax:* 6728-6405 (office). *E-mail:* koord1@tautas.lv (office). *Website:* www.tautaspartija.lv (office).

SKELEMANI, Phandu; Botswana lawyer and politician; *Minister of Foreign Affairs and International Co-operation;* b. 1945; ed Univ. of Botswana, Lesotho and Swaziland; joined civil service as State Counsel 1973, becoming Sr State Counsel 1975, Prin. State Counsel 1978, Deputy Attorney-Gen. 1980–82, Attorney-Gen. 1992–2003; mem. Parl. for Francistown East, mem. Botswana Democratic Party (BDP) (Domkrag); Minister of Presidential Affairs and Public Admin. 2004–07, of Justice, Defence and Security 2007–08, of Foreign Affairs and Int. Co-operation 2008–. *Address:* Ministry of Foreign Affairs and International Co-operation, Private Bag 00368, Gaborone, Botswana (office). *Telephone:* 3600700 (office). *Fax:* 3913366 (office). *E-mail:* csmaribe@gov.bw (office).

SKELTON, Carol; Canadian fmr politician; b. 12 Dec. 1945, Biggar, Sask.; m. Noel; three c.; fmr Co-ordinator Canadian Blood Services, Family Services Officer Canadian Red Cross; mem. Parl. (Conservative) for Saskatoon-Rosetown-Biggar 2000–08; fmr Deputy Health Critic, Critic for Social Devt, for Public Health, for Human Resources and Skills Devt (Social Economy), Sr Critic for Western Econ. Diversification; fmr Deputy House Leader, later Leader of the Official Opposition; Vice-Chair. Cttee for Persons with Disabilities; Minister of Nat. Revenue and of Western Economic Diversification 2006–07; mem. Security Intelligence Review Cttee 2011–; fmr mem. Bd Sask. Research Council, Canadian 4-H Council; fmr mem. Man. Cttee Sask. Party; fmr mem. Advisory Cttee on Alcohol. *Address:* Security Intelligence Review Committee, PO Box 2430, Station D, Ottawa, ON K1P 5W5, Canada. *E-mail:* info@sirc-csars.gc.ca. *Website:* www.sirc-csars.gc.ca.

SKELTON, H. Jay; American retail executive; b. 1938; began career with KPMG Peat Warwick, Jacksonville, Fla 1962, various positions including Man.-Pnr 1979–89; Pres. and CEO DDI Inc. (diversified holding co.) 1989–2004; Chair. Winn-Dixie Stores Inc. 2004–06; fmr mem. Bd of Dirs Patriot Transportation Holding Inc., Consolidated-Tomoka Land Co. *Address:* c/o Winn-Dixie Stores Inc., 5050 Edgewood Court, Jacksonville, FL 32254-3699, USA (office).

SKERRIT, Roosevelt, BA; Dominican politician; *Prime Minister and Minister of Finance, Foreign Affairs and Information Technology;* b. 8 June 1972, Vieille Case; ed New Mexico State Univ., Univ. of Mississippi, USA; mem. of Young Freedom Movt (youth arm of Dominica Freedom Party) while a student; fmr high school teacher; Lecturer, Clifton-Dupigny Community Coll. –1999; mem. House of Ass. 2000–; Minister of Educ., Sports and Youth Affairs 2000–04; Prime Minister of Dominica, Minister of Finance 2004–, also Minister of Nat. Security and Econ. Planning 2004–07, 2008–10, of Social Security and Foreign Affairs 2007–08, of Finance, Foreign Affairs and Information Tech. 2010–; mem. Dominica Labour Party (DLP), Leader 2004–. *Address:* Office of the Prime Minister, Government Headquarters, Kennedy Avenue, Roseau, Dominica (office). *Telephone:* 4482401 (office). *Fax:* 4485200 (office).

SKHIRI, Neji; Tunisian banker; b. 15 Feb. 1934, Monastir; m. Slimane Nebiha 1962; one s. three d.; ed Univ. of Tunis, Centre for Educ. of Bankers, Paris; Gen. Man. Cen. Bank of Tunisia 1958–80; Deputy Chair., Chair. Banque du Sud 1980–84; Deputy Chair. Union of Arab Banks 1980–89, Chair. 1989–92; Chair. Soc. Tunisienne de banque 1984–87, Union Int. de Banques 1987–89, Banque du Maghreb Arab 1989–91, Banque Tunisio-Qatari d'investissement 1991–95, NSK Finances 1996–, Tunisian-Italian Chamber of Commerce and Industry; Mayor of Monastir 1985–90; Officer Order of the Repub., Kt Order of Independence. *Leisure interests:* science and literature. *Address:* 3 rue Hamidi, Menzah I, 1004 Tunis, Tunisia. *Telephone:* 751-584. *Fax:* 232-363. *E-mail:* fmsk@hexabyte.tn (office).

SKIDELSKY, Baron (Life Peer), cr. 1991, of Tilton in the County of East Sussex; **Robert Jacob Alexander Skidelsky,** MA, DPhil, FBA, FRHistS, FRSL; British professor of political economy; *Emeritus Professor of Political Economy, University of Warwick;* b. 25 April 1939; s. of the late Boris Skidelsky and Galia Sapelkin; m. Augusta Hope 1970; two s. one d.; ed Brighton Coll. and Jesus Coll., Oxford; Research Fellow, Nuffield Coll. Oxford 1965; Assoc. Prof., Johns Hopkins Univ., USA 1970; Prof. of Political Economy, Univ. of Warwick 1990–, currently Emer. Prof.; Chair. Social Market Foundation 1991–2001; Chair. Hands Off Reading

Campaign 1994–97; Conservative Front Bench Spokesman on Culture, Media and Sport 1997–98, on Treasury Affairs 1998–99; mem. Lord Chancellor's Advisory Council on Public Records 1988–93; mem. Schools Examination and Assessment Council 1992–93; mem. Bd Manhattan Inst. 1994–, Moscow School of Political Studies 1999–, Janus Capital Group Inc. 2001–; mem. House of Lords Select Cttee on Econ. Affairs 2003–; Gov. Brighton Coll. 1998–; Chair. Wilton Park Academic Council 2004–; Hon. DLitt (Buckingham) 1997. *Publications:* Politicians and the Slump 1967, English Progressive Schools 1970, Oswald Mosley 1975, John Maynard Keynes, Vol. 1 Hopes Betrayed 1883-1920 1983, Vol. 2 The Economist as Saviour, 1920-1937 (Wolfson Prize for History) 1992, Vol. 3 Fighting for Britain, 1937-1946 (Duff Cooper Prize, James Tait Black Memorial Prize for Biography, Lionel Gelber Prize for Int. Relations, Arthur Ross Council on Foreign Relations Prize for Int. Relations) 2000, (single-vol. abridgement) 2003, Interests and Obsessions 1993, The World After Communism 1995, Beyond the Welfare State 1997, The Politics of Economic Reform 1998, Keynes: the return of the master 2009, A World by Itself: A History of the British Isles 2010, How Much is Enough?: Money and the Good Book (with Edward Skidelsky) 2012. *Leisure interests:* music, tennis. *Address:* House of Lords, London, SW1A 0PW (office); Tilton House, Firle, East Sussex, BN8 6LL, England (home). *Telephone:* (20) 7219-8721 (office); (1323) 811570 (home). *Fax:* (1323) 811017 (home). *E-mail:* skidelskyr@parliament.uk (office). *Website:* www.skidelskyr.com.

SKILBECK, Malcolm, AO, MA, PhD, FASSA; Australian educational researcher, consultant and author; *Professor Emeritus, Deakin University;* b. 22 Sept. 1932, Northam, WA; s. of Charles Harrison Skilbeck and Elsie Muriel Nash Skilbeck; m. 1st Elizabeth Robbins; one s. three d.; m. 2nd Dr Helen Connell 1984; one d.; ed Sydney Univ., Univ. of Illinois, USA, Univ. of London, UK; Prof. and Dean of Educ., Univ. of Ulster, NI 1971–75; Foundation Dir, Australian Curriculum Devt Centre 1975–81; Dir of Studies, Schools Council for Curriculum and Examinations for England and Wales 1981–83; Prof. of Curriculum Studies, Inst. of Educ., Univ. of London 1981–85; Vice-Chancellor and Prin. Deakin Univ. 1986–91, Prof. Emer. 1991–; Deputy Dir for Educ., Directorate of Educ., Employment, Labour and Social Affairs, OECD 1991–97; Dir Connell Skilbeck Int. Educ. Consultants 1997–; Consultant to OECD, UNESCO, nat. govts, British Council, Australian Int. Devt Assistance Bureau; Hon. DLitt. *Publications:* Culture and the Classroom 1976, A Core Curriculum for the Common School 1982, School Based Curriculum Development 1984, Evaluating the Curriculum for the Eighties 1984, Curriculum Reform 1990, The Vocational Quest 1994, Redefining Tertiary Education 1998, Access and Equity in Higher Education 2000, The University Challenged 2002. *Leisure interests:* gardens, books, art. *Address:* PO Box 278, Drysdale, Vic. 3222, Australia. *Telephone:* (3) 5253-3340. *E-mail:* skilbeck.connell@deakin.edu.au.

SKINNER, James (Jim) Alan; American food industry executive; *Non-Executive Chairman, Walgreen Company;* b. 1944; served in USN for ten years; began career with McDonald's as trainee restaurant man. 1971, then numerous man. positions including dir of field operations, restaurant man., regional Vice-Pres., US Sr Vice-Pres.; joined McDonald's int. man. team as Sr Vice-Pres. and Relationship Partner for Cen. Europe, the Middle East, Africa and India 1992, Exec. Vice-Pres. and Relationship Partner 1995–97, Pres. McDonald's Europe 1997–2001, fmr Pres. and COO for Europe/Asia/Pacific and the Middle East, fmr Pres. and COO McDonald's Restaurant Group, Vice-Chair. and CEO McDonald's Corpn 2004–12; mem. Bd of Dirs Walgreen Co. 2005–, Chair. (non-exec.) 2012–; mem. Bd Ronald McDonald House Charities, ITW (Illinois Tool Works), Catalyst; named by Dow Jones/Marketwatch as CEO of the Year 2007, named by Restaurants & Institutions magazine Executive of the Year 2007, named by Institutional Investor magazine as one of America's Best CEOs 2008, named by Chief Executive magazine as CEO of the Year 2009, named one of Barron's 30 Most Respected CEOs 2010. *Address:* Walgreen Company, 200 Wilmot Road, Deerfield, IL 60015, USA (office). *Telephone:* (847) 914-2500 (office). *Fax:* (847) 914-2804 (office). *E-mail:* info@walgreens.com (office). *Website:* www.walgreens.com (office).

SKINNER, Paul David, CBE, BA (Law), DpBA; British natural resources industry executive; *Non-Executive Chairman, Infrastructure UK;* b. 1944; m.; two s.; ed Univ. of Cambridge, Manchester Business School; joined The Royal Dutch/Shell Group of Cos 1966, sr appointments in UK, Greece, Nigeria, New Zealand and Norway, CEO Global Oil Products Business 1999–2003, Man. Dir Shell Transport and Trading Co. PLC 2000–03, also Group Man. Dir; Dir Rio Tinto plc and Rio Tinto Ltd 2001–09, Group Chair. 2003–09; Dir (non-exec.) Standard Chartered PLC 2003–, Tetra Laval Group 2005–, L'Air Liquide SA 2006–; Chair. Governing Body ICC (UK) 2004–08, Commonwealth Business Council 2007–09; Chair. (non-exec.), Infrastructure UK 2009–; mem. (non-exec.) Defence Bd, Ministry of Defence 2006–09; Pres. UK Chamber of Shipping 1997–98; mem. Bd INSEAD Business School 1999–2011. *Leisure interests:* skiing, other outdoor sports, opera, modern history. *Address:* Infrastructure UK, HM Treasury, 1 Horse Guards Road, London, SW1A 2HQ, England (office). *Telephone:* (20) 7270-5000 (office). *E-mail:* paul@skinnerlondon.com (office). *Website:* www.hm-treasury.gov.uk/infrastructure_about.htm (office).

SKINNER, Quentin Robert Duthie, MA, FBA; British historian and academic; *Barber Beaumont Professor of the Humanities, Queen Mary, University of London;* b. 26 Nov. 1940, Oldham, Lancs., England; s. of Alexander Skinner and Winifred Skinner (née Duthie); m. 2nd Susan James 1979; one s. one d.; ed Bedford School, Gonville and Caius Coll., Cambridge; Fellow, Christ's Coll., Cambridge 1962–2008, Vice-Master 1997–99, Hon. Fellow 2008–; Lecturer in History, Univ. of Cambridge 1967–78, Prof. of Political Science 1978–96, Regius Prof. of Modern History 1996–2008, Pro-Vice-Chancellor 1999; Barber Beaumont Prof. of the Humanities, Queen Mary, Univ. of London 2008–; mem. Inst. of Advanced Study, Princeton, New Jersey 1974–75, 1976–79; mem. Academia Europaea 1989; Foreign mem. American Acad. of Arts and Sciences 1986, American Philosophical Soc. 1997, Royal Irish Acad. 1999, Accad. Nazionale dei Lincei 2007, Österreichische Akad. der Wissenschaften 2009; Hon. DLitt (Chicago) 1992, (E Anglia) 1992, (Helsinki) 1997, (Oxford) 2000, (Leuven) 2004, (St Andrews) 2005, (Harvard) 2005, (Athens) 2007, (Aberdeen) 2007, (Santiago) 2009, Hon. LittD (Oslo) 2011; Wolfson Literary Award 1979, Balzan Prize 2006, Sir Isaiah Berlin Prize 2006. *Publications include:* The Foundations of Modern Political Thought, Vol. I The Renaissance 1978, Vol. II The Age of Reformation 1978, Machiavelli 1981, Philosophy in History (co-ed. and contrib.) 1984, The Return of Grand Theory in the Human Sciences (ed. and contrib.) 1985, The Cambridge History of Renaissance Philosophy (co-ed. and contrib.) 1988, Machiavelli: The Prince (ed. and introduction) 1988, Meaning and Context: Quentin Skinner and His Critics (ed. James Tully) 1988, Machiavelli and Republicanism (co-ed. and contrib.) 1990, Political Discourse in Early-modern Britain (co-ed. and contrib.) 1993, Milton and Republicanism (co-ed.) 1995, Reason and Rhetoric in the Philosophy of Hobbes 1996, Liberty before Liberalism 1998, Visions of Politics, Vol. I Regarding Method 2002, Vol. II Renaissance Virtues 2002, Vol. III Hobbes and Civil Science 2002, Republicanism: A Shared European Heritage (co-ed. and contrib.) Vol. I Republicanism and Constitutionalism in Early Modern Europe 2002, Vol. II The Values of Republicanism in Early Modern Europe 2002, States and Citizens (co-ed. and contrib.) 2003, Thomas Hobbes: Writings on Common Law and Hereditary Right (co-ed.) 2005, Hobbes and Republican Liberty 2008, Sovereignty in Fragments (co-ed. and contrib.) 2010. *Address:* Department of History, Queen Mary, University of London, Mile End Road, London, E1 4NS, England (office). *Telephone:* (20) 7882-8325 (office). *Fax:* (20) 8980-8400 (office). *E-mail:* q.skinner@qmul.ac.uk (office); qskinner@princeton.edu. *Website:* www .history.qmul.ac.uk (office).

SKOKOV, Yuri Vladimirovich, C.TECH.SC.; Russian politician; b. 16 June 1938, Vladivostok; ed Leningrad Electrotech. Inst.; mem. CPSU 1967–91; researcher then Deputy Dir Kalinin Research Inst. of Electric Sources, USSR Ministry of Defence 1969–75, Dir 1975–76; Deputy Dir-Gen. Research Production Union Quant 1977–86, Dir 1986–90; USSR People's Deputy 1989–91; People's Deputy of Russian Fed. 1990–; Chair. Bd of Concern Quantemp 1988–90, First Deputy Chair. Council of Ministers of RSFSR 1990–91; Econ. Counsellor to Pres. of Russia 1990–91; Sec. Council on Problems of Fed. and Territories 1991–92; Sec. Security Council 1992–93; Head of Fed. of Community Producers of Russian Fed. 1994; Chair. Bd Centre for Int. and Inter-regional Econ. Problems 1994; Chair. Bd Congress of Russian Communities 1995–99; f. AMBI-Bank 1998; Dir-Gen. Scientific Production Union Kvant-Co-operation 2000.

SKOL, Michael, BA; American diplomatist and business executive; b. 15 Oct. 1942, Chicago, Ill.; s. of Ted Skol and Rebecca Skol; m. Claudia Serwer 1973; ed Yale Univ.; joined US Foreign Service 1965, served in Buenos Aires, Saigon, Santo Domingo, Naples, Rome, San José and Bogotá (Deputy Chief of Mission) and as Desk Officer for Costa Rica, Paraguay and Uruguay, Deputy Dir for Policy Planning and Dir Andean Affairs, State Dept Bureau of Inter-American Affairs, Deputy Asst Sec. of State for S America, 1988–90, Amb. to Venezuela 1990–93,; Prin. Deputy Asst Sec. Latin American/Caribbean Dept of State 1993–95; Founding Chair. US-Colombia Business Partnership 1996–99; Sr Vice-Pres. Diplomatic Resolutions Inc., Washington, DC 1996–97; Founder and Pres. Skol and Assocs, Inc., Washington, DC 1998–; Sr Man. Dir for Latin America, DSFX, Washington, DC 1998–2005; Founder and Pres. Skol, Ospina & Serna LLC, Bogotá, Colombia 2000–03, Prin., Skol and Serna, Washington, DC and Bogotá 2003–12; Prin., Skol, Serna & Ruiz, Washington, DC, Bogotá and Medellín 2012–; Sr Assoc. Manchester Trade Ltd; mem. Council on Foreign Relations; Order of the Liberator (Venezuela) 1993, Order of Nat. Merit (Paraguay) 1995. *Television includes:* co-creator and first co-host 'Choque de Opiniones', CNN Spanish TV network 1997. *Address:* Manchester Trade Ltd, 1776 Eye Street, NW, 9th Floor, Washington, DC 20006 (office); 650 Park Avenue, Apartment 9A, New York, NY 10065, USA (home). *Telephone:* (202) 331-9464 (office). *E-mail:* michael.skol@skol -serna.net (office); michaelskol@skolsernaruiz.com (office). *Website:* ssadvisors.net (office).

ŠKOLČ, Jožef, Slovenian politician; b. 19 Aug. 1960, Breginje; ed Ljubljana Univ.; active in Socialist Youth League of Slovenia (ZSMS) 1979–84; mem. of Pres. Republican Conf. of Socialist Youth League (RKZSMS) 1984–, Pres. 1988–92; Chair. Cttee for Constitution 1990; Deputy Nat. Ass. for Ljubljana Moste-Polje (6) 1992–, Pres. Nat. Ass. 1994–96; Leader of ZSMS Deputies' Club (later Liberal Democratic Party) 1990–94; Co-ordinator of Liberal Democracy of Slovenia; Minister of Culture 1997–2000; Chair. Comm. for Mandates and Elections 2000; Leader, Deputy Club of Liberal Democracy 2007–; State Sec. responsible for non-governmental orgs 2008–11. *Address:* c/o Office of the Prime Minister, 1000 Ljubljana, Gregorčičeva 20, Slovenia (office).

SKOLIMOWSKI, Jerzy; Polish film director, artist and actor; b. 5 May 1938, Warsaw; m. Joanna Szczerbic; ed Warsaw Univ. and State Superior Film School, Łódź; wrote scripts for Wajda's Innocent Sorcerers, Polanski's Knife in the Water and Łomnicki's Poślizg; Special Prize, Venice Film Festival 1985. *Films:* Rysopis (Identification Marks: None) (also designer, author, editor, actor) 1964, Walkover (also screenwriter and actor) 1965, Bariera (Barrier) (also screenwriter) (Grand Prix, Int. Film Festival, Bergamo 1966) 1966, Le Départ 1967 Dialogue 20-40-60 1968, The Adventures of Gerard 1969, The Deep End 1971, King, Queen, Knave 1972, Lady Frankenstein (or Terminus) 1976, The Shout (Silver Palm, Cannes Film Festival 1978) 1978, Rece do góry (Hands Up!) (also screenwriter and actor) 1981, Moonlighting (British Film Award 1982) 1982, Success is the Best Revenge 1984, The Lightship 1985, Mesmerized (screenwriter) 1986, Torrents of Spring (screenwriter) 1989, Before and After Death 1990, 30 Door Key 1991, The Hollow Men, America 2008, A Short Film About Killing, Essential Killing 2011; as actor: Niewinni czarodzieje 1960, Boks 1961, Rysopis 1964, Walkower 1965, Sposób bycia 1966, Deep End 1971, Poslizg 1972, Rece do góry 1981, Die Fälschung 1981, White Nights 1985, Big Shots 1987, Torrents of Spring 1989, Mars Attacks! 1996, L.A. Without a Map 1998, Before Night Falls 2000, Eastern Promises 2007, Cztery noce z Anna (Four Nights with Anna) 2008, Avengers Assemble 2012. *Publications:* poetry: Gdzieś blisko siebie (Somewhere Close to Oneself); play: Ktoś się utopił (Somebody Got Drowned). *Address:* c/o Film Polski, ul. Mazowiecka 6/8, 00-048 Warsaw, Poland.

SKOLL, Jeffrey (Jeff) S., BS, MBA; American/Canadian business executive, foundation executive and film producer; *Chairman, Skoll Foundation;* b. 16 Jan. 1965, Montréal; ed Univ. of Toronto, Stanford Univ. Grad. School of Business; first job as gas pump attendant in North York, Ont.; f. Skoll Eng (consulting firm), Toronto 1987, Micros on the Move Ltd (computer hire firm) 1990; Man. Knight-Ridder Information (online news information) internet distribution channels 1995; Co-founder and Pres. eBay Inc. 1996–98, then Vice Pres., Strategic Planning and Analysis 1998; mem. Bd of Dirs eBay Foundation 1998–; Founder and Chair. Skoll Foundation 1999–; Founder and CEO Participant Productions (film production

co.), Los Angeles 2004–; f. Gandhi Project 2005; mem. Bd of Dirs Capricorn Man., Community Foundation Silicon Valley; mem. Advisory Bd Stanford Grad. School of Business; Hon. LLD (Univ. of Toronto) 2003; Leafy Award (Canada) 1999, Software Dent Forum Visionary Award 2001, Asscn of Fundraising Professionals Silicon Valley Chapter Outstanding Philanthropist Award 2002, Int. Asscn of Fundraising Professionals Outstanding Philanthropist Award 2003, Nat. Leadership Award for Commonwealth Club Silicon Valley 2004, Wired Magazine's Rave Award 2006. *Films produced:* House of D 2004, Good Night, and Good Luck 2005, North Country 2005, American Gun 2005, Syriana 2005, An Inconvenient Truth 2006, Fast Food Nation 2006, The World According to Sesame Street 2006, Chicago 10 2007. *Publications include:* numerous articles in popular and professional journals. *Address:* Skoll Foundation, 250 University Avenue, Suite 200, Palo Alto, CA 94301, USA (office). *Telephone:* (650) 331-1031 (office). *Fax:* (650) 331-1033 (office). *E-mail:* media@skollfoundation.org (office); info@participantproductions .com (office). *Website:* www.skollfoundation.org (office); www .participantproductions.com.

SKOMOROKHA, Viktor Yehorovych, Cand. of Law; Ukrainian judge; b. 1941, Matrosove Village, Solonyansk Dist, Dnipropetrovsk Region; m. Liudmyla Vasylivna; one s. one d.; ed Kharkiv Law Inst. (now Yaroslav Mudry Nat. Law Acad. of Ukraine); Judge, Krasny Luch Municipal Court, Luhansk Region 1967–70; mem. Luhansk Municipal Court 1970–76; Judge, Supreme Court of Ukraine 1976–96; Judge, Constitutional Court of Ukraine 1996, Chair. 1999–2002; Prof. 2003–; Order for Merits, Second Class 2000, First Class 2002; Cross of Honour for the Renaissance of Ukraine 2002; Veteran of Work Medal 1983, Distinguished Lawyer of Ukraine 1995. *Publications:* publs on Ukrainian constitutional issues, human rights and admin. reform. *Leisure interests:* history books, poetry, gardening. *Address:* c/o Constitutional Court, vul. Zhylianska 14, Kiev, Ukraine (office).

SKORTON, David J., BA, MD; American cardiologist, computer scientist and university administrator; *President, Cornell University;* b. 22 Nov. 1949, Milwaukee, Wis.; ed Northwestern Univ.; medical residency and cardiology fellowship, UCLA; Instructor, Univ. of Iowa 1980, Asst Prof. of Internal Medicine 1981, Asst Prof. of Electrical and Computer Eng 1982–84, Assoc. Prof. 1984–88, Prof. 1988–2003, Co-founder and Co-dir Adolescent and Adult Congenital Heart Disease Clinic, Univ. of Iowa Hosps and Clinics, Vice-Pres. for Research 1992, Interim Vice-Pres. for External Relations 2000–02, Vice-Pres. for Research and External Relations 2002–03, Pres. Univ. of Iowa 2003–06; Pres. Cornell Univ. 2006–15, held faculty appointments in Medicine and Medicine in Pediatrics at Weill-Cornell Medical Coll., New York City and in Biomedical Eng at Coll. of Eng on Ithaca campus; apptd Sec., Smithsonian Inst., Washington, DC 2014; Charter Past-Pres. Asscn for Accreditation of Human Research Protection Programs, Inc.; has served on bds and cttees of many other nat. orgs, including American Coll. of Cardiology, American Heart Asscn, American Inst. of Ultrasound in Medicine, American Soc. of Echocardiography, Asscn of American Univs, Council on Competitiveness, Korea America Friendship Soc.; Vice-Chair. Business-Higher Educ. Forum 2006–08, Chair. 2008–10; Life mem. Council on Foreign Relations, Advisory Council Nat. Inst. of Biomed Imaging and Bioengineering, NIH 2009–; Chair. Gov.'s Task Force on Diversifying the NY State Economy Through Industry-Higher Educ. Partnerships 2009, Advisory Council 10,000 Small Businesses 2009–, Council of Presidents, Univs Research Asscn 2010, NY Gov.-elect Andrew Cuomo's Transition Comm. on Econ. Devt and Labor 2010–11; Master, American Coll. of Cardiology. *Radio:* studied and played saxophone and flute in Iowa City and hosted a weekly jazz program, As Night Falls, on KSUI (Univ. of Iowa's public FM radio station). *Publications:* numerous articles, reviews, book chapters, and two major texts on cardiac imaging and image processing. *Address:* Office of the President, 300 Day Hall, Cornell University, Ithaca, NY 14853, USA (office). *Telephone:* (607) 255-5201 (office). *Fax:* (607) 255-9924 (office). *E-mail:* president@cornell.edu (office). *Website:* www.cornell.edu/president (office).

SKOTHEIM, Robert Allen, PhD; American historian and academic administrator; *President, Occidental College;* b. 31 Jan. 1933, Seattle, Wash.; s. of Sivert O. Skotheim and Marjorie F. Skotheim (née Allen); m. Nadine Vail 1953; one s. two d.; ed Univ. of Wash.; Prof. of History, Univ. of Wash., Wayne State Univ., UCLA, Univ. of Colorado 1962–72; Provost and Faculty Dean Hobart and William Smith Colls 1972–75; Pres. Whitman Coll. 1975–88; Dir Huntington Library, Art Collections, Botanical Gardens 1988–90, Pres. 1990–2001, now Pres. Emer.; Pres. Occidental Coll. 2008–; mem. Advisory Bd Thomas C. Wales Foundation; Guggenheim Memorial Fellowship 1967–68; numerous hon. degrees. *Publications:* American Intellectual Histories and Historians 1966, co-ed. Historical Scholarship in the United States and Other Essays 1967; ed. The Historian and the Climate of Opinion 1969, Totalitarianism and American Social Thought 1971, co-ed. American Social Thought: Sources and Interpretations (two vols) 1972. *Address:* Office of the President, Occidental College, 1600 Campus Road, Los Angeles, CA 90041, USA (office). *Telephone:* (323) 259-2691 (office). *Fax:* (323) 259-2907 (office). *E-mail:* rskotheim@oxy.edu (office). *Website:* www.oxy.edu (office).

SKOTNIKOV, Leonid Alekseyevich; Russian diplomatist and judge; *Judge, International Court of Justice;* b. 26 March 1951, Kalinin; m.; one s.; ed Moscow State Inst. of Int. Relations; mem. staff, Consular Dept Ministry of Foreign Affairs 1974–77; attaché, Perm. Mission to the UN 1977–81; mem. staff, Legal Dept, Ministry of Foreign Affairs 1981–91, Dir 1991–92, 1998–2001; Amb. to the Netherlands 1992–98; Amb. and Perm. Rep. to UN Office and other Int. Orgs in Geneva, the Disarmament Conf. 2001–05; Judge, Int. Court of Justice 2006–; Order of Friendship 2002. *Address:* International Court of Justice, Peace Palace, 2517 KJ The Hague, Netherlands (office). *Telephone:* (70) 302-23-23 (office). *Fax:* (70) 364-99-28 (office). *E-mail:* info@icj-cij.org (office). *Website:* www.icj-cij.org (office).

SKOU, Jens Christian, MD; Danish biophysicist and academic; *Professor Emeritus of Biophysics, University of Århus;* b. 8 Oct. 1918, Lemvig; s. of Magnus Martinus Skou and Ane Margrethe Skou; m. Ellen Margrethe Nielsen 1948; two d.; ed Univ. of Copenhagen; clinical appointments in surgery and orthopaedics 1944–47; Asst Prof. Inst. of Physiology, Univ. of Århus 1947, Assoc. Prof. 1954, Prof. and Chair. of Dept 1963, Prof. of Biophysics 1978–88, Prof. Emer. 1988–; mem. Royal Danish Acad. of Sciences, Deutsche Akad. der Naturforscher, Leopoldina, European Molecular Biology Org.; Foreign Assoc. NAS, Academia

Europaea, Int. Acad. of Humanism; Hon. mem. Japanese Biochemical Soc., American Physiological Soc., American Acad. of Arts and Sciences; Hon. DrMed (Copenhagen) 1986; Leo Prize 1959, Novo Prize 1964, Consul Carlsen Prize 1973, Anders Retzius Gold Medal 1977, Erik K. Fernström's Nordic Prize 1985, shared Nobel Prize for Chemistry 1997 (for identifying the first ion transporting enzyme, the Na,K-ATPase). *Publications:* scientific papers on the mechanism of action of local anaesthetics 1946–57; scientific publs on structure and function of the Na, K-pump, the transport system in the cell membrane responsible for the exchange of cations across membranes 1957–. *Leisure interests:* classical music, yachting, skiing. *Address:* Rislundvej 9, Risskov 8240, Denmark (home). *Telephone:* 86-17-79-18 (home). *Fax:* 86-12-95-99 (home).

SKOURAS, Thanos, PhD, FBIM; Greek economist and academic; *Professor Emeritus, Athens University of Economics and Business;* b. 21 Dec. 1943, Athens; s. of Spyros D. Skouras and Ismini Xanthopoulos; m. 1st Gella Varnara 1966 (divorced 1987); two s.; m. 2nd Savina Ioannides 1998; ed Athens Coll., King's Coll., Durham Univ. and London School of Econs, UK; Asst Lecturer, Lecturer, Sr Lecturer, Middlesex Polytechnic at Enfield, UK 1967–73; Prin. Lecturer and Head Econs Div., Thames Polytechnic 1974–77; Head Dept of Applied Econ. Studies, NE London Polytechnic (now Univ. of East London) 1978–86; Prof., Athens Univ. of Econs and Business 1986–2010, Prof. Emer. 2011–, Deputy Chair. Econs Dept 1987–89, Chair. Marketing and Communication Dept 2004–08, Vice-Rector 1989–92, Pres. Research Centre 1989–92; fmr Visiting Lecturer, Architectural Asscn School, London, Cambridge Univ., CEMI Beijing, Fudan Univ. Shanghai, Katholieke Univ. Leuven, Univ. of Athens; Adviser to Deputy Minister of Nat. Economy, Athens; mem. Council of Econ. Advisers 1986–88; Ed. Thames Papers in Political Economy 1974–86, British Review of Econ. Issues 1976–85; Assoc. Ed. Greek Econ. Review 1985–90; mem. Editorial Bd Int. Review of Applied Econs 1993–; Councillor Royal Econ. Soc., London 1982–86; mem. Governing Council Greek Centre of Planning and Econ. Research 1987–88; Chair. Cttee for Financing of Major Infrastructure Projects 1988; Council mem. Euro-China Research Asscn for Man. 1989–92; mem. Supreme Disciplinary Council, Econ. Chamber of Greece 1990–92; Consultant intra muros European Comm. DG XVI 1992–94; Chair. Abax Stockbroking 1991–94, Global New Europe Fund Portfolio Investments 2002–03, Credit M 2013–; mem. Bd Ergose 1996–97, Commercial Bank 1997, Greek Econ. Soc. 1998–99, Hellenic Centre for European Studies 2001–, Global New Europe Fund 2003–08, Acad. of Labour 2005–08, Greek State Scholarships Foundation 2008–09, Budget Cttee of European Univ., Florence 2008–09; Treas. Citizens' Movt for an Open Society 2007–10, Soc. for the Study of Greek History 2007–11; Hon. Research Fellow, Polytechnic of East London 1986–91. *Publications:* Land and its Taxation in Recent Economic Theory 1977, Post-Keynesian Economic Theory (co-ed.) 1985, The Greek Economy: Economic Policy for the 1990s (ed.) 1991, Production or Importation of Advanced Technology Manufactures? – The Case of Telecommunications Equipment (co-author) 1993, Economic Priorities on the Threshold of the 21st Century (co-ed.) 2000, The Economic Dimension of Mass Communication Media 2003; about 60 articles in professional journals. *Address:* Athens University of Economics and Business, 76 Patission Street, 104 34 Athens (office); 8 Chlois Street, 145 62 Athens, Greece. *Telephone:* (210) 8203432 (office). *Fax:* (210) 8082543 (office). *E-mail:* chlois@aueb.gr (office). *Website:* www.aueb.gr/gb (office).

SKOURIS, Vassilios; Greek judge; *President, Court of Justice of the European Union;* b. 1948; ed Free Univ., Berlin, Hamburg Univ., Germany; Asst Prof., Univ. of Hamburg, Germany 1972–77; Prof. of Public Law, Univ. of Bielefeld, Germany 1978, Univ. of Thessaloniki 1982; Minister of Internal Affairs 1989, 1996; Judge, Court of Justice of the European Communities (now EU) 1999–, Pres. 2003–; Dir Centre for Int. and European Econ. Law, Thessaloniki 1997–; mem. Acad. Council, Acad. of European Law, Trier 1995–; mem. Greek Nat. Research Cttee 1993–95, Scientific Cttee, Ministry of Foreign Affairs 1997–99; mem. Admin. Bd, Univ. of Crete 1983–87, Higher Selection Bd for Greek Civil Servants 1994–96, Admin. Bd, Greek Nat. Judges' Coll. 1995–96; Pres. Greek Asscn for European Law 1992–94, Greek Econ. and Social Council 1998; Dr hc mult.. *Address:* Court of Justice of the European Union, Ancien Palais de la Cour de Justice, Anneau, boulevard Konrad Adenauer, 2925 Luxembourg (office). *Telephone:* 4303-2209 (office). *Fax:* 4303-2736 (office). *E-mail:* vassilios.skouris@curia.europa.eu (office). *Website:* curia.europa.eu (office).

SKOVHUS, Bo; Danish singer (baritone); b. 22 May 1962, Ikast; s. of Freddy Jorgensen and Birthe Skovhus; one d.; ed Music Acad., Arhus, Royal Music Acad. and Opera School, Copenhagen, and in New York; debut in Don Giovanni, Vienna Volksoper 1988, debut as Silvio, Pagliacci Vienna Staatsoper 1991; regular guest singer with all major orchestras and opera cos including Metropolitan, New York, San Francisco, Houston, Munich State Opera, Hamburg State Opera, Berlin, Cologne, Covent Garden, Dresden, etc.; many recitals in Europe, USA and Japan; numerous lieder recitals with Helmut Deutsch, Stefan Vladar, Yefim Bronfman, Lief Ove Andsnes, Christoph Eschenbach and Daniel Barenboim; repertoire includes Don Giovanni, Almaviva in Le Nozze di Figaro, Guglielmo in Così fan tutte, Wolfram in Tannhauser, Olivier in Capriccio, Barber in Schweigsame Frau, Wozzeck, Hamlet, Billy Budd, Eugene Onegin, Yeletsky in Pique Dame, Danilo in Lustige Witwe, Eisenstein in Die Fledermaus, Mandryka in Arabella, Beckmesser in Die Meistersinger von Nürnberg, Kurwenal in Tristan und Isolde, Storch in Intermezzo; Kammersänger (Austria) 1997; Kt's Cross, Order of the Dannebrog. *Recordings include:* Don Giovanni (twice), Le Nozze di Figaro (three times), The Merry Widow, Britten's War Requiem, Carmina Burana, Fidelio, Das Lied von der Erde, Wozzeck, Mirror of Perfection (Blackford), I Pagliacci, Der Waffenschmied (Lortzing), Maskarade (Nielsen), Venus (Schoek), Die Schöne Müllerin, Schwanengesang (Schubert), Dichterliebe (Schumann), Liederkreis Op. 24 (Schumann), Eichendorff Lieder (Wolf), Italienisches Liederbuch (Wolf), Faust (Spohr), Oberon (Weber), Die Orchesterlieder (Strauss), Lyrische Sinfonie (Zemlinsky) (twice), Lieder (Zemlinski), arias by Britten, Gounod, Korngold, Verdi, Wagner, Thomas, Massenet and Tchaikovsky, Don Carlos, Tote Stadt, Brahms Requiem and Triumphlied, Mahler Knaben Wunderhorn/Klenau, Rilke, Scandinavian Orchestra Songs, Orchestra Songs by Schubert, Frühe lieder, Rückert lieder, Abschied, aus lied von der Erde (Mahler). *Address:* c/o Balmer & Dixon Management AG, Kreuzstrasse 82, 8032 Zurich, Switzerland (office). *Telephone:* (43) 2448644 (office). *Fax:* (43) 2448649 (office). *E-mail:* balmer@badix.ch (office). *Website:* www.badix.ch (office).

SKRINSKY, Aleksandr Nikolayevich, DSc; Russian physicist; b. 15 Jan. 1936, Orenburg; s. of Nikolay Alexandrovich Skrinsky and Galina Stepanovna Skrinskaya; m. Lydia Borisovna Golovanova; one s. one d.; ed Moscow State Univ.; Research Worker, Inst. of Nuclear Physics, Siberian Dept, USSR (now Russian) Acad. of Sciences, Head of Lab. 1959–, Deputy Dir 1971–77, Dir Budker Inst. of Nuclear Physics 1977–; Prof. Novosibirsk Univ. 1967–85; Corresp. mem. USSR (now Russian) Acad. of Sciences 1968–70, mem. 1970, Academician-Sec. Nuclear Physics Dept 1988–2002; mem. Int. Cttee for Future Accelerators (ICFA) 1983–90 (Chair. 1990–93), CERN Scientific Policy Cttee 1985–91; mem. Royal Swedish Acad. of Science 2002; Fellow American Physical Soc. 1999–; Lenin Prize 1967, USSR State Prize 1989, Robert R. Wilson Prize 2002, Karpinsky Prize 2002. *Publications:* more than 200 scientific works in the field of accelerator physics and technology, elementary particle physics. *Leisure interests:* ski-running, swimming, music. *Address:* Russian Academy of Sciences, Department of Physics, 117334 Moscow, Leninsky prosp. 32A, Russia. *Telephone:* (495) 938-07-53. *Fax:* (495) 938-54-24. *E-mail:* A.N.Skrinsky@inp.nsk.su; skrinsky@npd.ac.ru.

SKROWACZEWSKI, Stanisław; Polish/American conductor and composer; *Principal Guest Conductor, Deutsche Radio Philharmonie;* b. 3 Oct. 1923, Lwów (now in Ukraine); s. of Paweł Skrowaczewski and Zofia Skrowaczewska (née Karszniewicz); m. Krystyna Jarosz 1956 (died 2011); two s. one d.; ed Lwów Conservatoire and State Higher School of Music, Kraków; Conductor Wrocław Philharmonic Orchestra 1946–47; further composition studies with Nadia Boulanger and P. Klecki, Paris 1947–49; Artistic Dir and First Conductor, Silesian Philharmonic Orchestra, Katowice 1949–54; First Conductor, Kraków Philharmonic Orchestra 1955–56; Dir Nat. Philharmonic Orchestra, Warsaw 1957–59; Musical Dir Minnesota Orchestra 1960–79, now Conductor Laureate; Prin. Conductor and Musical Adviser, Hallé Orchestra 1984–91; Musical Adviser, St Paul Chamber Orchestra 1986–88, Milwaukee Symphony 1992–94; Prin. Conductor Yomiuri Nippon Symphony Orchestra, Tokyo 2007–10, Hon. Conductor Laureate 2010–; Prin. Guest Conductor Deutsche Radio Philharmonie; tours in Europe, N and S America, Israel, Japan, Australia; Commdr Cross of Polonia Restituta Order; Hon. DHL (Hamline Univ., St Paul, Minnesota) 1961; Hon. DMus (Macalester Coll., St Paul, Minn.) 1977; Dr hc (Univ. of Minnesota) 1979, (New England Conservatory of Music), (Univ. of Wrocław), (Karol Szymanowski Acad. of Music, Katowice); Second Prize for 'Overture 1947', Szymanowski Competition, Warsaw 1947, Second Prize, Int. Competition for String Quartet, Liège, Belgium 1953, State Prize (3rd Class) 1956, First Prize, Int. Conductor's Competition, Rome 1956, Conductor's Award of Columbia Univ., New York 1973, Third Prize, Kennedy Center Friedheim Award Competition (for Ricercari Notturni) 1978; 5 ASCAP Awards for imaginative programming with Minneapolis Symphony 1961–79, Gold Medal, Bruckner-Mahler Soc. 1999, McKnight Distinguished Artist Award 2004, Kilenyi Medal of Honor, Bruckner Soc. of America 2011. *Compositions include:* Symphony for String Orchestra, three other symphonies, Muzyka Nocą (Music by Night, suite of nocturnes), four string quartets, two overtures, Cantique des Cantiques (voice and orch.), Prelude, Fugue, Post-Ludium (orch.), English Horn Concerto 1969, Ricercari Notturni (orchestral), Clarinet Concerto, Violin Concerto 1985, Fanfare for Orchestra 1987, Sextet 1988, String Trio 1990, Triple Concerto 1992, Chamber Concerto 1993, Passacaglia Immaginaria 1995, Musica a quattro 1998, Concerto for Orchestra 1999, Trio for piano, clarinet and bassoon, six piano sonatas, Music for Winds 2009; also music for opera, ballet, film and theatre; recordings for Mercury, Philips, Angel, RCA Victor, IMP, Erato, Arte Nova, Vox, Albany. *Leisure interests:* alpinism, skiing, books, film, theatre. *Address:* c/o Intermusica Artists' Management Ltd, 36 Graham Street, Crystal Wharf, London, N1 8GJ, England (office). *Telephone:* (20) 7608-9900 (office). *Fax:* (20) 7490-3263 (office). *E-mail:* mail@intermusica.co.uk (office). *Website:* www.intermusica.co.uk (office); www.seekingtheinfinite.com (office).

SKULACHEV, Vladimir Petrovich; Russian biologist and academic; *Director, A. Belozersky Institute of Physico-Chemical Biology, Moscow State University;* b. 21 Feb. 1935, Moscow; s. of Petr Stepanovich Skulachev and Nadezhda Aronovna Skulacheva; m. Severina Inna Isaakovna; four s. one d.; ed Moscow State Univ.; jr researcher, Head of Div., Head of Lab. Moscow State Univ., Dir A. Belozersky Inst. of Physico-Chemical Biology, Dean Faculty of Bioengineering Bioinformatics; Corresp. mem. USSR (now Russian) Acad. of Sciences 1974, mem. 1990–; research in biochemistry, bioenergetics, investigation of molecular mechanisms of energy transformation in membranes of bacteria, mitochondria and chloroplasts; USSR State Prize. *Publications:* Energy Accumulation in Cells 1969, Energy Transformation in Biomembranes 1972, Membranes Bioenergies 1988; numerous other books and articles. *Leisure interests:* badminton, skiing. *Address:* A. N. Belozersky Institute of Physico-Chemical Biology, Moscow State University, 119992 Moscow, Russia (office). *Telephone:* (495) 939-55-30 (office); (495) 939-01-47 (office). *Fax:* (495) 939-03-38 (office). *E-mail:* skulach@belozersky.msu.ru (office). *Website:* www.genebee.msu.su (office).

SKURATOV, Yuri Ilyich, DJur; Russian lawyer and civil servant; b. 3 July 1952, Ulan-Ude; s. of Ilya I. Skuratov and Raisa G. Skuratova; m. Elena D. Besedina 1976; one s. one d.; ed Sverdlovsk Inst. of Law; teacher, Dean Sverdlovsk Inst. of Law 1977–89; Deputy Head of Div. on legis. initiatives and legal issues, CPSU Cen. Cttee 1989–91; Sr Consultant, Russian Ministry of Security 1991–92; Dir Research Inst. of Problems of Justice, Gen. Prosecutor's Office of Russia 1993–95; apptd Gen. Prosecutor 1995; dismissed by Pres. Yeltsin, but reinstated by Council of Fed.; dismissed again 1999; unsuccessful cand. for Pres. 2000. *Publications:* over 90 scientific works on problems of civil and criminal law. *Leisure interests:* chess, swimming.

SKWEYIYA, Zola Sidney Themba, LLD; South African politician, civil servant and diplomatist (retd); b. 14 April 1942, Simonstown; s. of Winnie Skweyiya; m. Edy Skweyiya; one c.; ed Lovedale High School, Univ. of Fort Hare, Univ. of Leipzig, Germany; mem. African Nat. Congress (ANC) 1956, mil. training, Lusaka 1965; Chief ANC Rep. at OAU, Addis Ababa 1980–85, ANC Rep. UN Comm. on Human Rights 1984–93; f. ANC Legal and Constitutional Dept 1985, Head 1985–94; returned from exile 1990; mem. ANC Nat. Exec. Cttee 1991–; MP 1994–2009; Minister of Public Services and Admin., Govt of Nat. Unity 1994–99, of Welfare and Population Devt 1999–2000, of Social Devt 2000–09; High Commr to UK 2009–13 (retd); Chair. and Trustee, Nat. Children's Rights Comm. 1990–; Trustee, SA Legal Defence Fund 1991–. *Leisure interests:* listening to jazz and classical music, reading. *Address:* Department of International Relations and Co-operation, Union Bldgs, East Wing, 1 Government Avenue, Arcadia, Pretoria 0002 (office); Department of International Relations and Co-operation, Private Bag X152, Pretoria 0001, South Africa (office). *Telephone:* (12) 3511000 (office). *Fax:* (12) 3291000 (office). *E-mail:* minister@foreign.gov.za (office). *Website:* www.dfa .gov.za (office).

SKYRMS, Brian, PhD; American academic; *UCI Distinguished Professor of Social Science, University of California, Irvine;* b. 11 March 1938, Pittsburgh, Pa; s. of Frederick John Skyrms and Marie Margaret Skyrms (née Schlipf); m. Pauline Jenkins 1972; two s.; ed Lehigh Univ., Univ. of Pittsburgh; Asst Prof., Calif. State Univ., Northridge 1964–65, Univ. of Del. 1965–66; Visiting Asst Prof., Univ. of Mich. 1966–67; Asst Prof. then Assoc. Prof., Univ. of Ill., Chicago 1967–70, Prof. 1970–80; Prof. of Philosophy, Univ. of Calif., Irvine 1980–97, Distinguished Prof. of Philosophy and Prof. of Econs 1997–, Dir Program in History and Philosophy of Science, UCI Distinguished Prof. of Social Sciences 1998–; mem. Governing Bd American Philosophical Asscn 1987–90, Philosophy of Science Asscn 1990–91, Pres. 2005–06; mem. several editorial bds including American Philosophical Quarterly and Philosophy of Science; Ed. Cambridge Studies in Probability, Induction and Decision Theory; Fellow Center for Advanced Study in the Behavioral Sciences 1993–94, American Acad. of Arts and Sciences 1994, NAS 1999; Guggenheim Fellow 1987–88; numerous science fellowships; Univ. of Calif. Pres.'s Research in the Humanities 1993–94; Pres. Pacific Div. American Philosophical Asscn 2000–01; FAAS 2004–; Lakatos Prize 1999, Paul Silverman Award 2006, Synthese Distinguished paper award 2010. *Publications:* Choice and Chance: An Introduction to Inductive Logic 1966, Causal Necessity 1980, Pragmatics and Empiricism 1984, The Dynamics of Rational Deliberation 1990, Evolution of the Social Contract 1996, The Stag Hunt and the Evolution of the Social Structure 2004, Signals: Evolution, Learning and Information 2010; ed. or co-ed. seven books; numerous articles in learned journals. *Address:* School of Social Sciences, Office 767 SST, 3151 Social Science Plaza, University of California, Irvine, Irvine, CA 92697-5100, USA (office). *Telephone:* (949) 824-6495 (office). *Fax:* (949) 824-2379 (office). *E-mail:* bskyrms@uci.edu (office). *Website:* www .humanities.uci.edu/philosophy (office).

SLACK, Paul Alexander, DPhil, DLitt, FBA; British historian and academic; *Professor Emeritus of Early Modern Social History, University of Oxford;* b. 23 Jan. 1943, Bradford, Yorks., England; s. of Isaac Slack and Helen Slack (née Firth); m. Diana Gillian Manby 1965 (deceased); two d.; ed Bradford Grammar School, St John's Coll., Oxford; Jr Research Fellow, Balliol Coll., Oxford 1966–69; Lecturer in History, York Univ. 1969–72; Fellow and Tutor in Modern History, Exeter Coll., Oxford 1973–96, Reader in Modern History, Univ. of Oxford 1990–96, Chair. Gen. Bd of Faculties 1995–96, Prin., Linacre Coll. Oxford 1996–2010, Prof. of Early Modern Social History, Univ. of Oxford 1999–2010, Prof. Emer. 2010–, Pro-Vice-Chancellor 1997–2000, Pro-Vice-Chancellor (Academic Services) 2000–05. *Publications:* The Impact of Plague in Tudor and Stuart England 1985, Poverty and Policy in Tudor and Stuart England 1988, The English Poor Law 1531–1782 1990, From Reformation to Improvement: Public Welfare in Early Modern England 1999. *Leisure interests:* opera, fell-walking. *Address:* Linacre College, Oxford, OX1 3JA, England (office). *Telephone:* (1865) 271650 (office). *Fax:* (1865) 271668 (office).

SLADE, Rt Hon. Sir Christopher John, Kt; British judge (retd); b. 2 June 1927, London; s. of the late George Penkivil Slade, KC and Mary A. A. Slade; m. Jane G. A. Buckley 1958; one s. three d.; ed Eton Coll. (Scholar) and New Coll., Oxford (Scholar); called to Bar 1951, QC 1965; in practice at Chancery Bar 1951–75; Judge, High Court of Justice, Chancery Div. 1975–82; Judge of Restrictive Practices Court 1980–82, Pres. 1981–82; Lord Justice of Appeal 1982–91; mem. Gen. Council of Bar 1958–62, 1965–69; mem. Senate of Four Inns of Court 1966–69; Bencher, Lincoln's Inn 1973; mem. Lord Chancellor's Legal Educ. Cttee 1969–71; Treas. Lincoln's Inn 1994. *Leisure interests:* multifarious. *Address:* 40 Rivermead Court, Ranelagh Gardens, London, SW6 3RX, England (home). *Telephone:* (20) 7731-0938 (home). *E-mail:* slade151@talktalk.net (home).

SLADE, Tuiloma Neroni, LLB; Samoan lawyer, diplomatist and judge; *Secretary-General, Pacific Islands Forum;* b. 8 April 1941; m.; two d.; ed Hague Acad. of Int. Law; qualified as solicitor and barrister, worked in law practice in Wellington, NZ 1967–68; legal counsel, Office of Attorney-Gen., Wellington 1969–73; Parl. Counsel 1973–75; Head of Del. UN Conf. on the Law of the Sea 1973–76; Attorney-Gen. of Western Samoa 1976–82, also Chief Justice for periods between 1980–82; Asst Dir Legal Div. Commonwealth Secr., London 1983–93; Amb. to USA 1993–2003, also Perm. Rep. to the UN, New York and High Commr to Canada; Chair. Alliance of Small Island States 1997–2003; Leader, Samoan del. to Preparatory Comm. for Int. Criminal Court, New York 1999–2002; Distinguished Diplomat in Residence, Temple Univ., Philadelphia 2003; Judge, Int. Criminal Court 2003–06; Sec.-Gen. Pacific Islands Forum 2008–; Chair. first S Pacific Law Conf. 1986; legal consultant S Pacific Forum Fisheries Agency 1989; UNITAR Fellowship, Hague Acad. of Int. Law and UN Legal Office; Order of Samoa (Poloaiga Sili a Samoa) 2005. *Address:* Office of the Secretary General, Pacific Islands Forum Secretariat, Private Mail Bag, Suva, Fiji (office). *Telephone:* 3312600 (office). *Fax:* 3220230 (office). *E-mail:* info@forumsec.org.fj (office). *Website:* www.forumsec.org (office).

SLAKTERIS, Atis; Latvian agricultural engineer and politician; b. 21 Nov. 1956, Code Pagasts, Bauska Dist; m.; two c.; ed Latvian Acad. of Agric., Univ. of Minnesota, USA; began career as mechanic, later Chief Engineer Code Co. 1980–89; First Deputy Man. Bauskas Lauktehnika (state-owned co.) 1989–90; Chief Engineer, Bauska Agric. Dept 1990–94, Head, Agric. Consultation Bureau 1994–96; Minister of State for Cooperation, Ministry of Agric. 1996–97; mem. 7th Saeima 1998–2002, serving as Chair. Cttee on Economy, Agricultural Environ-ment and Regional Policies 1998–99, Chair. Cttee on Privatisation 1999–2000; Parl. Sec., Ministry of Agric. 2000, Minister for Agric. 2000–02; Chair. People's Party 2002–08; Minister of Defence 2004, 2006–07, of Finance 2007–09. *Address:* c/o People's Party, Dzirnavu iela 68, Rīga 1919, Latvia.

SLANEY, Sir Geoffrey, Kt, KBE, MSc, ChM, FRCS; British surgeon (retd) and academic; *Professor Emeritus of Surgery, Queen Elizabeth Hospital, Birmingham;* b. 19 Sept. 1922, West Hallam; s. of Richard Slaney and Gladys L. Slaney; m. Josephine M. Davy 1956; one s. two d.; ed Univs of Birmingham, London and

Illinois; House Surgeon and Surgical Registrar, Gen. Hosp., Birmingham 1947–48; Capt., RAMC 1948–50; Surgical Registrar, Coventry, London and Hackney Hosps 1950–53; Surgical Registrar, Lecturer in Surgery and Surgical Research Fellow, Queen Elizabeth Hosp., Birmingham 1953–59; Hunterian Prof., Royal Coll. of Surgeons 1961–62; Prof. of Surgery, Univ. of Birmingham 1966–87; Barling Prof., Head Dept of Surgery, Queen Elizabeth Hosp., Birmingham 1971–86, now Emer.; Pres. Royal Coll. of Surgeons of England 1982–86, James IV Asscn Surgeons 1984–87, Int. Surgical Group 1985–86, Vascular Surgical Soc. 1974–75; Chair. Asscn Profs of Surgery 1979–81, Confed. of Royal Colls and Faculties in the UK 1984–86; Fellow, Asscn of Surgeons of GB and Ireland, American Surgical Asscn; Hon. Consulting Surgeon, United Birmingham Hosps and Regional Hosp. Bd 1959–, Royal Prince Alfred Hosp., Sydney 1981–; Hon. Consulting Surgeon Emer., City of London and Hackney Health Authority 1983–; Hon. FRACS, FACS, FRCA, FCSSL, FCSSA; Hon. Fellow, Royal Coll. of Surgeons in Ireland, Royal Coll. of Surgeons of Canada; Jacksonian Prize and Medal, Royal Coll. of Surgeons 1959, Pybus Memorial Medal 1978, Miles Memorial Medal 1984, Vanderbilt Univ. Medal 1987, Brooke Medal, Ileostomy Asscn of GB and Ireland 1990. *Publications:* Metabolic Derangements in Gastrointestinal Surgery (with B. N. Brooke) 1967, Cancer of the Large Bowel (co-author) 1991; numerous contribs to medical and surgical journals. *Leisure interests:* family, fishing. *Address:* 3 Mason's View, Laugherne Park, Martley, Worcs., WR6 6RQ, England (home). *Telephone:* (1886) 887890 (home).

SLATER, Christian; American actor; b. (Christian Michael Leonard Hawkins), 18 Aug. 1969, New York City; s. of Michael Gainsborough and Mary Jo Slater; m. Ryan Haddon 2000 (divorced 2006); one s. one d.; ed LaGuardia High School of Music, Art and Performing Arts; appeared at age of seven in TV series One Life to Live; professional stage debut at age of nine in touring production of The Music Man. *Stage appearances include:* Macbeth, David Copperfield, Merlin, Landscape of the Body, Side Man, One Flew Over the Cuckoo's Nest (Edinburgh Festival then Gielgud Theatre, London, Garrick Theatre, London 2006) (Theatregoers' Choice Award for Best Actor 2005) 2004–05, The Glass Menagerie (Ethel Barrymore Theatre, Broadway) 2005, Swimming with Sharks (Vaudeville Theatre, London) 2007. *Television appearances include:* Sherlock Holmes (film) 1981, Living Proof: The Hank Williams Jr. Story (film) 1983, The Haunted Mansion Mystery (film) 1983, Ryan's Hope (series) 1975, Secrets (film) 1986, Desperate for Love (film) 1989, Merry Christmas, George Bailey 1997, Prehistoric Planet (series) 2002, The West Wing (series) 2003, 2004, A Light Knight's Odyssey (film) 2004. *Films include:* The Legend of Billie Jean 1985, The Name of the Rose 1986, Twisted 1986, Tucker: The Man and his Dream 1988, Gleaming the Cube 1989, Heathers 1989, Beyond the Stars 1989, The Wizard 1989, Tales from the Darkside: The Movie 1990, Young Guns II: Blaze of Glory 1990, Pump up the Volume 1990, Robin Hood: Prince of Thieves 1991, Mobsters 1991, Star Trek VI: The Undiscovered Country 1991, Kuffs 1992, Ferngully: The Last Rainforest 1992, Where the Day Takes You 1992, Untamed Heart 1993, True Romance 1993, Jimmy Hollywood 1994, Interview with a Vampire 1994, Murder in the First 1995, Bed of Roses 1996, Broken Arrow 1996, Austin Powers: International Man of Mystery 1997, Julian Po 1997, Hard Rain (also prod.) 1998, Basil (also co-prod.) 1998, Very Bad Things (also prod.) 1998, Love Stinks 1999, The Contender 2000, 3000 Miles to Graceland 2001, Who is Cletis Tout? 2001, Run for the Money 2002, Windtalkers 2002, Masked and Anonymous 2003, The Good Shepherd 2004, Mindhunters 2004, Churchill: The Hollywood Years 2004, Pursued 2004, Alone in the Dark 2005, The Deal (also prod.) 2005, Hollow Man II 2006, Bobby 2006, Slipstream 2007, He Was a Quiet Man 2007, The Ten Commandments 2007, Igor (voice) 2008, Playback 2012. *Address:* c/o CAA, 9830 Wilshire Blvd., Beverly Hills, CA 90212, USA.

SLATER, Douglas, BSc, MD; St Vincent and the Grenadines physician and politician; b. 19 Aug. 1955, Clare Valley; m. Sherian Slater; two c.; ed Univ. of the West Indies, Univ. of Havana, Cuba; worked in medicine in Guyana, Jamaica and St Vincent and the Grenadines; Medical Officer of Health (Dir of Primary Health Care Service) 1994–98; Minister of Health and Environment –2010, of Foreign Affairs, Foreign Trade and Consumer Affairs 2010–13. *Address:* c/o Ministry of Foreign Affairs, Administrative Bldg, 3rd Floor, Bay St, Kingstown, St Vincent and the Grenadines.

SLATER, James (Jim) Derrick, FCA; British company director and author; b. 13 March 1929, Wirral, Cheshire; s. of Hubert Slater and Jessica Slater; m. Helen Wyndham Goodwin 1965; two s. two d.; ed Preston Manor County School; Dir, AEC Ltd 1959; Deputy Sales Dir, Leyland Motor Corpn 1963; acquired (with assocs) H. Lotery and Co., Ltd, later renamed Slater, Walker Securities Ltd, and apptd Chair. and Man. Dir 1964–72, Chair., CEO 1972–75; Dir, BLMC 1969–75; Chair., Salar Properties Ltd 1983. *Publications:* Return to Go (autobiog.) 1977; on investment: The Zulu Principle 1992, Investment Made Easy 1994, Pep Up Your Wealth 1994, Beyond the Zulu Principle 1996, How to Became a Millionaire 2000; children's books: Goldenrod, Goldenrod and the Kidnappers, Grasshopper and the Unwise Owl, The Boy Who Saved Earth, A. Mazing Monsters, Grasshopper and the Pickle Factory 1979, Roger the Robot Series 1980, Grasshopper and the Poisoned River 1981. *Leisure interests:* chess, backgammon, bridge, salmon fishing. *Address:* Field House, Smithwood Common, Cranleigh, Surrey, GU6 8QU, England (home). *Website:* www.jimslater.org.uk.

SLATER, Adm. Sir Jock (John Cunningham Kirkwood), Kt, GCB, LVO, DL; British naval officer; b. 27 March 1938, Edinburgh, Scotland; s. of James K. Slater, OBE, MD, FRCPE and M. C. B. Slater (née Bramwell); m. Ann Frances Scott 1972; two s.; ed Edinburgh Acad., Sedbergh School, Royal Naval Coll. Dartmouth; Lt, HMS Soberton 1965; Lt Commdr, Equerry to HM The Queen 1968–71; Commdr HMS Jupiter 1972–73; Capt., HMS Kent 1976–77; with Royal Coll. of Defence Studies 1978; Capt. HMS Illustrious 1981–83; Capt. School of Maritime Oper-ations, HMS Dryad 1983–85; Rear Adm., Asst Chief of Defence Staff 1985–87; Flag Officer, Scotland, NI, Naval Base Commdr Rosyth 1987–89; Vice-Adm., Chief of Fleet Support 1989–91; Adm., C-in-C of Fleet, Allied C-in-C Channel and Eastern Atlantic 1991–92; Vice-Chief of Defence Staff 1993–95, Chief of Naval Staff and First Sea Lord 1995–98; Dir Vosper Thornycroft Holdings 1999–2004; Dir and Sr Mil. Adviser to Lockheed Martin (UK) Ltd 1999–2008; consultant, Bristow Helicopters Ltd 2001–04; Chair. Imperial War Museum 2001–06, RN Club 1765–1785 2001–04, White Ensign Asscn 2002–05, Royal Nat. Lifeboat Inst. 2004–08; Pres. American Air Museum in Britain 2001–06, RN&RM Charity

2008–11, RM Asscn Concert Band 2007, Droxford and Dist Br. RBL 1999; Gov. Sedbergh School 1997–2002; DL Hants. 1999; Freeman of the City of London 1989; Elder Brother, Trinity House 1995; Prime Warden, Worshipful Co. of Shipwrights 2011–12; Commdr, US Legion of Merit 1997; Hon. DSc (Cranfield) 1998, (Univ. of Southampton) 2008; Sword of Honour and The Queen's Telescope, BRNC Dartmouth 1958, Cheetham Hill Memorial Prize, HMS Dryad 1966. *Achievements:* mem. Nat. Youth Orchestra 1955. *Publications:* articles in professional publs. *Leisure interest:* outdoor. *Address:* c/o Naval Secretary, Leach Building, Whale Island, Portsmouth, Hants., PO2 8BY, England. *E-mail:* jock.slater@talk21.com.

SLATER, Kelly; American professional surfer; b. (Robert Kelly Slater), 11 Feb. 1972, Cocoa Beach, Fla; s. of the late Steve Slater and of Judy Slater; one d.; joined professional surfing ranks in 1990; 11 times ASP World Champion 1992 (age 21, youngest ever), 1994, 1995, 1996, 1997, 1998, 2005, 2006, 2008, 2010, 2011; Winner, Mountain Dew Pipe Master, Hawaii 1999, Gotcha Tahiti Pro, Tahiti 2000, The Quiksilver, Hawaii 2002, Billabong Pro, Tahiti 2003, 2005, 2011, Billabong Pro, South Africa 2003, 2005, Billabong Pro Mundaka, Spain 2003, Nova Schin Festival, Brazil 2003, Snickers Australian Open 2004, Energy Australia Open 2004, The Globe WCT, Fiji 2005, Boost Mobile Pro, Calif. 2005, 2007, 2008, Quiksilver Pro, Australia 2006, 2008, 2011, Rip Curl Pro, Australia 2006, 2008, 2010, Glove Pro, Fiji 2008, Billabong Pro J-Bay, South Africa 2008, Billabong Pipeline Masters, Hawaii 2008, Hang Loose Pro, Brazil 2009, Hurley Pro, Calif. 2010, 2011, Rip Curl Pro, Portugal 2010, Rip Curl Search, Puerto Rico 2010, Nike US Open, Calif. 2011; first surfer ever to be awarded two perfect scores for a total 20 out of 20 points under the ASP two-wave scoring system 2005; most successful champion in the history of the sport; starred in TV series Baywatch early 1990s and in numerous surf movies; inspiration for Kelly Slater Pro Surfer video game; Laureus World Action Sportsperson of the Year 2012. *Leisure interests:* golf, fishing, music, playing the guitar. *Address:* c/o Shelby Meade, Fresh and Clean Media, 12701 Venice Boulevard, Los Angeles, CA 90066, USA (office). *Telephone:* (310) 313-7200 (office). *Fax:* (310) 313-0277 (office). *E-mail:* shelby@ freshcleanmedia.com (office). *Website:* www.freshcleanmedia.com (office); www .kellyslater.com.

SLATER, Rodney E., BS, JD; American lawyer and fmr government official; *Partner, Patton Boggs LLP;* b. 23 Feb. 1955, Tutwyler, Miss.; m. Cassandra Wilkins; one c.; ed Eastern Mich. Univ., Univ. of Arkansas; Asst Attorney-Gen., Ark. 1980–82; Special Asst to Gov. of Ark. for community and minority affairs 1983–85, Exec. Asst for econ. and community programs 1985–87, Dir Intergovernmental Relations Ark. State Univ. 1987–93; Admin. Fed. Highway Admin. US Dept of Transportation, Washington, DC 1993–97; US Sec. of Transportation 1997–2001; Ark. Liaison Martin Luther King Jr Fed. Holiday Comm. 1983–87; Pnr Patton Boggs LLP (law firm) 2001–; mem. Ark. Sesquicentennial Comm. 1986, Ark. State Highway and Transportation Comm. 1987–93, Chair. 1992–93; Pres. W. Harold Flowers Law Soc. 1985–92; Sec., Treasurer Ark. Bar Asscn 1989–93; Deputy Campaign Man., Sr Travelling Adviser Clinton for Pres. Campaign 1992; Deputy then Chair. Clinton/Gore Transition Team 1992–93; mem. Bd of Dirs Africane 2001–, Jt Center for Political and Econ. Studies 2001–. *Address:* Patton Boggs LLP, 2550 M Street, NW, Washington, DC 20037, USA (office). *Telephone:* (202) 457-5265 (office). *Fax:* (202) 457-6315 (office). *E-mail:* rslater@pattonboggs .com (office). *Website:* www.pattonboggs.com/rslater (office).

SLATKIN, Leonard Edward; American conductor and pianist; *Music Director, Detroit Symphony Orchestra;* b. 1 Sept. 1944, Los Angeles; s. of Felix Slatkin and Eleanor Aller; m. 4th Cindy McTee 2011; one s. from previous marriage; ed Indiana Univ., Los Angeles City Coll., Juilliard School; studied violin, piano, viola, composition, conducting; debut Carnegie Hall 1966; founder, Music Dir and Conductor St Louis Symphony Youth Orchestra 1979–80, 1980–81; Asst Conductor Youth Symphony of New York, Carnegie Hall 1966, Juilliard Opera, Theater and Dance Dept 1967, St Louis Symphony Orchestra 1968–71, Assoc. Conductor 1971–74, Prin. Guest Conductor Minn. Orchestra 1974–, Summer Artistic Dir 1979–80; Music Dir New Orleans Philharmonic Symphony Orchestra 1977–78; Music Dir Nat. Symphony Orchestra, Washington, DC 1996–2008; Prin. Conductor BBC Symphony Orchestra 2000–04; Prin. Guest Conductor Royal Philharmonic Orchestra 2005–, Pittsburgh Symphony Orchestra 2008–; Music Dir Detroit Symphony Orchestra 2008–; Music Dir Orchestre National de Lyon 2011–; guest conductor with orchestras worldwide, including most major US orchestras, Montréal, Toronto, Vienna, Vienna State Opera, London Symphony, London Philharmonia, English Chamber, Concertgebouw, Royal Danish, Stockholm, Scottish Nat., NHK Tokyo, Israel, Berlin, Stuttgart Opera; festivals include Tanglewood, Blossom, Mann Music Center, Mostly Mozart and Saratoga; five hon. degrees; four Grammy Awards. *Address:* Columbia Artists' Management Inc., 1790 Broadway, New York, NY 10019-1412, USA (office); Detroit Symphony Orchestra, Max M. Fisher Music Center, 3711 Woodward Avenue, Detroit, MI 48201, USA (office). *Telephone:* (212) 841-9512 (office). (313) 576-511 (office). *Fax:* (212) 841-9734 (office). (313) 576-5109 (office). *E-mail:* info@cami.com (office). *Website:* www.cami.com (office); www .detroitsymphony.com (office); www.leonardslatkin.com.

SLAVESKI, Trajko, PhD; Macedonian politician and academic; b. 1960, Ohrid; m.; two c.; ed SS Cyril and Methodius Univ., Skopje, State Univ. of Calif. and Harvard Univ., USA; Prof., Econs Faculty, SS Cyril and Methodius Univ., Skopje; Visiting Prof., Arizona State Univ., USA 1997, Nat. and Capodistrian Univ., Athens, Greece 1999–; Minister of Devt 1999–2000; Adviser to Minister of Finance and Nat. Co-ordinator for Poverty Reduction Strategy 2000–02; mem. Parl. 2006–; Minister of Finance 2006–09; mem. Exec. Cttee Internal Macedonian Revolutionary Org.-Democratic Party for Macedonian Nat. Unity (VMRO-DPMNE) 2003–, Vice-Pres. 2005–. *Address:* c/o Ministry of Finance, 1000 Skopje, Dame Gruev 14, Former Yugoslav Republic of Macedonia. *Telephone:* (2) 3117288. *E-mail:* finance@ finance.gov.mk. *Website:* www.finance.gov.mk.

SLAVITT, David Rytman, (David Benjamin, Henry Lazarus, Lynn Meyer, Henry Sutton), MA; American writer, poet, translator and academic; b. 23 March 1935, White Plains, NY; s. of Samuel Slavitt and Adele Slavitt; m. 1st Lynn Meyer 1956 (divorced 1977); two s. one d.; m. 2nd Janet Lee Abrahm 1978; ed Yale and Columbia Univs; Instructor in English, Georgia Inst. of Tech., Atlanta 1957–58; writer, Assoc. Ed., Newsweek 1958–65; Visiting Lecturer, Univ. of Maryland 1977; Visiting Assoc. Prof., Temple Univ. 1978–80; Lecturer in English and Comparative

Literature, Columbia Univ. 1985–86; teacher of creative writing, Rutgers Univ. 1987; Lecturer in English and Classics, Univ. of Pennsylvania 1991–97; Visiting Lecturer in Creative Writing, Princeton Univ. 1996; Lecturer in English, Bennington Coll. 2000; Assoc. Fellow, Trumbull Coll., Yale Univ.; has lectured widely at US univs and other academic insts; Pennsylvania Council on the Arts Award 1985, Nat. Endowment for Arts Fellowship in Translation 1988, Nat. Acad. and Inst. of Arts and Letters Award 1989, Rockefeller Foundation Artist's Residence, Bellagio 1989, Umhoefer Award in the Humanities 2007, Kevin Kline Theater Award 2010. *Publications include:* fiction: Rochelle, or Virtue Rewarded 1967, King Saul (play) 1967, Feel Free 1968, The Cardinal Sins (play) 1969, Anagrams 1970, ABCD 1972, The Outer Mongolian 1973, The Killing of the King 1974, King of Hearts 1976, Jo Stern 1978, Cold Comfort 1980, Ringer 1982, Alice at 80 1984, The Agent 1986, The Hussar 1987, Salazar Blinks 1988, Lives of the Saints 1990, Short Stories Are Not Real Life 1991, Turkish Delights 1993, The Cliff 1994, Get Thee to a Nunnery: Two Divertimentos from Shakespeare 1999, Aspects of the Novel: A Novel 2003, The Duke's Man 2011; as Henry Sutton: The Exhibitionist 1967, The Voyeur 1968, Vector 1970, The Liberated 1973, The Proposal 1980; as Lynn Meyer: Paperback Thriller 1975; as Henry Lazarus: That Golden Woman 1976; as David Benjamin: The Idol 1979; poetry: Suits for the Dead 1961, The Carnivore 1965, Day Sailing 1968, Child's Play 1972, Vital Signs: New and Selected Poems 1975, Rounding the Horn 1978, Dozens 1981, Big Nose 1983, Adrien Stoutenburg: Land of Superior Mirages: New and Selected Poems (ed.) 1986, The Walls of Thebes 1986, Equinox 1989, Eight Longer Poems 1990, Crossroads 1994, A Gift 1996, Epic and Epigram 1997, A New Pléiade: Seven American Poets 1998, PS3569.L3 1998, Falling from Silence: Poems 2001, Change of Address: Poems, New and Selected 2005, William Henry Harrison and Other Poems 2006, Seven Deadly Sins 2009; non-fiction: Understanding Social Life: An Introduction to Social Psychology (with Paul F. Secord and Carl W. Backman) 1976, Physicians Observed 1987, Virgil 1991, The Persians of Aeschylus 1998, Three Amusements of Ausonius 1998, The Book of Lamentations 2001, Re Verse: Essays on Poets and Poetry 2005; translator: The Eclogues of Virgil 1971, The Eclogues and the Georgics of Virgil 1972, The Tristia of Ovid 1985, Ovid's Poetry of Exile 1990, Seneca: The Tragedies 1992, The Fables of Avianus 1993, The Metamorphoses of Ovid 1994, The Twelve Minor Prophets 1999, The Voyage of the Argo of Valerius Flaccus 1999, Sonnets of Love and Death of Jean de Sponde 2001, The Elegies of Propertius 2001, The Poetry of Manuel Bandeira 2002, The Regrets of Joachim du Bellay 2004, The Phoenix and Other Translations 2004, Re Verse: Essays on Poets and Poetry 2005, Blue State Blues: A Republican in Cambridge 2006, William Henry Harrison and Other Poems 2006, Sophocles' Theban Plays 2007, De Rerum Natura of Lucretius 2008, Boethius' Consolation of Philosophy 2008, Ludovico Ariosto's Orlando Furioso 2009, George Sanders, Zsa Zsa, and Me: Essays on the Movies 2009, Dante's Vita Nuova 2010, The Latin Eclogues of Giovanni Boccaccio 2010, Poems from the Greek Anthology 2010, The Gnat and other minor poems of Virgin 2011, The Latin Poems of John Milton 2011, The Love Letters, Poems, and Remedies of Ovid 2011, The Sonnets and Short Poems of Petrarch 2012, The Poetry of Guido Cavalcanti 2012; contrib. of book reviews, articles in journals and magazines. *Address:* 35 West Street, #5, Cambridge, MA 02139, USA. *Telephone:* (617) 497-1219. *E-mail:* drslavitt@comcast.net.

SLEEP, Wayne, OBE; British dancer, actor and choreographer; b. 17 July 1948, Plymouth; ed Royal Ballet School (Leverhulme Scholar); joined Royal Ballet 1966, Soloist 1970, Prin. 1973; roles in: Giselle, Dancers at a Gathering, The Nutcracker, Romeo and Juliet, The Grand Tour, Elite Syncopations, Swan Lake, The Four Seasons, Les Patineurs, Petroushka (title role), Cinderella, The Dream, Pineapple Poll, Mam'zelle Angot, 4th Symphony, La Fille Mal Gardée, A Month in the Country, A Good Night's Sleep, Coppelia; also roles in operas: A Midsummer Night's Dream, Aida; choreography and lead role, The Point: co-starred in Song and Dance 1982, 1990, Cabaret 1986; f. DASH co. 1980; dancer and jt choreographer, Bits and Pieces 1989; numerous TV appearances including series The Hot Shoe Show 1983, 1984; Show Business Personality of the Year 1983. *Films include:* The Virgin Soldiers, The First Great Train Robbery, The Tales of Beatrix Potter. *Theatre includes:* Ariel in the Tempest, title role in Pinocchio, Genie in Aladdin, Soldier in The Soldier's Tale, Truffaldino in the Servant of Two Masters, Mr Mistoffelees in Cats. *Publications:* Variations on Wayne Sleep 1983, Precious Little Sleep (autobiog.) 1996. *Leisure interest:* entertaining. *Address:* c/o Nick Thomas Artists, Event House, Queen Margaret's Road, Scarborough, YO11 2SA; 22 Queensberry Mews West, London, SW7 2DY, England. *Telephone:* (1723) 500038.

SLEIMAN, Gen. Michel, BA; Lebanese politician, fmr army commander and head of state; *President;* b. 21 Nov. 1948, Amchit; m. Wafaa Sleiman; three c.; ed Lebanese Univ.; Chief Intelligence Br., Mount Lebanon 1990–91; Army Staff Sec.-Gen. 1991–93; Commdr 11th Infantry Brigade 1993–96, Sixth Infantry Brigade 1996–98; Commdr Lebanese Armed Forces 1998–2008; Pres. of Lebanon 2008–; Kt and Grand Cordon, Nat. Order of the Cedar; Lebanese Order of Merit (First, Second, Third and Extraordinary Grades); Grade of Excellence, Syrian Order of Merit; Collar of King Abdul Aziz; Grand Cross, Italian Order of Merit; Collar of Moubarak the Great; Khalifite Collar, Zayed Order; Oman Mil. Order; Grand Croix, Légion d'honneur; Collar, Nat. Order of the Star of Romania; Collar, Order of Isabella the Catholic; Collar, Order 'Pro Merito Melitensi'; Collar, Order of Makarios III; Grand Collar, Nat. Order of the Southern Cross; Grand Cordon, Nat. Order of Umayya; Qatari Necklace of Independence; Kt Grand Cross, Order of St Charles; Grand Cross, Order of Rio Branco, Armenian Order of Honour; Grand Star, Decoration of Honour; Grand Cross, Order of the Redeemer; Grand Cross, Nat. Order of the Lion, Grand Cross, Nat. Order of Ivory Coast; Medal of War, Medal of Nat. Unity, Medal of Mil. Pride (Silver), Medal of Mil. Valour (Silver), Medal of Honour of the Arab Fed. for Mil. Sports, Medal of the Pres. of Repub. of Ukraine, Medal of the Defence Ministry of Fed. Repub. of Russia, Mil. Medal, Medal of Internal Security, Medal of General Security, Medal of State Security, Medal of the Dawn of South, Commemorative Medal of Confs 2002, Prize of HH Patriarch Alexey II 2012. *Address:* Presidential Palace, Baabda, Lebanon (office). *Telephone:* (5) 900900 (office). *Fax:* (5) 900919 (office). *E-mail:* president_office@ presidency.gov.lb (office). *Website:* www.presidency.gov.lb (office).

ŠLESERS, Ainārs; Latvian politician; b. 22 Jan. 1970, Rīga; m.; two c.; ed Rīga Secondary School No. 25, Rīga Industrial Polytechnics, Christian Folk Coll., Norway, Latvian Christian Acad.; Pres. Latvian-Norwegian jt venture Latvian

Information and Commerce Centre, Norway 1992–96; Pres. Skandi Ltd 1993–96; Dir Gen. Varner Baltija Ltd 1994–98; Chair. Bd and Pres. JSC Supermarket Centres 1995–96, 1996–98; Dir Gen. Rimi Baltija Ltd 1996–97, Varner Hakon Invest Ltd 1996–98; mem. Saeima (Parl.) Oct.–Nov. 1998, 1999–2002, 2002–; Minister for Econs 1998–99; Deputy Prime Minister Nov. 2002–Jan. 2004, March–Dec. 2004; Minister of Transport 2004–09; Vice-Mayor of Rīga 2009–10; mem. Bd Latvian First Party (LPP) 2002–; mem. Bd Baltic Stability Fund 1996–; mem. Bd 'For Spiritual Renaissance in Latvia' 2001–. *Address:* c/o Ministry of Transport, Gogoļa iela 3, Rīga 1743, Latvia.

ŠLEŽEVIČIUS, Adolfas; Lithuanian politician and consultant; b. 2 Feb. 1948, Mirčiškės, Šiauliai Co.; ed Acad. of Nat. Econ., USSR Council of Ministers; Sr Engineer-Constructor, Chief Mechanic, Chief Engineer, Kaunas dairy factory 1971–77; Vice-Minister of Dairy and Meat Industry of Lithuania 1977–81; Chair. dairy production enterprise Pienocentras 1989–90; Vice-Minister of Agric. 1990–91; Pres. Lithuanian-Norwegian Jt Venture C. Olsen-Baltic 1991–93; Pres. Lithuanian Dairy Producers Asscn 1992–; mem. Democratic Labour Party; Prime Minister of Lithuania 1993–96, resgnd following corruption scandals; consultant to pvt. cos, including ATB-West. *Address:* c/o ATB-West, Rudaminos str. 1A, Vilnius 13275, Lithuania. *Telephone:* (5) 235-11-74. *Fax:* (5) 235-11-79. *E-mail:* info@atb-west.lt. *Website:* www.atb-west.lt.

SLICHTER, Charles Pence, AB, MA, PhD; American physicist and academic; *Research Professor of Physics and Center for Advanced Study Professor Emeritus of Physics and Chemistry, University of Illinois;* b. 21 Jan. 1924, Ithaca, NY; s. of Sumner Huber Slichter and Ada Pence Slichter; m. 1st Gertrude Thayer Almy 1952 (divorced 1977); three s. one d.; m. 2nd Anne FitzGerald 1980; two s.; ed Browne and Nichols School, Cambridge, Mass. and Harvard Univ.; Instructor, Univ. of Illinois 1949–51, Asst Prof. of Physics 1951–54, Assoc. Prof. 1954–55, Prof. of Physics 1955–97, mem. Center for Advanced Study, Univ. of Illinois 1968–, Prof. of Chem. 1986–97, Center for Advanced Study Prof. Emer. of Physics and Chem. 1997–, Research Prof. of Physics 1997–; mem. Bd of Dirs Polaroid Corpn 1975–97; Morris Loeb Lecturer, Harvard Univ. 1961; mem. Pres.'s Science Advisory Cttee 1965–69, Cttee on the Nat. Medal of Science 1969–74, Pres.'s Cttee on Science and Tech. 1976; Alfred Sloan Fellow 1957–63; mem. Corpn of Harvard Univ. 1970–95; mem. Comm. on Physical Sciences, Math. and Applications, Nat. Research Council 1993–96; Fellow, American Physical Soc., Int. EPR (ESR) Soc. 1998; mem. NAS, American Acad. of Arts and Sciences, American Philosophical Soc., Nat. Science Bd 1975–84; mem. Int. Soc. of Magnetic Resonance (ISMAR), Vice-Pres. 1983–86, Pres. 1987–90; Hon. mem. Corpn, Woods Hole Oceanographic Inst.; Hon. DSc (Waterloo) 1993, (Leipzig) 2010; Hon. LLD (Harvard) 1996; Langmuir Prize of American Physical Soc. 1969, ISMAR Triennial Prize 1986, Comstock Prize, NAS 1993, Buckley Prize, American Physical Soc. 1996, Nat. Medal of Science 2007, and other awards. *Publications:* Principles of Magnetic Resonance 1963, 1978, 1989, 1990, 1996; articles on solid state physics, chemical physics and magnetic resonance. *Address:* 311 Loomis Laboratory, Department of Physics, Univ. of Illinois at Urbana-Champaign, 1110 West Green Street, Urbana, IL 61801-3080 (office); 61 Chestnut Court, Champaign, IL 61822, USA (home). *Telephone:* (217) 333-3834 (office); (217) 352-8255 (home). *Fax:* (217) 244-7559 (office). *E-mail:* cslichte@illinois.edu (office). *Website:* physics.illinois.edu/people/profile .asp?cslichte (office).

SLIM DOMIT, Carlos, BBA; Mexican business executive; *Co-Chairman, América Móvil SAB de CV;* b. 1967; eldest s. of Carlos Slim Helú; m. María Elena Torruco 2010; ed Universidad Anáhuac; mem. Bd of Dirs Grupo Carso 1991–, currently Chair.; mem. Bd of Dirs Teléfonos de Mexico (Telmex) (Chair.), Grupo Sanborns (Chair.), America Móvil SAB de CV (Co-Chair. 2013–), Group7, América Telecom, Carso Global Telecom, US Commercial Corpn and some subsidiaries of Grupo Carso. *Address:* América Móvil SAB de CV, Lago Zurich No. 245 Edif. Telcel Piso 16, 11529 México DF, Mexico (office). *Telephone:* (55) 2581-3700 (office). *E-mail:* info@americamovil.com (office). *Website:* www.americamovil.com (office); www .carso.com.mx (office).

SLIM DOMIT, Patrick; Mexican telecommunications executive; *Co-Chairman, América Móvil SAB de CV;* b. 1969; s. of Carlos Slim Helú and Soumaya Domit; ed Univ. Anáhuac; Chair. América Móvil SAB de CV 2004–12, Co-Chair. (with Carlos Slim Domit) 2012–; Vice-Pres. Grupo Carso SAB de CV (fmr CEO); Vice-Chair. America Telecom –2004; fmr CEO Industrias Nacobre SAB de CV; Chair. Ferrosur SAB de CV; mem. Bd of Dirs Carso Global Telecom SAB de CV, Teléfonos de México SAB de CV (Telmex), Hoteles Calinda SAB de CV, Grupo Condumex SAB de CV, Empresas Frisco SAB de CV, Sears Roebuck de México SAB de CV, Cigarros La Tabacalera de México SAB de CV, Promotora Inbursa SAB de CV, Industrias Nacobre SAB de CV. *Address:* América Móvil SAB de CV, Lago Alberto 366, Colonia Anáhuac, 11320 Mexico DF, Mexico (office). *Telephone:* (55) 2581-3947 (office). *Fax:* (55) 2581-3948 (office). *E-mail:* info@americamovil.com (office). *Website:* www.americamovil.com (office).

SLIM HELÚ, Carlos; Mexican telecommunications industry executive and philanthropist; *Chairman, Teléfonos de México SA de C.V. (Telmex);* b. 28 Jan. 1940, Mexico City; s. of Julián Slim Haddad and Linda Helú; m. Soumaya Domit Gemayel (died 1999); six c.; ed Universidad Autónoma de México (UNAM); taught algebra and linear programming at UNAM while studying 1961; f. Grupo Carso 1961, expanded co. through series of acquisitions including Jarritos de Sur (bottling co.) 1970, Galas de México (cigarette manufacturer) 1976, Cigarrera La Moderna 1981, and many other cos, Chair. Teléfonos de México SA de C.V. (Telmex) 2002–, Grupo Financiero Inbursa, Hon. Lifetime Chair. Grupo Carso; Chair. Emer. América Móvil; fmr mem. Bd of Dirs Altria, SBC Communications –2004, Alcatel SA 2000–06; f. Fundación del Centro Histórico de la Ciudad de México A.C. 2000, Chair. Exec. Cttee for the Restoration of the Historic Centre 2001–; f. Instituto Carso para la Salud 2007; heads the Latin America Devt Fund project; mem. Exec. Bd RAND Corpn (Research and Devt) 2008–; Leopold II Commdr Medal (Belgium), Grand Officer, Nat. Order of the Cedar (Lebanon) 2008; Entrepreneurial Merit Medal of Honour, Mexican Chamber of Commerce 1985, CEO of the Year, Latin Trade magazine 2003, CEO of the Decade, Latin Trade magazine 2004, World Educ. and Devt Fund Award 2004, Alliance Award, Free Trade Alliance 2004, Hadrian Award, World Monuments Fund 2004, Real Estate Developers' Asscn Award 2004, Fashion Group Int. Prize for work in rescue of Historical Centre of Mexico City 2004, Galardon del Salon del Empresario,

Impulsa and Grupo Editorial Expansión 2006, Life Achievement Award, Worldwide Asscn of Mexicans Abroad (AMME) 2006, Golden Plate Award, American Acad. of Achievement 2007, Nat. Award to the Excellence Jaime Torres Bodet, Univ. Center Sun Group 2007, Industrialist of Year, Mexican Foundation for Health (Funsalud) 2007, recognized by Mexican Asscn of Professionals in Power of Attorney of Bottoms Chapter, Mexico City 2007, Man of the Year 2008, World Boxing Council 2009, ESADE award in recognition of his philanthropic and entrepreneurial management, ESADE Alumni, Barcelona 2009, George Washington Univ. Pres.'s Medal 2009, ranked by Forbes magazine amongst The World's Most Powerful People (sixth) 2009, (21st) 2010, (23rd) 2011, (11th) 2012, (12th) 2013. *Address:* Teléfonos de México SA de C.V., Parque Vía 190, Col Cuauhtémoc, 06599 México DF, Mexico (office). *Telephone:* (1) 5222-1212 (office). *Fax:* (1) 5545-5550 (office). *E-mail:* info@telmex.com.mx (office). *Website:* www.telmex.com.mx (office); www.carloslim.com.

SLIMANE, Hedi; French fashion designer, photographer and curator; *Creative Director, Saint Laurent Paris;* b. 5 July 1968, Paris; ed 'Hypokhagne' Prépa Sciences-Po, École du Louvre; discovered photography aged 11; began making own clothes aged 16; studied art history and completed a tailor apprenticeship at a men's design house; assisted fashion consultant Jean-Jacques Picart 1992–95; apptd ready-to-wear director of men's collections at Yves Saint Laurent 1996, later Artistic Dir; took up a residency at Kunst-Werke Inst. for Contemporary Art, Berlin 2000–02; Creative Dir for Dior Homme (menswear line of Christian Dior) 2000–07, in charge of launch of Dior Homme's first fragrance named Higher 2001; cr. stagewear for groups including The Libertines, Daft Punk, Franz Ferdinand and The Kills and artists including Mick Jagger, Beck, Jack White; returned to fashion and portrait photography 2007; Creative Dir for Saint Laurent Paris (fmrly Yves Saint Laurent) 2011–; CFDA Award for Int. Designer (first menswear designer) 2002. *Publications:* Intermission 1 2002, Berlin 2003, Stage 2004, London Birth of a Cult 2005, Interzone: The Hedi Slimane Book 2005, Portrait of a Performer: Courtney Love 2006, Costa Da Caparica 1989 (exhbn catalogue) 2007, Rock Diary 2008, American Youth (DVD box set) 2009, Anthology of a Decade 2011. *Address:* c/o Almine Rech Gallery, 19 rue Saintonge, 75003 Paris, France. *E-mail:* press@hedislimane.com (office). *Website:* www.hedislimane.com (office).

SLISKA, Lyubov Konstantinovna; Russian lawyer and politician; *First Deputy Chairman, State Duma;* b. 15 Oct. 1953, Saratov; m.; ed Saratov Inst. of Law; lawyer, Soyuzpechat Saratov 1977–89; on staff, regional trade cttee of heavy machine construction industry workers 1992–96; Perm. Rep. of Govt in Regional Duma, Deputy Chair. Regional Govt 1996–2000; mem. State Duma (Yedinstvo Movt List) 1999; First Deputy Chair. (Speaker) of State Duma 2000–; Order for Service to Motherland; Hon. PhD. *Leisure interests:* countryside, fishing. *Address:* State Duma, 103265 Moscow, Okhotny Ryad 1, Russia (office). *Telephone:* (495) 292-55-52 (office). *Fax:* (495) 292-86-00 (office). *E-mail:* sliska@duma.gov.ru (office). *Website:* www.duma.gov.ru (office).

SLIVA, Anatoly Yakovlevich, Cand.Jur.; Russian politician and judge; b. 10 Feb. 1940, Slavgorod, Belarus; m.; ed Moscow State Univ.; teacher and Dean, All-Union Juridical Inst. by correspondence; Sr Scientific Consultant, Deputy Head of Div. of local soviets, USSR Supreme Soviet 1988–92; Deputy Head of State Law Dept at Russian Presidency, concurrently Head of Div. on Interaction with Organs of Rep. and Exec. Power 1992–94; Official Rep. of Russian Pres. on legal problems to Supreme Soviet Russian Fed. 1992; mem. State Duma, Chair. Cttee on problems of local man. 1993–95; Rep. of Russian Pres. to Fed. Council 1996–98; Justice, Constitutional Court of Russian Fed. 1998–. *Address:* Constitutional Court, 103132, Moscow, Ilyinka str. 21, Russia. *Telephone:* (495) 206-92-25. *Website:* www .ksrf.ru.

SLONIMSKY, Sergey Michailovich, PhD; Russian composer, teacher and pianist; *Professor, St Petersburg Conservatoire;* b. 12 Aug. 1932, Leningrad (now St Petersburg); s. of Michail Slonimsky and Ida Slonimskaya (née Kaplan); m. Raisa Slonimskaya (née Zankisova) 1973; one s. one d.; ed Leningrad Conservatoire; mem. of Teaching Faculty, Music Theory and Composition, Leningrad (now St Petersburg) Conservatoire 1958–, Prof. 1976–; mem. Bd CIS Composers' Union (also mem. St Petersburg Br.); Cavalier of Commdr's Cross of Poland; RSFSR Glinka State Prize 1983, RSFSR People's Artist 1987, State Prize of Russia 2002. *Works include:* 13 symphonies 1958–2004, orchestral and vocal works, chamber works, opera, ballet, songs and choral pieces, including Carnival Overture 1957, Concerto Buffa, chamber orchestra 1966, Antiphones (string quartet) 1969, Virinea opera 1969, Icarus (ballet in three acts) 1973, Master and Margarita (chamber opera in three acts) 1970–85, Merry Songs for piccolo, flute and tuba 1971, Sonata for violoncello and piano 1986, Mary Stuart (opera performed at 1986 Edinburgh Festival, USSR and abroad), Hamlet (opera) 1990–94, Cerch: dell'Inferno secondo Dante 1992, 24 Preludes and Fugues for piano 1994, Ivan the Terrible 1994 (opera premiered at Samara 1998), 24 Preludes and Fugues for piano 1995, King Lear (opera after Shakespeare) 2001, The Magic Nut (ballet) 2005. *Recordings:* Requiem 2003, Magic Nut (ballet, libretto by Mihail Shemiakin) 2005. *Publications:* musicological study of Prokofiev's symphonies 1964, Burlesques, Elegies, Dithyrambs 2000, Free Dissonance 2005. *Leisure interest:* poetry, literature, painting. *Address:* St Petersburg Conservatoire of Music, 190000 St Petersburg, 3, Teatralnaya Square (office); 191186 St Petersburg, Canal Griboedova 9-97, Russia (home). *Telephone:* (812) 571-85-85 (home). *Fax:* (812) 571-58-11 (office). *E-mail:* sloh@rambler.ru (home). *Website:* eng.conservatory.ru (office).

SLOSAR, John Robert, BEcons; American airline industry executive; *Chairman, John Swire & Sons (HK) Ltd;* b. 1950, Ohio; ed Columbia Univ., Trinity Coll., Cambridge, UK; joined Swire Group (diversified group with interests in property, aviation, marine services, beverages, trade and industry) 1980, posted first to Thailand, then apptd Vice-Pres. for USA and Latin America, based in San Francisco, later Man. Dir, Hong Kong Aircraft Engineering Co. Ltd 1996–98, also Chair., Taikoo (Xiamen) Aircraft Engineering Co. (TAECO) 1996–98, Man. Dir, Swire Beverages Ltd 1998–2007, Chief Operating Officer, Cathay Pacific Airways Ltd 2007–11, also Chair., Swire Beverages, Hong Kong Dragon Airlines Ltd (Dragonair), CEO Cathay Pacific 2011–14, Chair. 2014–, also Chair. John Swire & Sons (HK) Ltd, Swire Pacific Ltd, Swire Properties Ltd, Hong Kong Aircraft Engineering Co. Ltd; mem. Bd of Dirs Swire Beverages 2006–, John Swire & Sons (HK) Ltd 2000–, Cathay Pacific Airways Ltd 2007–, Swire Pacific Ltd 2006–; Dir (non-exec.) Purecircle Ltd 2006–. *Address:* Cathay Pacific, One Pacific Place, 88 Queensway, Hong Kong Special Administrative Region, People's Republic of China (office). *Website:* www.swire.com (office).

SLOTA, Ján; Slovak engineer and politician; *President, Slovak National Party;* b. 14 Sept. 1953, Lietavská Lúčka; m.; three s. one d.; ed Faculty of Mining, Tech. Univ., Košice; Co-founder Slovak Nat. Party (SNS) 1990, Pres. 1994–99, 2003–; Mayor of Žilina 1990–2006; mem. Fed. Ass. of Czechoslovakia 1990–92; mem. Slovak Nat. Council –1992; mem. Parl. 2006–, mem. Cttee for Review of Decisions of Nat. Security Authority 2006–, Cttee on Human Rights, Minorities and Status of Women 2006–, Special Control Cttee of Activities of Slovak Intelligence Service 2006–; State Order of Andrej Hlinka (First Class), Cross of the Pres. (First Degree). *Address:* Slovak National Party (Slovenská národná strana), Šafárikovo nám. 3, 814 99 Bratislava, Slovakia (office). *Telephone:* (2) 5292-4260 (office). *Fax:* (2) 5296-6188 (office). *E-mail:* jan_slota@nrsr.sk (office); sns@sns.sk (office). *Website:* www .sns.sk (office).

SLOTOVER, Matthew, OBE; British publisher, entrepreneur and arts executive; *Director, Frieze Art Fairs;* b. 1968; s. of Robert Slotover and Jill Slotover; grandson of Richard Kravitz; m.; three c.; ed St Paul's School, London, Univ. of Oxford; first became interested in contemporary art after visiting Young British Artists art exhbn 'Modern Medicine' 1990; Co-Publr, with Amanda Sharp, Frieze magazine 1991–; Co-owner, with Amanda Sharp, Frieze Art Fair (int. contemporary art fair taking place annually in Oct.), Regent's Park, London 2002–, Randall's Island, New York 2012–, also Frieze Masters (London), a fair with a contemporary approach to pre-21st century art 2012–; Co-founder Counter Editions 1999; Chair. Bd of Trustees, South London Gallery; mem. Jury, Turner Prize 2000; hon. degree (Univ. of the Arts London) 2009. *Address:* Frieze, 1 Montclare Street, London, E2 7EU, England (office). *Telephone:* (20) 3372-6111 (office). *E-mail:* info@frieze.com (office). *Website:* friezelondon.com (office).

SLOVES, Marvin, BA; American advertising agency executive (retd); b. 22 April 1933, New York; s. of John H. Sloves and Evelyn S. Sloves (née Wishan); ed Brandeis Univ. and Oriental Inst., Univ. of Chicago; Staff Researcher, Leo Burnett Co., Chicago 1962; Dir of Research, Earle Ludgin Co., Chicago 1963–64; Account Exec. Ted Bates Co., New York 1965–67; Pres. and CEO, Scali, McCabe, Sloves, Inc., New York 1967–81, Chair. and CEO 1981–93; Vice-Chair. The Lowe Group 1993–95; Co-Chair. Lowe & Pnrs/Scali, McCabe, Sloves 1995–99 (retd). *Leisure interests:* boxing, memorabilia collecting. *Address:* PO Box 1745, Santa Fe, NM 87504, USA.

SLYNGSTAD, Yngve; Norwegian banking executive; *CEO, Norges Bank Investment Management;* b. 3 Nov. 1962; ed Univ. of Oslo, Norwegian School of Econs, Univ. of Paris, France, Univ. of California, Santa Barbara, USA; started career as Researcher, Norges Bank 1993; fmr Chief Investment Officer, Asian Equities, Storebrand Asset Management; Head of Equities, Norges Bank Investment Man. (NBIM) 1998–2007, CEO NBIM 2008–; ranked by Forbes magazine amongst The World's Most Powerful People (70th) 2013. *Address:* Norges Bank Investment Management, Bankplassen 2, PO Box 1179 Sentrum, 0107 Oslo, Norway (office). *Telephone:* 24-07-30-00 (office). *E-mail:* contact@nbim.no (office). *Website:* www .nbim.no (office).

SMALE, Stephen, PhD; American mathematician and academic; *Distinguished University Professor, Department of Mathematics, City University of Hong Kong;* b. 15 July 1930, Flint, Mich.; ed Univ. of Michigan; Instructor, Univ. of Chicago 1956–58; NSF Postdoctoral Fellowship, Inst. for Advanced Study, Princeton, NJ and Instituto de Mathematica Pura e Aplicada Rio de Janeiro, Brazil 1958–60; Alfred P. Sloan Research Fellow 1960–62; Assoc. Prof. of Math., Univ. of California, Berkeley 1960–61, Prof. 1964–94, Prof. without Stipend, Dept of Econs 1976–, Faculty Research Lectureship 1983, Prof. of Math. Emer. 1994–; Distinguished Univ. Prof., City Univ. of Hong Kong 1995–; Professorship, Columbia Univ., New York 1961–64; Research Prof., Miller Inst. for Basic Research in Science, Berkeley 1967–68, 1979–80, 1990; visiting mem. Institut des Hautes Etudes Scientifiques, Paris 1969–70, 1972–73, 1976; Visiting Prof., Univ. of Paris 1972–73, Yale Univ. 1974, Instituto de Matematica Pura e Aplicada, Rio de Janeiro 1976, 1988, 1994, Columbia Univ. 1987; Visiting Scientist, IBM Corpn, Yorktown Heights 1987; Visiting Corpn, Collège de France, Paris 1962; Foreign mem. Brazilian Acad. of Science 1964; mem. American Acad. of Arts and Sciences 1967, NAS 1970; Fellow, The Econometric Soc. 1983, Japan Soc. for the Promotion of Science 1993; hon. mem. Instituto de Matematica Pura e Aplicada, Rio de Janeiro 1990, Trinity Math. Soc., Dublin 1991–92, Moscow Math. Soc. 1997, London Math. Soc. 1998;; Hon. Prof., Univ. of Yunnan, Kunming 1997; Class of the Grand Cross of the Brazilian Nat. Order of Scientific Merit 1994; Hon. DSc (Univ. of Warwick, UK) 1974, (Queen's Univ., Kingston, Ont.) 1987, (Univ. of Mich.) 1996, (City Univ. of Hong Kong) 1997, (Rostov State Univ.) 1999; Dr hc (Université Pierre et Marie Curie, Paris) 1997; Veblen Prize for Geometry, American Math. Soc. 1965, Fields Medal, Int. Congress of Mathematicians, Moscow 1966, Univ. of Mich. Sesquicentennial Award 1967, American Math. Soc. Colloquium Lecturer 1972, Chauvenet Prize, Math. Asscn of America 1988, Von Neumann Award, Soc. for Industrial and Applied Math. 1989, Bishop Berkeley Lecturer, Trinity Coll., Dublin 1991, Distinguished Lecturer, Fields Inst., Waterloo, Canada 1992, Nat. Medal of Science 1996, Wolf Foundation Prize in Math. 2007. *Publications:* more than 100 articles in math. journals. *Address:* Department of Mathematics, City University of Hong Kong, 83 Tat Chee Avenue, Kowloon, Hong Kong Special Administrative Region, People's Republic of China (office). *Telephone:* (852) 2788 8646 (office). *Fax:* (852) 2788 8561 (office). *E-mail:* mago@cityu.edu.hk (office). *Website:* www.cityu.edu.hk (office).

SMALLMAN, Raymond Edward, CBE, PhD, DSc, FRS, FREng, FIMMM; British professor of metallurgy and materials science; *Professor Emeritus of Metallurgy and Materials, University of Birmingham;* b. 4 Aug. 1929, Wolverhampton; s. of David Smallman and Edith French; m. Joan D. Faulkner 1952; one s. one d.; ed Rugeley Grammar School and Univ. of Birmingham; Sr Scientific Officer, AERE Harwell 1953–58; Lecturer, Dept of Physical Metallurgy, Univ. of Birmingham 1958–63, Sr Lecturer 1963–64, Prof. of Physical Metallurgy 1964–69, Head, Dept of Physical Metallurgy and Science of Materials 1969–81, Feeney Prof. and Head, Dept of Metallurgy and Materials 1969–88, Prof. of Metallurgy and Materials 1988–93, Hon. Prof. 1993–2001, Prof. Emer. 2001–; Deputy Dean,

Faculty of Science and Eng 1981–84, Dean 1984–85, Dean of Eng 1985–87, Vice-Prin. Univ. of Birmingham 1987–92; Pres. Birmingham Metallurgical Asscn 1972–73; Vice-Pres. Metals Soc. 1980–84; Vice-Pres. Fed. of European Materials Socs 1992–94, Pres. 1994–96; Council mem., Science and Eng Research Council 1992–94, (Materials Comm. 1988–91); mem. Council Inst. of Materials (Chair. Int. Affairs Cttee 1993–97), Vice-Pres. 1995–99; Visiting Prof., Univ. of Pa 1961, Stanford Univ. 1962, NSW 1974, Cape Town 1976, Hong Kong 1990–; Van Horn Distinguished Lecturer, CASE Western Reserve Univ. 1978; Distinguished Lecturer, Hong Kong Univ. 1999; Warden Birmingham Assay Office 1994–98, Guardian 1997–2000; Foreign Assoc. Nat. Acad. of Eng, USA; mem. Lunar Soc. 1991–99; Royal Acad. of Eng, Inst. of Materials, Minerals and Mining; Hon. Foreign mem. China Ordnance Soc., Metal Science Soc. Czech Repub.; Hon. DSc (Wales) 1990, (Novi Sad) 1990, (Cranfield) 2001; Sir George Beilby Gold Medal, Inst. of Metals and Chemical Soc. 1969, Rosenhain Medal Inst. of Metals 1972, Elegant Work Prize, Metals Soc. 1979, Platinum Medal, Inst. of Metals 1989, Gold Medal and Prize, Acta Materialia 2004. *Publications:* Modern Physical Metallurgy 1961, Modern Metallography (jtly) 1968, Structure of Metals and Alloys (jtly) 1969, Defect Analysis in Electron Microscopy (jtly) 1975, Metals and Materials: Science, Processes and Applications (jtly) 1994, Modern Physical Metallurgy and Materials Engineering (jtly) 1999, Metals and Materials: The Development and History of the Department in the University of Birmingham 2006; over 300 scientific papers on relationship of microstructure of materials and properties in learned journals. *Leisure interests:* writing, travel, friendly golf, bridge, gardening. *Address:* Department of Metallurgy and Materials, School of Engineering, University of Birmingham, Edgbaston, Birmingham, B15 2TT (office); 59 Woodthorne Road South, Tettenhall, Wolverhampton, WV6 8SN, England (home). *Telephone:* (121) 414-5223 (office); (1902) 752545 (home). *Fax:* (121) 414-7368 (office); (1902) 752545 (home). *E-mail:* r.e.smallman@bham.ac.uk (office); ray.smallman@btopenworld .com (home).

SMART, George M.; American energy industry executive; *Chairman, First-Energy Corporation;* b. 1946; Chair. and Pres. Phoenix Packaging Corpn 1993–2001; Pres. Sonoco-Phoenix Inc. 2001–04; Dir FirstEnergy Corpn 1997–, Chair. (non-exec.) 2004–; mem. Bd of Dirs Ball Corpn, Unizan Financial Corpn 2000–, Ohio Edison Co. 1988–97. *Address:* FirstEnergy Corporation, 76 Main Street, Akron, OH 44308, USA (office). *Telephone:* (800) 646-0400 (office). *Fax:* (330) 384-3866 (office). *Website:* www.firstenergycorp.com (office).

SMART, Stephen Bruce, Jr, AB, SM; American business executive and fmr government official; b. 7 Feb. 1923, New York; s. of Stephen Bruce Smart and Beatrice Cobb; m. Edith Minturn Merrill 1949; one s. three d.; ed Harvard Coll. and Massachusetts Inst. of Tech.; served in US Army 1943–46, 1951–53; Sales Engineer, Permutit Co., New York 1947–51; joined Continental Group (fmrly Continental Can Co.) 1951, held various sales and gen. man. posts 1951–62, Vice-Pres. Cen. Div. 1962–65, Marketing and Corpn Planning 1965–68, Exec. Vice-Pres. Paper Operations 1969–73, Vice-Chair. 1973–75, Pres. and COO 1975–81, Chair. and CEO Continental Group 1981–85; Under-Sec. for Int. Trade, US Dept of Commerce 1985–88; Consultant, US Dept of State 1988; Sr Fellow, World Resources Inst. 1989–95, Dir 1993–2001. *Publications:* Beyond Compliance: A New Industry View of the Environment (ed.) 1992, Indian Summer: A Memoir 1999, A Community of the Horse: Partnerships 2003. *Leisure interests:* fishing, sailing, American decorative arts, thoroughbred horse breeding. *Address:* 20561 Trappe Road, Upperville, VA 20184, USA (home). *Telephone:* (540) 554-8302 (home).

SMEAL, Eleanor, MA; American feminist leader, political analyst and author; *President, Feminist Majority Foundation;* b. (Eleanor Marie Cutri), 30 July 1939, Ashtabula, OH; d. of Peter Anthony Cutri and Josephine E. Agresti; one s. one d.; ed Strong Vincent High School, Duke Univ., Univ. of Florida; joined Nat. Org. for Women 1970, Pres. 1977–82, 1985–87; Founder and Pres. Feminist Majority Foundation 1986–; Publr Ms. magazine (owned and published by Feminist Majority Foundation) 2001–; launched Feminist Majority Foundation Online (www.feminist.org) 1995; Hon. LLD (Duke Univ.); named by TIME Magazine as one of the "50 Faces for America's Future" 1979, chosen by The World Almanac as the fourth most influential woman in the USA 1983, featured as one of the six most influential Washington lobbyists in U.S. News and World Report. *Achievements include:* involved in several legislative initiatives, including Free Access to Clinic Entrances legislation (influenced by Madsen v. Women's Health Center) 1994, defeat of Proposition 209 in Calif., Pregnancy Discrimination Act, Equal Credit Act, Civil Rights Restoration Act, Violence Against Women Act, Freedom of Access to Clinic Entrances Act, Civil Rights Act 1991, and fight to amend Equal Rights Amendment. *Publications include:* How and Why Women Will Elect the Next President 1984. *Address:* Feminist Majority Foundation, 1600 Wilson Boulevard, Suite 801, Arlington, VA 22209, USA (office). *Telephone:* (703) 522-2214 (office). *Fax:* (703) 522-2219 (office). *E-mail:* info@feminist.org (office). *Website:* www .feminist.org (office).

SMIDT, Kristian, PhD; Norwegian academic; *Professor Emeritus of English Literature, University of Oslo;* b. 20 Nov. 1916, Sandefjord; s. of Bishop Johannes Smidt and Jofrid Smidt (née Grimstvedt); m. 1st Aagot Karner 1940 (divorced 1973); m. 2nd Anne Oulie-Hansen 1973; one s. two d.; ed Aske's Hatcham, London, Univ. of Oslo; Reader in English Literature Univ. of Oslo 1953–55, Prof. 1955–85, Prof. Emer. 1985–, Dir British Inst. 1955–73; Prof. of English Literature (temporary) Univ. of Tromsø 1973–76; Rockefeller Fellowship, Princeton Univ. 1951–52; Folger Shakespeare Library Fellowship, Washington, DC 1960–61; Visiting Fellowship, Clare Coll., Cambridge Univ. 1984; mem. Norwegian Acad. of Science and Letters, Vetenskaps-societen, Lund, Sweden, Norwegian Acad. of Language and Literature; Hon. OBE 1985; Nansen Award 1994. *Publications:* James Joyce and the Cultic Use of Fiction 1959, Poetry and Belief in the Work of T.S. Eliot 1961, Unconformities in Shakespeare's Plays (4 Vols) 1982–93, Shakespeare i norsk oversettelse 1994, Ibsen Translated 2000, Den mangfoldige Shakespeare 2000, The Importance of Recognition and Other Essays on T. S. Eliot 2001, Silent Creditors: Henrik Ibsen's Debt to English Literature 2004, Ed. Shakespeare's Richard III: Parallel Texts 1969. *Address:* Solveien 137, 1167 Oslo, Norway. *Telephone:* 22-28-86-42. *E-mail:* an-sm@online.no.

SMILEY, Jane Graves, MFA, PhD; American writer and academic; b. 26 Sept. 1949, Los Angeles; d. of James La Verne Smiley and Frances Nuelle Smiley (née

Graves); m. 1st John Whiston 1970 (divorced); m. 2nd William Silag 1978 (divorced); two d.; m. 3rd Stephen Mark Mortensen 1987 (divorced 1997); one s.; ed Vassar Coll. and Univ. of Iowa; Asst Prof., Iowa State Univ. 1981–84, Assoc. Prof. 1984–89, Prof. 1989–90, Distinguished Prof. 1992–96; Visiting Prof., Univ. of Iowa 1981, 1987; mem. American Acad. of Arts and Letters 2001–; Fulbright Grant 1976, Nat. Endowment for the Arts grants 1978, 1987; Friends of American Writers Prize 1981, O. Henry Awards 1982, 1985, 1988, Distinguished Alumni Award, Univ. of Iowa 2003. *Publications:* Barn Blind 1980, At Paradise Gate 1981, Duplicate Keys 1984, The Age of Grief 1987, Catskill Crafts: Artisans of the Catskill Mountains (non-fiction) 1987, The Greenlanders 1988, Ordinary Love and Goodwill 1989, A Thousand Acres (Pulitzer Prize in Fiction 1992, Nat. Book Critics Circle Award 1992, Midland Authors Award 1992, Heartland Prize 1992) 1991, Moo: A Novel 1995, The All-True Travels and Adventures of Lidie Newton 1998, Horse Heaven 2000, Dickens (biog.) 2002, Good Faith 2003, A Year at the Races 2004, Thirteen Ways of Looking at the Novel (non-fiction) 2006, Ten Days in the Hills 2007, The Georges and the Jewels (children's fiction) 2009, Private Life 2010, The Man Who Invented the Computer: The Biography of John Atanasoff, Digital Pioneer 2010. *Leisure interests:* cooking, swimming, playing piano, quilting. *Address:* c/o Knopf Publicity, Random House, 1745 Broadway, New York, NY 10019, USA (office).

SMIRNOV, Andrei Sergeyevich; Russian actor, film director and scriptwriter; b. 12 March 1941, Moscow; ed All Union State Inst. of Cinematography; numerous prizes at int. film festivals. *Films:* dir: Hey, Anybody! (with B. Yashin) 1962, An Inch of Land (with B. Yashin) 1964, A Little Joke (TV film with B. Yashin) 1966, Somebody Else's Pain (TV film) 1966, Jacqueline Francois Sings (TV film) 1966, Angel 1987, Belorussian Railway Station 1970, Fall 1974, By Trust and Truth 1979, Unwillful Striptease 1983; actor: Following, Chernov, Dreams of an Idiot, Mania of Giselle, Dnevnik ego zheny (Diary of His Wife) 2000, Persona non grata 2005, Elena 2011; scriptwriter: Autumn, Sentimental Journey, My Dear Relatives. *Television includes:* actor: Idiot (miniseries) 2003, Moskovskaya saga 2004, Master i Margarita (miniseries) 2005. *Plays directed:* Late Supper (Moscow Art Theatre) 1994, Turgenev's Month in a Village (Comedy Francaise) 1997. *Publications include:* plays: Autumn, Sentimental Journey; My Dear Relative. *Address:* 121019 Moscow, Suvirivski boulevard 8, Apt, Russia (office). *Telephone:* (495) 299-34-93 (office).

SMIRNOV, Igor Nikolayevich, DEconSc; Russian politician; b. 23 Oct. 1941, Petropavlovsk-Kamchatskii, Kamchatka Oblast (now Kamchatka Krai), Russian SFSR, USSR; s. of Nikolai Stepanovich Smirnov and Zinaida Grigor'evna Smirnova; m. Zhannetta Nikolayevna Lotnik; two s.; ed Zaporizhzhya Machine Construction Inst., Ukrainian SSR; mem. CPSU 1963–90; early career as engineer, chief engineer, chief of factory, dep.; Deputy Dir Novo-Kakhova Electromash plant, Ukrainian SSR; Dir Tiraspol Electromash plant 1987–1990, Moldavan SSR; Dir Tiraspol Jt Trade Union 1989–91, Chair. City Soviet and Tiraspol City Exec. Cttee 1990–91; Pres. Self-Declared 'Transnistrian Moldovan Repub.' (expelled from CPSU for separatism 1990) 1991–2011; People's Deputy of Moldova 1990–92; Academician, Ukrainian Economical-Cybernetics Acad.; mem. Int. Informatization Acad., Russian Acad. of Natural Sciences; Order of Repub. 1995, Medal, Order of Prince Daniyl of Moscow 1998, Order of Sergei Radonejski 1999, Order for Benefit of Motherland, Russian Acad. of Sciences, Order of World Distributing Univ., Cross for Faith and Motherland (3rd Degree), Cross for Defence of 'Transnistrian Moldovan Repub.', Cross for Service to the Cossacks, Order of Lenin, Star of Hero, Order of Glory of Russia 2000, Order for Personal Courage 2001; Medal for Labour Prowess, Medal on 10th anniversary of 'Transnistrian Moldovan Repub.'. *Publications:* Human Beings, Science and Technical Progress in a Century of Information 2000, In Favour of the Republic 2000, To Live on Our Land (Sholohov Prize) 2004. *Leisure interest:* hunting. *Address:* c/o Office of the President of the 'Transnistrian Moldovan Republic', 3300 Tiraspol, ul. 25 Oktyabrya 45, Moldova. *E-mail:* psp.pmr@mail.ru.

SMIRNOV, Igor Pavlovich, DPhilSc; Russian literary scholar and academic; *Professor Emeritus, University of Konstanz;* b. 19 May 1941, Leningrad (now St Petersburg); s. of Pavel Smirnov and Valentina Lomakina; m. 2nd Nadezda Grigoryeva 2011; ed Leningrad Univ.; Research Assoc., Leningrad Inst. of Russian Literature; left USSR 1981; Prof., Univ. of Konstanz, Germany 1981–2006, Prof. Emer. 2006–; Vjazemski Prize 1998, Andrey Bely Prize 2000. *Publications include:* Meaning in Art and the Evolution of Poetic Systems 1977, Diachronic Transformations of Literary Genres and Motifs 1981, Essays on the History of the Typology of Culture (with Johanna Smirnov) 1982, The Emergence of the Inter-text 1985, Towards a Theory of Literature 1987, Being and Creating 1990, On Old Russian Culture, Russian National Specificity and the Logic of History 1991, Psychohistory of Russian Literature from Romanticism to the Present Day 1995, A Novel of Secrets – Dr. Zhivago 1996, Homo homini philosophus 1999, Megahistory 2000, Philosophy for Everyday 2003, Philosophical Sociology of Revolution 2004, Genesis 2006, A (Hypo)Theory of Genres 2008, Semantic History of Cinema 2009, How Literature Refers to Philosophy 2010, Praxeology 2012. *Address:* Department of Russian, University of Konstanz, 78457 Konstanz (office); Kornblumenweg 14, 78465 Konstanz, Germany (home). *Telephone:* (7531) 882682 (office); (7531) 43583 (home). *Fax:* (7531) 4852 (office). *E-mail:* igor.smirnov@uni-konstanz.de (office).

SMIRNOV, Stanislav Konstantinovich, PhD; Russian mathematician and academic; *Professor, University of Geneva;* b. 3 Sept. 1970, Leningrad; ed St Petersburg Lyceum 239, St Petersburg State Univ., California Inst. of Tech., USA; has held research positions at Yale Univ., USA, Max Planck Inst. for Math., Germany, Inst. for Advanced Study, USA; at Royal Inst. of Tech., Stockholm, Sweden 1998–2003; Prof., Analysis, Math. Physics and Probability Group, Univ. of Geneva, Switzerland 2003–; also part-time at Chebyshev Lab., St Petersburg State Univ.; Fellow, American Math. Soc. 2012; jtly ranked first at Int. Math. Olympiad with perfect scores and gold medals on both occasions 1986, 1987, St Petersburg Math. Soc. Prize 1997, Clay Research Award 2001, Salem Prize (co-recipient) 2001, Göran Gustafsson Research Prize 2001, Rollo Davidson Prize 2002, Prize of European Math. Soc. 2004, Fields Medal (co-recipient) 2010. *Publications:* numerous papers in professional journals on complex analysis, dynamical systems and probability theory. *Address:* Section de mathématiques, University of Geneva, 2–4 rue du Lièvre, CP 64, 1211 Geneva 4, Switzerland (office). *Telephone:* (22)

3791149 (office). *Fax:* (22) 3791176 (office). *E-mail:* stanislav.smirnov@unige.ch (office). *Website:* www.unige.ch/~smirnov (office).

SMIRNOV, Vitaly Georgiyevich; Russian sports official; b. 14 Feb. 1935, Khabarovsk; m. Irina Aleksandrovna Smirnova; three s.; ed Cen. State Inst. of Physical Culture; instructor, Head Div. of Sports Moscow Comsomol Cttee 1958–60; First Sec. Kuntzevo Regional Comsomol Cttee; Moscow Region 1960; Chair. Moscow Regional Council, Union of Sports Socs and Orgs 1960–62; Second Sec., First Sec. Moscow Regional Comsomol Cttee 1962–68; First Sec. City Cttee of CPSU 1968–70; Deputy Chair., First Deputy Chair. USSR Cttee of Sports and Physical Culture 1970–75, Chair. Water Polo Fed. 1962–72; First Deputy Chair. Org. Cttee of Olympic Games 1980 in Moscow 1975–81; Chair. State Cttee on Sports and Physical Culture of Russian Fed. 1981–90; participant, IOC EB 1974–78, 1986–90, Vice-Pres. IOC 1978–82, 1991–95, 2001–05, mem. Int. Relations Comm. 2002–, Remuneration Working Group 2004–, 2009 Congress 2006–; Chair. USSR Olympic Cttee 1990–92, Pres. Olympic Cttee of Russia 1992–2001, Hon. Pres. 2001–; mem. Acad. of Creativity 1994–, Int. Acad. of Informatization, Peter's Acad. of Sciences and Arts; Order Sign of Honour 1966, 1970, 1976, Order Friendship of Nations 1980, Order Labour Red Banner 1985, Order of Honour 1994, Order For Services to Motherland 3rd degree 1966, Order for Services to Motherland 2nd degree 2001; orders and awards of international sports federations. *Publications:* numerous articles and papers on the devt of sports in Russia and the Olympic movt. *Leisure interests:* hunting, fishing, tennis. *Address:* c/o Russian Olympic Committee, 119992 Moscow, Luzhnetskaya emb. 8, Russia. *Telephone:* (495) 725-45-01 (office). *Fax:* (495) 637-02-55 (office). *E-mail:* smirnov@roc.ru (office). *Website:* www.roc.ru (office).

SMIRNOV, Vladimir Nikolaevich; Russian biochemist; b. 17 May 1937, Cheliabinsk; m. 1st Valeriana Kreier 1956 (divorced 1973); m. 2nd Galina Chernonsova 1976; one s.; ed Leningrad Univ.; mem. CPSU 1976–91; postgraduate 1959–64; Jr, Sr Research Fellow at USSR Acad. of Med. Science Inst. of Medical Radiology 1964–68; Head of Biochemical Section, Ministry of Health 1968–72; Corresp. mem. of USSR (now Russian) Acad. of Sciences 1981; Prof. of Biological Science 1977; Head of Lab. at All-Union Scientific Centre for Cardiology (br. of USSR (now Russian) Acad. of Medical Science) 1973–76, Dir 1976–82; Dir of Inst. of Experimental Cardiography of Acad. of Medical Sciences 1982–; Corresp. mem., then mem. Acad. of Medical Sciences 1984–; USSR State Prize 1978. *Publications:* works on molecular biology, biochem. of the heart, cellular and molecular athero- and trombogenesis. *Leisure interests:* hunting, fishing. *Address:* Institute of Experimental Cardiology, Cardiology Research Centre, 112552 Moscow, 3rd Cherepkovskaya 15A, Russia. *Telephone:* (495) 415-00-35 (office); (495) 203-84-83 (home). *Fax:* (495) 415-29-62.

SMISEK, Jeffery (Jeff) A., AB, JD; American airline industry executive; *Chairman, President and CEO, United Continental Holdings, Inc.;* b. 17 Aug. 1954, Washington, DC; m.; two d.; ed Princeton Univ., Harvard Law School; Pnr and Exec. Vice-Pres. Vinson & Elkins LLP, Houston 1983–95; Sr Vice-Pres. and Gen. Counsel, Continental Airlines Inc. 1995–96, Exec. Vice-Pres., Gen. Counsel and Sec. 1996–2001, Exec. Vice-Pres., Corp. 2001–03, Exec. Vice-Pres. 2003–04, Dir 2004–, Pres. 2004–10, COO 2008–09, Chair. and CEO Jan.–Oct. 2010, Pres. and CEO United Continental Holdings, Inc. (holding co. of United Airlines and Continental Airlines) Oct. 2010–, Chair. 2013–, Chair., Pres. and CEO United Airlines; mem. Bd of Dirs National Oilwell Varco Inc., Varco International Inc., Orbitz Inc.; named Aviation Week's Person of the Year 2010. *Address:* United Continental Holdings, Inc., c/o the Corporate Secretary's Office, Willis Tower, 233 South Drive, Chicago, IL 60606, USA (office). *Telephone:* (312) 997-8000 (office). *Fax:* (847) 700-2214 (office). *E-mail:* UALBoard@united.com (office). *Website:* www .unitedcontinentalholdings.com (office).

SMIT, John William; South African professional rugby union player; *Captain, South African National Rugby Union Team (Springboks);* b. 3 April 1978, Pietersburg (now Polokwane), Limpopo Prov.; ed Pretoria Boys High School (Head Prefect); plays as hooker and prop; played in First XV, Pretoria Boys High School 1994–96, Univ. of Natal 1997, Natal Sharks 1998, Sharks (Super 14) 1998–2007, 2008–11, Clermont 2007–08, Saracens 2011–, South African Nat. Rugby Union Team (Springboks) 2000–; played his first Springbok game 2000, played in a record 46 consecutive Test matches for South Africa 2003–07, Capt. 2004–; won Tri Nations 2004; captained South Africa to win Rugby World Cup, Paris 2007, series victory against British and Irish Lions 2009, Tri Nations 2009; currently most-capped capt. in int. rugby history; played his 100th Test (only the 15th player eve, and second South African) 2010. *Address:* Saracens Rugby Club, Kingsley House, Unit 3, Sandridge Park, Porters Wood, St Albans, Herts., AL3 6PH, England (office); c/o South African Rugby Union, PO Box 99, Newlands 7725, South Africa. *Telephone:* (1727) 792800 (office); (21) 6596700. *Fax:* (1727) 792801 (office); (21) 6863907. *E-mail:* info@saracens.com (office); yourview@sarugby.co.za. *Website:* www.saracens.com (office); www.sarugby.co.za.

SMITH, Ali; British writer; b. 1962, Inverness, Scotland; ed Univ. of Aberdeen, Univ. of Cambridge; fmr Lecturer, Univ. of Strathclyde; gave lecture on Angela Carter, Nat. Portrait Gallery, London 2004; Scottish Arts Council Award 1995; Hon. DLitt (Aberdeen) 2007, (Anglia Ruskin, Cambridge) 2008. *Publications:* Free Love and Other Stories (Saltire First Book Award) 1995, Like (novel) 1997, Other Stories and Other Stories 1999, Hotel World (novel) (Encore Prize, Scottish Arts Council Book Award, Scottish Arts Council Book of the Year 2002) 2001, The Whole Story and Other Stories 2003, The Accidental (novel) (Whitbread Novel of the Year 2005) 2004, The Reader 2006, Girl Meets Boy (SAC Sundial Novel of the Year 2008) 2007, The First Person and other stories 2008, There But For The 2011, Artful 2013; contrib. to TLS, The Scotsman, Guardian. *Address:* c/o Hamish Hamilton, c/o Penguin Books, 80 Strand, London, WC2R 0RL, England.

SMITH, Andrew David; British politician; b. 1 Feb. 1951; m.; one step-s.; ed Reading Grammar School and St John's Coll., Oxford; joined Labour Party 1973; mem. Oxford City Council 1976–87; MP for Oxford East 1987–; Opposition Spokesman on Higher Educ. 1988–92, on Treasury and Econ. Affairs 1992–94; Shadow Chief Sec. to HM Treasury 1994–96; Shadow Transport Sec. 1996–97; Minister of State, Dept for Educ. and Employment 1997–99; Chief Sec. to HM Treasury 1999–2002; Sec. of State for Work and Pensions 2002–04 (resgnd); Chair. Bd Oxford Brookes Univ. (fmrly Oxford Polytechnic) 1987–93. *Address:* House of

Commons, Westminster, London, SW1A 0AA (office); 4 Flaxfield Road, Blackbird Leys, Oxford, OX4 5QD, England (home). *Telephone:* (1865) 305080 (constituency office) (office). *Fax:* (1865) 305089 (office). *E-mail:* andrewsmith.mp@virgin.net (office). *Website:* www.andrewsmithmp.org.uk.

SMITH, Anthony David, CBE, MA; British administrator; b. 14 March 1938; s. of Henry Smith and Esther Smith; ed Brasenose Coll., Oxford; Current Affairs Producer, BBC 1960–71; Fellow, St Antony's Coll., Oxford 1971–76; Dir British Film Inst. 1979–88; Pres. Magdalen Coll., Oxford 1988–2005; mem. Bd of Dirs Channel Four TV 1980–84; mem. Acton Soc. Trust 1978–90; Chair. Writers and Scholars Educational Trust (Index on Censorship) 1989–99, Hill Foundation 1999–, Oxford-Russia Fund 2004–; mem. Arts Council 1990–94; Trustee, Prince of Wales Inst. of Traditional Arts 2005–09; Bd mem. The Sixteen Choir 2006–; mem. Council Royal Acad. of Dramatic Art 2007–; Hon. Fellow, Brasenose Coll. Oxford 1994, Magdalen Coll. Oxford 2005–; Dr hc (Oxford Brookes Univ., Univ. of Lincoln). *Publications:* The Shadow in the Cave: The Broadcaster, The Audience and the State 1973, British Broadcasting 1974, The British Press since the War 1976, Subsidies and the Press in Europe 1977, The Politics of Information 1978, Television and Political Life 1979, The Newspaper: An International History 1979, Newspapers and Democracy 1980, Goodbye Gutenberg – The Newspaper Revolution of the 1980s, The Geopolitics of Information 1980, The Age of the Behemoths 1991, From Books to Bytes 1993, The Oxford Illustrated History of Television 1995, Software for the Self: Culture and Technology 1996. *Address:* Albany, Piccadilly, London, W1J 0AX, England. *Telephone:* (20) 7734-5494.

SMITH, Brian (see SMITH, Sir E. Brian).

SMITH, Brian (see SMITH, Sir (Norman) Brian).

SMITH, Bruce Alfred, BS, MBA; American energy industry executive; b. 12 Oct. 1943, Coffeyville, Kan.; s. of George Alfred Smith and Isabel Smith (neé Andrews); m. 1st Cynthia Denton Smith (neé Doughat) 1969, divorced 1987; five s.; m. 2nd Gail Smith (neé Hutchison) 1990; ed Westminster Coll., Univ. of Kansas; served in US Army; worked as Financial Analyst, Ford Motor Co., Dearborn, Mich. 1967–69; Banking Officer, Metropolitan Div. Continental Ill. Nat. Bank and Trust Co., Chicago 1971–73, 2nd Vice-Pres. Multinational Div. 1973–75, Vice-Pres. Mining Div. 1975–77, Vice-Pres. and Section Man., Chicago and London 1977–80, Vice-Pres. and Man. Int. Energy Div., Chicago 1980–82, Vice-Pres. and Man. Southwest Group and Commercial Banking Houston 1983–86; Vice-Pres. and Treas. Valero Energy Corpn 1986–92; Chief Financial Officer Tesoro Corpn 1992–95, Exec. Vice-Pres. 1993–95, Pres. and CEO 1995–96, mem. Bd of Dirs 1995–2010, Chair., Pres. and CEO 1996–2010 (retd); mem. Bd of Dirs Noble Energy Inc., Nat. Petrochemical and Refiners Asscn. *Address:* c/o Tesoro Corporation, 300 Concord Plaza Drive, San Antonio, TX 78216-6999, USA.

SMITH, Carsten, DJur; Norwegian judge (retd); b. 13 July 1932, Oslo; s. of Oscar Smith and Julie Høyer; m. Lucy Dahl 1958; three d.; ed Univ. of Oslo; practised as attorney 1956–60; Deputy Judge 1960; Asst Prof., Univ. of Oslo 1957, Assoc. Prof. 1960, Prof. of Law 1964–91, Dir Inst. of Pvt. Law 1972–73, Dean, Faculty of Law 1977–79; Temporary Supreme Court Justice 1987, 1989–90; Chief Justice, Supreme Court of Norway 1991–2002; Chair. Saami Rights Comm. 1980–85, Comm. on Human Rights in Norwegian Legislation 1989–91, Comm. for reviewing Norwegian Court system 1996–99, Comm. on Nordic Saami Rights Convention 2003–05, Comm. on fishing rights in the ocean north of Norway for Saami People and other citizens 2006–08; mem. Permanent Court of Arbitration 1996–2004; mem. Norwegian Acad. of Science and Letters, Pres. 1991; mem. UN Perm. Forum on Indigenous Issues 2008–; Grand Cross of Royal Norwegian Order of St Olav 2003. *Publications include:* Law of Torts and Social Security (co-author) 1953, Law of Guarantees (Vols I–III) 1963–81, State Practice and Legal Theory 1978, Banking Law and State Regulations 1980, Contemporary Legal Reasoning 1992, The Law and the Life 1996; other books and articles in fields of int. law, constitutional law, admin. law and pvt. law. *Address:* c/o Secretariat of the Permanent Forum on Indigenous Issues, United Nations, 2 UN Plaza, Room DC2-1772, New York, NY, 10017, USA; Høyesterett, PO Box 8016 Dep, 0030 Oslo, Norway. *Telephone:* 22-03-59-05. *Fax:* 22-33-23-55.

SMITH, D. Orlando, OBE, FRCS; British Virgin Islands physician and politician; *Premier and Minister of Finance;* b. 28 Aug. 1944, Tortola; s. of Joshua Smith and Eldra Smith (née Davies); m. Lorna Smith; ed Univ. of the West Indies; trained as obstetrician; began medical career at Univ. Hosp. of the West Indies; intern, Princess Margaret Hosp., Nassau, Bahamas 1967–70; Chief Medical Officer of British Virgin Islands (BVI) 1979–96, also Surgeon, Peebles Hosp.; mem. Legis. Council (renamed House of Ass. 2007) 1999–; Leader of the Opposition 1999–2003; Chief Minister of British Virgin Islands 2003–07; Premier and Minister of Finance 2011–; Founding mem. and Leader Nat. Democratic Party 1998–; fmr Chair. British Virgin Islands Medical and Dental Asscn, Nat. Drug Advisory Council. *Address:* Office of the Premier, 33 Admin Dr., Wickham's Cay 1, Road Town, Tortola VG1110, British Virgin Islands (office). *Telephone:* 468-0026 (office). *Fax:* 468-6413 (office). *E-mail:* premieroffice@gov.vg (office).

SMITH, Dan F., BSc; American petrochemical industry executive; *Chairman, President and CEO, Lyondell Chemical Company;* m. Sandy Smith; two c.; ed Lamar Univ.; Engineer ARCO (Atlantic Richfield Co.) 1968–82, Planning Man. 1982–84, Vice-Pres., Planning and Control, ARCO Metals Co. 1984–85, Exec. Vice-Pres. and COO 1991–93; Vice-Pres., Control and Admin Lyondell Chemical Co. 1985, Vice-Pres. then Pres. of Mfg Operations 1985–88, Exec. Vice-Pres. and Chief Financial Officer 1988–91, 1993–94, Pres. 1994–, CEO 1996–, Chair. 2007–, CEO Partnership Governance Cttee, Equistar Chemicals LP 1997–, Millennium Chemicals Inc. 2004– (subsidiaries of Lyondell Chemical Co.); mem. Bd of Dirs Cooper Industries; mem. Lamar Univ. Coll. of Eng Advisory Council. *Address:* Lyondell Chemical Company, 1221 McKinney Street, Suite 700, Houston, TX 77010, USA (office). *Telephone:* (713) 652-7200 (office). *Website:* www.lyondell.com (office).

SMITH, Sir David Cecil, Kt, FRS, FRSE; British academic; b. 21 May 1930, Port Talbot, Wales; s. of William Smith and Elva Smith; m. Lesley Mutch 1965; two s. one d.; ed Colston's School, Bristol, St Paul's School, London and Queen's Coll. Oxford; Browne Research Fellow, Queen's Coll. Oxford 1956–59; Harkness Fellow, Univ. of Calif., Berkeley 1959–60; Univ. Lecturer, Dept of Agric. Science, Univ. of

Oxford 1960–74; Fellow and Tutor, Wadham Coll. Oxford 1964–74; Melville Wills Prof. of Botany, Univ. of Bristol 1974–80; Sibthorpian Prof. of Rural Econ. Univ. of Oxford 1980–87; Prin. and Vice-Chancellor, Univ. of Edin. 1987–94; Pres. Wolfson Coll., Oxford 1994–2000; Commdr Order of Merit (Italy), Order of Merit (Poland); Hon. DSc (Aberdeen) 1990, (Edin.) 1994 and numerous other hon. degrees. *Publication:* Biology of Symbiosis (with A. E. Douglas) 1987. *Leisure interest:* writing. *Address:* 13 Abbotsford Park, Edinburgh, EH10 5DZ, Scotland. *Telephone:* (131) 446-0230. *Fax:* (131) 446-0230. *E-mail:* smithsymbiosis@aol.com.

SMITH, Delia Ann, CBE, OBE, FRTS; British cookery writer and broadcaster; b. 18 June 1941, Woking, Surrey; m. Michael Wynn Jones; creator and presenter of several TV series since 1969; cookery writer, Evening Standard newspaper 1972–85; columnist, Radio Times; Consultant Food Ed., Sainsbury's Magazine; Dir Norwich City Football Club; UK's best-selling cookery author, with more than 21 million copies sold; signed, with Heston Blumenthal, by Waitrose supermarket chain to appear in a series of 40 commercials on UK television 2010; announced retirement from TV cookery programmes to concentrate on offering recipes online Feb. 2013; Hon. Fellow, St Mary's Coll., Univ. of Surrey 1996, John Moores Univ., Liverpool 2000; Dr hc (Nottingham) 1996, (East Anglia) 1999; Special Award, Andre Simon Memorial Fund 1994, BAFTA Special Award 2013. *Television:* Family Fare, Series 1 1973, Series 2 1974, Series 3 1975, Delia Smith's Cookery Course 1 1978–79, Delia Smith's Cookery Course 2 1980, Delia Smith's Cookery Course 3 1981, Delia Smith's One is Fun 1985, Delia Smith's Christmas 1990, Delia Smith's Summer Collection 1993, Delia Smith's Winter Collection 1995–96, Delia's Red Nose Collection 1997, Delia's How to Cook 1 1998, Delia's How to Cook 2 2000, Delia's How to Cook 3 2002, Delia's Chocolate C'Hunks 2001, Delia 2008, Delia's Classic Christmas 2009, Delia through the Decades 2010. *Publications:* How to Cheat at Cooking 1971, Country Fare 1973, Recipes from Country Inns and Restaurants 1973, Family Fare: Book 1 1973, Book 2 1974, Evening Standard Cookbook 1974, Country Recipes from Look East (regional TV programme) 1975, More Country Recipes from Look East 1976, Frugal Food 1976, Book of Cakes 1977, Recipes from Look East 1977, Food for Our Times 1978, Cookery Course: Part 1 1978, Part 2 1979, Part 3 1981, The Complete Cookery Course 1982, A Feast for Lent 1983, A Feast for Advent 1983, One is Fun 1985, Food Aid Cookery Book (ed.) 1986, A Journey into Prayer 1986, A Journey into God 1988, Delia Smith's Christmas 1990, Delia Smith's Summer Collection 1993, Delia Smith's Winter Collection 1995, Delia's Red Nose Collection 1997, How to Cook: Book 1 1998, How to Cook: Book 2 1999, How to Cook Book 3 2001, Delia's Chocolate Collection (for Comic Relief) 2001, Delia's Vegetarian Collection 2002, The Delia Collection: Soup, Fish, Chicken, Chocolate 2003, The Delia Collection: Pork, Italian 2004, The Delia Collection: Baking 2005, The Delia Collection: Puddings 2006, Delia's Kitchen Garden 2007, How to Cheat at Cooking (completely rewritten) 2008, Delia's Happy Christmas 2009. *Address:* c/o Deborah Owen Ltd, 78 Narrow Street, Limehouse, London, E14 8BP, England. *Telephone:* (20) 7987-5119. *Fax:* (20) 7538-4004. *E-mail:* do@deborahowen.co.uk (office). *Website:* www.deliaonline.com.

SMITH, Donnie; American business executive; *President and CEO, Tyson Foods Inc.;* joined Tyson Foods 1980, Sr Vice-Pres., Supply Chain Man. 2001–05, Sr Vice-Pres. and Chief Information Officer 2005–06, Sr Vice-Pres., Information Systems, Purchasing and Distribution 2006–07, Group Vice-Pres., Logistics and Operations Services 2007–08, Group Vice-Pres., Consumer Products 2008–09, Sr Group Vice-Pres., Poultry and Prepared Foods Jan.–Nov. 2009, Pres. and CEO Tyson Foods Inc. 2009–. *Address:* Tyson Foods Inc., 2200 Don Tyson Parkway, Springdale, AR 72762, USA (office). *Telephone:* (479) 290-4000 (office). *Fax:* (479) 290-4061 (office). *E-mail:* info@tysonfoodsinc.com (office). *Website:* www.tysonfoodsinc.com (office).

SMITH, Sir E. Brian, Kt, MA, PhD, DSc, FRSC; British scientist and university vice-chancellor (retd); b. 10 Oct. 1933, Mold, North Wales; s. of Eric Smith and Dilys Olwen Hughes; m. 1st Margaret Barr 1957 (divorced 1978); two s. one d.; m. 2nd Regina Arvidson Ball 1983; two step-d.; ed Alun Grammar School, Mold, Wirral Grammar School, Univ. of Liverpool; Fellow St Catherine's Coll. Oxford and Lecturer in Physical Chem., Univ. of Oxford 1960–88; Master St Catherine's Coll. 1988–93; Vice-Chancellor Cardiff Univ. 1993–2001; Dir ISIS Innovation Network 1988–97; mem. Bd Welsh Devt Agency 1998–2001, Wales European Centre 2001–03, Higher Educ. Funding Council for Wales 2002–; Gov. Univ. of Glamorgan 2002–06. *Publications:* Virial Coefficients of Pure Gases and Mixtures 1969, Basic Chemical Themodynamics 1973, Intermolecular Forces 1981, Forces Between Molecules 1986; papers in scientific journals. *Leisure interest:* mountaineering. *Address:* c/o Cardiff University, Park Place, Main Building, Cardiff, CF10 3AT, Wales (office). *Website:* www.cf.ac.uk (office).

SMITH, Elizabeth (Liz) A., BA, MBA; American business executive; *Chairman and CEO, Bloomin' Brands, Inc.;* ed Univ. of Virginia, Stanford Grad. School of Business; began career as a financial analyst at Paine Webber Inc. 1986; Asst Brand Man. Jell-O Ready-to-Eat-Snacks, Kraft Foods Inc. 1990–2000, also worked as Category Business Dir and Gen. Man. for Callard & Bowser-Suchard, Exec. Vice-Pres. and Gen. Man. Beverage Div. 2000–02, Pres. Beverages, Desserts and Cereals Group (div. of Kraft Foods Inc.) 2002–04, Group Vice-Pres. Kraft Foods North America and Pres. US Beverages and Grocery Sectors, Kraft Foods Inc. Jan.–Nov. 2004; joined American CareSource as Dir of Operations 2004, later Vice-Pres. of Operations, American Caresource Holdings, Inc.; Vice-Pres. of Field Operations, Furr's Restaurant Group Inc. from 2002; Exec. Vice-Pres. and Pres. N America and Global Marketing, Avon Products Inc. 2005–07, Pres. Avon Products Inc. 2007–09; mem. Bd of Dirs and CEO OSI Restaurant Partners LLC (now Bloomin' Brands, Inc.) 2009–, Chair. 2012–; fmr Business Services Man. for Visiting Nurse Asscn of Texas; Quality Man. for Tenet Healthcare Corpn –2004; mem. Bd of Dirs The William Carter Co. 2004–, Carter's Inc. 2004–08, Staples Inc. 2008–, Cosmetic, Toiletry & Fragrance Asscn, Personal Care Products Council; Dir of Big Brothers and Big Sisters of America; recognized by Advertising Age magazine as one of the top marketers in 1996, ranked by Fortune magazine amongst the 50 Most Powerful Women in Business in the US (42nd) 2007, (30th) 2008, (29th) 2009, ranked by Forbes magazine amongst The World's 100 Most Powerful Women (85th) 2009. *Address:* Bloomin' Brands, Inc., 2202 North West Shore Boulevard, 5th Floor, Tampa, FL 33607, USA (office). *Telephone:* (813) 282-1225 (office). *Fax:* (813) 282-1209 (office). *Website:* www.bloominbrands.com (office).

SMITH, Elizabeth Jean, OBE, MA (Hons); British broadcasting executive and international organization official; *Chairman, Commonwealth Media Group;* b. 15 Aug. 1936, Ajmer, India; d. of Sir Robert Hay and Lady Hay; m. Geoffrey Smith 1960; one s. one d.; ed Univ. of Edinburgh; Producer, Radio News, BBC 1960, Asst Head, Cen. Talks and Features, BBC World Service 1980, Head, Current Affairs 1984, Controller, English Programmes, BBC World Service 1987–94; apptd Sec.-Gen. Commonwealth Broadcasting Asscn 1994; currently Chair. Commonwealth Media Group; mem. Council of the Royal Commonwealth Society. Fellow, Radio Acad. *Publication:* Sambo Sahib (as Elizabeth Hay). *E-mail:* elizabeth@transformingbroadcasting.org.uk (office).

SMITH, Sir Francis Graham (See GRAHAM-SMITH, Sir Francis).

SMITH, Frank Thomas, DPhil, FRS; British mathematician and academic; *Goldsmid Professor of Applied Mathematics, University College London;* b. 24 Feb. 1948, Bournemouth, Dorset, England; s. of Leslie Maxwell Smith and Catherine Matilda Smith; m. Valerie Sheila Hearn 1972; three d.; ed Bournemouth School, Jesus Coll. Oxford, Univ. Coll. London; Research Fellow, Southampton Univ. 1972–73; Lecturer in Math., Reader then Prof., Imperial Coll. London 1973–84; Goldsmid Prof. of Applied Math., Univ. Coll. London 1984–; Visiting Prof., Univ. of Western Ontario, Canada 1978–79, Ohio State Univ. 1990. *Publications:* Boundary-Layer Separation (co-ed.); numerous scientific papers, mostly on theoretical and computational fluid dynamics, industrial and biomedical applications and math. modelling. *Address:* Mathematics Department, University College, Gower Street, London, WC1E 6BT (office); 9 Woodham Park Road, Woodham, Addlestone, Surrey, KT15 3ST, England (home). *Telephone:* (20) 7679-2837 (office); (1932) 352394 (home). *Fax:* (20) 7383-5519 (office). *E-mail:* frankmath@ucl.ac.uk (office). *Website:* www.ucl.ac.uk/Mathematics (office).

SMITH, George David William, MA, DPhil, FRS, FIMMM, FInstP, FRSC, CEng, CPhys; British metallurgist, materials scientist and academic; *Professor Emeritus of Materials Science, University of Oxford;* b. 28 March 1943, Aldershot, Hants., England; s. of George Alfred William Smith and Grace Violet Hannah Dayton Smith; m. Josephine Ann Halford 1968; two s.; ed Corpus Christi Coll., Oxford; SRC Research Fellow, Dept of Materials, Univ. of Oxford 1968–70, Research Fellow 1970–75, Sr Research Fellow 1975–77, Lecturer 1977–92, George Kelley Reader in Metallurgy 1992–96, Prof. of Materials Science 1996–2010, Prof. Emer. 2010–, Head of Dept 2000–05, Fellow, St Cross Coll., Oxford 1977–91 (Fellow Emer. 1991–), Trinity Coll., Oxford 1991–2010 (Fellow Emer. 2010–); Man. Dir Kindbrisk Ltd (renamed Oxford NanoScience Ltd 2000) 1987–2002, Chair. 2002–04; Chair. Polaron plc 2004–06; Chair. Int. Review Panel for RCUK Nanoscience Programme 2009; mem. Council Inst. of Materials 1998–2002 (Vice-Pres. 2002), UK Materials Foresight Panel 1998–2001, Council Inst. of Materials, Minerals and Mining 2003–05, Council Royal Soc. 2002–04, Scientific Advisory Panel, UK Environment Agency 2004, British Library Advisory Council 2004–11; Fellow, Inst. of Materials, Minerals and Mining; Liveryman of the Armourers' and Brasiers' Co.; Freeman of the City of London 1999; Hon. Fellow, Corpus Christi Coll. Oxford 2009; Beilby Medal and Prize 1985, Rosenhain Medal and Prize 1991, Nat. Award for Innovative Measurement 2004, Acta Materialia Gold Medal 2005, Inst. of Materials Platinum Medal 2006. *Publications:* Atom Probe Microanalysis (with M. K. Miller) 1989, Atom Probe Field Ion Microscopy (co-author) 1996; numerous contribs to scientific journals. *Leisure interests:* walking, fishing, bird watching, grandchildren. *Address:* Department of Materials, University of Oxford, Parks Road, Oxford, OX1 3PH, England (office). *Telephone:* (1865) 273700 (office). *Fax:* (1865) 273738 (office). *E-mail:* george.smith@materials.ox.ac.uk (office). *Website:* www-fim.materials.ox.ac.uk/people/smith.html (office).

SMITH, George E., BS, MS, PhD, FIEEE; American physicist and fmr inventor; b. 10 May 1930, White Plains, New York; m. E. Janet Carson 1955 (deceased); three c.; ed Univs of Pennsylvania and Chicago; served in Navy 1948–52; began career at Bell Labs in 1959, Head of Device Concepts Dept 1964, Head of VLSI Device Dept 1970–86 (retd); Founding Ed., IEEE Electron Device Letters; mem. Nat. Acad. of Eng; Fellow, American Physical Soc., Inst. for Electrical and Electronic Engineers (IEEE); IEEE Electron Devices Soc. Distinguished Service Award 1997, Stuart Ballentine Medal, Franklin Inst. (co-recipient) 1973, IEEE Morris N. Liebmann Memorial Award 1974, Progress Medal, Photographic Soc. of America 1986, IEEE Device Research Conf. Breakthrough Award 1999, Edwin H. Land Medal, Soc. for Imaging Science and Tech. 2001, C&C Prize (Computer and Communications), NEC Foundation, Tokyo 1999, Draper Prize (co-recipient) 2006, Nobel Prize in Physics (with Charles Kao and Willard S. Boyle) 2009. *Achievements include:* Co-inventor (with Willard S. Boyle) charge-coupled device (CCD) 1970; completed a 17-year cruise aboard his sailing vessel, Apogee 2006. *Publications include:* holds 31 US patents; more than 40 papers in professional journals on electronic and thermoelectric properties of semi metals, optical devices, the silicon-diode-array camera tube and charge-coupled devices. *Address:* 221 Teaneck Road, PO Box 787, Barnegat, NJ 08005, USA (office). *E-mail:* apogee2@comcast.net.

SMITH, Hon. Godfrey, BL; Belizean politician, lawyer and writer; *Deputy Leader, People's United Party;* m. Valerie Woods; two c.; ed Univ. of the W Indies; Assoc. Attorney, Barrow & Williams, Belize City 1994–97; Sec-Gen. People's United Party, Belize City 1997–98, Deputy Leader 2005–; Chief of Staff Office of the Prime Minister 1998–99; Attorney-Gen. 1999–2006, concurrently Minister of Information, then Minister of Foreign Affairs and Co-operation –2006; Minister of Tourism, and Nat. Emergency Man. 2006–08, of Information 2006–07; Founding Ed. Belize Law Reports, Belize Law Review, Belize Foreign Policy Yearbook; currently Lecturer, Univ. Coll. Belize; columnist Belize Times 2006–. *Publications include:* Belize Law Report (ed.), Practical Guide to Gross Receipt Tax. *Address:* People's United Party, 3 Queen St, Belize City, Belize. *Telephone:* 223-2428 (office). *Fax:* 223-3476 (office). *Website:* www.pupbelize.bz (office); www.flashpointbelize.com.

SMITH, Gordon Harold, BA, JD; American fmr politician; b. 25 May 1952, Pendleton, Ore.; s. of Milan Dale Smith and Jessica Smith (née Udall); m. Sharon Lankford; two s. one d.; ed Brigham Young Univ. and Southwestern Univ.; law clerk to Justice H. Vern Payne, New Mexico Supreme Court; pvt. practice in Ariz.; Owner, Smith Frozen Foods; mem. Ore. State Senate 1992–95, Pres. 1995–96; Senator from Ore. 1997–2009, mem. Budget Cttee, Chair. Sub-Cttee on Water and Power, mem. Sub-Cttee on Forests and Public Land Man., Sub-Cttee on Energy Rescheduling, Devt, Production and Regulation, mem. Energy and Natural Resources Cttee, Chair. Sub-Cttee on European Affairs, mem. Sub-Cttee on Near Eastern and S Asian Affairs, mem. Foreign Relations Cttee, mem. Sub-Cttee on E Asian and Pacific Affairs. *Address:* c/o 404 Russell Senate Office Building, Washington, DC 20510-3704, USA (office).

SMITH, Gordon Scott, PhD; Canadian diplomatist, academic and consultant; *Executive Director, Centre for Global Studies, University of Victoria;* b. 19 July 1941, Montreal, Que.; s. of the late G. Meredith Smith and Helen Scott; m. Lise G. Lacroix; three s. one d.; ed Lower Canada Coll. Montréal, McGill Univ., Univ. of Chicago and Massachusetts Inst. of Tech.; joined Defence Research Bd 1966, transferred to Dept of External Affairs 1967; mem. Canadian Del. to NATO 1968–70; Special Adviser to Minister of Nat. Defence 1970–72; joined Privy Council Office 1972; Deputy Sec. to Cabinet (Plans) 1978–79; Deputy Under-Sec. Dept of External Affairs 1979; Assoc. Sec. to Cabinet, Privy Council Office 1980–81; Sec. Ministry of State for Social Devt 1981–84; Assoc. Sec. to Cabinet and Deputy Clerk of Privy Council 1984; Deputy Minister for Political Affairs, Dept of External Affairs 1985; Amb. and Perm. Rep. of Canada to NATO 1985–90; Sec. to the Cabinet for Fed.-Provincial Relations, Govt of Canada 1990–91; Amb. to the EC 1991–94; Deputy Minister of Foreign Affairs 1994–97; Chair. Int. Devt Research Centre 1997–2007; Exec. Dir Centre for Global Studies and Adjunct Prof. of Political Science, Univ. of Vic. 1997–; Distinguished Fellow, Centre for Int. Governance Innovation (CIGI) 2010–; Visiting Prof., Diplomatic Acad. of the Univ. of Westminster, London; mem. Int. Advisory Bd Centre for Int. Governance Innovation, Waterloo, Ont.; Trudeau Mentor, Pierre Elliott Trudeau Foundation, Montréal; Pres. Gordon Smith Int. *Publication:* Altered States. *Leisure interests:* squash, tennis, sailing, skiing, antiques. *Address:* Centre for Global Studies, University of Victoria, POB 1700, STN CSC, Victoria, BC V8W 2Y2 (office); 2027 Runnymede Avenue, Victoria, BC V8S 2V5, Canada. *Telephone:* (250) 472-4726 (office). *Fax:* (250) 472-4830 (office). *E-mail:* gssmith@uvic.ca (office). *Website:* www.globalcentres.org (office).

SMITH, Graeme Craig; South African professional cricketer; b. 1 Feb. 1981, Johannesburg, Transvaal; s. of Graham Smith and Janet Smith; ed King Edward VII School; opening batsman; left-handed batsman; right-arm off-break bowler; plays for Gauteng 1990–2000, Western Prov. 2000–04, Hampshire 2000, S Africa 2002–14 (Capt. Test side 2003–14, ODI side 2003–11, T20I side 2005–10), Cape Cobras 2004–, Somerset 2005 (Capt. for part of season), Rajasthan Royals 2008–10, Pune Warriors India 2011, Surrey (Capt.) 2013–, ICC (Int. Cricket Council) World XI, Africa XI, United Cricket Bd of S Africa Invitation XI and Western Prov. Boland; First-class debut: 1999/2000; Test debut: South Africa v Australia, Cape Town 8–12 March 2002; One-Day Int. (ODI) debut: S Africa v Australia, Bloemfontein 30 March 2002; T20I debut: S Africa v NZ, Johannesburg 21 Oct. 2005; has played in 117 Tests, taken 8 wickets and scored 9,265 runs (27 centuries, 38 half-centuries), highest score 277, average 48.25, best bowling (innings) 2/145, (match) 2/145; ODIs: 197 matches, took 18 wickets and scored 6,989 runs, highest score 141, average 37.98, best bowling (innings) 3/30, (match) 3/30; T20Is: 33 matches, scored 982 runs, highest score 89 (not out), average 31.67; announced retirement from int. cricket March 2014; South African Cricketer of the Year 2001/02. *Achievements include:* made double centuries in consecutive Test matches: 277 at Edgbaston (highest individual innings ever made for S Africa) and 259 at Lord's (highest score ever made at Lord's by an overseas player) 2003; added 415 for first wicket with Neil McKenzie against Bangladesh (world record opening partnership) 2008. *Address:* c/o Surrey County Cricket Club, The Kia Oval, Kennington, London, SE11 5SS, England. *E-mail:* enquiries@surreycricket.com. *Website:* www.kiaoval.com.

SMITH, Hamilton O., MD; American medical scientist and academic; *Founder and Co-Chief Scientific Officer, Synthetic Genomics, Inc.;* b. 23 Aug. 1931, New York, NY; s. of Tommie Harkey and Bunnie Othanel Smith; m. Elizabeth Anne Bolton 1957; four s. one d.; ed Univ. of Illinois, Univ. of California at Berkeley, Johns Hopkins Univ. School of Medicine, Baltimore, Md; Internship, Barnes Hosp., St Louis, Mo. 1956–57; Lt in USNR, Sr Medical Officer 1957–59; Resident, Henry Ford Hosp., Detroit, Mich. 1960–62; Postdoctoral Fellow, Dept of Human Genetics, Univ. of Mich. 1962–64, Research Assoc. 1964–67; Asst Prof. of Microbiology, Johns Hopkins Univ. School of Medicine 1967–69, Assoc. Prof. 1969–73, Prof. of Microbiology 1973–81, Prof. of Molecular Biology and Genetics 1981, now Prof. Emer.; conducted work at Inst. for Genomic Research –1998; joined Celera Genomics 1998–2002; Scientific Dir Synthetic Biology and Biological Energy Groups, Venter Inst. 2002–; Founder and Co-Chief Scientific Officer Synthetic Genomics, Inc. 2005–; sabbatical year with Inst. für Molekular-Biologie, Univ. of Zurich, Switzerland 1975–76; Guggenheim Fellow 1975–76; shared Nobel Prize for Physiology and Medicine 1978 with Prof. Werner Arber (q.v.), and Dr Daniel Nathans for work on restriction enzymes; mem. NAS 1980, AAAS. *Leisure interests:* piano, classical music. *Address:* Synthetic Genomics, Inc., 9601 Blackwell Road, Suite 200, Rockville, MD 20850 (office); 8222 Carrbridge Circle, Baltimore, MD 21204, USA (home). *Telephone:* (240) 238-0800 (office); (301) 821-5409 (home). *Fax:* (240) 238-0888 (office). *E-mail:* info@syntheticgenomics.com (office). *Website:* www.syntheticgenomics.com (office).

SMITH, Henry Sidney, MA, FBA, DLit; British academic; *Professor Emeritus of Egyptology, University College London;* b. 14 June 1928, London; s. of Sidney Smith and Mary W. Smith (née Parker); m. Hazel Flory Leeper 1961 (died 1991); ed Merchant Taylors School, Sandy Lodge, Middx and Christ's Coll., Cambridge; Asst Lecturer in Egyptology, Faculty of Oriental Studies, Cambridge 1954–59, Lecturer 1959–63; Wallis Budge Fellow in Egyptology, Christ's Coll., Cambridge 1955–63; Field Dir Egypt Exploration Soc. Archaeological Survey of Nubia, Epigraphist at Nubian sites 1959–65; Reader in Egyptian Archaeology, Univ. Coll. London 1963–70, Edwards Prof. of Egyptology 1970–86, Prof. Emer. 1986–; Prin. Epigraphist and Site Supervisor, Egypt Exploration Soc., Saqqara, Egypt 1964–70, Field Dir, Sacred Animal Necropolis 1971–76, Anubieion 1976–81, Dir Memphis Project in Egypt 1981–88; Corresp. mem. Deutsches Archäologisches Institut; Medallist, Collège de France, Paris 1984. *Publications:* Preliminary Reports of the EES Archaeological Survey of Egyptian Nubia 1961, A Visit to Ancient Egypt: Memphis and Saqqara, c. 600–30 BC 1974, The Fortress of Buhen, II: The Inscriptions 1976, I: The Archaeological Report (with W. B. Emery and A. Millard)

1979, Saqqara Demotic Papyri I (with W. J. Tait) 1983, The Anubieion at Saqqara, Vols I and II (with D. G. Jeffreys and Lisa L. Giddy) 1988, 1992, The Sculpture from the Sacred Animal Necropolis at North Saqqara 1964–76 (with Elizabeth Anne Hastings) 1997, The Sacred Animal Necropolis at North Saqqara I: The Falcon Complex and Catacomb: The Archaeological Report II: The Main Temple Complex: The Archaeological Report (with Sue Davies) 2005, 2006, The Sacred Animal Necropolis at North Saqqara: The Mother of Apis Inscriptions (with C.A.R. Andrews and Sue Davies) (two vols) 2011; excavation reports, text publications and historical articles in int. journals. *Leisure interests:* varied. *Address:* Ailwyn House, High Street, Upwood, Huntingdon, Cambridgeshire, PE26 2QE, England (home). *Telephone:* (1487) 812196 (home).

SMITH, Ian William Murison, PhD, FRS, FRSC; British chemist and academic; *Research Fellow Emeritus, Department of Chemistry, University of Cambridge;* b. 15 June 1937, Leeds; s. of William Murison Smith and Margaret Moir Smith; m. Susan Morrish 1961; two s. two d.; ed Giggleswick School, Christ's Coll., Cambridge; Fellow, Christ's Coll., Cambridge 1963–85, Demonstrator in Physical Chem., Univ. of Cambridge 1966–71, Lecturer in Physical Chem. 1971–85, Tutor, Christ's Coll., Cambridge 1968–76, Dir of Studies 1972–85, Research Fellow Emer., Dept of Chem. 2002–; Prof. of Chem., Univ. of Birmingham 1985–91, Head, School of Chem. 1989–93, Mason Prof. of Chem. 1991, now Prof. Emer.; Millar Research Professorship, Univ. of California, Berkeley 1996; Stauffer Lectureship, Univ. Southern California 2000; Fellowship, Jt Inst. for Lab. Astrophysics, Univ. of Colorado 2000; Pres. Faraday Div. RSC 2001–03; Dr hc (Univ. of Duisberg-Essen); RSC Tilden Medal and Lectureship, RSC Special Award for Reaction Kinetics, Polanyi Medal 1990, EU Descartes Prize 2000, RSC Livesidge Lecturer 2002, Wilhelm Jost Memorial Lectures, Germany 2003. *Publications include:* Kinetics and Dynamics of Elementary Gas Reactions 1980, Modern Gas Kinetics (ed.) 1987, Low Temperatures and Cold Molecules (ed) 2008; more than 280 contrib. to scientific journals. *Leisure interests:* reading, theatre, walking, gardening under supervision. *Address:* The University Chemical Laboratory, University of Cambridge, Lensfield Road, Cambridge, CB2 1EW (office); 36 Grantchester Road, Cambridge, Cambs., CB3 9ED, England (home). *Telephone:* (1223) 336300 (office). *Fax:* (1223) 336362 (office). *E-mail:* iwms2@cam.ac.uk (office); i.w.m.smith@bham .ac.uk (office). *Website:* www.chem.bham.ac.uk/staff/smith (office).

SMITH, Ivor, MA, LLD, AA Dipl., RIBA; British architect; b. 27 Jan. 1926, Leigh-on-Sea, Essex; s. of H. S. Smith and F. E. Smith; m. Audrey Lawrence 1947; one s. three d.; ed Bartlett School of Architecture, Univ. Coll. London, Univ. of Cambridge School of Architecture, Architectural Asscn School of Architecture, London; with City Architects Dept, Sheffield 1951–61; in pvt. architectural practice 1961–87; Prof., Univ. Coll. Dublin 1969–73, Univ. of Bristol 1975–82, Heriot Watt Univ. 1982–90; Educational Consultant, Caribbean School of Architecture 1998–2001; Hon. LLD. *Leisure interests:* walking, drawing. *Address:* 28 Victoria Park, Cambridge, CB4 3EL, England (home). *Telephone:* (1223) 360365 (home). *E-mail:* ivor.arch@btinternet.com (home).

SMITH, Rt Hon Jacqueline Jill (Jacqui), PC, BA (Hons), PGCE; British teacher and politician; b. 3 Nov. 1962, London; m.; two s.; ed Dyson Perrins High School, Malvern, Worcs., Hertford Coll., Oxford, Univ. of Worcester; Business Studies and Econs teacher, Arrow Vale High School, Redditch 1986, Head, Econs Dept, Haybridge High School, Hagley –1997; Councillor, Redditch Borough Council 1991–97; MP for Redditch 1997–2010; Parl. Under-Sec. of State, Dept for Educ. and Employment 1999–2001; Minister of State with Responsibility for Social Services, Dept of Health 2001–03; Minister of State for Industry and the Regions and Deputy Minister for Women and Equality, Dept of Trade and Industry 2003–05; Minister of State for Schools and 14–19 Learners, Dept for Educ. and Skills 2005–06; Perm. Sec. to the Treasury and Chief Whip 2006–07; Sec. of State for the Home Dept 2007–09 (resgnd); mem. Treasury Select Cttee 1998–99; mem. Labour Departmental Cttees for Educ. and Employment 1997–2001, for the Treasury 1997–2001.

SMITH, Hon. James Herbert, MA; Bahamian politician and banker; b. 26 Oct. 1947, Nassau; s. of the late Bertram A. Smith and Rosalie B. Smith; m. Portia M. Campbell 1973 (deceased); two s. one d.; ed Ryerson Polytechnical Coll., Toronto and Univs of Windsor and Alberta, Canada; Deputy Perm. Sec., Ministry of Econ. Affairs 1977–79; Under-Sec., Cabinet Office 1980–84; Sec. for Revenue, Ministry of Finance 1984–85, Perm. Sec. 1985–86; fmr Chair. Bahamas Devt Bank; Gov. Cen. Bank of the Bahamas 1987–97; Amb. for Trade, Chief Negotiator, Free Trade Area of the Americas discussions 1997–2002; Minister of State for Finance 2002–07; fmr Chair. Bahamas Maritime Museum; Hon. doctorate. *Address:* c/o Ministry of Finance, Cecil V. Wallace Centre, West Bay Street, POB N-3017, Nassau, The Bahamas (office). *E-mail:* jp28451@hotmail.com (home).

SMITH, Jean Kennedy, BA; American foundation executive and diplomatist; b. 20 Feb. 1928, Massachusetts; d. of Joseph P. Kennedy and Rose Kennedy (née Fitzgerald); m. Stephen E. Smith 1956 (died 1990); two s. two d.; ed Manhattanville Coll., Purchase, NY; mem. Bd trustees Joseph P. Kennedy Jr Foundation 1964–, currently also Sec., John F. Kennedy Center for the Performing Arts 1964– (Chair. Educ. Cttee 1964–74 and Founder of Center's children's programs); fmr mem. Bd IRC; f. Very Special Arts (int. program for people with disabilities) 1974; Amb. to Ireland 1993–98; Hon. Irish Citizen; several hon. degrees; Jefferson Award for Outstanding Public Service, American Inst. for Public Service, Margaret Mead Humanitarian Award, Council of Cerebral Palsy Auxiliaries, Irish American of the Year Award, Irish America Magazine 1995, Rotary One Int. Award, Rotary Club of Chicago 1997, Terence Cardinal Cooke Humanitarian Award 1997, Hadassch Volunteer of the Year Award 2003, Presidential Medal of Freedom 2010. *Publication:* Chronicles of Courage: Very Special Artists 1993. *Leisure interests:* the arts, tennis, golf, sailing, reading. *Address:* 4 Sutton Place, New York, NY 10022, USA. *Telephone:* (212) 758-3610. *Fax:* (212) 813-1871.

SMITH, Dame Jennifer Meredith, DBE, JP; Bermudian politician; b. 14 Oct. 1947; d. of the late Eugene O. Smith and of Lillian E. Smith; began career as journalist; reporter, Bermuda Recorder 1970–74, Ed. 1974; on staff of Fame magazine, later Ed.; joined ZBM Radio and TV; art teacher at Sr Training School (attached to Bermuda Prison Service) for eight years; represented Bermuda as an artist at CARIFESTA in Jamaica; last exhbn in 1996; contested St George's N seat for Progressive Labour Party (PLP) in House of Ass. elections 1972, 1976, 1980;

mem. Senate 1980–89; fmr Shadow Minister for Educ.; mem. House of Ass. (PLP) 1989, 1993, 1998–, Deputy Speaker 2003–; Leader of PLP 1996–2003; Prime Minister of Bermuda 1998–2003; Minister of Educ. 2010–12; fmr Exec. mem. Commonwealth Parl. Asscn; Hon. DHumLitt (Mount St Vincent, Morris Brown Coll., Art Inst. of Pittsburgh); Outstanding Woman in Journalism Award 1972 and several other awards. *Publication:* Voice of Change 2003. *Leisure interests:* painting, dancing, reading, working with young people, writing, collecting match-book covers and first day stamp covers. *Address:* PO Box HM 2191, Hamilton HMHX, Bermuda (home). *Website:* voiceofchange.bm.

SMITH, Lt-Gen. (retd) Joseph Henry; Ghanaian army officer and politician; *Minister of Defence;* b. 9 Jan. 1945, Takoradi; m.; five c.; ed Ghana Mil. Acad.; Commdt Mil. Acad. and Training School 1992–93; Commdr 2nd Infantry Brigade Group 1993–96; Special Task Force Commdr to restore law and order in Northern Ghana 1994; Co. Commdr UNEF 1996; Commdr Ghana Army 1996–2001; Minister of Defence 2009–; fmr Chair. Bd of Dirs Nat. Insurance Comm.; mem. Nat. Security Bd 1996–2001, Ghana Armed Forces Command and Staff Coll. Control Bd 1996–2001; Companion of the Order of the Volta 2001, Legion of Merit (USA); Ghana/UN Peace Keeping Award 1976. *Address:* Ministry of Defence, Burma Camp, Accra, Ghana (office). *Telephone:* (21) 777611 (office). *Fax:* (21) 778549 (office). *E-mail:* kaddok@internetghana.com (office).

SMITH, Kevin Patrick; American director, film producer, screenwriter, author and actor; b. 2 Aug. 1970, Highlands, NJ; s. of Donald E. Smith and Grace Smith; m. Jennifer Schwalbach Smith 1994; one d.; ed Henry Hudson Regional High School, The New School, Vancouver Film School; Co-founder (with Scott Mosier) of View Askew Productions; Owner of Jay and Silent Bob's Secret Stash comic and novelty store in Red Bank, NJ; also hosts a weekly podcast with Scott Mosier known as SModcast. *Films include:* Mae Day: The Crumbling of a Documentary 1992, Clerks 1994, Mallrats 1995, Drawing Flies (producer) 1996, A Better Place (producer) 1996, Good Will Hunting (producer) 1996, Overnight Delivery (writer) 1997, Chasing Amy 1997, Supergman Lives (writer) 1998, Tail Lights Fade 1999, Big Helium Dog 1999, Dogma 1999, The Six Million Dollar Man (writer) 2000, Coyote Ugly (writer) 2000 Vulgar 2000, Scream 3 (actor) 2000, Jay and Silent Bob Strike Back 2001, The Concert for New York City 2001, The Flying Car 2001, Now You Know (actor) 2002, Daredevil (actor) 2003, Jersey Girl 2004, Reel Paradise (producer) 2005, Clerks II 2006, Small Town Gay Bar (producer) 2006, Doogal (actor) 2006, Bottoms Up (actor) 2006, Southland Tales (actor) 2006, Catch and Release (actor) 2007, Superman: Doomsday (actor) 2007, TMNT (actor) 2007, Degrassi Goes Hollywood (actor) 2007, Live Free or Die Hard (actor and writer) 2007, Zack and Miri Make a Porno 2008, Fanboys (actor) 2009, Cop Out 2010, Bear Nation (producer) 2010, 4.3.2.1 (actor) 2010, Red State 2011. *Television includes:* Hiatus (writer) 1996, Law & Order (actor) 2000, Clerks: The Animated Series (actor and producer) 2000, Duck Dodgers (actor) 2003, Yes, Dear (actor) 2004, Veronica Mars (actor) 2005, Joey (actor) 2005, Degrassi: The Next Generation (actor) 2005, Sucks Less with Kevin Smith (producer) 2006, Reaper (also producer) 2007, Phineas and Ferb (actor) 2010. *Music videos:* Can't Even Tell (Soul Asylum) as Silent Bob (also directed), Build Me Up Buttercup (The Goops) as Silent Bob, Because I Got High (Afroman) as Silent Bob, Kick Some Ass (Stroke 9) as Silent Bob. *Publications include:* books: Silent Bob Speaks, My Boring Ass Life, Shootin' the Sh*t with Kevin Smith; comics: Spider-Man/Black Cat: The Evil that Men Do (with Terry Dodson) 2002, 2005–06, Green Arrow: Quiver (with Phil Hester) 2001–02, Green Arrow: The Sound of Violence (with Phil Hester) 2002, Batman: Cacophony (with Walt Flanagan) 2008–09, Batman: The Widening Gyre (with Walt Flanagan) 2009–10, Green Hornet (with Jonathan Lau) 2010. *E-mail:* viewaskew@viewaskew.com (office). *Website:* www.viewaskew.com (office).

SMITH, Gen. (retd) Lance L., BA, MA; American army officer (retd); ed Virginia Polytechnic Inst., Cen. Michigan Univ., Air Command and Staff Coll., Ala, Army War Coll., Pa, Advanced Exec. Program, J.L. Kellogg Grad. School of Man., Northwestern Univ., Evanston, Ill.; entered USAF in 1970, commanded two fighter wings and led two air expeditionary force deployments to SW Asia: AEF III and the 4th Air Expeditionary Wing, served as Commdr of 7th Air Force, Pacific Air Forces, Air Component Commdr Repub. of Korea and US Combined Forces Command, Korea, Deputy Commdr US Forces, Korea, served two tours at the Pentagon and was Commdt of the NATO School at Supreme HQ Allied Powers Europe, Commdt of Air War Coll. and Commdr Air Force Doctrine Center, Deputy Commdr US Cen. Command, MacDill Air Force Base, Fla, Commdr US Jt Forces Command (USJFCOM) and NATO Supreme Allied Commdr for Transformation (ACT), Norfolk, Va 2005–07, retd 2008; flew more than 165 combat missions in SE and SW Asia in the A-1 Skyraider and the F-15E Strike Eagle, command pilot with more than 3,000 hours in the T-33, T-37, T-38, A-1, A-7, A-10, F-111F, F-15E and F-16 aircraft; rank of Second Lt 1970, First Lt, Capt. 1973, Maj. 1978, Lt-Col 1982, Col 1989, Brig.-Gen. 1995, Maj.-Gen. 1998, Lt-Gen. 2002, Gen. 2005; mem. Bd of Dirs North Carolina Military Foundation; Special Advisor, Rylex Consulting; Defense DSM, DSM, Silver Star with two oak leaf clusters, Defense Superior Service Medal, Legion of Merit with oak leaf cluster, DFC with two oak leaf clusters, Purple Heart, Meritorious Service Medal with three oak leaf clusters, Air Medal with one silver and four bronze oak leaf clusters, Aerial Achievement Medal with oak leaf cluster, Air Force Commendation Medal, Army Commendation Medal, Humanitarian Service Medal, Honor Cross of the Bundeswehr Medal (FRG), Order of Nat. Security Merit Gukseon Medal (Repub. of Korea), Order of Nat. Security Merit Cheonsu Medal (Repub. of Korea), Repub. of Viet Nam Gallantry Cross with Palm; Distinguished Achievement Award, Virginia Tech Univ. 2010. *Address:* c/o Rylex Consulting LLC. Landfall Executive Suites, 1213 Culbreth Drive, Wilmington, NC 28405, USA.

SMITH, Lanty Lloyd, BS, LLB; American lawyer and banking executive; *Chairman, Wachovia Corporation;* b. 11 Dec. 1942, Sherrodsville, Ohio; m. Margaret Smith; three d.; ed Wittenberg Univ., Duke Univ.; Assoc. Jones, Day, Cockley & Reavis (law firm), Cleveland 1967–73, Pnr, Jones Day, Reavis & Pogue 1974–77; Exec. Vice-Pres. and Sr Gen. Counsel Burlington Industries, Greensboro, N Carolina 1977–86, Pres. 1986–88; Chair. Precision Fabrics Group Inc. (est. to purchase existing businesses of Precision Fabrics Div. of Burlington Industries) 1988–; mem. Bd of Dirs Wachovia Corpn, Charlotte, N Carolina 1987–, lead Ind. Dir 2000–08, Chair. and interim CEO June–July 2008 Chair. July 2008–, Exec. Chair. Audit Cttee, Corp. Governance and Nominating Cttee; Co-founder and

Chair. Exec. Cttee of Bd of Dirs The Greenwood Group, Inc. 1992–; Chair. and CEO Tippet Capital (merchant banking firm), Raleigh, NC 2007–; Founder and Chair. Scion Neurostim (medical device devt co) 2007–; Pres. and CEO MediWave Star Tech Inc. 1999–; mem. Bd of Dirs Piedmont Pharmaceuticals 2007–, N Carolina Inst. of Medicine; f. Piedmont Angel Network; mem. Advisory Cttee Triad Health Project, Cen. N Carolina Chapter of Multiple Sclerosis Soc., Reading Connections; Americanism Award from Anti-Defamation League, Greensboro Outstanding Community Service Award, Class of 1914 Award, Wittenberg Univ. 2007. *Address:* 3105 Cone Manor Lane, Raleigh, NC 27613 (home); Wachovia Corpn, 301 South College Street, Suite 4000, One Wachovia Center, Charlotte, NC 28288-0013, USA (office). *Telephone:* (704) 590-0000 (office). *E-mail:* info@wachovia.com (office). *Website:* www.wachovia.com (office).

SMITH, Rt Hon. Sir Lockwood, Kt, KNZM, PhD; New Zealand diplomatist and fmr politician; *High Commissioner to UK;* m. Alexandra Smith; ed Auckland Grammar School, Massey Univ., Adelaide Univ. (Commonwealth Scholar); trained opera singer; ran a beef farming operation with his wife; fmr univ. lecturer; hosted educational children's TV shows in Australia and NZ; Marketing Man. for Cen. and SE Asia, New Zealand Dairy Board –1984; MP 1984–2013 (retd), Speaker, House of Reps 2008–13; served as a Sr Minister in various portfolios, including Educ., Agric. and Trade; also served as Deputy Minister of Finance, Minister of Forestry, Minister of Tourism, Minister Responsible for Contact Energy Ltd, Minister Responsible for the Educ. Review Office and Minister Responsible for the Nat. Library; High Commr to UK (also accred to Nigeria and Ghana and as Amb. to Ireland) 2013–. *Leisure interest:* sports and fitness. *Address:* New Zealand High Commission, New Zealand House, 80 Haymarket, London, SW1Y 4TQ, England (office). *Telephone:* (20) 7930-8422 (office). *Fax:* (20) 7839-4580 (office). *E-mail:* aboutnz@newzealandhc.org.uk (office); email@newzealandhc.org.uk (office). *Website:* www.nzembassy.com/united-kingdom (office).

SMITH, Dame Maggie Natalie, DBE; British actress; b. 28 Dec. 1934, Ilford, Essex; d. of Nathaniel Smith and Margaret Little; m. 1st Robert Stephens 1967 (divorced 1975, died 1995); two s.; m. 2nd Beverley Cross 1975 (died 1998); ed Oxford High School for Girls; first appeared with Oxford Univ. Dramatic Soc. (OUDS) in Twelfth Night 1952; appeared in revue New Faces New York 1956, Share My Lettuce 1957, The Stepmother 1958; with Old Vic Co. 1959–60 playing in The Double Dealer, As You Like It, Richard II, The Merry Wives of Windsor, What Every Woman Knows; other appearances include Rhinoceros 1960, Strip the Willow 1960, The Rehearsal 1961, The Private Ear and The Public Eye 1962, Mary, Mary 1963; with Nat. Theatre played in The Recruiting Officer 1963, Othello (Desdemona) 1964, The Master Builder 1964, Hay Fever 1964, Much Ado About Nothing 1965, Miss Julie 1965, A Bond Honoured 1966, The Beaux' Stratagem 1970, Hedda Gabler 1970, Three Sisters, Design for Living (Los Angeles) 1971, Private Lives, London 1972, USA 1974–75, Peter Pan 1973, Snap 1974; played 1976, 1977, 1978 and 1980 seasons, Stratford, Ont., Canada, Night and Day 1979, Virginia, London 1981, The Way of the World, Chichester Festival and London 1984–85, Interpreters, London 1985, The Infernal Machine 1986, Coming in to Land 1987, Lettice and Lovage, London 1987, New York 1990, The Importance of Being Earnest 1993, Three Tall Women 1994–95, Talking Heads 1996, A Delicate Balance 1997, The Lady in the Van 1999, The Breath of Life 2002, Talking Heads (Australian tour) 2004, The Lady from Dubuque 2007; Dir United British Artists 1992–; Hon. DLit (St Andrew's, Leicester) 1982, (Cambridge) 1993; Hon. DLitt (Bath) 1986; Evening Standard Best Actress Award 1962, 1970, 1982, 1985, 1994; Variety Club Actress of the Year 1963; LA Critics Award Best Actress 1970; Variety Club Award Best Stage Actress 1972 (plays); Acad. Award for Best Actress 1969, for Best Supporting Actress 1979; Best Actress Award from Soc. of Film and TV Arts (UK) 1969; Best Actress Award from Film Critics' Guild (USA) 1969 (films), BAFTA Award for Best Actress 1984, 1987, 1989, BAFTA Award for Lifetime Achievement 1992, BAFTA Award for Best Supporting Actress (for Tea with Mussolini); Tony Award 1990; Shakespeare Prize, FVS Foundation, Hamburg 1991. *Films include:* Child in the House (uncredited) 1956, Nowhere to Go 1958, Go to Blazes 1962, The V.I.P.s 1963, The Pumpkin Eater 1964, Young Cassidy 1965, Othello 1965, The Honey Pot 1967, Hot Millions 1968, The Prime of Miss Jean Brodie 1969, Oh! What a Lovely War 1969, Travels with My Aunt 1972, Love and Pain and the Whole Damn Thing 1973, Murder by Death 1975, Death on the Nile 1978, California Suite 1978, Quartet 1981, Clash of the Titans 1981, Better Late Than Never 1982, Evil Under the Sun 1982, Ménage à Trois 1982, The Missionary 1982, Lily in Live 1984, A Private Function 1984, A Room with a View 1985, The Lonely Passion of Judith Hearn 1987, Paris by Night 1988, Romeo-Juliet (voice) 1990, Hook 1991, Sister Act 1992, The Secret Garden 1993, Sister Act 2: Back in the Habit 1993, Richard III 1995, The First Wives Club 1996, Washington Square 1998, Tea with Mussolini 1999, Curtain Call 1999, The Last September 1999, Harry Potter and The Philosopher's Stone 2001, Gosford Park 2002, Divine Secrets of the Ya-Ya Sisterhood 2002, Harry Potter and the Chamber of Secrets 2002, Ladies in Lavender 2004, Harry Potter and the Prisoner of Azkaban 2004, Harry Potter and the Goblet of Fire 2005, Keeping Mum 2005, Becoming Jane 2007, Harry Potter and the Order of the Phoenix 2007, Harry Potter and the Half-Blood Prince 2009, From Time to Time 2009, Nanny McPhee and the Big Bang 2010, Gnomeo and Juliet 2011, Harry Potter and the Deathly Hallows: Part 2 2011, The Best Exotic Marigold Hotel 2011, Quartet 2012. *Television includes:* Kraft TV Theatre (Night of the Plague) 1957, Hay Fever 1960, Much Ado About Nothing 1967, Play of the Month (Man and Superman 1968, The Seagull 1968, The Merchant of Venice 1972, The Millionairess 1972, Mrs. Silly 1983, Talking Heads (mini-series) 1987, Memento Mori 1992, Suddenly, Last Summer 1993, All the King's Men 1999, David Copperfield 1999, My House in Umbria (Emmy Award for Best Actress) 2003, Capturing Mary 2007, Downton Abbey (series) (Emmy Award for Outstanding Supporting Actress in a Mini-series or Movie 2011, 2012, Golden Globe Award for Best Performance by an Actress in a Supporting Role in a Series, Mini-Series or Motion Picture Made for TV 2013, Screen Actors Guild Award for Outstanding Performance by a Female Actor in a Drama Series 2014) 2010–. *Leisure interest:* reading. *Address:* c/o Independent, Oxford House, 76 Oxford Street, London, W1D 1BS, England (office). *Telephone:* (20) 7636-6565 (office). *Fax:* (20) 7323-0101 (office). *E-mail:* info@independenttalent.com (office). *Website:* www.independenttalent.com (office).

SMITH, Martin (William) Cruz, BA; American writer; b. 3 Nov. 1942, Reading, Pa; s. of John Smith and Louise Lopez; m. Emily Arnold 1968; two d. one s.; ed Univ. of Pennsylvania; fmr newspaper reporter and ed.; CWA Golden Dagger Award 1981, Left Coast Crime Lifetime Achievement Award 2011. *Publications include:* The Indians Won 1970, Gypsy in Amber 1971, Analog Bullet 1972, Canto for a Gypsy 1972, Gorky Park (Gold Dagger Award, Crime Writers Asscn 1981) 1981, Nightwing 1977, Stallion Gate 1986, Polar Star 1989, Red Square 1992, Rose (Hammett Prize, Int. Asscn of Crime Writers 1996) 1996, Havana Bay (Hammett Prize, Int. Asscn of Crime Writers 1999) 1999, December 6 (aka Tokyo Station) 2002, Wolves Eat Dogs 2004, Stalin's Ghost 2007, Three Stations 2010, Tatiana 2013. *Address:* c/o Publicity Department, Simon & Schuster, Inc., 1230 Avenue of the Americas, New York, NY 10020, USA (office). *Website:* www.martincruzsmith.com.

SMITH, Michael, TD; Irish politician and fmr farmer; b. Nov. 1940, Roscrea, Co. Tipperary; m. Mary T. Ryan; one s. six d.; ed Univ. Coll. Cork; mem. Irish Farmers' Asscn 1969–; mem. Tipperary North Riding Co. Council 1967–88, Chair. 1986–87; mem. Dáil 1969–73, 1977–82 1987–2007; Minister of State, Dept of Agric. 1980–81; Senator 1982–87, Agric. Panel 1982–83, Culture and Educ. Panel 1983–87; Minister of State, Dept of Energy 1987–88; Minister for Energy 1988–89; Minister of State, Dept of Industry and Commerce 1989–91; Minister for the Environment 1992–94, for Defence 1997–2004; mem. Fianna Fáil. *Address:* Lismackin, Roscrea, Co. Tipperary, Ireland (home). *Telephone:* (505) 43157 (home).

SMITH, Michael Roger Pearson, OBE, BSc; British banker; *CEO, Australia and New Zealand Banking Group Ltd (ANZ);* b. 10 Sept. 1956; m.; three c.; ed City Univ., London; joined HSBC Group 1978, Man. Planning, Hongkong and Shanghai Banking Corpn Ltd, Hong Kong 1984–85, Man. Wholesale Banking, Australia 1985–87, State Man., New South Wales 1987–90, with Planning Dept, Midland Bank (now HSBC Bank), UK 1990–93, Man. Dir Int., Midland Bank 1993–95, Exec. Dir and Deputy CEO Hongkong Bank Malaysia Berhad (now HSBC Bank Malaysia Berhad) 1995–97, CEO HSBC Argentina Holdings SA 1997–2000, Chair. 2000–03, HSBC Group Gen. Man. 2000–07, Pres. and CEO Hongkong and Shanghai Banking Corpn Ltd 2004–07, Chair. HSBC Bank Malaysia Berhad 2004–07, Chair. Hang Seng Bank Ltd 2005–07; Exec. Dir and CEO Australia and New Zealand Banking Group Ltd (ANZ) 2007–; fmr mem. Bd Dirs Visa International Asia Pacific 2005–07; mem. Chongqing Mayor's Int. Econ. Advisory Council 2006–; Fellow, The Hong Kong Man. Asscn 2005–; Chevalier, Ordre du Mérite agricole 2007. *Leisure interests:* viniculture, golf, tennis, classic cars, art, antiques. *Address:* ANZ Centre, Level 9, 833 Collins Street, Docklands, Vic. 3008, Australia (office). *Telephone:* (3) 9683-9999 (office). *Fax:* (3) 9273-4875 (office). *E-mail:* media.relations@anz.com (office). *Website:* www.anz.com.au (office).

SMITH, Patti; American singer, songwriter, musician (guitar), poet and artist; b. 30 Dec. 1946, Chicago; d. of Grant Smith and Beverly Smith; m. Fred 'Sonic' Smith 1980 (died 1994); two s.; ed Glassboro State Teachers' Coll., NJ; avant-garde poet, singer and artist; performed in and co-wrote Cowboy Mouth with Sam Shepard 1971; fmr rock critic for Creem, Rock, Crawdaddy and Rolling Stone magazines 1970s; solo artist 1972–, forming Patti Smith Group 1974–; Artistic Dir, Meltdown Festival, South Bank Centre, London 2005; Commdr, Ordre des Arts et des Lettres 2005; inducted into Rock and Roll Hall of Fame 2007, ASCAP Founders Award 2010, Polar Music Prize, Royal Swedish Acad. of Music 2011, Katharine Hepburn Medal, Bryn Mawr Coll. 2013. *Recordings include:* albums: Horses 1975, Radio Ethiopia 1976, Easter 1978, Wave 1979, Dream Of Life 1988, Gone Again 1996, Peace And Noise 1997, Gung Ho 2000, Land 1975–2002 2002, Twelve 2007, The Coral Sea (with Kevin Shields) 2008, Banga 2012. *Publications:* Seventh Heaven (poems) 1971, Kodak (poems) 1972, Cowboy Mouth (play, with Sam Shepard) 1972, Witt (poems) 1973, Babel 1978, Early Work 1970–1979 (poems) 1980, Woolgathering (short stories) 1993, The Coral Sea (prose poems in memory of Robert Mapplethorpe) 1996, Auguries of Innocence (poems) 2006, Just Kids (Nat. Book Award for Non-Fiction) 2010. *Address:* c/o Ecco Press, HarperCollins, 10 East 53rd Street, New York, NY 10022, USA (office). *Fax:* (212) 207-7145 (office). *Website:* www.pattismith.net (home).

SMITH, Sir Paul Brierley, Kt, CBE; British fashion designer and retailer; b. 5 July 1946, Nottingham; s. of the late Harold B. Smith and Marjorie Smith; ed Beeston Fields School, Nottingham; first Paul Smith Shop opened, Nottingham 1970, others in London 1979, 1982, 1983, 1987, 1998, 2001, New York 1987, first Paul Smith franchise shop in Hong Kong 1990, flagship store Tokyo, Japan 1991 (now over 220 shops in Japan), first Milan shop 2001, first stand-alone accessories shop, London 2001, shop at London Heathrow Terminal 3 2002; first Paul Smith Collection Show, Paris 1976; launched Paul Smith for Women 1994; designed limited edn Mini 1998; launched fragrances range for men and women 2000, two fragrances 'Paul Smith Extreme' 2002, collection of furniture with Cappellini 2002; designed collection of rugs for The Rug Company 2002–03; launched collection of Swiss-made watches 2003, collection of writing instruments 2003; Royal Designer for Industry RCA 1991; Hon. MDes (Nottingham Polytechnic) 1991; Queen's Award for Industry 1995. *Address:* Paul Smith Ltd, 20 Kean Street, London, WC2B 4AS, England. *Telephone:* (20) 7836-7828. *Fax:* (20) 7379-0241. *E-mail:* press@paulsmith.co.uk. *Website:* www.paulsmith.co.uk.

SMITH, Richard, CBE; British artist; b. 1931, Letchworth, Herts.; m. Betsy Scherman; two s.; ed Luton School of Art, St Albans School of Art and Royal Coll. of Art; lived in New York 1959–61, 1963–65; teacher, St Martin's School of Art, London 1961–63; Artist-in-Residence, Univ. of Virginia 1967; Grand Prix São Paulo Bienal 1967; solo exhbns at the Kasmin Gallery 1963, 1967, Whitechapel Gallery 1966; participated in the Pittsburgh Int. 1961, New Shapes in Colour, Amsterdam, Berne and Stuttgart 1966–67 and in exhbns at Guggenheim Museum, Tate Gallery, etc.; works represented in Tate Gallery, Stuyvesant Foundation, Contemporary Art Soc., the Ulster Museum, Belfast, the Walker Art Centre, etc. *Address:* c/o Flowers East, 82 Kingsland Road, London E2 8DP, England (office). *Telephone:* (20) 7920-7777 (office). *Fax:* (20) 7920-7770 (office). *E-mail:* gallery@flowerseast.com (office).

SMITH, Robert Clinton, BA; American organization official and fmr politician; *President, Everglades Foundation;* b. 30 March 1941; s. of Donald Smith and Margaret Eldridge; m. Mary Jo Hutchinson 1966; two s. one d.; ed Lafayette Coll. and Long Beach State Univ.; Owner/man. Yankee Pedlar Realtors, Wolfeboro, New Hampshire 1975–85; mem. US 99th Congress from 1st Dist. of NH 1985–91; Senator from New Hampshire 1990–2002, fmr Chair. Cttee on Environment and

Public Works, Cttee on Armed Services, Cttee on the Judiciary, Select Cttee on Ethics; unsuccessful campaign for Republican nomination for Senator from Fla 2004; Pres. Everglades Foundation 2004–; Republican. *Address:* The Everglades Foundation, Inc, 1645 Palm Beach Lakes Boulevard, Suite 480, West Palm Beach, FL 33401, USA (office). *Telephone:* (561) 684-1061. *E-mail:* info@saveoureverglades.org (office). *Website:* www.saveoureverglades.org (office).

SMITH, Roberta, BA; American art critic; *Senior Art Critic, The New York Times*; b. New York City; d. of the late Thomas R. Smith and Eleanor Smith; ed Lawrence High School, Grinnell Coll.; participated in Whitney Museum's Ind. Study Program; became a studio asst to sculptor Donald Judd; also worked with Paula Cooper during early years of SoHo gallery devoted to contemporary art; began working as a professional art critic 1970s, writing for journals such as Arts, Artforum and Art in America 1976–80; Art Critic for the Village Voice 1981–85, for New York Times 1986–, now Sr Art Critic; served as guest curator and catalogue essayist for exhbn Four Artists and the Map at Kansas Univ.'s Spencer Museum of Art 1981; Frank Jewett Mather Award for Art Criticism, Coll. Art Assen 2003, Franklin D. Murphy Lecturer, Spencer Museum of Art and Kress Foundation Dept of Art History at Univ. of Kansas together with Nelson-Atkins Museum of Art, Kansas City 2004. *Address:* The New York Times, 620 Eighth Avenue, New York, NY 10018, USA (office). *Telephone:* (212) 556-1234 (office). *Fax:* (212) 556-7389 (office). *E-mail:* the-arts@nytimes.com (office). *Website:* www.nytimes.com (office); topics.nytimes.com/top/reference/timestopics/people/s/roberta_smith/index.html (office).

SMITH, Roland Hedley, CMG, MA; British fmr diplomatist; *Clerk, Wakefield & Tetley Trust;* b. 11 April 1943, Sheffield, Yorks., England; s. of Alan Hedley Smith and Elizabeth Louise Smith; m. Katherine Jane Lawrence 1971; two d.; ed King Edward VII School, Sheffield, Keble Coll. Oxford; joined Diplomatic Service 1967; Second Sec. Moscow 1969–71; Second, later First Sec., UK Del. to NATO, Brussels 1971–74; at FCO, London 1974–78; First Sec. and Cultural Attaché, Moscow 1978–80; at FCO 1980–83; mem. staff Int. Inst. for Strategic Studies 1983–84; Political Adviser, British Mil. Govt, Berlin 1984–88; at FCO 1988–92; Minister, UK Del. to NATO, Brussels 1992–95; Dir Int. Security, FCO 1995–98; Amb. to Ukraine 1999–2002; Dir St Ethelburga's Centre for Reconciliation and Peace, London 2002–04; Clerk, Wakefield (now Wakefield & Tetley) Trust 2004–. *Leisure interests:* music, especially choral singing, football (Sheffield United), trams. *Address:* Wakefield & Tetley Trust, Attlee House, 28 Commercial Street, London, E1 6LR, England (office). *Telephone:* (20) 7377-6614 (office). *E-mail:* roland.smith@wakefieldtrust.org.uk (office). *Website:* www.wakefieldtrust.org.uk (office).

SMITH, Gen. Sir Rupert Anthony, Kt, KCB, DSO, OBE, QGM; British army officer; b. 13 Dec. 1943; with Parachute Regt 1964; Deputy Commdt, Staff Col, Camberley 1989–90; Commdr 1st Armoured Div. BAOR, Gulf 1990–92; Asst Chief of Defence Staff (Operations) 1992–94; Commdr UN Protection Force, Bosnia-Herzegovina 1995; GOC and Dir of Mil. Operations, NI 1996–98; Deputy Supreme Allied Commdr in Europe 1998–2002; ADC Gen. to the Queen 2000–02. *Publication:* The Utility of Force: The Art of War in the Modern World 2005. *Address:* c/o RHQ The Parachute Regiment, Colchester, Essex, CO2 7SW, England (office).

SMITH, Stephen Francis, LLM; Australian politician; b. 12 Dec. 1955, Narrogin, WA; ed Univ. of Western Australia, London Univ., UK; solicitor, lecturer and tutor 1978–83; Prin. Pvt. Sec. to State Attorney-Gen., WA 1983–87; mem. Australian Labor Party Nat. Exec. 1987–90, Jr Vice-Pres. 1989–90; Adviser to Treas. P. J. Keating 1991, to Minister for Science and Tech. R. V. Free 1991, to Prime Minister P. J. Keating 1991–92; MP for Perth 1993–, Shadow Minister for Trade 1996–97, for Resources and Energy 1997–98, for Communications 1998–2001, for Health and Ageing 2001–04, for Industry, Infrastructure and Industrial Relations 2004–06, for Educ. and Training 2006–07, Minister for Foreign Affairs 2007–10, for Defence 2010–13. *Address:* Australian Labor Party (ALP), POB 6222, Kingston, ACT 2604, Australia (office). *Telephone:* (2) 6120-0800 (office). *Fax:* (2) 6120-0801 (office). *E-mail:* info@cbr.alp.org.au (office). *Website:* www.alp.org.au (office).

SMITH, Vernon L., BSEE, MA, PhD, FAAS; American economist and academic; *Professor of Economics and Law, George Mason University;* b. 1 Jan. 1927, Wichita; m. Candace Smith; ed Calif. Inst. of Tech., Univ. of Kansas and Harvard Univ.; Instructor in Econs Univ. of Kansas 1951–52; Economist, Harvard Econs Research Project 1954–55; mem. Man. Sciences Research Group, Purdue Univ. 1955–56, Asst Prof. 1956–58, Assoc. Prof. 1958–61, Prof. 1961–67, Krannert Outstanding Professorship 1964–67; Research Consultant Rand Corpn 1957–59; Contrib. Ed. Business Scope 1957–62; Visiting Prof. Stanford Univ. 1961–62; Prof. of Econs Brown Univ. 1967–68; Prof. of Econs Univ. of Mass. 1968–75; Visiting Prof. Univ. of Southern Calif. and Calif. Inst. of Tech. 1974–75; Prof. of Econs Univ. of Ariz. 1975–2001, Regents Prof. of Econs 1988–2001, McClelland Prof. of Econs 1998–; Research Dir Econ. Science Lab. 1986–2001; Prof. of Econs and Law George Mason Univ. (GMU), Arlington, Va 2001–, Dir and Research Scholar, Interdisciplinary Center for Econ. Science 2001–, Research Fellow Mercatus Center 2001–; Fellow Econometric Soc. 1988–, American Acad. of Arts and Sciences 1991; Distinguished Fellow American Econ. Assen 1992; mem. Editorial Bd American Econ. Review 1969–72, The Cato Journal, Journal of Economic Behavior and Organization (Assoc. Ed. 1985–), Journal of Risk and Uncertainty, Science 1988–91, Economic Theory, Economic Design 1994–, Games and Economic Behavior, Journal of Economic Methodology 1995–; mem. NAS 1995–; mem. Acad. Advisory Council, Inst. of Econ. Affairs, UK 1993–; Pres. Public Choice Soc. 1988–90, Econ. Science Assen (Founding Pres. 1986–87), Western Econ. Assen 1990–91, Assen for Pvt. Enterprise Educ. 1997, Int. Foundation for Research in Experimental Econs 1997; fmr Ford Foundation Faculty Research Fellow, Fellow Center for Advanced Study in the Behavioral Sciences 1972–73, Sherman Fairchild Distinguished Scholar, Calif. Inst. of Tech. 1973–74; Blue Ribbon Panel Mem. Nat. Electricity Rehabilitation Council 1997; consultant on privatization of electric power in Australia and NZ and participated in numerous pvt. and public discussions on energy deregulation in the USA; Hon. DrMan (Purdue) 1989; Andersen Consulting Prof. of the Year 1993, Assen for Pvt. Enterprise Educ. Adam Smith Award 1995, Distinguished Alumni Award, Calif. Inst. of Tech. 1996, Nobel Prize for Econs 2002. *Publications include:* Economics: An Analytical Approach (jtly with K. Davidson and J. Wiley) 1958, Investment and Production 1961, Economics of Natural and Environmental Resources 1977, Papers in Experimental

Economics (collected works) 1991, Experiments in Decision, Organization and Exchange 1993, Bargaining and Market Behavior: Essays in Experimental Economics (collected works) 2000; Research in Experimental Economics, Vols. 1–3 (ed.) 1979, 1982, 1985; Schools of Economic Thought: Experimental Economics (ed.) 1990; over 200 articles on capital theory, finance, natural resource econs and experimental econs. *Address:* Department of Economics, Interdisciplinary Center for Economic Science, George Mason University, 4400 University Blvd., MSN 1B2, Fairfax, VA 22030, USA (office). *Telephone:* (703) 993-4842 (office). *Fax:* (703) 993-4851 (office). *E-mail:* vsmith2@gmu.edu (office). *Website:* www.gmu.edu/departments/economics/facultybios/smith (office).

SMITH, Wilbur Addison, BComm; British novelist; b. 9 Jan. 1933, Zambia; m. 1st Danielle Antoinette Smith 1971 (died 1999); two s. one d.; m. 2nd Mokhiniso Rakhimova 2000; ed Michaelhouse, Natal and Rhodes Univ.; business exec. 1954–58; factory owner 1958–64; professional author 1961–. *Publications:* When the Lion Feeds 1964, The Dark of the Sun 1965, The Sound of Thunder 1966, Shout at the Devil 1968, Gold Mine 1970, The Diamond Hunters 1971, The Sunbird 1972, Eagle in the Sky 1974, The Eye of the Tiger 1975, Cry Wolf 1976, A Sparrow Falls 1977, Hungry as the Sea 1978, Wild Justice 1979, A Falcon Flies 1980, Men of Men 1981, The Angels Weep 1982, The Leopard Hunts in Darkness 1984, The Burning Shore 1985, Power of the Sword 1986, Rage 1987, The Courtneys 1987, The Courtneys in Africa 1988, A Time to Die 1989, Golden Fox 1990, Elephant Song 1991, River God 1993, The Seventh Scroll 1995, Birds of Prey 1997, Monsoon 1999, Warlock 2001, Blue Horizon 2003, The Triumph of the Sun 2005, The Quest 2007, Assegai 2009, Those in Peril 2011; contrib. to numerous journals and magazines. *Leisure interests:* fishing, wildlife, skiing, wing shooting. *Address:* c/o Charles Pick Consultancy Ltd, 21 Dagmar Terrace, London, N1 2BN, England (office). *Telephone:* (20) 7226-2779 (office). *Fax:* (20) 7226-2779 (office). *Website:* www.wilbursmithbooks.com; www.wilbursmith.net.

SMITH, Will; American actor and singer; b. (Willard Christopher Smith II), 25 Sept. 1968, Philadelphia, Pa; s. of Willard Smith, Sr and Caroline Smith; m. 1st Sheree Zampino 1992 (divorced); one s.; m. 2nd Jada Pinkett 1997; one s. one d.; ed Overbrook High School, Winfield, Pa; formed duo DJ Jazzy Jeff and the Fresh Prince; f. Overbrook Entertainment (production co.); developer and owner The Boom Boom Room (recording studio); with DJ Jazzy Jeff: Grammy Awards Best Rap Performance 1988, 1991; as solo artist: Grammy Awards Best Rap Solo Performance 1998, MTV Music Video Awards Best Male Video, Best Rap Video 1998, American Music Awards Favorite Pop/Rock Male Artist, Favorite Album, Favorite Male Soul/R&B Artist 1998, Favorite Pop/Rock Male Artist 2000; César d'honneur 2005, American Music Award for Favorite Male Pop/Rock Artist 2005, Kora All African Music Award for Best African American Diaspora Artist (for song, Switch) 2005. *Films include:* Where the Day Takes You 1992, Made in America 1993, Six Degrees of Separation 1993, Bad Boys 1995, Independence Day 1996, Men in Black 1997, Enemy of the State 1998, Wild Wild West 1999, Legend of Bagger Vance 2000, Ali 2002, Men in Black II: Alien Attack 2002, Bad Boys II 2003, Shark Tale (voice) 2004, I, Robot 2004, Hitch 2005, The Pursuit of Happyness 2006, I Am Legend 2007, Hancock 2008, Seven Pounds 2009, The Karate Kid (producer) 2010, Men in Black III 2012. *Television includes:* The Fresh Prince of Bel Air (series) 1990–96, Happily Ever After: Fairy Tales for Every Child (episode 'Pinocchio'; voice) 1997, All of Us Johnny (three episodes) 2003–04, Nur die Liebe zählt (episode) 2008. *Recordings include:* albums: as The Fresh Prince with DJ Jazzy Jeff: He's the DJ, I'm the Rapper 1988, And in This Corner… 1989, Homebase 1991, Rock the House 1991, Code Red 1993; solo: Big Willie Style 1997, Willennium 1999, Born to Reign 2002, Lost and Found 2005. *Publication:* Just the Two of Us (juvenile) 2005. *Address:* c/o Overbrook Entertainment, 450 North Roxbury Drive, 4th Floor, Beverly Hills, CA 90210 (office); c/o Ken Stovicz, Creative Artists Agency, 9830 Wilshire Boulevard, Beverly Hills, CA 90212, USA (office). *Telephone:* (310) 432-2400 (Overbrook) (office). *Fax:* (310) 432-2410 (Overbrook) (office). *Website:* www.overbrookent.com (office).

SMITH BASTERRA, Jaime, BA, MA; Spanish business executive; *CEO, Telefónica O2 Germany GmbH & Co;* b. 6 Sept. 1965; ed Univ. Comercial Deusto, Spain, Exeter Univ., UK; began career as telecommunications industry and Dir of Equity Research, Benito & Monjardin SVB SA, Madrid 1989–98; fmr Dir of Global Equities, Banesto (Banco Santander Group) 1989–99; Dir of Financial Planning, Telefónica Internacional 1999, Chief Financial Officer 1999–2000, Controller, Telefónica Group 2000–02, Chief Financial Officer, Telefónica de Espana 2002–05, Chair., Pres. and CEO Český Telecom a.s. 2005–07; CEO Telefónica O2 Germany GmbH & Co., Munich 2007–; Exec. Dir O2 plc, Telefónica Europe 2006–; mem. Bd of Dirs I+D, Telyco, TTP, Telfisa; mem. Presiding Cttee BITKOM. *Address:* Telefónica O2 Germany GmbH & Co., Georg-Brauchle-Ring 50, 80992 Munich, Germany (office). *Telephone:* (89) 24420000 (office). *Website:* www.o2online.de (office).

SMITH OF CLIFTON, Baron (Life Peer), cr. 1997, of Mountsandel in the County of Londonderry; **Trevor Arthur Smith,** Kt, BSc (Econ.), FRHistS, AcSS; British university vice-chancellor (retd) and business executive; b. 14 June 1937, London, England; s. of the late Arthur J. Smith and Vera G. Cross; m. 1st Brenda Eustace 1960 (divorced 1973); two s.; m. 2nd Julia Bullock 1979; one d.; ed London School of Econs; schoolteacher, London 1958–59; Asst Lecturer in Politics, Univ. of Exeter 1959–60; Research Officer, Acton Soc. Trust 1960–62; Lecturer in Politics, Univ. of Hull 1962–67; Lecturer, Queen Mary Coll. London 1967, Sr Lecturer, Head Dept 1972–85, Dean of Social Studies 1979–82, Prof. of Politics 1983–91, Pro-Prin. 1985–87, Sr Pro-Prin. 1987–89, Sr Vice-Prin., Queen Mary & Westfield Coll. 1989–91; Vice-Chancellor, Univ. of Ulster 1991–99 and Hon. Prof.; Visiting Prof., Univ. of York 1999–2003, Univ. of Portsmouth 2000–01; Dir Joseph Rowntree Reform Trust Ltd 1975–2006 (Chair. 1987–99); Chair. Political Studies Assen UK 1988–89, Vice-Pres. 1989–91, Pres. 1991–93; Dir Job Ownership Ltd 1978–85, New Society Ltd 1986–88, Statesman and Nation Publishing Co. Ltd 1988–90, Bell Educ. Trust Ltd 1988–93, Gerald Duckworth Ltd 1990–95; Deputy Pres. Inst. for Citizenship 1991–2001; Dir Irish Peace Inst. 1992–99; Pres. Belfast Civic Trust 1995–99; mem. Admin. Bd Int. Assen of Univs 1995–96, Editorial Bd Government and Opposition journal 1995–2013, Bd A Taste of Ulster 1996–99; mem. N Yorks Health Authority 2000–02; mem. (Liberal Democrat), House of Lords 1997–, Liberal Democrat Spokesman on NI 2000–11, British Irish Parl. Ass. 2000–11, Chair. Lords Select Cttee on Animals in Scientific Procedures 2001–02; Trustee

Stroke Asscn 2002–07; Academician Coll. of Learned Socs in the Social Sciences 2000; Hon. mem. of Senate (Fachhochschule Augsburg) 1994; Hon. Fellow, Queen Mary London 2003; Hon. LLD (Dublin) 1992, (Hull) 1993, (Belfast) 1995, (Nat. Univ. of Ireland) 1996; Hon. DHL (Alabama) 1998; Hon. DLitt (Ulster) 2002. *Publications:* Training Managers (with M. Argyle) 1962, Town Councillors (with A. M. Rees) 1964, Town and County Hall 1966, Anti-Politics 1972, The Politics of the Corporate Economy 1979, The Fixers (with Alison Young) 1996; contributed to numerous other publs. *Leisure interest:* water-colour painting. *Address:* House of Lords, Westminster, London, SW1A 0PW, England (office). *Telephone:* (20) 7219-5353 (office). *Fax:* (20) 7219-5979 (office). *E-mail:* smitht@parliament.uk (office). *Website:* www.parliament.uk/biographies/lords/lord-smith-of-clifton/3144 (office).

SMITH OF FINSBURY, Baron (Life Peer), cr. 2005, of Finsbury in the London Borough of Islington; **Rt Hon. Chris(topher) Robert Smith,** PC, PhD; British politician; *Chairman, Environment Agency;* b. 24 July 1951, Barnet, London, England; s. of Colin Smith and Gladys Smith (née Luscombe); ed George Watson's Coll., Edinburgh, Pembroke Coll., Cambridge, Harvard Univ. (Kennedy Scholar 1975–76), USA; Devt Sec., Shaftesbury Soc. Housing Asscn 1977–80; Devt Co-ordinator Soc. for Co-operative Dwellings 1980–83; Councillor, London Borough of Islington 1978–83, Chief Whip 1978–79, Chair. Housing Cttee 1981–83; Labour MP for Islington S and Finsbury 1983–2005, mem. Cttee on Standards in Public Life 2001–05; Opposition Spokesman on Treasury and Econ. Affairs 1987–92; Prin. Opposition Spokesman on Environmental Protection 1992–94, on Nat. Heritage 1994–95, on Social Security 1995–96, on Health 1996–97; Sec. of State for Culture, Media and Sport 1997–2001; Chair. Labour Campaign for Criminal Justice 1985–88, Tribune Group of MPs 1988–89; mem. (Non-Affiliated) House of Lords 2005–, Vice-Chair. British Museum Group 2005–; mem. Exec. Fabian Soc. 1990–96, Chair. 1996–97; Pres. SERA (Labour Environment Campaign) 1992–2007, Ramblers' Asscn 2004–08; Chair. Wordsworth Trust 2001–, Classic FM Consumer Panel 2001–07, Donmar Warehouse Theatre 2003–, Judges, Man Booker Prize for Fiction 2004, London Cultural Consortium 2004–08, Advertising Standards Authority 2007–, Environment Agency 2008–, Review of Film Policy for HM's Govt 2010–11, 2013; Dir Clore Cultural Leadership Programme 2003–08; Dir (non-exec.) PPL (Phonographic Performance Ltd) 2006–; Sr Assoc. Judge, Inst. in Man. Studies, Univ. of Cambridge 2001–07; Visiting Prof., Univ. of the Arts London 2002–; Visiting Fellow, Ashridge Business Coll. 2007–; Sr Fellow, RCA 2007; Vice-Pres. Christian Socialist Movt; Companion, Chartered Man. Inst. 2005–10; Trustee, The Sixteen 2013–; Patron The Food Chain, London; Hon. Life mem. BAFTA 2001; Hon. FRIBA 2001; Hon. Fellow, Pembroke Coll., Cambridge 2004, King's Coll., London 2008, Univ. of Cumbria 2010; Freedom of the Borough of Islington 2010; Dr hc (City Univ.) 2003 (Lancaster) 2011. *Publications:* Creative Britain 1998, Suicide of the West (co-author) 2006. *Leisure interests:* mountaineering (first MP to climb all the 3,000ft 'Munros' in Scotland), literature, theatre, music, art. *Address:* Environment Agency, Ergon House, Horseferry Road, London, SW1P 2AL (office); House of Lords, Westminster, London, SW1A 0PW, England. *Telephone:* (20) 3263-8188 (office); (20) 7492-2244 (office); (20) 7219-5119. *E-mail:* chris.smith@environment-agency.gov.uk (office); benedicta.moxon@environment-agency.gov.uk (office); smithcr@parliament.uk. *Website:* www .environment-agency.gov.uk (office); www.parliament.uk/biographies/lords/lord -smith-of-finsbury/186.

SMITH OF KELVIN, Baron (Life Peer), cr. 2008, of Kelvin in the City of Glasgow; **Rt Hon. Robert Haldane Smith,** Kt, CA; British business executive; *Chairman, SSE plc;* b. 8 Aug. 1944; m. Alison Marjorie Bell 1969; two d.; ed Allan Glen's School, Glasgow; accountant Robb Ferguson & Co., Glasgow 1963–68; with ICFC (later 3i Group PLC) 1968–82; with Royal Bank of Scotland 1983–85; Man. Dir Charterhouse Devt Capital Ltd 1985–89; BBC Nat. Gov. for Scotland and Chair. Broadcasting Council for Scotland 1999–2004; Chair. and CEO Morgan Grenfell Private Equity 2001, also CEO Morgan Grenfell Asset Man. (renamed Deutsche Asset Man. 1999), Chair. Deutsche Asset Man. 2000–02; Exec. Dir Scottish and Southern Energy plc 2003– (now SSE plc), Deputy Chair. 2003–05, Chair. 2005–, Chair. Nomination Cttee, mem. Remuneration Cttee; Chair. The Weir Group PLC 2002–; Chancellor Paisley Univ. 2003– (named changed to Univ. of the West of Scotland following merger with Bell Coll., Hamilton 2007); Chair. Glasgow 2014 Ltd; Chair. Bd of Trustees, Nat. Museums of Scotland 1993–2002; Dir (non-exec.) 3i Group PLC, Standard Bank Group Ltd, Aegon UK PLC; fmr mem. Bd of Dirs MFI Furniture Group PLC, Stakis PLC (also Chair. 1998–99), Bank of Scotland, Tip Europe PLC, Network Rail; Pres. British Asscn of Friends of Museums 1995–; fmr Pres. Inst. of Chartered Accountants of Scotland; mem. Financial Services Authority 1997–2000, Financial Reporting Council, Judicial Appointments Bd for Scotland, Council of Econ. Advisers to the First Minister of Scotland, Bd of Trustees The British Council; mem. Museums and Galleries Comm. 1988–98 (Vice-Chair. 1996–98); Patron Scottish Community Foundation; Dr hc (Glasgow, Edinburgh and Paisley). *Address:* SSE plc, Inveralmond House, 200 Dunkeld Road, Perth, PH1 3AQ, Scotland (office). *Telephone:* (1738) 456000 (office). *E-mail:* info@sse.com (office). *Website:* www.sse.com (office); www.hydro.co.uk (office).

SMITH PERERA, Roberto, PhD; Venezuelan politician and business executive; b. 1958, Barquisimeto; s. of Roberto Smith Camacho; m. Marina Pocaterra; three d.; ed Universidad Simón Bolívar and Harvard Univ., USA; early career working for telecommunications cos.; Coordinator of Govt's 8th Plan for the Nation 1989–90; Minister of Transport and Communications 1990–92; Amb. to EU, Belgium and Luxembourg 1992–95; Pres. Digitel Venezuela (telecoms co.) 1997–2002, f. Digicel in El Salvador and Guatemala (subsidiaries of Digitel) 1999; f. Microjuris.com (internet service); unsuccessful cand. in Vargas state gubernatorial elections 2004; Founder and Pres. Venezuela de Primera Party (Venezuela First) 2005–; unsuccessful cand. in presidential elections 2006. *Publications:* Venezuela, Vision or Chaos 1995. *Address:* c/o Microjuris.com Venezuela, Ave Las Acacias con Abraham Lincoln, Torre Lincon, PH –A Plaza Venezuela, Caracas, D.M., Venezuela. *Website:* www.venezueladeprimera.org.ve; www.robertosmith.org.

SMITHIES, Oliver, DPhil; American (b. British) biomedical scientist and academic; *Excellence Professor, Department of Pathology and Laboratory Medicine, School of Medicine, University of North Carolina;* b. 23 June 1925, Halifax; m. Nobuyo Maeda; ed Univ. of Oxford; Postdoctoral Fellowship, Univ. of Wisconsin 1951–53, Asst Prof., later Prof. Genetics and Medical Genetics 1960–63, Leon J.

Cole Prof. 1971–80, Hilldale Prof. 1980–88; Excellence Prof. of Pathology and Lab. Medicine, Univ. of North Carolina 1988–; Pres. Genetics Soc. of America; Foreign mem. Royal Soc. 1998; Hon. DSc (Chicago); Gairdner Foundation Int. Award 1990, 1993, Bristol-Myers Squibb Award for Distinguished Achievement in Cardiovascular/Metabolic Disease Research, CIBA Award for Hypertension Research 1996, jt recipient of American Heart Foundation Research Achievement Award for Distinguished Research in the Biomedical Sciences 1998, Int. Okamoto Award, Japan Vascular Disease Research Foundation 2000, Albert Lasker Award for Basic Medical Research 2001, Wolf Foundation Prize in Medicine 2002, Nobel Prize for Medicine (with Mario Capecchi and Sir Martin Evans) 2007 for the discovery of principles for introducing specific gene modifications in mice by the use of embryonic stem cells. *Publications:* over 240 publs. *Address:* Department of Pathology and Laboratory Medicine, School of Medicine, University of North Carolina, Chapel Hill, NC 27599, USA (office). *Telephone:* (919) 966-6913 (office). *E-mail:* oliver.smithies@pathology.unc.edu (office). *Website:* www.pathology.unc .edu/common/smithies.htm (office).

SMITS, Robert-Jan; Dutch EC official; *Director-General, Directorate-General for Research and Innovation, European Commission;* b. 1958; ed Utrecht Univ., Institut Universitaire d'Hautes Etudes Internationales, Switzerland, Fletcher School of Law and Diplomacy, USA; fmr Dir for European Research Area: Research Programmes and Capacity at EC's Directorate-Gen. for Research and Innovation (RTD), responsible for coordination of nat. research programmes, co-operation with intergovernmental research orgs (EIROforum, EUREKA, COST), Research Infrastructures, relations with European Investment Bank and the Structural Funds; Deputy Dir-Gen. Directorate-Gen. of Jt Research Centre, EC, responsible for Programmes and Stakeholder Relations, Resource Man., and Inst. for Energy, Inst. for Environment and Sustainability and Inst. for Prospective Technological Studies Feb.–June 2010; Dir-Gen. Directorate-Gen. for Research for Research and Innovation 2010–; Chair. several high-level cttees, including European Research Area Cttee (ERAC), Steering Cttee of the ERC (ERCEA). *Address:* Directorate-General for Research and Innovation, European Commission, Square Orban 8, 1050 Brussels, Belgium (office). *Telephone:* (2) 296-32-96 (office). *E-mail:* robert-jan.smits@ec.europa.eu (office). *Website:* ec.europa.eu/dgs/research (office).

SMOL, John P., BS, MSc, PhD, FRSC; Canadian biologist and academic; *Canada Research Chair in Environmental Change, Queen's University;* b. Montréal; ed McGill Univ., Brock Univ., Queen's Univ.; post-doctoral work with Geological Survey of Canada, High Arctic; joined faculty of Dept of Biology and School of Environmental Studies, Queen's Univ., Kingston 1984, Prof. 1991–, Canada Research Chair in Environmental Change 2000–; Founding Dir Paleoecological Environmental Assessment and Research Lab., Queen's Univ.; Founding Ed. Journal of Paleolimnology 1987–2007; Ed. Environmental Reviews, Developments in Paleoenvironmental Research; Distinguished Fellow, Geological Asscn of Canada; Hon. LLD (St Francis Xavier Univ.) 2003; Hon. PhD (Helsinki) 2007 numerous awards including Botanical Soc. of America Darbaker Prize 1992, Nat. Research Council Steacie Prize 1993, Miroslaw Romanowski Medal 2001, NSERC Herzberg Gold Medal 2004, W. A. Johnston Medal 2005, G. Evelyn Hutchinson Award 2007, Flavelle Medal 2008, Canada Council for the Arts Killam Prize 2009, Premier of Ont. Discovery Award 2009. *Publications:* over 350 journal articles and book chapters; 16 books, including Pollution of Lakes and Rivers: A Paleoenvironmental Perspective. *Address:* Department of Biology, Queen's University, Kingston, ON K7L 3N6, Canada (office). *Telephone:* (613) 533-6147 (office). *E-mail:* smolj@queensu.ca (office). *Website:* post.queensu.ca/~smolj/dper/dperjps.html (office).

SMOOT, George Fitzgerald, III, BS, PhD; American astrophysicist and cosmologist; *Professor of Physics and Director, Paris and Berkeley Centers for Cosmological Physics, University of California, Berkeley and Sorbonne Paris-Cité;* b. 20 Feb. 1945, Yukon, Fla; s. of George F. Smoot, Jr; ed Stetson Univ., Georgetown Univ., Massachusetts Inst. of Tech.; Postdoctoral researcher, MIT 1970; Research Physicist, Univ. of California, Berkeley Space Sciences Lab. 1971–74, jt appointment, Research Physicist, Lawrence Berkeley Nat. Lab. 1974–, Prof., Physics Dept, Univ. of California, Berkeley 1994–; Dir Berkeley Center for Cosmological Physics 2007–; Dir Inst. for the Early Universe and Distinguished Prof., Ewha Univ. and Acad. of Advanced Studies, Seoul, S Korea 2008–14; Chaire Blaise Pascal, Université de Paris, Diderot; Dir Paris Center for Cosmological Physics 2011–; Prof., Sorbonne Paris-Cité 2011–13; Dir Extreme Universe Lab., Moscow State Univ.; mem. American Physical Soc. Cttee on Safety of Commercial Nuclear Reactors 1974–75, Man. and Operations Working Group for Shuttle Astronomy 1976–80, Steering Group on Cosmic Background Explorer Satellite (Prin. Investigator on isotropy experiment—NASA) 1975–96, White Mountain Research Station Advisory Cttee 1982, Superconducting Magnet Facility for the Space Station Study Team 1985, Center for Particle Astrophysics at Univ. of California, Berkeley 1988, Radio Astronomy Lab. Advisory Cttee 1990; mem. American Physical Soc., American Astronomical Soc., AAAS, Int. Astronomical Union, NAS; Dr hc (Univ. of Marseille), (Reiko Univ.), (Miguel Hernandez Univ.), (Moscow State Univ.), (Bruno Giodano Global Shift Univ.), (Gustavus Adolphus Coll., Minn.); NASA Medal for Exceptional Scientific Achievement 1991, Popular Science Award 1992, Aerospace Laureate, Aviation Week & Space Technology 1993, Distinguished Scientist, ARCS Foundation, Inc. 1993, Kilby Award 1993, Gravity Research Foundation Essay First Award 1993, Productivity Group Award, Goddard Space Flight Center, NASA 1993, Golden Plate Award 1994, Lawrence Award 1995, Nobel Prize in Physics (with John C. Mather) 2006, Oersted Medal 2009. *Music:* Rhythms of the Universe with Mickey Hart and others. *Television:* The Big Bang Theory. *Publications:* Wrinkles in Time (co-author) 1993; more than 500 scientific papers in professional journals on astrophysics and cosmology. *Address:* Physics Department, University of California, Berkeley, 437 Old LeConte Hall, Berkeley, CA 94720-7300 (office); Ernest Orlando Lawrence Berkeley National Laboratory, 1 Cyclotron Road, Mail Stop 50R5005, Berkeley, CA 94720, USA (office). *Telephone:* (510) 486-5505 (office); (510) 486-5237 (office); (510) 642-9389 (office). *Fax:* (510) 486-7149 (office). *E-mail:* gfsmoot@lbl.gov (office). *Website:* www.physics.berkeley.edu/research/faculty/Smoot.html (office); aether.lbl.gov (office); pariscosmo.fr; ieu.ewha.ac.kr; bccp.lbl.gov (office).

SMOUT, Thomas Christopher, CBE, MA, PhD, FRSE, FBA, FSA (Scot.); British historian and academic; *Professor Emeritus of Scottish History, University of St Andrews;* b. 19 Dec. 1933, Birmingham; s. of Sir Arthur J. G. Smout and Lady Smout (Hilda Mount, née Follows); m. Anne-Marie Schøning 1959; one s. one d.; ed Leys School, Cambridge, Clare Coll., Cambridge; joined staff Edinburgh Univ. 1959, Prof. of Econ. History 1970–79; Prof. of Scottish History, Univ. of St Andrews 1980–91, Prof. Emer. 1991–; Dir St John's House Inst. for Advanced Historical Studies, Univ. of St Andrews 1992–97; Founder and Dir Inst. for Environmental History, Univ. of St Andrews 1992–2000; Visiting Prof., Univ. of Strathclyde 1991–95, Univ. of Dundee 1993–, Univ. of Stirling 1997–, Univ. of York 1998–99; Deputy Chair. Scottish Nat. Heritage 1992–97, mem. Bd 1992–98; Historiographer Royal in Scotland 1993–; mem. Bd Royal Comm. Ancient and Historical Monuments of Scotland 1986–2000, Nature Conservancy Council (Scotland) 1991–92, Royal Comm. on Historical Manuscripts 1999–2003, Advisory Council on Nat. Records and Archives 2003–04; Trustee Nat. Museums of Scotland 1991–94, Woodland Trust 1998–2004; Chair. Scottish Coastal Archaeology and the Problem of Erosion 2001–; Patron Scottish Native Woods 2004–; Hon. Fellow, Trinity Coll. Dublin 1994–; Dr hc (Queen's Univ., Belfast) 1995, (Edin.) 1996, (St Andrews) 1999, (Glasgow) 2001, (Stirling) 2002. *Publications:* Scottish Trade on the Eve of the Union 1963, History of the Scottish People, 1560–1830 1969, State of the Scottish Working Class in 1843 (with Ian Levitt) 1979, Scottish Population History from the 17th Century to the 1930s (with M.W. Flinn) 1976, Century of the Scottish People, 1830–1950 1986, Scottish Voices (with S. Wood) 1990, Prices, Food and Wages in Scotland (with A. Gibson) 1995, Nature Contested 2000, People and Woods in Scotland (ed.) 2002, History of the Native Woods of Scotland (with A. R. MacDonald and F. Watson) 2005. *Leisure interests:* birdwatching and other natural history, conservation, architecture. *Address:* Chesterhill, Shore Road, Anstruther, Fife, KY10 3DZ, Scotland. *Telephone:* (1333) 310330. *Fax:* (1333) 311193. *E-mail:* tcs1@st-andrews.ac.uk.

SMURFIT, Anthony P. J., BSc; Irish business executive; *President and Group Chief Operations Officer, Smurfit Kappa Group;* b. 19 Dec. 1963, Wigan; s. of Michael Smurfit; ed Univ. of Scranton, Pennsylvania, USA; mem. Bd Jefferson Smurfit Group (now Smurfit Kappa Group), Chief Exec. Smurfit France 1996, later Deputy Chief Exec. Smurfit Europe, then Chief Exec. Smurfit Europe –2002, Group COO 2002–05, Pres. and Group Chief Operations Officer Smurfit Kappa Group 2005–; Dir Irish Nat. Stud Co.; Hon. Consul of Mexico to Ireland 2003, Chevalier de la Légion d'honneur 2004. *Leisure interests:* golf, horse breeding. *Address:* Smurfit Kappa Group, Beech Hill, Clonskeagh, Dublin 4, Ireland (office). *Telephone:* (1) 202-7157 (office). *Fax:* (1) 202-7183 (office). *E-mail:* info@ smurfitkappa.com (office). *Website:* www.smurfitkappa.com (office).

SMURFIT, Michael, Jr, MBA; Irish business executive; s. of Michael Smurfit; ed Univ. Coll. Dublin; fmr Vice-Pres. World Purchasing, Jefferson Smurfit Group, Pres. and Chief Exec., Smurfit Packaging Corpn (now Smurfit-Stone Container Corpn) 1996; currently CEO SF Investments (pvt. investment co.), Dublin; mem. Bd of Dirs CNG Travel Group plc, GameAccount Global Limited, Escher plc, The K Club Limited, Irish Youth Foundation; mem. Irish Advisory Bd Michael Smurfit Grad. Business School, Univ. Coll. Dublin.

SMURFIT, Sir Michael William Joseph, Kt, KBE; Irish business executive (retd); b. 7 Aug. 1936, St Helens, England; m. 1st Norma Treisman (divorced); two s. two d.; m. 2nd Birgitta Beimark; two s.; joined Jefferson Smurfit & Sons Ltd 1955, f. Jefferson Smurfit Packaging Ltd (Lancs.) 1961, rejoined Jefferson Smurfit Group, Dir 1964, Jt Man. Dir 1967, Deputy Chair. 1979, Chair. and CEO Jefferson Smurfit Group PLC, Dublin 1977–2002, Chair. 2002–07, also Chair. Jefferson Smurfit Corpn & Container Corpn of America; mem. Irish Advisory Bd Michael Smurfit Grad. Business School, Univ. Coll. Dublin; fmr Chair. Telecom Eireann; Hon. LLD (Trinity Coll., Dublin), (Univ. of Scranton, Pennsylvania, USA). *Address:* Le Sardanapale, 2 Avenue Princesse Grace, Monte-Carlo 98000, Monaco (office). *Telephone:* (93) 157045 (office). *E-mail:* mwjsoffice@monaco.mc (office).

SNAPKOU, Mikalay H.; Belarusian economist and politician; *Minister of the Economy;* b. 1969, Mogilev (Mahiloŭ) Oblast; Chief of Financial Dept, Mogilev Oblast 2000–07, Deputy Head, Mogilev Oblast Exec. Cttee 2007–09; Deputy Chair. of Presidential Admin Jan.–Dec. 2009; Minister of the Economy Dec. 2009–. *Address:* Ministry of the Economy, 220050 Minsk, vul. Bersona 14, Belarus (office). *Telephone:* (17) 222-60-48 (office). *Fax:* (17) 200-37-77 (office). *E-mail:* minec@ economy.gov.by (office). *Website:* www.economy.gov.by (office).

SNEGUR, Mircea, DrAgriSc; Moldovan politician; b. 17 Jan. 1940, V. Trifăneşti, Soroca Dist; s. of Ion Snegur and Ana Snegur; m. Georgeta Snegur 1960; one s. one d.; ed Kishinau Inst. of Agric.; mem. CPSU 1964–90; work as agronomist, man. state and collective farms 1961–68, Chair. of Experimental Station 1968–73, Chief of Section Ministry of Agric. 1973–78; Dir-Gen. Research Production Asscn 'Selektsia', Balts 1978–81; Sec. CP Cttee, Yedinetsky Dist 1981–85; Sec. Cen. Cttee of CP of Moldavia 1985–89, Chair. Presidium of Supreme Soviet of Moldavia 1989–90; Pres. of Moldova 1990–96; Chair. Party of Resurrection and Accord (later Democratic Convention) 1995–2001; mem. of Parl. 1998, Constant Bureau of Parl. 1998–2001; Hon. Chair. Liberal Party 2002–; Order of the Repub. 2000. *Publications:* more than 100 articles on phytotechnical matters and the application of scientific procedures to production, Memories in Two Parts (monograph). *Leisure interests:* billiards, history and detective fiction, sports programmes, sport fishing. *Address:* 62A Puschin Street, Kishinau, Moldova. *Telephone:* 21-10-05 (office). *Fax:* 54-39-22 (office).

SNEH, Brig.-Gen. Ephraim, MD; Israeli politician, physician and army officer (retd); *Chairman, S. Daniel Abraham Center for Strategic Dialogue, Netanya Academic College;* b. 19 Sept. 1944, Tel-Aviv; s. of Dr Moshe Sneh; m.; two c.; ed Tel-Aviv Univ. Medical School; Research Fellow, Walter Reed Army Medical Center; rank of Brig.-Gen., army service includes Medical Officer of Paratroops Brigade 1972–74; Chief Medical Officer of the Paratroops and Infantry Corps 1974–78; Commdr of the Medical Teams during the Entebbe Rescue Operation 1976; Commdr Israel Defense Forces (IDF) elite unit 1978–80; Chief Medical Officer, IDF Northern Command 1980–81; Commdr of Security Zone in S Lebanon 1981–82; Head of the Civil Admin. of the West Bank 1985–87; mem. (Labor Party) of Knesset (Parl.) 1992– 2008; Minister of Health 1994–96, of Transportation 2001–02; Deputy Minister of Defence 1999–2001, 2006–07; est. Strong Israel Party

2008; Chair. S. Daniel Abraham Center for Strategic Dialogue, Netanya Academic Coll. 2008–; Pres. Silver Bullet Ltd. *Publication:* Navigating Perilous Waters 2005. *Address:* 6 Hachoshlim Street, PO Box 12006, Herzliya Pituach 46722 (office); 12 Hapalmach Street, Herzelia 46793, Israel (home). *Telephone:* (77) 6935612 (office). *Fax:* (77) 6935601 (office). *E-mail:* esneh@netvision.net.il (home). *Website:* sdc .netanya.ac.il (office); www.sneh.org.il.

SNELLGROVE, David Llewelyn, LittD, PhD, FBA; British academic and author; b. 29 June 1920, Portsmouth, Hants., England; s. of Lt-Commdr Clifford Snellgrove, RN and Eleanor M. Snellgrove; ed Christ's Hosp., Horsham, Southampton Univ. and Queen's Coll. Cambridge; war service in India –1946; Lecturer in Tibetan, SOAS, Univ. of London 1950–60, Reader in Tibetan, Univ. of London 1960–74, Prof. of Tibetan 1974–82, Prof. Emer. 1982–; has undertaken numerous expeditions to India and the Himalayas; Co-founder Inst. of Tibetan Studies (now Inst. of Buddhist Studies), Tring, Herts. 1966, fmr Chair. of Trustees; expeditions in Indonesia 1987–94, in Cambodia 1995–; Rockefeller Grant 1961–64, Leverhulme Grant 1978–81, The Burton Medal 2004. *Publications:* Buddhist Himalaya 1957, Himalayan Pilgrimage 1961, The Hevajra Tantra (two vols) 1959, The Nine Ways of Bon 1967, Four Lamas of Dolpo (two vols) 1967, A Cultural History of Tibet (with H. E. Richardson) 1968, The Cultural Heritage of Ladakh (with T. Skorupski) (two vols) 1979–80, Indo-Tibetan Buddhism, Indian Buddhists and their Tibetan Successors 1986, Asian Commitment 2000, Khmer Civilization and Angkor 2001, Angkor Before and After, A Cultural History of the Khmers 2004, Religion as History – Religion as Myth 2006; Gen. Ed. and major contrib. to The Image of the Buddha 1978. *Website:* www.dlsnellgrove.com.

SNIDER, Stacey, BA, JD; American film industry executive; *Co-Chairman and CEO, DreamWorks SKG;* b. 29 April 1961, Phila, Pa; m. Gary Jones; two c.; ed Univ. of Pennsylvania, Univ. of California, Los Angeles; began career in post room, Triad Agency, later Asst; Asst, Simpson-Bruckheimer Productions; joined Guber-Peters Entertainment Co. as Dir of Devt 1986–90, Exec. Vice-Pres. 1990–92; Production Pres. TriStar Pictures 1992–96; Co-Pres. of Production, Universal Pictures 1996–98, Head of Production April–Nov. 1998, Pres. of Production and Co-Chair. 1998, Chair. and CEO Universal Pictures 1999–2006; Co-Chair. and CEO DreamWorks SKG 2006–, also Prin. Partner; mem. Bd of Dirs City Year, Special Olympics of Southern California, American Film Inst.; Dorothy and Sherrill C. Corwain Human Relations Award, American Jewish Cttee 2004; named No. 2 on Power List in Women in Entertainment Report, The Hollywood Reporter 2003, ranked by Fortune magazine amongst 50 Most Powerful Women in Business in the US (20th) 2002, (18th) 2003, (28th) 2004, (33rd) 2005, (50th) 2006, ranked by Forbes magazine amongst 100 Most Powerful Women (60th) 2004, (59th) 2005, (94th) 2006, (87th) 2007, (63rd) 2009. *Address:* DreamWorks SKG, 1000 Flower Street, Glendale, CA 91201, USA (office). *Telephone:* (818) 733-7000 (office). *Fax:* (818) 695-7574 (office). *Website:* www.dreamworksstudios.com (office).

SNIPES, Wesley; American actor and producer; b. 31 July 1962, Orlando, Fla; one s.; ed High School for the Performing Arts, New York and State Univ. of New York, Purchase; fmr telephone repair man, New York; appeared in Martin Scorsese's video Bad 1987; Co-Founder Struttin Street Stuff puppet theatre mid-1980s; indicted on eight counts of US tax fraud Oct. 2006, convicted and sentenced to three years in prison 2008; ACE Award for Best Actor for Vietnam War Stories (TV) 1989, Best Actor for One Night Stand, Venice Film Festival. *Films:* Wildcats, Streets of Gold, Major League, Mo Better Blues 1990, Jungle Fever 1991, New Jack City, White Men Can't Jump, Demolition Man, Boiling Point, Sugar Hill, Drop Zone, To Wong Foo, Thanks for Everything, Julie Newmar 1995, The Money Train, Waiting to Exhale, The Fan 1996, One Night Stand, Murder at 1600, Blade (also producer) 1997, U.S. Marshals 1998, Down in the Delta (also producer) 1998, The Art of War 2000, Blade 2 2002, Undisputed 2002, Nine Lives 2004. *Broadway stage appearances:* Boys of Winter, Execution of Justice, Death and King's Horsemen. *Address:* c/o Amen Ra Films, 301 N Canon Drive, Beverly Hills, CA 90210, USA (office).

SNODGRASS, Anthony McElrea, DPhil, FBA, FSA, FRSA; British archaeologist and academic; *Laurence Professor Emeritus of Classical Archaeology, Faculty of Classics, University of Cambridge;* b. 7 July 1934, London, England; s. of Maj. W. M. Snodgrass and Kathleen M. Snodgrass; m. 1st Ann Vaughan 1959 (divorced 1978); three d.; m. 2nd Annemarie Künzl 1983; one s.; ed Marlborough Coll. and Worcester Coll., Oxford; Nat. Service, RAF 1953–55; Lecturer in Classical Archaeology, Univ. of Edin. 1961–68, Reader 1968–75, Prof. 1975–76; Laurence Prof. of Classical Archaeology, Univ. of Cambridge 1976–2001, now Prof. Emer.; Sather Prof. in Classics, Univ. of Calif. at Berkeley 1984–85; Geddes-Harrower Prof. Univ. of Aberdeen 1995–96; Fellow, Clare Coll. Cambridge 1977–; Vice-Pres. British Acad. 1990–92; mem. Humanities Research Bd 1994–95; Chair. British Cttee for the Reunification of the Parthenon Marbles 2002–10; Foreign mem. Russian Acad. of Sciences 2002; Hon. Fellow, Worcester Coll., Oxford 2000; Hon. Fellow, Archaeological Inst. of America 2010; Hon. DLitt (Edinburgh) 2008; Hon. DHumLitt (Chicago) 2009. *Publications:* Early Greek Armour and Weapons 1964, Arms and Armour of the Greeks 1967, The Dark Age of Greece 1971, Archaeology and the Rise of the Greek State 1977, Archaic Greece: the Age of Experiment 1980, An Archaeology of Greece 1987, Homer and the Artists 1998, Archaeology and the Emergence of Greece 2006. *Leisure interests:* mountaineering, skiing. *Address:* Clare College, Trinity Lane, Cambridge, CB2 1TL, England (office). *Telephone:* (1223) 313559 (home). *Fax:* (1223) 313559 (home). *E-mail:* ams1002@cam.ac.uk (office). *Website:* www.classics.cam.ac.uk/directory/anthony-snodgrass (office).

SNOOK, Hans; German business executive; b. 1948; m. Etta Lai Yee Lau; worked in hotel industry and in real estate sales in Canada; joined Young Generation paging group, Hong Kong 1984; co. bought by Hutchinson Whampoa 1986; Founder and CEO Orange 1994–2001; Chair. (non-exec.) Carphone Warehouse PLC 2002–05, Monstermob Group PLC 2005–07; Dir (non-exec.) DDD Group PLC 2006–. *Address:* c/o Board of Directors, DDD Group PLC, 3000 Ocean Park Blvd., Suite 1025, Santa Monica, CA 90405, USA (office).

SNOOP LION, (Snoop Dogg, Snoop Doggy Dogg); American rap artist; b. (Calvin Broadus), 20 Oct. 1971, Long Beach, Calif.; mem. 213 (with Warren G. and Nate Dogg) early 1990s, re-formed 2005; collaborations with Dr Dre, Rage Against the Machine, K-Ci, JoJo; numerous live appearances; Exec. Producer, satellite radio network, XM 2005–; MTV Europe Music Award for Best Hip-hop 2005. *Songs for* *film:* In Prison My Whole Life 2008. *Film appearances:* Half Baked 1998, Caught Up 1998, Ride 1998, Da Game of Life 1998, Urban Menace 1999, The Wrecking Crew 1999, Hot Boyz 1999, 3 the Hard Way 1999, Tha Eastsidaz 2000, Baby Boy 2001, Training Day 2001, Bones 2001, The Wash 2001, Crime Partners 2000 2001, Snoop Dogg's Hustlaz: Diary of a Pimp 2002, Malibu's Most Wanted (voice) 2003, Starsky & Hutch 2004, Soul Plane 2004, Racing Stripes (voice) 2005, Boss'n Up 2005, The Tenants 2006, Hood of Horror 2006, Arthur and the Invisibles (voice) 2006. *Recordings include:* albums: solo: Doggystyle 1993, Tha Doggfather 1996, Da Game Is To Be Sold, Not To Be Told 1998, Top Dogg 1999, The Last Meal 2000, Death Row's Greatest Hits 2001, Paid Tha Cost To Be Da Boss 2002, Rhythm & Gangsta: The Masterpiece 2004, The Blue Carpet Treatment 2006, Ego Trippin' 2008, Malice n' Wonderland 2009, Doggumentary 2011, Reincarnated (as Snoop Lion) 2013; with 213: The Hard Way 2005. *Address:* William Morris Agency, 1325 Avenue of the Americas, New York, NY 10019, USA (office). *Telephone:* (212) 586-5100 (office). *Fax:* (212) 246-3583 (office).

SNOUSSI, Ahmed, PhD; Moroccan fmr diplomatist; b. 22 April 1929, Meknès; m. Farida Snoussi; three c.; ed Faculté de Droit, Univ. de Paris and Inst. des Hautes Etudes Politiques; Dir of Public Information, Govt of Morocco and ed. various publs on foreign affairs 1958–60; Sec.-Gen. Ministry of Tourism, Information and Fine Arts 1963; Minister of Information 1967–71 (Moroccan Commr-Gen. Expo '67, Montréal); Amb. to Nigeria 1965, to Cameroon 1966, to Tunisia 1971, to Algeria 1973, to Mauritania and Envoy of the King to Heads of State 1978–79; Head of Moroccan del. UN Security Council 1992–94; Amb. and Perm. Rep. to UN, New York 1997–2001; fmr Chair. Exec. Bd Somathon Tuna Fishing and Packing Corpn, Lafarge Maroc Group; fmr Pres. Cinouca Corpn, Asscn of Deep Sea Fishing Fleets, Nat. Producers Asscn; Chevalier, Order of Ouissam Alaouite, Commdr, légion d'honneur. *Leisure interests:* poetry, painting, 'elucubrations de ma jeunesse'. *Address:* 3 Avenue de la Victoire, Rabat, Morocco (office). *Telephone:* (3) 7774141 (home). *Fax:* (3) 7777929 (home). *E-mail:* asnoussi51@yahoo.fr (home).

SNOW, David B., Jr, BSc, MS; American health care industry executive; *Chairman and CEO, Medco Health Solutions Inc.;* b. 1955; ed Bates Coll., Duke Univ.; began career working for Creighton Univ. Medical School, Memorial Hosp. of Burlington Co. then US Healthcare Inc.; Sr Vice-Pres. American Int. Healthcare 1988–89; Co-Founder, Pres. and CEO Managed Health Care Systems (later renamed AmeriChoice) 1989–93; Exec. Vice-Pres. Oxford Health Plans 1993–98; Pres. and COO WellChoice Inc. (fmrly named Empire BlueCross BlueShield) 1999–2003; Pres. and CEO Medco Health Solutions Inc. March–June 2003, Chair. and CEO June 2003–; ranked by Harvard Business Review as No. 27 on its list of the world's 50 Career Best-Performing CEOs 2010, named by Institutional Investor Best CEO in Health Care Tech. and Distribution in its All-America Exec. Team rankings 2011. *Address:* Medco Health Solutions Inc., 100 Parsons Pond Drive, Franklin Lakes, NJ 07417-2604, USA (office). *Telephone:* (201) 269-3400 (office). *Fax:* (201) 269-1109 (office). *E-mail:* info@medcohealth.com (office). *Website:* www.medcohealth.com (office).

SNOW, John W., LLB, PhD; American business executive and fmr government official; *Chairman, Cerberus Capital Management LP;* b. 2 Aug. 1939, Toledo, Ohio; ed Kenyon Coll., Univ. of Toledo, Univ. of Virginia, George Washington Univ.; Asst Prof. of Econs, Univ. of Maryland 1965–67; with Wheeler & Wheeler (law firm), Washington, DC 1967–72; Asst Gen. Counsel, US Dept of Transportation 1972–73; Adjunct Prof. of Law, George Washington Univ. Law School 1972–75; Deputy Asst Sec. for Policy, Plans and Int. Affairs 1973–74; Asst Sec. for Govt Affairs, US Dept of Transportation 1974–75, Deputy Under-sec. 1975–76; Admin., Nat. Highway Traffic Safety Admin. 1976–77; Visiting Prof. of Econs, Univ. of Virginia, 1977; Vice-Pres. of Govt Affairs, Chessie System Inc. (later part of CSX Corpn) 1977–80, Sr Vice-Pres. Corp. Services, CSX Corpn Richmond 1980–84, Exec. Vice-Pres. 1984–85, COO 1988–89, Pres. 1988–2001, CEO 1989–2003, Chair. 1991–2003; US Sec. of the Treasury 2003–06; Chair. Cerberus Capital Man. LP 2006–; Co-Chair. Nat. Comm. on Financial Inst. Reform, Recovery and Enforcement 1992–93; Chair. Business Roundtable 1995–96, now mem.; mem. Bd of Dirs Sapient Corpn, Verizon, Johnson & Johnson, US Steel, Asscn of American Railroads, Carmax; mem. Bd of Trustees Johns Hopkins Univ., The Business Council, Va Business Council, Nat. Coal Council; Co-Chair. Conf. Bd Blue-Ribbon Comm. on Public Trust and Pvt. Enterprise; Chair. Kennedy Center Corp. Fund Bd; Hon. LLD (Kenyon Coll.) 1993; Marco Polo Award, US–China Foundation for Int. Exchanges 2001. *Address:* Cerberus Capital Management LP, 299 Park Avenue, New York, NY 10171, USA (office). *Telephone:* (212) 891-2100 (office). *E-mail:* media@cerberuscapital.com (office). *Website:* www.cerberuscapital .com (office).

SNOW, Jonathan (Jon) George; British television journalist; b. 28 Sept. 1947; s. of Rt Rev. George Snow and Joan Snow; pnr Madeleine Colvin; two d.; ed St Edward's School, Oxford, Univ. of Liverpool; Voluntary Service Overseas, Uganda 1967–68; Co-ordinator New Horizon Youth Centre, London 1970–73 (Chair. 1986–); journalist, Independent Radio News, LBC 1973–76; reporter, ITN 1977–83, Washington Corresp. 1983–86, Diplomatic Ed. 1986–89; presenter, Channel Four News 1989–; Visiting Prof. of Broadcast Journalism, Nottingham Trent Univ. 1992–2001, Univ. of Stirling 2002–; Chair. Prison Reform Trust 1992–97; Trustee, Tate Modern Council 1999–2008, Nat. Gallery 1999–2008; Chancellor, Oxford Brookes Univ. 2001–08; Hon. FRIBA; Hon. DLitt (Nottingham Trent) 1994, Hon. DLitt (Open Univ.); Monte Carlo Golden Nymph Award, for Eritrea air attack reporting 1979, TV Reporter of the Year, for Afghanistan, Iran and Iraq reporting, Royal Television Soc. (RTS) 1980, Valiant for Truth Award, for El Salvador reporting 1982, Int. Award, for El Salvador reporting, RTS 1982, Home News Award, for Kegworth air crash reporting, RTS 1989, RTS Presenter of the Year 1994, 2002, BAFTA Richard Dimbleby Award 2005, RTS Journalist of the Year 2006. *Publications:* Atlas of Today 1987, Sons and Mothers 1996, Shooting History: A Personal Journey 2004; articles in The Guardian, Financial Times, Independent, Telegraph, New Statesman. *Leisure interests:* water colours, cycling. *Address:* Channel Four News, ITN, 200 Gray's Inn Road, London, WC1X 8HB, England. *Telephone:* (20) 7430-4237; (20) 7833-3000 (office). *Fax:* (20) 7430-4607. *E-mail:* jon.snow@itn.co.uk (office). *Website:* www.channel4.com/news (office).

SNOW, Peter John, CBE; British television presenter, reporter and author; b. 20 April 1938, Dublin, Ireland; s. of Brig. John F. Snow, CBE and Peggy Pringle; m. 1st Alison Carter 1964 (divorced 1975); one s. one d.; m. 2nd Ann MacMillan 1976;

one s. two d.; ed Wellington Coll. and Balliol Coll. Oxford; Second Lt, Somerset Light Infantry 1956–58; newscaster and reporter, ITN 1962–79, Diplomatic and Defence Corresp. 1966–79; Presenter BBC Newsnight 1979–97, Tomorrow's World 1997–2001, BBC Election Programmes 1983–2005, BBC Radio 4 Mastermind 1998–2000, Radio 4 Random Edition 1998–, Radio 4 Masterteam 2001–05, Battlefield Britain (BBC 2, jtly with s. Dan Snow) 2004, 20th Century Battlefields (jtly with s. Dan Snow) 2007; Judges' Award, Royal TV Soc. 1998. *Publications:* Leila's Hijack War (co-author) 1970, Hussein: A Biography 1972, Battlefield Britain 2004, The World's Greatest 20th Century Battlefields (with Dan Snow) 2007, To War with Wellington 2010, When Britain Burned the White House: The 1814 Invasion of Washington 2013. *Leisure interests:* sailing, skiing, model railways, photography. *Address:* c/o Lucas Alexander Whitley Ltd, 14 Vernon Street, London, W14 0RJ, England (office). *Telephone:* (20) 7 471-7900 (office). *Fax:* (20) 7471-7910 (office). *E-mail:* p.snow@btconnect.com (office).

SNOWDON, 1st Earl of, cr. 1961, Baron Armstrong-Jones, cr. 1999; **Antony Charles Robert Armstrong-Jones,** GCVO, FRSA, RDI; British photographer; b. 7 March 1930, London; s. of the late Ronald Owen Lloyd Armstrong-Jones, MBE, QC, DL and the Countess of Rosse; m. 1st HRH The Princess Margaret 1960 (divorced 1978, died 2002); one s. one d.; m. 2nd Lucy Lindsay-Hogg 1979; one d.; ed Eton Coll. and Jesus Coll., Cambridge; Consultant, Council of Industrial Design 1962–89; in charge of design of Investiture of HRH the Prince of Wales, Caernarfon 1969; Editorial Adviser, Design Magazine 1961–87; Artistic Adviser to The Sunday Times and Sunday Times Publs Ltd 1962–90; photographer Telegraph Magazine 1990–96; Constable of Caernarfon Castle 1963–; sits as Lord Armstrong-Jones in the House of Lords 1999–; Pres. Civic Trust for Wales, Contemporary Art Soc. for Wales, Welsh Theatre Co.; Vice-Pres. Univ. of Bristol Photographic Soc.; Sr Fellow, Royal Coll. of Art 1986, Provost 1995–2003; Fellow, Inst. of British Photographers, British Inst. of Professional Photography, Chartered Soc. of Designers, Royal Photographic Soc., Royal Soc. of Arts, Manchester Coll. of Art and Design; mem. Faculty Royal Designers for Industry; Hon. mem. North Wales Soc. of Architects, South Wales Inst. of Architects; Chair. Snowdon Report on Integrating the Disabled 1972; mem. Council, Nat. Fund for Research for the Crippled Child; Founder Snowdon Award Scheme for Disabled Students 1980; Pres. (England) Int. Year of Disabled People 1981; Patron British Disabled Water Ski Asscn; mem. The Prince of Wales Advisory Group on Disability 1983; Metropolitan Union of YMCAs, British Water Ski Fed., Welsh Nat. Rowing Club, Circle of Guide Dog Owners; designed Snowdon Aviary, London Zoo 1965 (Listed Grade II 1998), Chairmobile 1972; Dr hc (Bradford) 1989, (Portsmouth) 1989; Hon. LLD (Bath) 1989; Art Dirs Club of New York Certificate of Merit 1969, Soc. of Publication Designers Certificate of Merit 1970, The Wilson Hicks Certificate of Merit for Photocommunication 1971, Soc. of Publication Designers' Award of Excellence 1973, Design and Art Dirs' Award 1978, Royal Photographic Soc. Hood Award 1979, Silver Progress Medal, Royal Photographic Soc. 1986. *Television documentaries:* Don't Count the Candles (six awards, including two Emmys) 1968, Love of a Kind 1970, Born to be Small 1971, Happy being Happy 1973, Mary Kingsley 1975, Burke and Wills 1975, Peter, Tina and Steve 1977, Snowdon on Camera (presenter) 1981. *Publications:* London 1958, Malta (in collaboration with Sacheverell Sitwell) 1958, Private View (with John Russell and Bryan Robertson) 1965, Assignments 1972, A View of Venice (with Derek Hart) 1972, Inchcape Review 1977, Pride of the Shires (jointly) 1979, Personal View 1979, Tasmania Essay 1981, Sittings: 1979–83 1983, Israel: A First View 1986, My Wales (with Viscount Tonypandy) 1986, Stills 1983–87, 1987, Public Appearances 1987–1991 1991, Wild Flowers 1995, Snowdon on Stage 1996, Wild Fruit 1997, London Sight Unseen by Snowdon 1999, Photographs by Snowdon: A Retrospective 2000. *Leisure interests:* photography, gardening. *Address:* 22 Launceston Place, London, W8 5RL, England. *Telephone:* (20) 7937-1524 (office). *Fax:* (20) 7938-1727 (office). *E-mail:* lordsnowdon@aol.com (office).

SNOWE, Olympia Jean, BA; American politician; b. 21 Feb. 1947, Augusta, Me; d. of the late George Bouchles and Georgia Goranites Bouchles; m. John Rettie McKernan 1969; ed Edward Little High School, Auburn, Univ. of Maine; mem. Maine House of Reps 1973–76, Maine Senate 1976–78; mem. 96th–103rd Congresses from 2nd Maine Dist 1979–95; Deputy Republican Whip; Senator from Maine 1995–2013 (retd), mem. Cttee on Small Business & Entrepreneurship, Select Cttee on Intelligence, Cttee on Commerce, Science, & Transportation, Cttee on Finance; Counsel to Asst Majority Leader 1997; Republican; Hon. LLD (Husson Coll.) 1981, (Maine) 1982, (Bowdoin Coll.) 1985, (Suffolk) 1994, (Colby Coll.) 1996, (Bates Coll.) 1998; ranked by Forbes magazine amongst 100 Most Powerful Women (58th) 2004, (54th) 2005, numerous other awards and distinctions. *Address:* c/o 154 Russell Senate Office Building, Washington, DC 20510-1903, USA.

SNOWMAN, (Michael) Nicholas, MA; British music administrator; *General Director, Opera National du Rhin;* b. 18 March 1944, London; s. of the late Kenneth Snowman and Sallie Snowman (née Moghilevkine); m. Margo Michelle Rouard 1983; one s.; ed Hall School and Highgate School, London, Magdalene Coll., Cambridge; Asst to Head of Music Staff, Glyndebourne Festival 1967–69; co-founder and Gen. Man. London Sinfonietta 1968–72; Admin. Music Theatre Ensemble 1968–71; Artistic Dir Institut de Recherche et de Coordination Acoustique/Musique (IRCAM), Centre d'Art et de la Culture Georges Pompidou 1972–86; co-founder and Artistic Adviser Ensemble InterContemporain 1975–92, mem. Bd 1992–, Vice-Chair. 1998–; mem. Music Cttee Venice Biennale 1979–86; Artistic Dir Projects in 1980, 1981, 1983, Festival d'Automne de Paris; Programme Consultant Cité de la Musique, La Villette, Paris 1991–92; Gen. Dir (Arts) South Bank Centre, London 1986–92, Chief Exec. 1992–98; Gen. Dir Glyndebourne Opera 1998–2000, Opera Nat. du Rhin, Strasbourg 2002–(09); Chair. Wartski; mem. British Section, Franco-British Council 1995–; Trustee New Berlioz Edn 1996–; Gov. Royal Acad. of Music 1998–; Chevalier, Ordre nat. du Mérite, Officier, Ordre des Arts et des Lettres, Polish Order of Cultural Merit. *Publications:* The Best of Granta (co-ed.) 1967, The Contemporary Composers (series ed.) 1982–; papers and articles on music, cultural policy and France. *Leisure interests:* films, eating, spy novels. *Address:* c/o Wartski, 14 Grafton Street, London, W1X 4DE, England; 9 rue de Bain Finkwiller, 67000 Stasbourg, France (home). *Telephone:* (3) 88-75-48-64 (office); (6) 64-77-81-30 (home). *Fax:* (3) 88-25-52-59 (office). *E-mail:* wartski@wartski.com (office); nsnowman@onr.fr. *Website:* www.wartski.com; www.onr.fr.

SNOY, Bernard, DIur, PhD; Belgian economist, academic and international organization executive; *Professor, Institute of European Studies, Catholic Univer-*

sity of Louvain; ed Catholic Univ. of Louvain, Harvard Univ., USA; worked for World Bank 1974–86, Exec. Dir representing Austria, Belgium, Luxembourg, Turkey and countries in transition (Belarus, Czech Repub., Hungary, Kazakhstan, Slovakia and Slovenia) 1991–94; Econ. Adviser, EC 1986–88; Chief of the Cabinet, Belgian Minister of Finance, Philippe Maystadt 1988–91; mem. Bd of Dirs EBRD, London, representing Belgium, Luxembourg and Slovenia 1994–2002; Dir Working Table II (Econ. Reconstruction, Devt and Co-operation), Stability Pact for South Eastern Europe 2002–05; Co-ordinator OSCE Econ. and Environmental Activities 2005–08, Prof. Institute of European Studies, Catholic University of Louvain 2008–. *Publications include:* Taxes on Direct Investment Income in the E.E.C.: A Legal and Economic Analysis 1975, Fragility of the Int. Financial System: How Can We Prevent New Crises in Emerging Markets? (Int. Financial Relations) (co-author) 2002. *Address:* Institute of European Studies, Catholic University of Louvain, Deans Place, 1, 1348 Louvain-la-Neuve, Belgium (office). *Website:* www.uclouvain.be (office).

SNYDER, Allan Whitenack, DSc, FRS; American/Australian optical scientist and academic; *Foundation Director, Centre for the Mind, Australian National University and University of Sydney;* b. 28 Nov. 1940; s. of E. H. Snyder and Zelda Cotton; ed Cen. High School, Pennsylvania State Univ., Massachusetts Inst. of Tech., Harvard Univ. and Univ. Coll., London, UK; Greenland Ice Cap Communications Project 1961; Consultant, Gen. Telecommunications and Electricity Research Lab. 1963–67, British Post Office and Standard Telecommunications Lab. 1968–70; Sr Research Fellow, later Prof. Fellow, ANU 1971–79, Chair. Optical Physics and Visual Sciences Inst. for Advanced Studies 1978–, Head Applied Math. 1979–82, Founder and Head Optical Sciences Centre 1983–, Foundation Dir Centre for the Mind 1997, Peter Karmel Professorial Chair of Science and the Mind 1998–; Aniv Prof. of Science and the Mind, Univ. of Sydney 2000–; NSF Fellowship, Dept of Applied Physics, Yale Univ. Medical School, USA 1970–71; Guggenheim Fellow 1977, Foundation Fellow, Nat. Vision Research Inst. of Australia 1983, Royal Soc. Quest Research Fellow, Univ. of Cambridge, UK 1987; 150th Anniversary Chair of Science and the Mind, Univ. of Sydney; Assoc. Ed. Journal of Optical Soc. of America 1981–83; Clifford Patterson Lecturer, Royal Soc., London 2001; Research Medal, Royal Soc. of Vic. 1974, Thomas Rankin Lyle Medal, Australian Acad. of Science 1985, Edgeworth David Medal, Royal Soc. of NSW, Sutherland Memorial Medal, Australian Acad. of Technological Sciences 1991, CSIRO Research Medal 1995, Harrie Massey Medal and Prize, British Inst. of Physics 1996, Arthur E. Mills Oration and Medal, RACP 1966, Int. Australia Prize 1997, Marconi Int. Fellowship and Prize 2001, Centenary Medal 2003. *Publications include:* Photoreceptors Optics (co-author) 1975, Optical Waveguide Sciences (co-author) 1983, Optical Waveguide Theory (co-author) 1983, What Makes a Champion! (ed.). *Leisure interests:* art, thought and mind. *Address:* Centre for Mind, Main Quadrangle (A14), University of Sydney, Sydney, NSW 2006, Australia (office). *Telephone:* (2) 9351-8531 (office). *Fax:* (2) 9351-8534 (office). *E-mail:* allan@centreforthemind.com (office). *Website:* www .centreforthemind.com (office).

SNYDER, Barbara, BA, JD; American lawyer, academic and university administrator; *President, Case Western Reserve University;* b. 23 July 1955, Columbus, Ohio; m. Michael Snyder; two s. one d.; ed Ohio State Univ., Univ. of Chicago Law School; called to the Ill. Bar 1980; Legal Clerk, US Court of Appeals for Seventh Circuit, Chicago 1980–82; with Sidley & Austin (law firm), Chicago –1983; Asst Prof., Case Western Reserve School of Law, Cleveland 1983–86, Assoc. Prof. 1986–88, Pres. Case Western Reserve Univ. 2007–; Assoc. Prof., Moritz Coll. of Law, Ohio State Univ. 1988–90, Prof. 1990–2000, Joanne W. Murphy Prof. 2000–07, Interim Exec. Vice-Pres. and Provost, Ohio State Univ. 2003–04, Exec. Vice-Pres. and Provost 2004–07; mem. American Law Inst. 2007–; Moritz Coll. of Law Outstanding Professor Award 1997. *Publications:* co-author: Ohio Evidence 1996, The Ohio Rules of Evidence Handbook (annual 1996–2005). *Address:* Office of the President, Case Western Reserve University, 10900 Euclid Avenue, Cleveland, OH 44106-7001, USA (office). *Telephone:* (216) 368-4344 (office). *Fax:* (216) 368-4325 (office). *E-mail:* barbara.snyder@case.edu (office). *Website:* www .case.edu/president (office).

SNYDER, Richard Dale (Rick), BGS, MBA, JD; American business executive, politician and state governor; *Governor of Michigan;* b. 19 Aug. 1958, Battle Creek, Mich.; s. of Dale F. Snyder and Helen Louella 'Pody' Snyder; m. Sue Snyder 1987; one s. two d.; ed Stephen M. Ross School of Business, Univ. of Michigan, Univ. of Michigan Law School; with Coopers & Lybrand 1982–91, began in tax dept in Detroit office 1982, Partner 1988–89, Partner-in-Charge of mergers and acquisitions practice in Chicago office 1989–91; Exec. Vice-Pres. Gateway 1991–96, Pres. and COO 1996–97, Chair. 2005–07, interim CEO 2006 (co. sold to Acer Inc. of Taiwan 2007); Co-founder, Pres. and CEO Avalon Investments Inc. (venture capital co.), Ann Arbor, Mich. 1997–2000; Co-founder Ardesta LLC (venture capital firm), Ann Arbor 2000, Chair. and CEO –2010; mem. Bd of Dirs Henry Ford Museum, Michigan chapter of the Nature Conservancy and several bds tied to Univ. of Michigan; fmr Adjunct Asst Prof. of Accounting, Univ. of Michigan; Gov. of Michigan 2011–; Chair. Ann Arbor SPARK; mem. Bd Univ. of Michigan Coll. of Eng Nat. Advisory Cttee, mem. Tech. Transfer Nat. Advisory Cttee, Univ. of Michigan; mem. Gov. e-Michigan Advisory Council; mem. Advisory Bd Samuel Zell & Robert H. Lurie Inst. for Entrepreneurial Studies, NanoBusiness Alliance, Visiting Cttee Purdue Univ. School of Eng; mem. Michigan Bar Asscn, The Nature Conservancy, Michigan Chapter; Trustee, The Henry Ford Foundation; Republican. *Address:* Office of the Governor, State Capitol Building, PO Box 30013, Lansing, MI 48909, USA (office). *Telephone:* (517) 373-3400 (office). *Fax:* (517) 335-6863 (office). *Website:* www.michigan.gov/gov (office).

SNYDER, Richard E.; American publisher; b. 6 April 1933, New York; s. of Jack Snyder and Molly Rothman; m. 1st Otilie Freund 1963 (divorced); one s. one d.; m. 2nd Laura Yorke 1992; two s.; ed Tufts Univ., Medford; sales rep., Simon & Schuster 1961, Vice-Pres. Marketing 1966–69, Vice-Pres. Trade Books 1969–73, Exec. Vice-Pres. Trade and Educ. Admin 1973–75, Pres. and COO 1975–78, Pres. and CEO 1978–86, Chair. and CEO 1986–94, consultant 1994–95; Chair., CEO Golden Books Family Entertainment 1996–2001; Chair. PEN, NY Area 1988; Dir Reliance Group Holdings, Children's Blood Foundation; Trustee, New York Presbyterian Hosp.; Founder-mem. Nat. Book Foundation, Nat. Book Awards; mem. Council on Foreign Relations, Wildlife Conservation Soc., Econ. Club of NY.

SO, Augusto Ussumane; Guinea-Bissau politician; ed in USA; Minister, Ministry of Economy and Finance 2002–07; Pres. Asscn of Guineans, Bissau. *Address:* c/o Ministry of the Economy and Finance, CP 67, Avda 3 de Agosto, Bissau, Guinea-Bissau (office).

SO, John; Australian business executive and politician; *Chairman, Global Business Council, World Chinese Economic Forum;* ed Univ. of Melbourne; fmr JP; Councillor, City of Melbourne 1991–96, 1999–2001; Lord Mayor of Melbourne City Council 2001–08; Chair. World Chinese Economic Forum Global Business Council, Melbourne 2012–; mem. Cttee for Melbourne Bd, Cancer Council Bd, Shrine of Remembrance Bd, Victorian Community Council on Crime and Violence; fmr Vice-Pres. Melbourne Chinatown Traders Asscn; Patron Melbourne Jr Chamber of Commerce; Dr hc (Victoria Univ.) 2007; You Bring Charm to the World Award (among most influential Chinese in 2006) 2007. *Address:* Global Business Council, World Chinese Economic Forum, 1718, Jalan Ledang, Off Jalan Duta, 50480 Kuala Lumpur, Malaysia. *Telephone:* (3) 20935393. *E-mail:* info@ wceforum.org. *Website:* www.wceforum.org; www.johnso.com.au.

SOAMES, Rt Hon. Nicholas, PC; British politician; b. (Arthur Nicholas Winston Soames), 12 Feb. 1948; s. of the late Baron and Lady Soames and grandson of Sir Winston Churchill; m. 1st Catherine Weatherall 1981 (divorced 1988, 2nd Serena Smith 1993; two s. one d.; ed St Aubyns, Sussex and Eton Coll.; commissioned into 11th Hussars, served in Germany and UK, subsequently Equerry to HRH The Prince of Wales; worked as stockbroker 1972–74; Personal Asst to Sir James Goldsmith 1974–76; legislative asst on staff of US Senator Mark Hatfield, Washington DC 1976–78; Asst Dir Sedgwick Group 1979–81; joined firm of Lloyds Brokers as a Dir; MP (Conservative) for Crawley 1983–97, for Mid-Sussex 1997–; Parl. Sec. and Minister of Food, Ministry of Agriculture, Fisheries and Food 1992–94; Minister of State for the Armed Forces 1994–97; served on Countryside and Rights of Way Bill Cttee, Hunting Bill Cttee; fmr mem. Exec. of 1922 Committee; fmr Chair. Conservative Middle East Council; Shadow Sec. of State for Defence 2003–05; Pres. East Grinstead Target Shooting Club, Haywards Heath Dist Scout Council, Haywards Heath Rugby Football Club, Staplefield Cricket Club, South of England Hound Show; Vice-Pres. St Catherine's Hospice; fmr mem. Commonwealth War Graves Comm., Council of Royal United Services Inst., Court of Univ. of Sussex, Council of the South of England Agricultural Soc., Council for the Protection of Rural England, Burgess Hill Business Parks Asscn; Trustee Amber Foundation; Patron No. 24 Burgess Hill Detachment, Sussex Army Cadet Force; Hon. Pres. 172 Haywards Heath Squadron (air cadets). *Leisure interests:* reading, music, horse racing, country pursuits. *Address:* House of Commons, Westminster, London, SW1A 0AA, England (office). *Telephone:* (20) 7219-4143 (office). *Fax:* (20) 7219-2998 (office). *E-mail:* nicholas.soames.mp@parliament.uk (office). *Website:* www.nicholassoames.org.uk.

SOARES, Eugénio Lourenço; São Tomé and Príncipe politician and central banker; *Vice-Governor, Banco Central de São Tomé e Príncipe;* fmr MP from Mé-Zochi; Gov. São Tomé e Príncipe, ADB; Minister of Planning and Finance 2003–04; Vice-Gov. and mem. Council of Admin, Banco Central de São Tomé e Príncipe 2006–. *Address:* Banco Central de São Tomé e Príncipe, Praça da Independência, CP 13, São Tomé, São Tomé and Príncipe (office). *Telephone:* 221300 (office). *Fax:* 222777 (office). *E-mail:* bcstp@bcstp.st (office). *Website:* www.bcstp.st (office).

SOARES, Commdt Lúcio; Guinea-Bissau politician; b. 13 Dec. 1951, Bolama; m. Ana Maria Soares; five d.; Minister of Defence 2001, of the Interior 2009–11. *Address:* c/o Ministry of the Interior, Av. Unidade Africana, Bissau, Guinea-Bissau.

SOARES, Mário Alberto Nobre Lopes, LèsL, DenD; Portuguese politician, lawyer, historian and fmr head of state; *President, Mário Soares Foundation;* b. 7 Dec. 1924, Lisbon; s. of João Lopes Soares and Elisa Nobre Soares; m. Maria Barroso Soares 1949; one s. one d.; ed Univ. of Lisbon, Faculty of Law, Sorbonne, Paris; active opponent to Salazar's dictatorship; joined Anti-Facist Nat. Unity Movt 1943, f. Youth Movt of the Democratic Unity Movt 1946; mem. Presidential Candidature Cttee for Gen. Norton de Matos 1949, Gen. Humberto Delgado 1958; f. Portuguese Socialist Action 1964; deported to São Tomé March–Nov. 1968; rep. of Portuguese socialists at various European socialist congresses and 11th Congress of Socialist Int., Eastbourne, UK 1969; Portuguese rep. Int. League of Human Rights; imprisoned 12 times on political grounds; in exile in Paris 1970–74, returned to Portugal after coup April 1974; f. Partido Socialista 1973, Sec.-Gen. 1973–86; Vice-Pres. Socialist Int. 1976–86, Hon. Pres. 1986–; Minister of Foreign Affairs 1974–75; in charge of negotiations leading to independence of Portuguese colonies; Minister without Portfolio March–Aug. 1975; Deputy, Constituent Ass. 1975, Legis. Ass. 1976; mem. Council of State; Prime Minister of Portugal 1976–78, 1983–85; initiated negotiations in 1977 leading to Portugal joining EC, as Prime Minister signed Treaty of Accession June 1985; Leader of the Opposition 1978–83; Pres. of Portugal 1986–96; mem. European Parl. 1999–2004; Pres. Ind. World Comm. on the Oceans 1995–98, Portugal Africa Foundation 1997–, European Movt 1997–99 (Hon. Pres. 1999–), Steering Cttee World Water Contract 1997–, Cttee of Experts of the Council of Europe 1997–98, IPS Inter Press Int., Rome 2001–07 (mem. Int. Bd of Trustees 2008–), Inter-Parl. Del. for Relations with Israel 2002, Comm. for Religious Freedom 2007; Founder and Pres. Soares Foundation 1996–; mem. Club of Rome 1998, Euroamerica Foundation 1999–, Gen. Foundation of Salamanca Univ. 2000, Acad. of Latinity, Rio de Janeiro 2000, Foro Mundial de Redes, Barcelona 2001, Club of Madrid 2001, Club of Monaco 2002, World Political Forum (now New Policy Forum) 2002, 2010–, Green Cross Int. 2003, Grupo de Biarritz 2003, Group EU-Turkey Relations 2007, Centre for the Study of Global Governance 2007, Open Soc. Inst. 2007, Global Advisory Bd Global Climate Change, Human Security and Democracy, Univ. of Calif. 2010, Nat. Org. for the Blind, Madrid, Groupement d'etudes et de Recherches: Notre Europe (UNESCO), Peres Centre for Peace, Tel Aviv, Int. Project XXI Century: A Century of Global Challenges (Gorbachev Foundation); fmr Pres. Council of Europe; State Councillor; mem. Portuguese Soc. of Writers, Lisbon Acad. of Sciences; corresp. mem. Academia Brasileira de Letras, Acad. of the Kingdom of Morocco, Marine Acad. of France, Overseas Acad. of Sciences, France; 40 hon. doctorates including: Dr hc (Rennes, Hankuk, Lancaster, São Paulo, Brown, Salamanca, Princeton, Bologna, Turin, Sorbonne, Univ. Libre Bruxelles, Oxon., Leicester); Joseph Lemaire Prize 1975, Int. Prize of Human Rights 1977, Robert Schuman Prize 1987, Prince of Asturias Prize 1995, "Together" Prize of the Peace Foundation (Rome) 1997, Louis

Weiss Prize 1997, Adolph Bentinck Prize 1997, Int. Simón Bolivar Prize 1998, Pres.'s Medal, George Washington Univ. 1998, Stresemann Inst. Gold Medal 1999, Guy Trophy 2000, Univ. of California, Berkeley Gold Medal 2000, Schuman Foundation Honour Medal 2000, North-South Prize 2000, Roma per il Dialogo Prize 2001, Int. Special Press Prize 2001, Troféu Latino Prize 2005, Latinity Prize 2005, Portuguese Parl. Gold Medal for Human Rights 2008. *Publications:* As ideias político-sociais de Teófilo Braga 1950, Escritos Políticos 1969, Portugal's Struggle for Liberty 1972, Destruir o Sistema, Construir uma Vida Nova 1973, Caminho Difícil, do Salazarismo ao Caetanismo 1973, Escritos do Exílio 1975, Liberdade para Portugal (with Willy Brandt and Bruno Kreisky) 1975, Portugal, quelle Révolution? 1976, O Futuro será o Socialismo Democrático 1979, Resposta Socialista para o Mundo em Crise 1983, Persistir 1983, A Árvore e a Floresta 1985, Intervenções Vols I–VI 1987–92, Vols VII–VIII 1994, Moderador e Árbitro 1995, Democracia 1996, O Presidente 1996, Dois anos depois 1998, O mundo em português: um diálogo (with Pres. Fernando Henrique Cardoso) 1998, Português e Europeu 2000, Porto Alegre e Nova Iorque: um mundo dividido? 2002, Mémoire Vivante 2002, A Incerteza dos Tempos 2003, Incursões Literárias 2003, Um Mundo Inquietante 2003, Diálogo de Gerações (with Sérgio Sousa Pinto) 2004, Os Poemas da Minha Vida 2004, A Crise. E agora? 2005, O Que Falta Dizer 2005, Um Mundo em Mudança, O Elogio da Política, Em luta por um Mundo Melhor, No Centro do Furacão, Portugal Tem Saída (with Teresa de Sousa), Um Político Assumese – ensaio autobiográfico, político e ideológico; contribs. to República, Seara Nova, Ibéria (New York) etc. *Leisure interests:* books and collecting contemporary Portuguese paintings. *Address:* Rua Dr João Soares, 2-3, 1600 Lisbon, Portugal (home). *Website:* www.fmsoares.pt (office).

SOARES ALVES, Francisco José, MA; Portuguese archaeologist; *Chief of the Division of Nautical and Underwater Archaeology, IGESPAR (Portuguese Heritage), Ministry of Culture;* b. 18 April 1942, Lisbon; s. of José Augusto Ferreira Alves and Margaret Hellen Libbie Mason Soares; m. (divorced); one s.; ed D. João de Castro High School, Lisbon, Univ. of Paris, DEA—Institut d'Art et d'Archéologie, Paris; Prof. of Nautical and Underwater Archaeology, Universidade Nova de Lisboa, Faculdade de Ciências Sociais e Humanas; Dir archaeological campus, Braga (Bracara Augusta) 1976–80; Dir Portuguese Dept of Archaeology 1980–82; Dir Nat. Museum of Archaeology 1980–96; Dir Portuguese Centre for Underwater and Nautical Archaeology 1997–2007; Dir of underwater archaeology on sites of L'Océan (French flagship sunk in 1759) 1984, 15th Century shipwreck Ria de Aveiro A 1996–99, Senhora dos Mártires shipwreck (Indiaman lost in Tagus bar 1606) 1997–1998, Lima river dugouts (3rd century BC) 2003, Colab of the rescue and research of the 16th century Portuguese Oranjemund, Namibia shipwreck 2008–09; mem. Advisory Bd of State Parties of the Convention on the Protection of Underwater Cultural Heritage, UNESCO, Paris 2001; Franco Papo Award, 8th Rassegna di Archeologia, Italy. *Leisure interest:* diving. *Address:* IGESPAR, Palácio Nacional da Ajuda, Lisbon, Portugal (office). *E-mail:* falves@igespar.pt (office); franciscojsalves@gmail.com (home). *Website:* www.igespar.pt (office).

SOBEL, Dava; American science writer; b. 15 June 1947, New York, NY; s. of Samuel H. Sobel MD and Betty Sobel (née Gruber); divorced; one s. one d.; ed State Univ. of NY at Binghamton; fmr science reporter, New York Times; reported for several journals including Audubon, Discover, Life, The New Yorker; fmr Contributing Ed. Harvard Magazine; has lectured at The Smithsonian Inst., The Explorers Club, NASA Goddard Space Flight Center, Folger Shakespeare Library, Los Angeles Public Library, NY Public Library, Royal Geographical Soc. (London); numerous radio and TV appearances; mem. American Asscn of Univ. Women, Planetary Soc.; Fellow, American Geographical Soc.; Hon. DLit (Middlebury Coll., Vt) 2002, (Bath, UK) 2002; Nat. Media Award American Psychological Foundation 1980, Lowell Thomas Award Soc. of American Travel Writers 1992, Gold Medal Council for the Advancement and Support of Educ. 1994, Christopher Award 1999, Los Angeles Times Book Prize 2000, Nat. Science Bd Public Service Award 2001, Bradford Washburn Award Boston Museum of Science 2001, Nathaniel Bowditch Maritime Scholar 2003, Harrison Medal, Worshipful Co. of Clockmakers (UK) 2004, Klumpke-Roberts Award, Astronomical Soc. of the Pacific 2008. *Publications:* Is Anyone Out There? The Scientific Search for Extraterrestrial Intelligence (with Frank D. Drake) 1992, Longitude (several awards including Harold D. Vursell Memorial Award American Acad. of Arts and Letters 1996, UK Book of the Year 1996, Prix Faubert du Coton, Premio del Mare Circeo) 1995, Galileo's Daughter: A Historical Memoir of Science, Faith, and Love 1999, Letters to Father 2001, The Planets 2005, A More Perfect Heaven: How Copernicus Revolutionized the Cosmos 2011. *Address:* c/o Michael Carlisle, InkWell Management, 521 Fifth Avenue, 26th Floor, New York, NY 10175, USA (office). *E-mail:* dava@davasobel .com. *Website:* www.davasobel.com.

SOBERANES FERNÁNDEZ, José Luis, LicenDer, LLD; Mexican lawyer and academic; *President, Comisión Nacional de los Derechos Humanos (National Commission for Human Rights);* b. 10 Jan. 1950, Santiago de Querétaro, Querétaro; ed law degree from Universidad Nacional Autónoma de México (UNAM), Universidad de Valencia, Spain; Sec.-Gen. Latin American univs' asscn 1985–90; Dir Instituto de Investigaciones Jurídicas, UNAM 1990–98, full-time researcher at UNAM; Prof., Nat. Univ. of San Marcos (Peru); Visiting Prof. of the Social Sciences, Univ. of Toulouse, France; apptd by Congress Pres. Comisión Nacional de los Derechos Humanos (Nat. Comm. for Human Rights) 1999–; Academician and fmr Fellow, Royal Acad. of Jurisprudence, Spain; an expert on the origins of the Supreme Court in Mexico, religion and the law, and the colonial judicial system; Great Cross of San Raimundo de Peñafort (Spain). *Publications:* more than 20 books, including Los tribunales de la Nueva España 1980, Sobre el origen de la Suprema Corte de Justicia de la Nación 1987, Historia del sistema jurídico mexicano 1990, Los bienes eclesiásticos en la historia constitucional de México 1999; numerous papers in academic journals. *Address:* Edificio 'Héctor Fix Zamudio', Blvd Adolfo López Mateos 1922, 6° piso, Col. Tlacopac San Ángel, Delegación Álvaro Obregón, CP 01040, Mexico City, Mexico (office). *Telephone:* (55) 1719-2000 (office). *E-mail:* info@cndh.org.mx (office). *Website:* www.cndh.org .mx (office).

SOBERÓN VALDÉS, Francisco, PhD; Cuban politician and fmr central banker; b. 18 April 1945; fmr Prof. of Social Sciences and Econ. Planning; Founder and Leader, Unión de jóvenes Party (UJC) 1962–64; apptd mem. Cen. Cttee CP Party of Cuba 1970; fmr Deputy in Nat. Ass. of People's Power; Pres. Nat. Bank of Cuba

(renamed Cen. Bank of Cuba 1997) 1995–2009. *Address:* c/o Banco Central de Cuba, Calle Cuba, No 402, Aguiar 411, Habana Vieja, Havana, Cuba.

SOBERS, Sir Garfield (Gary) St Aubrun, Kt, AO; Barbadian/Australian fmr cricketer; b. 28 July 1936, St Michael; s. of Thelma Sobers and Shamont Sobers; m. Prudence Kirby 1969 (divorced 1990); two s. one adopted d.; ed Bay St School, Barbados; left-hand batsman, left-arm bowler, using all kinds of bowling; outstanding all-rounder; teams: Barbados 1952–74 (Capt. 1965–71), S Australia 1961–64, Notts. 1968–74 (Capt. 1968–71, 1973); Test debut: West Indies v England, Kingston 30 March–3 April 1954; only One-Day Int.: England v West Indies, Leeds 5 Sept. 1973; played in 93 Tests for W Indies 1953–74, 39 as Capt., scoring 8,032 runs (average 57.78) with 26 hundreds, including record 365 not out (record 1958–94), taking 235 wickets (average 34.03) and holding 109 catches, best bowling (innings) 6/73, (match) 8/80; scored First-class 28,314 runs (average 54.87) including 86 hundreds, took 1,043 wickets and held 407 catches, best bowling 9/49; hit six sixes in an over, Notts. vs Glamorgan at Swansea 1968; toured England 1957, 1963, 1966, 1969, 1973; Special Consultant Barbados Tourism Authority 1980; apptd tech. consultant to West Indies cricket coach 2004; became a dual Barbadian/Australian citizen through marriage in 1980; Hon. Life mem. MCC 1981; Order of the Caribbean Community 1998; West Indian Cricket Cricketer of the Year 1958–59, Wisden Cricketer of the Year 1964, The Cricket Soc. Wetherall Award for the Leading All-Rounder in English First-Class Cricket 1970, Walter Lawrence Trophy 1974, Barbados Nat. Hero 1998, selected as one of five Wisden Cricketers of the Century 2000, Sir Garfield Sobers Trophy inaugurated by Int. Cricket Council (ICC) 2004, selected retrospectively by Wisden as the Leading Cricketer in the World for the years 1958, 1960, 1962, 1964–66, 1968, 1970 2007. *Publications:* Cricket Advance 1965, Cricket Crusader 1966, King Cricket 1967 (with J. S. Barker), Cricket in the Sun (with J. S. Barker) 1967, Bonaventure and the Flashing Blade 1967, Sobers: Twenty Years at the Top 1988, Sobers: The Changing Face of Cricket (with Ivo Tennant) 1995. *Leisure interest:* golf. *Address:* 23 Highgate Gardens, St Michael, Barbados (home).

SOBHI, Col-Gen. Sedki; Egyptian army officer and government official; *Minister of Defence;* b. 12 Dec. 1955; ed Egyptian Mil. Acad., US Army War Coll., USA; joined Egyptian Army 1976, several command roles with Third Field Army, including Commdr, Mechanized Infantry Bn, Chief of Staff, Mechanized Infantry Brigade, Chief, Operations Br., Commdr, Third Field Army 2009; Chief of Staff, Egyptian Armed Forces 2012–14; Deputy Chair. Supreme Council of Armed Forces of Egypt 2012–14; Minister of Defence and Supreme Commdr of Armed Forces 2014–; attained rank of Maj.-Gen., Lt-Gen. 2012, Col-Gen. 2014; Fellow, Higher War Coll., Nasser Higher Mil. Acad. 2000; numerous mil. decorations including 25 April Decoration (Liberation of Sinai), Mil. Duty Decoration, First and Second Class, Liberation of Kuwait Medal, Golden Jubilee of 23 July Revolution, 25 Jan. Revolution Medal. *Address:* Ministry of Defence, Sharia 23 July, Kobri el-Kobba, Cairo, Egypt (office). *Telephone:* (2) 4032159 (office). *Fax:* (2) 2906004 (office). *E-mail:* mod@afmic.gov.eg (office).

SOBIROV, Ilgizar Matiakubovich, CandIur; Uzbekistani politician; *Chairman of the Senate;* b. 20 Feb. 1959, Urtaiap Kushkupir dist, Xorazm Viloyat; ed Law Faculty, Tashkent State Univ.; began career as mem. law collective, Kurshkupir dist; completed mil. service 1980; carried out pedagogical work in criminal law 1986–94; apptd Pro-Rector, Tashkent Legal Inst. 1994; fmr legal worker, Philosophy and Law Inst., Uzbek Acad. of Sciences; worked in Supreme Court, becoming Plenum Sec. and mem. Supreme Econ. Court; directed prov. admin of justice in Khorezm Prov.; Deputy, Oliy Majlis (Supreme Ass.) 2000–03, Deputy Chair. Cttee on Questions of Defence and Security 1999–2004, later Chair. Cttee on Legislation and Legal Questions; Hokim (Gov.), Kushkupir dist, Xorazm Viloyat 2003–05; elected Senator 2005–, Chair. Cttee on Questions of Defence and Security 2005–06, Chair. Senate 2006–. *Address:* Office of the Chairman of the Senate, 100029 Tashkent, Mustaqillik maydoni 6, Uzbekistan (office). *Telephone:* (71) 238-26-66 (office). *Fax:* (71) 238-29-01 (office). *E-mail:* info@senat.uz (office). *Website:* www.senat.uz (office).

SOBOLEV, Col-Gen. Valentin; Russian government official; *Deputy Secretary, Security Council of the Russian Federation;* b. 11 March 1947, Kyzyl-Atrek Dist (Turkmen SSR); ed V. Kuibyshev Inst. of Engineering and Construction, Moscow and Fed. Security Services Acad.; began career as construction worker, Aşgabat 1962; served in KGB; Deputy Dir Fed. Counterintelligence Service 1994–97; First Deputy Dir Fed. Security Service 1997–99; Deputy Sec., Security Council of the Russian Fed. 1999–, Acting Sec. 2007–08. *Address:* Office of the Deputy Secretary, Security Council of the Russian Federation, 103132 Moscow, Ipatyevskii per. 4/10, Russia. *Website:* www.scrf.gov.ru.

SOBOTKA, Bohuslav, BLL; Czech lawyer and politician; *Prime Minister;* b. 23 Oct. 1971, Telnice; m.; two c.; ed Masaryk Univ., Brno; mem. Czech Social Democratic Party (Česká strana sociálně demokratická—ČSSD) 1989–, Chair. Deputies Club 2001–02, Acting Chair. ČSSD 2010–11, Chair. 2011–14; mem. Parl. 1996–2002, 2002–06, 2006–; mem. Mandate (Proxy) and Immunity Cttee 1996–98; Chair. Sub-cttee for Financial and Capital Markets, Budget Cttee 1998–2001; mem. Municipal Council of Slavkov, nr Brno 1998–; Chair. Interim Comm. for Pension Reform 2001; Minister of Finance 2002–06; First Deputy Prime Minister 2005–06; Prime Minister 2014–. *Leisure interests:* history, literature, science fiction, film, travel. *Address:* Office of the Government, náb. E. Beneše 4, 118 01 Prague 1 (office); 9. května 21, 682 01 Vyškov, Czech Republic. *Telephone:* (2) 24002111 (office). *Fax:* (2) 57531283 (office). *E-mail:* posta@vlada.cz (office); info@ bohuslavsobotka.cz. *Website:* www.vlada.cz (office); www.bohuslavsobotka.cz.

SOBOTKA, Přemysl, MUDr; Czech doctor and politician; *Chairman, Senát (Senate);* b. 18 May 1944, Mladá Boleslav; s. of Zdeněk Sobotka and Eliška Sobotka; ed Charles Univ., Prague; physician 1968–; councillor, Liberec 1990–96; Chief Physician, Hosp. Liberec 1990–98; mem. Civic Democratic Party (Občanská demokratická strana—ODS); Senator, Vice-Chair. of Senát (Senate) 1996–2002, Chair. 2004–, mem. Cttee on Agenda and Procedure, Sub-cttee on Bestowing Decorations, Civic Democratic Party Caucus. *Publications:* papers in medical journals. *Leisure interests:* tennis, volleyball, travel. *Address:* Senát PČR, Valdštejnské nám. 4, 11801 Prague 1 (office); Nezvaolova 658, 460 16 Liberec, Czech Republic (home). *Telephone:* (2) 57072331 (office); (6) 02348371 (home). *Fax:*

(2) 57534509 (office). *E-mail:* sobotkap@senat.cz (office). *Website:* www.mfcr.cz (office); www.premyslsobotka.cz.

SOBTI, Atul, BEcons (Hons); Indian business executive; ed St Stephen's Coll., Univ. of Delhi, Indian Inst. of Man., Ahmedabad; has 30 years' experience in industries including durables, information tech. services, automobiles and pharmaceuticals; has worked for Xerox and Honda; Exec. Dir (Sales, Marketing, Finance and Human Resources) Hero Honda 1998–2005; Pres. (India, Middle East, Asia Pacific and the Global Consumer Healthcare Business) Ranbaxy Laboratories Ltd 2005–07, COO 2007–09, CEO and Man. Dir 2009–10 (resgnd). *Address:* c/o Ranbaxy Laboratories Ltd, Corporate Office, Plot 90, Sector 32, Gurgaon 122 001, Haryana, India.

SOBYANIN, Sergei Semenovich, PhD; Russian politician; *Mayor of Moscow;* b. 21 June 1958, Nyaksumvol, Berezovskii Dist, Khanty-Mansii Autonomous Okrug; m. Irina Sobyanina (divorced 2014); two d.; ed Kostroma State Inst. of Tech.; metalworker and then foreman at Chelyabinsk Pipe Plant 1980–82; Head of Admin. Dept Leninskii Dist Komsomol, Chelyabinsk 1982–84; party and admin. work in Khanty-Mansii Autonomous Okrug, Tyumen Oblast 1984–90; Head of State Tax Inspection Office, Kogalym, Khanty-Mansii Autonomous Okrug 1990–91; Mayor of Kogalym 1991–93; First Deputy Head Khanty-Mansii Autonomous Okrug 1993–94; Chair. Khanty-Mansii Autonomous Okrug Duma, mem. Fed. Council and Chair. Fed. Council Cttee on Constitutional Legislation and Judicial-Legal Matters 1994–2000; First Deputy to Presidential Plenipotentiary Envoy in Urals Fed. Dist 2000–01; Gov. of Tyumen Oblast 2001–05; Chief of Staff, Presidential Exec. Office 2005–08; Deputy Chair. of the Govt, in charge of co-ordinating Fed. Agencies, also Head of Govt Staff 2008–10; Mayor of Moscow 2010–13 (resgnd), 2013–; Chair. TVEL (state nuclear power co.) 2006–; Order of Merit, Medal For Services to the Fatherland (Second Degree), Church Second Stage Order of St Prince Danil Moscovskii, Medal of Honour in Educ., Ordre du Mérite Agricole (France) 2003; Russia's Man of the Year: Politician Prize 2003. *Address:* Office of the Mayor and Prime Minister of the Government of Moscow City, 125032 Moscow, ul. Tverskaya 13, Russia (office). *E-mail:* ud@mos.ru (office). *Website:* www.mos.ru/en/authority/ud (office).

SÓCRATES CARVALHO PINTO DE SOUSA, José; Portuguese politician; b. 6 Sept. 1957, Vilar de Maçada; divorced; two c.; Chair. Castelo Branco Fed., Partido Socialista (Socialist Party) 1983–96, mem. Partido Socialista Secr. 1991–, Spokesperson on Environmental Affairs 1991–95, Sec.-Gen. 2004–; mem. Parl. 1987–95; mem. Covilha Municipal Ass. 1989–96; Deputy Minister to the Prime Minister 1995–99; Minister of Environmental Affairs 1999–2002; mem. Parl. Comm. on National Defence 2002–; Prime Minister of Portugal 2005–11 (resgnd); Pres. World Conf. of Ministers Responsible for Youth 1998. *Address:* Partido Socialista, Largo do Rato 2, 1269-143 Lisbon, Portugal (office). *Telephone:* (21) 3822000 (office). *Fax:* (21) 3822049 (office). *E-mail:* info@ps.pt (office). *Website:* www.ps.pt (office).

SODANO, HE Cardinal Angelo, STD, JCD; Italian ecclesiastic; *Dean, College of Cardinals, Roman Curia;* b. 23 Nov. 1927, Isola d'Asti; s. of Hon. Giovanni Sodano and Delfina Brignolo; ed Pontifical Gregorian Univ., Rome, Pontifical Lateran Univ., Rome and Pontifical Ecclesiastical Acad., Rome; ordained priest, Asti 1950; Sec. Apostolic Nunciatures in Ecuador, Uruguay and Chile 1961–68; official, Council for Public Affairs of Church, Vatican City State 1968–77; apptd Titular Archbishop of Nova Caesaris 1977; Apostolic Nuncio to Chile 1978–88; Sec. Council for Public Affairs of the Church 1988–89; Sec. for Relations with States of Secr. of State 1989–90; Pro-Sec. of State to His Holiness Pope John Paul II 1990–91; cr. Cardinal-Priest of S. Maria Nuova 1991; Sec. of State 1991–2005 (resgnd), re-apptd 2005–06 (resgnd); apptd Cardinal-Bishop of Albano 1994–, Cardinal-Bishop of Ostia 2005–; mem. Congregations for the Doctrine of the Faith, for the Bishops, Pontifical Comm. for Vatican City State; Vice-Dean Coll. of Cardinals 2002–05, Dean 2005–; numerous honours and awards. *Address:* 00120 Vatican City, Rome, Italy (office).

SØDERBERG, Jess, MBA; Danish business executive; *Deputy Chairman of the Supervisory Board, Carlsberg Breweries A/S;* b. 1944; ed Copenhagen Business School; joined A.P. Møller 1970, various positions finance in USA and Denmark, Pnr 1986–93, Pnr and Group CEO A.P. Møller-Mærsk A/S 1993–2007; Vice-Chair. Mærsk Olie og Gas A/S 2004; Deputy Chair. Carlsberg Breweries A/S 2009–; Adviser to Permira; fmr Chair. Dansk Supermarked A/S, F. Salling A/S, Ejendomsaktieselskabet; mem. Advisory Council, Danske Bank; Kt, Order of Dannebrog, Order of Bernardo O'Higgins (Chile). *Address:* Carlsberg Breweries A/S, 100 Ny Carlsberg Vej, 1799 Copenhagen V, Denmark. *Website:* www.carlsberggroup.com (office).

SODERBERG, Nancy E., BA, MS; American academic, international organization official, fmr diplomatist and fmr government official; *Distinguished Visiting Scholar, Department of Political Science and Public Administration, University of North Florida;* b. 13 March 1958, San Turce, Puerto Rico; d. of Lars Olof Soderberg and Nancy Soderberg (née MacGilvrey); ed Vanderbilt Univ., Georgetown Univ. School of Foreign Service; budget and reports analyst, Bank of New England, Boston 1980–82; Research Asst Brookings Inst., Washington, DC 1982–83; Research Asst, US Agency for Int. Devt, Washington, DC 1983; Del. Selection Asst, Mondale-Ferraro Cttee, Washington, DC 1983, Foreign Policy Adviser 1984 (unsuccessful US presidential camgaign); Deputy Issues Dir, Foreign Policy, Dukakis for Pres. Cttee, Boston 1988; Foreign Policy Adviser to Senator Edward Kennedy, Washington, DC 1985–88, 1989–92; Foreign Policy Dir Clinton/Gore Transition, Little Rock 1992–93; Special Asst to Pres. for Nat. Security Affairs, Staff Dir Nat. Security Council, Washington, DC 1993–95, Deputy Asst to Pres. for Nat. Security Affairs 1995–2001; Alt. Rep. to UN with rank of Amb. 1997–2001; Vice-Pres. (Multilateral Affairs), Int. Crisis Group, New York 2001–05; Distinguished Visiting Scholar, Univ. of North Fla, Jacksonville 2006–; Adjunct Prof. Columbia Univ. School of Int. and Public Affairs 2004; foreign policy analyst for MSNBC; mem. Council for Foreign Relations; mem. Bd of Dirs Concern Worldwide; mem. Advisory Bd Nat. Cttee on American Foreign Policy, Tannenbaum Center; Pres. Sister Cities Program of the City of New York 2002–06. *Publications:* The Superpower Myth: The Use and Misuse of American Might 2005; numerous articles in professional journals. *Address:* 121 Lantern Wick Place, Ponte Vedra Beach, FL 32082; University of North Florida, Department of Political Science and

Public Administration, Jacksonville, FL 32224-2645, USA. *Telephone:* (904) 620-3926; (904) 620-1000 (office). *E-mail:* nsoderberg@aol.com; n00445553@unf.edu (office). *Website:* www.unf.edu/coas/polsci-pubadmin (office).

SODERBERGH, Steven; American film director, producer and screenwriter; b. 14 Jan. 1963, Atlanta; s. of Peter Andrew Soderbergh and Mary Ann Bernard; m. Elizabeth Jeanne Brantley 1989 (divorced 1994); m. 2nd Jules Asner 2003; ed high school and animation course at Louisiana State Univ.; aged 15 made short film Janitor; briefly ed. Games People Play (TV show); made short film Rapid Eye Movement while working as coin-changer in video arcade; produced video for Showtime for their album 90125; Co-founder Section Eight Productions 2001-07; signed six-film deal with 2929 Entertainment, releasing films simultaneously in cinemas, on DVD and on cable TV 2005–; Robert B. Aldrich Service Award, Dirs Guild of America 2014. *Films:* Winston (dir, screenplay) 1987, Sex, Lies and Videotape (dir, screenplay) (Cannes Palme d'Or) 1989, Kafka (dir) 1991, King of the Hill (dir, screenplay) 1993, Suture (exec. producer) 1993, Underneath (dir, screenplay) 1995, Gray's Anatomy (dir) 1996, Schizopolis (dir, screenplay) 1996, The Daytrippers (producer) 1996, Nightwatch (screenplay) 1997, Pleasantville (prod.) 1998, Out of Sight (dir) 1998, The Limey (dir) 1999, Erin Brockovich (dir) 2000, Traffic (dir) (Acad. Award for Best Dir) 2000, Ocean's Eleven (dir) 2001, Who is Bernard Tapie? (exec. producer) 2001, Tribute (exec. producer) 2001, Welcome to Collinwood (producer) 2002, Far from Heaven (exec. producer) 2002, Naqoyqatsi (exec. producer) 2002, Confessions of a Dangerous Mind (exec. producer) 2002, Insomnia (exec. producer) 2002, Full Frontal (dir) 2002, Solaris (dir, screenplay) 2002, Criminal (screenplay) 2004, Eros (dir, screenplay) 2004, Ocean's Twelve (dir) 2004, Able Edwards (exec. producer) 2004, Criminal (producer) 2004, Keane (producer) 2004, Bubble (dir, producer) 2005, The Big Empty (exec. producer) 2005, The Jacket (producer) 2005, Good Night and Good Luck (exec. producer) 2005, Rumor Has It (exec. producer) 2005, Syriana (producer) 2005, A Scanner Darkly (exec. producer) 2006, The Half Life of Timofey Berezin (producer) 2006, The Good German (dir, producer) 2006, Wind Chill (exec. producer) 2007, Ocean's Thirteen (exec. producer) 2007, Che 2008, The Informant! (dir) 2009, And Everything is Going Fine 2010, Haywire 2011, Magic Mike (dir) 2012. *Television as Director:* Fallen Angels (episode, The Quiet Room) 1993, K Street (series, also exec. producer) 2003, Unscripted (series pilot episode, also exec. producer) 2005, Behind the Candelabra (Outstanding Directorial Achievement in Movies for TV and Mini-Series, Dirs Guild of America 2014) 2013. *Address:* c/o Dollard Management & Productions, 21361 Pacific Coast Highway, #3, Malibu, CA 90265, USA.

SÕERD, Aivar; Estonian business executive and politician; b. 22 Nov. 1964, Haapsalu; pnr; three s.; ed Univ. of Tartu, Univ. of Oulu; Dir of Tartu Agency, AS Eesti Kindlustus 1990–93; Acting Head of Tax Policy Dept, Ministry of Finance 1993–96; Acting, then Perm. Gen. Dir Estonian Tax Bd 1996–2004; Chair. AS Vaba Maa 2004–05; Minister of Finance 2005–07, also Gov. of EIB for Estonia; Man. Dir Tallink Hotels 2007–11; mem. Riigikogu (Parl.) 2011–; mem. Estonian People's Union 2005–2010, Estonian Reform Party 2010–; Order of The White Star (Fourth Class) 2003; Global Finance Minister of the Year (Financial Times Group magazine The Banker Award) 2007. *Leisure interests:* recreational sports, music. *Address:* State Assembly (Riigikogu), Lossi plats 1a, 15165 Tallinn, Estonia (office). *E-mail:* Aivar.Soerd@riigikogu.ee (office). *Website:* www.riigikogu.ee (office); www.aivarsoerd.ee.

SOERYADJAYA, Edwin, BBA; Indonesian business executive; *President Commissioner, PT Saratoga Investama Sedaya Tbk;* s. of William Soeryadjaya; m.; three c.; ed Univ. of Southern California, USA; Vice-Pres. and Dir PT Astra International Tbk (conglomerate) 1981–93; f. PT Saratoga Investama Sedaya 1991, Pres. Commr 1997–; Commr PT Aria West International 1995–2003; Chair. and Founding Pnr, Saratoga Capital 1998–; Chair. L & M Group Investments Ltd, Singapore 2009–; Chair. PT Adaro Energy Tbk (coal mine), PT Sapta Indra Sejati (mining contractor), PT Indonesia Bulk Terminal (coal terminal), PT Pulau Seroja Jaya (dry bulk barging), PT Mitra Global Telekomunikasi Indonesia (telecom operator), PT Makmur Sejahtera Wisesa (power plant); Co-Propr Recapital Asia; Chair. Christian Univ. of Indonesia Foundation (Yayasan Universitas Kristen Indonesia). *Address:* PT Saratoga Investama Sedaya Tbk., Menara Karya, 15th Floor Jl. H.R. Rasuna Said Block X-5 Kav. 1-2, Jakarta 12950, Indonesia (office). *Website:* saratoga-investama.com.

SOEWANDI, Rini Mariani Soemarno, BEcons; Indonesian business executive and politician; b. 9 June 1958, Bethesda, Md, USA; m. Didik Soewandi; three c.; ed Wellesley Coll., USA; father worked for World Bank, Washington, DC; with Departemen Keuangan AS 1981; trainee, US Treasury Dept, Washington, DC, USA 1981–82; economist, Citibank 1982–89; Gen. Man. Finance Div., PT Astra International (Indonesia's main car maker) 1989, Dir of Finance 1990–98, Exec. Dir 1998–2000; Vice-Chair. Nat. Banking Penyehatan 1998; Vice-Pres. Commr PT United Tractors 1993; Commr Jakarta Stock Exchange 1995–2001; Commr PT Astra Agro Lestari 1995, Pres. Commr 1999; Pres. Commr PT Citra Motorindo 2000; Commr PT Agrakom 2000; Econ. Adviser to Minister of Finance 1997–98; Deputy Chair. Indonesian Bank Restructuring Agency April 1998; Minister of Industry and Trade 2001–04; Commr Aora TV 2008–. *Address:* AORA/PT Karyamegah Adijaya, Kantor Taman E3.3, Unit A 3A, Mega Kuningan, Jakarta 12950, Indonesia (office). *Telephone:* (21) 57948909 (office). *Fax:* (21) 5764526 (office). *E-mail:* info@aora.tv (office). *Website:* www.aora.tv (office).

SOFAER, Abraham David, LLD; American lawyer, fmr judge and academic; *George P. Shultz Senior Fellow in Foreign Policy and National Security Affairs, Hoover Institution, Stanford University;* b. 6 May 1938, Bombay, India; m. Marian Bea Scheuer 1977; five s. one d.; ed Yeshiva Coll. and New York Univ.; called to New York Bar 1965; law clerk, US Court of Appeals 1965–66, to Hon. J. Skelly and Hon. William J. Brennan, Jr, US Supreme Court 1966–67; Asst US Attorney, South Dist, New York 1967–69; Prof. of Law, Columbia Univ. 1969–79; Judge, US Dist Court for South Dist, New York 1979–85; Legal Adviser, State Dept, Washington, DC 1985–90; Partner, Hughes Hubbard & Reed 1991–94; George P. Shultz Distinguished Scholar, Sr Fellow in Foreign Policy and Nat. Security Affairs, Hoover Inst., Stanford Univ. 1994–, Prof. of Law (by Courtesy), Stanford Univ. 1996–; Distinguished Service Award, US State Dept 1988. *Publications:* War, Foreign Affairs and Constitutional Power: The Origins 1976; articles in legal journals. *Address:* Hoover Institution, Stanford University, Stanford, CA 94305-

6010 (office); 1200 Bryant Street, Palo Alto, CA 94301, USA (home). *Telephone:* (650) 725-3763 (office). *Fax:* (650) 723-8583 (office). *E-mail:* asofaer@stanford.edu (office). *Website:* (office); www.abesofaer.com.

SOGAVARE, Manasseh Damukana; Solomon Islands politician; *Leader, Ownership, Unity and Responsibility (OUR) Party;* b. 1954; m. Emmy Sogavare; mem. Nat. Parl. for East Choiseul 1997–, Minister of Finance 1998, Prime Minister of the Solomon Islands 2000–01, 2006–07; Pres. Ownership, Unity and Responsibility (OUR) Party. *Address:* Ownership, Unity and Responsibility (OUR) Party, c/o National Parliament, POB G19, Honiara, Solomon Islands (office).

SOGLO, Dieudonné Nicéphore, BA; Benin politician; *Mayor of Cotonou;* b. 29 Nov. 1934, Lomé, Togo; two c.; ed Univ. of Paris (Sorbonne) and Ecole nat. d'admin, Paris, France; fmr Inspector-Gen. of Finances, Tech. Adviser, Finance Ministry; Head Finance Dept 1963; fmr Chair. Nat. Monetary Comm., other financial insts; Gov. IMF 1964; Prime Minister of Benin 1990–91, Pres. of Benin 1991–96; Leader Parti de la Renaissance de Benin (renamed La Renaissance du Bénin), now Hon. Pres.; Mayor of Cotonou 2003–; Commander, Nat. Order of the Lion, Senegal 1986, Grand Croix, Légion d'Honneur 1995; Hon. DLitt (Clark Atlanta Univ.) 1995. *Address:* Zone Résidentielle, Lot G20, Les Cocotiers, Cotonou, Benin (home). *Telephone:* 21-32-36-76 (office). *Fax:* 21-32-40-23 (office). *E-mail:* ndsoglo@yahoo.fr (home); ndsoglo@hotmail.com (home); nicephore.soglo@wanadoo.fr (home).

SOHLMAN, Staffan A. R., BA; Swedish diplomatist and consultant; b. 21 Jan. 1937, Rome, Italy; s. of Rolf R. Sohlman and Zinaida Jarotskaja; m. Åsa Maria Carnerud 1961; one s. one d.; ed Sigtuna Humanistiska Laroverk, Washington and Lee Univ., USA, Stockholm and Lund Univs; Nat. Inst. for Econ. Research 1962–65; Ministry of Finance 1965–68; mem. Swedish Del. to OECD 1968–70; Ministry for Foreign Affairs, Dept for Devt Co-operation 1970–75, Head Multilateral Dept 1972, Project Leader Secr. for Futures Studies 1975–77, Head Transport Div. 1977–78; Deputy Dir-Gen. Nat. Bd of Trade 1978–84; Head Multilateral Dept of Ministry for Foreign Affairs Trade Dept 1984–88; Co-ordinator for Econ. Co-operation with Cen. and Eastern Europe, Ministry for Foreign Affairs 1989–90; Dir Cen. Bank 1989; Amb., Perm. Rep. Swedish Del. to OECD 1991–95, Acting Sec.-Gen. OECD Oct.–Nov. 1994; Chair OECD Steel Cttee 1986–88, OECD Liaison Cttee with Council of Europe 1992, OECD Council Working Party on Shipbuilding 1993–95, Wassenaar Arrangement on Export Control for Conventional Arms and Dual-Use Goods and Technologies 1996–99; Amb. and Insp. Gen. of Mil. Equipment, Ministry for Foreign Affairs 1995, Amb. and Insp. Gen., Head Nat. Inspectorate of Strategic Products 1996; Amb. and Defence Co-ordinator, Ministry of Defence 2000–03; currently manages Sohlman Senior Consultants; Chair Senior Power (think tank). *Publications:* Swedish Exports and Imports 1965–70, Resources, Society and the Future 1980, Swedish Defence Materials Administration 1996–2003, A Russian Family in Letters and memoirs 1886-1961. *Leisure interests:* music, art, architecture, literature. *Address:* Hornsgatan 51, 118 49 Stockholm, Sweden (home). *Telephone:* (8) 668-53-81. *E-mail:* staffan.sohlman@comhem.se (office); sasohlman@privat.utfors.se (office).

SOILIHI, Mohamed Ali; Comoran politician; *Vice-President, with responsibility for Finance, the Economy, the Budget and Investments and External Trading (Privatization);* Gov. World Bank 1997; Minister of Finance, Economy, Budget and Home Trade 1997, of Interior Jan.–March 2002, of Finance, Economy, Planning and Employment 2002–06, of Finance, Budget and Planning 2007, Vice-Pres., with responsibility for Finance, the Economy, the Budget and Investments and External Trading (Privatization) 2011–. *Address:* Ministry of Finance, the Budget and Investments, BP 324, Moroni, The Comoros (office). *Telephone:* 7744140 (office). *Fax:* 7744141 (office).

SOIRON, Rolf, PhD; Swiss business executive; *Chairman, Holcim Ltd;* b. 31 Jan. 1945; ed Univ. of Basel, Harvard Business School, USA; served in several positions in human resources, finance and man. at Sandoz Group 1972–83, Group Vice-Pres. Agribusiness USA 1988–92, COO 1992–93; CEO and Pres. Protek Group 1983–88; joined Jungbunzlauer Group, Basel 1993, Man. Dir 2002–03; mem. Bd of Dirs Holcim Ltd 1994–, Chair. 2003–, Chair. Governance, Nomination and Compensation Cttee, Chair. Advisory Bd Holcim Foundation for Sustainable Construction; mem. Bd of Dirs Synthes-Stratec 1995–; Chair. Nobel Biocare 2003–10, Lonza Group Ltd 2005–; Pres. (part-time) Univ. of Basel 1996–2005. *Address:* Holcim Group Support Ltd, Hagenholzstrasse 85, 8050 Zurich, Switzerland (office). *Telephone:* (58) 858-58-58 (office). *Fax:* (58) 858-54-59 (office). *E-mail:* info@holcim .com (office). *Website:* www.holcim.com (office).

SOISSON, Jean-Pierre Henri Robert, LenD; French politician; *Regional Counsellor for Burgundy;* b. 9 Nov. 1934, Auxerre (Yonne); s. of Jacques Soisson and Denise Soisson (née Silve); m. Catherine Lacaisse 1961; two s.; ed Lycée Jacques-Amyot, Auxerre, Faculté de Droit, Paris, Ecole nationale d'admin; auditor, Audit Office 1961; with del. to Algeria 1961–62; Lecturer, Institut d'Études Politiques de Paris 1962–68; tech. adviser to Sec.-Gen. of Merchant Navy 1964–65, to Sec. of State for Information, later for Foreign Affairs 1966–67, to Minister of Agric. 1967–68; Conseiller référendaire, Audit Office 1968–; Deputy to Nat. Assembly for Yonne 1968–74, 1978, 1981–88, 1993–; Deputy Sec.-Gen. Fédération nationale des républicains indépendants 1969–75, Vice-Pres. 1975–78; fmr Sec.-Gen. Parti Republicain; Co. Councillor, Auxerre sud-ouest 1970–76, Mayor 1971–98; Pres. Caisse d'Aide à l'équipement des collectivités locales 1973–74; fmr Pres. parl. group for rural Devt; Sec. of State for Univs 1974–76, for Professional Training 1976, to Minister of the Quality of Life (Youth and Sport) 1976–78; Minister for Youth, Sport and Leisure 1978–81, of Labour, Employment and Professional Training 1988–91, of State for the Civil Service and Admin. Reform 1991–92, of Agric. and Forests 1992–93; Vice-Pres., Conseil Général de l'Yonne 1982–88; Vice-Pres. Regional Council for Burgundy 1986–92, Pres. 1992–93, 1998–2004, Regional Counsellor 2004–; Pres. Comm. de surveillance de La Caisse des dépots et consignations; Sec.-Gen. United France 1991, Mouvement des Réformateurs 1992–2002; mem. Union pour un Mouvement Populaire 2002–; Croix de la valeur militaire; Commdr du Mérite agricole, des Palmes académiques, des Arts et Lettres; Grand Cross, German Order of Merit; Officer of various foreign orders. *Publications:* Le Piège (with Bernard Stasi and Olivier Stirn) 1973, La victoire sur l'hiver 1978, L'enjeu de la formation professionnelle 1987, Mémoires d'ouverture 1990, Politique en jachère 1992, #3, Voyage en Norvège 1995, Charles le Téméraire 1997, Charles Quint 2000, Marguerite, Princesse de Bourgogne 2002,

Philibert de Chalon, Prince d'Orange 2005, Paul Bert, l'idéal républicain 2008. *Leisure interests:* tennis, skiing. *Address:* Conseil Régional de Bourgogne, 17 Boulevard de la Trémouille, BP 1602, 21035, Dijon Cedex (office); Assemblée Nationale, 75355 Paris; 2 place Robillard, 89000 Auxerre, France (home). *Telephone:* (3) 86-52-00-98 (office). *E-mail:* jpsoisson@cr-bourgogne.fr (office); jpsoisson@assemblee-nationale.fr (home); jp.soisson@wanadoo.fr (home). *Website:* www.cr-bourgogne.fr (office); www.assemblee-nationale.fr (office).

SOJO GARZA-ALDAPE, Eduardo, PhD; Mexican economist, academic and government official; *President, Istituto Nacional de Estadística y Geografía;* b. 9 Jan. 1956, León, Guanajuato; ed Monterrey Inst. of Tech. and Advanced Studies, Univ. of Pennsylvania; fmr Researcher and Prof., Monterrey Inst. of Tech. and Advanced Studies, León; has held numerous positions in Fed. Public Admin including Tech. Dir and Short-Term Statistics Dir, Istituto Nacional de Estadística y Geografía (INEGI, Nat. Geography and Statistics Inst.) and Analyst Gen. Econ. and Social Policy Bureau 1979–82, currently Pres.; Coordinator Guanajuato State Govt Econ. Cabinet during Vicente Fox Quesada admin 1995–2000; Advisers Coordinator during Fox's presidential electoral campaign, then Pres. Elect's Transition Team Econ. Coordinator –2000, Chief Econ. Adviser and Chief, Presidential Office for Public Policy 2000–06; Sec. of Economy 2006–08; fmr Research Analyst, Univ. of Pa Link Project. *Publications include:* Guanajuato, Century XXI Study (co-author); numerous articles in professional journals and research on combined time series and econometric modeling. *Address:* Instituto Nacional de Estadística y Geografía, Av. Héroe de Nacozari Sur No. 2301, Edificio Sede, Jardines del Parque, CP 20270, 06170 México DF, Mexico. *Website:* www .inegi.org.mx (office).

SOK, An, BSc; Cambodian diplomatist and politician; *Deputy Prime Minister and Minister in Charge of the Council of Ministers;* b. 16 April 1950, Kirivong Dist, Takeo; m. Lok Chumteav Anny Sok An; four s. one d.; ed Royal Univ. of Phnom Penh, Nat. Sr Admin. School of Diplomacy; Sec.-Gen. and Cabinet Chief, Ministry of Foreign Affairs 1981–83; Sec.-Gen. Cambodian Nat. Peace Cttee 1983–85; Amb. to India 1985–88; Sec. of State, Ministry of Foreign Affairs 1988–91, Ministry of the Interior 1991; Co-Minister, Council of Ministers 1992–98, Sr Minister 1998–2004, Deputy Prime Minister and Minister in Charge of Council of Ministers 2004–; mem. Nat. Ass. for Takeiv 1993–; mem. Cambodian People Party, Cabinet Chief, Cen. Cttee 1991; Vice-Chair. Centralist Democratic Inst.; Head of Council of Admin. Reform, Apasara Authority, Nat. Cambodia Petroleum Authority, Nat. Land Dispute Authority, Cambodia Training Bd, Royal Acad., Khmer Rouge Tribunal, State Investment Bd on Rubber Enterprise; Hon. mem. Russian Acad. of Sciences 2002; Sena Medal, Thebdint Medal, Mohasena Medal, Mohasereyvathn Medal of Munisaraphond, Mohasereyvathn Medal of Suvathara, Cheatubkar Medal; Dr hc (Wesleyan Coll., Iowa) 1996, (Jeonú Univ., South Korea) 2005, (Kampuchea Univ.) 2006. *Address:* 70, Street 214, Sangkat Beung Rang, Khan Chamkarmom, Phnom Penh, Cambodia (office). *Telephone:* (23) 880628 (office).

SOKOLOFF, Louis, BA, MD; American physician and research scientist; *Scientist Emeritus, National Institute of Mental Health;* b. 14 Oct. 1921, Philadelphia, Pa; s. of Morris Sokoloff and Goldie Sokoloff; m. Betty Jane Kaiser 1947; one s. one d.; ed Univ. of Pennsylvania; Research Fellow, Instructor and Assoc. in Physiology and Pharmacology, Grad. School of Medicine, Univ. of Pennsylvania 1949–53; Assoc. Chief, Section on Cerebral Metabolism, Lab. of Neurochemistry, Nat. Inst. of Mental Health, Bethesda, Maryland 1953–56, Chief, Section on Cerebral Metabolism, Lab. of Clinical Science 1956–57, Chief 1957–68, Chief, Lab. of Cerebral Metabolism 1968–2004, Scientist Emer., Nat. Inst. of Mental Health 2004–; mem. NAS 1981, American Acad. of Arts and Sciences 1982, American Philosophical Soc. 2005; Hon. DSc (Yeshiva) 1982, (Glasgow) 1989, (Pennsylvania) 1997; Hon. ScD (Georgetown) 1992, (Michigan State) 1993; Hon. MD (Lund) 1980, (Rome) 1992; Dr hc (Philipps Univ. of Marburg) 1990; F.O. Schmitt Medal in Neuroscience 1980, Albert Lasker Clinical Medical Research Award 1981, Karl Spencer Lashley Award 1987, Distinguished Grad. Award, Univ. of Pennsylvania 1977, NAS Award in Neuroscience 1988, Cerebrovascular Disorder Research Promotion Award, Georg Charles de Hevesy Nuclear Medicine Pioneer Award 1988, Mihara 1988, Ralph Gerard Award, Soc. of Neuroscience 1996. *Publications include:* The Action of Drugs on the Cerebral Circulation (Pharmacological Review 11) 1959, The [14C] Deoxyglucose Method for the Measurement of Local Cerebral Glucose Utilization: Theory, Procedure and Normal Values in the Conscious and Anaesthetized Albino Rat (Journal of Neurochemistry, Vol. 28) 1977, The Relationship Between Function and Energy Metabolism: Its Use in the Localization of Functional Activity in the Nervous System (Neurosciences Research Program Bulletin 19 (2)) 1981, Metabolic Probes of Central Nervous System Activity in Experimental Animals and Man (Magnes Lecture Series, Vol. I) 1984, Brain Imaging and Brain Function (Proceedings of the Asscn for Research in Nervous and Mental Disease, Vol. 63) 1985, Imaging of Regional Functional Activities in the Nervous System (Bulletin of the American Acad. of Arts and Scientists) 1993, Energetics of Functional Activation in Neural Tissues (Neurochemical Research) 1999. *Leisure interests:* music, tennis, literature, history, travel. *Address:* National Institute of Mental Health, Building 49, Room 1B80, 49 Convent Drive, MSC 44415, Bethesda, MD 20892, USA (office). *Telephone:* (301) 496-1371 (office). *Fax:* (301) 402-0046 (office). *E-mail:* louissokoloff@mail.nih.gov (office). *Website:* intramural.nimh.nih.gov/research (office).

SOKOLOV, Aleksandr Sergeyevich, DFA; Russian politician and musicologist; b. 8 Aug. 1949, Leningrad; m. Larisa Sokolov; one d.; ed Moscow State Tchaikovsky Conservatory; Lecturer, Moscow State Tchaikovsky Conservatory 1977, Prof. of Musical Theory 1992, Prorector 1992–2001, Rector 2001–04; Minister of Culture and Mass Communications 2004–08; mem. Composers' Union of Russia; Order of the Hungarian Repub. with Star 2006, Order of St Sergiy Radonejsky 2006; Nat. Prize 2004. *Publications:* Music Around Us 1996, Musical Composition of the XX Century: Dialectic of Creation 2002 (Spanish trans. 2005), Introduction to the Musical Composition of the XX Century 2004. *Leisure interests:* music, hunting, tourism. *Address:* c/o Ministry of Culture and Mass Communications, Kitaigorodskii proyezd 7, build. 2, Moscow 109074, Russia (office).

SOKOLOV, Aleksandr (Sasha) Vsevolodovich; Russian writer; b. 6 Nov. 1943, Ottawa, Canada; s. of Vsevolod Sokolov and Lidia Sokolova; m. 2nd Johanna Steindl 1975; one s.; one d. from previous m.; ed Moscow Univ.; left USSR 1975 for

Austria, USA, Canada, France, Greece; returned to USSR 1989 (first emigré writer to do so); now lives in Moscow, retaining Canadian citzenship; works published in USSR 1989–. *Publications include:* School for Fools 1976, Entre Chien et Loup 1979, Palisandriia 1985, Vozhidanii nobeliia (Waiting for the Nobel) 1993. *Address:* c/o Ardis Publishers, One Overlook Drive, Woodstock, NY 12498, USA (office).

SOKOLOV, Grigory Lipmanovich; Russian pianist; b. 18 April 1950, Leningrad (now St Petersburg); ed Leningrad Conservatory (pupil of Moisey Halfin); numerous guest appearances in London, Paris, Vienna, Berlin, Madrid, Salzburg, Munich, Rome and New York; has worked with leading conductors including Myung-Whun Chung, Neeme Järvi, Herbert Blomstedt, Valery Gergiev, Sakari Oramo, Trevor Pinnock, Andrew Litton, Vassilly Sinajskij, Jukka-Pekka Saraste, Alexander Lazarev, John Storgards, Moshe Atzmon, Walter Weller and Evgeny Svetlanov; has performed with orchestras including New York Philharmonic, Montreal Symphony, Münchner Philharmoniker, Leipzig Gewandhaus, Philhannonia, Amsterdam Concertgebouw and Detroit Symphony; Prof., Leningrad (St Petersburg) Conservatory 1975–; Second Prize, All-Union Competition of Musicians 1965, First Prize, Int. Tchaikovsky Competition 1966, People's Artist of Russia 1988. *Recordings:* several live recordings including works by Bach, Beethoven, Brahms, Chopin, Rachmaninoff, Prokofiev, Schubert, Schumann, Scriabin and Tchaikovsky; DVD of 2002 Paris recital directed by Bruno Monsaingeon. *Address:* c/o Artists Management Co., Piazza R. Simoni 1, 37122 Verona, Italy (office). *Telephone:* (45) 8014980 (office). *E-mail:* office@amcmusic.com (office). *Website:* www.amcmusic.com (office).

SOKOLOV, Maksim Yur'yevich; Russian journalist; b. 1959, Moscow; m.; ed Moscow State Univ.; worked as programmer in All-Union Centre of Transport, USSR State Cttee on Science and Tech. 1981–83; All-Union Research Inst. of Patent Information 1983–84; All-Union Research Inst. for Man. of Coal Industry 1985–87; Research Inst. of Gen. Plan of Moscow 1988–89; journalist since late 1980s; contrib. Commersant (weekly) 1989–97; political observer, Izvestiya 1998–; publs in newspapers Nezavisimaya Gazeta, Atmoda, Segodnya, magazines Vek XX i Mir, Oktyabr, Soviet Analyst (UK); broadcaster Russian Public TV Co. ORT; commentator, TV programmes; special corresp., Soviet analyst; Gong 94 Journalism prize; Medal for the Defence of Free Russia 1991. *Leisure interests:* travelling, cooking, reading fiction, mushroom hunting. *Address:* Izvestiya, 103791 Moscow, Tverskaya str. 18, Russia. *E-mail:* m.sokolov@izvestia.ru (office).

SOKOMANU, George; Ni-Vanuatu politician; b. (George Kalkoa), 13 Jan. 1937, Vanuatu; m. Leitak Matautava 1960; four s. one d.; fmr Deputy Chief Minister and Minister of the Interior of New Hebrides; Pres. of Vanuatu 1980–88; arrested Dec. 1988; sentenced to six years' imprisonment March 1989, released April 1989; Sec.-Gen. South Pacific Comm. 1992–95; Deputy Prime Minister, Minister of Home Affairs, Local Govt, Police and Defence 1994–95; currently Chair. Red Cross Vanuatu; Patron, Pacific Peacebuilding Initiatives. *Address:* c/o Peacebuilders International, PO Box 256, Berowra, NSW 2081, Australia. *Telephone:* (2) 9086-9365. *Fax:* (2) 8078-3827. *Website:* www.peacebuilders.in.

SOKUROV, Alexander Nikolayevich; Russian film director; b. 14 June 1951, Irkutsk; ed Gorky (now Nizhny Novgorod) Univ., All-Union Inst. of Cinematography; worked in Gorky (now Nizhny Novgorod) TV, Lenfilm Studio, directed feature and documentary films; Founder and Dir Experimental School of Young Cinema Vanguard; various prizes at int. film festivals. *Films include:* A Solitary Voice of a Man (Bronze Leopard, Locarno Int. Festival 1978), Mournful Callousness, Days of Eclipse (FIPRESSI Prize—Montreal Int. Festival), A Sonata for Hitler, Second Round, Elegy (about F. Shalyapin), Moscow Elegy (dedicated to A. Tarkovsky) Soviet Elegy, Russian Elegy, The Quiet Pages, The Spiritual Voices (Sony Prize, Locarno Int. Festival 1995), Oriental Elegy (Grand Prix Oberhausen Festival 1996), Mother and Son (prizes at Int. Festivals of Berlin, Moscow 1997), The Knot: Solzhenitsyn 1998, Moloch 1999, Sonata for Hitler 2000, Calf 2001, Russian Ark 2003, The Sun (Best Director Eurasia Int. Film Festival) 2005, Alexandra 2007, Faust (Venice Film Festival Golden Lion) 2011. *Address:* 199048 St Petersburg, Smolenskaya nab. 4, Apt. 222, Russia.

SULAGH, Baqir, (Bayan Jabr); Iraqi politician; ed Baghdad Univ.; Sr Official Supreme Council for the Islamic Revolution in Iraq (SCIRI), fmr Head Damascus office; Minister of Construction and Housing 2003–04, of the Interior 2005–06, of Finance 2006–10; mem. United Iraqi Alliance. *Address:* c/o Ministry of Finance, Khulafa St, nr ar-Russafi Square, Baghdad, Iraq.

SOLANA MADARIAGA, (Francisco) Javier, PhD; Spanish fmr physicist, politician and international organization official; *President, Madariaga – College of Europe Foundation;* b. 14 July 1942, Madrid; brother of Luis Solana Madariaga; m. Concepción Giménez; one s. one d.; ed Colegio del Pilar, Universidad Compluense de Madrid; joined Spanish Socialist Party 1964; won Fulbright scholarship to study physical sciences in USA until 1968; Asst to Prof. Nicolas Cabrera, Univ. of Va 1968–71, then at Universidad Autónoma de Madrid (where contract was cancelled allegedly for political reasons); mem. Exec., Federación Socialista Madrileña and Federación de Trabajadores de la Enseñanza, Unión General de Trabajadores; Prof. of Solid State Physics, Universidad Complutense de Madrid 1977; mem. Congress of Deputies for Madrid; mem. Fed. Exec. Comm., Partido Socialista Obrero Español, fmr Press Sec. and Sec. for Research and Programmes; Minister of Culture 1982–88; Govt Spokesman 1985–88; Minister of Educ. and Science 1988–92, of Foreign Affairs 1992–95; Sec.-Gen. NATO 1995–99, responsible for NATO Defence and Foreign Policy 1999; Sec.-Gen. and High Rep. for Common Foreign and Security Policy, Council of the EU 1999–2009; Sec.-Gen. WEU 1999–2009; Pres. European Defence Agency 2004–; Pres. Madariaga –Coll. of Europe Foundation 1998–, Centre for Global Economy and Geopolitics, ESADE Business School, Barcelona 2009–; mem. Spanish Chapter of Club of Rome; Hon. KCMG 1999, Grand Cross of Isabel the Catholic, Kt of the Order of the Golden Fleece 2010; Manfred Wörner Medal, Ministry of Defence (Germany), Vision for Europe Award 2003, Statesman of the Year Award, EastWest Inst. 2003, Premio Carlomagno 2006, Carnegie-Wateler Peace Prize 2006, Charlemagne Prize 2007. *Publications:* more than 30 publs in field of solid-state physics. *Address:* Madariaga – College of Europe Foundation, Avenue de la Joyeuse Entrée, 14/2, 1040 Brussels, Belgium (office). *Telephone:* (2) 209-62-10 (office). *Fax:* (2) 209-62-11

(office). *E-mail:* info@madariaga.org (office); public.relations@consilium.eu.int. *Website:* www.madariaga.org (office).

SOLANKI, Sushil Kumar; Indian wrestler; b. 26 May 1983, Najafgarh, Delhi; s. of Diwan Singh Solanki and Kamla Devi Solanki; World Cadet Games (gold medal) 1998, Asian Jr Wrestling Championship (gold medal) 2000, Asian Wrestling Championships (bronze medal) 2003, Commonwealth Wrestling Championships (gold medal), Commonwealth Wrestling Championships (gold medal) 2003, 2005, 2007, Asian Wrestling Championships (bronze medal) 2008, Beijing Olympics 2008 (bronze medal), Asian Wrestling Championships (gold medal) 2010, FILA World Wrestling Championships (gold medal) 2010, Commonwealth Games (gold medal), Delhi 2010; currently Asst Commercial Man., Indian Railways; Arjuna Award 2006, Rajiv Gandhi Khel Ratna 2009. *Address:* Railway Complex, Shivaji Bridge, Behind Shankar Market, New Delhi 110 001 India (office). *Telephone:* (11) 23411173 (office); (11) 23413627 (office).

SOLBERG, Erna; Norwegian politician; *Prime Minister;* b. 24 Feb. 1961, Bergen; d. of Asbjørn Solberg and Inger Wenche Torgersen; m. Sindre Finnes; two c.; ed Univ. of Bergen; Deputy mem. Bergen city council 1979–83, 1987–89; mem. Storting (Parl.) for Hordaland 1989–; Minister of Local Govt and Regional Devt 2001–05; Prime Minister 2013–; mem. Høyre (Conservative party), Deputy Leader 2002–04, Leader 2004–; Commdr, Order of St Olav 2005. *Address:* Office of the Prime Minister, Glacisgt. 1, POB 8001 Dep., 0030 Oslo, Norway (office). *Telephone:* 22-24-90-90 (office). *Fax:* 22-24-95-00 (office). *E-mail:* postmottak@smk.dep.no (office). *Website:* www.regjeringen.no/smk (office).

SOLBERG, Monte; Canadian fmr politician; b. 17 Sept. 1958, Calgary; m. Debra LeClaire; two s.; fmr broadcaster and businessman; mem. Parl. for Medicine Hat, Alberta (Reform Party 1993–2001, Canadian Alliance 2001, then Conservative Party of Canada) 1993–2008, parl. positions held include Critic for Foreign Affairs, Nat. Revenue, Human Resources Devt, Vice-Chair. standing cttees on Finance, Human Resources Devt, Status of Persons with Disabilities, Foreign Affairs, Int. Trade; Minister of Citizenship and Immigration 2006–07, of Human Resources and Social Devt 2007–08; currently Sr Adviser, Fleishman-Hillard Inc. (public relations agency); Special Advisor, RCI Capital; columnist and contributor SUN News Network; fmr mem. Exec. Cttee Canada–USA Parl. Asscn; mem. Bd of Dirs Alberta Asscn of Broadcasters. *Address:* Fleishman-Hillard Inc., 540 Fifth Avenue SW, Suite 1410, Calgary, AB T2P 0M2, Canada.

SOLBES MIRA, Pedro, DPolSci; Spanish politician; b. 31 Aug. 1942, Pinoso, Alicante; m.; three c.; ed Univ. of Madrid, Inst. of European Studies of Free Univ., Brussels; civil servant, Ministry of Trade 1968–73, Commercial Counsellor to Spain's Perm. Mission to the EC 1973–78, Special Adviser to Minister for Relations with the EC 1978–79; Dir Gen. Commercial Policy, Ministry of Econs and Trade 1979–82; Gen. Sec. Ministry of Econs and Finance and mem. of task force for Spanish Accession negotiations to EC 1982–85; Sec. of State for Relations with the EC 1985; Pres. Internal Market Council during first Spanish presidency of EC 1989; Minister of Agric., Food and Fisheries 1991–93, of Economics and Finance 1993–96; Pres. Ecofin Council during Spanish presidency of EU 1995; mem. Spanish Parl. 1996; Pres. Jt Cttee of Spanish Parl. on EU 1996; European Commr for Econ. and Monetary Affairs 1999–2004; Second Deputy Prime Minister and Minister of the Economy and Finance 2004–09. *Address:* c/o Ministry of the Economy, Alcalá 9, 28014 Madrid, Spain.

SOLBRIG, Otto Thomas, PhD; American biologist and academic; *Bussey Professor of Biology, Emeritus, Herbaria, Harvard University;* b. 21 Dec. 1930, Buenos Aires, Argentina; s. of Hans Solbrig and Rose Muggleworth; m. Dorothy Crosswhite 1969; one s. one d.; ed Colegio Nacional de Mar de La Plata, Univ. Nacional de La Plata and Univ. of Calif., Berkeley; Research Asst Univ. of La Plata 1951–54; Teaching Fellow, Univ. of Calif., Berkeley 1956–58; Asst then Assoc. Curator, Gray Herbarium, Harvard Univ. 1960–66, Dir 1963–78; Assoc. Prof., Prof. Univ. of Mich. Ann Arbor 1966–69; Bussey Prof. of Biology Harvard Univ. 1969–, now Prof. Emer.; numerous professional appointments and affiliations etc.; Fellow, American Acad. of Arts and Sciences, AAAS; Guggenheim Fellow 1975–76; Hon. MA (Harvard) 1969; Extraordinary Prof. hc (Univ. of La Plata) 1991; Distinguished Prof. hc (Univ. of Buenos Aires) 1994; Cooley Prize 1961, Congressional Antarctic Medal 1967, Willdenow Medal, Berlin Botanical Gardens 1979. *Publications:* author or co-author of 16 books and more than 210 articles and chapters in books on plant population biology, cytology, ecology, evolution and taxonomy. *Leisure interest:* sailing. *Address:* Harvard University Herbaria, 22 Divinity Avenue, Cambridge, MA 02138, USA (office). *Telephone:* (617) 495-4302 (office). *Fax:* (617) 495-9484 (office). *E-mail:* solbrig@husc.harvard.edu (office). *Website:* www.huh.harvard.edu/research/staff/solbrig/solbrig (office).

SOLDI SOLDI, Rear-Adm. Héctor; Peruvian international organization official and fmr naval officer; *Secretary-General, Permanent Commission for the South Pacific;* ed Escuela Naval del Perú, Universidad Católica del Perú, Naval Postgraduate School, Monterey, Calif.; took part in Australian expedition to Antarctica as mem. scientific panel 1982; Peruvian rep. on Jacques Cousteau's expedition to Amazon on board ship Calypso 1982; Chief scientist for oceanography programme, first Peruvian expedition to Antarctica 1988, second expedition 1989; Head, Oceanography Dept, Peruvian Navy Directorate of Hydrography and Navigation, Lima 1985–90, Head, Dept of Environment 1992–93, Technical Dir 1994–97, Deputy Dir of Hydrography and Navigation 1998, Dir 2000–01; Commdr, Oceanographic research vessel Humboldt, Instituto del Mar de Peru 1990–91; Exec. Dir 12th Peruvian expedition to Antarctica 2000; Dir Escuela Naval del Perú (Peruvian Naval Acad.) 2002; Peruvian Naval Attaché to OAS and Head of Peruvian Del. to Inter-American Defense Bd, Washington, DC 2003–04; mem. Advisory Cttee, Ministry of Foreign Affairs 2005–09; Vice Chair. Intergovernmental Cttee, Global Oceans Observing System of Intergovernmental Oceanographic Comm. 2007–09; Pres. Multisectoral Comm., Nat. Focal Point Action Plan for Protection of Marine and Coastal Areas of S Pacific 2006–09; Pres. Nat. Cttee for Study of El Niño 2006–09; Chair. Instituto del Mar del Peru 2006–09; Sec.-Gen., Perm. Comm. for S Pacific, Ecuador 2010–. *Address:* Permanent Commission for the South Pacific, Av. Carlos Julio Arosemena, Km 3, Complejo Albán Borja, Edificio Classic, 2do piso, Guayaquil, Ecuador (office). *Telephone:* (4) 2221201 (office). *E-mail:* defnat@defense.tn (office). *Website:* www.cpps-int.org (office).

SOLEHOV, Mahmadnazar; Tajikistani government official; *Minister of Internal Affairs;* Chair. Constitutional Court 1998–2002; Minister of Internal Affairs 2002–03, 2006–; Chair. Council of Justice 2003–04; Head of Exec. Office of the Pres. 2004–06. *Address:* Ministry of Internal Affairs, 734025 Dushanbe, ul. Tekhron 29, Tajikistan (office). *Telephone:* (372) 21-17-40 (office). *Fax:* (372) 21-26-05 (office).

SOLH HAMADEH, Leila; Lebanese foundation executive; *Vice-President, Alwaleed Bin Talal Humanitarian Foundation;* b. Beirut; d. of Riad Al-Solh; m. Majed Hamadeh; ed St Joseph Univ., Beirut; Vice-Pres. Alwaleed Bin Talal Humanitarian Foundation 2003–; Minister of Industry 2004; Arab League Hon. Trophy 2008; Arab Women Medal, Arab Women Org. 2006, Pontifical Medal from Pope Benedict XVI 2008, Catholicos of All Armenians Gold Medal 2008, High Recognition Award, Arab Tender Forum, Abu Dhabi 2008, Union des Français de l'Etranger Order of Cedars of Lebanon 2009; Dr hc (Lebanese American Univ.) 2006, (Notre Dame) 2009, (Acad. française, Hagazian Univ. Service Shield); Vermeil Medal, St Joseph Univ. 2008, Woman of the Year 2008. *Publications:* Un Liban à retrouver (A Return to Lebanon) 2008, Les élections de 2009, Les enjeux culturels (2009 Elections, Cultural Issues) 2009. *Address:* Alwaleed Bin Talal Humanitarian Foundation, Osaily Building, 1st Floor, Riad El-Solh Square, Beirut, Lebanon (office). *Telephone:* (1) 966966 (office). *Fax:* (1) 966966 (office). *Website:* www.alwaleedbintalalfoundation.org (office).

SOLIS, Hilda Lucia, BA, MA; American politician and fmr government official; b. 20 Oct. 1957, Los Angeles; d. of Raul Solis and Juana Solis; m. Sam H. Sayyad 1982; ed California State Polytechnic Univ., Univ. of Southern California; interpreter, US Immigration and Naturalization Service, LA 1977–79; Ed.-in - Chief Office of Hispanic Affairs, White House, Washington, DC 1980–81; Man. Analyst, Civil Rights Div., Office of Man. and Budget 1981–82; Field Rep. Office of Assemblyman Art Torres, LA 1982; Dir Calif. Student Opportunity and Access Program 1982; mem. Rio Hondo Community Coll. Bd of Trustees 1985; mem. Calif. State Ass. for 57th Dist 1992–94; mem. Calif. State Senate from 24th Dist 1994–2000; mem. US House of Reps from 32nd Dist 2001–08, mem. Resouces Cttee, Energy and Commerce Cttee (Vice-Chair. Environment and Hazardous Materials Sub cttee, Select Cttee on Energy Independence and Global Warming; Co-Vice Chair. Democratic Steering and Policy Cttee, Sr Whip and Regional Whip for Southern California; Chair. Congressional Hispanic Caucus Task Force on Health and the Environment; mem. Comm. on Security and Cooperation in Europe 2007–08, Vice Chair. Gen. Cttee on Democracy, Human Rights and Humanitarian Questions; US Sec. of Labor, Washington, DC 2009–13; Democrat; Meritorious Service Award, US Dept of Defense 1981, Profile in Courage Award, John F. Kennedy Library Foundation 2000. *Address:* c/o Department of Labor, Frances Perkins Bldg, 200 Constitution Avenue, NW, Washington, DC 20210, USA.

SOLÍS, Ottón, MA; Costa Rican politician; b. 31 May 1954; m. Shirley Sanchez 1994; four c.; ed Univ. of Costa Rica, Univ. of Manchester, UK; has taught at Univs of Manchester and Reading, UK, Costa Rican univs, UN Univ. for Peace; Pres. Interamerican Econ. and Social Council, OAS 1987–88; Researcher Sustainable Devt Research Centre, Univ. of Costa Rica 2000; fmr Economist Cen. Bank of Costa Rica, Ministry of Planning and Econ. Policy; fmr Consultant ECLA, UNDP, SIDA; Founding Pres. Citizens Action Party (Partido Acción Ciudadana, PAC) 2000, unsuccessful presidential cand. 2006, 2010; Bacardi Family Eminent Scholar, Center for Latin American Studies, Univ. of Florida 2008; mem. Univ. Bd Open Univ. of Costa Rica 1990–93; mem. Special Cttee, La Amistad Park Trust Fund 1999, Cttee of Experts on Public Admin, UN 2002; mem. Team, Millennium Ecosystem Assessment 2001. *Address:* c/o Partido Acción Ciudadana (PAC), 25 San Pedro, 425 m sur del Templo Parroquial, San José, Costa Rica (office). *Telephone:* 281-2727 (office). *Fax:* 280-6640 (office). *E-mail:* pac2002@racsa.co.cr (office). *Website:* www.pac.or.cr (office).

SOLÍS CARRIÓN, Doris; Ecuadorean sociologist, teacher and politician; *Minister of Policy Coordination;* b. Cuenca; two s.; fmr Exec. Dir Service for an Alternative Devt of the South; Deputy Mayor of Cuenca 2000–02; Minister of Tourism 2003, Minister of Nat. and Cultural Heritage 2008–09, Minister/Head, Secr. of Peoples, Social Movts and Citizen Participation 2009–10, Minister of Policy Coordination 2011–; mem. faculty, Univ. of Cuenca, f. Gender Studies and Tourism programmes; Premio Valdivia, Nat. Congress 2001. *Address:* Government Services Cuenca, Sangurima 1456 y Coronel, Cuenca, Ecuador (office). *Telephone:* 22269173 (office). *Fax:* 22269010 (office).

SOLÍS RIVERA, Luis Guillermo, MA; Costa Rican politician and head of state; *President;* b. 25 April 1958, San José; s. of Freddy Solís Avendaño and Vivienne Rivera Allen; m. María Mercedes Peñas Domingo; six c.; ed Univ. of Costa Rica, Tulane Univ., USA; Assoc. Prof., Univ. of Costa Rica 1981–87; Fulbright Scholar, Univ. of Michigan 1983–85; Chief of Staff, Ministry of Foreign Affairs 1986–90, Amb. for Central American Affairs 1994–98; Coordinator, Center for Admin and Justice, also Researcher, Latin American and Caribbean Center, Florida Int. Univ. 1999; columnist, La República (daily newspaper) 1990s; Pres. of Costa Rica 2014–; fmr mem. Costa Rican dels to UN, OAS, EU and several other int. bodies; Consultant to UNDP; mem. Editorial Bd Foreign Affairs, Global Governance, Espacios; mem. Partido Liberación Nacional (PLN) 1977–2005, Dir of Int. Relations, Sec. Gen. 2002–03; mem. Partido Acción Ciudadana (PAC) 2009–. *Publications:* numerous essays and books on nat. and int. affairs. *Address:* Casa Presidencial, Zapote, San José, Costa Rica (office). *Telephone:* 2207-9170 (office). *Fax:* 2253-9078 (office). *Website:* www.presidencia.go.cr (office).

SOLLERS, Philippe, (pseudonym of Philippe Joyaux); French author and critic; b. 28 Nov. 1936, Bordeaux; s. of Octave Joyaux and Marcelle Molinié; m. Julia Kristeva 1967; one s.; ed Lycées Montesquieu and Montaigne, Bordeaux and Ecole Sainte-Geneviève, Versailles; co-f. and ran the avant garde journal Tel Quel (along with writer and art critic Marcelin Pleynet) 1960–82; Dir L'Infini (review) 1983–; mem. reading Cttee Editions Gallimard 1990–, Asscn of French Museums 1998–; Chevalier, Légion d'honneur, Officier, Ordre nat. du Mérite, Officier des Arts et des Lettres; Prix Médicis 1961, Grand Prix du Roman de la Ville de Paris 1988, Prix Paul-Morand (Académie française) 1992, Prix littéraire de la fondation Prince Pierre de Monaco 2006. *Publications include:* novels: Une Curieuse Solitude 1958, Le Parc 1961, Drame 1965, Nombres, Lois 1972, H 1973, Paradis, Vision à New York 1981, Femmes 1983, Portrait du joueur 1985, Paradis 2 1986, Le Coeur

absolu 1987, Les Surprises de Fragonard 1987, Les Folies françaises 1988, Le Lys d'or 1989, Carnet de nuit 1989, La Fête à Venise 1991, Le Secret 1993, Venise Éternelle 1993, La Guerre du Goût 1994, Femmes, Mythologies (co-author) 1994, Les Passions de Francis Bacon 1996, Studio 1997, L'Année du Tigre, Journal de l'année 1998, 1999, L'Oeil de Proust, les dessins de Marcel Proust 1999, Passion fixe 2000, La Divine Comédie 2000, L'Etoile des amants 2002, Illuminations à travers les textes sacrés 2003, Le Saint-Ane 2004, Logique de la fiction 2006, Une Vie Divine 2007, Un vrai roman: Mémoires 2007, Les Voyageurs du temps 2009, Trésor d'Amour 2011, L'Éclaircie 2012, Portraits de femmes 2013; essays: L'Intermédiaire 1963, Logiques 1968, L'Écriture et l'Expérience des Limites 1968 (published as Writing and the Experience of Limits 1982), Sur le Matérialisme 1974, Théorie des Exceptions 1985, De Kooning, vite 1988, Improvisations 1991, Sade contre l'Être suprême 1996, Les passions de Francis Bacon 1996, Picasso, le héros 1996, La Guerre du Goût 1994, Casanova l'admirable (Prix Elsa-Morante 1999) 1998, Francesca Woodman 1998, Francis Ponge 2001, Éloge de l'Infini 2001, Mystérieux Mozart 2001, Liberté du XVIIIème (Extract from La Guerre du Goût) 2002, Dictionnaire amoureux de Venise 2004, Poker 2005, Fleurs 2006, Guerres secrètes 2007, Vers le Paradis (with DVD) 2010, Discours Parfait 2010, Fugues 2012. *Address:* L'Infini, 5 rue Gaston-Gallimard, 75007 Paris, France (office). *Website:* www.philippesollers.net.

SOLOMIN, Yuri Mefod'yevich; Russian actor and theatre director; *Artistic Director, Maly Drama Theatre (National Theatre of Russia);* b. 18 June 1935, Chita; s. of Mefody Solomin and Zinaida Ryabtseva; m. Olga Nikolayevna Solomina; one d.; ed Shchepkin Higher School of Theatre Art; actor Maly Drama Theatre 1959–; Artistic Dir 1988–; teacher, then Prof. Shchepkin Theatre Coll. 1960–; Minister of Culture of Russian Fed. 1990–92; Pres. Asscn of Russian Drama Theatres; mem. Int. Acad. of Creative Arts; corresp. mem. Russian Acad. of Educ.; master-classes in USA, Japan, S Korea; Order For Service to Motherland (Fourth and Third Class), Order Friendship of Peoples, Order of Russian Orthodox Church, Order for Contrib. to Int. Culture (Japan), Int. K.S. Stanislavsky Prize; State Prize of Russian Fed., Prize Golden Aries, A.D. Popov Gold Medal, USSR Peoples' Artist, People's Artist of Russia and Kyrghyzia. *Film roles include:* Sleepless Night, Adjutant of His Highness, Dersu Ursala, Blockade, Ordinary Miracle, Dreams of Russia, There was Evening, There was Morning, Walking Through the Torments (serial), The Bat, The Farewell in June, Penitential Love, Native Land Waits, Moscow's Saga. *Plays include:* Inspector, Tsar Fedor Ioannovich, The Deep, Uncle Vanya, Cyrano de Bergerac, Seagull, Lady Windermere's Fan, Alive Corps. *Plays produced:* Forest (produced in Bulgaria and Russia), Perfidy and Love, Misfortune from Wit, Three Sisters, A Mysterious Box (vaudeville). *Publications:* From Adjutant to His Highness. *Leisure interest:* dogs and cats. *Address:* State Academic Maly Theatre of Russia, Teatralnaya pl. 1/6, Moscow, Russia (office). *Telephone:* (495) 925-98-68 (office). *Fax:* (495) 924-54-36 (office); (495) 921-03-50 (office). *E-mail:* theatre@maly.ru (office). *Website:* www.maly.ru (office).

SOLOMON, David H., MD; American professor of medicine; *Professor Emeritus, Geriatrics Center on Aging, University of California, Los Angeles;* b. 7 March 1923, Cambridge, Mass.; s. of Frank Solomon and Rose Roud Solomon; m. Ronda Markson 1946; two d.; ed Brown Univ. and Harvard Medical School; Medical House Officer, Peter Bent Brigham Hospital 1946–47; Research Fellow in Medicine, Peter Bent Brigham Hospital and Harvard Medical School 1947–48; Sr Asst Surgeon, US Public Health Service and Investigator, Gerontology Section, Nat. Heart Inst. 1948–50; Sr Asst Resident Physician, Peter Bent Brigham Hospital 1950–51; Fellow in Endocrinology, New England Center Hospital 1951–52; Instructor, School of Medicine, UCLA 1952–54, Asst Prof. 1954–60, Assoc. Prof. 1960–66, Prof. of Medicine 1966, Chief of Medicine (Harbor-UCLA Medical Center) 1966–71, Chair. Dept of Medicine 1971–81, Assoc. Dir Multi-campus Div. of Geriatric Medicine 1982–89, Dir UCLA Geriatrics Center on Aging 1991–96, Prof. Emer. UCLA 1993–; Consultant, Wadsworth Hosp., LA 1952–, Sepulveda Hosp. 1971–, RAND Corpn 1997–; several awards including John Phillips Memorial Award, American Coll. of Physicians 2002. *Publications:* co-author of three books, author of 202 scientific papers, 44 book chapters, 11 review articles and 122 published abstracts. *Leisure interests:* golf, running, reading, hiking, bridge. *Address:* 2103 Ridge Drive, Los Angeles, CA 90049, USA (home). *Telephone:* (310) 471-6346 (office); (310) 471-5256 (home). *Fax:* (310) 471-6346 (home). *E-mail:* davidsolomon@rand.org (office); d.solomon4@verizon.net (home).

SOLOMON, Edward I., PhD; American chemist and academic; *Monroe E. Spaght Professor in the School of Humanities and Sciences, Stanford University;* b. 20 Oct. 1946, New York; s. of Mordecai L. Solomon and Sally S. Solomon; m. Darlene J. Spira 1984; one s. one d.; ed Rensselaer Polytechnic Inst., Tory, New York, Princeton Univ.; Research Assoc., Princeton Univ., NJ 1972–73; Postdoctoral Fellow H.C. Ørsted Inst. 1973–74, Calif. Inst. of Tech. 1974–75; Asst Prof., MIT 1975–79, Assoc. Prof. 1979–81, Prof. 1981–82; Prof., Stanford Univ. 1982–, Spaght Prof. of Chem. 1991–; Invited Prof., Univ. of Paris, Tokyo Inst. of Tech., Tata Inst., India, Xiamen Univ., China, La Plata Univ., Argentina; First Glen Seaborg and other lectureships; Fellow AAAS, American Acad. of Arts and Sciences; Sloan Fellowship, NIH Merit Award., Japan Soc. for Promotion of Science Invitation Fellow, Dean's Award for Distinguished Teaching, Westinghouse Foundation Nat. Talent Search Award, Remsen Award 1994. *Publications:* three books; over 320 papers in scientific journals. *Leisure interests:* tennis, running, gourmet dining, int. travel. *Address:* Department of Chemistry, Stanford University, Stanford, CA 94305-5080, USA. *Telephone:* (650) 723-9104 (office). *Fax:* (650) 725-0259 (office). *E-mail:* Edward.Solomon@stanford.edu (office). *Website:* www.stanford.edu/dept/chemistry/faculty/solomon (office); www .stanford.edu/group/solomon (office).

SOLOMON, Sir Harry, Kt; British business executive; b. 20 March 1937, Middlesbrough, England; s. of Jacob Solomon and Belle Solomon; m. Judith D. Manuel 1962; one s. two d.; ed St Alban's School and Law Soc. School of Law; qualified solicitor 1960; in pvt. practice 1960–75; Man. Dir Hillsdown Holdings PLC 1975–84, Jt Chair. 1984–87, Chair. 1987–93, Dir (non-exec.) 1993–97; Chair. Harveys Holdings PLC 1994–2000; Dir Princedale Group PLC 1993–2000; Dir (non-exec.) Charterhouse European Holding Ltd 1993–2001, Frogmore Estates PLC 1993–2001, US Industries Inc. (now Jacuzzi Brands Inc.) 1995–2004, Falkland Islands Holdings PLC 1999–2009, Consolidated Land Investments Ltd 2000–09, The Portland Trust 2002–, Westcity Plc 2007–09, Portland Capital

2007–09, Monitor/Quest Ltd 2008–; Hon. FRCP. *Leisure interests:* jogging, tennis, theatre, collector of historical autographed letters. *Address:* Hillsdown House, 32 Hampstead High Street, London, NW3 1QD, England (office). *Telephone:* (20) 7431-7739 (office). *Fax:* (20) 7431-7740 (office). *E-mail:* harry@heathside.co.uk (office).

SOLOMONT, Alan D., BA, BS; American business executive, university administrator and fmr diplomatist; *Pierre and Pamela Omidayar Dean, Jonathan M. Tisch College of Citizenship and Public Service, Tufts University;* b. 1957, Boston, Mass; m. Susan Lewis; two d.; ed Tufts Univ., Univ. of Massachusetts, Lowell; Founder and CEO ADS Group (sold co. in 1996); Chair. Solomont Bailis Ventures 1998–; Co-founder HouseWorks; Founder and Man. Dir Angel Healthcare Investors; mem. Bd of Dirs Corpn for Nat. and Community Service 2000–09 (Chair. 2009), Boston Private Bank & Trust Co., Boston Medical Center, New Israel Fund, Israel Policy Forum, Univ. of Lowell, Univ. of Massachusetts, John F. Kennedy Presidential Library Foundation, WGBH Educational Foundation; Amb. to Spain (also accred to Andorra) 2010–13; Finance Chair. Democratic Nat. Cttee 1997–98; Trustee, Tufts Univ. 1999–2009, Pierre and Pamela Omidayar Dean, Jonathan M. Tisch Coll. of Citizenship and Public Service 2014–; Chair. Combined Jewish Philanthropies of Greater Boston and Hebrew Sr Life. *Address:* Jonathan M. Tisch College of Citizenship and Public Service, Lincoln Filene Hall, Tufts University, Medford, MA 02155, USA. *Telephone:* (617) 627-3453. *Fax:* (617) 627-3401. *E-mail:* activecitizen@tufts.edu. *Website:* activecitizen.tufts.edu/solomont.

SOLOVTSOV, Col-Gen. Nikolai; Russian army officer; *Commander, Strategic Missile Command;* b. 1 Jan. 1949, Zaysan, USSR Kazakh Repub.; m.; two c.; ed Rostov Higher Eng and Command School, Dzerzhinskiy Acad., Command Dept and General Staff Acad.; First Deputy Strategic Missile Command 1998–2001, Commdr 2001–; fmr Dean SMC Acad.; Order of Honours, Distinguished Service (3rd grade), Military Merits and ten medals. *Address:* Strategic Missile Command, Ministry of Defence, 105175 Moscow, ul. Myasnitskaya 37, Russia (office). *Telephone:* (495) 293-38-54 (office). *Fax:* (495) 296-84-36 (office). *Website:* www .mil.ru/eng/1862/12068/12088/12223/index.shtml (office).

SOLOVYEV, Sergey Aleksandrovich; Russian film director and scriptwriter; b. 25 Aug. 1944, Kem, Karelia; m. Tatyana Drubich (divorced); ed All-Union Inst. of Cinematography with Leningrad TV 1960–69; film dir Mosfilm Studio 1969–, artistic Dir Krug Film Union 1987–; Sec. USSR Union of Cinematographers 1986–90; Chair. Moscow Union of Cinematographers 1990–97; Co-Chair. Russian Union of Cinematographers 1990–92; Prof. All-Russian Inst. of Cinematography; debut as scriptwriter Look into the Face 1966, as film dir Family Happiness; worked as stage dir in Maly Theatre (Uncle Vanya) and Taganka Theatre (The Seagull). *Films include:* Yegor Bulychev and Others 1971, Station Inspector 1972, A Hundred Days After Childhood 1975 (Silver Bear, Berlin, Prize of All-Union Festival, Tunes of A White Night 1977), Rescuer 1980, Direct Heir 1982, Strange, White and Speckled 1986, Assa 1987, Black Rose: an Emblem of Sadness, Red Rose: an Emblem of Love 1989, The House Under the Starry Sky 1991, Three Sisters 1994, The Tender Age 2001. *Address:* Akademika Pilyugina, 117393 Moscow, str. 8, korp. 1, Apt. 330, Russia. *Telephone:* (495) 132-36-95 (home).

SOLOW, Robert Merton, PhD; American economist and academic; *Institute Professor Emeritus, Massachusetts Institute of Technology;* b. 23 Aug. 1924, Brooklyn, NY; s. of Milton Solow and Hannah Solow; m. Barbara Lewis 1945; two s. one d.; ed Harvard Univ.; Asst Prof. of Statistics, Mass. Inst. of Technology 1950–53, Assoc. Prof. of Econs 1954–57, Prof. of Econs 1958–73, Inst. Prof. 1973–95, Inst. Prof. Emer. 1995–; W. Edwards Deming Prof., New York Univ. 1996; Sr Economist, Council of Econ. Advisers 1961–62; Marshall Lecturer, Univ. of Cambridge, UK 1963–64; De Vries Lecturer, Rotterdam 1963, Wicksell Lecturer, Stockholm 1964; Eastman Visiting Prof., Univ. of Oxford, UK 1968–69; Killian Prize Lecturer, MIT 1978; Geary Lecturer, Univ. of Dublin, Ireland 1980; Overseas Fellow, Churchill Coll., Cambridge 1984; Mitsui Lecturer, Birmingham 1985; Nobel Memorial Lecture, Stockholm 1987 and numerous others in int. academic insts; mem. Nat. Comm. on Tech., Automation and Econ. Progress 1964–65, Presidential Comm. on Income Maintenance 1968–69; mem. Bd of Dirs Fed. Reserve Bank of Boston 1975–81, Chair. 1979–81; Fellow, Center for Advanced Study in Behavioral Sciences 1957–58, Trustee 1982–95; Vice-Pres. American Econ. Asscn 1968, Pres. 1979, Vice-Pres. AAAS 1970; Pres. Econometric Soc. 1964; Trustee Woods Hole Oceanographic Inst. 1988–, Alfred P. Sloan Foundation 1992–, Resources for the Future 1994–96, Urban Inst. 1994–, German Marshall Fund of US 1994–; Pres. Int. Econ. Asscn 1999–2002; mem. Nat. Science Bd 1995–2000; Fellow American Acad. of Arts and Sciences, mem. of Council, NAS 1977–80, mem. 1972–; Corresp. mem. British Acad.; mem. American Philosophical Soc.; Fellow, Acad. dei Lincei (Rome); Foundation Fellow, Russell Sage Foundation 2000–; Orden pour le mérite, Germany 1995; Hon. LLD (Chicago) 1967, (Lehigh) 1977, (Brown) 1972, (Wesleyan) 1982; Hon. LittD (Williams Coll.) 1974, (Rensselaer Polytechnic Inst.) 2003; Dr hc (Paris) 1975, (Geneva) 1982, (Conservatoire Nat. des Arts et Métiers, Paris) 1994, (Buenos Aires) 1999, (Pompeii Fabra, Barcelona) 2008; Hon. DLitt (Warwick) 1976, (Colgate) 1990, (Glasgow) 1992, (Harvard) 1992; Hon. ScD (Tulane) 1983; Hon. DScS (Yale) 1986, (Univ. of Mass., Boston) 1989, (Helsinki) 1990, (Boston Coll.) 1990, (Chile) 1992, (Rutgers Univ.) 1994; Hon. DSc in Business Admin. (Bryant Coll.) 1988; Hon. DEng (Colorado School of Mines) 1996; Hon. DHumLitt (New York) 2006; David A. Wells Prize, Harvard Univ. 1951, John Bates Clark Medal, American Econ. Asscn 1961, Killian Award, MIT 1977, Seidman Award in Political Econ. 1983, Nobel Prize for Econs 1987, Nat. Medal of Science 2000. *Publications:* Linear Programming and Economic Analysis 1958, Capital Theory and the Rate of Return 1963, Sources of Unemployment in the United States 1964, Price Expectations and the Behavior of the Price Level 1970, Growth Theory: An Exposition 1970, The Labor Market as a Social Institution 1989, Learning from "Learning by Doing" 1994, A Critical Essay On Modern Macroeconomic Theory (with Frank Hahn) 1995, Work and Welfare 1998, Inflation, Unemployment and Monetary Policy (with John B. Taylor) 1998; many journal articles. *Address:* 1010 Waltham Street, Apt. 328, Lexington, MA 02421-8057, USA (home). *Telephone:* (781) 538-5412 (home).

SOLT, Pál; Hungarian judge; b. 3 Oct. 1937, Szentendre; m.; one c.; ed Univ. of Eötvös Lóránd, Budapest; Asst Court Clerk, Cen. Dist Court of Pest 1960–63, Judge 1964–66; Head, Secr. of Supreme Court of Justice 1966–71, Judge 1980–87,

Chair. Panel 1987–89, 2002–, Pres. Supreme Court of Justice 1990–2002; Asst. Legal Dept, Secr. of Ministry of Finance 1971–80; mem. Constitutional Court 1989–; Pres. Nat. Council of Justice 1997–2002; Hon. LLD (San Beda Coll. of Law, Manila) 2001. *Address:* Supreme Court, Markó utca 16, 1055 Budapest, Hungary (office). *Telephone:* (1) 268-4575 (office). *Fax:* (1) 268-4603 (office). *E-mail:* solt@ legtelsobb.birosag.hu. *Website:* www.lb.hu (office).

SOLTANI, Bouguerra, (Abou Jarra), LèsL, DESS, PhD; Algerian academic and politician; *President, Harakat Mudjtamaa Silm (HMS);* b. 12 Jan. 1954, Chréa; m. Nedjwa Soltani; five c.; ed Constantine Univ.; Lecturer, Faculty of Humanities, Constantine Univ. 1980–94, Dept of Communications, Emir AbdelKader Univ. 1990–94; Ed.-in-Chief Al Tadhamoun magazine 1990–94; Chair. Consultative Cttee Hamas (now Mouvement de la société pour la paix–MSP) 1992–93, Pres. MSP 2003–; Sec. of State in charge of fishing 1992–93; mem. Nat. People's Ass. for Tébessa 1998–; Minister of Small and Medium-sized Enterprises and Handicrafts 1998–2000, of Labour and Social Security 2000–01; fmr Minister of State; Pres. Harakat Mudjtamaa Silm (Mouvement de la soc. pour la paix) 2010–. *Publications:* novel: La vache des orphelins 1970; poetry: L'épée de Al Hajjaj, Regards sur les liens entre le bien et le mal, Roses et Épines; essays: Feuillets Islamique 1979–89, Les écorces de la confrontation 1997, Les racines de la confrontation 1999, L'Algérie nouvelle- L'avancée vers la démocratie. *Address:* Mouvement de la société pour la paix, 63 rue Ali Haddad, Algiers (office); c/o Office of the Prime Minister, rue Docteur Saâdane, Algiers, Algeria (office). *Telephone:* (21) 27-35-02 (office). *Fax:* (21) 27-26-32 (office). *E-mail:* info@hmsalgeria.net (office). *Website:* www .hmsalgeria.net (office); www.cg.gov.dz (office).

SOLYMAR, László, MA, PhD, FRS, FIEE; British engineer and academic; *Visiting Professor, Department of Electrical and Electronic Engineering, Imperial College London;* b. 24 Jan. 1930, Budapest, Hungary; s. of Pál Solymar and Aranka Gold; m. Marianne Klopfer 1955; two d.; ed Tech. Univ., Budapest, Hungarian Acad. of Sciences; Lecturer, Tech. Univ., Budapest 1952–53; research engineer, Research Inst. for Telecommunications, Budapest 1953–56, Standard Telecommunications Labs Ltd, Harlow, Essex 1956–65; Lecturer, Dept of Eng Science, Univ. of Oxford 1966–86, Fellow Brasenose Coll. 1966–86, Donald Pollock Reader in Eng Science 1986–92, Fellow Hertford Coll. 1986–, Prof. of Applied Electromagnetism 1992–97, Leverhulme Emer. Fellow 1997–2001; Visiting Prof., Physics Lab., Ecole Normale Supérieure, Univ. of Paris 1965–66, Tech. Univ. of Denmark 1972–73, Dept of Physics, Univ. of Osnabrück 1987, Optical Inst., Tech. Univ., Berlin 1990, Dept of Materials, Autonomous Univ. of Madrid 1993, 1995, Tech. Univ., Budapest 1994, Dept of Electrical and Electronic Eng, Imperial Coll. London 2003–; Faraday Medal, IEE 1992. *Radio:* plays: Anaxagoras, Archimedes, Hypatia (with John Wain). *Publications:* The Rhineland War: 1936: The Way it Might Have Happened 2012; a book on the history of communications; various research and text books; several hundred papers in learned journals in the field of engineering and physics. *Leisure interests:* history, bridge, chess, swimming. *Address:* Department of Electrical and Electronic Engineering, Imperial College, Exhibition Road, London, SW7 2BT (office); 62 Hurst Rise Road, Oxford, OX2 9HQ, England (home). *E-mail:* laszlo.solymar@hertford.ox.ac.uk (office).

SOLYOM, Janos Paul; Swedish (b. Hungarian) concert pianist and conductor; b. 26 Oct. 1938, Budapest, Hungary; s. of Dr I. Solyom and M. Weill; m. Camilla Lundberg 1987; ed Franz Liszt Acad. of Music, Budapest, private studies with Ilona Kabos in London and Nadia Boulanger in Paris; int. concert career 1958–; mem. Royal Swedish Acad. of Music; Pro Patria Gold Medal; Royal Swedish Medal for Outstanding Artistic Merit 'Litteris et Artibus'. *Leisure interests:* architecture, hypnotherapy. *Address:* Norr Mälarstrand 54, 112 20 Stockholm, Sweden. *Telephone:* (8) 652-42-72. *E-mail:* pianos@solyom.com. *Website:* www.solyom.com.

SÓLYOM, László, LLD; Hungarian academic, judge, politician and fmr head of state; b. 3 Jan. 1942, Pécs; m. Erzsébet Nagy; one s. one d.; ed Univ. of Pécs, Friedrich Schiller Univ., Jena, Hungarian Acad. of Sciences; Lecturer in Civil Law, Univ. of Jena 1966–69; Research Fellow, Hungarian Acad. of Sciences 1969–82; Prof. of Law, Univ. of Budapest 1982–2002, Catholic Univ. of Budapest 1996–2012, Univ. of Cologne 1999–2000; Pres. Constitutional Court 1990–98; legal adviser to environmental groups and other civic movts 1982–89; Pres. of Hungary 2005–10; mem. Int. Comm. of Jurists, Geneva 1994–2001, scientific council, Wissenschaftskolleg zu Berlin Inst. for Advanced Study, Berlin 1995–2001, European Comm. for Democracy Through Law (The Venice Comm.) 1998–2005; Corresp. mem. Hungarian Acad. of Sciences 2001, Full mem. 2013; Grand Cross of Merit with Star (Germany) 1998; Grand Cross of Merit (Hungary) 1999; Hon. DJur (Cologne) 1999, (Frankfurt/Main) 2006, (Seoul) 2009; Humboldt Research Award 1998, Nagy Imre Prize (Hungary) 2003. *Publications:* The Decline of Civil Law Liability 1980, Die Persönlichkeitsrechte: Eine vergleichend-historische Studie über ihre Grundlagen 1984, Verfassungsgerichtsbarkeit in Ungarn: Analysen und Entscheidungssammlung 1990–93 (with Georg Brunner) 1995, Constitutional Judiciary in a New Democracy: The Hungarian Constitutional Court (with Georg Brunner) 2000, The Beginnings of Constitutional Justice in Hungary (in Hungarian) 2001, The Role of Constitutional Courts in the Transition to Democracy, 18(1) Int. Sociology 2003, Political Parties and Trade Unions in the Constitution (in Hungarian) 2004, Marks of a Presidency (in Hungarian) 2010, Worte des Hörers, in M.Stolleis (ed.), Herzkammern der Republik 2011, The Separation of Powers is Integral to the Fabric of Democracy, 7 Journal of Parliamentary and Political Law 2013, Normenhierarchie in der Verfassung und verfassungswidrige Verfassungsänderungen, Jahrbuch für Ostrecht 1/2014, The Rise and Decline of Constitutional Culture in Hungary, in A. von Bogdandy and P. Sonnevend (eds), Constitutional Crisis in the European Constitutional Area 2014. *Address:* c/o Office of the former President, 1118 Budapest, Kelenhegyi út 32, Hungary.

SOM, Peter; American fashion designer; *Creative Director, Women's Collection, Bill Blass;* ed Connecticut Coll., Parsons School of Design, New York; apprenticed with Michael Kors and Calvin Klein at Parson's School of Design, then worked Bill Blass design room; debut at Seventh on Sixth in Bryant Park tents with Spring 2001 Collection; returned to Bill Blass as Creative Dir Women's Collection 2007–; has designed for Scarlett Johansson, Claire Danes, Camilla Belle, Mandy Moore and Ginnifer Goodwin, among others; CFDA Scholarship Competition winner 1997, Parsons Gold Thimble for his work in the school's Designer Critic program, Lord & Taylor's Dress Competition winner. *Address:* Peter Som, Inc., 260 West 39th Street, 5th Floor, New York NY 10018, USA (office). *Telephone:* (212) 221-

5991 (office). *Fax:* (212) 221-1936 (office). *E-mail:* info@petersom.com (office). *Website:* www.petersom.com (office).

SOMARE, Rt Hon. Sir Michael Thomas, PC, CH, GCMG; Papua New Guinea politician; b. 9 April 1936, Rabaul, East New Britain Prov.; s. of Sana Ludwig Somare and Painari Betha; m. Veronica Bula Kaiap 1965; three s. two d.; ed Sogeri Secondary School, Admin. Coll.; teacher various schools 1956–64; Asst Area Educ. Officer, Madang 1962–63; Broadcasts Officer, Dept of Information and Extension Services, Wewak 1963–66, radio broadcaster and journalist 1966–67; mem. House of Ass. for East Sepik Regional 1968–; Parl. Leader Pangu Party 1968–38; Deputy Chair. Exec. Council 1972–73, Chair. 1973–75; Chief Minister Papua New Guinea 1974–75, Prime Minister 1975–80, 1982–85, 2002–11; Minister for Nat. Resources 1976–77, for Public Service Comm. and Nat. Planning 1977–80; Acting Minister for Police 1978–80; Leader of the Opposition 1980–82; Minister of Foreign Affairs 1988–94, 2000–01, 2006–07, also of Bougainville Affairs 2000–01, of Defence (acting) 2007, of Autonomy and Autonomous Regions 2007–, for Correctional Services (acting); Gov. E Sepik Prov. 1995–; Chair. Bd of Trustees, PNG; mem. Second Select Cttee on Constitutional Devt 1968–72, Australian Broadcasting Comm. Advisory Cttee; mem. Nat. Alliance Party, currently leader; Ancient Order of Sikatuna, Title of Rajah (Philippines) 1976, Grand Cross of Equestrian Order of St Gregory the Great 1993; six hon. degrees; Queen's Silver Jubilee Medal 1977, Pacific Man of the Year Award 1983. *Publication:* Sana: An Autobiography. *Leisure interests:* reading, golf, soccer, cricket, fishing. *Address:* Karan, Murik Lakes, East Sepik, Papua New Guinea (home).

SOMAVÍA, Juan O.; Chilean lawyer, diplomatist and international organization official; b. 21 April 1941; m. Adriana Santa Cruz; two c.; ed Catholic Univ. of Chile, Univ. of Paris; various posts in Ministry of Foreign Relations; Founder and Exec. Dir Latin American Inst. for Transnational Studies, Mexico; Co-ordinator Third World Forum; mem. Bd of Dirs and Vice-Pres. for Latin America of Inter-Press Service 1976–87; Sec.-Gen. South American Peace Comm. 1987; Pres. International Comm. of Chilean opposition No Campaign for Referendum 1988–89; Perm. Rep. to UN, New York 1990–99; Dir-Gen. ILO 1999–2012; fmr consultant to GATT and UNDP; mem. Bd of Dirs International Foundation for Devt Alternatives; mem. MacBride Comm. on communication problems; Laurea hc (Univ. of Turin) 2001, Dr hc (Connecticut Coll.) 1994, (Catholic Univ. of Lima) 1999, (Univ. of Paris I, Panthéon-Sorbonne) 2003; Leonidas Proaño Prize, Latin American Human Rights Asscn for contrib. to peace and regional security. *Address:* c/o International Labour Organization, 4 route des Morillons, 1211 Geneva 22, Switzerland.

SOMCHAI, Wongsawat, BL, MPA; Thai judge and politician; b. 31 Aug. 1947; m.; ed Thammasat Univ., Nat. Defence Coll. of Thailand, Nat. Inst. of Devt Admin; Asst Judge, Ministry of Justice 1974–75, Judge 1975–76; Judge, Chiangmai-Kwaeng Court 1976–77, Chiangmai Court 1977–83, Chiangrai Court 1983–86; Chief Justice, Pang-nga Court 1986–87, Rayong Juvenile Court 1987–88, Chonburi Court 1988–89, Nonthaburi Court 1989–90, Thonburi Criminal Court 1990–93; Justice, Court of Appeal Region II 1993–97, Chief Justice 1997–98; Deputy Perm. Sec., Ministry of Justice 1998–99, Perm. Sec. 1999–2006; Perm. Sec., Ministry of Labour March–Sept. 2006; mem. House of Reps 2007–08; Deputy Leader People Power Party 2007–08; Minister of Educ. Feb.–Sept. 2008; Prime Minister of Thailand 2008, also Minister of Defence, banned by Consitutional Court from holding public office for five years, Court also dissolved People Power Party after finding it committed electoral fraud; Kt Commdr, Most Noble Order of the Crown of Thailand (second class) 1980, (first class) 1986, (special class) 1992, Most Exalted Order of the White Elephant (second class) 1984, (first class) 1989, (special class) 1997; Chakrabarti Mala Medal 1999. *Address:* c/o Office of the Prime Minister, Government House, Thanon Nakhon Pathom, Bangkok 10300, Thailand (office).

SOMDY, Duangdy; Laotian government official; *Minister of Planning and Investment;* b. 1952, Savannakhet Prov.; ed Int. Admin. Inst., Paris, Donetsk Nat. Univ., Ukraine; Technical Officer, Dept of Gen. Planning, State Planning Cttee 1983–93, Dir-Gen., Dept of Gen. Planning, State Planning Cttee 1999–2002, Vice-Pres., Planning and Cooperation Cttee 2002–03; Vice-Minister of Finance 2003–07, Minister of Finance 2007–11, of Planning and Investment 2011–; fmr Vice-Chair. and Standing Mem. Poverty Reduction Fund Admin. Bd. *Address:* Ministry of Planning and Investment, rue Luang Prabang, Vientiane 01001, Laos (office). *Telephone:* (21) 218377 (office). *Fax:* (21) 215491 (office). *Website:* www.investlaos.gov.la (office).

SOMERVILLE, Christopher Roland, BSc, PhD, FRS, FRSC, FAAS; American (b. Canadian) biochemist and academic; *Professor of Plant and Microbial Biology, University of California, Berkeley;* b. 11 Oct. 1947; ed Univ. of Alberta; naturalized US citizen 1995; Research Assoc., Dept of Agronomy, Univ. of Illinois 1978-81; Asst Prof., Dept of Genetics, Univ. of Alberta 1981; Assoc. Prof., Dept of Botany and Plant Pathology, Michigan State Univ. (MSU) and MSU-DOE Plant Research Lab. 1982–86, Prof. 1986–93; Prof. of Biological Sciences, Stanford Univ. 1994–2007, Dir Dept of Plant Biology, Carnegie Inst. of Washington 1994–2007; Prof. of Plant and Microbial Biology, Univ. of California, Berkeley 2007–, Dir Energy Biosciences Inst. 2007–; Visiting Prof., Univ. of Glasgow, UK 1998–; mem. numerous editorial boards, advisory panels for NSF, NIH, US Dept of Agric. and other agencies and insts; consultant to many cos, including Unilever, DuPont, Monsanto, Eli Lilly, Pioneer, Dow, Mendel, Biotechnology, LS9; mem. Academia Europaea 2002, NAS 1996; Fellow, AAAS 2006; Hon. DSc (Queens) 1993, (Alberta) 1997, (Wageningen) 1998, Guelph (2006); NSF Young Presidential Investigator Award 1984, Schull Award, American Soc. of Plant Biologists 1987, MSU Distinguished Faculty Award 1992, Alexander von Humboldt US Sr Scientist Award 1992, Gibbs Medal, American Soc. of Plant Physiology 1993, Kumho Award Kumho Cultural Foundation 2001, Hopkins Award and Memorial Lecturer, Biochemical Soc. 2004, Mendel Medal, Genetics Soc. 2004, Balzan Prize, Int. Balzan Foundation (co-recipient) 2006. *Achievements include:* has pioneered the use of the small mustard plant, *Arabidopsis thaliana,* as model species for plant molecular genetics. *Publications:* Biochemistry and Molecular Biology of Membrane and Storage Lipids of Plants (co-ed.) 1993, Arabidopsis (co-ed.) 1994, The Arabidopsis Book (co-ed.) 2002; numerous papers in professional journals on plant genomics, embryo devt and the synthesis of structural and storage components of plant cells. *Address:* Energy Biosciences Institute, 130 Calvin Laboratory, University of

California, Berkeley, CA 94720-5230 (office); 161 Avenida Drive, Berkeley, CA 94708, USA (home). *Telephone:* (510) 643-6265 (office); (510) 665-6069 (office). *Fax:* (650) 325-6857 (office). *E-mail:* crs@berkeley.edu (office). *Website:* www.energybiosciencesinstitute.org (office); plantbio.berkeley.edu (office).

SOMERVILLE, Jane, MD, FRCP, FESC, FACC; British cardiologist and academic; *Professor Emeritus of Cardiology, Imperial College London;* b. (Jane Platnauer), 24 Jan. 1933, London, England; d. of Joseph Platnauer and Pearl Anne Backler; m. Walter Somerville (deceased); three s. one d.; ed Hill Crest Boys School, Wales, Queen's Coll., London, Guy's Hosp., London; est. Grown-Up Congenital Heart Disease (GUCH) Unit, Nat. Heart Hosp. (first specialist GUCH service in UK, led to new discipline in cardiology) 1975; Prof. of Cardiology, GUCH, Middlesex Hosp. and Univ. Coll. Hosp., London 1997–2002; Prof. Emer. of Cardiology, Imperial Coll. London; Chair. Council, Queen's Coll., Harley Street, London 2000–06; Consultant Cardiologist, Mater Dei Hosp., Malta; f. ESC Working Group, GUCH Patients' Asscn UK, World Congress of Pediatric Cardiology 1980; Fellow, European Soc. of Cardiology (ESC), American Coll. of Cardiology; Gold Medal, European Soc. of Cardiology 2008, Distinguished Service Award, American Coll. of Cardiology 2009, awarded LEGEND status of cardiovascular diseases, European Soc. of Cardiology 2007, American Coll. of Cardiology 2012; numerous int. guest lectures. *Publications:* 300 papers in medical journals. *Leisure interests:* collecting glass, Edwardian silver, mustard pots etc., opera, gardening, wild flowers. *Address:* 81–83 Harley Street, London, W1G 8PP, England (office). *Telephone:* (20) 7262-2144 (office). *Fax:* (20) 7724-5840 (office). *E-mail:* somerville.jane@btinternet.com (home).

SOMMARUGA, Cornelio, LLD; Swiss diplomatist and international organization official; *Chair, Geneva International Centre for Humanitarian Demining;* b. 29 Dec. 1932, Rome, Italy; s. of Carlo Sommaruga and Anna-Maria Valagussa; m. Ornella Marzorati 1957; two s. four d.; ed Rome, Paris, Univ. of Zürich; bank trainee, Zürich 1957–59; joined Diplomatic Service 1960; Attaché, Swiss Embassy, The Hague 1961; Sec., Swiss Embassy, Bonn 1962–64, Rome 1965–68; Deputy Head of Del. to EFTA, GATT and UNCTAD, Geneva 1969–73; Asst Sec.-Gen. EFTA 1973–75; Minister Plenipotentiary, Div. of Commerce, Fed. Dept of Public Economy, Berne 1976, Amb. 1977; del. to Fed. Council for Trade Agreements 1980–84; State Sec. for External Econ. Affairs 1984–86; Pres. ICRC 1987–99; Pres., UN Econ. Comm. for Europe 1977–78; Pres. Initiatives of Change Int., Caux 2000; Chair. J. P. Morgan (Suisse) SA, Geneva 2000–03 (mem. Bd 2003–), Geneva Int. Centre for Humanitarian Demining 2000, Karl Popper Foundation 2000; mem. Panel on UN Peace Operations, Int. Comm. on Intervention and State Sovereignty; Hon. mem. ICRC 2000; Commdr, Légion d'honneur; several other state honours from Italy, Belgium, The Holy See, Luxembourg, Lithuania, Iceland, Sweden; Hon. MD; Dr hc (Fribourg) 1985, (Minho) 1990, (Nice-Sophia Antipolis, Seoul Nat. Univ.) 1992; (Bologna) 1991, (Geneva) 1997, (Webster, St Louis) 1998; North-South Prize of the Council of Europe 2001; numerous awards from Red Cross Socs. *Address:* 7bis, avenue de la Paix, 1202 Geneva, Switzerland (office); 16 chemin des Crêts-de-Champel, 1206 Geneva, Switzerland (home). *Telephone:* (22) 906-16-97 (office); (22) 347-45-52 (home). *Fax:* (22) 906-16-90 (office); (22) 347-45-55 (home). *E-mail:* c.sommaruga@gichd.org (office); cornelio.sommaruga@bluewin.ch (home). *Website:* www.gichd.ch (office); www.chaux.ch.

SOMMARUGA, Simonetta; Swiss politician; *Vice-President and Head, Federal Department of Justice and Police;* b. 14 May 1960, Sins, Aargau; m. Lukas Hartmann; ed Conservatoire de Lucerne, Conservatoire de Fribourg, Fribourg Univ.; early career as concert pianist; mem. Grosser Rat (Great Council) of Bern (Social Democrat) 1981–90; Dir Swiss Consumer Protection Foundation 1993–2000, Pres. 2000–10; local councillor, Köniz 1997–2005; mem. Nationalrat (Nat. Council) 1999–2003; Rep. for Bern, Ständerat (Council of States) 2003–10; Pres. SWISSAID 2003–08; mem. Fed. Council 2010–, Head, Fed. Dept of Justice and Police 2010–; Vice-Pres., Swiss Confed. 2014–; Dir Concret AG 2010–; mem. Fondation Slow Food Suisse 2009–, Fondation Bärenpark Bern 2009–. *Leisure interests:* playing the piano, gardening, reading, walking. *Address:* Federal Department of Justice and Police, Bundeshaus West, 3003 Bern, Switzerland (office). *Telephone:* 313222111 (office). *Fax:* 313227832 (office). *E-mail:* info@gs-ejpd.admin.ch (office). *Website:* www.admin.ch (office) www.sommaruga.ch.

SOMMER, Alfred, MD, MHS; American epidemiologist and academic; *University Distinguished Professor and Dean Emeritus, Bloomberg School of Public Health, Johns Hopkins University;* b. 2 Oct. 1942, New York, NY; m. Jill Sommer; one s. one d.; ed Union Coll., Schenectady, NY, Harvard Medical School, Hopkins School of Public Health; Medical Intern and Resident, Beth Israel Hosp., Harvard Univ., Boston, Mass 1967–69; Attending Physician, Grady Memorial Hosp., Atlanta, Ga 1969–70; Fellow in Epidemiology, Johns Hopkins School of Hygiene and Public Health, Baltimore, Md 1972–73, Resident and Fellow in Ophthalmology, Wilmer Eye Inst. 1973–76, Instructor in Ophthalmology 1976–80, Active Staff, Ophthalmology 1980–, Asst Prof., Ophthalmology, Epidemiology, and Int. Health 1980–81, Assoc. Prof. 1981–85, Prof. 1985–, Prof. of Ophthalmology, Wilmer Eye Inst., Founding Dir Dana Center for Preventive Ophthalmology 1980–90, Dean, Johns Hopkins School of Hygiene and Public Health (now Bloomberg School of Public Health) 1990–2005, Dean Emer. 2005–, Univ. Distinguished Prof.; Visiting Prof. of Ophthalmology, Univ. of Padjadjaran; Dir Nutritional Blindness Prevention Research Program, Bandung, Indonesia 1976–79; Surgeon, Cicendo Eye Hosp., Bandung 1976–79; Visiting Fellow, Inst. of Ophthalmology, Univ. of London, UK 1979–80; Dir WHO Collaborating Center for the Prevention of Blindness 1980–90; Medical Adviser, Helen Keller Int., New York 1980–; Consulting Ophthalmologist, Loch Raven Veterans' Admin Hosp., Baltimore 1981–93; Corp. Dir Becton Dickenson & Co. 1998–, T. Rowe Price Group; Chair. Albert and Mary Lasker Foundation 2007–; Vice-Pres. Int. Council of Ophthalmology Foundation 2002–; mem. Bd of Dirs Int. Trachoma Initiative 2003–09 (also Trustee), Exec. Cttee Acad. for Educational Devt 1997–2007 (also Trustee); Chair. Advisory Bd Epidemiologic Reviews 1990–2005, Bd of Overseers American Journal of Epidemiology 1990–2005, Editorial Advisory Bd EyeNet Magazine 1999–; Editorial positions, American Journal of Ophthalmology, Archives Ophthalmology, American Journal of Epidemiology, Ophthalmology (TAAOO), New England Journal of Medicine, American Journal of Clinical Nutrition, Investigative Ophthalmology and Visual Science, Experimental Eye Research, American Journal of Public Health, Current

Eye Research Journal of the American Medical Assoc, Milbank Quarterly, Journal of the Royal Soc. of Medicine, Current Issues in Public Health, 1993–; mem. Royal Soc. of Medicine, UK 1979, Assoc for Research in Vision and Ophthalmology 1981, Soc. for Epidemiologic Research 1981, American Public Health Assoc 1982, American Ophthalmological Soc. 1983, American Glaucoma Soc. 1988, American Inst. of Nutrition/FASEB 1989, American Soc. for Clinical Nutrition 1989, Inst. of Medicine 1992, Academia Ophthalmologica Internationalis (19th Chair. 1997) 1997, NAS 2001, Int. Council of Ophthalmology 2002–; Trustee Foundation of the Int. Council of Ophthalmology; Fellow, American Acad. of Ophthalmology 1978, American Coll. of Preventive Medicine 1982; at forefront of research into vitamin A deficiency; Hon. Prof. of Ophthalmology, Peking Union Medical College, Beijing 1993; Hon. Prof. of Public Health, Sun Yat-sen Univ. of Medical Sciences, People's Repub. of China, 1998; First Hon. Prof., King Carlos III Nat. Inst. of Health, School of Public Health, Madrid; Helen Keller Blindness Prevention Award 1980, Honor Award 1986, Sr Honor Award 1996, American Acad. of Ophthalmology 1986, Charles A. Dana Award for Pioneering Achievements in Health 1988, First Dean's Alumni Award, Johns Hopkins Univ. School of Hygiene and Public Health 1988, Distinguished Service Award for Contribs to Vision Care, American Public Health Assoc 1988, Nat. Merit Award for Contribs to Public Health, Delta Omega (Public Health Honor Soc.) 1988, Award for Distinguished Contribs to World Ophthalmology, XXIVth Int. Congress of Ophthalmology, Int. Fed. of Ophthalmological Societies 1990, ACAM Achievement Award in Preventive Medicine 1990, Gold Medal for Contribs to World Ophthalmology, Saudi Ophthalmological Soc. 1991, Mericos H. Whittier Award in Ophthalmology, Mericos Eye Inst., Scripps Insts of Medicine and Science 1992, Joseph E. Smadel Award, Infectious Diseases Soc. of America 1992, 1st Recipient, Gesellschaft für angewandte Vitaminforschung Prize (Germany) 1995, Distinguished Alumnus Award, Johns Hopkins Univ., 1995, Albert Lasker Award for Clinical Medical Research 1997, Helmut Horten Medical Research Award 1997, Prince Mahidol Award for Int. Contribs to Medicine and Public Health (Thailand) 1997, Int. Gold Medal for Contribs to Ophthalmology, Singapore Nat. Eye Centre 1997, Int. Duke Elder Gold Medal, Int. Council of Ophthalmology 1998, Int. Blindness Prevention Award, American Acad. of Ophthalmology 1998, E.H. Christopherson Award, American Acad. of Pediatrics 2000, F. Parke Lewis Lifetime Achievement Professional Service Award, Prevent Blindness America 2001, Gold Jose Rizal Medal, Asia Pacific Acad. of Ophthalmology 2001, Bristol-Myers Squibb/Mead Johnson Award for Distinguished Achievement in Nutrition Research 2001, Danone Int. Prize for Nutrition 2001, Special Recognition Award for Leadership, Assoc for Research in Vision and Ophthalmology 2002, George Gehrmann Lecturer, American Coll. of Occupational and Environmental Medicine, Baltimore 2002, Howard S. Brode Lecturer in Science, Whitman Coll., Walla Walla, Washington 2002, Sir John Wilson Lecturer, Int. Congress of Ophthalmology, Sydney 2002, Pollin Prize in Pediatric Research 2004, Helen Keller Prize for Vision Research 2005, Gonin Medal 2006, Thomas Francis Medal in Public Health, Univ. of Michigan 2010, Laureate Award, American Acad. of Ophthalmology 2011, Ophthalmology Hall of Fame, American Soc. of Cataract and Refractive Surgery 2011. *Publications include*: Field Guide to the Detection and Control of Xerophthalmia 1978, Epidemiology and Statistics for the Ophthalmologist 1980, Nutritional Blindness: Xerophthalmia and Keratomalacia 1982, Periodic, Large Oral Doses of Vitamin A for the Prevention of Vitamin A Deficiency and Xerophthalmia (co-author) 1984, Vitamin A Deficiency: Health, Survival, and Vision (co-author) 1996, Getting What We Deserve: Health and Medical Care in America 2009; more than 80 book chapters and reviews and more than 200 articles in scientific journals. *Address*: Johns Hopkins Bloomberg School of Public Health, 615 N Wolfe Street, Baltimore, MD 21205-2179, USA (office). *Telephone*: (410) 502-4167 (office). *Fax*: (410) 502-4169 (office). *E-mail*: asommer@jhsph.edu (office). *Website*: www.jhsph.edu (office).

SOMMER, Elke; German actress and painter; b. (Elke Schletz), 5 Nov. 1940, Berlin; d. of Friedrich Schletz and Renate Schletz; m. Wolf Walther 1993; first film, L'Amico del Giaguaro 1958; since then has made more than 70 films including The Prize, The Victors, Shot in the Dark, The Oscar, Himmelsheim, Neat and Tidy, Severed Ties; hosted TV show Painting with Elke (PBS) 1985; Golden Globe Award 1965, Jefferson Award, Merit of Achievement Award 1990. *Leisure interests*: riding, art. *Address*: 540 N Beverly Glen Boulevard West, Los Angeles, CA 90024, USA. *Telephone*: (310) 724-8990. *Fax*: (310) 724-8993. *E-mail*: elkesommer@elkesommeronline.com. *Website*: www.elkesommeronline.com.

SOMMER, Ron; German business executive; *Chairman, Mobile TeleSystems OJSC;* b. 1949, Haifa, Israel; ed Univ. of Vienna, Austria; began career with Nixdorf Group in New York, Paris and Paderborn, Germany; Man. Sony Deutschland 1980, Chair. 1986; Pres., CEO Sony USA 1990; Pres., CEO Sony Europe 1993; CEO Deutsche Telekom AG 1995–2002; Chair. Mobile TeleSystems OJSC 2009–; mem. Bd of Dirs Motorola Inc. 2004–, Muenchener Rueckversicherung, AFK Sistema, Tata Consultancy Services, Weather Industries; mem. Int. Advisory Bd Blackstone Group; mem. Supervisory Bd Munich Re, Celanese AG 2004–06. *Address*: Mobile TeleSystems OJSC, 109147 Moscow, Bldg. 2, 5 Vorontsovskaya Street, Russia (office). *Website*: www.mtsgsm.com (office).

SOMMER, Theo, DPhil; German journalist; *Editor-at-Large, Die Zeit;* b. 10 June 1930, Constance; s. of Theo Sommer and Else Sommer; m. 1st Elda Tsilenis 1952; two s.; m. 2nd Heide Grenz 1976; two s.; m. 3rd Sabine Grewe 1989; one d.; ed Univ of Tübingen, Chicago and Harvard Univs; Local Ed. Schwäbisch-Gmünd 1952–54; Foreign Ed. Die Zeit 1958, Deputy Ed. 1968, Ed.-in-Chief 1973–92, Publr 1992–, Ed.-at-Large 2000–; Lecturer in Int. Relations, Univ. of Hamburg 1967–70; Chief of Planning Staff, Ministry of Defence 1969–70; mem. Deutsche Gesellschaft für Auswärtige Politik; mem. Council IISS 1963–76, 1978–87, German Armed Forces Structure Comm. 1970–72, Int. Comm. on the Balkans 1995–96, Ind. Int. Comm. on the Balkans 1999–2000; Deputy Chair. Comm. on the Future on the Bundeswehr 1999–2000; Chair. Comm. Investigating Effects of DU Ammunitions, Radar and Asbestos on German Armed Forces 2002; mem. Indo-German Consultative Group 1992– (Co-Chair. 1996–), German-Japanese Dialogue Forum 1993–; mem. Bd Deutsche Welthungerhilfe 1992–, Max-Bauer Preis 1992–, German-Turkish Foundation 1998–; mem. German Foreign Policy Assoc, IISS, Königswinter Conf., Advisory Council, Mil. History Inst.; Contributing Ed. Newsweek Int. 1968–90; regular contrib. to American, British, Japanese and Korean publs; commentator German TV, radio and moderator of monthly programmes; Hon. mem. Assoc of Anciens, NATO Defense Coll. 1971, Trilateral

Comm. 1993, Hon. Senator, Helmut-Schmidt-Universität 2012; Fed. Order of Merit (First Class) 1998, Gold Honor Cross, German Armed Forces 2002; Hon. LLD (Univ. of Maryland, USA) 1982; Theodor-Wolf Prize 1966, Int. Communications Award, People's Repub. of China 1991, Columbus Prize 1993. *Publications*: Deutschland und Japan zwischen den Mächten (Germany and Japan Between the Powers) 1935–40 1962, Vom Antikominternpakt zum Dreimächtepakt 1962, Reise in ein fernes Land 1964, Ed. Denken an Deutschland 1966, Ed. Schweden-Report 1974, Die chinesische Karte (The Chinese Card) 1979, Allianz in Umbruch (Alliance in Disarray) 1982, Blick zurück in die Zukunft (Look Back into the Future) 1984, Reise ins andere Deutschland (Journey to the Other Germany) 1986, Europa im 21. Jahrhundert 1989, Geschichte der Bonner Republik 1949–99 1999, Der Zukunft entgegen (Toward the Future) 1999, Phoenix Europe. The European Union: Its Progress, Problems and Prospects 2000, Hamburg 2004, 1945: Biographie eines Jahres 2005. *Address*: Die Zeit, Pressehaus, Speersort 1, 20079 Hamburg (office); 17 Zabelweg, 22359 Hamburg, Germany (home). *Telephone*: (40) 3280240 (office); (40) 6037300 (home). *Fax*: (40) 3280407 (office); (40) 6030044 (home). *E-mail*: sommer@zeit.de (office); tsommer01@aol.com (home). *Website*: www.zeit.de (office); www.theosommer.de.

SOMOGYI, Peter, PhD, FRS, FMedSci, FHAS; Hungarian/British professor of neurobiology; *Director, Medical Research Council Anatomical Neuropharmacology Unit, University of Oxford;* b. 27 Feb. 1950, Szentendre; ed Loránd Eötvös Univ., Budapest; research training in neurocytology and neuroanatomy at Semmelweis Univ. of Medicine, Budapest, in biochemistry and immunocytochemistry at the Univ. of Oxford, UK; postdoctoral fellowship at Flinders Medical Centre, South Australia; has trained research students since 1978; Assoc., later Co-Dir Anatomical Neuropharmacology Unit, MRC, Oxford, 1995–98, Dir 1998–; Prof. of Neurobiology, Univ. of Oxford 1996–; Distinguished Visiting Prof., Kyoto Univ., Japan 1998; Visiting Prof., Nat. Inst. of Physiological Sciences, Okazaki, Japan 2002; Nicholas Kurti Sr Research Fellow, Brasenose Coll., Oxford 2004–; Corresp. mem. Hungarian Acad. of Sciences 2004–; Assoc. of the Neuroscience Research Program, The Neuroscience Inst., San Diego, USA 2008–; Hon. PhD (József Attila Univ., Szeged) 1990; M. Lenhossek Prize, Assoc of Hungarian Anatomists and Embryologists 1982, Charles Judson Herrick Award, Assoc of American Anatomists 1984, Moruzzi Lecturer, European Neuroscience Assoc, Stockholm 1990, Krieg Cortical Discoverer Award, Cajal Club, American Anatomical Soc. 1991, Julian Tobias Memorial Lecture, Univ. of Chicago 1995, Yngve Zotterman Prize, Swedish Physiological Soc. 1995, Jerzy Olszewski Lecture, Montreal Neurological Inst. 2001, Janos Szentagothai Memorial Lecture, Budapest 2002, Wenner-Gren Foundation Distinguished Lecturer, Sweden 2003, Segerfalk Award Lecture, Lund, Sweden 2003, Special Plenary Lecture, 16th IFAA Conference, Kyoto, Japan 2004, 1st Janos Szentagothai Memorial Lecture, Univ. of California, Irvine 2005, Quastel Lecure, Otto Loewi Conf., Eilat, Israel 2006, Servier Conf. Lecture, Neuroscience Research Centre, Univ. of Montreal 2006, János Arany Medal, Hungarian Acad. of Sciences, Presidential Cttee for Contribution to Hungarian Science from Abroad 2006, István Báthory Award, Hungarian Nat. Council of Transylvania 2006, The IBRO Lecture Univ. of Debrecen, Hungary 2008, The 1st Hans Kosterlitz Lecture, Univ. of Aberdeen, Scotland 2008, The Feldberg Prize and Lectures, Feldberg Foundation, London 2009. *Address*: MRC Anatomical Neuropharmacology Unit, Mansfield Road, Oxford, OX1 3TH, England (office). *Telephone*: (1865) 271865 (office). *Fax*: (1865) 271648 (office). *E-mail*: peter.somogyi@pharm.ox.ac.uk (office). *Website*: mrcanu.pharm.ox.ac.uk (office).

SOMORJAI, Gabor Arpad, PhD, FAAS; American (b. Hungarian) chemist and academic; *Professor of Chemistry, University of California, Berkeley;* b. 4 May 1935, Budapest, Hungary; s. of Charles Somorjai and Livia Ormos; m. Judith Kaldor 1957; one s. one d.; ed Tech. Univ., Budapest, Univ. of California, Berkeley; mem. research staff, IBM, NY 1960–64; at Faculty, Dept of Chem., Univ. of California, Berkeley 1964–, Asst Prof. 1964–67, Assoc. Prof. 1967–72, Prof. 1972–; Faculty Sr Scientist, Materials Science Div. and Dir Surface Science and Catalysis Program, Lawrence Berkeley Lab., Berkeley, Calif. 1964–; Univ. Prof., Univ. of California System 2002–; numerous awards and visiting professorships in USA and UK, including Visiting Fellow, Emmanuel Coll. Cambridge 1969; mem. NAS 1979, ACS (Fellow 2009), American Physical Soc., American Acad. of Arts and Sciences 1983; Hon. mem. Hungarian Acad. of Sciences 1990, Chemical Soc. of Japan 2009; Hon. Fellow, Cardiff Univ. 2006; Dr hc (Tech. Univ., Budapest) 1989, (Univ. Pierre et Marie Curie) 1990, (Univ. Libre de Bruxelles) 1992, (Ferrara) 1998, József Attila Univ., Hungary) 1999 (Royal Inst. of Tech., Stockholm) 2000, (Manchester) 2001, (ETH Zurich) 2003, (Inst. of Chem., Chinese Acad. of Sciences—ICCAS) 2007, (Northwestern Univ.) 2010; Emmett Award American Catalysis Soc. 1977, ACS Colloid and Surface Chem. Award 1981, Centenary Lecturer, Royal Soc. of Chem., UK 1983, ACS Peter Debye Award 1989, ACS Adamson Surface Chemistry Award 1994, Hinshelwood Lecturer, Univ. of Oxford 1994, Linnett Lecturer, Univ. of Cambridge 1994, Von Hippel Award, Materials Research Soc. 1997, Wolf Prize 1998, ACS Catalysis Award 2000, Pauling Medal, Hungarian Acad. of Sciences 2000, Nat. Medal of Science 2002, Cotton Award 2003, Remsen Award, Maryland Section of ACS 2006, Langmuir Prize, American Physical Soc. 2007, Priestley Medal 2008, Miller Sr Fellow 2009, BBVA Frontiers of Knowledge Award in Basic Science 2010, ENI New Frontiers of Hydrocarbons Prize 2010, Honda Prize 2010, NAS Award in Chemical Sciences 2013. *Publications*: Principles of Surface Chemistry 1972, Chemistry in Two Dimensions 1981, Introduction to Surface Chemistry and Catalysis 1994, serves editorial bds of numerous scientific publs, more than 1,000 publs in major scientific journals. *Leisure interests*: swimming, walking. *Address*: Department of Chemistry, D58 Hildebrand, University of California, Berkeley, CA 94720-1460 (office); 665 San Luis Road, Berkeley, CA 94707, USA (home). *Telephone*: (510) 642-4053 (office). *Fax*: (510) 643-9668 (office). *E-mail*: somorjai@berkeley.edu (home). *Website*: www.cchem.berkeley.edu/gasgrp (office); chem.berkeley.edu/faculty/somorjai/ (office).

SOMPONG, Amornvivat, BBA, MA; Thai politician; b. 3 July 1941, Bangkok; m.; ed Curry Coll., Milton, Mass, USA, Chiangmai Univ.; mem. Exec. Cttee, Nat. Democracy Party 1981–82, Deputy Sec.-Gen. 1983–84, Sec.-Gen. 1984–88; Sec.-Gen. Ruam Thai Party 1988–89; Deputy Leader Unity Party 1988–89; Deputy Leader Chart Pathana Party 1992–93, mem. People's Power Party 1998–; mem. Parl. for Chonburi Prov. 1986–89, for Chiangmai Prov. 1992–93, 1994–96, 1999–2000; Vice-Chair. Industry Cttee, Nat. Ass. 1988–89; Deputy Minister of

Agric. and Cooperatives 1990–91, of Transport and Communications 1997; mem. Nat. Ass. 1991–; Minister of Industry 1992–93, of Labour and Social Welfare 1994–95, 1997, Minister to Prime Minister's Office 1996, Minister of Justice 2008, Deputy Prime Minister and Minister of Foreign Affairs 2008; adviser to Prime Minister 2001–05. *Address:* People's Power Party, 1770 Thanon Petchaburi Tat Mai, Bang Gapi, Huay Kwang, Bangkok 10310, Thailand (office). *Telephone:* (2) 686–7000 (office). *Website:* www.ppp.or.th (office).

SOMSAVAT, Lengsavat; Laotian politician; *Deputy Prime Minister;* b. 16 June 1945, Luangphrabang; m. Bounkongmany Lengsavad; one s. two d.; ed Nat. Org. for the Study of Policy and Admin; combatant in N Laos 1961–64; Officer, Cabinet of the Lao People's Revolutionary Party (LPRP) Cen. Cttee. 1964–76, Head of Secr. 1975–82; Deputy Chief, Council of Ministers 1982–88; fmr Deputy Minister; First Vice-Chair. LPRP History Research Comm. 1982–88, Chief of the Cabinet of LPRP and Cabinet of Ministers 1991–93; Amb. to Bulgaria 1989–91; Minister of Foreign Affairs 1993–2006; Deputy Prime Minister 1998–; Chair. Vientiane Cttee for Flood Control; Dr rer. pol (Ramkhamhaeng Univ., Thailand) 2000; Medal of Liberty Issara, Medal of Labour, Anti-Imperialist Cross, Revolutionary Medal, People's Repub. of Korea, Medal of Friendship Govts of Cuba and Bulgaria. *Leisure interests:* reading, golf, singing. *Address:* c/o Office of the Prime Minister, Ban Sisavat, Vientiane, Laos (office). *Telephone:* (21) 213653 (office). *Fax:* (21) 213560 (office).

SON, Kil-seung, BA; South Korean business executive; b. 1941; ed Seoul Nat. Univ.; joined Sunkyong Textiles Corpn (renamed SK Corpn) 1965, various Exec. Man. positions in Office of Corp. Man. and Planning, Group Pres. 1991, Pres. Daehan Telecom –1998, Chair. and CEO SK Corpn 1998–2003 (resgnd after conviction for accounting irregularities), also fmr Chair. and CEO SK Telecom, SK Shipping; Chair. Korean Business Council for the Arts, Korean Business Messena Asscn; fmr Chair. Fed. of Korean Industries (FKI); mem. Bd Dirs Forum Council; Hon. Citizen of China Award 2001, CEO of Korea Award, Korean Chamber of Commerce and Industry (KCCI) 2002, 2003, Korean Man. Award, Top Business Man. of Korea Award, KCCI. *Address:* c/o SK Group, 99 Seorin-dong, Jongru-Gu, Seoul 110-110, Republic of Korea (office).

SON, Masayoshi, BA (Econ); Japanese business executive; *Chairman, Sprint Corporation;* b. 11 Aug. 1957, Tosu, Saga Pref.; m.; one s. one d.; ed Univ. of California, Berkeley, USA; f. SoftBank 1981, Chair. and Pres. 1981–, CEO 1986–, serves in various capacities with SoftBank's portfolio of cos, including Pres. BB Technologies Corpn (currently SoftBank BB) 2001–, Chair. and CEO 2004–, Chair. Japan Telecom Co. Ltd (currently SoftBank Telecom Corpn) 2004–, and CEO 2006–, Chair. and CEO Vodafone K.K. (currently SoftBank Mobile Corpn) 2006–; Chair. Yahoo Japan Corpn (jt venture between SoftBank and Yahoo! Inc.) 1996–; Chair. Sprint Corpn (following acquisition of majority stake by SoftBank) 2013–; fmr Chair. Broadband Asscn in Japan, Great East Japan Earthquake Recovery Initiative Foundation. *Address:* Sprint Corporation, 6200 Sprint Parkway, Overland Park, KS 66251, USA (office). *Telephone:* (703) 433-4000 (office). *E-mail:* boardinquiries@sprint.com (office). *Website:* www.sprint.com (office).

SONDAKH, Peter; Indonesian business executive; *Chairman, PT Rajawali Corporation;* b. 1953, N Sulawesi; m. Eve Sondakh; three c.; joined family business (trading in coconut oil and timber) 1971, took over after death of father 1975; f. PT Rajawali Corpn (conglomerate) 1984, interests include cement, cigarettes, hotels, telecommunications, mining, plantations, retail and transportation; associated cos include PT Semen Gresik, PT Bentoel International, PT Excelcomindo Pratama; cos est. Taksi Express 1989, Lombok Tourism Devt Corpn 1989, Bank Pos 1989 (now merged with Bank Danamon Indonesia). *Address:* Office of the Chairman, PT Rajawali Corporation, Jl Mega Kuningan, Lot 5.1, Menara Rajawali Lt 27-28, Kuningan Timur, Setia Budi, Jakarta 12950, Indonesia (office). *Telephone:* (21) 5760808 (office). *Fax:* (21) 5761588 (office). *Website:* www.rajawali.com (office).

SONDECKIS, Saulius; Lithuanian conductor; b. 11 Oct. 1928, Šiauliai; s. of Jackus Sondeckis and Rozalija Sondeckienė; m. Silvija Sondeckienė; three s.; ed Lithuanian Conservatory as violinist, Moscow State Conservatory; Founder, Conductor and Artistic Dir Lithuanian Chamber Orchestra 1960–2004; tours fmr USSR, Europe, USA and Japan 1960–; teacher, Vilnius M. Čiurlionis School of Arts 1955–85, f. Youth Orchestra; Founder and Artistic Dir St Petersburg Camerata Chamber Orchestra (now Orchestra of Hermitage Museum) 1989–; Prof., Vilnius Conservatory (now Lithuanian Acad. of Music and Theatre) 1957–96, Chair. Strings Dept 1959–87; Prof., St Petersburg Conservatory 1989–91; f. (with G. Kremer) Kremerata Baltica Chamber Orchestra 1996; Chief Conductor Hellos Orchestra of Patras, Greece 1999–2004; conducted various European and Canadian orchestras; worked together with Rostropovich and many other distinguished soloists; first performance of chamber music by Alfred Schnittke, Sergey Slonimsky, Arvo Pärt, contemporary Lithuanian composers; Hon. Prof. N. A. Rimsky-Korsakov Conservatory, St Petersburg; Lithuanian Grand Duke First and Fifth Order of Gediminas Cavalier, First Grade Hon. Cross of Austria for Science and Arts 2003; Dr hc Lithuanian Acad. of Music and Theatre 2003; Lithuanian State Prize 1971, winner of Gold Medal at Herbert von Karajan Stiftung Competition in Berlin 1976, USSR People's Artist 1980, USSR State Prize 1987, State Prize of Lithuanian Govt 1998, WIPO Creativity Award, Gold Medal 2004. *Address:* Čiurlionio 28, Vilnius 03104, Lithuania (home). *Telephone:* (5) 2331557 (home). *Fax:* (5) 2332768 (home). *E-mail:* silvija@studiapro.lt (home).

SONDHEIM, Stephen Joshua, BA; American composer and lyricist; b. 22 March 1930, New York, NY; s. of Herbert Sondheim and Janet Fox; ed George School, Newtown, Pa, Williams Coll., Williamstown, Mass, private instruction; Pres. Dramatists' Guild 1973–81, Council mem. 1981–; Visiting Prof. of Drama and Musical Theatre, Univ. of Oxford Jan.–June 1990; mem. American Acad. and Inst. of Arts and Letters 1983–; Antoinette Perry Awards for Company 1971, Follies 1972, A Little Night Music 1973, Sweeney Todd 1979; Drama Critics' Awards 1971, 1972, 1973, 1976, 1979; Evening Standard Drama Award 1996; Grammy Awards 1984, 1986; Nat. Medal of Arts 1997, Praemium Imperial 2000. *Compositions:* television: Topper (co-author) 1953, Evening Primrose (music and lyrics) 1967; lyrics: West Side Story 1957, Gypsy 1959, Do I Hear a Waltz? 1965, Candide 1973; music and lyrics: A Funny Thing Happened on the Way to the Forum 1962, Anyone Can Whistle 1964, Evening Primrose 1966, Company 1970, Follies 1971, A Little Night Music 1973, The Frogs 1974, Pacific Overtures 1976, Sweeney Todd 1978,

Merrily We Roll Along 1981, Sunday in the Park with George 1984, Into the Woods (Drama Critics' Circle Award 1988) 1986, Follies 1987, Assassins 1991, Passion 1994, Bounce 2003 (renamed Road Show 2008); anthologies: Side by Side by Sondheim 1976, Marry Me a Little 1980, You're Gonna Love Tomorrow 1983, Putting It Together 1993; screenplays: (with Anthony Perkins) The Last of Sheila 1973, Birdcage 1996, Getting Away Murder 1996; film scores: Stavisky 1974, Reds 1981, Dick Tracy 1989; incidental music: The Girls of Summer 1956, Invitation to a March 1961, Twigs 1971, Company: A Musical 2007, Sweeney Todd 2007. *Publication:* Finishing the Hat 2010. *Address:* c/o John Breglio, 1285 Avenue of the Americas, New York, NY 10019, USA (office).

SONENBERG, Nahum, BSc, MSc, PhD, FRSC; Israeli biochemist and academic; *James McGill Professor, Department of Biochemistry, McGill University;* m.; two d.; ed Tel-Aviv Univ., Weizman Inst. of Science; early research position at Roche Inst. of Molecular Biology, NJ, USA; joined faculty at McGill Univ., Montreal, Canada 1979, currently James McGill Prof., Dept of Biochemistry, also Dir Sonenberg Lab.; Int. Research Scholar, Howard Hughes Medical Inst.; Distinguished Scientist, Canadian Insts of Health Research; Robert L. Noble Prize, Nat. Cancer Inst. of Canada 2002, Killiam Prize for Health Sciences 2005. *Publications:* numerous papers in scientific and medical journals. *Address:* McGill University, Room 807, McIntyre Medical Building, 3655 Promenade Sir William Osler, Montreal, Quebec H3G 1Y6, Canada (office). *Telephone:* (514) 398-7274 (office). *Fax:* (514) 398-7384 (office). *E-mail:* nahum.sonenberg@mcgill.ca (office). *Website:* www.med.mcgill.ca/nahum (office).

SONG, Baorui; Chinese politician; b. Dec. 1937, Shunyi Dist, Beijing; ed Tsinghua Univ., Beijing; joined CCP 1958; fmr Deputy Dir, Chief Engineer China Welding Rod Plant, Dir China Welding Rod Plant Inst. 1975–82; Man. China Welding Materials Manufacture Co. 1982–83; Deputy Sec. then Sec. CCP Zigong City Cttee 1983–86; fmr mem. Standing Cttee CCP Sichuan Prov. Cttee; Chair. Sichuan Prov. Comm. for Restructuring the Economy 1986–89, Exec. Deputy Sec. CCP Sichuan Prov. Cttee 1989–99; Gov. Sichuan Prov. 1996–99; Deputy Dir State Comm. for Restructuring Economy 2001–; Deputy Dir-Gen. CPPCC Sub-cttee for Handling Proposals 2003–; Alt. mem. 14th CCP Cen. Cttee 1992–97, mem. 15th CCP Cen. Cttee 1997–2002; Deputy 8th NPC. *Address:* Subcommittee for Handling Proposals, CPPCC, Beijing, People's Republic of China (office).

SONG, Fatang; Chinese politician; b. Dec. 1940, Tancheng, Shandong Prov.; ed Qufu Teachers' Univ.; joined CCP 1961; Cadre, Supervision Cttee, CCP Shandong Prov. Cttee 1964; Sec. Org. Dept, CCP Revolutionary Cttee, Shandong Prov. 1967; Deputy Div. Chief, Org. Dept, CCP Shandong Prov. Cttee 1973; Deputy Sec. CCP Tai'an Co. Cttee, Deputy Sec. CCP Tai'an Municipal Cttee, Shandong Prov. 1979–84, Sec. 1984, Mayor of Taian 1985–89; Vice-Gov. Shandong Prov. 1989–2000; Deputy Sec. CCP Shandong Prov. Cttee 1998–99; Deputy Gov., then Gov. Heilongjiang Prov. 2000–03; Sec. CCP Heilongjiang Prov. Cttee 2003–; Chair. Standing Cttee Heilongjiang Prov. People's Congress 2003–05; Alt. mem. 15th CCP Cen. Cttee 1997–2002, mem. 16th CCP Cen. Cttee 2002–07; Deputy, 9th NPC 1998–2003; Vice-Chair. Education, Science, Culture and Public Health Cttee, NPC 2005–. *Address:* Education, Science, Culture and Public Health Committee, National People's Congress, Beijing, People's Republic of China (office).

SONG, Jian, DSc; Chinese state official and academic; b. 29 Dec. 1931, Rongcheng Co., Shandong Prov.; s. of the late Song Zengjin and Jiang Yuxian; m. Wang Yusheng 1961; one s. one d.; ed Harbin Tech. Univ., Beijing Foreign Languages Inst., Bauman Eng Inst., Moscow and Moscow Univ., USSR; joined CCP 1947; Dir and Head, Lab. of Cybernetics, Inst. of Math., Acad. Sinica 1960–70; Dir Guided Missile Control Lab., 7th Ministry of Machine Bldg Industry 1962–70; Head, Chief Scientist, Space Science Div., Acad. of Space Tech. 1971–78, Vice-Pres., Deputy Science Dir, Acad. of Space Tech. 1978–81; Vice-Minister and Chief Eng Scientist, Ministry of Astronautics 1981–84; Researcher, China Aviation Industry Corpn; Research Prof., Beijing Inst. of Information and Control 1983–; Visiting Prof., MIT, Harvard, Univ. of Minn. 1980; Prof., Tsinghua Univ., Fudan Univ., Harbin Univ. of Tech. 1986–; Chair. State Science and Tech. Comm. 1984–98; State Councillor 1986–98, Chair. Environmental Protection Cttee; Vice-Chair. Three Gorges Project Construction Cttee; Head, State Leading Group for Man. of Intellectual Property Rights; mem. State Steering Group of Science, Tech. and Educ. 1998; Vice-Chair. State Academic Degrees Cttee 1999; Vice-Pres. China Soc. of Demographic Science 1982–86; Assoc. Chief Ed. System & Control Letters 1983–85; Chief Ed. Automatic Control & System Eng, Encyclopaedia of China 1983–; mem. Ed. Bd Encyclopaedia of China 1984–; Council mem. Int. Fed. of Automatic Control 1984–87; Vice-Pres. China System Eng Soc. 1985–87; Vice-Chair. Chinese People's Political Consultative Conf. 1998–; Pres. China-Japan Friendship Asscn 1998–; Alt. mem. 12th CCP Cen. Cttee 1982–87, mem. 13th CCP Cen. Cttee 1987–92, 14th CCP Cen. Cttee 1992–97, 15th CCP Cen. Cttee 1997–2002; Vice-Chair. 9th CPPCC Nat. Cttee 1998–2003; mem. Chinese Acad. of Sciences 1991–, Chinese Acad. of Eng 1994– (Pres. 1998–2002); Foreign mem. Russian Acad. of Sciences 1994, Royal Swedish Acad. of Eng Sciences 1994, Nat. Acad. of Eng, USA 2000, Argentine Acad. of Eng 2001, Yugoslav Acad. of Eng 2002; Corresp. mem. Nat. Acad. of Eng of Mexico 1985; Hon. Distinguished Visiting Prof. Washington Univ. 1986–; Hon. Pres. Chinese Asscn of Environmental Protection; Hon. DHumLitt (Houston) 1996; Nat. Natural Sciences Award, Nat. Award for Advancements in Science and Tech. 1987, Albert Einstein Award 1987, Int. Asscn for Mathematics 1987 and numerous other nat. and int. awards. *Publications:* Reference Frames in Space Flight 1963, Engineering Cybernetics (co-author) 1980, China's Population: Problems and Prospects 1981, Recent Development in Control Theory and Its Applications 1984, Population Projections and Control 1981, Population Control Theory 1985, Population Control in China: Theory and Applications 1985, Population System Control 1988, Science and Technology and Social System 1988; numerous articles. *Leisure interest:* swimming. *Address:* National Committee of Chinese People's Political Consultative Conference, 23 Taipingqiao Street, Beijing, People's Republic of China (office).

SONG, Lin, BEng; Chinese business executive; *Chairman, China Resources (Holdings) Co. Ltd;* b. 1963, Shanghai; ed Tongji Univ., Shanghai; joined China Resources Holdings Co. 1985, positions have included Pres. of the Co., Chair. China Resources Enterprise Ltd, China Resources Power Holdings Co. Ltd, China Resources Land Ltd, China Resources Cement Holdings Ltd, China Resources Logic Ltd (now China Resources Gas Group Ltd), China Resources Capital

Holdings Co. Ltd, Chair. and Gen. Man. China Resources Devt and Investment Co. Ltd, currently mem. Bd of Dirs and Chair. China Resources (Holdings) Co. Ltd, also Chair. China Resources Nat. Corpn; Deputy Chair. China Vanke Co. Ltd; Ind. Dir (non-exec.) Geely Automobile Holdings Ltd 2004–, The Bank of East Asia (China) Ltd. *Address:* China Resources (Holdings) Co. Ltd, Floor 49, CRC Building, 26 Harbour Road, Wanchai, Hong Kong Special Administrative Region, People's Republic of China (office). *Telephone:* 28797888 (office). *Fax:* 28275774 (office). *E-mail:* crc@crc.com.hk (office). *Website:* www.crc.com.hk (office).

SONG, Ping; Chinese party official; b. 1917, Juxian Co., Shandong Prov.; ed Inst. Marxism-Leninism, Yan'an; joined CCP 1937; Vice-Minister, Labour 1953; Vice-Chair. State Planning Comm. 1957–63; Sec. CCP Gansu and Vice-Chair. Gansu Revolutionary Cttee 1972, First Sec. CCP Gansu, Chair. Gansu Revolutionary Cttee, Second Political Commissar, PLA Lanzhou Mil. Region and First Political Commissar, Gansu Mil. Dist, PLA 1977–80; First Vice-Chair. State Planning Comm. 1981–83; Minister in charge of State Planning Comm. 1983–87; Chair. Family Planning Asscn 1990–; Deputy Sec.-Gen., First Session of the 7th NPC March 1988; Deputy Dir Leading Group for Co-ordinating Nat. Scientific Work 1983; State Councillor 1983–88; Vice-Chair. Environmental Protection Cttee State Council 1984–87, Nat. Agric. Zoning Cttee 1983–; Deputy Head Leading Group for Scientific Work, State Council 1983–92; Head Leading Group for Econ. Information Man., State Council 1986–92; Head Org. Dept Cen. Cttee CCP 1988–90; visited Pakistan 1991; mem. 11th Cen. Cttee CCP 1977, 12th Cen. Cttee CCP 1982–87, Political Bureau 1987–92, 13th Cen. Cttee (mem. Standing Cttee 1989–92); mem. Presidium 14th CCP Nat. Congress 1992; Hon. Pres. Chinese Asscn for Promotion of the Population Culture; Hon. Dir-in-Chief China Welfare Fund for the Handicapped; Hon. Adviser 'Happiness Project' Org. *Address:* Central Committee of CCP, Zhang Nan Hai, Beijing, People's Republic of China (office).

SONG, Gen. Qingwei; Chinese army officer and party official; b. 1929, Lingxian Co., Shandong Prov.; joined CCP 1945; Political Commissar of PLA Jinan Mil. Area Command 1987–95; rank of Lt-Gen. 1988, of Gen. 1994; mem. 14th CCP Cen. Cttee 1992–97; Vice-Chair. Foreign Affairs Cttee 9th NPC 1998. *Address:* c/o Standing Committee of National People's Congress, Beijing, People's Republic of China (office).

SONG, Ruixiang; Chinese politician; b. 1939, Jintan Co., Jiangsu Prov.; joined CCP 1959; Gov. of Qinghai Prov. 1985–93; Minister of Geology and Mineral Resources 1993–98, Party Group Sec. Ministry of Geology and Mineral Resources; Chair. Nat. Mineral Reserves Comm. 1995–96; Vice-Chair. Nat. Mineral Resources Cttee 1996–98; Deputy Dir State Gen. Admin. of Environment Protection 1998–2003; Dir China Seismological Bureau 2003–04; mem. 15th CCP Cen. Cttee 1997–2002; Del., 13th CCP Nat. Congress 1987–92. *Address:* c/o China Seismological Bureau, Beijing, People's Republic of China (office).

SONG, Sang-hyun, LLM, JSD; South Korean professor of law and judge; *President, International Criminal Court;* b. 21 Dec. 1941; m.; one s. one d.; ed Seoul Nat. Univ., Tulane Law School, New Orleans and Cornell Law School, Ithaca, NY, USA, Univ. of Cambridge, UK; called to the Bar, Repub. of Korea 1964; Mil. Prosecutor then Judge, Judge Advocate Office, Korean Armed Forces 1964–67; Attorney Haight, Gardner, Poor & Havens, New York 1970–72; Prof. of Law, Seoul Nat. Univ. 1972–2007, Dean Law School 1996–98; Lecturer in Law, Nat. Police Coll., Seoul 1983–2003; Judge (Appeals Div.), Int. Criminal Court (ICC), The Hague, Netherlands 2003–, Pres. ICC 2009–; Vice-Pres. UNICEF Korea 1998–2012; Pres. Korea Childhood Leukemia Foundation 1999–2009; has lectured at Univ. of Melbourne Law School, Harvard Law School and New York Univ.; Nat. Decoration of 2nd Highest Order (Moran), Govt of Repub. of Korea 1997, Nat. Decoration of the Highest Order (Mugunghwa), Govt of Repub. of Korea 2011; Most Distinguished Alumni Medal, Cornell Univ. 1994, Legal Culture Award, Korean Fed. Bar Asscn 1998. *Publications:* books: Introduction to the Law and Legal System of Korea 1983, An Introduction to Law and Economics 1983, Korean Law in the Global Economy 1996, The Korean Civil Procedure 2004; numerous articles in professional journals. *Address:* International Criminal Court, Maanweg 174, 2516 The Hague AB, Netherlands (office). *Telephone:* (70) 5158208 (office). *Fax:* (70) 5158620 (office). *E-mail:* pio@icc-cpi.int (office). *Website:* www.icc-cpi.int (office).

SONG, Yufang; Chinese business executive; currently Chair. China Railway Materials Commercial Corpn (now China Railway Materials Co. Ltd). *Address:* China Railway Materials Co. Ltd, 11 Huayuan Street, Xicheng District, Beijing 100032, People's Republic of China (office). *Telephone:* (10) 51895188 (office). *Fax:* (10) 51895028 (office). *E-mail:* crm@crmsc.com.cn (office). *Website:* www.crmsc .com.cn (office).

SONG, Zhaosu; Chinese politician; *Vice-Chairman, Environment and Resources Protection Committee, National People's Congress;* b. March 1941, Nanyang, He'nan Prov.; ed Zhengzhou Univ.; joined CCP 1965; Section Chief, Org. Dept, CCP Zhoukou Prefectural Cttee, He'nan Prov., later Deputy Sec. Zhoukou Prefectural Cttee; Deputy Sec. CCP Shangshui Co. Cttee, He'nan Prov.; Magistrate, Shangshui Co. (Dist) People's Court, He'nan Prov.; Sec. CCP Taikang Co. Cttee, He'nan Prov.; Sec. CCP Xuchang Prefectural Cttee, He'nan Prov.; Vice-Gov. He'nan Prov. 1988; Deputy Sec. CCP He'nan Prov. Cttee 1993–98, Sec. Political Science and Law Cttee; Acting Gov. Gansu Prov. 1998–99, Gov. 1999–2001; Deputy Sec. CCP Gansu Prov. Cttee 1998–2001, Sec. 2001–03; Chair. Standing Cttee, Gansu Prov. People's Congress 2003–04; Alt. mem. 15th CCP Cen. Cttee 1997–2002, mem. 16th CCP Cen. Cttee 2002–07; Vice-Chair. Environment and Resources Protection Cttee of NPC 2003–. *Address:* Environment and Resources Protection Committee, National People's Congress, Beijing, People's Republic of China (office).

SONG, Zhe, MA; Chinese diplomatist; b. April 1960; m.; one d.; Attaché, Third Sec., People's Inst. of Foreign Affairs 1983–88, Third, later Second Sec., Embassy in London 1988–92, Counsellor 2000–01, Second Sec., Deputy Dir, First Sec., Dir, Western European Dept, Ministry of Foreign Affairs 1992–2000, Counsellor 2001–02, Deputy Dir-Gen. 2002–03; Dir-Gen., Gen. Office of State Council 2003–08; Perm. Rep. and Head of Mission to EU, Brussels 2008–12. *Address:* Ministry of Foreign Affairs, 2 Chao Yang Men, Nan Dajie, Chao Yang Qu, Beijing 100701, People's Republic of China (office). *Telephone:* (10) 65961114 (office). *Fax:*

(10) 65962146 (office). *E-mail:* webmaster@mfa.gov.cn (office). *Website:* www .fmprc.gov.cn (office).

SONG, Zhiping; Chinese business executive; *Chairman, China National Building Materials Group;* successively held posts of Factory Dir Beixin New Building Materials Plant, Chair. and Sec. of Party Cttee, and Gen. Man. Beijing New Building Materials (Group) Co. Ltd, Gen. Man. and Deputy Sec. Party Cttee, China Nat. Building Materials Group Corpn, currently Outside Dir, Chair. and Sec. of Party Cttee. *Address:* China National Building Materials Group, 2 South Zi Zhu Yuan Road, Beijing 100048, People's Republic of China (office). *Telephone:* (10) 88416688 (office); (10) 68720842 (office). *Fax:* (10) 68422743 (office). *E-mail:* cnbmadmin@cnbm.com.cn (office). *Website:* www.cnbm.com.cn (office).

SONI, Rebecca; American swimmer; b. 18 March 1987, Freehold Borough, New Jersey; d. of Péter Sőni and Kinga Sőni; ed West Windsor-Plainsboro High School North, Plainsboro Township, New Jersey, Annenberg School for Communication, Univ. of Southern California; originally a gymnast, began swimming aged ten; six-time NCAA Champion 2006–09; 11-time All-American 2006–09; Summer Universiade, Izmir 2005: gold medal, 4×100m medley, silver medal, 100m breaststroke, 200m breaststroke; Olympic Games, Beijing 2008: gold medal, 200m breaststroke, silver medal, 100m breaststroke, 4×100m medley; World Championships (long course), Rome 2009: gold medal, 100m breaststroke, silver medal, 50m breaststroke, Shanghai 2011: gold medal, 100m breaststroke, 200m breaststroke, 4×100m medley, bronze medal, 50m breaststroke; World Championships (short course), Dubai 2010: gold medal, 50m breaststroke, 100m breaststroke, 200m breaststroke, silver medal, 4×100m medley; Pan Pacific Championships, Irvine 2010: gold medal, 100m breaststroke, 200m breaststroke, 4×100m medley; Olympic Games, London 2012: gold medal, 200m breaststroke, 4×100m medley relay (with Missy Franklin, Dana Vollmer, and Allison Schmitt), silver medal, 100m breaststroke; swims for Trojan Swim Club and Univ. of Southern California Trojans; coach: Dave Salo; spokeswoman for UN Foundation's Girl Up campaign 2010–; World Swimmer of the Year, Swimming World magazine 2010, 2011, American Swimmer of the Year, Swimming World magazine 2009, 2010, 2011. *Address:* c/o Wasserman Media Group, 10960 Wilshire Blvd, Suite 2200, Los Angeles, CA 90024, USA (office). *E-mail:* info@wmgllc.com (office). *Website:* www.rebsoni.com.

SONN, Franklin Abraham; South African diplomatist and academic; b. 11 Oct. 1939, Vosburg Dist; s. of Pieter (Pat) Sonn and Magdalene Kelin; m.; two c.; ed UNISA and Univ. of Western Cape; fmr Rector, Peninsula Technikon; fmr Chair. Comm. of Technikon Prins, Chair. Western Cape Foundation for Community Work, Mobil Foundation of S Africa, Inst. for Distance Educ.; Chair. Bd Trustees, Die Suid-Afrikaan Magazine, Nat. Educ. and Training Forum 1994; Vice-Chair. Urban Foundation; Dir Metropolitan M-Net 1994; mem. Bd Corp. Africa; Vice-Pres. Jt Council of Teachers Asscn of S Africa; Amb. to USA 1995–98; Chancellor Univ. of the Free State 2002–; Grand Counsellor, Order of the Baobab in Silver. *Publications include:* A Decade of Struggle 1986; numerous papers and official documents. *Leisure interests:* reading, walking, mountaineering, squash. *Address:* Office of the Chancellor, University of the Free State, POB 339, Bloemfontein 9300, South Africa (office). *Telephone:* (51) 401-9111 (office). *Fax:* (51) 401-2117 (office). *E-mail:* info@stiq.uovs.ac.za (home). *Website:* www.uovs.ac.za (office).

SONNENFELD, Barry; American cinematographer, film director and film producer; b. 1 April 1953, New York. *Films as cinematographer include:* Blood Simple 1984, Compromising Positions 1985, Three O'Clock High 1987, Raising Arizona 1987, Throw Momma from the Train 1987, Big 1988, When Harry Met Sally 1989, Miller's Crossing 1990, Misery 1990. *Films directed include:* The Addams Family 1991, For Love or Money 1993, Addams Family Values 1993, Get Shorty 1995, Men in Black 1997, Wild Wild West 1999, Big Trouble 2002, Men in Black II 2002, RV 2006, Men in Black III 2012. *Films produced include:* Get Shorty 1995, Out of Sight 1998, Wild Wild West 1999, The Crew 2000, Big Trouble 2002, The Ladykillers 2004, Lemony Snicket's A Series of Unfortunate Events 2004, Enchanted 2007, Space Chimps 2008. *Television:* Out of Step 1984 (Emmy Award for best cinematography 1984), Fantasy Island 1998, Secret Agent Man 2000, The Crew 2000, The Tick 2001, Karen Sisco 2003, Pushing Daisies 2007. *Address:* c/o CAA, 9830 Wilshire Boulevard, Beverly Hills, CA 90212; United Talent Agency, 9560 Wilshire Boulevard, Beverly Hills, CA 90212, USA.

SONNENFELDT, Helmut, MA; American international business consultant and fmr government official; *Guest Scholar, Brookings Institution;* b. 13 Sept. 1926, Berlin, Germany; s. of Dr Walther H. Sonnenfeldt and Dr Gertrud L. Sonnenfeldt; m. Marjorie Hecht 1953; two s. one d.; ed Univ. of Manchester, Johns Hopkins Univ.; went to USA 1944; mem. Counterintelligence Corps, US Army, Pacific and European Theaters; with Dept of State 1952–69, Policy Officer, US Disarmament Admin. 1960–61, Dir Office of Research and Analysis for the USSR and E Europe 1966–69; Sr Staff mem. for Europe and East–West Relations, Nat. Security Council 1969–74; Counselor of Dept of State 1974–77; Lecturer on Soviet Affairs, Johns Hopkins Univ. School of Advanced Int. Studies 1957–69; Trustee, Johns Hopkins Univ. 1974–, Visiting Scholar, School of Advanced Int. Studies, Johns Hopkins Univ. 1977–78; Guest Scholar, Brookings Inst., Washington, DC 1978–; Consultant Washington Center for Foreign Policy Research; Gov. and Dir UN Asscn of USA 1980; Dir Atlantic Council of USA 1978–; mem. IISS, London 1977–99, (mem. Exec. Cttee 1986–98), Council of Foreign Relations, Royal Inst. of Int. Affairs, London, Int. Advisory Council, Credit-Anstalt-Bankverein, Vienna 1983–98, Defense Policy Bd 2001–; Editorial Bd Politique Internationale (Paris) 1978–, Foreign Policy 1980–; Govt rep. to numerous confs and meetings abroad; consultant to int. investments firms and banks. *Publications:* Soviet Policy in the 1980s 1985, articles on int. issues in American and European journals. *Leisure interests:* tennis, music, reading biography. *Address:* Brookings Institution, 1775 Massachusetts Avenue, NW, Washington, DC 20036 (office); 5600 Wisconsin Avenue, #1505, Chevy Chase, MD 20815, USA (home). *Telephone:* (202) 797-6028 (office). *Fax:* (202) 797-6004 (office); (310) 656-6706 (home). *E-mail:* hsonnenfeldt@ brookings.edu (office); sonnenfeldt@cs.net (home). *Website:* www.brookings.edu/fp/ fp_hp.htm (office).

SONOKROT, Mazen, BEng; Palestinian business executive and fmr government minister; *CEO, Sinokrot Global Group;* b. 30 Nov. 1954, Jerusalem; s. of Mohammad Tawfique Sonokrot and Fatimah Sonokrot; four s.; ed Univ. of

Nottingham, UK; Chair. and CEO Sinokrot Global Group 1982–2005, CEO 2006–; Regional Dir Arab Food Industries Fed., Arab League 1982–97; Founder and fmr Chair. Palestinian Food Industries Asscn; Chair. Palestinian Fed. of Industries, Universal Group for Eng and Consulting, Industrial Modernization Center; Minister of Nat. Economy 2005–06; Chair. Palestinian Investment Promotion Agency, Palestinian Industrial Estates and Free Zones Area, Palestinian Standards Inst.; Sec. Pvt. Sector Coordinating Council; mem. Bd and Head, Investment Cttee, Palestine Investment Fund; mem. Palestinian Businessmen Asscn, Bd of Palestinian Economic Task Force, Bd Nat. Reform Cttee, Public-Pvt. Jt Econ. Cttee, Bd of Registry and Sanction, Ministry of Higher Educ.; mem. Higher Council of High Council for Tech. and Vocational Educ.; Assoc. mem. of all cttees in charge of formulating laws and legislation relating to the Palestinian economy; rep. of Palestinian pvt. sector in many local, regional and int. activities; contrib. to econ. trade agreements between Palestinian National Authority and USA, EU, Turkey, Arab and EFTA countries. *Address:* Sinokrot Global Group, PO 1410, Betuniah, Industrial Zone, Ramallah, Palestinian Autonomous Area (office). *Telephone:* (2) 2955701 (office). *Fax:* (2) 2955702 (office). *Website:* www.sinokrot .net (office).

SONOMPIL, Mishigiyn; Mongolian politician; b. 27 Jan. 1965; m.; two c.; fmr Commdr mil. unit; Dir Zaluu Mongol Corpn 1991–2004; mem. Democratic Party; mem. Parl. 2004–; Minister of Defence 2006–07. *Address:* c/o Democratic Party, Chingisiin, Örgön Chölöö 1, Ulan Bator, Mongolia (office).

SOOMRO, Mohammad Mian, BSc, MSc; Pakistani banker and politician; b. 19 Aug. 1950, Karachi, Sindh; s. of the late Ahmed Mian Soomro and Moula Bux Soomro; ed Forman Christian Coll., Lahore, Punjab Univ., Northrop Univ., USA; Head of Soomro tribe; mem. Pakistan Muslim League (PML); held various positions in nat. and int. orgs, including Bank of America; fmr Gen. Man. and CEO Int. Bank of Yemen, Faysal Islamic Bank of Bahrain, Muslim Commercial Bank, Agriculture Devt Bank of Pakistan, Fed. Bank of Cooperatives, Nat. Bank of Pakistan; Chair. Pakistan Banks Asscn 1997–2000; mem. Governing Council Inst. of Bankers in Pakistan 1997–2000; mem. Bd of Dirs Shell Pakistan Ltd, Pakistan Int. Airlines Corpn, Pakistan Refinery Ltd (Shell Petroleum Jt Venture), Pak Arab Refinery, Pak Arab Fertilizer, Bank Al-Jazira (Jeddah, Saudi Arabia), Nat. Investment Trust, Investment Co-operation of Pakistan, Nat. Discounting Services Ltd, Nat. Exchange Co. (Abu Dhabi), Nat. Bank Modaraba Man. Co. Ltd, First Women Bank Ltd, Consolidated Leasing Co., Nat. Construction Co., Pakistan Tourism Devt Corpn (all 1997–2000); helped establish micro-credit banking in Pakistan; Gov. of Sindh 2000–02; Senator 2003–, Chair. of Senate 2003–07, 2008–09, Chair. Finance Cttee; apptd caretaker Prime Minister 2007–08; Interim Pres. of Pakistan (following resignation of Pres. Pervez Musharraf) 18 Aug.–9 Sept. 2008. *Address:* c/o Senate of Pakistan, Parliament House, Islamabad, Pakistan. *Telephone:* (51) 9223475.

SOONG, James Chu-yul, PhD; Taiwanese politician; *Chairman, People First Party (PFP);* b. 16 March 1942, Hunan; m. Viola Chen; one s. one d.; ed Nat. Chengchi Univ., Taipei and Univ. of Calif., Berkeley, Catholic Univ. of America, Georgetown Univ., Washington, DC, USA; Sec. Exec. Yuan, Taiwan 1974–77; Deputy Dir-Gen. Govt Information Office 1977–79; Assoc. Prof., Nat. Taiwan Univ. 1975–79; Research Fellow, Inst. of Int. Relations, Nat. Chengchi Univ. 1974–; Personal Sec. to the Pres. 1978–89; Dir-Gen. Govt Information Office, Govt Spokesman 1979–84; mem. Cen. Cttee Kuomintang (KMT) 1981–2000, Dir/Gen. Dept of Cultural Affairs, KMT 1984–87; Deputy Sec.-Gen., KMT Cen. Cttee 1987–89, Sec.-Gen. 1989–93; mem. Cen. Standing Cttee 1988–2000; Gov., Taiwan Prov. Govt 1993–98; unsuccessful presidential cand. (ind.) 2000, then f. People First Party (PFP), Chair. 2000–; unsuccessful vice presidential cand. (PFP) 2004; Man. Dir China TV Co. 1984–93, Taiwan TV Enterprise 1984–93; Chair. Hua-hsia Investment Corpn; Distinguished Visiting Fellow Inst. of East Asian Studies, Univ. of Calif. 1999; Eisenhower Fellowship 1982; several decorations. *Publications:* A Manual for Academic Writers, How to Write Academic Papers, Politics and Public Opinions in the United States, Keep Free China Free. *Address:* People First Party, 1/F, 63 Chang-an East Road, Sec. 2, Taipei 10455, Taiwan (office). *Telephone:* (2) 25068555 (office). *Website:* www.pfp.org.tw (office).

SOPE, Barak; Ni-Vanuatu politician and diplomatist; *Chairman, Melanesian Progressive Party;* leading mem. Vanuaaku Pati (VP), Roving Amb.; mem. govts 1980–87; defected from VP, f. Melanesian Progressive Party 1987, Chair. 1987–; mem. coalition govts 1993–96; Prime Minister of Vanuatu 1999–2001 (resgnd); convicted of forgery and sentenced to three years in prison 2002, pardoned in 2003; Minister of Foreign Affairs 2004, of Agric., Quarantine, Forestry and Fisheries 2004–06. *Address:* Melanesian Progressive Pati, PO Box 39, Port Vila, Vanuatu (office). *Telephone:* 23485 (office). *Fax:* 23315 (office).

SOPHUSSON, Friðrik; Icelandic lawyer, politician and business executive; *Chairman, Íslandsbanki;* b. 18 Oct. 1943, Reykjavik; m. Dr Sigridur Duna Kristmundsdottir 1990; one d. (and five c. from first m.); ed Reykjavik Higher Secondary Grammar School and Univ. of Iceland; lawyer, part-time teacher Hlídaskóli School, Reykjavik 1963–67; Man. Icelandic Man. Asscn 1972–78; mem. Radio Council Icelandic State Broadcasting Service 1975–78; Nat. Research Council and Exec. Cttee of State Hosps 1984–87; Cen. Cttee Independence Party 1969–77, 1981–99, Vice-Chair. 1981–89, 1991–99; Pres. Independence Party's Youth Fed. 1973–77; MP for Reykjavik 1978–98; Minister of Industry and Energy 1987–88, of Finance 1991–98; mem. Bd of Dirs Nat. Bank of Iceland 1990–92, Icelandic Church Aid 1990–92, Enex 2001–06, Pharmaco 2002–03, Samorka (Fed. of Electricity and Waterworks) 2001–09, Icelandic Int. Chamber of Commerce 2001–09, Nordel 2001–03, Icelandic Chamber of Commerce 2002–09; Man. Dir Landsvirkjun (Nat. Power Co.) 1999–2009; Chair. Íslandsbanki 2010–. *Address:* Bjarkargata 10, 101 Reykjavik, Iceland (home). *E-mail:* islandsbanki@ islandsbanki.is (office). *Website:* www.islandsbanki.is (office).

SOPOANGA, Saufatu; Tuvaluan politician; fmr Special Ministerial Adviser, Ministry of Works, Communication and Transport; fmr Minister of Finance; Prime Minister of Tuvalu, Minister of Foreign Affairs and Labour 2002–04; Deputy Prime Minister and Minister of Works and Energy and of Communications and Transport 2004–06. *Address:* c/o Ministry of Works and Energy PMB, Vaiaku, Funafuti, Tuvalu (office).

SOPONRONNARIT, Somchart, PhD; Thai scientist and academic; *Professor of Energy Technology, King Mongkut's University of Technology Thonburi;* currently Prof. of Energy Tech., King Mongkut's Univ. of Tech., Thonburi Campus; mem. Academic Review Cttee, Sirindhorn Int. Inst. of Tech., Thammasat Univ.; mem. Asian Inst. of Tech.; Fellow, Royal Inst. of Thailand; UNESCO Science Prize 2003. *Publications:* Drying Grains and Some Types of Foods (seventh edn, in Thai) 1997; book chapters, research reports and more than 150 scientific papers in professional journals on thermal processes such as thermal application of solar energy, drying and storage of foods and cereal grains. *Address:* School of Energy, Environment and Materials, King Mongkut's University of Technology, Thonburi Campus, Suksawat 48 Road, Bangkok 10140 (office); 152 Banmore Road, Bangkok 10200, Thailand (home). *Telephone:* (2) 4708624 (office); (2) 4270039 (ext. 8624) (office); (2) 263838 (home). *Fax:* (2) 4279062 (office). *E-mail:* somchart.sop@kmutt.ac.th (office). *Website:* www2.kmutt.ac.th (office).

SORABJI, Richard Rustom Kharsedji, CBE, BPhil, MA, FBA; British academic; *Cyprus Global Distinguished Professor in the History and Theory of Justice, University of Texas;* b. 8 Nov. 1934, Brighton; s. of Prof. Richard Kakushru Sorabji and Mary Katherine Sorabji (née Monkhouse); m. Margaret Anne Catherine Tasker 1958; one s. two d.; ed Charterhouse, Pembroke Coll., Oxford Univ.; Assoc. Prof., Sage School of Philosophy, Cornell Univ. 1962–69; joined Dept of Philosophy, King's Coll. London 1970, Prof. of Ancient Philosophy 1981–2000, British Acad./Wolfson Research Prof. 1996–99, now Prof. Emer., Designer, First Dir King's Coll. Centre for Philosophical Studies 1989–91; Gresham Prof. of Rhetoric and mem. Sr Common Room, Pembroke Coll. 2000–03; Supernumerary Fellow, Wolfson Coll. Oxford 1996, now Hon. Fellow; Ranieri Distinguished Visiting Scholar, New York Univ. 2000–03, Cyprus Global Distinguished Prof. in the History and Theory of Justice 2008–; Adjunct Prof., Philosophy Dept, Univ. of Texas 2000–; Visiting Prof., CUNY 2004–07; Pres. Aristotelian Soc. 1985–86; Founder and organizer of int. project to translate ancient commentators on Aristotle in 50 vols 1985–; Dir Inst. of Classical Studies, London Univ. 1991–96; Foreign Hon. mem. American Acad. of Arts and Sciences 1997–. *Publications:* Aristotle on Memory 1972, Necessity, Cause and Blame 1980, Time, Creation and the Continuum 1983, Matter, Space and Motion 1988, Animal Minds and Human Morals 1993, Emotion and Peace of Mind 2001, Self: Ancient and Modern Insights about Individuality, Life and Death 2006, The Ethics of War: Shared Problems in Different Traditions (co-ed.) 2006, Greek and Roman Philosophy 100 BC to 200 AD (co-ed.) 2007; ed. numerous vols on commentators on Aristotle. *Leisure interests:* archaeology, architecture. *Address:* Wolfson College, Oxford, OX1 4LJ, England; Graduate School of Arts and Science, New York University, 6 Washington Square North, New York, NY 10003, USA (office). *Telephone:* (1865) 274100. *Fax:* (1865) 274125. *E-mail:* richard.sorabji@philosophy.oxford.ac.uk (office). *Website:* www .kcl.ac.uk/kis/schools/hums/philosophy/staff/r_sorabji (office).

SOREN, Hemant; Indian politician and government official; *Chief Minister of Jharkhand;* b. 10 Aug. 1975, Nemara, Ramgarh Dist, Bihar; s. of Shibu Soren and Roopi Soren; m. Kalpana Soren; two s.; mem. Jharkhand Mukti Morcha party; mem. Rajya Sabha 2009–10; Chief Minister of Jharkhand 2013–. *Address:* Office of the Chief Minister, Government of Jharkhand Secretariat, Project Building, 3 Kanke Road, Ranchi 834 008, Jharkhand, India (office). *Telephone:* (651) 2281500 (office). *Fax:* (657) 2281300 (office). *E-mail:* arjun.munda@gmail.com (office); dr.d.k .tiwari@live.in (office). *Website:* jharkhand.gov.in (office).

SOREN, Shibu; Indian politician; b. 11 Jan. 1944, Nemra village, Hazaribagh Dist, Jharkhand; s. of the late Shobaran Soren; m. Rupi Devi; three s. (one deceased) one d.; ed Gola High School; Gen. Sec. Jharkhand Mukti Morcha 1971–85, Pres. 1986–; mem. Lok Sabha (Parl.) 1980–96, 2002–04, 2009–; mem. Rajya Sabha (Parl.) 2001–02; Minister of Coal May–July 2004 (resgnd), reinstated 2006; Chief Minister of Jharkhand 2005, Aug. 2008–Jan. 2009, Dec. 2009–10; sentenced to life imprisonment on abduction and murder charges 2006, acquitted 2007; mem. Cttee on Coal and Steel 2009–, Jt Cttee on Salaries and Allowances of MPs 2009–. *Leisure interests:* archery, travelling, indoor games. *Address:* c/o Office of the Chief Minister, Government of Jharkhand, Secretariat, Ranchi 834 001, India.

SØRENSEN, Bengt Algot, DPhil; Danish academic; *Professor Emeritus of German Literature, University of Odense;* b. 24 Nov. 1927, Aarhus; s. of Christian Sørensen and Selma Mellquist; m. Agnes M. Pedersen 1954 (died 2005); one s. two d.; ed Århus, Hamburg and Tübingen Univs; Lecturer in Scandinavian Languages and Literature, Bonn, Germany 1955–60; Lecturer in German Literature, Arhus Univ. 1962–66; Prof. of German Literature, Odense Univ. 1966–97, Prof. Emer. 1997–; Visiting Prof. Univ. of Calif. at Irvine 1980, Univ. of Kiel 1983; Pres. Danish Research Council for the Humanities 1971–73; mem. Exec. Council European Science Foundation 1983–89; Vice-Pres. IVG (Int. Vereinigung der Germanistik) 1995–2000; mem. Royal Danish Acad. 1978–, Göttinger Akad. der Wissenschaften 1996–; Gold Medal, Univ. of Arhus 1953. *Publications:* Symbol und Symbolismus 1963, Allegorie und Symbol 1972, Herrschaft und Zärtlichkeit 1984, Jens Peter Jacobsen 1990, Geschichte der deutschen Literatur Bd I, II 1997, Funde und Forschungen. Ausgewählte Essays 1997; numerous articles about Danish and German literature. *Leisure interests:* fishing, gardening. *Address:* University of Odense, 5230 Odense M (office); Frederiksberg Alle 100, 1820 Frederiksberg, Denmark (home). *Telephone:* 65-50-32-16 (office); 66-17-64-99 (home). *Fax:* 65-93-16-64. *Website:* www.humaniora.sdu.dk (office).

SÓRENSEN, Jórgen Haugen; Danish sculptor; b. 1934; ed Coll. of Art and Design, Copenhagen; began as apprentice plasterer and potter; debut in Charlottenborg's Spring Exhbn 1953; exhbns at Museum of Modern Art New York, Yorks. Sculpture Park; works in collections in Denmark, England, Italy, Slovenia, Turkey, Olympic Sculpture Park, Seoul; Dir film JHS late 1960s; Prix de la Critique for JHS, Paris Biennale 1963. *Address:* Galleri Veggerby, Ny Østergade 34, 1101 København K, Denmark. *E-mail:* haugensorensen@FJRN -DETTEhotmail.com. *Website:* www.haugen-sorensen.dk.

SØRENSEN, Peter Ingemann Moesgaard, BA, MLaw; Danish lawyer and diplomatist; *Head of Delegation and Special Representative to Bosnia and Herzegovina, European Union;* b. 1967; m.; two c.; ed Arhus Univ.; worked as lawyer in Denmark and served as officer in Danish Army; appointments have included Political/Legal Advisor to UN Special Envoy to the Balkans and Head of

Political Affairs, OSCE Mission to Croatia; Legal Adviser to the High Rep., Sarajevo, Bosnia & Herzegovina, Carl Bildt and European Community Monitor Mission, Sarajevo 1996–97; Sr Adviser to the Special Rep. of UN Sec.-Gen. as well as to Deputy SRSG and Head of UNMIK EU Pillar IV, Kosovo 2001; Deputy Head of UNMIK EU Pillar IV and Dir of European Office 2002–06; EU High Rep.'s Personal Rep. in Belgrade, Serbia 2009–11; served as Head of EU Del. in Skopje, Former Yuguslav Repub. of Macedonia; Head of EU Del. and EU Special Rep. to Bosnia and Herzegovina 2011–. *Address:* Delegation of the European Union to Bosnia and Herzegovina and European Union Special Representative, 71000 Sarajevo, Skenderija 3A, Bosnia and Herzegovina (office). *Telephone:* (33) 254700 (Del.) (office); (33) 560800 (EU Special Rep.) (office). *Fax:* (33) 666037 (Del.) (office); (33) 668390 (EU Special Rep.) (office). *E-mail:* delegation-bih@eeas.europa.eu (office). *Website:* europa.ba (office).

SORENSTAM, Annika; Swedish fmr professional golfer; b. 9 Oct. 1970, Stockholm; d. of Tom Sorenstam and Gunilla Sorenstam; m. David Esch; ed Univ. of Arizona, USA; World Amateur Champion 1992; 72 career wins on LPGA tour including 10 major championships; victories include US Women's Open 1995, 1996, Safeway Classic 2003, Mizuno Classic 2003, LPGA Championship 2003, 2004, 2005, Women's British Open 2003, Kraft Nabisco Championship 2005; played on eight European Solheim Cup teams; first woman to shoot 59 in an LPGA Tour tournament 2001; first woman to win US $13 million in golf prize money, is LPGA career earnings leader with more than US$22 million; finished first on LPGA money list 2001–05 and eight times overall; first woman for 58 years to participate in a men's professional tour event, Bank of America Colonial Tournament, Fort Worth, Tex., May 2003; first int. player to be inducted into World Golf Hall of Fame, St Augustine, USA 2003; announced retirement 2008; f. Annika Course Design, ANNIKA Academy; Rookie of the Year 1994, Sports Personality of the Year, Sweden 1995, Vare Trophy Award 1995, 1996, 1998, 2001, 2002, Rolex Player of the Year Award 1995, 1997, 1998, 2001–05; Patty Berg Award 2003, Jerring Prize 2004; inducted into LPGA Hall of Fame 2003. *Leisure interests:* sports, music, cooking, skiing. *Address:* c/o Annika Sorenstam, IMG Center, Suite 100, 1360 East 9th Street, Cleveland, OH 44114, USA; c/o IMG Stureplan, 4C, 114 35 Stockholm, Sweden. *Website:* www.annikasorenstam.com; www.theannikaacademy.com.

SORINAS BALFEGÓ, Mateo, MSc; Spanish teacher and international organization executive; b. 13 March 1946, Tarragona; m.; two c.; ed Universidad Complutense, Madrid; Deputy Dir Boarding School, Universidad Laboral de Alcalá de Henares, Madrid 1967–69; teacher, Agüimes High School, Las Palmas, Gran Canaria 1969–70; mil. service 1970–71; teacher, Isabel de España High School, Las Palmas 1971–77; Pérez Galdós High School, Las Palmas 1977–78; Co-Sec. Cttee on Environment, Regional Planning and Local Authorities, Council of Europe 1978–86, Sec. Cttee on Migration, Refugees and Demography 1986–92, Sec. Political Affairs Cttee 1992–94, Political Counsellor, Pvt. Office of the Pres. 1992–96, Head of Cen. Div. 1994–97, Dir Political and Legal Affairs Dept 1997–2002, Dir-Gen. 2002–06, Sec.-Gen. Parl. Ass. 2006–11; mem. Nat. Cttee of Juventud Estudiante Católica (Young Catholic Students), Madrid 1963–67, Governing Bd Professional Asscn of Teachers on Sciences and Humanities, Las Palmas 1974–78; Orden del Mérito Civil: Cruz de Caballero 1988, Encomienda 1995, Cavaliere Grand'Ufficiale, Ordine di Sant'Agata (San Marino) 2007. *Address:* Secretariat of the Parliamentary Assembly, Council of Europe, avenue de l'Europe, 67075 Strasbourg Cedex, France (office). *Telephone:* (3) 88-41-20-00 (office). *Fax:* (3) 88-41-27-81 (office); (3) 88-41-27-82 (office). *E-mail:* webmaster .assembly@coe.int (office). *Website:* assembly.coe.int (office); www.coe.int (office).

SORIOT, Pascal, DrVetMed, MBA; French business executive; *Executive Director and CEO, AstraZeneca PLC;* ed École Nationale Vétérinaire, Maisons-Alfort, École des Hautes Études Commerciales – Institut Supérieur des Affaires; Financial Controller for the Asia-Pacific region, Roussel Uclaf 1986, held various management positions in finance and marketing at cos that later formed part of Sanofi-Aventis, Dist Sales Man., Roussel New Zealand 1987–89, Sales and Marketing Man., Roussel Australia from 1989, later Gen. Man., Div. Global Marketing Dir, Roussel Uclaf Pharmaceuticals 1994–96, Gen. Man. Hoechst Marion Roussel Australia 1996–97, Regional Vice-Pres., Asia Pacific, Hoechst Marion Roussel Tokyo 1997–2000, Sr Vice-Pres. and Head of Global Marketing and Medical Affairs, Aventis Bridgewater (USA) 2000–02, COO 2002–04, Sr Vice-Pres. Commercial Operations, USA 2004–06, Head of Strategic Marketing Pharma Div., Roche AG March–Dec. 2006, Head of Commercial Operations 2007–09, led successful merger with Genentech, San Francisco, CEO Genentech 2009–10, COO Pharmaceuticals Div., Roche AG 2010–12; Exec. Dir and CEO AstraZeneca PLC 2012–; Dir, Chugai Pharmaceutical Co. Ltd –2012. *Address:* AstraZeneca PLC, 2 Kingdom Street, London, W2 6BD, England (office). *Telephone:* (20) 7604-8000 (office). *E-mail:* info@astrazeneca.com (office). *Website:* www.astrazeneca.com (office).

SORKIN, Ihor Vyacheslavovych; Ukrainian central banker; b. 3 March 1967, Donetsk; m.; one s.; ed Baku Higher Combined-Arms Command School, Azerbaijan SSR, Donetsk State Univ., Donetsk Nat. Univ.; served in Soviet Army 1988–92, Nat. Guard of Ukraine 1992–96, successively, commdr landing assault platoon, reconnaissance bn and regimental intelligence chief of Nat. Guard; joined Nat. Bank of Ukraine 1996, successively, Economist of 1st Category, Leading Economist, Chief Economist, Head of Sector, Deputy Head of Dept, Head of Banking Supervision Dept in Office of Nat. Bank of Ukraine in Donetsk Oblast 2001–10, Deputy Gov. Nat. Bank of Ukraine 2010–11, 3rd ranking civil servant 2011, Acting Gov. 2012–13, Gov. 2013–14 (dismissed); mem. Nat. Security and Defence Council of Ukraine 2013–; Merited Economist of Ukraine 2011. *Address:* c/o Office of the Governor, Natsionalny Bank Ukrainy, 01601 Kyiv, vul. Institutska 9, Ukraine. *E-mail:* webmaster@bank.gov.ua.

SORO, Guillaume Kigbafori; Côte d'Ivoirian fmr rebel leader and politician; b. 8 May 1972, Diawala; two c.; ed univ. studies in France; Leader Ivorian Students' Fed. 1995–98; fmr Sec.-Gen. Mouvement patriotique de Côte d'Ivoire (MPCI); Leader, New Forces Rebels 2000–, led rebellion against Pres. Laurent Gbagbo that triggered Civil War 2002, controlled Northern Prov. of Côte d'Ivoire 2002; Minister of State for Communications 2003–05, of Reconstruction and Reinsertion 2005–07; Prime Minister 2007–12 (resgnd), also Minister of Defence –2012 (resgnd).

Address: Forces Nouvelles, Bouaké, Côte d'Ivoire. *Telephone:* 20-20-04-04. *E-mail:* senacom@fnci.info. *Website:* www.fnci.info.

SOROKIN, Vladimir Georgiyevich; Russian author, screenwriter, dramatist, librettist and painter; b. 7 Aug. 1955, Bykovo, Moscow Region; m. Irina Igorevna Sorokina; two d.; ed Moscow Inst. of Oil and Gas; worked as artist and writer in Moscow underground; not published in USSR until 1987; mem. Russian PEN Centre; scholarship of Deutsche Akademische Austauschung Dienst 1992; Andrey Beliy Prize 2003, Liberty Prize, USA 2005, Maxim Gorky Prize 2010. *Plays:* wrote 12 plays 1986–2009. *Screenplays:* Moskva 1995, Kopejka 1997, The Four 2000, Cashfire 2002, The Thing 2003, Exit 2004, The Target 2010. *Libretto:* opera 'The Children of Rosenthal' by Leonid Desyatnikov (performed at Bolshoi Theatre, Moscow) 2005. *Publications include:* Thirties Love of Marina 1982–84, The Queue (novel) 1983, The Norm 1984, Obelisk (short stories) 1980–84, Roman 1989, Four Stout Hearts (novel) 1991, Blue Lard 1999, The Feast 2001, The Ice (novel) 2002, Bro 2004, Trilogy 2005. *Leisure interests:* chess, cooking, table tennis. *Address:* 119333 Moscow, ul. Gubkina, d4 kv 47, Russia (home). *Telephone:* (499) 135-90-76 (home). *E-mail:* sornorma@mtu-net.ru (home). *Website:* www.srkn.ru (home); www.vladimirsorokin.ru (home).

SOROS, George; American (b. Hungarian) investment banker and philanthropist; *Chairman, Soros Fund Management LLC;* b. 12 Aug. 1930, Budapest; m.; five c.; ed London School of Econs; moved to England 1947; with Singer & Friedlander (merchant bankers), London; moved to New York 1956; est. pvt. mutual fund, Quantum Fund, registered in Curaçao 1969; since 1991 has created other funds, including Quasar Int., Quota, Quantum Emerging Growth Fund (merged with Quantum Fund to form Quantum Endowment Fund 2000), Quantum Realty Trust; Pres. and Chair. Soros Fund Man. LLC, New York 1973–; philanthropist since 1979, provided funds to help black students attend Cape Town Univ., SA; Founder, Open Soc. Fund (currently Chair. Open Soc. Inst.) 1979, Soros Foundation, Cen. European Univ., Budapest 1992; f. Global Power Investments 1994; Dr hc (New School for Social Research, Univ. of Oxford, Budapest Univ. of Econs, Yale Univ.); Laurea hc (Univ. of Bologna) 1995. *Publications include:* The Alchemy of Finance 1987, Opening the Soviet System 1990, Underwriting Democracy 1991, Soros on Soros – Staying Ahead of the Curve (jtly) 1995, The Crisis of Global Capitalism – Open Society Engendered 1998, Open Society – Reforming Global Capitalism 2000, George Soros on Globalization 2002, The Bubble of American Supremacy – Correcting the Misuse of American Power 2004, Soros on Freedom 2006, Soros Lectures 2010; numerous essays on politics, society and econs in major int. newspapers and magazines. *Address:* Soros Fund Management LLC, 888 7th Avenue, 33rd Floor, New York, NY 10106 (office); Open Society Institute, 400 West 59th Street, New York, NY 10019, USA. *Telephone:* (212) 548-0600. *Website:* www.georgesoros.com; www.soros.org.

SOROUSH, Abdolkarim, BSc; Iranian academic; *Researcher, Institute for Iranian Contemporary Historical Studies;* b. 1945, Tehran; ed Mortazavi High School, Alavi High School, Univ. of London and Chelsea Coll., London, UK; studied pharmacy and passed nat. entrance exams; left for London following graduation to continue studies; returned to Iran in 1979, and published book Knowledge and Value (Danesh va Arzesh); apptd Dir Islamic Culture Group, Teacher Training Coll., Tehran 1979; mem. Cultural Revolution Inst. 1980–83 (resgnd); Researcher, Inst. for Cultural Research and Studies (now the Inst. for Iranian Contemporary Historical Studies) 1983–; adviser to govt bodies; became more critical of political role played by Iranian clergy 1990s; co-founder monthly magazine Kiyan, and published his most controversial articles on religious pluralism, hermeneutics, tolerance, clericalism etc., magazine suppressed by direct order of supreme leader of Islamic Repub. 1998; more than 1,000 audio tapes of his speeches on various social, political, religious and literary subjects circulated world-wided, became subject to harassment and state censorship; Visiting Prof. teaching Islam and Democracy, Quranic Studies and Philosophy of Islamic Law, Harvard Univ., USA 2000–; Scholar-in-Residence, Yale Univ., USA; taught Islamic Political Philosophy at Princeton Univ. 2002–03; Visiting Scholar, Wissenschaftkolleg, Berlin, Germany 2003–04. *Publications include:* Dialectical Antagonism (in Persian) 1978, Philosophy of History (in Persian) 1978, What is Science, What is Philosophy (in Persian) (11th edn) 1992, The Restless Nature of the Universe (in Persian and Turkish) 1980, Satanic Ideology (in Persian) (fifth edn) 1994, Knowledge and Value (in Persian), Lectures in the Philosophy of Social Sciences: Hermeneutics in Social Sciences (in Persian) 1995, Sagaciousness, Intellectualism and Pietism (in Persian) 1991, The Tale of the Lords of Sagacity (in Persian) (third edn) 1996, Wisdom and Livelihood: A Commentary on Imam Ali's Letter to Imam Hasan (in Persian) (second edn) 1994, Sturdier than Ideology (in Persian) 1994, The Evolution and Devolution of Religious Knowledge in: Kurzman, Ch. (ed.), Intellectualism and Religious Conviction (in Persian), The World We Live (in Persian and Turkish), The Tale of Love and Servitude (in Persian), The Definitive Edition of Rumi's Mathnavi (in Persian) 1996, Tolerance and Governance (in Persian) 1997, Liberal Islam 1998, Political Letters (two vols) (in Persian) 1999, Expansion of Prophetic Experience (in Persian) 1999, Reason, Freedom and Democracy in Islam, Essential Writings of Adbolkarim Soroush (translated, ed with a critical introduction by M. Sadri and A. Sadri) 2000. *Address:* The Institute for Iranian Contemporary Historical Studies, PO Box 19395-1975, 128 Fayyazi (Fereshteh) Avenue, Elahieh, Tehran 19649, Iran (office). *Telephone:* (21) 264037-8 (office); (21) 2003490 (office). *Fax:* (21) 262096 (office). *E-mail:* info@drsoroush.com (office). *Website:* www.drsoroush.com (office); .

SORRELL, Sir John William, Kt, CBE, FCSD, FRSA; British designer; *Co-Founder, The Sorrell Foundation;* b. 28 Feb. 1945, London; s. of the late John William Sorrell and Elizabeth Jane Sorrell (née Taylor); m. Frances Mary Newell (q.v.) 1974; two s. one d.; ed Hornsey Coll. of Art; Designer Maine Wolff & Pnrs 1964; Pnr, Goodwin Sorrell 1964–71; Design Man. Wolff Olins 1971–76; Founder and Co-Chair. Newell and Sorrell 1976–97, Chair. Newell and Sorrell (now Interbrand Newell and Sorrell) 1983–2000; Vice-Pres. Chartered Soc. of Designers 1989–92; Chair. DBA 1990–92, Design Council 1994–2000; mem. British Rail Architecture and Design Panel 1991–93, RSA Design Advisory Group 1991–93, D & AD Strategic Planning Soc., Inst. of Design, New Millennium Experience Co. Creative Review Group 1998–2000 (and 'Godparent' for Identity Zone), Panel 2000, Dept of Trade & Industry's Encouraging Competitiveness Working Party 1998; Co-Founder and Chair. The Sorrell Foundation 1999–; Gov.

Design Dimension 1991–93; Chair. NHS London Design Advisory Group 2000–, Comm. for Architecture and the Built Environment 2004–, London Design Festival; Co-Chair. British Abroad Task Force 2000–; hon. mem. Romanian Design Centre, Hon. Fellow RIBA 2002–; Hon. DDesign (De Montfort) 1997, Dr hc (London Inst.) 1999; RSA's Bicentenary Medal 1998, D&AD Pres.'s Award 2008. *Publications:* Secret of Design Effectiveness 1995, Utopian Nights 1996, Utopian Papers 1996–, Creative Island 2002. *Leisure interests:* arboriculture, Arsenal Football Club, art, film. *Address:* The Sorrell Foundation, Somerset House, Strand, London WC2R 1LA, England (office). *Telephone:* (20) 7845-5860 (office). *Fax:* (20) 7845-5872 (office). *E-mail:* info@thesorrellfoundation.com (office). *Website:* www.thesorrellfoundation.com (office).

SORRELL, Sir Martin Stuart, Kt, MA, MBA; British advertising executive; *Chief Executive, WPP;* b. 14 Feb. 1945, London; ed Haberdashers' Aske's School, Christ's Coll. Cambridge and Harvard Business School, USA; consultant, Glendinning Assocs, Westport, Conn. 1968–69; Vice-Pres. Mark McCormack Org. 1970–74; Dir James Gulliver Assocs. 1975–77; Group Financial Dir Saatchi and Saatchi Co. PLC 1977–84; Founder and Group Chief Exec. WPP 1986–; Dir Storehouse PLC 1994–97; Dir (non-exec.) Colefax and Fowler Group PLC 1997–; mem. Advisory Bd Int. Grad. School of Man., Univ. of Navarra 1989–, Judge Inst. for Man. Studies, Univ. of Cambridge 1990–, IBM 1997–, Advisory Bd, ATP 2001–; mem. Bd Dirs of Assocs, Harvard Business School 1998–, Bd Dean's Advisors 1998–; Dir (non-exec.) Colefax & Fowler; FCO Amb. for British Business 1997–99, mem. Panel 2000 2000–; mem. Council for Excellence in Man. and Leadership; mem. Bd and Cttee Special Olympics 2000–, Corp. Advisory Group, Tate Gallery 2000–, Bd Nat. Asscn of Securities Dealers Automated Quotation System (NASDAQ) 2001–, Advisory Bd IESE, Spain, Dean's Advisory Council, Boston Univ., Bd Indian School of Business; Deputy Chair. and Gov. London Business School 1990–; Trustee Cambridge Foundation, Royal Coll. of Art Foundation; Patron Cambridge Alumni in Man., Queen Charlotte's Appeal at Hammersmith Hosp.; Hon. DBA (London Guildhall Univ.) 2001. *Leisure interests:* family, skiing, cricket. *Address:* WPP, 27 Farm Street, London, W1J 5RJ, England. *Telephone:* (20) 7408-2204 (office). *Fax:* (20) 7493-6819 (office). *Website:* www.wpp.com (office).

SORRENTINO, Paolo; Italian film director and screenwriter; b. 31 May 1970, Naples; m. Daniela D'Antonio; two c.; writer for various TV programmes including several episodes of The Team 2000; also directed TV commercials; mem. jury, Locarno Int. Film Festival 2008; Pres. jury, Turin Film Festival 2012. *Films include:* A Paradise (Un paradiso, short) 1994, Love has No Boundaries (L'amore non ha confini, short) 1998, One Man Up (L'uomo in più) 2001 (Nastro D'Argento for Best Young Dir), The Consequences of Love (Le conseguenze dell'amore) 2004, The Family Friend (L'amico di famiglia) 2006, Il divo 2008 (Jury Prize, Cannes Film Festival 2008, Italian Golden Globe for Best Screenplay 2009), The Slow Game (La partita lenta) 2009 (Raindance Festival Audience Award 2009), This Must Be the Place 2011, The Great Beauty (La grande bellezza) (BAFTA Award for Best Film not in the English Language 2014) 2013. *Publication:* Hanno tutti ragione (novel) 2010. *Address:* c/o Susan Norget Film Publicity, 198 Sixth Avenue, Suite 1, New York, NY 10013, USA (office). *Telephone:* (212) 431-0090 (office). *E-mail:* susan@norget.com (office). *Website:* www.norget.com (office).

SORU, Renato; Italian entrepreneur and politician; *President, Sardinia Region;* b. 16 Aug. 1957, Sanluri, Sardinia; ed Bocconi Univ., Milan; fmr derivatives trader; Founder, Chair. and CEO Tiscali internet service provider (ISP) 1998–2004, bought six small telecoms cos and ISPs in Germany, France, Switzerland, Belgium and Czech Repub.; Pres. Sardinia Region (Partito Democratico Sardo) with centre-left coalition 2004–. *Address:* Tiscali SpA, Sa Illetta, 09122 Cagliari, Italy (office). *Telephone:* 02309011 (office). *E-mail:* info@tiscali.com (office); info@pdsardo.it (office). *Website:* www.tiscali.com (office); www.pdsardo.it (office).

SORVINO, Mira, AB; American actress; b. 28 Sept. 1968; d. of Paul Sorvino; m. Christopher Backus 2004; two s. one d.; ed Harvard Univ. *Films include:* Amongst Friends 1993 (also assoc. producer), The Second Greatest Story Ever Told 1993, Quiz Show 1994, Parallel Lives 1994, Barcelona 1994, Tarantella 1995, Sweet Nothing 1995, Mighty Aphrodite (Acad. Award Best Supporting Actress 1996) 1995, The Dutch Master 1995, Blue in the Face 1995, Beautiful Girls 1996, Norma Jean and Marilyn 1996, Jake's Women 1996, Romy and Michele's High School Reunion 1997, The Replacement Killers 1997, Mimic 1997, Summer of Sam 1999, At First Sight 1999, Joan of Arc: The Virgin Warrior 2000, Lisa Picard is Famous 2001, The Great Gatsby 2001, The Triumph of Love 2001, Wisegirls 2002, The Grey Zone 2002, Gods and Generals 2003, The Final Cut 2004, Leningrad 2007, Reservation Road 2007, The Presence 2010, Jeremy Fink and the Meaning of Life 2011, Angels Crest 2011, Union Square 2011, Perfect Sisters 2012, The Trouble with Cali 2012, Smitty 2012, Trade of Innocents 2012, Space Warriors 2013. *Television includes:* The Great Gatsby 2000, Human Trafficking 2005, Covert One: The Hades Factor 2006, The Last Templar 2009, Finding Mrs. Claus (film) 2012, Trooper 2013. *Address:* c/o Michelle Stern, William Morris Endeavor, 1325 Avenue of the Americas, New York, NY 10019, USA.

SOSRODJOJO, Soegiharto; Indonesian business executive (retd); b. 1930; m.; five c.; f. Rekso Group 1950s (conglomerate with interests in tea and beverages, property, plantation, printing and packaging, wellness and food), subsidiary cos include Sinar Sosro, Gunung Slamat, Agropangan, among others. *Address:* c/o Rekso International, Graha Rekso Building, 10th Floor, Jl. Bulevar Artha Gading Kav A1, Sentra Bisnis, Artha Gading Kelapa Gading, Jakarta Utara 14240, Indonesia (office). *Telephone:* (21) 45856222 (office). *Fax:* (21) 45856201 (office). *E-mail:* info@reksointernational.com (office). *Website:* www.reksointernational.com (office).

SOTKILAVA, Zurab Lavrentievich; Georgian singer (tenor); b. 12 March 1937, Sukhumi; m.; two d.; ed Tbilisi Polytech. Inst., Tbilisi Conservatory; fmr professional football player in Dynamo, Tbilisi; soloist Tbilisi Opera Theatre 1965–74; Prof., Tbilisi Conservatory 1976–88; with Bolshoi Theatre 1974–; toured with Bolshoi and independently in Europe and America; Hon. Academician, Boston Acad. of Arts; People's Artist of USSR and Georgia; Grand Prize Gold Orpheus Festival (Bulgaria) 1986, Second Prize Int. Tchaikovsky Competition (1970), Grand Prix Barcelona Competition 1970. *Operatic roles include:* Vodemon (Iolanthe), Absalom (Absalom and Eteri), Cavaradossi (Tosca), Richard (Un Ballo in Maschera), Manrico (Il Trovatore), Radames (Aida), José (Carmen), Otello and

others. *Address:* Bolshoi Theatre, Teatralnaya pl. 1, Moscow, Russia. *Telephone:* (495) 244-07-31 (home). *Website:* www.bolshoi.ru.

SOTO ESTIGARRIBIA, Gen. Bernardino, PhD; Paraguayan army officer and government official; *Minister of National Defence;* b. 20 May 1952, Coronel Oviedo; ed Mariscal Francisco Solano López Mil. Acad.; fmr Instructor, US Army School of the Americas, USA; held numerous post in army, including Head of Operations, 6th Infantry Div., Head of Operations Div. Staff, Jt Commdr, 16th Infantry Regt, eventually becoming Commdr of Armed Forces; fmr Mil. Attaché, Embassy in Brazil; fmr Head of Mil. Cabinet of Presidency; took part in service comms in Brazil, Chile, Taiwan, Ecuador and USA; attained rank of Gen. 2007; Minister of Nat. Defence 2013–; Grand Cross, Order of Mariscal José Félix Estigarribia; numerous awards including Infantry Medal of Honour, Paraguayan Army Medal, Bernardo O'Higgins Medal (Chile), Medalla del Pacificador (Brazil), Medal of the Spanish Army. *Address:* Ministry of National Defence, Avda Mariscal López, esq. Vicepresidente Sánchez y 22 de Septiembre, Asunción, Paraguay (office). *Telephone:* (21) 21-0052 (office). *Fax:* (21) 21-1815 (office). *E-mail:* ministro@mdn.gov.py (office). *Website:* www.mdn.gov.py (office).

SOTOMAYOR, Javier; Cuban fmr athlete; b. 13 Oct. 1967, Limonar; m. María del Carmen García; first man to jump over 8 ft; set world indoor record (7 ft 11.5 in.) 1989 and world outdoor record (8 ft 0.5 in.) 1993; has cleared above 2.30m in 227 events; World Indoor Championships gold medallist 1989, 1993, 1995, 1999; Olympic gold medallist 1992, silver medallist 2000; World Championships gold medallist 1993, 1997, silver medallist 1991, 1995; achieved best height Pan-American Games, Winnipeg 1999; disqualified after failing cocaine test and prevented from competing again until Aug. 2000 by Int. Asscn of Athletics Feds. (IAAF); finished 5th in World Indoor Championships March 2001; retd Oct. 2001; voted Best Cuban Athlete of the Century.

SOTOMAYOR, Sonia, BA, JD; American lawyer, academic and judge; *Associate Justice, Supreme Court;* b. 25 June 1954, Bronx, New York; m. Kevin E. Noonan 1976 (divorced 1983); ed Blessed Sacrament School, Cardinal Spellman High School, New York, Princeton Univ., Yale Law School; born to Puerto Rican family that had moved to New York during World War II; Ed. Yale Law Journal and Man. Ed. Yale Studies in World Public Order; Asst Dist Attorney, New York Co. Dist Attorney's Office, Manhattan 1979–84; Assoc., Pavia & Harcourt (law firm), New York 1984–87, Partner 1988–92; Judge, US Dist Court, Southern Dist of NY (youngest mem. of court) 1992–98, Judge, US Court of Appeals for the Second Circuit (first Hispanic woman to serve on court) 1998–2009, Assoc. Justice, US Supreme Court 2009–; Adjunct Prof., New York Univ. Law School 1998–2007; Lecturer-in-Law, Columbia Univ. Law School 1999–; mem. ABA, New York Women's Bar Asscn, Puerto Rican Bar Asscn, Hispanic Nat. Bar Asscn, Asscn of Judges of Hispanic Heritage, Nat. Council of La Raza; fmr mem. Second Circuit Task Force on Gender, Racial and Ethnic Fairness in the Courts; fmr mem. Bd of Dirs New York Mortgage Agency, New York City Campaign Finance Bd, Puerto Rican Legal Defense and Educ. Fund; Hon. LLD (Herbert H. Hehman Coll.) 1999; Hon. JD (Princeton Univ.), (Brooklyn Law School); M. Taylor Pyne Prize (co-recipient), Princeton Univ., Award from Nat. Asscn of Women Lawyers, ranked by Forbes magazine amongst The World's 100 Most Powerful Women (19th) 2010. *Publication:* My Beloved World (autobiog.) 2013. *Address:* Supreme Court of the United States, 1 First Street, NE, Washington, DC 20543, USA (office). *Telephone:* (202) 479-3000 (office); (202) 479-3011 (Clerk's Office) (office); (202) 479-3211 (Public Information Office) (office). *E-mail:* info@supremecourt.gov (office). *Website:* www.supremecourt.gov (office).

SOUFLIAS, Georgios Ath.; Greek civil engineer and politician; b. 1941, Larisa; m. Marianna Koraka; two d.; civil engineer, Larisa 1966–74; mem. Parl. 1974–2000, Parl. Rep. of Nea Demokratia (New Democracy party) 1993–96, mem. Perm. Parl. Cttees of Foreign Affairs and Defence, Nat. Economy, Educ. and the Amendment of the Constitution 1993–2000, re-elected as Deputy at Large with Nea Demokratia 2004–; Deputy Minister of Interior Affairs 1977–80, of Nat. Economy 1980–81; Minister of Nat. Economy 1989; represented Nea Demokratia in tripartite cttee in charge of memorandum of co-operation that led to 'Ecumenical Govt' of Mr X. Zolotas 1989; Minister of Finance 1989–90, of Nat. Economy 1990, of Educ. 1991–93; cand. for presidency of Nea Demokratia 1997; expelled from Nea Demokratia Feb. 1998, returned to party on invitation of Pres. of Nea Demokratia during its Fifth Congress 2001, Head of Secr. of Political Planning and Program 2001–04; Minister for the Environment, Physical Planning and Public Works 2004–; Prof. Emer. of Human Studies, Greek Coll., Boston, USA 1993. *Address:* c/o New Democracy Party (Nea Demokratia), Odos Rhigillis 18, 106 74 Athens, Greece. *Telephone:* (210) 7418000. *Fax:* (210) 7418119. *E-mail:* ir@nd.gr. *Website:* www.nd.gr.

SOUHAIBI, Noman Taher as-, BA; Yemeni politician; b. 1965, Al-Sadda, Ibb; ed San'a Univ.; Deputy Chair. Tax Authority 2001–05, Chair. 2005–07; Minister of Finance 2007–11. *Address:* c/o Ministry of Finance, PO Box 190, San'a, Yemeni (office). *Telephone:* (1) 260370 (office). *Fax:* (1) 263040 (office).

SOULAGES, Pierre; French painter; b. 24 Dec. 1919, Rodez; m. Colette Llaurens 1942; ed Lycée de Rodez; exhibited abstract painting from 1947, in Salon des Surindépendants, Salon de Mai et Réalités Nouvelles; exhibited at int. festivals, including Documenta, Kassel, Biennales of Venice and São Paulo and the itinerary of the Guggenheim Collection, Carnegie Inst., Pittsburgh, The New Decade at Museum of Modern Art, New York, Tate Gallery, London, etc.; also décors for theatres and ballet, and lithographs and engravings; works in Museums of Modern Art, Paris and New York, Tate Gallery, London, Guggenheim Museum, New York, Phillips Gallery, Washington, Museum of Modern Art, Rio de Janeiro, L'Ermitage, St Petersburg, museums in many American cities, in Europe, Australia and Japan; Hon. mem. American Acad. of Arts and Letters; Commdr, then Grand Officier, Légion d'honneur; Grand Officier des Arts et des Lettres; Grand Croix, Ordre nat. du Mérite; Grand Prix, Tokyo Biennale 1957, Carnegie Prize, Pittsburgh, USA 1964, Grand Prix des Arts de la Ville de Paris 1975, Rembrandt Prize, Germany, 1976, Prix Nat. de Peinture, Paris 1986, Praemium Imperiale, Tokyo 1992, VII Premio Internacional Julio González, Valencia 2007, Prix Georges Pompidou, Paris 2007. *Publication:* subject of book 'Soulages, l'œuvre complet: Peintures' by P. Encrevé (three vols). *Address:* 12 rue Monge, 75005 Paris, France (home). *Fax:*

1-43-26-88-36 (office). *E-mail:* sec.soulages@wanadoo.fr (office). *Website:* www
.pierre-soulages.com.

SOULÉ MANA, Lawani; Benin government official; previously worked in West
African Devt Bank; Minister of Finance 2007–09. *Address:* c/o Ministry of Finance
And Economy Planning, BP 302, Cotonou, Benin (office).

SOULEY, Hassane (Bonto); Niger politician; Minister of Youth 2001–02, of Nat.
Defence 2002–07. *Address:* c/o Ministry of National Defence, BP 626, Niamey,
Niger (office).

SOULEZ-LARIVIÈRE, Daniel Joseph; French lawyer and writer; b. 19 March
1942, Angers (Maine-et-Loire); s. of Furcy Soulez-Larivière and Suzanne Soulez-
Larivière (née Larivière); m. Mathilde-Mahaut Nobecourt 1988; one s. with
Michèle Abbaye; ed Lycée Janson-de-Sailly, Collège Stanislas, Paris, Garden City
High School, New York, USA, Faculty of Law, Paris and Institut d'Etudes
Politiques, Paris; lawyer in Paris 1965–; Chargé de mission, Ministry of
Equipment and Housing 1966–67; f. Soulez Larivière & Associés 1969; Second
Sec. Conférence du stage 1969; mem. Conseil de l'Ordre 1988–90; mem.
Consultative Comm. for Revision of the Constitution 1992–93; mem. Advisory
Bd Centre de prospective de la gendarmerie; Municipal Counsellor for Chambellay
1995–; mem. Soc. of French Jurists; Chevalier, Légion d'honneur, Ordre nat. du
Mérite. *Publications include:* L'avocature 1982, Les juges dans la balance 1987, La
réforme des professions juridiques et judiciaires, vingt propositions 1988, Justice
pour la justice 1990, Du cirque médiatico-judiciaire et des moyens d'en sortir 1993,
Paroles d'avocat 1994, Grand soir pour la justice 1997, Dans l'engrenage de la
justice 1998, Lettres à un jeune avocat 1999, La justice à l'épreuve (with Jean-
Marie Coulon) 2002, Notre justice 2002, Le temps des Victimes (with Caroline
Eliacheff) 2007. *Leisure interest:* hunting. *Address:* Soulez Larivière & Associés, 22
avenue de la Grande Armée, 75017 Paris Cedex 17 (office); 6 rue des Fougères,
92140 Clamart (home); le Prieuré, 49220 Chambellay, France (home). *Telephone:*
1-47-63-37-22 (office); 1-45-34-56-50 (home). *Fax:* 1-42-67-83-05 (office); 1-46-26-
23-65 (office). *E-mail:* dsl@soulezlariviere.com (office). *Website:* www
.soulezlariviere.com.

SOUMARÉ, Cheikh Hadjibou; Senegalese politician; *President of the Commission, Union Economique et Monétaire Ouest Africaine (UEMOA);* b. 1951, Dakar;
ed Ecole Nationale d'Administration et de Magistrature, Univ. of Dakar; served as
municipal tax officer Kaolack, Sédhiou and Bambey 1981–85; Head Statistics Div.,
State Treasury 1985–90; Provisional Admin. Bank of Credit and Commerce Int.,
Senegal 1991–95; adviser to Minister for Finance 1995–96; Dir of the Budget
1996–2000; Dir-Gen. of Finance 2000–01; Deputy Minister for the Budget
2001–07; Prime Minister 2007–09 (resgnd); Pres., Comm. of the Union Economique et Monétaire Ouest Africaine (UEMOA) 2012–. *Address:* Union économique
et monétaire ouest-africaine (UEMOA), BP 543, Ouagadougou 01, Burkina Faso
(office). *Telephone:* 31-88-73 (office). *Fax:* 31-88-72 (office). *E-mail:* commission@
uemoa.int (office). *Website:* www.uemoa.int (office).

SOUSA, Manuel Inocêncio, MSc; Cape Verde politician; b. 1951; ed IST, Lisbon,
Portugal, IHE, Delft, Netherlands; fmr Minister of the Communities; Minister of
Foreign Affairs, Co-operation and Communities 2001–02; Sr Minister of Infrastructure and Transport (later Minister of State and of Infrastructure, Transport
and the Sea) 2002–11; unsuccessful cand. in presidential election Aug. 2011; mem.
Partido Africano da Independência de Cabo Verde. *Address:* c/o Partido Africano
da Independência de Cabo Verde, Av. Amílcar Cabral, CP 22, Praia, Santiago
(office); CP 376, Santo Vicente, Cape Verde (home). *Telephone:* (261) 9249 (home).
E-mail: inocenciosousa@hotmail.com (home).

SOUTER, Sir Brian, Kt; British business executive; *CEO, Stagecoach Group
PLC;* b. 1954; s. of Iain Souter and Catherine Souter; m. Elizabeth McGoldrick
1988; three s. one d.; ed Univs of Dundee and Strathclyde; fmrly trainee
accountant; f. Stagecoach Selkent bus co. with sister Ann Gloag (q.v.); Chair.
Stagecoach Group PLC 1980–2002, CEO 2002–; fmr Chair. ScotAirways Group
Ltd; Businessman of theYear, Insider Elite Awards 2004. *Address:* Stagecoach
Group PLC, 10 Dunkeld Road, Perth, PH1 5TW, Scotland (office). *Telephone:*
(1738) 442111 (office). *Fax:* (1738) 443076 (office). *E-mail:* info@stagecoachgroup
.com (office). *Website:* www.stagecoachgroup.com (office).

SOUTER, David Hackett, AB, MA, LLB; American lawyer and judge; *Associate
Justice, Supreme Court;* b. 17 Sept. 1939, Melrose, Mass; s. of Joseph A. Souter and
Helen A. Hackett; ed Harvard Univ., Univ. of Oxford, UK, Harvard Univ. Law
School; admitted to NH Bar 1967; Assoc., Orr & Reno, Concord 1966–68; Asst
Attorney-Gen. of NH 1968–71, Deputy Attorney-Gen. 1971–76, Attorney-Gen.
1976–78; Assoc. Justice, NH Superior Court 1978–83, NH Supreme Court
1983–90; Judge US Court of Appeals, 1st Circuit 1990; Assoc. Justice US Supreme
Court, Washington, DC 1990–; mem. ABA, NH Bar Asscn; Trustee Concord Hosp.
1972–85, NH Historical Soc. 1976–85; Fellow, American Acad. of Arts and
Sciences. *Address:* United States Supreme Court, One First Street, NE,
Washington, DC 20543, USA (office). *Telephone:* (202) 479-3211 (office). *Website:*
www.supremecourtus.gov (office).

SOUTHERN, Sir Edwin Mellor, Kt, FRS; British molecular biologist and
academic; *Founder, Chairman and Chief Scientific Officer, Oxford Gene Technology;* b. 1938; initiated some of the earliest DNA sequencing at MRC Mammalian
Genome Unit, Edinburgh 1967–79; Assoc. Dir MRC Clinical and Population
Cytogenetics Unit, where in 1979 he set up first project to map human genome
using molecular methods; Whitley Prof. of Biochemistry, Univ. of Oxford
1985–2009, Prof. Emer. 2009–; Fellow of Trinity Coll.; Founder, Chair. and Chief
Scientific Officer, Oxford Gene Technology 1995; Founder and Chair. The
Kirkhouse Trust (charity); Founder Edina Trust; Gairdner Foundation Int. Award
1990, Royal Medal, Royal Soc. of London 1998, Lasker Prize for Clinical Medical
Research (co-recipient) 2005, Asscn of Biomolecular Resource Facilities Award
2005. *Inventions include:* the Southern Blot, now a common laboratory procedure
used in DNA analysis for genetic fingerprinting and paternity testing. *Publications:* numerous articles in professional journals. *Address:* Oxford Gene Technology, The Hirsch Building, Begbroke Science Park, Sandy Lane, Yarnton,
Kidlington, OX5 1PF (office); Department of Biochemistry, University of Oxford,
South Parks Road, Oxford, OX1 3QU, England (office). *Telephone:* (1865) 275282
(office). *Fax:* (1865) 275283 (office). *E-mail:* contact@ogt.co.uk (office); ed

southern@bioch.ox.ac.uk/~southern (office). *Website:* www.ogt.co.uk (office); www
.bioch.ox.ac.uk (office).

SOUTO DE MOURA, Eduardo Elísio Machado; Portuguese architect; b. 25
July 1952, Porto; s. of José Alberto Souto de Moura and Maria Teresa Ramos
Machado; m. Luisa Penha; three d.; ed School of Fine Arts, Univ. of Porto; worked
in Atelier Alvaro Siza (architectural firm) 1975–79; worked for Serviço Ambula-
torio de Apojo local (interdisciplinary group est. to address Portugal's shortage of
affordable housing); Asst Prof., Univ. of Porto 1981–90, later Prof.; f. Atelier Souto
Moura Arquitectos Lda, Porto 1980; Visiting Prof. at architectural schools of
Geneva, Paris-Belleville, Harvard Univ., Dublin, ETH Zurich, Lausanne; mem.
Acad. of Arts Architecture Section, Berlin 2010; awards include António de
Almeida Foundation Prize 1980, Prémio Pessoa 1998, Academie d'Architecture de
France Architecture Medal 2010, Pritzker Prize 2011. *Works include:* more than 60
projects throughout Europe including Nevogilde houses, Porto 1983–88, Holiday
home, Quinta do Lago, Algarve 1984–89, Univ. of Aveiro Dept of Geosciences bldg
1990–94, Burgo Empreendimento (office buildings), Porto 1991, conversion of
Porto customs building to create the Museum of Transports and Communications
1993–2002, private house, Bom Jesus 1994, Trindade station, Porto Metro 1997,
Knowledge of the Seas Pavilion, Expo 98, Lisbon, Casa del Cinema Manoel de
Oliveira, Porto 1998–2002, Portugal Pavilion at Expo 2000, Hanover, Centro de
Arte Contemporânea, Bragança 2002–08, Braga Municipal Stadium 2003,
Serpentine Gallery Pavilion, London (with Alvaro Siza) 2005, Casa das Historias
Paula Rego, Cascais 2005–09, Burgo Tower, Porto 2007. *Address:* Atelier Souto
Moura Arquitectos Lda, Calçada do Ouro 1, 4150 Porto, Portugal (office).

SOVERN, Michael Ira, BA, LLB; American legal scholar, academic and fmr
university president; *President Emeritus and Chancellor Kent Professor of Law,
Columbia University;* b. 1 Dec. 1931, New York; m. 2nd Eleanor Lean 1963
(divorced 1974); m. 3rd Joan Wit 1974 (died 1993); m. 4th Patricia Walsh 1995; two
s. one d. from first m.; one d. from second m.; ed Columbia Coll., Columbia School of
Law; called to the Bar 1956; mem. Faculty, Columbia Law School 1957–, Prof. of
Law 1960–, Dean, Law School 1970–79, Chancellor Kent Prof. in Law 1977–, Univ.
Provost 1979–80, Pres. 1980–93, now Pres. Emer.; Chair. Japan Soc. 1993–,
American Acad., Rome 1993–, nat. advisory council Freedom Forum Media Studies
Center 1993–, Sotheby's 2000–; Pres. Schubert Foundation 1996–, also Dir
Schubert Org.; mem. Bd of Dirs Comcast Corpn 2002–, Chemical Bank 1981–96;
fmr mem. Bd of Dirs AT&T, GNY Insurance Group, Orion Pictures Corpn, Asian
Cultural Corpn; Fellow, American Acad. of Arts and Sciences; mem. American Law
Inst.; Hon. DPhil (Tel-Aviv), Hon. LL.D (Columbia) 1980, Commendatore, Order of
Merit (Italy) 1991, Alexander Hamilton Medal, Columbia Coll. 1993, Ctizens
Union Civic Leadership Award. *Publications:* Legal Restraints on Racial Discrim-
ination in Employment 1966, Law and Poverty 1969. *Address:* Office of the
President, The Shubert Foundation, 234 West 44th Street, New York, NY 10036;
School of Law, Columbia University, 435 West 116th Street, New York, NY 10027,
USA (office). *Telephone:* (212) 854-2640 (office). *Website:* www.shubertfoundation
.org; www.law.columbia.edu (office).

SØVNDAL, Villy; Danish politician; b. 4 April 1952, Linde; s. of Peter Søvndal
and Agnes Søvndal; m. Heidi Perto Søvndal; three c.; ed Kolding Coll. of Educ.;
teacher, Kolding school system 1980–92; mem. Kolding City Council 1982–94;
mem. Folketing (Parl.) for Vejle County constituency 1994–2007, for Copenhagen
greater constituency 2007–13; mem. Socialistisk Folkeparti (Socialist People's
Party), Party Chair. 2005–12; Minister for Foreign Affairs 2011–13. *Publication:*
Villys verden (Villy's World) 2008. *Address:* c/o Socialistisk Folkeparti (SF)
(Socialist People's Party), Christiansborg, 1240 Copenhagen K, Denmark.

SOW, Ahmedou Mostapha; Senegalese academic and physician; *Professor
Emeritus of Medicine, Dakar University;* b. 5 May 1931, Saint Louis; m.; ten c.; ed
Ecole Normale W. Ponty, Dakar, Dakar Univ.; studied medicine in Paris and
Sarajevo; Asst Lecturer in Histology and Embryology, Dakar Univ. 1963–66, Prof.
of Medicine 1976, Prof. Emer. 1988–; Head Physician, Diabetic Centre, Dakar,
Head Internal Medicine 1978–97; Dir urban centre for non-transmissible chronic
diseases; Consultant to OAU on Blood and Liver Diseases, to WHO on the Elderly
and Diabetes; Fellow Islamic Acad. of Sciences; Officer Palmes Académiques
Sénégalaises, Chevalier Ordre nat. du Lion, Commdr Ordre du Mérite, Senegal
Commdr Ordre des Palmes académiques, Commdr Ordre nat. du Mérite (France),
Distinction Prize in Medicine 1962. *Address:* Islamic Academy of Sciences, P.O.
Box 830036, Amman, Jordan (office). *Telephone:* 5522104 (office). *Fax:* 5511803
(office).

SOW, Ousmane; Senegalese sculptor; b. 1935, Dakar; moved to France 1957;
worked for 20 years as physiotherapist, Laennec Hosp., Paris; became full-time
sculptor at age of 50; best known for life-size statues of humans and groups of
humans; first major exhbn at Centre culturel français de Dakar 1988; has held solo
exhbns in Belgium, France, Germany, Italy, Japan, USA and Senegal; works
Nouba assis and Nouba debout displayed at Palazzo Grassi as part of Venice
Biennale 1995, and at Palais des Nations, Geneva and parl. buildings in Dakar and
Paris; major retrospective exhbns at Pont des Arts, Paris 1999 and Citadelle de
Besançon 2013; mem. Académie des Beaux-Arts (first African) 2013; Prince Claus
Award (Netherlands) 2008. *Works include:* Nouba wrestlers 1984–87, The Masai
1988–89, The Zulus 1990–91, Peulh 1993–94, Battle of Little Big Horn (35-piece
series) 1994–99, statue of Victor Hugo, Besançon 2001–02, L'Homme et l'Enfant
2013. *Address:* Le P'tit Jardin 84, rue des Entrepreneurs, 75015 Paris, France
(office). *Telephone:* (1) 45-58-45-32 (office). *Website:* www.ousmanesow.com (office).

SOW, Sadio Lamine; Malian journalist and politician; *Minister of Foreign Affairs
and International Co-operation;* b. 9 Aug. 1952, Kayes; m.; three c.; ed Université
de Paris X Nanterre; began career as journalist with Jeune Afrique early 1980s; 30
years in Burkina Faso, becoming Special Adviser to Pres. Blaise Compaoré;
Minister of Foreign Affairs and Int. Co-operation 2012–. *Address:* Ministry of
Foreign Affairs and International Co-operation, Koulouba, Bamako, Mali (office).
Telephone: 2022-8314 (office). *Fax:* 2022-5226 (office).

SOWRY, Hon. Roger; New Zealand fmr politician; b. 1958, Palmerston North;
m.; four c.; ed Victoria Univ. of Wellington; fmr Distribution Man., R. Hannah &
Co.; Nat. Party MP 1990–; apptd Jr Whip, then Sr Govt Whip 1993–96; Minister of
Social Welfare, Minister in Charge of War Pensions, Assoc. Minister of Health
1996–98 and Minister in Charge of Social Services, Work, Income, Welfare,

Housing, Employment and Leader of the House 1998–2000; Deputy Divisional Chair. Wellington Young Nationals 1979–80, Electorate Chair. Pencarrow 1982–86, Divisional Councillor 1985–96, Deputy Chair. Wellington Div. 1988–90, Wellington Rep. on NZ Nat. Exec. 1989–90; Deputy Leader Nat. Party 2001–03, Spokesman on Energy and Labour and Industrial Relations 2003–; mem. Commerce Select Cttee 2003–. *E-mail:* roger.sowry@xtra.co.nz (home).

SOYINKA, Akinwande Oluwole (Wole), BA; Nigerian playwright and academic; *Professor Emeritus of Comparative Literature, Obafemi Awolowo University;* b. 13 July 1934, Abeokuta; s. of Ayo Soyinka and Eniola Soyinka; m.; several c.; ed Univ. of Ibadan, Nigeria and Univ. of Leeds, UK; worked at Royal Court Theatre, London; Research Fellow in Drama, Univ. of Ibadan 1960–61; Lecturer in English, Univ. of Ife 1962–63; Sr Lecturer in English, Univ. of Lagos 1965–67; political prisoner 1967–69; Artistic Dir and Head, Dept of Theatre Arts, Univ. of Ibadan 1969–72; Research Prof. in Dramatic Literature, Univ. of Ife 1972, Prof. of Comparative Literature and Head of Dept of Dramatic Arts 1976–85; Goldwin Smith Prof. of Africana Studies and Theatre, Cornell Univ. 1988–92; passport seized Sept. 1994, living in France; charged with treason March 1997 in absentia; Woodruff Prof. Emer. of the Arts, Emory Univ., Atlanta 2004–; Prof. Emer. of Comparative Literature, Obafemi Awolowo Univ. 2007–; Prof. in Residence, Loyola Marymount Univ. 2007; Founder and Chair. The Democratic Front for a People's Federation 2010–; Ed. Ch'Indaba (fmrly Transition) Accra; Artistic Dir Orisun Theatre, 1960 Masks; Literary Ed. Orisun Acting Editions; Pres. Int. Theatre Inst. 1986–; Fellow, Churchill Coll. Cambridge 1973–74; mem. American Acad. of Arts and Letters, Int. Theatre Inst., Union of Writers of the African Peoples, Nat. Liberation Council of Nigeria; Fellow, Ghana Asscn of Writers, Pan-African Writers Asscn; Commdr, Légion d'honneur; Commdr, Fed. Repub. of Nigeria 1986; Commdr, Order of Merit (Italy) 1990; Hon. DLitt (Leeds) 1973, (Yale) 1981, (Morehouse), (Paul Valéry) (Bayreuth), (Ibadan), (Harvard); Hon. DScS (Edin.) 1977; Rockefeller Foundation Grant 1960, John Whiting Drama Prize 1966, Prisoner of Conscience Award, Amnesty Int., Jock Campbell-New Statesman Literary Award 1969, Nobel Prize for Literature 1986, George Benson Medal, RSL 1990, Writers Guild Lifetime Achievement Award 1996, Distinguished Scholar-in-Residence, New York Univ. 1999, and numerous other awards. *Plays:* The Invention 1955, The Lion and the Jewel 1959, The Swamp Dwellers 1959, A Dance of the Forests 1960, The Trials of Brother Jero 1961, The Strong Breed 1962, The Road 1964, Kongi's Harvest 1965, Madmen and Specialists 1971, Before the Blackout 1971, Jero's Metamorphosis 1973, Camwood on the Leaves 1973, The Bacchae of Euripides 1974, Death and the King's Horsemen 1975, Opera Wonyosi 1978, A Play of Giants 1984, Six Plays 1984, Requiem for a Futurologist 1985, From Zia, with Love 1992, A Scourge of Hyacinths (radio play) 1992, The Beatification of Area Boy 1995, King Baabu 2003. *Radio:* BBC Reith Lectures 2004. *Publications:* novels: The Interpreters 1964, The Forest of a Thousand Daemons (trans.), Season of Anomy 1973; poetry: Idanre and Other Poems 1967, Poems from Prison 1969, A Shuttle in the Crypt 1972, Poems of Black Africa (ed.) 1975, Ogun Abibman 1977, Mandela's Earth and Other Poems 1988, Samarkand and Other Markets I Have Known 2002; non-fiction: The Man Died (prison memoirs) 1972, Myth, Literature and the African World (lectures) 1972, Aké, The Years of Childhood (autobiog.) 1982, Art, Dialogue and Outrage 1988, Isara: A Voyage Round Essay 1990, Continuity and Amnesia 1991, Ibadan: The Pentelemes Years (memoir) 1994, The Open Sore of a Continent, A Personal Narrative of the Nigerian Crisis 1996, The Burden of Memory, The Muse of Forgiveness 1999, Conversations with Wole Soyinka 2001, You Must Set Forth at Dawn: A Memoir 2006. *Address:* Marymount Institute for Faith, Culture, and the Arts, Loyola Marymount University, 1 LMU Drive, Los Angeles, CA 90045, USA. *Website:* www .lmu.edu/libraries_research/marymountinstitute.htm.

SPACEK, Mary Elizabeth (Sissy); American actress; b. 25 Dec. 1949, Quitman, Tex.; d. of Edwin A. Spacek and Virginia Spacek; m. Jack Fisk 1974; two d.; ed Lee Strasberg Theater Inst. *Films:* Prime Cut 1972, Ginger in the Morning 1972, Badlands 1974, Carrie (Best Actress Nat. Soc. Film Critics) 1976, Three Women (Best Supporting Actress New York Film Critics) 1977, Welcome to LA 1977, Heart Beat 1980, Coal Miner's Daughter (Acad. Award for Best Actress, Best Actress New York and Los Angeles Film Critics, Foreign Press Asscn, Nat. Soc. Film Critics) 1980, Raggedy Man 1981, Missing 1982, The River 1984, Marie 1985, Violets are Blue 1986, Crimes of the Heart 1986, 'night Mother 1986, JFK 1991, The Long Walk Home, The Plastic Nightmare, Hard Promises 1992, Trading Mom 1994, The Grass Harp 1995, Streets of Laredo 1995, If These Walls Could Talk 1996, Affliction 1998, Blast From the Past 1999, In the Bedroom (Golden Globe for Best Actress 2002) 2001, Verna: USO Girl 2002, Tuck Everlasting 2002, Last Call 2003, A Home at the End of the World 2004, An American Haunting 2005, The Ring II 2005, Nine Lives 2005, Summer Running: The Race to Cure Breast Cancer 2005, North Country 2005, Gray Matters 2007, Hot Rod 2007, Lake City 2008, Four Christmases 2008, Get Low 2009, The Help 2011, Deadfall 2012. *Television:* The Girls of Huntington House 1973, The Migrants 1973, Katherine 1975, Verna, USO Girl 1978, A Private Matter (film) 1992, A Place for Annie (film) 1994, The Good Old Boys (film) 1995, Pictures of Hollis Woods (film) 2007, Gimme Shelter (film) 2010, Big Love (series) 2010. *Music includes:* Album of the Year Award (Country Music Asscn) for Coal Miner's Daughter 1980. *Publication:* My Extraordinary Ordinary Life (autobiog.) 2012. *Address:* c/o Steve Tellez, CAA, 2000 Avenue of the Stars, Beverly Hills, CA 90067, USA.

SPACEY, Kevin; American actor and theatre director; *Artistic Director, The Old Vic Theatre;* b. 26 July 1959, South Orange, NJ; ed Chatsworth High School, LA, Juilliard Drama School, NY; stage debut in Henry IV, Part I; Broadway debut in Ghosts 1982; mem. Bd of Trustees, Old Vic Theatre, London, Artistic Dir 2003–, also appearing there several productions; Co-Dir The Bridge Project, (theatre co. est. with Sam Mendes at Old Vic Theatre, London and Brooklyn Acad. of Arts, New York) 2007–; Cameron Mackintosh Visiting Prof. of Contemporary Theatre, St Catherine's Coll., Oxford 2008–; Hon. CBE 2010; Dr hc London South Bank Univ. 2005; Evening Standard Special Theatre Award 2008. *Films include:* Working Girl 1988, See No Evil, Hear No Evil 1989, Dad 1989, Henry and June 1990, Glengarry Glen Ross 1992, Consenting Adults 1992, Hostile Hostages 1994, Outbreak 1995, The Usual Suspects (Acad. Award for Best Supporting Actor) 1995, Se7en 1995, Looking for Richard 1996, A Time to Kill 1996, LA Confidential 1997, Midnight in the Garden of Good and Evil 1997, American Beauty (Acad. Award for Best Actor) 1999, Pay it Forward 2000, The Shipping News 2001, K-PAX 2001, The Life of

David Gale 2003, Beyond the Sea (also dir) 2004, Superman Returns 2006, Fred Claus 2007, 21 2008, Recount 2008, Telstar 2008, Shrink 2009, Moon (voice) 2009, The Men Who Stare at Goats 2009, Father of Invention 2010, Casino Jack 2010, Margin Call 2011, Horrible Bosses 2011, Inseparable 2011; dir Albino Alligator 1997. *Plays include:* theatre appearances include: Hurlyburly 1985, Long Day's Journey into Night, London 1986, Yonkers, NY (Tony Award), The Iceman Cometh, London 1998, National Anthems (Old Vic) 2005, Richard II (Old Vic) 2005, The Philadelphia Story (Old Vic) 2006, A Moon for the Misbegotten (Old Vic and Broadway) 2007, Speed the Plow (Old Vic) 2007. *Television includes:* Wiseguy 1988, House of Cards (series) 2013–14. *Address:* Polaris PR, 8135 West Fourth Street, Second Floor, Los Angeles, CA 90048, USA (office); c/o The Old Vic Theatre, The Cut, Waterloo, London, SE1 8NB, England (office). *Telephone:* (20) 7928-2651 (office). *Website:* www.oldvictheatre.com (office).

SPADER, James; American actor; b. 7 Feb. 1960, Boston; ed Phillips Acad. *Films include:* Endless Love 1981, The New Kids 1985, Pretty in Pink 1986, Baby Boom 1987, Less Than Zero 1987, Mannequin 1987, Jack's Back 1988, The Rachel Papers 1989, Sex, Lies and Videotape 1989, Bad Influence 1990, The Music of Chance 1993, Dream Lover 1994, Wolf 1994, Stargate 1994, Two Days in the Valley 1996, Crash 1997, Keys to Tulsa 1997, Critical Care 1997, Curtain Call 1998, Supernova 1998, Slow Burn 1999, Curtain Call 1999, Secretary 2002, I Witness 2003, Alien Hunter 2003, Shadow of Fear 2004, Shorts 2009, Lincoln 2012. *Television:* The Pentagon Papers 2003, The Practice (series) 2003–04, (Emmy Award for Outstanding Lead Actor in a Drama Series 2004), Boston Legal (series) 2004–08 (Emmy Award for Outstanding Lead Actor in a Drama Series 2005, 2007), The Office (series) 2011–12. *Address:* c/o ICM, 8942 Wilshire Boulevard, Beverly Hills, CA 90211, USA.

SPALDING, Alistair, CBE; British theatre executive; *Artistic Director and CEO, Sadler's Wells;* b. 25 Aug. 1957, Stotfold, Herts., England; programmer of film, classical music and visual arts, Hawth Theatre, Crawley 1988–94; Head of Dance and Performance, South Bank Centre, London 1994–2000; Dir of Programming, Sadler's Wells, London 2000–03, Interim Artistic Dir 2003–04, Artistic Dir 2004–, CEO 2004–; External Advisor, Validation Bd for Laban Centre degree courses, City Univ., London; Chair. Dance UK; mem. Advisory Panel, Arts Council of England Dance 1995–2003, Nat. mem. Arts Council of England Bd 2009–; Chevalier des Artes et des Lettres 2005; De Valois Award for Outstanding Achievement, Critics' Circle Dance Awards 2010. *Address:* Sadler's Wells, Rosebery Avenue, London, EC1R 4TN, England (office). *Telephone:* (20) 7863-8198 (office). *Fax:* (20) 7863-8199 (office). *Website:* www.sadlerswells.com (office).

SPALDING, D. Brian, ScD, PhD, FRS, FIMechE, FInstF, FREng; British scientist, academic and business executive; *Managing Director, Concentration, Heat and Momentum Ltd. (CHAM);* b. 9 Jan. 1923, New Malden, Surrey; s. of Harold Spalding and Kathleen Spalding; m. 1st Eda Ilse-Lotte Goericke; two s. two d.; m. 2nd Colleen King; two s.; ed King's Coll. School, Wimbledon, The Queen's Coll. Oxford and Pembroke Coll. Cambridge; Bataafsche Petroleum Matschapij 1944–45; Ministry of Supply 1945–47; ICI Research Fellow at Cambridge Univ. 1948–50, Demonstrator in Eng 1950–54; Reader in Applied Heat, Imperial Coll. of Science and Tech., London 1954–58, Prof. of Heat Transfer 1958–88, Prof. Emer. 1988–, Head of Computational Fluid Dynamics Unit 1981–88; Man. Dir Conduction Heat and Mass Transfer Ltd 1970–75, Concentration, Heat and Momentum Ltd 1975–; Chair. CHAM of N America Ltd 1977–91; mem. Royal Norwegian Soc., Russian Acad. of Sciences 1994, Ukrainian Nat. Acad. of Sciences 1994; Max Jakob Award 1978, Medaille d'Or 1980, Bernard Lewis Combustion Medal 1982, Luikov Medal 1986. *Publications:* Numerical Prediction of Flow, Heat Transfer Turbulence and Combustion (selected works) 1983, Heat Exchanger Design Handbook (jtly) 1982, Combustion and Mass Transfer 1979, GENMIX: A General Computer Program 1978, Mathematical Models of Turbulence (jtly) 1972, Heat and Mass Transfer in Recirculating Flows (co-author) 1967, Convective Mass Transfer (co-author) 1963, Engineering Thermodynamics (co-author) 1958, Some Fundamentals of Combustion 1955, Postscripts to Pushkin 2002; numerous scientific papers. *Leisure interests:* music, poetry reading. *Address:* Concentration, Heat and Momentum Ltd (CHAM), Bakery House, 40 High Street, Wimbledon, SW19 5AU, England (office). *Telephone:* (20) 8947-7651 (office). *Fax:* (20) 8879-3497 (office). *Website:* www.cham.co.uk (office).

SPALL, Timothy, OBE, FRSA; British actor; b. 27 Feb. 1957, London, England; s. of Joseph Spall and Sylvia Spall; m.; one s. two d.; ed Battersea Co. Comprehensive, Kingsway and Princeton Coll. of Further Ed., Royal Acad. of Dramatic Art, London. *Plays:* Merry Wives of Windsor, Nicholas Nickleby, The Three Sisters, The Knight of the Burning Pestle (RSC 1978–81), St Joan 1985, Mandragola 1985, Le Bourgeois Gentilhomme 1993, A Midsummer Night's Dream 1994 (Royal Nat. Theatre), This is a Chair 1996 (Royal Court). *Films include:* Quadrophenia 1978, Gothic 1986, The Sheltering Sky 1990, Life is Sweet 1990, Secrets and Lies 1996, The Wisdom of Crocodiles 1998, Still Crazy 1998, Topsy Turvy 1999, Clandestine Marriage 1999, Love's Labour's Lost 2000, Intimacy 2001, Lucky Break 2001, Rock Star 2001, Vanilla Sky 2001, All or Nothing 2002, Nicholas Nickleby 2002, Gettin' Square 2003, The Last Samurai 2003, Harry Potter and the Prisoner of Azkaban 2004, Lemony Snickett's A Series of Unfortunate Events 2004, Harry Potter and the Goblet of Fire 2005, Pierrepoint 2005, Enchanted 2007, Sweeney Todd 2007, Death Defying Acts 2007, Apaloosa 2008, The Damned United 2009, Harry Potter and the Half Blood Prince 2009, Heartless 2009, Desert Flower 2009, From Time to Time 2009, Alice in Wonderland (voice) 2010, Re-Uniting the Rubins 2010, Wake Wood 2010, My Angel 2010, Jackboots on Whitehall (voice) 2010, Harry Potter and the Deathly Hallows: Part I 2010, The King's Speech 2010, Harry Potter and the Deathly Hallows: Part 2 2011, My Angel 2011, Comes a Bright Day 2012, Sofia 2012, Upside Down 2012, Ginger & Rosa 2012, The Rise 2012, Love Bite 2012, The Love Punch 2013. *Television includes:* The Brylcream Boys 1978, Auf Wiedersehen Pet 1983, 1985, Roots 1993, Frank Stubbs Promotes 1994, 1995, Outside Edge 1994, 1995, Neville's Island 1997, Our Mutual Friend 1997, Shooting the Past 1999, The Thing About Vince 2000, Vacuuming Completely Nude in Paradise 2001, Perfect Strangers 2001, Auf Wiedersehen Pet (third series) 2002, My House in Umbria 2003, Cherished 2005, Mr Harvey Lights a Candle 2005, Mysterious Creatures 2006, A Room with a View 2007, The Street 2006–09, Oliver Twist 2007, Gunrush 2009, The Fattest Man in Britain 2009, 10 Minute Tales (Deep & Crisp & Even) 2009, The Syndicate (series) 2012, Blandings (series) 2013–14. *Leisure* *interests:* boating, drinking fine wines, reading. *Address:* c/o Markham & Froggatt, 4 Windmill Street, London, W1P 1HF, England (office); c/o Hofflund Palone, Suite 420, 9465 Wilshire Blvd, Beverley Hills, CA 90212, USA (office). *Telephone:* (20) 7636-4412 (London) (office); (310) 859-1971 (Beverley Hills) (office). *Fax:* (20) 7637-5233 (London) (office); (20) 8699-1657 (London) (office). *E-mail:* admin@markhamfroggatt.co.uk (office). *Website:* www.markhamfroggatt.com (office).

SPANIER, Graham B., BS, MS, PhD; American sociologist, academic and fmr university administrator; m. Sandra Spanier (née Whipple) 1971; one s. one d.; ed Iowa State Univ., Northwestern Univ.; Prof. and Assoc. Dean, Pennsylvania State Univ. 1973–82, Pres. 1995–2011; Vice-Provost for Undergraduate Studies, State Univ. of New York at Stony Brook 1982–86; Provost and Vice-Pres. for Academic Affairs, Oregon State Univ. 1986–91; Chancellor Univ. of Nebraska 1991–95; Chair. Nat. Asscn of State Univs and Land-Grant Colls (Co-Chair. Cttee on Higher Educ. and the Entertainment Industry), Nat. Security Higher Educ. Advisory Bd (mem. Nat. Counterintelligence Working Group), Big Ten Conference Council of Pres/Chancellors; Vice-Chair. Worldwide Univs Network; fmr Chair. Christian Children's Fund; fmr Pres. Nat. Council of Family Relations; mem. Bd of Dirs Jr Achievement Int. *Publications:* ten books and more than 100 scholarly publs. *Leisure interests:* magic, music, racquetball. *Address:* c/o Office of the President, Pennsylvania State University, University Park, PA 16802, USA.

SPANTA, Rangin Dadfar, PhD; Afghan academic and government official; *National Security Adviser;* b. 15 Dec. 1953, Herat prov.; m.; one c. one s. one d.; ed Kabul Univ., Aachen Univ., Germany; began living in Germany 1982; Prof., Inst. of Political Science, Tech. Univ. of Aachen 1992–2005, Dir Third World Studies Inst.; returned to Afghanistan to teach at Kabul Univ. 2005; Spokesperson Alliance for Democracy; adviser to Pres. on int. affairs 2005; Minister of Foreign Affairs 2006–10; Nat. Security Adviser 2010–. *Address:* c/o Office of the President, Gul Khana Palace, Presidential Palace, Kabul, Afghanistan (office). *E-mail:* president@afghanistangov.org (office). *Website:* www.president.gov.af (office).

SPAR, Debora L., BS, AM, PhD; American political scientist, academic and college administrator; *President, Barnard College;* m. Miltos Catomeris; two s. one d.; ed Georgetown and Harvard Univs; Grad. Assoc., Center for Int. Affairs, Harvard Univ. 1987–88, Crump Fellow, Energy and Environmental Policy Center, Kennedy School of Govt 1988, Research Fellow, Center for Business and Govt 1990, Asst Prof. of Business, Govt and Competition, Harvard Business School 1991–95, Assoc. Prof. 1995–99, Prof. 1999–2004, Chair. Business, Govt and the Int. Economy Unit, Sr Assoc. Dean, Recruiting 2004–05, Sr Assoc. Dean, Dir Div. of Research and Faculty Devt 2005–07, Spangler Family Prof., Harvard Business School 2005–08; Asst Prof., Dept of Political Science, Univ. of Toronto 1990–91; Pres. Barnard Coll. 2008–; Karl W. Deutsch Guest Prof., Wissenschaftszentrum, Berlin 2000; mem. Harvard Univ. Cttee on Human Rights 1995–, Chair. 2006–07; mem. Exec. Cttee, Weatherhead Center for Int. Affairs, Harvard Univ. 1995–, Cttee on African Studies, Harvard Univ. 2002–, Policy Advisory Cttee, Center for Int. Devt 2005–, Advisory Cttee on Honorary Degrees 2006–, Embryonic Stem Cell Research Org. 2006–, Policy Cttee, David Rockefeller Center for Latin American Studies, Harvard Univ. 1997–2002; Chair. Making Markets Work (exec. educ. programme for African officials) 2002–; mem. Bd Newton Schools Foundation 2002–04, Bd of Overseers, Newton Wellesley Hosp. 2007–; mem. Bd of Dirs Goldman Sachs 2011–; Univ. English Medal, Georgetown Univ. 1984, Dean's Citation, School of Foreign Service, Georgetown Univ. 1984, J. Raymond Trainor Citation for Excellence in the Study of Govt, School of Foreign Service, Georgetown Univ. 1984, DACOR Fellow 1984–86, Certificates of Distinction in Teaching, Harvard Coll. 1987–89, Distinguished Teaching Fellow Award, Govt Dept, Harvard Univ. 1988, Helen Dwight Reid Award, Best Doctoral Dissertation in Int. Relations, American Political Science Asscn 1991, Student Asscn Faculty Award for Outstanding Teaching, Harvard Business School 2000, Robert F. Greenhill Award for Outstanding Service, Harvard Business School 2005. *Publications:* Beyond Globalism: Remaking American Foreign Economic Policy (with Raymond Vernon) 1988, Iron Triangles and Revolving Doors: Cases in U.S. Foreign Economic Policymaking (with Raymond Vernon and Glenn Tobin) 1991, The Cooperative Edge: The Internal Politics of International Cartels 1994, Ruling the Waves: Cycles of Discovery, Chaos and Wealth from the Compass to the Internet 2001 (simultaneously published as Pirates, Prophets and Pioneers: Business and Politics Along the Technological Frontier, London 2001), Managing International Trade and Investment 2003, The Baby Business: How Money, Science, and Politics Drive the Commerce of Conception 2006; numerous book chapters and articles on the economics of the human fertility industry and the evolution of the Internet. *Address:* Office of the President, Barnard College, 3009 Broadway, New York, NY 10027, USA (office). *Telephone:* (212) 854-2021 (office). *E-mail:* dspar@barnard.edu (office). *Website:* www.barnard.edu (office).

SPARGO, Peter Ernest, BSc, MSc, Cert. Ed. (Cantab.), FRSSAf; South African academic; *Associate Professor Emeritus, University of Cape Town;* b. 7 June 1937, Johannesburg; s. of Alfred Hugh Spargo and Lilias McCall Spargo (née Fisher); m. Celia Rosamunde Key 1964; four d.; ed Jeppe High School, Univ. of the Witwatersrand, Johannesburg, Magdalene Coll. Cambridge, UK; Science Teacher, Jeppe High School, Johannesburg 1961–63; Lecturer in Science Educ., Johannesburg Coll. of Educ. 1964–71; Science Educ. Planner, Pretoria 1972–75; School of Educ., Univ. of Cape Town 1976–97, Dir Science Educ. Unit 1980–97, Hon. Research Assoc., Dept of Physics 1999–2012, Assoc. Prof. Emer. 2012–; Nat. Chair. SA Asscn of Teachers of Physical Science 1975–82; Trustee and Dir S African Science Educ. Project 1977–2008; Educ. Consultant to Shell Oil Co. (SA) 1977–89, Rössing Uranium Co. (Namibia) 1982–90; Nat. Pres. Fed. of Science and Math. Teachers Asscns of SA 1977–79, 1984–85; Gen. Sec. Royal Soc. of South Africa 1986–89, Fellow; Hon. Nat. Pres. South African Spelaeological Asscn 1996–; Medal of Honour, Fed. of Science and Math. Teachers Asscns of South Africa 1981. *Publications include:* numerous publs in the fields of science education, history of science and technology, author of science textbooks. *Leisure interests:* walking, reading, gardening. *Address:* PO Box 211, Rondebosch 7701; 10 Lochiel Road, Rondebosch, Cape Town, South Africa (home). *Telephone:* (21) 6864289 (home). *Fax:* (21) 5105979 (office). *E-mail:* peter@spargo.wcape.school.za.

SPARKS, Robert Stephen John, CBE, PhD, FRS; British geologist, volcanologist and academic; *Channing Willis Professor of Geology, Department of Earth Sciences, University of Bristol;* b. 15 May 1949, Harpenden, Herts., England; s. of

Kenneth Grenfell Sparks and Ruth Joan Rugman; m. Ann Elizabeth Talbot 1971; two s.; ed Imperial Coll., London; Fellow of Royal Comm. of Exhbn of 1851, Univ. of Lancaster 1974–76; NATO Post-doctoral Fellow, Univ. of Rhode Island, USA 1976–78; Lecturer, Univ. of Cambridge 1978–89, Fellow, Trinity Hall Cambridge 1980–89; Prof. of Geology, Univ. of Bristol 1989–, Channing Willis Prof. of Geology 1990–; Chief Scientist, Montserrat Volcano Observatory 1997–99; Prof. of Earth Sciences, Nat. Environment Research Council 1998–; Pres. Geological Soc. of London 1994–96, Int. Asscn of Volcanology and Chem. of Earth's Interior 1999–, VGP Section, American Geophysical Union 2008–12; Chair. of Environmental Sciences, Research Assessment Exercise 2008, Advisory Cttee on Math. Educ. UK 2012–(15); Dir Bristol Environmental Risk Research Centre (BRISK) 2008–11; European Research Council Advanced Researcher 2009–(14); Fellow, American Geophysical Union 1998; Hon. DSc (Lancaster) 2000; Dr hc (Univ. Blaise Pascal) 1999, (Univ. of Paris) 2003; Bakerian Lecture, Royal Soc. 2000; Bigsby Medal, Geological Soc. of London, Murchison Medal, Geological Soc. of London 1998, Arthur Day Medal, Geology Soc. of America 2000, Royal Soc. Wolfson Merit Award 2002, Arthur Holmes Medal, European Union of Geosciences 2004, Chiba Univ. Science Prize, Japan 2006, Thorarinsson Medal 2008. *Publications:* Volcanic Plumes 1997; more than 390 scientific articles and papers on volcanology (especially physics of volcanic eruptions), fluid mechanics, petrology and other geological topics. *Leisure interests:* music, travel, family. *Address:* Department of Earth Sciences, Wills Memorial Building, Room G17, Queen's Road, Bristol University, Bristol, BS8 1RJ (office); Walnut Cottage, 19 Brinsea Road, Congresbury, Bristol, BS49 5JF, England (home). *Telephone:* (117) 9545419 (office); (1934) 834306 (home). *Fax:* (117) 9253385 (office). *E-mail:* steve.sparks@bristol.ac.uk (office). *Website:* gfd.gly.bris.ac.uk (office); www.gly.bris.ac.uk/www/admin/personnel/RSJS.html (office).

SPASSKIY, Nikolay Nikolayevich, DPolSc; Russian diplomatist and government official; *Deputy Director-General, Rosatom;* b. 10 Aug. 1961, Sevastopol; s. of Nikolay Spasskiy and Rimma Spasskaya; m. Angela Maria Catalano; one d.; ed Moscow Inst. of Int. Relations; with USSR (later Russian) Ministry of Foreign Affairs 1983–; Deputy Head, First Deputy, Dept of N America 1992–94; Dir 1994–97; mem. Advisory Council, Ministry of Foreign Affairs 1995; Amb. to Italy (also accred to San Marino) 1997–2004; Deputy Sec., Nat. Security Council 2004–06, Deputy Head Rosatom Fed. Atomic Energy Agency 2006–08; Deputy Dir Gen. State Energy Corpn'Rosatam' 2008–. *Publications:* La Fine del Mondo e Altri Racconti Romani 1999, Il Complotto 2000, Il Bizantino 2002, Le Reliquie di San Cirillo 2004. *Leisure interests:* art, travel. *Address:* Rosatom, 119017 Moscow, Bolshaya Ordynka st 24, Russia (office). *Telephone:* (499) 949-24-05 (office). *Fax:* (495) 951-68-58 (office). *Website:* www.rosatom.ru/en (office).

SPASSKY, Boris Vasiliyevich; French/Russian chess player and journalist; b. 30 Jan. 1937, Leningrad (now St Petersburg); m. 1st Marina Shcherbacheva; m. 2nd; m. 3rd; ed Faculty of Journalism, Leningrad State Univ.; in Leningrad Section of Voluntary Sport Soc., Trud 1959–61; Trainer, Leningrad Section of Voluntary Sport Soc., Locomotiv 1964–79; played in numerous individual and command int. chess tournaments; USSR Grandmaster, Int. Grandmaster and World Chess Student Champion 1956, USSR Chess Champion 1962, World Chess Champion 1969–72 (when lost to Bobby Fischer); left USSR 1976; lost to Bobby Fischer in Yugoslavia 1992; works as a chess journalist; involved with World Chess Network; Hon. Pres. Kilkenny Chess Club, Ireland; several decorations including Honoured Master of the Sport 1965. *Website:* www.worldchessnetwork.com.

SPASSKY, Igor Dmitriyevich, DrTechSc; Russian engineer and academic; *Head, Central Design Bureau for Marine Engineering (RUBIN);* b. 2 Aug. 1926, Noginsk, Moscow Region; m.; one s. one d.; ed Dzerdjinsky Higher Naval Eng Coll.; service in Black Sea marine forces 1949–50; worked in enterprises of Ministry of Vessel Construction, Leningrad (now St Petersburg) 1950–; Head of Sector, Cen. Design Bureau for Marine Eng (RUBIN), then Deputy Chief Designer, Head and Chief Designer 1974–, Gen. Designer 1983–; Scientific and Tech. Leader of Kursk submarine recovery project; USSR Peoples' Deputy 1990–91; mem. USSR (now Russian) Acad. of Sciences 1987–; Hon. Citizen of St Petersburg; Red Banner of Labour 1963, Hero of Socialist Labour 1978, Order of Lenin 1970, 1978, Orders of October Revolution 1986, Order of Merit for Services to the Motherland 2002; 16 medals; Lenin Prize 1965, USSR State Prize 1983. *Publications:* ed. and contrib.: The Kurst 2000, Five Colours of Time, Submarines of the Tzarist Navy, History of National Shipbuilding (five vols), Submarines of Russia (three vols), Submarine Deisgn (collection of articles); more than 100 scientific works on designing atomic submarines, tech. of machine construction, construction mechanics, reliability and special energetics; articles in magazines Shipbuilding, Military Parade, Naval History, USA Naval Institute Proceedings. *Leisure interest:* fishing. *Address:* Central Design Bureau for Marine Engineering (RUBIN), 191119 St Petersburg, Marata str. 90, Russia (office). *Telephone:* (812) 113-51-32 (office). *Fax:* (812) 113-31-15 (office). *E-mail:* neptun@ckb-rubin.spb.su (office). *Website:* www.ckb-rubin.com (office).

SPÄTH, Lothar; German politician; b. 16 Nov. 1937, Sigmaringen; s. of Friedrich Späth and Helene Späth (née Lillich); m. Ursula Heinle 1962; one s. one d.; ed Gymnasium, Heilbronn, State School of Man., Stuttgart; mem. Landtag 1968–91; Chair. CDU group in Stuttgart Landtag 1972–78, Hon. Leader 1991–; Rep. of CDU for Baden-Württemberg 1977–91; Sec. of Interior Feb.–Aug. 1978, Minister-Pres. of Baden-Württemberg 1978–91; Pres. Bundesrat 1985–86; Chair. Jenoptik AG, Jena 1991–2003; Royal Norwegian Consul-Gen. of Thuringia and Saxony-Anhalt 1992–2003; Dr hc (Karlsruhe) 1984, (Pecs); Winner, John J. McCloy Prize 2000. *Publications:* Wende in die Zukunft 1985, 1992– Der Traum von Europa 1989, Natur und Wirtschaft 1992, Sind die Deutschen noch zu retten? 1993, Countdown für Deutschland 1995, Blühende Phantasien und harte Realitäten 1997, Die zweite Wende 1998, Die Stunde der Politik 1999, Jenseits von Brüssel 2001, Was jetzt getan werden muß 2002. *Leisure interests:* modern painting and graphics, card games, tennis. *Address:* Riedwiesenstrasse 1, 71229 Leonberg, Germany. *Telephone:* (7152) 907444. *Fax:* (7152) 907446. *E-mail:* mmueller@lotharspaeth.de (office).

SPAULDING, Winston, QC; Jamaican lawyer and fmr politician; b. 26 Aug. 1939; m.; five c.; called to the Bar, Inner Temple, London 1966; worked briefly in Jamaican and British civil service and practised law in the Bahamas; subsequently established legal practice in Jamaica; fmr mem. Nat. Exec. People's Nat.

Party; Deputy Leader Jamaica Labour Party 1977–83; Senator and Opposition Spokesman on Security and Justice 1977–80; MP for Cen. St James 1980–83 and for SE St Andrew 1983–89; Minister of Nat. Security and Justice and Attorney-Gen. 1980–86; Chair. Defence Bd 1980–86, Legislation Cttee 1980–86, Statute Law Commrs under the Law Revision Act 1980–86; mem. Council of Legal Educ. 1980–86; Founder-mem. Jamaica Council for Human Rights; Founder and First Chair. Human Rights Bureau of Jamaica Labour Party; as Minister of Justice initiated review of Gun Court Act which included abolition of mandatory life sentence; as Minister of Security initiated establishment of Police Staff Coll. *Address:* 21 Balmoral Avenue, Kingston 10, Jamaica (office). *Telephone:* 9298601. *Fax:* 9296196.

SPAVENTA, Luigi; Italian economist and academic; *Professor Emeritus of Economics, University of Rome;* b. 5 March 1934, Rome; s. of Renato Spaventa and Lydia De Novellis; m. Margaret Royce 1962; three c.; ed Univ. of Rome, King's Coll., Cambridge, UK; Prof. of Econ. Policy, Univ. of Palermo 1963–64; Prof. of Econs, Univ. of Perugia 1964–70, Univ. of Rome 1970–, now Prof. Emer.; mem. Italian Parl. (on leave from univ.) 1976–83; Visiting Fellow, All Souls' Coll., Oxford 1968–69; Visiting Scholar, IMF 1984; Luigi Einaudi Prof., Cornell Univ. 1989; Minister of the Budget 1993–94; Chair. Bd Finanza & Futuro SpA, Banca Monte dei Paschi di Siena SpA 1997–98; Chair. Consob (Securities Comm.) 1998–2003; Chair. MTS SpA, Sator Group; Trustee, Int. Accounting Standards Cttee Foundation –2010; Fellow, Centre for Econ. Policy Research; Kt Grand Cross, Order of Merit (Italy). *Publications:* essays and articles in specialized journals and books. *Leisure interest:* mountaineering. *Address:* Sator SpA, Via G. Carissimi 41, 00198 Rome (office); Via G.B. De Rossi 29, 00161 Rome, Italy (home). *Telephone:* (06) 858291 (office); (06) 85829202 (office); (06) 44238191 (home). *Fax:* (06) 85829306 (office); (06) 44236225 (home). *E-mail:* luigi.spaventa@satorgroup.com (office); luigi.Spaventa@fastwebnet.it (home). *Website:* www.satorgroup.com (office).

SPEARMAN, Thomas David, PhD, MRIA; Irish mathematician, academic and fmr university pro-chancellor; b. 25 March 1937, Dublin; s. of Thomas Spearman and Elizabeth Leadbeater; m. Juanita Smale 1961; one s. two d.; ed Greenlanes and Mountjoy Schools, Dublin, Trinity Coll., Dublin and St John's Coll., Cambridge, UK; Research Fellow, Univ. Coll. London 1960–61; Research Assoc., Univ. of Illinois, USA 1962–64; Lecturer in Theoretical Physics, Univ. of Durham, UK 1964–66; Univ. Prof. of Natural Philosophy, Trinity Coll. Dublin 1966–97, Fellow 1969–94, Sr Fellow 1994–97 (Fellow Emer. 1997–), Bursar 1974–77, Vice-Provost 1991–97, Pro-Chancellor Univ. of Dublin 2009–12; Prof. Associé, Univ. of Montpellier, France 1985–; Chair. Trustee Savings Bank, Dublin 1989–92; mem. Council, European Physical Soc. 1979–82; mem. European Space Science Cttee 1984–89; Vice-Pres. European Science Foundation 1983–89; Treas. Royal Irish Acad. 1980–88, Pres. 1999–2002; mem. Academia Europaea, Treas. 1989–2000; mem. European Science and Tech. Ass. 1994–98; mem. Bd Nat. Gallery of Ireland 1999–2002; mem. Governing Council European Science Foundation 2000–02; Chair. European Acads Science Advisory Council 2004–07. *Publications include:* Elementary Particle Theory (with A. D. Martin) 1970; numerous papers and articles on aspects of elementary particle physics, inverse problems and history of science. *Leisure interests:* walking, gardening, reading, listening to music, looking at pictures. *Address:* House No. 25, Trinity College, Dublin 2 (office); St Elmo, Marlborough Road, Glenageary, Co. Dublin, Ireland (home). *Telephone:* (1) 8962360 (office). *E-mail:* david.spearman@tcd.ie (office).

SPEARS, Britney Jean; American singer and entertainer; b. 2 Dec. 1981, McComb, Miss.; m. Kevin Federline 2004 (divorced 2007); two s.; raised in Kentwood, La; began performing as a child, landing acting roles in stage productions and TV shows; signed with Jive Records 1997, released debut album Baby One More Time 1999 (best-selling album by a teenage solo artist); presenter, Mickey Mouse Club; numerous tours, radio and TV appearances; judge, The X Factor (USA) 2012; owner of southern grill restaurant, Nyla; f. The Britney Spears Foundation; MTV Europe Music Awards for Best Female Artist 1999, 2004, for Best Song (for Baby One More Time) 1999, Best Breakthrough Act 1999, Best Pop Act 1999, several MTV Video Music Awards 1999, and Best Female Pop Vocal Performance 2000, Billboard Music Award 2000, American Music Award for Favourite New Artist 2000, Grammy Award for Best Dance Recording (for Toxic) 2005, MTV Video Music Award for Best Female Video (for Piece of Me) 2008, Best Celebrity Fragrance For Women – Cosmopolitan Fragrance Awards 2010, Best Celebrity Fragrance For Women – Readers' Award, Cosmopolitan Fragrance Awards 2011. *Tours:* Baby One More Time Tour 1999–2000, Oops! I Did It Again World Tour 2000–01, Dream Within a Dream Tour 2001–02, The Onyx Hotel Tour 2004, The M+M's Tour 2007, The Circus Starring Britney Spears 2009, Femme Fatale Tour 2011. *Films:* Longshot (cameo) 2000, Austin Powers in Goldmember (cameo) 2002, Crossroads 2002, Fahrenheit 9/11 (cameo) 2004. *Recordings include:* albums: Baby One More Time 1999, Oops! I Did It Again 2000, Britney 2001, In The Zone 2003, My Prerogative 2004, Blackout 2007, Circus 2008, Femme Fatale 2011, Britney Jean 2013. *Website:* www.britneyspears.com (office); www.britney .com.

SPEED, Malcolm Walter; Australian lawyer and sports administrator; b. 14 Sept. 1948; s. of Walter Speed and Audrey Speed; m. Alison Cutter 1971; three d.; ed Melbourne Univ.; solicitor 1971–81, called to Victoria Bar 1981, barrister 1981–94, Melbourne; Exec. Chair. Basketball Australia 1994–97; CEO Australian Cricket Bd 1997–2001, Int. Cricket Council 2001–08. *Leisure interests:* cricket, reading, walking, golf, history.

SPEIRN, Sterling, BSc, DIur; American foundation executive; *President and CEO, W. K. Kellogg Foundation;* b. 7 Feb. 1948, Detroit; m. Diana Aviv 2005; two s. (from previous m.); ed Stanford Univ., Univ. of Michigan Law School; taught high school in Cleveland, Ohio; law clerk, US Dept of Interior, Washington, DC; practised as lawyer; led Apple Computer's nat. computer grants program 1986–90; joined Peninsula Community Foundation, San Mateo, Calif. 1990, Pres. Chief Exec. 1992–2005; Pres. CEO W. K. Kellogg Foundation, Battle Creek, Mich. 2006–; fmr Chair. League of Calif. Community Foundations; mem. Bd of Advisors Pacific Community Ventures, Global Philanthropy Forum; taught seminar on philanthropy at Stanford Graduate School of Business 2000, 2001. *Address:* W. K. Kellogg Foundation, One Michigan

Avenue, East Battle Creek, MI 49017-4012, USA (office). *Telephone:* (269) 968-1611 (office). *Website:* www.wkkf.org (office).

SPELMAN, Rt Hon. Caroline Alice, PC, BA (Hons); British politician; b. (Caroline Alice Cormack), 4 May 1958, Bishop's Stortford, Herts., England; m. Mark Spelman 1987; two s. one d.; ed Herts and Essex Grammar School for Girls (now Hertfordshire and Essex High School), Bishop's Stortford, Queen Mary Coll., London; Sugar Beet Commodity Sec., Nat. Farmers Union 1981–84; Deputy Dir Int. Confed. of European Beetgrowers, Paris 1984–89; Research Fellow, Centre for European Agricultural Studies (part of Univ. of Kent and since 2000 known as Centre for European Agri-Environmental Econs) 1989–93; Dir, Spelman, Cormack & Assocs, Food and Biotechnology Consultancy, Dorridge, W Midlands 1989–2009; contested Bassetlaw constituency, Notts. 1992; MP (Conservative) for Meriden, W Midlands 1997–2010, for Meriden (revised boundary) 2010–, mem. Science and Tech. Select Cttee 1997–98, Environmental Audit Select Cttee 2013–, Parl. Jt Cttee on Slavery 2014–; Opposition Whip 1999–; Bd mem. Parl. Office of Science and Tech. 1997–2001; Opposition Spokesperson for Health 1999–2001, for Women's Issues 1999–2001; Shadow Sec. of State for Int. Devt 2001–03, Shadow Minister for Women 2001–04, Shadow Sec. of State for Environment 2003–04, for Local and Devolved Govt Affairs 2004–05, Shadow Office of Deputy Prime Minister/Communities and Local Govt 2005–07, 2009–10; Chair. Conservative Party 2007–09; Sec. of State for Environment, Food and Rural Affairs 2010–12; mem. Agricultural and Fisheries Council, Council of the EU 2010–12; Co-opted mem. Exec. Cttee Conservative Women's Nat. Council; mem. Bd of Dirs Governing Council, Conservative Christian Fellowship; Advisory Bd mem. Women2Win; Vice-Pres. Tearfund 2013–. *Address:* House of Commons, Westminster, London, SW1A 0AA (office); Constituency Office, 631 Warwick Road, Solihull, B91 1AR, England. *Telephone:* (20) 7219-4189 (London) (office); (121) 711-7029 (Solihull) (office). *E-mail:* caroline@carolinespelman.com (office); spelman@parliament.uk (office). *Website:* www.parliament.uk/biographies/commons/mrs-caroline -spelman/312 (office); www.carolinespelman.com.

SPENCE, A. Michael, MA, PhD; American economist and academic; *Philip H. Knight Professor Emeritus, Graduate School of Business, Stanford University;* ed Princeton Univ., Oxford Univ., UK, Harvard Univ.; Assoc. Prof., Harvard Univ. 1973–75, Chair. Advisory Cttee on Shareholder Responsibility 1978–79, Prof. 1979–86, Chair. Project in Industry and Competitive Analysis 1980–85, Chair. Business Econs PhD Program 1981–83, Chair. Dept of Econs 1983–84, Dean of Faculty 1984–90; Philip H. Knight Prof., Stanford Univ. 1990–2000, Dean 1990–99, Prof. Emer. 2000–; Pnr, Oak Hill Venture Pnrs, Menlo Park 1999–; Chair. Nat. Research Council Bd on Science, Tech. and Econ. Policy 1991–97; mem. Bd of Dirs Gen. Mills, Inc., Nike, Inc. 1995–2004, Siebel Systems, Inc. 1995–2004, Exult, Inc. 1999–2004, Blue Martini Software, Torstar, ITI Educ.; mem. American Econ. Assn; Fellow, AAAS, Econometric Soc.; John Bates Clark Medal, American Econ. Assn 1981, Nobel Prize in Econs 2001 (jt recipient); numerous other awards and prizes. *Address:* Oak Hill Venture Partners, 2775 Sand Hill Road, Menlo Park, CA 94025-7085; Graduate School of Business, 518 Memorial Way, Stanford University, Stanford, CA 94305-5015, USA (office). *Telephone:* (650) 723-2146 (office). *Website:* www.gsb.stanford.edu/news/spence_resume.html (office).

SPENCE, Jonathan Dermot, PhD, CMG; American historian, academic and writer; *Sterling Professor Emeritus of History, Yale University;* b. 11 Aug. 1936, Surrey, England; s. of Dermot Spence and Muriel Crailsham; m. 1st Helen Alexander 1962 (divorced 1993); two s.; m. 2nd Chin Annping 1993; ed Univ. of Cambridge, UK and Yale Univ.; Asst Prof. of History, Yale Univ. 1966–71, Prof. 1971–93, Sterling Prof. of History 1993–2008, Sterling Prof. of History Emer. 2008–; Visiting Prof., Univ. of Beijing 1987; Pres. American Historial Assocn 2004–05; mem. Bd of Govs Yale Univ. Press 1988–; mem. American Acad. of Arts and Sciences, American Philosophical Soc.; Guggenheim Fellow 1979–80; MacArthur Fellow 1987–92; Hon. LHD (Knox Coll.) 1984, (New Haven) 1989; Hon. LittD (Wheeling Coll.) 1985, (Chinese Univ. of Hong Kong) 1996, (Gettysburg) Coll. 1996, (Union Coll.) 2000, (Beloit Coll.) 2000, (Conn. Coll.) 2000; William C. DeVane Medal, Yale Chapter of Phi Beta Kappa 1978, Los Angeles Times History Prize 1982, Vursell Prize, American Acad. and Inst. of Arts and Letters 1983, Comisso Prize (Italy) 1987; Gelber Literary Prize (Canada) 1991. *Publications include:* Ts'Ao Yin and The K'Ang-Hsi Emperor 1966, To Change China 1969, Emperor of China 1974, The Death of Woman Wang 1978, The Gate of Heavenly Peace 1981, The Memory Palace of Matteo Ricci 1984, The Question of Hu 1988, The Search for Modern China 1990, Chinese Roundabout 1992, God's Chinese Son 1996, The Chan's Great Continent 1998, Mao Zedong 1999, Treason by the Book 2002, Return to Dragon Mountain: Memories of a Late Ming Man 2007. *Address:* 691 Forest Road, New Haven, CT 06515, USA (home). *E-mail:* jonathan.spence@yale.edu (office).

SPENCE, Michael James, BA (Hons), LLB (Hons), DPhil; Australian professor of law; *Vice-Chancellor and Principal, University of Sydney;* b. 10 Jan. 1962, Sydney, NSW; m. Beth Spence; five c.; ed Univ. of Sydney, Univ. of Oxford, UK; began career as lawyer with Mallesons Stephens Jacques, Sydney; lectured in Law at Univ. of Sydney –1988; also worked for the Australian Copyright Council; Fellow, St Catherine's Coll., Oxford and Lecturer, Univ. of Oxford 1992, becoming Head of Social Sciences Div.; trained for priesthood at St Stephen's House, Oxford; Vice-Chancellor and Prin. Univ. of Sydney 2008–. *Address:* Office of the Vice-Chancellor, University of Sydney, Sydney, NSW 2006, Australia (office). *Telephone:* (2) 9351-5051 (office). *Fax:* (2) 9351-4596 (office). *E-mail:* vice-chancellor@ vcc.usyd.edu.au (office); vice.chancellor@sydney.edu.au (office). *Website:* sydney .edu.au/about/leadership/vice-chancellor.shtml (office).

SPENCER, (Winston) Baldwin; Antiguan politician and trade union official; *Prime Minister and Minister of Foreign Affairs;* b. 8 Oct. 1948; m. Jacklyn Spencer; one s. one d.; Leader United Progressive Party; MP (UPP) for St John's Rural West constituency 1989–; fmr Leader of the Opposition; Prime Minister of Antigua and Barbuda 2004–, also Minister of Foreign Affairs 2005–. *Leisure interests:* football, cricket, basketball, listening to steel band music, reading, dancing. *Address:* Office of the Prime Minister, Queen Elizabeth Highway, St John's; United Progressive Party, Nevis Street, St John's (office); Cooks Estate, St John's, Antigua (home). *Telephone:* 462-4956 (office); 562-1049 (office); 462-1818; 461-4657 (home). *Fax:* 462-3225 (office); 462-5937 (office); 562-1065 (home). *E-mail:* pmo@candw.ag (office); upp@candw.ag (office). *Website:* www.antiguabarbuda.net/pmo (office); www.uppantigua.com (office).

SPENCER, Elizabeth, AB, MA; American writer; b. 19 July 1921, Carrollton, Miss.; d. of James L. Spencer and Mary James McCain; m. John A. B. Rusher 1956 (died 1998); ed Belhaven Coll. and Vanderbilt Univ.; Writer-in-Residence, Univ. of North Carolina 1969, Hollins Coll. 1973, Concordia Univ. 1977–78, Adjunct Prof. 1981–86; Visiting Prof., Univ. of North Carolina 1986–92; Vice-Chancellor Fellowship of Southern Writers 1993–97; mem. American Acad. of Arts and Letters; Hon. LittD (Southwestern Univ., Memphis) 1985, (Concordia Univ.) 1987, (Univ. of the South) 1992, (Univ. of North Carolina) 1998, (Belhaven Coll.) 1999; Guggenheim Foundation Fellow 1953, Rosenthal Foundation Award, American Acad. of Arts and Letters 1957, McGraw-Hill Fiction Award 1960, Award of Merit for short story, American Acad. of Arts and Letters 1983, Salem Award for Literature 1992, Dos Passos Award for Fiction 1992, NC Gov.'s Award for Literature 1994, Fortner Award for Literature 1998, Mississippi State Library Asscn Award for Non-fiction 1999, Thomas Wolfe Award, Univ. of NC 2002, NC Hall of Fame 2002, William Faulkner Award for Literary Excellence 2002, Lifetime Achievement Award, Mississippi Acad. of Arts and Letters 2009. *Film:* Light in the Piazza 1962. *Plays:* For Lease or Sale 1989, The Light in the Piazza (musical drama) 2006. *Publications:* Fire in the Morning 1948, This Crooked Way 1952, The Voice at the Back Door 1956, The Light in the Piazza 1960, Knights and Dragons 1965, No Place for an Angel 1967, Ship Island and Other Stories 1968, The Snare 1972, The Stories of Elizabeth Spencer 1981, Marilee 1981, The Salt Line 1984, Jack of Diamonds and Other Stories 1988, For Lease or Sale (play) 1989, On the Gulf 1991, The Night Travellers 1991, Landscapes of the Heart (memoir) 1998, The Southern Woman: New and Selected Fiction 2000; contrib. short stories in magazines and collections. *Leisure interests:* movies, theatre, travel. *Address:* 402 Longleaf Drive, Chapel Hill, NC 27517, USA (home). *Telephone:* (919) 929-2115 (home). *E-mail:* elizabeth0222@earthlink.net (home). *Website:* www.elizabethspencerwriter.com (home).

SPENCER, Octavia L., BS; American actress; b. 25 May 1970, Montgomery, Ala; ed Auburn Univ. *Films include:* A Time to Kill 1996, The Sixth Man 1997, Sparkler 1997, Never Been Kissed 1999, Live Virgin 1999, Being John Malkovich 1999, Blue Streak 1999, Everything Put Together 2000, What Planet Are You From? 2000, Big Momma's House 2000, Four Dogs Playing Poker 2000, The Journeyman 2001, The Sky Is Falling 2001, Spider-Man 2002, Legally Blonde 2: Red, White & Blonde 2003 S.W.A.T. 2003, Sol Goode 2003, Bad Santa 2003, Win a Date with Tad Hamilton! 2004, Breakin' All the Rules 2004, Coach Carter 2005, Pretty Persuasion 2005, Marilyn Hotchkiss' Ballroom Dancing & Charm School 2005, Miss Congeniality 2: Armed and Fabulous 2005, Beauty Shop 2005, Wannabe 2005, Pulse 2006, The Nines 2007, Next of Kin 2008, Pretty Ugly People 2008, Seven Pounds 2008, Love at First Hiccup 2009, Drag Me to Hell 2009, Jesus People: The Movie 2009, The Soloist 2009, Just Peck 2009, Halloween II 2009, Herpes Boy 2009, Small Town Saturday Night 2010, Dinner for Schmucks 2010, Peep World 2010, Girls! Girls! Girls! 2011, Flypaper 2011, The Help (Golden Globe Award for Best Supporting Actress 2012) 2011, Smashed 2012, The Trials and Tribulations of a Trailer Trash Housewife 2012, Lost on Purpose 2012. *Television includes:* Lansky (film) 1999, Missing Pieces (film) 2000, Follow the Stars Home (film) 2001, Little John (film) 2002, Titus (series) 2001-02, NYPD Blue (series) 2002-05, LAX (series) 2004-05, Ugly Betty (series) 2007, Halfway Home (series) 2007, The Minor Accomplishments of Jackie Woodman (series) 2006-07, The Looney Tunes Show (series, voice) 2011. *Address:* c/o TalentWorks, 3500 West Olive Avenue, Suite 1400, Burbank, CA 91505, USA (office). *E-mail:* info@talentworks (office). *Website:* www.talentworks.com (office).

SPERBER, Dan; French social sciences researcher; *Researcher, Institut Jean Nicod;* b. 20 June 1942, Cagnes; s. of the late Manès Sperber; ed Univ. of the Sorbonne, Paris and Univ. of Oxford, UK; researcher, CNRS 1965–, Dir of Research 1983, now Research Prof. and Researcher, Institut Jean Nicod; Co-f. EURO-EDU Asscn; Visiting Prof., LSE, Van Leer Inst., Jerusalem, Inst. for Advanced Study, Princeton Univ., Univ. of Michigan, Duxx School, Univ. of Hong Kong, Univ. of Cambridge, Univ. of Bologna; Annual Fellow, Templeton Research Lectures, Vanderbilt Univ. 2007–08; Rivers Memorial Medal, Royal Anthropological Inst. 1991. *Publications:* Rethinking Symbolism 1975, On Anthropological Knowledge 1982, Relevance: Communication and Cognition (with Deirdre Wilson) 1986, Explaining Culture 1996. *Address:* Institut Jean Nicod (EHESS/CNRS), 1bis av. Lowendal, 75007 Paris, France. *Telephone:* 1-53-59-32-89 (office). *E-mail:* dan@sperber.com (home). *Website:* www.institutnicod.org (office); www.dan.sperber.com.

SPERGEL, David Nathaniel, AB, MA, PhD; American astrophysicist and academic; *Charles A. Young Professor of Astronomy on the Class of 1897 Foundation, Professor of Astrophysical Sciences and Chairman, Department of Astrophysical Sciences, Princeton University;* b. 25 March 1961, Rochester, NY; ed John Glenn High School, Huntington, NY, Princeton and Harvard Univs; Visiting Scholar, Univ. of Oxford, UK 1983; Asst Prof., Princeton Univ. 1987–92, Assoc. Prof. 1992–97, Prof. 1997–2007, Charles A. Young Prof. of Astronomy on the Class of 1897 Foundation, Prof. of Astrophysical Sciences 2007–, Chair. Dept of Astrophysical Sciences 2006–, also Assoc. Faculty in Physics and Dept of Mechanical and Aerospace Eng; mem. Inst. for Advanced Study, Princeton, NJ, Keck Distinguished Visiting Prof. 2000–01; Co-founder and Prin. Investigator, Inst. for Physics and Math. of Universe, Univ. of Tokyo, Japan 2007–; Co-Chair. NAS Cttee on Astronomy and Astrophysics, NASA Science Definition Team for NRO 2.4m telescope; fmr Chair. NAS ASTRO 2010 Panel on Cosmology and Fundamental Physics, KITP Advisory Bd, NASA Astrophysics Subcommittee and numerous reviews; mem. NAS 2008; Fellow, American Acad. of Arts and Sciences 2012; Alfred P. Sloan Research Fellow 1988, NSF Presidential Young Investigator Award 1988, Helen B. Warner Prize, American Astronomical Soc. 1994, John T. and Helen D. MacArthur Fellowship 2001, Shaw Prize in Astronomy (co-recipient) 2010, Gruber Prize (as part of WMAP team) 2012, Pres.'s Distinguished Teaching Award 2013. *Publications:* more than 260 papers in peer-reviewed journals. *Address:* Astrophysical Sciences, 113 Peyton Hall, Princeton, NJ 08544, USA (office). *Telephone:* (609) 258-3589 (office). *Fax:* (609) 258-1020 (office). *E-mail:* dns@astro.princeton.edu (office). *Website:* www.princeton.edu/astro (office); www.astro.princeton.edu/~dns (office).

SPERLICH, Peter Werner, PhD; American political scientist, academic and legal consultant; *Professor Emeritus of Political Science and Law, University of California, Berkeley;* b. 27 June 1934, Breslau, Germany (now Wrocław, Poland); s. of Max Otto and Anneliese Gertrud Sperlich (née Greulich); ed Minnesota State Univ. at Mankato, Univ. of Michigan at Ann Arbor; arrived in USA 1956, naturalized 1961; joined Faculty of Univ. of California, Berkeley 1963, apptd Prof. of Political Science 1963, apptd Prof. in Law School 1980, now Prof. Emer.; has served as consultant to courts and law firms; cited by US Supreme Court and various state courts; Social Science Research Council Fellow 1966, Ford Foundation Fellow 1968; mem. American Legal Studies Asscn, Law and Soc. Asscn, Nat. Asscn for Dispute Resolution, Int. Soc. of Political Psychology, Soc. for Psychological Study of Social Issues, American, Int. and Western Political Science Asscns, Conf. Group on German Politics; research on law and politics in USA, Germany, Austria, Denmark, the Netherlands, Switzerland, the UK, Canada, Mexico, the USSR, Japan, Thailand, Hong Kong. *Publications:* Conflict and Harmony in Human Affairs 1971, Single Family Defaults and Foreclosures 1975, Trade Rules and Industry Practices 1976, Over-the-Counter Drug Advertisements 1977, Residing in a Mobile Home 1977, An Evaluation of the Emergency School Aid Act Nonprofit Organization 1978, Rotten Foundations – The Conceptual Basis of the Marxist-Leninist Regimes of East Germany and Other Countries of the Soviet Bloc 2002, Oppression and Scarcity – The History and Institutional Structure of the Marxist-Leninist Government of East Germany and Some Perspectives on Life in a Socialist System 2006, The East German Social Courts – Law and Popular Justice in a Marxist-Leninist Society 2007; numerous articles, including Easter Explained, in Free Inquiry Feb. 2012. *Address:* Department of Political Science, University of California, 581 Barrows Hall, Berkeley, CA 94720 (office); 35503 Vista del Luna, Rancho Mirage, CA 92270, USA (home). *Telephone:* (760) 770-0899 (office). *E-mail:* pws1934@gmail.com (home).

SPERLING, Gene B., BA, JD; American lawyer and government official; *Director, National Economic Council;* b. 24 Dec. 1958, Ann Arbor, Michigan; m. Allison Abner; two c.; ed Univ. of Minnesota, Yale Law School, Wharton School, Univ. of Pennsylvania; worked for New York Gov. Mario Cuomo 1990s; adviser to Pres. Bill Clinton 1993–2001; Deputy Dir Nat. Econ. Council 1993–96, Dir 1996–2000, 2011–; Chief Econ. Advisor to Hillary Clinton during her presidential campaign 2008; Counsellor to US Treasury Sec. Tim Geithner –2011; mem. Council on Foreign Relations 2000–, Sr Fellow for Econ. Policy and Dir Center on Universal Educ.; Visiting Fellow, Brookings Inst.; contributing ed. and columnist Bloomberg News; Sr Fellow, Center for American Progress; consultant and contributing writer for NBC's The West Wing (tv series); mem. Bd of Govs Philadelphia Stock Exchange; fmr advisor to Goldman Sachs. *Publications include:* The Pro-Growth Progressive, What Works In Girls' Education? (co-author); articles on universal education in Foreign Affairs, The New York Times, The Washington Post, The Los Angeles Times, The Financial Times. *Address:* National Economic Council, The White House, 1600 Pennsylvania Ave, NW, Washington DC 20500, USA (office). *Telephone:* (202) 456-1414 (office). *Website:* www.whitehouse.gov/administration/eop/nec (office).

SPETH, James Gustave (Gus), BA, MLitt, JD; American lawyer, scientist and academic; *Carl W. Knobloch, Jr Dean of the School of Forestry and Environmental Studies and Sara Shallenberger Brown Professor in the Practice of Environmental Policy, Yale University;* b. 4 March 1942, Orangeburg, SC; s. of James Gustave and Amelia St Clair Albergotti; m. Caroline Cameron Council 1964; two s. one d.; ed Yale Univ. and Univ. of Oxford, UK (Rhodes Scholar); barrister, Washington, DC 1969, Clerk, Supreme Court 1969–70; Sr Staff Attorney Nat. Resources Defence Council, Washington, DC 1977–79, mem. Bd of Dirs 1981–82, now Trustee; Chair. Council for Environmental Quality 1977–79; Prof. of Law, Georgetown Univ. 1981–82; Pres. and Founder World Resources Inst. 1982–93; joined UNDP 1982, Admin. 1993–99; Carl W. Knobloch, Jr Dean of the School of Forestry and Environmental Studies and Sara Shallenberger Brown Prof. in the Practice of Environmental Policy, Yale Univ. 1999–; mem. Bd of Dirs Center for Humans and Nature, World Resources Inst., Population Action International; Trustee, Rockefeller Brothers Fund; mem. India Council for Sustainable Devt; Hon. DIur (Clark Univ.) 1995, Vermont Law School 2005; Hon. Master of Philosophy (Coll. of the Atlantic) 2001; Hon. DS (Middlebury Coll.) 2007; Hon. DHumLitt (Univ. of South Carolina 2008); Resource Defense Award, Nat. Wildlife Fed. 1975, Nat. Leadership Award, Keystone Center 1991, Barbara Swain Award, Nat. Resources Council of America 1992, Special Recognition Award, Soc. for Int. Devt 1997, Special Leadership Award, Alliance for UN Sustainable Devt Programs 1998, Lifetime Achievement Award, Environmental Law Inst. 1999, Blue Planet Prize 2002, Global Environmental Award, Int. Asscn for Impact Assessment 2005, DeVane Lecturer, Yale Univ. 2007. *Publications:* Worlds Apart: Globalization and the Environment 2003, Red Sky at Morning: America and the Crisis of the Global Environment 2004, Global Environmental Governance (with Peter Haas) 2006, The Bridge at the Edge of the World: Capitalism, the Environment, and Crossing from Crisis to Sustainability 2008. *Address:* Yale School of Forestry and Environmental Studies, 195 Prospect Street, Sage Hall, New Haven, CT 06511 (office); 986 Forest Road, New Haven, CT 06515, USA (home). *Telephone:* (203) 432-5109 (office). *Fax:* (203) 432-3051 (office). *E-mail:* gus.speth@yale.edu (office). *Website:* www.yale.edu/forestry (office).

ŠPIDLA, Vladimír, PhDr; Czech politician; b. 22 April 1951, Prague; s. of Václav Špidla and Dagmar Spidlová; m. 1st; two s.; m. 2nd Viktorie Spidlová; one s. one d.; ed Charles Univ., Prague; fmr archaeologist, worker at historical monuments, sawmill, dairy and livestock industry; Vice-Pres. for Educ., Health Service, Social Affairs and Culture, Dist Cttee, Jindřichův Hradec 1990–91; Dir Labour Office, Jindřichův Hradec 1991–96; mem. Chamber of Deputies 1996–2004; Deputy Prime Minister and Minister of Labour and Social Affairs 1998–2002; Prime Minister of the Czech Repub. 2002–04 (resgnd); EU Commr for Employment, Social Affairs and Equal Opportunities 2004–10; Founding mem. Czech Social Democratic Party Br. in S Bohemia 1989, joined party leadership 1992, Vice-Chair. 1997–2001, Chair. 2001–04. *Leisure interests:* jogging, poetry, sports in nature, cross-country running, history and prehistory. *Address:* c/o European Commission, 200 Rue de la Loi, 1040 Brussels, Belgium. *Telephone:* (2) 299-11-11.

SPIEGLER, Marc, MJ; American/French journalist; b. 1968; m.; ed Medill School of Journalism, Univ. of Chicago; worked as a journalist in Chicago; moved to

Switzerland 1998, freelance art journalist and columnist writing for magazines and newspapers including The Art Newspaper, Monopol, Art and Auction Magazine, ARTnews Magazine, Artworld Salon, Neue Zürcher Zeitung, New York Magazine; Dir of Strategy and Devt, Art Basel 2007–. *Address:* Art Basel, c/o MCH Swiss Exhibition (Basel) Ltd, Messeplatz 10, 4005 Basel, Switzerland (office). *Telephone:* (58) 2062704 (office). *Fax:* (58) 2063130 (office). *E-mail:* info@artbasel.com (office); marc@marcspiegler.com (office). *Website:* www.artbasel.com (office); www.marcspiegler.com (office).

SPIELBERG, Steven, BA; American film director and producer; b. 18 Dec. 1947, Cincinnati, OH; s. of Arnold Spielberg and Leah Spielberg (née Posner); m. 1st Amy Irving (q.v.) 1985 (divorced 1989); two s.; m. 2nd Kate Capshaw; two d. (one adopted); ed Calif. State Coll., Long Beach; won film contest with war film Escape to Nowhere 1961; Dir episodes of TV series, including Night Gallery, Marcus Welby, MD, Columbo; directed 20-minute short Amblin'; Dir TV films Duel 1971, Something Evil 1972; Co-founder and Partner, Dreamworks SKG 1995–2005; Co-founder and Chair. Emer. Starlight Foundation; Artistic Adviser, 2008 Olympic Games in Beijing 2007–08 (resgnd); Hon. KBE (UK), Grosses Bundesverdienstkreuz 1998, Knight Grand Cross, Order of Merit of the Italian Repub. 2003, Legion d'honneur 2004; Dr hc (Univ. of Southern California) 1994, Hon. DLitt (Sussex) 1997; Directors Guild of America Award Fellowship 1986, Irving G. Thalberg Award 1987, Golden Lion Award (Venice Film Festival) 1993, BAFTA Award 1994, Acad. Award for Schindler's List 1994, David Lean (BAFTA), John Huston Award for Artists Rights 1995, American Film Inst. Lifetime Achievement Award 1995, James Smithson Bicentennial Medal 1999, Lifetime Achievement Award, Dir's Guild of America 1999, Britannia Award 2000, Lifetime Achievement Award, David di Donatello Awards 2004, Kennedy Center Honor 2006, Golden Globe Cecil B. DeMille Award 2009, Philadelphia Liberty Medal 2009. *Films directed include:* The Last Gun (short) 1959, Fighter Squad (short) 1961, Escape to Nowhere (short) 1961, Fireflight 1964, Slipstream (short, unfinished) 1967, Amblin' (short) 1968, The Sugarland Express 1974, Jaws 1975, Close Encounters of the Third Kind 1977, 1941 1979, Indiana Jones and the Raiders of the Lost Ark 1981, E.T.: The Extra-Terrestrial 1982, Twilight Zone: The Movie (segment 2) 1983, Indiana Jones and the Temple of Doom 1984, The Color Purple (also producer) 1985, Empire of the Sun 1987, Indiana Jones and the Last Crusade 1989, always 1989, The Visionary (video) (segment 'Par for the Course') 1990, Hook 1991, Jurassic Park 1993, Schindler's List 1993 (Acad. Award for Best Dir 1994, Golden Globe for Best Dir 1994), The Lost World: Jurassic Park 1997, Amistad 1997, Saving Private Ryan 1998 (Acad. Award for Best Dir 1999), The Unfinished Journey (documentary short) 1999, AI: Artificial Intelligence 2001, Minority Report 2002, Catch Me If You Can 2002, The Terminal 2004, War of the Worlds 2005, Munich 2005, Indiana Jones and the Kingdom of the Crystal Skull 2008, A Timeless Call (documentary short) 2008, The Adventures of Tintin: Secret of the Unicorn (also producer) (Golden Globe Award for Best Animated Feature Film 2012) 2011, War Horse (also producer) 2011, Lincoln (also producer) 2012. *Films produced include:* I Wanna Hold Your Hand 1978, Poltergeist (co-writer) 1982, Gremlins 1984, Young Sherlock Holmes (exec. producer) 1985, Back to the Future (co-exec. producer), The Goonies (writer and exec. producer) 1986, Batteries Not Included (exec. producer) 1986, The Money Pit (co-produced) 1986, An American Tail (co-exec. producer) 1986, Always 1989, Gremlins II (exec. producer), Dad (exec. producer), Joe versus the Volcano (exec. producer), Cape Fear (co-exec. producer) 1992, Casper 1995, Twister 1996, Deep Impact 1998, Eyes of the Holocaust (documentary) 2000, Shrek (uncredited) 2001, Evolution (uncredited) 2001, Jurassic Park III 2001, Men in Black II 2002, The Legend of Zorro 2005, Memoirs of a Geisha 2005, Monster House 2006, Spell Your Name (documentary) 2006, Flags of Our Fathers 2006, Letters from Iwo Jima 2006, The Big Bad Heist (short) 2007, Transformers 2007, Dance with the Devil (short) 2007, Eagle Eye 2008, Transformers: Revenge of the Fallen 2009, The Lovely Bones 2009, Hereafter 2010, True Grit 2010, Super 8 2011, Transformers: Dark of the Moon 2011, Cowboys & Aliens 2011, Real Steel 2011, Transformers: The Ride – 3D 2011, War Horse 2011, Men in Black III 2012, Delivery Man 2013. *Television includes:* Night Gallery (series) 1969–71, Marcus Welby, M.D. (series) 1970, The Name of the Game (series) 1971, The Psychiatrist (series) 1971, Columbo (series) 1971, Owen Marshall: Counselor at Law (series) 1971, Duel (film) 1971, Something Evil (film) 1972, Savage (film) 1973, Strokes of Genius (mini-series) (introductory segments, uncredited) 1984, Amazing Stories (series) 1985, Some Mother's Son 1996, Band of Brothers (mini-series) 2001, Semper Fi 2000, We Stand Alone Together (documentary) 2001, Broken Silence (mini-series documentary) 2002, Taken (mini-series) 2002, Burma Bridge Busters (documentary) 2003, Dan Finnerty & the Dan Band: I Am Woman (film) 2005, Into the West (mini-series) 2005, On the Lot (series) 2007, United States of Tara (series) 2009–11, The Pacific (mini-series) 2010, Locke & Key (film) (also exec. producer) 2011, Rising: Rebuilding Ground Zero (series documentary) 2011, Falling Skies (series) 2011, Terra Nova (series) 2011, Smash (series) 2012, The River (series) 2012. *Publication:* Close Encounters of the Third Kind (with Patrick Mann). *Address:* c/o Creative Artists Agency, 2000 Avenue of the Stars, Los Angeles, CA 90067, USA (office). *Telephone:* (424) 288-2000 (office). *Fax:* (424) 288-2900 (office). *Website:* www.caa.com (office); www.starlight.org.

SPIELMAN, Daniel Alan, BA, PhD; American computer scientist and academic; *Henry Ford II Professor of Computer Science, Mathematics and Applied Mathematics, Yale University;* ed Yale Univ., Massachusetts Inst. of Tech.; NSF Math. Sciences Postdoctoral Researcher, Div. of Computer Science, Univ. of California 1995–96; Asst Prof. of Applied Math., MIT 1996–2002, Assoc. Prof. 2002–05, Henry Ford II Prof. of Computer Science, Math. and Applied Math. 2005–; mem. Gödel Prize Cttee 2012–14; Assoc. Ed. SIAM Journal on Discrete Mathematics 2009–12; mem. Editorial Bd, Theory of Computing; mem. Connecticut Acad. of Science and Eng 2012; Fellow, Asscn for Computing Machinery (ACM) 2010; Best Student Paper at 26th ACM Symposium on Theory of Computing 1994, at 27th ACM Symposium on Theory of Computing 1995, MIT Lab. for Computer Science Thesis Award 1995, ACM Doctoral Dissertation Award 1995, NSF Career Award 1997, Alfred P. Sloan Foundation Research Fellowship 1998, Invited Speaker, Int. Congress of Mathematicians 2002, 2010, 2014, IEEE Information Theory Soc. Paper Award 2002, Gödel Prize, ACM and European Asscn for Theoretical Computer Science 2008, Fulkerson Prize, American Math. Soc. and Math. Programming Soc. 2009, Rolf Nevanlinna Prize, Int. Math. Union 2010, Best Paper at 43rd ACM Symposium on Theory of Computing 2011, Best Paper at 25th

Conf. on Learning Theory 2012, Simons Investigator 2012, MacArthur Fellowship 2012, Yale Science and Eng Asscn Award for Advancement of Basic and Applied Science 2013, Best Paper at 54th Annual IEEE Symposium on Foundations of Computer Science 2013. *Publications:* numerous papers in professional journals; five US patents. *Address:* AKW 201, Department of Computer Science, Yale University, PO Box 208285, 51 Prospect Street, New Haven, CT 06520-8285, USA (office). *Telephone:* (203) 436-1264 (office). *Fax:* (203) 432-0593 (office). *E-mail:* spielman@cs.yale.edu (office). *Website:* www.cs.yale.edu (office); www.cs.yale.edu/homes/spielman (office).

SPIELMANN, Alphonse, DenD; Luxembourg judge; b. 23 May 1931, Brattert; m. Catherine Hildgen 1961; three s.; ed Faculté de Droit and Inst. de Criminologie, Univ. of Paris and Centre Universitaire de Luxembourg; Attorney-Gen., Grand Duchy of Luxembourg; Judge, European Court of Human Rights 1985–98; numerous int. activities. *Publications:* Liberté d'expression ou censure? 1982, La Convention européenne des droits de l'homme et le droit luxembourgeois 1991. *Leisure interest:* history of the Second World War. *Address:* 12 Côte d'Eich, 1450 Luxembourg (office); 108 rue des Muguets, 2167 Luxembourg, Luxembourg (home).

SPIELVOGEL, Carl, BA; American advertising executive; *Chairman and CEO, Carl Spielvogel Associates Inc.;* b. 27 Dec. 1928, New York City; s. of Joseph Spielvogel and Sadie Spielvogel (née Tellerman); m. Barbara Lee Diamonstein 1981; two s. one d.; ed Baruch Coll.; reporter and columnist, New York Times 1950–60; with McCann Erickson, Inc., Interpublic Group of Cos, Inc., New York City 1960–74; Vice-Chair., Chair. Exec. Cttee and Dir Interpublic Group of Cos, Inc. 1974–80; Chair. and CEO Backer & Spielvogel Inc. 1980–87, Backer Spielvogel Bates Worldwide Inc. New York 1987–94; Chair., CEO United Auto Group 1994–97, Consultant –2000; Amb. to the Slovak Repub. 2000–01; currently Chair. and CEO Carl Spielvogel Assocs Inc., New York; mem. Bd of Dirs Apollo Investors Inc., Data Broadcasting Corpn (now Interactive Data Corpn) 1996–2000, 2001–, Asia Soc., Columbia Univ. Inst. for Study of Europe; fmr mem. Bd of Dirs Hasbro Inc., Barney's Inc.; Chair. Cttee Div., WNET-Public Broadcasting, Business Cttee; Trustee State Univ. of New York 2008–, Metropolitan Museum of Art, Lincoln Center for the Performing Arts; fmr Trustee Mount Sinai Hosp., Philharmonic Symphony Soc. of New York; mem.Council on Foreign Relations; mem. Exec. Cttee Council of American Ambs; fmr Fellow, John F. Kennedy School of Govt, Harvard Univ. *Address:* c/o Board of Directors, Interactive Data Corporation, 32 Crosby Drive, Bedford, MA 01730, USA (office).

SPIERKEL, Gregory M. E., BA, MBA; American electronics industry executive; ed Carleton Univ., Canada, Georgetown Univ., Institut Européen d'Admin des Affaires (INSEAD), Fontainebleau, France; Man. Dir Mitel Telecom, UK 1986–89, Gen. Man. for Far East, Hong Kong 1989–90, Pres. Mitel Inc., USA 1992–96, Vice-Pres. Global Sales and Marketing 1996–97; Pres. Ingram Micro Asia-Pacific 1997–99, Exec. Vice-Pres. Ingram Micro Inc. and Pres. Ingram Micro Europe 1999–2004, Corp. Pres. Ingram Micro Inc. 2004–05, CEO 2005–12; mem. Bd Dirs PACCAR Inc.; mem. Dean's Advisory Bd School of Business, Univ. of California, Irvine; mem. Bd of Counselors, George L. Argyros School of Business, Chapman Univ., Orange, Calif. *Address:* c/o Ingram Micro Inc., 1600 East St Andrew Place, PO Box 25125, Santa Ana, CA 92799-5125, USA. *E-mail:* info@ingrammicro.com.

SPIERS, Hon. Ronald Ian, BA, MPA; American diplomatist (retd); b. 9 July 1925, Orange, NJ; s. of Tomas Hoskins Spiers and Blanca Spiers (née De Ponthier); m. Patience Baker 1949; one s. three d.; ed Dartmouth Coll., Princeton Univ.; USN 1943–46; mem. US Del. to UN 1955–58; Dir Disarmament Affairs, State Dept, Washington 1958–62, NATO Affairs 1962–66; Political Counsellor, Embassy in London 1966–69, Minister 1974–77; Asst Sec. of State for Political-Mil. Affairs 1969–73; Amb. to the Bahamas 1973–74, to Turkey 1977–80; Asst Sec. for Intelligence and Research, Dept of State 1980–81; Amb. to Pakistan 1981–83; Under-Sec. for Man., Dept of State 1983–89; Under-Sec.-Gen. for Political and Gen. Ass. Affairs, UN, New York 1989–92; consultant to State Dept 1992–; mem. Council on Foreign Relations; Fellow, Nat. Acad. of Public Admin., American Acad. of Diplomacy; Presidential Distinguished Service Award 1984, 1986, Presidentially conferred with Rank of Career Amb. 1984, Woodrow Wilson Fellowship, Princeton Univ. *Leisure interests:* gardening, furniture making, classical music, opera. *Address:* 5 Timber Lane, Apt 312, Exeter, NH 03833, USA. *Telephone:* (603) 658-7069. *E-mail:* spiersronald1@gmail.com.

SPILIOTOPOULOS, Spilios P., LLM, MPhil; Greek politician and fmr air force pilot; b. 31 Oct. 1946, Pyrgos; m. Maria Tsouni; one d.; ed Univ. of Athens, Hellenic Air Force Acad., Inst. of S Florida, USA; mil. service with air force, becoming Aide de Camp to Pres. Constantine Caramanlis 1980–85, retd from air force with rank of Lt-Col; mem. Parl. (Nea Demokratia Party, NDP) for Achaia Dist 1989–; Deputy Minister for Nat. Defence 1992–93, also Deputy Sec.-Gen., NPD Parl. Ass. and mem. Educational Affairs Parl. Cttee, Foreign Affairs and Defence Parl. Cttee, Inter-parl. Cttee of Greece-Cyprus, Minister of Nat. Defence 2004–06, Chair. NDP Nat. Defence Cttee, NDP Political Council; fmr Dir Foundation of Political Studies and Educ.; fmr Head, Greek Del. to N Atlantic Ass. and mem. Political Cttee; fmr mem. Ass. WEU, OSCE, Org. for Black Sea Econ. Co-operation, Special Mediterranean Group; Grand Decoration of Honour in Silver (Austria), Commdr, Order of Merit (Cyprus, Egypt, Italy), Chevalier, Légion d'honneur, Commdr, Order of Merit and Golden Cross of Honour (Greece), Commdr, Mil. Order of Aviz (Portugal); First Air Acad. Graduation Award. *Publication:* Responsibilities of the National Air Carrier 1985; several articles. *Leisure interests:* sailing, sports, music. *Address:* 18 Dimikritoy str., 10673, Athens, Greece. *E-mail:* info@e-spilios .gr. *Website:* www.e-spilios.gr.

SPINDELEGGER, Michael, Dr iur.; Austrian politician; *Vice-Chancellor and Federal Minister of Finance;* b. 21 Dec. 1959, Mödling; m.; two c.; ed Univ. of Vienna; Asst Lecturer and Researcher, Inst. of Criminal Law, Univ. of Vienna 1982–83; Judges' Asst at several Courts of Law in Vienna 1983–84; civil servant, Fed. State Lower Austria 1984–87; mem. Cabinet of the Minister of Defence 1987–90; employed within the Secr. of the Bd, Strategic Man., GiroCredit (Austrian bank) 1993–94; speaker on European Relations, Employees' Asscn of the Austrian People's Party (ÖAAB) 1989–91, Deputy Head ÖAAB 1991–; mem. Fed. Chamber, Austrian Parl. 1992–93; mem. Nat. Ass. 1993–95; MEP (ÖVP-EVP), mem. of Parl. Cttee on Econs, Currency Issues and Industrial Policy, Deputy mem. Cttee for Social Issues and Employment 1995–96; ÖAAB Speaker on Foreign Affairs and Head of Parl. Cttee on Foreign Affairs 1996–2006; Chair. NÖAAB (ÖAAB of Lower Austria) 1998–; mem. Parl. Ass., Council of Europe 2000–07; Deputy Parl. Group Leader of the Austrian Peoples Party 2000–06; Head of the Austrian Del. to the Parl. Ass. of the Council of Europe 2002–2006; Second Pres. Austrian Nat. Council 2006–08; Fed. Minister for European and Int. Affairs 2008–13, for Finance 2013–, Vice-Chancellor 2011–; Party head, Austrian People's Party 2011–. *Address:* Federal Ministry for Finance, Hintere Zollamtstr. 2b, 1030 Vienna, Austria (office). *Telephone:* (1) 514-33-0 (office). *Fax:* (1) 514-33-50-57 (office). *E-mail:* buergerservice@bmf.gv.at (office). *Website:* www.bmf.gv.at (office).

SPINETTA, Jean-Cyril, LLB, BSc; French airline executive; *Honorary Chairman, Air France-KLM Group;* b. 4 Oct. 1943, Paris; s. of Adrien Spinetta and Antoinette Brignoll; m. Nicole Spinetta (née Ricquebourg); two s. two d.; ed Lycée Hoche, Versailles, Faculty of Law, Univ. of Paris, Institut d'études politiques (Sciences Po), Ecole nationale d'admin, Paris; teacher 1961–70; with Ecole nationale d'admin 1970–72; entered French civil service 1972, Head of Investments and Planning Dept, Ministry of Educ. 1972–76, seconded to Conseil d'Etat as Auditor 1976–78; served as Govt's Gen. Secr. 1978–81; Head of Information Dept, Office of Prime Minister Pierre Mauroy 1981–83; Dir, Ministry of Educ. 1983–84; Chief of Staff for Michel Delebarre 1984–90; successively Minister of Labour and Vocational Training, Minister of Social Affairs and Employment and Minister of Planning and Devt, Housing and Transport; joined Air Inter 1990, Pres. and CEO 1990–93; advisory posts to Pres. of France (including industrial matters) 1993–95; Admin. in charge of Public Service 1995–96; joined staff of Edith Cresson, European Commr for Science, Research and Educ. 1996–97; Chair. and CEO Air France SA 1997–2008, Chair. 2009–11, Chair. and CEO Air France-KLM Group 2004–08, 2011–13, Chair. 2009–11, Hon. Chair. 2013–; Chair. Assn European Airlines 2001–, Scientific Council, Inst. of Public Admin and Econ. Devt 2002–, Bd of Govs IATA 2004–05; Chair. Supervisory Bd Areva SA 2009–13; Dir (non-exec.) CNES 2002–, Unilever PLC and Unilever NV 2006–07; mem. Bd of Dirs Saint-Gobain 2005–13, Alcatel Lucent 2006–, Alitalia-Linee Aeree Italiane SpA –2007, GDF Suez 2008–, Le Monde Entreprises, Gaz de France SA; Officier, Ordre des Palmes Académiques; Commdr, Ordre nat. du Mérite, Légion d'honneur; Commdr, Order of Orange-Nassau (Netherlands). *Leisure interests:* tennis, skiing. *Address:* Groupe Air France, 45 rue de Paris, 95747 Roissy CDG Cedex, France (office). *Telephone:* 1-41-56-61-65 (office). *Fax:* 1-41-56-61-59 (office). *E-mail:* jcspinetta@airfrance.fr (office). *Website:* www.airfrance.com (office).

ŠPIRIĆ, Nikola, PhD; Bosnia and Herzegovina professor of economics and politician; *Minister of Finance and the Treasury;* b. 4 Sept. 1956, Drvar; m.; two c.; ed Univ. of Sarajevo; fmr Pres. Democratic Party for Banja Luka and Krajina; currently mem. Alliance of Ind. Social Democrats (SNSD); Prof. of Econs, Univ. of Banja Luka 1992–; mem. Parl. in House of Reps of Parl. Ass. of Bosnia and Herzegovina 1999–2000; Deputy Minister of Human Rights and Refugees, Council of Ministers of Bosnia and Herzegovina 2000; Chair. House of Peoples of Parl. Ass. of Bosnia and Herzegovina 2001–02; Chair./Deputy Chair. House of Reps 2002–06; Chair. State Council of Ministers (Prime Minister) Jan.–Nov. 2007 (resgnd), Dec. 2007–12; Minister of Finance and the Treasury 2012–. *Address:* Ministry of Finance and the Treasury, 71000 Sarajevo, trg Bosne i Hercegovine 1, Bosnia and Herzegovina (office). *Telephone:* (33) 205345 (office). *Fax:* (33) 202930 (office). *E-mail:* trezorbih@mft.gov.ba (office). *Website:* www.mft.gov.ba (office).

SPIRIN, Aleksandr Sergeyevich, PhD, DSc; Russian biochemist and molecular biologist; *Head of Laboratory of Protein Synthesis, Institute of Protein Research, Russian Academy of Sciences;* b. 4 Sept. 1931, Kaliningrad (now Korolev), Moscow Region; s. of Sergey Stepanovitch Spirin and Elena Abramovna Spirina (née Kalabekova); m. Tatiana Nikolayevna Fokina; ed Moscow State Univ.; mem. staff, Bakh Inst. of Biochemistry 1958–62, Head of Lab. 1962–73; Prof., Moscow State Univ. 1964–92, Prof. Emer. 1992–, Prof. and Chair of Molecular Biology 1973–; Head of Lab. of Protein Biosynthesis Mechanisms, Inst. of Protein Research 1967–, Dir Inst. 1967–2001; Chair. Bd Pushchino Scientific Centre 1990–2000; Corresp. mem. USSR (now Russian) Acad. of Sciences 1966–70, mem. 1970–, mem. Presidium 1988–2001, Adviser Presidium 2001–; mem. Deutsche Akad. der Naturforscher Leopoldina (now German Nat. Acad. of Sciences) 1974, Czechoslovak Acad. of Sciences 1988, Academia Europaea 1990, European Molecular Biology Org. 1991, Royal Physiographic Soc. (Lund) 1996, American Philosophical Soc. 1997, AAAS 1997, American Soc. for Biochemistry and Molecular Biology 2003; Two Orders of Lenin and other decorations; Dr hc (Granada) 1972, (Toulouse) 1999; Sir Hans Krebs Medal 1969, Lenin Prize 1976, State Prize of the USSR for Science 1988, Ovchinnikov Prize, Russian Acad. of Science 1992, Karpinskij Prize of FVS for Achievements in Science (Hamburg) 1992, State Prize of Russian Fed. for Science 2000, Belozersky Prize, Russian Acad. of Sciences 2000, Big Gold Lomonosov Medal, Russian Acad. of Sciences 2001, Science Prize, Russian Ind. Charity Foundation 'Triumph' 2005. *Publications include:* Macromolecular Structure of Ribonucleic Acids 1964, The Ribosome 1969, Ribosome Structure and Protein Biosynthesis 1986, Ribosomes 1999, Cell-Free Translation Systems (ed.) 2002. *Leisure interests:* hunting, breeding cats. *Address:* Institute of Protein Research, Russian Academy of Sciences, 142290 Pushchino, Moscow Region, Russia (office). *Telephone:* (495) 632-78-71 (office), (499) 137-39-20 (home). *Fax:* (495) 632-78-71 (office). *E-mail:* spirin@vega.protres.ru (office). *Website:* www .protres.ru (office); spirin.protres.ru (office).

SPIROIU, Lt-Gen. Niculae, PhD; Romanian international organization official, fmr government official and fmr army officer; *Executive Director, Euro-Atlantic Council Romania, NATO;* b. 6 July 1936, Bucharest; s. of Constantin Spiroiu and Paulina Spiroiu; m. 1963 (wife died 1991); one s. one d.; ed Tech. Mil. Acad.; scientific researcher with the Centre of Studies and Tests for Tanks and Autos Deputy Chief and Tech. Dept Chief; State Sec. and Head of the Army Supply Dept; Minister of Nat. Defence 1992–94; Counsellor Minister to UN 1994–2000; Sr Counsellor to Minister of Water and Environment Protection 2001–02; Exec. Dir Euro-Atlantic Council of Romania—Casa NATO 2005–; also currently Sr Research Fellow, EURISC Foundation; Co-Chair. US Action Comm., Center of Strategic and Int. Studies, Washington, DC 1997–99. *Leisure interests:* reading, symphonic music, motor cycling, motoring. *Address:* Euro-Atlantic Council Romania—Casa NATO, 82-88 M. Eminescu Str., ap. 19, Sector 2, Bucharest (office); EURISC Foundation, 82-88 Mihai Eminescu Street, Entrance B, app 19, Sector 2,

Bucharest, Sector 2, PO Box 2-101, Romania (office). *Telephone:* (21) 3193278 (Casa NATO) (office); (21) 2122102 (office). *Fax:* (21) 3193279 (Casa NATO) (office); (21) 3193279 (office). *E-mail:* office@casanato.org (office). *Website:* www.casanato .org (office); www.eurisc.org (office).

SPITERI, Lino, MA, DipSocStud; Maltese writer, journalist, financial consultant and fmr politician; b. 21 Sept. 1938, Qormi; s. of Emanuel Spiteri and Pauline Spiteri (née Calleja); m. Vivienne Azzopardi 1964; two s. two d.; ed Lyceum, Malta, Plater Coll. and St Peter's Coll. Oxford; teacher 1956–57; Clerk UK Mil. Establishment 1957–62; Deputy Ed. Il-Helsien (daily) 1962–64, It-Torca (weekly) 1964–66; Ed. Malta News 1967–68; Research Officer Malta Chamber of Commerce 1968–70; with Cen. Bank of Malta as Sr Research Officer, then Asst Head of Research 1971, Head of Research 1972, Deputy Gov. and Chair. Bd of Dirs 1974–81; Minister of Finance 1981–83, of Econ. Planning and Trade 1983–87; Opposition Spokesman on Econs and Finance 1989–96; Chair. Public Accounts Cttee 1995–96, Co-Chair, Malta-EU Jt Parl. Cttee 1996–98; Minister for Econ. Affairs and Finance 1996–97; mem. Malta Labour Party Gen. Exec. 1958–66; Gen. Sec. Labour League of Youth 1961–62; MP 1962–66; Malta Corresp. for Observer, Observer Foreign News Service, Guardian 1967–71; mem. Malta Broadcasting Authority 1968–70; mem. Comm. on Higher Educ. 1977–79; Chair. Students Selection Bd 1978–79; Pres. Qormi Football Club 1977–79; Chair. Bortex Group of Cos 2004–; Dir several cos; columnist, Times and Sunday Times of Malta and others; Companion, Malta Nat. Order of Merit 2008. *Publications:* Studies: The Development of Tourism in Malta 1968, The Development of Industry in Malta 1969; Fiction and poetry: Tad-Demm u l-Laham (short stories) 1968, Hala taz-Zghozija (short stories) 1970, Anatomija (short stories) 1978, Iz-Zewgt Ihbieb (short stories) 1979, Stqarrija (verses) 1979, Il-Halliel (short stories) 1979, Rivoluzzjoni do minore (novel) 1980, Jien Nimxi Wahdi (verses) 1987, Mal-Hmura tas-silla (short stories) 1993, Fejn Jixrob il-Qasab fis-sajf (short stories) 1996, Stejjer ghal Valentina (short stories) 1997, Ghaliex ix-Xewk (verses) 1998, Honourable People (short stories), Moods and Angles (collected articles) 1998, A Gentle Child 2004, Meta Jdellel il Qamar (short stories) 2005, Jien u Ghaddej fil-Politika (autobiog.) 2007, Island Faces 2011. *Leisure interests:* listening to other people's views, reading, writing. *Address:* 246, "Aurora", Triq Il-Linja, H'Attard, ATD 1232, Malta (home). *Telephone:* 21239894 (office); 21435089 (home). *Fax:* 21221076 (office). *E-mail:* linospiteri@bortexgroup.com (office); lspiteri@onvol.net (home).

SPITLER, Kenneth F., BA; American business executive; *Vice-Chairman, President and Chief Operating Officer, SYSCO Corporation;* b. 1949; ed Univ. of Tulsa; joined SYSCO Corpn 1986, Exec. Vice-Pres., Dallas 1986–92, Pres., Detroit 1992–95, Pres. and CEO, Houston 1995–2000, Sr Vice-Pres. of Operations, NE Region 2000–02, Exec. Vice-Pres. Redistribution and NE Region 2002–02, Exec. Vice-Pres. Foodservice Operations 2002–05, Exec. Vice-Pres. and Pres. N American Foodservice Operations 2005–07, Pres. and CEO 2007–09, Vice-Chair., Pres. and COO 2009–. *Address:* Sysco Corpn, 1390 Enclave Parkway, Houston, TX 77077-2099, USA (office). *Telephone:* (281) 584-1390 (office). *Fax:* (281) 584-2721 (office). *E-mail:* info@sysco.com (office). *Website:* www.sysco.com (office).

SPITZ, Lewis, MB, ChB, PhD, FRCS, FRCSE; British paediatric surgeon and academic; *Nuffield Professor Emeritus of Paediatric Surgery, Institute of Child Health, University College London;* b. 25 Aug. 1939, Pretoria, S Africa; s. of Woolf Spitz and Selma Spitz; m.; one s. one d.; ed Univ. of Pretoria, Univ. of the Witwatersrand; Consultant Paediatric Surgeon, Sheffield 1974–79; Nuffield Prof. of Paediatric Surgery, Inst. of Child Health, University Coll. London 1979–2004, Nuffield Prof. Emer. of Paediatric Surgery 2004–, Hon. Fellow, Inst. of Child Health; Consultant Paediatric Surgeon, Great Ormond St Hosp. for Children, London 1979–2006; Hunterian Prof., Royal Coll. of Surgeons (England) 2001–02; Hon. Fellow, American Acad. of Pediatrics, Royal Coll. of Surgeons in Ireland, Coll. of medicine, SA, Royal Coll. of Paediatrics and Child Health, American Coll. of Surgeons; Hon. MD (Sheffield) 2002, (Univ. of the Witwatersrand, South Africa) 2008; James Spence Medal, Royal Coll. of Paediatrics 2004, Clement-Price Thomas Award, Royal Coll. of Surgeons (England) 2004, Denis Browne Gold Medal, British Asscn of Paediatric Surgeons 2004, Rehbein Medal, German Assscn of Pediatric Surgeons, Rehbein Medal, European Assscn of Pediatric Surgeons, Ladd Medal, American Acad. of Pediatrics. *Publication:* Paediatric Surgical Diagnosis (co-ed. with M. Steiner and R. B. Zachary) 1981, Pediatric Surgery (co-ed. with A. G. Coran) 1995 (revised edn 2013), Great Ormond Street Colour Handbook of Paediatrics and Child Health: Papers on Oesophageal Atresia and Replacement and Conjoined Twins (co-ed. with S. Strobel, S. D. Marks, P. K. Smith, M. H. El-Habbal) 2007. *Leisure interests:* sport, food, drink. *Address:* Institute of Child Health, 30 Guilford Street, London, WC1N 1EH (office); 78 Wood Vale, London, N10 3DN, England (home). *Telephone:* (20) 8444-9985 (home). *E-mail:* l.spitz@ucl .ac.uk (office).

SPITZ, Mark (Andrew); American fmr swimmer; b. 10 Feb. 1950, Modesto, Calif.; s. of Arnold Spitz; m. Suzy Weiner; two s.; ed Indiana Univ.; won two gold medals in the team relay races (4×100m and 4×200m), Olympic Games, Mexico City 1968; became first athlete to win seven gold medals in a single Olympic Games, Munich 1972, in the 100m and 200m freestyle, 100m and 200m butterfly and as a team mem. of the 4×100m relay, 4×200m relay and 4×100m medley relay (all world records); unsuccessful comeback 1991; corporate spokesman, TV broadcaster, real-estate co. owner, now works as stock broker; mem. Int. Swimming Hall of Fame Selection Cttee; World Swimmer of the Year 1969, 1971, 1972, James E. Sullivan Award (for America's Outstanding Amateur Athlete) 1971, Associated Press Male Athlete of the Year 1972, Athlete of the Century (Water Sports) 1999; mem. Laureus World Sports Acad. *Leisure interests:* sailing, travel. *Address:* c/o Laura Cutler, Corporate Communications, Premier Management Group, LLC, 200 Merry Hill Drive, Cary, NC 27511, USA (office). *Telephone:* (919) 363-5105 (office). *E-mail:* laura@pmgsports.com (office). *Website:* www.markspitzusa.com (office).

SPITZER, Eliot Laurence, BA, JD; American lawyer, broadcaster, fmr government official and fmr politician; b. 10 June 1959; m. Silda Spitzer (née Wall); three d.; ed Princeton Univ. and Harvard Law School; fmr Ed. Harvard Law Review; Law Clerk for Hon. Robert W. Sweet, US Dist Court, Southern Dist of New York 1984–85; Assoc. Paul Weiss, Rifkind, Wharton & Garrison 1985–86; Asst Dist Attorney, Manhattan 1986–92, Chief Labor Racketeering Unit 1991–92; Assoc.

Skadden, Arps, Slate, Meagher & Flom 1992–94; Pnr, Constantine & Partners 1994–98; Attorney-Gen. of State of New York 1999–2007; columnist, Slate (online magazine) 2008–; Gov. of New York 2007–08 (resgnd); adjunct faculty mem. CUNY 2009–; Host, CNN's In the Arena (fmrly Parker Spitzer) 2010–11; Host, Viewpoint with Eliot Spitzer (Current TV) 2012–13; unsuccessful cand. for New York City Comptroller 2013; Democrat; named one of World's Most Influential People by Time magazine 2005; Paul H. Douglas Ethics in Govt Award, Univ. of Illinois 2004, Jacob J. Javits Public Service Award, American Psychiatric Assen 2005.

SPIVAK, Gayatri Chakravorty, MA, PhD; Indian literary theorist, academic and rural literacy and ecological agriculture activist; *University Professor, Columbia University;* b. 24 Feb. 1942, Kolkata; m. 1st Talbot Spivak (divorced); m. 2nd Basudeb Chatterji (divorced); ed Univ. of Calcutta, Univ. of Cambridge, Cornell Univ.; Asst Prof., then Prof. of Comparative Literature, Iowa Univ. 1965–77; Prof., Univ. of Texas 1978–83; Longstreet Prof. of English, Emory Univ. 1983–86; Andrew W. Mellon Prof. of English, Univ. of Pittsburgh 1986–91; Avalon Foundation Prof. in the Humanities, Columbia Univ., New York 1991–2007, Univ. Prof. 2007–, Dir Inst. for Comparative Literature and Soc. 2002–08; Visiting Prof., Brown Univ., Univ. of Texas, Univ. of California, Santa Cruz, Berkeley, Irvine, Université Paul Valery, Jawaharlal Nehru Univ., Stanford Univ., Univ. of British Columbia, Goethe Inst., Frankfurt, Riydah Univ.; Y.K. Pao Distinguished Visiting Prof. in Cultural Studies, Hong Kong Univ. of Science and Tech. 2001; translated the work of French philosopher Jacques Derrida 1976, Bengali writer Mahasweta Devi 2003; Distinguished Faculty Fellow, Maharaja Sayajirao Univ. of Baroda, India; fmr Fellow, Nat. Humanities Inst., Center for the Humanities at Wesleyan, Humanities Research Center, ANU, Canberra, Australia, Centre for the Study of the Social Sciences, Kolkata, Davis Center for Historial Studies, Princeton Univ., Rockefeller Foundation, Bellagio, Guggenheim Foundation; mem. Editorial Bd Cultural Critique, Diaspora, ARIEL, Re-thinking Marxism, Public Culture, Parallax, Interventions, etc.; mem. Global Agenda Council on Values, World Econ. Forum; Hon. PhD (Univ. of Toronto) 2000, (Univ. of London) 2003, Hon. DH (Oberlin Coll.) 2008; Guggenheim Fellowship, Sahitya Akademi Translation Prize, India 1997. *Publications include:* Myself I Must Remake: The Life and Poetry of W. B. Yeats 1974, Of Grammatology (trans. of Jacques Derrida) 1976, In Other Worlds: Essays in Cultural Politics 1987, Selected Subaltern Studies (co-ed.) 1988, The Post-Colonial Critic: Interviews, Strategies, Dialogues 1990, Outside in the Teaching Machine 1993, The Spivak Reader 1996, Don't Call Me Post-Colonial: From Kant to Kawakubo 1998, A Critique of Post-Colonial Reason: Toward a History of the Vanishing Present 1999, Death of a Discipline 2003, Other Asias 2005, An Aesthetic Education in the Era of Globalization 2012; chapters in books and articles in professional journals. *Address:* 602 Philosophy Hall, MC 4927, Columbia University, New York, NY 10027, USA (office). *Telephone:* (212) 851-0231 (office). *E-mail:* gcspiv@gmail.com (office). *Website:* www.columbia.edu/cu/english (office).

SPIVAKOV, Vladimir Teodorovich; Russian violinist and conductor; *Artistic Director and Principal Conductor, National Philharmonic of Russia;* b. 12 Sept. 1944, Ufa, Bashkortostan; m. Satinik Saakyants; three d.; ed Moscow State Conservatory, postgraduate with Yury Yankelevich; studied violin since age of six with B. Kroger in Leningrad; prize winner in several int. competitions including Tchaikovsky, Moscow; Founder and Conductor Chamber Orchestra Virtuosi of Moscow 1979–; Founder and Artistic Dir Music Festival in Colmar, France 1989–; Artistic Dir and Chief Conductor Russian Nat. Symphony Orchestra 1999–2003; Founder, Artistic Dir and Prin. Conductor Nat. Philharmonic of Russia 2003–; Guest Conductor of several orchestras including Chicago Symphony Orchestra, LA Philharmonic, London Symphony Orchestra, English and Scottish Chamber Orchestras; f. Int. Charity Foundation 1994; Les Insignes de Chevalier de la Légion d'Honneur 1994; USSR State Prize 1989, USSR People's Artist 1990, Triumph Prize, Nat. Cultural Heritage Award, Russia's Artist of the Year 2002, First Prize Montreal Competition, Marguerite Long St Jacques Thibaud Competition, Paris, Nicolo Paganini Int. Violin Competition, Genoa, Int. Tchaikovsky Competition, Moscow. *Recordings:* more than 20 CDs on Capriccio, RCA Victor Red Seal and BMG Classics including works by Brahms, Berg, Chausson, Franck, Prokoviev, Ravel, Tchaikovsky, Richard Strauss, Schubert, Sibelius, Shostakovich. *Leisure interest:* collecting paintings. *Address:* c/o Columbia Artists Management, 1790 Broadway, New York, NY 10019, USA; National Philharmonic of Russia, Moscow 115054, Office 208, 52/8 Kosmodamianskaya Embankment; Vspolny per. 17, Apt 14, Moscow, Russia. *Telephone:* (495) 290-23-24 (Moscow); 1-45-25-50-85 (Paris); (495) 730-1367 (Nat. Philharmonic). *Fax:* 1-45-25-04-60 (Paris); (495) 730-3778 (Nat. Philharmonic). *Website:* www.nfor.ru/eng.

SPOERRI, Philip, PhD; Swiss lawyer and international organization executive; *Director for International Law and Co-operation within the Movement, International Committee of the Red Cross;* b. 1963, Zurich; m.; one s.; ed Göttingen, Munich and Bielefeld Univs, Geneva Univ., Switzerland; worked as lawyer in pvt. firm in Munich; began career with ICRC in 1994, carried out first mission for ICRC in Israel (Occupied Territories), continued with missions in Kuwait and Yemen, Afghanistan and Democratic Repub. of Congo, headed legal advisers to Dept of Operations, Geneva, returned to Afghanistan as Head of Del. 2004–06, Dir for Int. Law and Co-operation within the Movt 2006–. *Address:* International Committee of the Red Cross, 9 avenue de la Paix, 1202 Geneva, Switzerland (office). *Telephone:* (22) 734-60-01 (office). *Fax:* (22) 733-20-57 (office). *E-mail:* press.gva@icrc.org (office). *Website:* www.icrc.org (office).

SPOGLI, Ronald P., AB, MBA; American investment banker and fmr diplomatist; *Partner, Freeman Spogli & Co.;* b. 1948, Los Angeles, Calif.; m. Georgia Spogli; one d. one step-s.; ed Stanford Univ., Harvard Business School; researcher, Stanford Univ. based in Milan, Italy 1972–73; fmr Man. Dir Investment Banking Div. Dean Witter Reynolds Inc.; Co-founder and Partner, Freeman Spogli & Co. (pvt. equity firm) 1983–; Amb. to Italy 2005–09 (also accred to San Marino 2006–09); apptd to US State Dept's Fulbright Foreign Scholarship Bd 2002; mem. Bd of Visitors, Stanford Univ.'s Inst. for Int. Studies 2000–; mem. Bd AFC Enterprises, Regents Bancshares, Winebow. *Address:* Freeman Spogli & Co., 11100 Santa Monica Boulevard, Suite 1900, Los Angeles, CA 90025 USA (office). *Telephone:* (310) 444-1822 (office). *Fax:* (310) 444-1870 (office). *E-mail:* info@freemanspogli.com (office). *Website:* www.freemanspogli.com (office).

SPONG, Rt Rev. John Shelby, AB, MDiv; American ecclesiastic and writer; b. 16 June 1931, Charlotte, NC; s. of John Shelby Spong and Doolie Griffith Spong; m. 1st Joan Lydia Ketner 1952 (died 1988); three d.; m. 2nd Christine Mary Bridger 1990; ed Univ. of North Carolina, Virginia Theological Seminary; Rector, St Joseph's, Durham, NC 1955–57, Calvary Church, Tarboro, NC 1957–65, St John's Church, Lynchburg, Va 1965–69, St Paul's Church, Richmond, Va 1969–76, Bishop, Diocese of Newark, NJ 1976–2000; Pres. NJ Council of Churches; Quatercentenary Fellow, Emmanuel Coll. Cambridge, UK 1992; William Belden Noble Lecturer, Harvard Univ. 2000; Visiting Lecturer, Univ. of The Pacific, Stockton, Calif. 2003; mem. of Faculty, Grad. Theological Union, Berkeley, Calif.; columnist, Beliefnet.com 1999–2000, AgoraMedia 2002–, Waterfront Media 2002–; Hon. DD (Virginia Theological Seminary), (St Paul's Coll.); Hon. DHL (Muhlenberg Coll.), (Holmes Inst., Chicago) 2004, (Univ. of North Carolina) 2007, (Lehigh Univ.) 2007, (Drew Univ.) 2010; Quartercentenary Scholar, Emmanuel Coll., Cambridge, UK 1992, David Frederick Strauss Award, Jesus Seminar 1999, Humanist of the Year, New York City 1999, John A. T, Robinson Award 2004, portrait hung in Hall of Honor in Martin Luther King Chapel, Morehead Coll., Atlanta, Ga for leadership in breaking the oppression of homosexual people 2010. *Radio:* Play by Play sportscaster in Tarboro NC and Lynchburg, Va 1960–65. *Publications include:* Honest Prayer 1973, This Hebrew Lord 1974, 1988, Dialogue: In Search of Jewish-Christian Understanding 1975, Christpower 1975, Life Approaches Death: A Dialogue on Medical Ethics 1976, The Living Commandments 1977, The Easter Moment 1980, Into the Whirlwind 1983, Beyond Moralism 1986, Consciousness and Survival 1987, Living in Sin? 1988, Rescuing the Bible from Fundamentalism 1991, Born of a Woman – A Bishop Rethinks the Virgin Birth and the Place of Women in a Male-Dominated Church 1992, Resurrection: Myth or Reality? 1994, Liberating the Gospels: Reading the Bible with Jewish Eyes 1996, Why Christianity Must Change or Die: A Bishop Speaks to Believers in Exile 1998, Here I Stand: My Struggle for a Christianity of Integrity, Love and Equality 2000, The Bishop's Voice 1999, A New Christianity for a New World 2001, Crossroads – The Sins of Scripture 2005, Eternal Life: A New Vision beyond Religion, Beyond Theism, Beyond Heaven and Hell 2009. *Leisure interests:* hiking, reading. *Address:* c/o Julie Rae Mitchell, HarperSanFrancisco, 353 Sacramento Street, Suite 500, San Francisco, CA, 94111, USA (office); 24 Puddingstone Road, Morris Plains, NJ 07950, USA (home). *Telephone:* (973) 538-9825 (home). *Fax:* (973) 540-9584 (home). *E-mail:* johnsspong@aol.com (home); cmsctm@aol.com (home). *Website:* www.johnshelbyspong.com.

SPONHEIM, Lars, MSc; Norwegian politician; *Leader, Liberal Party;* b. 23 May 1957, Halden; m.; three c.; consultant 1981–84; teacher, Statens Gartnerskule Hjeltnes 1984–88, Prin. 1992–; mem. local council, Ulvik Municipality 1984–95, Mayor 1988–91; mem. County Council, Hordaland Co. 1992–93; Dir of Agric., Ulvik and Granvin Municipalities 1993; mem. Parl. for Hordaland Co. to Storting (Parl.) 1993–, mem. Parl. Finance Cttee; Leader Venstre (Liberal) Party 1996–; Minister of Trade and Industry 1997–2000; Minister of Food and Agric. 2001–05; mem. Parl. Foreign Cttee 2005–. *Address:* Venstre, Stortinget, 0026 Oslo, Norway. *Telephone:* 23-31-33-62 (office). *Fax:* 23-31-38-72 (office). *E-mail:* lars.sponheim@stortinget.no (office); lars@venstre.no (office). *Website:* www.venstre.no (office).

SPRATT, Sir Greville Douglas, Kt, GBE, TD, JP, DL, DLitt, FRSA, FRGS; British business executive (retd); b. 1 May 1927, Westcliff-on-Sea, Essex, England; s. of Hugh D. Spratt and Sheelah I. Stace; m. Sheila F. Wade 1954 (died 2002); three d.; ed Leighton Park, Charterhouse and Sandhurst; served Coldstream Guards 1945–46; Commissioned Oxfordshire and Bucks Light Infantry 1946; seconded to Arab Legion 1946–48; joined HAC Infantry Bn 1950, CO 1962–65, Regimental Col 1966–70, mem. Court of Assistants 1960–70 and 1978–95; ADC to HM The Queen 1973–78; Lloyd's of London 1948–61, Underwriting Mem. 1950–; Man. Dir J. & N. Wade group 1972–76; Liveryman, Ironmongers' Co. 1977–, Master 1995–96; Alderman, Castle Baynard Ward 1978–95; Sheriff of City of London 1984–85; Lord Mayor of London 1987–88; Chancellor, City Univ. 1987–88; Dir Williams Lea Group, Craigie Taylor Int. Ltd; Chair. Governing Body, Charterhouse 1989–95; Chair. Forest Mere Ltd, Charterhouse Enterprises Ltd. 1992–95, Action Research for the Crippled Child 1989–99; Claremont and Kingsmead Underwriting Agency 1994–99; Regional Chair. Nat. Westminster Bank 1992–93; Vice-Pres. British Red Cross 1993–, Greater London TAVRA 1994–; holder of numerous civic, educational and charitable positions; Trustee Chichester Theatre and Cathedral; Hon. Col London Army Cadet Force 1983–98, Queen's Fusiliers 1988–92, London Regt 1992–95; Légion d'honneur, Ordre nat. du Mérite (France); Commdr Order of Lion (Malawi), Order of Aztec Eagle (Mexico), Order of Olav (Norway), Order of Merit (Senegal); KStJ; Hon. DLitt (City Univ.) 1988. *Leisure interests:* tennis, music, mil. history; stamp, coin and bank-note collecting.

SPRING, Richard (Dick), BA, BL; Irish business executive and fmr politician; *Executive Vice-Chairman, Fexco Ltd;* b. 29 Aug. 1950, Tralee, Co. Kerry; s. of Dan Spring and Anna Laide; m. Kristi Lee Hutcheson 1977; two s. one d.; ed Mount St Joseph Coll., Roscrea, Co. Tipperary, Trinity Coll. Dublin, King's Inns, Dublin; mem. Dáil Éireann (House of Reps) for Kerry North 1981–2002; Leader of Labour Party 1982–97; Tanaiste (Deputy Prime Minister) 1982–87 and Minister for the Environment 1982–83, for Energy 1983–87, Tanaiste and Minister for Foreign Affairs 1993–97; Chair. Gulliver Ireland; Exec. Vice-Chair. Fexco 2002–; Dir Realta (Irish Global HIV/AIDS Foundation); chair. or dir numerous public and pvt. cos; fmr Irish rugby union int.; Assoc. Fellow, Kennedy School of Govt, Harvard Univ. 1998–; Fellow, Salzburg Seminar 1998; mem. Council on Foreign Relations; Dr hc (Hartwick Coll., New York) 1998, (Misericordia Coll., Pennsylvania) 1999. *Leisure interests:* sport, reading, golf, swimming. *Address:* Fexco Ltd, 12 Ely Place, Dublin 2 (office); Fexco Ltd, Iveragh Road, Killorglin, Ireland (office). *Telephone:* (1) 6611800 (Dublin) (office); (66) 9761258 (Killorglin) (office); (87) 2391200 (mobile) (home). *E-mail:* dspring@fexco.com (office). *Website:* www.fexco.com (office).

SPRINGER, Timothy Alan, BA, PhD; American immunologist and academic; *Latham Family Professor of Pathology, Harvard Medical School;* b. 23 Feb. 1948, Fort Benning, Ga; ed Univ. of California, Berkeley, Harvard Univ., Mass; Biochemistry 10 Teaching Asst, Harvard Univ. 1972–74, Biochemistry 111 Teaching Asst 1974–75; NIH Research Fellow, Univ. of Cambridge, UK and MRC Lab. of Molecular Biology, Cambridge 1976–77; Asst Prof., Harvard Medical

School 1977–83, Assoc. Prof. 1983–89, Latham Family Prof. of Pathology 1989–, mem. Faculty Council, Harvard Univ. 1996–; Chief of Lab. of Membrane Immunochemistry, Dana Farber Cancer Inst. 1981–88; Vice-Pres. Center for Blood Research 1988–92; Councillor, Int. Leukocyte Workshop 1989–; mem. Scientific Review Bd, Howard Hughes Medical Inst. 1996–2000; Overseer, Bd of Overseers, CBR Inst. for Biomedical Research, Inc. 2002–; Visiting Prof., Univ. of Michigan 1990; Wellcome Visiting Prof., Wayne State Univ. 1997; consultant, Boehringer-Ingelheim 1989–95, LeukoSite, Inc. (Founder and Chair. Scientific Advisory Bd) 1992–99, Scientific Advisory Bd, Molecular Applications Group, Inc. 1997–, Millennium Pharmaceuticals 1999–2001, Sunesis Pharmaceuticals 2003–; Scientific Advisor, Canadian Vaccines and Immunotherapeutics Network 2001; Assoc. Ed. Journal of Immunology 1981–85, Molecular Biology of the Cell 1992–96; Advisory Ed. Journal of Experimental Medicine 1985–95; mem. Editorial Bd, Hybridoma 1981–, Regional Immunology 1988–, Cellular Immunology 1988–93, Journal of Clinical Immunology 1988–92, New Biologist 1989–92, Cell Regulation (Molecular Biology of the Cell) 1989–92, Immunological Reviews 1996–2001; mem. American Asscn of Immunologists 1979– (mem. Nomination Cttee 1993), Reticuloendothelial Soc. 1981–94 (Membership Chair. 1986, Chair. Program Cttee 1989), American Soc. of Biological Chemists 1982–, American Asscn of Pathologists 1989–, Soc. for Leukocyte Biology 1995–, NAS 1996– (Chair. Section 29, Biophysics and Computational Biology 2004–07); Fellow, American Acad. of Arts and Sciences 2001–; Nat. Merit Scholar 1966, Biochemistry Departmental Citation (awarded to most outstanding grad.) 1971, American Cancer Soc. Jr Faculty Research Award 1981, American Cancer Soc. Faculty Research Award 1984, NIH MERIT Grant Award 1988, 2004, Distinguished Lectureship, Vanderbilt School of Medicine 1992, American Heart Asscn Basic Research Prize 1993, Royal Soc. of Medicine Medal and Visiting Prof., UK 1994, William B. Coley Medal for Distinguished Research in Fundamental Immunology, Cancer Research Inst. 1995, Marie T. Bonazinga Award for Excellence in Leukocyte Biology Research, Soc. for Leukocyte Biology 1995, Crafoord Prize in Polyarthritis, Royal Swedish Acad. of Sciences (co-recipient) 2004, Fellowship, John Simon Guggenheim Memorial Foundation 2004. *Publications:* numerous scientific papers in professional journals on adhesion receptors of the immune system. *Address:* The CBR Institute for Biomedical Research, Inc., 200 Longwood Avenue, Room 251, Boston, MA 02115, USA (office). *Telephone:* (617) 278-3200 (office). *Fax:* (617) 278-3232 (office). *E-mail:* springer@cbr.med.harvard.edu (office). *Website:* www.cbrinstitute .org/labs/springer/tim_cv.html (office).

SPRINGSTEEN, Bruce; American singer, songwriter and musician (guitar); b. 23 Sept. 1949, Freehold, NJ; s. of Douglas Springsteen and Adele Springsteen; m. 1st Julianne Phillips 1985 (divorced 1990); m. 2nd Patti Scialfa 1991; two s. one d.; ed community coll.; performed in New York and NJ nightclubs; solo artist 1972–; numerous tours of USA and Europe; formed backing group the E-Street Band 1974; Grammy Award for Best Male Vocalist 1984, 1987, for Best Rock Performance by a Duo (jtly) 2004, BRIT Award for Best Int. Solo Artist 1986, Acad. Award for Best Original Song in a Film (for Streets of Philadelphia) 1994, MTV Best Video from a Film Award (for Streets of Philadelphia) 1994, Grammy Awards for Best Solo Rock Vocal Performance (for Devils & Dust) 2006, (for Radio Nowhere) 2008, (for Working on a Dream) 2010, for Best Rock Instrumental Performance (for Once Upon a Time in the West) 2008, for Best Rock Song (for Radio Nowhere) 2008, (for Girls in Their Summer Clothes) 2009, Golden Globe Award for Best Original Song (for The Wrestler) 2009, Kennedy Center Honor 2009. *Recordings include:* albums: Greetings from Asbury Park, New Jersey 1973, The Wild, The Innocent And The E-Street Shuffle 1973, Born To Run 1975, Darkness On The Edge Of Town 1978, The River 1980, Nebraska 1982, Born In The USA 1984, Bruce Springsteen And The E Street Band Live 1975–85 1986, Tunnel Of Love 1987, Chimes of Freedom 1988, Human Touch 1992, Lucky Town 1992, The Ghost Of Tom Joad 1995, The Rising (Grammy Award for Best Rock Album 2003) 2002, Roll Of The Dice 2003, Devils & Dust 2005, We Shall Overcome: The Seeger Sessions (Grammy Award for Best Traditional Folk Album 2007) 2006, Magic 2007, Working on a Dream 2009, Wrecking Ball 2012, High Hopes 2014. *Address:* Premier Talent Agency, 3 East 54th Street, New York, NY 10022, USA (office). *Website:* www.brucespringsteen.net.

SPRÜTH, Monika; German art gallery owner; Co-owner (with Philomene Magers) of Sprüth Magers galleries for contemporary art; opened gallery in Cologne 1983, London 2003, Berlin 2008. *Address:* Sprüth Magers, Hebbelstraße 93, 50968 Cologne (office); Sprüth Magers Berlin, Oranienburger Straße 18, 10178 Berlin, Germany (office); Sprüth Magers London, 7A Grafton Street, London, W1S 4EJ, England (office). *E-mail:* info@spruethmagers.com (office). *Website:* www .spruethmagers.com (office); spruethmagers.net (office).

SPUDICH, James A., BS, PhD; American biochemist and academic; *Douglass M. and Nola Leishman Professor of Cardiovascular Disease, Stanford University;* b. Benld, Ill.; m. Annamma (Anna) Spudich; two d.; ed Univ. of Illinois, Stanford Univ., Univ. of Cambridge, UK; Asst Prof., Dept of Biochemistry and Biophysics, Univ. of California, San Francisco 1971–74, Assoc. Prof. 1974–76, Prof. 1976–77; Prof., Dept of Structural Biology, Stanford Univ. School of Medicine 1977–92, Chair. 1979–84, Prof., Dept of Developmental Biology 1989–2011, Prof., Dept of Biochemistry 1992–, Chair. 1994–98, Douglass M. and Nola Leishman Prof. of Cardiovascular Disease 1987–, Co-founder and first Dir Interdisciplinary Program in Bioengineering, Biomedicine and Biosciences – Bio-X Stanford Univ. 1998–2002; Adjunct Faculty mem., Nat. Centre for Biological Sciences, Tata Inst. of Fundamental Research, Bangalore, India 2005–; Monitoring Ed., Proceedings of the National Academy of Sciences, USA 2000–; Ed. Cell 2009–; Co-founder Cytokinetics Inc., San Francisco; Pres. American Soc. for Cell Biology 1999; mem. NAS 1991; External Scientific mem. Max Planck Inst. for Biochemistry, Martinsried, Germany; Fellow, American Academy of Arts and Sciences 1997, AAAS 2001; Newhouse Foundation Fellow 1965–67, Dreyfus Teaching and Research Scholar 1976–77, Guggenheim Fellow 1978, Basic Research Prize, American Heart Asscn 1991, Alexander von Humboldt Research Award 1991, NIH Merit Award1991, Lifetime Research Career Award, Biophysical Soc. 1995, Lewis S. Rosenstiel Award for Outstanding Research Achievement in Field of Basic Medical Studies 1996, 1997 Repligen Award for Chem. of Biological Processes, ACS Div. of Biological Chem. 1996, Award for Outstanding Investigator in Field of Single Molecule Biology, Biophysics Soc. 2005 E.B. Wilson Medal, American Soc. for Cell Biology 2011, Albert Lasker Basic Medical Research Award (co-recipient)

2012. *Publications:* book chapters, reviews and more than 190 papers in professional journals. *Leisure interests:* flying small planes. *Address:* Spudich Lab, Department of Biochemistry, Beckman Center B405, Stanford, CA 94305-5307, USA (office). *Telephone:* (650) 723-7634 (office); (650) 723-6201 (office). *E-mail:* jspudich@stanford.edu (office). *Website:* med.stanford.edu/profiles/devbio/ faculty/James_Spudich (office); spudlab.stanford.edu (office).

SPURDZIŅŠ, Oskars; Latvian government official; b. 22 Aug. 1963, Aizpute; m.; two c.; ed Aizpute Secondary School, Univ. of Latvia; Chair. Deputies' Council and Bd Valmiera City Council 1990–94; consultant Latvian Asscn of Local Self-Govts 1994; Adviser, Ministry of Finance 1994–96; Adviser, Admin of Local Govt Affairs 1996–97; Man. Municipal Projects, Latvian Environmental Investment Fund 1997–99; Parl. Sec., Ministry of Educ. and Science 1999–2000, Ministry of Finance 2000–02, 2004–07; mem. 7th Saeima (Parl., People's Party, TP) 1999–2002; Project Man. Hipoteku Banka 2002–04. *Address:* People's Party, Basteja Bulvāris 1, Rīga 1050, Latvia (office). *Telephone:* 750-8808 (office). *Fax:* 750-8684 (office). *E-mail:* maija@tautaspartija.lv (office). *Website:* www.tautaspartija.lv (office).

SPYROU, Nicholas M., PhD; British physicist and academic; *Professor of Radiation and Medical Physics and Chairman of Medical Physics, University of Surrey;* currently Prof. of Radiation and Medical Physics and Chair. of Medical Physics, Univ. of Surrey, Dir for MSc Course in Medical Physics and BSc course in Physics with Medical Physics; mem. numerous int. cttees, including Int. Cttee of Activation Analysis, Nat. Health Group Knowledge Group-Network; Exec. mem. Biology and Medicine Div., American Nuclear Soc.; Hevesy Medal, Journal of Radioanalytical and Nuclear Chemistry 2005. *Publications:* more than 220 scientific publs. *Address:* Room 05BC04, School of Electronics and Physical Sciences, University of Surrey, Guildford, GU2 7XH, England (office). *Telephone:* (1483) 686802 (office). *Fax:* (1483) 686781 (office). *E-mail:* n.spyrou@surrey.ac.uk (office). *Website:* www.ph.surrey.ac.uk (office).

SQUIRE, Air Chief Marshal Sir Peter (Ted), GCB, DFC, AFC, DL, DSc, FRAeS; British air force officer; b. 7 Oct. 1945, Felixstowe, Suffolk, England; s. of the late Wing Commdr Frank Squire, DSO, DFC and Margaret Pascoe Squire (née Trump); m. Carolyn Joynson 1970; three s.; ed King's School, Bruton; with 20 Squadron, Singapore 1968–70, 4 FTS, Anglesey 1970–73, 3 (F) Squadron, Germany 1975–78; OC 1(F) Squadron 1981–83; Personal Staff Officer to Air Officer Commdg-in-Chief, Strike Command 1984–86; Station Commdr, RAF Cottesmore 1986–88; Dir Air Offensive 1989–91; SASO, RAF Strike Command 1991–93; Air Officer Commdg No. 1 Group 1993–94; ACAS 1994–96, DCDS (Programmes and Personnel), Ministry of Defence 1996–99; Air Officer Commdg-in-Chief, Strike Command and Commdr Allied Air Forces Northwestern Europe 1999–2000; Air ADC to HM The Queen 1999–2003; Chief of the Air Staff 2000–03; Commr Commonwealth War Graves Comm. 2003–08, Vice-Chair. 2005–08; Trustee, Imperial War Museum 2001–11 (Deputy Chair. 2004–06, Chair. 2006–11), American Air Museum in Britain 2002– (Pres. 2006–); Sr Warden King's School, Bruton 2004–11; Pres. Air Training Corps (Devon and Somerset) 2011–. *Leisure interests:* golf, cricket, gardening. *Address:* c/o National Westminster Bank, 5 South Street, Wincanton, Somerset, BA9 9DJ, England.

SQUYRES, Steven W., BA, PhD; American astronomer and academic; *Goldwin Smith Professor of Astronomy, Cornell University;* b. 1957, Wenonah, NJ; ed Gateway Regional High School, Woodbury Heights, NJ, Cornell Univ., Ithaca, NY; Postdoctoral Assoc. and Research Scientist at NASA Ames Research Center 1981–86; returned as faculty mem. to Cornell Univ. 1986, currently Goldwin Smith Prof. of Astronomy; has participated in several planetary space flight missions; Assoc. of Voyager imaging science team 1978–81, participated in analysis of imaging data from encounters with Jupiter and Saturn; radar investigator on Magellan mission to Venus; mem. Mars Observer gamma-ray spectrometer flight investigation team; co-investigator on Russian Mars '96 mission; currently Scientific Prin. Investigator for Mars Exploration Rover Project; co-investigator on Mars Express mission 2003, Mars Reconnaissance Orbiter's High Resolution Imaging Science Experiment 2005; mem. Gamma-Ray Spectrometer Flight Investigation Team for Mars Odyssey mission, imaging team for Cassini mission to Saturn; fmr Chair. NASA Space Science Advisory Cttee; mem. NASA Advisory Council; H.C. Urey Prize, Planetary Div. of American Astronomical Soc. 1987, ABC News Person of the Week 9 Jan. 2004, Carl Sagan Memorial Award 2004, World Tech. Award in Space, The World Tech. Network 2005, Wired Rave Award for Science for overseeing creation of Spirit and Opportunity that had, at the time, lasted 13 times longer than expected (1174 vs 90 martian days) 2005, Benjamin Franklin Medal in Earth and Environmental Science, Franklin Inst. 2007. *Publications:* Roving Mars: Spirit, Opportunity, and the Exploration of the Red Planet 2005; numerous scientific papers in professional journals on planetary sciences. *Address:* 428 Space Sciences Building, Cornell University, Ithaca, NY 14853, USA (office). *Telephone:* (607) 255-3508 (office). *Fax:* (607) 255-6918 (office). *E-mail:* squyres@astro.cornell.edu (office). *Website:* www.astro.cornell.edu (office).

ŠRAMKO, Ivan; Slovak fmr central banker and diplomatist; *Adviser on Central and Southeastern European operations, Intesa Sanpaolo SpA;* b. 3 Sept. 1957, Bratislava; m.; three c.; ed Univ. of Econs, Bratislava; worked in finance depts in several cos 1981–90; Deputy Dir VUB-ING Banking Co. 1990–91; Head VUB-Credit Lyonnais joint venture task force 1991–92; Gen. Man., then Deputy Chair., then Chair., Istrobanka 1992–98; Man. Tatra Banka 1998–2000, mem. Bd of Dirs 2000–02; Deputy Gov. Nat. Bank of Slovakia (Národná banka Slovenska) 2002–04, Gov. 2005–10; Amb. and Perm. Rep. to OECD, Paris, France 2010–11; Adviser on central and southeastern European operations, Intesa Sanpaolo SpA 2011–; mem. Gen. Council of European Cen. Bank 2009–10; Gov. IMF 2005–10; Alt. Gov. EBRD 2005–10; mem. Bd Slovak-Austrian Chamber of Commerce 1998; Chair. Man. Bd Univ. of Econs, Bratislava 2003–; Banker magazine European Central Banker of the Year 2006, Emerging Markets (newspaper) Central Bank Governor of the Year 2006, 2008. *Address:* Intesa Sanpaolo SpA., Piazza San Carlo 156, 10121 Turin, Italy (office). *Telephone:* (01) 15551 (office). *Fax:* (21) 28092124 (office). *E-mail:* info@intesasanpaolo.com (office). *Website:* www.intesasanpaolo.com (office).

SREEDHARAN, E.; Indian engineer; *Managing Director, Delhi Metro Rail Corporation;* b. 12 June 1932, Palakkad, Kerala; ed Basel Evangelical Mission Higher Secondary School, Victoria Coll., Palghat, Govt Eng Coll., Kakinada; Lecturer in Civil Eng, Govt Polytechnic, Kozhikode; Apprentice, Bombay Port

Trust; joined Indian Railways, Probationary Asst Engineer, Southern Railway 1954, eventually man. of numerous projects including implementation, planning and design for Kolkata Metro, retired 1990; Chair. and Man. Dir (on contract) Konkan Railway 1990; Man. Dir Delhi Metro Rail Corpn 2005–; mem. Advisory Bd Foundation for Restoration of National Values; Chevalier de la Légion d'Honneur 2005; Hon. DSc (Indian Inst. of Tech., Delhi), Hon. DLit (Rajasthan Tech. Univ.) 2009; Railway Minister's Award 1963, Padma Shri 2001, Man of the Year, The Times of India 2002, Shri Om Prakash Bhasin Award 2002, Juror's Award, Confed. of Indian Industry 2002-03, One of Asia's Heroes, TIME magazine 2003, All India Man. Asscn Award 2003, Bharat Shiromani Award, Shiromani Inst., Chandigarh 2005, CNN-IBN Indian of the Year 2007 (Public Service) 2008, Padma Vibhushan 2008. *Leisure interests:* yoga, reading the Bhagavad Gita. *Address:* Metro Bhawan, Fire Brigade Lane, Barakhamba Road, New Delhi 110 001, India (office). *Telephone:* (11) 23417910 (office). *Fax:* (11) 23417921 (office). *Website:* www .delhimetrorail.com (office).

SRINIVASAN, Krishnan, MA; Indian diplomatist, scholar and author; *Azad Fellow, Maulana Azad Institute of Asian Studies;* b. 15 Feb. 1937, Madras; s. of the late Capt. C. Srinivasan and Rukmani Chari; m. Brinda Srinivasan 1975; one s.; ed Bedford School, Christ Church, Oxford, UK; Chargé d'affaires, Libya 1969–71; High Commr in Zambia (also accred to Botswana) 1974–77, in Nigeria (also accred to Benin and Cameroon) 1980–82, in Bangladesh 1989–92; Amb. to Netherlands 1986–89; Perm. Sec. Foreign Ministry 1992–94, Foreign Sec. 1994–95; Deputy Sec.-Gen. (Political) Commonwealth 1995–2002; Visiting Fellow, Wolfson Coll., Cambridge 2002–05, Centre of Int. Studies, Cambridge 2002–05; Sr Fellow, Inst. of Commonwealth Studies, Univ. of London 2002–05; Visiting Prof., ASCI, Hyderabad, 2004–, Maulana Azad Inst. of Asian Studies, Calcutta 2006–; Chair. Kolkata (India) to Kunming (China) Forum; Fellow, Netherlands Inst. of Advanced Study 2003–04, Swedish Collegium for Advanced Studies 2008, 2012–13; Hon. mem. Christ Church Sr Common Room and High Table; Hind Ratna (India) 2001, Chevalier (Cameroon) 2007; Ramsden Sermon, Univ. of Oxford 2002, Rajiv Gandhi Memorial Lecturer, Hyderabad 2006, DC Pavate Memorial Lecturer, Dharwar 2010. *Publications include:* Tricks of the Trade 2000, The Rise, Decline and Future of the British Commonwealth 2005, The Jamdani Revolution 2008, Towards the New Horizon: World Order in the 21st Century 2009, Diplomatic Channels 2012; several novels, short stories and articles on int. affairs. *Leisure interests:* reading, music, watching sports. *Address:* Flat 8, Courtleigh, 126 Earls Court Road, London, W8 6QL, England.

SSEKANDI, Edward Kiwanuka, LLB; Ugandan lawyer and politician; *Vice-President;* b. 19 Jan. 1943, Masaka Dist; m.; ed Univ. of East Africa, Law Devt Centre, Kampala,; Llecturer, Law Devt Centre 1973–78, Acting Dir 1978–79; Lead Counsel, Comm. of Inquiry into Violations of Human Rights 1986–93; del. to Constitutional Ass. (responsible for drafting new Ugandan constitution) 1994–95; MP for Bukoto Co. Cen. 1996–, Deputy Speaker of Parl. 1996–2001, Speaker 2001–11; Vice-Pres. of Uganda 2011–; mem. Nat. Resistance Movt. *Address:* Office of the Vice President, Parliament Bldg, POB 7168, Kampala, Uganda (office). *Telephone:* (41) 4258441 (office). *E-mail:* aak@statehouse.go.ug (office). *Website:* www.statehouse.go.ug (office).

SSEMOGERERE, Paul Kawanga, DipEd, MPA; Ugandan politician; b. 11 Feb. 1932, Bumangi Ssese Islands, Kalangala Dist; s. of Yozefu Kapere and Maria Lwiza Nakirya; m. Dr Germina N. Ssemogerere; one s. four d.; ed St Mary's Coll., Kisubu, Makerere Univ. and Syracuse Univ., USA; teacher 1959–60; Leader Democratic Party (DP) 1977–2005; Leader of Opposition in Nat. Ass. 1981–85; Minister of Internal Affairs 1986–88, Second Deputy Prime Minister and Minister of Foreign Affairs 1988–94, of the Public Service 1994, of Regional Co-operation 1989; Chair. OAU Council of Ministers 1993–94; Cand. in 1996 Presidential elections; mem. Bd of Migration Policy Group 1999–; Hon. LHD (Alleghony Coll., USA) 1989. *Publications:* two book chapters on democracy and human rights in Africa. *Leisure interests:* seminars on politics and economics, eco-tourism, human rights advocacy, farming. *Address:* 401 Streicher Road, Cathedral Lubaga-Kampala, P.O. Box 548, Kampala, Uganda (home). *Telephone:* (41) 344155 (home). *E-mail:* ssemo2@africaonline.com (home).

SSENDAULA, Gerald; Ugandan politician (retd); *Chairman, Board of Directors, Private Sector Foundation Uganda;* b. 1943; mem. Bd of Govs African Capacity Building Foundation (ACBF); fmr Gov. Bank of Uganda; Minister of Finance, Planning and Econ. Devt 1998–2005; Sr Presidential Adviser on Financial Affairs 2005–; Chair. Bd of Dirs Pvt. Sector Foundation Uganda 2008–. *Address:* Private Sector Foundation Uganda, Plot 43, Nakasero Hill Road, PO BOX 7683, Kampala, Uganda (office). *Telephone:* (31) 2263850 (office). *Fax:* (41) 259109 (office). *E-mail:* psfu@psfuganda.org.ug (office). *Website:* www.psfuganda.org.ug (office).

STAAB, Heinz A., Dr rer. nat, DrMed; German scientist and academic; *Professor Emeritus of Chemistry, University of Heidelberg;* b. 26 March 1926, Darmstadt; m. Dr. Ruth Müller 1953; one s. one d.; ed Univs of Marburg, Tübingen and Heidelberg; research assoc., Max Planck Inst., Heidelberg 1953–59; Asst Prof. of Chem., Univ. of Heidelberg 1956–61, Assoc. Prof. 1961–62, Prof. 1963–, now Prof. Emer.; Dir Inst. of Organic Chem., Univ. of Heidelberg 1964–74; Dir Max Planck Inst. for Medical Research 1974–; Pres. Max Planck Soc. for the Advancement of Science, Munich 1984–90; mem. German Science Council 1976–79; Senator, Deutsche Forschungsgemeinschaft 1976–82 and 1984–90; mem. Bd of Govs Weizmann Inst. of Science, Israel 1977–; Pres. Gesellschaft Deutscher Naturforscher und Ärzte 1981–82; Pres. German Chem. Soc. 1984–85; mem. Heidelberg Acad. of Sciences (Pres. 1994–96), Acad. Leopoldina, Academia Europaea; Corresp. mem. Austrian Acad. of Sciences 1988, Bavarian Acad. of Sciences 1991; Hon. Prof., Chinese Acad. of Sciences 1992; Foreign mem. Russian Acad. of Sciences 1994; Hon. mem. Senate Max-Planck Soc. 1990, German Chem. Soc. 1998, Hon. Fellow Indian Acad. of Sciences 1988; Hon. PhD (Weizmann Inst. of Science) 1984; Adolf von Baeyer Award (German Chem. Soc.) 1979. *Publications:* Einführung in die theoretische organische Chemie 1959 (translations), Azolides in Organic Synthesis and Biochemistry (co-author); about 370/400 publications in professional journals. *Leisure interests:* travel, history, classical music. *Address:* Max-Planck-Institut für Medizinische Forschung, Jahnstrasse 29, 69120 Heidelberg (office); Schlosswolfsbrunnenweg 43, 69118 Heidelberg, Germany (home). *Telephone:* (6221) 4860 (office); (6221) 803330 (home). *Fax:* (6221) 486585 (office).

E-mail: heinz.staab@mpimf-heidelberg.mpg.de (office). *Website:* www.chemgeo .uni-hd.de/indexengl (office).

STABENOW, Deborah (Debbie) Ann, BS, MSW; American politician; *Senator from Michigan;* b. 29 April 1950, Gladwin, Mich.; d. of Robert Lee Greer and Anna Merle Greer (née Hallmark); one s. one d.; ed Michigan State Univ.; with Special Services, Lansing School Dist 1972–73; Co. Commr Ingham Co., Mason, Mich. 1975–78; State Rep. for Mich., Lansing 1979–2002; mem. Agric. Cttee, Science Cttee 105th–106th Congress from 8th Mich. Dist; Senator from Mich. 2003–, Chair. Cttee on Agric., Nutrition, and Forestry, mem. Cttee on the Budget, Cttee on Energy and Natural Resources, Cttee on Finance; Founder Ingham Co. Women's Comm.; Co-founder Council Against Domestic Assault; mem. Democratic Business and Professional Club, Mich. Democratic Women's Political Caucus, Grance United Methodist Church (fmr lay preacher, Chair. Social Concerns Task Force, Sunday School Music teacher), Lansing Boys' Club, Professional Advisory Cttee Lansing Parents Without Partners, Advisory Cttee Center for Handicapped Affairs, Mich. Council Family and Divorce Mediation Advisory Bd, Nat. Council for Children's Rights, Big Brothers/Big Sisters Greater Lansing Advisory Bd, Mich. Child Study Asscn Bd Advisers, Mich. Women's Campaign Fund; mem. Nat. Asscn for the Advancement of Colored People (NAACP), Lansing Regional Chamber of Commerce; awards include Service to Children Award, Council for Prevention of Child Abuse and Neglect 1983, Outstanding Leadership Award, Nat. Council of Community Mental Health Centers 1983, Snyder-Kok Award, Mental Health Asscn Mich., Awareness Leader of the Year Award, Awareness Communications Team Developmentally Disabled 1984, Communicator of the Year Award, Woman in Communications 1984, Lawmaker of the Year Award, Nat. Child Support Enforcement Asscn 1985, Distinguished Service Award, Lansing Jaycees 1985, Distinguished Service in Govt Award, Retarded Citizens of Mich. 1986. *Address:* 133 Hart Senate Office Building, Washington, DC 20510 (office); 2709 South Deerfield Avenue, Lansing, MI 48911-1783, USA (home). *Telephone:* (202) 224-4822 (home). *Fax:* (202) 224-2066 (office). *E-mail:* senator@stabenow.senate.gov (office). *Website:* stabenow.senate.gov (office).

STADEN, Berndt von; German diplomatist; b. 24 June 1919, Rostock; s. of Richard von Staden and Camilla von Voigt; m. Wendelgard von Neurath 1961; two s. one d.; ed Bonn and Hamburg Univs; mil. service 1940–45; jr barrister 1948–51; joined Foreign Ministry 1951, served in Brussels 1953–55, Dir, Soviet Affairs Desk, Bonn 1955–58; Staff mem., EEC Comm., Brussels, Head of Office of Pres. of Comm. 1958–63; Counsellor, Embassy in Washington, DC 1963–68, Deputy Asst State Sec., Foreign Office 1968–70, Asst State Sec., Head of Political Dept 1970–73, Amb. to USA 1973–79, Head of Dept for Foreign Relations and Security, Fed. Chancery 1979–81, State Sec., Foreign Office 1981–83; Co-ordinator for German-American Co-operation 1982–86; Prof. of Diplomacy, Georgetown Univ., Washington, DC 1985, 1988, 1990; Order of Merit (FRG), Order of Terra Mariana, First Class (Estonia). *Publications:* Erinnerungen aus der Vorzeit: Eine Jugend im Baltikum 1919–1939 1999, Ende, Anfang: Errinerungen 1939–1963 2001, Zwischen Eiszeit und Tauwetter 2005. *Leisure interests:* music, horse riding. *Address:* Leinfelderhof, 71665 Vaihingen, Germany (home). *Telephone:* (7042) 5440 (home). *Fax:* (7042) 98994 (home).

STADLER, Sergey Valentinovich; Russian violinist and conductor; *Chief Conductor, Symphony Orchestra of Russia;* b. 30 May 1962, Leningrad (now St Petersburg); s. of Valentin Raymundovich Stadler and Margarita Petrovna Stadler; m. Ilza Liepa (divorced); ed Leningrad State Conservatory, studied with Mikhail Vaiman, Boris Gutnikov in Leningrad Conservatory, with Leonid Kogan, Viktor Tretyakov in Moscow State Conservatory; has toured more than 50 countries since 1976; first performed music by Russian composers Rodion Shchedrin, Sergey Slonimsky, Boris Tishchenko and others; Prof., St. Petersburg State Conservatory 1984–89, fmr Artistic Dir and Chief Conductor N.A. Rimsky-Korsakov Saint-Petersburg State Conservatory of Opera and Ballet; began conducting 1996; Head of Competition Jury, Paganini Moscow Int. Violin Competition 2003–; Founder Hermitage Acad. of Music; Chief Conductor, Symphony Orchestra of Russia 2007–; People's Artist of Russia, winner, Concertino Contest, Prague 1976, winner, Concours Long-Thibaud 1979, second prize, Sibelius Competition 1980, winner, Tchaikovsky Competition 1982. *Address:* Symphony Orchestra of Russia, 105264 Moscow, 9 Parkovaia, 37/51, Russia (office). *Telephone:* (495) 179-01-70 (office). *Fax:* (495) 179-01-70 (office). *E-mail:* symor_orch@mail.ru (office). *Website:* www.symor.ru (office).

STADTMAN, Thressa (Terry) Campbell, BS, MS, PhD; American biochemist; *Section Head, Laboratory of Biochemistry, National Heart, Lung and Blood Institute, National Institutes of Health (NIH);* b. 12 Feb. 1920, Sterling, New York; d. of Earl Campbell and Bessie Campbell (née Waldron); m. Earl R. Stadtman 1943 (died 2008); ed Cornell Univ. and Univ. of California, Berkeley; Research Assoc., Univ. of California, Berkeley 1942–47; Research Assoc., Harvard Medical School, Boston 1949–50; Biochemist, Nat. Heart, Lung and Blood Inst., NIH 1950–, Section Head, Lab. of Biochemistry 1974–; Ed.-in-Chief Bio Factors (IUB-sponsored journal) 1987–; Senior Exec. Service 1988–; Pres. Int. Soc. of Vitamins and Related Bio Factors 1995; Helen Haye Whitney Fellow, Oxford Univ., England 1954–55; Rockefeller Foundation Grantee, Univ. of Munich, FRG 1959–60; mem. NAS, American Acad. of Arts and Sciences, Burroughs-Welcome Fund Toxicology Advisory Cttee 1994–97; Hillebrand Award, Chemical Soc. of Washington 1979, Rose Award, American Soc. of Biological Chemists 1987, Klaus Schwarz Medal 1988, Public Health Service Special Recognition Award 1991, L'Oréal-UNESCO Women in Science Lifetime Achievement Award 2000, Gabriel Bertrand Award, Fed. of European Socs of Trace Elements and Minerals 2001. *Publications:* original research papers in fields of Methane Biosynthesis, Amino Acid Metabolism, Vitamin B12 biochemistry, selenium biochemistry. *Leisure interests:* travel, gardening, skiing. *Address:* National Institutes of Health, Building 50, Loius B. Stokes Labs, Room 2120, Bethesda, MD 20892 (office); 16907 Redland Road, Derwood, MD 20855, USA (home). *Telephone:* (301) 496-3002 (office); (301) 869-1747 (home). *Fax:* (301) 496-0599 (office). *E-mail:* tcstadtman@nih.gov (office); stadtmat@nhlbi.nih.gov (office). *Website:* www.nhlbi.nih.gov (office).

STAEHELIN, Jenö C. A., Lic.Iur., LLM; Swiss lawyer and fmr diplomatist; *Partner, Brock Partners LLP;* b. 1940, Basel; ed Univ. of Berne, Harvard Law School; called to the Bar, Zurich 1968; fmr Clerk, Zurich Court then pvt law practice, Zurich 1968–69; joined Foreign Service 1969, overseas postings included at Embassies in Berne, Geneva and Stockholm 1969–71; Legal Adviser, Ministry of Foreign Affairs 1971–76; mem. Del. to OECD, Paris 1976–77; Vice-Pres. European Patent Office, Munich 1977–84; Minister and Deputy Dir for Int. Orgs, Ministry of Foreign Affairs 1984–87, Amb. in charge of European and N American Affairs 1987–93, also Amb. to Holy See 1991–93, Amb. to Japan 1993–97; Perm. Observer to UN, New York 1997–2002, Perm. Rep. to UN 2002–04; Pres. UNICEF 2003–04, Chair. UN Mine Action Support Group 2004; Pnr Brock Partners LLP (law firm), New York; f. Dr. Jenö Staehelin Foundation. *Address:* Brock Partners LLP, 622 Third Avenue, 12th Floor, New York, NY 10017, USA (office); Dr. Jenö Staehelin Foundation, Kantonsstrasse 46c, 8807 Freienbach, Switzerland. *Telephone:* (212) 209-3000 (office). *E-mail:* jstaehelin@brockfirm.com (office). *Website:* www .brockfirm.com (office).

STAFF, Joel, MBA; American business executive; *Chairman, Reliant Resources Inc.;* ed Univ. of Tex., Tex. A&M Univ.; began career with Baker Hughes Inc. (oil and gas industry supplier) 1976, served in various financial man. positions including Sr Vice-Pres. parent co. and Pres. Drilling and Production Groups –1993; Chair., Pres. and CEO Nat. OilWell Inc. 1993–2001; joined Reliant Resources Inc. 2002, mem. Bd Dirs 2002–, Interim Pres. Reliant Energy Retail Group, Chair. and CEO Reliant Resources 2003–07, Chair. 2007–; mem. Bd of Dirs Nat. OilWell Inc., Ensco Int. Inc.; Advisory Dir King Chapman & Broussard, Boys and Girls Club of Greater Houston; mem. Devt Bd Univ. of Tex. Health Science Center, Houston. *Address:* Reliant Resources Inc., 111 Louisiana, Houston, TX 77002, USA (office). *Telephone:* (715) 497-3000 (office). *Fax:* (713) 497-2319 (office). *Website:* www .reliant.com (office).

STAFFORD, HE Cardinal James Francis; American ecclesiastic; *Major Penitentiary of Apostolic Penitentiary, Roman Curia;* b. 26 July 1932, Baltimore; s. of F. Emmett Stafford and Mary Dorothy Stafford; ordained priest 1957; Auxiliary Bishop of Baltimore 1976–82; Bishop of Memphis 1982–86; Archbishop of Denver 1986–96, now Archbishop Emer.; cr. Cardinal (Cardinal-Deacon of Gesù Buon Pastore alla Montagnola) 1998–; Pres. Pontifical Council for the Laity 1998–; Major Penitentiary of Apostolic Penitentiary, Roman Curia 2003–. *Address:* Palazzo della Cancelleria, Piazza della Cancelleria, 1, 00186 Rome, Italy (office). *Telephone:* (06) 69887526 (office). *Fax:* (06) 69887557 (office). *E-mail:* vati877@ apostpnt.va (office).

STAFFORD, John Rogers, AB, JD; American lawyer and business executive; b. 24 Oct. 1937, Harrisburg, Pa; s. of Paul Henry Stafford and Gladys Lee Sharp; m. Inge Paul 1959; four d.; ed Montgomery Blair High School, Dickinson Coll., George Washington Univ. Law School; Assoc., Steptoe and Johnson 1962–66; Gen. Attorney, Hoffman-LaRoche 1966–67, Group Attorney 1967–70; Gen. Counsel, American Home Products Corpn (now Wyeth) 1970–74, Vice-Pres. 1974–77, Sr Vice-Pres. 1977–80, Exec. Vice-Pres. 1980–81, Pres. 1981–2001, Chair., Pres. and CEO 1986–2001, Chair. 2001–02; mem. Bd of Dirs Verizon 1997– (Dir NYNEX Corpn 1989–97), Honeywell Int. Inc., J.P. Morgan Chase & Co 1982–2005; fmr Dir Mfrs Hanover Corpn, Metropolitan Life Insurance Co., Cen. Park Conservancy, Pharmaceutical Mfrs Asscn, Project Hope, American Paralysis Asscn; mem. Bd of Trustees US Council for Int. Business; mem. ABA, DC Bar Asscn; mem. Advisory Bd Christopher Reeve Paralysis Foundation; Order of the Coif; Outstanding Achievement Alumnus Award 1981. *Leisure interests:* boating, golf. *Address:* c/o Board of Directors, Verizon Communications Inc., 1095 Avenue of the Americas, New York, NY 10036, USA.

STAFFORD-CLARK, Max; British theatre director; *Artistic Director, Out of Joint Theatre Company;* b. 17 March 1941; s. of David Stafford-Clark and Dorothy Stafford-Clark; m. 1st Carole Hayman 1971; m. 2nd Ann Pennington 1981; one d.; m. 3rd Stella Feehily 2010; one d.; ed Felsted School, Riverdale Country Day School, New York and Trinity Coll. Dublin; Artistic Dir Traverse Theatre, Edin. 1968–70; Dir Traverse Workshop Co. 1970–74; Founder and Artistic Dir Joint Stock Theatre Group 1974–79, English Stage Co. at Royal Court Theatre 1979–93; Founder and Artistic Dir Out of Joint Theatre Co. 1993–; Visiting Prof. Royal Holloway and Bedford Coll., Univ. of London 1993–94; Maisie Glass Prof. Univ. of Sheffield 1995–96; Visiting Prof., Univ. of Herts. 1999–, Univ. of York 2002–; Hon. Fellow, Rose Bruford Coll. 1996; Hon. DLitt (Oxford Brookes) 2000, (Herts.) 2000, (Warwick) 2006; Special Award, Evening Standard Theatre Awards 2004, TMA Special Award for Individual Achievement 2010, The Critics' Circle Centenary Award for Services to the Arts in Britain 2013. *Principal productions:* Fanshen 1975, Top Girls 1982, Tom and Viv, Rat in the Skull, Serious Money, Our Country's Good, The Steward of Christendom, Shopping And Fucking, Blue Heart, Some Explicit Polaroids, Rita Sue and Bob Too/A State Affair 2000, A Laughing Matter 2002, The Permanent Way 2003, Talking to Terrorists 2005, The Overwhelming 2006, O Go My Man 2006, The Convicts Opera 2008, Mixed Up North 2009, The Big Fella, Bang Bang Bang 2010, This May Hurt a Bit, Pitcairn 2014. *Publications:* Letters to George 1989, Taking Stock 2007, Page to Stage, Our Country's Good 2011, Journal of the Plague Year 2014. *Address:* Out of Joint, 7 Thane Works, Thane Villas, London N7 7NU (office). *Telephone:* (20) 7609-0207 (office). *E-mail:* ojo@outofjoint.co.uk (office). *Website:* www.outofjoint.co.uk (office).

STAGNO UGARTE, Bruno, BSc, MSc; Costa Rican politician; b. 8 April 1970, Paris, France; m. Laetitia Stagno; two c.; ed Princeton and Georgetown Univs, USA and Sorbonne, France; Consul-Gen. and Minister-Counsellor, Embassy in France 1994–98; Chef de Cabinet, Minister of Foreign Relations and Worship, San Jose 1998–2000; Prof., Universidad Latina 1999; Prof., School of Political Science, Univ. of Costa Rica 2000–02; adviser to legislative ass. 2000–02; Perm. Rep. to UN, New York 2002–06; Minister of Foreign Relations 2006–10; Vice-Chair. Bureau of CSD-11 (Comm. on Sustainable Devt), mem. CSD-12; mem. Inst. for Democracy and Electoral Assistance 1999–2000; Pres. Ass. of State Parties, Int. Criminal Court 2005–08; mem. Advisory Bd Parliamentarians for Global Action 2005–06; Del. Bureau Int. des Expositions, 29th session of UNESCO Gen. Conference 1995–98. *Address:* c/o Ministry of Foreign Relations, Avda 7 y 9, Calle 11 y 13, Apdo 10027, 1000 San José, Costa Rica (office).

STALLKAMP, Thomas J., BS, MBA; American business executive; *Industrial Partner, Ripplewood Holdings LLC;* b. 1946; ed Miami Univ., Ohio; with Chrysler Corpn, Detroit (now Chrysler Group LLC) for 20 years in various man. positions including Pres., mem. Man. Bd, then Vice-Chair. 1999; Vice-Chair. and CEO MSX Int. 2000–04; Industrial Pnr, Ripplewood Holdings LLC 2004–; mem. Bd of Dirs

Baxter Int. Inc., Visteon, MSX Int.; mem. Bd of Advisors, McDonough School of Business, Georgetown Univ.; Adjunct Prof. in Entrepreneurship, Babson Coll.; Trustee Babson Coll. *Address:* Ripplewood Holdings LLC, One Rockefeller Plaza, 32nd Floor, New York, NY 10020, USA (office). *Telephone:* (212) 582-6700 (office). *Fax:* (212) 582-4110 (office). *E-mail:* tstallkamp@babson.edu.

STALLONE, Sylvester Enzio; American actor and film director; b. 6 July 1946, New York; s. of Frank Stallone and Jacqueline Labofish; m. 1st Sasha Czach 1974 (divorced); two s.; m. 2nd Brigitte Nielsen 1985 (divorced 1987); m. 3rd Jennifer Flavin 1997; two d.; ed American Coll. of Switzerland, Univ. of Miami; has had many jobs including usher, bouncer, horse trainer, store detective, physical educ. teacher; now actor, producer and dir of own films; f. White Eagle Co.; Dir Carolco Pictures Inc. 1987–; mem. Screen Actors Guild, Writers Guild, Directors' Guild; Hon. mem. Stuntmans' Assocn; Officier, Ordre des Arts et des Lettres; Hon. César 1992, Golden Apple Male Star of the Year 1997, Hollywood Film Festival Lifetime Achievement Award 2010. *Films include:* Lords of Flatbush 1973, Capone 1974, Rocky (Donatello Award Best Foreign Actor 1976) 1976, F.I.S.T. 1978, Paradise Alley 1978, Rocky II 1979, Nighthawks 1980, Escape to Victory 1980, Rocky III 1981, First Blood, Rambo 1984, Rocky IV 1985, Cobra 1986, Over the Top 1986, Rambo II 1986, Rambo III 1988, Lock Up 1989, Set Up 1990, Tango and Cash 1990, Rocky V 1990, Isobar 1991, Stop or My Mom Will Shoot 1991, Oscar 1991, Cliffhanger 1992, Demolition Man 1993, Judge Dredd 1994, The Specialist 1994, Assassins 1995, Firestorm 1996, Daylight 1996, Cop Land 1997, An Alan Smithee Film: Burn Hollywood Burn 1998, Get Carter 2000, Driven (also screenwriter and producer) 2001, D-Tox 2002, Avenging Angelo 2002, Shade 2003, Spy Kids 3-D: Game Over 2003, Rocky Balboa 2006; films directed: Paradise Alley 1978, Rocky II 1979, Rocky III 1982, Staying Alive 1983, Rocky IV 1985, Rocky Balboa 2006, Rambo 2008, The Expendables (also dir and writer) 2010, The Expendables 2 (also sreenwriter) 2012. *Publications:* Paradise Alley 1977, The Rocky Scrapbook 1997. *Address:* William Morris Agency, One William Morris Place, Beverly Hills, CA 90212, USA. *Website:* www.sylvesterstallone.com.

STALS, Christian Lodewyk, DComm; South African fmr central banker and academic administrator; b. 13 March 1935; s. of Petrus J. Stals and Lilian Barnard; m. Hester Barnard 1958; three s. one d.; ed Afrikaans Hoër, Germiston and Univ. of Pretoria Extramural Div.; joined South African Reserve Bank 1955, Gen. Man. 1975, Deputy Gov. 1976, Sr Deputy Gov. 1981; Dir-Gen. Dept of Finance 1985; Special Econ. Adviser to Minister of Finance 1989; Gov. South African Reserve Bank 1989–99; Chancellor, Univ. of Pretoria 1997–2006; State President's Decoration for Distinguished Service. *Leisure interest:* golf. *Address:* c/o Office of the Chancellor, University of Pretoria, Pretoria 0002, South Africa (office).

STAMP, Gavin Mark, PhD, FSA; British architectural historian and writer; b. 15 March 1948, Bromley, Kent, England; s. of Barry Hartnell Stamp and Norah Clare Stamp (née Rich); m. Alexandra Artley 1982 (divorced 2006); two d.; ed Dulwich Coll., London, Gonville and Caius Coll., Cambridge; freelance writer and teacher –1990; Lecturer, Mackintosh School of Architecture, Glasgow School of Art 1990–99, Sr Lecturer and Hon. Prof. 1999–2003; Mellon Sr Fellow and Bye Fellow, Gonville and Caius Coll., Cambridge 2003–04, Hon. Prof., Univ. of Cambridge 2010–; ind. scholar 2004–; Chair. The Twentieth Century Soc. (fmrly The Thirties Soc.) 1983–2007; Founder and Chair. Alexander Thomson Soc. 1991–2003; Hon. Fellow, Royal Incorporation of Architects of Scotland 1994; Hon. FRIBA 1998. *Publications:* Robert Weir Schultz and his work for Marquesses of Bute 1981, The Great Perspectivists 1982, The Changing Metropolis 1984, The English House 1860–1914 1986, Telephone Boxes 1989, Greek Thomson (co-ed.) 1994, Alexander 'Greek' Thomson 1999, Edwin Lutyens' Country Houses 2001, An Architect of Promise: George Gilbert Scott Junior and the Late Gothic Revival 2002, Lutyens Abroad (co-ed.) 2002, The Memorial to the Missing of the Somme 2006, Britain's Lost Cities 2007, Lost Victorian Britain 2010, Anti-Ugly 2013. *Address:* 15 Belle Vue Court, 122D Devonshire Road, London, SE23 3SY, England (home). *E-mail:* gavin.stamp@btopenworld.com (home).

STAMP, Terence; British actor; b. 22 July 1938, Bow, London; s. of Thomas Stamp and Ethel Esther Perrott; m. Elizabeth O'Rourke 2002 (divorced 2008); ed Plaistow Co. Grammar School, Webber–Douglas Dramatic Acad.; theatre work before film debut in Peter Ustinov's film adaptation of Herman Melville's novel Billy Budd 1962; Hon. Dr of Arts (Univ. of East London) 1993; Amhurst Webber Memorial Scholarship 1957. *Music:* The Airborne Symphony (narrator). *Theatre:* Dracula, The Lady from the Sea. *Other films include:* Term of Trial 1962, The Collector 1965, Modesty Blaise 1966, Far From the Madding Crowd 1967, Poor Cow 1967, Blue 1968, Theorem 1968, Tales of Mystery 1968, The Mind of Mr. Soames 1969, A Season in Hell 1971, Hu-man 1975, The Divine Creature 1976, Striptease 1977, Meetings With Remarkable Men 1978, Superman 1978, Super-man II 1979 (Superman II: The Richard Donner Cut 2006), Death in the Vatican 1980, The Bloody Chamber 1982, The Hit 1984, Link 1985, Legal Eagles 1986, The Sicilian 1986, Wall Street 1988, Alien Nation 1988, Young Guns 1988, Prince of Shadows 1991, The Real McCoy 1992, The Adventures of Priscilla Queen of the Desert 1994, Limited Edition 1995, Tiré à part 1996, Bliss 1997, Love Walked In 1997, The Limey 1999, Star Wars: Episode I – The Phantom Menace 1999, Bowfinger 1999, Kiss the Sky 1999, Red Planet 2000, My Wife is an Actress 2000, Revelation 2001, Full Frontal 2002, My Boss's Daughter 2003, The Kiss 2003, The Haunted Mansion 2003, Dead Fish 2004, These Foolish Things 2004, Elektra 2005, Mr. & Mrs. Smith (scenes deleted) 2005, The Elder Scrolls IV: Oblivion (video game; voice) 2006, 9/11: The Twin Towers (narrator) 2006, September Dawn 2007, Wanted 2008, Get Smart 2008, Ultramarines: The Movie 2010. *Television includes:* Mindbender 1996, The Hunger – Anais 1997, Static Shock – Blast from the Past (voice) 2003, Smallville 2003–06. *Publications:* Stamp Album (memoirs, Vol. 1) 1988, Coming Attractions (memoirs, Vol. 2) 1988, Double Feature (memoirs, Vol. 3) 1989, The Night (novel) 1992, Stamp Collection Cookbook (jtly) 1997, The New Testament (audio book). *Leisure interest:* still tap dancing. *Address:* c/o Markham and Froggatt, 4 Windmill Street, London, W1P 1HF, England. *Telephone:* (20) 7636-4412. *Fax:* (20) 7637-5233. *E-mail:* admin@ markhamfroggatt.co.uk. *Website:* www.markhamfroggatt.com.

STAMPFER, Meir J., MD, DrPH; American nutritionist, epidemiologist and academic; *Professor of Nutrition and Epidemiology and Chairman, Department of Epidemiology, Harvard School of Public Health;* b. Lincoln, Neb.; ed Columbia Coll., New York Univ. School of Medicine, Harvard School of Public Health; Intern in Internal Medicine, Maimonides Hosp., Brooklyn, NY 1977–78; Resident, Community Medicine (Environmental), Mount Sinai School of Medicine, New York 1978–79; Resident, Preventive Medicine, Harvard School of Public Health, Boston, Mass 1979–81, Instructor in Medicine, Harvard Medical School 1982–85, Teaching Fellow, Dept of Epidemiology, Harvard School of Public Health 1982–85, Assoc. Physician, Brigham and Women's Hosp., Boston 1982–91, Consultant Physician, Veteran's Admin Hosp., Brockton, Mass 1984–85, Asst Prof. of Medicine, Harvard Medical School 1985–93, Assoc. Prof. of Epidemiology, Harvard School of Public Health 1988–93, Faculty mem. Div. of Biological Sciences, Harvard School of Public Health 1989–, Physician, Brigham and Women's Hosp. 1991–, Prof. of Nutrition and Epidemiology, Harvard School of Public Health 1993–, Assoc. Prof. of Medicine, Harvard Medical School 1993–2001, Chair. Dept of Epidemiology, Harvard School of Public Health 2000–, mem. Dana-Farber/Harvard Cancer Center 2000–, Prof. of Medicine, Harvard Medical School 2001–; Adjunct Prof., Karolinska Institutet, Stockholm, Sweden 2003–; Dozer Visiting Prof., Ben Gurion Univ., Israel; Assoc. Ed. American Journal of Epidemiology 1991–92, 1997, 2003–, Ed. 1992–97; mem. Editorial Bd American Fertility Soc. Menopause Publication 1992–94, Menopause (The Journal of the North American Menopause Soc.) 1993–, Journal of the American College of Nutrition 1994–, European Menopause Journal 1994–98, Journal of Women's Health 1998, American Journal of Medicine 1998; Tech. Reviewer, New England Journal of Medicine 1987–96; Int. Editorial Advisor, Journal of the British Menopause Society 2002–; mem. Soc. for Epidemiologic Research 1980–, Int. Soc. and Fed. of Cardiology, Council of Epidemiology and Prevention 1981–, American Epidemiological Soc. 1993–, American Asscn of Cancer Research 1999, Fellow, American Heart Asscn (Council of Epidemiology 1984, Council on Nutrition, Physical Activity and Metabolism 2003), American Coll. of Nutrition 1986; Jones Prize for Logic and Philosophy of Science, Columbia Univ. 1973, NIH Nat. Research Service Award 1979–82, Distinguished Alumnus Speaker, Maimonides Hosp. 1989, Duphar Lecturer, British Menopause Soc., UK 1994, Sr Investigator Award in Antioxidant Research, Comité Français de Coordination des Recherches sur l'Atherosclerose et le Cholesterol (France) 1994, Most-Cited Researchers in Clinical Medicine 1981–1998, Rank #1 in Epidemiology, #3 Overall ScienceWatch, Inst. for Scientific Information 1999, Frost Award, American Public Health Asscn 2000; Most-cited Scientist in Clinical Medicine 1995–2005, first overall, Inst. for Scientific Information 2005. *Publications:* more than 617 articles in medical journals on nutrition and chronic disease. *Address:* Department of Epidemiology, Harvard School of Public Health, Kresge Building, Room 904, 677 Huntington Avenue, Boston, MA 02115, USA (office). *Telephone:* (617) 432-6477 (office). *Fax:* (617) 566-7805 (office). *E-mail:* mstampfe@hsph.harvard.edu (office). *Website:* www.hsph.harvard.edu/faculty/meir-stampfe (office).

STANBURY, Hon. Robert Douglas George, PC, QC, BA, LLB, FID; Canadian business executive, lawyer and fmr politician; b. 26 Oct. 1929, Exeter, Ont.; s. of James George Stuart Stanbury and Elizabeth Jean Stanbury (née Hardy); m. Miriam Voelker 1952; two s. two d.; ed Exeter and St Catharines public schools, St Catharines Coll. Inst., Univ. of Western Ontario, Osgoode Hall Law School and York Univ.; Account Exec., Public & Industrial Relations Ltd, Toronto 1950–51; Pres. Canadian Univ. Liberal Fed. 1954; Partner, Hollingworth & Stanbury, Barristers and Solicitors, Toronto 1955–65; mem. North York Bd of Educ. 1961–64, Vice-Chair. 1962, Chair. 1963–64; mem. Metropolitan School Bd, Toronto 1963–64 and Metropolitan Toronto Planning Bd 1963; MP 1965–77; Chair. House of Commons Standing Cttee on Broadcasting, Films and Assistance to the Arts 1966–68; Parl. Sec. to Sec. of State of Canada 1968–69; Minister without Portfolio responsible for Citizenship 1969–71, for Information Canada 1970–71; Minister of Communications 1971–72, of Nat. Revenue 1972–74; Queen's Counsel 1974–; Del. to UN Gen. Ass. 1974, 1975, 1976, to UNESCO Conf., Paris 1969, UN Conf. on Crime, Kyoto 1970, UN Conf. on Apartheid, Lagos 1977, IDB meeting, Kingston 1977; Chair. Canadian Group IPU 1974–77; Founding Chair. Canadian Parl. Helsinki Group 1977; Pres. Hamilton Foundation 1982–83; Vice-Pres. Gen. Counsel and Dir, Firestone Canada Inc. 1977–83, Chair. and CEO 1983–85; Counsel, Inch Easterbrook & Shaker 1986–2000; Dir Art Gallery of Hamilton (Vice-Pres. 1982–86, Pres. 1986–87), mem. Bd of Govs 1988–2004, Dir Art Gallery of Hamilton Foundation 1996–2004; Dir Hamilton and Dist Chamber of Commerce 1980–85 (Pres. 1983–84), Dayton Tire Canada Ltd 1977–85, Canadian Chamber of Commerce 1982–86, Chedoke-McMaster Hosps 1983–92, (Vice-Chair. 1987–89), Workers' Compensation Bd of Ont. 1985–88, 1991–94 (Vice-Chair. 1991–94); mem. Canadian Broadcast Standards Council (Ont.) 1990– (Vice-Chair. 1996–99, Chair. 1991–), Nunavut Arbitration Bd 1994–2005, Advisory Council, Grad. School of Journalism, Univ. of Western Ont. 1994–97; Pres. Inst. of Corp. Dirs in Canada 1987–88; Chair. McMaster Univ. Business Advisory Council 1987–88, Employers' Council on Workers' Compensation 1996–98, Employers' Council of Ont. 1998–2000; Pres. and CEO Canadian Council for Native Business 1989–91; Conflict of Interest Commr, Territory of Nunavut 2000–01, Integrity Commr of Nunavut 2001; mem. Law Soc. of Upper Canada, Canadian Council of Admin. Tribunals, Int. Comm. of Jurists, UNA in Canada; Fellow, Inst. of Dirs 1985–; Canadian Centennial Medal 1967, Queen's Silver Jubilee Medal 1977, Confederation Medal 1993, Meredith Medal 1994, Queen's Golden Jubilee Medal 2002. *Address:* Inch, Easterbrook & Shaker, One Kings Street, West Suite 1500, Hamilton, ON L8P 4X8, Canada.

STANCLIFFE, Rt Rev. David Staffurth, MA, DD, FRSCM; British ecclesiastic; *Fellow of St Chad's College, Durham University;* b. 1 Oct. 1942, Devizes, Wilts., England; s. of Very Rev. Michael Stancliffe and Barbara Tatlow; m. Sarah Smith 1965; one s. two d.; ed Westminster School, Trinity Coll. Oxford and Cuddesdon Theological Coll.; ordained deacon 1967, priest 1968; Asst Curate, St Bartholomew's, Armley, Leeds 1967–70; Chaplain, Clifton Coll. Bristol 1970–77; Canon Residentiary, Portsmouth Cathedral 1977–82, also Dir of Ordinands and Lay Ministry Adviser, Diocese of Portsmouth 1977–82; Vicar, St Thomas of Canterbury, Portsmouth and Provost of Portsmouth 1982–93; Bishop of Salisbury 1993–2010; mem. Gen. Synod 1985–2010, Liturgical Comm. 1986–2005 (Chair. 1993–2005), Cathedral's Fabric Comm. 1991–2001; Pres. Council, Marlborough Coll. 1994–2010; Pres. The Ecclesiological Soc. 2010–; Conductor The Westron Wynd 1971–77, Apparatus Musicus 1977–93, The Bishop's Consort 1993–, Palatinate Voices 2012–; Fellow, Royal School of Church Music (Vice-Pres. 2005–), St Chad's Coll., Durham Univ. 2010–; Hon. Fellow, Guild of Church

Musicians 2005; Hon. Fellow, Trinity Coll., Oxford 2003, Sarum Coll., Salisbury 2012; Hon. DLitt (Portsmouth) 1993. *Publications include:* Liturgy for a New Century 1990 (contrib.), The Identity of Anglican Worship 1991, Enriching the Christian Year 1992, Celebrating Common Prayer—Pocket Version 1994, The Sense of the Sacramental 1995, New Soundings 1997 (contrib.), Flagships of the Spirit 1998 (contrib.), The Pilgrim Prayer Book 2003 (second edn 2007), God's Pattern 2003, The Lion Companion to Church Architecture 2008, The Gospels in Art, Music and Literature 2013. *Leisure interests:* old music, travel, Italy. *Address:* Butts House, Stanhope, Co. Durham, DL13 2UQ, England (office). *Telephone:* (1388) 526912 (office). *E-mail:* d.s.stancliffe@durham.ac.uk (office).

STANCZYK, Janusz Józef, PhD; Polish diplomatist; *Ambassador to the Netherlands;* b. 22 Jan. 1955, Tarnow; m.; two c.; ed Jagiellonian Univ., Kraków, Saint Louis Univ. and Univ. of Michigan, USA, Inst. of Legal Sciences, Polish Acad. of Sciences; Dir Legal and Treaties Dept, Foreign Ministry, Poland 1992–95, Dir Gen. for Legal Affairs 1995–97, Under-Sec. of State for Legal and Econ. Affairs and for relations with int. orgs (also responsible for ministry contact with nat. parl.) 1997–2000; mem. Del. UN Gen. Ass. 1992–96, 1998–2000; Perm. Rep. to UN, New York 2000–04; Deputy Minister for Foreign Affairs and Under-Sec. of State 2004–07; Amb. to Netherlands and Perm. Rep. OPCW 2007–12; Officer's Cross, Order of Polonia Restituta 2012. *Address:* Ministry of Foreign Affairs, 00-580 Warsaw, Al. Szucha 23, Poland (office). *Telephone:* (22) 5239201 (office). *Fax:* (22) 6257652 (office). *E-mail:* sm.sekretariat@msz.gov.pl (office). *Website:* www.msz .gov.pl (office).

STANDLEY, John T., BS; American business executive; *Chairman and CEO, Rite Aid Corporation;* m.; two c.; ed Pepperdine Univ.; fmr Sr Vice-Pres. Smith's Food and Drug, Salt Lake City; fmr Chief Financial Officer (CFO) Smitty's Supervalu Inc., Phoenix; Sr Vice-Pres. and CFO Ralphs Grocery Co. 1996–98; Sr Vice-Pres. Fred Meyer, Inc., Portland, Ore. 1998–99; Exec. Vice-Pres. and CFO Fleming Co., Inc., Oklahoma City May–Dec. 1999; joined Rite Aid Corpn 1999, Sr Exec. Vice-Pres. and Chief Admin. Officer 2002, CFO 2003–05, Pres. and COO Rite Aid Corpn 2008–10, Pres. 2010–13, CEO 2010–, Chair. 2012–; CEO Pathmark Stores 2005–07. *Address:* Rite Aid Corpn, PO Box 3165, Harrisburg, PA 17105 (office); Rite Aid Corpn, 30 Hunter Lane, Camp Hill, PA 17011, USA (office). *Telephone:* (717) 761-2633 (office). *Fax:* (717) 575-5871 (office). *E-mail:* contacttheboard@riteaid.com (office). *Website:* www.riteaid.com (office).

STANG, Peter J., BS, PhD; American chemist and academic; *Distinguished Professor of Chemistry, University of Utah;* b. 17 Nov. 1941, Nürnberg, Germany; ed DePaul Univ., Univ. of California, Berkeley; NIH Postdoctoral Fellow, Princeton Univ. 1967–68; Dept Chair., Univ. of Utah 1989–95, Distinguished Prof. of Chem. 1992–, Dean, Coll. of Science 1997–2007; Assoc. Ed. Journal of the American Chemical Society 1982–99, Ed. 2002–; Ed.-in-Chief, Journal of Organic Chemistry 2000–01; mem. NAS 2000; Foreign mem. Chinese Acad. of Sciences 2006, Hungarian Acad. of Sciences 2007; Fellow, American Acad. of Arts and Sciences 2002; Hon. Prof., CAS Inst. of Chem., Beijing 2010, Zheijiang Univ. 2010, East China Normal Univ. 2010, East China Univ. of Science and Tech. 2010; Dr hc (Russian Acad. of Sciences), (Lomonosov Moscow State Univ.) 1992; A. von Humboldt Sr Scientist Award 1977, 1997, Lady Davis Fellowship, Haifa, Israel 1986, 1997, Fulbright Hays Sr Scholar, Zagreb, Croatia 1988, JSPS Fellowship 1995, 1998, ACS James Flack Norris Award in Physical Organic Chem. 1998, ACS George A. Olah Award in Hydrocarbon Chem. 2003, Linus Pauling Medal 2006, Fred Basolo Medal for Outstanding Research in Inorganic Chem. 2009, Paul G. Gassman Distinguished Service Award, ACS Div. of Organic Chem. 2010, ACS F.A. Cotton Medal for Excellence in Chemical Research 2010, Nat. Medal of Science 2010, ACS Priestley Medal 2013. *Publications include:* Metal-catalyzed Cross-Coupling Reactions 1997, Templated Organic Synthesis (co-ed.) 1999. *Address:* Department of Chemistry, University of Utah, 315 South 1400 East, Room 2020, Salt Lake City, UT 84112-0850 (office). *Telephone:* (801) 581-8329 (office). *E-mail:* stang@chem.utah.edu (office). *Website:* www.chem.utah.edu/directory/faculty/stang.html (office).

STANISHEV, Sergey Dmitrievich, PhD; Bulgarian politician; *Chairman, Bulgarian Socialist Party;* b. 5 May 1966, Kherson, Ukrainian SSR; s. of Dimitar Stanishev and Dina Stanisheva; m. Monika Yosifova; one d.; ed Moscow State Univ., Moscow School for Political Studies, London School of Econs, UK; freelance journalist 1994–95; staff mem. Foreign Affairs Dept, Bulgarian Socialist Party (BSP) 1995, Chief Foreign Policy and Int. Relations Dept 1996–2001, elected mem. BSP Supreme Council (Chair. 2001–) and mem. Exec. Bureau 2000; mem. Bulgarian Nat. Ass. for Rousse constituency 2001–; mem. of the Presidency, Party of European Socialists (PES) 2002, Chair. PES Foreign Policy Network, Interim Pres. PES 2011–, Pres. PES 2012–; Prime Minister of Bulgaria 2005–09; Vice-Pres. Socialist International 2012–; voluntarily gave up his parl. immunity to be tried in court on a charge of losing seven classified documents while he was Prime Minister Oct. 2013. *Publications:* more than 50 publs on foreign policy issues. *Address:* Bulgarian Socialist Party (Bulgarska Sotsialisticheska Partiya), 1000 Sofia, ul. Positano 20, pb 382, Bulgaria (office). *Telephone:* (2) 810-72-00 (office). *Fax:* (2) 981-21-85 (office). *E-mail:* bsppress@bsp.bg (office). *Website:* www.bsp.bg (office).

STANISLAUS, Lamuel A., CBE, BSc, DDS; Grenadian/American diplomatist (retd) and oral surgeon; b. 22 April 1921, Petite Martinique; s. of Nathaniel Stanislaus and Margaret Belmar; m. Beryl R. Staniislaus; five c.; ed Howard Univ., USA; asst teacher, Petite Martinique RC School and St Patrick's RC School 1939–41; statistical clerk, Harbour and Wharves Dept, Port-of-Spain, Trinidad 1941–45; est. dental practice in New York 1956, now retd; Perm. Rep. to UN, New York 1985–90, 1998–2004; Founding mem. Grenada Nat. Party; mem. New Nat. Party, Mayor of New York's Advisory Council; mem. Bd of Advisers, Millennium Devt Goals Global Watch; Hon. Bd mem. and Advisor, West Indian-American Day Carnival Assen; Hon. DHumLitt (Univ. of St George's); Brooklyn Historical Soc. Award, District Attorney's Man of the Year Award, American Foundation of the Univ. of the West Indies Luminary Award, Trey Whitfield Award 2008. *Leisure interests:* swimming, public speaking, reading, writing. *Address:* 189 Montague Street, Suite 800D, Brooklyn, New York, NY 11225 (office); 22 Rutland Road, Brooklyn, New York, NY 11225-5313, USA (home). *Telephone:* (718) 857-6639 (office); (718) 282-9150 (home). *E-mail:* estanislausdds@msn.com (office).

STĂNIȘOARĂ, Mihai; Romanian engineer and politician; b. 11 June 1962, Craiova, Dolj co.; m. Codruța-Mirela Stănișoară; one s. one d.; ed Polytechnic Inst. of Timisoara, Nat. Defence Coll., Higher Coll. of Nat. Security, NATO Defence Coll., Rome; worked as engineer at measurement and control devices factory 1986–89; Asst. Tech. Univ. of Timisoara 1988–90; design engineer, Centre of Appliances Research and Technological Eng 1989–90; Sec. Gen., Chamber of Commerce and Industry, Mehedinti co. 1992–94, Chair. 1994–96; Sec. Gen. Ministry of Defence 2000; mem. Chamber of Deputies for Mehedinți Co. 2000–08 (Democratic Party), Pres. Parl. Del. to OSCE Parl. Ass. 2000–04, mem. Foreign Policy Cttee 2000–04, Chair. Defence, Public Order and Nat. Security Cttee 2004–07; Vice-Pres. Parl. Del. to NATO Parl. Ass. 2004–07; Presidential adviser on Nat. Security 2007–08; mem. Senate (Democratic Liberal Party) for Mehedinți Co. 2008–; Minister of Nat. Defence 2008–09. *Address:* Senate of Romania, 050711 Bucharest, Calea 13 Septembrie, nr 1–3, Sector 5, Romania (office). *Telephone:* (21) 414-1111 (office). *Fax:* (21) 315-6003 (Press) (office). *E-mail:* infopub@senat.ro (office). *Website:* www.senat.ro (office).

STANKEVIČIUS, Česlovas Vytautas; Lithuanian politician, engineer and diplomatist; *Adviser to the Minister of Foreign Affairs;* b. 27 Feb. 1937, Vilkaviskis Region; s. of Jonas Stankevičius and Uršulė Dubickaitė; m. Jadvyga Litvinaitė 1962; two s.; ed Kaunas Polytech. Inst.; engineer, Chief of Design, Chief Engineer, Kaunas Inst. of Urban Planning and Designing 1965–89; Chair. Kaunas Bd Sajūdis Movt 1989–90; elected Deputy and Vice-Pres. of Supreme Council, Repub. of Lithuania; signatory to March 11th Act on Re-establishment of Independence; Head official del. in negotiations with Russia 1990–93; Head, Lithuanian Parl. del. to N Atlantic Ass. 1991–92; mem. Seimas, Parl. Group of Christian Democrats 1996–2000; Minister of Defence 1996–2000; Amb. to Norway 2001–05; Adviser to the Minister of Foreign Affairs 2005–; co-author projects on nat. security and defence concept of Lithuania 1996, Law on Defence Org. 1997, Lithuanian defence strategy 2000; Order of Gediminas 2000. *Publications:* Enhancing Security of Lithuania and Other Baltic States in 1992–94 (monograph), Negotiations with Russia on Troop Withdrawal 2002. *Leisure interests:* literature, the arts. *Address:* Ministry of Foreign Affairs, J. Tumo-Vaizganto 9.2, 01511 Vilnius, Lithuania (office). *Telephone:* (5) 2362861 (office). *Fax:* (5) 2362405 (office). *E-mail:* ceslovas .stankevicius@urm.lt (office); cestan@takas.lt (home). *Website:* www.urm.lt (office).

STANKOVIĆ, Zoran, BA MA PhD; Serbian pathologist and politician; b. 9 Nov. 1954, Tegoviste, Vladicin Han Municipality; m.; two c.; ed Univ. of Niš, Mil. Medical Acad.; head of garrison first aid station, Peč 1982–85; commissioned Medical Corps Lt 1983; specialized training 1985–88; Forensic Assessor 1987; pathologist 1988–90, Head of Tissue Culture Dept 1990–96, Pathology and Forensic Medicine Inst., Mil. Medical Acad.; extraordinarily commissioned Maj. 1991; mem. Vukovar Ad Hoc Group, ICRC 1992–93; extraordinarily commissioned Lt-Col 1993; mem. Comm. Expert on Tracing Missing Persons of Republika Srpska Govt 1994; Prof., Faculty of Medicine, Banja Luka 1994–95; Visiting Prof. King's Coll., Cambridge 1995–; Prof. of Criminological Medicine, Belgrade Police Acad. 1996–; Head of Forensic Medicine Inst., Pathology and Forensic Medicine Inst. 1996–2001; commissioned Col 1997; Expert Officer, Comm. on Humanitarian Issues and Missing Persons of Fed. Repub. of Yugoslavia Govt 1997–; Expert Witness, The Hague Tribunal 1998–; extraordinarily commissioned Maj.-Gen. 2001 (retd in rank, 2005); Head of Pathology and Forensic Medicine Inst., Mil. Medical Acad. 2001–02; Pres. of the Cttee on Data Collection on Crimes Against Humanity and Int. Law of Fed. Repub. of Yugoslavia Govt 2002–03; mem. of Truth Comm. 2002; Head of Mil. Medical Acad. 2002–05; Minister of Defence 2005–06; Mil. Merits Medal 1988, "Bela Povelja" Award, Serbian Asscn of Doctors 1993, Public Health Service Org. Annual Award 1993, Cvijiceva Medal 1999. *Publications:* author or coauthor of over 40 scientific papers. *Address:* c/o Ministry of Defence, 11000 Belgrade, Birčaninova 5, Serbia (office).

STANLEY, Eric Gerald, MA, PhD, FBA; British professor of English; *Professor Emeritus, University of Oxford;* b. 19 Oct. 1923; m. Mary Bateman 1959; one d.; ed Queen Elizabeth's Grammar School, Blackburn, Univ. Coll., Oxford; Lecturer in English Language and Literature, Univ. of Birmingham 1951–62; Reader in English Language and Literature, Univ. of London, Queen Mary Coll. 1962–64, Prof. 1964–75; Prof. of English, Yale Univ. 1975–76; Rawlinson and Bosworth Prof. of Anglo-Saxon, Univ. of Oxford and Fellow Pembroke Coll. Oxford 1977–91, Prof. Emer. 1991–; mem. Medieval Acad. of America 1975–, Corresp. Fellow 2009–; Corresp. mem. Fryske Akad. 1991–, Bavarian Acad. of Science 1994–; Hon. DSL (Trinity Univ., Toronto) 2008, Hon. DLL (Toronto) 2008; Sir Israel Gollancz Memorial Lecturer, The British Acad. 1984. *Publications include:* books and academic articles, some of them in A Collection of Papers with Emphasis on Old English Literature 1987, In the Foreground: Beowulf 1994, Die angelsächsische Rechtspflege und wie man sie später aufgefasst hat 1999, Imagining the Anglo-Saxon Past 2000. *Leisure interest:* travel. *Address:* 18 Walton Street, Oxford, OX1 2HQ, England (home).

STANNARD, Robert William, CMG, BCom (NZ); New Zealand business executive; b. 16 Sept. 1926, Gisborne; s. of William C. Stannard and Clara Stannard; m. Shirley M. Sparkes 1956 (died 2012); one s. (deceased) two d.; ed Horowhenua Coll., Levin and Victoria Univ., Wellington; J. L. Arcus & Sons (chartered accountants), Wellington 1944–49; Peat, Marwick, Mitchell & Co. (chartered accountants), London and Singapore 1949–53; Pnr, Bowden, Bass & Cox (now KPMG), Wellington 1954–87; Statutory Man., Cornish Group 1974–90, Public Service Investment Soc. 1979–87; mem. Nat. Parks Centennial Comm. 1983–88; Chair., Databank Systems Ltd 1985–93, NZ Fishing Industry Bd 1988–93, Nat. Australia Bank (NZ) Ltd 1991–92, Overseas Investment Comm. 1978–97, Milburn NZ Ltd 1987–97, Trustees Executors 1991–2000, Bank of NZ 1993–96; Dir, Fiordland Travel Ltd 1973–97, Tower Trust Ltd (Local Bd) 1991–2002, Commercial Fisheries Services Ltd 1998–2003, Tower Safe Ltd 1999–2002; Distinguished Fellow, NZ Inst. of Dirs 2000; Rotary Paul Harris Fellow 1998; Trustee, Chatham Islands Enterprise Trust 1991–94; NZ 1990 Medal. *Leisure interests:* lawn bowls, mountain tramping, travel. *Address:* 36, Spencer Street, Crofton Downs, Wellington 6035, New Zealand (home). *Telephone:* (4) 479-3057 (home).

STANTON, Katie Jacobs, BA, MA; American business executive; *Vice-President, International Strategy, Twitter Inc.;* b. Peekskill, NY; m.; three c.; ed Rhodes Coll., Columbia Univ. School of Int. and Public Affairs; fmr producer for Yahoo! Finance; worked for Google on Google Moderator, Google Finance and Open Social initiative; first Dir of Citizen Participation, The White House, Washington, DC –2009; Special Adviser to the Office of Innovation, US Dept of State Jan.–July 2010, launched Text Haiti (mobile donation campaign for American Red Cross following earthquake in Haiti); Vice-Pres., Int. Strategy, Twitter Inc. 2010–; ranked by Forbes magazine amongst The World's 100 Most Powerful Women (56th) 2011. *Address:* Twitter Inc., 539 Bryant Street, Suite 402, San Francisco, CA 94107, USA (office). *Telephone:* (415) 896-2008 (office). *Website:* www.twitter.com (office).

STANZEL, Franz-Karl, DrPhil; Austrian academic; *Professor Emeritus of English, Karl-Franzens-Universität Graz;* b. 4 Aug. 1923, Molln; s. of Franz Stanzel and Luise Stanzel; m. Ina v. Navarini 1992; one d.; ed Univ. of Graz and Harvard Univ., USA; Lecturer in English, Karl-Franzens Univ. Graz 1949–50, 1951–57, Prof. of English 1962–93, Prof. Emer. 1993–, Dean, Faculty of Arts and Sciences 1967–68, Head, Dept of English 1962–78; Asst Prof., Univ. of Göttingen 1957–59; Prof., Univ. of Erlangen 1959–62; mem. Austrian Acad. 1972–2009; Bundesverdienstkreuz (Austria); Dr hc (Fribourg). *Publications include:* Typische Erzählsituationen im Roman 1955, Typische Formen des Romans 1964, Narrative Situations in the Novel 1969, Der literarische Aspekt unserer Vorstellungen vom Charakter fremder Völker 1974, Theorie des Erzählens 1979, A Theory of Narrative 1984, Englische und deutsche Kriegsdichtung, Sprachkunst 1987, Intimate Enemies (ed.) 1993, Europäer: Ein imagologischer Essay 1997, Europäischer Völkerspiegel (ed.) 1999, Unterwegs Erzähltheorie für Leser 2002, Telegonie-Fernzeugung. Macht und Magie der Imagination 2008, Welt als Text: Grundbegriffe der Interpretation 2011, Der Fall 'Laconia' und seine Folgen. Vergleich der BBC und ARD TV-Filme 2012. *Leisure interests:* cross-country skiing, gardening, travel. *Address:* Karl-Franzens-Universität Graz, Universitätsplatz 3, 8010 Graz (office); 511 Institut für Anglistik, Heinrichstrasse 36/II, 8010 Graz; Am Blumenhang 31/5, 8010 Graz, Austria (home). *Telephone:* (316) 380-2476 (office); (316) 47-55-56 (home). *Fax:* (316) 47-55-56 (home). *E-mail:* franzkarl .stanzel@kfunigraz.ac.at (office); franzkarl.stanzel@uni-graz.at (office). *Website:* www-gewi.uni-graz.at (office).

STANZEL, Volker, PhD; German diplomatist; *Ambassador to Japan;* b. 1948, Frankfurt; ed Frankfurt Univ., Kyoto Univ., Cologne Univ.; joined Foreign Service 1979, worked in Embassies in Rome, Tokyo, Aden, Beijing; Head of Press and Information Dept, Embassy in Beijing 1990–93; Head of Operation Center, Foreign Office in Bonn 1993–95, Head of Dept for Non-Proliferation and Civilian Use of Nuclear Energy 1999–2001; Foreign Policy Advisor to SPD, Bundestag 1995–98; Visiting Fellow, German Marshall Fund, Washington, DC 1998–99; Dir for Asian and Pacific Affairs, Ministry of Foreign Affairs 2001–02; Dir-Gen. for Political Affairs 2002–04; Amb. to People's Repub. of China 2004–07, to Japan 2009–; Political Dir Ministry of Foreign Affairs 2007–09; Hon. Prof. (Zhengzhou Univ.) 2006. *Publications:* Japan: Head of the Earth 1982, Winds of Change: East Asia's New Revolution 1997, A World of Warring States: China's Perception and Possibilities of Its International Role 1997, NATO after Enlargement 1998, Dealing with the Backwoods: New Problems in Transatlantic Relations 1999, Remembering and Forgetting: But Will the Past Forget About Us? 2001, China's Foreign Policy 2001, Germany's Defense at the Hindukush: The Experiment of Afghanistan 2005. *Address:* German Embassy, F4-5-10, Minami-Azabu, Minato-ku, Tokyo 106-0047 Japan (office). *Telephone:* (3) 5791-7700 (office). *Fax:* (3) 5791-7773 (office). *E-mail:* info@tokyo.diplo.de (office). *Website:* www.tokyo.diplo.de (office).

STAPLE, George Warren, CB, QC; British lawyer; *Consultant, Clifford Chance LLP;* b. 13 Sept. 1940, Bristol; s. of Kenneth Staple and Betty Staple; m. Olivia Lowry 1968; two s. two d.; ed Haileybury; qualified as solicitor 1963; Assoc., Condon & Forsyth, New York 1963; Pnr, Clifford-Turner, later Clifford Chance 1967–92, 1997–2001, consultant to Clifford Chance LLP 2001–; Dir, Serious Fraud Office 1992–97; Legal Assessor, Disciplinary Cttee Stock Exchange 1978–92; Dept of Trade & Industry Insp., Consolidated Goldfields 1986, Aldermanbury Trust 1988; a Chair., Authorization and Disciplinary Tribunals of Securities Asscn 1987–91, Securities and Futures Authority 1991–92; mem. Commercial Court Cttee 1977–92; mem. Council, Law Soc. 1986–2000; mem. Law Advisory Cttee of British Council 1998–2001; mem. Sr Salaries Review Body 2000–04; Chair., Review Bd for Govt Contracts 2002–09; Chair. Govs, Haileybury 2000–08; mem. Accountancy and Actuarial Disciplinary Tribunal; Gov., London Guildhall Univ. 1982–94; Fellow, Soc. for Advanced Legal Studies 1997; Trustee, Royal Humane Soc. 2007–, Romney Marsh Historic Churches Trust; Hon. QC 1997, Hon. Bencher, Inner Temple 2000. *Leisure interests:* cricket, hill walking, gardening. *Address:* Clifford Chance, 10 Upper Bank Street, London, E14 5JJ, England. *Telephone:* (20) 7006-1000. *Fax:* (20) 7006-5555. *Website:* www.cliffordchance.com (office).

STAPLETON, Craig Roberts, BA, MBA; American business executive and fmr diplomatist; *Senior Advisor, Stone Point Capital LLC;* b. Kansas City, Mo.; m. Dorothy Walker Stapleton; one s. one d.; ed Phillips Exeter Acad., Harvard Coll. and Harvard Business School; Pres. Marsh & McLennan Real Estate Advisors, New York 1982–2001; Partner with George W. Bush in ownership of Texas Rangers professional baseball team 1989–98; Conn. State Chair. for re-election campaign of Pres. George W. Bush 2004; mem. Bd of Dirs Allegheny Properties 2005, Metro PCS 2005, TB Woods & Winston Partners 2005, Abercrombie and Fitch; Amb. to Czech Repub. 2001–04, to France 2005–09 (also accred to Monaco 2006–09); Sr Advisor, Stone Point Capital LLC, Greenwich, Conn. 2009–; joined in ownership of St Louis Cardinals 2009–; Pres. Vaclav Havel Foundation; fmr mem. Visiting Cttee for Harvard Coll. and Cttee on Univ. Resources, Bd Peace Corps; Dir 9/11 Memorial Foundation; Trustee, George W. Bush Library and Foundation, Mona Bismark Foundation, de Touqueville/United Way Foundation, Cen. Europe for Research and Grad. Educ., Asscn Francois-Xavier Bagnoud; fmr Trustee Brunswick School, Greenwich, Conn.; Hon. Citizen of Deauville, Chateauneuf du Pape, Rocamadour and Vienne; Commdr, Légion d'honneur 2009; Jan Masaryk Medal for service to the Czech Repub. *Address:* Stone Point Capital LLC, 20 Horseneck Lane, Greenwich, CT 06830-6327 USA (office). *Telephone:* (203) 862-2900 (office). *Fax:* (203) 625-8357 (office). *E-mail:* CRSTAPLETON45@gmail.com (home). *Website:* www.stonepoint.com (office).

STAPLETON, Nigel John, MA; British business executive; b. 1 Nov. 1946, London; s. of Frederick E J. Stapleton and Katie M. Tyson; m. Johanna Molhoek 1982; one s. one d.; ed Univ. of Cambridge; internal auditor, Unilever Ltd 1968–70; Group Man. Internal Audit, Unilever Ltd 1970–73, Sr Auditor 1973–75; Corp. Planning Man. BOCM Silcock 1975–77, Devt Dir 1977–80; Commercial mem. N American office, Unilever PLC 1980–83; Vice-Pres. Finance, Unilever US Inc. 1983–86; Finance Dir Reed Int. PLC, London 1986–96, Deputy Chair. 1994–97, Chair. 1997–99, CEO 1999, Deputy Chair., Chief Financial Officer, Reed Elsevier 1994–97, Co-Chair. 1996–98; Chair. Veronis, Suhler Int. Ltd 1999–2002; Chair. Uniq PLC 2000–06; Dir (non-exec.) GEC 1997–99, Marconi PLC 1999, Axa UK PLC 2000–02, London Stock Exchange PLC 2001–10, JSC Kazpost 2008–14, Real Estate Fund Samruk Kazyna 2011–14, Samruk Kazyna JSC 2014–; Chair. Postal Services Comm. 2004–11; Chair. Mineworkers Pension Scheme 2008–, Coal Pension Trustees Ltd 2012–; Fellow, Chartered Inst. of Man. Accountants; Liveryman of the Worshipful Company of Stationers and Newspaper Makers; Hon. Fellow, Fitzwilliam Coll., Univ. of Cambridge 1997; Freedom of the City of London 1999. *Leisure interests:* gardening, classical music, opera, food and wine. *Address:* Mineworkers' Pension Scheme, Sutherland House, Russell Way, Crawley, RH10 1UH, England (office). *E-mail:* nigel.stapleton@btinternet.com (home). *Website:* www.mps-pension.org.uk (office).

STARCK, Christian, DrIur; German legal scholar and academic; *Professor Emeritus of Public Law, University of Göttingen;* b. 9 Jan. 1937, Breslau; s. of Walter Starck and Ruth Hubrich; m. Brigitte Edelmann 1965; one s. two d.; ed Univs of Kiel, Freiburg and Würzburg; clerk, Fed. Constitutional Court 1964–67; Govt official 1968–69; Lecturer, Univ. of Würzburg 1969–71; Prof. of Public Law, Univ. of Göttingen 1971–, currently Prof. Emer.; Rector Univ. of Göttingen 1976–77; Judge, Constitutional Court of Lower Saxony 1991–2006; Ed. Studien und Materialen zur Verfassungsgerichtsbarkeit 1973–; co-Ed. Juristenzeitung 1978–2006, Staatswissenschaften und Staatspraxis 1990–98, Beiträge zum ausländischen und vergleichenden öffentlichen Recht 1989–, Zeitschrift für Staats- und Europawissenschaften 2003–05; mem. TV Bd Zweites Deutsches Fernsehen 1978–92; mem. Asscn of German Profs of Public Law 1969– (Exec. Cttee 1988, 1989, Pres. 1998, 1999), Exec. Cttee Int. Asscn of Constitutional Law 1981–2004, Exec. Cttee German Asscn of Comparative Law 1985–; Pres. Societas Juris Publici Europaei 2003–07; Visiting Prof., Paris I (Panthéon-Sorbonne) 1987; mem. Acad. of Sciences and Humanities in Göttingen 1982– (Pres. 2008–12); Corresp. mem. Real Academia de Jurisprudencia y Legislación, Madrid 2010–; Fellow Inst. for Advanced Study, Berlin 1990–91; Hon. Pres. Int. Asscn of Constitutional Law 2004, Hon. Pres. Societas Iuris Publici Europeei 2007–, Hon. mem. Acad. of Sciences of Repub. of Korea. *Publications include:* Der Gesetzesbegriff des Grundgesetzes 1970, Rundfunkfreiheit als Organisationsproblem 1973, Das Bundesverfassungsgericht im politischen Prozess 1976; Bundesverfassungsgericht und Grundgesetz (two vols) (ed.) 1976, Vom Grund des Grundgesetzes 1979, El Concepto de Ley en la Constitución Alemana 1979, La Constitution, cadre et mesure du droit 1994, Praxis der Verfassungsauslegung Vol. I 1994, Vol. II 2006, Die Verfassungen der neuen deutschen Länder 1994, Der demokratische Verfassungsstaat 1995, Constitutionalism, Universalism and Democracy – A Comparative Analysis (ed.) 1999, Freiheit und Institutionen 2002, Verfassungen 2009, Grundgesetz Kommentar, 6th edn, Vol. I–III 2010, Jurisdicción constitucional y derechos fundamentales 2011. *Leisure interests:* architecture, literature, walking. *Address:* Schlegelweg 10, 37075 Göttingen, Germany (home). *Fax:* (551) 4882891 (home). *E-mail:* cstarck@gdwg.de (home). *Website:* www.jura.uni -goettingen.de/privat/c.starck.

STARCK, Philippe-Patrick; French designer; b. 18 Jan. 1949, Paris; s. of André Starck and Jacqueline Lanourisse; m. 1st Brigitte Laurent 1977 (deceased); two c.; m. 2nd Nori Vaccari-Starck; ed Inst. Notre-Dame de Sainte-Croix, Neuilly-sur-Seine, Ecole Nissim de Camondo, Paris; f. Starck Products 1979; Interior architecture: La Main-Bleue 1976, Les Bains-Douches 1978, pvt. apartments in Elysée Palace 1982, Le Café Costes 1984, La Cigale, Paris 1987, restaurants, housing and offices in Tokyo 1986–88, Royalton Hotel, New York 1988, Paramount Hotel, New York 1990, Teatriz Restaurant, Madrid 1990, Groningen Museum 1994, Peninsula Restaurant, Hong Kong 1994, Delano Hotel, Miami 1995, Theatron Restaurant, Mexico 1995, Mondrian Hotel, LA 1996, Asia de Cuba Restaurant, New York 1997, St Martin's Hotel, London 1999, Mikli glasses shop, Paris 1999, Restaurant BON, Paris 2000, Sanderson Hotel, London 2000, Hudson Hotel, New York 2000, Clift Hotel, San Francisco 2001, Miramar Hotel, Santa Barbara (in progress); architecture includes knife factory, Laguiole 1988, Asahi Nani Bldg, Tokyo 1989, bldgs in USA, Japan, France, Spain, Ecole Nat. des Arts Décoratifs, Paris 1995, air traffic control tower for Bordeaux Airport 1997, incineration plant, Paris/Vitry (2004); cr. furniture for Pres. of the Repub. 1982, for French, Italian, Spanish, Japanese and Swiss cos; designed boats for Bénéteau, vases for Daum, luggage for Vuitton, toothbrush for Fluocaril, urban furniture for Jean-Claude Decaux, Olympic Flame 1992, children's toys, Aprilia scooters, etc.; Worldwide Artistic Dir Thomson Consumer Electronics Group 1993–96; Artistic Dir Eurostar train 2001; Prof., Domus Acad., Milan, Italy, Ecole des Arts Décoratifs de Paris; Artistic Dir Int. Design Yearbook; exhbns at Georges Pompidou Museum and Decorative Arts Museum, Paris, Villa Medici, Italy, Deutsches Museum, Munich, Kunstmuseum, Düsseldorf, Museum of Modern Art, Kyoto, Japan, Design Museum, London and in Switzerland and USA; Vanity Case Exhbn travelling around the world; Commdr des Arts et des Lettres 1998, Chevalier Légion d'honneur 2000; numerous prizes, including Oscar du Luminaire 1980, three 1st prizes at Neocon, Chicago 1986, Delta de Plata, Barcelona 1986, Platinum Circle Award, Chicago 1987, Grand prix nat. de la Création Industrielle 1988; three awards for hotels in USA 1990, 1991, one for Hotel Paramount 1992, Disseny Barcelona 1995, Design-Zentrum Nordrhein Westfalen Award (Germany) for Duraint bathroom design 1995, Harvard Excellence in Design Award 1997, Prath Inst. Black Alumni Award 2001. *Leisure interest:* sailing. *Address:* Ubik, 18/ 20 rue de Faubourg du Temple, 75011 Paris; Starck-Ubik, 27 rue Pierre Poli, 92130 Issy les Moulineaux, France. *Telephone:* 1-48-07-54-54 (office); 1-41-08-82-82. *Fax:* 1-48-07-54-64 (office); 1-41-08-96-65. *E-mail:* press@starcknetwork.com (home); starck@starckdesign.com (office). *Website:* www.philippe-starck.com (office).

STARKEY, David Robert, CBE, MA, PhD, FSA, FRHistS; British historian, academic and broadcaster; b. 3 Jan. 1945, Kendal; s. of Robert Starkey and Elsie Lyon; ed Kendal Grammar School, Fitzwilliam Coll., Cambridge; Research Fellow,

Fitzwilliam Coll., Cambridge 1970–72, Visiting Fellow 1998–2001, Bye-Fellow 2001–06, Hon. Fellow 2006–; Lecturer in History, Dept of Int. History, LSE 1972–98; Visiting Vernon Prof. of Biography, Dartmouth Coll., NH, USA 1987, 1989; British Council Specialist Visitor, Australia 1989; mem. Editorial Bd History Today 1980–, Commemorative Plaques Working Group, English Heritage 1993–2006; Pres., Soc. for Court Studies 1995–2005; Patron, Tory Group for Homosexual Equality 1994–; Historical Adviser to Henry VIII Exhbn, Nat. Maritime Museum, Greenwich 1991; Guest Curator, Elizabeth I Exhbn, Nat. Maritime Museum 2003, Lost Faces – Identity and Discovery in Tudor Royal Portraiture Exhbn, Philip Mould Gallery 2006, Henry VIII: Man and Monarch Exhbn, British Library 2009; mem. Fitzwilliam Soc. (Pres. 2003–04); Hon. Assoc., Rationalist Press Asscn 1995–; Freeman, Worshipful Co. of Barbers 1992, Liveryman 1999; Hon. DLitt (Lancaster) 2004, (Kent) 2006; Medlicott Medal 2001. *Radio:* panellist, The Moral Maze (BBC Radio 4) 1992–2001, presenter, Talk Radio 1995–98. *Television:* presenter/writer, This Land of England (Channel 4) 1985, Henry VIII (Channel 4) (Indie Documentary Award 2002) 1998, Elizabeth (Channel 4) 2000, The Six Wives of Henry VIII (Channel 4) (New York Festival for int. TV programming and promotion silver medal) 2001, The Unknown Tudors (Channel 4) 2002, Re-Inventing the Royals 2002, Monarchy (Channel 4) 2004–07, Starkey's Last Word (More 4) 2006, Henry VIII: Mind of a Tyrant (Channel 4) 2009. *Publications:* This Land of England (with David Souden) 1985, The Reign of Henry VIII: Personalities and Politics 1985–86, Revolution Reassessed: Revisions in the History of Tudor Government and Administration (ed. with Christopher Coleman) 1986, The English Court from the Wars of the Roses to the Civil War (ed.) 1987, Rivals in Power: the Lives and Letters of the Great Tudor Dynasties (ed.) 1990, Henry VIII: A European Court in England 1991, The Inventory of Henry VIII, Vol. 1 (with Philip Ward) 1998, Elizabeth: Apprenticeship 2000 (WHSmith Award for Biog./Autobiog. 2001), Six Wives: The Queens of Henry VIII 2003, Monarchy: The Early Kings 2004, The History of England: Jane Austen and Charles Dickens 2006, Monarchy: From the Middles Ages to Modernity 2006, Henry: Virtuous Prince 2008, Crown & Country 2010; numerous articles in learned journals. *Leisure interests:* decorating, gardening. *Address:* Fitzwilliam College, Cambridge, CB3 0DG, England (office). *Telephone:* (1223) 332000 (office). *Website:* www.fitz.cam.ac.uk (office).

STAROBINSKI, Jean, PhD, MD; Swiss academic and writer; b. 17 Nov. 1920, Geneva; s. of Aron Starobinski and Szayndla Frydman; m. Jaqueline H. Sirman 1954; three s.; ed Univs of Geneva and Lausanne; Asst Prof., Johns Hopkins Univ., Baltimore, MD, USA 1953–56, Prof. of French Literature, History of Ideas 1958–85; Pres. Rencontres Int. de Geneva 1965–; mem. Accad. dei Lincei, British Acad., American Acad. of Arts and Sciences, Deutsche Akad.; Assoc. mem. Acad. des Sciences Morales et Politiques (France), Acad. Royale de Belgique; Soc. of Fellows, Johns Hopkins Univ.; Officier, Légion d'honneur 1980; hon. degrees from Univs of Lille 1973, Brussels, Lausanne 1979, Chicago 1986, Columbia (New York) 1987, Montreal 1988, Strasbourg 1988, Neuchâtel 1990, Nantes 1992, Oslo 1994, Turin 1994, Urbino 1995, Cluj 1995, ETH, Zürich 1998, Naples 2008; Prix Européen de L'Essai 1983, Balzan Prize 1984, Monaco Prize 1988, Goethe Prize 1994, Karl-Jaspers Prize 1999, Bellas Artes Prize 2009. *Publications include:* Jean Jacques Rousseau: la transparence et l'obstacle 1957, The Invention of Liberty (in trans.) 1964, La Relation critique 1970, Words upon Words (in trans.) 1971, 1789: Les Emblemes de la raison 1973, Montaigne en mouvement 1983, Le Remède dans le mal 1989, La Mélancolie au miroir 1989, Largesse 1994, Action et Réaction 1999, Les Enchanteresses 2005; contrib. to newspapers and journals. *Leisure interest:* music. *Address:* 51 avenue de Champel, 1206 Geneva, Switzerland (home). *Telephone:* (22) 3209864 (home).

STAROBINSKY, Aleksei A., MSc, PhD; Russian theoretical physicist and academic; *Principal Research Scientist, Landau Institute for Theoretical Physics;* b. 19 April 1948, Moscow; ed Moscow State Univ., Landau Inst. for Theoretical Physics, USSR (now Russian) Acad. of Sciences; Research Scientist, Sr Research Scientist, Landau Inst. for Theoretical Physics 1975–90, Science Sec. 1987–90, Head of Dept of Gravity and Cosmology and Leading Research Scientist 1990–97, Prin. Research Scientist 1997–, Co-Dir USSR-USA Summer Program for Young Investigators in Cosmology 1990, 1991, Deputy Dir of Inst. 1999–2003; Visiting Prof., Ecole Normale Superieure, Paris March–Sept. 1991, Yukawa Inst. for Theoretical Physics, Kyoto Univ., Japan 1993–94, Research Centre for Early Universe, Univ. of Tokyo, Japan 2000–01, Institut Henry Poincaré, CNRS, Paris Sept.–Dec. 2006, Yukawa Inst. for Theoretical Physics, Kyoto Univ. March–June 2007; mem. Int. Cttee on Gen. Relativity and Gravitation 1989–97, IUPAP Rep. 2004–10; mem. Astronomy Panel, Long-Term Research Grants Program, Int. Science Foundation 1993–94; mem. Editorial Bd, General Relativity and Gravitation 1989–97, JETP Letters (Russia) 1991–, Astronomy Letters (Russia) 1992–, International Journal of Modern Physics D 1992–, Classical and Quantum Gravity 1993–96, Gravitation and Cosmology (Russia) 1994–, Physical Review D 2001–03, Journal of Cosmology and Astroparticle Physics 2002–; mem. New York Acad. of Sciences 1995; Corresp. mem. Russian Acad. of Science 1997; Russian State Distinguished Scientific Fellowship 1994–97, A.A. Friedmann Prize for Research in Field of Gravity and Cosmology, Russian Acad. of Sciences 1996, Prize of Int. Academic Publishing Co. Nauka/Interperiodica for best work of the year published in its journals 2004, Klein Medal, Stockholm Univ., Tomalla Prize, Tomalla Foundation for Gravity Research, Switzerland (co-recipient), Amaldi Medal, Italian Soc. for Gen. Relativity and Gravitational Physics (co-recipient), Cosmology Prize, Peter Gruber Foundation (co-recipient) 2013. *Achievements include:* developed first working model of inflation and calculated the generation of gravitational waves during inflation 1979. *Publications:* more than 230 papers in professional journals. *Address:* Landau Institute for Theoretical Physics, 142432 Moscow Region, Chernogolovka, Akademika Semenova av., 1-A, Russia (office). *Telephone:* (495) 702-93-17 (office). *Fax:* (495) 702-93-17 (office). *E-mail:* office@itp .ac.ru (office). *Website:* www.itp.ac.ru (office).

STARODUBOV, Vladimir Ivanovich; Russian politician and surgeon; *Deputy Minister of Health and Social Development;* b. 17 May 1950, Kosoborodsk, Kurgan Region; m.; two d.; ed Sverdlovsk State Medical Inst.; surgeon, Head, Surgery Dept, Nizhny Tagil Hosp., Sverdlovsk Region 1973–77; asst. Chair of Surgery, Sverdlovsk State Inst. of Medicine 1977–80; Chief, Sverdlovsk town clinic 1980–81; instructor, Sverdlovsk Regional CP Cttee 1981–87; Deputy Head, Sverdlovsk Regional Dept of Public Health 1987–88; First Deputy Head, Main

Dept of Public Health, Sverdlovsk, Regional Soviet 1988–89; Head, Main Dept of Treatment and Prophylactics, Ministry of Public Health RSFSR 1989–90; Deputy Minister of Public Health Russian Fed. 1990–94; Head, Prof., Chair of Econs of Man., Russian Medical Univ. 1994–96; Deputy Minister of Public Health and Medical Industry 1996–98, Minister of Public Health 1998–99; Rep. of the Russian Fed. to WHO 1999–2001, 2004; Deputy Minister of Health and Social Devt 2005–, (acting Minister of Health and Social Devt 2007); Prof., Russian State Medical Univ. 1999–, Dir Cen. Public Health Research Inst. 1999–2004; Ed. Physician and Information Technology, Health Care Manager 2003–; mem. Russian Acad. Medical Sciences 2004; Honored Physician, Russian Federation 1999. *Publications:* articles: Methodological basics and mechanisms for health care quality assurance, (with O. Shchepin, A. Lindenbraten, G. Galanova) Moscow Medicine 2002, Clinical Management: theory and practice (with T. Lugovkina) 2003, Epidermilogy of tuberculosis (with I. Son, V. Litvinov, P. Seltsovsky) 2003, Health of Russian Population in social context of 1990s: problems and perspectives (ed with Y. Mikhailova, A. Ivanova) 2003; more than 250 publications. *Address:* Ministry of Health and Social Development 127994 Moscow, Rakhmanovskii per. 3/25 (office); 117587 Moscow, 9 Kirovogradskaya str., block 2 Apartment 169, Russia (home). *Telephone:* (495) 927-28-48 (office); (495) 315-39-26 (home). *Fax:* (495) 928-58-15 (office). *Website:* www.mzsrrf.ru (office).

STAROSTENKO, Vladimir Ivanovich; Russian government official; *Director, Moscow Railway;* b. 2 Sept. 1948, Tatarsk, Novosibirsk Region; m.; one s.; ed Tomsk Higher School of Railway Transport, Novosibirsk Inst. of Railway Eng; mem. of station staff, Tatarskaya W Siberian railway 1966–79, Station Man. 1970–75, inspector, Omsk Div. 1975–80, Station Man. Karbyshevo 1980–83, Head of Div. of Cargo, then Head of Div. of Transportation, Omsk Div. 1983–88, First Deputy Head of Omsk Div. 1988–90, Head of Novosibirsk Div. 1990–95, Deputy Head of West Siberian Railway 1995–96, Head 1997–99, Sept. 1999; Head of Kemerovo Railway 1996–97; Minister of Railways May–Sept. 1999; currently Dir Moscow Railway. *Address:* Moscow Railway, 107996 Moscow, 20 Krasnoprudnaya ul., Russia (office). *Telephone:* (495) 266-20-50 (office). *Fax:* (495) 264-51-77 (office). *E-mail:* press@mzd.ru (office). *Website:* www.mzd.ru (office).

STAROVOITOV, Gen. Aleksander Vladimirovich, DTechSc; Russian communications engineer; b. 18 Oct. 1940, Balashov, Saratov Region; m.; one s.; ed Penza Polytech. Inst., Higher Courses of Gen. Staff; numerous positions at Penza Research Electrotechnical Inst. 1962–86, including engineer, deputy head of workshop, sr engineer, head of lab., head of div., Prof., Deputy Dir, Dir-Gen., Kristall, Dir; Deputy Head, Dept of Govt Telecommunications 1986–91; Chair. Cttee on Govt Telecommunications of Pres. Gorbachev 1991; Dir-Gen. Fed. Agency of Govt Telecommunications and Information (FAPSI) 1991–98; Chair. Co-ordination Council of CIS on Security of System of Govt Telecommunications; Constructor-Gen. of Integrated State System of Confidential Telecommunications of Russia; mem. Vice-Pres. Acad. of Eng Sciences; mem. Vice-Pres. Acad. of Electrotechnical Sciences; mem. Acad. of Cryptography. *Publications:* over 150 articles and papers on problems of communications; several patents. *Address:* c/o FAPSI, 103031 Moscow, Bolshoi Kiselny per. 4, Russia.

STARR, Albert, MD; American cardiovascular surgeon and academic; *Medical Director, Providence Heart and Vascular Institute;* b. 1 June 1926, New York City; ed Columbia Coll. (now Columbia Univ.), Columbia Coll. of Physicians and Surgeons; completed internship at Johns Hopkins Hosp. and residency in gen. and thoracic surgery at Bellevue and Presbyterian Hosps of Columbia Univ.; Asst in Surgery, Columbia Univ. –1957; worked at Crippled Children's Div., Univ. of Oregon Medical School (now Oregon Health and Science Univ.) from 1957, later Instructor in Surgery, moved to Providence St Vincent Medical Center 1964; currently Medical Dir Providence Heart and Vascular Inst.; Dir Bioscience Research and Devt, Providence Health System, Ore.; Chair Holder, Albert Starr Academic Center for Cardiac Surgery; mem. Starr-Wood Cardiac Group of Portland; hon. degrees from Columbia Univ., Univ. of London, Reed Coll., Lewis and Clark Coll., American Coll. of Surgeons; Int. Heart Pioneer Award, Soc. de Chirurgie Thoracique Cardio-Vasculaire de Langue Francaise 2000, Albert Lasker Award for Clinical Medical Research, Lasker Foundation (co-recipient) 2007. *Achievements include:* co-inventor of first artificial heart valve (Starr heart valve), which he successfully implanted in 1960. *Publications:* numerous papers in professional journals. *Address:* Starr Wood Group, Suite 240, 9155 S.W. Barnes Road, Portland, OR 97225-6625, USA (office). *Telephone:* (503) 296-4027 (office). *Fax:* (503) 216-2488 (office). *E-mail:* astarr@starrwood.com (office). *Website:* www .starrwood.com (office). *Website:* www.providence.org (office).

STARR, Gregory B., BSc, MSc; American international organization official; *Director of Diplomatic Security Service and Principal Deputy Assistant Secretary for Diplomatic Security;* b. 3 Feb. 1953; m.; two c.; ed George Washington Univ.; Sr Regional Security Officer, Embassy in Tel-Aviv 1997–2000; also served as Regional Security Officer at embassies in Tunis, Dakar and Kinshasa; Dir Office of Physical Security Programs, Dept of State, Washington, DC 2000–04, Deputy Asst Sec. of State for Countermeasures 2004–07, Acting Asst Sec. for Diplomatic Security and Acting Dir of Office of Foreign Missions 2007–08, Dir Diplomatic Security Service and Prin. Deputy Asst Sec. for Diplomatic Security 2008–09, 2013–; Under-Sec.-Gen. for Safety and Security, UN 2009–13. *Address:* Bureau of Diplomatic Security, Department of State, Washington, DC 20522-2008, USA (office). *Website:* www.state.gov/m/ds (office).

STARR, Kenneth Winston, MA; American lawyer, academic and university administrator; *President, Baylor University;* b. 21 July 1946, Vernon, Texas; s. of W. D. Starr and Vannie M. Starr (née Trimble); m. Alice J. Mendell 1970; one s. two d.; ed George Washington, Brown and Duke Univs; law clerk, Court of Appeals (5th Circuit), Miami 1973–74, Supreme Court 1975–77; Assoc. Gibson, Dunn & Crutcher, LA 1974–75, Assoc. Pnr, 1977–81; counsellor to Attorney-Gen., US Justice Dept, Washington, DC 1981–83, Solicitor Gen. 1989–93; Judge Court of Appeals (DC Circuit) 1983; Pnr, Kirkland & Ellis, Washington, DC 1993–94; apptd ind. counsel for Whitewater Investigation as well as any collateral matters arising out of any investigation of such matters including obstruction of justice or false statements 1994; Prof. and Dean, Pepperdine Univ. School of Law 2004–10; Pres. Baylor Univ. 2010–. *Publications:* contrib. articles to legal journals. *Address:* Office of the President, Baylor University, Waco, TX 76798, USA (office). *Website:* www .baylor.edu (office).

STARR, Ringo, MBE; British musician (drums); b. (Richard Starkey), 7 July 1940, Dingle, Liverpool; m. 1st Maureen Cox 1965 (divorced 1975); two s. one d.; m. 2nd Barbara Bach 1981; ed Dingle Vale Secondary Modern School; fmrly an apprentice engineer; played with Rory Storme and The Hurricanes 1959–62; mem. The Beatles 1962–70; numerous performances and tours world-wide; attended Transcendental Meditation Course at Maharishi's Acad., Rishikesh, India Feb. 1968; formed Apple Corps Ltd, parent org. of The Beatles Group of Companies 1968; solo artist 1969–; BPI Award for Best British Group 1977, Lifetime of Peace and Love Award, David Lynch Foundation 2014. *Film appearances include:* with The Beatles: A Hard Day's Night 1964, Help! 1965, Magical Mystery Tour (TV film) 1967, Yellow Submarine (animated film) 1968, Let it Be 1970; solo: Candy 1968, The Magic Christian 1969, 200 Motels 1971, Blindman 1971, That'll be the Day 1973, Born to Boogie (also dir and producer) 1974, Son of Dracula (also producer) 1975, Lisztomania 1975, Ringo Stars 1976, Caveman 1981, The Cooler 1982, Give My Regards to Broad Street 1984. *Television:* narrator of Thomas the Tank Engine (children's programme) 1980s. *Recordings include:* albums: with The Beatles: Please, Please Me 1963, Introducing. . . The Beatles 1963, With The Beatles 1963, Meet The Beatles! 1964, A Hard Day's Night 1964, Something New 1964, Beatles For Sale 1965, Help! 1965, Rubber Soul 1966, Yesterday. . . And Today 1966, Revolver 1966, Sgt. Pepper's Lonely Hearts Club Band (BPI Award for Best British Album) 1967, Magical Mystery Tour 1967, The Beatles (White Album) 1968, Yellow Submarine 1969, Abbey Road 1969, Let It Be 1970, At The Beeb 1994, 1 2000; solo: Sentimental Journey 1969, Beaucoups Of Blues 1970, Ringo 1973, Goodnight Vienna 1974, Blasts From Your Past 1975, Ringo's Rotogravure 1976, Ringo The 4th 1977, Bad Boy 1977, Stop And Smell The Roses 1981, Old Wave 1983, All-Starr Band 1990, Time Takes Time 1992, Live From Montreaux 1994, Vertical Man 1998, I Wanna Be Santa Claus 1999, Ringo Starr & His All-Star Band: The Anthology 2001, King Biscuit Flower Hour 2002, Ringorama 2003, Anthology. . . So Far 2004, Choose Love 2005, Liverpool 8 2008, Y Not 2010, Ringo 2012 2012. *Address:* c/o Elizabeth Freund, Beautiful Day Media & Management LLC, 128 Coffey Street, 1R, Brooklyn, NY 11231, USA (office). *E-mail:* elizabeth@ beautifuldaymedia.com (office). *Website:* www.beautifuldaymedia.com (office); www.ringostarr.com.

STARSKI, Allan Mieczysław; Polish filmmaker and production designer; b. 1 Jan. 1943, Warsaw; m.; ed Fine Art Acad., Warsaw; mem. Acad. of Motion Picture Arts and Sciences, Polish Film Asscn; Gdańsk Film Festival Award 1979, Los Angeles Critics' Asscn Award, Polish Film Award for Polish Eagles 2000. *Films include:* The Shadow Line 1976, Man of Marble 1977, The Young Ladies of Wilko 1979, The Conductor 1979, Man of Iron 1981, Danton 1982, Eine Liebe in Deutschland 1983, Escape From Sobibor 1986, Korczak 1990, Europa, Europa 1990, Daens 1992, Papierowe malzenstwo (Paper Marriage) 1992, Schindler's List (Acad. Award 1994) 1993, Wielki tydzien (Holy Week) 1995, Historie milosne (Love Stories) 1997, Washington Square 1997, Pan Tadeusz (Pan Tadeusz: The Last Foray in Lithuania) 1999, Prawo ojca 2000, The Body 2000, The Pianist 2002, The I Inside 2003, EuroTrip 2004, Oliver Twist 2005, Hannibal Rising 2007. *Leisure interests:* cinema, ice skating.

STARZEWSKI, Tomasz; British/Polish fashion designer; b. 1961, London; ed St Martin's School of Design, London; began career designing eveningwear for royals and celebrities 1981; built up large business with distribution over UK, USA and Middle East; collections shown around the world as part of British Collections, group he f. in 1987; opened his first ready-to-wear boutique on Old Brompton Road, London 1989; opened House of Tomasz Starzewski, London 1991; American debut, New York 1999. *Address:* Tomasz Starzewski Studio, 97 Pimlico Road, London, SW1W 8PH, England (office). *Telephone:* (20) 7730-5559 (office). *Fax:* (20) 7730-5977 (office). *Website:* www.starzewski.com (office).

STARZL, Thomas Earl, BS, MS, MD, PhD; American neurophysiologist, physician and surgeon (retd); *Distinguished Service Professor of Surgery, School of Medicine, University of Pittsburgh;* b. 11 March 1926, Le Mars, Ia; ed Westminster Coll., Fulton, Mo., Northwestern Univ. Medical School, Chicago; known as "Father of Transplantation"; postgraduate work at Johns Hopkins Hosp., Baltimore, Md; fellowship and residencies at Johns Hopkins Hosp., Univ. of Miami and Veterans' Admin Research Hosp., Chicago; mem. faculty, Northwestern Univ. 1958–61; Assoc. Prof. of Surgery, Univ. of Colorado School of Medicine 1962–64, Prof. 1964, Chair. Dept of Surgery 1972–80; Prof. of Surgery, Univ. of Pittsburgh School of Medicine 1981, now Distinguished Service Prof. of Surgery, Univ. of Pittsburgh School of Medicine, Chief of Transplantation Services, Presbyterian Univ. Hosp. (now UPMC Presbyterian), Children's Hosp. of Pittsburgh and Veterans' Admin Hosp., Pittsburgh 1981–91, Dir Univ. of Pittsburgh Transplantation Inst. 1991, Inst. renamed Thomas E. Starzl Transplantation Inst. 1996, Dir Emer. 1996–; Pres. The Transplantation Soc.; Founding Pres. American Soc. of Transplant Surgeons, Transplant Recipients Int. Org.; mem. editorial boards of 40 professional publs; mem. more than 60 professional and scientific orgs; mem. Nat. French Acad. of Medicine 1992; has given more than 1,300 presentations at major meetings world-wide; Hon. mem. Acad. of Medical Sciences (Iran) 2004; 24 hon. doctorates from univs in USA and abroad; more than 200 awards and honours, including Markle Scholar in Medical Science, David M. Hume Memorial Award, Nat. Kidney Foundation, Brookdale Award in Medicine, American Medical Asscn Bd of Trustees and Brookdale Foundation, Bigelow Medal, Boston Surgical Soc., City of Medicine Award, Medallion for Scientific Achievement, American Surgical Asscn, William Beaumont Prize, American Gastroenterological Asscn, Peter Medawar Prize, The Transplant Soc., Jacobson Innovation Award, American Coll. of Surgeons, Lannelongue Int. Medal, Acad. Nationale de Chirurgie (France) 1998, King Faisal Int. Prize for Medicine 2001, Rhoads Medal, American Philosophical Soc., Prince Mahidol Award 2002, Presidential Nat. Medal of Science 2004, Roche Ernest Hodge Memorial Award (Highest Award), American Transplantation Soc. 2006, First Annual Tribute to Excellence Award, American Liver Foundation 2007, Castle Connolly Nat. Physician of the Year Award for Lifetime Achievement 2009, Diamond Award for Lifetime Achievement (Highest Distinction of Dept of Veterans Affairs Award for Lifetime Achievement) 2009, Gustav O. Lienhard Award, Inst. of Medicine, Washington, DC 2009, Carnegie Science Chair.'s Award 2010, Lasker-DeBakey Clinical Medical Research Award (co-recipient) 2012. *Achievements include:* successfully combined azathioprine (Imuran) and corticosteroids in allogenic kidney transplants performed in 1962 and 1963, leading to the largest series of kidney transplants and invigorating clinical attempts world-wide; performed world's first human liver transplant 1963 and first successful liver transplant 1967, both at Univ. of Colorado; he and his transplant team went on to perform approximately 1,000 kidney and 200 liver transplants at Colorado Gen. and Denver Veterans' Admin Hosps. *Publications:* The Puzzle People: Memoirs of a Transplant Surgeon 1992; author or co-author of four books, 300 book chapters and more than 2,200 scientific articles. *Address:* Thomas E. Starzl Transplantation Institute, UPMC Montefiore, 7 South 3459 Fifth Avenue, Pittsburgh, PA 15213, USA (office). *Telephone:* (412) 383-1346 (office). *Fax:* (412) 624-2010 (office). *E-mail:* mangantl@upmc.edu (office). *Website:* www.starzl.pitt.edu (office); www .stiresearch.health.pitt.edu (office).

STASHEVSKYI, Stanislav Telisforovych; Ukrainian politician and electrical engineer; b. 1943, Mar'yanivka, Vasylkivsky dist., Kiev region; ed Kiev Polytechnic Inst.; mil. service 1962–65; electrician, Specialized Planning Dept, Kyivelectromontazh Trust of Kyivmiskbud 1962, then Repairman, Foreman, Sr Foreman, Chief Engineer, Head of Dept 1965–79, then Deputy Head of co. and Chief Engineer 1979–87; Deputy Head, Holovkyivmiskbud 1987–92; First Vice-Pres. Kyivmiskbud Corpn (later Kyivmiskbud Holding Co.) 1992–96; First Deputy Head, Kyiv City Admin 1996–2001, Minister of Fuel and Energy 2001; People's Deputy, Verkhovna Rada (Parl.) 2002–05, Chair. Foreign Relations Cttee, Co-Chair. Inter-Parl. Comm. for Cooperation between Verkhovna Rada (Parl.) and Ass. of Russian Fed.; Head of Verkhovna Rada Perm. Del. to GUAM Parl. Ass., Chair. GUAM Parl. Ass. Cttee on Political and Legal Issues; mem. Ukraine-EU Co-operation Cttee, Deputy Chair., Exec. Cttee of Nat. Parl. Group of Ukraine at Inter-Parl. Union 2002–05; First Deputy Prime Minister 2005–06; mem. Kiev City Council and Nat. Political Council; Head of Pechersk Regional Org.; mem. Our Ukraine Party; I, II, and III Class Orders of Merit, II and III Class Orders of St Prince Volodymyr the Great, Arhistratig Michael Order; Diploma of the Verkhovna Rada. *Leisure interests:* riding, tennis. *Address:* Verkhovna Rada (Supreme Council), 01008 Kyiv, vul. M. Hrushevskoho 5, Ukraine (office). *Telephone:* (44) 255-21-15 (office). *Fax:* (44) 253-32-17 (office). *E-mail:* Stashevskyi.Stanislav@rada.gov.ua (office). *Website:* www.rada.gov.ua (office).

STASSE, François; French civil servant and economist; *Senior Member, Council of State;* b. 11 Jan. 1948, Neuilly-sur-Seine; s. of Roger Stasse and Christiane Stasse (née Deveaux); m. Nathalie Duhamel 1978; ed Inst. of Political Studies, Paris; with Ministry of Industry 1972–73; joined Gen. Bd of Planning 1974, Dir Commr's Office 1979–81; Tech. Adviser to Pres. of Rep. on Econs and Finance 1981–84; Counsel Council of State 1984, Sr mem. 1996–; Dir State Hosp. Paris 1989–93; Dir-Gen. Bibliothèque nationale de France 1998–2001. *Publications include:* La Morale de l'histoire 1994, La Véritable Histoire de la Grande Bibliotheque 2002, L'Heritage de Mendès France 2004; numerous articles in journals. *Address:* Conseil d'État, place du Palais Royal, 75100 Paris, France (office).

STAUDINGER, Ulrich; German publisher; b. 30 May 1935, Berlin; s. of Dr Wilhelm Staudinger and Elfriede Poth; m. Irmengard Ehrenwirth 1960 (died 1989); one s. two d.; ed Volksschule and Realgymnasium; publishing training 1954–57; Lingenbrinck Barsortiment, Hamburg 1957–58; Publicity and Sales, Ensslin & Laiblin, Jugendbuchverlag, Reutlingen 1958–59; Production, Carl Hanser Verlag, Munich 1959–60; Dawson & Sons, London 1960; Franz Ehrenwirth Verlag, Munich 1960; Partner, Ehrenwirth Verlag, Munich 1964–76; responsible for purchase of Franz Schneekluth Verlag KG, Darmstadt by Ehrenwirth Verlag 1967; purchased Schneekluth 1976, sold to Weltbild Verlag 1996; purchased Philosophia Verlag GmbH, Düsseldorf 1980; Perthes – Medaille des Börsenvereins des Deutschen Buchhandels e.V. Ehrenmitglied der Verwertungsgesellschaft Wort. *Address:* Philosophia Verlag GmbH, Gundelindenstraße 10, 80805 Munich, Germany (office). *Telephone:* (89) 299975 (office). *E-mail:* info@philosophiaverlag.com (office). *Website:* en.philosophiaverlag.com (office).

STAUNTON, Imelda Mary Philomena Bernadette, OBE; British actress; b. 9 Jan. 1956; d. of Joseph Staunton and Bridie McNicholas; m. Jim Carter 1983; one d.; ed La Sainte Union Convent, Highgate, London, RADA; repertory Exeter, Nottingham, York 1976–81; Olivier Award 1985, 1990, Screen Actors' Guild Award 1999. *Stage appearances include:* Guys and Dolls 1982, 1996, Beggar's Opera 1985, She Stoops to Conquer, Chorus of Disapproval 1985 (Olivier Award, Best Supporting Actress), The Corn is Green 1985, Fair Maid of the West 1986, Wizard of Oz 1986, Uncle Vanya 1988, Into the Woods 1990, Phoenix 1990 (Olivier Award, Best Actress in a Musical), Life x 3 2000, There Came a Gypsy Riding 2007. *Television appearances include:* The Singing Detective 1986, Yellowbacks 1990, Sleeping Life, Roots, Up the Garden Path 1990, Antonia and Jane, David Copperfield 1999, Victoria Wood Xmas Special 2000, Murder 2001, Cambridge Spies 2002, Strange 2002, Fingersmith 2005, A Midsummer Night's Dream 2005, Little Britain 2005, My Family and Other Animals 2005, Cranford (series) 2007–09, Clay 2008, Big and Small 2008, Psychoville 2010, Doctor Who 2011, The Girl 2012. *Film appearances include:* Comrades 1987, Peter's Friends 1992, Much Ado About Nothing 1993, Deadly Advice 1994, Sense and Sensibility, Twelfth Night, Remember Me 1996, Shakespeare in Love 1998, Another Life 1999, Rat 1999, Crush 2000, Bright Young Things 2002, Virgin of Liverpool 2002, Blackball 2002, Family Business 2002, Vera Drake (Best Performance by an Actress, British Ind. Film Awards, Best Actress, European Film Awards, Los Angeles Film Critics' Asscn, New York Film Critics' Circle, Evening Standard British Film Awards 2005, Best Actress in a Leading Role, BAFTA Awards 2005) 2004, Nanny McPhee 2005, 3 & 3 2005, Freedom Writers 2007, Harry Potter and the Order of the Phoenix 2007, Where Have I Been All Your Life? 2007, Three and Out 2008, A Bunch of Amateurs 2008, Taking Woodstock 2009, Harry Potter and the Deathly Hallows 2010, Another Year 2010, The Awakening 2011, Arthur Christmas (voice) 2011. *Address:* c/o ARG, 4 Great Portland Street, London, W1W 4PA, England.

STAVRAKIS, Charilaos, BA, MBA; Cypriot politician; b. 1956; ed Univ. of Cambridge, UK, Harvard Univ. Grad. School of Business Admin, USA; more than 25 years' experience in banking sector; undertook two-month consulting position at World Bank 1989; held various positions at Bank of Cyprus, including Head of Strategic Planning and Business Devt and Sr Man. of Treasury and Int. Services, Group Gen. Man. Int. Banking 1988–2004, Gen. Man. Cyprus Investment & Securities Corpn Ltd (CISCO) (investment banking arm of the Group) 2003–08; mem. Bd Dirs Cyprus Oil Refinery, Bank of Cyprus Australia, Bank of Cyprus

(Channel Islands) Ltd, Bank of Cyprus (AEDAK), Bank of Cyprus Mutual Funds Ltd, BOC Ventures Ltd, CEO-Cyprus and Deputy Group CEO 2005–08, assumed additional duties involving man. of subsidiary cos of the Group: BOC Factors, Bank of Cyprus Finance Corpn, General Insurance of Cyprus, Eurolife, The Cyprus Investment and Securities Corpn Ltd (CISCO), BOC Mutual Funds Ltd, Bank of Cyprus UK and the setting up of banks in Russia and Ukraine; Chair. Electricity Authority Cyprus 2005–08, Cyprus Bankers Employers' Asscn 2005–08; Minister of Finance (Ind.) 2008–11; mem. Chartered Inst. of Bankers (ACIB) 1988.

STAVRESKI, Zoran, BA, MA; Macedonian economist and politician; *Deputy Prime Minister and Minister of Finance;* b. 29 Oct. 1964, Ohrid; m.; one c.; ed Faculty of Econs, SS. Cyril and Methodious Univ., Skopje; Researcher, Research Directorate, Cen. Bank of Repub. of Macedonia 1993–97, Dir of Research Directorate 1997–2000; Under-Sec., Ministry of Finance 2000–01; Advisor to Exec. Dir in the Netherlands Constituency, World Bank 2001–04, Consultant in Europe and Cen. Asia Poverty Reduction and Econ. Man. Unit March–Aug. 2005, in Operational Policy and Country Services Units Sept. 2005–Feb. 2006, Sr Economist for Operational Policy and Country Services Units Feb.–Aug. 2006; Deputy Prime Minister, in charge of Econ. Affairs 2006–09, Deputy Prime Minister and Minister of Finance 2009–; Chair. Annual Meetings of the World Bank and IMF for 2008. *Address:* Ministry of Finance, 1000 Skopje, Mito Hadjivasilev Jasmin bb, Former Yugoslav Republic of Macedonia (office). *Telephone:* (2) 3117288 (office). *Fax:* (2) 3106779 (office). *E-mail:* finance@finance .gov.mk (office). *Website:* www.finance.gov.mk (office).

STAVRIDIS, Adm. James G., PhD, MALD; American naval officer and international organization official; *Chairman, US Naval Institute;* b. South Florida; m. Laura Stavridis; two d.; ed US Naval Acad. (distinguished grad.), Nat. War Coll. (distinguished grad.), Fletcher School of Law and Diplomacy, Tufts Univ.; Surface Warfare Officer, commanded Destroyer USS Barry (DDG-52) 1993–95, completed UN and NATO deployment to Haiti and Bosnia, and combat cruise to the Arabian Gulf, commanded Destroyer Squadron 21 1998, deployed to Arabian Gulf, commanded Enterprise Carrier Strike Group 2002–04, conducted combat operations in Arabian Gulf in support of both Operation Iraqi Freedom and Operation Enduring Freedom, commanded US Southern Command in Miami focused on Latin America and the Caribbean 2006–09; Supreme Allied Commdr, Europe, NATO 2009–13; Chair. US Naval Inst. 2013–; Dean, Fletcher School of Law and Diplomacy, Tufts Univ. 2013–; has served as a strategic and long-range planner on staffs of Chief of Naval Operations and Chair. of Jt Chiefs of Staff; also served as Exec. Asst to the Sec. of the Navy and as Sr Mil. Asst to the Sec. of Defense; Defense Distinguished Service Medal, Defense Superior Service Medal, five awards of the Legion of Merit; Gullion Prize, Fletcher School of Law and Diplomacy 1984, USS Barry won the Battenberg Cup as the top ship in the Atlantic Fleet under his command, John Paul Jones Award for Inspirational Leadership, Navy League 1998. *Publications include:* author or co-author of several books on naval ship-handling and leadership, including Command at Sea, Destroyer Captain, Partnership for the Americas about Latin America. *Leisure interests:* squash, tennis, cycling. *Address:* US Naval Institute, 291 Wood Road, Annapolis, MD 21402, USA (office). *Telephone:* (410) 268-6110 (office). *Fax:* (410) 571-1703 (office). *E-mail:* customer@usni.org (office). *Website:* www.usni.org (office).

STAVROPOULOS, William S., PhD; American chemical company executive (retd); b. 12 May 1939, Bridgehampton; m. Linda Stavropoulos; one s. one d.; ed Fordham Univ., Univ. of Washington; research chemist, Pharmaceutical Research Div., Dow Chemical Co. 1967, Diagnostics Product Research Div. 1970, Research Man. 1973, Diagnostic Products Business Man. 1976, Business Man. for polyolefins 1977, Dir of Marketing, Dow USA Plastics Dept 1979, Commercial Vice-Pres. Dow Latin America 1980, Pres. 1984, Commercial Vice-Pres. Dow USA, Basics and Hydrocarbons 1985, Group Vice-Pres. 1987, Pres. Dow USA 1990, Vice-Pres. The Dow Chemical Co. 1990, Dir 1990–, Sr Vice-Pres. 1991, Pres., COO 1993–95, Pres., CEO 1995–2000, 2002–04, Chair. 2002–06 (retd); mem. Bd of Dirs Dow Corning Corpn 1991, Marion Merrell Dow Inc. 1992, Dowell Schlumberger 1992, Chemical Bank; Trustees Midland Community Center and other bodies; Dr hc (Northwood Univ.) 1998; Man. of the Year Award from American Hellenic Education Progressive Association 1995, Man of the Year Award from Hellenic American Bankers Association 1997, Ellis Island Medal of Honor in 1998, CEO of the Year Kavaler Award 1999, Man of the Year Award from Hellenic American Chamber of Commerce 2000, Société de Chimie Industrielle's Palladium Medal Award 2001, Chemical Industry Medal Award, Soc. of Chemical Industry 2001, Institutional Investor magazine's award as one of Best CEOs in America in Chemicals/Commodity category (1998, 2003 and 2004), Soc. of Plastic Engineers Annual Business Man. Award 2003, Northwood Univ. 2004, Outstanding Business Leader Award, Junior Achievement of Central Michigan Business Hall of Fame 2005. *Address:* 8865 Bay Colony Drive, Naples, FL 34103, USA.

STEAD, C(hristian) K(arlson), CBE, ONZ, MA, PhD, LittD, FRSL, FEA; New Zealand writer and academic; *Professor Emeritus of English, University of Auckland;* b. 17 Oct. 1932, Auckland; s. of James Walter Ambrose Stead and Olive Ethel Stead (née Karlson); m. Kathleen Elizabeth Roberts 1955; one s. two d.; ed Mt Albert Grammar School, Auckland Univ. Coll. and Auckland Teachers' Coll., Univ. of Bristol, UK; Lecturer in English, Univ. of New England, NSW, Australia 1956–57; Michael Hiatt Baker Scholar, Univ. of Bristol 1957–59; Lecturer, Sr Lecturer, Assoc. Prof., Univ. of Auckland 1960–67, Prof. of English 1967–86, Prof. Emer. 1986–; writer 1986–; Nuffield Fellow, Univ. of London 1965, Hon. Fellow, Univ. Coll. London 1977, Sr Visiting Fellow, St John's Coll., Oxford 1996–97; Chair. NZ Literary Fund Advisory Cttee 1972–75, NZ Authors' Fund Cttee 1989–91; mem. NZ PEN (Chair. Auckland br. 1986–89, Nat. Vice-Pres. 1988–90), Creative New Zealand 1999; Fellow, English Asscn; Hon. DLetters (Bristol) 2001; Katherine Mansfield Prize 1960, Jessie Mackay Award for Poetry 1972, Katherine Mansfield Menton Fellowship 1972, New Zealand Book Award for Poetry 1976, New Zealand Book Award for Fiction 1985, 1995, Queen Elizabeth II Arts Council Scholarship in Letters 1988–89, Queen's Medal for Services to NZ Literature 1990, King's Lynn Award for poetry 2001, Michael King Fellowship 2005–06, Bogliasco Fellowship in Literature 2007, 2011, Prime Minister's Award for Literary Achievement (for fiction) 2009, Sunday Times EFG Private Bank Short Story Award 2010, Hippcrates Prize for Poetry and Medicine 2010. *Film:* Sleeping Dogs

1977. *Publications:* fiction: Smith's Dream 1972, All Visitors Ashore 1984, The Death of the Body 1986, Sister Hollywood 1989, The End of the Century at the End of the World 1992, The Singing Whakapapa 1994, Villa Vittoria 1997, Talking about O'Dwyer 2000, The Secret History of Modernism 2002, Mansfield: a novel 2004, My Name Was Judas 2006, Risk 2012; poetry: Whether the Will is Free 1964, Crossing the Bar 1972, Quesada 1975, Walking Westward 1978, Geographies 1982, Poems of a Decade 1983, Paris 1984, Between 1986, Voices 1990, Straw into Gold 1997, The Right Thing 2000, Dog 2002, The Red Tram 2004, The Black River 2007, Collected Poems 1951–2006 (Montana Book Award 2009) 2008, The Yellow Buoy 2013; short story collections: Five for the Symbol 1981, The Blind Blonde with Candles in Her Hair 1998; non-fiction: The New Poetic: Yeats to Eliot 1964, In the Glass Case: Essays on New Zealand Literature 1981, Pound Yeats Eliot and the Modernist Movement 1986, Answering to the Language: Essays on Modern Writers 1990, The Writer at Work 2000, Kin of Place: Essays on 20 New Zealand Writers 2002, Book Self: the reader as writer and the writer as critic 2008; editor: Oxford New Zealand Short Stories (2nd series) 1966, Measure for Measure, a Casebook 1971, Letters and Journals of Katherine Mansfield 1977, Collected Stories of Maurice Duggan 1981, The Faber Book of Contemporary South Pacific Stories 1994, Werner Forman's New Zealand 1994. *Leisure interests:* music, politics, swimming. *Address:* 37 Tohunga Crescent, Parnell, Auckland 1052, New Zealand. *Telephone:* (9) 379-9420. *E-mail:* ckstead1@xtra.co.nz.

STEADMAN, Alison, OBE; British actress; b. 26 Aug. 1946, Liverpool, Merseyside, England; d. of George Percival Steadman and Marjorie Evans; m. Mike Leigh (q.v.) (divorced 2001); two s.; partner Michael Elwyn; ed East 15 drama school, Loughton, Essex; began career in repertory theatre in Lincoln, Bolton, Liverpool, Worcester and Nottingham; Hon. Fellow, John Moores Univ., Liverpool; Hon. MA (East London); Hon. DLit (Liverpool) 2008; Dr hc (Essex) 2003; Evening Standard Best Actress Award 1977, Olivier Award for Best Actress 1993. *Stage appearances include:* Beverley in Abigail's Party, Mae-Sister Woman in Cat on a Hot Tin Roof, Nat. Theatre (NT) 1988, Uncle Vanya, Mari Hoff in The Rise and Fall of Little Voice, NT, David Edgar's Maydays, RSC, Tartuffe, RSC 1983, Joking Apart, Kafka's Dick, Royal Court, Marvin's Room 1993, The Plotters of Cabbage Patch Corner, The Provok'd Wife, Old Vic 1997, When We Are Married, Chichester and Savoy Theatres, The Memory of Water, Vaudeville Theatre, Entertaining Mr Sloane, Arts Theatre, The Woman Who Cooked Her Husband, New Ambassador Theatre, Losing Louis, Hampstead Theatre and Trafalgar Studios, London, Enjoy, UK tour and Gielgud Theatre, London, Blithe Spirit UK tour and Apollo Theatre, London 2010–11. *Films include:* Champions 1984, A Private Function 1984, Coming Through 1985, Clockwise 1986, Stormy Monday 1988, The Adventures of Baron Munchausen 1988, Wilt 1989, Shirley Valentine 1989, Life is Sweet 1990, Blame It On the Bellboy 1992, Secrets and Lies 1996, Topsy-Turvy 1999, Chunky Monkey 2001, Happy Now 2001, D.I.Y. Hard 2002, The Life and Death of Peter Sellers 2004, The Housewife 2005, Confetti 2006, Dead Rich 2006, Second Chance (short) 2009, French Exchange (short) 2011, The Day My Nan Died (short) 2012, (Notes) (short) 2012, Peterman 2014. *Radio includes:* Bette in Cousin Bette, Beyond Black 2009, My Mad Grandad 2009, Clarissa 2010, Miss Pross in Tale of Two Cities (BBC Radio 4) 2011. *Television includes:* Hard Labour 1973, Frost's Weekly (series) 1973, Girl 1974, The Wackers (series) 1975, Tarbuck and All That! (series) 1975, Through the Night 1975, Nuts in May 1976, Esther Waters 1977, Abigail's Party 1977, The Tartuffe or Imposter 1983, P'tang Yang Kipperbang 1984, Number One 1985, The Singing Detective (series) 1986, The Short and Curlies 1987, Virtuoso 1988, Monster Maker 1989, A Small Mourning 1989, The Finding 1990, Newshounds 1990, Gone to the Dogs (series) 1991, Selling Hitler (series) 1991, Gone to Seed (series) 1992, The Wimbledon Poisoner (series) 1994, Pride and Prejudice (series) 1995, The Snow Queen's Revenge (voice) 1996, No Bananas (series) 1996, Cold Lazarus (series) 1996, Karaoke (series) 1996, The Ugly Duckling (voice) 1997, The Missing Postman 1997, Crapston Villas (series, voice) 1998, Stressed Eric (series, voice) 1998, Santa's Last Christmas (voice) 1999, Let Them Eat Cake (series) 1999, Jack and the Beanstalk (voice) 2000, Fat Friends (series 1–4) 2000, Hans Christian Andersen: My Life as a Fairy Tale 2001, Adrian Mole: The Cappuccino Years 2001, Dalziel and Pascoe 2002, 2004, Comic Relief 2003: The Big Hair Do 2003, The Worst Week of My Life (series) 2004–06, Bosom Pals (voice) 2004, Twisted Tales – Fruitcake of the Living Dead 2005, Who Gets the Dog? 2006, The Worst Christmas of My Life: Part 1 2006, Part 2 2006, Part 3 2006, The Last Detective (series) 2007, Marple: Ordeal by Innocence (film) 2007, The Dinner Party (film) 2007, Fanny Hill (series) 2007, Who Gets the Dog? (film) 2007, The Omid Djalili Show (series) 2007, Gavin & Stacey (Series 1, 2 and 3) 2007–10, Gavin & Stacey Christmas Special 2008, Come Rain Come Shine (ITV drama) 2010, All Roads Lead Home (BBC) 2011, Playhouse Presents (series) – King of the Teds 2012, A Civil Arrangement (film) 2012, Inspector George Gently (series) – The Lost Child 2012, Little Crackers (series) 2012, Lewis (series) – Intelligent Design 2013, The Syndicate (series) 2013, Love & Marriage (series) 2013. *Address:* c/o Sue Latimer, Artists Rights Group Ltd, 4 Great Portland Street, London, W1W 8PA, England (office). *Telephone:* (20) 7436-6400 (office). *Fax:* (20) 7436-6700 (office). *E-mail:* info@argtalent.com (office). *Website:* www.argtalent.com (office).

STEADMAN, Ralph Idris; British cartoonist, writer and illustrator; b. 15 May 1936; s. of Raphael Steadman and Gwendoline Steadman; m. 1st Sheila Thwaite 1959 (divorced 1971); two s. two d.; m. 2nd Anna Deverson 1972; one d.; ed London School of Printing and Graphic Arts; with de Havilland Aircraft Co. 1952; cartoonist, Kemsley (Thomson) Newspapers 1956–59; freelance for Punch, Private Eye, Daily Telegraph during 1960s; political cartoonist, New Statesman 1978–80; designed set of stamps depicting Halley's Comet 1986; Artist-in-Residence, Leviathan (series of films, BBC 2) 1999; designer of set and costumes, The Crucible, Royal Ballet 2000; Hon. DLitt (Kent) 1995; Designers and Art Dirs Asscn Gold Award 1977, Silver Award 1977, Lifetime Achievement Award – Milton Caniff Award, Nat. Cartoonists Soc. (USA) 2005. *Written and illustrated:* Alice in Wonderland 1967, Alice Through the Looking Glass 1972, Sigmund Freud 1979, A Leg in the Wind and Other Canine Curses 1982, I, Leonardo 1983, That's My Dad 1986, The Big I Am 1988, No Room to Swing a Cat 1989, Near the Bone 1990, Tales of Weirrd 1990, Still Life with Bottle, Whisky According to Ralph Steadman 1994, Jones of Colorado 1998, Gonzo: The Art 1998, little.com 2000, The Joke's Over 2006. *Illustrator:* many books from 1961, including Friendship 1990 (in aid of John McCarthy), Adrian Mitchell, Heart on the Left, Poems 1953–84 1997, Roald Dahl, The Mildenhall Treasure 1999, Doodaa: The Balletic Art of Gavin Twinge 2002.

Publications include: Jelly Book 1968, Still Life with Raspberry: collected drawings 1969, The Little Red Computer 1970, Dogs Bodies 1971, Bumper to Bumper Book 1973, Two Donkeys and the Bridge 1974, Flowers for the Moon 1974, The Watchdog and the Lazy Dog 1974, America: drawings 1975, America: collected drawings 1977 (r.e. Scar Strangled Banger 1987), Between the Eyes 1984, Paranoids 1986, The Grapes of Ralph 1992, Teddy Where Are You? 1994, Sigmund Freud 1997, Untrodden Grapes 2005, Bruised Memories: Gonzo, Hunter Thompson and Me 2006, The Joke's Over 2007, The Devil's Dictionary (with Ambrose Bierce) 2008, Ralph Steadman's Book of Dogs 2011 Ralph Steadman's Book of Cats 2012, Ralph Steadman's Book of Extinct Boids 2012. *Leisure interests:* gardening, sheep husbandry, fishing, guitar, trumpet. *Address:* c/o Nat Sobel, Sobel Weber Associates, Inc., 146 East 19th Street, New York, NY 10003-2404, USA (office). *Telephone:* (212) 420-8585 (office). *Website:* www.sobelweber.com (office); www.ralphsteadman.com.

STEBBINS, Donald J., BSc, MBA; American business executive; b. 1958; ed Miami Univ., Univ. of Michigan; fmrly with Bankers Trust Co. and Citibank; joined Lear Corpn as Vice-Pres. Treas. 1992, then Sr Vice-Pres. Chief Financial Officer 1997, then COO Americas, Co-COO Europe, Asia and Africa; Pres. and COO Visteon Corpn 2005–08, Pres. and CEO 2008–12; mem. Bd of Dirs WABCO Holdings Inc., ITT Corpn 2012–, Allied Specialty Vehicles 2013–; mem. Business Advisory Council, Miami Univ.; Trustee Detroit Country Day School; mem. Business Leaders for Mich.

STEBBINS, Paul H.; American business executive; *Executive Chairman, World Fuel Services Corporation;* ed Georgetown Univ.; co-f., with Michael Kasbar, Trans-Tec Services, Inc. (global marine fuel services co.), acquired by World Fuel 1995, Exec. and Dir of World Fuel Services Corpn 1995–, Exec. Vice-Pres. and Pres. of marine segment 1995–2000, Pres. and COO World Fuel Services Corpn 2000–02, Exec. Chair. 2002–; mem. Bd of Dirs First Solar, Inc.; mem. Business Round Table; mem. Bd of Trustees, New World Symphony. *Address:* World Fuel Services Corporation, 9800 NW 41st Street, Suite 400, Miami, FL 33178, USA (office). *Telephone:* (305) 428-8000 (office). *E-mail:* info@wfscorp.com (office). *Website:* www.wfscorp.com (office).

STEEDS, John Wickham, PhD, FRS, FInstP; British physicist and academic; *Professor Emeritus of Physics, University of Bristol;* b. 9 Feb. 1940, London, England; s. of John Henry William Steeds and Ethel Amelia Steeds (née Tyler); m. Diana Mary Kettlewell 1969; two d.; ed Haberdashers' Aske's School, Univ. Coll. London, Univ. of Cambridge; Mullard Research Fellow, Selwyn Coll. Cambridge 1964–67; Lecturer, Physics Dept, Univ. of Bristol 1967–77, Reader 1977–85, Prof. of Electron Microscopy 1985–2007, Head of Dept 2001–05, Henry Overton Wills Prof. of Physics 2002–07, Prof. Emer. 2007–; fmr mem. Council European Pole Univ. of Lille; Chair. Emersons Innovations Ltd; Holweck Medal (Soc. Française de Physique and Inst. of Physics) 1996. *Publications:* Introduction to Anistropic Elasticity Theory of Dislocations 1973, Electron Diffraction of Phases in Alloys (with J. F. Mansfield) 1984, Thin Film Diamond (co-ed.) 1994. *Leisure interest:* tennis. *Address:* H.H. Wills Physics Laboratory, Room 3.20, Royal Fort Tyndall Avenue, University of Bristol, Bristol, BS8 1TL (office); Hall Floor Flat, 4 Codrinton Place, Bristol, BS8 3DE, England (home). *Telephone:* (117) 928-8730 (office); (117) 973-2183 (home). *Fax:* (117) 925-5624 (office). *E-mail:* J.W.Steeds@bristol.ac.uk (office). *Website:* www.phy.bris.ac.uk (office).

STEEL, Danielle Fernande Schüelein; American writer; b. 14 Aug. 1950, New York; d. of John Steel and Norma Schüelein-Steel (née Stone); m. 2nd Bill Toth 1977; m. 3rd John A. Traina Jr; four s. five d.; ed Lycée Français, Parsons School of Design, New York, Univ. of New York; worked as public relations and advertising exec., Manhattan, New York; published first novel 1973, then wrote advertising copy and poems for women's magazines; wrote first bestseller, The Promise 1979; Officier, Ordre des Arts et des Lettres. *Publications:* Going Home 1973, Passion's Promise 1977, Now and Forever 1978, Season of Passion 1978, The Promise 1979, Summer's End 1980, The Ring 1980, To Love Again 1981, Palomino 1981, Loving 1981, Remembrance 1981, Love: Poems 1981, A Perfect Stranger 1982, Once in a Lifetime 1982, Crossings 1982, Thurston House 1983, Changes 1983, Full Circle 1984, Having a Baby (contrib., non-fiction) 1984, Family Album 1985, Secrets 1985, Wanderlust 1986, Fine Things 1987, Kaleidoscope 1987, Zoya 1988, Star 1989, Daddy 1989, Heartbeat 1991, Message from Nam 1991, No Greater Love 1991, Jewels 1992, Mixed Blessings 1992, Vanished 1993, Accident 1994, The Gift 1994, Wings 1995, Lightning 1995, Five Days in Paris 1995, Malice 1995, Silent Honor 1996, The Ranch 1996, The Ghost 1997, Special Delivery 1997, His Bright Light (non-fiction) 1998, The Long Road Home 1998, The Klone and I 1998, Mirror Image 1998, Bittersweet 1999, Granny Dan 1999, Irresistible Forces 1999, The Wedding 2000, The House on Hope Street 2000, Journey 2000, Leap of Faith 2001, The Kiss 2001, Lone Eagle 2001, The Cottage 2002, Sunset in San Tropez 2002, Answered Prayers 2002, Dating Game 2003, Johnny Angel 2003, Safe Harbour 2003, Echoes 2004, Toxic Bachelors 2005, The House 2006, Impossible 2006, Miracle 2006, Coming Out 2006, HRH 2006, Bungalow 2 2007, Amazing Grace 2007, Sisters 2007, Honor Thyself 2008, A Good Woman 2008, Rogue 2008, One Day at a Time 2009, Summer's End 2009, Matters of the Heart 2009, Southern Lights 2009, Big Girl 2010, Family Ties 2010, Legacy 2010, Happy Birthday 2011, Hotel Vendome 2011, Betrayal 2012, Friends Forever 2012; eight children's books, one book of poetry. *Leisure interest:* my children. *Address:* c/o Random House Publicity Department, 1745 Broadway, New York, New York, NY 10019 (office); PO Box 1637, New York, NY 10156, USA (home). *E-mail:* atrandompublicity@randomhouse.com (office). *Website:* daniellesteel.com.

STEEL, Robert (Bob) K., BA, MBA; American banking executive and fmr government official; *President and CEO, Wachovia Corporation;* b. 3 Aug. 1951; m. Gillian Steel; three d.; ed Duke Univ., Univ. of Chicago; joined Goldman Sachs 1976, held several exec. positions including first as individual and institutional salesperson, then Man. Dir and Co-head of Equity Sales and Trading, Pnr, Head of Equities Div., New York, Co-Chief Operating Officer, Equities Div., Man. Dir and Head of Equities Div., Goldman Sachs Equities Europe 1988–94, Vice-Chair., Co-head of Equities Div. and Fixed Income 1998–2001, Head of Equities Div. 2001–02, Vice-Chair. 2002–04, Advisory Dir and Chair. (non-exec.) Securities 2004–06; Sr Fellow, John F. Kennedy School of Govt, Harvard Univ. 2004–06; Under-Sec. for Domestic Finance, US Dept of the Treasury, Washington, DC 2006–08; Pres. and CEO Wachovia Corpn 2008–; Chair. Bd of Trustees, Duke Univ.; fmr mem. Bd of

Dirs Barclays Bank PLC, Barclays PLC. *Address:* Wachovia Corpn, 301 South College Street, Suite 4000, One Wachovia Center, Charlotte, NC 28288-0013, USA (office). *Telephone:* (704) 590-0000 (office). *E-mail:* info@wachovia.com (office). *Website:* www.wachovia.com (office).

STEEL OF AIKWOOD, Baron (Life Peer), cr. 1997, of Ettrick Forest in the Scottish Borders; **David Martin Scott Steel,** KT, KBE, PC, MA, LLB, DL; Scottish politician, journalist and broadcaster; b. 31 March 1938, Kirkcaldy; s. of Very Rev. Dr David Steel; m. Judith Mary MacGregor 1962; two s. one d.; ed Prince of Wales School, Nairobi, Kenya, George Watson's Coll. and Univ. of Edinburgh; Pres., Edin. Univ. Liberals 1959; Past Pres., Students' Rep. Council 1960; Asst Sec., Scottish Liberal Party 1962–64; MP for Roxburgh, Selkirk and Peebles 1965–83, for Tweeddale, Ettrick and Lauderdale 1983–97; Scottish Liberal Whip 1967–70, Liberal Chief Whip 1970–75; Leader of Liberal Party 1976–88; Co-Founder, Social and Liberal Democrats 1988; Vice-Pres., Liberal Int. 1978–93, Pres. 1994–96; mem. Parl. del. to UN Gen. Ass. 1967; Sponsor, Pvt. Member's Bill to reform law on abortion 1966–67; Pres., Anti-Apartheid Movt of UK 1966–69; Chair., Shelter, Scotland 1969–73, Countryside Movt 1995–97; BBC TV Interviewer in Scotland 1964–65; Presenter of weekly religious programme for Scottish TV 1966–67, for Granada 1969, for BBC 1971–76; Dir, Border TV 1991–99; Rector, Univ. of Edin. 1982–85; MSP 1999–2003, Presiding Officer of Scottish Parl. 1999–2003; Chubb Fellow, Yale Univ., USA 1987; DL Ettrick and Lauderdale and Roxburghshire; Freedom of Tweeddale 1989, of Ettrick and Lauderdale 1990; Grand Cross of Order of Merit (Germany), Chevalier de la Légion d'honneur, Knight of the Thistle 2004; Dr hc (Stirling) 1991, (Heriot Watt) 1996; Hon. DLitt (Buckingham) 1994; Hon. LLD (Edin.) 1997, (Strathclyde) 2000, (Aberdeen) 2001, (St Andrews) 2003, (Glasgow Caledonian) 2004, (Brunel) 2010; Hon. DUniv (Open Univ.) 2001; Bronze Medal London-Cape Town Classic Car Rally 1998. *Publications include:* Boost for the Borders 1964, No Entry 1969, A House Divided 1980, Border Country 1985, Partners in One Nation 1985, The Time Has Come (with David Owen) 1987, Mary Stuart's Scotland (with Judy Steel) 1987, Against Goliath (autobiography) 1989. *Leisure interests:* angling, classic cars. *Address:* House of Lords, Westminster, London, SW1A 0PW, England (office); Ettrick Lodge, Selkirk, TD7 4LE, Scotland (home). *Telephone:* (20) 7219-4433 (office). *E-mail:* steeld@parliament.uk (office).

STEELE, Nickolas; Grenadian business executive and politician; *Minister of Foreign Affairs and International Business;* ed Northeastern Univ., USA; Owner, Steele's Auto Supplies Co. Ltd; fmr Shadow Minister of Trade and Investment; MP for Town of St George's 2013–; Minister of Foreign Affairs and Int. Business 2013–; organizer and country head, Caribbean Canada Emerging Leaders Org.; mem. numerous public bodies including Grenada Bd of Tourism, Grenada Chamber of Industry and Commerce, Westmorland School, Nat. Emergency Relief Org. (NERO); mem. New Nat. Party (NNP). *Address:* Ministry of Foreign Affairs and International Business, Ministerial Complex, 4th Floor, Botanical Gardens, Tanteen, St George's, Grenada (office). *Telephone:* 440-2640 (office). *Fax:* 440-4184 (office). *E-mail:* foreignaffairs@gov.gd (office).

STEELE, Tommy, OBE; British actor and singer; b. (Thomas Hicks), 17 Dec. 1936, Bermondsey, London; s. of Thomas Walter Hicks and Elizabeth Ellen Bennett; m. Ann Donoughue 1960; one d.; ed Bacon's School for Boys, Bermondsey; entered Merchant Navy 1952; first stage appearance Empire Theatre, Sunderland 1956, London debut 1957; roles include Buttons (Cinderella), London 1958/59, Tony Lumpkin (She Stoops to Conquer) 1960, Arthur Kipps (Half A Sixpence) 1963/64, New York 1965/66, Truffaldino (The Servant of Two Masters) 1968, title role in Hans Andersen, London 1974/75, 1977/78, 1981, Don Lockwood (Singin' in the Rain), London (also dir) 1983–85, 1989 Some Like it Hot (also dir) 1991, What a Show! 1995; film debut in Kill Me Tomorrow 1956; sculpted tribute to the Beatles' Eleanor Rigby 1982; Hon. DLitt (South Bank) 1998. *Films include:* The Tommy Steele Story, The Duke Wore Jeans 1957, Tommy the Toreador 1959, Light Up the Sky 1963, Its All Happening 1966, The Happiest Millionaire 1967, Half A Sixpence, Finian's Rainbow 1968, Where's Jack 1971; TV debut in Off the Record 1956, cabaret debut, Caesar's Palace, Las Vegas 1974; composed and recorded musical autobiog. My Life, My Song 1974. *Live performances include:* An Evening with Tommy Steele 1979, Tommy Steele in Concert 1998, lead role in Bill Kenwright's stage production of Scrooge (UK tour) 2003–04; Quincy's Quest (TV) 1979. *Publications include:* Hans Andersen (co-author, stage version), Quincy 1981, The Final Run 1983, Bermondsey Boy (autobiog.) 2006. *Leisure interests:* tennis, painting, sculpture. *Address:* c/o Laurie Mansfield, International Artistes, Suite 17, Adam House, 7-10 Adam Street, London, WC2N 6AA, England (office). *Telephone:* (20) 7520-9411 (office). *E-mail:* info@lmassocltd.com (office). *Website:* www.lauriemansfield.co.uk (office).

STEELE-PERKINS, Christopher Horace, BSc; British photographer; b. 28 July 1947, Burma; s. of Alfred Steele-Perkins and Mary Lloyd; m. 1st Jacqueline de Gier 1984 (divorced 1999); two s.; m. 2nd Miyako Yamada 1999; ed Christ's Hospital, Horsham, Sussex, Univ. of Newcastle; mem. Exit Group, London 1974–82; Assoc. Viva Agency, Paris 1976–79; mem. Photography Cttee, Arts Council of GB 1977–79; mem. Magnum Photos 1983–, Pres. 1996–98; Visiting Prof., Mushishino Art Univ., Tokyo 2000; World Press Oskar Barnack 1988, Tom Hopkinson Award for Photo-journalism 1988, Robert Capa Gold Medal 1989, Cooperative Award, One World Award (both for film Dying for Publicity) 1994, Naçion-Premier Photojournalism Award, World Press Daily Life First 2000. *Television films:* Dying for Publicity 1993, Afghan Taliban 1995. *Publications:* The Teds 1979, About 70 Photographs 1980, Survival Programmes 1982, Beirut: Frontline Story 1982, The Pleasure Principle 1989, St Thomas' Hospital 1992, Afghanistan 2000, Fuji 2002, Echoes 2004, England, My England 2009, Fading Light: Portraits of Centenarians 2012. *Leisure interests:* boxing, chess, photography, film, music, literature. *Address:* 49 St Francis Road, London, SE22 8DE,; Magnum Photos, 63 Gee Street, London, EC1V 3RS, England (office). *Telephone:* (20) 7490-1771 (office); (20) 8693-1114. *E-mail:* chrissteeleperkins@hotmail.com (office). *Website:* www.magnumphotos.com; chrissteeleperkins.com.

STEENBURGEN, Mary; American film actress; b. 8 Feb. 1953, Newport, Ariz.; m. 1st Malcolm McDowell 1980 (divorced); one s. one d.; m. 2nd Ted Danson (q.v.) 1995; ed Neighborhood Playhouse. *Films include:* Goin' South 1978, Time After Time 1979, Melvin and Howard (Acad. Award for Best Supporting Actress) 1980, Ragtime 1981, A Midsummer Night's Sex Comedy 1982, Romantic Comedy 1983,

Cross Creek 1983, Sanford Meisner – The Theatre's Best Kept Secret 1984, One Magic Christmas 1985, Dead of Winter 1987, End of the Line (also exec. producer) 1987, The Whales of August 1987, The Attic: The Hiding of Anne Frank 1988, Parenthood 1989, Back to the Future Part III 1989, Miss Firecracker 1989, The Long Walk Home 1990, The Butcher's Wife 1991, What's Eating Gilbert Grape 1993, Philadelphia 1993, Pontiac Moon 1994, Clifford 1994, It Runs in the Family 1994, My Family, Powder, The Grass Harp, Nixon, About Sarah 1995, Picnic (TV) 2000, Wish You Were Dead 2001, The Trumpet of the Swan 2001, Sunshine State 2002, Life as a House 2001, Nobody's Baby 2002, Casa de Los Babys 2003, Elf 2003, Hope Springs 2003, Marilyn Hotchkiss Ballroom Dancing & Charm School 2005, Inland Empire 2006, The Dead Girl 2006, Elvis and Anabelle 2007, Nobel Son 2007, Numb 2007, The Brave One 2007, Honeydripper 2007, Step Brothers 2008, Four Christmases 2008, In the Electric Mist 2009, The Proposal 2009, Did You Hear About the Morgans? 2009, Dirty Girl 2010, The Help 2011. *Television includes:* Joan of Arcadia (series) 2003–05, Curb Your Enthusiasm 2000–09, Robot Chicken 2011, Bored to Death 2011, Wilfred 2011–12, 30 Rock 2012. *Theatre appearances include:* Holiday (Old Vic, London) 1987, Candida (Broadway) 1993. *Address:* c/o Gersh Agency, 9465 Wilshire Blvd, 6th Floor, Beverly Hills, CA 90212, USA.

STEENSGAARD, Niels Palle, DPhil; Danish academic; *Professor, Faculty of the Humanities, Københavns Universitet;* b. 7 March 1932, Rødovre; s. of Knud Steensgaard and Kirstine Steensgaard (née Knop); m. Illa Frilis 1954; two d.; ed Univ. of Copenhagen, School of Oriental and African Studies, London, UK; Assoc. Prof., Inst. of History, Univ. of Copenhagen 1962, Dean, Faculty of Humanities 1974–76, Prof. 1977–; mem. Danish Research Council for the Humanities 1980–88, Chair. 1985–87; mem. Nordic Cttee Humanities Research Councils 1983–88, Chair. 1985–87; Danish Rep., Standing Cttee for the Humanities, European Science Foundation 1983–88; mem. Swedish Council for Research in the Humanities and Social Sciences 1992–96; Chair. Nat. Cttee of Danish Historians 1989; mem. Royal Danish Acad. of Sciences and Letters 1983, Academia Europaea 1989, Royal Historical Soc. 1997. *Publications:* The Asian Trade Revolution of the Seventeenth Century 1973, Verden På Opdagelsernes tid 1984, Verdensmarked og kulturmøter 1985. *Leisure interests:* losing my way in large books or towns. *Address:* Faculty of Humanities, Københavns Universitet, Njalsgade 80, 2300 Copenhagen (office); Lemnosvej 19, Copenhagen 2300 S, Denmark (home). *Telephone:* 35-32-80-60 (office). *Fax:* 35-32-80-52 (office). *E-mail:* hum-fak@fak.hum.ku.dk (office). *Website:* www.hum.ku.dk (office).

ȘTEFĂNESCU, I. Ștefan, PhD; Romanian historian; b. 24 May 1929, Goicea, Dolj Co.; s. of Ion Ștefănescu and Dumitra Ștefănescu; m. Teodora Ștefănescu 1958; one s. one d.; ed Coll. of History, Bucharest Univ. Lomonosov Univ. Moscow; researcher in history 1951–65; Head Romanian Medieval History Dept of the N Iorga Inst. of History of the Romanian Acad. 1965–66, Deputy Dir 1966–70, Dir 1970–90; Dean of the Coll. of History and Philosophy, Bucharest Univ. 1977–85; mem. Romanian Acad. of Social and Political Sciences 1970–90; corresp. mem. Romanian Academy 1974, mem. 1992; mem. Romanian Soc. for Historical Sciences (on main Bd), Int. Comm. for Hist. of State Ass., Comm. int. des études slaves; Vice-Chair. of the Nat. Cttee of Historical Sciences; Chair. of the Dept of History and Archaeology, Romanian Acad. of Social and Political Sciences 1970–90; mem. European Acad. of History 1981–; Deputy Nat. Ass. 1975–80, 1985–90; Order of Scientific Merit 1966, Star of the Repub. 1971; Prize of the Romanian Acad. 1967, Romanian Acad. Silver Medal 2003. *Works include:* The History of the Romanian People 1970, Medieval Wallachia from Basarab I the Founder until Michael the Brave, 1970, History of Dobrudja, Vol. III (with I. Barnea) 1971, Demography – a Dimension of History 1974, Encyclopedia of Romanian Historiography 1978, The Romanian Nation 1984, The Beginnings of Romanian Principalities 1991, The Romanian Principalities in the 14th–16th Centuries 1992, Romania's Economic History (co-author) 1994, History of the Romanians in the 17th Century 1996, Romania: Historical-Geographic Atlas (co-author) 1996, The Illustrated History of Craiova (co-author) 1996, The Romanian Principalities in the Eighteenth Century 1998, Studies of Economic History and History of Economic Thought (co-author) 1998, A History of the Romanians (Medieval History), Vol. III (co-author), Vol. IV (Ed.) 2001, Romania: Historical Landmarks (co-author) 2004. *Address:* 125 Calea Victoriei, 010071 Bucharest (office); 214 Calea Victoriei, Apt. 44, 010098 Bucharest, Romania (home). *Telephone:* (1) 2128640 (office); (1) 6593932 (home). *Fax:* (1) 2116608 (office). *E-mail:* msimionescu@acad.ro (office). *Website:* www.academiaromana.ro (office).

STEFANIUK, Franciszek Jerzy; Polish economist, politician and farmer; b. 4 June 1944, Drelów, Biała Podlaska Prov.; m.; five c.; ed Economic Tech. School, Międzyrzec Podlaski; manages own farm; Chair. Cooperative of Agricultural Circles, Drelów 1978–82; mem. United Peasant Party (ZSL) 1963–89, Polish Peasant Party (Polskie Stronnictwo Ludowe—PSL) 1989–, Chair. Party Commune Cttee, Drelów 1982–89; Chair. Party Voivodship Cttee, Biała Podlaska 1990–98, Vice-Chair. Bd Supreme Exec. Cttee 1992–97, Chair. Supervisory Bd PSL 2000–; Deputy to Sejm (Parl.) 1989–; Deputy Chair. PSL Parl. Caucus 1991–93; Vice-Marshal (Deputy Speaker) Sejm 1997–2001. *Leisure interests:* folklore, folk poetry, bee-keeping. *Address:* Biuro Poselskie w Białej Podlaskiej, 21-500 Biała Podlaska, ul. Janowska 3; Kancelaria Sejmu RP, 00-902 Warsaw, ul. Wiejska 4/6/8, Poland (office). *Telephone:* (22) 6942321 (office). *E-mail:* Franciszek.Stefaniuk@sejm.pl (office). *Website:* stefaniuk.sejm.pl.

STEFANOVIĆ, Nebojša, MEconSc, PhD; Serbian business executive and politician; *Minister of Internal Affairs;* b. 20 Nov. 1976, Belgrade; m. Ana Filipović; one d.; ed Mihajlo Petrović Alas Gymnasium No. 9, Belgrade, Faculty of Business Studies, Megatrend Univ.; worked in various pvt. firms, including computer equipment distribution and marketing; Marketing Dir, Intersped JSC 2004–08; Councillor, Belgrade City Ass. 2004–08, 2012–; Financial Man., Jabuka JSC 2008; mem. Serbian Radical Party −2008, left to found Serbian Progressive Party (SPP) 2008–, mem. Presidency, Vice-Pres. Main Bd and Pres. Belgrade City Bd; Deputy in Nat. Ass. of Serbia 2007–, Chair. Cttee on Trade and Tourism 2007–08, Pres. (Speaker), Nat. Ass. of Serbia 2012–14; Minister of Internal Affairs 2014–. *Address:* Ministry of Internal Affairs, 11070 Belgrade, bul. Mihaila Pupina 2, Serbia (office). *Telephone:* (11) 3112916 (office). *Fax:* (11) 3114650 (office). *E-mail:* info@mup.gov.rs (office). *Website:* www.mup.gov.rs (office).

STEFFEN, Will, PhD; Australian environmental scientist and academic; *Executive Director, Climate Change Institute, Australian National University;* ed Univ. of Florida, USA; began career as research chemist; fmr Researcher, Div. of Environmental Mechanics, CSIRO, Canberra; Exec. Dir Int. Geosphere-Biosphere Programme, Stockholm, Sweden 1998–2004; Visiting Fellow, Bureau of Rural Sciences, Dept of Agric., Fisheries and Forestry 2004–05; Dir Fenner School of Environment and Soc., also Pro Vice-Chancellor (Research), ANU, becoming Exec. Dir ANU Climate Change Inst.; Science Adviser to Australian Dept of Climate. *Address:* Climate Change Institute, Australian National University, Room 4027, Coombs Building, Canberra, ACT 0200, Australia (office). *Telephone:* (2) 6125-6599 (office). *E-mail:* will.steffen@anu.edu.au (office). *Website:* www.anu.edu.au/climatechange (office).

STEFFLER, John Earl, BA, MA; Canadian poet, writer and academic; b. 13 Nov. 1947, Toronto, Ont.; one s. one d.; ed Univ. of Toronto, Univ. of Guelph; Prof. of English, Sir Wilfred Grenfell Coll., Memorial Univ. of Newfoundland, Corner Brook Campus 1975–2005 (retd); Parl. Poet Laureate 2006–08; Scholar-in-Residence, Concordia Univ. 2007; mem. League of Canadian Poets, PEN, Writers' Alliance of Newfoundland and Labrador; Newfoundland Arts Council Artist of the Year Award 1992, Joseph S. Stauffer Prize 1993, Newfoundland and Labrador Poetry Award 1998, 2003. *Publications:* An Explanation of Yellow 1980, The Grey Islands 1985, The Wreckage of Play 1988, The Afterlife of George Cartwright (novel) (Smithbooks/Books in Canada First Novel Award 1992, Thomas Raddall Atlantic Fiction Award 1992) 1991, That Night We Were Ravenous (poems) (Atlantic Poetry Award) 1998, Helix 2003, Lookout 2010; contrib. to journals and periodicals. *Address:* c/o McClelland & Stewart Ltd, 75 Sherbourne Street, 5th Floor, Toronto, ON M5A 2P9, Canada.

ŠTEFKA, Maj.-Gen. Pavel; Czech army general; *Chief of the General Staff;* b. 15 Sept. 1954, Ruda nad Modravou; s. of Ludevít Štefka and Irena Štefka; m. Jirina; three d.; ed Mil. Coll., Vyskov, Mil. Acad., Warsaw, European Business School, Prague and American Nat. War Coll., Washington DC, USA; Chief of Staff of motorized bn., then Deputy Chief of Staff of motorized Regt, E Mil. Dist; Chief of Staff, later Commdr of motorized Regt, Bratislava; Chief of Operations in an armoured div.; tutor Mil. Acad. Brno 1991–94; Commdr 6th Mechanized Brigade, Brno 1994; Deputy Commdr 2nd Army Corps and Chief of Staff HQ Ground Forces, Olomouc 1994–98; Chief of Operations Section of the Gen. Staff, Army of the Czech Repub. 1998–99, Chief of the Gen. Staff 2002–; Cross of Merit of Minister of Defence (Czech Republic), Medal for Service to the Nation, NATO Medal for Service for Peace and Freedom, Commemorative Medal of Minister of Defence (Slovakia), Silver Medal of Polish Army, Commemorative Medal of Auxiliary Tech. Bns, Hon. Remembrance Badge of Fifty Years of NATO. *Leisure interests:* sport, film, travel. *Address:* c/o Ministry of Defence, Tychonova 1, 160 01 Prague 6, Czech Republic (office). *Telephone:* (2) 33041111 (office). *Fax:* (2) 3116238 (office). *E-mail:* stefkap@army.cz (office). *Website:* www.army.cz (office).

STEGER, Joseph A., PhD; American academic and fmr university administrator; b. 17 Feb. 1937, Philadelphia, Pa; s. of Joseph A. Steger and Georgianna Kirby; m. Carol R. Steger 1977; one s. one d.; ed Gettysburg Coll. and Kansas State Univ.; Sr Research Analyst, Prudential Insurance Co. 1964–66; Asst Prof., Assoc. Prof. Dept of Psychology, State Univ. of New York 1966–71; Prof., School of Man., Rensselaer Polytechnic Inst. 1971–74, Dean, School of Man. 1974–79, Dean and Vice-Pres. for Admin. and Budget 1977–78; Dean and Acting Provost 1978–79; Dir Organizational Devt and Human Resources, Colt Industries Inc. 1979–82; Sr Vice-Pres. and Provost, Univ. of Cincinnati 1982–84, Pres. 1984–2003; public comm. to review Cincinnati school finances 2004–; fmr Chair. Bd of Trustees Drake Center. *Publication:* Readings in Statistics for the Behavioral Scientist 1971. *Leisure interests:* sailing, golf. *Address:* c/o Office of the President, University of Cincinnati, PO Box 210063, Cincinnati, OH 45221-0063, USA.

STEHELIN, Dominique Jean Bernard, PhD; French research scientist; *Director of Research, Institute of Biology, Centre national de la recherche scientifique (CNRS);* b. 4 Sept. 1943, Thoisy; s. of Robert Stehelin and Berthe Zimmermann; m. 1st Liliane Fachan 1969 (divorced 1975); one d.; m. 2nd Monique Braun 2001; ed Lycée Fustel, Strasbourg and Univ. Louis Pasteur, Strasbourg; Perm. Researcher, sponsored by CNRS, at Louis Pasteur Univ. 1969–71; Postdoctoral studies at Institut de la Recherche Scientifique sur le Cancer with Dr A. Lwoff, Villejuif 1970–71; Visiting Scientist with J. M. Bishop at Univ. of Calif. Medical Center, San Francisco, USA 1972–75; Head of Molecular Oncology Research Unit, Institut Pasteur, Lille 1979–84, Prof. 1984–; Dir of Research CNRS 1985–; Founding Dir CNRS Inst. of Biology, Lille 1994–2000; Corresp. mem. Acad. of Sciences 1990–; mem. American Soc. of Microbiology, European Molecular Biology Org., Editorial Bd Oncogene; Chevalier, Ordre nat. du Mérite; Officier, Légion d'honneur; Grand Prix, Acad. des Sciences 1975, Louis Jeantet Award (Medicine), Geneva 1987 and four other awards. *Publications:* more than 300 int. publs on cancer research (cancer genes, retrovirus, angiogenesis). *Leisure interests:* skiing, diving, music. *Address:* CNRS Institut de Biologie, 1 rue Calmette, 59021 Lille (office); 36 rue Jacquemars Gielée, 59800 Lille, France (home). *Telephone:* (3) 20-87-11-08/09 (office); (3) 20-07-63-35 (home). *Fax:* (3) 20-87-11-11 (office). *E-mail:* dominique.stehelin@ibl.fr (office).

STEICHEN, René, DenD; Luxembourg business executive and fmr politician; *Chairman, SES Global;* b. 27 Nov. 1942; m.; three c.; ed Lycée Classique, Diekirch, Cours Supérieurs, Luxembourg, Faculties of Law, Aix-en-Provence and Paris and Inst. d'Etudes Politiques, Paris; lawyer, Diekirch 1969–84; mem. Diekirch Town Council 1969, Mayor 1974–84; Christian Social Deputy in Parl. 1979; Sec. of State for Agric. and Viticulture 1984, of Agric., Viticulture and Rural Devt and Minister-Del. for Cultural Research and Scientific Research 1989–93; Commr for Agric. and Rural Devt, EC 1993–95; Chair. Soc. Européenne des Satellites 1996–2000, SES Global 2001–. *Address:* SES Global SA, Château de Betzdorf, 6815 Betzdorf, RCS LuxembourgB, 81267 (office). *Telephone:* 7107251 (office). *Fax:* 710725227 (office). *Website:* www.ses.com (office).

STEIDEL, Charles (Chuck), AB, PhD; American astronomer and academic; *Lee A. DuBridge Professor of Astronomy, California Institute of Technology;* b. 14 Oct. 1962, Ithaca, NY; ed Princeton Univ., California Inst. of Tech.; Hubble Fellow, Univ. of California, Berkeley 1990–93; Asst Prof. of Physics, MIT 1993–95; Asst Prof. of Astronomy, California Inst. of Tech. 1995–97, Assoc. Prof. of Astronomy

1997–98, Prof. of Astronomy 1998–2004, Lee A. DuBridge Prof. of Astronomy 2004–; Tinsley Visiting Prof., Univ. of Texas 2010; mem. NAS 2006; Alfred P. Sloan Foundation Fellowship 1994–96, NSF Young Investigator Award 1994–99, ASCIT Undergraduate Teaching Award, California Inst. of Tech. 1997, Helen B. Warner Prize, American Astronomical Soc. 1997, David and Lucile Packard Foundation Fellowship 1997–2002, Lyman Spitzer Lecturer, Princeton Univ. 2001, MacArthur Fellowship 2002–07, Sackler Lecturer, Leiden Observatory (Netherlands) 2006, Medal of Institut d'Astrophysique, Paris 2008, Mohler Prize Lecturer, Univ. of Michigan 2009, Cosmology Prize, Gruber Foundation 2010. *Publications:* numerous papers in professional journals. *Address:* 252 Center for Astrophysics, Caltech 249-17, Pasadena, CA 91125, USA (office). *Telephone:* (626) 395-4168 (office). *E-mail:* ccs@astro.caltech.edu (office). *Website:* www.astro.caltech.edu/~ccs (office).

STEIGER, Paul E., BA; American journalist and editor; *Executive Chairman, ProPublica;* b. 15 Aug. 1942, Bronx, New York; ed Yale Univ.; staff writer, Los Angeles Times 1968, Econ. Corresp., Washington, DC Bureau 1971–78, apptd Business Ed. 1978; with Wall Street Journal, reporter for San Francisco Bureau 1966–68, Asst Man. Ed. 1983–85, Deputy Man. Ed. 1985–91, Man. Ed. 1991–2007, Ed.-at-Large 2007–, also Vice-Pres. Dow Jones & Co.; Ed.-in-Chief, Pres. and CEO ProPublica (ind. non-profit newsroom) 2008–12, Exec. Chair. 2013–; mem. Reporters Cttee for Freedom of the Press (mem. Steering Cttee); Trustee, John S. and James L. Knight Foundation; mem. Pulitzer Prize Bd 1998–2007 (Chair. 2007), Columbia Grad. School of Journalism Bd of Visitors; Poynter Fellow, Yale Univ. 2001–02; George Beveridge Ed. of the Year Award 2001, American Soc. of Newspaper Eds Leadership Award 2002, Gerald Loeb Award 2002, John Hancock Award 2002, Columbia Journalism Award 2002, Goldsmith Career Award for Excellence in Journalism, Harvard Univ. Joan Shorenstein Center on Press, Politics and Public Policy 2008. *Publications include:* The '70s Crash and How to Survive It 1970. *Address:* ProPublica, One Exchange Plaza, 55 Broadway, 23rd Floor, New York, NY 10006, USA (office). *Telephone:* (212) 514-5250 (office). *E-mail:* info@propublica.org (office). *Website:* www.propublica.org (office).

STEILMANN, Britta; German retail executive; *Founder, Britta Steilmann Design;* b. 1966, Wattenscheid; d. of Prof. Klaus Steilmann; one d.; Marketing and Product Man. Klaus Steilmann GmbH & Co. KG 1987–89, Chief Exec., Environment and Communications Dept 1993–96, Chair. Bd Dirs and CEO 2001–03; opened internet shop and launched website for services including living and interior design www.brittasteilmann.com 2003; f. B.S.S.D. GmbH & Co. KG 1992; Man. SG Wattenscheid 09 professional soccer team 1995; mem. Factor 10 Club, 100 Global Leaders for Tomorrow, World Econ. Forum, Innovation in Deutschland, Curator's Bd Fachhochschule für Technik und Wirtschaft Coll., Dresden Cultural Foundation, Curator's Bd Art of Nature, Bd German Fashion Institute DMI; Patron and Consultant, Big Sisters, AIESEC Meets EXPO 2000; Bundesverdienstkreuz; Capital Magazine Man. of the Year 1993, World-Wide Fund for Nature Eco-Manager of the Year 1993, Forbes Magazine Jr Man. of the Year 1994, Bavarian Communication Asscn Ecology and Communication First Prize 1995, ranked 40th by Fortune magazine amongst 50 Most Powerful Women in Business outside the US 2002. *Publication:* Millenium Moral. *Leisure interests:* hiking, horseback riding. *Address:* B.S.S.D. GmbH & Co. KG, Britta Steilmann | Design, Postfach 101011, 40839 Ratingen, Germany (office). *Telephone:* (2102) 875-0 (office). *Fax:* (2102) 87525 (office). *E-mail:* britta.steilmann@bssd.com (office). britta.steilmann@brittasteilmann.com (office). *Website:* www.brittasteilmann.com (office).

STEIN, Elias M., AB, MA, PhD; American mathematician and academic; *Professor, Department of Mathematics, Princeton University;* b. 13 Jan. 1931, Antwerp, Belgium; s. of Elkan Stein and Chana Goldman Stein; m. Elly Intrator 1959; one s. one d.; ed Univ. of Chicago; Instructor MIT 1956–58; Asst Prof. Univ. of Chicago 1958–61, Assoc. Prof. 1961–63; mem. Inst. for Advanced Study, Princeton 1962–63, 1984–85; Prof. Princeton Univ. 1963–, Chair. of Dept of Math. 1968–70, 1985–87; Guggenheim Fellow 1976–77, 1984–85; mem. American Acad. of Arts and Sciences, NAS, American Mathematical Soc.; Dr hc (Peking Univ.) 1988; Hon. DSc (Univ. of Chicago) 1992; AMS Steele Prize 1984, 2002, von Humboldt Award 1889–90, Shock Prize, Swedish Acad. of Sciences 1993, Wolf Prize for Math. (jtly) 1999, Nat. Medal of Science 2002. *Publications:* Singular Integrals and Differentiability Properties of Functions 1970, Topics in Harmonic Analysis Related to the Littlewood-Paley Theory 1970, Introduction to Fourier Analysis on Euclidean Spaces (with G. Weiss) 1971. *Address:* Department of Mathematics, Princeton University, 802 Fine Hall, Washington Road, Princeton, NJ 08544 (office); 132 Dodds Lane, Princeton, NJ 08544, USA (home). *Telephone:* (609) 452-3497 (office); (609) 924-9335 (home). *E-mail:* stein@math.princeton.edu (office). *Website:* www.math.princeton.edu (office).

STEIN, Peter Gonville, FBA; British legal scholar and academic; *Emeritus Regius Professor of Civil Law and Fellow, Queens' College, Cambridge;* b. 29 May 1926, Liverpool; s. of Walter O. Stein and Effie D. Walker; m. 1st Janet Chamberlain 1953, three d.; m. 2nd Anne Howard 1978; one step-s.; ed Liverpool Coll., Gonville and Caius Coll. Cambridge and Univ. of Pavia, Italy; served RN 1944–47; admitted solicitor 1951; Prof. of Jurisprudence, Univ. of Aberdeen 1956–68; Regius Prof. of Civil Law, Univ. of Cambridge 1968–93, now Prof. Emer., and Fellow, Queens' Coll., Cambridge 1968–; mem. Univ. Grants Cttee 1971–76; JP, Cambridge 1970–; Fellow, Winchester Coll. 1976–91; Pres. Soc. of Public Teachers of Law 1980–81; mem. US–UK Educational Comm. 1985–91; Fellow Academia Europaea 1989; Foreign Fellow, Accad. Nazionale dei Lincei, Accad. di Scienze Morali e Politiche di Napoli, Accad. degli Intronati di Siena, Kon. Akad. v. Wetenschappen, Brussels; Hon. Fellow, Gonville and Caius Coll., Cambridge; Hon. QC 1993; Hon. DrJur (Göttingen) 1980; Dott.Giur. hc (Ferrara) 1990, (Perugia) 2001; Hon. LLD (Aberdeen) 2000; Dr hc (Paris II) 2001. *Publications:* Regulae Iuris: from juristic rules to legal maxims 1966, Legal Values in Western Society (with J. Shand) 1974, Legal Evolution 1980, Legal Institutions 1984, The Character and Influence of the Roman Civil Law: essays 1988, The Teaching of Roman Law in England around 1200 (with F. de Zulueta) 1990, Notaries Public in England since the Reformation (ed. and contrib.) 1991, Römisches Recht und Europa 1996, Roman Law in European History 1999 (trans. into Spanish, Italian, Japanese, French, Hungarian and Basque). *Leisure interest:* gardening. *Address:*

Wimpole Cottage, 36 Wimpole Road, Great Eversden, Cambridge, CB23 1HR, England (home). *Telephone:* (1223) 262349 (home).

STEIN BARILLAS, Eduardo; Guatemalan politician; m. Myrna Coronado; five d.; ed Univ. of St. Louis, Northwestern Univ., USA; teaching positions at Universidad Rafael Landívar, Guatemala 1971–72, Universidad Centroamericana José Simeón Cañas, El Salvador 1972–80), Florida State Univ. Panama campus 1985–87; Resident Rep., Int. Org. for Migration (IOM), Panama 1993–95; Minister of Foreign Affairs 1996–2000; Vice-Pres. 2004–08; fmr Pres. Foundation of the Americas, Washington, DC; apptd by OAS to Head of Electoral Observation Mission, Presidential Elections in Peru 2000, resgnd, then returned as Head of Electoral Observation Mission 2001; consultant to IOM, Guatemala and UNDP, Panama; mem. Int. Crisis Group, Brussels, Inter-American Dialogue, Washington, DC; fmr mem. UN Int. Comm. on Intervention and State Sovereignty 2001; participated in several presidential and vice-presidential summits on Cen. American regional peace process including Esquipulas I and the San José Dialogue with EU. *Address:* c/o Inter-American Dialogue, 1211 Connecticut Avenue, NW, Suite 510, Washington, DC 20036, USA (office).

STEINBERG, Donald K., BA, M.Econ., MA; American diplomatist and international organization official; *Deputy President (Policy), International Crisis Group;* b. 25 March 1953, Los Angeles; s. of Warren Linnington and Beatrice Blass; ed Reed Coll., Portland, Ore., Univ. of Toronto, Canada, Columbia Univ.; joined Foreign Service, rising to rank of Minister-Counselor; postings in Brazil, Malaysia, Mauritius and Cen. African Repub.; acting Chief Textile Negotiator, Office of US Trade Rep. 1988–89; first Dir House Task Force on Trade and Competitiveness 1989, Sr Policy Adviser for Foreign Affairs and Defense to Leader of House of Reps 1989–90; Officer-in-Charge and Counselor for Econ. and Commercial Affairs, US Embassy, Pretoria 1990–93; Deputy Press Sec. for Nat. Security Affairs, White House 1993; Special Asst to fmr Pres. Clinton for W African Affairs and Sr Dir for African Affairs, Sr Dir for Public Affairs, Nat. Security Council; Amb. to Angola 1995–98; Special Haiti Coordinator, Dept of State 1999–2001, Special Rep. of Pres. and Sec. of State for Global Humanitarian Demining 1998, Deputy Asst Sec. of State for Population, Refugees and Migration 2000–01, Prin. Deputy Dir for Policy Planning 2001–03, Dir Jt Policy Council 2003–05; Sr Fellow, Jennings Randolph Fellowship Program, US Inst. of Peace 2004–05; Vice Pres. for Multilateral Affairs and Dir, New York office, Int. Crisis Group 2005, currently Deputy Pres. (Policy), Brussels; Pulitzer Fellowship and fellowships from American Political Science Asscn, Univ. of Toronto, Uma Chapman Fox Foundation and US Dept of State; Presidential Meritorious Honor Award 1994, Hough Award for Excellence in Print, three Superior Honor Awards, Distinguished Service Award 2002, Hunt Award for Advancing Women's Role in Policy Formation 2003 US Dept of State. *Publications:* many publs on US trade policies, Africa, landmines and the role of Congress in foreign affairs. *Address:* International Crisis Group, 149 Avenue Louise, Level 24, 1050 Brussels, Belgium (office). *Telephone:* (2) 502-90-38 (office). *Fax:* (2) 502-50-38 (office). *Website:* www.crisisgroup.org (office).

STEINBERGER, Jack, PhD; American/Swiss physicist; b. 25 May 1921, Germany; s. of Ludwig Steinberger and Bertha Steinberger (née May); m. 1st Joan Beauregard 1943; m. 2nd Cynthia Eve Alff 1962; three s. one d.; ed Univ. of Chicago; Visiting mem., Inst. of Advanced Study, Princeton 1948–49; Research Asst, Univ. of Calif., Berkeley 1949–50; Prof., Columbia Univ., New York 1950–71, Higgins Prof. 1967–71; staff mem., CERN 1968–; mem. NAS 1967–2002, Heidelberg Acad. of Sciences 1967–, American Acad. of Arts and Sciences 1969–, Acad. Nazionale dei Lincei 1997; Hon. Prof., Univ. of Heidelberg 1968; Hon. DLitt (Glasgow) 1990, Dr hc (IU Inst. of Tech., Dortmund, Columbia, Barcelona, Univ. Blaise Pascal); Nobel Prize in Physics (jtly) 1988, Pres.'s Science Medal, USA 1988, Mateuzzi Medal, Società Italiana delle Scienze 1991. *Publications include:* Muon Decay 1949, Pi Zero Meson 1950, Spin of Pion 1951, Parity of Pion 1954, 1959, Σ° Hyperon 1957, Properties of 'Strange Particles' 1957–64, Two Neutrinos 1962, CP Violating Effects in K° Decay 1966–74, High Energy Neutrino Physics 1975–83, Preparation of Lep Detector 1981, 3 Families of Matter 1989, Electroweak physics experiments 1989–97. *Leisure interests:* mountaineering, flute, cruising. *Address:* CERN, 1211 Geneva 23 (office); 25 chemin des Merles, 1213 Onex, Geneva, Switzerland (home). *Telephone:* (22) 7678125 (office); (22) 7934612 (home). *Fax:* (22) 7679425 (office).

STEINBRUCH, Benjamin; Brazilian business executive; *Chairman and CEO, Companhia Siderúrgica Nacional ADS;* b. 28 June 1953, Rio de Janeiro; s. of Mendel Steinbruch and Dorothéa Steinbruch; m. Carolina Steinbruch; four c.; ed Getulio Vargas Business Foundation; started work at Vicunha Siderurgia (family textiles and telecoms conglomerate) 1983, now Supt Officer; Chair. Companhia Siderúrgica Nacional ADS (steel producer) 1995–, CEO 2002–; Pres. Companhia Vale do Rio Doce (iron ore co.) 1997–2011; First Vice-Pres. Fiesp (Federação das Indústrias do Estado de São Paulo); regular columnist for Folha de São Paulo (newspaper); Vice-Pres., Treasury, Albert Einstein Soc. 2001–04; Admin. Emer., Regional Admin. Council of São Paulo 1997; mem. Superior Council for Infrastructure 2006–. *Leisure interests:* racehorse training. *Address:* Companhia Siderúrgica Nacional, Avenida Brigadeiro Faria Lima, 3400, 20° Andar, Itaim Bibi, 04538-132 São Paulo, Brazil (office). *Telephone:* (11) 3049-7591 (office). *E-mail:* invrel@csn.com.br (office). *Website:* www.csn.com.br (office).

STEINBRÜCK, Peer; German politician; b. 10 Jan. 1947, Hamburg; m.; three c.; ed Christian-Albrechts-Univ. zu Kiel; worked for Fed. Ministry of Planning 1974–76, Fed. Ministry of Research and Tech. 1976–77, Personal Asst to Minister 1977; mem. SPD Party; Chief of Staff for Minister-Pres., State of Nordrhein-Westfalen 1986–90; State Sec., Ministry of Natural Conservation, Environmental Protection and Regional Devt, State of Schleswig-Holstein 1990–92, State Sec., Ministry of Econs, Tech. and Transport 1992–93, State Minister of Econs, Tech. and Transport 1993–98; State Minister of Econs, Small Businesses, Tech. and Transport, State of Nordrhein-Westfalen 1998–2000, State Finance Minister 2000–02, Minister-Pres. 2002–05; Fed. Minister of Finance 2005–09; Chair. Bd of Supervisory Dirs, KfW Bankengruppe 2009. *Address:* c/o SPD, Willy-Brandt-Haus, Wilhelmstr. 141, 10963 Berlin, Germany (office). *Telephone:* (30) 259910 (office). *Fax:* (30) 25991410 (office). *Website:* www.spd.de (office).

STEINEM, Gloria, BA; American writer, journalist and editor; *Consulting Editor, Ms Magazine;* b. 25 March 1934, Toledo, Ohio; d. of Leo Steinem and Ruth Steinem (née Nuneviller); m. David Bale 2000; ed Smith Coll.; Chester Bowles Asian Fellow, India 1957–58; Co-Dir, Dir Ind. Research Service, Cambridge, Mass. and New York 1959–60; editorial asst, contributing, ed., freelance writer for various nat. and New York publs 1960–; Co-founder New York Magazine, contrib. 1968–72; Co-founder Ms Magazine 1972 (Ed. 1971–87, columnist 1980–87, consulting ed. 1987–); feminist lecturer 1969–; active various civil rights and peace campaigns including United Farmworkers, Vietnam War Tax Protest, Cttee for the Legal Defense of Angela Davis and political campaigns of Adlai Stevenson, Robert Kennedy, Eugene McCarthy, Shirley Chisholm, George McGovern; Co-founder and Chair Bd Women's Action Alliance 1970–; Convenor, mem. Nat. Advisory Cttee Nat. Women's Political Caucus 1971–; Co-Founder, Pres. Bd of Dirs Ms Foundation for Women 1972–; Founding mem. Coalition of Labor Union Women; Woodrow Wilson Int. Center for Scholars Fellow 1977, Women's Media Center 2004; mem. advisory bd Feminist.com; Penney-Missouri Journalism Award 1970, Ohio Gov.'s Award for Journalism 1972, named Woman of the Year, McCall's Magazine 1972, Missouri Honor Medal for Distinguished Service in Journalism 2004. *Publications include:* The Thousand Indias 1957, The Beach Book 1963, Outrageous Acts and Everyday Rebellions 1983, Marilyn 1986, Revolution From Within: A Book of Self-Esteem 1992, Moving Beyond Words 1994, Doing Sixty and Seventy 2006; contribs to various anthologies. *Address:* The Women's Media Center, 350 Fifth Avenue, Suite 901, New York, NY 10118, USA (office). *E-mail:* kathy@womensmediacenter.com (office). *Website:* www.womensmediacenter.com (office).

STEINER, Achim, BA, MA; German international organization executive; *United Nations Under-Secretary-General and Executive Director, United Nations Environment Programme;* b. 17 May 1961, Brazil; s. of Roland Steiner and Helga Steiner; m. Liz Riboy; ed Univs of Oxford and London, UK, German Devt Inst., Berlin, Harvard Business School, USA; Sr Policy Adviser, Global Policy Unit, Int. Union for the Conservation of Nature and Natural Resources (IUCN—The World Conservation Union), Washington, DC mid-1990s, worked in SE Asia as Chief Tech. Adviser on a programme for sustainable man. of Mekong River watersheds and community-based natural resources man., worked in IUCN's Southern Africa Regional Office, Dir-Gen. IUCN 2001–06; Sec.-Gen. World Comm. on Dams, based in SA 1998–2001; UN Under-Sec.-Gen. and Exec. Dir UNEP 2006–(14), also Dir-Gen. UNON (UN Office at Nairobi); Founding mem. Institut du developpement durable et des relations internationales (France); mem. several int. advisory bds including China Council for Inst. Cooperation on Environment and Devt, Environmental Advisory Council (ENVAC) of EBRD, UN Sec.-Gen.'s Advisory Council for the Global Compact, Int. Advisory Cttee of Global Environmental Action (Japan), Bd of Global Public Policy Inst. (Germany); Bruno H. Schubert-Stiftung Award, Steiger Award for Environment 2007, Tallberg Award for Environmental Leadership 2010. *Address:* United Nations Environment Programme, United Nations Avenue, Gigiri, PO Box 30552, 00100 Nairobi, Kenya (office). *Telephone:* (20) 7624001 (office). *Fax:* (20) 7624275 (office). *E-mail:* executiveoffice@unep.org (office). *Website:* www.unep.org (office).

STEINER, David P., BA, LLB; American lawyer and business executive; *CEO and Director, Waste Management Inc.;* ed Louisiana State Univ., Univ. of California, Los Angeles; began legal career with Jones, Walker, Waechter, Poitevent, Carrere & Denegre, New Orleans, La; fmr Assoc. Gibson, Dunn & Crutcher, San Jose, Calif.; Assoc. Phelps Dunbar, New Orleans –2000; Vice-Pres. and Deputy Gen. Counsel, Waste Man. Inc., Houston 2000–01, Sr Vice-Pres., Gen. Counsel and Corp. Sec. 2001–03, Chief Financial Officer 2003–04, CEO and Dir 2004–; mem. La and Calif. Bar Asscns. *Address:* Waste Management Inc., 1001 Fannin Street, Suite 4000, Houston, TX 77002, USA (office). *Telephone:* (713) 512-6200 (office). *Fax:* (713) 512-6299 (office). *Website:* www.wm.com (office).

STEINER, (Francis) George, DPhil, FBA, FRSL; American writer and scholar; b. 23 April 1929, Paris, France; s. of Dr Steiner and Mrs F. G. Steiner; m. Zara Shakow 1955; one s. one d.; ed Univ. of Paris, Univ. of Chicago, Harvard Univ. and Balliol Coll., Oxford, UK; mem. editorial staff, The Economist, London 1952–56; Fellow, Inst. for Advanced Study, Princeton 1956–58; Gauss Lecturer, Princeton Univ. 1959–60; Fellow and Dir of English Studies, Churchill Coll., Cambridge 1961–69, Extraordinary Fellow 1969–, Pensioner Fellow 1996–; Albert Schweitzer Visiting Prof., New York Univ. 1966–67; Visiting Prof., Yale Univ. 1970–71; Prof. of English and Comparative Literature, Univ. of Geneva 1974–94, Prof. Emer. 1994–; Visiting Prof., Collège de France 1992; First Lord Weidenfeld Visiting Prof. of Comparative Literature, Univ. of Oxford 1994–95; Charles Eliot Norton Prof. of Poetry, Harvard Univ. 2001–02; Pres. The English Asscn 1975–76; Corresp. mem. German Acad., Harvard Club, New York; Hon. mem. American Acad. of Arts and Sciences 1989; Hon. RA (London) 2004; Hon. Fellow, Balliol Coll., Oxford, St Anne's Coll., Oxford; Chevalier, Légion d'honneur, Commdr, Ordre des Arts et des Lettres 2001; Hon. DLitt (East Anglia) 1976, (Louvain) 1979, (Bristol) 1989, (Glasgow, Liège) 1990, (Ulster) 1993, (Kenyon Coll., USA) 1995, (Trinity Coll. Dublin) 1995, (Rome) 1998, (Sorbonne) 1998, (Salamanca) 2002, (Athens) 2004, (London) 2006, (Bologna) 2006; O. Henry Award 1958, Jewish Chronicle Book Award 1968, Zabel Prize of Nat. Inst. of Arts and Letters 1970, Le Prix du Souvenir 1974, Massey Lecturer 1974, Ransom Memorial Lecturer 1976, King Albert Medal of the Royal Belgian Acad. 1982, F.D. Maurice Lecturer, Univ. of London 1984, Leslie Stephen Lecturer, Univ. of Cambridge 1985, Robertson Lecturer, Courtauld Inst., London 1985, W.P. Ker Lecturer, Univ. of Glasgow 1986, Page-Barbour Lecturer, Univ. of Virginia 1987, Gifford Lecturer 1990, Priestley Lecturer, Univ. of Toronto 1995, Prince of Asturias Prize 2001, 2002, Alfonso Reyes Prize (Mexico) 2007. *Publications include:* Tolstoy or Dostoevsky: An Essay in the Old Criticism 1958, The Death of Tragedy 1960, Homer: A Collection of Critical Essays (co-ed. with Robert Flagles) 1962, Anno Domini: Three Stories 1964, The Penguin Book of Modern Verse Translation (ed.) 1966, Language and Silence 1967, Extraterritorial 1971, In Bluebeard's Castle: Some Notes Towards the Re-Definition of Culture 1971, The Sporting Scene: White Knights in Reykjavík 1973, Fields of Force 1974, A Nostalgia for the Absolute (Massey Lectures) 1974, After Babel: Aspects of Language and Translation 1975, Heidegger 1978, On Difficulty and Other Essays 1978, The Portage to San Cristóbal of A.H. 1981, Antigones 1984, George Steiner: A Reader 1984, Real Presences: Is There Anything in What We Say? 1989, Proofs and Three Parables 1992, The Deeps of the Sea 1996, Homer in English 1996, No Passion Spent 1996, Errata: An Examined Life 1998, Grammars of Creation 2001, Lessons of the Masters: The Charles Eliot Morton Lectures 2001–2002 2004, My

Unwritten Books 2008, The Poetry of Thought 2012. *Leisure interests:* chess, music, mountain walking. *Address:* 32 Barrow Road, Cambridge, CB2 8AS, England.

STEINER, Michael; German diplomatist, fmr government official and fmr UN official; *Ambassador to India;* b. 28 Nov. 1949, Munich, Bavaria; ed Univ. of Munich Law School, Univ. of Paris, France; Scientific Asst, Inst. of Int. Law, Univ. of Munich 1978–81; joined Diplomatic Service 1981, Counsellor for Econ. Collaboration, Embassy in Kinshasa 1983, with Int. Law Div., Ministry of Foreign Affairs 1983–86, Political Counsellor, Perm. Mission to UN, New York 1986–89, Political Counsellor, Embassy in Prague 1989–91, Head of Office for German Humanitarian Aid, Zagreb 1991–92, Head of Office of German Humanitarian Aid, Zagreb, Croatia 1991–92, Head of Labour Unit for Multilateral Efforts for Peace, Ministry of Foreign Affairs 1992–94, Head of Special Task Force for Peace Efforts in Bosnia and Herzegovina and Nat. Rep. at Int. Contact Group on the Balkans 1994–95, Contrib. Dayton Peace Talks 1995, Prin. Deputy High Rep. in Sarajevo 1996–97, Amb. to Czech Repub. 1998; Foreign Policy and Security Adviser to Chancellor 1998–2001; Special Rep. for Kosovo and Head of UN Interim Admin. Mission in Kosovo (UNMIK) 2002–03; Perm. Rep. to UN and Int. Orgs, Geneva 2003–07; Pres. Governing Council of UN Compensation Comm. for Iraq 2004; Amb. to Italy (also accred to San Marino) 2007–10, Amb. and Special Rep. to Afghanistan and Pakistan 2010–12, Amb. to India 2012–; Officer's Cross, Order of Merit. *Address:* German Embassy, 6/50g Shanti Path, Chanakyapuri, POB 613, New Delhi 110 021, India (office). *Telephone:* (11) 44199199 (office). *Fax:* (11) 26873117 (office). *E-mail:* info@new-delhi.diplo.de (office). *Website:* www.new-delhi.diplo.de (office).

STEINER, Sylvia Helena de Figueiredo, LLM; Brazilian judge; *Judge, Pre-Trial Division, International Criminal Court;* b. 19 Jan. 1953, São Paulo; m. (divorced); ed Univ. of São Paulo, Univ. of Brasilia; lawyer –1982; mem. Fed. Public Ministry 1982–95; fmr mem. and Vice-Pres. Penitentiary Council of São Paulo; Fed. Judge Regional, Court of Appeal of São Paulo 1995–2003; Judge, Pre-Trial Div., Int. Criminal Court (ICC) 2003–; mem. Brazilian Del. to Preparatory Comm. of ICC 1999–2001, to Experts' Conf. on Implementation of Humanitarian Law 2001, to Meeting on Implementation of ICC Statute 2001, to First Ass. of State Parties of ICC 2002; Founding Assoc. mem. Brazilian Inst. of Criminal Sciences; Deputy Dir Brazilian Criminal Sciences Journal; mem. Admin. Council Assen of Judges for Democracy, Exec. Council Brazilian Section of Int. Legal Comm., São Paulo Comm. for Peace and Justice; guest lecturer at numerous orgs, univs and insts. *Publications include:* A convenção americana sobre direitos humanos e sua integração ao processo penal brasileiro 2000; articles in professional journals. *Address:* International Criminal Court, PO Box 19519, 2500 CM The Hague, The Netherlands (office); Rua Estado de Israel, No. 181, Apt. 13, Vila Mariana, CEP 04022-000, São Paulo, Brazil (home). *Telephone:* (70) 515-85-15 (office); (11) 3311-4412 (home). *Fax:* (70) 515-85-55 (office); (11) 5572-3897 (home). *E-mail:* pio@icc-cpi.int (office); sylstein@uol.com.br (home); ssteiner@trf3.gov.br (home). *Website:* www.icp-cpi.int (office).

STEINFELD, Hailee; American actress; b. 11 Dec. 1996, Los Angeles; d. of Peter Steinfeld and Cheri Steinfeld; began acting at age eight; early supporting roles in several TV series and commercials. *Television includes:* Back to You 2007, Summer Camp 2010, Sons of Tucson 2010. *Films include:* She's a Fox 2009, True Grit (Alliance of Women Film Journalists Award for Best Supporting Actress, Austin Film Critics Assen Award for Best Supporting Actress, Broadcast Film Critics Assen Award for Best Young Performer, Central Ohio Film Critics Assen Award for Best Supporting Actress, Chicago Film Critics Assen Award for Best Supporting Actress, Houston Film Critics Soc. Award for Best Supporting Actress, Indiana Film Journalists Assen Award for Best Supporting Actress, Kansas City Film Critics Circle Award for Best Supporting Actress, Online Film Critics Soc. Award for Best Supporting Actress, Southeastern Film Critics Assen Award for Best Supporting Actress) 2010. *Address:* c/o ICM, 10250 Constellation Blvd, 9th Floor, Los Angeles, CA 90067, USA (office).

STEINHAFEL, Gregg W., BA, MBA; American business executive; *Chairman, President and CEO, Target Corporation;* b. Milwaukee, Wis.; m.; three c.; ed Carroll Coll., Kellogg Grad. School of Man., Northwestern Univ.; began career at Target as merchandising trainee 1979, has held various man. positions, Exec. Vice-Pres. of Merchandising, Target Stores, Inc. (subsidiary of Target Corpn) 1994–99, Pres. 1999–, mem. Bd of Dirs Target Corpn 2007–, CEO 2008–, Chair. 2009–; mem. Bd of Dirs The Toro Co. 1999–; mem. Bd The Retail Industry Leaders Assen, TreeHouse (Minnesota-based non-profit org.), Business Roundtable, Minnesota Business Partnership, Council for the Smithsonian Nat. Museum of African American History and Culture 2010–. *Address:* Target Corpn, 1000 Nicollet Mall, Minneapolis, MN 55403, USA (office). *Telephone:* (612) 304-6073 (office). *Fax:* (612) 696-3731 (office). *E-mail:* info@target.com (office). *Website:* www.target.com (office).

STEINHOFF, Janusz Wojciech, DTech; Polish politician; *Leader, Centre Party (Partia Centrum);* b. 24 Oct. 1946, Gliwice; m.; one d.; ed Silesian Tech. Univ., Gliwice; with Coal Industry Construction and Mechanization Plants, Gliwice 1974–75; Mining Dept Silesian Tech. Univ., Gliwice 1976–89, 1994–97; Chair. Higher Mining Office 1990–94; adviser, State Hard Coal Agency 1994–95; Vice-Chair. Regional Chamber of Commerce, Katowice 1996–97; Minister of the Economy 1997–2001, also Deputy Prime Minister; Co-Founder Solidarity Trade Union, Silesian Tech. Univ. 1980; underground Solidarity activist during martial law 1981–89; Solidarity expert on mining and protection of environment during Round Table debates, 1989; Deputy to Sejm (Parl.) 1989–93, 1997–2001; mem. Presidium Citizens Parl. Caucus (OKP) 1989–91; mem. Solidarity Election Action (AWS) Parl. Caucus 1997–2001; author of AWS programme for restructuring the mining sector; Co-Founder and Vice-Leader Christian Democratic Party; currently Leader Centre Party (Partia Centrum). *Address:* Centre Party (Partia Centrum), 00-057 Warsaw, pl. Dąbrowskiego 5, Poland (office). *Telephone:* (22) 8278442 (office). *Fax:* (22) 8278441 (office). *E-mail:* centrum@centrum.org.pl (office).

STEINITZ, Yuval, BA, MA, PhD; Israeli academic and politician; *Minister of Intelligence, of International Relations and of Strategic Affairs;* b. 10 April 1958; m.; three c.; ed Hebrew Univ., Jerusalem, Tel-Aviv Univ.; mil. serviced in Golani Brigade, reservist in Alexandroni Brigade; fmr mem. Peace Now movt; Prof. of

Philosophy, Haifa Univ. –1999; mem. Knesset (Likud Party) 1999–, Chair. Sub-Cttee for Defence, Planning and Policy 1999–2003, Sub-Cttee for Intelligence and Secret Services 2003–06, Cttee for Examination of Intelligence Services Following the War in Iraq 2003–06, Co-Chair. Jt Security Cttee between Knesset and US Congress 2003–, Sub-Cttee for State of Alert and Field Security 2006–, Sub-Cttee on Intelligence and Secret Services 2006–, mem. Foreign Affairs and Defence Cttee 1993– (Chair. 2003–06), Constitution Law and Courts Cttee 1999–2003; Minister of Finance 2009–13, of Intelligence, of Int. Relations and of Strategic Affairs 2013–; Pres. Assen for the Public's Right to Know 1999–2004. *Publications:* Invitation to Philosophy 1994, In Defense of Metaphysics 1995; articles in Israeli and Int. academic journals. *Address:* Knesset, Kiryat Ben-Gurion, Jerusalem 91008, Israel (office). *Telephone:* 2-6496115 (office). *Fax:* 2-6496579 (office). *E-mail:* ysteinitz@knesset.gov.il (office). *Website:* www.knesset.gov.il (office); yuvalsteinitz.ning.com.

STEINKÜHLER, Franz; German trade union official; b. 20 May 1937, Würzburg; m.; one c.; trained as toolmaker and became Chief of Production Planning 1951–60; joined IG Metall 1951, mem. Youth Group 1952, Chair. Youth Del. 1953, numerous local exec. positions 1953–63, Sec. Regional Exec. Bd, Stuttgart 1963–72, Dir Stuttgart Region 1972–83, Vice-Pres. IG Metall 1983–86, Pres. 1986–93; Pres. Int. Metalworkers' Fed. June 1987; mem. SPD 1951–, Vice-Pres. in Baden-Württemberg 1975–83, mem. Programme Cttee of Exec. Bd 1984; Workers' Rep. VW-AG, Wolfsburg Mannesmann AG, Supervisory Bd, Daimler Benz AG Super-visory Bd –1993, Thyssen AG; fmr Deputy Chair. Supervisory Bd Volkswagen AG; mem. State Tribunal of Baden-Württemberg 1983; currently business consultant; Hon. Senator Univ. of Konstanz 1983.

STEINMEIER, Frank-Walter; German politician and lawyer; *Federal Minister of Foreign Affairs;* b. 5 Jan. 1956, Detmold (Dist of Lippe); m.; one d.; ed secondary school in Blomberg, Justus Liebig Univ., Giessen; mil. service 1974–76; legal training in Frankfurt and Giessen 1983–86; Academic Asst to Chair of Public Law and Political Science, Dept of Law, Univ. of Giessen 1986–91; Desk Officer for Media Law and Policy, State Chancellery of Lower Saxony 1991, Chief-of-Staff, Office of the Minister-Pres., State of Lower Saxony 1993–94, Head of Directorate for Policy Guidelines, Inter-departmental Coordination and Planning 1994–96, State Sec. and Chief-of-Staff, Lower Saxony State Chancellery 1996–98; State Sec., Federal Chancellery and Commr for the Intelligence Services 1998–99, Fed. Chancellery Chief-of-Staff 1999–2005; Fed. Minister for Foreign Affairs 2005–09, 2013–, Vice-Chancellor 2007–09; mem. Sozialdemokratische Partei Deutschlands (SPD—Social Democratic Party), Chair. SPD Parl. Group (Leader of the Opposition) 2009–13; Pres. European Council 2007. *Address:* Federal Ministry of Foreign Affairs, Werderscher Markt 1, 10117 Berlin, Germany (office). *Telephone:* (30) 181-7 (office). *E-mail:* poststelle@auswaertiges-amt.de (office); frank-walter.steinmeier@bundestag.de (office). *Website:* www.auswaertiges-amt.de (office).

STEINMETZ, Pierre; French lawyer and politician; *Member, Conseil Constitutionnel;* b. 23 Jan. 1943, Sainte-Colombe (Rhône); s. of Emile Steinmetz and Marguerite Frossard; m. Daniele Sebi 1968; two s.; ed Ecole Nationale d'Administration, Institut d'études politiques de Paris; Civil Admin. second class Ministry of Depts and Territories Overseas, also with Ministry of Public Health and Social Security 1970; Dir Office of High Commr in Noumea 1972; Chargé de mission Gen. Secretariat 1975; Special Adviser in cabinet of Prime Minister Raymond Barre 1979–82; Chief Office of the Sec. Gen. of City of Paris 1982–87; Dir Econ. and Social Devt, Regional Council of Ile-de-France 1987; apptd to assess situation and restore dialogue in New Caledonia 1988; Prefect of Haute-Marne 1988; Chief, Office of Minister of Int. Cooperation and Devt 1989–91; Prefect of Pyrenees-Orientales 1992, of Haute-Savoie 1993, of Reunion 1994; Dir of Cabinet for Minister of Public Service, Reform of the State and Decentralization 1995; Prefect of Burgundy region, of defence zone of Cen. East, of Côte d'Or 1996, of Poitou-Charentes, of La Vienne 1997; Dir Nat. Gendarmerie 2000–02; Chief of Staff, Prime Minister's Office 2002–03; Mem. Conseil Constitutionnel 2004–; Chevalier de la légion d'honneur, Officier de l'ordre national du Mérite. *Leisure interests:* tennis, skiing. *Address:* Conseil Constitutionnel, 2 rue de Montpensier, 75001 Paris, France (office). *Telephone:* 1-40-15-30-00 (office). *Fax:* 1-40-20-93-27 (office). *E-mail:* relations-exterieures@conseil-constitutionnel.fr (office). *Website:* www.conseil-constitutionnel.fr (office).

STEINNES, Eiliv, DPhil; Norwegian environmental scientist and academic; *Professor Emeritus of Environmental Science, Norwegian University of Science and Technology;* b. 21 Sept. 1938, Elverum; s. of Eirik Steinnes and Aslaug Steinnes; m. Randi Surdal 1962; three d.; ed Univ. of Oslo; scientist, Norwegian Inst. for Atomic Energy 1964–68, Research leader 1969–79; Prof. of Environmental Science, Univ. of Trondheim Coll. of Arts and Science (now Norwegian Univ. of Science and Tech.) 1980–2008, Prof. Emer. 2008–, Rector 1984–90; mem. Norwegian Acad. of Tech. Sciences, Norwegian Acad. of Science and Letters, Royal Norwegian Soc. of Science and Letters; Hon. Prof., Univ. of Iasi, Romania 2000; Dr hc (Moldova State Univ.) 2002; Hevesy Medal (co-recipient) 2001, Guldberg-Waage Medal 2009. *Publications:* three books and more than 640 scientific papers. *Leisure interests:* outdoor life, in particular cross-country skiing and mountain tours. *Address:* Department of Chemistry, Norwegian University of Science and Technology, 7491 Trondheim (office); Sloreåsen 17A, 1257 Oslo, Norway (home). *Telephone:* 73-59-62-37 (office); 22-75-43-20 (home). *Fax:* 73-55-08-77 (office). *E-mail:* eiliv.steinnes@chem.ntnu.no (office). *Website:* www.chem.ntnu.no/english (office).

STEITZ, Joan Argetsinger, BS, PhD, FRSE; American biophysicist, biochemist and academic; *Sterling Professor of Molecular Biophysics and Biochemistry, School of Medicine, Yale University;* ed Antioch Coll., Harvard Univ.; NSF and Jane Coffin Childs Postdoctoral Fellowships, MRC Lab. of Molecular Biology, Cambridge, UK 1967–70; joined faculty, Yale Univ., New Haven, Conn. in 1970, currently Sterling Prof. of Molecular Biophysics and Biochemistry, School of Medicine, also Investigator, Howard Hughes Medical Inst. 1986–, and Dir Molecular Genetics Program, Boyer Center for Molecular Medicine; mem. Jury of 2004 L'Oréal USA Fellowships 2002, 2004; mem. American Acad. of Arts and Sciences 1982, NAS 1983, American Philosophical Soc. 1992; Fellow, American Acad. of Microbiology, Academia Europaea 2002; Hon. ScD (Brandeis Univ.) 2002, (Brown Univ.) 2003, (Princeton Univ.) 2003, (Watson School of Biological Sciences, Cold Spring Harbor Lab.) 2004; Passano Foundation Young Scientist Award 1975,

Eli Lilly Award in Biological Chemistry 1976, US Steel Foundation Award in Molecular Biology 1982, Lee Hawley, Sr Award for Arthritis Research 1983, Nat. Medal of Science 1986, Radcliffe Grad. Soc. Medal for Distinguished Achievement 1987, Dickson Prize for Science, Carnegie-Mellon Univ. 1988, Warren Triennial Prize 1989, Christopher Columbus Discovery Award in Biomedical Research 1992, first Weizmann Women and Science Award 1994, City of Medicine Award 1996, Novartis Drew Award in Biomedical Research 1999, L'Oréal-UNESCO For Women in Science Award 2001, Lewis S. Rosensteil Award 2002, FASEB Excellence in Science Award 2003, Howard Taylor Ricketts Award, Univ. of Chicago 2004, Caledonian Research Foundation Prize Lectureship 2004, RNA Soc. Lifetime Achievement Award 2004, Gairdner Award 2006. *Publications:* Molecular Biology of the Gene (Vol. II, 4th edn) (co-autor) 1987; numerous articles on molecular genetics, especially RNA structure and function. *Address:* Howard Hughes Medical Institute, Yale University, BCMM 136E, 295 Congress Avenue, PO Box 9812, New Haven, CT 06536-0812, USA (office). *Telephone:* (203) 737-4418 (office). *Fax:* (203) 624-8213 (office). *E-mail:* joan.steitz@yale.edu (office). *Website:* www .mbb.yale.edu/faculty/pages/steitzj.html (office).

STEITZ, Thomas A., BA, PhD; American molecular biologist and academic; *Sterling Professor of Molecular Biophysics and Biochemistry, Yale University;* b. 23 Aug. 1940, Milwaukee, Wis.; s. of Arthur Steitz and Catherine Steitz; m. Joan Steitz; one s.; ed Lawrence Coll., Harvard Univ.; Postdoctoral Fellow, Dept of Chem., Harvard Univ. 1966–67; Jane Coffin Childs Postdoctoral Fellow, MRC Lab. of Molecular Biology, Cambridge, UK 1967–1970; mem. Faculty, Yale Univ. 1970–, becoming Prof. of Chem., currently Sterling Prof. of Molecular Biophysics and Biochemistry; Macy Fellow, Max Planck Inst. for Biophysical Chem., Göttingen, Germany 1976–77; Fairchild Scholar, California Inst. of Tech. 1984–85; Investigator, Howard Hughes Medical Inst. 1986–; Visiting Prof., Univ. of Colorado, Boulder 1992–93; Co-founder and Chair. Scientific Advisory Bd, Rib-X Pharmaceuticals Inc.; mem. NAS 1990–; Foreign mem. Royal Soc., London 2011; Fellow, American Acad. of Arts and Sciences 1990, American Acad. of Microbiology; Hon. DSc (Lawrence Univ.) 1981; Pfizer Award in Enzyme Chem. 1980, Rosenstield Award for Distinguished Work in Basic Medical Research 2001, AAAS Newcomb Cleveland Prize 2001, Keio Medical Science Prize 2006, Gairdner Int. Award 2007, Nobel Prize in Chem. (with Venkatraman Ramakrishnan and Ada E. Yonath) 2009. *Address:* Yale University, Department of Molecular Biophysics and Biochemistry, Bass Center, Room 418, PO Box 208114, 266 Whitney Avenue, New Haven, CT 06520-8114, USA (office). *Telephone:* (203) 432-5619 (office). *Fax:* (203) 432-3282 (office). *E-mail:* thomas.steitz@yale.edu (office). *Website:* www.yale .edu/steitz (office).

STELLE, Kellogg Sheffield, PhD, FInstP; American physicist and academic; *Professor of Physics, Imperial College London;* b. 11 March 1948, Washington, DC; s. of Charles C. Stelle and Jane E. Kellogg; ed Phillips Acad. Andover, Mass., Harvard Coll. and Brandeis Univ.; Field Observer, Bartol Research Foundation, S Pole, Antarctica 1970–72; Lecturer in Math., King's Coll. London 1977–78; Research Fellow, Imperial Coll. London 1978–80, Advanced Fellow 1982–87, Lecturer in Physics 1987–88, Reader 1988–95, Prof. 1995–, Head of Theoretical Physics Group 2002–07; mem. Inst. for Advanced Study, Princeton, NJ 1986; Scientific Assoc., CERN, Geneva 1980–81, 1987, 1997–98; Programme Dir Institut Henri Poincaré, Paris 2000–01; Humboldt Visiting Prof., Albert Einstein Inst., Potsdam 2007–08; Ed. Classical and Quantum Gravity 1984–93; mem. London Math. Soc., AAAS, Fed. of American Scientists, Campaign for Science and Eng; Fellow, American Physical Soc.; Humboldt Research Award, Alexander von Humboldt Foundation 2006. *Publications:* numerous articles in scientific journals. *Address:* The Blackett Laboratory, Imperial College, H/519 Huxley Building, South Kensington Campus, Prince Consort Road, London, SW7 2AZ, England (office). *Telephone:* (20) 7594-7826 (office). *E-mail:* k.stelle@imperial.ac.uk (office). *Website:* www3.imperial.ac.uk/people/k.stelle (office).

STELMACH, Ed; Canadian politician; b. 11 May 1951, Andrew, Alberta; m. Marie Stelmach 1973; four c.; ed Univ. of Alberta; cut short his univ. educ. after death of brother and returned home to take over family homestead near Vegreville, Alberta; elected Lamont Co. Council 1986, apptd Reeve 1987; fmr Chair. Vegreville Health Unit Bd and mem. Archer Memorial Hosp. and Lamont Auxiliary Hosp. and Nursing Home Bds; MLA for Vegreville-Viking (now Fort Saskatchewan-Vegreville) 1993–2011, Deputy Whip, then Govt Caucus Whip 1995–97, Minister of Agric. 1997–99, of Infrastructure 1999–2001, of Transportation 2001–04, of Int. and Intergovernmental Affairs 2004–06; Leader, Progressive Conservative Party of Alberta 2006–11; Premier of Alberta 2006–11 (resgnd); fmr Chair. Alberta Agric. Research Inst.; fmr Leader Andrew 4-H Beef Club; fmr Pres. Lamont and District 4-H. *Address:* c/o Ed Stelmach Community Foundation, 20408-107 Avenue, Edmonton, Alberta T5S 1W9, Canada.

STELMAKH, Volodymyr, PhD; Ukrainian economist and fmr central banker; b. 18 Jan. 1939; joined Nat. Bank of Ukraine 1992, First Vice-Gov. 1993–2000, Gov. 2000–02, 2004–10; currently Adviser to Pres.; Hero of Ukraine 2007, Order of Yaroslav the Wise 2010. *Address:* c/o National Bank of Ukraine (Natsionalny Bank Ukrainy), 01008 Kyiv, vul. Institutska 9, Ukraine (office).

STEMBERG, Thomas G. (Tom), AB, MBA; American business executive and venture capitalist; *Managing General Partner, Highland Consumer Fund, Highland Capital Partners LLC;* b. 18 Jan. 1949, New Jersey; s. of Oscar Stemberg and Erika Ratzer Stemberg; pnr Katherine Chapman; six c.; ed Harvard Univ., Harvard Business School, Nichols Coll.; began career as corp. trainee, Jewel's Star Market 1973, Vice-Pres. Sales and Marketing –1980; joined First Nat. Supermarkets 1980, various sr man. positions including Pres. Edwards-Finast Div. –1986; f. Staples Inc. 1986, CEO 1986–2002, Chair. Bd of Dirs 1988–2002, Exec. Chair. 2002–04, Chair. (non-exec.) and Assoc. (part-time) 2004–05, Chair. Emer. 2005–; Man. Gen. Pnr, Highland Consumer Fund, Highland Capital Pnrs LLC 2005–; Founder Olly Shoes; mem. Bd of Dirs CarMax, Inc., Guitar Center, lululemon athletica, PETsMART, Inc., Pharmaca; Co-Chair. Friends of Harvard Basketball; mem., Harvard Business School Bd of Dean's Advisers; mem. Faculty of Arts and Sciences Financial Aid Task Force; Trustee Boston Symphony Orchestra; George F. Baker Scholar, Harvard Business School 1972; Hon. DBA; inducted into Babson Coll. Entrepreneurial Hall of Fame, SPARC Retail Hall of Fame 2005, Harvard Business School Alumni Achievement Award. *Publication:* Staples for Success 1996. *Leisure interests:* skiing, squash. *Address:* Highland Capital Partners LLC,

92 Hayden Avenue, Lexington, MA 02421, USA (office). *Telephone:* (781) 861-5500 (office). *Fax:* (781) 861-5499 (office). *E-mail:* tstemberg@hcp.com (office). *Website:* www.hcp.com/highland_consumer_fund (office).

STEMPLOWSKI, Ryszard Maria, LLM, PhD, DHabil (Hist); Polish academic, lawyer, historian and diplomatist; *Professor, Institute of Political Science, Akademia Ignatianum, Kraków;* b. 25 March 1939, Wygoda-Witwica; s. of Kazimierz Stemplowski and Eugenia Białecka; m. Irena Zasłona 1975; two d.; ed Tech. Lycée, Bydgoszcz, Dept of Ecological Eng, Wrocław Univ. of Tech., Dept of Law, Wrocław Univ., Inst. of History, Polish Acad. of Sciences, Warsaw; Research Fellow, Inst. of History, Polish Acad. of Sciences 1973–90; Chief, Chancellery of Sejm (Parl.) 1990–93; Amb. to UK 1994–99; Dir Polish Inst. of Int. Affairs 1999–2004; Prof., Warsaw School of Econs 2001–04; Prof. of History and Politics, Jagiellonian Univ., Kraków 2005–10; Prof., Inst. of Political Science, Akademia Ignatianum 2010–; Ed. Polish Diplomatic Review 2000–04; Co-founder and mem. Polish Soc. of Studies of Latin America 1978–; Visiting Fellow, St Antony's Coll. Oxford 1974; Alexander von Humboldt Research Fellow, Univ. of Cologne 1981–82; mem. Polish Historical Soc. 1975– (Sec.-Gen. 1976–78), Academia Europaea 2013; Gran Croce di Merito del Ordine Constantiniano di S. Giorgio 1997; Kt, Order of Polonia Restituta 2000; Interfaith Gold Medallion Peace Through Dialogue, Int. Council of Christians and Jews 1999. *Publications:* more than 180 articles; 25 books, including (in Polish) Argentina and the Rivalries among the United States, United Kingdom and Germany 1930–46 1975, State Socialism in the Actually Existing Capitalism: Chile 1932 1996 (second edn 2013), An Introduction to the Polish Foreign Policy Analysis (two vols) 2006 (second edn 2007), Philosophical Foundations of Integration of European States in the 20th and 21st Centuries 2012, Poles, Ruthenians, Ukrainians, Argentines in Misiones (Argentina) 1892–2009 2011 (second edn 2013) (English edn: On the State of Latin American States – Approaching the Bicentenary 2009), Europe – Latin America: Looking at Each Other 2010. *Leisure interests:* music, cosmology, poetry in translation. *Address:* Institute of Political Science, Akademia Ignatianum, ul. Kopernika 26, 31-501 Kraków (office); ul. Sulkowskiego 4 M. 3, 01-602, Warsaw, Poland (home). *Telephone:* 50-9928193 (mobile) (office). *E-mail:* ryszard@stemplowski.pl (home). *Website:* www.ignatianum.edu.pll (office); www.stemplowski.pl (home).

STENBÄCK, Pär Olav Mikael, MPolSci; Finnish international administrator and fmr politician; b. 12 Aug. 1941, Porvoo (Borgå); s. of Arne Mikael Stenbäck and Rakel Stenbäck (née Granholm); m. Liv Sissel Lund 1970; two s.; ed Helsinki Univ.; Ed. with Finnish Broadcasting Co. 1962–68; Chair. Svensk Ungdom (youth org. of Swedish People's Party of Finland) 1967–70; mem. Parl. 1970–85; Chair. Swedish People's Party 1977–85; Minister of Educ. 1979–82, of Foreign Affairs 1982–83; Man. Dir Hanaholmen Swedish-Finnish Culture Centre 1974–85; Sec.-Gen. Finnish Red Cross 1985–88, Pres. 1996–99; Sec.-Gen. Int. Fed. (fmrly League) of Red Cross and Red Crescent Socs, Geneva 1988–92; Sec.-Gen. Nordic Council of Ministers, Copenhagen 1992–96; mem. Esbo City Council 2005–08; Pres. Foundation for Swedish Culture in Finland 1996–2002; Chair. Norwegian-Swedish Comm. preparing new Reindeer Grazing Convention 1998–2001, Finnish Children and Youth Foundation 2001–, Finnish-Swedish Cultural Foundation 2005–10; Vice-Pres. for Europe, Int. Youth Foundation, Geneva USA 1996–2005; mem. Bd Int. Crisis Group 1995–, Mehiläinen Pvt. Hosp. Corpn 2001–06, Deutsche Kinder-und Jugendstiftung 2001–11, Bd ICTI-Care Foundation 2008–, UWC Int. Council 2013–; Monitor, Int. Red Cross and Red Crescent Movt (Israel/Palestine) 2007–13, mem. Standing Comm. of the Int. Red Cross and Red Crescent Movt 2011–; numerous other professional appointments; Hon. Minister (Finland) 1999; Grand Cross, Royal Order of Northern Star (Sweden), Grand Cross of the Falcon (Iceland), Grand Cross St Olav (Norway), Grand Cross of Dannebrog (Denmark), Commdr of the Order of the Lion, Commdr (First Class), White Rose (Finland), Grand Cross of Santa Miranda (Venezuela) and numerous other foreign and Red Cross decorations; Dr hc (Petrozavodsk State Univ.) 2000; Helsinki Univ. Medal; Henri Dunant Medal 2009. *Publications:* Vision och verklighet (Vision and Reality) 2003, När världen öppnade sig (When the World Opened Up) 2007, Kriser och katastrofer (Crises and Disasters, memoirs) 2009 (edns in Swedish and Finnish). *Leisure interests:* literature, fishing, history, African colonial stamps. *Address:* Hirbölebågen 15, 02160 Esbo, Finland. *Telephone:* 50-5252060 (mobile). *Fax:* (9) 4128725. *E-mail:* par@stenback.fi. *Website:* www.stenback.fi.

STENBECK, Cristina, BSc; Swedish business executive; *Chairman, Investment AB Kinnevik;* b. 1977; d. of the late Jan Stenbeck; m. Alexander Fitzgibbons; three d.; ed Georgetown Univ., USA; worked for Polo Ralph Lauren, New York, USA for two years; mem. Bd Invik & Co. AB 1997–, Vice-Chair. Invik & Co. AB and Industriförvaltnings AB Kinnevik 2003–2007, Chair. 2007–, cos merged to form Investment AB Kinnevik 2003; mem. Bd of Dirs Metro International SA, Millicom International Cellular SA, Modern Times Group MTG AB, Tele2, Transcom WorldWide SA, Emesco AB; ranked by the Financial Times amongst Top 25 Businesswomen in Europe (11th) 2005, (13th) 2006, (12th) 2007, ranked by Fortune magazine amongst 50 Most Powerful Women in Business outside the US (47th) 2008. *Address:* Investment AB Kinnevik, PO Box 2094, 103 13 Stockholm, Sweden (office). *Telephone:* (8) 56200000 (office). *Fax:* (8) 203774 (office). *E-mail:* info@kinnevik.se (office). *Website:* www.kinnevik.se (office).

STENFLO, Jan Olof, MS, PhD; Swedish/Swiss astronomer; b. 10 Nov. 1942, Sweden; s. of Carl Stenflo and Signe Röden; m. Joyce E. Tucker 1971; two s.; ed Univ. of Lund; Asst Prof., Univ. of Lund 1969–75; Research Scientist, Swedish Natural Science Research Council 1975–80; Prof. of Astronomy, ETH, Zürich and Univ. of Zürich 1980–2007, Dir Inst. of Astronomy, ETH 1980–2006; Pres. LEST Foundation 1983–97; mem. Royal Swedish Acad. of Sciences, Norwegian Acad. of Science and Letters, Royal Physiographic Soc. Lund; Edlund Prize, Royal Swedish Acad. of Sciences 1974, Minor planet named 70737 Stenflo 2007, Prix Janssen, Soc. Astronomique de France 2008. *Publications:* Solar Magnetic Fields 1994; more than 260 scientific papers on astronomy in int. journals. *Leisure interests:* classical music, mountain hiking, skiing. *Address:* Institute of Astronomy, ETH, 8093 Zürich, Switzerland (office). *Telephone:* (44) 6323804 (office). *Fax:* (44) 6321205 (office). *E-mail:* stenflo@astro.phys.ethz.ch (office). *Website:* www.astro.phys.ethz .ch (office).

STENGEL, Richard, BA; American editor and government official; *Under Secretary of State for Public Diplomacy and Public Affairs;* b. 2 May 1955, New York, NY; m. Mary Pfaff; two c.; ed Princeton Univ., Christ Church Coll., Oxford,

UK; worked for MSNBC TV; staff writer, Time magazine, New York 1981–83, Assoc. Ed. 1984–88, sr writer and essayist 1989–98; Ferris Prof. of Journalism, Princeton Univ. 1998–99; Sr Advisor and chief speechwriter for presidential candidate Bill Bradley 1999; Man. Ed., Time.com 2000, Cultural Ed., Time magazine, then Nat. Ed. and Asst Man. Ed. –2004; Pres. and CEO, Nat. Constitutional Center, Philadelphia 2004–06; Man. Ed., Time magazine 2006–13; UnderSec. of State for Public Diplomacy and Public Affairs, US State Dept 2013–. *Film:* Mandela (producer, documentary) 1995. *Publications include:* January Sun: One Day, Three Lives, a South African Town 1990, Long Walk to Freedom (with Nelson Mandela) 1993, You're Too Kind: A Brief History of Flattery 2000, Mandela's Way: Fifteen Lessons on Life, Love and Courage 2010; contrib. articles to The New Yorker, The New Republic, New York Times and others. *Address:* Department of State, 2201 C Street, NW, Washington, DC 20520, USA (office). *Telephone:* (202) 647-4000 (office). *Fax:* (202) 647-6738 (office). *Website:* www.state.gov (office).

STENLUND, Bengt Gustav Verner, MSc (Eng), DTech; Finnish professor of polymer technology (retd); b. 17 Aug. 1939, Kristinestad; s. of Gustav Stenlund and Linda Hofman; m. Kerstin Ottosson 1964; one s.; Research Assoc. The Finnish Pulp and Paper Research Inst. 1965–77; Acting Prof. of Polymer Tech., Abo Akad. 1977–79, Prof. 1979–2002, Dean. Faculty of Chemical Eng 1982–85, Vice-Rector 1985–88, Rector 1988–97; mem. Research Council of Tech. Finish Acad. of Sciences 1983–85, Chair. and Bd mem. 1986–88; Chair. Finnish Rectors' Council 1990–92; Chair. LC Working Group on EC Research Policy 1993–95; Chair. Steering Group, Baltic Univ. Programme 1995–98; Head of Lab. of Polymer Tech. 1997–2002; mem. Scientific Del. of Finnish Chemical Industry 1985–90; mem. Bd Nordic Foundation of Tech. 1987–90; mem. Steering Cttee Finnish Centres of Expertise 1996–98; mem. Bd CRE 1994–98; Chair. Swedish Acad. of Eng of Finland 2001–04, Evaluation Cttee The Bank of Sweden Tercentenary Foundation 2002–04; mem. European Univ. Evaluation Team 1998–, Int. Selection Cttee, The Millenium Tech. Prize 2003–06, Int. Expert Cttee of Vinnova, Sweden 2006, Bd Resource Centre of Math., Science and Tech. 2006–; mem. European Science and Tech. Asscn 1994–97, Finnish Acad. of Eng, Finnish Soc. of Science and Letters, Royal Swedish Acad. of Eng, ACS 1997–2001, Japanese Inst. of Finland 1997–2002; Hon. mem. Swedish Acad. of Eng Sciences of Finland; Commdr, Order of the White Rose of Finland; Hon. DTech (Karlstad) 2000. *Publications:* Gel Chromatography of Lignosulfonates 1970; about 50 publs about natural and synthetic polymers. *Leisure interests:* art, society activities, grandchildren. *Address:* Peltolantie 6 B 61, 20700 Abo (home); Abo Akademi University, Biskopsgatan 8, 20500 Abo, Finland (office). *Telephone:* (400) 521556 (home). *E-mail:* bengt.stenlund@abo.fi (office). *Website:* www.abo.fi/fak/tkf (office).

STEPANIUC, Victor, DHist; Moldovan politician; *Deputy Prime Minister;* b. 13 July 1958, Ialoveni; m.; three c.; ed State Univ. of Moldova, Free Int. Univ. of Moldova; teacher of Russian language and literature, Hansca Village School, Ialoveni 1975–86, Dir of School 1986–96; mem. Parl. 1996–, mem. Juridical Comm. on Nominations and Immunities 1996–98, Chair. Parl. Comm. for Youth, Sport and Tourism 1998–2001, for Culture, Science, Educ., Sport, Tourism and Media 2005–08, Chair. CP Parl. Group 1998–2005, mem. Perm. Bureau 1998–; Deputy Prime Minister of Moldova 2008–. *Address:* Office of the Council of Ministers, 2033 Chișinău, Piața Marii Adunări Naționale 1, Moldova (office). *Telephone:* (22) 25-01-04 (office). *Fax:* (22) 24-26-96 (office). *E-mail:* anteprim@moldova.md (office). *Website:* www.gov.md (office).

STEPANKOV, Valentin Georgievich; Russian lawyer; b. 17 Sept. 1951, Perm; s. of Georgii Vassilyevich Stepankov and Antonina Andreyevna Klopova; m. 2nd Irina Vasilevna Martynova 2000; one s. from first m.; ed Perm State Univ.; investigator, Office of Public Prosecutor, Sverdlovsk Dist 1975–76, Perm Region 1976–77; Public Prosecutor of town of Gubakh Perm Region 1977–81; instructor, Div. of Regional Cttee of CPSU 1981–83; Public Prosecutor of Perm 1983–87; Deputy-Dir Investigation Dept Office of Public Prosecutor of USSR 1987–88; Public Prosecutor of Khabarovsk Region 1986–90; First Deputy Public Prosecutor of RSFSR 1990–91; Procurator-Gen. of Russia 1991–93; Deputy Head of Admin., Perm Region 1994–96; mem. State Duma (Parl.) 1996–99; Deputy Rep. of Russian Pres. to Volga Fed. Dist 2000; Deputy Sec. Security Council of Russia 2003; Deputy Minister of Natural Resources 2004–06; mem. Bd of Dirs Permskiye Motory (Perm Engines) 1999–2000; Honoured Lawyer of Russian Fed. 2001–. *Publications:* monograph on Kremlin conspiracy and numerous articles. *Leisure interests:* painting, reading, walks in the forest. *Address:* c/o Ministry of Natural Resources, ul. B. Gruzinskaya 4/6, 123812 Moscow, Russia (office).

STEPANOV, Petr Petrovich; Moldovan (b. Russian) politician; b. 2 Jan. 1959, Sankino village, Krasnochetaiskii region, Chuvash Autonomous Okrug, USSR; m.; two c.; ed Superior Tech. School 'A.D. Baumann', Moscow, VUZ Inst. of Higher Educ.; worked as engineer at natural gas compression stations in city of Surgut, Tyumen Oblast, transferred to Yamalo-Nenets Autonomous Okrug 1982–85, Head of gas compression station 1985–87; worked at Petr Stepanov man. co. providing gas from Tiraspol 1987–96, held positions of engineer in charge of checking tech. condition of the pipes; Gen. Man. Tiraspoltransgaz 1996–2005, CEO Tiraspol-transgaz-Pridnestrovie 2005–07; Minister of Industry of self-proclaimed 'Trans-nistrian Moldovan Republic' 2007–12; Chair. of the Govt, 'Transnistrian Moldovan Republic' 2012–13; Order of Honour, Order 'Labour Glory', Order 'For Merit' Grade II, Medal 'for hard work' and other medals of anniversary of breakaway Repub. of Transnistria; Gold Reserve 2000, Man of the Year 2003. *Address:* c/o Office of the Chairman of the Government, 3300 Tiraspol, ul. 25 Oktyabrya 45, Moldova.

STEPASHIN, Col.-Gen. Sergey Vadimovich, CandHist, LLD; Russian security official; *Chairman, Accounts Chamber of the Russian Federation;* b. 2 March 1952, Port Arthur; m.; one s.; ed Higher Political Coll., USSR Ministry of Internal Affairs, Mil. Acad., Financial Acad. under Russian Fed. Govt; service in Interior Forces 1973–90; Lecturer, Higher Political Coll., Leningrad 1981–90; Deputy to RSFSR Supreme Soviet 1990–93; after attempted coup Aug. 1991 Head of Cttee on Defence and Security of the Russian Fed. Supreme Soviet; author programme of reorganization of state security system; Chief, Leningrad Fed. Security Agency; Admin. and Deputy Chair. Russian Fed. Security Agency 1991–92; First Deputy Dir Fed. Counter-Intelligence Service (later Fed. Security Service) 1993–94, Dir 1994–95; Head of Admin, Dept of Govt 1995–97; Minister of Justice 1997–98, of Internal Affairs 1998–99; First Deputy Chair. of Govt April–May 1999, Chair. of

Govt (Prime Minister) May–Aug. 1999; Chair. Exec. Council of Russia and Belarus Union May–Aug. 1999; joined Yabloko Movt 1999; mem. State Duma (Parl.) 1999–2000; Chair. Accounts Chamber of Russian Fed. 2000–; Pres. European Org. of Supreme Audit Insts 2002–; Prof., Russian Fed. State Counsellor of Justice; Order of Fortitude 1998, Order 'For Merits Before Fatherland', Third Degree 2002, Légion d'honneur, Commodore degree 2005, Order 'For Services to the Father-land', Second Degree 2007. *Publication:* Personal and Social Security (Political and Legal Issues) 1994. *Leisure interests:* sports, literature, theatre. *Address:* Accounts Chamber of the Russian Federation, 119992 Moscow, Zubovskaya Str. 2, Russia. *Telephone:* (495) 986-05-09 (office). *Fax:* (495) 986-09-52 (office). *E-mail:* info@ach .gov.ru (office). *Website:* www.ach.gov.ru (office).

STEPHANOPOULOS, George Robert, AB,MA; American broadcast journalist and fmr government official; b. 10 Feb. 1961, Fall River, Mass.; s. of Robert Stephanopoulos and Nikki C. Stephanopoulos; ed Columbia Univ., Univ. of Oxford, UK (Rhodes Scholar); fmrly admin. asst to US Rep. Edward Feighan, Washington, DC; Deputy Communications Dir, Dukakis-Bentsen Presidential Campaign 1988; fmr Exec. Floor Man. to US Rep. Richard Gephardt (later House Majority Leader); Sr Adviser to Pres. of USA 1993–96; Communications Dir, Clinton-Gore Presidential Campaign 1992; Communications Dir, The White House 1992–96, also Sr Adviser for Policy and Strategy; Visiting Prof. of Political Science, School of Int. and Public Affairs, Columbia Univ. 2001–02; contrib. and corresp., ABC News 1997–2002, Host and Chief Political Analyst, This Week with George Stephano-poulos (public affairs TV programme) 2002–09, Co-anchor Good Morning America 2009–; Medal of Excellence, Columbia Univ. 1993. *Publication:* All Too Human 1999. *Address:* Good Morning America, Times Square Studios, 1500 Broadway, New York, NY 10036, USA (office). *Website:* abcnews.go.com/GMA (office).

STEPHANOPOULOS, Konstantinos; Greek lawyer, politician and fmr head of state; b. 1926, Patras; s. of Demetrius Stephanopoulos and Vrisiis Stephanopoulos; m. Eugenia El. Stounopoulou 1959; two s. one d.; ed Univ. of Athens; pvt. law practice 1954–74; mem. Parl. for Achaia (Nat. Radical Union) 1964, (New Democracy) 1974, 1977, 1981, 1985, (Democratic Renewal) 1989; Under-Sec. of Commerce July–Nov. 1974; Minister of the Interior 1974–76, of Social Services 1976–77; in Prime Minister's Office 1977–81; Pres. of Greece 1995–2005; Parl. Rep., New Democracy Party 1981–85, Pres. Party of Democratic Renewal 1985–94; American Hellenic Inst. Hellenic Heritage Nat. Public Service Award 2005. *Address:* Valaoritou 9B, 10671 Athens (office); Dafnis 0, 15452 Psyhico, Greece (home). *Telephone:* (210) 3602212 (office); (210) 6773190 (home). *Fax:* (210) 3602212 (office). *E-mail:* stephan@otenet.gr (office).

STEPHEN, Marcus; Nauruan politician, fmr head of state and fmr weightlifter; b. 1 Oct. 1969; s. of Lawrence Stephen and Sunshine Stephen; m. Amanda Stephen; one s. two d.; ed St Bede's Coll., Mentone, Vic. and Royal Melbourne Inst. of Tech., Australia (Diploma of Accounting); participated as weightlifter for Samoa at Olympic Games, Barcelona 1992, for Nauru at Olympic Games, Atlanta 1996, Sydney 2000; in Commonwealth Games won one gold and two silver medals at Auckland 1990, three gold medals in Victoria 1994, three gold medals in Kuala Lumpur 1998, three silver medals at Manchester 2002; retd from sport in 2002; mem. Parl. from Ewa and Anetan 2003–07, held positions of Minister of Finance, for Sport, Telecommunications and Transport; Pres. of Nauru 2007–11 (resgnd); Rep. at Int. Whaling Comm. 2005; Pres. Nauru Olympic Cttee 2009–. *Address:* c/o Office of the President, Yaren, Nauru.

STEPHEN, Baron (Life Peer), cr. 2011, of Lower Deeside in the City of Aberdeen; **Nicol Stephen,** LLB; British politician and business executive; b. 23 March 1960, Aberdeen, Scotland; ed Robert Gordon's Coll., Aberdeen, Univs of Aberdeen and Edinburgh; Dip. Legal Practice 1981; trainee solicitor, C & P H Chalmers 1981–83; Solicitor, Milne & Mackinnon 1983–88; Sr Man., Touche Ross Corp. Finance 1988–91; Dir, Glassbox Ltd 1992–99; Councillor, Grampian Regional Council 1982–92; contested Kincardine and Deeside in gen. elections 1987, 1992; MP for Kincardine and Deeside 1991–92; Scottish Liberal Democrat Spokesperson for Health 1995–97; contested Aberdeen South 1997; MSP (Liberal Democrat) 1999–2011, Party Spokesperson for Educ. and Heritage, Team Leader; held several Ministerial posts, including Deputy First Minister of Scotland 2005–07; Leader of Scottish Liberal Democrats 2005–08; mem. Cttee of the Regions 2002–05, Alt. mem. 2010–; mem. (Liberal Democrat) House of Lords 2011–; Dir, Renewable Energy Ventures Ltd, Grampian Youth Orchestra. *Address:* House of Lords, Westminster, London, SW1A 0PW, England (office). *Telephone:* (20) 7219-2964 (office). *E-mail:* stephenn@parliament.uk (office).

STEPHEN, Rt Hon. Sir Ninian Martin, KG, AK, GCMG, GCVO, KBE, KStJ; Australian lawyer and international official; b. 15 June 1923, Oxford, UK; s. of the late Frederick Stephen and Barbara Stephen (née Cruickshank); m. Valery Mary Sinclair 1949; five d.; ed George Watson's School, Edinburgh Acad., St Paul's School, UK, Chillon Coll., Switzerland, Scotch Coll., Melbourne, Melbourne Univ.; served World War II, Australian Army; admitted as barrister and solicitor, Victoria 1949; QC 1966; Judge, Supreme Court, Victoria 1970; Justice, High Court, Australia 1972–82; Gov.-Gen. of Australia 1982–89; Chair. Nat. Library of Australia 1989–94; Amb. for the Environment 1989–92; Chair. Strand Two, Northern Ireland Talks 1992, UN Group of Experts on Cambodia, Australian Citizenship Council; Judge, International Criminal Tribunals for Yugoslavia 1993–97, for Rwanda 1995–97; mem. Ethics Comm. International Olympic Cttee 2000–; Chair. ILO High Level Team to Myanmar 2001; Hon. Bencher Gray's Inn 1981; Commdr, Légion d'honneur 1993. *Address:* 4 Treasury Place, Melbourne, Vic. 3002 (office); Flat 13/1, 193 Domain Road, South Yarra, Vic. 3141, Australia (home). *Telephone:* (3) 9650-0266 (office); (3) 9820-2787 (home). *Fax:* (3) 9650-0270 (office). *E-mail:* ninian.stephen@dpmc.gov.au (office).

STEPHENS, Toby; British actor; b. 21 April 1969, London; s. of Sir Robert Stephens and Dame Maggie Smith; m. Anna-Louise Plowman 2001; ed London Acad. of Music and Dramatic Art. *Plays:* Measure for Measure (RSC), A Midsummer Night's Dream (RSC), Unfinished Business (playing Young Beamish, RSC), Wallenstein (RSC), All's Well That Ends Well (playing Bertram, RSC), Anthony and Cleopatra (playing Pompey, RSC), Coriolanus (playing Coriolanus, RSC) (Sir John Gielgud Award for Best Actor 1994, Ian Charleson Award 1995), Britannicus, Phedre (Almedia & Brooklyn Acad., New York), A Streetcar Named Desire (The Haymarket), Tartuffe (playing Damis, Playhouse Theatre), Ring

Around the Moon (Lincoln Center Theater, New York) 1999, Betrayal (Donmar Warehouse, London) 2007. *Films:* Orlando 1992, Twelfth Night 1996, Sunset Heights 1997, Photographic Fairies 1997, Cousin Bette 1998, Onegin 1999, The Announcement 2000, Space Cowboys 2000, Possession 2002, James Bond: Die Another Day 2002, Terkel in Trouble (voice) 2004, The Rising Ballad of Mangal Pandey 2005, Midsummer Dream (voice) 2005, Severance 2006, Dark Corners 2006, One Day 2007. *Television:* The Camomile Lawn 1992, Tenant of Wildfell Hall 1996, The Great Gatsby 2000, Perfect Strangers 2001, Napoléon 2002, Cambridge Spies 2003, Poirot (episode, Five Little Pigs) 2003, London 2004, The Queen's Sister 2005, The Best Man 2005, Sharpe's Challenge 2006, Jane Eyre (miniseries) 2006, Robin Hood (series). *Address:* c/o ICM, Oxford House, 76 Oxford Street, London, W1N 0AX, England.

STEPHENSON, Hugh; British journalist and academic; b. 18 July 1938, Simla, India; s. of the late Sir Hugh Stephenson and Lady Stephenson; m. 1st Auriol Stevens 1962 (divorced 1987); two s. one d.; m. 2nd Diana Eden 1990; ed New Coll. Oxford, Univ. of California, Berkeley, USA; served in diplomatic service in London and Bonn 1964–68; with The Times, London 1969–81, Ed., The Times Business News 1971–81; Ed. The New Statesman 1982–86; Prof. of Journalism, City Univ. 1986–2003, Prof. Emer. 2003–; Dir History Today Ltd 1981–; Dir European Journalism Centre, Maastricht 1992–2008, Chair. 1995–2002; currently crossword ed. The Guardian newspaper. *Publications include:* The Coming Clash 1972, Mrs. Thatcher's First Year 1980, Claret and Chips 1982, Libel and the Media (with others) 1997, Secrets of the Setters 2005, also various series of crosswords collections. *Address:* c/o The Guardian, Kings Place, 90 York Way, London, N1 9GU, Englnad (office). *Telephone:* (20) 3353-2000 (office). *E-mail:* hugh .stephenson@guardian.co.uk (office). *Website:* www.guardian.co.uk/crosswords (office).

STEPHENSON, Randall L., BSc, MA; American telecommunications executive; *Chairman and CEO, AT&T Inc.;* b. 22 April 1960, Oklahoma City; m. Lenise H. Stephenson; ed Central State Univ., Okla, Univ. of Oklahoma; began career with Southwestern Bell Telephone, Oklahoma City (later SBC) 1982, various man. roles in finance, becoming Dir of Finance SBC Int., Mexico City 1992–96, Controller SBC Communications, San Antonio 1996–97, Sr Exec. Vice-Pres. and Chief Financial Officer 2001–04, COO SBC Communications Inc. 2004–05, COO AT&T Inc. (following merger of SBC and AT&T Corpn 2005) 2005–07, mem. Bd of Dirs AT&T Inc. 2005–, Chair. and CEO 2007–; Dir Cingular Wireless 2001–06, Chair. 2003–04; Dir Emerson Electric Co. 2006–; Chair. United Way of Metropolitan Dallas Campaign 2011; mem. Nat. Exec. Bd, Boy Scouts of America. *Address:* AT&T Inc., 208 South Akard Street, Dallas, TX 75202, USA (office). *Telephone:* (210) 821-4105 (office). *Fax:* (210) 351-2071 (office). *E-mail:* info@att.com (office). *Website:* www.att.com (office).

STEPHENSON, Thomas F., AB, MBA, JD; American business executive and diplomatist; b. 1942, Wilmington, Del.; m.; four c.; ed Harvard Coll., Harvard Business School, Boston Coll. Law School; has served on numerous pvt. and public corp. bds; fmr securities analyst, Fidelity Management Co., helped found Fidelity Ventures, Pres. Fidelity Ventures 1977–87; Pnr, Sequoia Capital (Silicon Valley venture capital co.) 1987–2006; Amb. to Portugal 2007–09; mem. Bd of Overseers and Exec. Cttee, Harvard Univ.; fmr mem. Exec. Cttee of Bd of Overseers of Hoover Inst., Stanford Univ., Bd of Advisors of Stanford Inst. for Econ. Policy Research, Bd of Dirs of Conservation Int., Wilson Center Council; fmr Corp. Fund Vice-Chair. The Kennedy Center; fmr mem. bds and cttees Tufts New England Medical Center, Boston. *Address:* Sequoia Capital, 3000 Sand Hill Road, 4-250, Menlo Park, CA 94025, USA (office). *Telephone:* (650) 854-3927 (office). *Fax:* (650) 854-2977 (office). *E-mail:* stephenson@sequoiacap.com (office). *Website:* www.sequoiacap.com (office).

STEPIN, Vyacheslav Semenovich; Russian academic; *Director, Institute of Philosophy, Russian Academy of Sciences;* b. 19 Aug. 1934, Bryansk; s. of Semen Nikolaievich Stepin and Antonina Grigorievna (née Petrova) Stepina; m. Tatiana Ivanovna Vagranova 1957; ed Belorussia State Univ.; Prof., Chair.; Dir Inst. of History of Natural Sciences and Tech. 1987–88; Dir Inst. of Philosophy, Russian Acad. of Sciences 1988–; Corresp. mem. USSR (now Russian) Acad. of Sciences 1987, mem. 1994; research in theory of cognition, philosophy of science and tech., history of science; Vice-Pres. Philosophy Soc.; Pres. Asscn For Humanitarian Dialogue; foreign mem. Nat. Acad. of Sciences, Repub. of Belarus 1998, Ukraine 2000; Hon. Consulting Prof., Inst. of Int. Law and Econs, Hong Kong 1994, Hon. mem. Acad. of Sciences and Educ., Karlsruhe, Germany; Dr hc (Univ. of Karlsruhe) 1999. *Publications include:* Contemporary Positivism and Science 1963, Practical Nature of Cognition and Methodical Problems of Contemporary Physics 1970, Methods of Scientific Cognition 1974, Scientific Revolutions in Dynamics of Culture 1987, Philosophical Anthropology and Philosophy of Science 1992, Scientific Picture of the World in the Culture of Technogenic Civilization 1994, Philosophy of Science and Technics 1995, Age of Changes and Scenarios of the Future 1996, Civilization. Science. Culture 2002. *Address:* Institute of Philosophy, Russian Academy of Sciences, 199991 Moscow, Volkhonka str. 14 (office); DM Ulianov str. 3, Ap. 130, Moscow, Russia (home). *Telephone:* (495) 203-95-69 (office). *Fax:* (495) 200-32-50. *E-mail:* stepin@iph.ras.ru. *Website:* ru .philosophy.kiev.ua.

STERLING, Sir Michael John Howard, Kt, PhD, DEng, FIEE, FRSA; British engineer, academic and university vice-chancellor; b. 9 Feb. 1946, Paddock Wood, Kent, England; s. of Richard Howard Sterling and Joan Valeria Sterling (née Skinner); m. Wendy Karla Anstead 1969; two s.; ed Hampton Grammar School, Middx, Univ. of Sheffield; student apprentice, AEI 1964–68; GEC Research Engineer 1968–71; Lecturer in Control Eng, Univ. of Sheffield 1971–78, Sr Lecturer 1978–80; Prof. of Eng, Univ. of Durham 1980–90; Vice-Chancellor and Prin., Brunel Univ. 1990–2001; Vice-Chancellor, Univ. of Birmingham 2001–09; mem. Council IEE 1991–93, Vice-Pres. 1997–2001, Deputy Pres. 2001–02, Pres. 2002–03; Chair. OCEPS Ltd 1990–, Higher Educ. Statistics Agency 1992–, Higher Educ. Funding Council Steering Cttee on Performance Indicators 1992–95 (mem. Quality Assessment Cttee 1992–95), WASMACS Ltd 1994–, MidMAN 2001; Dir COBUILD Ltd 2001–, UCAS 2001–, Universitas 21 2001–; mem. Science & Eng Research Council Eng Bd 1989–92, Electricity Research Council 1987–89, Royal Acad. of Eng Standing Cttee for Educ., Training and Competence to Practise 1993–97, Cttee 2 for Int. Co-operation in Higher Educ., British Council 1991–96,

AWM Broadband Steering Group 2002–, Bd WMHEA 2001–; Fellow, Inst. of Measurement and Control (Pres. 1988, Council mem. 1983–91); Fellow, Royal Acad. of Engineering; Pres. Elmhurst School for Dance 2002–; Trustee, Barber Inst. of Fine Art 2001–; Gov. Burnham Grammar School 1990–, Hampton School 1991– (Chair. of Govs 1997–); Freeman City of London 1996, Liveryman Worshipful Co. of Engineers 1998; Hon. DEng (Sheffield) 1995, Hon. DUniv (Tashkent, Uzbekistan) 1999, Dr hc (West Bohemia, Czech Repub.) 2001; Inst. of Measurement and Control ICI Prize 1980, IEE Hartree Premium 1985, Commemorative Medal 2000. *Publications:* Power Systems Control 1978; over 200 tech. papers and book contribs. *Leisure interests:* gardening, DIY, computers, model eng. *Address:* c/o Vice-Chancellor's Office, Birmingham University, Edgbaston, Birmingham, B15 2TT, England.

STERLING OF PLAISTOW, Baron (Life Peer), cr. 1990, of Pall Mall in the City of Westminster; **Jeffrey Maurice Sterling,** GCVO, CBE; British business executive; b. 27 Dec. 1934, London; s. of Harry Sterling and Alice Sterling; m. Dorothy Ann Smith 1985; one d.; ed Reigate Grammar School, Preston Manor County School and Guildhall School of Music, London; Paul Schweder & Co. (Stock Exchange) 1955-57; G. Eberstadt & Co. 1957–62; Financial Dir General Guarantee Corpn 1962–64; Man. Dir Gula Investments Ltd 1964–69; Chair. Sterling Guarantee Trust PLC 1969–85 (merged with P&O 1985), P&O Steam Navigation Co. 1983, P&O Asia 1992, P&O Princess Cruises 2000–03, currently Life Pres.; Special Adviser to Sec. of State for Industry 1982–83, to Sec. of State for Trade and Industry 1983–90; mem. British Airways Bd 1979–82; mem. Exec., World Org. for Rehabilitation by Training Union 1966–, Chair. Org. Cttee 1969–73, Chair. ORT Tech. Services 1974, Vice-Pres. British ORT 1978; Pres. Gen. Council of British Shipping 1990–91, EC Shipowners' Asscns 1992–94; Deputy Chair. and Hon. Treasurer London Celebrations Cttee Queen's Silver Jubilee 1975–83; Chair. Young Vic Co. 1975–83; f. Motability (charity) 1977, Vice-Chair. and Chair. of Exec. 1977–94, Chair. 1994–; Chair. of the Govs Royal Ballet School 1983–99; Chair. Queen's Golden Jubilee Weekend Trust 2001–02; Fellow, ISVA 1995; Gov. Royal Ballet 1986–99; Hon. Capt. RNR 1991–; Elder Brother Trinity House 1991; Hon mem. Royal Inst. of Chartered Surveyors 1993; Freeman City of London; Hon. Fellow Inst. of Marine Engineers 1991, Inst. of Chartered Shipbrokers 1992, Royal Inst. of Chartered Shipbrokers 1992, Royal Inst. of Naval Architects 1997; KStJ 1998; Hon. DBA (Nottingham Trent) 1995; Hon. DCL (Durham) 1996. *Leisure interests:* music, swimming, tennis. *Address:* House of Lords, London, SW1A 0PW, England. *Telephone:* (20) 7219-4819. *Website:* www.motability.co.uk.

STERN, Ernest, MA, PhD; American economist and academic; *Partner and Senior Advisor, The Rohatyn Group;* b. 25 Aug. 1933, Frankfurt, Germany; s. of Henry Stern; m. Zina Gold 1957; ed Queens Coll., New York and Fletcher School of Law and Diplomacy; Economist, US Dept of Commerce 1957–59; Program Economist, USAID 1959–63; Instructor, Middle East Tech. Univ. 1960–61; Economist, Office of Pakistan Affairs, USAID 1963–64; Officer in Charge of Pakistan Affairs 1964–64, Asst Dir for Devt Policy USAID India 1965–67, Deputy Dir USAID Pakistan 1967–68, Deputy Staff Dir Comm. on Int. Devt (Pearson Comm.) 1968–69; Lecturer, Woodrow Wilson School of Public and Int. Affairs, Princeton, NJ 1971; Sr Staff mem. Council on Int. Econ. Policy, The White House 1971; joined World Bank 1972, various posts including Deputy Chair. Econ. Cttee, Sr Adviser on Devt Policy, Dir Devt Policy, then Vice-Pres. S Asia until 1978, Vice-Pres. Operations, World Bank July 1978, Sr Vice-Pres., Operations 1980–87, Sr Vice-Pres., Finance 1987, Man. Dir 1991–95 (retd); Man. Dir JP Morgan Chase 1995; currently Partner and Sr Advisor, The Rohatyn Group, New York; mem. Bd Advisors Inst. for Int. Econs, Washington, DC; mem. Bd of Overseers, Int. Center for Econ. Growth, Calif.; fmr mem. Bd of Dirs Center for Global Devt, US-Russian Business Council, Commonfund; mem. Council on Foreign Relations, Group of Thirty Consultative Group on Int. Econ. and Monetary Affairs, Inc. (G-30), Washington, DC; William A. Jump Memorial Foundation Meritorious Award 1964, 1966. *Address:* c/o The Group of Thirty, 1726 M Street NW, Suite 200, Washington, DC 20036, USA. *Telephone:* (212) 984-2900 (New York) (office); (202) 331-2472 (Washington, DC). *E-mail:* info@group30.org. *Website:* www.group30.org.

STERN, Fritz, PhD; American historian and academic; *University Professor Emeritus, Columbia University;* b. 2 Feb. 1926, Breslau, Germany; s. of Rudolf A. Stern and Catherine B. Stern; m. 1st Margaret J. Bassett 1947 (divorced 1992); one s. one d.; m. 2nd Elisabeth Niebuhr Sifton 1996; ed Bentley School, New York, Columbia Univ.; Lecturer and Instructor, Columbia Univ. 1946–51; Acting Asst Prof., Cornell Univ. 1951–53; Asst Prof., Columbia Univ. 1953–57, Assoc. Prof. 1957–63, Full Prof. 1963–67, Seth Low Prof. 1967–92, Univ. Prof. 1992–96, Univ. Prof. Emer. 1997–; Provost 1980–83; Visiting Prof., Free Univ. of Berlin 1954, Yale Univ. 1963, Fondation Nationale des Sciences Politiques, Paris 1979; Perm. Visiting Prof., Konstanz Univ. 1966–; Consultant US State Dept 1966–67; Guggenheim Fellowship 1969–70; mem. OECD team on German Educ. 1971–72; Netherlands Inst. for Advanced Study 1972–73; Trustee German Marshall Fund 1981–99, Aspen Inst. Berlin 1983–2000; Sr Advisor, US Embassy in Bonn 1993–94; mem. American Acad. of Arts and Sciences 1969–, Trilateral Comm. 1983–90, American Philosophical Soc. 1988, German-American Academic Council 1993–97; Corresp. mem. Deutsche Akad. für Dichtung und Sprache 1988; Senator, Deutsche Nationalstiftung 1993–; Hon. Senator, Deutsche Nationalstiftung 2008–; Orden pour le Mérite (Germany) 1994, Knight Commdr's Cross (Germany) 2004; Hon. DLitt (Oxford) 1985; Hon. LLD (New School for Social Research, New York) 1997, (Columbia Univ.) 1998, (Wrocław) 2002; Hon. DHumLitt (Princeton) 2007; Dr hc (Carl von Ossietzky Universität, Oldenburg) 2013; Lionel Trilling Book Award 1977, Lucas Prize (Tübingen) 1984, Kulturpreis Schlesien (Wrocław) 1996, Peace Prize of the German Book Trade 1999, Alexander-von-Humboldt Research Prize 1999, Bruno Snell Medal, Univ. of Hamburg 2002, Lifetime Achievement Award, American Historical Asscn 2007, Jacques Barzun Prize, American Philosophical Soc. 2007, Annual Prize for Tolerance and Reconciliation, Jewish Museum, Berlin 2007, Lifetime Achievement Award, American Historical Asscn 2007, Marion Dönhoff Prize for reconciliation 2009, Volkmar and Margret Sander Prize, Deutsches Haus, New York Univ. 2013. *Publications:* The Politics of Cultural Despair: A Study in the Rise of the Germanic Ideology 1961, Gold and Iron: Bismarck, Bleichroeder and the Building of the German Empire 1977, The Failure of Illiberalism: Essays in the Political Culture of Modern Germany 1972, Dreams and Delusions: The Drama of German History 1987; ed. The Varieties of History from Voltaire to the Present 1956, Der Nationalsozialismus als Versuchung, in

Reflexionen Finsterer Zeit 1984, Verspielte Grösse: Essays zur deutschen Geschichte 1996, Das Feine Schweigen: Historische Essays 1999, Einstein's German World 1999, Grandeurs et Defaillances de l'Allemagne du XXème Siècle 2001, Five Germanys I Have Known 2006, Der Westen im 20. Jahrhundert: Selbstzerstörung, Wiederaufbau, Gefährdungen der Gegenwart 2008, Helmut Schmidt-Fritz Stern: Unser Jahrhundert, Ein Gespräch 2010, Joschka Fischer-Fritz Stern: Gegen den Strom: Ein Gespräch über Geschichte und Politik 2013, Elisabeth Sifton-Fritz Stern: No Ordinary Men: Dietrich Bonhoeffer and Hans von Dohnanyi, Resisters Against Hitler in Church and State 2013. *Leisure interests:* reading, hiking, cross-country skiing. *Address:* 15 Claremont Avenue, New York, NY 10027, USA. *Telephone:* (212) 666-2891. *Fax:* (212) 316-0370. *E-mail:* fs20@ columbia.edu.

STERN, Howard Allan, BA; American radio broadcaster, television host, author, actor and photographer; b. 12 Jan. 1954, Jackson Heights, Queens, New York; s. of Ben Stern and Rae Stern; m. 1st Alison Berns 1978 (divorced 2001); three d.; m. 2nd Beth Ostrosky 2008; ed Boston Univ.; disc jockey with WRNW, Briarcliff Manor, NY 1976–78, WCCC, Hartford, Conn. 1978–79, WWWW, Detroit 1979–80, WWDC, Washington, DC 1980–82, WNBC, New York 1982–85, WXRK, New York 1985–2005; syndicated in several other radio markets with Clear Channel 1986, with Infinity Broadcasting Corpn 1998–2005; The Howard Stern Show, Sirius XM Radio 2006–; judge on TV talent show America's Got Talent (replaced Piers Morgan) 2012–; Libertarian cand. for Gov. of NY 1994. *Television includes:* Petey Greene's Washington 1981, Late Night with David Letterman 1984–93, Nightlife 1987, The New Hollywood Squares 1988, The Howard Stern Show (WOR-TV) 1990–92, 1992 MTV Video Music Awards 1992, The Howard Stern 'Interview' 1992–93, The Larry Sanders Show 1993, The Jon Stewart Show 1993, Howard Stern 1994–2005, Saturday Night Live 1997, The Magic Hour 1998, The Roseanne Show 1998, The Howard Stern Radio Show 1998–2001, The Concert for New York City 2001, Extra 2004, Howard TV 2005–, Piers Morgan Tonight 2011, The Daily Show with Jon Stewart 2011, Late Show with David Letterman 2011, America's Got Talent (judge) 2012–; as producer: Son of the Beach (also writer) 2000, Doomsday (also writer) 2002, Howard Stern: The High School Years 2003. *Recordings include:* 50 Ways to Rank Your Mother 1982, Crucified by the FCC 1991, Private Parts: The Album 1997. *Publications:* Private Parts 1993, Miss America 1995. *Address:* c/o Don Buchwald & Associates, 10 East 44th Street, New York, NY 10017, USA (office). *Website:* www.howardstern.com.

STERN, Jacques; French engineer, business executive and fmr academic; b. 21 March 1932, Paris; m. Janine Riemer 1956; three s.; ed Ecole Polytechnique, Ecole Nationale supérieure de l'Aéronautique, Harvard Univ., USA, Institut des Hautes Etudes de la Defense Nationale; in charge of design and devt of French Air Defence computer system (STRIDA), French Air Force 1958–64; Founder and Pres. Soc. d'Etudes des Systèmes d'Automation (SESA) 1964; apptd Chair. and CEO Bull 1982, Chair. Honeywell Bull Inc. 1987, Hon. Pres. Bull 1989–; Founder and Pres. Sycomore 1989–; Founder, Stern Systèmes d'information 1998–; Founder and Pres. Synesys 1998–2001; Vice-Pres. Fyssen Foundation 1994; mem. Bd of Dirs Planet Finance, Air France, Thomson Group; Bd mem. Ecole Polytechnique, Fondation des Sciences Politiques et Sociales (representing Prime Minister), Conseil Perfectionnement de l'ENST; mem. Comité Consultatif Banque de France, Comité Nat. Evaluation de la Recherche; Prof., various univs and eng schools; Hon. mem. Acad. des Technologies; Officier, Ordre nat. du Mérite, Chevalier, Légion d'honneur. *Publications include:* several tech. books. *Address:* 1 rue Le Notre, 75016 Paris, France (home). *Telephone:* 1-45-27-35-11 (office). *E-mail:* jj.stern@ free.fr (home).

STERN, Klaus, DrIur; German legal scholar, academic and judge; *Professor Emeritus, Institute für öffentliches Recht und Verwaltungslehre, University of Cologne;* b. 11 Jan. 1932, Nuremberg; m. Helga Stern 1976; ed Humanistisches Gymnasium, Nuremberg and Univs of Erlangen and Munich; Dozent, Univ. of Munich 1961; Prof., Berlin Univ. 1962; Prof. and Dir Inst. für öffentliches Recht und Verwaltungslehre, Univ. of Cologne 1966–, now Prof. Emer., Rector 1971–73, Pro-Rector 1973–75; Head of Studies, Verwaltungs- und Wirtschaftsakademie, Düsseldorf 1966–; Judge, Constitutional Court, Nordrhein-Westfalen 1976–2000; mem. Rheinland-Westfalische Akad. der Wissenschaften 1978–; Hon. mem. Japan Acad. 2006; Dr hc (Univ. of Breslau, Poland) 1987, (Fed. Univ. Ceara of Fortaleza, Brazil) 1991, (Univ. of Verona) 2005; Grosses Bundesverdienstkreuz 1989, Austrian Ehrenkreuz for Research and Art 1998, Verdienstorden, NRW 2000, Verdienstorden, City of Düsseldorf 2002. *Publications:* Staatsrecht der Bundesrepublik Deutschland (four vols); many other books and articles on constitutional and admin. law. *Address:* Institut für Rundfunkrecht an der Universität zu Köln, Aachener Straße 197–199, 50931 Cologne (office); Institut für öffentliches Recht und Verwaltungslehre, Universität zu Köln, Albertus-Magnus-Platz, 50931 Cologne, Germany. *Telephone:* (221) 9415465 (office). *Fax:* (221) 9415466 (office). *E-mail:* klaus.stern@uni-koeln.de (office); mail@klaus-stern.net. *Website:* www .jura.uni-koeln.de (office); www.klaus-stern.net.

STERN, Robert Arthur Morton, BA, MArch, FAIA; American architect and academic; *J.M. Hoppin Professor of Architecture and Dean, School of Architecture, Yale University;* b. 23 May 1939, New York; s. of Sidney Stern and Sonya Stern (née Cohen); m. Lynn G. Solinger 1966 (divorced 1977); one s.; ed Columbia and Yale Univs.; Program Dir Architectural League New York 1965–66; designer, Richard Meier, architect, New York 1966; consultant Small Parks Program, Dept of Parks, New York 1966–70; urban designer, Housing and Devt Admin. New York 1967–70; partner Robert AM Stern & John S. Hagmann, Architects, New York 1969–77, Prin. Robert AM Stern Architects 1977–89, Sr Partner 1989–; lecturer to Prof. of Architecture, Columbia Univ. 1970–72, Prof. 1982–98; J.M. Hoppin Prof. of Architecture and Dean, School of Architecture, Yale Univ. 1998–; Acting Dir Historical Preservation Program, Columbia Univ. School of Architecture 1991–98; mem. Bd of Regents American Architecture Foundation 1989–91, Bd of Dirs Chicago Inst. for Architecture and Urbanism 1990–93, Bd of Dirs. Preservation League of NY, Exec. Cttee, Architectural League of New York 1977– (Pres. 1973–77); Dir (non-exec.) Walt Disney Co. 1992–2003; numerous awards including AIA Nat. Honor awards 1980, 1985, 1990; President's Medal from Architectural League of NY 2002. *Television:* hosted Pride of Place: Building the American Dream, an eight-part, eight-hour documentary series on PBS 1986. *Publications include:* New Directions in American Architecture 1969, The House that Bob Built

1991, The American Houses of Robert A. M. Stern 1991, New York 1960 (with Thomas Mellins and David Fishman) 1995; also co-authored series New York 1880, New York 1900, New York 1930, New York 1960. *Address:* Office of the Dean, Yale School of Architecture, 180 York Street, New Haven, CT 06511 (office); Robert A.M. Stern Architects, 460 West 34th Street, New York, NY 10001, USA (office). *Telephone:* (203) 432-2279 (Yale) (office); (212) 967-5100 (NY) (office). *Fax:* (203) 432-7175 (Yale) (office); (212) 967-5588 (NY) (office). *Website:* www.architecture .yale.edu (office); www.ramsa.com (office).

STERN OF BRENTFORD, Baron (Life Peer), cr. 2007, of Elsted in the County of West Sussex and of Wimbledon in the London Borough of Merton; **Nicholas Herbert Stern,** PhD; British economist, academic and fmr government official; *IG Patel Chair in Economics and Government, London School of Economics;* b. 1946, London; m. Susan Stern; three c.; ed Latymer Upper School, Peterhouse Coll., Univ. of Cambridge; taught at Univ. of Oxford, Univ. of Warwick, LSE, Sorbonne, MIT; Chief Economist, EBRD 1993–99; Sr Vice-Pres. and Chief Economist, World Bank 2000–03; Second Perm. Sec., Man. Dir, Budget and Public Finances, Treasury of the UK 2003–04, Head of Govt Econ. Service 2003–07 (retd); commissioned to compile Stern Review on the Econs of Climate Change 2005, published 2006; IG Patel Chair in Econs and Govt, LSE 2007–, Dir India Observatory, Asia Research Centre; Fellow, British Acad., Econometrics Soc.; Hon. Fellow, American Acad. of Arts and Sciences; Hon. DSc (Warwick) 2006. *Publications:* Palanpur: The Economy of an Indian Village (with C. J. Bliss) 1982, The Theory and Practice of Tax Reform in Developing Countries (with E. Ahmad) 1991, A Strategy for Development 2002. *Leisure interests:* reading, travelling, watching Wimbledon Football Club. *Address:* House of Lords, London, SW1A 0PW; Asia Research Centre, 10th Floor, Tower 2, London School of Economics, Houghton Street, London, WC2A 2AE, England. *Telephone:* (20) 7219-5353 (House of Lords). *Fax:* (20) 7107-5285. *E-mail:* arc@lse.ac.uk. *Website:* www .lse.ac.uk/collections/IndiaObservatory (office); www.lse.ac.uk/collections/ asiaResearchCentre.

STERNBERG, Robert Jeffrey, BA, PhD; American psychologist, writer, editor and academic; *Provost, Senior Vice-President and Professor of Psychology, Oklahoma State University;* b. 8 Dec. 1949, Newark, NJ; m. Alejandra Campos 1991; one s. one d.; ed Yale Univ., Stanford Univ.; Asst Prof., Yale Univ. 1975–80, Assoc. Prof. 1980–83, Prof. 1983–86, IBM Prof. of Psychology and Education 1986–2005, Dir Center for the Psychology of Abilities, Competencies and Expertise 2000–05; Dean, School of Arts and Sciences, Tufts Univ. 2005–10, Dir Center for the Psychology of Abilities, Competencies and Expertise 2006–10; Provost, Sr Vice-Pres. and Prof. of Psychology, Oklahoma State Univ. 2010–; Ed. Psychological Bulletin 1991–96, Contemporary Psychology 1999; Distinguished Assoc., The Psychometrics Centre, Univ. of Cambridge; Pres. Eastern Psychological Asscn 2007–08, International Asscn for Cognitive Education and Psychology 2009–11, Federation of Asscns in Behavioral and Brain Sciences 2012–13; Ed.-in-Chief, Educational Psychology Series, Lawrence Erlbaum Assocs 1996–; mem. American Acad. of Arts and Sciences, AAAS, American Educational Research Asscn, American Psychological Soc., International Council of Psychologists, National Asscn for Gifted Children, Psychonomic Soc., Soc. for Research in Child Development, Soc. of Multivariate Experimental Psychology, American Psychological Asscn (Pres. 2003); Hon. Prof., Univ. of Heidelberg; Dr hc (Complutense Univ., Madrid) 1994, (Univ. of Paris V, France) 2000, (Univ. of Cyprus) 2000, (Univ. of Leuven, Belgium) 2001, (Constantine the Philosopher Univ., Slovakia) 2004, (Durham Univ., UK) 2006, (St Petersburg State Univ., Russia) 2006, (Tilburg Univ.) 2007, (Ricardo Palma Univ., Peru) 2008, (Eureka Coll.) 2008, (Univ. of Connecticut) 2009, (De la Salle Univ., Philippines) 2011, (Univ. of Huelva, Spain) 2012; Distinguished Scholar Award, National Asscn for Gifted Children 1985, Outstanding Book Award, American Educational Research Asscn 1987, Sylvia Scribner Award 1996, Guggenheim Fellowship 1985–86, Award for Excellence, Mensa Education and Research Foundation 1989, G. Stanley Hall Distinguished Lecturer, American Psychological Asscn 1997, E. L. Thorndike Award for Career Achievement in Educational Psychology 2003, Farnsworth Award, American Psychological Asscn 2003, Arthur W. Staats Award, American Psychological Foundation and the Soc. for General Psychology 2003, Anton Jurovsky Award, Slovak Psychological Soc. 2004, Arnheim Award, American Psychological Asscn 2005, Interamerican Psychologist Award, Interamerican Soc. of Psychology 2005, E. Paul Torrance Award, National Asscn for Gifted Children 2006, Sir Francis Galton Award, International Asscn of Empirical Aesthetics 2008, Presidential Award for Distinguished Lifetime Contributions to the Public Understanding of Psychology, American Psychological Asscn Division of Media Psychology 2008, Distinguished Service Award, International Asscn for Cognitive Education and Psychology 2011. *Publications include:* Intelligence, Information Processing, and Analogical Reasoning: The Componential Analysis of Human Abilities 1977, Beyond IQ: A Triarchic Theory of Human Intelligence 1985, Intelligence Applied: Understanding and Increasing Your Intellectual Skills 1986, What is Intelligence? (with D. K. Detterman) 1986, The Psychologist's Companion, second edn 1988, The Triangle of Love 1988, The Triarchic Mind: A New Theory of Human Intelligence 1988, Metaphors of Mind: Conceptions of the Nature of Intelligence 1990, Love the Way You Want It 1991, Tacit Knowledge Inventory for Managers (with R. K. Wagner) 1991, For Whom Does the Bell Curve Toll?: It Tolls for You 1995, In Search of the Human Mind 1995, Defying the Crowd: Cultivating Creativity in a Culture of Conformity (with T. I. Lubart) 1995, Off Track: When Poor Readers Become Learning Disabled (with L. Spear-Swerling) 1996, Cognitive Psychology 1996, Successful Intelligence 1996, Introduction to Psychology 1997, Pathways to Psychology 1997, Thinking Styles 1997, Successful Intelligence 1997, Cupid's Arrow: The Course of Love Through Time 1998, Love is a Story 1998, Perspectives on Learning Disabilities: Biological, Cognitive, Contextual (with L. Spear-Swerling) 1999, Our Labeled Children: What Every Parent and Teacher Needs to Know About Learning Disabilities (with E. L. Grigorenko) 1999, Teaching for Successful Intelligence (with E. L. Grigorenko) 2000, Psychology: In Search of the Human Mind 2001, Educational Psychology (with W. M. Williams) 2001, Dynamic Testing (with E. L. Grigorenko) 2002, Psychology 101½: Psychology for Success in Academia 2004, The Nature of Leadership 2004, A Brief History of Intelligence 2004, Wisdom, Intelligence and Creativity Synthesized 2007, The Nature of Hate (with K. Sternberg) 2008, College Admissions for the 21st Century 2010, Explorations of the Nature of Giftedness (with L. Jarvin, L. and E. L.

Grigorenko) 2011; other: ed. of many books; contributions: numerous scholarly books and journals. *Address:* Department of Psychology, Oklahoma State University, 116 North Murray, Stillwater, OK 74078-3064, USA. *Telephone:* (405) 744-6027. *Fax:* (405) 744-8067. *E-mail:* robert.sternberg@okstate.edu. *Website:* psychology.okstate.edu.

STERNBERG, Seymour G. (Sy); American insurance executive; *Chairman, New York Life Insurance Company;* b. 1943, New York City, NY; Sr Vice-Pres. Insurance Dept, New York Life Insurance Co. 1989–91, Exec. Vice-Pres. and Vice-Chair. Bd 1991–95, Pres. and COO 1995–97, Chair. and CEO 1997–2001, Chair., Pres. and CEO 2001–03, Chair. and CEO 2003–08, Chair. 2008–; mem. Bd Dirs Express Scripts Inc. 1992–; US Rep. to Asia-Pacific Econ. Co-operation Business Advisory Council 2001; Pnr and mem. New York City Partnership and Chamber of Commerce, Co-Chair. Breakthrough for Learning Initiative; Vice-Chair. Kennedy Center Corp. Fund; mem. The Business Roundtable, Lincoln Center Consolidated Corp. Fund Leadership Cttee, Bd Govs United Way of Tri-State; mem. Bd Trustees Big Brothers and Big Sisters of New York City; New Yorker for New York Award, Citizens Cttee of New York 2001. *Address:* New York Life Insurance Company, 51 Madison Avenue, New York, NY 10010, USA (office). *Telephone:* (212) 576-7000 (office). *Fax:* (212) 576-8145 (office). *E-mail:* info@newyorklife.com (office). *Website:* www.newyorklife.com (office).

STERNBERG, Sir Sigmund, Kt, FRSA, JP; British business executive; *Chairman, Martin Slowes Estates Ltd;* b. 2 June 1921, Budapest, Hungary; s. of the late Abraham Sternberg and Elizabeth Sternberg; m. Hazel Everett Jones 1970; one s. one d. and one s. one d. from a previous m.; Chair., Martin Slowe Estates Ltd 1971–; Deputy Chair., Labour Finance and Industry Group 1972–93, Hon. Life Pres. 2002–; Life Vice-Pres. Royal Coll. of Speech and Language Therapists 2002–; Life Pres. Sternberg Centre for Judaism 1996–; Founder Three Faiths Forum (Christian, Muslim and Jewish Dialogue Group) 1997; Pres. Movt for Reform Judaism 1998–; Sr Religious Advisor, World Econ. Forum 2002–; Life mem. Magistrates' Asscn 1965; Vice-Pres. Keston Inst.; mem. Bd John Templeton Foundation 1998; Paul Harris Fellow, Rotary Foundation of Rotary Int. 1989; Gov., Hebrew Univ. of Jerusalem; Life mem. Royal Soc. of Medicine 2002; Patron Int. Council of Christians and Jews, Anne Frank Trust UK; Freeman, City of London; Hon. Fellow, Univ. Coll. London 2001; Hon. DUniv (Essex) 1996, (Open Univ.) 1998, (Hebrew Union Coll., Cincinnati) 2000; Hon. DHumLitt (Richmond American Int. Univ.) 2008; Kt Commdr with Star, Order of St Gregory the Great 1985, Order of St John of Jerusalem 1988, Order of the Gold Star (Hungary) 1990, Commdr, Order of Civil Merit (Spain) 1993, Commdr, Order of Honour (Greece) 1996, Commdr, Royal Order of Polar Star (Sweden) 1997, Commdr's Cross with Star, Order of Merit (Poland) 1999, Order of Commendatore (Italy) 1999, Gran Oficial, Orden de Mayo al Merito (Argentina) 1999, Grand Cross, Order of Bernardo O'Higgins (Chile) 2000, Václav Havel Memorial Medal (Ukraine) 2001, Commdr, Order of Merit (Portugal) 2000, Order of the White Two-Armed Cross (Slovakia) 2003, Officier de la Légion d'honneur 2003, Order of the Madara Horseman (Bulgaria) 2003, Order of Francisco de Miranda (Venezuela) 2004, Commdr's Cross, Order of Merit (Hungary) 2004, Kt Grand Cross, Royal Order of Francis I 2005, Kt Commdr's Cross, Order of Merit (Germany) 2006, Order Pentru Merit (Romania) 2007, Alawite Officer Wissam (Morocco) 2009, and numerous other decorations; Medal of Merit, Warsaw Univ. 1995, Rotary Int. Award of Honour 1998, Templeton Prize 1998, Wilhelm Leuschner Medal, Wiesbaden 1998, (jtly) St Robert Bellarmine Medal, Gregorian Univ. 2002, (jtly) Distinguished Service Award, Int. CCJ 2005, St Mellitus Medal 2008, The FIRST Lifetime Achievement Award 2008. *Publication:* Sir Sigmund Sternberg – The Knight With Many Hats (biog. by Emma Klein). *Leisure interests:* swimming. *Address:* Star House, 104 Grafton Road, London, NW5 4BA, England (office). *Fax:* (20) 7485-4512 (office).

STETTER, Karl Otto, Dr rer. nat (habil.); German microbiologist and academic; *Professor Emeritus, University of Regensburg;* b. 16 July 1941, Munich, Bavaria; ed Staatliche Luitpold-Oberrealschule, Munich, Technical Univ., Munich, Ludwig Maximilians Univ., Munich; Postdoctoral Fellow, Dept of Molecular Biology, Max Planck Inst. for Biochemistry, Martinsried 1973–75; Lecturer, Botanical Inst. 1975–77; Asst Prof. ('Privatdozent' and 'Oberassistent'), Faculty of Biology, Ludwig Maximilians Univ., Munich 1977–80; Prof. of Microbiology and Head of Dept of Microbiology ('Ordinarius') and Archaeencenter, Univ. of Regensburg 1980–2002, Prof. Emer. 2002–; mem. (Prof. Above Scale) Dept of Microbiology and Molecular Genetics and Inst. of Geophysics and Planetary Science, Faculty of Life Sciences, UCLA, USA 1989–; Co-founder DIVERSA Corpn, San Diego, Calif., USA 1994 (merged with Celunol to form Verenium Corpn 2007); mem. Editorial Bd Systematic and Applied Microbiology 1992–, Extremophiles – Microbial Life Under Extreme Conditions 1996–, Geobiology 2000–; mem. Gesellschaft für Biologische Chemie 1970–, American Soc. of Microbiology 1974–, Deutsche Gesellschaft für Hygiene und Mikrobiologie 1979–, German Univ. Soc. 1981–, Int. Cttee on Environmental Biogeochemistry (ISEB) 1984–, Vereinigung für Allgemeine und Angewandte Mikrobiologie 1986–, Soc. of German Scientists and Physicians 1986–, Int. Cttee on Systematic Bacteriology 1986–, Int. Inst. of Biotechnology 1992–, Gesellschaft Deutscher Chemiker 1994–, Deutsche Akad. der Naturforscher Leopoldina, 1995–, Int. Soc. for the Study of the Origin of Life 1996–, Royal Netherlands Acad. of Arts and Sciences 1999–, Bayerische Akad. der Wissenschaften 2002–; Hon. mem. Botanical Soc. of Regensburg 2001; Annual Award, German Soc. of Hygiene and Microbiology 1985, Gottfried Wilhelm Leibniz Award, German Science Foundation (Highest German Award for Research Excellence) 1988, Medal Lecture, Int. Inst. of Biotechnology 1994, Bergey Medal, Bergey's Manual Trust 1999, Leeuwenhoek Medal, Royal Netherlands Acad. of Arts and Sciences (in recognition for the most influential work in microbiology in the previous decade) 2003; approx. 330 invited lectures 1987–2007. *Major discovery: Nanoarchaeum equitans,* an archaeal microorganism containing world's smallest known genome, discovered in hydrothermal vent off coast of Iceland 2002. *Television:* contrib. to and appearance in more than 30 nat. and int. films and documentaries, including Life is Impossible (BBC TV Horizon, UK) 1993, The Secret of Life – The Immortal Thread (WGBH, USA) 1993, The Origin of Life (ARTE, France and Germany) 1994, Planet of Ocean (NHK TV, Japan) 1998, Intimate Strangers (PBS, USA) 1999, Die Jagd nach den Feürzwergen (Hunting the Fire Dwarfs; ZDF, Germany) 2001. *Publications:* author or co-author of more than 330 scientific publs. *Address:* Lehrstuhl für Mikrobiologie, Universität

Regensburg, Universitätstraße 31, 93343 Regensburg, Germany (office). *Telephone:* (941) 943-1821 (office); (941) 943-3161 (office); (89) 68096548 (home). *Fax:* (941) 943-3243 (office); (89) 68096580 (home). *E-mail:* karl.stetter@biologie.uni-r .de (office). *Website:* www.biologie.uni-regensburg.de/Mikrobio/Stetter (office).

STEVENS, Anne L., BEng; American business executive; *Chairman, President and CEO, Carpenter Technology Corporation;* b. Reading, Pa; ed Drexel Univ. and Rutgers Univ.; held various eng, mfg and marketing positions at Exxon Chemical Co.; marketing specialist in Plastic Products Div., Vehicle Exterior Systems, Ford Motor Co. 1990–92, Man. Quality Services Dept, Saline, Mich. 1992–95, Mfg Man., Plastic and Trim Products Operations 1995, Plant Man., Enfield Plant, UK (Ford's first female plant man. in Europe) 1995–97, Asst Vehicle Line Dir Small Car Vehicle Centre, Ford Automotive Operations, Dunton, UK 1997–99, Dir Mfg Business Office for Ford in N America 1999–2001, Exec. Dir Vehicle Operations in N America 2000–01, Vice-Pres. N America Ass. Operations 2001, Vice-Pres. N America Vehicle Operations 2001–03, Group Vice-Pres. Canada, Mexico and S America 2003–06, Exec. Vice-Pres. and COO The Americas 2006 (retd); Chair., Pres. and CEO Carpenter Technology Corpn, Reading, Pa 2006–; mem. Bd of Dirs Lockheed Martin 2002–; mem. Bd Council of the Americas; mem. Advisory Bd Mexico Inst. of the Woodrow Wilson Int. Center for Scholars; mem. Exec. Advisory Bd Juran Center for Leadership in Quality, Univ. of Minnesota; mem. Shingo Prize Bd of Govs; mem. Nat. Acad. of Eng 2004; Trustee, Drexel Univ., Women's Automotive Asscn Int; ranked by Fortune magazine amongst 50 Most Powerful Women in Business in the US (27th) 2000, (41st) 2002, (49th) 2004, (22nd) 2005, Shingo Leadership Award 2000, Soc. of Mfg Engineers Eli Whitney Award 2003, Automotive Hall of Fame Distinguished Service Citation 2003, named by Automotive News as a Leading Woman in the North American Automotive Industry 2005, one of only two women nominated by Motor Trend to the Power List (car magazine's list of the top 50 people in the automotive industry) (41st) 2006. *Leisure interest:* car racing. *Address:* Carpenter Technology Corporation, PO Box 14662, Building #L05, Reading, PA 19612-4662, USA (office). *Telephone:* (610) 208-2000 (office). *Fax:* (610) 208-3716 (office). *Website:* www.cartech.com (office).

STEVENS, Cat (see ISLAM, Yusuf.)

STEVENS, Glenn, BEcons, MA; Australian economist and central banker; *Governor, Reserve Bank of Australia;* b. 23 Jan. 1958, Sydney; m.; two c.; ed Univ. of Sydney, Univ. of Western Ont., Canada; joined Research Dept, Reserve Bank of Australia 1980, Head, Econ. Analysis Dept 1992–95, Head, Int. Dept 1995–96, Asst Gov. (Econ.) 1996–2001, Deputy Gov. 2001–06, Gov. 2006–, also Chair. Payments System Bd; Chair. Council of Financial Regulators, Foundation for Children; Visiting Scholar, Fed. Reserve Bank of San Francisco 1990; mem. Bd of Dirs Anika Foundation; fmr mem. Advisory Bd Melbourne Inst. for Applied Econ. and Social Research, Hong Kong Inst. for Monetary Research. *Publications include:* numerous articles on monetary policy and other econ. matters. *Address:* Reserve Bank of Australia, GPO 3947, Sydney, NSW 2001, Australia (office). *Telephone:* (2) 9551-9507 (office). *Fax:* (2) 9551-8030 (office). *E-mail:* governor@rba.gov.au (office). *Website:* www.rba.gov.au (office).

STEVENS, Sir Jocelyn Edward Greville, Kt, CVO, FRSA; British publisher; b. 14 Feb. 1932, London; s. of Major C.G.B. Stewart-Stevens and Betty Hulton; m. 1st Jane Armyne Sheffield 1956 (dissolved 1979); one s. two d. (one s. deceased); m. 2nd Emma Cheape 2008; ed Eton Coll., Univ. of Cambridge; mil. service with Rifle Brigade 1950–52; journalist, Hulton Press 1955–56; Chair. and Man. Dir Stevens Press Ltd, Ed. Queen Magazine 1957–68; Personal Asst to Chair., Beaverbrook Newspapers 1968, Dir 1971–81, Man. Dir 1974–77; Man. Dir Evening Standard Co. Ltd 1969–72, Daily Express 1972–74; Deputy Chair. and Man. Dir Express Newspapers 1974–81; Ed. and Publr The Magazine 1982–84; Dir Centaur Communications 1982–84; Gov. Imperial Coll. of Science, Tech. and Medicine 1985–92, Winchester School of Art 1986–89; Rector and Vice-Provost RCA 1984–92; Chair. The Silver Trust 1990–93, English Heritage 1992–2000, Prince of Wales's Phoenix Trust 2000–03, Prince's Regeneration through Heritage Trust 2002–03; Deputy Chair. Independent TV Comn. 1991–96; Dir (non-exec.) The TV Corpn 1996–2002, Asprey & Co. –2002, Garrard & Co. –2002; Pres. The Cheyne Walk Trust 1989–93; Trustee, Eureka! The Children's Museum 1990–2000, Butrint Foundation 2000–05; Hon. DLitt (Loughborough) 1989, (Buckingham) 1998; Hon. FCSD 1990, Sr Fellow RCA 1990. *Leisure interest:* skiing.

STEVENS, John Paul, AB JD; American lawyer and judge; b. 20 April 1920, Chicago, Ill.; s. of Ernest James Stevens and Elizabeth Street; m. 1st Elizabeth Jane Sheeren 1942; one s. three d.; m. 2nd Maryan Mulholland Simon 1979; ed Univ. of Chicago, Northwestern Univ. School of Law; served USN (awarded Bronze Star Medal) 1942–45; Co-Ed. of Law Review, Northwestern Univ. School of Law 1947; Law Clerk to Supreme Court Justice Wiley Rutledge 1947; with Poppenhusen, Johnston, Thompson and Raymond (law firm) 1948–51, 1952; Pnr, Rothschild, Stevens, Barry and Myers 1952–70; Circuit Judge, Seventh Circuit Court of Appeals 1970–75; Assoc. Justice, US Supreme Court 1975–2010 (retd); Assoc. Counsel, Monopoly Power Sub-Cttee of US House of Reps Judiciary Cttee 1951; mem. Attorney Gen.'s Nat. Cttee on Antitrust Laws 1953–55; part-time teacher, Northwestern Univ. School of Law, later Univ. of Chicago Law School 1952–56; admitted to Ill. Bar 1949, to US Supreme Court 1954; mem. American Law Inst.; Presidential Medal of Freedom 2012. *Publications:* numerous articles on commercial monopoly affairs. *Address:* c/o United States Supreme Court, One First Street, NE, Washington, DC 20543, USA.

STEVENS, Robert Bocking, MA, DCL, LLM; British lawyer and academic; b. 8 June 1933; s. of John S. Stevens and Enid Dorothy Bocking Stevens; m. 1st Rosemary Wallace 1961 (divorced 1983); m. 2nd Katherine Booth 1985; one s. two d.; ed Keble Coll. Oxford and Yale Univ., USA; mem. Essex Court Chambers, Lincoln's Inn Fields 1965–, Midland Circuit 1962–76; Asst Prof. of Law, Yale Univ., USA 1959–61, Assoc. Prof. 1961–65, Prof. 1965–76, Fellow, Jonathan Edwards Coll. 1963–76; Prof. of Law and Adjunct Prof. of History, Tulane Univ., New Orleans, USA 1976–78, Provost 1976–78; Pres. Haverford Coll., Pa, USA 1978–87; Prof. of History, Univ. of California, Santa Cruz 1987–93, Chancellor 1987–91; Counsel, Covington & Burling (law firm), Washington, DC, London 1991–; mem. Council, Justice (UK Br., Int. Comm. of Jurists) 1992–98; Master, Pembroke Coll. Oxford 1993–2001; Chair. Sulgrave Manor (Home of Washington Family) Bd 2002–; Bencher, Gray's Inn 1999; Hon. Fellow, Keble Coll. Oxford

1983, Pembroke Coll. Oxford 2001; several hon. degrees. *Publications include:* Law and Politics: The House of Lords as a Judicial Body 1800–1976 1978, The American Law School: Legal Education in America 1850–1980 1983, The Independence of the Judiciary: The View from the Lord Chancellor's Office 1993, The English Judges 2002, From University to Uni 2004; co-author and ed. of other books on law, history and welfare; articles and monographs. *Leisure interests:* politics, history, talking, claret. *Address:* Covington & Burling, 265 Strand, London, WC2R 1BH (office); 19 Burgess Meade, Oxford, OX2 6XP, England (home). *Telephone:* (20) 7067-2000 (office); (1865) 558420 (home). *Fax:* (20) 7067-2222 (office); (1865) 558420 (home). *E-mail:* rstevens@cov.com (office). *Website:* www.cov.com (office).

STEVENS, Robert J., MEng, MBA; American business executive; *Executive Chairman, Lockheed Martin Corporation;* b. McKeesport, Pa; ed Slippery Rock Univ., Polytechnic Univ. of New York, Columbia Univ. (Fairchild Fellowship), Dept of Defense Systems Man. Coll.; served in US Marine Corps; various man. positions in program man., finance, mfg and operations, Loral Systems Mfg Co., Vice-Pres. and Chief Financial Officer –1988, Gen. Man. 1988–93; Exec. Vice-Pres. and Chief Financial Officer, Lockheed Martin Air Traffic Man. 1993–96, Pres. Lockheed Martin Air Traffic Man. 1996–98, Pres. and COO Lockheed Martin Energy and Environment Sector 1998–99, Vice-Pres. Strategic Devt Org., Lockheed Martin Corpn 1998–99, Chief Financial Officer 1999–2001, Pres. and COO 2001–04, Pres. and CEO 2004–10, Chair. 2005–12, CEO 2010–12, Exec. Chair. 2013–; Lead Dir Monsanto Co.; mem. Bd of Dirs Congressional Medal of Honor Foundation; mem. US Pres. Bush's Comm. to examine the Future of the US Aerospace Industry 2001–02; mem. Int. Advisory Bd Atlantic Council, British-American Business Council, Council on Foreign Relations; mem. Bd of Govs Aerospace Industries Asscn; apptd by Pres. Obama to the Advisory Cttee for Trade Policy and Negotiations 2012; Fellow, American Astronautical Soc., AIAA (Hon. Fellow 2012), Royal Aeronautical Soc., Int. Acad. of Astronautics; Distinguished Alumni Award, Slippery Rock Univ., Exec. of the Year, Nat. Man. Asscn 2004, Industry Executive of the Year, Government Computer News, Private Sector Council Leadership Award, Partnership for Public Service, Globe and Anchor Award, Marine Corps Scholarship Foundation, inaugural LeJeune Recognition for Exemplary Leadership, Marine Corps Heritage Foundation 2010, James Forrestal Industry Leadership Award, Nat. Defense Industrial Asscn 2011, Hispanic Engineer Nat. Achievement Awards Corporation's Chairman's Award 2012, Wright Brothers Memorial Trophy, Nat. Aeronautic Asscn 2012, Circle of Honor Award, Congressional Medal of Honor Foundation 2013, Semper Fidelis Award, Marine Corps Scholarship Foundation 2013. *Address:* Lockheed Martin Corporation, 6801 Rockledge Drive, Bethesda, MD 20817-1877, USA (office). *Telephone:* (301) 897-6000 (office). *Fax:* (301) 897-6704 (office). *E-mail:* info@lockheedmartin.com (office). *Website:* www.lockheedmartin.com (office).

STEVENS OF KIRKWHELPINGTON, Baron (Life Peer), cr. 2005, of Kirkwhelpington in the County of Northumberland; **John Arthur Stevens,** QPM, MPhil, LLB, CIMgt, FRSA, DL; British police officer (retd) and business executive; *Chairman, Quest Limited;* b. 21 Oct. 1942; s. of C. J. Stevens and S. Stevens; m.; two s. one d.; ed St Lawrence Coll., Ramsgate, Univ. of Leicester, Univ. of Southampton; mem. Metropolitan Police 1963–83, staff Police Staff Coll. 1983–84, Deputy Commr 1998–99, Commr 2000–05 (retd); Asst Chief Constable of Hants. Constabulary 1986–89, Deputy Chief Constable of Cambs. Constabulary 1989–91; Chief Constable of Northumbria 1991–96; HM Inspector of Constabulary 1996–98; currently Chair. Quest Ltd (pvt. security co.); has chaired numerous enquiries including Stevens Enquiry on NI 1989–2003, Operation Paget into deaths of Diana, Princess of Wales and Dodi Fayed 2003–06, inquiry into football corruption 2006; Dir (non-exec.) BAA 2007–; Adviser, Forensic Science Service; Visiting Prof., Univ. of Cambridge 1984–85, City Univ. of New York 1984–85; Chancellor, Univ. of Northumbria 2005–; Visiting Lecturer, Int. Crime Prevention Centre, Canada 1998; Adviser to Prime Minister of Romania 2002–; patron, various charities in Romania and London; DL Greater London 2001; Hon. Fellow, Wolfson Coll. Cambridge 2000; KStJ; Hon. LLD (Leicester) 2000; Hon. DCL (Northumbria) 2001. *Leisure interests:* flying, rugby, walking, cricket, charity work. *Address:* Quest Limited, 8 Frederick's Place, London, EC2R 8HY (office); Quest Limited, Selous House, 5-12 Mandela Street, London, NW1 0DU; House of Lords, London, SW1A 0PW, England. *Telephone:* (20) 7387-7993 (office). *Fax:* (20) 7387-7994 (office). *E-mail:* info@quest.co.uk (office). *Website:* www.quest.co.uk (office).

STEVENS OF LUDGATE, Baron (Life Peer), cr. 1987, of Ludgate in the City of London; **David Robert Stevens,** MA; British business executive; b. 26 May 1936; s. of (Arthur) Edwin Stevens; m. 1st Patricia Rose (divorced 1971); one s. one d.; m. 2nd Melissa Milicevich 1977 (died 1989); m. 3rd Meriza Giori 1990; ed Stowe School and Sidney Sussex Coll. Cambridge; man. trainee, Elliott Automation 1959; Dir Hill Samuel Securities 1959–68, Drayton Group 1968–74; Chair. City & Foreign (now Alexander Proudfoot PLC) 1976–95, Drayton Far East 1976–93, English & Int. 1976–79, Consolidated Venture (fmrly Montagu Boston) 1979–93, Drayton Consolidated 1980–92, Drayton Japan 1980–93, Econ. Devt Cttee for Civil Eng 1984–86; Dir United News & Media PLC (fmrly United Newspapers PLC) 1974–99, Chair. 1981–99; CEO INVESCO MIM 1980–87, Deputy Chair. 1987–89, Chair. 1989–93; Chair. MIM Britannia Ltd (fmrly Montagu Investment Man. Ltd) 1980–92 (CEO 1980–87), Express Newspapers 1985–99, PNC Telecom (fmrly Personal Number Co.) 1998–. *Leisure interests:* golf, gardening. *Address:* House of Lords, London, SW1A 0PW, England.

STEVENSON, Hon. Adlai E., III; American lawyer, investment banker and fmr politician; *Chairman, SC&M Investment Management Corporation;* b. 10 Oct. 1930, Chicago, Ill.; s. of the late Adlai Stevenson II (fmr Gov. of Illinois, presidential candidate and Amb. to UN); great-grandson of Adlai E. Stevenson (Vice-Pres. of USA 1893–97); m. Nancy L. Anderson 1955; two s. two d.; ed Milton Acad., Mass. and Harvard Univ.; law clerk to a justice of Ill. Supreme Court 1957; joined Chicago law firm of Mayer, Brown and Platt 1958–66, pnr 1966–67, 1981–83, of Counsel 1983–91; elected to Ill. House of Reps. 1964; State Treas. of Ill. 1966–70; Senator from Illinois 1970–81; Democratic Cand. for Gov. of Ill. 1982, 1986; Chair. SC&M Int. Ltd (now SC&M Investment Man. Corpn) 1991–95, Pres. 1995–98, Chair. 1998–; Co-Chair. Huamei Capital Co., Inc. 2005–; Co-Chair. Stevenson, Melamed & Assocs; mem. Bd of Dirs Stonewater Control Systems Inc.; Order of the Sacred Treasure, Gold and Silver Stars (Japan); numerous awards, hon. degrees and directorships. *Address:* HuaMei Capital Company, Inc., 71 South Wacker Drive, Suite 2760, Chicago, IL 60606 (office); 4302 South Blandings Road, Hanover, IL 61041, USA (home). *Telephone:* (312) 957-4260 (office). *Fax:* (312) 957-4261 (office). *E-mail:* info@huameicapital.com (office). *Website:* www.huameicapital.com (office).

STEVENSON, Juliet, CBE; British actress; b. 30 Oct. 1956; d. of Michael Guy Stevens and Virginia Ruth Marshall; one s. one d. two step-s.; ed Hurst Lodge School, Berks., St Catherine's School, Surrey, Royal Acad. of Dramatic Art; with RSC (now Assoc. Artist), Royal Nat. Theatre, Royal Court Theatre, film, TV, radio, audiobooks; Bancroft Gold Medal, Royal Acad. of Dramatic Art 1977, Time Out Award for Best Actress 1991, Evening Standard Film Award for Best Actress 1992, Lawrence Olivier Theatre Award for Best Actress 1992. *Plays include:* Measure for Measure 1978, Henry IV Parts 1 and 2 1980, A Midsummer Night's Dream 1981, The Witch of Edmonton 1981, Breaking the Silence 1984, As You Like It 1985, Troilus and Cressida 1985, Les Liaisons Dangereuses 1986 (all for RSC), Not I, Footfalls Money, Burn This (West End) 1990, Death and the Maiden (Royal Court and West End) (Olivier Award 1992) 1991, The Duchess of Malfi (Greenwich Theatre and West End) 1995, Yerma 1987, Hedda Gabler 1989, The Caucasian Chalk Circle 1997, The Country (Royal Court) 2000, Private Lives 1999, The Seagull (Nat. Theatre) 2006, Other Worlds, A Little Night Music (New York City Opera), Duet for One 2009. *Films include:* Drowning by Numbers, Ladder of Swords, Truly Madly Deeply, The Trial, The Secret Rapture, Emma, The Search for John Gissing, Who Dealt?, Beckett's Play, Bend It Like Beckham, Food of Love, Nicholas Nickleby, Mona Lisa Smile, Being Julia, Pierrepoint 2006, Breaking and Entering 2006, When Did You Last See Your Father? 2007, Dustbin Baby 2008, The Secret of Moonacre 2008, Desert Flower 2009, Shell Shock 2009, Diana 2013. *Radio includes:* To the Lighthouse, Volcano, Albertina, House of Correction, Hang Up, Cigarettes and Chocolate, A Little Like Drowning, Victory, The Pallisers, Mary Poppins, The Lovers of Viorne. *Television includes:* Miss Marple, Hear the Silence, The Road From Coorain, Play (Beckett), Trial by Fire, Cider with Rosie, Stone Scissors Paper, The Politician's Wife, A Doll's House (Nora), Life Story, Antigone, The March, Maybury, Thomas and Ruth, Aimée, The Mallens, Living With Dinosaurs, The Hour (series) 2011, White Heat (series) 2012, The Village (series) 2013; wrote and fronted BBC documentary Great Journeys. *Publications:* Clamorous Voices (jtly) 1988, Shall I See You Again? (jtly), Players of Shakespeare (jtly). *Leisure interests:* piano, travelling, gardening, reading, tennis. *Address:* c/o Markham and Froggatt Ltd, Julian House, 4 Windmill Street, London, W1P 1HF, England.

STEVENSON OF BALMACARA, Baron, (Life Peer), cr. 2010, of Little Missenden in the County of Buckinghamshire; **Robert Wilfrid (Wilf) Stevenson,** MA, FCCA; British public affairs consultant; b. 19 April 1947, Lochalsh, Ross-shire, Scotland; s. of James Stevenson and Elizabeth Macrae; m. 1st Jennifer Grace Antonio 1972 (divorced 1979); m. 2nd Elizabeth Ann Minogue 1991; one s. two d.; ed Edinburgh Acad., Univ. Coll., Oxford, Napier Coll., Edinburgh; Research Officer, Univ. of Edinburgh Students Asscn 1970–74; Sec. and Acad. Registrar, Napier Polytechnic, Edinburgh 1974–87; Deputy Dir BFI 1987–88, Dir 1988–97; Dir The Smith Inst. 1997–2008; Sr Policy Adviser to the Prime Minister 2008–10; mem. (Labour), House of Lords 2010–, Opposition Whip 2011–, Opposition Spokesperson for Business, Innovation and Skills 2011–, Culture, Media and Sport 2011–; Chair. StepChange Debt Charity 2010–, Consumer Credit Counselling Service Ltd; Dir, StepChange (Voluntary Arrangements) Ltd, StepChange (Equity Release) Ltd (wholly owned subsidiary of Foundation for Credit Counselling, a registered charity); Gov., Chiltern Way Fed., Bucks. (special school for 11–19-year-old boys and girls); Hon. DArts (Napier Univ., Edinburgh) 2008. *Publications:* Gordon Brown Speeches 1997–2006 (ed.) 2006, Moving Britain Forward (ed.) 2006, The Change We Choose (ed.) 2010. *Leisure interests:* cinema, bee keeping. *Address:* House of Lords, Westminster, London, SW1A 0PW (office); Missenden House, Little Missenden, Amersham, Bucks., HP7 0RD, England (home). *Telephone:* (20) 7219-8194 (office); 7778-465103 (mobile) (office); (1494) 890689 (home). *E-mail:* stevensonw@parliament.uk (office); wilf@wilfstevenson.co.uk (home). *Website:* www.parliament.uk/biographies/lords/lord-stevenson-of-balmacara/4175 (office).

STEVENSON OF CODDENHAM, Baron (Life Peer), cr. 1999, of Coddenham in the County of Suffolk; **Henry Dennistoun Stevenson,** Kt, CBE; British business executive and business consultant; b. 19 July 1945, Edinburgh, Scotland; s. of Alexander James Stevenson and Sylvia Florence Stevenson (née Ingleby); m. Charlotte Susan Stevenson (née Vanneck); four s.; ed Glenalmond School and King's Coll., Cambridge; Chair. SRU Group of cos 1972–96; Chair. GPA, then AerFi, Group 1993–2000; Chair. Pearson plc 1997–2005 (Dir 1986–97); Dir, Halifax plc 1999–2009; Chair. HBOS plc 2001–09; Gov., Bank of Scotland 2006–09; Dir, British Technology Group 1979–89, Tyne Tees TV 1982–87, Manpower Inc. (fmrly Blue Arrow) 1988–2006, Thames Television plc 1991–93, J. Rothschild Assurance plc 1991–97, J. Rothschild Assurance Holdings plc 1991–99, English Partnerships 1993–99, BSkyB Group plc 1994–2000, Lazard Bros 1997–2000, Whitehall Trust Ltd 1997–2004, St James's Place Capital 1997–2002 (Hon. Pres. 2002–04), Economist Newspapers 1998–2011, Western Union Co. 2006–12, Loudwater Investment Partners Ltd 2007–12, Culture and Sport Glasgow 2007–09, Cloaca Maxima Ltd 2010–13, Waterstones Holdings Ltd 2011–; Chair. of Trustees, Tate Gallery 1989–98, Inter Mediate 2011–; Chair. Newton Aycliffe and Peterlee New Town Devt Corpn 1971–80, Intermediate Technology Devt Group 1983–90; Dir, Nat. Building Agency 1977–81, LDDC 1981–88; mem. (Crossbench), House of Lords 1999–, Chair. Appointments Comm. 2000–09, Arts and Media Honours Cttee 2008–12, mem. Works of Art Cttee 2009–; Chair. Govt working party on role of voluntary movements and youth in the environmtent 1971, '50 Million Volunteers' (HMSO), Ind. Advisory Cttee on Pop Festivals 1972–76, 'Pop Festivals, Report and Code of Practice' (HMSO), Advisory on Agricultural Marketing to Minister of Agric. 1979–83, Special Advisory to Prime Minister and Sec. of State for Educ. on use of IT in Educ. 1997–2000; mem. Panel on Takeovers and Mergers 1992–2000, Bd British Council 1996–2003, Standards Cttee, Westminster City Council 2008–12; Chair. NAYC 1973–81, Sinfonia 21 (fmrly Docklands Sinfonietta) 1989–99, Aldeburgh Music (fmrly Aldeburgh Productions) 2000–12; Pres. Aldeburgh Music 2012–; MQ, Transforming Mental Health 2010–; Dir, Glyndebourne Productions 1998–, London Music Masters 2011–, Inst. for Govt 2008–13; Trustee, Tate Gallery Foundation 1998–, Horse's Mouth 2006–; mem. Admin. Council, Royal Jubilee Trusts 1978–80; Chancellor,

Univ. of the Arts London (fmrly London Inst.) 2000–10; Gov., LSE 1995–99, London Business School 1999–2002; DL, Suffolk 2008. *Publication:* Information and Communications Technology in UK Schools (The Stevenson Report) 1997. *Address:* House of Lords, Westminster, London, SW1A 0PW, England. *Website:* www.parliament.uk/biographies/lords/lord-stevenson-of-coddenham/2474.

STEWART, Alec James, OBE; British fmr professional cricketer; b. 8 April 1963, Merton, London; s. of Michael James Stewart (fmr Surrey Capt. and Test player) and Sheila Stewart; m. Lynn Blades 1991; one s. one d.; ed Tiffin Boys' School, Kingston upon Thames; right-hand opening batsman; wicket-keeper; Surrey 1981–2003 (Capt. 1992–97); played in 133 Tests for England 1990–2003, 14 as Capt. 1993 (deputized), 1998–99, scoring 8,463 runs (average 39.54, highest score 190) including 15 hundreds; played in 170 One-Day Ints, scored 4,677 runs (average 31.60, highest score 116) including four hundreds; played in 447 First-class matches, scored 26,165 runs (average 40.06, highest score 271 not out) including 48 hundreds; held 11 catches, equalling world first-class record, for Surrey vs Leicestershire, Leicester 19–22 Aug. 1989; toured Australia 1990–91, 1994–95, 1998–99 (Capt.); overtook record (118 Tests) of Graham Gooch to become England's most-capped cricketer, Lords July 2002; retd 2003; Dir of Business, Surrey County Cricket Club 2003–, rejoined Surrey as mem. coaching staff specializing in batting, wicket keeping and mentoring 2009–; Founding Dir Arundel Promotions, with specific responsibility for player man. and representation 2004–; cricket columnist, Daily Mirror; Wisden Cricketer of the Year 1993. *Publications:* Alec Stewart: A Captain's Diary (co-author) 1999, Playing for Keeps 2003. *Leisure interests:* Chelsea Football Club, spending time with his family. *Address:* Surrey County Cricket Club, The Brit Oval, Kennington, London, SE11 5SS, England (office). *Telephone:* (871) 246-1100 (office). *Fax:* (20) 7735-7769 (office). *E-mail:* enquiries@surreycricket.com (office). *Website:* www.britoval.com/home/surrey-cricket (office).

STEWART, Sir Brian John, Kt, CBE, MSc, CA; British brewery executive; b. 9 April 1945, Stirling, Scotland; s. of Ian M. Stewart and Christina McIntyre; m. Seonaid Duncan 1971; two s. one d.; ed Perth Acad., Edinburgh Univ.; joined Scottish & Newcastle Breweries (now Scottish and Newcastle PLC) 1976, Corp. Devt Dir 1985–88, Group Finance Dir 1988–91, Group Chief Exec. 1991–2000, Deputy Chair. 1997–2000, Exec. Chair. 2000–03, Chair. (non-exec.) 2003–08 (after acquisition of Scottish & Newcastle by a consortium of Carlsberg and Heineken); Dir (non-exec.) Booker 1993–99; Dir (non-exec.) Standard Life Assurance Co. 1993–2007, Chair. (non-exec.) 2003–07 (retd); mem. Bd of Dirs (non-exec.) C & C Group PLC 2010–. *Leisure interests:* skiing, golf.

STEWART, David (Dave) A.; British musician (guitar, keyboards) and songwriter; b. 9 Sept. 1952, Sunderland; m. 1st Pam Stewart (divorced); m. 2nd Siobhan Fahey 1987 (divorced); two s.; fmr mem., Harrison and Stewart (with Brian Harrison); Founder mem. Longdancer 1973; Founder mem. The Catch 1977, later renamed The Tourists 1979–80; Founder mem. Eurythmics (with Annie Lennox) 1980–89, 1999–, live appearances worldwide; solo artist 1990–; Founder mem. The Spiritual Cowboys 1990–92; mem. Vegas 1992–93; f. record label Anxious Records 1988; produces and directs films, including computer-enhanced films; writes film soundtracks; owner of recording studio, The Church 1992; producer and session musician for artists, including Mick Jagger, Bob Dylan, Tom Petty, Daryl Hall, Bob Geldof, Boris Grebenshikov, Sinead O'Connor, Feargal Sharkey; Hon. DMus (Westminster) 1998; Ivor Novello Award for Songwriter of the Year (for Sweet Dreams, with Annie Lennox) 1984, MTV Music Award for Best New Artist Video (for Sweet Dreams (Are Made Of This)) 1984, Ivor Novello Award for Best Song (for It's Alright (Baby's Coming Back, with Annie Lennox) 1987, Grammy Award for Best Rock Performance (for Missionary Man) 1987, BRIT Awards for Best Producer 1986, 1987, 1990, for Oustanding Contribution 1999, Golden Globe Award for Best Original Song (with Mick Jagger, for Old Habits Die Hard, from the film Alfie) 2005. *Compositions for film and television:* Rooftops 1989, De Kassière (with Candy Dulfer) 1989, Jute City (BBC1) 1991, GFI (TV series, with Gerry Anderson) 1992, No Worries 1993, The Ref 1994, Showgirls 1995, Beautiful Girls 1996, Crimetime 1996, Cookie's Fortune 1999, Honest 2000, Le Pont du trieur 2000, Chaos 2002, Around the World in 80 Days 2004; contrib. songs to numerous other films. *Film directed:* Honest 2000. *Recordings include:* albums: with The Tourists: The Tourists 1979, Reality Affect 1979, Luminous Basement 1980; with Eurythmics: In The Garden 1981, Sweet Dreams 1982, Touch 1983, Be Yourself Tonight 1985, Revenge 1986, Savage 1987, We Too Are One 1989, Eurythmics Live 1983–89 1992, Peace 1999; with The Spiritual Cowboys: Dave Stewart And The Spiritual Cowboys 1990; with Vegas: Vegas 1992; solo: Greetings From The Gutter 1994. *Address:* 19 Management Ltd, Unit 3, Ransomes Dock, 35–37 Park Gate Road, London, SW11 4NP, England (office). *Telephone:* (20) 7801-1919 (office). *Fax:* (20) 7801-1920 (office). *Website:* www.davestewart.com; www.eurythmics.com.

STEWART, Donald A., BA, FIA, FCIA; British insurance industry executive; b. 1946, Glasgow, Scotland; ed Univ. of Glasgow, Harvard Business School, USA; joined Sun Life Financial, London 1969–74, Head of Canadian Pension Div., Toronto, Canada 1980–86, Head Project Team to Est. Mutual Fund Operation 1986, Pres. Spectrum Investments (mutual funds) 1986–87, Head of Information Tech., Sun Life Financial 1987–92, Chair. and CEO Sun Life Financial Trust 1992–95, Sr Vice-Pres. and Chief Actuary 1995–96, Pres. and COO 1996–98, Pres. and CEO Sun Life Insurance Co. of Canada 1998–99, Chair. and CEO 1999–2000, Chair. and CEO Sun Life Financial Inc. 2000–05, CEO 2005–11 (retd), Chair. and CEO Sun Life Assurance Co. of Canada 2000, also Chair. Sun Life Insurance and Annuity Co. of NY; benefits consultant, William M. Mercer, Toronto 1974–80; mem. Bd of Dirs MFS Investment Man., Novelis Inc., Canadian Life and Health Insurance Assccn, The Geneva Assccn (think tank); Chair. Canada's Nat. Task Force on Financial Literacy 2009–. *Address:* c/o Sun Life Financial Inc., 150 King Street West, Toronto, ON M5H 1J9, Canada. *E-mail:* boarddirectors@sunlife.com.

STEWART, John M.; British banker; *Chairman, Legal & General Group Plc;* joined Woolwich 1977, served in numerous exec. positions, Group Operations Dir 1995–96, CEO 1996–2000, Deputy Group CEO Barclays Bank (after acquisition of Woolwich by Barclays) 2000–03; CEO and Prin. Bd mem. Nat. Australia Group Europe 2003–04, Man. Dir and Group CEO Nat. Australia Bank Ltd 2004–08; Chair. Legal & General Group Plc 2010–; Dir (non-exec.) Telstra Corpn; mem. Scottish Enterprise's Int. Advisory Bd, Court of the Bank of England, Australian Fed. Attorney Gen.'s Business-Govt Advisory Group on Nat. Security; fmr mem. Australian Prime Minister's Task Group on Emissions Trading; Assoc. Chartered Insurance Inst. *Address:* Legal & General Group Plc, One Coleman Street, London, EC2R 5AA, England (office). *Telephone:* (20) 3124-2000 (office). *Fax:* (20) 7528-6222 (office). *E-mail:* info@legalandgeneralgroup.com (office). *Website:* www .legalandgeneralgroup.com (office).

STEWART, Sir John Young (Jackie), Kt, OBE; British fmr racing driver; b. 11 June 1939, Milton, West Dunbartonshire, Scotland; s. of the late Robert Paul Stewart and Jean Clark Young; m. Helen McGregor 1962; two s.; ed Dumbarton Acad.; mem. British Clay Pigeon Shooting Team 1956–62; first raced 1961; competed in four meetings driving for Barry Filer, Glasgow 1961–62; drove for Ecurie Ecosse and other private entrants, winning 14 out of 23 starts 1963, 28 wins out of 53 starts 1964; drove Formula 1 for British Racing Motors (BRM) 1965–67, for Ken Tyrrell 1968–73; has won Australian, New Zealand, Swedish, Mediterranean, Japanese and many other non-championship major int. Grands Prix; set new world record by winning his 26th World Championship Grand Prix (Zandvoort) 1973, 27th (Nürburgring) 1973; third in World Championship 1965, 2nd in 1968 and 1972, World Champion 1969, 1971, 1973; retd 1973; involved with son, Paul, in operation of Paul Stewart Racing and Stewart Grand Prix, a Formula One team cr. 1996, sold to Ford Motor Co. in 1999 who ran the operation as Jaguar Racing from start of 2000 season; Chair. and CEO Jaguar Racing 1999–2000; Vice-Pres. British Dyslexia Asscn 1998–; Pres. British Racing Drivers' Club 2000–06; RBS Global Amb. 2004–12; Pres. Dyslexia Scotland 2004–; Freedom of West 2009; Hon. Prof., Univ. of Stirling 1998; Hon. Dr Aut. Eng (Lawrence Inst. of Tech., USA) 1986; Dr hc (Glasgow Caledonian) 1993, (Stirling Univ.) 2001, (Edinburgh Univ.) 2006; Hon. DEng (Heriot-Watt Univ.) 1996, (Glasgow Univ.) 2001; Hon. DSc (St Andrews Univ.) 2008; British Automobile Racing Club Gold Medal 1971, 1973, Daily Express Sportsman of the Year 1971, 1973, BBC Sports Personality of the Year 1973, Scottish Sportsman of the Year 1973, Sports Illustrated American Sportsman of the Year 1973, World Sportsman of the Year 1973, ABC Sports Personality of the Year 1973, Seagrove Trophy 1973, 1999. *Film:* Weekend of a Champion 1972. *Publications:* World Champion (with Eric Dymock) 1970, Faster! (with Peter Manso) 1972, On the Road 1983, Jackie Stewart's Principles of Performance Driving (with Alan Henry) 1986, The Jackie Stewart Book of Shooting 1991, Winning is Not Enough (auto-biog.) 2007. *Leisure interests:* shooting (clay pigeon champion), golf, tennis. *Telephone:* (1296) 620913 (office). *Fax:* (1296) 620049 (office). *Website:* www.sirjackiestewart.com (office).

STEWART, Jon; American comedian, actor, writer and producer; b. (Jonathan Stuart Leibowitz), 28 Nov. 1962, New York City; m. Tracey McShane 2000; one s. one d.; ed Coll. of William and Mary; numerous early jobs, including contingency planner for New Jersey Dept of Human Services, contract admin. for CUNY, puppeteer for children with disabilities, and bartender at local Franklin Corner Tavern, stand-up comedian; moved to New York City 1986; began hosting TV network Comedy Central's Short Attention Span Theater 1989; hosted You Wrote It, You Watch It on MTV 1992; appeared several times in HBO's The Larry Sanders Show 1992–2001; host, The Jon Stewart Show on MTV (first talk show on that network) 1993–95; host, Comedy Central's The Daily Show with Jon Stewart 1999–; host, Acad. Awards ceremony 2006, 2008; Hon. DArts (Coll. of William and Mary) 2004; Peabody Awards for coverage of 2000 and 2004 US presidential elections on The Daily Show, keynote speaker at Commencement Ceremony, Princeton Univ. 2004, recipient of 10 Emmy Awards. *Films include:* Mixed Nuts 1994, Wishful Thinking 1997, Half Baked 1998, The Faculty 1998, Playing by Heart 1999, Big Daddy 1999, The Office Party 2000, Jay and Silent Bob Strike Back 2001, Death to Smoochy 2002. *Television includes:* as writer: The Sweet Life (series) 1989, The Jon Stewart Show (series) 1993, The Daily Show (series) (also co-exec. producer) 1996–; Since You've Been Gone 1998, The Colbert Réport (series) (exec. producer) 2005. *Recordings:* The Daily Show with Jon Stewart Presents Earth (The Audiobook) (Grammy Award for Best Spoken Word Album 2011) 2010. *Publications:* The Daily Show with Jon Stewart Presents America (The Book): A Citizen's Guide to Democracy Inaction 2004, Earth (The Book): A Visitor's Guide to the Human Race 2010. *Address:* Comedy Partners, 1175 Broadway, 10th Floor, New York, NY 10019 USA (office). *Telephone:* (212) 767-8600 (office). *Fax:* (212) 767-8592 (office). *Website:* www.thedailyshow.com (office).

STEWART, Kirstine; Canadian television executive; *Executive Vice-President, English Services, Canadian Broadcasting Corporation;* b. 1968, Toronto, Ont.; m. Ken Layfield (divorced); two d.; fiancé Zaib Shaikh 2011; ed Univ. of Toronto, Global Leadership in the 21st Century Program, Kennedy School of Govt, Harvard Univ., USA; worked as receptionist at Paragon Entertainment following graduation 1988, rose to become Pres. of Distribution; fmr Gen. Man. and Vice-Pres. Programming Trio/Newsworld International (CBC/Power Corpn jt venture); later joined US-based Hallmark Entertainment as Sr Vice-Pres. of Programming; Sr Vice-Pres. Programming, Alliance Atlantis Communications 2003–06; joined CBC as Gen. Man., Television 2006, Exec. Dir of Network Programming, CBC Television 2006–10, Exec. Vice-Pres. of English Services, CBC (first woman) 2011–; mem. Forum of Young Global Leaders, selected to advise World Econ. Forum; Founding Bd mem. Culture Days; mem. Bd Banff Television and Film Festival, White Knights, Amfar; named Canadian Women in Communications Woman of the Year 2010, recognized by Women's Exec. Network as one of Canada's Top 100 Most Powerful Women, named one of Canada's Top 40 Under 40 2006, her role recognized by Marketing Magazine in naming CBC Media Player of the Year 2009. *Address:* CBC/Radio-Canada Corporate Communications, PO Box 3220, Station C, Ottawa, ON K1Y 1E4, Canada (office). *Telephone:* 613-288-6033 (General) (office). *E-mail:* liaison@radio-canada.ca (office). *Website:* www.cbc.ca (office); www.cbc.radio-canada.ca (office).

STEWART, Martha Helen Kostyra, BA; American editor, writer and business executive; b. 3 Aug. 1941, Jersey City, NJ; d. of the late Edward Kostyra and Martha Kostyra (née Ruszkowski); m. Andy Stewart 1961 (divorced 1989); one d.; ed Barnard Univ.; fmr model, stockbroker, caterer; Owner and Ed.-in-Chief Martha Stewart Living magazine 1990–; Founder, Chair. and CEO Martha Stewart Living Omnimedia 1997–2003, mem. Bd –2004, Founding Editorial Dir (non-exec.) March 2004–; also appears in cooking feature on NBC's Today Show; mem. Bd NY Stock Exchange June–Oct. 2002; mem. Bd Revlon Inc. –2004; under investigation for alleged insider trading June 2002, found guilty of conspiracy, making false statements and obstruction of justice March 2004, sentenced to prison and released March 2005; moved to cable TV's Hallmark Channel to offer eight hours of weekday programming Sept. 2010; ranked by Fortune magazine amongst the 50 Most Powerful Women in Business in the US (21st) 2005, (28th) 2006, ranked by Forbes magazine amongst The World's 100 Most Powerful Women (99th) 2010. *Television:* host of TV show Martha 2005–, starred in The Apprentice: Martha Stewart 2005. *Publications include:* (with Elizabeth Hawes) Entertaining 1982, Weddings 1987; (as sole author) Martha Stewart's Hors d'Oeuvres: The Creation and Presentation of Fabulous Finger Food 1984, Martha Stewart's Pies and Tarts 1985, Martha Stewart's Quick Cook Menus 1988, The Wedding Planner 1988, Martha Stewart's Gardening: Month by Month 1991, Martha Stewart's New Old House: Restoration, Renovation, Decoration 1992, Martha Stewart's Christmas 1993, Martha Stewart's Menus for Entertaining 1994, Holidays 1994, The Martha Rules 2005, Martha Stewart's Homekeeping Handbook 2006, Martha Stewart's Dinner at Home 2009. *Leisure interests:* avid animal lover, pets include champion show Chow Chow dogs, French Bulldogs, Himalayan cats and Friesian horses. *Address:* Martha Stewart Living Omnimedia, 11 West 42nd Street, 25th Floor, New York, NY 10036 (office); Martha Stewart, 19 Newton Toke, Suite 6, Westport, CT 06880; 10 Saugatuck Avenue, Westport, CT 06880, USA (home); c/o Susan Magrino Agency, 40 West 57th Street, 31st Floor, New York, NY 10019. *Telephone:* (212) 827-8000 (office). *Fax:* (212) 827-8204 (office). *Website:* www.marthastewart.com (office); www.themarthablog.com.

STEWART, Sir Patrick, OBE; British actor and producer; *Professor of Performing Arts, University of Huddersfield;* b. 13 July 1940, Mirfield, W Yorks.; s. of Alfred Stewart and Gladys Stewart; m. 1st Sheila Falconer 1966; one s. one d.; m. 2nd Wendy Neuss 2002 (divorced); m. 3rd Sunny Ozell 2013; ed Bristol Old Vic Theatre School; mem. various local drama groups from about age 12; left school at 15 to work as jr reporter on local newspaper; acting experience with various repertory cos; spent year as furniture salesman, saving cash to attend drama school 1957; professional debut in Repertory in Lincoln 1959; performed at Manchester Library Theatre and toured around the world with Old Vic Co. early 1960s; joined RSC 1966, Assoc. Artist 1967–87; spell with Royal Nat. Theatre in mid-1980s; went to Los Angeles to star in Star Trek: The Next Generation, playing role of Capt. Jean-Luc Picard 1987–94; Founding Dir ACTER (A Centre for Theatre Educ. and Research); Dir Flying Freehold Productions, Paramount Studios, Los Angeles 1998–; Cameron Mackintosh Visiting Prof. of Contemporary Theatre, St Catherine's Coll. Oxford 2007–08, now Fellow Emer.; Chancellor, Univ. of Huddersfield 2004–, Prof. of Performing Arts 2008–. *Films include:* Hedda 1975, Excalibur 1981, Dune 1984, Lady Jane 1986, LA Story 1991, Robin Hood – Men in Tights 1993, Gunmen 1994, Jeffrey 1995, Star Trek: First Contact 1996, Conspiracy Theory 1997, Masterminds 1997, Moby Dick 1998, Dad Savage 1998, Star Trek: Insurrection 1999, X-Men 2000, Star Trek: Nemesis 2002, X-Men: X2 2003, Boo, Zino and the Snurks (voice) 2004, Chicken Little (voice) 2005, Bambi II (voice) 2006, X-Men: The Last Stand 2006, TMNT (voice) 2007, X-Men Origins: Wolverine (uncredited) 2009, Castlevania: Lords of Shadow (voice) 2010, Match 2012, Ted (voice, narrator) 2012, Hunting Elephants 2013. *Theatre includes:* Antony and Cleopatra (Olivier Award, Soc. of West End Theatre Award) 1979, 2006, Henry IV 1984, Who's Afraid of Virginia Woolf (London Fringe Award) 1987, A Christmas Carol (Drama Desk Award, Olivier Award 1992) 1988–1996, The Tempest 1995, Othello 1997, The Ride Down Mount Morgan 1998, The Master Builder 2003, A Christmas Carol 2005, Macbeth (London Evening Standard Award for Best Actor 2007) 2007, Waiting for Godot 2009, Bingo: Scenes of Money and Death 2010, A Life in the Theatre 2010, The Merchant of Venice 2011, The Improvised Shakespeare Co. 2013. *Television includes:* Star Trek: The Next Generation, The Mozart Inquest, Maybury, I Claudius, Tinker, Tailor, Soldier, Spy, Smiley's People, The Lion in Winter 2003, Mysterious Island 2005, The Snow Queen (voice) 2005, Family Guy (voice, three episodes) 2005–07, Eleventh Hour 2006, American Dad! (numerous episodes) 2005–09, Hamlet (as Claudius/Ghost) 2009, Macbeth 2011, Richard II 2012. *Music:* narrative on Peter and the Wolf (Grammy Award) 1996. *Address:* c/o Independent Talent Agency, Oxford House, 76 Oxford Street, London, W1B 1DS, England. *Telephone:* (20) 7231-1964; (20) 7636-6565.

STEWART, Roderick (Rod) David, CBE; British singer; b. 10 Jan. 1945, London; m. 1st Alana Collins 1979 (divorced 1984), one s. one d.; one d. with Kelly Emberg; m. 2nd Rachel Hunter 1990 (divorced), one d. one s.; m. Penny Lancaster 2007, one s.; singer with Steampacket, Shotgun Express, Jeff Beck Group 1968–69, Faces 1969–75; solo artist 1971–; Rolling Stone Magazine Rock Star of the Year 1971, British Rock and Pop Award for Lifetime Achievement 1992, BRIT Lifetime Achievement Award 1993. *Recordings include:* albums: two with Jeff Beck, four with Faces; solo: Every Picture Tells a Story 1971, Never a Dull Moment 1972, Atlantic Crossing 1975, A Night On The Town 1976, Foot Loose and Fancy Free 1977, Blondes Have More Fun 1978, Foolish Behaviour 1980, Tonight I'm Yours 1981, Camouflage 1984, Love Touch 1986, Out of Order 1988, The Best Of 1989, Downtown Train 1990, Vagabond Heart 1991, Lead Vocalist 1992, Unplugged. . . and Seated 1993, A Spanner In The Works 1995, When We Were the New Boys 1998, Human 2000, It Had To Be You. . . The Great American Songbook 2002, The Story So Far: The Best of Rod Stewart 2003, Thanks for the Memory 2005, Still the Same 2006, Some Guys Have All the Luck 2008, Songbook 2009, Merry Christmas, Baby 2012, Time 2013. *Publication:* Rod: The Autobiography 2012. *Website:* www.rodstewart.com.

STEWART, S. Jay, BS, MBA; American business executive; b. 18 Sept. 1938; s. of Virgil Harvey Stewart and Lena Rivers Repair; m. Judith Daniels 1961; one s. two d.; ed Univ. of West Virginia and Univ. of Cincinnati; Eng Marketing and Mfg, Monsanto Corpn 1961–73; Dir of Devt, Dir of Marketing, Gen. Man. Ventron Div., Thiokol Corpn 1973–79, Pres. Dynachem Div. 1979–82, Group Vice-Pres. for Chemicals 1982; Pres. Thiokol Chemical Div., Morton Thiokol, Inc. 1982–83, Group Vice-Pres. Chemicals 1983–86, Pres., COO and Dir 1986–89; Pres., COO and Dir Morton Int. Inc. 1986–94, Chair. and CEO 1994–99 (Morton Int. acquired by Rohm and Haas Co. 1999); mem. Bd of Dirs Autoliv, Inc. 1997–, Chair. 2001–07; mem. Bd of Dirs HSBC North America Holdings Inc.; mem. Advisory Bd Nat. Foundation for History of Chem. 1991–; mem. ACS, AIChE, Commercial Devt Asscn. *Address:* Autoliv, Inc., World Trade Center, Klarabergsviadukten 70, Section E, 107 24 Stockholm, Sweden. *Telephone:* (8) 587-20-600. *Fax:* (8) 411-70-25. *Website:* www.autoliv.com.

STEWARTBY, Baron (Life Peer), cr. 1992, of Portmoak in the District of Perth and Kinross; **Bernard Harold Ian Halley Stewartby,** PC, LittD, FBA, FRSE; British banker and fmr politician; b. 10 Aug. 1935, London; s. of the late Prof. H. C. Stewart and Dorothy Stewart (née Lowen); m. Deborah Charlotte Buchan 1966; one s. two d.; ed Haileybury Coll. and Jesus Coll., Cambridge; Lt-Commdr RNR; Brown Shipley & Co. Ltd 1960–82; Conservative MP for Hitchin/N Herts. 1974–92; Econ. Sec. to the Treasury 1983–87; Minister of State for the Armed Forces 1987–88, for NI 1988–89; Chair., Throgmorton Trust PLC 1990–2005; Dir, Financial Services Authority 1993–97; Deputy Chair., Standard Chartered PLC 1993–2004; Deputy Chair., Amlin PLC 1995–2006; Chair., Treasure Valuation Cttee 1996–2001; Hon. Fellow, Jesus Coll., Cambridge 1994, Hon. Keeper of Medieval Coins, Fitzwilliam Museum, Cambridge 2008; Medallist, Royal Numismatic Soc. 1996, Royal Naval and Royal Marine Forces Reserve Decoration. *Publications:* The Scottish Coinage 1955, Coinage in Tenth-Century England 1989, English Coins 1180–1551 2009. *Leisure interests:* archaeology, tennis. *Address:* House of Lords, London, SW1A 0PW, England (office); Broughton Green, Broughton, Peeblesshire, ML12 6HQ, Scotland (home). *Telephone:* (20) 7219-6418 (office). *Fax:* (20) 7821-6455 (office).

STEYN, Hon. Jan Hendrik, BA, BLL; South African lawyer; b. 4 March 1928, Cape Town; s. of H.P.M. Steyn and Zerilda Steyn; ed Jan van Riebeeck School, Univ. of Stellenbosch; began practising as lawyer, Cape Town 1950, took Silk 1963, apptd. Justice of Supreme Court, Cape Prov. Div. 1964, retd 1981; apptd First Exec. Dir The Urban Foundation 1977 (on leave of absence from Supreme Court), now Hon. Chair.; Chair. Ind. Devt Trust 1990–94, SA Media Council 1989; Judge, Court of Appeal, Lesotho 1992, Botswana 1994; Acting Judge of Cape Supreme Court; Jt Ombudsman to Life Assurance Industry 1996–2003; Chair. Bd of Investigation into Saldanha Steel Project 1995, Comm. of Enquiry into Remuneration of Election Reps; Dir First Nat. Bank, Anglo-American Corpn, Barlow Rand Ltd, Metropolitan Life of SA Ltd; Founder The Inst. of Criminology, Univ. of Cape Town; Trustee of numerous charitable orgs; four hon. degrees; Businessman of the Year Award, SA Inst. of Housing 1984, Paul Harris Fellowship Award, Rotary Int., Harvard Business School Business Statesman Award 1985. *Publications:* Crime and Punishment in South Africa (co-ed.); numerous publns on crime and its control. *Leisure interest:* golf. *Address:* c/o Court of Appeal, Maseru, Lesotho.

STEYN, Baron (Life Peer), cr. 1995, of Swafield in the County of Norfolk; **Johan Van Zyl Steyn,** PC, QC, MA; British judge; b. 15 Aug. 1932, Stellenbosch, S Africa; s. of Van Zyl Steyn and Janet Steyn (née Blignaut); m. Susan Leonore Lewis; two s. two d. by previous m.; one step-s. one step-d.; ed Jan van Riebeeck School, Cape Town, S Africa, Univ. of Stellenbosch, S Africa, Univ. Coll. Oxford; began practising at S African Bar 1958; Sr Counsel of Supreme Court of S Africa 1970; settled in UK; began practising at English Bar 1973, Bencher, Lincoln's Inn 1985, QC 1979; a Presiding Judge, Northern Circuit 1989–91; Judge of the High Court 1985–91; a Lord Justice of Appeal 1992–95, a Lord of Appeal in Ordinary 1995–2005; mem. Supreme Court Rule Cttee 1985–89; Chair. Race Relations Cttee of the Bar 1987–88; mem. Lord Chancellor's Advisory Cttee on Legal Educ. and Conduct 1994–96; Pres. British Insurance Law Asscn 1992–94; Hon. Fellow, Univ. Coll. Oxford 1995; Hon. mem. American Law Inst.; Hon. LLD (Queen Mary and Westfield Coll., London) 1997, (Univ. of East Anglia) 1997. *Publications:* Democracy Through Law 2004. *Address:* House of Lords, Westminster, London, SW1A 0PW, England (office). *Telephone:* (20) 7219-5353 (office). *Fax:* (20) 7219-6156 (office).

STICH, Michael; German business executive and fmr professional tennis player; b. 18 Oct. 1968, Pinneberg; m. 1st Jessica Stockmann 1992 (divorced 2003); m. 2nd Alexandra Rikowski 2005; ed studied history of art; Nat. Jr Champion 1986; turned professional 1988; semi-finalist, French Open 1990; mem. W German Davis Cup Team 1990; won first professional title, Memphis 1990; winner, Men's Singles Championship, Wimbledon 1991; Men's Doubles (with John McEnroe q.v., 1992; won ATP World Championship 1993; retd 1997; won 28 professional titles and more than 12 million dollars in prize money; UN Amb. 1999–; German Davis Cup team Capt. Oct. 2001–Sept. 2002; mem. Senior tour; CEO Hanseatik Rückenzentrum, Michael Stich Foundation; Tournament Dir, German Tennis Open, Hamburg and NORD/LB Braunschweig. *Television:* game show (PRO 7) 2000, commentator, BBC and Eurosport. *Leisure interests:* golf, horses, sports, painting. *Address:* Magdalenstr. 42–43B, 20148 Hamburg, Germany.

STICH, Stephen Peter, PhD; American professor of philosophy and cognitive science; *Board of Governors Professor, Rutgers University;* b. 9 May 1943, New York; s. of Samuel J. Stich and Sylvia L. Stich; m. Judith Ann Gagnon 1971; one s. one d.; ed Univ. of Pennsylvania, Princeton Univ.; mem. staff, Univs of Michigan 1968–78, Maryland 1978–86, California, San Diego 1986–89; Prof. of Philosophy and Cognitive Science, Rutgers Univ. 1989–, Bd of Govs Prof. 1998–, Dir Research Group on Evolution and Higher Cognition; Adjunct Prof., CUNY Grad. Center 1994–97; Pres. Soc. for Philosophy and Psychology 1982–83; Fulbright Sr Research Scholar 1978–79; Fellow, Center for Advanced Study in the Behavioral Sciences 1983–84; Visiting Fellow, Research School of Social Sciences, ANU 1992; Erskine Fellow, Canterbury Univ., Christchurch, NZ 1996; Clark-Way-Harrison Distinguished Visiting Prof., Dept of Philosophy, Washington Univ. in St Louis 2007; Fellow, American Acad. of Arts and Sciences 2009–; Hon. Prof. of Philosophy, Univ. of Sheffield 2005–; Jean Nicod Prize, Institut Jean Nicod, Paris 2007. *Publications:* From Folk Psychology to Cognitive Science 1983, The Fragmentation of Reason 1990, Philosophy and Connectionist Theory (co-author) 1991, Deconstructing The Mind 1996, Mindreading (co-author) 2003. *Address:* Department of Philosophy, Davison Hall, Douglass Campus, Rutgers University, New Brunswick, NJ 08901 (office); 55 Liberty Street, Apt 8-A, New York, NY 10005, USA (home). *Telephone:* (732) 932-9861 (office). *Fax:* (212) 571-4838 (office); (732) 932-8617 (home). *E-mail:* stich@ruccs.rutgers.edu (office). *Website:* ruccs.rutgers.edu/archivefolder/research%20group/research.html (office); www.rci.rutgers.edu/~stich/ (home).

STIELER, Frank, DrJur; German lawyer and business executive; *Chairman of the Executive Board and CEO, Hochtief AG;* b. 13 Dec. 1958; m.; five c.; ed Johann Wolfgang Goethe Univ., Frankfurt; held various positions with Lurgi AG, including Chief Financial Officer Lurgi Energie and Umwelt GmbH 1994–97 and CEO Lurgi Bamag GmbH 1997–99; Sr Vice-Pres., Azurix (subsidiary of Enron), Houston, USA 1999–2001; moved to Siemens 2001, responsible for

Industrial Application div., Power Generation Group, CEO Siemens Oil & Gas Div. 2008–11; mem. Exec. Bd Hochtief AG 2009–, CEO 2011–, also responsible for the HOCHTIEF Europe and HOCHTIEF Asia Pacific divs and the Public-Pvt. Partnership segment. *Address:* Hochtief AG, Opernplatz 2, 45128 Essen, Germany (office). *Telephone:* (201) 824-0 (office). *Fax:* (201) 824-2777 (office). *E-mail:* info@conti-online.com (office). *Website:* www.hochtief.com (office).

STIGLITZ, Joseph Eugene, PhD, FBA; American economist and academic; *Professor of Economics and Finance, Graduate School of Business, Columbia University;* b. 9 Feb. 1943, Gary, Ind.; s. of Nathaniel D. Stiglitz and Charlotte Fishman; m. 1st 1978; two s. two d.; m. 2nd Anya Schiffrin 2004; ed Amherst Coll., Mass. Inst. of Tech. and Univ. of Cambridge (Fulbright Scholar); Prof. of Econs, Cowles Foundation, Yale Univ. 1970–74; Visiting Fellow, St Catherine's Coll. Oxford 1973–74; Prof. of Econs, Stanford Univ. 1974–76, Sr Fellow, Hoover Inst. 1988–2001, Joan Kenney Prof. of Econs 1992–2001; Drummond Prof. of Political Econ., Univ. of Oxford 1976–79; Oskar Morgenstern Distinguished Fellow, Inst. of Advanced Studies, Princeton 1978–79; Prof. of Econs, Princeton Univ. 1979–88; Stern Visiting Prof., Columbia Univ. 2000, Prof. of Econs and Finance, Grad. School of Business 2000, Co-Founder and Pres. Initiative for Policy Dialogue 2000–, Univ. Prof. 2000–, Chair. Cttee on Global Thought 2006–; mem. Pres.'s Council of Econ. Advisers 1993–95, Chair. (mem. of cabinet) 1995–97; Special Adviser to Pres. of World Bank, Sr Vice-Pres. and Chief Economist 1997–2000; Chair. Man. Bd and Dir Grad. Summer Programs, Brooks World Poverty Inst., Univ. of Manchester 2006–; Special Adviser, Bell Communications Research, numerous consultancies in public and pvt. sector; Sr Fellow, Brookings Inst. 2000; Fellow, American Acad. of Arts and Sciences, NAS, Econometric Soc., American Philosophical Soc., Inst. for Policy Research (Sr Fellow 1991–93); Hon. DHL (Amherst Coll.) 1974; Dr hc (Univ. of Leuven, Ben Gurion Univ.), (Oxford) 2004; Guggenheim Fellow 1969–70; John Bates Clark Award, American Econ. Asscn 1979, Int. Prize, Accad. dei Lincei, Rome 1988, UAP Scientific Prize, Paris 1989; Nobel Prize for Econs (jt recepient) 2001. *Film appearance:* Four Horseman (documentary) 2012. *Publications include:* Globalization and its Discontents, Economics of the Public Sector 2000, Principles of Economics 1997, Rethinking the East Asia Miracle (co-ed.) 2001, The Roaring Nineties 2003, Fair Trade for All (co-author), 2005, Making Globalization Work 2006, The Three Trillion Dollar War: The True Cost of the Iraq Conflict (co-author) 2008, Freefall: America, Free Markets and the Sinking of the World Economy 2010, The Price of Inequality: The Avoidable Causes and Invisible Costs of Inequality 2012; other books and more than 300 papers in learned journals. *Address:* Uris Hall, Room 814, Columbia University, 3022 Broadway, New York, NY 10027, USA (office). *Telephone:* (212) 854-1481 (office). *Fax:* (212) 662-8474 (office). *E-mail:* jes322@columbia.edu (office). *Website:* www.josephstiglitz.com.

STIGWOOD, Robert Colin; Australian impresario; b. 16 April 1934, Adelaide, SA; s. of Gordon Stigwood and Gwendolyn Stigwood (née Asbury); ed Sacred Heart Coll., Adelaide; relocated to UK 1954; est. Robert Stigwood Org. (RSO) 1967; f. RSO Records 1973; Founder, Music for UNICEF 1979; TV producer in England and USA of The Entertainer and The Prime of Miss Jean Brodie; Chair. Stigwood group of cos; Key to Cities of Los Angeles and Adelaide; Int. Producer of the Year, ABC Interstate Theatres Inc. *Stage musicals produced:* Hair, Oh! Calcutta, The Dirtiest Show in Town, Pippin, Jesus Christ Superstar, Evita (Tony Award for Best Musical 1980), Grease (London) 1993, Saturday Night Fever, Sweeney Todd, Sing a Rude Song, John Paul George Ringo and Bert. *Films produced:* Jesus Christ Superstar 1973, Tommy 1975, Bugsy Malone (exec. producer) 1976, Saturday Night Fever 1977, Grease 1978, Sgt. Pepper's Lonely Hearts Club Band 1978, Moment by Moment 1978, Times Square 1980, Gallipoli 1981, The Fan 1981, Grease 2 1982, Staying Alive 1983, Young Alive 1984, Evita 1996. *Television produced:* Traitor's Gate 1962, Cucumber Castle (exec. producer) 1970, The Virginia Hill Story 1974. *Leisure interests:* tennis, swimming, sailing, reading. *Address:* c/o Robert Stigwood Organisation, Barton Manor, East Cowes, Isle of Wight, PO32 6LB, England.

STIHL, Hans Peter; German business executive; b. 18 April 1932, Stuttgart; s. of Andreas Stihl and Maria Giersch; m.; ed Technische Hochschule, Stuttgart; Chair. and Pnr, Andreas Stihl Fabrik; Pres. Deutsche Industrie und Handelstag, Bonn 1988–2000, Hon. Pres. 2001–; Vice-Pres. Inst. of German Economy, Cologne 1983–88, Treas. 1983–88; Pres. IHK Stuttgart 1990–2001, Hon. Pres. 2001–; Chair. Advisory Bd Stihl Holding AF & Co. KG and Chair. Supervisory Bd Stihl AG 2002–; mem. Man. Bd Verein Deutscher Maschinen- und Anlagenbau (VDMA) –1988; Hon. Consul-Gen. of Singapore 2002–; Grand Cross with Star for Distinguished Service of the Order of Merit of FRG 2002; Hanns Martin Schleyer Award 2003. *Address:* Stihl Holding AG & Co., Badstr. 115, 71336 Dieburg, Germany. *E-mail:* hon.konsulat-singapur.stgt@stihl.de.

STILLER, Ben; American actor and film director; b. 30 Nov. 1965, New York; s. of Jerry Stiller and Ann Meara; m. Christine Taylor; two c.; ed Univ. of California, Los Angeles. *Films:* Empire of the Sun 1988, Reality Bites (also dir) 1994, Happy Gilmore 1996, Flirting with Disaster 1996, The Cable Guy (also Dir) 1996, Zero Effect 1998, Your Friends and Neighbors 1998, There's Something About Mary 1998, Permanent Midnight 1998, Mystery Men 1999, Black and White 1999, Meet the Parents 2000, Keeping the Faith 2000, Zoolander (also dir) 2001, The Royal Tenenbaums 2001, Duplex 2003, Nobody Knows Anything 2003, Along Came Polly 2004, Starsky & Hutch 2004, Envy 2004, Dodgeball 2004, Anchorman 2004, Meet the Fockers 2004, Madagascar (voice) 2005, Danny Roane: First Time Director 2006, School for Scoundrels 2006, Tenacious D: The Pick of Destiny 2006, Night at the Museum 2006, The Heartbreak Kid 2007, Tropic Thunder (also dir) 2008, Madagascar: Escape 2 Africa (voice) 2008, Night at the Museum: Battle of the Smithsonian 2009, The Marc Pease Experience 2009, Greenberg 2010, Little Fockers 2010, Tower Heist 2011, Madagascar 3: Europe's Most Wanted (voice) 2012, The Watch 2012. *Television includes:* The Ben Stiller Show (Emmy Award) 1990–93, Heat Vision and Jack 1999, Freaks and Geeks 2000, Arrested Development 2004–06, Phineas and Ferb 2010. *Address:* c/o United Talent Agency, 9560 Wilshire Boulevard, Suite 500, Beverly Hills, CA 90212, USA (office).

STILWELL, Richard Dale, MusB; American singer (baritone); b. 6 May 1942, St Louis; s. of Otho John Clifton and Tressie Stilwell (née Parrish); m. 1st Elizabeth Louise Jencks 1967 (divorced); m. 2nd Kerry M. McCarthy 1983; ed Anderson Coll., Univ. of Indiana; with Metropolitan Opera Co., New York 1970–; appear-

ances in major roles Washington Opera Soc., Marseilles Opera Co., Santa Fe Opera, San Francisco Opera Co., Paris Opera Co., La Scala, Covent Garden, Hamburg State Opera, Glyndebourne Opera Festival, Van. Opera Co., Chicago Opera Co., Tanglewood Festival, Israel Philharmonic, Boston Symphony, LA Philharmonic, etc.; soloist with Nat. Symphony, Washington, Chicago Symphony, American Symphony, Carnegie Hall, Boston Symphony, LA Philharmonic, etc.; mem. American Guild Musical Artists; Nat. Soc. of Arts and Letters Award 1963, Fisher Foundation award Metropolitan Opera Auditions 1965. *Address:* Columbia Artists Management, 1790 Broadway, New York, NY 10019-1412, USA (office). *Telephone:* (212) 841-9500 (office). *Fax:* (212) 841-9744 (office). *E-mail:* info@cami.com (office). *Website:* www.cami.com (office).

STINCO, Antoine; French architect; b. 1934, ; ed Ecole Nationale Supérieure des Beaux-Arts, Paris (studio of Edouard Albert-Paul Herbe, Jean Prouvé); worked on light and mobile architecture and particularly on inflated structures; exhibited inflated structure in ARC (Museum of Modern Arts of Paris) 1968; participated with GAU (Urban Architecture Group) in renewal of urban architecture in France 1974; est. own architectural firm 1984; fashion design artist with Christiane Bailly Assocs 1970–90; taught in Sculpture Dept at Beaux-Art, Paris 1993–99. *Major works include:* Jeu de paume, Nat. Gallery, Jardin de Tuileries, Paris 1991, Musée du Louvre, Paris, six kiosks in Jardin de Tuileries 1995–97, Ecole du Louvre and Aile de Flore, Louvre Museum 1997–98, Musée d'art moderne et contemporain Les Abattoirs, Toulouse (with R. Papillault) 2000, Musée des Beaux Arts, Angers 2003, MC2 Arts Centre extension, Maison de la Culture, Grenoble 2004, Le Théâtre nat. de Bretagne 2008. *Publications:* Le Territoire de L'Architecture – Suivi de Vingt-Quatre Projets et Realisations (with Vittorio Gregotti) 1982, Les Abattoirs, Histoires et Transformation 2000. *Address:* SA Antoine Stinco, 73 boulevard de Sebastopol, 75002 Paris, France (office). *Telephone:* 1-45-08-18-66 (office).

STING, CBE; British singer, musician (bass guitar), songwriter and actor; b. (Gordon Matthew Thomas Sumner), 2 Oct. 1951, Wallsend, Newcastle upon Tyne; s. of the late Ernest Sumner and Audrey Sumner (née Cowell); m. 1st Frances Tomelty 1976 (divorced 1984); one s. one d.; m. 2nd Trudie Styler 1992; two s. two d.; ed St Cuthbert's High School, Newcastle upon Tyne, Univ. of Warwick, Coventry, Northern Counties Coll. of Educ.; worked as bus conductor, construction labourer and tax officer –1971; primary school teacher, St Paul's First School, Cramlington, Newcastle 1975–77; played with local jazz bands, including Phoenix Jazzmen, the Newcastle Big Band, and Last Exit; mem., with Stewart Copeland and Henry Padovani (replaced by Andy Summers), and lead singer of rock group, The Police 1977–84, re-formed to tour 2007–08; solo artist 1985–; numerous tours, TV and radio broadcasts in Europe and USA; Chevalier, Ordre des Arts et Lettres 2007; Hon. DMus (Northumbria) 1992; Ivor Novello Awards for Best Song (for They Dance Alone) 1989, four BMI songwriting awards 1998, BMI Award for Int. Achievement 2002, BRIT Award for Best Male Artist 1994, for Outstanding Contribution to Music 2002, Emmy Award for Best Performance (Sting in Tuscany... All This Time) 2002, 14 Grammy Awards (with The Police and solo), Grammy Award for Best Pop Collaboration with Vocals (for Whenever I Say Your Name, with Mary J. Blige) 2004, MusiCares Foundation Person of the Year 2003, Billboard Music Century Award for Creative Achievement 2003. *Stage appearance:* The Threepenny Opera (Broadway) 1989, Twin Spirits 2009. *Film appearances include:* Quadrophenia 1979, Radio On 1980, Artemis 81 (BBC TV) 1981, Brimstone and Treacle 1982, Dune 1984, The Bride 1985, Plenty 1985, Bring on the Night 1985, Giulia and Giulia 1987, The Adventures of Baron Munchausen 1988, Stormy Monday 1988, The Grotesque 1995, Lock, Stock and Two Smoking Barrels 1998, The Tulse Luper Suitcases: The Moab Story 2003, Bee Movie 2007. *Recordings include:* albums: with the Police: Outlandos D'Amour 1977, Regatta De Blanc 1979, Zenyatta Mondatta 1980, Ghost In The Machine 1981, Synchronicity 1983, Every Breath You Take: The Classics 1995, Sting & The Police—The Very Best Of 1997, 2002, The Police 2007; solo: The Dream of The Blue Turtles 1985, Bring On The Night 1986, Nothing Like The Sun 1987, The Soul Cages 1991, Ten Summoner's Tales 1994, Mercury Falling 1996, Brand New Day 1999, All This Time 2001, Sacred Love 2003, Songs of Love 2003, My Funny Valentine 2005, Songs From The Labyrinth 2007, Songs for Tibet – The Art of Peace 2008, If On a Winter's Night 2009, Symphonicities 2010, The Last Ship 2013. *Publications:* Jungle Stories: The Fight for the Amazon 1989, Escape Artist (memoir) 2003. *Address:* Kathryn Shenker Associates, 12th Floor, 1776 Broadway, New York, NY 10019, USA (office); c/o Publicity Department, Polydor Records, 72 Black Lane, London, W6, England (office). *Telephone:* (20) 8910-4800 (office). *Website:* www .sting.com.

STINSON, William W.; Canadian insurance industry executive; CEO Canadian Pacific Ltd 1985–96; apptd mem. Bd of Dirs Sun Life Financial Inc. 1985, Lead Dir 1999–2003, Chair. (non-exec.) Sun Life Financial Inc. and Sun Life Assurance Co. 2003–05 (retd); currently Chair. and CEO Westshore Terminals Inc., Chair. Westshore Terminals Income Funds; mem. Bd of Dirs Grant Forest Products Inc. 2003–, CHC Helecopter Corpn 2003–; Trustee Fording Canadian Coal Trust. *Address:* Westshore Terminals Income Fund, 1800-1067 Cordova Street West, Vancouver BC V6C 1C7, Canada (office).

STIPE, (John) Michael; American musician and songwriter; b. 1 April 1960, Decatur, Ga; ed Univ. of Georgia; Founder mem. and lead singer, R.E.M. 1980–2011; Owner, C-00 (film co.) and Single Cell Pictures 1987–; Owner, Grit vegetarian restaurant, Athens, Ga; numerous MTV Music Video Awards, Earth Day Award 1990, Billboard Award for Best Modern Rock Artist 1991, BRIT Awards for Best Int. Group 1992, 1993, 1995, Grammy Awards for Best Pop Performance, Best Music Video 1992, Atlanta Music Awards for Act of the Year, Video of the Year 1992, IRMA Award for Int. Band of the Year 1993, Rolling Stone Critics Award for Best Band 1993. *Recordings:* albums: Chronic Town 1982, Murmur 1983, Reckoning 1984, Fables Of The Reconstruction 1985, Life's Rich Pageant 1986, Dead Letter Office 1987, Document 1987, Eponymous 1988, Green 1988, Out Of Time (Billboard Award for Best World Album, Q Award for Best Album) 1991, Automatic For The People (Grammy Award for Best Alternative Music Album, Atlanta Music Award for Rock Album, Q Award for Best Album, Rolling Stone Critics Award for Best Album 1993) 1992, Monster 1994, New Adventures In Hi-Fi 1996, Up 1998, Star Profiles 1999, Reveal 2001, Bad Day Pt 1 and 2 2003, Glastonbury 1999 2003, Around The Sun 2004, Accelerate 2008,

Collapse into Now 2011. *Address:* REM/Athens Ltd, 250 West Clayton Street, Athens, GA 30601, USA (office). *Website:* www.remhq.com.

STIPRAIS, Eduards; Latvian diplomatist, government official and economist; *Under-Secretary of State and Political Director, Ministry of Foreign Affairs;* b. 19 Feb. 1969, Rīga; m. Zanda Grauze; ed Univ. of Latvia; mil. service 1988–89; trainee, Ministry of Social Maintenance May–July 1991, Dept of Foreign Econ. Relations, Council of Ministers 1991–92; Desk Officer, Ministry of Foreign Trade 1992–93; EC Desk Officer, Ministry of Foreign Affairs 1993, Head EC/EFTA Relations Div. 1993–94, Deputy Dir Dept of Int. Econ. Relations 1994–95, Sec. Latvian del. for the negotiations on the Agreement on Free Trade and Trade Related Matters with the EU 1993–94, for the negotiations on the Europe Agreement 1994–95, Advisor on Secondment to OECD/EU SIGMA Programme, Paris 1995, Second Sec., Latvian Mission to the EU, Brussels March–Oct. 1995, First Sec. 1995–98, Head, task force for preparation of EU accession negotiations 1998–99, Deputy Chief Negotiator EU accession negotiations 1999–2003, Deputy Head 2003–04, Deputy Perm. Rep. 2004, Perm. Rep. 2004–07; Head of Chancery of Pres. of Latvia 2007–08; Amb. and Dir Gen. for Bilateral Relations, Ministry of Foreign Affairs 2009; Amb. to UK 2009–13; Under-Sec. of State and Political Dir, Ministry of Foreign Affairs 2013–; mem. Latvian European Movt; Officer, Order of Three Stars (Fourth Class) 2004, Kt, Order of Merits (Second Class) (Ukraine) 2009; State Sec.'s Award, Ministry of Foreign Affairs 2000, Silver Award of Honour, Ministry of Interior 2003, Certificate of Recognition, Cabinet of Ministers 2003. *Address:* Ministry of Foreign Affairs, K. Valdemāra iela 3, Rīga 1395, Latvia (office). *Telephone:* 6701-6201 (office). *Fax:* 6782-8121 (office). *E-mail:* mfa.cha@mfa.gov.lv (office). *Website:* www.mfa.gov.lv (office).

STIRLING, Sir Angus Duncan Aeneas, Kt; British arts administrator; b. 10 Dec. 1933, London; s. of Duncan Alexander Stirling and Lady Marjorie Stirling; m. Armyne Morar Helen Schofield 1959; one s. two d.; ed Eton Coll., Trinity Coll., Cambridge, Univ. of London; mem. staff, Christie, Manson & Woods Ltd 1954–57, Lazard Bros. and Co. Ltd 1957–66; Asst Dir Paul Mellon Foundation for British Art 1966–69, Jt Dir 1969–70; Deputy Sec.-Gen. Arts Council of GB 1971–79; Deputy Dir-Gen. The Nat. Trust 1979–83, Dir-Gen. 1983–95; Sr Policy Adviser Nat. Heritage Memorial Fund 1996–97; Dir Royal Opera House, Covent Garden 1979–96, Chair. 1991–96, Chair. Friends of Covent Garden 1981–91, Deputy Chair. Royal Ballet Bd 1988–91; Chair. Greenwich Foundation for the Royal Naval Coll. 1996–2003, Policy Cttee, Council for Protection of Rural England 1996–2001, Jt Nature Conservation Cttee 1997–2002; mem. Crafts Council 1980–85, Council of Man. Byam Shaw School of Art 1965–89, Advisory Council London Symphony Orchestra 1979–, Bd of Govs Live Music Now 1982–89, Govt Task Force on Tourism and the Environment 1991, Court of the Fishmongers' Co. 1991– (Prime Warden 2004–05), ICOMOS UK Tourism Cttee 1993–2003 (Chair. IUCN/ICOMOS UK Liaison Cttee 2003–07), Council Royal School of Church Music 1996–98, Bd of Govs Gresham School 1999–2007, Fabric Advisory Cttee, Wells Cathedral 2001–, City & Guilds of London Art School 2003–10; mem. Bd of Dirs Courtauld Inst. of Art 1981–83, 2002–, currently Trustee; Trustee, Theatres Trust 1983–91, Heritage of London Trust 1983–95, Samuel Courtauld Trust 1984–, World Monuments Fund UK 1996–2008, Stowe House Preservation Trust 1998–; Vice-Patron Almshouses Asscn 1998–2009; Hon. Fellow, Trinity Coll. of Music; Hon. DLitt (Greenwich, Leicester). *Leisure interests:* music, travel, walking, painting. *Address:* 30 Upper Addison Gardens, London, W14 8AJ, England (home). *Telephone:* (20) 7610-5432 (office).

STIRN, Olivier, LenD; French politician; *Executive Adviser, Union pour un Mouvement Populaire;* b. 24 Feb. 1936, Boulogne-Billancourt; s. of Alexandre Stirn and Geneviève Dreyfus; m. Evelyn Toledano 1989; one s. one d. (and two s. from previous m.); ed Univ. of Paris, Institut de Sciences Politiques; Chief of Cabinet for Prefect of La Meuse 1961–64, Chargé de mission 1964; Chief of Cabinet for Minister of State in charge of Overseas Depts and Territories 1964, for Sec. of State for Foreign Affairs 1966–67, for Sec. of State for Social Affairs 1967–68; Deputy for Calvados 1968–73, 1981–86 (Gen. Councillor 1970–88, 1994–2001), for Manche 1986–88; Councillor Gen., Mayor of Vire 1971; Pres., Urban Community of Cherbourg 1989–90; Sec. of State for Parl. Relations 1973–74, for Overseas Territories 1974–78, for Foreign Affairs 1978–81, for Defence 1980–81; Minister Del. for Overseas Territories May–June 1988, Minister Del. attached to Minister of Industry and Territorial Devt 1988–89, to Minister of Industry, Territorial Devt and Tourism (with special responsibility for Tourism) 1989–90; Chair. Dialogue 2000 1988–; Amb. to Council of Europe, Strasbourg 1991–93; Business Consultant 1993–; Consultant to Rothschild & Cie 1998–2001; Editorial Dir Editions du Félin 2005–; Executive Adviser, Union pour un Mouvement Populaire (UMP) 2004–; founder, Mouvement des sociaux-libéraux 1977; Vice-Pres., Parti radical socialiste 1977; co-founder, Carrefour social-démocrate 1977; founder and Pres., Union centriste et républicaine 1984; Nat. Del., Parti socialiste 1986; Chevalier, Légion d'honneur, and many foreign decorations. *Publications:* Le piège (with Bernard Stasi and J. P. Soisson) 1973, Une certaine idée du centre 1985, Tourisme: chance pour l'économie, risque pour les sociétés?, Mes Présidents: 50 ans au service de la 5e République 2004. *Leisure interests:* tennis, golf, history. *Address:* 55 rue la Boétie, 75008 Paris (office); 14 Avenue Pierre 1er de Serbie, 75116 Paris, France (home). *Telephone:* 1-47-20-41-93 (office); 1-47-20-41-57 (home). *Fax:* 1-40-76-60-44 (office); 1-47-20-41-93 (home). *E-mail:* evestirn.sic@free.fr (office).

STIRRUP, Baron (Life Peer), cr. 2011, of Marylebone in the City of Westminster; **Graham Eric (Jock) Stirrup,** Kt, GCB, AFC, ADC, DSc, FRAeS, FCMI, RAF; British air force officer; b. 4 Dec. 1949; s. of William Hamilton Stirrup and Jacqueline Brenda Stirrup (née Coulson); m. Mary Alexandra Elliot 1976; one s.; ed Merchant Taylors' School, Northwood, RAF Coll., Cranwell, Jt Service Defence Coll., Royal Coll. of Defence Studies; qualified flying instructor 1971–73; loan service, Sultan of Oman's Air Force 1973–75; fighter reconnaissance pilot 1976–78; exchange pilot, USAF 1978–81; Flight Commdr 1982–84; Officer Commdr No. II (Army Co-operation) Squadron 1985–87; Dir Air Force Plans and Programmes, Ministry of Defence 1994–97; Air Officer Commdr No. 1 Group 1997–98; Asst Chief of Air Staff 1998–2000; Deputy C-in-C, Stike Commdr, Commdr NATO Combined Air Operations Centre 9 and Dir European Air Group 2000–02; Deputy Chief of Defence Staff (Equipment Capability) 2002–03; Chief of Air Staff 2003–06, Chief of Defence Staff 2006–10; mem. (Crossbench) House of Lords 2011–. *Leisure interests:* golf, music, theatre, history. *Address:* c/o Ministry of Defence, Main

Building, Whitehall, London, SW1A 2HB (office); House of Lords, Westminster, London, SW1A 0PW, England. *Telephone:* (20) 7219-5979 (House of Lords). *E-mail:* stirrupg@parliament.uk (office). *Website:* www.mod.uk (office); www.parliament.uk/biographies/lords/graham-stirrup/17769 (office).

STITZER, H. Todd; American business executive; m. Marenda Stitzer; two c.; ed Harvard and Columbia Univs; Asst Gen. Counsel Cadbury Schweppes Beverages N America 1983, Vice-Pres. and Gen. Counsel, Worldwide Beverages Stream 1988, Group Devt Dir responsible for Strategic Planning and External Devt, UK 1991–93, Vice-Pres. Marketing and Strategic Planning N America 1993–95, COO N America 1995–97; Pres. and CEO Dr Pepper/Seven Up 1997–2000; Chief Strategy Officer, Cadbury Schweppes (now Cadbury plc) 2000–02, Deputy CEO 2002–03, CEO 2003–10; mem. Bd of Dirs Diageo plc 2004–; mem. Bd of Trustees Business in the Community 2008–. *Address:* c/o Cadbury plc, Cadbury House, Sanderson Road, Uxbridge Business Park, Uxbridge, London, UB8 1DH, England (office).

STOCK, Carlos Olímpio; São Tomé and Príncipe politician; fmr Dir Studies and Documentation Office, Ministry of Justice; Minister of Defence and Public Security 2010–12; mem. Acção Democrática Independente (ADI). *Address:* c/o Ministry of Defence and Public Security, Avenue 12 de Julho, CP 427, São Tomé, São Tomé and Príncipe.

STOCKING, Dame Barbara, DBE; British charity administrator; *Chief Executive, Oxfam GB;* b. 28 July 1951, Rugby, Warwicks.; m. Dr John MacInnes; two s.; fmr regional dir in the Nat. Health Service (NHS); Chief Exec. Oxfam GB (first woman) 2001–; Vice-Chair. Steering Cttee for Humanitarian Response (alliance made up of CEOs of nine humanitarian networks or agencies (Care International, Caritas Internationalis, International Cttee of the Red Cross, Int. Fed. of Red Cross and Red Crescent Socs, Int. Save the Children Alliance, Lutheran World Fed., Oxfam, WCC and World Vision International). *Address:* Oxfam GB, Oxfam House, John Smith Drive, Cowley, Oxford OX4 2JY, England (office). *Telephone:* 0300-200130 (within UK only) (office); (1865) 473727 (office). *E-mail:* enquiries@oxfam.org.uk (office). *Website:* www.oxfam.org.uk (office).

STOCKTON, 2nd Earl of; Alexander Daniel Alan Macmillan, FBIM, FRSA; British publisher, farmer and politician; *District Councillor, South Bucks District Council;* b. 10 Oct. 1943, Oswestry; s. of the late Maurice Victor Macmillan (Viscount Macmillan of Ovenden) and of Dame Katherine Macmillan (Viscountess Macmillan of Ovenden), DBE; grandson of the late 1st Earl of Stockton (fmrly, as Harold Macmillan, Prime Minister of UK 1957–63); m. 1st Hélène Birgitte Hamilton 1970 (divorced 1991); one s. two d.; m. 2nd Miranda Elizabeth Louise Nultall 1995 (divorced 2010); ed Eton Coll. and Paris and Strathclyde Univs; Sub-Ed., Glasgow Herald 1963–65; Reporter, Daily Telegraph 1965–67, Foreign Corresp. 1967–68, Chief European Corresp., Sunday Telegraph 1968–70; Dir, Birch Grove Estates Ltd 1969–86, Chair. 1983–89; Dir, Macmillan and Co. Ltd 1970–76, Deputy Chair. 1976–80, Chair. 1984–90, Pres. 1990–; Chair., Macmillan Publrs Ltd 1980–90 (Pres. 1990–), St Martin's Press, New York 1983–88 (Dir 1974–90), Sidgwick and Jackson 1989–90; mem. MEP (Conservative) for SW of England 1999–2004, Vice Pres. (Defence), European Parl. Foreign Affairs Cttee 2000–04, mem. Convention on the Future of Europe (Rep. of European Peoples' Party) 2003–04; District Councillor, South Bucks. District Council 2011–; Chair., Cen. London Training & Enterprise Council 1990–95; Pres., Ludwig von Mises Institut UZW 2005–; Dir, Book Trade Benevolent Soc. 1976–88, Chair., Booktrust Appeal 1978–86; Dir, United British Artists Ltd 1984–90 (Chair. 1985–90); mem. Lindemann Fellowship Cttee 1979– (Chair. 1983–), British Inst. of Man. 1981–, Council of Publrs Asscn 1985–88, Carlton Club Political Cttee 1975–88 (Chair. 1984); Gov., Archbishop Tenison's School 1979–86, Merchant Taylor's School 1980–82, 1990–, English Speaking Union 1980–84, 1986–93; Liveryman, Worshipful Co. of Merchant Taylors 1972, Court Asst 1987, Master 1991–92; Liveryman, Worshipful Co. of Stationers 1973, Court Asst 1989; Hon. DLitt (De Montfort) 1993, (Westminster) 1995; Hon. DUniv (Strathclyde) 1993; Schumann Medal 2004. *Leisure interests:* fishing, aviation. *Address:* The Priory, Denham Village, Bucks., UB9 5AS, England (home). *Telephone:* (1895) 834181 (home). *E-mail:* thepriory@dbac.co.uk (home).

STODDART, Brian, BA, MA, PhD; New Zealand university administrator; ed Univ. of Canterbury, Univ. of Western Australia; fmr Pro Vice-Chancellor (Asia), RMIT Univ., Dir of Int. Programmes, RMIT Univ., Pro Vice-Chancellor (Research and Int.), Univ. of New England, Pro Vice-Chancellor (Int.), Victoria Univ., Acting Deputy Vice-Chancellor, Victoria Univ.; joined La Trobe Univ. as Deputy Vice-Chancellor (Research) 2004, Vice-Chancellor and Pres. 2005–06 (resgnd); mem. Australian Vice-Chancellors' Cttee (AVCC); fmr mem. numerojus editorial bds including Journal of Sport and Social Issues, Australian Soc. for Sports History; Australia-New Zealand Foundation Award. *Publications:* Saturday Afternoon Fever: Sport in the Australian Culture 1986, Liberation Cricket: Caribbean Cricket Culture 1995, The A–Z of Australian Cricketers 1997, The Imperial Game: Cricket, Culture and Society 1998, Soundings in Modern Sports Culture 2006; contribs to Sport Report, Pro News, World of Cricket, Action, The Australian, Sunday Herald, The Age, and over 35 articles in refereed journals and collections. *Address:* c/o Office of the Vice-Chancellor, La Trobe University, Plenty Road, Bundoora, Vic. 3086, Australia (office).

STODDART, Sir James Fraser, Kt, PhD, DSc, FRS; British chemist and academic; *Board of Trustees Professor of Chemistry, Northwestern University;* b. 24 May 1942, Edinburgh, Scotland; two c.; ed Univ. of Edinburgh; NRC Postdoctoral Fellow, Queens' Univ., Kingston, Ont., Canada 1967–70; ICI Research Fellow, Univ. of Sheffield 1970, Lecturer in Chem. 1970–78, Reader 1981–90; Researcher, ICI Corp. Lab., Runcorn 1978–81; Prof. of Organic Chem., Univ. of Birmingham 1990–97, Head of School of Chem. 1993–97; Winstein Chair, Dept of Chem. and Biochemistry, UCLA 1997–2003, Dir California NanoSystems Inst. 2002–07, Fred Kavli Chair in NanoSystems Sciences, UCLA 2003–08; Bd of Trustees Prof. of Chem., Northwestern Univ. 2008–; visiting prof. at numerous int. univs, including as Carnegie Centenary Visiting Prof., Scottish Univs 2005, World Class Univ. Faculty, Korea Inst. of Science and Tech. 2011, 2012; mem. Editorial Bd Crystal Growth and Design, Journal of Organic Chemistry, Organic Letters, Angewandte Chemie, Chemistry-A European Journal, Synthesis, Bioorganic Chemistry Reviews; Pres. Chemical Section, BAAS 1996; mem. American Acad. of Arts and

Sciences 2012; Fellow, German Acad. of Natural Sciences Leopoldina, AAAS 2005; Hon. Prof., East China Univ. 2005, Jilin Univ. 2012; hon. lecturer at numerous int. univs; Hon. FRSE; Hon. FRSC; Hon. DSc (Birmingham) 2005, (Twente) 2006, (Sheffield) 2008, (Trinity Coll. Dublin) 2009, (St Andrews) 2010; numerous awards, including Univ. of Edinburgh Hope Prize in Chem. 1964, Humboldt Fellowship 1998, Izatt-Christensen Award 1993, ACS Cope Scholar Award 1999, UCLA Herbert Newby McCoy Award 2000, Nagoya Gold Medal 2004, Univ. of Edinburgh Alumnus of the Year 2005, AAAS Fellowship 2005, King Faisal Int. Prize 2007, Albert Einstein World Prize 2007, Tetrahedron Prize for Creativity 2007, Feynman Prize 2007, ACS Arthur C. Cope Award 2008, Davy Medal, Royal Soc. 2008, Royal Medal, Royal Soc. of Edinburgh 2010, Int. Soc. for Nanoscale Science, Computation, and Eng Award, Foundations of Nanoscience (FNANO) 2010, Undergraduate Chem. Council Teacher of the Year, Northwestern Univ. 2011, Distinguished Citizen Award, Illinois St Andrews Soc. 2012. *Publications:* more than 1,000 publs in scientific journals. *Address:* Department of Chemistry, Northwestern University, 2145 Sheridan Road, Evanston, IL 60208-3113, USA (office). *Telephone:* (847) 491-3793 (office). *Fax:* (847) 491-1009 (office). *E-mail:* stoddart@northwestern.edu (office). *Website:* stoddart.northwestern.edu (office).

STOFILE, Rev. Makhenkesi Arnold, MA, MTheol; South African academic, politician and diplomatist; *Ambassador to Germany;* b. 27 Dec. 1944, Winterburg, Adelaide Dist, Eastern Cape; s. of Simon Stofile and Miriam Stofile; m. Nambita Stofile 1977; two s. (deceased) two d.; ed Univ. of Fort Hare, Princeton Univ., USA; worked as farm labourer and machine operator 1965–68; part-time tutor with African Ind. Churches Asscn Seminary 1971–72; Sr Lecturer in Theology and Philosophy, Univ. of Fort Hare 1973–86; convicted under Ciskeian Internal Security Act and sentenced to 11 years imprisonment 1987; Sr Lecturer in Theology, Univ. of Transkei 1991; MP 1994–96, (Govt Chief Whip 1994–96), 2004–; ANC Treas. Gen. 1995–97; Premier of Eastern Cape 1997–2004; Minister of Sport and Recreation 2004–10; Amb. to Germany 2011–; Dr hc (Univ. of Port Elizabeth) 2000. *Achievement:* (with wife) Ballroom Dancing Champions for Black S African Univs. *Leisure interests:* rugby, boxing. *Address:* Embassy of South Africa, Tiergartenstr. 18, 10785, Berlin, Germany (office); 143 Queens Road, King Williams Town 5600, South Africa (home). *Telephone:* (30) 220730 (office). *Fax:* (30) 22073190 (office). *E-mail:* berlin.info@foreign.gov.za (office); Nobulali1@sport1.pwv.gov.za (office). *Website:* www.suedafrika.org (office).

STOIBER, Edmund, DJur; German lawyer and politician; b. 1941, Oberaudorf; m. Karin Stoiber; three c.; ed Univ. of Munich and Hochschule für Politische Wissenschaft; personal counsellor to Bavarian State Minister for Devt 1972–74, Dir of Ministerial Office 1974; entered Bavarian Parl. 1974; admitted socialist 1978; Gen. Sec. Christian Social Union (CSU) 1978–83, Chair. CSU 1999–2007, Hon. Chair. 2007–; Campaign Man. for Franz Josef Strauss, Fed. Elections 1980; State Sec. and Dir Bavarian State Chancellery 1982–86, State Minister and Dir 1986–88; Bavarian State Minister for Internal Affairs 1988–93, Minister-Pres. of Bavaria 1993–2007; Chair, EU High Level Group of Independent Stakeholders on Admin. Burdens 2007–12; cand. in Chancellery elections 2002; mem. Bd Bayern Munich (football team); Bayerischer Verdienstorden 1984, Grosses Bundesverdienstkreuz mit Stern und Schulterband 1999, Grosskreuz des Verdienstordens der Bundesrepublik Deutschland 2004, Verdienstorden des Landes Baden-Württemberg 2009. *Publications:* Politik aus Bayern 1976, Der Hausfriedensbruch im Licht akt. Probleme 1984. *Leisure interests:* skiing, football. *Address:* Wagmüllerstraße 18, 80538 Munich, Germany. *E-mail:* info@stoiber.de. *Website:* www.stoiber.de.

STOKER, Richard, FRAM, ARAM, ARCM; British composer, actor, conductor, writer and poet and painter; b. 8 Nov. 1938, Castleford, Yorks., England; s. of Bower Morrell Stoker and Winifred Stoker; m. Gillian Patricia Watson 1986; ed Breadalbane House School, Castleford, Univ. of Huddersfield with Harold Truscott, Coll. of Art, Royal Acad. of Music and Drama, composition with Sir Lennox Berkeley, conducting with Maurice Miles, pvt. study with Nadia Boulanger in Paris (Mendelssohn Scholarship), Arthur Benjamin, Eric Fenby, Benjamin Britten; performance debut with BBC Home Service 1953, Nat. and Int. Eisteddfods, Wales 1955–58; conducting debut 1956; Asst Librarian, London Symphony Orchestra 1962–63; Prof. of Composition, RAM 1963–87 (tutor 1970–80); composition teacher, St Paul's School 1972–74, Magdalene Coll., Cambridge 1974–76; Ed. The Composer magazine 1969–80; Magistrate, Inner London Comm. 1995–2003, Crown Court 1998–2003; Adjudicator, Royal Philharmonic Soc. Composer's Award, Cyprus Orchestral Composer's Award from the Ministry of Culture 2001–, BBC Composer's Awards; mem. Composers' Guild 1962– (mem. exec. cttee 1969–80); Founder mem. RAM Guild Cttee 1994– (Hon. Treas. 1995–); Founder mem. European-Atlantic Group 1993–; mem. Byron Soc. 1993–2000, Magistrates' Asscn 1995–2003, English and Int. PEN 1996–2005; mem. and Treas. Steering Cttee Lewisham Arts Festival 1990, 1992; Founder mem. Atlantic Council 1993, RSL, Creative Rights Alliance 2001–; concert appearances as pianist including Queen Elizabeth Hall, Purcell Room, Leighton House, RAM, Pizza on the Park, Barnet Festival; mem. RAM Guild; BBC Music Award 1952, Eric Coates Award 1962, Dove Prize 1962, Nat. Library of Poetry (USA) Editors' Choice Award 1995, 1996, 1997. *Compositions include:* four symphonies 1961, 1976, 1981, 1991; 12 nocturnes; two jazz preludes; overtures: Antic Hay, Feast of Fools, Heroic Overture; three string quartets, three violin sonatas, Partita for Violin and Harp or Piano, Sonatina for Guitar, two piano sonatas, three piano trios, A York Suite for piano, Piano Variations, Piano Concerto, Partita for Clarinet and Piano, Wind Quintet; organ works: Partita, Little Organ Book, Three Improvisations, Symphony; Monologue, Passacaglia, Serenade, Petite Suite, Nocturnal, Festival Suite; choral works and song cycles: Benedictus, Ecce Homo, Proverb, Psalms, Make Me a Willow Cabin, Canticle of the Rose, O Be Joyful, A Landscape of Truth; piano works: Zodiac Variations, Regency Suite, A Poet's Notebook; vocal works: Music That Brings Sweet Sleep, Aspects of Flight, Four Yeats Songs, Four Shakespeare Songs, Johnson Preserv'd (three-act opera), Thérèse Raquin (in preparation), Chinese Canticle, Birthday of the Infanta; music for film and stage includes Troilus and Cressida, Portrait of a Town, Garden Party, My Friend – My Enemy. *Recordings:* appearances on numerous CDs and records. *Films:* appearances include Red Mercury Rising, Woken, Daddy's Girl, Portrait of a Town, Lear and Goneril, The Shrink, Bedtime Story, The Usual, The End of the Line, The Queen, The Da Vinci Code, Ancient Cataclysms, Vagabond Shoes, Encounter, Bouquet, Interval, Home Guard Ron,

Pirates of the Caribbean IV. *Television:* Mary Tudor (four-part series), Comment (Channel 4), Europe, Dirty Weekend in Hospital, Happiness (BBC), Troilus and Cressida. *Radio:* interviews and discussions on BBC Radio 3, 4, World Service, Radio Leeds, New York Times Radio, Radio New York, Wall Street Radio, Radio Algonquin. *Publications include:* Portrait of a Town 1970, Words Without Music 1974, Strolling Players 1978, Open Window – Open Door (autobiog.) 1985, Tanglewood (novel) 1990, Between the Lines 1991, Diva (novel) 1992, Collected Short Stories 1993, Sir Thomas Armstrong: A Celebration 1998, Turn Back the Clock 1998, A Passage of Time 1999; contrib. to anthologies, including Triumph, Forward, Outposts, Spotlight, Strolling Players, American Poetry Soc. publs, reviews and articles for periodicals, including Records and Recording, Books and Bookmen, Guardian, Performance, The Magistrate, poems in numerous anthologies and internet publs; contrib. to Oxford Dictionary of Nat. Biography (nine entries) 2004, 2006 (adviser 2003–). *Leisure interests:* squash, skiing, tennis, swimming, yoga, golf, windsurfing, judo. *Telephone:* 7906-843812 (mobile). *E-mail:* r_stoker@btinternet.com. *Website:* www.richardstoker.co.uk.

STOKES, Kerry Matthew, AC, FAIM; Australian business executive; *Chairman, Seven Network Ltd;* b. 13 Sept. 1940, Vic.; s. of M. P. Stokes; m. 2nd Christine Simpson 2003; two s.; ed St George's CBC, Western Australia Tech. Coll.; Chair. Australian Capital Equity Pty Ltd (Dir 1981–), Austrim Ltd, Golden West Network (TV), Westrac Equipment Pty Ltd; Chair. Canberra Theatre Trust 1981–86, Dir 1989–91; Chair. Art Gallery Foundation, WA 1989–91; Chair. The Fed. Capital Press Pty Ltd (Canberra Times), Seven Network Ltd 1995–, Chair. Seven Network Ltd 1995–99, Exec. Chair. 1999–; Dir 1989–91; Pres. Appeal Campaign for Inst. for Child Health Research; Founder-mem. Council Nat. Gallery of Australia, Chair. 1996–2000; Hon. Life Mem. RSL Australia 1993–, Hon. Fellow, Murdoch Univ. 2000; WA Citizen of the Year Award 1994, Centenary Medal 2003, Western Australia's Australian of the Year 2012. *Publications:* Boyer Lectures (Advance Australia Where) 1994, Andrew Olle Memorial Lecture 2001. *Leisure interests:* photography, sailing, scuba diving. *Address:* Seven Network Ltd, Wharf 17, Pirrama Road, Pyrmont, NSW 2009 (office); c/o Australian Capital Equity Pty Ltd, Level 3, 30 Kings Park Road, West Perth, WA 6005, Australia. *Telephone:* (2) 87777102 (office). *Fax:* (2) 87777149 (office). *Website:* www.yahoo!7.com.au (office).

STOKES, Patrick T., BS, MBA; American brewery industry executive; *Chairman, Anheuser-Busch Companies, Inc.;* b. 11 Aug. 1942, Washington, DC; m. Anna-Kristina Stokes; ed Boston Coll., Columbia Univ.; Financial Analyst, Shell Oil Co. 1966–67; began career in corp. planning, Anheuser-Busch 1969, held various positions including mem. Policy Cttee 1974, Vice-Pres. Raw Materials Acquisition 1976–81, Vice-Pres. and Group Exec. 1981–86; COO Campbell Taggert Inc. (subsidiary), Dallas 1986–90, CEO 1990–2002; Sr Exec. Vice-Pres. Anheuser-Busch Cos Inc. 2000–02, Pres. and CEO 2002–06, Chair. 2006–, Pres. Anheuser-Busch Int. Inc. 1990–99. *Address:* Anheuser-Busch Companies, Inc., 1 Busch Place, St Louis, MO 63118, USA (office). *Telephone:* (314) 577-2000 (office). *Fax:* (314) 577-2900 (office). *Website:* www.anheuser-busch.com (office).

STOL, Marten; Dutch academic; *Professor Emeritus of Akkadian (Assyriology), Ugaritic and History of Ancient Near East, Free University of Amsterdam;* b. 10 Nov. 1940, Oldekerk; m. Rose C. van Wyngaarden 1968; one s. one d.; ed Gymnasium, Middelburg and Univ. of Leiden; Research Assoc., Univ. Leiden 1968–70, Asst Prof. 1970–82; Research Assoc., Chicago Assyrian Dictionary, Oriental Inst., Univ. of Chicago 1973–74; Prof. of Akkadian (Assyriology), Ugaritic and History of Ancient Near East, Free Univ. Amsterdam 1983–2005, Prof. Emer. 2005–; Sr Researcher, Nederlands Instituut voor het Nabije Oosten, Leiden 2006–; Gen. Sec., Soc. Ex Oriente Lux 1973–99; mem. Royal Netherlands Acad.; Hon. mem., American Oriental Soc. 1999, Ex Oriente Lux 2003. *Publications:* Studies in Old Babylonian History 1976, On Trees, Mountains and Millstones in the Ancient Near East 1979, Letters from Yale 1981, Letters from Collections in Philadelphia, Chicago and Berkeley 1986, Epilepsy in Babylonia 1993, Langs's Heeren wegen 1997, Birth in Babylonia and the Bible 2000, Die Altbabylonische Zeit 2004, Vrouwen van Babylon 2012. *Address:* Heivlinder 27, 2317 JS Leiden, Netherlands.

STOLER, Andrew L., BS, MBA; American/Australian international organization official and academic; b. 20 Aug. 1951; ed George Washington Univ., Georgetown Univ.'s School of Foreign Service; with Office of Int. Trade Policy, US Dept of Commerce, Washington, DC 1975–79; Dir for Canada, Australia and NZ, US Trade Rep. Office 1980–81, MTN Codes Co-ordinator, Geneva 1982–87, Deputy Asst US Trade Rep. for Europe and the Mediterranean, Washington, DC 1988–89, Deputy Chief of Mission, Geneva 1989–99 (concurrently Deputy Perm. Rep. to WTO); Deputy Dir-Gen. WTO 1999–2002; Exec. Dir Inst. for Int. Trade, Univ. of Adelaide, Australia 2002–11, also Adjunct Prof. of Int. Trade; mem. Aid Advisory Council (Australia) 2004–, Advisory Cttee of Shanghai WTO Affairs Consultation Centre; Sr Advisor, Shenzhen WTO Affairs Centre; Assoc. Commr, Australian Productivity Comm. 2009–10; *Telephone:* 41-2586063 (mobile). *E-mail:* andrewlstoler@gmail.com.

STOLFI, Fiorenzo; San Marino lawyer and politician; b. 11 March 1956; m. Luana Dorina Console; two s.; ed Univ. degli Studi di Urbino; mem. San Marino Socialist Party 1978–, fmr Vice-Pres. and Sec.-Gen.; mem. Great Council of San Marino (Parl.) 1983–, Chair. 2003–06; Sec. of State for Tourism, Commerce, Sport and Agric. 1983–86, for Industry, Handicrafts and Econ. Co-operation 1992–2000, for Internal Affairs, Posts and Telecommunications, Home Affairs and Civil Defence 2001–02, for Finance and the Budget, Transport and Relations with the Azienda Autonoma di Stato Filatelica e Numismatica (AASFN) June–Dec. 2002, for Foreign and Political Affairs, Planning and Econ. Co-operation Dec. 2002–03, for Foreign Affairs, Political Affairs and Econ. Planning 2006–08; Vice-Gov. IMF for San Marino 1993–2000, Gov. 2002–03; Gov. World Bank for San Marino 2001–02. *Address:* c/o Secretariat of State for Foreign and Political Affairs, Planning and Economic Co-operation, Palazzo Begni, Contrada Omerelli, 47890 San Marino (office).

STOLKER, Carel J. J. M., PhD; Dutch judge, academic and university administrator; *Rector Magnificus and President, University of Leiden;* b. 23 June 1954, Leiden; ed Univ. of Leiden; taught liability law at Hastings School of Law, Univ. of California, San Francisco, USA; published regularly on issues relating to liability law, in co-operation with Hastings' colleague David Levine; mem. Faculty, Civil Law Dept, Univ. of Leiden, Vice-Dean for Research 2000–05, Dean of the Law

School 2005–11, Rector Magnificus and Pres. Univ. of Leiden 2013–; mem. Chief Editorial Staff, Tekst & Commentaar series; Ed.-in-Chief Onrechtmatige Daad (Negligence); has served in numerous public posts, including as mem. of two nat. audit cttees of the Dutch Judiciary 2005, Co-Chair. 2010; Deputy Judge, Court of Haarlem; Deputy Justice, Court of Appeal of 's-Hertogenbosch. *Publications include:* dissertation (published as a book) on the liability of medical doctors, in particular in wrongful birth cases 1988, a study on medical liability crisis in USA 1989, vol. on Dutch Civil Code (ed.); numerous publs on private law and comparative law. *Address:* Office of the Rektor, A.2.05, The Old Library, University of Leiden, Rapenburg 70, PO Box 9500, 2311 EZ Leiden, Netherlands (office). *Telephone:* (71) 527-31-43 (office). *E-mail:* cjjmstolker@cvb.leidenuniv.nl (office). *Website:* www.leidenuniv.nl (office).

STOLL, Jean-François; French civil servant; *Head of General Treasury Office (Yvelines departement);* b. 19 Jan. 1950, Isle-Adam; m. Noëlle Nicolas 1976; four c.; ed Institut des Etudes politiques, Paris, Ecole Nat. d'Admin; joined Ministry of Econ., Commercial Attaché Indonesia 1982–84, Tech. Adviser 1982–86, Commercial Adviser Mexico 1987–90, Tech. Adviser for Int. Affairs, Office of the Prime Minister 1990–93, Head Service for Promotion of External Trade 1993, Dir External Econ. Relations Dept 1998–2003; Head, Gen. Treasury Office (Seine-Saint-Denis departement) 2003–11, (Yvelines departement) 2011–; Dir Electricité de France (EDF) 1999–2003; Chevalier, Ordre Nat. du Mérite. *Address:* Préfecture des Yvelines, 1 rue Jean Houdon, 78010 Versailles Cedex (office); 6 rue d'Ulm, 75005 Paris, France (home). *Telephone:* 1-39-49-78-00 (office); 1-48-96-60-01 (home). *E-mail:* pref-communication78@yvelines.gouv.fr (office). *Website:* www.minefi.gouv.fr (office).

STOLLEY, Paul David, MD, MPH; American physician and professor of medicine; b. 17 June 1937, Pawling, New York; s. of Herman Stolley and Rosalie Chertock; m. Jo Ann Goldenberg 1959; one s. two d.; ed Lafayette Coll., Cornell Univ. Medical School and Johns Hopkins School of Public Health; medical officer, US Public Health Service 1964–67; Asst and Assoc. Prof. of Epidemiology, Johns Hopkins School of Public Health 1968–76; Herbert C. Rorer Prof. of Medical Science, Univ. of Pennsylvania School of Medicine 1976–90; Prof. and Chair. Dept of Epidemiology, Univ. of Maryland 1991–99, currently Prof. Emer.; fmr mem. Editorial Bd New England Journal, Milbank Quarterly; fmr Assoc. Ed. Clinical Pharmacology and Therapeutics; Pres. American Coll. of Epidemiology 1987–88; mem. Inst. of Medicine, NAS, Soc. for Epidemiologic Research (Pres. 1984), Int. Epidemiology Asscn (fmr Treas.), Johns Hopkins Soc. of Scholars, Science Advisory Cttee to Fed. Drugs. Admin. Commr 1993; Hon. MA (Pennsylvania) 1976. *Publications include:* Case Control Studies (co-author) 1982, Foundations of Epidemiology (co-author) 1994, Epidemiology 1994, Investigating Disease Patterns 1995 (received American Medical Writers Asscn Award 1996) and numerous articles on epidemiological subjects. *Leisure interests:* classical music, history, literature.

STOLOJAN, Theodor Dumitru, PhD, DEcon; Romanian economist and politician; b. 24 Oct. 1943, Tîrgoviste; s. of Theodor Stolojan and Nadejda Stolojan; m. Elena Stolojan; one s. one d.; ed Acad. of Econ. Studies, Coll. of Finances, Credit and Accountancy, Bucharest; worked as economist, Ministry of the Food Industry 1966–72; first as economist and then as Chief of Division, State Budget Dept, Ministry of Finance 1972–82, then Deputy Dir, Dir of Dept Foreign Currencies and Int. Financial Relations 1982–87, Gen. Insp. Dept of State Revenues 1988–89, First Deputy Minister of Finance 1989–90, Minister of Finance 1990–91; Pres. of Nat. Agency of Privatization –1991; Prime Minister of Romania 1991–92; Economist, later Sr Economist, IBRD 1992–98; Pres. Tofan Corporated Finance 1999–2000; Pnr, Strategic Consulting Ltd; Prof., Univ. of Transylvania, Braşov 2002–; Pres. Nat. Liberal Party 2002–04; Adviser to the Pres. 2004–06; Co-founder and Chair. Liberal Democratic Party (Partidul Liberal Democrat) 2006–07, First Vice-Chair. 2008–; MEP 2007–, mem. European People's Party (Christian Democrats) and European Democrats; apptd Prime Minister by Pres. of Romania 10 Dec. 2008, withdrew acceptance 15 Dec.; mem. Bd of Dirs Romanian-American Investment Fund, Bucharest; mem. Int. Inst. of Public Finance 1978–. *Publications:* Integration and European Fiscal Policy 2002; numerous studies. *Leisure interests:* skiing, travelling in mountains, jogging. *Address:* European Parliament, Bât. Willy Brandt 04M121, 60, rue Wiertz, 1047 Brussels, Belgium (office); Liberal Democratic Party (Partidul Liberal Democrat), Bucharest (office); Aurel Vlaicu 42-44, Apt 3, Sector 2, Bucharest, Romania. *Telephone:* (2) 284-56-70 (office). *Fax:* (2) 284-96-70 (office). *Website:* www.europarl.europa.eu (office).

STOLPE, Manfred; German politician; b. 16 May 1936, Stettin, Germany (now Szczecin, Poland); m. Ingrid Ehrhardt; one d.; legal studies in Jena and Berlin; fmly in charge of organizational work of Protestant Church in East Germany; Consistorial Pres. Berlin-Brandenburg Church 1982–90; active in human rights movt; joined SPD 1990; Minister-Pres. of Brandenburg 1990–2002; Fed. Minister of Transport, Building and Housing 2002–05; Order of Merit of the State of Brandenburg 2006; Dr hc (Univ. of Dokkyo, Japan) 1989, (Ernst-Moritz-Arndt Univ., Greifswald) 1989, (Univ. of Zürich) 1991, (Univ. of Szczecin) 1996; Carlo-Schmid Prize 1991. *Address:* c/o Sozialdemokratische Partei Deutschlands, Wilhelmstr. 141, 10963 Berlin, Germany.

STOLPER, Edward M., AB, MPhil, PhD; American geologist, academic and university administrator; *Interim President, California Institute of Technology;* b. 16 Dec. 1952; m. 1973; ed Harvard Coll., Univ. of Edinburgh, UK, Harvard Univ.; Asst Prof. of Geology, California Inst. of Tech. 1979–82, Assoc. Prof. 1982–83, Prof. 1983–, named William E. Leonhard Prof. of Geology 1990, Chair. Div. of Geological and Planetary Sciences 1994–2004, Interim Provost 2004, Provost 2007–, Interim Pres. 2013–; Scholar, QRI (Quantum Resevoir Impact); Bateman Visiting Scholar, Yale Univ. 1988, 2005; Miller Visiting Research Prof., Univ. of California, Berkeley 1990; Fellow, American Acad. of Arts and Sciences, Geological Soc. of America, Geochemical Soc., European Asscn for Geochemistry, Mineralogical Soc. of America, American Geophysical Union, Meteoritical Soc.; mem. NAS, Mineralogical Soc. of America, Academia Europaea, Royal Soc. of London; Dr hc (Univ. of Edinburgh) 2008, (Hebrew Univ. of Jerusalem) 2012; Newcomb Cleveland Prize, American AAAS 1984, F.W. Clarke Medal, Geochemical Soc. 1985, James B. Macelwane Award, American Geophysical Union 1986, Arthur Holmes Medal, European Union of Geosciences 1997, Arthur L. Day Medal, Geological Soc. of America 2004, V.M. Goldschmidt Medal, Geochemical Soc. 2012. *Publications:*

numerous papers in professional journals on the origin and evolution of igneous rocks on the earth and other planets. *Address:* Office of the President, California Institute of Technology, 1200 East California Blvd, M/C 204-31, Pasadena, CA 91125, USA (office). *Telephone:* (626) 395-6301 (office). *Fax:* (626) 449-9374 (office). *Website:* president.caltech.edu (office); provost.caltech.edu (office).

STOLTE, Dieter; German business executive, newspaper publisher and academic; *Chairman of the Supervisory Board, Ströer Out-of-Home Media AG;* b. 18 Sept. 1934, Cologne; ed Univs of Tübingen and Mainz; Head of Science Dept, Saarländischer Rundfunk 1961–62; Personal adviser to Dir-Gen. of Zweites Deutsches Fernsehen (ZDF) 1962, Controller, Programme Planning Dept 1967, Programming Dir 1976–82, Dir-Gen. ZDF March 1982–2002; Publisher, Die Welt and Berliner Morgenpost (newspapers) 2002–05; mem. Supervisory Bd Ströer Out-of-Home Media AG, Cologne 2002–, currently Chair.; Dir and Deputy Dir Gen., Südwestfunk 1973; Prof., Univ. of Music and Presentation Arts, Hamburg 1980–; mem. Admin. Council, German Press Agency (dpa), Hamburg, European Broadcasting Union (EBU); Chair. Admin. Council TransTel, Cologne; Chair. DeutschlandRadio, Cologne; mem. Bd of Dirs Axel Springer Foundation 2004–; mem. Int. Broadcast Inst., London; mem. Council, Nat. Acad. of TV Arts, New York, Int. Acad. of Arts and Sciences, New York; Hon. Citizen of State of Tenn., USA; Bundesverdienstkreuz, Officer's Cross, Golden Order of Merit (Austria), Bavarian Order of Merit; Int. Emmy Directorate Award 1997, Köckritz Prize 1998, Verdienstorden, Berlin 1999, Robert Geissendorfer Prize 2001. *Publications:* ed. and co-author of several books on programme concepts and function of television, etc.; several essays on subjects relating to the philosophy of culture and the science of communication. *Address:* Office of the Chairman of the Supervisory Board, Ströer Out-of-Home Media AG, Ströer Allee 1, 50999 Cologne, Germany (office). *E-mail:* ir@stroeer.de (office). *Website:* www.stroeer.com (office).

STOLTENBERG, Jens; Norwegian politician and international organization official; *Secretary-General designate, NATO;* b. 16 March 1959, Oslo; m. Ingrid Schulerud; two c.; ed Univ. of Oslo; journalist, Arbeiderbladet (nat. daily) 1979–81; Information Sec., Oslo Labour Party 1981; Exec. Officer, Statistics Norway 1989–90; Lecturer in Econs, Univ. of Oslo 1989–90; mem. Cen. Bd, Labour Youth League (AUF) 1979–89, Leader, AUF 1985–89; Vice-Pres. Int. Union of Socialist Youth 1985–89; mem. Cen. Bd, Norwegian Labour Party (Arbeiderpartiet) 1985–, Leader Oslo Labour Party 1990–92, Deputy Leader Labour Party 1992–2002, Leader 2002–14; Deputy mem. Storting (Parl.) 1989–93, mem. for Oslo 1993–; mem. Standing Cttee Social Afairs 1991–93, on Oil and Energy Affairs 1997–2000, on Foreign Affairs 2001–05; Sec., Ministry of Environment 1990–91; Minister of Trade and Energy 1993–96, of Finance 1996–97; Prime Minister of Norway 2000–01, 2005–13; Sec.-Gen. designate NATO, Brussels Oct. 2014–; Head, Govt Comm. on Male Roles 1986; mem. Norwegian Defence Comm. 1990–92; mem. Bd Global Vaccine Fund 2001–05; apptd UN Special Envoy on Climate Change 2013. *Address:* Office of the Secretary-General, NATO, Blvd Léopold III, 1110 Brussels, Belgium (office). *Telephone:* (2) 707-41-11 (office). *Fax:* (2) 707-45-79 (office). *E-mail:* natodoc@hq.nato.int (office). *Website:* www.nato.int (office).

STOLTENBERG, Thorvald; Norwegian politician and diplomatist; b. 8 July 1931, Oslo; s. of Emil Stoltenberg and Ingeborg Stoltenberg; m. Karin Stoltenberg 1957; one s. two d.; joined Foreign Service 1959; served in San Francisco, Belgrade, Lagos and Foreign Ministry; Int. Sec. Norwegian Fed. of Trade Unions 1970–71; Under-Sec. of State, Foreign Ministry 1971–72, 1976–79; Under-Sec. of State, Ministry of Defence 1973–74, Ministry of Commerce 1974–76; Minister of Defence 1979–81, of Foreign Affairs 1987–89, 1990–93; Amb. to UN, New York 1989–90; UN High Commr for Refugees 1989–90; Special Rep. for UN Sec.-Gen. in fmr Yugoslavia 1993–94; Co-Chair. Steering Cttee, Int. Conf. on the Fmr Yugoslavia 1993–96; Amb. to Denmark 1996–99; Pres. Norwegian Red Cross 1999–2008; Chair. Bd of Int. Inst. for Democracy and Electoral Assistance 2003. *Address:* c/o Norwegian Red Cross, PO Box 1, Groenland, 0133 Oslo, Norway (office).

STONE, (Isaac) 'Biz'; American internet company executive; *Co-founder and Creative Director, Twitter Inc.;* b. 10 March 1974; m. Livia Stone; ed Wellesley High School, Northeastern Univ., Univ. of Massachusetts; Designer, Little, Brown and Co. 1994–97; Creative Dir Xanga Inc. 1999–2001; Sr Specialist, Google Inc. 2003–05; Dir Community Odeo Inc. 2005–06; Co-founder (with Jack Dorsey) Obvious Corpn 2006 (spun off Twitter Inc. 2006), Twitter Inc., San Francisco 2007, Creative Dir 2007–; strategic adviser for social impact, Huffington Post 2011–; named one of The World's Most Influential People, TIME magazine 2009, 40 Under 40 Rising Stars, Fortune magazine 2009. *Publications:* Blogging: Genius Strategies for Instant Web Content 2002, Who Let the Blogs Out? 2004. *Address:* Twitter Inc., 539 Bryant St, Suite 402, San Francisco, CA 94107, USA (office). *Telephone:* (415) 896-2008 (office). *Website:* twitter.com (office); www.bizstone.com (office).

STONE, John Owen, BA (Hons), BSc (Hons); Australian politician, financial executive, public servant and columnist; b. 31 Jan. 1929, Perth; s. of Horace Stone and Eva Stone (née Hunt); m. Nancy Hardwick 1954; four s. one d.; ed Univ. of Western Australia and New Coll., Oxford, UK; Rhodes Scholar 1951; Asst to Australian Treasury Rep. in London 1954–56, Australian Treasury Rep. in London 1958–61; in Research and Information Div., Gen. Financial and Econ. Policy Br., Dept of Treasury, Canberra 1956–57, in Home Finance Div. 1961–62, Asst Sec. Econ. and Financial Surveys Div. 1962–66; Exec. Dir for Australia, New Zealand and South Africa, IMF and IBRD 1967–70, for Swaziland and Lesotho, IMF 1969–70; First Asst Sec., Revenue, Loans and Investment Div., Treasury 1971; Sec., Australian Loan Council; Sec., Australian Nat. Debt Comm. 1971; Deputy Sec. (Econ.), Treasury 1971–76, Deputy Sec. Treasury 1976–78, Sec. 1979–84; Visiting Prof., Centre of Policy Studies, Monash Univ., Melbourne 1984; consultant, Potter Partners, Stockbrokers 1985–87; weekly columnist, Melbourne Herald, Sydney Morning Herald 1985–87, The Australian 1987–89, Sunday Telegraph 1989, The Australian Financial Review 1990–98, Adelaide Review 1998–2003; regular contrib. to National Observer quarterly 2002–09, Quadrant Magazine 1985–2013; Ed. and Publr Proceedings of The Samuel Griffith Soc. 1992–2010; Dir Sperry (Australia) Ltd 1985–87, Peko-Wallsend Ltd 1986–87; Chair. J.T. Campbell & Co. Ltd 1994–96; Senator for Queensland, Leader of Nat. Party in the Senate and Shadow Minister for Finance 1987–90; mem. Defence Efficiency Review 1996–97; Sr Fellow, Inst. of Public Affairs, Melbourne 1985–87, 1990–95; Fellow, Acad. of the Social Sciences of Australia 1976–81 (resgnd); mem. Mont Pelerin Soc.

2008–; James Webb Medley Prize, Univ. of Oxford 1953. *Publications include:* Upholding the Australian Constitution, Proceedings of The Samuel Griffith Society (vols 1–21) 1992–2009 (Ed. and Publr). *Leisure interests:* reading, wine and food. *Address:* 17 Fitzsimmons Avenue, Lane Cove, NSW 2066, Australia. *Telephone:* (2) 9428-1311. *Fax:* (2) 9420-0063. *E-mail:* j_o_stone@bigpond.com.

STONE, Matthew (Matt) Richard; American screenwriter, film director and producer; b. 26 May 1971, Houston, Tex.; s. of the late Gerald Whitney Stone, Jr and of Sheila Lois Belasco; m. Angela Howard; one s.; collaborated with Trey Parker on short animation, Jesus vs Frosty 1992, later remade as animated Christmas card for FoxLab, titled The Spirit of Christmas 1995; Co-creator and Exec. Producer, South Park animation (with Trey Parker) 1997–, and other films and TV series. *Films include:* Jesus vs Frosty (writer, dir) 1992, Your Studio and You (writer) 1995, The Spirit of Christmas (writer, dir) 1995, Alferd Packer: The Musical (aka Cannibal! The Musical) (writer, producer) 1996, Orgazmo (writer, dir, producer) 1997, South Park: Bigger Longer & Uncut (writer, producer) (Los Angeles Film Critics Award, New York Film Critics Award, MTV Movie Award) 1999, How's Your News? (exec. producer) 1999, Team America: World Police (writer, producer) 2004. *Television includes:* South Park (series writer, producer) 1997–, That's My Bush! (series writer, producer) 2001, Kenny vs. Spenny (producer) 2007. *Film appearances include:* BASEketball 1998, provides voices for many characters in his animation films and television series. *Recordings include:* albums: Chef Aid: The South Park Album, South Park: Bigger, Longer and Uncut (soundtrack), Mr Hankey's Christmas Classics, Timmy and the Lords of the Underworld, The Book of Mormon (Grammy Award for Best Musical Theater Album 2012) 2011. *Play:* Book of Mormon (Tony Award for Best Musical 2011, WhatsOnStage Award for Best New Musical 2014, Olivier Award for Best New Musical 2014) 2011. *Address:* c/o Paramount Studios, 5555 Melrose Avenue, Hollywood, CA 90038, USA. *E-mail:* news@southparkstudios.com. *Website:* www.southparkstudios.com.

STONE, Norman, MA; British historian and academic; *Professor of International Relations and Director, Center for Russian Studies, Bilkent University;* b. 8 March 1941, Glasgow; s. of the late Norman Stone and Mary Robertson Stone (née Pettigrew); m. 1st Marie-Nicole Aubry 1966 (dissolved 1977); two s.; m. 2nd Christine Booker (née Verity) 1982; one s.; ed Glasgow Acad. and Gonville & Caius Coll., Cambridge; research student, Christ's Coll., Cambridge attached to Austrian and Hungarian insts 1962–65; Research Fellow, Gonville & Caius Coll. 1965–67; Asst Lecturer, Faculty of History, Univ. of Cambridge 1967–72, lecturer in History (Russian) 1973–84; Fellow, Jesus Coll., Cambridge and Dir of Studies in History 1971–79; Fellow, Trinity Coll. Cambridge 1979–84; Prof. of Modern History, Univ. of Oxford and Fellow, Worcester Coll. Oxford 1984–97; Prof. of Int. Relations, Bilkent Univ., Ankara 1997–, also Dir Center for Russian Studies; Order of Merit (Poland) 1993; Wolfson Prize 1976. *Publications:* The Eastern Front 1914–17 1976, Hitler 1980, Europe Transformed 1878–1919 1982, Czechoslovakia: Crossroads and Crises (Ed.) 1989, The Other Russia (with Michael Glenny) 1990, World War One 2009, The Atlantic and Its Enemies: A Personal History of the Cold War 2010, articles in the press. *Leisure interests:* music, Eastern Europe, languages, Turkey. *Address:* Center for Russian Studies, Department of International Relations, Bilkent University, 06800 Bilkent, Ankara, Turkey (office); 22 St Margaret's Road, Oxford, OX2 6RX England (home). *Telephone:* (312) 2901249 (office); (1865) 439481 (home). *Fax:* (312) 2664326 (office). *E-mail:* CRS@bilkent.edu.tr (office). *Website:* www.bilkent.edu.tr/~crs (office).

STONE, Oliver, BFA; American film director, producer and screenwriter; b. 15 Sept. 1946, New York; s. of Louis Stone and Jacqueline Goddet; m. 1st Najwa Sarkis (divorced); m. 2nd Elizabeth Stone (divorced); m. 3rd Sun-jung Jung 1996; ed Yale Univ. and New York Univ. Film School; teacher, Cholon, Viet Nam 1965–66; US Merchant Marine 1966, US Army, Viet Nam 1967–68. *Films include:* Writer: Midnight Express (Acad. Award for best screenplay adapted from another medium) 1978, Conan the Barbarian 1982, Scarface 1983; Writer and Dir: Seizure 1973, The Hand 1981, Year of the Dragon (with Michael Cimino) 1985, Salvador (co-writer) 1986, Platoon (Acad. Award for Best Film and Best Dir) 1986, Wall Street 1987, Talk Radio (co-writer) 1988, Born on the Fourth of July (Acad. Award for Best Dir 1990) 1989, No One Here Gets Out Alive 1990, The Doors 1991, JFK 1991, Heaven and Earth 1993, Natural Born Killers 1994, Nixon 1995, A Child's Night Dream 1997, U-Turn 1998, Saviour 1998; Producer: Reversal of Fortune, Iron Maze, South Central, Zebrahead, Wild Palms (TV series) 1993, New Age 1994, The People vs Larry Flynt; Writer, Dir and Producer: Any Given Sunday 2000, Comandante (documentary) 2003, Alexander 2004, World Trade Center 2006, South of the Border 2009, Wall Street: Money Never Sleeps 2010; as director: W. 2008, Savages 2012. *Address:* Ixtlan Productions, 12233 West Olympic Blvd, Suite 322, Los Angeles, CA 90064, USA (office). *Telephone:* (310) 826-7080 (office). *Fax:* (310) 826-7090 (office).

STONE, Roger W.; BS (Econ); American business executive; *CEO and Chairman, KapStone Paper and Packaging Corporation;* b. 16 Feb. 1935, Chicago, Ill.; s. of Marvin Stone and Anita Masover; m. Susan Kessert 1955; three d.; ed Wharton School of Finance, Univ. of Pennsylvania; joined Stone Container Corpn 1957, Vice-Pres. Gen. Man. Container Div. 1970–75, Pres. and COO 1975–79, Pres., CEO 1979–98, Chair. 1983–98, Pres., CEO Smurfit Stone Container Corpn 1998–99; Chair. and CEO Box USA Group, Inc. 2000–04; Man. Stone-Kaplan Investments, LLC (pvt. investment co.) 2004–07; CEO and Chair. KapStone Paper and Packaging Corpn, Northbrook, Ill. 2007–; mem. Bd of Dirs McDonalds Corpn, Autoliv, Inc.; fmr mem. Bd of Dirs Morton Int., Option Care Inc.; mem. Advisory Council for Econ. Devt. *Leisure interest:* golf. *Address:* Kapstone Paper and Packaging Corporation, 1101 Skokie Blvd, Suite 300, Northbrook, IL 60062-4124, USA (office). *Telephone:* (847) 239-8800 (office). *Fax:* (847) 205-7551 (office). *E-mail:* information@kapstonepaper.com (office). *Website:* www.kapstonepaper.com (office).

STONE, Sharon; American actress; b. 10 March 1958, Meadville, Pa; m. 1st George Englund Jr; m. 2nd Michael Greenburg 1984 (divorced 1987); m. 3rd Phil Bronstein 1998 (divorced 2004); two adopted s.; ed high school in Pennsylvania and Edinboro Coll.; Chevalier, Ordre des Arts et Lettres. *Films include:* Above the Law, Action Jackson, King Solomon's Mines, Allan Quatermain and the Lost City of Gold, Irreconcilable Differences, Deadly Blessing, Personal Choice, Basic Instinct, Diary of a Hit Man, Where Sleeping Dogs Lie, Sliver, Intersection, The Specialist,

The Quick and the Dead, Casino, Last Dance, Diabolique 1996, Sphere, The Mighty 1999, The Muse 1999, Simpatico 1999, Gloria 1999, Beautiful Joe 2000, Cold Creek Manor 2003, A Different Loyalty 2004, Catwoman 2004, Jiminy Glick in La La Wood 2004, Broken Flowers 2005, Alpha Dog 2006, Basic Instinct 2 2006, Bobby 2006, If I Had Known I Was a Genius 2007, When a Man Falls in the Forest 2007, Democrazy 2007, The Year of Getting to Know Us 2008, Five Dollars a Day 2008, Streets of Blood 2009, The Burma Conspiracy 2011, The Mule 2012, Lovelace 2013, Fading Gigolo 2013. *Television appearances include:* Bay City Blues (series), Tears in the Rain (film), War and Remembrance (mini-series), Calendar Girl Murders (film), The Vegas Strip Wars (film), Huff (series) 2006, Law & Order: Special Victims Unit (series) 2010. *Address:* William Morris Endeavour, 1 William Morris Place, Beverly Hills, CA 90212; c/o Guy McElwaine, PO Box 7304, North Hollywood, CA 91603, USA.

STONECIPHER, Harry Curtis, BS; American aircraft industry executive (retd); b. May 1936, Scott Co., Tenn.; ed Tenn. Poly tech. Inst.; with General Electric 1960–61, 1962–86, Martin Aircraft Co. 1961–62; Exec. Vice-Pres. Sundstrand Corpn 1987, Pres. and COO 1987–88, Pres. and CEO 1988–94, Chair. 1991–94; Pres. and CEO McDonnell-Douglas Corpn, St Louis 1994–97; apptd Pres. and CEO Boeing Co., Seattle 1997, COO Boeing Corpn (later Boeing Co.) 1997–2002, Pres. and CEO 1997–2002, 2003–05 (resgnd); mem. Bd of Dirs Milacron, Inc.; Fellow, Royal Aeronautical Soc.; John R. Allison Award 1996, Rear Adm. John J. Bergen Leadership Medal Nay League 1996. *Address:* 4973 Bacopa Lane South, St Petersburg, FL 33715-2638 USA (office).

STONEHAM OF DROXFORD, Baron (Life Peer), cr. 2011, of the Meon Valley in the County of Hampshire; **Ben Stoneham,** BA, MA, Advanced Manager Program; British political activist, fmr company director, fmr newspaper director and fmr manager; *Chairman, Housing 21;* b. 24 April 1948, Tunbridge Wells, Kent; s. of Maj. B.J.R. Stoneham and Mrs B.M. Stoneham; m. Anne Kirstine Mackintosh 1975; two s., one d.; ed Christ's Coll., Univ. of Cambridge, Univ. of Warwick, London Business School; Dir and Man. Dir Portsmouth and Sunderland Newspapers Ltd 1987–89; Group Production Dir and Personnel Dir News International 2000–03; Operations Dir, Liberal Democrat HQ 2003–10; Chair. Portsmouth Harbour Renaissance Ltd 1996–2005, First Wessex Housing Group 2007–, Housing 21 2011–; Dir Thames Gateway Thurrock Urban Devt Corpn 2004–10. *Leisure interests:* gardening, sport, war history. *Address:* House of Lords, Westminster, London, SW1A 0PW, England. *Telephone:* (20) 7219-5353 (House of Lords). *Fax:* (20) 7219-5979 (House of Lords).

STONESIFER, Patricia Q. (Patty), BA; American foundation executive; b. 1956, Indianapolis; m. 2nd Michael Kinsley; two c. (from previous m.); ed Indiana Univ.; several sr man. positions with Microsoft Corpn 1988–96, most recently Sr Vice-Pres. Interactive Media Div.; man. consultant 1996–97; Pres. and Chair. Gates Learning Foundation 1997–99, Pres. and Co-Chair. Bill and Melinda Gates Foundation 1999–2006, CEO 2006–08; apptd mem. Bd of Dirs amazon.com 1997, Viacom 2000; mem. Bd The Vaccine Fund; mem. Bd of Regents Smithsonian Inst., Washington, DC, Chair. 2009–12; Chair. White House Council on Community Solutions 2010–; fmr mem. US Del. to UN Gen. Ass. Special Session on AIDS; Dr hc (Indiana Univ.) 2007, (Tufts Univ.) 2009; ranked by Forbes magazine amongst 100 Most Powerful Women (52nd) 2004. *Address:* c/o White House Council for Community Solutions, Corporation for National and Community Service, 1201 New York Avenue, NW, Washington, DC 20525, USA (office). *Website:* www.serve .gov/council_home.asp (office).

STOPFORD, Michael, MA; American public relations executive and fmr international civil servant; *Group Director, Corporate Reputation, The Coca-Cola Company;* b. 22 June 1953, London; s. of Edward Stopford and Patricia Carrick; m. Susan Navrat; two s. one d.; ed Oxford Univ.; fmr mem. HM Diplomatic Service, served at Perm. Mission to UN, New York, Second Sec. and Press Attaché, Embassy in Vienna; Assoc. then Second Officer, Exec. Office of Sec.-Gen. of UN 1979–83, Special Projects Officer, Dept of Public Information 1983–87, Chef de Cabinet to Dir-Gen., UN Office in Geneva and Under-Sec.-Gen. for Human Rights 1987–91, Chef de Cabinet to Exec. Del. of Sec.-Gen. for Inter-Agency Humanitarian Programme in Iraq, Kuwait and Iraq–Turkey and Iraq–Iran border areas 1991–92, with Dept for Humanitarian Affairs 1992, Special Asst to UnderSec.-Gen. for Public Information, Dept of Public Information, UN, New York 1992, Dir UN Information Center, Washington, DC, 1992–95; Chief of Media and Public Relations, Int. Financial Corpn 1996–97; Sr Asst to Pres. for Int. Affairs, American Univ., Washington, DC 1997; Sr Issues Adviser, Exxon Mobil Corpn, USA 2000–01; Head of Global Public Affairs and Govt Relations, Syngenta International AG, Basel, Switzerland 2002–06; Group Dir, Corp. Reputation, The Coca-Cola Company, Atlanta, Ga 2006–; Hon. LLD (New England Coll.) 1998. *Publication:* The UN and Global Intervention: Delusions of Grandeur (co-author) 1997. *Leisure interests:* opera, art, sailing, skiing. *Address:* The Coca-Cola Company, PO Box 1734, Atlanta, GA 30301 (office); 723 Rock Springs Court, NE, Atlanta, GA 30306-2328, USA (home). *Telephone:* (404) 717-2653 (office). *E-mail:* m.stopford@gmx.ch (home). *Website:* www.thecoca-colacompany.com (office).

STOPPARD, Sir Tom, Kt, OM, CBE, FRSL; British writer; b. (Thomas Straussler), 3 July 1937, Zlin, Czechoslovakia; s. of the late Dr Eugene Straussler and Martha Straussler; step-s. of Kenneth Stoppard; m. 1st Jose Ingle 1965 (divorced 1972); two s.; m. 2nd Dr Miriam Moore-Robinson 1972 (divorced 1992); two s.; ed Pocklington Grammar School, Yorks.; journalist, Bristol 1954–60, freelance journalist, London 1960–64; mem. Cttee of the Free World 1981–; mem. Royal Nat. Theatre Bd 1989–; Hon. MLitt (Bristol), (Brunel); Hon. LittD (Leeds) 1979, (Sussex) 1980, (Warwick) 1981, (London) 1982; Dr hc (Kenyon Coll.) 1984, (York) 1984; John Whiting Award, Arts Council 1967, Italia Prize (radio drama) 1968, New York Drama Critics Best Play Award 1968, Antoinette Perry Awards (Tony Awards) 1968, 1976, 2007, Evening Standard Awards 1967, 1972, 1974, 1978, 1982, 1993, 1997, 2006, Sony Award 1991, Olivier Award 1993, Dan David Prize 2008, Sunday Times Award for Literary Excellence 2008, Praemium Imperiale 2009, PEN Pinter Prize 2013. *Plays:* Rosencrantz and Guildenstern are Dead 1967, The Real Inspector Hound 1968, Enter a Free Man 1968, After Magritte 1970, Dogg's Our Pet 1972, Jumpers 1972, Travesties 1975, Dirty Linen 1976, New-Found-Land 1976, Every Good Boy Deserves Favour (with music by André Previn, 1978, Night and Day 1978, Dogg's Hamlet, Cahoots Macbeth 1979,

Undiscovered Country 1980, On the Razzle 1981, The Real Thing 1982, Rough Crossing 1984, Dalliance (adaption of Schnitzler's Liebelei) 1986, Hapgood 1988, Arcadia (Evening Standard Award for Best Play) 1993, Indian Ink 1995, The Invention of Love 1997, The Seagull (trans. 1997), The Coast of Utopia (trilogy: Part One: Voyage, Part Two: Shipwreck, Part Three: Salvage) (Tony Award for Best Play 2007) 2002, Rock 'N' Roll (London Critics' Circle Award for Best New Play) 2006. *Screenplays:* The Romantic Englishwoman (co-author) 1975, Despair 1977; film scripts: The Human Factor 1979, Brazil (with Terry Gilliam, and Charles McKeown) 1984, Crown 1987, Empire of the Sun 1987, Rosencrantz and Guildenstern are Dead (also dir) 1989, The Russia House 1989, Billy Bathgate 1990, Shakespeare in Love (co-author) 1998 (jt winner Acad. Award for Best Original Screenplay 1999), Enigma 2001, Anna Karenina 2012. *Radio plays:* The Dissolution of Dominic Boot 1964, M is for Moon among Other Things 1964, Albert's Bridge 1967, If You're Glad I'll be Frank 1968, Where are They Now? 1970, Artist Descending a Staircase 1972, The Dog It Was That Died 1983, In the Native State 1991. *Television plays:* Professional Foul 1977, Squaring the Circle 1984, The Television Plays 1965–84 1993, Parade's End 2012. *Publications include:* Lord Malquist and Mr Moon (novel) 1966, Introduction 2 (short stories) 1963, The Plays for Radio 1964–91 (radio plays) 1994. *Address:* c/o United Agents Ltd, 12–26 Lexington Street, London, W1F 0LE, England (office). *Telephone:* (20) 3214-0800 (office). *Fax:* (20) 3214-0801 (office). *E-mail:* info@unitedagents.co.uk (office). *Website:* www.unitedagents.co.uk (office).

STORARO, Vittorio; Italian cinematographer; b. 24 June 1940, Rome; ed Centro Sperimentale; mem. Italian Asscn of Cinematographers 1971–, Vice-Pres. 1977–78, Pres. 1988–90; mem. Acad. of Motion Picture Arts and Sciences 1980–, American Soc. of Cinematographers 1988–, European Acad. of Motion Picture Arts and Sciences 1999–; teacher, Acad. of Motion Picture Arts and Sciences of Image, L'Aquila, Italy 1994; Lifetime Achievement Award, American Soc. of Cinematographers 2001, Coolidge Award 2005. *Films include:* Giovinezza, Giovinezza 1968, Delitto al Circolo del Tennis, La Strategia del Rango 1969, Il Conformista, L'Eneide 1970, Addio Fratello Crudele 1971, Giornata Nera per l'Ariete 1971, Orlando Furioso 1971, Last Tango in Paris 1972, Bleu Gang…, Malizia 1972, Giordano Bruno 1973, Le Orme 1974, Novecento 1974, Scandalo 1975, Agatha, La Luna 1978, Apocalypse Now (Acad. Award for Best Cinematography 1980) 1979, Reds (Acad. Award for Best Cinematography 1981) 1982, Tarzan, the Ape Man 1980, One from the Heart 1981, Wagner 1982, Ladyhawke 1983, The Last Emperor (Acad. Award for Best Cinematography 1988,) 1987, Tucker: The Man and His Dream 1988, New York Stories (Life Without Zoe) 1989, Dick Tracy 1990, The Sheltering Sky 1990, Tosca (TV) 1992, Little Buddha 1993, Roma!, Imago Urbis, Flamenco (de Carlos Saura) 1995, Taxi 1996, Tango, no me dejes nunca (Cannes Film Festival Award) 1998, Bulworth 1998, Goya en Burdeos (Goya in Bordeaux) 1999, Mirka 2000, Picking up the Pieces 2000, La Traviata (TV) 2000, Zapata: El sueño del héroe 2004, Exorcist: The Beginning 2004, Dominion: Prequel to the Exorcist 2005, All the Invisible Children 2005. *E-mail:* vittorio@ storarovittorio.com. *Website:* storarovittorio.com.

STORCH, Marcus, MSc; Swedish business executive; b. 28 July 1942, Stockholm; s. of Hilel Storch and Anna Storch; m. Gunilla Berglund 1972; one d.; ed Royal Inst. of Tech., Stockholm; Dept Head, AGA AB, Welding 1968–72, Pres. Welding Div. AGA AB 1972–75, Pres. Gas Div. 1975–81, Exec. Vice-Pres. AGA AB 1978–81, Pres. and CEO 1981–96; Chair. Nobel Foundation; Vice-Chair. A. Johnson AB, AXFOOD AB, Mekonomen; mem. Bd Nordstjernan AB, Oresund AB; Hon. Dr Med. (Karolinska Institutet). *Address:* Linnégatan 8, 114 47 Stockholm, Sweden (office). *Telephone:* (8) 679-97-00 (office). *E-mail:* storch@telia.com (office).

STØRE, Jonas Gahr, BSc; Norwegian politician and diplomatist; *Minister of Health and Care Services;* b. 25 Aug. 1960; m.; three c.; ed Royal Norwegian Naval Acad., Institut d'Etudes Politiques de Paris, France; Teaching Fellow, Harvard Law School, USA 1986; Researcher, Norwegian School of Man. 1986–89; Special Adviser, Office of the Prime Minister 1989–95, Dir.-Gen., Int. Dept 1995–98, State Sec. and Chief of Staff 2000–01; Perm. Rep. to UN, Geneva 1998; Chief of Staff, WHO 1998–2000; Working Chair., ECON Analysis 2002–03; Sec.-Gen., Norwegian Red Cross 2003–05; Minister of Foreign Affairs 2005–12, of Health and Care Services 2012–; mem. Det norske Arbeiderparti (Norwegian Labour Party). *Address:* Ministry of Health and Care Services, Einar Gerhardsens pl. 3, POB 8011 Dep., 0030 Oslo, Norway (office). *Telephone:* 22-24-90-90 (office). *E-mail:* postmottak@hod.dep.no (office). *Website:* www.regjeringen.no/hod (office).

STOREY, David Malcolm; British author and playwright; b. 13 July 1933, Wakefield, Yorkshire; s. of Frank Richmond Storey and Lily Storey (née Cartwright); m. Barbara Hamilton 1956; two s. two d.; ed Queen Elizabeth Grammar School, Wakefield, Wakefield Coll. of Art and Slade School of Art; Fellow, Univ. Coll. London 1974; Los Angeles Drama Critics Award 1969, Writer of the Year Award, Variety Club of GB 1969. *Publications include:* novels: This Sporting Life (Macmillan Award) 1960, Flight into Camden (John Llewellyn Rhys Memorial Prize 1961, Somerset Maugham Award 1963) 1960, Radcliffe 1963, Pasmore (Faber Memorial Prize 1972) 1972, A Temporary Life 1973, Edward 1973, Saville (Booker Prize 1976) 1976, A Prodigal Child 1982, Present Times 1984, A Serious Man 1998, As It Happened 2002, Thin-Ice Skater 2004; plays: The Restoration of Arnold Middleton (Evening Standard Award 1967), In Celebration 1969 (also film), The Contractor (New York Critics' Prize 1974) 1969, Home (Evening Standard Award, New York Critics' Prize) 1970, The Changing Room (New York Critics' Prize) 1971, Cromwell 1973, The Farm 1973, Life Class 1974, Night 1976, Mother's Day 1976, Sisters 1978, Dreams of Leaving 1979, Early Days 1980, The March on Russia 1989, Stages 1992; poems: Storey's Lives: Poems 1951–1991 1992. *Address:* c/o A.M. Heath and Co. Ltd, 6 Warwick Court, Holborn, London, WC1R 5DJ, England (office).

STOREY, Baron (Life Peer), cr. 2011, of Childwall in the City of Liverpool; **Mike Storey,** OBE, CBE, BEd (Hons); British politician and headteacher; m.; one d.; ed St Katharine's Coll., Liverpool, Chester Coll.; fmr Head Teacher, Plantation Primary School, Halewood, Knowsley; Councillor (Liberal Democrat) for Wavetree Ward, South Cen. Dist, Liverpool City Council 1973–2011, became youngest Chair. of Educ. in history of Liverpool 1980–83, Deputy Leader of Council 1980–83, Leader 1998–2005, involved in Liverpool's successful bid to become European Capital of Culture 2008; Lord Mayor of Liverpool 2010. *Address:* House of Lords,

Westminster, London, SW1A 0PW, England (office). *Telephone:* (20) 7219-1972 (office). *E-mail:* storeym@parliament.uk (office).

STORK, Gilbert, PhD; American chemist and academic; *Eugene Higgins Professor Emeritus of Chemistry, Columbia University;* b. 31 Dec. 1921, Brussels, Belgium; s. of Jacques Stork and Simone Weil; m. Winifred Elizabeth Stewart 1944 (died 1992); one s. three d.; ed Univ. of Wisconsin; Instructor, Harvard Univ. 1946–48, Asst Prof. 1948–53; Assoc. Prof., Columbia Univ. 1953–55, Prof. 1955–67, Eugene Higgins Prof. of Chem. 1967–92, Prof. Emer. 1992–, Chair. of Dept 1973–76; mem. NAS 1961, American Acad. of Arts and Sciences 1962, American Philosophical Soc. 1995; Foreign mem. Royal Soc. of Chem. (UK) 1983, Acad. des Sciences (France) 1989, Royal Soc. 1999, Chemical Soc. of Japan 2002; Hon. DSc (Lawrence Coll.) 1961, (Paris) 1979, (Rochester) 1982, (Emory) 1988, (Columbia) 1993, (Wisconsin) 1997; ACS Award in Pure Chem. 1957, ACS Baekeland Medal, New Jersey Section 1961, Harrison Howe Award 1962, Edward Curtis Franklin Memorial Award of Stanford Univ. 1966, ACS Award in Synthetic Organic Chem. 1967, Nebraska Award 1973, Roussel Prize 1978, Nichols Medal 1980, ACS Arthur C. Cope Award 1980, NAS Award in Chemical Sciences 1982, Willard Gibbs Medal 1982, Nat. Medal of Science 1983, Tetrahedron Prize 1985, Roger Adams Award 1991, George Kenner Award 1992, Robert Welch Award 1993, Wolf Prize (co-recipient) 1995, first Barton Gold Medal, Royal Soc. of Chem. 2002, Noyori Prize (Japan) 2004, H.C. Brown Award 2005; numerous other awards. *Publications include:* Stereospecific Synthesis of Cantharidin 1951, The Enamine Alkylation 1954, Stereochemistry of Polyene Cyclization 1955, Enolate Trapping Alkylation 1965, Stereospecific Synthesis of Reserpine 1989, Stereoselective Synthesis of Quinine 2001. *Leisure interest:* tennis. *Address:* Department of Chemistry, Columbia University, Chandler Hall, New York, NY 10027 (office); 188 Chestnut Street, Englewood Cliffs, NJ 07632, USA (home). *Telephone:* (212) 854-2178 (office); (201) 871-4032 (home). *Fax:* (212) 932-1289 (office). *E-mail:* gjs8@columbia .edu (office); gstork@nj.rr.com. *Website:* www.columbia.edu/cu/chemistry (office).

STORM, Kornelis (Kees), MA, CPA; Dutch business executive; *Chairman of the Supervisory Board, KLM NV;* b. 12 June 1942, Amsterdam; m.; two c.; ed Univ. of Rotterdam; chartered accountant, Moret & Limperg 1970–76; mem. Exec. Bd Kon. Scholten-Honig NV 1976–78, AGO 1978–83; mem. Exec. Bd AEGON NV 1983–93, Chair. 1993–2002, currently mem. Supervisory Bd; Chair. Supervisory Bd KLM NV, PON Holding BV; mem. Bd of Dirs Unilever NV, Baxter International; Ind. Dir, Anheuser-Busch InBev, Chair. 2012–. *Publication:* Management With a Smile. *Address:* c/o Supervisory Board, AEGON NV, Aegonplein 50, PO Box 202, 2501 The Hague (office); Zwaluwenweg 2, 2111 HC Aerdenhout, Netherlands (home). *Telephone:* (70) 3448287 (office); (23) 5242619 (home). *Fax:* (70) 3448593 (office); (23) 5248076 (home). *E-mail:* kees.storm@aegon.com (office). *Website:* www .aegon.com (office).

STÖRMER, Horst Ludwig, PhD; German physicist and academic; *I. I. Rabi Professor of Physics and Professor of Applied Physics, Columbia University;* b. 6 April 1949, Frankfurt am Main; s. of Karl-Ludwig Stormer and Marie Ihrig; m. Dominique A. Parchet 1982; ed Univ. of Stuttgart; with tech. staff AT&T Bell Labs 1977–83, head of Dept 1983–91, Dir Physics Research Lab. 1992–; Prof. of Physics and Applied Physics, Columbia Univ. 1998–, now I. I. Rabi Prof. of Physics and Prof. of Applied Physics; Adjunct Physics Dir Lucent Technologies 1997–; Bell Labs Fellow 1982; Fellow, American Physics Soc., American Acad. of Arts and Sciences; Officier, Légion d'honneur 1999; Buckley Prize, American Physics Soc. 1984, Otto Klug Prize, Germany 1985, Nobel Prize in Physics (jtly) 1998, NYC Mayor's Award 2000. *Address:* Department of Physics, Columbia University, 922 Schapiro CEPSR, MC 5206, New York, NY 10027 (office); Lucent Technologies, 700 Mountain Avenue, New Providence, NJ 07974, USA. *Telephone:* (212) 854-3279 (office); (908) 582-3380 (office). *E-mail:* horst@phys.columbia.edu (office). *Website:* www.ap.columbia.edu (office).

STORR, Robert, MFA; American author, curator and academic; *Professor of Painting/Printmaking and Dean of the School of Art, Yale University;* b. 1949; ed Swarthmore Coll., Pa, School of the Art Inst. of Chicago and studies in Europe and Mexico; Curator of Painting and Sculpture, Museum of Modern Art (MOMA), New York 1990–98, Sr Curator of Contemporary Art 1999–2002; Rosalee Solow Prof. of Modern Art, Inst. of Fine Arts, New York Univ. 2002–06; fmr mem. Faculty, Center for Curatorial Studies, Bard Coll.; Prof. of Painting/Printmaking and Dean of the School of Art, Yale Univ. 2006–; also currently Consulting Curator of Modern and Contemporary Art, Philadelphia Museum of Art; Curator Venice Biennale 2007; Visiting Artist, Critic and Lecturer, Univ. of Pennsylvania, Ruskin School of Drawing, Oxford, UK, School of the Art Inst. of Chicago, Rhode Island School of Design, RCA, London, UK, Grad. Painting Program, Hunter Coll.; Grad. School and Univ. Center, CUNY, Harvard Univ.; Contributing Ed. Art in America, Grand Street; mem. Editorial Bd Art Journal 1985–95; Chevalier des Arts et des Lettres 2000; Dr hc School of the Art Institute of Chicago and the Maine College of Art; First Prize, American Inst. of Commemorative Art 2002, American Chapter of Int. Asscn of Art Critics Award, AICA Award for Distinguished Contribution to the Field of Art Criticism, ICI Agnes Gund Curatorial Award, Lawrence A. Fleischman Award for Scholarly Excellence in the Field of American Art History, Smithsonian Institution's Archives of American Art. *Publications include:* prin. author or ed. of 35 books and monographs, including Philip Guston 1986, Modern Art Despite Modernism 2000, Gerhard Richter: October 18, 1977 2000, Gerhard Richter: 40 Years of Painting 2002; author of essays for exhbn catalogues and books on Louise Bourgeois, Chuck Close, Felix Gonzalez-Torres, Philip Guston, David Hammons, Eva Hesse, Ilya Kabakov, Alex Katz, Ellsworth Kelly, Steve McQueen, Elizabeth Murray, Bruce Nauman, Jim Nutt, Raymond Pettibon, Martin Puryear, Susan Rothenberg, Peter Saul, and Nancy Spero, among others; other publs include articles, interviews, and exhbn reviews for Art in America, Art/Press, Paris, Artforum, Grand Street, Parkett, The Art Journal, Washington Post BookWorld, and other journals and newspapers. *Address:* Yale University School of Art, 1156 Chapel Street, New Haven, CT 06511, USA (office). *Telephone:* (203) 432-2600 (office). *Website:* art.yale.edu/RobertStorr (office).

STOTHARD, Sir Peter M., Kt, MA; British journalist, writer and newspaper editor; *Editor, The Times Literary Supplement;* b. 28 Feb. 1951, Chelmsford, Essex, England; s. of Wilfred Stothard and Patricia Savage; m. Sally Ceris Emerson 1980; one s. one d.; ed Brentwood School, Essex and Trinity Coll., Oxford; journalist, BBC 1974–77; Shell Petroleum 1977–79; business and political writer,

Sunday Times 1979–80; Features Ed. and leader writer, The Times 1980–85; Deputy Ed. The Times 1985–92, US Ed. 1989–92, Ed. 1992–2002; Ed. The Times Literary Supplement 2002–; Chair. of judging panel for Man Booker Prize 2012; Pres. Classical Asscn –2012; Hon. Fellow, Trinity Coll. Oxford 2000–; Pres.'s Medal, British Acad. 2013. *Publications:* Thirty Days: A Month at the Heart of Blair's War 2003, On the Spartacus Road: A Spectacular Journey through Ancient Italy 2010, Alexandria: The Last Nights of Cleopatra 2013. *Leisure interests:* ancient and modern literature. *Address:* The Times Literary Supplement, 3 Thomas More Square, London, E98 1XY, England (office). *Telephone:* (20) 7782-4960 (office). *E-mail:* editor@the-tls.co.uk (office). *Website:* www.the-tls.co.uk (office).

STOTT, Kathryn Linda, ARCM; British pianist; *Artistic Director, Manchester Chamber Concerts Society;* b. 10 Dec. 1958, Nelson, Lancs.; d. of Desmond Stott and Elsie Cheetham; m. 1st Michael Ardron 1979 (divorced 1983); m. 2nd John Elliot 1983 (divorced 1997); one d.; ed studied at Yehudi Menuhin School under Marcel Ciampi, Vlado Perlemuter and Louis Kentner and at Royal Coll. of Music, London under Kendall Taylor; debut, Purcell Room, London 1978; has since performed extensively in recitals and concertos both in UK and in Europe, Far East, Australia, Canada and USA; ten appearances at Henry Wood Promenade concerts; Dir Fauré and the French Connection Festival, Manchester 1995, Piano 2000, Manchester 2000, Piano 2003, Manchester 2003, Chopin and his Legacy, Leeds 2005; Artistic Dir Manchester Chamber Concerts Soc. 2008–; Martin Scholarship 1976, Churchill Scholarship 1979, Croydon Symphony Award, Chappell Medal, Royal Amateur Orchestral Soc. Silver Medal 1979; Chevalier, Ordre des Arts et des Lettres 1996. *Recordings:* 30 recordings, including premieres of concertos by George Lloyd and Michael Nyman. *Leisure interests:* horse-riding, travel, film noir. *Address:* c/o Jane Ward, 60 Shrewsbury Road, Oxton, Merseyside, CH43 2HY, England. *Telephone:* (151) 513-2716. *Fax:* (151) 513-2716. *E-mail:* jane@kathrynstott.com. *Website:* www.kathrynstott.com.

STOURNARAS, Ioannis, BEcons, MPhil, DPhil; Greek economist, academic and government official; *Minister of Finance;* b. 10 Dec. 1956, Athens; ed Univ. of Athens, Univ. of Oxford, UK; Research Fellow and Lecturer, St Catherine's Coll., Oxford 1982–86, worked at Oxford Inst. for Energy Studies; mil. service 1986; Special Adviser to Ministry of Economy and Finance on Public Enterprises and Incomes Policy 1986–89, to Bank of Greece on Monetary Policy 1989–94; represented Bank of Greece as alt. mem. in Meetings of the Govs of EU Cen. Banks; Prof. of Econs, Dept of Econs, Univ. of Athens 1989–, teaches Macroeconomics and Econ. Policy; Chair. Council of Econ. Advisors, Ministry of Economy and Finance 1994–2000; represented Ministry of Economy and Finance at Monetary Cttee (now Econ. and Financial Cttee) of the EU; participated in negotiations for Greek entry into Econ. and Monetary Union; responsible for consultations with int. orgs including IMF, EC and OECD; Vice-Chair. Public Gas Corpn 1994–97; mem. Bd of Dirs Public Debt Man. Office 1998–2000; Chair. and CEO Emporiki Bank 2000–04; Vice-Chair. Asscn of Greek Banks 2000–04; Man. Dir Kappa Securities 2005–08; Trustee, Gennadius Library 2005–; Dir Gen. Foundation for Econ. and Industrial Research (IOBE) 2008–; Minister for Devt, Competitiveness and Shipping in caretaker govt of Panagiotis Pikrammenos May–June 2012; Minister of Finance (following formation of coalition govt between New Democracy (Nea Demokratia), Panhellenic Socialist Movt (PASOK) and Democratic Left) July 2012–. *Publications:* articles in academic journals on macroeconomics, optimum taxation theory, public debt dynamics, Economic and Monetary Union, energy economics, monetary policy, distortions of financial systems. *Address:* Ministry of Finance, Karageorgi Servias 10, 105 62 Athens (office); Department of Economics, School of Law, University of Athens, Odos Pesmazoglou 8, 10509 Athens, Greece (office). *Telephone:* (210) 3375000 (Ministry) (office); (210) 3243525 (Univ. of Athens) (office). *Fax:* (210) 3332608 (Ministry) (office); (210) 3228538 (Univ. of Athens) (office). *E-mail:* kataggelies@sdoe.gr (office); ystourn@econ.uoa.gr (office). *Website:* www.minfin.gr (office); www.econ.uoa.gr (office).

STOWE, Madeleine; American actress; b. 18 Aug. 1958, Los Angeles; d. of the late Robert Stone and Mireya Mora; m. Brian Benben 1986; one d.; ed Univ. of Southern California; began acting career at Solari Theatre, Beverly Hills; appeared in TV series The Gangster Chronicles, mini-series Beulah Land and TV films The Nativity, The Deerslayer, Amazons, Blood and Orchids. *Films include:* Stakeout 1987, Tropical Snow 1989, Worth Winning 1989, Revenge 1990, The Two Jakes 1990, Closet Land 1991, Unlawful Entry 1992, The Last of the Mohicans 1992, Short Cuts 1993, Blink 1994, China Moon 1994, Twelve Monkeys 1995, Playing by Heart 1998, The Proposition 1998, The General's Daughter 1999, Imposter 2001, We Were Soldiers 2002, Avenging Angelo 2002, Octane 2003. *Television includes:* The Magnificent Ambersons 2002, Saving Milly 2005, Raines (series) 2007, The Christmas Hope (film) 2009, Revenge (series) 2011–13. *Address:* c/o David Schiff, UTA, 9560 Wilshire Boulevard, Suite 500, Beverly Hills, CA 90212, USA.

STOWELL OF BEESTON, Baroness (Life Peer), cr. 2011, of Beeston in the County of Nottinghamshire; **Tina Stowell,** MBE; British fmr business executive and fmr civil servant; *Government Whip;* b. Nottingham, Notts.; civil servant for ten years, worked at Ministry of Defence, Embassy in Washington, DC and in No. 10 Downing Street Press Office; Deputy Chief of Staff to William Hague as Leader of HM Opposition and Leader of Conservative Party –2001; Deputy Sec. BBC 2001–03, Head of Communications for BBC Trust 2003–08, Head of Corp. Affairs, BBC 2008–10; Govt Whip 2011–; fmr Chair. Tina Stowell Associates –2011; also worked at Granada Media and for Sir David Frost at Paradine Productions. *Address:* House of Lords, Westminster, London, SW1A 0PW, England (office). *Telephone:* (20) 7219-5353 (office). *Fax:* (20) 7219-5979 (office). *E-mail:* stowellt@parliament.uk (office). *Website:* www.tinastowell.co.uk (office).

STOYANOV, Petar Stefanov; Bulgarian lawyer and fmr head of state; b. 25 May 1952, Plovdiv; m. Antonina Stoyanova; one s. one d.; ed St Kliment Ohridski Univ. of Sofia; divorce lawyer 1978–90; became active in politics 1989; mem. Union of Democratic Forces (UDF), Spokesman in Plovdiv 1990, Pres. UDF Legal Council 1993, Deputy Chair. UDF responsible for domestic policy 1995, Chair. 2005–07 (resgnd), mem. Nat. Exec. Council; Deputy Minister of Justice 1992–93; mem. Parl. 1994–96, 2005–07, Chair. UDF Parl. Group Parl. Comm. on Youth, Sports, and Tourism; presidential cand. 1996; Pres. of Bulgaria 1997–2002; Special Envoy

for Moldova of OSCE Chair-in-Office 2004. *Address:* Blvd V. Levski 54, 1000 Sofia, Bulgaria (office). *Telephone:* 888-80-10-92 (mobile) (office). *Fax:* (2) 988-40-47 (office).

STOYKOV, Gen. Zlatan Kirilov; Bulgarian military officer; b. 17 March 1951, Tsarvaritsa; m.; two d.; ed Vasil Levski Army Acad., Nat. War Coll., Gen. Staff Coll., Russia; Platoon Commdr, 19th Motorrifle Regt 1973–74; Co. Commdr, First Motorrifle Div. 1974–78; Service Support and Guard Battalion Commdr and Commdt, First Army 1980–81, Asst Chief of Operations Dept 1981–82, Sr Asst 1982–83; Asst Chief of Operations Dept, Operations Directorate, Land Forces Command 1983–84, Sr Asst 1984–87, Deputy Chief 1987–88; Chief of Operations Dept and Deputy Chief of Staff, First Army 1988–92, Deputy Chief of Staff 1992–93; Third Motorrifle Div. Commdr 1995–98; Chief Rapid Reaction Forces HQ 1998–2000; Second Army Corps Commdr 2000–02; Deputy Chief of Gen. Staff, Armed Forces for Resources 2002–03; Chief of Land Forces HQ 2003–06; promoted to Gen. 2006; Chief of Gen. Staff 2006–09. *Address:* Ministry of Defence, 3 Dyakon Ignatiy ul, 1000 Sofia, Bulgaria (office). *Telephone:* (2) 922-09-66 (office). *Fax:* (2) 922-09-68 (office). *E-mail:* presscntr@mod.bg (office). *Website:* www.md.government.bg (office).

STRAARUP, Peter, BCom; Danish banking executive; b. 19 July 1951; m. Rickie Retchin; two c.; joined Den Danske Bank 1968, Arbitrage Dealer 1975; Loan Admin Man. Scandinavian Bank Ltd, London 1976–77; Vice-Pres. Den Danske Bank 1977–81, Rep. Houston Rep. Office 1981–83, Head of Foreign Banking Relations, Copenhagen 1983, Gen. Man. Singapore Br. 1984–85, New York 1985–86, mem. Exec. Bd, Copenhagen 1986, CEO, Chair. Exec. Bd and Chair. Exec. Cttee Danske Bank Group 1998–2012; Chair. Forsikringsselskabet Danica, Skadeforsikringsaktieselskab af 1999–, Danica Pension, Livsforsikringsaktieselskab, Danica Liv III, Livsforsikringsaktieselskab, Danica Pension I, Livsforsikringsaktieselskab, DDB Invest AB; mem. Bd of Dirs Denmark-America Foundation; mem. Int. Monetary Conf., Institut Int. d'Etudes Bancaires. *Address:* c/o Danske Bank Group, Danske Bank A/S, Holmens Kanal 2-12, 1092 Copenhagen, Denmark.

STRÅBERG, Hans, MSE; Swedish business executive; *President and CEO, AB Electrolux;* b. 22 Feb. 1957, Västervik; m.; two c.; ed Chalmers Univ. of Technology, Gothenborg; early position as Asst to Scientific Counsellor, Swedish Embassy in Washington, DC; joined AB Electrolux 1983, held various exec. positions including Exec. Vice Pres. of Operations at American subsidiary Frigidaire Home Appliances –1998, Exec. Vice Pres. Electrolux Group and Pres. Floor Care and Light Appliances Business Sector 1998, Pres. and CEO 2002–; mem. Bd of Dirs Asscn of Swedish Eng. Industries, AB Ph. Nederman & Co., Nederman Holding AB, Roxtec AB. *Leisure interests:* tennis, hunting, cars, family. *Address:* Office of the Chief Executive, AB Electrolux, St Göransgatan 143, Stockholm, Sweden (office). *Telephone:* (8) 7386000 (office). *Fax:* (8) 7387640 (office). *Website:* www.electrolux.com (office).

STRACHAN, Sir Ian Charles, Kt, MA, MPA; British business executive; b. 7 April 1943, Oldham; s. of Dr Charles Strachan and Margaret Craig; m. 1st Diane Shafer 1967 (divorced 1987); one d.; m. 2nd Margaret Auchincloss 1987; one step-s. one step-d.; ed Fettes Coll. Edinburgh, Christ's Coll. Cambridge and Princeton and Harvard Univs; Assoc. Ford Foundation, Malaysia 1967–69; various positions in Exxon Corpn 1970–86; Sr Vice-Pres. and Chief Financial Officer, Johnson & Higgins, New York 1986–87; Finance Dir RTZ Corpn PLC (now Rio Tinto) 1987–91, Deputy Chief Exec. 1991–95; Man. Dir BTR PLC July–Dec. 1995, Chief Exec. 1996–99; Deputy Chair. Invensys PLC 1999–2000; Chair. Instinet Group LLC 2003–05; mem. Bd of Dirs (non-exec.) Transocean Inc. 2000–, Johnson Matthey PLC, Xstrata PLC 2003–, Rolls-Royce Group PLC, Commercial Union 1992–95, Thomson-Reuters PLC 2000–. *Leisure interests:* tennis, golf, reading, oriental antiques. *Address:* c/o Board of Directors, Thomson-Reuters PLC, The Reuters Bldg., South Colonnade, Canary Wharf, London, E14 5EP, England (office). *Website:* www.thomsonreuters.com (office).

STRACHE, Heinz-Christian; Austrian politician; *Chairman, Freiheitliche Partei Österreichs (Freedom Party);* b. 12 June 1969; divorced; two c.; trained as a dental technician; active in local Vienna politics since 1991; Chair. Freiheitliche Partei Österreichs (FPÖ—Die Freiheitlichen) (Freedom Party) 2005–; Chair. Parl. Group of FPÖ in Austrian Parl. *Address:* Freiheitliche Partei Österreichs (Die Freiheitlichen), Friedrich-Schmidt Pl. 4, 1080 Vienna (office); Freiheitlicher Parlamentsklub Reichsratsstraße 7/20, 1017 Vienna, Austria. *Telephone:* (1) 512-35-35-0 (office); (40110) 7012. *Fax:* (1) 513-35-35-9 (office). *E-mail:* bgst@fpoe.at (office). *Website:* www.fpoe.at (office); www.hcstrache.at.

STRAHL, Charles (Chuck); Canadian politician; b. 1957, British Columbia; m. Deb Strahl 1975; four c.; ed Trinity Western Univ.; fmr Pnr road construction and logging contracting firm; elected MP 1993 as Reform Party mem., re-elected 1997 (Reform Party), 2000 (Canadian Alliance), 2004, 2006 (Conservative Party), represented constituencies of Fraser Valley East 1993–97, Fraser Valley 1997–2004, Chilliwack—Fraser Canyon 2004–11; fmr Official Opposition Whip and House Leader; Deputy Speaker of House and Chair., Cttees of the Whole 2004; Minister of Agric. and Agri-Food and Minister for Canadian Wheat Bd 2006–07, of Indian Affairs and Northern Devt and Federal Interlocutor for Métis and Non-Status Indians 2007–10, of Transport, Infrastructure and Communities 2010–11. *Address:* c/o Indian and Northern Affairs Canada, Terrasses de la Chaudière, 10 Wellington, North Tower, Gatineau, ON K1A 0H4, Canada. *Website:* www.chuckstrahl.com (home).

STRAHLMAN, Ellen, MD, MHSc; American ophthalmologist and pharmaceutical industry executive; *Chief Medical Officer, GlaxoSmithKline North American Pharmaceuticals;* ed Harvard Univ., Johns Hopkins Univ. School of Medicine, Bloomberg School of Public Health; fmr CEO Virogen Ltd; fmr Chief Medical Officer and Global Head of Research and Devt, Bausch & Lomb; fmr Sr Medical Officer, Nat. Eye Inst., NIH; fmrly held sr positions at Merck and Novartis; Vice-Pres. of Licensing and Worldwide Business Devt, Pfizer –2008; Chief Medical Officer, GlaxoSmithKline North American Pharmaceuticals 2008–; mem. Columbia Univ. Medical and Science Tech. Council; Bd mem. Foundation of American Acad. of Ophthalmology. *Address:* GlaxoSmithKline North American Pharmaceuticals, One Franklin Plaza, Philadelphia, PA 19102, USA (office). *Telephone:* (215) 751-4638 (office). *Website:* us.gsk.com (office).

STRAKER, Louis, BA, MA, KCMG; Saint Vincent and the Grenadines politician; b. 23 Feb. 1944, Layou; ed Hunter Coll., City Univ. New York, Long Island Univ.; 25 years with Chemical Bank of New York (now Chase Manhattan); MP for Central Leeward Constituency 1994–; Deputy Prime Minister of Saint Vincent and the Grenadines, Minister of Foreign Affairs, Commerce and Trade 2001–05, Deputy Prime Minister and Minister of Transport, Works and Housing May–Dec. 2005; Deputy Prime Minister and Minister of Foreign Affairs, Commerce and Trade 2005–10; mem. Unity Labour Party. *Address:* c/o Ministry of Foreign Affairs, Administrative Building, 3rd Floor, Bay Street, Kingstown, Saint Vincent and the Grenadines.

STRAKHOV, Vladimir Nikolayevich, D.Phys.Math.Sc.; Russian physicist; b. 3 May 1932; ed Moscow Inst. of Geological Prospecting; sr engineer, researcher, Head of Lab. Prof. O. Schmidt Inst. of Earth Physics, USSR (now Russian) Acad. of Sciences 1959–89, Dir-Gen. 1989–; Corresp. mem. USSR (now Russian) Acad. of Sciences 1987, mem. 1992; main research in math., geophysics, gravitational and magnetic methods of prospecting mineral deposits, magnetic anomalies of oceans; went on hunger strike in protest at the state of scientific research and its financing 1996; mem. Russian Acad. of Natural Sciences. *Address:* c/o Russian Academy of Sciences, 119991 Moscow, Leninskii avenue, 14, Russia (office). *Telephone:* (495) 938-03-09 (office).

STRAND, Mark, AB, BFA, MA; American poet, writer and academic; *Professor of English and Comparative Literature, Columbia University;* b. 11 April 1934, Summerside, PEI, Canada; m. 1st Antonia Ratensky 1961 (divorced 1973); one d.; m. 2nd Julia Rumsey Garretson 1976 (divorced 1998); one s.; ed Antioch Coll., Yale Univ., Univ. of Iowa; instructor, Univ. of Iowa 1962–65; Fulbright Lecturer, Univ. of Brazil 1965; Asst Prof., Mount Holyoke Coll. 1966; Visiting Prof., Univ. of Washington 1967, Univ. of Virginia 1977, California State Univ. at Fresno 1977, Univ. of California, Irvine 1978, Wesleyan Univ. 1979–80; Adjunct Prof., Columbia Univ. 1968–70, Prof. of English and Comparative Literature 2005–; Visiting Lecturer, Yale Univ. 1969–70, Harvard Univ. 1980–81; Assoc. Prof., Brooklyn Coll., CUNY 1971; Bain Swiggett Lecturer, Princeton Univ. 1972; Fanny Hurst Prof. of Poetry, Brandeis Univ. 1973; Prof., Univ. of Utah 1981–86, Distinguished Prof. 1986–94; Poet Laureate of the USA 1990–91; Elliot Coleman Prof. of Poetry, Johns Hopkins Univ. 1994–97; fmr Andrew MacLeish Distinguished Service Prof., Univ. of Chicago; Writer-in-Residence, American Acad., Rome 1982; mem. American Acad. and Inst. of Arts and Letters 1980–, Nat. Acad. of Arts and Sciences 1995–; Fulbright Scholarship to Italy 1960–61, Ingram Merrill Foundation Fellowship 1966, Nat. Endowment for the Arts grants 1967–68, 1977–78, Rockefeller Fellowship 1968–69; Edgar Allan Poe Prize 1974, Guggenheim Fellowship 1974–75, Nat. Inst. of Arts and Letters Award 1975, Acad. of American Poets Fellowship 1979, John D. and Catherine T. MacArthur Foundation Fellowship 1987–92, Utah Gov.'s Award in the Arts 1992, Bobbitt Nat. Prize for Poetry 1992, Bollingen Prize for Poetry 1993, Bingham Prize for Poetry 1998, Pulitzer Prize 1999, Wallace Stevens Prize, Acad. of American Poets 2004, Gold Medal for Poetry, American Acad. for Arts and Letters 2009. *Publications:* poetry: Sleeping With One Eye Open 1964, Reasons for Moving 1968, Darker 1970, Halty Ferguson: 18 Poems from the Quechua (trans.) 1971, Rafael Alberti: The Owl's Insomnia (trans.) 1973, The Sargentville Notebook 1973, The Story of Our Lives 1973, Carlos Drummond de Andrade: Souvenir of the Ancient World (trans.) 1976, Another Republic: 17 European and South American Writers (co-ed. with Charles Simic) 1976, The Late Hour 1978, Selected Poems 1980, Travelling in the Family: The Selected Poems of Carlos Drummond de Andrade (trans.) 1986, The Continuous Life 1990, The Best American Poetry (ed.) 1991, Dark Harbor 1993, The Golden Ecco Anthology (ed.) 1994, Blizzard of One (Pulitzer Prize in Poetry 1999) 1998, Man and Camel 2006, New Selected Poems 2007, Almost Invisible 2012; prose: The Monument 1978, The Planet of Lost Things (juvenile) 1982, The Art of the Real 1983, Mr and Mrs Baby (short stories) 1985, The Night Book (juvenile) 1985, Rembrandt Takes a Walk (juvenile) 1986, William Bailey 1987, Hopper 1994; contrib. of poems, book reviews, art reviews, essays on poetry and painting, and interviews in numerous periodicals; contribs to numerous anthologies. *Address:* 602 Philosophy Hall, Department of English and Comparative Literature, Columbia University, New York, NY 10027 (office); 2700 Broadway (8B), New York, NY 10025, USA (home). *Telephone:* (212) 854-7468 (office); (646) 478-8704 (home). *E-mail:* ms3091@columbia.edu (office). *Website:* www.columbia.edu/cu/english (office).

STRANGE, Curtis Northrop; American professional golfer; b. 30 Jan. 1955, Norfolk, Va; s. of Thomas Wright Strange, Jr and Nancy Neal; m. Sarah Jones; two s.; ed Wake Forest Univ.; turned professional 1976; won Pensacola Open 1979, Sammy Davis Jr Greater Hartford Open 1983, LaJel Classic 1984, Honda Classic, Panasonic-Las Vegas Int. 1985, Canadian Open 1985, Houston Open 1986, Canadian Open, Fed. Express-St Jude Classic, NEC Series of Golf 1987, Sandway Cove Classic, Australia 1988, Ind. Insurance Agent Open, Memorial Tournament, US Open, Nabisco Championships 1988, US Open, Palm Meadows Cup, Australia 1989, Holden Classic, Australia 1993; mem. PGA Tour Charity Team, Michelob Championship, Kingsmill 1996; Capt. US Ryder Cup Team 2002 after playing on five Ryder Cup Teams; apptd golf analyst for ABC Sports 1997; Golfer of the Year 1986, 1987, inducted into World Golf Hall of Fame 2007, inducted into Hampton Roads Sports Hall of Fame 2009. *Leisure interests:* hunting, fishing, Harley-Davidson motorcycles. *Address:* c/o IMG, 1 Erieview Plaza, Suite 1300, Cleveland, OH 44114, USA.

STRANGFELD, John R., Jr, BS, MBA; American business executive; *Chairman and CEO, Prudential Financial, Inc.;* b. 27 Dec. 1953; m. Mary Kay Strangfeld; ed Susquehanna Univ., Darden School of Business, Univ. of Virginia; joined Prudential 1977, served in various exec. positions, including Chair. PRICOA Capital Group, London, UK 1989–95, Sr Man. Dir, Pvt. Asset Man. Group 1995–98, CEO Prudential Investment Man. of Prudential Insurance 1998–2002, Chair. and CEO Prudential Securities (renamed Prudential Equity Group LLC) 2000, Exec. Vice-Pres. Prudential Financial 2001–02, Vice-Chair. Prudential Financial, Inc. 2002–07, Pres. and CEO 2007–08, mem. Bd Dirs, Chair. and CEO 2008–; mem. Bd of Mans Wachovia Securities Financial Holdings LLC (jt venture of Prudential and Wachovia) 2003–; mem. Financial Services Forum, Financial Services Roundtable, Business Roundtable, Geneva Asscn, American Council of Life Insurers; mem. Exec. Cttee of the Bd of Dirs New Jersey Performing Arts

Center, Newark; Vice-Chair. Bd of Trustees, Susquehanna Univ.; Pres. Bd of Trustees, Darden Foundation, Univ. of Virginia. *Address:* Prudential Financial, Inc., 751 Broad Street, Newark, NJ 07102-3777, USA (office). *Telephone:* (973) 802-6000 (office). *Fax:* (973) 802-4479 (office). *E-mail:* info@prudential.com (office). *Website:* www.prudential.com (office).

STRÁNSKÝ, Jiří; Czech writer; b. 12 Aug. 1931, Prague; m. Jitka Balíková; one s., one d.; ed High School; manual worker –1989; political prisoner 1950–58, 1970–72; began publishing work after 'Velvet Revolution' 1989–, mem. of Confed. of Political Prisoners, Pres. of Czech Centre of Int. PEN 1992–98; Chair. M. Havel Foundation; mem. Council for TV, Council for Grants and Devt of Czech Cinematography 2000–; Chevalier, Ordre des Arts et des Lettres 2002; Egon Hostovský Prize 1991, Medal for Merit 2001, Karel Čapek Prize, Czech PEN 2006. *Publications include:* Za plotem, psáno ve vězení, Štěstí 1969, Zdivočelá země 1970, Aukce 1989, Přelet 2001, Povídačky pro moje slunce 2002, Povídačky pro Klárku 2004, Perlorodky 2005, Srdcerváč 2005, Stařec a smrt 2007; script for film Boomerang 1996 (Czech Literary Fund Prize 1998), script for TV play The Uniform 2000. *Leisure interests:* scouting, riding. *Address:* c/o Czech Centre of International PEN, PO Box 123, Klementinum 190 /5. patro, 110 00 Prague 1, Czech Republic (office). *E-mail:* centrum@pen.cz (office). *Website:* www.pen.cz (office).

STRASBURGER, Baron (Life Peer), cr. 2011, of Langridge in the County of Somerset; **Paul Strasburger;** British business executive and philanthropist; m. Evelyn S. Strasburger; f. Safe Estates Services Ltd; mem. Liberal Democrat party. *Address:* House of Lords, Westminster, London, SW1A 0PW, England (office). *Telephone:* (20) 7219-5353 (office). *Fax:* (20) 7219-5979 (office).

STRĂTAN, Andrei, DEcon; Moldovan government official; b. 3 Sept. 1966, Chişinău; m.; two c.; ed Chişinău Polytechnic Inst., Moldova State Univ.; served in Soviet Customs Control Dept 1991–92, Repub. of Moldova Customs Dept 1992–2002, Head of Div. 1992–95, Deputy Dir-Gen. 1995–97, Prime Deputy Dir-Gen. 1997–99, Dir-Gen. 1999–2002; served on special missions with rank of Amb. including Head, Nat. Bureau of Stability Pact, Ministry of Foreign Affairs 2002–03; Deputy Prime Minister and Minister of Foreign Affairs 2003–04; Minister of Foreign Affairs 2004; Deputy Prime Minister and Minister of Foreign Affairs and European Integration 2005–09. *Address:* c/o Ministry of Foreign Affairs, 2012 Chişinău, str. 31 August 80, Moldova.

STRATAS, Teresa Anastasia Strataki, OC; Canadian singer (soprano); b. (Anastasia Stratakis), 26 May 1938, Toronto, Ont.; d. of Emmanuel Stratas and Argero Stratakis; m. Tony Harrison; ed Univ. of Toronto; began singing career in nightclubs in Toronto; debut at Toronto Opera Festival 1958; won audition to Metropolitan Opera, New York 1959; performances there include Berg's Lulu, Jenny in Brecht and Weill's Mahagonny, Suor Angelica, Lauretta and Giorgetta in Il Trittico; major roles in opera houses worldwide include Paris (Lulu 1979), Brussels (Lulu 1988), Boston (Mimi 1989), Chicago (Mélisande 1992); appeared as Violetta in Zeffirelli's film of La Traviata 1983; appeared in Broadway musical Rags 1986; cr. role of Marie Antoinette in Ghosts of Versailles, premiered Metropolitan Opera, NY 1992; Il Tabarro and Pagliacci at the Met 1994; Hon. LLD (McMaster Univ.) 1986, (Toronto) 1994, (Rochester) 1998, (Juilliard School of Music), (Royal Conservatory of Music); Hon. DLitt (York Univ.) 2000; Canadian Music Council Performer of the Year 1979, Drama Desk Award for Leading Actress in a Musical on Broadway 1986–87, Gemini Award for Best Supporting Actress (for Under the Piano) 1997, three Grammy Awards, Opera Canada Award for Creative Artist 2003. *Address:* Vincent & Farrell Associates, 157 West 57th Street, Suite 502, New York, NY 10019, USA (office).

STRATHAIRN, David Russell; American actor; b. 26 Jan. 1949, San Francisco, Calif.; s. of Thomas Scott Strathairn, Jr and Mary Frances Strathairn (née Frazier); m. Logan Goodma 1980; two s.; ed Redwood High School, Larkspur, Calif., Williams Coll.; studied clowning at the Ringling Brothers and Barnum & Bailey Clown Coll., Venice, Fla; worked briefly as a clown in a travelling circus. *Theatre includes:* has performed several roles in stage plays by Harold Pinter, including two consecutive New York Classic Stage Co. (CSC) productions of The Birthday Party 1988, 1989 and dual roles of prison Officer and Prisoner in Mountain Language 1989; workshop production of A House Divided by W. Stuart McDowell at The Players 1989; Kerner in Tom Stoppard's Hapgood 1994; Devlin in Pinter's Ashes to Ashes in New York premiere by the Roundabout Theatre Co. 1999. *Films include:* Return of the Secaucus Seven 1979, Lovesick 1983, Enormous Changes at the Last Minute 1983, Silkwood, Iceman 1984, The Brother from Another Planet 1984, When Nature Calls 1985, At Close Range 1986, Matewan 1987, Nicky and Gino 1988, Stars and Bars 1988, Call Me 1988, Eight Men Out 1988, The Feud 1989, Memphis Belle 1990, City of Hope 1991, Big Girls Don't Cry... They Get Even 1992, A League of Their Own 1992, Bob Roberts 1992, Sneakers 1992, Passion Fish 1992, Stand Off 1993, Lost in Yonkers 1993, The River Wild 1994, Losing Isaiah 1995, Dolores Claiborne 1995, Home for the Holidays 1995, Mother Night 1996, Song of Hiawatha 1997, L.A. Confidential 1997, Bad Manners 1997, The Climb 1998, With Friends Like These... 1998, Simon Birch 1998, Meschugge 1998, A Midsummer Night's Dream 1999, Limbo 1999, A Map of the World 1999, A Good Baby 2000, Harrison's Flowers 2000, The Victim (short) 2001, Ball in the House 2001, Speakeasy 2002, Blue Car 2002, The Root 2003, Twisted 2004, Missing in America 2005, Good Night, and Good Luck (Best Actor, Venice Int. Film Festival 2005) 2005, The Notorious Bettie Page 2005, Steel Toes 2006, The Shovel (short) 2006, Heavens Fall 2006, The Sensation of Sight 2006, We Are Marshall 2006, Fracture 2007, Racing Daylight 2007, My Blueberry Nights 2007, The Bourne Ultimatum 2007, Matters of Life and Death (short) 2007, The Spiderwick Chronicles 2008, Kisses Over Babylon (short) 2009, Cold Souls 2009, The Uninvited 2009, Howl 2010, The Tempest 2010, The Whistleblower 2010, No God, No Master 2012, The Bourne Legacy 2012, Lincoln 2012, Maladies 2013. *Television includes:* Miami Vice (series) – Out Where the Buses Don't Run 1985, Broken Vows (film) 1987, Spenser: For Hire (series) – One for My Daughter 1987, Another World (series) 1987, The Days and Nights of Molly Dodd (series) 1988–91, The Equalizer (series) – Sea of Fire 1988, Day One (film) 1989, Wiseguy (series) 1990, Heat Wave (film) 1990, Judgment (film) 1990, Son of the Morning Star (film) 1991, Without Warning: The James Brady Story (film) 1991, Lethal Innocence (film) 1991, O Pioneers! (film) 1992, The American Clock (film) 1993, American Masters (series documentary) (narrator) 1993–2005, Beyond the Call (film) 1996, In the Gloaming (film) 1997, Evidence of Blood (film) 1998,

Freedom Song (film) 2000, The Miracle Worker (film) 2000, Big Apple (series) 2001, Lathe of Heaven (film) 2002, Master Spy: The Robert Hanssen Story (film) 2002, Paradise (film) 2004, The Sopranos (series) 2004, Take 3 (film) 2006, The Supreme Court (series) (narrator) 2007, Monk (series) – Mr. Monk and the Genius 2008, Diese American Experience (series documentary) – The Trials of J. Robert Oppenheimer 2009, Matadors (film) 2010, Temple Grandin (film) (Outstanding Supporting Actor in a Miniseries or a Movie, Acad. of Television Arts and Sciences 2010) 2010, House (series) – Lockdown 2010, Alphas (series) 2011–12, Hemingway & Gellhorn (film) 2012. *Address:* c/o Celebrity Talent International, PO Box 2240, Carlsbad, CA 92018, USA (office).

STRATHCLYDE, 2nd Baron, cr. 1955; **Rt Hon. Thomas Galloway Dunlop du Roy de Blicquy Galbraith**, PC; British politician; b. 22 Feb. 1960, Glasgow, Scotland; s. of the late The Hon. Sir Thomas (Tam) Galbraith, KBE and Simone Galbraith (née du Roy de Blicquy); m. Jane Skinner 1992; three d.; ed Sussex House, London, Wellington Coll., Univs of East Anglia and Aix-en-Provence; insurance broker, Bain Clarkson Ltd (fmrly Bain Dawes) 1982–88; Conservative cand. in European Election, Merseyside E 1984; Govt Whip, House of Lords 1988–89; Govt Spokesman for Dept of Trade and Industry 1988–89, Parl. Under-Sec. of State Dept of Employment (Tourism) 1989–90, Dept of Environment July–Sept. 1990, 1992, Scottish Office 1990–92; Minister for Agric., Fisheries, Highlands and Islands 1990–92; Chief Govt Whip 1994–97, Opposition Chief Whip 1997–98, Deputy Speaker 1997–98, Leader of the Opposition 1998–2010, Leader of the House of Lords 2010–13; Chancellor of the Duchy of Lancaster 2010–13; Dir, Auchendrane Estates Ltd; Gov., Wellington Coll., Berks. *Address:* House of Lords, Westminster, London, SW1A 0PW, England (office). *Telephone:* (20) 7219-5353 (office). *Fax:* (20) 7219-3051 (office). *Website:* www.parliament.uk/biographies/lords/thomas-galbraith/26626 (office).

STRAUB, Elek, BEng; Hungarian telecommunications industry executive; b. 1944; ed Budapest Tech. Univ.; Head of Information Tech. Dept, Ministry of Labour 1970–80; Head of Information Tech. Div. and later Vice-Pres., Cen. Statistical Office 1980–90, also Govt Adviser, Information Tech. Devt Cttee; Gen. Man. IBM Hungary 1990–95; CEO Matáv 1995–2005, mem. Bd 1995–2005, Chair. 1996–2000, Chair. Man. Cttee 2000–05, (Matáv renamed Magyar Telekom 2005), Chair. and CEO Magyar Telekom 2005–06 (resgnd); mem. Bd of Dirs Graphisoft SE; currently Pres. Hungarian Yachting Asscn; Chair. German-Hungarian Chamber of Commerce 2004–06; 1st Class Cross of Distinction of Order (FRG) 2004, Order of Merit of Republic of Hungary, Officer's Cross 2004. *Address:* Magyar Vitorlás Szövetség (Hungarian Yachting Association), 1146 Budapest, Istvánmezei út 1-3, Hungary (office). *Telephone:* (1) 4606925 (office). *Fax:* (1) 4606926 (office). *E-mail:* hunsail@hunsail.hu (office). *Website:* www.hunsail.hu (office).

STRAUJUMA, Laimdota; Latvian economist and politician; *Prime Minister;* b. 24 Feb. 1951; ed Univ. of Latvia; mem. People's Party from 1998, Unity 2014–; Sec. of State, Ministry for Agric. 2000–06, Ministry for Regional Devt and Local Govt 2007–10; Minister of Agric. 2011–14; Prime Minister of Latvia (first woman) 2014–; mem. Latvian Acad. of Sciences. *Address:* Office of the Cabinet of Ministers, Brivibas Blvd 36, Rīga 1520, Latvia (office). *Telephone:* 6708-2800 (office). *Fax:* 6728-0469 (office). *E-mail:* vk@mk.gov.lv (office). *Website:* www.mk.gov.lv (office).

STRAUME, Janis; Latvian politician; b. 1962, Sigulda; m.; one s. two d.; ed Rīga State Medical Inst.; physician, Rīga City clinic, endoscopist, Latvian Diagnostics Centre 1986–90; mem. Latvian Human Rights Group Helsinki 86 (Rīga Chapter), Latvian Nat. Independence Movt, Citizen's Congress of Latvian Repub., Union of 18th Nov.; mem. Saeima 1990–2006, Chair. 1999–2002, Deputy Chair. 2002–06, mem. Foreign Affairs Cttee, Nat. Security Cttee; Chair. Union for Fatherland and Freedom Faction (LNNK) 1998–2002, For Fatherland and Freedom Union/Latvian Nat. Independence Movt (TB/LNNK) 2002. *Address:* c/o For Fatherland and Freedom Union/Latvian National Independence Movement (Apvienība 'Tēvzemei un Brīvībai'/Latvijas Nacionālās Neatkarības Kustība), Jēkaba iela 20/22–9, Rīga 1050, Latvia.

STRAUSS, Andrew John, OBE, MBE; British (b. South African) fmr professional cricketer; b. 2 March 1977, Johannesburg, Transvaal, South Africa; m. Ruth McDonald 2003; one s. one d.; ed Caulfield Grammar School, Melbourne, Australia, Caldicott School, Radley Coll., Hatfield Coll., Durham Univ.; moved to England aged six; left-handed opening batsman; left-arm medium bowler; played for Durham Univ. cricket team and Middx second XI; played for Middx 1998–2012 (Capt. 2002–04), MCC 2002, Northern Dists 2007–08, England 2004–12 (Test Capt. 2006 (deputized), 2009–12, ODI Capt. –2011); First-class debut: 1998; Test debut: England v New Zealand, Lord's 20–24 May 2004; One-Day Int. (ODI) debut: Sri Lanka v England at Dambulla 18 Nov. 2003; T20I debut: England v Australia, Southampton 13 June 2005; played in 100 Tests and scored 7,037 runs (21 centuries and 27 fifties), highest score 177, average 40.91; ODIs: 127 matches, scored 4,205 runs, average 35.63, highest score 158; First-class: 241 matches, 17,046 runs, average 42.72, highest score 241 not out; only fourth batsman to score a century at Lord's on his Test debut 2004; only fifth player to have scored their first Test and ODI hundreds on same ground; first England batsman to score two hundreds in a Test in India 2008; only second England capt. in two decades to regain the Ashes 2009; Capt. England Ashes-winning Test team 2009, 2010–11; holds the record for most catches (121) by an outfield player for England, going past Ian Botham and Colin Cowdrey at Lord's against South Africa Aug. 2012; announced retirement from all forms of the game 29 Aug. 2012; commentator, Sky TV cricket 2013–; Pres. Primary Club Juniors (charity that helps fund blind cricket). *Address:* c/o Middlesex County Cricket Club, Lord's Cricket Ground, St John's Wood, London, NW8 8QN, England. *Telephone:* (20) 7289-1300. *Fax:* (20) 7286-5453. *E-mail:* enquiries@middlesexccc.com. *Website:* www.middlesexccc.com.

STRAUSS, Botho; German playwright and novelist; b. 2 Dec. 1944, Naumburg; ed Cologne and Munich; moved with family to Remscheid, Ruhr region; on staff of Theater heute, West Berlin; Dramaturg at Schaubühne Theater, West Berlin 1970–75; mem. PEN; Schiller Prize Baden-Württemberg 1977, Literaturpreis, Bayerische Akademie der Schönen Künste 1981, Mülheimer Drama Prize 1982, Jean Paul Prize 1987, Georg Büchner Prize 1989, Berlin Theatre Prize 1993, Lessing Prize 2001, Schiller Memorial Prize 2007. *Plays include:* Die Hypochonder (first play, 1971, winner Hannover Dramaturgie Award), Trilogie des Wiederse-

hens 1976, Gross und Klein 1978, Kalldeway Farce 1981, Der Park 1983, Das Gleichgewicht 1994, Theaterstücke in zwei Banden 1994. *Publications:* Bekannte Gesichter, gemischte Gefühle (jtly) 1974, Die Widmung (novel) 1979, Rumor (novel) 1980, Paare, Passanten (novel) 1981, Der Junge Mann (novel) 1984, Diese Erinnerung an einen, der nur einen Tag zu Gast War 1985, Die Fremdenführerin 1986, Niemand Anderes (novel) 1987, Besucher 1988, Kongress: Die Kette der Demütigungen 1989, Beginnlosigkeit. Reflexionen 1992, Anschwellender 1993, Wohnen Dammern Lügen 1994, Die Fehler des Kopisten 1997, Das Partikular 2000, Der Narr und seine Frau heute abend in Pancomedia 2001, Die Nacht mit Alice, als Julia ums Haus schlich 2003, Der Untenstehende auf Zehenspitzen 2004, Mikado 2006. *Address:* Rowohlt Verlage, Hamburgerstrasse 17, London 21465 Reinbek, Germany (office). *Telephone:* (40) 72720 (office). *Fax:* (40) 7272319 (office). *E-mail:* info@rowohlt.de (office). *Website:* www.rowohlt-theaterverlag.de (office).

STRAUSS-KAHN, Dominique Gaston André; French economist, lawyer, politician and international organization executive; b. 25 April 1949, Neuilly-sur-Seine; s. of Gilbert Strauss-Kahn and Jacqueline Fellus; m. 3rd Anne Sinclair 1991; one s. three d. from fmr marriages; ed Paris Inst. for Political Studies, École des Hautes Études Commerciales; Lecturer, Univ. of Nancy II 1977–80; Scientific Counsellor Nat. Inst. of Statistics and Econ. Studies (INSEE) 1978–80; Dir Cerepi (CNRS) 1980–; Prof., Univ. of Paris-X Nanterre 1981; Chief of Financial Services Commissariat Gen., Plan, Asst Commr Plan 1984–86; elected Socialist Deputy Val-d'Oise 1988–91, 1997, 2001–02; Pres. of Comm. on Finances, Assemblée Nationale 1988, Minister Del. of Industry and Foreign Trade to the Minister of State, Minister of the Economy, Finance and Budget 1991–92; Minister of Industry and Foreign Commerce under Minister of Economy, Finance and Budget 1992–93, Minister of Economy, Finance and Industry 1997–99; mem. Socialist Party Cttee of Dirs 1983–, Nat. Sec. 1984–89; mem. Socialist Party Bureau 1995–; Mayor City of Sorcelles (Val d'Oise) 1995–97, apptd First Deputy Mayor 1997; Chair. Scientific Cttee Jean-Jaurès Foundation 2000; Special Councellor to Sec.-Gen. OECD 2000; Visiting Prof., Stanford Univ., USA 2000–01; fmr Dir of Research, Paris Inst. of Political Studies and Prof. of Econs; fmr Prof., École des Hautes Études Commerciales (HEC School of Man.); Co-founder A gauche en Europe (think-tank) 2003; Chair. Exec. Bd and Man. Dir IMF 2007–11 (resgnd); unsuccessful cand. for Socialist Party nomination in presidential election 2007; Head of Bilderberg Group 2010; ranked by Forbes magazine amongst The World's Most Powerful People (47th) 2009, (37th) 2010. *Publications include:* Inflation et partage des surplus: le cas des ménages (co-author) 1975, La richesse des Français 1977, Économie de la famille et accumulation patrimoniale 1977, L'epargne et la retraite 1982, Pierre Bérégovoy: une volonté de réforme au service de l'économie 1984–1993 2000, La Flamme et la Cendre 2002, Pour l'égalité réelle: Eléments pour un réformisme radical 2004, Lettre ouverte aux enfants d'Europe 2004, DVD pour le Oui à la constitution 2005, 365 jours, journal contre le renoncement 2006. *Leisure interests:* piano, cinema, skiing, rugby. *Address:* c/o International Monetary Fund, 700 19th Street, NW, Washington, DC 20431, USA.

STRAUSS-LAHAT, Ofra, LLB; Israeli business executive; *Chairperson, Strauss Group;* b. 22 Aug. 1960; ed Tel-Aviv Univ.; began career in int. marketing services and training programme at Estée Lauder, USA, Area and Marketing Man. 1987–89; joined family-owned Strauss Ice-cream Co. 1989, Organized Market Man., Strauss Sales Div. 1989–90, Marketing Man. 1991–93, Gen. Man. Strauss Salads 1993–95, Deputy Pres. and CEO 1996–2001, Chair. 2001–04, Chair. Strauss Group 2004–; Chair. Ametz Lochem 1992–97; mem. Supervisory Bd Numico NV 2006–; Chair. Donations Apparatus, WIZO Israel 1995; Co-Chair. Israel, United Jewish Communities Gen. Ass.; mem. Bd of Trustees, The Jewish Agency for Israel, Chair. Babayit Beyachad project 2005; ranked by Fortune magazine amongst the 50 Most Powerful Women in Business outside the US (46th) 2002, (48th) 2003, (45th) 2004, (42nd) 2005, (47th) 2006, (46th) 2007–08, (45th) 2009. *Address:* Strauss Group, 84 Arlozorov Street, PO Box 19, 52100 Ramat Gan (office); 49 Hasivim Street, PO Box 194, 49517 Petach Tikva, Israel (office). *Telephone:* (3) 6752111 (office). *Fax:* (3) 6752366 (office). *E-mail:* peril@elite.co.il (office); Service@Strauss-Group.com (office). *Website:* www.elite.co.il (office).

STRAW, Rt Hon. John (Jack) Whitaker, PC, MP; British lawyer and politician; b. 3 Aug. 1946, Buckhurst Hill, Essex, England; s. of Walter A. W. Straw and Joan S. Straw; m. 1st Anthea L. Weston 1968 (divorced 1978); one d. (deceased); m. 2nd Alice E. Perkins 1978; one s. one d.; ed Brentwood School, Univ. of Essex and Univ. of Leeds School of Law; Pres. Nat. Union of Students 1969–71; mem. Islington Borough Council 1971–78, Inner London Educ. Authority 1971–74 (Deputy Leader 1973–74); called to Bar, Inner Temple 1972, Bencher 1997, practised as barrister 1972–74; special adviser to Sec. of State for Social Services 1974–76, to Sec. of State for Environment 1976–77; on staff of Granada TV (World in Action) 1977–79; MP for Blackburn 1979–; Opposition Treasury Spokesman 1980–83, Environment 1983–87; mem. Parl. Cttee of Labour Party (Shadow Cabinet) 1987–97; Shadow Sec. of State for Educ. 1987–92, for the Environment (Local Govt) 1992–94; Shadow Home Sec. 1994–97; Home Sec. 1997–2001; Sec. of State for Foreign and Commonwealth Affairs 2001–06; Leader of the House of Commons and Lord Privy Seal 2006–07; Lord Chancellor and Sec. of State for Justice 2007–10; mem. Council, Inst. for Fiscal Studies 1983–2000, Lancaster Univ. 1989–92; Vice-Pres. Asscn of District Councils; Visiting Fellow, Nuffield Coll. Oxford 1990–98; Visiting Prof., Univ. Coll. London 2011–; Gov. Blackburn Coll. 1990–, Pimlico School 1994–2000 (Chair. 1995–98); Fellow, Royal Statistical Soc. 1995–; Labour; Hon. LLD (Leeds) 1999, (Brunel) 2007. *Publications:* Policy and Ideology 1993, Last Man Standing 2012; contribs to pamphlets, newspaper articles. *Leisure interests:* walking, cooking puddings, music. *Address:* House of Commons, Westminster, London, SW1A 0AA, England. *Telephone:* (20) 7219-3000; (1254) 52317 (constituency office) (office). *Fax:* (20) 7219-2310 (office). *E-mail:* jack.straw@blackburnlabour.org (office).

STREEP, Meryl (Mary Louise), AB, MFA; American actress; b. 22 June 1949, Summit, NJ; d. of Harry Streep, Jr and Mary W. Streep; partner John Cazale 1976 (died 1978); m. Donald J. Gummer 1978; one s. three d.; ed Vassar Coll., Yale School of Drama, singing studies with Estelle Liebling; professional acting debut in New York in The Playboy of Seville at Cubiculo Theatre 1971; Broadway debut in New York in Trelawny of the Wells at Vivian Beaumont Theater, Lincoln Center 1975; appeared in 27 Wagons Full of Cotton, New York 1976; took part in Henry V and Measure for Measure at New York Shakespeare Festival 1976; also acted in

Happy End (musical), The Taming of the Shrew, Wonderland (musical), Taken in Marriage and numerous other plays; Hon. mem. American Acad. of Arts and Letters 2010; Officer, Ordre des Arts et des Lettres 2000; Commdr, Ordre des Arts et des Lettres 2003; Dr hc (Dartmouth) 1981, (Yale) 1983, (Lafayette) 1985; Hon. DFA (Princeton) 2009; Hon. Dr of Arts (Harvard) 2010; People's Choice Award for Favorite Motion Picture Actress 1984–90, Favorite All-Around Female Entertainer 1986, World-Favorite Motion Picture Actress 1990, Aftonbladet TV Prize for Best Foreign TV Personality – Female (Bästa utländska kvinna) 1987, received a star on the Hollywood Walk of Fame 1998, Women in Film Crystal Award 1998, Bette Davis Lifetime Achievement Award 1998, Special Award, Berlin Int. Film Festival 1999, Hon. César Award, Acad. des Arts et Techniques du Cinéma 2003, American Film Inst. Lifetime Achievement Award 2004, Stanislavsky Award, Moscow Int. Film Festival 2004, 27 May 2004 proclaimed 'Meryl Streep Day' by Manhattan Borough Pres. C. Virginia Fields 2004, inducted into New Jersey Hall of Fame 2008, Honoree, 34th Annual Kennedy Center Honors 2011, Hon. Golden Bear, Berlin Int. Film Festival 2012. *Plays include:* The Playboy of Seville 1971, Trelawny of the Wells 1975, Measure for Measure 1976, 27 Wagons Full of Cotton 1976, A Memory of Two Mondays 1976, Alice in Concert 1978, 1980–81, The Seagull 2001, Mother Courage and her Children 2006, Soho Rep Spring Gala 2007. *Films include:* Julia 1976, The Deer Hunter (Best Supporting Actress Award from Nat. Soc. of Film Critics) 1978, Manhattan 1979, The Seduction of Joe Tynan (New York Film Critics Circle Award for Best Supporting Actress) 1979, The Senator 1979, Kramer vs. Kramer (New York Film Critics Circle Award for Best Supporting Actress 1979, Acad. Award for Best Supporting Actress 1980, Golden Globe Award for Best Motion Picture Actress in a Supporting Role 1980) 1979, The French Lieutenant's Woman 1981 (BAFTA Film Award for Best Actress 1982), Sophie's Choice (New York Film Critics Circle Award for Best Actress 1982, Acad. Award for Best Actress in a Leading Role 1983, Golden Globe Award for Best Actress in a Motion Picture – Drama 1983) 1982, Still of the Night 1982, Silkwood 1983, Plenty 1984, Falling in Love 1984, Out of Africa 1985, Heartburn 1985, Ironweed 1987, A Cry in the Dark (Best Actress Award, New York Critics 1988, Cannes 1989) 1988, Evil Angels (Best Actress, Cannes Film Festival 1989) 1988, The Lives and Loves of a She Devil 1989, Hollywood and Me 1989, Postcards from the Edge 1991, Defending Your Life 1991, Death Becomes Her 1992, The House of the Spirits, The River Wild 1994, The Bridges of Madison County 1995, Before and After, Marvin's Room, One True Thing 1998, Dancing at Lughnasa 1999, Music of the Heart 1999, The Hours 2002 (Silver Berlin Bear Award for Best Actress with Nicole Kidman and Julianne Moore), Adaptation (Golden Globe for Best Supporting Actress 2003) 2002, The Manchurian Candidate 2004, Lemony Snicket's A Series of Unfortunate Events 2004, Prime 2005, The Ant Bully (voice) 2006, The Devil Wears Prada (Golden Globe for Best Actress Musical or Comedy 2007) 2006, A Prairie Home Companion (Best Supporting Actress Nat. Soc. of Film Critics 2007, Best Actress, London Film Critics' Circle Awards 2007) 2006, Evening 2007, Rendition 2007, Lions for Lambs 2007, Mamma Mia! 2008, Doubt 2008, Julie and Julia (Golden Globe for Best Performance by an Actress in a Motion Picture— Comedy or Musical 2010) 2009, Fantastic Mr Fox (voice) 2009, It's Complicated 2009, Higglety Pigglety Pop! or There Must Be More to Life (video short) (voice) 2010, The Iron Lady (Golden Globe Award for Best Performance by an Actress in a Motion Picture – Drama 2012, BAFTA Film Award for Leading Actress 2012, Australian Acad. of Cinema and Television Arts Int. Award 2011, Acad. Award for Best Performance by an Actress in a Leading Role 2012) 2011, Hope Springs 2012, To the Arctic 3D (documentary) (narrator) 2012, August: Osage County 2013, The Homesman 2014, Into the Woods 2014. *Television includes:* The Deadliest Season 1977, Holocaust (Emmy Award) 1978, Uncommon Women 1979, Velveteen Rabbit, First Do No Harm 1997, Angels in America (Golden Globe for Best Actress in a Miniseries or TV Movie 2004, Screen Actors Guild Award for Best Actress in a Miniseries 2004, Emmy Award for Outstanding Lead Actress in a Miniseries or Movie 2004) 2003, Web Therapy (series) 2012. *Leisure interests:* peace and anti-nuclear causes, gardening, skiing, raising family, visiting art galleries and museums. *Address:* c/o Kevin S. Huvane, Creative Artists Agency, 2000 Avenue of the Stars, Los Angeles, CA 90067, USA (office). *Telephone:* (424) 288-2000 (office). *Fax:* (424) 288-2900 (office). *Website:* www.caa.com (office).

STREET, Hon. Anthony Austin; Australian business executive and fmr politician; b. 8 Feb. 1926, Melbourne, Vic.; s. of Brig. the Hon. Geoffrey Austin Street, MC and Evora Francis Street (née Currie); m. Valerie Erica Rickard 1951; three s.; ed Melbourne Grammar; Royal Australian Navy; primary producer; mem. for Corangamite, House of Reps 1966–84; Sec. Govt Mems Defence and Wool Cttees 1967–71; mem. Jt Parl. Cttee on Foreign Affairs 1969; Chair. Fed. Rural Cttee of Liberal Party 1970–74; mem. Fed. Exec. Council 1971–; Asst Minister for Labour and Nat. Service 1971–72; mem. Liberal Party Shadow Cabinet for Social Security, Health and Welfare 1973, for Primary Industry, Shipping and Transport 1973–74, for Science and Tech. and ACT 1974–75, for Labour 1975; Minister for Labour and Immigration Nov.–Dec. 1975; Minister Assisting the Prime Minister in Public Service Matters 1975–77; Minister for Employment and Industrial Relations 1975–78, for Industrial Relations 1978–80, for Foreign Affairs 1980–83; resgnd from Parl. 1984; now Man. and Co. Dir. *Leisure interests:* flying, cricket, golf, tennis. *Address:* 153 The Terrace, Ocean Grove, Vic. 3226, Australia (home).

STREET, Sir Laurence Whistler, AC, KCMG, LLB, QC; Australian judge and commercial mediator; b. 3 July 1926, Sydney, NSW; s. of the late Sir Kenneth Street and Jessie Street; m. 1st Susan Gai Watt 1952, two s. two d.; m. 2nd Penelope Patricia Ferguson 1989, one d.; ed Cranbrook School, Sydney, Univ. of Sydney; served in Royal Australian Navy 1943–47; barrister, NSW 1951; Lecturer, Univ. Sydney Law School 1962–65; QC 1963; Commdr and Inaugural Sr Officer RANR Legal Br. 1964–65, Pres. Courts Martial Appeal Tribunal 1971–74; Judge Supreme Court NSW 1965–88; Judge Court of Appeal 1972–74; Chief Judge in Equity 1972–74; Chief Justice of NSW 1974–88; Lt-Gov. NSW 1974–89; Pres. Cranbrook School Council 1966–74, St John Ambulance Australia (NSW) 1974–; Chair. Inaugural Planning Cttee, Australian Commercial Disputes Centre 1985–86; Fellow UTS Sydney 1990; mem. London Court of Int. Arbitration 1988–2003; Pres. LCIA Asia-Pacific Council 1989–; Chair. Advisory Bd Dispute Resolution Centre, Bond Univ. 1989–99, UTS Centre for Dispute Resolution 1991–2001; Pres. Australian Br. Int. Law Asscn 1990–94, World Pres. 1990–92, Life Vice-Pres. 1992–; Pres. Sydney Univ. Law School Foundation 1990–; Chair.

Australian Govt Int. Legal Services Advisory Council 1990–2009, Govt Relations Australia Ltd 2000–04; Dir John Fairfax Holdings Ltd 1991–94, Chair. 1992–97; mem. WIPO Arbitration Consultative Comm., Geneva 1994–2003; Chair. Judiciary Appeals Bd NSW Rugby League 1998–; Australian Govt Designated Conciliator to ICSID, Washington, DC 1995–; ADR Consultant to Australian Defence Legal Office 1999–; Mediator Court of Arbitration for Sport, Lausanne 2000–; Fellow, Chartered Inst. of Arbitrators (UK) 1992, Australian Inst. of Co. Dirs 1992; Life Fellow, Australian Centre for Int. Commercial Arbitration 2004; Patron Sir Laurence Street Annual Negotiation Competition inaugurated by Australian Law Students Asscn 2006; conducted first mediation over the return to Australia of aboriginal human remains held by Natural History Museum, London, UK 2007; chaired inquiry which led to an agreed procedural protocol between Australian Fed. Police, Australian Intelligence and Security Org. and Commonwealth Dir of Prosecutions governing the investigation and prosecution of terrorism activities 2008; chaired in-depth inquiry est. by Chief of Defence into the Defence Force Disciplinary System 2008; has carried out several other public assignments, including as senior probity auditor for Defence Dept on $8 billion air warfare destroyer project 2005–, as senior probity auditor for Department of Immigration and Citizenship on the Immigration Detention facilities project 2007–, for the Inquiry for the Queensland Govt into the Palm Island aboriginal death in custody 2008; Hon. Col 1st/15th Royal NSW Lancers 1986–96; Hon. Fellow, Inst. of Arbitrators Australia (Grade I) 1989, Australian Inst. of Building 2003; KStJ 1976; Grand Officer of Merit, Order of Malta 1977; Hon. LLD (Sydney), (Macquarie), (Univ. of Tech.); Hon. DEcon (New England Univ.) 1996. *Publication:* Mediation – A Practical Outline (5th edn) 2003, Australian chapter, in Mediators on Mediation (CEDR Excellence in ADR Publication Award 2006) 2005. *Address:* Level 12, 233 Macquarie Street, Sydney, NSW 2000 (office); 1 Wolseley Crescent, Point Piper, NSW 2027, Australia (home). *Telephone:* (2) 9223-0888 (office); (2) 9363-1480 (home). *Fax:* (2) 9223-0588 (office); (2) 9327-8871 (home). *E-mail:* lstreet@laurencestreet.com.au (office). *Website:* www.laurencestreet.com.au (office).

STREET, Robert, AO, PhD, DSc, FAA; Australian physicist and academic; *Honorary Research Fellow, Department of Physics, University of Western Australia;* b. 16 Dec. 1920, Wakefield, England; s. of Joe Street and Edith Elizabeth Street; m. Joan Marjorie Bere 1943; one s. one d.; ed Univ. of London; Scientific Officer, Dept of Supply, UK 1942–45; Lecturer, Dept of Physics, Univ. of Nottingham 1945–54; Sr Lecturer, Dept of Physics, Univ. of Sheffield 1954–60; Foundation Prof. of Physics, Monash Univ., Melbourne, Victoria 1960–74; Dir Research School of Physical Sciences, ANU 1974–77; Vice-Chancellor Univ. of Western Australia 1978–86, Dir Magnetics Group, Research Centre for Advanced Materials and Minerals Processing 1991, now Hon. Research Fellow; fmr Pres. Australian Inst. of Nuclear Science and Eng; mem. and Chair. Australian Research Grants Cttee 1970–76; Chair. Nat. Standards Comm. 1967–78; FAA 1973, Treas. 1976–77; Pres. Int. Inst. of Business and Tech., Perth, Western Australia 1987–90; Chair. Child Health Research Foundation of Western Australia 1988–93; Consultant, CRA Advanced Tech. Devt 1992–96. *Publications:* scientific papers on magnetism in learned journals. *Address:* The University of Western Australia, Department of Physics, 35 Stirling Highway, Crawley, WA 6009, Australia (office). *Telephone:* 6488-2718 (office). *E-mail:* street@physics.uwa.edu.au (office). *Website:* www.physics.uwa.edu.au (office).

STREET-PORTER, Janet, FRTS; British writer, broadcaster and fmr newspaper editor; *Editor-at-Large, The Independent on Sunday;* b. (Janet Bull), 27 Dec. 1946, London, England; m. 1st Tim Street-Porter 1967 (divorced 1975); m. 2nd A. M. M. Elliott 1976 (divorced 1978); m. 3rd Frank Cvitanovich (divorced 1988, died 1995); ed Lady Margaret Grammar School and Architectural Asscn; columnist, Petticoat Magazine 1968, Daily Mail 1969–71, Evening Standard 1971–73; own show, LBC Radio 1973; presenter of youth programmes, late night talk shows and factual series, London Weekend Television 1975–83; Head of Youth and Entertainment Features, BBC TV 1988–94, Head of Ind. Production for Entertainment 1994; Head of Live TV, Mirror Group TV 1994–95; Ed. The Independent on Sunday 1999–2001, Ed.-at-Large 2001–; presenter, Bloomberg TV 2001–05; currently Columnist, Daily Mail; Pres. Ramblers' Asscn 1994–97 (now Vice-Pres.); Trustee, Science Museum 2008; Assoc. RIBA; Patron Inst. of Contemporary Arts; Prix Italia 1992, BAFTA Award for Originality 1988, European Cedefop Award (twice), Food and Farming Industry Award 2008. *Television includes:* as series presenter: London Weekend Show 1975–79, Saturday Night People 1978–80, Six O'Clock Show 1982–83, Design Awards, Travels with Pevsner, Coast to Coast, The Midnight Hour, As The Crow Flies (series), Cathedral Calls, J'Accuse, The Internet, Men Talking, Demolition, The F Word; presented two series on teaching and nursing for Channel 5 and various documentaries for Sky, The Genius of British Art, Channel 4 2009; writer and producer: The Vampire (opera for BBC 2); as producer: Network 7 (co-producer, Channel 4) 1987. *Publications:* Scandal 1980, The British Teapot 1981, Coast to Coast 1998, As the Crow Flies 1999, Baggage – My Childhood 2004, Fall Out 2006, Life's too F***ing Short 2008, Don't Let the B*****ds Get You Down 2009. *Leisure interests:* walking, modern art. *Address:* c/o Rosemary Scoular, United Agents, 12–26 Lexington Street, London, W1P 0LE, England (office). *Telephone:* (20) 3214-0893 (office). *E-mail:* rscoular@unitedagents .co.uk (office). *Website:* www.janetstreetporter.com.

STREETER, Stephanie A.; American business executive; *CEO, Libbey Inc.;* b. 1957; m. Ed Streeter; one s. one d. (twins); ed Stanford Univ.; worked in product devt, market analysis and sales man. for several software and office equipment cos; spent 14 years with Avery Dennison Corpn in a variety of product and business man. positions, including as Group Vice-Pres. of Worldwide Office Products 1996–2000; Pres. and COO Banta Corpn (printing and supply chain man. services) 2001–02, Pres. and CEO 2002–07, Chair. 2004–07 (until its acquisition by R.R. Donnelley & Sons); mem. Bd of Dirs US Olympic Cttee 2004–09, Acting CEO 2009–10; mem. Bd of Dirs and CEO Libbey Inc. (manufacturer of glassware and tableware) 2011–; mem. Bd of Dirs Goodyear Tire and Rubber Co., Kohl's Corpn, Green Bay Packers (professional football team), Catalyst. *Address:* Libbey Inc., 300 Madison Avenue, PO Box 10060, Toledo, OH 43699-0060, USA (office). *Telephone:* (419) 325-2501 (office). *Fax:* (419) 325-2585 (office). *E-mail:* info@libbey .com (office). *Website:* www.libbey.com (office); corporate.libbey.com (office).

STREIFF, Christian; French automotive industry executive; b. 21 Sept. 1954, Sarrebourg; m.; three c.; ed Ecole Nationale Supérieure de Mines, Paris; joined Saint-Gobain Group 1979, served in various mfg positions and as Corp. Planning Man., Gen. Man. Gevetex GmbH 1988–91, Gen. Man. Vetrerie Italaine SpA, Italy 1991–94, CEO Saint-Gobain Emballage 1994–97, Pres. Pipe Div. and Chair. and CEO Pont-a-Mousson SA 1997–2001, Sr Vice-Pres. Saint-Gobain Group and Pres. Abrasives and Ceramics and Plastics Div. 2001–03, Deputy CEO Saint-Gobain Group 2003–05; Pres. and CEO Airbus S.A.S. July–Oct. 2006; Special Advisor, reporting to Chair. Man. Bd PSA Peugeot Citroën SA 2006–07, Chair. Man. Bd 2007–09; Dir (non-exec.) Thyssen-Krupp AG, Continental AG; mem. Supervisory Bd Prysmian SpA (Italy). *Address:* c/o PSA Peugeot Citroën SA, 75 avenue de la Grande-Armée, 75116 Paris, France (office).

STREISAND, Barbra Joan; American singer and actress; b. 24 April 1942, Brooklyn, New York; d. of Emanuel Streisand and Diana Streisand (née Rosen); m. 1st Elliot Gould 1963 (divorced 1971); one s.; m. 2nd James Brolin 1998; ed Erasmus Hall High School; nightclub debut at Bon Soir 1961; appeared in off-Broadway revue Another Evening with Harry Stoones 1961; appeared at Caucus Club, Detroit and Blue Angel New York 1961; played in musical comedy I Can Get It for You Wholesale 1962; began recording career with Columbia records 1963; appeared in musical play Funny Girl, New York 1964, London 1966; TV programme My Name is Barbra shown in England, Holland, Australia, Sweden, Bermuda and the Philippines, winning five Emmy awards; second programme Color Me Barbra also shown abroad; numerous concert and nightclub appearances; f. Barwood Films (film production co.) 1972; Commdr des Arts et Lettres 1984; New York, Critics Best Supporting Actress Award 1962, Grammy Awards for Best Female Pop Vocalist 1963, 1964, 1965, 1977, 1986, London Critics' Musical Award 1966, American Guild of Variety Artists' Entertainer of the Year Award 1970, Nat. Medal of Arts, Emmy Award for Best Individual Performance in a Music or Variety Programme (for Barbra Streisand: Timeless) 2001, American Film Inst. Lifetime Achievement Award 2001, Kennedy Center Honor 2008. *Recordings include:* albums: The Barbra Streisand Album 1963, The Second Barbra Streisand Album 1963, The Third Album 1964, My Name Is Barbra 1965, People 1965, Color Me Barbra 1966, Je m'appelle Barbra 1967, Barbra Streisand: A Happening In Central Park 1968, What About Me? 1969, Stoney End 1970, Barbra Joan Streisand 1972, Classical Barbra 1974, The Way We Were 1974, Lazy Afternoon 1975, A Star Is Born 1976, Superman 1977, Songbird, 1978, Wet 1979, Guilty (with Barry Gibb) 1980, Memories 1981, Emotion 1984, The Broadway Album 1986, One Voice 1986, Til I Loved You 1989, Just For The Record 1991, Butterfly 1992, Back To Broadway 1993, Barbra Streisand – The Concert 1994, The Concert – Highlights 1995, Mirror Has Two Faces 1996, Higher Ground 1997, A Love Like Ours 1999, Timeless 2000, Christmas Memories 2001, The Essential Barbra Streisand 2002, Duets 2002, The Movie Album 2003, Guilty Pleasures 2005, Love is the Answer 2009, One Night Only 2010, What Matters Most 2011, Release Me 2012; soundtracks include: Funny Girl 1968, Yentl 1983, Nuts 1987, The Prince of Tides 1991. *Films include:* Funny Girl (Acad. Award (Oscar) 1968) 1968, Hello Dolly 1969, On a Clear Day You Can See Forever 1969, The Owl and the Pussycat 1971, What's up Doc? 1972, Up the Sandbox 1973, The Way We Were 1973, For Pete's Sake 1974, Funny Lady 1975, A Star is Born 1977, Yentl 1983 (also dir and producer), Nuts 1987, Sing 1989, Prince of Tides 1990 (also dir, co-producer), The Mirror Has Two Faces (also dir) 1996, Meet the Fockers 2004. *Address:* c/o Martin Erlichman Associates, 5670 Wilshire Boulevard, Suite 2400, Los Angeles, CA 90036, USA (office); Barwood Films, 330 West 58th Street, Suite 301, New York, NY 10019, USA (office). *Telephone:* (212) 762-7191 (office). *Website:* www .barbrastreisand.com.

STREISSLER, Erich W., DrIur; Austrian economist and academic; *Professor Emeritus of Economics, Econometrics and Economic History, University of Vienna;* b. 8 April 1933, Vienna; s. of Albert Streissler and Erna Leithe; m. Monika Ruppe 1961; two s. (one deceased) three d.; ed Vienna Law School, Univ. of Vienna, Univ. of Oxford, UK, Hamilton Coll., New York, USA; studied also in France and Spain; Prof. of Statistics and Econometrics, Univ. of Freiburg Br., Germany 1962–68, twice Dean of Law and Social Science Faculty 1965–67; Prof., Univ. of Vienna 1968, now Prof. Emer., Dean of Law and Social Science Faculty 1973–74; apptd Vice-Pres. Austrian Inst. of Econ. Research 1990; Distinguished Austrian Visiting Prof., Stanford Univ., USA 1983; Pres. Austrian Econs Asscn 1988–94, Pres. Confed. of European Econ. Asscns 1990–91; mem. Bd of Control, Vienna Stock Exchange 1990–98; Treas. Int. Econ. Asscn 1992–99; mem. Austrian Acad. of Sciences; Hon. mem. Hungarian Acad. of Sciences, Bavarian Acad. of Sciences; various science prizes. *Publications:* numerous articles in scientific journals on econ. growth, distribution, monetary matters, analysis of econ. systems and especially on the history of thought in econs. *Leisure interests:* hiking, history. *Address:* Faculty of Social Sciences and Economics, Vienna University, Hohenstaufeng 9, 1010 Vienna (office); 18 Khevenhuellerstrasse 15, 1180 Vienna, Austria (home). *Telephone:* 4277-374-25 (office); 44-05-770 (home). *Fax:* 4277-9374 (office). *E-mail:* Erich.Streissler@oeaw.ac.at (office).

STREITWIESER, Andrew, Jr, AB, MA, PhD; American scientist and academic; *Professor Emeritus of Chemistry, University of California, Berkeley;* b. 23 June 1927, Buffalo, NY; s. of Andrew Streitwieser and Sophie Streitwieser; m. 1st Mary Ann Good 1950 (died 1965); m. 2nd Suzanne Cope 1967 (died 2006); m. 3rd Joyce Hessel 2007; one s. one d.; ed Stuyvesant High School and Columbia Univ.; Atomic Energy Comm. Postdoctoral Fellow, MIT 1951–52; Instructor in Chem., Univ. of Calif., Berkeley 1952–54, Asst Prof. 1954–59, Assoc. Prof. 1959–63, Prof. of Chem. 1963, Prof. Emer. 1993–, Prof. Grad. School 1995–98; consultant to industry 1957–; Guggenheim Fellow 1969; mem. NAS, American Acad. of Arts and Sciences, Bavarian Acad. of Sciences; ACS awards: Calif. Section 1964, Award in Petroleum Chem. 1967; Humboldt Sr Scientist Award (Bonn) 1976, Humboldt Award (Bonn) 1979, Norris Award in Physical Organic Chem. 1982, Cope Scholar Award 1989, Sr Scientist Mentor, Camille and Henry Dreyfus Foundation 2008, Roger Adams Award in Organic Chem. 2009. *Publications include:* Molecular Orbital Theory for Organic Chemists 1961, Solvolytic Displacement Reactions 1962, Supplemental Tables of Molecular Orbital Calculations (with J. I. Brauman) Vols I and II 1965, Progress in Physical Organic Chemistry (co-ed.) Vols I–XI 1963–74, Dictionary of π-Electron Calculations (with C. A. Coulson) 1965, Orbital and Electron Density Diagrams (with P. H. Owens) 1973, Introduction to Organic Chemistry (with C. H. Heathcock) 1976, 1981, 1985, (also with E. L. Kosower) 1992, Solutions Manual

and Study Guide for Introduction to Organic Chemistry (with C. H. Heathcock and P. A. Bartlett) 1985 (third edn), A Lifetime of Synergy with Theory and Experiment 1996. *Leisure interests:* music (especially opera), wine, photography. *Address:* 1160 Miller Avenue, Berkeley, CA 94708, USA (office); Department of Chemistry, 325B Lewis, University of California, Berkeley, CA 94720-1960, USA (office). *Telephone:* (510) 841-6877 (office); (510) 642-2204 (home). *E-mail:* astreit@ berkeley.edu (office). *Website:* chem.berkeley.edu/faculty/emeriti/streitwieser.php (office).

STRENGER, Hermann-Josef; German business executive; *Honorary Chairman of the Supervisory Board, Bayer AG;* b. 26 Sept. 1928, Cologne; m. Gisela Buchholtz 1956; two s. two d.; joined Bayer AG as commercial trainee 1949; Chemical Sales Dept –1954; assigned to subsidiary, Brazil 1954–57, to Bayer subsidiary, AB Anilin Kemi, Sweden 1958–61; Head, Sales Dept for raw materials for surface coatings, Leverkusen 1961–65; Head, Polyurethanes Dept 1965–69, Dir 1969–70; Commercial Head, Polyurethanes Div. 1970–72, mem. Bd of Man. 1972–; Deputy Chair. Man. Bd Bayer AG 1978–84, Chair. and Chief Exec. 1984–92, Chair. Supervisory Bd, CEO 1992–2002, now Hon. Chair.; Chair. Supervisory Bd VEBA AG; apptd Chair. Carl Duisberg Gesellschaft 1987; Chair. Supervisory Bd Linde AG 1996; mem. Supervisory Bd Hapag-Lloyd AG 1983, Karstadt AG 1983. *Address:* c/o Bayer AG, 51368 Leverkusen, Germany.

STREPPEL, J. B. M. (Joseph Bonifatius Maria); Dutch business executive; *Chairman of the Supervisory Board, Royal KPN;* ed Tilburg Univ.; CEO Labouchere 1991–95; CEO FGH Bank 1995; Chief Financial Officer AEGON NV 1998–2009; mem. Supervisory Bd Royal KPN 2003–, Chair. 2010–, Chair. Nominating and Corp. Governance Cttee, mem. Remuneration and Organizational Devt Cttee; mem. Supervisory Bd Van Lanschot NV; mem. Cttee of Listed Cos of Euronext (Amsterdam); Chair. Shareholders Communication Channel, Monitoring Cttee Corp. Governance Code, Duisenberg School of Finance, Holland Financial Centre. *Address:* Royal KPN, Maanplein 55, 2516 CK The Hague, Netherlands (office). *Telephone:* (70) 451-01-00 (office). *Fax:* (70) 451-01-01 (office). *E-mail:* ad.scheepbouwer@kpn.com (office). *Website:* (office).

STRETTON, James, BA; British business executive; *Chairman, Lammermuir Festival;* b. 16 Dec. 1943, Peterborough, Cambs., England; m. Isobel Christine Robertson 1968; two d.; ed Laxton Grammar School, Oundle, Worcester Coll., Oxford; Deputy Man. Dir Standard Life Assurance Co. 1988–94, Chief Exec. UK Operations 1994–2001; Dir Bank of England 1998–2003, Chair. Bank of England Pension Trustee Co. 2001–04; fmr Chair. The Wise Group; mem. Scottish Business Forum 1998–99, Court of Univ. of Edinburgh 1996–2002 (apptd Rector's Assessor 2003), Franchise Bd of Lloyds 2002–09 (Chair. Lloyd's Pension Scheme Trustees) 2010–14; fmr Disciplinary Bd of Actuarial Profession; Dir Edinburgh Int. Festival Ltd 1997–2004; Trustee, Lamp of Lothian Collegiate Trust 2003–; Chair. Lammermuir Festival 2010–. *Address:* 15 Letham Mains, Haddington, East Lothian, EH41 4NW, Scotland.

STRICKER, Steven (Steve) Charles; American professional golfer; b. 23 Feb. 1967, Edgerton, Wis.; m. Nicki Stricker; one d.; ed Univ. of Illinois; grew up playing golf at Lake Ripley Country Club and Edgerton Towne Country Club; turned professional 1990; began career on Canadian Professional Golf Tour, won two tournaments; first joined PGA Tour 1994; first successes at top level include Kemper Open 1996, Motorola Western Open 1996, and seven top-ten finishes on way to finishing fourth on PGA Tour money list 1996; has won eleven tournaments on PGA Tour including WGC-Accenture Match Play Championship 2001 and two FedEx Cup playoff events; winner The Barclays 2007, Crowne Plaza Invitational at Colonial 2009, John Deere Classic 2009, 2010, 2011, Deutsche Bank Championship 2009, Northern Trust Open 2010, Memorial Tournament 2011, Hyundai Tournament of Champions 2012; other wins include Wisconsin State Open (as an amateur) 1987, Victoria Open (Canada) 1990, Wisconsin State Open 1990, 1991, 1998, 2000, Canadian PGA Championship 1993, The Shark Shootout (with Jerry Kelly) 2009; results in major championships: tied for fifth at US Open 1998, second at PGA Championship 1998, fifth at US Open 1999, tied for tenth at US Masters 2001, tied for sixth at US Open 2006, tied for seventh at PGA Championship 2006, tied for eighth at British Open 2007, tied for seventh 2008, tied for sixth at US Masters 2009; mem. US team at Dunhill Cup 1996 (winners), US team at Presidents Cup 1996 (winners), 2007 (winners), 2009 (winners), US team at Ryder Cup 2008 (winners), 2010, 2012; inducted into Wisconsin State Golf Asscn Hall of Fame 2007. *Address:* c/o The PGA of America, 100 Avenue of the Champions, Palm Beach Gardens, FL 33410, USA.

STRICKLAND, John Estmond, MA, JP; British business executive; *Chairman, Octopus Holdings Ltd;* b. 23 Oct. 1939; s. of William F. Strickland and Nora N. Strickland; m. Anthea Granville-Lewis 1963; three s.; ed Jesus Coll., Univ. of Cambridge; early positions with IBM in UK and Control Data in USA; Asst Gen. Man. TSV, Hongkong and Shanghai Banking Corpn 1980–82, Gen. Man. TSV 1983–88, Exec. Dir Services 1989–96, Chair. 1996–99; Dir HSBC Holdings PLC 1988, Marine Midland Bank 1991–96, Midland Bank PLC 1993–96; Chair. Hongkong Bank Malaysia Berhad 1996–98; Vice-Chair. Hang Seng Bank Ltd 1996; Chair. Octopus Holdings Ltd 2011–; Chair. Hong Kong Cyberport Management Co. Ltd 2003–10; Pres. Outward Bound Trust of Hong Kong; mem. Bd of Dirs Airport Authority Hong Kong, Hong Kong Exchanges and Clearing Ltd 2000–, Esquel Enterprises Ltd 2001–; mem. Council Outward Bound Trust of Hong Kong; Hon. Fellow, Univ. of Hong Kong; Hong Kong Computer Soc., Hong Kong Inst. of Bankers, Hong Kong Man. Asscn; Dr hc (City Univ. of Hong Kong), (Hong Kong Polytechnic Univ.). *Leisure interests:* mountaineering, reading. *Address:* Octopus Cards Limited, 46/F, Manhattan Place, 23 Wang Tai Road, Kowloon Bay, Kowloon, Hong Kong Special Administrative Region, People's Republic of China (office). *Website:* www.octopus.com.hk (office).

STRICKLAND, Theodore (Ted), BA, MA, PhD, MDiv; American psychologist, politician and fmr state governor; *Member, Governors' Council, Health Project, Bipartisan Policy Center;* b. 4 Aug. 1941, Lucasville, Ohio; s. of Orville Strickland and Carrie Strickland; m. Frances Smith; ed Asbury Coll., Wilmore, Ky, Univ. of Kentucky, Lexington, Asbury Theological Seminary; Consulting Psychologist, Southern Ohio Correctional Facility 1985–92, 1994–96; Dir of Social Services, Kentucky Methodist Home (children's home); Asst Prof. of Psychology, Shawnee State Univ., Portsmouth, Ohio 1988–92, 1994–96; also served as United Methodist

Minister; briefly Assoc. Pastor, Wesley United Methodist Church (now Cornerstone United Methodist Church), Portsmouth; cand. for 6th Congressional Dist of Ohio 1976, 1978, 1980; mem. US House of Reps for 6th Congressional Dist of Ohio 1993–95, 1997–2007; Gov. of Ohio 2007–11; mem. Govs' Council, Health Project, Bipartisan Policy Center, Washington, DC 2011–; Co-Chair. Appalachian Regional Comm. 2009; Chair. Midwest Govs' Asscn 2010; mem. American Psychological Asscn, Ohio Psychological Asscn; Democrat; Outstanding Psychologist Award, Nat. Alliance for the Mentally Ill (co-recipient) 2004. *Address:* Bipartisan Policy Center, Suite 1000, 1225 I Street NW, Washington, DC 20005, USA (office). *Telephone:* (202) 204-2400 (office). *Fax:* (202) 637-9220 (office). *E-mail:* bipartisaninfo@bipartisanpolicy.org (office). *Website:* www.bipartisanpolicy.org (office); www.tedstrickland.com.

STRINA, Luisa; Brazilian gallery owner, art dealer and collector; art dealer 1970–; f. Galeria Luisa Strina, São Paulo 1974; first Latin-American gallery invited to participate in Basel Art Fair 1992. *Address:* Rua Padre João Manuel 755 – loja 02, Cerqueira César, São Paulo, 01411–001 Brazil (office). *Telephone:* (11) 3088-2471 (office). *Fax:* (11) 3064-6391 (office). *E-mail:* info@galerialuisastrina .com.br (office). *Website:* www.galerialuisastrina.com.br.

STRINGER, Sir Howard, Kt, MA; American/British electronics industry executive and broadcasting executive; b. 19 Feb. 1942, Cardiff, Wales; s. of Harry Stringer and Marjorie Mary Pook; m. Jennifer A. Kinmond Patterson 1978; two c.; ed Oundle School, Northants., Merton Coll., Oxford; emigrated to USA 1965; served with US Army in Viet Nam 1965–67; researcher and producer, CBS News 1967–76; Exec. Producer, CBS Reports 1976–81, CBS Evening News 1981–84; naturalized US citizen 1985; Exec. Vice-Pres. CBS News 1984–86, Pres. 1986–88; Pres. CBS Broadcast Group 1988–95; Chair. and CEO Tele-TV 1995–97; Pres. Sony Corpn of America 1997, Chair. and CEO 1998–2012, Pres. and CEO Sony Corpn 2005–12, Chair. 2005–12, Chair. of the Bd of Sony Corpn 2012–13; Vice-Chair. American Film Inst. –1999, Chair. Bd of Trustees 1999–; mem. Bd of Dirs Six Continents PLC, BBC 2013–; Gov. Motion Picture and TV Fund Foundation; Trustee, Presbyterian Hosp., Museum of TV and Radio; Hon. Fellow, Merton Coll., Oxford 2000, Royal Welsh Coll. of Music and Drama 2001; US Army Commendation Medal; Dr hc (Univ. of Glamorgan, Univ. of the Arts, London); nine Emmy Awards for: The Rockefellers, The Palestinians, A Tale of Two Irelands, The Defense of the United States, The Boat People, The Boston Goes to China, The Fire Next Door, and The CIA's Secret Army 1974–76; First Amendment Leadership Award, Radio and Television News Dirs Foundation 1996, inducted into Broadcasting and Cable Hall of Fame 1996, Steven J. Ross Humanitarian Award, UJA-Fed. of New York 1999, inducted into Royal Television Soc.'s Welsh Hall of Fame 1999, Visionary Award for Innovative Leadership in Media and Entertainment, Museum of Television and Radio 2007, honoured by Lincoln Center, Big Brothers Big Sisters and New York Hall of Science. *Television includes:* CBS Reports (exec. producer) 1976–81, CBS Evening News with Dan Rather (exec. producer) 1981–84.

STRITCH, Elaine; American actress and singer; b. 2 Feb. 1926, Detroit, Mich.; d. of George J. Stritch and Mildred Stritch (née Tobe); m. John Bay 1973 (died 1982); ed Sacred Heart Convent, Detroit, Drama Workshop, New School for Social Research; Broadway debut as Pamela Brewster in Loco 1946; other performances include Three Indelicate Ladies 1947, Yes M'Lord 1949, Melba Snyder in revival of Pal Joey 1952, Bus Stop 1955, Mimi Paragon in Sail Away, New York 1961, London 1962, Martha in Who's Afraid of Virginia Woolf? 1962, 1965, Joanne in Company, New York 1970, London 1971, Love Letters, London 1990, Elaine Stritch At Liberty (tour) 2002. *Films include:* The Scarlet Hour 1956, Three Violent People 1956, A Farewell to Arms 1957, The Perfect Furlough 1958, Who Killed Teddy Bear 1965, Pigeons 1971, September 1988, Cocoon: The Return, Cadillac Man 1990, Out to Sea 1997, Screwed 2000, Small Time Crooks 2000, Autumn in New York 2001, Monster-in-Law 2005, Romance & Cigarettes 2005. *Television includes:* My Sister Eileen 1962, Two's Company (British series) 1975–76, 1979, Stranded 1986, Life's a Bitch (series) 2003, Elaine Stritch: At Liberty (Emmy Award for Outstanding Individual Performance in a Variety or Music Programme 2004), Paradise 2004, 30 Rock 2007. *Publication:* Am I Blue? – Living With Diabetes and, Dammit, Having Fun 1984. *Address:* c/o The Blake Agency, 23441 Malibu Road, Malibu, CA 90265, USA. *E-mail:* blakeagency@aol.com.

STROE, Radu; Romanian engineer and politician; b. 31 Aug. 1949, Iași Co.; m. Victoria Stroe (divorced); ed Civilian Marine Inst., Constanța, Univ. of Law, Bucharest; marine and naval officer in merchant fleet, Navrom, Constanța 1972–74; Chief Engineer III with Dept of Naval Transportation, Ministry of Transport and Communications 1974–85; Chief Engineer, Admin of Danube-Bucharest Canal 1986–90; Gen. Dir, Ministry of Transport 1991–93, Minister's Counsellor 1993–94, Chief Engineer 1994–97; Deputy Sec. Gen. and Sec. Gen. of the Govt 1997–2000; mem. Nat. Liberal Party; mem. Camera Deputaților (Chamber of Deputies) for Maramureș Co. 2001–04, for Bucharest 2010–; Minister for Co-ordinating the Gen. Secr. of Govt 2005–08; mem. Senate for Maramureș Co. and Pres. Parl. Comm. for Overseeing and Controlling the Romanian Intelligence Service 2005–08; Project Man., Frontal Communication SRL 2009–10; Minister-Del. for Admin, Ministry of Admin and Interior Aug.–Dec. 2012; Minister of Internal Affairs Dec. 2012–14; Officer, Order 'Star of Romania'. *Address:* c/o Ministry of Internal Affairs, 010086 Bucharest 1, Piața Revoluției 1A, Romania. *E-mail:* petitii@mai.gov.ro.

STROHAL, Christian, DrIur; Austrian diplomatist and international organization executive; *Permanent Representative, Organization for Security and Co-operation in Europe, Vienna;* b. 1 May 1951, Vienna; m.; three c.; ed schools in Vienna, studies in law, econs and int. relations in Vienna, London and Geneva; with Ministry for Foreign Affairs (MFA) since 1976, postings to London, Geneva and Deputy Head of Mission to Rabat 1981–85, Head of Human Rights Office, MFA, Minister and Deputy Perm. Rep., Austrian Mission to UN and int. orgs, Geneva 1988–92, Amb. and Special Rep. for World Conf. on Human Rights 1992–93, Dir for Human Rights, Int. Humanitarian Law, and Minority and Gender Issues, MFA 1994–2000, Amb. to Luxembourg 2000–03, Amb. and Dir Office for Democratic Insts and Human Rights, OSCE 2003–08, Perm. Rep. to UN, Geneva 2008–13, to OSCE, Vienna 2013–; del. to numerous int. confs in framework of UN, Council of Europe and OSCE; Vice-Chair. UN Comm. on Human Rights 1997–98, UN Human Rights Council 2011–12; Pres. Governing Council, UN Security Council Compensation Comm. 2009–10, Governing Bodies, Int. Org. for

Migration 2011–12, lecturer at various insts; Felix Ermacora Prize for Human Rights. *Publications:* several publs on int. human rights issues. *Address:* Ministry for European and International Affairs, Minoritenplatz 8, 1014 Vienna, Austria (office). *Telephone:* (5) 011-50-0 (office). *Fax:* (5) 011-59-0 (office). *E-mail:* christian .strohal@bmeia.gv.at (office). *Website:* www.bmeia.gv.at (office).

STRØM-ERICHSEN, Anne-Grete; Norwegian computer engineer and politician; b. 1949; m.; two c.; mem., Bergen City Council 1991–2005, mem. Exec. Bd 1991–2000, Deputy Mayor, City of Bergen 1998–99, Mayor 1999–2000, Chief Commr, City of Bergen 2000–03, Commr 2003–, Councillor and Chair., Standing Cttee on Environmental Affairs and Urban Devt, City of Bergen 2003–05; Deputy Leader, Labour Party in Bergen 1992, Leader, Hordaland Labour Party 1997–99, mem. Det norske Arbeiderparti (Norwegian Labour Party) Cen. Council 2001–; Minister of Defence 2005–09, 2012–13, Minister of Health and Care Services 2009–12. *Address:* c/o Ministry of Defence, Glacisgt. 1, POB 8126 Dep., 0032 Oslo, Norway (office).

STRÖMHOLM, Stig Fredrik, LLD, DJur; Swedish university vice-chancellor (retd); b. 16 Sept. 1931, Boden; s. of Major Frederik Strömholm and Gerda Jansson; m. Gunilla M. Forslund 1958; one s. two d.; ed Univs of Uppsala, Cambridge and Munich; clerk, Southern Dist Court of Uppsala 1958–60; Jr Judge, Stockholm Court of Appeal 1961; Asst Prof. of Comparative Law, Uppsala Univ. 1966, Prof. of Jurisprudence 1969, Dean, Faculty of Law 1973–79, Deputy Vice-Chancellor 1978–89, Vice-Chancellor 1989–97; Pres. Royal Swedish Acad. of Letters, History and Antiquities 1985–93, Academia Europaea, London 1997–2002; mem. several Swedish and foreign acads; Orden pour le Mérite (FRG) and other decorations; Dr hc at several Swedish and foreign univs; several prizes. *Publications:* 25 vols of legal science including Le droit moral de l'auteur, three vols 1967–73, A Short History of Legal Thinking in the West 1985; some 20 vols of criticism and fiction. *Leisure interests:* reading, travelling. *Address:* Flogstavägen 5CI, 752 73 Uppsala, Sweden. *Telephone:* (18) 515045. *E-mail:* gunilla.stromholm@telia.com.

STROMINGER, Jack L., MD; American physician, biochemist and academic; *Higgins Professor of Biochemistry, Department of Molecular and Cellular Biology, Harvard University;* b. 7 Aug. 1925, New York; m.; four c.; ed Harvard and Yale Univs; Intern, Barnes Hosp., St Louis 1948–49; Research Fellow, American Coll. of Physicians, Dept of Pharmacology, Washington Univ. School of Medicine, St Louis 1949–50, Research Asst 1950–51; Sr Asst Surgeon, Public Health Service, Nat. Inst. of Arthritis and Metabolic Diseases, Bethesda 1951–54; leave of absence, Carlsberg Laboratory, Copenhagen, Denmark and Molteno Inst., Cambridge Univ., England, Commonwealth Fund Fellow 1955; Asst Prof. of Pharmacology, Dept of Pharmacology, Washington Univ. School of Medicine, Markel Scholar in Medical Science 1958–60, Prof., 1960–61, Forsyth Faculty Fellow 1960, Prof. of Pharmacology and Microbiology, Depts of Pharmacology and Microbiology 1961–64; Prof. of Pharmacology and Chemical Microbiology, Univ. of Wis. Medical School, Madison, Chair. Dept of Pharmacology, mem. Univ. Cttee on Molecular Biology 1964–68; Prof. of Biochemistry, Dept of Biochemistry and Molecular Biology, Harvard Univ., Cambridge, Mass. 1968–83, Chair. Dept of Biochemistry and Molecular Biology 1970–73, Higgins Prof. of Biochemistry 1983–, Dir of Basic Sciences, Sidney Farber Cancer Center 1974–77; Head of Tumor Virology Div., Dana–Farber Cancer Inst., Boston 1977–; mem. Steering Cttee Biomedical Sciences Scientific Working Group, WHO; mem. NAS 1970–, American Acad. of Arts and Sciences, Nat. Inst. of Medicine 1975–, AAAS, American Soc. of Biological Chemists, of Microbiologists, of Pharmacology and Experimental Therapeutics, American Asscn of Immunologists, ACS; Hon. DSc (Trinity Coll., Dublin) 1975; Guggenheim Fellowship 1974–75, John J. Abel Award in Pharmacology 1960, Paul-Lewis Laboratories Award in Enzyme Chem. 1962, NAS Award in Microbiology in Honour of Selman Waxman 1968, Rose Payne Award, American Soc. for Histocompatibility and Immunogenetics 1986, Pasteur Medal 1990, Albert Lasker Award for Basic Medical Research 1995, Paul Ehrlich Prize 1996, Klemperer Award, New York Acad. of Medicine 1999, Japan Prize, Science and Technology Foundation of Japan 1999. *Address:* Dana-Farber Cancer Institute, 44 Binney Street, Dana 1410, Boston, MA 02115; Department of Molecular and Cell Biology, Harvard University, Room 407, 7 Divinity Avenue, Cambridge, MA 02138, USA (office). *Telephone:* (617) 632-3083 (office). *Fax:* (617) 632-2662. *E-mail:* jlstrom@ fas.harvard.edu (office). *Website:* www.mcb.harvard.edu/Faculty/Strominger.html (office); www.people.fas.harvard.edu/%7Ejlstrom (office).

STRONACH, Hon. Belinda C., PC; Canadian politician and business executive; b. 2 May 1966, Newmarket, Ont.; d. of Frank Stronach; two c.; ed York Univ.; joined family-owned Magna Int. Inc. (automotive components supplier) 1988, mem. Bd of Dirs 1988–, held various sr positions including Vice-Pres. 1995–98, Exec. Vice-Pres. 1998–2001, CEO 2001–02, Pres. and CEO 2002–04, Exec. Vice-Chair. 2006–2010; resgnd from Magna in 2004 to run for leadership of Conservative Party of Canada, which she lost, also resgnd as Chair. Bd of Dirs Decoma Int. Inc., Tesma Int. Inc.; MP (Conservative) for Newmarket-Aurora and trade critic 2004–05, MP (Liberal) May 2005–08; Minister of Human Resources and Skills Devt and Minister responsible for Democratic Renewal 2005–06; Critic for Competitiveness and the New Economy 2006–07, Chair. Women's Caucus 2006–07; Founder and Chair. Belinda Stronach Foundation 2008–; fmr mem. Bd of Dirs Intier Automotive Inc.; Founding mem. Canadian Automotive Partnership Council; Dir Yves Landry Technological Endowment Fund, US Chamber of Commerce 2003–; mem. Dean's Council, John F. Kennedy School of Govt, Harvard Univ., Dean's Advisory Council, Joseph L. Rotman School of Man., Univ. of Toronto; mem. Ont. Task Force on Productivity, Competitiveness and Econ. Progress; Hon. LLD (McMaster Univ.) 2003, Dr hc (Brock Univ.) 2009; ranked by Time Magazine as one of the world's 100 most influential people 2004, ranked 77th by Forbes magazine amongst 100 Most Powerful Women 2004, Paul Harris Award 2008. *Address:* The Belinda Stronach Foundation, 236 Avenue Road, Suite 300, Toronto, ON M5R 2J4, Canada (office). *Telephone:* (416) 531-1919 (office). *Fax:* (416) 531-1918 (office). *E-mail:* info@tbsf.ca (office). *Website:* www.tbsf.ca (office); www.belindastronach.ca.

STRONACH, Frank, CM; Austrian/Canadian automotive industry executive and politician; *Founder and Honorary Chairman, Magna International Inc.;* b. (Franz Strohsack), 6 Sept. 1932, Kleinsemmering, Styria, Austria; m. Elfriede Sallmutter; one s. one d. Belinda C. Stronach (q.v.); tool and die apprentice in Weiz, Austria;

emigrated to Montreal, Canada 1954; various jobs including machinist, dish-washer and golf course asst, Kitchener and Toronto, Ont. 1954–57; Co-founder (with Tony Czapka) Multimatic Investments Ltd 1957, merged with Magna Electronics Co. Ltd 1969, renamed Magna International Inc. 1973, Chair. 1969–2011, Hon. Chair. 2011–; cand. for Liberal Party, Fed. Elections 1988; Pnr, Stronach & Co. (consulting firm); Owner Magna Entertainment Corpn specializing in horse-racing entertainment and owns and operates several US racetracks; entered Austrian politics, founding Stronach Inst. 2011, campaigned against the euro, f. Team Stronach for Austria political party 2012; Hon. Prof. of Practical Business Man., Graz Univ. of Tech. 2004; Hon. PhD (Haifa Univ.), Hon. LLD (Univ. Coll. of Cape Breton), Hon. DComm (St Mary's Univ., Halifax), Hon. DEng (Kettering Univ.) 1997; inducted into Canadian Business Hall of Fame 1996, Business Leader of the Year Award, Richard Ivey School of Business 1997, Entrepreneur of the Year Award, Univ. of Michigan 1998, Sovereign Award for Outstanding Owner nine times, Eclipse Award for Outstanding Owner 1998, 1999, 2000, Eclipse Award for Outstanding Breeder 2000, 2004, 2005, 2006, Entrepreneur of the Year Lifetime Achievement Award, Ernst & Young 2000, 2001, Canadian Int. Exec. of the Year, Canadian Council for Int. Business 2002, Gold Medal for meritorious service from Austria 2002, Person of the Year Award, Yves Landry Foundation 2004, B'nai Brith Canada Award of Merit 2005. *Leisure interest:* thoroughbred horse breeding. *Address:* Magna International Inc., 337 Magna Drive, Aurora, ON L4G 7K1, Canada (office). *Telephone:* (905) 726-2462 (office). *Fax:* (905) 726-7164 (office). *E-mail:* info@magna.com (office). *Website:* www.magnaint.com (office); www.magna.com (office).

STRONG, David F., PhD, FRSC; Canadian geologist and university president; *President, University Canada West; b.* 26 Feb. 1944, Botwood, Newfoundland; m. Lynda Joan Marshall; two d.; ed Memorial Univ. of Newfoundland, Lehigh Univ., Pa, USA, Univ. of Edinburgh, Scotland; Asst Prof., Dept of Geology, Memorial Univ. of Newfoundland 1970–72, Assoc. Prof. 1972–74, Acting Head of Dept 1974–75, Prof., Dept of Earth Sciences 1974–90, Univ. Research Prof. 1985–90, Special Adviser to Pres. 1986–87, Vice-Pres. (Academic) 1987–90; Pres. and Vice-Chancellor Univ. of Vic. 1990–2000, Pres. Emer. 2000–; Chair. and CEO LearningWise Inc. 2002–; Pres. Univ. Canada West 2005–; Visiting Prof. Université de Montpellier, France 1976–77; W. F. James Prof. of Pure and Applied Sciences, St Francis Xavier Univ., Nova Scotia 1981–82; mem. Bd of Dirs Seabright Corpn Ltd 1986–; Assoc. Ed. Canadian Journal of Earth Sciences 1977–83, Transactions of the Royal Soc. of Edinburgh 1980–; Chair. Natural Sciences and Eng Research Council of Canada 1983–86, mem. 1982–88; mem. Research Council, Canadian Inst. of Advanced Research 1986–, Newfoundland and Labrador Advisory Council on Science and Tech. 1988–, Governing Council, Nat. Research Council of Canada 1999– (mem. Exec. Cttee 2002–); Fellow Geological Asscn of Canada, Geological Soc. of America, Soc. of Econ. Geologists; mem. Canadian Inst. of Mining and Metallurgy, Mineralogical Asscn of Canada; Univ. of Edin. Swiney Lecturer 1981; Hon. Fellow Geological Asscn of Canada; Hon. DSc (Memorial Univ., Newfoundland) 1990; Hon. LLD (St Francis Xavier Univ.) 1992; APICS Young Scientist Award (now the Frazer Medal) 1973, Foreign Exchange Fellowships to Japan 1976, to France 1976–77, Canadian Inst. of Mining and Metallurgy Distinguished Service Award 1979, Geological Asscn of Canada Past Pres.'s Medal 1980. *Publications:* about 200 scientific and technical papers. *Leisure interests:* reading, music, gardening. *Address:* Office of the President, University Canada West, 950 Kings Road, Victoria, BC V8T 1W6 (office); LearningWise Inc., Suite 135A, R-Hut, McKenzie Avenue, PO Box 3075 STN CSC, Victoria, BC V8W 3W2, Canada (office). *Telephone:* (250) 978-1800 (office); (250) 472-4331. *Fax:* (250) 978-1801 (office); (250) 721-6497. *E-mail:* david.strong@universitycanadawest.ca (office); dfstrong@learningwise.com (office). *Website:* www.universitycanadawest.ca (office); www.learningwise.com (office).

STRONG, Liam (Gerald Porter), BA; British business executive; *Chairman, Virtual IT Ltd; b.* 6 Jan. 1945, Enniskillen, Northern Ireland; s. of Gerald James Strong and Geraldine Crozier Strong; m. Jacqueline Gray 1970; one s. one d.; ed Trinity Coll., Dublin; joined Procter & Gamble, Newcastle-upon-Tyne 1967–71; Household Man., Reckitt & Colman 1971, moved to Corp. Planning Unit, London 1973, Marketing and Sales Dir, then Gen. Man. Reckitt & Colman 1975–80, Vice-Pres. Sunset Designs, Calif., USA 1980–82, Head Int. Pharmaceuticals Div., Reckitt & Colman 1982–86, Pres. Durkee French, USA 1986–89; Dir of Marketing, British Airways 1989–90, Dir Marketing and Operations 1990–91; Chief Exec. Sears PLC 1991–97; CEO Worldcom International 1997–2001; Pres. CEO Teleglobe International Holdings Ltd. 2003–06; currently Pnr, Cerberus European Capital Advisors LLP; Chair. (non-exec.) Virtual IT Ltd, London; mem. Bd of Dirs Skystream Inc. 2000–; mem. Bd of Govs Ashridge (Bonar Law Memorial) Trust. *Leisure interests:* reading, shooting, opera. *Address:* Virtual IT Ltd, The Lime House, Quadrant Business Centre, Salusbury Road, London, NW6 6RJ, England (office). *Telephone:* (20) 7644-2800 (office). *Fax:* (20) 7644-2801 (office). *E-mail:* info@virtualit.biz (office). *Website:* www.virtualit.biz (office).

STRONG, Rt Hon. Maurice F., PC, CC, OM, LLD, FRS, FRSA, FRSC; Canadian environmentalist, international organization official and business executive; *b.* 29 April 1929, Oak Lake, Man.; s. of Frederick Milton Strong and Mary Fyfe Strong; m. 1st Pauline Olivette Williams 1950 (divorced 1980); two s. two d. one foster d.; m. 2nd Hanne Marstrand 1981; ed Oak Lake High School, Manitoba; served in UN Secr. 1947; Pres. or Dir of various Canadian and int. corpns 1954–66; also involved in leadership of various pvt. orgs in field of devt and int. affairs; Dir-Gen. External Aid Office of Canadian Govt 1966 (now Canadian Int. Devt Agency); Chair. Canadian Int. Devt Bd; Alt. Gov. IBRD, ADB, Caribbean Devt Bank; UN Under-Sec. Gen. with responsibility for environmental affairs 1970–72, Chief Exec. for 1972 Conf. on Human Environment, Stockholm, June 1972; Montague Burton Prof. of Int. Relations, Univ. of Edin. 1973; Exec. Dir UNEP 1973–75; Chair. Petro Canada 1976–78; Pres. Stronat Investments Ltd 1976–80; Chair. Bd of Govs Int. Devt Research Centre 1977–78; Chair. Strovest Holdings Inc., Procor Inc. 1978–79, AZL Resources Inc. 1978–83, Int. Energy Devt Corpn 1980–83, NS Round Table Soc. for Int. Devt, Canadian Devt Investment Corpn 1982–84, Supercritical Combustion Corpn, Int. Advisory Group, CH2M Hill Cos Ltd; Chair. and Dir Tech. Devt Corpn; Dir or mem. numerous business and conservation groups in Canada and internationally including Foundation Bd World Econ. Forum, Leadership for Environment and Devt, Zenon Environmental, Inc., The Humane Soc. of the US; UnderSec.-Gen., UN 1985–87, 1989; Pres. World Fed.

UNA 1987, The Baca Corpn; Dir Better World Soc. 1988; Chair., Pres. American Water Devt Inc., Denver 1986–89; Sec.-Gen. UN 1992 Conf. on Environment and Devt; Chair. Ontario Hydro 1992–95, World Resources Inst.; Sr Adviser to Pres. of World Bank 1995–; Under-Sec.-Gen. and Exec. Co-ordinator for UN Reform 1997; Under-Sec.-Gen. and Sr Adviser to Sec.-Gen. of UN 1998–2005 (resgnd); Pres. Council UN Univ. for Peace, San José, Costa Rica 2001–; Chair. Earth Council Foundation; mem. Bd of Dirs UN Foundation, Int. Advisory Bd, Toyota Motor Corpn, Int. Advisory Bd, Center of Int. Devt at Harvard Univ., Int. Advisory Council, Liu Centre for the Study of Global Issues at Univ. of British Columbia, Lamont-Doherty Observatory Advisory Bd; Distinguished Fellow, Int. Inst. for Sustainable Devt; Fellow, Royal Architectural Inst. of Canada; Hon. Bd mem. David Suzuki Foundation; hon. degrees from 49 univs; Nat. Order of the Southern Cross (Brazil), Commander of the Order of the Golden Ark (Netherlands), Royal Order of the Polar Star (Sweden 1996, Henri Pittier Order of Venezuela 1997; Tyler Evironmental Prize 1974, Nat. Audubon Soc. Award 1975, Charles A. Lindbergh Award 1981, Pearson Peace Medal 1989, Alexander Onassis Delphi Prize 1993, Int. St Frances Prize for the Environment 1993, Jawaharlal Nehru Award for Int. Understanding 1994, Blue Planet Prize, Asahi Glass Foundation 1994, IKEA Environmental Award 1995, Millennium Award, The Princes' Award Foundation, Denmark 2000, Global Steering Wheel Int. Prize, Russia 2001, Global Environment Leadership Award 2002, Candlelight Award, Carriage House Center on Global Issues 2002, NAS Public Welfare Medal (first non-US citizen) 2004 and numerous other awards, prizes and decorations. *Publications:* The Great Building Bee (with Jacques Hébert) 1980, A Life for the Planet 1999, Where On Earth Are We Going?; various articles in journals. *Address:* S3 Holdings Inc., 150 Isabella Street, Suite 100, Ottawa, ON K15 1V7, Canada (office). *Telephone:* (613) 232-1222 (office). *Fax:* (613) 569-4667 (office). *E-mail:* info@mauricestrong.org (office). *Website:* www.mauricestrong.net (office).

STRONG, Sir Roy Colin, Kt, PhD, FSA, FRSL; English historian, writer and fmr museum director; *b.* 23 Aug. 1935, London; s. of George Edward Clement Strong and Mabel Ada Smart; m. Julia Trevelyan Oman 1971 (died 2003); ed Queen Mary Coll., Univ. of London and Warburg Inst.; Asst Keeper, Nat. Portrait Gallery, London 1959–67, Dir 1967–73; Dir, Victoria and Albert Museum, London 1974–87; Vice-Chair., South Bank Bd (now South Bank Centre) 1985–90; Dir, Oman Productions Ltd, Nordstern Fine Art Insurance 1988–2001; organizer of exhbns including The Elizabethan Image (Tate Gallery) 1969, The Destruction of the Country House (Victoria and Albert Museum) 1974, Artists of the Tudor Court (Victoria and Albert Museum) 1983; mem. Arts Council of GB 1983–87 (Chair., Arts Panel 1983–87), Council, RCA 1979–87; Patron, Pallant House, Chichester 1986–; Fellow, Queen Mary Coll., Univ. of London, Royal Soc. of Literature 1999; High Bailiff and Searcher of the Sanctuary of Westminster Abbey 2000; Pres., Garden History Soc. 2000–06; Hon. MA (Worcester) 2004; Hon. DLitt (Leeds) 1983, (Keele) 1984; Shakespeare Prize (FVS Foundation, Hamburg) 1980, President's Award Royal Photographic Soc. of Great Britain 2003. *Television:* Royal Gardens (series) 1992, The Diets Time Forgot (series) 2008, Visions of England 2010. *Radio:* numerous series. *Publications:* Portraits of Queen Elizabeth I 1963, Leicester's Triumph (with J. A. Van Dorsten) 1964, Holbein and Henry VIII 1967, Tudor and Jacobean Portraits 1969, The English Icon: Elizabethan and Jacobean Portraiture 1969, Elizabeth R (with Julia Trevelyan Oman) 1971, Van Dyck: Charles I on Horseback 1972, Inigo Jones: The Theatre of the Stuart Court (with S. Orgel) 1972, Mary Queen of Scots (with Julia Trevelyan Oman) 1972, Splendour at Court: Renaissance Spectacle and The Theatre of Power 1973, An Early Victorian Album (with Colin Ford) 1974, Nicholas Hilliard 1975, The Cult of Elizabeth: Elizabethan Portraiture and Pageantry 1977, And When Did You Last See Your Father? The Victorian Painter and British History 1978, The Renaissance Garden in England 1979, Britannia Triumphans, Inigo Jones, Rubens and Whitehall Palace 1980, Holbein 1980, The English Miniature (with J. Murdoch, J. Murrell and P. Noon) 1981, The English Year (with Julia Trevelyan Oman) 1982, The English Renaissance Miniature 1983, Artists of the Tudor Court (with J. Murrell) 1983, Glyndebourne, A Celebration (contrib.) 1984, Art and Power, Renaissance Festivals 1450–1650 1984, Strong Points 1985, Henry Prince of Wales and England's Lost Renaissance 1986, C. V. Wedgwood Festschrift (contrib.) 1986, Creating Small Gardens 1986, Gloriana, Portraits of Queen Elizabeth I 1987, The Small Garden Designers Handbook 1987, Cecil Beaton: the Royal Portraits 1988, Creating Small Formal Gardens 1989, Lost Treasures of Britain 1990, A Celebration of Gardens 1991, Small Period Gardens 1992, Royal Gardens 1992, Versace Theatre 1992, William Larkin 1994, A Country Life 1994, Successful Small Gardens 1994, The Tudor and Stuart Monarchy 1995, The Story of Britain 1996, The English Arcadia 1996, Country Life 1897–1997 1997, The Roy Strong Diaries 1967–1987 1997, On Happiness 1997, The Tudor and Stuart Monarchy 1998, The Spirit of Britain 1999, Garden Party 2000, The Artist and the Garden 2000, Ornament in the Small Garden 2001, Feast – A History of Grand Eating 2002, The Laskett – The Story of a Garden 2003, Coronation: A History of Kingship and the British Monarchy 2005, Passions Past and Present 2005, A Little History of the English Country Church 2007, Visions of England 2011; numerous articles in newspapers and periodicals. *Leisure interests:* gardening, cooking, weight training. *Address:* The Laskett, Much Birch, Hereford, HR2 8HZ, England (home). *E-mail:* strong@ereal.net (home).

STROPNICKÝ, Martin; Czech actor, theatre director, diplomatist and politician; *Minister of Defence; b.* 19 Dec. 1956, Prague; ed Theatre Faculty of Acad. of Performing Arts, Prague, Diplomatic Acad., Vienna, Austria; worked at Prague Municipal Theatres and Vinohrady Theatre 1980–90; worked at Ministry of Foreign Affairs from 1990, Amb. to Portugal 1993–94, to Italy 1994–97, to the Holy See (Vatican) 1999–2002; mem. caretaker govt as Minister of Culture 1998; Artistic Dir, Vinohrady Theatre 2003–12; mem. Parl. (ANO 2011) 2013–; Minister of Defence 2014–. *Address:* Ministry of Defence, Tychonova 1, 160 01 Prague 6, Czech Republic (office). *Telephone:* (973) 201111 (office). *Fax:* (973) 200149 (office). *E-mail:* info@army.cz (office). *Website:* www.army.cz (office).

STROSSEN, Nadine, BA, JD; American lawyer and academic; *Assistant Professor of Clinical Law, New York Law School; b.* 18 Aug. 1950, Jersey City; d. of Woodrow John Strossen and Sylvia Strossen; m. Eli Michael Noam 1980; ed Harvard Law School, Radcliffe Coll.; Assoc. Attorney, Sullivan & Cromwell 1978–83; Partner, Harvis & Zeichner 1983–84; mem. Nat. Bd of Dirs American Civil Liberties Union 1983–, Pres. 1991–2008, mem. Advisory Cttee on Reproductive Freedom Project 1983–, Nat. Exec. Cttee 1985–, Nat. Gen. Council 1986–91; Asst Prof. of Clinical Law, New York Law School 1989–; Adjunct Prof. Grad. School of Business Univ. of Columbia 1990–; mem. Exec. Cttee Human Rights Watch 1989–91; mem. Bd Dirs Coalition to Free Soviet Jewry 1984–; mem. Asia Watch 1987–, Vice-Chair. 1989–91; mem. Nat. Coalition Against Censorship 1988, Middle East Watch 1989–91, The Fund for Free Expression 1990–; mem. Steering Cttee New York Legal Council for Soviet Jewry 1987–. *Publications include:* Regulating Campus Hate Speech – A Modest Proposal? 1990, Recent US and International Judicial Protection of Individuals Rights: A Comparative Legal Process Analysis and Proposed Synthesis 1990, In Defense of Pornography: Free Speech and the Fight for Women's Rights 1995, numerous articles in professional journals. *Leisure interests:* singing, skiing, travel. *Address:* New York Law School, 57 Worth Street, New York, NY 10013-2960 (office); 450 Riverside Drive, #51, New York, NY 10027, USA (home). *Telephone:* (212) 431-2375 (office). *Fax:* (212) 431-1992 (office). *E-mail:* nadine.strossen@nyls.edu (office). *Website:* www.nyls.edu (office).

STROTHOTTE, Willy; German mining industry executive; *Chairman, Xstrata plc;* b. 23 April 1944; apprentice Frank & Schulte 1961–64; joined C Tennant 1966; various positions trading in metals and minerals in Germany, Belgium and USA 1961–78; joined Glencore International 1978, becoming Head of Metals and Minerals 1984–93, CEO 1993–94, CEO and Chair. 1994–2001, currently Chair. Glencore International AG, also Chair. Xstrata AG 1994–2002, Xstrata plc 2002–; mem. Bd of Dirs Century Aluminium Corpn, Minara Resources Ltd 2000–, KKR Financial Holdings LLC 2007–. *Address:* Xstrata plc, Bahnhofstrasse 2, PO Box 102, 6301 Zug, Switzerland (office). *Telephone:* (41) 726-60-70 (office). *Fax:* (41) 726-60-89 (office). *E-mail:* info@xstrata.com (office). *Website:* www.xstrata.com (office).

STROUT, Elizabeth; American writer; b. Portland, Me; one d.; ed Bates Coll., Syracuse Univ. Coll. of Law; fmr faculty mem., Bard Coll., Warren Wilson Coll., Manhattan Community Coll.; currently Faculty mem., Creative Writing Program, Queens Univ. of Charlotte. *Publications include:* Amy and Isabelle (Los Angeles Times Art Siedenbaum Award for First Fiction, Chicago Tribune Heartland Prize) 1998, Abide With Me 2006, Olive Kitteridge (short stories) (Pulitzer Prize for Fiction 2009) 2008, The Burgess Boys 2013. *Address:* Creative Writing Program, Queens University of Charlotte, 1900 Selwyn Avenue, Charlotte, NC 28274, USA (office). *Telephone:* (704) 337-2499 (office). *Fax:* (704) 337-2503 (office). *E-mail:* mbraeckel@randomhouse.com. *Website:* www.queens.edu (office); elizabethstrout .com.

STROYEV, Yegor Semyonovich, DEcons; Russian politician; b. 25 Feb. 1937, Stroyevo, Khotynetsky, Orel Region; s. of Semyon Fedorovich Stroyev and Anna Ivanovna Stroyeva; m. Nina Semvyovna Stroyeva; one d.; ed I.V. Michurin Horticultural Inst., Acad. of Social Sciences, Moscow; mem CPSU 1958–91; worked at Progress collective farm, Khotynetsky Dist; Sec. Khotynetsky CPSU Dist Cttee, Chair. Exec. Cttee Pokrovsky Dist Soviet of People's Deputies, First Sec. Pokrovsky CPSU Dist Cttee, Sec., First Sec. Orel CPSU Regional Cttee 1985–89; Sec. CPSU Cen. Cttee 1989–91; mem. Politburo of CPSU Cen. Cttee 1990–91; resgnd after Aug. coup d'état; fmr People's Deputy of USSR; mem. Council of Fed. Ass. of Russian Fed. 1995–2001, Chair. 1996–2001, Hon. Chair. 2001–; Chair. Council of Inter-parl. Ass. of CIS Mem. States 1996–; Head of Admin. Orel Oblast 1993–2009; Dir All-Russia Scientific Research Inst. of Fruit Crop Breeding 1991–93; Academician, Russian Acad. of Agricultural Sciences; Hon. mem. Russian Acad. of Literature; Order of the Oct. Revolution 1973, Order of the Red Banner of Labour 1987, Order of St Prince Vladimir 1997 and other awards. *Publications include:* Methodology and Practices of Agrarian Restructuring 1994, To Give a Chance to the Peasant 1995, Land Issue 1999, Self-determination of Russia and Global Modernization 2001, In A Rapid River 2003, Agricultural Complex of Russian Chernozem Land 2003. *Leisure interest:* recreation in the countryside. *Address:* c/o Governor's Office, Lenina pl. 1, 30200 Orel, Russia.

STRUBE, Jürgen Friedrich, DJur; German business executive; *Honorary Chairman of the Supervisory Board, BASF SE;* b. 1939, Bochum; m.; one d.; ed Univs of Freiburg, Geneva, Switzerland and Munich; joined BASF 1969, several posts, then with BASF Brasileira SA, São Paulo 1974–85, Head, Glasurit do Brasil Ltda 1980–, Head, Brazil Regional Div. 1982–, in charge of Information Systems and Fibres Operating Divs. and Regional Divs in N America 1985–88, of Foams, Polyolefins and PVC and Information Systems Operating Divs and Brazil and Latin American Regional Divs 1988–90, mem. Bd Exec. Dirs BASF AG, Ludwigshafen, Germany 1985–, Chair. 1990–2003, Chair. Supervisory Bd BASF AG (renamed BASF SE Jan. 2008) 2003–09, Hon. Chair. 2009–; Chair. Supervisory Bd Fuchs Petrolub AG 2003–11; mem. Supervisory Bd Allianz Deutschland AG, BMW Group 2001–10 (currently Deputy Chair.), Bertelsmann AG (Deputy Chair. 2004–), Commerzbank AG –2008, Hapag-Lloyd AG, Linde AG –2008; Pres. Asscn of Chemical Industry (VCI) 1996–97, UNICE 2003–; mem. Int. Advisory Cttee New York Stock Exchange Euronext, Inc.; mem. Econ. Advisory Bd RWE AG; Hon. Senator, Deutsche Hochschule für Verwaltungswissenschaften, Speyer 1997, Hon. Prof. 1999; Hon. Senator, Univ. of Mannheim 1998, Univ. of Heidelberg 2003; Order of Merit, 1st Class of FRG 2000; Dr hc (Univ. of Maryland) 1995, (European Business School, Oestrich-Winkel) 2003, Centenary Medal, Soc. of Chemical Industry 1999, John J. McCloy Award, American Council on Germany 2001, Rhine-Neckar Regional Award 2003, Medal of Merit (Rhineland-Palatinate) 2003, Int. Palladium Medal Award, Soc. de Chimie Industrielle (American Section) 2005. *Address:* BASF SE, Carl-Bosch-Str. 38, 67056 Ludwigshafen, Germany (office). *Telephone:* (621) 60-0 (office); (621) 60-99938 (office). *Fax:* (621) 60-42525 (office); (621) 60-20129 (office). *E-mail:* presse.kontakt@basf.com (office). *Website:* www .basf.com (office).

STRUNK, Klaus Albert, DPhil; German professor of linguistics; b. 22 Aug. 1930, Düsseldorf; s. of Albert Strunk and Hedwig Schäfer; m. Marion Kriegeskotte 1957; two s. one d.; ed Univs of Cologne and Bonn; Prof., Univ. of Saarland and Dir, Inst. of Indo-European Linguistics and Indo-Iranian Philology 1967–77; Prof., Univ. of Munich and Dir, Inst. of Gen. and Indo-European Linguistics 1977–98, Dean Dept I (Linguistics and Literature) 1985–87; Ed., Kratylos review 1969–83; Co-Ed., Glotta review 1974–2000, series Studies in Indo-European Language and Culture (Berlin and New York) 1985–, Muenchener Studien zur Sprachwissenschaft review 1992–2002; Pres., Indogermanische Gesellschaft 1983–92; mem. Bayer-

ische Akademie der Wissenschaften 1979–, Sec., Philosophy and History section 1989–2004; mem. Société de Linguistique de Paris 1978–, Philological Soc., London 1993–. *Publications:* Die sogenannten Aeolismen der homerischen Sprache 1957, Nasalpraesentien und Aoriste. Ein Beitrag zur Morphologie des Verbums im Indo-Iranischen und Griechischen 1967, Probleme der lateinischen Grammatik (Ed.) 1973, Lachmanns Regel für das Lateinische 1976, Generative Versuche zu einigen Problemen in der historischen Grammatik indogermanischer Sprachen 1976, Typische Merkmale von Fragesätzen und die altindische Pluti 1983, Zum Postulat 'vorhersagbaren' Sprachwandels bei unregelmässigen oder komplexen Flexionsparadigmen 1991, Kleine Schriften 2005, Zur Geschichte der Sprachwissenschaft im 19 Jahrhundert – Briefe Johannes Schmidts an August Schleicher 1865–1868 2013; numerous articles and reviews on Greek, Latin, Indo-Iranian and Indo-European linguistics. *Leisure interests:* reading books on history, literature, classical music, sport. *Address:* Ringbergstrasse 11, 83707 Bad Wiessee, Germany. *Telephone:* (8022) 82198.

STRUZIK, Adam; Polish physician and politician; *Marshal of Mazovian Voivodeship;* b. 1 Jan. 1957, Kutno; m.; one s. one d.; ed Medical Acad., Łódź; Councillor, Municipal Council of Duninów 1986–90, City and Commune of Gąbin 1990–; Dir Voivodeships Jt Hosp. in Płock 1990–97; Marshal (Speaker) of Nat. Regional Council of Territorial Self-Govt 1994–98; Councillor, Regional Council of Mazovian Voivodeship 1998–, Marshal of Mazovian Voivodeship 2001–; mem. Solidarity Trade Union 1980–; mem. Polish Peasant Party (PSL) 1989–, Exec. Council; Senator (Płock Voivodeship) 1991–2001, Marshal of Senate 1993–97; Vice-Pres. Nat. Ass. that adopted Constitution of Repub. of Poland 1997; Pres. Council of Mazovian Sickness Foundation 1999–2001, Council for Nat. Asscn of Sickness Foundations 1999–2001; Co-founder Aid Foundation for Voivodeship Hosp., Płock; mem. Programming Bd TVP SA; mem. supreme authorities of govt coalition party (PSL) 2007–, Cttee on Devt (DEVE), Cttee of The Regions, RELEX Cttee; mem. Polish Hunting Asscn, Płock Scientific Soc., Polish Haematology Soc.; Commdr's Cross, Order of Leopold (Belgium). *Leisure interests:* politics, literature, tourism. *Address:* Urząd Marszałkowski Województwa Mazowieckiego, ul. Jagiellońska 26, 03-719 Warsaw, Poland. *Telephone:* (22) 5907804 (office). *Fax:* (22) 5907875 (office). *E-mail:* a.struzik@mazovia.pl (office). *Website:* www .mazovia.pl (office).

STRZEMBOSZ, Adam Justyn, DrIur; Polish lawyer, judge and government official; b. 11 Nov. 1930, Warsaw; s. of Adam Strzembosz and Zofia Strzembosz (née Gadomska); m. Zofia Strzembosz 1957; two s. two d.; ed Jagiellonian Univ., Cracow, Warsaw Univ.; legal adviser, Ministry of Labour and Social Security 1953–56; judge, Co. Court 1956–68, Prov. Court 1968–81; researcher, Research Inst. of Judicial Law 1974–81; Head of Solidarity Group, Ministry of Justice 1980–81; Asst Prof. and Head of Dept of Penal Law, Catholic Univ. of Lublin 1982–89, Prof. 1986–; Vice-Minister of Justice 1989–90; judge and First Pres. Supreme Court 1990–98 (retd); Head of Tribunal of State 1990–98; mem. Bd Solidarity Mazowsze Region 1980; Del. to 1st Solidarity Conf., Jt Leader Appeal Comm., Gdańsk Oliwa 1981; Co-Founder Soc. for Promotion and Propagation of Sciences; mem. Catholic Univ. of Lublin Scientific Asscn, Penal Law Asscn; Krzyż Wielki, Order Odrodzenia Polski 2008, Knightly Order of St. Gregory the Great (Holy See) 2010. *Publications:* six books and more than over 200 treatises and articles. *Leisure interests:* cycling, literature. *Address:* ul. Stanisława Augusta 73 m.20, 03-846 Warsaw, Poland (home).

STUART, Freundel Jerome, BA, LLB, LLM, QC; Barbadian lawyer and politician; *Prime Minister;* b. St Philip; ed Univ. of the West Indies; practising attorney 1984–; mem. House of Ass. (Parl.) for St Philip South 1994–99, for St Michael South 2008–; Senator 2003–07; fmr Attorney-Gen. and Minister of Home Affairs; Acting Prime Minister of Barbados May–Oct. 2010, Prime Minister Oct. 2010–; mem. Democratic Labour Party. *Address:* Office of the Prime Minister, Government HQ, Bay St, St Michael, Barbados. *Telephone:* 436-6435 (office). *Fax:* 436-9280 (office). *E-mail:* info@primeminister.gov.bb (office). *Website:* www.primeminister.gov.bb (office).

STUART, Sir Kenneth Lamonte, Kt, MD, FRCP, FACP, FFPM, FFPHM; Barbadian physician (retd); b. 16 June 1920, Barbados; s. of Egbert Stuart and Louise Stuart; m. Barbara Cecille Ashby 1958; one s. two d.; ed Harrison Coll., Barbados, Queen's Univ., Belfast, Northern Ireland; Rockefeller Foundation Fellow in Cardiology, Mass. Gen. Hosp., Boston, USA 1956–57; Wellcome Research Fellow, Harvard Univ. 1960–61; Prof. of Medicine, Univ. of West Indies 1966–76, Dean of Medical School 1969–73, Head of Dept of Medicine 1972–76; Commonwealth Medical Adviser 1976–85; Consultant Adviser, Wellcome Tropical Inst. 1985–95; Gresham Prof. of Physics, Gresham Coll., London 1988–94; mem. Bd of Govs Liverpool School of Tropical Medicine 1980–96, Int. Research Centre of Canada 1985–90; Chair. Court of Govs, London School of Hygiene and Tropical Medicine 1983–86, Commonwealth Caribbean Medical Research Council 1988, Errol Barrow Memorial Trust 1989–99; mem. Council and Trustee The London Lighthouse 1994–2001, Council Royal Overseas League 1994–2000, United Medical and Dental Schools of Guy's and St Thomas's Hosps 1994–98, Guy's, King's and St Thomas's Hosp. Medical and Dental School 1998, King's Coll. London 1998–2002; Trustee, Schools Partnership Worldwide 1990–, Int. Medical Educ. Trust 2000 1998–; Hon. Medical and Scientific Adviser, Barbados High Comm., London 1991–, Freeman of City of London 1992; Hon. DSc (Queen's, Belfast) 1986. *Leisure interests:* tennis, literature. *Address:* 3 The Garth, Cobham, Surrey, KT11 2DZ, England (home). *Telephone:* (1932) 863826 (home). *Fax:* (1932) 860427 (office). *E-mail:* kenstuart@lineone.net (home).

STUBB, Cai-Göran Alexander, BA, MA, PhD; Finnish journalist, politician and academic; *Minister for European Affairs and Foreign Trade;* b. 1 April 1968, Helsinki; m. Suzanne Innes-Stubb; one s. one d.; ed Mainland High School, Daytona Beach, Fla, USA, Gymnasiet Lärkan, Helsinki, Furman Univ. (golf scholarship), USA, Univ. of Paris (Sorbonne), Coll. of Europe, Belgium, London School of Econs, UK; mil. service; researcher, Ministry of Foreign Affairs 1995–97, Finnish Acad. 1997–99; columnist for various newspapers, including APU, Ilta-Sanomat, Blue Wings, various papers in Suomen Lehtiyhtymä group, Nykypäivä and Hufvudstadsbladet 1997–; special researcher, Finland's representation to EU, Brussels 1999–2001, mem. Finnish Govt's del. to intergovernmental negotiations for Treaty of Nice; Prof., Coll. of Europe, Brussels 2000–07; adviser to Pres. of EC 2001–03, mem. Comm. Task Force on European Convention; mem. Finland's representation to EU as a special expert and to intergovernmental negotiations for European Constitution 2003–04; mem. European Parl. (European People's Party) 2004–08, Vice-Pres. Cttee on Internal Market and Consumer Protection, mem. Cttee on Budgetary Control, Substitute mem. Cttee on Constitutional Affairs, Substitute mem. Del. to EU-Turkey Jt Parl. Cttee; Minister for Foreign Affairs 2008–11, for European Affairs and Foreign Trade 2011–; mem. (Nat. Coalition) Eduskunta (Parl.) 2011–. *Publications:* 11 books about the EU; several articles in academic journals. *Address:* Ministry of Foreign Affairs, Merikasarmi, Laivasto-katu 22, PO Box 176, 00023 Helsinki, Finland (office). *Telephone:* (295) 350000 (office). *E-mail:* ekmi@formin.fi (office). *Website:* formin.finland.fi (office); www .alexstubb.com.

STUBBE, JoAnne, BS, PhD; American chemist and academic; *Novartis Professor of Chemistry and Professor of Biology, Massachusetts Institute of Technology;* b. Champagne, Ill.; ed Univ. of Pennsylvania, Univ. of California, Berkeley; Postdoctoral Researcher, UCLA 1971–72; Asst Prof., Dept of Chem., Williams Coll. 1972–77; Asst Prof., Dept of Pharmacology, Yale Univ. 1977–80; Asst Prof., Dept of Biochemistry, Univ. of Wisconsin 1980–87; Prof., Dept of Chem., MIT 1987–, now Novartis Prof. of Chem. and Prof. of Biology; mem. NAS 1992; Fellow, American Acad. of Arts and Sciences 1991, American Philosophical Soc.; Hon. DSc (Harvard) 2013; Myron L. Bender and Muriel S. Bender Distinguished Summer Lecturer, Northwestern Univ. 1992, ACS F.A. Cotton Medal for Excellence in Chemical Research 1998, NSF Nat. Medal of Science 2009, ACS Nakanishi Prize 2009, Benjamin Franklin Medal in Chem. 2010, Welch Award in Chem. (co-recipient) 2010, Killian Faculty Achievement Award, MIT 2012. *Publications:* numerous papers in professional journals. *Address:* Room 18-598, Department of Chemistry, Massachusetts Institute of Technology, 77 Massachusetts Avenue, Cambridge, MA 02139, USA (office). *Telephone:* (617) 253-1814 (office). *E-mail:* stubbe@mit.edu (office). *Website:* chemistry.mit.edu (office); biology.mit.edu/ people/joanne_stubbe (office).

STUBBS, Imogen Mary, MA; British actress; b. 20 Feb. 1961, Rothbury; d. of late Robin Stubbs and Heather McCracken; m. Trevor Nunn (q.v.) 1994; one s. one d.; ed St Paul's Girls School, London, Exeter Coll. Oxford and Royal Acad. of Dramatic Art; Gold Medal, Chicago Film Festival. *Plays as actress:* appeared with RSC in The Rover, Two Noble Kinsmen, Richard II 1987–88, Othello 1991, Heartbreak House 1992, St Joan 1994, Twelfth Night 1996, Blast from the Past 1998, Betrayal 1998, The Relapse 2001, Three Sisters 2002, Fallujah 2007, Alphabetical Order 2009, The Glass Menagerie 2010, Private Lives 2011, Little Eyolf 2011. *Play as author:* We Happy Few (Gielgud Theatre, London) 2004. *Television appearances include:* The Browning Version 1985, The Rainbow 1988, Fellow Traveller 1989, Pasternak 1990, Othello 1990, Relatively Speaking 1990, Sandra, c'est la vie 1993, Anna Lee (series) 1993, Mothertime 1997, Blind Ambition 2000, Big Kids (series) 2000, So What Now? 2001, Marple: The Moving Finger 2006, Brief Encounters 2006, New Tricks 2009, The Adventures of Daniel 2010, Injustice 2011. *Films:* Privileged 1982, Nanou 1986, A Summer Story 1988, Deadline 1988, Erik the Viking 1989, True Colors 1991, The Wanderer (voice) 1991, A Pin for the Butterfly 1994, Jack and Sarah 1995, Sense and Sensibility 1995, Twelfth Night: Or What You Will 1996, Collusion 2003, Dead Cool 2004, Stories of Lost Souls 2006, Behind the Director's Son's Cut 2007. *Leisure interests:* writing, skiing, collecting junk. *Address:* c/o Nick Hern Books Ltd, The Glasshouse, 49a Goldhawk Road, London, W12 8QP, England.

STUCKY, Steven, BM, MFA, DMA; American composer, conductor and academic; b. 7 Nov. 1949, Hutchinson, Kan.; s. of Victor Eugene Stucky and Louise Doris Trautwein; two c.; ed Baylor Univ., Cornell Univ. with Karel Husa, studied conducting with Daniel Sternberg; mem. Faculty, Cornell Univ. 1980–2014, Chair. Music Dept 1992–97, also Given Foundation Prof. of Composition; mem. Faculty, Juilliard School 2014–; Composer-in-Residence, Los Angeles Philharmonic Orchestra, later consulting composer for new music 1988–2009; Composer-in-Residence, Aspen Music Festival and School 2001, 2010, 2013, Dir Aspen Contemporary Ensemble 2005; Visiting Prof. of Composition, Eastman School of Music 2001–02; Ernest Bloch Visiting Prof. of Music, Univ. of California, Berkeley 2003; Co-Dir Seal Bay Festival of American Chamber Music, Me; mem. Bd of Dirs Koussevitzky Foundation, Bogliasco Foundation, Aaron Copland Fund for Music; Barr Inst. Composer Laureate, Univ. of Missouri, Kansas City 2007; mem. American Acad. of Arts and Sciences 2006, American Acad. of Arts and Letters 2007; Trustee, American Acad. in Rome; Guggenheim Foundation Fellowship 1986, Bogliasco Fellowship 1997, Goddard Lieberson Fellowship, American Acad. of Arts and Letters 2002, Pulitzer Prize for Music 2005. *Compositions include:* Notturno 1981, Two Holy Sonnets of Donne for mezzo, oboe and piano 1982, Sappho Fragments for mezzo and ensemble 1982, Voyages for voice and wind orchestra 1984, Double Concerto for violin, oboe and chamber orchestra 1985, Concerto for Orchestra 1987, Threnos for wind ensemble 1988, Son et Lumière for orchestra 1988, Angelus for orchestra 1989, Serenade for wind quintet 1989, Impromptus for orchestra 1991, Four Poems of A. R. Ammons for baritone and ensemble 1992, Funeral Music for Queen Mary (arrangement of Purcell) 1992, Ancora for orchestra 1994, Fanfares and Arias for wind ensemble 1994, Concerto for two flutes and orchestra 1994, Pinturas de Tamayo for orchestra 1995, Cradle Songs 1997, Concerto Mediterraneo 1998, Ad Parnassum 1998, American Muse 1999, Nell'ombra, nella luce 2000, Partita-Pastorale 2000, Etudes (concerto for recorder and chamber orchestra) 2000, Skylarks 2001, Noctuelles (orchestration of Ravel) 2001, Concerto for percussion and wind orchestra 2001, Album Leaves 2002, Whispers 2002, Colburn Variations 2002, Spirit Voices for percussion and orchestra 2002–03, Second Concerto for Orchestra (Pulitzer Prize for Music 2005) 2003, Jeu de timbres 2003, Sonate en forme de préludes 2003–04, Piano Quartet 2004–05, New Motets 2005, Hue and Cry 2006, Dialoghi 2006, Radical Light 2006–07, August 4, 1964 2007–08, Rhapsodies 2008, Chamber Concerto 2009, Piano Quintet 2010, Silent Spring 2011, Symphony 2012, Take Him, Earth 2012, Say Thou Dost Love Me 2012, Rain Shadow 2012, The Stars and the Roses 2013, The Classical Style (opera) 2013–14, Sonata for Violin and Piano 2014. *Publications include:* Lutosławski and his Music (ASCAP-Deems Taylor Prize 1982) 1981. *Address:* c/o 21C Media Group, 162 West 56th Street, Suite 506, New York, NY 10019, USA (office). *Telephone:* (212) 245-2110 (office). *E-mail:* jlustig@ 21cmediagroup.com (office). *Website:* www.stevenstucky.com.

STUDER, Cheryl; American singer (soprano); *Professor of Voice, Hochschule für Musik, Würzburg;* b. 24 Oct. 1955, Midland, Mich.; m. 3rd Michalis Doukakis; two d. (by previous m.); ed Interlochen Arts Acad., Oberlin Coll., Univ. of Tennessee, Hochschule für Musik, Vienna; studied singing with Gwendolyn Pyke, at Berkshire Music Centre, at Tanglewood with Phyllis Curtin and at Hochschule für Musik, Vienna with Hans Hotter; engaged for concert series with Boston Symphony Orchestra by Seiji Ozawa 1979; opera debut as the First Lady in The Magic Flute, Munich 1980–82; with Darmstadt State Theatre, Germany 1982–84, Deutsche Oper, Berlin 1984–86; US debut as Micaela in Carmen, Lyric Opera of Chicago 1984; debut at Bayreuth 1985, Royal Opera House, Covent Garden 1987, Metropolitan Opera, New York 1988; sings wide variety of roles, especially Wagner, Verdi, Mozart and Strauss; Prof. of Voice, Hochschule für Musik Würzburg 2003–; Chair., Maria Callas Prize; Hon. Prof., Beijing Central Conservatory; Int. Music Award 1993, Vocalist of the Year (USA) 1994, Grammy Awards. *Address:* Encompass Arts, LLC, 119 West 72nd Street, New York, NY 10023, USA (office). *Telephone:* (212) 439-8055 (office). *E-mail:* kathy@encompassarts.com (office). *Website:* encompassarts.com/artist/cheryl-studer (office).

STUHR, Jerzy; Polish actor, film director and academic; *Rector, Ludwik Solski State School of Drama;* b. 18 April 1947, Kraków; s. of Tadeusz Stuhr and Maria Stuhr; m. 1971; one s. one d.; ed Jagiellonian Univ. and Ludwik Solski State School of Drama, Kraków; main theatrical roles at Stary Theatre, Kraków with Andrzej Wajda (q.v.), notably Hamlet 1982, Dostoevsky's The Possessed and Crime and Punishment 1984, P. Süskind's Double Bass (actor and dir) 1985–, Le Bourgeois Gentilhomme 1993, Harold Pinter's Ashes to Ashes 1996, Merry Wives of Windsor (dir) 1998; dir, actor and teacher, Italy 1980–; Rector, Ludwik Solski State School of Drama, Kraków 1990–97, 2002–, Lecturer 1998–; Lecturer, Faculty of Radio and Television, Silesia Univ. 1998–; mem. European Film Acad. 1998–; Chief Judge, Odessa International Film Festival 2011; Dr hc (Silesia Univ.); Best Actor, Chicago Festival 1978, Premio della Critica Teatrale 1982, Premio Fiprescii for Love Stories, Venice Film Festival 1997, Grand Prix for Love Stories, Polish Film Festival, Gdynia 1997, Nastro d'Argento 1997, Big Anima Special Jury Prize, Karlovy Vary 2000, Emerging Master, Int. Film Festival, Seattle 2001. *Film roles include:* Zycie za zycie (Life for Life) 1991, Uprowadzenie Agaty (Hijacking of Agata) 1993, Decalogue X, Three Colours – White 1994, Spis cudzoloznic (List of Lovers) 1995, Matka swojej matki 1996, Historie milosne (Love Stories) 1997, Kiler 1997, Kilerów 2-óch 1999, Tydzien z zycia mezczyzny (A Week in the Life of a Man) 1999, Down House 2000, La Vita altrui 2000, Duze zwierze (Big Animal) 2000, Weiser 2001, Show 2003, Pogoda na jutro (Tomorrow's Weather) 2003, Persona non grata 2005, Doskonale popoludnie 2005, Il Caimano 2006, The Making of Parts 2006, Korowód 2007, Habemus Papa 2011. *Films directed include:* Spis cudzoloznic (List of Lovers) (also screenwriter) 1995, Historie milosne (Love Stories) (also screenwriter) 1997, Tydzien z zycia mezczyzny (A Week in the Life of a Man) (also screenwriter) 1999, Duze zwierze (Big Animal) 2000, Pogoda na jutro (Tomorrow's Weather) (also screenwriter) 2003, Korowód (also screenwriter) 2007, We Have a Pope 2011. *Publications include:* Heart Illness, or My Life in Art (autobiography) 1992, Big Animal 2000, True Pretender 2000. *Leisure interests:* literature, sport. *Address:* Office of the Rector, Ludwik Solski State School of Drama, ul. Straszewskiego 21–22, 31-109 Kraków, Poland (office). *Telephone:* (12) 4228196 (office). *Fax:* (12) 4220209 (office). *E-mail:* sekretariat@pwst.krakow.pl (office). *Website:* www.pwst.krakow.pl (office).

STUIVER, Minze, PhD; American geologist and academic; *Professor Emeritus, Department of Earth and Space Sciences, University of Washington;* b. 25 Oct. 1929, Vlagtwedde, Netherlands; s. of Albert Stuiver; ed Univ. of Groningen; Research Assoc., Yale Univ. 1959–62; Sr Research Assoc. and Dir Radiocarbon Lab. 1962–69; Prof. of Geological Sciences and Zoology, Univ. of Washington, Seattle 1969–82, Prof. of Geological Sciences and Quaternary Sciences 1982–98, now Prof. Emer., Dir Quaternary Isotope Lab. 1972–98; Ed. Radiocarbon 1976–88; mem. Geological Soc. of America, American Quaternary Asscn; Alexander von Humboldt Sr Scientist, FRG 1983; Hon. DSc (Queen's Univ., Belfast) 2009; Pomerance Award, Archaeological Inst. of America 1993, Distinguished Career Award in Quaternary Science, AMQUA 2000, Penrose Medal, Geological Soc. of America 2005. *Achievements include:* second-most-cited scientist in the field of Geosciences in 1990s, Incites. *Address:* University of Washington, Department of Earth and Space Sciences, 035 QRC/ATG, Seattle, WA 98195-1310, USA (office). *E-mail:* minze@u.washington.edu (office). *Website:* depts.washington.edu/qil (office).

STUMP, Nicholas (Nick) Withrington, BAppSc, MAppSc, FAusIMM; Australian business executive; *Chairman, GroundProbe Pty Ltd;* b. 16 Dec. 1941, Adelaide, S Australia; s. of Stanley Withrington and Dorothy Ellen; m. Alison Goode 1966; one s. two d.; ed Scotch Coll. Adelaide, Unley High School, Univ. of Adelaide and S Australian Inst. of Tech.; worked for CRA Group 1970–95; held several tech. and operating man. positions with Zinc Corpn Broken Hill 1970–77; transferred to Mary Kathleen Uranium Ltd (CRA subsidiary) 1977; Man. Planning and Evaluation, CRA Group, Melbourne 1980; Gen. Man. CRA's Sulphide Corpn zinc smelter, Cockle Creek, NSW 1983–85; Man. Dir Comalco Rolled Products, Sydney 1985–87; Pres. Commonwealth Aluminum Corp Ltd USA 1988; Chief Exec. Comalco Ltd and Group Exec. CRA Ltd 1991–95; Chief Exec. MIM Holdings Ltd 1995–2001; Chair. Sustainable Minerals Inst., Univ. of Queensland; Chair. GroundProbe Pty Ltd; mem. Bd of Dirs John Holland Group Pty Ltd, Ludowici Ltd, Australia 21 Ltd; mem. Senate, Univ. of Queensland 1996–; Pres. Minerals Council of Australia 1997–99 (mem. 1995–); Vice-Pres. Queensland Mining Council Ltd 1995; Fellow, Australasian Inst. of Mining and Metallurgy; Arthur F. Taggart Award, American Inst. of Mining Engineers (co-recipient) 1975. *Leisure interests:* cruising and offshore yacht racing. *Address:* GroundProbe Pty Ltd, 8 Hockings Street, South Brisbane, Queensland 4101, Australia (office). *Telephone:* (7) 3010-8999 (office). *Fax:* (7) 3010-8988 (office). *E-mail:* info@groundprobe.com (office). *Website:* www.australia21.org.au (office).

STUMPF, John G., BA, MBA; American banker; *Chairman, President and CEO, Wells Fargo & Company;* b. Pierz, Minn.; ed St Cloud State Univ., Univ. of Minnesota; joined Norwest Corpn 1982, served in numerous exec. positions including Sr Vice-Pres. and Chief Credit Officer, Norwest Bank NA, Minneapolis 1982–89, Exec. Vice-Pres. Southwestern Banking 1989–91, Regional Pres. Norwest Banks Colo/Ariz. 1991–94, Regional Pres. Norwest Banks Texas

1994–98, Head of Southwestern Banking Group (after merger of Norwest Corpn and Wells Fargo & Co.) 1998–2000, Head of Western Banking Group 2000–02, Group Exec. Vice-Pres. of Community Banking 2002–05, Pres. Wells Fargo & Co. 2005–, mem. Bd of Dirs 2006–, CEO 2007–, Chair. 2010–; Chair. Visa USA 2005–; mem. Bd of Dirs The Clearing House, Financial Services Roundtable, Target Corpn, Chevron Corpn; mem. California Business Roundtable; Trustee, San Francisco Museum of Modern Art. *Address:* Wells Fargo & Co., PO Box 63750, San Francisco, CA 94163 (office); Wells Fargo & Co., 420 Montgomery Street, San Francisco, CA 94104, USA (office). *Telephone:* (866) 878-5865 (office). *Fax:* (626) 312-3015 (office). *E-mail:* BoardCommunications@wellsfargo.com (office). *Website:* www.wellsfargo.com (office).

ŠTURANOVIĆ, Željko; Montenegrin politician; b. 31 Jan. 1960, Nikšić; m.; two c.; ed Faculty of Law, Podgorica; early career working at Nikšić Steel Factory as Sr Officer and Head, Legal Dept; Rep. House of Citizens, Fed. Parl. 1993–2001; mem. Parl. of Repub. of Montenegro 2001–06, Minister of Justice 2001–06, Prime Minister 2006–08 (resgnd); Chair. Comm. for Human Resources; mem. Democratic Party of Socialists of Montenegro (DPSM). *Address:* c/o Democratic Party of Socialists of Montenegro (Demokratska Partija Socijalista Crne Gore), 81000 Podgorica, Jovana Tomaševića 33, Montenegro. *Telephone:* (81) 225830. *Fax:* (81) 242101. *E-mail:* webmaster@dps.cg.yu. *Website:* www.dps.cg.yu.

STURRIDGE, Charles, BA; British director, writer and producer; b. 24 June 1951, London, England; s. of Jerome Sturridge and Alyson Sturridge (née Burke); m. Phoebe Nicholls; three c.; ed Univ. Coll., Oxford; fmr mem. Nat. Youth Theatre; fmr Pres. Oxford Univ. Dramatic Soc.; worked as actor and theatre dir; debut as professional dir in musical version of Hard Times, Belgrade Theatre, Coventry; joined Granada TV 1974; freelance dir/writer/producer 1979–; Chair. Directors UK; numerous awards for feature films and TV documentaries. *Theatre includes:* Dir and Co-writer Hard Times, Belgrade Theatre, Coventry 1974; Dir own trans. (with Tania Alexander) of The Seagull, Queens Theatre, London 1985, Endgame, Gate Theatre/Barbican 2006; trans. (with Tania Alexander) of Uncle Vanya. *Films include:* Runners 1982, Contrib. Dir to Aria (La Vergine degli angeli from La Forza del Destino) 1987, A Handful of Dust (writer/dir) 1988, Where Angels Fear to Tread (writer/dir) 1991, Fairytale – A True Story (co-writer) (BAFTA Best Children's Film 1998) 1997, Lassie 2005 (writer/dir), The Scapegoat (writer/dir) 2012. *Television documentaries and dramas include:* Coronation Street, World In Action, Brideshead Revisited (17 awards including BAFTA award for Best Series, two American Golden Globe awards, Grand Award of New York Film and TV Festival), Soft Targets (BBC 1) 1982, The Storyteller 1988, Gulliver's Travels 1996 (12 int. awards, including Humanitas Prize and five US Primetime Emmys), A Foreign Field, Longitude (writer/dir, Channel 4) 2000 (five BAFTA Awards including Best Series), Shackleton (writer/dir, Channel 4) (BAFTA Award for Best Series and two Emmy Awards), Ohio Impromptu (Beckett on Film, Channel 4) (LWT South Bank Award for Best TV Drama), No. 1 Ladies Detective Agency (Mirage/BBC/HBO/Weinstein Co.) 2009, The Road to Coronation Street (ITV/BBC 4) (BAFTA and RTS Awards for Best Single Drama, New York Film and TV Festival Gold Medal) 2010, Astonish Me (WWF) 2010, Dates (series) 2013, The Ends of The Earth 2013, Da Vinci's Demons (series) 2014. *Address:* c/o Independent Talent Group Ltd, Oxford House, 76 Oxford Street, London, W1D 1BS, England (office). *Telephone:* (20) 7636-6565 (office). *Fax:* (20) 7323-0101 (office). *E-mail:* info@independenttalent.com (office). *Website:* www.independenttalent .com (office).

STURUA, Robert Robertovich; Georgian theatre director; *Artistic Director, Shota Rustaveli Professional State Drama Theatre;* b. 31 July 1938, Tbilisi; s. of the late Robert Ivanovich Sturua; m. Dudana Kveselava 1968; two s.; ed Shota Rustaveli Theatre and Film, Georgian State Inst.; joined Rustaveli Theatre, Tbilisi 1962, Dir 1979–80, Artistic Dir 1982–2011; Artistic Dir, Shota Rustaveli Professional State Drama Theatre 2013–; first Guest Dir at Saarbrücken State Theatre; has staged over 100 productions, including operas; Hon. Citizen of Tbilisi 1996; Order of Merit (Georgia) 1998, Order of Friendship (Russian Fed.) 2008; Albert Schweiter Prize, Germany 1975, Honoured Art Worker of Georgian Soviet Repub. 1976, Kote Marjanishvili Award (for the production "Kvarkvare" by P. Kakabadze) 1976, State Award of USSR (for "The Caucasian Chalk Circle" by B. Brecht) 1979, People's Artist of Georgia 1980, The English Critic's Prize 1980, The Italian Critics' Prize 1981, Shota Rustaveli Prize for Richard III 1981, People's Artist of the USSR 1982, Prize of the State Univ. of Argentina 1988, The Shakespeare's International Society included the production of Hamlet at the Riverside Studio on its list of the ten best productions of Hamlet of the 20th century 1992, State Prize of Georgia 1996, Grand Prize at Rustavi Festival "Golden Mask" for Macbeth 1996, Mikheil Tumanishvili Prize 1997, Georgian Theatre Soc. Prize for The Best Production of the Year/Best Stage Directing for The Snake Lady 1998, Gold Medal at Rustavi Festival "Golden Mask" 1998, Chaplin Club Award and Grand Prize at Russian Festival "Baltic House" for the production of What if the Wet Lilac is Wet 1998, Alexandre Kazbegi Prize 1999, State Prize of the Russian Fed. 1999, Gold Medal at Rustavi Festival "Gold Mask" 2000, "Patriarch of the Theatre", VI Ceremony of Awarding the Theatre Prize "Chaika" (Seagull) 2001, Stanislavski Int. Prize for contributing to the development of the theatrical art, Moscow 2002, Polikarpe Kakabadze Prize 2002, Prize "Zolotaya Moskva" (Golden Moscow) for the production of Sior Todero Brontolon at Theatre Satiricon 2003, Grand Prize for Hamlet at the Rustavi Festival 2003, Best Stage Dir for the production of The Styx, Faces magazine 2005, Grand Prize, Eighth Int. Theatre Festival "Baltic House" 2006, Sergo Parajanov Int. Prize 2006, Asscn of Theatre Historians and Critics of Argentina acknowledged the San Martine Theatre production of The Resistable Rise of Arturo Ui as the best in 7 nominations 2006, Giorgi Tovstonogov Prize, St Petersburg br. of the Theatrical Artists' Union of the Russian Fed. 2009, Special Prize of the Journalists' Int. Fund "Gold Pen" 2009, Ilia Chavchavadze Medal 2009, "Hit of the Season" (The Tempest), Theatre "ET CETERA", Russian Theatre Soc. Award) 2012 Grand Prize of ("Hunting Season", best productions of 2010–11) 2012, Theatre Prize "Duruji" for Best Direction "Hunting Season" 2012, "Golden Mask" (Zolotaya Maska) 2013, Special Prize from His Holiness Beatitude Ilia II, Archbishop of Mtskheta-Tbilisi and Catholicos-Patriarch of All Georgia on his 75th birthday 2013. *Theatre productions:* Rustaveli Theatre: The Third Desire (V. Blazek) 1963, Before the Supper (V. Rozov, Georgian version by G. Chakviani) 1963, The Accusation (R. Sturua, G. Kavtaradze) 1964, The Trial of Salem (Miller, original title The Crucible) 1964, Marie-Octobre (J. Rober) 1965, The Sunny Night

(N. Dumbadze) 1965, Khanuma (A. Tsagareli) 1969, The Good Woman of Sezuan (Brecht) 1969, 1993, The Stepmother of Samanishvili (D. Kldiashvili) 1969, The Georgian Poetry Evening 1970, The Children of the World (S. Jgenti) 1970, Salamura (A. Sulakauri) 1971, Medea (Anouilh) 1971, Our Melodies (G. Kancheli) 1972, Doctor Stockman (Enemy of Society) (Ibsen) 1973, The Verdict (N. Dumbadze) 1973, The Chairman of Raikom (R. Tabukashvili) 1974, Kvarkvare (P. Kakabadze) 1974, The Betrayal (A. Sumbatashvili) 1976, The Caucasian Chalk Circle (Brecht) 1975, The Beginning (A. Gellman) 1981, The Dragon (E. Schwartz) 1976, Grandmother, Iliko, Ilarion and Myself (N. Dumbadze) 1977, The Contemporary Man (E. Gabrilovich, I. Reisman) 1977, Richard III (Shakespeare) 1979, The Role for the Young Actress (T. Chiladze) 1980, Blue Horses on the Red Grass (M. Shatrov) 1980, Variations on Contemporary Theme (R. Sturua, L. Popkadze, A. Varsimashvili) 1981, The Charm of Amherst (W. Luis) 1981, Funerals in California (R. Ibraginbekov) 1983, From 3 till 6 (A. Chkhaidze) 1984, The Day of Hundred Ergasterum (M. Kveselava) 1985, The Concert for Two Violins Accompanied by Oriental Instruments (R. Sturua, A. Chichinadze) 1987, King Lear (Shakespeare) 1987, The Mother of God (liturgy, composer G. Kancheli) 1989, The Dialogues for the Play in Two Acts (D. Turashvili) 1990, Life is a Dream (P. Calderon) 1992, Gospel According to Jacob (R. Sturua) 1994, Macbeth (Shakespeare) 1995, Lamara (G. Robakidze) 1996, Does It Matter if Wet Lilac Is Wet (L. Tabukashvili, co-dir D. Khinikadze) 1997, The Serpent-Woman (C. Gozzi, co-dir D. Sakvarelidze) 1998, The Day of Meeting (T. Chiladze, co-dir G. Tavadze) 1999, Is He Human?! (I. Chavchavadze) 2000, Twelfth Night or What You Will (Shakespeare) 2001, Hamlet (Shakespeare) 2001, Waiting for Godot (Beckett) 2003, The Styx (G. Kancheli) 2003, Soldier, Love, Bodyguard and... the President (L. Bugadze) 2005, The Misfortune of Darispan (D. Kldiashvili) 2006, Sweet, Sad Scent of Vanilla (I. Samsonadze) 2006, The Mask of Foe (A. Nothomb, original title La cosmetique de l'ennemi) 2007, Twelve Angry Man (R. Rose) 2007, Birdie Died in Glen (T. Chiladze) 2007; overseas: The Stepmother of Samanishvili D. Kldiashvili, The Saarbrucken Municipal Theatre 1974, The Wild Money (A. Ostrovsky), Schauspielhaus, Düsseldorf 1977, As You Like It (Shakespeare), Schauspielhaus, Düsseldorf 1980, Electra (Sophocles), Theatre Athenaeum, Festival of Ancient Greek Drama, Athens 1986, The Brest Piece (M. Shatrov), Vakhtangov Theatre, Moscow 1987, Mother Courage (Brecht), Cervantes Nat. Theatre, Buenos Aires 1988, Oedipus Rex (Sophocles), Theatre Athenaeum, Festival of Ancient Greek Drama, Athens 1989, Tartuffe (Molière), Habima Theatre, Tel-Aviv 1989, Three Sisters (Chekhov), Queen's Theatre, London 1990, Eugene Onegin (Tschaikhovsky), Teatro Communale di Bologna 1991, The Comedy of Errors (Shakespeare), Nat. Theatre, Helsinki 1991, Hamlet (Shakespeare), Riverside Studios, London 1992, Antigone (Sophocles), Istanbul Municipal Theatre 1994, The Seagull (Chekhov), The London King Theatre 1995, Mouth Open (Hanoch Levin), Tel-Aviv Chamber Theatre 1995, Measure for Measure (Shakespeare), Nat. Theatre, Helsinki 1995, The Visions of Simone Machard (Brecht), Alvares Theatre, Argentina 1997, Hamlet (Shakespeare), The Satirikon Theatre, Moscow 1998, Coriolanus (Shakespeare), Irodio Theatre, Acropolis, Athens 1999, The Merchant of Venice (Shakespeare), Moscow Theatre Et Cetera 1999, The Merchant of Venice (Shakespeare), Moscow Theatre Et Cetera 2000, Twelfth Night or What You Will (Shakespeare), Ivan Vazov Nat. Theatre, Sofia 2001, Signor Todero (Goldoni), Satirikon Theatre, Moscow 2002, Krapp's Last Tape (Beckett), Et Cetera Theatre, Moscow 2002, Oedipus Rex (Sophocles), Kiev 2003, Hamlet (Shakespeare), State Theatre, Ankara 2004, Romeo and Juliet (Shakespeare), Pushkin Theatre, Moscow 2004, The Resistible Raise of Arturo Ui (Brecht), President Alvares Theatre, Buenos Aires 2005, King Lear (Shakespeare), Chamber Theatre, Israel 2006, The Tempest (Shakespeare), Theatre Et Cetera, Moscow 2010, The Taming of the Shrew (Shakespeare), Athens 2011, You have found a good place for feeding dogs (Tarik Noui), Theatre Et Cetera, Moscow 2012, The Comedy of Errors (Shakespeare), Theatre Et Cetera, Moscow 2013. *Opera productions:* And it was on eighth year, Tbilisi State Opera, 1983, Music for the Living (G. Kancheli, libretto R. Sturua), Tbilisi State Opera 1984, Barbale (V. Dolidze, interpreted by V. Kakhidze, libretto R. Sturua and D. Akhobadze) 1986, Eugene Onegin (Tschaikhovsky), Teatro Communale di Bologna, Italy 1990, Othello (Verdi), Tbilisi State Opera 1991, Angel of Fire (Prokofiev), Tbilisi State Opera 1990, Carmen (Bizet), Tbilisi State Opera 1992, The Visions of Ivan the Terrible (S. Solimski), Samara State Academic Opera Theatre, conductor M. Rostropovich (world premiere) 1999, Music for the Living (G. Kancheli, libretto R. Sturua), Tbilisi State Opera 1999, Lady in the Dark, Teatro dell'Opera di Roma (Costanzi Theatre), Italy 2002, Mazeppa (Tchaikovsky), Bolshoi Theatre, Moscow 2004. *Address:* Shota Rustaveli Theatre, Tbilisi, Georgia (office). *E-mail:* info@rustavelitheatre.ge (office). *Website:* www.rustavelitheatre.ge (office).

STÜTZLE, Walther K. A., Dr rer. pol; German journalist; *Senior Distinguished Fellow. German Institute for International and Security Affairs;* b. 29 Nov. 1941, Westerland-Sylt; s. of the late Moritz Stützle and Annemarie Ruge; m. Dr H. Kauper 1966; two s. two d.; ed Westerland High School and Univs of Berlin, Bordeaux and Hamburg; Researcher, IISS, London 1967–68, Foreign Policy Inst. Bonn 1968–69; Desk Officer, Ministry of Defence, Planning Staff, Bonn 1969–72, Pvt. Sec. and Chef de Cabinet, 1973–76, Head, Planning Staff, Under-Sec. of Defence, Plans and Policy 1976–82; mem. editorial staff, Stuttgarter Zeitung 1983–86; Dir Stockholm Int. Peace Research Inst. (SIPRI) 1986–91; Ed.-in-Chief Der Tagesspiegel 1994–98; Perm. Sec., Ministry of Defence 1998–2002, Visiting Prof., Potsdam Univ. 2004–; Sr Distinguished Fellow, German Inst. for Int. and Security Affairs 2004–. *Publications include:* Adenauer and Kennedy in der Berlinkrise 1961–62 1972, Politik und Kräftverhältnis 1983, Europe's Future – Europe's Choices (co-author) 1967, ABM Treaty – To Defend or Not to Defend 1987, SIPRI Yearbook (ed.) 1986–90, From Alliance to Coalition: The Future of Transatlantic Relations (contributor) 2004. *Leisure interests:* history, reading, sailing, mountain walking. *Address:* Stiftung Wissenschaft und Politik, Deutsches Institut für Internationale Politik und Sicherheit, Ludwigkirchplatz 3-4, 10719 Berlin, Germany (office). *Telephone:* (30) 880070 (office). *Fax:* (30) 88007100 (office). *E-mail:* walther.stuetzle@swp-berlin.org (office). *Website:* www.swp-berlin .org (office).

STYLIANIDIS, Evripidis, PhD; Greek lawyer and politician; b. 8 April 1966, Maroneia, nr Komotini, Rhodope Pref. of Thrace; m. Stergioula Papachristou; ed Democritus Univ. of Thrace, Komotini, Univ. of Hamburg, Germany; worked at Gen. Consulate in Hamburg, Germany 1991–94; served in Artillery Corps of the

Hellenic Army 1994–95; adviser to Pres. of New Democracy party on youth affairs and cultural diplomacy 1995–96; Fellow, European Public Law Centre 1997–98, Researcher 1997–2000; taught in Master's degree programme in public law at Law School of Nat. and Capodistrian Univ. of Athens; first entered politics with New Democracy (Nea Demokratia) as mem. European Parl. nominee 1994; ran for Parl. 1996; elected mem. Hellenic Parl. for Rhodope Pref. 2000–; New Democracy's Alt. Co-ordinator for Foreign Affairs 2001–04; fmr mem. NATO Parl. Ass. and Vice-Pres. Greece-Brazil and Greece-Germany and mem. Greece-Russia Parl. Friendship Cttees; Minister for Nat. Educ. and Religious Affairs 2007–09, for Transport and Communications Jan.–Oct. 2009; Minister for the Interior following formation of coalition govt with Panhellenic Socialist Movt (PASOK) and Democratic Left (Dimokratiki Aristera) 2012–13. Address: New Democracy (Nea Demokratia), Leoforos Syngrou 340, Kallithea, 176 73 Athens, Greece (office). Telephone: (210) 9444000 (office). Fax: (210) 7251491 (office). E-mail: ndpress@nd.gr (office). Website: www.nd.gr (office).

STYMIEST, Barbara, HBA, MBA, FCA; Canadian business executive and fmr banking executive; *Chairman, BlackBerry;* ed Richard Ivey School of Business, Univ. of Western Ontario; started career as partner at Ernst & Young; Exec. Vice-Pres. and Chief Financial Officer Investment Banking Div., Bank of Montreal –2000; CEO (first woman) TSX (Toronto Stock Exchange) Group 2000–05; COO RBC (Royal Bank of Canada) Financial Group 2004–11 (retd); mem. Bd of Dirs Research In Motion Ltd 2007–, Chair. 2012– (name changed to BlackBerry 2013); Dir, George Weston Ltd, Sun Life Financial Inc., University Health Network, Canadian Inst. for Advanced Research; mem. or fmr mem. Royal Ont. Museum, Toronto Rehabilitation Inst. Foundation, Hincks-Dellcrest Children's Centre, United Way Campaign Cabinet; Fellow, Inst. of Chartered Accountants of Ont.; ranked by Fortune magazine amongst 50 Most Powerful Women in Business outside the US (34th) 2005, (27th) 2006, (30th) 2007, (15th) 2008. Address: BlackBerry, 295 Phillip Street, Waterloo, ON N2L 3W8, Canada (office). Telephone: (519) 888-7465 (office). Fax: (519) 888-7884 (office). E-mail: info@blackberry.com (office). Website: www.blackberry.com (office).

SU, C. Y., Taiwanese business executive; *Chairman, Formosa Oil (Asia Pacific) Corporation;* b. (Su Chi-yi), Dir, Formosa Petrochemical Corpn, Pres. –2011, Chair. Formosa Oil (Asia Pacific) Corpn; Dir Nat. Petroleum Corpn. Address: Formosa Petrochemical Corporation, 1-1, Formosa Plastics Group Industrial Zone, Mailiao, Yunlin (office); Formosa Oil (Asia Pacific) Corporation, Second Floor 6, 54 Sector 4, Minsheng East Road, Songshan District, Taipei 10574, Taiwan (office). Telephone: (2) 27122211 (Yunlin) (office); (2) 87129988 (Taipei) (office). Fax: (2) 87128050 (Yunlin) (office); (2) 87705283 (Taipei) (office). E-mail: fpccpre@fpcc.com .tw (office). Website: www.fpcc.com.tw (office); www.fpg.com.tw (office).

SU, Chi, PhD; Taiwanese government official and academic; b. 1 Oct. 1949, Taichung; s. of Chan-Wu Su and Kuo-Yin Ni; m. Chen Yue-ching (Grace Chen); one s. one d.; ed Nat. Chengchi Univ., Johns Hopkins and Columbia Univs, USA; Assoc. Prof., Dept of Diplomacy, Nat. Chengchi Univ. 1984–90, Prof. 1990–, Deputy Dir Inst. of Int. Relations 1990–93; Sec. Gen., Office of the Univ. Pres. 1989–90; mem. Exec., Yuan Research, Devt and Evaluation Comm. 1990–94; Sec.-Gen., China Political Science Asscn 1990–91; Deputy Dir, Kuomintang Cen. Cttee, Dept of Mainland Affairs 1992–93; Vice-Chair Exec., Yuan Mainland Affairs Council 1993–96; Dir-Gen., Govt Information Office 1996–97; mem. Exec., Yuan Minister of State 1997; Nat. Policy Adviser to Pres. of Repub. 1997, Deputy Sec.-Gen. to Pres. 1997–99; Chair., Mainland Affairs Council 1999; Prof., Inst. of China Studies, Tamkang Univ. and Convener, Nat. Security Div., Nat. Policy Foundation 2000–05; Legislator 2005–08; Sec.-Gen. Nat. Security Council 2008–10 (resgnd). Publications: The Normalization of Sino-Soviet Relations, Taiwan's Relations with Mainland China: A Tail Wagging Two Dogs; over 20 papers and articles. Address: 122, Sec. 1, Chung-Ching 5 Road, Taipei 10048, Taiwan.

SU, Guaning, BSc, MS, PhD; Singaporean engineer and university administrator; *President Emeritus, Nanyang Technological University;* ed Univ. of Alberta, Canada, California Inst. of Tech., Stanford Univ., Harvard Business School; began career as Research and Devt Engineer, Ministry of Defence; CEO Defence Science and Tech. Agency 2000–02; Pres. Nanyang Tech. Univ. 2003–11, Pres. Emer. 2011–; Adviser, Bitwave Pte Ltd; Dir Singapore Cable Vision, DSO Nat. Labs, Agency for Science, Tech. and Research, Biomedical Research Council; mem. Science and Eng Research Council, Nat. Science and Tech. Bd 1991–2001, Econ. Devt Bd Exec. Cttee; mem. Bd of Trustees Singapore Nat. Research Foundation, Business China; Founder Chair. Global Alliance of Technological Univs 2009; Fellow, Inst. of Engineers, Singapore (Pres. 1994–96); Chevalier de Legion d'Honneur 2005; Public Admin Medal (Silver) 1989, Public Service Medal 1997, Public Admin Medal (Gold) 1998, Long Service Medal 1998, Nat. Science and Tech. Medal 2003. Address: Nanyang Technological University, Nanyang Avenue, Singapore, 639798, Singapore (office). Telephone: 6790-4769 (office). Fax: 6791-8494 (office). E-mail: ntu@edu.sg (office). Website: www.ntu.edu.sg (office).

SU, Rong; Chinese politician; *Secretary, Jiangxi CCP Provincial Committee;* b. Oct. 1948, Taonan, Jilin Prov.; ed Jilin Univ.; joined CCP 1970; Deputy Sec., later Sec. CCP Party Cttee, Najin Commune, Tao'an Co., Jilin Prov. 1974, Sec. Najin Commune 1975, Lingxia Commune 1975; Deputy Sec. CCP Tao'an Co. Cttee 1980; Sec. CCP Fuyu Co. Cttee, Jilin Prov. 1983; mem. Standing Cttee, CCP Baicheng Prefectural Cttee, Jilin Prov. 1983, Deputy Sec. CCP Baicheng Prefectural Cttee 1985–87, Commr Prefectural Admin. Office 1985, Sec. CCP Baicheng Prefectural Cttee 1987; Sec. CCP Siping City Cttee, Jilin Prov. 1989, Chair. Standing Cttee, Siping City People's Congress 1990; mem. Standing Cttee, CCP Jilin Prov. Cttee 1992–93, Sec.-Gen. Jilin Prov. Cttee 1992–93, Deputy Sec. 1996–2001; Sec. Yanbian Korean Autonomous Prefecture Cttee 1995–97, Qinghai Prov. Cttee 2001–03 (mem. Standing Cttee 2001–03), CCP Gansu Prov. Cttee 2003–06; Chair. Standing Cttee, Gansu Prov. People's Congress 2004–06; Exec. Vice-Pres. CCP Cen. Cttee Party School 2006–07; Alt. mem. 14th CCP Cen. Cttee 1992–97, 15th CCP Cen. Cttee 1997–2002, mem. 16th CCP Cen. Cttee 2002–07, 17th CCP Cen. Cttee 2007–; Sec. CCP Jianqxi Prov. Cttee 2007–. Address: Jianqxi Provincial People's Government, Jianqxi Province, People's Republic of China (office).

SU, Shulin, BSc, MSc; Chinese government official, petroleum engineer and business executive; *Governor, Fujian Province;* b. 1962, Dong'e Co., Shandong Prov.; ed Daqing Petroleum Inst., Harbin Inst. of Tech.; sr engineer with

experience in China's oil and gas industry; Deputy Dir, later Dir Petroleum Admin, Daqing, Heilongjiang Prov. 1998–99; Vice-Pres. and Gen. Man. and Chair. PetroChina Co. Ltd, Daqing Oilfield Co. Ltd, Daqing 1999–2003, Dir, PetroChina Co. Ltd 2002–06; Chair. China Petrochemical Corpn (Sinopec Group) 2007–11, Sec. Party Cttee 2007–11; Deputy Sec., CCP, Prov. Cttee Fujian Prov. 2011–; Acting Gov., then Vice-Gov., then Gov. People's Govt, Fujian Prov. 2011–; Sec. Leading Party Group, CCP, People's Govt, Fujian Prov. 2011–; Alt. mem. 16th CCP Cen. Cttee 2002–07, 17th CCP Cen. Cttee 2007–12, mem. 18th CCP Cen. Cttee 2012–. Address: Fujian Provincial People's Government, Fuzhou, Fujian Province, People's Republic of China (office). E-mail: info@fujian.gov.cn (office). Website: www.fujian.gov.cn (office).

SU, Shuyang, (Su Yang, Yu Pingfu); Chinese writer; b. 1938, Baoding, Hebei Prov.; ed Renmin Univ.; fmr teaching asst, Dept of CCP History, Renmin Univ.; Lecturer, Beijing Teachers' Coll.; worker, Baoding Voltage Transformer Factory; Lecturer, Beijing Coll. of Chinese Medicine; currently playwright, Beijing Film Studio; Vice-Chair. China Film Asscn; mem. Bd of Dirs Chinese Writers Asscn. Publications include: Song of Loyal Hearts (play), Wedding, Masquerade, The Death of Lao She, The Moon Goddess, I Am a Zero, Big Family Matter, Flying Moth, Taiping Lake, Sunset Boulevard: Selected Screenplays by Su Shuyang, Homeland (novel), About Love (poetry), A Reader on China 2007, A Reader on Tibet 2009. Address: Chinese Writers Association, No.25, East Tucheng Road, Chaoyang District, Beijing 100013, People's Republic of China.

SU, Tong; Chinese writer; b. (Tong Zhonggui), 23 Jan. 1963, Suzhou, Jiangsu Prov.; ed Beijing Normal Univ.; fmrly Lecturer, Nanjing Acad. of Arts; Ed. Zhongshan Magazine; Writer-in-Residence, Univ. of Iowa Int. Writing Program 2001; mem. Jiangsu Provincial Writers' Asscn. Publications include: (titles in translation) The Eighth Is a Bronze Sculpture, The Escape of 1934, The Mournful Dance, The Lives of Women, Wives and Concubines 1990, Raise the Red Lantern (three novellas) 1991, Blush 1994, Rice 1995, Jasmine Woman 2004, My Life as an Emperor 2006, Binu – The Myth of Meng Jiang Nu 2007, The Boat to Redemption (Man Asian Literary Prize) 2009. Address: c/o Canongate Books, 14 High Street, Edinburgh, EH1 1TE, Scotland (office).

SU, Tseng-chang; Taiwanese lawyer and politician; b. 28 July 1947, Pingtung; m. Su Jan Shiow-ling; three d.; ed Nat. Taiwan Univ.; practised as lawyer 1973–83; joined Taipei Jr Chamber 1973, Pres. 1978; Vice-Pres. Jr Chamber International Taiwan 1979; elected mem. Taiwan Prov. Ass. 1981; Magistrate, Pingtung Co. 1989–94, Taipei Co. 1997–2004; Sec.-Gen. Democratic Progressive Party, Chair. 2005; Sec.-Gen. Office of the Pres. 2004–05; Premier of Taiwan 2006–07; unsuccessful cand. for Vice-Pres. of Taiwan 2008; Most Outstanding Chapter in Asia Award 1978, Outstanding LOM Pres. of the World Award 1978. Address: c/o Democratic Progressive Party, 10/F, 30 Beiping East Road, Taipei 10051, Taiwan.

SUÁREZ COPPEL, Juan José, BA, PhD; Mexican business executive, economist and academic; b. 1959; ed Instituto Tecnológico Autónomo de México (ITAM), Univ. of Chicago, USA; fmr Prof. of Econs, ITAM, Univ. Autónoma de Barcelona, Spain, Brown Univ., USA; fmr Chief of Staff to Sec. of Finance and Public Credit; fmr Corp. Treas., Grupo Televisa; Dir of Derivatives Trading Desk, Banco Nacional de México SA (Banamex) 2001; Chief Financial Officer, Petróleos Mexicanos (PEMEX) 2001–06, Dir Gen. 2009–12; Chief Financial Officer, Grupo Modelo –2009; Dir, El Cid Resorts, Jacobs Engineering Group Inc. 2013–; fmr Dir I.I.I. Servicios SA de CV, Instalaciones Inmobiliarias para Industrias SA de CV, Mexicana de Lubricantes SA de CV, Instituto Mexicano del Petróleo. Address: c/o Corporate Secretary, Jacobs Engineering Group Inc., 155 North Lake Avenue 91101, PO Box 7084, Pasadena, CA 91109-7084, USA. Telephone: (877) 522-6272 (office). E-mail: presiding.director@jacobs.com (office). Website: www.jacobs.com (office).

SUÁREZ PERTIERRA, Gustavo, LLD; Spanish academic and fmr politician; *Professor, Universidad Nacional de Educación a Distancia;* b. 1949, Cudillero, Oviedo; m.; one s. one d.; ed Univs of Oviedo, Valladolid and Munich; Prof. in Canon Law, Complutense Univ., Madrid 1978, also sometime Vice-Dean of Law and mem. Academic Council of Human Rights Inst.; Dir-Gen. of Religious Matters, Ministry of Justice and Pres. of Advisory Comm. on Religious Freedom 1982; Deputy Sec., Ministry of Defence 1984; Sec. of State for Mil. Admin. 1990–93; Minister of Educ. and Science 1993–95, of Defence 1995–96; Pres. Parl. Comm. for Public Admin. 1996–2000; Prof., Universidad Nacional de Educación a Distancia 2000–; Dir Instituto Universitario Gen. Gutiérrez Mellado 2001–05; Chair. Real Instituto Elcano (research inst.), Madrid 2002–12. Address: Facultad de Derecho, Calle Obispo Trejo 2, 28040 Madrid, Spain (office). E-mail: gsuarezpertierra@gmail.com (office).

SUBAEY, Ahmed A. Al-; Saudi Arabian oil industry executive; *CEO, S-Oil Corporation;* fmr Pres. and CEO Saudi Petroleum International Inc. (US subsidiary of Saudi Aramco), fmr Pres. Saudi Petroleum Ltd (Japanese unit of Saudi Aramco); CEO S-Oil Corpn (jt venture between Saudi Arabia's state-run oil co. and Hanjin Group) 2008–. Address: S-Oil Corpn, Yeouido PO Box 758, 63rd Floor Building, 60 Yeouido-dong Yeongdungpo-gu, Seoul 150-607, South Korea (office). Telephone: (2) 3772-5151 (office). E-mail: info@s-oil.com (office). Website: www.s-oil.com (office).

SUBBA ROW, Raman, CBE, MA; British company director, public relations consultant and fmr cricketer; b. 29 Jan. 1932, Streatham, London, England; s. of the late Panguluri Venkata Subba Row and of Doris Pinner; m. Anne Harrison 1960; two s. one d.; ed Whitgift School, Croydon and Trinity Hall, Cambridge; Pilot Officer, RAF 1956–58; left-hand opening batsman; played for Univ. of Cambridge 1951–53, Surrey 1953–54, Northants. 1955–61 (Capt. 1958–61); Test debut: England v NZ, Manchester 24–29 July 1958; played in 13 Tests for England 1958–61, scored 984 runs (average 46.85, highest score 137) including three hundreds; toured Australia 1958–59; played in 260 First-class matches, scored 14,182 runs (average 41.46, highest score 300) including 30 hundreds; Assoc. Dir W.S. Crawford Ltd 1963–69; Man. Dir Management Public Relations Ltd 1969–92; Chair. Surrey Co. Cricket Club 1974–79, Test and County Cricket Bd 1985–90; Int. Cricket Council (ICC) referee (41 Tests, 119 One-Day Ints) 1992–2001; apptd to work with ICC on reform of int. umpiring and refereeing panels; mem. Inst. of Dirs; Wisden Cricketer of the Year 1961. Leisure interests: golf, sports generally.

Address: Leeward, 13 Manor Way, South Croydon, Surrey, CR2 7BT, England (home). *Telephone:* (20) 8688-2991 (home). *Fax:* (20) 8688-2991 (home).

SUBBARAO, Duvvuri, BSc (Hons), MSc, MS (Econs), PhD; Indian economist and fmr central banker; b. 11 Aug. 1949, Eluru, AP; m. Urmila Rao; two s.; ed Indian Inst. of Tech., Kharagpur, Indian Inst. of Tech., Kanpur, Ohio State Univ., USA, Andhra Univ.; came top in All India Civil Service examination for entry into Indian Admin. Service and Indian Foreign Service 1972; Humphrey Fellow, MIT, USA 1982–83; Jt Sec., Dept of Econ. Affairs 1988–93; Finance Sec., Govt of AP 1993–98; Lead Economist, World Bank 1999–2004; Sec. to Prime Minister's Econ. Advisory Council 2005–07; Finance Sec., Ministry of Finance 2007–08; Gov. Reserve Bank of India 2008–13. *Publications:* has written extensively on issues in public finance, decentralization and political economy of reforms. *Address:* c/o Reserve Bank of India, Central Office, Shahid Bhagat Singh Road, POB 10007, Mumbai 400 001, India.

SUBOTNICK, Morton Leon, MA; American composer and academic; b. 14 April 1933, Los Angeles; s. of Jack Jacob Subotnick and Rose Luckerman; m. 1st Linn Pottle 1953 (divorced 1971); one s. one d.; m. 2nd Doreen Nelson 1976 (divorced 1977); m. 3rd Joan La Barbara 1979; one s.; ed Univ. of Denver, Mills Coll.; Co-founder San Francisco Tape Music Center 1961–65; fmr Music Dir Ann Halprin's Dance Co. and San Francisco Actors' Workshop, fmr Music Dir Lincoln Center Repertory Theatre; Dir of electronic music at original Electric Circus, St Mark's Place, New York 1967–68; Artist-in-Residence, New York Univ. School of the Arts 1966–69; apptd Co-Dir Center for Experiments in Art, Information and Tech., California Inst. of Arts, Valencia 1969, also Co-Chair. Composition Dept; Visiting Prof. in Composition, Univ. of Maryland 1968, Univ. of Pittsburgh 1969, Yale Univ. 1982, 1983; Composer-in-Residence DAAD, West Berlin 1981, MIT 1986; Brandeis Award for Music 1983, American Acad. of Arts and Letters Composer Award, SEAMUS Lifetime Acheivement Award 1998, ASCAP John Cage Award, ACO Lifetime Achievement Award. *Compositions include:* Silver Apples of the Moon, The Wild Bull, Trembling, The Double Life of Amphibians, The Key to Songs, Return: The Triumph of Reason (electronic composition in honour of the return of Halley's Comet) 1986, In Two Worlds 1987–88, And The Butterflies Begin to Sing 1988, A Desert Flowers 1989, All my Hummingbirds have Alibis, Jacob's Room (opera) 1993, Making Music 1996, Intimate Immensity 1997, Echoes from the Silent Call of Girona 1998. *Address:* 25 Minetta Lane, Apt 4B, New York, NY 10012, USA. *E-mail:* morts@creatingmusic.com. *Website:* www.mortonsubotnick .com.

SUBRAMANIAM, A.; Indian social worker and educationalist; b. 18 Oct. 1925, Kodungallur, Kerala State; s. of Ananthanarayanan Ammal and Lakshmi Ammal; jailed for six months in 1942 for participating in Quit India Movt; trade union worker; Tamil Nadu State Sec. of Socialist Party for several years; headed trade unions in textiles, eng, road transport, ports and docks, papermaking, tea plantations, heavy electricals; Nat. Pres. Hind Mazdoor Sabha for two terms, has represented Hind Mazdoor Sabha on visits to UK, USA, USSR, China, Japan, South Africa, Sri Lanka, Singapore, Malaysia, Germany, France, Italy and Switzerland; Sec. Thiagi N. G. Ramaswarny Memorial Higher Secondary School and Nursery School; mem. of Tamil Nadu Legis. Ass. 1971–76. *Leisure interest:* reading. *Address:* Thiagi NGR Bhavan, 248 (Old 2112) Trichy Road, Singanallur, Coimbatore 641 005 (office); Thamarai, 42 (Old 65) 2nd Street, Lal Bahadur Nagar, Coimbatore 641 004, India (home). *Telephone:* (422) 2573145 (office); (422) 2574460 (home); (422) 2574140. *Fax:* (422) 2574140. *E-mail:* ayess_25@rediffmail .com (office).

SUBRAMANYAN, Kalpathi Ganapathi; Indian artist, sculptor and academic; b. 5 Feb. 1924, Kerala; s. of K. P. Ganapathi and Alamelu Ammal; m. Susheela Jasra 1951; one d.; ed Univ. of Madras, Kalabhavana, Visvabharati and Slade School of Art, London; Lecturer in Painting, Faculty of Fine Arts, M. G. Univ., Baroda 1951–59, Reader 1961–66, Prof. 1966–80, Dean, Faculty of Fine Arts 1968–74; Prof. of Painting, Kala Bhavana, Visva Bharati, Santiniketan 1980–89, Prof. Emer. 1989–2004; Deputy Dir (Designs), All India Handloom Bd, Bombay 1959–61, Design Consultant 1961–65; Visiting Lecturer, Canada 1976; Visiting Fellow, Visvabharati, Santiniketan 1977–78; Christensen Fellow, St Catherine's Coll., Oxford 1987–88; JDR III Fund Fellowship, New York 1967–68; Fellow, Lalit Kala Acad. 1993; Hon. DLitt (Rabindra Bharati Univ., Calcutta) 1992, (Banaras Hindu Univ., Varanasi) 1997; Governor's Prize, Bombay Art Soc. 1957, Maharashtra State Award 1961, Hon. Mention (São Paulo Biennale) 1961, Nat. Award 1965, Gold Medal, 1st Indian Triennale 1968, Padma Shri 1975, Kalidas Samman 1981, Shiromani Puraskar 1994, Kala Ratna, All India Fine Arts and Crafts Soc., New Delhi 1999, Abanindra Puraskar 2000, Jadunath Sarkar Gold Medal, Asiatic Soc., Kolkata 2000, Gana Krishti Puraskar 2001, Manaviyam Ravi Varma Award, Govt of Kerala 2001, Lalit Kala Ratna Puraskar 2004, Lifetime Achievement Award, Acad. of Fine Arts, Kolkata 2005, Padma Bhushan 2006; numerous other awards. *Publications:* Moving Focus (essays on art) 1978, Living Tradition 1985, Creative Circuit (collection of lectures) 1991. *Leisure interests:* reading, handicraft. *Address:* c/o Kala Bhavana, Santiniketan, 731 235, West Bengal (office); Kailas, 13 Purvapalli, Santiniketan, 731 235, West Bengal, India (home). *Website:* www.visva-bharati.ac.in (office).

SUCHET, David, CBE, OBE; British actor; b. 2 May 1946, London, England; s. of the late Jack Suchet and Joan Suchet (née Jarché); m. Sheila Ferris 1976; one s. one d.; ed Wellington School, Somerset, London Acad. of Music and Dramatic Art; fmr mem. Nat. Youth Theatre, Chester Repertory Co.; joined RSC 1973; Assoc. Artist, Birmingham Rep., Connaught Theatre, Worthing, Northcott Theatre, Exeter, Liverpool Rep., Chichester Festival Theatre, Theatre Royal, Bath; Visiting Prof. of Theatre, Univ. of Neb., USA 1975; mem. Fight Dirs Asscn; Freedom of the City of London 2009; hon. degree from Univ. of Kent, Canterbury 2010; awards for Salieri in Amadeus 2000, Melmotte in The Way We Live Now 2002, Maxwell 2009. *Roles for RSC include:* Tybalt in Romeo and Juliet 1973, Orlando in As You Like It 1973, Tranio in Taming of the Shrew 1973, Zamislov in Summerfolk 1974, 1975, Wilmer in Comrades 1974, The Fool in King Lear 1974, 1975, Pisanio in Cymbeline 1974, Hubert in King John, Ferdinand King of Navarre in Love's Labour's Lost 1975, Shylock in The Merchant of Venice 1978, Grumio in Taming of the Shrew 1978, Sir Nathaniel in Love's Labour's Lost 1978, Glougauer in Once in a Lifetime 1978, Caliban in The Tempest 1978, Sextus Pompey in Antony and Cleopatra 1978, Angelo in Measure for Measure 1979, Iago in Othello, Every Good Boy Deserves

Favour, Bolingbroke in Richard II 1981, Achilles in Troilus and Cressida, Mercutio in Romeo and Juliet, Iago in Othello 1985. *Other stage roles include:* Lucio in Measure for Measure 1977, Thomas Gilthead in The Devil is an Ass 1977, The Kreutzer Sonata 1978, Tsaravitch and George Wochner in Laughter! 1978, Joe Green in Separation 1987, This Story of Yours, Litvanoy in The Wedding Feast, Estragon in Waiting for Godot, John Aubrey in Brief Lives, Mole in Toad of Toad Hall, Timon in Timon of Athens 1991, John in Oleanna (Variety Club Best Actor Award 1994) 1993, Sid Field in What a Performance 1994, George in Who's Afraid of Virginia Woolf? (Critic's Circle Best Actor Award 1997) 1996, Salieri in Amadeus (Variety Club Best Actor Award 1998, South Bank Award and Backstage Theatre Award 2000) 1998–2000, Gregor Antonescu in Man and Boy, Duchess Theatre, London 2005, Once in a Lifetime, Royal Nat. Theatre 2006, All My Sons, Apollo Theatre, London (Best Actor, Olivier Awards, Critics' Circle Award) 2010, Long Day's Journey into Night, London 2012. *Films include:* Tale of Two Cities 1978, Schiele in Prison 1980, The Missionary 1982, Hunchback of Notre Dame 1982, Red Monarch (Best Actor, Marseilles Film Festival 1983) 1983, Trenchcoat 1983, Greystoke: The Legend of Tarzan, Lord of the Apes 1984, Little Drummer Girl 1984, Song for Europe (video title Cry for Justice) (Best Actor, Royal TV Soc. Performance Awards 1986) 1985, Thirteen to Dinner 1985, Falcon and the Snowman 1985, Gulag 1985, Iron Eagle 1986, Murrow 1986, Big Foot and The Hendersons 1986, Stress (Best Actor Award, British Industry/Scientific Film Asscn 1986) 1986, Crime of Honor 1987, The Last Innocent Man 1987, A World Apart 1988, To Kill a Priest (also known as Popielusko) 1988, The Lucona Affair, When the Whales Came 1990, Executive Decision 1995, Deadly Voyage 1995, Sunday 1996, A Perfect Murder 1997, RKO 1999, Sabotage 1999, Live From Baghdad 2002, The In-Laws 2003, Foolproof 2003, Flood 2006, Flushed Away (voice) 2006, Flood 2007, The Bank Job 2008, Act of God 2009, Effie 2010. *Work for radio includes:* The Kreutzer Sonata (one-man show) (Best Radio Actor of the Year 1979), Shylock in The Merchant of Venice, Bolingbroke in Richard II, First Night Impression, Rosenberg in the Trenches, Chimes at Midnight, The Isaac Babel Stories, Super Cannes (Book at Bedtime) and numerous other parts. *Television includes:* role of Hercule Poirot in dramatization of 65 Agatha Christie Poirot novels (for LWT) Series 1989–, 100th Anniversary Special: The Mysterious Affair at Styles 1990, Oppenheimer 1978, Being Normal, Saigon – the Last Days, Time to Die, The Life of Freud (Best Actor, Royal TV Soc. Performance Awards 1986), Blott on the Landscape (Best Actor, Royal TV Soc. Performance Awards 1986), Oxbridge Blues 1986, Playing Shakespeare 1983, Master of the Game 1984, Reilly – Ace of Spies 1984, Mussolini: The Untold Story 1985, James Joyce's Ulysses, Cause Célèbre 1988, The Life of Agatha Christie 1990, Once in a Lifetime, Bingo, Long Ago and Far Away 1989, Days of Majesty 1994, Fighting Fund (episode of The Protectors), Separation 1990, Secret Agent, Kings and Castles, Nobody Here but Us Chickens 1989, The Cruel Train, The Curious 1994, Moses 1995, Solomon 1997, See Saw 1997, The Way We Live Now 2001, National Crime Squad 2001–02, The First Lady 2003, Henry VIII 2003, Space Odyssey (voice) 2004, A Bear Named Winnie 2004, Dracula (film) 2006, Maxwell (film) 2007, Diverted (film) 2009, Going Postal (film) 2010, Hidden (series) 2011, Richard II (film) 2012 In The Footsteps of St Paul (documentary) 2012. *Achievements include:* brown belt in Aikido; a First Master of Japanese Samurai. *Publications:* essays in Players of Shakespeare 1985. *Leisure interests:* photography, clarinet, ornithology, theology, boating on inland waterways. *Address:* c/o Ken McReddie Associates Ltd, 36-40 Glasshouse Street, London, W1B 5DL, England (office). *Telephone:* (20) 7439-1456 (office). *Fax:* (20) 7734-6530 (office). *E-mail:* email@kenmcreddie.com (office).

SUCHOCKA, Hanna, DrIur; Polish lawyer, politician and diplomatist; b. 3 April 1946, Pleszew; d. of Adam Mickiewicz Univ., Poznań; scientific worker, Dept of Constitutional Law of Adam Mickiewicz Univ., Poznań 1968–69, 1972–90, Catholic Univ. of Lublin 1988–92, Polish Acad. of Science 1990–; mem. Democratic Party (SD) 1969–84, Democratic Union 1991–94, Freedom Union 1994–; Deputy to Sejm (Parl.) 1980–85, 1989–2001; mem. Civic Parl. Caucus 1989–91, mem. Democratic Union Parl. Caucus (now Freedom Union) 1991–, Deputy Chair. Parl. Legis. Cttee 1989–92; Chair. Council of Ministers (Prime Minister) 1992–93; Minister of Justice and Attorney-Gen. 1997–99; mem. Pontifical Acad. of Social Sciences, Rome 1994; Amb. to the Holy See 2001–13; Dr hc (Oklahoma); Max Schmidtheiny Prize 1994, Foyer Prize 2004. *Publications:* author of reports and articles for professional publs and int. confs.

SUDAN, Madhu, PhD; Indian mathematician and academic; *Fujitsu Chair Professor, Department of Electrical Engineering and Computer Science, Massachusetts Institute of Technology;* b. 12 Sept. 1966; ed Indian Inst. of Tech. and Univ. of California, Berkeley, USA; student researcher, IBM Almaden Research Center 1990, mem. Research Staff, Math. Sciences Dept, IBM Thomas J. Watson Research Center, Yorktown Heights, NY 1992–97; Assoc. Prof., Dept of Electrical Eng and Computer Science, MIT 1997–2002, Prof. 2003–05, Fujitsu Chair Prof. 2005–, mem. Computer Science and AI Lab. (CSAIL), Theory of Computing (TOC) Group, CSAIL, Algorithms, Complexity, and Cryptography and Information Security subgroups, TOC; Fellow, Radcliffe Inst. for Advanced Study 2003–04; Ed. Society for Industrial and Applied Math. (SIAM) Journal on Discrete Mathematics 1997–, SIAM Journal on Computing 2000–03, Information and Computation 2000–03; Guest Ed. Journal of Computer and System Sciences (special issue devoted to papers from Complexity '2001) 2001–02; Ed.-in-chief Foundations and Trends in Theoretical 2004–; mem. Asscn for Computing Machinery, IEEE, Society for Industrial and Applied Math., American Math. Soc.; Sakrison Memorial Award for PhD Thesis, Dept of Electrical Eng and Computer Science, Univ. of California, Berkeley 1993, ACM Doctoral Dissertation Award 1993, Sloan Foundation Fellowship 1998, NSF Career Award 1999, Information Theory Paper Award 2000, Gödel Prize 2001, Nevanlinna Prize 2002. *Publications include:* Efficient Checking of Polynomials and Proofs and the Hardness of Approximation Problems 1996, Complexity Classifications of Boolean Constraint Satisfaction Problems (co-author) 2001; more than 90 articles in scientific journals on theoretical computer science, algorithms, computational complexity, optimization and coding theory. *Address:* Stata Center, Massachusetts Institute of Technology, Room G640, 32 Vassar Street, Cambridge, MA 02139, USA (office). *Telephone:* (617) 253-9680 (office). *Fax:* (617) 258-8682 (office). *E-mail:* madhu@mit.edu (office). *Website:* theory.csail.mit.edu/~madhu (office); people.csail.mit.edu/madhu (office).

SUDARSONO, Juwono, PhD; Indonesian government official, diplomatist and academic; m.; two s. one d.; ed Univ. of Indonesia, Univ. of California, Berkeley,

USA, London School of Econs, UK; Visiting Prof., Columbia Univ. 1986–87; Dean of Social and Political Science, Univ. of Indonesia 1988–94; Vice-Gov. Indonesian Defence Coll. 1995–98; apptd Minister of Environment 1998, then Minister of Educ.; served as first civilian Minister of Defence 1999; returned to Univ. of Indonesia teaching part-time; fmr Commr Strategic Intelligence; Amb. to UK and Repub. of Ireland 2003–04; Minister of Defence 2004–09. *Address:* c/o Ministry of Defence, Jalan Medan Merdeka Barat 13–14, Jakarta Pusat, Indonesia (office).

SÜDHOF, Thomas Christian, MD; German/American neuroscientist and academic; *Avram Goldstein Professor in the School of Medicine and Professor, by courtesy, of Neurology and of Psychiatry and Behavioral Sciences, Stanford University;* b. 22 Dec. 1955, Göttingen; m. Lu Chen; ed Univ. of Göttingen, Harvard Univ., USA; Postdoctoral Researcher, Max Planck Inst. for Biophysical Chemistry, Göttingen –1982; Postdoctoral Fellow, Univ. of Texas SW Medical Center, Dallas 1983, headed own lab. 1986–2008, Prof., Faculty for Molecular Genetics 1991; Investigator, Howard Hughes Medical Inst. 1986–; Scientific mem. and Dir Max Planck Inst. for Experimental Medicine, Göttingen 1995–98; moved to Stanford Univ. 2008, currently Avram Goldstein Prof. in the School of Medicine and Prof., by courtesy, of Neurology and of Psychiatry and Behavioral Sciences; mem. NAS 2002, Inst. of Medicine 2008, American Acad. of Arts and Sciences 2010; Kavli Prize in Neuroscience, Kavli Foundation 2010, Lasker DeBakey Basic Medical Research Award, Albert and Mary Lasker Foundation 2013, Nobel Prize in Physiology or Medicine (jtly with James Rothman and Randy Schekman) 2013. *Address:* Stanford University School of Medicine, Department of Molecular and Cellular Physiology, Beckman Center, Room B100, 279 Campus Drive, Stanford, CA 94305-5345, USA (office). *Fax:* (650) 725-8021 (office). *E-mail:* tcs1@stanford .edu (office). *Website:* med.stanford.edu/profiles/neuroscience/researcher/ Thomas_Sudhof (office).

SUDJIC, Deyan, OBE; British architecture critic and arts administrator; *Director, The Design Museum;* b. 6 Sept. 1952, London; s. of the late Miša J. Sudjic and of Ceja Sudjic (née Pavlovic); m. Sarah Miller; one d.; ed Latymer Upper School, London and Univ. of Edin.; chose not to practise as an architect; Architecture Corresp. Sunday Times 1980–85; fmr Critic London Daily News; Critic Sunday Correspondent 1989–90; Architecture Critic The Guardian 1991–97; Visiting Prof. of Design Theory and History, Hochschule für Angewandte Kunst, Vienna 1993–97; Dir Glasgow 1999 UK City of Architecture and Design; Ed. Domus Magazine 2000–04; Architecture Critic The Observer 2000–; Dir 8th Venice Architectural Biennale 2002; Dir The Design Museum, London 2006–; Visiting Prof. of Design, Royal Coll. of Art; Founder Ed., later Editorial Dir Blueprint magazine, also f. Tate and Eye magazines. *Publications include:* Cult Objects 1985, New British Architecture: The Design of Richard Rogers, Norman Foster and James Stirling 1986, Rei Kawakubo: A Monograph of the Japanese Fashion Designer 1990, Cult Heroes: An Investigation of the Mechanics of Celebrity 1990, The Hundred Mile City: A Study of the Rapidly Evolving Modern City 1992, The Architecture of Richard Rogers 1995, The Architecture of Erick van Egeraat 1997, Ron Arad: A Monograph 1999, John Pawson Works 2000, Architecture and Democracy 2001, The Edifice Complex: How the Rich and Powerful Shape the World 2005, The Language of Things 2008, Norman Foster: A Life in Architecture 2010. *Address:* The Design Museum, 28 Shad Thames, London, SE1 2YD, England (office). *Telephone:* (870) 909-9009 (office). *E-mail:* info@designmuseum.org (office). *Website:* www.designmuseum.orgus (office).

SUDO, Fumio; Japanese steel industry executive; b. 3 March 1941; ed Hokkaido Univ.; joined Kawasaki Steel Corpn 1964, Gen. Man., Steelmaking, Mizushima 1988, mem. Bd of Dirs 1994–, Exec. Officer 1994–2000, Exec. Vice-Pres. 2001, Pres. and CEO 2001–03, Pres. and CEO JFE Steel Corpn 2003–05, mem. Bd of Dirs JFE Holdings Inc. (following merger of Kawasaki Steel Corpn with Nihon Kōkan Kabushiki-gaisha) 2002–10, Pres. and CEO 2005–10, Pres. Nihon Keizai Shimbun (now called The Nikkei) of JFE Holdings, Inc. 2005–08, Chair. JFE 21st Century Foundation. *Address:* c/o JFE Holdings, Inc., 1-5-1 Marunouchi, Chiyoda-ku, Tokyo 100-6527, Japan. *Telephone:* (3) 3217-4049. *Website:* www.jfe-holdings.co.jp.

SUEBWONGLEE, Surapong; Thai physician and politician; fmr Communist rebel; trained as a medical doctor before entering politics; fmr mem. Thai Rak Thai party; Govt Spokesman 2005; Minister of Information and Communications Tech. –2006 (Govt of Prime Minister Thaksin Sinawatra deposed in mil. coup Sept. 2006); Sec.-Gen. People's Power Party 2007–08 (party dissolved by Constitutional Court); Deputy Prime Minister and Minister of Finance Sept. 2008; to face trial for abuse of power 2011.

SUGA, Yoshihide, LLB; Japanese politician; *Chief Cabinet Secretary;* b. 6 Dec. 1948, Akita Pref.; ed Hosei Univ.; Sec. to Rep. Hikosaburo Okonogi 1975, Sec. to Minister for Int. Trade and Industry 1984–87; mem. Yokohama City Council 1987; mem. House of Reps 1996–, Parl. Sec. for Land, Infrastructure and Transport 2002–03, for Int. Trade and Industry 2003–04; Deputy Sec.-Gen. LDP 2001–, Chair. Diet Affairs Cttee 2004, Sr Vice-Minister for Internal Affairs and Communications 2005–06, Minister of Internal Affairs and Communications and Minister of State for Privatization of Postal Services 2006–07; Chief Cabinet Sec. 2012–, also Minister in charge of Strengthening Nat. Security. *Address:* Cabinet Office, 1-6-1, Nagata-cho, Chiyoda-ku, Tokyo 100-8968 (office); Liberal-Democratic Party (Jiyu-Minshuto), 1-11-23, Nagata-cho, Chiyoda-ku, Tokyo 100-8910, Japan (office). *Telephone:* (3) 5253-2111 (office); (3) 3581-6211 (office). *E-mail:* koho@ldp .jimin.or.jp (office). *Website:* www.cao.go.jp (office); www.jimin.jp (office); www .sugayoshihide.gr.jp.

SUGAR, Baron (Life Peer), cr. 2009, of Clapton in the London Borough of Hackney; **Alan Michael Sugar;** British business executive and government official; b. 24 March 1947, London, England; s. of Nathan Sugar and Fay Sugar; m. Ann Simons 1968; two s. one d.; ed Brooke House School, London; Chair. and Man. Dir Amstrad PLC 1968–97, CEO –1993, Chair. 1997–2001, Chair. and CEO 2001–; Owner and Chair. Tottenham Hotspur PLC 1991–2001; Chair. Viglen PLC 1997–; Govt Enterprise Champion 2009–10; Trustee, Alan Sugar Foundation; Empire Partner, The Hackney Empire (charity); Hon. DSc (City Univ.) 1988; Hon. Fellow, City and Guilds of London Inst. *Television:* star of The Apprentice (BBC) 2005–, Young Apprentice (Junior Apprentice in series 1) (BBC) (BAFTA Award for Best Reality & Constructed Factual 2012) 2010–. *Publications:* The Apprentice Revisited 2006, What You See is What You Get: My Autobiography 2010. *Leisure*

interest: tennis. *Address:* Amstrad PLC, Brentwood House, 169 King's Road, Brentwood, Essex, CM14 4EF (office); House of Lords, Westminster, London, SW1A 0PW, England. *Telephone:* (1277) 228888 (office); (20) 7219-5353 (House of Lords). *Fax:* (1277) 211350 (office). *E-mail:* info@amstrad.com (office). *Website:* www.amstrad.com (office); www.parliament.uk/biographies/lords/alan-sugar/ 58862; www.bbc.co.uk/apprentice.

SUGAR, Ronald D., BEng, MSc, PhD; American defence industry executive; b. July 1948, Toronto, Ont., Canada; m.; two c.; ed Univ. of California, Los Angeles, Stanford Univ., Univ. of Pennsylvania, Harvard Univ.; began career in tech. and man. positions at Hughes Aircraft Co., Argosystems Inc. and The Aerospace Corpn 1970s; joined TRW Aerospace and Information Systems 1970s, held various sr positions including Vice-Pres. Space Communications Div., Chief Financial Officer, Exec. Vice-Pres., Gen. Man. Global Automotive Electronics –1990s; Pres. and COO Litton Industries 2000–01, Pres. and COO Northrup Grumman Corpn (following acquisition of Litton by Northrup 2001) 2001–03, Chair., Pres. and CEO 2003–06, Chair. and CEO 2006–10 (retd); mem. Bd Dirs Chevron Corpn 2005–, LA Philharmonic Asscn; apptd by Pres. of USA to Nat. Security Telecommunications Advisory Cttee; Gov. Aerospace Industries Asscn; Nat. Fundraising Chair. Pearl Harbor Memorial Fund; fmr Chair. Aerospace Industries Asscn; Nat. Trustee Boys & Girls Clubs of America; Trustee, Cleveland Inst. of Music, Nat. Defense Industrial Asscn, Univ. of Southern California; Fellow, AIAA; FRAeS; mem. Nat. Acad. of Eng; Engineering Alumnus of the Year, UCLA 1996, Daniel J. Epstein Eng Man. Award, Univ. of Southern Calif. 2003, Semper Fidelis Award, Marine Corps Foundation, John R. Alison Leadership to Nat. Defense Award, Air Force Asscn, Eisenhower Distinguished Citizen Award, Army Distaff Foundation. *Address:* c/o Northrop Grumman Corpn, 1840 Century Park East, Los Angeles, CA 90067-2199, USA.

SUGISAKI, Shigemitsu; Japanese financial industry executive, international organization official and fmr civil servant; *Vice-Chairman, Goldman Sachs Japan Company, Ltd;* b. 1941, Tokyo; ed Univ. of Tokyo, Columbia Univ.; positions with Ministry of Finance 1964–76, 1979–94 including mem. Minister's Secr., Deputy Vice-Minister of Finance for Int. Affairs 1990–91, Deputy Dir-Gen. Int. Finance Bureau 1991–92, Commr Tokyo Regional Taxation Bureau 1992–93, Sec.-Gen. Exec. Bureau Securities and Exchange Surveillance Comm. 1993–94; Personal Asst to Pres. Asian Devt Bank 1976–79; Special Adviser to Man. Dir IMF 1994–97, Deputy Man. Dir 1997–2004; Chair. Sompo Japan Research Inst.; Vice-Chair. Goldman Sachs Japan Co. Ltd 2006–. *Address:* Goldman Sachs Japan Co. Ltd, Roppongi Hills, Mori Tower, Level 43-48, 10-1, Roppongi 6-chome, Minato-ku, Tokyo 106-6147, Japan (office). *Telephone:* (3) 6437-1000 (office). *Website:* www2 .goldmansachs.com/japan (office).

SUGIURA, Seiken, BEcons; Japanese lawyer and politician; b. 26 July 1934, Okazaki-city, Aichi Pref.; m. Toshiko Sugiura; one s. one d.; ed Univ. of Tokyo; began career with Kawasaki Steel Corpn 1957; called to the Bar 1972; Vice-Pres. Tokyo First Bar Asscn 1982; mem. House of Reps 1986–2009, Parl. Vice-Minister, Ministry of Agric., Forestry and Fisheries 1990–92, Parl. Vice-Minister, Nat. Land Agency 1992–96, Chair. House of Reps Judicial Affairs Cttee 1998, Sr Vice-Minister for Foreign Affairs 2001–02, Deputy Chief Cabinet Sec. 2004–06, also Minister of Justice 2005–06; several sr posts in LDP including Deputy Chair. of Gen. Council 1999, Deputy Chair. Policy Research Council 2000; Assoc. Mem. InterAction Council (of Former Heads of State and Government). *Leisure interests:* golf, walking, classical music. *Address:* InterAction Council, 3-16-13 Roppongi, Minato-ku, 106-0032 Tokyo, Japan. *Telephone:* (3) 5549-2950. *Fax:* (3) 5549-2955. *E-mail:* interact@vega.ocn.ne.jp. *Website:* www.interactioncouncil.org.

SUH, Kyung-bae, MBA; South Korean business executive; *Chairman and CEO, AmorePacific Corporation;* b. 1963; s. of Suh Sung-whan; m.; two c.; ed Cornell Univ., USA; joined family business AmorePacific Corpn (cosmetics co.) 1980s, Pres. and CEO 1997, now Chair. and CEO; Korea's Best CEO, Ernst & Young 2010. *Address:* AmorePacific Corpn, 181, Hangangno 2-ga, Yongsan-gu, Seoul 140-012, South Korea (office). *Telephone:* (2) 709-6006 (office). *Fax:* (2) 709-6029 (office). *Website:* www.amorepacific.com (office).

SUH, Kyung-suk; South Korean business executive; *Vice-Chairman, GS Holdings;* began career in Ministry of Finance, Man. Ulsan Tax Office 1971–75, Sr Officer, Ministry of Finance 1975–89, Vice-Dir Tax Court 1989–90; Financial Commr, Embassy in Japan 1990–91; moved to LG Group as Finance Advisor to Chair. LG Group 1991–92, Vice-Pres. 1992–94, Sr Vice-Pres. 1994–96, Exec. Vice-Pres. LG Strategic Business Devt Dept 1996, Exec. Vice-Pres. LG Investment Trust 1996–97, Pres. and CEO LG Investment Trust 1997–98, Pres. and CEO LG Capital 1998–2000, Pres. and CEO Kukdong City Gas 2000–01, Pres. and CEO LG Investment Securities 2001–04, mem. Exec. Bd, Pres. and CEO GS Holdings (spun off from LG Group in 2004) 2004–09, Vice-Chair. 2009–. *Address:* GS Holdings Corpn, 23 F, GS Tower, 679 Yoksam Dong, Gangnam Gu, Seoul, South Korea (office). *Telephone:* (2) 2005-1114 (office). *Fax:* (2) 2005-8181 (office). *E-mail:* info@ gsholdings.com (office). *Website:* www.gsholdings.com (office); www.gs.co.kr (office).

SUHAIBI, Noman Taher as-; Yemeni politician; b. 1965; ed San'a Univ.; Dir Gen Office of the Prime Interest 1995–2001; Chair. Tax Dept 2005–07; Minister of Finance 2007–. *Address:* Ministry of Finance, PO Box 190, Yemen (office). *Telephone:* (1) 260365 (office). *Fax:* (1) 263040 (office). *E-mail:* support@mofyemen .net (office). *Website:* www.mof.gov.ye (office).

SUHL, Harry, PhD; American physicist and academic; *Professor Emeritus of Physics, University of California, San Diego;* b. 18 Oct. 1922, Leipzig, Germany; s. of Bernhard Suhl and Klara Bergwerk; m. 1949 (deceased); ed Univ. Coll., Cardiff and Oriel Coll., Oxford, UK; Temp. Experimental Officer, Admiralty, London 1943–46; Tech. Staff, Bell Labs, NJ 1948–60; Prof. of Physics, Univ. of California, San Diego 1961, now Prof. Emer. Inst. for Pure and Applied Physical Sciences; Consultant, Aerospace Corpn 1961–, Exxon Research and Eng, NJ 1977–; Co-Ed. Magnetism 1961–74; Solid State Communications 1961–; Nat. Science Foundation Fellow 1971; Alexander V. Humboldt Sr Fellow 1991; Fellow, American Physics Soc., NAS, American Acad. of Arts and Sciences; Guggenheim Fellow 1968–69. *Publication:* Magnetism – A Treatise on Modern Theory and Materials (with G.T. Rado) 1966. *Address:* Physics Department, University of California, San Diego, 9500 Gilman Drive, La Jolla, CA 92093, USA (office). *Telephone:* (619) 534-4748 (office). *Fax:* (619) 534-0173 (office). *E-mail:* suhl@physics.ucsd.edu (office). *Website:* ipaps.ucsd.edu (office).

SUI, Anna; American fashion designer; *Founder and Designer, Anna Sui Corporation;* b. 4 Aug. 1955, Dearborn, Mich.; d. of Paul Sui and Grace Sui; ed Parsons School of Design, New York; Founder and Designer, Anna Sui Corpn 1988–; launched first collection 1991; established reputation with 'baby-doll' collection 1993; designer Sui Anna Sui 1995–; launched new line of special-occasion gowns 1997; CFDA Perry Ellis Award for New Fashion Talent 1993, Geoffrey Beene Lifetime Achievement Award 2009. *Address:* c/o KCD Inc., 450 West 15th Street, Suite 604, New York, NY 10011; Anna Sui Corporation, 275 West 39th Street, Floor 9, New York, NY 10018 (office); 113 Green Street, New York, NY 10012, USA (office). *Telephone:* (212) 768-1951 (office). *E-mail:* contactus@annasui.com. *Website:* www.annasui.com.

SUI, Lt-Gen. Mingtai; Chinese army officer; b. 1942, Zhaoyuan Co., Shandong Prov.; ed Political and Mil. Coll. and Univ. of Nat. Defence; joined PLA 1960, CCP 1962; Deputy Political Commissar, later Political Commissar, Zhouqiao Regt 1976–82; Deputy Political Commissar, Eng Corps, PLA Services and Arms 1982–83 (also Dir Political Dept); Deputy Political Commissar, 2nd Artillery Force, PLA Services and Arms 1983–86 (Dir Political Dept 1983–86, 1994–97, Deputy Dir 1990–94), Political Commissar 1997–2007 (retd); mem. 15th CCP Cen. Cttee 1997–2002, 16th CCP Cen. Cttee 2002–07; rank of Maj.-Gen. 1988, Lt-Gen. 1996. *Address:* c/o People's Liberation Army Second Artillery Force Headquarters, Beijing, People's Republic of China.

SUI, Gen. Yongju; Chinese army officer; *Political Commissar, Second Artillery Force, Services and Arms, People's Liberation Army;* b. Nov. 1932, Dalian City; engaged in secret communist activities while still at school as mem. New Democratic Youth; joined CCP 1950, PLA 1950; Clerk Luda Garrison Command responsible for Communist Youth League work; Sec. Political Office Public Security Militia Luda Border Defence Regt 1953; Co. Political Guidance Officer Eng Regt Second Artillery, Regt Org. Section Chief, Div. Chief Political Dept 1969, Political Commissar, Dir Base Political Dept, Asst Political Commissar, Base Political Commissar; elected. mil. rep. 7th NPC 1988; selected as activist to study Mao's works 1968; trained Second Artillery Eng Acad. 1985, Dir Political Office Second Artillery 1988; Second Asst Political Commissar, Second Artillery 1985–92, Political Commissar 1992–; mem. Cen. Comm. for Disciplinary Inspection; rank of Maj.-Gen. 1988, Lt-Gen. 1990, Gen. 1996; Del., 15th CCP Nat. Congress 1997–2002; mem. 9th Standing Cttee of NPC 1998–2003. *Address:* People's Liberation Army, Ministry of National Defence, Jingshanqian Jie, Beijing, 100009, People's Republic of China (office).

ŠUICA, Dubravka, BA; Croatian teacher and politician; b. 20 May 1957, Dubrovnik; m. Capt. Stijepo Šuica; one d.; ed Univ. of Zagreb, Univ. of Buffalo, USA; taught English and German in Lapad Elementary School, Dubrovnik 1981–88, Centar za odgoj i usmjereno obrazovanje High School, Dubrovnik 1988–90; Prof. of English and German, Luka Sorkočević School of Arts, Dubrovnik 1990–92; Asst, Maritime Faculty, Dubrovnik 1992–94; Prof. of English, Polytechnic of Dubrovnik 1994–2000; Prin. Gimnazija Dubrovnik Classical Academic High School 1996–2000; Prof. of German, American Coll. of Man. and Tech., Dubrovnik 1998–2000; mem. Exec. Bd Municipality of Dubrovnik in charge of educ. 1991–93; Mayor of Dubrovnik 2001–09; mem. Croatian Democratic Union (HDZ) 1990–, Pres. City Cttee and mem. HDZ's Cen. Cttee 1998–, Vice-Pres. HDZ 2012–; mem. Croatian Parl. 2000–, mem. Inter-Parl. Cooperation Cttee 2000–04, Cttee on Local and Regional Self-Govt 2000–04, Deputy mem. Del. in OSCE Parl. Ass. 2000–04, Pres. Cttee for Family, Youth and Sport 2000–04; mem. European Parl. (EPP) 2013–; Pres. Croatian Del. to Congress of Local and Regional Authorities of Council of Europe (CLRAE) 2004, First Vice-Pres. Chamber of Local Authorities of CLRAE 2004; Councillor, Dubrovnik-Neretva Co. Ass. 1997–2001, 2006–; mem. Bd Union of Asscn of Towns of Repub. of Croatia 2002, European Asscn of Historic Towns and Regions 2004, Union of Asscn of Towns and Asscn of Municipalities of Repub. of Croatia 2005; Kt, Order of European Wine Kts 2005, Croatian Kts' Consulate–Order of European Wine Kts 2005; named Croatia's Mayor of the Year 2005, 'Tourist Flower – Quality for Croatia' Award 2005, named one of Top 10 World Mayors 2006, World Mayor Award, City Mayors 2006. *Address:* European Parliament, 60 Rue Wiertz, Altiero Spinelli 04F259, 1047 Brussels, Belgium.

SUISSA, Eliyahu (Eli); Israeli politician and fmr army officer; b. 1956, Afula, Morocco; m.; four c.; career officer in Israel Defense Forces (IDF) and Army Chaplain of IDF Northern Command; Dist Commr (Jerusalem), Ministry of the Interior 1986–96, Ministry of the Interior and of Religious Affairs 1996–99; mem. Knesset (Shas) 1999–2003; Minister of Nat. Infrastructure 1999–2000 (resgnd), Minister without Portfolio, responsible for Jerusalem Affairs 2001–03. *Address:* c/o Ministry of the Interior, PO Box 6158, 2 Rehov Kaplan, Kiryat Ben-Gurion, Jerusalem 9108, Israel.

SUKARNOPUTRI, Megawati (see MEGAWATI, Sukarnoputri).

ŠUKER, Ivan, DiplEcon; Croatian politician and economist; b. 12 Nov. 1957, Livno; m. Andrea Šuker; one s. one d.; ed Univ. of Zagreb; Chief Accountant, City Council, Velika Gorica 1984–86, Financial Dir 1986–1990, Head of Fiscal Office 1990–2000, Deputy Mayor 1990–91, Chief of Gen. Staff, Velika Gorica (during war) 1991–92; mem. City Council, Zagreb 1993–97, Deputy Mayor 1997–2000; elected to Sabor (Parl.) for Croatian Democratic Union (Hrvatska demokratska zajednica–HDZ) 2000–, mem. Finance and Budget Cttee, Pres. HDZ, Velika Gorica 2000–03, mem. HDZ Nat. Bureau 2000–, Deputy Chair. HDZ 2002–; Minister of Finance 2003–10, Deputy Prime Minister 2009–10; fmr Chair. Croatian Basketball Asscn. *Leisure interest:* basketball. *Address:* c/o Ministry of Finance, 10000 Zagreb, ul. Katančićeva 5, Croatia.

ŠUKYS, Raimondas, DCL; Lithuanian lawyer and politician; b. 27 Oct. 1966, Šiauliai; m. Adelė Šukys; one s. one d.; ed Janonio Secondary School (now J. Janonio Gymnasium), Šiauliai, Vilnius State Univ. (now Vilnius Univ.); mil. service 1985–87; lawyer, Šiauliu kraštas (daily newspaper) 1991–92; lawyer, Verslo raktas (advisory co.) 1992–94; asst, Civil Law and Civil Process Dept, Law Faculty, Vilnius Univ. 1992–2004; referent, Fraction of Lithuanian Democratic Working Party (LDDP) 1993–94; adviser, Seimas (Parl.) Comm. on Econ. Crime Investigation 1994–97; mem. Lithuanian Liberal Party 1997–2003, Liberal and

Centre Union 2003–; mem. election HQ of cand. for presidency, Valdas Adamkus 1997; solicitor, UAB BNA group 1998–99; adviser for civil law, Legal Dept, Office of the Govt 1999–2000; mem. Seimas (Lithuanian Liberal Party) for Fabijoniškes Election Dist No. 5, mem. Cttee on Legal Affairs 2000–04, re-elected to Seimas for Liberal and Centre Union 2004–; Attorney of Pres. Valdas Adamkus for elections 2004; Minister of the Interior 2006–07, of Health 2010–12; mem. Vilnius City Bd 2002–03. *Leisure interests:* gardening, literature, music, fishing. *Address:* Liberal and Centre Union, Vilniaus g. 22/1, Vilnius 01402, Lithuania (office). *Telephone:* (5) 231-3264 (office). *Fax:* (5) 261-9363 (office). *E-mail:* info@lics.lt (office). *Website:* www.lics.lt (office).

SULAIMAN, Lama al-, BSc, MSc, PhD; Saudi Arabian business executive; *Vice-President, Jeddah Chamber of Commerce and Industry;* b. 11 Sept. 1966, Beirut; ed King Abdulaziz Univ., King's Coll., Univ. of London; Consultant (part-time), Nutrition Laboratory, King Fahad Research Centre, King Abdulaziz Univ. Hospital 1990–2002; Owner, Chamelle Health Club for Women, Jeddah 2000–; Deputy Chair. Jeddah Chamber of Commerce and Industry 2005–, also currently Vice-Pres.; Pres. Al-Sayedah Khadija Bint Khouaylid Center for Business Women 2005–; mem. Young Arab Leaders 2003, Nat. Inst. of Health Services 2005–, Saudi French Business Consulate 2007–, ILO Saudi Delegation 2009–; mem. Bd of Dirs Nat. Home Health Care Foundation 1999–2008, Rolaco Holdings, Luxembourg 2000–, Saudi Inst. for Health Services 2005–; mem. Bd of Trustees Jeddah Social and Economic Circle 2004; ranked by Arabian Business amongst the Power 500: The Worlds's Most Influential Arabs (41st) 2011, (63rd) 2012. *Address:* Jeddah Chamber of Commerce and Industry, King Khalid Street, Ghurfa Building, PO Box 9549, Jeddah, 21423, Saudi Arabia (office). *Telephone:* (2) 6518028 (office); (2) 6534280 (home). *Fax:* (2) 6601802 (home); (2) 6674335. *E-mail:* info@jcci.org.sa (office); nutrilama@yahoo.co.uk (home). *Website:* www.jcci.org.sa/jcci/en (office).

SULAYEM, Sultan Ahmed bin, BS; United Arab Emirates business executive; *Chairman, DP World;* b. 1955; ed Temple Univ., Phila, USA; began career as customs inspector, Dubai Port late 1970s; Chair. Jebel Ali Free Zone 1985; Chair. and Man. Dir Dubai Ports Authority 1991; f. Nakheel (property developer), Chair. –2010; Chair. Dubai World (holding co. for govt investments) –2010; Chair. DP World (operates more than 60 container-handling terminals across six continents) 2007–; mem. Bd Dubai Exec. Council; Chair. Tejari.com; f. Istithmar (pvt. equity fund); Dir Investment Corpn of Dubai –2009, Seven Tides International; Chair. UAE Br., Chartered Inst. of Logistics and Transport; mem. World Export Processing Zones Asscn; Assoc. mem. French Business Council; Dr hc (Middlesex Univ., Dubai) 2008; Arabian Hotel Investment Conf. Leadership Award 2008, named by World Econ. Forum as Global Leader for Tomorrow, ranked by Arabian Business amongst the Power 500: The Worlds's Most Influential Arabs (23rd) 2012. *Leisure interests:* endurance racing, deep-sea diving. *Address:* DP World, 5th Floor, JAFZA 17, Jebel Ali Free Zone, PO Box 17000, Dubai, United Arab Emirates (office). *Telephone:* (4) 8811110 (office). *Fax:* (4) 8811331 (office). *E-mail:* info@dpworld.com (office). *Website:* www.dpworld.com (office).

SULEIMAN, Mohamud Hassan; Somali politician; Minister of Finance and the Treasury 2012–. *Address:* Ministry of Finance and the Treasury, 1 Villa Somalia, 2525 Mogadishu, Somalia (office). *Telephone:* (5) 404240 (office). *Website:* www.mof .somaligov.net (office).

SULEIMAN, Omar; Egyptian government official and fmr intelligence officer; *Vice-President;* b. 2 July 1936, Qena; ed Mil. Acad., Cairo, Frunze Mil. Acad., USSR, Ain Shams Univ.; fmr mil. officer and mil. intelligence officer, becoming Deputy Head of Mil. Intelligence 1986, Dir 1991; Minister without Portfolio and Dir Egyptian Gen. Intelligence Directorate 1993–2011; Vice-Pres. of Egypt 2011–. *Address:* Office of the Vice-President, Cairo, Egypt (office).

SULEMAN, Rao Qamar, MA; Pakistani air force officer; *Chief of Air Staff;* b. 1954, Okara, Okara Dist, Punjab Prov.; ed Pakistan Air Force Public School, Sargodha (belonged to 17th entry, 851-Sabre House), Flying Instructors' School, Combat Commanders' School, PAF Air War Coll., Faisal, Nat. Defence Coll., Islamabad; joined Pakistan Air Force (PAF) Acad., Risalpur 1972, commissioned in PAF as fighter pilot in 59th GD(P) Course 1975, has commanded No. 15 Squadron, No. 31 (Fighter) Wing at Samungli, PAF Base, Peshawar and Southern Air Command, also served in UAE Air Force on deputation, directed staff at PAF Air War Coll., later served as Commdt there, Deputy Dir at Operations Br., Asst Chief of Staff (Plans), Asst Chief of Air Staff (Evaluation), Deputy Insp. Gen. of PAF at Air HQ, sr staff appointments include Dir-Gen. Air Force Strategic Command and Deputy Chief of Air Staff (Operations) at Air HQ, Islamabad, promoted to Air Vice-Marshal 2003, to Air Marshal 2007, Chief of the Air Staff 2009–; Tamgha-e-Imtiaz (Mil.), Sitara-e-Basalat Sitara-e-Imtiaz (Mil.), Hilal-e-Imtiaz (Mil.), Nishan-e-Imtiaz (Mil.) . *Address:* Office of the Chief of the Air Staff, Ministry of Defence, Pakistan Secretariat, No. II, Rawalpindi 46000, Pakistan (office). *Telephone:* (51) 9271107 (office). *Fax:* (51) 9271113 (office).

SULEYMANOGLU, Naim; Turkish weightlifter; b. (Naim Suleimanov), 23 Jan. 1967, Ptchar, Bulgaria; defected to Turkey in 1986; youngest world record breaker (16 years, 62 days) when he set records for clean and jerk (160 kg) and combined total (285 kg); triple Olympic gold medallist; 22 gold, one silver and one bronze in Sr World Championships (twice for Bulgaria); retd 1996; fmr Vice-Pres. Int. Weightlifting Fed.; launched clothing and leather goods business; inducted into Int. Weightlifting Hall of Fame 2000, 2004, voted one of the 25 greatest athletes of the 20th century by Int. Sports Journalist Asscn. *Address:* c/o Turkiye Halter Federasyonu, Ulus Ishani A Blok, Ulus 06050 Ankara, Turkey.

SULEYMENOV, Olzhas Omarovich; Kazakhstani politician, diplomatist and writer; *Ambassador and Permanent Delegate to United Nations Educational, Scientific and Cultural Organization (UNESCO);* b. 1936; ed Kazak State Univ., Maxim Gorky Inst. of Literature in Moscow; mem. CPSU 1989–90; debut as writer in 1960; Ed.-in-Chief Studio Kazakhfilm 1962–71; head of div. Prostor (magazine) 1971–; Sec. Bd Kazakh Writers' Union 1971–; Chair. Kazakh Cttee on relations with writers of Asia and Africa 1980–; actively participates in ecological movt, actions of protest against nuclear tests in Semipalatinsk since late 1980s; Deputy to USSR Supreme Soviet 1984–89; People's Deputy, mem. USSR Supreme Soviet 1989–91; Founder and Leader of People's Progress Party of Kazakhstan 1992–95; Amb. to Italy 1995–2001; Amb. and Perm. Del. to UNESCO, Paris 2001–; USSR Komsomol Prize, State Abai Prize of Kazakh SSR. *Publications:* collections of poetry including Argamaki 1961, Sunny Nights 1962, The Night of Paris 1963, The Kind Time of the Sunrise 1964, The Year of Monkey 1967, Above White Rivers 1970, Each Day – Morning 1973, Repeating in the Noon 1973, A Round Star 1975, Definition of a Bank 1976 and others. *Address:* Permanent Delegation of Kazakhstan to UNESCO, 59 rue Pierre Charron, 75008 Paris, France (office). *Telephone:* 1-42-25-02-10 (office). *Fax:* 1-42-25-11-11 (office). *E-mail:* Unescokz@wanadoo.fr (office).

SULÍK, Richard; Slovak economist, business executive and politician; *Chairman, Freedom and Solidarity;* b. 22 Jan. 1968, Bratislava, Czechoslovakia; four c.; ed Ludwig Maximilian Univ., Germany, Univ. of Econs, Bratislava; emigrated with parents to Pforzheim, FRG 1980; returned to Czechoslovakia 1991; f. co. FaxCOPY; Special Adviser to Minister of Finance Ivan Miklos *c.* 2003 whom he convinced to take his master thesis as a blueprint for the 2004 Slovak tax reform, remained on Advisory Bd of the Ministry; CEO of municipal waste disposal co. 2004–06; returned as Special Adviser to Ministry of Finance under Ján Počiatek; Founder and Chair. Freedom and Solidarity (Sloboda a Solidarita—SaS) party 2009–; mem. Nat. Council of the Slovak Repub. (Národná rada Slovenskej republiky) 2010–, Chair. (Speaker) 2010–11. *Address:* National Council of the Slovak Republic (Národná rada Slovenskej republiky), nam. Alexandra Dubčeka 1, 812 80 Bratislava (office); Freedom and Solidarity (Sloboda a Solidarita), Priemyselná 8, 821 09 Bratislava, Slovakia (office). *Telephone:* (2) 5972-1111 (Nat. Council) (office); (2) 5245-4089 (SaS) (office). *Fax:* (2) 5441-9529 (Nat. Council) (office). *E-mail:* richard@sulik.sk; info@nrsr.sk (office); sas@strana-sas.sk (office). *Website:* www.nrsr.sk (office); www.strana-sas.sk (office); richardsulik.blog.sme.sk; web.sulik.sk.

SULLIVAN, Andrew, PhD; British journalist; b. 20 Aug. 1963, Godstone, Surrey; pnr Aaron Tone; ed Magdalen Coll., Oxford, Kennedy School of Govt, Harvard Univ., USA; intern, Centre For Policy Studies, London; intern, New Republic magazine 1986, returned to Harvard and taught in Govt Dept 1987, returned as Assoc. Ed. New Republic 1987, Deputy Ed. 1990, Acting Ed. 1991, Ed. 1991–96; contributing writer and columnist, New York Times Magazine, contrib. New York Times Book Review –2002; weekly columnist for Sunday Times of London; est. andrewsullivan.com's Daily Dish blog 2000 at Time magazine, moved to TheAtlantic.com 2007–11, with Daily Beast 2011–13, est. Dish Publishing LLC to offer subscription service. *Publications include:* Virtually Normal: An Argument About Homosexuality 1995, Love Undetectable: Notes on Friendship, Sex, and Survival 1999, The Conservative Soul 2006, Intimations Pursued: The Voice of Practice in the Conversation of Michael Oakeshott 2007; as ed.: Same-Sex Marriage Pro & Con: A Reader 1997 (2nd edition 2004). *Website:* dish.andrewsullivan.com.

SULLIVAN, Barry F., MBA; American business executive and fmr government official; *Vice-Chairman, K Road Acquisition Corporation;* b. 21 Dec. 1930, Bronx, NY; m.; four s. one d.; ed Columbia Univ., Georgetown Univ., Univ. of Chicago; served in US Army in Korea; with Chase Manhattan Bank 1957–80, mem. Man. Cttee 1974–80; Chair. and CEO First Chicago Corpn, First Nat. Bank of Chicago 1980–91; apptd Deputy Mayor, Finance and Econ. Devt, New York City 1992; Vice-Chair. Sithe Energies Inc. 1995–2003; Pres. and COO K Road Power Management LLC (pvt. investment co.) 2003–, Vice-Chair. Man. Bd K Road Acquisition Corpn 2003–; Dir and COO EBG 2006–07; fmr Vice-Pres. Exec. Cttee, Chicago Asscn of Commerce and Industry; mem. Bd of Dirs Liati Group LLC, Liati Capital LLC, Omega Tools Inc., Perftech Inc., Hilliard Farber & Co. Inc., Power Generating Co. 2007–; mem. Pres.'s Council, Graduate Theological Union; Trustee and mem. Exec. Cttee, Univ. of Chicago, also Chair. of Council of Graduate School of Business; Trustee, Art Inst. of Chicago, Gregorian Univ. Foundation; Dr hc (Univ. of Chicago) 1994; John Jay Award, Columbia Coll. 1996. *Address:* K Road Acquisition Corporation, 330 Madison Avenue, 25th Floor, New York, NY 10017, USA. *Telephone:* (212) 351-0535.

SULLIVAN, Dennis Parnell, BA, PhD; American mathematician and academic; *Albert Einstein Chair in Science, City University of New York;* b. 12 Feb. 1941, Port Huron, Mich.; three s. two d.; ed Rice and Princeton Univs; NATO Fellow, Univ. of Warwick, UK 1966; Miller Fellow, Univ. of California, Berkeley 1967–69; Sloan Fellow of Math., MIT 1969–72, Prof. of Math. 1972–73; Prof. Perm., Institut des Hautes Etudes Scientifiques, Paris, France 1973–96; Albert Einstein Chair in Science, Queens Coll. and Grad. School, CUNY, New York 1981–; concurrently Distinguished Prof. of Math., State Univ. of New York at Stony Brook; fmr Vice-Pres. American Math. Soc.; mem. NAS, New York Acad. of Sciences; Fellow, AAAS, American Acad. of Arts and Sciences 1991, American Math. Soc. 2012; Dr hc (Warwick) 1984; Oswald Veblen Prize in Geometry 1971, Elie Cartan Prix en Géométrie, French Acad. of Sciences 1981, King Faisal Int. Prize of Science 1994, New York City Mayor's Award for Excellence in Science and Tech. 1997, Nat. Medal of Science 2004, Steele Prize, American Math. Soc. 2006, Wolf Prize in Math. 2010. *Publications:* several papers in math. journals. *Leisure interest:* people. *Address:* Mathematics PhD Program, City University of New York, The Graduate Center, 365 Fifth Avenue, Room 4214-12, New York, NY 10016-4309 (office); Mathematics Department, 5-114 Mathematics Building, SUNY, Stony Brook, NY 11794-3651, USA. *Telephone:* (212) 817-8578 (office); (631)-632-8359 (Stony Brook). *Fax:* (212) 817-1527; (631)-632-7631 (Stony Brook). *E-mail:* dsullivan@gc.cuny.edu; dennis@math.sunysb.edu (office). *Website:* www.gc.cuny.edu/Page-Elements/Academics-Research-Centers-Initiatives/Doctoral-Programs/Mathematics/Faculty-Bios/Dennis-Sullivan (office); www.math.sunysb.edu (office).

SULLIVAN, Janice; American business executive; *CEO, Edun Americas, Inc.;* fmr exec. with Donna Karan; joined DKNY Jeans and DKNY Active licence divs, Liz Claiborne 1997, Pres. 2005–07, Pres. Narciso Rodriguez LLC 2007; Pres. Calvin Klein Jeans Div., Warnaco Group, Inc. 2007–09; CEO Edun Americas, Inc. 2010–. *Address:* Edun Americas Inc., 107 Grand Street, 3rd Floor, New York, NY 10013, USA (office). *Telephone:* (212) 274-1521 (office). *Fax:* (212) 226-4656 (office). *Website:* www.edun.com (office).

SULLIVAN, Louis Wade, BS, MD; American physician, academic and fmr government official; *President Emeritus, School of Medicine, Morehouse College;* b. 3 Nov. 1933, Atlanta; s. of Walter Wade Sullivan and Lubirda Elizabeth Sullivan (née Priester); m. Eve Williamson 1955; three c.; ed Morehouse Coll., Atlanta,

Boston Univ.; Intern, New York Hosp.-Cornell Medical Centre, New York 1958–59, resident in internal medicine 1959–60; Fellow in Pathology, Mass. Gen. Hosp., Boston 1960–61; Research Fellow, Thorndike Memorial Lab., Harvard Medical School, Boston 1961–63, Instructor of Medicine 1963–64; Asst Prof. Medicine, NJ Coll. Medicine 1964–66; Co-Dir Haematology, Boston Univ. Medical Centre 1966, Assoc. Prof. 1968–74, Prof. of Medicine and Physiology 1974–75; Dir of Hematology, Boston City Hosp.; Founder and Dean, School of Medicine, Morehouse Coll. 1975–89, Pres. 1981–89, 1993–2002, Pres. Emer. 2002–; Sec., US Health and Human Services Admin., Washington, DC 1989–93; mem. Bd of Dirs Gen. Motors 1993–2002, Henry Schein 2002–, Points of Light Foundation 2004–, United Therapeutics Corpn, Emergent BioSolutions Inc., Inhibitex, Inc., 3M Corpn, Bristol-Myers Squibb Co., Cigna Corpn, Georgia Pacific Corpn, Africare, Callaway Gardens; mem. Sickle Cell Anaemia Advisory Cttee, NIH 1974–75, Medical Advisory Bd, Nat. Leukemia Asscn 1968–70, (Chair. 1970); mem. American Soc. of Hematology, American Soc. of Clinical Investigation, Inst. of Medicine; mem. Pres.'s Bd of Advisors on Historically Black Colls and Univs, Presidential Advisory Council on HIV/AIDS; Founding Pres. Asscn of Minority Health Professions Schools; Chair. Nat. Health Museum, Sullivan Alliance to Transform America's Health Professions; more than 55 hon. degrees. *Publications:* numerous papers in professional journals. *Address:* c/o Office of the President, Morehouse School of Medicine, 720 Westview Drive, SW, Atlanta, GA 30310, USA (office).

SULLIVAN, Martin J., OBE; British insurance executive and business executive; *Chairman and CEO, Willis Global Solutions;* b. 1955; m.; two d.; joined Finance Dept, American Int. Underwriters (AIU), part of American Int. Group (AIG) 1971, with Property Dept 1974, Property Man. UK 1983, later Regional Property Man. UK/Ireland, Man. AIU London and Regional Marketing Man. UK/Ireland 1988, Asst Man. Dir AIG Europe (UK) Ltd 1989, COO 1991, Pres. UK/Ireland Div., AIU and Man. Dir AIG Europe (UK) Ltd 1993, Sr Vice-Pres., Foreign Gen. Insurance 1996, Exec. Vice-Pres. 1998, COO AIU New York 1996, Pres. 1997, mem. Bd AIG Inc. 2002–08, Vice-Chair. and Co-COO AIG Inc. 2002–05, Chair. and CEO AIG Inc. 2005–08; Deputy Chair. Willis Group Holdings PLC, Chair. and CEO Willis Global Solutions, London 2010–; Dir International Insurance Soc., Geneva Asscn, Young Audiences Inc., Friends of London Youth Inc.; mem. Bd of Dirs Transatlantic Holdings (apptd Chair. 2006); mem. Business Advisory Cttee, St George's Soc., British Memorial Garden Trust; mem. Bd of Trustees, American Assocs of the Royal Acad. Trust; assoc. mem. Chartered Insurance Inst.; mem. Chartered Man. Inst.; Fellow, Inst. of Leadership and Man.; Dr hc (Hofstra Univ.) 2008; The American Ireland Fund Leadership Award 2007. *Address:* Willis Global Solutions, London, England (office). *Telephone:* (20) 3124-6000 (office). *Website:* www.willis.com (office).

SULLIVAN, Michael J., BSc, JD; American lawyer, diplomatist and fmr politician; *Partner, Rothgerber Johnson & Lyons LLP;* b. 22 Sept. 1939, Omaha, Neb.; s. of Joseph B. Sullivan and Margaret Hamilton; m. Jane Metzler 1961; one s. two d.; ed Univ. of Wyoming; Assoc., Brown, Drew, Apostolos, Barton & Massey (law firm), Casper, Wyo. 1964–67, Partner 1967–; Gov. of Wyo. 1987–95; Amb. to Ireland 1998–2001; Partner, Rothgerber Johnson & Lyons LLP 2001–; mem. ABA; Democrat. *Leisure interests:* jogging, tennis, golf, fly-fishing, reading. *Address:* Rothgerber Johnson & Lyons LLP, 123 West First Street, Suite 200, Casper, WY 82601-2480, USA (office). *Telephone:* (307) 232-0222 (office). *Fax:* (307) 232-0077 (office). *E-mail:* msullivan@rothgerber.com (home). *Website:* www.rothgerber.com (office).

SULLIVAN, Teresa A., PhD; American sociologist, academic and university administrator; *President, University of Virginia;* m. Douglas Laycock; two s.; ed St Joseph's High School, Jackson, Miss., James Madison Coll. at Michigan State Univ., Univ. of Chicago; Summer Research Assoc., Survey Research Laboratory, Univ. of Illinois, Urbana 1970; Admin. Intern, Office of the President, Michigan State Univ. 1970–71; Instructor to Asst Prof. of Sociology, Population Research Center, Univ. of Texas at Austin 1975–76, Faculty Research Assoc., Population Research Center 1981, Assoc. Prof. of Sociology 1981–87, Training Dir Population Research Center 1982–87, Dir of Women's Studies 1985–87, Prof. of Sociology 1987–2006, Prof. of Law 1988–2006, Asst Chair. Dept of Sociology 1988–89, Assoc. Dean, Office of Grad. Studies 1989–90, 1992–95, Chair. Dept of Sociology 1990–92, Vice-Provost, Office of the Exec. Vice-Pres. and Provost Univ. of Texas at Austin 1994–95, Vice-Pres. and Grad. Dean 1995–2003, Exec. Vice-Chancellor for Academic Affairs 2002–06, Prof. Emer. of Sociology and Law 2006–10; Asst Prof. of Sociology and the Coll., Faculty Research Assoc., Population Research Center, Univ. of Chicago 1977–81; Prof. of Sociology, Provost and Exec. Vice-Pres. for Academic Affairs, Univ. of Michigan, Ann Arbor 2006–10; George M. Kaufman Presidential Prof. of Sociology and Pres. Univ. of Virginia 2010– (resgnd then reinstated June 2012); Research Fellow, East-West Population Inst., Honolulu, HI 1986; Visiting Scholar, Population Studies Center, Univ. of Michigan 1990; Faculty mem., Man. Devt Seminar, Univ. of Chicago Grad. School of Business, Vail, Colo Summers 1991–93; fmr Chair. US Census Advisory Cttee; Fellow, AAAS 1995; mem. Sociological Research Asscn 1990, Philosophical Soc. of Texas 1997; General Mills Scholarship 1967–68, Michigan State Univ. Merit Scholar 1967–70, Presidential Fellow, Michigan State Univ. 1970–71 (Carnegie Foundation), Maria Leonard Honor Fellow, Nat. Alpha Lambda Delta 1971–72, Sparks Memorial Honor Fellow, Nat. Phi Kappa Phi 1971–72, NSF Grad. Fellow 1971–74, Liberal Arts Council Teaching Excellence Award 1985, Dean's Merit Award for Community Service 1985, UtmosT Magazine 'Ten Best Professors' Poll 1987, Pres.'s Associates Teaching Excellence Award 1989–90, Faculty Fellowship in Law, Cox & Smith, Inc. 1991–94, 1995–2006, UtmosT Magazine 'Best Professor Hall of Fame' 1992, Students' Asscn Teaching Excellence Award 1992, Distinguished Scholarly Publ. Award, American Sociological Asscn 1992, Distinguished Scholarly Paper Award, Southwestern Sociological Asscn 1993, Leadership Texas, Class of 1994, Faculty Fellowship in Law, Locke, Harrell, Raine, Purcell 1994–95, Fellow, Woodrow Wilson Foundation Award for Innovation in Grad. Educ. 2000, Sister Agnes McPhee Award for contribs to educ. 2002, Distinguished Alumna Award, James Madison Coll. 2004. *Publications:* Marginal Workers, Marginal Jobs: The Underutilized American Worker 1978, Young Catholics in the United States and Canada (co-author) 1981, The Dilemma of American Immigration: Beyond the Golden Door (co-author) 1983, Underemployment, in International Journal of Sociology and Social Policy (special issue) (ed.) 1987, As We Forgive Our Debtors:

Bankruptcy and Consumer Credit in America (co-author) (ABA Silver Gavel Award 1990) 1989, The Social Organization of Work (co-author) 1990 (fifth edn 2012), Instructor's Manual to Accompany Hodson and Sullivan's Social Organization of Work 1995, The Fragile Middle Class: Americans in Debt (co-author) (Writing Award, American Coll. of Financial Services Lawyers 2000) 2000, Instructor's Manual with Test Bank for Hodson and Sullivan's The Social Organization of Work (third edn 2002), Instructor's Resource Manual with Test Bank for Hodson and Sullivan's The Social Organization of Work (fourth edn 2008); more than 80 scholarly articles and chapters on social demography, especially labour force and ethnic groups, sociology of cultural insts (science, educ., law, religion). *Address:* Office of the President, University of Virginia, Madison Hall, PO Box 400224, Charlottesville, VA 22904-4224, USA (office). *Telephone:* (434) 924-3337 (office). *Fax:* (434) 924-3792. *E-mail:* jbg@virginia.edu (office). *Website:* www.virginia.edu/president (office).

SULSTON, Sir John Edward, Kt, PhD, FRS; British scientist; b. 27 March 1942, Fulmer, Bucks., England; s. of the late Rev. Canon Arthur Edward Aubrey Sulston and Josephine Muriel Frearson Blocksidge; m. Daphne Edith Bate 1966; one s. one d.; ed Merchant Taylor's School and Pembroke Coll., Cambridge; Postdoctoral Fellowship at Salk Inst., Calif. 1966–69; staff scientist, MRC Lab. of Molecular Biology, Cambridge 1969–2003; Dir The Sanger Centre 1992–2000; Chair. Inst. for Science Ethics and Innovation, Univ. of Manchester 2007–; mem. Human Genetics Comm. 2001–09; mem. European Molecular Biology Org. 1989–, Academia Europaea 2001–; Hon. Fellow, Pembroke Coll., Cambridge 2000, Royal Soc. of Chemisty 2003, Acad. of Medical Sciences 2003, hon. mem. Biochemical Soc. 2002, Physiological Soc. 2002, Freedom of Merchant Taylors' Co. 2004; Hon. DSc (Trinity Coll., Dublin) 2000, (Essex) 2002, (Cambridge) 2003, (Royal Holloway) 2003, (Exeter) 2003, (Newcastle) 2004, (British Columbia) 2009, (Liverpool) 2009, (Manchester) 2009, Hon. LLD (Dundee) 2005; Officier, Légion d'honneur 2004; W. Alden Spencer Award (jtly) 1986, Gairdner Foundation Award (jtly) 1991, 2002, Darwin Medal, Royal Soc. 1996, Rosenstiel Award (jtly) 1998, Pfizer Prize for Innovative Science 2000, Genetics Soc. of America George W. Beadle Medal 2000, Biochemical Soc. Sir Frederick Gowland Hopkins Medal 2000, Edinburgh Medal 2001, City of Medicine Award, Durham, NC 2001, Prince of Asturias Award, Spain 2001, Robert Burns Humanitarian Award 2002, Daily Mirror Pride of Britain Award 2002, Medical Soc. of London Fothergillian Medal 2002, Tel-Aviv Univ. Dan David Prize 2002, General Motors Sloan Prize 2002, Nobel Prize in Physiology or Medicine (jtly) 2002, Dawson Prize in Genetics, Trinity Coll., Dublin 2006. *Television:* Royal Inst. Christmas Lectures (Channel 4) 2001. *Publications:* The Common Thread – A Story of Science, Politics, Ethics and the Human Genome (jtly) 2002; papers in scientific journals. *Leisure interests:* gardening, walking. *Address:* 39 Mingle Lane, Stapleford, Cambridge, CB22 5SY, England. *Telephone:* (1223) 842248. *E-mail:* jes@sanger.ac.uk (office).

SULTAN, Donald Keith, BFA, MFA; American painter, printmaker and sculptor; b. 5 May 1951, Asheville, NC; s. of Norman Sultan and Phyllis Sultan; m. Susan Reynolds 1978; one s. one d.; ed Univ. of North Carolina, Art Inst. of Chicago; represented by Willard Gallery 1979–82, Blum Helman Gallery 1982–89, M. Knoedler Gallery New York 1989; work in collections: Art Inst. of Chicago, Hirsh Museum and Sculpture Garden, Washington DC, The Metropolitan Museum of Art, New York, The Museum of Fine Arts, Boston, The Museum of Modern Art, New York, The Solomon R. Guggenheim Museum, New York, Walker Art Center, Minneapolis, Bibliothèque Nationale, Paris 1992; Public Service Grant NY State 1978–79, Nat. Endowments for the Arts 1980–81; Dr hc (Corcoran School of Art, Washington, DC) 2000, (New York Acad. of Art) 2002, (Univ. of North Carolina) 2007. *Address:* c/o Knoedler & Company, 19 East 70th Street, New York, NY 10021, USA.

SULTAN, Fouad, BSc; Egyptian banking executive and fmr government official; b. 26 Jan. 1931; s. of Abdel Latif Sultan and Farida Torky; m. Ferial Fikry 1956, one s. one d.; ed Univ. of Cairo; worked for 21 years with Cen. Bank of Egypt; seconded to IMF, North Yemen 1971–74; CEO Misr-Iran Bank 1974–85; head of several cttees in Fed. of Egyptian Banks; Minister of Tourism and Civil Aviation 1985–93; fmr Chair. and CEO El Ahly Development and Investment Co.; mem. Bd of Dirs Crédit Agricole Egypt; apptd Chair. Heliopolis Sporting Club 1989;. *Leisure interests:* rowing, tennis, swimming. *Address:* c/o Board of Directors, Crédit Agricole Egypt, 2/ 4/ 6, Hassan Sabry Street, 11511 Cairo, Egypt.

SULTANGAZIN, Umirzak Makhmutovich; Kazakhstani scientist and academic; b. 10 April 1936, Kustanai Region; s. of Sultangazy Makhmutov and Nurila Makhmutova; m. Raikhan Meirmanova 1958, two c.; ed Kazakh State Univ. and USSR (now Russian) Acad. of Sciences, Novosibirsk; Asst Prof., Kazakh State Univ. 1958–60, Assoc. Prof. 1960–64, Prof. of Math. 1972–78; Dir Inst. of Math. and Mechanics, Acad. of Sciences of Kazakh SSR 1978–88, Vice-Pres. of Acad. 1986–88, Pres. 1988–94, Dir Space Research Inst. of Kazhakhstan 1991–95; Visiting Prof., Karlov Univ., Czechoslovakia 1972, Kyoto Univ., Japan 1994–95; Chair. Fed. of Cosmonautics 1985, Peace Fund of Kazakh SSR 1987, Math Cttee of Kazakhstan 1994; Corresp. mem. Acad. of Sciences of Kazakh SSR 1975, mem. 1983; mem. CPSU 1968–91, Cen. Cttee 1989–91; mem. Parl. Kazakh SSR 1987–89, Parl. of USSR 1989–91; Korolev's Medal 1986, State Prize of USSR for Science and Tech. 1987, Red Banner Order 1987, Prize of Acad. of Sciences of USSR and Czechoslovakia for Nat. Sciences 1988. *Publications include:* Concentrated Capacity in the Problems of Heat Physics and Microelectronics 1972, Method of Spherical Harmonics in Kinetic Transport Theory 1979, Mathematical Problems of Kinetic Transport Theory 1986, Discrete Nonlinear Models of Boltzmann Equation 1987, Ecological and Economical Model of Kazakhstan 1995; 150 articles on mathematical physics, numerical mathematics and ecology. *Leisure interests:* history, mountain tourism. *Address:* c/o National Academy of Sciences of the Republic of Kazakhstan, PO 480021, 28 Shevchenko Street, Almaty, Kazakhstan. *Telephone:* (727) 262-38-96 (office); (727) 261-68-53. *Fax:* (727) 249-43-55. *E-mail:* usultan@academset.kz.

SULTANOV, Bakhyt Turlykhanuly; Kazakhstani economist and politician; *Deputy Prime Minister and Minister of Finance;* b. 29 Nov. 1971, Almaty; ed Kazakh Nat. Tech. Univ.; several years with Ministry of Finance, including as Deputy Dir, Budget Dept 1997, Dir, Public Procurement Dept 1998, Deputy Dir, Dept of the Treasury 1999, Dir of State Budget 2002, Dir, Dept of Fiscal Policy and Planning, Ministry of Econ. Affairs and Budget Planning 2002–03, Deputy

Minister of Economy and Budget Planning 2003–06, Chair. Statistical Agency 2006–07, Deputy Minister of Finance Jan.–Aug. 2007, Minister of Econ. Affairs and Budget Planning 2007–10, Asst to Pres. 2010, Deputy Head, Admin of the Pres. 2012–13, Deputy Prime Minister and Minister of Finance 2013–; Astana 10 Year Anniversary Medal. *Address:* Ministry of Finance, 010000 Astana, Zhenis d-ly 11, Kazakhstan (office). *Telephone:* (7172) 71-77-64 (office). *Fax:* (7172) 71-77-85 (office). *E-mail:* administrator@minfin.kz (office). *Website:* www.minfin.kz (office).

SULTANOV, Marat Abdyrazakovich; Kyrgyzstani politician; b. 5 Dec. 1960, Frunze (Bishkek); m.; two d.; ed Moscow State Univ.; Prof., Kyrgyz Nat. Univ. 1987–92; Deputy Chair. Nat. Bank of the Kyrgyz Repub. (Kyrgyz Respublikasynyn Uluttuk Banky) 1992–94, Chair. 1994–98; Minister of Finance Jan.–June 1999, 2009–10; mem. Parl. 2000–, Speaker, Zhogorku Kenesh (Supreme Council) 2006–09; Head, Defence and Security Dept in Presidential Admin 2004. *Address:* c/o Ministry of Finance, 720040 Bishkek, pr. Erkindik 58, Kyrgyzstan (office).

SULTANOV, Otkir S.; Uzbekistani fmr politician; b. 14 July 1939; m.; one d.; ed Tomsk State Polytech. Inst.; electrician, Tomsk plant of cutting metals 1963; with Tashkent Aviation Production Union 1964–85, numerous positions including Master, Head of Lab., Head of Production Automatization, Deputy Chief Engineer, Deputy Dir-Gen.; Head of Scientific Production Unit, Vostok 1985–91; Chair. State Cttee for Foreign Trade and Int. Relations 1991–92; Minister of External Econ. Relations, Deputy Prime Minister 1992–95; Prime Minister of Uzbekistan 1995–2003; fmr Deputy Prime Minister in charge of Industry; People's Deputy of Uzbekistan; Mekhnat Shukhradi; Merited Engineer Repub. of Uzbekistan. *Address:* c/o Office of the Cabinet of Ministers, Mustaqillik maydoni 5, 100078 Tashkent, Uzbekistan (office).

SULZBERGER, Arthur Ochs, Jr, BA; American newspaper publisher; *Chairman, The New York Times Company;* b. 22 Sept. 1951, Mount Kisco, NY; s. of the late Arthur Ochs Sulzberger and Barbara Winslow Grant; m. Gail Gregg 1975; one s. one d.; ed Tufts Univ., Harvard Univ. Business School; reporter, The Raleigh Times, N Carolina 1974–76; corresp., Associated Press, London, UK 1976–78; Washington, DC bureau corresp., The New York Times 1978–81, city hall reporter 1981, Asst Metro Ed. 1981–82, Group Man., Advertising Dept 1983–84, Sr Analyst, Corp. Planning 1985, Production Co-ordinator 1985–87, Asst Publr 1987–88, Deputy Publr 1988–92, Publr 1992–, Chair. The New York Times Co. 1997–; mem. Bd New York City Outward Bound Center; RIT Isaiah Thomas Award in Publishing 2003, Nat. Book Award 'Literarian Award for Outstanding Service to the American Literary Community' 2012. *Address:* The New York Times Company, 620 Eighth Avenue, New York, NY 10018, USA (office). *Telephone:* (212) 556-1234 (office). *E-mail:* publisher@nytimes.com (office). *Website:* www .nytco.com (office).

SUMAIDA'IE, Samir Shakir Mahmood, BSc; Iraqi business executive and diplomatist; b. 1944, Baghdad; m.; five c.; ed Durham Univ., UK; left Iraq after Saddam Hussein seized power 1973; Middle East Man., Nixdorf Computers, Paderborn, Germany 1973–74; Middle East Man., Logica Ltd, London 1974–78; Man. Dir Tenda Ltd, London 1978–82; Man. Dir Turath Ltd, London 1982–90; Man. Dir Samir Design Ltd, London 1991–96; Man. Dir China Business Int., Beijing 1996–2003; returned to Baghdad and was apptd mem. Iraq Governing Council July 2003; Minister of the Interior April–Aug. 2004; Perm. Rep. to UN, New York 2004–06, Amb. to USA 2006–11; participant, Beirut and Vienna Opposition Confs 1991, NY Iraqi Opposition Conf. 1992; Co-founder, manifesto, Democratic Party of Iraq 1993; mem. Governing Council of Iraq 2003, fmr Chair. Media Cttee, Cttee on Provs, fmr Deputy Chair. Foreign Affairs Cttee, fmr mem. Security, Finance and Public Service Cttees. *Publication:* The Night of the Long Lament: A Day in the Life of an Iraqi Dissident, Ahmed Al-Habboubi (trans). *Leisure interests:* writing Arabic poetry in classical form, calligraphy and design in the Islamic decorative medium. *Address:* Ministry of Foreign Affairs, opp. State Org. for Roads and Bridges, Karradat Mariam, Baghdad, Iraq (office). *Telephone:* (1) 537-0091 (office). *E-mail:* press@iraqmofa.net (office). *Website:* www.mofa.gov .iq (office); www.sumaidaie.com.

SUMAYE, Frederick; Tanzanian politician; b. 29 May 1950, Hanang Dist, Arushah; ed Egerton Coll., Kenya, Edward S. Mason Program, Kennedy School of Govt, Harvard Univ., USA; Tutor, MATI–Nyegezi 1973–76; Eng Section Man. Kilombero Sugar Co. 1976–80; Head of Rural Energy Dept, CARMATEC 1980–82; mem. Parl. for Hanang constituency 1985–2005; Deputy Minister of Agric. 1987–94, Minister of Agric. 1995; Prime Minister of Tanzania 1995–2005; mem. Chama Cha Mapinduzi (Party for Democracy and Progress), mem. Cen. Cttee –2007; mem. Bd of Dirs Nyanya Project. *Address:* c/o Chama Cha Mapinduzi, (Revolutionary Party of Tanzania), Kuu Street, POB 50, Dodoma, Tanzania.

SUMI, Shuzo, BEng; Japanese insurance executive; *Chairman and Representative Director, Tokio Marine Holdings, Inc.;* b. 11 July 1947; ed Waseda Univ.; joined Tokio Marine 1970, Dir and Chief Rep., Overseas Div. of Tokio Marine, London, UK 2000–01, Dir, Gen. Man. and Chief Rep., Overseas Div. of Tokio Marine, London 2001–02, Man. Dir Tokio Marine 2002–04, Man. Dir Tokio Marine & Nichido 2004–05, Sr Man. Dir June–Dec. 2005, Sr Man. Dir and Gen. Man. Drastic Reform Promotion Dept, Tokio Marine & Nichido 2005–06, Sr Man. Dir Tokio Marine & Nichido 2006–07, Pres. and Rep. Dir Tokio Marine & Nichido 2007–13, Chair. and Rep. Dir 2013–, Pres. and Rep. Dir Tokio Marine Holdings, Inc. 2007–13, Chair. and Rep. Dir 2013–. *Address:* Tokio Marine Nichido Building Shinkan, 1-2-1 Marunouchi, Chiyoda-ku, Tokyo, 100-0005, Japan (office). *Telephone:* (3) 6212-3333 (office). *E-mail:* ir@tokiomarinehd.com (office). *Website:* www .tokiomarinehd.com (office).

SUMMERS, Lawrence H., PhD; American economist, academic, fmr government official and fmr university administrator; b. 30 Nov. 1954, New Haven, Conn.; s. of Dr Robert Summers and Anita Summers; one s. two d.; ed Mass. Inst. of Tech and Harvard Univ.; domestic policy economist, US Council of Econ. Advisers 1982–83; Prof. of Econs Harvard Univ. 1983–93, 2002, Nathaniel Ropes Prof. of Political Economy 1987, Pres. Harvard Univ. 2002–06, Charles W. Eliot Univ. Prof. 2006–; Chief Economist and Vice-Pres. of Devt Econs IBRD 1991–93; fmr Econ. Adviser to Pres. Bill Clinton; Treasury Under-Sec. for Int. Affairs 1993–95; Deputy Treasury Sec. 1995–99; Sec. of Treasury 1999–2001; Arthur Okun Distinguished Fellow in Econs, Globalization and Governance, Brookings Inst. 2001–02; Pres. Harvard Univ. 2002–06; Dir Nat. Econ. Council, The White House,

Washington, DC 2009–10; Fellow, American Acad. of Arts and Sciences; mem. Nat. Acad. of Sciences 2002–; Hon. DJur (Harvard) 2007; Alan T. Waterman Award, Nat. Science Foundation 1987, John Bates Clark Medal 1993, Alexander Hamilton Medal 2001. *Publications:* Understanding Unemployment, Reform in Eastern Europe (co-author), more than 100 articles. *Leisure interests:* skiing, tennis. *Address:* Department of Economics, Harvard University, Littauer Center 242, 1875 Cambridge Street, Cambridge, MA 02138, USA. *Telephone:* (617) 495-0436 (office). *Fax:* (617) 495-8550 (office). *E-mail:* lawrence_summers@harvard.edu (office). *Website:* www.economics.harvard.edu (office).

SUMNER, Gordon Matthew (see STING).

SUMPTION, Jonathan Philip Chadwick, OBE, MA; British barrister, judge and author; *Judge of the Supreme Court of the United Kingdom;* b. 9 Dec. 1948, London, England; s. of A. J. Sumption and H. Sumption; m. Teresa Mary Whelan 1971; one s. two d.; ed Eton Coll., Magdalen Coll., Oxford; Fellow in History, Magdalen Coll., Oxford 1971–75; called to Bar (Inner Temple) 1975; Recorder 1993–2001; Judge of Courts of Appeal of Guernsey and Jersey 1995–2011; mem. Brick Court Chambers; Judge, Supreme Court of the UK 2011–; Gov. RAM. *Publications:* Pilgrimage: An Image of Medieval Religion 1975, The Albigensian Crusade 1979, The Hundred Years War (Vol. 1) 1989, (Vol. 2) 1999, (Vol. 3) 2010. *Leisure interests:* music, history. *Address:* Supreme Court, Parliament Square, London, SW1P 3BD, England (office). *Telephone:* (20) 7960-1500 (office). *Fax:* (20) 7960-1901 (office). *E-mail:* enquiries@supremecourt.gsi.gov.uk (office). *Website:* www.supremecourt.gov.uk (office).

SUN, Chunlan; Chinese party official and fmr trade union official; *Secretary, Tianjin Municipal CCP Committee;* b. 1950, Hebei Prov.; ed Anshan Industrial Tech. Acad.; joined CCP 1973; began career at Anshan Clock Factory; leading positions in provincial women's fed., provincial and nat. trade unions including Chair., Liaoning Provincial Fed. of Trade Unions 1994, Vice-Chair., All-China Fed. of Trade Unions 2005–09; Mayor, Dalian City, Liaoning Prov. 2001–05; Sec., Fujian CCP Provincial Cttee 2009–12, Chair. Cttee, Fujian Provincial People's Congress 2010–12; Sec., Tianjin Municipal CCP Cttee (only female provincial-level party chief in China) 2012–; alt. mem. 15th CCP Cen. Cttee 1997–2002, 16th CCP Cen. Cttee 2002–07, mem. 17th CCP Cen. Cttee 2007–12, 18th CCP Cen. Cttee 2012–, also mem. 18th CCP Cen. Cttee Politburo 2012–. *Address:* Chinese Communist Party Politburo, Quanguo Renmin Diabiao Dahui, Zhongguo Gongchan Dang, 1 Zhongnanhai, Beijing, People's Republic of China. *Website:* cpc .people.com.cn (office).

SUN, Honglie, BSc, MSc; Chinese agronomist; b. 2 Jan. 1932, Puyang, Henan Prov.; m. Wu Huanning 1956; one s. one d.; ed Beijing Agricultural Univ., Shenyang Inst. of Forestry and Soil Science, Chinese Acad. of Sciences; Research Fellow, Comm. for Integrated Survey of Natural Resources (Chinese Acad. of Sciences) 1961–, Dir 1983; Head Multi-disciplinary Expedition of Qinghai-Tibet Plateau 1973; Visiting Scholar, Inst. of Alpine and Arctic Research, Colorado Univ. 1981–82; Vice-Pres. Chinese Acad. of Sciences 1984–92; Vice-Pres. International Council of Scientific Unions 1993–96. Chair. Academic Cttee of Antarctic Research of China 1986; Chair. Nat. Cttee of China for MAB, UNESCO; Vice-Chair. Int. Mountain Soc., State Antarctic Cttee; a Vice-Pres. Social Devt Science Soc. 1992–; Dir Cttee for Comprehensive Survey of Natural Resources; Fellow, Third World Acad. of Sciences 1987; mem. Gen. Cttee of ICSU 1990; mem. Div. of Earth Sciences, Chinese Acad. of Sciences 1992–, mem. 4th Presidium of Depts 2000–; mem. Standing Cttee of 8th Nat. People's Congress 1993; mem. Credentials Cttee, Environmental and Resources Protection Cttee; mem. 21st Century Cttee for China-Japan Friendship; Special Prize, Chinese Acad. of Sciences 1986, First Prize, State Natural Sciences Awards 1987, Chen Jiagen Prize 1989. *Publications include:* The Soil of Heilongjiang River Valley 1960, The Land Resources Assessment of North-East China, Inner Mongolia and West China 1966, The Soils of Tibet 1970, Land Types of Qinghai-Tibet Plateau and the Principles of Agricultural Assessment 1980, Land Resources and Agricultural Utilization in Tibet Autonomous Region, Mountain Research and Development 1983, Integrated Scientific Survey on Tibetan Plateau (series) 1983–89. *Leisure interest:* photography. *Address:* Chinese Academy of Sciences, 52 Sanlihe Road, Beijing 100864, People's Republic of China (office).

SUN, Jiadong; Chinese scientist; b. 7 April 1948, Fuxian, Liaoning Prov.; ed Harbin Univ. of Tech., USSR Ruchkovski Air Force Eng Inst.; Dir of Design Section, Vice-Dir Overall Design Dept, No. 5 Research Inst. of Ministry of Defence; Vice-Pres. No. 5 Research Inst. of Seventh Ministry of Machine Bldg Industry; Pres. Chinese Space Tech. Research Inst.; Dir Science and Tech. Cttee, Chief Engineer, fmr Vice-Minister of Ministry of Aerospace Industry; fmr Researcher, Sr Science and Tech. Adviser, China Aviation Industry Corpn; Chief Designer, Chinese Lunar Exploration Program 2003–; Fellow, Chinese Acad. of Sciences; mem. International Acad. of Astronautics; Meritorious Service Medal, CCP Cen. Cttee, State Council and Cen. Mil. Comm. 1999, Nat. Science and Tech. Award 2009. *Achievements include:* instrumental in devt of China's first atomic bomb and hydrogen bomb; presided over the overall design of China's first medium-range missile, first satellite and first telecommunications satellite. *Address:* Chinese Academy of Sciences, 52 Sanlihe Road, Beijing 100864, People's Republic of China. *Website:* www.clep.org.cn.

SUN, Jiazheng; Chinese politician; b. March 1944, Siyang, Jiangsu Prov.; ed Nanjing Univ., May 7th Cadre School, Jilin Prov.; joined CCP 1966; sent to do manual labour, Liuhe Co., Jilin Prov.; fmr Deputy Head, Chinese People's Armed Police Force, Fanji Commune; Deputy Head, Work Group, CCP Revolutionary Cttee, Liuhe Co. 1971; Sec. Liuhe Co. Cttee CCP Communist Youth League of China 1971; Sec. CCP Party Cttee, Ma'an Commune, Liuhe Co. 1971; mem. Standing Cttee CCP Liuhe Co. Cttee 1975; Vice-Chair. CCP Revolutionary Cttee, Liuhe Co. 1975; Sec. Jiangsu Prov. Cttee CCP Communist Youth League of China 1978; mem. Standing Cttee CCP Jiangsu Prov. Cttee 1983–89, Sec.-Gen. Jiangsu Prov. Cttee 1983–89, Head, Publicity Dept 1988; Sec. CCP Xuzhou City Cttee, Jiangsu Prov. 1984–86; Minister of Radio, Film and TV 1984–88; Minister of Culture 1998–2007; Pres. China Fed. of Literary and Art Circles 2006–; Alt. mem. 12th CCP Cen. Cttee 1982–87, 13th CCP Cen. Cttee 1987–92, 14th CCP Cen. Cttee 1992–97, mem. 15th CCP Cen. Cttee 1997–2002, 16th CCP Cen. Cttee 2002–07; Vice-Chair. 11th CPPCC Nat. Cttee 2008–13; Hon. Chair. Bd of Dirs Beijing Film

Coll. *Address:* China Federation of Literary and Art Circles, On Court North, Chaoyang District, Beijing 100029, People's Republic of China. *Telephone:* (10) 64025528. *E-mail:* webmaster@cflac.org.cn.

SUN, Laiyan, PhD; Chinese engineer; *Chairman, Supervision and Administration Commission, Ministry of Supervision;* b. Oct. 1957, Beijing; m.; one d.; ed Xian Communication Univ., Univ. de Paris 6ème; Eng Team Leader/Deputy Div. Dir Beijing Inst. of Satellite Environment Eng 1982–87, Acting Deputy Dir, later Dir, Prof. 1993–99; Vice Admin. China Nat. Space Admin (CNSA) 1999–2004, Admin. 2004–10; Sec. Gen. Comm. of Science, Tech. and Industry for Nat. Defence (COSTIND) 2001–04, Vice Minister 2004–08, Dir COSTIND State Aerospace Industry Bureau 2008–10; Chair. Supervision and Admin Comm., Ministry of Supervision 2010–; numerous ministerial and nat. awards. *Address:* Supervision and Administration Commission, Ministry of Supervision, 4 Zaojunmiao, Haidian Qu, Beijing 100081, People's Republic of China (office). *Telephone:* (10) 62114181 (office). *Fax:* (10) 62217692 (office). *Website:* www.mos.gov.cn (office).

SUN, Li; Chinese engineer and business executive; *President and General Manager, China National Aviation Fuel Group Corporation;* ed Tsinghua Univ., Capital Univ. of Econs and Business, Beijing, Party School of Cen. Cttee of CCP, corp. man. training with IBM, ENSPM (France), ICI (UK); joined Liaoyang Petrochemical & Fibre Co. 1975, promoted several times until Deputy Gen. Man. –1998; Deputy Dir Refinery Dept, China Nat. Petroleum Corpn 1998–99; Gen. Man. PetroChina Lanzhou Petrochemical Co. 1999–2002; Gen. Man. PetroChina Chemical and Sales Co. 2002–05; Deputy Pres. China Nat. Aviation Fuel (CNAF) Group Corpn (fmrly China Aviation Oil Holding Co.) 2005–07, Pres. and Gen. Man. 2007–, Chair. CNAF Corpn Ltd and CNAF Land Oil Co. Ltd; mem. Bd of Dirs and Deputy Chair. (non-exec.) China Aviation Oil Singapore Corpn Ltd 2007–10, Chair. (non-exec.) 2010–. *Address:* China National Aviation Fuel Group Corporation, 2 Madian Road, Haidian District, Beijing 100088, People's Republic of China (office). *Telephone:* (10) 59890754 (office). *Fax:* (10) 59890766 (office). *E-mail:* info@cnaf.com (office). *Website:* www.cnaf.com (office).

SUN, Mingbo, PhD, MBA; Chinese business executive; *Chairman, Tsingtao Brewery Group;* b. Dec. 1956; ed Tongji Univ., Fudan Univ., Washington Univ., St Louis, USA; following graduation assigned to Shandong Xintai Xingtai Brewery, becoming Brewery Technician, Workshop Dir, Deputy Dir; transferred to Tsingtao Brewery 1993, positions included Deputy Factory Man., Chief Engineer, Asst to Gen. Man., Vice-Chief Engineer, Exec. Vice-Pres., Pres., Tsingtao Brewery Group Co. Ltd 2008–12, Chair. 2012–. *Address:* Tsingtao Brewery Group, Tsingtao Beer Tower, May 4th Square, Hong Kong Road, Qingdao 266071, People's Republic of China (office). *Telephone:* (532) 571-1119 (office). *Fax:* (532) 85713240 (office). *Website:* www.tsingtaobeer.com (office).

SUN, Shu; Chinese geologist; *Academician, Institute of Geology and Geophysics, Chinese Academy of Sciences;* b. 23 July 1933, Jintan, Jiangsu Prov.; ed Nanjing Univ.; Research Fellow, Inst. of Geology and Geophysics, Chinese Acad. of Sciences, currently Academician; Deputy Dir Nat. Natural Science Foundation of China; Vice-Pres. Chinese Petroleum Soc., Chinese Soc. of Mineralogy, Petrology and Geochemistry, Geological Soc. of China; mem. 4th Presidium, Chinese Acad. of Sciences 2000; Academician, International Eurasian Acad. of Sciences; Fellow, Third World Acad. of Sciences; Hon. Fellow, Geological Soc. of London; Earth Sciences Prize. *Publications:* Geological Changes of Precambian Period in the South of North China Fault Block (ed.), The Geology of Xiaoxing'anling, Wandashan and Zhangguangchailing (jtly), over 50 research papers and research reports. *Address:* Institute of Geology and Geophysics, Chinese Academy of Sciences, No. 19, Beitucheng Western Road, Chaoyang District, Beijing 100029, People's Republic of China (office). *Telephone:* (10) 82998001 (office). *Fax:* (10) 62010846 (office). *E-mail:* shusun@163bj.com (office). *Website:* www.igcas.ac.cn (office).

SUN, Wenjie; Chinese engineer and construction industry executive; *Chairman, China State Construction Engineering Corporation;* ed Tongji Univ.; joined China State Construction Engineering Corpn (CSCEC) 1968, posted to Hong Kong 1981, subsequently Chair. China Overseas Holdings Ltd, Pres. CSCEC 2001–09, Chair. 2009–, also Deputy Sec. Leading Party Mems' Group; Rep. 15th and 16th CCP Cen. Cttees. *Address:* China State Construction Engineering Corporation, CSCEC Mansion, 15 Sanlihe Road, Haidian District, Beijing 100037, People's Republic of China (office). *Telephone:* (10) 88082888 (office). *Fax:* (10) 88082888 (office). *E-mail:* info@cscec.com (office). *Website:* www.cscec.com (office).

SUN, Wensheng; Chinese government official; *Secretary, Ministry of Land and Resources;* b. Feb. 1942, Weihai City, Shandong Prov.; ed Shandong Metallurgical Inst. and CCP Cen. Cttee Cen. Party School; joined CCP 1966; workshop dir, Zhuzhou Smeltery 1963–81, Deputy Dir 1981–83; Sec. CCP Zhuzhou City Cttee 1983; Vice-Dir Org. Dept CCP Hunan Prov. Cttee 1984, Dir 1985, Vice-Sec. 1989; Vice-Sec. CCP Shanxi Prov. Cttee, Vice-Gov., Acting Gov. of Shanxi Prov. 1993–94, Gov. 1994–98; Vice-Minister of Land and Resources 1999–2003, Minister of Land and Resources 2003–07; Deputy Sec. CCP Leading Party Group, Ministry of Land and Resources 1999–2003, Sec. 2003–; mem. Com. Comm. for Discipline Inspection, CCP Cen. Cttee 2002–; Alt. mem. 12th CCP Cen. Cttee 1982–87, 13th CCP Cen. Cttee 1987–92, mem. 14th CCP Cen. Cttee 1992–97, 15th CCP Cen. Cttee 1997–2002. *Address:* Ministry of Land and Resources, 3 Guanyingyuanxiqu, Xicheng Qu, Beijing 100035, People's Republic of China (office).

SUN, Wook; South Korean business executive; fmr Pres. and CEO Samsung Human Resources Devt Centre; CEO Nongshim Co. Ltd; mem. Bd of Dirs and Chair. POSCO 2009–12, Chair. Evaluation and Compensation Cttee, mem. Audit Cttee, Insider Trading Cttee. *Address:* POSCO Head Office, 1 Goedong-dong, Nam-gu, Pohang, Kyongsangbuk-do, 790-600; POSCO, POSCO Centre, 892 Daechi-4-dong, Kangnam-ku, Seoul 135-777, South Korea. *E-mail:* info@posco.com.

SUN, Yafang; Chinese business executive and fmr government official; *Chair-woman, Huawei Technologies Company Ltd;* b. 1955; ed Chengdu Univ. of Electronic Science and Tech., Harvard Business School, USA; worked as a technician at state-owned Xinxiang Liaoyuan Radio Factory 1982–83, teacher at China Research Inst. of Radio Wave Propagation 1983–85, engineer at Beijing Research Inst. of Information Tech. 1985–89; joined Huawei 1989, has held several exec.-level positions, including Pres. of Marketing and Sales, Pres. of Human

Resources, Pres. of Strategy and Marketing Cttee, Pres. Huawei Univ., Co-founder Huawei Technologies 1992, Chair. 1999–; ranked by Fortune magazine amongst the 50 Most Powerful Women in Business outside the US (25th) 2006, (27th) 2007, (26th) 2008, (20th) 2009, (21st) 2010, (17th) 2011, (18th) 2012, ranked by Forbes magazine amongst The World's 100 Most Powerful Women (90th) 2010, (91st) 2012, (77th) 2013. *Address:* Huawei Technologies Co. Ltd, Bantian, Longgang District, Shenzhen 518129, People's Republic of China (office). *Telephone:* (755) 28780808 (office). *E-mail:* hwtech@huawei.com (office). *Website:* www.huawei.com (office).

SUN, Yang; Chinese swimmer; b. 1 Dec. 1991, Hangzhou, Zhejiang; ed Hangzhou Chenjinglun Sports School; mem. Zhejiang Prov. Sports Team 2003–, Nat. Team 2006–; winner, 400m, 1,500m freestyle, Nat. Winter Championships 2006, 10km freestyle, Nat. Marathon Swimming Tournament 2006, 1,500m freestyle, Nat. Championships 2007, 1,500m freestyle, Nat. Intercity Games 2007; runner-up, 400m, 1,500m freestyle, Nat. Champions Tournament 2007; competed for China at Beijing Olympics 2008; World Championships (long course), Rome 2009: bronze medal, 1,500m freestyle; Asian Games, Guangzhou 2010: gold medal, 1,500m freestyle, 4×200m freestyle, silver medal, 200m freestyle, 400m freestyle; World Championships (long course), Shanghai 2011: gold medal, 800m freestyle, 1,500m freestyle, silver medal, 400m freestyle, bronze medal, 4×200m freestyle; broke Grant Hackett's (and longest-held) world record in swimming in 1,500m freestyle at World Championships, Shanghai 2011 (only men's swimming record not to have been beaten during the techsuit era); Olympic Games, London 2012: gold medal, 400m freestyle, 1,500m freestyle, silver medal, 200m freestyle, bronze medal, 4×200m freestyle; World Championships (long course), Barcelona 2013: gold medal, 400m freestyle, 800m freestyle, 1,500m freestyle; coach: Zhu Zhigen; named the Rookie of the Year at CCTV Sports Awards 2010, Pacific Rim Swimmer of the Year 2011. *Address:* Chinese Swimming Association, Beijing, People's Republic of China. *Website:* swimming.sport.org.cn.

SUN, Ying; Chinese academic and politician; *Director, Party History Research Center, Communist Party of China Central Committee;* b. Nov. 1936, Tianjin, Baodi Co.; ed Shanxi Teachers' Coll. 1958; joined CCP 1956; fmr Deputy Sec. CCP Communist Youth League of China, Shanxi Univ.; fmr Dir Political Dept, Taiyuan Eng Inst., Shanxi Prov.; fmr Deputy Sec. Shanxi Prov. Cttee CCP Communist Youth League of China; fmr Vice-Chair. Shanxi Prov. Science and Tech. Asscn; fmr mem. Standing Cttee CCP Shanxi Prov. Cttee; Deputy Sec. CCP Taiyuan City Cttee, Sec. 1985; Deputy Sec. CCP Gansu Prov. Cttee 1988–98, Sec. 1998–2001, Standing Cttee CCP Gansu Prov. Cttee 1998–2001; Vice-Gov. Gansu Prov. 1996–97, Gov. 1997–98; Dir Party History Research Centre of CCP Cen. Cttee 2001–; mem. 15th CCP Cen. Cttee 1997–2002; Deputy, 9th NPC 2002–. *Address:* Central Committee of Chinese Communist Party, Beijing, People's Republic of China (office).

SUN, Zhengcai, DAgric; Chinese agricultural scientist and politician; *Secretary, Chongqing Municipal CCP Committee;* b. Sept. 1963, Rongcheng Co., Shandong Province; joined CCP 1988; began career as researcher in agricultural science, Beijing; Head, Shunyi Dist People's Govt, Beijing 2002–06, also Sec.-Gen., Beijing Municipality CCP Cttee 2002–06; Minister of Agric. 2006–09, also Sec., CCP Leading Party Group 2006–09; Sec., Jilin CCP Provincial Cttee 2009–12; Chair. Standing Cttee, Jilin Provincial People's Congress 2010–12; Sec., Chongqing Municipal CCP Cttee 2012–; mem. 17th CCP Cen. Cttee 2007–12, 18th CCP Cen. Cttee 2012–, also mem. 18th CCP Cen. Cttee Politburo 2012–. *Address:* Chinese Communist Party Politburo, Quanguo Renmin Diabiao Dahui, Zhongguo Gong-chan Dang, 1 Zhongnanhai, Beijing, People's Republic of China. *Website:* cpc .people.com.cn (office).

SUN, Zhenyu; Chinese economist, government official and diplomatist; b. 1946, Fengrun, Hebei Prov.; ed Beijing Foreign Languages Inst.; joined Ministry of Foreign Trade 1973, served as Deputy Dir, Dir and Deputy Dir-Gen. Regional Policy Dept; fmr Vice-Pres. China Nat. Cereals, Oils and Foodstuffs Import and Export Corpn 1985–90; Dir-Gen., Dept of American and Oceanic Affairs, Ministry of Foreign Trade and Econ. Cooperation 1990–94, Vice-Minister 1994–2002, Amb. and Perm. Rep. to WTO, Lausanne, Switzerland 2002–10; currently Chair. China Soc. for WTO Studies. *Publications:* Decision Making in the WTO 2004, Multilateralism and Regionalism 2005, China's Performance in the WTO 2007. *Address:* c/o Permanent Mission of China to the World Trade Organization, 228 rue de Lausanne, 1292 Chambéry, Switzerland (office).

SUNDERLAND, Sir John Michael, Kt, MA; British business executive; *Chairman, Merlin Entertainments Group Ltd;* b. 24 Aug. 1945, Oxford; m.; three d. one s.; ed King Edward VII School, Lytham, Lancs., Queen's Coll., Univ. of St Andrews, Scotland; joined Cadbury Ltd 1968, apptd. mem. Bd Cadbury Ireland 1978, Cadbury Schweppes SA 1981, Marketing Dir, then Man. Dir Schweppes Ltd UK 1983, Founding Dir Coca-Cola & Schweppes Beverages 1987, Man. Dir Trebor Bassett 1989, Cadbury Schweppes Confectionery and Cadbury Schweppes Main Bd Dir 1993, Group CEO Cadbury Schweppes PLC (now Cadbury PLC) 1996–2003, Chair. 2003–08; Chair. Merlin Entertainments Group 2009–; Deputy Pres. CBI 2003, 2007, Pres. 2004–06; mem. Bd of Dirs Financial Reporting Council; Dir (non-exec.) Barclays; Adviser, CVC Capital Pnrs (pvt. equity firm), London; mem. Advisory Group Bd Trinsum Group (fmrly Marakon and IFL); Asscn mem. BUPA; Fellow, RAM; Gov. Court of Henley Man. Coll., Reading Univ.; Pres. Food and Drink Fed. 2002–04, Inc. Soc. of British Advertisers 2002–05, Confed. of British Industry 2004–06, Chartered Man. Inst. 2007–08; Chancellor, Aston Univ. 2011–; Hon. LLD St Andrews Univ. 2007, Hon. DLitt Aston Univ. 2011. *Leisure interests:* sport, history, theatre. *Address:* Merlin Entertainments Group Ltd, 3 Market Close, Poole, BH15 1NQ, England (office). *Telephone:* (1202) 666900 (office). *E-mail:* enquiries@merlinentertainments.biz (office). *Website:* www .merlinentertainments.biz (office).

SUNDQUIST, Donald (Don) Kenneth, BA; American business executive and fmr politician; *Founding Partner, Sundquist Group;* b. 15 March 1936, Moline, Ill.; s. of Kenneth Sundquist and Louise Rohren; m. Martha Swanson 1959; one s. two d.; ed Augustana Coll. Rock Island, Ill.; Div. Man. Josten's Inc. 1961–72; Exec. Vice-Pres. Graphic Sales of America, Memphis 1973, Pres. 1973–82; mem. US House of Reps from 7th Tenn. Dist 1983–95; Gov. of Tennessee 1995–2003; Founding Pnr, Sundquist Anthony LLC (now Sundquist Group), Washington, DC

2004–; Chair. Medicaid Advisory Comm., US Dept of Health and Human Services 2005–06; Founding mem. and Hon. Co-Chair. Japan-America Soc. of Tenn.; Republican. *Leisure interests:* golf, reading. *Address:* Sundquist Group, 51 Louisiana Avenue, NW, Washington, DC 20001, USA (office). *Telephone:* (202) 347-3900 (office). *Fax:* (202) 347-4448 (office). *E-mail:* dh@sundquistgroup.com (office). *Website:* sundquistgroup.com (office).

SUNDQVIST, Ulf Ludvig, MPolSc; Finnish business consultant and fmr politician; *Senior Associate, Business Environment Europe;* b. 22 Feb. 1945, Sipoo; s. of Karl Eric Sundqvist and Helga Linnea Lönnkvist; m. Eine Kristiina Joki 1969; one s. one d.; ed Helsinki Univ.; Asst Lecturer, Faculty of Political Science, Helsinki Univ. 1968–70; mem. Parl. 1970–83; Minister of Educ. 1972–75, of Trade and Industry 1979–81; Gen. Sec. Finnish Social Democratic Party 1975–81, Chair. 1991–93; mem. Supervisory Bd Neste Ltd 1970–, Chair. 1976–94; Deputy Chief Gen. Man. STS-Bank Ltd 1981, Chief Gen. Man. 1982–91, mem. Bd 1992–94; pvt. consultant 1993–; Sr Adviser Ergo Consult Oy; Sr Assoc. Business Environment Europe SA, Brussels; Hon. PhD (Kuopio). *Leisure interests:* music, literature. *Address:* Business Environment Europe, Rue d' l'Industrie, 42 bte 16, 1040 Brussels, Belgium (office). *Telephone:* (2) 2308360 (office). *Fax:* (2) 2308370 (office). *E-mail:* info@bee.be (office). *Website:* www.bee.be (office).

SUNG, Chul-yang, BA, MA, PhD; South Korean academic, politician and diplomatist; *Distinguished Professor, Korea University;* b. 20 Nov. 1939; m. Daisy Lee Yang; one s. one d.; ed Seoul Nat. Univ., Univ. of Hawaii and Univ. of Kentucky, USA; served in Korean Army 1960–62; taught at Eastern Kentucky Univ. and Univ. of Kentucky Fort Knox Center, USA 1970–75, Prof. of Political Science, Lexington 1978; Visiting Prof., Northwestern Univ., Pembroke State Univ., Indiana Univ., USA and Seoul Nat. Univ.; taught at Grad. Inst. of Peace Studies (GIP), Kyung Hee Univ., Seoul 1986, Dean of Academic Affairs at GIP 1987–94; mem. Korean Nat. Ass. 1996–2000, Vice-Chair. Unification and Foreign Affairs Cttee; Amb. to USA 2000–03; currently Distinguished Prof., Korea Univ.; Sec.-Gen. Asscn of Korean Political Scientists in N America; Pres. Korean Asscn of International Studies; mem. Advisory Cttee, Ministry of Foreign Affairs, Ministry of Nat. Defence, Nat. Unification Bd; Chair. Advisory Cttee Kim Dae-jung Peace Foundation; Presidential Award 1964, Distinguished Service to Korean Community in Kentucky Award 2001. *Publications include:* North and South Korean Political Systems: A Comparative Analysis, Polemics and Foibles: Fragments on Korean Politics, Society and Beyond, numerous articles and essays. *Address:* Korea University, Anam-dong Seongbuk-gu, Seoul 136-70, South Korea (office). *Telephone:* (2) 3290-1152 (office). *Website:* www.korea.edu (office).

SUNG, Joseph J. Y., MB BS, PhD, MD, FRCPE, FRACP; Hong Kong medical scientist, academic and university administrator; *Vice-Chancellor and President, The Chinese University of Hong Kong;* ed Univ. of Hong Kong, Univ. of Calgary, Canada, Chinese Univ. of Hong Kong; Medical Officer, Prince of Wales Hosp. 1985–92; Lecturer, Dept of Medicine, Shaw Coll. 1992–98, Chair. Dept of Medicine and Therapeutics 1999–2010, Assoc. Dean (Clinical), Faculty of Medicine 2002–04, Assoc. Dean (Gen. Affairs) 2004–09, Head of Shaw Coll. 2008–10; Prof. of Medicine and Therapeutics, Chinese Univ. of Hong Kong 1998–, Mok Hing Yiu Prof. of Medicine 2007–, Vice-Chancellor and Pres. 2010–; mem. Medical Council of Hong Kong 2007–, Research Council, Food and Health Bureau, Hong Kong Special Admin. Region (HKSAR) 2007–; Academician, Chinese Acad. of Eng 2011; Fellow, Royal Coll. of Glasgow, Royal Coll. of London, Royal Coll. of Thailand, American Coll. of Gastroenterology, American Gastroenterological Asscn, Hong Kong Coll. of Physicians, Hong Kong Acad. of Medicine; JP, HKSAR Govt 2012; Hon. Prof., Li Ka Shing Faculty of Medicine, Univ. of Hong Kong 2007–09; Hon. mem. American Soc. for Gastrointestinal Endoscopy; Outstanding Staff and Team Award, Hosp. Authority 1998, Eminent Scientist of the Year, Int. Research Promotion Council 2003, Vice-Chancellor's Exemplary Teaching Award, CUHK 2003, Silver Bauhinia Star, HKSAR Govt 2004, Cheung Kong Achievement Award, Ministry of Educ., People's Repub. of China (PRC) and Li Ka Shing Foundation 2006, The Most Outstanding Contrib. Award (Clinical Therapeutics), Food and Health Bureau, HKSAR Govt 2007, State Scientific and Technological Progress Award, Second-Class Award, Nat. Office for Science and Tech. Awards, PRC 2007, Marshall and Warren Lecture Award 2009, Endoscopy Award, German Soc. of Gastroenterology 2009, Ho Leung Ho Lee Advancement Prize, The Ho Leung Ho Lee Foundation 2011. *Publications:* numerous papers in professional journals on intestinal bleeding, *Helicobacter pylori*, peptic ulcer, hepatitis B and colorectal cancer. *Address:* Office of the Vice-Chancellor, 1/F, Room 101, University Administration Building, The Chinese University of Hong Kong, Shatin, NT, Hong Kong Special Administrative Region, People's Republic of China (office). *Telephone:* 3943-8600 (office). *Fax:* 2603-7301 (office). *E-mail:* js_vcoffice@cuhk.edu.hk (office). *Website:* www.cuhk.edu.hk (office).

SUNGURLU, Mahmut Oltan; Turkish lawyer and politician; b. 1936, Gümüşhane; m.; one c.; ed Bursa Lycée, Istanbul Univ.; began practising law in Gümüşhane 1963; f. Anavatan Partisi (Motherland Party) prov. org. in Gümüşhane 1983; mem. Parl. for Gümüşhane 1983–99; Minister of Justice 1986–87, 1987–88, 1989–92, 1997–98; Deputy Chair. Anavatan Partisi (Mother-land Party) June 1988; currently Chair. Bd of Trustees Istanbul Şehir Univ. *Address:* c/o Board of Trustees, Istanbul Şehir University, Kuşbakışı Caddesi No: 27 34662, Altunizade, Üsküdar, Istanbul, Turkey.

SUNUNU, John E., BS, MS, MBA; American business executive and fmr politician; *Senior Policy Advisor, Akin Gump Strauss Hauer & Feld LLP;* b. 10 Sept. 1964, Salem, NH; s. of John H. Sununu; m. Kitty Sununu; three c.; ed Salem High School, Massachusetts Inst. of Technology and Harvard Grad. School of Business; worked for REMEC, Inc. 1987; man. and operations specialist with Pittiglio, Rabin Todd & McGrath 1990–92; Chief Financial Officer and Dir of Operations Teletrol Systems, Inc. 1992–96; mem. US House of Reps for First Congressional Dist, NH 1996–2002, mem. Commerce, Science, and Transportation Cttee, Finance Cttee, Homeland Security and Governmental Affairs Cttee, Jt Econ. Cttee; Senator from New Hampshire 2003–09; Sr Policy Advisor, Akin Gump Strauss Hauer & Feld LLP 2010–; mem. Bd of Dirs Time Warner Cable Inc. 2009–, Boston Scientific Inc.; mem. Bd of Dirs Mans ConvergEx Holdings. *Address:* Akin Gump Strauss Hauer & Feld LLP, Robert S. Strauss Building 1333 New Hampshire Avenue, NW, Washington, DC 20036-1564, USA (office). *Telephone:*

(202) 887-4140 (office). *Fax:* (202) 887-4288 (office). *E-mail:* jsununu@akingump .com (office). *Website:* www.akingump.com (office).

SUNUNU, John H., PhD; American business consultant and fmr politician; *President, JHS Associates, Ltd;* b. 2 July 1939, Havana, Cuba; m. Nancy Hayes 1958; five s. including John E. Sununu; three d.; ed Massachusetts Inst. of Tech.; Founder and Chief Engineer, Astro Dynamics 1960–65; Pres. JHS Engineering Co. and Thermal Research Inc., Salem, NH 1965–82; Assoc. Prof. of Mechanical Eng, Tufts Univ. 1966–82, Assoc. Dean, Coll. of Eng 1968–73; mem. NH House of Reps 1973–74, Govt Energy Council; Chair. Govt Council on NH Future 1977–78; mem. Govt Advisory Cttee on Science and Tech. 1977–78; Gov. of NH 1983–89; Chair. coalition of NE Govs 1985–86; White House Chief of Staff, Washington, DC 1989–91, Counsellor to the Pres. 1991–92; Chair. Task Force on Tech.; Pres. JHS Assoc. Ltd 1992–; host, Crossfire (CNN nightly news/public affairs discussion program) 1992–98; fmr Pnr, Trinity Int. Pnrs; Vice-Chair. Alliance for Acid Rain Control; Chair. Emer. NH Republican Party GOP; mem. Hon. Council of Advisors, US-Azerbaijan Chamber of Commerce; fmr Chair. Republican Gov.'s Asscn, New England Gov.'s Asscn; Vice-Chair. Advisory Comm. on Intergovernmental Relations. *Address:* JHS Associates Ltd, 49 Linden Road, Hampton Falls, NH 03844 (office), JHS Associates Ltd, 815 Connecticut Avenue, NW, Suite 1200, Washington, DC 20006, USA (office). *Telephone:* (603) 890-1630 (office). *Fax:* (603) 890-1634 (office). *Website:* www.jhsassociates.com (office).

SUNYAEV, Rashid Alievich; Russian astrophysicist and research institute director; *Chief Scientist, Space Research Institute, Russian Academy of Sciences;* b. 1 March 1943; m.; three s. one d.; ed Moscow Inst. of Physics and Tech.; Jr Researcher, Inst. of Applied Math., USSR (now Russian) Acad. of Sciences 1968–71, Sr Researcher 1971–74, Head of Lab. of Theoretical Astrophysics, Space Research Inst. 1974–82, Head of Dept of High Energy Astrophysics 1982–2002, Chief Scientist 1992–, Corresp. mem. USSR (now Russian) Acad. of Sciences 1984, mem. 1992; Prof., Moscow Inst. of Physics and Tech. 1975–2001; Scientific mem. Max Planck Inst. for Astrophysics, Garching, Germany 1995–, Dir 1996–; Adjunct Prof., Columbia Univ., USA; Maureen and John Hendricks Visiting Prof., Inst. for Advanced Study, Princeton, NJ, USA 2010–; Scientific Head, Int. Orbital Observatory ROENTGEN on complex space station Mir, Orbital Observatory GRANAT; Vice-Pres. COSPAR (ICSU Cttee on Space Research) 1986–94; Ed.-in-Chief, Astronomy Letters 1985, Astrophysics and Space Physics Reviews 1979–2005; mem. Editorial Bd, Space Science Reviews 1988–2007; mem. Advisory Bd on Astrophysics and Space Physics, Springer (previously Kluwer) Scientific Publrs 1995–; mem. Int. Astronomical Union 1968, European Acad. of Sciences, Int. Acad. of Astronautics, European Astronomical Soc. 1991 (Vice-Pres. 1991–93), American Physical Soc. 1993, German Acad. of Natural Scientists Leopoldina 2003; Foreign Assoc. NAS 1991, American Acad. of Arts and Sciences 1992; Scientific mem. Max-Planck Soc. 1995; Foreign mem. Royal Netherlands Acad. of Arts and Sciences 2004, Royal Soc. 2009; Int. mem. American Philosophical Soc. 2007; Foreign Fellow, Royal Astronomical Soc. 1993; Hon. mem. American Astronomical Soc. 1992; Bundesverdienstkreuz 2010; Bruno Rossi Prize 1988, Bruce Medal 2000, State Prize of Russian Fed. 2000, Alexander Friedman Prize, Russian Acad. of Sciences 2002, Dannie Heineman Prize for Astrophysics 2003, Gruber Prize in Cosmology 2003, Int. Astronomical Union Gold Medal for Cosmology, Crafoord Prize (jtly) 2008, Henry Norris Russell Award, American Astronomical Soc. 2008, Karl Schwarzschild Medal, German Astronomische Gesellschaft 2008, King Faisal Int. Prize for Science (Physics) and Gold Medal (co-recipient) 2009, Antoinette de Vaucouleurs Medal, Univ. of Texas, Austin 2009, Kyoto Prize and Gold Medal, Inamori Foundation (co-recipient) 2011, Benjamin Franklin Medal in Physics, Franklin Inst. 2012. *Publications include:* Black Holes in Double Systems 1973, Observation of Relict Irradiation as Method of Studying the Nature of X-ray Irradiation of Galaxy Clusters 1973, Comptonization of X-ray Irradiation in Plasma Clouds: characteristic spectra 1980; numerous articles. *Address:* Space Research Institute, Russian Academy of Sciences, 117997 Moscow, Profsoyuznaya Street 84/32, Russia (office); Room 130, Max-Planck-Institut für Astrophysik, Karl-Schwarzschild-Str. 1, 85748 Garching, Germany. *Telephone:* (495) 333-33-73 (office); (89) 300002244; (495) 331-38-05 (home). *Fax:* (495) 233-53-77; (89) 300002899. *E-mail:* rs@star.iki.rssi.ru (office); sunyaev@mpa-garching .mpg.de (office); iki@cosmos.ru. *Website:* arc.iki.rssi.ru/eng/index.htm (office).

SUNYE, Gilbert Saboya, BEcons; Andorran economist and politician; *Minister of Foreign Affairs;* b. 1966, Andorra la Vella; ed Univ. of Social Sciences, Toulouse, France; began career in banking sector, as CEO, Asset Management BIBM UAA, later Deputy Dir-Gen. of BIBM responsible for Private Banking and Asset Man. 1991–2009; f. Savoy AlfaQuest Advisors (ind. financial consultancy) 2010; Minister of Foreign Affairs 2011–; Dir-Gen. Agrupament Nacional Democràtic (AND) 1994–97, also Pres. Parl. Econ. Comm.; Founding mem. Partit Demòcrata 2002, Nou Centre 2008; currently mem. Bd of Man. Partit Reformista d'Andorra. *Leisure interests:* music, reading, travel, football, computer technology. *Address:* Ministry of Foreign Affairs, Carrer Prat de la Creu 62–64, Edif. Administratiu, Andorra la Vella AD500, Andorra (office). *Telephone:* 875704 (office). *Fax:* 869559 (office). *E-mail:* exteriors.gov@andorra.ad (office). *Website:* www.mae.ad (office).

SUOMINEN, Ilkka Olavi, MPolSci; Finnish business executive and fmr politician; b. 8 April 1939, Nakkila; s. of Leo Suominen and Anna Suominen; m. Riitta Suhonen 1977; one s. two d.; Dept Head, J.W. Suominen Oy 1960–72, Deputy Man. Dir 1972–74, Man. Dir 1975–79, mem. Man. Bd; mem. Parl. 1970–75, 1983–94; Leader Nat. Coalition Party 1979–91; Vice-Chair. European Democrat Union 1986–93; Speaker of Parl. 1987, 1991–96; Minister of Trade and Industry 1987–91; Pres. CSCE Parl. Ass. 1992–94; mem. European Parl. 1999–2004; Chair. Admin. Bd Oy Alko AB 1980–88, 1991–94, Gen. Man. 1994; Chair. Bd of Dirs ICL Data (Finland) 1992–96; Vice-Chair. Confed. of Finnish Industries 1978–79; Pres. Finnish Biathlon Asscn 1998–2003; Chevalier, Ordre nat. du Mérite 1983; Commdr, Order of Lion 1986, Grand Cross 1993; Grand Cross, Order of Merit (Hungary) 1992; Grand Cross, Order of Merit (Norway) 1993; Grand Cross, Order of Merit (Italy) 1993; Dr hc (Tampere Univ. of Technology) 1992. *Leisure interests:* hunting, fishing. *Address:* Ruoholahdenkatu 6 A 15, 00180 Helsinki, Finland. *Telephone:* 405066145 (mobile). *E-mail:* ilkka@suominen.net.

SUOD, Husnu, LLB, LLM; Maldivian lawyer and politician; *Senior Partner, Suood & Anwar LLP;* ed Int. Islamic Univ., Malaysia, Univ. of Queensland, Australia; Asst to Attorney-Gen. 1988–94, State Attorney at Attorney-Gen.'s Office

1994–97; Chief Judge of Civil Court, Malé 1997–99; Pnr, Muizzu Suood and Co. (law firm), Malé 1999–2009, Man. Pnr 2008–09; Attorney Gen. 2009–10; Chair. Nat. Law Reform Comm. 2009–10; currently Sr Pnr, Suood & Anwar LLP (law firm); mem. Maldives Law Comm. 1994–2002; lecturer in business law and Maldives legal system at Faculty of Man. and Computing and Faculty of Sharia Law, Maldives Coll. of Higher Educ. and Inst. of Islamic Studies, Malé; mem. Human Rights Comm. of the Maldives; mem. Maldivian Democratic Party; Nat. Award of Excellence for Outstanding Services in the field of law/legal services 2011. *Address:* Suood & Anwar LLP, Level 2, Orchid Maage Ameer Ahmed Magu, Malé 20095, The Maldives (office). *Telephone:* 3344-911 (office). *E-mail:* info@ suoodanwar.com (office). *Website:* www.suoodanwar.com (office).

SUPAMONGKOL, Kantathee, MA, PhD; Thai government official and academic; *Visiting Professor of Law and Diplomacy, University of California, Los Angeles;* b. 3 April 1952; m.; ed Univ. of California, Los Angeles, Univ. of Southern California, American Univ., Washington, DC, USA; fmr Prof. of Law and Int. Relations; joined Ministry of Foreign Affairs 1984, with Perm. Mission to UN, New York 1988–92; Adviser on Foreign Affairs to Speaker of House of Reps 1992; Dir Policy and Planning Div., Ministry of Foreign Affairs 1993–94; mem. Parl. 1995, 2001, mem. Cttee on Foreign Affairs, Cttee on Tourism, House of Reps; Adviser on Foreign Affairs to Prime Minister 1996; Trade Rep. of Thailand 2001–05; Adviser to Minister of Industry; Special Envoy of the Prime Minister; Adviser on Foreign Affairs to Minister of Foreign Affairs; Minister of Foreign Affairs 2005–06; Prof., UCLA, USA 2007–09, currently Visiting Prof. of Law and Diplomacy and Sr Fellow, Burkle Center for International Relations; Chair. Human Security Network, Kanta Enterprise International; fmr Dir Post Publishing Public Co.; Kt Grand Cordon (Special Class) of the Most Noble Order of the Crown of Thailand. *Address:* 11359 Bunche Hall, Box 951487, Los Angeles, CA 90095-1487, USA (office). *Telephone:* (310) 206-6365 (office). *Fax:* (310) 206-3555 (office). *E-mail:* Kantathi@ucla.edu (office). *Website:* www.international.ucla.edu (office); www .kantagroup.com.

SUPANDJI, Hendarman; Indonesian lawyer and government official; *Attorney-General;* b. 6 Jan. 1947, Klaten, Cen. Java; ed Univ. of Diponegoro; began career with Dist Prosecutor's Office, Cen. Jakarta 1979–81; with Cen. Intelligence Operation, Office of the Attorney-Gen. 1982–83, Prosecutor's Attaché, Embassy in Bangkok 1990–95, Civil and State Admin Asst, Chief's Prosecutor Office, Palembang 1996–97, Staff Expert Adviser to Attorney-Gen. 1998, Head of Financial Bureau, Attorney-Gen.'s Office 1998–2002, Chief Prosecutor in Yogyakarta and Sec. to Deputy Attorney for Supervision 2002–04, Head of Corruption Eradication Team 2005, Deputy Attorney-Gen. for Special Crimes 2005–07, Attorney-Gen. 2007–; Dr hc (Diponegoro) 2009. *Address:* Office of the Attorney-General, Jalan Sultan Hasanuddin 1, Kebayoran Baru, Jakarta, Indonesia (office). *Telephone:* (21) 7221377 (office). *Fax:* (21) 7392576 (office). *E-mail:* postmaster@kejaksaan.go.id (office). *Website:* www.kejaksaan.go.id (office).

SUPPES, Patrick, BS, PhD, FAAS; American scientist and academic; *Lucie Stern Professor Emeritus of Philosophy, Stanford University;* b. 17 March 1922, Tulsa, Okla; m. 1st Joan Farmer 1946 (divorced 1970); one s. two d.; m. 2nd Joan Elizabeth Sieber 1970 (divorced 1979); one s. one d.; ed Univ. of Chicago and Columbia Univ.; Lecturer (part-time), Columbia Univ. 1948–50; Asst and Assoc. Prof., Dept of Philosophy, Stanford Univ. 1950–59, Prof. 1959–92, Dir, Inst. for Math. Studies in the Social Sciences 1959–92, Prof. (by courtesy), Dept of Statistics 1960–92, Chair., Dept of Philosophy 1963–69, Prof. (by courtesy), School of Educ. 1967–92, Prof. (by courtesy), Dept of Psychology 1973–92, Lucie Stern Prof. of Philosophy 1975–92, Prof. Emer. 1992–, Dir and Faculty Advisor, Educ. Program for Gifted Youth 1992–; Pres. Computer Curriculum Corpn 1967–90; Fellow, American Psychological Asscn, Asscn for Computing Machinery 1994; mem. Nat. Acad. of Educ. (Pres. 1973–77), American Acad. of Arts and Sciences, Finnish Acad. of Science and Letters, NAS, European Acad. of Sciences and Arts; Corresp. mem. Yugoslav Acad. of Sciences and Arts 1990; Foreign mem. USSR (now Russian) Acad. of Pedagogical Sciences, Norwegian Acad. of Science and Letters; Hon. mem. Chilean Acad. of Sciences; Dr hc (Nijmegen) 1979, (Acad. de Paris, Univ. René Descartes) 1982, (Regensburg) 1999, (Bologna) 1999; Palmer O. Johnson Memorial Award, American Educational Research Asscn 1967, Distinguished Scientific Contribution Award, American Psychological Asscn 1972, Columbia Univ. Teachers College Medal for Distinguished Service 1978, E.L. Thorndike Award for Distinguished Psychological Contrib. to Educ., American Psychological Asscn 1979, Nat. Medal of Science 1990, Louis Robinson Award, Educom 1993. *Publications include:* Introduction to Logic 1957, Decision Making: An Experimental Approach (with D. Davidson and S. Siegel) 1957, Axiomatic Set Theory 1960, Markov Learning Models for Multiperson Interactions (with R. C. Atkinson) 1960, First Course in Mathematical Logic (with S. Hill) 1964, Experiments in Second-Language Acquisition (with E. Crothers) 1967, Computer Assisted Instruction: Stanford's 1965–66 Arithmetic Program (with M. Jerman and D. Brian) 1968, Studies in the Methodology and Foundations of Science 1970, A Probabilistic Theory of Causality 1970, Foundations of Measurement (with D. Krantz, R. D. Luce, A. Tversky) Vol. I 1971, Vol. II 1989, Vol. III 1990, Computer-assisted Instruction at Stanford, 1966–68 (with M. Morningstar); Probabilistic Metaphysics 1974, The Radio Mathematics Project: Nicaragua 1974–1975 (with B. Searle and J. Friend) 1976, Logique du Probable 1981, Estudios de Filosofía y Metodología de la Ciencia 1988, Language for Humans and Robots 1991, Models and Methods in the Philosophy of Science 1993, Language and Learning for Robots (with C. Crangle) 1994, Foundations of Probability with Applications (with M. Zanotti) 1996, Representation and Invariance of Scientific Structures 2002; and over 300 articles in professional journals. *Address:* Center for the Study of Language and Information, Ventura Hall, Stanford University, Stanford, CA 94305-4115 (office); 678 Mirada Avenue, Stanford, CA 94305, USA. *Telephone:* (650) 725-6030 (office). *E-mail:* suppes@csli .stanford.edu (office). *Website:* www.stanford.edu/~psuppes (office).

SUPPLE, Barry Emanuel, CBE, PhD, FRHistS, FBA; British economic historian and academic; b. 27 Oct. 1930, London, England; s. of Solomon Supple and Rose Supple; m. 1st Sonia Caller 1958; two s. one d.; m. 2nd Virginia McNay 2003; ed Hackney Downs Grammar School, LSE and Christ's Coll. Cambridge; Asst Prof. of Business History, Grad. School of Business Admin., Harvard Univ., USA 1955–60;

Assoc. Prof. of Econ. History, McGill Univ. 1960–62; Lecturer in Econ. and Social History, Univ. of Sussex, Reader, then Prof. 1962–78, Dean, School of Social Sciences 1965–68, Pro-Vice-Chancellor (Arts and Social Studies) 1968–72, Pro-Vice-Chancellor 1978; Reader in Recent Social and Econ. History, Univ. of Oxford 1978–81, Professorial Fellow, Nuffield Coll. 1978–81; Prof. of Econ. History Univ. of Cambridge 1981–93, Prof. Emer. 1993–, Professorial Fellow, Christ's Coll. 1981–83, Hon. Fellow 1984; Master of St Catharine's Coll., Cambridge 1984–93, Hon. Fellow 1993; Dir Leverhulme Trust 1993–2001; Pres. Econ. History Soc. 1992–95, Foreign Sec. British Acad. 1995–99; mem. Social Science Fellowship Cttee, Nuffield Foundation 1974–94; Co-Ed. Econ. History Review 1973–82; Academic Consultant, Lisbet Rausing Charitable Fund (renamed Arcadia) 2001–07; Hon. Fellow, Worcester Coll., Oxford 1986; Hon. FRAM 2001; Hon. DLitt (Sussex) 1998, (Leicester) 1999, (Warwick) 2000, (Bristol) 2001. *Publications:* Commercial Crisis and Change in England, 1600–42, 1959, The Experience of Economic Growth (ed.) 1963, Boston Capitalists and Western Railroads 1967, The Royal Exchange Assurance: a history of British insurance 1720–1970, 1970, Essays in Business History (ed.) 1977, History of the British Coal Industry, Vol. IV (1914–46), The Political Economy of Decline 1987, The State and Economic Knowledge: the American and British Experience (ed.) 1990, The Rise of Big Business (ed.) 1992, Doors Open 2008, Six Days in Poland 2010, articles and reviews in learned journals. *Leisure interests:* tennis, photography. *Address:* 3 Scotts Gardens, Whittlesford, Cambridge, CB22 4NR, England (home). *Telephone:* (1223) 830606 (home). *E-mail:* barrysupple@gmail.com (home).

SUR, Pierre-Olivier, BA; French lawyer; b. 19 July 1963, Paris; s. of Bernard Sur and Marie-Claude Pellerin; two d.; ed Lycée Montaigne, Paris, Univs of Paris IV-Sorbonne and Paris II-Panthéon Assas, Inst. of Political Studies (IEP), Paris; attorney, Court of Appeal, Paris 1985–, Bar Phnom Penh, Cambodia 2008; Sec. Conférence du stage 1990; Prof., IEP 2001–, mem. Bd 1997–2000, Dauphin 2012–13; Pres. of the Paris Bar 2014–, mem. Ethics Cttee 2001–09; Dir Victims Guarantee Fund 2002–10, Nat. Inst. of Advanced Studies of Safety and Justice 2010–; Judicial Observer to Sarajevo 1994; mem. Cercle du Bois de Boulogne (clay pigeon shooting), Compagnia della vela de Venise; Chevalier, Légion d'honneur, Ordre nat. du Mérite. *Publications:* Droit pénal général (co-author) 1997, Nul n"est censé ignorer la loi 2004, Dans les yeux du bourreau 2010. *Leisure interests:* tennis, sailing. *Address:* SCP Fischer, Tandeau de Marsac, Sur & associés, 67 boulevard Malesherbes, 75008 Paris, France (office). *E-mail:* posur@ftms-a.com (office).

SURANCHIYEV, Abdulda Shergaziyevich; Kyrgyzstani politician; *Acting Minister of Internal Affairs;* b. 1950, Tuzovka village, Yssyk-Atin dist, Chui Oblast; ed Kyrgyz State Univ.; rank of Police Maj. Gen.; Insp. of Correctional Labour Insts, Ministry of Internal Affairs, Kyrgyz SSR 1970–71; Investigator in internal affairs section of Djet-Oguz Dist Exec. Cttee, Yssyk-Kul Oblast 1973; served in interior forces of USSR Ministry of Internal Affairs 1973-76, Insp., Deputy Head of Criminal Investigation Dept of Internal Affairs section, Sverdlovsk Dist Exec. Cttee, Frunze City (now Bishkek) 1976–81; Sr Insp., Head of Dept, Criminal Investigation Dept of Internal Affairs, Frunze City Exec. Cttee 1981–85; Deputy Head of Internal Affairs section, Pervomai Dist, Frunze City Exec. Cttee 1985–89; Head of Criminal Investigations Section, Ministry of Internal Affairs, Kyrgyz SSR and Kyrgyz Repub. 1989–93; Deputy Head of Criminal Investigations Dept, Ministry of Internal Affairs 1993; Head of Internal Affairs Section, Pervomai Dist, Bishkek City 1993–96; Head of Internal Affairs Section, Bishkek City 1996–2002; Deputy Minister of Internal Affairs 2002–05; worked for Ministry of Internal Affairs 2005–08, Deputy Head of Section for Defence and Security of the Admin of the Pres. 2008; transferred to mil. reserve 2009; Acting Minister of Internal Affairs Feb. 2013–; mem. Social Democratic Party of Kyrgyzstan (SDPK—Kyrgyzstandyn Sotsial-Demokratiyalyk Partiyasy); 'Dank' Medal. *Address:* Ministry of Internal Affairs, 720040 Bishkek, Frunze 469, Kyrgyzstan (office). *Telephone:* (312) 66-24-50 (office). *Fax:* (312) 26-62-80 (office). *E-mail:* pressa@mvd.kg (office). *Website:* www.mvd.kg (office).

SURANI, Azim, CBE, PhD, FRS, FMedSci; British biologist and academic; *Mary Marshall and Arthur Walton Professor of Physiology and Reproduction, The Wellcome Trust / Cancer Research UK Gurdon Institute, University of Cambridge;* b. 13 Jan. 1945, Kisumu, Kenya; s. of Habib Surani and Sherbanu Surani; m. Nuria Surani; one s. three d.; ed Univs of London and Cambridge; currently Mary Marshall and Arthur Walton Prof. of Physiology and Reproduction, The Wellcome Trust/Cancer Research UK Gurdon Inst. of Cancer and Developmental Biology, Univ. of Cambridge and Dept of Physiology, Devt and Neuroscience; Rosenstiel Award, Gabor Award, Royal Medal, Royal Soc. 2010. *Publications:* numerous papers on embryonic devt, genomic imprinting, specification of germ cells, epigenetic reprogramming, and pluripotent stem cells. *Leisure interests:* reading, hiking, music. *Address:* The Wellcome Trust/Cancer Research UK Gurdon Institute, Henry Wellcome Building of Cancer and Developmental Biology, University of Cambridge, Tennis Court Road, Cambridge, CB2 1QN, England (office). *Telephone:* (1223) 334136 (office). *Fax:* (1223) 334089 (office). *E-mail:* a.surani@gurdon.cam.ac.uk (office); as10021@mole.bio.cam.ac.uk (office). *Website:* www.gurdon.cam.ac.uk/~suranilab (office); www.stemcells.cam.ac.uk/researchers/principal-investigators/azim-surani (office).

SURÁNYI, György, PhD, DEcon; Hungarian economist and banking executive; *Chairman, Central European International Bank Limited;* b. 3 Jan. 1954, Budapest; m.; two c.; ed Univ. of Economics, Budapest, Hungarian Acad. of Sciences; Research Fellow and Head of Dept, Financial Research Inst., Budapest 1977–86; consultant, World Bank, Washington, DC 1986–87; Counsellor to Deputy Prime Minister, Council of Ministers 1988–89; Sec. of State, Nat. Planning Office 1989–90; Pres. Nat. Bank of Hungary 1990–91; Man. Dir Cen. European Int. Bank Ltd 1992–95, Chair. 2001–; Pres. Nat. Bank of Hungary 1995–2001; Head of Multinational Banking, IntesBci Group, Italy 2001–; Pres. Supervisory Bd Privredna Banka, Zagreb 2001–; mem. Supervisory Bd VUB, Bratislava 2001–; Prof. of Finance, Corvinus Univ. of Economics, Central European Univ., Budapest; mem. Bd of Dirs Bruegel (econ. research inst.), EastWest Inst., New York; mem. PCG Principles Consultative Group; Global Leader for Tomorrow, World Econ. Forum 1993, Leadership in Econ. Transition, EastWest Inst., New York 2001. *Publications:* author of several articles and books on monetary and financial issues. *Address:* Central European International Bank Ltd, Medve u. 4-14, 1027

Budapest, Hungary (office). *Telephone:* (1) 423-2924 (office). *Fax:* (1) 489-6226 (office). *E-mail:* gsuranyi@cib.hu (office). *Website:* www.cib.hu (office).

SURAPONG, Tovichakchaikul, BA, MA, PhD; Thai politician; b. 1 May 1953; ed Khon Kaen Univ., Youngstown State Univ., Univ. of Akron, USA; mem. House of Reps 1996–2000; Chair. Standing Cttee on Monetary Affairs, Finance, Banking and Financial Insts 2000; Minister of Foreign Affairs 2011–14; mem. Puea Thai; Kt Grand Cross (First Class), Most Noble Order of Crown of Thailand. *Address:* c/o Ministry of Foreign Affairs, 443 Sri Ayudhya Road, Bangkok 10400, Thailand (office).

SURDO BONETTI, Vittorio Claudio; Italian diplomatist; b. 1943, Libya; m. Roya Mirtolouei Surdo; began Foreign Service career in Cairo 1973–76, other overseas postings include Embassy in Paris 1976–78, in Tehran 1981–85, in Bonn 1985–89, Amb. to Ukraine 1992–96, to Turkey 1999–2004, to Russia (also accred to Turkmenistan) 2006–10; Adviser, ENEL Group 2012–; Commendatore dell'Ordine al merito della Repubblica italiana 1995, Grande Ufficiale 2004, Cavaliere 2010, Order of Friendship (Russia) 2010. *Address:* Enel SpA, Viale Regina Margherita 137, 00198 Rome, Italy (office).

SUREAU, Claude, LèsSc, MD; French obstetrician and gynaecologist; b. 27 Sept. 1927, Paris; s. of Maurice Sureau and Rita Jullian; m. Janine Murset 1956; one s. two d.; ed Paris Univ., Columbia Presbyterian Medical Center; Asst Prof., Paris Univ. 1956–61, Assoc. Prof. 1961–74; Prof. and Chair., Dept of Obstetrics and Gynaecology, St Vincent de Paul Hosp., Paris 1974–76, Univ. Clinique Baudelocque 1976–89; Pres., Int. Fed. of Obstetricians and Gynaecologists 1982–85, Pres., Standing Cttee on Ethical Aspects of Human Reproduction 1985–94; Pres. European Assen of Gynaecology and Obstetrics 1988–91; Dir Unit 262, Physiology and Physiopathology of Reproduction, Nat. Inst. of Health and Medical Research 1983–90; Active Staff mem. American Hosp. of Paris 1989–93, Chief of Gynaecological Unit 1990–93, Medical Dir American Hosp. of Paris 1994–95; Pres. Theramex Inst. 1996–2008; mem. Nat. Acad. of Medicine of France 1978–, Vice-Pres. 1999, Pres. 2000; Vice-Pres. Observatory of the Precautionary Principle 2007; mem. High Council on Population and Family 1996–2003, Nat. Ethics Advisory Cttee 2005–; Commdr Ordre nat. du Mérite 1996, Légion d'honneur. *Publications:* Le danger de naître 1978, Ethical Dilemmas in Assisted Reproduction 1996, Alice au pays des clones 1999; Co-ed.: Clinical Perinatology 1980, Immunologie de la réproduction humaine 1983, Aux débuts de la vie 1990, Ethical Aspects of Human Reproduction 1995, Ethical Problems in Obstetrics and Gynaecology 2000, Fallait-il tuer l'enfant Foucault? et Humanisme médical 2003, Son nom est personne 2005, Contemporary Ethical Dilemmas in Assisted Reproduction, l'Erreur médicale et De la sanction à la prévention de l'erreur médicale 2006. *Address:* 16 rue d'Aubigny, 75017 Paris, France (home).

SURESH, Subra, MS, ScD; Indian engineer, materials scientist, academic and university administrator; *President, Carnegie Mellon University;* b. 30 May 1956; m. Mary Delmar 1986; two d.; ed Indian Inst. of Tech., Madras, Iowa State Univ., Massachusetts Inst. of Tech.; Postdoctoral Researcher, Univ. of California, Berkeley and Lawrence Berkeley Lab. 1981–83; Asst Prof. of Eng, Brown Univ. 1983–89, Prof. 1989–93; R.P. Simmons Prof. of Materials Science and Eng, MIT 1993, Head of Dept of Materials Science and Engineering 2000–06, Ford Prof. of Eng 2002–10, later Vannevar Bush Prof. of Eng, Dean, School of Eng 2007–10; Dir NSF 2010–13; Pres. Carnegie Mellon Univ. 2013–; Clark B. Millikan Endowed Chair for Visiting Professorship, California Inst. of Tech. 1999–2000; Founding Chair, Program on Advanced Materials, Singapore-MIT Alliance; Founding Dir Global Enterprise for Micromechanics and Molecular Medicine; mem. NAS, Nat. Acad. of Eng 2002, American Acad. of Arts and Sciences 2004, Indian Nat. Acad. of Eng 2004, German Nat. Acad. of Sciences 2007, Spanish Royal Acad. of Sciences, Spanish Royal Acad. of Eng, Royal Swedish Acad. of Eng Sciences, Acad. of Sciences of the Developing World, Indian Acad. of Sciences; elected a fellow or hon. mem. of all the major materials research societies in USA and India; Dr hc (Sweden Royal Inst. of Tech. and univs in USA, Switzerland, Spain, China and India); selected by Technology Review magazine as a top-ten researcher whose research "will have a significant impact on business, medicine or culture" 2006, Acta Materialia Gold Medal 2006, European Materials Medal, Fed. of European Materials Socs 2007, Eringen Medal, Soc. of Eng Science 2008, Gen. Pres.'s Gold Medal, Indian Nat. Science Congress 2011, Padma Shri Award 2011, Nadai Medal 2011, ASME Timoshenko Medal 2012, R.F. Mehl Award, Minerals, Metals and Materials Soc. 2012, Benjamin Franklin Medal in Mechanical Eng and Materials Science 2013. *Publications:* Fatigue of Materials 1991, Fundamentals of Functionally Graded Materials (co-author) 1998, Thin Film Materials: Stress, Surface Evolution and Failure (co-author) 2003. *Address:* Office of the President, Carnegie Mellon University, 5000 Forbes Avenue, Pittsburgh, PA 15213, USA (office). *Telephone:* (412) 268-2000 (office). *Website:* www.cmu.edu/leadership (office).

SURIE, Nalin, MA; Indian diplomatist (retd); b. 24 July 1951; m. Poonam Surie; two d.; ed Univ. of Delhi, Delhi School of Econs; joined Indian Foreign Service 1973, served in Missions in Hong Kong, Brussels, Dar-es-Salaam and Thimphu; served at HQ UN Div., Ministry of External Affairs 1977–79; Dir Dept of Econ. Affairs, Ministry of Finance 1989–91; Jt Sec., East Europe, Ministry of External Affairs HQ 1991–94, Jt Sec./Additional Sec., East Asia 2000–03, Sec. (West) 2004–09; Deputy Perm. Rep. to UN 1994–97; Amb. to Poland 1997–2004, to People's Repub. of China 2003–06; High Commr to UK 2009–11; Life mem. Indian Gymkhana Club 2011. *Address:* c/o Ministry of External Affairs, South Block, New Delhi 110 011, India. *Telephone:* (11) 23011127. *E-mail:* eam@mea.gov.in.

SURJÁN, László, MD, PhD; Hungarian physician and politician; b. 7 Sept. 1941, Kolozsvár (now Cluj, Romania); s. of László Surján and Margit Surján (née Göttinger); m. Zsófia Stverteczky 1966; one s. two d.; ed Roman Catholic Theologic Acad. Semmelweis Univ. Medical School, Budapest; Lecturer, Semmelweis Medical Univ. 1969–70, Post-grad. Medical School 1970–90; joined Hungarian Christian Democratic Party (Chair. 1990–95); elected mem. Hungarian Parl. (Magyar Polgári Szövetség—Fidesz) 1990, Pres. Employment and Labour Affairs Cttee of Parl. 1994–98, Vice-Chair. Foreign Affairs Cttee 1998–2002, Deputy Speaker 2000–01; Minister of Welfare 1990–94; Head, Hungarian Del. to Parl. Ass. of Council of Europe and Vice-Chair. Foreign Affairs Cttee 1998–2004; mem. European Parl. (Group of the European People's Party—Christian Democrats and European Democrats) 2004–, mem. Cttee on Budgets, Substitute mem. Cttee on

Regional Devt, mem. Temporary Cttee on Policy Challenges and Budgetary Means of the Enlarged Union 2007–2013, Vice-Chair. Del. to EU-Chile Jt Parl. Cttee, Substitute mem. Del. to EU-Romania Jt Parl. Cttee; Chair. WHO Regional Cttee for Europe 1992–93; Vice-Chair. European Union of Christian Democrats 1992–99; mem. numerous socs. *Publications:* author of 48 scientific publs. *Address:* European Parliament, Bâtiment Altiero Spinelli, 12E246, 60 rue Wiertz, 1047 Brussels, Belgium (office). *Fax:* (2) 284-9835 (office). *E-mail:* lsurjan@europarl.eu .int (office).

SURKIS, Grigoriy; Ukrainian politician, business executive and international organization executive; *Honorary President, Football Federation of Ukraine;* b. 4 Sept. 1949, Odessa; m.; one s. one d.; ed Kyiv Technological Inst. of Food Industry; worked for Trest Kievzhilstroymontazh 1974–88; held exec. positions with Kiev City Council 1988–91; Pres. Slavutich (holding co.) 1993–98; Owner, Dynamo Kiev Football Club, Pres. 1993–98; Pres. Professional Football League and Vice-Pres. Football Fed. of Ukraine 1996–2000, Pres. 2000–12, Hon. Pres. 2012–; mem. Parl. 1998–2006; mem. UEFA Professional Football Cttee 2002–04; mem. UEFA Exec. Cttee 2004–; mem. FIFA Nat. Asscns Cttee; Amb. to Council of Europe for Sport; mem. Nat. Olympic Cttee of Ukraine; mem. Bd of Trustees Jewish Confed. of Ukraine; Order of Merit (Third Degree) 1996, (Second Degree) 1999, (First Degree) 2004, Commdr, Order of the Italian Repub., Order of Prince Yaroslav Mudry The Wise (Fifth Degree) 2006), Order of Ukrainian Orthodox Church 'Apostale Prince Volodymyr' (First Degree) 2006, (Fourth Degree) 2012; Businessman of the Year 1996, 1998, Man of the Year 1997. *Leisure interests:* fitness. *Address:* Football Federation of Ukraine, 7-A Laboratornyi provulok, PO Box 293, Kiev 03150, Ukraine (office). *Telephone:* (44) 521-05-21 (office). *Fax:* (44) 521-05-50 (office). *E-mail:* info@ffu.org.ua (office). *Website:* www.ffu.org.ua (office).

SURKOV, Vladislav Yuryevich, MSc; Russian (Chechen) business executive and government official; *Aide to the President;* b. (Aslambek Dudayev), 21 Sept. 1964; s. of Andarbek (Yuriy) Danil'bekovich Dudayev and Zinaida Antonovna Surkova; m. 1st Yuliya Vishnevskaya; one s.; m. 2nd (civil ceremony) Natalya Dubovitskaya 1998; two s.; ed Moscow Inst. of Steel and Alloys, Moscow Inst. of Culture, Moscow Int. Univ.; name changed to Vladislav Surkov 1969; army service 1983–85; Dir Metapress Agency (communications) 1990–92; Head of Advertising Dept Menatep Credit and Financial Enterprises Asscn (later Menatep Bank) 1992–94, Deputy Head of Client Services Dept 1992–94, Deputy Head of Public Relations Dept 1994–96, Vice-Pres. State Orgs Relations Dept 1996–97, mem. Bd of Dirs 1996–97; Deputy Head, Head of Public Relations, Rosprom 1996–97; First Deputy Council Chair. Commercial Innovation Bank Alfa Bank 1996–97; First Deputy Dir-Gen., then Public Relations Dir Public Russian TV (ORT) 1998, First Sec., Supervisory Bd 1998–99; Aide to Chief of Staff, Presidential Admin 1999, Deputy Chief of Staff, Presidential Admin 1999–2008, Aide to the Pres. 2004–08, 2013–, First Deputy Chief of Staff, Presidential Admin 2008–11; Deputy Chair. of the Govt (in charge of econ. modernization), Head of the Govt Admin 2011–13 (resgnd); State Councillor of the Russian Fed. (First Class), Order of Merit for the Fatherland (Third Class) 2003, Gratitude of the Pres. of the Russian Fed. 2003, 2004, 2010, Medal of P.A. Stolypin (Second Class) 2011; Diploma of the Cen. Election Comm. of the Russian Fed. 2008. *Leisure interests:* playing the guitar, writing music. *Address:* Office of the President, 103132 Moscow, Staraya pl. 4, Russia. *Telephone:* (495) 625-35-81. *Fax:* (495) 606-07-66. *E-mail:* president@gov .ru. *Website:* www.kremlin.ru.

SURLYK, Finn C., Cand. scient., PhD, Dr scient.; Danish geologist and academic; *Professor, Department of Geography and Geology, University of Copenhagen;* b. 17 March 1943, Copenhagen; s. of C. Surlyk and K. Surlyk; m. Nanna Noe-Nygaard; two s.; Asst Prof., Univ. of Copenhagen 1968–69, Assoc. Prof. 1971–80, Research Prof., Dept of Geography and Geology 1984–89, Prof. (Geology of Sedimentary Basins) 1989–; Head, Dept of Petroleum Geology, Geological Survey of Greenland, Copenhagen 1981–84; Chair. Danish Nat. Cttee of Geology 1976–86; Gen.-Sec. Int. Asscn of Sedimentologists 1986–90, Pres. 1990–94; Sec. Subcommission on Cretaceous Stratigraphy, Int. Union of Geological Sciences 2005–10; mem. Bd Govs, Geological Survey of Denmark 1979–81, Geological Survey of Denmark and Greenland 1988–91, 1991–94; mem. Cttee for Petroleum-Related Research, Ministry of Energy 1986–90, Danish Natural Science Research Council 1992–98; mem. Sedimentary and Geochemical Processes Panel, Ocean Drilling Programme/ JOIDES Resolution (Jt Oceanographic Insts for Deep Earth Sampling) 1991–98, European Science Foundation Man. Cttee for the Ocean Drilling Programme (EMCO), Havarikommission for Nordsøen, Bd of Dansk Ekspeditionsfond (Galathea 3); Ed.-in-Chief Palaeogeography, Palaeoclimatology, Palaeoecology; mem. Editorial Bd Norwegian Journal of Geology; Head of FNU-sponsored Cretaceous Research Centre, SedBas PhD School (Geology of Sedimentary Basins); Co-convenor of six int. congresses and symposia; mem. scientific evaluation cttees in Norway, Sweden, France, Portugal, UK, USA; reviewer for the research councils in Norway, Sweden, Finland, Portugal, UK, USA, Canada, the Netherlands; reviewer for numerous scientific journals; participant or leader of more than 20 expeditions to East and North Greenland; participant in the Galathea 3 expedition as a scientist on one leg and as cruise leader on two legs; field work in Denmark, Faroe Islands, Norway, Sweden, Germany, Poland, France, UK, Ireland, Switzerland, Croatia, Italy, Spain, Portugal, Greece, Tunisia, Australia, USA, Canada; mem. Royal Danish Acad. of Arts and Letters 1986; Hon. Fellow, Geological Soc. of London 1991; Kt of the Dannebrog 2001, (First Degree) 2012; Gold Medal, Univ. of Copenhagen 1969, Recipient First Jubilee Prize, Danish Nat. Oil and Gas Co., Danmarks Geologipris 2003. *Television:* Magasin-program 2008. *Publications:* about 200 papers, particularly on the geology of Greenland. *Leisure interests:* jazz, bass-playing, outdoor life. *Address:* Department of Geography and Geology, University of Copenhagen, Øster Voldgade 10, 1350 Copenhagen K (office); Islandsvej 11, 2800 Lyngby, Denmark (home). *Telephone:* 35-32-24-53 (office); 21-65-35-25 (home). *E-mail:* finns@geol.ku.dk (office). *Website:* geo.ku.dk (office).

SURMA, John P., Jr, BS; American steel industry executive; *Chairman and CEO, United States Steel Corporation;* b. 25 May 1954, Pittsburgh, Pa; ed Pennsylvania State Univ.; joined Price Waterhouse LLP 1976–81, Man. 1981–85, Sr Man. 1985–87, Partner 1987–97; Exec. Staff Asst to Vice-Chair. Fed. Reserve Bd (as part of Pres.'s Exec. Exchange Program) 1983; Sr Vice-Pres. Finance and Accounting, Marathon Oil Co. 1997, Pres. Speedway SuperAmerica LLC

1998–2000, Sr Vice-Pres. Supply and Transportation, Marathon Ashland Petroleum LLC 2000, Pres. 2001; Vice-Chair. and Chief Financial Officer, United States Steel Corpn 2002–03, Pres. and COO 2003–04, Pres. and CEO 2004–06, Chair. and CEO 2006–; Chair. International Iron and Steel Inst. 2006–07, Vice-Chair. 2007–; mem. Bd of Dirs American Iron and Steel Inst. (fmr Chair. and Vice-Chair.), Bank of New York, Mellon Corpn, Calgon Carbon Corpn, Nat. Asscn of Mfrs, International Iron and Steel Inst., Allegheny Conf. on Community Devt (also mem. Exec. Cttee), Nat. Petroleum Council; Chair. Allegheny County (Pa) Parks Foundation; mem. Bd of Visitors, Univ. of Pittsburgh Katz Grad. School of Business; mem. Bd of Trustees, Pennylvania State Univ. (also mem. Smeal Coll. of Business's Bd of Visitors); mem. American Inst. of CPAs; Hon. mem. Nat. Soc. of Black Engineers 2006; Elbert Gary Medal, American Iron and Steel Inst. 2006. *Address:* United States Steel Corpn, 600 Grant Street, Pittsburgh, PA 15219-2800, USA (office). *Telephone:* (412) 433-1121 (office). *Fax:* (412) 433-5733 (office). *E-mail:* info@ussteel.com (office). *Website:* www.ussteel.com (office).

SURTEES, John, OBE; British fmr racing motorcyclist and driver; b. 11 Feb. 1934, Tatsfield, Surrey, England; s. of John Norman Surtees and Dorothy Cynthia Calla Surtees; m. Jane Sparrow 1987; one s. (died 2009) two d.; ed Ashburton Secondary School, London; only man to win both world motorcycling and world motor racing championships; began motorcycle road racing 1950, 350cc World Champion 1958, 1959 and 1960, 500cc World Champion 1956, 1958, 1959 and 1960; began car racing 1960, World Champion 1964, runner-up 1966, CanAm Champion 1966; Grand Prix wins (motorcycling): won 32 World Championship motor cycle Grand Prix and six Isle of Man TT races; (motor racing): 1963 German (Ferrari), 1964 German (Ferrari), 1964 Italian (Ferrari), 1966 Belgian (Ferrari), 1966 Mexican (Cooper-Maserati), 1967 Italian (Honda); racing car constructor and team owner (F5000, F2 and F1); closed down racing operation Team Surtees 1978; Founder-mem. Constructers' Asscn; drives for Mercedes Benz and Honda in historic demonstration events; motor sport consultant, journalist and property developer, Man. Dir John Surtees Ltd 1979–; Vice-Pres. British Racing Drivers' Club; mem. Worshipful Co. of Carmen. *Publications:* Speed 1963, John Surtees – World Champion 1991. *Leisure interests:* restoration of period property, Grand Prix motor cycles and cars, antiques, food and wine. *Address:* John Surtees Ltd, Monza House, Fircroft Way, Edenbridge, Kent, TN8 6EJ, England (office). *Telephone:* (1732) 865496 (office). *Fax:* (1732) 866945 (office). *E-mail:* johnsurtees@johnsurtees.com (office). *Website:* www.johnsurtees.com (office).

SURTY, Mohamed Enver, BA, LLM; South African lawyer and politician; *Deputy Minister of Basic Education;* b. 15 Aug. 1953; m.; ed Univ. of Durban-Westville, Univ. of South Africa, Univ. of Western Cape; cand. attorney, Johannesburg 1975, gen. practitioner and human rights lawyer 1977–94; Prov. and Programming Whip for NW Prov. 1994–99; mem. Senate, then Nat. Council of Provs 1994–2004, Chief Whip 1999–2004; mem. Man. Cttee, Constitutional Ass., negotiator for African Nat. Congress (ANC) on the Bill of Rights 1994–96, observer mem. ANC Nat. Exec. Council 1999–2007; Deputy Minister of Educ. 2003–04; Minister of Justice and Constitutional Devt 2008–09; Deputy Minister of Basic Educ. 2009–. *Leisure interests:* soccer, cricket, squash reading. *Address:* Ministry of Basic Education, Sol Plaatje House, 123 Schoeman Street, Private Bag X603, Pretoria 0002, South Africa (office). *Telephone:* (12) 3125501 (office). *Fax:* (12) 3235989 (office). *Website:* www.education.gov.za (office).

SURUMA, Ezra, PhD, MA, BSc; Ugandan economist; *Senior Adviser to President of Uganda on Finance and Economic Planning;* b. 11 Nov. 1945; s. of Sulimani Balirenwa and Esiteri; m. Specioza Suruma; four s.; ed Fordham Univ., Univ. of Conn.; previous positions include Dir of Econ. Affairs, Movement Sec., Chair. and Man. Dir, Uganda Commercial Bank, Deputy Gov. and Dir of Research, Bank of Uganda; Minister of Finance, Planning and Econ. Devt 2005–09; Sr Adviser to Pres. of Uganda on Finance and Economic Planning 2009–; Visiting Fellow, Brookings Inst., Washington, DC 2010. *Address:* c/o Ministry of Finance, Planning and Economic Development, Appollo Kaggwa Road, Plot 2/4, POB 8147, Kampala, Uganda (office).

SURUR, Ahmad Fathi, BSc, MA, LLM, PhD; Egyptian politician and academic; *Speaker, Majlis Ash-sha'ab (People's Assembly);* b. 9 July 1932, Kena; s. of Mostafa Kamel Surur and Fatma Ali Hassan; m. Zeinab El-Housseiny; one s. two d.; ed Cairo Univ., Univ. of Mich; Deputy Attorney Gen. 1953–59; Prof. of Criminal Law, Cairo Univ. 1959–, Head of Dept 1978–83, Dean of Faculty of Law 1983–85, Vice-Rector Cairo Univ. 1985–86; Chair. Supreme Council of Univs 1986–90; Cultural Attaché, Embassy in Switzerland 1964, Cultural Counsellor, Embassy in France 1965–67; Minister of Educ. 1986–90; Mem. Majlis Ash-sha'ab (People's Ass.) 1987–, Speaker 1990–; mem. Political Bureau Nat. Democratic Party 1990–; Pres. Union of African Parls 1990–91; Pres. Inter-parl. Union 1994–97; Pres. Arab Parl. Union 1998–2000; Pres. Union of Islamic Parls. 2000–; Chair. Egyptian Soc. for Criminal Law 1989–, Egyptian Soc. of Francophone affiliated Jurists 1992–, Int. Inst. for Law in the totally or partially Francophone countries, Paris 1994–, Conf. of Euro-Mediterranean Speakers, Alexandria 2000–; Vice Chair. Int. Soc. for Criminal Law, Paris 1989–; Hon. Chair. Inst. for Higher Studies in Criminal Science, Sicily 2000–; Dr hc (Constantin Univ., USA) 2001; Sciences and Art Medal 1964, 1983, Highest Homala Decoration of Alawi Throne, Morocco 1987, Ordre de la Pleiade, Assemblée Internationale des Parlementaires des Francophones 1992; Highest Distinction Award in Social Sciences 1993. *Publications:* Theory of Nullity 1959, Offences Against Public Interest 1963, Penal Law (parts I and II) 1980, Criminal Procedures Law 1993, Constitutional Legality and Human Rights 1995, Constitutional Protection of Rights and Liberties 2000, Criminal Constitutional Law 2001. *Address:* 11583 Maglis Al-Shaab, Cairo, Egypt (office). *Telephone:* (2) 7943130 (office). *Fax:* (2) 7943116 (office). *E-mail:* parli@idsc.gov.eg (office). *Website:* www.parliament.gov.eg.

SUSCHITZKY, Wolfgang; British (b. Austrian) cameraman and photographer (retd); b. 29 Aug. 1912, Vienna, Austria; s. of Wilhelm Suschitzky and Mrs Suschitzky (née Bauer); m. three times; two s. one d.; ed Graphische Lehr- und Versuchsanstalt Vienna; started in documentary films with Paul Rotha 1937; first feature film No Resting Place 1950; freelance cameraman, exhbns London 1982, 1988, 1989, 1995, 1997, 2000, 2001, 2007, Edin. 2002, Amsterdam 1982, 2006, Vienna 1999, 2006; mem. British Soc. of Cinematographers, BAFTA, Royal Zoological Soc.; Hon. mem. Asscn of Cinematograph, Television and Allied Technicians, Royal Photographic Soc., British Soc. of Cinematographers; City of

Vienna Gold Medal, The Amateur Photographer's Award for Exceptional Achievement in Photography 2008, Gold Medal of Merit for Lifetime Achievement (Austria) 2008, BAFTA Special Award for Creative Contrib. 2012. *Films as cameraman include:* The Small World of Sammy Lee 1962, Ulysses 1966, Entertaining Mr Sloan 1969, Get Carter 1970, Staying On 1980; numerous documentaries and commercials. *Publications:* Photographing Animals 1941, Photographing Children 1942, Kingdom of the Beasts (with Julian Huxley) 1956, Charing Cross Road in the Thirties 1980, Photos 2006, Wolf Suschitzky Photos 2006, Wolf Suschitzky Films 2010. *Leisure interests:* photography, film, music, literature, travel. *Address:* Flat 11, Douglas House, 6 Maida Avenue, London, W2 1TG, England (home). *Telephone:* (20) 7723-6269 (home).

SUSMAN, Louis B., BA, LLB; American lawyer, diplomatist and investment banking executive; *Chairman, DJE Holdings;* b. 19 Nov. 1938, Chicago, Ill.; m. Marjorie Sachs; two c.; ed Univ. of Michigan, Washington Univ., St Louis; practised law in St Louis, Mo. for 27 years, Sr Partner, Thompson & Mitchell law firm 1981–89; served in leadership positions with Salomon Brothers 1989–98; Chair. N American Customer Cttee, Citibank and Citigroup Inc. 1998–2000, Vice-Chair. Citigroup Global Markets, Chicago 2000–09 (retd); Amb. to UK 2009–13; Chair. DJE Holdings 2013–; Special Adviser, BDT Capital Partners 2013–, Henry Crown & Co. 2013–; mem. Democratic Nat. Cttee 1972–82; Nat. Finance Chair. John Kerry for Pres. 2003–04; Co-Chair. Finance Cttee Bill Bradley for Pres. 1999–2000; Finance Chair. (Mo.) Dick Gephardt for Pres. 1998; mem. Bd of Dirs and Man. Cttee St Louis Cardinals professional baseball team 1975–89; mem. Chair.'s Circle of the Chicago Council on Global Affairs; mem. Bd Art Inst. of Chicago, Northwestern Children's Memorial Hosp.; mem. US Advisory Comm. on Public Diplomacy 1988; fmr Dir Center for Nat. Policy, Washington, DC. *Address:* DJE Holdings/Edelman, 200 East Randolph Street, 63rd Floor, Chicago, IL 60601, USA (office). *Website:* www.edelman.com (office).

SUŠNIK, Janez; Slovenian transport industry executive and government official; *President, Adria Kombi;* b. 18 Sept. 1942, Golnik; m.; two c.; ed Tech. Coll., Ljubljana; Pres. Admin. Bd Alpe Tour (forwarding agency) –2001; Asst Man. Viator–Vektor (forwarding agency) 2002; Pres. Nat. Council of Slovenia 2002–08; Pres. Adria Kombi (intermodal transport co.), Ljubljana 2008–; mem. Exec. Cttee Chamber of Commerce and Industry of Slovenia (CCIS), Transport Section 1995–2003, Exec. Cttee Regional Chamber for Gorenska Region at CCIS 1995–2003; apptd Chair. Supervisory Bd Adtla Kaubl (nat. authority for combining traffic) 1990, Supervisory Bd Automehaniza (road enterprise) 1998–2002; First Prize, Dance Contest, Bled 1959, Silver Plaquette of Community Kranw 1982, Praise of the Fed. Traffic Ministry of Yugoslavia 1984, Acknowledgement of the Presidency of the Yugoslav Repub. Traffic Agency 1988. *Leisure interests:* cycling, skiing, swimming, mountaineering, reading. *Address:* Adria Kombi, Tivolska 50, 1000 Ljubljana, Slovenia (office). *Telephone:* (1) 2345280 (office). *Fax:* (1) 2345290 (office). *E-mail:* infor@adriakombi.si (office). *Website:* www.adriakombi.si (office).

SUSSANGKARN, Chalongphob, BA, PhD; Thai economist and government official; b. 16 April 1950; ed Univ. of Cambridge, UK; Lecturer in Econs, Univ. of Calif., Berkeley, USA 1977–79; Economist, World Bank 1979–85; Research Fellow, Macroeconomic Policy Program, Thailand Devt Research Inst. 1985–86, Dir Human Resources and Social Devt Program 1987–95, Pres. 1996–2007, Researcher 2008–; Minister of Finance 2007–08; mem. Bd Econ. Soc. of Thailand, Exec. Cttee Global Devt Network –2005, Exec. Cttee Nat. Centre for Genetic Eng and Biotechnology; Law Devt Cttee, Office of the Council of State; mem. Advisory Bd Asia-Pacific Development Journal, ASEAN Economic Bulletin, Asian Development Review, Asian Economic Policy Review; apptd Regional Co-ordinator, East Asian Devt Network 2004; Nat. Outstanding Researcher Award, Nat. Research Council of Thailand 2004. *Publications:* numerous research papers and contribs to professional journals. *Address:* Thailand Development Research Institute, 565 Ramkhamaeng 39 (Thepleela) Wangthonglang, Bangkok, 10310, Thailand.

SUSSKIND, Leonard, BS, PhD; American physicist and academic; *Felix Bloch Professor of Physics, Stanford University;* b. 1940, South Bronx, New York City; m. 1st 1960; four c.; m. 2nd; ed City Coll. of New York, Cornell Univ., Ithaca, NY; began working as a plumber aged 16; NSF Post-doctoral Fellow, Cornell Univ. 1965–66; Asst Prof. of Physics, Belfer Grad. School of Science, Yeshiva Univ., New York City 1966–68, Assoc. Prof. of Physics 1968–70, Prof. of Physics 1970–79; Prof. of Physics, Univ. of Tel-Aviv, Israel 1971–72; Prof. of Physics, Stanford Univ., Calif. 1979–, Felix Bloch Prof. of Physics 2000–; Assoc. Faculty mem. Perimeter Inst. for Theoretical Physics, Waterloo, Ont., Canada 2007; Distinguished Prof., Korea Inst. for Advanced Study; mem. NAS, American Acad. of Arts and Sciences; Pregel Award, New York Acad. of Science 1975, Loeb Lecturer, Harvard Univ. 1976, J.J. Sakurai Prize in Theoretical Particle Physics 1997. *Achievements include:* widely regarded as one of the fathers of string theory for his early contributions to the String Theory model of particle physics; one of at least three physicists who independently discovered, during or around 1970, that Veneziano dual resonance model of strong interactions could be described by a quantum mechanical model of strings. *Publications:* The Cosmic Landscape: String Theory and the Illusion of Intelligent Design 2005, The Black Hole War 2008; numerous scientific papers in professional journals on models of internal structure of hadrons, gauge theories, quark confinement, symmetry breaking, instantons, quantum statistical mechanics, baryon production in the universe, model for fermion masses, gravity in lower dimensions and quantum cosmology. *Address:* Room 332, Varian Physics Building, 382 Via Pueblo Mall, Stanford, CA 94305-4060, USA (office). *Fax:* (650) 723-2686 (office). *E-mail:* susskind@stanford.edu (office). *Website:* www.stanford.edu/dept/physics (office).

SÜSSMUTH, Rita, DPhil; German politician; *President, German Adult Education Association;* b. (Rita Kicknuth), 17 Feb. 1937, Wuppertal; m. Prof. Hans Süssmuth; one d.; ed Univs of Münster, Tübingen and Paris; academic career includes Prof., Int. Comparative Educ. Science, Univ. Bochum 1969; Prof. of Educ., Univ. of Dortmund 1971; Dir Research Inst. Frau und Gesellschaft (Woman and Soc.), Hanover 1982–85; mem. Scientific Advisory Cttee on Family Affairs, Fed. Ministry for Youth, Family Affairs and Health 1971–85; mem. 3rd Comm. on Family Affairs; Head of 7th Comm. on Youth; Fed. Minister for Family Affairs, Youth and Health 1985–88; Fed. Minister for Youth, Family Affairs, Women and Health 1986–88; Pres. German Fed. Parl.; mem. Bundestag representing

Göttingen 1987–2002; mem. CDU Bd 1987–98; Fed. Chair. Women's Union of CDU 1986–2001; Pres. European Movt Germany; apptd Vice-Pres. German Asscn of Adult Educ. Centres 1997 (now German Adult Educ. Asscn), currently Pres.; mem. Advisory Council, Bertelsmann Stiftung 1997–; Vice Pres. Parl. Asscn of OSCE 2000–2003; Chair. Ind. Comm. on Migration to Germany 2000–01; Chair. Ind. Council of Experts on Immigration and Integration 2002–; Hon. Prof., Univ. of Göttingen 2003–; Steering Cttee on Intercultural Conflict and Societal Integration, Social Science Research Centre, Berlin 2004; mem. Advisory Bd German Foundation for World Population; Dr hc (Hildesheim) 1988, (Bochum) 1990, (Veliko Tärnovo, Czech Repub.) 1994, (Timişoara, Romania) 1995, (Sorbonne Nouvelle) 1996, (Johns Hopkins) 1998, (Ben Gurion, Israel) 1998; Magnus Hirschfeld Medal 2006. *Publications include:* Frauen: Der Resignation keine Chance 1985, Aids: Wege aus der Angst 1987, Kämpfen und Bewegen: Frauenreden 1989, Wenn der Zeit der Rhythmus ändert 1991, Die planlosen Eliten (jtly) 1993, Wer nicht kämpft, hat schon verloren 2000, Mut zur Macht in Frauenhand. *Leisure interest:* tennis. *Address:* German Adult Education Association, Obere Wilhelmstraße 32, 53225 Bonn, Germany (office). *Telephone:* (228) 97569 (office). *Fax:* (228) 97555 (office). *E-mail:* info@dvv-international.de (office). *Website:* www.rita-suessmuth.de (office).

ŠUŠTERŠIČ, Janez, PhD; Slovenian economist, academic and politician; *Vice-President, Civic List;* b. 29 Dec. 1966, Ljubljana; ed Univ. of Ljubljana, Univ. of Zurich, Switzerland; Dir Office for Macroeconomic Analyses and Devt 2001–07; Founding mem. Slovenian Econ. Forum 2003; Vice-Pres. Econ. Policy Cttee, EU Council (Ecofin) 2005–07; Prof., Faculty of Man., Univ. of Primorska and School of Advanced Social Studies, Nova Gorica; Assoc. Prof. of Econs, Faculty of Man., Univ. of Primorska, Koper; fmr Visiting Lecturer, Int. School of Business and Social Studies, Celje; Vice-Chair. Econ. Policy Cttee, ECOFIN 2005–07; fmr Vice-Chair. Govt's Reforms Cttee; Nat. Lisbon Strategy Co-ordinator; mem. Gregor Virant's Civic List (renamed Civic List April 2012) Vice-Pres. 2011–; Minister of Finance 2012–13. *Address:* Civic List (Državljanska lista), 1000 Ljubljana, Ukmarjeva ulica 2, Slovenia (office). *Telephone:* (51) 352467 (office). *E-mail:* info@d-l.si (office). *Website:* www.d-l.si (office).

SUTALINOV, Murat; Kyrgyzstani politician; b. 24 April 1963, Frunze; ed Higher School of USSR Ministry of Internal Affairs; held numerous positions in USSR Ministry of Internal Affairs in Kyrgyzstan; Deputy Head of Internal Affairs Dept, Bishkek 2000–01; Head of Internal Affairs Dept in Chuy Region 2001–02; Chief Criminal Investigation and Head of Dept of Ministry of Internal Affairs 2002–03; Head of Internal Affairs Dept in Osh Region 2003–04; Head of Defence and Security, Dept of Presidential Admin. 2004–05; Attorney-Gen. March–May 2005; Minister of Internal Affairs May 2005–06 (resgnd); Chair. State Cttee for Nat. Security 2006–10. *Address:* c/o Ministry of Internal Affairs, 720040 Bishkek, ul. Frunze 469, Kyrgyzstan (office).

ŠUTANOVAC, Dragan; Serbian politician; b. 24 July 1968, Belgrade; m. Marija Šutanovac; two s.; ed Faculty of Mechanical Eng, Univ. of Belgrade, Marshall Centre for Security Studies, Germany; mem. European Parl. April–May 2000; Deputy, Belgrade City Ass. 2000–; Special Adviser, Ministry of Internal Affairs 2000–01; mem. Nat. Ass. (Parl.) 2000–, Pres. Parl. Cttee for Defence and Security 2002–03; Deputy Minister of the Interior 2001–06; Minister of Defence 2007–12; Vice-Pres. Democratic Party (Demokratska Stranka). *Address:* c/o Ministry of Defence, 11000 Belgrade, Bírčaninova 5, Serbia.

SUTANTO, Harjo; Indonesian business executive (retd); b. 1926; m.; four c.; co-f. Wings Group (consumer products co.), Surabaya 1948, now retd; fmrly controlled PT Bank Ekonomi. *Address:* c/o Wings Group, Kawasan Perluasan Utara, PT JIEP, Jalan Tipar Cakung Kav F 5-7, Jakarta 13910, Indonesia (office). *Telephone:* (21) 4602696 (office). *Fax:* (21) 4603494, (office). *Website:* www.wingscorp.com (office).

SUTCLIFFE, James H.; British business executive; *Chairman, Sun Life Financial Inc.;* Sr Exec. with Prudential plc –2000; joined Old Mutual plc 2000, Group CEO –2008; Ind. mem. Bd of Dirs Sun Life Financial Inc. 2009–, Chair. 2011–, Chair. Risk Review Cttee; Dir, Lonmin plc and of several public cos; Chair. UK Bd for Actuarial Standards; Dir, UK Financial Reporting Council; Trustee, Buffelshoek Trust, The Nelson Mandela Legacy Trust (UK) 2005–08; Fellow, UK Inst., Faculty of Actuaries. *Address:* Sun Life Financial Inc., 150 King Street West, Toronto, ON M5H 1J9, Canada (office). *Telephone:* (416) 979-9966 (office). *Fax:* (416) 597-9108 (office). *E-mail:* boarddirectors@sunlife.com (office). *Website:* www .sunlife.com (office).

SUTHERLAND, Donald McNichol, OC; Canadian actor; b. 17 July 1935, St John, NB; s. of Frederick McLae Sutherland and Dorothy Isabel Sutherland (née McNichol); m. 1st Lois May Hardwick 1959; m. 2nd Shirley Jean Douglas 1966 (divorced); one s. Kiefer Sutherland (q.v.) one d.; m. 3rd Francine Racette 1971; three s.; ed Bridgewater High School, NS, Univ. of Toronto; appeared on TV (BBC and ITV) in Hamlet, Man in a Suitcase, The Saint, Gideon's Way, The Avengers, Flight into Danger, Rose Tattoo, March to the Sea, Lee Harvey Oswald, Court Martial, Death of Bessie Smith, Max Dugan Returns, Crackers, Louis Malle, The Disappearance; Pres. McNichol Pictures Inc.; Officier, Ordre des Arts et des Lettres; Hon. PhD. *Plays:* Lolita (Broadway) 1981, Enigmatic Variations 2000. *Films include:* The World Ten Times Over 1963, Castle of the Living Dead 1964, Dr Terror's House of Horrors 1965, Fanatic 1965, The Bedford Incident 1965, Promise Her Anything 1966, The Dirty Dozen 1967, Billion Dollar Brain 1967, Oedipus Rex 1968, Interlude 1968, Joanna 1968, The Split 1968, Start the Revolution Without Me 1969, Act of the Heart 1970, M*A*S*H* 1970, Kelly's Heroes 1970, Little Murders 1970, Alex in Wonderland 1971, Klute 1971, Johnny Got His Gun (as Christ) 1971, Steelyard Blues 1972, Lady Ice 1972, Alien Thunder 1973, Don't Look Now 1973, S*P*Y*S* 1974, The Day of the Locust 1975, 1900 1976, Casanova (Fellini) 1976, The Eagle Has Landed 1977, The Great Train Robbery 1978, Blood Relatives 1978, Bear Island 1979, Ordinary People 1980, Lolita 1981, Eye of the Needle 1981, Threshold 1982, Winter of Our Discontent, Ordeal by Innocence 1984, Revolution 1985, Gauguin 1986, The Wolf at the Door 1987, A Dry White Season 1988, Bethune: The Making of a Hero 1989, Lock Up 1989, Apprentice to Murder 1989, Lost Angels 1989, The Railway Station-man 1991, Scream from Stone 1991, Faithful 1991, JFK 1991, Backdraft, Agaguk, Buffy the Vampire Slayer, Shadow of the Wolf 1993, Benefit of the Doubt, Younger and Younger 1993,

Six Degrees of Separation 1993, The Puppet Masters, Disclosure, Outbreak, Hollow Point, The Shadow Conspiracy, A Time to Kill, Virus 1999, Instinct 1999, Toscano 1999, The Art of War 2000, Panic 2000, Space Cowboys 2000, Uprising 2001, The Big Herst 2001, Final Fantasy: The Spirits Within 2001, Big Shot's Funeral 2001, Five Moons Plaza 2003, Italian Job 2003, Baltic Storm 2003, Cold Mountain 2003, Aurora Borealis 2005, Fierce People 2005, Pride and Prejudice 2005, Land of the Blind 2005, An American Haunting 2005, Ask the Dust 2006, Sleepwalkers 2007, Reign Over Me 2007, Puffball 2007, Fool's Gold 2008, Astro Boy (voice) 2009, The Con Artist 2010, The Mechanic 2011, The Hunger Games 2012, Sofia 2012, Dawn Rider 2012, The Best Offer 2013, Jappeloup 2013, The Hunger Games: Catching Fire 2013. *Television includes:* Hamlet, Man in a Suitcase, The Saint, Gideon's Way, The Avengers, Flight into Danger, Rose Tattoo, March to the Sea, Lee Harvey Oswald, Court Martial, Death of Bessie Smith, Max Dugan Returns, Crackers, Louis Malle, The Disappearance, The Path To War (Golden Globe for Best Supporting Actor in a TV series or TV movie 2003) 2002, Salem's Lot 2004, Human Trafficking 2005, Commander in Chief (series) 2005–06, Land of the Blind 2006, Dirty Sexy Money 2007–09, The Pillars of the Earth (mini-series) 2010, Crossing Lines (series) 2013. *Leisure interests:* sailing, baseball, Montreal. *Address:* c/o Katherine Olin, Creative Artists Agency, 2000 Avenue of the Stars, Los Angeles, CA 90067, USA. *Telephone:* (424) 288-2000. *Fax:* (424) 288-2900. *Website:* www.caa.com.

SUTHERLAND, Grant Robert, AC, PhD, DSc, FRS, FAA; Australian geneticist and academic; *Geneticist Emeritus, Women's and Children's Hospital, Adelaide;* b. 2 June 1945, Bairnsdale, Vic.; s. of John Sutherland and Hazel Wilson Mason McClelland; m. Elizabeth Dougan 1979; one s. one d.; ed Numurkah High School, Univ. of Melbourne and Univ. of Edinburgh, UK; Dir Dept of Cytogenetics and Molecular Genetics, Women's and Children's Hosp., Adelaide 1975–2002, Foundation Research Fellow 2002–07, Geneticist Emer. 2007–; Affiliate Prof., Dept of Paediatrics, Univ. of Adelaide 1991–, School of Molecular and Biomedical Science 1996–2001, 2006–; Int. Research Scholar, Howard Hughes Medical Inst., Bethesda, Md, USA 1993–97; Pres. Human Genetics Soc. of Australasia 1989–91, Human Genome Org. 1996–97; Co-founder and Co.-Chair., Scientific Advisory Bd of Bionomics Ltd; mem. Bd of Dirs Thesan PLC, Beef CRC Ltd; Hon. Fellow, Royal Coll. of Pathologists of Australasia 1994; Hon. mem. European Cytogenetics Asscn 2005; Hon. MD (Adelaide) 2013; co-recipient Australia Prize in Molecular Genetics 1998, Nat. Australia Day Council Australian Achiever Award 2001, Ramaciotti Medal for Excellence in Biomedical Research 2001, Thompson ISI Australian Citation Laureate 2004, Major Lecture, Annual Scientific Meeting of the Human Genetics Soc. of Australasia (named the Grant Sutherland Lecture 2005–) 2005. *Publications include:* two books and more than 480 papers in medical and scientific journals on human genetics. *Leisure interest:* gardening, reading. *Address:* Women's and Children's Hospital, Adelaide, SA 5006 (office); PO Box 1635, Victor Harbor, SA 5211, Australia (home). *Telephone:* (8) 7516-3121 (home). *E-mail:* grant.sutherland@adelaide.edu.au (office). *Website:* www.adelaide.edu.au/mbs (office); www.wch.sa.gov.au (office).

SUTHERLAND, Ivan Edward, BSc, MSc, PhD; American electrical engineer, computer scientist and academic; *Senior Researcher, Asynchronous Research Center, Portland State University;* b. 16 May 1938, Hastings, Neb.; m. Marly Roncken 2006; one s. one d.; ed Scarsdale High School, NY, Carnegie Inst. of Tech. (now Carnegie Mellon Univ.), California Inst. of Tech., Massachusetts Inst. of Tech.; commissioned as First Lt in US Army, served as electrical engineer at Nat. Security Agency 1963–64, then as researcher at Defense Advanced Research Projects Agency 1964–65; Assoc. Prof. of Electrical Eng. Harvard Univ. 1965–68; Prof. of Computer Science, Univ. of Utah 1968–74; Fletcher Jones Prof. of Computer Science, California Inst. of Tech. 1974–81; Visiting Scholar, Computer Science Div., Univ. of California, Berkeley 2005–08; Visiting Scientist, Asynchronous Research Center, Portland State Univ. 2008–; co-f. (with David C. Evans) Evans & Sutherland, Salt Lake City, Utah 1968, Vice-Pres. and Chief Scientist; also worked as consultant for RAND Corpn 1976–80; co-f. Sutherland, Sproull & Assoc. 1980 (acquired by Sun Microsystems, Inc. and formed core of Sun Microsystems Labs 1990), Vice-Pres. and Tech. Dir, Fellow 2001; mem. Nat. Acad. of Eng 1972, NAS 1978; Fellow, Asscn for Computing Machinery (ACM) 1994, Computer History Museum 2005; first Zworykin Award, Nat. Acad. of Eng 1972, IEEE Emanuel R. Piore Award 1986, Leadership Award, Computerworld Honors Program 1987, A.M. Turing Award 1988, ACM Software System Award 1993, EFF Pioneer Award, Electronic Frontier Foundation 1994, Certificate of Merit, The Franklin Inst. 1996, Smithsonian Computer World Award 1996, IEEE John von Neumann Medal 1998, R&D 100 Award (team) 2004, Kyoto Prize in Advanced Tech. (co-recipient) 2012. *Publications:* SketchPad (software); more than 60 patents. *Address:* Asynchronous Research Center, Maseeh College of Engineering and Computer Science, Portland State University, PO Box 751, 1900 SW Fourth Avenue, Suite 105, Portland, OR 97201, USA (office). *E-mail:* marly .roncken@gmail.com (office). *Website:* www.pdx.edu (office).

SUTHERLAND, John Andrew, PhD, FRSL; British academic and writer; *Emeritus Lord Northcliffe Professor of Modern English Literature, University College London;* b. 9 Oct. 1938; s. of Jack Sutherland and Elizabeth Sutherland (née Salter); m. Guilland Watt 1967; one s.; ed Colchester Royal Grammar School, Univs of Leicester and Edinburgh; nat. service, 2nd Lt, Suffolk Regt 1958–60; Lecturer in English, Univ. of Edin. 1965–72; Lecturer in English, Univ. Coll. London 1972–84, Lord Northcliffe Prof. of Modern English Literature 1992–2004, Prof. Emer. 2004–; columnist, The Guardian; Hon. DLitt (Leicester) 1998. *Publications include:* Thackeray at Work 1974, Victorian Novelists and Publishers 1976, Fiction and the Fiction Industry 1978, Bestsellers 1980, Offensive Literature 1982, The Longman Companion to Victorian Fiction 1989, Mrs Humphry Ward 1992, The Life of Walter Scott: A Critical Biography 1995, Victorian Fiction: Writers, Publishers, Readers 1995, Is Heathcliffe a Murderer? 1996, Can Jane Eyre be Happy? 1997, Where Was Rebecca Shot? 1998, Who Betrays Elizabeth Bennet? 1999, Henry V, War Criminal ? 1999, Last Drink to LA 2000, The Literary Detective 2000, Literary Lives 2001, Reading the Decades 2002, Stephen Spender: The Authorised Biography 2004, How to Read a Novel: A User's Guide 2006, Bestsellers: A Very Short Introduction 2007, Curiosities of Literature 2008, Magic Moments 2008, Love, Sex, Death and Words (with Stephen Fender) 2010, Lives of the Novelists: A History of Fiction in 294 Lives 2012. *Leisure interest:* walking.

Address: c/o Department of English, University College London, Gower Street, London, WC1E 6BT, England.

SUTHERLAND, Kiefer; American actor; b. 21 Dec. 1966, London, England; s. of Donald Sutherland (q.v.) and Shirley Douglas; m. 1st Camelia Kath 1987 (divorced 1990); two d.; m. 2nd Kelly Winn 1996 (divorced 2008); two step-s.; debut with LA Odyssey Theatre in Throne of Straw aged 9. *Films include:* Max Dugan Returns 1983, The Bay Boy 1984, At Close Range 1986, Crazy Moon 1986, Stand By Me 1986, The Lost Boys 1987, The Killing Time 1987, Promised Land 1987, Bright Lights, Big City 1988, Young Guns 1988, Renegades 1989, Chicago Joe and the Showgirl 1990, Flashback 1990, Flatliners 1990, The Nutcracker Prince (voice) 1990, Young Guns II 1990, Article 99 1991, Twin Peaks: Fire Walk With Me 1992, A Few Good Men 1992, The Vanishing 1993, The Three Musketeers 1993, The Cowboy Way, Teresa's Tattoo, Eye for an Eye, A Time to Kill 1996, Truth or Consequences NM (also Dir) 1997, Dark City 1997, Ground Control 1998, The Breakup 1998, Woman Wanted 1999, The Red Dove 1999, Hearts and Bones 1999, Beat 2000, Picking up the Pieces 2000, The Right Temptation 2000, Cowboy Up 2001, To End All Wars 2001, Desert Saints 2002, Dead Heat 2002, Behind the Red Door 2002, Phone Booth 2002, Paradise Found 2003, Taking Lives 2004, Jiminy Glick in La La Wood 2004, River Queen 2005, The Sentinel 2006, Mirrors 2008, Marmaduke (voice) 2010, The Reluctant Fundamentalist 2012, Pompeii 2014. *Television appearances include:* Amazing Stories, Trapped in Silence, Brotherhood of Justice, Last Light (also Dir) 24 (Golden Globe for Best Actor in a TV Series 2002, Screen Actors Guild Best Actor in a Drama Series Award 2004, 2006) 2001–10, Touch (series) 2012–13, 24: Live Another Day (series) 2014. *Address:* c/o Creative Artists Agency, 2000 Avenue of the Stars, Los Angeles, CA 90607, USA.

SUTHERLAND, Peter Denis, BCL; Irish international civil servant, lawyer, politician, business executive and UN official; *Special Representative of the Secretary-General for Migration, United Nations;* b. 25 April 1946; s. of W. G. Sutherland and Barbara Sutherland; m. Maria del Pilar Cabria Valcarcel 1971; two s. one d.; ed Gonzaga Coll., Univ. Coll. Dublin and King's Inns; called to Irish Bar (King's Inns), English Bar (Middle Temple) and New York Bar; admitted to Bar of the Supreme Court of the United States; practising mem. of Irish Bar 1968–81; Tutor in Law, Univ. Coll., Dublin 1968–71; apptd. Sr Counsel 1980; Attorney-Gen. 1981–82, 1982–84; mem. Strategy Cttee Fine Gael Party 1978–81, Dir Policy Programme, 1981 Gen. Election; mem. Comm. of the European Communities (responsible for Competition and Relations with the European Parl.) 1985–89; Dir-Gen. GATT (later World Trade Org.) 1993–95; Chair. Allied Irish Banks 1989–93; mem. Bd of Dirs British Petroleum Co. PLC (now BP plc), Deputy Chair. 1995–97, Chair. 1997–2009; Chair. (non-exec.) Goldman Sachs International 1995–; Chair. London School of Econs 2008–; Special Rep. of UN Sec.-Gen. for Migration 2006–; mem. advisory group to José Manuel Barroso, Pres. of EC, on energy and climate change issues 2007–; Chair. Trilateral Comm. (Europe); Vice-Chair. European Roundtable of Industrialists; Pres., Federal Trust; mem. Foundation Bd, World Econ. Forum; mem. Advisory Council, European Policy Center; Consultor, Admin of the Patrimony of the Holy See; Goodwill Amb. UNIDO; Visiting Fellow, Kennedy School of Govt, Harvard Univ. 1989; Visiting Prof., Univ. Coll. Dublin; mem. Royal Irish Acad.; Hon. Bencher, King's Inns Dublin 1995, Hon. Fellow, London Business School 1997, Oxford Univ. Inst. of Econs, Bencher, Middle Temple 2002, Hon. KCMG, Kt Commdr of the Order of St Gregory 2008, Hon. Vice-Pres. Law Soc., Univ. Coll. Dublin 2011; Grand Cross of Civil Merit (Spain) 1989, Grand Cross of King Leopold II (Belgium) 1989, Chevalier Légion d'honneur 1993, Commdr du Wissam (Morocco) 1994, Order of Rio Branco (Brazil) 1996, Grand Cross of Order of Infante Dom Henrique (Portugal) 1998, Medal of Merit of Baden-Württemburg (Germany) 2008; Hon. LLD (St Louis, Nat. Univ. of Ireland, Coll. of Holy Cross, Bath Univ., Suffolk Univ., USA, Open Univ., Trinity Coll. (Dublin), Reading, Nottingham, Exeter, Queen's Univ. Belfast, Univ. of Notre Dame, Univ. of Sussex); Hon. DPhil (Dublin City Univ., Koc Univ., Turkey); European Person of the Year 1988, Gold Medal of European Parl. 1988, First European Law Prize Paris 1988, Irish People of the Year Award 1989, Robert Schuman Medal 1989, New Zealand Centenary Medal 1990, Consumer for World Trade Annual Award 1994, Dean's Medal, Wharton School, Univ. of Pennsylvania 1996, David Rockefeller Int. Leadership Award 1998, Lifetime Achievement Award, Ireland Chamber of Commerce 2009. *Publications include:* 1^{er}janvier 1993 – ce qui va changer en Europe 1989; and numerous articles in law journals. *Leisure interests:* reading, sport. *Address:* Goldman Sachs International, Peterborough Court, 133 Fleet Street, London, EC4A 2BB, England (office). *Telephone:* (20) 7774-4141 (office). *Fax:* (20) 7774-4001 (office).

SUTHERLAND, Dame Veronica Evelyn, DBE, MA; British college president and fmr diplomatist; b. 25 April 1939, York, Yorks., England; d. of the late Lt-Col Maurice G. Beckett and of Constance M. Cavenagh-Mainwaring; m. Alex J. Sutherland 1981; ed Royal School, Bath, Univs of London and Southampton; joined diplomatic service 1965, Second Sec., then First Sec. Embassy in Copenhagen 1967–70, Embassy in New Delhi 1975–78; with FCO 1970–75, 1978–80, Counsellor 1981, 1984–87, Asst Under-Sec. of State (Personnel) 1990–95; Perm. Del. to UNESCO 1981–84; Amb. to Côte d'Ivoire 1987–90, to Ireland 1995–99; Deputy Sec.-Gen. of the Commonwealth 1999–2002; Pres. Lucy Cavendish Coll., Cambridge 2001–08; Chair. Airey Neave Trust 2001–11; Hon. LLD (Trinity Coll., Dublin) 1998.

SUTHERLAND OF HOUNDWOOD, Baron (Life Peer), cr. 2001, of Houndwood in the Scottish Borders; **Stewart Ross Sutherland,** Kt, KT, MA, FBA, FRSE; British university vice-chancellor and company director (non-executive); b. 25 Feb. 1941, Scotland; s. of George Sutherland and Ethel Masson; m. Sheena Robertson 1964; one s. two d.; ed Woodside School, Robert Gordon's Coll., Univ. of Aberdeen and Corpus Christi Coll. Cambridge; Asst Lecturer in Philosophy, Univ. Coll. of N Wales 1965; Lecturer in Philosophy, Univ. of Stirling 1968, Sr Lecturer 1972, Reader 1976; Prof. of History and Philosophy of Religion, King's Coll. London 1977–85, Vice-Prin. 1981–85, Prin. 1985–90, Fellow 1983; Vice-Chancellor Univ. of London 1990–94; HM Chief Insp. of Schools 1992–94; Vice-Chancellor and Prin. Univ. of Edin. 1994–2002; non-party political mem. House of Lords 2001–; mem. Council of Science and Tech. 1993–2000; Chair. Royal Comm. on Long-term Care of the Elderly 1997–99, Univ. Grants Cttee (Hong Kong) 1996–2004, House of Lords Select Cttee on Science and Tech.; Liveryman, Goldsmiths Co. 1991, Courts Asst 2002; Chair. YTL Education (UK) 2003–; Provost Gresham Coll. 2003–08;

Hon. Fellow, King's Coll., London 1984, Corpus Christi Coll. Cambridge 1989, Univ. Coll. at Bangor 1991, Inst. of Educ., London 2003, Royal Coll. of Gen. Practitioners 2003, Faculty of Actuaries 2004, Birbeck, London 2004; Hon. LHD (Coll. of Wooster, Ohio) 1986, (Commonwealth Univ. of Va) 1992, (New York Univ.) 1996; Hon. LLD (Aberdeen) 1991, (Nat. Univ. of Ireland) 1992; Hon. DUniv (Stirling) 1993; Hon. DLitt (Richmond Coll.) 1995, (Univ. of Wales) 1996, (Glasgow) 1999, (Warwick) 2001, (St Andrews) 2002, (McGill) 2003, (London) 2004, (Queen Margaret Univ. Coll.) 2004, (Edin.) 2004; Dr hc (Uppsala) 1995. *Publications:* Atheism and the Rejection of God 1977, The Philosophical Frontiers of Christian Theology (ed. with B. L. Hebblethwaite) 1983, God, Jesus and Belief 1984, Faith and Ambiguity 1984, The World's Religions (ed.) 1988, Religion, Reason and the Self (jtly) 1989; articles in books and learned journals. *Leisure interests:* Tassie medallions, theatre, jazz. *Address:* House of Lords, Westminster, London SW1A 0PD, England (office). *Telephone:* (7753) 489643 (mobile). *E-mail:* sutherlands@parliament.uk (office).

SUTJIPTO, Adm. (retd) Widodo Adi; Indonesian government official and fmr naval officer; b. 1 Aug. 1944; fmr Head of Armed Forces; Co-ordinating Minister for Political, Legal and Security Affairs 2004–09. *Address:* c/o Office of the Co-ordinating Minister for Political, Legal and Security Affairs, Jalan Medan Merdeka Barat 15, Jakarta 10110, Indonesia (office).

SUTLEY, Nancy, BA, MA; American government official; *Chair, White House Council on Environmental Quality;* b. 20 April 1962, New York City; ed Cornell Univ., Kennedy School of Govt, Harvard Univ.; fmr Special Asst to Admin. US Environmental Protection Agency (EPA), Washington, DC; Deputy Sec. for Policy and Intergovernmental Relations, Calif. Environmental Protection Agency 1999–2003; Energy Adviser to Calif. Gov. Gray Davis 1999–2003; Deputy Mayor for Energy and Environment, Los Angeles; mem. Calif. State Water Resources Control Bd 2003–05; mem. Bd Metropolitan Water Dist of Southern Calif.; Chair. White House Council on Environmental Quality, Washington, DC 2009–. *Address:* White House Council on Environmental Quality, 722 Jackson Place, NW, Washington, DC 20503, USA (office). *Telephone:* (202) 395-5750 (office). *Fax:* (202) 456-6546 (office). *Website:* www.whitehouse.gov/ceq (office).

SUTRISNO, Gen. (retd) Try; Indonesian army officer (retd) and politician; b. 15 Nov. 1935; s. of Subandi Sutrisno and Mardiyah Sutrisno; m. Tuti Sutiawati; seven c.; early career as mil. engineer; ADC to Pres. 1974–78; Army Chief of Staff 1986–88; Commdr of the Armed Forces 1988–93; Vice-Pres. of Indonesia 1993–97; left Golkar Party to join Justice and Unity Party 1998; mem. Indonesian-Malaysian Eminent Persons Group (est. by govts of Indonesia and Malaysia to advise on jt issues) 2008–. *Address:* c/o Dewan Perwakilan Rakyat, Jalan Gatot Subroto 16, Jakarta, Indonesia.

SUTTER, Joos, Lic. oec. HSG; Swiss business executive; *Chairman of the Executive Committee and CEO, Coop Genossenschaft;* b. 1964; ed Swiss diploma in auditing; Chair. Exec. Cttee and CEO Coop Genossenschaft 2011–, Head of Retail Business Unit, Interim Head of Finance/Services Business Unit; Dir, Coop Vitality AG, Berne, Coop ITS-Travel AG, Wollerau (Chair.), Coopernic SCRL, Brussels, Palink UAB, Lithuania/Palink SIA (Latvia). *Address:* Coop Genossenschaft, Thiersteinerallee 12, Postfach 2550, 4002 Basel, Switzerland (office). *Telephone:* (61) 3366666 (office). *Fax:* (61) 3366040 (office). *E-mail:* info@coop.ch (office). *Website:* www.coop.ch (office).

SUTTON, Cecilia (Cece) Stewart, BA, MBA; American banking executive; *President, US Consumer and Commercial Banking, Citigroup Inc.;* b. 1956, Charlotte, North Carolina; two c.; ed Univ. of South Carolina, Winthrop Univ.; joined First Union Corpn 1978, Br. Man., Raleigh, N Carolina 1984–86, Consumer Banking Man., Greenville, S Carolina 1986–89, Consumer Bank Training Dir Charlotte, N Carolina 1988–89, Area Exec. Rock Hill, S Carolina 1989–92, 1993–95, Head of S Carolina Gen. Banking Group, Greenville 1992–93, Exec. Vice-Pres. 2001; Exec. Vice-Pres. and Head of Retail and Small Business Banking, Wachovia Corpn (following merger with First Union Corpn), Charlotte 2001–08; Pres. Retail Banking Group, Morgan Stanley, New York 2008–10; Pres. US Consumer and Commercial Banking, Citigroup Inc. 2011–; Chair. Consumers Bankers Asscn 2006–; mem. Bd of Dirs United States Cellular Corpn 2013–; ranked by Fortune magazine amongst 50 Most Powerful Women in Business in the US (28th) 2007, (33rd) 2008. *Address:* Citigroup Inc., 399 Park Avenue, New York, NY 10022, USA (office). *Telephone:* (212) 559-1000 (office). *Website:* www.citigroup.com (office).

SUTTON, Philip John, RA; British artist; b. 20 Oct. 1928, Poole, Dorset, England; s. of L. L. Sutton and Anne Sutton; m. Heather Cooke 1954; one s. three d.; ed Slade School of Fine Art and Univ. Coll., London; Lecturer, Slade School of Fine Art, Univ. Coll. 1954–; Artist-in-Residence, Fulham Pottery 1987–; solo exhbns bi-annually at Roland Browse & Delbanco and Browse & Darby 1956–84; Leeds City Art Gallery retrospective 1960; travelled in Australia and Fiji painting landscapes 1963–64; retrospective exhbn, Diploma Gallery, Royal Acad. 1977; toured Israel with 10 British artists 1979; visited Australia 1980; designed Post Office Greeting Stamps 1989; moved to Manorbier, Wales 1989; worked on ceramics with Jean-Paul Landreau in Wales and visited Italy painting watercolours 1990. *Publications:* Philip Sutton RA – His Family & His Friends 1998, Philip Sutton – Life and Art & Work 2008, Philip Sutton – An Artist's View 2009. *Leisure interests:* swimming, running. *Address:* 3 Morfa Terrace, Manorbier, Tenby, Pembrokeshire, SA70 7TH, Wales. *Telephone:* (1834) 871474. *E-mail:* sutton.cooke@dogglemail.com. *Website:* philipsuttonra.com.

SUWAIDI, Sultan bin Nasser as-, BS; United Arab Emirates central banker and business executive; *Governor, Central Bank of the United Arab Emirates;* joined Abu Dhabi Investment Authority 1978, later Deputy Dir –1982; Gen. Man. Abu Dhabi Investment Co. 1982–84; Gen. Man. Gulf International Bank, Bahrain 1984–85; Man. Dir and CEO Abu Dhabi Commercial Bank 1985–91; Gov. Cen. Bank of the UAE 1991–; Central Bank Gov. of the Year Award 2006, ranked by Arabian Business amongst the Power 500: The World's Most Influential Arabs (54th) 2012, (32nd) 2013. *Address:* Central Bank of the United Arab Emirates, PO Box 854, Abu Dhabi, United Arab Emirates (office). *Telephone:* (2) 6652220 (office). *Fax:* (2) 6667494 (office). *E-mail:* admin@cbuae.gov.ae (office). *Website:* www.centralbank.ae (office).

SUWANNATHAT, Air Chief Marshall Sukampol; Thai politician and fmr air force officer; ed Armed Forces Academies Preparatory School; several years' service in Royal Thai Air Force, including fmr F5 jet pilot, fmr Asst Chief of Staff of Royal Thai Air Force, Insp.-Gen., Ministry of Defence –2011; Minister of Transport 2011–12, of Defence 2012–13. *Address:* c/o Ministry of Defence, Thanon Sanam Chai, Bangkok 10200, Thailand.

SUZMAN, Dame Janet, DBE, BA; South African/British actress and director; b. 9 Feb. 1939, Johannesburg, South Africa; d. of Saul Suzman and Betty Sonnenberg; m. Trevor Nunn (q.v.) 1969 (divorced 1986); one s.; ed Kingsmead Coll., Univ. of the Witwatersrand, London Acad. of Music and Dramatic Art; moved to UK 1960; The Spencer Memorial Lecture, Harvard Univ. 1987; The Tanner Lectures, Brasenose Coll., Oxford 1995, The Drapers Lecture, Queen Mary and Westfield Coll., Univ. of London 1996, The Morell Lecture, Univ. of York 1999; Pres. Shakespeare's Birthday Celebrations 2010–11; Pres. Conf. of Drama Schools; Vice-Pres. London Acad. of Music and Dramatic Art; Hon. Assoc. Artist RSC; Hon. Patron the Market Theatre, The Baxter Theatre, Cape Town; Hon. Lecturer in the Shakespeare Inst., Stratford, Univ. of Birmingham; Hon. Fellow, School of Arts Univ. of Liverpool; Queen's Silver Jubilee Medal 1977; Hon. MA (Open Univ.) 1984; Hon. DLit (Warwick) 1990, (Leicester) 1992, (Queen Mary and Westfield Coll.) 1997, (Southampton) 2002, (Middlesex) 2003, (Kingston) 2006, (Cape Town) 2010, (Liverpool John Moore's Univ.) 2011; Best Actress, Evening Standard Drama Award 1973, 1976, Plays and Players Award 1976, Best Production Award, Liverpool Echo 1993, Barclays TMA Award for Best Dir 1997, Best Dir Award, Liverpool Echo 2010, The Pragnell Prize for Services to Shakespeare 2011. *Roles for RSC and West End include:* Lady Anne, La Pucelle, Lady Percy, Luciana, Ophelia, Beatrice, Rosalind 1962–70, Lulu in The Birthday Party 1963–64, Portia, Rosalind (RSC) 1965, Carmen in The Balcony, She Stoops to Conquer (Oxford Playhouse) 1966, Katharina, Celia, Berinthia in The Relapse 1967, Cleopatra and Lavinia (RSC) 1972–73, Hester in Hello and Goodbye (Kings Head) 1973, Masha in Three Sisters (Cambridge Theatre) 1976, The Death of Bessie Smith (Market Theatre, Johannesburg) 1976, Shen Te in The Good Woman of Setzuan (Tyneside Theatre Co.) 1976, at Royal Court Theatre 1977; Hedda Gabler (Duke of York's Theatre) 1977, Duchess of Malfi 1978, The Greeks (Aldwych) 1980, Boesman and Lena (Hampstead) 1984, Vassa (Greenwich Theatre) 1985, Andromache (Old Vic) 1987, Another Time (Wyndhams) 1989–90, Hippolytus (Almeida) 1991, The Sisters Rosensweig (Old Vic) 1994, The Retreat from Moscow (Chichester) 1999, The Free State (Birmingham Repertory and tour) 2000, The Hollow Crown (tour of Far East) 2003, Whose Life is it Anyway (Comedy) 2005, Frobishers Gold (The Shaw) 2006, Volumnia in Coriolanus (RSC) 2007, The Dream of the Dog (Finborough Theatre, Trafalgar Studios) 2010, Solomon and Marion (Baxter Theatre) 2011. *Plays directed:* Othello, (Market Theatre, Johannesburg) 1987, Othello (Channel Four) 1988, A Dream of People (The Pit) 1990, The Cruel Grasp (Edinburgh Festival) 1991, No Flies on Mr. Hunter (Chelsea Centre) 1992, Death of a Salesman (Theatr Clwyd) 1993, The Deep Blue Sea (Theatr Clwyd) 1996, The Good Woman of Sharkville (Market Theatre, Johannesburg) 1996 and UK tour 1997, The Cherry Orchard (Birmingham Rep.) 1997, The Snow Palace (tour 1998) and Tricycle Theatre 1998, The Free State – A South African Response to The Cherry Orchard (Birmingham Repertory) and UK tour 2000, The Guardsman 2000, Measure for Measure (Guildhall) 2004, Hamlet (Grahamstown Festival and The Complete Works Festival, Stratford-on-Avon) 2006, Master Harold and the Boys (LAMDA) 2009, Antony and Cleopatra (Liverpool Playhouse) (Liverpool Echo Best Production Award 2010) 2010, Antony and Cleopatra (Chichester Festival Theatre) 2012, Much Ado About Nothing (LAMDA) 2012. *Film appearances:* A Day in the Death of Joe Egg 1970, Nicholas and Alexandra 1971, Nijinsky 1978, The Black Windmill 1979, The House on Garibaldi Street 1979, Priest of Love 1981, The Draughtsman's Contract 1981, E la Nave Va 1982, A Dry White Season 1988, Nuns on the Run 1990, Leon the Pig-Farmer 1992, Max 2001, Fairy Story 2002, Felix 2013. *Radio:* Latest: Miss Haversham, Mrs. Klein, Life and Fate. *Television includes:* The Family Reunion 1967, Saint Joan 1968, The Three Sisters 1969, Macbeth 1970, Hedda Gabler 1972, Twelfth Night 1973, Shakespeare or Bust 1973, Antony and Cleopatra (RSC) 1974, Miss Nightingale, Clayhanger (serial) 1975–76, Robin Hood (CBS TV) 1983, Mountbatten: The Last Viceroy 1985, The Singing Detective 1986, The Miser 1987, Revolutionary Witness 1989, Masterclass on Shakespearian Comedy 1990, Masterclass from Haymarket Theatre (Sky TV) 2001, White Clouds (BBC) 2002, Hiroshima (movie) 2005, Trial & Retribution (series) 2006, The Colour of Magic (film) 2008, Midsomer Murders (series) – The Sword of Guillaume 2010, Tinga Tinga Tales (series) (voice of Ostrich) 2011, Sinbad (series) 2012, Labyrinth (series) 2012, Moominland Tales: The Life of Tove Jansson (film) 2012. *Publications:* Hedda Gabler: The Play in Performance 1980, Acting with Shakespeare: Three Comedies 1996, The Free State 2000 (republished 2011), A Commentary on Antony and Cleopatra 2001, Not Hamlet 2012, Antony and Cleopatra (ed.) 2012. *Leisure interests:* not climbing Everest or rowing the Atlantic. *Address:* c/o Steve Kenis and Co., Royalty House, 72–74 Dean Street, London, W1D 3SG, England (office). *Telephone:* (20) 7434-9055 (office). *Fax:* (20) 7287-6328 (office). *E-mail:* sk@sknco.com (office).

SUZUKI, Akira, PhD; Japanese chemist and academic; *Professor Emeritus, Hokkaido University;* b. 12 Sept. 1930, Mukawa, Hokkaido; ed Hokkaido Univ., Sapporo; apptd Asst Prof., Dept of Chemical Process Eng, Faculty of Eng, Hokkaido Univ. 1961, Prof., Dept of Applied Chem. 1973–94, Prof. Emer. 1994–; Prof., Okayama Univ. of Science 1994–95, Univ. of Science and the Arts 1995–2002; postdoctoral research with Herbert Charles Brown at Purdue Univ., USA 1963–65; Person of Cultural Merit 2010, Order of Culture 2010; Weissberger-Williams Lectureship Award 1986, Korean Chemical Soc. Award 1987, Chemical Soc. of Japan Award 1989, DowElanco Lectureship Award 1995, The H.C. Brown Lecture Award 2000, Japan Acad. Prize 2003, Nobel Prize in Chem. (jtly with Richard Heck and Ei-ichi Negishi) "for palladium-catalyzed cross couplings in organic synthesis" 2010. *Achievements include:* first published the Suzuki reaction, the organic reaction of an aryl- or vinyl-boronic acid with an aryl- or vinyl-halide catalysed by a palladium(0) complex 1979. *Publications:* numerous papers in professional journals. *Address:* Faculty and Graduate School of Engineering, Hokkaido University, Kita 13, Nishi 8, Kita-ku, Sapporo 060-8628, Hokkaido, Japan (office). *E-mail:* info@eng.hokudai.ac.jp (office). *Website:* www.eng.hokudai.ac.jp (office).

SUZUKI, David Takayoshi, OC, BA, PhD; Canadian broadcaster, geneticist and academic; *Chairman, David Suzuki Foundation;* b. 24 March 1936, Vancouver, BC; s. of Kaoru Carr Suzuki; m. 2nd Tara Cullis; two c.; ed Amherst Coll., Univ. of Chicago; Biologist, Dept of Lands & Forests, Sudbury, Ont. 1958; Teaching Asst, Dept of Biology, Amherst Coll., Amherst, Mass 1957–58; Research Asst for Dr W. K. Baker, Univ. of Chicago 1958–59, Teaching Asst, Dept of Zoology, Univ. of Chicago 1959–61; Asst Prof., Dept of Genetics, Univ. of Alberta 1962–63; Asst Prof., Dept of Zoology, Univ. of BC 1963–65, Assoc. Prof. 1965–69, Prof. 1969–93, Prof. Emer. 2001–; Visiting Prof., Univ. of Calif., Berkeley 1966, 1969, 1976, 1977, Univ. of Puerto Rico 1972, Univ. of Toronto 1978; f. David Suzuki Foundation 1990, now Chair.; Fellow, Royal Soc. of Canada 1978–84, AAAS 1980–; has produced and hosted many CBC and other TV series and specials on science topics; Order of BC 1995; Hon. LLD (Univ. of Prince Edward Island) 1974, (Trent Univ., Ont.) 1981, (Univ. of Calgary) 1986, (Queen's Univ. in Kingston, Ont.) 1987; Hon. DSc (Univ. of Windsor, Ont.) 1979, (Acadia Univ., NS) 1979, (Lakehead Univ., Ont.) 1986, (McMaster Univ., Ont.) 1987, (Carleton Univ., Ont.) 1987, (Amherst Coll., Mass) 1988, (Griffith Univ., Queensland, Australia) 1997, (Whitman Coll., Washington, DC) 1999, (York Univ., Ont.) 2005, (UQAM, PQ) 2005, (Flinders Univ., S Australia) 2006, (Univ. of Montreal, PQ) 2007, (Univ. of Western Ont.) 2007; Hon. DHL (Governors State Univ., Ill.) 1986; Hon. DDL (Open Univ., Canada) 1998, (Simon Fraser Univ., BC) 2001; Hon. Doctor of Environmental Science (Unity Coll., ME) 2000; Hon. Doctor of Communication (Ryerson Univ., Ont.) 2007; numerous awards including Oustanding Japanese-Canadian of the Year Award 1972, Broadcaster of the Year, Canadian Broadcasters League 1976, Sanford Fleming Medal, Royal Canadian Inst. 1981, Japan Times Prize 1983, Medal of Honor, Canadian Asscn 1984, Gold Medal Award, Biological Council of Canada 1986, UNESCO Kalinga Prize 1986, Wiegand Award for Canadian Excellence, Univ. of Waterloo 1990, Lifetime Achievement Award, Univ. of BC Alumni 2000, John Drainie Award for Excellence in Broadcast Journalism 2002, Queen Elizabeth II Golden Jubilee Medal 2002, Lindbergh Award 2004, voted one of 10 Greatest Canadians by CBC viewers 2004, Bradford Washburn 2006, Right Livelihood Award 2009. *Radio includes:* Quirks and Quarks 1974–79, It's a Matter of Survival 1989. *Television includes:* Science Magazine 1974–79, Suzuki on Science 1979, The Nature of Things 1979–, A Planet for the Taking (UNEP Medal) 1985, From Naked Ape to Superspecies. *Publications:* more than 45 books, including An Introduction to Genetic Analysis (with A. F. Griffiths) 1976, The Japan We Never Knew 1996, The Sacred Balance: Rediscovering Our Place in Nature (with A. McConnell) 1997, A Glimpse of Canada's Future 1997, Tree Suitcase 1998, Earth Time 1998, From Naked Ape to Superspecies 1999, You Are the Earth 1999, Eco-Fun 2000, Good News for a Change 2001, When the Wild Comes Leaping Up 2002, Genetics – A Beginner's Guide (co-author) 2002, Sacred Balance – A Visual Celebration 2002, The Salmon Forest 2002, David Suzuki Reader 2003, Tree – A Life Story 2004, Grassroots Rising 2006, David Suzuki: The Autobiography (British Columbia Booksellers' Choice Award in Honour of Bill Duthie 2007) 2006. *Address:* c/o Elois Yaxley, David Suzuki Foundation, Suite 219, 2211 West 4th Avenue, Vancouver, BC V6K 4S2, Canada (office). *Telephone:* (604) 732-4228 (office). *Fax:* (604) 730-9672 (office). *Website:* www.davidsuzuki.org (office).

SUZUKI, Haruo, LLB; Japanese business executive; b. 31 March 1913, Hayama, Kanagawa Pref.; s. of Chuji Suzuki and Masu Suzuki; m. Ito Hibiya 1941; two d.; ed Tokyo Imperial Univ.; with Nomura Securities Co. Ltd 1936–38; joined Showa Denko KK 1939, Exec. Vice-Pres. 1959–71, Pres. 1971–81, Chair. 1981–87, Hon. Chair. 1987–2000, apptd Sr Counsellor 2000; Chair. Japan Chemical Industry Asscn 1976–78, New Materials Study Group 1983, Japan Fine Ceramics Asscn 1986–91; Perm. Trustee, Japan Cttee for Econ. Devt 1945; Dir Int. Primary Aluminium Inst. 1974–76, 1980–82; Exec. Dir Fed. of Econ. Orgs 1972–87; Chair. Japan-Southern US Asscn 1984–90; fmr Dir and Sr Counsellor, Japan Econ. Research Inst.; Chair. Asscn for Corp. Support for the Arts in Japan 1990–94, Hon. Chair. 1994–; apptd Consultant, Village Shonan Inc. 1996; mem. Industrial Structure Council of Ministry of Int. Trade and Industry (MITI) 1972–92, Industrial Property Council, Patent Office, MITI 1983–91; mem. Legis. Council, Ministry of Justice 1982–92; mem. Comité de réflexion sur l'avenir des relations franco-japonaises, Ministry of Foreign Affairs 1982–84; First Class Order of the Sacred Treasure 1979, Officier, Légion d'honneur 1995; Hon. DEcon (Humboldt Univ., Berlin) 1975. *Publications include:* Chemical Industry 1968, What the Classics Have Taught Me 1979 and others. *Leisure interests:* reading, art appreciation, painting, travelling. *Address:* c/o Showa Denko KK, 13-9, Shiba Daimon 1-chome, Minato-ku, Tokyo, Japan.

SUZUKI, Ichiro; Japanese professional baseball player; b. 22 Oct. 1973, Kasugai; m. Yumiko Suzuki; ed Aikoudai Meiden, Aichi Pref.; outfielder; with Japanese Pacific League team Orix Blue Wave 1994–2000; set Japanese records for continuous games and batting average; signed with Seattle Mariners Nov. 2000–2012, traded to New York Yankees 2012–; set American League record for singles (190) in a season 2001; American League batting champion 2001, 2004; set major league record for hits (262) 2004; Matsutaro Shoriki Award 1994–95, 2004, American League Most Valuable Player 2001, American League Rookie of the Year 2001, Gold Glove Award 2001, 2002, 2003, 2004. *Address:* New York Yankees, Yankee Stadium, 1 East 161st Street, Bronx, New York, NY 10451, USA. *Website:* newyork.yankees.mlb.com.

SUZUKI, Kunio; Japanese business executive; b. 27 Aug. 1939; joined Osaka Shosen Kaisha (renamed Mitsui OSK Lines Ltd 1964) 1962, Gen. Man. Tanker Div. 1988–91, Dir and Gen. Man. Tanker Div. 1991–93, Dir 1993–94, Man. Dir 1994–95, apptd Rep. Dir 1995, Sr Man. Dir 1995–98, Vice-Pres. 1998–2000, Pres. 2000–04, Chair. and CEO Mitsui OSK Lines Ltd 2004–06, apptd Chair. 2006; Chair. Japanese Shipowners' Assan; apptd Dir (non-exec.) Dah Sing Financial Holdings Ltd 2003. *Address:* c/o Mitsui OSK Lines Ltd, 1-1 Toranomon, 2-chome, Tokyo 105-8688, Japan.

SUZUKI, Nobuya, BSc; Japanese insurance company executive; *Chairman and Representative Director, Meiji Yasuda Life Insurance Company;* b. 1950; ed Kyoto Univ.; joined Meiji Yasuda Life Insurance Co. 1979, Gen. Man. Yamagata Regional Office 1999–2001, Gen. Man. Strategic Research Office 2001–04, Gen. Man. Risk Man. Control Dept 2004–06, Gen. Man. Product Devt Dept 2006–08, Exec. Officer and Gen. Man. Product Devt Dept 2008–10, Man. Exec. Officer 2010–13, Chair. and Rep. Dir 2013–. *Address:* Meiji Yasuda Life Insurance Co., 1-1, Marunouchi 2-

chome, Chiyoda-ku, Tokyo 100-0005, Japan (office). *Telephone:* (3) 3283-8293 (office). *Fax:* (3) 3215-8123 (office). *E-mail:* info@meijiyasuda.co.jp (office). *Website:* www.meijiyasuda.co.jp (office).

SUZUKI, Osamu; Japanese business executive; *Chairman, President, CEO and COO, Suzuki Motor Corporation;* b. 30 Jan. 1930, Gero, Gifu; s. of Shunzo Suzuki and Toshiko Suzuki; m. Shoko Suzuki 1958; two s. one d.; ed Chuo Univ.; joined Suzuki Motor Co. Ltd 1958, Dir 1963–66, Jr Man. Dir 1967–72, Sr Man. Dir 1973–77, Pres. and CEO 1978–2000 (name changed to Suzuki Motor Corpn 1990), Chair. and CEO 2000–, Pres. and COO 2008–; Exec. Officer, Narita Int. Airport Corpn; Exec. Officer, later Man. Dir Exec. Officer Mitsui OSK Lines Ltd –2005, Man. Dir MOL (Asia) Ltd –2005, Pres. and CEO MOL (America) Inc. (subsidiary of Mitsui Osk Lines Ltd) 2005–08; fmr Gen. Man. Keihanshin region of Daito Trust Construction Co. Ltd; Dir (non-exec.) Maruti Suzuki India Ltd; Chair. Suzuki Foundation; Dir, Yamada Corpn 2010–; Sitara-i-Pakistan (Pakistan) 1985, Medal of Honour with Blue Ribbon 1987, Mil. Cross of Order of Repub. of Hungary 1993, Middle Cross with Star Order of Merit (Hungary) 2004, Padma Bhushan (India) 2007. *Leisure interest:* golf. *Address:* Suzuki Motor Corpn, 300 Takatsuka-cho, Minami-ku, Hamamatsu-shi, Shizuoka 432-8611, Japan (office). *Telephone:* (53) 440-2023 (office). *Fax:* (53) 440-2776 (office). *E-mail:* info@suzuki.co.jp (office). *Website:* www.globalsuzuki.com (office); www.suzuki.co.jp (office).

SUZUKI, Seijun; Japanese film director and actor; b. (Seitaro Suzuki), 24 May 1923, Nihonbashi, Tokyo; after service in Japanese navy during World War II enrolled in film dept, Kamakura Acad.; Asst Dir Shochiku studios –1954, then Dir Nikkatsu studios 1954–1967. *Films directed include:* Minato no Kanapi (Harbour Toast) 1956, Hozuna wa utau (Pure Emotions of the Sea) 1956, Akuma no Machi (Satan's Town) 1956, Ukigusa no yado (Inn of the Floating Weeds) 1957, Rajo to Kenju (The Naked Woman and the Gun) 1957, Hachijikan no Kyofu (Eight Hours of Terror) 1957, Kagenaki koe (Voice Without a Shadow) 1958, Fumihazushita Haru (The Boy Who Came Back) 1958, Aoi Chibusa (Young Breasts) 1958, Ankokugai no bijo (Beauty of the Underworld) 1958, Suppadaka no Nenrei (Age of Nudity) 1959, Love Letter 1959, Ankoku no Ryoken (Passport to Darkness) 1959, Subete Ga Kurutteru (Everything Goes Wrong) 1960, Kutabare Gurentai (Fighting Delinquents) 1960, Kemono no Nemuri (Sleep of the Beast) 1960, Clandestine Zero Line 1960, Tokyo Kishitai (Tokyo Nights) 1961, Toge O Wataru Wakai Kaze (The Wind-of-Youth Group Crosses the Mountain Pass) 1961, Sandanju no Otoko (Man With a Shotgun) 1961, Muteppo-daisho 1961, Hell of a Guy 1961, Blood-Red Water in the Channel 1961, Ore ni Kaketa Yatsura (Guys Who Put Money on Me) 1962, Hai Tiin Yakuza (High-Teen Yakuza) 1962, Yaju no Seishun (Youth of the Beast) 1963, Tantei Jimusho 23 (Detective Bureau 2-3) 1963, Kanto Mushuku (Kanto Wanderer) 1963, Akutaro (The Bastard) 1963, Nikutai no Mon (Gate of Flesh) 1964, Oretachi no chi ga Yurusanai (Our Blood Will Not Forgive) 1964, Hana to Doto (The Flower and the Angry Wave) 1964, Shunpu Den (Story of a Prostitute) 1965, Irezumi ichidai (Tattooed Life) 1965, Akutaroden: Waruihoshi no Shita Demo (Stories of Bastards) 1965, Kawachi Karumen 1966, Tokyo Nagaremono (Tokyo Drifter) 1966, Kenka Erejii (The Born Fighter) 1966, Koroshi no Rakuin (Branded to Kill) 1967, Otoko no Naka ni wa Tori Ga Iru (There's a Bird Inside a Man) 1969, Hishu Monogatari (Tale of Sorrow and Sadness) 1977, Ana no Kiba (The Fang in the Hole) 1979, Tsigoineruwaizen 1980, Kageroza (Heat Shimmer Theatre) 1981, Kapone oi ni Naku (Capone Cries a Lot) 1985, Rupan Sansei: Babiron no Ogon Densetsu (Lupin III: The Golden Legend of Babylon) 1985, Yumeji 1991, Kekkon 1993, Pistol Opera 2001, Princess Raccoon 2005. *Films as actor include:* Yaju no Seishun (Youth of the Beast) 1963, Kuraku naru-made Matenai! 1975, Marilyn ni Aitai (Shiro and Marilyn) 1988, Pachinko Graffiti 1992, Cold Fever 1995, Ki no ue no Sogyo 1997, Fuyajo (Sleepless Town) 1998, Pupu no Monogatari 1998, Kôfuku no Kane (Blessing Bell) 2002.

SUZUKI, Tadashi; Japanese theatre director and producer; *Artistic Director, Suzuki Company of Toga;* b. 20 June 1939, Shimizu City; m. Hiroko Takeuchi 1969; one s.; ed Kitazono High School and Waseda Univ.; f. Waseda Sho-Gekijo 1966; apptd. Artistic Dir Iwanami Hall 1974; built Toga Theatre, Toga Village, Toyama Pref. 1976; Guest Prof. at Juilliard School, Univ. of Wis. (Milwaukee), Univ. of Calif. (San Diego), Univ. of Del., Central Acad. of Drama (Beijing), Shanghai Theatre Acad. and others; founded Japan Performing Arts Center 1982–99; began annual Toga Int. Arts Festival 1982, Toga Int. Actor Training Programme 1983; Artistic Dir Acting Co. Mito (ACM) Theatre 1989–94; Gen. Artistic Dir Shizuoka Performing Arts Center 1995–2007; Artistic Dir Suzuki Co. of Toga; Chair. Japan Performing Arts Foundation 2000–10; mem. Int. Cttee Theatre Olympics 1994; several awards for services to the arts. *Work includes:* own texts On the Dramatic Passions I 1969, II 1970, III 1970, Night and Clock 1975, Greek tragedies and plays by Chekhov and Shakespeare, adaptations of Edmond Rostand's Cyrano de Bergerac, Yukio Mishima's Madame de Sade and Junichiro Tanizaki's Okuni to Gohei. *Publications:* The Sum of the Internal Angles 1973, Dramatic Language 1977, On the Dramatic Passions 1977, Horizon of Deception 1980, Force that Crosses the Border 1984, The Way of Acting 1986, What Theatre Is 1988, The Way of Directing 1994, Dramatic Language II 1999, The Sum of the Internal Angles II 2003. *Leisure interest:* collecting costumes (especially hats). *Address:* Japan Performing Arts Foundation, 3-19-17-402, Takanawa, Minato-ku, Tokyo 108-0074, Japan (office). *Telephone:* (3) 3445-8010 (office). *Fax:* (3) 3445-8012 (office). *E-mail:* engekijin@jpaf.or.jp (office). *Website:* www.jpaf.or.jp (office); www.scot -suzukicompany.com (office).

SUZUKI, Toshifumi; Japanese retail executive; *Chairman and CEO, Seven & i Holdings Co. Ltd;* b. 1933; opened first convenience store (konbini) 1974; fmr labour union leader; f. Seven-Eleven Japan Co. (imported name and concept from US to Japan 1970s); Pres. Ito Yokado Co. Ltd (supermarket chain) 2000–03, Chair. and CEO 2003–05, Chair. and CEO Seven & i Holdings Co. Ltd (holding co. of Ito Yokado, Seven Eleven Japan, Denny's Japan and other operating cos) 2005–, Chair. 7-Eleven Inc. (after acquisition by Seven & i Holdings) 2005–; Pres. Keiranden Cttee on Distribution 2000–. *Address:* Seven & i Holdings Co. Ltd, 8-8 Nibancho, Chiyoda-ku, Tokyo 102-8455, Japan (office). *Telephone:* (3) 6238-3711 (office). *E-mail:* info@7andi.com (office). *Website:* www.7andi.com (office).

SUZUKI, Tsuneo; Japanese politician; b. 10 Feb. 1941; ed Faculty of Political Science and Econs, Waseda Univ.; mem. House of Reps (Kanagawa Pref. 7th Dist) 1986–; joined LDP 1986, Dir Environment Div., LDP 1997, Deputy Chair. Research Comm. on the Educ. System 1998, Research Comm. on Fundamental

Environmental Issues 1999, Policy Research Council 2000–01, Vice-Chair. Party Org. HQ 2001, Chair. Special Cttee on Foreign Students 2001–03, Deputy Chair. Diet Affairs Cttee 2003–04, Chair. Cttee on Nat. Capital Area 2004–05, Dir-Gen. Information Research Bureau 2006–07, Chair. Special Cttee on Public Safety 2007; Parl. Sec. of Educ. 1992–96, of Environment 1996–97; Chair. Cttee on Educ., House of Reps 1999, Special Cttee on Political Ethics and Election Law 2005, Cttee on Disasters 2007–08; Sr State Sec. for Educ., Science, Sports and Culture 2000; Minister of Educ., Culture, Sports, Science and Tech. 2008–10. *Address:* c/o Ministry of Education, Culture, Sports, Science and Technology, 3-2-2, Kasumigaseki, Chiyoda-ku, Tokyo 100-8959, Japan.

SUZUMURA, Kotaro, BA, MA, PhD; Japanese economist and academic; *Professor Emeritus of Public Economics, Institute of Economic Research, Hitotsubashi University;* b. 7 Jan. 1944, Tokoname, Aichi Pref.; s. of Hidetaro Suzumura and Sumie Suzumura; three d.; ed Hitotsubashi Univ.; Lecturer, Dept of Econs, Hitotsubashi Univ. 1971–73, apptd Prof. of Public Econs, Inst. of Econ. Research 1984, now Prof. Emer.; Assoc. Prof., Inst. of Econ. Research, Kyoto Univ. 1973–82; Lecturer, LSE 1974–76; Visiting Assoc. Prof. of Econs, Stanford Univ. 1979–80; Visiting Fellow, Dept of Econs, Univ. of Pennsylvania 1987, All Souls Coll., Oxford, UK 1988; Dir-Gen. Tokyo Centre for Econ. Research 1990–92; Pres. Japanese Econ. Asscn 1999–2000, Soc. for Social Change and Welfare 2000–01; Chair. Far Eastern Standing Cttee, Econometric Soc. 1995–2000, Fellow 1990–, mem. Council 1995–2000; Ed.-in-Chief Japanese Economic Review 1995–97; mem. Council Soc. for Social Choice and Welfare, Science Council of Japan 2000–03; Medal with Purple Ribbon 2004, Japan Acad. Prize 2006. *Publications include:* Rational Choice, Collective Decisions and Social Welfare (Nikkei Econs Book Prize 1984) 1983, The Economic Analysis of Industrial Policy (Nikkei Econs Book Prize 1988) 1988, Competition, Commitment and Welfare 1995, Social Choice Re-examined (co-ed. two vols) 1996, 1997, Development Strategy and Management of the Market Economy (jtly) 1997, Handbook of Social Choice and Welfare vol. I (co-ed.) 2002. *Leisure interests:* reading novels. *Address:* Institute of Economic Research, Hitotsubashi University, Naka 2–1, Kunitachi, Tokyo 186-8603 (office); 1-29-3 Asagaya Minami, Suginami-ku, Tokyo, Japan (home). *Telephone:* (42) 580-8353 (office); (3) 3311-5110 (home). *Fax:* (42) 580-8353 (office); (3) 3311-5110 (home). *E-mail:* suzumura@ier.hit-u.ac.jp (office). *Website:* www.ier.hit-u.ac.jp (office).

SVANBERG, Carl-Henric, BSc, MSc; Swedish business executive; *Chairman, BP plc; Chairman, AB Volvo;* b. 29 May 1952, Porjus; m. Agneta Svanberg 1983; three c.; ed Univ. of Uppsala, Linköping Inst. of Tech.; fmr ice hockey player with IF Björklöven, Umeå; various foreign assignments in project exports, Asea Brown Boveri 1977–85; joined Securitas (security co.) 1986, Exec. Vice-Pres. 1990–94; Pres. and CEO Assa Abloy Group 1994–2003, Deputy Chair. 2003–; Dir (non-exec.) Telefonaktiebolaget L. M. Ericsson 2003–12, Pres. and CEO 2003–09, Chair. Sony Ericsson Mobile Communications AB 2003–09; Dir (non-exec.) BP plc 2009–, Chair. 2010–, Chair. Chair.'s Cttee, Nomination Cttee; Chair. AB Volvo 2012–; mem. Bd Dirs Melker Schörling AB; mem. Bd Confed. of Swedish Enterprise, Bd Univ. of Uppsala, Steering Cttee Global Alliance for Information and Communication Technologies and Devt, External Advisory Bd Earth Inst. at Columbia Univ., Bd Djurgårdens IF Hockey; mem. Advisory Bd Harvard Kennedy School; Dr hc (Linköping Univ.) 2006, (Luleå Univ. of Tech.); King of Sweden's Medal. *Leisure interests:* sailing, working with Boy Scouts. *Address:* BP plc, International Headquarters, 1 St James's Square, London, SW1Y 4PD, England (office); AB Volvo, 405 08 Gothenburg, Sweden (office). *Telephone:* (20) 7496-4000 (London) (office); (31) 660000 (Gothenburg) (office). *Fax:* (20) 7496-4630 (London) (office); (31) 545772 (Gothenburg) (office). *Website:* www.bp.com (office); www.volvo.com (office).

SVANHOLM, Poul Johan, LLB; Danish banker and business executive; b. 7 June 1933, Aalborg; s. of Poul Svanholm and Gerda Svanholm (née Stougaard); m. Lise Andersen 1957; one s. one d.; ed Univ. of Copenhagen; Pres. Vingaarden, Odense 1962–72; Pres. Carlsberg A/S, Copenhagen 1972–82, CEO Carlsberg Group 1982–96; Chair. Danske Bank 1983–2003; mem. Bd D/S Svendborg (A.P. Moeller Group) 1978–2003, Vice-Chair. A.P. Moeller-Maersk A/S 2003–; mem. European Advisory Cttee to New York Stock Exchange 1986–2005; Chair. Thomas B. Thrige Foundation 1979–2008; Grand Cross of Order of Dannebrog 1997, Hon. CBE 1997. *Leisure interest:* Ravnborg Estate. *Address:* 15 Helleruplund Allé, 2900 Hellerup, Denmark (home). *Telephone:* 39-62-23-45 (home). *Fax:* 39-62-75-46 (home). *E-mail:* poul.svanholm@privat.dk (home).

SVANIDZE, Nikolay Karlovich; Russian historian and broadcast journalist; b. 2 April 1955, Moscow; m. Marina Svanidze; one s.; ed Moscow State Univ.; Researcher, Inst. of USA and Canada, USSR (now Russia) Acad. of Sciences 1978–91; on staff, Russian TV 1992–, commentator, Vesti 1991–94, host, Zerkalo 1996–2007, Deputy Dir of Information Programmes and Head of Studio Information and Analytical Programmes 1996–97; Deputy Chair., then Chair. All Russian State TV and Radio Co. 1996–98; mem. Public Chamber; Teffi Prize, Russian Acad. of TV. *Publication:* Medvedev 2008. *Address:* All-Russian State Television and Radio Broadcasting Company, 125040 Moscow, ul. 5-aya Yamskogo Polya 19/21, Russia (office). *Telephone:* (495) 745-39-78 (office). *Fax:* (495) 975-26-11 (office).

ŠVANKMAJER, Jan; Czech stage designer and film director; b. 4 Sept. 1934, Prague; m. Eva Švankmajerová 1960; one s. one d.; ed Theatrical Acad. of Performing Arts, Prague 1954–58; freelance artist 1958–; numerous drawings, graphic sheets, collages, stage sets and (with his wife) art pottery; Prix Special ASIFA 1990, Award for Lifetime Work UK 1995, Freedom Prize (Berlin) 2001, Czech Lion Prize 2002. *Films directed include:* Dimensions of Dialogue 1982, Down to the Cellar 1982, The Pendulum, The Pit and Hope 1983, Alice 1987, Virile Games 1988, Another Kind of Love 1988, Meat Love 1988, Darkness-Lightness-Darkness 1989, The Death of Stalinism in Bohemia 1990, Food 1992, The Faust Lesson 1994, Conspirators of Pleasure 1996, Otesánek (Little Otik) (Czech Lion) 2001, Lunacy 2005, Surviving Life 2010. *Publications:* Hmat a imaginace 1994, Animus Anima Animation (co-author) 1998, Power of Imagination 2001, Transmutation of the Senses 2004. *Address:* Athanor Lld, Film Production Company, Jaromir Kallista & Jan Svankmajer, U 5.baterie 21/1034, 162 00 Prague 6, Czech Republic (office). *Telephone:* (2) 33322905 (office). *Fax:* (2) 24313383 (office). *E-mail:* athanor@nextra.cz (office). *Website:* www.athanor.cz (office).

SVARTVIK, Jan, PhD; Swedish academic; *Professor Emeritus of English, Lund University;* b. 18 Aug. 1931, Torsby; s. of Gustaf Svartvik and Sigrid Svartvik; m. Gunilla Berner 1958; two s. one d.; ed Uppsala Univ.; Research Asst and Asst Dir Survey of English Usage, Univ. Coll. London 1961–65; Lecturer, Univ. of Gothenburg 1965–70; Visiting Prof., Brown Univ., USA 1969; Prof. of English, Lund Univ. 1970–95, now Prof. Emer.; Pres. Asscn Int. de Linguistique Appliquée 1981–84; Chair. Org. Cttee, Nobel Symposium on Corpus Linguistics 1991; Chair. Steering Cttee for Evaluation of Linguistics in Sweden 1990–92; mem. Royal Acad. of Letters, History and Antiquities, Royal Swedish Acad. of Sciences, Academia Europaea, Societas Scientarum Fennica; Dr hc (Bergen) 1996, (Masaryk Univ.) 1998, (Helsinki) 2000. *Publications:* On Voice in the English Verb 1966, The Evans Statements 1968, A Grammar of Contemporary English (co-author) 1972, A Comprehensive Grammar of the English Language (co-author) 1985, The London-Lund Corpus of Spoken English: Description and Research 1990, Directions in Corpus Linguistics: Proceedings of Nobel Symposium 82 1992 (ed.), Words, Proceedings (ed.) 1996, Engelska – öspråk världsspråk, trendspråk (August Prize for Swedish Non-fiction Book of the Year) 1999, Handbok i engelska (co-author) 2001, Politikens bog om engelsk 2001, A Communicative Grammar of English 2002, English: One Tongue, Many Voices (co-author) 2006. *Address:* Tumlaregränden 7, 22651 Lund, Sweden.

SVEDBERG, Bjoern, MSc; Swedish business executive; *Managing Director, Prêt à Porter AB;* b. 4 July 1937, Stockholm; s. of Inge Svedberg and Anna-Lisa Svedberg; m. Gunnel Nilsson 1960; four c.; ed Royal Inst. of Tech., Stockholm and Man. Devt Inst., Univ. of Lausanne; Man. Eng Telephone Exchange Div., L.M. Ericsson Telephone Co. 1972–76, Sr Vice-Pres. of Research and Devt 1976–77, Pres. 1977–90, Chair. 1990; apptd Chair. Nefab AB 1999; Chair. Mo och Domsjo AB 1991–92; currently Man. Dir Prêt à Porter AB; mem. Bd of Dirs AB Volvo 1994, ABB Ltd –1999, Stora AB, Investor 1998–2007; mem. Royal Swedish Acad. of Eng Sciences (fmr Chair.); fmr Pres. Canada/Sweden Business Asscn; fmr mem. Bd Fed. of Swedish Industry. *Address:* Prêt à Porter Group AB, Petersbergsgatan 19, 501 10 Borås, Sweden (office). *Telephone:* (3) 317-60-00 (office). *Fax:* (3)317-60-97 (office). *E-mail:* mail@pretaporter.se (office). *Website:* www.pretaporter.se (office).

SVEDMAN, Sven-Erik, MBA; Norwegian diplomatist; *Ambassador to Germany;* b. 13 Oct. 1946; m. Gunilla Svedman; three c.; ed Lund Univ., Sweden; with Ministry of Foreign Affairs, Oslo 1973–76, Attaché, Embassy in Reykjavik 1976–78, Embassy Sec., Norwegian Del. to OECD, Paris 1978–81, Ministry of Foreign Affairs 1981–82, World Bank, Washington, DC 1982–84, Embassy Sec. (Political Affairs), Embassy in Bonn 1984–88, Political Adviser, Ministry of Foreign Affairs 1988–89, Sec. of State, Ministry of Foreign Affairs 1989–90, Minister and Deputy Amb., Embassy in Washington, DC 1990–94, Amb. to Israel 1994–97, Man. Dir, Oil & Gas 1997–99, Dir Gen., Ministry of Foreign Affairs 1999–2003, Amb. to France (also Perm. Rep. to UNESCO) 2003–05, Perm. Sec. Gen., Ministry of Foreign Affairs 2005–07, Amb. to Germany 2007–; Commdr, Royal Norwegian Order of Merit 2000, Grand Officer, Order of St Olav 2005, Commdr de la Légion d'honneur 2003, Italian, Spanish and German Grand Cross. *Address:* Royal Norwegian Embassy, Rauchstr. 1, 10787 Berlin, Germany (office). *Telephone:* (30) 505050 (office). *Fax:* (30) 505055 (office). *E-mail:* emb.berlin@mfa .no (office). *Website:* www.norwegen.no (office).

SVEJGAARD, Arne, MD, DSc; Danish scientist, immunologist and academic; *Professor of Clinical Immunology, University of Copenhagen;* b. 13 March 1937, Odense; m. Else Lyngsoe 1960; two s. one d.; ed Univ. of Arhus Medical School and Univ. Hosp. of Arhus; Dir Tissue Typing Lab., Univ. Hosp. of Copenhagen 1970–87, apptd Dir Dept of Clinical Immunology 1987; Prof. of Clinical Immunology, Univ. of Copenhagen 1991–; apptd Councillor Int. Histocompatibility Workshops 1975; apptd Chair. Danish Cttee for Immunology 1985; mem. Royal Danish Acad. of Sciences and Letters 1981–; Chair. Alfred Benzon Foundation 1996, Danish Medical Research Council 1997–2002; Kt of Dannebrog 1994; Tsuji Memorial Lecture 1981; Gaardon Prize 1980, Novo Prize 1981, Hess Thaysen Prize 1989, Europe and Medicine Senior Prize 2002. *Publications include:* Iso-antigenic Systems of Human Blood Platelets 1969, The HLA System (with others) 1975, HLA and Disease (with J. Dausset) 1977, numerous scientific articles in professional journals. *Address:* Department of Clinical Immunology, Section 7631, University Hospital of Copenhagen, Blegdamsvej 9, 2100 Copenhagen 0 (office); Skovvang 67, 3450 Allerød, Denmark. *Telephone:* 35-45-76-30 (office); 48-17-32-11 (home). *E-mail:* arnesvej@post4.tele.dk (office).

SVENSSON, Åke, MSc; Swedish business executive; *President, Teknikföretagen (Association of Swedish Engineering Industries);* b. 1952; joined Saab Group 1976, held several exec. positions including Project Man., Gen. Man. Saab Aerosystems, Gen. Man. Future Products and Tech., Sr Vice-Pres. Saab Aerospace 2000–03, Pres. and CEO Saab AB 2003–10; mem. Bd of Dirs Gripen International (Saab jt venture), Copenhagen Malmö Port AB 2001–10; Pres. Teknikföretagen (Asscn of Swedish Eng Industries) 2010–; apptd Chair. AeroSpace and Defence Industries Asscn of Europe 2007; mem. Royal Swedish Acad. of War Sciences. *Address:* Teknikföretagen, Storgatan 5, PO Box 5510, 114 85 Stockholm, Sweden (office). *Website:* www.teknikforetagen.se

SVĚRÁK, Jan; Czech film director; b. 6 Feb. 1965, Žatec; m.; three c.; ed Film Acad. of Arts; pnr in film production co. Luxor 1996; Co. Biograf Jan Svěrák Pictures 1996–; mem. Acad. of Motion Picture Arts and Sciences, Czech Film Acad.; numerous awards including Acad. Award for best foreign student film 1989, Czech Lion Awards for Direction 1996, 1997, 2001, Time for Peace Prize 1997. *Film roles:* Kulový blesk (Ball Lightning) (uncredited) 1978, Nejistá sezóna (An Uncertain Season) 1988, Valka barev 1993, Rebelové (The Rebels) 2001, Tmavomodrý svet (Dark World Blue) (uncredited) 2001, Román pro zeny 2005. *Films directed include:* Sbohem, nadrazicko 1984, Vsak su vinar 1985, Ropáci (Oil Gobblers) 1988, Obecná skola (The Elementary School) 1991, Akumulátor 1 1994, Jizda (The Ride) 1994, Kolya (Golden Globe Award, Acad. Award and Czech Lion Award) 1996, Tmavomodrý svet (Dark World Blue) 2001, Tatínek (video) 2004, Vratné lahve 2007, Kuky se vrací 2010. *Leisure interest:* painting. *Address:* c/o Fandango Portobello Sales, Eardley House, 4 Uxbridge Street, Notting Hill Gate, London, W8 7SY, England; PO Box 33, 155 00 Prague 515, Czech Republic. *Telephone:* (20) 7908-9890 (London). *E-mail:* biograf@sverak.cz. *Website:* www .sverak.cz.

SVERDLOV, Yevgeny Davidovich; Russian biochemist; *Councillor, Institute of Molecular Genetics, Russian Academy of Sciences;* b. 16 Nov. 1938, Dneprope-trovsk, Ukrainian SSR; ed Moscow State Univ.; Sr Lab., Jr, Sr Researcher, Inst. of Bio-organic Chem. 1965–88; Dir, then Scientific Dir, then Councillor, Inst. of Molecular Genetics, USSR (now Russian) Acad. of Sciences 1988–; Ed.-in-Chief Molekulyarnaya Genetika, Mikrobiologiya i Virusologiya (Molecular Genetics, Microbiology and Virology); mem. Scientific Council of Biotechnology, Russian Acad. of Sciences; Corresp. mem. USSR (now Russian) Acad. of Sciences 1984, mem. 1994; mem. Russian Acad. of Agricultural Sciences 1994, German Acad. of Sciences Leopoldina, Academia Europaea; Lenin Prize, USSR State Prize. *Publications include:* Organic Chemistry of Nucleic Acids 1970; more than 300 scientific articles. *Address:* Institute of Molecular Genetics, 123182 Moscow 2, Kurchatov Square, Russia (office). *Telephone:* (499) 196-00-00 (office). *Fax:* (499) 196-02-21 (office). *E-mail:* img@img.ras.ru (office); edsverd@gmail.com.

SVERRISDÓTTIR, Valgerður; Icelandic politician; b. 23 March 1950; m. Arvid Kro; three d.; ed Reykjavík Women's School; Sec., Agricultural Research Labs 1967–68; Sec. to Man. Dir KEA Cooperative 1969–70; Sec., Akureyri Regional Hosp. 1970–71; teacher, Grenivík School, 1972–82; has worked as farmer 1974–; Deputy Mem. Althingi (Parl.) 1984–87, mem. for NE Iceland constituency 1987–, Second Deputy Speaker 1988–89, 1990–91, Deputy Speaker 1992–95; Minister of Industry and Commerce 1999–2005, for Nordic Cooperation 2004–05, of Foreign Affairs 2006–07; mem. Progressive Party NE Iceland Constituency Cttee 1983–87, Chair. 1985-86, mem. Cen. Cttee 1983–, Deputy Sec. 1990–92, Parl. Group Leader 1995–99; mem. Nordic Council 1987–90, 1995–99, Chair. Parl. Group 1995–99; mem. Bd of Dirs KEA Cooperative 1981–92, SÍS (Fed. of Iceland Cooperative Socs) 1985–92, Akureyri Ship Repair Yard 1989–91, Bifröst Cooperative Coll. 1990–96 (Chair. 1995–96), Nordic Cultural Fund 1991–93, 1995–99 (Chair. 1995). *Address:* Framsóknarflokkurinn (Progressive Party), Hverfisgata 33, POB 453, 121 Reykjavík, Iceland (office). *Telephone:* 5630500 (office). *E-mail:* valgsv@althingi.is.

SVILANOVIČ, Goran, LLM; Serbian politician and lawyer; *Co-ordinator of Economic and Environmental Activities, Organization for Security and Co-operation in Europe;* b. 22 Oct. 1963, Gnjilane, Kosovo; m.; two c.; ed Belgrade Univ., Inst. of Law, Strasbourg, Saarbrücken Univ., European Univ. of Peace, Austria; worked as Asst Researcher, Belgrade Univ. 1986–98, discharged following protest against controversial univ. law 1998; collaborator with Yugoslavian Forum on Human Rights 1989–93; head of telephone service for rescue of victims of nat., ethnic, religious and other discrimination, Centre for Anti-war Action 1993–97; Chair. Council on Human Rights 1996–98; Official Rep. of Civic Alliance of Serbia (Građanski savez Srbije—GSS) 1997, Vice-Pres. 1998, Pres. 1999, left party 2004; Fed. Minister of Foreign Affairs 2000–04; mem. Parl. (nominated for Democratic Party) 2004–; Chair. Working Table I, Stability Pact for South Eastern Europe 2004–08; Co-ordinator of Econ. and Environmental Activities, OSCE 2008–; mem. Int. Comm. on the Balkans. *Publications:* Civil and Civil Process Law; books and numerous articles on the situation of refugees and problems of citizenship. *Address:* Office of the Co-ordinator of Economic and Environmental Activities, Organization for Security and Co-operation in Europe, Kärntner Ring 5–7, 1010 Vienna, Austria (office). *Telephone:* (1) 514-36-151 (office). *Fax:* (1) 514-36-96 (office). *E-mail:* info@osce.org (office). *Website:* www.osce.org (office).

SVINAROV, Nikolai Avramov, LLB; Bulgarian lawyer and politician; b. 6 May 1958, Shuman; m.; two d.; ed Univ. of Sofia St Kliment Ohridsky; lawyer practising penal law, Turgoviste 1984–85, civil and commercial law, Sofia 1985–2001; mem. Council, Lawyer's League, Sofia 1992–96; mem. and Chief Sec., Supreme Lawyer's Council 1998–2001; apptd mem. Parl., 39th Nat. Ass. (Nat. Movt Simeon the Second) 2001; Minister of Defence 2001–05. *Address:* c/o Ministry of Defence, Aksakov Str. 1, 1000 Sofia, Bulgaria.

SVOBODA, Cyril, JUDr; Czech politician and lawyer; *Chairman, Christian Democratic Union-Czecheslovak People's Party (KDU-CSL);* b. 24 Nov. 1956, Prague; m. Věnceslava Svoboda; four s.; ed Charles Univ., Prague, Pan American Inst. for Int. Studies, Notre Dame Univ., USA; legal officer, Transgas 1980–93; Adviser to Deputy Prime Minister for Human Rights, Restitution and Relations Between the State and the Church 1990–92; Deputy Chair. Legis. Council, Czech Govt 1992–98; Deputy Minister of Justice 1992–96; Deputy Minister of Foreign Affairs for issues related to accession to the EU 1996–98; Minister of the Interior Jan.–July 1998; Chair. Petition Cttee, Chamber of Deputies 1998–2002; Deputy Prime Minister and Minister of Foreign Affairs 2002–04; Minister of Foreign Affairs 2002–06; mem. Chamber of Deputies 2006–; Chair. Govt Legis. Council 2007–; joined Christian Democratic Union-Czechoslovak People's Party (KDU-CSL) 1995, First Deputy Chair. 1999–2001, Chair. 2001–03, 2009–, Deputy Chair. 2003–06; Leader of Coalition of Four Jan.–March 2001; mem. European Comm. for Democracy through Law 1994–, Deputy Chair. 1997–; Chair. Cttee for the Rules of Procedure and Immunity of the Parl. Ass., Council of Europe 2001–; Grosses Verdienstkreuz mit Stern und Schulterband (Germany) 2008. *Publications include:* Annotations on the Constitution of the Czech Republic (co-author), The Act on Out-of-Court Rehabilitation in Questions and Answers; numerous articles and studies on legislation and foreign policy. *Leisure interests:* literature, sport (running, skiing, swimming, cycling). *Address:* KDU-CSL, Karlovo náměstí 5, 128 01 Prague 2, Czech Republic (office). *Telephone:* (2) 26205111 (office). *Fax:* (2) 26205100 (office). *E-mail:* predseda@kdu.cz (office). *Website:* www.kdu.cz (office).

SVOBODA, Jiří, MgA; Czech film director and academic; *Professor, University of Finance and Administration;* b. 5 May 1945, Kladno; s. of Dr Jiří Svoboda and Bozena Svobodova (née Procházková); m. Milena Niznanska 1973; two d.; ed Film Acad. of Performing Arts, Prague (FAMU); studied drama at Acad. of Performing Arts, Prague, expelled for political reasons 1963; worked as warehouseman and driver 1963–66; dir and scriptwriter, Film Studios Barrandov 1971–93; freelance film dir and scriptwriter 1994–; mem. CP of Czechoslovakia 1975–90; Deputy Chair. Film Union of Czech Artists 1987–90; Chair. CP of the Czechlands and Moravia 1990–93; Deputy to House of Nations, Fed. Ass. of CSFR 1990–92; seriously wounded in attempt on his life Dec. 1992; Sr Lecturer, Acad. of Performing Arts; Prof., Film and TV and New Media, Univ. of Finance and Admin (VSFS) 2009–, Univ. of J.A. Komensky 2011–; mem. European Film Acad., Czech Film and TV Acad., Franz Kafka Soc.; Merited Artist 1986; Grand Prize Karlovy Vary 1982, San Remo 1982, Jury Prize Cannes 1983, Prix CIRCOM 2009, Grand Prix CIRCOM 2010. *Films include:* (as dir or scriptwriter): Hostage 1975, A Mirror

for Christine 1975, House on the Embankment 1976, The Break Time 1977, The Blue Planet 1979, Girl with a Shell 1980, The Chain 1981, A Meeting with Shadows 1982, The End of the Lonely Berhof Farmstead 1983, The Lancet, Please 1985, Papilio 1986, The World Knows Nothing 1987, A Curse on the Hajnůs' House 1988, Only About Family Orders (about political trials in 1950s) 1989, Bolt from the Blue 2004, Sametoví vrazi 2005, The Wave 2007, Irreversible Man 2009, Dominant Women 2010. *Television:* wrote and directed more than 25 TV films and plays and part of series 10 Centuries of Architecture 1999–2000, Blow Up 2001, (Udelení milosti se zamítá) The Act of Grace is Disproved 2002, The Visionary 2003, Billow (Parts 1–3) 2005, Rainbow of God 2007, The Irredeemable Man 2009, Pretty Women and Monster 2010, Domina 2010. *Publication:* Killers from the Velvet (novel). *Leisure interests:* philosophy, political theory, literature. *Address:* The University of Finance and Administration, 101 00 Prague 10, Estonska 500 (office); Na Balkáně 120, Prague 3, Czech Republic (home). *Telephone:* 77-7211324 (mobile). *E-mail:* jiri@jiri-svoboda.cz (home). *Website:* www.vsfs.cz (office); www .svobodajiri.euweb.cz.

SWAGER, Timothy M., BS, PhD; American chemist and academic; *John D. MacArthur Professor of Chemistry and Head, Department of Chemistry, Massa-chusetts Institute of Technology;* b. 7 Jan. 1961, Sheridan, Mont.; m.; two c.; ed Calif. Inst. of Tech., Mont. State Univ.; IBM Graduate Fellow 1984–87; Asst Prof. of Chem., Univ. of Pennsylvania 1990–96, Prof. 1996; Prof. of Chem., MIT 1996–2005, John D. MacArthur Prof. and Head, Dept of Chem. 2005–; Founder Iptyx Corpn; Clare Hall Visiting Fellow, Univ. of Cambridge, UK 2005; has served on panels for Nat. Research Council, Defense Science Bd, Nat. Science Foundation, US Senate Commerce Cttee; mem. Science Advisory Bd, ICx Technologies, Nomadics Inc., Collegium Pharmaceutical Inc., Plextronics Inc., Nano-C Inc.; Assoc. Ed. Synfacts 2005–; mem. Editorial Advisory Bd Accounts of Chemical Research, Journal of Polymer Science, Supramolecular Chemistry, Advanced Synthesis & Catalysis, Journal of Supramolecular Chemistry, Journal of Materials Chemistry; Alfred P. Sloan Research Fellow 1994–96; Fellow, American Acad. of Arts and Sciences 2006–; mem. Nat. Acad. of Arts and Sciences 2008–; Dr hc (Montana State Univ.) 2007; Merck Index Undergraduate Chem. Award 1983, Most Outstanding Senior Chem. Major, American Inst. of Chemists 1983, Herbert Newby McCoy Award For Outstanding Graduate Research, California Inst. of Tech. 1988, Office of Naval Research Young Investigator 1992–95, DuPont Young Faculty Award 1993–96, ACS Philadelphia Section Award 1996, Union Carbide Innovation Recognition Award 1998, ACS Cope Scholar Award 2000, Vladimir Karapetoff Award, MIT 2000, Carl S. Marvel Creative Polymer Chem. Award, ACS-Polymer Div. 2005, Christopher Columbus Foundation Homeland Security Award 2005, Lemelson-MIT Award for Inventorship 2007. *Publications:* more than 200 publs in scientific books and journals. *Address:* Massachusetts Institute of Technology, Department of Chemistry, Cambridge, MA 02139, USA (office). *Telephone:* (617) 253-4423 (office). *Fax:* (617) 253-7929 (office). *E-mail:* tswager@ mit.edu (office). *Website:* web.mit.edu/tswager/www (office).

SWAN, Sir John William David, KBE, BA, JP; Bermudian business executive; *Chairman, Swan Group of Companies;* b. 3 July 1935; s. of John Nicholas and Margaret Swan; m. Jacqueline Roberts 1965; one s. two d.; ed Cen. School and Howard Acad., Bermuda and W. Virginia Wesleyan Coll.; Real Estate Salesman with Rego Ltd 1960–62; Founder, CEO and Chair. John W Swan Ltd 1962–, Chair. Swan Group of Cos 1996–; mem. Parl. (United Bermuda Party) 1972–95, Minister for Marine and Air Services, Labour and Immigration 1977–78, Home Affairs 1978–82, Premier of Bermuda 1982–95; fmr Parl. Sec. for Finance, Chair. Bermuda Hosp. Bd, Chair. Dept of Civil Aviation; mem. Chief Execs Org. and World Business Council; mem. and Fellow, Senate, Jr Chamber Int. 1992; Eminent Professional Mem. Royal Inst. of Chartered Surveyors 2006–; Trustee Bermuda Inst. of Ocean Sciences; Hon. Freeman City of London 1985; Hon. LLD (Tampa Univ.) 1986, (W Va Wesleyan Coll.) 1987, (Atlantic Union Coll., Mass.) 1991; St Paul's Anniversary Citation 1969, Outstanding Young Man of the Year 1969, Int. Medal of Excellence (first recipient), Poor Richard Club of Phila 1987 and other awards. *Leisure interests:* tennis, sailing, reading. *Address:* Swan Building, 26 Victoria Street, Hamilton, HM12 (home); 11 Grape Bay Drive, Paget PG06, Bermuda (home). *Telephone:* (441) 295-1785 (office); (441) 236-1303 (home). *Fax:* (441) 295-6270 (office); (441) 236-7935 (home). *E-mail:* sirjohn@challengerbanks .bm (office). *Website:* sirjohnswan.webs.com.

SWAN, Wayne Maxwell, BA; Australian academic and politician; b. 30 June 1954, Nambour, Queensland; m. 2nd Kim Swan; one s. two d.; ed Nambour State High School, Univ. of Queensland; Lecturer in Public Admin, Queensland Inst. of Tech. 1976–77, 1981–82, 1985–88; Policy Analyst, Office of Youth Affairs 1978; adviser to Leader of the Opposition, Bill Hayden 1978–80, to Fed. Labor Ministers, Mick Young and Kim Beazley 1983, to Minister for Foreign Affairs, Bill Hayden 1984; mem. Australian Labor Party (ALP) Admin. Cttee (Queensland) 1984–90, Del., ALP Nat. Conf. 1986, 1988, 1990, Campaign Dir 1989–, State Sec. Queensland Br. of ALP 1991–93, Deputy Leader of ALP 2010–13; Treas. and Labor MP for Lilley, Brisbane 1993–96, 1998–; Shadow Minister for Family and Community Services 1998–2000, 2001–04, Man. of Opposition Business in the House 2001–03; Shadow Treas. 2004–07; Treas. of Australia 2007–13; Deputy Prime Minister 2010–13. *Publication:* Postcode: The Splintering of a Nation 2005. *Address:* c/o Department of the Treasury, Langton Crescent, Parkes, ACT 2600, Australia (office). *E-mail:* wayne.swan.mp@aph.gov.au (office). *Website:* www.swanmp.org (office).

SWANK, Hilary; American actress; b. 30 July 1974, Bellingham, Wash.; m. Chad Lowe 1997 (divorced 2006). *Films include:* Buffy the Vampire Slayer 1992, The Next Karate Kid 1994, Sometimes They Came Back... Again 1996, Heartwood 1997, Boys Don't Cry (numerous awards including Best Actress, Acad. Awards, Boston Soc. of Film Critics Award for Best Actress, Chicago Film Critics Asscn Award for Best Actress, Las Vegas Film Critics Soc. Award for Best Actress, Golden Globe Award for Best Actress) 1999, The Gift 2000, Affair of the Necklace 2000, Insomnia 2002, The Core 2003, 11:14 2003, Red Dust 2004, Million Dollar Baby (Best Dramatic Actress, Golden Globe Awards 2005, Best Actress, Screen Actors Guild Awards 2005, Best Actress, Acad. Awards 2005) 2004, Black Dahlia 2006, Freedom Writers 2007, The Reaping 2007, P.S. I Love You 2007, Birds of America 2008, Amelia (Hollywood Film Festival Best Actress) 2009, Conviction 2010, The Resident 2011, New Year's Eve 2011. *Television includes:* Terror in the Family 1996, Leaving LA 1997.

SWANN, Kathryn (Kate) Elizabeth, BSc; British business executive; *CEO, SSP Group;* ed Univ. of Bradford; fmrly in retail marketing, Tesco Plc, Coca-Cola Schweppes, Homepride Foods and Dixons Stores Group; fmr Marketing Dir Currys PLC; Marketing Dir then Man. Dir Homebase, J Sainsbury PLC –2000; Man. Dir Argos PLC 2000–03; CEO WH Smith PLC 2003–13; CEO SSP Group 2013–Dir (non-exec.) Lambert Howarth Group PLC 2000–06, The British Land Co. PLC 2006–; Dr hc (Bradford) 2007; ranked by Fortune magazine amongst the 50 Most Powerful Women in Business outside the US (tenth) 2004, (20th) 2005, (34th) 2006, (32nd) 2007, (39th) 2008, (31st) 2009, (35th) 2010, ranked by the Financial Times amongst the Top 25 Businesswomen in Europe (17th) 2005, (21st) 2006, (17th) 2007. *Address:* 169 Euston Road, London, NW1 2AE, England (office). *Telephone:* (20) 3714-5243 (office). *Website:* www.foodtravelexperts.com (office).

SWANNELL, Robert; British lawyer, chartered accountant and business executive; *Chairman, Marks and Spencer Group plc;* ed Rugby School; with Schroders investment bank (acquired by Citigroup 2000) 1977–2010, later Chair. Citigroup 2007–10, Vice-Chair. CitiEurope –2008; Chair. HMV 2009–11, Dir (non-exec.) –2011; Dir (non-exec.) Marks & Spencer 2010–, Chair. 2011–; Chair. Governing Body, Rugby School; Sr Ind. Dir The British Land Company plc 1999–2010, 3i Group plc –2010; fmr Dir and Trustee Career Academies UK 2003–10; fmr mem. Regulatory Decisions Cttee of FSA, Industrial Advisory Bd of BIS (Dept for Business, Innovation and Skills); Dir and Trustee, Career Academies UK 2003–10. *Address:* Marks and Spencer Group plc, Waterside House, 35 North Wharf Road, London, W2 1NW, England (office). *Telephone:* (20) 7935-4422 (office). *Fax:* (20) 7487-2679 (office). *E-mail:* retailcustomer.services@marksandspencer .com (office). *Website:* www.marksandspencer.com (office).

SWANSON, William H., BEng, FRAeS; American business executive; *Chairman and CEO, Raytheon Company;* b. 1949, Calif.; m. Cheryl Swanson; ed Calif. Polytechnic State Univ., Golden Gate Univ.; joined Raytheon Co. 1972, various man. positions including Exec. Vice-Pres. and Chair. and CEO Raytheon Systems Co. 1998–2000, Exec. Vice-Pres. and Pres. Electronic Systems Div. 2000–02, Pres. 2002–03, Pres., Dir and CEO Raytheon Co. 2003–04, Chair. and CEO 2004–; mem. Bd Congressional Medal of Honor Foundation; mem. Advisory Council Calif. Polytechnic State Univ. School of Eng, Bd of Regents Pepperdine Univ., Bd of Visitors Graziadio School of Business and Man., CIA Officers Memorial Foundation Bd of Advisors, Pres.'s Nat. Security Telecommunications Advisory Cttee; mem. Bd Dirs Cal Poly Foundation, John F. Kennedy Library Foundation, Bd Govs' Exec. Cttee, Aerospace Industries Asscn; Vice-Chair. Business-Higher Educ. Forum, Co-Chair. Securing America's Leadership in Science, Tech., Eng and Math. Initiative; mem. Editorial Advisory Bd The Journal of Electronic Defense; mem. Nat. Defense Industrial Asscn, Asscn of the United States Army, the Navy League, Air Force Assc'n; a Regent of Pepperdine Univ.; Trustee, Assc'n of the US Army; Fellow, AIAA; Hon. Chair. MATHCOUNTS®; Hon. LLD (Pepperdine Univ.) 2002, Hon. DrSc (California Polytechnic State Univ.); Outstanding Industrial Eng Grad. 1972, Hon. Alumnus Award, Calif. Polytechnic State Univ. School of Eng 1991, Semper Fidelis Award, Marine Corps Scholarship Foundation, Aviation Week & Space Technology Laurel Award for "significant contributions" to the field of aeronautics/propulsion, named "California Manufacturer of the Year" by California Manufacturing & Tech. Assc'n, Navy League Fleet Adm. Chester W. Nimitz Award, NDIA James Forrestal Industry Leadership Award, John W. Dixon Award, Assc'n of the United States Army, Diversity Best Practices CEO Diversity Leadership Award, Inst. of Industrial Engineers' Captains of Industry Award, Six Sigma Premier Leader Award, Int. Soc. of Six Sigma Professionals, Woodrow Wilson Award for Corp. Citizenship, Kennedy Greenway Vision Award. *Address:* Raytheon Co., Mail Stop 2335, 870 Winter Street, Waltham, MA 02451-1449, USA (office). *Telephone:* (781) 522-3000 (office). *Fax:* (781) 522-3001 (office). *E-mail:* info@raytheon.com (office). *Website:* www.raytheon.com (office).

SWAR AD-DAHAB, Field Marshal (see DAHAB, Field Marshal Abdul-Rahman Swar ad-).

SWARAJ, Sushma, BA, LLB; Indian politician; *Leader of the Opposition, Lok Sabha;* b. 14 Feb. 1952, Ambala Cantonment; m. Swaraj Kaushal 1975; one d.; ed Punjab Univ., Chandigarh; Advocate, Supreme Court of India 1973–; mem. (Janata Party) Haryana Legis. Ass. 1977–82, (Bharatiya Janata Party–BJP) 1987–90; All-India Sec. BJP 1985–87, 1990–92, All-India Gen. Sec. and Official Spokesperson 1992–96; Cabinet Minister 1977–78; Minister for Educ. 1987–89; mem. Parl. (Rajya Sabha) 1990–96, 2000–, Chair. Cttee on Petitions 1994–96; mem. Parl. (Lok Sabha) for S Delhi 1996–98, 1998–2000, for Vidisha 2009–, Leader of the Opposition 2009–; mem. Delhi Legis. Ass. 1998; Chief Minister of Delhi 1998; Minister of Information and Broadcasting 1996–98, 2000–03, with additional charge of Ministry of Communications 1998; Minister of Health and Family Welfare and of Parl. Affairs 2003–04; Head of BJP 2009 poll campaign cttee. *Address:* Bharatiya Janata Party, 11 Ashok Road, New Delhi 110 001 (office); Daga House, in front of Raja Bhoj Airport, Bhopal, India (home). *Telephone:* (11) 23382234 (office). *Fax:* (11) 23782163 (office). *E-mail:* bjpco@vsnl.com (office). *Website:* www.bjp.org (office).

SWEDISH, Joseph R., BA, MA; American business executive; *CEO, WellPoint, Inc.;* ed Univ. of North Carolina, Charlotte, Duke Univ.; has worked in health care industry since early 1970s; has served as CEO for a range of major health systems since 1989; Pres. and CEO Trinity Health Corpn 2004–13; CEO WellPoint, Inc. 2013–; mem. Bd of Dirs Blue Cross Blue Shield Assc'n, Nat. Inst. for Health Care Man., America's Health Insurance Plans, Catholic Health Assc'n; mem. Nat. Quality Forum, Health Research and Educational Trust. *Address:* WellPoint, Inc., 120 Monument Circle, Indianapolis, IN 46204, USA (office). *Telephone:* (317) 532-6000 (office). *Fax:* (317) 488-6028 (office). *E-mail:* boardofdirectors@wellpoint.com (office). *Website:* www.wellpoint.com (office).

SWEENEY, Anne Mary, BA, EdM; American media executive; *Co-Chair, Media Networks and President, Disney-ABC Television Group, The Walt Disney Company;* b. 4 Nov. 1957, Kingston, NY; m. Philip Miller; two c.; ed The Coll. of New Rochelle, NY and Harvard Univ.; various exec. positions at Nickelodeon/Nick at Nite 1981–93, most recently Sr Vice-Pres. Program Enterprises; Chair. and CEO FX Networks Inc. 1993–96; Pres. Disney Channel and Exec. Vice-Pres. Disney/ABC Cable Networks, The Walt Disney Co. 1996–2000, Pres. ABC Cable Networks Group and Disney Channel Worldwide 2000–04, Co-Chair. Media Networks and

Pres. Disney-ABC Television, The Walt Disney Co. 2004–; mem. Bd of Dirs Lifetime Television, The Museum of Radio & Television, Special Olympics, Women in Cable and Telecommunications, Walter Kaitz Foundation; Hon. Chair. Cable Positive; Women in Cable Exec. of the Year 1994, American Women in Radio and Television STAR Award 1995, inducted into American Advertising Fed.'s Advertising Hall of Achievement 1996, Women in Cable Woman of the Year 1997, Women in Cable Advocate Leader Award, Southern Calif. chapter 1998, Women in Film's Lucy Award 2002, Cable Television Public Affairs Assc'n's Pres.'s Award 2004, New York Women in Film & Television Muse Award 2004, named by The Hollywood Reporter "The Most Powerful Woman in Entertainment", inducted into the Broadcasting & Cable Hall of Fame 2005, ranked by Fortune magazine amongst 50 Most Powerful Women in Business in the US (39th) 2002, (35th) 2003, (18th) 2004, (16th) 2005, (13th) 2006, (15th) 2007, (12th) 2008, (16th) 2009, (15th) 2010, (14th) 2011, (12th) 2012, ranked by Forbes magazine amongst The World's 100 Most Powerful Women (27th) 2004, (33rd) 2005, (15th) 2006, (77th) 2007, (30th) 2008, (52nd) 2009, (69th) 2010, (25th) 2011, (22nd) 2012, (24th) 2013. *Address:* 500 S Buena Vista Street, Burbank, CA 91521-9722, USA (office). *Telephone:* (818) 560-1000 (office). *Fax:* (818) 560-1930 (office). *Website:* www .disneyabctv.com (office).

SWEENEY, John Joseph, BSc; American trade union official; *President Emeritus, AFL-CIO;* b. 5 May 1934, Bronx, New York; s. of John Sweeney and Patricia Sweeney; m. Maureen Power; one s. one d.; ed Iona Coll.; with IBM (Int. Business Machines Corpn); researcher, Int. Ladies Garment Workers Union; Contract Dir Building Service Employees Int. Union (later Service Employees Int. Union) New York City Local 32B 1960–80, Pres. 1980; Vice-Pres. AFL-CIO (American Fed. of Labor-Congress of Industrial Orgs) 1980–95, Pres. 1995–2009 (retd), Pres. Emer. 2009–; Presidential Medal of Freedom 2010. *Publication:* America Needs a Raise 1996. *Address:* c/o AFL-CIO, 815 16th Street, NW, Washington, DC 20006, USA (office).

SWEENEY, Ed, CBE, BA, MSc; British; *Chairman, Advisory, Conciliation and Arbitration Service;* ed Univ. of Warwick, London School of Econs; Research Officer Nat. Union of Bank Employees (NUBE) 1977, various roles in finance, becoming Deputy Gen. Sec. Banking Insurance and Finance Union (BIFU) 1991–96, Gen. Sec. 1996–2000, Gen. Sec. UNIFI 2000–04, Deputy Gen. Sec. Amicus (following merger) 2004–07; Chair. Advisory, Conciliation and Arbitration Service 2007–; mem. TUC Gen. Council, TUC Exec. Cttee; Chair. TUC Int. Devt Group; Jt Chair. DfID/TUC Forum; mem. TUC Superannuation Cttee, TUC Learning and Skills Task Group; TUC Skills for Life Advocate; mem. Trade Union Sustainable Devt Cttee; mem. Council Inst. of Employment Rights; mem. British Del. to WTO Ministerial Confs 2001, 2003; Reviewer on Occupational Pensions De-Regulation Review; Visiting Prof., Leeds Business School. *Address:* Advisory, Conciliation and Arbitration Service, 22nd Floor, Euston Tower, 286 Euston Road, London, NW1 3JJ, England (office). *E-mail:* esweeney@acas.org.uk (office). *Website:* www.acas.org.uk (office).

SWENSEN, Joseph Anton; American conductor, composer and violinist; *Founder and Director, U-HAC International;* b. 4 Aug. 1960, New York, NY; m. 2nd Kristina Algot-Sörensen; three s. (one from previous m.); ed Juilliard School; Prin. Guest Conductor Stockholm Chamber Orchestra 1994–97, Lahti Symphony Orchestra 1995–2000; Prin. Conductor Scottish Chamber Orchestra (SCO) 1996–2005, Conductor Emer. 2005–; Prin. Guest Conductor BBC Nat. Orchestra of Wales 2000–03; Prin. Conductor Malmö Opera och Musikteater 2006–11; Prin. Guest Conductor and Artistic Advisor Ensemble Orchestral de Paris 2009–12; Founder and Dir Habitat4Music 2012–; toured Japan with SCO 1995, USA 1999; debut at Edinburgh Int. Festival with SCO 1998; cycle of Beethoven performances to mark 25th anniversary of SCO 1999; conducted new production of The Marriage of Figaro at the Royal Danish Opera 1999; Guest Conductor with City of Birmingham Symphony, Finnish Radio Symphony, Hallé Orchestra, Orchestra Nat. du Capitole de Toulouse; Prof. of Music, Indiana Univ. Jacobs Schooll of Music 2013–; own orchestral works have been performed by various orchestras; Dr hc (St Andrew's, Scotland) 2001; Leventritt Foundation Scholarship 1978, Avery Fisher Career Grant 1982. *Recordings include:* Mendelssohn, Sibelius, Brahms, Prokofiev, Dvořák. *Address:* c/o Victoria Rowsell Artist Management Ltd, 34 Addington Square, London, SE5 7LB, England (office). *Telephone:* (20) 7701-3219 (office). *Fax:* (20) 7701-3219 (office). *E-mail:* management@victoriarowsell.co.uk (office). *Website:* www.victoriarowsell.co.uk (office); www.josephswensen.com.

SWETT, Richard Nelson, BA, FAIA; American architect, business consultant, diplomatist and fmr politician; *CEO, Climate PROSPERITY Enterprise Solutions, LLC;* b. 1 May 1957, Lower Merion, Pa; s. of the late Philip Eugene Swett Sr and of Ann Parkhurst Swett; m.; three s. four d.; ed Yale Univ.; licensed architect in several states; has worked in real estate devt, alternative energy devt, energy conservation, industrial devt and export promotion; mem. US House of Reps from 2nd Congressional Dist of NH, Washington, DC 1990–95, mem. several Congressional Cttees, co-author Congressional Accountability Act, author, Transportation for Livable Communities Act; Amb. to Denmark 1998–2001; fmr Sr Counselor, APCO Worldwide Inc.; fmr Pres. Swett Assocs Inc.; Co-founder and CEO Climate PROSPERITY Enterprise Solutions, LLC 2011–; mem. Board of Advisors, H.C. Andersen Foundation; mem. Bd of Peers overseeing design quality issues for US Gen. Services Admin for US Govt bldg portfolio; Founding mem. Advisory Bd European Center of Calif. 2001–06; mem. Bd Sunrise Capital Partners 2001–04, CATCH (Concord Area Trust for Community Housing); fmr State Chair. US Olympic Cttee 2001; Fellow, AIA; Sr Fellow, Design Futures Council; Grand-Croix of the Order of the Dannebrog (Denmark) 2001; Hon. LLD (Franklin Pierce Coll.) and several other hon. degrees; Presidential Citation, AIA. *Publications:* A Nation Reconstructed, A Quest to Make Cities All That They Can Be (co-author), Leadership by Design: Creating an Architecture of Trust. *Leisure interests:* tennis, reading, piano, sailing, skiing, running, basketball, golf, painting, travel, family. *Address:* CPES, 5 South State Street, Suite 1, Concord, NH 03301 (office); 1 Putney Road, Bow, NH 03304, USA (home). *Telephone:* (603) 226-1072 (office). *Fax:* (603) 226-1071 (office). *E-mail:* jwasag@ClimatePROSPERITYSolutions.com (office). *Website:* www.climateprosperitysolutions.com (office).

ŚWIĘCICKI, Marcin, DEconSc; Polish politician and economist; *Director, UNDP Blue Ribbon Analytical and Advisory Centre, Kyiv;* b. 17 April 1947, Warsaw; s. of Andrzej Święcicki and Jadwiga Święcicka; m. Joanna Szyr 1969; three s., one d.; ed

Warsaw Univ.; Asst. Econ. Sciences Inst., Warsaw Univ. 1971–72; Councillor, then Chief Specialist in Planning Comm. attached to the Council of Ministers 1972–82; Dir for study and analysis matters 1982–87, Gen. Sec. of Consultative Econ. Council 1987–89; mem. PZPR 1974–90, PZPR Cen. Cttee 1989–90, Sec. PZPR Cen. Cttee Aug.–Sept. 1989; participant Round Table debates, mem. group for economy and social policy Feb.–April 1989; Deputy to Sejm (Parl.) 1989–91, 1993–96; Minister for Foreign Econ. Co-operation 1989–91; Deputy Chair. Sejm Cttee on Foreign Econ. Relations 1993–95; Mayor of Warsaw 1994–99; Co-Chair. Govt and Territorial Self-Govt Jt Comm. 1994–99; Adviser to Lithuanian Govt 1993; Co-Founder Tax Reform Movt 1993–; Co-Founder Cen. European Forum 1995–; Pres. Union of Polish Metropolises 1994–99; mem. Polish Econ. Soc. 1978–; Co-Founder Consensus Dialogue Group 1986–90, mem. Secr. 1986–89; Co-Founder and Treas. Polish Asscn for the Club of Rome 1987–91; scientific worker, Inst. of Econ. Sciences, Polish Acad. of Sciences 1991–93; ind. adviser 1991–94, 2001–; Under-Sec. of State, Ministry of the Economy 1999; mem. Negotiating Team, Polish Accession to EU 1999–2000; Adviser to Pres. of Lithuania 1999–2000; Co-ordinator of OSCE Econ. and Environmental Activities 2002–05; Dir UNDP Blue Ribbon Analytical and Advisory Centre, Kyiv, Ukraine 2007–; mem. Democratic Union (now Freedom Union) 1991–2009 (mem. Council, Warsaw br. 1991–93, mem. Nat. Council 1993–2009); Co-Founder and Vice-Pres. Polish Fulbright Alumni Asscn 1993–96; Pres. Polish Cttee of Support for Museum of the History of Polish Jews 1997–; Fellowship, George Washington Univ., Washington, DC 1975–76, Harvard Univ. 1984–85; Hon. mem. Union of Warsaw Uprising Veterans (Związek Powstańców Warszawskich); Gold and Bronze Cross of Merit; Bronze Medal in long jump, European Jr Athletic Championship, Odessa 1966, Labour and Wages Comm. Award 1971, Award of Chair. of Radio and TV Cttee 1988, Daily Trybuna Ludu Award 1989. *Publications include:* Perspektywiczne programowanie problemowe w Polsce 1978, Revolution in Social Sciences and Future Studies Movement 1978, Rozwój sytuacji i polityki gospodarczej (Ed.) 1985, Reforma własnościowa 1989, The Economy of Ukraine (with Stanisław Wellisz) 1993, Demographic and Financial Preconditions for Pension Reform in Ukraine 2010. *Leisure interests:* mountain hiking, jogging, volleyball, political books, memoirs, essays. *Address:* Węgrzyna 29, 00-769 Warsaw, Poland (home); UNDP Blue Ribbon Analytical and Advisory Centre, 1/14 Sadova St., 4th floor, 01021 Kyiv, Ukraine (office). *Telephone:* (22) 6423651 (Warsaw) (home); (44) 2535866 (Kyiv) (office). *Fax:* (22) 6422722 (Warsaw) (home); (44) 2535611 (Kyiv) (office). *E-mail:* marcin.swiecicki@undp.org (office); m.swiecicki@melog.com (office). *Website:* www.un.org/brc (office); www.swiecicki.pl (home).

SWIFT, Graham Colin, FRSL; British writer; b. 4 May 1949, London, England; s. of Lionel Allan Stanley Swift and Sheila Irene Swift (née Bourne); ed Dulwich Coll., Queens' Coll., Cambridge, Univ. of York; Hon. Fellow, Queens' Coll. Cambridge 2005; Hon. LittD (East Anglia) 1998; Hon. DUniv (York) 1998; Hon. DLit (London) 2003; Geoffrey Faber Memorial Prize, Guardian Fiction Prize, RSL Winifred Holtby Award 1983, Premio Grinzane Cavour (Italy) 1987, Prix du meilleur livre étranger (France) 1994, Booker Prize, James Tait Black Memorial Prize 1996. *Publications include:* novels: The Sweet Shop Owner 1980, Shuttlecock 1981, Waterland 1983, Out of This World 1988, Ever After 1992, Last Orders 1996, The Light of Day 2003, Tomorrow 2007, Wish You Were Here 2011; short stories: Learning to Swim and Other Stories 1982, England and Other Stories 2014; anthology: The Magic Wheel (co-ed. with David Profumo) 1986; non-fiction: Making an Elephant: Writing from Within 2009. *Leisure interest:* fishing. *Address:* c/o AP Watt at United Agents LLP, 12–26 Lexington Street, London, W1F 0LE, England (office). *Telephone:* (20) 3214-0800 (office). *Fax:* (20) 3214-0801 (office). *E-mail:* info@unitedagents.co.uk (office). *Website:* www.apwatt.co.uk (office).

SWIFT, Taylor Alison; American singer and songwriter; b. 13 Dec. 1989, Wyomissing, Pa; d. of Scott Swift and Andrea Swift; began songwriting 2001; solo artist 2006–; CMA Horizon Award 2007, CMT Award for Female Video of the Year 2008, Acad. of Country Music Awards for Best New Female Vocalist 2008, for Entertainer of the Year 2011, 2012, for Video of the Year (for Highway Don't Care) 2014, CMA Awards for Female Vocalist of the Year 2009, for Entertainer of the Year 2009, 2011, for Music Video of the Year 2009, for Int. Achievement 2009, American Music Awards for Artist of the Year 2009, 2013, for Favorite Female Artist 2009, for Favorite Pop/Rock Female Artist 2009, 2013, for Favorite Adult Contemporary Artist 2009, for Favorite Country Female Artist 2013, for Musical Event of the Year (for Highway Don't Care) 2013, CMA Pinnacle Award 2013, Grammy Awards for Best Female Country Vocal Performance (for White Horse) 2010, for Best Country Song (for White Horse) 2010, for Country Solo Performance (for Mean) 2012, for Country Song (for Mean) 2012, for Best Song Written for Visual Media (for Safe & Sound) 2013, Woman of the Year, Billboard magazine 2011, MTV Europe Music Award for Best Female 2012, for Best Live Act 2012, for Best Look 2012, Billboard Music Awards for Top Artist 2013, for Top Female Artist 2013, for Top Country Artist 2013, for Top Billboard 200 Artist 2013, for Top Digital Songs Artist 2013, for Top Country Song (for We Are Never Ever Getting Back Together) 2013, American Country Award for Single of the Year: Vocal Collaboration (for Highway Don't Care) 2013, for Worldwide Artist of the Year 2013, MTV Video Music Award for Best Female Video (for I Knew You Were Trouble) 2013. *Recordings include:* albums: Taylor Swift 2006, Sound of the Season 2007, Fearless (Acad. of Country Music Award for Best Album 2009, CMA Award for Album of the Year 2009, American Music Award for Favorite Country Album 2009, Grammy Award for Album of the Year 2010, Grammy Award for Best Country Album 2010) 2008, Speak Now 2010, Red (Billboard Music Awards for Top Billboard 200 Album 2013, for Top Country Album 2013, American Music Award for Favorite Country Album 2013) 2012. *Film appearances:* Valentine's Day 2010, Dr Seuss' The Lorax (voice) 2012. *Address:* c/o Big Machine Records, 1219 16th Avenue South, Nashville, TN 37212, USA. *Website:* www.bigmachinerecords.com; www.taylorswift.com.

SWINBURNE, Richard Granville, MA, BPhil, FBA; British academic; *Nolloth Professor Emeritus of the Philosophy of the Christian Religion, University of Oxford;* b. 26 Dec. 1934, Smethwick, West Midlands, England; s. of William H. Swinburne and Gladys E. Swinburne; m. Monica Holmstrom 1960 (separated 1985); two d.; ed Univ. of Oxford; Fereday Fellow, St John's Coll., Oxford 1958–61; Leverhulme Research Fellow in History and Philosophy of Science, Univ. of Leeds 1961–63; Lecturer in Philosophy, Univ. of Hull 1963–72; Prof. of Philosophy, Univ. of Keele 1972–84; Nolloth Prof. of the Philosophy of the Christian Religion, Univ. of

Oxford 1985–2002, Prof. Emer. 2002–; Visiting Assoc. Prof., Univ. of Maryland 1969–70; Visiting Prof., Syracuse Univ. 1987, Univ. of Rome 2002, Catholic Univ. of Lublin 2002, Yale Univ. 2003, St Louis Univ. 2003. *Publications:* Space and Time 1968 (second edn) 1981, The Concept of Miracle 1971, An Introduction to Confirmation Theory 1973, The Coherence of Theism 1977 (revised edn 1993), The Existence of God 1979 (second edn) 2004, Faith and Reason 1981 (second edn) 2005, Personal Identity (with S. Shoemaker) 1984, The Evolution of the Soul 1986, revised edn 1997), Responsibility and Atonement 1989, Revelation 1991 (second edn) 2007, The Christian God 1994, Is There a God? 1996 (revised edn) 2010, Providence and the Problem of Evil 1998, Epistemic Justification 2001, The Resurrection of God Incarnate 2003, Was Jesus God? 2008, Mind, Brain, & Free Will 2013. *Address:* 50 Butler Close, Oxford, OX2 6JG, England (home). *Telephone:* (1865) 514406 (home). *E-mail:* richard.swinburne@oriel.ox.ac.uk (office).

SWING, William Lacy, BA, BD; American diplomatist and international organization official; *Director-General, International Organization for Migration;* b. 11 Sept. 1934, Lexington, N Carolina; s. of Baxter D. Swing and Mary F. Swing (née Barbee); m. Yuen Cheong 1993; one s. one d. from previous m.; ed Catawba Coll., Yale Univ., Tübingen Univ., Harvard Univ.; Vice-Consul, Port Elizabeth, S Africa 1963–66; int. economist, Bureau of Econ. Affairs, Dept of State 1966–68; Consul, Hamburg 1968–72; Desk Officer for FRG, Dept of State 1972–74; Deputy Chief of Mission, Embassy in Bangui, Cen. African Repub. 1974–76; Sr Fellow, Center for Int. Affairs, Harvard Univ. 1976–77; Deputy Dir, Office of Cen. African Affairs, Dept of State 1977–79; Amb. to Repub. of the Congo 1979–81, to Liberia 1981–85, to S Africa 1989–92, to Nigeria 1992–93, to Haiti 1993–98, to Democratic Repub. of the Congo 1998–2001; Dir Office of Foreign Service Assignments and Career Devt 1985–87; Deputy Asst Sec. for Personnel 1987–89; Special Rep. of UN Sec.-Gen. for Western Sahara 2001–03, Democratic Repub. of the Congo 2003–08; Dir-Gen. Int. Org. for Migration 2008–; Fellow, Harvard Univ.; Hon. Fellow, Univ. of Oxford 2013; Hon. LLD (Catawba Coll.) 1980; Hon. DHumLitt (Hofstra) 1994; Presidential Distinguished Service Award 1985; Distinguished Honor Award 1994, Award for Valor 1995, Presidential Meritorious Service Award 1987, 1990, 1994, 1998, Presidential Certificate of Commendation 1998, Award for Lifetime Contribs to American Diplomacy, American Foreign Service Asscn 2012. *Publications:* Education for Decision 1963, U.S. Policy Towards South Africa: Dilemmas and Priorities 1977, Liberia: The Road to Recovery 1982, Haiti: In Physical Contact with History 1994; book chapter in Challenges of Peace Implementation 2004. *Leisure interests:* tennis, squash, golf. *Address:* International Organization for Migration, 17 route des Morillons, CP 71, 1211 Geneva 19, Switzerland (office). *Telephone:* (22) 717-9111 (office). *Fax:* (22) 798-6150 (office). *E-mail:* hq@iom.int (office). *Website:* www.iom.int (office).

SWINNERTON-DYER, Sir (Henry) Peter Francis, Bt, KBE, MA, FRS; British mathematician and academic; *Professor Emeritus, Department of Pure Mathematics and Mathematical Statistics, University of Cambridge;* b. 2 Aug. 1927, Ponteland; s. of the late Sir Leonard Dyer; m. Dr Harriet Crawford 1983; ed Eton Coll. and Trinity Coll., Cambridge; Research Fellow, Trinity Coll. 1950–54; Commonwealth Fund Fellow, Univ. of Chicago 1954–55; Coll. Lecturer in Math., Trinity Coll. 1955–71, Dean 1963–70; Lecturer in Math., Cambridge Univ. 1960–71, Prof. of Math. 1971–88, now Prof. Emer., Master of St Catharine's Coll. 1973–83; Vice-Chancellor, Cambridge Univ. 1979–81; Chair. Univ. Grants Cttee 1983–89, Chief Exec. Univs Funding Council 1989–91; apptd Chair. European Scientific and Tech. Ass. 1994; Chair. Sec. of State for Nat. Heritage's Advisory Cttee, Library and Information Services Council 1992–95; mem. Advisory Bd for Research Councils 1977–90; Vice-Pres. Inst. of Manpower Studies 1983; Visiting Prof. Harvard Univ. 1970–71; Chair. Cttee on Acad. Org., Univ. of London 1980–81; mem. Advisory Council on Science and Tech. 1987–89; Hon. Fellow, Worcester Coll., Oxford 1980, St Catharine's Coll., Cambridge 1983, Trinity Coll., Cambridge 1983; Hon. DSc (Bath) 1981, (Wales) 1991, Hon. ScD (Ulster) 1991, (Birmingham) 1992, (Nottingham) 1992, Hon. LLD (Aberdeen) 1991, Dr hc (Oslo) 2003; Sylvester Medal 2006. *Publications:* Analytic Theory of Abelian Varieties 1974, A Brief Guide to Algebraic Number Theory 2002 and papers in learned journals. *Leisure interest:* gardening. *Address:* The Dower House, Thriplow, Royston, Herts., SG8 7RJ; Department of Pure Mathematics and Mathematical Statistics, Centre for Mathematical Sciences, University of Cambridge, Wilberforce Road, Cambridge, CB3 0WB, England (office). *Website:* www.dpmms.cam.ac.uk (office).

SWINNEY, John Ramsay, MA; Scottish politician and management specialist; *Cabinet Secretary for Finance and Sustainable Growth;* b. 13 April 1964, Edin., Scotland; s. of Kenneth Swinney and Nancy Swinney (née Hunter); m. 1st Lorna Ann King 1991 (divorced 1998); one s. one d.; m. 2nd Elizabeth Quigley 2003; one s.; ed Univ. of Edinburgh; Sr Man. Consultant, Devt Options Ltd 1988–92; Strategic Planning Prin., Scottish Amicable 1992–97; MP (Scottish Nat. Party—SNP) for N Tayside 1997–2001; MSP (SNP) for N Tayside 1999–2011, for Perthshire N 2011–; Leader of the Opposition 2000–04, Convener Enterprise and Lifelong Learning Cttee 1999–2000, Convener European and External Relations Cttee 2004–05; Nat. Sec. SNP 1986–92, Vice-Convener for Publicity 1992–97, Treasury Spokesperson 1995–2000, Sr Vice-Convener (Deputy Leader) 1998–2000, Nat. Convener (Leader) 2000–04; Shadow Minister for Finance and Public Services 2005–07; Cabinet Sec. for Finance and Sustainable Growth 2007–. *Leisure interests:* hill walking, cycling, running. *Address:* 35 Perth Street, Blairgowrie, PH10 6DL, Scotland (office). *Telephone:* (1250) 876576 (office). *Fax:* (1250) 876991 (office). *E-mail:* john.swinney.msp@scottish.parliament.uk (office). *Website:* johnswinneymsp.com.

SWINTON, Tilda, BA (Hons); British actress; b. (Katherine Mathilda Swinton), 5 Nov. 1960, London, England; d. of Maj.-Gen. Sir John Swinton, KCVO, OBE, DL and Judith Balfour, Lady Swinton (née Killen); partner John Byrne 1989–2005; two c. (twins); partner Sandro Kopp 2004–; ed Queen's Gate School, London, West Heath Girls' School, Fettes Coll., New Hall, Cambridge; known for both avant-garde and mainstream films; mem. Jury, 38th Berlin Int. Film Festival 1988; performance art appearance sleeping in a glass case, Serpentine Gallery, London 1996; f. Ballerina Ballroom Cinema Of Dreams film festival 2008; Dr hc (Royal Scottish Acad. of Music and Drama, Glasgow) 2006. *Films:* Caravaggio 1986, Egomania – Insel ohne Hoffnung 1986, Aria 1987, Friendship's Death 1987, Das andere Ende der Welt 1988, Degrees of Blindness 1988, L'ispirazione (short) 1988, The Last of

England 1988, War Requiem 1989, Play Me Something 1989, The Garden 1990, Edward II 1991, The Party: Nature Morte 1991, Orlando 1992, Wittgenstein 1993, Blue (voice) 1993, Remembrance of Things Fast: True Stories Visual Lies 1994, Female Perversions 1996, Conceiving Ada 1997, Love is the Devil: Study for a Portrait of Francis Bacon 1998, The War Zone 1999, The Protagonists 1999, The Beach 2000, Possible Worlds 2000, The Deep End 2001, Vanilla Sky 2001, Teknolust 2002, Adaptation 2003, Young Adam (Scottish BAFTA Award for Best Actress 2004) 2003, The Statement 2003, Thumbsucker 2004, Broken Flowers 2005, Constantine 2005, Absent Presence (short) 2005, The Chronicles of Narnia: The Lion, the Witch and the Wardrobe 2005, Stephanie Daley 2006, Deep Water (voice) 2006, The Man from London 2007, Sleepwalkers 2007, Michael Clayton (Acad. Award for Best Supporting Actress 2008) 2007, Burn After Reading 2008, The Chronicles of Narnia: Prince Caspian 2008, Julia 2008, The Curious Case of Benjamin Button 2008, The Limits of Control 2009, Io Sono l'Amore (I Am Love) 2009, The Chronicles of Narnia: The Voyage of the Dawn Treader 2010, We Need to Talk about Kevin (several awards for Best Actress including Austin Film Critics Asscn Award, European Film Award, Houston Film Critics Award, Nat. Bd of Review Award, Online Film Critics Soc. Award, San Francisco Film Critics Circle Award) 2011, Genevieve Goes Boating (video short) (narrator) 2011, Moonrise Kingdom 2012, Snowpiercer 2013, Only Lovers Left Alive 2013, The Zero Theorem 2013. *Television:* Zastrozzi: A Romance (mini-series) 1986, Your Cheatin' Heart (series) 1990, Screenplay (series) – Man to Man: Another Night of Rubbish on the Telly 1992, Shakespeare: The Animated Tales (series) – Hamlet 1992, Das offene Universum (film) 1993, The Somme (film) 2005, Getting On (series) 2012. *Address:* c/o Christian Hodell, Hamilton Hodell Ltd, Fifth Floor, 66–68 Margaret Street, London, W1W 8SR, England (office). *Telephone:* (20) 7636-1221 (office). *Fax:* (20) 7636-1226 (office). *E-mail:* info@hamiltonhodell.co.uk (office). *Website:* www.hamiltonhodell.co.uk (office).

SWIRE, Sir Adrian (Christopher), Kt, MA; British business executive; *Honorary President, John Swire & Sons;* b. 15 Feb. 1932, London; s. of the late John Kidston Swire and Juliet Richenda Barclay; m. Lady Judith Compton 1970; two s. one d.; ed Eton, Univ. Coll., Oxford; served Coldstream Guards 1950–52; fmrly with RAFVR and Royal Auxiliary Air Force; joined Butterfield & Swire in Far East 1956; Dir, John Swire & Sons Ltd 1961–2004, Deputy Chair. 1966–87, Chair. 1987–97, 2002–04, Exec. Dir 1998–2002, Hon. Pres. 1998–; Dir, Swire Pacific 1978–2008; Pro-Chancellor, Southampton Univ. 1995–2004; Dir, Cathay Pacific Airways 1965–2005, Brooke Bond Group 1972–82, Navy, Army and Air Force Insts 1972–87, HSBC Holdings PLC 1995–2002; Pres., Gen. Council of British Shipping 1980–81; Chair., Int. Chamber of Shipping 1982–87; mem. Gen. Cttee Lloyds Register 1967–99, Int. Advisory Council, China Int. Trust and Investment Corpn 1995–2005; Chair., RAF Benevolent Fund 1996–2000; Pres., Spitfire Soc. 1996–2009; Trustee, RAF Museum 1983–91; Hon. Air Commodore Royal Auxiliary Air Force 1987–2000; DL Oxfordshire 1989; Hon. Fellow, Nuffield Coll., Oxford 1998; Hon. DSc (Cranfield) 1995, Hon. DUniv (Southampton) 2002; Air League Founder's Medal 2006. *Address:* Swire House, 59 Buckingham Gate, London, SW1E 6AJ, England (office). *Telephone:* (20) 7834-7717 (office). *Fax:* (20) 7630-0380 (office). *E-mail:* acs@jssldn.co.uk (office).

SWITKOWSKI, Zygmunt (Ziggy) Edward, BSc, PhD; Australian (b. German) scientist and business executive; b. 21 June 1948, Rheine, Germany; m. Jadzia Teresa 1970; one s. one d.; ed St Bernardo's Coll., Univ. of Melbourne; Sr Research Scientist, Eastman Kodak Co., New York 1978–80, Man. Research and Devt 1980–82, Sales Man. 1982–83, Marketing Man. Consumer Products 1983–85, Dir Business Planning 1985–88; Deputy Man. Dir Kodak (Australasia) Ltd 1988–92, Chair., Man. Dir 1992–96; Dir Amcor Ltd 1995–99; Chair., Acting CEO Optus Vision Pty Ltd 1996–97, CEO Optus Communications Pty Ltd 1996–97; Group Man. Dir Business Int. Div. Telstra Corpn Ltd 1997–99, CEO 1999–2004 (resgnd); Chair. Australian Nuclear Science and Tech. Org. 2007–10; Chair. Opera Australia 2008–; Chancellor Royal Melbourne Inst. of Tech. 2011–; Dir (non-Exec.) Suncorp, Tabcorp, Oil Search, Lynas; fmr Chair. Australian Quality Council; Fellow, Australian Inst. of Co. Dirs; mem. Business Council of Australia. *Address:* c/o Opera Australia, 480 Elizabeth Street, Surry Hills, NSW 2010, Australia (office). *Website:* www.opera-australia.org.au (office).

SY, Henry, Sr; Philippine retail executive; *Chairman, SM Prime Holdings Inc.;* b. 25 Oct. 1924, Xiamen, China; m.; six c.; ed Far Eastern Univ., Manila; moved to Philippines 1936; worked in father's convenience store from age 12; opened shoe shop in Quiapo 1946; opened first ShoeMart (SM) store 1958, first dept store 1972, first mall in Quezon City Dist, Manila 1985; Chair. SM Prime Holdings Inc. 1994–; Chair. SM Land Inc. (fmrly Shoemart Inc.); Chair. and CEO SM Investments Corpn, SM Development Corpn, Highlands Prime Holdings Inc.; Chair. Emer. Banco de Oro Unibank Inc.; Hon. Chair. China Banking Corpn. *Address:* SM Corporate Offices, Building A, J.W. Diokno Boulevard, Mall of Asia Complex, Pasay City 1300, Philippines (office). *Telephone:* (2) 8311000 (office). *Fax:* (2) 8341800 (office). *E-mail:* info@smprime.com (office). *Website:* www.smprime.com (office).

SY-COSON, Teresita T., AB-BSc; Philippine retail executive; *Executive Vice-President and Advisor, SM Prime Holdings Inc.;* b. 19 Oct. 1950, Manila; d. of Henry Sy, Sr; m. Louis Coson (died 2003); three c.; ed Assumption Coll.; Pres. Shoemart 1990, mem. Bd of Dirs and Exec. Vice-Pres. SM Prime Holdings Inc. 1994–, Advisor 2008–, Vice-Chair. Investments Corpn (SM Group's holding co.); fmr Chair. and Chief Exec. Banco de Oro Universal, Chair. Banco de Oro Unibank, Inc. –2005, (following merger with Equitable PCI Bank) 2007–, Vice-Chair. June–July 2007; Dir and Exec. Vice-Pres. First Asia Realty Devt Corpn; Pres. SM Mart, Inc.; Pres. and Chair. ShoeMart, Inc., Supervalue, Inc.; Chair. BDO Realty Corpn, BDO Leasing & Finance, Inc. (Dir 2005–); Vice-Chair. Generali Pilipinas Holding Co., Inc., Equitable PCI Bank 2006–; Dir, Multi-Realty Devt Corpn, Supervalue, Inc., Asia-Pacific Computer Tech. Center, Inc., BDO Capital Insurance Brokers, Inc., SM Keppel Land, Inc., PCI Leasing & Finance, Inc. 2005–, PCI Capital Corpn, Equitable Card Network, Inc., Equitable Savings Bank, Inc., EBC Investments, Inc., and other pvt. insts; Ind. Dir, Philippine Long Distance Telephone Co. 2004–06; mem. APEC Business Advisory Council; Trustee and Treas. SM Foundation Inc. 2003–; ranked by Fortune magazine amongst the 50 Most Powerful Women in Business outside the US (39th) 2002, (45th) 2003, (47th) 2004, (46th) 2005–06, (41st) 2007, (48th) 2008, (40th) 2009, (42nd) 2010, selected by Forbes magazine as one of Top 50 International Power Women 2003, Excellence in

Retail Banking Award, The Asia Banker 2004. *Leisure interest:* reading business books. *Address:* SM Prime Holdings Inc., Building A, SM Corporate Offices, J.W. Diokno Blvd, Mall of Asia Complex, Pasay City 1300, Philippines (office). *Telephone:* (632) 831-1000 (office). *Fax:* (632) 833-8991 (office). *E-mail:* info@smprime.com (office). *Website:* www.smprime.com (office).

SYAL, Meera, MBE, BA; British writer and actress; b. 27 June 1963, Wolverhampton; d. of Surendra Syal and Surrinder Syal; m. 1st 1989; one d.; m. 2nd Sanjeev Bhaskar 2005; one s.; ed Queen Mary's High School for Girls, Walsall, Univ. of Manchester; actress in one-woman comedy One of Us after graduation (Nat. Student Drama Award); fmr actress Royal Court Theatre, London; writer of screenplays and novels; actress and comedienne in theatre, film and on TV; contrib. to The Guardian newspaper; Scottish Critics Award for Most Promising Performer 1984, Woman of the Year in the Performing Arts, Cosmopolitan Magazine 1994, Chair.'s Award, Asian Women of Achievement Awards 2002, Women in Film and TV Creative Originality Award 2002. *Plays include:* Serious Money (London and Broadway, New York) 1987, Stitch 1990, Peer Gynt 1990, Bombay Dreams (story to musical) 2001, Rafta Rafta (Royal Nat. Theatre) 2007. *Radio includes:* Legal Affairs 1996, Goodness Gracious Me 1996–98, The World as We Know It 1999. *Film appearances include:* Sammie and Rosie Get Laid 1987, A Nice Arrangement, It's Not Unusual, Beautiful Thing 1996, Girls' Night 1997, Jhoom Barabar Jhoom 2007, Mad Sad & Bad 2009. *Television appearances include:* The Real McCoy (five series) 1990–95, My Sister Wife (BBC series) 1992, Have I Got News For You 1992, 1993, 1999, Sean's Show 1993, The Brain Drain 1993, Absolutely Fabulous 1995, Soldier Soldier 1995, Degrees of Error 1995, Band of Gold 1995, Drop the Dead Donkey 1996, Ruby 1997, Keeping Mum (BBC sitcom) 1997–98, The Book Quiz 1998, Goodness Gracious Me (first UK Asian TV comedy sketch show; co-writer) 1998–2000, Room 101 1999, The Kumars at No. 42 2002–06, Jekyll 2006, Beautiful People 2008, Holby City 2009. *Written works include:* A Nice Arrangement (short TV film) 1991, My Sister Wife (TV film; Best TV Drama Award, Comm. for Racial Equality, Awards for Best Actress and Best Screenplay, Asian Film Acad. 1993) 1992, Bhaji on the Beach (film) 1994, Anita and Me (novel and adapted for TV) (Betty Trask Award) 1996, Goodness Gracious Me (comedy sketch TV show; co-writer) 1999, Life Isn't All Ha Ha Hee Hee (novel) 1999. *Leisure interests:* singing in jazz quintet, netball. *Address:* c/o Rochelle Stevens, 2 Terretts Place, Islington, London, N1 1QZ, England (office). *Telephone:* (20) 7359-3900 (office).

SYBERBERG, Hans-Jürgen, DrPhil; German film director, film producer, theatre director and writer; b. 8 Dec. 1935, Nossendorf, Pomerania; m.; ed studies in literature and history of art at Munich; made over 80 short TV films 1963–65; later work includes documentaries, feature films and theatre; several Bundesfilmpreise and other awards including Bayerischer Filmpreis. *Films:* Fritz Kortner Rehearses Schiller's Intrigue and Love 1965, Shylock Monolog 1966, The Counts Pocci 1967, How Much Earth Does a Man Need 1968, Sexbusiness Made in Passing 1969, San Domingo 1970, After My Last Removal (Brecht) 1971, Ludwig—Requiem for a Virgin King 1972, Ludwig's Cook 1972, Karl May—In Search of Paradise Lost 1974, The Confessions of Winifred Wagner 1975, Hitler, A Film from Germany 1977, Parsifal (Kritiker Preis, Berlin 1983) 1982, Die Nacht 1984, Edith Clever liest Joyce-Molly 1985, Fräulein Else 1987, Penthesilea 1988, Marquise von O 1990, Ein Traum, was sonst? 1994, Höhle der Erinnerung 1997. *Plays include:* (in collaboration with E. Clever) Die Nacht 1984, Penthesilea 1988, Die Marquise von O... 1989, Ein Traum, was sonst? 1990. *Publications include:* The Film as the Music of the Future 1975, Syberbergs Filmbuch 1976, Die Kunst als Rettung aus der deutschen Misere (essay) 1978, Die freudlose Gesellschaft 1981 Der Wald steht schwarz und schweiget 1984, VomUnglück und Glück der Kunst in Deutschland nach dem letzten Kriege 1990, Der verlorene Auftrag 1994. *Address:* Genter Strasse 15A, 80805 Munich, Germany. *Telephone:* (89) 3614882. *Fax:* (89) 3614905. *E-mail:* film@syberberg.de; hjs@syberberg.de. *Website:* www.syberberg.de.

SYCHOV, Alyaksandr; Belarusian diplomatist; *Ambassador to Austria;* b. 19 Sept. 1951, Gomel, Byelorussian SSR; m. Natalia Vedmedenko 1976; one s. one d.; ed Moscow State Inst. of Int. Relations; Third then Second Sec., Ministry of Foreign Affairs 1979–84; Del. Perm. Mission of the Repub. of Belarus to UN office and other int. orgs, Geneva 1984–90; Head Dept of Foreign Econ. Relations, Ministry of Foreign Affairs 1991–92, Deputy Minister for Foreign Affairs 1992–94; Perm. Rep. to UN, New York 1994–2000; Deputy Minister of Foreign Affairs 2000–05; Amb. to Austria 2005–, also Perm. Rep. to OSCE, JCG, OSCC and other int. orgs in Vienna; Chair. First Cttee of the 51st session of the UN Gen. Ass., 19th Special Session 1996–97; Vice-Pres. ECOSOC 1998–99. *Publications:* numerous articles on Belarus foreign policy and int. affairs. *Leisure interests:* art, opera, tennis, soccer. *Address:* Embassy of Belarus, Hüttelbergstr. 6, 1140 Vienna, Austria (office). *Telephone:* (1) 419-96-30-11 (office). *Fax:* (1) 416-96-30-30 (office). *E-mail:* mail@byembassy.at (office). *Website:* www.austria.belembassy.org (office).

SYDOW, Max von; French (b. Swedish) actor; b. 10 April 1929, Lund, Sweden; s. of Carl W. von Sydow and Greta Rappe; m. 1st Kerstin Olin 1951 (divorced 1979); two s.; m. 2nd Catherine Brelet 1997; two s.; ed Royal Dramatic Theatre School, Stockholm; Norrköping-Linköping Theatre 1951–53, Hälsingborg Theatre 1953–55, Malmö Theatre 1955–60, Royal Dramatic Theatre, Stockholm 1960–74, 1988–94; film work in Sweden 1949–95; int. productions 1962–; Commdr Ordre des Arts et Lettres; Golden Beetle Award for Best Actor 1987, 1996, for Best Dir 1988, Litteris et Artibus (medal) 1978 (Sweden). *Plays acted in include:* Peer Gynt, Henry IV (Pirandello), The Tempest, Le misanthrope, Faust, Ett Drömspel, La valse des toréadors, Les sequestrés d'Altona, After the Fall, The Wild Duck, The Night of the Tribades 1977, Duet for One 1981, The Tempest 1988, Swedenhielms 1990, And Give Us the Shadows 1991, The Ghost Sonata 1994. *Films include:* Bara en mor (Only a Mother) 1949, Fröken Julie (Miss Julie) 1951, Ingen mans kvinna 1953, Rätten att älska 1956, Det sjunde inseglet (The Seventh Seal) 1957, Smultronstället (Wild Strawberries) 1957, Prästen i Uddarbo 1957, Nära livet (So Close to Life) 1958, Spion 503 1958, Ansiktet (The Face) 1958, Jungfrukällan (The Virgin Spring) 1960, Bröllopsdagen (The Wedding Day) 1960, Såsom i en spegel (Through a Glass Darkly) 1961, Nils Holgerssons underbara resa (Wonderful Adventures of Nils) 1962, Älskarinnan (The Mistress) 1962, Nattvardsgästerna (Winter Light) 1963, The Greatest Story Ever Told 1965, 4 × 4 1965, The Reward 1965, Hawaii 1966, The Quiller Memorandum 1966, Här har du ditt liv (This Is Your Life) 1966, Vargtimmen (Hour of the Wolf) 1968, Svarta palmkronor (Black

Palm Trees) 1968, Skammen (Shame) 1968, Made in Sweden 1969, En passion (A Passion) 1969, The Kremlin Letter 1970, The Night Visitor 1971, Utvandrarna (The Emigrants) 1971, Beröringen (The Touch) 1971, Äppelkriget (The Apple War) 1971, Embassy 1972, Nybyggarna (The New Land) 1972, The Exorcist 1973, Steppenwolf 1974, Cuore di cane (Dog's Heart) 1975, Ägget är löst! (Egg! Egg! A Hardboiled Story) 1975, Trompe-l'oeil 1975, Three Days of the Condor 1975, The Ultimate Warrior 1975, Cadaveri eccellenti (aka Illustrious Corpses) 1976, Foxtrot (aka The Far Side of Paradise) 1976, Il deserto dei Tartari (The Desert of the Tartars) 1976, Voyage of the Damned 1976, Gran bollito (aka Black Journal) 1977, Exorcist II: The Heretic 1977, March or Die 1977, Brass Target 1978, Hurricane 1979, Bugie bianche (aka Footloose, and Venetian Lies) 1980, La mort en direct (Death Watch) 1980, Flash Gordon 1980, Victory 1981, Jugando con la muerte (aka Hit Man, USA) 1982, Conan the Barbarian 1982, Ingenjör Andrées luftfärd (The Flight of the Eagle) 1982, Le cercle des passions (aka Circle of Passions), The Adventures of Bob & Doug McKenzie: Strange Brew 1983, Never Say Never Again 1983, A Soldier's Tale 1984, The Ice Pirates 1984, Dreamscape 1984, Dune 1984, Code Name: Emerald (aka Deep Cover, USA TV title) 1985, Il pentito (The Repenter) 1985, The Second Victory 1986, Hannah and Her Sisters 1986, Oviri (The Wolf at the Door) 1986, Duet for One 1986, Pelle erobreren (Pelle the Conqueror) (Bodil Award Best Actor, European Film Award for Best Actor, Guldbagge Award Best Actor, Robert Festival Best Actor) 1987, Una vita scellerata (A Violent Life) 1990, Father 1990, Awakenings 1990, Mio caro dottor Gräsler (aka The Bachelor, USA) 1991, A Kiss Before Dying 1991, Europa (voice) 1991, Bis ans Ende der Welt (Until the End of the World) 1991, Oxen 1991, Den goda viljan (The Best Intentions) 1992, Dotkniecie reki (The Silent Touch) 1992, Morfars resa (Grandpa's Journey) 1993, Needful Things 1993, Time Is Money 1994, Dypets ensomhet (Depth Solitude) 1995, Judge Dredd 1995, Truck Stop 1996, Hamsun (Swedish Guldbagge Award for Best Actor 1997) 1996, Jerusalem 1996, What Dreams May Come 1998, Snow Falling on Cedars 1999, Non ho sonno (aka Sleepless, USA) 2001, Vercingétorix 2001, Intacto (Intact) 2001, Les amants de Mogador 2002, Minority Report 2002, Heidi 2005, Le Scaphandre et le papillon 2007, Rush Hour 3 2007, Emotional Arithmetic 2007, The Diving Bell and the Butterfly 2007, Shutter Island 2010, Truth & Treason 2011; Dir Katinka 1987, Extremely Loud & Incredibly Close 2011. Television includes: Herr Sleeman kommer 1957, Rabies 1958, The Diary of Anne Frank 1967, I havsbandet (mini-series) 1971, Kvartetten som sprängdes (mini-series) 1973, Le dernier civil 1983, Samson and Delilah 1984, Quo Vadis? (mini-series) 1985, The Last Place on Earth (mini-series) 1985, Kojak: The Belarus File 1985, Christopher Columbus (mini-series) 1985, Gösta Berlings saga (mini-series, segments 1–3) 1986, Red King, White Knight 1989, Hiroshima: Out of the Ashes 1990, Den goda viljan (mini-series) 1991, Och ge oss skuggorna 1993, Onkel Vanja 1994, A che punto è la notte 1995, Citizen X 1995, Radetzkymarsch (mini-series) Radetzky March) 1995, Samson and Delilah (voice, uncredited) 1996, Enskilda samtal (Private Conversations) 1996, Profiler (series) 1997, Hostile Waters 1997, La principessa e il povero (The Princess and the Pauper) 1997, Solomon 1997, Nuremberg (mini-series) 2000, La fuga degli innocenti (Hidden Children: The Flight of the Innocents) (mini-series) 2004, Ring of the Nibelungs 2004, L'Inchiesta 2007, The Tudors 2009. Publication: Loppcirkus (with Elisabeth Sörenson) 1989. Leisure interests: nautical history, environment preservation, Baroque music. Address: c/o Diamond Management, 31 Percy Street, London, W1T 2DD, England (office); c/o Agence Anne Alvares Correa, 18 rue Troyon, 75017 Paris, France (office).

SYKES, Lynn R., PhD; American geologist and academic; *Higgins Professor Emeritus of Earth and Environmental Sciences, Lamont-Doherty Geological Observatory, Columbia University;* b. 16 April 1937, Pittsburgh, Pa; s. of Lloyd A. Sykes and Margaret Woodburn Sykes; m. 1st Meredith Henschkel (divorced); m. 2nd Katherine Flanz 1986 (died 1996); m. 3rd Kathleen Mahoney 1998; ed Massachusetts Inst. of Tech. and Columbia Univ.; Research Asst, Lamont-Doherty Geological Observatory, Columbia Univ. 1961–64, Research Assoc. 1964–66, Adjunct Asst Prof. of Geology 1966–68, Head of Seismology Group 1973–83, apptd Higgins Prof. of Earth and Environmental Sciences 1978, now Prof. Emer.; main areas of interest are seismology, tectonics and arms control, earthquake prediction and the detection and identification of underground atomic tests; Chair. Nat. Earthquake Prediction Evaluation Council; mem. NAS, American Acad. of Arts and Sciences, Geological Soc. of London, Arms Control Assocn; Fellow, American Geophysical Union, Geological Soc. of America, Royal Astronomical Soc., AAAS; Walter H. Bucher Medal of American Geophysical Union for original contribs. to basic knowledge of earth's crust 1975, Public Service Award, Fed. of American Scientists 1986, John Wesley Powell Award, US Geological Survey 1990, Vetleson Award for devt and testing of plate tectonics 2000. Publications: more than 315 papers in scientific journals. Leisure interests: hiking, canoeing, opera, travel. Address: Lamont-Doherty Earth Observatory, Columbia University, PO Box 1000, 230C Seismology Building, 61 Route 9W, Palisades, NY 10964-8000 (office); 100 Washington Spring Road, Palisades, NY 10964-8000, USA. Telephone: (845) 365-8880 (office). Fax: (845) 365-8150 (office). E-mail: sykes@ldeo.columbia.edu (office). Website: www.ldeo.columbia.edu/~sykes (office).

SYKES, Sir Richard (Brook), Kt, PhD, DSc, FRS, FMedSci; British research microbiologist, business executive and university administrator; *Chairman, The Royal Institution of Great Britain;* b. 7 Aug. 1942, Huddersfield, Yorks.; s. of the late Eric Sykes and of Muriel Mary Sykes; m. Janet Mary Norman 1969; one s. one d.; ed Queen Elizabeth Coll., London, Bristol Univ., London Univ.; Head of Antibiotic Research Unit, Glaxo Research Ltd 1972–77; Asst Dir, Dept of Microbiology, Squibb Inst. for Medical Research, Princeton 1977, Dir of Microbiology 1979, Vice-Pres. Infectious and Metabolic Diseases 1983–86; Deputy Chief Exec., Glaxo Group Research Ltd 1986, Group Research and Devt Dir, Glaxo PLC and Chair. and Chief Exec., Glaxo Group Research Ltd 1987, Deputy Chair. and Chief Exec., Glaxo PLC 1993, Chair., Glaxo Wellcome PLC 1997–2001, CEO 1997; Chair. (non-exec.), GlaxoSmithKline 2001–02; Chair., Metabometrix Ltd 2004–, Merlion Pharmaceuticals Pte Ltd 2005–, Omnicyte Ltd 2006–, Circassia Ltd 2007–, NHS London 2008–10, The Royal Institution of Great Britain 2010–; Rector, Imperial Coll. of Science, Tech. and Medicine 2001–08; Visiting Prof., King's Coll., London and Univ. of Bristol; Pres., British Asscn for the Advancement of Science 1998–99; Dir (non-exec.), Rio Tinto PLC 1997–, Lonza Group Ltd 2003–, Imperial Coll. Healthcare NHS Trust 2007–, Eurasian Natural Resources Corpn 2007–; Chair., UK Stem Cell Foundation 2005–; mem. Council for Science and

Tech. 1993–2002; mem. Bd of Trustees Nat. History Museum 1996–2005, Bd Higher Educ. Funding Council for England 2002–, UK India Business Council 2007–; Fellow, Imperial Coll. School of Medicine; Fleming Fellow, Lincoln Coll., Oxford 1992; Hon. mem. Nat. Acad. of Medicine, Brazil; Hon. Fellow Royal Coll. of Physicians, Univ. of Wales, Cardiff, Royal Pharmaceutical Soc.; Hon. FRSC; Hon. Citizen of Singapore 2004; Companion of the Most Admirable Order of Direkgunabhom (Thailand) 2006; Hon. DPharm (Madrid) 1993, Hon. DSc (Brunel, Hull, Herts.) 1994, (Bristol, Newcastle) 1995, (Huddersfield, Westminster) 1996, (Leeds) 1997, (Edin., Strathclyde) 1998, (Cranfield, Leicester, Sheffield, Warwick) 1999, Hon. MD (Birmingham) 1995, Hon. LLD (Nottingham) 1997, Dr hc (Sheffield Hallam, Surrey); Hamao Umezawa Memorial Award (Int. Soc. of Chemotherapy) 1999, Singapore Nat. Day Public Service Star Award 1999. Leisure interests: tennis, swimming, opera, skiing. Address: The Royal Institution of Great Britain, 21 Ablemarle Street, London, W1S 4BS (office); Flat 11, Hale House, 34 De Vere Gardens, London W8 5AQ, England (home). Telephone: (20) 7409-2992 (office). E-mail: ri@ri.ac.uk (office). Website: www.rigb.org (office).

SYLLA, Yvette; Malagasy politician; *Minister of Foreign Affairs;* b. (Yvette Rakoto), m. Jacques Hugues Sylla, fmr Prime Minister of Madagascar (died 2009); four c.; Pres. Madagasikara Mandroso (Mother – Madagascar Devt) party 2010–; Minister of Foreign Affairs 2011–. Address: Ministry of Foreign Affairs, BP 836, Anosy, 101 Antananarivo, Madagascar (office). Telephone: (20) 2221198 (office). Fax: (20) 2234484 (office). E-mail: contact@madagascar-diplomatie.net (office). Website: www.madagascar-diplomatie.net (office).

SYLVA CHARVET, Érika; Ecuadorean academic and politician; *Minister of Culture;* m. Rafael Quintero López; two s.; ed Universidad Católica del Ecuador, Universidad Central de Quito, Universidad FLACSO, Mexico; Researcher and later Prof., Ecuadorian Vocational Training Service and Faculdad Latinoamericana de Ciencias Sociales; Prof. of Sociology, Universidad Católica del Ecuador 1980–81; Minister of Culture 2010–; fmr columnist, El Telegrafo. Publications include: Nación, Clase y Cultura 1984, Ecuador: una Nación en Ciernes 1991, Los Mitos de la Ecuatorianida 1992, Identidad Nacional y Pode 2004, Feminidad y Masculinidad en la cultura afroecuatoriana. El caso del norte de Esmeralda 2010. Address: Ministry of Culture, Avenida Colón E5-34 y Juan León Mera, Quito, Ecuador (office). Telephone: (2) 381-4550 (office). E-mail: comunicacion@ministeriodecultura.gov.ec (office). Website: www.ministeriodecultura.gov.ec (office).

SYMON, Lindsay, CBE, TD, MB, ChB, FRCS, FRCSE; British professor of neurological surgery; b. 4 Nov. 1929, Aberdeen, Scotland; s. of William L. Symon and Isabel Symon; m. Pauline Barbara Rowland 1954; one s. two d.; ed Aberdeen Grammar School and Univ. of Aberdeen; House Physician/Surgeon, Aberdeen Royal Infirmary 1952–53, Surgical Registrar 1956–58; Clinical Officer/Jr Specialist in Surgery, British troops in Austria 1953–55; Clinical Research Fellow, MRC 1958–61; Major in charge, No. 2 Mobile Neurosurgical Team, TA, RAMC 1960–68; Rockefeller Travelling Fellow, Wayne State Univ., Detroit, Mich., USA 1961–62; Sr Registrar, Neurosurgery, Nat. Hosps 1962–65, Consultant Neurosurgeon 1965–78, Prof. of Neurological Surgery and Sr Surgeon 1978–95; mem. External Staff MRC 1965–78; Hon. Consultant Neurosurgeon, St Thomas's Hosp., London 1973–95, Hammersmith Hosp., London 1978–95, Royal Nat. Throat, Nose and Ear Hosp. 1979–95, The Italian Hosp. 1981–89; Adjunct Prof., Dept of Surgery, Southwestern Medical School, Dallas, Tex. 1982–95; Civilian Adviser in Neurosurgery, RN 1979–95; Pres. World Fed. of Neurosurgical Socs 1979–93, Hon. Pres. 1993–; Pres. Harveian Soc., London 1997–98, Trustee 1999–; mem. Ukrainian Acad. of Science 1992–; Hon. FACS 1994, Hon. mem. Soc. of Neurological Surgeons; Jamieson Medal, Australasian Neurosurgical Soc. 1982, John Hunter Medal, Royal Coll. of Surgeons 1985, Joachim Zulch Prize, Max Planck Inst. 1993, Otfrid Förster Medal, German Soc. Neurosurgery 1998, Medal of Honour, Soc. of British Neurological Surgeons 2008, Samii Medal of Honour, World Fed. of Neurological Socs 2013. Publications include: texts on cerebrovascular surgery, physiology of the cerebral circulation, surgery of acoustic neuroma, general neurosurgical topics. Leisure interests: golf, prehistory. Address: Maple Lodge, Rivar Road, Shalbourne, nr Marlborough, Wilts., SN8 3QE, England (home). Telephone: (1672) 870501 (home). Fax: (1672) 870501 (home). E-mail: lindsaysymon@tiscali.co.uk.

SYMONENKO, Petro Mykolayovych; Ukrainian politician; *First Secretary of Central Committee, Communist Party of Ukraine;* b. 1 Aug. 1952, Donetsk; m. 1st Svetlana; two s.; m. 2nd Oksana Vashchenko; one d.; ed Donetsk State Polytechnical Inst. and Kyiv Inst. of Political Science and Social Admin; joined Komsomol 1975; joined CPSU 1978, fmr Deputy Sec. Donetsk regional CP Cttee; Deputy Dir Ukrvuhlemash machine-building co. 1991–93; First Sec. Cen. Cttee of CP of Ukraine 1993–; mem. Verkhovna Rada (Parl.) 1994–, Chair. CP Parl. faction; mem. Parl. Ass. of the Council of Europe 1997–; cand. in presidential elections 1999, 2004, 2010. Address: Communist Party of Ukraine (Komunistychna Partiya Ukrainy), 04070 Kyiv, vul. Borysohlibska 7, Ukraine (office). Telephone: (44) 238-93-76 (office). E-mail: symonenko.petro@rada.gov.ua (office); press@kpu.net.ua (office). Website: www.rada.gov.ua (office); www.kpu.ua (office).

SYMONETTE, Theodore Brent; Bahamian barrister, real estate developer and politician; b. 2 Dec. 1954, Nassau; s. of Sir Roland Symonette and Lady Margaret Symonette; m. Robin Mactaggart; one s. two d.; ed St Andrew's School, Nassau, Leys School, Cambridge, Brunel Univ., London, UK; called to Bahamas Bar 1978; fmr Senator; mem. House of Ass. for St Anne; fmr Minister of Tourism; fmr Attorney-Gen.; Deputy Leader, Free Nat. Movt; Deputy Prime Minister and Minister of Foreign Affairs 2007–12, also responsible for Immigration 2008–12; fmr Chair. Hotel Corpn, Airport Authority, Public Accounts Cttee. Address: c/o Ministry of Foreign Affairs, East Hill Street, PO Box N-3746, Nassau, The Bahamas.

SYMONS OF VERNHAM DEAN, Baroness (Life Peer), cr. 1996, of Vernham Dean in the County of Hampshire; **Elizabeth Conway Symons,** MA, FRSA; British politician; b. 14 April 1951; d. of Ernest Vize Symons and Elizabeth Megan Symons (née Jenkins); pnr, Philip Alan Bassett; one s.; ed Putney High School for Girls, Girton Coll., Cambridge; Admin. Trainee, Dept of the Environment 1974–77; Asst Sec., Inland Revenue Staff Fed. 1977–88, Deputy Gen. Sec. 1988–89; Gen. Sec., Asscn of First Div. Civil Servants 1989–96; Parl. Under-Sec. of State, FCO

1997–99; Minister of Defence Procurement, Ministry of Defence 1999–2001; apptd Minister of State (Minister for Trade), FCO and Dept of Trade and Industry 2001; Deputy Leader of House of Lords 2001–05; Minister of State for the Middle East, FCO and Dept of Trade and Industry 2003–05; mem. Gen. Council, TUC 1989–96, Council, RIPA 1989–97, Exec. Council, Campaign for Freedom of Information 1989–97, Hansard Soc. Council 1992–97, Advisory Council, Civil Service Coll. 1992–97, Council, Industrial Soc. 1994–97, Council, Open Univ. 1994–97; Employment Appeal Tribunal 1995, Equal Opportunities Comm. 1995–97; Exec. mem. Involvement and Participation Asscn 1992; Gov. Polytechnic of N London 1989–94, London Business School 1997; Trustee, Inst. for Public Policy Research 1993; Hon. Assoc. Nat. Council of Women 1989. *Leisure interests:* gardening, reading. *Address:* House of Lords, Westminster, London, SW1A 0PW, England (office).

SYMS, Sylvia, OBE; British actress and director; b. 6 Jan. 1934, London; m. Alan Edney 1957 (divorced 1989); one s. one d.; ed Royal Acad. of Dramatic Art; Founder-mem. and Artistic Dir Arbela Production Co.; numerous lectures, including Dodo White McLarty Memorial Lecture 1986; mem. The Actors' Centre 1986–91, Arts Council Drama Panel 1991–96, Council for RADA 1992–2010; Variety Club Best Actress in Films Award 1958, Ondas Award for Most Popular Foreign Actress (Spain) 1966, Manchester Evening News Best Actress Award. *Theatre includes:* Dance of Death, Much Ado About Nothing, An Ideal Husband, Ghosts, Entertaining Mr. Sloane (Best Actress Award, Manchester Evening News) 1985, Who's Afraid of Virgina Woolf? 1989, The Floating Lightbulb 1990, Antony and Cleopatra 1991, For Services Rendered 1993, Funny Money 1996, Ugly Rumours 1998, Mothers and Daughters 1999–2003, Love Lust 2003, We All Make Mistakes 2003. *Films include:* Ice Cold in Alex 1953, The Birthday Present 1956, The World of Suzie Wong 1961, Run Wild Run Free 1969, The Tamarind Seed 1974, Chorus of Disapproval 1988, Shirley Valentine 1989, Shining Through 1991, Dirty Weekend 1992, Staggered 1994, Food for Love 1996, Mavis and the Mermaid 1999, Deep Down 2001, What a Girl Wants 2002, I'll Sleep When I'm Dead 2003, The Queen 2006, Is There Anybody There? 2008. *Television includes:* Love Story 1964, The Saint 1967, My Good Woman 1972–73, Nancy Astor 1982, Ruth Rendell Mysteries 1989, Dr. Who 1989–90, May to December 1989–90, The Last Days of Margaret Thatcher 1991, Natural Lies, Mulberry, Peak Practice, Ruth Randell Mysteries 1993, 1997–98, Ghost Hour 1995, Heartbeat 1998, At Home with the Braithwaites 2000–03, The Jury 2002, Where the Heart Is 2003, Born and Bread 2003, The Poseidon Adventure 2005, Child of Mine 2005, Eastenders 2007–10. *Radio includes:* Little Dorrit, Danger in the Village, Post Mortems, Joe Orton, Love Story, The Change 2001, 2003. *Plays and television directed:* Better in My Dreams 1988, The Price 1991, Natural Lies 1991–92. *Leisure interests:* gardening, dogs. *Address:* c/o Brown & Simcocks, 1 Bridge House Court, 109 Blackfriars Road, London, SE1 8HW, England (office). *Telephone:* (20) 7928-1229 (office). *Fax:* (20) 7928-1909 (office). *E-mail:* barryandcarrig@lingone.net (office); sylviasymsedney@aol.com (home). *Website:* www.sylviasyms.co.uk (home).

SYRON, Richard (Dick) Francis, PhD; American economist, banking executive and academic; b. 25 Oct. 1943, Boston; s. of Dominick Syron and Elizabeth Syron (née McGuire); m. Margaret Mary Garatoni 1972; one s. one d.; ed Boston Coll., Tufts Univ.; Deputy Dir Commonwealth of Mass 1973–74; Vice-Pres. and Economist Fed. Reserve Bank of Boston 1974–82, Sr Vice-Pres. and Econ. Adviser 1982–85, Pres. and CEO 1989–94; Exec. Asst to US Sec. of Treasury, Washington, DC 1979–80, Deputy Asst to Sec. for Econ. Policy 1980–81; Asst to Chair. Volcker, Fed. Reserve System, Washington, DC 1981–82; Pres. Fed. Home Loan Bank of Boston 1986–88; Chair. American Stock Exchange 1994–99; Chair. and CEO Thermo Electron, Mass. 1999–2002; Chair. and CEO Freddie Mac (Fed. Home Loan Mortgage Corpn), Washington, DC 2003–08; Adjunct Prof. of Finance, Carroll School of Management, Boston College; mem. Bd of Dirs Genzyme Corpn 2006–; Trustee, Boston Coll., Woods Hole Oceanographic Inst. *Address:* c/o Board of Directors, Genzyme Corporation, 500 Kendall Street, Cambridge, MA 02142, USA.

SYRYJCZYK, Tadeusz Andrzej, DTech; Polish politician and consultant; *Senior Expert, Transport Consultants Group TOR Ltd;* b. 9 Feb. 1948, Kraków; m. Barbara Syryjczyk; ed AGH Univ. of Science and Tech., Kraków; Lecturer, AGH Univ. of Science and Tech. y, Kraków 1971–89; mem. Solidarity Trade Union 1980–89; interned during state of martial law 1981–82; mem. Presidium Małopolska Region 1981; mem. regional authorities in Kraków 1982–84; with ABAKS, Kraków 1987–89; Minister of Industry 1989–91; Chief of Prime Minister's team of advisers and Under-Sec. of State in Council of Ministers 1992–93; Minister of Transport and Maritime Economy 1998–2000; Deputy to Sejm (Parl.) 1991–2001, mem. Parl. Comm. for Privatization, Econ. System and Industry 1991–92, Parl. Comm. for Econ. Policy, Budget and Finances 1993–97, Parl. Comm. for Public Finances 1997–98, Parl. Comm. for Nat. Defence 1998; mem. Democratic Union Parl. Caucus 1991–94, Freedom Union Parl. Caucus 1994–2001, Chair. 1997–98; mem. Democratic Union 1991–94; mem. Freedom Union 1994–, Nat. Council and Regional Council, Kraków 1983–2001; Vice-Pres. Freedom Union 1995–2001; Co-founder Cracow Industrial Soc., Kraków 1987, Pres. 1990–; mem. Polish Tourist Country-Lovers' Asscn, Polish Informatics Soc. *Publications:* papers on automatics and informatics, articles in nat. magazines. *Leisure interest:* tourism, mountaineering. *Address:* Aleja Kijowska 24/80, 30-079 Kraków, Poland. *Telephone:* (12) 6336427; (60) 1471870 (mobile). *E-mail:* tadeusz@syryjczyk.krakow.pl. *Website:* www.syryjczyk.krakow.pl.

SYSTROM, Kevin, BS; American software engineer; *CEO and Co-Founder, Instagram;* b. 30 Dec. 1983, Holliston, Mass; s. of Douglas Systrom and Diane Systrom; ed Stanford Univ.; internship at Odeo (search website); spent two years at Google, Inc., worked on Gmail, Google Reader and other products, later with Corporate Devt team; co-f. Instagram (photo-sharing service), currently CEO; co-f. Burbn (HTML5-based location-sharing service) 2010. *Address:* Instagram, 181 South Park Street, San Francisco, CA 94107, USA. *Telephone:* (415) 857-3369 (office). *Website:* instagram.com (office).

SYSUYEV, Oleg Nikolayevich; Russian banker and fmr politician; *First Deputy Chairman of the Board of Directors, Alfa-Bank;* b. 23 March 1953, Kuybyshev (now Samara); m.; one s. one d.; ed Kuybyshev Moscow Aviation Inst.; Master, Head of Tech. Div., engineer and Sec., CP Cttee at Kuibyshev aviation team 1976–87; Sec., Krasnoglinsk Dist CP Cttee of Kuybyshev 1987–91; del. to 18th CP Congress; Head

of Samara Admin. 1991–94; Mayor of Samara 1994–97; participant in Russia Our Home movt; Co-Chair. Union of Mayors of Russian Towns 1995–97; Deputy Head of Russian Govt, Minister of Labour and Social Devt 1997–98; Co-ordinator Russian Comm. on Regulation of Trade-Social Relations 1997–98; First Deputy Head of Admin. of Pres. Yeltsin 1998–99; First Deputy Chair. of Bd Alfa-Bank 1999–; Pres. Congress of Municipalities of Russia 2000–; mem. Presidential Council for Local Govt; Deputy Chair. Presidential Cttee for Literature and the Arts. *Leisure interests:* playing guitar, piano, violin. *Address:* Alfa-Bank, 27 Kalanchevskaya Str., 107078 Moscow, Russia (office). *Telephone:* (495) 620-91-91 (office). *E-mail:* mail@alfabank.ru (office). *Website:* www.alfabank.com (office).

SZABAD, György, PhD; Hungarian politician and historian; b. 4 Aug. 1924, Arad, Romania; s. of Erzsébet Blantz; m. Andrea Suján; one d.; ed Loránd Eötvös Univ., Budapest; served in forced labour camp 1944; mem. staff, Nat. Archives 1949, Univ. Asst Lecturer 1954, Lecturer 1956, Prof. 1970; mem. Revolutionary Cttee 1956; Founding mem. and Nat. Bd mem. Hungarian Democratic Forum 1987; Founding mem. Hungarian Democratic People's Party; Speaker of Hungarian Parl. 1990–94, mem. Parl. 1994–98; Pres. Cttee of Hungarian and Polish Historians; Corresp. mem. Hungarian Acad. of Sciences 1982, mem. 1998–; Grand Cross of Honour of the Repub. of Hungary 2000; Hungarian Acad. of Sciences Award 1965, 1973, Council of Europe Pro Merito 1991. *Publications include:* Kossuth on the Political System of the United States of America 1975, Hungarian Political Trends between the Revolution and the Compromise 1849–1867 1977, Conceptualization of a Danubian Federation 1998. *Address:* Kelenhegyi ut. 40/B, 1118 Budapest, Hungary (home). *Telephone:* 385-3761 (home). *E-mail:* aszabad@t-online.hu (home).

SZABO, Denis, OC, DèsSc, FRSC, OQ; Canadian/Belgian criminologist and academic; *Professor Emeritus of Criminology and Chairman, International Centre for Comparative Criminology, University of Montreal;* b. 4 June 1929, Budapest, Hungary; s. of Jenő Denes and Catherine Zsiga; m. Sylvie Grotard 1956; two d.; ed Univs of Budapest, Louvain and Paris; Asst Univ. of Louvain 1952–56; lecturer in Sociology, Catholic Univ. of Paris and Lyon 1956–58; Asst Prof. Univ. of Montreal 1958–59, Assoc. Prof. 1959–66, Prof. of Criminology 1966–95, Prof. Emer. 1995–; Founder and Dir School of Criminology, Univ. of Montreal 1960–70; Founder and Dir Int. Center for Comparative Criminology, Univ. of Montreal 1969–84, now Chair. of Bd; founder Quebec Soc. of Criminology; Pres. Asoc. Internationale des Criminologues de Langue Française, Geneva 1989–2002 (Hon. Pres. Liége 2002); consultant to Canadian, US, French, Hungarian and UN comms and bodies on crime prevention; mem. Hungarian Acad. of Sciences 1993–, Romanian Soc. of Criminology 2003–; Corresponding mem. Acad. des Sciences Morales et Politiques, Institut de France 2004; Hon. Pres. Int. Soc. of Criminology, Hon. mem. Basque Inst. of Criminology (Spain) 2003; Commdr Ordre Nat. du Mérite, Côte d'Ivoire 1986, Commdr Ordre du Mérite Répub., Hungary 1996, Chevalier des Arts et des Lettres, France 1996, Officier Ordre nat. du Québec 1998 and other decorations; Dr hc (Siena, Budapest, Aix-Marseille, Panteios-Athens, Bucharest); Sutherland Award, American Soc. of Criminology 1968, Golden Medal Beccaria, German Soc. of Criminology 1970 and other awards. *Publications:* Crimes et villes 1960, Criminologie et politique criminelle 1978, The Canadian Criminal Justice System (with A. Parizeau), Science et crimes 1986, Criminologie empirique au Québec (ed. with Marc Le Blanc), De l'anthropologie à la criminologie comparée 1993, Traité de criminologie empirique (ed. with Marc Le Blanc) 1994, Vols II and III 2002–04. *Leisure interests:* gardening, swimming. *Address:* International Centre for Comparative Criminology, Pav.M.Caron-L.Groulx-3200 J.B., bureau C-4103, University of Montreal, C.P. 6128, Montreal, H3C 3J7 (office); 66, Square Copp, Georgeville, J0B 1T0, Canada (home). *Telephone:* (514) 343-6111 (office); (819) 843-4343 (home). *Fax:* (514) 343-2269 (office); (514) 343-2269 (office). *E-mail:* denis .szabo@umontreal.ca (office). *Website:* www.cicc.umontreal.ca (office).

SZABO, Gabriela; Romanian professional athlete; *Vice-President, Romanian Athletics Federation;* b. 14 Nov. 1975, Bistrita; m. Gyonyossy Zsolt 1999; fmr indoor European record-holder and outdoor World record-holder in 5,000m; silver medal, 1,500m, Olympic Games, Atlanta 1996; world's fastest at 1,500m, one mile, 2,000m, 3,000m and 5,000m 1998; gold medal, 5,000m Olympic Games, Sydney 2000, bronze medal, 1,500m, Sydney 2000; set new world records for indoor 5,000m in Feb. 1999, 3,000m. Birmingham, England, Feb. 2001; gold medal, 1,500m World Championships 2001; silver medal, European Championships 5,000m 1998, 1,500m 2002; retd 2005; currently Vice-Pres. Romanian Athletics Fed.; first female track athlete to make US $1 million in prize money in one season; European Athlete of the Year 1999, IAAF Athlete of the Year 1999. *Address:* Romanian Athletics Federation, 2, dr. Primo Nebiolo, 71323 Bucharest, Romania (office). *Telephone:* (21) 2232229 (office). *Fax:* (21) 2232227 (office). *E-mail:* gabi@gabiszabo .com; fra.teh@ew.ro (office). *Website:* www.gabiszabo.com; www.fra.ro (office).

SZABÓ, István, DLA; Hungarian film director, writer and academic; b. 18 Feb. 1938, Budapest; s. of Dr István Szabó and Mária Vita; m. Vera Gyürey; ed Budapest Acad. of Theatre and Film Arts; started as mem. Balázs B. Studio, Budapest; leading mem. Hungarian Film Studios; Tutor, Coll. of Theatre and Film Arts, Budapest; mem. Acad. of Motion Picture Arts and Sciences, Akad. der Künste, Berlin; Béla Balázs Prize 1967, Kossuth Prize 1975. *Productions:* short films: Concert 1961, Variations upon a Theme 1961, Te (You) (Grand Prix de Tours) 1963, Budapest, amiért szeretem (Budapest, Why I Love It) 1971; series: Álom a házról (Dream About the House) (Main Prize of Oberhausen) 1971; documentaries: Kegyelet (Piety) 1967, Várostérkép (City Map) (Grand Prix of Oberhausen) 1977, Steadying the Boat 1996; TV plays: Osbemutató (Première) 1974, Katzenspiel (Cat Play) 1982, Bali 1983; TV films: Der grüne Vogel (The Green Bird) 1979, Offenbach 1995; full-length films: Álmodozások kora (The Age of Day-Dreaming) (Silver Prix, Locarno) 1964, Apa (Father) (Grand Prix, Moscow) 1966, Szerelmesfilm (A Film of Love) 1970, Tüzoltó utca 25 (No. 25 Fireman's Street) (Grand Prix of Locarno) 1973, Budapesti mesék (Budapest Tales) 1976, Bizalom (Confidence) (Silver Bear of Berlin 1981) 1979, Mephisto (Acad. Award 1982, David di Donatello Prize (Italy), Italian Critics' Prize, Critics' Prize, UK) 1981, Colonel Redl (BAFTA Award 1986, Best West German Film—Golden Band) 1985, Hanussen 1988, Meeting Venus 1990, Sweet Emma, Dear Böbe (Silver Bear of Berlin, European Acad. Award for Best Screenplay) 1991, Steadying the Boat (BBC) 1996, Sunshine (European Acad. Award for Best Screenplay, Canadian Acad. Award for Best Film) 1999, Taking Sides 2001, Being Julia 2003, Relatives

2005, The Door 2011; operas: Tannhäuser, Paris 1987, Boris Godunov, Leipzig 1993, Il Trovatore, Vienna 1993, The Three Sisters, Budapest 2000 (also Kassel 2002). *Address:* 1132 Budapest, Váci-6, Hungary (home). *Telephone:* (1) 340-5559 (home). *Fax:* (1) 340-5559 (home). *E-mail:* islfilm@t-online.hu.

SZABÓ, Miklós, PhD, DSc; Hungarian archaeologist and academic; *Director, Archaeological Institute, Eötvös Loránd University of Arts and Sciences;* b. 3 July 1940, Szombathely; s. of Dezső Szabó and Irén Süle; m. Ágnes Molnár; three s.; ed Eötvös Loránd Univ. of Arts and Sciences (ELTE); with Dept of Archaeology, Hungarian Nat. Museum 1963–66; with Dept of Antiquities Museum of Fine Arts 1966–85, Deputy Dir Gen. 1985–87; Asst Prof., Dept of Classical Archaeology of ELTE 1983–89, Prof. and Head of Dept 1989, Gen. Vice-Rector 1991–93, Rector 1993–99; research into Ancient Greek and Celtic archaeology, involved in excavations in Greece by the French Inst. of Archaeology in Athens 1970–78; in France 1978, led the Hungarian excavation expedition in Bibracte, France 1988–; Visiting Prof., Univ. of Paris (Sorbonne) 1980–81, Ecole normale supérieure, Paris 1985, Coll. de France 1989, 2000–01, Univ. of Burgundy 2003; Pres. Archaeological Cttee Hungarian Acad. of Sciences 1994; Corresp. mem. Hungarian Acad. of Sciences 1995 (mem. 2001–), German Archaeological Inst. 1977–, Royal Acad. of Barcelona 1997–, Acad. française 2002–; Ed. Dissertationes Pannonicae; mem. Editorial Bd Acta Archaeologica and Études Celtiques; Hon. mem. Greek Archaeological Soc. 1998; Chevalier, Ordre nat. du Mérite 1995, Commdr, Légion d'honneur 2001, Ordre des Arts et Lettres 2001; Dr hc (Burgundy) 1997, (Dijon) 1997, (Bologna) 1999; Kuzsinszky Medal 1984, Collège de France Medal 1989, Rómer Flóris Commemorative Medal 1990, City of Dijon Commemorative Medal 1991. *Publications include:* The Celtic Heritage in Hungary 1971, Hellász fénykora (The Golden Age of Greece) 1972, Világtörténelem képekben I, (World History in Pictures I, co-author) 1972, A keleti kelta művészet (Eastern Celtic Art, co-author) 1974, Les Celtes (co-author) 1978, Les Celtes en Pannonie. Contribution à l'histoire de la civilisation celtique dans la cuvette des Karpates 1988, I Celti (co-author) 1991, Les Celtes de l'Est: Le second âge du fer dans la cuvette des Karpates 1992, Decorated Weapons of the La Tène Iron Age in the Carpathian Basin (co-author) 1992, Archaic Terracottas of Boeotia 1994, Storia d'Europa II (co-author) 1994, A la frontière entre l'Est et l'Ouest (co-author) 1998, Prähistorische Goldschätze im Ungarischen Nationalmuseum (co-author) 1999, Trésors pré-historiques de Hongrie (co-author) 2001, Celtes de Hongrie (co-author) 2001, Celtas y Vettones (co-author) 2001. *Address:* Eötvös Loránd University of Arts and Sciences, Múzeum krt. 4/B, 1088 Budapest, Hungary (office). *Telephone:* (1) 411-6554 (office); (1) 200-1743 (home). *Fax:* (1) 411-6553 (office). *E-mail:* archinst@ludens.elte.hu (office).

SZCZUREK, Mateusz, DEcon, MEconSc, PhD; Polish economist and politician; *Minister of Finance;* b. 11 Aug. 1975; m.; five c.; ed Univ. of Warsaw, Univ. of Sussex, UK, Int. Centre for Money and Banking Studies, Geneva and London, Columbia Univ., USA; Economist with ING Barings 1997–2011, becoming Chief Economist, ING Bank Slaski; Lecturer in Econs, School of Econs, Warsaw, Univ. of Sussex, Goethe Business School, Frankfurt; Minister of Finance 2013–; mem. Asscn of Polish Economists. *Leisure interests:* photography, cycling. *Address:* Ministry of Finance, 00-916 Warsaw, ul. Swiętokrzyska 12, Poland (office). *Telephone:* (22) 6945555 (office). *Fax:* (22) 6944177 (office). *E-mail:* kancelaria@mofnet.gov.pl (office). *Website:* www.mf.gov.pl (office).

SZÉKELY, Gábor, MA; Hungarian theatre director and academic; *Faculty Director, University of Drama, Film and Television, Budapest;* b. 26 May 1944, Jászbrény; s. of late Árpád Székely and of Irma Csuka; m. Erika Székely 1967; one s. two d.; ed Könyves Kálmán Grammar School, Budapest, Budapest Acad. of Dramatic and Cinematic Art; Asst Dir, Szolnoki Szigligeti Theatre 1968–71, Prin. Dir 1971–72, Theatre Man. and Prin. Dir 1972–78; Prin. Dir Budapest Nat. Theatre 1978–82, apptd Theatre Man. 1982; Theatre Man. Budapest Katona József Theatre 1982–89; teacher of dramatic art and theatre direction, Acad. of Dramatic and Cinematic Art 1972–, apptd Head, Theatre Dirs' Faculty 1990; has directed in Novi Sad, Stuttgart, Prague Nat. Theatre; invited to direct at Deutsches Theater, Berlin, Comédie Française, Paris 1991, Helsinki City Theatre 1993; Dir Uj Szinház Theatre 1993–97; univ. prof. 1991–; guest teacher, Paris Acad. of Dramatic and Cinematic Art 1993; Rector Univ. of Drama, Film and TV, Budapest 2001–06, Faculty Dir 2007–; Dr hc (Tirgu Mures Univ.); Jászai Mari Prize, Merited Artist, Outstanding Artist, Kossuth Prize, critics' prize for best theatre performance and best theatre direction, several times. *Plays directed include:* As You Like It, Troilus and Cressida, Timon of Athens (Shakespeare), Georges Dandin, L'impromptu de Versailles, Don Juan (Molière), The Death of Tarelkin (Kobilin), The Death of Danton, Woyzeck (Büchner); guest performances abroad with Budapest Nat. and Katona József theatres (among others): Cat's Play (Orkény), Family Toth (Orkény), Moscow, Bucharest, Prague, Helsinki; Catullus (Fust), Vienna, Paris (Odeon), Zürich; Le Misanthrope (Molière), Moscow; Coriolanus (Shakespeare), Berlin; The Escape (Bulgakov), Prague. *Leisure interests:* architecture, fine arts. *Address:* Jókai u. 36. II/12, 1066 Budapest, Hungary. *Telephone:* (1) 332-4284.

SZEKERES, Imre, PhD; Hungarian engineer and politician; b. 9 Sept. 1950, Szolnok; m.; two c.; ed Veszprém Univ. of Chemical Eng; sec. of communist youth org. at Univ.; Asst Lecturer, Cybernetics Inst., Veszprém Univ. 1974–77; mem. Veszprém City Council 1986, later Deputy Chair. responsible for culture and finances; co-f. Reformkörök movt; Chair. Hungarian Socialist Party (HSP) Org. in Veszprém Co. 1989, headed electoral list during first parl. elections 1990, Nat. Sec. 1990, Vice-Chair. 1990–2004, Deputy Chair. 2004–, electoral campaign chief 1994, mem. Parl. for Jászapáti 1994–2002, 2006–, for co. party list of Jász-Nagykun-Szolnok Co. 2002–06, Head, HSP parl. group 1994–98; Chair. Parl. Budget and Finance Cttee 1998–2002; Political State Sec., Cabinet of Prime Minister 2002–04; Minister of Defence 2006–10; Pres. Hungarian Triathlon Asscn 2003–; mem. Jász Ass001 ('The people of Jászság Ass002') and other social orgs of Jászság (geographical region of Hungary); Freeman of Jászapáti. *Leisure interest:* triathlon. *Address:* c/o Ministry of Defence, 1055 Budapest, Balaton u. 7–11, Hungary. *Telephone:* (1) 474-1114. *E-mail:* media@hm.gov.hu. *Website:* www.szekeresimre.hu.

SZEMERÉDI, Endre, PhD; Hungarian/American mathematician, computer scientist and academic; *State of New Jersey Professor of Computer Science, Rutgers University;* b. 21 Aug. 1940, Budapest, Hungary; m.; five c.; ed Eötvös Loránd Univ., Moscow State Univ., USSR; Visiting Prof., Stanford Univ. 1974,

McGill Univ., Canada 1980, Univ. of South Carolina 1981–83, Univ. of Chicago 1985–86; State of New Jersey Prof. of Computer Science, Rutgers Univ. 1986–; Perm. Research Fellow, Rényi Inst. of Math., Budapest; mem. Inst. for Advanced Study, Princeton, NJ; Fairchild Distinguished Scholar, California Inst. of Tech. 1987–88; Eisenbud Prof., MSRI Berkeley 2008; Aisenstadt Chair, CRM, Univ. of Montreal; Corresp. mem. Hungarian Acad. of Sciences 1982, 1987; mem. NAS 2010; Dr hc (Charles Univ., Prague); Grünwald Prize 1967, 1968, Rényi Prize 1973, Pólya Prize for Achievement in Applied Math., Soc. for Industrial and Applied Math. 1975, Prize of Hungarian Acad. of Sciences 1979, Leroy P. Steele Prize for Seminal Contrib. to Research, American Math. Soc. 2008, Rolf Schock Prize in Math. 2008, Abel Prize, Norwegian Acad. of Science and Letters 2012. *Achievements include:* his proof of an old conjecture of Paul Erdős and Paul Turán 1975 (now known as Szemerédi's theorem). *Publications:* more than 200 papers in professional journals on discrete mathematics, theoretical computer science, arithmetic combinatorics and discrete geometry. *Address:* SAS – Computer Science, 110 Frelinghuysen Road, Piscataway, NJ 08854-8019, USA (office). *Telephone:* (732) 445-2001 (office). *E-mail:* endre.szemeredi@rutgers.edu (office). *Website:* sas.rutgers.edu (office).

SZENES, Gen. (retd) Zoltán, MSc, PhD, CSc; Hungarian army officer (retd) and academic; *Professor and Head, Department of International and Security Studies, National University of Public Service;* b. 23 July 1951, Kócsk; m. Dr Ibolya Gáspár; one d.; ed Mil. Tech. Acad., Budapest, War Coll. of Logistics and Transportation, Leningrad (now St Petersburg), Russia, Hungarian Acad. of Science, Budapest Univ. of Econs, Royal Coll. of Defence Studies, London, UK; joined Hungarian People's Army 1969; assigned to 25th Tank Regt, Tata 1973–74; staff officer, 11th Tank Div. 1974–75; Chief of Staff for Logistics, 9th Mechanized Div., Kaposvár 1979–82; Sr Lecturer, Dept of Logistics, Zrínyi Miklós Nat. Defence Univ., Budapest 1985–86 (became Nat. Univ. of Public Service through merger with Police Coll. and Faculty of Public Admin of Corvinus Univ. of Budapest in 2012), Assoc. Prof. 2007–09, Prof. 2009–; Head of Logistics Dept 1986–91; Chief of Supply Services of Defence Command 1991–92; Fellow, Royal Coll. of Defence Studies, London 1995; Head of Educ. and Science Dept, Ministry of Defence 1996–98; Mil. Rep. to NATO and WEU, Brussels, Belgium 1998–99; ACOS Logistics, AFSOUTH HQ, Naples, Italy 1999–2002; Dir of Defence Staff 2002–03, Chief of Defence Staff 2003–05; apptd Maj.-Gen. 2002, Lt-Gen. 2003, Gen. (retd) 2008; Visiting Prof., Baltic Defence Coll., Tartu, Estonia; Guest Lecturer, NATO Defence Coll. 2010–; Chair. Mil. Science Cttee, Hungarian Acad. of Sciences; Co-Pres. Budapesti Honvéd Sport Club 2003–10; mem. Hungarian Logistics Asscn, Hungarian Soc. of Mil. Sciences, Hungarian Mil. Science Asscn, IISS, London 1995–2005; Cross of the Legion of Honour (Officer Grade) 2004, Commdr's Cross, Order of Merit (Mil. Div.) 2004; Meritorious Service Award, Pro Scientia Gold Medal, Tanárky Sándor Price Award, Hungarian Asscn of Mil. Sciences, Budapest, Hungarian NATO Enlargement Medal, NATO KFOR and SFOR Medals, Officer Service Medal (First Class), Andrássy Gyula Price Award 2001, NATO Service Award for the Period 1998–2002 2004, Defence Service Award (First Class) 2010, Medal of Merit, Baltic Defence Coll. 2010. *Publications:* The Implications of NATO for Civil-Military Relations in Hungary 2001, Future of NATO (in Academic and Applied Research in Military Science journal) 2005, The Effects of Peacekeeping on the HDF (in Peacekeeping Today and Tomorrow) 2006, Ten Years in NATO (with Peter Tálas) 2009, On the Hungarian Military Science (article) in Military Science Quarterly 2011, 1, UN Peacekeeping NUPS 2013. *Leisure interests:* photography, reading, running and gardening. *Address:* National University of Public Service, 1101 Budapest, Hungária krt. 9–11, Hungary (office). *Telephone:* (1) 432-9331 (office); 30-2428914 (mobile). *Fax:* (1) 432-9331 (office). *E-mail:* szenes.zoltan@uni-nke.hu (office); szenes@hotmail.com (home). *Website:* www.uni-nke.hu (office).

SZENTIVÁNYI, Gábor; Hungarian economist and diplomatist; *Ambassador for Nordic-Baltic Issues;* b. 9 Oct. 1952, Vaskút; s. of József Szentiványi and Ilona Fejes; m. Gabriella Gönczi; one s. one d.; ed Univ. of Econ. Sciences, Budapest; joined Foreign Service 1975, positions in Baghdad 1976–81, Washington, DC 1986–91; mem. staff Protocol Dept, Ministry of Foreign Affairs 1982–85, Spokesman and Dir-Gen. for Press and Int. Information Dept 1994–97, Deputy State Sec. 2002–04, State Sec. and Political Dir 2007–09; Amb. to UK 1997–2002, to the Netherlands 2004–07, to Sweden 2009–13; Amb. for Nordic-Baltic Issues 2013–; Man. Dir Burson-Marsteller's Budapest office 1991–94; mem. Hungarian Foreign Affairs Soc., Hungarian Atlantic Council; Freeman, City of London, UK 2000; Hon. GCVO, Officer, Order of Prince Henry the Navigator 1982, Grand Cross of Merit (Chile) 2002, Middle Cross of the Order of Merit 2004, Kt Grand Cross, Order of Oranje-Nassau (Netherlands) 2007. *Leisure interests:* boating, reading. *Address:* Ministry of Foreign Affairs, Bem rkp. 47, 1027 Budapest, Hungary (office). *Telephone:* (1) 458-1545 (office). *Fax:* (1) 214-8059 (office). *E-mail:* gszentivanyi@mfa.gov.hu (office). *Website:* www.kormany.hu/en/ministry-of-foreign-affairs (office).

SZILI, Katalin, DJur; Hungarian lawyer, political scientist and politician; b. 13 May 1956, Barcs; m. Miklós Molnár 1977; raising two c. of friends who died in an accident; ed Nagy Lajos Grammar School, Pécs, Janus Pannonius, Univ. of Pécs, Eötvös Loránd Univ., Budapest; Counsellor of Tutelage Affairs, then Head of Section, Pécs City Council 1981–85; legal counsellor, Water Directorate, South Transdanubian Region, then Admin. Head of Dept, then Leader of Authority Dept of Environment and Water Directorate, then of Environment Supervisory Authority 1985–92; mem. of Local Govt of Pécs 1992–94; expert, Parl. Group of Hungarian Socialist Party (MSZP) 1993–94; Political Sec. of State, Ministry for Environment and Regional Devt 1994–98; mem. MSZP 1989–, Baranya Co. Pres. of MSZP 1997–2001, Pres. Nat. Women's Asscn of MSZP 1998–2000, Nat. Vice-Pres. MSZP 2000–; mem. Gen. Ass. of Co. of Baranya 1998–99; mem. (MSZP) Hungarian Nat. Ass. for Pécs 1994–2010, Ind. mem. 2010–, Deputy Speaker 1998–2002, Speaker 2002–09, mem. Cttee on Sustainable Devt 2010– (Chair. 2013–), Vice-Chair. Parl. Cttee of Nat. Cohesion 2011–13, Chair. Sub-cttee on Autonomy 2012–, Chair. Community of Social Justice 2013–; nominated as cand. for presidential election 2005; Chair. Global Centre for ICT in Parl. 2008–09, Forum of Hungarian Reps from the Carpathian Basin 2002–09, Nat. Council for Sustainable Devt 2008 (Hon. Chair. 2009–); Founder and Chair. Forum of Nat. and Ethnic Minorities in Hungary 2009; Founder Social Union Party 2010; Hon. Assoc. Prof., Univ. of Pécs 2008; Hon. Citizen of Barcs, Dejtár, Kazincbarcika, Kővágószőlős and Szügy; Grand Cross of Belgium 2003, Grand Cross, Order of

Merit (Germany) 2004, Commdr, Légion d'honneur 2005, Grand Gold Service Medal with Ribbon (Austria), Congressional Great Cross of Peru 2005, Commdr's Cross, Order of Merit with Star (Poland) 2006, Order of Merit (Mongolia) 2006, Hon. Certificate and Hon. Medal of the Bulgarian Pres. 2007, Spanish Legion of Honour Grand Cross 2007, Grand Officer, Order of the Star of Italian Solidarity 2009, Order of White Rose (Finland) 2012; Dr hc (L.N. Gumilev Eurasian Univ., Kazakhstan) 2007; Appreciative Title of the Chamber 'Pro economy of Baranya' 1998, 18 Trees in the Yad Vashem Memorial Park, Israel 2005, Medal of Honour, Asscn of Displaced Persons for achievements in human rights issues 2007, Pro Urbe Award, Tirgu-Mures (Romania) 2008, Báthory Award, Hungarian Nat. Council of Transylvania 2008, Tolerance Award, Ass. of the Autonomous Prov. of Vojvodina 2009. *Leisure interests:* environmental protection, minority issues. *Address:* Országgyűlés (National Assembly), 1054 Budapest, rkp. 19, Hungary (office). *Telephone:* (1) 441-4000 (office); (1) 441-5012 (office). *Fax:* (1) 441-5010 (office). *E-mail:* katalin.szili@parlament.hu (office). *Website:* www.parlament.hu (office); www.szilikatalin.hu.

SZILVÁSY, György, PhD; Hungarian politician; b. 29 April 1958, Budapest; ed Karl Marx Univ. of Econs, Loránd Eötvös Univ. of Arts and Sciences; Govt Chief Consultant, Office of Council of Ministers 1989; Deputy Minister, Office of the Prime Minister 1989–90, also Sec., Bd of Supervision of Hungarian TV and Radio; Deputy Sec. of State, Office of the Prime Minister 1990–95; Sec. of State, Ministry of Environment and Regional Devt 1995–98, of Children, Youth and Sports 2002–03, of Culture 2003–04, of the Interior 2004–05; Titular Sec. of State and Chief of Cabinet, Office of the Prime Minister 2005–06, Political Sec. of State 2006, Minister in charge of Prime Minister's Office 2006–07, Minister without Portfolio in charge of Civilian Nat. Security Services 2007–10; Dir Altus Investment and Assets Man. Inc. 1998–2000; CEO Perfekt Inc. 2000–02. *Address:* c/o Office of the Prime Minister, 1055 Budapest, Kossuth Lajos tér 1–3, Hungary (office).

SZINETÁR, Miklós; Hungarian theatre and film director; b. 8 Feb. 1932, Budapest; m. Ildikó Hámori, one s. one d.; ed High School of Dramatic Art; Producer, Budapest Operetta Theatre, then Chief Producer 1953–60; Chief Producer, Hungarian TV, Artistic Dir then Chief Artistic Dir 1962, Deputy Chair. of Hungarian TV 1979–90; Man. Dir Budapest Operetta Theatre 1993–96; Chief Man. Dir Hungarian State Opera House 1996–2001, apptd Gen. Dir 2002; Golden Nympha, Monte Carlo 1970, Best Director, Prague TV Festival 1976–79, Silver Asterix, Trieste 1980, Pro urbe Budapest 2001. *Films include:* Déliáb minden mennyiségben 1961, Janos Háry 1965, Baleset 1967, Csárdás Fürstine (The Csardas Princess, UK) (also adaptation) 1971, Az erőd (The Fortress) (also screenwriter) 1979. *Television:* Éjszakai repülés 1963, Halálnak halála 1969, Az ember tragédiája (The Tragedy of the Man, USA) 1969, Igéző 1969, Rózsa Sándor (mini-series) 1979, A Kékszakállú herceg vára (Bluebeard's Castle) 1981, Der Kronprinz 1988, Così fan Tutte, Fidelio, The Barber of Seville, The Life of Franz Liszt. *Publications:* Kalandsaim 1987, Igy Kell Ezt 2003. *Address:* Bethlen Gábor u. 16, 2011 Budakalász, Hungary (home). *Telephone:* (36) 26343000 (home). *Fax:* (36) 26540380 (home). *E-mail:* szini1@axelero.hu.

SZOKA, HE Cardinal Edmund Casimir, BA; American ecclesiastic; b. 14 Sept. 1927, Grand Rapids, Mich.; s. of Casimir Szoka and Mary Wolgat; ordained priest 1954, Bishop of Gaylord, Mich. 1971–81; Bishop of Detroit 1981–90, Archbishop Emer. 1990–; Cardinal-Priest of Ss. Andrea e Gregorio al Monte Celio 1988–; Pres. of Pref. of Econ. Affairs of Holy See, Roman Curia 1990–97; Pres. of Governatorate of Vatican City State, Roman Curia 1997–2006, Pres. Emer. 2006–; Pres. of Vatican City State, Roman Curia 2001–06; Second Sec. Council for Relations with States; mem. Congregations for the Causes of Saints, for the Bishops, for the Evangelization of Peoples, for the Clergy, for Insts of Consecrated Life and for Socs of Apostolic Life. *Address:* c/o Secretariat of State, Palazzo Apostolico Vaticano, 00120 Città del Vaticano, Rome, Italy.

SZŐNYI, Erzsébet; Hungarian musician; b. 25 April 1924; d. of Jenő Szőnyi and Erzsébet Piszanoff; m. Dr. Lajos Gémes 1948; two s.; ed Music Acad., Budapest and Paris Conservatoire; teacher of music at a Budapest grammar school 1945–48, Music Acad., Budapest 1948–; leading Prof. of Music Acad. 1960–81; Vice-Pres. Int. Soc. for Music Educ. 1970–74; Co-Chair. Hungarian Kodály Soc. 1978–2003, Chair. 2007–, Co-Chair. Bárdos Soc. 1988–, Forum of Hungarian Musicians 1995–; Hon. Pres. Hungarian Choir Asscn 1990–; Gen. adviser on methodology, Int. Kodály Soc. 1979–; mem. Chopin Soc. of Warsaw, Liszt Soc. of Hungary; mem. Hungarian Acad. of Art 1992–, Hungarian Composers' Soc. 1999–; Dr hc (Duquesne Univ., Pittsburgh) 2006; Erkel Prize 1959, Hungarian Repub. Medal 1993, Apácai Csere János Prize 1994, Bartók-Pásztory Prize 1995, 2004, Prize for Artistic Excellence 2000, Zoltán Kodály Prize 2001, Hungarian Heritage Prize 2004, Hungarian Choir Asscn Medal 2004, Kossuth Prize 2006, Prima Prize 2011. *Compositions include:* Concerto for Organ and Orchestra; symphonic works: Musica Festiva, Divertimento 1 and 2, Prelude and Fugue, Three Ideas in Four Movements; operas: Tragedy of Firenze, A Gay Lament, Break in Transmission, Elfrida (madrigal opera) 1987–, several children's operas; chamber music, oratorios, vocal compositions, etc. *Publications:* Methods of Musical Reading and Writing, Kodály's Principles in Practice, Travels in Five Continents, Twentieth-Century Musical Methods. *Leisure interests:* gardening, cooking. *Address:* Ormódi-utca 13, 1124 Budapest XII, Hungary (home). *Telephone:* (1) 356-7329 (home).

SZOSTAK, Jack William, BS, PhD; Canadian/American molecular biologist and academic; *Professor of Genetics, Harvard Medical School;* b. 9 Nov. 1952; ed McGill Univ., Canada, Cornell Univ.; Asst Prof., Sidney Farber Cancer Inst. and Dept of Biological Chemistry, Harvard Medical School 1979–83, Assoc. Prof., Dana Farber Cancer Inst. and Dept of Biological Chem. 1983–84, Assoc. Prof., Dept of Genetics 1984–87, Prof. 1988–, Prof. of Chem. and Chemical Biology, Harvard Univ.; Assoc. Molecular Biologist, Dept of Molecular Biology, Massachusetts Gen. Hosp. 1984–87, Molecular Biologist 1988–, Alex A. Rich Distinguished Investigator 2000–; Investigator, Howard Hughes Medical Inst. 1998–; Co-Chair. Nat. Research Council Cttee on the Origin and Evolution of Life 2003–; mem. NAS 1998–; Fellow, New York Acad. of Sciences 1999–; mem. Editorial Bd Chemistry and Biology 1994–; Penhallow Prize in Botany, McGill Univ. 1972, NAS Award in Molecular Biology 1994, Louis Vuitton-Moet Hennesey 'Vinci of Excellence' Award 1996, Hans Sigrist Prize, Univ. of Bern, Switzerland 1997, Genetics Soc. of America Medal 2000, ACS Harrison Howe Award 2003, Albert Lasker Award for

Basic Medical Research (with Elizabeth Blackburn and Carol Greider) 2006, Dr H.P. Heineken Prize for Biochemistry and Biophysics 2008, Nobel Prize in Physiology or Medicine (with Elizabeth Blackburn and Carol Greider) 2009. *Publications:* more than 170 papers in scientific journals. *Address:* Szostak Lab, CCIB 7215, Simches Research Center, 185 Cambridge Street, Boston, MA 02114 (office); Department of Molecular Biology, Massachusetts General Hospital, Wellman 9, Fruit Street, Boston, MA 02114, USA (office). *Telephone:* (617) 726-5102 (Lab.) (office); (617) 726-5981 (Hosp.) (office). *Fax:* (617) 643-3328 (Lab.) (office); (617) 726-6893 (Hosp.) (office). *E-mail:* szostak@molbio.mgh.harvard.edu (office). *Website:* molbio.mgh.harvard.edu/szostakweb (office).

SZOSTEK, Andrzej Ryszard, BPhil; Polish ecclesiastic and academic; b. 9 Nov. 1945, Grudziądz; ed Catholic Univ. of Lublin; ordained priest 1974; with Dept of Ethics, Catholic Univ. of Lublin 1970–04, scientific worker 1971–04, Extraordinary Prof. 1992–99, Ordinary Prof. of Ethics and Philosophy 2000–04, Head of Dept of Ethics, mem. man. team Inst. of John Paul II 1983–98, Pro-Rector 1992–98, Rector 1998–2004; Lecturer, Superior Monastic House, Lublin 1987–90; Provincial Councillor Marians 1987–93; mem. Cttee of Formation of Marians 1975–90, Scientific Soc., Catholic Univ. of Lublin 1980–, Polish Philosophical Soc., Lublin 1982, Int. Cttee of Theology, Vatican Congregation of Religious Studies 1992–98, Lublin Scientific Soc. 1998–2001 (Distinguished mem. 2001–), Pontificia Academia Pro Vita 2001–; Hon. Fellow, St Mary's Coll., London 2000; Order of Merit 2001, Palmes Académiques 2001, Kawaler Orderu Odrodzenia Polski 2005; Medal, Comm. of Nat. Educ. 2001, Brązowe Odznaczenie, Za zasługi w obronności kraju 2002, Honorowe Odznaczenie (Premium Honorificum) Lubelskiego Towarzystwa Naukowego 2003, Nagroda naukowa im Wł, Pietrzaka 2003, Nagroda Rektora KUL I stopnia 2005, Wyróżnienie Lubelskiego Towarzystwa Naukowego Resolutio pro Laude Academica 2005. *Publications include:* Rules and Exceptions – Philosophical Aspects of the Discussion about Absolute Norms in Contemporary Theology 1980, Nature–Reason–Freedom. Philosophical Analysis of the Concept of Creative Intellect in Contemporary Moral Theology 1989, Talks on Ethics 1993, On Dignity, Truth and Love 1995 and numerous other publs. *Leisure interests:* mountaineering, music, chess. *Address:* c/o Katolicki Uniwersytet Lubelski, Katedra Etyki, Al. Racławickie 14, 20-950 Lublin, Poland.

SZUMSKI, Henryk; Polish army officer; b. 6 April 1941, Potulice; m. Wiesława Jawor; three s. one d.; ed Officer's School, Poznan, Gen. Staff Acad. Polish Armed Forces, Warsaw, Gen. Staff Acad. Armed Forces of USSR, Moscow; career soldier 1964–; commdr section and co. of brigade 1964–68, Chief of Staff and Commdr 1971–76, Chief of Staff and Commdr of 16th Armoured Div. 1976–78, Commdr 12th Mechanized Div., Szczecin 1980–84, Chief of Staff of Pomeranian Mil. Dist 1984–86, Deputy Chief of Gen. Staff for Operational Matters, 1986–87, Commdr Silesian Mil. Dist 1987–89, First Deputy Chief of Gen. Staff, 1989–90, Chief of Main Bd of Combat Training, 1990–92; Brig.-Gen. 1983, Maj.-Gen. 1988, Lt-Gen. 1997; Inspector of Leadership of Gen. Staff 1993–97, Chief of Gen. Staff 1997–2000; mem. Nat. Security Council 2000–05; Commandory Cross with Star (Poland), Legion d'Honneur, Legion of Merit (USA). *Leisure interests:* history, literature, sport. *Address:* 05-806 Komorów, ul. Bugai 14A, Poland (home). *Telephone:* (22) 7989487 (home). *Fax:* (22) 6826488 (home).

SZŰRÖS, Mátyás, PhD; Hungarian politician and diplomatist; b. 11 Sept. 1933, Püspökladány; ed Moscow Univ. Inst. of Int. Relations, Budapest Univ. of Econ. Sciences; on staff of Foreign Ministry 1959–65; staff mem. HSWP 1965–74, Deputy Leader Foreign Dept HSWP Cen. Cttee 1974–75, Head 1982–83; Amb. to GDR 1975–78, to USSR 1978–82; mem. Cen. Cttee HSWP 1978, Secr. 1983–89; mem. Parl. 1985–, Chair. Foreign Relations Parl. Cttee 1985–89 (mem. 1998–), Pres. of Parl. March–Oct. 1989, Acting Pres. 1989–90, Deputy Speaker 1990–94; Chair. Hungarian Group of IPU 1989–90, 1994–2002, mem. Exec. Cttee IPU 1994–96; Gen. Pres. SDP 2003–05; Chair. Ópusztaszer Historical Commemorative Cttee 1989–98, Bd Trustees Illyés Foundation 1994–99, Trustee 1999–; mem. Council of Hundreds (World Fed. of Hungarians) 1997–; Freeman of Püspökladány 1996, of Beregszász 1997; Bocskai Award 1996. *Publications:* Hazánk és a nagyvilág (Homeland and World) 1985, Hazánk és Európa (Homeland and Europe) 1987, Magyarságról-Külpolitikáról (On Being Hungarian and on Foreign Policy) 1989, Cselekvő politikával a magyarságért-Politikai portré (1988–96) (Active policy for Hungary, portrait of a politician) 1996, Köztársaság született harangszavú délben (1989. október 23) (The Republic Was Born and the Bells Rang at Noon, 23 October 1989) 1999, National Politics and Joining. Questions of Integration 2001, Hoggan tovább a rögös utakon (How Much Marching Further on the Thorny Way) 2003. *Address:* Hungarian National Assembly, 1055 Budapest, Kossuth Lajos tér 1-3, Hungary (office). *Telephone:* (1) 441-5067 (office); (1) 441-5068 (office). *Fax:* (1) 441-5972 (office). *E-mail:* secretariate@ipu.parlament.hu (office).

SZYMANCZYK, Michael E., BS; American business executive; *Chairman and CEO, Altria Group, Inc.;* ed Indiana Univ.; joined Proctor & Gamble 1971, served in several sales and marketing positions –1987; Vice-Pres. of Sales, Kraft Inc. 1987–88, Vice-Pres. Retail Operations 1988, Sr Vice-Pres. Swift-Eckrich Inc. 1989; Sr Vice-Pres. of Sales, Philip Morris USA, New York 1990–97, COO July-Nov. 1997, Pres. and CEO 1997–2008, Chair. 2002–08, Chair. and CEO Altria Group Inc. (parent co.) 2008–; mem. Bd of Trustees Univ. of Richmond, Virginia Commonwealth Univ. School of Eng Foundation, United Negro Coll. Fund, Richmond Performing Arts Center; fmr Chair. and current mem. Dean's Advisory Council for Indiana Univ. Kelley School of Business; fmr mem. Bd Futures for Children. *Address:* Altria Group, Inc., 120 Park Avenue, New York, NY 10017, USA (office). *Telephone:* (917) 663-4000 (office). *Fax:* (917) 663-2167 (office). *E-mail:* info@altria.com (office). *Website:* www.altria.com (office).

SZYMCZYK, Adam; Polish gallery curator; *Director and Chief Curator, Kunsthalle Basel;* b. 1970, Piotrków Trybunalski; ed Univ. of Warsaw; Co-founder and Curator, Foksal Gallery Foundation, Warsaw 1997–2003; Dir and Chief Curator Kunsthalle Basel 2003–; co-curated, with Elena Filipovic, When Things Cast No Shadow, 5th Berlin Biennale for Contemporary Art 2008; Walter Hopps Award for Curatorial Achievement 2011. *Publications:* numerous exhbn catalogues; contrib. to Parkett, Frieze, Flash Art, Fluid, Kunstbulletin, Spike. *Address:* Kunsthalle Basel, Steinberg 7, 4051 Basel, Switzerland (office). *Telephone:* (61) 2069900 (office). *Fax:* (61) 2069919 (office). *E-mail:* info@kunsthallebasel.ch (office). *Website:* www.kunsthallebasel.ch (office).

T

TABACHNYK, Dmytro Volodimirovych, DS; Ukrainian politician and historian; *Minister of Education and Science and Youth and Sport;* b. 26 Nov. 1964, Kiev; s. of Volodomir Igorovich Tabachnyk and Alla Viktorovna Tabachnyk; m. Tetyana Evgenyovna Nazarova; ed Kiev State Univ.; fmr copyist, then restorer, Cen. State Archives of Cinematography, Documents of Ukraine; jr researcher, Inst. of History of Ukraine, Ukrainian Acad. of Sciences, leading researcher, Inst. of Politology 1997–; Deputy, Kiev City Soviet 1990–94; Deputy Head Kiev City Exec. Comsomol Cttee 1991–92; Head of Press Service, Cabinet of Ministers 1992–93; First Deputy Head, State Cttee on Publishing, Polygraphy and Book Trade 1993–94; Head of Admin., Presidency 1994–96, Counsellor 1997–98, Head, Constitution Comm. 1994–96; People's Deputy of Ukraine of III, IV Convocations 1998–2003, Deputy of Verkhovna Rada (Party of the Regions), Crimean Autonomous Repub. 2006; Vice-Prime Minister of Ukraine 2002–05, responsible for Humanitarian Issues 2006–07; mem. Verkhovna Rada (Parl.) 2007–; Minister of Educ. and Science and Youth and Sports 2010–; Dir Nat. Expert Inst. of Ukraine 2005–; Prof., Ukrainian Acad. of State Man. 1995–; Corresp. mem. Acad. of Juridical Sciences. *Publications:* over 400 papers. *Leisure interests:* collecting art, theatre, books. *Address:* Ministry of Education and Science, and Youth and Sport, 01135 Kiev, pr. Peremohi 10, Ukraine (office). *Telephone:* (44) 486-24-42 (office). *Fax:* (44) 236-10-49 (office). *E-mail:* ministry@mon.gov.ua (office). *Website:* www.mon.gov.ua (office).

TABAI, Ieremia T., CMG; I-Kiribati fmr head of state and international organization official; b. 1950, Nonouti; m.; two c.; ed King George V School, Tarawa, St Andrew's Coll., Christchurch, NZ, Victoria Univ., Wellington, NZ; mem. Gilbert Islands (later Kiribati) House of Ass. 1974–91; fmr Leader of the Opposition; Chief Minister of the Gilbert Islands 1978–79, also Minister of Local Govt; Pres. of Kiribati and Minister of Foreign Affairs (fmrly Gilbert Islands) 1979–91; Sec.-Gen. South Pacific Forum 1991–98; Chair. Commonwealth Observer Group 2001; Co-Owner New Star newspaper; Hon. LLD (Vic. Univ. of Wellington). *Address:* c/o Ministry of Foreign Affairs, PO Box 68, Bairiki, Tarawa, Kiribati.

TABAKOV, Oleg Pavlovich; Russian actor and director; *Artistic and Managing Director, Moscow Art Theatre of A.P. Chekhov;* b. 17 Aug. 1935, Saratov; s. of Pavel K. Tabakov and Maria A. Beresovskaya; m. 1st Lyudmila Krilova 1959 (divorced); one s. one d.; m. 2nd Marina V. Zudina 1995; one s. one d.; ed Moscow Arts Theatre Studio-School; Co-founder and actor with Sovremennik Theatre 1957–83; with Moscow Arts Theatre 1983–; stage debut 1956; film debut 1957; mem. CPSU 1965–91; master of theatre training 1976–; Assoc. Prof., State Inst. of Theatre Arts (GITIS) 1976–85; Prof., Moscow Arts Theatre Studio School 1985–, Chancellor 1986–; Founder and Producer, Moscow Theatre Studio (now Oleg Tabakov Theatre) 1974–; directed and taught in numerous countries; f. and teacher Stanislavsky Summer School, Cambridge, Mass, USA 1992–; Founder and Pres. Russian-American Performing Arts Center 1992–; Artistic Dir Moscow Art Theatre of A.P. Chekhov 2000–; Hon. mem. Russian Acad. of Arts 2008; People's Artist of the USSR 1987, Order of Merit for Fatherland I Degree 2010; Dr hc (Czech Acad. of Fine Arts) 2007; State Prize for Acting 1967, European Cultural Prize 'Trebbia' 2011. *Stage roles include:* Misha in Always Alive 1956, Aleksandr in The Same Old Story 1966, Brother Lymon in The Ballad of Sad Café 1966, Klava in Always on Sale 1965, Major in Tooth, Others and Major 1971, Balalaykin in Balalaykin and Co. 1974, Anchugin in Provincial Anecdotes 1975, 1996, Malvolio in Twelfth Night 1975, Peter Stockman in Dr. Stockman 1979, Salieri in Amadeus 1983, Hailmayer in Judgers 1985, Sorin in Seagull 1987, Buton in Cabal of Hippocrates 1989, Tacker in I Ought to be in Pictures 1990, Meyer Volf in My Big Land 1991, Famusov in Woe from Wisdom 1992, Uncle in The Same Old Story 1993, Tallyran in Le Souper 1994, Ivan Kolomiytsev in The Last Ones 1995; has directed Champions, Every Wise Man has a Fool in his Sleeve, The Same Old Story, Goldoni's Revenge, Copenhagen 2003, The Last Victim 2003, Tartuffe 2004, The Adventure Based on the Dead Souls 2006, The Marriage of Figaro 2009, The Seagull 2011, The Year When I Wasn't Born 2012. *Films include:* The Tight Knot 1956, War and Peace 1967, Noisy Day 1960, Light My Star, Light 1969, Kashtanka 1975, Unfinished Play for Mechanical Piano 1977, A Few Days of I. I. Oblomov's Life (Oxford Int. Festival Prize for best male actor 1980) 1979, Flights of Fancy 1983, The Art of Living in Odessa 1989, The Inner Circle 1991, The Shadows 1991, Shirli-Myrli 1995, Moskovskiye kanikuly 1995, The White Dunes 1996, Three Stories 1997, Sympathy Seeker 1997, Prezident i yego vnuchka 2000, Taking Sides 2001, Statski sovetnik 2005, Andersen – Life without Love 2006, Melody for a Street Organ 2008, Lions, Eagles and Partridges 2010. *Publications:* My Real Life, Touch to the Miracle. *Leisure interest:* driving a car. *Address:* Moscow Art Theatre of A.P. Chekhov, 125009 Moscow, Kamergurskiy per. 3, Russia (office). *Telephone:* (495) 629-33-12 (office). *Fax:* (495) 692-75-36. *E-mail:* tabakov@theatre.ru (office); tabakov@mxat.ru (office). *Website:* www.mxat.ru (office); www.tabakov.ru.

TABAKOVIĆ, Jorgovanka, MA, PhD; Serbian economist, politician and central banker; *Governor, National Bank of Serbia;* b. 21 March 1960, Vučitrn; widowed; three c.; ed Univ. of Priština; began career as econs teacher, Secondary Econs School, Priština 1981–89; Financial Dir, Grmija trading co. 1990–92; Gen. Man. Priština banka AD 1992; various posts in domestic banking –1999; mem. Nat. Ass. (parl.) (Serbian Radical Party) 1993–2000, (Serbian Progressive Party) 2008–12, May–Aug. 2012; Minister of Econ. and Ownership Transformation 1998–2000; joined Telekom Srbija (telecoms co.) 1999, Gen. Man., Logistics Dept 2005–08; Lecturer, Faculty of Man., Univ. of Novi Sad 2006–07; Gov. Nat. Bank of Serbia (central bank) 2012–; mem. Serbian Progressive Party 2008–, Vice-Pres. 2012–. *Publications:* several studies on privatization and financial markets. *Address:* Office of the Governor, National Bank of Serbia, 11000 Belgrade, Kralja Petra 12, POB 1010, Serbia (office). *Telephone:* (11) 3027194 (office). *Fax:* (11) 3027394 (office). *E-mail:* kabinet@nbs.rs (office). *Website:* www.nbs.rs (office).

TABAKSBLAT, Morris; Dutch business executive; b. Rotterdam; m.; two s. one d.; ed Leiden Univ.; joined Unilever 1964, mem. Bd 1984, mem. Unilever Special Cttee 1992–99, Chair. and CEO 1994–99; Chair. Reed Elsevier Group plc and Reed Elsevier plc 1999–2005, Chair. Supervisory Bd 1999–2005; Pres. Aegon NV 2000–; Chair. European Round Table of Industrialists –2001; Deputy Chair. European

Culture Foundation –2009; mem. Bd of Govs. Leiden Univ. Medical Centre, Mauritshuis Museum, The Hague; Vice-Chair. USA Conf. Bd; Chair. Supervisory Bd, AEGON NV, TNT Post Group NV, TPG NV; mem. Int. Advisory Bd Salomon Smith Barney, Renault Nissan; Hon. KBE. *Address:* c/o European Cultural Foundation, Jan van Goyenkade 5, 1075 HN, Amsterdam, Netherlands.

TABINAMAN, John; Papua New Guinea politician; mem. Regional House of Reps 2005–; Vice-Pres. Autonomous Govt of Bougainville 2007–, additional ministerial portfolios for Public Service, Planning and Implementation and Peace and Autonomy 2007–, Acting Pres. Autonomous Govt of Bougainville 2008–09. *Address:* c/o Autonomous Bougainville Government, House of Representatives, PO Box 322, Buka, Autonomous Region of Bougainville, Papua New Guinea (office). *E-mail:* abghausparl@datec.net.pg (office).

TABONE, Anton; Maltese politician; b. 15 Nov. 1937; s. of Anton Tabone; m. Margerite Stivala; three s.; ed St Aloysius Coll.; employee, Nat. Bank of Malta 1955–66; mem. Parl. for Gozo (Nationalist Party) 1966–98; mem. Gozo Civic Council 1966–73; Party Spokesman for Agric. and Fisheries, later for Gozo Affairs 1973–87; Minister for Gozo 1987–96; Shadow Minister for Gozo 1996–98; Speaker House of Reps 1998–2008; Companion of the National Order of Merit 2008. *Address:* c/o House of Representatives, The Palace, Valletta, Malta.

TABOR, Harry Zvi, PhD, FInstP; British/Israeli fmr research physicist; b. 7 March 1917, London; s. of Charles Tabor and Rebecca Tabor; brother of David Tabor; m. Vivienne Landau 1947; two d.; ed Quintin Hogg School, London, Univ. of London and Hebrew Univ. of Jerusalem; research physicist in UK instrument industry (including defence-related research and devt 1939–45) 1939–49; Research Council of Israel 1949–74; Dir Nat. Physical Lab. of Israel 1950–74; Chair. and Scientific Dir Scientific Research Foundation, Jerusalem 1969; mem. research cttees Ministry of Science & Tech., Ministry of Energy and Infrastructure 1975; Pres. Int. Solar Energy Soc. (ISES) 1981–83; guest lecturer NAS 1961 and at numerous univs; consultant to UNESCO and WEC; Dr hc (Weizmann Inst.) 1992; Royal Soc. Gold Medal Energy Award 1975 for pioneering work on exploitation of solar energy, Diesel Gold Medallist 1977, Farrington Daniels Award (ISES) 1981, Alfred Krupp Energy Prize 1981, Quality of Life Award (Knesset, Israel) 1995. *Publications:* selected reprints of papers by Harry Zvi Tabor, Solar Energy Pioneer (ed. by Morton B. Prince) 1999, book chapters and some 90 papers in scientific journals. *Leisure interests:* music, theatre, study of social problems (non-party). *Address:* PO Box 3745, Jerusalem 91036, Israel. *Telephone:* 2-6435785. *Fax:* 2-6437470. *E-mail:* taborh@zahav.net.il.

TABUNSCIC, Gheorghe, PhD; Moldovan politician; b. 1 Jan. 1949, Copciac; m.; two c.; ed Chişinău Agricultural Inst.; agronomist and Vice-Chair. Victory collective farm, Taraclia rayon 1962–75; fmr Leader, Moldovan CP Comrat Br., advocate for autonomy of Gagauz region; elected Başkan (Gov.) of Gagauz-Yeri following autonomy 1995–99, re-elected 2002–06. *Address:* c/o Office of the Başkan, Gagauz-Yeri, 3800 Comrat, Moldova (office).

TACHA, Deanell Reece, JD; American lawyer, federal judge and university administrator; *Duane and Kelly Roberts Dean and Professor of Law, School of Law, Pepperdine University;* b. 26 Jan. 1946, Goodland, Kan.; ed Univ of Kansas and Univ of Michigan Law School; Special Asst to US Sec. of Labor, Washington, DC 1971–72; Assoc. Hogan and Hartson (law firm) 1973, Thomas J. Pitner 1973–74; Dir Douglas Co. Legal Aid Clinic, Lawrence, Kan. 1974–77; Assoc. Prof. of Law Univ. of Kansas 1974–77, Prof. 1977–85, Assoc. Dean 1977–79, Assoc. Vice-Chancellor 1979–81, Vice-Chancellor 1981–85; Judge US Court of Appeals, 10th Circuit 1985–2001, 2007–11, Chief Judge 2001–07; Duane and Kelly Roberts Dean and Prof. of Law, School of Law, Pepperdine Univ. 2011–; mem., US Sentencing Comm. 1994-1998. *Address:* Office of the Dean, School of Law, Pepperdine University, 24255 Pacific Coast Highway, Malibu, CA 90263, USA (office). *Telephone:* (310) 506-4611 (office). *Fax:* (310) 506-4266 (office). *Website:* law.pepperdine.edu (office).

TADDZHUDDIN, Talgat Safich; Russian (Tartar) ecclesiastic; *Head, Central Spiritual Directorate of Russian Muslims;* b. 12 Oct. 1948, Kazan, Tatarstan, Russia; m.; five c.; ed El-Azkhar Theological Univ., Cairo; First Imam-Khatyb, mufti and Chair. of Sacred Bd Mosque El-Mardjani; Chair. Dept of Int. Relations of Muslim Orgs of the USSR 1990; Supreme Mufti of Russia and European countries of CIS; awarded the sacred title Sheik-iul-Islam; Official Rep. of Muslims of Russia to maj. foreign and public Muslim orgs., Org. of Islam Confed., UNESCO, European League of Muslims; currently Head, Central Spiritual Directorate of Russian Muslims. *Publications:* The Wild East 1999, Limit of Rationality 1998, and numerous scientific works on political and religious culture. *Leisure interest:* foreign languages. *Address:* Vypolzov per. 7, 129090 Moscow, Russia (office). *Telephone:* (095) 281-49-04 (office).

TADIĆ, Boris; Serbian politician, psychologist and fmr head of state; b. 15 Jan. 1958, Sarajevo, Bosnia and Herzegovina; s. of Ljuba Tadić and Nevenka Tadić; m. 1st Veselinka Zastavniković 1980 (divorced 1996); m. 2nd Tatjana Rodić; two d.; ed Univ. of Belgrade; convicted for student political activities; several positions as prof. of psychology, army clinical psychologist, researcher on devt and social psychology projects; Prof. of Politics and Advertising, Univ. for Drama and Arts, Belgrade 2003; Founder and Dir Centre for the Devt of Democracy and Political Skills 1997–2002; mem. Democratic Party 1990–2014, later Sec. of Gen. Cttee, Vice-Pres. Exec. Bd, Acting Pres. Exec. Bd, Vice-Pres. of Democratic Party (twice), Pres. 2004–12, Hon. Pres. 2012–14 (resgnd); mem. New Democratic Party 2014–; Rep. to Nat. Ass. 1996–97; mem. Council for Science and Tech.; Rep. in Council of Fed. Ass. 2000; Minister of Telecommunications, Fed. Repub. of Yugoslavia 2002–03; Minister of Defence, Council of Ministers of Serbia and Montenegro 2003–04; elected Rep. to Ass. of Serbia and Montenegro 2003, Acting Head of Group of Democratic Party Reps; Pres. of Serbia 2004–12 (resgnd); mem. Bd for Defence and Security; first Pres. Comm. for the Supervision of Security Service; Order of the Republika Srpska 2012; Dr hc (Dimitrie Cantemir Christian Univ.) 2009; European Prize for Political Culture, Ringier Group, Zurich 2007, Medal For the Contrib. to the Victory of Russian Fed. 2008, The Courage of Perseverance

Quadriga Award, Werkstatt Deutschland, Berlin 2008, Golden Keys of the City of Madrid 2009, Steiger Award of Rhine-Ruhr 2010, North-South Prize of the Council of Europe 2011, Ilyas Afandiyev Int. Prize (Azerbaijan) 2012. *Address:* c/o Democratic Party (Demokratska Strana), Krunska 69, Belgrade, Serbia (office). *E-mail:* info@ds.org.rs.

TADLAOUI, Mohammed, BSc; Moroccan engineer; *President, Socoplan;* b. 1939, Meknès; m.; two s. one d.; ed Imperial Coll. London and Inst. of Civil Engineers, UK, Sorbonne, Paris; research engineer, UK 1963, project engineer Arup and Partners 1966; consulting engineer Morocco 1973; Founder, Pres. and Gen. Dir Socoplan (consulting engineers) 1975–; co-founder and mem. Moroccan Fed. of Consulting Engineers (FMCI) 1976–; Gen. Sec. Ismailia Asscn of Micro Credit; Founding mem. Regional Asscn Grande Ismailia, Meknès; mem. Moroccan Nat. Fed. of Micro-Credit. *Leisure interests:* swimming, tennis, history, literature. *Address:* Socoplan, Residence Royale, av. Moulay Slimane, Rabat 10000, Morocco (office). *Telephone:* (7) 721020 (office). *Fax:* (7) 735663 (office). *E-mail:* socoplan@iam.net.ma (office).

TADROS, Tharwat Fouad, MSc, PhD; British/Egyptian scientist, academic and consultant; *Consultant and Visiting Professor, Imperial College London;* b. 29 July 1937, Kena, Egypt; s. of Fouad Tadros Mikhail and Rosa Wasif El-Gouhary; m. Jantina Lodewijka Buter 1969; two s.; ed secondary school, Luxor, Egypt, Alexandria Univ.; Lecturer in Physical Chem., Faculty of Science, Alexandria Univ. 1962–66; Agric. Univ. Wageningen, Netherlands 1966–68; research worker Lab. for Applied Research, Delft, Netherlands 1968–69; Tech. Officer ICI 1969–74, Sr Research Officer 1974–78, Research Assoc. 1978–89, Sr Research Assoc. 1989–; Visiting Prof., Univ. of Bristol 1983–84; Consultant and Visiting Prof., Imperial Coll. London 1988–; industrial lecturer; Past Pres. Int. Asscn of Colloid and Interface Science; RSC Colloid and Surface Chem. Award and Medal, Silver Medal 1990. *Publications:* author of four books, editor of ten books and more than 250 scientific articles in learned journals; ed two scientific journals. *Leisure interests:* chess, reading, debates. *Address:* 89 Nash Grove Lane, Wokingham, Berks., RG40 4HE, England. *Telephone:* (118) 973-2621. *E-mail:* tharwat@tadros.fsnet.co.uk.

TAFAJ, Myqerem, MSc, PhD, PhD; Albanian politician and academic; b. 14 Nov. 1957, Diber; ed Agricultural Univ. of Tirana, Univ. of Hohenheim, Stuttgart, Germany; Asst. Agricultural Univ. of Tirana 1982–88, Lecturer 1989–91, Prof. 1997–, expert in fields of systems of educ., educational legislation, governance and man., curriculum devt, higher educ.; Lecturer, Univ. of Stuttgart-Hohenheim 1999–2005, Guest Scientist (under auspices of the Alexander von Humboldt Foundation); Dir Gen. of Science, Ministry of Higher Educ. 1996–97, Minister of Higher Educ. and Science March–July 1997; Educ. and Science Adviser to the Prime Minister 2005–09; mem. Democratic Party 1991, mem. Cttee, Political Orientation 2005; mem. Democratic Party of Albania 2005–; Sec. Gen. Council of Ministers 2006–07; mem. Parl. for Tirana Dist 2009–; Minister of Educ. and Science 2009–13; Deputy Prime Minister April–Sept. 2013; Chair. Group of Experts on Reform of Science; fellowship from German Foundation for Int. Devt 1990. *Address:* Kuvendi Popullor, Bulevardi Dëshmorët e Kombit 4, Tirana, Albania (office). *E-mail:* tafaj@uni-hohenheim.de (office); info@parlament.al (office). *Website:* www.parlament.al (office).

TAFT, Robert (Bob) Alphonso II, BA, MA, JD; American politician and fmr state official; b. 8 Jan. 1942; s. of the late Robert Taft Jr, fmr Senator from Ohio, grand-s. of the late Robert Taft, fmr Senator from Ohio, great grand-s. of the late William Howard Taft, fmr US Pres.; m. Hope Taft; one d.; ed Yale Univ, Princeton Univ, Univ of Cincinnati Law School; served as volunteer teacher for US Peace Corps in East Africa; mem. Ohio House of Reps 1976–80; Commr Hamilton Co., Ohio 1981–90; Sec. of State of Ohio 1990–99; Gov. of Ohio 1999–2007; Distinguished Research Assoc., Univ. of Dayton 2007–; mem. Bd of Dirs Alliance for the Great Lakes 2008–. *Address:* c/o University of Dayton, 300 College Park, Dayton, OH 45469, USA (office).

TAGAREV, Todor, MSc, PhD; Bulgarian politician; b. 18 April 1960, Stamboliyski; ed Air Force Acad., Dolna Mitropolia, NE Zhukovsky Air Force Eng Acad., Moscow, Russia, US Air Command and Staff Coll., Air Univ., Alabama, USA; 12 years of field, teaching and man. experience in Bulgarian Air Force; Researcher, Bulgarian Acad. of Sciences Inst. of Control and Systems Research 1994–97 and Space Research Inst. 1997–98; Head, IT for Security Dept and Centre for Security and Defence Man., Inst. of Information and Communication Technologies 2008; Sr Research Assoc, Inst for Security and Int. Studies 1995–; Dir Defence Planning Directorate, Ministry of Defence 1998–2001, also Dir Armaments Policy Directorate and Nat. Armaments Dir May–Sept. 2001, Adviser to Minister of Defence 2009–10, Minister of Defence (in caretaker govt) March–May 2013; Head of Security and Defence Man. Dept, G.S. Rakovski Nat. Defence Acad., Sofia 2004–08; mem. NATO Research and Tech. Bd and Nat. Rep. to System Analysis and Studies Panel 2005–08. *Address:* c/o Ministry of Defence, 1092 Sofia, ul. Dyakon Ignatiy 3, Bulgaria.

TAGAYEV, Aitibai Sultanovich; Kyrgyzstani economist and politician; b. 30 April 1958, Naukat Dist, Osh Oblast; m.; three s.; ed Kyrgyz State Univ.; started career at Chapayev Collective Farm, Naukat Dist, Osh Oblast 1974; Deputy Head Accountant, Construction Materials Factory, Kyzylkiya town 1981, becoming Head Accountant and Deputy Dir of Financial and Econ. Questions; Deputy Dir for Commercial Matters, Nur KM Building Materials Co., Kyzylkiya town, Batken Oblast 1993–94, Man. Dir 1994–98, Asst Chair., later Chair. 1998–2005; Deputy, Zhogorku Kenesh (Parl.) 2005–, mem. Econs, Budget and Finance Cttee 2005–, Chair. Zhogorku Kenesh (Speaker) 2008–09; mem. Bright Road People's Party (Ak Zhol) 2007–; Hon. Scholar of the Kyrgyz Repub. 2003. *Address:* c/o Zhogorku Kenesh, 720053 Bishkek, ul. Abdymomunov 207, Kyrgyzstan (office). *E-mail:* zs@kenesh.gov.kg (office). *Website:* www.kenesh.kg (office).

TAGIYEV, Tachberdy; Turkmenistani engineer and politician; b. 1955, Etrek dist; ed Turkmen Polytechnic Inst.; Minister of the Petroleum Industry and Mineral Resources 2002–03; Gov. Balkan Velayat 2003; Head of Turkmenbashi oil refinery 2006–07; Deputy Chair. of the Govt (Deputy Prime Minister), responsible for Petroleum and Natural Gas 2007–09, also Dir-Gen. Turkmengaz (state-run gas monopoly). *Address:* c/o Office of the President and the Council of Ministers, 744000 Aşgabat, Turkmenistan.

TAGLE, HE Cardinal Luis Antonio Gokim, BA, MA, STD; Philippine ecclesiastic and academic; *Archbishop of Manila;* b. 21 June 1957, Manila; s. of Manuel Topacio Tagle and Milagros Gokim; ed St Andrew's School, Parañaque, San José Seminary, Ateneo de Manila Univ., Loyola School of Theology, Catholic Univ. of America, doctrinal courses at Inst. of Pope Paul VI Univ.; ordained priest, Archdiocese of Imus 1982; Parochial Vicar of San Agustín Parish – Méndez-Núñez, Cavite 1982–83, Spiritual Dir 1982–83; Rector diocesan seminary of Imus 1983–85; studies in Rome 1985–92; Episcopal Vicar for Religious 1993–95; Parish Priest and Rector of Nuestra Señora del Pilar Cathedral-Parish, Imus 1998–2001; taught Theology at San Carlos Seminary 1982–85 and Divine Word Seminary, Tagaytay, Cavite; mem. Int. Theological Comm. 1997–2002; mem. Editorial Bd History of Vatican II project led by Alberto Melloni, Bologna 1995–2001; Bishop of Imus 2001–11; Archbishop of Manila 2011–; cr. Cardinal (Cardinal-Priest of San Felice da Cantalice a Centocelle) 2012; currently Chair. Episcopal Comm. on Doctrine of Faith of the Philippines; mem. Congregation for Catholic Educ. 2012–; named a Synod Father for 13th Ordinary Gen. Ass. of Synod of Bishops on New Evangelization 2012; mem. Presidential Cttee of Pontifical Council for the Family 2013–, Pontifical Council for Pastoral Care of Migrants and Itinerants 2013–; Prof. of Dogmatic Synthesis, Grad. School of Theology, San Carlos Seminary, Archdiocesan Major Seminary of Manila; Assoc. Prof. of Systematic Theology, Loyola School of Theology, Ateneo de Manila Univ. *Television:* presenter, The Word Exposed; co-presenter, Kape't Pandasal (Coffee and Prayer) (ABS-CBN). *Address:* 121 Arzobispo Street, Intramuros, PO Box 132, 1099 Manila, Philippines (office). *Telephone:* (2) 521-6501 (office). *Fax:* (2) 527-3955 (office). *Website:* www.rcam.org (office).

TAGORE, Sharmila; Indian actress; b. 8 Dec. 1946, Hyderabad; d. of Gitindranath Tagore; m. Mansoor Ali Khan Pataudi (deceased 2011) 1969; three c.; began career as actress 1959; Chair. Cen. Bd of Film Certification 2004–11; UNICEF Goodwill Amb. 2005–; Ordre des Arts et des Lettres 2004; Filmfare Lifetime Achievement Award 1997, Star Screen Lifetime Achievement Award 2002, Lifetime Achievement Nat. Award, Journalist Asscn of India 2007. *Films include:* Apur Sansar 1959, Devi 1960, Nirjan Saikatey 1963, Kashmir Ki Kali 1964, Waqt 1965, Devar 1966, Nayak 1966, An Evening in Paris 1967, Aradhana (Filmfare Best Actress Award) 1969, Aranyer Din Ratri 1970, Seemabaddha 1971, Chhoti Bahu 1971, Amar Prem 1972, Daag 1973, Aa Gale Lag Jaa 1973, Chupke Chupke 1975, Mausam (Nat. Film Award for Best Actress) 1975, Amanush 1977, Desh Premee 1982, Sunny 1984, Mississippi Masala 1991, Aashiq Awara 1993, Mann 1999, Dhadkan 2000, Shubho Mahurat 2003, Abar Aranye (Best Supporting Actress) 2004, Viruddh: Family Comes First 2005, Eklavya: The Royal Guard 2006, Fool and Final 2007, Tasveer 8*10 2008, Morning Walk 2009. *Address:* c/o Central Board of Film Certification, Bharat Bhavan 91-E Walkeshwar Road, Mumbai 400 006, India.

TAHA, Ali Osman Mohamed; Sudanese politician; b. 1947, Khartoum; ed Univ. of Khartoum; mem. Khartoum Univ. Student Union (Kusu) 1966–71, Pres. 1969–70; organizer sha'ban movement 1973; in judiciary 1972–76; Minister of Social Planning. 1973; Minister of Foreign Affairs 1996–98; First Vice-Pres. of Sudan 1998–2005; Second Vice-Pres. 2005–11, First Vice-Pres. 2011–13. *Address:* c/o People's Palace, POB 281, Khartoum, Sudan (office). *Fax:* 183-771025.

TAHER, Abdulhadi H., PhD; Saudi Arabian business executive and fmr government official; b. 1930, Medina; ed Ain Shams Univ., Egypt, Univ. of California, Berkeley, USA; entered Saudi Arabian Govt service 1955; Dir-Gen. Ministry of Petroleum and Mineral Resources 1960; Gov., Gen. Petroleum and Mineral Org. (PETROMIN), Riyadh 1962–86; Man. Dir Saudi Arabian Fertilizers Co. (SAFCO) 1966–76, Jeddah Oil Refinery 1970; Chair. Arab Maritime Petroleum Transport Co. –1981; f. Aal Taher Group, Abdul Hadi H. Taher & Partners Co., Ltd; fmr mem. Bd of Dirs Saudi Arabian American Oil Co., Saudi Govt Railways Corpn; has lectured in Business Admin at King Saud Univ., Riyadh; Trustee, Coll. of Petroleum and Minerals; mem. Industrial Research and Devt Centre, Saudi Arabia; Hon. mem. American Soc. of Petroleum Engineers. *Publications include:* Income Determination in the International Petroleum Industry 1966, Development and Petroleum Strategies in Saudi Arabia (Arabic) 1970, Energy: A Global Outlook 1980, Saudi Arabian Hydrocarbons and World Affairs (co-author) 2013; lectures and papers on econ. and petroleum affairs. *Address:* Abdul Hadi H. Taher & Partners Co., Ltd. (CIC), PO Box 7232, Jeddah 21462, Saudi Arabia (office). *E-mail:* info@cictg.com (office). *Website:* www.cictg.com (office).

TAHER, Nahed, BS, MA, MSc, PhD; Saudi Arabian banker and economist; *CEO, Gulf One Investment Bank;* ed King Abdulaziz Univ., Jeddah, Lancaster Univ., UK; Co-owner and Financial Advisor, Bullhide Liner (polyurethane coating) franchise, Jeddah 1987–97; Financial Advisor, Minara (support services co.), Jeddah 1993–2002; Lecturer, later Asst Prof. of Econs and Head of Accounting Dept, King Abdulaziz Univ.; Sr Strategic Economist and Chair. Portfolio Man. Cttee, Nat. Commercial Bank, Jeddah (first woman to hold such a position in a bank in Saudi Arabia) 2002–05; Founder and CEO Gulf One Investment Bank, Bahrain (first Saudi woman to head a bank in Gulf region) 2005–; consultant to Saudi Cultural Summit; mem. Saudi Econ. Asscn, Center for Strategic Studies of Mekkah Emirate, Businesswomen's Cttee of Jeddah Chamber of Commerce, Saudi Cttee of Eisenhower Fellowship; mem. Bd Int. Inst. for Man. Devt (Switzerland) (first mem. from Middle East) 2008–, Advisory Bd King Abdulaziz Univ. 2010–; ranked by Forbes magazine amongst 100 Most Powerful Women (72nd) 2006, Businesswoman of the Year Award (Saudi Arabia) 2007, ranked by Arabian Business amongst Power 100: World's Most Influential Arabs (45th) 2008, (66th) 2009, Professorship Award, Lancaster Univ. 2011. *Address:* Gulf One Investment Bank BSC, Bahrain Financial Harbour, West Tower, Level 15, PO Box 11172, Manama, Bahrain (office). *Telephone:* 17102555 (office). *Fax:* 17100063 (office). *E-mail:* info@gulf1bank.com (office). *Website:* www.gulf1bank.com (office).

TAHIJA, George Santosa, BSc, MBA; Indonesian business executive; *President Director, PT Austindo Nusantara Jaya;* b. 1958; s. of the late Julius Tahija and Jean Tahija; brother of Sjakon George Tahija; ed Trisakti Univ., Jakarta, Darden School, Univ. of Virginia, USA; Pres. Dir PT Austindo Nusantara Jaya and CEO Austindo Group; Commr Freeport Indonesia; Dir Arc Exploration 1998–; Founder and Chair. Coral Triangle Center; mem. Founding Bd PSKD Mandiri School; mem. Advisory Bd The Nature Conservancy Indonesia Chapter; mem. Bd of Supervisors, Endeavor Indonesia; mem. Bd of Trustees Asia Business Council, Darden School,

Univ. of Virginia; mem. Plenary Cttee Trisakti Univ. Foundation. *Achievements include:* has summited Mount Kilimanjaro, Tanzania, Carstensz Pyramid, Indonesia, Mount Elbrus, Russia. *Publications:* A Walk In the Clouds 2005, Land of Water 2006. *Address:* PT Austindo Nusantara Jaya, Graha Irama, 3rd Floor, Jl.H.R.Rasuna Said Kav. 1-2, Jakarta 12950, Indonesia (office). *Telephone:* (21) 5261415 (office). *Fax:* (21) 5261416 (office). *E-mail:* contact@austindogroup .com (office). *Website:* www.austindogroup.com (office).

TAHIJA, Sjakon George, MD; Indonesian ophthalmologist, eye surgeon and business executive; *Medical Director, Klinik Mata Nusantara;* b. 1953; s. of Julius Tahija and Jean Tahija; brother of George Santosa Tahija; ed Univ. of Indonesia, Lions Eye Inst., Perth, Australia, Univ. of Wisconsin, Madison, USA; mem. Bd of Commrs PT Austindo Nusantara Jaya 1986–, Pres. Dir PT Austindo Nusantara Jaya Healthcare Services Div.; Medical Dir and Vitreoretinal Consultant, Klinik Mata Nusantara; mem. European Soc. of Cataract and Refractive Surgeons, American Acad. of Ophthalmology, Indonesian Ophthalmologists Asscn. *Publications:* numerous publications in the field of ophthalmology. *Address:* PT Austindo Nusantara Jaya, Graha Irama, 3rd Floor, Jl.H.R.Rasuna Said Kav. 1-2, Jakarta 12950, Indonesia (office). *Telephone:* (21) 5261415 (office). *Fax:* (21) 5261416 (office). *E-mail:* contact@austindogroup.com (office). *Website:* www.austindogroup .com (office).

TAHIR-KHELI, Shirin, BA, MA, PhD; Pakistani/American political scientist, academic, government official and fmr UN official; b. 24 Aug. 1944, Hyderabad, India; d. of Dr Muhammad Raziuddin Siddiqui; m.; two c.; ed Wesleyan Univ., Univ. of Pennsylvania; grew up in Pakistan; began career as Academic Advisor in Office of the Dean, Temple Univ., Philadelphia 1972–73, Asst Prof. of Political Science 1973–79, Assoc. Prof. 1980–82; mem. Policy Planning Staff in Office of US Sec. of State, Washington, DC 1982–84; Dir for Political-Military Affairs, Nat. Security Council, The White House 1984–86, Dir for Near East and South Asia 1986–88; Adjunct Prof., School for Advanced Int. Studies, Johns Hopkins Univ. 1988–89, also Dir South Asia Inst.; US Rep. for Special Political Affairs, UN, New York 1990–93, Sr Dir for Democracy, Human Rights and Int. Operations, UN Security Council 2003–05; fmr Sr Advisor to US Sec. of State on UN Reform; Fellow, Princeton Univ. Center of Int. Studies; Co-Chair. Council on Foreign Relations Study Group on India and Pakistan; fmr mem. Presidential Comm. on the Public Service; fmr mem. Bd of Trustees, The Aga Khan Univ., Pakistan; fmr Sr Fellow, Foreign Policy Research Inst., Philadelphia; mem. Council on Foreign Relations, US Comm. on Int. Religious Freedom, IISS. *Address:* c/o Council on Foreign Relations, Harold Pratt House, 58 East 68th Street, New York, NY 10065, USA (office). *Telephone:* (212) 434-9771 (office). *Fax:* (212) 434-9800 (home). *Website:* www.cfr.org (office).

TAHIRI, Saimir, MPL; Albanian lawyer and politician; *Minister of the Interior;* b. 30 Oct. 1979, Tirana; ed Faculty of Law, Univ. of Tirana; External Lecturer, Faculty of Law, Univ. of Tirana 2006–08 and in several other higher educational insts; practising lawyer 2008–; mem. Parl. (Socialist Party) for Tirana Dist 2009–, Deputy Chair. Parl. Group, mem. Cttee on Legal Affairs, Public Admin and Human Rights 2009–13; Acting Pres. Socialist Party of Tirana 2011–; Minister of the Interior 2013–. *Address:* Ministry of the Interior, Sheshi Skënderbej 3, Tirana, Albania (office). *Telephone:* (4) 2228167 (office); (4) 2247155 (office). *E-mail:* minister@moi.gov.al (office). *Website:* www.moi.gov.al (office).

TAIANA, Jorge; Argentine academic, politician and diplomatist; b. 31 May 1950, Buenos Aires; m.; three c.; ed Bachiller Colegio Nacional, Buenos Aires, Univ. of Buenos Aires; Adjunct Prof., Univ. of Buenos Aires 1985–91; Titular Prof., Univ. of Lomas de Zamora 1987; Prof., Univ. Rafael Landívar, Guatemala 1994; Titular Prof., Nat. Univ. of Quilmes 1995–2001; Head of Cabinet, Ministry of Education 1973–74; Under-Sec., Ministry of Economy 1974–75; Regional Dir Servicio Universitario Mundial (non-Govt Org.) 1986–89; advisor to Foreign Affairs Cttee, Chamber of Deputies 1987–89; Under-Sec. for Foreign Policy, Ministry of Foreign Affairs 1989–90, Dir Int. Orgs 1990–91; Amb. to Guatemala and Belize 1992–96; Exec.–Sec. Inter-American Comm. on Human Rights, OAS 1996–2001; Sec. for Human Rights, Govt of Buenos Aires Province 2002–03; Vice-Minister of Foreign Affairs 2003–05, Minister of Foreign Affairs, Int. Trade and Worship 2005–10; Grand Cross, Order of Quetza (Guatemala) 1996, Order of El Sol del Peru (Peru) 2003, Order of Antonio José de Irisarri (Guatemala) 2003, Order of Baron de Rio Branco (Brazil) 2005, Officer, Order of Wissam Al Alaoui (Morocco) 2004. *Publications:* author of several publications on human rights and labour movements. *Address:* c/o Ministry of Foreign Affairs, International Trade and Worship, Esmerelda 1212, 1007 Buenos Aires, Argentina (office).

TAIBU, Tatenda; Zimbabwean professional cricketer; b. 14 May 1983, Harare; ed Churchill Boys High School; wicketkeeper; right-handed batsman; right-arm off-break/right-arm medium pace bowler; plays for Mashonaland 2000–05, Zimbabwe 2001– (Capt. 2003/04–05), Cape Cobras 2005–06, Namibia 2006–07 (List A Capt. 2006), Kolkata Knight Riders 2008–, Mashonaland A, Mountaineers Franchise Team, Northerns (Zimbabwe), Africa XI; First-class debut: 1999/2000; Test debut: Zimbabwe v West Indies, Bulawayo 19–22 July 2001; One-Day Int. (ODI) debut: Zimbabwe v West Indies, Harare 23 June 2001; T20I debut: Australia v Zimbabwe, Cape Town 12 Sept. 2007. *Achievements include:* became youngest Test capt. in history when given Zimbabwean captaincy April 2004. *Address:* c/o Zimbabwe Cricket, Harare, Zimbabwe. *E-mail:* info@zimcricket.org. *Website:* www .zimcricket.org.

TAILLANDIER, François Antoine Georges, MA; French writer; b. 20 June 1955, Chamalières; s. of Henri Taillandier and Denise Ducher; three c.; teacher 1980–83; full-time writer 1984–, also contrib. Le Figaro (newspaper), La Montagne (newspaper), L'Humanité (newspaper), L'Atelier du Roman (periodical); Admin., Soc. des Gens de Lettres de France; Prix Roger Nimier 1992, Acad. française Prix de la critique 1997. *Publications:* fiction: Personnages de la rue du Couteau 1984, Tott 1985, Benoît ou les contemporains obscurs 1986, Les Clandestins (Prix Jean-Freustié 1991) 1990, Les Nuits Racine 1992, Fan et le jouet qui n'existe pas (with Charles Barat) 1993, Mémoires de Monte-Cristo 1994, Des hommes qui s'éloignent 1997, Anielka (Grand Prix du roman de l'Académie française 1999) 1999, Le cas Gentile 2001, La Grande Intrigue: Vol. 1 Option Paradis 2005, Vol. 2 Telling 2006, Il n'y a personne dans les tombes 2007; non-fiction: Tous les secrets de l'avenir 1996, Aragon 1997, Journal de Marseille 1999, N6, la route de l'Italie 1999, Les

Parents lâcheurs 2001, Borges, une restitution du monde 2002, Pour ou contre Jacques Chirac (with Joseph Macé-Scaron) 2002, Un Autre langue 2004, Balzac (biog.) 2005. *Address:* c/o Editions Stock, 31 rue de Fleurus, 75006 Paris, France (office).

TAILLEFER, Louis, PhD, FRSC; Canadian quantum physicist and academic; *Professor of Physics and Canada Research Chair in Quantum Materials, University of Sherbrooke;* ed Univ. of Cambridge, UK; Post-doctoral Fellow, Univ. of Cambridge; later worked at CNRS, Grenoble, France; Research Fellow, Alfred P. Sloan Foundation 1993–97; Prof. of Physics, McGill Univ. –2002, Univ. of Toronto –2002; Prof. of Physics and Canada Research Chair in Quantum Materials, Univ. of Sherbrooke 2002–, Dir Quantum Materials programme, Canadian Inst. for Advanced Research (CIFAR); Fellow, American Physical Soc. 2003; numerous awards, including Prix Urgel-Archambault, Asscn francophone pour le savoir 1998, E.W.R. Steacie Memorial Fellowship, Natural Sciences and Eng Research Council of Canada 1998–2000, Herzberg Medal, Canadian Asscn of Physicists (CAP) 1998, Premier's Research Excellence Award, Govt of Ontario 2000–03, Scientist of the Year, Radio-Canada 2002, Canada Research Chair (Level I) 2002–09, Prix Marie-Victorin, Govt of Québec (youngest recipient) 2003, CAP Brockhouse Medal 2003, CAP Medal of Achievement 2008, Institutional Prize for Research and Creation, Univ. of Sherbrooke 2012, Killam Prize (co-recipient), Canada Council for the Arts 2012. *Publications:* numerous papers in professional journals. *Address:* Local D2-1084-2, Département de physique, Faculté des sciences, 2500 boulevard Université, Sherbrooke, PQ J1K 2R1 (office); Canadian Institute for Advanced Research, 180 Dundas Street West, Suite 1400, Toronto, ON M5G 1Z8, Canada (office). *Telephone:* (819) 821-8000 (ext. 62051) (Sherbrooke) (office); (416) 971-4251 (Toronto) (office). *Fax:* (819) 821-8046 (Sherbrooke) (office); (416) 971-6169 (Toronto) (office). *E-mail:* louis.taillefer@usherbrooke.ca (office). *Website:* www.physique.usherbrooke.ca/taillefer (office); www.cifar.ca/louis -taillefer (office).

TAILLIBERT, Roger René; French architect; *Managing Director, Taillibert International Sarl;* b. 21 Jan. 1926, Châtres-sur-Cher; s. of Gaston Taillibert and Melina Benoit; m. Béatrice Pfister 1965; one d.; ed school in Châtres sur Cher, École Nat. des Beaux-Arts, Paris; own practice 1969–; Chief Architect, Public Buildings for Govt 1967, civil buildings and nat. palaces; Curator Grand Palais 1977–82, Palais de Chaillot 1983–86; Chair. Taillibert International Sarl, Taillibert Gulf International (UAE), TGE, Doha 2007–; mem. Acad. des Beaux-Arts (Pres. 2005, 2010–), Inst. de France, Acad. d'Architecture 2000, Acad. des Sports, des Arts de la Rue, New Thinking group, RSA; Commdr, Légion d'honneur 1983, Ordre nat. du Mérite 1983, des Arts et des Lettres 1983, des Palmes Académiques 1983, Ordre du Mérite pour le Commerce et l'Industrie 2000; Ecole Nat. Supérieure des Beaux-Arts, Diplôme d'Architecture (DPLG) décerné par le Gouvernement Français 1955; Médaille d'argent décerné par l'Acad. d'Architecture pour ses recherches et ses applications pratiques 1971, Grand Médaille du Sport 1972, Prix Nat. des Arts et de la Littérature 1973, Prix Européen 1973, Médaille d'or de la Créativité Architecturale 1973, Grand Prix Cembureau 1974–76, Médaille des Structures 1976, Grand Prix Nat. d'Architecture 1976, Premier Prix Nat. d'Architecture 1977, Grand Prix des Arts, Canada 1977, Prix Elphège Baude 1977, Médaille de l'Acad. Nat. des Sports, Italie 1977, Grand Prix du Rayonnement Français 1982, Laureat du Prix Européen d'Architecture Métallique 2000, Médaille de Vermeil de la Ville de Paris 2000, Médaille d'Or du Sport 2000, Grand Prix of Europe Timber Structures, IAKS Award 2007, Int. Architecture Award 2012. *Main works:* numerous including: sporting facilities: Deauville Swimming-Pool 1966, Parc des Princes Stadium Paris 1972, Olympic Complex, Montréal, Canada 1976, Olympic Complex, Lille, France 1977–81, Sporting and cultural facilities at Kirchberg Luxembourg 1984, Khalifa Stadium, Qatar 2002, Bamenda Stadium Cameroon, Ice Skating-Ring, Abu Dhabi, Stadia for Soccer World Cup 2006, Morocco, velodromes at Bordeaux 1987, Poitiers 1997, Vannes 2001, Astana (Kazasthan) 2004; also: Nat. Geographic Centre, Amman, Jordan; Officers' Club, Abu Dhabi, UAE; sports complex, Baghdad, Guests' Palace, Bahrain, univ. bldgs, Sousse, Gabès, Tunisia, sports and golf club houses, Yamoussoukro and Abidjan, 'La Riviera' Hotel and Leisure Complex, Côte d'Ivoire; in France: secondary schools in Tours, Vauréal, Dreux, Argenton sur Creuse, School of Pharmacy, Toulouse, Coca-Cola plant, Grigny, pharmaceutical lab. P. Fabre, Castres, DAF plant, Survilliers, skiing and mountaineering nat. school, Chamonix, Nat. Inst. for Sports and Physical Educ., Paris, pre-Olympic centre, Font-Romeu, nuclear plants Penly and Civaux, Thomson CSF (now EADS – Elancourt/France), Pierre Centre, St Julien en Genevoix, swimming complex at Nogent-sur-Oise 1995,Lycée Raspail, Paris 1995, Commercial and residential complex, St-Quentin-en-Yvelines 1995, Pierre Fabre Lab., Lavaur, 'Les Pyramides' Sport and Leisure Complex, Port-Marly, La Porte Océane, La Rochelle, Aspire, Pierre Fabre Canceropole, Toulouse, Crèche in Montauban, 'Besselue' Villas, La Rochelle; studies for projects in Iraq and Lebanon; feasibility studies for projects in Argentina and Uruguay (hotels, sports facilities, leisure parks, etc.); armed forces Officers' club (Abu Dhabi/UAE), Mercure Grand Hotel, Jebel Hafeet, Al ain (UAE), 'd'Coque' Nat. Sports and Cultural Complex (Luxembourg), Silhouette Tower and Conf. Centre, Doha (Qatar), New Baniyas Stadium (UAE), Coca-Cola extension, Aspire Acad. extension. *Publications:* Montréal – Jeux Olympiques 1976, Construire l'avenir 1977, Roger Taillibert (autobiog.) 1978, Taillibert Architect I and II 1985, 1997, Transluscent City 2000, Notre Cher Stade Olympique 2005, Roger Taillibert-Réalisations Vols 1 and 2 2006, Evasions Chromatiques/Roger Taillibert's Paintings 2007, Roger Taillibert: Constructions Vols 1 and 2 2008, Le Parc des Princes 2009, Roger Taillibert Architecte (in French and English) 2010, Entrée Principale 2010, Main Entrance '76' 2011, Montréal mythes et scandales (in French and English) 2011, Book of Sketches 2011, Le Parc Olympique de Montréal 2011; numerous articles and conference presentations for Acad. des Beaux-Arts/Institut de France and other publs. *Leisure interests:* painting, photography, music, sport (especially football). *Address:* Taillibert International Sarl, 163 rue de la Pompe, 75116 Paris, France (office); Taillibert Gulf Environment, PO Box 25418, Bin Hamoodah Bldg 603, Sheikh Khalifa Street, Abu Dhabi, UAE (office); Taillibert Gulf (Doha), PO Box 20218, Doha, Qatar. *Telephone:* 1-47-04-29-92 (Paris) (office); (2) 627-3667 (Abu Dhabi) (office); 4436-0297 (Doha) (office). *Fax:* 1-47-55-84-82 (Paris) (office); 1-42-27-37-71 (Doha) (office); 4436-6415 (Doha) (office); (2) 627-4012 (Abu Dhabi) (office). *E-mail:*

rtaillibert-1@dial.oleane.com (office); tailgulf@emirates.net.ae (office); taillibert .qa@hotmail.com (office). *Website:* www.agencetaillibert.com (office).

TAIPALE, Vappu Tuulikki, DM; Finnish politician and psychiatrist; b. 1 May 1940, Vaasa; m. Ilkka Taipale 1965; two s. two d.; psychiatrist, Aurora Youth Polyclinic 1970–74; Paediatric Clinic 1975–79; Asst Prof. of Child Psychiatry, Kuopio Univ. 1980–83, Tampere Univ. 1983–; First Minister of Social Affairs and Health 1982–83, Second Minister 1983–84; Dir-Gen. Nat. Bd of Social Welfare 1984–90; Dir-Gen. Nat. Agency for Welfare and Health 1991–92, Nat. Research and Devt Centre for Welfare and Health 1992–2008; Chair. COST A5 Ageing and Tech. Int. Soc. for Gerontechnology, EAG Key Action 6, EU 5th FP; mem. SDP, UNU Council 2001–; Dr hc (Univ. of Vaasa) 1998, (Univ. of Jyväskylä) 2004.

TAIT, Marion, CBE; British ballet mistress and dancer; *Assistant Director, Birmingham Royal Ballet;* b. 7 Oct. 1950, London, England; d. of Charles Tait and Betty Hooper; m. David Morse 1971; ed Royal Acad. of Dancing and Royal Ballet School; joined Royal Ballet School aged 15, graduating to Royal Ballet's touring co. (later known as Sadler's Wells Royal Ballet, now Birmingham Royal Ballet); Prin. Dancer 1974; danced all the classics and other prin. roles including Juliet, Elite Syncopations, Las Hermanas, The Invitation, Hobson's Choice, The Dream, The Burrow, Lizzie Borden in Fall River Legend and Hagar in Pillar of Fire; cr. many roles for Kenneth MacMillan and David Bintley; guest appearances world-wide; Ballet Mistress (to both co. and students), and still performs character roles, Birmingham Royal Ballet 1995–, Asst Dir to David Bintley 2011–; Dancer of the Year 1994, Evening Standard Ballet Award 1994, Critics' Circle Award with Desmond Kelly for TV programme Ballet Hoo!. *Leisure interest:* needlework, garden. *Address:* Birmingham Royal Ballet, Thorp Street, Birmingham, B5 4AU, England (office). *Telephone:* (121) 245-3500 (office). *Website:* www.brb.org.uk (office).

TAITTINGER, Anne-Claire, MA; French business executive; *Chairman of the Executive Board, Groupe Taittinger;* d. of Jean Taittinger and Corinne Deville; m.; two s.; ed Inst. d'Etudes Politiques de Paris and Centre for Advanced Business Courses; fmr urban planner; fmrly held positions within several Soc. du Louvre cos, Head Soc. du Louvre 1997–2006, Pres. and CEO 2003–06; Chair. Bd Baccarat 1993–2005, Vice-Pres. 2005–06, mem. Bd of Dirs 2006–07; Chair. Exec. Bd Groupe Taittinger 2003–; Dir Dexia 2001. *Address:* Groupe Taittinger, 9, place Saint-Nicaise, 51100 Reims, France (office). *Telephone:* (3) 26-85-45-35 (office). *Fax:* (3) 26-50-14-30 (office). *Website:* www.taittinger.fr (home).

TAJ, Lt-Gen. Nadeem; Pakistani military and intelligence officer; fmr Mil. Sec. to fmr Pres. Musharraf; fmr Dir-Gen. of Mil. Intelligence; fmr Gen. Officer Commdt, Lahore; Commdt Pakistan Mil. Acad., Kakul –2007; Dir Inter-Services Intelligence (Pakistan's largest intelligence agency) 2007–08, promoted to Lt-Gen. *Address:* c/o Ministry of Defence, Pakistan Secretariat, No. II, Rawalpindi 46000, Pakistan.

TAJANI, Antonio; Italian journalist, politician and international organization official; *Vice-President and Commissioner for Industry and Entrepreneurship, European Commission;* b. 4 Aug. 1953, Rome; m.; two c.; ed La Sapienza Univ., Rome, Scuola di Guerra Aerea, Florence; fmr Officer in Italian Air Force; fmr Air Defence Controller and Head of Operations Room, 33rd Air Force Radar Centre; fmr professional and parl. journalist; Ed. Il Settimanale (weekly newspaper) 1982; Presenter, radio news programme, RAI Uno 1982; Head of Rome editorial office, Il Giornale (daily newspaper) 1983; Co-f. Forza Italia 1993; mem. European Parl. 1994–2008, Vice-Pres., European People's Party 2002–, Head of Forza Italia European Parl. Del. 1999–2008; mem. Rome City Council 2001; Vice-Pres. EC and Commr for Transport 2008–10, Vice-Pres. EC and Commr for Industry and Entrepreneurship 2010–. *Address:* European Commission, rue de la Loi 200, 1049 Brussels, Belgium (office). *Telephone:* (2) 299-11-11 (office). *Fax:* (2) 295-01-38 (office). *Website:* ec.europa.eu (office).

TAKABWEBWE, Michael, LLB; I-Kiribati lawyer; b. 11 Nov. 1945, Tabiteuea North; s. of Teababa Taumeang and Nei Ana Neaua; m. Tebaniman Tito 1979; three d.; ed Univ. of Melbourne, Australia; State Advocate 1979–81, Sr State Advocate 1981–83; Attorney-Gen. of Kiribati 1983–2002; prin. legal adviser to Kiribati govt on constitution and all other Kiribati laws 1983–2002; mem. Parl. and Cabinet 1983–2002; Puisne Judge 2002–05; Judge, High Court of Kiribati 2002–05; Rep. to Commonwealth Law Ministers Meetings 1986, 1990, 1993, 1996; Rep. to Int. Bar Asscn Meeting, Fiji 2002; mem. Int. Bar Asscn 2004; Rep. to Int. Bar Conference Auckland 2004. *Publications include:* Kiribati, Asia–Pacific Constitutional Yearbook 1995. *Leisure interests:* gardening, listening to pop and classical music, reading. *Address:* c/o Justice's Chambers, High Court of Kiribati, POB 501, Betio, Tarawa, Kiribati (office). *Telephone:* (686) 21849 (home).

TAKÁCS-NAGY, Gábor; Hungarian/Swiss violinist and conductor; *Music Director, Verbier Festival Chamber Orchestra* and *Manchester Camerata;* b. 17 April 1956, Budapest, Hungary; s. of László Takács-Nagy and Matild Pataki; m. Lesley de Senger (née Townson) 1991; two d.; ed Béla Bartók Conservatory, Franz Liszt Music Acad. of Budapest; f. Takács String Quartet 1976, Takács Piano Trio 1996, Mikrokosmos String Quartet 1998, Camerata Bellerive 2005; concert tours from 1980 every year throughout Europe, every other year in Australia, USA, Japan, South America; Prof. Haute Ecole de Musique, Geneva 1997–; Music Dir, Verbier Festival Chamber Orchestra 2007–, Weinberger Kammer Orchestra 2007–, MAV Symphony Orchestra, Budapest 2010–12, Manchester Camerata 2011–; Prin. Guest Conductor Budapest Festival Orchestra 2012–; Prin. Artistic Partner, Irish Chamber Orchestra 2013–; Hon. RAM; First Prize Evian Competition 1977, Menuhin Competition (Portsmouth) 1981, Scholarship Award, Banff School of Fine Arts, Franz Liszt Prize 1983. *Leisure interests:* sport, theatre, hiking, reading. *Address:* Case postale 186, 1245 Collonge-Bellerive, Switzerland. *E-mail:* ldstn@ hotmail.com. *Website:* www.bellerive-festival.ch; www.gabortakacsnagy.com.

TAKAHAGI, Mitsunori; Japanese business executive; *Executive Consultant, JX Holdings, Inc.;* b. 3 Dec. 1940, Kanagawa Pref.; ed Faculty of Law, Hitotsubashi Univ.; joined Nippon Mining Co. Ltd 1964, Gen. Man. Products Export Dept, Petroleum Group 1988–89, Gen. Man. Marketing Dept, Petroleum Group 1990–91, Deputy Gen. Man., Chita Oil Refinery, Japan Energy Corpn 1991–94 (Nippon Mining Co. merged with Kyodo Oil Co. in 1992 to create Nikko Kyodo, renamed Japan Energy Corpn 1993), Dir in charge of Industry Energy Dept 1994–96, Dir

and Gen. Man. Osaka Br. Office 1996–98, Man. Dir and Gen. Man. Tokyo Br. Office 1998–99, Dir, Exec. Corp. Officer, Gen. Man. of Managerial Staff Group 1999–2001, Dir and Sr Exec. Corp. Officer 2001–02, Pres., Rep. Dir and Dir Nippon Mining Holdings, Inc. 2002–06, Pres. and CEO 2006–10, Pres., CEO and Rep. Dir JX Holdings, Inc. (following incorporation of Nippon Oil Corpn and Nippon Mining Holdings in JX Holdings, Inc. through a share transfer) 2010–12, Exec. Consultant 2012–. *Address:* JX Holdings, Inc., 2-6-3, Ote-machi, Chiyoda-ku, Tokyo 100-0004, Japan (office). *Telephone:* (3) 3502-1131 (office). *Fax:* (3) 3502-9352 (office). *E-mail:* info@hd.jx-group.co.jp (office). *Website:* www.hd.jx-group.co .jp (office).

TAKAHASHI, Genichirō; Japanese writer, critic and academic; b. 1 Jan. 1951, Onomichi, Hiroshima; ed Yokohama Nat. Univ.; participated in student movt 1960s and early 70s, imprisoned for six months; worked as labourer until 1981; novelist and essayist 1982–; currently Prof. of Literature, Meiji Gakuin Univ.; Visiting Fellow, Donald Keene Center of Japanese Culture, Columbia Univ., USA 2002. *Publications include:* novels: Sayonara Gyangutachi (Gunzō New Writers' Award) (first novel to be translated into English, as Sayonara, Gangsters 2004) 1982, Ōbaa za reinbō (Over the Rainbow) 1984, Oyogu Otoko (The Swimming Man) 1984, Jon Renon tai kaseijin (John Lennon Versus the Martians) 1985, Yūga de kanshōteki Nihon yakkyū (Japanese Baseball: Languid and Happy) (Mishima Yukio Award 1988) 1987, Penguin mura ni hi ga Ochite (Sundown in Penguin Town) 1989, Wakusei P-13 no himitsu (The Secret of Planet 13) 1990, Gosutobasutazu (Ghostbusters) 1997, Godzilla 2001, The Rise and Fall of Japanese Literature (Itoh Sei Literature Award) 2001, May Your Reign Last Forever and Ever 2002, Some Stories on Sex and Love 2005, Miyazawa Kenji's Greatest Hits 2005, Until The Day We Ride the Soul Train 2008, Battling Evil 2010, A Nuclear Reactor in Love 2011, Goodbye, Christopher Robin (Tanizaki Prize 2012) 2012; numerous collections of essays include Bungaku ga konna ni wakatte ii kashira (Is it Okay to Understand Literature So Well?) 1989. *Address:* Faculty of International Studies, Meiji Gakuin University, 1-2-37 Shirokanedai, Minato-ku, Tokyo 108-8636, Japan.

TAKAHASHI, Hiroaki; Japanese energy industry executive; *Chairman and Representative Director, Tohoku Electric Power Company, Inc.;* ed Tohoku Univ.; joined Tohoku Electric Power Co., Inc. 1963, served in various exec. positions, including Man. of Sec.'s Office, Man. Dir, Vice-Pres. and Chief Dir of Customer Service, Pres. and Rep. Dir –2010, Chair. and Rep. Dir 2010–; mem. Bd of Dirs The Energy Conservation Centre, Japan. *Address:* Tohoku Electric Power Company, Inc., 1-7-1 Honcho, Aoba-ku, Sendai, Miyagi 980-8550, Japan (office). *Telephone:* (22) 225-2111 (office). *Fax:* (22) 225-2550 (office). *Website:* www.tohoku-epco.co.jp (office).

TAKAHASHI, Kozo; Japanese business executive; *President and CEO, Sharp Corporation;* joined Sharp Corpn 1980s, served as its Exec. Officer and Group Gen. Man. in Health and Environment Systems Group, served as part of man. team of Sharp Electronics Corpn's business-to-business group 1997–2001, Dir of Sharp Electronics Corpn 2010–, Chair. and CEO Sharp Electronics Corpn 2010–12, Group Gen. Man. North and South America Group 2010–12, Chief Officer of Products Business Group, Chief Products Officer of Sharp Corpn 2012–13, Exec. Vice-Pres. 2012–13, Chief Officer of Sales and Marketing 2012–13, Group Gen. Man. Global Business Group, Pres. and CEO Sharp Corpn 2013–. *Address:* Sharp Corpn, 22-22 Nagaike-cho, Abeno-ku, Osaka 545-8522, Japan (office). *Telephone:* (6) 6621-1221 (office). *Fax:* (6) 6627-1759 (office). *E-mail:* info@sharp.co.jp (office). *Website:* sharp-world.com (office); www.sharp.co.jp (office).

TAKAHASHI, Takako; Japanese writer; b. 1932, Kyoto; m. Takahashi Kazumi (died 1971); ed Kyoto Univ.; writer of novels and short stories 1972–1985; trans. of French writers including Mauriac; retd from writing to become a Roman Catholic nun first in Paris, then Japan; returned to writing during 1990s. *Publications:* Sojikei (Congruent Figures) 1972, Sora no hate made (To the End of the Sky) 1973, Botsuraku Fusei (Falling Scenery) 1974, Yuwakusha (The Temptress) 1976, Ningyo no ai (Doll Love) 1976, Ronrii uuman (trans. as Lonely Woman) 1977, Ten no Mizumi 1977, Yomigaeri no ie (The House of Rebirth) 1980, Yosoi seya, waga tamashii yo (Gird up Thyself, Oh My Soul) 1982, Ikari no ko (Child of Wrath; Yomiuri Prize) 1985, Tochi no Chikara 1992, Takahashi Kazumi to iu hito: Nijugonen no nochi ni 1997, Kirei na hito 2003, Haka no hanashi 2006. *Address:* c/o Kodansha International Ltd, Otowa Building, 1-17-14 Otowa, Bunkyo-ko, Tokyo, 112-8652, Japan (office).

TAKAKURA, Ken; Japanese actor; b. (Oda Toshimasa), 16 Feb. 1931, Kita Kyushu, Fukuoka; made screen debut 1956, actor in more than 130 films in Japan and USA; Japanese Acad. Awards 1978, 1981, 1982, Best Actor, Montreal World Film Festival 1999. *Films include:* Denko Karate Uchi (Lightning Karate Blow) 1956, Nippon G-men 1956, Gyangu series of films 1961–64, Abashiri Bangaichi (Abashiri Prison) series of films 1963–72, Koya no toseinin (Drifting Avenger) 1968, Gion Matsuri (The Day the Sun Rose) 1968, Too Late the Hero 1970, The Yakuza 1975, Shinkansen daibakhua (Bullet Train) 1975, Hakkodasen 1977, Shiawase no kiiroi hankachi (The Yellow Handkerchief) 1978, Haruka naru yama no yobigoe (Distant Cry from Spring) 1980, Eki Station (Station) 1981, Nankyoku Monogatari (Antarctica) 1983, Umi e (See You) 1988, Black Rain 1989, Mr Baseball 1992, Shiju Shichinin no Shikaku (47 Ronin) 1994, Poppoya (Railroad Man) 1999, Hotaru (The Firefly) 2001, Riding Alone for Thousands of Miles 2005.

TAKAMATSU, Shin, PhD; Japanese architect; b. 5 Aug. 1948, Shimane Pref.; s. of Toshio Takamatsu and Yuriko Takamatsu; m. Toshiko Hariguchi 1970; two d.; ed Ohda High School, Kyoto Univ.; Prin. Architect, Shin Takamatsu Architects and Assocs, Kyoto 1980; mem. Nihon Kenchiku Gakai (Japan Architecture Inst.) 1989–, Japan Inst. of Architecture 1993–; work exhibited at Venice Biennale 1985, Kirini Plaza, Paris 1988, Killing Moon, London 1988, Nîmes 1989, Berlin 1991, San Francisco Museum of Modern Art 1992, Kyoto Municipal Museum of Art 1995; Hon. Fellow, AIA 1995; Japan Architects Asscn Prize 1984, Venice Biennale Prize 1985, Second Int. Interior Design Award 1987, Architectural Inst. of Japan Prize 1989, Grand Prize, Journal of Japanese Soc. of Commercial Space Designers 1989, Architectural Inst. of Japan Prize 1990, Kyoto Pref. Meritorious Cultural Service Award 1994, Art Encouragement Prize, Ministry of Educ. 1996, Public Architecture Prize 1998. *Publications:* Works-Shin Takamatsu 1984, Architecture and Nothingness 1996, To the Poetic Space 1998. *Leisure interests:* architecture, furniture design. *Address:* Shin Takamatsu Architects and Associates, 195 Jobodaiin-cho Takeda, Fushimi-ku, Kyoto 612, Japan. *Telephone:* (7) 5621-6002 (office). *Fax:* (7) 5621-6079 (office). *E-mail:* syntax@takamatsu.co.jp (office). *Website:* www.takamatsu.co.jp (office).

TAKASHIMA, Tatsuyoshi; Japanese advertising industry executive; *Chairman, President and CEO, Dentsu Inc.;* joined Dentsu Inc. (advertising agency) 1966, has held several man. positions including Sr Man. Dir, Exec. Vice-Pres. –2007, Pres. and COO 2007–09, Rep. Dir 2007–11, Pres. and CEO 2009–11, Chair., Pres. and CEO 2011–; Exec. Dir Japan Marketing Asscn; mem. Supervisory Bd Publicis Groupe SA 2008–; mem. Bd of Dirs Tokyo Broadcasting System Holdings Inc. 2009–; mem. Foundation Bd, International Inst. for Man. Devt. *Address:* Dentsu Inc., 1-8-1, Higashi-shimbashi, Minato-ku, Tokyo 105-7001, Japan (office). *Telephone:* (3) 6216-5111 (office). *Website:* www.dentsu.com (office).

TAKEBE, Tsutomu; Japanese politician; ed Waseda Univ.; mem. Hokkaido Ass. 1971–; elected to House of Reps 1986; Vice Minister Hokkaido Devt Agency 1990–92, Vice Minister, Ministry of Transport 1992–94, apptd Chair. Commerce and Industry Cttee 1996, Judicial Affairs Cttee 1999, Rules and Admin Cttee 2003; apptd Dir Transport Div., Liberal Democratic Party (LDP) 1994, Dir Cabinet Div. 1994, Deputy Sec.-Gen. 1998, Deputy Chair. Policy Research 2000, Chief Deputy Chair. Policy Research 2002, Sec.-Gen. 2004–06. *Address:* Liberal Democratic Party, 1-11-23 Nagata-cho, Chiyoda-ku, Tokyo 100-8910, Japan (office). *Telephone:* (3) 3581-6211 (office). *E-mail:* koho@ldp.jimin.or.jp (office). *Website:* www.jimin.jp (office).

TAKEICHI, Masatoshi, MSc, PhD; Japanese cell biologist and academic; *Director, RIKEN Kobe Institute and Centre for Developmental Biology;* b. 27 Nov. 1943, Nagoya; ed Nagoya and Kyoto Univs; Asst Prof., Dept of Biophysics, Faculty of Science, Kyoto Univ. 1970–78, Assoc. Prof. 1978–86, Prof. 1986–99, Head, Centre for Molecular and Developmental Biology 1993–98, Prof., Dept of Cell and Developmental Biology, Grad. School of Biostudies 1999–2002; Visiting Prof., Nat. Inst. for Basic Biology 1992–97; Dir RIKEN Kobe Inst. and Centre for Developmental Biology, Kobe 2000–; Assoc. Ed. Cell Structure and Function 1983–, Neuron 1988–, Molecular Biology of the Cell 1989–97, Development, Growth and Differentiation 1990–, Developmental Biology 1991–95 (mem. Editorial Bd 1995–), Developmental Cell 2001–; Reviewing Ed. Science 1996–99; mem. Advisory Bd Development 1987–; mem. Editorial Bd Differentiation 1988–, Current Opinion in Cell Biology 1989–, Cell 1991–94, Trends in Genetics 1994–, Cell Adhesion and Communication 1994–, Genes and Development 1995–, Molecular and Cellular Neuroscience 1995–, Genes to Cells 1996–, Developmental Dynamics 1996–, Journal of Cell Biology 1998–2000, Journal of Neuroscience 1998–; mem. Japan Acad. 2000–, Japanese Soc. of Developmental Biologists (Pres. 1999–), Japan Soc. for Cell Biology (Bd mem.), Molecular Biology Soc. of Japan, Japan Neuroscience Soc. 2001, Japanese Cancer Asscn (Bd mem. –2000), Japanese Biochemical Soc., Japanese Soc. for Molecular Biology, American Soc. for Cell Biology, Int. Soc. of Developmental Biologists (Bd mem.); Toray Science and Tech. Grant 1984, Asahi Gakujyutsu Grant 1985, Naito Foundation Special Project Grant 1988–90, Tsukahara Nakaakira Award 1989, Chunichi Culture Award 1992, Dunham Lecturer, Harvard Medical School 1993, Osaka Science Award 1993, Keith Porter Lecturer, 33rd Annual Meeting of American Soc. of Cell Biology 1993, Asahi Award, Asahi Shimbun 1994, Jean Brachet Lecturer, 8th Congress of Int. Soc. of Differentiation 1994, Academic Prize, The Princess Takamatsu-miya Cancer Research Foundation 1995, Japan Acad. Prize 1996, Uehara Award 1996, Ross Harrison Prize, Int. Soc. of Developmental Biologists 2001, Keio Medical Science Prize 2001, Person of Cultural Merits 2004, co-recipient Japan Prize, Science and Tech. Foundation of Japan 2005. *Publications:* numerous articles in scientific journals. *Address:* RIKEN Kobe Institute and Centre for Developmental Biology, 2-2-3 Minatojima-minamimachi, Chuo-ku, Kobe 650-0047, Japan (office). *Telephone:* (78) 306-0111 (office). *Fax:* (78) 306-0101 (office). *E-mail:* takeichi@cdb .riken.jp (office). *Website:* www.cdb.riken.go.jp (office).

TAKEMURA, Masayoshi; Japanese politician (retd); b. 26 Aug. 1934, Youkaichi City, Shiga Pref.; ed Tokyo Univ.; joined Ministry of Home Affairs 1962, at Saitama Pref. offices 1967–70, Research Counsellor to Minister of Home Affairs 1970–71; Mayor of Youkaichi City, Shiga Pref. 1971–74, Gov. of Shiga Pref. 1974–86; Pres. New Party Sakigake (Harbinger) 1993–96; Minister of State, Chief Cabinet Sec. 1993–94; Minister of Finance 1994–96; mem. House of Reps, Shiga Pref. 1986–2000 (Chair. Environment Cttee).

TAKENAKA, Heizo, PhD; Japanese economist, academic and government official; *Director, Global Security Research Institute, Keio University;* b. 3 March 1951; ed Hitotsubashi Univ. and Osaka Univ.; joined Japan Devt Bank 1973, Research Inst. of Capital Formation 1977; Visiting Scholar, Harvard Univ., USA 1981, Visiting Assoc. Prof. 1989; Visiting Scholar, Univ. of Pennsylvania 1981; Assoc. Prof., Faculty of Econs, Osaka Univ. 1987; Visiting Fellow, Inst. of Int. Econs 1989; Assoc. Prof., Faculty of Policy Man., Keio Univ. 1990, Prof., Faculty of Policy Man. 1996, 2006–, Dir Global Security Research Inst. 2004, 2001, 2004, 2006–; Dir The Tokyo Foundation (fmrly Global Foundation for Research and Scholarship) 1997, Exec. Dir 1998, Pres. 1999; mem. Econ. Strategy Council 1998, IT Strategy Council 2000, IT Strategy HQ 2001; Minister of State for Econ. and Fiscal Policy 2001–05, for Information Tech. Policy 2001–02, for Financial Services Agency 2002–04, for Privatization of the Postal Services 2004–06, of Internal Affairs and Communications 2005–06; mem. House of Councillors, Diet, Tokyo 2004–05. *Publications:* in Japanese: The Economics of Business Investment 1984, The Macroeconomic Analysis of External Imbalances 1987, The Economics of US–Japan Friction 1991, The Globalization of the Japanese Economy and Corporate Investment 1993, Wealth of People 1994, The Economy in Which Fast Movers Win 1998; in English: Contemporary Japanese Economy and Economic Policy 1991; popular writing includes a cartoon book explaining economics. *Address:* Office of the Director, Global Security Research Institute, Keio University, 2-15-45 Mita, Minato-ku, Tokyo 108-8345, Japan (office). *E-mail:* gsec@info.keio.ac.jp (office). *Website:* www1.gsec.keio.ac.jp/english.php (office); takenakaheizo.cocolog-nifty .com.

TAKENAKA, Kyoji; Japanese manufacturing industry executive; *Head, Robot Business Promotion Council;* b. 28 Nov. 1946; joined Fuji Heavy Industries Ltd 1969, Staff Gen. Man. Product Planning Office 1998–91, Staff Gen. Man. Product

Planning Div. 1991–95, Project Gen. Man. Subara Devt and Eng Div. 1995–99, Vice-Pres., Project Gen. Man. of Product Planning Office and Gen. Man. Special Version Devt Dept 1999–2000, Vice-Pres., Sr Gen. Man. of Corp. Planning Div. and Gen. Man. Alliance Promotion Office 2000–01, Pres. and COO 2001–03, Pres. and CEO Fuji Heavy Industries Ltd 2003–06; currently Head of Robot Business Promotion Council, Japan Robot Asscn. *Address:* Robot Business Promotion Council, c/o Japan Robot Association, Kikaishinko Bldg., 3-5-8 Shiba-koen, Minato-ku, Tokyo 105-0011, Japan. *Telephone:* (3) 3434-2919. *Fax:* (3) 3578-1404. *Website:* www.jara.jp/e.

TAKEYAMA, Minoru, BArch, MArch; Japanese architect and academic; *Principal, Minoru Takeyama architect & U/A;* b. 15 March 1934, Sapporo; ed Waseda Univ., Harvard Univ., USA; began career with Josep Lluis Sert, Mass, USA 1960–61, Harrison Abramovitz, New York 1961, Jorn Utzon, Arne Jacobsen and Henning Larsen, Copenhagen, Denmark 1962–64; returned to Japan and est. Minoru Takeyama architect & United Actions, Prin. 1965–, opened second office in Sapporo 1975; Prof. of Architecture, Musashino Art Univ., Tokyo 1975–, currently Prof. of Architectural and Urban Design; Visiting Prof., Royal Danish Acad. of Fine Arts, Copenhagen 1962–63, Univ. Manitoba 1979, Univ. of Hong Kong 1981, Nat. Univ. of Singapore 1983, Univ. of California, Berkeley 1986, 1979, 1978, 1977, Harvard Univ. 1987, Univ. of Illinois, Ubana-Champaign 1989–90, Tech. Univ. of Liberec, Czech Repub. 2006; mem. Architectural Inst. of Japan, Japan Inst. of Architects; Hon. Fellow, AIA 1993–, Soc. of Czech Architects 2006–; Special Prize, First World Biennale of Architecture, Bulgaria 1981, Annual Design Award 1987, Int. Illumination Design Award 1992, Honour Award of Waterfront Design 1993, Tokyo Design Award 1993. *Buildings include:* Ichiban-kan, Number One Bldg 1969, Niban-kan, Number Two Bldg 1970, Hotel Beverley Tom, Hokkaido 1973, Atelier Indigo studio, Sapporo 1976, Nakamura Hospital, Sapporo 1978, Sweet Factory, Nara 1985, Renaissance Bldg, Kyoto 1986, Tokyo Port Terminal 1991, Crematorium, Cemetery and Memorial Complex, Yokohama 2001, Central Railway Station Complex, Seoul 2002; co-f. post-modernist group ARCHITEXT 1971. *Publications:* Blue Nirvana 1972, Autobiography of an Architect 1973, Street Semiology 1975, Meaning of Streets 1977, Language in Architecture 1983, Tokyo Urban Language 1984. *Address:* Minoru Takeyama architect & U/A, Uehara Side Park 102, 3-42-4 Uehara Shibuya-ku, Tokyo (office); Musashino Art University, 1-736 Ogawa-cho, Kodaira-shi, Tokyo 187-8505, Japan. *Telephone:* (3) 5790-6268 (office). *Fax:* (3) 5454-8531 (office). *E-mail:* info@m-take.com (office). *Website:* www .m-take.com (office); www.musabi.ac.jp.

TAKHAR, Bonnie; American business executive; *CEO and President, Halston LLC;* has held managerial positions with Donna Karan and Nicole Farhi Group; joined Earl Jean, Inc., CEO of Earl Jean Europe, London 1999–2002, Global Pres. of Earl Jean, New York (following acquisition of Earl Jean, Inc. by Nautica Enterprises) 2002–04; Advisor to CEO of Jimmy Choo Ltd on business devt 2004–06, Chief Commercial Officer, Jimmy Choo Ltd 2006–07; CEO and Pres. Halston LLC 2007–. *Address:* Halston LLC, 1350 Avenue of the Americas, Suite 2025, New York, NY 10019, USA (office). *Telephone:* (212) 282-1200 (office). *Fax:* (212) 786-6775 (office). *E-mail:* info@halston.com (office). *Website:* www.halston .com (office).

TAKIZAKI, Takemitsu; Japanese business executive; *Chair, Keyence Corporation;* b. 1946; m.; f. Lead Electric Co. (mfr of electronic sensors) 1974, later renamed Keyence Corpn, becoming Pres. and Rep. Dir, Chair. and Rep. Dir 2000–. *Address:* Office of the Chairman, Keyence Corporation, 1-3-14 Higashi-nakajima, Higashi-Yodogawa, Osaka, Japan (office). *Telephone:* (6) 6379-1111 (office). *Website:* www.keyence.com (office).

TAKUMIYA, Osamu; Japanese health care industry executive; *Chairman and Representative Director, Mediceo Corporation;* Vice-Pres. Kuraya Sanseido Inc. 2001, Vice-Pres. and Exec. Dir of Sales 2003, Chair. and Rep. Dir Kuraya Sanseido Inc. (following separation of pharmaceutical distribution from purchasing businesses to form new Kuraya Sanseido Inc. and Mediceo Holdings Co. Ltd, as parts of Mediceo Group) 2004–09, Chair. and Rep. Dir Mediceo Corpn (after merger of several Mediceo Group cos) 2009–. *Address:* Mediceo Corporation, 7-15 Yaesu 2-chome, Chuo-ku, Tokyo 104-8464, Japan (office). *Telephone:* (3) 3517-5800 (office). *Fax:* (3) 230-5566 (office).

TAL, Hisham; Jordanian lawyer, judge and government official; b. 1943, Irbid; ed Damascus Univ.; lawyer –1991; Judge, Court of Cassation and Higher Court of Justice 1991–94; Deputy Prime Minister and Minister of Political Devt and Parl. Affairs 2005; Pres. Legislation and Opinion Bureau 2009–10; Minister of Justice 2010–11. *Address:* c/o Ministry of Justice, POB 6040, Amman 11118, Jordan (office).

TALABANI, Jalal; Iraqi politician and head of state; *President;* b. 1933, Kelkan; ed high schools in Erbil and Kirkuk; f. secret student asscn at age of 13; mem. Kurdish Democratic Party 1947, elected to Cen. Cttee 1951; denied admission to medical school by govt due to political activities; allowed to enter law school 1953; forced to go into hiding to escape arrest for founding and becoming Sec.-Gen. of Kurdistan Student Union 1956; following overthrow of Hashemite monarchy, returned to law school 1958; pursued career as journalist and ed. of Khabat and Kurdistan; mil. service 1959, later Commdr of tank unit; organized and led Kurdish revolt against Govt in Mawat, Rezan and Karadagh regions 1961; rep. Kurdish leadership on numerous diplomatic missions in Europe and Middle East 1960s; Founder and Sec.-Gen. Patriotic Union of Kurdistan 1975–; apptd mem. Iraqi Governing Council 2003; President of Iraq 2005–. *Address:* Office of the President, Baghdad, Iraq (office).

TALAGI, Grace Sisilia Tupou, BSc; Niuean civil servant and diplomatist; b. 27 Feb. 1952, Niue; m. Takili Talagi; one s. three d.; food technologist 1976–81, food industry trainer 1981–83; Agric. Projects Man. and Exports Promoter 1983–88; Dir of Agric. and Fisheries 1988–94; Asst Head of External Affairs 1994–99; Sec. to the Govt 1999–2005; High Commr to NZ (first woman diplomatist) 2005–11. *Leisure interests:* research reading, golf, watching sports. *Address:* PO Box 175, Alofi, Niue (home).

TALAGI, Toke Tufukia, BSA; Niuean politician; *Premier and Minister of Finance;* b. 9 Jan. 1951, Alofi; s. of Siona Talagi and Pelenita Talagi; m. Emeline Fifitaloa Peleni; three c.; ed Nelson Coll., Massey Univ., New Zealand; elected to

Nat. Ass. 1999; fmr Deputy Prime Minister, Minister of Educ.; Premier 2008–, also Chair. of Cabinet and Minister responsible for Premier's Dept, Civil Aviation, Crown Law Office, Planning, Econ. Devt and Statistics, External Affairs, Niue Public Service Comm., Finance, Customs and Revenue, Govt Assets, Police and Nat. Security, Environment, Meteorological Services and Climate Change, Tourism, Immigration and Population, Private Sector Devt, and Youth and Sports; Chair. Pacific Islands Forum 2008; Pres. Niue Rugby Union. *Leisure interest:* reading. *Address:* Office of the Premier, PO Box 40, Fale Fono, Alofi, Niue (office). *Telephone:* 4200 (office).

TALAL, Prince Walid ibn, BSc, MA; Saudi Arabian business executive; *Founder and Chairman, Kingdom Holding Company;* b. 7 March 1955, Riyadh; s. of HRH Prince Talal ibn Abd al-Aziz as-Sa'ud and Princess Mona as-Solh; nephew of HM King Abdullah ibn Abd al-Aziz as Sa'ud; m. 1st Dalal bint Saud bin Abdul Aziz, one s. one d.; m. 4th Princess Ameerah al Taweel; ed Menlo Coll., Calif., Syracuse Univ., NY, USA; began building investment portfolio 1979; Chair. United Saudi Bank 1988–99; Founder and Chair. Kingdom Holding Co. 1980– (now one of the largest and most diversified private investment cos in the world); investments in numerous int. cos, including Citigroup Inc., News Corpn, Euro Disney SCA, Planet Hollywood chain of restaurants, Apple Computers, Fairmont Hotels & Resorts, PepsiCo Inc., Procter & Gamble, Kodak, Motorola, Compaq Computer Group, Savoy Hotel, London, Twitter, Beijing Jingdong Trading Co. (Chinese online retailer) etc.; unveiled plans to construct the world's tallest building, Kingdom Tower in Jeddah 2011; also struck deal with Bloomberg to launch own news channel 2011; investments in Nigeria through Kingdom Zephyr Africa Management 2012; Hon. Citizen of 19 cities 1998–2009; numerous decorations, including Grand Officer, Nat. Cedar Medal (Lebanon) 2002, Nat. Order of the Lion (Senegal) 2003, Officer, Order of Orange Nassau (Netherlands) 2003, Hilal i Pakistan Medal 2006, Commdr, Légion d'honneur 2006, Grand Officer, Order of the Golden Heart (Philippines) 2007, Order of the Brilliant Star with Grand Cordon Medal (Taiwan) 2007, Pontifical Medal (Vatican) 2008; 20 hon. doctorates from univs in USA, UK, Bosnia and Herzegovina, Bulgaria, Central Africa Republic, Egypt, Ghana, Indonesia, Korea, Lebanon, Madagascar, Malaysia, Palestine, Philippines, Tunisia and Uganda; Presidential Medal, Univ. of New Haven, Conn., USA 1999, ranked no 1. by Arabian Business amongst the Power 500: The World's Most Influential Arabs 2004–13, Vermeil Medal, St Joseph's Univ. (Lebanon) 2010. *Address:* Kingdom Holding Co., PO Box 1, Riyadh 11321, Saudi Arabia (office). *Telephone:* (1) 211-1111 (office). *Fax:* (1) 211-1112 (office). *E-mail:* media&info@ kingdom.com.sa (office). *Website:* www.kingdom.com.sa (office); www .alwaleedfoundations.org.

TALAT, Mehmet Ali, MSc; Turkish Cypriot politician; b. 6 July 1952, Kyrenia; m.; one s. one d.; ed Middle East Tech. Univ., Ankara, Eastern Mediterranean Univ., Famagusta; began career as self-employed electrical engineer; active in Turkish Cypriot orgs, Co-founder and first Chair. Cypriots Educ. and Youth Fed. (KÖGEF), Turkey; joined youth div. Republican Turkish Party (Cumhuriyetçi Türk Partisi, CTP), mem. CTP Party Council, and Cen. Exec. Cttee, also CTP Sec., becoming Chair. 1996–; Minister of Educ. and Culture 1994, later Minister of State and Deputy Prime Minister; mem. Parl. for Nicosia 1998–; Prime Minister of 'Turkish Repub. of Northern Cyprus' 2004–05, Pres. 2005–10. *Address:* Mersin Cad 9, Kyrenia, Turkish Republic of Northern Cyprus (home). *Telephone:* (392) 2293242 (home). *E-mail:* mat@defne.net.

TALBAKOV, Ismoil; Tajikistani economist and politician; *Secretary of Central Committee, Communist Party of Tajikistan;* m.; four c.; ed Tajik State Univ.; fmr officer in Soviet Army; mem. Majlisi Namoyandagon (Parl.); Sec., Cen. Cttee, CP of Tajikistan; unsuccessful cand. in presidential elections 2006. *Address:* Communist Party of Tajikistan, 734002 Dushanbe, Kuchai F. Niyazi 37, Tajikistan (office). *Telephone:* (372) 21-77-87 (office). *Website:* www.kpt.freenet.tj (office).

TALBOTT, Strobe; American journalist and fmr government official; *President, The Brookings Institution;* b. 25 April 1946, Dayton, Ohio; s. of Nelson S. Talbott and Josephine Large; m. Brooke Lloyd Shearer 1971; two s.; ed Hotchkiss School, Connecticut, Yale Univ. and Univ. of Oxford, UK; joined Time magazine, Diplomatic Corresp., White House Corresp., Eastern Europe Corresp., Washington Bureau Chief 1984–89, Ed.-at-Large 1989–94; Amb.-at-Large, US State Dept Feb.–Dec. 1993, Deputy Sec. of State 1994–2001; Pres. The Brookings Inst. 2002–; Chair. Foreign Affairs Policy Bd, US State Dept 2011–; Rhodes Scholar, Univ. of Oxford 1969; Dir Carnegie Endowment for Int. Peace; mem. Council on Foreign Relations; Fellow, American Acad. of Arts and Sciences 2009–; Dr hc (Monterey Inst., Trinity Coll., Georgetown Univ., Washington Univ. in St Louis, Fairfield Univ.). *Publications include:* Khrushchev Remembers 1970, Khrushchev Remembers: The Last Testament (jtly) 1974, Endgame: The Inside Story of Salt II 1979, Deadly Gambits: The Reagan Administration and the Stalemate in Nuclear Arms Control 1984, The Russians and Reagan 1984, Reagan and Gorbachev (jtly) 1987, The Master of the Game: Paul Nitze and the Nuclear Peace 1988, At the Highest Levels: The Inside Story of the End of the Cold War (jtly) 1993, The Age of Terror: America and The World After September 11 (co-ed.) 2001, The Russia Hand: A Memoir of Presidential Diplomacy 2002, Engaging India 2005, The Great Experiment 2008, Fast Forward: Ethics and Politics in the Age of Global Warming (with William Antholis) 2010. *Address:* The Brookings Institution, 1775 Massachusetts Avenue, NW, Washington, DC 20036, USA (office). *Telephone:* (202) 797-6000 (office). *Fax:* (202) 797-6004 (office). *E-mail:* communications@brookings.edu (office). *Website:* www.brookings.edu (office).

TALENT, James (Jim) Matthes; American politician; *Distinguished Fellow, Heritage Foundation;* b. 18 Oct. 1956, Des Peres, Mo.; s. of Milton Talent and Marie Talent (née Matthes); m. Brenda Talent 1984; two s. two d.; ed Kirkwood High School, Washington Univ., St Louis and Univ. of Chicago Law School; clerk to Judge of US Court of Appeals 1982–83; elected (Republican) to Mo. House of Reps 1984–92, later Minority Leader –1992; elected to Congress (Second Dist, Mo.) 1992–2000, later Asst Minority Leader; mem. Armed Services Cttee 1992–2000, Small Business Cttee 1992–2000 (Chair. 1997), Educ. Cttee; Senator from Missouri 2003–07; Distinguished Fellow, Heritage Foundation, Washington, DC 2007–; Arnold J. Lien Prize for Most Outstanding Undergrad. in Political Science, Nat. Asscn of Women Business Owners' Nat. Public Policy Award (first male recipient), named Legislator of the Year by Dept of Missouri Veterans of Foreign Wars, Int. Franchise Asscn and Ind. Electrical Contractors, Vietnam Veterans of

America's Lifetime Achievement Award 2000. *Address:* Heritage Foundation, 214 Massachusetts Ave, NE, Washington, DC 20002-4999 (office); 9433 Olive Blvd, St Louis, MO 63132, USA (home). *Telephone:* (314) 453-0344 (home). *Fax:* (314) 453-0805 (home). *E-mail:* staff@heritage.org (office). *Website:* www.heritage.org/about/ staff/t/jim-talent (office).

TALIBOV, Vasif Yusif oğlu, PhD; Azerbaijani politician; *Chairman, Ali Mäclis (Supreme Assembly) of the Autonomous Republic of Naxçıvan;* b. 14 Jan. 1960, Aralig, Ilyich (now Şarur) Dist, Naxçıvan ASSR, Azerbaijan SSR; s. of Yusif Talibov and Minaye Talibova; m. Sevil Sultanova; two s. one d.; ed Naxçıvan State Pedagogical Inst., Baku State Univ.; began career with Sharur Dist Public Educ. Dept 1976; secondary school teacher, village of Damirchi, Şarur Dist 1981–82; Cadre Inspector, Naxçıvan Knitted Goods Factory 1982; Sr Asst, Ali Mäclis (Supreme Ass.) of Autonomous Repub. of Naxçıvan 1991–94, First Deputy for Econ. Links 1994–95, Deputy (mem. Parl.) 1995–, Chair. Ali Mäclis 2005–; Founder-mem. New Azerbaijan Party (NAP), Chair. 1995–; mem. Co-ordinating Council, Congress of Azerbaijanis Worldwide 2001–; Medal of Glory 2010. *Address:* Ali Mäclis (Supreme Assembly) of the Autonomous Republic of Naxçıvan, 7000 Naxçıvan, H. Aliyev pr. 50, Azerbaijan (office). *Telephone:* (36) 544-01-01 (office). *Fax:* (36) 544-01-01 (office). *E-mail:* info@alimeclis.az (office). *Website:* www .alimeclis.az (office).

TALLAWY, Mervat Mehani Ahmed; Egyptian diplomatist and international organization official; b. 1 Dec. 1937, Menya; d. of Mehani Tallawy and Soraya Abdel-Hamid; m. Dr Ali Abdel-Rahman Rahmy 1964; one d.; ed American Univ. Cairo, Inst. for Diplomatic Studies, Cairo and Grad. Inst. of Int. Studies, Geneva, Harvard Law School, USA; joined Ministry of Foreign Affairs 1963; served Geneva, New York and Caribbean countries, Vienna and Tokyo; Deputy Dir UN Inst. for the Advancement of Women 1982–85; Amb. to Austria and Resident Rep. to IAEA, UNIDO and UN Centre for Social and Humanitarian Affairs 1988–91; Dir of Int. Econ. Dept, Ministry of Foreign Affairs 1991; Asst Minister for Int. Political and Econ. Affairs 1992–93; Amb. to Japan 1993–97; Minister of Insurance and Social Affairs 1997–99; Sec.-Gen. Nat. Council for Women 2000; UN Under-Sec.-Gen. and Exec. Dir UN Econ. and Social Comm. for Western Asia (ESCWA) 2000–07; Rapporteur-Gen. UN Conf. on Adoption of Int. Convention on Prevention of Illicit Drug Trafficking, Vienna 1988; Co-ordinator-Gen. for the Arab Econ. and Social Summit, Kuwait 2009; mem. UN Cttee on Elimination of Discrimination against Women (CEDAW) (Chair. 1990–92); Chair. UN Comm. on Status of Women 1991–93; Chair. workshop on Women and Violence leading to adoption of UN Declaration on Elimination of Violence Against Women, Vienna 1992; Chair. Working Group on Health, UN Int. Conf. for the Advancement of Women, Beijing 1995; Head Egyptian Del. to Multilateral Middle East Peace Talks Working Group on Econ. Regional Co-operation, Brussels 1992, Paris 1992, Rome 1993 and to Steering Cttee of Multilateral Middle East Talks, Tokyo 1994; Head Egyptian Del. to UN World Conf. on Natural Disasters, Yokohama 1994; Del. to UN Environment Conf., Rio de Janeiro 1992; Head of Negotiation Group to UN Int. Conf. on Population and Devt, Cairo 1994; initiator of proposal leading to adoption of UN Declaration for the Protection of Women and Children in Time of Armed Conflicts 1974; founder mem. Egyptian Social Democratic Party 2011; Chair. Egyptian Nat. Council of Women 2012; Head, Egyptian Del. to UN Comm. on the Status of Women 2013; mem. Club of Rome; Amb. of the Year (Austria) 1991, Nat. Order of the Cedar (Lebanon). *Leisure interests:* theatre, classical music, walking, reading, painting. *Address:* 8 El-Kamel Mohammed, El Zamalek, 11211 Cairo, Egypt (home). *Telephone:* (2) 738-3422 (home). *Fax:* (2) 735-8102 (home). *E-mail:* tallawy@hotmail.com (office).

TALLING, J(ohn) F(rancis), PhD, FRS; British biologist; b. 23 March 1929, Grange Town; s. of Frank Talling and Miriam Talling; m. Ida Björnsson 1959; one s. one d.; ed Sir William Turner's School, Coatham, Yorks., Univ. of Leeds, Univ. of London; Lecturer in Botany, Univ. of Khartoum 1953–56; Postdoctoral Fellow, Univ. of California, USA 1957; Biologist, Freshwater Biological Asscn 1958–89, Sr Research Fellow 1991–2008; Visiting Prof., Univ. of Lancaster 1992–98; Naumann-Thienemann Medal, Int. Asscn of Limnology 1989. *Publications:* Ecological Dynamics of Tropical Inland Waters (with J. Lemoalle) 1998; about 100 scientific papers. *Leisure interests:* archaeology. *Address:* Hawthorn View, The Pines, Bongate, Appleby, Cumbria CA16 6HR, England (home).

TALMACI, Leonid; Moldovan economist and banker; b. 26 April 1956, Reteni; m. Nina Talmaci 1977; one d.; ed Financial Banking Coll., Chişinău, Financial-Econ. Inst. Leningrad (now St Petersburg); Prin. Economist Stroibank USSR 1984–88; Deputy Head Dept, Promstroibank USSR 1988, Chair. Energomash Bank 1988–91; Gov. Nat. Bank of Moldova 1991–2009 (resgnd); Deputy Chair. Russia Bank Asscn 1990–92. *Address:* c/o National Bank of Moldova, 7 Renaşterii Avenue, 2006 Chişinău, Moldova.

TALMI, Igal, DrScNat; Israeli physicist and academic; *Professor Emeritus, Department of Particle Physics, Weizmann Institute of Science;* b. 31 Jan. 1925, Kiev, Ukraine; s. of Moshe Talmi and Lea Talmi (née Weinstein); m. Chana Talmi (née Kivelewitz) 1949; one s. one d.; ed Herzlia High School, Hebrew Univ. of Jerusalem and Swiss Fed. Inst. of Tech.; served in Israeli Defence Forces 1947–49; Research Fellow, Princeton Univ. 1952–54, Visiting Assoc. Prof. 1956–57, Visiting Prof. 1961–62, 1966–67; apptd Prof. of Physics, Weizmann Inst. of Science 1958, Prof. Emer. 1995–, Head, Dept of Nuclear Physics 1967–76, Dean Faculty of Physics 1970–84; mem. Israel Acad. of Sciences and Humanities 1963–, Chair. Div. of Sciences 1974–80; Weizmann Prize of the Tel-Aviv Municipality 1962, Israel Prize (with A. de Shalit) 1965, Rothschild Prize, 1971, Hans A. Bethe Prize, American Physical Soc. 2000, EMT Prize 2003. *Publications include:* Nuclear Shell Theory (with A. de Shalit) 1963, Simple Models of Complex Nuclei 1993, numerous publs on theoretical nuclear physics. *Leisure interest:* bird watching. *Address:* Department of Particle Physics, Weizmann Institute of Science, Rehovot 76100, Israel (office). *Telephone:* (8) 9342060 (office); (8) 9468166 (home). *Fax:* (8) 9344106 (office). *E-mail:* igal.talmi@weizmann.ac.il (office). *Website:* www.weizmann.ac.il/ (office).weizmann.ac.il/physics/staff/Talmi.htm (office).

TALPES, Ioan, PhD; Romanian politician and fmr army officer; b. 24 Aug. 1944, Topleţ, Caraş-Severin Co.; m.; one c.; ed Faculty of History and Philosophy and School of Active Officers 'Nicolae Balcescu', Sibiu; scientific research mil. officer, Centre of Historical Studies and Researches and Mil. Theory of the Defence

Ministry 1970–88; Ed.-in-Chief Mil. Publishing House 1988–90, Dir March–July 1990; worked for secret service –1989; Presidential Adviser, Romanian Presidency 1990–92; Dir Foreign Intelligence Service with ministerial rank 1994–97; Amb. to Bulgaria 1997–98; Chief Adviser on Security Matters to the Pres. and Head of Presidental Admin 2000–, Minister of State responsible for Defence, European Integration and Justice and Head of Nat. Security Dept 2004; mem. Senatul (Senate) 2004–. *Publications:* numerous articles, studies and books published in Romania and abroad. *Address:* Senatul, 050711 Bucharest 5, Calea 13 Septembrie 1–3, Romania (office). *Telephone:* (21) 4021111 (office). *Fax:* (21) 3121184 (office). *E-mail:* csava@senat.ro (office). *Website:* www.senat.ro (office).

TALU, Umur E., BA; Turkish journalist; b. 7 Aug. 1957, Istanbul; s. of M. Muvakkar and G. Güzin; m. Şule Talu 1987; two d.; ed Galatasaray High School and Bosphorus Univ.; educ. specialist, Railway Workers' Union 1977–78; Int. Econ. Cooperation Sec. Union of Municipalities 1978–80; Econ. Corresp. Günaydin (newspaper) 1980–82; Chief, Econ. Dept Günes (newspaper) 1982–83; Ed. with Cumhuriyet (newspaper) 1983–85; Chief, Econ. Dept Milliyet (newspaper) 1985–86, News Ed. 1986–87, 1988–92, Ed.-in-Chief 1992–94, columnist 1994; currently columnist, Gazete Haberturk; Ed. Hürriyet (newspaper) 1987–88; Freedom of the Press Award, Turkish Journalists' Asscn 1996. *Publications:* Social Democracy in Europe (co-author) 1985, Keynes (trans.) 1986, Mr Uguran's Post Office 1996. *Leisure interests:* sport, music, films. *Address:* c/o Gazete Haberturk, Abdülhakhamit Cad. No: 25, Beyoğlu, Istanbul, Turkey. *E-mail:* utalu@htgazete.com.tr. *Website:* www.haberturk.com/htyazar/umur-talu.

TALWAR, Rana Gurvirendra Singh, BA; Indian banker and investment industry executive; *Chairman, Sabre Capital Worldwide Inc.;* b. 22 March 1948; s. of R. S. Talwar and Veera Talwar; m. 1st Roop Som Dutt 1970 (divorced); one s. one d.; m. 2nd Renuka Singh 1995; one s.; ed Lawrence School, Sanawar, St Stephen's Coll., Delhi, Delhi Univ.; exec. trainee, Citibank 1969–70, numerous operational, corp. and institutional banking assignments, India 1970–76, Group Head for Treasury and Financial Inst. 1976, Regional Man. for Eastern India 1977, Group Head of Treasury and Financial Insts Group, Saudi American Bank, Jeddah 1978–80, Regional Consumer Business Man., Singapore, Malaysia, Indonesia, Thailand and India 1982–88, Div. Exec., Asia Pacific 1988–91, Exec. Vice-Pres. and Group Exec., Consumer Bank, Asia Pacific, Middle East and Eastern Europe 1991–95, Exec. Vice-Pres. Citicorp and Citibank, responsible for USA and Europe 1996–97; Group Exec. Dir Standard Chartered PLC 1997–98, CEO 1998–2001; Chair. Centurion Bank of Punjab 2004–08 (Centurion acquired by HDFC Bank Ltd); currently Co-Founder and Chair. Sabre Capital Worldwide Inc., London; mem. Bd of Dirs (non-exec.) Pearson PLC 2000–07, Fortis SA 2004–09, Schlumberger Ltd 2005–08; Patron Nat. Soc. for Prevention of Cruelty to Children 2005; mem. Governing Body London Business School; fmr mem. Indian School of Business. *Leisure interests:* bridge, golf, tennis, travel. *Address:* Sabre Capital Worldwide Inc., 2nd Floor, Berkeley Square House, Berkeley Square, London, W1J 6BD, England (office).

TAM, Yiu Chung, JP; Chinese trade union official and government official; *Chairman, Democratic Alliance for Betterment of Hong Kong;* b. 15 Dec. 1949, Hong Kong; m. Lai Xiang Ming; two c.; ed Australian Nat. Univ., London School of Econs, UK; trade union officer; Vice-Chair. Hong Kong Fed. of Trade Unions; Chair. Employees' Retraining Bd, Elderly Comm., fmr mem. Preparatory Cttee for Hong Kong Special Admin. Region; mem. Exec. Council Hong Kong Special Admin. Region 1997–2002, Legis. Council Hong Kong Special Admin. Region 1998–; mem. Vocational Training Council, Standing Comm. on Civil Service Salaries and Conditions of Service, Ind. Comm. Against Corruption Complaints Cttee, Services Promotion Strategy Unit; fmr Vice-Chair. Democratic Alliance for Betterment of Hong Kong, Chair. 2007–; Hon. Life Fellow Inst. of Commercial Man., UK; Gold Bauhinia Star. *Address:* 12F SUP Tower, 83 King's Road, North Point, Hong Kong (office); Executive Council Secretariat, 1st Floor, Main Wing, Central Government Offices, Central, Hong Kong Administrative Region, People's Republic of China. *Telephone:* 25286888 (office). *Fax:* 25282326 (office). *E-mail:* yctam@dab.org.hk (office). *Website:* www.yctam.org (office).

TAMAKOSHI, Ryosuke; Japanese banking executive; b. 10 July 1947; joined Sanwa Bank Ltd 1970, mem. Bd of Dirs 1997–2002, Sr Exec. Officer 1999–2000, Pres. 2000–01; Pres. United Calif. Bank 2001–02; Sr Exec. Officer UFJ Bank Ltd 2002, Deputy Pres. 2002–04, Head, Global Banking and Trading Div. 2003, Chair. 2004, Pres. and CEO UFJ Holdings Inc. 2004, Chair. UFJ Holdings Inc. and UFJ Bank Ltd 2004–05, Chair. Mitsubishi UFJ Financial Group (after merger with Mitsubishi Tokyo Financial Group, Inc.) 2005–10, Deputy Chair. Bank of Tokyo-Mitsubishi UFJ Ltd 2006–08; Dir, Mitsubishi UFJ Financial Group, Inc. 2005–, The Kansai Electric Power Co., Inc. 2006–; Dir (non-exec.) Dah Sing Financial Holdings Ltd 2003–05. *Address:* Mitsubishi UFJ Financial Group, Inc., 7-1, Marunouchi 2-Chome, Chiyoda-ku, Tokyo 100-8330 (office); The Kansai Electric Power Co. Inc., 6-16, Nakanoshima 3-chome, Kita-ku, Osaka 530-8270, Japan (office). *Telephone:* (3) 3240-8111 (Tokyo) (office); (6) 6441-8821 (Osaka) (office). *Fax:* (3) 3240-8203 (Tokyo) (office); (6) 6447-7174 (Osaka) (office). *E-mail:* info@mufg.jp (office); info@kepco.co.jp (office). *Website:* www.mufg.jp (office); www.kepco.co.jp (office).

TAMARÓN, Marqués de Santiago de Mora-Figueroa, 9th Marqués de Tamarón; Spanish diplomatist; *Ambassador of Spain for Cultural Diplomacy;* b. 18 Oct. 1941, Jerez de la Frontera; s. of José de Mora-Figueroa, 8th Marqués de Tamarón, and Dagmar Williams; m. Isabelle de Yturbe 1966; one s. one d.; ed Univ. of Madrid and Escuela Diplomática; Lt Spanish Marine Corps 1967; Sec. Embassy, Nouakchott 1968–70, Paris 1970–73; Banco del Noroeste 1974; Counsellor, Copenhagen 1975–80; Minister-Counsellor, Ottawa 1980–81; Pvt. Sec. to Minister of Foreign Affairs 1981–82; Head of Studies and Deputy Dir Escuela Diplomática 1982–88; Dir Inst. de Cuestiones Internacionales y Política Exterior (INCIPE) 1988–96; Dir Instituto Cervantes 1996–99; Amb. to UK 1999–2004; Vice-Pres., Spanish section, Hispano–American Cttee 2004–11; Amb. of Spain for Cultural Diplomacy 2012–; mem. Trilateral Comm. 1989–96; Commdr Order of Carlos III, Officier, Ordre nat. du Mérite (France), Commdr Order of Dannebrog, Commdr Order of Merit (Germany), Gran Cruz Mérito Naval (Spain). *Publications:* Pólvora con Aguardiente 1983, El Guirigay Nacional 1988, Trampantojos 1990, El Siglo XX y otras Calamidades 1993, El Peso de la Lengua Española en el Mundo (co-author)

1995, El Rompimiento de Gloria 2003. *Leisure interests:* philology, mountain walking, gardening.

TAMAZAWA, Tokuichiro; Japanese politician; mem. House of Reps (LDP) 1976–2009; fmr Dir-Gen. Defence Agency; fmr Parl. Vice-Minister for Agric., Forestry and Fisheries, Minister 1999–2001; Pres. East Asian Friendship Asscn; Order of Brilliant Star with Grand Cordon 2008.

TAMBUNTING, Jesus P., BS; Philippine banking executive and diplomatist; *Chairman and CEO, Planters Development Bank;* b. 1937; m. Margarita Tambunting; four c.; ed Ateneo de Manila Univ., Culver Mil. Acad., Ind., Univ. of Maryland, USA; began career as asst cashier with Philippine bank, becoming Sr Vice-Pres. and Treas.; bought small thrift bank, Malolos, Bulacan; acquired Bulacan Devt Bank 1972, renamed Planters Devt Bank (Plantersbank) 1976 (now largest devt bank in Philippines), currently Chair. and CEO; Amb. to UK 1993–98; Chair. Micro Enterprise Bank of the Philippines; Co-Chair. Philippine-British Business Council; Dir Philam Asset Management Inc., Globe Telecom, Philam Fund Inc., Philam Strategic Growth Fund Inc., Philam Bond Fund Inc., Philam Dollar Bond Fund Inc.; fmr Chair. Asscn of Devt Financing Insts in Asia and the Pacific; fmr Pres. Management Asscn of the Philippines, Chamber of Thrift Banks, Devt Bankers Asscn of the Philippines; mem. Bd Philippine Business for Social Progress, Carlos P. Romulo Foundation; Knight, Equestrian Order of the Holy Sepulchre of Jerusalem (Vatican) 2004; Asian Bankers Asscn Lifetime Achievement Award 2005, Ernst & Young Philippines Entrepreneur of the Year 2009. *Address:* Planters Development Bank, Plantersbank Building, 314 Sen. Gil Puyat Avenue, Makati City, Philippines (office). *Telephone:* (2) 8847600 (office). *E-mail:* info@plantersbank.com.ph (office). *Website:* www.plantersbank.com.ph (office).

TAMEN, Pedro, LLB; Portuguese poet and translator; b. 1 Dec. 1934, Lisbon; s. of Mário Tamen and Emília Tamen; m. Maria da Graça Seabra Gomes 1975; two s. two d.; ed Lisbon Univ.; Dir Moraes Publishing House 1958–75; Pres. Portuguese PEN Club 1987–90, Vice-Pres. 1991–2002; Trustee, Calouste Gulbenkian Foundation, Lisbon 1975–2000; mem. Bd of Dirs Portuguese Asscn of Writers; D. Diniz Prize 1981, Grand Prix for Translation 1990, Critics Award 1993, INAPA Prize for Poetry 1993, Nicola Prize for Poetry 1998, Press Poetry Prize 2000, PEN Club Poetry Prize 2000, Inês de Castro Prize 2006, Luis Miguel Nava Prize 2006, Correntes de Escritas Prize 2007. *Publications include:* 12 books of poetry since 1958; Retábulo das Matérias (Collected Works) 2001, Analogia e Dedos (Prémio Literário Inês de Castro 2008) 2006, O Livro do Sapateiro (Poetry Prize, Portuguese Asscn of Writers 2011, Correntes de Escritas Prize 2011) 2010, Um Teatro às Escuras 2011. *Address:* Apartado 47, EC Palmela, 2951-901 Palmela, Portugal (home). *Telephone:* (21) 233-1144 (office). *Fax:* (21) 233-2203 (office). *E-mail:* ptamen@gmail.com (home). *Website:* www.arscives.com/pedrotamen.

TAMIM, Lt-Gen. Dahi Khalfan; United Arab Emirates police officer and government official; *Commander-in-Chief, Dubai Police Force;* b. 1 Oct. 1951; m.; two s. three d.; ed Royal Police Acad., Amman, Jordan; joined Dubai Police Force 1970, becoming Head of Financial and Admin. Affairs, Deputy Commdr-in-Chief 1979–80, Commdr-in-Chief 1980–; attained rank of Lt-Gen. 2004; rose to worldwide fame when he led the investigation into the assassination of Mahmoud al-Mabhouh, a Hamas operative killed by a hit squad in a hotel in Dubai 2010; mem. Dubai Exec. Cttee; Chair. Hamdan Bin Mohammed e-Univ. (fmrly e-TQM Coll.), Dubai; est. an orphanage in Dubai and launched the Khalfan School for teaching the Holy Quran; Service Order (First Class); Dubai Police Medal of Appreciation (First Class) twice, Dubai Police Distinguished Service Medal three times, Dubai Police Good Conduct Medal three times, Best Man. Dir Award in the public sector at the GCC level 1983, Nat. Security Medal (Saudi Arabia), Social Defence Medal, HH Ruler of Sharjah, UN Most Prominent Arab Figure Award in the field of Narcotics Control 2000, Middle East Regional Exec. CEO Personality Award 2004, ranked by Arabian Business amongst the Power 500: The World's Most Influential Arabs (second) 2010, (12th) 2012, (14th) 2013. *Address:* Dubai Police Headquarters, PO Box 1493, Dubai, United Arab Emirates (office). *Telephone:* (4) 269-2222 (office). *Fax:* (4) 217-1430 (office). *E-mail:* mail@dubaipolice.gov.ae (office). *Website:* www.dubaipolice.gov.ae (office).

TAMM, Ditlev, DJur, DPhil, R; Danish historian, academic and legal scholar; *Professor of Legal History, Faculty of Law, University of Copenhagen;* b. 7 March 1946, Copenhagen; s. of Henrik Tamm and Lizzie Knutzen; m. 1st Maria Pilar Lorenzo 1973 (separated 1987); two d.; ed Univ. of Copenhagen and in Germany and France; Prof. of Legal History, Univ. of Copenhagen 1978–; mem. Royal Danish Acad., Academia Europea and several other Danish and int. scientific bds and cttees; Dr Jur hc (Helsinki) 2000; A.S. Orsted Award 1974, Sarton Medal 2005. *Publications:* Fra lovkyndighed til retsvidenskab 1976, Retsopgøret efter besaettelsen 1984, Roman Law 1997, Bournonville 2005; several books and articles on Danish and European legal history, political history and cultural history. *Leisure interests:* languages, opera, bicycling. *Address:* Studiegården, Studiestraede 6, 1455 Copenhagen (office); Dantes Plads 3, 3, th, 1556 Copenhagen V, Denmark (home). *Telephone:* 35-32-31-67 (office); 39-29-93-92 (home). *E-mail:* ditlev.tamm@jur.ku.dk (office). *Website:* jur.ku.dk/english (office).

TAMM, Peter; German publisher; *Chairman, International Maritime Museum, Hamburg;* b. 12 May 1928, Hamburg; s. of Emil Tamm; m. Ursula Weisshun 1958; one s. four d.; ed Univ. of Hamburg; Shipping Ed., Hamburger Abendblatt 1948–58; Man. Dir Ullstein GmbH (Publr) Berlin 1960–62; Man. Dir Bild-Zeitung Hamburg 1962–64; Man. Dir Verlagshaus Axel Springer and Ullstein Verlag Berlin 1964–68, Chair. and CEO Axel Springer Verlag 1968–82, Chair. Bd 1982–91; Vice-Pres. Bundesverband Deutscher Zeitungsverleger 1982–91; currently Chair. of Bd Int. Maritime Museum, Hamburg, Peter Tamm Sen. Foundation; Bayerischer Verdienstorden 1976, Bundesverdienstkreuz I. Klasse 1986, Grosses Verdienstkreuz des Verdienst-ordens der Bundesrepublik Deutschland 1993, Cavaliere Ufficiale: Orden für die Verdienste um die Italienische Republik 1994, Grosses Verdienstkreuz mit Stern 1998, Gold Ehrenkreuz der Bundeswehr 2001, Commdr Order of the White Rose of Finland 2003; Hamburger Bürgerpreis 1996, Vasco da Gama Naval Medal 1997, Seewartmedaille in Silber 1998, Bismarckmedaille in Gold 1999, Professoren-Titel durch die Stadt Hamburg 2002, Hamburg Citizen of the Year 2004. *Publication:* Maler der See 1980. *Leisure interests:* model ships, marine books, maritime and naval history. *Address:* Koreastrasse 1, 20457 Hamburg, Germany (office). *Telephone:* (30) 092300 (office).

Fax: (30) 0923045 (office). *E-mail:* A.Reineward@peter-tamm-sen.de (office). *Website:* www.imm-hamburg.de.

TAMUERA, Tekiree; I-Kiribati politician; b. 16 Feb. 1940, Maiana; s. of Tamuera Timau and Era Iobi; m. Raratu Rouatu; three s.; ed King George V School, Tarawa Teachers Coll., Geelong Teachers Coll., Australia, South Devon Tech. Coll., UK; fmr teacher; fmr Chair. Public Services Comm.; interim Chair. Council of State 24–28 May 1994; Speaker of Parl. 1998–2003. *Leisure interests:* cutting toddy, fishing. *Address:* Betio, Tarawa, Kiribati (home).

TAMURA, Norihisa; Japanese politician; *Minister of Health, Labour and Welfare;* b. 15 Dec. 1964, Mie Pref.; ed Chiba Univ.; started career at Nippon Doken Co. (construction co.), Tsu, Mie Pref. 1987; Sec. to MP Hajime Tamura 1994–96; mem. House of Reps (lower house of Parl.) for Mie Pref. Dist No. 4 (LDP) 1996–, Dir Cttee on Rules and Admin 2005, Cttee on Health, Labour and Welfare 2007, 2010 (Chair. 2008); Parl. Sec. of Health, Labour and Welfare 2002, of Educ., Culture, Sports, Science and Tech. 2003; Vice-Minister for Internal Affairs and Communication 2006; Minister of Health, Labour and Welfare 2012–; Deputy Sec.-Gen. LDP 2005, Acting Chair. Research Comm. on Social Security System 2007, Deputy Chair. Policy Research Council 2009, Dir Health, Labour and Welfare Div., Policy Research Council 2010. *Address:* Ministry of Health, Labour and Welfare, 1-2-2, Kasumigaseki, Chiyoda-ku, Tokyo 100-8916, Japan (office). *Telephone:* (3) 5253-1111 (office). *Fax:* (3) 3501-2532 (office). *E-mail:* www-admin@mhlw.go.jp (office). *Website:* www.mhlw.go.jp (office).

TAN, Amy Ruth, MA, LHD; American writer; b. 19 Feb. 1952, Oakland, Calif.; d. of John Yuehhan and Daisy Ching Tan (née Tu); m. Louis M. DeMattei 1974; ed San José State Univ., Univ. of California, Berkeley, Dominican Coll., San Rafael; specialist in language devt, Alameda Co. Asscn for Mentally Retarded 1976–80; Project Dir MORE, San Francisco 1980–81; freelance writer 1981–88; Marian McFadden Memorial Lecturer, Indianapolis-Marion Co. Public Library 1996; Best American Essays Award 1991. *Film:* The Joy Luck Club (screenwriter, producer) 1993. *Publications include:* The Joy Luck Club (Commonwealth Club and Bay Area Book Reviewers' Best Fiction Award 1990) 1989, The Kitchen God's Wife 1991, The Hundred Secret Senses 1995, The Bonesetter's Daughter 2000, Saving Fish from Drowning 2005, Rules for Virgins 2011; for children: The Moon Lady 1992, The Chinese Siamese Cat 1994; non-fiction: The Opposite of Fate: A Book of Musings (autobiog.); numerous short stories and essays. *Address:* Steven Barclay Agency, 12 Western Avenue, Petaluma, CA 94952, USA (office); c/o Ecco Books/HarperCollins Publishers, 10 East 53rd, New York, NY 10022, USA. *Website:* www .amytanauthor.com.

TAN, Andrew L., BS; Philippine real estate executive; *Chairman and CEO, Alliance Global Group Inc.;* b. 1952, Fujian Prov., People's Repub. of China; m.; four c.; ed Univ. of the East, Manila; f. Megaworld Corpn 1989, currently Chair., also Pres. Megaworld Foundation Inc.; Chair. and CEO Alliance Global Group Inc. 2006–; CEO and Pres. Yonghe King Brand 2007–; Pres. Richmonde Hotel Group International Ltd; Treas. Empire East Land Holdings Inc. 1994–98, Chair. 1994, currently Prin. Exec. Officer; Vice-Chair. and Treas. Golden Arches Devt Corpn; Co-owner Resort World Manila (casino); dir of numerous cos; mem. European and Philippine Chambers of Commerce; Quezon City Businessman of the Year 2004. *Address:* Alliance Global Group Inc., 20/F IBM Plaza, Eastwood City CyperPark, 188 E. Rodriguez Jr. Avenue, Bagumbayan, Quezon City 1110, Philippines (office). *Telephone:* (2) 9112949 (office). *Fax:* (2) 4210851 (office). *Website:* allianceglobalinc .com (office).

TAN, Chorh Chuan, MD, FRCP, FRCPE, FRACP, FACP, FRGS; Singaporean renal physician, academic and university administrator; *President, National University of Singapore;* ed Nat. Univ. of Singapore, Inst. of Molecular Medicine, Oxford, UK; fmr Commonwealth Medical Fellow and Wellcome Fellow, Univ. of Oxford, fmr Visiting Scholar, Wolfson Coll., Oxford; Dean of Nat. Univ. of Singapore (NUS) Faculty of Medicine 1997–2000, Provost of NUS, then Sr Deputy Pres. 2004–08, Pres. NUS 2008–; Dir of Medical Services, Ministry of Health 2000–04, led public health response to the 2003 SARS epidemic; Chair. Nat. Univ. Health System; Deputy Chair. Agency for Science, Tech. and Research (A*STAR); helped establish Duke-NUS Grad. Medical School, in his capacity as Deputy Chair. Governing Bd NUS 2004–07, now Sr Advisor to Governing Bd; mem. Bd of Dirs Monetary Authority of Singapore; inaugural Chief Exec. Nat. Univ. Health System 2008; mem. World Econ. Forum's Global Univ. Leaders Forum 2008–, mem. World Econ. Forum's Science Advisory Cttee; Chair. Int. Alliance of Research Univs 2008–12; Fellow, Polish Acad. of Medicine; Hon. MD (King's Coll. London); Hon. DSc (Duke Univ., USA, Loughborough Univ., UK); Dr John Yu Medal, George Inst. for Global Health (Australia), Albert Schweitzer Gold Medal, Polish Acad. of Medicine, Achievement Medal, Singapore Soc. of Nephrology, Singapore Youth Award 1996, Public Service Star for outstanding contribs to overcoming SARS in Singapore 2003, Public Admin Gold Medal 2004, Nat. Science and Tech. Medal 2008. *Publications:* numerous papers in professional journals. *Address:* Office of the President, National University of Singapore, 21 Lower Kent Ridge Road, Singapore 119077 (office). *Telephone:* 65161200 (office). *E-mail:* uprtancc@nus.edu .sg (office). *Website:* www.nus.edu.sg/president (office).

TAN, Dun, MA; Chinese composer; b. 18 Aug. 1957, Si Mao, Hunan Province; s. of Tan Xiang Qiu and Fang Qun Ying; m. Jane Huang 1994; ed Cen. Conservatory of Music, Beijing and Columbia Univ., USA; violist, Beijing Opera Orchestra 1976–77; Vice-Pres. Cen. Conservatory of Music 1978–; works performed by major orchestras in China and at festivals world-wide; has conducted orchestras including Royal Concertgebouw, London Symphony, New York Philharmonic, Berlin Philharmonic, BBC Symphony and Filarmonica della Scala; four recordings of his major orchestral works, oriental instrumental music, chamber music and electronic music issued by China Nat. Recording Co.; works also include 14 film scores for US and Chinese films, six modern ballet scores, music for several stage plays; orchestral piece commissioned by Inst. for Devt of Intercultural Relations Through the Arts, USA for Beijing Int. Music Festival 1988; Artistic Dir Fire Crossing Water Festival, Barbican Centre, London 2000; composed music for Olympic Games medal ceremonies, Beijing 2008; commissioned by Google/YouTube to compose internet Symphony Eroica; named UNESCO Goodwill Amb. 2013; second place Weber Int. Chamber Music Composition Competition, Dresden 1983, Suntory Prize 1992, Grawemeyer Award 1998, Musical America

Composer of the Year 2003. *Film scores:* Aktion K 1994, Nanjing 1937 1995, Fallen 1997, In the Name of the Emperor 1998, Wo hu cang long (Crouching Tiger Hidden Dragon) (Grammy Award 2001, Acad. Award 2001, British Acad. Film Award 2001, Classical BRIT Contemporary Music Award 2001) 2000, Ying xiong (Hero) 2002. *Compositions:* orchestral works: Li Sao (symphony) 1979, Five Pieces in Human Accent for piano 1980, Feng Ya Song for string quartet 1982, Fu for two sopranos, bass and ensemble 1982, Piano Concerto 1983, Symphony in two movements 1985, On Taoism for orchestra 1985, Traces for piano 1989, Eight Colours for string quartet 1989, Silk Road for soprano and percussion 1989, Orchestral Theatre I: Xun 1990, Soundshape 1990, Silent Earth 1991, Elegy: Snow in June 1991, Jo-Ha-Kyu 1992, Death and Fire: Dialogue with Paul Klee 1992, Orchestral Theatre II: Re 1992, CAGE for piano 1993, Circle for four trios, conductor and audience 1993, The Pink 1993, Autumn Winds for instruments and conductor ad lib 1993, Memorial Nineteen for voice, piano and double paper 1993, Orchestral Theatre III: Red 1993, Yi concerto for cello 1994, Ghost Opera 1994, Marco Polo 1995, A Sinking Love 1995, Heaven, Earth, Mankind symphony for the 'Bian Zhong' bronze bells (composed in celebration of the Hong Kong handover) 1997, Concerto for Six 1997, Heaven Earth Mankind 1997, Peony Pavilion 1998, 2000 Today: A World Symphony for the Millennium: A Musical Odyssey for the Ages 1999, Water Passion after St Matthew 2000, Crouching Tiger Concerto 2000, The Map concerto for cello, video and orchestra 2003, Eight Memories in Watercolor 2003, Secret Land: for Orchestra and 12 Violoncelli 2004; opera: Out of Beijing 1987, Nine Songs 1989, Marco Polo 1994, Peony Pavilion 1998, Tea 2002, Eight Memories in Watercolor 2003, The First Emperor (opera score, libretto co-writer) 2006. *Leisure interests:* painting in ink, calligraphy. *Address:* 367 W 19th Street, Suite A, New York, NY 10011, USA (office). *Telephone:* (212) 627-0410 (office). *Fax:* (917) 606-0247 (office). *E-mail:* tan_dun@hotmail.com (office). *Website:* www.tandunonline.com (office); www.youtube.com/tandun (office).

TAN, Kim, BSc, PhD; Malaysian biotechnology entrepreneur; *Chairman, Spring-Hill Management Ltd;* Chair. Spring Hill Man. Ltd, Fund Man. Spring Hill Bioventures Sdn Bhd; Dir (non-exec.) Active Capital Investment Trust. *Publications include:* over 40 scientific pubs. *Address:* SpringHill Management, PO Box 822, Guildford, Surrey, GU5 0ZR, England (office). *Telephone:* (1483) 890574 (office). *Fax:* (1483) 894333 (office). *E-mail:* info@springhilluk.com (office). *Website:* www.springhilluk.com (office).

TAN, Lucio C., BS; Philippine business executive; *Chairman and CEO, Philippine Airlines Inc.;* b. 17 July 1934, Amoy, Fujian province, China; m.; six c.; ed Far Eastern Univ., Manila; f. Fortune Tobacco 1966; f. Asian Breweries 1970s; acquired Allied Banking Corpn 1977; Chair. and CEO Philippine Airlines Inc. 1995–; acquired Philippine National Bank, other cos under Lucio Tan Group of Cos include Foremost Farms Inc., Shareholdings Inc. *Address:* Philippine Airlines Inc., PAL Corporate Communications Department, PAL Center, Ground Floor, Legazpi Street, Legaspi Village, Makati City, Metro Manila, 0750, The Philippines (office). *Telephone:* (2) 8171234 (office). *Fax:* (2) 8136715 (office). *E-mail:* rgeccd@pal.com.ph (office). *Website:* www.philippineairlines.com (office).

TAN, Melvyn, FRCM; British concert pianist; b. 13 Oct. 1956, Singapore; s. of Tan Keng Hian and Wong Sou Yuen; ed Anglo-Chinese School, Yehudi Menuhin School, Royal Coll. of Music, London; has been performing on concert stage since early 1980s; following graduation, made a name performing on historical instruments, culminating in original recordings of Beethoven sonatas for EMI and a tour on Beethoven's own piano in Europe and UK; has devoted time to extending repertoire and returned to the modern piano to explore later and contemporary repertoire 1995–; tours regularly and extensively in Europe, Australia, the Far East and USA; has performed in most major venues and music festivals world-wide; returned to Singapore after a self-imposed exile of nearly 32 years for a homecoming concert 2011, continues to visit Singapore regularly to perform and encourage young musical talent; Artist-in-Residence, Yong Siew Toh Conservatory of Music, Singapore. *Recordings include:* Debussy Préludes 2005, Beethoven Complete Piano Concertos with London Classical Players under Sir Roger Norrington, Beethoven and Schubert piano works, Mozart Piano Concert K414, Beethoven Concerto No. 2 with London Chamber Orchestra directing from keyboard. *Television:* featured extensively on the BBC soundtrack of Pride and Prejudice with music by Carl Davis. *Leisure interests:* keeping fit, good cuisine and being able to visit places without having to perform. *Telephone:* 7919-138428 (mobile) (office). *E-mail:* dtoennesmann@gmail.com (office). *Website:* www.msbuhl .com (office); www.melvyntan.com.

TAN, Royston; Singaporean filmmaker; ed Temasek Polytechnic; writer and dir of numerous short films and one feature film 1999–; work has been showcased at over 20 int. film festivals; ASEAN Dir of the Year Award 2001, Young Artist of the Year, Singapore Nat. Arts Council 2002, Asia's Most Promising Talents, Netpac Jury 2003. *Films:* short films: Sons (Best Short Film, Singapore Int. Film Festival 2000) 1999, Hock hiap leong (Merit Award, Tampere Int. Film Festival) 2001, Mother (Voice Award, Singapore Shorts Film Festival) 2001, 24 Hours 2002, 4A Florence Close, AIDS documentary for Channel News Asia; feature film: 15 (Netpac-Frespesci Award, Singapore Int. Film Festival) 2003. *Address:* c/o The Substation, 45 Armenian Street, 179936 Singapore (office).

TAN, Tan Sri Dato' Seri Vincent; Malaysian entrepreneur; *Chairman and CEO, Berjaya Corporation Berhad;* b. (Tan Chee Yioun), 1952; m.; 11 c.; family originated from Yongchun Pref., Fujian Prov., China; began career as McDonald's franchisee; acquired major controlling stake in share capital of Berjaya Kawat Berhad, currently Chair. and CEO Berjaya Corpn Berhad, businesses include golfing, property, resorts and gambling; operates MiTV, pay-TV service in Malaysia launched 2005; acquired controlling share in Cardiff City Football Club 2010; Co-owner 289-foot yacht, Asean Lady. *Leisure interest:* scuba diving. *Address:* Berjaya Corporation Berhad, Lot 13-01A, Level 13 (East Wing), Berjaya Times Square, No. 1 Jalan Imbi, 55100 Kuala Lumpur, Malaysia (office). *Telephone:* (3) 2149-1999 (office). *Fax:* (3) 2143-1685 (office). *E-mail:* info@berjaya.com.my (office). *Website:* www.berjaya.com (office).

TAN, Yuan Yuan; Chinese ballet dancer; b. 1976, Shanghai; ed Shanghai Dancing School, John Cranko School, Stuttgart, Germany; enrolled Shanghai Dance School 1987; briefly studied in Stuttgart, Germany; joined San Francisco Ballet as a soloist 1995, promoted to Prin. Ballerina 1997; Guest Prin. Dancer,

Hong Kong Ballet May 2008; Silver Medal, Jr Female Div., Second Int. Ballet Competition, Helsinki 1991, Gold Medal, Jr Female Div., 5th Int. Ballet Competition, Paris 1992, Gold Medal, Jr Female Classical Div. and Nijinsky Award, 1st Japan Int. Ballet and Modern Dance Competition 1993, MOVADO Award for Outstanding Contrib. to Arts and Culture in China 1998, named by Dance magazine as one of Top 100 Elite Dancers of the 20th Century 2000, World Journal Outstanding Youth Award 2003, honoured by Time magazine (Asia edn) as one of Asia's Heroes 20 Under 40 2004, The Bund magazine City of Heart award, Shanghai 2007. *Ballet roles:* Giselle in Giselle (Tomasson), Juliet in Romeo & Juliet (Tomasson), Odette/Odile in Swan Lake (Tomasson), Kitri in Don Quixote (Tomasson/Possokhov), Nanna in Nanna's Lied (Tomasson), cr. role in 7 for Eight (Tomasson), Aurora, Lilac Fairy, and Enchanted Princess in The Sleeping Beauty (Tomasson), cr. lead role in Sylvia (Morris), Desdemona in Othello (Lubovitch), Sugar Plum Fairy and Snow Queen in Nutcracker (Christensen/Tomasson), cr. title role in Chi-Lin, cr. prin. role in Silver Ladders, cr. pas de deux in Pandora Dance, Schoenberg variation prin. in Criss-Cross, pas de deux and second movt prin. in Prism, pas de trois in Tuning Game, Prin. in Handel – a Celebration, Valses Poeticos, and Beads of Memory (Tomasson), second movt prin. in Symphony in C, Angel and Waltz Couple in Serenade, fourth movt prin. in Western Symphony, Prin. in Theme and Variations, Prin. and Soloist in Concerto Barocco, demi-soloist in Ballo Delia Regina, Aria II in Stravinsky Violin Concerto, Siren in Prodigal Son and Prin. in Bugaku, pas de deux in Emeralds, soloist in Rubies, Terpsichore in Apollo, second aria in Stravinsky Violin Concerto, and Prin. in Diamonds (Balanchine), Maninyas, La Cathedrale Engloutie, Spirit in Taiko, and cr. prin. role in Tu Tu (Welch), Thais Pas de Deux (Ashton), cr. role in Continuum and Polyphonia (Wheeldon), cr. role of Princess in Damned (Possokhov), cr. role in Study in Motion (Possokhov), The Waltz Project (Martins), Prin. in Raymonda, Act III (Nureyev after Petipa), Elite Syncopations (MacMillan), La Esmeralda pas de deux (Perrot), first and second pas de deux in Without Words (Duato), Italian Ballerina in Gala Performance (Tudor), Prin. in Etudes (Lander), Prin. and Soloist in Glass Pieces, Mauve and Pink in Dances at a Gathering, and first pas de deux in In the Night (Bobbins), Prin. in Paquita and Nikiya and third variation in La Bayadere, Act II (Makarova after Petipa), cr. prin. role in Magrittomania (Possokhov), Angelo (Adam), Grand Pas Classique (Gsovsky). *Address:* Hong Kong Ballet, G/F 60 Blue Pool Road, Happy Valley, Hong Kong Special Administrative Region, People's Republic of China (office). *Website:* www .hkballet.com (office).

TAN KENG YAM, Tony, PhD; Singaporean academic, banker, government official, business executive and head of state; *President;* b. 7 Feb. 1940, Singapore; s. of the late Tan Seng Hwee and of Lim Neo Swee; m. Mary Chee Bee Kiang 1964; four c.; ed St Patrick's School, St Joseph's Inst., Univ. of Singapore, Mass. Inst. of Tech., USA and Univ. of Adelaide, Australia; Lecturer in Math., Univ. of Singapore 1967–69; Sub-Man. Overseas Chinese Banking Corpn 1969, Gen. Man. 1978; MP 1979–; Sr Minister of State (Educ.) 1979; Minister of Educ. 1980, concurrently Vice-Chancellor, Nat. Univ. of Singapore; Minister for Trade and Industry, concurrently Minister in charge of Nat. Univ. of Singapore and Nanyang Tech. Inst. 1981–83; Minister of Finance 1983–85, of Educ. and Health Jan.–April 1985, for Trade and Industry 1985–86, of Educ. 1985–91; Chair. People's Action Party Cen. Exec. Cttee 1993; Chair. and CEO Oversea-Chinese Banking Corpn Ltd 1992; Deputy Prime Minister of Singapore Aug. 1995–, concurrently Minister of Defence 1995–2003, Coordinating Minister for Security and Defence 2003–05; Pres. of Singapore 2011–; Dir. Singapore Press Holdings Ltd 2005–, currently Chair.; Deputy Chair. and Exec. Dir Govt of Singapore Investment Corpn Pte Ltd (GIC); Chair. Nat. Research Foundation; Deputy Chair. Research, Innovation and Enterprise Council; Chair. Ministry of Educ.'s Int. Academic Advisory Panel. *Leisure interests:* swimming, golf and walking. *Address:* Office of the President, The Istana, Orchard Rd, Singapore 238823, Singapore (office). *E-mail:* istana_general_office@istana.gov.sg (office). *Website:* www.istana.gov.sg (office).

TANAI, Shahnawaz; Afghan politician and fmr army general; *Leader, Da Afghanistan Da Solay Ghorzang Gond (Afghanistan Peace Movement);* b. 1950, Dargai, Khost Prov.; m.; two s. one d.; apptd Chief of Mil. Intelligence 1978, served as Chief of Army Staff and Minister of Defence in Soviet-backed Democratic Repub. of Afghanistan 1988–90; led mil. coup against Pres. Mohammad Najibullah 1990, after failure of coup went into exile in Pakistan 1990–2005; returned to Afghanistan 2005 as Leader, Da Afghanistan Da Solay Ghorzang Gond (Afghanistan Peace Movt). *Address:* Da Afghanistan Da Solay Ghorzang Gond (Afghanistan Peace Movement), Kolola Poshta (adjacent to Dost Hotel), Kabul, Afghanistan (office).

TANAKA, Hisao, BEcons; Japanese business executive; *Representative Executive Officer, President and CEO, Toshiba Corporation;* b. 20 Dec. 1950; ed Kobe Univ. of Commerce; joined Toshiba Corpn 1973, Sr Vice-Pres., Toshiba Information Equipment (Philippines) Corpn 1996–2000, Gen. Man. and Deputy Man. Dir Toshiba (UK) Co. Ltd 2000–01, Toshiba Information Systems (UK) Ltd 2001–02, Gen. Man., Procurement Div., Digital Media & Network Co. 2002–04, Gen. Man., Procurement Div., PC & Network Co. 2004–05, Chief Production Exec., PC & Network Co. 2005–06, Exec. Vice-Pres. and Chief Production Exec. April–June 2006, Officer, Corp. Vice-Pres., Exec. Vice-Pres. and Chief Production Exec. 2006–07, Exec. Officer, Vice-Pres., Man., Corp. Procurement Div. 2007–08, Exec. Officer, Corp. Sr Vice-Pres., Gen. Man., Procurement Group 2008–09, Exec. Officer, Corp. Exec. Vice-Pres., Gen. Exec., Procurement & Logistics Group 2009–11, Dir, Rep. Exec. Officer, Corp. Sr Exec. Vice-Pres., Gen. Exec., Quality Div., Procurement & Logistics Group, Productivity & Environment Group 2011–12, Dir, Rep. Exec. Officer, Corp. Sr Exec. Vice-Pres., Gen. Exec., Strategic Planning & Communications Group, Procurement & Logistics Group, Productivity & Environment Group 2012–13, Dir, Rep. Exec. Officer, Pres. and CEO Toshiba Corpn 2013–. *Address:* Toshiba Corpn, 1-1, Shibaura 1-chome, Minato-ku, Tokyo 105-8001, Japan (office). *Telephone:* (3) 3457-4511 (office). *Fax:* (3) 3455-1631 (office). *E-mail:* info@toshiba.co.jp (office). *Website:* www.toshiba.co.jp (office).

TANAKA, Koichi, BEng; Japanese chemist; *Assistant Manager, Life Science Laboratory, Shimadzu Corporation;* b. 3 Aug. 1959, Toyama City; ed Tohoku Univ.; joined Cen. Research Lab., Shimadzu Corpn 1983, seconded to subsidiary Kratos Group PLC, UK 1992, joined R&D Dept of Analytical Instruments Div., Japan 1992, seconded to Shimadzu Research Lab. (Europe) Ltd, UK 1997,

seconded to Kratos Group PLC, UK 1999, Asst Man. Life Science Lab., Shimadzu Corpn, Kyoto 2002–; Nobel Prize in Chemistry (co-recipient) 2002. *Address:* Shimadzu Corporation, 1 Nishinkyo Kuwabaracho, Nakagyou-ku, Kyoto 604-8511, Japan (office). *Website:* www.shimadzu.com (office).

TANAKA, Makiko; Japanese politician; b. 14 Jan. 1944; d. of Kakuei Tanaka (fmr Prime Minister of Japan); m. Naoki Tanaka; ed Waseda Univ.; fmr Deputy Dir-Gen. LDP Int. Bureau; Minister of State, Dir-Gen. Science and Tech. Agency 1994–95; Ministry of Foreign Affairs 2001–02; mem. House of Reps for Nigata –2002 (resgnd), 2003–12; Minister of Education, Culture, Sports, Science and Technology Oct.–Dec. 2012; mem. House Cttee on Health and Welfare; mem. Democratic Party of Japan 2009–. *Address:* Democratic Party of Japan, 1-11-1, Nagata-cho, Chiyoda-ku, Tokyo 100-0014, Japan (office). *Telephone:* (3) 3595-9988 (office). *Fax:* (3) 3595-9961 (office). *E-mail:* dpjenews@dpj.or.jp (office). *Website:* www.dpj.or.jp (office).

TANAKA, Naoki; Japanese politician; b. (Naoki Suzuki), 19 June 1940, Kanazawa, Ishikawa; m. Makiko Tanaka; mem. House of Reps 1983–96, House of Councillors from Niigata Pref. 1998–; Minister of Defence Jan.–June 2012; mem. Democratic Party of Japan. *Address:* Democratic Party of Japan, 1-11-1, Nagata-cho, Chiyoda-ku, Tokyo 100-0014, Japan (office). *Telephone:* (3) 3595-9988 (office). *Fax:* (3) 3595-9961 (office). *E-mail:* dpjenews@dpj.or.jp (office). *Website:* www.dpj .or.jp (office); www.naoki-tanaka.jp.

TANAKA, Nobuo, MBA; Japanese international organization official; *Global Associate for Energy, Security and Sustainability, Institute of Energy Economics;* b. 3 March 1950; m. Gloria Tanaka; two c.; ed Univ. of Tokyo, Case Western Reserve Univ., Ohio, USA; began career with Ministry of Economy, Trade and Industry (METI) 1973, held posts including Deputy Dir Gen. Affairs Div., Machinery and Information Industries Bureau, Personnel Div., Dir of Int. Nuclear Energy Affairs, Natural Resources and Energy Agency, Dir for Industrial Finance Div. and Dir for Policy Planning and Coordination Div. 1995–98, Dir-Gen. Multilateral Trade System Dept 2002–04; Deputy Dir for Science, Tech. and Industry, OECD 1989–91, Dir for Science, Tech. and Industry 1991–95, 2004–07, also Head Steering Group of Centre for Entrepreneurship 2004–07; Minister for Energy, Trade and Industry, Embassy in Washington, DC 1998–2000; Exec. Vice-Pres. Research Inst. of Economy Trade and Industry, Japan 2000–02; Exec. Dir IEA 2007–11; Global Assoc. for Energy Security and Sustainability, Inst. of Energy Economics 2011–. *Address:* Institute of Energy Economics, Inui Kachidoki Building, 1-13-1 Kachidoki, Chuo-ku, Tokyo 104-0054, Japan (office). *Telephone:* (3) 5547-0222 (office). *Fax:* (3) 5547-0223 (office). *Website:* www.eneken.ieej.or.jp (office).

TANAKA, Shoji, PhD; Japanese scientist and academic; *Professor Emeritus, University of Tokyo;* b. 19 Sept. 1927, Odawara, Kanagawa; m. Kimiko Tanaka 1956; one s.; ed Univ. of Tokyo; Lecturer, Faculty of Eng, Univ. of Tokyo 1955–58, Assoc. Prof. 1958–68, Prof. 1968–88, Prof. Emer. 1988–; Prof., Tokai Univ. 1988–93; Vice-Pres. Int. Superconductivity Tech. Center (ISTEC) 1988–2008, Advisor 2008–; Dir Superconductivity Research Lab. 1988–2008, Advisor 2008–; Consultant Prof., Shanghai Univ., People's Repub. of China; Order of Merit of the Rising Sun (Third Class) 1999; Hon. DSc (Purdue Univ., USA) 1999; Purple Ribbon Medal 1990 and other awards. *Publications:* Research of Semiconductor Physics 1950–75, Research of Superconductivity 1975, High-Temperature Superconductivity 1991, Industry Technology are the World of the Future 1994. *Leisure interests:* golf, reading. *Address:* Superconductivity Research Laboratory, 1-10-13, Shinonome, Koto-ku, Tokyo 135-0062 (office); 2-5-26, Ichigaya kaga-cho, Shinjuku-ku, Tokyo 162-0062, Japan (home). *Telephone:* (3) 3536-5700 (office); (3) 3260-5500 (home). *Fax:* (3) 3536-5717 (office); (3) 3260-9398 (home). *E-mail:* tanaka@istec.or .jp (office). *Website:* www.istec.or.jp (office).

TANAKA, Takashi; Japanese business executive; *General Manager, Corporate & Marketing Communications Sector and President, KDDI Corporation;* b. 26 Feb. 1957; mem. Bd of Dirs, Assoc. Sr Vice-Pres., Gen. Man., Solution Business Sector, KDDI Corpn 2007–10, Assoc. Sr Vice-Pres., Solution Business, Consumer Business, and Product Devt Sector April–June 2010, Sr Vice-Pres. June–Dec. 2010, Pres. KDDI Corpn Dec. 2010–13, Gen. Man. Corp. & Marketing Communications Sector and Pres. KDDI Corpn 2013–. *Address:* KDDI Corpn, Garden Air Tower, 3-10-10, Iidabashi, Chiyoda-ku, Tokyo 102-8460, Japan (office). *Telephone:* (3) 6678-0692 (office). *Fax:* (3) 6678-0305 (office). *E-mail:* info@kddi.com (office). *Website:* www.kddi.com (office).

TANAKA, Yasuo; Japanese writer and politician; *Leader, New Party Nippon;* b. 1956; ed Univ. of Hitotsubashi; community activist, Kobe, following 1995 earthquake; elected first ind. Gov. of Nagano Pref. 2000–06; mem. House of Councillors for Hyogo 8th Dist 2006– Co-founded New Party Nippon (Shinto Nippon) 2005, Leader 2005–. *Publications:* Nantonaku Kurisutaru (Somehow Crystal, Bungei Prize) 1983. *Address:* New Party Nippon, 1-7-11, Hirakawa-cho, Chiyoda-ku, Tokyo 102-0093, Japan (office). *Telephone:* (3) 5213-0333 (office). *Fax:* (3) 5213-0888 (office). *Website:* www.love-nippon.com (office).

TANAKA, Yoshikazu, BL; Japanese business executive; *Founder and CEO, GREE Inc.;* b. 1977, Mitaka-City, Tokyo; ed Nihon Univ.; worked at So-net Entertainment Corpn and Rakuten, Inc.; while at the latter, began developing SNS GREE in his spare time 2003, opened SNS GREE to the public as a personal website Feb. 2004; Founder, CEO, Pres. and Rep. Dir GREE, Inc. (social network service) Dec. 2004–; mem. Bd of Dirs GREE International, Inc.; ranked by Forbes ASIA as Asia's Youngest Self-Made Billionaire under the age of 35 2010, selected as the World's Second-Youngest Self-Made Billionaire after Mark Zuckerberg 2010, youngest founder whose company is listed on the TSE first section 2010. *Address:* GREE, Inc., Roppongi Hills Mori Tower, 6-10-1 Roppongi, Minato-ku, Tokyo 106-6151, Japan (office). *E-mail:* pr@gree.co.jp (office); inquiry@gree-corp .com (office). *Website:* www.gree.jp (office); www.gree.co.jp/en (office); www.gree -corp.com (office).

TANASESCU, Mihai Nicolae; Romanian politician; b. 11 Jan. 1956, Bucharest; m.; two c.; ed Acad. of Econ. Studies, Bucharest, Int. Inst. for Public Admin, Paris, France, Int. Monetary Fund Inst., Vienna, Austria, Harvard Business School, USA; Head of Accounting Dept, ICRAL (Constructions, Repairs and Locative Admin Enterprise), Bucharest 1978–83; Exec., Dept for State Incomes, Ministry of

Finance 1990–92, Dept for the State Budget 1992–93, Dept for Public Debt 1993–97; Alt. Exec. Chair. IBRD for group of 12 East European countries, Washington, DC 1997–2000; Minister of Public Finance 2000–04. *Publications:* scientific research papers on econs, financial analysis and forecasting in Romanian and foreign journals. *Address:* c/o Ministry of Public Finance, Str. Apolodor 17, 70663 Bucharest, Romania (office). *Telephone:* (21) 4103400 (office). *Fax:* (21) 3122077 (office).

TANAYEV, Nikolai Timofeyevich; Kyrgyzstani politician; b. 5 Nov. 1945, Penza Oblast, Russia; ed Dzhambul Hydroengineering Inst. (Kazakh SSR); Head of Osh Regional Water Canal Directorate 1984; Head of Chuipromstroi (Chui Industrial Construction) Trust 1985; apptd Chair. State Agency on Architecture and Construction 2000; fmr First Deputy Prime Minister 2001; Head of Special Comm. investigating deaths of demonstrators shot by police March 2002; Acting Prime Minister of Kyrgyzstan May 2002, Prime Minister 2002–05. *Address:* c/o Office of the Prime Minister, 720003 Bishkek, Dom Pravitelstva, Kyrgyzstan (office).

TANCOCK, Liam John; British swimmer; b. 7 May 1985, Exeter, Devon; s. of Tony Tancock and Kim Tancock; pnr Caitlin McClatchey; ed St Luke's High School, Exeter, Loughborough Univ.; began swimming career at Exeter City Swimming Club and continued at Loughborough Univ.; Summer Universiade, Izmir 2005: gold medal, 50m backstroke; World Championships (long course), Montreal 2005: bronze medal, 50m backstroke, Melbourne 2007: bronze medal, 50m backstroke, 100m backstroke, Rome 2009: gold medal, 50m backstroke, Shanghai 2011: gold medal, 50m backstroke; World Championships (short course), Manchester 2008: gold medal, 100m backstroke, silver medal, 50m backstroke, 200m medley, bronze medal, 100m medley; European Championships (long course), Budapest 2006: bronze medal, 4×100m medley, Budapest 2010: silver medal, 50m backstroke, bronze medal, 100m backstroke; European Championships (short course), Trieste 2005: bronze medal, 50m backstroke, 4×50m medley, 4×50m freestyle; Commonwealth Games (competing for England), Melbourne 2006: gold medal, 100m backstroke, silver medal, 50m backstroke, 4×100m medley, Delhi 2010: gold medal, 50m backstroke, 100m backstroke, silver medal, 4×100m freestyle, bronze medal, 4×100m medley); swims for Loughborough Univ. SC; coaches: Jon Randall 1995–2002, Ben Titley 2003–. *Leisure interests:* sports, cinema. *Address:* c/o Ian Armiger, Director of Swimming, Loughborough Swimming, Loughborough, Leics., LE11 3TU, England. *Telephone:* (1509) 226206. *E-mail:* i.c.armiger@lboro.ac.uk. *Website:* www.loughboroughswimming.com; www.liamtancock.com.

TANDJA, Col Mamadou; Niger army officer (retd) and fmr head of state; b. 1938, Maine-Soroa; m.; 10 c.; participated in mil. junta that ousted Pres. Diori 1974, apptd mem. Supreme Mil. Council; Prefect of Maradi region 1976–79; Minister of the Interior 1979–81, 1990–91; Prefect of Tahoua region 1981–88; Amb. to Nigeria 1988–90; Chair. Mouvement national pour la société de développement—Nassara 1991–; Pres. of Niger 1999–2010 (ousted in coup 18 Feb.); fmr Chair. Econ. Community of West African States. *Address:* c/o Mouvement national pour la société de développement—Nassara (MNSD—Nassara), rue Issa Beri 30, cnr blvd de Zarmaganda, porte 72, BP 881, Niamey, Niger (office).

TANDJUNG, Akbar; Indonesian politician; b. 14 Aug. 1945, Sibolga, N Sumatera; m. R.A. Krissnina Maharani; four c.; ed Univ. of Indonesia; mem. Functional Devt Faction, House of Reps 1977–88, Deputy Chair. 1997–, Speaker House of Reps 1999–2004; State Minister for Youth and Sports 1988–93, for People's Housing 1988–98, for People's Housing and Settlement 1998, Minister State Sec. 1998; found guilty of embezzling state funds Sept. 2002, conviction dismissed Feb. 2004; mem. People's Consultative Ass. 1992–97; Chair. Cen. Bd Golkar Party 1998–2004; Mahaputra Adiprandana Star. *Leisure interest:* swimming. *Address:* c/o House of Representatives, Jalan Gatot Subroto 16, Jakarta, Indonesia (office).

TANG, Ching W., BS, PhD; American scientist and academic; *Doris Johns Cherry Professor of Chemical Engineering and Professor of Chemistry, University of Rochester;* ed Univ. of British Columbia, Canada, Cornell Univ.; joined Eastman Kodak as Research Scientist 1975, Sr Research Scientist 1981–90, Research Assoc. 1990–98, Sr Research Assoc. 1998–2003, Distinguished Fellow, Kodak Research Laboratories, Eastman Kodak Co. 2003; Doris Johns Cherry Prof. of Chemical Eng, Univ. of Rochester 1996–, jt appointments in Dept of Chem. and Dept of Physics and Astronomy, Chair. Chemical Eng Dept 2011–; mem. Nat. Acad. of Eng 2006; Fellow, American Physical Soc. 1998, Soc. for Information Display 2002; Hon. Prof., Shanghai Univ. 2002, South China Univ. of Tech. 2002; Dr hc (Shanghai Univ., South China Univ. of Tech.); numerous awards, including Eastman Kodak Distinguished Inventor 1994, Eastman Kodak Team Achievement Award 1999, Eastman Kodak Innovation Award 2000, Jack Rajchman Prize, Soc. of Information Display 2001, ACS Carothers Award 2001, ACS Northeast Regional Innovation Award 2001, Rochester Law Asscn Inventor of the Year Award 2002, ACS Award for Team Innovation 2003, Humboldt Research Award 2005, Lifetime Achievement Award, Hajim School of Eng and Applied Sciences, Univ. of Rochester 2010, Wolf Prize in Chem. (co-recipient) 2011, Eduard Rhein Award 2013. *Achievements include:* recognized for invention of high-efficiency Organic Light Emitting Diodes (OLED). *Publications:* numerous papers in professional journals on chemical and condensed matter physics and, in particular, on organic electronics. *Address:* Department of Chemical Engineering, 206 Gavett Hall, RC 270166, University of Rochester, Rochester, NY 14627-0166, USA (office). *Telephone:* (585) 275-3552 (office). *Fax:* (585) 273-3237 (office). *E-mail:* chtang@ chem.rochester.edu (office); ching.tang@rochester.edu (office). *Website:* www.chem .rochester.edu/faculty/faculty.php?name=tang (office).

TANG, Dengjie, MBA; Chinese engineer and business executive; *President, China South Industries Group Corporation;* b. 1964, Jianhu Co., Jiangsu Prov.; ed Tongji Univ.; Vice-Mayor of Shanghai Municipality 2003–; served successively as Head of Control Section and Man. of Industrial Eng Section of Production Project Dept, Shanghai Volkswagen Automotive Co. Ltd, Deputy Man. of Project and Devt Dept, Shanghai Automotive Industry General Co. (Group), Gen. Man. Shanghai ZF Steering Co. Ltd, Vice-Pres. Shanghai Automotive Industry Co. (Group), Deputy Party Sec. and Pres. Shanghai Electrical General Co. (Group), Deputy Party Sec. Shanghai Party Work Cttee for Industry and Dir of Shanghai Econ.

Comm.; Pres. China South Industries Group Corpn 2012–. *Address:* China South Industries Group Corpn, 10 Chedaogou, 69 Zizhuyuan Road, Haidian District, Beijing 100089, People's Republic of China (office). *Telephone:* (10) 68963764 (office). *Fax:* (10) 68963765 (office). *E-mail:* info@chinasouth.com.cn (office). *Website:* www.csgc.com.cn (office); www.chinasouth.com.cn (office).

TANG, Gen. Fei; Taiwanese politician and air force officer (retd) and government official; b. 15 March 1932, Jiangsu; m. Chang, Ming-tsan; one s. two d.; ed Air Force Preparatory School, Chinese Air Force Acad.; air force pilot 1953–60, Operations Officer 1960–61, Flight Leader 1961–65, Squadron Commdr 1968–72, Asst Air Attaché, Embassy in USA 1972–75, Chief, Operations Section, 3rd Wing 1975–76, Group Commdr 1976–78, Mil. Attaché, Embassy in S. Africa 1979–83, Wing Commdr 1983–84, C/S/Planning, GHQ, ROCAF 1984–85, Supt, Air Force Acad. 1985–86, Dir, Political Warfare Dept, GHQ, ROCAF 1986–89, CG, Combat Air Commdr 1989, Vice C-in-C ROCAF 1989–91, Insp.-Gen., MND 1991–92, C-in-C ROCAF 1992–95, Vice Chief of Gen. Staff (Exec.), MND 1995–98, Chief of Gen. Staff, MND 1998–99, Gen., ROCAF (retd); Minister of Defence 1999–2000; Premier of Taiwan 2000; Sr Adviser to Pres. 2000; Visiting Fellow, Hoover Inst., Stanford Univ. 2004.

TANG, Ignacio Milam; Equatorial Guinean politician and diplomatist; *Vice-President, in charge of Presidential Affairs;* b. 1940; Minister of Justice and Worship 1996–98, of Youth and Sports 1998–99; fmr Second Vice-Pres. Chamber of People's Reps 1999–2001; Deputy Prime Minister for the Civil Service and Admin. Coordination 2001–03; Sec.-Gen. of the Presidency 2003–06; Amb. to Spain 2006–08; Prime Minister 2008–12; Vice-Pres., in charge of Presidential Affairs 2012–; mem. Democratic Party of Equatorial Guinea. *Address:* Office of the Vice-President, Malabo, Equatorial Guinea (office).

TANG, Jiaxuan; Chinese diplomatist; *President, China-Japan Friendship Association;* b. Jan. 1938, Zhenjiang City, Jiangsu Prov.; ed Fudan Univ., Shanghai, Peking Univ.; intern, State Broadcasting Admin 1962; staff mem., Translation and Interpretation Dept, Ministry of Foreign Affairs 1964–70; mem. Council and Deputy Div. Chief Chinese People's Asscn for Friendship with Foreign Countries 1970–78; mem. Council Sino-Japanese Friendship Asscn 1970–78; joined CCP 1973; Second Sec., then First Sec. Embassy, Tokyo, Japan 1978–83, Minister-Counsellor 1988–91, Minister 1988–91; First Secretary, then Deputy Dir Asian Affairs Dept, Ministry of Foreign Affairs 1983–88; Asst to Minister of Foreign Affairs 1991–93, Vice-Minister 1993–98, Minister 1998–2003; State Councillor 2003–08; mem. 15th CCP Cen. Cttee 1997–2002, 16th CCP Cen. Cttee 2002–07; currently Pres. China-Japan Friendship Asscn. *Publication:* Heavy Storm & Gentle Breeze: A Memoir of China's Diplomacy 2011. *Address:* China-Japan Friendship Association, No.1, Taijichang Avenue, Dongcheng District, Beijing, People's Republic of China (office). *E-mail:* office@zryx.org.cn (office). *Website:* www.zryx.org.cn (office).

TANG, Shubei; Chinese government official; b. Jan. 1931, Shanghai; m. Liang Wenfeng; one s. one d.; joined CCP 1949; fmrly official Shanghai Fed. of Trade Unions; Ed., Head of Reporters Cttee, Fujian Daily 1955; Chief, Editorial Dept, New Vietnamese-Chinese News 1955–57; Sec., then Deputy Dir, Dir China News Service 1957–69; Deputy Div. Chief Dept of Consular Affairs 1971–78; First Sec. Tokyo Embassy 1978–82; Div. Chief Dept of Consular Affairs 1982–83; Consul-Gen., San Francisco 1983–86; Amb. to USA 1986–88; Dir Office for Taiwan Affairs of Foreign Ministry 1988–89, Deputy Dir for Taiwan Affairs of State Council 1989–2000; Deputy Dir CCP Cen. Cttee Taiwan Affairs Office 1991–; Exec. Vice-Chair. Asscn for Relations Across the Taiwan Straits 1991–2000; Deputy Dir CPPCC Cen. Cttee Coordinating Cttee for Reunification of the Motherland 1993–98; mem. Standing Cttee 8th CPPCC Nat. Cttee 1993–98, 9th CPPCC Nat. Cttee 1998–2003, Vice-Chair. CPPCC Sub-cttee for Hong Kong, Macao and Taiwan Compatriots and Overseas Chinese 1998–2003; mem. Hong Kong Special Admin. Region Preparatory Cttee 1995–97. *Address:* Office for Taiwanese Affairs, c/o State Council, Beijing, People's Republic of China (office). *Telephone:* (10) 68332419 (office). *Fax:* (10) 68332824 (office).

TANG, Gen. Tianbiao; Chinese army officer; b. Oct. 1940, Shimen Co., Hunan Prov.; ed Harbin Inst. of Mil. Eng, Inst. of PLA Engineer Corps, Propaganda and Theoretical Cadre Training Course of CCP Cen. Cttee Party School and Univ. of Nat. Defence; joined CCP 1961; held various posts in Guangzhou Mil. Region; Deputy Dir Propaganda Dept Guangzhou Mil. Region 1983; Deputy Office Head and Deputy Dir Cadre Dept of PLA Gen. Political Dept; Deputy Dir PLA Navy's Political Dept; Dir Cadre Dept of Gen. Political Dept; Deputy Dir Leading Group for the Placement of Demobilized Army Officers 1993–; Asst Dir PLA Gen. Political Dept 1993–95, Deputy Dir 1995–; rank of Lt-Gen. 1994, Gen. 2000; Deputy to 8th NPC 1993–98; mem. 15th CCP Cen. Cttee 1997–2002, 16th CCP Cen. Cttee 2002–07. *Address:* c/o Ministry of National Defence, Jingshanqian Jie, Beijing, People's Republic of China (office). *Telephone:* (10) 6370000 (office).

TANG, Xiaowei; Chinese physicist; b. Oct. 1931, Wuxi Co., Jiangsu Prov.; ed Tsinghua Univ., Beijing; Researcher, later Prof. Inst. of High Energy Physics, Beijing (IHEP) 1981–; Prof. Zhejiang Univ., Univ. of Science and Tech. of China (USTC); mem. Dept Math. and Physics, Academia Sinica 1985–; Del. 12th and 13th CCP Nat. Congress; mem. Chinese Acad. of Sciences 1980–; Nat. Scientific Prize of China. *Publications:* author or co-author of more than 400 papers. *Address:* Institute of High Energy Physics (IHEP), POB 918, Beijing 100039, People's Republic of China (office).

TANG, Yiau-Ming, BSc; Taiwanese army officer (retd) and government official; b. 29 Nov. 1938; m. Liu, Hsiu; two s. one d.; ed Mil. Acad., Army Command and Gen. Staff Coll., Armed Forces Univ., Armed Forces War Coll., Armed Forces Univ.; Div. Commdr in army 1984–86, Corps Commdr 1988–90, Deputy Field Army Commdr 1990–93, Field Army Commdr 1993–95, Deputy C-in-C 1995–96, C-in-C 1996–99; Chief of Gen. Staff, Ministry of Nat. Defense 1999–2002; Minister of Nat. Defence 2002–04; Sr Adviser to Pres. 2004. *Address:* c/o Office of the President, 122 Chungking South Road, Sec. 1, Taipei 100, Taiwan (office).

TANG, Yuanyou; Chinese business executive; currently Man. Dir Henan Coal and Chemical Industry Group Co. Ltd. *Address:* Henan Coal and Chemical Industry Group Co. Ltd, Guo Long Mansion, Zhengzhou 450046, Hebei Province,

People's Republic of China (office). *E-mail:* info@hnccgc.com (office). *Website:* www
.hnccgc.com (office).

TANG YING YEN, Henry, JP, GBS; Hong Kong business executive and
government official; b. 6 Sept. 1952, Jiangsu Province, Wuxi City; m. Lisa Kuo;
one s. three d.; ed Univ. of Michigan, USA; Man. Dir Peninsula Knitters Ltd;
Chair. Fed. of Hong Kong Industries 1995–2001; Dir Meadville Ltd; Hong Kong
Affairs Adviser to Chinese Govt; mem. Legis. Council 1991–98; mem. Exec.
Council, Hong Kong Special Admin. Region July 1997–2002, Sec. for Commerce,
Industry and Technology July 2002–Aug. 2003, Financial Sec. Aug. 2003–2007,
Chief Sec. for Admin 2007–11 (resgnd); mem. Selection Cttee for First Govt of
Hong Kong Special Admin. Region, CPPCC Shanghai Cttee, Hong Kong Trade
Devt Council, Liberal Party; Dr hc (Hong Kong Polytechnic Univ.); Hon. DIur (City
Univ. of Hong Kong); Young Industrialist Award 1989, Global Leader for
Tomorrow, World Economic Forum 1993. *Address:* c/o Central Government
Offices, Lower Albert Road, Central, Hong Kong Special Administrative Region,
People's Republic of China.

TANGNEY, Lt.-Gen. (retd) William Patrick, BA, MA; American army officer
(retd) and business executive; *Senior Vice-President for Intelligence, Future
Technologies, Inc.;* b. 7 Oct. 1945, Worcester, Mass.; ed The Citadel, Syracuse
Univ., US Naval Coll.; joined US Army 1968, advanced to rank of Lt.-Gen. 1998;
Operational Staff Officer G-3 Training Div., US Army John F. Kennedy Center for
Mil. Assistance, Fort Bragg 1972–74; Exec. Officer, 2nd Special Forces Bn, 7th
Special Forces Group 1974, 5th Special Forces Group 1981–83; Deputy Asst Chief
of Staff G-3 1983–85; Commdr 3rd Bn 5th Special Forces Group 1985–87; Chief of
Special Forces, US Total Army Personnel Command, Alexandria, Va 1987–88;
Commdr 10th Special Forces Group, Fort Devens, Mass. 1990–92; Commanding
Gen. Special Operations, MacDill Air Force Base, Fla 1993–94; Deputy Com-
manding Gen., Chief of Staff, US Army Special Operations Command, Fort Bragg
1994–95; Commanding Gen. US Army Special Forces Command (Airborne), Fort
Bragg 1995–97, US Army John F. Kennedy Special Warfare Center, Fort Bragg
1996–98; Deputy Commdr in Chief, Special Operations Command, MacDill Air
Force Base, Fla 2000–02 (retd); currently Sr Vice-Pres. for Intelligence, Future
Technologies, Inc.; Distinguished Service Medal, Defense Superior Service Medal
(with Oak Leaf Cluster), Legion of Merit (with Oak Leaf Cluster), Bronze Star
Medal with V Device, Bronze Star Medal (with 2 Oak Leaf Clusters), Defense
Meritorious Service Medal. *Address:* Future Technologies, Inc., 3877 Fairfax Ridge
Road, Suite 110N, Fairfax, VA 22030, USA (office). *Telephone:* (703) 278-0199
(home). *Fax:* (703) 385-0886 (office). *Website:* www.ftechi.com (office).

TANIGAKI, Sadakazu, LLB; Japanese lawyer and politician; *Minister of Justice;*
b. 7 March 1945, Tokyo; ed Univ. of Tokyo; passed Nat. Bar Examination 1979;
Attorney-at-Law 1984; mem. House of Reps (lower house of Parl.) for Kyoto No. 5
constituency (LDP) 1983–, Chair. Standing Cttee on Communications 1991,
Standing Cttee on Rules and Admin 1995; Vice-Minister of Posts and Telecom-
munications 1988, of Defence 1990; Minister of State for Science and Tech. 1997,
State Sec. for Finance 1998; Minister of State for Industrial Revitalization Corpn
2002; Minister of Finance 2003–06, of Land, Infrastructure and Transport 2008, of
Justice 2012–; Chair. Financial Reconstruction Comm. 2000, Nat. Public Safety
Comm. 2002, Food Safety Comm. 2002; Vice-Chair. LDP Nat. Diet Cttee 1987, Dir-
Gen. LDP Election Bureau 1996, Chair. Policy Research Council 2007, LDP Pres.
2009–12. *Leisure interests:* mountaineering, cycling, wine tasting. *Address:*
Ministry of Justice, 1-1-1, Kasumigaseki, Chiyoda-ku, Tokyo 100-8977, Japan
(office). *Telephone:* (3) 3580-4111 (office). *Fax:* (3) 3592-7011 (office). *E-mail:*
webmaster@moj.go.jp (office). *Website:* www.moj.go.jp (office).

TANIGAKI, Sadakazu; Japanese politician; *Minister of Justice;* b. 7 March 1945,
Kyoto; m.; two d.; ed Univ. of Tokyo; first elected to House of Reps 1983; Vice-
Minister for Post and Telecommunications 1988–89, for Defence 1990; Chair. Parl.
Cttee on Communications 1991–93, Rules and Admin 1995–96; Minister for
Science and Tech. 1997–98; State Sec. for Finance 1998–99; Chair. Financial
Reconstruction Comm. 2000; Minister for Food Safety Comm. 2002–03; Chair. Nat.
Public Safety Comm. 2002–03; Minister for Industrial Revitalization Corpn
2002–03, of Finance 2003–06, of Land, Infrastructure, Transport and Tourism,
Ocean Policy 2008–09; mem. LDP, Chief Policymaker 2007–09, Pres. 2009–12;
Minister of Justice 2012–. *Address:* Ministry of Justice, 1-1-1, Kasumigaseki,
Chiyoda-ku, Tokyo 100-8977 (office); Liberal-Democratic Party, 1-11-23, Nagata-
cho, Chiyoda-ku, Tokyo 100-8910, Japan (office). *Telephone:* (3) 3580-4111 (office);
(3) 3581-6211 (office). *Fax:* (3) 3592-7011 (office); (3) 3581-1910 (office). *E-mail:*
webmaster@moj.go.jp (office). *Website:* www.moj.go.jp (office); www.jimin.jp
(office).

TANIGUCHI, Yoshio; Japanese architect; *Principal, Taniguchi and Associates;*
b. 1937, Tokyo; ed Keio Univ., Tokyo, Grad. School of Design, Harvard Univ., USA;
worked in studio of Kenzo Tange 1964–72; Prin. Taniguchi Associates, Tokyo
1979–; has taught architecture at Harvard Univ., UCLA, Univ. of Tokyo.
Achievements include: won competition to design expansion of Museum of Modern
Art, New York 1998, completed 2004. *Address:* Taniguchi and Associates, 4-1-40
Toranomon, Minato-ku, Tokyo 105-8529, Japan. *Telephone:* (3) 3438-1506. *Fax:* (3)
3438-1248.

TANIN, Zahir, MD; Afghan journalist, physician and diplomatist; *Permanent
Representative, United Nations;* b. 1 May 1956; m. Dr Zarghoona Sediq Tanin; two
c.; ed Kabul Medical Univ.; began career as journalist in Kabul 1980; freelance
writer in France 1992–93; fmr Ed.-in-Chief Afkbar-e-Haftah and Sabawoon
Magazine; Research Fellow, Int. Relations Dept, LSE, England 1994–95; Producer, BBC World Service 1995–2000, Sr Producer 2000–01, Ed. Afghanistan and
Cen. Asia (Persian Section) 2001–03, Persian/Pashto Section in Afghanistan
2003–06; Amb. and Perm. Rep. to UN, New York 2006–, apptd Vice-Chair. Bureau
on the Inalienable Rights of the Palestinian People 2006, Vice-Pres. 63rd Session of
UN Gen. Ass. 2008–09, chaired several plenary meetings, including part of High
Level Meeting on Interfaith and Intercultural Dialogue 2008, apptd Chair
intergovernmental negotiations on Security Council reform on behalf of Pres. of
Gen. Ass. 2009, Vice-Chair. Open Ended Working Group on the Question of
Equitable Representation of and an Increase in Membership of the Security
Council and Other Related Matters. *Radio:* The Oral History of Afghanistan in the
20th Century (BBC). *Publications include:* The Communist Regime in Afghanistan

(co-author), Afghanistan in the Twentieth Century. *Address:* Permanent Mission
of Afghanistan to United Nations, 633 Third Avenue, 27th Floor, New York, NY
10017, USA (office). *Telephone:* (212) 972-1212 (office). *Fax:* (212) 972-1216 (office).
E-mail: info@afghanistan-un.org (office). *Website:* www.afghanistan-un.org
(office).

TANJUNG, Chairul, MBA; Indonesian business executive; *Founder and Chair-
man, CT Corporation;* b. 1962, Jakarta; m.; two c.; ed Univ. of Indonesia, Institut
Pendidikan and Pengembangan Manajemen (Educ. and Man. Devt Inst.); Founder
and Chair. Para Group (PT Para Inti Holtindo, now CT Corpn) 1987–); extensive
business interests in banking, media, property, lifestyle and entertainment; Chair.
Indonesia Forum Foundation, Nat. Kidney Foundation Indonesia; Dir Pacific
Basin Econ. Council; mem. Bd of Dirs Indonesian Cttee for Humanitarian
Program, Indonesian Red Cross, Jakarta Art Foundation; Cttee mem. Jakarta
Initiative (The Company Restructuring Agency); fmr Chair. Badminton Asscn of
Indonesia. *Address:* CT Corporation, Menara Bank Mega, 24th Floor. Jl. Kapt. P.
Tendean Kav. 12 –14 A, Jakarta 12790, Indonesia (office). *Telephone:* (21)
79175533 (office). *Fax:* (21) 79193300 (office). *Website:* www.ctcorpora.com (office).

TANKARD, Meryl; Australian choreographer, director and designer; b. 8 Sept.
1955, Darwin, NT; d. of (Mick) Clifford Tankard and Margot Tankard; m. Regis
Lansac; ed Australian Ballet School, Australian Film Television and Radio School
(Grad. Diploma in Directing); dancer with Australian Ballet Co. 1975–78; solo
dancer with Pina Bausch Wuppertal Tanztheater, Germany 1978–84, Guest
Performer and Choreographer 1984–89; Artistic Dir Meryl Tankard Co., Canberra
1989–92, Meryl Tankard Australian Dance Theatre 1993–99, freelance dir/
choreographer 1999–; Canberran of the Year 1992, Sidney Myer Performing
Arts Award for Individual Achievement 1993, Victoria Green Room Awards 1993,
1994, Betty Pounder Award for Original Choreography 1994, 'Age' Performing
Arts Award for Best Collaboration (Dance) 1995, Mobil Pegasus Award for Best
Production 1997, Australian Dance Awards' Lifetime Achievement Award 2003,
Centenary Medal Australia, Australia Council Fellowship, Australian Dance
Awards outstanding achievement in choreography 2010. *Major works choreo-
graphed include:* Echo Point (Australia) 1984, 1990, Travelling Light (UK and
Australia) 1986–87, Two Feet (Australia, NZ, Japan and Germany) 1988–94, VX
18504 (Australia) 1989–95, Court of Flora (Australia) 1990–93, Nuti & Kikimora
(Italy, Indonesia, Australia, China and Germany) 1990–94, Chants of Marriage I
and II (Australia) 1991–92, Furioso (Australia and overseas) 1993–99, O Let Me
Weep (Australia) 1994, Aurora (Australia) 1994–96, Orphée et Eurydice
(Australia) 1995–96, Possessed (Australia, France and Germany) 1995–99, The
Deep End (Australia) 1996, Rasa 1996, Inuk 1997 (Australia, Germany), Bolero
(France, USA, Hong Kong) 1999, The Beautiful Game (UK) 2000, Sydney Olympic
Opening Ceremony 'Deep Sea Dreaming', Merryland (Netherlands, Switzerland,
Germany) 2002, The Wild Swans (Australian Ballet) 2003, @North (Berlinballet,
Berlin) 2004, Petrushka for Netherlands Dance Theatre I (Den Haag) 2004,
Tarzan for Disney Productions 2006, Kaidan (Sydney Opera House) 2007, Inuk 2
(Sydney Dance Co.), The Oracle (Sydney Opera House) 2009. *Films:* Moth, Mad
2010. *Leisure interest:* designing. *Address:* PO Box 3129, Bellevue Hill, NSW 2023,
Australia (office). *Telephone:* (2) 9300-6811 (office). *Fax:* (2) 9300-6811 (office).
E-mail: meryltankard@iprimus.com.au (office). *Website:* www.meryltankard.com
(office).

TANKSLEY, Steven D., BS, PhD; American agronomist, geneticist and aca-
demic; *Liberty Hyde Bailey Professor of Plant Breeding and Chairman of the
Genomics Initiative Task Force, Cornell University;* b. Hattiesburg, Miss.; ed
Colorado State Univ., Univ. of California, Davis; Postdoctoral Fellow, Univ. of
California, Davis 1979–81; Asst Prof., New Mexico State Univ., Las Cruces
1981–85; Assoc. Prof. of Plant Breeding, Cornell Univ. 1985–94, Full Prof. 1994–,
currently Liberty Hyde Bailey Prof. of Plant Breeding and Chair. Genomics
Initiative Task Force; mem. NAS 1995–; Alexander von Humboldt Foundation
Award, Martin Gibbs Medal, American Soc. of Plant Biologists, Wolf Prize in
Agric., Wolf Foundation (co-recipient) 2004. *Achievements include:* mem. of team of
Cornell Univ. scientists who successfully cloned first gene for disease resistance in
tomato, using technique known as map-based cloning developed for Human
Genome Project 1993. *Publications:* numerous scientific papers in professional
journals. *Address:* Department of Plant Breeding and Genetics, 248 Emerson,
Cornell University, Ithaca, NY 14853, USA (office). *Telephone:* (607) 255-1673
(office). *Fax:* (607) 255-6683 (office). *E-mail:* sdt4@cornell.edu (office). *Website:*
plbrgen.cals.cornell.edu (office).

TANNER, Alain; Swiss film director; b. 6 Dec. 1929, Geneva; ed in London; made
numerous documentaries before directing feature films. *Films include:* Charles
Dead or Alive 1969, Salamander 1971, The Middle of the World, Jonah Who Will be
25 in the Year 2000 1976, Messidor 1979, Light Years Away (Special Jury Prize,
Cannes Film Festival 1985) 1981, In the White City 1983, No Man's Land 1985,
Une Flamme Dans Mon Coeur 1987, The Woman of Rose Hill 1989, The Man Who
Lost His Shadow 1991, The Diary of Lady M 1993, Les Hommes du port 1995,
Fourbi 1996, Requiem 1998, Jonas et Lila, Á demain 1999, Fleurs de sang 2002,
Paul s'en va 2004.

TANNER, Lindsay, MA; Australian politician; b. 26 April 1956, Orbost, Vic.; m.
Andrea Tanner; two d.; ed Univ. of Melbourne; Articled Clerk and Solicitor,
Holding Redlich 1982–85; Electorate Asst for Senator Barney Cooney 1986; Asst
Sec., Federated Clerks Union, Vic. 1987–88, State Sec. 1988–93; MP (Australia
Labor Party) for Melbourne 1993–, Shadow Minister for Transport 1996–98, for
Finance and Consumer Affairs 1998, for Communications 2001–04, for Finance
2005–07, Minister for Finance and Deregulation 2007–10. *Publications:* The
Politics of Pollution (jt author) 1978, The Last Battle 1996, Open Australia 1999,
Crowded Lives 2003; numerous articles in journals and newspapers. *Leisure
interests:* reading, playing piano, sport. *Address:* c/o Department of Finance and
Administration, John Gorton Building, King Edward Terrace, Parkes ACT 2600,
Australia. *E-mail:* Lindsay.Tanner.MP@aph.gov.au. *Website:* www.lindsaytanner
.com.

TANNER, Roger Ian, PhD, FRS, FAA; British engineer and academic; *P.N.
Russell Professor of Mechanical Engineering, University of Sydney;* b. 25 July
1933, Wells, Somerset, England; s. of R. J. Tanner and E. Tanner; m. Elizabeth
Bogen 1957; two s. three d.; ed Univs of Bristol and Manchester, Univ. of

California, Berkeley, USA; eng apprentice, Bristol Aero Engines 1950–53; Lecturer in Mechanical Eng, Univ. of Manchester 1958–61; Sr Lecturer, Reader, Univ. of Sydney, Australia 1961–66, P.N. Russell Prof. of Mechanical Eng 1975–, Pro-Vice-Chancellor (Research) 1994–97; Prof., Brown Univ. Providence, RI, USA 1966–75; Fellow, Australian Acad. of Tech. Science and Eng 1977; Edgeworth David Medal 1966, Australian Soc. of Rheology Medallion 1993, A.G.M. Michell Medal 1999, British Soc. of Rheology Gold Medal 2000. *Publications include:* Engineering Rheology 1985, 2000, Rheology: An Historical Perspective 1998. *Leisure interests:* golf, opera. *Address:* Department of Aerospace, Mechanical and Mechatronic Engineering, University of Sydney, Sydney, NSW 2006 (office); Marlowe, Sixth Mile Lane, Roseville, NSW 2069, Australia (home). *Telephone:* (2) 9351-7153 (office). *Fax:* (2) 9351-7060 (office). *E-mail:* roger.tanner@sydney.edu.au (office).

TANOESOEDIBJO, Hary, BCom, MBA; Indonesian business executive; *Group President and CEO, PT Global Mediacom Tbk;* b. 26 Sept. 1965, Surabaya; m.; five c.; ed Carleton Univ., Canada, Univ. of Ottawa; co-f. PT Bhakti Investama Tbk, Surabaya 1989, Pres. Commr 1989–2009, Pres. Dir 2009–, Pres. Dir PT Global Mediacom Tbk 2002–, currently Group Pres. and CEO, CEO MNC Group 2004–; Commr PT Mobile 8 Telecom 2004–, PT MNC Sky Vision 2006–; Pres. Dir PT Rajawali Citra Televisi 2003–08; Dir MNC International Ltd 2007–; Chair. and CEO Linktone Ltd 2008–; co-f. Indonesia Recovery Co. Ltd; other holdings include Bimantara Citra, Indomilk, SCTV; mem. Partai NasDem 2011–13, Partai Hati Nurani Rakyat (Hanura) 2013–. *Address:* PT Global Mediacom Tbk, Floor 27, Kebon Sirih Tower, Kebon Sirih Street, Lot 17-19, Jakarta 10340, Indonesia (office). *Telephone:* (21) 3900885 (office). *Fax:* (21) 3909207 (office).

TANOTO, Sukanto, (Chen Jianghe); Indonesian business executive; *Founder, Chairman and CEO, RGE Pte Ltd;* b. 25 Dec. 1949; m.; four c.; ed INSEAD, France, Harvard Univ. and Wharton Business School, USA; left school aged 17 to join family business supplying parts to oil and gas cos, Medan; f. Raja Garuda Mas (RGM) (plywood mfr) 1973, later RGM Int., renamed RGE (Royal Golden Eagle) Pte Ltd 2009, (conglomerate with interests in paper, palm oil, construction, energy), associated cos include Pacific Oil & Gas Ltd, Asia Pacific Resources Int. Holdings Ltd; f. Tanoto Foundation 1984; mem. INSEAD Int. Council, World Pres Org., Wharton Bd of Overseers; named Outstanding Contributor among Asia-Pacific Chinese Entrepreneurial Leaders with the Strongest Social Responsibility 2009, Wharton School Dean's Medal Award. *Address:* RGE Pte Ltd, 80 Raffles Place, #50-01 UOB Plaza 1, Singapore 048624, Singapore (office). *Telephone:* 62169368 (office). *Fax:* 65384668 (office). *Website:* www.rgei.com (office); www .sukantotanoto.net.

TANTAWI, Field Marshal Muhammad Hussain; Egyptian army officer and government official; *Adviser to the President;* b. 1935; served as infantry officer in Suez war 1956, six-days war 1967, October 1973 war; Minister of Defence and Mil. Production 1991–2012; apptd Gen. Commdr for Armed Forces 1995; Chair., Supreme Council of the Armed Forces and de facto Head of State (following resignation of Pres. Hosni Mubarak) 2011–12; Adviser to Pres. 2012–; Order of the Nile 2012. *Address:* c/o Ministry of Defence and Military Production, Sharia 23 July, Kobri el-Kobba, Cairo, Egypt.

TANTI, Tulsi R., BCom, DipEng; Indian energy industry executive; *Chairman and Managing Director, Suzlon Energy;* b. Rajkot, Gujarat; m.; three c.; ed Rajkot Coll.; began career in textile industry, Gujarat; co-f. Suzlon Energy (wind power venture) 1995, currently Chair. and Man. Dir; Solar Energy Soc. of India (SESI) Business Leadership Award 2002, World Wind Energy Award 2003, SESI Lifetime Achievement Award as Best Renewable Man of the Decade 2006, Time magazine Hero of the Environment 2007. *Address:* Suzlon Energy, 5th Floor, Godrej Millennium 9, Koregaon Park Road, Pune 411 001, Maharashtra, India (office). *Telephone:* (20) 40122000 (office). *Fax:* (20) 40122100 (office). *E-mail:* pune@suzlon .com (office). *Website:* www.suzlon.com (office).

TANTOCO, Bienvenido R., Sr; Philippine retail executive and diplomatist; b. 7 April 1921; m. Gliceria Tantoco (deceased); six c.; ed Jose Rizal Univ., Mandaluyong; opened first retail outlet with wife 1951; fmr Chair. Rustan Commercial Corpn, Rustan Supermarkets Inc., Rustan Int. Trading Corpn, Rustan Marketing Corpn, Royal Duty Free Shops, Tourist Duty Free Shops Inc., Stores Specialists Inc., Rustan Coffee Corpn, Rustan Supercenters Inc., Sta Elena Golf Club, Sta Elena Properties Inc.; Amb. of Philippines to Holy See 1983–86; Pres. Philippine–Italian Asscn 1977–86; fmr Pres. Philippine Retailers Asscn, Shopwise; Commdr, Order of Merit of the Repub. of Italy, Order of Merit of the Repub. of Portugal, Kt, Grand Cross of the Order of Pius IX 1985 Hon. DH (Jose Rizal Univ.). *Address:* c/o Rustan's Department Store, Ayala Avenue, Makati City 1224, Philippines (office).

TANZI, Vito, BA, MA, MA, PhD; American/Italian economist; *Independent Scholar and Honorary President, International Institute of Public Finance;* b. 29 Nov. 1935, Italy; s. of Luigi Tanzi and Maria Tanzi; m. Maria T. Bernabé 1997; three s.; ed George Washington and Harvard Univs; Chair. of Econs Dept, American Univ., Washington, DC 1971–74, Prof. of Econs 1970–74; Head of Tax Policy Div., IMF 1974–81, Dir Fiscal Affairs Dept 1981–2000; Pres. Int. Inst. of Public Finance 1990–94, now Ind. Scholar and Hon. Pres.; Sr Assoc. Carnegie Endowment for Int. Peace 2001; Under-Sec. of State, Ministry of Economy and Finance, Italy 2001–03; Sr Consultant in Trade and Integration, IDB 2003–07; Commendatore della Repubblica Italiana; Dr hc (Córdoba, Argentina) 1998, (Liège, Belgium) 1999, (Turin, Italy) 2001, (Bari, Italy) 2003, (Lisbon, Portugal) 2007; various awards. *Publications:* 20 books, including Government versus Markets 2011, Italica 2012, Dollars, Euros and Debt 2013; more than 300 articles in professional journals. *Leisure interests:* naïf art, African art, photography, music, travel, collecting old keys and old locks. *Address:* 5912 Walhonding Road, Bethesda, MD 20816, USA. *Fax:* (301) 229-4106. *E-mail:* vitotanzi@msn.com.

TAO, Gen. Bojun; Chinese army officer; b. 1936, Yongji Co., Jilin Prov.; joined PLA 1951, CCP 1961; Chief, Wuhan Mil. Dist (Combat Div., Artillery HQ), PLA Guangzhou Mil. Region 1976–77, Dir Artillery HQ 1983; Deputy Army Commdr PLA Chengdu Mil. Region 1983–85, Chief-of-Staff 1985–92, Commdr 2000; Chief of Staff Guangzhou Mil. Region 1992, Deputy Commdr 1993–96, Commdr 2000; Commdr Guangdong Mil. Region 1996–2001; rank of Maj.-Gen. 1988, Lt-Gen. 1991, Gen. 2000; Del., 13th CCP Cen. Cttee 1987–92, 14th CCP Cen. Cttee

1992–97, mem. 15th CCP Cen. Cttee 1997–2002. *Address:* People's Liberation Army, c/o Ministry of National Defence, Jingshanqian Jie, Beijing, People's Republic of China (office).

TAO, Ho; Chinese artist and architect; b. 1936; ed Williams Coll. and Harvard Univ., Mass, USA; worked with architect Walter Gropius; in practice as architect in Hong Kong; art work includes acrylic paintings, lithographs, pen-and-ink sketches and sculptures in marble, wood and rusty scrap iron; works exhibited at Hong Kong Univ. Museum; f. TAOHO Design 1968; World Economic Forum Crystal Award 1997. *Buildings include:* Hong Kong Arts Centre 1977. *Designs include:* Bauhinia emblem, flag of Hong Kong Special Administrative Region, Synergy of Dynamic Energy (displayed at West Hall area, Hong Kong International Airport). *Address:* Taoho Design Architects Ltd, 4 Suffolk Road, Kowloon, Hong Kong Special Administrative Region, People's Republic of China (office). *Website:* www.taoho.com (office).

TAO, Siju; Chinese party official; *Commissioner General, Chinese People's Armed Police Force;* b. 1935, Jingjiang Co., Jiangsu Prov.; joined CCP 1949; Vice-Minister of Public Security 1984–90, Minister 1990–98; Vice-Chair. Internal Affairs and Judicial Cttee 9th NPC 1998–; Chair. Nat. Narcotics Control Comm. 1993–; First Political Commissar, Chinese People's Armed Police Force 1990–, Commr-Gen. 1992–; mem. Cen. Comm. of Political Science and Law; mem. 14th CCP Cen. Cttee 1992–97, 15th CCP Cen. Cttee 1997–2002; mem. 9th Standing Cttee of NPC 1998–2003. *Address:* c/o Standing Committee of National People's Congress, Beijing, People's Republic of China (office). *Telephone:* (10) 65122831 (office).

TAO, Terence, BSc, MSc, PhD, FRS; Australian mathematician and academic; *James and Carol Collins Professor of Mathematics, University of California, Los Angeles;* b. 17 July 1975, Adelaide, South Australia; s. of Dr Billy Tao and Grace Tao; m. Laura Tao; one s. one d.; ed Flinders Univ. of South Australia, Princeton Univ.; began learning calculus aged seven, progressed to univ.-level calculus aged 11, apptd Full Prof. aged 24; Hedrick Asst Prof. then Prof. of Math., UCLA 1996–; Visiting Prof., Univ. of New South Wales 2000; Corresponding mem. Australian Acad. of Sciences; Foreign mem. NAS; Fellow, American Acad. of Arts and Sciences 2009, American Math. Soc.; Hon. Prof., ANU 2001–03; Bronze, Silver and Gold Medals (youngest ever Gold medallist) Int. Math. Olympiads, Salem Prize 2000, Bôcher Memorial Prize 2002, Clay Research Award 2003, Australian Math. Soc. Medal 2005, Ostrowski Prize 2005, Levi L. Conant Prize, American Math. Soc. (jtly) 2005, Fields Medal, Int. Congress of Mathematicians 2006, SASTRA Ramanujan Prize 2006, MacArthur Fellowship Award 2006, Alan T. Waterman Award 2008, Onsager Medal 2008, King Faisal Int. Prize (co-recipient) 2010, Nemmers Prize in Math. 2010, Polya Prize 2010, Crafoord Prize (co-recipient) 2012, Simons Foundation Award 2012, Joseph I. Lieberman Award 2013. *Publications:* 17 books, including Solving Mathematical Problems: A Personal Perspective 2006, Analysis, Vols I and II 2006, Additive Combinatorics (co-author) 2006, Nonlinear Dispersive Equations: Local and Global Analysis 2006, Structure and Randomness: Pages from Year One of a Mathematical Blog 2008, Poincaré's Legacies: Pages from Year Two of a Mathematical Blog, Vols I and II 2009, An Introduction to Measure Theory 2011, An Epsilon of Room, I: Real Analysis: Pages from Year Three of a Mathematical Blog 2011, An Epsilon of Room, II: Pages from Year Three of a Mathematical Blog 2011, Topics in Random Matrix Theory 2012, Higher-order Fourier Analysis 2012, Compactness and Contradiction 2013; more than 250 articles in professional journals. *Address:* Mathematical Sciences 6183, Department of Mathematics, UCLA, Los Angeles, CA 90095-1555, USA (office). *Telephone:* (310) 206-4844 (office). *Fax:* (310) 206-6673 (office). *E-mail:* tao@math .ucla.edu (office). *Website:* www.math.ucla.edu/~tao (office); terrytao.wordpress .com.

TAPAGARARUA, Willie Jimmy; Ni-Vanuatu politician and fmr diplomatist; *President, Liberal Democratic Party;* ed Malapoa Coll.; Freight and Traffic Officer, Air Melanesia 1989; Receptionist and Reservations Officer, Radisson Palms and Casino 1992; Asst Chief Security Officer, Club Vanuatu 1993; Compliance and Freight Officer, Ifira Shipping Agencies 1994–95; Private Business (real estate) 1997–2004; MP for Efate 2004–08, currently for Port Vila Town; fmr Deputy Prime Minister and Minister for Industry and Commerce; Amb. to China 2009; Minister of Finance and Econ. Man. March–May 2013; Pres. Liberal Democratic Party 2012–. *Address:* c/o Ministry of Finance, PMB 058, Port Vila, Vanuatu.

TAPIA ROA, Ruth Esperanza; Nicaraguan government official and diplomatist; *Ambassador to France;* b. 21 Nov. 1960, Masaya; ed Centre d' Etudes Diplomatiques et Strategiques, Universidad Centroamericana, Managua; First Sec., Embassy in Paris 1985–90; Spokesperson, Supreme Court of Justice 2002–07; Sec.-Gen. Ministry of Nat. Defence 2007–12; Amb. to France 2012–. *Address:* Embassy of Nicaragua, 34, avenue Bugeaud, 75116, Paris, France (office). *Telephone:* 1-44-05-93-07 (office). *Fax:* 1-44-05-92-42 (office). *E-mail:* contact@ amb-nicaragua.fr (office). *Website:* www.amb-nicaragua.fr (office).

TAPLIN, Guy Christie; British artist; b. 5 March 1939, London; s. of George Frederick Taplin and Gladys Lillian Taplin (née Peters); m. Robina Dunkery Jack 1989; one s. one d.; ed Norlington Secondary Modern School, Leyton; self-taught artist (sculptor) 1978–; fmrly worked as window cleaner; Post-Office messenger 1954–58, meat porter 1960, driver 1961, ladies' hairdresser 1961–62, lifeguard 1962–68, cook 1964, birdkeeper Regent's Park 1970–76; also had own fashion business during 1960s. *Publications:* books on his work: Birds of Creation, Bird on Wire (by Ian Collins). *Leisure interests:* life, art, folk art, travel, chance.

TAPPER, Colin Frederick Herbert, MA, BCL; British lawyer and academic; *Emeritus Fellow, Magdalen College, University of Oxford;* b. 13 Oct. 1934, West Drayton, London Borough of Hillingdon, England; s. of H. F. Tapper and F. G. Tapper (née Lambard); m. Margaret White 1961; one d.; ed Magdalen Coll., Oxford; teacher, LSE 1959–65; barrister, Grays Inn 1961; tutor, Magdalen Coll. 1965–79, Fellow 1965–2002 (Vice-Pres. 1991–92) Emer. Fellow 2002–, All Souls Reader in Law 1979–94; Prof. of Law 1992–2002; mem. Bd of Dirs Butterworth Group 1979–84, Butterworth Telepublishing 1979–89; consultant to Masons (solicitors) 1990–2003. *Publications:* Computers and the Law 1973, Computer Law 1978, Cross on Evidence (ed.) 1990, Handbook of European Software Law (ed.) 1995, Cross and Tapper on Evidence (ed.) 1999. *Leisure interests:* computing, reading, writing. *Address:* Magdalen College, Oxford, OX1 4AU (office); Corner Cottage, Woodstock Road, Stonesfield, Witney, Oxon., OX29 8QA, England (home).

Telephone: (1865) 276055 (office); (1993) 891284 (home). *Fax:* (1865) 276103 (office); (1993) 891395 (home). *Website:* www.ox.ac.uk/colleges/colleges_and_halls_az/magdalen.html (office).

TARAND, Andres; Estonian politician; b. 11 Jan. 1940, Tallinn; s. of Helmut Tarand and Leida Tarand; m. Mari Tarand (née Viiding) 1963; two s.; ed Tartu State Univ.; hydrometeorologist 1963; Research Asst, Tallinn Botanical Gardens 1965–68, Sr Engineer 1970–73, Sr Researcher 1973–76, Sector Dir 1976–79, 1981–88, Dir of Research 1979–81, Dir Tallinn Botanical Gardens 1988–90; researcher, Antarctic Expedition 1968–70; Chair. Environment Cttee Supreme Soviet Estonian SSR 1990; mem. Council of Estonia 1990–92; mem. Constitutional Ass. 1991–92; mem. Riigikogu (Parl.) 1992, 1995–2004; Minister for the Environment 1992–94, 1994–95; Prime Minister of Estonia 1994–95; mem. People's Party Moderates (Rahvaerakond Mõõdukad, renamed Sotsiaaldemokraatlik Erakond 2004) 1996–, Chair. 1996–2002, Chair. Cttee of Foreign Affairs 1999–2002; mem. European Parl. (Socialist Group) 2004–, mem. Cttee on Industry, Research and Energy, Del. for Relations with the Korean Peninsula, Substitute mem. Cttee on the Environment, Public Health and Food Safety, Del. for Relations with Australia and NZ; Regional Vice-Pres. Globe International Europe 1999–; mem. Estonian Geographical Asscn 1966–; Bd Estonian Inst. for Sustainable Devt, Stockholm Environment Inst.'s Centre, Tallinn 1988–, Bd Univ. of Tartu 1996–, Bd Estonian Nature Fund 1998–; Badge of the Order of Nat. Coat of Arms (Second Class) 2001, Commdr, Légion d'honneur 2001; Panda Award, Danish Section of WWF 1998. *Publications:* Neljakümne kiri 1991, Cassiopeia 1992, Kiri ei Põle Ära 2005; numerous articles on climatology, urban ecology, politics. *Leisure interests:* chess, ornithology, traditional style gardening. *Address:* European Parliament, Bâtiment Altiero Spinelli, 12G165, 60 rue Wiertz, 1047 Brussels, Belgium (office); Harju 1-1, 10 146 Tallinn, Estonia. *Telephone:* (2) 284-5429 (office). *Fax:* (2) 284-9429 (office). *E-mail:* andres.tarand@europarl.europa.eu (office). *Website:* www.europarl.europa .eu (office); www.atarand.eu.

TARANDA, Gediminas Leonovich; Russian/Lithuanian ballet dancer; b. 26 Feb. 1961, Kaliningrad; ed Moscow Acad. of Choreography, Moscow Acad. of Dance; joined Bolshoi Theatre as dancer 1980, Soloist 1982, Leading Soloist 1985–93, dismissed after conflict with admin.; Founder (with M. Plisetskaya) and Dir Imperial Russian Ballet Co. 1994–; Co-organizer European Culture Centre (under patronage of European Parl.); First Prize, USSR Championship Ballet Competition 1980. *Leading roles include:* classical and contemporary Russian repertoire including Espado (Don Quixote), Corregidor (Carmen), Forest Warden (Giselle), Kuman (Prince Igor), Severyan (Stone Flower), Yashka (Golden Age), Kurbsky (Ivan the Terrible), Abderakhman (Raimonda), Vizir (Legend of Love) and others. *Address:* Imperial Russian Ballet Company, 103001 Moscow, Trekhprudny per. 11/13, building 2B, Office 45, Russia. *Telephone:* (495) 299-13-98.

TARANTINO, Quentin Jerome; American film director, actor, screenwriter and producer; b. 27 March 1963, Knoxville, Tenn.; s. of Tony Tarantino and Connie McHugh; fmrly worked in Video Archives, Manhattan Beach, Calif.; Officier, Ordre des Arts et des Lettres, Order of Merit of the Hungarian Repub. 2010; Career Achievement Award, Casting Soc. of America 2004, Empire Film Award for Icon of the Decade 2005, Golden Eddie Filmmaker of the Year Award, American Cinema Editors 2007, Lifetime Achievement Award, Cinemanila Int. Film Festival 2007, Filmmaker on the Edge Award, Provincetown Int. Film Festival 2008, Hon. César, Acad. des Arts et Techniques du Cinéma 2011. *Films include:* My Best Friend's Birthday (actor, dir, producer) 1987, Reservoir Dogs (actor, dir) 1992, Past Midnight (assoc. producer) 1992, Siunin Wong Fei-hung tsi titmalau (producer) 1993, Eddie Presley (actor) 1993, Sleep With Me (actor) 1994, Killing Zoe (exec. producer) 1994, Somebody to Love (actor) 1994, Pulp Fiction (actor, dir) (Golden Palm, Cannes Film Festival, Acad. Award for Best Screenplay 1995) 1994, Destiny Turns on the Radio (actor) 1995, Desperado (actor) 1995, Four Rooms (actor, dir, exec. producer) 1995, Red Rain (producer) 1995, Girl 6 (actor) 1996, From Dusk Till Dawn (actor, exec. producer) 1996, Curdled (actor, exec. producer) 1996, Jackie Brown (dir) 1997, God Said, 'Ha!' (exec. producer) 1998, 40 Lashes (dir) 2000, Little Nicky (actor) 2000, Kill Bill Vol. I (dir, producer) 2003, Kill Bill Vol. II (dir, producer) 2004, Daltry Calhoun (exec. producer) 2005, Hostel (exec. producer) 2005, Freedom's Fury (exec. producer) 2006, Grindhouse (actor) 2007, Death Proof (writer, producer, dir, actor) 2007, Planet Terror (actor) 2007, Sukiyaki Western Django (actor) 2007, Diary of the Dead (voice) 2007, Planet Terror (producer) 2007, Hell Ride (exec. producer) 2008, Inglourious Basterds (actor and dir) 2009, Django Unchained (dir) 2012. *Film screenplays:* My Best Friend's Birthday 1992, Reservoir Dogs 1992, True Romance 1993, Natural Born Killers 1994, Pulp Fiction 1994, Four Rooms (segment: The Man from Hollywood) 1995, From Dusk Till Dawn 1996, Jackie Brown 1997, 40 Lashes (dir) 2000, Kill Bill (also novel) 2003, Inglourious Basterds 2009, Django Unchained (Golden Globe Award for Best Screenplay 2013, BAFTA Award for Best Original Screenplay 2013, Academy Award for Best Original Screenplay 2013) 2012. *Television includes:* ER (dir, episode 'Motherhood') 1994, Alias (actor, one episode) 2004, CSI: Crime Scene Investigation (dir, writer two episodes) 2005, Alias (actor, four episodes) 2006. *Address:* c/o WME Entertainment, 9601 Wilshire Boulevard, Beverly Hills, CA 90210-5213, USA; 6201 Sunset Boulevard, Suite 35, Los Angeles, CA 90028, USA. *Telephone:* (310) 285-9000. *Fax:* (310) 285-9010. *Website:* www.wma.com.

TĂRANU, Cornel, DMus; Romanian composer and conductor; b. 20 June 1934, Cluj; s. of Francisc Țăranu and Elisabeta Țăranu; m. Daniela Mărgineanu 1960; one d.; ed Cluj Conservatory; Prof. of Composition, Cluj Conservatory; Conductor of Ars Nova, contemporary music ensemble; Vice-Pres. Romanian Composers' Union 1990–; Artistic Dir Modern Festival Cluj; mem. Romanian Acad. 1993–; Chevalier, Ordre des Arts et des Lettres 2002; Prize of the Romanian Composers' Union 1972, 1978, 1981, 1982, 2001, Grand Prize 2005, Prize of the Romanian Acad. 1973, The Koussevitsky Prize 1982. *Works include:* Sonatas for flute, oboe, clarinet and percussion, Sonata for double bass solo, viola sonata, one piano concerto, cantatas, four symphonies, Séquences, Incantations, Symmétries, Alternances, Raccords for orchestra, two Sinfoniettas for strings, Garlands for chamber orchestra, Don Giovanni's Secret for chamber opera, Chansons nomades (oratorio), Chansons sans amour (lieder), Sempre Ostinato for saxophone and ensemble, Chansons sans réponse, Hommage à Paul Célan, Memento and Dedications (cantatas), Miroirs for saxophone and orchestra, Prolégomènes for

chamber orchestra, Orpheus (cantata), Tombeau de Verlaine for mixed choir, Mosaïques for saxophone and ensemble, Testament for choir 1988, Chansons interrompues for voice and ensemble 1993, Cadenze Concertante for cello and chamber orchestra 1993, Trajectoires for ensemble 1994, Crisalide for saxophone, tape and ensemble, Five Tzara Songs for voice and piano, Remembering Bartók for oboe and ensemble, Enescu's 'Caprice Roumain' for violin and orchestra (new arrangement) 1995, Responsorial for clarinet 1996, Antiphona for flute and orchestra 1996, Flaine Quintette for winds 1997, Laudatio per Clusium for voice and instruments 1997, Saturnalii for baritone and ensemble 1998, Three Labiş Poems for bass and piano 1998, Cadenze per Antiphona for flute and solo 1998, Siciliana Blues for piano and chamber orchestra 1998, Concerto for oboe and strings 1998, Oreste-Oedipe (chamber opera) 1999–2001, Concerto Breve for flute orchestra 2001, Modra Rijeka for choir 2002, Shakespeare Sonnets for voice and ensemble 2003, Baroccoco for baroque ensemble 2004, Rimembranza for orchestra 2004, Sinfonia da Requiem for choir and orchestra 2005, Sax-Sympho for saxophone and orchestra 2006, Madrigals (verse by Blaga, Vinea, Attila, Ady); also film and theatre music. *Publication:* Enesco dans la conscience du présent 1981. *Leisure interest:* chess. *Address:* 'Gh. Dima' Music Academy, str. I. I. C. Bratianu 25, 400079 Cluj (office); Str. Nicolae Iorga 7, 400063 Cluj-Napoca, Romania (home). *Telephone:* (264) 593879 (office); (264) 443283 (home). *Fax:* (264) 593879 (office). *E-mail:* corneltaranu@yahoo.com (office). *Website:* www .corneltaranu.com.

TARAR, Muhammad Rafiq; Pakistani politician, lawyer and fmr head of state; b. 2 Nov. 1929, Pir Kot, Gujranwala Dist; m.; three s. one d.; ed Govt Islamia High School, Gujranwala, Guru Nanak Khalsa Coll., Gujranwala, Punjab Univ. Law Coll.; legal practice, Gujranwala; Additional Sessions Judge, Gujranwala, Bahawalnagar, Sargodha; mem. Lahore High Court 1974, Chief Justice of Punjab 1989; mem. Electoral Comm. of Pakistan 1980–89; mem. Supreme Court 1991–94; Senator, Pakistan Muslim League March–Dec. 1997; Pres. of Pakistan 1998–2001. *Address:* House 457, G-3, Johar Town, Lahore, Pakistan.

TARASCON, Jean-Marie, MS, PhD; French physicist and academic; *Professor and Director, CNRS Laboratory of Reactivity and Solid State Chemistry, Amiens;* b. 21 Sept. 1953; ed Univ. of Bordeaux; Post-Doctoral Fellow, Cornell Univ., Ithaca, NY, USA 1980–81; Post-Doctoral Fellow, Bell Labs, Murray Hill, NJ, USA 1982–83; mem. Tech. Staff, Bellcore Solid State Chem. Div., Red Bank, NJ, USA 1983–89, Dir Energy Storage Group 1989–94, Bellcore Fellow 1990–; Prof. and Dir, CNRS Lab. of Reactivity and Solid State Chem., Amiens 1995–; Co-Ed. Journal of Solid State Ionics, Journal of Solid State Electrochemistry, Journal of Materials Chem., International Journal of Inorganic Materials; mem. Academie des Sciences 1999–; mem. ACS, Electrochemical Soc., Materials Research Soc., Institut Universitaire de France 2002–; Bellcore Award of Excellence 1987, Bellcore President Award 1993, Industry Week Best Tech. of the Year Award 1994, R and D 100 Award 1994, 1995, Popular Mechanics Design and Eng Award 1995, Int. Battery Asscn Research Award 1995, Electrochemical Soc. Battery Tech. Award 1997, Thomas Alva Edison Patent Award 2001, Volta Medal Award 2002, ISI Award 2004, Prix du rayonnement français 2004. *Address:* Laboratoire de Réactivité et de Chimie des Solides, Université de Picardie Jules Verne, UMR-CNRS 6007, 33, rue Saint-Leu, 80039 Amiens, Cedex 1, France (office). *Telephone:* (3) 22-82-75-71 (office). *Fax:* (3) 22-82-75-90 (office). *E-mail:* jean-marie.tarascon@sc.u-picardie.fr (office). *Website:* www.u-picardie.fr/labo/lrcs/jean-marie_tarascon .htm (office).

TARASOV, Gennady Pavlovich; Russian diplomatist and UN official; *Inspector, Joint Inspection Unit, United Nations;* b. 14 Sept. 1947, Moscow; m. Elena Tarasov; ed Moscow State Inst. of Int. Relations; on staff, Ministry of Foreign Affairs 1970–, worked in Egypt, USSR Perm. Mission to UN, New York and several other posts –1986; Deputy Head of Dept of Near E and N African Countries, USSR Ministry of Foreign Affairs 1986–90, Amb. of USSR, then of Russian Fed. to Saudi Arabia 1990–96, Dir Dept of Information and Press, Ministry of Foreign Affairs 1996–98, Amb. to Portugal 1998–2001, to Israel 2002–07; UN Sec.-Gen.'s High-Level Co-ordinator for compliance by Iraq on its obligations regarding Kuwait 2008–12, Insp., Jt Inspection Unit 2013–. *Address:* Palais des Nations, 1211 Geneva 10, Switzerland (office). *Telephone:* (22) 9173041 (office). *Fax:* (22) 9170627 (office). *E-mail:* tarasovg@un.org (office). *Website:* www.un.org (office).

TARASSOVA, Elvira; Russian ballet dancer; *First Soloist, Kirov Ballet;* b. 5 Aug. 1969, St Petersburg; ed Vaganova Acad.; joined Kirov Ballet 1988, First Soloist 1996–; Best Partner, Moscow Competition 1997, Honored Artist of Russia. *Repertoire includes:* Cinderella (Coppelia, Krivlaka), Don Quixote (Kitri), Faust (Vakhanka), Giselle (Myrtha), La Bayadère (Gamzatti), Le Corsaire (Medora, Gulnara), Sleeping Beauty (Brilliant Fairy), Symphony in C (Allegro Vivace). *Address:* Kirov Ballet, c/o Maryinsky Theatre, One Theatre Square (Teatralnaya Ploshchad), St Petersburg 190000, Russia (office). *Telephone:* (812) 114-12-11 (office). *Fax:* (812) 314-17-44 (office). *E-mail:* elvira@kirov.com (office). *Website:* www.kirov.com (office).

TARASYUK, Borys Ivanovych; Ukrainian politician and diplomatist; *Chairman, Narodnyi Rukh Ukrainy (People's Movement of Ukraine-Rukh);* b. 1 Jan. 1949, Dzerzhynsk, Zhytomyr Oblast; m.; one s. two d.; ed Kyiv State Univ.; attaché, Third, Second, First Sec., Ukrainian Ministry of Foreign Affairs 1975–81; Second, First Sec., Perm. Mission of Ukrainian SSR to UN, New York 1981–86; First Sec., Div. of Int. Orgs, Ukrainian Ministry of Foreign Affairs 1986–87; instructor, Div. of Foreign Relations, Ukrainian CP Cen. 1987–90; Head, Dept of Political Analysis and Planning, Ministry of Foreign Affairs 1991–92; Deputy, First Deputy Minister of Foreign Affairs, Head, Nat. Cttee on Disarmament Problems 1992–95; Amb. to Belgium (also accred to Netherlands, Luxembourg) 1995–98; Head, Mission to NATO, Brussels 1997–98; Minister of Foreign Affairs 1998–2000, 2005–07 (resgnd); mem. Nat. Security Defence Council; Chair. Narodnyi Rukh Ukrainy (People's Movt of Ukraine-Rukh) 2003–; mem. Bd of Dirs East-West Inst. 1993–2001; Chair. Cttee on European Integration 2002–; Dir Inst. of Social Studies and Int. Relations 2001–02; Founder and Dir Inst. of Euro-Atlantic Co-operation 2001–; State Order 'For Merits', III Grade 1996, II Grade 1999, I Grade 2005; Dr hc (Rivne Int. Econ. and Humanitarian Univ.) 2000, (Ivan Franko Nat. Univ. of Lviv) 2004, (Int. Personnel Acad.) 2002; state awards from Argentina, Brazil, France, Lithuania, Portugal, Sweden, Venezuela. *Leisure interests:* table tennis, fishing, woodwork. *Address:* Narodnyi

Rukh Ukrainy, 01034 Kyiv, vul. O. Honchara 33, Ukraine (office). *Telephone:* (44) 246-47-67 (office). *Fax:* (44) 531-30-42 (office). *E-mail:* org@nru.org.ua (office). *Website:* www.nru.org.ua (office); www.ieac.org.ua.

TARFUSSER, Cuno Jakob, DJur; Italian lawyer, public prosecutor and judge; *Second Vice-President, International Criminal Court;* b. 11 Sept. 1954, Merano; m. Gerda Amplatz; ed Innsbruck Univ., Padua Univ.; Deputy Public Prosecutor, Bolzano, Southern Tyrol 1987–2001, Chief Prosecutor 2001–09; Judge, Pre-Trial Div., Int. Criminal Court (ICC), The Hague, Netherlands 2009–, Second Vice-Pres. ICC 2012–. *Address:* International Criminal Court, PO Box 19519, 2500 CM The Hague, The Netherlands (office). *Telephone:* (70) 515-85-15 (office). *Fax:* (70) 515-85-55 (office). *E-mail:* pio@icc-cpi.int (office); otp.informationdesk@icc-cpi.int (office). *Website:* www.icc-cpi.int (office).

TARHOUNI, Ali Abdussalam, PhD; Libyan economist, academic and government official; b. 1951; m. Mary Li; four c.; ed Al Fateh Univ., Tripoli, Michigan State Univ., USA; in exile in USA 1973–2011; Asst Prof. of Business Econs, Michael G. Foster School of Business, Univ. of Washington, Seattle 1984–85, Sr Lecturer 1985–2011; fmr Consultant, FAO; returned to Libya Feb. 2011; Minister of Finance and Oil (apptd by Nat. Transitional Council following overthrow of Mu'ammar Gaddafi) March–Nov. 2011, also Chair. Supreme Security Cttee, interim Prime Minister of Libya Oct.–Nov. 2011. *Address:* c/o Ministry of Finance and Oil, Tripoli, Libya (office).

TARIN, Shaukat Fayaz Ahmed, MBA; Pakistani economist, banker and government official; *Advisor to Chairman, Silkbank Limited;* b. 1 Oct. 1953, Multan; s. of Jamshaid Ahmed Tarin and Mumtaz Tarin; m. Razalia Tarin; one s. two d.; ed Punjab Univ., Lahore; joined Citibank as trainee in 1975; Sr Head of Country Operations Support, Citibank NA, Dubai 1985–87, Gen. Man. Citibank Gulf 1987–90, Gen. Man. Citibank Pakistan 1991–95, Gen. Man. Citibank Thailand 1995–97; Pres. and CEO Habib Bank 1997–2000; Pres. and Group CEO Union Bank 2000–06; est. consortium, along with Sadeq Sayeed, Bank-Muscat, Nomura Holdings Inc. and International Finance Corpn to acquire 85.09% stake in bank from Saudi Pak Industrial and Agricultural Investment Co. Ltd 2008, Pres. Saudi Pak Commercial Bank –2008; Advisor to Prime Minister on Finance (with status of fed. minister) 2008–10 (resgnd), also Head of Exec. Cttee of Nat. Econ. Council and Econ. Co-ordination Cttee; elected unopposed mem. of Senate from Sindh July 2009–; fmr Chair. Karachi Stock Exchange; Advisor to Chair., Silkbank Ltd 2010–; Quaid-e-Azam Gold Medal Award 2005, Sitara-e-Imtiaz 2007. *Address:* Silkbank Ltd, Silkbank Building, I.I. Chundrigar Road, Karachi 74200, Pakistan (office). *Telephone:* (21) 32460001 (office). *Fax:* (21) 32460464 (office). *E-mail:* shaukat.tarin@silkbank.com.pk (office). *Website:* www .silkbank.com.pk (office).

TARISA, Watanagase, BA, MA, PhD; Thai economist and fmr central banker; b. 30 Nov. 1949; m.; one d.; ed Keio Univ., Japan, Univ. of Washington, AMP program at Harvard Univ., USA; joined Bank of Thailand 1975, economist, Financial Inst. Analysis Section, Dept of Econ. Research 1975–78, Chief Analyst, Banking Analysis Section, Banking Dept 1979, study leave 1979–83, Section Chief, Policy Section, Dept of Financial Insts Supervision and Examination 1984–85, Deputy Div. Chief, Financial Insts Supervision Div. 1986–87, Asst Dept of Econ. Research 1987, Deputy Dir Dept of Bank Supervision and Examination and Head of Payment System Devt Task Force 1991–93, Dir Payment System Devt Office 1993–96, Dir Payment System Dept 1996–97, Dir Financial Insts Regulations Dept 1997–98, Asst Gov., Financial Insts Regulation and Examination Group 1998–99, Asst Gov., Financial Insts Policy Group 1999–2001, Asst Gov., Financial Markets Operations Group 2001–02, Deputy Gov. Financial Insts Stability 2002–07, also mem. Bd, Financial System Policy Cttee, Monetary Policy Cttee, Gov. Bank of Thailand (first woman) 2006–10; economist, Cen. Banking Dept, IMF, Washington, DC 1988–91; fmr mem. Bd of Dirs Securities Analysts Asscn; Commdr (Third Class), The Most Noble Order of The Crown of Thailand; Outstanding Leadership Award, Bank of Thailand 2001, Outstanding Individual Research Award, Nat. Defence Coll. of Thailand 2006. *Leisure interests include:* watercolour painting, yoga. *Address:* c/o Bank of Thailand, 273 Samsen Road, Bangkhunprom, Bangkok 10200, Thailand (office).

TARJAN, Robert Endre, PhD, FAAS; American computer scientist and academic; *James S. McDonnell Distinguished University Professor of Computer Science, Princeton University;* b. 30 April 1948, Pomona, Calif.; s. of George Tarjan and Helen Emma Tarjan; three d.; ed California Inst. of Tech., Stanford Univ.; Asst Prof. of Computer Science, Cornell Univ., Ithaca, NY 1972–73; Miller Research Fellow, Univ. of California, Berkeley 1973–75; Asst Prof. of Computer Science, Stanford Univ. 1974–77, Assoc. Prof. 1977–80; mem. tech. staff, AT&T Bell Labs, Murray Hill, NJ 1980–89; Adjunct Prof. of Computer Science, New York Univ. 1981–85; James S. McDonnell Distinguished Univ. Prof. of Computer Science, Princeton Univ. 1985–, Co-Dir NSF Center for Discrete Math. and Theoretical Computer Science 1989–94, 2001–; Fellow, NEC Research Inst., Princeton 1989–97; Visiting Scientist, MIT 1996; Chief Scientist, InterTrust and Sr Research Fellow, STAR Labs, InterTrust Technologies Corpn, Sunnyvale, Calif. 1997–2001; Corp. Fellow, Compaq Computer Corpn, Houston, Tex. 2002; Chief Scientist, Hewlett Packard Corpn, Palo Alto, Calif. 2002–03; Sr Fellow 2003–; mem. Nat. Advisory Bd Computer Professionals for Social Responsibility 1987–, Bd of Govs Inst. for Math. and its Applications 1988–91; Ed. Princeton University Press Series in Computer Science 1985–, John Wiley Series in Discrete Mathematics 1987–97, Transactions on Mathematical Software 1978–80, Journal of the Association for Computing Machinery 1979–83, SIAM Journal on Computing 1979–83, Journal of Graph Theory 1985–88, Journal of Algorithms 1983–90, Discrete and Computational Geometry 1985–, Journal of the American Mathematical Society 1986–91, European Journal of Combinatorics 1988–91; Correspondent, Mathematical Intelligencer 1991–; mem. NAS 1987, Nat. Acad. of Eng 1988, American Philosophical Soc. 1990; Foundation Fellow, Inst. for Combinatorics and its Applications 1991; Fellow, American Acad. of Arts and Sciences 1985, Asscn for Computing Machinery (ACM) 1994, New York Acad. of Sciences 1994, Soc. of Ind. and Applied Math. 2009; Miller Research Fellowship, Univ. of California, Berkeley 1973–75, Guggenheim Fellowship 1978–79, Nevanlinna Prize in Information Science 1983, NAS Award for Initiatives in Research 1984, Lanchester Prize (Hon. Mention), Operations Research Soc. of America 1984, 1993, Distinguished mem. of Technical Staff, AT&T Bell Labs 1985, A.M. Turing Award,

Asscn for Computing Machinery 1986, ACM Paris Kanellakis Award in Theory and Practice 1999, Edelman Prize, Inst. for Operations Research and Man. Sciences (INFORMS) 2009. *Publications:* Data Structures and Network Algorithms 1983, Notes on Introductory Combinatorics 1983; 19 patents and more than 275 articles and reports in scientific journals. *Address:* Department of Computer Science, Princeton University, 35 Olden Street, Room 324, Princeton, NJ 08544-2087 (office); 4 Constitution Hill East, Princeton, NJ 08540, USA (home). *Telephone:* (609) 258-4797 (Princeton) (office); (650) 857-2497 (Palo Alto) (office); (609) 921-0132 (home). *Fax:* (609) 258-1771 (Princeton) (office). *E-mail:* ret@cs .princeton.edu (office). *Website:* www.cs.princeton.edu/~ret (office).

TARKOWSKI, Andrzej K., MSc, PhD, DSc; Polish zoologist, embryologist and academic; *Professor, Institute of Zoology, Warsaw University;* b. 4 May 1955, s. of Władysław Tarkowski and Janina Tarkowska de domo Osuchowska; m. Teresa Tarkowska; one d.; ed Warsaw Univ.; a world leader in research on early devt of mammals; Asst and Adjunct, Inst. of Zoology, Warsaw Univ. 1955–64, Assoc. Prof. 1960–61, Head, Dept of Embryology 1964–2003, Dir Inst. of Zoology 1972–81 1987–2003, Prof. 1978–; Visiting Prof. of the Royal Soc., Dept of Zoology, Univ. of Oxford, UK 1984–85; mem. Polish Acad. of Sciences 1974–, Polish Acad. of Arts and Sciences 1990–, Academia Europaea 1991–; Foreign mem. French Acad. of Sciences 1984–; Foreign Assoc. NAS 2003–; Dr hc (Jagiellonian Univ., Kraków) 2000, (Medical Univ., Łódź) 2005; Albert Brachet Prize, Royal Acad. of Belgium 1980, Polish Nat. Award 1980, Alfred Jurzykowski Foundation (USA) Award 1984, Embryo Transfer Pioneer Award, Int. Embryo Transfer Soc. 1991, Japan Prize, Science and Tech. Foundation of Japan 2002. *Publications:* numerous articles in scientific journals. *Leisure interest:* photography. *Address:* Zakład Embriologii, Instytut Zoologii, Wydział Biologii, Uniwersytet Warszawski, Miecznikowa 1, 02-096 Warsaw, Poland (office). *Telephone:* (22) 5541208 (office); (22) 5541209 (office). *Fax:* (22) 5541210 (office). *E-mail:* akt@biol.uw.edu.pl (office). *Website:* www.biol .uw.edu.pl (office).

TARLEV, DTechSci; Moldovan business executive and politician; b. 9 Oct. 1963, Başcalia, Basarabeasca Dist; m.; three c.; ed Chişinău Polytechnical Inst.; worked as tractor driver; served in army of USSR 1981–83; Chief Mechanic, Bucuria confectionery factory, Chief Engineer Bucuria SA 1991–93, First Deputy Dir-Gen. 1993–95, Chair. Bd of Admin., Dir-Gen. 1995–2001; studied int. marketing and trade man. in USA; fmr mem. Supreme Econ. Council of Pres., Econ. Council of Govt; mem. Repub. Comm. on Collective Negotiations between Businessmen and Trade Unions 1998–99; mem. Party of Communists of the Repub. of Moldova; Prime Minister of Moldova 2001–08; fmr Chair. Nat. Asscn of Mfrs 1995–2001; mem. Council Int. Union of Mfrs, Int. Acad. of Sciences and Computing Systems 1998–; mem. Int. Acad. of Sciences and Informational Systems 1998; Order of Work Glory 1997; Businessman of the Year (six times) 1995–2000, Gold Medal for Efficient Man., Int. Acad. of Human Resources 2000, several medals for tech. inventions shown at int. exhbns 1997–. *Achievements include:* holds five patents on tech. inventions. *Publications:* more than 30 scientific publs. *Address:* Party of Communists of the Republic of Moldova, 2012 Chişinău, N. Iorga Str. 11, Moldova (office). *Telephone:* (22) 23-46-14 (office). *Fax:* (22) 23-36-73 (office). *E-mail:* info@ pcrm.md (office). *Website:* www.pcrm.md (office).

TARNOPOLSKI, Vladimir Grigor'yevich; Russian composer; *Professor of Composition, Moscow Conservatory;* b. 30 April 1955, Dniepropetrovsk, Ukrainian SSR, USSR; m. Irina Ivanovna Snitkova; one s.; ed Moscow State Tchaikovsky Conservatory; freelance composer 1988–; co-f. Moscow Asscn of Contemporary Music 1989; Prof. of Composition, Moscow Conservatory 1992–, Founder and Artistic Dir first Russian Centre for Contemporary Music 1993–; f. Studio for New Music Ensemble 1993–, Moscow Forum –Int. Festival of Contemporary Music 1994–; Prof., Founder and Head of Dept for Contemporary Music, Tchaikovsky Conservatory 2003–; works performed by Ensemble Modern, Intercontemporain, Klangforum Wien, Musikfabrik Ensemble, Schonberg Ensemble, Ensemble Recherche, Bayerische Rundfunk Symphony Orchestra in major European and US festivals; Dmitry Shostakovich Prize, Moscow 1991, Paul Hindemith Prize, Plon 1991, Rostrum 2001. *Compositions include:* operas: Wenn die Zeit ueber die Ufer tritt (Munich 1999), Jenseits der Schatten (Bonn 2006), Cinderella (children's opera on text by Roald Dahl); music parodies: Three Graces 1987 (St Petersburg 1988), Ah, ces russes... ou l'Elexir Magic (Evian 1993); ballet: Ins Theater 1998, Boxing Pushkin (a scene within a collective dance-performance); chorus and orchestral/instrumental: Psalmus poenitentialis for violin, choir and organ 1986; orchestral: Cello Concerto 1980, The Breath of the Exhausted Time 1994...Le vent des mots qu'il n'a pas dits for cello and orchestra 1996, Feux follets 2003, Foucault's Pendulum 2004, Eastanbul 2008; large ensemble/chamber orchestra: Choral Prelude 'Jesus, Your Deep Wounds' 1987, Cassandra 1991, Landscape after the Battle (with bass or bass choir on the text by Reiner Maria Rilke) 1995; ensemble: Chevengur for voice and ensemble (text by Andrey Platonov) 2001, Last and Lost 2011; wind band: Welt voll Irrsinn on texts by K. Schwitters 1993; chamber music: Troïsti muziki for piano trio with singing on text by Grigory Skovoroda 1989, Echoes of the Passing Day for clarinet, cello and piano 1990, O, PART – OP ART 1992, Amoretto for soprano and ensemble (text by E. Spenser) 1992, Scenes from the Real Life for soprano and three instruments on texts by E. Jandl 1995, Impression-Expression III for piano and ensemble 1996. *Address:* Centre for Contemporary Music, Tchaikovsky Conservatoire, of. 316, Bolshaya Nikitskaya str. 13, 125009 Moscow (office); Arbat str., N 51, Apt 41-a, 119002 Moscow, Russia (home). *Telephone:* (495) 690-51-81 (office). *Fax:* (495) 690-51-81 (office). *E-mail:* vladimir.tarnopolski@ccmm.ru (home). *Website:* www.tarnopolski.ru.

TARR, Béla; Hungarian film director, screenwriter and producer; b. 21 July 1955, Pécs; ed Budapest Film Acad.; began making amateur films aged 16 and later worked as caretaker at nat. House for Culture and Recreation; amateur work brought him to attention of Bela Balazs Studios which helped fund his feature debut Családi tűzfészek 1979; founding mem. Tarsulas Film Studio 1981–85, TT Filmmühely Kft 2003–; Commdr, Cross of the Hungarian Repub., Kossuth Decoration of the Hungarian Repub.; Andrzej Wajda Freedom Award, France Culture Award, Lifetime Achievement Award, Jerusalem, Giraldillo Award, Seville. *Films include:* Hotel Magnezit 1978, Családi tüzfészek (Family Nest) (also screenplay) 1979, Szabadgyalog (The Outsider) (also screenplay) 1981, Panelkapcsolat (The Prefab People, USA) (also screenplay) 1982, Őszi almanach (Almanac of Fall) (also screenplay) 1985, Szörnyek évadja (Season of Monsters,

USA) (actor) 1987, Kárhozat (Damnation) (also screenplay) 1987, The Last Boat (short feature, also screenwriter) 1989, City Life 1990, Sátántangó (Satan's Tango) (also screenplay) 1994, Journey on the Plain 1995, Szenvedély (Passion) (screenplay) 1998, Werckmeister harmóniák (Werckmeister Harmonies) (also assoc. producer and screenwriter) 2000, Château de sable (artistic supervisor) 2000, Visions of Europe (segment 'Prologue') 2004, A Halál kilovagolt Perzsiából (producer) 2005, The Man from London 2007. *Television includes:* Macbeth (also screenplay) 1982. *Address:* c/o TTF Kft, Róna u. 174, Budapest 1145, Hungary. *Fax:* (1) 251-9969. *E-mail:* ttfilmmuhely@t-online.hu.

TARSCHYS, Daniel, PhD; Swedish politician and political scientist; *Professor Emeritus of Political Science and Public Administration, University of Stockholm;* b. 21 July 1943, Stockholm; s. of Bernhard Tarschys and Karin Alexanderson; m. Regina Rehbinder 1970; two d.; ed Univ. of Stockholm, Univ. of Leningrad, USSR, Princeton Univ., USA; Prof. of Political Science and Public Admin., Univ. of Stockholm 1985–2010, Prof. Emer. 2010–; City Councillor in Lidingö 1970–76; adviser with Ministry of Finance 1976–78, 1979–83; Sec. of State, Prime Minister's Office 1978–79; Prof. of Soviet and E European Studies, Uppsala Univ. 1983–85; mem. Parl. 1976–82, 1985–94; Chair. Parl. Social Affairs Cttee 1985–91, Foreign Affairs Cttee 1991–94; Vice-Pres. Liberal International 1992–94, Int. Political Science Asscn 2006–09; mem. Council of Europe Parl. Ass. 1986–94, Alt. mem. 1981–83; Sec.-Gen. Liberal, Democratic and Reformers Group (LDR) 1987–91, Chair. 1991–94; Sec.-Gen. Council of Europe 1994–99; Chair. Swedish Nat. Council on Medicine and Ethics 2001–11; Chair. Edita and Ira Morris Hiroshima Foundation 2004–, Bank of Sweden Tercentenary Foundation 2006–14, European Humanities Univ. 2012–, Swedish Research Inst., Istanbul 2013–; mem. Royal Swedish Acad. of Sciences 2008–; Sr Fellow, Zentrum für Europäische Integrationsforschung, Univ. of Bonn, 2009; mem. Bd of Trustees European Studies Inst., Moscow 2007–, Eurasia Partnership Foundation, Tbilisi 2008–; Grand Crosses of Germany, Liechtenstein, Romania, San Marino and Spain; Herbert Tingsten Award (jtly with Ingemar Hedenius) 1976, Nagrada Sloboda (Prix liberté), Centre Int. pour la Paix, Sarajevo 1995, Gold Medal, Comenius Univ. of Bratislava 1997, King's Medal (Sweden) 2004, Karl Staaff Gold Medal 2009. *Publications:* books and articles on political philosophy, budgetary policy, public admin. and comparative politics. *Address:* Department of Political Science, University of Stockholm, 106 91 Stockholm, Sweden (office). *E-mail:* daniel.tarschys@statsvet.su.se (office). *Website:* www.statsvet.su.se/forskning/vara-forskare/daniel-tarschys (office).

TARTAKOVSKY, Vladimir Aleksandrovich; Russian chemist; b. 10 Aug. 1932; m.; one d.; ed Moscow State Univ.; worked as researcher, teacher; Head of Lab., Inst. of Organic Chem., USSR (now Russian) Acad. of Sciences 1955–86, Dir N.D. Zelinsky Inst. of Organic Chem. 1988–2002, now mem. Academic and Scientific Councils, Corresp. mem., USSR (now Russian) Acad. of Sciences 1987, mem. 1992; main research in organic synthesis, chem. of nitro-compounds; Lenin Prize 1976, AM Butlerov Prize, Lomonosov Gold Medal, Russian Acad. of Sciences 2011. *Address:* N.D. Zelinsky Institute of Organic Chemistry, 119991 Moscow, Leninsky prosp. 47, Russia (office). *Telephone:* (495) 137-29-44 (office). *Fax:* (495) 135-5328 (office). *E-mail:* secretary@ioc.ac.ru (office). *Website:* www.ioc.ac.ru (office).

TARTT, Donna; American writer; b. 23 Dec. 1963, Greenwood, Miss.; ed Univ. of Mississippi, Bennington Coll.; published first sonnet in a Miss. literary review 1976; WHSmith Literary Award 2003. *Publications include:* novels: The Secret History 1992, The Little Friend 2002, The Goldfinch 2013 (Pulitzer Prize for Fiction 2014); short stories include: A Christmas Pageant (Harper's) 1993, A Garter Snake (GQ) 1995, True Crime (audio book) 1996; contrib. articles to magazines. *Address:* c/o Amanda Urban, ICM Partners, 730 Fifth Avenue, New York, NY 10019, USA (office). *Telephone:* (212) 556-5600 (office). *E-mail:* MSouthard@icmtalent.com (office). *Website:* www.icmtalent.com (office); www .curtisbrown.co.uk/donna-tartt (office).

TARUTA, Sergey A.; Ukrainian steel industry executive; *Chairman, Industrial Union of Donbass;* fmr Head, Dept of Foreign Econ. Relations, AzovStal Steel Mill; mem. Bd of Dirs Industrial Union of Donbass (ISD) 1995, Chair. 2001–; Chair. Supervisory Bd, JSC Khartsyzsk Pipe Mill; mem. Supervisory Bd OJSC AzovStal; owner Metallurg Donetsk football team. *Address:* Industrial Union of Donbass, Shorsa str. 48, Donetsk 83050, Ukraine. *Telephone:* (62) 381-40-02 (office). *Fax:* (62) 381-40-30 (office). *Website:* www.isd.com.ua (office).

TARUTOKO, Shinji; Japanese politician; b. 6 Aug. 1959, Shimane Pref.; ed Osaka Univ., Matsushita Inst. of Govt and Man.; mem. House of Reps (Parl.) (Japan New Party, later DPJ) for Osaka No.12 constituency 1993–2012, Chair. Environment Cttee 2009, Fundamental Nat. Policies Cttee 2010; Minister for Internal Affairs and Communications Oct.–Dec. 2012, also of Regional Revitalization, Minister of State for Okinawa and Northern Territories' Affairs and for Promotion of Local Sovereignty Oct.–Dec. 2012; mem. Democratic Party of Japan (DPJ) 1998–, Chair. Community Interaction Cttee 2004, Diet Affairs Cttee 2010, Acting Sec.-Gen. 2011. *Address:* Democratic Party of Japan, 1-11-1, Nagata-cho, Chiyoda-ku, Tokyo 100-0014, Japan (office). *Telephone:* (3) 3595-9988 (office). *Fax:* (3) 3595-9961 (office). *Website:* dpjnews@dpj.or.jp (office); www.tarutoko.jp.

TARZI, Nanguyalai, PhD; Afghan diplomatist; *Ambassador to Switzerland;* m.; one s. one d.; ed Kabul Univ. and Faculté de Droit et Sciences Économiques, Paris, France; Prof. of Law and Political Science, Kabul Univ. 1964–70; joined Ministry of Foreign Affairs 1970; Political Observer of OIC, Perm. Mission to UN 1979–86; Deputy Perm. Observer of OIC to UN, New York 1986–92; Perm. Observer of OIC to UN, Geneva 1992–2000; Dir UN Information Centre, Tehran 2001–02; mem. Emergency Loya Jirga 2002; Amb. to Pakistan 2002–06; Amb. to Switzerland and Perm. Rep. to UN and other Int. Orgs, Geneva 2007–10, 2012–; Amb. to India (also accred to Bhutan, the Maldives, Nepal and Sri Lanka) 2010–12. *Address:* Embassy of Afghan, 23 Avenue de France, 1202 Geneva, Switzerland (office). *Telephone:* (22) 731-16-16 (office). *Fax:* (22) 731-45-10 (office). *E-mail:* ambassador@mission -afghanistan.ch (office); mission.afghanistan@bluewin.ch (office). *Website:* www .mission-afghanistan.ch (office).

TASCA, Catherine, LenD; French politician and government official; *Senator from Yvelines;* b. 13 Dec. 1941, Lyons; d. of Angelo Tasca and Alice Naturel; one d.; ed Inst. d'Etudes Politiques, Paris and Ecole Nat. d'Admin; civil servant, Ministry of Culture 1967; Dir Maison de la Culture de Grenoble 1973; Gen. Man. Ensemble Intercontemporain 1978; Co-Dir Théâtre de Nanterre-Amandiers 1982; mem.

Comm. Nat. de la Communication et des Libertés (CNCL) 1986; Minister Del. attached to the Minister of Culture and Communications 1988–91; Sec. of State for Francophone Countries and External Cultural Relations 1992–93; Minister of Culture and Communications 2000–02; Conseiller d'Etat en service extraordinaire 2003–04; Senator from Yvelines 2004–; Pres. Admin. Bd Canal+Horizons 1993–97; Deputy to Nat. Ass. from Yvelines 1997–, mem. Socialist Party; Ordre des Arts et des Lettres, Chevalier, Légion d'honneur. *Publication:* Un Choix de vie 2002. *Address:* Sénat, 15 rue de Vaugirard, 75291 Paris (office); 21 rue Saint-Amand, 75015 Paris, France (home). *Telephone:* 42-34-28-18 (office). *E-mail:* c.tasca@senat .fr (office). *Website:* www.senat.fr (office).

TASHIYEV, Kamchybek; Kyrgyzstani politician, lawyer, engineer and chemist; *Chairman, Homeland Idealistic Democratic Political Party (Ata-Jurt);* b. Jalal-Abad Prov.; ed Kyrgyz Nat. State Univ.; Asst Chief of Staff, Office of the Prime Minister 2002–03; Deputy Head of Lenin Dist Admin, Bishkek City Admin 2003–05; Deputy to Jogorku Kenesh (Parl.), Chair. Cttee on Fuel and Energy Sector and Water Resources 2005–07; Minister of Emergency Situations 2007–09; Chair. Homeland Idealistic Democratic Political Party (Ata-Jurt); rank of Maj.-Gen. 2009; arrested on charges including attempting to overthrow the Govt Oct. 2012, cleared by Bishkek City Court June 2013, decision reversed by Supreme Court Aug. 2013, sentenced to 18 months' imprisonment. *Address:* c/o Homeland Idealistic Democratic Political Party (Ata-Jurt), 720000 Bishkek, Chygysh-5 33/3, Kyrgyzstan. *Telephone:* (312) 89-01-50. *E-mail:* iyikatajurt@gmail.com. *Website:* www.atajurt.org.

TASHMUHAMEDOVA, Dilorom Hafurjanovna, MD; Uzbekistani physician and politician; *Speaker, Qonunchilik palatasi (Legislative Chamber);* b. 19 Feb. 1962, Tashkent Oblast; m. P. Tashmuhamedov; four c.; ed Tashkent State Medical Inst., Faculty of Intergovernmental Relations and External Econ. Relations, Acad. of State and Social Construction; early career as teacher, Tashkent State Medical Inst.; f. Farmed (pharmaceuticals co.) 1994; Deputy, Oly Majlis (Supreme Ass.) 2001–04, Deputy Qonunchilik palatasi (Legis. Chamber) 2004–, mem. Cttee for Int. Affairs and Inter-parl. Communication, Deputy Speaker 2007–08, Speaker 2008–; mem. Adolat (Justice) Social Democratic Party, First Sec. Political Council 2005–, also leader of parl. faction; unsuccessful cand. in presidential election 2007; Dustlik (Friendship) Order 2006. *Publications include:* series of academic works about medicine; numerous articles about socio-political reform, the development of a multi-party system and of democratic institutions and the increasing involvement of women in social life. *Address:* Office of the Speaker, Qonunchilik palatasi, 100035 Tashkent, Bunyedkor ko'ch. 1, Uzbekistan (office). *Telephone:* (71) 239-87-07 (office). *Fax:* (71) 239-41-51 (office). *E-mail:* info@parliament.gov.uz (office). *Website:* www.parliament.gov.uz (office).

TASMAGAMBETOV, Imangali Nurgaliyevich; Kazakhstani politician; *Mayor of Astana;* b. 9 Dec. 1956; s. of Nurgali Tasmagambetov and Mataevna Kokanova; m. Klara Bekkulova; one s. two d.; ed Pushkin Pedagogical Inst., Oral; began career as geography teacher 1979; served in various govt positions including Chair. State Cttee on Youth Affairs 1991–93; Asst to Pres. 1993–94; apptd Atyrau oblast akim (Gov.) 1998; Deputy Prime Minister for Cultural Affairs 1991–93, in charge of Social and Ethnic Policy 2000–02; Prime Minister of Kazakhstan 2002–03; State Sec. 2003–04; Mayor of Almaty 2004–08, of Astana 2008–; Order of Parasat 1998, Order of the First Pres. of Kazakhstan Nursultan Nazarbayev 2004, Astana 10-Year Medal 2008, Order of Barys, Second Class 2010, Order of Friendship (Russian Fed.), Order of Holy Prince Daniel of Moscow, Order of St Seraphim of Sarov, Second Class 2010. *Publications:* several scientific papers and articles on socio-economic devt and political science. *Leisure interests:* history, literature. *Address:* Office of the Mayor, 473000 Astana, Kazakhstan (office). *Website:* en.government.kz (office).

TASSLER, Nina, BFA; American television executive; *President, CBS Entertainment;* m. Jerry Levine; two c.; ed Boston Univ.; following graduation, moved to New York City and worked for Roundabout Theatre Co.; moved to Los Angeles, Calif. and worked as talent agent at Triad Artists for five years; Dir, Movies and Mini-Series, Lorimar/Warner Bros. Television from 1990, Vice-Pres., Drama Devt, Warner Bros. Television –1997; Vice-Pres., Drama, CBS Productions 1997–98, Sr Vice-Pres., Drama Devt, CBS Entertainment 1998–2003, Exec. Vice-Pres., Drama Series Devt 2003–04, Pres. CBS Entertainment 2004–; Creative Achievement Award 2005. *Films include:* Frankie and Johnny Are Married (actress) 2003, The Optimist (producer) 2013. *Address:* CBS Corporation, 51 West 52nd Street, New York, NY 10019-6188, USA (office). *Telephone:* (212) 975-4321 (office). *Website:* www.cbscorporation.com (office).

TATA, Jamshed Rustom, DSc, FRS; British medical research scientist; *Senior Research Scientist Emeritus, Medical Research Council;* b. 13 April 1930, Bombay, India; s. of Dr Rustom J. Tata and Gool Tata (née Contractor); m. Renée S. Zanetto 1954; two s. one d.; ed Univ. of Bombay, Indian Inst. of Science, Bangalore, Coll. de France and Univ. of Paris (Sorbonne), Paris, France; Postdoctoral Fellow, Sloan-Kettering Inst., New York, USA 1954–55; Beit Memorial Fellow, Nat. Inst. for Medical Research, London 1956–60; Visiting Scientist, Wenner-Gren Inst., Univ. of Stockholm, Sweden 1960–62; mem. Scientific Staff, MRC, Nat. Inst. for Medical Research, London 1962–96, Sr Research Scientist 1996–, Head, Lab. of Developmental Biochemistry 1973–96; Visiting Prof., Univ. of California, Berkeley, USA 1969–70, Ecole Normale Superieure, Lyon, France; Fogarty Int. Scholar, NIH, Bethesda, Md, USA 1983–89, Visiting Scientist 1997; Chair. Cell and Molecular Panel, Wellcome Trust 1990–92, Int. Relations Group 1997–2004; Dir (non-exec.) Biotech Analytic 2000–04; mem. Indian Nat. Acad. of Sciences; Corresp. mem. Soc. de Biologie, France; Fellow, Third World Acad. of Sciences; Chair. and Trustee, Oxford Int. Biomedical Centre 1996–2007; several interviews and reports on BBC Radio and one documentary on BBC TV; ed. of several science journals and publs; Dr hc (Ecole Normale Superieure, Paris) 2009; various awards. *Publications:* The Thyroid Hormones 1959, Chemistry of Thyroid Diseases 1960, Metamorphosis 1972, The Action of Growth and Developmental Hormones 1983, Metamorphosis 1986, Hormonal Signalling and Post-embryonic Development 1998; more than 250 original scientific papers and reviews. *Leisure interests:* gardening, reading, travel, tennis. *Address:* 15 Bittacy Park Avenue, Mill Hill, London, NW7 2HA, England (home). *Telephone:* (20) 8816-2108 (office); (20) 8346-6291 (home). *Fax:* (20) 8906-4477 (office). *E-mail:* jtata@nimr.mrc.ac.uk (office); jrtata134@clara.co.uk (home).

TATA, Ratan N., GBE, BSc; Indian business executive; b. 28 Dec. 1937, nephew of J. R. D. Tata; ed Cornell Univ., Harvard Business School, USA; joined Tata Group 1962, Chair. Tata Industries 1981–2012, Chair. Tata Sons Ltd (holding co. comprising 80 cos) 1991–2012, also Chair. various cos in Tata Group, including Tata Steel, Tata Motors Ltd, Tata Engineering & Locomotive Co. Ltd, Tata Industries Ltd, Tata Chemicals Ltd, The Indian Hotels Co. Ltd, Tata Tea Ltd, Tata IBM Ltd, Information Technology Park Ltd, Tata Lucent Technologies Ltd, Tata Trustee Co. Ltd, Tata International AG Zug, Switzerland, Tata Ltd, London, UK, Tata Inc., New York, USA, Tata Technologies (Pte) Ltd, Singapore, Tata Communications Ltd, Tata Hydro Electric Power Supply Co. Ltd, The Andhra Valley Power Supply Co. Ltd, The Tata Power Co. Ltd, Corus (following acquisition of Corus by Tata Steel in April 2007) 2007–12; mem. Bd of Dirs The Bombay Dyeing & Mfg Co. Ltd, Haldia Petrochemicals Ltd, Antrix Corpn Ltd, Varuna Overseas Ltd, UK; Chair. Indian Investment Comm.; mem. Indian Prime Minister's Council on Trade and Industry, Nat. Hydrogen Energy Bd, Nat. Mfg Competitiveness Council, Global Business Council on HIV/AIDS, The Reserve Bank of India, Nat. Council of Applied Econ. Research; mem. International Advisory Council, Singapore Econ. Devt Bd; mem. International Investment Council, Repub. of South Africa; mem. International Advisory Bd Mitsubishi Corpn, American International Group, JP Morgan Chase; Trustee, Rand Corpn, Cornell Univ., Univ. of Southern California, Foundation Bd, Ohio State Univ.; Hon. Fellow, LSE, London, UK; Hon. DBA (Ohio State Univ.), Hon. DTech (Asian Inst. of Tech., Bangkok), Hon. DSc (Univ. of Warwick); Padma Bhushan 2000, ranked by Forbes magazine amongst The World's Most Powerful People (59th) 2009, (61st) 2010, Padma Vibhushan 2008. *Address:* c/o Tata Sons Ltd, Bombay House, 24 Homi Mody Street, Mumbai 400 001, India.

TATARINOV, Leonid Petrovich; Russian palaeontologist and zoologist; *Adviser, Russian Academy of Sciences;* b. 12 Nov. 1926, Tula; s. of Petr Lukich Tatarinov and Anna Nikolayevna Tatatrinova; m. Bułat Susanna Gurgenovna 1941; two d.; ed Moscow Univ.; mem. CPSU 1964–91; served in Soviet Army 1943–44; mem. staff USSR Acad. of Sciences Inst. of Palaeontology (jr research fellow, then head of lab. and sr research fellow) 1955–73, Dir 1975–92, Vice-Sec. Dept of Gen. Biology of USSR (now Russian) Acad. of Sciences 1975–, currently Adviser; Chair. Council for Study of Palaeobiology and Evolution 1981; mem. Council Russian Acad. of Sciences 1992–; Scientific Chief of Jt Soviet- (now Russian-) Mongolian Palaeontological Expedition 1975–96; Ed.-in-Chief Palaeontology Journal 1978–88, 1993–2001, Zoological Journal 1988–93; Corresp. mem. USSR (now Russian) Acad. of Sciences 1974, mem. 1981–; Foreign mem. Linnean Soc., London; USSR State Prize 1978, Order of Merit for the Fatherland 1999. *Publications:* Sketches on the Theory of Evolution 1987, Palaeontology and Evolutionary Doctrine 1989, Sketches on the Evolution of Reptiles 2006, and other works on origins and early evolution of tetrapods. *Leisure interests:* music, history. *Address:* Palaeontological Institute, Academy of Sciences, Profsoyunaya str. 123, 117321 Moscow, Russia (office); Leninskij pr. 18, ap. 71, 117019 Moscow, Russia (home). *Telephone:* (495) 339-07-00 (office); (495) 438-12-94 (home). *Fax:* (495) 339-12-66. *E-mail:* tatarin@paleo.ru (office). *Website:* www.paleo.ru (office).

TATE, Jeffrey Philip, CBE, MA, MB, BChir; British conductor; *Principal Conductor, English Chamber Orchestra and Hamburger Symphoniker;* b. 28 April 1943, Salisbury, Wilts.; s. of Cyril H. Tate and Ivy Ellen Naylor (née Evans); ed Farnham Grammar School, Christ's Coll. Cambridge and St Thomas's Hosp. London; trained as medical doctor 1961–67; joined London Opera Centre 1969; joined staff of Royal Opera House, Covent Garden 1970; made recordings as harpsichordist 1973–77; Asst to Pierre Boulez (q.v.) for The Ring, Bayreuth 1976–81; Asst to Sir John Pritchard, Cologne Opera 1977; conducted Gothenburg Opera, Sweden 1978–80; Metropolitan Opera début 1979; Covent Garden debut 1982; Chief Guest Conductor, Geneva Opera 1983–95; Prin. Conductor, English Chamber Orchestra 1985–, Royal Opera House, Covent Garden 1986–91; Prin. Guest Conductor, Royal Opera House, Covent Garden 1991–94, Orchestre Nat. de France 1989–98; Chief Conductor and Artistic Dir Rotterdam Philharmonic Orchestra 1991–94; Chief Conductor Minnesota Orchestra Summer Festival 1997–; Prin. Guest Conductor Teatro La Fenice 1999; Musical Dir Teatro di San Carlo, Naples 2005–12; Principal Conductor, Hamburger Symphoniker 2008–; appears with maj. orchestras in Europe and America; numerous recordings with English Chamber orchestra; Pres. Asscn for Spina Bifida and Hydrocephalus 1989–, Music Space Trust 1991–; other charitable positions; Hon. DMus (Leicester) 1993; Hon. Fellow Christ's Coll. Cambridge, St Thomas's and Guy's Hosp. Medical School; Grand Prix du Disque (for complete recording of opera Lulu) 1995, Premio della Critica Musicale 'Franco Abbiati' Spettacolo prize (for Königskinder, with Paul Curran) 2003; Officier, Ordre des Arts et des Lettres 1995, Chevalier, Légion d'honneur 1999. *Leisure interests:* church-crawling, with gastronomic interludes. *Address:* Fondazione Teatro di San Carlo, Via San Carlo 98/F, 80132 Naples, Italy (office). *Telephone:* (081) 7972331 (office). *Fax:* (081) 400902 (office). *Website:* www.teatrosancarlo.it (office).

TATE, John Torrence, Jr, PhD; American mathematician and academic; *Sid W. Richardson Foundation Regents Chair Emeritus in Mathematics and Professor Emeritus, University of Texas;* b. 13 March 1925, Minneapolis, Minn.; ed Harvard Coll. and Princeton Univ.; Research Asst and Instructor, Princeton Univ., NJ 1950–53; Visiting Prof., Columbia Univ., New York 1953–54; Prof., Harvard Univ., Cambridge, Mass 1954–90; Prof. and Sid W. Richardson Foundation Regents Chair in Math., Univ. of Texas, Austin 1990–, now Emer.; mem. NAS 1969; Foreign mem. Acad. des sciences 1992, Norwegian Acad. of Science and Letters; Hon. mem. London Math. Soc. 1999; Cole Prize, American Math. Soc. 1956, Sloan Fellowship 1959–61, Guggenheim Fellowship 1965–66, Leroy P. Steele Prize for Lifetime Achievement 1995, Wolf Prize in Math. Wolf Foundation 2003, Abel Prize, Norwegian Acad. of Science and Letters 2010. *Publications:* numerous articles in math. journals on arithmetic algebraic geometry. *Address:* Department of Mathematics, College of Natural Sciences, University of Texas, 1 University Station Stop C1200, Austin, TX 78712, USA (office). *Telephone:* (512) 471-7107 (office); (512) 471-7711 (office). *Fax:* (512) 471-9038 (office). *E-mail:* tate@math .utexas.edu (office). *Website:* www.ma.utexas.edu/people/emeritus_faculty (office).

TATISHVILI, Tsisana Bezhanovna; Georgian singer (soprano); b. 30 Dec. 1939, Tbilisi; m. Giorgi Totibadze; ed V. Sarandzhishvili Conservatoire, Tbilisi; joined Tbilisi (now Georgian) State Opera as soloist 1963; has toured Germany, Poland,

fmr Czechoslovakia and other countries; roles have included Tatiana in Eugene Onegin, Liza in Queen of Spades, Aida, Leonora in Il Trovatore, Donna Anna in Don Giovanni, Ortrud in Lohengrin, Salome, Desdemona in Otello, Santuzza in Cavalleria Rusticana, Eteri in Paliashvili's Absalom and Eteri; Prof. V. Saradjishvili Tbilisi State Conservatoire 1985–; vocal consultant at Georgian State Opera 1999–; mem. Artistic Council 2001–; Fellow, Georgian Acad. of Humanitarian Sciences; Order of Nat. Merit of Georgia; People's Artist of Georgian SSR 1973, Paliashvili Prize 1979, 1987, People's Artist of USSR 1979, Presidential Order of Excellence (Georgia) 2012; Order of Honour. *Address:* c/o V. Saradjishvili Tbilisi State Conservatoire, 8 Griboedov str., 0108 Tbilisi, Georgia.

TATOLA, Col Benando; Chadian army officer and government official; *Minister-delegate at the Presidency of the Republic, responsible for National Defence and War Veterans;* ed Air Command and Staff Coll., Montgomery, Ala, USA; fmr Mil. Chief of Staff to Pres.; currently Minister-delegate at the Presidency of the Repub., responsible for Nat. Defence and War Veterans. *Address:* Ministry of National Defence, BP 916, N'Djamena, Chad (office). *Telephone:* 22-52-35-13 (office). *Fax:* 22-52-65-44 (office).

TATUM, Beverly Daniel, MA, PhD; American clinical psychologist, academic and university administrator; *President, Spelman College;* m. Travis Tatum; two s.; ed Wesleyan Univ., Conn., Univ. of Mich., Hartford Seminary, Conn.; clinical psychologist, ind. practice 1988–98; Dissertation Fellow, Center for Black Studies, Univ. of Calif., Santa Barbara 1980–81, Lecturer, Dept of Black Studies 1982–83; Asst Prof. Dept of Psychology, Westfield State Coll., Mass 1983–86, Assoc. Prof. 1986–89; Assoc. Prof. Dept of Psychology and Educ., Mount Holyoke Coll., Mass 1989–96, Prof. 1996–, Dept Chair 1997–98, Dean of Coll. and Vice-Pres. for Student Affairs 1998–2002, Acting Pres. 2002; Pres. Spelman Coll., Atlanta, Ga 2002–; Visiting Scholar, Wellesley Coll., Mass 1991–92; mem. Bd of Dirs Smith Child Care Center at Sunnyside, Mass 1985–92, Equity Inst., Mass 1988–90; mem. Bd of Trustees, Williston Northampton School 1999–; mem. Bd of Incorporators, Hartford Seminary 2000–; Chair. Human Subjects Cttee, Psychology Dept, Mount Holyoke Coll. 1989–90; Chair. Coll. Cttee on Fellowships 1998–; mem. African-American Studies Steering Cttee, Multicultural Community and College Life Cttee, Academic Policies Cttee; Faculty Adviser, Psychology Club, Mount Holyoke Club 1990–91; Westfield State Coll. Campus Rep., Mass Teachers Asscn 1986–89; mem. American Psychological Asscn, American Educational Research Asscn, American Coll. Personnel Asscn, American Asscn of Univ. Women, Nat. Asscn of Multicultural Educ.; Elder, Martin Luther King Community Presbyterian Church 1994–97; Rackham Opportunity Fellowship, Univ. of Mich. 1975–78; Fellow American Psychological Asscn; Ford Foundation Postdoctoral Fellow 1991–92; Nat. Achievement Award 1971–72, Distinguished Service Award, Westfield State Coll. 1986, 1987, Commonwealth Citation for Meritorious Service, Westfield State Coll. 1988, Asscn of Women in Psychology Publ. Award 1994, Nat. Asscn of Multicultural Educ. Book of the Year Award 1998. *Publications:* Assimilation Blues: Black Families in a White Community 1987, Why Are All the Black Kids Sitting Together in the Cafeteria? and Other Conversations About Race 1997, Can We Talk About Race? and Other Conversations in an Era of Resegregation 2007. *Address:* Office of the President, Spelman College, 350 Spelman Lane, SW, Atlanta, GA 30314-4399, USA (office). *Telephone:* (404) 270-5001 (office). *Fax:* (404) 270-5010 (office). *E-mail:* btatum@spelman.edu (office). *Website:* www.spelman .edu/administration/office (office).

TAUBES, Clifford Henry, PhD; American mathematician and academic; *William Petschek Professor of Mathematics, Harvard University;* b. 1954, Rochester, NY; ed Cornell Univ., Princeton Univ., Harvard Univ.; currently William Petschek Prof. of Math., Harvard Univ.; mem. NAS 1996; Fellow, American Acad. of Arts and Sciences 1995; four-time speaker at Int. Congress of Mathematicians 1986, 1994 (plenary), 1998, 2010 (plenary; selected, but did not speak), Veblen Prize, American Math. Soc. 1991, Elie Cartan Prize, Acad. des sciences 1993, Clay Research Award 2008, NAS Award in Math. 2008, Shaw Prize in Math. (co-recipient) 2009. *Publications:* Modeling Differential Equations in Biology, The L Squared Moduli Spaces on Four Manifold with Cylindrical Ends (Monographs in Geometry and Topology), Metrics, Connections and Gluing Theorems (CBMS Regional Conf. Series in Math.); numerous papers in professional journals. *Address:* Mathematics Department, Harvard University, SC 504, Cambridge, MA 02138, USA (office). *Telephone:* (617) 495-5579 (office). *E-mail:* chtaubes@math.harvard.edu (office). *Website:* www.math.harvard.edu (office).

TAUBIRA-DELANNON, Christiane, DSci; French politician; *Minister of Justice and Keeper of the Seals;* b. 2 Feb. 1952, Cayenne, French Guiana; Founder and Pres. Walwari (political movt) 1993; Deputy to Nat. Ass. for French Guiana (1st constituency) 1993–2012; mem. European Parl. (Group of the European Radical Alliance, Énergie Radicale) 1994–99; mem. Parti Guyanais de Centre Gauche; mem. Cttee on Devt and Co-operation, Del. for relations with the countries of S America; joined the Socialist Party (PS) 1997; commissioned by Prime Minister Lionel Jospin for a report on gold discovery in Guiana; gave her name to the 21 May 2001 law recognizing the Atlantic slave trade and slavery as a crime against humanity; a Left Radical Party (PRG) cand. for the presidency though not belonging to the party 2002, Vice-Pres. Left Radical Party 2002–; Regional Councillor of French Guiana 2010–; Minister of Justice and Keeper of the Seals 2012–. *Publications:* Peche en Fiches (Guyane) 1993, Mes météores : combats politiques au long cours 2012, Paroles de liberté 2014. *Address:* Ministry of Justice, 13 place Vendôme, 75042 Paris Cedex 01, France (office). *Telephone:* 1-44-77-60-60 (office). *Fax:* 1-44-77-60-00 (office). *E-mail:* cyberjustice@justice.gouv.fr (office). *Website:* www.justice.gouv.fr (office).

TAUBMAN, A. Alfred; American business executive; b. 31 Jan. 1925, Pontiac, Mich.; s. of Philip Taubman and Fannie Taubman; m. 1st Reva Kolodney 1949 (divorced 1977); two s. one d.; m. 2nd Judith Mazor 1982; ed Univ. of Michigan, Lawrence Inst. of Tech.; Chair. and CEO The Taubman Co. (now Taubman Centers Inc.), Bloomfield Hills, Mich. (specializing in shopping-centre design, planning and devt) 1950–; Chair. Sothebys Holdings 1983–2000, owner of Sotheby's (art auctioneers) 1983–2000; sentenced to one year and one day's imprisonment for price-fixing 2002, released after 10 months. *Publication:* Threshold Resistance 2007. *Website:* www.thresholdresistance.com.

TAUR MATAN RUAK; Timor-Leste head of state and fmr army officer; *President;* b. (José Maria Vasconcelos), 10 Oct. 1956, Baguia, Baucau region; s. of António de Vasconcelos and Albertina Amaral; m. Isabel da Costa Ferreira; one s. two d.; joined guerrilla group Falintil (resisting Indonesian occupation) 1975, rising through ranks to become Company Commdr 1979, Asst Chief of Staff 1981, mil. adviser to Deputy Chief of Staff of Falintil 1983, responsible for all mil. operations throughout Timor-Leste 1986, Deputy Chief of Staff 1986–92, Chief of Staff 1992–98, Commdr of Falintil 1998–2001, rank of Brig.-Gen. 2001, Chief of Staff of East Timor Defence Force (Falintil-ETDF) 2002–11 (following restoration of independence 2002), rank of Maj.-Gen. 2009, demobilised from Falintil 2011; Pres. of Timor-Leste 2012–; Portuguese Parl. Human Rights Prize 1999. *Address:* Office of the President, Palácio das Cinzas, Caicoli, Dili, Timor-Leste (office). *Telephone:* 3339011 (office). *Website:* presidenttimorleste.tl (office).

TAURAN, HE Cardinal Jean-Louis Pierre, MA, DCnL; Vatican ecclesiastic and diplomatist; *President, Pontifical Council for Interreligious Dialogue;* b. 5 April 1943, Bordeaux, France; ed Gregorian Univ., Rome, Institut Catholique, Toulouse, France; ordained priest 1969, served as parish priest in Bordeaux 1969–72; joined Diplomatic Service of the Holy See 1975, served in various positions including Embassies in Dominican Repub. and Lebanon, joined Council for the Public Affairs of the Church (now Section for Relations with States), Rome 1983, apptd Under-Sec. 1988, Sec. for the Holy See's Relations with States 1990–2003; ordained Titular Archbishop of Thelepte 1991; cr. Cardinal (Cardinal-Deacon of Sant'Apollinare alle Terme Neroniane-Alessandrine) 2003; Archivist of Vatican Secret Archives and Librarian of Vatican Library 2003–07; Pres. Pontifical Council for Interreligious Dialogue, Roman Curia 2007–13, 2013–; participated in Papal Conclave 2005, 2013; Pres.'s Medal, Catholic Univ. of America 1999. *Address:* Office of the President, Pontifical Council for Interreligious Dialogue, Roman Curia, Via dell'Erba, 1, 00193, Rome, Italy (office). *Telephone:* (06) 69884321 (office). *Fax:* (06) 69884494 (office). *Website:* www .vatican.va/roman_curia (office).

TAUREL, Sidney, MBA; American (b. Spanish) pharmaceuticals industry executive; *Chairman Emeritus, Eli Lilly & Company;* b. 9 Feb. 1949, Casablanca, Morocco; ed École des Hautes Études Commerciales, Paris, France, Columbia Univ., New York; joined Eli Lilly Int. Corpn 1971, Marketing Assoc. 1971–72, Marketing Plans Man., Brazil 1971–76, marketing and sales assignments in E Europe and France 1976–81, Gen. Man., Brazil 1981–83, Vice-Pres. Lilly European Operations, London, UK 1983–86, Pres. Eli Lilly Pres. Pharmaceutical Div. 1991–93, mem. Lilly Bd Dirs 1991–, Exec. Vice-Pres. Eli Lilly & Co. and Pres. Pharmaceutical Div. 1993–96, Pres. 1996–2005, COO 1996–98, CEO 1998–99, Chair. and CEO 1999–2008, Chair. Emer. 2009–; mem. Bd of Dirs IBM Corpn, McGraw-Hill Cos Inc., RCA Tennis Championships; mem. Exec. Cttee Pharmaceutical Research and Mfrs of America (PhRMA), Exec. Cttee Business Council; apptd to Pres.'s Homeland Security Advisory Council 2002–03, to Pres.'s Export Council 2003–06, Advisory Cttee for Trade Policy and Negotiations 2007–; mem. Bd of Overseers Columbia Business School; Trustee, Indianapolis Museum of Art; US citizen 1995; Chevalier, Légion d'honneur 2001. *Address:* Eli Lilly & Co., Lilly Corporate Center, Indianapolis, IN 46285, USA (office). *Telephone:* (317) 276-2000 (office). *Fax:* (317) 277-6579 (office). *E-mail:* info@lilly.com (office). *Website:* www .lilly.com (office).

TAUS, Josef, LLD; Austrian banker, business executive and fmr politician; b. 8 Feb. 1933, Vienna; s. of Josef Taus and G. Schinko; m. Martha Loibl 1960; ed Univ. of Vienna, Hochschule für Welthandel; early career as journalist and served in law practice; with Austrian Inst. of Econ. Research; joined Girozentrale und Bank der Österreichischen Sparkassen AG as Sec. and Head of Econ. Div. 1958, mem. Man. Bd 1967–68, Chair. and Man. Dir 1968–75; fmr Man. Sparinvest-Kapitalanlage GmbH; mem. Parl. 1975–91; State Sec., Fed. Ministry of Communications and Nationalized Enterprises 1966–67; Fed. Chair. Austrian People's Party (ÖVP) 1975–79; Man. Pnr, Constantia Industrieverwaltungs GesmbH. 1979–86; mem. Supervisory Bd Management Trust Holding AG, Vienna 1989–; mem. Bd of Dirs Constantia Industrieholding AG 1986–89, ECO TRUST Holding AG 1989, Trust Invest AG 1990–; Man. Dir Fremdenverkehrsbetriebe GesmbH and Co. OHG. *Leisure interests:* skiing, music, reading, swimming. *Address:* Management Trust Holding AG, Argentinierstraße 42, 1040 Vienna (office); Zahnradbahnstrasse 17, 1190 Vienna, Austria (home). *Telephone:* (1) 535-61-03 (office). *Fax:* (1) 535-61-03 (office). *E-mail:* office@mth-gruppe.at (office). *Website:* www.mth-gruppe.at (office).

TAUTOU, Audrey; French actress; b. 9 Aug. 1978, Beaumont, Puy de Dôme, Auvergne; began acting lessons, Cours Florent, Paris; film debut in Vénus beauté (Institut) 1999. *Films include:* Vénus beauté (institut) (Venus Beauty Salon) (César Award for Most Promising Actress, Lumière Award for Most Promising Young Actress) 1999, Triste à mourir 1999, Épouse-moi 1999, Voyous Voyous (Pretty Devils) 2000, Le battement d'ailes du papillon (Happenstance) 2000, Le fabuleux destin d'Amélie Poulain (Amélie) (Chicago Film Critics Asscn Award for Most Promising Performer, Lumière Award for Best Actress, Sant Jordi Award for Best Foreign Actress) 2001, Dieu est grand, je suis toute petite (God Is Great, And I'm Not) 2001, À la folie... pas du tout (He Loves Me... He Loves Me Not) 2002, L'auberge espagnole (The Spanish Apartment) 2002, Dirty Pretty Things 2002, Pas sur la bouche 2003, Nowhere to Go But Up 2003, Les Marins perdus (Lost Seamen) 2003, Un long dimanche de fiançailles 2004, Les poupées russes 2005, The Da Vinci Code 2006, Hors de prix 2006, Ensemble, c'est tout 2007, Coco avant Chanel 2009, De vrais mensonges 2010, La Délicatesse 2011, Thérèse D 2012. *Address:* c/o Claire Blondel, Artmedia, 20 avenue Rapp, 75007 Paris, France (office). *Telephone:* 1-43-17-33-23 (office). 1-45-51-13-00. *E-mail:* info@artmedia.fr (office); bcgpresse@wanadoo.fr (office). *Website:* www.artmedia.fr (office). *Fax:* 1-45-51-18-19.

TAVERNE, Suzanna, BA; British company director; *Trustee, British Broadcasting Corporation;* b. 3 Feb. 1960, London, England; d. of Dick Taverne and Janice Taverne; m.; Marc Vlessing 1993; one s. one d.; ed Pimlico School, Westminster School, Balliol Coll., Oxford; with S.G. Warburg & Co. Ltd 1982–90; Finance Dir, Newspaper Publishing PLC 1990–94; consultant to Saatchi & Saatchi PLC 1994–95; Dir of Strategy and Devt, Pearson PLC 1995–98; Man. Dir British Museum, London 1999–2001; Dir of Operations, Imperial Coll. London 2002–05; Chair. Nat. Council for One Parent Families 2002–07, Gingerbread 2007–10; Dir

(non-exec.) Nationwide Building Society 2005–12, FCE Bank plc 2008–; mem. Advisory Bd Manchester Business School 2010–; Trustee, Design Museum 2006–11, StepChange Debt Charity 2009–, Shakespeare Schools Festival 2011–, BBC 2012–. *Address:* 35 Camden Square, London, NW1 9XA, England (home). *Telephone:* (20) 7482-5710 (office). *E-mail:* taverne@vlessing.com (home).

TAVERNER, Sonia, ARAD; Canadian ballerina and dance teacher; b. 18 May 1936, Byfleet, Surrey, England; d. of Herbert F. Taverner and Evelyn N. Taverner; ed Elmhurst Ballet School, Royal Ballet School, London and Ballet Arts and American Ballet Theater Schools, New York; joined Royal Ballet 1954, toured USA and Canada; joined Royal Winnipeg Ballet 1956, leading dancer 1957, ballerina 1962–66; appeared with Royal Winnipeg Ballet, Commonwealth Arts Festival, London 1964; joined Les Grands Ballets Canadiens as Prin. Dancer 1966–74; appeared as guest artist with the Boston Ballet Co., in Swan Lake 1967; Guest Teacher, Les Grands Ballets Canadiens Summer School 1970; Prin. Artist, The Pennsylvania Ballet 1971–72; Head of Ballet Div., Grant MacEwan Community Coll. 1975–80; Dir Professional Program Devt, Alberta Ballet School 1981–82; f. School of Classical Ballet, Spruce Grove, Alberta 1982–97; producer, own concert Variations 1977; Guest Artist, Vancouver Opera 1977, Les Grands Ballets Canadiens in Giselle and The Nutcracker 1977, 1978, Alberta Ballet Co. in The Nutcracker and Raymonda 1978, 1979; Guest Teacher, Alberta Ballet Summer School 1975, 1976, Pacific Ballet Theatre Summer School 1979; Guest Artist with Toronto, Winnipeg and Vancouver Symphony Orchestras; Guest Teacher, Penticton, BC 1984–85; Royal Acad. of Dance (RAD) Teaching Diploma 1993; Guest Teacher, Edmonton Dance Centre 1998–2002; has toured extensively in N America, Jamaica and UK; registered mem. RAD (Life mem. 2002, Assoc. 2003), Actors Equity Asscn, American Guild of Musical Artists; Dame Adeline Genée Silver Medal 1954, Canada Council Exploration Grant 1977. *Principal roles include:* classical: Swan Lake, Sleeping Beauty, Giselle, Nutcracker, Raymonda and Les Sylphides; Balanchine: Symphony in C, Allegro Brilliante, Theme and Variations, Raymonda Variations; Pas de Deux from Don Quixote, Black Swan Pas de Deux from Act III of Swan Lake, Tchaikovsky Pas de Deux, choreographed by George Balanchine, Flames of Paris Pas de Deux, choreographed by Alexander Vainonen. *Leisure interests:* cooking, reading, gardening, sewing, currently writing my memoirs of my life in dance. *Address:* PO Box 2039, Stony Plain, AB T7Z 1X6, Canada (home). *Telephone:* (780) 963-5567 (home). *E-mail:* taverner@ telusplanet.net (home).

TAVERNIER, Bertrand René Maurice; French film director; b. 25 April 1941, Lyon; s. of René Tavernier and Geneviève Dumond; m. Claudine O'Hagan 1965; one s. one d.; ed Ecole St-Martin de Pontoise, Lycées Henri-IV, Fénelon, Paris, Univ. de Paris (Sorbonne); press attaché and journalist, then film dir; mem. Société des réalisateurs de films, APR; Pres. Inst. Lumière 1982–. *Films include:* Le baiser de Judas, Une charge explosive, La chance et l'amour, L'horloger de Saint-Paul (Louis Delluc prize 1973), Que la fête commence (César Best Screenplay, Best Direction) 1975, Le juge et l'assassin (César Best Screenplay 1976) 1976, Des enfants gâtés 1977, La mort en direct (Foreign Press Award 1979) 1979, Une semaine de vacances 1980, Coup de torchon 1981, Mississippi Blues 1983, Un dimanche à la campagne (Best Dir Award, Cannes Film Festival, NY Critics Award) 1984, Autour de minuit 1986, La passion béatrice 1987, La vie et rien d'autre 1988 (European Film Festival Special Prize 1988), Daddy nostalgie 1990, La guerre sans nom 1991, L.627 1991, La fille d'Artagnan 1994, L'Appât 1995, De l'autre côté du periph (TV documentary) 1997; jt screenplay La trace 1983; (producer) Veillées d'Armes 1994, Capitaine Conan 1996 (Méliès Prize for Best French Film 1996, César for Best Dir 1997), Ça commence aujourd'hui 1999 (Prix de la Fipresci, Berlin, Prix du Public, San Sebastian and Tübingen, Prix Photogramas de Plata for Best Foreign Language Film, Spain), Histoires de vies brisées 2001, Laissez-passer 2002 (Best Film, Best Dir Fort Lauderdale 2002), Holy Lola 2004, In the Electric Mist 2008, The Princess of Montpensier 2010. *Publications:* 30 ans de cinéma américain (jtly) 1970, 50 ans de cinéma américain (jtly) 1991, Qu'est-ce qu'on attend? 1993, Amis américains 1994 and other books. *Leisure interests:* jazz, food, literature, movies. *Address:* Institut Lumière, 25 rue du Premier Film, 69008 Lyon (office); Little Bear, 7–9 rue Arthur Groussier, 75010 Paris, France. *Telephone:* 1-42-38-06-55 (office). *Fax:* 1-42-45-00-33 (office). *E-mail:* contac@institut-lumiere.org (office). *Website:* www.institut-lumiere.org (office).

TAVIANI, Paolo; Italian film director; b. 8 Nov. 1931, San Miniato; brother of Vittorio Taviani (q.v.); ed Univ. of Pisa. *Films:* co-dir (with Vittorio Taviani): Un uomo da bruciare 1963, I fuorilegge del matrimonio 1963, Sovversivi 1967, Sotto il segno dello scorpione 1969, San Michele aveva un gallo 1971, Allonsanfan 1974, Padre Padrone (Cannes Film Festival Palme d'Or, FIPRESCI Prize) 1977, The Meadow 1979, La notte di San Lorenzo (The Night of the Shooting Stars) (Cannes Film Festival Grand Prix du Jury) 1981, Xaos 1984, Good Morning, Babylon 1988, Il Sole anche di Notte 1990, Fiorile 1993, The Elective Affinities 1996, 1998 Two Kidnappings 1998, The Lark Farm 2007.

TAVIANI, Vittorio; Italian film director; b. 20 Sept. 1929, San Miniato; brother of Paolo Taviani (q.v.); ed Univ. of Pisa. *Films:* co-dir Un uomo da Bruciare 1963, I fuorilegge del metraimonio 1963, Sovversivi 1967, Sotto il segno dello scorpione 1969, San Michele aveva un gallo 1971, Allonsanfan 1974, Padre Padrone (Cannes Film Festival Palme d'Or, FIPRESCI Prize) 1977, The Meadow (Italian-French) 1979, La notte di San Lorenzo (The Night of the Shooting Stars) (Cannes Film Festival Grand Prix du Jury) 1981, Xaos 1984, Good Morning, Babylon 1988, Il Sole Anche di Notte 1990, Fiorile 1993, The Elective Affinities, Tu Ridi (You Laugh) 1998, Lark Farm 2007. *Television:* Resurrezione (Resurrection) (film) 2001, Luisa Sanfelice (miniseries) 2004.

TAVOLA, Kaliopate, MAgrSc; Fijian government official, economist and diplomatist; b. 10 Oct. 1946, Dravuni; m. Helen Tavola; one s. two d.; ed Massey Univ., New Zealand, Australian Nat. Univ., Australia; Agric. Officer, Ministry of Primary Industries 1973–77, Sr Agric. Officer 1977–79, Prin. Economist 1979, Prin. Agric. Officer Eastern Div./Projects 1980, Chief Economist 1980–81, 1982–84, Dir of Agric. (acting) 1981–82, later Minister of Primary Industries; London Rep. Fiji Sugar Marketing Co. Ltd 1984–88, Deputy CEO 1998–2000, in Suva 2000–08; Commercial Counsellor, Fiji High Comm. 1984–88; Head of Mission to EU, Brussels 1988–98; Amb. to Belgium (also accred to Luxembourg, Netherlands, France, Italy, Spain, Portugal, Greece) 1988–98; Perm. Rep. to UNESCO, Paris, also to FAO, WTO, WCO, OPCW; responsible for IFAD, MFO, PCA 1988–98;

Commr-Gen. South Pacific Pavilion, EXPO '92, Seville, Spain 1992; Minister of Foreign Affairs and External Trade 2000–06; mem. Senate. *Leisure interests:* reading, gardening, music, golf. *Address:* c/o The Senate, Parliament of Fiji Islands, Government Buildings, Suva, Fiji (office). *E-mail:* ktavola@govnet.gov.fj.

TAWADA, Yoko, MA; Japanese novelist; b. 23 March 1960, Tokyo; ed Waseda Univ., Univ. of Hamburg, Germany; based in Germany 1982–, writes in German and Japanese; Writer-in-Residence, Villa Aurora, Pacific Palisades, USA 1997; lectured on poetry at Univ. of Tübingen 1998; Max Kade Distinguished Visitor and Writer-in-Residence, Foreign Languages and Literatures Section, MIT 1999; Writer-in-Residence, Univ. of Kentucky 2004, Washington Univ. in St.Louis 2008, Stanford Univ. 2009, Cornell Univ. 2009; City of Hamburg Prize in Literature 1990, Gunzo Prize for new writers 1991, Lessing Prize 1994, Adelbert von Chamisso Prize 1996, Izumi Kyooka Literature Prize 2000, Punkamura Prix Des Deux Magots 2002, Ito Sei Literature Prize 2003, Tanizaki Junichiro Prize 2003, Goethe Medal 2005. *Publications include:* Nur da wo du bist da ist nichts (poems and stories) 1987, Das Bad (novel) 1989, Missing Heels (short story) 1991, Wo Europa anfaengt (Where Europe Begins, poems and stories) 1991, Sanninkankei (short stories) 1991, Inumukoiri (The Bridegroom was a Dog, short stories) (Akutagawa Prize) 1993, Ein Gast (novel) 1993, Arufabetto no kizuguchi (novel) 1993, Tintenfisch auf Reisen (short stories) 1994, Gottoharutotetsudo (short stories) 1996, Talisman (essays) 1996, Seijodensetsu (novel) 1996, Aber die Mandarinen muessen heute abend noch geraubt werden (poems) 1997, Kitunetsuki (poems) 1998, Hikon (novel) 1998, Verwandlungen (essays) 1998, Katakoto no uwagoto (essays) 1999, Hikari to zerachin no raipuchihhi (short stories) 2000, Opium fuer Ovid (novel) 2000, Hinagiku no ocha no baai (short stories) 2000, Yogisha no yakoressha 2002, Kyukeijikan 2002, Exophonie (essays) 2003, Tabi wo suru hadaka no me (novel) 2004, Uni ni otoshita namae 2006, Ameika 2006, Tokeru machi sukeru toori 2007, Students of the Snow (Noma Literary Prize) 2011. *Address:* c/o konkursbuch Verlag Claudia Gehrke, PF 1621, 72006, Tübingen, Germany. *E-mail:* office@konkursbuch.com; tawadaoo@yahoo.co.jp. *Website:* www.konkursbuch.com/html/tawada.html; yokotawada.de.

TAWARA, Machi, BA; Japanese poet; b. 1962, Osaka; ed Waseda Univ.; worked as a high school teacher 1985–89; writer of tanka poetry 1987–, over three million copies of first collection in print; 32nd Kadokawa Tanka Award 1986. *Publications include:* poetry collections: Sarada kinenbi (Salad Anniversary) (Modern Japanese Poets Asscn Award 1988) 1987, Chokoreeto kakumeri (The Chocolate Revolution) 1997; translations of classic poetry into contemporary Japanese: Man'yoshu (10,000 Leaves), Taketori Monogatori (The Tale of the Bamboo Cutter), Chokoreeto-go yaku midaregami (Tangled Hair in Chocolate Language) 1998; several popular travel and photography books, numerous essays for newspapers and magazines. *Address:* c/o Kodansha International Limited, Otowa YK Building, Bunkyo-ku, Tokyo 112-8652, Japan (office). *Website:* www.gtpweb.net/twr/indexe.htm.

TAXELL, (Lars Evald) Christoffer, LLM; Finnish business executive and fmr politician; *Chairman, Finnair oyj;* b. 14 Feb. 1948, Turku; s. of Lars Erik Taxell and Elna Hillevi Brunberg; m. Rachel Margareta Nygård 1974; two d.; Chair. Youth Org., Swedish People's Party 1970–72, Party Chair. 1985–90; Political Sec. 1970–71; Asst Lecturer, School of Econ., Abo Akademi, Turku 1973–75; mem. Parl. 1975–91; Minister of Justice 1979–87, of Educ. and Science 1987–90; mem. Bd of Dirs Partek Corpn 1984–2002, Pres. and CEO 1990–2002; Chair. Confed. of Finnish Industries EK 2005–06; Chair. Finnair Oyj 2003–, Stockmann Oyj 2007–; mem. Bd of Dirs Sampo plc 1998–, Raisio plc 2003–, Nordkalk Corpn 2003–, Luvata Group 2005–; Chair. European Services Forum, Brussels 2007–; Chancellor, Abo Akademi Univ. 2004–; Dr hc (Abo Akademi Univ.) 1998. *Address:* Office of the Chairman, Finnair Oyj, Tietotie 11 A, Vantaa Airport 01053, Finnair, Finland (office); European Services Forum, Avenue de Cortenbergh 168, 1000 Brussels, Belgium. *Telephone:* (9) 81881 (office). *Fax:* (9) 8184092 (office). *E-mail:* esf@esf.be. *Website:* www.finnair.com (office); www.esf.be/new.

TAY, Simon SC, LLB, LLM; Singaporean academic; *Chairman, Singapore Institute of International Affairs;* s. of the late Tay Seow Huah and of Cheong Keong Hin; m. Siow Jin Hua; one s.; ed Nat. Univ. of Singapore, Harvard Univ., USA; served as Nominated Mem. of Parl. 1997–2001; Chair. Nat. Environment Agency 2002–08; Visiting Prof., Harvard Law School 2003; currently Prof. of Int. Law and Public Policy, Nat. Univ. of Singapore and Lee Kuan Yew School of Public Policy and Visiting Prof., Yale Univ., USA; mem. numerous expert panels, ASEAN Regional Forum, APEC Ind. Experts, Energy City Center Int. Advisory Bd; Ind. Bd mem. and adviser to several large cos with regional interests; Fulbright Fellow, Harvard 1993–94; Laylin Prize, Harvard 1994, Singapore Young Artist of the Year 1995, Eisenhower Fellowship 2002, Nat. Day Award PBM 2006, Bernard Schwartz Fellow, Asia Soc., New York 2009. *Publications:* Stand Alone 1993, Asian Dragons and Green Trade 1996, Reinventing ASEAN 2001, The Enemy Within: Combating Corruption in Asia 2003, Sketching Regional Futures 2005, A Mandarin and the Making of Public Policy 2006, Elections in Asia: Making Democracy Work 2006, Climate Change Negotiations 2008, City of Small Blessings 2009, Asia Alone 2010. *Address:* Singapore Institute of International Affairs, 2 Nassim Road, Singapore, 258370 (office). *Telephone:* 67349600 (office). *Fax:* 67336217 (office). *E-mail:* chairman@siiaonline.org (office). *Website:* www.siiaonline.org (office).

TAYA, Col Maawiya Ould Sid'Ahmed; Mauritanian politician; fmr army officer and fmr head of state; b. 1943; served in Saharan War 1976–78, Chief of Mil. Operations, then commdr garrison at Bir Mogkrein; Minister of Defence 1978–79; Commdr nat. gendarmerie 1979–80; Minister in charge of Perm. Secr., Mil. Cttee for Nat. Recovery 1979–81; Army Chief of Staff 1980–81, March–Dec. 1984; Prime Minister and Minister of Defence 1981–84, 1984–92; Pres. of Mauritania and Chair. Mil. Cttee for Nat. Salvation 1984–92, elected Pres. of Mauritania 1992–2005 (deposed in bloodless coup). *Address:* c/o Présidence de la République, BP 184, Nouakchott, Mauritania.

TAYLOR, Allan Richard, OC; Canadian banker; b. 14 Sept. 1932, Prince Albert, Sask.; s. of Norman Taylor and Anna Lydia Norbeck Taylor; m. Shirley Irene Ruston 1957; one s. one d.; joined Royal Bank of Canada 1949, Dir, Head Int. Div. 1977–83, Pres. and COO 1983–86, CEO 1986–94, Chair. 1986–95; Dir Canadian Inst. for Advanced Research, Toronto, Neuroscience Network, Montréal; Pres. Int. Monetary Conf. 1992–93; Chair. Canadian Bankers Asscn 1984–86; mem. Council

of Patrons, Canadian Outward Bound; mem. Advisory Council Canadian Exec. Service Overseas; mem. Advisory Bd, Canadian Journalism Foundation, Advisory Bd, Canadian Foundation for AIDS Research; Exec. Adviser, Public Policy Forum; Hon. DJur (Univ. of Regina) 1987, (Concordia Univ.) 1988, (Queen's Univ.) 1991; Hon. DBA (Laval) 1990; Dr hc (Ottawa) 1992; inducted into Canadian Business Hall of Fame 2006. *Leisure interests:* golf, tennis, fishing. *Address:* Suite 2915, South Tower, Royal Bank Plaza, Toronto, ON M5J 2J5, Canada (office). *Telephone:* (416) 974-4041 (office). *Fax:* (416) 974-8713 (office). *E-mail:* allan.taylor@rbc.com (office).

TAYLOR, Andrew Dawson, OBE, BSc, DPhil; British physicist and academic; *Executive Director, National Laboratories, Science and Technology Facilities Council, Rutherford Appleton Laboratory;* b. 1 March 1950, Falkirk, Scotland; m.; four c.; ed St John's Coll., Oxford; joined Rutherford Lab. as part of team promoting accelerator-based neutrons sources as tools to investigate microscopic structure and dynamics of condensed matter, Dir ISIS facility, Science and Tech. Facilities Council (STFC), Rutherford Appleton Lab., Didcot, Oxon. 1992–2012, Exec. Dir STFC's Nat. Labs 2012–; also worked at Los Alamos, NM, USA; Hon. Fellow, Mansfield Coll., Oxford 2011; Hon. DSc (Glasgow) 2010 (London) 2012; Glazebrook Medal, Inst. of Physics 2006. *Publications:* numerous scientific papers in professional journals on pulsed neutron source instrumentation and science. *Address:* Science and Technology Facilities Council, Rutherford Appleton Laboratory, Harwell Science and Innovation Campus, Harwell, Oxford, OX11 0QX, Oxon., England (office). *Telephone:* (1235) 446681 (office). *Fax:* (1235) 445383 (office). *E-mail:* andrew.taylor@stfc.ac.uk (office). *Website:* www.scitech.ac.uk (office).

TAYLOR, Ann (see TAYLOR, Rt Hon. (Winifred) Ann).

TAYLOR, Baroness (Life Peer), cr. 2005, of Bolton in the County of Greater Manchester; **(Winifred) Ann Taylor,** PC; British politician; b. 2 July 1947, Motherwell; m. David Taylor 1966; one s. one d.; ed Bolton School and Univs of Bradford and Sheffield; fmr teacher and part-time tutor, Open Univ.; MP for Bolton West 1974–83, for Dewsbury 1987–2005; Parl. Pvt. Sec. to Sec. of State for Educ. and Science 1975–76, to Sec. of State for Defence 1976–77; an Asst Govt Whip 1977–79; Opposition Spokesman on Educ. 1979–81, on Housing 1981–83, on Home Affairs 1987–90, on Environment 1990–92, on Educ. 1992–94; Shadow Leader of House of Commons 1994–97; Pres. of the Council and Leader of the House of Commons 1997–98; Chief Whip 1998–2001; Chair. Select Cttee on Modernization 1997–98; Spokesperson on Citizen's Charter 1994–95; mem. Select Cttee on Standards and Privileges 1995–97; fmr Deputy Chair. Ind. Football Comm.; Vice-Chair. Forestry Group, House of Lords 2005–, Parl. Under-Sec. of State and Govt Spokesperson, Ministry of Defence 2007–; mem. Bd of Dirs Thales SA France; mem. Labour Party; Hon. Fellow, Birkbeck Coll. London. *Address:* House of Lords, London, SW1A 0PW, England (office). *Telephone:* (20) 7219-5183 (office). *E-mail:* taylora@parliament.uk (office).

TAYLOR, Arthur Robert, MA; American business executive and fmr university president; b. 6 July 1935, Elizabeth, NJ; s. of Arthur Earl Taylor and Marion Hilda Scott; m. Marion McFarland 1959 (divorced); three d.; m. 2nd Kathryn Pelgrift; ed Brown Univ.; Asst Dir of Admissions, Brown Univ. 1957–60; with The First Boston Corpn 1961–70, Vice-Pres. Underwriting Dept 1966–70, Dir 1970; Vice-Pres. (Finance), Int. Paper Co. 1970–71, Exec. Vice-Pres. 1971–72, Dir 1971–72; Pres. and Dir CBS Inc. 1972–76; Chair. Arthur Taylor & Co., New York 1977–; fmr mem. Bd of Dirs Travelers Corpn, Rockefeller Center Inc., American Friends of Bilderberg, Pitney Bowes Inc., Louisiana Land and Exploration, Eastern Airlines, Nomura Pacific Basin Fund; Vice-Chair. Forum Corpn, Boston, Mass 1988–; Dean, Faculty of Business, Fordham Univ. 1985–89; Pres. Muhlenberg Coll., Pa 1992–2002; mem. Council on Foreign Relations, Nat. Cttee on American Foreign Policy, Center for Inter-American Relations, Japan Soc.; Trustee, Brown Univ., Franklin Savings Bank, New York Hosp., William H. Donner Foundation; Commr Trilateral Comm. *Publications:* article in Harvard Review of Business History 1971, chapter in The Other Side of Profit 1975. *Address:* Main Street, Salisbury, CT 06068, USA (home).

TAYLOR, Charles, CC, OQ, BA, MA, DPhil, FBA; Canadian academic; *Professor Emeritus of Philosophy, McGill University;* b. 5 Nov. 1931, Montréal; s. of Walter Margrave Taylor and Simone Beaubien; m. Alba Romer 1956 (deceased), five d.; m. 2nd Aube Billard; ed McGill Univ., Univ. of Oxford, UK; Fellow, All Souls Coll. Oxford 1956–61, Asst Prof. of Political Science and Philosophy, Univ. of Oxford 1961, Prof. of Political Science and Prof. of Philosophy 1973–76, Chichele Prof. of Social and Political Theory and Fellow, All Souls Coll. 1976–81; Prof. of Philosophy, Univ. of Montréal 1962–71; Prof. of Political Science, then of Philosophy, McGill Univ. 1982–2006, Prof. Emer. 2006–; Bd of Trustees Prof. of Law, Northwestern Univ. 2002–08; mem. RSC; Corresp. mem. American Acad. of Arts and Sciences; Grand Officier, Ordre Nat. de Québec 2000; John Locke Prize, Oxford 1955, Templeton Prize 2007, Kyoto Prize 2008. *Publications:* The Explanation of Behaviour 1964, Hegel 1975, Hegel and Modern Society 1979, Human Agency and Language 1985, Philosophy and the Human Sciences 1985, Sources of Self 1989, The Malaise of Modernity 1991, Philosophical Arguments 1995, Varieties of Religion Today 2002, Modern Social Imaginaries 2004, A Secular Age 2007, Dilemmas and Connections: Selected Essays 2011. *Leisure interests:* skiing, swimming, hiking. *Address:* Department of Philosophy, McGill University, Stephen Leacock Building, Room 908, 855 Sherbrooke Street W, Montréal, PQ H3A 2T7 (office); 6603 Jeanne Mance, Montréal, PQ H2V 4L1, Canada (home). *Telephone:* (514) 398-6060 (office). *E-mail:* cmt1111111@aol.com (home). *Website:* www.mcgill.ca/philosophy (office).

TAYLOR, Charles Ghankay; Liberian fmr head of state; b. 1948; m. 3rd Jewel Taylor (divorced); m. 4th Victoria Addison-Taylor; three d.; Leader Nat. Patriotic Front of Liberia (NPFL), part of combined rebel force which overthrew fmr Pres. Samuel Doe; engaged in civil insurrection 1991–96; mem. Transitional Exec. Council of State 1996–97; Pres. of Liberia 1997–2003; indicted for war crimes in Sierra Leone 2003; in exile in Nigeria 2003, arrested March 2006, extradited to The Hague 2006; convicted by Special Court for Sierra Leone, based in The Hague, of 11 counts of aiding and abetting war crimes and crimes against humanity 26 April 2012, sentenced to 50 years in prison.

TAYLOR, Charles Margrave, CC, OQ, BA, MA, DPhil, FRSC; Canadian academic; *Board of Trustees Professor of Law and Philosophy, Northwestern University;* b. 5 Nov. 1931, Montréal; ed McGill Univ., Balliol Coll., Oxford; Fellow, All Souls Coll., Oxford 1956–61; Asst Prof., Dept of Political Science, McGill Univ., Montréal 1961–62, Prof. 1962–97, Prof. Emer. 1998–; Bd of Trustees Prof. of Law, Northwestern Univ. 2002–; Prof., Univ. of Montréal 1962–71; Chichele Prof. of Social and Political Theory, Univ. of Oxford 1976–81; Mills Visiting Prof., Univ. of California, Berkeley 1974, 1983; Alan B. Plaunt Memorial Lecturer, Carleton Univ., Ottawa 1978; Alex Corry Lecturer, Queen's Univ., Kingston, Ont. 1980; B.N. Ganguli Lecturer, Centre for the Study of Developing Socs, Delhi 1981; Suhrkamp Lecturer, Univ. of Frankfurt 1984; Guest Prof., J.W. Goethe Univ., Frankfurt 1984; Visiting Prof. of Political Science and Philosophy, Hebrew Univ. of Jerusalem 1985; Massey Lecturer, CBC 1991; Tanner Lecturer, Stanford Univ. 1992; Max Horkheimer Lecturer, Univ. of Frankfurt 1996; Storrs Lecturer, Yale Univ. 1998; Templeton Prize 2007, Kyoto Prize 2008. *Publications:* The Explanation of Behaviour 1964, The Pattern of Politics 1970, Erklärung und Interpretation in den Wissenschaften vom Menschen 1975, Hegel 1975, Hegel and Modern Society 1979, Social Theory As Practice 1983, Human Agency and Language: Philosophical Papers 1 1985, Philosophy and the Human Sciences: Philosophical Papers 2 1985, Negative Freiheit? Zur Kritik des neuzeitlichen Individualismus 1988, Sources of the Self: The Making of the Modern Identity 1989, The Malaise of Modernity 1991, Multiculturalism and 'The Politics of Recognition' 1992, Rapprocher les solitudes: crits sur le fédéralisme et le nationalisme au Canada 1992, Roads to Democracy: Human Rights and Democratic Development in Thailand 1994, Philosophical Arguments 1995, A Catholic Modernity? 1999, Wieviel Gemeinschaft braucht die Demokratie? Aufsätze zur politische Philosophie 2002, Varieties of Religion Today: William James Revisited 2002, Modern Social Imaginaries 2004, A Secular Age 2007. *Address:* Department of Philosophy, Northwestern University, Kresge Hall, Campus Drive, Evanston, IL 60208-2214, USA (office). *Telephone:* (847) 491-3656 (office). *Fax:* (847) 491-2547 (office). *E-mail:* charles-taylor@law.northwestern.edu (office). *Website:* www.philosophy .northwestern.edu (office).

TAYLOR, Grace Oladunni L., PhD; Nigerian biochemist and academic; ed Univ. of London, UK and Univ. of Ibadan; Prof. of Chemical Pathology, Univ. of Ibadan (retd); has taught medicine in Nigeria and other African countries; mem. Third World Org. for Women in Science; L'Oréal-UNESCO For Women in Science Award 1998. *Publications:* numerous articles in scientific journals on lipid metabolism. *Address:* c/o Department of Chemical Pathology, University of Ibadan, Ibadan, Nigeria (office). *Website:* www.ui.edu.ng (office).

TAYLOR, Graham, OBE; British professional football manager and fmr professional footballer; b. 15 Sept. 1944, Worksop, Notts., England; s. of Tommy Taylor; m. Rita Cowling 1965; two d.; ed Scunthorpe Grammar School; player, Grimsby Town 1962–68 (won Lincolnshire Sr Cup 1967/68), Lincoln City 1968–72 (won Lincolnshire Sr Cup 1968/69, 1969/70); Man. Lincoln City 1972–77 (won Lincolnshire Sr Cup 1974/75), Watford FC 1977–87, 1996, 1997–2001 (Football League First Div. play-off winner 1998/99), Aston Villa 1987–90, 2002–03, England nat. team 1990–93, Wolverhampton Wanderers 1994–95; Dir (nonexec.) Aston Villa 2001–03, Watford FC 2009–; Vice-Pres. Scunthorpe United 2003–; football commentator, BBC Radio Five Live, Sky TV 2004–; has managed a team of celebrities for Sky One's annual series, The Match; Celebrity Amb. for Sense Enterprise Bd, Birmingham; Patron, Lincoln City FC. *Address:* Scunthorpe United Football Club, Glanford Park, Doncaster Road, Scunthorpe, Lincolnshire DN15 8TD, England (office). *Telephone:* (1724) 848077 (office). *E-mail:* admin@ scunthorpe-united.co.uk (office). *Website:* www.scunthorpe-united.co.uk (office).

TAYLOR, Gregory Frank, AO, BEcons; Australian civil servant and economist; b. 1 July 1942, Adelaide; s. of Frank Taylor and Constance Rischbieth; m. Jill Beatrice Bodman 1967; one s. one d.; ed Univ. of Adelaide; Chair. Industries Assistance Comm., Canberra 1988; CEO Dept of Employment Educ. and Training 1989–94, Dept of Primary Industries and Energy 1993–95, Dept of Industry, Tech. and Commerce 1996; Exec. Dir IMF, Washington, DC 1997–2000; Chair. Australian Mathematics Trust Bd. *Leisure interest:* skiing. *Address:* c/o Australian Mathematics Trust, University of Canberra, ACT 2601, Australia.

TAYLOR, John B., BA, DEcon; American economist and government official; *Mary and Robert Raymond Professor of Economics, Stanford University;* b. 8 Dec. 1946, Yonkers, NY; m. Allyn Taylor; two d.; ed Princeton Univ., Stanford Univ.; Mary and Robert Raymond Prof. of Econs, Stanford Univ., also Sr Fellow, Hoover Inst., fmr Dir Stanford Inst. for Econ. Policy Research, fmr Dir Introductory Econs Center, fmr Chair. Stanford Cttee on Undergraduate Studies; Sr Staff Economist and mem. Presidential Council of Econ. Advisers under Pres Gerald Ford and George Bush, Sr; Under-Sec. of Treasury for Int. Affairs 2001–05; mem. California Council of Econ. Advisers under Gov. Arnold Schwarzenegger 2005–; Fellow, American Acad. of Arts and Sciences; Medal of Repub. of Uruguay 2005; Hoagland Prize 1992, Lilian and Thomas B. Rhodes Prize 1997, Alexander Hamilton Award 2005, George Shultz Award 2005, Adam Smith Award 2007. *Address:* Stanford University, Department of Economics, Stanford, CA 94305, USA (office). *Telephone:* (650) 723-9677 (office). *E-mail:* JohnBTaylor@stanford.edu (office). *Website:* www.stanford.edu/~johntayl (office).

TAYLOR, Rt Rev. John Bernard, KCVO, MA; British ecclesiastic; b. 6 May 1929, Newcastle upon Tyne, England; s. of George Taylor and Gwendoline Taylor; m. Linda Courtenay Barnes 1956; one s. two d.; ed Watford Grammar School, Christ's and Jesus Colls Cambridge, Hebrew Univ. of Jerusalem and Ridley Hall, Cambridge; RAF service 1952–54; ordained deacon 1956, priest 1957; Vicar of Henham and Elsenham, Essex 1959–64; Vice-Prin. Oak Hill Theological Coll. London 1964–72; Vicar of All Saints' Woodford Wells, Essex 1972–75; Archdeacon of West Ham 1975–80; Bishop of St Albans 1980–95; Chair. Council, Wycliffe Hall, Oxford 1985–99; Lord High Almoner to HM the Queen 1988–97; Pres. The Bible Soc. 1997–2004; Pres. and Chair. of Council, Haileybury 1980–95; Pres. Hildenborough Evangelistic Trust 1986–2000, Garden Tomb Asscn 1987–2010, Church's Ministry Among Jewish People 1996–2010; Chair. Council, Tyndale House, Cambridge 1996–2004; Hon. LLD. *Publications include:* Tyndale Commentary on Ezekiel 1969, Preaching through the Prophets 1983, Preaching on God's Justice 1994. *Leisure interests:* bird-watching, walking. *Address:* 22 Conduit Head Road, Cambridge, CB3 0EY, England. *Telephone:* (1223) 313783.

TAYLOR, John Bryan, PhD, FRS; British physicist and academic; *Consultant, Culham Centre for Fusion Energy;* b. 26 Dec. 1928, Birmingham; s. of Frank H. Taylor and Ada Taylor (née Stinton); m. Joan M. Hargest 1951; one s. one d.; ed Oldbury Co. High School and Univ. of Birmingham; served in RAF 1950–52; physicist, Atomic Weapons Research Establishment, Aldermaston 1955–59, 1961–62; Harkness Fellow, Univ. of California 1959–60; on staff of UKAEA, Culham Lab. 1962–89, Head of Theory Div. 1963–81, Chief Physicist, Culham Lab. 1981–89, Consultant 1994–; Fondren Foundation Prof. of Plasma Theory, Univ. of Texas at Austin 1989–94; Consultant Culham Centre for Fusion Energy 1994–; mem. Inst. for Advanced Study, Princeton, New Jersey 1969, 1980, 1981; Fellow, American Physical Soc.; Maxwell Medal, Inst. of Physics 1971, Max Born Prize and Medal, German Physical Soc. 1979, Award for Excellence in Plasma Research, American Physical Soc. 1986, James Clerk Maxwell Prize, American Physical Soc. 1999, Hannes Alfvén Prize, European Physical Soc. 2004. *Publications:* contribs to scientific learned journals. *Leisure interests:* gliding, model engineering. *Address:* Culham Centre for Fusion Energy, Culham Science Centre, Abingdon, OX14 3DB (office); Radwinter, Winterbrook Lane, Wallingford, OX10 9EJ, England (home). *Telephone:* (1235) 528822 (office). *E-mail:* bryan.taylor@ccfe.ac.uk (office). *Website:* www.ccfe.ac.uk (office).

TAYLOR, John Russell, (Charles Graham, William Hall, Brian Brooke), MA; British writer, broadcaster, editor and academic; b. 19 June 1935, Dover, Kent, England; s. of Arthur Russell Taylor and Kathleen Mary Taylor (née Picker); civil partner Ying Yeung Li; ed Dover Grammar School, Jesus Coll. Cambridge, Courtauld Inst. of Art; Sub-Ed., Times Educ. Supplement 1959–60; Editorial Asst, Times Literary Supplement 1960–62; Film Critic, The Times 1962–73; Dir of Film Studies, Tufts Univ. in London 1970–72; Prof., Div. of Cinema, Univ. of Southern Calif., USA 1972–78; Art Critic, The Times 1978–2005; Ed. Films and Filming 1983–90; Art Critic, Radio Two Arts Programme 1990–2000; Friend of the Festival Award, Chicago Int. Film Festival 2010. *Film:* Charles Chaplin Makes The Countess from Hong Kong 1966. *Television:* Feet Foremost 1968, The Imposter 1969, Dracula 1969, Curse of the Mummy 1970, A Letter to David 1971, A Quiet Place in the Country 1971. *Publications:* Joseph L. Mankiewicz 1960, Anger and After 1962 (USA: The Angry Theatre 1969), Anatomy of a Television Play 1962, Cinema Eye, Cinema Ear 1964, Penguin Dictionary of the Theatre 1966, The Art Nouveau Book in Britain 1966, Art in London 1966, The Rise and Fall of the Well-Made Play 1967, The Art Dealers 1969, Harold Pinter 1969, The Hollywood Musical 1971, The Second Wave 1971, Peter Shaffer 1974, David Storey 1974, Directors and Directions 1975, The Revels History of Drama in English Vol. VII 1978, Hitch 1978, Impressionism 1981, Strangers in Paradise 1983, Ingrid Bergman 1983, Alec Guinness 1984, 2000, Vivien Leigh 1984, Hollywood 1940s 1985, Portraits of the British Cinema 1986, Orson Welles 1986, Edward Wolfe 1986, Great Movie Moments 1987, Post-War Friends 1987, Robin Tanner 1989, Bernard Meninsky 1990, John Copley 1990, Impressionist Dreams 1990, Liz Taylor 1991, Muriel Pemberton 1993, Ricardo Cinalli 1993, Igor Mitoraj 1993, Claude Monet 1995, Bill Jacklin 1997, The World of Michael Parkes 1998, Antonio Saliola 1998, The Sun is God 1999, Michael Parkes: The Stone Lithographs 2000, Peter Coker 2002, Roberto Barnardi 2002, Roboz: The Painter's Paradox 2005, One Hand, Two Fingers 2005, Philip Sutton Woodcuts 2006, The Art of Michael Parkes 2006, Adrian George 2006, The Michael Winner Collection of Donald McGill 2006, Carl Laubin 2007, The Art of Jeremy Ramsey 2007, Randy Klein: Road 2008, The Glamour of the Gods 2008, Philip Sutton 2008, Exactitude 2009, Roboz: Face to Face 2011, High Relief 2013; edited: Let the Children Write 1961, Three Plays by John Arden 1964, New English Dramatists 8 1965, Look Back in Anger: A Casebook 1968, The Pleasure Dome (USA: Graham Greene on Film) 1972, Masterworks of British Cinema 1974, The Wizard of Oz 50th Anniversary Edn 1989. *Leisure interest:* buying books, talking to strange dogs. *Address:* c/o The Times, 1 Pennington Street, London, E98 1TT, England (office). *Telephone:* (20) 7782-5000 (office). *Website:* www.timesonline.co.uk (office).

TAYLOR, Joseph Hooton, Jr, PhD; American radio astronomer, physicist and academic; *Emeritus James McDonnell Distinguished Professor of Physics, Princeton University;* b. 29 March 1941, Philadelphia; s. of Joseph Taylor and Sylvia Evans; m. Marietta Bisson 1976; one s. two d.; ed Haverford Coll. and Harvard Univ.; Research Fellow and Lecturer, Harvard Univ. 1968–69; Asst Prof. of Astronomy, Univ. of Mass., Amherst 1969–72, Assoc. Prof. 1973–77, Prof. 1977–81; Prof. of Physics, Princeton Univ. 1980–2006, James McDonnell Distinguished Prof. of Physics 1986–2006, Prof. Emer. 2006–, Dean of Faculty 1997–2003; Fellow, American Acad. of Arts and Sciences; mem. NAS, American Astronomy Soc., Int. Scientific Radio Union, Int. Astronomy Union; Hon. DSc (Chicago) 1985, (Mass) 1994; Wolf Prize in Physics 1992, shared Nobel Prize for Physics 1993 and other awards and distinctions. *Publication:* Pulsars 1977. *Address:* Department of Physics, Princeton University, 215 Jadwin Hall, PO Box 708, Princeton, NJ 08544 (office); 272 Hartley Avenue, Princeton, NJ 08540, USA (home). *E-mail:* jtaylor@princeton.edu (office).

TAYLOR, Lance Jerome, BS, PhD; American economist and academic; *Arnhold Professor of International Co-operation and Development, New School University;* b. 25 May 1940, Montpelier, Idaho; s. of W. Jerome Taylor and Ruth R. Taylor; m. Yvonne S. M. Taylor 1963; one s. one d.; ed Calif. Inst. of Tech., Harvard Univ.; Asst then Assoc. Prof., Harvard Univ. 1968–74; Prof., MIT 1974–93; Arnhold Prof. of Int. Co-operation and Devt, New School for Social Research (now New School Univ.), New York 1993–, also Dir Center for Econ. Policy Analysis –2008, now Faculty Research Fellow; Visiting Prof., Univ. of Brasília 1973–74, Delhi School of Econs 1987–88, Stockholm School of Econs 1990; consultant for UN agencies and over 25 govts and agencies; Marshall Lecturer, Univ. of Cambridge 1987; V. K. Ramaswamy Lecturer, Delhi School of Econs 1988. *Publications:* Structuralist Macroeconomics 1983, Varieties of Stabilization Experience 1988, Income Distribution, Inflation and Growth 1991, The Market Meets its Match: Restructuring the Economies of Eastern Europe 1994, Global Finance at Risk 2000, Reconstructing Macroeconomics 2003. *Leisure interest:* raising cashmere goats. *Address:* Center for Economic Policy Analysis, New School University, 80 Fifth Avenue 5th Floor, Room 509, New York, NY 10011 (office); 15 Old County Road, P.O. Box 378, Washington, ME 04574, USA (home). *Telephone:* (212) 229-5901 ext. 352 (office); (207) 845-2722 (home). *Fax:* (212) 229-5903 (office); (207) 845-2589 (home). *E-mail:* taylorl@newschool.edu (office); lance@blacklocust.com (home). *Website:* www .newschool.edu/cepa (office).

TAYLOR, Martin; British banker and business executive; *Chairman, Syngenta AG;* b. 8 June 1952; m. Janet Davey 1976; two d.; ed Eton Coll. and Balliol Coll., Oxford; joined Reuters news agency as journalist in Paris; subsequently ed. Lex comment column, Financial Times, London; Personal Asst to Chair. of Courtaulds, later Dir Courtaulds Clothing Div., CEO Courtaulds PLC 1990–93, Chair. 1993; CEO Barclays Bank PLC 1994–98; mem. Bd of Dirs (non-exec.) WH Smith Group PLC 1993–98, Chair. 1999–2003; adviser to Goldman Sachs Int. 1999–2005; currently Chair. Syngenta AG, Basel, Switzerland, also Chair. Syngenta Foundation for Sustainable Agric.; Vice Chair. RTL Group SA; mem. UK Ind. Banking Comm.; fmr mem. UK Council for Science and Tech.; fmr Chair. UK Inst. of Public Policy Research Comm. on public/private partnerships. *Address:* Office of the Chairman, Syngenta AG, Schwarzwaldallee 215, Basel 4058, Switzerland (office). *Telephone:* 613231111 (office). *Fax:* 613231212 (office). *Website:* www.syngenta .com (office); www.syngentafoundation.org.

TAYLOR, Martin, MBE; British jazz musician (guitar) and composer; b. 20 Oct. 1956, Harlow, Essex; s. of William 'Buck' Taylor; ed Passmore Comprehensive School, Harlow; began playing aged four, playing in local bands aged 12, professional musician 1972–; support act for Count Basie and his Orchestra, QE2; performed and recorded regularly with violinist Stéphane Grappelli; formed Martin Taylor's Spirit of Django 1994–; played and recorded with Bill Wyman's Rhythm Kings 1998, 1999; featured on Prefab Sprout album Andromeda Heights; recordings (with Steve Howe) of guitars from Chinery Collection; Freeman of the City of London 1998; Dr hc (Paisley) 1999, (Royal Scottish Acad. of Music and Drama) 2010; Music Retailers Assen Award for Excellence 1985, British Jazz Award for Best Guitarist 1987, 1988, 1989, 1990, 1991, 1993, 1995, 1997, 1999, 2001, British Acad. of Composers & Songwriters Gold Badge of Merit 1999, Pioneer to the Life of the Nation 2003, BBC Radio 2 Jazz Award 2007, British Jazz Award 2007, Scottish Jazz Award 2012, Lifetime Achievement Award, Ards Int. Guitar Festival 2012. *Recordings include:* albums: Taylor Made 1978, Skye Boat 1981, Sarabanda (with John Patitucci and Paulinho Da Costa) 1987, Don't Fret 1990, Change Of Heart 1991, Artistry 1993, Reunion (with Stéphane Grappelli) 1993, Spirit of Django (British Jazz Awards for Best Album 1995) 1994, Portraits 1995, Years Apart 1996, Gypsy 1998, Two's Company 1999, I'm Beginning To See The Light 1999, Kiss & Tell 1999, In Concert (live) 2000, Stepping Stones 2000, Nitelife 2001, Solo (Int. Guitar Foundation Award for Best Album) 2002, Valley 2005, Gypsy Journey 2005, Freternity 2007, Double Standards 2008, Last Train to Hauteville 2010. *Film soundtracks include:* (with Stéphane Grappelli) Milou en Mai, Dirty Rotten Scoundrels. *Publication includes:* Martin Taylor: Autobiography of a Travelling Musician, The Martin Taylor Guitar Method. *Leisure interests:* cooking, walking, painting, cartoons, caricatures. *Address:* P3 Music Ltd, Incheoch, Alyth, Perthshire, PH11 8HJ, Scotland (office). *E-mail:* management@ p3music.com (office); martin@martintaylor.com. *Website:* www.p3music.com (office); www.martintaylor.com.

TAYLOR, (John) Maxwell (Percy); British insurance industry executive; *Chairman, Mitsui-Sumitomo Insurance London Companies;* b. 17 March 1948; s. of Harold Guy Percy Taylor and Anne Katherine Taylor (née Stafford); m. Dawn Susan Harling 1970; one s. one d.; joined Willis Faber & Dumas as jr aviation broker 1970; Dir Willis Faber, then Willis Corroon Group PLC, Chair. and Chief Exec. Willis, Faber & Dumas, Group Exec. Dir 1997; elected to Council of Lloyd's 1997, Chair. of Lloyd's 1998–2000; mem. Aon Corpn Group Exec. Cttee and Deputy Chair. UK Operations 2001–09 (retd), now Adviser; Chair. Mitsui-Sumitomo Insurance London Cos 2009–; mem. Bd of Dirs Qatarlyst (fmrly Qatar Insurance Services); Dir Financial Services Compensation Scheme 2007–; Chair. British Insurance Brokers Assen; Chair. Council of Univ. of Surrey; fmr Chair. Lloyd's Insurance Brokers' Cttee, London Insurance Market Network, Vice-Pres. Insurance Inst. of London. *Leisure interests:* music, skiing, golf, travelling. *Address:* Mitsui Sumitomo Insurance Group, 25 Fenchurch Avenue, London, EC3M 5AD, England (office). *Telephone:* (20) 7977-8321 (office). *Fax:* (20) 7977-8300 (office). *E-mail:* enquiries@msilm.com (office). *Website:* www.msilm.com (office).

TAYLOR, Rev. Michael Hugh, OBE, BD, MA, DLitt, STM; British minister of religion, charity administrator and academic; *Professor Emeritus of Social Theology, University of Birmingham;* b. 8 Sept. 1936, Northampton, Northants., England; s. of Albert Taylor and Gwendolen Taylor; m. Adele May Dixon 1960; two s. one d.; ed Northampton Grammar School, Univ. of Manchester, Union Theological Seminary, New York; Baptist Minister, North Shields, Northumberland and Hall Green, Birmingham 1960–69; Prin. Northern Baptist Coll., Manchester 1970–85; Lecturer in Theology and Ethics, Univ. of Manchester 1970–85; Examining Chaplain to Bishop of Manchester 1975–85; Dir Christian Aid 1985–97; Pres. Selly Oak Colls, Birmingham 1998–99; Prof. of Social Theology, Univ. of Birmingham 1999–2004, Prof. Emer. 2004–; Dir World Faiths Devt Dialogue 2002–04; Chair. Audenshaw Foundation Trustees 1979–93; mem. Comm. on Theological Educ., WCC 1972–91, Vice-Moderator 1985–91; mem. Council, Overseas Devt Inst. 1986–2000; mem. Comm. IV: Sharing and Service WCC; Chair. Assen of Protestant Devt Agencies in Europe 1991–94; Pres. Jubilee 2000 UK Coalition 1997–2001; Chair. Burma Campaign –2000, Health Unlimited 2002, Worcester Diocesan Bd for Social Responsibility 2009–; Commr High Pay Comm. 2010–; Chair. of Govs Fircroft Coll., Birmingham 2006–; Trustee, Mines Advisory Group 1998 (Chair. 2000–), Responding to Conflict 2005– (Chair. 2007–); Trustee and Vice-Chair. St Philip's Centre, Leicester 2002–; Patron, Jubilee Debt Campaign 2001–, Student Christian Movt 2005–; broadcast talks on radio; Hon. mem. of Foundation, Worcester Cathedral 2002–07; Fulbright Travel Award 1969. *Publications:* Variations on a Theme 1971, Learning to Care 1983, Good for the Poor 1990, Christianity and the Persistence of Poverty 1991, Not Angels but Agencies 1995, Jesus and the International Financial Institutions 1996, Past their Sell-By Date? The Role of Northern NGOs in the Future of Development 1998, Poverty and Christianity 2000, Christianity, Poverty and Wealth in the 21st Century 2003, Eat Drink and Be Merry for Tomorrow We Live 2005, Border Crossings 2006, Sorting out Believing 2011. *Leisure interests:* walking, theatre, music, cinema, cooking. *Telephone:* (121) 443-5618 (office). *E-mail:* mhandamtaylor@btinternet.com (office). *Website:* www.birmingham.ac.uk/ research/activity/globalethics/staff/taylor-michael.aspx (office).

TAYLOR, Paul B.; American dancer, choreographer and author; *Artistic Director, Paul Taylor Dance Company;* b. 29 July 1930, Allegheny Co., Pa; s. of Paul B. Taylor and Elizabeth P. Rust; ed Virginia Episcopal School, Syracuse Univ., Juilliard School, Metropolitan School of Ballet and Martha Graham School of Contemporary Dance; fmr dancer with the cos of Martha Graham, George Balanchine, Charles Weidman, Anna Sokolow, Merce Cunningham, Katherine Litz, James Waring and Pearl Lang; Dancer-Choreographer-Dir Paul Taylor Dance Co. 1954–; co. has performed in 520 cities in more than 60 countries; choreographed 138 dances, many of them taken up by more than 50 other dance cos world-wide; Hon. mem. American Acad. and Inst. of Arts and Letters 1989; Commdr des Arts et des Lettres 1990, Légion d'honneur 2000; Hon. Dr Fine Arts (Connecticut Coll.), (Duke Univ.) 1983, (Syracuse Univ.) 1986, (State Univ. of New York at Purchase) 1988, (The Juilliard School) 1988, (California Inst. of the Arts) 1989, (Skidmore Coll.) 1995, (Adelphi Univ.) 2008; Guggenheim Fellowship 1961, 1965, 1983, Centennial Achievement Award, Ohio State Univ. 1970, Brandeis Univ. Creative Arts Award gold medal 1978, Dance Magazine Award 1980, Samuel H. Scripps/American Dance Festival Award 1983, MacArthur 'Genius' Award 1985, New York State Governor's Award 1987, New York City Mayor's Award of Honor for Art and Culture 1989, Kennedy Center Honor 1992, Nat. Medal of Arts 1993, Award from Chicago Int. Film Festival 1993, Algur H. Meadows Award for Excellence in the Arts 1995, Lifetime Achievement Award, Americans for the Arts 2004, Lifetime Achievement 'Bessie' Award 2012. *Choreography includes:* Jack and the Beanstalk 1954, Circus Polka 1955, Little Circus 1955, 3 Epitaphs 1956, The Least Flycatcher 1956, Untitled Duet 1956, Tropes 1956, Obertura Republicana 1956, The Tower 1957, Seven New Dances 1957, May Apple 1958, Rebus 1958, Images and Reflections 1958, Meridian 1960, Option 1960, Tablet 1960, The White Salamander 1960, Junction 1961, Fibers 1961, Insects and Heroes 1961, Tracer 1962, Piece Period 1962, Aureole 1962, La Negra 1962, Party Mix 1963, Scudorama 1963, Poetry in Motion 1963, The Red Room 1964, Duet 1964, From Sea to Shining Sea 1965, Nine Dances with Music by Corelli 1965, Post Meridian 1965, Orbs 1966, Agathes' Tale 1967, Lento 1967, Public Domain 1968, Private Domain 1969, Churchyard 1969 Duets 1969, Foreign Exchange 1970, Big Bertha 1970, Fêtes 1971, Book of Beasts 1971, Guests of May 1972, So Long Eden 1972, Noah's Minstrels 1973, West of Eden 1973, American Genesis 1973, Untitled Quartet 1974, Sports and Follies 1974, Esplanade 1975, Runes 1975, Cloven Kingdom 1976, Polaris 1976, Images 1976, Dust 1977, Aphrodisiamania 1977, Airs 1978, Diggity 1978, Nightshade 1979, Profiles 1979, Le Sacre du Printemps (The Rehearsal) 1980, Arden Court 1981, House of Cards 1981, Lost, Found and Lost 1982, Mercuric Tidings 1982, Sunset 1983, Snow White 1983, Musette 1983, Equinox 1983, Byzantium 1984, Roses 1985, Last Look 1985, Musical Offering 1986, Ab Ovo Usted Ad Mala (From Soup to Nuts) 1986, Syzygy 1987, Kith and Kin 1987, Brandenburgs 1988, Counterswarm 1988, Danbury Mix 1988, Speaking in Tongues (Emmy Award 1991) 1988, Minikin Fair 1989, The Sorcerer's Sofa 1989, Of Bright & Blue Birds & The Gala Sun 1990, Company B 1991, Fact and Fancy (3 Epitaphs and All) 1991, Oz 1992, A Field of Grass 1993, Spindrift 1993, Moonbine 1994, Funny Papers 1994, Offenbach Overtures 1995, Eventide 1997, Prime Numbers 1997, Piazzolla Caldera 1997, The Word 1998, Fiddlers Green 1998, Oh, You Kid! 1999, Cascade 1999, Arabesque 1999, Fiends Angelical 2000, Dandelion Wine 2000, Black Tuesday 2001, Antique Valentine 2001, Promethean Fire 2002, Dream Girls 2002, In the Beginning 2003, Le Grand Puppetier 2004, Dante Variations 2004, Klezmerbluegrass 2004, Spring Rounds 2005, Banquet of Vultures 2005, Troilus and Cressida (reduced) 2006, Lines of Loss 2007, De Suenos (Of Dreams) 2007, De Suenos que se Repiten (Of Recurring Dreams) 2007, Changes 2008, Beloved Renegade 2008, Also Playing 2009, Brief Encounters 2009, Phantasmagoria 2010, Three Dubious Memories 2010, The Uncommitted 2011, Gossamer Gallants 2011, House of Joy 2012, To Make Crops Grow 2012, Perpetual Dawn 2013. *Television:* eight different programmes on Dance in America (PBS). *Publications:* Private Domain (autobiog.) 1987, Facts and Fancies 2013. *Leisure interests:* gardening, jigsaw puzzles. *Address:* Paul Taylor Dance Company, 551 Grand Street, New York, NY 10002, USA (office). *Telephone:* (212) 431-5562 (office). *Fax:* (212) 966-5673 (office). *E-mail:* jt@ptdc.org (office). *Website:* www.ptdc .org (office).

TAYLOR, Philip (Phil); British professional darts player; b. 13 Aug. 1960, Stoke-on-Trent; s. of Douglas Taylor and Elizabeth Taylor; m. to Yvonne Taylor; one s. three d.; ed Milfield Middle School, Stanfield Tech. High School; fmr sheet metal worker; numerous tournament victories including: Embassy World Championship 1990, 1992, World Master 1990, European Cup Singles Championship 1992, PDC World Championship 1995, 1996, 1997, 1998, 1999, 2000, 2001, 2002, 2004, 2005, 2006, PDC World Matchplay 1995, 1997, 2000, 2001, 2002, News of the World Championship 1997, PDC World Grand Prix 1998, 1999, 2000, 2002, 2003, Quebec Open 2001, North American Cup 2001, 2002, 2003, JP Sports Pro Singles 2002, Montréal Open 2002, Las Vegas Desert Classic 2002, UK Open 2003, Bobby Bourn Memorial Trophy 2003, Stan James World Matchplay 2003; first unranked player to win a major tournament (Canadian Open 1990); unbeaten for nearly two years in televised matches 1999–2001; nine-dart finish at Stan James World Matchplay 2002 (1st since 1990 in televised match). *Publications:* (with Sid Waddell) The Power: My Autobiography 2003. *E-mail:* philtaylor@premiumtv.co.uk. *Website:* www.philthepower.com.

TAYLOR, Richard Edward, CC, PhD, FRS, FRSC; Canadian physicist and academic; *Professor Emeritus, Stanford Linear Accelerator Center;* b. 2 Nov. 1929, Medicine Hat, Alberta; s. of Clarence Richard Taylor and Delia Alena (née Brunsdale) Taylor; m. Rita Jean Bonneau 1951; one s.; ed Univ. of Alberta, Edmonton, Stanford Univ., Calif., USA; Boursier, Laboratoire de l'Accélérateur Linéaire, Orsay, France 1958–61; physicist, Lawrence Berkeley Lab., Berkeley, Calif. 1961–62; staff mem. Stanford Linear Accelerator Center, Calif. 1962–68, Assoc. Prof. 1968–70, Prof. 1970–2003, Prof. Emer. 2003–, Assoc. Dir Research Div. 1982–86, Lewis M. Terman Prof. 1993–99; mem. American Acad. of Arts and Sciences, Canadian Assen of Physicists; Foreign Assoc. NAS; Fellow, American Physical Soc., AAAS; Hon. DSc (Alberta) 1991, (Lethbridge, Alberta) 1993, (Victoria, BC) 1994, (Liverpool) 1999, (Queen's, Ont.) 2000; Hon. LLD (Calgary, Alberta) 1993; Dr hc (Paris-Sud) 1980, (Blaise-Pascal) 1997, (Carleton Univ., Ont.) 1999; Guggenheim Fellow 1971–72, A. von Humboldt Sr Scientist Award 1982, W.K.H. Panofsky Prize (with H.W. Kendall and J.I. Friedman) 1989, Nobel Prize in Physics (with H. W. Kendall and J. I. Friedman) 1990, Canadian Science and Eng Hall of Fame. *Publications:* numerous scientific papers. *Address:* Stanford Linear Accelerator Center (SLAC), Mail Stop 43, 2575 Sand Hill Road, Menlo

Park, CA 94025 (office); 757 Mayfield Avenue, Stanford, CA 94305, USA (home). *Telephone:* (650) 926-2417 (office); (650) 857-1345 (home). *Fax:* (650) 926-2987 (office). *E-mail:* retaylor@slac.stanford.edu (office). *Website:* www.slac.stanford .edu (office).

TAYLOR, Richard Lawrence, BA, PhD, FRS; British mathematician and academic; *Herchel Smith Professor of Mathematics, Harvard University;* b. 19 May 1962; s. of John C. Taylor (physicist); m. Christine Taylor; one s. one d.; ed Clare Coll., Cambridge, Princeton Univ., USA; fmr research student of Andrew Wiles, returned to Princeton Univ. to help Wiles complete proof of Fermat's last theorem 1995; Savilian Chair of Geometry, Univ. of Oxford and Fellow, New Coll. Oxford 1995–96; currently Herchel Smith Prof. of Math., Harvard Univ., USA; Whitehead Prize 1990, Fermat Prize 2001, Ostrowski Prize 2001, Cole Prize, American Math. Soc. 2002, Shaw Prize in Math. Sciences for his work on the Langlands program with Robert Langlands 2007, Clay Research Award, Clay Math. Inst. (co-recipient) 2007. *Publications:* numerous math. papers in professional journals. *Address:* Department of Mathematics, Faculty of Arts and Sciences, Harvard University, One Oxford Street, Cambridge, MA 02138, USA (office). *Telephone:* (617) 495-2171 (office). *Fax:* (617) 495-5132 (office). *E-mail:* rtaylor@math.harvard.edu (office). *Website:* www.math.harvard.edu (office).

TAYLOR, Stuart Ross, MA, PhD, DSc, FAA; New Zealand geochemist and academic; b. 26 Nov. 1925, Ashburton; s. of the late T. S. Taylor; m. Noel White 1958; three d.; ed Ashburton High School, Canterbury Univ. Coll., Univ. of New Zealand and Indiana Univ., USA; Lecturer in Mineralogy, Univ. of Oxford 1954–58; Sr Lecturer in Geochemistry, Univ. of Cape Town 1958–60; Professorial Fellow, Research School of Earth Science, Australian Nat. Univ. (ANU) 1961–90, Visiting Fellow, Research School of Physical Sciences 1991, 1993–99, also currently; mem. Council, ANU 1971–76; mem. Lunar Sample Preliminary Examination Team, Houston, Texas 1969–70, Prin. Investigator, Lunar Sample Analysis Program 1970–90; Visiting Prof., Univ. of Vienna 1992, 1996; Foreign Assoc. NAS (USA); Fellow, Geochemical Soc., American Geophysical Union; Hon. Fellow, UK and Indian Geological Socs, Royal Soc. of New Zealand, Hon. AC 2008; Goldschmidt Medal, Geochemical Soc. 1993, Gilbert Award, Geological Soc. of America 1994, Leonard Medal, Meteoritical Soc. 1998, Bucher Medal, American Geophysical Union 2002. *Achievements include:* Asteroid 5670 named Ross Taylor. *Publications include:* Spectrochemical Analysis (jtly) 1961, Moon Rocks and Minerals (jtly) 1971, Lunar Science: A Post-Apollo View 1975, Planetary Science: A Lunar Perspective 1982, The Continental Crust: Its Composition and Evolution (jtly) 1985, Solar System Evolution: A New Perspective 1992, Destiny or Chance: Our Solar System and Its Place in the Cosmos 1998, Planetary Crusts (with Scott McLennan) 2009; some 240 papers in scientific journals. *Leisure interests:* reading history, gardening, classical music. *Address:* 18 Sheehan Street, Pearce, ACT 2607, Australia.

TAYLOR, Wendy Ann, CBE, FZS, FRBS, FRSA; British sculptor; b. 29 July 1945, Stamford, Lincs., England; d. of Edward P. Taylor and Lilian M. Wright; m. Bruce Robertson 1982; one s.; ed St Martin's School of Art; mem. Fine Art Bd Council of Acad. Awards 1980–85, Specialist Adviser 1985–93; Specialist Adviser, Cttee for Art and Design 1988–93; mem. Cttee for Art and Design, Council of Nat. Acad. Awards; mem. Royal Fine Art Comm. 1981–99; mem. Council, Morley Coll. 1984–89; mem. Court RCA; design consultant, New Towns Comm. (Basildon) 1985–88; design consultant, London Borough of Barking and Dagenham 1989–93, 1997–2003; Advisory Bd, London Docklands Devt Corpn 1989–93; mem. Advisory Group of the Polytechnics and Colls Funding Council 1989–90; mem. Council, Royal Soc. of British Sculptors 1999–2000; Fellow, Queen Mary and Westfield Coll. (London Univ.); Trustee, Leicestershire's Appeal for Music and the Arts 1993–2010; mem. Design Panel, Thames Gateway Area 2005–07; Walter Neurath Award 1964, Pratt Award 1965, Sainsbury Award 1966, Arts Council Award 1977, Duais Na Ríochta Gold Medal, Eire 1977, Arts Council Award 1991, Civic Trust Partnership Award 2002, Building of the Year Award, Architectural Sculpture 2004. *Television:* South Bank Show (LWT) 1988. *Leisure interest:* gardening. *Address:* 73 Bow Road, London, E3 2AN, England (home). *Telephone:* (20) 8981-2037 (home). *E-mail:* wendytaylorsculptor@gmail.com (office); wendy-taylor@ fsmail.net (home). *Website:* wendytaylorsculpture.co.uk (office).

TAYLOR, Sir William, Kt, CBE, BSc (Econ), PhD; British academic; *Visiting Professor, University of Winchester;* b. 31 May 1930, Crayford, Kent; s. of Herbert Taylor and Maud Taylor; m. Rita Hague 1954; one s. two d.; ed London School of Econs, Univ. of London Inst. of Educ.; fmr school teacher and deputy head teacher, Kent; later worked in two colls of educ. and Dept of Educ., Univ. of Oxford; Prof. of Educ., Univ. of Bristol 1966; Dir London Inst. of Educ. 1973–83; Prin. Univ. of London 1983–85, Chair. of Convocation 1994–97; Vice-Chancellor Univ. of Hull 1985–91; Vice-Chancellor Univ. of Huddersfield 1994–95, Thames Valley Univ. 1998–99; Visiting Prof., Univ. of Oxford 1991–97, Univ. of Southampton 1998–10, Univ. of Winchester 2010–; Gov. Univ. of Glamorgan 1992–2002, Christ Church, Univ. Coll., Canterbury 1996–2004; Interim Head, Winchester School of Art, Univ. of Southampton 2004; Chair. Council for Accreditation of Teacher Educ. 1984–93; Chair. Bd NFER/Nelson publishing co. 1988–99; Pres. Soc. for Research in Higher Educ. 1996–2001; Specialist Adviser, House of Commons Educ. and Skills Cttee 2000–07; Chair. NI Cttee for Teacher Educ. 1994–2003; mem. Council, Hong Kong Inst. of Educ. 1998–2003; Charter Fellow, Coll. of Preceptors; Hon. Fellow, Westminster Coll. Oxford, Thames Polytechnic, Commonwealth Council for Educ. Admin., Inst. of Educ.; Dr hc (Aston, Bristol, Leeds, London, Kent, Loughborough, Open Univ., Huddersfield, Hull, Kingston, Plymouth, Oxford Brookes, Univ. of West of England, Ulster, Queen's Univ. Belfast, Southampton, Leicester, Glamorgan, Essex, Hong Kong Inst. of Educ.). *Publications include:* The Secondary Modern School, Society and the Education of Teachers, Planning and Policy in Post-secondary Education, Heading for Change, Research and Reform in Teacher Education, The Metaphors of Education, Universities under Scrutiny. *Leisure interest:* books and music. *E-mail:* william.taylor@winchester.ac.uk (office). *Website:* www.winchester.ac.uk (office).

TAYLOR-WOOD, Sam, OBE; British artist, photographer and filmmaker; b. 1967; m. Jay Jopling (divorced 2008); two d.; partner Aaron Johnson; one d.; ed Hastings Coll. of Art and Tech., Goldsmiths Coll., London; uses highly choreographed photographic sequences; first solo exhbn, London 1994. *Works include:* Fuck, Suck, Spank, Wank 1993, Slut 1993, Killing Time (film) 1994, Method in

Madness (film) 1994, Five Revolutionary Seconds XI 1997, Atlantic 1997, Five Revolutionary Seconds XIII 1998, Soliloquy I 1998, Soliloquy V 1998, Self Portrait in a Single Breasted Suit with Hare 2001, Hummmm 2001, Mute (film) 2001, Breach (film) 2001, Still Life (film) 2001, Self Portrait as a Tree, Strings (film) 2003, Ascension (film) 2003, David (video portrait) 2004, Crying Men 2004, Self Portrait Suspended 2004. *Solo exhibitions include:* White Cube², London 1995–96, Fundació 'la Caixa', Barcelona 1997, Hirshhorn Museum and Sculpture Garden, Washington, DC 1999, Musée d'art contemporain, Montreal, Matthew Marks Gallery, New York, The State Russian Museum, St Petersburg, Kunsthalle, Zurich, Louisiana Museum of Modern Art in Denmark, White Cube², London 2001, Stedelijk Museum, Amsterdam 2001, Hayward Gallery, London (retrospective) 2001, White Cube, London 2004. *Film:* Nowhere Boy (dir) 2009. *Publications include:* Contact 2001, Crying Men 2004. *Address:* c/o Regen Projects, 633 North Almont Drive, Los Angeles, CA 90069, USA. *Telephone:* (310) 276-5424. *Fax:* (310) 276-7430.

TAYYEBNIA, Ali, PhD; Iranian academic, economist and government official; *Minister of Economic Affairs and Finance;* b. 1960, Isfahan; ed Tehran Univ., London School of Econs, UK; fmr mem. Faculty, Dept of Econs, Tehran Univ.; Sec., Econ. Comm. 1997–2000, 2005–07; Deputy Head, Presidential Office for Planning 2001–05; Minister of Econ. Affairs and Finance 2013–. *Address:* Ministry of Economic Affairs and Finance, Sour Esrafil Ave, Nasser Khosrou Street, Tehran 11149-43661, Iran (office). *Telephone:* (21) 22553401 (office). *Fax:* (21) 22581933 (office). *E-mail:* info@mefa.gov.ir (office). *Website:* mefa.gov.ir (office).

TAZAKI, Masamoto; Japanese engineer and business executive; *Advisor, Kawasaki Heavy Industries Ltd;* b. 1935, Manchuria; ed Kyushu Univ.; joined Kawasaki Aircraft Co. Ltd (now Kawasaki Heavy Industries Ltd) in 1958, has served in various exec. and man. positions including Exec. Man.-Dir and Sr Gen.-Man. Consumer Products and Machinery Group, Pres. Kawasaki Heavy Industries USA 1989–96, mem. Bd of Dirs Kawasaki Heavy Industries 1992–2009, Sr Vice-Pres. 1996–97, Sr Exec. Vice-Pres. 1997–2000, Pres. 2000–05, Chair. 2005–09, Advisor 2009–; Pres. Japan Ship Exporters Asscn 2009–. *Address:* Kawasaki Heavy Industries Ltd, Kobe Crystal Tower, 1-3 Higashikawasaki-cho 1-chome, Chuo-ku, Kobe 650-8680, Japan (office). *Telephone:* (7) 8371-9530 (office). *Fax:* (7) 8371-9568 (office). *Website:* www.khi.co.jp (office).

TAZHIN, Marat Muhanbetkaziyevich, PhD; Kazakhstani politician; b. 8 April 1960, Aktubinsk; ed Almaty Inst. of Nat. Economy, Kazakh State Univ.; began career as scientific researcher –1992; First Deputy Head, then Head of Internal Policy Dept, Deputy Chief of Presidential Apparatus, Head of Information and Analysis Center, Office of the Pres. 1992–94; State Adviser to Pres. 1994–95; Deputy Head, Admin of Pres. and Head, Analysis and Strategic Research Center 1995–99; Nat. Security Asst to Pres. 1999–2001, 2002, 2006–07; Sec. Security Council 1999–2001, Dec. 2001–Aug. 2002, April 2006–Jan. 2007, Chair. Nat. Security Cttee May–Dec. 2001; First Deputy Chief, Admin of Pres. 2002–06; Minister of Foreign Affairs 2007–09; Order of Kurmet, Order of Barys. *Address:* c/o Ministry of Foreign Affairs, 010000 Astana, Tauelsizdik 31, Kazakhstan (office).

TCHAIKOVSKY, Aleksandr Vladimirovich; Russian composer and pianist; b. 19 Feb. 1946, Moscow; m. 1st; one s. one d.; m. 3rd; one d.; ed Moscow State Conservatory; performs as pianist and chamber musician 1967–; teacher, Moscow P. I. Tchaikovsky Conservatory 1976, Prof. 1994–, currently Composition Chair, Composition Dept; Artistic Consultant, Mariinsky Theatre, St Petersburg 1996–; Artistic Dir Moscow State Philharmonia 2003–; mem. Bd of Dirs Pervyi Kanal; winner Hollybush Festival Prize (USA) 1987, People's Artist of Russia 1998. *Compositions include:* operas: Grandfather Is Laughing 1976, Three Sisters (after A. Chekhov) 1994; ballets: Inspector 1960, Battleship Potemkin 1988; symphonies 1985, 1991 (Aquarius), two piano concertos, two viola concertos, Distant Dreams of Childhood for violin and viola 1990, Concerto-Buff for violin and marimba 1990, Triple Concerto for piano, violin and cello 1994, folk operas Tsar Nikita and Motya and Savely for two soloists and folk instruments, Quartet (after A. Pushkin) 1997–99; chamber music, incidental music to theatre and film productions. *Leisure interests:* collecting models of cars, table hockey. *Address:* Composition Department, Moscow P. I. Tchaikovsky Conservatory, 125009 Moscow, Bolshaya Nikitskaya St 13/6 (office); 125040 Moscow, Leningradsky prosp. 14, Apt. 4, Russia (home). *Telephone:* (495) 629-32-74 (office); (495) 551-54-18 (home). *E-mail:* spravka@mosconsv.ru (office). *Website:* www.mosconsv.ru (office).

TCHEN, Christina (Tina) M., BA, JD; American lawyer and government official; *Assistant to the President and Chief of Staff to the First Lady;* b. 25 Jan. 1956, Columbus, Ohio; one s. one d.; ed Harvard Univ., Northwestern Univ. School of Law; Assoc., Skadden, Arps, Slate, Meagher & Flom LLP, Chicago 1984–92, Pnr 1992–2009; Deputy Asst to Pres. and Dir Office of Public Engagement, The White House 2009–11, Asst to Pres. and Chief of Staff to First Lady Michelle Obama 2011–; mem. Bd of Trustees Univ. of Chicago Medical Center; mem. Bd of Dirs Chicago Public Library 2003–, Harvard Alumni Asscn, Chicago Bar Foundation, Chicago Area Foundation Legal Services; Chair. Field Foundation Illinois 2004–; mem. ABA, Women's Bar Asscn of Illinois. *Publications include:* numerous articles in professional journals. *Address:* The White House, 1600 Pennsylvania Avenue, NW, Washington, DC 20500, USA (office). *Website:* www.whitehouse.gov/ administration/first-lady-michelle-obama (office).

TCHIKAIDZE, Aleksandre; Georgian police chief and government official; *Minister of Internal Affairs;* b. 6 June 1985, Tbilisi; m.; two c.; ed Ivane Javakhishvili Tbilisi State Univ.; rank of Police Col; employed at various police units in Gldani-nadzaladevi and Vake-Saburtalo Police Div. 2008–09, Asst to Detective Investigators, Gldani-nadzaladevi Police Div. 2009, Detective Investigator, Gldani-Nadzaladevi Police Div. 2010–11, Head of Gldani-Nadzaladevi Police Div., Tbilisi Police Main Div. 2011–12, Chief of Kakheti Regional Main Div. 2012–13, Head of Tbilisi Police Main Div. May–Nov. 2013; Minister of Internal Affairs Nov. 2013–. *Address:* Ministry of Internal Affairs, 0114 Tbilisi, Gulua 10, Georgia (office). *Telephone:* (32) 274-62-50 (office). *Fax:* (32) 241-10-17 (office). *E-mail:* monitoringi@mia.gov.ge (office). *Website:* www.police.ge (office).

TCHIMANGOA, Gen. Thomas Théophile; Central African Republic army officer and government official; *Minister of National Defence;* served for many years in Central African Armed Forces (FACA), including as Commdr, Amphibious Bn, Head, Inst. Protection and Security   Bn 2010, Project Man. and Head of

Operational Command Centre 2013; Minister of Nat. Defence, in charge of Reorganization of Armed Forces, Fmr Combatants, War Victims, Disarmament, Demobilization and Reintegration 2014–. *Address:* Ministry of National Defence, Bangui, Central African Republic (office). *Telephone:* 21-61-00-25 (office).

TCHONGÓ DOMINGOS, Salvador; Guinea-Bissau politician; m.; two c.; ed Instituto Superior de Economia, Lisbon, Portugal and Universidade Católica, Lisbon; teacher of secondary education, Portugal 1981–92; founding mem. Resistência da Guiné-Bissau—Movimento Bah-Fatah, Sec.-Gen. 1987–92, 1993–95, Vice-Pres. 1992–93, 1995–2002, Pres. 2002; Vice-Pres. Assembléia Nacional Popular 1994–99; unsuccessful presidential candidate 1999; Sec.-Gen. Presidência da República da Guiné-Bissau 2000–05. *Address:* c/o Assembléia Nacional Popular, Bissau, Guinea-Bissau.

TCHUKHONTSEV, Oleg Grigoryevich; Russian poet; b. 8 March 1938, Pavlov Posad, Moscow Region; m. Irina Igorevna Povolotskaya; ed Moscow Pedagogical Inst.; poetry section, mem. Editorial Bd Novy Mir; published in Druzhba Narodov, Yunost, Molodaya Gvardiya, Novy Mir; State Prize of Russia 1993. *Publications:* From Three Notebooks (cycles Posad, Name, Sparrow's Night) 1976, The Dormer Window 1983, Poetry 1989, By Wind and Heat 1986, Passing Landscape 1997 and other books of poetry; translations of Goethe, Warren, Frost, Kits and numerous other poets. *Address:* Bolshoi Tishinsky per. 12, Apt. 10, 123557 Moscow, Russia (home). *Telephone:* (495) 253-51-95 (home).

TCHURUK, Serge; French engineer and business executive; b. 13 Nov. 1937, Marseille; s. of Georges Tchurukdichian and Mathilde Dondikian; m. Hélèna Kalfus 1960; one d.; ed Lycée Thiers à Marseille, Ecole nationale supérieure de l'armement, Ecole Polytechnique, Paris; various refining and research positions Mobil/Oil BV Rotterdam 1964–68, Dir French research centre 1968–70, Dir of Information, France 1971–73, attaché int. planning, New York and dir plans and programmes France 1973–77, Dir social and external relations 1977–79, Pres. and Dir-Gen. 1979–80; Dir-Gen. fertilizer div. Rhône-Poulenc Inc. 1981, Asst Dir-Gen. Rhône-Poulenc Group 1982, Dir-Gen. special chemicals 1983, Dir-Gen. Rhône-Poulenc Group 1983; Pres. Bd Dirs CdF Chimie 1986, Pres. Dir-Gen. 1987–90 (became Orkem 1988); mem. Bd Dirs Total 1989, 1995–, Pres. 1990–95; Chair. and CEO Alcatel Alsthom (later Alcatel) 1995–2006, Chair. Alcatel-Lucent (after Alcatel acquisition of Lucent) 2006–08; mem. Bd of Dirs Inst. Pasteur 2001–, Total, Thales; Officier, Légion d'honneur, Officier, Ordre nat. du Mérite; Manager of the Year Award, Le Nouvel Economiste 2000. *Leisure interests:* music, skiing, tennis. *Address:* c/o Alcatel-Lucent, 54 rue de la Boétie, 75008 Paris, France. *Telephone:* 1-40-76-10-10. *E-mail:* execoffice@alcatel-lucent.com.

TE KANAWA, Dame Kiri Jeanette Claire, ONZ, DBE, AC; New Zealand singer (soprano); b. (Claire Mary Teresa Rawstron), 6 March 1944, Gisborne, North Island; adopted d. of Thomas Te Kanawa and Nell Te Kanawa; m. Desmond Park 1967 (divorced 1997); one s. one d.; ed St Mary's Coll., Auckland, London Opera Centre; first appearance at Royal Opera, Covent Garden, London 1970, Santa Fe Opera, USA 1971, Lyons Opera, France 1972, Metropolitan Opera, New York, USA 1974; appeared at Australian Opera, Royal Opera House Covent Garden, Paris Opera during 1976–77 season; appeared at Houston Opera, USA and Munich Opera 1977; debut La Scala, Milan 1978; Salzburg Festival 1979; San Francisco Opera Co. 1980; Edinburgh Festival, Helsinki Festival 1980; sang at wedding of HRH the Prince of Wales 1981; sang the premiere of Paul McCartney's Liverpool Oratorio, written by Carl Davis, at Liverpool Cathedral and in London 1991; voice of the theme of the Rugby World Cup, performing first recorded version of World in Union 1991; appeared in 2000 Today on 1 January 2000; returned to the Cologne Opera House for two final performances of the Marschallin in Rosenkavalier 2010; final opera performance before retirement was a cameo role in La fille du régiment at Royal Opera House, London 2014; appeared in ITV's Downton Abbey playing Dame Nellie Melba, an Australian operatic soprano 2013; Founding Trustee and Chair. Kiri Te Kanawa Foundation 2004–; Hans Christian Andersen Amb. 2005–; Patron Ringmer Community Coll.; Hon. Fellow, Somerville Coll., Oxford 1983, Wolfson Coll., Cambridge 1997; Hon. Mem. RAM; Hon. LLD (Dundee) 1982; Hon. DMus (Durham) 1982, (Oxford) 1983, (Nottingham) 1992, (Waikato) 1995, (Cambridge) 1997; Hon. DLitt (Warwick) 1989, (Sunderland) 2003, (Auckland), (Chicago); Classical Brit Award for Lifetime Achievement 2010. The Kiri Prize competition to find a gifted opera singer of the future est. in her honour 2010, Edison Classical Music Award 2012, World Class New Zealand Award 2012. *Operas include:* Boris Godunov 1970–71, Parsifal 1971, The Marriage of Figaro (Countess) 1971, 1972, 1973, 1976, 1979, 1986, 1991, 1997, Otello 1972, 1973, 1974, 1987, 1988, 1991, 1992, Simon Boccanegra 1973, 1974, 1975, 1976, 1977, 1979, 1980, 1986, 1988, 1991, 1995, 1997, Carmen 1973, Don Giovanni 1974, 1975, 1976, (film) 1979, 1981, 1983, 1988, 1996, Faust 1974, The Magic Flute 1975, 1980, La Bohème 1975, 1976, 1977, 1979, 1980, 1989, 1991, Eugene Onegin 1975, 1976, Così fan tutte 1976, 1981, 1986, 1987, 1988, Arabella 1977, 1980, 1981, 1983, 1984, 1990, 1993, 1994, 1995, Die Fledermaus 1978, 1984, 1986, 1987, La Traviata 1978, 1980, 1983, 1984, Der Rosenkavalier 1981, 1984, 1985, Manon Lescaut 1983, Samson 1986, Don Carlos 1984, Capriccio 1990, 1991, 1993, 1998, Vanessa 2001, 2002, 2004. *Recordings include:* Don Giovanni (as Elvira), Così fan tutti (as Fiordiligi), Carmen (as Micha), Mozart Vespers, Mozart C Minor Mass, The Magic Flute (Pamina), Siegfried (Woodbird), The Marriage of Figaro, Hansel and Gretel, La Bohème, Capriccio, Otello, Die Fledermaus, French and German arias and songs, Maori songs 1999, Strauss songs with orchestra, Songs of the Auvergne, West Side Story, The Very Best of ... 2003, Kiri Sings Karl 2006. *Publications:* Land of the Long White Cloud (children's book) 1989, Opera for Lovers (with Conrad Wilson) 1997. *Leisure interests:* golf, swimming, cooking. *Address:* c/o Kiri Te Kanawa Foundation, PO Box 38387, Howick, Auckland 2045, New Zealand (office); c/o Kiri Te Kanawa Foundation (UK), 23B Prince of Wales Mansions, Prince of Wales Drive, London, SW11 4BQ, England (office). *Telephone:* (9) 5349398 (Auckland) (office); (20) 8332-9829 (London) (office). *Fax:* (9) 5340629 (Auckland) (office); (20) 8332-7049 (London) (office). *E-mail:* foundation@ kiritekanawa.org (office); gillian.newson@btopenworld.com (office). *Website:* www .kiritekanawa.org (office).

TEA BANH, Gen.; Cambodian politician; *Deputy Prime Minister and Minister of Defence;* b. 5 Nov. 1945, Koh Kong Prov.; s. of the late Tea Toek and Nou Pheng Chenda; m. Tao Toeun 1955; three c.; platoon Commdr Koh Kong Prov. 1962–69, Co. Commdr 1969–70, Mil. Commdr and Dir Training 1973–79; Deputy Chief of

Staff in charge of Telecommunications and Air Force 1979–80, Deputy Minister of Nat. Defence in charge of Telecommunications and Air Force 1980–82; Minister of Communications, Transport and Posts 1982–87; Vice-Chair. Council of Ministers 1984–88; mem. Parl. for Siem Reap Prov. 1988–; Minister of Nat. Defence 1987–88, 1993–94, 2006–, Deputy Minister 1988–93, Co-Minister 1994–2006; Deputy Prime Minister 2006–; Co-Deputy C-in-C Nat. Armed Forces 1994–95. *Leisure interest:* golf. *Address:* Ministry of National Defence, blvd Confederation de la Russie, cnr rue 175, Phnom-Penh, Cambodia (office). *Telephone:* (23) 883184 (office). *Fax:* (23) 366169 (office). *E-mail:* info@mond.gov.kh (office). *Website:* www.mond.gov.kh (office).

TEANNAKI, Teatao; I-Kiribati politician; *Leader, National Progressive Party;* Vice-Pres. of Kiribati 1979–91; Pres. of Kiribati 1991–94; mem. Parl. for Abiang 1994–; currently Leader Nat. Progressive Party. *Address:* National Progressive Party, Tarawa, Kiribati.

TEBBIT, Baron (Life Peer), cr 1992, of Chingford in the London Borough of Waltham Forest; **Norman Beresford Tebbit,** PC, CH; British politician; b. 29 March 1931, Enfield; s. of Leonard Tebbit and Edith Tebbit; m. Margaret Elizabeth Daines 1956; two s. one d.; ed Edmonton Co. Grammar School; RAF Officer 1949–51; commercial pilot and holder of various posts, British Air Line Pilots' Asscn 1953–70; MP for Epping 1970–74, for Chingford 1974–92; Parl. Pvt. Sec. Dept of Employment 1972–73; Under-Sec., Dept of Trade 1979–81; Minister of State, Dept of Industry Jan.–Sept. 1981; Sec. of State for Employment 1981–83, for Trade and Industry 1983–85; Chancellor of the Duchy of Lancaster 1985–87; Chair., Conservative Party 1985–87; Life Peer, House of Lords 1992–; Dir, BET PLC 1987–96, British Telecom PLC 1987–96, Sears PLC 1987–99, Spectator Ltd; Co-Presenter, Target, Sky TV 1989–97; columnist, The Sun 1995–97, Mail on Sunday 1997–2001; blogger, Daily Telegraph 2010–. *Publications:* Upwardly Mobile 1988, Unfinished Business 1991, The Game Cook 2009. *Leisure interests:* peace and quiet, shooting, gardening. *Address:* House of Lords, Westminster, London, SW1A 0PW, England (office). *Telephone:* (20) 7219-3000 (office). *E-mail:* tebbitn@parliament.uk (office).

TÉCHINÉ, André Jean François; French author and filmmaker; b. 13 March 1943, Valence, Tarn-et-Garonne. *Films:* Paulina s'en va 1969, Souvenirs d'en France 1975, Barocco 1976, Les Sœurs Brontë 1979, Hôtel des Amériques 1981, Rendez-vous 1985 (Prize for Best Director, Cannes Int. Film Festival 1985), Le Lieu du crime 1986, Les Innocents 1987, J'embrasse pas 1991, Ma Saison préférée 1993, Les Roseaux sauvages 1994 (Prix Louis-Delluc 1994, César for Best French Film, Best Dir and Best Original Screenplay or Adaptation 1995), Les Voleurs 1996, Alice et Martin 1998, Loin 2001, Les Égarés (Strayed) 2003, Les Temps qui changent 2004, Les Témoins 2007, The Girl on the Train 2009. *Television:* La Matiouette

TEER, Kees, DSc, FIEEE; Dutch scientist; b. 6 June 1925, Haarlem; m. Jozina A. Kas 1951; three c.; ed Tech. Univ. Delft; joined Philips Research Labs, Eindhoven 1950, Sr Researcher, Deputy Head of Acoustics, 1958, Deputy Dir 1966, Man. Dir 1968, Chair. Man. Cttee 1982–85; Prof. Tech. Univ. Delft 1987–91; mem. Netherlands Scientific Council for Govt 1985–88; mem. Bd of Dirs Royal Dutch PTT 1988–97, Nedap Industries 1985–97; mem. Royal Netherlands Acad. of Sciences 1977–; Officer, Order of Orange Nassau 1984; C. T. de Groot plaquette 1992. *Publications:* several publs on electro-acoustics, TV systems, electronic principles, information tech. and society, R&D man. etc. *Leisure interests:* philosophy, writing, society versus technology. *Address:* Hoge Duinlaan 3, 5582 KD Waalre, Netherlands. *Telephone:* (40) 2216861. *Fax:* (40) 2219222. *E-mail:* k.teer@wxs.nl.

TEGELTIJA, Zoran, PhD; Bosnia and Herzegovina economist and politician; *Minister of Finance of Republika Srpska;* b. 29 Sept. 1961; m.; two c.; ed Sarajevo Univ.; began career working in oil refinery, Bosanski Brod; worked with Tax and Customs Admin of Republika Srpska, Deputy, Nat. Ass. of Republika Srpska 2000–02; Mayor of Mrkonjic Grad 2004; fmr Chair. Bosnia and Herzegovina State Border Comm.; Sr Asst, Dept of Public Finance and Monetary Econs, Univ. of Business and Man. Eng, Banja Luka, later Asst Prof.; Minister of Finance of Republika Srpska 2010–; mem. Alliance of Independent Social Democrats, head of party electoral team 2006. *Address:* Ministry of Finance, 78000 Banja Luka, Trg Republike Srpske 1, Bosnia and Herzegovina (office). *Telephone:* (51) 339768 (office). *Fax:* (51) 339645 (office). *E-mail:* mf@mf.vladars.net (office). *Website:* www .vladars.net/sr-SP-Cyrl/Vlada/Ministarstva/mf (office).

TEGUEDI, Ahmed Ould; Mauritanian diplomatist; *Minister of Foreign Affairs;* b. 15 Sept. 1954, Chinguetti; m. Chekrada Mint Ahmed Ould Labeid; ed Acad. of Econ. Studies, Bucharest, Romania; joined Ministry of Foreign Affairs 1981, apptd Head, Western Europe, Eastern Europe, Americas and European Econ. Community, African-Caribbean-Pacific Divs 1981, Second Counsellor, Embassy in Washington, DC 1987–88, First Counsellor, Embassy in Cairo 1988–90, Chargé d'affaires a.i. 1990, First Counsellor and Chargé d'affaires a.i., Embassy in Sana 1991–93, in Rabat 1993–95, Head of Office responsible for Mauritanian interests in Tel-Aviv, Israel 1995–99, Amb. to Israel 1999–2009, Amb. and Perm. Rep. to UN, New York 2012–13; Minister of Foreign Affairs 2013–. *Address:* Ministry of Foreign Affairs and Co-operation, BP 230, Nouakchott, Mauritania (office). *Telephone:* 45-25-26-82 (office).

TEH, Tan Sri Dato' Hong Piow, PhD; Malaysian banker; *Chairman, Public Bank Berhad;* b. 14 March 1930, Singapore; m. Puan Sri Tay Sock Noy 1956; four c.; ed Anglo-Chinese School, Singapore, Pacific Western Univ., Clayton Univ., Univ. of Malaya; began career as bank clerk in Overseas-Chinese Banking Corpn Ltd 1950, promoted to bank officer 1955–60; Man. Malayan Banking Berhad 1960–64, Gen. Man. 1964–66; est. Public Bank 1966, currently Chair. Public Bank Berhad. *Address:* Public Bank Berhad, Menara Public Bank 146, Jalan Ampang, 50450 Kuala Lumpur, Malaysia (office). *Telephone:* (3) 2176-6000 (office). *Fax:* (3) 2161-9307 (office). *E-mail:* info@publicbank.com.my (office). *Website:* www .pbebank.com (office); www.publicbank.com.my (office).

TEICH, Malvin Carl, PhD; American academic; *Professor of Electrical and Computer Engineering, Professor of Biomedical Engineering, Professor of Physics, Boston University;* b. 4 May 1939, New York, NY; s. of Sidney R. Teich and Loretta K. Teich; ed Massachusetts Inst. of Tech., Stanford and Cornell Univs; Research

Scientist, MIT Lincoln Lab., Lexington, Mass 1966–67; Prof. of Eng Science and Applied Physics, Columbia Univ., New York 1967–96, Prof. Emer. 1996–, Chair. Dept of Electrical Eng 1978–80, mem. Columbia Radiation Lab.; Prof. of Electrical and Computer Eng, Prof. of Biomedical Eng, Prof. of Physics, Boston Univ. 1995–, Distinguished Scholar 2009, mem. Photonics Center, Hearing Research Center, Center for Adaptive Systems, Program in Neuroscience; Deputy Ed. Journal of European Optical Society B: Quantum Optics 1988–92; mem. Bd of Editors Optics Letters 1977–79, Journal of Visual Communication and Image Representation 1989–92, Jemná Mechanika a Optika 1994–; Fellow, IEEE, AAAS, American Physical Soc., Optical Soc. of America, Acoustical Soc. of America; IEEE Browder Thompson Memorial Prize 1969, John Simon Guggenheim Memorial Foundation Fellow 1973, Citation Classic Award, Inst. for Scientific Information 1981, Memorial Gold Medal, Palacký Univ. 1992, IEEE Morris E. Leeds Award 1997. *Publications:* Fundamentals of Photonics (with B. E. A. Saleh) 1991, 2007, Fractal-Based Point Processes (with S. B. lowen) 2005; 350 articles in tech. journals; six US patents. *Address:* Department of Electrical and Computer Engineering, Boston University, 8 Saint Mary's Street, Boston, MA 02215, USA (office). *Telephone:* (617) 353-1236 (office). *Fax:* (617) 353-6440 (office). *Website:* people.bu.edu/teich (office); www.bu.edu/bme/people/joint/teich (office).

TEISSIER, Guy; French politician; b. 4 April 1945, Marseilles; ed Ecole de Notariat de Marseilles; mem. Parti Républicain (Union pour un Mouvement Populaire from 2002); Conseiller Général for Bouches de Rhône 1982–2004; Mayor 9th and 10th arrondissements, Marseilles 1983–; mem. Conseil Municipal de Marseilles 1983–; elected Deputy to Nat. Ass. for Bouches-du-Rhône 1988 (invalidated by Conseil Constitutionel) re-elected 1993–; Sec. Nat. Ass. 1997–99, 2002;, mem. Comm. of Cultural, Family and Social Affairs 1988; mem. Comm. of Nat. Defence 1993–2002, Sec. 1994–95, Pres. 2002–07. *Address:* Mairie des 9e et 10e arrondissements, 150 boulevard Paul-Claudel, 13009 Marseille (office); Assemblée Nationale, 33, rue Saint-Dominique, 75 007 Paris (office); Nouveau Parc Sevigne, 15 place Mignard, 13009 Marseilles, France (home). *Telephone:* 4-91-14-63-50 (office); 1-40-63-73-83 (office); 4-91-23-39-28 (home). *Fax:* 4-91-14-63-44 (office); 1-40-63-79-63 (office); 4-91-23-36-14 (office). *E-mail:* gteissier@assemblee-nat.fr (office). *Website:* www.guyteissier.com (office).

TEITELBAUM, Philip, PhD; American psychologist and academic; *Graduate Research Professor in Psychology, University of Florida;* b. 9 Oct. 1928, Brooklyn, New York; s. of Bernard Teitelbaum and Betty Schechter; m. 1st Anita Slavsal 1955; m. 2nd Evelyn Satinoff 1963; m. 3rd Osnat Boné 1985; five s.; ed Johns Hopkins Univ.; Instructor and Asst Prof. in Psychology, Harvard Univ. 1954–59; Assoc., Full Prof., Univ. of Pa 1959–73; Prof., Univ. of Ill. 1973–85, Emer. Prof. 1985–; Fellow, Center for Advanced Studies, Univ. of Ill. 1979–85; Grad. Research Prof. in Psychology, Univ. of Fla 1984–; mem. NAS, AAAS; Guggenheim Fellow; Fulbright Fellow; American Psychology Asscn Scientific Contrib. Award. *Publications:* Fundamental Principles of Physiological Psychology 1967, Vol. on Motivation, Handbook of Behavioral Neurobiology (with Evelyn Satinoff) 1983. *Address:* Psychology Department, 337 PSY, University of Florida, Gainesville, FL 32611; 2239 NW 17th Avenue, Gainesville, FL 32605, USA (home). *Telephone:* (352) 273-2180 (office); (352) 372-5714 (home). *Fax:* (352) 392-7985 (office). *E-mail:* teitelb@ufl.edu (office); teitelb@hotmail.com (home). *Website:* www.psych.ufl.edu/~teitelb (office).

TEIXEIRA, Jose, LLB, BA; Timor-Leste lawyer and politician; ed Univ. of Queensland, Univ. of New England, Australia; left East Timor aged 11; worked as lawyer in Brisbane, Australia; returned to East Timor 2002; fmr Sec. of State for Tourism, Environment and Investment, Minister for Natural Resources, Minerals and Energy Policy; currently mem. Nat. Parl.; Spokesman Frente Revolucionária do Timor Leste Independente (Fretilin). *Address:* Frente Revolucionária do Timor Leste Independente (Revolutionary Front for an Independent East Timor), Rua dos Mártires da Pátria, Dili, Timor-Leste. *Telephone:* 3321409. *Website:* fretilin-rdtl.blogspot.com.

TEIXEIRA DA CRUZ, Paula; Portuguese lawyer and politician; *Minister of Justice;* b. 1 June 1960, Luanda, Angola; m. Paulo Teixeira Pinto (divorced); two c.; ed Free Univ. of Lisbon; teacher of Admin. Law, Free Univ. of Lisbon 1983–87, Inst. of Financial and Fiscal Studies –1992; mem. Social Democratic Party (PSD) 1995–, mem. PSD Nat. Political Cttee 1997–98, Vice-Pres. 2005–06; worked in govt of Cavaco Silva 1990s; City Councillor, Lisbon 1998–2002, Pres. Municipal Ass. 2005–09; Pnr, F. Castelo Branco & Associados 2006–; Minister of Justice 2011–; mem. Gen. Council, Bar Asscn 2002–05; mem. Portuguese Asscn of European Law, Asscn for the Progress of Law. *Address:* Ministry of Justice, Praça do Comércio, 1149-019 Lisbon (office); F. Castelo Branco & Associados, Avenida de a Liberdade 249, 1st Floor, 1250–143 Lisbon, Portugal. *Telephone:* (21) 3222300 (office). *Fax:* (21) 3479208 (office). *E-mail:* gmj@mj.gov.pt (office); paulateixeiradacruz-9782@adv.oa.pt. *Website:* www.mj.gov.pt (office).

TEIXEIRA DOS SANTOS, Fernando, PhD; Portuguese economist and government official; b. 13 Sept. 1951; m. Maria Clementina Pereira Nunes Teixeira dos Santos; ed Univ. of Porto, Univ. of SC, USA; Chair. Exec. Cttee, Int. Org. of Securities Comms 2000–04, Chair. European Regional Cttee 2004–05; Chair. Instituto Iberoamericano de Mercado de Valores, Cttee of European Securities Regulators Expert Group, Portuguese Securities Exchange Comm.; Prof. of Economics, Univ. of Porto 1986–95; Sec. of State for the Treasury and Finance 1995–99; Pres. Comissão do Mercado de Valores Mobiliários 2000–05; Minister of State and Finance 2005–11; Gov. for Portugal, EIB; Grand Official of the Order Infante D. Henrique 2005. *Address:* c/o Ministry of Finance and Public Administration, Av. Infante D. Henrique 1, 1149-009 Lisbon, Portugal (office). *Website:* www.min-financas.pt (office).

TEIXEIRA PINTO, Elsa Maria Neto d'Alva Teixeira de Barros; São Tomé and Príncipe politician; Sec. of State for Reform of the State and Public Admin 2002–03, 2003–04, Minister of Justice 2004–08, of Public Admin and Parl. Affairs 2004–05, of Nat. Defence 2008–10, also Minister of Internal Order, Justice and Parl. Affairs; mem. Movimento de Libertação de São Tomé e Príncipe—Partido Social Democrata (MLSTP—PSD). *Address:* Assembleia Nacional, Palácio dos Congressos, CP 181, São Tomé, São Tomé and Príncipe (office).

TEIXEIRA PINTO, Paulo Jorge; Portuguese academic and banker; *Chairman, Banco Activobank (Portugal), SA;* b. 10 Oct. 1960, Angola; m. Paula da Cruz; two c.;

ed Univ. of Lisbon, Univ. of Madrid, INSEAD, Fontainebleau; Lecturer in Law, Univ. of Lisbon and Free Univ. 1983–88; Under-Sec. of State of the Presidency of the Council of Ministers 1991–92, Sec. of State of the Presidency 1992–95; Head of Legal Dept, Banco Comercial Português SA (BCP) 1995–2000, Gen. Man. 2000–05, Co. Sec. 2000–05, Chair. 2005–07; Gen. Sec. Millennium bcp Foundation 2004–05, Chair. 2005–07, currently Chair. Banco Activobank (Portugal), SA (bank cr. by BCP and Banco Sabadell); Vice-Chair. Portuguese Banking Asscn; mem. Opus Dei 1986–; mem. Supervisory Bd Energias de Portugal; Pres. Causa Real 2008–. *Address:* Office of the Chairman, Banco Activobank (Portugal), SA Rua Augusta 84, 1149-023 Lisbon, Portugal (office). *Telephone:* (21) 4232673 (office). *Fax:* (21) 0066883 (office). *E-mail:* ab7_dop@activobank7.pt (office). *Website:* www.activobank7.pt (office).

TEJPAL, Tarun J.; Indian newspaper editor and writer; *CEO and Editor-in-Chief, Tehelka;* fmr reporter for The Indian Express and The Telegraph, ed. with India Today and India Express Group; has written for numerous int. publications, including The Paris Review, The Guardian, Financial Times and Prospect; co-f. India Ink publishing house; fmr Managing Ed. Outlook news magazine –2000; Founding CEO and Ed.-in-Chief, Tehelka newspaper 2000–, initially web-only news site, relaunched as nat. weekly newspaper 2004–. *Publications:* The Alchemy of Desire (novel) (Prix Millepages) 2005, The Story of My Assassins 2009, The Valley of Masks 2011. *Address:* Tehelka, M-76, Second Floor, M-Block Market, Greater Kailash Part 2, New Delhi 110 048, India (office). *Telephone:* (11) 40575757. *E-mail:* editor@tehelka.com (office). *Website:* www.tehelka.com (office); www.taruntejpal.com.

TEKLE, Afewerk, OM, MA; Ethiopian painter, sculptor and architect; b. 22 Oct. 1932, Ankober, Shoa Prov.; s. of Weizero Feleketch Yematawork and Ato Tekle Mamo; divorced; ed Cen. School of Arts and Crafts and Slade School of Art, Univ. of London, UK, Accad. di Michelangelo, Florence Italy; sent to England to become a mining engineer 1947; artistic studies 1947–54; solo exhbns world-wide; has also produced drawings and designs for stamps, playing cards, posters, flags and nat. ceremonial dress; designed his own house, studio and gallery 'Villa Alpha'; exhibited and lectured in fmr USSR, USA, Senegal, Turkey, Zaïre, UAE, Bulgaria, Munich, Germany (XX Olympiad), Kenya and Algeria; mem. French Int. Acad. of Arts 1997, Russian Acad. of Fine Arts 1999; Hon. Citizen of USSR 1989; Grand Order of Cyril and Methodius (Bulgaria) 1968, Order of Merit (Senegal), Kt Commdr, Order of St Sylvester (Holy See); Haile Selassie I Prize for Fine Arts 1964, Int. Gold Mercury Award, Italy 1982, American Golden Acad. Award 1992, Cambridge Order of Excellence, UK 1992, Council of the ABI World Laureate, 27th Int. Millennium Congress on the Arts and Communication, Washington, DC 2000, Grand Amb. of the Fine Arts and Int. Peace Award, Int. World Forum 2008, Lifetime Greatness Award for Services to the Fine Arts of the World 2009; numerous other awards, medals and decorations by heads of state. *Works include:* King Solomon meets the Queen of Sheba, St George's Cathedral, Addis Ababa, Equestrian Statue of Ras Makonnen, Harar, The Struggles and Aspirations of the African People (stained glass), Africa Hall, UN Building 1960, Meskel Flower (considered to be his masterpiece) 1961, Mural of St Paul's Hosp. 1972, Last Judgment, Adigrat Cathedral, Tigrai, northern Ethiopia, Unity Triptych: (a) The Disunity of Man, (b) Towards the Unity of Man, (c) Symbol of Human Unity (Gold Medal, Algiers Int. Festival 1977), Self Portrait (first African painting to be included in perm. collection of Uffizi Gallery, Florence, Italy) 1981, The Victory of Ethiopia over Evil Forces 1992, The Chalice and the Cross in the Life of the African People (First Prize, Biennale of Aquitaine 1997) 1997, The Sun of Senegal 1997, Mother Ethiopia, The Simien Mountains, three projects for public Squares to be done in Ethiopia and one in any of the countries of Africa (Lifetime Achievement Award (UK) and Gold Medal for Ethiopia (USA), World Forum 2009). *Leisure interests:* reading, fencing, walking, mountaineering. *Address:* Villa Alpha 22, Yetebeb Godanna, PO Box 5651, Addis Ababa, Ethiopia (office). *Telephone:* 71-59-41 (office). *Fax:* 71-59-41 (office). *E-mail:* hmal.afewerk.tekle@ethionet.et (office).

TELAVI, Willy, MA; Tuvaluan politician and fmr police officer; ed Univ. of the South Pacific, Northern Territory Univ. (now Charles Darwin Univ.), Australia; long career with Tuvalu Police Force, becoming Police Commr 1993–2009; MP for constituency of Nanumea 2006–, Minister of Home Affairs 2006–10, Prime Minister and Minister of Home Affairs 2010–13. *Address:* c/o Office of the Prime Minister, PMB, Vaiaku, Funafuti, Tuvalu.

TELEFONI RETZLAFF, Misa, LLB, CPA; Samoan lawyer and politician; b. 21 May 1952; ed King's Coll., Auckland and Auckland Univ., NZ; with Jackson Russell Tunks and West, Auckland, NZ 1974–76; admitted to Bar as Barrister and Solicitor of the Supreme Court, NZ 1975, Western Samoa 1976; pvt. legal practice as H. T. Retzlaff, Apia, Western Samoa 1976–92 (closed office on appointment as Minister of State); apptd Attorney-Gen. 1986–88, resgnd on running as MP; elected MP for Falelatai and Samatau Dist 1988–2011, served as Opposition MP 1988–91; Minister of State with portfolios of Agric., Forests, Fisheries and Meteorology and Minister of Shipping 1992–96, of Health 1996–2001; Deputy Prime Minister and Minister of Finance 2001–06; Deputy Prime Minister and Minister of Commerce, Tourism, Industry and Labour 2006–11 (retd); Vice-Pres. WHO 1999; Chair. FAO Asia/Pacific Regional Conf. and Inaugural Meeting, FAO Ministers 1995; admitted as CPA Samoa 1977, apptd Pres. of Samoa Chamber of Commerce 1977–79; Dir Retzlaff Group of Cos 1975–86, also of eight cos in Western Samoa, one in NZ and Suva, Fiji (resgnd from all 1992); Pro-Chancellor Nat. Univ. of Samoa 1986–98; elected to Komiti Tumau (Standing Cttee) of Methodist Church of Samoa 1996–; mem. Inaugural Council of Piula Theological Coll. 1998–; Signatory Latimer House Rules on Good Governance, The Commonwealth; spoke at numerous univs and int. confs including ESCAP 1994, Commonwealth Law Conf., Kuala Lumpur 1999; Order of Merit, Chile 1994; Kellock Fellows Scholarship, NZ 1969, Sr Prize in Law, Auckland Univ., World Food Day Medal 2005. *Publications:* Love and Money 2005, To Thine Own Self be True. *Address:* c/o Department of Commerce, Industry and Labour, Apia, Samoa.

TELIČKA, Pavel; Czech diplomatist, lawyer and university teacher; *Partner, BXL Consulting;* b. 24 Aug. 1965, Washington, USA; m. Eva Teličková; one s. one d.; ed Charles Univ., Prague; joined Ministry of Foreign Affairs 1986, mem. of del. for talks on Czech membership of EU 1991, with Czech Standing Mission to EU 1991–95, Deputy Amb. to Brussels 1993–95; Dir of Dept in Ministry of Foreign Affairs 1995–98, Dir-Gen. Dept for EU and NATO 1998; Deputy Chair. Comm. for

Czech Integration to EU 1998, Chief Negotiator 1998–99; Deputy Minister for Foreign Affairs 1998–99; apptd State Sec. for European Affairs 1999; Amb. and Head, Perm. Mission of Czech Repub. to European Communities 2003–04, EU Commr without Portfolio 2004; currently Co-founder and Pnr, BXL Consulting (consults on EU affairs); Sr External Adviser, European Policy Centre; mem. Admin. Council, Notre Europe Foundation, Paris; mem. Europe-USA-Asia Trilateral Comm.; Hon. mem. Man. Bd Nat. Training Fund 1999–2003, Centre of Good Will 2001–; mem. Bd Govs Univ. of Tomase Bati 2001–03; mem. Tomáš Bata Foundation 1997–, High Level Group of Ind. Stakeholders on Admin. Burdens; Pres. Václav Havel Commemorative Medal 2003, Commemorative Medal of King Jiří z Poděbrad 2003. *Publications:* (with K. Barták) How Were We Entering the EU? 2003. *Leisure interests:* playing rugby and squash, fitness, cross-country skiing, biking, roller-skating, music, travel, driving. *Address:* BXL Consulting, Rond-Point Schuman 11, 1040 Brussels, Belgium (office). *Telephone:* (2) 256-75-15 (office). *Fax:* (2) 256-75-03 (office). *E-mail:* office@bxl.cz (office). *Website:* www.bxl.cz (office).

TELITO, Rev. and Rt Hon. Sir Filoimea, GCMG, MBE; Tuvaluan government official; b. Vaitupu Island; fmr school prin. and church pastor; Gov.-Gen. of Tuvalu 2005–10. *Address:* c/o Office of the Governor-General, Private Mail Bag, Vaiaku, Funafuti, Tuvalu (office).

TELLEM, Nancy; American media executive; *President, Entertainment and Digital Media, Microsoft;* b. 1954; m. Arn Tellem; three c.; ed Univ. of California; began career as TV industry lawyer; with Warner Bros TV (then Lorimar TV) 1987–97, Exec. Vice-Pres. of Business and Financial Affairs; Exec. Vice-Pres. of Business Affairs for CBS Entertainment and Exec. Vice-Pres. CBS Productions 1997–98, Pres. CBS Entertainment 1998–2004, Pres. CBS Paramount Network Television Entertainment Group 2004–10; Pres. Entertainment and Digital Media, Microsoft 2012–; Dir ThirdAge Media Inc. 2000, Artful Style Inc. 2000; ranked by Forbes Magazine amongst 100 Most Powerful Women (75th) 2006, (49th) 2007, (32nd) 2008. *Address:* Microsoft Production Studios, 520 Broadway, Santa Monica, CA 90401, USA (office). *Website:* www.microsoft.com/en-us/productionstudios (office).

TELLEP, Daniel Michael, MS; American business executive (retd); b. 20 Nov. 1931, Forest City, Pa; m. Pat Tellep; six c.; ed Univ. of California, Berkeley and Harvard Univ.; with Lockheed Missiles & Space Co. 1955–, Chief Eng Missile Systems Div. 1969–75, Vice-Pres., Asst Gen. Man. Advanced Systems Div. 1975–83, Exec. Vice-Pres. 1983–84, Pres. 1984–86, Pres. Lockheed Missiles and Space Group 1986–89, Chair. and CEO Lockheed Corpn 1989–95 (merged with Martin Marietta to form Lockheed Martin 1994), Chair., CEO Lockheed Martin 1996–97 (retd); mem. Interstate Bancorp Bd 1991–, Bd of Govs Music Center LA Co. 1991–95, Calif. Business Round Table 1992–; Fellow, AIAA, American Astronautical Soc.; mem. Nat. Acad. of Eng; James V. Forrestal Award 1995, Calif. Mfrs Award 1996, Nat. Eng Award 1996, Karman Wings Award 1997 and numerous other awards. *Address:* c/o Lockheed Martin Corporation, 6801 Rockledge Drive, Bethesda, MD 20817, USA.

TELLER, Juergen; German photographer; b. 28 Jan. 1964, Erlangen; pnr, Venetia Scott; one d.; ed Bayerische Staatslehranstalt für Photographie, Munich; living and working in London 1986–; Citibank Photography Prize 2003. *Publications:* Go Sees 1999, Tracht 2001, More, Stephanie Seymour 2001. *Address:* 1 Telford Road, London, W10 5SH, England (office). *Telephone:* (20) 8964-0966 (office). *Fax:* (20) 8964-0790 (office). *E-mail:* juergenteller@ukf.net (office).

TELLIER, Paul M., PC, CC; Canadian business executive and former public official; b. 1939, Joliette, Québec; ed Université Laval and Univ. of Oxford, UK; admitted to Bar, Québec 1963; Deputy Minister for Indian Affairs and Northern Devt 1979–82; Deputy Minister of Energy, Mines and Resources 1982–85; Clerk of the Privy Council and Sec. to Cabinet of Govt of Canada 1985–92; Pres. and CEO Canadian Nat. Railway Co. (CN) 1992–2003; Pres. and CEO Bombardier Inc. 2003–04; Chair. GCT Global Container Terminals Inc. 2007–; Dir Alcan Aluminium Ltd, Bell Canada Enterprises Inc./Bell Canada 1999–, McCain Foods Ltd; fmr Chair. Conf. Bd of Canada, Co-Chair. Canada–Japan Business Council; Vice-Chair. Canadian Council of Chief Execs, Co-Chair. N America Policy Cttee; mem. Bd Dans la rue 2000–03; Hon. LLD (Univ. of Alberta) 1996; Hon. PhD (Univ. of Ottawa) 2000; Hon. DComm (St Mary's Univ.) 2001; Public Policy Forum Outstanding Performance Award 1988, Gov. Gen.'s Outstanding Achievement Award 1990, Transportation Person of the Year Award, Nat. Transportation Week 1997, Grand Montréalais 1998, Canada's Outstanding CEO of the Year 1998, B'nai Brith Canada Award of Merit 2000, Les Affaires newspaper Personality of the Year 2000, McCullogh Logistics Exec. of the Year Award, Nat. Industrial Transportation League and Logistics Management & Distribution Report 2001, Industry Achievement Award, Canadian Railway Hall of Fame 2002, Fellowship Award, Inst. of Corp. Dirs 2003, Distinguished Canadian Leadership Award 2004; second St Clair tunnel named in his honour 2004. *Address:* Bell Canada Enterprises, 1000 de La Gauchetière Ouest, Bureau 3700, Montréal, Québec H3B 4Y7, Canada (office). *Telephone:* (888) 932-6666 (office). *Fax:* (514) 870-4385 (office). *E-mail:* bcecomms@bce.ca (office).

TELLKAMP, Uwe; German writer and physician; b. 28 Oct. 1968, Dresden; m.; one s.; practising doctor –2004; Uwe Johnson Prize 2008, German Nat. Prize 2009. *Publications:* novels: Der Hecht, die Träume und das Portugiesische Café 2000, Der Schlaf in den Uhren (Ingeborg Bachmann Prize) 2004, Der Eisvogel 2005, Zimorodek 2006, Der Turm (German Book Prize 2008, Konrad Adenauer Foundation Literature Prize 2009) 2008, Der Zitronenrabe 2009, Die Schwebebahn: Dresdner Erkundungen 2012; other: Die Sandwirtschaft: Leipziger Poetikvorlesungen 2007; contrib. articles to literary journals and anthologies. *Address:* c/o Suhrkamp Verlag, Postfach 101945, 60019 Frankfurt, Germany (office). *E-mail:* geschaeftsleitung@suhrkamp.de (office). *Website:* www.suhrkamp .de (office).

TELMER, Frederick Harold, MA; Canadian business executive; b. 28 Dec. 1937, Edmonton, Alberta; s. of Ingar Telmer and Bernice Telmer; m. Margaret Goddard Hutchings; three s.; ed Garneau High School, Edmonton, Univ. of Alberta; joined Industrial Relations Dept, Stelco Inc. 1963, various man. positions in Marketing Div., subsequently Gen. Man. Field Sales, apptd Gen. Man. Corp. Affairs and Strategic Planning 1984, Vice-Pres. 1985, Pres. Stelco Steel 1988, Dir

Stelco Inc. 1989, Chair. and CEO 1991–97, Chair. 1997–2003; Founding Dir Japan Soc. *Leisure interests:* golf, tennis, skiing. *Address:* 4451 Lakeshore Road, Burlington, ON L7L 1B3, Canada (home).

TELTSCHIK, Horst; German business executive and fmr politician; b. 14 June 1940, Klantendorf; s. of Richard Teltschik and Anna Teltschik; m. Gerhild Ruff 1967; one s. one d.; ed Gymnasium Tegernsee and Freie Univ. Berlin; Asst Prof., Otto-Suhr-Inst., Freie Univ. Berlin 1968–70; Head of Int. Policy and Intra-German Relations Group, CDU Fed. HQ, Bonn 1970–72; Exec. Ministerial Counsellor to Prime Minister, Rhineland-Palatinate State Chancellery 1972–76; Chief of Staff of Chair. of CDU/CSU Parl. Group, Bundestag, Bonn 1977–82; Ministerial Dir Fed. Chancellery, Head of Directorate-Gen. for Foreign and Intra-German Relations, Devt Policy, External Security 1982–90; Deputy Chief of Staff of Fed. Chancellery 1983–90; CEO Bertelsmann Foundation 1991–92; mem. Bd of Man., Econ. and Governmental Affairs, BMW AG 1993–2000, BMW Rep. of Bd of Man. for Cen. and Eastern Europe, Asia and Middle East 2000–03, Chair. BMW Foundation Herbert Quandt 1993–2003; Lecturer and Hon Prof, Pres. Boeing Germany 2003–06; Founding Pres., Korean German Inst. of Tech., Seoul 2006–09; Pres. Soc. of Munich Philharmonic Orchestra 1993–2003; Pres. German-Israeli Business Asscn 2002–11; mem. Bd of Dirs Roche Holding Ltd 2002–10; mem. German-Japanese Dialogue Forum 1991–2003, German-Indian Consultative Group 1992–2003, Univ. Council, Munich Acad. of Arts 2000–07, Senate of German Nat. Foundation 2000–, German Council on Foreign Relations (DGAP) 2000, Steering Cttee of SWP-Foundation, German Inst. for Int. Politics and Security Affairs 2000–10, German-Russian Raw Material Forum 2008–, Korea-Germany Jt Consultation Cttee on Nat. Unification 2011–; mem. Int. Advisory Bd Council on Foreign Relations, New York 2000–10; mem. Bd of Trustees Eugen Biser Foundation; organizer, Munich Conf. on Securities Policy 1999–2008; Hon. Gen. Consul of India for Bavaria and Thuringia 1992–2002; Hon. Prof. and Lecturer, Technical Univ. Munich 1996–2007; Diplompolitologe; Großen Bundesverdienstkreuz ausgezeichnet 2008, Bundesverdienstkreuz am Bande, Verdienstkreuz 1. Klasse des Verdienstordens der Bundesrepublik Deutschland, Verdienstorden des Freistaates Bayern, Das Große Verdienstkreuz des Verdienstordens der Bundesrepublik Deutschland, Commdr, Légion d'honneur, Grande Ufficiale (Italy), Commdr (Luxembourg), Bavarian Verdienstorden, Manfred Wörner Medaille 2011; also orders and distinctions from Argentina, Spain, Mexico, Cameroon, Nepal, Portugal, Finland, Tunisia, Austria, Poland, Russian Federation, Hungary, Bulgaria; Hon. DUniv (Budapest) 1991, (Sogang, Seoul) 1997; Soziale Ordnung Magazine Future-Award 1999, SCOPUS Award, Hebrew Univ. of Jerusalem 2005, British-German Community Medal, British Chamber of Commerce in Germany 2009. *Publication:* 329 Tage – Innenansichten der deutschen Einigung. *Leisure interests:* literature, tennis. *Address:* Karl-Theodor Strasse 38, 83700 Rottach-Egern, Germany. *Telephone:* (8022) 26677. *Fax:* (8022) 662849. *E-mail:* horstmt@t-online.de.

TEMARU, Oscar Manutahi; French Polynesian politician and fmr head of state; b. 1 Nov. 1944, Faa'a Dist, Tahiti; m. Marie Temaru; seven c.; in French Navy 1961–63; customs officer 1964–99; f. Front de Libération de la Polynésie—FLP (Polynesia Liberation Front) 1977 (changed party name to Tavini Huiraatira no te ao maohi—Serve the Polynesian People 1983); Mayor of Faa'a 1983; elected mem. Territorial Ass. 1986; mem. UPD Party (Union for Democracy); Pres. of French Polynesia June–Oct. 2004, 2005–06, 2007–08, Feb.–Nov. 2009, 2011–13. *Leisure interest:* golf. *Address:* Tavini Huiraatira, rue des Remparts, Papeete, French Polynesia (office). *Telephone:* 424902. *Fax:* 434209. *E-mail:* contact@tavinihuiraatira.com. *Website:* www.tavinihuiraatira.com.

TEMBO, Akihiko; Japanese oil industry executive; ed Tokyo Univ.; joined Idemitsu Kosan Co. Ltd 1964, Man. Dir, Idemitsu International Europe PLC 1988–91, Dir and Gen. Man. Treasury Dept, Idemitsu Kosan Co. Ltd 1991–98, Man. Dir Idemitsu Kosan Co. Ltd 1998–2000, Sr Managing Man. Dir 2000–02, Pres. and Rep. Dir 2002–09, Chair. and Rep. Dir 2009–13; fmr Vice-Pres. Petroleum Asscn of Japan, later Pres. *Address:* c/o Idemitsu Kosan Co. Ltd, 1-1, Marunouchi 3-chome, Chiyoda-ku, Tokyo 100-8321, Japan. *E-mail:* info@idemitsu .com.

TEMERLIN, (Julius) Liener, BFA; American advertising executive (retd); b. 27 March 1928, Ardmore, Okla; s. of S. Pincus Temerlin and Julie Kahn Temerlin; m. Karla Samuelsohn 1950; two d.; ed Ardmore, Okla High School, Univ. of Oklahoma; COO Glenn Advertising 1970–74; Pres. Glenn, Bozell & Jacobs 1974–79; Chair. of Bd Bozell & Jacobs 1979–85; Chair. Bozell, Jacobs, Kenyon & Eckhardt 1985–88, Bozell 1989–92; Chair. Temerlin McClain Advertising 1992–2001, Chair. Emer. 2001–; Founder and Pres. Temerlin Consulting, Dallas –2009 (retd); consultant, The Richards Group 2005–09; Founder, Chair. and Festival Dir AFI Dallas Int. Film Festival 2007–08; Algur H. Meadows Distinguished Prof. of Advertising, Meadows School of the Arts, Southern Methodist Univ.; Chair. Dallas Museum of Art Devt Cttee 1993–96; Pres. Council Dallas Symphony Asscn 1989–; mem. Bd of Dirs Madison Council, Library of Congress 1991–2002, East-West Inst. 1999–; mem. Steering Cttee for Capital Campaign, KERA (Public TV Council) 2000–01; Trustee, American Film Inst. 1992–2000, Hon. Trustee 2000–; mem. in support of Innovations in Medicine Campaign, Southwestern Medical Foundation Leadership Council 2002–, Community Advisory Cttee for Clinical Services 2003–; Bill D. Kerss Award, Dallas Advertising League 1983, Nat. Conf. of Christians and Jews Brotherhood Award 1984, Susan G. Komen Foundation for Breast Cancer Research 1989, Community Service Award, Jas. K. Wilson Silver Cup Award, Dallas 1990, Linz Award for civic service 1990, Volunteer Fundraiser of the Year 1991, Silver Medal Award, Dallas Advertising League 1991, Father of the Year 1991, Best Man in Advertising Award 1992, Servant Leader Award, Volunteer Center of Dallas 2001, Temerlin Advertising Inst., Southern Methodist Univ. named after him 2001, inducted into Southwest Advertising Hall of Fame Inaugural Class 2008. *Telephone:* (972) 739-7480 (office). *Fax:* (972) 739-7483 (office). *E-mail:* connie.beebe@temerlinconsulting.com (office).

TEMIRKANOV, Yuri Khatuyevich; Russian conductor; *Music Director and Principal Conductor, St Petersburg Philharmonic Orchestra;* b. 10 Dec. 1938, Nalchik, Repub. of Kabardino-Balkaria; s. of Khatu Sagidovich Temirkanov and Polina Petrovna Temirkanova; m. Irina Guseva (deceased); one s.; ed Leningrad Conservatoire; First Violinist with Leningrad Philharmonic Orchestra 1961–66;

Conductor for Maly Theatre and Opera Studio, Leningrad 1965–68; Chief Conductor, Leningrad Philharmonic Orchestra 1968–76, Kirov Opera and Ballet Co. 1976–88; Prof. Leningrad Conservatoire 1979–88; Artistic Dir State Philharmonia 1988–; Prin. Guest Conductor Royal Philharmonic Orchestra and Philadelphia Orchestra; Chief Conductor Royal Philharmonic Orchestra 1992–97; Prin. Guest Conductor, Danish Radio Orchestra 1997–2008; Music Dir Baltimore Symphony Orchestra 1999–2007, Music Dir Emer. 2007–; Music Dir and Prin. Conductor St Petersburg Philharmonic Orchestra 2007–; Prin. Guest Conductor Bolshoi Theatre, Russia 2007–; Music Dir Teatro Regio di Parma 2009–; guest conductor of major orchestras in Europe and Asia, including the Berlin Philharmonic, Vienna Philharmonic, Dresden Staatskapelle, London Philharmonic, London Symphony, Royal Concertgebouw Orchestra, Santa Cecilia, Rome and La Scala and in USA the major orchestras in New York, Philadelphia, Boston, Chicago, Cleveland, San Francisco and Los Angeles; USSR People's Artist 1981, Glinka Prize, USSR State Prize 1976, 1985. *Opera productions include:* Porgy and Bess (at Maly), Peter the Great (at Kirov), Shchedrin's Dead Souls (at Bolshoi and Kirov), Tchaikovsky's Queen of Spades and Eugene Onegin (Kirov) 1979. *Address:* c/o IMG Artists, The Light Box, 111 Power Road, London, W4 5PY, England (office). *Telephone:* (20) 7957-5800 (office). *Fax:* (20) 7957-5801 (office). *E-mail:* nmathias@imgartists.com (office). *Website:* www.imgartists.com (office).

TEMÍSTOCLES MONTÁS, Juan, PhD; Dominican Republic politician; *Secretary of State for the Economy, Planning and Development;* b. 1950; m. Carmen Artero; two s. one d.; ed Univ. Autónoma de Santo Domingo, Univ. Politécnica de Madrid, Spain; mem. Nat. Congress (Parl.) 1986–90; Admin. Corporación Dominicana de Electricidad (now Corporación Dominicana de Empresas Eléctricas Estatales) 1996–98; Tech. Sec. to the Presidency 1998–2000, 2004–06; Exec. Dir Global Foundation for Democracy and Devt 2000–04; Sec. of State for Economy, Planning and Devt 2007–; mem. Partido de la Liberación Dominicana. *Address:* Secretariat of State for the Economy, Planning and Development, Palacio Nacional, Avda México, esq. Dr Delgado, Bloque B, 2°, Santo Domingo, Dominican Republic (office). *Telephone:* 695-8028 (office). *Fax:* 695-8432 (office). *E-mail:* informacion@economia.gov.do (office). *Website:* www.economia.gov.do (office).

TEMPEST, Brian W., PhD; British pharmaceuticals executive; *Strategy Advisor, Hale & Tempest Company Ltd;* b. 13 June 1947, Morecambe, Lancs., England; s. of Bill Tempest and Joan Tempest; m. Jasmin Tempest; three s.; ed Lancaster Univ.; fmrly with Beecham and GD Searle, various positions in sales, marketing and man.; Regional Dir for Africa, Far East and Middle East, Glaxo Holdings 1985–93; Worldwide Commercial Operations Dir, Fisons plc 1993–95; Regional Dir for Europe, CIS and Africa, Ranbaxy Laboratories Ltd 1995–2000, Worldwide Pres., Pharmaceuticals 2000–04, CEO and Man. Dir July 2004–Dec. 2005, Chief Mentor and Exec. Vice-Chair. 2006–07; Strategy Advisor, Hale & Tempest Co. Ltd 2008–; Chair. Advisory Bd Lancaster Univ. Man. School; mem. Scrip Global Awards Panel; mem. Editorial Bd Journal of Generic Medicine 2007–; mem. RSC, Royal Soc. of Medicine; Hon. Prof., Lancaster Univ. 2007–. *Telephone:* (98) 10091192 (India; mobile) (office); (7852) 268530 (mobile) (office). *Fax:* (5) 67-20-64-44 (France) (office). *E-mail:* brian.tempest@clara.co.uk (home). *Website:* www .briantempest.com (home).

TEMPLEMAN, Baron (Life Peer), cr. 1982, of White Lackington in the County of Somerset; **Sydney William Templeman,** PC, QC, MBE, MA; British fmr judge; b. 3 March 1920, London; s. of Herbert W. Templeman and Lilian (née Pheasant) Templeman; m. 1st Margaret Rowles 1946 (died 1988); two s.; m. 2nd Sheila Barton Edworthy 1996 (died 2009); ed Southall Grammar School and St John's Coll. Cambridge; served 4/1st Gurkha Rifles 1941–46; mem. Middle Temple 1946–, Treas. 1987–; mem. Bar Council 1961–65, 1970–72; QC 1964; Attorney-Gen., Duchy of Lancaster 1970; Judge, Chancery Div., 1972; Pres., Senate of Inns of Court and Bar 1974; mem., Royal Comm. on Legal Services 1976; Lord Justice of Appeal 1978–82; Lord of Appeal in Ordinary 1982–95; Visitor, Essex Univ. 1990; Pres., Bar European Group 1987–95, Asscn of Law Teachers 1997–; Hon. Fellow, St John's Coll. Cambridge 1982; Hon. mem. Canadian Bar Asscn 1976, American Bar Asscn 1976, Newfoundland Law Soc. 1984; Hon. DLitt (Reading) 1980, Hon. LLD (Birmingham) 1986, (Exeter) 1991, (Huddersfield Polytechnic) 1989, (West of England) 1993, (Nat. Law School of India) 1994. *Address:* House of Lords, London, SW1A 0PW, England. *Telephone:* (1392) 275428 (home).

TEMPLETON, Richard (Rich) K., BSc; American electronics industry executive; *Chairman, President and CEO, Texas Instruments Inc.;* b. 1958; m.; three c.; ed Union Coll., NY; joined Texas Instruments Inc. (TI) 1980, held various positions including Exec. Vice-Pres. semiconductor business 1996–2004, COO TI 2000–04, mem. Bd of Dirs 2003–, Pres. and CEO 2004–08, Chair., Pres. and CEO 2008–; mem. Bd of Dirs Semiconductor Industry Asscn; mem. Business Roundtable, Dallas Chief Exec. Roundtable. *Address:* Texas Instruments Inc., 12500 TI Boulevard, Dallas, TX 75266-4136, USA (office). *Telephone:* (972) 995-2011 (office). *Website:* www.ti.com (office).

TEMU, Sir Puka, KBE, CMG; Papua New Guinea physician and politician; *Minister of Public Service;* worked for six years at Royal Melbourne and Royal Prince Alfred hosps, Australia; fmr Head of Papua New Guinea Health Dept; fmr Minister of Public Service, of State Enterprise and Commerce; Deputy Prime Minister and Minister of Lands, Physical Planning and Mining 2007–10; led unsuccessful vote of no confidence against Prime Minister Michael Somare July 2010; Leader of the Opposition 2010–11; Minister of Agric. and Livestock 2011–12, of Public Service 2012–; MP for Abau Dist; mem. Nat. Alliance Party. *Address:* Department of Public Service, Waigani 131, NCD, Papua New Guinea (office).

TEN HOLT, Friso; Dutch painter and etcher; b. 6 April 1921, Argelès-Gazost, France; m. A. Taselaar 1946; two s. one d.; ed Rijksakademie van Beeldende Kunsten, Amsterdam; paintings mainly of swimmers, landscapes and nudes, portraits and figures; Prof. of Painting, Rijksakademie van Beeldende Kunsten, Amsterdam 1969–83; solo exhbns in Netherlands since 1952, London 1959, 1962, 1963, 1965, 1969, 1973; group exhbns at Beaverbrook Art Gallery, Canada and Tate Gallery, London 1963, Biennale Salzburg 1964, Carnegie Inst., Pittsburgh 1964, Netherlands travelling exhbn 1957–58; works in collections in Netherlands, Sweden, UK, France and USA. *Major works:* stained-glass windows for churches in Amsterdam and The Hague and for Haarlem Cathedral. *Leisure interest:*

reading. *Address:* Abbestede 1, 1759 NC Callantsoog, Netherlands. *E-mail:* info@ frisotenholt.nl. *Website:* www.frisotenholt.nl.

TENDULKAR, Sachin Ramesh; Indian fmr professional cricketer; b. 24 April 1973, Bombay (now Mumbai); s. of the late Ramesh Tendulkar and of Rajni Tendulkar; m. Anjali Mehta; one s. one d.; ed Sharadashram Vidyamandir (High School); right-hand batsman, right-arm off-break, leg-break bowler (over 100 One-Day Ints (ODI) wickets); teams: Bombay 1988–96 (renamed Mumbai) 1997–2013, Yorks. 1992, India 1989–2013 (Capt. 1996–98, 1999–2000), ICC (Int. Cricket Council) World ODI XI 2004, 2007, Mumbai Indians (Indian Premier League) 2008–13; First-class debut for Bombay cricket team aged 14, scored a century on debut 1988; Test debut (cap 187): India v Pakistan, Karachi 15–20 Nov. 1989; ODI debut (cap 74): Pakistan v India, Gujranwala 18 Dec. 1989; played in 200 Tests (25 as Capt.), scored 15,921 runs (average 53.78), 51 centuries, 68 half-centuries; set new record for most runs scored by a batsman in Test cricket Oct. 2008; 463 ODIs (73 as Capt.), scored 18,426 runs (average 44.83), 49 centuries, 96 half-centuries; First-class: 310 matches, 25,396 runs (average 57.84), 81 hundreds, 116 half-centuries; highest scores: 248 not out (Test), 200 not out (ODI); balls bowled: 4,240 (Test), 8,054 (ODI); wickets taken: 46 (Test), 154 (ODI); bowling average: 54.17 (Test), 44.48 (ODI); best bowling 3/10 (Test), 5/32 (ODI); catches: 115 (Test), 140 (ODI); highest run scorer in both Test matches and ODIs and also the batsman with the most centuries in either form of the game; first player to score 50 centuries in all int. cricket combined; first player to score a double century in an ODI (v S Africa in Gwalior) 24 Feb. 2010; first batsman to score 12,000, 13,000, 14,000 and 15,000 runs in Test cricket; passed 30,000 runs in int. cricket 20 Nov. 2009; became the most-capped Test cricketer in history after taking field for his 169th match v Sri Lanka, Colombo 3 Aug. 2010; only person to hit 50 Test centuries (scored 50th v S Africa 19 Dec. 2010); first cricketer to score 2,000 ODI World Cup runs v Netherlands, Delhi 9 March 2011; first and only player to score 100 centuries in int. cricket (51 Test and 49 ODI centuries) at Mirpur against Bangladesh in the Asia Cup 16 March 2012; nominated to Rajya Sabha (Upper House of Parl.) 2012; retd 2013; UNICEF Brand Amb. for South Asia 2013–; owns two restaurants, Tendulkar's, Colaba, Mumbai and Sachin's, Mulund, Mumbai, in partnership with Sanjay Narang of Mars Restaurants; also owns restaurant in Bangalore called Sachin's; Hon. Group Capt., Indian Air Force (first sportsperson and first personality without an aviation background) 2010; Hon. mem. Order of Australia 2012; Arjuna Award 1994, Wisden Cricketer of the Year 1997, Rajiv Gandhi Khel Ratna Award 1998, Padma Shri Award 1999, Maharashtra Bhushan Award 2001, rated by Wisden as the second greatest Test batsman after Sir Donald Bradman, and the second greatest ODI batsman behind Sir Vivian Richards 2002 (ratings revised to leave Tendulkar ranked No. 1 and Richards at No. 2 2003), Player of the Tournament, Cricket World Cup 2003, ICC World ODI XI 2004, 2007, 2010, Rajiv Gandhi Awards – Sports 2005, mentioned in TIME magazine as "the greatest living exponent of his craft" 2006, ICC World Test XI 2009, 2010, 2011, Sir Garfield Sobers Trophy for Cricketer of the Year, ICC Awards 2010, Wisden Leading Cricketer in the World 2010, LG People's Choice Award 2010, Outstanding Achievement in Sport and the People's Choice Award, The Asian Awards, London 2010, Castrol Indian Cricketer of the Year Award 2011, BCCI Cricketer of the Year Award 2011, Wisden India Outstanding Achievement Award 2012, Padma Vibhushan 2008, Bharat Ratna 2014. *Address:* Rajya Sabha, Parliament House Annexe, New Delhi 110 001 (office); Dorab Villa, 19-A, Perry Cross Road, Opposite Joggers' Park, Bandra, Mumbai 400 050, India (home). *Telephone:* (11) 23034695 (office), (22) 26457576 (home). *Fax:* (11) 23792940 (office). *E-mail:* ast1@vsnl.net.

TENET, George J., MIA; American academic, investment industry executive and fmr government official; *Managing Director, Allen & Company LLC;* b. New York; m. A. Stephanie Glakas; one s.; ed Georgetown Univ. School of Foreign Service, School of Int. Affairs, Columbia Univ.; Research Dir American Hellenic Inst. 1978–79; Legis. Asst, Legis. Dir, staff of US Senator John Heinz 1982–85; fmr head of supervision of arms control negotiations between USSR and USA, subsequently Staff Dir, US Senate Select Cttee on Intelligence 1988–93; Special Asst to Pres. and Sr Dir for Intelligence Programs, Nat. Security Council 1993–95; Deputy Dir of CIA 1995–96, Acting Dir 1996–97, Dir 1997–2004 (resgnd); Distinguished Prof. in the Practice of Diplomacy, Edmund A. Walsh School of Foreign Service and Sr Research Assoc., Inst. for the Study of Diplomacy, Georgetown Univ. 2004–; Man. Dir Allen & Co., New York 2008–; mem. Bd of Dirs QinetiQ Group plc, UK 2006–08; Egyptian Order of Merit (First Class); Canadian Security Intelligence Service Gold Medal, Presidential Medal of Freedom 2004, America's Democratic Legacy Award from Anti-Defamation League 2005. *Publications:* The Ability of US Intelligence to Monitor the Intermediate Nuclear Force Treaty, At the Center of the Storm 2007. *Address:* Allen & Company LLC, 711 5th Ave., 9th Floor, New York, NY 10022 (office); Edmund A. Walsh School of Foreign Service, 301 InterCultural Center, 37th and O Streets, NW, Washington, DC 20057, USA. *Telephone:* (212) 832-8000 (NY) (office); (202) 687-5696. *Fax:* (212) 832-8023 (NY) (office); (202) 687-1431. *Website:* www.georgetown.edu/sfs.

TENG, Teng; Chinese politician; b. 1930, Jiangyin Co., Jiangsu Prov.; ed Tsinghua Univ., Beijing and in USSR; joined CCP 1948; Deputy Dir Chemical Eng Dept, Tsinghua Univ. 1960–66, Prof., Vice-Pres. Tsinghua Univ. 1980–84; Vice-Minister in charge of State Science and Tech. Comm. 1985–86; Deputy Head, Propaganda Dept CCP Cen. Cttee 1986–87; Vice Minister in charge of State Educ. Comm. 1988–93; Vice-Chair. Exec. Bd UNESCO 1991–93; Dir Sustainable Devt Research Centre; Pres. Chinese Ecological Econs Council; Vice-Pres. Chinese Acad. of Sciences 1986–87, Chinese Acad. of Social Sciences 1993–98; mem. 8th and 9th Standing Cttee NPC 1993–2003, mem. Educ., Science, Culture and Public Health Cttee 1993–98; Pres. Chinese and Ecological Econs Council 1998–2005; Govt Prize of Science and Tech. 1978. *Publication:* Future Outlook for the Environment and Sustainable Development 2002. *Leisure interest:* classical music. *Address:* 5th Jianguomennei Dajie, Beijing 100732 (office); Cuiweisili 1-2-401, Beijing 100036, People's Republic of China (home). *Telephone:* (10) 65137697 (office); (10) 68258097 (home). *Fax:* (10) 65137815 (office); (10) 68252720 (home). *E-mail:* tengteng@cass.org.cn (office); tengcass@yahoo.com (home).

TENG, Wensheng; Chinese writer and politician; b. 1940, Changning Co., Hunan Prov.; ed Chinese People's Univ.; joined CCP 1965; Research Fellow, Research Office, Secr. of CCP Cen. Cttee; Vice-Dir, later Dir Policy Research Office of CCP Cen. Cttee; Deputy Sec.-Gen. CCP Cen. Advisory Comm. 1988–92; Dir CCP Cen.

Cttee Literature Research Office 2002–; mem. 15th CCP Cen. Cttee 1997–2002, 16th CCP Cen. Cttee 2002–07; fmr chief speech writer for Pres. Jiang Zemin. *Publication:* book on evolution of Mao Zedong thought. *Address:* Policy Research Office of Chinese Communist Party Central Committee, 1 Zhong Nan Hai, Beijing, People's Republic of China (office).

TENNANT, Emma Christina, FRSL; British writer; b. 20 Oct. 1937; d. of 2nd Baron Glenconner and Elizabeth Lady Glenconner; one s. two d.; ed St Paul's Girls' School; fmr freelance journalist; Founder, Ed., Bananas 1975–78; Gen. Ed., In Verse 1982–, Lives of Modern Women 1985–; Hon. DLitt (Aberdeen) 1996. *Television includes:* Frankenstein's Baby, Screen One. *Publications:* The Colour of Rain (as Catherine Aydy) 1963, The Time of the Crack 1973, The Last of the Country House Murders 1975, Hotel de Dream 1976, Bananas Anthology (ed.) 1977, Saturday Night Reader (ed.) 1978, The Bad Sister 1978, Wild Nights 1979, Alice Fell 1980, The Boggart (with M. Rayner) 1981, The Search for Treasure Island 1981, Queen of Stones 1982, Woman Beware Woman 1983, The Ghost Child 1984, Black Marina 1985, The Adventures of Robina by Herself (ed.) 1986, Cycle of the Sun: The House of Hospitalities 1987, A Wedding of Cousins 1988, The Magic Drum 1989, Two Women of London 1989, Faustine 1992, Tess 1993, Pemberley 1993, Emma in Love 1996, An Unequal Marriage 1994, Strangers: A Family Romance 1998, Girlitude 1999, Burnt Diaries 1999, The Ballad of Sylvia and Ted (contrib.) 2001, A House in Corfu 2001, Felony 2002, Corfu Banquet 2003, Heathcliff's Tale 2005, The Harp Lesson 2005, The French Dancer's Bastard 2006, The Autobiography of the Queen (with Hilary Bailey) 2007, Seized 2008, Diana: The Ghost Biography (with Hilary Bailey) 2008, The Beautiful Child 2010. *Leisure interest:* walking in Greece. *Address:* c/o Marsh Agency, 50 Ablemarle Street, London, W1S 4BD, England (office). *Telephone:* (20) 7493-4361 (office). *Fax:* (20) 7495-8961 (office). *Website:* www.marsh-agency.co.uk (office).

TENNEKES, Hendrik, DS (Eng); Dutch meteorologist; b. 13 Dec. 1936, Kampen; s. of the late Cornelis Tennekes and of Harmpje Noordman; m. Olga Vanderpot 1964 (divorced 1998); one s. one d.; ed Delft Tech. Univ.; Asst Prof., Assoc. Prof., Prof. of Aerospace Eng, Pennsylvania State Univ. 1965–77, currently Adjunct Prof.; Dir of Research, Royal Netherlands Meteorological Inst. 1977–90, Dir of Strategic Planning 1990–95; Prof. of Meteorology, Free Univ., Amsterdam 1977–2001; Visiting Prof., Univ. of Washington, Seattle 1976–77; Visiting Sr Scientist, Nat. Center for Atmospheric Research, Boulder, Colo 1987; mem. Royal Netherlands Acad. of Arts and Sciences; mem. Advisory Bd Royal Palace Foundation, Amsterdam 1990–2001. *Publications:* A First Course in Turbulence (with J. L. Lumley) 1972, The Simple Science of Flight 1996; numerous publs on turbulence, predictability, chaos, boundary-layer meteorology and environmental philosophy. *Leisure interests:* poetry, landscape painting. *Address:* Velperweg 30-19, 6824 BJ Arnhem, Netherlands (home). *Telephone:* (30) 379-2247 (home). *E-mail:* henktennekes@kpnplanet.nl (home).

TENORIO, Pedro Pangelinan; American politician (retd); b. 18 April 1934, Saipan, Northern Mariana Islands; s. of the late Blas Pangelinan Tenorio and of Guadalupe Sablan Pangelinan; m. Sophia Pangelinan 1959; four s. four d.; ed George Washington High School, Guam; mem. House of Reps, Congress of Micronesia; Senator Marianas Dist Legislature; Vice-Pres. The Senate, Northern Mariana Commonwealth Legislature 1978–80, Pres. 1980–82; Gov. Commonwealth of the Northern Mariana Islands 1982–91, 1998–2001; Hon. LLD (Univ. of Guam) 1998. *Leisure interest:* golf. *Address:* c/o Office of the Governor, Caller Box 10007, Capitol Hill, Saipan, MP 96950, Commonwealth of the Northern Mariana Islands.

TENZIN, Daw; Bhutanese central banker; *Governor, Central Bank of Bhutan;* b. 1956; ed Australia Nat. Univ.; worked in Ministry of Information and Communications; fmr Sec., Planning Comm.; Man. Dir Royal Monetary Authority (cen. bank of Bhutan) 2003–10, Gov. 2010–, also Chair. Credit Information Bureau of Bhutan. *Address:* Royal Monetary Authority, Post Box No. 154, Thimphu, Bhutan (office). *Telephone:* (2) 323111 (office). (2) 323112 (office). *Fax:* (2) 322847 (office). *Website:* www.rma.org.bt (office).

TEO, Rear-Adm. (retd) Chee Hean, MSc, MPA; Singaporean politician and fmr naval officer; *Deputy Prime Minister, Co-ordinating Minister for National Security and Minister for Home Affairs;* b. 27 Dec. 1954; m. Chew Poh Yim; one s. one d.; ed St Michael's School, St Joseph's Inst., Singapore Armed Forces Training Inst., UMIST, Manchester, Imperial Coll., London, Kennedy School of Govt, Harvard Univ.; various command and staff appointments in Repub. of Singapore Navy and Jt Staff 1977–86, Chief of Navy 1991, rank of Rear-Adm. 1991, retd 1992; Littauer Fellow, Harvard Univ. 1986; MP for Marine Parade Group Representation Constituency 1992–97, for Pasir Ris Group Representation Constituency 1997–, becoming Minister of State in Ministries of Finance, Communications and Defence, Acting Minister for Environment and Sr Minister of State for Defence 1995–96, Minister for Environment and Second Minister for Defence 1996–97, Minister for Educ. and Second Minister for Defence 1997–2001, Minister for Defence 2003–11, Deputy Prime Minister 2009–, also Co-ordinating Minister for Nat. Security, Minister for Home Affairs and Minister in charge of the Civil Service 2011–; Pres.'s Scholarship, Singapore Armed Forces Scholarship 1973. *Address:* Ministry of Home Affairs, New Phoenix Park, 28 Irrawaddy Road, Singapore 329560, Singapore (office). *Telephone:* 64787010 (office). *Fax:* 62546250 (office). *E-mail:* mha_feedback@mha.gov.sg (office). *Website:* www.mha.gov.sg (office).

TEO, Michael Eng Cheng, BBA, MA; Singaporean diplomatist and air force officer (retd); b. 19 Sept. 1947, Sarawak; s. of Teo Thian Lai and Lim Siew Kheng; m. Joyce Teo (née Ng Sinn Toh); one s. one d.; ed Auburn Univ., Fletcher School of Law and Diplomacy, Tufts Univ., USAF War Coll., USA; joined Repub. of Singapore Air Force 1968, Commdr 1985, Brig.-Gen. 1987, Chief of Air Force 1990 (retd); joined Diplomatic Service 1993, High Commr to NZ 1994–96, Amb. to Repub. of Korea 1996–2001, High Commr to UK (also accred as Amb. to Ireland) 2002–11; The Most Noble Order of the Crown (Thailand) 1981, Legion of Merit, Degree of Commdr (USA) 1991, Order of Diplomatic Service Merit Gwanghwa Medal (Repub. of Korea) 2002; Public Admin Medal (Singapore) 1989, Outstanding Achievement Award (Philippines) 1989, Bintang Swa Bhuana Paksa Utama (Indonesia) 1991. *Leisure interests:* golf, hiking, reading. *Address:* c/o Singapore High Commission, 9 Wilton Crescent, Belgravia, London, SW1X 8SP, England.

TEODORO, Gilberto ('Gilbert') Cojuangco, Jr, BSc, LLB, LLM; Philippine lawyer, politician and air force officer; b. 14 June 1964, Manila; s. of Gilberto Teodoro, Sr and Mercedes Cojuangco; m. Monica Prieto-Teodoro; one s.; ed Xavier School, De La Salle Univ., Univ. of the Phillipines (UP), Harvard Law School, USA, Air Command and Staff Coll. of the Philippine Air Force, Jt Command and Staff Coll.; Pres. Kabataang Barangay for Cen. Luzon 1980–85, for Prov. of Tarlac 1980–85; mem. Sanguniang Panlalawigan, Prov. of Tarlac 1980–86; called to the Phillipines Bar 1989; lawyer, EP Mendoza Law firm 1990–97; admitted to State Bar of NY, USA 1997; Congressman of First Dist of Tarlac 1998–, Asst Majority Leader (11th Congress), Head of Nationalist People's Coalition House mems and mem. House contingent to Legis.-Exec. Devt Advisory Council; Sec. of Nat. Defense (youngest Sec. to hold Defense portfolio) 2007–10; licensed commercial pilot; Col, Philippine Air Force, 0-133104 E (Reserve Force); Asst Faculty mem. Command and Gen. Staff Course; Lecturer, Air Command Staff Coll.; Chair. Philippine Nat. Police Foundation Inc.; mem. Integrated Bar of the Philippines, UP Alumni Assn, UP Law Alumni Assn, Harvard Alumni Assn, Harvard Law Alumni Assn; Lifetime mem. Armor-Cavalry Assn of the Philippines; Hon. Command Pilot, Philippine Air Force; Hon. mem. PMA Alumni Assn Sponsoring Class – '76, Philippine Air Force Aviation Cadet Alumni Assn Sponsoring Class – '80, Assn of Chiefs of Police of the Philippines, Inc.; Mil. Merit Medal, Philippine Air Force Gen. Staff Course Badge, Presidential Flight Crew Badge, Mil. Civic Action Medal (Plain), Mil. Civic Action Medal with Bronze Service Star, Mil. Civic Action Medal with Second Service Star; Dean's Medal for Academic Excellence, Univ. of the Phillipines 1989, Leadership and Seminar Academic Excellence Awardee, Air Command and Staff Coll. of the Philippine Air Force 2001, Leadership Award, Jt Command and Staff Coll. 2003; numerous mil. awards and commendations, including Basic RASS Aeronautical Badge, Caliber .45 Pistol Expert Marksmanship Badge, M-16 Rifle Marksmanship Badge. *Address:* c/o Department of National Defense, DND Building, 3rd Floor, Camp Aguinaldo, Quezon City, 1100 Metro Manila, The Philippines.

TEODOROVICI, Eugene Orlando, BA, MA, PhD; Romanian politician; *Minister of EU Funds;* b. 12 Aug. 1971; ed Spiru Haret High School, Bucharest, Faculty of Commerce, Acad. of Econ. Studies, Nat. School of Political and Admin. Studies, Dept for Int. Relations and European Integration; referee, Directorate Gen. of Man., Marketing, Prognosis and Human Resources, Ministry of Transport 1991–97, expert, Gen. Directorate for European Integration 1997–99; expert, Dept for European Integration Feb.–June 1999, Dir June–Dec. 1999; Dir Dept for European Affairs, Ministry of Foreign Affairs Jan.–Dec. 2000; Dir, Co-ordination Directorate of ISPA and SAPARD, Ministry of European Integration 2000–04; Dir Gen. Man. Authority for Cohesion Fund, Ministry of Economy and Finance 2004–05; Dir Gen., Infrastructure Man. Authority, Ministry of Finance 2005–07; Sec. of State, Ministry of Economy and Finance 2007–09; Dir Gen., ISPA Man. Authority, Ministry of Public Finance Jan.–June 2009; Dir, Audit Authority, Court of Accounts of Romania 2009–12; State Advisor, Body of Advisers to Prime Minister May–Dec. 2012; Senator, Romanian Parl. Dec. 2012–; Minister of EU Funds Dec. 2012–; Pres. Inter-Ministerial Cttee on Financing, Guaranteeing and Insuring Local Authorities (within Ministry of Public Finance), Inter-Ministerial Cttee on Financing, Guaranteeing and Insuring the Pvt. Sector (within EXIM Bank); Romanian Rep. on Bd of Dirs of EIB; Nat. Coordinator of HIPERB Programme; Rep. of Ministry of Public Finance in Export Council; expert co-ordinator in project of institutional twinning between Romania and Moldova ('Harmonization of Public Procurement Legislation in the Republic of Moldova'); mem. Bd CEC Bank SA. *Address:* Ministry of EU Funds, Bucharest, Tower Center, Blvd Ion Mihalache 15–17, Sector 1, Romania (office). *Telephone:* (372) 838500 (office). *Fax:* (372) 838501 (office). *E-mail:* contact.minister@fonduri-ue.ro (office). *Website:* www.fonduri-ue.ro (office).

TEPPERMAN, Jonathan D., BA, MA,0 LLM; Canadian journalist and editor; *Managing Editor, Foreign Affairs;* b. 10 Aug. 1971, Windsor, Ont.; s. of Bill Tepperman and Rochelle Tepperman; ed Yale Univ., Univ. of Oxford, UK, New York Univ. School of Law; fmr speechwriter for US Amb. to UN 1994–95; journalist writing for Forward 1996, Jerusalem Post 1997; Assoc. Ed. and Production Man. Foreign Affairs (journal of Council on Foreign Relations) 1998–2001, Sr Ed. 2001–04, Deputy Man. Ed. 2004–07, Man. Ed. 2011–; Deputy Ed. Newsweek International, New York 2007–09; Man. Ed. and Dir EurasiaGroup 2010. *Publications include:* numerous contributions to publications including New York Times, Newsweek, LA Times, Christian Science Monitor, Wall Street Journal, New Republic. *Address:* Foreign Affairs, Editorial Department, 58 East 68th Street, New York, NY 10065, USA (office). *Telephone:* (212) 434-9696 (office). *E-mail:* jtepperman@cfr.org (office); jt@jonathantepperman.com. *Website:* www .foreignaffairs.com (office); jonathantepperman.com (office).

TER-MINASSIAN, Teresa, MS (Econs); Italian economist and international organization official; *Director, Fiscal Affairs Department, International Monetary Fund;* ed Univ. of Rome, Harvard Univ., USA; began career in Research Dept, Cen. Bank of Italy 1967–78; seconded to IMF as economist in Fiscal Affairs Dept 1971, Deputy Dir 1988–97, Dir 2001–, also fmr Chief, Southern European Div., European Dept and Deputy Dir Western Hemisphere Dept 1997–2001. *Publication:* Fiscal Federalism in Theory and Practice 1997. *Address:* International Monetary Fund, 700 19th Street, NW, Washington, DC 20431, USA (office). *Telephone:* (202) 623-8844 (office). *Fax:* (202) 623-4259 (office). *E-mail:* tterminassian@imf.org (office). *Website:* www.imf.org (office).

TER-PETROSSIAN, Levon, DLit; Armenian politician and philologist; b. 9 Jan. 1945, Aleppo, Syria; m. Lyudmila Pletnitskaya; one s.; ed Yerevan State Univ., Leningrad Inst. of Orientology; family moved to Armenia in 1946; jr researcher, Armenian Inst. of Literature 1972–78, sr researcher, then Scientific Sec. Matenadaran Archive 1978–90; took part in dissident movt, arrested 1966, 1988–89; mem. Chair. Karabakh Cttee in Matenadaran 1988; Deputy, Supreme Soviet of Armenian SSR 1989, Chair. 1990–91; mem. Bd, Pan-Armenian Nat. Movt 1989–2013 (fmr Chair.), party spearheaded formation of Armenian Nat. Congress (ANC), coalition of 18 opposition parties in opposition to ruling govt coalition; Pres. of Armenia 1991–98; took leading role in protests as part of a wave of regional unrest 2011; led ANC during the parl. election 2012, alliance transformed into a single political party 2013. *Publications:* six books and more than 70 papers on the history of Armenia. *Leisure interests:* reading, chess. *Address:* 0009 Yerevan,

Koyun Street 19A; 0010 Yerevan, Tsitsernakaberd Highway, Armenia (home). *Telephone:* (10) 52-09-74; (10) 52-09-57. *E-mail:* aladtp@arminco.com (office). *Website:* www.levonpresident.am.

TERASAWA, Yoshio, BA (Econs); Japanese banker and business executive; b. 3 Oct. 1931, Tokyo; s. of Tsunesaburo Terasawa and Kura Terasawa; m. 1960; one s. three d.; ed Waseda Univ., Wharton Business School, Univ. of Pennsylvania, USA; Pres. Nomura Securities Int. 1970–80, Chair. 1980–85, Exec. Vice-Pres. Nomura Securities, Tokyo 1985–88; Dir-Gen. Econ. Planning Agency May–June 1994; Chair. Foreign Policy Cttee 1996–97; Sr Adviser Price Waterhouse 1998–99; Chair. Lone Star Japan Acquisitions 1999–2001; Chair. Tokyo Star Bank, 2001–08 (retd); Exec. Vice-Pres. Multilateral Investment Guarantee Agency 1988; Dir English-Speaking Union of Japan; fmr Fulbright Scholar; Hon. Citizen New York City 1972. *Publications:* Night and Day on Wall Street, Windblown on Wall Street, Think Big!!, From the Window of Washington, DC. *Address:* c/o Tokyo Star Bank, 6-16, Akasaka 1-chome, Minato-ku, Tokyo, Japan.

TERBIL, Fathi; Libyan lawyer and human rights activist; *Minister of Youth and Sports;* b. 1972; ed Garyounis Univ., Benghazi; human rights lawyer; represents relatives of over 1,000 prisoners allegedly killed by Libyan security forces in Abu Salim Prison in 1996; arrested in Benghazi, Feb. 2011, which sparked initial protests against Ghaddafi regime; mem. Nat. Transitional Council 2011; Minister of Youth and Sports 2011–; Ludovic-Trarieux Int. Human Rights Prize 2011. *Address:* Ministry of Youth and Sports, Tripoli, Libya (office).

TERENGGANU, HM The Sultan of; Tuanku Mizan Zainal Abidin; Malaysian fmr head of state; *Sultan of Terengganu;* b. 22 Jan. 1962, Kuala Terengganu; s. of the late Sultan Mahmud Al Muktafi Billah Shah and Bariah binti Hishamuddin Alam Shah; m. Permaisuri Nur Zahirah Cik Puan Seri Rozita Adil Bakeri 1996; two s. two d.; apptd Heir Apparent Yang di-Pertuan Muda of Terengganu 1979; 16th Sultan of Terengganu 1998–; Timbalan Yang di-Pertuan Agong (Deputy Supreme Head of State) 1999–2006; 13th Yang di-Pertuan Agong (Supreme Head of State) 2006–11; Col-in-Chief Royal Armoured Corps; Chancellor Universiti Malaysia Terengganu 2001–06. *Address:* Istana Badariah, 20500 Kuala Terengganu, Malaysia (office).

TERENIUS, Lars Yngve, PhD; Swedish medical research scientist and academic; *Professor Emeritus of Experimental Alcohol and Drug Dependence Research, Karolinska Institute;* b. 9 July 1940, Örebro; s. of Yngve Terenius and Margareta Hallenborg; m. 1st Malin Åkerblom 1962 (divorced 1986); m. 2nd Mona Hagman 1989; two s.; ed Faculties of Science and Medicine, Uppsala Univ.; Asst Prof. of Pharmacology, Medical Faculty, Uppsala Univ. 1969–79, Prof. of Pharmacology, Faculty of Pharmacy 1979–89; Prof. of Experimental Alcohol and Drug Dependence Research, Karolinska Inst. 1989–2008, Prof. Emer. 2008–; Visiting Scientist Nat. Inst. for Medical Research, London 1972–73, Univ. of Aberdeen, Scotland 1975, Hebrew Univ., Jerusalem 1983, 1986; Fogarty Scholar, NIH, USA 1988–89; mem. Royal Swedish Soc. of Sciences, Royal Swedish Acad. of Sciences, Academia Europaea, American Acad. of Arts and Sciences, IPSEN Award 2000; Dr hc (Uppsala) 1981, (Trondheim) 1983; Olof Rudbeck Prize 1999; Pacesetter Award 1977, Gairdner Award 1978, Jahre Award 1980, Björkén Award of Uppsala Univ. 1984, IPSEN Award 2000. *Publications:* 400 papers on experimental endocrinology, cancer research, neurobiology. *Address:* Department of Clinical Neuroscience, Karolinska Institute, universitetssjukhuset, 171 76, Stockholm (office); Kyrkogårdsgatan 29, 753 12 Uppsala, Sweden (home). *Telephone:* (8) 5177-48-60 (office). *Fax:* (8) 34-19-39 (office). *E-mail:* Lars .Terenius@ki.se (office). *Website:* www.ki.se (office).

TERESHCHENKO, Sergei, BSc; Kazakhstani politician; b. 30 March 1951, Lesozavodsk, Primorskiy Region; s. of Aleksandr Ivanovich Tereshchenko and Tamara Ivanovna Tereshchenko; m. Yevgenya Tsykunova; two d.; ed Alma-Ata Inst. of Agric., Moscow Univ. of Commerce; held offices in state power organs of Chimkent Region 1986–89, Chair. of the Exec. Cttee of Chimkent Region 1990–91; First Deputy-Chair. Council of Ministers of Kazakh Soviet Repub. 1989–90; Vice-Pres. of Kazakhstan April–May 1991; Prime Minister of Kazakhstan 1991–94; Minister of Foreign Affairs 1994–95; Chair. Bd of Dirs Integrazia Fund 1994–; Vice-Chair. Republican (Otan) Party 1999–2002, Deputy Chair. Ass. of the Peoples of Kazakhstan Oct. 2002–; Order of Dostyk (First Class) 1999; State Prize for Peace and Spiritual Content 1999. *Publications include:* Kazakh Land is My Cradle 1999, Kazakhstan, Reforms, Market 2000. *Leisure interests:* hunting, swimming, fashion, travelling. *Address:* 92 Maoulenov str., 480012 Almaty (office); 121-18 Kounaev str., 480100 Almaty, Kazakhstan (home). *Telephone:* (727) 262-40-57 (office); (727) 263-36-18 (home). *Fax:* (727) 262-14-96 (office). *E-mail:* tyelena@ nursat.kz (home).

TERESHKOVA, Maj.-Gen. Valentina Vladimirovna, CandTechSc; Russian politician and fmr cosmonaut; b. 6 March 1937, Maslennikovo, Yaroslavl Region; d. of the late Vladimir Aksyonovich Tereshkov and Elena Fyodorovna Tereshkova; m. 1963 (divorced); one d.; ed Yaroslavl Textile Coll. and Zhukovsky Air Force Engineering Acad.; fmr textile worker, Krasny Perekop textile mill, Yaroslavl; Textile Mill Sec., Young Communist League 1960; joined Yaroslavl Air Sports Club 1959 and started parachute jumping; mem. CPSU 1962–91, Cen. Cttee CPSU 1971–90; began cosmonaut training March 1962; made 48 orbits of the Earth in spaceship Vostok VI 16–19 June 1963; first woman in world to enter space; Deputy to USSR Supreme Soviet 1966–90; USSR People's Deputy 1989–91; Chair. Soviet Women's Cttee 1968–87; mem. Supreme Soviet Presidium 1970–90; Head Union of Soviet Socs. for Friendship and Cultural Relations with Foreign Countries 1987–92; Chair. then Dir of Presidium, Russian Asscn of Int. Co-operation (now Russian Centre of Int. Scientific and Cultural Co-operation) 1992–; Pres. Moscow House of Europe 1992–; Head Russian Centre for Int. Scientific and Cultural Co-operation 1994–2004; Pilot-Cosmonaut of USSR, Hero of Soviet Union, Joliot-Curie Gold Medal, World Peace Council 1966, Order of the Nile (Egypt) 1971 and numerous other int. decorations. *Address:* c/o Russian Centre of International Co-operation, 103885 Moscow, Vozdvizhenka Str. 14–18, Russia.

TERFEL, Bryn, CBE; British singer (bass-baritone); b. (Bryn Terfel Jones), 9 Nov. 1965, Pantglas, Snowdonia, Wales; s. of Hefin Jones and Nesta Jones; m. Lesley Halliday 1987; three s.; ed Ysgol Dyffryn Nantlle, Penygroes, Gwynedd and Guildhall School of Music and Drama; debut, WNO as Guglielmo 1990; sang Mozart's Figaro at Santa Fe Opera and ENO 1991; Royal Nat. Opera, Covent

Garden debut as Masetto in Don Giovanni 1992, repeated on tour to Japan; sang at Salzburg Festival as the Spirit Messenger in Die Frau ohne Schatten, and as Jochanaan in Salome 1992; Leporello in Don Giovanni 1994; further appearances at Vienna Staatsoper as Mozart's Figaro 1993, at Chicago as Donner in Das Rheingold, debuts at New York Metropolitan Opera 1994, Sydney Opera House 1999; frequent guest soloist with Berlin Philharmonic Orchestra; sang in the Brahms Requiem under Colin Davis and at Salzburg Easter Festival under Abbado (Herbert von Karajan In Memoriam) 1993; sang Nick Shadow in The Rake's Progress for WNO 1996, Figaro at La Scala 1997, Scarpia for Netherlands Opera 1998, Falstaff at the reopening of the Royal Opera House, Covent Garden 1999; four male roles in Les Contes d'Hoffmann and Don Giovanni, both at Metropolitan Opera, New York, and Nick Shadow in The Rake's Progress for San Francisco Opera 1999–2000; baritone roles in Les Contes d'Hoffmann at the Opéra Bastille, Sweeney Todd in Chicago, and Falstaff and Don Giovanni at Covent Garden 2002–03; Mephistopheles in Faust, Wotan in Das Rheingold and Die Walküre at Covent Garden 2004; Scarpia and the Flying Dutchman for the Royal Opera House 2009; Die Meistersinger von Nürnberg, Welsh Nat. Opera 2010; Wotan in Das Rheingold, Metropolitan Opera, New York 2010, Die Walküre 2010; many concert appearances in Europe, USA, Canada, Japan and Australia; Pres. Nat. Youth Choir of Wales, Festival of Wales; Vice-Pres. Llangollen Int. Eisteddfod; Founder, Faenol Festival 2000–; Hon. Fellow, Univ. of Wales, Aberystwyth, Welsh Coll. of Music and Drama, Univ. of Wales, Bangor; Hon. DMus (Glamorgan) 1997; White Robe, Gorsedd; recipient Kathleen Ferrier Scholarship 1988, Gold Medal Award 1989, Lieder Prize Cardiff Singer of the World Competition 1989, Gramophone magazine Young Singer of the Year 1992, British Critics Circle Award 1992, Int. Classical Music Awards Newcomer of Year 1993, Classical BRIT Award for Male Artist of the Year 2004, 2005, Nordoff-Robbins Silver Clef Classical Award 2006, Queen's Medal for Music 2006. *Recordings include:* Salome, Le nozze di Figaro, An Die Musik, Wagner Arias, Britten's Gloriana, Beethoven's Ninth Symphony, Brahms' Requiem, Schwanengesang, Cecilia and Bryn, If Ever I Would Leave You, Handel Arias, Vagabond (Caecilia Prize 1995, Gramophone People's Award 1996) 1995, Opera Arias (Grammy Award for best classical vocal performance) 1996, Something Wonderful (Britannia Record Club Members' Award) 1997, Don Giovanni 1997, Bryn (Classical BRIT Award for Best Album 2004) 2003, Simple Gifts (Grammy Award for Best Classical Crossover Album 2007) 2005, Tutto Mozart! 2006, First Love: Songs from the British Isles 2008, Elgar's The Dream of Gerontius (Gramophone Award for Best Choral Recording) 2009, Bad Boys 2009, At His Very Best 2010, Carols & Christmas Songs 2010. *Leisure interests:* golf, collecting fob watches, supporting Manchester United. *Address:* c/o Harlequin Agency, 203 Fidlas Road, Cardiff, CF14 5NA, Wales. *Telephone:* (29) 2075-0821 (office). *Fax:* (29) 2075-5971 (office). *E-mail:* doreen@harlequin-agency.co.uk (office). *Website:* www .harlequin-agency.co.uk (office).

TERIUM, Peter; Dutch business executive; *CEO, RWE AG;* b. 26 Sept. 1963, Nederweert; ed Nederlands Instituut voor Registeraccountants, Amsterdam; trainee tax auditor, Tax Dept, Ministry of Finance, ind. tax auditor working for Ministry of Finance 1984–85; Audit Supervisor, KPMG, Eindhoven 1985–90; various positions at Schmalbach-Lubeca AG 1990–2002; plant controller at PET Containers Germany, Head of Controlling for White Cap Germany and Product Group Controller for White Cap Europe, Vice-Pres., Finance and Accounting, White Cap Europe and Asia, Vice-Pres., Finance and Accounting, PET Containers Europe and Asia Head of Group Controlling, RWE AG, Essen 2003–05, mem. Exec. Bd RWE Umwelt AG, Viersen 2004–05, CEO RWE Trading GmbH, Essen 2005–08, Chief Financial Officer and in dual role mem. Group Business Cttee up to its termination –2007, RWE Supply & Trading GmbH (RWEST), Essen 2008–09, Programme Man., Essen April–Oct. 2009, CEO Essent NV 2009–11, mem. Exec. Bd and CEO Bd of RWE AG, Essen 2011–12, CEO RWE AG 2012–. *Address:* RWE AG, Opernplatz 1, 45128 Essen, Germany (office). *Telephone:* (201) 1215025 (office). *Fax:* (201) 1215265 (office). *E-mail:* info@rwe.com (office). *Website:* www .rwe.com (office).

TEROKHIN, Serhiy Anatolijovych; Ukrainian politician; *Deputy Head of Committee on Public Finances, Verkhovna Rada (Parliament);* b. 29 Sept. 1963, Kyiv; m. Svitlana Terokhina; one s. one d.; ed Nat. Taras Shevchenko Univ. of Kyiv; joined Army 1986–88; Asst Chair., Head of Marketing, Ukrainian Republican Bank, Bank for Foreign Trade of USSR 1988–91; Head of Monetary and Financial Dept, Minister of Foreign Econ. Relations 1991–92; Chief, Dept of Monetary and Financial Policy, Econ. Bd, State Duma of Ukraine June–Nov. 1992; Deputy Minister of the Economy and Head of Dept of Financial and External Econ. Activity 1992–93; Dir Ukrainian Fund on Support of Reforms 1993–94; mem. Parl. (Fatherland—Batkivshchyna) 1994–, Head of Tax and Customs Cttee 2007–10, Deputy Head of Cttee on Public Finances 2010–; Scientific Researcher, Harvard Univ. 1995; Minister of the Economy 2005; Co-Chair. Open Society Inst. 1997–; Head of Asscn of Tax Payers of Ukraine 1999. *Address:* Verkhovna Rada, 01008 Kyiv, vul. M. Hrushevskoho 5, Ukraine (office). *Telephone:* (44) 255-28-07 (office). *Fax:* (44) 255-25-91 (office). *E-mail:* Teriokhin.Serhii@rada.gov.ua (office). *Website:* www.rada.gov.ua (office).

TERRAGNO, Rodolfo H., DJur; Argentine lawyer, politician and writer; b. 16 Nov. 1943, Buenos Aires; m. Sonía Pascual Sánchez; two s.; ed Univ. de Buenos Aires; Ed.-in-Chief Confirmado magazine, Buenos Aires 1967–68; Pres. Terragno SA de Industrias Químicas 1970–76; Ed. Magazine Survey, Buenos Aires 1973–76; Asst Prof., Univ. de Buenos Aires 1973–80; Exec. Vice-Pres. El Diario de Caracas SA 1976–80; researcher, Inst. of Latin American Studies, London 1980–82, LSE 1980–82; Vice-Pres. ALA Enterprises Inc., Miami and New York, USA 1982–86; Minister of Works and Public Services 1987–89; mem. Parl. 1993–95, 1997–99, Vice-Pres. Budget and Finance Cttee 1997–99, mem. Group of Five who led alliance govt 1997–99; Pres. UCR 1995–97; Chief of Cabinet of Ministers of the Nat. Exec. 1999–2000; Nat. Senator for City of Buenos Aires 2001–07; Dir Letters SAH, Luxembourg 1982–86, Latin American Newsletters Ltd, London and Paris 1982–86; rep. at int. conferences, including dispute with UK over Falkland Islands 1983–85; Pres. Fundación Argentina Siglo 21 1986–87; Ordre National du Mérite 1987, Cavaliere di Gran Croce (Italy) 1987, Medalha Mérito Maua (Brazil). *Publications:* Los dueños del poder 1972, Los 400 días de Perón 1974, Contratapas 1976, Muerte y resurreción de los políticos 1981, La Argentina del Siglo 21 1985, The Challenge of Real Development 1987, Proyecto 95 1993, El Nuevo Modelo

1994, Bases para un Modelo de Crecimiento, Empleo y Bienestar (ed.) 1996, Maitland & San Martín 1998, Falklands/Malvinas 2002, El peronismo de los 70 2005, La Simulación 2005, Historia y futuro de las Malvinas 2006, Diario íntimo de San Martín 2009. *E-mail:* rodolfo@terragno.org.ar. *Website:* www.terragno.org.ar.

TERRAZAS SANDOVAL, HE Cardinal Julio, C.Ss.R.; Bolivian ecclesiastic; *Archbishop of Santa Cruz de la Sierra;* b. 7 March 1936, Vallegrande; ed Emacas Univ.; ordained priest of the Congregation of the Most Holy Redeemer 1962; Auxiliary Bishop of La Paz 1978–82; Bishop of Oruro 1982–91; Archbishop of Santa Cruz de la Sierra 1991–; cr. Cardinal (Cardinal-Priest of San Giovanni Battista de' Rossi) 2001; participated in Papal Conclave 2005, 2013; elected Pres. Bolivian Episcopal Conf. 1985, re-elected 1988, 2001; named one of the 100 most important people in the world by El Pais newspaper 2008. *Address:* Arzobispado, Casilla 25, Calle Ingavi 49, Santa Cruz, Bolivia (office). *Telephone:* (3) 32-4286 (office). *Fax:* (3) 33-0181 (office). *E-mail:* asc@scbbs-bo.com (office).

TERRY, (John) Quinlan, FRIBA; British architect; b. 24 July 1937, London; s. of the late Philip Terry and Phyllis Terry; m. Christina de Ruttié 1961; one s. four d.; ed Bryanston School, Architectural Asscn; joined late Raymond Erith RA 1962–73; work includes Kingswalden Bury, the New Common Room Bldg at Gray's Inn, the restoration of St Mary's Church on Paddington Green; Partner, Erith and Terry 1967–, in pvt. practice (latterly under name Quinlan and Francis Terry) 1973–, work includes large classical pvt. houses in stone erected in England, USA and Germany including six pvt. villas in Regent's Park for Crown Estate Commrs, offices, shops and flats at Richmond Riverside, new Lecture Theatre, Jr Common Room, Library and residential bldgs for Downing Coll. Cambridge, Brentwood Cathedral, restoration of the three State Rooms at No. 10 Downing Street, restoration of St Helen's Church, Bishopsgate, new commercial bldg 20–32 Baker Street, new retail bldg at Merchant Square, Colonial Williamsburg, Va; mem. Royal Fine Art Comm. 1994–97; Rome Scholar 1969, Prix Int. de la Reconstruction 1983, Building of the Year Award 1994, Georgian Groups' Award for Best Modern Classical House 2005, Richard H. Driehaus Prize 2005. *Publications include:* Architectural Monographs 1991, Architects Anonymous 1993, Radical Classicism 2006. *Leisure interest:* theology. *Address:* Quinlan and Francis Terry LLP, Old Exchange, High Street, Dedham, Colchester, Essex, CO7 6HA, England (office). *Telephone:* (1206) 323186 (office); (1206) 322370 (office). *Fax:* (1206) 323759 (office). *E-mail:* quinlan@qftarchitects.com (office). *Website:* www.qftarchitects.com (office).

TERZIĆ, Adnan, BA; Bosnia and Herzegovina politician; b. 1960, Zagreb; ed Univ. of Sarajevo; mem. Party of Democratic Action 1991–, Vice-Chair. 2001; served in army 1992–95; Gov. Cen. Bosnia canton 1997–98, 2000–01; Prime Minister 2002–2007, Head of SDA Club of Reps, House of Reps 2000–02, concurrently Minister of European Integration. *Address:* Party of Democratic Action, Mehmeda Spahe 14, 71000 Sarajevo, Bosnia and Herzegovina (office). *Telephone:* (33) 472192 (office). *Fax:* (33) 650429 (office). *Website:* www.sda.ba (office).

TESAURO, Giuseppe; Italian professor of international law and judge; *Judge, Constitutional Court;* b. 15 Nov. 1942, Naples; m. Paola Borrelli 1967; three c.; ed Liceo Umberto, Naples, Univ. of Naples, Max Planck Inst. Volkerrecht-Heidelberg; Asst Prof. of Int. Law, Univ. of Naples 1965–71; Prof. of Int. Law and Int. Org., Univs of Catania, Messina, Naples, Rome 1971–88; Dir EEC Law School, Univ. of Rome 1982–88; mem. Council Legal Affairs, Ministry of Foreign Affairs 1986–; Judge, First Advocate Gen. European Court of Justice 1988–98; Pres. Italian Competition Authority 1998–2004; Judge, Constitutional Court 2005–. *Publications:* Financing International Institutions 1968, Pollution of the Sea and International Law 1971, Nationalizations and International Law 1976, Movements of Capital in the EEC 1984, Course of EEC Law 2012. *Leisure interests:* tennis, football, sailing. *Address:* Constitutional Court, Piazza del Quirinale 41, 00187 Rome, Italy (office). *Telephone:* (06) 46981 (office). *Fax:* (06) 4698916 (office). *E-mail:* ccost@cortecostituzionale.it (office). *Website:* www.cortecostituzionale.it (office).

TESFAMARIAM, Yohannes Gebremeskel; Ethiopian UN official; *Head of Mission and Force Commander, United Nations Interim Security Force for Abyei (UNISFA);* b. 1960, Tigray; m.; three c.; ed Addis Ababa Univ.; served as Head of Peacekeeping Dept, Head of Mil. Intelligence Dept, Ministry of Nat. Defence, Commdr, Army Corps; fmr Commr, UN Mission in Ethiopia and Eritrea (UNMEE); Deputy Force Commdr, UN Interim Security Force for Abyei (UNISFA) 2012–13, Head of Mission and Force Commdr 2013–. *Address:* United Nations Interim Security Force for Abyei (UNISFA), Department of Peacekeeping Operations, United Nations, New York, NY 10017, USA (office). *Telephone:* (212) 963-1234 (office). *Fax:* (212) 963-4879 (office). *Website:* www.un.org/en/peacekeeping/missions/unisfa (office).

TESFAY, Lt-Gen. Tadesse Werede, MBA; Ethiopian army officer and UN official; b. 13 July 1958; m.; four c.; joined Nat. Defence Forces, held several posts including Head of Jt Training Dept, Commdr Army Corps, mem. Defence Commdrs Council; Head of Mission and Force Commdr, UN Interim Security Force for Abyei (UNISFA) 2011–13. *Address:* c/o United Nations Interim Security Force for Abyei (UNISFA), Department of Peace-keeping Operations, Room S-3727-B, United Nations, New York, NY 10017, USA.

TESHABAEV, Muxammadyusuf M.; Uzbekistani politician; *Chairman, Movement of Entrepreneurs and Businessmen—Liberal Democratic Party of Uzbekistan;* b. 27 Nov. 1954, Andijon; m.; three c.; ed Tashkent Nat. Econ. Inst.; Deputy Head of Trade for the Andijan region and Chair. JSC Andizhongazmol 1989–96; Head of Directorate of Strategic Planning and Internal Trade, UzDaewooAuto 1996–2002; with Noldkomeksrim Co. Ltd (food import-export co.) 2003–05; Deputy Council of People's Deputies for Andijan region 1990–94; mem. Movt of Entrepreneurs and Businessmen—Liberal Democratic Party of Uzbekistan (Tadbirkorlar va Ishbilarmonlar Harakati—O'zbekiston Liberal Demokratik Partiyasi) (O'zlidep), Vice-Chair. Exec. Cttee 2003–05, Chair. Exec. Cttee 2005–; mem. Legis. Chamber (Qonunchilik palatasi) Oliy Majlis 2005–, Chair. Cttee on Agric. and Water Man. *Address:* Movement of Entrepreneurs and Businessmen—Liberal Democratic Party of Uzbekistan (O'zlidep), 100015 Tashkent, Mirobod tumani, Nukus ko'ch. 73A, Uzbekistan (office). *Telephone:* (71) 255-27-99 (office). *Fax:* (71) 255-62-11 (office). *E-mail:* uzlidep@intal.uz (office). *Website:* www.uzlidep.uz (office).

TESHOME WIRTU, Mulato; Ethiopian politician, diplomatist and head of state; *President;* b. 1956, Arjo, Welega Prov. (now Oromo Region); one s.; ed Peking Univ., People's Repub. of China; Deputy Minister of Econ. Devt and Cooperation during mid-1990s, Minister of Agric. 2001–03; Speaker, House of Fed. (upper house of parl.) 2002–05; fmr Amb. to People's Repub. of China and Japan, Amb. to Turkey 2006–13; Pres. of Ethiopia 2013–. *Address:* Office of the President, POB 1031, Addis Ababa, Ethiopia (office). *Telephone:* (11) 1551000 (office). *Fax:* (11) 1552030 (office).

TESSON, Philippe, DèsSc; French journalist and publishing executive; b. 1 March 1928, Wassigny (Aisne); s. of Albert Tesson and Jeanne Ancely; m. Dr Marie-Claude Millet 1969; one s. two d.; ed Coll. Stanislas, Inst. of Political Studies, Paris; Sec. of Parl. Debates 1957–60; Ed.-in-Chief, Combat 1960–74; candidate in legis. elections 1968; Diarist and Drama Critic, Canard Enchaîné 1970–83; Co-Man. and Dir Soc. d'Editions Scientifiques et Culturelles 1971, Pres. 1980; Founder, Man. Dir and Ed.-in-Chief, Quotidien de Paris 1974–94; Dir Nouvelles Littéraires 1975–83; Drama Critic, L'Express Paris 1986; Dir and Co.-Man. Quotidien du Maire 1988; Animator (TV programme with France 3) A Quel Titre 1994–96; Ed. Valeurs actuelles 1994–; Drama Critic, Revue des deux Mondes 1990–, Figaro Magazine 1995–; literary and theatre Corresp. Rive Droite/Rive Gauche (TV) 1997–2004; Dir Avant-scène Théâtre 2001–; Chevalier, Légion d'honneur 1987, Officier, Légion d'honneur 2009. *Publication:* De Gaulle 1er 1965, Où est passée l'autorité? 2000. *Address:* L'Avant-scène Théâtre, 75 rue des Saints-Pères, 75006 Paris, France (office). *Telephone:* 1-53-63-80-60 (office). *Fax:* 1-53-63-88-75 (office). *E-mail:* contact@avant-scene-theatre.com (office). *Website:* www.avant-scene-theatre.com (office).

TESTER, Jonathan (Jon), BS; American organic farmer and politician; *Senator from Montana;* b. 21 Aug. 1956, Havre, Mont.; m. Sharla Tester; one s. one d.; ed Coll. of Great Falls; worked as custom butcher operator; fmr music teacher, Big Sandy School Dist; now grows organic wheat, barley, lentils, peas, millet, buckwheat and alfalfa (lucerne); fmr Chair. Sandy School Bd of Trustees; served on Big Sandy Soil Conservation Service Cttee, Chouteau Co. Agricultural Stabilization and Conservation Service Cttee; elected to Mont. State Senate 1998, Minority Whip 2001, Minority Leader 2003, Pres. Mont. Senate 2005–06; Senator from Montana 2007–, mem. Banking, Housing and Urban Affairs Cttee, Energy and Natural Resources Cttee, Homeland Security and Govt Affairs Cttee, Veterans' Affairs Cttee, Small Business and Entrepreneurship Cttee, Indian Affairs Cttee; Democrat. *Address:* 724 Hart Senate Office Building, Washington, DC 20510-2604, USA (office). *Telephone:* (202) 224-2644 (office). *Fax:* (202) 224-8594 (office). *Website:* tester.senate.gov (office).

TESTINO, Mario; Peruvian fashion photographer; b. 1954, Lima; portfolio includes Madonna for Versace, Princess of Wales for Vanity Fair 1997, advertising campaign for Gucci, Sir Hardy Amies, John Galliano, Jade Jagger, Naomi Campbell, Devon Aoki and Alexander McQueen for Vogue's Millennium souvenir issue 2000; work exhibited in Nat. Portrait Gallery, London 2001–02. *Publications include:* Visionaire 35: Man 2000, Mario Testino: Portraits 2003, Mario Testino: Kids 2003, Let Me In 2007. *Address:* c/o Art Partner New York, 155 Sixth Avenue, 15th Floor, New York, NY 10013, USA (office). *Telephone:* (212) 343-9889 (office). *Fax:* (212) 343-9891. *E-mail:* info@mariotestino.com. *Website:* www.mariotestino.com.

TETANGCO, Amando M., Jr, AB (Econ), MA; Philippine central banker; *Governor, Bangko Sentral ng Pilipinas (Central Bank of the Philippines);* b. 14 Nov. 1952; m. Elvira Ma. Plana; one s. two d.; ed Ateneo de Manila Univ., Univ. of Wisconsin-Madison, USA (Central Bank scholar); worked with Man. Services Div. of SGV & Co. 1973–74; joined Bangko Sentral ng Pilipinas (BSP—Cen. Bank of the Philippines) 1974, Deputy Gov. BSP in-charge of Banking Services Sector, Econ. Research and Treasury –2005, represented BSP at Nat. Econ. and Devt Authority Bd, Nat. Food Authority Council, Industrial Guarantee and Loan Fund Review Cttee, also served as Alt. Exec. Dir IMF, Washington, DC 1992–94, closely involved with various int. and regional orgs including Exec. Meeting of East Asia and Pacific Cen. Banks, ASEAN and ASEAN +3, South East Asia Cen. Banks (SEACEN) and APEC, Gov. BSP 2005–. *Address:* Bangko Sentral ng Pilipinas, A. Mabini Street, cnr Pablo Ocampo Street, Malate, 1004 Metro Manila, Philippines (office). *Telephone:* (2) 7087011 (office). *Fax:* (2) 7087208 (office); (2) 7087416 (office). *E-mail:* bspmail@bsp.gov.ph (office). *Website:* www.bsp.gov.ph (office).

TETT, Gillian, PhD; British journalist and author; *Assistant Editor, Financial Times;* b. 1967; ed Clare Coll., Cambridge; joined Financial Times 1993, worked in fmr USSR and Europe and in Econs Dept, Bureau Chief, Tokyo 1997–2003, Deputy Head of Lex column 2003, fmr Asst Ed. and US Managing Ed., currently markets and finance commentator and an Asst Ed.; Wincott Prize 2007, British Business Journalist of the Year 2008, British Press Awards Journalist of the Year 2009, British Acad. President's Medal 2011. *Publications:* Saving the Sun: How Wall Street mavericks shook up Japan's financial system and made billions 2004, Fool's Gold: How Unrestrained Greed Corrupted a Dream, Shattered Global Markets and Unleashed a Catastrophe (Spear's Book Awards Financial Book of the Year 2009) 2009. *Address:* The Financial Times Newspaper Group, 1330 Avenue of the Americas, New York, NY 10019-5436, USA (office). *E-mail:* gillian.tett@ft.com (office). *Website:* www.ft.com/comment/columnists/gillian-tett (office).

TETTAMANZI, HE Cardinal Dionigi; Italian fmr ecclesiastic; *Apostolic Administrator of Vigevano;* b. 14 March 1934, Renate; ordained priest 1957; consecrated Bishop 1989; Metropolitan Archbishop of Ancona-Osma 1989–1991; Pres. Episcopal Conf., Marche region 1989; Pres. Bishops' Comm., CEI 1990, Sec.-Gen. CEI 1991, Vice-Pres. 1995–2000; Metropolitan Archbishop of Genoa 1995–2002; cr. Cardinal (Cardinal-Priest of Santi Ambrogio e Carlo) 1998; Archbishop of Milan 2002–11, Archbishop Emer. 2011–; participated in Papal Conclave 2005, 2013; Apostolic Admin. of Vigevano, Italy 2012–. *Address:* c/o Archdiocese of Milan, Palazzo Arcivescovile, Piazza Fontana 2, 20122 Milan, Italy.

TEUFEL, Erwin; German politician; b. 4 Sept. 1939, Rottweil; m.; four c.; Dist Admin. Rottweil and Trossingen municipality 1961–64; Mayor of Spaichingen 1964–72; mem. State Parl. of Baden-Württemberg 1972–; Leader CDU Parl. Group 1978–91; Minister-Pres. of Baden-Württemberg 1991–2005; Chair. CDU-Baden-Württemberg 1991–2005; mem. Fed. Cttee of CDU. *Address:* Dreifaltigkeitsberg-strasse 44, 78549 Spaichingen, Germany (home).

TEVES, Margarito B., BA, MSc; Philippine government official and economist; ed Universidad Cen. de Madrid, Spain, Williams Coll., USA; mem. Congress 1987–98, Chair. Cttee on Rural Devt, on Econ. Affairs; Chair. and CEO Think Tank Inc. 1998–2000; Pres. and CEO Land Bank of the Philippines 2000–05; Sec. of Finance 2005–10; Chair. People's Credit and Finance Corpn, Philippine Crop Insurance Corpn; mem. Bd Manila Electric Co., PhilEquity Fund Inc.; mem. Council, Nat. Food Authority, Food Terminal Inc.; f. Corporate Planning Soc. of the Philippines; fmr Pres. Philippine Econ. Soc.; fmr Trustee Philippine Futuristics Soc. *Address:* c/o Department of Finance, DOF Building, Roxas Boulearvd, cnr Pablo Ocampo Street, 1004 Metro Manila, Philippines.

TÉVOÉDJRÈ, Albert, LèsL; Benin politician and international civil servant; *Ombudsman, Presidential Mediation Board;* b. 10 Nov. 1929, Porto Novo; s. of Joseph Tévoédjrè and Jeanne Singbo Tévoédjrè; m. Isabelle Ekué 1953; three s.; ed Toulouse Univ., France, Fribourg Univ., Switzerland, Institut Universitaire de Hautes Etudes Internationales, Geneva, Sloan School of Management and MIT, USA; teaching assignments include Lycée Delafosse, Dakar, Senegal 1952–54, Ecole Normale d'Institutrices, Cahors, France 1957–58, Lycée Victor Ballot, Porto Novo 1959–61, Geneva Africa Inst. 1963–64, Georgetown Univ., Washington, DC 1964; Sec. of State for Information 1961–62; Sec.-Gen. Union Africaine et Malgache (UAM) 1962–63; Research Assoc., Center for Int. Affairs, Harvard Univ. 1964–65; joined Int. Labour Office 1965, Regional Dir for Africa March 1966, Asst Dir-Gen. 1969–75, Deputy Dir-Gen. 1975; Dir Int. Inst. for Labour Studies 1975–84; Sec.-Gen. World Social Prospects Asscn (AMPS) 1980–; fmr Chief Ed. L'Etudiant d'Afrique Noire; Minister of Planning and Employment Promotion 1997–99; Chair. Millennium for Africa Comm. –2002; Special Envoy of the UN Sec.-Gen. in Ivory Coast 2003–05; Ombudsman, Presidential Mediation Bd (OPM) 2006–; Founding mem. Promotion Africaine (soc. to combat poverty in Africa); Founding mem. Nat. Liberation Movt and mem. Cttee 1958–60; Deputy Sec.-Gen. of Nat. Syndicate of Teachers, Dahomey 1959–60; Visiting Prof., Sorbonne, Paris 1979–, Univ. des Mutants, Dakar 1979–, Nat. Univ. of Côte d'Ivoire 1979–, Northwestern Univ. 1980; Int. Humanitarian Medal 1987. *Publications:* L'Afrique revoltée 1958, La formation des cadres africains en vue de la croissance économique 1965, Pan-Africanism in Action 1965, L'Afrique face aux problèmes du socialisme et de l'aide étrangère 1966, Une stratégie du progrès social en Afrique et la contribution de l'OIT 1969, Pour un contrat de solidarité 1976, La pauvreté—richesse des peuples 1978, etc. *Address:* Place de la République, 01BP, 1501 Port-Novo, Benin (office). *Telephone:* 20-21-20-22 (office). *Fax:* 20-21-44-36 (office). *E-mail:* webmaster@mediateur.gouv.bj (office). *Website:* www.mediateur.gouv.bj (office).

TEWARI, Manish, BA, LLB; Indian lawyer and politician; *Minister of State for Information and Broadcasting;* b. 8 Dec. 1965, Chandigarh; s. of the late Dr Vishwanath Tewari and Amrit Kaur; m. Naaznin B. Shafa 1996; one d.; ed Punjab Univ., Chandigarh, Univ. of Delhi; Coll. Unit Pres., Nat. Students' Union of India (NSUI), DAV Coll., Chandigarh 1981–82, Gen.-Sec., NSUI, Chandigarh 1982–83, Jt Sec., NSUI Nat. Cttee 1984, Gen.-Sec., NSUI Nat. Cttee 1985, Nat. Pres. NSUI 1988–93; mem. All India Congress Cttee 1991, Sec. 1997–98, 2004, Nat. Spokesperson 2008; Pres. Int. Union of Students 1992–93; Nat. Pres. Indian Youth Congress 1998–2000; elected to 15th Lok Sabha (lower house of Parl.) for Ludhiana (Punjab) constituency 2009–; Union Cabinet Minister of State (Ind. Charge) for Information and Broadcasting 2012–. *Leisure interests:* swimming, running, reading history books. *Address:* Ministry of Information and Broadcasting, 'A' Wing, Shastri Bhavan, Dr Rajendra Prasad Road, New Delhi 110 001, India (office). *Telephone:* (11) 23382639 (office). *Fax:* (11) 23386530 (office). *E-mail:* secy-in@nic.in (office). *Website:* mib.gov.in (office).

TEYSSEN, Johannes, DrIur; German business executive; *Chairman of the Board of Management and CEO, E.ON SE;* b. 10 Sept. 1959, Hildesheim; ed Univs of Freiburg and Göttingen; doctoral studies scholarship in Boston, Mass, USA 1984; Research Asst, Univ. of Göttingen 1984–86; law clerk, State Superior Court, Celle, Bar examination (Assessorexamen) 1986–89; Head of Energy and Corp. Law Dept, PreussenElektra AG, Hanover 1991–94, Head of Legal Affairs (Regional Utilities) 1994–98; mem. Bd of Man. HASTRA AG, Hanover 1998–99; Chair. Bd of Man. AVACON AG, Helmstedt 1999–2001; mem. Bd of Man. E.ON Energie AG, Munich 2001–03, Chair. 2003–07, mem. Bd of Man. E.ON AG, Düsseldorf 2004–08, Vice-Chair. 2008–10, Chair. (CEO) 2010– (E.ON SE from 2012). *Address:* E.ON SE, E.ON-Platz 1, 40479 Düsseldorf, Germany (office). *Telephone:* (211) 45790 (office). *Fax:* (211) 4579501 (office). *E-mail:* info@eon.com (office). *Website:* www.eon.com (office).

THABANE, Motsoahae Thomas, BA; Lesotho politician and civil servant; *Prime Minister;* b. 28 May 1939, Maseru; m.; two s. two d.; ed Univ. of South Africa; worked as civil servant for 26 years, First Clerk Asst to Senate and Deputy to Clerk of the Senate, Parl. of Lesotho 1966–70, Asst Sec. (Admin), Ministries of Health and Education 1970–72, Prin. Sec. in various govt ministries including Justice 1972–76, Health 1978–83, Foreign Affairs 1983–85 and Interior 1985–86, Sec. to ruling Mil. Council and also political adviser to the Mil. 1986–88, Govt Sec. 1988–90; Minister of Foreign Affairs, Information and Broadcasting 1990–91; escaped to South Africa following mil. coup in April 1991, worked as devt consultant; following April 1993 democratic elections, re-opened an office as devt consultant and commodities broker 1994–95; joined Ind. Electoral Comm. as Prov. Office Admin. for Free State region, South Africa–June 1994; Special Political Adviser to Prime Minister Ntsu Mokhehle 1995–98; elected mem. Parl. (Abia constituency) 1998; Minister of Foreign Affairs 2001–02, of Home Affairs and Public Safety 2002–04, of Communications, Science and Tech. 2005–07; Prime Minister 2012–; Pres. All Basotho Convention party 2007–. *Leisure interests:* politics, reading, physical fitness, walking, light classic and traditional music, jazz rhythm and blues. *Address:* Office of the Prime Minister, POB 527, Maseru 100, Lesotho (office). *Telephone:* 22311000 (office). *Fax:* 22320662 (office). *Website:* www.gov.ls/pm (office).

THAÇI, Hashim, PhD; Kosovo politician and fmr guerrilla leader; *Prime Minister;* b. 24 April 1968, Burojë; m.; one s.; ed Univ. of Prishtina, Univ. of Zurich, Switzerland; student leader and first student pres. of parallel Albanian Univ. of Prishtina 1989; joined Albanian political émigré group in Switzerland 1993, Co-founder People's Movt of Kosovo (LPK), a Marxist-Leninist political party devoted to Albanian popular nationalism; became mem. inner circle of Kosovo Liberation Army (KLA), later Commdr KLA, and Dir Political Group; Chair. Democratic Party of Kosovo (PDK) 2000–, mem. Parl. Group 2006–; mem. and Prime Minister, Interim Admin. Council, Kosovo 1999–2000, Prime Minister of Kosovo 2008–; Hon. Dr of Int. Relations (Geneva School of Diplomacy) 2012; received a copy of the key of the city of Tirana on the occasion of his state visit to Albania 2008. *Address:* Office of the Prime Minister, 10000 Prishtina, Rruga Nënë Terezë (office); Democratic Party of Kosovo (Partia Demokratike e Kosovës), 10000 Prishtina, Rruge Nënë Terezë 20; Arbëria, Rruge Metush Krasniqi 22, 10000 Prishtina, Kosovo. *Telephone:* (38) 20114635 (office); (38) 224262. *Fax:* (38) 211202 (office); (38) 223769. *E-mail:* info_pmo@ks-gov.net (office); pdk@pdk-ks.org. *Website:* www.kryeministri-ks.net (office); www.pdk-ks.org.

THACKER, Charles (Chuck) P., BS; American computer scientist; b. 26 Feb. 1943, Pasadena, Calif.; ed Univ. of California, Berkeley; left univ. to form the Berkeley Computer Corpn and designed the processor and memory system, group became the core technologists at Computer Systems Lab. at Xerox Palo Alto Research Center (PARC) during 1970s and 1980s, served as project leader of Xerox Alto personal computer system (first computer to use a mouse-driven Graphical User Interface), co-inventor of Ethernet LAN, contributed to numerous other projects, including first laser printer; Co-founder Systems Research Center, Digital Equipment Corpn 1983; joined Microsoft Research to help establish Microsoft Research Cambridge in Cambridge, UK 1997; designed hardware for Microsoft's Tablet PC, and later the Lectrice, a pen-based hand-held computer; a Microsoft Technical Fellow; Fellow Asscn for Computing Machinery (ACM) 1994, Computer History Museum 2007; Dr hc (Swiss Fed. Inst. of Tech.); Distinguished Alumnus in Computer Science, Univ. of California, Berkeley 1996, Charles Stark Draper Prize (co-recipient) 2004, IEEE John von Neumann Medal 2007, ACM A.M. Turing Award for 2009. *Address:* Microsoft Research Redmond, One Microsoft Way, Redmond, WA 98052-6399, USA (office). *Website:* research.microsoft.com (office).

THADA-THAMRONGVECH, Suchart, BSc, MSc, PhD; Thai politician; *Minister of Education;* b. 8 Aug. 1952; ed Thammasat Univ., London School of Econs, UK, McMaster Univ., Canada, Nat. Defence Coll.; Vice Chancellor of Int. Relations and Research Div., Ramkhamhaeng Univ. 1991–93; mem. Prov. Waterworks Authority 1992–95; mem. Audit Cttee, Bangkok Metropolitan Bank PLC 1998–2002; mem. Bd of Dirs Bank for Agric. and Agricultural Cooperatives 2001; mem. Metropolitan Waterworks Authority 2001–02; adviser to Minister for Commerce 2003, to Minister for Energy 2003–05; Deputy Minister of Finance 2008, Minister of Finance 2008, of Educ. 2012–; fmr mem. Securities and Exchange Comm.; fmr mem. and Chair. Examination Cttee Ratchaburi Electricity Generating PLC, PTT PLC, Siam City Bank PLC, Pan Asia Footwear PLC. *Address:* Ministry of Education, Wang Chankasem, Thanon Ratchadamnoen Nok, Bangkok 10300, Thailand (office). *Telephone:* (2) 281-9264 (office). *Fax:* (2) 281-1753 (office). *E-mail:* website@emisc.moe.go.th (office). *Website:* www.moe.go.th (office).

THAHANE, Timothy T., BComm, MA; Lesotho government official and diplomatist; *Minister of Energy, Meteorology and Water Affairs;* b. 2 Nov. 1940, Leribe; s. of Nicodemus Thahane and Beatrice Thahane; m. Dr Edith Mohapi 1972; one s. one d.; ed Lesotho High School, Univs of Newfoundland and Toronto, Canada; Asst Sec., Prin. Asst Sec., Cen. Planning Office 1968–70, Dir of Planning 1968–73; Amb. to EEC for Negotiations of Lomé Convention 1973–74; Alt. Exec. Dir (Africa Group 1) World Bank 1974–76, Exec. Dir 1976–78, representing 15 African countries and Trinidad and Tobago; Vice-Chair. and Chair., Jt Audit Cttee of World Bank Group 1976–78; Amb. to the USA 1978–80; Vice-Pres. UN Affairs, IBRD 1990–96; Deputy Gov. South African Reserve Bank 1996–2002; Minister of Finance and Devt Planning 2002–12, Minister of Energy, Meteorology and Water Affairs 2012–; mem. Nat. Ass. for Likhetlane Constituency No 16 2012–; Dir Bd of Global Coalition for Africa, Washington 1992–; mem. Bd of Lesotho Bank (Vice-Chair. 1972–73), Third World Foundation, Centre for Econ. Devt and Population Activities, Washington, DC; mem. Lesotho Congress for Democracy (LCD). *Publications:* articles on econ. planning and investment in Lesotho, Southern Africa and Africa in general. *Leisure interests:* reading, music. *Address:* Ministry of Energy, Meteorology and Water Affairs, Maseru 100, Lesotho (office).

THAIN, John A., BS, MBA; American business executive; *Chairman and CEO, CIT Group Inc.;* ed Massachusetts Inst. of Tech., Harvard Univ.; Chief Financial Officer and Head of Operations, Tech. and Finance The Goldman Sachs Group LP 1994–99, also Co-CEO for European Operations 1995–97, Dir 1998–2003, Pres. and Co-COO 1999, Pres. and Co-COO Goldman Sachs Inc. 1999–2003, Pres. and COO 2003; CEO New York Stock Exchange (NYSE) 2004–07 (NYSE Euronext, Inc. following merger of NYSE Group and Euronext NV in June 2006); Chair. and CEO Merrill Lynch & Co., Inc. 2007–09 (resgnd); Chair. and CEO CIT Group Inc. 2010–; mem. Bd of Dirs Blackrock Inc.; mem. several visiting cttees at MIT Sloan School of Management, Int. Advisory Panel of Monetary Authority of Singapore, US Nat. Advisory Bd of INSEAD (Institut Européen d'Admin des Affaires), Bd of Mans of New York Botanical Garden, Bd of Mans of New York-Presbyterian Hosp., Harvard Business School Bd of Dean's Advisors, Partnership for New York City. *Address:* CIT Group Inc., 11 West 42nd Street, New York, NY 10036, USA (office). *Telephone:* (212) 461-5200 (office). *Website:* www.cit.com (office).

THAKSIN SHINAWATRA, PhD; Thai business executive and politician; b. 26 July 1949, Chiangmai; brother of Yingluck Shinawatra; m. Pojaman Shinawatra (divorced 2008); three c.; ed Police Cadet Acad., Eastern Kentucky Univ., Sam Houston State Univ., USA; joined Royal Thai Police Dept 1973, Lt-Col 1987, resgnd 1987; Chair. Shinawatra Computer and Communications Group 1987–94; Minister of Foreign Affairs 1994–95; Leader Palang Dharma Party 1995–96; Deputy Prime Minister in charge of Traffic and Transportation in Bangkok 1995–96, Deputy Prime Minister 1997; Prime Minister of Thailand 2001–06 (re-elected 2005, briefly resigned position 4 April–23 May 2006, ousted in bloodless coup by army generals led by Gen. Sonthi Boonyaratglin for alleged "corruption and devisiveness" while abroad visiting UN Gen. Ass. in New York 19 Sept. 2006; Founder and Leader Thai Rak Thai Party 1998–2006; Founder and Vice-Chair. THAICOM Foundation for Secondary Educ. 1993; Pres. Northerners' Asscn of Thailand 1998; Chair. Manchester City Football Club 2007–08; special adviser to Cambodian govt 2009–10; convicted in absentia 2008, sentenced to two years in prison; family assets frozen by Supreme Court 2010; granted Montenegrin citizenship 2009; Hon. (External) mem. Police Cadet Acad. Council 1996–, Hon.

mem. Asscn Ex-Mil. Officers 1998–; 1992 ASEAN Businessman of the Year Award, Lee Kuan Yew Exchange Fellowship 1994 and other awards.

THAKUR, Mahantha; Nepalese politician; *President, Terai Madhes Loktantrik Party;* fmr Nepal Congress leader; Minister for Science and Tech. –2007 (resgnd); Pres. Terai Madhes Loktantrik Party 2007–. *Address:* Terai Madhes Loktantrik Party, Kathmandu, Nepal (office). *Telephone:* (1) 4462398 (office).

THAKUR, Rameshwar, LLB, MA, FCA; Indian chartered accountant and politician; b. 28 July 1927, Thakur Gangti village, Godda Dist, Jharkhand; m. Narmada Thakur; two s. two d.; ed Bhagalpur, Patna Univ., Calcutta Univ., Inst. of Chartered Accountants of India, New Delhi; actively participated in Quit India Movt 1942, remained underground for nearly six months in Raj Mahal Hills, Santhal Parganas, arrested and detained in Cen. Jail, Dum Dum, Calcutta in connection with nat. movt 1946; took active part in healthcare, educational and social reforms and rural reconstruction activities, particularly in Santhal Parganas, Jharkhand; chartered accountant since 1953; Lecturer, City Coll., Calcutta Univ. 1955–60; Visiting Prof., Delhi Univ. 1960–73; mem. Rajya Sabha (Indian Nat. Congress) 1984–96; Union Minister of State for Finance (Revenue), Rural Devt and Parl. Affairs 1991–94; Gov. of Orissa 2004–07, of Andhra Pradesh (Additional Charge) 2006–07, of Karnataka 2007–09, of Madhya Pradesh 2009–11; Pres. Inst. of Chartered Accountants of India 1966–67; Nat. Pres. All India Bharat Scouts & Guides 1998–2001, 2004–; Chair. Study Group on Banking Costs, Banking Comm., Govt of India 1978–82, Associated Journals Ltd 1987–91, Thakur Research Foundation, New Delhi, Rajenda Bhawan Trust, New Delhi; Dir, Unit Trust of India four years, Export Credit and Guarantee Corpn three years, Punjab Nat. Bank 1978–82, Punjab, Haryana and Delhi Chambers of Commerce three years, Bd Govs Man. Devt Inst., Gurugaon, Haryana; Sec. Sanjay Gandhi Memorial Trust, Amethi, UP; Group Leader Indian Del. to World Congress of Scouts, Brussels 1964, Int. Congress of Accountants, Mexico 1982; Deputy Leader Indian Parl. Union Conf., Geneva 1984; Leader, 15th Asia Pacific Gathering, Colombo 1984, Indian Del. to 17th Gen. Ass., Coventry, UK 1987; Chair. World Congress of Scouts & Guides Fellowship 1999; Trustee Hari Devi Smarak Nidhi and Gadadhar Mishra Smarak Nidhi public charitable trusts; engaged in Khadi & Village Industries, Rural Devt Programmes, Godda Dist, Jharkhand since 1965. *Address:* c/o Raj Bhavan, Bhophal, Madhya Pradesh, India.

THAM, Khai Meng, BA, MA; Singaporean advertising executive; *Worldwide Creative Director and Chairman, World Wide Creative Council, Ogilvy & Mather Worldwide;* ed Central Saint Martins and Royal Coll. of Art, London, UK; worked in London and Chicago before returning to Asia; taught at RCA, London; Co-Chair. and Regional Exec. Creative Dir, Ogilvy & Mather Asia Pacific 1999–2008, Worldwide Creative Dir and Chair. World Wide Creative Council (first Asian) 2008–, mem. Worldwide Bd and Exec. Cttee; mem. Bd New York's Agencies In Action (coalition of US advertising agencies to alleviate hunger in the city); Chair. Clio Jury 2005–; named Creative Dir of the Year by Campaign Brief Asia, Pres.'s Award, Pres. S. R. Nathan 2009. *Publication:* The Ugly Duckling: A Cautionary Tale of Creativity. *Address:* Ogilvy & Mather, The Chocolate Factory, 636 11th Avenue, New York, NY 10036, USA (office). *Telephone:* (212) 237-4000 (office). *E-mail:* info@ogilvy.com (office). *Website:* www.ogilvy.com (office).

THAMMAVONG, Thongsing; Laotian politician; *Prime Minister;* b. 12 April 1944, Xoneneua village, Viengthong Dist; military medical student 1958, served on battlefield in Laos–Vietnam border area 1959–60; attended cultural training 1960–63; Deputy Dir Xamneua Secondary School 1963, Dir Lower Secondary School and Dir Educ. Dept, Xiengkhor Dist, Huaphan Prov., Dir Upper Secondary School and Teacher Training School, Sopbao, Viengxay Dist 1971–76, several positions with Ministry of Educ. 1976–79; mem. Phak Pasason Pativat Lao (Lao People's Revolutionary Party—LPRP) 1967–, Standby mem. Party Cen. Cttee 1981, Pres. Newspaper and Radio Cttee and Deputy Head, Party Propaganda and Training Bd 1982–83, mem. Politburo and Head, Party Cen. Cttee Office 1991–; Minister of Culture 1983–88; Vice-Pres. Nat. Ass. 1989–91, Acting Pres. 1991–92, Pres. 2006–10; Mayor of Vientiane 2002; Prime Minister 2010–. *Address:* Office of the Prime Minister, Ban Sisavat, Vientiane, Laos (office). *Telephone:* (21) 213653 (office). *Fax:* (21) 213560 (office).

THAN, Field Marshal Shwe; Myanma politician, army officer and fmr head of state; b. 2 Feb. 1933, Kyaukse; m. Daw Kyaing Kyaing; joined army aged 20; positions included time spent in dept of psychological warfare; several other positions in army after mil. coup that ousted Prime Minister U Nu in 1962, including promotion to Lt-Col 1972, to Col 1978, to Commdr of Mil. Dist of South West 1983, Asst Man. of Gen. Staff of the Army, Brig.-Gen. and Vice-Minister of Defence 1985, Maj.-Gen. 1986; mem. Cen. Exec. Cttee 1986; Prime Minister 1992–2003, Minister of Defence 1992–; Chair. State Law and Order Restoration Council (SLORC) 1992–97, Chair. State Peace and Devt Council (SDP) 1997–2011 (council dissolved). *Address:* c/o Ministry of Defence, Ahlanpya Phaya Street, Yangon, Myanmar. *Telephone:* (1) 281611.

THAN NYEIN, U; Myanma economist and central banker; *Governor, Central Bank of Myanmar;* Gov. Central Bank of Myanmar 2007–; Gov. for Myanmar, IMF; Chair. Myanmar Banks Asscn. *Address:* Office of the Governor, Central Bank of Myanmar, Office 55, Nay Pyi Taw, Myanmar (office). *Telephone:* (67) 418203 (office). *Fax:* (67) 418270 (office). *E-mail:* director.admin.cbm@mptmail.net.mm (office). *Website:* www.cbm.gov.mm (office).

THANAJARO, Gen. Chettha; Thai politician; *Leader, Ruam Jai Thai Chart Pattana (Thais United National Development);* fmr Deputy Army Commander, later C-in-C; fmr Minister of Science and Tech.; Minister of Defence 2004–05; currently Leader, Ruam Jai Thai Chart Pattana (Thais United Nat. Devt); Pres. Olympic Cttee of Thailand. *Address:* Ruam Jai Thai Chart Pattana (Thais United National Development), c/o House of Representatives, Bangkok, Thailand (office).

THANHAWLA, Lal, BA; Indian politician; *Chief Minister of Mizoram;* b. 19 May 1942, Durtlang, Aizawl, Mizoram; s. of H. P. Sailo and Lalsawmliani; m. Lal Riliani 1970; one s. two d.; ed Gauhati Univ.; joined Indian Nat. Congress 1967, mem. All India Congress Cttee 1973–, Pres. Mizoram Pradesh Congress Cttee 1973–2014; mem. Mizoram Legis. Ass. 1978, 1979, 1984, 1987, 1989, 1993, 2003–08, Chief Minister 1984–87, 1989–93, 1993–98, 2008–13, 2014–, Leader of Opposition 1978–84, 1987–89, 2003–08; mem. Congress Working Cttee; mem. 9th

Finance Comm. of India; Chair. NE Olympic Comm.; Founder-Ed. Remna Arsi & Mizo Aw (daily newspaper); Chair. Literary Cttee of Nat. Devt Council; Pres. Mizoram Olympic Asscn; mem. Nat. Interpretation Council; Life mem. YMCA, Evangelical Fellowship of India, Bible Soc. of India; 12 nat. and int. awards for contribs to peace and social work. *Leisure interests:* gardening, reading. *Address:* Chief Minister's Office, McDonald Hill, Zarkawt, Aizawl 796 001, Mizoram (office); A/14 Zarkawt Main Street, Aizawl 796 001, Mizoram, India (home). *Telephone:* (389) 2322150 (office); (389) 2343461 (home). *Fax:* (389) 2322245 (office); (389) 2342898 (home). *E-mail:* cm-mizoram@nic.com (office); hawla19@yahoo.com (office). *Website:* mizoram.nic.in (office).

THANI, Abdallah al-; Libyan politician; *Minister of Defence;* b. 1954; ed Bengasi Mil. Acad.; fmr mem. Nat. Transitional Council, now Gen. Nat. Congress (Parl.); Minister of Defence 2013–, also Acting Prime Minister April–May 2014. *Address:* Ministry of Defence, Tripoli, Libya (office). *Telephone:* (21) 4800734 (office). *Fax:* (21) 4800168 (office). *E-mail:* info@defense.gov.ly (office). *Website:* www.defense.gov.ly (office).

THANI, Sheikh Abdul Aziz ibn Khalifa ath-, BS; Qatari politician, international official and petroleum industry executive; b. 12 Dec. 1948, Doha; one s. three d.; ed Northern Indiana Univ., USA; Deputy Minister of Finance and Petroleum June–Dec. 1972, Minister of Finance and Petroleum, State of Qatar 1972; Chair. State of Qatar Investment Bd 1972–89, Qatar Nat. Bank 1972, Qatar Gen. Petroleum Corpn 1973; Gov. IMF and IBRD (World Bank) 1972; rep. at numerous int. confs including OPEC, OAPEC and Arab, Islamic and non-aligned summit confs; resident in France. *Leisure interest:* scuba diving.

THANI, Sheikh Abdullah bin Khalifa ath-; Qatari politician; b. 25 Dec. 1959, Doha; six s.; ed Royal Mil. Acad., Sandhurst UK; various positions within Qatar Armed Forces 1976–89; Minister of the Interior 1989–96; Deputy Prime Minister 1995–96; Prime Minister of Qatar 1996–2007 (resgnd); Chair. Qatari Olympic Cttee 1979–89. *Address:* c/o Office of the Prime Minister, PO Box 923, Doha, Qatar.

THANI, Sheikh Abdullah bin Nasser bin Khalifa ath-; Qatari government official; *Prime Minister and Minister of the Interior;* b. 1959; s. of Nasser bin Khalifa ath-Thani; m.; six c.; ed Beirut Arab Univ.; fmr Commdr, Ministry of Interior Security Force and Chair. Nat. Anti-Terrorism Cttee; Asst Dir Special Security Force Dept for Operations Affairs 2001–04; Head of Security Cttees for Doha Asian Games 2006 and Qatar World Cup 2022; Minister of State for Internal Affairs 2005–13; Prime Minister and Minister of the Interior 2013–. *Address:* Ministry of the Interior, POB 115, Doha, Qatar (office). *Telephone:* 44330000 (office). *Fax:* 44322927 (office). *E-mail:* info@moi.gov.qa (office). *Website:* www.moi.gov.qa (office).

THANI, Sheikh; Abdullah bin Saoud al-, BA (Econ), MBA (USA), MBA (UK); Qatari central banker; *Governor, Qatar Central Bank;* b. (Abdulla Saoud Al-Thani), 1 Jan. 1957, Doha; worked in Foreign Exchange Dept, Qatar Central Bank 1982–89, Deputy Gov. 1990–2001, Gov. 2006–; Chair. Qatar Devt Bank 1996–; Chair. State Audit Bureau 2001–06; Pres. Gen. Retirement and Pension Authority 2006–; mem. Bd of Dirs Coll. of Business and Economy, Qatar Univ. 2006–; Chair. QFC Regulatory Authority 2012–, Islamic Financial Services Bd 2013–, Int. Islamic Liquidity Man. Corpn; Arab Banking Personality of the Year 2011. *Address:* Qatar Central Bank, PO Box 1234, Doha, Qatar (office). *Telephone:* 44456400 (office); 44456456 (office). *Fax:* 44415587 (office). *E-mail:* g@qcb.gov.qa (office). *Website:* www.qcb.gov.qa (office).

THANI, Sheikh Ahmed bin Jassim bin Mohamed ath-; Qatari oil engineer, business executive and politician; *Minister of Business and Trade;* ed Imperial Coll. of Science, Tech. and Medicine, UK, Delft Univ. of Tech., The Netherlands, Carnegie Mellon Tepper School of Business, USA; served at different levels at Qatargas and became its COO (Engineering and Ventures), mem. decision-making body and also managed around 250 capital projects for the co., both onshore and offshore; worked at Total in La Defense, Paris, for more than a year; external posting at Mobil Research Center, Meptec, Dallas, Tex., USA; Dir Gen. Al Jazeera Network 2011–13; Minister of Business and Trade 2013–; Chair. Tech. Cttee of Gas Processing Centre, Qatar Univ. Research Centre; mem. Industrial Advisory Bd Coll. of Engineering, Qatar Univ.; ranked by Arabian Business amongst the Power 500: The Worlds's Most Influential Arabs (31st) 2012. *Address:* Ministry of Business and Trade, POB 1968, Doha, Qatar (office). *Telephone:* 4945555 (office). *Fax:* 44945000 (office). *E-mail:* mbt@mbt.gov.qa (office). *Website:* www.mbt.gov.qa (office).

THANI, Sheikh Hamad bin Jasim bin Jaber ath-; Qatari politician; *Prime Minister and Minister of Foreign Affairs;* b. 1959; Dir Office of the Minister of Municipal Affairs and Agric. 1982–89, Minister of Municipal Affairs and Agric. 1989–92; Deputy Minister of Electricity and Water 1990–92; Minister of Foreign Affairs 1992–; First Deputy Prime Minister 2003–07; Prime Minister 2007–; Head Perm. Cttee for the Support of Al Quds 1998–; mem. Supreme Defence Council 1996–, Parl. Constitution Cttee 1999–, Ruling Family Council 2000–; CEO Supreme Council for the Investment of the Reserves of State (Qatar Investment Authority) 2000–; fmr Chair. Qatar Electricity and Water Co.; fmr Pres. Cen. Municipal Council, Special Emiri Projects Office; fmr Dir Special Emiri Projects Office; fmr mem. Bd of Dirs Qatar Petroleum, Supreme Council for Planning. *Address:* Ministry of Foreign Affairs, POB 250, Doha (office); Qatar Investment Authority, PO Box 23224, Doha, Qatar. *Telephone:* 4334334 (office). *Fax:* 4442777 (office). *E-mail:* webmaster@mofa.gov.qa (office). *Website:* www.mofa.gov.qa (office).

THANI, Sheikh Hamad bin Khalifa ath-; royal; b. 1 Jan. 1952, Doha; s. of Sheikh Khalifa bin Hamad ath-Thani; m. Sheikha Mozah bint Nasser al-Missned; five s. (including Amir of Qatar Sheikh Tamim bin Hamad bin Khalifa ath-Thani) two d.; ed Royal Mil. Coll., Sandhurst, UK; apptd Heir-Apparent May 1977; Commdr First Mobile Bn (now Hamad Mobile Bn); Maj., then Maj.-Gen., C-in-C Armed Forces of Qatar; Minister of Defence 1977–2013; Amir of Qatar 1995–2013 (abdicated); Prime Minister 1995–96; fmr Supreme Pres. Higher Planning Council; Pres. Higher Youth Council 1979–91; f. Mil. Sports Fed.; mem. Int. Mil. Sports Fed.; Pres. Qatari Nat. Olympic Cttee 2000–; mem. IOC, mem. Sports for All Cttee; Chair. Organizing Cttee 15th Asian Games 2006; Head, Upper Council of Environment and Natural Sanctuaries; Nishan-i-Pakistan 1999, Nat. Order of

Merit (Malta) 2009, Grand Order of King Tomislav with Sash and Great Morning Star (Croatia) 2009, Grand Collar of the Order of the Liberator Simon Bolivar (Venezuela) 2010; Orders of Merit from Cote D'Ivoire, Cuba, Dominican Republic, Egypt, Finland, France, Germany, Greece, Indonesia, Italy, Lebanon, Morocco, Oman, Portugal, Romania, Saudi Arabia, Senegal, Tunis, UK, Yemen. *Leisure interest:* sports. *Address:* c/o The Royal Palace, PO Box 923, Doha, Qatar. *Website:* www.diwan.gov.qa.

THANI, Sheikh Khalid bin Khalifa bin Jassim ath-; Qatari business executive; *CEO, QatarGas;* Dir of Ras Laffan Industrial City –2010; CEO QatarGas 2010–; ranked by Arabian Business amongst the Power 500: The World's Most Influential Arabs (70th) 2012. *Address:* Qatargas Doha Head Office, Omar Al-Mukhtar Street, West Bay, Doha, Qatar (office). *Telephone:* 44736000 (office). *Fax:* 44736666 (office). *E-mail:* infos@qatargas.com.qa (office). *Website:* www.qatargas.com (office).

THANI, Sheikh Khalifa bin Hamad ath-, (fmr Amir of Qatar); b. 1932, Doha; s. of the late Heir Apparent Sheikh Hamad bin Abdullah bin Jassim ath-Thani; son, Sheikh Hamad bin Khalifa ath-Thani; ed Royal Mil. Coll., Sandhurst, UK; apptd Heir Apparent 1948; served successively as Chief of Security Forces, Chief of Civil Courts, Minister of Educ., Finance and Petroleum; Deputy Ruler 1960–72, also Minister of Educ. 1960–70; Prime Minister 1970–72, Minister of Finance 1970–72; Chair. Investment Bd for State Reserves 1972; deposed his cousin Sheikh Ahmad and took office as Amir of Qatar 1972, deposed by his son June 1995.

THANI, Sheikh Tamim bin Hamad bin Khalifa ath-, (Amir of Qatar); Qatari; b. 3 June 1980, Doha; s. of fmr Amir of Qatar Sheikh Hamad bin Khalifa ath-Thani and Sheikha Mozah bint Nasser al-Missned; m. 1st Sheikha Jawahar bint Hamad bin Sohaim ath-Thani 2005; two s. two d.; m. 2nd Sheikha Anoud bint Mana al-Hajri 2009; one s. one d.; ed Sherborne School, Dorset, Harrow School and Royal Mil. Acad. Sandhurst, UK; commissioned as a Second Lt in Qatar Armed Forces 1998, Deputy C-in-C of the Armed Forces 2009, later C-in-C; proclaimed Heir Apparent when his elder brother Sheikh Jassim bin Hamad bin Khalifa ath-Thani renounced his right to the throne 5 Aug. 2003, Amir of Qatar (following abdication of his father) 25 June 2013–; Head of Upper Council of the Environment and Natural Sanctuaries; Chair. Qatar Investment Authority; fmr Chair. Supreme Council for the Environment and Natural Reserves, Supreme Educ. Council, Supreme Council of Information and Communication Tech., Public Works Authority (Ashghal), Urban Planning and Devt Authority, Bd of Regents of Qatar Univ., Ruling Family Council; fmr Deputy Chair. High Cttee for Co-ordination and Follow Up; fmr Vice-Pres. Supreme Council for Econ. Affairs and Investment; Pres. as-Sadd Sports Club 1999–2000; Chair. Qatar Nat. Olympic Cttee 2000–, Organizing Cttee Asian Games, Doha 2006; mem. IOC, Supreme Educ. Council; Chair. ictQATAR programme 2005–; headed Doha's bid for the 2020 Olympics; Necklace of Merit 2003, Issa bin Salman al-Khalifa Order of Merit-Excellence Class (Bahrain) 2004, Collar of the Order of Zayed (UAE) 2005, Grand Officier, Légion d'honneur 2010; Sheikh Essa Bin Salman Al Khalifa Medal (Bahrain) 2004, Sheikh Zayed bin Sultan al-Nahyan Medal of Honour (UAE) 2004, voted Best Sport Personality in the Arab World in popular Egyptian newspaper Al Ahram 2006, OCA Award of Merit, Olympic Council of Asia 2007. *Address:* The Royal Palace, PO Box 923, Doha, Qatar. *Website:* www.diwan.gov.qa.

THANIN KRAIVICHIEN (see Kraivichien, Thanin).

THAPA, Gen. (retd) Pyar Jung, BA; Nepalese army officer; b. 15 Sept. 1946; ed St Xavier High School, Tribhuvan Univ., Royal Mil. Acad., Sandhurst, UK, US Army War Coll., USA; joined Royal Nepalese Army 1964, Second Lt Singh Nath Battalion, promoted to rank of Maj.-Gen. 1998, Asst Chief of Army Staff 1998–2002, Dir Integrated Security and Devt Program, promoted to rank of Lt-Gen. 2001, Chief of Army Staff 2002–06 (retd); Battalion Commdr UN Interim Force in Lebanon 1986, Deputy Sector Commdr Sector West, UN Protection Forces in Fmr Yugoslavia 1992. *Address:* c/o Army Headquarters, Singha Durbar, Kathmandu, Nepal (office).

THAPA, Ram Bahadur, (Badal); Nepalese politician and fmr guerrilla commander; b. 1955; s. of Karn Bahjadur Thapa Magar and Nanda Kumari Thapa Magar; mem. Cen. Cttee CP of Nepal (Maoist), coordinator of cen. advisory council of Magar cen. Liberation Front; coordinator of cand. selection cttee for Constituent Ass. election 2008; Minister of Defence 2008–09. *Address:* c/o Ministry of Defence, Singha Durbar, Kathmandu, Nepal (office).

THAPA, Surya Bahadur; Nepalese politician; b. 20 March 1928, Muga, East Nepal; s. of Bahadur Thapa; m. 1953; one s. three d.; ed Allahabad Univ., India; House Speaker, Advisory Ass. to King of Nepal 1958; mem. Upper House of Parl. 1959; Minister of Forests, Agric., Commerce and Industry 1960, of Finance and Econ. Affairs 1962; Vice-Chair. Council of Ministers, Minister of Finance, Econ. Planning, Law and Justice 1963; Vice-Chair. Council of Ministers, Minister of Finance, Law and Gen. Admin. 1964–65; Chair. Council of Ministers, Minister of Palace Affairs 1965–69; Prime Minister of Nepal and Minister of Palace Affairs 1979–83; Minister of Finance 1979–80, of Defence 1980–81, 1982–83, of Foreign Affairs 1982; Prime Minister of Nepal 1997–98, Prime Minister and Minister of Royal Palace Affairs, of Defence, of Home Affairs, of Foreign Affairs, of Industry, Commerce and Supplies, of Law, Justice and Parl. Affairs, of Agric. and Co-operatives, of Population and the Environment, of Water Resources, of Land Reforms and Man., of Women, Children and Social Welfare, of Forest and Soil Conservation, of Science and Tech., of Labour and Transport Man., of Gen. Admin, of Local Devt and of Health, Interim Govt 2003–04 (resgnd); Pres. Rashtriya Prajatantra Party 1990–2002; Pres. Rashtriya Janashakti Party (split from Rashtriya Prajatantra Party Nov. 2004) 2005–; mem. Royal Advisory Cttee 1969–72; arrested and released 1972, 1975; Hon. DLitt (Kurukshetra Univ.); Tri-Sahkti-Patta 1963, Gorkha Dakshinbahu I 1965, Om Rama Patta 1980; several Nepalese and foreign awards. *Address:* Rashtriya Janashakti Party (National People's Power Party), Ramalphokhari, Kathmandu, Nepal (office). *Telephone:* (1) 4437063 (office). *Fax:* (1) 4437064 (office).

THAPAR, Gautam; Indian chemical engineer and business executive; *Chairman, Ballarpur Industries Ltd;* b. 7 Dec. 1960, nephew of Lalit Mohan Thapar; ed Doon School, St Stephen's Coll., Delhi, Pratt Inst., USA; joined family co. Ballarpur Industries Ltd (BILT) 1986, held positions successively in paper mills and pulp

unit, chemicals and foods businesses, Head of Finance 1997–98, CEO 1998–99, Man.-Dir Andra Pradesh Rayons (APR) Ltd 1999, Jt Man.-Dir BILT 1999–2001, Vice-Chair. and Man.-Dir BILT 2001–06, Chair. 2006–; Chair. Crompton Greaves Ltd 2004–, Confederation of Indian Industry; Vice-Chair. Governing Body and General Body, Thapar Center for Industrial Research and Development; mem. Bd of Dirs Asahi India Safety Glass Ltd 2002–, Pratham India Educ. Initiative 2003–, Compass Limited, CG Capital & Investments Ltd, Greaves Cotton Ltd, Global Green Company Ltd, KCT Papers Ltd, KCT Chemicals & Electricals Ltd, Solaris Chemtech Ltd, Osian's Connoisseurs of Art Pvt Ltd; mem. Bd of Trustees Patiala Technical Education Trust, Aspen India; mem. Bd of Govs Thapar Inst. of Engineering and Technology; mem. Man. Cttee of Associate Chambers of Commerce and Industries. *Address:* Ballarpur Industries Limited, First India Place, Tower C, Mehrauli – Gurgaon Road, Gurgaon, Haryana 122 002, India (office). *Telephone:* (124) 280424243 (office). *Fax:* (124) 280426061 (office). *E-mail:* corpcom@bilt.com (office). *Website:* www.bilt.com (office).

THAROOR, Shashi, MA, MALD, PhD; Indian UN official, politician and author; *Minister of State for Human Resource Development;* b. 9 March 1956, London, England, UK; s. of Chandran Tharoor and Lily Tharoor; m. Sunanda Pushkar Tharoor (died 2014); twin s. one step-s.; ed St Stephen's Coll., Delhi Univ., Fletcher School of Law and Diplomacy, Tufts Univ., USA; joined UN 1978, with UNHCR, served at Geneva HQ, Head of Office in Singapore; Special Asst for UN Peace-keeping operations; Exec. Asst to UN Sec.-Gen. 1997–98, Dir Communications and Special Projects, Office of the Sec.-Gen. 1998–2000; Interim Head of Dept of Public Information 2001–02, Head and Under-Sec.-Gen. for Public Information 2002–07; mem. Lok Sabha 2009–; Minister of State for External Affairs 2009–10, for Human Resource Development 2012–; Chair., Afras Ventures (investment co.) 2008–; mem. Bd of Overseers Fletcher School of Law and Diplomacy, Bd of Trustees, Aspen Inst. India, Advisory Bd World Policy Journal, Advisory Bd Virtue Foundation, Advisory Bd Breakthrough (human rights org.); Fellow, New York Inst. of the Humanities; Hon. DLitt; Pravasi Bharatiya Samman 2004; Commonwealth Writers' Prize, several journalism and literary awards; named Global Leader of Tomorrow by World Econ. Forum, Davos, Switzerland 1998. *Publications include:* Reasons of State 1981, The Great Indian Novel 1989, The Five Dollar Smile and Other Stories 1990, Show Business 1992, India: From Midnight to the Millennium 1997, Riot 2001, Kerala: God's Own Country 2002, Nehru: The Invention of India 2003, Bookless in Baghdad 2005, The Elephant, the Tiger and the Cellphone: Reflections on India in the 21st Century 2007, Pax Indica: India and The World of the 21st Century 2012. *Leisure interests:* cricket, theatre, literature, cinema. *Address:* Ministry of Human Resource Development, Shastri Bhavan, Dr Rajendra Prasad Road, New Delhi 110 001, India (office). *Telephone:* (11) 23384073 (office). *Fax:* (11) 23381567 (office). *E-mail:* shashi.tharoor@nic.in (office); office@tharoor.in (office). *Website:* www.mhrd.gov.in (office); www.tharoor.in.

THARP, Twyla, BA; American dancer and choreographer; b. 1 July 1941, Portland, Ind.; ed Pomona Coll., Barnard Coll.; studied with Richard Thomas, Merce Cunningham, Igor Schwezoff, Louis Mattox, Paul Taylor, Margaret Craske, Erick Hawkins; with Paul Taylor Dance Co. 1963–65; freelance choreographer with own modern dance troupe Twyla Tharp Dance and other cos, including Joffrey Ballet and American Ballet Theater 1965–87, The Paris Opera Ballet, The Martha Graham Dance Company; Artistic Assoc. Choreographer American Ballet Theatre, New York 1988–91; re-formed Twyla Tharp Dance periodically between 1991 and present; Hon. mem. American Acad. of Arts and Letters 1997; more than 15 hon. degrees; two Emmy Awards and numerous other awards including Dance Magazine Annual Award 1981, Laurence Olivier Award 1991, Doris Duke Awards for New Work 1999, Astaire Award 2003, The Drama League Award for Sustained Achievement in Musical Theatre, the Outer Critics Circle Award for Outstanding Choreography, Kennedy Center Honor 2008. *Major works choreographed include:* Tank Dive 1965, Re-Moves 1966, Forevermore 1967, Generation 1968, Medley 1969, Fugue 1970, Eight Jelly Rolls 1971, The Raggedy Dances 1972, As Time Goes By 1974, Sue's Leg 1975, Push Comes to Shove 1976, Once More Frank 1976, Mud 1977, Baker's Dozen 1979, When We Were Very Young 1980, The Catherine Wheel (with music by David Byrne) 1981, Nine Sinatra Songs 1982, Amadeus 1984, White Nights 1985, Singin' in the Rain 1985, In the Upper Room 1986, Rules of the Game 1989; choreographed Cutting Up 1993 for US tour, Demeter and Persephone 1993, 1994, Waterbaby Bagatelles 1994, Red White and Blues 1995, How Near Heaven 1995, Mr. Worldly Wise 1996, Movin' Out (Tony Award 2003), Even the King 2003, The Times They Are A Changin' 2006, Armenia 2008, Nightspot 2008, Rabbit and Rogue 2008, Come Fly With Me (later renamed Come Fly Away) 2009; films Hair 1979, Ragtime 1980, Amadeus 1984, White Nights 1985, I'll Do Anything 1994; videotape Making Television Dance (Chicago International Film Festival Award) 1977, CBS Cable Confessions of a Corner Maker 1980, Baryshnikov by Tharp (two Emmy Awards, Director's Guild for America Award for Outstanding Director of Achievement. *Publications:* Push Comes to Shove (autobiog.) 1992, The Creative Habit: Learn it and Use it for Life 2003, The Collaborative Habit: Life Lessons for Working Together 2009. *E-mail:* jah@twylatharp.org (office). *Website:* www.twylatharp.org (office).

THAUGSUBAN, Suthep; Thai politician; b. 7 July 1949, Surat Thani Prov.; fmr mem. Ratha Sapha (Parl.) for Surat Thani Prov. (resgnd 2009); fmr Minister of Agric., of Transport and Communications; Deputy Prime Minister and Minister for Security Affairs 2008–11; Sec. Gen. Prachatipat (Democrat Party) –2011. *Address:* c//o Office of the Prime Minister, Government House, Thanon Nakhon Pathom, Bangkok 10300, Thailand (office).

THAWLEY, Michael, AO; Australian business executive and fmr diplomatist; *Senior Vice-President, Capital Strategy Research Inc. and Capital Research and Management Company;* b. 16 April 1950, London, England, UK; joined Foreign Affairs Dept 1972, served in Rome, Moscow, Tokyo; Int. Adviser to the Prime Minister 1996–99; fmr staff mem. Office of Nat. Assessments, Dept of Prime Minister and Cabinet; Amb. to USA 2000–05; Sr Vice-Pres. Capital Strategy Research Inc., Washington, DC 2005–, Capital Research and Management Co. 2007–; mem. Bd, Vice-Chair. and Prin. Exec. Officer World Growth and Income Fund; mem. Bd and Vice-Chair. American Funds Global Balanced Fund; mem. Bd of Dirs US Studies Centre, Univ. of Sydney, Lowy Inst. for Int. Policy, Sydney. *Address:* Capital Strategy Research Inc., 3000 K Street NW, Suite 230, Washington, DC 20007-5140, USA (office). *Telephone:* (202) 945-6300 (home).

THÉ, Guy Blaudin de (see DE THÉ, Guy Blaudin).

THEEDE, Steven M., BS; American oil industry executive; b. 1952, Hutchison, Kan.; ed Kan. State Univ.; trained as mechanical engineer; joined Conoco, Houston, Tex. 1974, worked in production, pipelines, refining, marketing, and int. relations, held positions successively as Gen. Dir Assessment and Tech. Devt, Gen. Dir Planning and Admin, Int. Refining and Marketing, Pres. Conoco Pipeline Co., CEO and Gen. Dir Conoco Ltd (UK), Gen. Dir Exploration & Production (E&P) for S and N America, Vice-Pres. Human Resources, Pres. of E&P for Europe (following merger of co. to form ConocoPhilips 2002) 2002–03, for Europe, Russia and the Caspian 2002–03; COO OAO NK Yukos (Yukos Oil Co.), Moscow, Russia 2003–04, CEO 2004–06 (resgnd); mem. Bd of Dirs Serica Energy; fmr Chair. Energy Cttee, US–Russia Business Council 2003. *Address:* 5498 Lynbrook Drive, Houston, TX 77056, USA.

THEIN SEIN, Gen. U; Myanma army officer, politician and head of state; *President;* m. Daw Khin Khin Win; ed Defence Services Acad. 9; held positions of Second and First Sec. in ruling State Peace and Devt Council junta; also served as Chair. govt-sponsored Nat. Convention Convening Comm.; Acting Prime Minister April–Oct. 2007, Prime Minister 2007–11; Pres., Repub. of the Union of Myanmar 2011–; promoted to rank of full Gen. from Lt-Gen. (Myanmar's fourth-highest ranking gen.) 2007. *Address:* Office of the President, Yangon, Myanmar (office). *Telephone:* (office).

THÉMEREAU, Marie-Noëlle; New Caledonian politician; b. 1949; m.; two c.; served as Rep. in Southern Prov. and Congrès 1989–2001, 2004–07, Vice-Pres. Congrès 1999–2001; Vice-Pres. Southern Prov. 1996–99; also fmr Head of Admin; Pres. New Caledonia 2004–07 (resgnd); mem. L'Avenir Ensemble party. *Address:* c/o L'Avenir Ensemble, 2 bis blvd Vauban, Nouméa, New Caledonia. *Telephone:* 281179. *Fax:* 281011. *E-mail:* avenirensemble@lagoon.nc. *Website:* www .avenirensemble.nc.

THEOCHARIS, Reghinos D., PhD; Cypriot economist and academic; *Professor Emeritus, Athens University of Economics and Business;* b. 10 Feb. 1929, Larnaca; s. of Demetrios Theocharis and Florentia Theocharis; m. Madeleine Loumbou 1954; one s. one d.; ed Athens School of Econs, Univ. of Aberdeen and London School of Econs; Insp. of Commercial Educ., Cyprus 1953–56; at LSE 1956–58; Bank of Greece, Athens 1958–59; Minister of Finance in Cyprus Provisional Govt 1959–60; Minister of Finance 1960–62; Gov. of Bank of Cyprus 1962–75; Prof., Athens Univ. of Econs and Business 1975–96, Prof. Emer. 1996–; Dir-Gen. Centre of Planning and Econ. Research (KEPE), Athens 1978–81; Hon. Fellow, LSE 1971. *Publications:* On the Stability of the Cournot Solution on the Oligopoly Problem 1960, Early Developments in Mathematical Economics 1983, The Development of Mathematical Economics: From Cournot to Jevons 1993. *Leisure interests:* chess, gardening. *Address:* 2 Raidestou Street, Kessariani, Athens, 16122, Greece (home). *Telephone:* 2107214531 (home).

THEODORAKIS, Mikis; Greek composer; b. 29 July 1925, island of Chios; s. of Georges Michel Theodorakis and Aspasia Poulaki; m. Myrto Altinoglou 1953; one s. one d.; ed Athens Conservatoire and Paris Conservatoire; joined resistance against German occupation of Greece 1942; arrested and deported during civil war 1947–52; moved to Paris 1953 and studied under Olivier Messiaen; first public concert Sonatina (for pianoforte), Paris 1954; set to bouzouki music the poem Epitaphios by Iannis Ritsos 1958–59 and subsequently wrote numerous other successful songs; Ballet music for Antigone (first performed in London by Dame Margot Fonteyn), Stuttgart Ballet, etc.; returned to Greece 1962; leader Lambrakis youth movt; MP 1963; imprisoned for political activities 1967, released April 1970; lived in Paris 1970–74; resgnd from CP March 1972; MP 1981–1986 (resgnd), 1989–93 (resgnd), Minister of State 1990–92 (resgnd); f. Cttee for Greek-Turkish Friendship 1986; Gold Medal, Moscow Shostakovich Festival 1957, Copley Prize, USA 1957, First Prize Athens Popular Song Festival 1961, Sibelius Award, London 1963, Gold Medal for Film Music, London 1970, Socrates Prize, Stockholm 1974, First Literary Prize, Athens 1987; Lenin Int. Peace Prize 1982. *Works include:* Sinfonia (oratorio) 1944, Love and Death (voice, strings) 1945–48, Assi-Gonia (orchestra) 1945–50, Sextet for Flute 1946, Oedipus Tyrannus (strings) 1946, Greek Carnival (ballet suite) 1947, First Symphony (orchestra) 1948–50, Five Cretan Songs (chorus, orchestra) 1950, Orpheus and Eurydice (ballet) 1952, Barefoot Battalion (film) 1953, Suite No. 1 (four movements, piano and orchestra) 1954, Poèmes d'Eluard (Cycle 1 and Cycle 2) 1955, Suite No. 2 (chorus, orchestra) 1956, Suite No. 3 (five movements, soprano, chorus, orchestra) 1956, Ill Met by Moonlight (film) 1957, Sonatina No. 1 (violin, piano) 1957, Les amants de Teruel (ballet) 1958, Piano Concerto 1958, Sonatina No. 2 (violin, piano) 1958, Antigone (ballet) 1958, Epitaphios (song cycle) 1959, Deserters (song cycle) 1958, Epiphania (song cycle) 1959, Honeymoon (film) 1960, Phoenician Women – Euripides (theatre music) 1960, Axion Esti (pop oratorio) 1960, Electra-Euripides (film), Phaedra (film) 1962, The Hostage (song cycle) 1962, The Ballad of the Dead Brother (musical tragedy) 1962, Zorba the Greek (film), The Ballad of Mauthausen (song cycle) 1965, Romiossini (song cycle) 1965, Lisistrata – Aristophanes (theatre music) 1966, Romancero Gitano (Lorca) (song cycle) 1967, Sun and Time (song cycle) 1967, Arcadias Nos. 1–10 (song cycles) 1968–69, Canto General (Pablo Neruda) (pop oratorio) 1972, Z (film), Etat de Siège (film) 1973, Ballads (song cycle) 1975, Symphony No. 2 (orchestra and piano) 1981, Messe Byzantine (Liturgie) 1982, Symphony No. 3 (orchestra, chorus, soprano) 1982, Sadoukeon Passion (cantata for orchestra, chorus, soloists) 1983, Liturgie No. 2 1983, Symphony No. 7 (orchestra, chorus, soloists) 1983, Requiem 1985, Kostas Kariotakis (opera in two acts) 1985, Beatrice (song cycle) 1987, Faces of the Sun (song cycle) 1987, Symphony No. 4 1987, Memory of Stone (song cycle) 1987, Like an Ancient Wind (song cycle) 1987, Canto Olympico (symphony) 1991, Medea (opera) 1990, Electra (opera) 1993. *Publications include:* La Dette, Journals of Resistance 1972, Ballad of the Dead Brother, Culture and dimensions politiques 1973, Star System, Antimanifeste, Les chemins de l'Archange (autobiog.), 4 vols 1986–92. *Address:* Epifanous 1, Akropolis, 117 42 Athens, Greece. *Telephone:* (1) 9214863. *Fax:* (1) 9236325. *Website:* en.mikis-theodorakis.net.

THÉODORE, Jean-François; French stock exchange executive; *Global Head of Technology, NYSE Euronext;* b. 5 Dec. 1946, Paris; s. of Charles Théodore and Aimée Chevallier; m. Claudine Lefèbvre 1976; one s. two d.; ed Lycées Montaigne and Louis-le-Grand, Faculty of Law, Paris, Institut d'études politiques de Paris;

Ecole nat. d'admin 1971–74; civil servant, Ministry of Econ. and Finance 1974–78, Crédit nat. 1978–80, Head, Bureau des états africains et de la zone franc 1980–82, Head, Bureau des investissements étrangers en France et français à l'étranger 1982–84, Asst Dir Etablissements de crédit 1984–86, Deputy Dir, Head of Funding and Investment Dept, Treasury 1986–90; Gen. Man. Soc. des bourses françaises 1990–91, Chair. and CEO 1991–; Pres. Int. Fed. of Stock Exchanges 1993–94, Fed. of European Stock Exchanges 1998–; Vice-Pres. Soc. interprofessionelle de compensation des valeurs mobilières (Sicovam) 1992, Chair. 1993–; Pres. Matif SA 1998–; Chair. Euronext 2000–07, Deputy CEO NYSE Euronext (after acquisition of Euronext by New York Stock Exchange) 2007–09, Global Head of Tech. 2009–; Chevalier, Ordre nat. du Mérite, Légion d'honneur; Prix Andese du financier 2000. *Leisure interests:* opera, American cinema, theatre. *Address:* NYSE Euronext, Société des bourses françaises, 39 rue Cambon, 75001 Paris, France (office). *Telephone:* 1-49-27-10-00 (office). *Fax:* 1-49-27-14-33 (office). *E-mail:* d.lande@ euronext.fr (office). *Website:* www.euronext.fr (office); www.nyse.com (office).

THEOPHILOS, Theophilou V., MA; Cypriot lawyer and fmr diplomatist; b. 9 Sept. 1946, Limnia, Famagusta; ed Athens Univ., Stanford Univ., USA; lawyer in Famagusta 1971–73; Attaché, Cultural Div., Ministry of Foreign Affairs 1974, Head of EEC Desk 1974–76, Sec., Political Affairs Div. (Question of Cyprus) 1977–78, Head of Cyprus Question Desk 1979–81, Deputy Dir Political Div. 1985–86, Dir Office of Minister of Foreign Affairs 1993, Dir European Div. 1993–96; Consul Gen., New York, USA 1981–84; in charge of Orgs of NAM Foreign Ministers Conf., Nicosia 1987–88; High Commr to India with concurrent accreditation to nine other countries 1989–93; Amb. to Germany (also accred to Poland and the Holy See) 1996–2000; Perm. Rep. to EU 2000–04; mem. Bd of Dirs Laiki Group 2005; mem. Cyprus Bar Asscn. *Publications:* numerous articles in Cypriot newspapers and magazines. *Address:* 16 Panteli Katelari, Diagoras Bldg, Nicosia 1306, Cyprus (office). *Telephone:* 22660767 (office). *Fax:* 22678777 (office). *E-mail:* montanios@montanioslaw.com.cy (office).

THEOPHILUS III, His Beatitude Patriarch of the Holy City of Jerusalem and all Palestine, Syria, beyond the Jordan river, Cana of Galilee and Holy Zion (Ilija Jannopoulos); Greek ecclesiastic; b. 1952, Messinia, Greece; ed Univ. of Athens, Durham Univ.; entered Brotherhood of Holy Sepulchre 1964; attended Patriarchal school in Jerusalem 1964–70; tonsured monk with name of Theophilus 1970; ordained deacon 1970; ordained priest 1975; attended Athens Univ. and later worked in Jerusalem at Gen. Secr. of the Holy Synod, Patriarchal School, and St Charalampy's Monastery; elevated to rank of archimandrite 1978; apptd mem. Editorial Bd Nea Zion journal 1981; sent to UK to study at Durham Univ. 1981; Sec. for Foreign Relations, Holy Synod of the Patriarchate of Jerusalem 1986–88; Rep. Patriarchate of Jerusalem in Cen. Cttee, World Council of Churches 1988–91; hegumen, Monastery of St George the Victorious, Cana Galilee 1991–96; Rep. of Patriarchate of Jerusalem with Patriarch of Moscow and All Russia and Rector, Jerusalem Representation Church, Moscow 2001–03; Patriarchal epitrop, Doha Qatar 2003–04; Senior Custodian Holy Sepulchre and mem. Holy Synod of Patriarchate of Jerusalem 2004–05; Archbishop of Mount Tabor Feb. 2005; elected Patriarch of Jerusalem Aug., enthroned Nov. 2005. *Address:* Greek Orthodox Patriarchate, PO Box 14518, 91145 Jerusalem, Israel (office). *Telephone:* 2-6271657 (office). *Fax:* 2-6261283 (office). *E-mail:* patriarch .theophilos@jerusalem-patriarchate.info (office). *Website:* www.jerusalem -patriarchate.org (office).

THERON, Charlize; South African actress; b. 7 Aug. 1975, Benoni, SA; trained as ballet dancer; went to Milan aged 16 to become a model; moved to New York to dance with Joffrey Ballet; knee injury ended dancing career; moved to Los Angeles to take up acting; appointed UN Messenger of Peace 2008–; Los Angeles Film Festival Spirit of Independence Award 2006. *Films include:* Children of the Corn III 1994, Two Days in the Valley 1996, That Thing You Do! 1996, Trial and Error 1997, Hollywood Confidential 1997, Devil's Advocate 1997, Cop Land/The Yards 1997, Mighty Joe Young 1998, Celebrity 1998, The Cider House Rules 1999, The Astronaut's Wife 1999, The Yards 2000, Reindeer Games 2000, Men of Honor 2000, The Legend of Bagger Vance 2000, Navy Diver 2000, Sweet November 2001, The Curse of the Jade Scorpion 2001, 15 Minutes 2001, The Yards/Nightwatch 2002, Waking Up in Reno 2002, Trapped 2002, 24 Hours 2002, Sweet Home Alabama (exec. producer) 2002, The Italian Job 2003, Monster (Golden Globe Award, Best Dramatic Actress 2004, Critics' Choice Award, Best Actress 2004, Screen Actors Guild Best Actress Award 2004, Acad. Award, Best Actress 2004) 2003, The Life and Death of Peter Sellers 2004, Head in the Clouds 2004, North Country 2005, Aeonflux 2005, In the Valley of Elah 2007, Battle in Seattle 2007, Hancock 2008, The Burning Plain 2008, Young Adult 2011, Snow White and the Huntsman 2012, Prometheus 2012. *Address:* c/o Spanky Taylor, 3727 West Magnolia, Burbank, CA 91505 (office); c/o United Talent Agency, Inc., 9560 Wilshire Blvd., Suite 500, Beverly Hills, CA 90212, USA.

THEROUX, Paul Edward, BA, FRSL, FRGS; American writer; b. 10 April 1941, Medford, Mass; s. of Albert Eugene Theroux and Anne Dittami Theroux; m. 1st Anne Castle 1967 (divorced 1993), two s.; m. 2nd Sheila Donnelly 1995; ed Univ. of Massachusetts; Lecturer, Univ. of Urbino, Italy 1963, Soche Hill Coll., Malawi 1963–65, Makerere Univ., Kampala, Uganda 1965–68, Univ. of Singapore 1968–71; Writer-in-Residence, Univ. of Va 1972; Hon. DLitt (Tufts Univ., Trinity Univ.) 1983, (Univ. of Mass.) 1988; Playboy magazine Editorial Awards 1972, 1976, 1977, 1979. *Play:* The White Man's Burden 1987. *Screenplay:* Saint Jack 1979, Chinese Box (story) 1997. *Publications:* fiction: Waldo 1967, Fong and the Indians 1968, Girls at Play 1969, Murder in Mount Holly 1969, Jungle Lovers 1971, Sinning with Annie 1972, Saint Jack 1973, The Black House 1974, The Family Arsenal 1976, The Consul's File 1977, Picture Palace (Whitbread Award) 1978, A Christmas Card 1978, London Snow 1980, World's End 1980, The Mosquito Coast (James Tait Black Memorial Prize 1982, Yorkshire Post Best Novel Award 1982) 1981, The London Embassy 1982, Doctor Slaughter 1984, O-Zone 1986, My Secret History 1988, Chicago Loop 1990, Dr. DeMarr 1990, Millroy the Magician 1993, My Other Life 1996, Kowloon Tong 1997, Collected Stories 1997, Collected Short Novels 1998, Hotel Honolulu 2000, The Stranger at the Palazzo d'Oro (short stories) 2002, Telling Tales (contrib. to charity anthology) 2004, Blinding Light 2005, The Elephanta Suite 2007, A Dead Hand: A Crime in Calcutta 2009, The Lower River 2012; non-fiction: V. S. Naipaul (criticism) 1973, The Great Railway Bazaar (travel) 1975, The Old Patagonian Express (travel) 1979, The Kingdom by the Sea (travel) 1983, Sailing through China (travel) 1983, Sunrise with Sea Monsters (travel) 1985, Riding the Iron Rooster: By Train Through China (travel) (Thomas Cook Prize for Best Literary Travel Book 1989) 1988, Travelling the World (travel) 1990, The Happy Isles of Oceania: Paddling the Pacific (travel) 1992, The Pillars of Hercules (travel) 1995, Sir Vidia's Shadow: A Friendship Across Five Continents (travel) 1998, Fresh-Air Fiend (travel) 1999, The Worst Journey in the World 2000, Nurse Wolf and Dr Sacks 2000, Dark Star Safari: Overland from Cairo to Cape Town (travel) 2002, Ghost Train to the Eastern Star (travel) 2008, The Tao of Travel 2011, The Last Train to Zona Verde: My Ultimate African Safari 2013. *Leisure interest:* rowing. *Address:* Hamish Hamilton Ltd, 80 Strand, London, WC2, England (office); The Wylie Agency, 250 West 57th Street, New York NY 10107, USA (office).

THEVENOUX, Sophie; Monegasque politician and diplomatist; *Ambassador to France;* m.; two c.; Head of Admin and Finance, Seigneurie Caraïbes, Elf Group, Guadeloupe 1981–82; Financial Officer, Gen. Mills Toys and Games, France 1982–86; Deputy Dir of the Budget and Treasury 1995–99, Dir 1999–2005, Dir-Gen. Dept of Finance and the Economy 2005–09, Govt Councillor for Finance and the Economy 2009–11; Amb. to France 2011–; Officier, Ordre de Saint-Charles. *Address:* Embassy of Monaco, 22 boulevard Suchet, 75116 Paris, France (office). *Telephone:* 1-45-04-74-54 (office). *Fax:* 1-45-04-45-16 (office). *E-mail:* ambassade .en.france@gouv.mc (office).

THEWLIS, David; British actor; b. 20 March 1963; s. of Alec Raymond Wheeler and Maureen Wheeler (née Thewlis); m. Sara Jocelyn Sugarman 1992 (divorced 1993); ed Highfield High School, Blackpool, St Anne's Coll. of Further Educ., Guildhall School of Music and Drama, London. *Theatre includes:* Buddy Holly at the Regal, Ice Cream, Lady and the Clarinet (winner Edin. Fringe First), The Sea. *Television includes:* Valentine Park (series) 1985, The Singing Detective (mini-series) 1986, The Short and Curlies (film) 1987, Skulduggery (film) 1989, Bit of a Do (series) 1989, Oranges Are Not the Only Fruit (film) 1990, Journey to Knock (film) (Best Actor, Rheims Film Festival 1992) 1991, Filipina Dreamgirls (film) 1991, Prime Suspect 3 1993, Dandelion Dead (miniseries) 1994, Endgame (film) 2000. *Films include:* Road 1987, Vroom 1988, Little Dorrit 1988, Resurrected 1989, Life is Sweet 1990, Afraid of the Dark 1991, Damage 1992, The Trial 1993, Naked (Best Actor, Cannes Film Festival, Nat. Soc. of Film Critics Awards Best Actor 1994, New York Film Critics Circle Awards Best Actor 1993) 1993, Black Beauty 1994, Total Eclipse 1995, Restoration 1995, James and the Giant Peach (voice) 1996, Dragonheart 1996, The Island of Dr Moreau 1996, Seven Years in Tibet 1997, Divorcing Jack 1998, The Big Lebowski 1998, Besieged 1998, Whatever Happened to Harold Smith 1999, Gangster No. 1 2000, Timeline 2003, Harry Potter and the Prisoner of Azkaban 2004, Kingdom of Heaven 2005, All the Invisible Children 2005, The New World 2005, Basic Instinct 2 2006, The Omen 2006, The Inner Life of Martin Frost 2007, Harry Potter and the Order of the Phoenix 2007, The Boy in the Striped Pyjamas 2008, Harry Potter and the Half-Blood Prince 2009, Harry Potter and the Deathly Hallows: Part 1 2010, War Horse 2011, The Lady 2011. *Publication:* The Late Hector Kipling (novel) 2007. *Leisure interest:* painting.

THIAM, Tidjane, MBA; French/Côte d'Ivoirian business executive; *Group Chief Executive, Prudential plc;* b. 29 July 1962, Côte d'Ivoire; ed École Polytechnique, Paris, École Nationale Supérieure des Mines de Paris, Institut Européen d'Admin des Affaires (INSEAD), World Bank's Young Professionals Program, USA; moved with family to Morocco aged four; brought up in France; studied engineering in France before joining McKinsey & Co. (man. consultants), Paris, London and New York 1986; Chief Exec. then Chair. Nat. Bureau for Tech. Studies and Devt in Côte d'Ivoire 1994–97; Pres. Nat. Council on Information Superhighways and Nat. Soc. for Human Resources Devt 1997–98; Minister of Planning and Devt 1998–99; arrested and held for several weeks following mil. coup 1999; returned to France to become a Pnr with McKinsey & Co. 2000–02; apptd CEO Europe, Aviva 2002, later Group Strategy and Devt Dir and Man. Aviva International –2008; Exec. Dir Prudential plc 2008–, Chief Financial Officer –2009, Group Chief Exec. 2009–; Chair. G20 High Level Panel for Infrastructure Investment Jan.–Nov. 2011; Dir (non-exec.) Arkema (France) –2009; mem. External Advisory Council of World Bank Inst. 1999–, Africa Progress Panel chaired by Kofi Annan 2007–, Council of the Overseas Devt Inst., London, Bd of Asscn of British Insurers (Chair. 2012–), Int. Business Council of World Econ. Forum, European Financial Round Table 2013–; sponsor of Opportunity International; Chevalier, Légion d'honneur 2011; named by World Econ. Forum, Davos as one of the annual 100 Global Leaders for Tomorrow 1998, as a mem. of the Dream Cabinet 1999, named by The Observer amongst The 100 powerful black Britons who are changing the world (fifth) 2007, (second) 2008. *Address:* Prudential plc, Laurence Pountney Hill, London, EC4R 0HH, England (office). *Telephone:* (20) 7548-3901 (office). *Fax:* (20) 7548-3631 (office). *E-mail:* info@prudential.co.uk (office). *Website:* www.prudential.co.uk (office).

THIBAUDET, Jean-Yves; French pianist; b. 7 Sept. 1961, Lyon; ed Paris Conservatoire, Lyon Conservatory of Music; now based in LA and Paris; appears with major orchestras in USA and Europe including Royal Concertgebouw, London Philharmonic, Royal Philharmonic, Orchestre Nat. de France etc.; regular visitor to major US and European music festivals; in recital has collaborated with mezzo-sopranos Brigitte Fassbaender and Cecilia Bartoli, Renee Fleming and cellist Truls Mørk; debut, BBC Promenade Concerts 1992, regular appearances since then; records exclusively for Decca (over 20 recordings); Chevalier, Ordre des Arts et des Lettres 2001; Prix du Conservatoire, Paris Conservatory 1976, winner, Young Concert Artists Auditions 1981, Echo Award 1990, 1998, Schallplattenpreis 1992, Gramophone Award 1998, Edison Prize 1998, Choc de la Musique 1999, 2003, Diapason d'Or for his recordings of works by Debussy 2000, Premio Pegasus 2002, Echo Classical Music Awards 2002. *Films:* Portrait of a Lady 1997, Bride of the Wind 2001. *Television:* Piano Grand! (PBS/Smithsonian Special) 2000. *Leisure interests:* tennis, swimming, riding, water-skiing, museums, movies, racing cars. *Address:* c/o IMG Artists, Carnegie Hall Tower, 152 West 57th Street, 5th Floor, New York, NY 10019 (office); c/o M. L. Falcone Public Relations, 155 West 68th Street, Suite 1114, New York, NY 10023, USA (office). *E-mail:* artistsny@imgartists.com (office).

THIBAULT, Bernard; French trade union official; b. 2 Jan. 1959, Paris; m.; two c.; ed station of Noisy-le-Sec; apprentice, Société Nationale des Chemins de fer Français (SNCF) 1974–76; joined Confédération Générale du Travail (CGT) 1977, responsible for the Youth Cttee, Sec. syndicat de son dépôt 1980–82, Sec. CGT railway Paris-Est 1982–87, joined Fed. Bureau of CGT railway 1987, Deputy Sec.-Gen. 1990–93, Gen. Sec. CGT railway 1993–99, Sec.-Gen. CGT 1999–2013; joined Parti communiste français (PCF) 1987, mem. Nat. Council of PCF 1997–2001. *Publications:* Qu'est-ce que la CGT? 2002, Ma voix ouvrière: entretiens avec Pierre-Marie Thiaville et Marcel Trillat 2004. *Address:* c/o Confédération Générale du Travail, 263 rue de Paris, 93 516 Montreuil Cedex, France. *E-mail:* info@cgt.fr.

THICH, Quang Do; Vietnamese Buddhist leader; b. (Dang Phuc Tue), 27 Nov. 1928, Thai Binh Prov.; in exile in India and Sri Lanka; taught Buddhist philosophy in Saigon in the 1960s and 1970s; fmr leader Unified Buddhist Church of Vietnam, currently Deputy Leader; imprisoned by Communist authorities; released 1998, launched Appeal for Democracy in Vietnam plan and was placed under house arrest in Thanh Minh Temple 2001; shared Homo Homini Award for human rights activism, People in Need (Czech Repub.) 2002, Thorolf Rafto Memorial Prize 2006, chosed by A Different View magazine as one of the 15 Champions of World Democracy 2008. *Address:* Thanh Zinh Zen Monastery, Ho Chi Minh City, Viet Nam.

THIEBAUD, Wayne, MA; American artist and academic; *Professor Emeritus, University of California, Davis;* b. 15 Nov. 1920, Mesa, Ariz.; m. 1st Patricia Patterson 1945 (divorced 1959); two d.; m. 2nd Betty Jean Carr 1959; one s. one step s.; ed Frank Wiggins Trade School, Long Beach Jr Coll., San. José State Coll. (now San José State Univ.), California State Coll. (now California State Univ.); worked as commercial artist and freelance cartoonist from 1938; served USAAF 1942–45; started career as painter 1947; Asst Prof., Dept of Art, Univ. of Calif., Davis 1960, Assoc. Prof. 1963–67, apptd Prof. 1967, Faculty Research Lecturer 1973–, currently Prof. Emer.; co-founder Artists Co-operative Gallery (now Artists Contemporary Gallery), Sacramento 1958; numerous one-man exhbns in USA since 1950; one-man exhbn Galleria Schwarz, Milan, Italy 1963; represented USA at São Paulo Bienal, Brazil 1968; commissioned to do paintings of Wimbledon tennis tournament, England 1968; selected as Nat. Blazer for Nat. Endowment for the Arts, Washington, DC 1972; commissioned by US Dept of Interior to paint Yosemite Ridge Line for Bicentennial Exhbn, America 1976; mem. American Acad., Inst. of Arts and Letters, New York City 1985; Nat. Acad. of Design, New York City; Award of Distinction, Nat. Art Schools Asscn and Special Citation Award, Nat. Asscn of Schools of Art and Design 1984, Nat. Medal of the Arts 1994. *Publication:* Wayne Thiebaud: Private Drawings—The Artist's Sketchbook 1987. *Address:* Department of Art, University of California, 1 Shields Avenue, Davis, CA 95616, USA (office). *Telephone:* (530) 752-3135 (office). *Website:* art.ucdavis.edu (office).

THIELEN, Gunter, DEng; German business executive; *Chairman, Supervisory Board, Bertelsmann SE Co. KGaA;* b. 4 Aug. 1942, Quierschied, Saarland; ed Tech. Univ. of Aachen; various man. positions with BASF, Ludwigshafen 1970; Tech. Dir Wintershall Refinery, Kassel 1976; joined Bertelsmann AG as CEO Maul Belser printing co., Nuremberg 1980, mem. Exec. Bd Bertelsmann AG 1985, Head Print and Industrial Operations Div. (renamed Bertelsmann Arvato AG) 1985–2002, Chair. and CEO 2002–07, mem. Bertelsmann SE Co. KGaA Supervisory Bd 2002–, Chair. 2007–; Chair. Bertelsmann Stiftung (Foundation), Gütersloh 2001, 2007–; Chair. Bertelsmann Verwaltungsgesellschaft mbH (BVG) 2001; Johns Hopkins Univ. Global Leadership Award 2005. *Address:* Supervisory Board, Bertelsmann SE Co. KGaA, Carl-Bertelsmann-Str. 270, 33311 Gütersloh, Germany (office). *Telephone:* (5241) /80-0 (office). *Fax:* (5241) 80-62321 (office). *Website:* www.bertelsmann.com (office).

THIEMANN, Bernd, PhD; German banker and business executive; *Chairman of the Supervisory Board, Hypo Real Estate Holding AG;* ed Univs of Münster and Freiburg; early man. positions with German Sparkasse org.; mem. Man. Bd Nord/LB 1976, Chair. 1981–91; Chair. Man. Bd and CEO DG Bank 1991–2001; Pnr, Man. Dir and Sr Adviser, Leonardo & Co. GmbH & Co. KG (fmrly Drueker & Co. GmbH & Co. KG) 2005–09; Chair. Supervisory Bd Rothschild GmbH 2001–, Constantin Medien AG (fmrly EM.Sport Media AG) 2001–, Celanese AG of Celanese Corpn 2004–, Hypo Real Estate Holding AG 2009–, Deputy Chair. Advisory Bd Wurth Group; fmr Deputy Chair. Supervisory Bd Berentzen-Gruppe AG; mem. Supervisory Bd Nordland Papier AG –2002, VEBA Oel AG –2002, Deutsche Euroshop AG 2004–, M.M. Warburg Bank & Co. KGaA, ThyssenKrupp Stainless AG; fmr mem. Supervisory Bd Suedzucker AG; mem. Econ. Advisory Group, Fraport AG. *Address:* Hypo Real Estate Holding AG, Unsöldstrasse 2, 80538 Munich, Germany (office). *Telephone:* (89) 2030-070 (office). *Fax:* (89) 2030-077-72 (office). *E-mail:* info@hyporealestate.com (office). *Website:* www.hyporealestate.com (office).

THIEME, Reiner; German business executive; *Chairman of the Supervisory Board, ZF Friedrichshafen AG;* Chair. Keiper Recaro Group 1979–87; joined Wilhelm Karmann GmbH, Osnabrück 1987, Chair. Bd of Man. 1990–2003; Chair. Supervisory Bd ZF Friedrichshafen AG 2003–; fmr Vice-Pres. German Automobile Industry Asscn (VDA). *Address:* ZF Friedrichshafen AG, Graf-von-Soden-Platz 1, 88046 Friedrichshafen, Germany (office). *Telephone:* (7541) 77-0 (office). *Fax:* (7541) 77-908000 (office). *E-mail:* postoffice@zf.com (office). *Website:* www.zf.com (office).

THIER, Samuel Osiah, MD; American physician and academic; *Professor Emeritus of Medicine and Health Care Policy, Harvard Medical School;* b. 23 June 1937, Brooklyn, NY; s. of Sidney Thier and May H. Thier; m. Paula Dell Finkelstein 1958; three d.; ed Cornell Univ., State Univ. of New York, Syracuse; Intern, Massachusetts Gen. Hosp. 1960–61, Asst Resident 1961–62, 1964–65, Postdoctoral Fellow 1965, Chief Resident in Medicine 1966, Pres. 1994–97; Clinical Assoc. Nat. Inst. of Arthritis and Metabolic Diseases 1962–64; Instructor to Asst Prof., Harvard Medical School 1967–69, Prof. of Medicine and Health Care Policy 1994–2007, Prof. Emer. 2006–; Assoc. Prof. then Prof. of Medicine, Univ. of Pennsylvania Medical School 1969–74; Prof. and Chair. Dept of Medicine, Yale Univ. School of Medicine and Chief of Medicine, Yale-New Haven Hosp. 1975–85; Pres. Inst. of Medicine, NAS 1985–91; Pres. and Prof., Brandeis Univ. 1991–94; Pres. Partners Healthcare System Inc. 1994–2002, CEO 1996–2002. *Publications:* numerous articles and chapters in medical journals and textbooks. *Address:* Massachusetts General Hospital, 55 Fruit Street, Bulfinch 370, Boston, MA 02114,

USA (office). *Telephone:* (617) 726-1811 (office). *Fax:* (617) 726-1900 (office). *E-mail:* sthier@partners.org (office).

THIERSE, Wolfgang; German politician; b. 22 Oct. 1943, Breslau; ed Humboldt Univ.; fmr typesetter; teaching asst, Dept of Cultural Theory and Aesthetics, Humboldt Univ., Berlin 1964; mem. staff, Ministry of Culture, GDR 1975–76, Cen. Inst. for History of Literature, Acad. of Sciences, GDR 1977–90; Chair. Social Democratic Party, GDR (which later factioned) 1990; mem. Bundestag (Parl.) 1990–, Pres. 1998–2005, Vice-Pres. 2005–13. *Publications include:* The Right Life in a False System, The Future of the East. *Address:* Bundestag, Platz der Republik 1, 11011 Berlin (office); Hagenauer Straße 3, 10435 Berlin, Germany. *Telephone:* (30) 22777028 (office). *Fax:* (30) 22776928 (office). *E-mail:* wolfgang.thierse@ bundestag.de (office). *Website:* www.bundestag.de (office); www.thierse.de.

THIESSEN, Gordon, OC, BA, MA, PhD; Canadian economist, company director and fmr central banker; b. 14 Aug. 1938, South Porcupine, Ont.; m. Annette Hillyar 1964; two c.; ed Univ. of Saskatchewan, London School of Econs, UK; joined Bank of Canada 1963; Visiting Economist, Reserve Bank of Australia 1973–75; Adviser to Gov. Bank of Canada 1979, Deputy Gov. responsible for econ. research and financial analysis 1984, Sr Deputy Gov. 1987, Chair. Bd of Dirs, mem. Exec. Cttee 1987, Gov. 1994–2001; fmr Exec.-in-Residence, Univ. of Ottawa School of Man.; Chair. Canadian Public Accountability Bd 2003–; mem. Bd of Dirs IPSCO Inc., Inst. for Research on Public Policy, Univ. of Saskatchewan; Swedish Order of the Polar Star, Commdr, Order of the North Star; Dr hc (Univ. of Saskatchewan, Univ. of Ottawa). *Leisure interests:* skiing, sailing.

THIJS, Johan, MSc; Belgian business executive; *Group CEO, KBC Group NV;* b. 1965; ed Catholic Univ. of Louvain; various actuarial functions in life and non-life insurance, ABB Insurance 1988–95, Head of Non-life Dept, Limburg regional office, ABB Insurance 1995–98; Prov. Man., Limburg and Eastern Belgium, KBC Insurance 1998–2001, Sr Gen. Man., Non-life Insurance, KBC Insurance 2001–09, mem. Exec. Cttee KBC Group, CEO Belgium Business Unit 2009–12, Group CEO KBC Group NV 2012–. *Address:* KBC Group NV, Havenlaan 2, Brussels 1080, Belgium (office). *Telephone:* (2) 429-50-45 (office). *Fax:* (2) 429-63-40 (office). *E-mail:* johan.thijs@kbc.be (office). *Website:* www.kbc.be (office).

THIKEO, Lien; Laotian politician; *Minister of Finance;* several years with Ministry of Finance, including as Vice-Pres., Planning and Investment Cttee and Vice-Pres., Planning and Cooperation Cttee, fmr Deputy Minister of Industry and Handicraft, Minister of Finance 2014–; Gov. Sayabouri Prov. and Sec., Sayabouri LPRP Party Cttee 2006–14; mem. Lao People's Revolutionary Party (LPRP), mem. Cen. Cttee. *Address:* Ministry of Finance, 23 rue Singha, Ban Phonxay, BP 24, Vientiane, Laos (office). *Telephone:* (21) 900798 (office). *Fax:* (21) 900798 (home). *E-mail:* ict@mof.gov.la (office). *Website:* www.mof.gov.la (office).

THINLEY, Jigmi Yozer, MA; Bhutanese politician; b. 1952, Bumthang; ed St Stephen's Coll., India, Pennsylvania State Univ., USA; mem. civil service 1954–1983, Head, Royal Civil Service Comm. Secr., Dir Educ. Dept; fmr Perm. Rep. to UN, New York; Chair. Council of Ministers 1998–99; Minister of Foreign Affairs 1998–2003; Prime Minister, Chair. and Minister of Home and Cultural Affairs 2003–04; Minister of Home and Cultural Affairs 2004–07 (resgnd); Founder-Pres. Druk Phuensum Tshogpa (DPT) party 2007–13; Prime Minister 2008–13; Red Scarf 1987, Druk Thuksey and Coronation Medals 1999, Druk Wangyal Medal 2008. *Address:* Druk Phuensum Tshogpa (DPT), Chang Lam, Thimphu, Bhutan (office). *Telephone:* (2) 336336 (office). *Fax:* (2) 335845 (office). *E-mail:* dpt@druknet.bt (office). *Website:* www.dpt.bt (office).

THINOT, Dominique Pierre; French painter, teacher and diplomatist; *Professor and Director of Programmes for Public Art, École Nationale Supérieure des Arts Décoratifs;* b. 3 Oct. 1948, Paris; s. of Pierre Thinot and Y. Hervé; m. Claire Moreau 1977; two s.; ed Diplômé d'études supérieures, Paris; Prof., École Nationale Supérieure des Arts Décoratifs, Paris 1972–, Dir of Programmes for Public Art; has taught at various univs in Asia 1980–; leader of several cultural missions to Japan, Singapore, Korea and China 1985–; Pres. Asscn of Artists of the Bateau-Lavoir, Paris; mem. Gruppe Sieben, Germany 1975–; currently Chargé de Misson pour l'Asie, Int. Relations; Prof., Xi'an Acad. of Fine Arts, China; ECPD Special Counsellor, European Centre for Peace and Devt, Univ. for Peace est. by the UN; Artistic Dir Socs de construction européennes et asiatiques; dir of public art projects; adviser to artistic projects at univs; Chevalier, Ordre des Tastevins (Clos de Vougeot); Prix de la Création Artistique, Ministry of Cultural Affairs 1971, 1974, Prix de l'Acad. des Beaux-Arts 1983, Distinction du Govt de la République Arabe d'Egypte 1996. *Television:* numerous reports for TV networks in France, Japan, Korea, China and Taiwan. *Leisure interests:* music, oenology. *Address:* Bateau-Lavoir, 13 place Emile Goudeau, 75018 Paris (home); 13 route des Vieilles-Vignes, 17880 Les Portes, Ile-de-Ré, France (home). *Telephone:* 1-78-11-30-08 (home). *E-mail:* artpublic3000@gmail.com (office); contact@dominiquethinot.com (home). *Website:* www.ensad.fr (office).

THODEY, David I., BA, FAICD; Australian business executive; *CEO, Telstra Corporation Ltd;* b. Perth, WA; ed Victoria Univ., NZ, Kellogg Post-Grad. School Gen. Man. Program, Northwestern Univ., USA; began as systems engineer at IBM, held several sr exec. positions in marketing and sales across Asia Pacific, CEO IBM Australia/NZ –2001; Group Man. Dir Telstra Mobiles, Telstra Corpn Ltd 2001–02, Group Man. Dir Telstra Enterprise and Govt 2002–09, responsible for corp., govt and large business customers in Australia, TelstraClear in NZ and int. sales div., Chair. TelstraClear New Zealand 2003–09, CEO Telstra Corpn Ltd 2009–; Chair. Basketball Australia 2008–10, Sensis Pty Ltd 2009–; mem. Bd GSM Asscn 2013–; Fellow, Australian Inst. of Co. Dirs. *Address:* Telstra Corporation Ltd, 242 Exhibition Street, Melbourne, Vic. 3000, Australia (office). *Telephone:* (3) 9634-6400 (office). *Fax:* (3) 9632-3215 (office). *E-mail:* info@telstra.com.au (office). *Website:* www.telstra.com.au (office).

THOHIR, Garibaldi, BBA, MBA; Indonesian coal mining executive; *President Director, PT Adaro Energy Tbk;* b. 1 May 1965, Jakarta; m. Alinda G. Thohir; one s. two d.; ed Univ. of Southern California, Northrop Univ., Los Angeles, USA; began career by forming holding co. for family business 1991; entered coal mining industry with acquisition of minority interest in PT Allied Indo Coal (small coal jt venture), S Sumatra 1991, bought out jt venture pnr 1998, currently Pres. Dir; acquired PT Padangbara Sukses Makmur 2003, currently Pres. Dir; acquired

Adaro Indonesia (coal mining co.) 2005, currently Pres. Dir PT Adaro Energy Tbk; f. PT Wahana Ottomitra Multiartha (PT WOM Finance TbK) 1997, currently Pres. Commr; Pres. Dir PT Trinugraha Thohir, PT Alam Tri Abadi, PT Dianlia Setyamukti, PT Jasapower Indonesia; Pres. Commr PT Trinugraha Food Industri, PT Wahanaartha Harsaka, PT Wahanaartha Motorent, PT Makmur Sejahtera Wisesa, PT Karunia Barito Sejahtera; Dir PT Indonesia Bulk Terminal. *Leisure interests:* sports, travelling with family. *Address:* PT Adaro Indonesia, Menara Karya, 22nd floor, Jln. H.R. Rasuna Said, Blok X-5, Kav. 1-2, Jakarta 12950, Indonesia (office). *Telephone:* (21) 5211265 (office). *Fax:* (21) 5211266 (office). *Website:* www.adaro.com (office).

THOMAS, Betty; American film director and actress; b. 27 July 1948, St Louis, Mo.; ed Ohio Univ., Chicago Art Inst., Roosevelt Univ.; fmr mem. Second City improvisation group, Chicago; performed at the Comedy Store, Los Angeles. *Films include:* actress: Tunnelvision 1976, Chesty Anderson: US Navy 1976, Jackson County Jail 1976, Loose Shoes 1980, Used Cars 1980, Homework 1982, Troop Beverly Hills 1989; director: Only You 1992, The Brady Bunch Movie 1995, Private Parts 1997, Dr Dolittle 1998, 28 Days 2000, I Spy (also producer) 2002, R3 2003, John Tucker Must Die 2006; producer: Can't Hardly Wait 1998, Surviving Christmas 2004; exec. producer: Charlie's Angels 2000. *Television include:* director: (series) Doogie Howser MD, Dream On (Emmy Award 1993), Hooperman, Mancuso FBI, Arresting Behavior, Couples; (film) My Breast; (documentary drama) The Late Shift (Directors' Guild of America Award 1997); (actress) (series) Hill Street Blues (Emmy Award 1985); (films) Outside Chance, Nashville Grab, When Your Lover Leaves, Prison for Children. *Address:* c/o Creative Artists Agency, 2000 Avenue of the Stars, Los Angeles, CA 90067, USA (office).

THOMAS, Chantal; French essayist; *Director of Research, Centre National de la Recherche Scientifique (CNRS);* b. 1945, Lyon; specialist in eighteenth century history; biographical publs on Sade, Casanova, Thomas Berhard and Marie-Antoinette; debut novel Adieux à la Reine sold over 110,000 copies and translated into German, English, Korean, Greek, Italian, Japanese, Dutch and Portugese 2002; currently Dir of Research, CNRS. *Publications include:* Marquis de Sade: L'Oeil de la letter 1978, Casanova: Un Voyage libertine 1985, The Wicked Queen: The Origins of the Myth of Marie-Antoinette 2001, Coping with Freedom: Reflections on Ephemeral Happiness 2001, Adieux à la Reine (Farewell to the Queen, Prix Femina 2002) 2002, Le Lectrice-Adjointe 2003, L'île flottante 2004, Apolline ou L'école de la Providence 2005, Le Palias de la Reine 2005, Chemins de sable 2006, Jardinière Arlequin 2006, Cafés de la Mémoire 2008, Le Testament d'Olympe 2010, L'esprit de conversation 2011. *Address:* CNRS Headquarters, 3, rue Michel-Ange, 75794 Paris cedex 16 (office); c/o Editions du Seuil, 27 rue Jacob, 75006 Paris, France (office). *Telephone:* 1-44-96-40-00 (CRNS) (office); 1-40-46-50-50 (office). *Fax:* 1-44-96-53-90 (CRNS) (office); 1-40-46-43-00 (office). *E-mail:* contact@seuil.com (office). *Website:* www.cnrs.fr (office).

THOMAS, Clarence, BA, JD; American judge; *Associate Justice, Supreme Court;* b. 23 June 1948, Pinpoint, Savannah, Ga; ed Conception Seminary, Conception Junction, Mo., Holy Cross Coll. and Yale Law School; admitted to bar in Mo. 1974, served as Asst Attorney-Gen. Mo. 1974–77; pvt. legal practice as an attorney for Monsanto Co. 1977–79; Legislative Asst to Mo. Senator John Danforth, US Senate 1979–81; Asst Sec. for Civil Rights, US Dept of Educ. 1981–82; Chair. US Equal Employment Comm. 1982–90; Judge US Court of Appeals for DC Circuit 1990–91; Assoc. Justice US Supreme Court 1991–. *Publication:* My Grandfather's Son 2007. *Address:* United States Supreme Court, One First Street, NE, Washington, DC 20543, USA (office). *Telephone:* (202) 479–3211 (office). *Website:* www .supremecourtus.gov (office).

THOMAS, David; British singer (bass); b. 26 Feb. 1943, Orpington, Kent, England; m. Veronica Joan Dean 1982; three d.; ed St Paul's Cathedral Choir School, London, King's School, Canterbury, Choral Scholar, King's Coll., Cambridge; began singing as boy chorister in St Paul's Cathedral Choir, London; repertoire from Baroque and Classical, and includes works by Walton, Tippett, Britten, Stravinsky, Schoenberg and Schnittke; tours to Europe, USA and Japan; appearances at int. festivals, including Tanglewood, Salzburg, Edinburgh, Lucerne, Stuttgart, Aldeburgh and BBC Promenade Concerts; has appeared with many of the major symphony orchestras and ensembles in UK, including City of Birmingham Symphony, London Philharmonic, Royal Philharmonic, Philharmonia, Hallé, Royal Liverpool Philharmonic, Chamber Orchestra of Europe, London Classical Players, Scottish Chamber Orchestra, Manchester Camerata, Northern Sinfonia, Taverner Consort, Acad. of Ancient Music and London Baroque, and has worked regularly with conductors including Simon Rattle, John Eliot Gardiner, Nicholas McGegan and Christopher Hogwood; notable engagements in UK include TV recording of Beethoven's 9th Symphony with London Classical Players conducted by Roger Norrington, Handel's Orlando at BBC Proms conducted by Christopher Hogwood and Die Schöpfung with Chamber Orchestra of Europe and Frans Bruggen; regular concerts with soprano Emma Kirkby and lutenist Anthony Rooley; sang Sarasto in Covent Garden Festival's production of Die Zauberflöte and the Commendatore in Don Giovanni and General Spork in Cornet Cristoph Rilke's Song of Love and Death for Glyndebourne Touring Opera; other engagements have included performances of the Christmas Oratorio in Leipzig and Berlin, a series of Messiahs in Italy and concerts with the Orchestre de la Suisse Romande, Fundaçao de Sao Carlos in Lisbon, Wiener Akademie, with Kammerchor Stuttgart in concerts in Göttingen, and Handel's Serse and Resurrezione in Brighton and Göttingen; engagements in USA have included Messiah with Los Angeles Philharmonic in the Hollywood Bowl, Haydn's Creation with Boston Symphony Orchestra and Simon Rattle, Messiah at Lincoln Center with Acad. of Ancient Music, Schubert's Winterreise at Cornell University and Handel's Judas Maccabaeus, Susanna and Theodora with Philharmonia Baroque and Nicholas McGegan; teaches at Trinity Coll. of Music, London. *Recordings include:* more than 100 records, including Handel's Serse (Hanover Band/Nicholas McGegan), Handel's Susanna, Apollo and Daphne and Judas Maccabeus (Philharmonia Baroque/Nicholas McGegan), Handel's Semele, Purcell's Fairy Queen and Bach's Magnificat (Monteverdi Choir/English Baroque Soloists/John Eliot Gardiner), Handel's Messiah, Orlando, Athalia, etc. (Acad. of Ancient Music/Christopher Hogwood), Handel's Acis, Galatea e Polifemo (London Baroque/Charles Medlam), Handel's Messiah and Israel in Egypt, Bach's B Minor Mass and St John Passion (Taverner Consort & Players/Andrew Parrot), Handel's

Messiah (Bach Collegium, Japan/Masaaki Suzuki), Coffee Cantata with Emma Kirkby, Mozart's Requiem (Hanover Band/Roy Goodman), Stravinsky's Pulcinella (City of London Sinfonia/Richard Hickox) and The Creation (City of Birmingham Orchestra/Simon Rattle), Beethoven Choral Symphony (American Bach Soloists/ Jeffrey Thomas); solo record Arias for Montagnana, Handel. *Leisure interests:* the island of Dominica, Koi carp. *Address:* c/o Allied Artists, 42 Montpelier Square, London, SW7 1JZ (office). *Telephone:* (20) 7589-6243 (office). *Fax:* (20) 7581-5269 (office). *Website:* www.alliedartists.co.uk (office). *E-mail:* davidthomas@london .com (home).

THOMAS, Sir Derek Morison David, KCMG, MA; British fmr diplomatist and business consultant; b. 31 Oct. 1929, London; s. of K. P. D. Thomas and Mali Thomas; m. Lineke Van der Mast 1956; one s. one d.; ed Radley Coll. and Trinity Hall, Cambridge; articled apprentice, Dolphin Industrial Developments Ltd 1947; entered HM Foreign Service 1953; RNVR 1953–55; appointments overseas included Moscow, Manila, Sofia, Ottawa, Paris, Washington, DC; Deputy Under-Sec. of State for Europe and Political Dir FCO 1984–87; Amb. to Italy 1987–89; European Adviser to NM Rothschild and Sons Ltd 1990–2003, Dir 1991–99; Dir Rothschild Italia 1990–97, Christow Consultants Ltd 1990–99, Rothschild Europe 1991–97; Dir, Assoc. CDP Nexus 1990–92; Dir New Court Int. Ltd, Moscow, Consilium Spa, Prague 1994–2001; mem. Export Guarantees Advisory Council 1991–97; Chair. British Invisibles Lotis Cttee 1992–96, Council S.O.S. Sahel 1991–2000, Council Royal Inst. of Int. Affairs 1994–97, Council Reading Univ. 1990–99; Chair. British Inst. of Florence 1996–2002; Hon. Fellow, Trinity Hall, Cambridge 1998; Hon. LLD (Leicester) 2003. *Leisure interests:* exploring the past and present, music, theatre, wines, reading when there is time, grandchildren, gardening. *Address:* Flat 1, 12 Lower Sloane Street, London, SW1W 8BJ, England (home). *Telephone:* (20) 7730-1473 (home). *E-mail:* derekthomas@gmail.com (home).

THOMAS, D(onald) M(ichael0, MA; British novelist and poet; b. 27 Jan. 1935, Redruth, Cornwall; s. of Harold Redvers Thomas and Amy Thomas (née Moyle); m. Angela Thomas; two s. one d.; ed Redruth Grammar School, Univ. High School, Melbourne, New Coll., Oxford; English teacher, Teignmouth, Devon 1959–63; Lecturer, Hereford Coll. of Educ. 1963–78; full-time author 1978–; Gollancz/Pan Fantasy Prize, PEN Fiction Prize, Cheltenham Prize, Los Angeles Times Fiction Prize, Cholmondeley Award for Poetry, Orwell Prize for Biography. *Play:* Hell Fire Corner 2004. *Publications:* Two Voices 1968, Logan Stone 1971, Love and Other Deaths 1975, Honeymoon Voyage 1978, The Flute-Player 1978, Birthstone 1980, The White Hotel 1981, Dreaming in Bronze 1981, Ararat 1983, Selected Poems 1983, Swallow 1984, Sphinx 1986, Summit 1987, Memories and Hallucinations 1988, Lying Together 1989, Flying in to Love 1992, The Puberty Tree (new and selected poems) 1992, Pictures at an Exhibition 1993, Eating Pavlova 1994, Lady with a Laptop 1996, Alexander Solzhenitsyn (biog.) 1998, Charlotte 2000, Dear Shadows 2003, Not Saying Everything 2006, Bleak Hotel 2008. *Leisure interests:* travel, Russia, Cornwall, the life of the imagination. *Address:* The Coach House, Rashleigh Vale, Truro, Cornwall, TR1 1TJ, England. *Telephone:* (1872) 261724. *E-mail:* dmthomas@btconnect.com. *Website:* www.don-whitehotel.blogspot.com.

THOMAS, Sir Eric Jackson, Kt, MD, FRCOG, FMedSci, FRCP; British physician, academic and university administrator; *Vice-Chancellor, University of Bristol;* b. 24 March 1953, Hartlepool, Cleveland, England; s. of Eric Jackson Thomas and Margaret Mary Murray; m. Narell Marie Ronnard 1976; one s. one d.; ed Ampleforth Coll., Univ. of Newcastle upon Tyne; Lecturer in Obstetrics and Gynaecology, Univ. of Sheffield 1985–87; Sr Lecturer in Obstetrics and Gynaecology, Univ. of Newcastle upon Tyne 1987–90; Consultant, Obstetrician and Gynaecologist, Newcastle Gen. Hosp. 1987–2000; Prof. of Obstetrics and Gynaecology, Univ. of Southampton 1991–2001, Head School of Medicine 1995–98, Dean Faculty of Medicine, Health and Biological Sciences 1998–2000, Consultant, Obstetrician and Gynaecologist, Southampton Univ. Hosps Trust 1991–2001, Dir (non-exec.) Southampton Univ. Hosps Trust 1997–2000, Southampton and SW Hants. Health Authority 2000–01; Vice-Chancellor Univ. of Bristol 2001–; Exec. Sec. Council of Heads of Medical Schools 1998–2000; mem. Council Royal Coll. of Obstetricians and Gynaecologists 1995–2001, Bd South West Regional Sports 2003–06, Bd South West Regional Devt Agency 2003–08, CASE Europe 2007– (Chair. 2010–); mem. Bd Universities UK 2006–, Chair. Research Policy Cttee 2006–, England and Northern Ireland Council 2009–11, Vice-Pres. Universities UK 2009–11, Pres. 2011–13; Hon. LLD (Bristol) 2004; Hon. DSc (Southampton) 2006, (Teeside) 2008, (West of England) 2010; William Blair Bell Memorial Lecturer, Royal Coll. of Obstetricians and Gynaecologists 1987. *Publications:* Modern Approaches to Endometriosis (co-author) 1991; publs on endometriosis and reproductive medicine. *Address:* Office of the Vice-Chancellor, University of Bristol, Senate House, Tyndall Avenue, Bristol, BS8 1TU, England (office). *Telephone:* (117) 928-7499 (office). *E-mail:* jami.west@bris.ac.uk (office). *Website:* www.bris.ac.uk (office).

THOMAS, Gareth, PhD; American scientist and academic; *Professor Emeritus, University of California, Berkeley;* b. 9 Aug. 1932, Maesteg, Wales; s. of David Basset Thomas and Edith May Gregory; m.; one s.; ed Univ. of Wales, Univ. of Cambridge, UK; with Univ. of Calif., Berkeley 1960–, Prof. 1967, now Prof. Emer.; Assoc. Dean, Grad. Div. 1968–69, Asst to Chancellor 1969–72, Acting Vice-Chancellor, Acad. Affairs 1971–72, Chair. Faculty of Coll. of Eng 1977–78, Sr Faculty Scientist, Materials and Molecular Research Div., Scientific Dir. Nat. Center for Electron Microscopy, Prof., Dept of Materials and Mineral Eng 1982–93; mem. NAS, Nat. Acad. of Eng and numerous cttees; Hon. ScD (Cambridge) 1969, (Lehigh Univ.) 1978, (Kraków Univ., Poland) 1999 and numerous other awards. *Publications:* several books and 600 research papers. *Leisure interests:* squash, skiing, cricket. *Address:* c/o Department of Materials Science and Engineering, 481 HMMB, University of California, Berkeley, CA 94720, USA. *E-mail:* garth@ berkeley.edu. *Website:* www.mse.berkeley.edu.

THOMAS, Harvey, CBE, FRSA; British international public relations consultant; b. 10 April 1939, London; s. of the late John Humphrey Kenneth Thomas and Olga Rosina Thomas; m. Marlies Kram 1978; two d.; ed Westminster School, London, Northwestern Coll., Minn., USA, Univ. of Minnesota, Univ. of Hawaii, Honolulu; articled in law 1957–60; Billy Graham Evangelistic Assoc 1960–75, N of England Mission 1960–61, Direct Mail, Minneapolis 1961–63, Press Relations, Southern California Mission 1963, KAIM Radio, Honolulu 1963–64, London

Missions 1965–67, World Congress on Evangelism, Berlin 1966, Australasian Missions 1967–69, Dir Euro 70 Crusades 1969–70, Dir European Congress on Evangelism, Amsterdam 1970–71, research in 80 countries for 1974 Int. Congress on World Evangelization Lausanne 1971–72, SPRE-E 73, London 1973, Dir Billy Graham LAUSTADE Rally, Lausanne 1974, Gen. Sec. EUROFEST Brussels 1975; int. public relations and presentation consultant 1976–; Co-ordinator Int. Exposition for Tech. Transfer 1984; Public Relations, Luis Palau Mission to London 1984; Dir of Presentation, Conservative Party 1978; Field Dir Prime Minister's Election Tour 1987; Chair. Fellowship of European Broadcasters; mem. Bd London Cremation Co. PLC; Chair. Trans World Radio UK; Fellow, Chartered Inst. of Public Relations, Chartered Inst. of Journalists; mem. Inst. of Dirs; int. political consultant; conf. speaker and moderator; broadcaster and commentator on politics, religion and media; exec. coach; Individual Achievement Int. Broadcasting Award 2000. *Publications:* In the Face of Fear 1985, Making an Impact 1989, If They Haven't Heard It – You Haven't Said It 1995. *Leisure interests:* family, travel, broadcasting, public speaking, trains. *Address:* 23 The Service Road, Potters Bar, Herts., EN6 1QA, England (home). *Telephone:* (1707) 649910 (home). *Fax:* (1707) 662653 (home). *E-mail:* harvey@hthomas.net (office). *Website:* www.hthomas.net (office).

THOMAS, Iwan, MBE, BSc; British athlete; b. 5 Jan. 1974, Farnborough, Hants.; ed Stamford School, Brunel Univ.; fourth-ranked BMX rider, Europe 1988; Fifth, Olympic Games 400m 1996, Silver Medal 4×400m relay; Gold Medal, Amateur Athletics Asscn Championships 400m 1997 (British record, 44.36 seconds), 1998; Silver Medal, World Championships 4×400m relay 1997; Gold Medal, European Championships 400m 1998, World Cup 400m 1998, Commonwealth Games 400m 1998; Patron Norwich Union Startrack Scheme; British Athletics Writers' Male Athlete of the Year 1998. *Leisure interests:* music, Playstation, socializing with friends. *Address:* Nuff Respect (Agent), 107 Sherland Road, Twickenham, Middx, TW1 4HB, England (office). *Telephone:* (20) 8891-4145 (office). *Fax:* (20) 8891-4140 (office). *E-mail:* nuff_respect@msn.com (office). *Website:* www.nuff-respect.co.uk (office); www.iwanthomas.co.uk.

THOMAS, Dame Jean Olwen, CBE, DBE, SCD., FRS, CChem, FMedSci; British scientist and academic; *Professor of Macromolecular Biochemistry and Master, St Catharine's College, University of Cambridge;* b. 1 Oct. 1942; d. of John Robert Thomas and Lorna Prunella Thomas (née Harris); ed Llwyn-y-Bryn High School for Girls, Swansea, Univ. Coll., Swansea, Univ. of Wales; Beit Memorial Fellow 1967–69, Univ. of Cambridge 1967–69, demonstrator in Biochemistry 1969–73, Lecturer 1973–87, Reader in the Biochemisry of Macromolecules 1987–91, Prof. of Macromolecular Biochemistry 1991–, Chair. Cambridge Centre for Molecular Recognition 1993–2003, Fellow, New Hall 1969–2006, tutor 1970–76, Vice-Pres. 1983–87, Master, St Catharine's Coll. 2007–; Fellow, Royal Soc. 1986–, mem. Council 1990–02, Biological Sec. and Vice-Pres. 2008–; Pres. Biochemical Soc. 2000–05; mem. European Molecular Biology Org. 1982–, Academia Europaea 1991–, Council and Scientific Advisory Cttee Imperial Cancer Research Fund 1994–2000, Scientific Advisory Cttee Lister Inst. 1994–2000, Internal Merit Promotion Panel of Research Councils (Chair. 2006–), Royal Soc. of Chem.; Fellow, Acad. of Medical Sciences 2002–; Gov. Wellcome Trust Ltd 2000–; Trustee British Museum 1994–2004; Hon. Fellow, UCW Swansea 1987, Cardiff Univ. 1998, Hon. Mem. Biochemical Soc. 2008; Hon. DSc (Wales) 1992, (East Anglia) 2002; Ayling Prize 1964, Hinkel Research Prize 1967, K. M. Stott Research Prize, Newnham Coll., Cambridge 1976. *Publications:* Companion to Biochemistry: Selected Topics for Further Study Vol. 1 1974, Vol. 2 1979 (jt and contrib.); numerous papers in scientific journals. *Leisure interests:* reading, music, walking. *Address:* St Catharine's College, Trumpington Street, Cambridge, CB2 1RL (office); Department of Biochemistry, 80 Tennis Court Road, Cambridge, CB2 1QW (office); 26 Eachard Road, Cambridge, CB3 0HY, England (home). *Telephone:* (1223) 338347 (St Catharine's) (office); (1223) 333670 (office); (1223) 362620 (home). *E-mail:* master@caths.cam.ac.uk (office). *Website:* www.caths.cam.ac.uk (office).

THOMAS, Jeremy, CBE; British film producer; *Owner, Recorded Picture Company;* b. 26 July 1949, London, England; s. of Ralph Thomas and Joy Thomas; m. 1st Claudia Frolich 1977 (divorced 1981); one d.; m. 2nd Vivien Coughman 1982; two s.; began work in film-processing lab., later worked as asst and in cutting room; worked with Dir Philippe Mora, editing Brother Can You Spare a Dime; went to Australia where he produced first film Mad Dog Morgan 1974, then returned to England in 1976 to produce Jerzy Skolimowski's The Shout; f. Recorded Picture Co. Ltd 1975; Chair. BFI 1992–97; set up own film distribution co. Recorded Releasing 1985; f. Hanway Films 1998; Vittorio de Sica Prize 1986, Special Award, Evening Standard Film Awards 1991, Michael Balcon BAFTA Award 1991, BFI Fellowship, Screen International Prize for World Cinema Achievement, European Film Awards 2006. *Films include:* Mad Dog Morgan 1976, The Shout (Grand Prix de Jury, Cannes Film Festival) 1978, The Great Rock'n'Roll Swindle 1979, The Kids are Alright (Special Consultant) 1979, Bad Timing 1980, Eureka 1982, Merry Christmas Mr Lawrence 1982, The Hit 1983, Insignificance 1984, The Last Emperor (winner of nine Academy Awards including Best Picture) 1987, Everybody Wins 1990, The Sheltering Sky 1990, The Naked Lunch 1991, Let Him Have It (exec. producer) 1991, Little Buddha 1993, Rough Magic (exec. producer) 1994, Victory (exec. producer) 1994, Stealing Beauty 1995, The Ogre (exec. producer) 1996, The Brave (exec. producer) 1996, Crash (exec. producer) (Grand Prix de Jury, Cannes Film Festival) 1996, Blood and Wine 1996, All The Little Animals (Dir) 1998, The Cup (exec. producer) 1999, Gohatto 2000, Brother 2000, Sexy Beast 2001, Rabbit Proof Fence (exec. producer) 2002, Triumph of Love (exec. producer) 2002, Young Adam 2003, Travellers and Magicians (exec. producer) 2003, The Dreamers (producer) 2003, Dreaming Lhasa (exec. producer) 2004, Heimat 3 (exec. producer) 2004, Don't Come Knocking (exec. producer) 2004, Tideland 2004, Glastonbury (exec. producer) 2005, Fast Food Nation 2005, Mister Lonely (exec. producer) 2006, Joe Strummer: The Future is Unwritten (exec. producer) 2007, Franklyn 2008, Creation 2009, 13 Assassins (exec. producer) 2010, Essential Killing (exec. producer) 2010, Pina (exec. producer) 2011, A Dangerous Method (producer) 2011, Hara-Kiri: Death of a Samurai (producer) 2011, Vara: A Blessing (exec. producer) 2012, Kon-Tiki (producer) 2012. *Address:* Recorded Picture Co. Ltd, 24 Hanway Street, London, W1T 1UH, England (office). *Telephone:* (20) 7636-2251 (office). *Fax:* (20) 7636-2261 (office). *E-mail:* kp@recordedpicture.com (office). *Website:* www.recordedpicture.com (office).

THOMAS, (John David) Ronald, (J. D. R. Thomas), DSc, CChem, FRSC; British chemist and academic; *Professor Emeritus of Chemistry and Applied Chemistry, University of Wales and Cardiff University;* b. 2 Jan. 1926, Carnaugwynion, Gwynfe, Wales; s. of John Thomas and Betty Thomas (née Watkins); m. Gwyneth Thomas 1950; three d.; ed Llandovery Grammar School and Univ. of Wales, Cardiff (now Cardiff Univ.); RAMC blood transfusion training, Clifton Coll. and South-mead Hosp., Bristol 1944; served in RAMC, India 1944–47; Tech. Asst British Resin Products Ltd Tonbridge 1948; analytical chemist, Spillers Ltd, Cardiff 1950–51, Glamorgan Co. Council 1951–53; Asst Lecturer, Cardiff Coll. of Tech. 1953–56; Lecturer, South East Essex Tech. Coll. 1956–58; Sr Lecturer, Newport and Monmouthshire Coll. of Tech. 1958–61; Sr Lecturer and Reader, Univ. of Wales Inst. of Science and Tech. (UWIST) and Univ. of Wales, Cardiff 1961–90; Counsellor, Open Univ. 1970–71; Prof., Univ. of Wales, Cardiff (now Cardiff Univ.) 1990–93, Prof. Emer. 1994–; mem. Court Univ. of Wales 1989–2001, 2002–08, Council 1997–2001; mem. Council UWIST, Cardiff 1976–79, Univ. of Wales Coll. of Medicine 1993–99; mem. Court Aberystwyth Univ. 1995–; Royal Soc. sponsored invitee to Iranian Chemical Soc. Third Int. Congress and Iranian univs 1975; British Council sponsored invitee to Asian Chemical Congress '87, Seoul and univs at Taejon and Ulsan, S Korea 1987; Foreign Expert, Academia Sinica (Nanjing), Hunan (Changsha), North West (Xian) and Shanghai Teachers Univs 1983, 1985; Visiting Prof., Japan Soc. for the Promotion of Science 1985, NEWI (now Glyndwr Univ.), Wrexham 1995–96; Assessor, Univ. Pertanian Malaysia 1992–94, 1997–99, Univ. Sains Malaysia 1996–98, Universidade Nova de Lisboa and Universidade do Porto 1998–99, Hong Kong Research Grants Council 1996–2009; RSC Schools Lecturer in Analytical Chem. 1985–86; Distinguished Visiting Fellow, La Trobe Univ., Australia 1989; mem. Govt High-Level Mission on Analytical Instrumen-tation to Japan 1991; Adviser to RSC on privatization of UK Lab. of Govt Chemist 1995–97; Vice-Pres. Soc. for Analytical Chem. and Analytical Div. Chem. Soc. 1974–76, mem. Council Chem. Soc. 1976–79; Hon. Sec. Analytical Div. RSC 1987–90, Pres. 1990–92, mem. Council RSC 1990–2005; Chair. Analytical Editorial Bd RSC 1985–90; Sec. Baptist Union of Wales Superannuation Appeal 1976–78; mem. Council, Baptist Union of Wales 1994–97; lectured widely in UK, Europe, Middle and Far East, Australia, USA; Hon. Ed. Newsletter, Analytical Div., RSC 1995–2007; Hon. Prof., Univ. 'Politehnica', Bucharest, Romania 1996–; Hon. Course Adviser, Hong Kong Baptist Univ. 1991–2009; Hon. Mem. Romanian Soc. of Analytical Chem. 1994–, Romanian Chem. Soc. 1999–; Commonwealth Foundation Lecturer, CSMC Research Inst., Bhavnagar, India 1978, RSC Electroanalytical Chem. Medal and Award 1981, E.A. Moelwyn-Hughes Lecturer, Univ. of Cambridge 1988, Ion-Selective Electrodes Lecturer, Third Chemical Congress of N America, Toronto, Canada 1988, J. Heyrovsky Centenary Medal, Czechoslovak Acad. of Sciences 1990, RSC symposium in his honour, Cardiff 1994, White Robe, Gorsedd of Bards 2000, RSC L.S. Theobald Lectureship, 2001, Enric Casassas Memorial Lecturer, Univ. of Barcelona 2002, Most Visited Article Award of Inst. d'Estudis Catalans 2005, Distinguished Service Award Analytical Div. RSC 2006, Medal and Award for Service to RSC 2009. *Achievements include:* famed for PVC-based ion sensors and electrochemical sensors for biomedical and technological roles. *Publications:* ed.: Selective Electrode Reviews, Vols 1–14 1979–92; Trans. Ed.: Membrane Electrodes in Drug Substances Analysis (Cosofret) 1982; author: History of the Analytical Division, Royal Society of Chemistry 1999; co-author: Calculations in Advanced Physical Chemistry 1962–83 (Hungarian trans. 1979), Noble Gases and their Compounds 1964, Selective Ion-Sensitive Electrodes 1971 (Chinese trans. 1975, Japanese 1977), Dipole Moments in Inorganic Chemistry 1971 (Spanish trans. 1974), Practical Electrophoresis 1976, Chromatographic Separations and Extraction with Foamed Plastics and Rubbers 1982; more than 300 articles in scientific journals on chemical and bio-sensors, reaction kinetics, separation chem. and environmental matters. *Leisure interests:* travel, reading (current affairs and history), browsing and things of Wales, genealogy. *Address:* 4 Orchard Court, Gresford, Wrexham, LL12 8EB, Wales (home). *Telephone:* (1978) 856771 (home). *E-mail:* jdrthomas@aol.com (home).

THOMAS, Sir John Meurig, Kt, MA, DSc, LLD, FRS; British scientist and academic; *Professorial Research Fellow, Davy Faraday Research Laboratory;* b. 15 Dec. 1932, Llanelli, Wales; s. of David J. Thomas and Edyth Thomas; m. Margaret Edwards 1959 (died 2002); two d.; ed Gwendraeth Grammar School, Univ. Coll., Swansea, Queen Mary Coll., London; Scientific Officer, UKAEA 1957–58; Asst Lecturer, Lecturer, Sr Lecturer then Reader, Dept of Chem., Univ. Coll. of N Wales, Bangor 1958–69; Prof. and Head Dept of Chem., Univ. Coll. of Wales, Aberystwyth 1969–78; Head of Dept of Physical Chem., Univ. of Cambridge, Professorial Fellow of King's Coll. 1978–86, Master of Peterhouse 1993–2002, Distinguished Hon. Research Fellow, Dept of Materials Science, 1993–2002, Hon. Prof. in Solid State Chem. 2002–; Cabinet Office Advisory Cttee on Applied Research and Devt 1982–85; Dir Royal Inst. of GB 1986–91, Resident Prof. 1986–88, Fullerian Prof. of Chem. 1988–94, Prof. of Chem. and Professorial Research Fellow 1994–; Deputy Pro-Chancellor Univ. of Wales 1991–94; Dir Davy Faraday Research Labs 1986–91; Chair. Chem. Research Applied to World Needs, IUPAC 1987–95; Pres. Chem. Section, BAAS 1988–89; Hon. Visiting Prof. of Physical Chem., Queen Mary Coll., London 1986–, Prof. of Chem., Imperial Coll., London 1986–91, Miller Prof., Univ. of Calif., Berkeley 1998; Distinguished Visiting Prof., Ecole Nat. Supérieure de Chimie Paris 1991; Visiting Prof., Scuola Normale Superiore Pisa 2003; Trustee British Museum (Natural History) 1986–91, Science Museum 1989–95; Commr, 1851 Royal Exhbn 1995– (Chair. Scientific Research Cttee 1996–2005); Tetelman Fellow, Yale Univ. 1997; mem. Academia Europaea 1989; Rutherford Memorial Lecturer of Royal Soc. in New Zealand 1997; Hon. Professorial Fellow Academia Sinica (Shanghai), Imperial Coll. London, Queen Mary Coll. London; Hon. FREng; Hon. FRSE; Hon. Fellow, Indian Acad. (Bangalore), Indian Acad. (Delhi), UMIST, Univ. Coll. Swansea, American Acad. of Arts and Science, American Philosophical Soc., Venezuelan Acad. of Sciences, Russian Acad. of Sciences, Inst. of Physics; Hon. Foreign Fellow, Eng Acad. Japan 1991, Hungarian and Polish Acad. of Sciences 1998, Royal Spanish Acad. of Sciences 1999, Göttingen Acad. of Sciences 2003–, Hon. Bencher, Gray's Inn 1986; Hon. DSc (Heriot-Watt Univ.) 1989, (Birmingham) 1991, (Claude Bernard Univ., Lyon) 1994, (Compluterose Univ., Madrid) 1994, (Western Univ., Ont.) 1995, (Eindhoven Univ., Netherlands) 1996, (Aberdeen, Surrey) 1997, (American Univ. Cairo) 2002, (Sydney, Clarkson, NY) 2005, (Osaka) 2006; Hon. DUniv (Open Univ.) 1992; laureate hc (Turin Univ.) 2004; Baker Lecturer,

Cornell Univ. 1983, Bakerian Prize Lectureship, Royal Soc. 1990, Rutherford Lecturer, Royal Soc. NZ 1997, Centennial Karl Ziegler Lecturer Max Planck Inst. Mülheim 1998, Linus Pauling Lectureship, Calif. Inst. of Tech. 1999, John C. Polanyi Nobel Laureate Lecturer, Univ. of Toronto 2000, Dreichamer Lecturer, Univ. of Illinois–Urbana 2004, Ipatieff Lecturer, Northwestern Univ. 2004, Golden Jubilee Distinguished Lecturer, Hong Kong Baptist Univ. 2006, Woodward Lecturer, Yale Univ. 2006; numerous awards including Faraday and Longstaff Medals, RSC 1990, Messel Gold Medal, Soc. of Chemical Industry 1992, Davy Medal, Royal Soc. 1994, ACS Willard Gibbs Gold Medal 1995, Hon. Medal, Polish Acad. of Sciences, Warsaw 1996, Semonov Centenary Medal, Russian Acad. of Sciences 1996, ACS Award for Creative Research in Catalysis 1999, Linus Pauling Gold Medal for Advances in Science, Stanford Univ. 2003, Giulionatta Gold Medal for Contributions to Catalysis, Italian Chem. Soc. 2003; new mineral meurigite named in his honour 1995; symposium in his honour organized by Microscopy and Microanalysis Soc. of America, Philadelphia 2000 and by RSC London 2002, Sir George Gabriel Stokes Gold Medal for Analytical Science, Royal Soc. of Chem. 2005. *Television:* Royal Inst. Christmas Lectures on Crystals 1987–88; many Welsh language broadcasts. *Radio:* BBC Annual Lecture in Welsh 1978. *Publi-cations:* Principles of Heterogeneous Catalysis 1967, Characterization of Catalysts 1980, Heterogeneous Catalysis: Principles and Practice 1997, Michael Faraday and the Royal Institution: The Genius of Man and Place 1991, Perspectives in Catalysis (with K. I. Zamaraev) 1992; Pan Edrychwyf ar y Nefoedd (Welsh Radio Lecture) 1978; Founding Co-Ed.-in-Chief Catalysis Letters 1988–, Topics in Catalysis 1992–, Current Opinion in Solid State and Materials Science; over 950 articles on catalysis solid-state and surface science. *Leisure interests:* walking, Welsh literature, ancient civilizations, birdwatching, popularization of science, listening to music. *Address:* Dept of Materials Science, Cambridge, CB2 3QZ (office); Davy Faraday Research Laboratory, The Royal Institution, 21 Albemarle Street, London, W1S 4BS, England (office). *Telephone:* (1223) 334300 (Cambridge) (office); (20) 7670-2928 (London) (office). *Fax:* (1223) 740360 (Cambridge) (home); (20) 7670-2958 (London) (office). *E-mail:* jmt@ri.ac.uk (office). *Website:* www.ri.ac .uk/DFRL (office).

THOMAS, Sir Keith Vivian, Kt, MA, FBA; British historian and academic; *Fellow, All Souls College, Oxford;* b. 2 Jan. 1933, Wick, Glamorgan, Wales; s. of Vivian Thomas and Hilda Thomas; m. Valerie June Little 1961; one s. one d.; ed Barry Co. Grammar School and Balliol Coll., Oxford (Brackenbury Scholar); nat. service in Royal Welch Fusiliers 1950–52; Fellow, All Souls Coll., Oxford 1955–57, 2001–, St John's Coll. Oxford 1957–86, Tutor 1957–85; Reader in Modern History, Univ. of Oxford 1978–85, Prof. 1986, Pres. Corpus Christi Coll. 1986–2000, Pro-Vice-Chancellor, Univ. of Oxford 1988–2000, Fellow, All Souls Coll. 2001–; Del., Oxford Univ. Press 1980–2000; mem. Econ. and Social Research Council 1985–90, Reviewing Cttee on Export of Works of Art 1990–92, Royal Comm. on Historical Manuscripts 1992–2002; Trustee, Nat. Gallery 1991–98, British Museum 1999–2008; Pres. British Acad. 1993–97; Chair. Supervisory Cttee, Oxford Dictionary of Nat. Biography 1992–2004, British Library Advisory Cttee for Arts, Humanities and Social Sciences 1997–2002, Advisory Cttee, Warburg Inst., Univ. of London 2000–08; Hon. Fellow, Balliol Coll. Oxford 1984, St John's Coll. Oxford 1986, Univ. of Cardiff 1995, Corpus Christi Coll. Oxford 2000, Warburg Inst., Univ. of London 2008; Hon. Vice-Pres. Royal Historical Soc. 2001–; Foreign Hon. mem. American Acad. of Arts and Sciences 1983, Japan Acad. 2009; Cavaliere Ufficiale, Ordine al Merito della Repubblica Italiana 1991; Hon. DLitt (Kent) 1983, (Wales) 1987, (Hull) 1995, (Leicester) 1996, (Sussex) 1996, (Warwick) 1998, (London) 2006, (Columbia) 2011; Hon. LittD (Sheffield) 1992, (Cambridge) 1995; Hon. LLD (Williams) 1988, (Oglethorpe, Atlanta, Ga) 1996, (Uppsala) 2014; mem. Academia Europaea 1993; Wolfson Literary Award for History 1971, G.M. Trevelyan Lecturer, Univ. of Cambridge 1979, Ford's Lecturer, Univ. of Oxford 2000, Norton Medlicott Medal, Historical Asscn 2003. *Publications:* Religion and the Decline of Magic 1971, Puritans and Revolutionaries (co-ed with Donald Pennington) 1978, Man and the Natural World 1983, The Oxford Book of Work (ed.) 1999, Roy Jenkins: A Retrospective (co-ed with Andrew Adonis) 2004, Changing Conceptions of National Biography 2005, The Ends of Life: Roads to Fulfilment in Early Modern England 2009, The Wolfson History Prize: an Informal History 2012. *Leisure interest:* looking for second-hand bookshops. *Address:* All Souls College, Oxford, OX1 4AL (office); The Broad Gate, Broad Street, Ludlow, Shropshire, SY8 1NJ, England (home). *Telephone:* (1865) 279379 (office); (1584) 877797 (home). *Fax:* (1865) 279299 (office). *E-mail:* keith.thomas@all-souls.oxford .ac.uk (home).

THOMAS, Michael Tilson (see Tilson Thomas, Michael).

THOMAS, Robert Kemeys, MA, DPhil, FRS; British chemist and academic; *Professor, Physical and Theoretical Chemistry Laboratory, University of Oxford;* b. 25 Sept. 1941, Harpenden; s. of Rev. Herbert Thomas and Agnes Thomas (née McLaren); m. Pamela H. Woods 1968; one s. two d.; ed St John's Coll., Oxford; researcher Univ. of Oxford 1968–78, Fellow, Merton Coll. 1975–78, Lecturer in Physical Chem. 1978–, Fellow and tutor Univ. Coll. 1978–; Tilden Lecturer, Royal Soc. of Chem.; Hon. Prof., Inst. of Chem., Chinese Acad. of Sciences, Beijing 1999–. *Publications:* papers in scientific journals. *Leisure interests:* music, flora, fungi, Chinese language. *Address:* Physical and Theoretical Chemistry Laboratory, South Parks Road, Oxford, OX1 3QZ, England (office); University College, High Street, Oxford, OX1 4BH. *Telephone:* (1865) 275422 (office); (1865) 276602 (office). *Fax:* (1865) 275410 (office). *E-mail:* robert.thomas@chem.ox.ac.uk (office). *Website:* rkt.chem.ox.ac.uk (office); www.chem.ox.ac.uk/researchguide/rkthomas.html (office).

THOMAS, Hon. Tillman Joseph, (Uncle Tilly), BEcons; Grenadian lawyer and politician; *Leader, National Democratic Congress;* b. 13 June 1945, Hermitage, St Patrick; m. Sandra Thomas; ed Fordham Univ., USA, Univ. of the West Indies, Hugh Woodling Law School, Trinidad; fmr political prisoner under govt of Maurice Bishop early 1980s; mem. House of Reps for St Patrick E 1984–90, 2003–; Jr Minister, Ministry of Legal Affairs 1984–90; Founder-mem. Nat. Democratic Congress Party 1987, Asst Gen. Sec. 1987–90, Leader 2000–; Leader of Opposition 2003–08; Prime Minister 2008–13, was also Minister of Nat. Security, Foreign Affairs, Public Admin, Information, Information Communications Tech., Legal Affairs and Nat. Mobilization. *Film:* The Island President (documentary) 2011. *Address:* National Democratic Congress, NDC Headquarters, Lucas Street, St

George's, Grenada (office). *Telephone:* 440-3769 (office). *E-mail:* ndcgrenada@ndcgrenada.org (office). *Website:* www.ndcgrenada.org (office).

THOMAS-GRAHAM, Pamela, BA, MBA, JD; American business executive and author; *Chief Talent, Branding and Communications Officer, Credit Suisse AG;* b. 1963, Detroit, Mich.; m. Lawrence Otis Graham; three c.; ed Detroit Lutheran West High School, Harvard-Radcliffe Coll., Harvard Business School, Harvard Law School; fmr Ed. Harvard Law Review; joined McKinsey & Co. 1989, Partner 1995–99, leader of Media and Entertainment practice –1999; Pres. and CEO CNBC.com 1999–2001, Pres. and CEO CNBC 2001–05, Chair. 2005; Group Pres. Better and Moderate Apparel, Liz Claiborne Inc. 2006–07; Man. Dir Angelo, Gordon and Co. (pvt. investment man. firm), New York 2008–09; Chief Talent, Branding and Communications Officer, Credit Suisse AG 2010–, mem. Exec. Bds Credit Suisse Group AG and Credit Suisse AG; mem. Bd of Dirs Clorox Co. 2005–, Idenix Pharmaceuticals Inc. 2005–, New York Philharmonic, Parsons School of Design; mem. Council on Foreign Relations, Economic Club of New York; fmr mem. US Sec. of State Condoleezza Rice's Advisory Cttee on Transformational Diplomacy; Capt. Jonathan Fay Prize. *Publications:* A Darker Shade of Crimson 1998, Blue Blood 2000, Orange Crushed 2004. *Address:* Credit Suisse AG, 11 Madison Avenue, New York, NY 10010-3629, USA (office). *Telephone:* (212) 325-2000 (office). *Fax:* (212) 325-6665 (office). *Website:* www.credit-suisse.com (office).

THOMAS OF SWYNNERTON, Baron (Life Peer), cr. 1981, of Notting Hill in Greater London; **Hugh Swynnerton Thomas,** MA, FRHistS; British historian; b. 21 Oct. 1931, Windsor; s. of Hugh Whitelegge and Margery (née Swynnerton) Thomas; m. Vanessa Jebb 1962; two s. one d.; ed Sherborne School, Queens' Coll., Cambridge and Sorbonne, Paris; Foreign Office 1954–57; Sec. UK Del. to UN Disarmament Sub-cttee 1955–56; Lecturer, Royal Mil. Acad., Sandhurst 1957; worked for UNA 1959–61; Prof. of History, Univ. of Reading 1966–76; Chair. Grad. School of European Studies 1973–76, Centre for Policy Studies 1979–91; King Juan Carlos I Prof. New York Univ. 1995; Visiting Prof. of History, Boston Univ. 1996, Univ. Prof. 1997–; Corresp. mem. Real Academia de la Historia, Madrid; Hon. Fellow, Queens' Coll., Cambridge 2007; Order of the Aztec Eagle 1995, Grand Cross, Order of Isabel la Católica, Spain 2001, Commdr Ordre des Arts et des Lettres, France 2008; Somerset Maugham Prize 1962, Arts Council Nat. Book Award for History 1980, Nonino Prize, Udine 2009, Bocaccio Prize, Italy 2009, Gabarron Prize 2009, Calvo Serer Prize 2009, Joaquín Romero Murube Prize 2013. *Publications include:* The Spanish Civil War 1961, The Suez Affair 1966, Cuba or the Pursuit of Freedom 1971, Goya and the Third of May 1808 1973, John Strachey 1973, An Unfinished History of the World 1979, The Case for the Round Reading Room 1983, Havannah! (novel) 1984, Armed Truce: The Beginnings of the Cold War 1945–46 1986, Klara (novel) 1988, Madrid: A Traveller's Companion (ed.) 1988, Ever Closer Union: Britain's Destiny in Europe 1991, The Conquest of Mexico 1993, The Slave Trade 1997, The Future of Europe 1998, Who's Who of the Conquistadors 2000, Rivers of Gold 2003, Beaumarchais in Seville 2007, Don Eduardo 2007, The Golden Age: Charles V and his Spanish Empire 2010, The Golden Rule: Philip II and the Spanish Empire 2013. *Address:* House of Lords, London, SW1A 0PW; 29 Ladbroke Grove, London, W11 3BB, England. *Telephone:* (20) 7219-5353 (House of Lords).

THOMPSON, Alan Eric, MA, PhD, FRSA, FSA (Scot); British economist and academic; *Professor Emeritus of Economics, Heriot-Watt University;* b. 16 Sept. 1924; s. of Eric Thompson and Florence Thompson; m. Mary Heather Long 1960; three s. one d.; ed Univ. of Edin.; Lecturer in Econs, Univ. of Edin. 1953–59, 1964–71; Labour MP for Dunfermline 1959–64; Econ. Consultant, Scotch Whisky Asscn 1965–70; Visiting Prof., Graduate School of Business, Stanford Univ., Calif. 1966, 1968; A. J. Balfour Prof. of Econs of Govt, Heriot-Watt Univ., Edin. 1972–84, Prof. Emer. 1984–; mem. Scottish Council for Adult Educ. in HM Forces 1973–98; mem. Local Govt Boundaries Comm. for Scotland 1975–82; mem. Joint Mil. Educ. Cttee, Edin. and Heriot-Watt Univs 1975–2004; mem. Court, Heriot-Watt Univ. 1980; Chair. Northern Offshore Maritime Resources Study 1974–84; BBC Nat. Gov. for Scotland 1976–79; mem. Royal Fine Art Comm. for Scotland 1975–80, Scottish-Russian Co-ordinating Cttee for Trade and Industry 1985–90; Parl. Adviser to Scottish TV 1966–76, to Pharmaceutical Gen. Council (Scotland) 1985–99; Adviser, Robert Burns Memorial Trust 1995–97; Chair. Bd of Govs, Newbattle Abbey Coll. 1980–82; mem. Bd of Dirs Scottish AIDS Research Foundation 1991–96; Hon. Vice-Pres. Asscn of Nazi War Camp Survivors 1960–. *Publications:* The Development of Economic Doctrine (with Alexander Gray) 1980; contributions to learned journals. *Address:* 11 Upper Gray Street, Edinburgh, EH9 1SN, Scotland (home).

THOMPSON, Sir Clive Malcolm, Kt, BSc; British business executive; *Deputy Chairman, Strategic Equity Capital plc;* b. 4 April 1943, Bristol; s. of H. L. Thompson and P. D. Thompson (née Stansbury); m. Judith Howard 1968; two s.; ed Clifton Coll., Bristol and Birmingham Univ.; Marketing Exec. Royal Dutch Shell Group 1964–67; Marketing Exec. and Gen. Man. Boots Co. PLC 1967–70; Gen. Man. Jeyes Group Ltd 1970–78; Man. Dir Health and Hygiene Div., Cadbury Schweppes 1978–82; Chief Exec. Rentokil Initial PLC 1983–2003, Chair. (non-exec.) 2003–04; Pres. CBI 1998–2000; Deputy Chair. Financial Reporting Council; fmr Dir (non-exec.) Wellcome PLC, Sainsbury PLC, Seeboard PLC, Caradon PLC, BAT Industries PLC; fmr Chair. Kleeneze PLC, European Home Retail (EHR) 2002–06; Deputy Chair. Strategic Equity Capital plc, London 2005–; mem. Hampel Cttee on Corp. Governance 1998; Hon. DSc (Birmingham) 1999. *Leisure interests:* the stock market, current affairs, walking, golf. *Website:* www.strategicequitycapital.com (office).

THOMPSON, Daley (Francis Morgan), CBE; British fmr athlete; b. 30 July 1958, Notting Hill, London; m. Tisha Quinlan 1987; one c.; Sussex Schools 200 m title 1974; first competitive decathlon, Welsh Open Championship June 1975; European Junior Decathlon Champion 1977; European Decathlon silver medallist 1978, gold medallist 1982 and 1986; Commonwealth Decathlon gold medallist 1978, 1982 and 1986; Olympic Decathlon gold medallist 1980 (Moscow) and 1984 (LA); World Decathlon Champion 1983; est. new world record for decathlon (at Olympic Games, LA), set four world records in all and was undefeated between 1978 and 1987; retd July 1992; invited to run leg of the Olympic Torch relay at the opening of the Sydney Olympic Games 2000. *Publications:* Going for Gold 1987, The Greatest 1996. *Address:* Church Row, Wandsworth Plain, London SW18, England.

THOMPSON, Don, BS (ElecEng); American business executive; *President and CEO, McDonald's Corporation;* m. Liz Thompson; two c.; ed Purdue Univ.; began career at McDonald's as an electrical engineer 1990, has since held several leadership positions, including Div. Pres., Exec. Vice-Pres. and US COO, Pres. McDonald's USA –2011, Pres. and COO McDonald's Corpn 2011–12, Pres. and CEO 2012–; mem. Bd of Dirs Exelon Corpn, Northwestern Memorial Hosp., Purdue Univ.; mem. Civic Cttee of the Commercial Club, The Economic Club, World Business Chicago, Brazier Foundation; Dr hc (Excelsior Coll., Albany, NY) 2008; Purdue Univ. Outstanding Electrical and Computer Eng Award, named a Purdue Univ. Old Master Fellow 2006, named by Black Enterprise as Corp. Exec. of the Year 2007, Corp. Exec. Award, Trumpet Foundation 2008, Presidential Inspiration Award, Alpha Phi Alpha fraternity 2009, Achievement Award, Exec. Leadership Council 2010, Humanitarian Award, Illinois Holocaust Museum 2012. *Address:* McDonald's Corporation, 2915 Jorie Blvd, Oak Brook, IL 60523, USA (office). *Telephone:* (630) 623-3000 (office). *Fax:* (630) 623-7056 (office). *Website:* www.mcdonalds.com (office).

THOMPSON, Dorothy Carrington, CBE, BSc (Hons), MSc; British energy industry executive; *CEO and Executive Director, Drax Group;* two c.; ed London School of Econs; early career in banking; Asst Group Treas. Powergen 1993–98; joined InterGen NV 1998, later Head of European Business; CEO and Exec. Dir Drax Group Ltd 2005–; Dir (non-exec.) Johnson Matthey plc; ranked by the Financial Times amongst Top 25 Businesswomen in Europe (16th) 2006, (19th) 2007, ranked by Fortune magazine amongst the 50 Most Powerful Women in Business outside the US (50th) 2010. *Address:* Drax Power Ltd, Drax Power Station, Selby, N Yorks., YO8 8PH, England (office). *Telephone:* (1757) 618381 (office). *Fax:* (1757) 618504 (office). *Website:* www.draxgroup.plc.uk (office).

THOMPSON, Emma; British actress and screenwriter; b. 15 April 1959; d. of Eric Thompson and Phyllida Law; m. 1st Kenneth Branagh 1989 (divorced); m. 2nd Greg Wise 2003; one d.; ed Camden Girls' School and Newnham Coll. Cambridge; appeared with Cambridge Footlights; Chair. Bd of Trustees Helen Bamber Foundation; Int. Amb. ActionAid (charity). *Stage appearances include:* The Cellar Tapes, Edin. Festival 1981–82 (Perrier Pick of the Fringe Award 1981), A Sense of Nonsense (revue tour) 1983, Short Vehicle, Edin. Festival 1984, Me and My Girl, Adelphi 1984–85, Look Back in Anger, Lyric 1989, A Midsummer Night's Dream (world tour) 1990, King Lear (world tour) 1990. *Films:* The Tall Guy 1988, Henry V 1989, Impromptu 1989, Howards End 1991 (eight awards for Best Actress, including New York Critics, LA Critics, Golden Globe, Acad. Award, BAFTA, Nat. Bd of Review; David di Donatella Award for Best Foreign Actress (Italy)), Dead Again 1991, Peter's Friends 1992, Much Ado About Nothing 1993, Remains of the Day 1993 (David di Donatella Award for Best Foreign Actress (Italy)), In the Name of the Father 1993, Junior 1994, Carrington 1995, Sense and Sensibility (nine awards for Best Screenplay, including Acad. Award, Golden Globe, LA Film Critics, New York Film Critics, Writers Guild of America, Evening Standard British Film Award; awards for Best Actress from BAFTA and Nat. Bd of Review), The Winter Guest 1996 (Panisetti Award for Best Actress, Venice Film Festival), Primary Colors 1997, Judas Kiss 1997, Imagining Argentina 2003, Love Actually 2003, Harry Potter and the Prisoner of Azkaban 2004, Nanny McPhee (also screenplay writer) 2005, Stranger Than Fiction 2006, Harry Potter and the Order of the Phoenix 2007, Last Chance Harvey 2008, Brideshead Revisited 2008, The Boat that Rocked 2009, An Education 2009, Nanny McPhee and the Big Bang 2010, Harry Potter and the Deathly Hallows Part 2 2011, Brave (voice) 2012, Men in Black III 2012. *Television appearances include:* Emma Thompson Special, Channel 4 1983, Alfresco (two series), Granada 1983–84, The Crystal Cube, BBC 1984, Tutti Frutti, BBC (BAFTA Award for Best Actress) 1986, Fortunes of War, BBC (BAFTA Award for Best Actress) 1986–87, Thompson 1988, Knuckle, BBC 1988, The Winslow Boy, BBC 1988, Look Back in Anger, Thames 1989, Cheers 1992, Blue Boy, BBC Scotland 1994, Ellen, Touchstone TV/ABC (Emmy Award for Outstanding Guest Actress in a Comedy Series) 1998, Wit (Best Actress Award, Semana Internacional de Cine de Valladolid) 2000, Angels in America (miniseries) 2003, The Song of Lunch 2010. *Address:* c/o Hamilton Hodell Ltd, 5th Floor, 66–68 Margaret Street, London, W1W 8SR, England (office). *Telephone:* (20) 7636-1221 (office). *Fax:* (20) 7636-1226 (office). *E-mail:* info@hamiltonhodell.co.uk (office). *Website:* www.hamiltonhodell.co.uk (office).

THOMPSON, Francis Michael Longstreth, CBE, DPhil, FBA; British historian and academic; *Professor Emeritus of History, University of London;* b. 13 Aug. 1925, Purley, Surrey; s. of Francis Longstreth-Thompson; m. Anne Challoner 1951; two s. one d.; ed Bootham School, York and The Queen's Coll., Oxford; Lecturer in History, Univ. Coll. London 1951–63, Reader in Econ. History 1963–68; Prof. of Modern History, Univ. of London and Head of Dept of History, Bedford Coll. London 1968–77, Prof. of History and Dir, Inst. of Historical Research 1977–90, Prof. Emer. 1990–; Ford's Lecturer, Univ. of Oxford 1993–94; Pres., Econ. History Soc. 1983–86, Hon. Vice-Pres. 1986–; British mem., Standing Cttee for Humanities, European Science Foundation 1983–93; Pres., Royal Historical Soc. 1988–92; Pres., British Agric. History Soc. 1988–92. *Publications:* English Landed Society in the 19th Century 1963, Chartered Surveyors: The Growth of a Profession 1968, Victorian England: The Horse-Drawn Society 1970, Hampstead: Building a Borough, 1650–1964 1974, Countrysides (in The Nineteenth Century; ed. Asa Briggs) 1970, Britain (in European Landed Elites in the Nineteenth Century; ed. David Spring) 1977, Landowners and Farmers (in The Faces of Europe; ed. Alan Bullock) 1980, The Rise of Suburbia (ed.) 1982, Horses in European Economic History (ed.) 1983, The Rise of Respectable Society: A Social History of Victorian Britain 1988, The Cambridge Social History of Britain 1750–1950, three vols (ed.) 1990, The University of London and the World of Learning 1836–1986 (ed.) 1990, Landowners, Capitalists and Entrepreneurs (ed.) 1994, Gentrification and the Enterprise Culture: Britain, 1780–1980 2001. *Leisure interests:* gardening, walking, carpentry. *Address:* Holly Cottage, Sheepcote Lane, Wheathampstead, Herts., AL4 8NJ, England. *Telephone:* (158) 283-3129 (home).

THOMPSON, Fred Dalton, BA, JD; American lawyer, politician and actor; b. 19 Aug. 1942, Sheffield, Ala; m. 1st Sarah Elizabeth Lindsey 1959 (divorced 1985); three c.; m. 2nd Jeri Kehn 2002; one s. one d.; ed Vanderbilt Univ., Memphis State Univ.; practiced law 1967–69; Asst US District Attorney 1969–72; Minority Counsel, Senate Select Cttee on Presidential Campaign Activities ('Watergate

Cttee') 1973–74; Special Counsel to Tenn. Gov. Lamar Alexander 1980; Special Counsel, Senate Cttee on Foreign Relations 1980–81; Special Counsel, Senate Cttee on Intelligence 1982; mem. Tenn. Appellate Court Nominating Comm. 1985–87; Senator from Tenn. 1994–2003; Chair. Senate Cttee to Investigate Fund Raising during 1996 Presidential Election 1997; Chair. Senate Governmental Affairs Cttee 1997–2001; campaign chair. for John McCain in 2000 Republican presidential primary; fmr Visiting Fellow, American Enterprise Inst.; Special Program Host and Sr Analyst for ABC News Radio; Republican; unsuccessful cand. for Republican nomination for US Pres. 2007; host, The Fred Thompson Show (radio talk show) 2009–. *Films include:* No Way Out 1987, Feds 1988, Fat Man and Little Boy 1989, Hunt for Red October 1990, In the Line of Fire 1993, Days of Thunder 1990, Die Hard 2 1990, Class Action 1991, Necessary Roughness 1991, Curly Sue 1991, Cape Fear 1991, Aces: Iron Eagle III 1992, Thunderheart 1992, Born Yesterday 1993, In the Line of Fire 1993, Baby's Day Out 1994, and others. *Television includes:* Law and Order 2002–07. *Publication:* At That Point in Time: The Inside Story of the Senate Watergate Committee 1975. *Address:* Fred Thompson Show, c/o Westwood One, 1166 Avenue of the Americas, 10th Floor, New York, NY 10036, USA. *Telephone:* (212) 641-2000. *Website:* fredthompsonshow.com.

THOMPSON, G. Kennedy (Ken), BA, MBA; American business executive; b. 25 Nov. 1950, Rocky Mount, NC; ed Univ. of NC, Wake Forest Univ.; joined First Union Corpn 1976, various man. and exec. positions including Pres. First Union Ga, Sr Vice-Pres. and Head First Union Human Resources, Pres. First Union Fla, Vice-Chair. of Corpn and Head Global Capital Markets 1998–99, Chair., Pres. and CEO First Union Corpn 1999–2001, Pres. and CEO Wachovia Corpn (after merger of First Union and Wachovia) 2001–08; mem. Bd of Dirs Fla Rock Industries Inc., Carolinas Healthcare System; mem. Financial Services Forum, The Business Council, Bd Financial Services Roundtable; Vice-Chair. NY Clearing House; mem. Bd Teach for America, NC Blumenthal Performing Arts Center, Charlotte Latin School, YMCA Metropolitan Bd, United Way of Cen. Carolinas Inc., Charlotte Inst. for Tech. Innovation; Co-Chair. Advantage Carolina; mem. Bd Trustees Wake Forest Univ. *Address:* c/o Wachovia Corporation, 301 South College Street, Suite 4000, Charlotte, NC 28288-0013, USA (office).

THOMPSON, Gregory (Greg) Francis, BA, BEd; Canadian fmr politician; b. 28 March 1947, St Stephen, NB; m. Linda Thompson; two s.; ed St Thomas Univ.; fmr teacher and financial planner; MP (Conservative) for Carleton–Charlotte 1988–93, for New Brunswick SW 1997–2011, has served as Critic for Atlantic Canada Opportunities Agency, Public Accounts, Health, Regional Devt, Treasury Bd and Human Resources Devt, fmr mem. Cttees for Fisheries and Oceans, Health, Public Accounts and Sub-cttees for Whistleblowing, Non-Medicinal use of Drugs, Combatting Corruption, Agenda and Procedure; Co-Chair. Canada-US Inter-Parl. Group 2004–06; Minister of Veterans Affairs 2006–10 (resgnd); mem. Bd of Dirs Theatre New Brunswick, Charlotte County Hosp., New Brunswick Drug and Alcohol Dependency Comm.

THOMPSON, Harold Lindsay, AM, MB, BS, FRACGP; Australian medical practitioner; b. 23 April 1929, Aberdeen, Scotland; s. of Harold Thompson and Johan D. Thompson; m. 1st Audrey J. Harpur 1957 (died 1996); three s. two d.; m. 2nd Jennifer Manton 1997; ed Aberdeen, Melbourne and Sydney Grammar Schools and postgrad. training in UK; Surgeon-Lt Royal Australian Navy 1956–60; now in gen. practice in Lakemba, NSW; Exec. Dir Canterbury Div. of Gen. Practice 1996–2002; Assoc. Prof., Faculty of Medicine, Univ. of Sydney 1996–; fmr Chair. Diagnostic Medical Cooperative Ltd; Fellow Australian Medical Asscn 1973, Pres. 1982–85; Pres. Confed. of Medical Asscns of Asia and Oceania 1985–87; Immediate Past Pres. 1987–89; Chair. Australian Urban Divs of Gen. Practice 1995–2000; Vice-Chair. Australian Council on Healthcare Standards 1985–89; Vice-Pres. Australian Council of Professions 1985–87, Pres. 1989–91; Assoc. Prof., Faculty of Medicine, Univ. of Sadmer 1996; mem. Council, World Medical Asscn 1984–90, Pres. 1988–89; mem. Econ. Planning Advisory Cttee 1989–91, Bd Southern Sydney Area Health Service 1991–95; Chair. Council Confed. of Medical Asscns of Asia and Oceania 1989–95, GP Advisory Cttee NSW Health 1997–2002, Chair. 1998–2002; Gold Medal, Australian Medical Asscn 1986; Medal, Australian Council on Healthcare Standards 1990, Distinguished Service Award, Confed. of Medical Asscns of Asia and Oceania 1987, Award of Merit 1989, 1995, Gusi Peace Prize 2008. *Leisure interests:* croquet, fishing, bridge. *Address:* 601/2 Roseby Street, Drummoyne, NSW 2047 (office); 4/100 Milsom Road, Cremorne, NSW 2090, Australia (home). *Telephone:* (2) 9719-8391 (office); (2) 9908-2980 (home). *E-mail:* hlindsaythompson@bigpond.com.

THOMPSON, James R., JD; American lawyer and fmr politician; *Senior Chairman, Winston & Strawn LLP;* b. 8 May 1936, Chicago, Ill.; s. of Dr J. Robert Thompson and Agnes Thompson; m. Jayne Carr 1976; one d.; ed Univ. of Illinois, Washington Univ., St Louis, Missouri, Northwestern Univ. Law School; admitted to Illinois Bar 1959; Prosecutor, State Attorney's Office, Cook County, Ill. 1959–64; Assoc. Prof., Northwestern Univ. Law School 1964–69; Chief, Dept of Law Enforcement and Public Protection, Office of Ill. Attorney-Gen. 1969–70; First Asst US Attorney 1970–71, US Attorney for Northern Dist of Ill. 1971–75; Counsel, Winston & Strawn (law firm), Chicago 1975–77, Pnr and Chair. Exec. Cttee 1991–2006, Chair. and CEO 1993–2006, Sr Chair. 2006–; Gov. of Ill. 1977–91; mem. Exec. Cttee Nat. Govs' Asscn 1980–82, Chair. 1983–84; Co-Chair. Attorney-Gen.'s Task Force on Violent Crime 1981; Chair., Pres.s Intelligence Oversight Bd 1989–93; mem. Presidential Advisory Cttee on Federalism 1981, Advisory Bd of Fed. Emergency Man. Agency 1991–93; Chair. Republican Govs' Asscn, Mid-western Govs' Conf., Nat. Govs' Asscn Task Force on Job Creation and Infrastructure 1982; Chair. Council of Great Lakes Govs 1985; Vice-Chair. Martin Luther King Jr Nat. Holiday Cttee 1985; Chair. Public Review Bd of UNITE-HEREIU Union, Ill. Math. and Science Foundation; US Chair. Midwest US-Japan Asscn; Co-Chair. Rare Isotope Accelerator Task Force, CLEAR (Illinois Criminal Code Revision), ABA Cttee on Sentencing Reform; Commr Nat. Comm. on Terrorist Attacks Upon the US (9-11 Comm.) 2003–04; mem. Bd of Dirs JBT Corpn, Navigant Consulting Group, Inc., Maximus, Inc.; Republican; Hon. LLD (Lincoln Coll.) 1975, Hon. DHumLitt (Roosevelt Univ.) 1979, Hon. DJur (North-western Univ. and Illinois Coll.) 1979, Hon. LLD (Monmouth Coll.) 1981, (Marshall Law School) 1984, (Elmhurst Coll.) 1985, Dr hc (Pratt Inst.) 1984; Justice in Legislation Award, American Jewish Congress 1984, Distinguished

Public Service Award, Anti-Defamation League 1984, Swedish-American of the Year, Vasa Order of America 1985, Laureate Award of the ISBA Acad. of Illinois Lawyers 2000, Justice John Paul Stevens Award 2003. *Publications:* co-author of four textbooks including Cases and Comments on Criminal Procedure; numerous articles in professional journals. *Address:* Winston & Strawn LLP, 35 W Wacker Drive, Suite 4200, Chicago, IL 60601-9703, USA (office). *Telephone:* (312) 558-7400 (office). *Fax:* (312) 558-5700 (office). *E-mail:* jthompson@winston.com (office). *Website:* www.winston.com (office).

THOMPSON, Jennifer (Jenny), BSc, MD; American physician and fmr swimmer; b. 26 Feb. 1973, Danvers, Mass; ed Stanford Univ., Columbia Univ.; mem. Badger Swim Club, NY 2001–; won 19 Nat. Collegiate Athletic Asscn (NCAA) titles, most in NCAA female swimming history; 26 nat. medals, 85 medals from int. competition including 14 from World Championships; competed at Olympic Games 1992, 1996, 2000, 2004 (third female swimmer to qualify for four Olympics); most decorated swimmer in Olympic history with 12 medals (eight gold medals); most Olympic gold medals among US women; holds world records 100m. butterfly, 50m. butterfly, 100m. individual medley; intern, Memorial Sloan-Kettering Cancer Center, New York; currently resident anesthesiologist, Brigham and Women's Hosp., Boston; US All-Star swimming team 1989, 1992–95, 1997–2000, 2002–04, USA Swimming Swimmer of the Year 1993, 1998, Female Swimmer of the Meet, World Short Course Championships 1999, Female Swimmer of the Meet, Pan Pacific Championships 1999, Sports Foundation's Sportswoman of the Year 2000. *Address:* Department of Anesthesiology, Perioperative and Pain Medicine, Brigham and Women's Hospital, 75 Francis Street, Boston, MA 02115, USA (office). *Telephone:* (617) 732-8210 (office). *Website:* www.brighamandwomens .org/anesthesiology (office).

THOMPSON, John Griggs, PhD, FRS; American mathematician and academic; *Graduate Research Professor Emeritus, Department of Mathematics, University of Florida;* b. 13 Oct. 1932, Ottawa, Kan.; ed Yale Univ., Univ. of Chicago; with Inst. of Defense Analysis 1959–60; Asst Prof., Harvard Univ. 1961–62; Prof., Univ. of Chicago 1962–68; Fellow, Univ. Coll., Cambridge, UK 1968–70, Rouse Ball Prof. of Pure Math. 1970–93, Prof. Emer. 1993–; Grad. Research Prof., Univ. of Florida 1993–, now Prof. Emer.; mem. NAS 1971, Norwegian Acad. of Science and Letters; Dr hc (Illinois) 1968, (Yale) 1980, (Chicago) 1985, (Oxford) 1987, (Ohio State); Cole Prize, American Math. Soc. 1965, Fields Medal, Int. Congress of Mathematicians, Nice 1970, American Math. Soc. Colloquium Lecturer 1974, Senior Berwick Prize, London Math. Soc. 1982, Sylvester Medal, Royal Soc. 1985, Wolf Prize (Israel) 1992, Poincaré Prize, Acad. des sciences (France) 1992, Nat. Medal of Science (jtly) 2000, Abel Prize (jtly), Norwegian Acad. of Science and Letters 2008. *Publications:* numerous articles in math. journals on group theory. *Address:* Department of Mathematics, University of Florida, 365 Little Hall, corner of SW 13th Street and SW 2nd Avenue, PO Box 118105, Gainesville, FL 32611-8105, USA (office). *Telephone:* (352) 392-0281 (ext. 228) (office). *Fax:* (352) 392-8357 (office). *E-mail:* jthomps@math.ufl.edu (office). *Website:* www.math.ufl.edu/fac/thompson.html (office).

THOMPSON, John M.; Canadian banker and business executive; m.; three c.; ed Univ. of Western Ontario, Richard Ivey Business School at Univ. of Western Ontario and Kellogg Grad. School, Northwestern Univ., USA; joined IBM Canada Ltd as a systems engineer 1966, later Marketing Man., Pres. and CEO 1986, Corp. Vice-Pres., Marketing and Services, IBM Corpn 1991, Head AS/400 Server business, Sr Vice-Pres. and Group Exec. IBM Software Group 1995, Vice-Chair. 2000–02; mem. Bd Dirs Toronto-Dominion Bank 1988–, Chair. (non-exec.) TD Bank Financial Group 2003–10; mem. Bd of Dirs Thomson Reuters Corpn, Atlantic Salmon Fed.; Vice-Chair. Supervisory Bd Philips Electronics NV, Hosp. for Sick Children; Chancellor Univ. of Western Ontario 2008–; fmr Dir Conf. Bd of Canada, Canadian Council of Chief Exec.; served on past Premier of Ontario's Councils for educ. reform, human resources reform and industrial policy; Hon. LLD (Univ. of Western Ontario) 1994. *Leisure interests:* being with his grandchildren, fly-fishing, boating, golf. *Address:* c/o TD Bank Financial Group, Toronto-Dominion Centre, King Street West and Bay Street, Toronto, ON M5K 1A2, Canada.

THOMPSON, John W., BBA, MBA; American computer industry executive; *Independent Chairman, Microsoft Corporation;* b. 24 April 1949, Fort Dix, NJ; ed John F. Kennedy High School, Riviera Beach, Fla (now Suncoast Community High School), Florida A&M Univ., Sloan Fellows Program of MIT Sloan School of Man.; began career with IBM Corpn 1971, held sr exec. positions in sales, marketing and software devt, latterly as Gen. Man. IBM Americas as well as membership of Worldwide Man. Council –1999; Chair. and CEO Symantec Corpn 1999–2009, Chair. 2009–11; mem. Bd of Dirs Virtual Instruments 2009–, CEO 2010–; Ind. Dir, Microsoft Corpn 2012–, Ind. Chair. 2014–; mem. Bd of Dirs UPS, Seagate Technology, Florida A&M Univ. Cluster, Ill. Gov.'s Human Resource Advisory Council, Teach for America; mem. Nat. Infrastructure Advisory Cttee 2002–, Financial Crisis Inquiry Comm. 2009–; bought 20% share of Golden State Warriors NBA professional basketball team under the umbrella of Bay Area Basketball Partners, LLC 2005; Dr hc (Univ. of Notre Dame, Mendoza Coll. of Business) 2008; David Packard Medal of Achievement, TechAmerica Foundation, Business Hall of Fame Laureate, Junior Achievement 2008, Pioneer Business Leader Award, Silicon Valley Educ. Foundation 2010, Spirit of Silicon Valley Lifetime Achieve-ment Award, Silicon Valley Leadership Group 2012. *Address:* Microsoft Corpor-ation, 1 Microsoft Way, Redmond, WA 98052-8300 (office); Virtual Instruments, 25 Metro Drive, San Jose, CA 95110 USA (office). *Telephone:* (425) 882-8080 (Redmond) (office); (408) 579-4000 (San Jose) (office). *Fax:* (425) 936-7329 (Redmond) (office); (408) 579-4001 (San Jose) (office). *E-mail:* info@microsoft.com (office); info@virtualinstruments.com (office). *Website:* www.microsoft.com (office); www.virtualinstruments.com (office).

THOMPSON, Julie Dawn, PhD; British biologist, biochemist and academic; *Senior Researcher, Institut de Génétique et de Biologie Moléculaire et Cellulaire, Centre National de la Recherche Scientifique;* with Vickers Shipbuilding and Eng Ltd 1984–86; with Singer Link Miles Ltd 1986–88; with Rediffusion Simulation Ltd 1988–90; European Molecular Biology Lab., Heidelberg, Germany 1991–94; Sr Researcher, Institut de Génétique et de Biologie Moléculaire et Cellulaire (CNRS/Institut Nat. de la Santé et de la Recherche Médicale—INSERM/Université Louis Pasteur), Illkirch, France 1995–; collaborated in creation of CLUSTAL W program for nucleic acid and protein sequences; Cristal du CNRS 2005, prix Madeleine

Lecoq 2007. *Publications:* numerous articles in scientific journals on nucleic acid and protein multiple sequence alignment programs. *Address:* Institut de Génétique et de Biologie Moléculaire et Cellulaire, 1 rue Laurent Fries, BP10142, 67404 Illkirch Cedex, France (office). *Telephone:* (3) 88-65-32-00 (office). *Fax:* (3) 88-65-32-01 (office). *E-mail:* thompson@unistra.fr (office). *Website:* www.igbmc.fr (office).

THOMPSON, Kenneth (Ken) Lane, BS, MS; American computer scientist; *Distinguished Engineer, Google Inc.;* b. 4 Feb. 1943, New Orleans, La; ed Univ. of California, Berkeley; worked with Dennis Ritchie on Multics operating system during 1960s, cr. Bon programming language; worked at Bell Labs –2000; Fellow, Entrisphere, Inc. 2000–06; Distinguished Engineer, Google Inc. 2006–, co-invented the Go programming language; mem. Nat. Acad. of Eng 1980; Fellow, Computer History Museum 1997; Turing Award (co-recipient with Dennis Ritchie) 1983, IEEE Richard W. Hamming Medal (co-recipient with Dennis Ritchie) 1990, Nat. Medal of Tech. (co-recipient with Dennis Ritchie) 1998, first IEEE Tsutomu Kanai Award 1999, Japan Prize for Information and Communications (co-recipient with Dennis Ritchie) 2011. *Achievements include:* prin. creator (with Dennis Ritchie) of Unix operating system, also invented B programming language (direct predecessor to C programming language), one of the creators and early developers of Plan 9 operating systems. *Publications:* several patents. *E-mail:* ken@google.com (office).

THOMPSON, Mark Edward, BS, PhD; American chemist and academic; *Professor of Chemistry, University of Southern California;* ed Univ. of California, Berkeley, Univ., California Inst. of Tech.; Visiting Scientist, E.I. duPont deNemours & Co., Wilmington, Del. 1983; Science and Eng Research Council (SERC) Research Fellow, Inorganic Chem. Lab., Univ. of Oxford, UK, worked with Prof. Malcolm L.H. Green studying electronic and nonlinear-optical properties of organometallic materials 1985–87; Asst Prof., Princeton Univ., Princeton, NJ 1987–95; Assoc. Prof., Dept of Chem., Univ. of Southern California 1995–99, Prof. of Chem. 2000–, Chair. Dept of Chem. 2005–; mem. Editorial Bd Chemistry of Materials 1998–2003; Distinguished Inventor of the Year, Intellectual Property Owners Asscn 1998, Thomas Alva Edison Patent Award, Research and Devt Council of NJ 1998, Raubenheimer Outstanding Faculty Award, Coll. of Letters, Arts and Science, Univ. of Southern California 2004, Jan Rajchman Prize for Outstanding Research in Flat Panel Displays, Soc. for Information Display 2006, MRS Medal, Materials Research Soc. 2006. *Publications:* more than 200 scientific papers in peer-reviewed journals on organic light emitting diodes (OLEDs), organic photovoltaic devices (OPVs or solar cells), devt of nano-biotic sensors and abiotic–biotic interfaces; 71 US patents. *Address:* Room 268, Laird J. Stabler Laboratories (LJS), Chemistry Department, University of Southern California, 840 West 36th Place/Downey Way, Los Angeles, CA 90089-0744, USA (office). *Telephone:* (213) 740-6402 (office). *Fax:* (213) 740-0930 (office); (213) 740-8594 (office). *E-mail:* met@usc.edu (office). *Website:* chem.usc.edu/faculty/Thompson.html (office); met.usc.edu (office).

THOMPSON, Mark John, MA, FRTS, FRSA; British media executive; *President and CEO, The New York Times Company;* b. 31 July 1957, London, England; s. of Duncan John Thompson and Sydney Columba Thompson (née Corduff); m. Jane Emilie Blumberg 1987; two s. one d.; ed Stonyhurst Coll., Merton Coll., Oxford; Research Asst Trainee, BBC TV 1979–1980, Asst Producer Nationwide 1980–1982, Producer Breakfast Time 1982–84, Output Ed. London Plus 1984–85, Newsnight 1985–87, Ed. Nine O'Clock News 1988–90, Panorama 1990–92, Head of Features 1992–94, Head of Factual Programmes 1994–96, Controller BBC2 1996–98; Dir of Nat. and Regional Broadcasting 1998–2000; Dir of TV, BBC 2000–02; CEO Channel 4 2002–04; Dir-Gen. BBC 2004–12; Pres. and CEO The New York Times Co., New York 2012–; mem. Bd of Trustees, Media Trust 2002–12; Patron Art Room (charity), Oxford; ranked 65th by Forbes magazine amongst The World's Most Powerful People 2009. *Leisure interests:* walking, cooking. *Address:* The New York Times Company, 620 8th Avenue, New York, NY 10018, USA. *Telephone:* (212) 556-1234. *Website:* www.nytco.com.

THOMPSON, Sir Michael Warwick, Kt, DSc, FInstP; British physicist, academic and university vice-chancellor; *Emeritus Professor, University of Birmingham;* b. 1 June 1931; s. of Kelvin W. Thompson and Madeleine Walford; m. 1st Sybil N. Spooner 1956 (died 1999); two s.; m. 2nd Jenny Mitchell 2000; ed Rydal School and Univ. of Liverpool; Research Scientist, AERE, Harwell, Reactor Physics and Metallurgy 1953–65; Prof. of Experimental Physics, Univ. of Sussex 1965–80, Pro-Vice-Chancellor 1972–78; Vice-Chancellor, Univ. of E Anglia 1980–86; Vice-Chancellor and Prin., Univ. of Birmingham 1987–96, Emer. Prof. 1996–; Chair. Council John Innes Research Inst. 1980–86, British Council Cttee for Academic Research Collaboration with Germany 1988–; mem. SRC Physics Cttee (also Chair.) 1972–79, E Sussex Educ. Cttee 1973–78, E Sussex Area Health Authority 1973–80, W Midlands Regional Health Authority 1987–90 (non-exec. Dir 1990–96), Council for Nat. Academic Awards 1988–91, Council of Asscn of Commonwealth Univs 1990–95, Council for Industry and Higher Educ. 1991–96; mem. Bd of Dirs COBUILD Ltd 1987–96, TPIC Ltd 1987–; mem. Council of the Cttee of Vice-Chancellors and Prins 1989–96 (Chair. Medical Cttee 1994); Trustee, Barber Inst. of Fine Art 1987–2007, St Bartholomew's Medical Coll. 1998–2000; Grosses Bundesverdienstkreuz (Germany) 1997; Hon. LLD (Birmingham) 1997; Hon. DSc (Sussex) 1998; CV Boys Prize, Inst. of Physics. *Publications:* Defects and Radiation Damage in Metals 1968; over 100 papers in scientific journals on the interaction of radiation with solids. *Leisure interests:* sailing, the arts. *Address:* Stoneacre, The Warren, Polperro, Cornwall, PL13 2RD, England (home).

THOMPSON, (Rupert) Julian (de la Mare), MA; British art consultant; b. 23 July 1941; s. of Rupert Spens Thompson and Florence Elizabeth Thompson (née de la Mare); m. Jacqueline Julie Ivimy 1965; three d.; ed Eton Coll. and King's Coll., Cambridge; joined Ceramics Dept, Sotheby's 1963, Head of Chinese Art Dept 1969, Chair. Sotheby's UK and Sotheby's International 1982–86, Deputy Chair. 1987–92, Chair. Sotheby's Asia 1992–2004 (retd); currently Chief Investment Officer, China Fund. *Address:* Crossington Farm, Upton Bishop, Ross-on-Wye, Herefordshire, HR9 7UE, England. *Telephone:* (1989) 780-471.

THOMPSON, Scott, BA; American business executive; *CEO, ShopRunner;* ed Stonehill Coll., Boston, Mass; worked with Coopers and Lybrand delivering information tech. solutions to financial services clients; fmr Chief Information Officer, Barclays Global Investors; fmr Exec. Vice-Pres. of Tech. Solutions, Inovant (subsidiary of Visa formed to oversee global technology); Sr Vice-Pres. and Chief Tech. Officer, PayPal (div. of eBay Inc.) –2008, Pres. PayPal 2008–11; mem. Bd of Dirs and CEO Yahoo! Inc. 2012; CEO ShopRunner (members-only shopping service) 2012–; mem. Bd of Dirs F5 Networks Inc., Zuora Inc.; Ernst & Young Entrepreneur Of The Year Award 2011. *Address:* ShopRunner, 225 Washington Street, 3rd floor, Conshohocken, PA, 19428, USA (office). *Website:* www.shoprunner.com (office).

THOMPSON, Tommy George, BS, JD; American lawyer and fmr politician; *Partner, Akin Gump Strauss Hauer & Feld LLP;* b. 19 Nov. 1941, Elroy, Wis.; s. of Allan Thompson and Julie Dutton; m. Sue Ann Mashak 1969; one s. two d.; ed Univ. of Wisconsin; political intern in office of US Rep. Thomson, Washington, DC 1963; legis. messenger, Wis. State Senate 1964–66; with Elroy and Mauston, Wis. 1966–87; self-employed real estate broker, Mauston 1970; mem. Dist 87 Wis. State Ass. 1966–87, Asst Minority Leader 1972–81, Floor Leader 1981–87; Gov. of Wisconsin 1987–2001; US Sec. Health and Human Services, Washington, DC 2001–05; Pnr, Akin Gump Strauss Hauer & Feld LLP, Washington, DC 2005–; Chair. Republican Govs' Asscn 1991–92; Chair. Bd of Dirs Amtrak 1998–99; fmr mem. Exec. Cttee Nat. Govs' Asscn; mem. ABA; Nature Conservancy Award 1988, Thomas Jefferson Freedom Award (American Legis. Exchange Council) 1991; Leadership in Natural Energy Conservation Award, US Energy Asscn 1994, Horatio Alger Award, and numerous other awards. *Leisure interests:* hunting, fishing, sports. *Address:* Akin Gump Strauss Hauer & Feld LLP, Robert S. Strauss Building, 1333 New Hampshire Avenue, NW, Washington, DC 20036-1564, USA (office). *Telephone:* (202) 887-4080 (office). *Fax:* (202) 887-4288 (office). *E-mail:* tthompson@akingump.com (office). *Website:* www.akingump.com (office).

THOMSEN, Niels Jørgen, DPhil; Danish historian and academic; b. 21 April 1930, Copenhagen; s. of the late Sigurd Thomsen and Gudrun Kirkegaard; m. Birgit Nüchel Petersen 1953; two s.; ed Univ. of Copenhagen; Dir Danish Press Museum, Århus 1958–65; Lecturer, School of Journalism, Århus 1962–65; Asst Prof. of Econ. History, Univ. of Copenhagen 1965–71, Asst Prof. of Political Science 1971–73, Prof. of Modern History 1973–2000; Danish Ed. Pressens Årbog 1968–82; Chair. Soc. for History and Econs, Copenhagen 1980–83; Chair. Soc. for Contemporary History 1982–; mem. Royal Danish Acad. of Science and Letters. *Publications:* Partipressen 1965, Dagbladskonkurrencen 1870–1970 I–II 1972, Københavns Universitet 1936–66 1986, De danske aviser 1634–1989 (with Jette Søllinge) I–III 1987–91, Industri, stat og samfund 1870–1939 1991, Hovedstrømninger 1870–1914 1998; about 80 articles on political and media history in professional journals. *Address:* Institute of History, University of Copenhagen, Njalsgade 102, 2300 Copenhagen S (office); Vitus Berings Allé 15, 2930 Klampenborg, Denmark (home). *Telephone:* 35-32-82-43 (office); 39-64-33-16 (home). *Fax:* 35-32-82-41 (office). *E-mail:* n.thomsen@mail.tele.dk (home). *Website:* www.hum.ku.dk (office).

THOMSON, Sir Adam McClure, Kt, KCMG, CMG; British diplomatist; *Permanent Representative-designate, North Atlantic Treaty Organization;* m. Fariba Shirazi Thomson; three c.; joined FCO 1978, Asst Desk Officer, Defence Dept 1978–79, Desk Officer, E European and Soviet Dept 1980–81, Third, later Second Sec. (Political), Embassy in Moscow 1981–83, Second, later First Sec. Political, Econ. and CEP Cttees, UK Del. to NATO 1983–86, Head of Israel/Lebanon Team, Near East and N Africa Dept, FCO 1986–89, seconded to Cabinet Office, Assessments Staff 1989–91, First Sec., Politico-Mil., Embassy in Washington, DC 1991–95, Political Counsellor, High Comm., New Delhi 1995–98, Head of Security Policy Dept, FCO 1998–2002, Amb. and Deputy Perm. Rep., UK Mission to UN, New York 2002–06, Dir S Asia and Afghanistan Directorate, FCO 2006–09, High Commr to Pakistan 2009–13; Amb. and Perm. Rep.-designate NATO 2014–. *Address:* UK Delegation to NATO, Blvd Leopold III, 1110 Brussels, Belgium (office). *Telephone:* (2) 707-75-01 (office). *Fax:* (2) 707-75-96 (office). *E-mail:* ukdel.natogeneralenquiries@fco.gsi.gov.uk (office). *Website:* www.gov.uk/government/world/uk-joint-delegation-to-nato (office).

THOMSON, Brian Edward, AM; Australian theatre designer; b. 5 Jan. 1946, Sydney; s. of Austin Thomas Thomson and Andoree Gertrude Thomson; ed Applecross Sr High School, Perth Tech. Coll., Univ. of New South Wales; Supervising Designer, closing ceremony of Olympic Games, Sydney 2000; Production Designer, Centennial of Fed. Ceremony 2001; Designer, opening and closing ceremonies, Rugby World Cup 2003; Australian Film Inst. Award for production design, Rebel 1985, Ground Zero 1987, Sydney Theatre Critics' Award for Best Designer 1989, 1992, 1993, 1994, Mo Award 1994, 1995. *Musicals:* Hair, Jesus Christ Superstar (London and Australia), The Rocky Horror Show (original London production and worldwide), Chicago, The Stripper, Company, Chess, The King and I (Broadway production 1996 (Tony Award), London Palladium), How to Succeed in Business Without Really Trying, South Pacific, Hello, Dolly!, Merrily We Roll Along, Grease, Happy Days. *Theatre:* Housewife Superstar!!! (London and New York); The Threepenny Opera (opening season, Drama Theatre, Sydney Opera House); Big Toys (the Old Tote); A Cheery Soul, Chinchilla, Macbeth, The Doll Trilogy, The Ham Funeral, A Midsummer Night's Dream, The Crucible, The Homecoming, Uncle Vanya, Death and the Maiden, Coriolanus, Falsettos, King Lear, Arcadia, Medea, Mongrels, Third World Blues, After the Ball, White Devil (also at Brooklyn Acad. of Music), Up for Grabs (all for Sydney Theatre Co.); Arturo Ui, Rock-Ola (Nimrod); Lulu, Shepherd on the Rocks Crow (State Theatre Co. of S Australia); Ghosts, The Tempest, The Master Builder, Buzz, Frogs, Aftershocks, Radiance, Up the Road, Burnt Piano, The Laramie Project (Company B Belvoir); Angels in America (Melbourne Theatre Co.); Soulmates, One Day of the Year (Sydney Theatre Co.), My Zinc Bed, Buried Child (Company B Belvoir), Dame Edna Back With A Vengeance, Broadway 2004, Three Furies, Sydney Festival 2005. *Film and television:* Barlow and Chambers, Shadow of the Cobra (both miniseries); Shirly Thompson vs. the Aliens, The Rocky Horror Picture Show, Starstruck, Rebel, Night of Shadows (also dir), Ground Zero, Turtle Beach, Frauds. *Dance:* Synergy, Fornicon (Sydney Dance Co.), Tivol (Sydney Dance Co. and Australian Ballet). *Opera:* Death in Venice, The Makropulos Affair (Adelaide Festival); Turandot, Aida, Summer of the Seventeenth Doll (Vic. State Opera);

Voss, Death in Venice, Tristan und Isolde, Katya Kabanova, The Eighth Wonder (The Australian Opera); Billy Budd (Welsh Nat. Opera, Opera Australia, Canadian Nat. Opera), Sweeney Todd (Lyric Opera of Chicago). *Leisure interests:* movies, sport (Aussie rules, cricket, tennis). *Address:* 5 Little Dowling Street, Paddington, NSW 2021, Australia. *Telephone:* (2) 9331-1584 (office); (4) 1164-3323 (home). *E-mail:* bt@brianthomson.biz (office). *Website:* www.brianthomson.biz (office).

THOMSON, James Alan, BS, MS, PhD; American business executive and security expert; *President and CEO, RAND Corporation;* b. 21 Jan. 1945, Boston, Mass; m. Darlene Thomson; ed Univ. of New Hampshire and Purdue Univ.; Research Fellow, Univ. of Wisconsin, Madison 1972–74; Systems Analyst, Office of Sec. of Defense, US Dept of Defense, Washington, DC 1974–77; staff mem. Nat. Security Council, Washington, DC 1977–81; Vice-Pres. RAND Corpn, Santa Monica, Calif. 1981–88, Pres. and CEO 1989–; Dir LA World Affairs Council, Object Reservoir Inc., AK Steel Holdings Corpn; mem. Int. Inst. for Strategic Studies (UK), Council on Foreign Relations 1985–, Bd Los Angeles World Affairs Council; Hon. DSc (Purdue) 1992, (New Hampshire); Hon. LLD (Pepperdine) 1996. *Publications:* Conventional Arms Control and the Security of Europe 1988; articles on defence issues. *Address:* RAND Corporation, 1776 Main Street, Santa Monica, CA 90401, USA (office). *Telephone:* (310) 451-6936 (office). *Fax:* (310) 451-6972 (office). *E-mail:* thomson@rand.org (office). *Website:* www.rand.org (office).

THOMSON, James (Jamie) Alexander, BS, VMD, PhD; American developmental biologist and academic; *John D. MacArthur Professor, School of Medicine and Public Health, University of Wisconsin-Madison;* b. 20 Dec. 1958, Oak Park, Ill.; ed Univs of Illinois and Pennsylvania; board certified in veterinary pathology 1995; Post-doctoral Research Fellow, Primate In Vitro Fertilization and Experimental Embryology Lab., Oregon Nat. Primate Research Center 1988–90; joined Univ. of Wisconsin-Madison 1990, currently John D. MacArthur Prof., Univ. of Wisconsin-Madison School of Medicine and Public Health, Dir of Regenerative Biology, Morgridge Inst. for Research, Faculty mem. Genome Center of Wisconsin, has conducted pioneering work in isolation and culture of non-human primate and human embryonic stem cells; Adjunct Prof., Molecular, Cellular, and Developmental Biology Dept, Univ. of California, Santa Barbara; Co-founder and Chief Scientific Officer, Cellular Dynamics International, Madison; Chief Pathologist, Wisconsin Nat. Primate Research Center; mem. NAS; Hon. DSc (Univ. of Illinois, Urbana-Champaign) 2013; featured on the cover of TIME magazine's America's Best in Science & Medicine feature 2001, named by TIME magazine as one of the world's 100 most influential people 2008, King Faisal Int. Prize in Medicine (co-recipient) 2011, Albany Medical Center Prize (co-recipient) 2011. *Publications:* numerous articles in professional journals; several patents. *Address:* Department of Cell and Regenerative Biology, School of Medicine and Public Health, Morgridge Institute for Research, University of Wisconsin-Madison, 330 North Orchard Street, Madison, WI 53715, USA (office). *Telephone:* (608) 316-4348 (office). *E-mail:* jthomson@morgridgeinstitute.org (office). *Website:* discovery.wisc.edu/home/ morgridge/about-morgridge/leadership/james-thomson/ (office); ink.primate.wisc .edu/~thomson (office).

THOMSON, Jennifer Ann, PhD; South African microbiologist, molecular biologist and academic; *Professor of Microbiology, Department of Molecular and Cell Biology, University of Cape Town;* ed Univ. of Cape Town, Univ. of Cambridge, UK, Rhodes Univ.; Post-doctoral Fellow, Harvard Univ., USA; Visiting Scientist, MIT –1983; Lecturer, later Assoc. Prof., Dept of Genetics, Univ. of Witwatersrand 1983; Dir Lab. for Molecular and Cell Biology, CSIRO; Head, Dept of Microbiology, Univ. of Cape Town 1988, Prof. of Microbiology, Dept of Molecular and Cell Biology (formed by merger of Depts of Biochemistry and Microbiology) 2001–; expert adviser, WHO; addressed UN Gen. Ass. on theme of genetically modified crops for developing countries 2002; Co-founder South African Women in Science and Eng; fmr Vice-Pres. Acad. of Science of South Africa; fmr mem. African Acad. of Sciences Policy Cttee; Fellow, Royal Soc. of South Africa; L'Oréal-UNESCO For Women in Science Award 2004. *Publications:* Genes for Africa 2002; numerous articles in scientific journals on biological control of plant pests and diseases, genetically modified plants to improve agricultural productivity and food quality in developing countries and molecular genetics of industrially and medically important anaerobic bacteria. *Address:* Department of Molecular and Cell Biology, University of Cape Town, Private Bag Rondebosch, 7701 Cape Town, South Africa (office). *Telephone:* (21) 650-3256 (office). *Fax:* (21) 689-7573 (office). *E-mail:* jat@science .uct.ac.za (office). *Website:* www.mcb.uct.ac.za (office).

THOMSON, Sir John Adam, GCMG, MA; British diplomatist (retd); *Research Affiliate, Science, Technology and Global Security Working Group, Massachusetts Institute of Technology;* b. 27 April 1927, Aberdeenshire; s. of the late Sir George Thomson, FRS and Kathleen Smith; m. 1st Elizabeth Anne McClure 1953 (died 1988); three s. one d.; m. 2nd Judith Ogden Bullitt 1992; ed Philips Exeter Acad., NH, USA, Aberdeen Univ., Trinity Coll., Cambridge; Third Sec., Embassy in Jeddah 1951, Damascus 1954; Foreign Office 1955; Private Sec. to Perm. Under-Sec. 1958; First Sec., Embassy in Washington, DC 1960; Foreign Office 1964; Acting Head of Planning Staff 1966; Counsellor, Head of Planning Staff 1967; seconded to Cabinet Office as Chief of Assessment Staff 1968; Minister, Deputy Perm. Rep. to NATO 1972; Asst Under-Sec. of State, Foreign and Commonwealth Office 1973; High Commr in India 1977–82; Perm. Rep. to UN 1982–87; Leader CSCE Humanitarian Mission to Bosnia-Herzegovina 1992; Prin. Dir, 21st Century Trust 1987–90; Research Affiliate, Science, Tech. and Global Security Working Group, MIT 2004–; Chair. Minority Rights Group Int. 1991–99, Flemings Emerging Markets Investment Trust 1991–98; int. adviser, ANZ Grindlays Bank 1996–97 (Dir 1987–96); mem. Council IISS, Governing Body Inst. of Devt Studies, Sussex, Council Overseas Devt Inst., London, Howie Cttee for Secondary Educ. in Scotland 1990–92; Trustee Nat. Museums of Scotland 1991–99; Assoc. mem. Nuffield Coll., Oxford 1988–91; Hon. Foreign Mem., American Acad. of Arts and Sciences 2010; Hon. LLD (Ursinus Coll.) 1984, (Aberdeen) 1986. *Publication:* Crusader Castles (with Robin Fedden) 1956. *Leisure interests:* castles, oriental carpets, walking. *Address:* Science, Technology and Global Security Working Group, Massachusetts Institute of Technology, 70 Memorial Drive, Building E51-163, Cambridge, MA 02142, (office). *Telephone:* (617) 452-3976 (office). *Website:* web.mit.edu/stgs (office).

THOMSON, Peter William, AO, CBE; Australian professional golfer; b. 23 Aug. 1929, Melbourne, Vic.; m. Stella Mary 1960; one s. three d.; turned professional 1949; British Open Champion 1954, 1955, 1956, 1958, 1965 (only player to win three successively since Open became 72-hole event 1892); won British PGA Match-Play Championship four times and 16 major tournaments in Britain; Australian Open Champion 1951, 1967, 1972, NZ Open Champion nine times; won open titles of Italy, Spain, Hong Kong, Philippines, India and Germany; played 11 times for Australia in World Cup (won twice); won World Seniors Championship 1984, PGA Seniors Championship of America 1984; Capt. Pres.'s Cup Int. Team 1996, 1998, 2000; fmr Pres. Professional Golfers' Assçn of Australia; Dir Thomson Perrett & Lobb; mem. James McGrath Foundation, Vic.; Hon. DBA (Queen Margaret Univ. Coll. Edin.) 2002, Hon. DIur (St Andrews) 2005, Dr hc (Victoria) 2006. *Leisure interests:* classical music, literature, discussing politics. *Address:* Kerkin Court, 1–107 Mathoura Road, Toorak, Vic. 3142, Australia (home). *Telephone:* (3) 86 988000 (office). *E-mail:* peter@thomsonperrett.com.au (office).

THOMSON, Richard Murray, OC, BASs (Eng), MBA; Canadian banker (retd); b. 14 Aug. 1933, Winnipeg, Man.; s. of H. W. Thomson and Mary Thomson; m. Heather Lorimer 1959; ed Univ. of Toronto, Harvard Business School, Queen's Univ., Kingston, Ont.; joined Toronto-Dominion Bank, Head Office 1957, Sr Asst Man., St James & McGill, Montreal 1961, Asst to Pres., Head Office 1963, Asst Gen. Man. 1965, Chief Gen. Man. 1968, Vice-Pres., Chief Gen. Man., Dir 1971, Pres. 1972–79, Pres. and CEO 1977–79, CEO 1978–97, Chair. 1978–98. *Leisure interests:* golf, tennis, skiing. *Address:* TD Bank Group, TD Centre, 55 King Street, PO Box 1, Toronto, ON M5K 1A2, Canada (office). *Telephone:* (416) 982-8356 (office). *Fax:* (416) 983-8607 (office). *Website:* www.td.com (office).

THOMSON, Robert James; Australian journalist, newspaper editor and business executive; *Chief Executive, News Corp;* b. 11 March 1961, Torrumbarry; m. Wang Ping; two s.; financial and gen. affairs reporter, then Sydney Corresp. The Herald, Melbourne 1979–83; sr feature writer Sydney Morning Herald 1983–85; corresp. for the Financial Times, Beijing 1985–89, Tokyo 1989–94, Foreign News Ed., London 1994–96, Asst Ed. Financial Times and Ed. Weekend FT 1996–98, US Man. Ed. Financial Times 1998–2002; Ed. The Times (UK) 2002–07, Publr, Wall Street Journal 2007–08, Man. Ed. 2008–13, Man. Ed. and Ed.-in-Chief, Dow Jones 2008–13, mem. Bd of Dirs and Chief Exec. News Corp (following restructuring of News Corporation to spin off its publishing assets into similarly named News Corp while existing News Corporation renamed 21st Century Fox and its legal successor) 2013–; mem. Knight-Bagehot Fellowship Bd, Columbia Univ.; Dr hc (RMIT) 2010; Business Journalist of the Year, The Journalist and Financial Reporting Group (TJFR) 2001. *Television:* regular appearances on ABC News, CNN, Fox News Channel. *Publications:* The Judges: A Portrait of the Australian Judiciary, The Chinese Army (co-author), True Fiction (ed.). *Leisure interests:* cinema, tennis, reading. *Address:* News Corp, 1211 Avenue of the Americas, New York, NY 10036, USA (office). *Telephone:* (212) 416-3012 (office). *Fax:* (212) 416-2790 (office). *Website:* newscorp.com (office).

THOMSON, William Reid, BSc, MSc, MPhil (Econs); British economist, geopolitical adviser, pension fund expert and writer; *Chairman, Private Capital Limited, Hong Kong;* b. 10 Aug. 1939, London, England; s. of the late Wing-Commdr W. Thomson and Nellie Hendry Thomson; m. 1st Mary Cormack 1967 (divorced 1986); m. 2nd Jeannette Vinta 1987; two s. one d.; ed George Washington Univ., Univ. of Washington, USA, Univ. of Manchester; economist and operations analyst with various cos 1961–72; investment analyst, Legg Mason & Co. 1973–74; Sr Economist, US Treasury Dept 1974–85, Office of Debt Analysis and Office of Int. Devt Banks; Exec. Dir African Devt Bank 1982–83; Alt. Exec. Dir Asian Devt Bank 1985–90, Vice-Pres. 1990–94; Sr Counsellor to Pres. 1994–95; Sr Adviser Franklin Templeton Investments Asia 1995–2008; Chair. Yamamoto Int. Co (Japan) (venture capital) 1996–, Siam Recovery Fund 1997–2005, PEDCA LLC 1997–2005, Momentum Asia Ltd (hedge funds) 1998–2003, Private Capital Ltd Hong Kong 2005–; Dir Finavestment Ltd, London 2008–; adviser, Axiom Alternative Fund 2004–09; Visiting Prof., Nihon Univ., Tokyo; writer on Asian political/ econ. affairs, Asia Asset Management, Asia and Pacific Review, Asia Times, The Standard Hong Kong and also for many websites. *Publication:* Confidential Inside Asia Report 1996–2001, Asia Asset Management 2003–; many others. *Leisure interests:* jogging, cricket, reading, writing. *Address:* 184 London Road, Guildford, GU1 1XR, England (home); Private Capital Ltd, 16/F Shun Ho Tower, 24–30 Ice House Street, Central, Hong Kong Special Administrative Region, People's Republic of China (office). *Telephone:* 2869-1996 (Hong Kong) (office); 811-8181 (Manila) (office); (1483) 440825 (home). *Fax:* 28110-9521 (Hong Kong) (office); 814-0130 (Manila) (office); (1483) 440825 (home). *E-mail:* wrthomson@private-capital .com.hk (office); wrthomson@btconnect.com (home); bill_thomson2003@yahoo.com (home). *Website:* www.private-capital.com.hk (office); www.finavestment.com (office).

THOMSON OF FLEET, 3rd Baron Thomson of Fleet; **David Kenneth Roy Thomson,** MA; Canadian business executive; *Chairman, Thomson Reuters;* b. 12 June 1957; s. of the late Kenneth Thomson, 2nd Baron Thomson of Fleet and of Nora Marilyn Lavis Thomson; m. 1st; two d.; m. 2nd (divorced); one s.; one d. with Kelly Rowan; ed Upper Canada Coll., Selwyn Coll., Cambridge, UK; has held several positions in cos controlled by his family, including Man. The Bay store at Cloverdale Mall, Etobicoke, Ont. and Pres. of Zellers (retailer); f. real estate firm Osmington Inc. (owned and operated outside of Thomson group); mem. Bd of Dirs Thomson Corpn 1988–, Chair. 2002–, now Chair. Thomson Reuters (following merger with Reuters), Chair. The Woodbridge Co. Ltd (Thomson family investment co.); Patron Art Gallery of Ontario; succeeded to title of 3rd Baron Thomson of Fleet 12 June 2006. *Address:* Thomson Reuters, 3 Times Square, New York, NY 10036, USA (office). *Telephone:* (646) 223-4000 (office). *E-mail:* info@ thomsonreuters.com (office). *Website:* www.thomsonreuters.com (office).

THONDAMAN, (Savumiamoorthy) Arumugam Ramanathan; Sri Lankan politician; *Minister of Livestock and Rural Community Development;* b. 29 May 1964; m.; ed Royal Coll., Colombo; advocate for Indian Tamils of Sri Lanka; MP for Nuwara Eliya Dist; fmr Minister of Livestock Devt and Estate Infrastructure; Minister of Housing and Plantation Infrastructure –2004; Pres. and Gen. Sec. Ceylon Workers' Congress (affiliated with United People's Freedom Alliance); Minister of Youth Empowerment and Socio-Economic Devt 2007–10, of Livestock and Rural Community Devt 2010–. *Address:* Ministry of Livestock and Rural

Community Development, 45 St Michael's Road, PO Box 562, Colombo 3 (office); No. 09 2/2, Rajakeeya Mawatha, Mayfair Flats, Colombo 7, Sri Lanka (home). *Telephone:* (11) 2541369 (office). *Fax:* (11) 2430365 (office). *E-mail:* geethacb@hotmail.com (office). *Website:* www.livestock.gov.lk (office).

THONGLOUN, Sisolit; Laotian politician; *Deputy Prime Minister and Minister of Foreign Affairs;* b. 10 Nov. 1945; ed Pedagogical Coll., Neo Lao Hak Sat, Houaphanh, Pedagogical Inst., St Petersburg, Russia, Acad. of Social Science, Moscow; Staff Officer, Educational Div., Neo Lao Hak Sat (Lao Nat. Patriotic Front), Houaphanh Prov. 1967–69; Staff Officer, Rep. Office, Neo Lao Hak Sat (LNPE), Hanoi 1969–73; Instructor, Vientiane Univ. 1978–79; Sec. to Ministry of Educ. and Chief, External Relations Div., Ministry of Educ. 1979–81; Dir Public Research Dept, Ministry Council Bd, Office of the Prime Minister 1985–86; Vice-Minister, Ministry of Foreign Affairs 1987–92; Minister of Labour and Social Welfare 1993–97; mem. Parl. 1998–2000; Deputy Prime Minister of Laos 2001–, Minister of Foreign Affairs 2006–; Pres. Cttee for Planning and Cooperation, Cttee for Investment and Cooperation, Lao Nat. Cttee for Energy; Hon. Pres., SOS of Lao PDR1–. *Address:* Ministry of Foreign Affairs, rue That Luang 01004, Ban Phonxay, Vientiane, Laos (office). *Telephone:* (21) 413148 (office). *Fax:* (21) 414009 (office). *E-mail:* souknivone@mofa.gov.la (office). *Website:* www.mofa.gov.la (office).

't HOOFT, Gerardus, PhD; Dutch physicist and academic; *Professor of Theoretical Physics, University of Utrecht;* b. 5 July 1946, Den Helder; s. of H. 't Hooft and M. A. van Kampen; m. Albertha A. Schik 1972; two d.; ed Dalton Lyceum Gymnasium beta, The Hague, Rijks Universiteit, Utrecht; Fellow, CERN (Theoretical Physics Div.), Geneva 1972–74; Asst Prof., Univ. of Utrecht 1974–77, Prof. of Theoretical Physics 1977–; mem. Koninklijke Acad. van Wetenschappen, Letteren en Schone Kunsten v. België, Koninklijke Nederlandse Acad. van Wetenschappen, Koninklijke Hollandsche Maatschappij der Wetenschappen 1983; Foreign Assoc. NAS; Fellow and CPhys, Inst. of Physics, London, UK 2000; Amb., Mars One Project 2012; Foreign Hon. mem. American Acad. of Arts and Sciences, Acad. des Sciences; Commdr, Nederlandse Leeuw 1999, Hon. Medal, Astana (Kazakhstan) 2000, Officier, Légion d'honneur 2001, and others; Dr hc (Chicago) 1981, (Leuven) 1996, (Bologna) 1998, (Cape Town) 2001, (Hofstra Univ.) 2001, (Marseille) 2001, (Columbus, Ohio) 2003, (Hefei) 2004, (Salamanca) 2006 and others; W. Prins Prize 1974, Akzo Prize 1977, Dannie Heineman Prize 1979, Wolf Foundation Prize in Physics, 1981, Spinoza Premium 1995, Pius XI Medal 1983, Lorentz Medal 1986, Franklin Medal 1995, G.C. Wick Medal 1997, High Energy Physics Prize, European Physical Soc. 1999, Nobel Prize for Physics (jtly) 1999, Erice Prize 2009, Asteroid 9491 Thooft named in his honour, Lomonosov Gold Medal, Russian Acad. of Sciences 2010. *Publications include:* Under the Spell of the Gauge Principle 1994, In Search of the Ultimate Building Blocks 1996, Playing with Planets 2008, Tijd in Machten van Tien 2011; papers on Renormalization of Yang-Mills Fields, magnetic monopoles, Instantons, Gauge theories, quark confinement, quantum mechanics, quantum gravity and black holes. *Address:* Faculty of Physics and Astronomy, University of Utrecht, Prinetonplein 5, 3584 CC Utrecht (office); University of Utrecht, Spinoza Institute, PO Box 80.195, 3508 TD Utrecht, Netherlands (office). *Telephone:* (30) 2535928 (office). *Fax:* (30) 2539282 (office); (30) 2535937 (office). *E-mail:* g.thooft@uu.nl (office). *Website:* www.staff.science.uu.nl/~hooft101 (office).

THORENS, Justin Pierre; Swiss professor of law and attorney; b. 15 Sept. 1931, Collonge-Bellerive; s. of Paul L. Thorens and Germaine Falquet; m. Colette F. Vecchio 1963; one s. one d.; ed Univ. of Geneva, Freie Univ. Berlin and Univ. Coll. London; attorney-at-law, Geneva Bar 1956–2011; Alt. Pres. Jurisdictional Court, Geneva 1971–78; Lecturer, Faculty of Law, Univ. of Geneva 1967, Assoc. Prof. 1970, Prof. 1973–96, Dean 1974–77, Hon. Prof. 1996–; Rector, Univ. of Geneva 1977–83; Visiting Scholar, Stanford Univ. 1983–84, Univ. of Calif., Berkeley 1983–84; Guest Prof., Univ. of Munich, Germany 1984; mem. Cttee European Centre for Higher Educ. (CEPES), Bucharest 1981–95, Pres. 1986–88; mem. Admin. Council Asscn des Universités Partiellement ou Entièrement de Langue Française (AUPELF), Montreal 1978–87, Vice-Pres. 1981–87, Hon. Vice-Pres. 1987–, mem. Gov. Council 1987–; Pres. Bd Int. Asscn of Univs (AIU), Paris 1985–90, Hon. Pres. 1990–; Vice-Pres. UNDL Foundation, Geneva 2001–; Pres. Int. Latsis Foundation 1989–2013; Bd mem. Fondation des Archives historiques de l'Abbaye de Saint-Maurice 2007–; mem. Council UN Univ. Tokyo 1986–92, Pres. 1988–89; mem. UNESCO Swiss Nat. Comm. 1989–2001, mem. Int. Acad. of Estate and Trust Law; mem. Soc. of Trust and Estate Practitioners, also mem. of many other nat. and int. asscns in the legal and cultural fields; various prizes, awards and distinctions. *Publications:* publs on pvt. law, civil procedure, arbitration, Anglo-American property law, univ. politics, cultural questions. *Leisure interests:* history and all its aspects, both European and the rest of the world; interaction of cultures of various times and regions. *Address:* 18 chemin du Nant d'Aisy, 1246 Corsier, Switzerland (home). *Telephone:* (22) 751-80-81 (office); (22) 751-12-62 (home). *Fax:* (22) 751-80-82 (office); (22) 751-80-82 (home). *E-mail:* justin.thorens@bluewin.ch.

THORNBURGH, Richard (Dick) Lewis, BEng, LLB; American lawyer and fmr politician; *Counsel, K&L Gates LLP;* b. 16 July 1932, Pittsburgh, Pa; s. of Charles G. Thornburgh and Alice Sanborn; m. Virginia W. Judson 1963; four s.; ed Yale Univ. and Univ. of Pittsburgh; admitted to Pa Bar 1958, US Supreme Court Bar 1965; attorney, Kirkpatrick & Lockhart LLP (now K&L Gates LLP), Pittsburgh 1959–79, 1977–79, 1987–88, 1994– (in Washington, DC); US attorney for Western Pa, Pittsburgh 1969–75; Asst Attorney-Gen. Criminal Div. US Justice Dept 1975–77; Gov. of Pennsylvania 1979–87; Dir Inst. of Politics, J.F. Kennedy School of Govt, Harvard Univ. 1987–88; Attorney-Gen. of USA 1988–91; UnderSec. Gen. for Admin. and Man. UN 1992–93; Founding Chair. State Science and Tech. Inst.; Chair. Legal Policy Advisory Bd, Washington Legal Foundation; Vice-Chair. World Cttee on Disability; mem. American Law Inst.; Trustee, Urban Inst.; mem. Nat. Acad. of Public Admin.; Lifetime Nat. Assoc., Nat. Acads of Science and Eng 2001–; Fellow, American Bar Foundation; Republican; 32 hon. degrees; Special Medallion Award, Fed. Drug Enforcement Admin. 1973, Distinguished Service Medal, American Legion 1992, Wiley E. Branton Award, Washington Lawyers' Cttee 2002, American Lawyer Magazine Lifetime Achievement Award 2006. *Publications:* Where the Evidence Leads (autobiography) 2003, Report of the Independent Review Panel on the September 8, 2004 '60 Minutes Wednesday' Segment "For the

Record" Concerning President Bush's Texas Air National Guard Service (with Louis D. Boccardi) 2005, Puerto Rico's Future: A Time to Decide 2007. *Address:* K&L Gates LLP, 1800 Massachusetts Avenue NW, Washington, DC 20036-1221, USA (office). *Telephone:* (202) 778-9080 (office). *Fax:* (202) 778-9100 (office). *E-mail:* dick.thornburgh@klgates.com (office). *Website:* www.klng.com (office).

THORNE, David, BA, MA; American business executive and fmr diplomatist; b. 16 Sept. 1944; s. of Landon Thorne, Jr; twin brother of Julia Thorne; m. Rose Thorne; two c.; ed Yale and Columbia Univs; moved with family to Rome when his father was apptd by Pres. Eisenhower to administer Marshall Plan for Italy 1953; served in USN 1966–70; Co-founder Adviser Investments (specializes in Vanguard and Fidelity mutual funds and exchange-traded funds); has been an investor in several business ventures, including marketing consulting, real estate, publishing and financial services; sold publishing business to Martha Stewart Omnimedia; Amb. to Italy (also accred to San Marino) 2009–13; fmr Pres. and current Bd mem. Inst. of Contemporary Art, Boston; Public Service Award, Columbia Univ.; Cavaliere di Gran Croce dell'ordine al Merito. *Publication:* The New Soldier 1971. *Leisure interest:* plays league soccer in New England. *Address:* Adviser Investments, 85 Wells Avenue, Suite 109, Newton, MA 02459, USA (office). *E-mail:* dthorne@adviserinvestments.com (office). *Website:* www.adviserinvestments.com (office).

THORNE, Kip Stephen, BS, PhD; American research physicist, academic and writer; *Feynman Professor of Theoretical Physics Emeritus, California Institute of Technology;* b. 1940, Logan, Utah; s. of David Wynne Thorne and Alison Comish; m. 1st Linda Jeanne Peterson 1960 (divorced 1977); one s. one d.; m. 2nd Carolee Joyce Winstein 1984; ed California Inst. of Tech. and Princeton Univ.; Postdoctoral Fellow, Princeton Univ. 1965–66; Research Fellow in Physics, Calif. Inst. of Tech. 1966–67, Assoc. Prof. of Theoretical Physics 1967–70, Prof. 1970–, William R. Kenan Jr Prof. 1981–91, Richard P. Feynman Prof. of Theoretical Physics 1991–2009, Emer. 2009–; Prof. of Physics, Univ. of Utah 1971–98; Fulbright Lecturer, France 1966; Visiting Prof., Moscow Univ. 1969, 1975, 1978, 1981, 1982, 1986, 1988, 1990, 1998; Andrew D. White Prof.-at-Large, Cornell Univ. 1986–92; Chair. Topical Group on Gravity of American Physical Soc. 1997–98; Alfred P. Sloan Research Fellow 1966–68; Guggenheim Fellow 1967; mem. Int. Cttee on Gen. Relativity and Gravitation 1971–80, 1992–, Cttee on US-USSR Co-operation in Physics 1978–79, Space Science Bd, NASA 1980–83; Foreign mem. Russian Acad. of Sciences 1999; mem. American Philosophical Soc. 1999; mem. NAS 1973; Fellow, American Acad. of Arts and Sciences, American Physical Soc., AAAS; Hon. DSc (Illinois Coll.) 1979, (Utah State Univ.) 2000, (Glasgow) 2001; Dr hc (Moscow State Univ.) 1981; Hon. DHumLitt (Claremont Grad. Univ.) 2002; American Inst. of Physics Science Writing Award in Physics and Astronomy 1969, 1994, Priroda (USSR) Readers' Choice Award 1989, 1990, Phi Beta Kappa Science Writing Award 1994, Julius Edgar Lilienfeld Prize, American Physical Soc. 1996, Karl Schwarzschild Medal, German Astronomical Soc. 1996, 24th Annual Award for Excellence in Teaching, Associated Students of the California Inst. of Tech. (undergraduates) 1999–2000, Robinson Prize in Cosmology, Univ. of Newcastle 2002, California Scientist of the Year 2004, Student Council Mentoring Award 2004, Commonwealth Award in Science 2005, J.D. Jackson Award for Excellence in Graduate Educ. (American Asscn of Physics Teachers) 2012. *Publications:* co-author: Gravitation Theory and Gravitational Collapse 1965, High Energy Astrophysics, Vol. 3 1967, Gravitation 1973, Black Holes: The Membrane Paradigm 1986; sole author: Black Holes and Time Warps: Einstein's Outrageous Legacy 1994. *Address:* California Institute of Technology, MS 130-33 Theoretical Astrophysics, 1200 East California Boulevard, Pasadena, CA 91125-0001, USA (office). *Telephone:* (626) 395-4598 (office). *Fax:* (626) 796-5675 (office). *E-mail:* kip@tapir.caltech.edu (office). *Website:* www.its.caltech.edu/~kip (office).

THORNE LEÓN, Jaime; Peruvian lawyer and politician; ed Univ. Pontificia Católica del Perú; fmr Prof. of Law, Univ. de Lima; pvt. legal practice with Estudios Montoya, Thorne Abogados y Thorne, Echeandía & Asociados Abogados SCR Ltda; fmr Arbitrator, Centro de Arbitraje Nacional e Internacional de la Cámara de Comercio de Lima; Legal Adviser to Grupo Piaggio and Corporación Unique-Yanbal; Dir Hierro-Perú (mining co.); Sec., Jurado Provincial de Elecciones (regional election comm.); Pres. Nat. Inst. for the Defence of Competition and the Protection of Intellectual Property –2010; Minister of Defence 2010–11. *Address:* c/o Ministry of Defence, Edif. Quiñones, Avda de la Peruanidad s/n, Jesús María, Lima 1, Peru (office).

THORNING-SCHMIDT, Helle, MA, MSc; Danish politician; *Prime Minister;* b. 14 Dec. 1966, Rødovre; d. of Holger Thorning-Schmidt Grete Thorning-Schmidt; m. Stephen Kinnock; ed Univ. of Copenhagen, Coll. of Europe, Bruges; Int. Consultant, Danish Trades Union Congress (LO) 1997–99; Head, Socialdemokraterne (Social Democrats) Secr., European Parl. 1994–97, MEP 1999–2004; Leader, Socialdemokraterne 2005–; Prime Minister 2011–; mem. Bd of Dirs Danmarks Nationalbank 2005–. *Publications include:* En dollar om dagen (A Dollar a Day) (co-author) 2001, Forsvar for Fællesskabet (In Defence of Fellowship) (co-author) 2002. *Address:* Prime Minister's Office, Christiansborg, Prins Jørgens Gård 11, 1218 Copenhagen K (office); Socialdemokraterne (Social Democrats), Danasvej 7, 1910 Frederiksberg C, Denmark (office). *Telephone:* 33-92-33-00 (Copenhagen) (office); 72-30-08-00 (Frederiksberg) (office). *Fax:* 33-11-16-65 (Copenhagen) (office); 72-30-08-50 (Frederiksberg) (office). *E-mail:* stm@stm.dk (office); s@socialdemokraterne.dk (office). *Website:* www.stm.dk (office); www.socialdemokraterne.dk (office); www.thorning-schmidt.dk.

THORNTON, Billy Bob; American actor, director and writer; b. 4 Aug. 1955, Hot Springs, Ark.; m. 1st Melissa Lee Gatlin (divorced 1980); one d.; 2nd Toni Lawrence (divorced 1988); 3rd Cynda Williams (divorced 1992); 4th Pietra Dawn Chernak (divorced 1997); two s.; 5th Angelina Jolie (q.v.) 2000 (divorced 2003); one adopted s.; one d. with Connie Angland. *Films include:* Sling Blade (also dir, screenplay; Acad. Award for Best Adapted Screenplay 1996, Chicago Film Critics Award for Best Actor, Independent Spirit Awards), U-Turn 1997, A Thousand Miles 1997, The Apostle 1997, A Gun A Car A Blonde, Primary Colors 1997, Homegrown 1998, Armageddon 1998, A Simple Plan 1998, Pushing Tin 1998, The Man Who Wasn't There 2001, Bandits 2001, Monster's Ball 2001, Love Actually 2003, Intolerable Cruelty 2003, Bad Santa 2003, The Alamo 2004, Friday Night Lights 2004, Bad News Bears 2005, The Ice Harvest 2005, School for Scoundrels 2006, The Astronaut Farmer 2007, Mr Woodcock 2007, Eagle Eye 2008, The

Informers 2008, The Smell of Success 2009, Faster 2010, Puss in Boots (voice) 2011, Jayne Mansfield's Car 2012. *Television:* The 1,000 Chains, Don't Look Back (actor, writer), The Outsiders (series), Hearts Afire. *Address:* c/o Creative Artists Agency, 2000 Avenue of the Stars, Los Angeles, CA 90067, USA.

THORNTON, Dame Janet Maureen, DBE, CBE, PhD, FRS; British molecular biologist and academic; *Director, European Bioinformatics Institute;* b. 23 May 1949; d. of Stanley James McLoughlin and Kathleen Barlow; m. Alan Thornton 1970; one s. one d.; ed Nottingham Univ., King's Coll. London, Nat. Inst. of Medical Research; tutor, Open Univ. 1976–83; molecular pharmacologist, Nat. Inst. of Medical Research 1978; Science and Eng Research Council Advanced Fellow 1979–83, Lecturer 1983–89, Sr Lecturer 1989–90, Bernal Chair. of Crystallography 1996–; Dir Biomolecular Structure and Modelling Unit, Univ. Coll. London 1990–, Prof. of Biomolecular Structure 1990–; consultant, European Molecular Biology Lab., European Bioinformatics Inst. (EMBL-EBI) 1994–2000, Dir EMBL-EBI 2000–; Head Jt Research School in Molecular Sciences, Univ. Coll. London and Birkbeck Coll. 1996–2000; Fellow, Churchill Coll. Cambridge; Hon. Prof., Dept of Chem., Univ. of Cambridge; Hans Neurath Award, Protein Soc., USA 2000, Dorothy Hodgkin Award, Protein Soc., Zurich 2009. *Publications:* numerous articles in scientific journals. *Leisure interests:* reading, music, gardening, walking. *Address:* EMBL-EBI, Wellcome Trust Genome Campus, Hinxton, Cambridge, CB10 1SD, England (office). *Telephone:* (1223) 494648 (office); (1223) 494444 (office). *Fax:* (1223) 494468 (office). *E-mail:* doffice@ebi.ac.uk (office); thornton@ebi.ac.uk (office). *Website:* www.ebi.ac.uk/Thornton (office).

THORNTON, John Lawson; American business executive and academic; *Professor and Director of Global Leadership, Tsinghua University;* b. 2 Jan. 1954, New York; ed Hotchkiss School, Harvard Coll., Oxford Univ., UK, Yale School of Org. and Man.; joined Goldman Sachs 1980, f. and built merger and acquisition business for co. in Europe 1983–91, pnr 1988 with exec. responsibility for operations in Europe, Middle East and Africa, mem. Bd of Dirs 1996, Pres., Co-COO 1999–2003; Prof. and Dir of Global Leadership Tsinghua Univ., China 2003–; mem. Bd Dirs Ford Motor Co., News Corpn, Intel, Inc., China Unicom Ltd, HSBC Holdings plc, HSBC North America Holdings Inc.; fmr mem. Bd Dirs Goldman Sachs Group, Inc., British Sky Broadcasting, Laura Ashley Holdings PLC, Hughes Electronics Corpn, Pacific Century Group Inc.; Chair. Brookings Inst. Bd of Trustees; mem. Council on Foreign Relations; mem. Advisory Bd Asia Society, Goldman Sachs Foundation, Hotchkiss School, Morehouse Coll., Tsinghua Univ. School of Econs and Man. (Beijing), Yale Univ. Investment Cttee, Yale School of Man. *Address:* Tsinghua University, 1 Qinghuayuan, Beijing 100084, People's Republic of China (office). *Telephone:* (10) 62782015 (office). *Fax:* (10) 62770349 (office). *E-mail:* info@tsinghua.edu.cn (office). *Website:* www.tsinghua.edu.cn/eng/index.htm (office).

THORP, Holden, BSc, PhD; American chemist, academic and university administrator; *Provost and Executive Vice-Chancellor for Academic Affairs, Washington University in St Louis;* b. 16 Aug. 1964, Fayetteville, NC; m. Patti Worden Thorp; one s. one d.; ed Univ. of North Carolina, California Inst. of Tech.; Postdoctoral Asst, Yale Univ. 1989–90; Asst Prof. of Chem., North Carolina State Univ. 1990–92; Asst Prof. of Chem., Univ. of North Carolina 1992–99, Prof. 1999–, Kenan Prof. and Chair. Dept of Chem. 2005, Dean Coll. of Arts and Sciences 2007–08, Chancellor Univ. of North Carolina 2008–13, Dir Morehead Planetarium and Science Center 2001–05; Provost and Exec. Vice-Chancellor for Academic Affairs, Washington Univ. in St Louis 2013–, holds an endowed professorship with appointments in chemistry and medicine; co-f. Viamet Pharmaceuticals Inc. 2005; mem. Nat. Advisory Council for Innovation and Entrepreneurship, Nat. Security Higher Educ. Advisory Bd; Chair. Cttee for the NAS charged with establishing and promoting a culture of safety in academic laboratory research; numerous awards, including Ruth and Philip Hettleman Prize for Artistic and Scholarly Achievement 1996, Tanner Award for Excellence in Undergraduate Teaching, Nat. Science Foundation's Presidential Young Investigator Award. *Publications:* more than 130 scholarly publications on the electronic properties of DNA and RNA. *Leisure interests:* playing jazz bass and keyboard. *Address:* Office of the Provost, 229 North Brookings Hall, One Brookings Drive, Campus Box 1072, St Louis, MO 63130-4899, USA (office). *Telephone:* (314) 935-3000 (office). *E-mail:* provost@wustl.edu (office). *Website:* provost.wustl.edu (office).

THORPE, Ian James; Australian swimmer; b. 13 Oct. 1982, Sydney; s. of Kenneth William Thorpe and Margaret Grace Thorpe; ed East Hills Boys Technical High School; winner three gold medals, two silver medals, Olympic Games, Sydney 2000; set new world record in 400m freestyle and 4×200m relay; winner 11 World Championship gold medals 1998–2003; won 10 gold medals and broke own 400m freestyle world record, Commonwealth Games; won nine titles including five gold medals, Pan-Pacific Games, Yokohama 2002; winner two gold medals, one silver medal, one bronze medal, Olympic Games, Athens 2004; world-record holder for 200m and 400m freestyle; retd from competitive swimming 2006; numerous awards including NSW Athlete of the Year 1998, three times Australian Swimmer of the Year, four times World Swimmer of the Year, Swimming World Magazine 1998, 1999, Male Athlete of the Year, Australian Sports Awards 2000, Young Australian of the Year 2000, The Sport Australia Hall of Fame's 'Don Award' 2000, Jesse Owens American Int. Athlete Trophy Award 2001, China Sports Daily's Most Popular World Athlete 2002. *Achievements:* Ian Thorpe's Fountain for Youth launched Nov. 2000. *Publications:* The Journey, Live Your Dreams, This is Me (autobiog.) 2012. *Leisure interests:* surfing, cooking, movies, dinner, water skiing, computer games, music, TV. *Address:* c/o Grand Slam International Pty Ltd, PO Box 402, Manly, NSW 1655, Australia (office). *Telephone:* (2) 9949-1356 (office). *Fax:* (2) 8214-3426 (office). *E-mail:* gsi@grandslamint.com (office). *Website:* www.grandslamint.com (office).

THORPE, Rt Hon. (John) Jeremy, PC; British politician; b. 29 April 1929; m. 1st Caroline Allpass 1968 (died 1970); one s.; m. 2nd Maria (Marion) Stein, fmr Countess of Harewood, 1973; ed Rectory School, Eton Coll. and Trinity Coll., Oxford; barrister, Inner Temple 1954; MP for N Devon 1959–79; Treas. UN Parl. Group 1962–67; Hon. Treas. Liberal Party 1965–67, Leader 1967–76; Pres. N Devon Liberal Asscn 1987–; Consultant, Stramit; Chair. Jeremy Thorpe Assocs Ltd 1984–; Hon. Fellow, Trinity Coll., Oxford Univ.; Hon. DCL (Exeter). *Publications:* To All Who Are Interested in Democracy 1951, Europe: The Case for Going In 1971, In My Own Time (autobiography) 1999. *Leisure interests:*

collecting Chinese ceramics, music. *Address:* 2 Orme Square, Bayswater, London, W2 4RS, England. *Telephone:* (20) 7727-8181.

THORPE, Nigel James, CVO, BA; British diplomatist (retd); b. 3 Oct. 1945; three d.; ed East Grinstead Co. Grammar School, Cardiff Univ.; joined Diplomatic Service 1969, served in various positions including at Embassy in Warsaw 1970–72, High Comm., Dhaka 1973–74, at FCO 1975–79, High Comm., Ottawa 1979–81; seconded to Dept of Energy, London 1981–82; Deputy Head Southern Africa Dept, FCO 1982–85, Deputy Head of Mission, Embassy in Warsaw 1985–88, Deputy High Commr, Harare 1989–92, Head of Cen. European Dept, FCO 1992–96, Sr Directing Staff, Royal Coll. of Defence Studies, London 1996–98, Amb. to Hungary 1998–2003 (retd); Pres. Vodafone Hungary Foundation 2003–08. *Publication includes:* Harmincad Utca 6: A Twentieth Century History of Budapest. *Leisure interests:* family, his dog, music.

THOTTUNKAL, HE Cardinal Moran Mor Baselios Cleemis, BPhil, BTh, MTh, PhD; Indian ecclesiastic; *Major Archbishop of Trivandrum (Syro-Malankarese) and Catholicos of the Syro-Malankara Catholic Church;* b. (Isaac Thottunkal), 15 June 1959, Mukkoor, nr Mallappally Town, Pathanamthitta dist, Kerala; s. of Mathew Thottunkal and Annamma Thottunkal; ed Minor Seminary Formation, Tiruvalla, St Joseph's Pontifical Inst., Mangalapuzha, Aluva, Papal Seminary, Pune, Dharmaram Coll., Bangalore, Pontifical Univ. of St Thomas Aquinas (Angelicum), Rome; ordained priest, Archdiocese of Battery (Bathery) (Syro-Malankarese) 1986; Vicar Gen. (Proto Syncellus) of the Eparchy of Bathery 1997–2001; apptd Titular Bishop of Chaialum 2001; Auxiliary Bishop of Trivandrum (Syro-Malankarese) 2001–03; Bishop of Tiruvalla (Syro-Malankarese) 2003–06; Archbishop of Tiruvalla (Syro-Malankarese) 2006–07; Major Archbishop of Trivandrum (Syro-Malankarese) 2007–; cr. Cardinal (Cardinal-Priest of San Gregorio VII) 2012; mem. Congregation for Oriental Churches 2013–, Pontifical Council for Interreligious Dialogue 2013–. *Address:* Major Archbishop's House, Pattom, Thiruvananthapuram 695 004, Kerala, India (office). *Telephone:* (471) 2541642 (office). *Fax:* (471) 2541635 (office).

THOULESS, David James, PhD, FRS; American (b. British) physicist and academic; *Professor Emeritus of Physics, University of Washington;* b. 21 Sept. 1934, Bearsden, Scotland; s. of Robert Thouless and Priscilla Thouless (née Gorton); m. Margaret Scrase 1958; two s. one d.; ed Winchester Coll., Trinity Hall, Cambridge, UK, Cornell Univ.; physicist, Lawrence Radiation Lab., Berkeley, Calif. 1958–59; ICI Research Fellow, Univ. of Birmingham 1959–61, Prof. of Math. Physics 1965–79; Lecturer, Univ. of Cambridge and Fellow of Churchill Coll. 1961–65, Royal Soc. Research Prof. and Fellow of Clare Hall, Cambridge 1983–86; Prof. of Applied Science, Yale Univ. 1979–80; Prof. of Physics, Univ. of Washington 1980–2003, now Prof. Emer.; mem. NAS 1995; Fellow, American Physical Soc. 1987; Maxwell Prize 1973, Holweck Medal 1980, Fritz London Award 1984, Wolf Prize for Physics 1990, Dirac Prize 1993, Onsager Prize 2000. *Publications:* Quantum Mechanics of Many-Body Systems 1961 (revised edn 1972), Topological Quantum Numbers in Nonrelativistic Physics 1998. *Address:* Department of Physics, B423, University of Washington, Seattle, WA 98195, USA (office). *Telephone:* (206) 685-2393 (office). *E-mail:* thouless@phys.washington.edu (office). *Website:* www.phys.washington.edu (office).

THRIFT, Nigel John, PhD, FBA; British geographer, academic and university administrator; *Vice-Chancellor and President, University of Warwick;* b. 12 Oct. 1949, Bath; ed Nailsea School, Univ. of Wales, Aberystwyth, Univ. of Wales, Lampeter, Univs of Bristol and Oxford; fmr Head of Life and Environmental Sciences Div., Univ. of Oxford, later Pro-Vice-Chancellor for Research; Vice-Chancellor Univ. of Warwick 2006–; Chair. Centre for Research on Socio-Cultural Change (CRESC) Advisory Bd; Commr, Marshall Aid Comm.; mem. Bd Higher Educ. Statistics Agency, Coventry and Warwickshire Local Enterprise Partnership Bd, European Inst. of Innovation and Tech. Governing Bd; mem. Nat. Curriculum Review Advisory Cttee; Trustee, Council for Industry and Higher Educ.; Hon. LLD (Bristol) 2010; Victoria Medal, Royal Geographical Soc. 2003, Distinguished Scholarship Honors, Asscn of American Geographers 2007, Gold Medal, Royal Scottish Geographical Soc. 2008. *Publications:* Spatial Formations 1996, Knowing Capitalism (Theory, Culture and Society) 2005, Non-Representational Theory 2007; co-editor of more than 20 books; numerous papers in professional journals on int. finance, cities and political life, non-representational theory, affective politics and the history of time; contribs to Times Higher Education, Chronicle of Higher Education. *Address:* Office of the Vice-Chancellor and President, University of Warwick, Coventry, Warwicks., CV4 8UW, England (office). *Telephone:* (24) 7652-3630 (office). *E-mail:* vcpa@warwick.ac.uk (office). *Website:* www2.warwick.ac.uk/services/vco (office).

THRUN, Sebastian Burkhard, BSc, MSc, PhD; German computer scientist and academic; *Research Professor of Computer Science, Stanford University;* b. 14 May 1967, Solingen; m. Petra Dierkes-Thrun 1995; ed Univ. of Hildesheim, Univ. of Bonn; Research Asst, German Nat. Research Centre for Information Tech., Sankt Augustin 1989–91; Research Computer Scientist, Carnegie Mellon Univ. 1995–98, Asst Prof. of Computer Science, Robotics and Automated Learning and Discovery 1998–2001, Assoc. Prof. 2001–03; Assoc. Prof. of Computer Science, Stanford Univ. 2003–07, also of Electrical Eng 2006–07, Prof. of Computer Science and Electrical Eng 2007–11, Research Prof. of Computer Science 2011–, also Dir Stanford Artificial Intelligence Lab. (SAIL) 2004–; co-founder Udacity (online private educ. org.) 2012; Prin. Engineer, Google, Inc. 2007–, Google Fellow 2011–; Sr Adviser, Charles River Ventures 2009–; mem. Deutsche Akademie der Naturforscher Leopoldina (German Acad. of Sciences) 2007, Nat. Acad. of Eng 2007; Braunschweig Research Prize 2007, Max Planck Research Award 2011, Asscn for the Advancement of Artificial Intelligence Ed Feigenbaum Prize 2011. *Achievements include:* led devt of robotic vehicle Stanley, winner of Defense Advanced Research Projects Agency (DARPA) Grand Challenge 2005; involved in devt of Google's self-driving car. *Address:* Gates Building 154, 353 Serra Mall, Stanford Artificial Intelligence Lab, Stanford, CA 94305-9010, USA (office). *Telephone:* (650) 723-2797 (office). *Fax:* (650) 725-1449 (office). *E-mail:* thrun@stanford.edu (office). *Website:* robots.stanford.edu (office).

THRUSH, Brian Arthur, MA, ScD, FRS; British scientist and academic; *Professor Emeritus of Physical Chemistry, University of Cambridge;* b. 23 July 1928, London; s. of late Arthur Thrush and Dorothy Thrush; m. Rosemary C. Terry

1958; one s. one d.; ed Haberdashers' Aske's Hampstead School and Emmanuel Coll., Cambridge; Univ. Demonstrator, Asst Dir of Research, Lecturer, Reader in Physical Chem. Univ. of Cambridge 1953–78, Prof. of Physical Chem. 1978–95, now Prof. Emer.; Head Dept of Chem., Univ. of Cambridge 1988–93; Fellow, Emmanuel Coll., Cambridge 1960–, Vice-Master 1986–90; mem. Natural Environment Research Council 1985–90; Visiting Prof. Chinese Acad. of Sciences 1980–; mem. Council, Royal Soc. 1989–91, Academia Europaea 1992–98; Tilden Lecturer (Royal Soc. of Chem.) 1965; M. Polanyi Medal (Royal Soc. of Chem.) 1980, Rank Prize for Opto-Electronics 1992. *Publications:* papers on spectroscopy, gas reactions and atmospheric chemistry in learned journals. *Leisure interests:* wine, gardens. *Address:* Department of Chemistry, University of Cambridge, Lensfield Road, Cambridge, CB2 1EW (office); Brook Cottage, Pemberton Terrace, Cambridge, CB2 1JA, England (home). *Telephone:* (1223) 763137 (office); (1223) 357637 (home). *Fax:* (1223) 336362.

THUBRON, Colin Gerald Dryden, CBE, FRSL; British writer; *President, Royal Society of Literature;* b. 14 June 1939, London; s. of Brig. Gerald Ernest Thubron and Evelyn Kate Dryden; m. Margreta de Grazia 2011; ed Eton Coll.; mem. editorial staff, Hutchinson & Co. Publishers Ltd 1959–62; freelance documentary film maker 1963–64; Production Ed., The Macmillan Co., USA 1964–65; freelance author 1965–; Vice-Pres., Royal Soc. of Literature 2003–10, Pres. 2010–; Fellow, Royal Asiatic Soc. 1991; Hon. DLitt (Warwick) 2002; Silver Pen Award of PEN 1985, Thomas Cook Award 1988, Hawthornden Prize 1988, Mungo Park Medal, Royal Scottish Geographical Soc. 2000, Lawrence of Arabia Medal, Royal Soc. of Asian Affairs 2001, Soc. of Authors Travel Award 2008, Prix Bouvier 2010, Ness Award, Royal Geographical Soc. 2011. *Scenario:* The Prince of the Pagodas (ballet at The Royal Opera House, Covent Garden). *Publications:* Mirror to Damascus, The Hills of Adonis, Jerusalem, Journey into Cyprus, Among the Russians, Behind the Wall, The Lost Heart of Asia, In Siberia, Shadow of the Silk Road 2006, To a Mountain in Tibet 2011; novels: The God in the Mountain, Emperor, A Cruel Madness, Falling, Turning Back the Sun, Distance, To the Last City. *Address:* 28 Upper Addison Gardens, London, W14 8AJ, England (home). *Telephone:* (20) 7602-2522 (home). *E-mail:* Thubron@hotmail.com (home).

THULASIDAS, V., MA; Indian airline industry executive; b. 25 March 1948, Allepey dist, Kerala; ed Inst. of English, Thiruvananthapuram; fmr lecturer, Kerala; various positions in Tripura including Commr of Taxes, Dir of Settlement and Land Records, of Food and Civil Supplies; fmr Under-Sec., Ministry of Civil Aviation; fmr Jt Sec. (Air), Ministry of Defence; Chief Sec. of Tripura –2003; Chair. and Man. Dir Air-India 2003–08. *Address:* c/o Air-India Ltd, Air India Building, Nariman Point, Mumbai 400 021; 22B Sterling Apartments, 38 Peddar Road, Mumbai 400 026, India (home). *Telephone:* (22) 22796666. *Fax:* (22) 22024897.

THULIN, Inge G.; Swedish business executive; *Chairman, President and CEO, 3M Company;* b. 9 Nov. 1953, Malmö; ed Gothenburg Univ./IHM Business School, School of Econs and Commercial Law; various Sales and Marketing positions, 3M Sweden 1979–87, Group Man., Life Sciences Sector 1987–91, Business Man., Vision Care and Orthopedic Products, 3M Europe 1991–93, European Business Unit Man., Surgical Devices 1993–95, Man. Dir 3M Russia 1995–97, Skin Health Business Unit Dir, Skin Health Div. 1997–98, Marketing Operations Dir, Skin Health Div. 1998–99, Gen. Man., Skin Health Div. 1999–2000, Div. Vice-Pres., Skin Health Div. 2000–02, Vice-Pres., Europe and Middle East 2002–03, Exec. Vice-Pres., Int. Operations 2003–11, Exec. Vice-Pres. and COO 3M Company 2011–12, Chair., Pres. and CEO 2012–; mem. Int. Programs Advisory Council, Carlson School of Man., Univ. of Minnesota 2003–; mem. Bd Toro Co. 2007–12. *Address:* 3M Corporate Headquarters, 3M Center, St Paul, MN 55144-1000, USA (office). *Telephone:* (651) 733-1110 (office). *Fax:* (651) 733-9973 (office). *E-mail:* info@mmm.com (office). *Website:* www.mmm.com (office).

THUN, Matteo; Italian architect and designer; b. 1952, Bolzano; ed Salzburg Acad. under Oskar Kokoschka, Univ. of Florence; moved to Milan 1978; Co-founder and fmr Partner, Sottsass Associati, Milan; co-f. Memphis Group 1981; Chair of Product Design and Ceramics, Vienna Acad. for Applied Arts 1982; f. Matteo Thun studio 1984; Creative Dir Swatch 1990–93; Applied Art Chair, Vienna; mem. RIBA; numerous awards including ADI Compasso d'Oro Award (three times), Design of the Year Award for Via col Vento 1987, Forum Design Award 1989, Design Award, North Rhine-Westphalia 1994, Baden Württemberg Int. Design Award for 'O Sole Mio' 1997, IF Contract world Award for Missoni Shop System 2000, Industrial Design Forma Forum for 'Heidis' 2000, IF Contract world Award for Fila Shop 2000, Side Hotel in Hamburg chosen as Hotel of the Year 2001, Architecture and Tech. Innovation Prize and Good Design Award for 'Thun' 2003, ADI Design System: Architecture and Tech. Int. Prize for 'Girly' 2004, ADI Design System: Architecture and Tech. Int. Prize for 'Isy' 2004, Vigilius Mountain Resort won the Wallpaper Design Award 2004, inducted into Interior Hall of Fame, New York 2004, Red Dot Award for Product Design for Porsche Design Store 2005, Radisson SAS, Frankfurt chosen as the best hotel opened in the year, Worldwide Hospitality Awards 2005, Panda d'oro Award for Vigilius Mountain Resort 2005, Design Plus Award for 'Archetun' 2006, IF Product Design Award for 'Roma' 2006, Legambiente/Regione Lombardi Award for Vigilius Mountain Resort 2006, Good Design Award for 'Roma' 2007, Prix Acier Construction for Strategic Unit by Hugo Boss 2007, Bronze Medal for 'Valverde' 2008, Water Innovation Award 2008, IF Product Design Award for 'Muse' 2008, Good Design Award for Rapsel 'Il bagno che non c'è' 2009, Editors Awards, ICFF, New York for Rapsel 'Il bagno che non c'è' 2009, Wallpaper* Design Award for Rapsel 'Ofurò' 2010, Wallpaper* Design Award for TVS 'Terra' 2010, iF Product Design Award for Zumtobel 'Ciria' Lighting 2010, Green Good Design Award for Belux 'Arba' Lighting 2010, Green Good Design Award for Rapsel 'Ofurò' 2010, Best Bath & Material Design 2010, Best of Year Interior Design USA for Rapsel 'Ofurò' 2010, Green Good Design Award for Zucchetti 'Isy' 2011, Hon. Mention, Compasso d'Oro for TVS 'Terra' 2011, Simon Taylor Award for Lifetime Achievement 2011, Good Design award for Antrax Serie Theater 2013. *Architecture projects include:* Vigilius Mountain Resort, S. Tyrol, Hugo Boss Concept Store, New York, shop interiors for Missoni 1998–2002, Fila 2001, Porsche Design 2005–06, Radisson Blu Harbour Hotel, Dusseldorf (room design), Side Hotel, Hamburg (room design), Heidis Low-Energy Prefab House System. *Design projects include:* Rapsel Ofurò (bathroom accessories), CIRIA by Zumtobel Lighting, Savoy Zucchetti (bathroom fittings), Girly (bathroom fittings), Roma (bathroom fittings). *Address:* Via Appiani 9, 20121

Milan, Italy (office). *Telephone:* (02) 6556911 (office). *Fax:* (02) 6570646 (office). *E-mail:* info@matteothun.com (office). *Website:* www.matteothun.com (office).

THUNE, John, BA, MBA; American politician; *Senator from South Dakota;* b. Murdo, SDak; m. Kimberley Weems; two d.; ed Biola Univ., Univ. of South Dakota; started career in Washington, DC working for US Senator Jim Abdnor; served in US Small Business Admin; returned to SDak as Exec. Dir of local Republican Party 1989; State Railroad Dir 1991–93; Exec. Dir SDak Municipal League 1993–96; mem. House of Reps, Washington, DC 1996–2004, served on House Transportation and Agric. Cttees; Senator from South Dakota 2005–, mem. Agric., Nutrition and Forestry Cttee, Budget Cttee, Commerce, Science and Transportation Cttee, Finance Cttee, Chair. Senate Republican Policy Cttee 2009–11, Chair. Senate Republican Conf. *Leisure interests:* spending time with his family, pheasant hunting, running. *Address:* 511 Dirksen Senate Office Building, Washington, DC 20510, USA (office). *Telephone:* (202) 224-2321 (office). *Fax:* (202) 228-5429 (office). *Website:* thune.senate.gov (office).

THUNELL, Lars H., PhD; Swedish international organization executive; m.; three c.; ed Univ. of Stockholm; Pres. and CEO Securum (asset man. co.), Stockholm 1992–94; CEO Trygg-Hansa insurance co. 1992–97; CEO Skandinaviska Enskilda Banken AB 1997–2005; CEO and Exec. Vice-Pres. IFC (mem. World Bank Group) 2006–12; Vice-Chair. (non-exec.) and mem. Bd of Dirs Sithe Global Power LLP 2012–; mem. Bd of Dirs Standard Chartered PLC 2012–, Kosmos Energy 2012–, Middle East Investment Initiative; Sr Adviser, Centre for Strategic and International Studies (US foreign policy think-tank); fmr Chair. IBX Integrated Business Exchange AB; fmr Deputy CEO Nordbanken. *Publications include:* author of books and articles on risk and risk man. in int. business. *Address:* c/o Board of Directors, Sithe Global, 277 Park Avenue, 40th Floor, New York, NY 10172, USA.

THURAU, Klaus Walther Christian, MD; German physiologist; b. 14 June 1928, Bautzen; s. of Walther Thurau and Helene Engel; m. Antje Wiese 1957; two s.; ed High School, Berlin and Univs of Erlangen and Kiel; Lecturer in Physiology, Univ. of Göttingen 1955–65; Chair. Dept of Physiology, Univ. of Munich 1968–; Visiting Prof. American Heart Asscn 1964; Gilman Prof., Dartmouth Medical School 1968; Visiting Prof., American Kidney Foundation 1980; Pres. Int. Soc. of Nephrology; Treas. and Councillor Int. Union of Physiological Science; mem. Exec. Bd Int. Council of Scientific Unions; Chair. Verum-Foundation, German UNESCO Comm. on Natural Sciences; mem. German Physiological Soc., Soc. for Clinical Investigation, American Soc. of Physiology, Int. Soc. for Hypertension, Int. Soc. of Nephrology; Emer. Ed. European Journal of Physiology (Pflügers Archiv.). *Publications:* various papers on renal function (in medical journals). *Leisure interest:* music. *Address:* Department of Physiology, University of Munich, 12 Pettenkoferstr., 80336 Munich (office); Josef-Vötterstrasse 6, 81545 Munich, Germany (home). *Telephone:* (89) 218075558 (office); (89) 6422618 (home). *Fax:* (89) 218075532 (office); (89) 64254517 (home). *E-mail:* klaus.thurau@med.uni -muenchen.de (office).

THURLEY, Simon John, CBE, MA, PhD, FSA, FRHistS; British foundation executive and museum administrator; *Chief Executive, English Heritage;* b. 29 Aug. 1962, Huntingdon, Cambs., England; s. of the late Thomas Manley Thurley and Rachel Thurley (née House); m. 2nd Anna Keay 2008; one s. one d.; ed Kimbolton School, Cambs., Bedford Coll. and Courtauld Inst. of Art, London; Insp. of Ancient Monuments, Crown Buildings and Monuments Group, English Heritage 1988–90; Curator Historic Royal Palaces 1990–97; Dir Museum of London 1997–2002; CEO English Heritage 2002–; Chair. Cttee Soc. for Court Studies 1996–; Pres. City of London Archaeological Soc. 1997–2002, Huntingdon-shire Local History Soc.; Visiting Prof. of Medieval History and Hon. Fellow, Royal Holloway Coll., Univ. of London; Visiting Prof. of Built Environment, Gresham Coll.; mem. Council St Paul's Cathedral; Hon. mem. Royal Inst. of Chartered Surveyors; Hon. RIBA. *Television:* Lost Buildings of Britain (Channel 4) 2004, The Buildings that Made Britain (Channel 5) 2006. *Publications:* Henry VIII: Images of a Tudor King (co-author) 1989, The Royal Palaces of Tudor England 1993, Whitehall Palace 2000, Lost Buildings of Britain 2004, Hampton Court 2004, Somerset House 2009; frequent contribs to historical publs. *Leisure interest:* ancient buildings. *Address:* English Heritage, 1 Waterhouse Square, 138–142 Holborn, London, EC1N 2ST, England (office). *Telephone:* (20) 7973-3000 (office). *E-mail:* simon@kingstaithe.com (office). *Website:* www.english-heritage.org.uk (office); www.simonthurley.com.

THURMAN, Uma; American actress; b. 29 April 1970, Boston, Mass; d. of Robert Thurman and Nena Schlebrugge; m. 1st Gary Oldman (q.v.) 1991 (divorced 1992); m. 2nd Ethan Hawke (q.v.) 1997 (divorced 2004); two d. one s.; worked as model; Chevalier, Ordre des Arts et des Lettres 2006. *Films:* The Adventures of Baron Munchhausen 1988, Dangerous Liaisons 1988, Even Cowgirls Get the Blues, Final Analysis, Where the Heart Is, Henry and June, Mad Dog and Glory 1993, Pulp Fiction 1994, Robin Hood, Dylan, A Month by the Lake 1995, The Truth About Cats and Dogs 1996, Batman and Robin 1997, Gattaca 1997, The Avengers 1998, Les Misérables 1998, Vatel 2000, The Golden Bowl 2001, Chelsea Walls 2002, Kill Bill Vol. I 2003, Kill Bill Vol. II 2004, Be Cool 2005, The Producers: The Movie Musical 2005, Prime 2005, My Super Ex-Girlfriend 2006, The Life Before Her Eyes 2008, The Accidental Husband (also prod.) 2008, Motherhood 2009, Percy Jackson & the Olympians: The Lightning Thief 2010, Bel Ami 2012, Playing for Keeps 2012. *Television includes:* Hysterical Blindness (Golden Globe for Best Actress in a mini-series or TV movie 2003) 2002. *Address:* c/o Brian Lourd, CAA, 9830 Wilshire Boulevard, Beverly Hills, CA 90212, USA.

THURSTON, William Paul, PhD; American mathematician and academic; *Jacob Gould Schurman Professor of Mathematics, Cornell University;* b. 30 Oct. 1946, Washington, DC; ed New Coll., Sarasota, Fla, Univ. of California, Berkeley; at Inst. for Advanced Study, Princeton NJ 1972–73; Asst Prof. of Math., MIT 1973–74; Prof. of Math., Princeton Univ. 1974–96, Univ. of California, Davis 1996–2003, Cornell Univ., Ithaca, NY 2003–, now Jacob Gould Schurman Prof. of Math.; Alfred P. Sloan Foundation Fellowship 1974–75, Oswald Veblen Geometry Prize, American Math. Soc. 1976, Alan T. Waterman Award 1979, Fields Medal, Gen. Ass. of Int. Math. Union, Warsaw 1982 (presented 1983), American Math. Soc. Colloquium Lecturer 1989. *Publications:* numerous articles in math. journals on topology. *Address:* Department of Mathematics, 533 Malott Hall, Cornell

University, Ithaca, NY 14853-4201, USA (office). *Telephone:* (607) 255-2334 (office). *Fax:* (607) 255-7149 (office). *E-mail:* wpt@math.cornell.edu (office). *Website:* www.math.cornell.edu (office).

THWAITE, Anthony Simon, OBE, MA, DLitt, FRSL, FSA; British writer and poet; b. 23 June 1930, Chester, Cheshire; s. of Hartley Thwaite and Alice Thwaite (née Mallinson); m. Ann Barbara Thwaite (née Harrop) 1955; four d.; ed Kingswood School, Bath, Christ Church, Oxford; Visiting Lecturer in English Literature, Univ. of Tokyo 1955–57; radio producer, BBC 1957–62; Literary Ed., The Listener 1962–65; Asst Prof. of English, Univ. of Libya, Benghazi 1965–67; Literary Ed., New Statesman 1968–72; Co-Ed., Encounter 1973–85; Editorial Dir, Editorial Consultant, André Deutsch 1986–95; Hon. Lay Canon, Norwich Cathedral 2005; Hon. DLitt (Hull) 1989, (East Anglia) 2007; Richard Hillary Memorial Prize 1968, Cholmondeley Award 1983. *Publications:* poetry: Home Truths 1957, The Owl in the Tree 1963, The Stones of Emptiness 1967, Inscriptions 1973, New Confessions 1974, A Portion for Foxes 1977, Victorian Voices 1980, Poems 1953–1983 1984, revised edn as Poems 1953–1988 1989, Letter from Tokyo 1987, The Dust of the World 1994, Selected Poems 1956–1996 1997, A Different Country: New Poems 2000, A Move in the Weather 2003, The Ruins of Time (ed.) 2006, Collected Poems 2007, Late Poems 2010; other: Contemporary English Poetry 1959, The Penguin Book of Japanese Verse (co-ed. with Geoffrey Bownas) 1964, Japan (with Roloff Beny) 1968, The Deserts of Hesperides 1969, Poetry Today 1973, The English Poets (co-ed. with Peter Porter) 1974, In Italy (with Roloff Beny and Peter Porter) 1974, New Poetry 4 (co-ed. with Fleur Adcock) 1978, Twentieth Century English Poetry 1978, Odyssey: Mirror of the Mediterranean (with Roloff Beny) 1981, Larkin at Sixty (ed.) 1982, Poetry 1945 to 1980 (co-ed. with John Mole) 1983, Six Centuries of Verse 1984, Philip Larkin: Collected Poems (ed.) 1988, Selected Letters of Philip Larkin (ed.) 1992, Philip Larkin: Further Requirements (ed.) 2001, Poet to Poet: John Skelton 2008, Philip Larkin: Letters to Monica (ed.) 2010. *Leisure interests:* archaeology, antiquarian beachcombing. *Address:* The Mill House, Low Tharston, Norwich, Norfolk, NR15 2YN, England (home). *Telephone:* (1508) 489569 (home).

THYS, Willy Lucien Ghislain; Belgian trade union official and international organization official; b. 18 July 1943, Le Roeulx; m. Micheline Berteau; three c.; ed FOPES/UCL Inst. for Adult Educ.; shop steward, ACV-CSC at Belgian Rail 1963, mem. Exec. Cttee railway workers' fed. in ACV-CSC 1970; Sec.-Gen. Belgian Christian Fed. of Communication and Cultural Workers 1976–87; Nat. Sec. ACV-CSC 1987; Sec.-Gen. World Confed. of Labour (WCL) 1996–2006 (after WCL merged with Int. Confed. of Free Trade Unions and eight nat. trade union orgs to form Int. Trade Union Confed.—ITUC). *Address:* c/o International Trade Union Confederation (ITUC), 5 blvd Roi Albert II, 1210 Brussels, Belgium.

TIAN, Chengping; Chinese politician; b. 1940, Daming, Hebei Prov.; s. of Tian Ying; ed Tsinghua Univ., Beijing; joined CCP 1964; sent to do manual labour, Huoqiucheng (Xihu Army Farm), Anhui Prov. 1968; Sec. Publicity Section, Shengli Chemical Plant, Shandong Prov. 1970; Sec. CCP Communist Youth League of China, Beijing Gen. Petrochemical Works 1970; Deputy Sec. CCP Party Cttee, Qianjin Chemical Plant, Beijing Yanshan Petrochemical Corpn 1974, Deputy Sec. CCP Party Cttee, Beijing Yanshan Petrochemical Corpn 1983; Sec. CCP Xicheng Dist Cttee, Beijing 1984; Deputy Sec. CCP 8th Qinghai Prov. Cttee 1988–97, Sec. 1997–99; Gov. of Qinghai Prov. 1993–97; Chair. Standing Cttee Qinghai Prov. People's Congress 1998–99; mem. Standing Cttee CCP Shanxi Prov. Cttee 1999–2005, Sec. CCP Shanxi Prov. Cttee 1999–2005; Chair. Standing Cttee Shanxi Prov. People's Congress 2003–05; Minister of Labour and Social Security 2005–07; Alt. mem. 13th Cen. Cttee CCP 1987–91, 14th CCP Cen. Cttee 1992–97, mem. 15th CCP Cen. Cttee 1997–2002, 16th CCP Cen. Cttee 2002–07, 17th CCP Cen. Cttee 2007–12; Deputy, 8th NPC 1993–98, 9th NPC 1998–2003. *Address:* c/o Ministry of Labour and Social Security 12 Hepinglizhong Jie, Dongcheng Qu, Beijing 100716, People's Republic of China (office).

TIAN, Congming; Chinese politician; b. May 1943, Fugu, Shaanxi Prov.; ed Beijing Normal Univ.; joined CCP 1965; clerk, Political Department, Bayannur League, Inner Mongolia Autonomous Region People's Govt 1970–74; corresp., Xinhua News Agency Nei Monggol Br. 1974–80; Deputy Dir Policy Research Office, CCP Inner Mongolia Autonomous Regional Cttee 1980–83, mem. Standing Cttee CCP Inner Mongolia Autonomous Regional Cttee 1983–84, Sec.-Gen. CCP Inner Mongolia Autonomous Regional Cttee 1983–84, Deputy Sec. CCP Inner Mongolia Autonomous Regional Cttee 1984–88; Deputy Sec. CCP Tibetan Autonomous Regional Cttee 1988–90; Vice-Minister of Radio, Motion Picture and TV 1990–98 (Deputy Sec. CCP Leading Party Group 1990–98); Dir State Gen. Admin of Radio, Motion Picture and TV 1998–2000 (Sec. CCP Leading Party Group 1998–2000); Pres. Xinhua News Agency 2000–08; mem. 14th CCP Cen. Cttee 1992–97 (mem. Cttee for Discipline Inspection 1992–97), 15th CCP Cen. Cttee 1997–2002, 16th CCP Cen. Cttee 2002–07. *Address:* c/o Xinhua News Agency, 57 Xuanwumen Xidajie, Beijing 100803, People's Republic of China (office). *Telephone:* (10) 63071114 (office). *Fax:* (10) 63071210 (office). *Website:* www .xinhuanet.com (office).

TIAN, Fengshan; Chinese fmr politician; b. Oct. 1940, Zhaoyuan Co., Heilongjiang Prov.; ed Second Artillery Tech. Coll., Xi'an City, Shaanxi Prov.; joined CCP 1970; teacher, Zhaoyuan Co.; Sec. CCP Party Cttee, Zhaoyuan People's Commune; Chair. CCP Revolutionary Cttee, Zhaoyuan Co.; Deputy Sec. CCP Zhaoyuan Co. Cttee; Deputy Magistrate, later Magistrate Zhaoyuan Co. (Dist) People's Court; Deputy Commr Suihua Prefectural Admin. Office, Heilongjiang Prov. 1983–85, Commr 1985–88 (Deputy Sec. CCP Party Cttee); Sec. CCP Mudanjiang Municipal Cttee 1988–89; Vice-Gov. Heilongjiang Prov. 1989–94, Acting Gov. 1994–95, Gov. 1995–2000; Sec. CCP Leading Party Group, Ministry of Land and Resources 1999–2003, Minister of Land and Resources 2000–03 (removed from post); Deputy Sec. CCP Heilongjiang Prov. Cttee; Sec. CCP Harbin Municipal Cttee 1992; Alt. mem. 13th CCP Cen. Cttee 1987–92, 14th CCP Cen. Cttee 1992–97, mem. 15th CCP Cen. Cttee 1997–2002, 16th CCP Cen. Cttee 2002–04 (expelled from CCP 2004); Deputy to 8th NPC from Heilongjiang Prov. 1996; sentenced to life imprisonment for accepting bribes Dec. 2005.

TIAN, Guoli, BA; Chinese economist and business executive; *Chairman, Bank of China Limited;* b. Dec. 1960; ed Capital Construction Dept, Hubei Coll. of Econs (later Zhongnan Univ. of Econs and Law); held various positions at China

Construction Bank (CCB), including sub-br. gen. man., deputy br. gen. man., department gen. man. of CCB Head Office, and Asst Pres. of CCB 1983–99; served successively as Vice-Pres. then Pres. China Cinda Asset Management Co., later Chair. China Cinda Asset Management Corpn 1999–2010; Vice-Chair. and Pres. CITIC Group 2010–13, also Chair. and Dir (non-exec.), China CITIC Bank; Chair. Bank of China Ltd 2013–; Chair. and Dir (non-exec.), BOCHK (Holdings) 2013–. *Address:* Bank of China Ltd, 1 Fuxingmen Nei Dajie, Beijing 100818, People's Republic of China (office). *Telephone:* (10) 66596688 (office). *Fax:* (10) 66593777 (office). *E-mail:* info@boc.cn (office). *Website:* www.boc.cn (office).

TIAN, Huiyu, MA; Chinese economist and business executive; *President and CEO, China Merchants Bank Company Limited;* ed Columbia Univ., USA; has served in a range of banks in various posts, including as Vice-Pres., Bank of Shanghai, Deputy Man. Dir, China Construction Bank (CCB), Shanghai, Man. Dir, CCB, Shenzhen, Retail Business Dir, CCB, Man. Dir, CCB, Beijing; Exec. Dir, Pres. and CEO China Merchants Bank Co. Ltd 2013–. *Address:* China Merchants Group Ltd, 40th Floor, China Merchants Building, 168–200 Conaught Road, Central, Hong Kong Special Administrative Region (office); China Merchants Bank Co. Ltd, 7088 Shen Nan Road, Futian District, Shenzhen 518040, Guangdong, People's Republic of China (office). *Telephone:* 25428288 (Hong Kong) (office); (755) 83198888 (Shenzhen) (office). *Fax:* 25448851 (Hong Kong) (office); (755) 83195109 (Shenzhen) (office). *E-mail:* cmhk@cmhk.com (office). *Website:* www.cmhk.com (office); www.cmbchina.com (office).

TIAN, Jiyun; Chinese politician; b. June 1929, Feicheng Co., Shandong Prov.; joined CCP 1945; teacher, Guiyang People's Revolutionary Univ., Guizhou Prov.; Admin. Cadre, Prov. Training Class for Financial Cadres, Guizhou Prov.; Section Chief, later Div. Chief, later Deputy Dir Finance Dept, Guizhou Prov.; Deputy Dir, later Dir Financial Bureau, Sichuan Prov. 1969; Deputy Sec.-Gen. State Council 1981–83, Sec.-Gen. 1983–88; Dir Nat. Afforestation Cttee; Chair. China Cttee of the Int. Decade for Natural Disaster Reduction 1983–87; Vice-Premier, State Council 1983–93; Head, Commodity Prices Group, State Council 1984–93; mem. Secr. CCP Cen. Cttee 1985–87; Dir State Flood Control and Drought Relief HQ 1988–93, Cen. Forest Fire Prevention HQ 1987–93; mem. 12th CCP Cen. Cttee 1982–87, 13th CCP Cen. Cttee 1987–92, 14th CCP Cen. Cttee 1992–97, 15th CCP Cen. Cttee 1997–2002, mem. Politburo 1985–2002, Politburo Secr. 1985–87; Vice-Chair. 8th Standing Cttee of NPC 1993–98, 9th Standing Cttee of NPC 1998–2003. *Address:* c/o Standing Committee of National People's Congress, Beijing, People's Republic of China (office).

TIAN, Zengpei; Chinese diplomatist and politician; b. 1930, Raoyang Co., Hebei Prov.; ed Nankai Univ.; joined CCP 1947; joined Ministry of Foreign Affairs, becoming Section Chief and Dir, Political Dept, later Deputy Dir, Dir, and Deputy Dir-Gen. Dept of Soviet Union and Eastern Europe Affairs, Counsellor, Chinese Embassy, Moscow, USSR 1976–81; Minister-Counsellor, Embassy in Yugoslavia 1982–84, Amb. to Czechoslovakia 1984–85, to Yugoslavia 1986–88, Vice-Minister of Foreign Affairs 1988–96; mem. 14th CCP Cen. Cttee 1992–97; Del., 15th CCP Nat. Congress 1997–2002; mem. Standing Cttee 9th CPPCC Nat. Cttee 1998–2003, Chair. Foreign Affairs Sub-cttee 1998–2003. *Address:* c/o National Committee of Chinese People's Political Consultative Conference, Taipingqiao Street, Beijing, People's Republic of China (office). *Telephone:* (10) 553831 (office).

TIAN, Zhaowu; Chinese scientist and university administrator; b. 1927, Fuzhou City, Fujian Prov.; ed Xiamen Univ., Fujian Prov.; Prof., Xiamen Univ., Pres. 1982–89; Pres. China Chem. Asscn 1986; Vice-Pres. Int. Electrochemistry Asscn 1996; mem. Dept of Chem., Academia Sinica 1980–, Third World Acad. of Sciences 1996–; advanced the Feature Current idea of multi-hole electrode polarization and the Uneven Liquid Film model; also promoted electrochemical tech., including a new generation of ion chromatogram suppressers, corrosion measurement systems, and the first domestic electrochemical comprehensive testers; mem. Standing Cttee 8th CCP Nat. Cttee 1993–98; Dr hc (Univ. of Wales, UK) 1984; Hon. Nat. Prize of Sciences 1987. *Address:* c/o Xiamen University, Xiamen, Fujian Province, People's Republic of China.

TIANGAYE, Nicolas; Central African Republic lawyer and politician; b. 13 Sept. 1956, Bocaranga; ed Univ. Bedél Bokassa, Bangui, Univ. of Orleans, France; mem. Bangui Bar 1983, Bar Asscn of CAR 1994–98; served as lawyer for numerous years, including as defence lawyer for Jean-Bedél Bokassa (deposed emperor of Central African Repub.) 1986–87 and for Pres. François Bozizé 1989; lawyer with Int. Criminal Tribunal for Rwanda, Arusha, Tanzania 1996–98; Chair. Nat. Transitional Council (Parl.) of CAR 2003–05; took part in drafting of new constitution 2004; Spokesman, Forces of Change Collective 2010; Prime Minister and Head of Govt 2013–14; Founder mem. Inter-African Union of Human Rights, Vice-Pres. 1992–98; mem. Int. Asscn of Young Lawyers 1986–2001; Grand Officier, Ordre du Mérite Centrafricain, Grand Officier, Ordre de la Reconnaissance Centrafricain.

TIAO, (Beyon) Luc-Adolphe, MSc; Burkinabè journalist, diplomatist and politician; *Prime Minister;* b. 4 June 1954, Tenkodogo; m.; four c.; ed Univ. of Dakar, Senegal, Univ. of Ouagadougou, Univ. of Montreal, Canada, Centre for Diplomatic and Strategic Studies, Paris, France; Dir of Newspapers, Directorate-Gen. of the Press 1984–85; Dir and Chief Publr state-owned daily newspaper Sidwaya 1987–90; Sec.-Gen., Ministry of Communication and Culture 1990–92; Press Attaché, Embassy in Paris 1992–96; Adviser, Mission of Dept of Communication at Prime Minister's Office 1996–2001; Pres. Superior Council of Communication (media regulator) 2001–08; Amb. to France 2008–11; apptd Prime Minister of Burkina Faso by Pres. Blaise Compaoré following protests by students, mil. personnel and police April 2011; mem. Congress for Democracy and Progress party; Founding mem. and fmr Pres. Journalists Asscn of Burkina Faso; Founding mem. and Sec. Gen. Asscn of Devt'Earth-Schools' 1991; mem. several nat. and int. asscns, including Burkinabe Movt for Human Rights and Peoples' Rights (MBDHP); Expert and Rapporteur Gen. Conf. of Information Ministers of Mem. States of Econ. Community of West African States (ECOWAS) 1989; mem. Cttee of Experts of Panos Inst. of Paris and Union of Journalists of West Africa (WAJA) charged to reflect pluralism of the press in Africa at start of democratic processes 1990–91; Communications Adviser (Strategy-Media) to Pres. of Organizing Cttee of African Cup of Nations Jan.–April 1998; consultant to Nat. Comm. for Decentralization Sept. 1998; Sr Consultant to Supreme Council of Information for org. and conduct of seminar on Media, Democracy and Nat. Languages Oct. 1998; consultant to FAO Project TCP/BKF on project for a nat. communication policy for rural devt Feb.–March 1999. *Publications include:* The Politics of Communication in Black Africa (research report) 1987, The Committees for the Defense of the Revolution and the Process of Mobilization for Development in Burkina Faso (thesis) 1987, The Process of Democratic Transition in South Africa from the Sahara, from Burkina Faso 1994. *Leisure interests:* jogging, reading, cinema. *Address:* Office of the Prime Minister, 03 BP 7027, Ouagadougou 03, Burkina Faso (office). *Telephone:* 50-32-48-89 (office). *Fax:* 50-33-05-5. *E-mail:* webmaster@primature.gov.bf (office). *Website:* www.gouvernement.gov.bf (office).

TIBAIJUKA, Anna Kajumulo, DSc; Tanzanian agricultural economist and United Nations official; *Minister of Lands, Housing and Human Settlements Development;* m. Wilson Tibaijuka (died 2000); five c. (one adopted); ed Swedish Univ. of Agricultural Sciences, Uppsala; Assoc. Prof. of Econs, Dar-es-Salaam Univ. 1993–98; Founding Chair. Tanzanian Nat. Women's Council; UNCTAD Special Co-ordinator for Least Developed Countries, Landlocked and Small Island Developing Countries 1998–2000; Exec. Dir UN Centre for Human Settlements (UN-HABITAT) 2000–10, Under-Sec.-Gen. 2002–10, Dir-Gen. UN Office, Nairobi (UNON) 2006–10; currently Minister of Lands, Housing and Human Settlements Devt; mem. Tanzanian Govt del. to several UN Summits, including World Summit for Social Devt, Copenhagen 1995, Fourth World Conf. on Women, Beijing 1995, UN Conf. on Human Settlements, Istanbul 1996, World Food Summit, Rome 1996 (elected Co-ordinator for Eastern Africa in Network for Food Security, Trade and Sustainable Devt—COASAD); mem. Bd Int. Scientific Advisory Bd, UNESCO 1997–; Exec. Sec. for Third UN Conf. on Least Developed Countries, Brussels, Belgium 2001; mem. Comm. for Africa 2004–05; apptd UN Special Envoy to study impact of Zimbabwean Govt's campaign (known as Operation Murambatsvina) to evict informal traders and people deemed to be squatting illegally in certain areas 2005. *Address:* Ministry of Lands, Housing and Human Settlements Development, Kivukoni Front, Ardhi House, POB 9132, Dar es Salaam, Tanzania (office). *Telephone:* (22) 2121241 (office). *Fax:* (22) 2124576 (office). *Website:* www.ardhi.go.tz (office).

TIBERI, Jean, LenD; French politician; b. 30 Jan. 1935, Paris; s. of Charles Tiberi and Hélène Pallavicini; m. Xavière Casanova; one s. one d.; ed Coll. Sainte-Barbe, Lycées Montaigne and Louis-le-Grand and Faculté de Droit, Paris; Acting Judge, Colmar 1958; Deputy Public Prosecutor, Metz 1959, Meaux 1959; Judge, Beauvais 1959, Nantes 1960; Chancellery 1960–63; Dir of Studies, Faculté de Droit, Paris 1961–; Conseiller de Paris 1965–; First Vice-Pres. Conseil de Paris 1983–95; Deputy to Mayor of Paris 1977–83, First Deputy 1983–95; Deputy to Nat. Ass. 1968–; fmr Sec. of State at Ministries of Agric., Industry and Research; Mayor of 5th arrondissement of Paris 1983–95; Sec. Paris RPR 1985–2000; Mayor of Paris 1995–2000; Deputy of Paris 2002–; Mayor of 5th arrondissement of Paris 2000–. *Publications:* Le quartier latin, Paris capitale des siècles 1988, La nouvelle Athènes, Paris capitale de l'esprit 1992. *Address:* Mairie du 5th arrondissement, 21 place du Panthéon, 75231, Paris Cedex 5 (office); Assemblée Nationale, 126 rue de l'Université, 75007 Paris (office); 1 place du Panthéon, 75005 Paris, France (home). *Telephone:* 1-40-63-62-84 (office). *Fax:* 1-40-63-62-96 (office). *E-mail:* jtiberi@assemblee-nationale.fr (office). *Website:* www.assemblee-nationale.fr/12/tribun/fiches_id/2816.asp (office).

TIBILOV, Leonid; Georgian politician; *President of 'Republic of South Ossetia';* b. 28 March 1952, Verkhnyi Dvan, Znaur Dist, South Ossetian Autonomous Oblast, Georgian SSR, USSR; began career as physics teacher before joining KGB in 1981; South Ossetian Minister of State Security and Head of KGB 1992–98; played role in internationally mediated efforts to resolve conflict between South Ossetia and Tbilisi 1990s; apptd First Deputy Prime Minister 2006; co-chaired a Georgian-Ossetian peacekeeping comm.; unsuccessful cand. in presidential election 2006; Pres. 'Republic of South Ossetia' 19 April 2012–; Ind. *Address:* Office of the President of the 'Republic of South Ossetia', 100001 Tskhinvali, ul. Khetgurova 1, South Ossetia, Georgia (office). *Telephone:* (9974) 45-00-01 (office). *Fax:* (9974) 45-47-63 (office). *E-mail:* ospress@yandex.ru (office).

TICHENOR, Warren W., BS; American business executive and diplomatist; b. 1960, Harlingen, Tex.; s. of McHenry Taylor Tichenor, Jr; m. Rhonda S. Tichenor; one s.; ed Univ. of Southern California; early career working in various positions in family's media co. Tichenor Media System, Inc. (later renamed Hispanic Broadcasting Corpn, merged with Univision Communications 2003, sold 2007); Pres. W.W. Tichenor & Co., Inc. (pvt. investment firm), San Antonio, Tex. –2006; Dir Hispanic Campaign 2000 (served in similar capacity in George W. Bush's re-election campaign for Gov. of Tex. 1998); has served on bds and in other capacities of various charitable, political, business and civic orgs; Amb. and Perm. Rep. to UN and other Int. Orgs, Geneva 2006–09. *Address:* W.W. Tichenor & Co., Inc., 45 NE Loop 410, Suite 265, San Antonio, TX 78216, USA (office). *Website:* wwtichenorco.com (office).

TICKELL, Sir Crispin (Charles Cervantes), GCMG, KCVO; British fmr university chancellor and fmr diplomatist; b. 25 Aug. 1930, London, England; s. of Jerrard Tickell and Renée Haynes; m. 1st Chloë Gunn 1954 (divorced 1976); two s. one d.; m. 2nd Penelope Thorne Thorne 1977; ed Westminster School and Christ Church, Oxford; entered HM Diplomatic Service 1954, served at Embassy in The Hague 1955–58, Embassy in Mexico 1958–61, Embassy in Paris 1964–70; Pvt. Sec. to Chancellor of Duchy of Lancaster 1970–72; Head of Western Orgs Dept 1972–75; Fellow, Centre for Int. Affairs, Harvard Univ. 1975–76; Chef de Cabinet to Pres. of Comm. of EC 1977–81; Visiting Fellow, All Souls Coll. Oxford 1981; Amb. to Mexico 1981–83; Deputy Under-Sec. of State 1983–84; Perm. Sec. Overseas Devt Admin. 1984–87; Perm. Rep. to UN, New York 1987–90; Warden, Green Coll., Oxford 1990–97, Dir Green Coll. Centre for Environmental Policy and Understanding 1992–2006; Chancellor Univ. of Kent 1996–2006; Chair. Trustees, St Andrew's Prize for the Environment 1998–; Dir Policy Foresight Programme, The James Martin 21st Century School, Univ. of Oxford 2006–10; Adviser at Large to Pres. of Arizona State Univ. 2004–; Dir (non-exec.) IBM UK 1990–95 (mem. IBM Advisory Bd 1995–2000), Govett Mexican Horizons Investment 1991–96, Govett American Smaller Companies Trust 1996–98, Govett Enhanced Income Investment Trust 1999–; mem. Friends Provident Stewardship Cttee of Reference 1999–2002; Dir BOC Foundation 1990–2003; Pres. Royal Geographical Soc. 1990–93 (Vice-Pres. 1993–2002), Hon. Vice-Pres. 2002), Marine Biological Asscn 1990–2001 (Vice-Pres.

2001–), Earth Centre 1996–2000, Nat. Soc. for Clean Air 1997–99, Tree Aid 2007–; Chair. Int. Inst. for Environment and Devt 1990–94, Earthwatch Europe 1990–97, Climate Inst. of Washington, DC 1990–2002, 2012–, Advisory Cttee on Darwin Initiative for the Survival of Species 1992–99, Gaia Soc. 1998–2001, Advisory Cttee on the Environment of Int. Council for Science 1999–2004, Gaia Special Interest Group of Geological Soc. of London 2000–; Convenor Govt Panel on Sustainable Devt 1994–2000; mem. Govt Task Force towards an Urban Renaissance 1998–99, on Potential Risks from Near Earth Objects 2000, Copenhagen Climate Council 2008–09; Trustee, Nat. History Museum 1992–2001, World Wildlife Fund (UK) 1993–99, Royal Botanic Garden, Edinburgh 1997–2001, Thomson-Reuters Foundation 2000–, TERI Europe 2003–; Sr Inaugural Visiting Fellow, Harvard Univ. Center for the Environment 2002–03; Fellow, Geological Soc. of London 2000–, Linnean Soc. of London 2008–; mem. ASU Council for the Global Inst. for Sustainablility; Co-founder Sir Crispin Tickell High Altitude Climate Observatory in Mexico and the associated Tickell Interaction Network in Mexico and beyond 2010–; Hon. Fellow, Anglo American School, New York 1990, Westminster School 1993, St Edmund's Coll., Cambridge 1995, Green Coll., Oxford 1997, Royal Scottish Geographical Soc. 1992, Chartered Inst. of Water and Environmental Man. 1996, Royal Inst. of GB 2002, Soc. for the Environment 2013; Hon. FRIBA 2000; Hon. Sr mem. Darwin Coll., Cambridge 1997; Officer, Order of Orange-Nassau (Netherlands) 1958, Chevalier, Nat. Order of Mali 1979, Orden Academica del Derecho, de la Cultura, y de la Paz 1989, Order of Aztec Eagle with Sash (Mexico) 1994; Dr hc (Academia Mexicana de Derecho Internacional) 1983, (Univ. of Stirling) 1990, (Sheffield Hallam Univ.) 1996, (Univ. of East London) 1998, (Open Univ.) 2006, (Univ. Juarez Autonoma de Tabasco) 2011; Hon. LLD (Univ. of Massachusetts, USA) 1990, (Univ. of Birmingham) 1991, (Univ. of Bristol) 1991; Hon. DSc (Univ. of East Anglia) 1990, (Univ. of Sussex) 1991, (Cranfield Univ.) 1992, (Loughborough Univ. of Tech.) 1995, (Univ. of Exeter) 1999, (Univ. of Hull) 2001, (Univ. of Plymouth) 2001, (Univ. of St Andrews) 2002, (Univ. of Southampton) 2002, (Oxford Brookes Univ.) 2002, (Université du Littoral Cote d'Opale) 2002; Hon. DLitt (Polytechnic of Cen. London (now Univ. of Westminster) 1990; Hon. DCL (Univ. of Kent at Canterbury) 1996; Hon. DHumLitt (American Univ. of Paris) 2003; Hon. DJur (Univ. of Nottingham) 2003; Hon. DrScs (Univ. of Brighton) 2006; mem. The Global 500: Roll of Honour for Environmental Achievement of UNEP 1991, Global Environmental Leadership Award, Climate Inst. of Washington, DC 1996, Distinguished Lecturer, British Geological Survey 1994, Centennial Lecturer, Arizona State Univ. 1995, Melchett Medallist, Inst. of Energy 1996, Kelvin Medallist, Royal Philosophical Soc. of Glasgow 1996, first Happold Medallist, Nat. Construction Industry Council 1998, Patron's Medal, Royal Geographical Soc. 2000, Distinguished Environmental Lecturer, Harvard Univ. 2001, Award for Int. Co-operation on Environment and Devt, China Council for Int. Co-operation on Environment and Devt 1996, Award for Int. Co-operation on Environmental Protection, Chinese State Environmental Protection Agency (SEPA) 2003, CAB Int. Bioscience Fellow 2004, Friendship Award, Govt of People's Repub. of China 2004, Minor Planet named No. 5971 Tickell 2006. *Publications include:* Climatic Change and World Affairs 1977, Mary Anning of Lyme Regis 1996; contribs to many books and papers. *Leisure interests:* climatology, palaeohistory, art (especially pre-Colombian), mountains. *Address:* Ablington Old Barn, Ablington, Cirencester, Glos., GL7 5NU, England (office). *Telephone:* (1285) 740569 (office). *E-mail:* ct@crispintickell.net (office), penelopetickell@googlemail.com (office). *Website:* www.crispintickell.net.

TICKNER, Robert, LLM, BEcons; Australian lawyer, organization official and fmr politician; *CEO, Australian Red Cross;* b. 24 Dec. 1951, Sydney; m. Jody Tickner; one c.; ed Univ. of Sydney; Lecturer, Faculty of Business Studies, NSW Inst. of Tech. 1974–78, Faculty of Law 1978–79; Prin. Solicitor, Aboriginal Legal Service, Redfern, Sydney 1979–83; Alderman, Sydney City Council 1977–84; MP for Hughes, NSW 1984–96; Minister for Aboriginal and Torres Strait Islander Affairs 1990–96; CEO Job Futures Ltd 2000–05; CEO Australian Red Cross 2005–; Office holder, Fed. Electorate Council and other Australian Labor Party bodies; Pres. NSW Soc. of Labor Lawyers; Cttee mem. NSW Council for Civil Liberties; Founding Cttee mem. Citizens for Democracy; Convenor Labor Parliamentarians for Nuclear Free Australia; fmr Chair. Parl. Group of Amnesty Int. *Leisure interests:* golf, tennis. *Address:* Australian Red Cross National Office, PO Box 196, Carlton South, Vic. 3053, Australia (office). *Telephone:* (3) 9345-1800 (office). *Fax:* (3) 9348-2513 (office). *E-mail:* natinfo@redcross.org.au (office). *Website:* www.redcross.org.au (office).

TIDIANE SOUARÉ, Ahmed; Guinean politician; b. 1951; mem. Cttee for Implementation of Econ., Financial and Admin. Reforms of Presidency 1989–90, Coordinator, Office for Monitoring and Evaluation of Presidency 1990–94; Head of Cabinet, Ministry of Econ. and Financial Control 1994–96, Ministry Del. to the Prime Minister in charge of the budget 1996–97, Ministry of Economy and Finance 1997–2002; Insp. Gen. of Finances 2002–05; Minister of Mines and Geology 2005–06, also Chair. Bd of Dirs Compagnie des Bauxites de Guinée; Minister of State for Higher Educ. and Scientific Research 2006–07; Prime Minister of Guinea May–Dec. 2008 (replaced following coup d'état); arrested on charge of misuse of funds June 2009.

TIE, Ning; Chinese writer; *President, Chinese Writers' Association;* b. 1957, Beijing; d. of Tie Yang and Xu Zhi-ying; Council mem. Chinese Writers' Asscn 1985–, Vice-Pres. 2001–06, Pres. (first woman) 2006–; Alt. mem. 16th CCP Cen. Cttee 2002–07, 17th CCP Cen. Cttee 2007–12, mem. 18th CCP Cen. Cttee 2012–. *Publications:* Path in the Night 1980, Xiangxue (Nat. Short Story Prize) 1982, Red Shirt With No Buttons (Nat. Fiction Prize) 1984, Rose Gate 1988, Cotton Stack 1988, Hay Stack (short stories) 1991, Women's White Night (non-fiction) 1991, Straw Ring (non-fiction) 1992, For Ever and Ever 1999, The Great Bather 2000, The Bathing Women 2012. *Leisure interests:* music, gourmet cooking. *Address:* Chinese Writers' Association, No.25, East Tucheng Road, Chaoyang District, Beijing 100013, People's Republic of China. *Telephone:* (10) 64221865 (office). *Fax:* (10) 64222240. *Website:* www.chinawriter.com.cn (office).

TIEFENSEE, Wolfgang; German politician; b. 1955, Gera; skilled telecommunications worker 1974; mil. service 1975, as a conscientious objector served in a construction unit; graduated as an industrial electronics engineer 1979; Research and Devt Engineer, VEB Communications Works, Leipzig 1979–86; studied part-time for a postgraduate degree in computer science in the construction industry

1982; Devt Engineer, Technische Hochschule Leipzig 1986–90; studied part-time for a degree in electrical eng 1988; engaged in politics with Leipzig Round Table, Deputy Mayor without portfolio and mem. City Council 1989–90, Head of School Admin Office 1990, Deputy Mayor for Schools and Educ. 1992–94, Deputy Mayor for Youth, Schools and Sport and Vice-Mayor 1994, Mayor of Leipzig 1998–2005; mem. SPD 1995–; Fed. Minister of Transport, Building and Urban Affairs and Fed. Govt Commr for the New Fed. States 2005–09; Vice-Pres. Saxon Asscn of Cities and Towns 2001–; Pres. Eurocities 2002–04; mem. Exec. Cttee German Asscn of Cities. *Address:* c/o SPD, Willy-Brandt-Haus, Wilhelmstr. 141, 10963 Berlin, Germany (office). *Telephone:* (30) 259910 (office). *Fax:* (30) 25991410 (office). *Website:* www.spd.de (office).

TIEMANN, Susanne, DJur; German lawyer, politician and academic; b. 20 April 1947, Schwandorf; d. of Hermann Bamberg and Anna-Maria Bamberg; m. Burkhard Tiemann 1969; one s. two d.; ed Ludwig-Maximilian Univ. Munich; called to the Bar, Munich 1975; served as lawyer in Cologne 1980; Prof. for Social and Admin. Law, Univ. of Bonn, Catholic Univ. of Cologne, now Prof. Emer.; mem. Bundestag (CDU/CSU) 1994–2002; Chair. 1992–94; mem. Bd German Fed. of Liberal Professions 1988–; mem. Exec. Bd and Vice-Pres. European Secr. of the Liberal, Intellectual and Social Professions (SEPLIS) 1988, Pres. 1989–95; Chair. German Taxpayers' Asscn 1992–94; Hon. Prof., Katholische Fachhochschule Nordrhein-Westfalen 1998–; Frauen für Europa Prize 1993. *Address:* Stefan-Lochner-Straße 11, 50999 Cologne, Germany.

TIEN, Hung-Mao, MA, PhD; Taiwanese academic and diplomatist; b. 7 Nov. 1938, Tainan; m. Amy Tien; one s. one d.; ed Tunghai Univ. and Univ. of Wisconsin, USA; fmr Prof. of Political Science, Univ. of Wisconsin; Pres. Inst. for Nat. Policy Research 1991–; mem. Nat. Unification Research Council, Office of Pres. of Taiwan 1994–; Nat. Policy Adviser to Pres. of Taiwan 1996–; Dir Foundation for Int. Co-operation and Devt 1996–, Minister of Foreign Affairs 2000–02; Rep. to UK 2002. *Publications include:* Government and Politics in Kuomintang China 1927–37, The Great Transition, Social and Political Change in the Republic of China, Taiwan's Electoral Politics and Democratic Transition: Riding the Third Wave 1995. *Leisure interests:* golf, tennis, table-tennis. *Address:* #225, Tung-shih Street, Hsi-chih, Taipei County, Taiwan (home).

TIETMEYER, Hans, Dr rer. pol; German banker, economist and civil servant; *Senior Adviser, Lazard Asset Management (Deutschland) GmbH;* b. 18 Aug. 1931, Metelen; s. of Bernhard Tietmeyer and Helene Tietmeyer; m. 1st Marie-Luise Tietmeyer (died 1978); m. 2nd Maria-Therese Tietmeyer 1980; one s. one d.; ed Univs of Münster, Bonn and Cologne; Sec. Bischöfliche Studienforderung Cusanuswerk 1959–62; Fed. Ministry of Econs 1962–82, Head of Div. of Gen. Econ. Policy 1973–82; mem. Econ. Policy Cttee of EC and OECD 1972–82; Sec. of State, Ministry of Finance 1982–89; mem. Bd of Dirs, Bundesbank 1990, Vice-Pres. 1991–93, Pres. 1993–99; Hon. Prof. of Public Econ. of Halle-Wittenberg 1996–; Monetary Policy Adviser to IMF 2002; Sr Adviser, Lazard Asset Man., Frankfurt 2003–; Grosses Bundesverdienstkreuz; Dr hc (Münster) 1994, (Maryland) 1997. *Publications:* The Social Market Economy and Monetary Stability 1999; more than 100 articles on economics. *Leisure interests:* sport, rambling. *Address:* Lazard Asset Management (Deutschland) GmbH, Alte Mainzer Gasse 37, 60311 Frankfurt, Germany (office). *Telephone:* (69) 506060 (office). *Fax:* (69) 50606100 (office). *Website:* www.lazardnet.com (office).

TIGERMAN, Stanley, MArch, FAIA; American architect; *Partner, Tigerman McCurry Architects;* b. 20 Sept. 1930, Chicago, Ill.; s. of Samuel B. Tigerman and Emma L. Stern; m. Margaret I. McCurry 1979; one s. one d.; ed Yale Univ.; architectural draughtsman, George Fred Keck, Chicago 1949–50; Skidmore Owings & Merrill, Chicago 1957–59; Paul Rudolph, New Haven 1959–61; Harry Weese 1961–62; Pnr Tigerman & Koglin, Chicago 1962–64; Prin. Stanley Tigerman & Assoc. Chicago 1964–82; Pnr Tigerman Fugman McCurry, Chicago 1982–88, Tigerman McCurry Architects, Chicago 1988–; Co-Founder Archeworks Design Lab. Chicago 1993; Prof. of Architecture Univ. of Ill., Chicago 1967–71, 1980–93, Dir School of Architecture 1985–93; Davenport Prof. of Architecture, Yale Univ. 1979, 1993, Bishop Prof. 1984; Architect-in-Residence, American Acad. Rome 1980; Visiting Prof. Univ. of Cincinnati 1980, Univ. of Houston 1981, Tulane 1981, Univ. of Nebraska 1981, Univ. of North Carolina, Charlotte 1982, Harvard 1982, Iowa State 1985 Univ., Univ. of Rotterdam 1985; Visiting Scholar, American Acad. in Rome 1985; mem. Advisory Cttee Princeton Univ. 1997; 55 nat.,and local AIA awards, 96 various other awards, AIA Illinois Gold Medal in recognition of outstanding lifetime service 2008, AIA/ACSA Topaz Medallion for Excellence in Architectural Educ. 2008. *Publications:* Chicago's Architectural Heritage: A Romantic Classical Image... & Work of the Current Generation of Chicago Architects 1979, VERSUS: An American Architect's Alternatives 1982, Stanley Tigerman Architoons 1988, The Architecture of Exile 1988, Stanley Tigerman, Buildings & Projects 1966–89 1989. *Leisure interests:* drawing, reading. *Address:* Tigerman McCurry Ltd, 444 North Wells Street, Suite 206, Chicago, IL 60654, USA (office). *Telephone:* (312) 644-5880 (office). *Fax:* (312) 644-3750 (office). *E-mail:* tma@tigerman-mccurry.com (office). *Website:* www.tigerman-mccurry .com (office).

TIGYI, József; Hungarian biophysicist and academic; b. 19 March 1926, Kaposvár; s. of András Tigyi and Julianna Mátrai; m. Anna Sebes; two s.; ed Medical Univ. of Pécs; Prof. and Dir of Biophysical Inst., Medical Univ. of Pécs 1971–91, Vice-Rector 1967–73, Rector 1973–79, now Prof. Emer.; corresp. mem. Hungarian Acad. of Sciences 1967–76, mem. 1976–, Vice-Pres. 1988, Pres. Regional Cttee, Pécs 1996–; Pres. Acad. Section No. 8 (Biological Sciences) 1980–88; Pres. Hungarian Biophysical Soc. 1972–91, Hon. Pres. 1991–; Pres. UNESCO European Collaboration in Biophysics 1976–86; Chief Ed. Acta Biochimica et Biophysica 1981–91; mem. Royal Soc. of Medicine, New York Acad. of Sciences 1980–, European Acad. of Arts, Sciences and Humanities, Paris 1990–, WHO Exec. Bd 1972–75, Int. Council of Scientific Unions (ICSU) Gen. Cttee, Cttee on the Teaching of Science 1986–93, Gesellschaft für mathematische u. physikalische Biologie (GDR), Biophysical Soc. of Romania, of India; Gen. Sec. Int. Union of Pure and Applied Biophysics (IUPAB) 1984–93, Co-Chair. Special Cttee on Radiation and Environmental Biophysics 1993–; Labour Order of Merit (Silver) 1966, (Gold) 1970, 1979. *Publications:* Application of Radioactive Isotope in Experimental Medicine 1965, Biophysics: Theory of Bioelectric Phenomena,

Biological Semi-conductors, Energetics of Cross-Striated Muscle 1977, Physical Aspects of the Living Cell 1991. *Address:* Biophysical Institute, University of Pécs, Szigeti ut 12, 7643 Pécs, Hungary (office). *Telephone:* (72) 536-263 (office). *Fax:* (72) 536-261 (office). *E-mail:* jozsef.tigyi@aok.pte.hu (office). *Website:* www.aok.pte.hu (office).

TIHIĆ, Sulejman; Bosnia and Herzegovina politician; *Chairman, Party of Democratic Action (PDA) (Stranka Demokratske Akcije) (SDA);* b. 26 Nov. 1951, Bosanski Šamac; m.; two s. one d.; ed Univ. of Sarajevo; judge and public prosecutor, Bosanski Samac 1975–83, lawyer 1983–92; imprisoned for three months by Bosnian Serb forces in Bosanski Samac and other towns during Bosnian War of 1992–95; Head Consular Dept, Embassy of Bosnia and Herzegovina, Berlin, Germany 1994–96; Adviser to Minister of Foreign Affairs on Consular Affairs 1996–99; mem. Parl. Republika Srpska 1996–2002, Deputy Speaker 2000–02, nominated by UN High Rep. in Bosnia and Herzegovina as mem. of Parl. Cttee on Constitutional Issues 2001; Founding mem. Party of Democratic Action, Chair. 2001–; mem. of the Presidency (tripartite) 2002–06, Chair. Presidency March–Oct. 2004, Feb.–Oct. 2006; mem. House of Peoples (Parl.) 2011–, currently Deputy Speaker. *Address:* Party of Democratic Action (PDA) (Stranka Demokratske Akcije) (SDA), 71000 Sarajevo, Mehmeda Spahe 14, Bosnia and Herzegovina (office). *Telephone:* (33) 216906 (office). *Fax:* (33) 650429 (office). *E-mail:* sda@bih .net.ba (office). *Website:* www.sda.ba (office).

TIHIPKO, Serhiy Leonidovych; Ukrainian banker and politician; b. 13 Feb. 1960; m.; one d.; ed Dnipropetrovsk Metallurgical Inst.; Head of Dept of Agitation and Propaganda, Young Communist League during late 1980s; Chair. Bd Privatbank 1992–97; Deputy Prime Minister responsible for Privatization and Econ. Devt 1997–99, apptd Minister of Economy 1999; elected to Verkhovna Rada (Parl.) June 2000; elected Leader Working Ukraine party Nov. 2000 (party reconstituted as A Strong Ukraine 2009, merged with Party of the Regions 2011); Gov. Nat. Bank of Ukraine 2002–05 (resgnd); campaign man. for Viktor Yanukovych during presidential election 2004; cand. in presidential election 2010; Deputy Prime Minister, responsible for Econ. Affairs March–Dec. 2010, Deputy Prime Minister and Minister of Social Policy 2010–12; mem. Verkhovna Rada (Parl.) 2012–. *Address:* c/o Ministry of Social Policy, 01001 Kyiv, vul. Esplanadna 8/10, Ukraine (office).

TIIK, Simmu; Estonian diplomatist; *Ambassador to Russia;* b. 19 Feb. 1959, Tartu; m.; one d.; ed Univ. of Tartu, Univ. of Copenhagen, Denmark; worked at Cen. Library, City of Tartu 1980–89; with Dept of Policy Planning, Ministry of Foreign Affairs, Tallinn 1993–96, Embassy in Copenhagen 1997–99, Adviser in Foreign Affairs, Prime Minister's Office 1999–2003, Chef de Cabinet to Minister of Foreign Affairs 2003, Amb. to Ireland 2003–06, Dir-Gen. Third Political Dept, Ministry of Foreign Affairs 2006–08, Amb. to Russia 2008–12. *Address:* Embassy of Estonia, 125009 Moscow, M. Kislovskii per. 5, Russia (office). *Telephone:* (495) 737-36-40 (office). *Fax:* (495) 737-36-46 (office). *E-mail:* embassy.moskva@estemb.ru (office). *Website:* www.estemb.ru (office).

TIILIKAINEN, Teija Helena; Finnish political scientist, academic and research institute director; *Director, Finnish Institute of International Affairs;* b. 22 April 1964, Lohja; ed Abo Akademi Univ.; Lecturer in Social Sciences, Univ. of Turku 1989–90, Acting Departmental Asst 1990–91, Lecturer in Political Sciences and Int. Relations 1993–96; Acting Departmental Asst, Dept of Political Science, Abo Akademi Univ. 1992–93, 1996; Research Fellow, 'Citizens Europe' Research Project, financed by Acad. of Finland 1993–95; Ed.-in-Chief, Politiikka (Politics; Finnish journal of Political Science) 1995–96; Researcher, Dept of Strategic Studies, Nat. Defence Coll. 1996–98; Lecturer in European Politics 1998–; Gen.-Sec., Forum for European Security 1997–99 (Chair. 1999–2001); Researcher, Coordinator of Programme on European Policy-Making, Dept of Political Science, Univ. of Helsinki, Mar–Aug. 1998, 1999–2000, Acting Prof. in Int. Relations Sept.–Dec. 1998; Lecturer, Perm. Course in European Political Integration, European Comm., Jean Monnet Project 1998–2005; Project Coordinator, Nordic Research Programme in Security Policy 1999–; Dir of Research, Centre for European Studies, Univ. of Helsinki 2001–03, Dir Network for European Studies 2003–07, 2009; State Sec., Ministry for Foreign Affairs 2007–08; Vice-Chair. Finnish Inst. of Int. Affairs 2007–, currently Dir; Lecturer, Finnish Defence Courses 2004–; Chair. Finnish Int. Studies Asscn 1994–96, Organization Europpanaiset (Women in Europe) 2005–07; mem. Editorial Bd Ulkopolitiikka (Finnish Journal of Foreign Affairs) 1994–2001 (currently Dir and Ed.-in-Chief); mem. Bd of Dirs Parl. Library 1999–, Foreign and Security Policy Research, Swedish Inst. of Int. Affairs, Stockholm 2000–, British Council Awards 2001–, Foundation for Finnish Foreign Policy Research 2001; mem. Cttee for Liberal Adult Education, Univ. of Helsinki 1999–, Acad. Bd EUROPEAUM 2004–, Tanner Acad. 2005–, Nat. Bd of Econ. Defence 2000–08, Asscn Cttee, Finnish Cultural Foundation 2006–; columnist, Hufvudstadsbladet (Swedish newspaper in Finland) 1997, Turun Sanomat 1999–, Etelä-Suomen Sanomat 1999–, Suomen Kuvalehti 2000–01, MTV News 2002–; Swedish-Finnish Cultural Foundation Annual Award 2001, Univ. of Helsinki Annual J.V. Snellman Award 2002, Finnish Social Scientist Asscn Social Scientist of the Year Award 2002, Tanner Award 2005. *Publications include:* numerous articles in Finnish and int. journals. *Leisure interests:* sports, reading. *Address:* Finnish Institute of International Affairs, PO Box 400, 00161 Helsinki, Finland (office). *Telephone:* (9) 432-7701 (office). *Fax:* (9) 432-7799 (office). *E-mail:* teija.tiilikainen@fiia.fi (office). *Website:* www.fiia.fi (office).

TIJDEMAN, Robert; Dutch mathematician and academic; *Professor of Mathematics, University of Leiden;* b. 30 July 1943, Oostzaan; m. Alberdina Broertjes; two d.; ed Univ. of Amsterdam; scientific worker, Univ. of Amsterdam 1967–70; mem. Inst. for Advanced Study, Princeton, NJ 1970–71; Reader, Univ. of Leiden 1971–75, Prof. of Math. 1975–, Dir Thomas Stieltjes Inst. for Math. 1999–, Chair. Dept of Math. and Computer Science 1991–93; Visiting Prof., Univ. of Cambridge 1976, Univ. of Michigan 1976, ETH 1980, Univ. of Pisa 1975, Univ. of New South Wales 1985, Univ. of Waterloo, Canada 1987, Keio Univ. 1989, Tata Inst., Mumbai 1991, 2000, MSRI 1993, Nihon Univ. 1996, Univ. Diderot (Paris 7) 2001; Vice-Pres. Dutch Math. Soc. 1982–84, Pres. 1984–86; Chair. Akademie Raad voor Wiskunde 2003–; mem. Wiskundig Genootschap 1966–, American Math. Soc. 1971–, London Math. Soc. 1977–, Royal Netherlands Acad. of Arts and Sciences 1987–, Societé Mathématique de France 1988–, Deutsche Mathematiker Verein 1990–,; Dr hc

(Debrecen, Hungary) 1999. *Publication:* Exponential diophantine equations (with T. N. Shorey) 1986. *Address:* Mathematical Institute, University of Leiden, POB 9512, 2300 RA Leiden, Netherlands. *Telephone:* (71) 5277138. *Fax:* (71) 527 7101. *E-mail:* tijdeman@math.leidenuniv.nl (office). *Website:* www.math.leidenuniv.nl/~tijdeman (office).

TIJERINO PACHERO, José Maria; Costa Rican lawyer and politician; *Minister of Governance, Police and Public Security;* b. 11 Nov. 1947; s. of José María Tijerino Rojas and Clara Pachero Chaverri; m. Olga Cristina Picado Gatgens 1972; one s. one d.; ed Univ. de Costa Rica, Univ. de Valencia, Spain; Public Prosecutor, Cañas, Guanacaste Prov. 1976; fmr Deputy Public Prosecutor and Trial Attorney, Alajuela Prov.; fmr Deputy Head of Public Prosecutor's Office, also Co-ordinator, Third Tribunal Superior Penal, San José; Attorney-Gen. of Costa Rica 1990–95; pvt practice as lawyer, Tribunales de la República de Costa Rica 1995–; Prof. of Law, Univ. de Costa Rica; Minister of Governance, Police and Public Security 2010–; mem. Partido Liberación Nacional. *Address:* Ministry of Governance, Police and Public Security, Apdo 55, 4874 San José,, Costa Rica (office). *Telephone:* 2227-4866 (office). *Fax:* 2226-6581 (office). *Website:* www.msp.go.cr (office).

TIKHONOVSKY, Maj.-Gen. Pyotr; Belarusian army officer; *Chief of General Staff;* b. 8 June 1958, Sidorovka, Klimovichi Dist, Mogilyov Region; ed Leningrad Combined Arms Command School, Mil. Acad., Russian Gen. Staff Acad., Moscow; platoon Commdr 1980, later company Commdr, Exec. Officer and Deputy Chief of Staff of motorised infantry regt, Sr Officer 1991, becoming leader of operations section, tank army staff, later Sr Officer and leader of planning team, Operations Directorate, Gen. Staff HQ, Belarusian Armed Forces, promoted to Deputy Chief, Operations Directorate 1999, later Deputy Chief of Gen. Staff, Chief of Main Operations Directorate and First Deputy Chief of Gen. Staff –2009, Chief of Gen. Staff and First Deputy Minister of Defence 2009–. *Address:* Ministry of Defence, 220034 Minsk, vul. Kamunistychnaya 1, Belarus (office). *Telephone:* (17) 297-12-12 (office). *Fax:* (17) 289-19-74 (office). *E-mail:* milcoop@mod.mil.by (office). *Website:* mod.mil.by (office).

TILEY, John, CBE, LLD, FBA; British lawyer and academic; *Professor Emeritus of Law of Taxation, University of Cambridge;* b. 25 Feb. 1941, Leamington Spa, Warwicks.; s. of the late William Tiley OBE and Audrey Tiley; m. Jillinda Draper 1964; two s. one d.; ed Winchester Coll. and Lincoln Coll. Oxford; called to the Bar, Inner Temple 1964, Hon. Bencher 1993; Recorder 1989–97; Lecturer, Lincoln Coll. Oxford 1963–64, Univ. of Birmingham 1964–67; Fellow, Queens' Coll. Cambridge 1967–; Asst Lecturer, Univ. of Cambridge 1967–72, Lecturer 1972–87, Reader 1987–90, Prof. of Law of Taxation 1990–2008, Prof. Emer. 2008–, Leverhulme Trust Fellow Emer. 2008–10, Chair. Faculty Bd of Law 1992–95, currently Deputy Dir Centre for Tax Law; Pres. Soc. of Public Teachers of Law 1995–96; Visiting Prof., Dalhousie Univ., Canada 1972–73, Univ. of Auckland 1973, Univ. of Western Ontario 1978–79, Univ. of Melbourne 1979, Case Western Reserve Univ. 1985–86, 1996, 2002; Hon. QC; Hon. Fellow, Chartered Inst. of Taxation 2009. *Publications:* Revenue Law 1976 (sixth edn 2008); ed. of various works on taxation and contribs to legal journals. *Leisure interests:* walking, visits to art galleries, listening to music. *Address:* Queens' College, Cambridge, CB3 9ET, England (office). *Telephone:* (1223) 335511 (office). *Website:* www.queens.cam.ac.uk (office).

TILGHMAN, Shirley Marie, BSc, PhD, FRS; Canadian biologist, academic and fmr university president; *President Emerita, Princeton University;* b. 17 Sept. 1946; one s. one d.; ed Queen's Univ., Temple Univ., USA; secondary school teacher, Sierra Leone 1968–70; Fogarty Int. Fellow, NIH 1975–77; Asst Prof., Fels Research Inst., Temple Univ. School of Medicine 1978–79; mem., Inst. for Cancer Research 1979–86; Adjunct Assoc. Prof. of Human Genetics and Biochemistry and Biophysics, Univ. of Pennsylvania 1980–86; Howard A. Prior Prof. of the Life Sciences, Princeton Univ. 1986–2001, Dir Lewis-Sigler Inst. for Integrative Genomics, Princeton Univ. 1998, Pres. Princeton Univ. 2001–13, Pres. Emer. and Prof. of Molecular Biology 2013–, Chair. Council on Science and Tech. 1993–2000; investigator, Howard Hughes Medical Inst. 1988; Adjunct Prof., Dept of Biochemistry, Univ. of Medicine and Dentistry of NJ (UMDNJ) – Robert Wood Johnson Medical School 1988; Foreign assoc., NAS; mem. American Acad. of Arts and Sciences; mem. Nat. Advisory Council, Nat. Center for Human Genome Research 1991–96; mem. Editorial Bd, Genes and Development (journal); mem. Bd of Dirs Rockefeller Univ., NIH, Jackson Laboratory, Whitehead Inst. for Biomedical Sciences of MIT, Google Inc. 2005–; Trustee, Amherst Coll. 2013–; Princeton Pres.'s Award for Distinguished Teaching 1996, L'Oréal-UNESCO Women in Science Award 2002, Lifetime Achievement Award, Soc. of Developmental Biology 2003, Genetics Soc. of America Medal 2007, Henry G. Friesen Int. Prize in Health Research 2010. *Address:* Carl Icahn Lab, 240, Lewis-Sigler Institute of Integrative Genomics, Washington Road, Princeton, NJ 08544-1014, USA (office). *Telephone:* (609) 258-2900 (office). *E-mail:* smt@princeton.edu (office). *Website:* molbio.princeton.edu (office).

TILL, James Edgar, OC, MA, PhD, FRS, FRSC; Canadian biophysicist; *Senior Scientist Emeritus and University Professor Emeritus, Prevention/Statistics, Ontario Cancer Institute;* b. Lloydminster, Sask.; ed Univ. of Sask. and Yale Univ.; post-doctoral fellowship, Connaught Medical Research Labs; mem. Faculty, Dept of Medical Biophysics, Univ. of Toronto 1958, Univ. Prof. 1984–97, Assoc. Dean (Life Sciences) School of Grad. Studies for three years, Sr Scientist Ontario Cancer Inst. 1957–96, Sr Scientist Emer., Prevention/Statistics 1996–, Univ. Prof. Emer. 1997–; mem. Nat. Bd Canadian Breast Cancer Foundation, Bd of Ethics Cttee, Stem Cell Network, Editorial Bd Journal of Medical Internet Research, Editorial Bd BMC Medical Informatics and Decision Making, Coll. of Reviewers, Canada Research Chairs Program; Pres. (Volunteer) Nat. Cancer Inst. of Canada 1998–2000, Past Pres. (Volunteer) 2000–01; Chair. Man. Cttee Cancer Information Service, Canadian Cancer Soc. 1998–99, Knowledge Man. Cttee Stem Cell Network 2001–04; Vice-Chair. Institutional Advisory Bd Inst. of Cancer Research, Canadian Insts of Health Research 2001–04; mem. Research Advisory Cttee Canadian Breast Cancer Research Alliance 2001–05, Clinical Trials Network Advisory Cttee, Ontario Cancer Research Network 2002–03, Research Action Group, Canadian Strategy for Cancer Control 2002–05, Jt Preventive Oncology and Research Bd Cttee, Cancer Care Ontario 2002–05; Hon. DSc (Toronto) 2004; co-recipient Gairdner Foundation Int. Award 1969, co-recipient RSC Thomas W. Eadie Medal 1991, Robert L. Noble Prize, Nat. Cancer Inst. of Canada 1993, Ernest McCulloch & James Till Award est. by American Soc. for Blood and Marrow

Transplantation for the best scientific paper by a new investigator published in its journal 1999, R. M. Taylor Medal, Canadian Cancer Soc./Nat. Cancer Inst. of Canada 2001, inducted into The Canadian Medical Hall of Fame 2004, co-recipient Albert Lasker Basic Medical Research Award, Albert and Mary Lasker Foundation 2005, co-recipient Biomedical Science Ambassador Award, Partners in Research 2005, co-recipient Centenary Medal, Royal Soc. of Canada 2005. *Achievements include:* with Ernest McCulloch was first to discover stem cells in bone marrow. *Publications:* numerous articles in scientific journals. *Address:* Princess Margaret Hospital, 9th Floor Room 416, 610 University Avenue, Toronto, ON M5G 2M9, Canada (office). *Telephone:* (416) 946-2948 (office). *Fax:* (416) 946-2024 (office). *E-mail:* till@uhnres.utoronto.ca (office). *Website:* medbio.utoronto.ca/faculty/till.html (office); myprofile.cos.com/tillj16 (office).

TILL, Jeremy, MA, DipArch, RIBA; British architect and academic; *Dean, School of Architecture and the Built Environment, University of Westminster;* b. 5 April 1957, Cambridge, England; s. of Barry Till and Shirley Philipson; partner Sarah Wigglesworth; ed Univ. of Cambridge, Polytechnic of Cen. London, Middlesex Univ.; Pnr, Peter Currie Architects 1985–92; Dir Sarah Wigglesworth Architects 1992–; Sr Lecturer, Kingston Univ. 1986–92; Sr Lecturer and Sub-Dean of Faculty, The Bartlett School of Architecture, Univ. Coll. London 1992–98; Prof. of Architecture and Head School of Architecture Univ. of Sheffield 1999–2008; Dean, School of Architecture and the Built Environment, Univ. of Westminster 2008–; Curator British Pavilion, Venice Architecture Biennale 2006; Fulbright Arts Fellowship 1990, Civic Trust Award 2002, RIBA Award 2004, RIBA Sustainability Prize 2004, RIBA Pres.'s Award for Research 2007, 2009. *Radio includes:* Shaping Our Spaces (two-part series, BBC Radio 4), contrib. to Talking Allowed (Radio 4), Front Row (Radio 4). *Television includes:* Grand Designs 2002. *Publications include:* Architecture and the Everyday 1997, 9 Stock Orchard Street: A Guidebook 2002, Architecture and Participation 2005, Flexible Housing 2007, Architecture Depends 2009. *Leisure interests:* cooking, eating, drinking. *Address:* School of Architecture and the Built Environment, University of Westminster, 35 Marylebone Road, London, NW1 5LS (office); 9 Stock Orchard Street, London, N7 9RW, England (home). *Telephone:* (20) 7911-5130 (office). *Fax:* (20) 7911-5171 (office). *E-mail:* j.till@westminster.ac.uk (office). *Website:* www.wmin.ac.uk (office).

TILLERSON, Rex W., BS; American energy industry executive; *Chairman and CEO, Exxon Mobil Corporation;* b. Wichita Falls, Tex.; m. Renda St Clair; four c.; ed Univ. of Texas, Austin; joined Exxon Co. as Production Engineer 1975, held several eng, tech. and supervisory roles 1975–87, including Business Devt Man., Natural Gas Dept 1987–89, Gen. Man. Cen. Production Div. 1989–92, moved to Dallas, Tex. as Production Advisor to Exxon Corpn and then to Florham Park, NJ as Coordinator of Affiliate Gas Sales, Exxon Corpn Int. 1992–95; Pres. Exxon Yemen Inc. and Esso Exploration and Production Khorat Inc. 1995–98, Vice-Pres. Exxon Ventures (CIS) Inc. and Pres. Exxon Neftegas Ltd 1998–99, Exec. Vice-Pres. ExxonMobil Devt Co. 1999–2001, Sr Vice-Pres. Exxon Mobil Corpn 2001–04, Pres. and mem. Bd of Dirs 2004–06, Chair. and CEO 2006–; mem. Bd of Dirs American Petroleum Inst. (Chair. Exec. Cttee and Policy Cttee), US-Russia Business Council; fmr Dir, United Negro Coll. Fund; mem. Exec. Bd and Nat. Pres. Boy Scouts of America 2010–12; mem. Nat. Petroleum Council, Business Roundtable (and its Energy Task Force), Emergency Cttee for American Trade; mem. Chancellor's Council and Eng Advisory Bd for Univ. of Texas at Austin, Soc. of Petroleum Engineers; Vice-Chair. Ford's Theatre Soc.; Trustee, Center for Strategic and Int. Studies; mem. Exec. Cttee The Business Council 2011–12; mem. Nat. Acad. of Eng 2013; Hon. Trustee, Business Council for Int. Understanding; Hon. PhD (Eng) (Worcester Polytechnic Inst.); ranked by Forbes magazine amongst The World's Most Powerful People (22nd) 2009, (49th) 2010, (46th) 2011, (22nd) 2012, (16th) 2013. *Address:* ExxonMobil Corporation, 5959 Las Colinas Blvd, Irving, TX 75039-2298, USA (office). *Telephone:* (972) 444-1000 (office). *Fax:* (972) 444-1350 (office). *Website:* www.exxonmobil.com (office).

TILLMAN, Robert (Bob) L.; American retail executive (retd); began career as store man., Lowe's Cos 1962, various man. positions including Exec. Vice-Pres. and COO, Exec. Vice-Pres. Merchandising, Sr Vice-Pres. Merchandising and Marketing, mem. Bd of Dirs 1994–, Pres. and CEO 1996–98, Chair. and CEO Lowe's Cos Inc. 1998–2005 (retd), Chair. and CEO Emer. 2005–; mem. Bd of Dirs Bank of America 2005–09. *Address:* c/o Lowe's Companies Inc., 1000 Lowe's Boulevard, Mooreville, NC 28117, USA (office).

TILLMANS, Wolfgang; German artist; b. 1968, Remscheid; s. of Karl A. Tillmans and Elisabeth Tillmans; ed Bournemouth and Poole Coll. of Art and Design, UK; Artist Trustee, Bd of Tate Gallery, London 2009–14; Turner Prize 2000, Kulturpreis, German Soc. of Photography 2009. *Publications:* Wolfgang Tillmans, 1995, For When I'm Weak I'm Strong, exhbn catalogue 1996, Burg 1998, Soldiers: The Nineties 1999, Portraits 2001, View from Above, If one thing matters, everything matters 2002, Freischwimmer 2004, Truth Study Center 2005, Manual 2007, Lighter 2008, Wako Book 4 2008, Wolfgang Tillmans, Serpentine Gallery 2010, Abstract Pictures 2011, Neue Welt 2012, Wolfgang Tillmans, Moderna Museet 2012. *Address:* c/o Maureen Paley, 21 Herald Street, London, E2 6JT, England. *Telephone:* (20) 7729-4112. *Fax:* (20) 7729-4113. *E-mail:* info@maureenpaley.com. *Website:* www.maureenpaley.com.

TILMAN, G(eorge) David, PhD; American biologist and academic; *Munzer Professor of Developmental Biology and Biochemistry, Regents' Professor and McKnight Presidential Chair in Ecology, University of Minnesota;* b. 22 July 1949, Aurora, Ill.; ed Univ. of Michigan; during doctoral research on algae, worked on math. model to predict outcome of resource competition, continued to work on model after appointment at Univ. of Minnesota, currently Munzer Prof. of Developmental Biology and Biochemistry, Regents' Prof. and McKnight Presidential Chair in Ecology, also Dir Univ.'s Cedar Creek Ecosystem Science Reserve; mem. Bd NSF, Nat. Research Council; mem. NAS 2002; Fellow, American Acad. of Arts and Sciences 1995; W.S. Cooper Award, Ecological Soc. of America 1989, MacArthur Award, Ecological Soc. of America 1997, designated by ISI Essential Science Indicators the Most Highly Cited Environmental Scientist of the Decade (1990–2000) 2000, (1996–2006) 2006, Int. Prize for Biology, Japan Soc. for the Promotion of Science 2008, Dr A.H. Heineken Prize for Environmental Sciences 2010. *Publications:* numerous papers in professional journals. *Address:* Ecology/Evolution/Behavior, Room 100 Ecology, 6098A (Campus Delivery Code), 1987

Upper Buford Circle, St Paul, MN 55108, USA (office). *Telephone:* (612) 625-5740 (office); (612) 625-5743 (office). *Fax:* (612) 624-6777 (office). *E-mail:* tilman@umn .edu (office); dirccgdt@umn.edu (office). *Website:* umn.edu/home/tilman (office); www.cbs.umn.edu/explore/field-stations/cedarcreek (office).

TILMANT, Michel; Belgian banking executive; b. 21 July 1952; ed Univ. of Louvain, Louvain School for European Affairs; with Morgan Guaranty Trust Co., New York 1977–91, held various positions including Head of European Investor Services, Paris and London, Head of Operations Services, New York, Gen. Man., Brussels br.; Vice-Chair. and COO, Banque International à Luxembourg 1991–92; mem. Exec. Cttee, Bank Brussels Lambert (BBL) 1992–2000, CEO 1997–2000; mem. Exec. Bd, ING Groep NV (after acquisition of BBL by ING) 1998–2009, Chair., ING Barings 1998–99, Vice-Chair., ING Groep 2000–04, Chair. Exec. Cttee, ING Europe 2000–04, Chair. Exec. Bd, ING Groep 2004–09; Chair., European Financial Services Round Table, Institut Int. d'Etudes Bancaires; mem. Bd, Belgian Governance Inst., Koninklijk Concertgebouworkest, Inst. of Int. Finance, Inc., Geneva Asscn; Trustee, Univ. of Louvain.

TILSON, Joseph (Joe), ARCA, RA; British artist; b. 24 Aug. 1928, London; s. of Frederick Albert Edward Tilson and Ethel Stapley Louise Saunders; m. Joslyn Morton 1956; one s. two d.; ed St Martin's School of Art, Royal Coll. of Art, British School, Rome; Visiting Lecturer, Slade School, Univ. of London, 1962–63, King's Coll., Univ. of Durham 1962–63, exhibited at Venice Biennale 1964; Lecturer, School of Visual Arts, New York 1966, Staatliche Hochschule, Hamburg 1971–72; Rome Prize 1955, Grand Prix Fifth Biennale, Kraków 1974, Henry Moore Prize, Bradford 1984, Grand Prix, 15th Biennale, Ljubljana 1985 and 21st Biennale 1995. *Art exhibitions:* retrospective exhbn, Boymans van Beuningen Museum, Rotterdam 1973, Sackler Galleries, Royal Acad., London 2002. *Address:* c/o Alan Cristea Gallery, 31 Cork Street, London, W1X 2NU, England; c/o Waddington Galleries, 11 Cork Street, London, W1S 3LT, England. *Telephone:* (20) 7439-1866; (20) 7851-2200; (20) 7259-0024 (home). *Fax:* (20) 7734-4146; (20) 7734-1549. *E-mail:* info@alancristea.com; mail@waddington-galleries.com. *Website:* www.alancristea.com; www.waddington-galleries.com.

TILSON THOMAS, Michael, (MTT); American conductor, pianist and composer; *Music Director, San Francisco Symphony Orchestra;* b. 21 Dec. 1944, Los Angeles; s. of Theodor Thomas and Roberta Thomas; ed Univ. of Southern California; conductor, Young Musicians' Foundation Orchestra, Los Angeles 1963–67; conductor and pianist, Monday Evening Concerts 1963–68; musical Asst Bayreuth 1966–67; Asst Conductor, Boston Symphony Orchestra 1969, Assoc. Conductor 1970–71, Prin. Guest Conductor 1972–74; New York debut 1969; London debut with London Symphony Orchestra (LSO) 1970; Dir Young People's Concerts, New York Philharmonic 1971–77; Music Dir Buffalo Philharmonic 1971–79; Prin. Guest Conductor, Los Angeles Philharmonic 1981–85; Music Dir Great Woods Inst. 1985, Music Dir Great Woods Festival 1987–88; Prin. Conductor, LSO 1988–95, Prin. Guest Conductor 1995–; Founder and Artistic Dir New World Symphony 1988–; Music Dir San Francisco Symphony Orchestra 1995–; Artistic Dir Pacific Music Festival; Dir YouTube Symphony Orchestra 2009–; guest conductor with orchestras and opera houses in USA and Europe; Chevalier, Ordre des Arts et des Lettres; Tanglewood Koussevitzky Prize 1968, Ditson Award for contrib. to American music 1994, Musical America Conductor of the Year 1994, American Music Center Award 2001, two Gramophone Awards, seven Grammy Awards including Best Classical Album 2004, 2007, 2010, Classic FM Gramophone Award for Artist of the Year 2005, Nat. Medal of Arts 2010. *Compositions include:* Poems of Emily Dickinson, premiered by Renée Fleming and San Francisco Symphony Orchestra. *Recordings include:* Mahler Symphonies 1, 3 and 6 (with San Francisco Symphony Orchestra), four-hand version of Stravinsky's Rite of Spring (with Ralph Grierson), Charles Ives' 2nd Symphony (with Concertgebouw Orchestra), complete works of Carl Ruggles (with Buffalo Philharmonic), various musicals by Weill and Gershwin, works of Bach, Beethoven, Prokofiev, Reich and Cage, Mahler's Seventh Symphony (with San Francisco Symphony Orchestra) 2007, Mahler's Eighth Symphony and Adagio from Symphony No. 10 2009, Adams' Harmonielehre & Short Ride In A Fast Machine (with San Francisco Symphony Orchestra) (Grammy Award for Best Orchestral Performance 2013) 2012. *Address:* MTT Inc., 1745 Broadway, 18th Floor, New York, NY 10019 (office); c/o San Francisco Symphony, Davies Symphony Hall, 201 Van Ness Avenue, San Francisco, CA 94102 (office). *Telephone:* (212) 246-7726 (New York) (office). *Fax:* (212) 489-5217 (New York) (office). *E-mail:* skashiyama@sfsymphony.org (office). *Website:* www.sfsymphony.org (office); www.michaeltilsonthomas.com.

TILTON, Glenn F.; American airline industry executive; *Chairman of the Midwest and Member of the Executive Committee, JPMorgan Chase;* b. 1948; m. Jackie Tilton; two c.; joined Texaco Inc. 1970, served in various marketing, corp. planning and European downstream assignments, Pres. US Refining and Marketing –1989, Vice-Pres. Texaco Inc. 1989–91, Chair. Texaco Ltd 1991–92, Pres. Texaco Europe 1992–95, Pres. Texaco USA 1995, Sr Vice-Pres. Texaco Inc. 1995–97, apptd Pres. Texaco Global Business Unit 1997, Chair. and CEO Texaco Inc. 2001, Vice-Chair. ChevronTexaco Corpn (following merger between Texaco and Chevron) 2001–02; Chair. Dynegy Inc. 2002; Chair., Pres. and CEO United Airlines (UAL) Corpn and United Airlines 2002–10, Chair. (non-exec.) United Continental Holdings, Inc. (holding co. of United Airlines and Continental Airlines) 2010–13; Chair. of the Midwest for JPMorgan Chase and mem. of its company-wide Exec. Cttee 2011–; named by Pres. Obama to the Presidential Export Council 2010–, by US Transportation Sec. Ray LaHood to the Future of Aviation Advisory Cttee 2010–, by Chicago Mayor Richard Daley to the O'Hare Express Blue Ribbon Cttee 2010–; mem. Bd of Dirs Abbott Laboratories, Corning Inc., Northwestern Memorial Hosp.; Chair. American Cancer Soc.'s nat. programme, CEOs against Cancer 2011–; mem. Bd Field Museum, Museum of Science and Industry, World Business Chicago Exec. Cttee, Commercial Club of Chicago Civic Cttee, Econ. Club of Chicago, Executives' Club of Chicago, Big Shoulders Fund, After School Matters, British American Chamber of Commerce; owns a ranch in Santa Fe, NM. *Leisure interest:* horse riding. *Address:* JPMorgan Chase & Co., 270 Park Avenue, New York, NY 10017-2070, USA (office). *Telephone:* (212) 270-6000 (office). *Fax:* (212) 270-1648 (office). *E-mail:* info@jpmchase.com (office). *Website:* www.jpmorganchase.com (office).

TIMBERLAKE, Justin Randall; American singer, songwriter and actor; b. 31 Jan. 1981, Memphis, Tenn.; m. Jessica Biel (q.v.) 2012; started vocal training aged

eight; guest appearance at Grand Ole Opry 1991; early TV appearances include Star Search 1992, The Mickey Mouse Club 1993–94; mem. *NSYNC vocal quintet 1995–, first headline US tour 1998; also solo artist 2002–; f. Justin Timberlake Foundation, a charity to fund music and art programmes in schools; founder, Chair. and CEO Tennman Records 2007–; American Music Awards for Favorite Pop/Rock Band, Duo or Group 2002, for Favorite Pop/Rock Male Artist 2007, 2013, for Favorite Soul/R&B Male Artist 2013, MOBO Award for Best R&B Act 2003, MTV Award for Best Pop Video (for Cry Me A River) 2003, BRIT Award for Best Int. Male Solo Artist 2004, 2007, Grammy Awards for Best Male Pop Vocal Performance (for Cry Me A River) 2004, (for What Goes Around...Comes Around) 2008, for Best Dance Recording (for Sexy Back) 2007, (for LoveStoned/I Think She Knows) 2008, for Best Rap/Sung Collaboration (with T.I.) 2007, (for Holy Grail, with Jay-Z) 2014, for Best R&B Song (for Pusher Love Girl) 2014, MTV Europe Music Award for Best Male Artist, for Best Pop Act 2006, Meteor Ireland Music Award for Best Int. Male Artist 2007, MTV Video Music Award for Best Male Artist 2007, for Best Video (for Mirrors) 2013, MTV Video Music Michael Jackson Video Vanguard Award 2013. *Film appearances:* Longshot 2000, On the Line 2001, Edison 2005, Alpha Dog 2006, Southland Tales 2006, Black Snake Moan 2006, Shrek the Third (voice) 2007, The Open Road 2009, The Social Network 2010, Bad Teacher 2011, Friends with Benefits 2011, In Time 2011, Trouble with the Curve 2012, Runner, Runner 2013, Inside Llewyn Davis 2013. *Recordings include:* albums: with *NSYNC: *NSYNC 1998, Home For The Holidays 1998, The Winter Album 1998, No Strings Attached 2000, Celebrity 2001; solo: Justified (Grammy Award for Best Pop Vocal Album, BRIT Award for Best Int. Album 2004) 2002, FutureSex/LoveSounds (American Music Award for Favorite Soul/R&B Album 2007) 2006, The 20/20 Experience (American Music Award for Favorite Soul/R&B Album 2013) 2013, The 20/20 Experience 2 of 2 2013. *Publication:* Justin Timberlake (autobiography) 2004. *Address:* Wright Entertainment Group, PO Box 590009, Orlando, FL 32859-0009, USA (office). *Website:* www .justintimberlake.com; www.nsync.com.

TIMKEN, William Robert, Jr, BA, MBA; American business executive and diplomatist; b. Canton, OH; m. Sue Timken; six c.; ed Phillips Acad., Stanford Univ. and Harvard Business School; various exec. positions, including Pres. and CEO Timken Co. 1962–2003, Chair. 1973–2003, Chair. (non-exec.) 2004–05 (retd); mem. Bd of Dirs numerous public cos; fmr Chair. Nat. Asscn of Mfrs, The Manufacturing Inst., Ohio Business Roundtable; fmr mem. Advisory Council, Stanford Univ. School of Business; fmr mem. US-Japan Business Council; apptd by Pres. George W. Bush as Chair. Securities Investor Protection Corpn 2003; Amb. to Germany 2005–08; Hon. Citizen of Colmar, France; Chevalier, Légion d'honneur; Woodrow Wilson Award for Corp. Citizenship, Adam Smith Award, Ellis Island Medal of Honor, named Ohio Business Statesman of the Year, Ohio Gov.'s Award. *Address:* 2321 Brentwood Road, NW, Canton, OH 44706-1301, USA.

TIMMERMANS, Frans Cornelis Gerardus Maria; Dutch diplomatist and politician; *Minister of Foreign Affairs;* b. 6 May 1961, Maastricht; m.; four c.; ed Radboud Univ., Nijmegen, Univ. of Nancy, France; began career as official with Ministry of Foreign Affairs 1987, Policy Officer, European Integration Dept 1988–90, Second Sec., Embassy in Moscow 1990; fmr Deputy Head, EC Affairs Section, Ministry for Devt Cooperation; mem. staff of European Commr Hans van de Broek 1994–95; Adviser and Private Sec. to Max van der Stoel, High Commr on Nat. Minorities, OSCE 1995–98; mem. House of Reps (lower house of Parl.) (PvdA) 1998–2007, 2010–12; Minister for European Affairs 2007–10, Minister of Foreign Affairs 2012–; fmr Guest Lecturer, Netherlands Inst. of Int. Relations, Clingendael, Netherlands Defence Coll.; mem. Exec. Cttee European Movement; mem. Partij van de Arbeid (Labour Party) 1990–. *Address:* Ministry of Foreign Affairs, Bezuidenhoutseweg 67, POB 20061, 2500 EB The Hague, Netherlands (office). *Telephone:* (70) 3486486 (office). *Fax:* (70) 3484848 (office). *Website:* www .rijksoverheid.nl/ministeries/bz (office).

TIMMS, Rt Hon. Stephen C., MA, MPhil; British business consultant and politician; *Shadow Minister for Employment;* b. 29 July 1955, Oldham, Lancs., England; s. of Ronald James Timms and Margaret Joyce Timms (née Johnson); m. Hui-Leng 1986; ed Farnborough Grammar School, Emmanuel Coll., Cambridge; worked as consultant in computer and telecommunications industries for Logica then Ovum 1978–94; Councillor, London Borough of Newham 1984–97, Chair. Planning Cttee 1987–90, Leader Newham Council 1990–94; MP for Newham North East (by-election) 1994–97, for East Ham 1997–; Parl. Pvt. Sec. to Andrew Smith MP as Minister of State, Dept for Educ. and Skills 1997–98; joint Parl. Pvt. Sec. to Marjorie Mowlam MP as Sec. of State for NI 1998; Parl. UnderSec. of State, Dept of Social Security 1998–99, Minister of State 1999; Financial Sec., HM Treasury 1999–2001, 2004–05, 2008–10; Minister of State for School Standards, Dept for Educ. and Skills 2001–02; Minister of State for Energy, E-Commerce and Postal Services, Dept of Trade and Industry 2002–04; Minister of State (Pensions Reform), Dept for Work and Pensions 2005–06; Chief Sec. to the Treasury 2006–07; Minister for Competitiveness, Dept for Business, Enterprise and Regulatory Reform 2007–08; Minister of State for Employment, Dept for Work and Pensions 2008; Minister for Digital Britain 2009–10; Govt Adviser on Faith 2007–10; Shadow Minister for Employment 2010–; mem. Commons Select Cttees for Treasury 1996–97 and Public Accounts 2004–05; Sec., Parl. Labour Party Treasury Cttee 1997–98; mem. Labour Party Departmental Cttees for Educ. and Employment 1997–2001, Environment, Transport and the Regions 1997–2001, the Treasury 1997–2001, Labour Party Faith Envoy 2007–; Chair. Christians on the left 2012–, Traidcraft Foundation Trustees 2012–; Vice-Pres. Tear Fund 2012–; mem. Bd East London Partnership (now East London Business Alliance) 1990–2006; mem. Stratford Devt Partnership 1992–94; Dr hc (Univ. of East London) 2002; Computing Magazine Award for Outstanding Contrib. to UK IT 2007. *Publication:* Broadband Communications: The Commercial Impact 1986. *Address:* House of Commons, Westminster, London, SW1A 0AA, England (office). *Telephone:* (20) 7219-4000 (office). *Fax:* (20) 7219-2949 (office). *E-mail:* stephen@stephentimms.org.uk (office); timmss@parliament.uk (office). *Website:* www .stephentimms.org.uk (office).

TIMOFTI, Nicolae Vasilyevich; Moldovan judge, politician and head of state; *President;* b. 22 Dec. 1948, Ciutulești, Moldavian SSR, USSR; s. of Vasile Timofti and Elenda Timofti; m. Margareta Timofti; three s.; ed Moldova State Univ.; Soviet Army service 1974–76; Judge, Frunze Dist Court, Chișinău 1976–80, Supreme

Court of the Moldavian SSR 1980–90, Deputy Chair. Supreme Court of Justice and Chair. Judicial Bd 1990–96, Chair. Appeals Chamber of Repub. of Moldova 1996–2001, Judge, Supreme Court of Moldova 2005–, Chair. Supreme Council of Magistrates 2011; Pres. of Moldova 23 March 2012–; Chair. Asscn of Judges and mem. Supreme Council of Magistrates 1996–2001. *Address:* Office of the President, 2073 Chişinău, bd. Ştefan cel Mare 154, Moldova (office). *Telephone:* (22) 25-02-44 (office). *Website:* www.president.md (office).

TIMON, Clay S., BS; American business executive (retd); b. 20 May 1943, Chicago, Ill.; m. Barbara Timon; two c.; ed Leed School of Business Univ. of Colo; fmr Bd Dir, Man. Supervisor (Paris) Macam-Erickson, Man. Services Dir (Tokyo), Sr Vice-Pres./Man. Supervisor; fmr Sr Vice-Pres. Int. Doyle Dane Bernbach; fmr Vice-Pres./Dir Worldwide Advertising Colgate-Palmolive; fmr Regional Vice-Pres. Saatchi & Saatchi, Paris; Chair., Pres., CEO Landor Assocs 1994–2004 (retd); World Pres. Int. Advertising Asscn 1988–90; fmr Chair. Int. Cttee of American Asscn of Advertising Agencies; mem. Business Advisory Council Leeds School of Business, Univ. of Colorado; mem. Bd of Dirs LifeMasters Supported SelfCare, Inc. 2006–, Music in the Vineyards (the Napa Valley Summer Chamber Music Festival); fmr mem. Bd of Dirs WebWare Corpn (now ClearStory Systems) 2001; Outstanding Speaker Award, Leeds School of Business, Univ. of Colo 2002. *Leisure interests:* travel, reading, tennis, vintage automobiles.

TIN AUNG MYINT, Lt-Gen U; Myanmar politician and fmr army officer; b. 29 May 1950; ed Defence Services Acad., Pyin Oo Lwin; fmr army officer, roles included Quartermaster-Gen. and Commdr, NE Region 1997; fmr Chair. Burmese Trade Council and Minister of Military Affairs; elected to House of Reps for Pobbathiri constituency, Nay Pyi Taw Region 2010; First Sec., State Peace and Devt Council (junta) –2011; Vice-Pres., Repub. of Union of Myanmar 2011–12; mem. Union Solidarity and Devt Party. *Address:* c/o Office of the Vice-President, Yangon, Myanmar.

TINARI, Philip, BA, AM; American editor, institute director and academic; *Director, Ullens Center for Contemporary Art;* b. 1979; ed Duke and Harvard Univs, Peking Univ., Beijing, People's Repub. of China; has run Office for Discourse Engineering (publishing imprint, editorial office, translation studio) 2007–; Contributing Ed. Artforum; Founding Ed. and Acting Publr LEAP, The International Art Magazine of Contemporary China, Modern Media Group 2010–; Dir Ullens Center for Contemporary Art, Beijing 2011–; Adjunct Prof., Coll. of Humanities, China Cen. Acad. of Fine Arts; also serves as China Rep. to Art Basel and Art Basel Miami Beach art fairs; Fulbright Fellow, Peking Univ. *Publications:* has written on contemporary art in China, for publs including The Wall Street Journal, The New York Times Magazine, Dushu. *Address:* Ullens Center for Contemporary Art, 798 Art District, 4 Jiuxianqiao Lu, Chaoyang District, Beijing 100015 (office); LEAP, Modern Media Group, 1106 China View No. A2, Gongti Donglu, Chaoyang District, Beijing 100027, People's Republic of China (office). *Telephone:* (10) 57800200 (Ullens) (office); (10) 65615550 (LEAP) (office). *Fax:* (10) 57800220 (Ullens) (office). *E-mail:* visitor@ucca.org.cn (office); info@leapleapleap .com (office). *Website:* www.ucca.org.cn (office); leapleapleap.com (office); philtinari .com.

TINDEMANS, Leo; Belgian politician; b. 16 April 1922, Zwyndrecht; s. of Frans Tindemans and Margaret Vercruyssen; m. Rosa Naesens 1960; two s. two d.; ed State Univ. of Ghent, Catholic Univ. of Louvain, Univ. of Antwerp; mem. Chamber of Deputies 1961–89; Mayor of Edegem 1965–76; Minister of Community Affairs 1968–71; Minister of Agric. and Middle Class Affairs 1972–73; Deputy Prime Minister and Minister for the Budget and Institutional Problems 1973–74; Prime Minister 1974–78; Minister of Foreign Affairs 1981–89, Minister of State 1992; Vice-Pres. European Union of Christian Democrats, Leader 1992–94; Pres. European People's Party 1976–85; mem. European Parl. 1979–81, 1989–99; Pres. Group of European People's Party, European Parl. 1992–94; Pres. Belgian Christian People's Party (CVP) 1979–81; Pres. Antwerp Business School; Christian Democrat; Hon. Prof., Faculty of Social Sciences, Catholic Univ., Louvain; Hon. DLitt (City Univ., London) 1976, Dr hc (Heriot-Watt Univ., Edin.) 1978, (Georgetown Univ.) 1984, (Deusto Univ., Bilbao) 1991; Charlemagne Prize 1976, St-Liborius-Medaille für Einheit und Frieden 1977, Stresemann Medal 1979, Robert Schuman Prize 1980. *Publications:* Ontwikkeling van de Benelux 1958, L'autonomie culturelle 1971, Regionalized Belgium, Transition from the Nation State to the Multinational State 1972, Een handvest voor woelig België 1972, Dagboek van de werkgroep Eyskens 1973, European Union 1975, Europe, Ideal of Our Generation 1976, Open Brief aan Gaston Eyskens 1978, Atlantisch Europa 1980, Europa zonder Kompas 1987, L'Europe de l'Est vue de Bruxelles 1989, Duel met de Minister 1991, De toekomst van een idee 1993, Cain in the Balkans 1996. *Leisure interests:* reading, writing, walking. *Address:* Jan Verbetlei 24, 2650 Edegem, Belgium (home). *Fax:* (3) 455-66-58.

TINDLE, David, RA; British artist; b. 29 April 1932, Huddersfield, Yorks; m. 1st Jillian Evans 1953 (divorced) 1957); one s. one d.; m. 2nd Sheila Pratt 1957 (divorced 1969); three s. one d.; m. 3rd Janet Trollope 1969 (divorced 1992); one s. two d.; ed Coventry School of Art; worked as scenic artist for theatre until moving to London in 1951; numerous exhbns in London and provinces since 1952; works in many public and private collections including Tate Gallery, Nat. Portrait Gallery; designed and painted set for Iolanta (Tchaikovsky), Aldeburgh Festival 1988; Visiting Tutor, Royal Coll. of Art 1973–83, Fellow 1981, Hon. Fellow 1984; Ruskin Master of Drawing, St Edmund Hall, Oxford 1985–87; lives and works in Italy; Hon. Fellow St Edmund Hall, Oxford 1988–; Hon. mem. Royal Birmingham Soc. of Artists; Hon. MA (St Edmund Hall, Oxford) 1985; Critics Award 1962, RA Johnson Wax Award 1983. *Television:* contrib. on egg tempura to A Feeling for Paint 1980. *Leisure interests:* music, films, cats and dogs, visiting the towns and museums of Italy. *Address:* c/o The Redfern Gallery, 20 Cork Street, London, W1S 3HL, England. *Telephone:* (20) 7734-1732. *E-mail:* art@redfern-gallery.com. *Website:* www.redfern-gallery.com.

TINE, Augustin; Senegalese dental surgeon and politician; *Minister of the Armed Forces;* b. Fandène, Thiès region; m.; three s. three d.; ed Univ. Cheikh Anta Diop, Dakar; early training as priest, Ngazobil seminary; dental surgeon, El hadji Ibrahima Niasse Hosp., Kaolack 1980–95; pvt. dental practice, Saloum 1995–97; fmr mem. local council, Fandène; Minister of the Armed Forces 2012–; mem. Parti démocratique sénégalais 1999–2007, Alliance pour la République (APR) 2007–,

later APR regional co-ordinator, Thiès region; mem. Conseil national des chirurgiens dentistes du Sénégal. *Leisure interest:* football. *Address:* Ministry of the Armed Forces, Bldg Administratif, 8e étage, ave Léopold Sédar Senghor, BP 4041, Dakar, Senegal (office). *Telephone:* 33-849-7612 (office). *Fax:* 33-823-6338 (office). *Website:* www.forcesarmees.gouv.sn (office).

TING, Samuel Chao Chung, BSE, PhD; American physicist and academic; *Thomas Dudley Cabot Professor of Physics, Massachusetts Institute of Technology;* b. 27 Jan. 1936, Ann Arbor, Mich.; s. of Prof. Kuan Hai Ting and Prof. Tsun-Ying Wang; m. 2nd Susan Carol Marks 1985; one s. two d.; two d. (from previous marriage); ed primary and secondary schools in China, Univ. of Michigan; Ford Foundation Fellow, European Org. for Nuclear Research (CERN), Geneva 1963; Instructor, Columbia Univ., New York 1964, Asst Prof. 1965–67; Group Leader, Deutsches Elektronen Synchrotron (DESY), Hamburg, FRG 1966; Assoc. Prof. of Physics, MIT 1967–68, Prof. 1969–, Thomas Dudley Cabot Inst. Prof. 1977–; Programme Consultant, Div. of Particles and Fields, American Physical Soc. 1970; Assoc. Ed. Nuclear Physics B 1970; mem. Editorial Bd Nuclear Instruments and Methods 1977, Mathematical Modelling, Chinese Physics; Fellow, American Acad. of Arts and Sciences 1975; mem. American, Italian and European Physical Socs; Foreign mem. Academia Sinica, Taiwan 1975, Pakistani Acad. of Science 1984, USSR (now Russian) Acad. of Sciences 1989, Academy of Sciences 1993; mem. NAS 1977–, Deutsche Akademie der Naturforscher Leopoldina 1996; Hon. Prof. Beijing Normal Coll., China 1984, Jiatong Univ., Shanghai, China 1987; Hon. ScD (Michigan) 1978, (Chinese Univ. of Hong Kong) 1987, (Bologna) 1988, (Columbia) 1990, (Univ. of Science and Tech., China) 1990, (Moscow State Univ.) 1991, (Bucharest) 1993, (Tsinghua Taiwan) 2002, (Nat. Tiaotong Univ. Taiwan) 2003; Ernest Orlando Lawrence Award 1976, Nobel Prize for Physics (jtly with Burton Richter q.v.) for discovery of the heavy, long-lived 'J' (or 'psi') particle 1976, Eringen Medal, Soc. of Eng Scientists 1977, De Gasperi Gold Medal for Science, Italy 1988, Gold Medal for Science, City of Brescia, Italy 1988, Forum Engelberg Prize 1996, NASA Public Service Award 2001. *Address:* Massachusetts Institute of Technology, 77 Massachusetts Ave., Bldg 44-114, Cambridge, MA 02139, USA (office). *Telephone:* (617) 253-8326 (office). *E-mail:* ting@lns.mit.edu (office). *Website:* web.mit.edu/physics (office).

TINY, Carlos Alberto Pires; São Tome and Príncipe politician; fmr Minister of Health; fmr Pres. Assembleia Nacional; unsuccessful cand. for Pres. 2001; Minister of Foreign Affairs, Co-operation and Communities 2008–10; mem. Movimento de Libertação de São Tomé e Príncipe—Partido Social Democrata. *Address:* c/o Ministry of Foreign Affairs, Co-operation and Communities, Av. 12 de Julho, CP 111, São Tomé, São Tomé and Príncipe (office).

TIONG, Tan Sri Datuk Hiew King; Malaysian/Chinese business executive; *Executive Chairman, Rimbunan Hijau Group;* m.; four c.; Founder and Chair. Rimbunan Hijau Group (timber co.) 1975–, with logging operations in Papua New Guinea and Russia, also controls Sin Chew Jit Poh and Guang Ming Daily (Chinese nat. daily newspapers in Malaysia), The National Daily, Papua New Guinea, and Ming Pao Holdings Ltd, Hong Kong; mem. Sarawak United People's Party (major party of ruling coalition govt in Sarawak). *Address:* Rimbunan Hijau Group, PO Box 454, No. 66–78 Pusat Suria Permata, Jalan Upper Lanang, Sibu 96000, Sarawak, Malaysia (office). *Telephone:* (84) 216155 (office). *Fax:* (84) 215217 (office). *E-mail:* info@rhg.com.my (office). *Website:* www.rhg.com.my (office).

TIRAVANIJA, Rirkrit; Thai artist; b. 1961, Buenos Aires, Argentina; m. Elizabeth Peyton (divorced); ed Art Inst. of Chicago, USA; co-founder The Land Foundation, Chiang Mai, Thailand; Prof., School of the Arts, Columbia Univ.; Solomon R. Guggenheim Foundation Hugo Boss Prize 2004. *Works include:* Untitled (Free) 1992, Untitled (Still) 1994, Utopia Station (50th Venice Biennale) 2003, Untitled (the air between the chainlink fence and the broken bicycle wheel) 2005, Untitled (Pay Attention) 2009. *Address:* c/o Gavin Brown's Enterprise, 620 Greenwich Street, New York, NY 10014, USA (office). *E-mail:* theland@ thelandfoundation.org (office). *Website:* www.thelandfoundation.org (office).

TIRIMO, Martino, FRAM, FRSAMD, Dip RAM, ARAM; British concert pianist and conductor; *Professor, Trinity Laban Conservatoire of Music & Dance;* b. 19 Dec. 1942, Larnaca, Cyprus; s. of Dimitri Tirimo and Marina Tirimo; m. Mione J. Teakle 1973; one s. one d.; ed Bedales School, England (Cyprus Govt Scholarship), Royal Acad. of Music, London, Vienna State Acad.; first public recital, Cyprus 1949; conducted seven performances of La Traviata with singers and musicians from La Scala, Milan, at Cyprus Opera Festival 1955; London debut, Wigmore Hall 1965; gave first public performance of complete Schubert sonatas (including unfinished ones with own completions), London 1975; first public performance of Beethoven piano concertos cycle directed from keyboard in two consecutive evenings, Dresden 1985, London 1986; first performance of Tippett piano concerto in several European countries 1986–2013; concerto performances with major orchestras world-wide as well as recitals, radio and TV appearances in Europe, USA, Canada, SA and the Far East 1965–; four series of performances of complete Beethoven piano sonatas 2000, two series devoted to the major piano works of Robert and Clara Schumann 2001; six-concert series devoted to the major piano works of Chopin 2002; Mozart piano concertos series, directing from keyboard 2001–; f. Rosamunde Trio with violinist Ben Sayevich and cellist Daniel Veis 2002; performed with Vienna Philharmonic during Olympics, Athens Festival 2004, Olympic Games torch bearer 2004; performed complete Mozart solo piano works in several series of eight concerts, including at Cadogan Hall, London 2006; performed Chopin entire works in ten concerts in various countries, including at King's Place, London 2010; Tchaikovsky series at King's Place, London 2012; Prof., Trinity Coll. of Music (now Trinity Laban Conservatoire of Music & Dance) 2003–; mem. jury in various int. piano competitions 1995–; Hon. Prof., Middlesex Univ. 2004–; prizewinner, Int. Beethoven Competition, Vienna 1965, Liszt Scholarship, Boise Foundation Scholarship, Gulbenkian Foundation Fellowship 1967–69, Jt Winner, Munich Int. Piano Competition 1971, Winner, Geneva Int. Piano Competition 1972, Gold Medal, Associated Bd of Royal Schools of Music 1959, Macfarren Medal, Royal Acad. of Music 1964, Silver Disc 1988 and Gold Disc 1994 for recording of Rachmaninov 2nd Concerto and Paganini Rhapsody, Nemitsas Foundation Prize 2011, and other prizes and awards. *Film score:* The Odyssey 1998. *Recordings:* more than 50 albums, including complete piano works of Mozart, Beethoven, Debussy and Janáček; Brahms piano concertos, Chopin concertos, Tippett piano concerto, Rachmaninov concertos, complete Schubert piano sonatas, complete Mendelssohn works for piano and cello, Tchaikovsky, Shostakovich and Dvořák piano trios (Rosamunde Trio), several other recordings with mixed repertoire. *Television:* live performance of Tippett piano concerto from Coventry Cathedral for BBC TV in celebration of composer's 90th birthday and 50th birthday of UN. *Publications include:* urtext edn of complete Schubert piano sonatas in three vols 1997–99. *Leisure interests:* chess, reading, self-knowledge, theatre, badminton. *Address:* c/o International Music Amphictyony (office); 1 Romeyn Road, London, SW16 2NU, England. *Telephone:* (210) 6015224 (Athens) (office); (20) 8677-4847. *Fax:* (210) 6994520 (Athens) (office). *E-mail:* deskaps@otenet.gr (office); martino@tirimo.fslife.co.uk. *Website:* www.martinotirimo.com.

TIRKEY, Dilip; Indian professional field hockey player; b. 24 Nov. 1977, Sawnamara, Sundergarh, Orissa; s. of Vincent Tirkey; ed Bhanwani Shankar School; belongs to Oraon tribe of Chota Nagpur; fmr Asst Man., Indian Airlines; trained in NIS Patiala under coach A. K. Basal; started his career as inside forward but developed into defender; int. debut in Test Series vs Australia 1994; Vice-Capt. Jr World Cup, Milton Keynes, UK 1997, selected in World XI Team; Gold Medal, SAF Games, Chennai 1995, Bangkok Asian Games 1998, Prime Minister's Gold Cup 2001; Silver Medal, Asian Games, Busan 2002; Bronze Medal, Asia Cup, Kuala Lumpur, Malaysia 1999; first Adivasi captain of ind. Indian nat. team and second in Indian history; youngest Olympian when capped at Atlanta, USA 1996; signed to play with Klein Zwitserland hockey club, Netherlands 2005; currently Capt. with Orissa Steelers; Ekalavya Puraskar 1996, ONGC-Hockey Year Book Award 1998, Arjuna Award 2002, Padma Shri 2004. *Leisure interests:* music, dance.

TIROLE, Jean, PhD; French economist and academic; *Scientific Director, Institut d'Économie Industrielle (IDEI);* b. 9 Aug. 1953; ed Université Paris IX-Dauphine, Massachusetts Inst. of Tech., USA; researcher, CERAS, École Nationale des Ponts et Chaussées 1981–84; Prof. of Econs, MIT 1984–91; Sr Fellow, Inst. for Policy Reform 1990–95; Prof., École Polytechnique 1994–96; Dir of Accumulative Studies, École des Hautes Etudes en Sciences Sociales 1995–; mem. Conseil d'Analyse Économique (Prime Minister's Council of Econ. Advisors) 1999–2006; currently Dir Fondation Jean-Jacques Laffont, Toulouse School of Econs; also currently Scientific Dir Institut d'Économie Industrielle (IDEI), Toulouse; Founder-mem. and Fellow, European Corp. Governance Inst. 2002–; Visiting Prof. at Harvard, Stanford, Princeton, Lausanne, Wuhan Univs; Pres. European Econ. Asscn 2001; mem. Econometric Soc. (mem. Exec. Cttee 1993–99, Pres. 1998), French High Council for Science and Tech. 2006–, European Research Council panel 2007–; Foreign Hon. mem. American Acad. of Arts and Sciences 1993, American Econ. Asscn 1993; Chevalier, Légion d'honneur 2007; Dr hc (Université Libre de Bruxelles) 1989, (London Business School) 2007; Sloan Fellow 1985, Guggenheim Fellow 1988, Yrjo Jahnsson prize, European Econ. Asscn 1993, Center for Econ. Studies Prize 1996, Public Utility Research Center Distinguished Service Award, Univ. of Florida 1997, John von Neumann Award, Budapest Univ. 1998, Distinguished Fellow Award, Industrial Org. Soc. 1999, Gold Medal, CNRS 2002, 2007, Prix Dargélos de l'Ecole Polytechnique 2002, Thomson Prize in Econs, Inst. of Scientific Information 2004, BBVA Foundation Frontiers of Knowledge Award in the Econs, Finance and Man. category 2008, named amongst the most influential economists in the world according to IDEAS/RePEc 2011; lectures include Hicks Lecture, Univ. of Oxford 1992, Walras-Pareto Lectures, Lausanne 1992, Schumpeter Lecture, European Econ. Asscn 1993, Pazner Lecture, Tel-Aviv 1993, Walras-Bowley Lecture, Econometric Soc. 1994, Munich Lectures, Munich 1996, JMCB Lecture 1999, Wicksell Lectures 1999, Baffi Lectures, Bank of Italy 2000, Scribner Lectures and the Frank Graham Lecture, Princeton Univ. 2002, Marshall Lectures, Univ. of Cambridge 2003, Tinbergen Lecture, Amsterdam 2003, David Kinley Lectures, Univ. of Illinois 2005, inaugural JEEA Lecture 2005, inaugural Telecom Italia Lecture, Milan 2005, Snyder Lecture, Univ. of California, Santa Barbara 2005, Rosenthal Lecture 2006. *Publications include:* Concurrence Imparfaite (in French) 1985, The Theory of Industrial Organization, Game Theory (with Drew Fudenberg) 1988, A Theory of Incentives in Procurement and Regulation (with Jean-Jacques Laffont) 1993, The Prudential Regulation of Banks (with Mathias Dewatripont) 1994, Competition in Telecommunications (with Jean-Jacques Laffont), Financial Crises, Liquidity and the International Monetary System, The Theory of Corporate Finance (Award for Excellence, Asscn of American Publrs 2006) 2005; more than 180 articles in journals. *Address:* IDEI, Université des Sciences Sociales, Manufacture des Tabacs, Aile Jean-Jacques Laffont, Accueil MF 404, 21 allée de Brienne, 31000 Toulouse, France (office). *Telephone:* (5) 61-12-86-42 (office). *Fax:* (5) 61-12-86-37 (office). *E-mail:* tirole@cict.fr (office). *Website:* idei.fr (office).

TISA SABUNI, Aggrey, BSc, MEconSc; South Sudanese politician; *Minister of Finance, Commerce and Economic Planning;* b. Kajo Keji County, Eastern Equatoria State; ed Univ. of Khartoum, Univ. of Glasgow, UK; fmr Under-Sec. of Econ. Planning; Econ. Adviser to Pres. 2011–13; Minister of Finance, Commerce and Econ. Planning 2013–; mem. Sudan People's Liberation Movt. *Address:* Ministry of Finance, Commerce and Economic Planning, Juba, South Sudan (office). *Telephone:* (256) 477126466 (mobile) (office). *E-mail:* kitoundo@hotmail.com (office). *Website:* www.commerce-goss.org (office).

TISCH, Andrew H., BS, MBA; American business executive; *Chairman of the Executive Committee, Member of the Office of the President and Co-Chairman of the Board, Loews Corporation;* b. 14 Aug. 1949, Asbury Park, NJ; s. of the late Laurence Tisch and of Wilma Tisch; m. Ann Tisch (née Rubenstein); four c.; ed Cornell and Harvard Univs; joined Loews Corpn 1971, mem. Bd of Dirs 1985–, Chair. Exec. Cttee, mem. Office of the Pres. and Co-Chair. Bd 2006–; Pres. Bulova Corpn 1979–90, currently Chair.; CEO and Chair. Lorillard Inc. 1990–95; mem. Bd of Dirs Canary Wharf Group PLC, Zale Corpn, K12 Inc., CNA Financial Corpn 2006–. *Address:* Loews Corpn, 667 Madison Avenue, New York, NY 10021-8087, USA (office). *Telephone:* (212) 521-2000 (office). *Fax:* (212) 521-2525 (office). *E-mail:* info@loews.com (office). *Website:* www.loews.com (office).

TISCH, James S., MBA; American business executive; *President, CEO and Member of the Office of the President, Loews Corporation;* b. 2 Feb. 1953, Atlantic City, NJ; s. of the late Laurence Tisch and Wilma Tisch; m. Merryl Tisch (neé Hiat); two s. one d.; ed Cornell Univ., Wharton Business School, Univ. of Pennsylvania; joined Loews 1977 (hotel chain est. by Lawrence Tisch 1946), various exec. positions including Dir Loews Corpn, Pres. 1998–, COO 1998–99,

CEO 1999–, also Mem. Office of the Pres.; Chair. and CEO Diamond Offshore Drilling Inc.; Dir, Educational Broadcasting Corpn 2003–, Chair. 2006–; mem. Bd of Dirs CAN Financial Corpn, Vail Resorts Inc.; mem. Bd of Overseers Univ. of Pennsylvania; mem. Council on Foreign Relations. *Address:* Loews Corpn, 667 Madison Avenue, New York, NY 10021-8087, USA (office). *Telephone:* (212) 521-2000 (office). *Fax:* (212) 521-2525 (office). *E-mail:* info@loews.com (office). *Website:* www.loews.com (office).

TISCH, Jonathan Mark, BA; American business executive; *Co-Chairman and Member of the Office of the President, Loews Corporation;* b. 7 Dec. 1953, Atlantic City, NJ; s. of the late Preston Robert Tisch and Joan T. Tisch (née Hyman); cousin of James Tisch (q.v.) and Andrew Tisch (q.v.); m. Lizzie Rudnick 2007; ed Tufts Univ.; worked as cinematographer and producer at WBZ-TV, Boston 1976–79; Sales Man. Loews Hotels, New York 1980–81, Dir of Devt 1981–82, Vice Pres. 1982–85, Exec. Vice-Pres. 1985–86, Pres. 1986, CEO 1989–, also Chair., mem. Bd of Dirs Loews Corpn 1986–, mem. Office of the Pres. 1998–, Co-Chair. 2006–; Chair. Travel Business Roundtable 1995–; Co-Chair. NYC & Co. tourism agency; Treas. and mem. Bd of Dirs, NY Giants football team 1991–; mem. Bd of Dirs Elizabeth Glaser Paediatric AIDS Foundation, Tribeca Film Inst., Business Council for the Metropolitan Museum of Art; mem. Bd of Trustees and Patron, Jonathan M. Tisch Coll. of Citizenship and Public Service, Tufts Univ.; mem. US Dept of Commerce US Travel and Tourism Advisory Bd 2003–; fmr Chair. New York Rising, American Hotel and Lodging Asscn; fmr Vice-Chair. Welfare to Work Partnership; Travel Agent magazine Hotel Person of the Year, Business Travel Industry's Most Influential Executives, Business Travel News, 25 Most Influential People in the Meetings Industry, Meeting News magazine, Tufts Alumni Asscn Distinguished Alumni Award 1996. *Television:* host, Open Exchange: Beyond the Boardroom. *Publications:* The Power of We: Succeeding Through Partnerships 2004, Chocolates on the Pillow Aren't Enough: Reinventing the Customer Experience 2007. *Address:* Loews Corpn, 667 Madison Avenue, New York, NY 10021-8087, USA (office). *Telephone:* (212) 521-2000 (office). *Fax:* (212) 521-2525 (office). *E-mail:* info@loews.com (office). *Website:* www.loews.com (office).

TISCH, Thomas J., BA, LLB; American business executive and university administrator; *Managing Partner, Four Partners;* b. 1955; ed Brown Univ., New York Univ.; Man. Partner, Four Partners (pvt. investment co.) 1992–; mem. Bd of Trustees, Brown Univ. 2002–, Chancellor 2007–; mem. Bd of Dirs Sears Holdings Corpn, Infonxx Inc.; mem. Bd of Trustees New York Univ. Medical Center, KIPP Acad., Manhattan Inst. for Public Policy Research. *Address:* c/o Office of the Chancellor, Brown University, One Prospect Street, Campus Box 1860, Providence, RI 02912, USA (office).

TISHKOV, Valery Aleksandrovich, DHist; Russian historian and anthropologist; *Director, Institute of Ethnology and Anthropology, Russian Academy of Sciences;* b. 6 Nov. 1941; m.; one s.; ed Moscow State Univ.; teacher, Magadan State Pedagogical Inst. 1964–66; aspirant, Moscow State Pedagogical Inst. 1966–69; docent, Dean, Magadan State Pedagogical Inst. 1969–72; researcher, Inst. of Gen. History USSR (now Russian) Acad. of Sciences, Scientific Sec., Div. of History, USSR Acad. of Sciences, also Head of Dept, Inst. of Ethnography; Deputy Dir, Inst. of Ethnology and Anthropology Russian Acad. of Sciences 1972–89, Dir 1989–; Fed. Minister for Nationalities, Russian Govt 1992; Vice-Pres. Int. Union of Ethnological and Anthropological Sciences 1993 (re-elected 1998); mem. Public Chamber of Russia, Chair. Cttee on Tolerance and Freedom of Faith 2006–10; Full mem. Russian Acad. of Sciences 2008; Order of Honour 2009; Distinguished Scholar of the Russian Fed. 1998, State Prize in Science and Art 2001. *Publications:* Ethnicity, Nationalism and Conflict in and after the Soviet Union. The Mind Aflame 1997, Peoples and Religions of the World (Russian Encyclopaedia) 1998, Chechnya: Life in a War-Torn Society 2004, Tundra and Sea: Chukotka Ivory Art 2008, Peoples of Russia: Atlas of Cultures and Religions 2008. *Leisure interests:* fishing, collection of Arctic ivory art. *Address:* Institute of Ethnology and Anthropology, Russian Academy of Sciences, Leninsky prosp. 32A, 119334 Moscow, Russia (office). *Telephone:* (495) 938-17-47 (office). *Fax:* (495) 938-06-00 (office). *E-mail:* tishkov@ethno.msk.ru, tishkov@iea.ras.ru (home). *Website:* www.valerytishkov.ru.

TITARENKO, Mikhail Leontyevich, PhD; Russian academic; *Director, Institute of Far East Studies, Russian Academy of Sciences;* b. 27 April 1934, Bryansk region; s. of the late Leonty Titarenko and Maria Titarenko; m. Galina Titarenko 1957 (died 1997); two s.; ed Moscow State Univ., Beijing Univ., Fudan Univ., Shanghai; diplomatic service 1961–65; researcher and consultant in govt bodies 1965–85; Dir Inst. of Far East Studies, Russian Acad. of Sciences 1985–; mem. Editorial Bd, Far Eastern Affairs 1986–; Chair. Academic Council on Problems of Modern China, Russian Acad. of Sciences 1987–; Pres. All-Russian Asscn of Sinologists 1988–; Corresp. mem. Russian Acad. of Sciences 1997–, Academician 2003–; mem. Russia Acad. of Natural Sciences, Int. Acad. of Informatization; Honour of the Russian Fed. 1994, Merited Scholar of Russia 1995, 200 Years of Russian Foreign Service Medal 2002, Russian Federation Nat. Award in Science and Technology 2010. *Publications:* Anthology of Ancient Chinese Philosophy (two vols), Ancient Chinese Philosopher Mo Di 1985, Development of Productive Forces in China 1989, History of Chinese Philosophy 1989, Economic Reform in China: Theory and Practice 1990, Russia and East Asia: Issues of International and Cross-Civilization Relations 1994, Russia Towards Asia 1998, China: Civilization and Reforms 1999, Russia's Co-operative Security: East Asian Vector 2003; and numerous articles. *Leisure interests:* collecting stamps, matchboxes, skiing, mushroom hunting. *Address:* Institute of Far East Studies, Russian Academy of Sciences, 32 Nakhimovsky pr., 117218 Moscow, Russia (office). *Telephone:* (495) 124-01-17 (office); (495) 198-55-38 (home). *Fax:* (495) 718-96-56 (office). *E-mail:* ifes@cemi.rssi.ru (office). *Website:* www.ifes-ras.ru (office).

TITIKPINA, Col Atcha Mohammed; Togolese army officer and politician; *Chief of General Staff;* b. 1955; m.; ed Officer Training School, Côte d'Ivoire, Inst. des hautes études de Défense nationale, Paris, France; Commdr, Airborne Troops Training Centre 1987–94; Commdr, Presidential Guard 1994–2005; Aide de camp to Pres. 2005–06; Minister of Security and Civil Protection; currently Chief of Gen. Staff. *Address:* c/o Ministry of Security and Civil Protection, rue Albert Sarraut, Lomé, Togo (office). *E-mail:* info@republicoftogo.com (office).

TITO, Teburoro, BSc; I-Kiribati politician and fmr head of state; b. 25 Aug. 1953, Tabiteuea North; m. Nei Keina; one c.; ed King George V Secondary School, Univ. of South Pacific, Suva, Papua New Guinea Admin. Coll.; student co-ordinator, Univ. of South Pacific Students' Asscn 1977–79; scholarship officer, Ministry of Educ. 1980–82, Sr Educ. Officer 1983–87; mem. Maneaba ni Maungatabu (Parl.) and Leader of Opposition 1987–94; mem. Parl. Public Accounts Cttee 1987–90; Pres. of Kiribati 1994–2003, also Minister of Foreign Affairs; and Int. Trade mem. CPA Exec. Cttee for Pacific Region 1989–90; Chair. Kiribati Football Ass. 1980–94; Dr of World Peace (Maharishi Univ. of World Peace) 2001. *Leisure interests:* sports, especially soccer, tennis and table tennis. *Address:* c/o Office of the President, PO Box 68, Bairiki, Tarawa (office); Tabuarorae, Eita Village, South Tarawa, Kiribati (home). *Telephone:* 21183. *Fax:* 21145.

TITOV, Konstantin Alekseyevich, CandEconSc; Russian politician; b. 30 Oct. 1944, Moscow; m. Natalia Borisovna Titova; one s.; ed Kuybyshev (now Samara) Aviation Inst., Kuybyshev Inst. of Planning; milling-machine operator, Kuybyshev aviation factory 1962–63; flight engineer 1968–69, Deputy Sec. Komsomol Cttee 1969–70; Deputy Head Students Div., Kuybyshev City Komsomol Cttee 1970–73; Sec. Komsomol Cttee, Jr, Sr Researcher, Head of Group, Head Research Lab. Kuybyshev Inst. of Planning 1973–88; Deputy Dir Research Cen. Informatika (Samara br.) 1988–90; Chair. Samara City Council 1990–91; Head of Admin. Samara Region 1991–96; Gov. Samara Region 1996–2007; mem. Council of Fed. of Russia 1993–2001, Chair. Cttee on Budget, Taxation Policy, Finance and Customs Regulation 1996–2001; Pres. Interregional Asscn of Econ. Interaction 'Bolshaya Volga' 1994; Deputy Chair. 'Our Home Is Russia' political movt 1995; Chair. of Council, Union of Right Forces 1998–; Cand. for Pres. of Russian Fed. 2000; Chair. Russian Party of Social Democracy 2000, Co-Founder Union of Social Democratic Parties 2001; mem. Russian Acad. of Natural Sciences; Golden Mask Prize, Russian Theatre Artists Union; Order of St Faithful Prince Daniil Moskovsky (3rd Degree), Order of St Grand Duke Vladimir (2nd Degree); Order of Friendship, Green Man of the Year, Russian Ecological Union 1996, Honoured Economist of the Russian Fed., Gov. of the Year 1998, Nat. Prize of Peter the Great 2002, Order Glory of Russia 2002, Nat. Olympus Laureate 2003. *Leisure interests:* football, photography, music, painting, reading.

TITOV, Col Vladimir Georgievich, MBA; Russian business executive and fmr cosmonaut; *General Director of Russian Operations, Excalibur Almaz Limited;* b. 1 Jan. 1947, Sretensk, Chita Region; s. of the late Georgie Titov and of Vera Titova; m. Alexandra Kozlova; one s. one d.; ed Chernigov Higher Mil. Aviation School, Yuriy Gagarin Air Force Acad., International Univ., Moscow; pilot instructor, Commdr of aviation unit 1970–76; mem. cosmonauts' team since 1976; Commdr of space flights on spacecraft Soyuz T-8 1983 and record-breaking flight on Soyuz TM-4 and space station MiR; Deputy Head Dept of Man. Centre of Cosmonauts' Training 1988–99; apptd Dir for Space and Communications, Russia and CIS, Boeing Corpn, Moscow 1999; currently Gen. Dir Russian Operations, Excalibur Almaz Ltd (pvt. int. space exploration co.); Hero of the Soviet Union, Order of Lenin 1983, 1988, Commdr de la Légion d'honneur 1988; US Harmon Prize 1990. *Address:* Excalibur Almaz Ltd, 15–19 Athol Street, Douglas, Isle of Man, IM1 1LB, British Isles (office). *E-mail:* contact@excaliburalmaz.com (office). *Website:* excaliburalmaz.com (office).

TITOV, Yuriy Evlampievich; Russian fmr gymnast; b. 27 Nov. 1935, Omsk; s. of Evlampiy Titov and Marina Titova; m. Valerie Kouzmenko 1960; one s. one d.; ed Kiev Inst. of Physical Culture; all-round champion of USSR 1958, 1961, of Europe 1959 and the world 1962; Honoured Master of Sports 1956; Olympic gymnastics champion 1956; won 13 gold medals at European, World Championships and Olympic Games; int. class judge 1968; mem. CPSU 1969–91; Vice-Pres. Int. Gymnastic Fed. 1972–76, Pres. 1976–96, Hon. Life Pres. 1996–; Head of Dept of Gymnastics, USSR State Sports Cttee 1968–87; Lecturer, Moscow Acad. of Physical Culture 1980–, Leningrad (now St Petersburg) Acad. of Physical Culture 1988–, Prof. 1993–; Pres. Russian Gymnastics Fed. 2004–; Sec. Nat. Olympic Cttee 1987–88, mem. Int. Olympic Cttee (IOC) Working Group on Women and Sport 1995–, ex officio mem. IOC 1995–96; Hon. Pres. Fédération Internationale de Gymnastique Olympic Order 1992, inducted into Int. Gymnastics Hall of Fame 1999. *Publications:* The Sum of Points 1971, The Ascent 1982, The Notes of the President 1984, Rhythmic Gymnastics (jtly) 1998; works on methodology of gymnastics. *Leisure interests:* history, carpentry, doing nothing with pleasure. *Address:* Kolokolnikov per. 6, Apt. 19, 103045 Moscow, Russia.

TITS, Jacques Léon, DrSc; French mathematician and academic; *Honorary Professor of Mathematics, Collège de France;* b. 12 Aug. 1930, Uccle, Belgium; s. of Léon Tits and Louisa Tits (née André); m. Marie-Jeanne Dieuaide 1956; ed Univ. of Brussels; with Belgian Nat. Fund for Scientific Research 1948–56; Asst, Univ. of Brussels 1956–57, Assoc. Prof. 1957–62, Prof. 1962–64; Prof., Univ. of Bonn 1964–74; Assoc. Prof., Collège de France, Paris 1973–74, Prof. of Group Theory 1975–2000, Hon. Prof. 2000–; Visiting Teacher and Prof., Eidgenössische Technische Hochschule, Zürich, Switzerland 1950, 1951, 1953, Inst. for Advanced Study, Princeton, USA 1951–52, 1963, 1969, 1971–72, Univ. of Rome, Italy 1955, 1956, Univ. of Chicago, USA 1963, Univ. of California, Berkeley, USA 1963, Univs of Tokyo and Kyoto, Japan 1971, Yale Univ., USA 1966–67, 1976, 1980, 1984, 1990, 1995, 2002; mem. editorial bds of periodicals and scientific collections; Ed.-in-Chief Math. Publs of IHES 1980–99; Guest Speaker at Int. Congresses of Mathematicians, Stockholm 1962, Nice 1970, Vancouver 1974; lecture tours in USA, UK, Israel, etc.; mem. Deutsche Akad. der Naturforscher Leopoldina 1977, American Acad. of Arts and Sciences 1992, NAS 1992, Norwegian Acad. of Science and Letters; Founding mem. Academia Europaea; Corresp. mem. Acad. des Sciences, Paris 1977, mem. 1979; Foreign mem. Royal Netherlands Acad. of Arts and Sciences 1988; Foreign Assoc. Royal Belgian Acad. 1991; Hon. mem. London Math. Soc. 1993; Chevalier, Légion d'honneur, Commdr des Palmes académiques, Officier, Ordre nat. du Mérite; Dr hc (Utrecht) 1970, (Ghent) 1979, (Bonn) 1987, (Louvain) 1992; Prix scientifique Interfacultaire L. Empain 1955, Prix Wettrems, Acad. de Belgique 1958, Grand Prix des Sciences mathématiques et physiques, Acad. des Sciences 1976, Wolf Prize 1993, Cantor Medal, Deutsche Mathematiker-Vereinigung (German Math. Soc.) 1996, Abel Prize (co-recipient) 2008. *Publications:* more than 150 scientific papers. *Leisure interests:* languages, literature, arts. *Address:* Collège de France, 11 place Marcelin Berthelot, 75231

Paris Cedex 05, France (office). *Fax:* 1-44-27-17-04 (office). *E-mail:* jacques.tits@ college-de-france.fr (office).

TIWARI, Shri Narayan Dutt, LLB, MA; Indian politician, social worker and journalist; b. 18 Oct. 1925, Balyuti, Nainital Dist, Uttaranchal; s. of the late Shri Poornanand Tiwari; m. Dr (Smt.) Sushila Tiwari 1954 (deceased); ed M.B. School, Haldwani, E.M. High School, Bareilly, C.R.S.T. High School, Nainital, Allahabad Univ., Uttar Pradesh (UP); joined Indian Freedom Movt aged 13; joined 'Quit India' Movt 1942; imprisoned for 15 months; Pres. Allahabad Univ. Students' Union 1947; Sec. Political Sufferers' Distress Relief Soc.; mem. Uttar Pradesh Legis. Ass. 1952–62, 1969–79 1984–85, 1988–89, 1991–92, Leader of the Opposition 1960–61, 1977–79, 1988–89, 1990–91; Chair. Public Accounts Cttee 1961–62, mem. UP Police Comm. and Panchayati Raj Comm. 1961–62; Pres. Indian Youth Congress 1965–69; Minister of Labour, Planning and Panchayati Raj, UP 1969, of Finance and Parl. Affairs 1970, of Finance, Power, Heavy Industries, Irrigation, Labour, Sugarcane, Excise, Panchayati Raj and Parl. Affairs 1971, of Finance, Industry, Irrigation, Labour, Sugarcane, Excise and Parl. Affairs 1973, of Finance, Heavy Industries, Hill Devt and Planning 1974–75; Chief Minister of UP 1976–77, 1984–85, 1988–89; elected to Lok Sabha 1980, re-elected 1996, elected to 13th Lok Sabha from Nainital Constituency 1999; Union Minister of Planning and Deputy Chair. Planning Comm. (held additional Charge of Labour Ministry) 1980–81; Union Minister for Industry (held additional charge of Ministry of Steel and Mines) 1981–84 (1982–83); Union Minister for Industry (held additional charge of Ministry of Petroleum & Natural Gas) 1985–86; mem. Rajya Sabha 1985–88; Union Minister for External Affairs 1986–87; Leader Congress (I) Party in Rajya Sabha May–June 1987; Union Minister of Finance and Commerce 1987–88; Pres. All India Indira Congress (Tiwari) 1995–96; Leader Parl. Party, AIIC (T) May–Dec. 1996, party merged with Indian Nat. Congress 1997; first elected Chief Minister of newly created Uttaranchal State (now Uttarakhand) 2002–07; Gov. of Andhra Pradesh 2007–09; Ed. Prabhat (monthly); Special Corresp., National Herald; est. Jana Vidyapeeth (People's Coll.) in Haldwani 1962, Jawahar Lal Nehru Nat. Youth Centre 1967. *Publications:* European Miscellany (collection of articles) 1964; contributed numerous articles in Amrit Bazar Patrika, Leader, Deshdoot, National Herald, Pioneer, Blitz etc. *Leisure interests:* music, reading books on modern topics, econs, planning, int. relations. *Address:* c/o Office of the Chief Minister, Government of Andhra Pradesh, 'C' Block, 4th Floor, AP Secretariat, Hyderabad, India (office); Mohalla Ganj, Kashipur, Distt. Udham Singh Nagar, Uttaranchal; B-315, Dr Sushila Tiwari Marg, Mahanagar, Lucknow, Uttar Pradesh, India.

TIZARD, Dame Catherine (Anne), ONZ, GCMG, GCVO, DBE, OBE, QSO, BA; New Zealand public official (retd); b. 4 April 1931, Auckland; d. of Neil Maclean and Helen Montgomery Maclean; m. Robert James Tizard 1951 (divorced 1983); one s. three d.; ed Matamata Coll. and Auckland Univ.; Tutor in Zoology, Univ. of Auckland 1963–83; mem. Auckland City Council 1971–83, Auckland Regional Authority 1980–83, Mayor of Auckland (first woman) 1983–90; JP 1980–86; Gov.-Gen. of New Zealand (first woman) 1990–96; Chair. NZ Worldwide Fund for Nature 1996–2000, NZ Historic Places Trust 1996–2002, Sky City Charitable Trust 1996–2002, Cancer Control Council, Kiri te Kanawa Foundation; Dir NZ Symphony Orchestra Trust Bd; occasional radio, TV and newspaper commentator and columnist; public speaker and debater; numerous community activities including roles with Auckland War Memorial Inst. and Museum, Library Council of NZ, Auckland Univ. Council, Local Govt Asscn of NZ, Royal NZ Ballet Trust; Dir XIV Commonwealth Games Ltd, America's Cup Village Bd; Hon. Fellow, Lucy Cavendish Coll. Cambridge, UK and Winston Churchill Fellow 1981, Hon. Freeman, Worshipful Co. of Butchers 1990, Freedom, City of London 1990, Hon. Capt., Royal NZ Navy 1997, Hon. Col Auckland (Countess of Ranfurly's Own) and Northland Bn Group 2007; Hon. LLD (Auckland) 1992; New Zealand Medal 1990, Suffrage Centennial Medal 1993. *Publication:* Cat Amongst the Pigeons 2010. *Leisure interests:* music, reading, drama, scuba diving. *Address:* 12A Wallace Street, Herne Bay, Auckland 1, New Zealand. *Telephone:* (9) 376-2555. *E-mail:* cath.tizard@xtra.co.nz (home).

TJANDRANEGARA, Eka; Indonesian business executive; *Founder, Mulia Group;* b. 1946; s. of Tjandra Kusuma; m. f. Java Marine Lines Pte Ltd 1981, renamed Jaya Holdings Ltd, Dir, later Chair.; f. Mulia Group (real estate co.), also Pres. Dir Mulia Industrindo (glass mfr); Commr Royale Jakarta Golf Club. *Address:* Wisma Mulia, Floor 56th, Jalan Jenderal Gatot Subroto No. 42, Jakarta 12710, Indonesia (office). *Telephone:* (21) 5200888 (office). *Fax:* (21) 5200872 (office). *E-mail:* enquiry@mulialand.com (office). *Website:* www.mulialand.com (office).

TJEKNAVORIAN, Loris; Iranian composer and conductor; b. 13 Oct. 1937, Iran; s. of Haikaz Tjeknavorian and Adriné Tjeknavorian; m. 1st Linda Pierce 1964 (divorced 1979); one s.; m. 2nd Julia Cory Harley-Green 1986; m. 3rd Naira 2004; ed Tehran Conservatory of Music, Iran, Vienna Acad. of Music, Salzburg Mozarteum, Univ. of Michigan, USA; several works published in Vienna following graduation 1961; given scholarship to study with the late Carl Orff 1963–64; lived in Salzburg and worked on opera Rostam and Sohrab; began studying conducting in USA 1965; Composer-in-Residence, Concordia Coll., Moorhead, Minn. 1966–67; Head of Instrumental and Opera Departments, Moorhead Univ., Minn. 1966–70; signed conducting contract with RCA recording co. 1975–; numerous recordings with leading orchestras, including London Symphony Orchestra, Royal Philharmonic Orchestra, London Philharmonic Orchestra; works have been performed by major orchestras, including Vienna Symphony, London Philharmonic, American Symphony; Prin. Conductor and Artistic Dir Armenian Philharmonic Orchestra 1989–2000, numerous recordings for ORF (Austria) and ASV recording co.; Order of Homayoun; Austrian Presidential Gold Medal for Artistic Merit 2010, Highest Medal of the Repub. of Armenia, Highest Order of Arts of the Iranian Islamic Repub. *Compositions:* more than 80 works (five symphonies, five operas, a requiem, chamber music, concerto for piano, violin, guitar, cello and pipa (Chinese lute), ballet music, choral works and an oratorio, and more than 40 film scores), including Requiem for the Massacred 1975, Simorgh (ballet music), Lake Van Suite, Erebouni for 12 strings 1978, Credo Symphony Life of Christ (after medieval Armenian chants) 1976, Liturgical Mass, Violin Concerto, oratorios Lucifer's Fall and Book of Revelation, Mass in Memoriam 1985, Othello (ballet), ballet suites for

orchestra, five symphonies. *Address:* Vogelsanggasse 39–41/30, 1050 Vienna, Austria. *E-mail:* ltjeknavorian@yahoo.com. *Website:* www.loristjeknavorian.com.

TKACH, Robert, BS, MS, PhD; American physicist; *Director, Transmission Systems and Networks Research, Bell Labs, Alcatel-Lucent;* ed Univ. of Cincinnati, Cornell Univ.; with Bell Labs (now Bell Labs, Alcatel-Lucent) 1984–96, Dir of Transmission Systems and Networks Research 2006–; with AT&T Labs 1996–2000; with Celion Networks 2000–06; Chair. Optical Fiber Communications (OFC) Conf. Steering Cttee, fmr Gen. Co-Chair. OFC; mem. Tech. Advisory Bd, Optoelectronics Industry Data Asscn; fmr Vice-Pres. Optical Internetworking Forum; fmr Assoc. Ed. Journal of Lightwave Technology; fmr mem. IEEE LEOS Bd Govs; mem. Nat. Acad. of Eng 2009; Fellow, Optical Soc. of America, IEEE, AT&T; Thomas Alva Edison Patent Award, Research and Devt Council of NJ, John Tyndall Award, Optical Soc. of America and IEEE 2008, Marconi Prize and Fellowship (co-recipient) 2009, IEEE Alexander Graham Bell Medal (co-recipient) 2013. *Publications:* numerous papers in professional journals. *Address:* Bell Labs, Alcatel-Lucent, 600 Mountain Avenue, Murray Hill, NJ 07974-0636, USA (office). *Telephone:* (908) 582-8500 (office). *Website:* www.alcatel-lucent.com/bell-labs (office).

TKACHENKO, Oleksander Mikolayevich, CandTechSc; Ukrainian politician; b. 7 March 1939, Shpola, Cherkassy Region; m. Larissa Mitrofanivna Tkachenko; one d.; ed Belotsekivski Agric. Inst., Higher Party School, CPSU Cen. Cttee; worked as First Sec., Tarashansk Comsomol Cttee 1966–70, then Ukrainian CP functionary in agric. sector 1970–82; State Minister, Head of Cttee on Agric. Policy and Food Ukrainian SSR 1985–91; Head of Agric. Asscn Zemlya i Lyudi 1992–94; Leader, Ukrainian Farmers' Party; mem. Verkhovna Rada (Parl.) 1994–, First Vice-Chair. Verkhovna Rada 1994–98, Chair. (Speaker) 1998–2000; unsuccessful cand. for Pres. 1991. *Address:* Verkhovna Rada, M. Hrushevskoga str. 5, 252008 Kiev, Ukraine. *Telephone:* (381) 226-28-25 (office).

TKESHELASHVILI, David, LLM; Georgian politician; *Chief of President's Administration;* b. 16 Oct. 1969, Tbilisi; m. Nino Tkeshelashvili; one s. one d.; ed Tbilisi State Univ., Emory Univ., USA; mil. service 1987–89; Head of Regional Dept of the Citizens' Union's Youth Arm 1993–95, also Political Sec. and Deputy Chair., Press Sec. 1994–95, Chair. Youth Arm of Citizens' Union 1998–2002; elected mem. Parl. (Citizens' Union) 1995, served as Deputy Majority Leader (re-elected 1999, re-elected for Nat. Movt-Democrats 2004), Chair. Sub-cttee for Relations with Media and Non-governmental Orgs for Human Rights Cttee 1999–2003; Minister of Environmental Protection and Natural Resources 2006–07, of Labour, Health and Social Affairs 2007–08, State Minister for Regional Issues 2008–09, Minister of Regional Devt and Infrastructure 2008–10, also First Deputy Prime Minister 2009–10, Chief of Pres.'s Admin 2010–; Edmund Muskie Scholarship 2005. *Address:* Office of the President, 0105 Tbilisi, P. Ingorovka 7, Georgia (office). *Telephone:* (32) 99-00-70 (office). *Fax:* (32) 99-88-87 (office). *E-mail:* secretariat@admin.gov.ge (office). *Website:* www.president.gov.ge (office).

TKESHELASHVILI, Ekaterine (Eka), LLM; Georgian lawyer and government official; b. 23 May 1977, Tbilisi; m.; four c.; ed Tbilisi State Univ., Univ. of Notre Dame, USA; Chief Specialist, Centre for Foreign Policy Research and Analysis, Ministry of Foreign Affairs 1997–99; field officer, Int. Cttee of Red Cross 1998–2000; intern, Appeals Office, Int. Tribunal of fmr Yugoslavia 2001–02; lawyer and Dir Institutional Reform and Non-governmental Sector, IRIS Georgia (Tbilisi office of Univ. of Maryland's Center for Institutional Reform and the Informal Sector) 2002–04; Deputy Minister of Justice 2004–05; Deputy Minister of Internal Affairs 2005–06; Chair. Tbilisi Court of Appeals 2006–07; Minister of Justice 2007–08; Prosecutor Gen. Feb.–May 2008; Minister of Foreign Affairs May–Dec. 2008; Sec. Nat. Security Council 2008–10; Deputy Prime Minister and State Minister, responsible for Reintegration 2010–12. *Address:* c/o Office of the State Minister, responsible for Reintegration, 0105 Tbilisi, P. Ingorovka 7, Georgia. *E-mail:* mg@smr.gov.ge.

TLASS, Lt-Gen. Mustafa el; Syrian politician and army officer; b. 11 May 1932, Rastan City, Mouhafazat, Homs; m. Lamyaa al-Jabri 1958; two s. two d.; ed Mil. and Law Colls. and Voroshilov Acad., Moscow; active mem. Baath Arab Socialist Party 1947–, Sec. of Rastan Section 1951; Sports teacher, Al-Kraya School, Mouhafazat al-Soueda 1950–52; attended Mil. Coll. 1952–54; seconded to Egyptian army 1959–61; Insp. Ministry of Supply 1962; mem. Free Officers' Movement 1962–63, detained 1962–63; Commdr Tank Bn and Chief of Cen. Region of Nat. Security Court 1963; Chief of Staff, 5th Armoured Brigade 1964–66; mem. Regional Command, Regional Congress of Baath Arab Socialist Party 1965, 1968, 1969, 1975, of Politbureau 1969–, of Nat. Council of Revolution 1965–71; participated in movt of 23 Feb., promoted to Commdr of Cen. Region and of Fifth Armoured Brigade; rank of Maj.-Gen. 1968, Chief of Staff of Armed Forces 1968–70, First Deputy Minister of Defence 1968–72; participated in coup installing Pres. Hafez Al-Assad Nov. 1970; First Deputy C-in-C Armed Forces 1970–72, Deputy C-in-C 1972; mem. People's Council 1971–; Minister of Defence 1972–2004, also Deputy Prime Minister; Deputy Chief of Jt Supreme Mil. Council of Syrian and Egyptian Armed Forces 1973; rank of Lt-Gen. 1978; 33 orders and medals. *Publications include:* Guerilla War, Military Studies, An Introduction to Zionist Strategy, The Arab Prophet and Technique of War, The Armoured Brigade as an Advanced Guard, Bitter Memories in the Military Prison of Mezzah, The Fourth War between Arabs and Israel, The Second Chapter of the October Liberation War, Selections of Arab Poetry, The Steadfastness Front in Confrontation with Camp David, The Algerian Revolution, Art of Soviet War, American Policy under the Carter Regime, The Technological Revolution and Development of the Armed Forces. *Leisure interests:* reading and writing books, military and historical studies, photography. *Address:* c/o Ministry of Defence, Place Omayad, Damascus, Syria.

TLUSTÝ, Vlastimil; Czech politician; b. 19 Sept. 1955; early career as Researcher, Agricultural Machinery Research Inst.; Asst Lecturer, Agricultural Univ. of Prague 1990; mem. Parl. 1991–2009, mem. Civic Democratic Party (Občanská demokratická strana—ODS), Deputy Chair., Chair. ODS Parl. Club, Vice Chair. Finance Cttee; Chair. Supervisory Bd CKA (Czech Consolidation Agency) –2006; Minister of Finance June–Oct. 2006 (resgnd); fmr Chair. Union of

Land Owners and Pvt. Farmers of Czech Repub. *Address:* c/o Ministry of Finance, Lětenská 15, 118 00 Prague 1, Czech Republic (office).

TOAFA, Maatia; Tuvaluan politician; *Minister of Finance and Economic Development;* b. 1954; began career with Pacific Islands Forum Secr., Suva, Fiji; Deputy Prime Minister of Tuvalu, Minister for Works, Communications and Transport –2004; acting Prime Minister Aug.–Oct. 2004, Prime Minister and Minister of Foreign Affairs and Labour, Oct. 2004–06, Leader of the Opposition 2006–10, Prime Minister Sept.–Dec. 2010, Minister of Finance and Econ. Devt 2013–. *Address:* Ministry of Finance and Economic Development, PMB, Vaiaku, Funafuti, Tuvalu (office). *Telephone:* 20202 (office). *Fax:* 20210 (office). *E-mail:* secfin@tuvalu.tv (office).

TOAN, Barrett A., MA; American business executive; b. 1947, Briarcliff Manor, NY; m. Polly Toan; one d. one s.; ed Kenyon Coll., Wharton School, Univ. of Pennsylvania; began career in Bureau of the Budget, Office of the Gov. of Ill.; fmr consultant to state and local govts for Price Waterhouse & Co., Washington, DC; budgetary adviser to Ark. Attorney-Gen. Bill Clinton, 1979; Commr Ark. Div. of Social Services 1980–81; Dir Mo. Dept of Social Services 1982; Exec. Dir and COO Sanus Corp. Health Systems Inc. (renamed GenCare) 1985–1991; joined Express Scripts Inc. (pharmacy benefit man. co.) 1992, mem. Bd of Dirs 1992–, Pres. and CEO –2000, Chair., Pres. and CEO 2000–05, Chair. 2005–06 (retd); mem. Bd of Dirs Sigma-Aldrich Corpn, Genworth Financial, Inc.; Mentor St Louis, Kenyon Coll.; mem. Investors Council and Leadership Circle, Regional Chamber and Growth Asscn. *Leisure interests:* history, literature. *Address:* c/o Board of Directors, Express Scripts Inc., 13900 Riverport Drive, Maryland Heights, MO 63043, USA (office).

TOBGAY, Lyonchhen Tshering, BS, MPA; Bhutanese politician; *Prime Minister;* b. 19 Sept. 1965, Haa; ed Univ. of Pittsburgh, Harvard Univ., USA; began career as program officer, Tech. and Vocational Section, Dept of Educ. 1991, promoted Officer-in-Charge, later Head of Nat. Tech. Training Authority; Dir Dept of Human Resources –2007 (resgnd); carried out groundwork to form People's Democratic Party (PDP); trained in Cambodia, Thailand, USA, Philippines, S Korea, UK and Italy; fmr mem. Bd Royal Univ. of Bhutan, Council for Higher Educ., Bhutan Bd of Examinations and several others; mem. Parl. representing Sombaykha constituency in Haa, Leader of Opposition in Nat. Ass. –2013; Pres. People's Democratic Party 2009–; Prime Minister 2013–. *Address:* Cabinet Secretariat, Tashichhodzong, PO Box 1011, Thimphu (office); People's Democratic Party, PO Box 835, Thimphu, Bhutan (office). *Telephone:* (2) 321437 (Cabinet) (office); (2) 327137 (PDP) (office); (17) 110546 (mobile). *Fax:* (2) 321438 (Cabinet) (office); (2) 335757 (PDP) (office). *E-mail:* cabinet@druknet.bt (office); tsheringtobgay@pdp.bt (office); tsheringtobgay.blog@gmail.com. *Website:* www.cabinet.gov.bt (office); www.tsheringtobgay.com.

TOBGYE, Lyonpo Sonam; Bhutanese judge; *Chief Justice of Bhutan;* Chief Justice, High Court –2009, Supreme Court 2009–; Chair. Nat. Judicial Comm. 2003–; Pres. South Asian Asscn for Regional Cooperation in Law (SAARCLAW) 2011–. *Address:* High Court (Thrimkhang Gongma), Thimphu, Bhutan (office). *Telephone:* 322344 (office). *Fax:* 322921 (office). *E-mail:* judiciary@druknet.bt (office). *Website:* www.judiciary.gov.bt (office).

TOBIA, Maguid, BSc; Egyptian writer; b. 25 March 1938, Minia; teacher of math. 1960–68; mem. Higher Council of Arts and Literature 1969–78; mem. staff Ministry of Culture 1978–; mem. Writers' Union, Chamber of Cinema Industry, Soc. of Egyptian Film Critics, Fiction Cttee of Supreme Council of Culture; Medal of Science and Arts (First Class); several literary prizes. *Film scripts include:* Story of Our Country 1967, Sons of Silence 1974, Stars' Maker 1978, Harem Cage 1981. *Play:* International Laugh Bank 2001. *Television:* Friendly Visit (series) 1980. *Publications:* collections of short stories: Vostock Reaches the Moon 1967, Five Unread Papers 1970, The Coming Days 1972, The Companion 1978, The Accident Which Happens 1987, 23 Short Stories 2001; novels: Circles of Impossibility 1972, The They 1973, Sons of Silence 1974, The Strange Deeds of Kings and the Intrigues of Banks 1976, The Room of Floor Chances 1978, The Music Kiosk 1980, Hanan 1981, West Virgin 1986, The Emigration to the North Country of Hathoot's Tribe (three vols: To the North Country 1987, To the South Country 1992, To the Lakes Country 2005), The Story of Beautiful Reem 1991, The Great History of Donkeys 1996, Amosis Case 2005; contribs to Al Ahram and several Arabic magazines. *Leisure interests:* reading, travel. *Address:* 15 El-Lewaa Abd El Aziz Aly, Heliopolis, 11361, Cairo, Egypt (home). *Telephone:* 2917801 (home). *Fax:* 2917801 (home).

TOBIAS, Randall L., BS; American business executive and government official; b. 20 March 1942, Lafayette, Ind.; m. 1st Marilyn Jane Salyer 1966 (died 1994); one s. one d.; m. 2nd Marianne Williams 1995; one step-s. one step-d.; ed Indiana Univ.; served in US Army 1964–66; numerous positions, Indiana Bell 1964–81, Illinois Bell 1977–81; Vice-Pres. (residence marketing, sales and service) AT&T 1981–82; Pres. American Bell Consumer Products 1983–84, Sr Vice-Pres. 1984–85, Chair. and CEO AT&T Communications, New York 1985–91, AT&T International, Basking Ridge, NJ 1991–93, Vice-Chair. AT&T, New York and Chair. 1986–93; Chair., Pres. and CEO Eli Lilly & Co., Indianapolis 1993–98, Chair. Emer. 1999–; Amb. and Coordinator US Govt Activities to Combat HIV/AIDS Globally 2003–06; Dir of Foreign Assistance and Admin., USAID 2006–07 (resgnd); fmr mem. Bd of Dirs Eli Lilly & Co., Kimberly-Clark, Knight-Ridder, Phillips Petroleum; fmr Chair. Bd of Trustees Duke Univ.; fmr Vice-Chair. Colonial Williamsburg Foundation; mem. Council on Foreign Relations, numerous other appointments; Dr hc (Indiana Univ., Wabash Coll., Butler Univ., Gallaudet Univ., Ball State Univ.); Hon. DEng (Rose-Hulman Inst. of Tech.); Pharmaceutical Industry CEO of the Year 1995, named CEO of the Year by Working Mother magazine 1996, named as one of Top Twenty-Five Mans of the Year by Business Week Magazine 1997, Norman Vincent Peale Humanitarian of the Year 1997, Indiana Univ.-Purdue Univ.-Indianapolis (IUPUI) Urban Univ. Medal, Positive Ally Award, Nat. Asscn of People with AIDS 2005. *Publication:* Put The Moose On The Table (with Todd Tobias) 2003. *Leisure interests:* skiing, shooting.

TOBIN, Brian V., PC, OC; Canadian businessman and fmr politician; *Senior Business Adviser, Fraser Milner Casgrain LLP;* b. 21 Oct. 1954, Stephenville, Newfoundland; s. of Patrick Tobin and Mary Frye; m. Jodean Smith 1977; two s. one d.; ed Memorial Univ., St John's, Newfoundland, Inst. of Corporate Directors,

Univ. of Toronto; worked as a journalist; MP for Humber-St Barbe-Baie Verte 1980–96; MP for Bonavista-Trinity-Conception 2000–02, Parl. Sec. to Minister of Fisheries and Oceans 1980; Minister of Fisheries and Oceans 1993; Premier of Newfoundland 1996–2000; Minister of Industry and Minister responsible for the Atlantic Canada Opportunities Agency and for Western Econ. Diversification and Francophonie and for the Econ. Devt Agency of Canada for the Regions of Québec 2000–02; currently Sr Business Adviser, Fraser Milner Casgrain LLP, Toronto; Sr Fellow, Fraser Inst. 2006–10; Chair. Nat. Liberal Caucus 1989; mem. numerous House of Commons Cttees; Chair. New Flyer Industries, Market Resource Corpn; mem. Bd of Dirs Aecon Group Inc., Norvista Resources, Cline Mining Corpn; Dr hc (St Francis Xavier 2001, Brock 2004). *Address:* Fraser Milner Casgrain LLP, 77 King Street West, Suite 400, Toronto, ON M5K 0A1, Canada (office). *Telephone:* (416) 863-4511 (office). *Fax:* (416) 863-4592 (office). *Website:* www.fmc-law.com (office).

TODD, Damian Roderic (Ric), BA; British diplomatist; b. 29 Aug. 1959, Crawley, West Sussex; s. of the late George Todd and Annette Todd; m. Alison Todd; one s. two d.; ed Worcester Coll., Oxford; with Defence Dept, FCO 1980–81, Third then Second Sec., Cape Town and Pretoria 1981–84, EC Dept 1984–87, First Sec. and Consul, Embassy in Prague 1987–89, Econ. Relations Dept 1989–91, First Sec. (Econ.), Embassy in Bonn 1991–95; seconded to HM Treasury, London 1995–97, Head, Agric. Spending Team, HM Treasury 1995–97, Agricultural Team 1996–97; EU Coordination and Strategy Team 1998–2001; Amb. to Slovakia 2001–04, FCO Finance Dir 2004–13, Amb. to Poland 2007–11, Gov. Turks and Caicos Islands 2011–13. *Address:* c/o Foreign and Commonwealth Office, King Charles Street, London, SW1A 2AH (office).

TODD, Sir David, Kt, CBE, MD, FAM, FRCP, FRCPE, FRCPGlas, FRACP, FRCPath; British professor of medicine; *Professor Emeritus, University of Hong Kong;* b. 17 Nov. 1928, China; s. of Paul J. Todd and Margaret S. Todd; ed Univ. of Hong Kong; Prof. Dept of Medicine, Univ. of Hong Kong 1972–96, Head, Dept of Medicine 1974–89, Sub-Dean, Faculty of Medicine 1976–78, Pro-Vice-Chancellor 1978–80, now Prof. Emer.; consultant (medicine) to Govt of Hong Kong 1974–89; Pres. Hong Kong Acad. of Medicine 1992–96, Council for AIDS Trust Fund, Hong Kong 1993–96; Hon. Mem. Chinese Medical Asscn 1995; Hon. DSc (Chinese Univ. of Hong Kong) 1990, (Hong Kong Univ.) 1992, Hon. LLD (Lingnan Univ. Hong Kong). *Publications:* numerous articles in professional journals. *Leisure interests:* classical music, stamp collecting, swimming. *Address:* D12 Breezy Court, 2A Park Road, Mid-levels, Hong Kong Special Administrative Region, People's Republic of China (home). *E-mail:* dtodd@hkucc.hku.hk (office).

TODD, Olivier René Louis, LèsL, MA; French writer; b. 19 June 1929, Neuilly; s. of Julius Oblatt and Helen Todd; m. 1st Anne-Marie Nizan 1948; m. 2nd France Huser 1982; two s. two d.; ed Sorbonne, Corpus Christi Coll., Cambridge, UK; teacher, Lycée Int. du Shape 1956–62; Univ. Asst, St-Cloud 1962–64; reporter, Nouvel Observateur 1964–69; Ed. TV Programme Panorama 1969–70; Asst Ed. Nouvel Observateur 1970–77; columnist and Man. Ed. L'Express 1977–81; worked for BBC (Europa, 24 Hours) and ORTF 1964–69; Chevalier, Légion d'honneur, Commdr, Ordre des Arts et des Lettres; Hon. PhD (Stirling, Bristol), Hon. DLitt (Edinburgh) 2005; Prix Cazes 1981, Prix France Télévision 1997, Prix du Mémorial 1997. *Publications:* Une demi-campagne 1957, La traversée de la Manche 1960, Des trous dans le jardin 1969, L'année du Crabe 1972, Les canards de Ca Mao 1975, La marelle de Giscard 1977, Portraits 1979, Un fils rebelle 1981, Un cannibale très convenable 1982, Une légère gueule de bois 1983, La balade du chômeur 1986, Cruel Avril 1987, La négociation 1989, La Sanglière 1992, Albert Camus, une vie 1996, André Malraux, une vie 2001, Catre d'identités, souvenirs 2005. *Leisure interests:* walking, Luxembourg Gardens. *Address:* 8 rue du Pin, 83310 La Garde Freinet, France (home). *Telephone:* 4-94-43-63-34 (home).

TODMAN, Michael, BSBA; American business executive; *President, Whirlpool North America;* b. St Thomas, US Virgin Islands; ed Georgetown Univ.; various man. roles with Wang Laboratories Inc. and Price Waterhouse & Co. –1993; Finance Dir Whirlpool UK 1993, later Gen. Man. N Europe and Vice-Pres. Consumer Services, Whirlpool Europe, Controller N America 1995, Vice-Pres. Product Man. 1996, Vice-Pres. Sears Sales and Marketing 1997, Sr Vice-Pres. Sales and Marketing, N America 1999, Exec. Vice-Pres. N America, also mem. Exec. Cttee Whirlpool Corpn 2001, Exec. Vice-Pres. and Pres. Whirlpool Europe 2001, Pres. Whirlpool International 2006–07, 2010–, mem. Bd of Dirs Whirlpool Corpn 2006–, Pres. Whirlpool N America 2007–10; mem. Bd of Dirs Newell-Rubbermaid, Georgetown University, Economic Club of Southwestern Michigan; mem. Loyola Univ. Council of Regents. *Address:* Whirlpool Corporation, 2000 North M-63 States, Benton Harbor, MI 49022-2692, USA (office). *Telephone:* (269) 923-5000 (office). *Fax:* (269) 923-3722 (office). *Website:* www.whirlpoolcorp.com (office).

TODORIĆ, Ivica, BEcons; Croatian business executive; *President, Agrokor Group;* b. 1951; m. Vesna Bašic; two s. one d.; ed Faculty of Econs, Zagreb Univ.; est. co. trading in flowers 1976, expanded in 1980s to include grains, oil, fruit and vegetables, f. Agrokor (jt stock co.) 1989, now Pres., Agrokor Group, acquired numerous cos including Jaska vino d.d. 1998, Kiseljak 2000, Alastor d.o.o., Frikom 2003, also owns retail chain Konzum; Co-founder and Pres. Croatian Employers Asscn 1993. *Address:* Agrokor d.d., Trg D. Petrovića 3, 10000 Zagreb, Croatia (office). *Telephone:* (1) 4894111 (office). *Fax:* (1) 4894080 (office). *E-mail:* predsjednik@agrokor.hr (office); agrokor@agrokor.hr (office). *Website:* www .agrokor.hr (office).

TODOROVSKY, Valery Petrovich; Russian filmmaker; b. 8 May 1962, Odessa; s. of Piotr Yefimovich Todorovsky and Maiya Grigoriyevna Todorovskaya; ed All-Union Inst. of Cinematography; began career as scriptwriter; producer several TV series. *Films include:* A Man of the Retinue, Cynics, Live (UNICEF Prize, Chicago Film Festival), Moscow Nights (Green Apple Prize, Golden Leaf), Katafalk (dir) 1990, Lyubov (Love) (writer, dir) 1991, Otdushina (A Vent) (writer) 1991, Hearse (dir) (Mannheim Film Festival Prize 1991), Nad tyomnoy vodoy (Above Dark Water) 1993, Katya Ismailova (dir) 1994, Strana glukhikh (Country of the Deaf) (writer, dir) 1998, Lyubovnik (The Lover) (dir) 2002, Moy svodnyy brat Frankensteyn (My Step Brother Frankenstein) (dir) 2004. *Television includes:* Kamenskaya, Morskoy volk (The Sea Wolf) (writer) 1991. *Address:* Ramenki str. 11, korp. 2, Apt. 272, 117607 Moscow, Russia. *Telephone:* (495) 931-56-63.

TOELLE, Michael, BS; American business executive and farmer; ed Minnesota State Univ., Moorhead, Certificate of Dir Educ., Nat. Asscn of Corp. Dirs Dir Professionalism course; operates a family grain and hog farm near Browns Valley, Minn.; served on Bd of Country Pnrs Cooperative, Browns Valley, Minn. for 15 years, Chair. for 10 years; first elected to Bd of Dirs of CHS to represent Minnesota mems 1992, Chair. CHS 2002–11, fmr mem. Finance and Investment Cttee CHS Cooperatives Foundation; actively involved in numerous agric. and commodity groups. *Address:* CHS, PO Box 64089, St Paul, MN 55164-0089 (office); CHS, 5500 Cenex Drive, Inver Grove Heights, MN 55077, USA (office). *Telephone:* (651) 355-6000 (office). *E-mail:* michael.toelle@chsinc.com (office). *Website:* www.chsinc.com (office).

TOENNIES, Jan Peter, PhD; German physicist and academic; *Director Emeritus, Max-Planck-Institut für Dynamik und Selbstorganization;* b. 3 May 1930, Philadelphia, USA; s. of Gerrit Toennies and Dita Jebens; m. Monika Zelesnick 1966; two d.; ed Amherst Coll., Brown Univ.; Asst, Bonn Univ., FRG 1962–65, Privat Dozent 1965–67, Dozent 1967–69; Scientific mem. and Dir Max-Planck-Inst. für Strömungsforschung (now Max-Planck Inst. für Dynamik und Selb-storganisation) 1969–98, Acting Dir 1998–2001, currently Dir Emer., Emer. Scientific Mem., Max-Planck-Soc. 2002–05, Admin. Dir 2001–02; Assoc. Prof., Dept of Physics, Göttingen Univ. 1971–; Visiting Miller Prof. of Chem. and Physics, Univ. of California, Berkeley 2005; Corresp. mem. Acad. of Sciences, Göttingen; mem. German Acad. of Natural Sciences 'Leopoldina'; Hon. Prof., Bonn Univ. 1971–; Hon. DPhil (Gothenburg) 2000, Hon. DSci (Amherst Coll.) 2007; Physics Prize, Göttingen Acad. of Sciences 1964, Gold Heyrovsky Medal of the Czechoslovak Acad. of Sciences 1991, Hewlett-Packard Europhysics Prize (for outstanding achievement in condensed matter research) 1991, Max Planck Prize, Alexander von Humboldt Foundation 1992, Stern-Gerlach Medal, German Physical Soc. 2002, Kolos Medal, Univ. of Warsaw 2005, Benjamin Franklin Medal for Physics (co-recipient) 2006, Herschbach Award (co-recipient) 2013. *Publications include:* Chemical Reactions in Shock Waves (with E. F. Greene) 1964, A Study of Intermolecular Potentials with Molecular Beams at Thermal Energies (with H. Pauly) in Advances in Atomic and Molecular Physics 1965, Molecular Beam Scattering Experiments, contribution in Physical Chemistry, An Advanced Treatise 1974, Rotationally and Vibrationally Inelastic Scattering of Molecules (Chem. Soc. Review) 1974, Scattering Studies of Rotational and Vibrational Excitation of Molecules (with M. Faubel) 1977, Advances in Atomic and Molecular Physics 1977, The Study of the Forces between Atoms of Single Crystal Surfaces 1988, Annual Review of Physical Chemistry, Serendipitous Meanderings and Adventures with Molecular Beams 2004, Angewandte Chemie (Int. Ed.), Superfluid Helium Droplets: A Uniquely Cold Nanomatrix for Molecules and Molecular Complexes (with A. Vilesov) 2004; more than 700 publs in scientific journals. *Leisure interest:* sailing, hiking, physics toys. *Address:* Max-Planck-Institut für Dynamik und Selbstorganisation, Am Fassberg 17, 37077 Göttingen (office); Ewaldstrasse 7, 37085 Göttingen, Germany (home). *Telephone:* (551) 5176600 (office); (551) 57172 (home). *E-mail:* jtoenni@gwdg.de (office). *Website:* wwwuser.gwdg.de/~mpisfto (office).

TOEWS, Miriam, BA; Canadian writer and journalist; b. 1964, Steinbach, Manitoba; ed Univ. of Manitoba, Univ. of King's Coll., Halifax; John Hirsch Award for Most Promising Manitoba Writer 1996, Gold Medal for Humour, Nat. Magazine Award 1999. *Film:* as actor: Luz silenciosa 2007. *Publications include:* novels: Summer of My Amazing Luck 1996, A Boy of Good Breeding (McNally Robinson Book of the Year Award) 1998, A Complicated Kindness (Margaret Laurence Award for Fiction, McNally Robinson Book of the Year, Canadian Booksellers Asscn Fiction Book of the Year 2005, Gov. Gen.'s Award for Fiction 2005) 2004, The Flying Troutmans (Rogers Writers' Trust Fiction Prize) 2008, Travails with an Aunt 2009, Irma Voth 2011; other: Swing Low: A Life (memoir) 2000. *Address:* c/o Knopf Canada, 210-33 Yonge Street, Toronto, ON M5E 1G4, Canada (office).

TOFFLER, Alvin, BA; American writer; b. 4 Oct. 1928, New York, NY; m. Adelaide Elizabeth (Heidi) Toffler (née Farrell) 1950; one d.; ed New York Univ.; Assoc. Ed., Fortune Magazine 1959–61; Visiting Scholar, Russell Sage Foundation 1969–70; f. (with wife) Toffler Associates (consultancy) 1996; Fellow, AAAS; mem. American Soc. of Journalists and Authors, IISS, World Future Studies Fed.; Officier, Ordre des Arts et Lettres; several hon. doctorates; American Soc. of Journalists and Authors Author of the Year, Prix de Meilleur Livre Étranger. *Publications:* The Schoolhouse in the City 1968, The Eco-Spasm Report 1975; with Heidi Toffler: The Culture Consumers 1964, Future Shock 1970, The Futurists (ed.) 1972, Learning for Tomorrow (ed.) 1973, The Third Wave 1980, Previews and Premises 1983, The Adaptive Corporation 1984, Power Shift 1990, War and Anti-War 1993, Creating a New Civilization 1994–95, Revolutionary Wealth 2006; contrib. to newspapers, journals and periodicals. *Address:* Toffler Associates, 1775 Wiehle Avenue, Reston, VA 20190, USA (office). *Telephone:* (703) 674-5480 (office). *Fax:* (703) 674-5494 (office). *Website:* www.toffler.com (office).

TOHÁ MORALES, Carolina Montserrat, PhD; Chilean politician and government official; *Mayor of Santiago;* b. 12 May 1965; d. of the late José Tohá (fmr Vice-Pres. of Chile under Salvador Allende); m. Fulvio Rossi; ed Universidad de Chile, Univ. of Milan, Italy; played role in re-establishment of Federación de Estudiantes de la Universidad de Chile (FECH) 1984, Vice-Pres. 1987; mem. Partido por la Democracia (PPD), Vice-Pres. 1999; worked on presidential campaign of Ricardo Lagos 1999; Under-Sec. to Govt Spokesperson 2000–06; mem. Nat. Congress (PPD) for Santiago 2001–09 (re-elected 2005), Pres. 2010–; managed presidential runoff campaign of Eduardo Frei Ruiz-Tagle 2009; apptd Govt Spokesperson (first woman) 2009–10; Mayor of Santiago 2012–. *Address:* Ilustre Municipalidad de Santiago, Plaza de armas S/N, Casilla 52-D, Santiago, Chile (office). *E-mail:* alcaldesa@munistgo.cl (office). *Website:* www.municipalidaddesantiago.cl (office).

TÓIBÍN, Colm, FRSL; Irish journalist and writer; b. 30 May 1955, Enniscorthy, Co. Wexford; s. of Micheál Tóibín; ed Christian Brothers School, Enniscorthy, Univ. Coll., Dublin; in Spain 1975–78; Features Ed., In Dublin 1981–82; Ed. Magill (political and current affairs magazine) 1982–85; journalist and columnist, Dublin Sunday Independent 1985–; Hon. DLitt (Univ. of Ulster) 2008; American Acad. of Arts and Letters E.M. Forster Award 1995, Center for Scholars and Writers Fellowship, New York Public Library, Soc. of Authors Travelling Scholarship 2004, 38th annual AWB Vincent American Ireland Fund Literary Award 2010, Irish PEN Award 2011. *Plays:* Beauty in a Broken Place 2003. *Publications:* fiction:

Infidelity (contrib.), The South (Irish Times First Novel Award 1991) 1990, The Heather Blazing (Encore Award) 1993, The Story of the Night 1996, The Blackwater Lightship 1999, Finbar's Hotel (contrib.) 1999, The Master (Los Angeles Times Novel of the Year 2004, Stonewall Book Award 2004, Lambda Literary Award 2004, Int. IMPAC Dublin Literary Award 2006) 2004, Mothers and Sons 2006, Brooklyn (Costa Book Award for Best Novel) 2009, The Empty Family 2010, The Testament of Mary 2012; non-fiction: Seeing is Believing: Moving Statues in Ireland 1985, Walking along the Border (with T. O'Shea) 1987, Homage to Barcelona 1990, Dubliners 1990, The Trial of the Generals: Selected Journalism 1980–90 1990, Bad Blood 1994, Sign of the Cross 1994, The Kilfenora Teaboy 1997, The Irish Famine 1999, Love in a Dark Time 2001, Lady Gregory's Toothbrush 2002, New Ways to Kill Your Mother: Writers and Their Families 2012; editor: SOHO Square VI: New Writing from Ireland 1993, Enniscorthy: History & Heritage 1998, Penguin Book of Irish Fiction 1999, The Modern Library 1999, New Writing II 2002; contrib. articles. *Address:* c/o Rogers, Coleridge and White Ltd, 20 Powis Mews, London, W11 1JN, England (office). *Telephone:* (20) 7221-3717 (office). *Fax:* (20) 7229-9084 (office). *E-mail:* info@rcwlitagency.co.uk (office). *Website:* www.rcwlitagency.co.uk (office); www.colmtoibin.com.

TOIVO, Andimba Toivo ya; Namibian politician; b. 22 Aug. 1924, Omangundu, Ovamboland; s. of Andimba Toivo ya Toivo and Nashikoto Elizabeth; m. 2nd Vicki Lynn Erenstein 1990; three s. two d.; ed St Mary's Mission School, Odimbo; taught at St Mary's Mission School, Odimbo; served in SA Army 1942–43; worked in SA gold mines and on railways; mem. African National Congress and Modern Youth Soc.; deported to Ovamboland 1958; f. (with Sam Nujoma) SW African People's Org. (SWAPO), mem. Politburo –2007; arrested 1966; sentenced to 20 years' imprisonment, Robben Island 1968; released in Windhoek, Namibia 1984; mem. Politburo and Sec.-Gen. SWAPO 1984–91; Minister of Mines and Energy 1990–98, Minister of Labour 1999–2003; Minister of Prisons and Correctional Services 2003–06; Leader SWAPO del. to UN 1984. *Leisure interests:* volleyball, tennis, jogging, swimming and reading. *Address:* c/o SWAPO Party of Namibia (SWAPO), POB 1071, Windhoek, Namibia.

TOKAYEV, Kassym-Jomart, DPolSci; Kazakhstani diplomatist, politician and fmr UN official; *Chairman (Speaker), Senate;* b. 17 May 1953, Almaty; s. of the late Kemel Tokayev and of Turar Shabarbayeva; m. Nadezhda Tokayeva 1983; one s.; ed Moscow State Inst. of Int. Relations, Beijing Language Inst., People's Repub. of China, Diplomatic Acad., Ministry of Foreign Affairs of USSR, Moscow; joined Ministry of Foreign Affairs of USSR 1975, posted to Soviet Embassy in Singapore 1975–79, Attaché, Third Sec., Ministry of Foreign Affairs 1979–83, Second Sec. of Dept 1984–85, Second, then First Sec., then Counsellor, Soviet Embassy in Beijing 1985–91, Deputy Foreign Minister of Kazakhstan 1992–93, First Deputy Foreign Minister 1993–94, Minister of Foreign Affairs 1994–99, Deputy Prime Minister March–Oct. 1999, Prime Minister of Kazakhstan Oct. 1999–2002 (resgnd), Sec. of State – Minister of Foreign Affairs 2002–07; Chair. (Speaker) of the Senate 2007–11, 2013–; Dir-Gen. UN Office at Geneva (UNOG), UnderSec.-Gen. and Personal Rep. of UN Sec.-Gen. to Conf. on Disarmament 2011–13; also served as Sec.-Gen. Conf. on Disarmament; signed Comprehensive Nuclear-Test-Ban Treaty (CTBT), New York 1996, Treaty on a Nuclear-Weapons-Free Zone in Cen. Asia (CANWFZ), Semipalatinsk 2005; Hon. Prof., Dr of the Diplomatic Acad. and mem. Bd of Trustees, Ministry of Foreign Affairs of Russian Fed.; Hon. Dean of Geneva School of Diplomacy; Parasat (Nat. Award) 1996, Astana Medal, Independence Medal, First Pres. (Nat. Award) 2004, Friendship (Russia) 2004, Yaroslav Mudry (Ukraine) 2007. *Publications:* How it Was... Disturbance in Beijing 1993, United Nations: Half a Century of Serving for Peace 1995, Under the Banner of Independence 1997, Kazakhstani Foreign Policy in the Context of Globalisation 2000, Diplomacy of the Republic of Kazakhstan 2001, Meeting up the Challenge 2003, Light and Shadow – Essays of the Diplomat 2007. *Leisure interests:* reading, playing tennis, listening to modern music. *Address:* Office of the President, Senate (Senat), 010000 Astana, Abay d-ly 33, Parliament House, Kazahkhstan (office). *Telephone:* (7172) 15-33-76 (office). *Fax:* (7172) 33-31-18 (office). *E-mail:* smimazh@ parlam.kz (office). *Website:* www.parlam.kz (office).

TŐKÉS, Very Rev. László; Romanian ecclesiastic; b. 1 April 1952, Cluj/ Kolozsvár; s. of István Tőkés and Erzsébet Vass; m. Edit Joó 1985; two s. one d.; ed Protestant Theological Inst. Cluj; asst minister at Braşov/Brassó, then at Dej/ Dés 1975–84; discharged for political reasons and suspended from church service 1984–86; reinstated as chaplain then pastor, Timişoara/Temesvár 1986–89; banished to small parish of Mineu/Menyő, threatened with eviction; demonstration by supporters was beginning of revolution that overthrew Communist Govt 1989; Oradea Bishop of Királyhágómellék Diocese, Nagyvárad 1990–; MEP 2007–, Vice-Pres. European Parl. 2010–; mem. Temporary Nat. Salvation Council; Co-Chair. Hungarian Reformed Synod of Romania; Pres. Reformed Hungarian World Fed.; Hon. Pres. Hungarian Democratic Alliance of Hungarians in Romania, Hungarian World Fed.; Freeman Cities of Sárospatak amd Székelyudvarhely and of 5th and 11th dists of Budapest; mem. European Senate of Honour 1992, Kt of Johannit Order 1993, Grand Cross of the Order of the Hungarian Repub. 1999; Dr hc (Theological Acad. of Debrecen) 1990, (Regent Univ., Va Beach, USA) 1990, (Hope Coll., Holland, Mich.) 1991; Berzsenyi Prize, Hungary 1989, Roosevelt Prize of The Netherlands 1990, Bethlen Gábor Prize, Hungary 1990, Geuzenpenning Prize, Netherlands 1991, Pro Fide Prize, Finland 1993, Bocskay Prize, Hungary 1995, Hungarian Heritage Prize 1996, Minority Prize of Catalan CIEMEN Centre, Spain 1996, Leopold Kunschak Prize, Austria 1998, Fidelity Prize (Hungary) 1999. *Publications:* Where the Lord's Soul, there Freedom (selections of sermons) 1990, The Siege of Timişoara '89 1990, With God for the People 1990, There is a Time to Speak (with David Porter) 1993, A Phrase – And What is Behind 1993, In the Spirit of Timişoara – Ecumenism and Reconciliation 1996, Hope and Reality – Selected Writings 1999, Timişoara Memento – Self Confessions 1999, Timişoara Siege 1999; sermons, articles in ecclesiastical and secular publs. *Address:* European Parliament, Bât. Altiero Spinelli, 12E217, 60, rue Wiertz, 1047 Brussels, Belgium (office); Str. Craiovei 1, 3700 Oradea, Romania. *Telephone:* (2) 284-58-01 (office). *Fax:* (2) 284-98-01 (office). *E-mail:* laszlo.tokes@europarl.europa.eu (office). *Website:* www.europarl.europa.eu (office).

TOKHI, Hamidullah; Afghan politician; Gov. of Zabul Prov. 2002–03, of Wardak Prov.–Aug. 2003; mem. Hizb-i-Islami party; currently mem. Parl.

TOKIWA, Toshiji; Japanese retail executive; ed Keio Univ.; Dir and Gen. Man., New York Br., Dai-Ichi Kangyo Bank, Ltd 1993–95, Sr Man. Dir Dai-Ichi Kangyo Bank, Ltd 1995–96; Pres. and CEO Chuo Real Estate Co., Ltd. 1996–2000; Chair. AEON Co. Ltd 2000–06, Corp. Adviser 2006–, mem. Bd of Dirs (non-exec.), Vice-Chair. then Chair. Jusco Stores (Hong Kong) Co. Ltd (subsidiary) 2003–06; mem. Bd of Dirs Talbots Inc. (subsidiary) 2000–06. *Address:* c/o AEON Company Ltd, 1-5-1 Nasake, Mihami-ku, Chiba 261-8515, Japan (office).

TOKODY, Ilona; Hungarian soprano; b. 27 April 1953, Szeged; d. of András Tokody and Ilona Nagy; ed Liszt Ferenc Music Acad., Budapest; won Kodály singing competition 1972, Erkel competition of Inter-konzert Agency 1973, Ostend competition operatic category 1976; joined State Opera, Budapest 1976; regular guest performer Staatsoper Wien and Deutsche Oper West-Berlin; appearances in opera houses and concert halls worldwide, including Metropolitan Opera House, Royal Opera House Covent Garden, Vienna State Opera, San Francisco Opera, Teatro Colón, Buenos Aires, Liceo, Barcelona, Bavarian State Opera, San Carlo, Naples, Rome Opera, Bolshoi, Carnegie Hall, New York, Musikverein, Vienna, Royal Opera, Copenhagen; Life Mem., Halhatatlanok Társulata; Franz Liszt Prize 1980, Artist of Merit of Repub. of Hungary Award 1983, Kossuth Prize 1985, Repub. of Hungary Outstanding Artist Award 1990, Bartók-Pásztory Prize 2010, Hazám-díj 2012. *Operatic roles include:* leading roles in La Forza del Destino, Don Carlos, Suor Angelica, Madama Butterfly, Il Trovatore, Aida, La Juive, La Bohème, Manon Lescaut, Nedda in I Pagliacci, Micaela in Carmen, Alice in Falstaff, Giselda in I Lombardi, Desdemona in Otello. *Recordings include:* Suor Angelica, Nerone, La Fiamma, Brahms Requiem, Il Tabarro, Guntram, Iris, Ilona Tokody – Portrait Of The Artist 1995, Beethoven – Symphony No. 9 2000. *Leisure interests:* cooking, badminton, gymnastics, table tennis, reading. *Address:* c/o Hungarian State Opera, Andrássy ut 22, 1062 Budapest, Hungary.

TOKURA, Masakazu; Japanese business executive; *President, Sumitomo Chemical Company Ltd;* ed Univ. of Tokyo; began career at Sumitomo Chemical Co. Ltd 1974, Man. Exec. Officer in charge of Planning and Coordination Office and Quality Assurance Office of IT-related Chemicals Sector 2006–08, Dir and Man. Exec. Officer in charge of IT-related Chemicals Sector 2008–09, Dir and Sr Man. Exec. Officer 2009–11, Pres. Sumitomo Chemical Co. Ltd 2011–. *Address:* Sumitomo Chemical Co. Ltd, 27-1, Shinkawa 2-chome, Chuo-ku, Tokyo 104-8260, Japan (office). *Telephone:* (3) 5543-5102 (office). *Fax:* (3) 5543-5901 (office). *E-mail:* info@sumitomo-chem.co.jp (office). *Website:* www.sumitomo-chem.co.jp (office).

TOKURA, Yoshinori, PhD; Japanese physicist and academic; *Professor, Department of Applied Physics, University of Tokyo;* ed Univ. of Tokyo; Assoc. Prof., Dept of Physics, Univ. of Tokyo 1986–93, Prof. 1994–95, Prof., Dept of Applied Physics 1995–; mem. Physical Soc. of Japan, American Physical Soc., Japan Soc. of Applied Physics; Nishina Memorial Prize 1990, IBM Japan Science Prize 1990, Bernd Matthias Prize 1991, Nissan Science Prize 1998, Asahi Prize 2001, James C. McGroddy Prize for New Materials, American Physical Soc. 2005. *Publications:* more than 500 articles in scientific journals. *Address:* Department of Applied Physics, School of Engineering, University of Tokyo, Hongo 7-3-1, Bunkyo-ku, Tokyo 113-8656, Japan (office). *Telephone:* (3) 5841-6870 (office). *Fax:* (3) 5841-6839 (office). *E-mail:* uchida@cmr.t.u-tokuo.ac.jp (office). *Website:* www.ap.t.u -tokyo.ac.jp (office).

TOLAND, John Francis, PhD, FRS, FRSE; British/Irish mathematician, academic and research institute director; *N.M. Rothschild & Sons Professor of Mathematical Sciences and Director, Issac Newton Institute for Mathematical Sciences, University of Cambridge;* Prof. of Math., Univ. of Bath 1982–2011; Eng and Physical Sciences Research Council Sr Research Fellowship 1997–2002; N.M. Rothschild & Sons Prof. of Math. Sciences and Dir Issac Newton Inst. for Math. Sciences, Univ. of Cambridge 2011–, Fellow of St John's Coll.; Scientific Dir Int. Centre for Math. Sciences 2002–10; Pres. London Math. Soc. 2005–07; Chair. Math. Sciences panel for Research Excellence Framework by Higher Educ. Funding Council for England 2010–; mem. Exec. Cttee, Int. Math. Union; Hon. Fellow, Univ. Coll. London 2008; Hon. DSc (Queen's University Belfast) 2000, (Edinburgh) 2007, (Heriot-Watt) 2007, (Essex) 2009; Senior Berwick Prize, London Math. Soc. 2000, Sylvester Medal, Royal Soc. 2012. *Publications:* numerous papers in professional journals. *Address:* Issac Newton Institute for Mathematical Sciences, 20 Clarkson Road, Cambridge, CB3 0EH, England (office). *Telephone:* (1223) 335980 (office), (1223) 335982 (Sec.) (office); (1223) 765235 (St John's Coll., evenings). *Fax:* (1223) 330508 (office). *E-mail:* jft26@newton.ac.uk (office). *Website:* www.newton.ac.uk (office).

TOLEDANO, Sidney; French fashion industry executive; *CEO, Christian Dior SA;* b. 25 July 1951, Casablanca, Morocco; s. of Boris Toledano, fmr industrial and Pres. of the Jewish community in Casablanca, and Ines Benezra; m. Katia Assous 1981; one s. two d.; ed École Centrale Paris; began career as researcher and marketing consultant, A.C. Nielsen, spent some time in Brazil; moved to Kickers; joined Lancel (handbag mfr) 1983–93; joined Christian Dior SA 1993, Pres. 1998–2003, CEO 2003–, also responsible for overseeing strategy at Fendi, also currently Pres. and CEO Christian Dior Couture, Acting Pres. Galliano 2006, Man. Christian Dior GmbH (Germany), Christian Dior Espanola (Spain), Christian Dior Puerto Banus (Spain), Christian Dior Couture Maroc (Morocco), Calto, Srl (Italy), Gen. Dir Christian Dior Couture RUS (Russia), Christian Dior Couture Stoleshnikov (Russia), Christian Dior Couture S.de RL de CV (Mexico), Chair. Fendi France, Bopel (Italy), Christian Dior Inc. (USA), Christian Dior Italia S.r.l. (Italy), Christian Dior Saipan, Les Jardins d'Avron LLC (USA), Mardi SpA (Italy), Lucilla S.r.l. (Italy), Sole Dir Christian Dior Puerto Banus (Spain), John Galliano, SA (France), Christian Dior Australia Pty Ltd, Christian Dior Couture Korea, Christian Dior Guam Ltd, Christian Dior Far East Ltd (China), Christian Dior Fashion (Malaysia) Sdn Bhd (Malaysia), Christian Dior Hong Kong Ltd, Christian Dior KK (Japan), Christian Dior New Zealand, Christian Dior Singapore Pte, Christian Dior Taiwan Ltd, Christian Dior UK Ltd, Fendi Adele S.r.l. (Italy), Fendi International BV, Fendi Industria S.r.l., Fendi Italie S.r.l., Fendi SA (Luxembourg), Fendi S.r.l.; mem. Exec. Cttee Chambre Syndicale de Haute Couture; Dir Comité Colbert, French Inst. of Fashion; Pres. Cercle Saint-Roch; Chevalier, Légion d'honneur 2005. *Address:* Christian Dior SA, 30 avenue Montaigne, 75008 Paris, France (office). *Telephone:* 1-44-13-24-98 (office). *Fax:* 1-44-13-27-86 (office). *E-mail:* info@dior.com (office). *Website:* www.dior.com (office).

TOLEDO, Francisco; Mexican artist; b. 17 July 1940, Juchitán, Oaxaca; two s. three d.; first solo exhbn Mexico City 1959; travelled to Paris to work at Cite Universitaire 1960, returned to Mexico 1965; worked at Casa de la Cultura, Juchitán and Inst. de Artes Gráficas, Oaxaca; associated with Museo de Arte Contemporaneo de Oaxaca, Jorge Luis Borges Library for the Blind, Cine El Pochote, Centro Cultural de Santo Domingo. *Website:* www.franciscotoledo.net.

TOLEDO MANRIQUE, Alejandro ('Cholo'), PhD; Peruvian economist, international organization official and fmr politician; *President, Global Center for Development and Democracy;* b. 28 March 1946, Cabana, Ancash Prov.; m. Eliane Karp; ed Univs of Stanford and San Francisco, USA; fmr mem. staff World Bank; adviser to UN, World Bank, IDB, ILO and OECD; Research Fellow, Inst. for Int. Devt, Harvard Univ., 1991–94; Perm. Prof. of ESAN, Univ. Lima; Visiting Prof., Univ. of Waseda and Japan Foundation, Tokyo; Founder-mem. and Leader Perú Posible party (opposition alliance); presidential cand. 2000, subsequently boycotted election; Pres. of Peru 2001–06; Distinguished Scholar in Residence, Center for Advanced Study in the Behavioral Sciences, Stanford Univ. 2006–08, Payne Distinguished Visiting Lecturer, Freeman Spogli Inst. for Int. Studies 2007–08, also Visiting Scholar, Center on Democracy, Devt and the Rule of Law; Founder and Pres. Global Center for Devt and Democracy; currently Distinguished Visiting Scholar, School of Advanced Int. Studies, Johns Hopkins Univ., Washington, DC; also Non-Resident Sr Fellow in Foreign Policy and Global Economy and Devt, Brookings Inst. *Publications:* Las Cartas sobre la Mesa, Social Inversion for Growth, Economic Structural Reforms, Peru's Challenge: The Transition to Sustained Economic Growth; and several books on econs and devt. *Address:* Global Center for Development and Democracy, 505 9th Street, NW, Suite 1000, Washington, DC 20004, USA; Global Center for Development and Democracy, Av. De la Aviación 545 Miraflores, Lima, Peru; Perú Posible, Bajada Balta 131, Miraflores, Lima. *Telephone:* (202) 776-7801. *E-mail:* contacto@cgdd.org. *Website:* www.cgdd.org.

TOLENTINO ARAÚJO, Jorge Homero; Cape Verde politician and diplomatist; *Minister of National Defence;* Minister in Assistance to Prime Minister's Office and Minister of Culture and Sports 2003–04; Amb. to Germany (also accred to Finland and Poland) 2008–10, to Spain 2010; Minister of Nat. Defence 2011–. *Address:* Ministry of National Defence, Praia, Santiago, Cape Verde (office).

TOLGFORS, Sten, BSc; Swedish politician; b. 17 July 1966, Forshaga; ed Karlberg Upper Secondary School, Oakcrest High School, USA, Örebro Univ., Amål; mem. Örebro City Ass. 1991–94; Special Adviser, Ministry of Defence 1992–93, Ministry of Industry and Commerce 1992–94; mem. Nat. Bd Moderate Party Youth Org. 1990–95, Nat. Exec. 2002–, Spokesperson for Social Insurance 2002–03, Spokesperson for Educ. 2003–06; mem. Riksdag (Parl.) 1994–, Alt. mem. Cttee on Educ. 1994–2002, Cttee on Foreign Affairs 1994–98, Cttee on Industry and Trade 1998–2002, Del. to OSCE Parl. Ass. 1998–2002; mem. Del. to Nordic Council 1998–2002, Cttee on Foreign Affairs 1998–2002, Cttee on Social Insurance 2002–03, Cttee on Educ. 2003–06, Advisory Council on Foreign Affairs 2006; Minister for Trade 2006–07, for Defence 2007–12 (resgnd). *Address:* c/o Ministry of Defence, Jakobsgatan 9, 103 33 Stockholm, Sweden.

TOLLETT, Leland E.; American business executive; joined Tyson Foods Inc. 1959, mem. Bd of Dirs 1984–2008, Pres. and CEO 1991–98, Chair. 1995–98, Consultant 1998–, Interim Pres. and CEO Jan.–Nov. 2009; mem. Bd of Dirs Worthen Banking Corpn 1988–, JB Hunt Transport Services Inc. (fmrly Hunt J B Transport Services Inc.) 2001–. *Address:* Tyson Foods Inc., 2200 Don Tyson Parkway, Springdale, AR 72762-6999, USA (office). *Telephone:* (479) 290-4000 (office). *Fax:* (479) 290-4061 (office). *E-mail:* info@tysonfoodsinc.com (office). *Website:* www.tysonfoodsinc.com (office).

TOLLI, Abbas Mahamat; Chadian politician; Sec. of State –2005; Minister of Finance and Information Tech. 2005–08, Minister of Infrastructure and Equipment 2011; Sec.-Gen. Banque des Etats de l'Afrique centrale 2008–10. *Address:* c/o Ministry of Infrastructure and Equipment, N'Djamena, Chad (office).

TOLNAY, Lajos, PhD; Hungarian business executive; *Chairman, MAL Company Ltd;* b. 27 Sept. 1948, Sajószentpéter; m.; four c.; ed Heavy Industries Tech. Univ., Miskolc and Budapest Univ. of Econs; various positions DIMAG Co. Ltd 1971–92, Gen. Dir 1989–92; Man. Dir Dunaferr Trading House Ltd 1992–93; Pres.-Man. Dir PTW Investment Co. Ltd 1993–95; Man. Dir Rákóczi Bank 1994, Pres. 1994–; Pres. Hungarian Chamber of Commerce 1990–93, Hungarian Chamber of Commerce and Industry 1994; Man. Dir Inota Aluminium Co. Ltd 1996–; Chair. Bd Magyar Aluminium Ltd (now MAL Co. Ltd) 1997–; Chair. Controlling Cttee Életút First Nat. Pension Fund; Chair. NAT Hungarian Accreditation Bd; mem. Exec. Bd ICC, Hon. Chair. ICC Hungary; mem. Supervisory Bd Hungexpo Co. Ltd, Bankár Investment Co. Ltd; various awards and decorations. *Address:* MAL Co. Ltd, Termelő és Kereskedelmi Rt., 1012 Budapest, Hungary (office). *E-mail:* mal@mal .hu (office). *Website:* www.mal.hu (office).

TOLSTAYA, Tatyana Nikitichna; Russian writer; b. 3 May 1951, Leningrad (now St Petersburg); d. of Mikhail Lozinsky; great-grandniece of Leo Tolstoy and granddaughter of Alexei Tolstoy; m. Andrey V. Lebedev; two s.; ed Univ. of Leningrad; Ed. of Eastern Literature Nauka Publishing, Moscow 1987–89; fmr Assoc. Prof. of English, Skidmore Coll., NJ, USA; co-host The School for Scandal TV interview show (Telekanal Kultura); Triumph Prize 2001. *Publications:* On the Golden Porch (short story) 1983, Sleepwalker in a Fog 1992, Night 1995, Day 1997, Kys 1998, Two of Them 2001, The Slynx 2007, White Walls 2007. *Address:* c/o Telekanal Kultura (Television Channel Culture), 123995 Moscow, ul. M. Nikitskaya 24, Russia (office). *Telephone:* (495) 780-56-01 (office). *E-mail:* web@ tv-culture.ru (office). *Website:* www.tvkultura.ru (office).

TOMALIA, Donald A., BA, PhD; American chemist, entrepreneur and academic; *Distinguished Professor and Research Scientist, Department of Chemistry and Director of the National Dendrimer and Nanotechnology Center, Central Michigan University;* b. 1938; ed Univ. of Michigan, Michigan State Univ.; worked for many years at Dow Chemical Co.; co-f. Dendritech, Inc. (first commercial producer of dendrimers) 1992, Founding Pres. and Chief Scientist 1992–2000; Vice-Pres. of Tech., MMI 1998–2000; Scientific Dir for the Biologic Nanotechnology Center, Univ. of Michigan Medical School 1998–2000; f. Dendritic Nanotechnologies, Inc. (DNT), Mount Pleasant, Mich. (jt venture with Starpharma Pooled Development,

Melbourne, Australia) 2002, DNT Prin. Investigator in MIT/Inst. for Soldier Nanotechnologies (MIT/ISN) 2003; currently Distinguished Prof. and Research Scientist, Dept of Chem. and Dir Nat. Dendrimer Center, Cen. Michigan Univ., Mount Pleasant; F1000 Faculty mem. 2005–; Dr hc (Cen. Michigan Univ.) 2002; IR-100 Award 1978, 1986, 1991, Leonardo da Vinci Award (France) 1996, Award for Outstanding Achievement in Polymer Science and Tech., Soc. of Polymer Science (Japan) 2002, Dow/Karabatsos and Distinguished Alumni Lectureship Award 2005, Frost & Sullivan Innovation of the Year Award (Nanomaterials for Advanced Medical Applications Tech.) 2005, Chevron Lectureship, Texas A&M, College Station, Tex. 2009. *Achievements include:* discovered dendrimers (dentritic architecture) 1979, jtly invented and developed dendritic polymers. *Publications:* Dendrimers and Other Dendritic Polymers; more than 200 peer-reviewed publs and more than 110 US patents. *Address:* National Dendrimer and Nanotechnology Center, Central Michigan University, 2625 Denison Drive, Mount Pleasant, MI 48859, USA (office). *Telephone:* (989) 774-2424 (office). *E-mail:* cartmkt@cmich.edu (office). *Website:* www.dendrimercenter.org (office); www.cst.cmich.edu/chemistry (office).

TOMALIN, Claire, MA, FRSL; British writer; b. 20 June 1933, London; d. of Emile Delavenay and Muriel Emily Herbert; m. 1st Nicholas Osborne Tomalin 1955 (died 1973); two s. three d. (one d. and one s. deceased); m. 2nd Michael Frayn (q.v.) 1993; ed Hitchin Girls' Grammar School, Dartington Hall School, Newnham Coll., Cambridge; publr's reader and Ed. 1955–67; Asst Literary Ed. New Statesman 1968–70, Literary Ed. 1974–77; Literary Ed. Sunday Times 1979–86; Vice-Pres. English PEN 1997, Royal Literary Fund 2000; mem. London Library Cttee 1997–2000, Advisory Cttee for the Arts, Humanities and Social Sciences, British Library 1997–2000, Council RSL 1997–2000; Trustee, Nat. Portrait Gallery 1992–2002, Wordsworth Trust 2004; Hon. mem. Magdalene Coll. Cambridge 2003, Hon. Fellow, Lucy Cavendish Coll. Cambridge 2003, Newnham Coll. Cambridge 2003; Hon. DLitt (East Anglia) 2005, (Birmingham) 2005, (Greenwich) 2006, (Cambridge) 2007, (Open Univ.) 2008, (Goldsmiths Coll.) 2009, (Roehampton) 2010, (Portsmouth) 2012; Whitbread Prize 1974, James Tait Black Prize 1990, NCR Book Award 1991, Hawthornden Prize 1991, Samuel Pepys Award 2003, Rose Mary Crawshay Prize 2003. *Plays include:* The Winter Wife 1991. *Publications include:* The Life and Death of Mary Wollstonecraft 1974, Shelley and his World 1980, Katherine Mansfield: A Secret Life 1987, The Invisible Woman 1990, The Winter Wife 1991, Mrs Jordan's Profession 1994, Jane Austen: A Life 1997, Maurice by Mary Shelley (ed.) 1998, Several Strangers: Writing from Three Decades 1999, Samuel Pepys: The Unequalled Self (Whitbread Awards for Book of the Year and Best Biog.) 2002, Thomas Hardy: The Time-Torn Man 2006, Selected Poems of Thomas Hardy 2006, Charles Dickens (Galaxy Nat. Book Award for Biography of the Year) 2011. *Leisure interests:* music, gardening, walking. *Address:* c/o David Godwin, David Godwin Associates, 55 Monmouth Street, London, WC2H 9DG, England (office). *Telephone:* (20) 7240-9992 (office). *Fax:* (20) 7395-6110 (office). *E-mail:* david@davidgodwinassociates.co.uk (office). *Website:* www.davidgodwinassociates.co.uk (office); www.clairetomalin.co.uk.

TÓMASDÓTTIR, Halla, BBA, MBA; Icelandic business executive; *Co-Founder and Executive Chairman, Auður Capital;* early career in USA working with M&M/ Mars, later Human Resources Dept, Pepsi Cola; spent six years at Reykjavík Univ. as Asst Prof., also Dir for Exec. Educ. and Female Entrepreneurship; Man. Dir Iceland Chamber of Commerce –2007; Co-founder Auður Capital (financial services co.) 2007, currently Exec. Chair.; Co-founder Sisters Capital (sustainable investment co.) 2012; Chair. Veritas Capital (sales and marketing co. in pharmaceutical and medical device sector), TAL (mobile communication co.); Vice-Chair. Olgerdin; fmr mem. Bd of Dirs of several orgs including Icelandic Stock Exchange, Sjóvá, Vistor, Calidris; Cartier Women's Initiative Award 2009. *Leisure interest:* fly fishing. *Address:* Auður Capital, Borgartún 29, 105 Reykjavík, Iceland (office). *Telephone:* 585-6500 (office). *Fax:* 585-6515 (office). *E-mail:* audur@audur .is (office). *Website:* www.audurcapital.is (office).

TOMBINI, Alexandre Antonio, PhD; Brazilian economist and central banker; *President, Banco Central do Brasil;* b. 9 Dec. 1963, Porto Alegre; ed Univ. de Brasília, Univ. of Illinois, USA; Gen. Coordinator for Int. Affairs, Econ. Policy Secretariat, Ministry of Finance 1991–92, Gen. Coordinator for External Affairs 1992–95; Sr Adviser, Foreign Trade Bd, Office of Chief of Staff of Pres. of Brazil 1995–98; Adviser to Bd, Banco Central do Brasil 1998–99, Head, Dept of Studies and Research 1999–2001, Deputy Gov. for Financial System Regulation and Org. 2006–10, Pres. Banco Central do Brasil 2011–; Sr Adviser to Exec. Dir and mem. Exec. Bd Brazilian Office, IMF, Washington, DC 2001–05; Visiting Prof., Univ. de Brasília 1993–94. *Address:* Banco Central do Brasil, SBS, Quadra 03, Mezanino 01, Bloco B, 70074-900, Brasília DF, Brazil (office). *Telephone:* (61) 3414-1414 (office). *Fax:* (61) 3223-1033 (office). *E-mail:* secre.surel@bcb.gov.br (office). *Website:* www.bcb.gov.br (office).

TOMBLIN, Earl Ray, BS, MBA; American politician and state governor; *Governor of West Virginia;* b. 15 March 1952, Logan Co.; s. of Earl Tomblin and Freda M. Tomblin (née Jarrell); m. Joanne Jaeger 1979; one s.; ed Univ. of West Virginia, Marshall Univ., Univ. of Charleston; self-employed business exec. and fmr school teacher; mem. W Va House of Dels 1974–80, W Va Senate 1980–2011, Senate Pres. 1995–2011; Lt-Gov. of W Va 2000–10, Acting Gov. of West Virginia 2010–11, Gov. of West Virginia 2011–; Vice-Chair. Nat. Council of State Govts 2004, Chair. 2005; Democrat; Dr hc (South West Virginia Community and Tech. Coll.); Nat. Bulger Award for Legislative Leadership 2009. *Address:* Office of the Governor, State Capitol, 1900 Kanawha Boulevard East, Charleston, WV 25305, USA (office). *Telephone:* (304) 558-2000 (office). *Fax:* (304) 342-7025 (office). *Website:* www.governor.wv.gov (office).

TOMBRELLO, Thomas Anthony, Jr, BA, MA, PhD; American physicist and academic; *William R. Kenan, Jr Professor of Physics, California Institute of Technology;* b. 20 Sept. 1936, Austin, Tex.; s. of the late Thomas A. Tombrello and Jeanette M. Tombrello; m. Stephanie Merton Tombrello; one s. three d. (one deceased); ed Rice Univ., Houston, Tex.; joined Physics Dept, Calif. Inst. of Tech. (Caltech) 1961, Prof. of Physics 1971–, William R. Kenan Jr Prof. of Physics 1997–, Tech. Assessment Officer 1996–, and Chair., Div. of Physics, Math. and Astronomy 1998–2008; fmr Faculty mem., Yale Univ.; Vice-Pres. and Dir of Research, Schlumberger-Doll Research 1987–89; fmr mem. Vice-Pres.'s Space Policy Advisory Bd; mem. US Nuclear Physics Del. to People's Repub. of China; mem. NAS

Panel on Future of Nuclear Science; Assoc. Ed. Nuclear Science Applications; fmr Assoc. Ed. Radiation Effects; mem. Visiting Cttees, Lawrence Livermore Nat. Lab.; mem. Scientific Advisory Bd Rice Univ. Center for Nanoscience and Tech.; Consultant, Applied Minds Inc., Arrowhead Research, Trillience Research, Form Factor Inc., Schlumberger Ltd, Glenair Inc.; Distinguished Alumnus, Rice Univ. 1998; Hon. PhD (Uppsala) 1997; Von Humboldt Award 1983, Richard P. Feynman Prize for Excellence in Teaching 1994. *Address:* Department of Physics, California Institute of Technology, 201 Sloan Annex, Pasadena, CA 91125, USA (office). *Telephone:* (626) 395-4581 (office). *Fax:* (626) 577-8442 (office). *E-mail:* tat@caltech .edu (office). *Website:* www.pma.caltech.edu/GSR/tombrello.html (office).

TOMBS, Baron (Life Peer), cr. 1990, of Brailes in the County of Warwickshire; **Francis Leonard Tombs,** Kt, BSc, LLD, DSc, FREng; British engineer; b. 17 May 1924, Walsall, West Midlands, England; s. of Joseph Tombs and Jane Tombs; m. Marjorie Evans 1949 (died 2008); three d.; ed Elmore Green School, Walsall, Birmingham Coll. of Tech.; with British Electricity Authority 1948–57; Gen. Man., Gen. Electric Co. Ltd 1958–67; Dir and Gen. Man. James Howden and Co. 1967–68; Dir of Eng, South of Scotland Electricity Bd 1969–73, Deputy Chair. 1973–74, Chair. 1974–77; Chair. Electricity Council for England and Wales 1977–80; Dir N.M. Rothschild & Sons Ltd 1981–94; Chair. The Weir Group Ltd 1981–83; Chair. T&N PLC 1982–89; Dir Rolls-Royce Ltd 1982–92, Chair. 1985–92; Chair. Old Mutual SA Fund 1994–99; Dir Shell (UK) Ltd 1983–94; Chancellor Univ. of Strathclyde 1991–97; Chair. Eng Council 1985–88; Hon. FICE; Hon. FIMechE; Hon. FIChemE; Hon. FIEE (and fmr Pres.); Hon. FRSE 1996; Papal Knighthood of the Order of St Gregory 2002; Hon. DSc (Aston) 1979, (Lodz, Poland) 1980, (Cranfield Inst. of Tech.) 1985, (City Univ., London) 1986, (Bradford) 1986, (Queen's Univ., Belfast) 1988, (Surrey) 1988, (Nottingham) 1989, (Cambridge) 1990, (Warwick) 1990; Hon. DUniv (Strathclyde) 1991; Hon. DTech (Loughborough) 1979; Dr hc (CNAA) 1988. *Publications:* Nuclear Energy Past, Present and Future—Electronics and Power 1981, Reversing the Decline in Manufacturing Industry (Mountbatten Lecture 1993), Power Politics 2010. *Leisure interest:* music. *Address:* Honington Lodge, Honington, Shipston on Stour, Warwicks., CV36 5AA, England (home). *E-mail:* tombsf@parliament.uk (office). *Website:* www.parliament .uk/biographies/lords/lord-tombs/27057 (office).

TOMÉ, Carol B., BA, MBA; American business executive; *Executive Vice-President, Corporate Services and Chief Financial Officer, Home Depot, Inc.;* b. Wyo.; ed Univ. of Wyoming, Univ. of Denver, Colo; began career as commercial lender with United Bank of Denver (now Wells Fargo); spent several years as Dir of Banking for Johns-Manville Corpn; Vice-Pres. and Treas. Riverwood Int. Corpn –1995; joined Home Depot, Inc., Atlanta, Ga in 1995, Chief Financial Officer 2001–, Exec. Vice-Pres. of Corp. Services 2007–; mem. Bd of Dirs United Parcel Service (UPS), Chair. Audit Cttee) 2003–, Fed. Reserve Bank of Atlanta 2008– (currently Chair.), High Museum of Art, Atlanta Botanical Garden; Chair. Advisory Bd Metropolitan Atlanta Arts Fund, The Metropolitan Atlanta Chamber of Commerce 2012–; mem. The Committee of 200; named by The Wall Street Journal as one of 50 Women to Watch 2007, ranked by Forbes magazine amongst 100 Most Powerful Women (16th) 2008, Lettie Pate Whitehead Evans Award, BDN Network 2009, CFO of the Year Award, CFO Roundtable 2009, Distinguished Alumna Award, Univ. of Wyoming 2011, ranked by The Wall Street Journal as No. 2 on its list of the best Chief Financial Officers in corporate America 2012, ranked by Fortune magazine amongst the 50 Most Powerful Women in Business in the US (44th) 2012. *Address:* Home Depot Inc., 2455 Paces Ferry Road NW, Atlanta, GA 30339, USA (office). *Telephone:* (770) 433-8211 (office). *Fax:* (770) 384-2805 (office). *E-mail:* info@homedepot.com (office). *Website:* www.homedepot.com (office).

TOMEING, Litokwa; Marshall Islands politician and fmr head of state; b. 1939, Ratak Chain; m.; seven c.; traditional tribal chief; Mayor, Wotje Atoll 1965–69; apptd Minister for Ratak 1997; mem. Nitijela (Parl.) for Wotje Atoll 1969–, Vice-Speaker 1992–95, Speaker 2000–07; fmr mem. United Democratic Party, mem. United People's Party 2007–; Pres. Marshall Islands 2008–09. *Address:* c/o Office of the President, Government of the Republic of the Marshall Islands, POB 2, Majuro MH 96960, Marshall Islands.

TOMESCU, Constantina; Romanian athlete; b. (Constantina Diță), 23 Jan. 1970, Turburea, Gorj Co.; m. Valeriu Tomescu (her coach); long-distance runner, specializes mainly in half marathon and marathon; competed at World Half Marathon Championships, Palermo 1999; finished 10th in marathon at World Championships, Edmonton 2001; finished seventh in 10,000m at European Championships Munich 2002; finished fifth at World Half Marathon Championships, Vilamoura, Portugal 2003, third at World Half Marathon Championships, New Delhi 2004; won Chicago Marathon 2004 (personal best time of 2:21:30); Bronze Medal, marathon, World Championships, Helsinki 2005; won women's half marathon at World Half Marathon Championships, Edmonton 2005; finished second in 20km at World Road Running Championships, Debrecen, Hungary 2006; finished third in London Marathon 2007; Gold Medal, women's marathon, Olympic Games, Beijing 2008 (time of 2:26:44, oldest Olympic marathon champion in history). *Address:* c/o Federatia Romana de Atletism, 2 dr. Primo Nebiolo, 71323 Bucharest, Romania. *Telephone:* (21) 2232229. *Fax:* (21) 2232227. *E-mail:* fra.teh@ ew.ro. *Website:* www.fra.ro.

TOMIĆ, Dragan; Serbian engineer, business executive and politician; b. 9 Dec. 1935, G. Bukovica; s. of Boško Tomić and Mitra Tomić; m. Milica Tomić 1964; two d.; ed Univ. of Belgrade; held various positions at Rekord Rubber Works, Rakovica 1962–86, Gen. Dir 1986; Pres. Eng Soc. of Yugoslavia; Gen. Dir NIS–Jugopetrol Co.; Chair. Man. Bd RTV Politika Co. 1993–; mem. Nat. Parl. (Skupština) of Serbia 1994–97, Speaker 1997–2001, Acting Pres. of Serbia July–Dec. 1997; Chair. Union of Yugoslav Engineers and Technicians 1993–. *Leisure interests:* chess, walking with his dog.

TOMITA, Tetsuro; Japanese business executive; *President and CEO, East Japan Railway Company;* has held numerous exec. positions at East Japan Railway Co., including, Head of Corp. Planning HQ and Head of Health and Welfare Dept, Chief Financial Officer and Man. Dir, Head of Personnel Dept and Head of Finance Dept, Exec. Vice-Pres. Corp. Planning HQ 2008–12, Exec. Dir, Pres. and CEO 2012–. *Address:* East Japan Railway Company, 2-2-2 Yoyogi, Shibuya-ku, Tokyo 151-8578, Japan (office). *Telephone:* (3) 5334-1150 (office). *Fax:* (3) 5334-1110 (office). *E-mail:* info@jreast.co.jp (office). *Website:* www.jreast.co.jp (office).

TOMIZAWA, Ryuichi, LLB; Japanese chemical industry executive; *Senior Advisor, Mitsubishi Chemical Holdings Corporation;* b. Tokyo; m.; two s.; ed Tokyo Univ. Faculty of Law; began career with Mitsubishi Chemical Corpn (MCC), assignments in Malaysia 1990–92, Germany 1992–95, involved in cr. of Mitsubishi Tokyo Pharmaceuticals, various positions including Gen. Man., Dir, Exec. Vice-Pres. Mitsubishi Pharma Corpn –2002, Pres. and CEO Mitsubishi Chemical Holdings Corpn 2002–07, mem. Bd of Dirs and Chair. 2007–12, Sr Advisor 2012–; Exec. Dir, Taiyo Nippon Sanso Corpn; Outside Dir, Tokyo Gas Co. Ltd 2011–; Dir, Chi Mei Corpn. *Leisure interest:* golf. *Address:* Mitsubishi Chemical Holdings Corporation, 14-1 Shiba 4-chome, Minato-ku, Tokyo 108-0014, Japan (office). *Telephone:* (3) 6414-4870 (office). *Fax:* (3) 6414-3745 (office). *E-mail:* info@ mitsubishichem-hd.co.jp (office). *Website:* www.mitsubishichem-hd.co.jp (office).

TOMKA, Peter, LLM, PhD; Slovak diplomatist, lawyer, arbitrator and judge; *Judge and President, International Court of Justice;* b. 1 June 1956, Banska Bystrica; s. of Ján Tomka and Kornélia Tomková; m. Zuzana Halgasová 1990; one s. one d.; ed Faculty of Law, Charles Univ., Prague, Faculty of Int. Law and Int. Relations, Ukraine, Law Inst. of Peace and Devt, France, Inst. of Int. Public Law and Int. Relations, Greece, Hague Acad. of Int. Law; Asst, Faculty of Law, Charles Univ., Prague 1980–84, Lecturer 1985–86, Adjunct Lecturer 1986–91; Asst Legal Adviser, Ministry of Foreign Affairs, Czechoslovakia 1986–90, Head of Public Int. Law Div. 1990–91; Counsellor and Legal Adviser, Czechoslovakian Mission to the UN 1991–92; Deputy Perm. Rep. of Slovakia to the UN 1993–97, Perm. Rep. 1999–2003; Agent of Slovakia before the Int. Court of Justice (ICJ) 1993–2003, Judge, ICJ 2003–, Vice-Pres. 2009–12, Pres. 2012–; Legal Adviser to Slovak Ministry of Foreign Affairs 1997–99; Chair. UN Legal Cttee 1997, Cttee of Advisers on Public Int. Law, Council of Europe 2001–02; mem. Perm. Court of Arbitration, The Hague 1994–, UN Int. Law Comm. 1999–2003, American Soc. of Int. Law 2000–, European Soc. of Int. Law 2004–; Arbitrator in the Iron Rhine case (Belgium/Netherlands) 2003–05, in Kishenganga Court of Arbitration (Pakistan versus India) 2010–, in Annex VII to the UN Convention on the Law of the Sea 2004–, and in Int. Centre for Settlement of Investment Disputes 2005–; mem. Bd of Eds Právník (The Lawyer) 1990–91; Assoc. mem. Inst. of Int. Law 2011; mem. Curatorium of the Hague Acad. of Int. Law 2013–; Hon. Pres. Slovak Soc. of Int. Law 2003–; Hon. Bencher of the Middle Temple 2013. *Publications:* numerous articles in professional journals. *Address:* International Court of Justice, Peace Palace, Carnegieplein 2, 2517 KJ The Hague, Netherlands (office). *Telephone:* (70) 302-23-23 (office). *Fax:* (70) 302-24-20 (office). *E-mail:* p.tomka@icj-cij.org (office). *Website:* www.icj-cij.org (office).

TOMKO, HE Cardinal Jozef, DTheol, DrIur, DScS; Slovak ecclesiastic; *President Emeritus of the Pontifical Committee, International Eucharistic Congresses;* b. 11 March 1924, Udavské, Humenné; s. of Andrej Tomko and Anna Tomko; ordained priest 1949; consecrated Bishop (Titular See of Doclea) 1979; cr. Cardinal (Cardinal-Deacon of Gesù Buon Pastore alla Montagnola) 1985, (Cardinal-Priest of S. Sabina) 1996; Sec.-Gen. of Synod of Bishops 1979–85; mem. Comm. for Admin. of State of Vatican 1985–2004; Prefect of the Congregation for the Evangelization of Peoples 1985–2001; Adviser, Sec. of Vatican State 1996–2004; Pres. Pontifical Cttee for Int. Eucharistic Congresses (retd) 2001–07, now Emer.; numerous missions world-wide; Gran Cruz de la Orden del Libertador San Martín (Argentina) 1989, Order of the White Double Cross, First Class (Slovak Repub.) 1995; Prize of Grand Duchy of Luxembourg 1988. *Publications include:* Light of Nations 1972, Christianity and the World 1974, Christ Yesterday and Today 1976, Ecumenism 1977, Sinodo dei Vescori 1985, La Missione verso il terzo millennio 1998, On Missionary Roads (trans. as Sulle strade della Missione 2008) 2006. *Address:* 00120 Città del Vaticano (office); Via della Conciliazione 44, 00193 Rome, Italy (home). *Telephone:* (06) 698-824-24 (home). *E-mail:* jozef.tomko@tin.it (home).

TOMKYS, Sir (William) Roger, Kt, KCMG, DL, MA; British diplomatist and academic; b. 15 March 1937, Bradford, W Yorks.; s. of Arthur Tomkys and Edith Tomkys; m. Margaret Abbey 1963; one s. one d.; ed Bradford Grammar School and Balliol Coll., Oxford; entered HM Diplomatic Service 1960, served in Amman, Benghazi, Athens, Rome, Amb. to Bahrain 1981–84, to Syria 1984–86, Asst Under-Sec., later Deputy Under-Sec. of State, FCO 1986–90, High Commr in Kenya 1990–92; Master of Pembroke Coll., Cambridge 1992–2004, Chair. Arab-British Chamber of Commerce 2004–10; Commendatore dell'Ordine al Merito 1980, Order of Bahrain First Class 1984. *Leisure interests:* travel, books, golf, shooting. *Address:* Croydon House Farm, Lower Road, Croydon, Royston, Cambs., SG8 0EF, England (home). *Telephone:* (1223) 207343 (home). *Fax:* (1223) 207339 (home). *E-mail:* r.tomkys@btinternet.com (home).

TOMLINSON, Sir John Rowland, CBE; British singer (bass); b. 22 Sept. 1946, Accrington, Lancs.; s. of Rowland Tomlinson and Ellen Greenwood; m. Moya Joel 1969; one s. two d.; ed Accrington Grammar School, Manchester Univ. and Royal Manchester Coll. of Music; debut at Glyndebourne Festival 1972, ENO 1974, Royal Opera House, Covent Garden 1976; since then has appeared in many operas throughout Europe and N America, including Parsifal, Tristan und Isolde and Lohengrin; has sung role of Wotan/Wanderer in The Ring Cycle, Bayreuth Festival 1988–98; other significant roles include Boris in Boris Godunov, ENO (Manchester) 1982, Don Basilio in Il Barbiere di Siviglia, Covent Garden 1985, Moses, ENO 1980, Fiesco in Simon Boccanegra, ENO 1988, Mephistopheles in Damnation of Faust, Santiago, Chile 1990, Attila, Opera North 1990, Filippo II in Don Carlos, Opera North 1992, König Marke in Tristan and Isolde, Bayreuth Festival 1993, Mephistopheles in Damnation of Faust, La Fenice, Venice 1993, Claggart in Billy Budd, Covent Garden 1994, Hans Sachs in Die Meistersinger, Berlin Staatsoper 1995, Kingfisher in Midsummer Marriage, Covent Garden 1996, Bluebeard in Bluebeard's Castle, Berlin Philharmonic 1996, Four Villains in Tales of Hoffmann, ENO 1998, Moses in Moses and Aaron, New York Metropolitan Opera 1999, Golaud in Pelléas et Mélisande, Glyndebourne 1999, Mephistopheles in Damnation of Faust, Munich Staatsoper 2000, Hagen in Götterdämmerung, Bayreuth 2000, Baron Ochs in Rosenkavalier, Staatsoper Dresden 2000, Borromeo in Palestrina, Covent Garden 2001, Gurnemanz in Parsifal, New York Metropolitan 2001; numerous broadcasts, recordings, opera videos and concert performances; Hon. FRNCM; Hon. DMus (Sussex) 1997, (Manchester) 1998; Singer of the Year, Royal Philharmonic Soc. 1991, 1998, 2008, Evening Standard Opera Award 1998, Soc. of London Theatre's Special Award, Olivier Awards 2007. *Address:* Music

International, 13 Ardilaun Road, Highbury, London, N5 2QR, England (office). *Telephone:* (20) 7359-5183 (office).

TOMLINSON, Lindsay Peter, OBE, MA, FIA; British financial executive; *Vice Chairman, Europe, Barclays Global Investors Ltd.;* b. 7 Oct. 1951, Derby; s. of P. Tomlinson and J. M. Tomlinson; m. Sarah Caroline Anne Martin 1973; four s. one d.; ed Clifton Coll., St John's Coll., Cambridge; actuarial student Commercial Union Assurance Co. 1973–77; sr pensions consultant Metropolitan Pensions Asscn 1977–81; Sr Investment Man. Provident Mutual Managed Pension Funds 1981–87; CEO (Europe) Barclays Global Investors (fmrly BZW Investment Man.) 1987–2003, now Vice Chair. *Address:* Barclays Global Investors Limited, Murray House, 1 Royal Mint Court, London, EC3N 4HH (office); Investment Management Association, 65 Kingsway, London, WC2B 6TD, England (office). *Telephone:* (20) 7668-8866 (office). *Fax:* (20) 7668-6866 (office). *Website:* www.barclaysglobal.com (office); www.investmentuk.org (office).

TOMLINSON, Mel Alexander, BFA; American dancer; b. 3 Jan. 1954, Raleigh, NC; s. of Tommy W. A. Tomlinson and Marjorieline Henry Tomlinson; ed F. J. Carnage Jr High School, J. W. Ligon High School, North Carolina Gov.'s School and North Carolina School of the Arts; Prin., Agnes DeMille's Heritage Dance Theater 1973, Dance Theatre of Harlem Inc. 1974–77, Alvin Ailey American Dance Theatre 1977–78, Dance Theatre of Harlem Inc. 1978–81; mem. corps de ballet, New York City Ballet 1981, soloist 1982–87; mem. faculty, North Carolina School of Arts 1987–91; dancer, Boston Ballet 1991–, also teacher in CITYDANCE program. *Leisure interests:* knitting, swimming, gymnastics, reading, sewing, games.

TOMNITZ, Donald J., BA, MBA; American construction industry executive; *Vice-Chairman, President and CEO, D. R. Horton Inc.;* b. 1948, St Louis; m. Sharon Tomnitz; two c.; ed Westminster Coll., Western Illinois Univ.; served as capt. in US Army; fmr Vice-Pres. Republic Bank of Dallas, Crow Development Co.; joined D. R. Horton Inc. as Vice-Pres. 1983, Pres. Homebuilding Div. 1996–98, CEO and Vice-Chair. 1998–, Pres. 2000–. *Address:* D.R. Horton, Inc., 301 Commerce Street, Suite 500, Fort Worth, TX 76102, USA (office). *Telephone:* (817) 390-8200 (office). *Fax:* (817) 436-6717 (office). *Website:* www.drhorton.com (office).

TOMONO, Hiroshi; Japanese business executive; *Representative Director, President and COO, Nippon Steel & Sumitomo Metal Corporation;* fmr Vice-Pres. and Pres. in Sumitomo Metal Industries Ltd (merged with Sumitomo Metal Industries, Ltd to become Nippon Steel & Sumitomo Metal Corpn 2012), Rep. Dir, Pres. and COO Nippon Steel & Sumitomo Metal Corpn 2012–. *Address:* Nippon Steel & Sumitomo Metal Corpn, Marunouchi Park Building, 6-1, Marunouchi 2-chome, Chiyoda-ku, Tokyo 100-8071, Japan (office). *Telephone:* (3) 6867-4111 (office). *Fax:* (3) 6867-5607 (office). *E-mail:* info@www.nsc.co.jp (office). *Website:* www.nsc.co.jp (office); www.worldsteel.org (office).

TOMOS; Chinese artist; b. 26 Nov. 1932, Tumed Banner, Inner Mongolia (Nei Monggol); s. of Yun Yao and Xing Yu; m. Xiahe-xiou 1967; two s.; ed Cen. Inst. of Fine Arts, Beijing; Assoc. Prof. of Fine Arts, Inner Mongolia Normal Coll.; Dean of Fine Arts, Inner Mongolia Teachers' Training Coll. 1984–; Adviser on Fine Arts to Children's Palace, Huhehot, Inner Mongolia; Vice-Chair. Inner Mongolian Branch of Chinese Artists' Asscn 1980–; Dir Standing Cttee, Chinese Artists' Asscn 1985–, mem. Oil Art Cttee 1985–; mem. Selection Cttee for Sixth Nat. Art Exhbn of oil paintings; mem. Art Educ. Cttee of Nat. Educ. 1986–; Dir Inner Mongolia branch of China External Cultural Exchange Asscn; Dir Cheng's Style Tai-Chi Chuan Asscn 1993–; Chair. Judges' Cttee for 8th Annual Chinese Art Exhbn, Inner Mongolia 1994, 8th Annual Best Chinese Artwork Exhbn 1994; Consultant, The Watercolour Asscn, Inner Mongolia 1994; Dir China Oil Painting Asscn 1995–; Chair. Inner Mongolian Artists' Asscn 1996–; Head of Del. of Inner Mongolian painters to Hong Kong 1993; First Prize for Art, Inner Mongolia, Merit of Art Educ. Award, Wu Zuo Ren Int. Art Foundation 1990, Expert and Scholar award of Govt 1991 and medals awarded for individual paintings. *Works include:* Mine, Wind on the Grasslands, Having a Break, Dawn, Milkmaid, A Woman Hay-making, At Dusk, Polo, Spring Wind, White Horse and Wind, At Dark and many others. *Publications:* Selection of oil-paintings, Tomos's Album of Paintings (sketches and oil paintings) 1993, The Techniques of Oil Painting 1999. *Leisure interests:* Chinese Gongfu, Peking opera, Chinese medicine. *Address:* Art Department, Normal College, Nei Monggol Autonomous Region, People's Republic of China (office).

TOMOWA-SINTOW, Anna; Bulgarian singer (soprano); b. 22 Sept. 1943, Stara Zagora, Bulgaria; m. Albert Sintow; one d.; ed Nat. Conservatory of Sofia with Zlatew Tscherkin and Katja Spiridonowa; debut at Leipzig Opera 1967; joined Deutsche Staatsoper, Berlin 1973; guest engagements at all leading European and US opera houses, with conductors including Karajan, Böhm, Haitink, Kleiber, Solti, Abbado, Muti, Maazel, Mehta, Levine, Chailly, Davis, Barenboim, Thielemann; N America debut in San Francisco 1974, at Met, New York 1978, Chicago 1981; numerous tours in Japan, also with La Scala and Berlin Philharmonic under von Karajan; regular guest at Salzburg Festival 1973–91; Dr hc; Kammersängerin, Vienna and Berlin, two Grammy Awards for Ariadne and Don Giovanni/Donna Anna, three Orphée d'Or awards. *Recordings include:* Lohengrin, Le Nozze di Figaro, Don Giovanni, Die Zauberflöte, Der Rosenkavalier, Ariadne auf Naxos, Madame Butterfly, La Traviata, Tosca, Eugene Onegin, Aida, Otello, Capriccio, Andrea Chénier, Simon Boccanegra, Prince Igor, Mozart Coronation Mass, Mozart Requiem, Bach Magnificat, Brahms German Requiem, Verdi Requiem, Strauss Four Last Songs (Orphée d'Or) and Capriccio monologue, Beethoven Missa Solemnis and 9th Symphony, recitals of Verdi arias and of Italian and German arias. *Major roles include:* Arabella, Ariadne, Marschallin, Salome, Madelaine in Capriccio, Agyptische Helena, Countess Almaviva, Fiordiligi, Donna Anna, Elsa in Lohengrin, Elisabeth in Tannhäuser, Sieglinde, Aida, Traviata, Leonora in La Forza del Destino, Amelia in Ballo, Simone Boccanegra, Elisabetta in Don Carlo, Yaroslavna in Prince Igor, Tatjana in Onegin, Tosca, Madama Butterfly, Turandot, Manon Lescaut, Norma, Santuzza, Das Wunder der Heliane, etc. *Leisure interests:* nature, reading books, singing. *Address:* c/o Silvana Sintow-Behrens International Promotions, Schleibingerstrasse 8, 81669 Munich, Germany (office). *Telephone:* (89) 44218900 (office). *Fax:* (89) 44218903 (office). *E-mail:* ats@sintow-behrens.com (office); office@sintow-behrens.com (office). *Website:* www .sintow-behrens.com (office).

TOMUR, Dawamat; Chinese party official; b. 1927, Toksun, Xinjiang Uygur Autonomous Region; s. of Ziweidihan Dawamat; m. Gulzirahan 1944; five s. two d.; ed Cen. Nationalities Coll., Beijing; village chief 1950–54; joined CCP 1952; Magistrate, County (Dist) People's Court, Toksun, Xinjiang Uygur Autonomous Region 1954–64; Sec. CCP Cttee, Toksun Cttee, Tunpan Basin 1956, First Sec. 1960; Vice-Chair. Xinjiang Autonomous Region 1964–78; Deputy for Xinjiang, 3rd NPC; mem. Standing Cttee, Autonomous Regional Revolutionary Cttee, Xinjiang 1968; Deputy for Xinjiang, 5th NPC 1978; Deputy Sec. CCP Cttee Xinjiang 1978–; Vice-Minister of State Nationalities Affairs Comm., State Council 1979–89; Chair. Autonomous Regional People's Congress, Xinjiang 1978–85; mem. 12th Cen. Cttee, CCP 1982; Gov. Xinjiang Autonomous Region 1986–93; Vice-Sec. Xinjiang Autonomous Regional CCP Cttee 1985; mem. 13th Cen. Cttee, CCP 1987–92, 14th Cen. Cttee CCP 1992–97; mem. Standing Cttee 5th NPC 1978–83, Vice-Chair. Standing Cttee 8th NPC 1993–98, 9th NPC 1998–2003. *Publications:* Footprints of my Life (poetry) 2005. *Leisure interests:* writing poetry, playing Chinese Checkers. *Address:* Standing Committee of National People's Congress, Beijing, People's Republic of China (office).

TONEGAWA, Susumu, PhD; Japanese immunologist, neuroscientist and academic; *Director, Picower Institute for Learning and Memory, Massachusetts Institute of Technology;* b. 5 Sept. 1939, Nagoya; s. of Tsutomu Tonegawa and Miyuko Tonegawa; m. Mayumi Yoshinari 1985; three c.; ed Kyoto Univ. and Univ. of Calif., San Diego; postgraduate work at Dept of Biology, Univ. of Calif., San Diego 1968–69, The Salk Inst., San Diego 1969–70; mem. Basle Inst. for Immunology, Basle, Switzerland 1971–81; Prof. of Biology, Center for Cancer Research and Dept of Biology, MIT 1981–, now Picower Prof. of Biology and Neuroscience, Depts of Brain and Cognitive Sciences and Biology, Biology Alumni Investigator, Howard Hughes Medical Inst. 1988–, Dir Picower Inst. for Learning and Memory, MIT 1994–, also Alumni Investigator and Dir RIKEN–MIT Center for Neural Cicuit Genetics; mem. American Acad. of Arts and Sciences; Foreign Assoc. mem. NAS; Hon. mem. American Asscn of Immunologists, Scandinavian Soc. for Immunology; Bunkakunsho Order of Culture 1984; numerous awards and prizes including Avery Landsteiner Prize 1981, Gairdner Foundation Int. Award 1983, Robert Koch Prize 1986, Lasker Prize 1987, Nobel Prize for Medicine 1987. *Address:* Picower Institute for Learning and Memory, Massachusetts Institute of Technology, 77 Massachusetts Avenue, Building 46, Room 4235, Cambridge, MA 02139-4307, USA (office). *Telephone:* (617) 324-1660 (office). *Website:* mit.edu/picower (office).

TONELLI, Gilles; Monegasque civil servant, politician and diplomatist; *Ambassador to Belgium;* m.; three c.; ed Ecole des Travaux Publiques; engineer in Paris 1983–84, section head at public works service 1984–87; Official Rep. at Dept of Public Works and Social Affairs 1987–90, Dir of Urban Planning and Construction 1990–93, Dir-Gen. Dept Public Works and Social Affairs 1993–95, 1995–99; Tech. Adviser, Dept of Finance 1995; Gen. Controller of Expenditure 1999–2000; Sec.-Gen. Ministry of State 2000–05; Govt Counsellor for Facilities, the Environment and Urban Planning 2005–06, 2009–11, for Finance and the Economy 2006–09; Amb. to Belgium 2012–. *Address:* Embassy of Moncao, 17 place Guy d'Arezzo, 1180 Brussels, Belgium (office). *Telephone:* (2) 347-49-87 (office). *Fax:* (2) 343-49-20 (office). *E-mail:* ambassade.monaco@skynet.be (office).

TONG, Anote, MSc; I-Kiribati politician and head of state; *President and Minister for Foreign Affairs and Immigration;* b. 1952; s. of Chinese migrant who settled in Gilbert Islands following World War II; m. Meme Bernadette Tong; eight c.; ed Univ. of Canterbury, Christchurch, NZ, LSE, UK; Sr Asst Sec., Ministry of Educ. 1976–77; Sec. Ministry of Communication and Works 1980–82; Minister for Natural Resources Devt 1994–96; mem. Parl. for Maiana Island 1996–2003; Sr mem. Boutokaan Te Koaua Party 1996–2003; Beretitenti (Pres.) of Kiribati and Minister for Foreign Affairs and Immigration 2003–; fmr Chair. National Fishing Co., Development Bank of Kiribati, Otintai Hotel Ltd, Air Tungaru Co-operative. *Address:* Office of the President (Beretitenti), POB 68, Bairiki, Tarawa, Kiribati (office). *Telephone:* 21183 (office). *Fax:* 21145 (office).

TONG, Yin Chu; Chinese politician; b. 1915, Hefei City, Anhui Prov.; ed Shanghai Jiaotong Univ.; lived in Indonesia 1938–47; joined China Democratic Construction Asscn 1948; Chair. Cen. Cttee China Zhi Gong Dang (political party) 1988–97, Hon. Chair. 1997; Vice-Chair. 8th Nat. Cttee CPPCC 1993–98; Adviser, China Council for Promotion of Peaceful Nat. Reunification, All China Fed. of Returned Overseas Chinese. *Address:* c/o National Committee of Chinese People's Political Consultative Congress, 23 Taiping Qiao Street, Beijing, People's Republic of China (office).

TONG, Zengyin; Chinese banker; b. 1934, Yinxian, Zhejiang Prov.; joined CCP 1954; Vice-Gov. People's Bank of China –1993; fmrly Vice-Chair. China Securities Regulatory Cttee; Founding Pres. Minsheng Bank (China's first privately owned nat. bank) 1996; currently Chair. TRAC Financial Talents Cttee. *Address:* TRAC Financial Talents Committee, No.6-302 Famous Garden 77, Fucheng RD, Haidian District, Beijing 100006, People's Republic of China (office). *Website:* www.ft.org .cn/en/ (office).

TONG, Zhiguang; Chinese international official and professor of economics; b. 21 Jan. 1933, Hebei Prov.; ed Beijing Inst. of Foreign Trade and Univ. of Int. Business and Econs, Bombay Univ., India; joined CCP 1973; Deputy Head State Council Leading Group for Right to Intellectual Property 1991–; Vice-Minister of Foreign Trade and Econ. Co-operation 1991–93; Chair. Bd The Export-Import Bank of China 1994–99; Chair. WTO Research Soc. of China 2001–; Vice-Chair. China-UK Friendship Group; mem. China-US Inter-parliamentary Exchange Group of the NPC; fmr Chief Negotiator and Del. Leader for China's accession to GATT/WTO and Sino-US Trade Negotiations; fmr sr diplomatist to India, Myanmar, USA and UN; fmr Adviser to Chinese Del. of UN Gen. Ass.; fmr Pres. and CEO of China Resources (Holdings) Co. Ltd, Hong Kong; mem. 8th Standing Cttee NPC 1993–98, mem. NPC Foreign Affairs Cttee, del. of Hebei Prov. to 8th NPC 1993–98, 9th Standing Cttee NPC 1998–2003; Del., 15th CCP Nat. Congress 1997–2002; Lifelong Hon. Adviser, China Soc. for WTO Studies. *Publications:* several articles on foreign trade, int. econs and the WTO. *Leisure interests:* golf, classical music, Chinese calligraphy. *Address:* 2212, 28 Dong Holi Xiang, Anwai Beijing 100710 (office); 7202 Yin Zha Hu Tong, Xicheng Qu, Beijing (home); c/o The Export-Import Bank of China, 75 Chongnei Street, Beijing 100005, People's Republic of China (office). *Telephone:* (10) 84255121 (office); (10) 64259703 (home). *Fax:* (10) 84255122 (office). *E-mail:* wtori@sina.com.cn (office); info@chinawto.org.cn (office). *Website:* (office).

TONG HON, HE Cardinal John, MA, PhD; Hong Kong ecclesiastic; *Bishop of Hong Kong [Xianggang];* b. 31 July 1939, Hong Kong; ed Chinese Univ. of Hong Kong, Pontifical Urbaniana Univ., Rome; spent ten years living in Huadu, Guangzhou before returning to Hong Kong; ordained priest, Diocese of Hong Kong [Xianggang] 1966; served with Holy Spirit Study Center, Congregation for the Evangelization of Peoples, Hong Kong for 24 years; apptd Auxiliary Bishop of Hong Kong [Xianggang] and Titular Bishop of Bossa 1996; Coadjutor Bishop of Hong Kong [Xianggang] 2008–09, Bishop of Hong Kong [Xianggang] 2009–; cr. Cardinal (Cardinal-Priest of Regina Apostolorum) 2012; participated in Papal Conclave 2013; mem. Congregation for the Evangelization of Peoples 2003–; travelled to Guangzhou as Rep. of the Pope, along with other Hong Kong religious leaders 2005. *Address:* Catholic Diocese Centre 12/F, 16 Caine Road, Hong Kong Special Administrative Region, People's Republic of China (office). *Telephone:* 2522-3677 (office); 3589-2428 (office); 2843-4679 (office). *Fax:* 2522-3749 (office); 2525-4707 (office). *E-mail:* hkcsco@catholic.org.hk (office). *Website:* www.catholic.org.hk (office).

TONG SANG, Gaston, DipEng; French Polynesian engineer, politician and fmr head of state; b. 7 Aug. 1949, Bora Bora; two c.; ed Collège La Mennais, Papeete, Lycée Montaigne, Bordeaux, Ecole des Hautes études industrielles (HEI), Centre des Hautes Etudes de la Construction, Paris; engineer, Road Infrastructure Dept, Polynesian Dept of Works 1976–80, Head, Maritime Works Dept 1980–82; Cabinet Dir for Govt Counsellors 1982–84; Cabinet Dir for Minister of Works 1984–86; Minister of Works, Supplies, Energy and Mines 1986–89; Mayor of Bora Bora 1989–91; Regional Councillor for Iles sous le Vent and Minister of Supplies, Urban Areas, Works and Energy 1991–95; Minister of Works, Energy and Ports 1995–96, of Housing, Territories, Urban Areas and Real Estate 1996–98, of Property Affairs, Land Man. and Urban Areas 1998–2000, of Land Man. and Land Redistribution 2001–04, of Energy, Commerce, Industry and Small Businesses 2004–07; Pres. of French Polynesia 2007, 2008–09 (resgnd), also Minister for External Relations, Int. Transport and Communication; mem. To Tatou Ai'a party; Chevalier de l'ordre Nat. du Mérite 1996, Chevalier des Palmes académiques 2000, Chevalier de la Légion d'honneur 2004. *Address:* c/o Office of the President of the Government, BP 2551, 98713 Papeete, French Polynesia (office).

TONKIN, Peter Frederick, BSc (Arch) (Hons), BArch (Hons), LFAIA; Australian architect; *Director, Tonkin Zulaikha Greer Architects;* b. 10 Jan. 1953, Blayney, NSW; s. of John Ebenezer Tonkin and Veronica Mariea Tonkin (née Perry); m. Ellen Claire Woolley; one s. one d.; ed Univ. of Sydney; in practice with Lawrence Nield and Partners 1979–81; ind. practice 1981–, Co-founder Tonkin Zulaikha 1987, Tonkin Zulaikha Greer 1988–; Visiting Design Tutor, Sydney Univ., Univ. of New South Wales, Univ. of Tech., Sydney; Adjunct Prof. of Architecture, Univ. of Queensland 2003–13, Univ. of Canberra; Fellow, Royal Australian Inst. of Architects (fmr Vice-Pres. and Chair. of Practice and Design Bds), Historic Houses Trust Exhbns Cttee; Trustee, Historic Houses Trust NSW 2003–13; Licentiate Fellow, AIA; numerous awards and prizes, including Royal Australian Inst. of Architects Merit Awards 1988, 1991, 1993, 1996, 2000, 2001, 2003 and every year 2007–13, Winner, Vietnam Memorial Competition 1990, Tomb of the Unknown Soldier Competition 1993, Master Builders Asscn Merit Award 1993, ACEA Engineering Excellence Award 1999, Property Council of NSW Devt of the Year 1999, Int. Royal Inst. of Chartered Surveyors Award for Conservation 2000, Winner, Nat. Gallery of Australia Competition 2000, Winner, Australian War Memorial London Competition 2003, Winner, Canberra Int. Arboretum Competition 2005, Winner, Australian Memorial NZ Competition 2012. *Achievements:* design projects include refurbishment of Sydney Customs House, Fed. Museum and Library, Tenterfield, Royal Blind Soc. Library, Nat. Memorial to Australian Vietnam Forces, Tomb of the Unknown Australian Soldier, Canberra, Australian War Memorial, London, Craigieburn Bypass, Hume Freeway, Melbourne, Carriageworks Performing Arts Centre, Sydney, Paddington Reservoir Gardens Sydney, Glebe Town Hall refurbishment, Nat. Arboretum, Canberra. *Publications:* numerous books, articles, papers and essays. *Leisure interests:* mountain sports, motorcycling. *Address:* Tonkin Zulaikha Greer Architects, 117 Reservoir Street, Surry Hills, NSW 2010, Australia (office). *Telephone:* (2) 9215-4900 (office). *Fax:* (2) 9215-4901 (office). *E-mail:* peter@tzg.com.au (office). *Website:* www.tzg.com.au (office).

TØNNESSON, Stein, CandPhil, DPhil; Norwegian peace researcher; *Research Professor, Peace Research Institute Oslo (PRIO);* b. 2 Dec. 1953, Copenhagen, Denmark; s. of Kåre Tønnesson and Birgit Tønnesson; one s.; ed Univ. of Arhus, Denmark, Univ. of Oslo; taught Norwegian and History at Univ. of Oslo 1983; historian for Norwegian Asscn of Sports 1983–85; wrote doctoral thesis on Vietnam Revolution of 1945 1986–92; Research Fellow, Peace Research Inst. Oslo (PRIO) 1990–92, Dir 2001–09, Research Prof. 2009–; Research Prof. Nordic Inst. of Asian Studies 1992–95, Sr Research Fellow 1995–98; consultant to Statoil 1996–2000; Prof. of Human Devt Studies, Univ. of Oslo 1998–2001; Randolph Jennings Sr Fellow, US Inst. of Peace 2010–11; Adjunct Prof. and Leader, East Asian Peace Programme, Uppsala Univ. 2011–(16); mem. Bd NORFUND 2007–; Bd Institute for Security and Devt Policy 2011–, Bd Inst. of Social Research 2011–; CAS Book Prize for best study in the humanities 2011. *Publications include:* The Vietnamese Revolution of 1945 1991, Imperial Policy and Southeast Asian Nationalism 1930–1957 (co-ed.) 1995, Asian Forms of the Nation (co-ed.) 1996, Vietnam 1946: How the War Began 2010. *Address:* Jacob Aalls gt. 13, 0368 Oslo (home); PRIO, PO Box 9229, Grønland, 0134 Oslo, Norway (office). *Telephone:* 22-54-77-31 (office). *Fax:* 22-54-77-01 (office). *E-mail:* stein@prio.no (office); stein.tonnesson@pcr.uu.se (office). *Website:* www.prio.no (office); www.pcr.uu.se (office); www.cliostein.com (office).

TOOLEY, Sir John, Kt, MA; British arts administrator and arts consultant; b. 1 June 1924, Rochester, Kent, England; s. of the late H. R. Tooley; m. 1st Judith Craig Morris 1951 (divorced 1965); three d.; m. 2nd Patricia J. N. Bagshawe 1968 (divorced 1990); one s.; m. 3rd Jennifer Anne Shannon 1995 (divorced 2003); ed Repton School and Magdalene Coll., Cambridge; Sec. Guildhall School of Music and Drama 1952–55; Asst to Gen. Admin., Royal Opera House, Covent Garden 1955–60, Asst Gen. Admin. 1960–70, Gen. Admin. 1970–80, Gen. Dir 1980–88;

Chair. Almeida Theatre 1990–97, Fabric Advisory Cttee Salisbury Cathedral 1992–2005, Salisbury Cathedral Girl Choristers Trust 1995–2006, Nureyev Foundation 1995–2008; Pres. Salisbury Festival 1988–2005; Chair. Monument Insurance Brokers Ltd 1997–2002; consultant, Int. Man. Group 1988–97, Ballet Opera House, Toronto 1989–90, Istanbul Foundation for Culture and Arts 1993–, Antelope Films 1993–; Dir London Philharmonic Orchestra 1998–, Britten Estate 1989–96, South Bank Bd 1991–97, Compton Verney Opera Project 1991–97, Welsh Nat. Opera 1992–2000, David Gyngell Holdings Ltd 1996–97; Gov. Royal Ballet 1994–97; adviser, Borusan Philharmonic Orchestra, Istanbul 2005–08; Trustee Britten Pears Foundation 1988–99, Walton Trust 1988–2000, Wigmore Hall 1989–2001, Almeida Theatre 1990–2002, Performing Arts Labs 1992–97, Cardiff Bay Opera House 1995–96, Sidney Nolan Trust 1995–, Mozartfest, Bath 2001–; Hon. FRAM; Hon. FGSM; Hon. FRNCM; Hon. mem. Incorporated Soc. of Musicians; Hon. Fellow, Magdalene Coll. Cambridge 2005; Commendatore of Italian Repub. 1976; Hon. DUniv (Univ. of Central England) 1996; Queen Elizabeth II Coronation Award 2005. *Publication:* In House 1999. *Leisure interests:* walking, theatre. *Address:* 18 Grange Court, Cambridge, CB3 9BD, England (home). *Telephone:* (1223) 358737 (office); (1223) 351995 (home). *Fax:* (1223) 358737 (office). *E-mail:* tooley@btinternet.com (home).

TOOMEY, Patrick Joseph (Pat), AB; American business executive and politician; *Senator from Pennsylvania;* b. 17 Nov. 1961, Providence, RI; m. Kris Ann Duncan 1997; two s. one d.; ed La Salle Acad. (scholarship), Harvard Univ.; investment banker, Chemical Bank, New York 1984–86; Vice-Pres. and Dir, US subsidiary, Morgan, Grenfell & Co. 1986–91; financial consultant, Hong Kong, 1990–91; Co-founder Toomey Enterprises, Inc., Allentown, Pa 1991–, opened, with two younger brothers, Rookie's Restaurant, Allentown 1991; elected to Allentown's newly est. Govt Study Comm. 1994; mem. US House of Reps for 15th Congressional Dist of Pa 1999–2005; unsuccessful cand. for US Senate 2006; Pres. and CEO Club for Growth, Washington, DC 2004–09; Senator from Pennsylvania 2011–, mem. Banking, Housing and Urban Affairs Cttee, Budget Cttee, Commerce, Science and Transportation Cttee, Jt Econ. Cttee; mem. Bd of Dirs Commonwealth Foundation for Public Policy Alternatives 2007–; Republican; named Man of the Year, US Marine Corps 1999, Honor Roll Award, Concord Coalition 2000. *Address:* 502 Hart Senate Office Building, Washington, DC 20510, USA (office). *Telephone:* (202) 224-4254 (office). *Fax:* (202) 228-0284 (office). *Website:* toomey.senate.gov (office).

TOOPE, Stephen J., LLB, BCL, PhD; Canadian university administrator; *President and Vice-Chancellor, University of British Columbia;* m. Paula Rosen; three c.; ed Trinity Coll., Cambridge, UK, McGill Univ., Harvard Univ., USA; served as Law Clerk to Chief Justice of Canada 1986–87; Research Dir, Office of the Special Rep., Royal Comm. on Aboriginal Peoples 1991; Asst Prof. of Law, McGill Univ. 1987–93, Assoc. Prof. 1993–99, Prof. 1999–2006, Assoc. Dean (Grad. Studies and Research), Faculty of Law 1991–94, Dean 1994–99; Pres. and Vice-Chancellor Univ. of British Columbia 2006–; consultant on int. law, int. human rights and legal reform to Depts of Foreign Affairs and Justice, Int. Devt Agency 1988–; Dir World Univ. Service of Canada 2004–; Chair. Research Univs Council of BC 2009–11; mem. Bd of Dirs Canadian Human Rights Foundation (now Equitas) 2001–06; mem. UN Working Group on Enforced or Involuntary Disappearances (Chair. and Rapporteur 2004–06) 2003–07; mem. Int. Advisory Bd, Faculty of Law, Nat. Univ. of Singapore 2001–, Journal of Int. Law and Int. Relations 2004–; mem. Academic Council, Inst. for Transnational Arbitration, USA 2001–, Research Council, Canadian Inst. for Advanced Research 2004–, Advisory Council, Minister of Justice 2005–06, Social Sciences and Humanities Research Council 2005–, Order of Canada Advisory Council 2011–15; mem. Exec. Cttee Asscn of Univs and Colls of Canada 2006–, Vice-Chair. 2010–11, Chair. 2011–13; Lead negotiator for the Govt of Canada, Manuge v. The Queen 2012; mem. Bd Conf. Bd of Canada 2009–, Public Policy Forum of Canada 2012–; BC Business Council 2006–; Council mem., Social Sciences and Humanities Research Council of Canada 2005–08; Fern Gertrude Kennedy Prize in Jurisprudence (jtly) 1982, F.R. Scott Prize in Constitutional Law 1983, Casimar Bielski QC Prize in Int. Law 1983, Ballon Medal 1983, Douglas J. Sherbaniuk Distinguished Writing Award, Canadian Tax Foundation (jtly) 1995, Francis Deák Publication Award, American Soc. of Int. Law (jtly) 1998, David L. Johnston Award for Distinguished Service, McGill Alumni Asscn 1997, John W. Durnford Teaching Excellence Award, McGill Univ. 2001, McGill Univ. Scarlet Key Award, Queen Elizabeth II Diamond Jubilee Medal 2012. *Publications:* Mixed International Arbitration 1990; articles in American Journal of International Law, Columbia Journal of Transnational Law, Harvard Journal of International Law, McGill Law Journal and many other int. journals in N America and Europe. *Address:* Office of the President, University of British Columbia, 1958 Main Mall, Vancouver, BC V6T 1Z2, Canada (office). *Telephone:* (604) 822-8300 (office). *Fax:* (604) 822-5055 (office). *E-mail:* presidents.office@ubc.ca (office). *Website:* president.ubc.ca (office).

TOPALLI, Jozefina Çoba, MPA; Albanian politician; b. 26 Nov. 1963, Shkodër; m.; two c.; ed Luigj Gurakuqi Univ., Shkodra, Univ. of Padua, Italy and Tirana Univ.; civil servant, Chamber of Commerce, Shkodra 1992–95; Lecturer and Chancellor, Luigj Gurakuqi Univ., Shkodra 1995–98; mem. Democratic Party of Albania—Partia Demokratike e Shqipërisë, Vice-Chair. 1997–; mem. Kuvendi Popullor (People's Ass.) 1996–, Deputy Speaker 1997–2005, Speaker 2005–13, fmr Deputy Pres. Parl. Children's Cttee, fmr mem. Social Work, Health and Family Cttee; mem. Council of Europe 2002–; mem. monitoring missions during gen. elections held in Ukraine and Palestinian Autonomous Areas 2004–05; active participant in campaigns for the Objectives of the Millennium Devt; Honorary Citizen of Çair Municipality, Macedonia 2012; Mediterranean Award, Int. Mediterranean Forum for Peace, consigned by Senator Gergio De Gregori, Pres. of Italian Parl. Del. to Ass. of NATO 2010, declared First Amb. of UNICEF for the protection of children's rights in Albania, Medal of Honour from Chair. of Legis. Ass. of St Petersburg, Millennium Peace Award: Cavaliere per la Pace, Int. Peace Union, Sacro Cuore Univ., Italy. *Address:* Kuvendi Popullor, Bulevardi Dëshmorët e Kombit 4, Tirana, Albania (office). *E-mail:* info@parlament.al (office). *Website:* www.parlament.al (office); www.jozefinatopalli.al.

TOPALOV, Veselin; Bulgarian chess master; b. 15 March 1975, Rousse; winner, World Under-14 Chess Championship, Puerto Rico 1989, silver medal, World Under-16 Championship, Singapore 1990; named Grandmaster 1992; reached last

16 in FIDE World Chess Championship 1999, quarter-finals 2000, last 16 2001, semi-finals 2004, World Champion 2005; losing finalist, Cands Tournament, Dortmund 2002; jt first place with Gary Kasparov, Linares 2005; winner, M-tel Masters 2005, 2006; lost title reunification match against Vladimir Kramnik 2006; unsuccesful challenger versus world champion Viswanathan Anand in World Chess Championship 2010. *Achievements include:* in Oct. 2006 had the second-highest Elo rating of all time (2813). *Address:* c/o Bulgarian Chess Federation, PO Box 927, 1000 Sofia, Bulgaria. *Telephone:* (2) 930-08-18. *E-mail:* federation@chessbg.com. *Website:* www.chessbg.com.

TOPBAŞ, Kadir, PhD; Turkish architect and politician; *Mayor of Istanbul;* b. 1945, Artvin; m.; two s. one d.; ed Marmara Univ., Mimar Sinan Univ., Univ. of Istanbul; worked as architect, Istanbul Metropolitan Municipality; adviser to Recep Tayyip Erdogan, Mayor of Istanbul Metropolitan Municipality 1994–98, also served as Deputy Dir Istanbul 1st Cultural Heritage Protection and Monuments Cttee of Ministry of Culture; Mayor of Beyoğlu 1999–2004; Mayor of Istanbul 2004–; mem. Supervisory Bd TAC Foundation; mem. Adalet ve Kalkınma Partisi—AKP (Justice and Development Party); Co-Pres. UCLG 2007–10, Pres. 2010–; Pres. Union of Municipalities of Turkey 2009–, UN Advisory Cttee of Local Authorities 2011; mem. Proposal Group for Local Govts Reform Project, Bd of Trustees and Bd of Dirs TAÇ (History and Environment Foundation). *Publications include:* Beyoglu: Kültürleri Buluşturan Kent, Geçmişten Günümüze Beyoglu I-II, Anılarda Beyoglu. *Address:* Istanbul Büyükşehir Belediye Başkanlığı, Şehzadebaşı Cad. No. 25, Saraçhane, Istanbul, Turkey (office). *Telephone:* (212) 4551400 (office). *Fax:* (212) 4552185 (office). *E-mail:* baskan@ibb.gov.tr (office); irelations@ibb.gov.tr (office). *Website:* www.ibb.gov.tr (office).

TOPCHEYEV, Yuriy Ivanovich, DTech Sc; Russian cyberneticist and academic; *Emeritus Professor, International G. Soros Science Education Programme;* b. 26 Sept. 1920, Yaroslavl; s. of Ivan Yakovlevich Topcheyev and Vera Aleksandrovna Topcheyeva; m. Inna Ivanovna Smirnova 1965; one s.; ed Moscow Aviation Inst.; mem. CPSU 1948–91; Chief Dept of Scientific Research Inst. of Automatic Systems 1943–72; mem. staff and Prof., Inst. of Physical Eng, Moscow 1968–89, Chief of Faculty 1972–88; Prof. Int. G. Soros Science Educ. Programme 1996–97, Emer. Prof. 1997–; mem. Comm. of Co-ordination Cttee on Computers of USSR (now Russian) Acad. of Sciences 1978–85, Co-ordination Cttee on Robotics 1980–87; Chair. Council on Systems of Automated Design, Ministry of Higher Educ. 1977–87; mem. Council Specialized Scientific and Technological Activities of USSR (now Russian) Acad. of Sciences 1989–, Russian Cosmonautics 1992–; World Innovation Foundation 2001–, Prof. and Grand Doctor of Philosophy, Acad. Européenne d'Informatisation (Belgium) 2003–; Order of Labour Banner 1950, State Prize 1972, Korolev Medal 1977, Gagarin Medal 1981, Gold Medal, Russian Exhbn Centre 2005. *Publications include:* Encyclopaedia for Automatic Regulation Systems Design 1989; (co-author) Basics of Automatic Regulation 1954, Modern Methods of Automatic Control System Design (ed. and co-author) 1967, Technical Cybernetics (4 Vols) 1967–89, Philosophy of Nonlinear Control Systems 1990, Nonlinear Systems of Automatic Control (Vols 1–9) 1970–92, People and Robotics (Vol. 1) 1995, (Vol. 2) 1998, Development of Robotics 2000, Robotics: A Historical Overview 2001, Robotics – History and Perspectives 2002, Robotic Assisted Human's Activity (A History of Development) 2004, Biography of Mstislav Vsevolodovich Keldysh 2002, biographies of Vladimir Mikhailovich Myasischev and Pavel Osypovich Sukhoi 2003, Robotics – Assisted Human's Activity (A History of Development) (co-author) 2005, Biography of Vladimir Mikhailovich Petlyakov 2005, History of Domestic Aviation Arms 2005; over 310 articles, including 12 on great contemporary Russian scientists in A History of Science Engineering 2002, and 2 pieces on contemporary biosphere ecology. *Leisure interests:* nonlinear systems design, the history of the development of automatic systems and robotics. *Address:* 125212 Moscow, Leningradskoye sch. 31, Apt. 147, Russia. *Telephone:* (495) 156-63-06. *E-mail:* fsg100@yandex.ru (home).

TÖPFER, Klaus, PhD; German politician and international organization official; b. 29 July 1938, Waldenburg, Silesia; m.; three c.; ed Univs of Mainz, Frankfurt am Main and Munster; family expelled from Silesia, settled in Höxter/Weser 1945; Head, Political Economy Dept, Inst. of Devt Planning, Munster 1970–71; Head, Planning and Information Section, Saarland State Chancellery, Saarbrücken; Lecturer, Coll. of Admin., Speyer 1971–78; Prof. Ordinarius, Hanover Univ., Dir Inst. of Environmental Research and Regional Planning 1978–79; Hon. Prof. Mainz Univ. 1985–; joined CDU 1972, CDU Dist Chair., Saarbrücken, mem. CDU State Exec., Saar 1977–79; State Sec., Rhineland Palatinate Ministry of Social Affairs, Health and Environment, Mainz 1978–85; Deputy Chair. CDU Fed. Cttee of Experts on the Environment 1983; Minister of Environment and Health, Rhineland Palatinate 1985–87; CDU Dist Chair., Rhein-Hunsrück 1987–; Fed. Minister for the Environment, Nature Conservation and Nuclear Safety 1987–94, of Regional Planning, Housing and Urban Devt 1994–98; Exec. Dir UNEP, Nairobi 1998–2006; Acting Dir UN Centre for Human Settlements (Habitat) 1998–2000; Chairman of the Energy Efficiency in Buildings (EEB) Assurance Group, an initiative of the World Business Council for Sustainable Development (WBCSD); Founding Dir Inst. for Advanced Sustainability Studies, Potsdam 2009–; mem. Advisory Bd German Foundation for World Population, Holcim Foundation for Sustainable Construction 2004–; strategic advisor to Desertec Industrial Initiative (Dii); Order of Merit of the Federal Republic of Germany (1986) and the Grand Cross of the Order of Merit of the Federal Republic of Germany; TÜV Environment Prize 2000, German Environment Prize 2002, Bruno H Schubert Environment Prize 2002.

TOPI, Bamir Myrteza, PhD, DrSc; Albanian biologist, politician and fmr head of state; *Leader, New Democratic Spirit;* b. 24 April 1957, Tirana; m. Teuta Mema; two d.; ed Veterinary Medicine Faculty, Agricultural Univ. of Tirana; Scientific Researcher, Inst. for Veterinary Studies, Tirana 1984–87, Dir 1990–96; elected to Nat. Ass. 1996, re-elected twice; Minister of Agric. and Food 1996–97; Pres. of Albania 2007–12; fmr Deputy Chair. Democratic Party, resgnd on taking office 2007; Founder and Leader, New Democratic Spirit 2012–; Hon. Pres. KF Tirana football club 2005–07, Hon. Citizen of Prishtina, Kosovo 2008, of Rrëshen, of Burrel, of Gjakova, Kosovo; Kt Grand Cross, Grand Order of King Tomislav (Croatia) 2009; Dr hc (Univ. of Prishtina) 2008; Goddess on the Throne Gold Medal, Prishtina 2009. *Address:* New Democratic Spirit (Fryma e Re Demokratike), Rruga George W. Bush, Pallati i Kasmeve 15/1, Tirana, Albania (office).

Telephone: (4) 2242444 (office). *Fax:* (4) 2242444 (office). *Website:* www.frd.al (office).

TOPOL, Chaim; Israeli actor, producer and director; b. 9 Sept. 1935, Tel-Aviv; s. of Yaakov Topol and Rela Goldman; m. Galia Finkelstein 1956; one s. two d.; joined entertainment unit during army service 1953; f. The Green Onion satirical theatre 1956, Municipal Theatre of Haifa 1959; starred in stage productions of Fiddler on the Roof in London 1967, 1983, 1994, on Broadway, New York 1990, in Melbourne 1998, in Sydney 2005, in Wellington, NZ 2007, USA tour 2009, in Ziegfield 1988; further roles include The Caucasian Chalk Circle, Romanov and Juliet, Othello, A View From The Bridge, Chichester Festival Theatre, Gigi, London 2008,; actor, producer, dir for the Genesis Project, filming the Bible, New York 2003; Chair. Jordan River Village, Galilee 2011– (holiday facility for children with life-threatening or chronic illnesses); Golden Globe Award 1972, San Francisco Film Festival Winner 1972, David Donatello Award 1972. *Films include:* Cast A Giant Shadow 1965, Sallah 1966, Before Winter Comes 1969, A Talent for Loving, Fiddler on the Roof 1971, The Public Eye 1972, Galileo 1974, Flash Gordon 1972, For Your Eyes Only 1980, The Winds of War 1981, A Dime Novel, Queenie, Left Luggage 1997, Time Elevator 1998, War and Remembrance 1989, Mr Know All 1988; several TV films. *Albums include:* Fiddler on the Roof (cast album), It's Topol, War Songs, Topol 68, Fiddler on the Roof (film album), Topol's Israel. *Publication:* Topol by Topol (autobiography) 1981, To Life! (A Treasury of Jewish Wisdom, Wit and Humour) 1995. *Leisure interests:* book illustrations and portrait drawings. *Address:* c/o Diamond Management, 31 Percy Street, London, W1T 2DD, England (office); 22 Vale Court, Maida Vale, London, W9 1RT, England. *Telephone:* (20) 7631-0400 (office). *E-mail:* agents@diman.co.uk (office); fbvandoren@aol.com (office). *Fax:* (20) 7266-2155.

TOPOL, Eric J., MD; American cardiologist and academic; *Director, Scripps Translational Science Institute;* b. 26 June 1954, Queens, New York; m. Susan Leah Merriman 1979; one s. one d.; ed Univ. of Virginia, Charlottesville, Univ. of Rochester School of Medicine and Dentistry, NY; at Univ. of Rochester School of Medicine and Dentistry 1975–79; Intern in Medicine, Moffitt Hosp., Univ. of California, San Francisco 1979–80, Asst and Sr Resident in Medicine 1980–82; Fellow in Cardiovascular Medicine, Johns Hopkins Hosp., Baltimore, Md 1982–85; Sr Fellow, Coronary Angioplasty, San Francisco Heart Inst. 1984; Asst Prof. of Internal Medicine, Univ. of Michigan School of Medicine, Ann Arbor 1985–87, Assoc. Prof., 1987–90, Prof. 1990–91; Consulting Prof. of Medicine, Duke Univ. School of Medicine, Durham, NC 1991–2002; Prof. of Medicine, Cleveland Clinic Health Sciences Center, Ohio State Univ. School of Medicine 1991–2002; Provost and Prof. of Medicine, Cleveland Clinic Lerner Coll. of Medicine, Case Western Reserve Univ. 2002–06; Co-Dir Cleveland Clinic Heart Center 1991–2006, Chair. Dept of Cardiovascular Medicine, Cleveland Clinic Foundation 1991–2006, Provost, Chief Academic Officer and mem. Bd of Govs Cleveland Clinic Foundation 2001–06, Vice-Chair. Dept of Molecular Cardiology, Cleveland Clinic Research Institute 1991–2006, Dir Joseph J. Jacobs Center for Thrombosis and Vascular Biology 1991–2006; Dir Scripps Translational Science Inst., Scripps Research Inst. 2007–, Chief Academic Officer, Scripps Health 2007–, Sr Consultant, Div. of Cardiology, Scripps Clinic 2007–, Prof. of Molecular and Experimental Medicine 2007–, Founding Dean, Scripps School Medicine 2008–; Co-founder and Vice-Chair. West Wireless Health Inst.; Amon G. Carter Professorship, Univ. of Texas Health Science Center 1988; Donald and Lois Roon Visiting Professorship, Scripps Clinic and Research Foundation 1992; Barnet Berris Visiting Professorship, Univ. of Toronto 1992; Goldberg Visiting Professorship, Cedars-Sinai Medical Center 1994; Edward Massie Visiting Professorship, Washington Univ. School of Medicine 1995; Simon Dack Visiting Professorship, Mount Sinai Cardiovascular Inst. 1995; Marjorie and Gaye Grollman Visiting Professorship, Univ. of Virginia 1995; Isadore Rosenfeld Visiting Professorship, Cornell Univ. Medical School 1995; John J. Sampson Visiting Professor, Univ. of California, San Francisco Medical Center 1998; mem. Bd of Dirs Rhone-Poulenc-Rorer, Inc. 1997, Quintiles Transnational, Inc. 1997–; Ed. Current Opinion in Cardiology 1994–96, Scientific American Medicine 1995–98, Cardiology Website: TheHeart.Org 2000–; mem. Editorial Bd American Journal of Cardiology 1988–, Journal of the American College of Cardiology 1989–93, 1995–99, 2001–03, Coronary Artery Disease 1989–, International Journal of Cardiac Imaging 1990–, Cardiology 1990–, Trends in Cardiovascular Medicine 1990–, Choices in Cardiology 1990–, Clinical Cardiology 1990–, Circulation 1991– (Consulting Ed. 2001–), Cardiology in the Elderly 1991–, British Heart Journal 1992–, Journal of Myocardial Ischemia 1992–, Current Literature 1993–, Cardiovascular Drug Therapy 1993–, Primary Cardiology 1994–, Clinics in Interventional Cardiology 1995–, Journal of Women's Health 1995–, European Heart Journal 1996–, Seminars in Interventional Cardiology 1996–, Revista Espanola de Cardiologia 1996–, American Heart Journal 1996–, Journal of Clinical and Experimental Cardiology 1997–, Acute Coronary Syndromes 1997–, American Journal of Medicine 1998–, Journal of Clinical and Basic Cardiology 1998–, Current Treatment Options in Cardiovascular Diseases 1998–, Heart Disease: A Journal of Cardiovascular Medicine 1998–, Current Opinion in Cardiovascular, Renal and Pulmonary Investigational Drugs 1998–, International Journal of Cardiology 1999–, Heart Drug Journal 1999–, Cardiovascular Therapeutics 2000–, ASEAN Heart Journal 2001–; editorial consultant/manuscript reviewer for numerous journals; mem. NAS, AAAS, American Soc. of Clinical Investigation 1990, Best Doctors in America 1992–2003, American Asscn of Physicians 1995, Johns Hopkins Soc. of Scholars 1999, Int. Soc. for Fibrinolysis and Thrombolysis, American Fed. for Clinical Research, Asscn of Univ. of Cardiologists, Asscn of Profs in Cardiology, Inst. of Medicine 2004; Fellow, American Heart Asscn 1983–85, American Coll. of Chest Physicians, Soc. of Cardiac Angiography and Interventions (also Trustee), European Soc. of Cardiology, American Coll. of Cardiology, American Coll. of Physicians; Hon. mem. Columbian Soc. of Cardiology, Polish Cardiac Soc.; Outstanding Medical Specialist in the US, Town and Country 1989, Sir William Osler Award, Univ. of Miami School of Medicine 1989, 4th Annual Virginia Heart Center Award, Virginia Heart Center 1992, Distinguished Teacher Award, Cleveland Civic Foundation 1992, Best Doctors in America, American Health Magazine 1996, Distinguished Teacher Award, Cleveland Civic Foundation 1997, Most Cited Researchers in Cardiology, Science Watch 1999, Top Docs-Medicine's Most Cited, Science Watch 1999, Scientific Achievement in Clinical Research, Cleveland Clinic Foundation 2000, Innovator of the Year, American Coll. of Cardiovascular Administrators and

Alliance of Cardiovascular Professionals 2001, Top 0.5% Cited Researcher, Inst. for Scientific Information 2001, America's Top Doctors, Castle Connolly Medical Publishers 2001, American Heart Asscn's Top Ten Research Advances 2001, Gill Heart Inst. Award for Outstanding Contribs to Cardiovascular Medicine 2002, Dr William Beaumont Award in Medicine, American Medical Asscn 2002, Andreas R. Gruntzig Award, Swiss Soc. of Cardiology 2002, one of Top 10 Most Cited Researchers in Medicine, In-Cites, ISI 2003, Silver Medal for Outstanding Physician/Scientist, European Soc. of Cardiology 2004. *Publications:* ed. of 30 medical books and author of more than 1,600 articles in medical and scientific journals. *Leisure interests:* family, golf, travel, reading. *Address:* Scripps Translational Science Institute, 3344 North Torrey Pines Court, Suite 300, La Jolla, CA 92037, USA (office). *Telephone:* (858) 554-5708 (office). *Website:* www.stsiweb.org.

TOPOLÁNEK, Mirek; Czech politician; b. 15 May 1956, Vsetín; m.; three c.; ed mil. high school in Opava, Brno Univ. of Tech.; Project Designer, later Ind. Designer, OKD Ostrava 1980–87; Head Designer Specialist, Energoproject Praha, Ostrava Works 1987–91; Exec. Dir then Man. Dir VAE Ltd (later VAE Inc.) 1991–96, Chair. 1996; active in citizens forum 1989; mem. Municipal Corpn of Ostrava-Poruba 1990–94; Senator 1995–2004; mem. Civic Democratic Party (ODS) 1994–, Vice-Chair. 1996–98, Chair. 2002–10; mem. Cttee for Economy, Agric. and Transport, Org. Cttee and Chair. Sub-cttee for Power Eng, Vice-Pres. of Senate 2002–04; Chair. ODS Senate Club 1990–2002; Prime Minister June–Oct. 2006 (resgnd), reinstated Jan. 2007–09 (resgnd); mem. Bd Asscn for Restoration and Devt of Northern Moravian Region and Silesia, Mining Coll., Univ. of Tech., Ostrava, Jagello Asscn. *Address:* Civic Democratic Party (Občanská demokratická strana), Polygon House, Doudlebská 1699/5, 140 00 Prague 4, Czech Republic (office). *Telephone:* (2) 34707111 (office). *Fax:* (2) 34707103 (office). *E-mail:* mirek .topolanek@ods.cz (office). *Website:* www.topolanek.cz.

TOPORNIN, Boris Nikolayevich; Russian legal specialist and academic; *Director, Institute of State and Law, Russian Academy of Sciences;* b. 29 Dec. 1929; m.; two s.; ed Moscow Inst. of Int. Relations; Jr, then Sr Researcher and Scientific Sec., Inst. of Law, USSR (now Russian) Acad. of Sciences 1955–62; Deputy Chief Scientific Sec., Presidium of USSR Acad. of Sciences 1962–67; Head of Div., First Deputy Dir Inst. of State and Law, USSR Acad. of Sciences 1967–89, Dir 1989–; Corresp. mem. USSR (now Russian) Acad. of Sciences 1987, mem. 1991, Acad. Sec., Dept of Philosophy and Law; Deputy Pres. Int. Asscn of Constitutional Law; mem. Int. Acad. of Law; Humboldt Inst. Prize 1999, Femida Prize 2000. *Publications include:* Political Foundation of Socialism 1972, New Constitution of USSR 1980, Development of Socialist Democracy 1985, Foreign Policy and Science 1990. *Publications:* Federalismus zwischen Integration und Sezession. Chancen und Risiken bundesstaatlicher Ordnung 1993, Legal Foundation of Russian Economy 2000. *Address:* Institute of State and Law, Russian Academy of Sciences, 119841 Moscow, Znamenka str. 10, Russia (office). *Telephone:* (495) 291-87-56 (office); (495) 203-92-12 (office). *E-mail:* igpran@igpran.ru (office). *Website:* www .igpran.ru/engl (office).

TOPOYEV, Maj.-Gen. Esen; Kyrgyzstani politician and army officer; fmr Minister of Defence. *Address:* c/o Ministry of Defence, 26 Logvinenko str., Bishkek, 710001, Kyrgyzstan.

TOPPO, HE Cardinal Telesphore Placidus, DD; Indian ecclesiastic; *Archbishop of Ranchi;* b. 15 Oct. 1939, Jhargaon, Gumla Dist, Jharkhand; s. of Ambrose Toppo and Sofia Xalxo; ed Lievens Barway Boys' Secondary School, Chainpur, St Xavier's Coll., Ranchi, Pontifical Urban Univ., Rome, Italy, Univ. of Ranchi; ordained priest 1969; f. apostolic school for cands to priesthood from Munda Tribe; Prof. and Asst to Dir of St Joseph's High School, Torpa; Bishop of Dumka 1978; Coadjutor Archbishop of Ranchi 1984, Archbishop of Ranchi 1985–; attended Eighth Ordinary Ass. of World Synod of Bishops, Vatican City 1990, Special Ass. for Asia of World Synod of Bishops, Vatican City 1998, Second Special Ass. for Europe of World Synod of Bishops, Vatican City 1999, Tenth Ordinary Ass. of World Synod of Bishops, Vatican City 2001; cr. Cardinal (Cardinal Priest of Sacro Cuore di Gesù agonizzante a Vitinia) (first tribal cardinal of India—Oraon of Kurukh tribe) 2003; participated in Papal Conclave 2005, 2013; Pres.-Del. 11th Gen. Ordinary Ass. of World Synod of Bishops 2005; fmr Vice-Pres. Conf. of Catholic Bishops of India, Pres. 2004–06, mem. Special Comm. for Evangelization, Comm. for Inter-religious Dialogue; mem. Pontifical Council for Inter-Religious Dialogue, Bishops' Friends of the Focalare Movt, Cen. Cttee Fed. of Asian Bishops' Confs, Advisory Council Margareta Weisser Foundation for Indigenous Tribal Peoples in Asia, Governing Body Indo-German Social Service Soc., New Delhi, Nat. Educ. Group; Chair. Regional Bishops' Council, Jharkhand Bishops and Major Superiors Forum; fmr Chair. Office of Peace and Harmony of the FABC; Chancellor Faculty of Theology, Ranchi; mem. Governing Body Vikas Maitri, Ranchi, St Xavier's Coll., Ranchi, Nirmala Coll., Hinoo, Ursuline BEd Coll., Lohardaga; Pres. Chotanagpur Catholic Mission Co-operative Credit Soc., Catholic Charities, Ranchi; Patron Sarva Dharma Milan Parishad, Ranchi, Citizens' Forum, Ranchi; Managing Trustee Jharkhand Antyodaya Public Charitable Trust; Jharkhand Ratan, Lok Sewa Samity, Ranchi 2002. *Address:* Archbishop's House, PO Box 5, Purulia Road, Ranchi 834 001, Jharkhand, India (office). *Telephone:* (651) 204728 (office). *Fax:* (651) 304844 (office). *E-mail:* rca_ranch@ hotmail.com; telestoppo@rediffmail.com. *Website:* www.ranchiarchdiocese.com (office).

TOPTAN, Köksal; Turkish politician; b. 2 Sept. 1943, Rize; m.; three c.; ed Law Faculty, Istanbul Univ.; mem. Büyük Millet Meclisi (Grand Nat. Ass., Parl.) from Zonguldak 1977–91, 2007–, from Bartin 1991–2002, fmr Chair. Parl. Justice Cttee, Parl. Speaker 2007–09; Minister of State 2007–09; Minister of Educ. 1991–93; Minister of Culture Oct. 1995; Head, Türkiyem (charity); mem. Dogru Yol Party 1986–99; mem. Justice and Development Party (AKP) 2002–. *Address:* Büyük Millet Meclisi (Grand National Assembly), 06543 Bakanlýklar, Ankara, Turkey. *Telephone:* (312) 4205290. *Fax:* (312) 4205296. *E-mail:* koksal.toptan@tbmm.gov.tr (home); info@koksaltoptan.net. *Website:* www.tbmm.gov.tr; www.koksaltoptan .com.

TORFS, Henri Maria Dymphna André Laurent (Rik), PhD; Belgian canon law scholar, academic and university administrator; *Rector, Katholieke Universiteit Leuven;* b. 16 Oct. 1956, Turnhout; ed Sint-Gummaruscollege (Lier), Katholieke Universiteit Leuven (Catholic Univ. of Louvain), Univ. of Strasbourg,

France; fmr Senator for Christian Democratic and Flemish party in Belgian Fed. Parl.; Asst Prof., Faculty of Canon Law, Katholieke Universiteit Leuven 1988–96, Prof. 1996–, Dean of the Faculty 1994–2003, 2009–13, Rector Katholieke Universiteit Leuven 2013–; Guest Prof., Univ. of Stellenbosch, Univ. of Paris, Univ. of Nijmegen, Univ. of Strasbourg; mem. Academic Bd Int. Center for Law and Religion Studies, Brigham Young Univ., USA; mem. Bd of Experts, Int. Religious Liberty Asscn; fmr Pres. and Bd mem. European Consortium for Church and State Research; Founder and Bd mem. Working Group Nederlandstalige Canonisten (Dutch-speaking Canonists); mem. Comm. for Intercultural Dialogue 2005–, Commissie ter invulling van de cursus maatschappelijke oriëntatie 2006–, Les Assises de l'Interculturalité 2009–; adviser to Govt of Romania regarding the protection of religious minorities. *Publications include:* Het huwelijk als levensgemeenschap. Een kerkrechtelijke benadering 1990, Mensen en rechten in de Kerk 1993, De kardinaal heeft verdriet 2002, Voor het zinken de kerk uit 2004, Religie, vrede en onvrede 2005, Lof der lankmoedigheid 2006, Het hellend vla 2008, Wie gaat er dan de wereld redden? (Liberales Prize) 2009. *Address:* Rectorial Offices, Naamsestraat 22, Box 5000, 3000 Leuven, Belgium (office). *Telephone:* (16) 324067 (office). (16) 324066 (office). *Fax:* (16) 324196 (office). *E-mail:* rik.torfs@ kuleuven.be (office). *Website:* www.kuleuven.be (office); www.riktorfs.be (office).

TORIBIONG, Johnson, LLM, DIur; Palauan lawyer, diplomatist, politician and fmr head of state; b. 22 July 1946; m. Valeria Toribiong; ed Univ. of Washington Law School, USA; fmr Amb. to Taiwan; Pres. of Palau 2009–13. *Address:* c/o Office of the President, POB 6051, Koror, PW 96940, Palau.

TORIHARA, Mitsunori; Japanese business executive; *Chairman, Tokyo Gas;* b. 12 March 1943; joined Tokyo Gas 1967, Rep. Dir, Exec. Vice-Pres., Chief Exec. of Strategic Planning Div. and in charge of Internal Audit Dept and Compliance Dept 2003–04, Rep. Dir, Exec. Vice-Pres., Chief Exec. of Corp. Communication Div. and in charge of Compliance Dept 2004–06, Rep. Dir, Pres. and Exec. Pres. 2006–10, mem. Bd of Dirs and Chair. 2010–. *Address:* Tokyo Gas, 1-5-20 Kaigan, Minato-ku, Tokyo 105-8527, Japan (office). *Telephone:* (3) 5400-3888 (office). *E-mail:* tgir@ tokyo-gas.co.jp (office). *Website:* www.tokyo-gas.co.jp (office).

TORKUNOV, Anatoly Vasilyevich, Cand Hist, DrPolSci; Russian academic and diplomatist; *Rector, Moscow State Institute of International Relations;* b. 26 Aug. 1950, Moscow; m.; one d.; ed Moscow State Inst. of Int. Relations (MGIMO Univ.); teacher Moscow State Inst. of Int. Relations 1974–, Pro-Rector 1977–, Dean Chair. of Int. Relations, then First Pro-Rector 1986–; diplomatic service in People's Democratic Repub. of Korea 1971–72, in USA 1983–86; Rector, Moscow State Inst. of Int. Relations 1992–; Pres. Russian UN Asscn; mem. Expert Analytical Council, Attestation Bd Ministry of Russian Asscn of Int. Studies, Scientific Council of Security Council of Russian Fed., Russian Acad. of Nat. Sciences, Acad. of Sciences of Higher Schooling, Nat. Russian Cttee on problems of UNESCO; mem. Editorial Bd journals Global Gov. (USA), Mezhdunarodnaya Zhizn, Moscovsky Zhurnal Mezhdunarodnogo Prava, Bisnes i Politika; mem. Russian Acad. of Sciences; Order of Friendship between Peoples, Order of Merit, Order of Honour, Order of Diplomatic Merit (Repub. of Korea); Medals for Labour Merit, 850th Anniversary of Moscow, 300 Years of Russian Navy. *Publications:* seven monographs and over 170 scientific publs on int. relations, problems of Russian foreign policy, Asian-Pacific Region, Korea including: The War in Korea 1950–1953 Tokyo 2000, History of Korea, Moscow 2003, Contemporary International Relations and Russian Foreign Policy, Moscow 2004. *Leisure interests:* theatre, music. *Address:* Office of the Rector, Moscow State Institute of International Relations, 117454 Moscow, Vernadskogo prosp. 76, Russia (office). *Telephone:* (495) 434-00-89 (office). *Fax:* (495) 434-90-61 (office). *E-mail:* tork@mgimo.ru (office). *Website:* www.mgimo.ru (office).

TÖRMÄLÄ, Pertti, DPhil; Finnish scientist and academic; *Chairman and Chief Scientific Officer, Bioretec Limited;* b. 26 Nov. 1945, Tampere; s. of Matti Törmälä and Elma Virtanen; m. 1st Kirsti Miettinen 1967 (dissolved); two d.; m. 2nd Mirja Talasoja 1995; Assoc. Prof. of Non-Metallic Materials, Tampere Univ. of Tech. 1975, Prof. of Fibre Raw Materials, Prof. of Plastics Tech. and Head Inst. of Plastics Tech. 1985–95; fmr Research Prof., Acad. of Finland, Acad. Prof. and Head of Inst. of Biomaterial Tech. 2001–2005; Chair. and Chief Scientific Officer Bioretec Ltd 2005–; Hon. DMed; Nat. Inventor Prize 1986, Nordic Tech. Prize 1988. *Publications include:* eight textbooks, 150 patents and more than 800 scientific papers. *Leisure interests:* exercise, music. *Address:* Bioretec Ltd, Saarchkarjenknja 5, 33300 Tampere, Finland (office). *Telephone:* (40) 5146944 (office). *E-mail:* pertti.tormala@bioretec.com (office). *Website:* www.bioretec.com (office).

TORNATORE, Giuseppe; Italian filmmaker; b. 27 May 1956, Bagheria, Palermo, Sicily; debut as dir at age 16, with short film Il Carretto. *Television films include:* Ritratto di un Rapinatore, Incontro con Francesco Rosi, Scrittori Siciliani e Cinema: Verga, Pirandello, Brancati and Sciascia and Il Diario di Guttuso. *Feature films include:* writer and dir: Il Camorrista (The Professor) 1987, Cinema Paradiso (Special Jury Prize, Cannes Festival 1989) 1988, Stanno Tutti Bene (Everybody's Fine) 1991, Una Pura formalità (A Pure Formality) 1994, Uomo delle Stelle (Starmaker) 1995, La Leggenda del pianista sull'oceano (The Legend of the Pianist on the Ocean) 1998, Malèna 2000, The Unknown Woman 2006, Baarìa 2009. *Documentaries include:* Ethnic Minorities in Sicily (Best Documentary, Salerno Film Festival 1982), L'ultimo gattopardo: Ritratto di Goffredo Lombardo 2010.

TÖRNUDD, Klaus, PhD; Finnish diplomatist (retd) and academic; b. 26 Dec. 1931, Helsinki; s. of Allan Törnudd and Margit Niininen; m. Mirja Siirala 1960; one s. one d.; ed Univ. of Helsinki, Univ. of Paris and School of Advanced Int. Studies, Johns Hopkins Univ., Washington, DC; joined Foreign Service 1958, served at Perm. Mission to UN, New York 1961–64, Embassy in Cairo 1964–66, Embass in Moscow 1971–73, CSCE 1973–74; Prof. of Int. Politics, Univ. of Tampere 1967–71; Deputy Dir of Political Affairs, Ministry for Foreign Affairs 1974–77, Dir 1977–81, Under-Sec. of State for Political Affairs 1983–88; Perm. Rep. to the UN, New York 1988–91; Fellow, Harvard Univ., USA 1991–92; Sr Adviser, Ministry for Foreign Affairs 1992–93; Amb. to France and to UNESCO 1993–96; mem. Sr Faculty, Geneva Centre for Security Policy 1997–98; Visiting Prof., Nat. Defence Coll. of Finland 1998–2003; Ed. Co-operation and Conflict (Nordic Journal of Int. Politics) 1968–70, mem. Editorial Bd 1976–79; mem.

Editorial Bd of Ulkopolitiikka-Utrikespolitik 1983–87; Chair. of Bd Tampere Peace Research Inst. 1978–82; Chair. UN Study Group on Nuclear Weapon-Free Zones 1983–85; mem. Bd of Trustees UNITAR 1984–88; mem. of Bd of Govs IAEA 1985–87; mem. UN Sec.-Gen.'s Advisory Bd on Disarmament Matters 1991–96; Dr hc (Åbo Akademi Univ., Finland) 2002. *Publications:* several books on Finnish politics and int. affairs. *Address:* Tempelgatan 8 A, 00100 Helsinki, Finland. *Telephone:* (9) 490159. *E-mail:* klaus.toernudd@kolumbus.fi.

ToROBERT, Sir Henry Thomas, KBE, BEcons; Papua New Guinea banker; b. 1942, Kokopo; ed Univ. of Sydney, Australia; Asst Research Officer, Reserve Bank of Australia, Port Moresby 1965, Deputy Man. 1971–72, Man. 1972; Gov. and Chair. Bank of Papua New Guinea 1973–93; Chair. Credit Corpn (PNG) Ltd 1993–2007 (resgnd); Pnr, Deloitte Touche Tohmatsu 1993–; Chair. Papua New Guinea Inst. of Applied Social and Econ. Research 1975–82; Chair. Man. Bd Bankers' Coll. 1973–; Chair. Govt Super Task Force on Project Implementation 1994–; Pres. Amateur Sports Fed. and PNG Olympic and Commonwealth Games Cttee 1980–. *Address:* c/o Credit Corporation (PNG) Ltd, PO Box 1787, Port Moresby, Papua New Guinea.

TÖRÖK, László, DTech, DSc; Hungarian archaeologist and academic; *Research Professor Emeritus, Archaeological Institute, Research Centre for Humanities, Hungarian Academy of Sciences;* b. 13 May 1941, Budapest; s. of László Török and Mária Giesz; m. Erzsébet Szödy 1984 (died 2012); ed Budapest Univ. of Tech. Sciences, Eötvös Loránd Univ.; Research Fellow, Archaeological Inst., Hungarian Acad. of Sciences 1964, Sr Research Fellow 1985, Adviser 1991, Research Prof. 2004–12, Research Prof. Emer. 2012–; Lecturer, Eötvös Loránd Univ. of Arts and Sciences, Dept of Egyptology 1972, Hon. Prof. 1992–; Visiting Prof., Dept of Classics, Univ. of Bergen, Norway 1980, 1989–92, 1994–99; Overseas Visiting Scholar, St John's Coll. Cambridge 1998; Vice-Pres. of the Int. Soc. for Nubian Studies 1990–2002; Gen. Ed. of Antaeus (periodical) 1984–99; mem., Norwegian Acad. of Science and Letters 1994; mem., Hungarian Acad. of Science 2004; Albert Reckitt Archaeological Lecture, British Acad. 1995; research into ancient history and archaeology of Middle Nile Region and Hellenistic and late antique art of Egypt; Dr hc (Univ. of Bergen, Norway) 2000. *Publications:* Economic Offices and Officials in Meroitic Nubia 1978, Der meroitische Staat 1986, The Royal Crowns of Kush 1987, Late Antique Nubia 1988, Coptic Antiquities I–II 1993, Fontes Historiae Nubiorum I 1994, II 1996, III 1998, IV 2000 (with co-authors), Hellenistic and Roman Terracottas from Egypt 1995, The Birth of an Ancient African State 1995, Meroe City: An Ancient African Capital 1997, The Kingdom of Kush: Handbook of the Napatan-Meroitic Civilization 1997, The Hunting Centaur 1998, The Image of the Ordered World in Ancient Nubian Art 2002, Transfigurations of Hellenism: Aspects of Late Antique Art in Egypt AD 250–700 2005, Between Two Worlds: The Frontier Region Between Ancient Nubia and Egypt 3700 BC – 500 AD 2009, Hellenizing Art in Ancient Nubia 300 BC – AD 250 and its Egyptian Models: A Study in Acculturation 2011, Adoption and Adaptation: The Sense of Culture Transfer between Ancient Nubia and Egypt 2011, Herodotus in Nubia 2014; over 100 articles. *Leisure interest:* reading (belles-lettres). *Address:* MTA Bölcsészettudományi Kutatóközpont Régészeti Intézet, 1014 Budapest, Úri utca 49, Hungary (office). *Telephone:* 70-322-1140 (mobile). *Fax:* (1) 224-6719 (office). *E-mail:* tl.napata@freemail.hu (office).

TOROSSIAN, Tigran, PhD, DPolSci; Armenian engineer and politician; b. 14 April 1956, Yerevan; m.; one d.; ed Yerevan Polytechnic Inst.; Engineer, then Leading Engineer, Yerevan Scientific Research Inst. of Math. Machines 1978–88, Subdivision Head, then Scientific Assoc. 1988–95; mem., Cen. Electoral Comm. 1996–98; Ed.-in-Chief, Republican Party newspaper 1997–98; Deputy, Nat. Ass. (Republican Party of Armenia) 1999–, Vice-Chair. Azgayin Zhoghov (Nat. Ass.) 1999–2006, Chair. 2006–08, Chair. ad hoc Cttee on Constitutional Amendments 2001–03, ad hoc Cttee on Matters of Integration in European Structures 2003–08; Head of Armenian Del., Parl. Ass. of Council of Europe, Vice-Chair. Parl. Ass. of the Council of Europe European Democrat Group 2004–07; Vice-Chair. Cttee on the Honouring of Obligations and Commitments by Mem. States of Council of Europe 2006–07; mem. Party Bd Republican Party of Armenia 1993–2008, Deputy Chair. 1998–2005, Deputy Chair. Republican Party of Armenia 2005–08; Medal for Exceptional Services to Motherland 2006, Oder of St M. Mashtots of NKR 2007; Hon. DSc (Univ. of Artsakh); First Prize for The Best Scientific Work (Social Sciences), Competition of Nat. Science Acad. 2009. *Achievements include:* holder of ten eng patents. *Publications:* more than 30 scientific studies in math., four monographs and more than 40 scientific studies in political science and about 200 articles. *Telephone:* (10) 51-34-47 (office). *E-mail:* toros@parliament.am (office); t.tigran@yahoo.com (office).

TORP, Niels A., DipArch; Norwegian architect; *Principal, Niels Torp Arkitekter MNAL;* b. 8 March 1940, Oslo; s. of Ernst Torp and Nini Torp (née Butenschøn); m. Bente Poulsson; one s. three d.; ed Norges Tekniske Høgskole, Trondheim, The Norwegian Inst. Rome; joined Torp & Torp Arkitekter MNAL 1965, Partner 1970, Man. 1974, Man., Prin. Niels Torp Arkitekter MNAL 1984–; visiting lecturer at architectural schools in Norway and other European countries; major works: Giskehagen residential homes 1986, Scandinavian Airlines System (SAS) HQ, Stockholm 1987, Aker Brygge (dockland devt Oslo) 1988, HQ Den Norske Bank 1988, Hamar Olympiahall 1991, Alna Shopping Centre, Oslo 1996, railway station/ bus terminal, Gothenburg 1996, Christiania Qvartalet 1996, BA HQ, London 1997, Colosseum Park, Oslo 1997, Oslo Airport Gardermoen (with Aviaplan) 1998, airport control tower and airport hotel, Oslo 1998, Papendrop – Utrecht, The Netherlands, five office bldgs 1999, NSB (Norwegian Railway) HQ, Oslo 1999, devt plans for towns Larvik, Sandefjord, Drammen, Ås, Elverum, Hamar and Bodø, Masterplan Tjuvholmen, Oslo 2002, Nydalen Campus BI business school, Oslo 2005, Culture Centre Larvik 2007, AkerHus office bldg, Oslo 2008, The Soloist office bldg, Belfast 2009, Værnes Hotel, Trondheim 2009, Hotel Park Inn, Oslo Airport 2010, Vulkan Hotel, Oslo 2011, Tjuvholmen F1 South, Oslo 2011, NMD Oslo 2011, Jordan Airlines HQ, Amman 2012; A.C. Houens Legacy, Sundts Prize for Architectural Merits, Awards from the Stone Asscn, Fine Art Award (Oslo City Council), Carl M. Egers Legacy, Europa Nostra Awards, Prize for Built Environment (Norwegian Dept of Environment), Kasper Salin Prize (Sweden), European Award for Steel Structures, Swedish Stone Asscn Award, Concrete Award (Norway), British Construction Industry Award 1998, Brunel Award 1998, Aesthetic Counsel Diploma, Bærum, Norway 1998, Parelius Scholarship 1998,

Glulam Award 1999 (with Aviaplan), RIBA Award for Architecture 1999, Jacob Award for Design 1999, Civic Trust Award 2000, Oslo Council Jubilee Prize 2006, Int. Property Prize, Int. Real Estate Fed. (FIABCI) 2008, Houen Fonds Diploma 2008, European Commercial Property Awards 2010, City Prize 2012, Concrete Award 2012. *Leisure interests:* music, playing piano, sailing. *Address:* Industrigaten 59, PO Box 5387, 0304 Oslo, Norway (office). *Telephone:* 23-36-68-00 (office). *Fax:* 23-36-68-01 (office). *E-mail:* firmapost@nielstorp.no (office). *Website:* www .nielstorp.no (office).

TORRANCE, Sam, MBE, OBE; British professional golfer; b. 24 Aug. 1953, Largs; s. of Bob Torrance and June Torrance; m. Suzanne Torrance 1995; one s. two d.; professional golfer 1970–; has played in eight Ryder Cups (European Capt. 2002) and represented Scotland on numerous occasions; winner Scottish PGA Championship 1978, 1980, 1985, 1991, 1993; mem. Dunhill Cup team (eight times), World Cup team (11 times), Hennessy Cognac Cup team (five times), Double Diamond team (three times); Capt. winning European team in Asahi Glass Four Tours Championship, Adelaide 1991; Capt. winning British Ryder Cup Team 2002; winner of 28 tournaments worldwide since 1972 including Italian Open 1987, Germany Masters 1990, Jersey Open 1991, Kronenbourg Open 1993, Catalan Open 1993, Honda Open 1993, Hamburg Open 1993, British Masters 1995, French Open 1998; played US Sr Tour 2003–04, returned to European Sr Tour 2004–, winner Travis Perkins Senior Masters 2004, Irvine Whitlock Seniors Classic 2005, De Vere PGA Seniors Championship 2005, Bendinat London Seniors Masters 2005, Sharp Italian Seniors Open 2006, AIB Irish Seniors Open 2006, PGA Seniors Championship 2006, Scottish Seniors Open 2006; winner European Seniors Tour's Order of Merit 2005, 2006. *Publications:* Sam: The Autobiography of Sam Torrance 2003. *Leisure interests:* snooker, tennis. *Address:* c/o CSA, 90 High Street, Burnham, Bucks., SL1 7JT, England (office).

TORRES DE COLOM, Sandra, MPolSci; Guatemalan politician; b. Melchor de Mencos; m. Alvaro Colom Caballeros (divorced); four c.; ed Univ. San Carlos de Guatemala, Univ. Rafael Landívar; spent most of her career working on policies and projects promoting social devt, especially for women, children and people with special needs; mem. and Dir Unidad Nacional de la Esperanza (UNE), UNE Nat. Coordinator for Women and Pres., Social Cohesion Council; chosen as UNE nominee for 2011 presidential elections, divorced Alvaro Colom Caballeros April 2011 in order to run for Pres. of Guatemala following her husband's tenure, move ruled illegal by Supreme Court July 2011. *Address:* Unidad Nacional de la Esperanza, 2a Avenida 5-11, Zona 9, Guatemala City, Guatemala (office). *Telephone:* 232-4685 (office). *E-mail:* ideas@une.org.gt (office). *Website:* www .guatemala.gob.gt/primeradama.php (office).

TORRES-PEIMBERT, Silvia, PhD; Mexican astronomer and academic; *Professor Emerita, Institute of Astronomy, Universidad Nacional Autónoma de México (UNAM);* ed Univ. of California, Berkeley, USA; Prof., Faculty of Sciences and Inst. of Astronomy, Universidad Nacional Autónoma de México (UNAM), Head of Grad. Programme of Astronomy, now Prof. Emer., also Coordinator of Physical, Math. and Eng Sciences 2009; Ed. Revista Mexicana de Astronomia y Astrofisica for over 20 years; mem. American Astronomical Soc., Int. Astronomical Union (fmr Vice-Pres.); mem. UNESCO Global Scientific Cttee; Fellow, Acad. of Sciences for the Developing World; L'Oréal-UNESCO Women in Science Award (Latin America) 2011. *Radio:* producer of radio programme on the academic activity of UNAM. *Address:* Universidad Nacional Autonoma de Mexico, Inst de Astronomía, Circuito exterior s/n Ciudad Universitaria, México DF 04510, Mexico (office). *Telephone:* (55) 5622-3945 (office). *Fax:* (55) 5622-3945 (office). *E-mail:* silvia@astro.unam.mx (office). *Website:* www.astroscu.unam.mx/IA/index .php?option=com_content&view=article&id=463&Itemid=88&lang=en (office).

TORRICELLI, Robert G., JD, MPA; American business executive and fmr politician; *Partner, Panepinto Properties;* b. 26 Aug. 1951, Paterson, NJ; ed Rutgers and Harvard Univs; called to the Bar, NJ 1978; Deputy Legis. Counsel, Office of Gov. of NJ 1975–77; counsel to Vice-Pres. Mondale, Washington, DC 1978–81; pvt. legal practice, Washington, DC 1981–82; mem. US House of Reps 1983–97; Senator from New Jersey 1996–2002; currently Partner, Panepinto Properties; Democrat. *Address:* Panepinto Properties, Harborside Plaza 10, 3 Second Street, Suite 1203, Jersey City, NJ 07311, USA (office). *Telephone:* (201) 521-9000 (office). *Fax:* (201) 434-3218 (office). *E-mail:* info@panprop.com (office). *Website:* www.panepintoproperties.com (office).

TORRIJOS ESPINO, Martin; Panamanian business executive, politician and fmr head of state; b. 18 July 1963, Panama City; s. of Gen. Omar Torrijos; m. Vivian de Torrijos; one s.; ed Texas A&M Univ., USA; fmr man. McDonald's, Chicago, USA; Sec.-Gen. Democratic Revolutionary Party (PRD) 1999–; cand. for presidential elections 1999; Pres. of Panama 2004–09; Vice-Pres. Conference of Political Parties of Latin America and the Caribbean (COPPAL) 2002–. *Address:* c/o Partido Revolucionario Democrático (PRD), Calle 42 Bella Vista, entre Avda Perú y Avda Cuba, bajando por el teatro Bella Vista, Panamá 9, Panama (office).

TORRY, Sir Peter James, GCVO, KCMG; British consultant and fmr diplomatist; b. 1948, Berlin, Germany; m. Angela Torry; three d.; ed Dover Coll., New Coll., Oxford; joined FCO 1970, Third Sec., Embassy in Havana 1971–73, Second Sec. (Econ.), Embassy in Jakarta 1974–77, First Sec., FCO 1977–81, 1985–89 (later also Counsellor), First Sec. (Political), Embassy in Bonn 1981–85, Counsellor, Embassy in Washington, DC 1989–93, Dir for Personnel and Security, FCO 1993–98, Amb. to Spain 1998–2003, to Germany 2003–07; Sr Adviser, Centrica PLC, Betfair PLC, Celesion AG, White Owl Capital; f. Peter Torry Consultancy Ltd; mem. Advisory Bd Lloyds Pharmacy, Global Econ. Symposium, Kiel Inst.; Policy Fellow, Bonn Inst. for Employment. *Leisure interests:* golf, walking, skiing, books, antique furniture. *Address:* Peter Torry Consultancy Ltd, Flat 17, 192 Emery Hill Street, London, SW1P 1PN, England (office). *E-mail:* info@petertorry.co.uk (office). *Website:* www.petertorry.co.uk (office).

TORSHIN, Aleksander Porfiryevich; Russian politician; *Deputy Chairman, Sovet Federatsii (Federation Council);* b. 27 Nov. 1953, Mitoga, Kamchatsk region; m. Nina Valer'yevna Torshina; two d.; ed All Union Inst. of Law, Moscow State Univ.; teacher, Docent, Acad. of Public Sciences, fmr functionary, Cen. CPSU Cttee; Deputy Head Div. on Public Relations with Chambers, Factions and Public Orgs, Fed. Ass. of Russian Fed. 1993–95; Statistics Sec., Deputy Chair. Cen. Bank 1995–98; Deputy Chair. Admin of Russian Fed. Govt, Rep. of Russian Fed. Gov. to

State Duma (Parl.) 1998–99; Deputy Dir-Gen. Statistics-Sec., State Corp. Agency on Restructuring of Credit Orgs (ARKO) 1999–2001; mem. Sovet Federatsii (Fed. Council) representing Mari-El Repub. 2001–, Deputy Chair. 2002–, Acting Chair. 2011; Deputy Chair. Parl. Union of Russia and Byelorussia Union 2004–; mem. Cttee on Agrarian-Food Policy, Comm. on Regulation and Organization of Parl. Activities, Comm. on Controlling Council of Fed. Activities; Rep. of Govt of Mari-El Repub. to Fed. Ass. *Address:* Federation Council, 103426 Moscow, Bolshaya Dmitrovka str. 26 (office); Leninsky prosp. 29, Office 114, Yoshkar-Ola, 424001 Republic of Mari-El, Russia (office). *Telephone:* (495) 292-59-21 (office). *Fax:* (495) 292-76-03 (office). *Website:* www.council.gov.ru (office).

TORSTENDAHL, Rolf, PhD; Swedish historian and academic; *Professor Emeritus of History, Uppsala University;* b. 9 Jan. 1936, Jönköping; s. of Torsten Torstendahl and Ragnhild Torstendahl (née Abrahamsson); m. 1st Anna-Maria Ljung 1960 (died 1987); two s.; m. 2nd Tamara A. Salycheva 1996; ed Uppsala Univ.; Lecturer, Dept of History, Uppsala Univ. 1964–67, Assoc. Prof. 1968–78, Sven Warburg Prof. of History 1978–80, Stockholm Univ.; Prof., Uppsala Univ. 1981–2000, Prof. Emer. 2001–; Prof., Mälardalen Univ. 2002–03; Dir Swedish Collegium for Advanced Study in the Social Sciences 1985–90, Dean of Faculty 1994–99; mem. Royal Swedish Acad. of Letters, History and Antiquities 1982, Norwegian Acad. of Science and Letters 1989, Academia Europaea 1989, Russia Acad. of Sciences, Urals Div. 1995; Dr hc (Russian State Univ. for the Humanities) 2006; Björnstiernas Prize, Royal Swedish Acad. of Letters, History and Antiquities 1976. *Publications include:* Teknologins nytta 1975, Dispersion of Engineers in a Transitional Society 1975, Professions in Theory and History (ed.) 1990, The Formation of Professions (ed.) 1990, Bureaucratization in Northwestern Europe 1880–1985 1991, State Theory and State History (ed.) 1992, History-making (ed.) 1996, State Policy and Gender System (ed.) 1999, An Assessment of Twentieth-Century Historiography (ed.) 2000, Zarozhdenie demokraticheskoi kultury 2005 (English edn 2012), Gjort, tänkt, känt (memoirs) 2011. *Address:* Department of History, Uppsala University, PO Box 628, 751 26 Uppsala (office); St Olofsgatan 4, 75 312 Uppsala, Sweden (home). *Telephone:* (18) 471-15-29 (office); (18) 12-52-98 (home); 700-980452 (mobile). *E-mail:* rolf.torstendahl@hist.uu.se (office). *Website:* www.hist.uu.se (office).

TORTELIER, Yan Pascal; French conductor and violinist; b. 19 April 1947, Paris; s. of the late Paul Tortelier and of Maud Tortelier; m. Sylvie Brunet-Moret 1970; two s.; ed Paris Conservatoire and Berks. Music Centre, music studies with Nadia Boulanger, studies in conducting with Franco Ferrara; debut as concert violinist, Royal Albert Hall 1962; has since toured extensively world-wide; Konzertmeister, Assoc. Conductor of Orchestre du Capitole de Toulouse 1974–82; Prin. Conductor and Artistic Dir, Ulster Orchestra 1989–92; Prin. Conductor, BBC Philharmonic 1992–2003, Conductor Laureate 2003–10, Conductor Emer. 2010–; Prin. Guest Conductor, Pittsburgh Symphony Orchestra 2005–08; Prin. Conductor, Orquestra Sinfónica de São Paulo 2009–11, Hon. Guest Conductor 2012–; guest conducting with San Francisco Symphony, Dresden Philharmonic, London Philharmonic, Minnesota Orchestra, Baltimore Symphony, St Petersburg Philharmonic, Sydney Symphony, Melbourne Symphony etc.; Hon. DLitt (Ulster) 1992; Dr hc (Lancaster) 1999; First Prize for Violin, Paris Conservatoire 1961. *Recordings include:* Ravel/Debussy/Massenet (BBC Music Magazine Orchestral Award 2012). *Publication:* première orchestration of Ravel's Piano Trio (world première concert 1992). *Leisure interests:* skiing, windsurfing, scuba diving, nature. *Address:* c/o IMG Artists, The Light Box, 111 Power Road, London, W4 5PY, England (office). *Telephone:* (20) 7957-5800 (office). *Fax:* (20) 7957-5801 (office). *E-mail:* nmathias@imgartists.com (office). *Website:* www .imgartists.com (office).

TORVALDS, Linus Benedict, MSc; Finnish/American computer software developer; *Fellow, The Linux Foundation;* b. 28 Dec. 1969, Helsinki; s. of Nils Torvalds and Anna Torvalds; m. Tove Monni; three d.; ed Univ. of Helsinki; fmr teacher and research asst; cr. the Linux kernel and oversaw open source devt of the widely used Linux operating system; with Transmeta 1997, later Transmeta Fellow –2003; Fellow, Open Source Devt Labs Inc. (consortium formed by high-tech cos including IBM, Hewlett-Packard, Intel, AMD, RedHat, Novell and many others, OSDL merged with The Free Standards Group to become The Linux Foundation 2007) 2003–; remains the ultimate authority on what new code is incorporated into the standard Linux kernel; Dr hc (Stockholm) 1999, (Helsinki) 2000; asteroid 9793 Torvalds named in his honour 1996, EFF Pioneer Award 1998, Lovelace Medal, British Computer Soc. 2000, InfoWorld Award for Industry Achievement 2000, Takeda Award for Social/Econ. Well-Being (co-recipient) 2001, named by TIME mazazine as one of the most influential people in the world 2004, Vollum Award, Reed Coll. 2005, inducted into Hall of Fellows of the Computer History Museum, Mountain View, Calif. 2008, C&C Prize, NEC Corpn 2010, Millennium Tech. Prize, Technology Acad. Finland (co-recipient) 2012, an inaugural inductee into the Internet Hall of Fame 2012. *Publications:* Just for Fun (with David Diamond) 2001; 35 patents world-wide. *Address:* The Linux Foundation, 660 York Street, Suite 102, San Francisco, CA 94110, USA (office). *Telephone:* (415) 723-9709 (office). *Fax:* (415) 723-9709 (office). *E-mail:* info@ linuxfoundation.org (office). *Website:* www.linuxfoundation.org (office).

TORVILL, Jayne, OBE; British ice skater; b. 7 Oct. 1957; d. of George Torvill and Betty Torvill (née Smart); m. Philip Christensen 1990; ed Clifton Hall Grammar School for Girls; insurance clerk 1974–80; British Pair Skating Champion (with Michael Hutchinson) 1971; British Ice Dance Champion (with Christopher Dean q.v.) 1978–83, 1994; European Ice Dance Champion (with Christopher Dean) 1981–82, 1984, 1994; World Ice Dance Champion (with Christopher Dean) 1981–84; World Professional Ice Dance Champion (with Christopher Dean) 1984, 1985, 1990, 1995, 1996; Olympic Ice Dance Champion (with Christopher Dean) 1984; Olympic Ice Dance Bronze Medal (with Cristopher Dean) 1994; Tours include: Australia and NZ 1984, Royal Variety Performance London 1984, world tour with own co. of int. skaters 1985, guest artists with IceCapades 1987, world tour with co. of skaters from Soviet Union 1988, Australia as guests of S Australian Govt 1991, GB with co. of skaters from Ukraine 1992, Torvill & Dean, Face the Music, World Tour, UK, Australia and N America 1994, Stars on Ice tour in USA and Canada 1997, Torvill & Dean Ice Adventures in UK 1997–98, Stars on Ice Tour in USA and Canada 1997–98; choreography includes Stars on Ice in USA 1998–99, 1999–2000, O'Connor and O'Dougherty 1999–2000, GB Nat. Champion Synchro-

nized Skating Team 1999–2000; Hon. MA (Nottingham Trent) 1994; BBC Sportsview Personality of the Year (with Christopher Dean) 1983–84; Figure Skating Hall of Fame (with Christopher Dean) 1989. *Television:* Path of Perfection (Thames Television video) 1984, Fire & Ice (also video) 1986, World Tour (video) 1988, Bladerunners (BBC documentary) 1991, Great Britain Tour (TV special and video) 1992, The Artistry of Torvill and Dean (ABC) 1994, Face the Music (video) 1995, Torvill & Dean: The Story So Far (video) 1996, Bach Cello Suite (with Yo-Yo Ma) 1996, Dancing on Ice. *Publications:* (with Christopher Dean) Torvill and Dean: An Autobiography 1984, Torvill and Dean: Fire on Ice (with Christopher Dean) 1984, Torvill and Dean: Face the Music and Dance 1995, Facing the Music (with Christopher Dean) 1995. *Leisure interests:* theatre, ballet, dogs. *Address:* POB 32, Heathfield, East Sussex, TN21 0BW, England. *Website:* www.torvillanddean.com/ jayne.html.

TOSATTI, Erio, PhD; Italian physicist and academic; *Professor and Head of Condensed Matter Theory Group, International School For Advanced Studies (SISSA);* ed Univ. of Modena, CERN, Geneva, Scuola Normale Superiore, Pisa; served as Second Lt, Weather Forecast Service, Italian Air Forces 1970–71; staff mem. Italian Research Council, Univ. of Rome 1971–77; Royal Soc./NATO Fellow, Cavendish Lab., Univ. of Cambridge, UK 1972–73; Deutsche Forschungsgemeinschaft Visitor, Univ. of Stuttgart, Germany 1974; Sr NATO Fellow, Stanford Univ., USA 1977; sr staff mem. Italian Research Council and Lecturer, Univ. of Trieste 1977–80; Co-founder and consultant Condensed Matter Programme, Int. Centre for Theoretical Physics, Trieste 1977–, Deputy Head 1990–, Acting Dir 2002–03, Permanent Bd Mem., Trieste and Adriatico Research Confs; Prof. and Head, Condensed Matter Theory Group, Int. School For Advanced Studies (SISSA), Trieste 1980–; Visiting Scientist, RCA Zürich and IBM Zürich Research Labs 1984–85; Visiting Prof., Universite' Pierre et Marie Curie, Paris 1994, 1996, 2002, 2003, Univ. of NSW, Australia 1999, Donostia Int. Physics Centre, San Sebastian, Spain 2001, Universite' Pierre et Marie Curie, Paris, France 2002, 2003, Chinese Acad. of Sciences, Beijing and Fudan Univ., Shanghai, China 2004, Raman Research Inst., Bangalore, India 2006, Fudan Univ., Shanghai 2006, Renmin Univ., Beijing and Univ. of Hong Kong 2007, Universite' Paris-Sud, Orsay, France 2008; mem. Scientific Advisory Cttee, Elettra Synchrotron, Trieste 2002–; mem. Italian Physical Soc., American Physical Soc., European Physical Soc.; Corresp. mem. Accademia Nazionale dei Lincei, Rome 2006; Eli Burstein Lecture Award, Univ. of Pa 1994, Francesco Somaini Triennial Physics Prize 1997, Lamina Aurea di Redu' 1999, US Physics Medal for Int. Leadership 2006. *Publications:* co-ed.: Physics of Intercalation Compounds 1981, Fractals in Physics 1986, High-Temperature Superconductors 1987, Towards the Theoretical Understanding of High-Temperature Superconductors 1988, Strongly Correlated Electron Systems I 1990, Strongly Correlated Electron Systems II 1991, Strongly Correlated Electron Systems III 1993, Clusters and Fullerenes 1993, The Physics of Sliding Friction 1996; contrib.: over 460 articles and reviews in int. journals. *Address:* International School For Advanced Studies (SISSA), via Beirut 2–4, 34014 Trieste, Italy (office). *Telephone:* (40) 3787438 (office). *Fax:* (40) 3787528 (office). *Website:* www .sissa.it/~tosatti (office).

TOSIC, Momir, BEcons; Bosnia and Herzegovina politician and economist; ed Univ. of Belgrade; Head of Investments, Sipad Planinski, Han Pijesak 1979–83; Man. OOUR Dept, Centrotrans (transport co.) 1983–87; Chair. Exec. Bd, Han Pijesak municipality 1987–93; Gen. Dir Sipad Komerc, Sokolac 1993–95; Pres. Bd of Dirs Elektroprivreda Republika Srpska 1995; Dir Srpske Sume (Serb Forests) 1992–98; Rep., Ass. of Bosnia and Herzegovina, also Nat. Ass. of Republika Srpska; Del. and First Chair. House of People (Parl. Ass.); mem. Bosnia and Herzegovina parl. del. to Council of Europe, Strasbourg; mem. SDS (Serbian Democratic Party) Main Bd –2004, conditionally removed from office by High Rep. Paddy Ashdown 30 June 2004; Deputy Minister of Foreign Trade and Econ. Relations 2003–04, conditionally removed from office by High Rep. Paddy Ashdown 30 June 2004. *Address:* c/o Ministry of Foreign Trade and Economic Relations, trg Oktobra bb, 71000 Sarajevo, Bosnia and Herzegovina (office). *Telephone:* (33) 445750 (office).

TOŠOVSKÝ, Josef, BCom; Czech banker; *Chairman, Financial Stability Institute;* b. 28 Sept. 1950, Náchod; m. Bohdana Světlíková; two d.; ed Univ. of Econs Prague; Assoc. Prof., Univ. of Econs, Prague; banker with Czechoslovak State Bank 1973–, Deputy Dir 1978–, consultant to Bank Chair. 1982; Chief Economist, Živnostenská banka, London 1984–85, Deputy Dir June–Dec. 1989; Consultant to Bank Chair., Prague 1986–89; Chair. Czechoslovak State Bank 1989–92, Gov. 1992, for Czech Nat. Bank 1993–97, 1998–2000; Prime Minister of Czech Repub. 1997–98; Chair. Financial Stability Inst., BIS, Basel, Switzerland 2000–; Dr hc (Mendelova Univ. Brno) 2002; Central Banker of the Year, IMF 1993, European Man. of the Year, European Business Press Fed. 1994, Karel Engliš Prize 1994, European Banker of the Year, Group 20+1 1996, East-West Inst. Award for Leadership in Transition (USA) 2001. *Publications:* numerous articles in professional press. *Leisure interest:* tennis. *Address:* Financial Stability Institute, Bank for International Settlements, Centralbahnplatz 2, 4002 Basel, Switzerland (office). *Telephone:* (61) 2808074 (office). *Fax:* (61) 2809100 (office). *E-mail:* josef .tosovsky@bis.org (office). *Website:* www.bis.org (office).

TOSUNYAN, Garegin A., CandPhys, Math, Sciences, DrJur; Russian banker; *President, Association of Russian Banks;* b. 1955, Yerevan; m.; two d. one s.; ed Moscow State Univ., All-Union Jurist Inst. (by correspondence), Acad. of Nat. Economy, Govt of Russian Fed.; worked in United Inst. of Nuclear Studies in Dubna Moscow region; Researcher, All-Union Electrotechnology Inst., Moscow 1977–88, later Sr Researcher, Head of Div.; Chief Expert, Head of Div., Head of Dept, Chief of Dept on Sciences and Tech., Moscow City Council of Deputies 1988–90; Founder and Pres. Technobank 1990–98; first Vice-Pres. Asscn of Russian Banks 1990, Pres. 2002–; Chair. Bd of Dirs Interbanking Finance Corpn 1992–; Head of Dept, Acad. of Nat. Economy 1997–; Head, Banking Law Centre, Inst. of State and Law, Russian Acad. of Sciences 1999–; mem. Council of Banking Reps, Office of Mayor of Moscow 1994–; mem. Consultative Council on Banking Activities, Govt of Russian Fed. 1996–; adviser to Mayor of Moscow on financial and banking problems 1997–, to Chair. of Fed. Council of Fed. Ass. of Russian Fed. 2004–; Adviser to Chair. Govt of Russian Fed. 1998–2000. *Publications include:* more than 170 scientific works and articles on problems of the banking system and banking law, and 37 studies, including Banking Business and Banking Law in Russia: Experience, Problems, Perspectives 1995, State Management in the Field of Finance and Credits in Russia (textbook) 1997, Money and Power 2000, Banking Law of the Russian Federation 1999–2002, Market of Self Regulation 2004. *Address:* Association of Russian Banks, Skatertny per. 20 bldg 1, PO Box 41, Moscow 121069, Russia (office). *Telephone:* (495) 291-66-30 (office). *Fax:* (495) 291-66-66 (office). *E-mail:* arb@arb.ru (office). *Website:* www.arb.ru (office).

TOTSKY, Gen. Konstantin Vasilyevich; Russian army officer, diplomatist and government official; *Deputy Head of Service, Federal Service on Supervision in Nature Management;* b. 23 Feb. 1950, Kagan, Uzbekistan; m.; two d.; ed Higher Frontier Mil. School, Frunze Mil. Acad., Gen. Staff Mil. Acad.; army service in Pacific, Cen. Asian, Transcaucasian, NW Border Dist 1977–89; participated in mil. operations in Afghanistan; Head, Acad. of Fed. Border Service of Russian Fed. 1996–; Dir Fed. Border Service 1998; Chair. Council of Border Forces of CIS Countries 1998–2003; rank of Amb.; Head of Mission of Russian Fed. to NATO 2003–08; Deputy Head of Service, Fed. Service on Supervision in Nature Man. 2009–; more than 30 orders and medals. *Address:* 4/6 Bolshaya Gruzinskaya Street, Moscow 123995, Russia (office). *Telephone:* (499) 615-99-43 (office); (499) 611-12-04 (office); (495) 254-61-65 (office); (499) 611-21-41 (office). *Fax:* (495) 254-62-33 (office). *E-mail:* info@rpn.gov.ru (office). *Website:* rpn.gov.ru (office).

TÖTTERMAN, Richard Evert Björnson, DPhil, JurLic; Finnish diplomatist; b. 10 Oct. 1926, Helsinki; s. of B. Björn Tötterman and Katharine Clare Wimpenny; m. Camilla S. Veronica Huber 1953; one s. one d.; ed Univ. of Helsinki, Brasenose Coll., Oxford, UK; joined Ministry for Foreign Affairs 1952, diplomatic posts in Stockholm 1954–56, Moscow 1956–58, at Ministry of Foreign Affairs 1958–62, Berne 1962–63, Paris 1963–66; Deputy Dir, Ministry of Foreign Affairs 1966; Sec.-Gen., Office of Pres. of Finland 1966–70; Sec. of State, Ministry of Foreign Affairs 1970–75, Amb. to UK 1975–83, to Switzerland 1983–90, also accred to the Holy See 1988–90; Chair., Multilateral Consultations preparing CSCE 1972–73; Hon. Fellow, Brasenose Coll., Oxford 1982; Hon. GCVO, Hon. OBE; Kt Commdr, Order of the White Rose of Finland; Grand Cross, Order of the Dannebrog (Denmark), Order of Merit (Austria), Order of Orange-Nassau (Netherlands), Order of the Pole Star (Sweden), Order of the Falcon (Iceland), Order of St Olav (Norway), Order of Merit (Poland), Order of the Lion (Senegal), Order of the Banner (Hungary); Grand Officier, Ordre de la Couronne (Belgium); Commdr, Ordre nat. du Mérite; Kt, Order of Vasa (Sweden). *Leisure interests:* music, int. relations. *Address:* Parkgatan 9A, 00140 Helsinki, Finland (home). *Telephone:* (9) 627721 (home).

TOTTI, Francesco; Italian professional footballer; b. 27 Sept. 1976, Porta Metronia, Rome; s. of Enzo Totti and Fiorella Totti; m. Ilary Blasi 2005; one s. one d.; striker/attacking midfielder; youth player for Fortitudo 1984, Smit Trastevere 1984–86, Lodigiani 1986–89, Roma 1989–92; sr player for AS Roma 1993– (430 appearances, 187 goals), Capt. 1998–, won Serie A 2001, Supercoppa Italiana 2001, 2007, Coppa Italia 2007, 2008; mem. Italy U-16-15 team 1991–92, Italy U-18 team 1993–95, Italy U-19 team 1995–97, Italy U-21 team 1997 (won UEFA European Under-21 Football Championship 1996, Mediterranean Games 1997), Italy 1998–2006 (58 caps, nine goals, won World Cup, Germany 2006); leading all-time scorer for AS Roma; Good-Will Amb., UNICEF 2003–, FIFA/SOS Children's Villages 2006–; runs football school, Number Ten, and owns motorcycle racing team Totti Top Sport; Cavaliere Ordine al Merito della Repubblica Italiana (Fifth Class) 2000, (Fourth Class) 2006; Serie A Young Footballer of the Year 1999, Euro 2000 Team of the Tournament 2000, Serie A Footballer of the Year 2000, 2003, Italian Footballer of the Year 2000, 2001, 2003, 2004, 2007, ESM Team of the Year 2000/01, 2003/04, 2006/07, named in FIFA 100 2004, FIFA World Cup All-Star Team 2006, Serie A Top Scorer 2006/07, European Golden Shoe 2006/07, USSI Silver Ball (Serie A Fair Play award) 2007/08, Roma all-time leading scorer, Roma all-time highest number of appearances. *Publications:* Tutto Totti: Mo je faccio er cucchiaio (autobiography), published two best-selling joke books (some of the jokes were filmed in short sketches featuring himself with friends and nat. team-mates in a short show called La sai l'ultima di Totti). *Leisure interest:* collects jerseys from sports teams around the world. *Address:* c/o AS Roma, Via di Trigoria Km 3,600, 00128 Rome, Italy. *Telephone:* (06) 501911. *Fax:* (06) 5061736. *E-mail:* info@asromastore.it. *Website:* www.asroma.it; www.francescototti.com.

TOTTIE, Thomas, FilLic; Swedish fmr librarian; b. 3 July 1930, Waxholm; s. of the late John Tottie and Gerda Tottie (née Willers); m. 1st; two d.; m. 2nd Marianne Sandels 1972; two s.; ed Stockholm Univ.; Asst Librarian, Royal Library, Stockholm 1961; Sec. Swedish Council of Research Libraries 1966–73; Deputy Dir Stockholm Univ. Library 1975–76; Dir Library of Royal Carolingian Medico-Chirurgical Inst., Stockholm 1977; Chief Librarian, Uppsala Univ. 1978–96; mem. and official of various professional orgs; Dr hc (Uppsala) 1994. *Publications:* two books and numerous articles and reports on librarianship. *Leisure interests:* biography, sailing. *Address:* University Publications from Uppsala, Uppsala University Library, PO Box 510, 751 20 Uppsala (office); Kyrkogardsgatan 5A, 753 10 Uppsala, Sweden (home). *Telephone:* (18) 471-20-39 (office); (18) 12-32-00 (home). *E-mail:* thomas.tottie@ub.uu.se (office). *Website:* www.ub.uu.se/upu (office).

TOUADÉRA, Faustin-Archange, BSc, MSc, PhD; Central African Republic mathematician, university vice-chancellor and politician; b. 21 April 1957, Bangui; ed Barthelemy Boganda Coll., Bangui, Univ. of Bangui, Univ. of Abidjan, Côte d'Ivoire, Lille Univ. of Science and Tech. (Lille I), France, Univ. of Yaoundé I, Cameroon; Asst Lecturer in Math., Faculty of Science, Univ. of Bangui 1987, Vice-Dean Faculty of Science 1989–92, apptd Dir Coll. for Training of Teachers (ENS) 1992, Vice-Chancellor Univ. of Bangui 2004–08; mem. Inter-state Cttee for Standardization of Math. Programmes in French-speaking countries and Indian Ocean (CIEHPM) 1992–2002, Pres. CIEHPM 2001–03; mem. African Network of Math. and Applications for Devt (RAMAD) 2001–; Vice-Pres. Math. Union of Cen. African Repub. (UMAC) 2003–; Prime Minister of Cen. African Repub. 2008–12 (dismissed); Chevalier of the Order, Officer of the Order, Kt of the Order (all for services to educ.). *Address:* c/o Office of the President, Palais de la Renaissance, Bangui, Central African Republic.

TOUBERT, Pierre Marcel Paul, PhD; French academic; *Professor of Medieval History, Collège de France;* b. 29 Nov. 1932, Algiers; s. of André Toubert and Paola Garcia y Planes; m. Hélène Poggioli 1954; one s.; ed Ecole Normale Supérieure, Paris, Ecole des Hautes-Etudes, Paris, Univ. of Paris and Ecole Française d'Archéologie, Rome; mem. Ecole Française, Rome 1958–61; Dir of Studies, École

des Hautes-Etudes 1964–92; Prof. Dept of History, Univ. of Paris (Sorbonne) 1969–92; Prof. Coll. de France 1991–; mem. Nat. Council for Scientific Research, CNRS 1992–; mem. Acad. des Inscriptions et Belles-Lettres, Inst. de France, Academia Europaea 1989–, Nat. Cttee of Evaluation of Univs 1996–, High Council of Technological Research 1999–, Accademia Nazionale dei Lincei, Rome 2000–, Instituto Lombardo, Milan 2003–; Officier, Légion d'honneur, Commdr, Ordre nat. du Mérite 2010, Ordre des Arts et Lettres; Commdr des Palmes académiques; Dr hc (Siena) 1999, (Liège) 2002. *Publications include:* Les structures du Latium médiéval 1973, Etudes sur l'Italie médiévale 1976, Histoire du haut Moyen Age et de l'Italie médiévale 1987, Castillos señores y campesinos en la Italia medieval 1990, Dalla terra ai castelli nell'Italia medioevale 1994, L'Europe dans sa première croissance 2004, Moyen Age et Renaissance au Collège de France 2009, Remploi, citation et plagiat: conduites et pratiques médiévales 2009; many other books and publs on medieval Italy, econ. and social history of the Middle Ages. *Address:* Collège de France, 11 place Marcelin Berthelot, 75231 Paris Cedex 05 (office); 34 rue Guynemer, 75006 Paris, France (home). *Telephone:* 1-44-27-10-32 (office). *Fax:* 1-44-27-10-89 (office). *E-mail:* pierre.toubert@college-de-france.fr (office).

TOUBIANA, Serge; French editor, organization executive and university administrator; *Chairman, Ecole nationale supérieure d'architecture de Paris-Malaquais;* b. 15 Aug. 1949, Sousse, Tunisia; ed high school in Grenoble, Université Paris 3-Sorbonne Nouvelle (Centre Censier); family moved to Grenoble 1962; Co-Ed. Les Cahiers du Cinema magazine 1973–81, Ed. of relaunced edn 1981–92; Dir Cinémathèque française 2003–; Chair. École nationale supérieure d'architecture de Paris-Malaquais 2009–; fmr Lecturer in Cinema (part-time), Univs of Paris III and Paris VII; mem. Jury, Prix Louis Delluc 1986–2001, Cannes Int. Film Festival 1992; mem. Advances sur recette 1985, Vice-Pres. 1989, 1990; Pres. Comm. d'aide à la distribution 1992; Editorial Dir, Dept DVD at MK2 2000–01. *Publications:* Persévérance (with Serge Daney) 1994, L'arrière-mémoire -Entretien avec Micheline Presle 1994, Le cinéma vers son deuxième siècle 1995, François Truffaut (with Antoine De Baecque) 1996, Simenon 2003, Le cinéma d'Amos Gitai, Exils et territoires 2003. *Address:* École nationale supérieure d'architecture de Paris-Malaquais, 14, rue Bonaparte, 75272 Paris Cedex 06 (office); Cinémathèque française, 51 rue de Bercy, 75012 Paris, France (office). *Telephone:* 1-55-04-56-50 (École) (office); 1-71-19-33-33 (Cinémathèque française) (office). *E-mail:* info@paris-malaquais.archi.fr (office); info@cinematheque.fr (office). *Website:* www.paris-malaquais.archi.fr (office); www.cinematheque.fr (office).

TOUBLANC, Yves; French business executive; *Chairman of the Supervisory Board, Groupe BPCE;* began career in Saint-Gobain group 1972, held positions of responsibility in IT, management control and in Finance Dept; joined Poliet Group 1982, Chair. Bollon Point P Co., Chambéry 1994; took over and managed cos active in the transformation of cardboard 1994–2001, sold co.; Founder and Chair. Châtel Participations 2002–; mem. Steering and Supervisory Bd Caisse d'Epargne des Alpes 1993–, Chair. 2003–07, Chair. Steering and Supervisory Bd Caisse d'Epargne Rhône-Alpes (savings bank created from merger of Caisse d'Epargne Rhône-Alpes Lyon and Caisse d'Epargne des Alpes) and Vice-Chair. Supervisory Bd BPCE 2007–12, Chair. Supervisory Bd BPCE 2012–. *Address:* Groupe BPCE, 50 avenue Pierre Mendès France, 75201 Paris Cedex 13, France (office). *Telephone:* 1-58-40-41-42 (office). *E-mail:* info@bpce.fr (office). *Website:* www.bpce.fr (office).

TOUBON, Jacques, LenD; French politician; b. 29 June 1941, Nice; s. of Pierre-Constant Toubon and Yolande (Molinas) Toubon; m. 1st Béatrice Bernascon; m. 2nd Lise Weiler 1982; ed Lycée Masséna, Nice, Lycée Jean Perrin, Lyon, Faculté de Droit, Lyon, Inst. d'Etudes Politiques, Lyon and Ecole Nat. d'Admin; civil servant 1965–76, Chef de Cabinet, to Minister of Agric. 1972–74, to Minister of Interior 1974, Tech. Adviser, Office of Prime Minister 1974–76; Asst Sec.-Gen. Rassemblement pour la République (RPR) 1977–81, Sec.-Gen. 1984–88; Deputy to Nat. Ass. 1981–93; Mayor 13th Arrondissement, Paris 1983–2001, Deputy Mayor of Paris 1983–2001; Pres. Club 89 1993–; Minister of Culture and the French Language 1993–95, of Justice 1995–97; adviser to Pres. Jacques Chirac 1997–98; mem. European Parl. 2004–09; Dir Fondation Claude Pompidou 1970–77, Pres. Eurimages, Council of Europe 2002–09; Sec. Gen. for anniversary of African Independence 2010; Pres. Advisory Cttee, Centre for History of Immigration; mem. HADOPI; Chevalier du Mérite Agricole, Chevalier, Légion d' Honneur, Commdr des Arts et letters. *Publication:* Pour en finir avec la peur 1984. *Leisure interests:* collecting modern art, opera. *Address:* 86, rue Notre Dame des Champs, 75006, Paris (home); Quai d' Orsay, 75007 Paris, France (office). *Telephone:* 1-46-33-58-30 (home); 1-43-17-57-92 (office).

TOULOUSE, Gérard, DSc; French scientist; *Research Scientist, Laboratoire de Physique de l'Ecole Normale Supérieure, Le Centre national de la recherche scientifique (CNRS);* b. 4 Sept. 1939, Vattetot-sur-mer; s. of Robert Toulouse and Thérèse Toulouse (née Tiret); m. Nicole Schnitzer 1970; one s. one d.; ed Ecole Normale Supérieure, Ulm, Orsay; research scientist, CNRS 1965–, Laboratoire de Physique de l'Ecole Normale Supérieure 1976–; Post-doctoral Fellow, Univ. of California, San Diego, La Jolla 1969–71; Vice-Pres. Cttee of Exact and Natural Sciences (French nat. comm. for UNESCO) 1997 (Pres. 1999); Sec.-Gen. Foundation La Ferthé 1996; Vice-Pres. Pugwash France 1998; Visitor, Ecole Supérieure de Physique et Chimie, Paris 1985–86; Fellow, Inst. for Advanced Studies, Jerusalem 1987–88; Vice-Pres. European Acad. of Sciences, Arts and Letters 2004; mem. Acad. of Sciences, Paris 1990; Founding mem. French Nat. Acad. of Tech., Paris 2000; Foreign Hon. Mem. American Acad. of Arts and Sciences 1996; Hon. Mem. Palestine Acad. of Science and Tech.; Chevalier, Ordre nat. du Mérite; Langevin Prize 1976, Triossi Prize 1979, Holweck Prize 1983, CEA Prize 1989; Cecil Powell Medal 1999. *Publications:* Introduction au groupe de renormalisation 1975, Biology and Computation: a Physicist's Choice 1994, Regards sur l'éthique des sciences 1998, Les scientifiques et les droits de l'homme 2003, Quelle éthique pour les sciences? 2005. *Address:* Laboratoire de physique de l'Ecole Normale Supérieure, 24 rue Lhomond, 75231 Paris, France (office). *Telephone:* 1-44-32-34-87 (office). *Fax:* 1-43-36-76-66 (office). *E-mail:* toulouse@physique.ens.fr (office). *Website:* www.lpt.ens.fr/~toulouse (office).

TOUMA, Ahmad Saleh; Syrian dentist and political activist; b. 1965, Deir el-Zor Prov.; long-time political opponent of Assad regime; detained numerous times by Syrian govt, fmrly sentenced to two-and-half years in prison; spent time in exile in

Turkey; mem. Syrian Nat. Coalition (SNC) opposition group, elected Prime Minister by SNC Sept. 2013; *Website:* www.etilaf.org/en.

TOUMAZOU, Christofer (Chris), BSc, PhD, DEng, FRS, FREng, FIET, FIEEE, FRSM, CEng; British computer scientist and academic; *Chief Scientist of the Institute of Biomedical Engineering, Director of the Centre for Bio-Inspired Technology and Professor of Biomedical Circuit Design, Imperial College London;* b. 5 July 1961; ed Oxford Brookes Univ., also in collaboration with UMIST (now Univ. of Manchester); Research Fellow, Dept of Electrical and Electronic Eng, Imperial Coll. London 1986, Prof. of Circuit Design 1995–, Head of Circuits and Systems Group, then Head of Dept of Bioengineering 2001, cr. Inst. of Biomedical Eng 2003, first Dir and Chief Scientist, also Dir Centre for Bio-Inspired Tech., Regius Professorship 2013, Winston Wong Chair, Biomedical Circuits; Chair. Royal Soc. Panel for Theo Murphy Blue Skies Award, UK EPSRC Healthcare Panel, UK EPSRC Electronics and Photonics Panel; mem. Wellcome Trust Tech. Transfer Challenge Cttee; fmr mem. of several govt cttees, including the Foresight Cttee on Infectious Diseases, Ministry of Defence Strategic Advisory Cttee on Critical Technologies; Ed.-in-Chief Electronics Letters; Sr Adviser, Bd of Grace Semiconductor, Taiwan; Int. Adviser on medical devices to Govt of Singapore; Chair. and CEO DNA Electronics Ltd, Toumaz Holdings Ltd, GeneOynx; f. Applied Bionics PTE, Future Waves; mem. Academia Europaea 2007; Fellow, Inst. of Eng and Tech., City and Guilds Inst. 2010; Hon. DEng (Oxford Brookes Univ.) 2010; IEE Rayleigh Best Book Award 1991, IEEE CAS Outstanding Young Author Award 1992, IEEE Electronics Letters Premium Award 1993, Clifford Paterson Lecturer, Royal Soc. 2003, IEEE CAS Educ. Award 2005, Silver Medal, Royal Acad. of Eng 2007, World Technology Network Award for Health and Medicine 2009, J.J. Thompson Medal for Electronics, Inst. of Eng and Tech. 2011, Gabor Medal, Royal Soc. 2013. *Publications:* more than 320 research papers in professional journals in the field of radio frequency and low power electronics; 23 int. patents. *Address:* 405 Bessemer Building, Department of Electrical and Electronic Engineering, Imperial College London, South Kensington Campus, London, SW7 2AZ, England (office). *Telephone:* (20) 7594-6255 (office). *Fax:* (20) 7581-4419 (office). *E-mail:* c.toumazou@imperial.ac.uk (office). *Website:* www3 .imperial.ac.uk/people/c.toumazou (office); www3.imperial.ac.uk/circuitssystems (office).

TOUMI, Khalida, (Khalida Messaoudi); Algerian politician; b. 1958; ed Univ. of Algiers; Co-founder Algerian League of Human Rights 1985, Asscn for Equality of Men and Women Before the Law 1985, Ind. Asscn for the Triumph of Women's Rights (also Pres.) 1990, SOS Women in Distress 1991, Asscn of Solidarity and Support to Families of Victims of Terrorism 1992; mem. Nat. Consultative Comm. 1992–93; Co-founder Mouvement pour la République 1992, Vice-Pres. 1992–97; mem. Rassemblement pour la Culture et la Démocratie (RCD) 1997–2001, Vice-Pres. 1998–2000; Deputy for Algiers 1997–2001, Head of RCD Parl. Group 2000; Vice-Pres. Nat. Comm. for Educ. Reform 2000; Minister of Communication and Govt Spokesperson 2002–14, of Culture 2004–14; Hon. Citizen Commune de Caltabellotta, Italy 1997; Dr hc (Catholic Univ. of Louvain, Belgium) 1998; Alexander Langer Int. Prize 1997, Freedom Prize 1998, Pisa Donna Prize 1998, Telamone Peace Prize 1998, City of Ferrarra Prize 1999, Liberty Prize (Sociéta Libera, Milan) 2004, Gamayung Award 2004. *Address:* c/o Ministry of Culture, BP 100, Palais de la Culture 'Moufdi Zakaria', Plateau des Annassers, Kouba, Algiers, Algeria.

TOUNGUI, Paul; Gabonese politician; s.-in-law of the late Pres. Omar Bongo; m. Pascaline Bongo; fmr Univ. Prof. of Math.; Minister of Mines, Energy Resources, Oil and Hydro Resources 2001; Minister of State for Econ. Affairs, Finance, the Budget and Privatization 2002–08; Minister of Foreign Affairs, Int. Co-operation and Francophone Affairs 2008–12; First Vice-Chair. IMF Intergovernmental Group of 24 on Int. Monetary Affairs and Devt; mem. Bd of Govs African Devt Bank, Islamic Devt Bank. *Address:* c/o Ministry of Foreign Affairs, International Co-operation and Francophone Affairs, BP 2245, Libreville, Gabon (office).

TOUQAN, Umayya Salah, MBA, PhD; Jordanian fmr central banker, economist and diplomatist; b. 1946, Amman; m. Lina Izziddine Mufti; ed American Univ., Beirut, Univ. of Oxford, UK, Columbia Univ., USA; joined Cen. Bank of Jordan 1967, fmr Head Econ. Research Dept, Gov. and Chair. 2001–10; Perm. Rep. to UN, New York 1973–78; Amb. to The Netherlands, Belgium, Luxembourg and the EU 1996–2000; Senator, Upper House of Parl. 2010–; Minister of Finance 2011–12; fmr Econ. Adviser to the Prime Minister; fmr Dir-Gen. Jordan Stock Exchange; fmr Sr Economist, Arab Monetary Fund, Abu Dhabi; Grand Order of Al-Istiklal (Independence) 1995, Grand Order of Al-Kawkab (Jordan) 2001, Grand Cross, Order of the Crown (Belgium) 2001; Central Banker of the Year, The Banker, London. *Address:* c/o Ministry of Finance, PO Box 85, Amman 11118, Jordan (office).

TOURAINE, Agnès, MBA; French business executive; *Founder and President, Act III Consultants, Act III Gaming;* b. 18 Feb. 1955, Neuilly-sur-Seine; d. of René Touraine and Eliane Touraine (née Bertolus); m. Joël Cordier 1987; one s. one d.; ed Institut d'Études Politiques (Diplome Sc Po), Paris, Columbia Business School, New York, USA; consultant then Project Man., McKinsey & Co. 1981–85; Sr Vice-Pres. for Strategy then Head of Consumer Publishing Div., Hachette 1985–95; Founding Pres. and CEO Liris Interactive 1995–97, renamed Havas Interactive 1997, Exec. Vice-Pres. Consumer Products 1998–2000, Vice-Chair. and CEO Havas 2000–01, renamed Vivendi Universal Publishing 2001, Chair. and CEO Vivendi Universal Publishing 2001–03; f. Act III Consultants (man. consultancy), Paris 2003, Act III Gaming, Paris 2009; Venture Partner, JVP Israel-Paris 2009, ITV, London, Néopost Fondation de France; Chevalier, Ordre nat. du Mérite, Chevalier de la Légion d'honneur; ranked 26th by Fortune magazine amongst 50 Most Powerful Women in Business outside the US 2002. *Leisure interests:* contemporary art, reading, skiing, tennis. *Address:* Act III Consultants, 44 avenue des Champs Elysées, 75008 Paris, France (office). *Telephone:* 1-58-56-19-04 (office); 1-46-33-38-66 (home). *Fax:* 1-58-56-18-78 (office). *E-mail:* atouraine@ act3consultants.com (office). *Website:* www.act3consultants.com (office); www .act3gaming.com (office).

TOURAINE, Alain Louis Jules François, DèsSc; French sociologist; *Founder and Director of Studies, Centre d'Analyse et d'Intervention Sociologiques;* b. 3 Aug. 1925, Hermanville; s. of Albert Touraine and Odette Cleret; m. Adriana Arenas

1957 (deceased); one s. one d.; ed Lycées Montaigne and Louis-le-Grand, Paris and Ecole Normale Supérieure; Dir of Studies, Ecole Pratique des Hautes Etudes (now Ecole des Hautes Etudes en Sciences Sociales) 1960–, Founder and Dir of Studies, Centre d'Analyse et d'Intervention Sociologiques (CADIS) 1980–; Prof., Faculté des Lettres de Paris-Nanterre 1966–69; f. Lab. de Sociologie Industrielle (now Centre d'Etude des Mouvements Sociaux) 1958–80; mem. Haut Conseil à l'Intégration 1994–96; mem. Academia Europaea, American Acad. of Arts and Sciences, Polish Acad. of Sciences 1991, Mexican Acad. of Sciences 1998, Brazilian Acad. of Letters 1998, Fundación Academia Europea de Yuste 2004; Officier Légion d'honneur, Officier des Arts et des Lettres, Officier, Ordre O'Higgins (Chile), several Ordres d'honneur; 25 hon. doctorates. *Publications:* Sociologie de l'Action 1965, La Société post-industrielle 1969, Production de la société 1973, Pour la sociologie 1974, La voix et le regard 1978, Mort d'une gauche 1979, L'après-socialisme 1980, Solidarité 1982, Le mouvement ouvrier (with Dubet and Wieviorka) 1984, Le retour de l'acteur 1984, La parole et le sang. Politique et société en Amérique Latine 1988, Critique de la modernité 1992, Qu'est-ce que la démocratie? 1994, Lettre à Lionel, Michel, Jacques, Martine, Bernard, Dominique ... et vous 1995, Le Grand refus, réflexion sur la grève de décembre 1995 (with Dubet, Khosrokhavar, Lapeyronnie and Wieviorka), Pourrons-nous vivre ensemble? Egaux et différents 1997, Comment sortir du libéralisme? 1999, La recherche de soi. Dialogue sur le sujet (with F. Khosrokhavar) 2000, Un nouveau paradigme, pour comprendre le monde d'aujourd'hui 2005, Le monde des femmes 2006, Penser autrement 2007, Si la gauche veut des idées, Ségolène Royal et Alain Touraine 2008, La crise entre deux avenirs 2010. *Leisure interest:* Latin America. *Address:* CADIS, 54 blvd Raspail, 75006 Paris (office); 32 blvd de Vaugirard, 75015 Paris, France (home). *Telephone:* 1-49-54-24-57 (office); 1-43-20-04-11 (home). *Fax:* 1-42-84-05-91 (office); 1-45-38-54-05 (home). *E-mail:* touraine@ehess.fr (office). *Website:* www.ehess.fr/centres/cadis (office).

TOURAY, Omar Alieu, MA, PhD; Gambian diplomatist; *Secretary of State for Foreign Affairs;* b. 5 Nov. 1965, Farafenni; m.; three c.; ed Grad. Inst. of Int. Studies, Univ. of Geneva; joined diplomatic corps as Sr Asst Sec., Ministry of External Affairs 1995, served at Embassy in Brussels and at Mission to EU 1995–2002; Amb. to Ethiopia, Perm. Rep. to African Union and High Commr to South Africa and Kenya 2002–07; Perm. Rep. to UN, New York 2007–08; Sec. of State, Ministry of Foreign Affairs 2008–. *Publications:* The Gambia and the World: A History of the Foreign Policy of Africa's Smallest State, 1965–1995 2000; numerous papers on int. econ. relations. *Address:* Department of State for Foreign Affairs, 4 Marina Parade, Banjul, Gambia (office). *Telephone:* 4223577 (office). *Fax:* 4223578 (office).

TOURÉ, Lt-Col Amadou Toumani; Malian army officer and fmr head of state; b. 4 Nov. 1948, Mopti; m.; two d.; ed Ecole Normale Secondaire de Badalabougou, Bamako; with Armed Forces of Mali, Lt 1974–78, Capt. 33rd Parachute Bn 1978–84, Commdr 1984–88, rank of Lt-Col 1988, Brigade Gen. 1992–96, Army Gen. 1996–; Commdr Presidential Guard 1981–84; led coup which overthrew Gen. Moussa Traoré (q.v.) March 1991; Leader Nat. Reconciliation Council 1991–92; Chair. Transition Cttee for the Salvation of the People (acting Head of State) 1991–92; participated in diplomatic initiatives in Rwanda, Burundi, Togo 1996, Cen. African Repub. 1997; Head Inter-African Mission to Monitor the Implementation of the Bangui Agreements 1997–; Pres. of Mali 2002–12 (ousted in military coup then resgnd); Rotary Int. Paul Harris Fellow; Chevalier, Nat. Order of Mali 1981, Grand Cross 1993, Gold Medal of Independence, Mali 1992, Commander, Légion d'Honneur 1994, Grand Officier 1998, Grand Officier, Central African Order of Merit 1996, Grand Officer, Order of Merit of Chad 1997, Grand Medal, Int. Order of Lawyers 2005; Laureate Prize for the Promotion of Democracy in Africa, Observatoire Panafricain de la Démocratie (OPAD) 1996, Prix du Ciwara d'Exception 1997, Prix Chaba Sangare 2001. *Address:* c/o Office of the President, B.P. 1463, Koulouba, Bamako, Mali.

TOURÉ, Aminata; Senegalese human rights activist and politician; *Prime Minister;* b. 12 Oct. 1962, Dakar; m. Oumar Sarr (divorced); ed Univs of Dijon and Aix-en-Provence, France; began career in Marketing Dept, SOTRAC (public transport co.), Dakar 1988; fmr Programme Dir, Asscn sénégalaise pour le bien-être familial (Senegalese family planning asscn); five years with United Nations Population Fund (UNFPA) 1995–2000, including positions as Sr Technical Adviser to Ministry of Family and Social Action, Burkina Faso, later UNFPA Regional Adviser for Francophone African Countries, Program Coordinator on Gender and HIV in West Africa for UN Fund for Women Regional Office, becoming Dir UNFPA Human Rights Dept, New York 2003–10; head of electoral campaign for Landing Savané in presidential election 1993; Chief of Staff to presidential cand. Macky Sall 2010; Minister of Justice 2012–13; Prime Minister 2013–; mem. Alliance pour la République (APR—Yaakaar). *Address:* Office of the Prime Minister, Bldg Administratif, 9e étage, ave Léopold Sédar Senghor, BP 4029, Dakar, Senegal (office). *Telephone:* 33-889-6969 (office). *Fax:* 33-823-4479 (office). *Website:* www .gouv.sn (office).

TOURÉ, Hamadoun, PhD; Malian electrical engineer, international organization official and politician; *Minister of Communication, Posts and New Technologies;* b. 3 Sept. 1953; m.; four c.; ed Tech. Inst. of Electronics and Telecommunications of Leningrad, Univ. of Electronics, Telecommunications and Informatics, Moscow, Russia; worked at PANAFTEL microwave terminal 1979; worked at International Switching Centre, Bamako 1980, Engineer in charge of operation and maintenance of the International Satellite earth station, Bamako 1981–84; Group Dir and Regional Dir Int. Telecommunications Satellite Org. (INTELSAT), Washington, DC 1985–96; Dir Gen. Africa Region, ICO Global Communications 1996–98; Dir Telecommunications Devt Bureau (BDT), Int. Telecommunication Union (ITU), Geneva 1998–2006, Sec.-Gen. ITU 2007–12; Minister of Communication, Posts and New Technologies 2012–, also Govt Spokesman; mem. IEEE 1986–, Asscn of Satellite Professionals 1990–, Int. Telecommunications Acad. 1999–, Royal Swedish Acad. of Eng Sciences 2010–; Kt of Nat. Order of Mali, Officer, Nat. Order of Côte d'Ivoire, Grand Officer, Nat. Order of the Dominican Republic, 2009; Dr hc (tate Odessa Nat. Acad. of Telecommunications, Ukraine), (Univ. of Belarus) 2009, (Nat. Univ. of Moldova) 2010, (Russian–Armenian (Slavonic) Univ., Armenia) 2010, (Kigali Inst. of Science and Tech.) 2010, (Wroclaw Univ. of Tech., Poland) 2010. *Address:* Ministry of Communication, Posts and New Technologies, ave de l'Yser, Quartier du Fleuve,

BP 116, Bamako, Mali (office). *Telephone:* 2022-2054 (office). *Fax:* 2022-2054 (office).

TOURÉ, Modibo, BSc, MBA; Malian UN official; *Special Adviser to the Special Envoy of the Secretary-General to the Great Lakes Region, United Nations;* m.; three c.; ed Ecole Nationale d'Admin, Bamako, Vanderbilt Univ., USA; consultant with Shell Oil, Mali 1982–84; Inspecteur des Finances, Bamako 1984–87; Man. United Parcel Service, Nashville, Tenn., USA 1989–90; UNDP Program Officer and later Asst Resident Rep., Burkina Faso 1991–94, Deputy Resident Rep., Djibouti 1994–97, Program Man., New York 1997–98, Sr Deputy Resident Rep., Rwanda 1998–99, Sr Country Program Man., New York 1999–2001, Special Adviser to Dir, Regional Bureau for Africa, New York 2000–01, UN Resident Coordinator, Humanitarian Coordinator and UN Resident Rep., Chad 2001–04, UNDP Resident and Humanitarian Coordinator, Ethiopia 2004–05, mem. UNDP Transition Team 2005–06; Dir UN Mine Action Service 2005–06; Sec.-Gen. African Devt Bank (ADB) 2006–10; Special Adviser to the Special Envoy of the Sec.-Gen. to the Great Lakes Region, UN 2013–. *Address:* Office of the Secretary-General, United Nations, New York, NY 10017, USA (office). *Telephone:* (212) 963-1234 (office). *Fax:* (212) 963-4879 (office). *Website:* www.un.org/sg (office).

TOURÉ, Sanoussi, PhD; Malian politician; ed Univ. of Paris X, France; Dir-Gen. of Finance Control, Ministry of Economy and Finance 1978–87, Dir-Gen. of Budget 1987–91, tech. adviser to Minister of the Economy and Finance 1991–94; consultant to the World Bank, Canadian Co-operation, US-Aid 1995–2000; Dir of Public Finances, W African Econ. and Monetary Union 2001–05, consultant 2005–; Minister and Dir of Cabinet Office 2008–09; Minister of Economy and Finance 2009–11; Lecturer in Finance and Fiscal Studies, Univ. of Mali 1980–2000. *Address:* c/o Ministry of the Economy and Finance, Bamako, Mali (office).

TOURÉ, Sidia; Guinean politician; *President, Union des forces républicaines;* fmr Dir Office of the Prime Minister of Côte d'Ivoire; Prime Minister of Guinea 1996–99, Minister of Economy, Finance and Planning 1996–97; Pres. Union des forces républicaines; cand. in presidential elections 2010. *Address:* Union des forces républicaines (UFR), Immeuble 'Le Golfe', 4e étage, BP 6080, Conakry, Guinea (office). *Telephone:* 45-42-38 (office). *Fax:* 45-42-31 (office). *E-mail:* ufrguinee@yahoo.fr (office).

TOURÉ, Younoussi; Malian politician; b. 27 Dec. 1941, Niodougou, Timbuktu Region; s. of Singoro Touré and Santadji Tamoura; m. Alimata Traore 1970; two s. three d.; studied in Dakar, Senegal and Abidjan, Côte d'Ivoire; joined Cen. Bank of Mali 1969, Dir Gen. 1983; rep. at Banque Centrale des états de l'Afrique de l'ouest (BCEAO); Prime Minister 1992–93; Special Adviser to Gov. of BCEAO 1993–94; Commr, West African Econ. and Monetary Union (UEMOA) 1994; mem. Nat. Ass. (URD) for Niafunké Dist 2007–, First Vice-Pres. Nat. Ass. 2007–; mem. Union pour la République et la démocratie (URD), fmr Pres. *Leisure interests:* reading, sport. *Address:* Union pour la République et la démocratie, Niaréla, rue 268, porte 41, Bamako, Mali. *Telephone:* 2021-8642. *E-mail:* contact@urd-mali.net. *Website:* www.urd-mali.net.

TOURET, Jacques Léon Robert; French geologist and academic; *Guest Scientist, ABC Mines (Ecole des Mines), Paris;* b. 2 Jan. 1936, Fumay; s. of the late Martial Touret and Suzanne Gouilly; m. 1st Christiane Poinsignon 1960 (divorced 1972); one s. two d.; m. 2nd Lydie Mohammed 1974; one d.; ed Lycée Chanzy, Charleville, Ecole Nat. Supérieure de Géologie Appliquée, Nancy and Univ. of Nancy; Asst, Ecole Nat. Supérieure de Géologie, Nancy 1958–64, Asst Lecturer in Geology 1964–69; Lecturer in Geology, Univ. of Nancy 1969–74; Prof., Univ. of Paris 7 1974–80; Prof., Earth Science Inst., Free Univ., Amsterdam, Netherlands 1980–2001, Prof. Emer. 2001–; currently Guest Scientist, Ecoles des Mines, Paris; Invited Prof., Ecole Normale Supérieure, Paris 1994–97; Chargé de mission, CNRS, Paris 1978–80; mem. Royal Netherlands Acad. of Sciences, Norwegian Acad. of Science and Letters, Academia Europaea; Hon. Fellow, European Union of Geologists; Chevalier, Ordre nat. du Mérite; Dr hc (Liège Univ., Belgium) 2001; Prix Carrière, Acad. des Sciences, Paris 1970, Dumont Medal (Belgian Geological Soc.) 1992, Van Waterschoot van der Gracht Medal (Netherlands) 1996. *Publications include:* Le Socle précambrien de Norvège méridionale 1969, The deep Proterozoic Crust in the North Atlantic province (with A. C. Tobi) 1985. *Leisure interests:* classical music, French literature. *Address:* Musée de Minéralogie, Ecole des Mines, 60 blvd Saint Michel, 75006 Paris, France (office). *Telephone:* 1-40-51-93-11 (office).

TOURNIER, Michel, LèsL, LenD, DPhil; French writer; b. 19 Dec. 1924, Paris; s. of Alphonse Tournier and Marie-Madeleine Tournier (née Fournier); ed Saint-Germain-en-Laye, Univ. of Paris (Sorbonne), Univ. of Tübingen, Germany; radio and TV production 1949–54; press attaché, Europe No. 1 1955–58; head of literary services, Editions Plon 1958–68; contrib. to Le Monde, Le Figaro; mem. Acad. Goncourt 1972–2011, Hon. mem. 2011–; Officier, Légion d'honneur, Commdr, Ordre nat. du Mérite; Dr hc (Univ. Coll. London) 1997; Goethe Medal 1993. *Publications:* fiction: Vendredi, ou les limbes du Pacifique (trans. as Friday) 1967 (Grand Prix de l'Acad. Française), Le Roi des Aulnes (trans. as The Ogre) (Prix Goncourt) 1970, Vendredi, ou la vie sauvage (trans. as Friday and Robinson: Life on Esperanza Island) 1971, Les Météores 1975, Le Coq de bruyère 1978, Pierrot, ou les secrets de la nuit 1979, Gaspard, Melchior et Balthazar (trans. as The Four Wise Men) 1980, Gilles et Jeanne 1983, Le Vagabond immobile 1984, Journal de voyage au Canada 1984, La Goutte d'or (trans. as The Golden Droplet) 1986, Le Médianioche amoureux (trans. as The Midnight Love Feast) 1989, La Couleuvrine 1994, Eléazar, ou la source et le buisson 1996, Barbedor 2003, La Famille Adam 2003, Telling Tales (contrib. to charity anthology) 2004, Journal extime 2004, Mephisto 2006, Vendredi ou la vie sauvage: D'après Vendredi ou les limbes du Pacifique 2007; non-fiction: Le Vent paraclet (trans. as The Wind Spirit: An Autobiography) 1977, Des clefs et des serrures 1979, Le Vol du vampire 1981, Le Tabor et le Sinaï 1989, Le Crépuscule des masques 1992, Le Miroir des idées 1994, Le Pied de la lettre 1994, Célébrations 1999, Les vertes lectures 2006, Le bonheur en Allemagne? 2004. *Leisure interest:* photography. *Address:* Le Presbytère, Choisel, 78460 Chevreuse, France (home). *Telephone:* 1-30-52-05-29 (home).

TOUSIGNANT, Claude, OC; Canadian artist; b. 23 Dec. 1932, Montreal, PQ; s. of Alberic Tousignant and Gilberte Hardy-Lacasse; m. Judith Terry 1968; two d.; ed School of Art and Design, The Montreal Museum of Fine Arts; numerous solo and group nat. and int. exhbns 1956–; works included in major N American public and

pvt. collections; First Prize, Salon de la jeune peinture 1962, First Prize, Painting, Art Gallery of Ont. 1967, Canadian Inst. in Rome Award 1973, Prix Paul-Emile Borduas 1989. *Address:* 181 rue Bourget, Montreal, PQ H4C 2M1(Studio); 460 avenue Bloomfield, Outremont, PQ H2V 3R8, Canada (home). *Telephone:* (514) 934-3012 (Studio); (514) 948-1463 (home).

TOVAR FAJA, Roberto; Costa Rican politician; b. 1945; ed Univ. of Barcelona, Spain; Deputy 1978–82, 1990–94; Pres. Legis. Ass. 1992–93; Head of Faction, Unidad Social Cristiana (USC—Christian Social Unit) 1991–92, fmr Sec.-Gen.; Pres. Comm. of Econ. Subjects 1978–79; mem. Bd of Dirs Consultant Inter-American Inst. of Human Rights; fmr Minister of the Presidency and Planning; Minister of Foreign Relations 2002–06. *Address:* c/o Ministry of Foreign Affairs, Avda 7 y 9, Calle 11 y 13, Apdo 10027, 1000 San José, Costa Rica (office).

TOWNE, Robert; American screenwriter; b. 23 Nov. 1934, Los Angeles; m. Luisa Towne; two c.; ed Pomona Coll. *Screenplays include:* The Tomb of Ligeia 1964, Villa Rides 1967, The Last Detail 1967, Chinatown 1974, Shampoo (with Warren Beatty) 1974, The Yazuka (jtly) 1975, Personal Best (also producer-dir 1984), Greystoke 1984, Tequila Sunrise 1988, Days of Thunder, The Two Jakes, The Firm (co-screenwriter) 1993, Love Affair (co-screenwriter), Mission Impossible (co-screenwriter), Without Limits (also dir) 1998, Mission Impossible 2 2000, Ask the Dust (also dir) 2006. *Address:* c/o CAA, 9830 Wilshire Boulevard, Beverly Hills, CA 90212, USA.

TOWNES, Charles Hard, BA, MS, PhD; American physicist and academic; *Professor Emeritus of Physics, University of California, Berkeley;* b. 28 July 1915, Greenville, South Carolina; s. of Henry Keith Townes and Ellen Sumter Hard; m. Frances H. Brown 1941; four d.; ed Furman and Duke Univs, California Inst. of Tech.; Asst, California Inst. of Tech. 1937–39, Trustee 1979–; mem. Tech. staff, Bell Telephone Labs 1939–47; Assoc. Prof. of Physics, Columbia Univ., New York 1948–50, Prof. 1950–61; Exec. Dir Radiation Lab. 1950–52, Chair. Dept of Physics 1952–55; Vice-Pres. and Dir of Research, Inst. for Defense Analyses 1959–61; Provost and Prof. of Physics, MIT 1961–66, Inst. Prof. 1966–67; Univ. Prof., Univ. of California 1967–86, Prof. Emer. 1986–94, Prof. in the Grad. School 1994–; mem. Bd of Dirs Perkin-Elmer Corpn 1966–85, Gen. Motors 1973–86, Bulletin of the Atomic Scientists 1964–69; Chair. Science and Tech. Advisory Comm. for Manned Space Flight, NASA 1964–69; Chair. Space Science Bd, NAS 1970–73; mem. Pres.'s Science Advisory Cttee 1966–70, Vice-Chair. 1967–69; mem. Bd of Dirs Grad. Theological Union 1993–96, Center for Theology and the Natural Sciences 1989–; mem. Bd of Advisors, Templeton Foundation Humility Theology Center 1993–; mem. Editorial Bd Review of Scientific Instruments 1950–52, Physical Review 1951–53, Journal of Molecular Spectroscopy 1957–60; Foreign mem. Royal Soc. 1976, Nat. Acad. of Sciences, India, Indian Nat. Science Acad.; mem. Astronomical Soc. of the Pacific 1989–, American Acad. of Arts and Sciences, American Philosophical Soc., American Astronomical Soc., Space Program Advisory Council, NASA, NAS (Council mem. 1967–72, 1978–81), Pontifical Acad. of Science 1983, Russian Acad. of Sciences 1993, Nat. Acad. of Eng; Guggenheim Fellow 1955–56; Fellow, American Physical Soc. (Council mem. 1959–62, 1965–71, Pres. 1967), IEEE, Californian Acad. of Sciences; mem. Bd of Trustees, Carnegie Inst. of Washington 1965–, RAND Corpn 1965–70, Pacific School of Religions 1983–93; Trustee, California Inst. of Tech. 1979–; Hon. mem. Optical Soc. of America, Hon. Fellow, Rozhdestvensky Optical Soc. of Russia 1995; Officier, Légion d'honneur; numerous hon. degrees include DLitt, ScD, LLD, LHD; lectures: Fulbright Lecturer, Paris 1955–56, Tokyo 1956; Richtmeyer Lecturer, American Physical Soc. 1959, Scott Lecturer, Cambridge 1963, Centennial Lecturer, Univ. of Toronto 1967, Jansky Lecturer, Nat. Radio Astronomy Observatory 1971, Lincoln Lecturer 1972–73, Halley Lecturer, Oxford 1976, Schiff Memorial Lecturer, Stanford 1982, Michelson Memorial Lecturer, US Naval Acad. 1982, Faculty Research Lecturer, Univ. of California, Berkeley 1986, Beckman Lecturer, Univ. of Illinois 1986, Schultz Lecturer, Yale Univ. 1987, Fulbright Fellow Lecturer, Collège de France 1987, Darwin Lecturer, Univ. of Cambridge 1988, Houston Memorial Lecturer, Rice Univ., Houston 1990, VanVleck Lecturer, Univ. of Minnesota 1990, K.S. Krishnan Memorial Lecture, Nat. Physical Lab., India 1992, Golden Jubilee Lecture, Council of Scientific and Industrial Research, India 1992, Nishina Lecturer, Tokyo, Japan 1992, Rajiv Gandhi Lecture, New Delhi, India 1997, Weinberg Lecture, Oak Ridge Nat. Lab., Tenn. 1997, Henry Norris Russell Lectureship, American Astronomical Soc. 1998, Sackler Lecturer, Univ. of Leiden 1999, Loeb Lecturer, Harvard Univ. 2000, Hamilton Lecturer, Princeton Univ. 2000, Bunyan Lecturer, Stanford Univ. 2000, Ford/Nobel Lecture, MIT 2001, Karl Schwarzschild Lecture, Astronomische Gesellschaft 2002, Schroedinger Lecture, Centre for Philosophy and Foundations of Science, New Delhi 2003, Birla Lecture, Birla Science Centre, Hyderabad 2003; awards: NAS Comstock Award 1959, Stuart Ballantine Medal, Franklin Inst. 1959, 1962, Rumford Premium, American Acad. of Arts and Sciences 1961, AIEE David Sarnoff Award in Electronics 1961, NAS John A. Carty Medal 1962, Thomas Young Medal and Prize, Inst. of Physics and Physical Soc., UK 1963, Nobel Prize for Physics 1964, NASA Distinguished Public Service Medal 1969, IEEE Medal of Honor 1967, Wilhelm Exner Award 1970, Plyler Prize, American Physical Soc. 1977, Niels Bohr Int. Gold Medal 1979, LeConte Medal 1980, Nat. Medal of Science 1982, L.W. Frolich Award 1986, Berkeley Citation 1986, Nat. Inventors' Hall of Fame 1976, Eng and Science Hall of Fame 1983, Commonwealth Award 1993, ADION Medal, Observatory of Nice 1995, Frederick Ives Medal, Optical Soc. of America 1996, Frank Annunzio Award 1999, Rabindranath Tagore Centenary Plaque 1999, Founder's Award, Nat. Acad. of Eng 2000, Author of Best Science Book of the Year, American Physical Soc. 2000, Lomonosov Gold Medal, Russian Acad. of Sciences 2001, Karl Schwarzschild Medal, Astronomische Gesellschaft 2002, Templeton Prize 2005, Vannevar Bush Medal 2006, Lifetime Achievement Award, Laser Inst. of America 2010, Nancy DeLoye Fitzroy and Ronald V. Fitzroy Medal, American Soc. of Mechanical Engineers 2012, Fizeau Prize, Observatoire de la Côte d'Azur 2012, Golden Goose Award 2012. *Achievements include:* holder of patents in electronics, including fundamental patents on masers and lasers, etc. *Publications include:* Microwave Spectroscopy 1955, Quantum Electronics 1960, Quantum Electronics and Coherent Light 1964, Making Waves 1995, How the Laser Happened; Adventures of a Scientist 1999; other scientific papers on microwave spectroscopy, molecular and nuclear structures, radio and infra-red astronomy, masers and lasers, etc. *Leisure interests:* natural history, music. *Address:* University of California, Department of Physics, 366 LeConte, #7300, Berkeley, CA 94720, USA (office). *Telephone:* (510)

642-1128 (office); (510) 433-0446 (home). *Fax:* (510) 643-8497 (office). *E-mail:* cht@ ssl.berkeley.edu (office). *Website:* physics.berkeley.edu (office).

TOWNSHEND, Peter (Pete) Dennis Blandford; British composer, musician (guitar), publisher and author; b. 19 May 1945, Isleworth, London, England; s. of Clifford Townshend and Betty Townshend; m. Karen Astley 1968; one s. two d.; ed Acton Co. Grammar School and Ealing Art Coll.; mem. rock group, The Detours, renamed The Who 1964– (various reunion tours and recordings); solo artist 1979–; appearances include: Nat. Jazz and Blues Festival 1965, 1966, 1969, Monterey Pop Festival 1967, Woodstock 1969, Rock at the Oval 1971, Farewell tour 1982–83, Live Aid, Wembley 1985, Reunion tour 1989, Quadrophenia 1996/1997, Concert for NYC 2001, Live8 2005; owner Eel Pie Recording Productions Ltd and Eel Pie Publishing Ltd 1972–; est. Eel Pie (bookshops and publishing co.) 1976–83; est. Meher Baba Oceanic (UK archival library) 1976–; Ed., Faber & Faber (publrs) 1983–; Gold Ticket Madison Square Garden 1979, Ivor Novello Award for Contribution to British Music 1982, British Phonographic Industry Award 1983, BRIT Lifetime Achievement Award 1983, BRIT Award for Contribution to British Music 1988, International Rock Living Legend Award 1991, Q Lifetime Achievement Award 1997, Ivor Novello Lifetime Achievement Award 2001, BMI Pres.'s Award 2002, BMI TV Music Awards 2004, 2005, 2006, 2007, Silver Clef Award 2005, The Who were inducted into the UK Music Hall of Fame in 2005, Q Legend Award 2006, South Bank Show Outstanding Achievement Award 2007, Kennedy Center Honor 2008, Les Paul Award 2013. *Compositions include:* Tommy (rock opera) (Tony Award for score 1993, Grammy Award for original cast recording 1993, Dora Mavor Moore Award 1994, Olivier Award 1997) 1969, Quadrophenia (rock opera) 1973, The Boy Who Heard Music (rock opera) 2007. *Recordings include:* albums: with The Who: My Generation 1965, A Quick One 1966, Happy Jack 1967, The Who Sell Out 1967, Magic Bus 1968, Tommy 1969, Live At Leeds 1970, Who's Next 1971, Meaty Beefy Big And Bouncy 1971, Quadrophenia 1973, The Who By Numbers 1975, The Story Of The Who 1976, Who Are You 1978, The Kids Are Alright (live) 1979, Face Dances 1981, Hooligans 1982, It's Hard 1982, Rarities Vols. 1 and 2 1983, Who's Last (live) 1984, Two's Missing 1987, Join Together (live) 1990, Live At The Isle Of Wight Festival 1970 1996, The BBC Sessions 2000, Moonlighting 2005, Endless Wire 2006; solo: Who Came First 1972, Rough Mix 1977, Empty Glass 1980, All The Best Cowboys Have Chinese Eyes 1982, Scoop 1983, White City: A Novel 1985, Another Scoop 1987, The Iron Man: A Musical 1989, Psychoderelict 1993, Pete Townshend Live 1999, Lifehouse Chronicles 2000, The Oceanic Concerts 2001, Live: La Jolla 2001, Live: Sadler's Wells 2001, The Kids Are Alright 1979. *Films:* music for: Tommy 1975, Quadrophenia 1979, The Kids Are Alright 1979. *Television:* music for CSI: Miami and CSI: Crime Scene Investigation. *Publications:* The Story of Tommy (with Richard Barnes), Horse's Neck 1985, Tommy: The Musical 1995, London 1996. *Leisure interest:* sailing. *Address:* Trinifold Management, 12 Oval Road, Camden, London, NW1 7DH, England (office); Eel Pie Publishing Ltd, 4 Friars Lane, Richmond, Surrey, TW9 1NL, England (office). *Telephone:* (20) 7419-4300 (office); (20) 8940-8171 (office). *Fax:* (20) 7419-4325 (office); (20) 8940-8172 (office). *E-mail:* trinuk@globalnet.co.uk (office); nic@eelpie.com (office). *Website:* www.trinifold.co.uk (office); www.eelpie .com (office); www.thewho.com.

TOYBERG-FRANDZEN, Jens Anders; Danish UN official; *Executive Representative of the Secretary-General and Head, United Nations Integrated Peacebuilding Office in Sierra Leone (UNIPSIL);* b. 1950; m.; ed Aarhus Univ.; has served as Acting UN Resident Coordinator, UNDP Resident Rep. in Yemen, Resident Coordinator and Resident Rep. in Bosnia and Herzegovina, also served with UN in Bhutan, Iraq, Nepal and Turkey; Exec. Rep. of Sec.-Gen. and Head of the UN Integrated Peacebuilding Office in Sierra Leone (UNIPSIL) 2012–. *Address:* United Nations Integrated Peacebuilding Office in Sierra Leone (UNIPSIL), Cabenda Hotel, 14 Signal Hill Road, PO Box 5, Freetown, Sierra Leone (office). *Website:* www.unipsil.unmissions.org (office).

TOYE, John, BA, MA, MSc, PhD; British development economist and academic; *Chair of the Advisory Panel, Department of International Development, Queen Elizabeth House, University of Oxford;* b. 7 Oct. 1942, Wisbech, Cambs.; s. of John Redmond Toye and Adele Toye (née Francis); m. Janet Toye (née Reason); one s. one d.; ed Univ. of Cambridge, School of Oriental and African Studies, Univ. of London; Asst Principal, UK Home Civil Service, Her Majesty's Treasury 1965–68; Research Fellow in Economics, School of Oriental and African Studies, Univ. of London 1970–72, currently Professorial Research Assoc.; Fellow and Tutor, Wolfson Coll., Cambridge 1972–80; Grad. Asst Centre of South Asian Studies, Univ. of Cambridge 1972–74, Research Officer, Overseas Studies Cttee 1975–77, Asst Dir of Development Studies 1977–80; Consultant on Third World Studies, Open Univ. 1981–83; Dir of Research Coordination, Commodities Research Unit Ltd, London and New York 1980–82, Dir (non-exec.) 1982–85; Prof. of Development Policy and Planning, Univ. of Wales 1982–87, also Dir; Dir Inst. of Development Studies, Univ. of Sussex, Brighton 1987–97, Professorial Fellow 1987–97; Dir Globalization and Development Strategies Div., UN Conf. on Trade and Development, Geneva 1998–2000; Dir Centre for the Study of African Economies, Dept of Economics, Univ. of Oxford 2000–03, Sr Research Assoc. and Visiting Prof., Dept of International Development, Queen Elizabeth House 2003–09, currently Chair of the Advisory Panel; Visiting Fellow, St Antony's Coll., Oxford 2000–03; fmr Dir Centre for the Study of African Economies, Oxford; Chair. Bd of the Journal of Development Studies 1976–2006; Bd mem. Bd of Contemporary South Asia 1989–99, Journal of International Development 1989–2007, World Development 1994–97, European Journal of Development Research 1995–2007; Man. Ed. Journal Oxford Development Studies 2005–; Fellow, Human Development and Capability Asscn 2010–; Hon. Fellow, School of Public Policy, Univ. of Birmingham 1989–92, Hon. Pres. Development Studies Asscn of Great Britain and Ireland 1994–96, Hon. Trustee, Inst. of Development Studies, Sussex Univ. 2005–, Hon. Professorial Assoc., School of Oriental and African Studies 2010–12. *Publications include:* Taxation and Economic Development (ed.) 1978, Trade and Poor Economies (co-ed.) 1979, Public Expenditure and Indian Development Policy 1960–70 1981, Dilemmas of Development: Reflections on the Counter-Revolution in Development Theory and Policy 1987, 1993, Indo-European Cooperation in an Interdependent World (ed.) 1989, Does Aid Work in India? A Country Study of Official Development Assistance (co-author) 1990, Aid and Power: The World Bank and Policy-Based Lending in the 1980s (two vols, co-author) 1991, 1995, Structural Adjustment and Employment Policy: Issues and

Experience 1995, Challenging the Orthodoxies (co-ed.) 1996, A World Without Famine? (co-ed.) 1997, Keynes on Population 2000, Trade and Development: Directions for the Twenty-first Century (ed.) 2003, The UN and Global Political Economy: Trade, Finance and Development (co-author) 2004; numerous book chapters, book reviews, commissioned reports, and articles in professional journals. *Address:* Department of International Development, Queen Elizabeth House, University of Oxford, 3 Mansfield Road, Oxford, OX1 3TB, England (office). *Telephone:* (0)1865-281835 (office). *Fax:* (0)1865-281801 (office). *E-mail:* john .toye@economics.ox.ac.uk (office). *Website:* www.qeh.ox.ac.uk (office); www .johntoye.net.

TOYODA, Akio, MBA; Japanese automotive industry executive; *President and Representative Director, Toyota Motor Corporation;* b. 3 May 1956, Nagoya; grandson of Kiichiro Toyoda; m. Hiroko Toyoda; two c.; ed Keio Univ., Tokyo, Babson Coll., Mass, USA; joined Toyota Motor Corpn 1984, Vice-Pres. New United Motor Manufacturing Inc., Calif., USA, mem. Bd of Dirs Toyota Motor Corpn 2000–, Man. Dir 2002–03, Sr Man. Dir and Chief Asia and China Operations Officer 2003–05, Exec. Vice-Pres. 2005–09, Pres. and Rep. Dir 2009–, Head of team that developed Gazoo.com (Toyota web site) 1996; ranked by Forbes magazine amongst The World's Most Powerful People (28th) 2009, (43rd) 2012, (44th) 2013. *Address:* Toyota Motor Corpn, 1 Toyota-Cho, Toyota City, Aichi Prefecture 471-8571, Japan (office). *Telephone:* (5) 6528-2121 (office). *Fax:* (5) 6523-5800 (office). *Website:* www.toyota-global.com (office); www.toyota.co.jp (office).

TOYODA, Kanshiro; Japanese automotive industry executive; *Chairman, Aisin Seiki Company Ltd;* s. of Eiji Toyoda and Kazuko Toyoda; m. Akiko Toyoda; fmr Man. Shinkawa Seiki Co. Ltd; Pres. Aisin Seiki Co. Ltd (automotive component mfr) –2005, Chair. 2005–, Dir Aisin AW Co. Ltd, Aisin Chemical Co. Ltd, ADVICS Co. Ltd. *Address:* Aisin Seiki Co. Ltd, 2-1 Asahi-machi, Karlya, Aichi 448-8650, Japan (office). *Telephone:* (5) 6624-8239 (office). *Fax:* (5) 6624-8003 (office). *E-mail:* info@aisin.com (office). *Website:* www.aisin.com (home).

TOYODA, Shoichiro, DEng; Japanese automotive industry executive; *Honorary Chairman, Toyota Motor Corporation;* b. 27 Feb. 1925, Nagoya; s. of Kiichiro Toyoda and Hatako Toyoda; m. Hiroko Mitsui 1952; one s. one d.; ed Nagoya and Tohoku Univs; joined Toyota Motor Corpn 1952, Man. Dir 1961, Sr Man. Dir 1967, Exec. Vice-Pres. 1972, Pres. Marketing Org. 1981, Pres., Toyota Motor Corpn 1982, Chair. 1992–99, Hon. Chair. 1999–, Sr Adviser and mem. Bd 1996–; Chair., Japanese Automobile Mfrs Asscn 1986–90; Vice-Chair., Keidanren (Fed. of Econ. Orgs) 1990–94, Chair. 1994–2002, Hon. Chair. 2002–; Chair., Japan Asscn for 2005 World Exposition 1997–2006, Pres., Kaiyo Acad. 2006–; Hon. KBE 1995, Commdr, Légion d'honneur (France) 1998, Order of Merit (Turkey) 1998, Commdr's Cross of the Order of Merit (Germany) 2001, Grand Cordon of the Order of the Rising Sun (Japan) 2002, Knight Grand Cordon (First Class) of the Most Admirable Order of the Direkgunabhorn (Thailand) 2004, Grand Cordon, Order of the Paulownia Flowers (Japan) 2007, Cavaliere di Gran Croce decorato di Gran Cordone (Italy) 2007, numerous other hons; Deming Prize (Japan) 1980, Medal with Blue Ribbon for Outstanding Public Service (Japan) 1984, FISITA Medal (France) 2000. *Leisure interests:* traditional Japanese music, gardening, golf. *Address:* Toyota Motor Corporation, 1 Toyota-cho, Toyota, Aichi 471-8571, Japan (office).

TOYODA, Tetsuro, BMechEng, MBA; Japanese automotive industry executive; *President, Toyota Industries Corporation;* b. 1 June 1929, Nagoya; s. of Kiichiro Toyoda and Hatako Iida; m. Shimizu Ayako; one s. one d.; ed Univ. of Tokyo, New York Univ., USA; joined Toyota Motor Corpn 1953, apptd Dir 1974, supervised creation of New United Motor Mfg Inc. (NUMMI), jt venture with General Motors in Calif., USA 1984, Pres. NUMMI 1984–86; Sr Man. Dir Toyota 1986–88, Exec. Vice-Pres. 1988–92, Pres. 1992–95, Vice-Chair 1995–96, Sr Adviser to the Bd 1996–, Pres. and Rep. Dir, Toyota Industries Corpn 2005–; fmr Chair. Japan Automobile Mfrs' Asscn; Vice-Chair. Japan Asscn of Corp. Execs (Keizai Doyukai); Grand Cordon of the Orders of the Sacred Treasure 1999. *Leisure interest:* listening to music. *Address:* Toyota Industries Corpn, 2-1, Toyota-cho, Kariya-shi, Aichi 448-8671, Japan (office). *Telephone:* (566) 222511 (office). *Fax:* (566) 275650 (office). *E-mail:* info@toyota-industries.com (office). *Website:* www.toyota -industries.com (office).

TOZAKA, Milner, OBE; Solomon Islands politician and fmr diplomatist; b. 21 Oct. 1951; m. Jane Tozaka; ed Univ. of South Pacific, Suva, Fiji; Chair. Nat. Disaster Council 1984–85; UNDP Consultant, Ministry of Prov. Govt 1995; Chair. Prov. Govt Review Cttee 1999; High Commr to Australia 2000–05; mem. Parl. for North Vella Lavella Constituency 2006–, Chair. Constitution Review Cttee 2006–07; Minister for Public Service April–May 2006, 2007–10. *Address:* c/o Ministry of Public Service, Honiara, Solomon Islands (office).

TOZOUN, Biossey Kokou; Togolese politician; *President, Haute autorité de l'audiovisuelle et de la communication;* Minister of Foreign Affairs and Co-operation 2003–05, of Communication and Civil Affairs 2005–06, Keeper of the Seals, Minister of Justice 2007; currently Pres. Haute autorité de l'audiovisuelle et de la communication; fmr Pres. Société Nationale des Editions du Togo (publr). *Address:* Haute autorité de l'audiovisuelle et de la communication, Lomé, Togo. *Website:* www.haactogo.tg (office).

TRABER, Peter G., BS, MD; American gastroenterologist and college administrator; *President Emeritus, Baylor College of Medicine;* m. Bobbi Traber; one s. one d.; ed Univ. of Michigan, Wayne State Univ. Medical School, Northwestern Univ. School of Medicine; mem. of faculty, Univ. of Michigan School of Medicine 1987–92; Chief of Gastroenterology, Univ. of Pennsylvania School of Medicine 1992–97, Chair., Dept of Internal Medicine 1997–2000, also CEO Univ. of Pennsylvania Health System and Interim Dean; Sr Vice-Pres. for Clinical Devt and Medical Affairs and Chief Medical Officer, GlaxoSmithKline 2000–03; Pres. and CEO Baylor Coll. of Medicine 2003–08, Pres. Emer. 2008–; Fellow, AAAS 2003–; mem. American Soc. of Clinical Investigation; Dir Alkek Foundation, BCM Technologies, BioHouston, Federal Reserve Bank of Dallas (Houston Br.), Greater Houston Partnership, Houston Tech. Center, Nat. Space Biomedical Research Inst.; Sr Ed. Handbook of Gastroenterology; Assoc. Ed. Kelly Textbook of Internal Medicine; Wayne State Univ. School of Medicine Distinguished Alumnus Award 1999, American Gastroenterological Asscn Outstanding Service Award 2006. *Address:* Baylor College of Medicine, One Baylor Plaza, Houston, TX 77030, USA (office).

Telephone: (713) 798-4951 (office). *E-mail:* pgtraber@bcm.tmc.edu (office). *Website:* www.bcm.edu (office).

TRABUCO CAPPI, Luiz Carlos; Brazilian business executive; *CEO, Banco Bradesco SA;* b. 1951, Marília, São Paulo; ed São Paulo Univ. of Philosophy, Science and Languages, Fundação Escola de Sociologia e Política de São Paulo; joined Banco Bradesco SA 1969, Departmental Dir 1984–92, Pres. Bradesco Vida e Previdência SA 1992–98, elected Man. Dir Banco Bradesco 1998, apptd Vice-Pres. 1999, later Exec. Vice-Pres., Dir and Pres. Grupo Bradesco Seguros 2003–, CEO Banco Bradesco SA 2009–, mem. Bd of Dirs Banco Bradesco SA and several cos of Bank Bradesco SA Group; Chair. Odontoprev SA; Pres. Nat. Asscn for Pvt. Pension Plans (ANAPP) 1994–2000; mem. Deliberative Council of Federação Brasileira de Bancos (FEBRABAN); Pres. Associação Nacional da Previdência Privada (ANAPP) 1994–2000; fmr CEO Bradesco Vida e Previdência, Grupo Segurador, Marketing and Capitation Cttee of Associação Brasileira das Entidades de Crédito Imobiliário e Poupança (ABECIP), Federação Nacional de Saúde Suplementar (FENA-SAÚDE); fmr Vice-Chair. Bd of Reps of Confederação Nacional das Instituições Financeiras (CNF); mem. Deliberative Council of Associação Brasileira das Companhias Abertas (ABRASCA) 2000–03; fmr mem. Bd of Dirs Banco Espírito Santo, SA, Lisbon, Portugal, ArcelorMittal Brasil (ex: Companhia Siderúrgica Belgo-Mineira); fmr mem. Superior Bd and Vice-Pres. Confederação Nacional das Empresas de Seguros Gerais, Previdência Privada e Vida, Saúde Suplementar e Capitalização (CNSeg); fmr Sitting mem. Asscn Internationale pour l'Étude de l'Economie de l'Assurance –Asscn de Genève, Geneva, Switzerland; fmr mem. Hon. Council of Academia Nacional de Seguros e Previdência. *Address:* Banco Bradesco SA, Cidade de Deus, Prédio Novo, Osasco, São Paulo 06029-900, Brazil (office). *Telephone:* (11) 3684-9229 (office); (11) 3684-3749 (office). *Fax:* (11) 3684-4570 (office); (11) 3684-2714 (office). *E-mail:* info@bradesco.com.br (office). *Website:* www.bradesco.com.br (office).

TRACHTENBERG, Stephen Joel, JD, MPA; American lawyer, academic and university administrator; *President Emeritus and University Professor of Public Service, George Washington University;* b. 14 Dec. 1937, Brooklyn, New York; s. of Oscar Trachtenberg and Shoshana Weinstock; m. Francine Zorn 1971; two s.; ed Columbia, Yale and Harvard Univs; admitted New York Bar 1964, US Supreme Court Bar 1967; attorney, Atomic Energy Comm. 1962–65; Special Asst to US Educ. Comm., Health, Educ. and Welfare, Washington, DC 1966–68; Assoc. Prof. of Political Science, Boston Univ. 1969–77, Assoc. Dean 1969–70, Dean 1970–74, Assoc. Vice-Pres., Co-Counsel 1974–76, Vice-Pres. Academic Services 1976–77; Pres., Prof. of Law, Univ. of Hartford, Conn. 1977–88; Pres. George Washington Univ., Washington, DC 1988–2007, Pres. Emer. 2007–, also Univ. Prof. of Public Service; Chair. Educ. Specialty Practice, Korn/Ferry International 2007–; 20 hon. degrees; numerous awards, including Sabin Vaccine Inst. Prize 2005. *Address:* The Trachtenberg School, George Washington University, MPA Building, 805 21st Street, NW, Suite 600, Washington, DC 20052 (office); Korn/Ferry International, 1700 K Street, NW, Suite 700, Washington, DC 20006, USA (office). *Telephone:* (202) 994-6500 (office); (202) 822-9444 (office). *E-mail:* trachtenberg@gwu.edu (office). *Website:* www.gwu.edu; www.kornferry.com (office).

TRAHAR, Anthony (Tony) John, BComm, CA (SA); South African business executive; b. 1 June 1949, Johannesburg; m. Patricia Trahar; one s. one d.; ed St. John's Coll., Univ. of the Witwatersrand; qualified CA 1973; man. trainee, Anglo American Corpn 1974–76, Personal Asst to Chair. of Exec. Cttee 1976–77, Exec. Dir 1991–2000, CEO 2000–07 (retd), Chair. Anglo Forest Products, Anglo Industrial Minerals Div., Financial Dir Anglo American Industrial Corpn 1982–92, Deputy Chair. 1992–2007; Man. Dir Mondi 1986–89, Exec. Chair. 1989, Chair. Mondi Europe 1993–2003; Chair. Anglo American Corpn of SA, Paleo Anthropological Scientific Trust; Dir Anglo Platinum, Anglo Gold, DB Investments; Kt Grand Commdr, Gold Cross with Star (First Class) (Austria) 2004; Hon. LLD. *Leisure interests:* shooting, fishing, gym, classic cars and music. *Address:* c/o Anglo American PLC, 20 Carlton House Terrace, St James's, London, SW1Y 5AN, England. *E-mail:* ajtrahar@angloamerican.co.za.

TRAILL, Sir Alan, KStJ, GBE, QSO, MA, DMus; British arbitrator and insurance consultant; b. 7 May 1935, London; s. of George Traill and Margaret (Matthews) Traill; m. Sarah Jane Hutt 1964; one s.; ed Charterhouse and Jesus Coll., Cambridge; Dir Morice Tozer Beck (insurance brokers) 1958–73; Underwriting mem. Lloyd's 1963–89; Founder Dir Traill Attenborough (Lloyd's brokers) 1973, Chair. 1980; Man. Dir Colburn Traill Ltd 1989–96; Div. Dir First City Insurance Brokers Ltd 1996–2000; Dir City Arts Trust Ltd 1978–, Grandactual Ltd 1993–97, Int. Disputes Resolution Centre (IDRC) 2002–, Cayman Islands Monetary Authority 2003–06; Bd mem. ARIAS (Insurance Arbitration Soc.) 1997–; mem. Pathfinder Team Consulting 1992–; mem. Advisory Council and Educ. Cttee, London Symphony Orchestra 1997–; Chair. UK/NZ 1990 Cttee 1989–90; Chair. Trustees, Waitangi (Link) Foundation 1991–99; Trustee, St Paul's Cathedral Choir School Foundation 1985–2010, Morden Coll. 1995–; Hon. Gov. Christ's Hosp. 1980–, Chair. Gov. Menuhin School; Patron Lord Mayor Treloar Trust 1985–; mem. Court of Common Council (of City of London) 1970–2005, Alderman 1975–2005, Sheriff 1982–83, Lord Mayor of London 1984–85; Master Worshipful Co. of Musicians 2000; Vice-Pres. Bridewell Royal Hosp. 2003–06; Commemorative Medal NZ 1990. *Leisure interests:* DIY, travel, opera, music, assisting with education. *Address:* Wheelers Farm, Thursley, Godalming, Surrey, GU8 6QE, England (home). *Telephone:* (7714) 328204 (mobile); (1252) 703271 (home). *Fax:* (1252) 703271 (home). *E-mail:* atraill.granary@btinternet.com (office).

TRAINOR, Sir Richard Hughes (Rick), KBE, BA, MA, DPhil, FRHistS, AcSS, FKC; American/British historian, academic and university administrator; *Rector, Exeter College, Oxford;* b. 31 Dec. 1948, Camden, NJ, USA; s. of the late William Richard Trainor and the late Sarah Hughes Trainor; m. Marguerite Dupree 1980; one s. one d.; ed Brown Univ. and Princeton Univ., USA, Merton and Nuffield Colls Univ. of Oxford, UK; Jr Research Fellow, Wolfson Coll., Univ. of Oxford 1977–79; joined Dept of Econ. History, Univ. of Glasgow 1979, later becoming Prof., Dean of Social Sciences and Vice-Prin.; Vice-Chancellor and Prof. of Social History, Univ. of Greenwich 2000–04; Pres., Prin. and Prof. of Social History, King's Coll. London 2004–14; Rector, Exeter Coll., Oxford Oct. 2014–; Chair. Advisory Council, Inst. of Historical Research 2004–09; Pres. Universities UK 2007–09; mem. UK-US Fulbright Comm. 2003–09 (Patron 2010–), Arts and Humanities Research Council 2006–11, Inst. of Public Policy Research Comm. on the Future of Higher Educ.

2012–13, Review Bd of the Higher Educ. Funding Council for England's Review of Philanthropic Support for Higher Educ. throughout the UK 2012–13; Hon. Sec. Econ. History Soc. 1998–2004, Pres. 2013–; Gov. St Paul's School 2012–; Gov. RAM 2013–; Hon. Fellow, Merton Coll. Oxford, Trinity Coll. of Music, Inst. of Historical Research; Hon. DCL (Kent) 2009, Hon. DHL (Rosalind Franklin Univ. of Medicine and Science) 2012. *Publications:* History and Computing III: Historians, Computers and Data: Applications in Research and Teaching (co-ed.) 1991, Towards an International Curriculum for History and Computing (co-ed.) 1992, Black Country Elites: The Exercise of Authority in an Industrialized Area 1830–1900 1993, The Teaching of Historical Computing: An International Framework (co-ed.) 1993, University, City and State: The University of Glasgow on Gilmorehill since 1870 (with J. F. Munro and M. S. Moss) 2000, Urban Governance: Britain and Beyond since 1750 (co-ed.) 2000; book chapters and articles in peer-reviewed journals. *Address:* James Clerk Maxwell Building, King's College London, 57 Waterloo Road, London, SE1 8WA, England (office). *Telephone:* (20) 7848-3434 (office). *Fax:* (20) 7848-3430 (office). *E-mail:* principal@kcl.ac.uk (office). *Website:* www.kcl.ac .uk/aboutkings/principal/ricktrainor.aspx (office).

TRAIRATVORAKUL, Prasarn, BEng, MEng, MBA, DBA; Thai economist and central banker; *Governor, Bank of Thailand;* b. 20 Aug. 1952; m. Nisarat Trairatvorakul; ed Chulalongkorn Univ., Asian Inst. of Tech., Thai Nat. Defence Coll., Harvard Univ., USA; Research Fellow, Int. Food Policy Research Inst., Washington, DC 1981–83; joined Bank of Thailand (central bank) as Economist, Dept of Econ. Research 1983, becoming Section Chief, Dept of Bank Supervision and Examination, later Deputy Dir, Dept of Financial Insts Supervision and Examination –1992, Gov. Bank of Thailand 2010–; Deputy Sec.-Gen., Securities and Exchange Comm. of Thailand 1992–99, Sec.-Gen. 1999–2003; Pres. KASI-KORNBANK Public Co. Ltd 2004–10; Chair. KFactoring Co. Ltd 2005–09, KLeasing Co. Ltd 2005–10; Vice-Chair. Muangthai Life Assurance Co. Ltd 2010, Muangthai Group Holding Co. Ltd 2010; Exec. Dir Thai Red Cross Soc. 1998–; mem. Council Chulalongkorn Univ. 2008; Dir Financial Reform Advisory Cttee, Ministry of Finance 1998–2000; Dir State Enterprises Capital Policy Cttee 2000–03; Chair. Thai Bankers Asscn 2010; Commdr (Third Class), Most Noble Order of the Crown of Thailand, Commdr (Third Class), Most Exalted Order of the White Elephant; Central Bank Governor of the Year for Asia, Emerging Markets Magazine 2011, Financier of the Year, Money & Banking Magazine 2012. *Address:* Office of the Governor, Bank of Thailand, 273 Thanon Samsen, Wat Sam Phraya, Phra Nakhon, Bangkok 10200, Thailand (office). *Telephone:* (2) 283-5010 (office). *Fax:* (2) 280-0609 (office). *E-mail:* PrasarnT@bot.or.th (office). *Website:* www.bot.or .th (office).

TRAN, Duc Luong; Vietnamese politician, fmr head of state and fmr mining engineer; b. 5 May 1937, Quang Ngai Prov.; m. Nguyen Thi Vinh; moved to Hanoi after leaving school 1955; studied geology and was employed as a cartographer; joined Dang Cong san Viet Nam (CP of Viet Nam) 1959, held several party roles in 1970s, mem. Politburo 1996–97; apptd Deputy Prime Minister 1987; Pres. of Viet Nam 1997–2006. *Address:* c/o Dang Cong san Viet Nam, 1 Hoang Van Thu, Hanoi, Viet Nam.

TRAN, Rev. Tam Tinh, (Hoang Tam), PhD, FRSC; Vietnamese/Canadian archaeologist and academic; *Professor Emeritus of Classical Archaeology, Université Laval;* b. 16 April 1929, Nam Dinh; ed Séminaire Pontifical, Università Laterano, Université de Fribourg, Ecole Pratique des Hautes Etudes, Paris, CNRS; ordained priest 1956; excavations at Soli, Cyprus 1965–74, Pompeii and Herculaneum 1969–76; Co-founder Fraternité Vietnam 1976; Prof. of Classical Archaeology, Université Laval 1964–71, Sr Prof. 1971–94, Prof. Emer. 1994–; Tatiana Warscher Award for Archaeology, American Acad. at Rome 1973, Prix G. Mendel, Acad. des Inscriptions et Belles-Lettres, France 1978. *Publications include:* Le culte d'Isis à Pompéi 1964, Le culte des divinités orientales à Herculaneum 1971, Le culte des divinités orientales en Campanie 1972, Isis lactans 1973, Catalogue des peintures romaines au musée du Louvre 1974, Tôi vê Hanoi 1974, Tro vê nguôn 1974, I cattolici nella storia del Vietnam 1975, Dieu et César 1978, Sérapis debout 1983, Soloi I, La Basilique 1985, La casa dei Cervi à Herculaneum 1988, Corpus des lampes antiques conservées au Québec I 1991, Corpus des lampes à sujets asiatiques du musée gréco-romain d'Alexandrie 1993, Xin thay day con cau nguyen 2004, Loan bao tin mung 2004, Lay Cha 2004, Ong la ai? 2004; and numerous articles on classical iconography and religion. *Address:* Université Laval, Cité Universitaire, Québec City, PQ G1K 7P4 (office); 2995 Maricourt, Suite 300, Québec City, PQ G1W 4T8, Canada (home). *Telephone:* (418) 653-3513 (office). *E-mail:* vinhsont2005@yahoo.ca. *Website:* www.ulaval.ca (office).

TRAN, Trong Toan, MA; Vietnamese diplomatist and international organization official; b. 12 Oct. 1952, Ha Tay Prov. (now Ha Noi); s. of Tran Trong An and Pham Thi Lan; m. Le Thi Lai; two d.; ed Faculty of Orientalistics, Tashkent State Univ., Uzbekistan; official, S Asia Dept, Ministry of Foreign Affairs 1975–80, Embassy of Viet Nam, New Delhi 1980–83, Foreign Minister's Secr. and Asst Dir-Gen. Foreign Ministry's Secr. 1984–89, Acting Dir-Gen. S Asia Dept 1990–92, Minister Counsellor, New Delhi 1992–95, Dir-Gen. Dept of Econ. Affairs 1996–2000, Vice-Chair. Viet Nam Nat. Cttee for the Pacific Econ. Co-operation Council 1996–2000, 2004–05, Viet Nam Sr Official to APEC 1999; Amb. to Malaysia 2000–03, Dir-Gen. Foreign Minister's Advisory Bd, then Dir-Gen. Dept of Multilateral Econ. Co-operation, Ministry of Foreign Affairs 2003–04, mem. Govt Negotiation Team for Int. Econ. Integration, Amb. and Deputy Exec. Dir APEC Secr. 2005, Amb. and Exec. Dir 2006; Standing Vice-Chair. Cttee for Overseas Vietnamese, Ministry of Foreign Affairs 2007–09; Amb. to S Korea 2010–13, Ministry of Foreign Affairs 2013–; State Order of Labour, Pres. of Viet Nam 2007; awards from Minister of Foreign Affairs. *Publications:* several books and a series of articles, including The Asia-Pacific Economic Cooperation Forum (APEC) (author and Chief Ed.) 1998, Globalization and Vietnam's International Economic Integration (author and Chief Ed.) 1999, APEC Glossaries 2006, Collection of My Speeches as APEC Secretariat Executive Director 2006, Stories on President Ho Chi Minh and Vietnamese Diplomacy (Chief Ed.) 2010, Selective Poems of Vietnamese Diplomats (Chief Ed.) 2010. *Leisure interests:* volleyball, badminton, table tennis, golf. *Address:* Ministry of Foreign Affairs, 1 Ton That Dam, Ba Dinh District, Hanoi, Viet Nam (office). *Telephone:* (4) 37992000 (office). *Fax:* (4) 38231872 (office). *E-mail:* tttoantt@yahoo.com (office); banbientap@mofa.gov.vn (office). *Website:* www.mofa.gov.vn (office).

TRAORÉ, Abou-Bakar; Malian government official; Minister of the Economy and Finance 2004–07, of Finance 2007–09. *Address:* c/o Ministry of the Economy and Finance, BP 234, Koulouba, Bamako, Mali (office).

TRAORÉ, Gen. Moussa; Malian politician and army officer; b. 25 Sept. 1936, Kayes; ed Training Coll., Fréjus, Cadets Coll., Kati; became NCO in French Army; returned to Mali 1960; promoted Lt 1964, Col 1971, Brig.-Gen. 1978; at Armed Forces Coll., Kati until 1968; led coup to depose Pres. Modibo Keita Nov. 1968; Pres. Mil. Cttee for Nat. Liberation (Head of State) and C-in-C of the Armed Forces 1968–91, also Prime Minister 1969–80; Pres. of Mali 1979–91; Minister of Defence and Security 1978–86, of the Interior 1978–79, of Nat. Defence 1988–90 (overthrown in coup, under arrest); Chair. OAU 1988–89; Sec.-Gen. Nat. Council Union Démocratique du Peuple Malien 1979–80, fmr mem. Cen. Exec. Bureau; Pres. Conf. of Heads of State, Union Douanière des Etats de l'Afrique de l'Ouest 1970; overthrown March 1991; stood trial Nov. 1992; sentenced to death for mass murder Feb. 1993; sentence commuted to life imprisonment 1997; charged with embezzlement Oct. 1998; sentenced to death Jan. 1999; sentence commuted to life imprisonment Sept. 1999; officially pardoned 2002.

TRAPATTONI, Giovanni; Italian professional football manager and fmr footballer; b. 17 March 1939, Cusano Milanino, Milan; defender/midfielder; sr player, AC Milan 1959–71 (274 appearances, three goals, won Serie A 1961/62, 1967/68, Italian Cup 1966/67, European Cup 1963, 1969, UEFA Cup Winners' Cup 1967/68, Intercontinental Cup 1969), Varese 1971–72, Italy 1960–64 (17 caps, one goal); Man. AC Milan 1974, 1976, Juventus 1976–86 (won Serie A 1976/77, 1977/78, 1980/81, 1981/82, 1983/84, 1985/86, Italian Cup 1978/79, 1982/83, European Cup 1984/85, UEFA Cup Winners' Cup 1984, UEFA Cup 1977, 1993, European Super Cup 1984, Intercontinental Cup 1985), Inter 1986–91 (won Serie A 1988/89, UEFA Cup 1991), Bayern Munich 1994–95, 1996–98 (won German League 1996/97, German Cup 1998), Cagliari 1995–96, Fiorentina 1998–2000, Italy nat. team 2000–04; Head Coach, Benfica, Portugal 2004–05 (won Portuguese League 2004/05), VfB Stuttgart 2005–06, Red Bull Salzburg, Austria 2006–08 (won Austrian League 2006/07); Man. Repub. of Ireland nat. team 2008–13; one of only two coaches, alongside Ernst Happel, to have won the league title (ten times) in four different countries (Italy, Germany, Portugal and Austria); fourth coach with most int. competitions for clubs won in the world (second in Europe) with seven titles in eight finals, including Intercontinental Cup final (mainly with Juventus); only coach, alongside Udo Lattek, to have won all three major European club titles; only coach to have won all UEFA club competitions and World Club title; also has record of three UEFA Cup wins; UEFA Cup Winning Coach 1976–77, 1990–91, 1992–93, UEFA Cup Winners' Cup Winning Coach 1983–84, European Cup Winning Coach 1984–85. *Publication:* Fischia il Trap (biog.). *Website:* www.trapattoni.de.

TRAUNER, Sergio; Italian lawyer and business executive; b. 9 March 1934, Athens, Greece; s. of Livio Trauner and Nada Mandich; m. (divorced); ed Univ. of Trieste; lawyer in pvt. practice; counsellor to Trieste Municipality 1962–75, 1982–; to Friuli Venezia Giulia Region 1964–78; Dir Finmare Co. (IRI Group) 1981–84, EFIM 1984–87; mem. Presidential Cttee and Bd of Dirs IRI 1986–91; Pres. ILVA SpA 1991–; Pres. Società Ginnastica Triestina 2009–; Commendatore of Italian Repub., Officer, Order of Merit of Italian Repub. *Publications:* books on art and history. *Leisure interests:* reading, travel. *Address:* c/o Società Ginnastica Triestina, Via della Ginnastica, 47, 34142 Trieste, Italy. *E-mail:* sgt_trieste@virgilio.it. *Website:* www.ginnasticatriestina.com.

TRAUTMAN, Andrzej; Polish theoretical physicist and academic; *Professor Emeritus, Warsaw University;* b. 4 Jan. 1933, Warsaw; s. of Mieczysław Trautman and Eliza Trautman (née André); m. Róża Michalska 1962; two s.; ed Warsaw Univ. of Tech., Warsaw Univ.; asst, Inst. of Radiolocation, Warsaw Univ. of Tech. 1952–53, Inst. of Applied Math. 1953–55; postgraduate studies, Inst. of Physics, Polish Acad. of Sciences (PAN) 1955–58, doctorate 1959; lecturer 1959; scientific training, Imperial Coll., King's Coll., London, Univ. of Syracuse, USA 1959–61; scientist, Inst. of Theoretical Physics, Warsaw Univ. 1961–, Asst Prof. and Head of Dept Electrodynamics and Theory of Relativity 1962–68, Extraordinary Prof. 1964–71, Ordinary Prof. 1971–2004, Prof. Emer. 2004–; Deputy Dir Inst. of Theoretical Physics 1968–74, Dir 1975–85; Corresp. mem. Polish Acad. of Sciences 1969–76, mem. 1977–, mem. Presidium 1972–83, Vice-Pres. 1978–80, Chair. Cttee of Physics; Corresp. mem. Polish Acad. of Arts and Science, Kraków; Deputy Chair. Gen. Bd of Polish Physics Asscn 1970–73, Foreign mem. Czechoslovak Acad. of Sciences 1980–90; mem. Int. Cttee of Theory of Relativity and Gravitation 1965–80, Int. Journal of Theoretical Physics, Journal of Geometry and Physics; Visiting Prof., American Math. Soc., Santa Barbara 1962, Coll. de France, Paris 1963 and 1981, Brandeis Univ., USA 1964, Univ. of Chicago 1971, Univ. of Pisa, Italy 1972, The Schrödinger Professorship, Univ. of Vienna 1972, State Univ. of NY at Stony Brook 1976–77, Univ. of Montreal 1982, 1990, Univ. of Texas at Dallas 1985, 1986; Gold Cross of Merit, Officer's Cross of Order of Polonia Restituta; Dr hc (Silesian Univ., Czech Repub.) 2001; State Prize 1st Class 1976, Alfred Jurzykowski Foundation Award in Physics 1984. *Publications:* Differential Geometry for Physicists 1984, The Spinorial Chessboard (with P. Budinich) 1988, Space Time and Gravitation (with W. Kopczyński) 1992; and numerous works on theory of gravitational waves, energy of gravitation field, modern methods of differential geometry and their application in physics, Einstein-Cartan's Theory, Dirac operator and spin structures on manifolds. *Leisure interest:* chess. *Address:* Instytut Fizyki Teoretycznej UW, ul. Hoża 69, 00-681 Warsaw, Poland (office). *Telephone:* (22) 5532295 (office). *Fax:* (22) 6219475 (office). *E-mail:* andrzej.trautman@fuw.edu.pl (office). *Website:* www.fuw.edu.pl (office).

TRAUTZ, Volker, Dr rer. nat; German business executive; b. 1945; ed Univ. of Stuttgart; worked as asst at Univ. of Stuttgart –1974; joined BASF AG 1974, served several man. positions, including 14 years in S America, Pres. BASF's Consumer Products Div. 1991–95, mem. Bd Exec. Dirs BASF 1995–2000, responsible for all polymers, including eng resins, PVC and polyurethanes, and for BASF's activities in Asia; CEO Basell (renamed LyondellBasell Industries following acquisition by Basell of Lyondell Chemical Co. Dec. 2007) 2000–09 (retd). *Address:* c/o LyondellBasell Industries, PO Box 2416, 3000 CK Rotterdam. *E-mail:* info@lyondellbasell.com.

TRAVIS, Randy; American country singer, songwriter and musician (guitar); b. (Randy Bruce Traywick), 4 May 1959, Marshville, North Carolina; m. Lib Hatcher (Mary Elizabeth Robertson) 1991; played local clubs with brothers; resident at Charlotte nightclub (owned by Lib Hatcher) 1977; early recordings as Randy Traywick; resident singer, as Randy Ray, Nashville Palace 1992; solo artist as Randy Travis 1985–; Acad. of Country Music Top Male Vocalist 1985, 1986, 1987, 1988, Grammy Award for Best Country Newcomer 1986, CMA Horizon Award 1986, Acad. of Country Music Song of the Year (for On the Other Hand) 1986, (for Forever and Ever Amen) 1987, (for Three Wooden Crosses) 2004, CMA Single of the Year (for Forever and Ever Amen) 1987, Music City News Male Artist of the Year, Star of Tomorrow and Single of the Year (for On the Other Hand) 1987, CMA Male Vocalist of the Year 1987, 1988, Music City News Entertainer of the Year, Male Artist of the Year, Single of the Year (for Forever and Ever Amen) and Entertainer of the Year 1989, Grammy Award for Best Album Collaboration (for Same Old Train 1998, CMA Song of the Year (for Three Wooden Crosses) 2003, Grammy Award for Best Country Collaboration with Vocals (for I Told You So with Carrie Underwood) 2010, also awards from Performance magazine, AMOA Jukebox, Country Music Round Up, NECMA, TNN Viewers Choice Awards, Rolling Stone magazine, Playboy magazine, Billboard Music Awards, BBC Radio Two, Dove Awards, Christian Country Music Awards. *Recordings include:* albums: Storms Of Life (Acad. of Country Music Album of the Year 1986, Music City News Album of the Year 1986) 1986, Always And Forever (Grammy Award 1987, CMA Album of the Year 1987, Music City News Album of the Year 1988) 1987, Old 8x10 (Grammy Award 1988) 1988, An Old Time Christmas 1989, No Holdin' Back 1989, Heroes And Friends 1990, High Lonesome 1991, Wind In The Wire 1993, This Is Me 1994, Full Circle 1996, You And You Alone 1998, A Man Ain't Made Of Stone 1999, Inspirational Journey 2000, Randy Travis Live 2001, Anthology 2002, Rise And Shine (Grammy Award 2004) 2002, Worship & Faith (Grammy Award 2005) 2003, Passing Through 2004, Glory Train (Grammy Award for Best Southern, Country, Or Bluegrass Gospel Album 2007) 2005, Songs of the Season 2007, Around the Bend 2008, Blessed Assurance 2011, Influence, Vol. 1: The Man I Am 2013. *Address:* Elizabeth Travis Management, 1610 16th Avenue South, Nashville, TN 37212, USA (office). *Telephone:* (615) 383-7258 (office). *Fax:* (615) 269-7828 (office). *E-mail:* webmaster@randytravis.com. *Website:* www.randytravis.com.

TRAVKIN, Nikolai Ilyich; Russian politician; b. 19 March 1946, Novo-Nikolskoe, Moscow region; m.; two s.; ed Kolomna Pedagogical Inst., Higher Party School; mem. CPSU 1970–90; worker, brigade-leader, Head of the Dept of Glavmosstroi; initiator self-financing and self-man. into construction industry 1969–; Deputy Head of construction union 1967–89; mem. of the movt Democratic Russia 1988–; People's Deputy of the USSR 1989–91; People's Deputy of Russia 1990–93; Co-founder and Chair. Democratic Party of Russia 1990–94; Chair. of the Sub cttee, Supreme Soviet of the USSR (supervising local soviets and devt of self-man.) 1989–90; Chair. Cttee Supreme Soviet of Russia; supervising local soviets and devt of self-man. May–Dec. 1990; head of local admin. Shakhovskoy Dist 1991–96; Co-leader Civic Union coalition 1992–93; mem. State Duma (Parl.) Yabloko group (now Union of Right Forces faction) 1993–2003; Minister without Portfolio 1994–96; mem. Cttee on Problems of Fed. and Regional Politics 1996–; Pres. Fund in Support of Farmers; Hero of Socialist Labour 1986. *Leisure interests:* theatre, literature. *Address:* c/o Yabloko Russian United Democratic Party (Rossiiskaya obyedinennaya demokraticheskaya partiya 'Yabloko'), 119017 Moscow, ul. Pyatnitskaya 31/2, Russia.

TRAVOLTA, John; American actor; b. 18 Feb. 1954, Englewood, NJ; s. of Salvatore Travolta and the late Helen (née Burke) Travolta; m. Kelly Preston 1991; one s., one s. deceased, one d.; TV series Welcome Back Kotter 1975–77; Billboard Magazine Best New Male Vocalist Award 1976, Male Star of the Year, Nat. Asscn of Theatre Owners 1983, Alan J. Pakula Prize 1998, Lifetime Achievement Award, Palm Springs Int. Film Festival 1999. *Films:* Carrie 1976, The Boy in the Plastic Bubble (for TV) 1976, Saturday Night Fever (Nat. Bd of Review Award for Best Actor) 1977, Grease 1978, Moment by Moment 1978, Urban Cowboy 1980, Blow-Out 1981, Staying Alive 1983, Two of a Kind 1983, Perfect 1985, The Experts 1988, Chains of Gold 1989, Look Who's Talking 1989, Look Who's Talking Now 1990, The Tender 1991, All Shook Up 1991, Look Who's Talking 3 1994, Pulp Fiction 1994, White Man's Burden 1995, Get Shorty (American Comedy Award, Golden Globe Award for Best Actor) 1995, Broken Arrow 1996, Phenomenon 1996, Michael 1997, Face Off 1997, She's So Lovely 1997, Primary Colors 1998, A Civil Action 1998, The General's Daughter 1999, Battlefield Earth 2000, Lucky Numbers 2000, Swordfish 2001, Domestic Disturbance 2001, Basic 2003, The Punisher 2004, A Love Song for Bobby Long 2004, Ladder 49 2004, Be Cool 2005, Lonely Hearts 2006, Wild Hogs 2007, Hairspray 2007, The Taking of Pelham 1 2 3 2009, Old Dogs 2009, From Paris with Love 2010, Savages 2012. *Recordings include:* John Travolta 1976, Travolta Fever 1978, Grease 1978, Let Her In: The Best of John Travolta 1996, Hairspray 2007. *Publications:* Staying Fit 1984, Propeller One-Way Night Coach (juvenile) 1998. *Leisure interest:* flying. *Address:* William Morris Agency, One William Morris Place, Beverly Hills, CA 90212, USA (office); William Morris Endeavor, 9601 Wilshire Blvd, Beverly Hills, CA 90212, USA. *Telephone:* (310) 859-4000 (office). *Fax:* (310) 859-4462 (office). *Website:* www.wma.com (office).

TREACY, Philip, MA, RCA; Irish milliner; b. 26 May 1967, Ballinsoe, Co. Galway; s. of the late James Vincent Treacy and Katie Agnes Treacy; ed Nat. Coll. of Art and Design, Dublin, Royal Coll. of Art, London; while a student worked for designers including Rifat Ozbek, John Galliano and Victor Edelstein; f. Philip Treacy Millinery, London 1991; house milliner for Marc Bohan at Hartnell and for Victor Edelstein; has collaborated with Karl Lagerfeld, Chanel's couture and ready-to-wear shows 1991–; his own ready-to-wear range sold in New York and London 1991–; designed head dresses for Pola John's production of My Fair Lady 1992; presented own show, London 1993; launched accessory range 1997; first show in New York 1997; Interior Design Dir The G (hotel) 2005; British Accessory Designer of the Year award 1991, 1992, 1993, 1996, 1997, Irish Fashion Oscar 1992, Haute Couture Paris 2000, Moet & Chandon Award 2002, Int. Designer of the Year, China Fashion Awards 2004. *Address:* Philip Treacy London Head Office, 1 Havelock Terrace, London, SW8 4AS, England (office). *Telephone:* (20) 7738-8080 (office). *Fax:* (20) 7738-8545 (office). *E-mail:* admin@philiptreacy.co.uk (office). *Website:* www.philiptreacy.co.uk (office).

TRECHSEL, Stefan, DIur, PD; Swiss lawyer and judge (retd); b. 25 June 1937, Berne; s. of Manfred F. Trechsel and Steffi Friedlaender; m. Franca Julia Kinsbergen 1967; two d.; ed Univ. of Berne and Georgetown Univ., Washington, DC; Asst and Main Asst for Criminal Law, Univ. of Berne 1964–71; Swiss Fed. Dept for Tech. Cooperation 1966–67; Public Prosecutor, Dist of Bern-Mittelland 1971–75; Guest Prof. of Criminal Law and Procedure, Univ. of Fribourg 1975–77; Prof., Hochschule St Gallen 1979–99; Prof. of Criminal Law and Legal Criminal Procedure, Univ. of Zurich 1999–2004, Prof. Emer. 2004–; Judge ad litem, Int. Criminal Tribunal for the Fmr Yugoslavia, The Hague, Netherlands 2006–13; mem. European Comm. of Human Rights 1975–99 (2nd Vice-Pres. 1987, Chamber Pres. 1993–94), AIDP 2013–, FIPP 2013–; Council of Europe Medal pro merito 2004; Dr hc (New York Univ. Law School) 1975; ASIL award for Human Rights in Criminal Proceedings 1995. *Publications:* Der Strafgrund der Teilnahme 1967, Die Europäische Menschenrechtskonvention, ihr Schutz der persönlichen Freiheit und die Schweizerischen Strafprozessrechte 1974, Strafrecht Allgemeiner Teil I (6th edn of textbook by Peter Noll) 1994, Schweizerisches Strafgesetzbuch, Kurzkommentar 1997, Human Rights in Criminal Proceedings 2005, Praxiskommentar StGB 2008 (second edn 2012). *Leisure interests:* music, literature, art, chamber music (cello). *Address:* Rabbentalstr. 63, 3013 Berne, Switzerland (home). *Telephone:* (31) 3328449 (home). *E-mail:* trechsel@gmx.net (office).

TREDE, Michael, BA, MD, BChir; German surgeon; b. 10 Oct. 1928, Hamburg; s. of Hilmar Trede and Gertrud Trede (née Daus); m. Ursula Boettcher 1956; one s. four d.; ed The Leys School, Cambridge and Univ. of Cambridge; Surgeon-in-Training, Freie Universität, Berlin 1957–62, Heidelberg Univ. 1962–72; Prof. and Chair. Dept of Surgery, Klinikum Mannheim, Univ. of Heidelberg, now Prof. Emer. and Chair.; Pres. Deutsche Gesellschaft für Chirurgie, Int. Surgical Soc. 1993–95; Hon. mem. Austrian, American, Swiss, Italian and Portuguese Surgical Asscns; Hon. FRCS (England, Ireland, Glasgow, Edin.); Hon. FACS; Dr hc (Edinburgh) 1995. *Publications:* Surgery of the Pancreas (with D. C. Carter), The Art of Surgery 1999, Der Rückkehrer. Skizzenbuch eines Chirurgen 3rd edn 2003; 500 articles on surgery in scientific journals. *Leisure interests:* painting, violinplaying, mountaineering, skiing. *Address:* Nadlerstrasse 1A, 68259 Mannheim, Germany. *Telephone:* (621) 383-2728 (office); (621) 796301.

TREGLOWN, Jeremy Dickinson, BLitt, MA, PhD, FRSL; British author, journalist and academic; *Professor of English, University of Warwick*; b. 24 May 1946, Anglesey, N Wales; s. of the late Rev. G. L. Treglown and Beryl Treglown; m. 1st Rona Bower 1970 (divorced 1982); one s. two d.; m. 2nd Holly Eley (née Urquhart) 1984 (died 2010); one d. with Jennifer Lewis; ed Bristol Grammar School, St Peter's Coll., Oxford; Lecturer in English Literature, Lincoln Coll. Oxford 1973–76, Univ. Coll., London 1976–79; Asst Ed. The Times Literary Supplement 1979–81, Ed. 1982–90; Prof. of English, Univ. of Warwick 1993– (Chair. Dept of English and Comparative Literary Studies 1995–98); Chair. of Judges, Booker Prize 1991, Whitbread Book of the Year Award 1998; Co-Ed. Liber: A European Review of Books 1989; Contributing Ed., Grand Street magazine, New York 1991–98; Visiting Fellow, All Souls Coll., Oxford 1986; Fellow, Huntington Library 1988; Mellon Visiting Assoc., California Inst. of Tech. 1988; Ferris Visiting Prof., Princeton Univ. 1992; Jackson Brothers Fellow, Beinecke Library, Yale Univ. 1999; Leverhulme Research Fellow 2001–03; Margaret and Herman Sokol Fellow, Cullman Center for Scholars and Writers, New York Public Library 2002–03; Fellow in History, Bogliasco Foundation 2011; Fellow, Rockefeller Foundation, Bellagio 2011; mem. Council, RSL 2010–; Hon. Research Fellow, Univ. Coll. London 1991–. *Publications:* The Letters of John Wilmot, Earl of Rochester (ed.) 1980, Spirit of Wit: Reconsiderations of Rochester (ed.) 1982, Roald Dahl: A Biography 1994, Grub Street and the Ivory Tower: Literary Journalism, and Literary Scholarship from Fielding to the Internet (co-ed. with Bridget Bennett) 1998, Romancing: The Life and Work of Henry Green 2000, VS Pritchett: A Working Life 2004, Essential Stories/V.S. Pritchett (ed.) 2005, Roald Dahl: Collected Stories (ed.) 2006; contrib. of introductions to recent edns of R. L. Stevenson's In the South Seas, Robert Louis Stevenson's The Lantern Bearers, the complete novels of Henry Green; various articles on poetry, drama and literary history. *Address:* English and Comparative Literary Studies, Room H526, University of Warwick, Coventry, CV4 7AL, England (office). *Telephone:* (24) 7652-3323 (office). *Fax:* (24) 7652-4750 (office). *E-mail:* jeremy.treglown@warwick .ac.uk (office). *Website:* www2.warwick.ac.uk/fac/arts/english (office).

TREHAN, Naresh Kumar, MD; Indian cardiovascular surgeon; *Chairman and Managing Director, Medanta-The Medicity*; b. 12 Aug. 1946; m. Madhu Trehan; ed King George's Medical Coll., Lucknow, American Bd of Surgery and American Bd of Cardiothoracic Surgery, USA; Teaching Asst and Clinical Instructor, New York Univ. Medical Center, USA 1971–74, Attending Cardiothoracic Surgeon 1979–88, Asst Prof. of Surgery 1981–88; Attending Cardiothoracic Surgeon, New York Infirmary-Beekman Downtown Hosp., St Vincent's Hospital and Medical Center, Bellevue Hospital, New York 1979–88; Chief Thoracic and Cardiovascular Surgery, Veterans Administration Hosp., New York; Personal Surgeon to Pres. of India 1991–; est. Escorts Heart Inst. and Research Centre 1988, Exec. Dir and Chief Cardiovascular Surgeon, Escorts Heart Inst. and Research Centre 1988–2007; Sr Cardiovascular and Thoracic Surgeon, Apollo Hospitals 2007–09; currently Chair. and Man. Dir Medanta-The Medicity, Haryana; Pres. Indian Health Care Fed., Int. Soc. for Minimally Invasive Cardiac Surgery 2004–05; Chair. Healthcare Industry Cttee, Confed. of Indian Industries; Fellow, Royal Soc. of Medicine, London, American Coll. of Surgeons, Int. Medical Sciences Acad.; mem. Soc. of Thoracic Surgeons of America, Asscn of Thoracic and Cardiovascular Surgeons of Asia, Scientific Council, American Coll. of Angiology, European Asscn for Cardio-thoracic Surgery, Key Advisory Group, Ministry of Health and Family Welfare, Inst. Body of Sanjay Gandhi Post Grad. Inst. of Medical Sciences, Lucknow 1996–2001, Governing Council, Sri Jayadeva Inst. of Cardiology, Bangalore; mem. Bd of Dirs Int. Soc. for Minimally Invasive Cardiac Surgery; mem. Editorial Bd Heart Surgery Forum (journal); Hon. Consultant to Cromwell Hospital, London, UK 1994, Cardiothoracic Surgery to Armed Forces Medical Services 1997, Hon. Visiting Prof., Cardiovascular Surgery, LPS Inst. of Cardiology, Kanpur 1996, Bangladesh Medical Coll., Dhaka 2000, Hon. Fellow, Royal Australasian Coll. of Surgeons 2002; Hon. DSc (Banaras Hindu Univ.) 1996, (Chhatrapati Shahu Ji Maharaj Univ., Kanpur) 2004, (King George's Medical Univ., Lucknow) 2007; Nagrik Club Jaipur Award 1991, Joshi Award, Delhi Medical Asscn 1989, Alumni Award, KG Medical Coll., Lucknow 1989, Nat.

Integration Council Award 1988, Padma Shri 1991, Nat. Inst. of Punjab Studies Bhai Vir Singh Int. Award, Yuva Shakti Org. Jaipur Award 1992, Shiromani Award 1992, T.P. Jhunjhunwala Foundation Award 1992–93, Mother India Int. Award, NRI Inst. 1992, Distinguished Service Award, Indian Medical Asscn Acad. of Medical Specialities 1993, Distinguished Service Award, Acad. of Medical Specialities 1994, Sushruta Award 1994, Samajshree Award, Indian Council of Man. Exec., Bombay 1995, Rajiv Gandhi Nat. Unity Award 1995, Lok Seva Award 1995, India Int. Gold Award, NRI Inst. 1995, Rotary Ratna Award, Rotary Int. 1996, Life Time Achievement Award, Int. Medical Integration Council 1999, Dr K. Sharan Cardiology Excellence Award, Indian Medical Asscn 2000, Indira Gandhi Millennium Award, All India Feroze Gandhi Memorial Soc. 2000 AMA Physician's Recognition Award, CME Alliance at ISMICS, Germany 2001, Padma Bhushan Award 2001, Rashtriya Ratan Award 2001, Ernst & Young Entrepreneur Award, Jewel of India in the Millennium, Int. Award Cttee, Wisitex Foundation 2002, Life Time Achievement Award, Int. Soc. of Cardiovascular Ultrasound 2002, Dr B.C. Roy Nat. Award 2005, Lal Bahadur Shastri Nat. Award 2005. *Address:* Medanta-The Medicity, Sector 38, Gurgaon, Haryana 122 001, India (office). *Telephone:* (124) 4834 333 (office). *Fax:* (124) 4834 222 (office). *E-mail:* naresh.trehan@ medanta.org (office); ntrehan@vsnl.com (office). *Website:* www.drnareshtrehan .com (office).

TREICHL, Andreas; Austrian banking executive; *Chairman of the Management Board,, Erste Group Bank AG;* b. 1952; ed studied econs in Vienna; began career with Chase Manhattan Bank, New York 1977; joined Erste Bank in 1983 for three years, rejoined bank and apptd to Man. Bd 1994, Chair. 1997–, responsible for Group Communication, Group HR, Strategic Group Devt, Group Secr., Group Audit, Group Marketing, Group Investor Relations, Group Identity, good.bee – banking for the unbanked. *Address:* Erste Bank der oesterreichischen Sparkassen AG, Graben 21, 1010 Vienna, Austria (office). *Telephone:* (50) 100-10100 (office). *Fax:* (50) 100-13112 (office). *E-mail:* investor.relations@erstebank.at (office). *Website:* www.erstebank.com (office).

TREICHL, Heinrich, LLD; Austrian business executive; b. 31 July 1913, Vienna; s. of Dr Alfred Treichl and Dorothea Treichl (née Baroness Ferstel); m. Helga Ross 1946; two s.; ed Univs of Frankfurt, Germany and Vienna; Dir, Banque des Pays de l'Europe Centrale, Paris, Mercur Bank AG and Länderbank Wien AG, Vienna 1936–39; Pnr, Ullstein and Co., Vienna 1946–55; Dir, Österreichische Industrie- und Bergbauverwaltungs GmbH, Vienna 1956–58; Dir, Creditanstalt-Bankverein, Vienna 1958, Chair. of Man. Bd 1970–81 (merged with Bank Austria 1998); fmr Pres. F.A. v Hayek Inst., Vienna; Hon. Pres. Austrian Red Cross Soc.; Hon. Chair. Supervisory Bd Bank für Kärnten und Steiermark AG, Bank für Oberösterreich und Salzburg, Bank für Tirol und Vorarlberg AG; Grande Ufficiale Ordine del Merito (Italy), Commdr, Order Homayoun, Commdr, Légion d'honneur, Kt Commdr, Order of St Gregory, Grand Decoration of Honour in Gold for Services to Repub. of Austria, Grand Decoration in Silver with Star for Services to Repub. of Austria. *Leisure interests:* literature, hunting, skiing. *Address:* Salmgasse 2, 1030 Vienna, Austria (home). *Telephone:* (1) 713-31-50 (home). *Fax:* (1) 713-31-50 (home). *Website:* www.hayek-institut.at.

TREISMAN, Anne, BA, DPhil, FRS; British/American psychologist and academic; *James S. McDonnell Distinguished Professor of Psychology, Princeton University;* b. 27 Feb. 1935, Wakefield, Yorks., England; m. Daniel Kahneman; four c.; ed Univs of Cambridge and Oxford; Research Asst to Prof. R.C. Oldfield, Dept of Experimental Psychology, Univ. of Oxford 1961–63, mem. MRC Psycholinguistics Research Unit 1963–66; Visiting Research Scientist, Behavioral Sciences Dept, Bell Telephone Labs, New Jersey, USA 1966–67; Fellow, St Anne's Coll., Oxford 1967–78, Univ. Lecturer in Psychology, Univ. of Oxford 1967–78; Fellow, Center for Advanced Study in Behavioral Sciences, Stanford Univ., California 1977–78; Prof. of Psychology, Univ. of British Columbia 1978–86; Fellow, Canadian Inst. for Advanced Research 1984–86; Prof. of Psychology, Univ. of California, Berkeley 1986–94; Visiting Scholar, Russell Sage Foundation, New York 1991–92; Prof. of Psychology, Princeton Univ. 1993–, James S. McDonnell Distinguished Univ. Prof. of Psychology 1995–; Fellow, American Psychological Soc.; mem. Asscn for Research in Vision and Ophthalmology, Soc. of Experimental Psychologists 1979–, Cognitive Neuroscience Soc., Psychonomic Soc., British Experimental Psychology Soc., American Philosophical Soc., American Acad. of Arts and Sciences, NAS; Killam Sr Fellowship 1982–83; Hon. Prof., Inst. of Psychology, Chinese Acad. of Sciences 2004; Hon. DSc (Univ. of British Columbia) 2004, (Univ. Coll. London) 2006; British Experimental Psychology Soc. Spearman Medal 1963, Soc. of Experimental Psychologists Howard Crosby Warren Medal 1990, Cognitive Neuroscience Soc. George Miller Award, American Psychological Asscn Distinguished Scientific Contribution Award 1990, Minerva Foundation Golden Brain Award 1996, Univ. of Louisville Grawemeyer Award in Psychology 2009, Nat. Medal of Science 2012. *Address:* Department of Psychology, Green Hall, Princeton University, Princeton, NJ 08544-1010, USA (office). *Telephone:* (609) 258-4648 (office). *Fax:* (609) 258-1113 (office). *E-mail:* psych@princeton.edu (office). *Website:* psych.princeton.edu (office).

TREITEL, Sir Guenter Heinz, Kt, QC, MA, DCL, FBA; British academic; *Professor Emeritus of English Law, University of Oxford;* b. 26 Oct. 1928, Berlin, Germany; s. of Dr Theodor Treitel and Hanna Treitel (née Levy); m. Phyllis M. Cook 1957; two s.; ed Kilburn Grammar School and Magdalen Coll., Oxford; came to UK 1939; Asst Lecturer, LSE 1951–53; Lecturer, Univ. Coll., Oxford 1953–54; Fellow of Magdalen Coll., Oxford 1954–79, Fellow Emer. 1979–; All Souls Reader in English Law 1964–79; Vinerian Prof. of English Law, Univ. of Oxford and Fellow of All Souls Coll. 1979–96, Prof. Emer. and Fellow Emer. 1996–; Visiting Lecturer, Univ. of Chicago 1963–64, Visiting Prof. 1968–69, 1971–72; Visiting Prof., Univ. of Western Australia 1976, Univ. of Houston 1977, Southern Methodist Univ. 1978, 1988–89, 1994, Distinguished Visiting Prof. 2000, 2003; Visiting Prof., Univ. of Va 1978–79, 1983–84, Univ. of Santa Clara 1981; Visiting Scholar, Ernst von Caemmerer Gedächtnisstiftung 1990; Clarendon Lecturer in Law, Univ. of Oxford 2001; consultant to Law Comm. on law of contract 1972–84; Trustee, British Museum 1983–98; mem. Council Nat. Trust 1984–93; Hon. Bencher, Gray's Inn. *Publications:* The Law of Contract (11 edns) 1962–2003, Chitty on Contracts (nine edns as jt ed.) 1968–2012, An Outline of the Law of Contract (six edns) 1975–2004, Remedies for Breach of Contract: A Comparative Account 1988, Unmöglichkeit, "Impracticability" und "Frustration" im angloamerikanischen Recht 1991, Frustration and Force Majeure (three edns) 1994–2014, Benjamin's Sale of Goods (eight edns as co-author) 1974–2010, English Private Law (two edns as co-author) 2000–07, Carver on Bills of Lading (three edns as co-author) 2001–11, Some Landmarks of Twentieth Century Contract Law 2002 (Chinese trans. 2010); ed. of other law books. *Leisure interests:* reading, music. *Address:* All Souls College, Oxford, OX1 4AL, England. *Telephone:* (1865) 279379. *Fax:* (1865) 279299.

TREKI, Ali Abdessalam, BA, PhD; Libyan politician, diplomatist and UN official; b. 10 Oct. 1938, Misrata; s. of Abdussalem Treki and Amna Treki; m. Aisha Dihoum 1969; one s. three d.; ed Garyounes Univ., Benghazi, Toulouse Univ., France; joined Foreign Ministry 1970, Dir of Political Admin. 1970–73, Dir of African Admin. 1973–74, Asst Deputy for Political Affairs 1974–76, Minister of Foreign Affairs 1976–82, 1984–86, Perm. Rep. to UN, New York 1982–84 (Vice-Pres. 37th Session of UN Gen. Ass. 1982, Chair. Gen. Ass.'s Fourth Cttee (Decolonization) and represented Libya on UN Comm. on Human Rights), 1986–90, 2003–09; Perm. Rep. to League of Arab States, Cairo, Egypt 1991–94; Amb. to France 1995–99; Sec. for African Affairs 1999–2003; Special Adviser to Libyan leader Muammar al-Gaddafi 2004, began a tour of African countries, acting as Gaddafi's special envoy, to work toward solutions for several African conflicts and disputes, notably in the Sudan, Chad, Ethiopia-Eritrea and Djibouti-Eritrea 2005, named Sec. for African Union (AU) Affairs by the Gen. People's Congress of Libya 2005–09; unsuccessful cand. for Chairmanship of AU Comm. at AU summit in Addis Ababa 2008; Pres. 64th Session of UN Gen. Ass. 2009–10; Co-Chair. Pakistan-Libya Jt Econ. Comm. 2010; headed Libyan del. to summits and confs of the League of Arab States, chaired the League's Council of Ministers 1976–77; led Libyan del. to summits and ministerial confs of OIC and chaired the Council of Ministers of Islamic States; headed Libyan del. to ministerial meetings of the Non-Aligned Movt, as well as to the Movt's summit conf. in Cuba 1979; helped mediate several conflicts in Bosnia and Herzegovina, Cyprus and the Philippines; resgnd and went to Egypt 31 March 2011; decorations from several countries, including the Hilal-i-Pakistan 2010; Dr hc from univs in USA, Europe, Africa and Asia.

TRELFORD, Donald Gilchrist, MA, FRSA; British journalist, editor and academic; b. 9 Nov. 1937, Coventry, West Midlands, England; s. of T. S. Trelford and Doris Gilchrist; m. 1st Janice Ingram 1963 (divorced 1978); two s. one d.; m. 2nd Katherine Louise Mark 1978 (divorced 1998); one d.; m. 3rd Claire Elizabeth Bishop 2001; one s.; ed Bablake School, Coventry, Selwyn Coll., Cambridge; pilot officer, RAF 1956–58; worked on newspapers in Coventry and Sheffield 1961–63; Ed. Times of Malawi and corresp. in Africa, The Times, Observer, BBC 1963–66; joined Observer as Deputy News Ed. 1966, Asst Man. Ed. 1968, Deputy Ed. 1969–75, Dir and Ed. 1975–93, CEO 1992–93; Dir Optomen Television 1988–97, Observer Films 1989–93, Cen. Observer TV 1990–93; Dir, Prof., Dept of Journalism Studies, Univ. of Sheffield 1994–2000, Visiting Prof. 2001–; Chair. Soc. of Gentlemen, Lovers of Musick 1996–2002, London Press Club 2002–07 (Pres. 2007–); mem. British Exec. Cttee, Int. Press Inst. 1976–, Asscn of British Eds 1984–, Guild of British Newspaper Eds 1985– (mem. Parl. and Legal Cttee 1987–91); Vice-Pres. British Sports Trust 1988–2002; Ind. Assessor BBC TV Regional News 1997; mem. Council, Media Soc. 1981–2003 (Pres. 1999–2002), Judging Panel, British Press Awards 1981– (Chair. 2003–05), Scottish Press Awards 1985, Olivier Awards Cttee, SWET 1984–93, Defence, Press and Broadcasting Cttee 1986–93, Cttee, MCC 1988–91, Competition Comm.'s Newspaper Panel 1999–, Council Advertising Standards Authority 2002–; Vice-Pres. Newspaper Press Fund 1992– (Chair. Appeals Cttee 1991); Acting Ed. The Oldie 1994; Judge, Whitbread Literary Awards 1992, George Orwell Prize 1998; sports columnist Daily Telegraph 1993–; Dir St Cecilia Int. Festival of Music 1995–2002; Freeman of the City of London 1988; Hon. DLitt (Sheffield); Granada Newspaper of the Year Award 1983, 1993, commended, Int. Ed. of the Year (World Press Review) 1984. *Radio:* presenter, LBC Breakfast News 1994; regular panellist, BBC Radio Five Live. *Television:* presenter of sports and current affairs series, Channel 4 and BBC 2. *Publications include:* Siege 1980, Snookered 1986, Child of Change (with Garry Kasparov) 1987, Saturday's Boys 1990, Fine Glances 1990; (contrib.) County Champions 1982, The Queen Observed 1986, Len Hutton Remembered 1992, World Chess Championships (with Daniel King) 1993, W. G. Grace 1998; Ed.: Sunday Best 1981, 1982, 1983, The Observer at 200 1992; contrib. to Animal Passions 1994. *Leisure interests:* golf, snooker. *Address:* Flat 3, 6 River Terrace, Henley-on-Thames, Oxon., RG9 1BG, England. *Telephone:* 7850-131742 (mobile). *E-mail:* donaldtrelford@yahoo.co.uk.

TREMAIN, (Edwin) Garrick; New Zealand landscape artist and cartoonist; b. 4 Feb. 1941, Wellington; s. of Edwin Rex Tremain and Linda Joyce Tremain; m. Jillian Mary Butland; two d.; ed Palmerston North Boys' High School; worked as shepherd; then as artist and art director for advertising agencies in NZ, UK and Malaysia; full-time artist 1973–; syndicated cartoonist 1988–; NZ Commemorative Medal 1990, Cartoonist of the Year 1996, 1999. *Publications:* Nursery Rhymes Mother Never Read You 2005, Twenty Years of Tremain 2007, The Trouble with Golf 2011, The Arrowtown Collection 2011. *Leisure interests:* golf, piano, jazz music. *Address:* Stonebridge, 188 Domain Road, RDI Queenstown, Otago, New Zealand. *Telephone:* (3) 409-8244. *E-mail:* tremain@queenstown.co.nz. *Website:* garricktremain.com.

TREMAIN, Rose, CBE, BA, FRSL; British writer; b. (Rosemary Jane Thomson), 2 Aug. 1943, London; d. of the late Keith Thomson and Viola Mabel Thomson; m. 1st Jon Tremain 1971; one d.; m. 2nd Jonathan Dudley 1982 (dissolved 1990); pnr Richard Holmes; ed Univ. of Paris (Sorbonne) and Univ. of East Anglia; novelist and playwright 1971–; part-time tutor Univ. of East Anglia 1988–95; mem. judging panel, Booker Prize 1988, 2000; Hon. DLitt (East Anglia) 2001, (Essex) 2005, (Open Univ.) 2010, Hon. Fellowship (Goldsmiths Coll., London) 2012; Univ. of Essex Fellowship 1979–80; one of Granta's Best Young British Novelists 1983, Giles Cooper Award 1985, Angel Literary Award 1986, Sony Award 1996. *Plays for radio include:* Temporary Shelter 1985, Who Was Emily Davison? 1996, The End of Love 1999, One Night in Winter 2001. *Television:* A Room for the Winter 1979, Daylight Robbery 1982. *Publications:* fiction: Sadler's Birthday 1976, Letter to Sister Benedicta 1978, The Cupboard 1981, The Swimming Pool Season 1984, Restoration (Sunday Express Book of the Year Award) 1989, Sacred Country (James Tait Black Memorial Prize 1993, Prix Fémina Etranger 1994) 1992, The Way I Found Her 1997, Music and Silence (Whitbread Novel of the Year) 1999, The

Colour 2003, The Road Home (Orange Broadband Prize for Fiction 2008) 2007, Trespass 2010, Merivel: A Man of His Time 2012; for children: Journey to the Volcano 1985; short story collections: The Colonel's Daughter (Dylan Thomas Short Story Prize 1984) 1982, The Garden of the Villa Mollini 1988, Evangelista's Fan 1994, Collected Short Stories 1996, The Darkness of Wallis Simpson and Other Stories 2005; non-fiction: The Fight for Freedom for Women 1971, Stalin: An Illustrated Biography 1974. *Leisure interests:* yoga, gardening. *Address:* 2 High House, South Avenue, Thorpe St Andrew, Norwich, NR7 0EZ, England (home). *Telephone:* (1603) 439682 (home).

TREMAINE, Scott Duncan, BSc, MA, PhD, FRS, FRSC; Canadian astrophysicist and academic; *Professor, Institute for Advanced Study, Princeton;* b. 25 May 1950, Toronto, Ont.; s. of Vincent Tremaine and Beatrice Tremaine (née Sharp); m. Marilyn Tremaine; ed McMaster Univ., Hamilton, Ont., Princeton Univ., NJ; mem. Inst. for Advanced Study 1978–81; Assoc. Prof., MIT 1981–85; Prof., Univ. of Toronto 1985–97; Dir Canadian Inst. for Theoretical Astrophysics 1985–96; Prof. and Chair. Dept of Astrophysical Sciences, Princeton Univ. 1998–2006; Prof., Inst. for Advanced Study, Princeton 2007–; mem. NAS 2002; Foreign Hon. mem. American Acad. of Arts and Sciences 1992; Hon. DSc (McMaster Univ., St Mary's Univ., Univ. of Toronto); Warner Prize, American Astronomical Soc. 1983, Steacie Prize 1989, Rutherford Medal in Physics 1990, Carlyle S. Beals Award 1990, Heinemann Prize for Astrophysics 1997, Dirk Brouwer Award 1997, Tomalla Prize 2013. *Publication:* Galactic Dynamics (with J. Binney) 1987 (second edn 2008). *Address:* School of Natural Sciences, Institute for Advanced Study, Einstein Drive, Princeton, NJ 08540, USA (office). *Telephone:* (609) 734-8191 (office). *Fax:* (609) 924-7592 (office). *E-mail:* tremaine@ias.edu (office). *Website:* www.sns.ias.edu (office).

TREMBLAY, Marc-Adélard, OC, MA, LSA, PhD, FRSC, GOQ; Canadian social anthropologist and academic; *Professor Emeritus of Social Anthropology, Laval University;* b. (Joseph Adélard), 24 April 1922, Les Eboulements; s. of Wellie Tremblay and Lauretta Tremblay; m. Jacqueline Cyr 1949; one s. five d.; ed Montreal, Laval and Cornell Univs; research assoc., Cornell Univ. 1953–56; Asst Prof., Dept of Sociology and Anthropology, Laval Univ. 1956, Prof. of Social Anthropology 1963–93, Prof. Emer. 1994–; Founding Pres., Canadian Sociology and Anthropology Asscn 1965–67; Pres. Canadian Ethnology Soc. 1976–77, Royal Soc. of Canada 1981–84, Asscn of Canadian Univs for Northern Studies 1985–87, Québec Council for Social Research 1987–91; Dir Groupe d'études Inuit et Circumpolaires 1990–94; mem. Nunavik Comm. 1999–2001; Special Adviser Fed. Negotiating Team for Establishment of a Nunavik Govt; mem. many other professional and scientific orgs; Grand Officier Ordre Nat. du Québec 1995; Dr hc (Ottawa) 1982, (Guelph) 1984, (Univ. of N British Columbia) 1994, (Carleton) 1995, (Ste-Anne) 1997, (McGill) 1998; Prix de la Province de Québec 1964, Innis-Gérin Medal, Royal Soc. of Canada 1979, Molson Prize, The Canada Council 1987, Marcel Vincent Prize, French Canadian Asscn for the Advancement of Science 1988. *Publications:* People of Cove and Woodlot: communities from the viewpoint of social psychiatry 1960, Les comportements économiques de la famille salariée 1964, Initiation à la recherche dans les sciences humaines 1968, Famille et Parenté en Acadie 1971, Communities and culture in French Canada 1973, Patterns of Amerindian Identity 1976, L'identité québécoise en péril 1983, Conscience et Enquête 1983, L'Anthropologie à l'Université Laval: Fondements historiques, pratiques, académiques, dynamismes d'évolution 1989, Les Fondements historiques et pratiques de l'anthropologie appliquée 1990; 25 books and monographs and 200 articles. *Leisure interests:* gardening, cross-country skiing, classical music, skating. *Address:* Département d'Anthropologie, Université Laval, Cité Universitaire, Ste-Foy, Québec (office); 835 rue Nouvelle-Orléans, Ste-Foy, Québec, G1X 3J4, Canada (home). *Telephone:* (418) 653-5411 (home). *Fax:* (418) 653-9865. *E-mail:* matremgt@globetrotter.net (home). *Website:* pages.globetrotter .net/matrem (home).

TREMBLAY, Michel; Canadian writer; b. 25 June 1942, Montréal; ed Graphic Arts Inst. of Québec; worked as linotypist 1963–66; Officier, Ordre des Arts et des Lettres, Chevalier de la Legion d'Honneur 2008; Dr hc (Concordia, McGill, Stirling, Windsor); first prize for young writers sponsored by CBC (for play Le Train, written 1959) 1964, Gov.-Gen.'s Performing Arts Award 1999. *Film scripts include:* Françoise Durocher, Waitress 1972, Il était une fois dans l'Est 1973, Parlez-nous d'amour 1976, Le Soleil se lève en retard 1977. *Plays include:* Les Belles sœurs 1968, En pièces detachées 1969, La Duchesse de Langeais 1969, Les Paons 1971, Hosanna 1973, Bonjour Là, bonjour 1974, Ste Carmen de la Main 1976, Damnée Manon, Sacrée Sandra 1977, L'Impromptu d'outremont 1980, Les Grandes vacances 1981, Les Anciennes odeurs 1981, Albertine en cinq temps 1984, Le Vrai monde? 1987, La Maison suspendue 1990, Nelligan (opera libretto, Opéra de Montréal) 1990, Marcel poursuivi par les chiens 1992, Messe solennelle pour une pleine lune d'été 1996, Encore une fois, si vous permettez 1998, L'État des lieux 2002, Le Passé antérieur 2003. *Radio plays include:* Le Cœur découvert 1986, Le Grand Jour 1988, Six Heures au plus tard 1988. *Television:* Le Cœur découvert 2000. *Publications:* Contes pour buveurs attardés 1966, La Cité dans l'œuf 1969, C't'à ton tour, Laura Cadieux 1973, La Grosse femme d'à côté est enceinte 1973, Thérèse et Pierrette à l'école des Saints-Anges 1980, La Duchesse et le roturier 1982, Des Nouvelles d'Edouard 1984, Le Cœur découvert 1986, Le Premier quartier de la lune 1989, Les Vues animées 1991, Douze coups de théâtre 1992, Le Cœur éclaté 1995, Un Ange cornu avec des ailes de tôle 1996, L'Homme qui entendait siffler une bouilloire 2001, Bonbons assortis 2002, Le Cahier noir 2003, Le Cahier rouge 2004, Le Cahier Bleu 2005, Le Trou dans le mur 2006, La Traversée du continent 2007, La Traversée de la Ville 2008, La traversée des sentiments 2009, Le passage obligé 2010, La grande mêlée 2011. *Leisure interest:* painting water colours. *Address:* Agence Goodwin, 839 Sherbrooke Street East, Suite 200, Montréal, PQ H2L 1K6, Canada (office). *Telephone:* (514) 598-5252 (office). *Fax:* (514) 598-1878 (office). *E-mail:* artistes@goodwin.agent.ca (office). *Website:* www.agencegoodwin.com (office).

TREMLETT, David Rex; British artist; b. 13 Feb. 1945, Cornwall, England; s. of Rex Tremlett and Dinah Tremlett; m. Laure Florence 1987; one s. two d.; ed St Austell Grammar School, Falmouth Art Coll., Birmingham Coll. of Art and Royal Coll. of Art; exhibited widely in UK, USA, Europe, Africa, Australia, Mexico, Japan etc.; recent projects include: walls of Law Courts, Amsterdam, two rooms at Benesse Guesthouse, Naoshima Island, Japan, façade of St Denis Univ., Paris, main hall of BBL Bank Kortrijk, Belgium, walls and ceiling at Eaton Hall, Chester, UK, walls of castle of Marchese di Barolo, Barolo, Italy, lobby of Cen. Landesbank, Dresden, Germany, Chapel of Barolo, Italy, interior wall at ABN AMRO HQ, Amsterdam, Netherlands, walls of British Embassy Berlin, walls at Obayashi HQ, Tokyo, Japan, walls and floor of Palazzo Fantuzzi, Bologna, Italy, wall for the Grosvenor Estates, London, walls of Rione Alto metro station, Naples, Italy, walls, ceiling and floor of Chapel of Santa Maria dei Carcerati Bologna, wall drawings for British Council Centre, Nairobi, Kenya, walls of Esserheem Penitentiary, N Holland, all 25 stained glass windows of St Peter and St Paul Church, Villenauxe-la-Grande, France, Villa Caldogno (Palladio) Vicenza, Italy (one room of wall drawings), Zamosc Synagogue wall drawings, Zamosc, Poland, Villa Amista (Byblos Hotel) ceilings, Verona, Italy, The Qube (Atrium), Tottenham Court Road, London, two entrance rooms, Castello di Formigine, Formigine, Italy, walls of Chapelle Notre-Dame des Fleurs, Moric, Brittany, France, entrance wall of Palazzo Mantegazza, Lugano, Switzerland, portico ceiling of Beata Vergine Assunta Church, Mortorone, Italy, ceiling of Forte di Bard, Aosta, Italy, wall for the Paladian Villa Pisani, Vicenza, Italy, walls of A La Cruz restaurant, London, stained glass windows for Chapelle Notre-Dame des Fleurs, Moric, Brittany, hallway and staircase of Manton Hall, Tate Britain, London, walls for three rooms of Fernandez and Wells Bar, Somerset House, London, 3 Fernandez and Wells Bars in Soho, London, Reception Area of 26 Finsbury Square London, 'Artists House' at Roche Court Sculpture Park, Salisbury. *Films:* Non-Improvisation (b/w) 1971, No Title 1995. *Music:* Hand Up/Too Bad (CD), A Journey with David Tremlett (soundtrack). *Television:* A Journey with David Tremlett (satellite) 2003. *Publications include:* selected artists books: Some Places to Visit 1974, On the Waterfront 1978, Scrub 1978, On the Border 1979, Restless 1983, Rough Ride 1985, Ruin 1987, Sometimes We All Do 1988, Tremlett-West Bengal 1990, Internal 1991, From Wall to Wall 1991, Mjimwema Drawings 1991, Abandoned Drawings 1993, Casa de Dibujos 1993, Nouveaux Plans 1994, Columns 1995, How Far in that Direction 1996, Walls and their Drawings 1997, Pages (Eritrea) 1998, Clear and Fuzzy 1999, If Things Could Talk 2002, Black as Midnight with the Eyes Shut 2002, Between You and Me (with John Haldane and Laure Genillard) 2006, Texas 2007, D.T. 2008; selected catalogues: Dates/Differents 1987, Written Form 1990, A Quiet Madness 1992, PAC Catalogue 1993, Rooms in Vienne 1994, Walls at the Palais Jacques Coeur, Bourges 1994, Wall Drawings 1969–1995, Passa Dentro 2000, If Walls Could Talk 2001, A New Light 2003, 37 Wall Drawings in Issoire 2003, David Tremlett – British Council Nairobi 2005, David Tremlett-Retrospectve Musée des Beaux Arts, Grenoble France/Pecci Museum, Prato, Italy 2006, Lumière – The Stained Glass Windows of St Peter and St Paul Church, Villenauxe-la-Grande, France 2006, Between You and Me 2006, David Tremlett: A Dialogue Between Past and Present 2008, D.T. 2008, David Tremlett – Drawn, Rubbed, Smeared 2009, Walls (Forte di Bard) 2010, Place and Material, MAMAC, Nice 2010, David tremlett – Drawing Rooms, Hamburg Kunsthalle 2010, David Tremlett at Villa Pisani 2010, David Tremlett – The Thinking in Space, David Tremlett – Architecte de Lumière. *Leisure interests:* Davidson glass, African music, Saharan architecture, cross-country running. *Address:* Broadlawns, Chipperfield Road, Bovingdon, Hemel Hempstead, HP3 0JR, England. *E-mail:* tremlett@tremlett.demon.co.uk. *Website:* www.davidtremlett.com.

TREMONTI, Giulio; Italian politician and lawyer; b. 18 Aug. 1947, Sondrio, Lombardy; ed Univ. of Pavia; teacher of tax law, Univ. of Pavia; fmr Sr Teaching Fellow, Inst. of European and Comparative Law, Univ. of Oxford, UK; mem. Camera dei Deputati (Parl.) (Forza Italia) 1994–, mem. Parl. Special Cttee for Reform of Italian Constitution; Minister of Finance 1994–95, 2008–11, of Economy and Finance 2001–04 (resgnd), Sept. 2005–06, Deputy Prime Minister 2005–06; Pres. Comm. for Monetary Reform 1994–95; 1994–95; fmr Vice-Pres. Aspen Inst. Italia; mem. Italy/Vatican Cttee for Treaty on Financing of Ecclesiastical Insts, Comm. on Deregulation; Ed. Rivista di Diritto Finanziario e Scienza delle Finanze; regular contrib., Corriere della Sera. *Publications:* several books on tax and public policy. *Address:* c/o Ministry of Finance, Via XX Settembre 97, 00187 Rome, Italy (office).

TRENDAFILOVA, Ekaterina Panayotova, PhD; Bulgarian barrister and judge; *Judge, Pre-Trial Division, International Criminal Court;* b. 20 June 1953, Sofia; m. Emil Roussev Bachvarov; one d.; ed Sofia Univ. 'St Kliment Ohridski'; legal internship, Sofia City Court 1977–78; Deputy Dist Attorney, Sofia Dist Court 1985–89; specialization at Inst. of State and Law, Moscow, USSR 1983, 1985; Prof., Faculty of Law, Sofia Univ. 'St Kliment Ohridski' 1984–, Assoc. Prof. (Docent) 1996–2001, Full Prof. 2001–; Prof., Faculty of Law, Veliko Turnovo Univ. 'Sts Cyril and Methodius' 1995–; Visiting Prof., Tokai Univ., Japan 1993; called to the Bar of Bulgaria 1995; advised the Ministry of Foreign Affairs on the establishment of the Int. Criminal Court (ICC) and served as an expert to the Ministry of Justice, Ministry of Interior, Constitutional Court, Supreme Court of Cassation and Parl. of Bulgaria where she chaired the Criminal Div. of the Legis. Consultative Council; Judge, Pre-Trial Div., ICC 2003–; mem. Intergovernmental Comm. entrusted with the preparation of the ratification of the European Convention on Human Rights and Fundamental Freedoms 1991; Bulgarian Rep. to UN Comm. for Crime Prevention and Criminal Justice, Vienna 1992–94; Chair. Program and Analytical Center for European Law 1999–, Modern Criminal Procedure Foundation 1999–; Vice-Pres. Specialized Scientific Council on Legal Science 2003–04; mem. Comm. for Social Sciences at the Higher Accreditation Agency with the Council of Ministers of Bulgaria 2000–03, Legal Comm. Nat. Higher Attestation Comm. with the Council of Ministers of Bulgaria 2004–05; scientific advisor, Students' Internship Program between the American Govt and Bulgarian Parl. 2000–05; Head, Criminal Div. Legis. Consultative Council with the Speaker of the Bulgarian Parl. 2001–05; Middle-term expert under the PHARE Twinning project (Bulgaria–Austria) 2002–03; mem. Consultative Council Open Soc. Inst. Project 'Access to Justice' 2002–05, Advisory Bd Open Soc. Inst. Int. Project 'Independence and Accountability of Prosecution' 2003–05; European expert within EC CARDS Regional Project 2004–; Head of Working Group on Judicial Reform, Open Soc. Inst. Project Strategy for the Socio-econ. and Political Devt of Bulgaria 2005–2010 2004–05; mem. Editorial Bd Human Rights Review 2003–; mem. Union of Bulgarian Lawyers 1980–, Union of Bulgarian Scholars 1984– (Chair. legal section 2001–03), Bulgarian Humboldt Soc. 1994–, Bulgarian Fulbright Soc. 1997–, Women with Int. Societal Expertise (WISE), Paris 2004–; Fulbright Scholarship, Univ. of California, USA 1997; Hon. mem. European Correspondents Scientific

Cttee, Centre Int. Constats et Prospective, Paris 1991; Best Young Lecturer of the Year Award, Nat. Soc. for Dissemination of Legal Knowledge 1984, Alexander von Humboldt Scholarship, Augsburg Univ., Germany 1993–94, Author of the Year Award for contrib. to the legal literature 2000, Legal Initiative for Training and Devt Award 2004. *Publications:* more than 70 publs in Bulgaria, USA, France, Italy and the Netherlands in the field of human rights law, criminal procedural law, int. criminal procedural law, comparative law and constitutional law. *Address:* International Criminal Court, PO Box 19519, 2500 CM The Hague (office); International Criminal Court, Maanweg 174, 2516 AB The Hague, Netherlands (office). *Telephone:* (70) 515-85-15 (office). *Fax:* (70) 515-85-55 (office). *E-mail:* eptrend@abv.bg (office); pio@icc-cpi.int (office). *Website:* www.icc-cpi.int (office).

TRENTHAM, David R., BA, PhD, FRS; British medical research scientist and academic; *Visiting Professor, Randall Division of Cell and Molecular Biophysics, King's College London;* b. 22 Sept. 1938, Solihull, West Midlands, England; s. of John A. Trentham and Julia A. M. Trentham; m. Kamalini Bhargava 1966; two s.; ed Uppingham School and Univ. of Cambridge; MRC Jr Research Fellow, Lecturer and Reader, Dept of Biochemistry, Univ. of Bristol 1966–77; Chair. and Edwin M. Chance Prof., Dept of Biochemistry and Biophysics, School of Medicine, Univ. of Pennsylvania, Phila, USA 1977–84; Head, Div. of Physical Biochemistry, MRC Nat. Inst. for Medical Research, London 1984–2003, Visiting Worker 2003–; Visiting Prof., Randall Div. of Cell and Molecular Biophysics, King's Coll. London 2003–; Hon. Prof., Randall Div., King's Coll. London 2001; Colworth Medal, Biochemical Soc. 1974, Wilhelm Feldberg Prize 1990. *Publications:* numerous articles in biochemical and academic journals. *Address:* Randall Division of Cell and Molecular Biophysics, King's College London, School of Biomedical Sciences, New Hunt's House, Guy's Campus, London, SE1 1UL, England (office). *E-mail:* drtrentham@aol.com (home). *Website:* www.kcl.ac.uk/biohealth/research/divisions/randall (office).

TRESCHOW, Michael, MEng; Swedish business executive; *Chairman, Unilever NV and Unilever PLC;* b. 1943, Helsingborg; ed Inst. of Tech., Lund; divisional man. roles in Scandinavia and France with Bahco Ventilation 1970–76; joined Atlas Copco AB 1976, Pres. and CEO 1991–97; Pres. and CEO AB Electrolux 1997–2002, Chair. 2004–07; Chair. Ericsson (Telefonaktiebolaget L.M. Ericsson) 2002–11; Chair. (non-exec.) Unilever NV and Unilever PLC 2007–; mem. Bd of Dirs B-Business Partners 2001–, Knut and Alice Wallenberg Foundation; Dir (non-exec.) SKF 1992, Saab 1992, Parker-Hannifin Corp. 1996; mem. Bd Dirs ABB Ltd 2003–; mem. European Advisory Bd Eli Lilly & Co. 2008–; Chair. Swedish Trade Council 1996, Confed. of Swedish Enterprise 2004–07; mem. Royal Acad. of Eng Sciences; King's Medal of 12th Dimension and Ribbon of Order of Seraphims (Sweden) 2000, Gran Cruz de la Orden del Mérito Civil (Spain) 2000, Chevalier, Légion d'honneur 2002, Commr Order of the Crown (Belgium) 2004. *Leisure interests:* golf, hunting. *Address:* Unilever PLC, Unilever House, 100 Victoria Embankment, London, EC4Y 0DY, England (office). *Telephone:* (20) 7822-5252 (office). *Fax:* (20) 7822-5511 (office). *E-mail:* press-office.london@unilever.com (office). *Website:* www.unilever.com (office).

TRETHEWEY, Natasha, AB, MA, MFA; American poet and academic; *Poet Laureate;* b. 26 April 1966, Gulfport, Miss.; d. of Eric Trethewey and the late Gwendolyn Ann Turnbough; m. Brett Gadsden; ed Univ. of Georgia, Hollins Univ., Univ. of Massachusetts, Amherst; Lehman Brady Jt Chair Prof. of Documentary and American Studies, Duke Univ. and Univ. of North Carolina 2005–06; currently Charles Howard Candler Prof. of English and Creative Writing, Emory Univ.; Louis D. Rubin Writer-in-Residence, Hollins Univ. 2012; Poet Laureate of Miss. 2012; US Poet Laureate 2012–; James Weldon Johnson Fellow in African American Studies, Beinecke Library, Yale Univ. 2009; Dr hc (Delta State Univ.) 2007, (Hollins Univ.) 2010; Nat. Endowment for the Arts Literature Fellowship 1999, Bunting Fellowship for Radcliffe Inst. for Advanced Study, Harvard Univ. 2000, Lillian Smith Book Award 2001, 2007, Miss. Inst. of Arts and Letters Book Prizes 2001, 2003, 2007, John Simon Guggenheim Memorial Foundation Fellowship 2003, Rockefeller Foundation Fellowship 2004. *Publications include:* Domestic Work (Cave Canem Foundation Poetry Prize 1999) 2000, Bellocq's Ophelia 2002, Native Guard (Pulitzer Prize for Poetry 2007) 2006, Beyond Katrina: A Meditation on the Mississippi Gulf Coast 2010, Thrall 2012. *Address:* c/o Alison Granucci, Blue Flower Arts, PO Box 1361, Millbrook, NY 12545, USA (office); Creative Writing Program, N209 Callaway Center, Emory University, 537 Kilgo Circle, Atlanta, GA 30322, USA (office). *Telephone:* (845) 677-8559 (office); (404) 727-4683 (office). *Fax:* (845) 677-6446 (office); (404) 727-4672 (office). *E-mail:* Alison@blueflowerarts.com (office); creativewriting@emory.edu (office). *Website:* www.blueflowerarts.com (office); www.creativewriting.emory.edu/faculty/trethewey.html (office); www.loc.gov/poetry.

TRETYAK, Vladislav A.; Russian ice hockey player (retd) and politician; b. 25 April 1952, Orudyevo, Moscow region; s. of Alexander D. Tretyak and Vera P. Tretyak; one s. one d.; m. Tatyana Ye Tretyak; ed Moscow State Inst. of Physical Culture, Lenin Mil. Political Acad.; ice hockey player 1967–84; (13 times USSR champion); hockey goalkeeper Central Army Sports Club and USSR nat. team (10 times world champion, nine times European champion); as a nat. team player played in 117 games in world, European championships and Olympic games; fmr Pres. Int. Sports Acad.; served as goalkeeper consultant to Chicago Black Hawks professional ice hockey team in 1990s; mem. State Duma (faction United Russia) 2003–; Pres. Ice Hockey Fed. of Russia 2006–; Gen. Man. of Russian 2010 Winter Olympic ice hockey team; inducted into Hockey Hall of Fame 1989, named Best Russian Hockey Player of the 20th Century 2000. *Publications include:* four books. *Address:* State Duma, 103265 Moscow, Okhotnyi ryad 1, Russia (office). *Website:* www.duma.ru (office); www.fhr.ru.

TRETYAKOV, Viktor Viktorovich; Russian violinist; b. 17 Oct. 1946, Krasnoyarsk; m. Natalia Likhopoi; one d.; ed Moscow Conservatory (pupil of Yury Yankelevich); First Prizes, All-Union Competition of Violinists 1965, Int. Tchaikovsky Competition 1966; concert career since mid-1960s, soloist of Moscow Philharmonic 1969; tours Europe, USA, Japan; participant in numerous European music festivals; Artistic Dir and Conductor, Moscow (now Russian) Chamber Orchestra 1983–90; Prof. and Head of Chair of Violin, Tchaikovsky Moscow State Conservatory 1979–; Prof., Hochschule für Musik, Cologne 1996–; Lenin Komsomol Award 1967, People's Artist of the RSFSR 1979, Glinka State Award of the RSFSR 1981, USSR People's Artist 1987, Shostakovich Premium 1997, Triumph Prize 2003. *Address:* Berliner Konzertagentur Monika Ott, Dramburger, Str. 46, 12683 Berlin; Burgblick 9b, 53177 Bonn, Germany (home). *Fax:* (228) 9329641 (home).

TRETYAKOV, Vitaly Toviyevich; Russian journalist; b. 2 Jan. 1953, Moscow; m.; one s.; ed Moscow State Univ.; jr ed. to Ed. Press Agency Novosti (APN) 1976–88; reviewer, political reviewer, Deputy Ed.-in-Chief Moskovskiye Novosti (weekly) 1988–90; f. Nesavisimaya Gazeta (newspaper) 1990, Ed.-in-Chief 1990–2000; Dir-Gen. Independent Publishing Group 2001–04; Ed.-in-Chief, Moskovskiye Novosti 2004–07; currently Ed.-in-Chief, Politicheskii Klass; mem. Exec. Bd Council on Foreign and Defence Policy. *Publications include:* Philanthropy in Soviet Society 1989, Gorbachev, Ligachev, Yeltsin: Political Portraits on the Perestroika Background 1990, Titus of Sovietologists: Their Struggle for Power: Essays on Idiotism of Russian Policy 1996. *Leisure interests:* theatre, collecting of art albums. *Address:* Politicheskii Klass, 119002 Moscow, per. Sivtsev Vrazhek 29/16/415, Russia (office). *Telephone:* (495) 241-43-67 (office). *E-mail:* info@politklass.ru (office). *Website:* politklass.livejournal.com (office).

TREVES, Vanni E., CBE, MA, LLM; British/Italian business executive; b. 3 Nov. 1940, Italy; s. of the late Giuliano Treves and of Marianna Treves; m. Angela Treves; two s. one d.; ed St Paul's, London, Univ. Coll. Oxford, Univ. of Illinois; joined Macfarlanes (law firm) as articled clerk 1963, qualified 1965, Asst Solicitor 1965–68, Visiting Attorney, White & Case, New York 1968–69, Partner, Macfarlanes 1970–2002, Sr Partner 1987–99; Chair. Equitable Life Assurance Soc. 2001–09; Chair. Intertek Group plc 2002–12; Chair. Channel Four Television Corpn 1998–2004, Korn/Ferry Int. UK, BBA Group PLC 1989–2000, McKechnie PLC 1991–2000; mem. . Bd of Dirs Amplifin; Chair. NSPCC Justice for Children Appeal 1997–2000; Gov. Coll. of Law 1999–, Sadler's Wells Foundation 1999–; Trustee, J. Paul Getty Charitable Trust; mem. Devt Bd Nat. Art Collections Fund; mem. Law Soc. *Leisure interests:* art, walking, food.

TREVINO, Lee Buck; American professional golfer; b. 1 Dec. 1939, Dallas, Tex.; s. of Joe Trevino and Juanita Barrett; m. Claudia Bove 1983; three s. three d.; professional 1960–; US Open Champion 1968, 1971; British Open Champion 1971, 1972; Canadian Open Champion 1971 and numerous other championships 1965–80; US PGA Champion 1974, 1984; Champion US Sr Open 1990, PGA Sr Championship 1994; won Australian PGA Sr Championship 1996; Chair. Bd Lee Trevino Enterprises, Inc. 1967–; US PGA Player of the Year 1971, Sr Tour Player of the Year 1990, 1992, 1994. *Publication:* Super Mex (autobiog.) 1983. *Leisure interest:* fishing. *Address:* Lee Trevino Enterprises, Inc., 1901 West 47th Place, Suite 200, Mission, KS 66205, USA.

TREVOR, William, CLit, BA; Irish writer; b. 24 May 1928, Mitchelstown, Co. Cork; s. of James William Cox and Gertrude Cox; m. Jane Ryan 1952; two s.; ed St Columba's Coll., Dublin, Trinity Coll., Dublin; mem. Irish Acad. of Letters; Hon. KBE 2002; Hon. DLitt (Exeter) 1984, (Dublin) 1986, (Queen's Univ., Belfast) 1989, (Nat. Univ., Cork) 1990; Hawthornden Prize 1965, Royal Soc. of Literature Prize 1978, Whitbread Prize for Fiction 1978, Allied Irish Banks Award for Services to Literature 1978, Whitbread Prize for Fiction 1983, Whitbread Book of the Year 1994, Sunday Express Book of the Year Award 1994, David Cohen British Literature Prize 1999, PEN Prize for Short Stories 2001, Irish Times Prize for Irish Fiction 2001, Listowel Prize 2002, Int. Nonino Prize 2008, Lifetime Achievement in Literary Ireland Award 2008. *Publications include:* The Old Boys 1964, The Boarding House 1965, The Love Department 1966, The Day We Got Drunk on Cake 1967, Mrs Eckdorf in O'Neill's Hotel 1968, Miss Gomez and the Brethren 1969, The Ballroom of Romance 1970, Elizabeth Alone 1972, Angels at the Ritz 1973, The Children of Dynmouth 1977, Lovers of Their Time 1979, Other People's Worlds 1980, Beyond the Pale 1981, Fools of Fortune 1983, A Writer's Ireland: Landscape in Literature 1984, The News from Ireland 1986, Nights at the Alexandra 1987, The Silence in the Garden 1988, Family Sins and Other Stories 1989, The Oxford Book of Irish Short Stories (ed.) 1989, Two Lives 1991, William Trevor: The Collected Stories 1992, Juliet's Story 1992, Excursions in the Real World (essays) 1993, Felicia's Journey 1994, Ireland: Selected Stories 1995, After Rain 1996, Cocktails at Doney's and Other Stories 1996, Death in Summer 1998, The Hill Bachelors 2000, The Story of Lucy Gault 2002, A Bit on the Side (short stories) 2004, Cheating at Canasta 2007, Love and Summer 2009, The Collected Stories 2009, Beyond the Pale and Other Stories 2010, Selected Stories 2011. *Address:* PFD, Drury House, 34–43 Russell Street, London, WC2B 5HA, England (office). *Telephone:* (20) 7344-1000 (office). *Fax:* (20) 7836-9543 (office). *E-mail:* info@pfd.co.uk (office). *Website:* www.pfd.co.uk (office).

TRICHET, Jean-Claude, LèsSc; French fmr central banker; *Chairman, Bruegel;* b. 20 Dec. 1942, Lyon; s. of Jean Trichet and Georgette Vincent-Carrefour; m. Aline Rybalka 1965; two s.; ed Ecole des Mines, Nancy, Univ. of Paris, Inst. d'Etudes Politiques, Paris, Faculté Sciences Economiques, Paris and Ecole Nat. d'Admin; Engineer, competitive sector 1966–68, Insp. of Finances 1971–76; assigned to Gen. Inspectorate of Finance 1974, assigned to Treasury Dept 1975, Sec.-Gen. Business Restructuring Interministerial Cttee 1976–78; Adviser, Minister of Economic Affairs 1978; Adviser to Pres. of Repub. 1978–81; Head of Devt Aid Office and Deputy Dir of Bilateral Affairs, Treasury Dept 1981, Head of Int. Affairs, Treasury Dept 1985; Chief of Staff to Minister of Finance 1986–87; Dir Treasury Dept 1987; Alternate Gov. IMF and World Bank 1987, Under-Sec. of Treas. and Censor Bank of France 1987–93; Gov. Bank of France 1993–2003; Chair. Paris Club 1985–93; mem. Bd of Dirs BIS 1993–2003, EMI 1994–98; Gov. IBRD 1993–95; Vice-Gov. IMF 1995–2003; Chair. Monetary Cttee of EC 1992–93; Dir European Cen. Bank 1998–2003, Pres. 2003–11 (retd); Chair. Group of Ten Cen. Bank Govs 2003–11; Chair. Bruegel (think tank), Brussels 2012–; Commdr, Légion d'honneur, Ordre nat. du Mérite, decorations from Austria, Argentina, Belgium, Brazil, Ecuador, Germany, Ivory Coast and Yugoslavia; hon. doctorates from several univs; Policy Maker of the Year, Int. Economy Magazine 1991, Int. Prize Zebilli Marimo, Acad. des Sciences Morales et Politiques 1999, Int. Prize Pico della Mirandola 2002, Prix franco-allemand de la Culture/Deutsch-Französischer Kulturpreis 2006, ranked by Forbes magazine amongst The World's Most Powerful People (25th) 2009, (15th) 2010. *Publications include:* various articles on finance and economy. *Leisure interest:* poetry. *Address:* Office of the Chairman, Bruegel, rue de la Charité 33, 1210 Brussels, Belgium (office). *Telephone:* (2) 227-42-10 (office). *Website:* www .bruegel.org (office).

TRICOIRE, Jean-Pascal, MBA; French business executive; *President and CEO, Schneider Electric SA;* b. 11 May 1963; m.; three c.; ed Ecole Supérieure d'Electronique de l'Ouest Grad. School of Eng, Angers, CESMA Business School, Lyon; began career with Alcatel, Schlumberger and St Gobain 1985–86; joined Merlin Gerin 1986; various exec. roles with Schneider Electric SA 1988–99 including posts in Italy, China and S Africa, becoming Head of Global Strategic Accounts 1999–2001, Exec. Vice-Pres. Int. Div. 2002–03, COO 2003–06, Chair. Man. Bd (Pres.) and CEO 2006–; Chair. France-China Cttee of Mouvement des Entreprises de France (MEDEF) 2009–. *Leisure interests:* multi-cultural teams, commitment, humour, curiosity, travelling off the beaten path, whitewater sports, new technologies. *Address:* Schneider Electric SA, 43–45 boulevard Franklin Roosevelt, 92500 Rueil-Malmaison, France (office). *Telephone:* 1-41-29-70-00 (office). *Fax:* 1-41-29-71-00 (office). *E-mail:* info@schneider-electric.com (office). *Website:* www.schneider-electric.com (office).

TRIESMAN, Baron (Life Peer), cr. 2004, of Tottenham in the London Borough of Haringey; **David Maxim Triesman,** BA, MA, FRSA, FRSS; British economist, politician, trade union official and company director; *Shadow Foreign and Commonwealth Minister, House of Lords;* b. 30 Oct. 1943, Herts., England; s. of Michael Triesman and Rita Triesman (née Lubran); m. Lucy Hooberman 2004; one d.; ed Stationers' Co. School, London, Univ. of Essex and King's Coll., Cambridge; Sr Research Officer in Addiction, Inst. of Psychiatry 1970–74; secondment to Asscn of Scientific, Tech. and Managerial Staff 1974–75; Sr Lecturer and Co-ordinator Post grad. Research, Polytechnic of the South Bank 1975–84; Deputy Sec.-Gen. (Nat. Negotiating Sec.) Nat. Asscn of Teachers in Further and Higher Educ. 1984–93; Gen. Sec. Asscn of Univ. Teachers 1993–2001; Gen. Sec. Labour Party 2001–03, Govt Whip and Lord-in-Waiting 2004–05; Parl. Under-Sec. of State for Foreign and Commonwealth Affairs 2005–07; Govt Spokesman on Higher Educ., Trade and Industry, Foreign Affairs and Aid 2004–; Prime Minister's Special Envoy on Returns 2007–08; Under-Sec. of State for Innovation, Univs and Skills, Minister for Intellectual Property and Higher Educ. 2007–08; Chair. The Football Asscn and England 2018 FIFA World Cup Bid 2008–10 (resgnd); Shadow Foreign and Commonwealth Minister 2010–; Chair. (non-exec.) Mortgage Credit Corpn 1978–2001, Victoria Management Ltd 2000–01; Chair. Usecolor Foundation 2001, Triesman Assocs 2010–, Templewood Merchant Bank 2010–13; Dir, Salamanca Group 2013–; Dir (non-exec.) The Social Homes Corpn 2013–, Havin Bank 2013–; Visiting Prof. in Social Econs, St Lawrence Univ. 1977; Visiting Fellow in Econs, Wolfson Coll., Cambridge 2000–; Sr Visiting Fellow, Univ. of Warwick 2003–; Visiting Fellow, LSE 2004–; mem. Greater London Manpower Bd 1981–86, Home Office Consultative Cttee on Prison Educ. 1980–83, Burnham Further and Higher Educ. Cttee 1980–84, Univ. Entrance and Schools Exams Bd for Social Science 1980–84, Standing Cttee on Business and the Community, Higher Educ. Funding Council for England 1999–; mem. Kensington, Chelsea and Westminster Area Health Authority 1976–82; mem. Industrial Relations Public Appointments Panel, Dept of Trade and Industry 1996–2001, Ind. Review of Higher Educ. Pay and Conditions 1998–99, Cabinet Office Better Regulation Task Force 2000–03, Treasury Public Services Productivity Panel 2000–03, British N American Cttee 1999–2013; mem. Fabian Soc. 1974–, Charles Rennie Mackintosh Soc., Glasgow 1986–, Highgate Literary and Scientific Inst. 1990–; mem. Council, Ruskin Coll., Oxford 2000–03, Univ. of Northamptonshire; Trustee, The Football Foundation 2008–10; Fellow, Royal Statistical Soc.; Hon. LLD (London South Bank Univ.); Hon. DUniv (Essex); Hon. Fellow, Univ. of Northampton 1995. *Publications include:* The Medical and Non-Medical Use of Drugs 1969, Football Mania (with G. Viani) 1972, Football in London 1985, College Administration (co-author) 1988, Managing Change 1991, Can Unions Survive (Staniewski Memorial Lecture) 1999, Higher Education for the New Century 2000; 18 academic papers on epidemiology, drug addiction and related statistical method. *Leisure interests:* football, art, reading, blues guitar, hill walking. *Address:* House of Lords, Westminster, London, SW1A 0PW, England (office). *Telephone:* (20) 7219-3000 (office). *E-mail:* triesmand@parliament.uk (office).

TRIGUBOFF, Harry Oscar, AO; Australian property developer; *Chairman and Managing Director, Meriton Apartments Pty Ltd;* b. 3 March 1933, Darien, People's Repub. of China; s. of Moishe Triguboff and Freda Triguboff; m. 1st Hana Postel 1959 (divorced 1976); two d.; m. 2nd Rhonda Eileen 1980; ed Scots Coll., Sydney, Univ. of Leeds, UK; immigrated to Australia 1947; early jobs included driving a taxi and owning a milk run; Founder, Chair. and Man. Dir Meriton Apartments Pty Ltd 1963–; Sir Phillip Lynch Award, Housing Ind. Asscn 1995, Property Man of the Year Award 2003, Ernst & Young Entrepreneur of the Year 2008, Property Person of the Year, Urban Taskforce Australia 2009. *Address:* Meriton Apartments Pty Ltd, Level 11, 528 Kent Street, Sydney, NSW 2000, Australia (office). *Website:* www.meriton.com.au (office).

TRILLO-FIGUEROA MARTÍNEZ-CONDE, Federico, DIur, PhD; Spanish politician, jurist and diplomatist; *Ambassador to UK;* b. 23 May 1952, Cartagena, Murcia; s. of Federico Trillo-Figueroa and Eloísa Martínez-Conde; m. María José Molinuevo; five c.; ed Univ. of Salamanca, Univ. Complutense of Madrid; Sec.-Gen. Partido Popular (PP) Parl. Group (Conservative Party) 1982–89; mem. Nat. Exec. Cttee, PP 1987–; Chief of Staff to Manuel Fraga Iribarne, Leader of the PP and Adjunct Gen. Sec. of the Party 1989–90; mem. Parl. (PP) for Alicante 1989–2012, Deputy Speaker of the Congress 1989–96, Speaker of the Congress and Nat. Ass. 1996–2000, Speaker of the Constitutional Comm. of the Spanish Parl. 2004–08; Sec. of State for Defence 2000–04; Amb. to UK 2012–; Grand Cross, Carlos Tercero, Grand Cross, Isabel La Católica, Grand Cross of Civil Merit, Grand Cross, San Raimundo de Peñafort Judicial Merit, Grand Cross of Naval Merit, Chevalier, Légion d'honneur, Grand Cross, Order of the Italian Repub., Grand Cross Enrique el Navegante (Portugal), Golden Grand Cross (Austria). *Publications include:* Pregones y Semblanzas 1997, El poder político en los dramas de Shakespeare (Political Power in Shakespeare's Dramas) 1999, Memoria de Entreguerras 2005. *Leisure interests:* reading, music, cycling. *Address:* Embassy of Spain, 39 Chesham Place, London, SW1X 8SB, England (office). *Telephone:* (20) 7235-5555 (office). *Fax:* (20) 7259-5392 (office). *E-mail:* emb.londres@maec.es (office). *Website:* www .exteriores.gob.es/embajadas/londres/en/Pages/inicio.aspx (office).

TRIMBLE OF LISNAGARVEY, Baron (Life Peer), cr. 2006, of Lisnagarvey in the County of Antrim; **David Trimble,** PC, LLB; British politician, barrister and university lecturer; b. 15 Oct. 1944, Belfast; s. of the late William Trimble and of

Ivy Jack; m. 1st Heather McComb (divorced); m. 2nd Daphne Orr 1978; two s. two d.; ed Bangor Grammar School and Queen's Univ. Belfast; Lecturer in Law, Queen's Univ. Belfast 1968–77, Sr Lecturer 1977–90; mem. N Ireland Constitutional Convention 1975–76; mem. Parl. for Upper Bann 1990–2005; Leader Ulster Unionist Party (UUP) 1995–2005; First Minister, Northern Ireland Ass. 1998–2000, 2001–02 (Ass. suspended Oct. 2002); mem. N Ireland Ass. for Upper Bann 1998–; Chair. Lagan Valley Unionist Asscn 1985–90, Ulster Soc. 1985–90; left UUP and joined Conservative Party 2007; hon. degrees include Hon. LLD (Queen's) 1999, (New Brunswick) 2000, (Wales) 2002; shared Nobel Peace Prize 1998. *Publications:* To Raise up a New Northern Ireland 2001, Misunderstanding Ulster 2007. *Leisure interests:* music, reading, opera. *Address:* House of Lords, London, SW1A 0PW England (office). *Telephone:* (20) 7219-3000 (office). *Fax:* (20) 7219-5979 (office). *E-mail:* trimbled@parliament.uk (office). *Website:* www.davidtrimble.org (office).

TRINTIGNANT, Jean-Louis Xavier; French actor; b. 11 Dec. 1930, Piolenc (Vaucluse); s. of Raoul Trintignant and Claire Tourtin; m. 1st Colette Dacheville (Stéphane Audran (q.v.)) 1954 (divorced); m. 2nd Nadine Marquand (q.v.) 1961 (divorced 1997); one s. two d. (both deceased); ed Faculté de Droit, Aix-en-Provence; theatre debut 1951; film roles 1955–; Officier des Arts et des Lettres; Prix d'interprétation de l'Acad. du Cinéma (for Mata Hari, Agent H21) 1965; Prize, Cannes Festival (for Z) 1969; Prix David de Donatello, Taormina Festival 1972;. *Plays include:* Macbeth, Jacques ou la Soumission (Ionesco), Hamlet, Bonheur, impaire et passe (Sagan), Deux sur la balançoire, Art 1998, Poèmes à Lou 1999, Comédie sur un quai de gare 2001, Moins deux 2005. *Films include:* Et Dieu créa la femme 1956, Club de femmes 1956, Les liaisons dangereuses 1959, L'été violent 1959, Austerlitz 1959, La millième fenêtre 1959, Pleins feux sur l'assassin 1960, Coeur battant 1960, Le jeu de la vérité 1961, Horace 62 1961, Les sept péchés capitaux 1961, Il sorpasso 1962, Il successo 1962, Chateau en Suède 1963, La bonne occase 1964, Mata Hari, Agent H21 1964, Angélique marquise des anges 1964, Meurtre à l'italienne 1965, La longue marche 1965, Le 17e ciel 1965, Paris brûle-t-il? 1965, Un homme et une femme 1966, Safari diamants 1966, Trans-Europ-Express 1966, Mon amour, mon amour 1967, L'homme qui ment 1967, Les biches 1968, Le voleur de crimes 1968, Z 1969, Ma nuit chez Maud 1969, Disons un soir à diner 1969, L'Américain 1969, La mort a pondu un oeuf 1969, Le conformiste 1970, Si douces, si perverses 1970, Le grand silence 1971, Une journée bien remplie (author and dir) 1973, Le train 1973, Les violins du bal 1973, Le mouton enragé 1974, Le secret 1974, Le jeu avec le feu 1975, Shattering 1977, Le désert des Tartares 1977, The French Way 1978, L'argent des autres 1978, Le maitre nageur 1979 (also dir), La terrasse 1980, Je vous aime 1980, La femme d'à côté 1981, Un assassin qui passe 1981, Malevil 1981, Passion d'amour 1981, Une affaire d'hommes 1981, Eaux profondes 1981, Le grand-pardon 1982, Boulevard des assassins 1982, Le bon plaisir 1983, Vivement dimanche! 1983, La crime 1983, Le bon plaisir, Femmes de personne 1984, Under Fire, Viva la vie 1984, L'été prochain, Partir, revenir 1985, Rendez-vous, David, Thomas et les autres 1985, L'homme aux yeux d'argent 1985, Un homme et une femme: vingt ans déja 1986, La femme de ma vie 1986, La vallée fantôme 1987, Le Moustachu 1987, Bunker Palace Hotel 1989, 'Merci la vie' 1991, Le Grand Pardon II (narrator) 1992, L'Instinct de l'ange 1993, L'oeil écarlate 1993, Three Colours: Red 1994, Regarde les hommes tomber 1994, The City of Lost Children (voice) 1995, Fiesta 1995, Un homme est tombé dans la rue 1996, C'est jamais loin 1996, Un héros très discret 1996, Tykho Moon 1996, Ceux qui m'aiment prendront le train 1998, Janis et John 2003, Immortel (ad vitam) (voice, uncredited) 2004, Amour 2012. *Television:* Pour un oui ou pour un non (film) 1990, Julie de Carneilhan (film) 1990, La controverse de Valladolid (film) 1992, L'interdiction (film) 1993, Rêveuse jeunesse (film) (voice) 1994, L'insoumise (film) 1996, Julie ou L'amour de Dieu (film) 2005. *Address:* c/o Artmédia, 20 avenue Rapp, 75007 Paris (office); c/o Viens voir les comédiens (Talent Agency) 40, rue de La Folie Régnault, 75011 Paris (office); 30 rue des Francs-Bourgeois, 75003 Paris, France (home).

TRINTIGNANT, Nadine; French film director, screenwriter and writer; b. 11 Nov. 1934, Nice, Alpes-Maritimes; d. of Jean Marquand and Lucienne Marquand (née Cornillad); m. 1st Jean-Louis Trintignant (q.v.) 1961 (divorced 1997); two d. (both deceased) one s.; m. 2nd Alain Corneau 1998 (died 2010); ed Lycée Molière, Inst. Fénelon and Cours Lamartine, Paris; trainee, LTC Lab. 1952, trainee film ed. 1953–54, Asst Film Ed. 1954–58, Chief Ed. and Continuity Person 1958–64; Dir TV programmes in the Le Cinéma and Les Femmes Aussi series 1965–66; writer and dir of films and TV programmes; Officier Ordre des Arts et Lettres, Chevalier Ordre nat. du Mérite. *Films include:* Dir: Fragilité, ton nom est femme (Festival de Hyères Prize, Salonika Festival Prize, Greece) 1965, L'île bleue 2000; Writer and Dir: Mon amour, mon amour 1967, Le voleur de crimes 1969, Ça n'arrive qu'aux autres 1971, La semaine des quatre jeudis 1972, Défense de savoir 1973, Le voyage de noces 1976, Madame le Juge, L'innocent 1977, Premier voyage 1980, Portrait de Mikis Theodorakis, L'été prochain 1984, La maison de jade 1988, Fugueuses 1994, L'insoumise 1996. *Television includes:* film: Le tiroir secret 1985, Lucas 1988, Rêveuse jeunesse 1992, Les inséparables; Dir: Qui c'est ce garçon? (series) 1986, Victoire 1998 (Sept d'or de la mise en scène), L'île bleue 2000, Colette 2003. *Publications:* Ton chapeau au vestiaire 1998, Combien d'enfant 2000, La jeune-homme de la rue de France 2002, Ma fille Marie 2003, Marie Trintignant 2004, J'ai été jeune un jour 2006, Une étrange peine 2007. *Leisure interests:* music, travelling. *Address:* 30 rue des Francs-Bourgeois, 75003 Paris, France. *Telephone:* (1) 42-74-47-01. *Fax:* (1) 42-74-55-03. *E-mail:* nadine.trintignant@wanadoo.fr.

TRIPPE, Thomas G., PhD; American particle physicist; ed Univ. of California, Los Angeles; mem. Particle Data Group, Lawrence Berkeley Nat. Lab., Berkeley, Calif. 1970–2008; research work at Bevatron, CERN, SLAC and Fermilab (retd). *Publication:* Particle Physics: One Hundred Years of Discoveries: An Annotated Chronological Bibliography 1996, Review of Particle Physics, biennial 2010. *Leisure interests:* windsurfing, gardening, photography. *Address:* 1551 La Vereda Road, Berkeley, CA 94708, USA (home). *Telephone:* (510) 841-0262 (home) *Fax:* (510) 548-8435 (home). *E-mail:* trippe@dslextreme.com (home).

TRITTIN, Jürgen; German politician; b. 25 July 1954, Bremen; one d.; worked as journalist 1973; business man. Alternative-Greens-Initiative List (AGIL) group Göttingen City Council 1982–84; press spokesman for Green Party group Lower Saxony Landtag 1984–85, Chair. 1985–86, 1988–90, Deputy Chair. Alliance '90/Greens group 1994–95, spokesman Fed. Exec. 1994–98; mem. Lower Saxony Landtag 1985–90, 1994–95, Lower Saxony Minister for Fed. and European Affairs 1990–94, also head of state mission to fed. insts in Bonn; mem. Bundestag 1998–; Fed. Minister for the Environment, Nature Conservation and Nuclear Safety 1998–2005. *Address:* Bundestag, Platz der Republik 1, 11011 Berlin (office); Room 2.533, Dorotheenstr.101, 10117 Berlin, Germany (office). *Telephone:* (30) 22772253 (office). *Fax:* (30) 22776203 (office). *E-mail:* juergen.trittin@bundestag.de (office). *Website:* www.trittin.de.

TRIVEDI, Ram Krishna, MA; Indian state governor (retd); b. 1 Jan. 1921, Myingyan, Burma (now Myanmar); s. of Pandit Mahavir Trivedi and Rama Trivedi; m. Krishna Trivedi 1944 (deceased); four s. one d.; joined civil service 1943; Dist Magistrate, Tehri Garhwal, Faizabad, Allahabad and Kanpur; Vice-Prin., IAS Training School, Delhi 1957–58, Acting Prin. 1958–59, Deputy Dir Nat. Acad. of Admin. 1959–62; Sec. Medical and Health Dept Govt of Uttar Pradesh 1968–70; Commr and Sec. Dept of Finance 1968–71; Commr Allahabad 1970–71; Chair. UP State Electricity Bd 1972–73; Sec. Dept of Civil Supplies and Cooperation 1974–75; Dept of Personnel & Admin. Reforms, Govt of India 1975–77; Chair. and Man. Dir STC 1978; Vice-Chancellor, Bundelkhand Univ. 1979; Adviser to Gov. of Madhya Pradesh; Chair. British India Corpn Kanpur 1980; Central Vigilance Commr Govt of India 1980–82; Chief Election Commr of India 1982–85; Gov. of Gujarat 1986–90; fmr Vice-Pres. Exec. Council, Indian Inst. of Public Admin.; mem. Gov. Body, Asian Centre for Devt Admin. Kuala Lumpur; Pres. Ramkrishna Mission, Lucknow; Hon. DLitt (Lucknow), Hon. LLD (Bundelkhand); Padma Bhushan Award 1986. *Publication:* The Greening of Gujarat. *Leisure interests:* yoga, serious reading, philately, photography. *Address:* Anand Niwas, B-7, Niralanagar, Lucknow, UP 226 020, India (home). *Telephone:* (522) 2787180 (home).

TROCKEL, Rosemarie; German artist and academic; b. 13 Nov. 1952, Schwerte; ed Kölner Werkschulen under Prof. Werner Schriefers; numerous solo exhbns in USA, especially at Museum of Modern Art (MoMA), New York 1980s and all over Europe; 'knitting pictures', produced in 1980s and 1990s; cr. Memorial Frankfurter Engel, Frankfurt am Main 1995; Prof., Staatliche Kunstakademie, Düsseldorf 1998–; lives and works in Cologne; Arbeitsstipendium der Stiftung Kunstfonds zur Förderung der zeitgenössischen bildenden Kunst, Bonn 1984, Stipendium, Kulturkreis der deutschen Wirtschaft, Cologne 1985, Karl Ströher Prize, Frankfurt am Main 1989, Günter Fruhtrunk Prize, Akad. der Bildenden Künste, Munich 1991, Konrad von Soest Prize, Münster 1992, Preisträgerstipendium, Günther-Peill-Stiftung, Düren 1996, Nordrhein-Westphalia State Prize 1998, Int. Arts Prize, Kulturstiftung Stadtsparkasse, Munich 1999, German Pavilion, Venice Biennale 1999, Kulturpreis, Cologne 2001, Wolfgang Hahn Prize, Gesellschaft für Moderne Kunst am Kölner Museum Ludwig 2004, Westfälische Ehrengalerie 2006, Arts Prize, Landeshauptstadt Düsseldorf 2008, Peter Weiss Prize, City of Bochum 2010, Kaiserring der Stadt Goslar 2011, Roswitha-Haftmann Prize, Zurich 2014. *Publications:* Jedes Tier ist eine Künstlerin 1993, Pro Test, mit einem Text von Rosemarie Trockel 2002, Löffel + Mirabelle 1995, Rosemarie Trockel präsentiert: Pierre Klossowski, Pierre Zucca – Lebendiges Geld (Edn Exlibris Nr 4, Gerhard Teewen (ed.)) 2005, Mutter (with Marcus Steinweg) 2006, Duras (with Marcus Steinweg) 2008. *Address:* c/o Sprüth Magers Berlin, Oranienburger Straße 18, 10178 Berlin (office); c/o Friederike Schuler, Sprüth Magers, Hebbelstraße 93, 50968 Cologne, Germany (office); c/o Sprüth Magers London, 7A Grafton Street, London, W1S 4EJ, England (office). *Telephone:* (30) 28884030 (Berlin) (office); (221) 937297513 (Cologne) (office); (20) 7408-1613 (London) (office). *Fax:* (30) 288840352 (Berlin) (office); (221) 937297517 (Cologne) (office); (20) 7499-4531 (London) (office). *E-mail:* fs@spruethmagers.com (office); info@spruethmagers.com (office). *Website:* www.spruethmagers.com (office).

TROE, Jürgen, Dr rer. nat; German chemist and academic; *Niedersachsenprofessor for Research, Georg-August-Universität Göttingen;* b. 4 Aug. 1940, Göttingen; ed Univ. of Göttingen; Prof. of Physical Chem., Ecole Polytechnique Fédérale de Lausanne, Switzerland 1971–75, Hon. Prof. 1976–; Prof. of Physical Chem., Inst. for Physical Chem., Univ. of Göttingen 1975–2008, Prof. Emer. 2008–, Niedersachsenprofessor for Research 2008–, Chair. Lab. for Laser Tech. 1987, Dir Max-Planck-Inst. for Biophysical Chem., Göttingen 1990–2008, Prof. Emer. 2008–; Pres. Deutsche Bunsen-Gesellschaft für Physikalische Chemie 1999–2002; Editorial Chair. Physical Chem./Chemical Physics 2000–03; mem. Deutsche Akademie der Naturforscher Leopoldina 1980–, Akademie der Wissenschaften zu Göttingen 1982–, Academia Europaea, London 1989–, Berlin-Brandenburgische Akademie der Wissenschaften 2000–; mem. Senate, Deutsche Forschungsgemeinschaft 2002– (Chair. Physical Chem. and Chem. Sections 1984–92); mem. Nat. Science Bd of Germany 1993–98; Fellow, American Physical Soc. 2010; Foreign hon. mem. American Acad. of Arts and Science 1989–; Honorary Member, Bunsen-Gesellschaft 2009; Hon. DSc (Bordeaux) 1995, (Karlsruhe) 1995; Deutsche Bunsen-Gesellschaft für Physikalische Chemie Bodenstein Award 1971, Walther-Nernst-Denkmünze 1998, Royal Soc. of Chem. Centenary Medal 1980, Polanyi Medal 1992, Alexander von Humboldt Foundation Max-Planck Research Award 1993, Deutsche Akademie der Naturforscher Leopoldina Carus Medal 1995, Int. Combustion Inst. Bernard Lewis Gold Medal 1996. *Address:* Institut für Physikalische Chemie, Georg-August-Universität Göttingen, Tammannstrasse 6, 37077 Göttingen, Germany (office). *Telephone:* (551) 393122 (office). *Fax:* (551) 393150 (office). *E-mail:* shoff@gwdg.de (office). *Website:* www.uni-pc.gwdg.de/troe (office).

TROISGROS, Pierre Emile René; French hotelier and restaurateur; b. 3 Sept. 1928, Châlon-sur-Saône; s. of Jean-Baptiste Troisgros and Marie Badaut; m. Olympe Forte 1955; two s. one d.; ed Lycée Bourgneuf, Roanne; worked Roanne-Etretat 1944–45, Armenonville, Paris 1946, St Jean de Luz 1947; mil. service, Tunisia 1948; at Lucas Carton, Paris 1950–52, Point, Vienne 1954, then Maxim's and Retour à Roanne; now Pres. Supervising Cttee Restaurant Troisgros SA, Roanne; Ordre Nat. du Mérite 1969, Officier des Arts et des Lettres 1985, Chevalier, Légion d'honneur 1987. *Publications:* Cuisiniers à Roanne (with Jean Troisgros) 1977, Toc et Toque 1983, Les Petits Plats des Troisgros (with Michel Troisgros) 1985, Cuisine de famille chez Les Troisgros (jtly) 1998. *Leisure interests:* tennis, basketball. *Address:* Place Jean Troisgros, 42300 Roanne; 20 route de Commelle, 42120 Le Coteau, France (office). *Telephone:* 4-77-71-66-97. *Fax:* 4-77-70-39-77 (office). *E-mail:* info@troisgros.com (office). *Website:* www.troisgros.fr (office).

TROLLOPE, Joanna, (Caroline Harvey), OBE, MA, DL; British writer; b. 9 Dec. 1943; d. of Arthur Trollope and Rosemary Hodson; m. 1st David Potter 1966; two d.; m. 2nd Ian Curteis 1985 (divorced 2001); two step-s.; ed Reigate Co. School and St Hugh's Coll., Oxford; Information and Research Dept Foreign Office 1965–67; various teaching posts, including Farnham Girl's Grammar School, Daneshill School 1967–79; Chair. Betty Trask Prize for Soc. of Authors 1993, Advisory Cttee on Nat. Reading Initiative, Dept of Nat. Heritage 1996–97; mem. Advisory Cttee on Nat. Year of Reading, Dept of Educ. 1998, Council of Soc. of Authors 1997–, Campaign Bd St Hugh's Coll. Oxford, Council of West Country Writer's Asscn; Vice-Pres. Trollope Soc.; Judge, Costa Book Awards 2002, Chair. Advisory Bd 2007; mem. International PEN, Romantic Novelists' Asscn; Trustee, Joanna Trollope Charitable Trust 1995–; Patron County of Glos. Community Foundation 1994–2004, March Foundation, Mulberry Bush, For Dementia; Chair. Nat. Portrait Gallery Fund Raising Gala 2009; DL for Co. of Glos. 2002–08; Judge, The Melissa Nathan Awards 2005–11, The Sunday Times EFG Private Bank Short Story Award 2011–12; Chair. Orange Prize for Fiction 2012, Review Panel for UK Dept for Culture, Media & Sport (DCMS) into e-lending in libraries, Report Panel for UK DCMS, Role of Public Libraries 2013–; Trustee, Nat. Literacy Trust 2013–; Lifetime Achievement Award, Romantic Novelists Asscn 2010. *Publications include:* as Caroline Harvey: Eliza Stanhope 1978, Parson Harding's Daughter (aka Mistaken Virtue) (Historical Novel of the Year Award, Romantic Novelists' Asscn 1979, Elizabeth Goudge Historical Award 1980) 1979, Leaves from the Valley 1980, The City of Gems 1981, The Steps of the Sun 1983, The Taverners' Place 1986, Legacy of Love 1992, A Second Legacy 1993, A Castle in Italy 1993, The Brass Dolphin 1997; as Joanna Trollope: Britannia's Daughters: A Study of Women in the British Empire 1983, The Choir 1988, A Village Affair 1989, A Passionate Man 1990, The Rector's Wife 1991, The Men and the Girls 1992, A Spanish Lover 1992, The Best of Friends 1992, The Country Habit: An Anthology (ed.) 1993, Next of Kin 1996, Faith 1996, Other People's Children 1998, Marrying the Mistress 2000, Girl from the South 2002, Brother and Sister 2004, Second Honeymoon 2006, The Book Boy 2006, Britannia's Daughters 2007, Friday Nights 2008, The Other Family 2010, Daughters in Law 2011, The Soldier's Wife 2012; contribs to newspapers and magazines. *Leisure interests:* reading, conversation, very long baths. *Address:* c/o United Agents, 12–26 Lexington Street, London, W1F 0LE, England (office). *Telephone:* (20) 3214-0800 (office). *Fax:* (20) 3214-0801 (office). *E-mail:* info@unitedagents.co.uk (office); joanna@joannatrollope.com (office). *Website:* unitedagents.co.uk (office); www.joannatrollope.com

TRONCHETTI PROVERA, Marco; Italian business executive; *Chairman, Pirelli & C. SpA;* b. 1948, Milan; three c.; ed Bocconi Univ., Milan; worked in family maritime transport business 1973–86; joined Pirelli Group as Partner, Pirelli & C. 1986, Man. Dir and Gen. Man. Soc. Int. Pirelli SA, Basle 1988–92, Man. Dir and Gen. Man. (Finance and Admin. and Gen. Affairs) Pirelli SpA 1991–92, Exec. Deputy Chair. and Man. Dir Pirelli SpA 1992–96, Deputy Chair. Pirelli & C. 1995–99, Chair. and CEO Pirelli SpA 1996–, Chair. Pirelli & C. 1999–; Chair. Olivetti 2001–; Chair. Bd and Exec. Cttee CAMFIN SpA, Milan; Chair. Telecom Italia SpA 2001–06 (resgnd); Chair. Bd Il Sole 24 Ore; Deputy Chair. Confindustria (nat. employers' org.), Chair. 2000–; mem. Bd Mediobanca, Banca Commerciale Italiana, Banca Intesa, GIM, RAS, Università Commerciale Luigi Bocconi, FC Internazionale Milano; mem. European Round Table of Industrialists, Int. Advisory Bd of Allianz, Int. Council of J. P. Morgan, New York Stock Exchange Advisory Cttee, Italian Group of Trilateral Comm. *Address:* Office of the Chairman, Pirelli SpA, Viale Sarca 202, 20126, Milan (office); CONFINDUSTRIA, Viale dell'Astronomia 30, EVR, 00144 Rome, Italy. *Telephone:* (02) 64422650 (office); (06) 59031. *Fax:* (02) 64423733 (office); (06) 5919615. *E-mail:* confindustria@confindustria.it (office). *Website:* www.confindustria.it (office).

TROŠKA, Zdeněk, MA; Czech film and theatre director and scriptwriter; b. 18 May 1953, Strakonice; s. of Václav Troška and Růžena Troška; ed Lycée Carnot, Dijon, France, Acad. of Film and Musical Arts; Prin./Head Prize for Luck From Hell II, St Petersburg, Russia 2002. *Films:* Jak rodí chlap (How a Man Gives Birth) 1980, Bota jménem Melichar (Boot) 1983, Slunce, seno, jahody (The Sun, Hay and Strawberries) 1984, Poklad hrabete Chamaré (The Treasure of Count Chamaré) 1984, O princezne Jasněnce a létajícim sevci (About Princess Jasněnka) 1987, Flying Shoemaker 1987, Slunce, seno a pár facek (The Sun, Hay and Some Slaps) 1989, Zkouskové období (The Time of Examinations) 1990, Slunce, seno, erotika (The Sun, Hay and Erotics) 1991, Princezna ze mlejna (The Princess from the Mill) 1994, Z pekla stestí (Helluva Good Luck) 1999, Princezna ze mlejna 2 2000, Z pekla stesti 2 (Goblins and Good Luck 2) 2001, Andelská tvár 2002, Kamenák 2003, Kamenák 2 2004, Kamenák 3 2005, Nejkrasnejsi hadanka 2008, Doktor od jezera hrochu 2010. *Plays:* Don Carlos (Nat. Theatre, Prague) 1989, Rusalka, Hamlet (musical version) 2000, Luck From Hell 2000, Luck From Hell II 2001. *Leisure interests:* literature, music: piano and organ, cooking, mushrooming, hiking. *Address:* Hoštice u Volyně 77, 387 01 Volyně, Czech Republic (office).

TROST, Barry Martin, PhD; American scientist and academic; *Tamaki Professor of Humanities and Science, Department of Chemistry, Stanford University;* b. 13 June 1941, Philadelphia, Pa; s. of Joseph Trost and Esther Trost; m. Susan Paula Shapiro 1967; two s.; ed Univ. of Pennsylvania and Massachusetts Inst. of Tech.; Asst Prof. of Chem., Dept of Chem., Univ. of Wis. 1965–68, Assoc. Prof. 1968–69, Prof. 1969–76, Helfaer Prof. 1976–82, Vilas Prof. 1982–87; Prof. of Chem., Stanford Univ. 1987–, Tamaki Prof. of Humanities and Sciences 1990–; consultant, E.I. du Pont de Nemours and Merck, Sharp & Dohme; mem. ARCO Science Bd; mem. Cttee on Chemical Sciences, NAS 1980–83; mem. and Chair. NIH Medicinal Chem. Study Section 1982–; Commr, Nat. Research Council Comm. on Eng and Tech. Systems; Ed.-in-Chief Comprehensive Organic Synthesis (Vols 1–9) 1991, Chair. 1996–; Ed. Chemical Tracts/Organic Chem.; mem. NAS, American Chemical Soc., AAAS; Dr hc (Univ. Claude Bernard, Lyon, Technion, Israel); ACS Award in Pure Chem. 1977, for Creative Work in Synthetic Organic Chem. 1981, Backland Award 1981, AIC Chemical Pioneer Award 1983, Alexander von Humboldt Award (Fed. Repub. of Germany) 1984, Cope Scholar Award of ACS 1989, ACS Guenther Award 1990, Dr Paul Janssen Prize for Creativity in Organic Synthesis 1990, Merit Award, NIH 1988, Roger Adams Award 1995, Herbert C. Brown Award 1999, Nichols Medal 2000, Elsevier Boss Award 2000, Yamada Prize 2001, Signature Award for Grad. Educ. in Chem. 2002, ACS Arthur C. Cope Award 2004, John Scott Award 2004, Nagoya Medal 2008. *Publications:* Problems in Spectroscopy 1967, Sulfur Ylides 1974, Organic Synthesis Today and Tomorrow

(ed.) 1981, Selectivity: a Goal for Synthetic Efficiency (ed.) 1984; more than 850 scientific articles in leading chemical journals. *Address:* Department of Chemistry, Stanford University, Stanford, CA 94305-5080, USA (office). *Telephone:* (650) 723-3385 (office). *Fax:* (650) 725-0002 (office). *E-mail:* bmtrost@stanford.edu (office). *Website:* chemistry.stanford.edu/faculty/barry-trost (office); www.stanford.edu/group/bmtrost (office).

TROTMAN-DICKENSON, Sir Aubrey Fiennes, Kt, DSc; British university vice-chancellor and principal (retd); b. 12 Feb. 1926, Wilmslow, Cheshire, England; s. of Edward Trotman-Dickenson and Violet Murray (née Nicoll); m. Danusia Hewell 1953; two s. one d.; ed Winchester Coll., Balliol Coll. Oxford and Univs of Manchester and Edin.; Fellow, Nat. Research Council, Ottawa, Ont. 1948–50; Asst Lecturer, ICI Fellow, Univ. of Manchester 1950–53; E.I. Du Pont de Nemours, Wilmington, USA 1953–54; Lecturer, Univ. of Edin. 1954–60; Prof. of Chem., Univ. Coll. of Wales, Aberystwyth 1960–68; Prin. Univ. of Wales Inst. of Science and Tech. 1968–88, Univ. Coll., Cardiff 1987–88, Univ. of Cardiff 1988–93; Vice-Chancellor Univ. of Wales 1975–77, 1983–85, 1991–93; Chair. Kingswood Conservative Asscn 1996–98, Chair. Kingswood Liberal Democrats 2004–; Hon. LLD (Wales); Tilden Lecturer 1963. *Publications:* Gas Kinetics 1955, Free Radicals 1959, Tables of Biomolecular Gas Reactions 1967, Comprehensive Inorganic Chemistry (ed. 1973); more than 150 contribs to learned journals. *Address:* Siston Court, Bristol, BS16 9LU, England. *Telephone:* (117) 937-2109.

TROVOADA, Miguel dos Anjos da Cunha Lisboa; São Tomé and Príncipe fmr head of state; fmrly in charge of foreign relations for the São Tomé e Príncipe Liberation Movt (MLSTP), fmr mem. Political Bureau; Prime Minister of São Tomé e Príncipe 1975–78, also Minister of Defence and Foreign Affairs July–Dec. 1975, of Econ. Co-ordination, Co-operation and Tourism 1975–78, of Trade, Industry and Fisheries 1978–79; arrested and imprisoned 1979, released 1981, then in exile in Lisbon; Pres. and C-in-C of the Armed Forces of São Tomé e Príncipe 1991–95 (deposed in coup 15 Aug. 1995), reinstalled 1995–2001. *Address:* c/o Office of the President, São Tomé, São Tomé e Príncipe.

TROVOADA, Patrice Emery; São Tomé and Príncipe politician; b. 18 March 1962, Libreville, Gabon; s. of Miguel Trovoada, Pres. of São Tomé and Príncipe 1991–2001; Minister of Foreign Affairs 2001–02; oil adviser to Pres. Fradique de Menezes –2005 (sacked by Pres.); Sec.-Gen. Independent Democratic Action (ADI) Party; cand. in presidential election July 2006; Prime Minister Feb.–June 2008, 2010–12. *Address:* Acção Democrática Independente, Av. Marginal 12 de Julho, Edif. C. Cassandra, São Tomé, São Tomé and Príncipe (office). *Telephone:* 222201 (office).

TRPEVSKI, Ljube, MSc, PhD; Macedonian politician, banker and academic; b. 3 Aug. 1947, Velmej, Ohrid; m.; one s. one d.; ed Univ. of St Cyril and St Methodius, Skopje, Univ. of Tallahassee, Fla; teaching Asst, Faculty of Econs, Univ. of St Cyril and St Methodius, Skopje 1970–77, lecturer 1977–80, Docent 1980–85, Assoc. Prof. 1985–91, Prof. 1991; Deputy Gov. Nat. Bank of Macedonia 1987–91, Gov. 1997–2004; Minister, Pres. Securities and Exchange Comm. 1992–95; Vice-Pres. of Macedonia 1996; indicted for breach of duty and embezzlement 2007, sentenced to four years in jail 2008; released from prison after Supreme Court overturned judgment Jan. 2010; currently Prof., Faculty of Econs, Sts Cyril and Methodius Univ., Skopje. *Publications:* Lexicon of Contemporary Market Economy (co-author, ed.) 1993, Money and Banking 1995, The Republic of Macedonia (co-author) 1996 and numerous articles. *Address:* University Sts Cyril and Methodius, Faculty of Economics, Blvd Goce Delchev 9V, 1000 Skopje (office); Mile Pop Jordanov 52, 91000 Skopje, Republic of Macedonia (home). *E-mail:* ljubet@eccf .ukim.edu.mk (office).

TRUBETSKOI, Kliment Nikolayevich; Russian geochemist; *Adviser, Research Institute of Comprehensive Exploitation of Mineral Resources, USSR (now Russian) Academy of Sciences;* b. 3 July 1933; m.; two c.; ed Moscow Inst. of Nonferrous Metals and Gold; Jr, then Sr Researcher, Research Inst. of Comprehensive Exploitation of Mineral Resources, USSR (now Russian) Acad. of Sciences 1961–81, Head of Lab. 1981–87, Deputy Dir 1987, Dir 1987–2003, Prof. of Geotechnology 2003, now Adviser; Chair. Russian State Geological Exploration Univ. 2003; Corresp. mem. USSR (now Russian) Acad. of Sciences 1987–91, mem. 1991–; Vice-Pres. Acad. of Mining Sciences; USSR State Prize 1990, N. Melnikov Gold Medal and Prize 1989, 2004, Russian State Prize 1999, 2000, Prize of the Pres. of Russia 2001. *Achievements include:* took part in devt of tech. to save resources in quarries, developed theoretical fundamentals of projecting, prognosis and tech. of complex utilization of mineral deposits. *Publications:* author of 30 books and 600 scientific articles in periodicals. *Leisure interests:* chess, swimming, photography, travelling. *Address:* Research Institute of Comprehensive Exploitation of Mineral Resources, 111020 Moscow, Krukovsky tupik 4, Russia. *Telephone:* (495) 360-89-60 (office); (495) 331-52-55 (home). *Fax:* (495) 360-89-60 (office). *E-mail:* trubetsk@ipkonran.ru (office). *Website:* www.ipkonran.ru (office).

TRUBETSKOV, Dmitry Ivanovich, DPhys-MathSc; Russian physicist and academic; *Head Chair of Electronics, Oscillations and Waves, Saratov State University;* b. 14 June 1938, Saratov; s. of Ivan Trubetskov and Varvara Trubetskova; m. Sofya Vasilyeva 1962; one s.; ed Saratov State Univ.; aspirant 1960–64; teacher 1961–68; docent 1968; Prof., Saratov State Univ. 1981–, Head, Chair of Electronics and Wave Processes 1981–, Rector 1994–2003; mem. IEEE Electron Devices Soc. 1995; Corresp. mem. USSR (now Russian) Acad. of Sciences 1991; Educ. Award of the Pres. of Russian Fed. 2001. *Publications include:* Analytical Methods of Calculation in Microwave Electronics (with V. N. Shevchik) 1970, Electronics of Backward-Wave Tubes 1975, Introduction into the Theory of Oscillations and Waves 1984, Oscillations and Waves in Linear and Non-linear Systems (with M. I. Rabinovich) 1989, Nonlinear Dynamics in Action (with A. A. Koronovsky) 1995, Lectures on Microwave Vacuum Microelectronics (with A. G. Rozjenev and D. V. Sokolov) 1996, Nonlinear Waves (with N. M. Ryskyn) 2000, Linear Oscillators and Waves (with A. G. Rozjenev) 2001, The Trace of Inspiration and Patient Labour 2001, Linear Oscillations and Waves, Problems (with A. P. Kuznetsov and A.G. Rozjenev) 2001, Introduction into the Theory of Self-Organization Open Systems (with E. S. Mchedlova and L. V. Krasichkov) 2002, Lectures on Microwave Electronics for Physicists, Vol. 1 (with A. Hramov) 2003, Introduction to Synergetics, Oscillations and Waves 2003, Lectures on Microwave Electronics for Physicists Vol. 2 (with A. Hramov) 2004, Introduction to

Synergetics, Chaos and Patterns 2004, The Way to Synergetics (with B. Bezruchko, A. Koronovsky and A. Hramov) 2005, Synchronization: Scientist and Time 2006, Higher Education in Russia from the Point of Vew of Nonlinear Dynamics (with M. Strikhanov, A. Koronovsky, U. Sharaevsky and A. Hramov) 2007. *Leisure interest:* reading. *Address:* Saratov State University, Astrakhanskaya str. 83, 410011 Saratov, Russia (office). *Telephone:* (8452) 512-107 (office); (8452) 231-993 (home). *Fax:* (8452) 512-107 (office). *E-mail:* trubetskovdi@nonlin .sgu.ru (office).

TRUBNIKOV, Gen. (retd) Vyacheslav Ivanovich; Russian security officer, politician and diplomatist (retd); b. 25 April 1944, Irkutsk; m.; one d.; ed Moscow State Inst. of Int. Relations; served in USSR KGB (First Main Directorate, intelligence) 1967–91; staff mem. HQ of First Main Dept (intelligence) 1977–84; KGB station officer in India (as corresp. Press Agency Novosti) 1971–77; mem. Union of Journalists 1973; resident in Bangladesh and India 1984–90; Head Div. of America KGB 1990–92; First Deputy Dir Russian Intelligence Service 1992–96, Dir 1996–2000; mem. Security Council, Defence Council and Foreign Policy Council of Russia 1996; First Deputy Minister of Foreign Affairs 2000–04; Amb. to India 2004–09 (retd). *Address:* c/o Ministry of Foreign Affairs, 119200 Moscow, Smolenskaya-Sennaya pl. 32/34, Russia.

TRUDEAU, Garry B., BA, MFA; American cartoonist; b. 21 July 1948, New York; m. Jane Pauley 1980; three c.; ed Yale Univ. School of Art and Architecture; cr. comic strip Doonesbury at Yale 1969, now syndicated nationwide; Fellow, American Acad. of Arts and Sciences; Pulitzer Prize for Editorial Cartooning 1975, 12th Annual John S. Knight Lecturer 2000; hon. degrees from Yale Univ., Colgate Univ., Williams Univ., Duke Univ. and 18 other univs. *Plays include:* Doonesbury 1983, Rapmaster Ronnie, A Partisan Review (with Elizabeth Swados) 1984. *Films:* A Doonesbury Special for NBC-TV 1977 (Special Jury Prize at Cannes Film Festival). *Television:* conceived (with Robert Altman) Tanner '88 1988. *Publications include:* Any Grooming Hints for Your Fans, Rollie, But the Pension Fund was Just Sitting There, The Doonesbury Chronicles, Guilty, Guilty, Guilty, We Who are about to Fry, Salute You: selected cartoons in In Search of Reagan's Brain, Vol. 2, Is This Your First Purge, Miss ?, Vol. 2, It's Supposed to be Yellow, Pinhead: selected cartoons from You Ask for Many, Seetle for June, Vol. 1, The Wreck of the Rusty Nail, Dressed for Failure 1983, Confirmed Bachelors are Just So Fascinating 1984, Sir I'm Worried About Your Mood Swings 1984, Doonesbury Dossier: The Reagan Years 1984, Check Your Egos at the Door 1986, Talking 'Bout My G-G-Generation 1988, We're Eating More Beets 1988, Read My Lips, Make My Day, Eat Quiche and Die 1989, Recycled Doonesbury 1990, You're Smoking Now Mr Butt! 1990, In Search of a Cigarette Holder Man: A Doonesbury Book 1994, Doonesbury Nation 1995, Flashbacks 1995; The Portable Doonesbury 1993; contribs. to The People's Doonesbury and many others. *Website:* doonesbury.slate .com.

TRUDEAU, Justin Pierre James, BA, BEd; Canadian politician; *Leader, Liberal Party of Canada;* b. 25 Dec. 1971, Ottawa; s. of the late Pierre Elliott Trudeau (fmr Prime Minister) and Margaret Sinclair Trudeau Kemper; m. Sophie Grégoire; one s. one d.; ed McGill Univ., Univ. of British Columbia; began career as teacher, West Point Grey Acad. and Sir Winston Churchill Secondary School, Vancouver; mem. House of Commons (Liberal) for Papineau constituency 2008–, mem. Parl. Cttees on Environment and Sustainable Devt and Citizenship and Immigration; Leader, Liberal Party of Canada 2013–. *Radio:* panellist on Canada Reads (CBC Radio) 2003–04. *Address:* Liberal Party of Canada, 81 Metcalfe Street, Suite 600, Ottawa, ON K1P 6M8, Canada (office). *Telephone:* (613) 237-0740 (office). *Fax:* (613) 235-7208 (office). *E-mail:* info@liberal.ca (office). *Website:* www .liberal.ca (office). justin.ca.

TRUE, Baron (Life Peer), cr. 2010, of East Sheen in the County of Surrey; **Nicholas Edward True,** CBE; British politician and fmr civil servant; *Leader of the Council, London Borough of Richmond-upon-Thames;* b. 31 July 1951; mem. Conservative Research Dept 1976–82; Personal Asst to Lord Whitelaw 1978–82; Special Adviser to Sec. of State, Dept of Health and Social Security 1982–86; Dir Public Policy Unit Ltd 1986–90; Deputy Head of Prime Minister (PM)'s Policy Unit 1990–95; Ministerial nominee to English Sports Council 1996–97; Special Adviser to PM's Office 1997; Pvt. Sec. to Leader of the Opposition, House of Lords 1997–2010; Councillor, Richmond upon Thames 1986–90, 1998–, Deputy Leader 2002–06, Leader of the Opposition 2006–10, Leader of the Council 2010–; mem. Leaders' Cttee, London Councils (fmrly ALG); mem. (Conservative) House of Lords 2010–; Trustee, Sir Harold Hood's Charitable Trust 1996–, Richmond Civic Endowment Trust 2006–10, Royal Parks Bd 2012–. *Leisure interests:* books, cricket, Italy, Byzantium. *Address:* London Borough of Richmond upon Thames, Civic Centre, 44 York Street, Twickenham, TW1 3BZ (office); House of Lords, Westminster, London, SW1A 0PW (office); 114 Palewell Park, East Sheen, SW14 8JH, England (home). *Telephone:* (20) 8487-5001 (Richmond upon Thames) (office); (20) 7219-2562 (House of Lords) (office); (20) 8876-9628 (home). *E-mail:* Cllr .LordTrue@richmond.gov.uk (office). *Website:* www.richmond.gov.uk (office).

TRUJILLO, Solomon Dennis (Sol), BS, MBA; American telecommunications industry executive; b. 17 Nov. 1951, Cheyenne, Wyo.; ed Univ. of Wyoming; began career with Mountain Bar Telephone 1974; Pres. and CEO USWest Dex Inc. 1992–95, Pres. and CEO US est Communications 1995–98, CEO and Chair. USWest Inc. 1999–2000; Chair., Pres. and CEO Graviton Inc., La Jolla, Calif. 2000; mem. Exec. Bd Orange SA 2001–04, CEO 2003–04; mem. Bd of Dirs and CEO Telstra Corpn Ltd, Australia 2005–09 (resgnd); mem. Chair.'s Council, Alcatel 2000–03; mem. Bd of Dirs Target, GSMA 2008–; fmr mem. Bd of Dirs Pepsi Co., Gannet, Bank of America, Electronic Data Systems Corpn (EDS), Tomas Rivera Policy Inst.; mem. Advisory Bd UCLA School of Public Affairs; fmr Gov. World Econ. Forum, mem. World Econ. Forum's Steering Cttee on Climate Change 2008; fmr Trustee, Boston Coll., UCLA's School of Public Policy; fmr trade policy adviser in Clinton and Bush admins; Dr hc (Univ. of Wyoming, Univ. of Colorado). *Address:* c/o Telstra Corporation Ltd, 242 Exhibition Street, Melbourne, Vic. 3000, Australia. *Telephone:* (3) 9634-6400. *Fax:* (3) 9632-3215. *E-mail:* info@telstra.com .au.

TRUMAN, Edwin Malcolm, BA, MA, PhD; American economist and academic; *Senior Fellow, Peterson Institute for International Economics;* b. 6 June 1941, Albany, NY; s. of David B. Truman and Elinor G. Truman; m. Tracy P. Truman;

one s. one d.; ed Amherst Coll., Yale Univ.; trained as economist; Prof., Yale Univ. 1967–74; joined Div. of Int. Finance, Bd of Govs of Fed. Reserve System 1972, Dir (later Staff Dir) 1977–98; Asst Sec., US Treasury for Int. Affairs 1998–2001, Asst Sec. (Int. Affairs) and Counsellor to Sec. of the Treasury 2009; taught at Amherst Coll. 2006, 2008, 2010, Williams Coll. 2008, 2010, 2012, 2014; Sr Fellow, Peterson Inst. for Int. Econs, Washington, DC 2001–; mem. G-7 Working Group on Exchange Market Intervention 1982–83, G-10 Working Group on the Resolution of Sovereign Liquidity Crises 1995–96, G-10-sponsored Working Party on Financial Stability in Emerging Market Econs 1996–97, G-22 Working Party on Transparency and Accountability 1998, Financial Stability Forum's Working Group on Highly Leveraged Insts 1999–2000; Hon. LLD (Amherst Coll.) 1988. *Publications:* Inflation Targeting in the World Economy 2003, Chasing Dirty Money: The Fight Against Money Laundering (co-author) 2004, A Strategy for IMF Reform 2006, Sovereign Wealth Funds: Threat or Salvation? 2010; numerous articles on int. monetary econs, int. debt problems, econ. devt and European econ. integration. *Address:* Peterson Institute for International Economics, 1750 Massachusetts Avenue NW, Washington, DC 20036-1903, USA (office). *Telephone:* (202) 237-1730 (home). *Fax:* (202) 659-3225 (office). *E-mail:* ttruman@piie.com (office); tnttruman@yahoo.com (home). *Website:* www.iie.com (office).

TRUMKA, Richard Louis, JD; American lawyer and trade union official; *President, AFL-CIO;* b. 24 July 1949, Nemacolin, Pa; s. of Frank Richard Trumka and Eola Elizabeth Bertugli; m. Barbara Vidovich 1982; one s.; ed Philadelphia State Univ., Villanova Univ.; served at bar US Dist Court 1974, US Court of Appeals 1975, US Supreme Court 1979; Attorney United Mine Workers of America, Washington 1974–77, 1978–79; Miner-Operator Jones and Loughlin Steel, Nemacolin, Pa 1977–78, 1979–81, mem. Int. Exec. Bd Dist 4, Masontown, Pa 1981–83, Int. Pres., Washington 1982–95, Pres. Emer. 1995–; Sec. Treas. AFL-CIO, Washington 1995–2009, Pres. 2009–; Dir Nat. Bank, Washington 1983–85, Dinamo Corpn 1983–; mem. Bd of Dirs American Coal Fund 1983–; Trustee Philadelphia State Univ.; Labor Responsibility Award, Martin Luther King Center for Non-Violent Social Change 1990. *Address:* AFL-CIO, 815 16th Street, NW, Washington, DC 20006, USA (office). *Telephone:* (202) 637-5000 (office). *Fax:* (202) 637-5058 (office). *Website:* www.aflcio.org (office).

TRUMP, Donald John, Sr, BS; American business executive, property developer, television producer and author; *Chairman and President, The Trump Organization;* b. 14 June 1946, Queens, New York; s. of Fred C. Trump and Mary Anne Trump (née MacLeod); m. 1st Ivana Zelnicek 1977 (divorced 1991); two s. one d.; m. 2nd Marla Maples 1993 (divorced 1999); one d.; m. 3rd Melania Knauss 2005; ed New York Mil. Acad., Fordham Univ., Wharton School of Finance, Univ. of Pennsylvania; worked for father's real-estate firm, Elizabeth Trump & Son, while attending univ., joined firm in 1968, given control 1971, renamed it The Trump Organization, currently Chair. and Pres.; Founder Trump Entertainment Resorts; Chair. Trump Plaza Assocs, LLC, Trump Atlantic City Assocs; holdings include: (New York) Trump Tower on Fifth Avenue; (Fla) Mar-A-Lago at Palm Beach, Trump Plaza; (Atlantic City) Trump Plaza Hotel Casino, Trump Castle Casino, Trump Taj Mahal Casino Resort; acquired 50 per cent stake in Empire State Bldg 1994; mem. Bd of Dirs Police Athletic League; mem. Advisory Bd Lenox Hill Hosp. and United Cerebral Palsy; Dir Fred C. Trump Foundation; Founder-mem. cttee to complete construction of Cathedral of St John the Divine and Wharton Real Estate Center; fmr Co-Chair. New York Vietnam Veterans Memorial Fund; Hotel and Real Estate Visionary of the Century, UJA Fed. 2000. *Radio:* Clear Channel Radio broadcasts 2004. *Television:* host and co-exec. producer, The Apprentice 2004–. *Publications:* Trump – The Art of the Deal 1989, Trump: Surviving at the Top 1990, Trump 1997, The Art of the Comeback 1997, The America We Deserve 2000, How to Get Rich 2004, Think Like a Billionaire 2004, Trump: Think Like a Billionaire: Everything You Need to Know about Success, Real Estate, and Life 2005, Why We Want You to Be Rich: Two Men – One Message 2006, Trump University Real Estate 101: Building Wealth with Real Estate Investments 2006, Trump 101: The Way to Success 2006, Trump: How to Get Rich 2008, Trump – Never Give Up: How I Turned My Biggest Challenges into Success 2008, Trump University Commercial Real Estate 101: How Small Investors Can Get Started and Make it Big 2008, Think Like a Champion: An Informal Education in Business and Life 2010, Think BIG: Make It Happen in Business and Life 2012, Time to Get Tough 2012. *Address:* Office of the Chairman, The Trump Organization, 725 Fifth Avenue, New York, NY 10022, USA (office). *Telephone:* (212) 832-2000 (office). *Fax:* (212) 755-3230 (office). *Website:* www.trump.com (office).

TRUONG, My Hoa; Vietnamese politician; b. 8 May 1945, Tien Giang Prov.; sister of Truong Tan Sang, Pres. of Viet Nam; m. 1975; two d.; joined People's Army aged 15; mem. CP of Vietnam 1963–; captured aged 19 and imprisoned for 11 years; Party Sec. and Chair. People's Cttee, Tan Binh dist of Ho Chi Minh City 1986–91; Pres. Nat. Cttee for the Advancement of Women 1995; Pres. The Women's Union 1995; Vice-Chair. Nat. Ass. 1994–2002; Vice-Pres. Socialist Repub. of Viet Nam 2002–07; fmr Vice-Chair. Nat. Cttee for Population and Family Planning; fmr mem. Exec. Bd Cen. Party Cttee, Congress Party del. *Address:* c/o National Committee for Population and Family Planning, 12 Ago Tat To, Dong Da, Hanoi, Viet Nam.

TRUONG, Tan Sang, LLB; Vietnamese politician and head of state; *President;* b. 21 Jan. 1949, My Hanh, Duc Hoa, Long An, French Indochina (now Viet Nam); joined CP 1969; taken prisoner by S Vietnamese Govt 1971, held in Bien Hoa Prison, Phu Quoc island dist, released under Paris Peace Treaty 1973; headed Ho Chi Minh City's Forestry Dept as well as city's New Econ. Zone Devt Dept 1983–86; promoted to Standing Bd of city's Party Cttee 1986; Party Chair. for Ho Chi Minh City 1992; mem. Politburo 1996–; Party Sec. for Ho Chi Minh City 1996–2000; promoted to 10th position in nat. party at a congress April 2001; also apptd Head of party's Econ. Comm.; promoted to fifth position in party at a congress April 2006, also appointed Head of party's Secr.; promoted to party's number two slot between congresses Oct. 2009; ranked as the party's number one leader following 11th Nat. Congress, Hanoi Jan. 2011; Pres. of Viet Nam July 2011–. *Address:* c/o Dang Cong San Viet Nam (Communist Party of Viet Nam), 1 Hoang Van Thu, Hanoi, Viet Nam. *E-mail:* cpv@hn.vnn.vn. *Website:* www.cpv.org.vn.

TRUSS, Warren Errol; Australian farmer and politician; *Deputy Prime Minister and Minister for Infrastructure and Regional Development;* b. 8 Oct. 1948, Kingaroy, Queensland; m. Lyn Truss; mem. Kingaroy Shire Council 1976–90, fmr

Chair.; mem. House of Reps (Parl.) (Nat. Party of Australia) for Wide Bay constituency 1990–, Nat. Party Parl. Leader 2007–; Minister for Customs and Consumer Affairs 1997–98, for Community Services 1998–99, for Agric., Fisheries and Forestry 1999–2005, for Transport and Regional Services 2005–06, for Trade 2006–07; Shadow Minister for Infrastructure and Transport 2010–13; Deputy Prime Minister 2013–, also Minister for Infrastructure and Regional Devt 2013–; Chair. Fraser Coast-South Burnett Regional Tourism Bd 1985–89; Deputy Chair. Bulk Grains Queensland 1985–90; fmr Deputy Chair. Queensland Grain Handling Authority; Pres. Australian Council of Rural Youth 1973–74; fmr Pres. Burnett District Local Govt Asscn, Lutheran Youth of Queensland; mem. State Council, Queensland Graingrowers Asscn 1979–90; mem. Nat. Party of Australia, Leader 2007–; Centenary Medal 2001. *Address:* Department of the Prime Minister and Cabinet, 1 National Circuit, Barton, ACT 2600, Australia (office). *Telephone:* (2) 6271-5111 (office). *Fax:* (2) 6271-5414 (office). *Website:* www.dpmc.gov.au (office); www.warrentruss.com.

TRUSZCZYŃSKI, Jan, MA; Polish politician, diplomatist and international organization official; *Director-General for Education and Culture, European Commission;* b. 30 July 1949, Warsaw; m.; two c.; ed Warsaw School of Commerce, Institut für Internationale Beziehungen, Potsdam, Germany, Polish Inst. of Int. Affairs, Warsaw; trainee, then desk officer in Human Resources and Training Dept, Ministry of Foreign Affairs 1972–78; Second Sec., Embassy in The Hague 1978–82; European Integration Desk Officer, Western Europe Dept, Ministry of Foreign Affairs 1982–88; Counsellor, Embassy in Brussels (in charge of bilateral and EC matters) 1988–89; Deputy Head of Polish Mission to the European Communities, Brussels 1989–93; corresp. banking officer, then Head of Investor Relations, Bank Inicjatyw Gospodarczych (BIG) SA, Warsaw 1993–94; Head of Rep. Office of Kredietbank NV in Poland 1995–96; Amb. and Perm. Rep. to EU, Brussels 1996–2001 (mem. of Poland's EU accession negotiation team 1998–2001); Undersecretary of State, Chancellery of the Pres. of Poland (acting as Chief Adviser to the Pres. on European integration) Feb.–Oct. 2001; Undersecretary of State, Ministry of Foreign Affairs 2001–05, Govt's Plenipotentiary for Negotiations on Accession of Poland to the EU 2001–03; Sec. of State, Ministry of Foreign Affairs Jan.–Oct. 2005; Man. Dir Foundation for Polish-German Co-operation in Warsaw 2005–07; Deputy Dir-Gen. for Enlargement, EC 2007–09, Deputy Dir-Gen. for Educ. and Culture 2009–10, Dir-Gen. for Educ. and Culture 2010–. *Address:* Office of the Director-General for Education, Training, Culture and Youth, Directorate-General for Education and Culture, European Commission, 1049 Brussels, Belgium (office). *E-mail:* eac-info@ec.europa.eu (office). *Website:* ec.europa.eu/dgs/education_culture/index_en.htm (office).

TRUTNEV, Yurii Petrovich; Russian politician; *Deputy Prime Minister and Presidential Representative to Far Eastern Federal Okrug;* b. 1 March 1956; m.; two s.; ed Perm Polytechnic Inst.; engineer, Perm Scientific Research Inst. of Oil 1978–81; instructor Regional Komsomol Cttee and Sport Cttee 1981–88; Pres. EKS Int. (food business) 1996, Dir 2000–; Deputy, Perm City Duma (parl.) 1994–96, Chair. Cttee on Econ. Policy and Taxation; Mayor of Perm 1996–2000; Gov. of Perm Oblast 2000–04; Minister of Natural Resources and Ecology 2004–12; Asst to the Pres. of Russia 2012–13; Deputy Prime Minister and Presidential Rep. to the Far Eastern Fed. Okrug 2013–. *Leisure interests:* karate, wrestling, rally racing. *Address:* Office of the Presidential Representative, 680030 Khabarovsk, ul. Sheronova 22, Russia (office). *Telephone:* (4212) 31-39-78 (office). *Fax:* (4212) 31-38-04 (office). *Website:* www.dfo.gov.ru (office); www.trutnev.ru.

TSACHEVA DANGOVSKA, Tsetska, LLB; Bulgarian jurist and politician; b. 24 May 1958, Dragana, Ugarchin Municipality, Lovech Prov.; m. Rumen Dangovski; one s.; ed Pleven High School of Math., Sofia Univ.; mem. Bulgarian CP –1989 (resgnd); practised as lawyer and was subsequently a head legal adviser to Pleven Municipality 1999–2007; mem. Citizens for European Devt of Bulgaria (GERB) 2007–, Deputy Chair. GERB Party 2013–; joined Pleven Municipal Council as GERB mem. 2007; GERB cand. for Mayor of Pleven 2007; headed GERB's voting list in Pleven Prov. in parl. elections and was also party's proportional cand. for that constituency 2009; mem. Narodno Sobraniye (Nat. Ass.) for 15-Pleven 2009–, Chair. 2009–13; mem. Pleven Bar Asscn. *Address:* Citizens for European Development of Bulgaria (Grazhdani za evropeysko razvitie na Balgariya) 1463 Sofia, pl. Balgariya 1, NDK Administration Building 17, Bulgaria (office). *Telephone:* (2) 490-13-13 (office). *Fax:* (2) 490-09-51 (office). *E-mail:* pr@gerb.bg (office). *Website:* www.gerb.bg (office).

TSAI, Eng-Meng; Taiwanese business executive; *Chairman and CEO, Want Want China Holdings Ltd;* m.; one s.; joined Want Want China Holdings Ltd 1976, Gen. Man. I Lan Foods Industrial Co. Ltd (subsidiary), Taiwan –1987, Chair., Exec. Dir and CEO Want Want China Holdings Ltd, Shanghai 1987–, Chair. and CEO Want Want Holdings Ltd 1987–; Chair. and controlling shareholder of San Want; fmr mem. Council Standing Cttee of Taiwan Confectionery, Biscuit and Floury Food Industry Asscn, Food Devt Asscn of Taiwan; Hon. Prof. (Nanjing Normal Univ.) 1995. *Address:* Want Want China Holdings Ltd, 1088 East Hong Song Road, Shanghai 201103, People's Republic of China (office). *Telephone:* (21) 61151111 (office). *Fax:* (21) 61151777 (office). *E-mail:* info@www.want-want.com (office). *Website:* www.want-want.com (office).

TSAI, Hong-tu, BA, JD; Taiwanese insurance industry executive; *Chairman, Cathay Life Insurance Company Ltd;* s. of the late Tsai Wan-lin and Tsai Chou Pao-chin; ed Nat. Taiwan Univ., Southern Methodist Univ., USA; Man. Dir and Vice-Chair. Cathay Life Insurance Company Ltd –1980, Chair. 1980–, also Chair. Cathay Financial Holding Co. Ltd (parent co. Lin-Yuan Group est. by father Tsai Wan-lin); mem. Life Insurance Asscn of Repub. of China; Chair. Life Insurance Asscn of Repub. of China. *Address:* Cathay Life Insurance Co. Ltd, 296 Jen Ai Road, Section 4, Taipei 10639, Taiwan (office). *Telephone:* (22) 755-1399 (office). *Fax:* (22) 704-1485 (office). *E-mail:* info@cathlife.com.tw (office); service@cathayholdings.com.tw (office). *Website:* www.cathlife.com.tw (office).

TSAI, Ing-wen, LLB, LLM, PhD; Taiwanese politician and professor of law; b. 31 Aug. 1956; ed Nat. Taiwan Univ., Cornell Univ., USA and LSE, UK; assoc. Prof., Law Dept, Nat. Chengchi Univ. 1984–90, Prof., Grad. School of Law 1990–91, Prof. of Law, Grad. Inst. of Int. Trade 1993–2000 (mem. Int. Trade Comm.); Prof., Grad. School of Law, Soochow Univ. 1991–93; Adviser on Int. Econ. Orgs, Ministry of Econ. Affairs 1992–2000; Convener, Drafting/Research Group on 'Statute Gov-

erning Relations with Hong Kong and Macao' 1994–95; mem. Advisory Cttee Mainland Affairs Council, Exec. Yuan 1994–98, Chair. 2000–04; Nat. Policy Adviser to Pres. 2004–06; Vice-Pres. of Exec. Yuan 2006–07 (resgnd); Chair. TaiMedBiologics (biotechnology firm) 2007–08; Chair. Democratic Progressive Party 2008–12; mem. Fair Trade Comm., Exec. Yuan 1995–98, Advisory Cttee of Copyright Comm., Ministry of Interior 1997–99; Sr Adviser Nat. Security Council 1999–2000; unsuccessful cand. (DPP) in presidential election 2012. *Address:* Democratic Progressive Party, 10/F, 30 Beiping East Rd, Taipei 10051, Taiwan (office). *Telephone:* (2) 23929989 (office). *Fax:* (2) 23929989 (office). *E-mail:* foreign@dpp.org.tw (office). *Website:* www.dpp.org.tw (office).

TSAI, Michael Ming-hsien, PhD; Taiwanese politician and diplomatist; ed California Western School of Law, USA; mem. Parl. (Progressive Democratic Party), served as a legislator for two terms and as Deputy Rep. to USA; fmr Vice-Minister of Nat. Defense, adviser to Ministry of Nat. Defense –2008, Minister of Nat. Defense 2008; mem. Democratic Progressive Party. *Publications include:* Defending Taiwan – The Future Vision of Taiwan's Defence Policy and Military Strategy (co-ed.) 2002, Submarines and Taiwan's Defense (co-author) 2004, Taiwan's Security and Air Power (co-author) 2004, (co-author of book on Taiwanese defence reform) 2006. *Address:* Democratic Progressive Party, 10/F, 30 Beiping East Road, Taipei 10051, Taiwan (office). *Telephone:* (2) 23929989 (office). *Fax:* (2) 23929989 (office). *E-mail:* foreign@dpp.org.tw (office). *Website:* www.dpp.org.tw (office).

TSAI, Ming-Liang; Taiwanese film director. *Films include:* Rebels of the Neon God 1992, Vive l'Amour (Venice Golden Lion Award 1994) 1994, The River (Berlin Silver Bear Award 1996) 1996, Tian bian yi duo yun 2005, The Hole, Last Dance, Dong, I Don't Want to Sleep Alone 2006, Visage 2009.

TSAI, Wan-tsai; Taiwanese banker; b. 5 Aug. 1929, brother of Tsai Wan-lin; uncle of Tsai Hong-tu; m.; four c.; Founder and fmr Chair. Fubon Group, now retd; fmr legislator of Legis. Yuan (Parl.). *Address:* Fubon Financial Holding Co. Ltd, 237 Chien Kuo South Road Section 1, Taipei, Taiwan (office). *Telephone:* (2) 6636-6636 (office). *Fax:* (2) 6636-0111 (office). *E-mail:* ir@fubon.com (office). *Website:* www.fubongroup.com (office).

TSANG, Sir Donald Yam-kuen, Kt, KBE, JP, MPA; Chinese government official; b. (Tsang Yam-kuen), 7 Oct. 1944, Hong Kong; m.; two s.; ed in Hong Kong and Harvard Univ., USA; joined Govt of Hong Kong 1967; served in various govt depts and brs of Govt Secr.; attached to Asian Devt Bank, Manila 1977; Dist Officer, Shatin; Deputy Dir of Trade responsible for trade relations with N America; Deputy Sec. of Gen. Duties Br. responsible for Sino-British Jt Declaration 1985–89; Dir of Admin. Office of Chief Sec. 1989–91; Dir-Gen. of Trade 1991–93; Sec. for the Treasury 1993–95; Financial Sec. 1995–2001; Chief Sec. for Admin. 2001–05, Acting Chief Exec. March–May 2005 (resgnd to campaign for election as Chief Exec.), Chief Exec. 2005–12; Grand Bauhinia Medal 2002; Hon. LLD 1999; Hon. DBA 1999; Dr hc (Chinese Univ. of Hong Kong, Hong Kong Polytechnic Univ., Univ. of Hong Kong). *Leisure interests:* hiking, swimming, bird-watching, music. *Address:* c/o Office of the Chief Executive, 5/F Main Wing, Central Government Offices, Lower Albert Rd, Central, Hong Kong Special Administrative Region, People's Republic of China (office).

TSANG, John Chun-wah, JP, MPA; Chinese government official; *Financial Secretary, Hong Kong Special Administrative Region;* b. 1951; m.; two c.; ed La Salle Coll., Hong Kong, Boston State Coll., Massachusetts Inst. of Tech., Kennedy School of Govt, Harvard Univ., USA; began career working in Boston Public Schools, USA; joined Hong Kong civil service 1982, Admin. Asst to the Financial Sec. 1987–91, Asst Dir-Gen. of Trade 1991–95, Pvt. Sec. to Gov. Chris Patten 1995–97, Dir-Gen. Econ. and Trade Office, London 1997–99, Commr of Customs and Excise 1999–2002, Perm. Sec. for Housing, Planning and Lands 2002–03, Sec. for Commerce, Industry and Tech. 2003–06; Dir Office of the Chief Exec. of Hong Kong 2006–07, Financial Sec. 2007–, mem. Exec. Council, Hong Kong Special Admin. Region; Chair. Sixth Ministerial Conference (MC6), WTO 2005. *Address:* Executive Council, Central Government Offices, Lower Albert Road, Central, Hong Kong Special Administrative Region, People's Republic of China (office). *Telephone:* 28102545 (office). *Fax:* 28450176 (office). *Website:* www.gov.hk (office).

TSANG, Yok-Sing; Hong Kong politician; *Legislative Councillor, Hong Kong Special Administrative Region;* Founding Chair. Democratic Alliance for the Betterment of Hong Kong 1992–2003 (resgnd); currently Legis. Councillor, Special Admin. Region of Hong Kong, People's Repub. of China, apptd mem. Exec. Council (Cabinet) 2002, Chair. Cttee on Rules of Procedure, Panel on Educ.; mem. political section, Preparatory Cttee for Hong Kong Special Admin. Region (SAR); mem. Bd of Dirs Airport Authority; mem. Comm. on Strategic Devt, ICAC Complaints Cttee, Disaster Relief Fund Advisory Cttee. *Address:* Executive Council Secretariat, 1/F, Main Wing, Central Government Offices, Lower Albert Road, Central, Hong Kong Special Administrative Region, People's Republic of China (office). *Telephone:* 28102581 (office). *Fax:* 28450176 (office). *E-mail:* ceo@ceo.gov.hk (office). *Website:* www.ceo.gov.hk (office); www.dab.org.hk (office).

TSAO, Robert H.C., MS; Taiwanese electronics industry executive; *Chairman Emeritus, United Microelectronics Corporation;* b. 24 Feb. 1947, Shantung; ed Nat. Univ. of Taiwan, Nat. Chiao Tung Univ.; Deputy Dir Electrical Research Service Org. 1979–81; Vice-Pres. United Microelectronics Corpn 1980, Pres. 1981–91, Chair. 1991–2006 (resgnd), now Chair. Emer.; indicted for allegedly making illegal investments in a Chinese foundry 2006, found not guilty of charges by Hsinchu Dist. Court 2007; Chair. Unipac Microelectronics Corpn 1989; Vice-Chair. TECO Information System Co. Ltd 1995; mem. Standing Bd Chinese Nat. Fed. of Industry, Chair. Intellectual Property Protection Cttee 1991–94; Chair. Asscn of Allied Industries in Science-Based Industry Park 1987–93. *Address:* United Microelectronics Corporation Ltd, No. 3, Li-Hsin 2nd Road, Hsinchu Science Park, Hsinchu, Taiwan (office). *Telephone:* (35) 782258 (office). *Fax:* (35) 779392 (office). *E-mail:* foundry@umc.com (office). *Website:* www.umc.com (office).

TSAPOGAS, Makis Joakim, MD, DSc, MCh, PhD, MRCS, LRCP, FACS; Greek professor of vascular diseases, medical scientist and academic; *Professor of Vascular Diseases, New York University and University of London;* m. Lily Philossopoulou; ed Univs of Athens, London and New York; Lecturer, King's Coll. Hosp. Medical School, London 1961–63, Sr Lecturer 1963–67; Hunterian Prof.,

Royal Coll. of Surgeons, UK 1964; Assoc. Prof., Albany Medical Coll. Union Univ. New York 1967–70, Prof. 1970–75; Adjunct Prof. Rensselear Polytechnic Inst. New York 1970–75; Prof., Rutgers Medical School, NJ 1976; Prof. of Vascular Diseases, State Univ. of New York, Stony Brook 1977–; adviser, WHO 1986–; consultant, UN, New York 1993–; Prof. of Vascular Diseases, Univs of NY and London; Visiting Prof. in many univs in Europe and N America; Physician in charge of the Pres. of Greece and the Ecumenical Orthodox Patriarchate, Constantinople; corresp. mem. Acad. of Athens; Fellow, Archaeological Soc. of Athens; adviser to several medical schools 2009–; Hon. mem. Parnassos Literary Soc. and over 30 medical, research and bio-medical scientific socs, Hon. citizen of Nea Smyrni and Kos; Hon. MD (Nice Univ.), (Athens Univ.), (Patras Univ.); Hon. PhD; Red Cross Gold Medal, Gold Medal and Cross of the Ecumenical Patriarchate, Medal of the towns of Heraklion and Alexandroupoulis. *Publications include:* Atherosclerosis in the Lower Limb 1959, Treatment of Thrombosis 1965, Management of Vascular Diseases 1985, Medical Education 1992, Venous Thrombosis and Pulmonary Embolism 2001, Biomedical Progress and Society 2004, Hypertension 2006, Lipids and Cardiovascular Disease 2007, Post-Graduate Medical Education 2008, Athersclerosis in Women 2009, Recent Advances in Medicine 2009, Molecular Biology in Medicine (contrib.) 2009, Prevention of Vascular Diseases 2009, Cardiovascular Diseases in Children 2010, Hypertension in Young People 2010, The Role of Lipids in Health and Disease 2010; over 200 articles in scientific medical journals. *Leisure interests:* classical music, reading, travelling. *Address:* 8 Merlin Street, Kolonaki, 106 71 Athens, Greece (home). *Telephone:* (21) 03390988 (home). *Fax:* (21) 03390989 (home).

TSCHIRA, Klaus; German software industry executive; *Managing Director, European Media Laboratory;* b. Freiburg; with IBM Germany as systems engineer Mannheim –1972; Co-founder of Systemanalyse + Programmentwicklung (later SAP AG) 1972, now mem. Supervisory Bd 1998–; f. Klaus Tschira Foundation 1995; founder and Man. Dir European Media Lab. 1997–; mem. IBM European Software Vendors Advisory Council 1990–92; Chair. Friends of FZI (Forschungszentrum für Informatik) Karlsruhe; mem. Supervisory Bd GMD (Forschungszentrum für Informatik) St. Augustin; mem. GI Praesidium of German Informatics Society 1991–96; Hon. mem. Senate of Heidelberg Univ. 1996, Senate of Mannheim Univ. 1999 Dr hc (Klagenfurt Univ., Austria) 1995. *Address:* Villa Bosch, Schloss-Wolfsbrunnen-Weg 33, 69118 Heidelberg (office); SAP AG, PO Box 1461, 69185 Walldorf, Germany (office). *Telephone:* (6227) 747474 (SAP) (office). *Fax:* (6227) 757575 (SAP) (office). *Website:* www.eml.villa-bosch.de (office); www .kts.villa-bosch.de (office); www.sap.com (office).

TSCHÜTSCHER, Klaus, LLM, DrIur; Liechtenstein politician and academic; b. 8 July 1967; m. Jeanette Tschütscher; two c.; ed Univs of St Gallen and Zurich, Switzerland; Leader, Liechtenstein Fiscal Admin Sept. 1995; mem. Exec. Cttee Liechtenstein Steuerwaltung 1996–; Dozent, Univ. of Liechtenstein 1998–; mem. Vaterländische Union (Patriotic Union); mem. Liechtenstein Del. to OECD (Harmful Tax Practices) 1999, to EU (EU tax topics, in particular EU interest taxation) 1999, for legal aid negotiations with USA 2001; Chair. Standing Working Group 'International Developments of the Tax Law' 2001–; mem. MWS Mixed Comm. 2001–; mem. Future Finance Plan Liechtenstein 2002; Deputy Prime Minister and Minister of Econ. Affairs, of Justice and of Sports 2005–09, Prime Minister of Liechtenstein 2009–13, also Minister of Gen. Govt Affairs, Finance, Family Affairs and Gender Equality 2009–13. *Address:* c/o Regierungsgebäude, Postfach 684, 9490 Vaduz, Liechtenstein (office).

TSEKOA, Mohlabi Kenneth, BEd, MA; Lesotho politician, educator and diplomatist; *Minister of Foreign Affairs and International Relations;* b. 13 Aug. 1945; m.; two s. one d.; ed Nat. Univ. of Lesotho, Univ. of Botswana, Lesotho and Swaziland, Univ. of Newcastle-upon-Tyne, Univ. of London, UK, Univ. of Mass, USA; teacher, Hlotse High School 1970–74; Deputy Headmaster, St Agnes High School 1974–76; Sr Educ. Officer, Lesotho Distance Teaching Centre 1976–78, Dir 1978–84; Deputy Prin. Sec., Ministry of Educ. 1984–86, Prin. Sec. 1986–89; High Commr to UK and Amb. to Ireland, Spain and Portugal 1989–96; Govt Sec. and Head of the Public Service 1996–2001; Minister of Finance and Devt Planning 2001–02, of Foreign Affairs 2002–04, of Educ. and Training 2004–07, of Foreign Affairs and Int. Relations 2007–. *Address:* Ministry of Foreign Affairs and International Relations, POB 1387, Maseru 100, Lesotho (office). *Telephone:* 22311746 (office). *Fax:* 22310527 (office). *E-mail:* dps@foreign.gov.ls (office). *Website:* www.lesotho.gov.ls/foreign (office).

TSELKOV, Oleg; Russian artist; b. 1934, Moscow; ed Moscow secondary art school, Minsk Inst. of Theatre Art and Leningrad Acad. of Art; expelled from school for 'formalism'; later graduated from Leningrad Theatre Inst. as stage-designer 1958; designed numerous productions; mem. of Artists' Union; left USSR 1977, now lives in Paris.

TSEPKALO, Valery V.; Belarusian academic, government official and fmr diplomatist; *Director, High-Tech Park Administration;* b. 22 Feb. 1965, Grodno; m. Veronika Tsepkalo; ed Belarus Technological Inst., Moscow State Inst. of Int. Relations, Russia; mil. service 1984–86; with Embassy of USSR in Finland 1991; joined Ministry of Foreign Affairs, Repub. of Belarus 1992–93, First Deputy Minister for Foreign Affairs 1994–97; Adviser to Exec. Sec. of CIS 1994; lecturer on int. relations, geopolitics and neo-conservatism; Amb. to USA 1997–2002; Sr Adviser to Pres. of Belarus 2002–, Rep. of Pres. to Nat. Ass. 2005–; currently also Dir High-Tech Park Admin. *Publications include:* By The Road of the Dragon 1994, numerous articles on int. security, foreign policy and world economy. *Address:* Office of the President, Minsk, K. Marksa 38, Dom Urada, 220016 Minsk, Belarus (office). *Telephone:* (17) 222-60-06 (office). *Website:* www.president.gov.by (office).

TSERETELI, Zurab Konstantinovich; Georgian sculptor and artist; *President, Russian Academy of Arts;* b. 4 Jan. 1934, Tbilisi; m. Inessa Andronikashvili (deceased); one d.; ed Dept of Painting, Tbilisi Acad. of Arts; Chief Designer, Ministry of Foreign Affairs 1970–80; Prof. Brockport Univ. New York USA 1979; Chief Designer, Summer Olympic Games, Moscow 1980; Prof. Acad. of Arts, Tbilisi 1981; Deputy, Supreme Council of Georgia 1985–89; Chair. Union of Designers of Georgia 1987–91; Sec. USSR Union of Designers; USSR People's Deputy 1989–91; Pres. Moscow Int. Foundation for Support to UNESCO Russia 1992–; Chief Designer, War Memorial, Moscow 1995; Chief Designer, interior and exterior decoration of Cathedral of Christ the Saviour, Moscow 1995–2000; UNESCO

Goodwill Amb. 1996–; Chief Designer, Manezh Square and the underground shopping mall, Moscow 1997; Vice-Pres. Russian Acad. of Informatics 1998; Dir Moscow Museum of Modern Art 1999–; Dir Tsereteli Art Gallery, Moscow 2000–; mem. Russian Acad. of Arts 1989–, Pres. 1997–, Head Dept of Design; mem. Georgian Acad. of Arts 1996, Acad. of World Elite 1997, Acad. of Art of Kyrgyzstan 1998; corresp. mem. Spanish Royal Acad. of Fine Arts, Madrid, Spain 1998, French Acad. of Fine Arts, Paris, France; Vice-Pres. Russian Acad. of Creativity; author of numerous sculptures, mosaics, monumental murals, stained-glass windows, revived old technique of traditional Georgian enamel; creator of numerous monuments including Friendship in Moscow (with poet A. Voznesensky), Kindness Wins over Evil (New York, UN Bldg), Happiness for Children of the World (Univ. of Fine Arts, Brockport), Columbus (Miami), Birth of a New Man (London), Moment of Victory (Moscow), Peter the Great (Moscow), Tear of Grief (To the Struggle Against World Terrorism), Bayonne, New Jersey, and others in Tbilisi, Tokyo, Seville, Osaka, Brasília; Hero of Socialist Labour USSR 1991, Order, Friendship of Peoples, Russia 1994, Order for Services to the Fatherland (3rd Class, Russia) 1996, Hon. Cross Combattant Volontaire, Asscn of Veterans, French Resistance, France 2000, Order, Glory of Russia 2003, Int. Peace Prize, Jt Convent of Figures of Culture, USA 2003, Order for Services to the Fatherland (2nd Class) 2006, (1st Class) 2010, Chevalier, Légion d'honneur 2012; numerous awards including Lenin Prize 1976, State Prize of USSR 1978, 1983, People's Artist of Georgia 1978, of USSR 1979, of Russia 1994, Picasso Prize 1994, State Prize of Russia 1996, Vermeil Medal, Paris, France 1998, Prize of Modern Art 2000, Int. Recognition, Golden Hand (France) 2000, Medal for Services and Homeland, Russia 2003, Jewish Nat. Fund Tree of Life 2005. *Leisure interests:* collecting works of art. *Address:* Office of the President, Russian Academy of Arts, 21 Prechistenka str., 119034, Moscow (office); Bolshaya Gruzinskaya str. 17, 123557, Moscow, Russia (office). *Telephone:* (495) 201-36-65 (office), (495) 254-77-67 (home). *E-mail:* info@ tsereteli.ru. *Website:* en.rah.ru (office); www.mmoma.ru (office); www.tsereteli.ru (home).

TSHERING, Lyonpo Dago; Bhutanese diplomatist and politician; *Special Envoy of the Prime Minister and Foreign Policy Adviser to the Prime Minister;* b. 17 July 1941, Paro; ed Univ. of Bombay, Indian Admin. Service Training, Mussoorie and Indian Audit and Accounts Service Training, Simla, India, Univ. of Manchester, UK, Nat. Admin, Tokyo; Asst, Ministry of Devt 1961–62; Asst, Office of the Chief Sec. 1962–63; returned to Ministry of Devt 1963, Sec. 1965–71; mem. Nat. Ass. 1968–1990; mem. Royal Advisory Council 1968–70; First Sec., Bhutan Embassy in India 1971–73; Deputy Perm. Rep. to UN 1973–74, Perm. Rep. 1974–80, 1984–85; Amb. to Bangladesh 1980–84; Minister of Home Affairs 1985–98; Amb. to India 1998–2009; currently Special Envoy of the Prime Minister and Foreign Policy Adviser to the Prime Minister; Orange Scarf, Excellence in Diplomacy Award, India-Bhutan Friendship Asscn 2004. *Address:* Cabinet Secretariat, Tashichhodzong, Thimphu, Bhutan. *Telephone:* (2) 321437. *Fax:* (2) 321438. *Website:* www .cabinet.gov.bt.

TSHERING, Goonglon Wogma (Maj.-Gen.) Dozin Batoo; Bhutanese army officer; *Chief Operations Officer, Royal Bhutan Army;* b. Nov. 1951, Toebesa, Thimphu; ed Indian Mil. Acad., Dehradun, Defence Services Staff Coll., Wellington, India; completed Young Officer's Course, Commando Course, Intelligence Staff Officer's Course, Jr Command Course and Sr Command Course; commissioned into Royal Bhutan Army 1971, has held various command posts, apptd Operations and Training Officer 1976, commanded Wing 4 and Wing 7, apptd Commdt of mil. training centre 1988, Deputy Chief Operations Officer 1991, Commdr Command Centre 1997, promoted to rank of Dozin (Brig.) 1997; Deputy Chief Operations Officer Royal Bhutan Army Feb.–Nov. 2005, Chief Operations Officer Nov. 2005–; Druk Yurgyal Medal, Drakpoi Wangyal Medal, Drakpoi Thugsey Medal, Drakpoi Khorlo Medal. *Address:* Royal Bhutan Army Headquarters, Thimphu, Bhutan (office).

TSHERING, Kinga, BSc, MBA; Bhutanese banking executive; *CEO, DHI Infra Limited;* ed Univ. of Kansas, USA, School of Business, Pepperdine Univ., USA; Asst Engineer, Transmission Unit, Dept of Power 1994–96, Exec. Engineer 1996–99; Nat. Project Man. Water Resource Man. and Power Systems Master Plan Update Project Feb.–Oct. 2002; Gen. Man. Bhutan Power Corpn 2002–05; Head of Div., Renewable Energy Div., Dept of Energy, Ministry of Trade and Industry 2005–06; CEO Bhutan Electricity Authority, Ministry of Trade and Industry 2006–07; CEO Bank of Bhutan Ltd 2007–10; mem. Bd of Dirs Druk Holding and Investments Ltd 2007–08, CEO 2007–10, Project Dir Druk Holding and Investments Educ. City Project 2010, CEO DHI Infra Ltd 2011–; apptd mem. Bd of Dirs Bhutan Ferro Alloys Ltd 2007; Dispute Resolution Fellow, School of Law, Pepperdine Univ., USA 1999–2001. *Address:* DHI Infra Limited, POB 980, Thimphu, Bhutan (office). *Telephone:* (2) 331852 (office). *Fax:* (2) 332057 (office). *Website:* www.dhiinfra.bt (office).

TSHERING, Tashi, BSc, MSc; Bhutanese mining engineer, business executive and politician; *CEO, Penden Cement Authority Limited;* ed univs in USA; fmr Jt Dir of Geology and Mines, Ministry of Trade and Industry; fmr Deputy Man. Dir, later Officiating Man. Dir Dungsam Cement Project Authority (DCPA), fmr consultant to DCPA and other proposed cement plants; CEO Penden Cement Authority Ltd 2010–; fmr Resource Person for the Study on Strategic Partnership between PCAL and DCPA; campaigned for Nat. Council seat from Trashigang Dzongkag 2007. *Address:* Penden Cement Authority Ltd, Gomtu, Pagli Gewog, Samste, Dzongkhag, Bhutan (office). *Telephone:* (5) 371013 (office). *Fax:* (5) 371015 (office).

TSHERING, Lyonpo Ugyen, BA; Bhutanese politician and diplomatist; b. 8 Aug. 1954, Thimphu; m.; ed Univ. of California, Berkeley, USA; joined Govt Planning Comm. 1978, apptd Co-ordinator bilateral and multilateral assistance to Govt 1983, Project Co-ordinator, Computer Support Centre 1984, apptd Sec. Computerization Cttee 1983, Dir Planning Comm. 1986–89, now Vice-Chair.; Perm. Rep. to UN, New York 1989–98; apptd Editorial Adviser to Nat. Ass. 1980; fmr Chair. Asian Devt Bank; apptd Chair. World Bank Projects Implementation Cttee 1984; Chair. Tech. Cttee on Rural Devt, SAARC 1988–89; Sec., Ministry of Foreign Affairs 2001–03; Minister of Labour and Human Resources 2003–07 (resgnd), of Foreign Affairs 2008–13; Red Scarf 1998. *Address:* c/o Ministry of Foreign Affairs, Convention Centre, PO Box 103, Thimphu, Bhutan.

TSHISEKEDI WA MULUMBA, Etienne; Democratic Republic of the Congo politician; *Leader, Union pour la démocratie et le progrès social;* Prime Minister of Zaïre (now Democratic Repub. of the Congo) and C-in-C of Armed Forces Sept.–Oct. 1991, Prime Minister 1992–93 (dismissed by Pres. Mobutu March 1993), April 1997; Leader, Union pour la démocratie et le progrès social. *Address:* Union pour la démocratie et le progrès social (UDPS), 546 ave Zinnia, Limete, Kinshasa, Democratic Republic of the Congo (office). *Telephone:* 813140685 (office). *E-mail:* udps@globalserve.net. *Website:* www.udps.net.

TSHULTIM, Dasho Jigme, BA; Bhutanese diplomatist and politician; ed St Joseph's Coll., Darjeeling, India, Univ. of Manchester, UK; served in Govt as Head of Tourism, Dzongda and Zhung Dronyer (Chief of Protocol); Amb. to Bangladesh (also accred to Pakistan, Maldives, Sri Lanka and S Korea) 2004–07; mem. Bhutan People's Unity Party; mem. Parl. for Radhi-Sakteng constituency, Trashigang 2008–, Speaker of Nat Ass. 2008–13. *Address:* National Assembly Secretariat, Gyelyong Tshokhang, PO Box 139, Thimphu, Bhutan (office). *E-mail:* jtshultim@nab.gov.bt (office).

TSIEN, Roger Y., PhD; American chemical biologist and academic; *Professor of Pharmacology, School of Medicine and Professor of Chemistry and Biochemistry, University of California, San Diego;* b. 1 Feb. 1952, New York, NY; ed Livingston High School, Harvard Coll. and Univ. of Cambridge, UK; Postdoctoral Fellow, Gonville and Caius Coll., Cambridge; fmr Faculty mem., Univ. of California, Berkeley; Prof. of Pharmacology, School of Medicine and Prof. of Chem. and Biochemistry, Univ. of California, San Diego 1989–; Investigator, Howard Hughes Medical Inst. 1989–; mem. Inst. of Medicine, NAS; Hon. FRSC 2008; Hon. Academician, Academia Sinica 2008; Hon. DSc (Univ. of Hong Kong) 2009, (Chinese Univ. of Hong Kong) 2009; Searle Scholar 1983, Gairdner Foundation Int. Award 1995, Artois-Baillet-Latair Health Prize 1995, ACS Creative Invention Award 2002, Protein Soc. Anfinsen Award 2002, Dr A.H. Heineken Prize in Biochemistry 2002, Royal Netherlands Acad. of Sciences Award, Wolf Prize in Medicine (jtly) 2004, Keio Medical Science Prize 2004, Rosenstiel Award 2006, E.B. Wilson Medal 2008, Nobel Prize in Chem. (jtly) 2008, Distinguished Science and Technology Award, The 2009 Asian American Engineers of the Year Award 2009, Lifetime Innovation Award, Univ. of California, San Diego 2009, AHA Distinguished Scientists, American Heart Asscn 2009, Molecular Imaging Research Award, Soc. of Molecular Imaging 2009, Gen. Pres. Gold Medal, 97th Indian Science Congress 2010, RSC Spiers Memorial Award 2010. *Publications:* numerous articles in scientific journals on signal transduction, especially in neurons and cancer cells, with the help of designed molecules, imaging, and photochemical manipulation. *Address:* Tsien Laboratory, Howard Hughes Medical Insititute, 9500 Gilman Drive, CMM West Room 310, La Jolla, CA 92093-0647, USA (office). *Telephone:* (858) 534-4891 (office); (858) 534-7009 (Lab.) (office). *Fax:* (858) 534-5270 (office). *E-mail:* rtsien@ucsd.edu (office). *Website:* www.tsienlab.ucsd.edu (office).

TSIPRAS, Alexis; Greek politician; *Leader, Coalition of the Radical Left (SYRIZA);* b. 28 July 1974, Athens; partner Peristera Baziana; two s.; ed Ampelokipoi Br. High School, Nat. Tech. Univ. of Athens (NTUA); worked as civil engineer in construction industry; joined Communist Youth of Greece late 1980s, active in student uprising in early 1990s; mem. Exec. Bd Students' Union, Civil Eng School, NTUA, student rep. at Univ. Senate; elected rep. on Cen. Council of Nat. Students Union of Greece (EFEE) 1995–97; left party to remain in coalition following departure of CP of Greece from Synaspismós coalition of radical parties; first person to hold position of Political Sec. of youth wing of Synaspismós Neolaia Syn 1999–2003; elected mem. Synaspismós party's Cen. Political Cttee and to its Political Secr. 2004; ran for Municipality of Athens on the Anoihti Poli (Open Town) Coalition of the Radical Left (Synaspismós Rhizospastikís Aristerás–SYRIZA) ticket in local elections 2006; Chair. Synaspismós 2008–; mem. Vouli (Parl.) for the Athens A' constituency 2009–; elected unanimously by Secr. of SYRIZA as Head of the Coalition of the Radical Left (SYRIZA) parl. group, SYRIZA came second in legis. election May 2012, mandated by Pres. Karolos Papoulias to form a coalition govt 8 May 2012, announced he had failed to form a coalition the following day; Leader of the Opposition June 2012–; Party of the European Left nominee for Pres. of the EC in 2014 European Parl. election. *Leisure interest:* supports Panathinaikos Football Club. *Address:* Synaspismós – Coalition of the Left of Movements and Ecology, Pl. Eleftherias 1, 105 53 Athens (office); Coalition of the Radical Left (SYRIZA), Odos Valtetsiou 39, 10681 Athens, Greece (office). *Telephone:* (210) 3378522 (Synaspismós) (office); (210) 3829910 (SYRIZA) (office). *Fax:* (210) 3219914 (Synaspismós) (office); (210) 3217003 (Synaspismós) (office); (210) 3829911 (SYRIZA) (office). *E-mail:* foreignpolicy@syn.gr (office); info@syriza.gr (office). *Website:* www.syn.gr (office); www.syriza.gr (office).

TSISKARIDZE, Nikolai; Georgian ballet dancer; b. 31 Dec. 1973, Tbilisi; s. of Maxim Tsiskaridze and Lamara Tsiskaridze; ed Tbilisi Ballet School, Bolshoi Ballet Acad., Moscow Choreographic Inst.; joined the Bolshoi Ballet 1992, prin. dancer –2013; numerous prizes including Silver Medal, 7th Japan World Ballet Competition, Osaka 1995, Soul of Dance Rising Star Nat. Prize 1995, First Prize and Gold Medal, 8th Moscow Int. Ballet Competition 1997, Merited Artist of Russia 1997, La Sylphide Russian Nat. Dance Org. Diploma Dancer of the Year 1997, Gold Mask, Russian Nat. Award for Best Male Role 1999, 2000, Benois de la Danse Int. Award, Dancer of the Year 1999, Mayor of Moscow Prize in Literature and Art 2000. *Dance:* roles in numerous ballets including Sleeping Beauty, Gisèle, Raymonda, La Sylphide, La Bayadère, The Nutcracker, Swan Lake, Romeo and Juliet, Legend of Love, Narcissus, Pharaoh's Daughter, etc. *Leisure interest:* reading. *Address:* Komsomolsky Prospekt 35, Apt. 106, Moscow 119146, Russia (home). *Telephone:* (495) 242-29-79 (home).

TSOHATZOPOULOS, Apostolos-Athanasios; Greek politician and civil engineer; b. 1939, Athens; m. Mrs Vassiliki Stamati; two s. one d.; ed Tech. Univ. of Munich, FRG; deprived of citizenship by mil. dictatorship 1969; active in Panhellenic Liberation Movt, mem. Nat. Council during dictatorship; returned to Greece 1974; mem. Cen. Cttee and Exec. Office PASOK 1974–90, Gen. Sec. 1990–95, mem. Exec. Office 1995–; mem. Parl. 1981–; Minister of Public Works 1981–84, to the Prime Minister 1986–87, of the Interior 1987–89, of Transport and Communications 1989, of the Interior 1993–94, 1995–96, of Nat. Defence 1996–2001, of Devt 2002–04. *Address:* Komna Traka 3, 11257 Athens (office); Omirou 8, 10564 Athens, Greece. *Telephone:* (210) 3216059 (office). *Fax:* (210)

3246070 (office). *E-mail:* tsoha-ath@ath.forthnet.gr (office). *Website:* www.akis.gr (office).

TSONEV, Nikolai Georgiev, PhD; Bulgarian economist, academic, politician and fmr army officer; b. 9 June 1956, Pernik; ed Nat. Artillery Mil. School, Shumen, Vassilyevski Air Defence School, Kyiv, Ukrainian SSR, Univ. for Nat. and World Economy, Sofia, Sofia Univ. St Kliment of Ohrid; officer in Bulgarian Army 1978–92; man. of several limited liability firms 1992–99; Dir Public Procurement Directorate, Ministry of Defence 1999–2000, adviser to Minister of Defence 2001–02, Dir of Social Activities Directorate 2002–08, Minister of Defence 2008–09; charged by prosecuting magistrates for equipment purchase deal alleged to have lost the public purse 12.9 million leva ($9 million) Nov. 2009; Prof. of Strategic Planning, Civic Admin and European Integration Inst. 2002–; Prof., Univ. for Nat. and World Economy, Sofia 2004–. *Address:* c/o Ministry of Defence, 1000 Sofia, ul. Dyakon Ignatiy 3, Bulgaria (office).

TSONGA, Jo-Wilfried; French professional tennis player; b. 17 April 1985, Le Mans; s. of Didier Tsonga and Évelyne Tsonga; ed Univ. of Maine, USA; won US Open Juniors title against Marcos Baghdatis in the final 2003; also reached semifinals of other three Grand Slam events; turned professional 2004; suffered several injuries that kept him from playing 2004–06; won first ATP Masters Series championship at Paris Masters 2008; qualified for Tennis Masters Cup, Shanghai 2008; winner, Bangkok, Thailand 2008, Johannesburg 2009, Marseille 2009, 2013, Tokyo 2009, Metz, France 2011, Vienna 2011; semifinalist, French Open 2013; finalist, ATP World Tour Finals 2011; mem. Tennis Club de Paris; lives in La Rippe, Switzerland. *E-mail:* agence@interactive-one.fr (office). *Website:* www.interactive-one.fr (office); www.jowiltsonga.fr.

TSUDA, Hiroshi; Japanese automotive industry executive; fmr Sr Man. Dir Suzuki Motor Corpn, Pres. and COO 2003–08, Sr Advisor 2008–. *Address:* Suzuki Motor Corpn, 300 Takatsuka-cho, Minami-ku, Hamamatsu-shi, Shizuoka 432-8611, Japan (office). *Telephone:* (53) 440-2023 (office). *Fax:* (53) 440-2776 (office). *E-mail:* info@suzuki.co.jp (office). *Website:* www.suzuki.co.jp (office); www.globalsuzuki.com (office).

TSUGA, Kazuhiro, BS, MS; Japanese business executive; *President and Representative Director, Panasonic Corporation;* ed Osaka Univ., Univ. of California, Santa Barbara, USA; joined Panasonic (then known as Matsushita Electric Industrial Co. Ltd) 1979, held positions of increasing responsibility, including Head of Advanced Appliances Devt Centre for Audiovisual Technologies 2001–04, Exec. Officer 2004–08, Pres. Automotive Systems Co. and Man. Exec. Officer, Panasonic Corpn 2008–11, Head of Overseas R&D Centres and Digital Network Strategic Planning Office, Pres. AVC Networks Co. 2011–12, also Sr Man. Dir and mem. Bd, Pres. and Rep. Dir Panasonic Corpn 2012–. *Address:* Panasonic Corporation, Corporate Headquarters, 1006 Oaza Kadoma, Kadoma-shi, Osaka 571-8501, Japan (office). *Telephone:* (6) 6908-1121 (office). *Fax:* (6) 6908-2351 (office). *E-mail:* info@panasonic.net (office). *Website:* www.panasonic.net (office).

TSUI, Daniel C., PhD; American (b. Chinese) physicist and academic; *Arthur LeGrand Doty Professor of Electrical Engineering, Princeton University;* b. 1939, Henan, China; ed Univ. of Chicago; Arthur LeGrand Doty Prof. of Electrical Eng, Princeton Univ. 1982–; mem. NAS, Acad. Sinica, American Acad. of Arts and Sciences, Chinese Acad. of Sciences; Fellow, American Physics Soc.; Nobel Prize in Physics for discovery of fractional quantum Hall effect (jtly with Robert B. Laughlin and Horst L. Störmer) 1998, Benjamin Franklin Medal 1998. *Publications:* numerous articles in scientific journals. *Address:* Room B-426, Engineering Quadrangle, Princeton University, Olden Street, Princeton, NJ 08544, USA (office). *Telephone:* (609) 258-2544 (office). *Fax:* (609) 258-6279 (office). *E-mail:* tsui@princeton.edu (office). *Website:* www.ee.princeton.edu (office).

TSUI, Lap-Chee, OC, OOnt, BSc, MPhil, PhD, FRS, FRSC; Canadian geneticist, academic and university administrator; b. 21 Dec. 1950, Shanghai, China; s. of Jing Lue Hsue and Hui Ching Wang; m. (Ellen) Lan Fong 1977; two s.; ed The Chinese Univ. of Hong Kong, Univ. of Pittsburgh, USA; staff geneticist, Dept of Genetics and scientist, The Research Inst., Hosp. for Sick Children, Toronto, Canada 1983–88, Sr Research Scientist 1988–89, Sellers Chair in Cystic Fibrosis Research 1989–, Geneticist-in-Chief 1996–2002; Asst Prof. Depts of Medical Genetics and Medical Biophysics, Univ. of Toronto 1983–88, Assoc. Prof. 1988–90, Prof., Dept of Molecular and Medical Genetics 1990–2006, Univ. Prof. 1994–2006, H.E. Sellers Chair in Cystic Fibrosis 1998–2006; Vice-Chancellor and Pres., The Univ. of Hong Kong 2002–13; Howard Hughes Int. Scholar 1991–96; Assoc. Ed. Clinical Genetics 1991–; Ed. Int. Journal of Genome Research 1990, Assoc. Ed. Genomics 1994–; mem. Editorial Bd several scientific journals; Adviser, European Journal of Human Genetics 1992–; Dir American Soc. of Human Genetics, Mon Sheong Foundation, Educ. Foundation, Fed. of Chinese Canadian Professionals; Foreign Assoc., NAS 2004; Foreign mem., Chinese Acad. of Science 2009–; Pres. The Human Genome Org.; Lee Kuan Yew Distinguished Visitor, Singapore 2000; Foreign Mem. Chinese Academy of Science 2009; Hon. Pres., Prix Galien 1998, Hon. mem. World Innovation Foundation 2001, Hon. FRCP (UK) 2005, Hon. Fellow, Hong Kong Coll. of Physicians 2005, Hong Kong Coll. of Pathologists 2005, Hong Kong Coll. of Pathologists 2006, Univ. of Cambridge 2012; Chevalier, Légion d'honneur 2007, Gold Bauhinia Star of the Hong Kong SAR 2011; Dr hc (St Francis Xavier Univ., Antigonish, NS) 1994, (York Univ., Toronto) 2001, (Tel-Aviv Univ.) 2005, (King's Coll. London) 2009, (Univ. of Edinburgh) 2010, (Fudan Univ.) 2013; Hon. DSc (Univ. of New Brunswick) 1991, (Chinese Univ. of Hong Kong) 1992, (Univ. of Toronto) 2007, (Univ. of Aberdeen) 2007, (Western Univ.) 2013; Hon. DCL (Univ. King's Coll.) 1991; numerous prizes and awards, including Scientist Award, Medical Research Council (Canada) 1989–93, Gold Medal of Honour, Pharmaceutical Mfrs Asscn of Canada 1989, RSC Centennial Award 1989, Award of Excellence, Genetic Soc. of Canada 1990, Gairdner Int. Award 1990, Canadian Achiever Award 1991, Sarstedt Research Prize 1993, XII San Remo Int. Award for Genetic Research 1993, J.P. Lecocq Prize 1994, Henry Friesen Award, Canadian Soc. of Clinical Investigation and Royal Coll. of Physicians and Surgeons of Canada 1995, Medal of Honour, Canadian Medical Asscn 1996, Distinguished Scientist Award, MRC 2000, Zellers Senior Scientist Award, Canadian Cystic Fibrosis Foundation 2001, Killam Prize, Canada Council 2002, Queen's Golden Jubilee Medal 2002, Distinguished Achievement Award, Chinese American Physicians Soc. 2004, European Cystic Fibrosis Soc. Award 2009, Laureate, Canadian Medical

Hall of Fame 2012. *Achievements include:* identified the defective gene (viz. Cystic Fibrosis Transmembrane Regulator (CFTR)) that causes cystic fibrosis. *Publications include:* numerous scientific papers and reviews. *Leisure interests:* travel, good food. *Address:* c/o Vice-Chancellor's Office, The University of Hong Kong, 10/F Knowles Building, Pokfulam Road, Hong Kong Special Administrative Region, People's Republic of China. *E-mail:* tsuilc@hku.hk.

TSUJII, Akio; Japanese transport industry executive; *Chairman, Kinki Nippon Railway Company;* Pres. Kinki Nippon Railway Co. Ltd –2003, apptd CEO 2003, Chair. 2003–. *Address:* Kinki Nippon Railway Company Ltd, 6-1-55 Uehommachi Tennoji-ku, Osaka 543-8585, Japan (office). *Telephone:* (6) 6775-3465 (office). *Fax:* (6) 6775-3467 (office). *Website:* www.kintetsu.co.jp (office).

TSUKAMOTO, Hiroshi; Japanese national organization official and fmr government official; *President, Institute for International Studies and Training;* b. 10 March 1946; ed Kyoto Univ.; joined Ministry of Int. Trade and Industry—MITI (now Ministry of Economy, Trade and Industry) 1968, First Sec., Embassy in Jakarta 1979–82, Dir for Int. Petroleum Affairs, Petroluem Dept, Natural Resources and Energy Agency April–Dec. 1982, Dir Middle East Office, West Europe-Africa-Middle East Div., Int. Trade Policy Bureau, Nat. Land Agency 1982–84, Office Dir Regional Devt Bureau 1984–86; Visiting Research Fellow, Royal Inst. of Int. Affairs (now Chatham House), London 1986; Dir-Gen. for Gen. Coordination Dept, MITI Osaka Bureau 1987–89, Dir Fiber and Spinning Div., Consumer Goods Industry Bureau 1989–91, Dir Policy Planning Office, Minister's Secr. 1991–92, now Special Adviser; Pres. Japan External Trade Org. (JETRO), New York 1992–94, Pres. JETRO, Tokyo 2002–07; Pres. Inst. for Int. Studies and Training 2007–; Commr Gen. of Japan Pavilion, Expo 2010, Shanghai 2010; mem. Bd of Dir NHK International, Inc.; Deputy Dir-Gen. for Global Environment Affairs (MITI) 1994–95; Exec. Dir People's Finance Corpn 1995–97; Pres. Electronic Industries Asscn of Japan (later Japan Electronics and Information Tech. Industries Asscn) 1997–2002. *Address:* Office of the President, Institute for International Studies and Training, Toranomon Jitsugyokaikan 2F, 1-1-20 Toranomon, Minato-ku, Tokyo 105-0001, Japan (office). *Telephone:* (3) 3503-6621 (office). *Fax:* (3) 3501-0550 (office). *E-mail:* info@iist.or.jp (office). *Website:* (office).

TSUKAMOTO, Takashi; Japanese business executive; *Chairman, Mizuho Financial Group, Inc.;* b. 2 Aug. 1950; joined Dai-Ichi Kangyo Bank Ltd 1974; Exec. Officer/Gen. Man. Human Resources Div., Mizuho Corp. Bank Ltd 2002–03, Man. Exec. Officer/Head of Risk Man. Group, Head of Human Resources Group and Gen. Man. Post-retirement Counselling, Mizuho Financial Group, Inc. 2003–04, Man. Exec. Officer/Head of Risk Man. Group and Head of Human Resources Group Feb.–April 2004, Man. Exec. Officer/Head of Europe, Middle East and Africa, Mizuho Corp. Bank Ltd 2004–06, Man. Dir/Chief Strategy Officer and Chief Financial Officer 2006–07, Deputy Pres. 2007–08, Deputy Pres.-Exec. Officer/Head of Financial Control and Accounting Group, Mizuho Financial Group, Inc. April 2008, Pres. and CEO Mizuho Financial Strategy Co. Ltd 2008–09, Deputy Pres./Head of Financial Control and Accounting Group, Mizuho Financial Group, Inc. 2008–09, Pres. and CEO/Head of Human Resources Group 2009–10, Pres. and CEO 2010–11, Chair. 2011–, Pres. and CEO Mizuho Bank Ltd 2011–. *Address:* Mizuho Financial Group, Inc., Marunouchi 2-chome Building, 2-5-1, Marunouchi, Chiyoda-ku, Tokyo 100-8333, Japan (office). *Telephone:* (3) 5224-1111 (office). *Fax:* (3) 3215-4616 (office). *E-mail:* info@mizuho-fg.co.jp (office). *Website:* www.mizuho-fg.co.jp (office).

TSUKANOV, Nikolay; Russian politician; *Governor of Kaliningrad;* b. 22 March 1965, Lipovo; m. Svetlana Tsukanov; one s.; ed Moscow Higher School of Privatization and Entrepreneurship, Kazan Tupolev State Technical Univ.; served in army 1983–85; Mayor of Gusev 2005–09, Head of Gusev municipal area 2009–10; mem. United Russia (Yedinaya Rossiya), Head of Kaliningrad Br. July 2010–; Gov. of Kaliningrad 2010–. *Leisure interests:* hunting, fishing. *Address:* Office of the Governor, 236007 Kaliningrad, ul. D. Donskogo 1, Russia (office).

TSUKIOKA, Takashi; Japanese business executive; *CEO and Representative Director, Idemitsu Kosan Company Limited;* joined Idemitsu Kosan Co. Ltd in 1975, Man. of Kobe Br. 2002–05, Man. of Chubu Br. 2005–07, Exec. Officer of Man. Supply and Demand Dept 2007–08, Man. Exec. Officer and Man. Supply and Demand Dept 2008–09, Rep. Dir 2009–, Man. Dir, later Exec. Vice-Pres., Pres. Idemitsu Kosan Co. Ltd –2013, CEO 2013–. *Address:* Idemitsu Kosan Company Ltd, 1-1, Marunouchi 3-chome, Chiyoda-ku, Tokyo 100-8321, Japan (office). *Telephone:* (3) 3213-3115 (office). *Fax:* (3) 3213-9354 (office). *E-mail:* info@idemitsu .com (office). *Website:* www.idemitsu.com (office).

TSUKUDA, Kazuo, BS, MS; Japanese engineering industry executive; *Senior Corporate Advisor, Mitsubishi Heavy Industries;* b. 1 Sept. 1943; m. Yoshiko Kazuo; ed Univ. of Tokyo; joined Mitsubishi Heavy Industries 1968, engineer 1968–79, liaison to Westinghouse 1979–81, steam-turbine engineer 1982–95, Deputy Gen. Man., Takasago Machinery Works 1995–99, Gen. Man., Nagoya Machinery Works 1999–2000, Gen. Man., Industrial Machinery Div. 2000–02, Man. Dir and Gen. Man., Global Strategic Planning and Operations HQ 2002–03, Pres. and CEO Mitsubishi Heavy Industries 2003–08, Chair. 2008–13, Sr Corp. Advisor 2013–, Dir Mitsubishi Research Inst., Inc. 2010–. *Address:* Mitsubishi Heavy Industries, 16-5, Konan 2-chome, Minato-ku, Tokyo 108-8215, Japan (office). *Telephone:* (3) 6716-3111 (office). *Fax:* (3) 6716-5800 (office). *E-mail:* info@ mhi.co.jp (office). *Website:* www.mhi.co.jp (office).

TSUMBA, Leonard Ladislas, PhD; Zimbabwean economist, academic and banker; *Chairman, Dairibord Holdings Zimbabwe Limited (DHZL);* b. 27 June 1943, Harare; s. of Ladislus Million Tsumba and Regina Tsumba; m. Nola Arne Yasinski 1969; two d.; ed Georgetown Univ., Howard Univ., Virginia Polytechnic Inst. and State Univ. (Virginia Tech), Blacksburg, Va, USA; Instructor in Econs, Hampton Inst., USA 1970–72; Asst Prof. of Econs, Trinity Coll., USA 1975–77, 2007; consultant, Money and Finance Div. UNCTAD 1979; with CitiBank NA, USA 1977–81; Exec. Asst to Gov. Reserve Bank of Zimbabwe 1981–82, Gen. Man. 1982–86, Deputy Gov. 1986–87, Group Chief Exec. 1987–83, Gov. 1993–2003; Chief Exec. and Man. Dir Finhold/Zimbabwe Banking Corpn 1987–93; Chair. Central African Bldg Soc. 2004–; Chair. Dairibord Holdings Zimbabwe Ltd (DHZL) 2012–. *Leisure interest:* golf. *Address:* Dairibord Holdings Limited, ZB Life Towers, 77 Jason Moyo Avenue/Sam Nujoma Streets, PO Box 587, Harare (office); 23 Shawasha Hills, PO Box Ch 147, Chisipite, Harare, Zimbabwe (home). *Telephone:*

(4) 790801-8 (office); (91) 282791 (home). *Fax:* (4) 795220 (office); (4) 582791 (home). *E-mail:* zwtsumba@zol.co.zw. *Website:* www.dairibord.com (office).

TSUSHKO, Vasyl Petrovych; Ukrainian economist and politician; *Chairman, Socialist Party of Ukraine;* b. 1 Feb. 1963, Nadrichne, Tarutynsky Dist, Odesa Oblast; m.; one s. one d.; ed Izmayil Tech. School of Agric., Odesa Agric. Inst. and Nat. Univ. of Internal Affairs; served in Soviet Army 1983–85; Deputy Dir and Dir of various state farms 1988–97; Gov. Odesa Regional State Admin 2005–06; Minister of Internal Affairs 2006–07, of the Economy March–Dec. 2010; mem. Parl. and Leader Parl. faction Socialist Party of Ukraine (Sotsialistychna Partiya Ukrainy—SPU) –2006, Chair. SPU 2010–. *Address:* Socialist Party of Ukraine (Sotsialistychna Partiya Ukrainy), 02100 Kyiv, vul. Bazhova 12, Ukraine (office). *Telephone:* (44) 296-68-27 (office). *Fax:* (44) 296-68-27 (office). *E-mail:* zegal@ socialist.in.ua (home). *Website:* www.spu.in.ua (office).

TSUTSUI, Yoshinobu, BA; Japanese business executive; *President and Representative Director, Nippon Life Insurance Company;* b. 30 Jan. 1954, Hyogo Pref.; ed Kyoto Univ.; joined Nippon Life Insurance Co. 1977, Gen. Man. Nagaoka Br. 1999–2001, Gen. Man. Public Affairs Dept 2001–03, Gen. Man. Corp. Planning Dept 2003–04, Dir and Gen. Man. 2004–07, Dir, Exec. Officer and Gen. Man. Corp. Planning Dept and Risk Man. Dept Jan.–March 2007, Dir, Man. Exec. Officer and Gen. Man. Legal Office, Head of Corp. Admin Sector (Corp. Planning, Public & Investors Relations, Planning and Research, Actuarial, and Legal related) 2007–09, Dir and Sr Man. Exec. Officer 2009–10, Dir and Sr Man. Exec., Head of Investment Man. Sector (Credit, and Securities Operation related) and Corp. Admin Sector 2010–11, Pres. and Rep. Dir Nippon Life Insurance Co. 2011–; Ind. Dir, Imperial Hotel Ltd 2011–. *Address:* Nippon Life Insurance Co., 3-5-12 Imabashi, Chuo-ku, Osaka 541-8501, Japan (office). *Telephone:* (6) 6209-5525 (office). *Fax:* (3) 5510-7340 (office). *E-mail:* info@nissay.co.jp (office). *Website:* www .nissay.co.jp (office).

TSUYA, Masaaki, BA (Econ), MBA; Japanese business executive; *Chairman, CEO and Representative Director, Bridgestone Corporation;* ed Hitotsubashi Univ., Univ. of Chicago, USA; Dir Div. of Int. Relations and Licenses, Bridgestone Corpn Co. Ltd 2004, served as Dir of Internal Auditing Office, Office of Group CEO and Vice-Pres. Bridgestone Corpn, served as Chief Compliance Officer, Chief Human Rights Officer, Chief Risk-Management Officer, Vice-Pres. and Sr Officer, Bridgestone Corpn, Chair. Bridgestone Americas, Inc. Jan.–March 2011, CEO Bridgestone Corpn 2012–, Chair. 2013–; Dir, Inoue Rubber Vietnam Co. Ltd; Ind. Dir, Inoue Rubber Thailand Public Co. Ltd 2001–09. *Address:* Bridgestone Corporation, 10-1, Kyobashi 1-chome, Chuo-ku, Tokyo 104-8340, Japan (office). *Telephone:* (3) 3567-0111 (office). *Fax:* (3) 3535-2553 (office). *E-mail:* info@ bridgestone.co.jp (office). *Website:* www.bridgestone.co.jp (office).

TSVANGIRAI, Morgan Richard; Zimbabwean trade union official and politician; b. 1952, Gutu, Masvingo; m. 1st Susan Tsvangirai 1978 (died 2009); six c.; m. 2nd Elizabeth Macheka 2011; ed Silveria and Gokomere High Schools, Harvard Univ., USA; with Mutare Clothing Co. 1972–74; mem. local textile union; rose from plant operator to foreman Trojan Nickel Mine, Bindura 1974–84; mem. Associated Mine Workers' Union, apptd Br. Chair. 1984; fmr exec. mem. Nat. Mine Workers' Union; elected Sec.-Gen. Zimbabwe Congress of Trade Unions (ZCTU) 1988; charged with being a spy for SA, imprisoned for six weeks 1989; Founder and Chair. Nat. Constitutional Ass.; organized series of anti-Govt strikes against tax rises 1997; Founder and Pres. Movement for Democratic Change (MDC) 1999–; Parl. Opposition Leader 2000–09; unsuccessful Presidential cand. 2002, 2008, 2013; charged with treason Feb. 2002 and put on trial for allegedly plotting the assassination of Pres. Robert Mugabe (q.v.), acquitted Oct. 2004; Prime Minister 2009–13. *Leisure interests:* reading, spending time with family. *Address:* Movement for Democratic Change, Harvest House, 6th Floor, cnr Angwa St and Nelson Mandela Ave, Harare, Zimbabwe (office). *Website:* www.mdczimbabwe.org (office).

TSVETANOV, Tsvetan Genchev; Bulgarian politician; *Deputy Chairperson, Citizens for European Development Board;* b. 8 April 1965, Sofia; m. Desislava Tsvetanova; three d.; ed Nat. Sports Acad., Sofia, Inst. of Postgraduate Studies with Univ. of Nat. and World Economy, Sofia; Specialist, Inspector, Sr Inspector, Chief Inspector, Team Leader, Ministry of the Interior (MoI) Cen. Information, Analysis and Org. Service and at MoI Information Tech. and Automation of Man. Service 1987–2001; Sr Expert, sector Nat. Services, Specialized and Gen. Admin, Schools, Research Insts, R&D Insts and Specialized Anti-Terrorism Unit, Human Resource Man. Div., MoI, 7th Sr Rank 1997–2001; Head of Dept/Operational Asst to MoI Sec. Gen./MoI Cen. Admin 2001–05; Deputy Mayor for Public Order and Security, Sofia Municipality Nov. 2005; mem. 41st Nat. Ass. (Citizens for European Devt of Bulgaria—GERB) for Veliko Turnovo Constituency 2009–, Deputy Chair. 2014–; Deputy Prime Minister and Minister of the Interior 2009–13; govt cand. for presidential election 2011; Silver Cross of the Order of Merit of the Spanish Civil Guard 2014; numerous awards from man. of Ministry of the Interior 1987–2005, White Cross of Law Enforcement Merit Medal, Spanish Nat. Police, Ministry of the Interior of Spain 2005, Certificate for outstanding int. operational police cooperation, Dir of Europol 2009, Insignia of Honour for outstanding performance of official duties, Minister of the Interior of Lithuania 2009. *Address:* Citizens for European Development of Bulgaria (GERB), NPC Office Building, floor 17, Pl. 1, 1000 Sofia, Bulgaria (office). *Telephone:* (2) 490-13-13 (office). *Fax:* (2) 490-09-51 (office). *E-mail:* pr@gerb.bg (office). *Website:* www.gerb.bg (office).

TSVETKOV, Aleksey, PhD; Russian poet and critic; b. 2 Feb. 1947, Stanislaw (now Ivano-Frankivsk), Ukraine; s. of Petr Tsvetkov and Bella Tsvetkov (née Tsyganov); m. Olga Samilenko 1978; ed Odessa Univ., Moscow Univ., Univ. of Michigan, USA; journalist in Siberia and Kazakhstan; poetry recitals and participant in Volgin's Moscow Univ. literary soc. Luch 1970–75; emigrated to USA 1974; co-f Russkaya zhizn', San Francisco 1976–77; Prof. of Russian Language and Literature, Dickinson Coll., Pa 1981–85; broadcaster, Voice of America (to Germany and Czech Republic); poetry has appeared in Kontinent, Ekho, Vremya i my, Apollon, Glagol and elsewhere; Dr hc (Univ. of Mich.) 1977. *Publications include:* A Collection of Pieces for Life Solo 1978, Three Poets: Kuzminsky, Tsvetkov, Limonov 1981, Dream State 1981, Eden 1985, Simply Voice 1991, The Last Continent 2012. *Leisure interest:* collecting baroque opera records.

TSZYU, Kostya; Australian (b. Russian) professional super-lightweight boxer; b. 19 Sept. 1969, Serov, Russia; youngest person to win Russian National Championships (aged 16); six times Russian champion, three times European champion; won gold medal World Amateur Championships, Sydney 1991; emigrated to Australia 1991; won International Boxing Federation (IBF) World Super-Lightweight Championship Jan. 1995, lost title to Vince Phillips May 1997; won World Boxing Asscn (WBA) and World Boxing Council (WBC) World Super-Lightweight Championships Feb. 2001 v. Sharmba Mitchell; won Undisputed World Super-Lightweight Championship Nov. 2001 v. Zab Judah, became first in 40 years to unify the division, one of only three undisputed champions, two defences; stripped of WBA title for failing to make mandatory defence June 2004; beat Sharmba Mitchell again to retain WBC and IBF titles; won 30 fights, including 24 knock-outs, one defeat; rated 4th best pound-for-pound boxer by USA Today Oct. 2003; trainer Johnny Lewis. *Address:* c/o Sports Management Australia, POB 66, Miller's Point, NSW 2000, Australia (office). *Fax:* (2) 9548-5789. *E-mail:* webmaster@kostyatszyu.com; mwatt@smagroup.com.au (office).

TU, Youyou, BSc, PhD; Chinese medical scientist, pharmaceutical chemist and academic; *Chief Scientist, China Academy of Chinese Medical Sciences;* b. 30 Dec. 1930, Ningbo, Zhejiang Prov.; m.; ed Peking Univ. School of Medicine (Medical School became ind. Beijing Medical Coll., renamed Beijing Medical Univ. 1985, latter merged with Peking Univ. to become Peking Univ. Health Science Centre); studied at Dept of Pharmaceutical Sciences, graduated 1955; trained for two and a half years in traditional Chinese medicine; worked at Acad. of Chinese Medicine (now China Acad. of Chinese Medical Sciences), Beijing following graduation, promoted to tenured researcher (as grad. tutor) 1980, promoted to academic adviser for doctorate cands 2001, currently Chief Scientist; best known for discovering artemisinin (also known as Qinghaosu) and dihydroartemisinin, used for treating malaria; Nat. Science Congress Prize 1978, Albert Einstein World Science Prize, World Culture Council 1987, (one of the) Ten Science and Technology Achievements in China, State Science Comm. 1992, (one of the) Ten Great Public Health Achievements in New China 1997, GlaxoSmithKline Outstanding Achievement Award in Life Science 2011, Lasker-DeBakey Clinical Medical Research Award 2011, Outstanding Contrib. Award, China Acad. of Chinese Medical Research 2011, (one of the Ten) Nat. Outstanding Females 2012. *Publications:* numerous papers in professional journals. *Address:* China Academy of Chinese Medical Sciences, Beijing 100700, People's Republic of China (office). *Telephone:* (10) 6401-4356 (office). *E-mail:* info@catcm.ac.cn (office). *Website:* www .catcm.ac.cn (office).

TUBAYYEB, Samir A., BEng, PhD, MBA; Saudi Arabian petroleum industry executive; *CEO, S-Oil Corporation;* ed King Fahad Univ. of Petroleum and Minerals, Univ. of Calif., Berkeley, Harvard Business School; in various positions over 25 years with Saudi Aramco, including Project Man., Jt Venture and Planning; Rep. Dir and CEO S-Oil Corpn 2005–; Maeil Business Economy CEO of the Year 2007. *Address:* S-Oil Corporation, PO Box 758, 60 Yoido-dong, Yeongdungpo-gu, Seoul 150-607, Republic of Korea (office). *Telephone:* (2) 3772-5151 (office). *Fax:* (2) 783-7993 (office). *Website:* www.s-oil.com (office).

TUBMAN, Winston; Liberian lawyer, diplomatist and politician; ed London School of Econs and Univ. of Cambridge, UK and Harvard Law School, USA; taught law at Univ. of Liberia and at univs in USA 1968–72; est. Tubman Law Firm, Monrovia 1968, Man. and Sr Partner until late 1980s; Prin. Legal Officer, Office of Legal Affairs 1973–75, 1991–96, UNEP 1975–77; served in Ministry of Foreign Affairs and Ministry of Planning and Economic Affairs 1977–79; Amb. to UN, New York (also accred to Cuba and Mexico) 1979–81; Justice Minister 1982–83; Chair. Legal and Constitutional Cttee of the group of Liberian political leaders meeting in Banjul, Gambia that established an interim govt in Liberia (later Foreign Minister and Minister of State) 1990; Exec. Sec. Comm. of Inquiry into ambushing and killing of Pakistani peace-keepers in Mogadishu 1993; assigned to UN Peace Office in Zagreb, Croatia and UN Peace-keeping Mission in Eastern Slavonia (UNTAES) –1998; Sr Adviser to Commdr UN Iraq–Kuwait Observation Mission (UNIKOM) 1998–; Head of UN Political Office for Somalia (UNPOS) 2002–05; Leader and unsuccessful presidential cand. (Nat. Democratic Party of Liberia) 2005; unsuccessful presidential cand. (Congress for Democratic Change) 2011 mem. Bar of Supreme Court of Liberia. *Address:* Congress for Democratic Change, Tubman Blvd, POB 2799, Monrovia, Liberia (office). *Website:* www.cdcforliberia.org (office).

TUCCI, HE Cardinal Roberto; Italian ecclesiastic and broadcasting official; b. 19 April 1921, Naples; ordained priest; fmr Ed. La Civiltà Cattolica; Vice-Pres. Italian Catholic Union of the Press 1961–82; Gen. Sec. Italian Province of the Jesuits 1967–69; consultor to Pontifical Council for Social Communications 1965–89; apptd Gen. Man. Vatican Radio 1973, Chair. Admin. Cttee 1986–2001; cr. Cardinal 2001. *Address:* c/o Radio Vaticana, Palazzo Pio, Piazza Pia 3, 00193 Rome, Italy (office).

TUCCI, Stanley, BFA; American actor; b. 11 Nov. 1960, Peekskill, New York; s. of Stanley Tucci Sr and Joan Tucci (née Tropiano); m. Kate Tucci 1995 (died 2009); three c.; ed Purchase Coll., State Univ. of New York. *Films include:* Prizzi's Honor 1985, Monkey Shines 1988, Slaves of New York 1989, Billy Bathgate 1991, Beethoven 1992, The Public Eye 1992, It Could Happen to You 1994, Mrs Parker and the Vicious Circle 1994, Kiss of Death 1995, Big Night (also writer, dir and co-producer) (Boston Soc. of Film Critics Awards for Best New Dir and Best Screenplay, Independent Spirit Award for Best First Screenplay, New York Film Critics Circle Awards for Best New Dir, Sundance Film Festival Waldo Salt Screenwriting Award) 1996, A Life Less Ordinary 1997, The Impostors (also writer, dir and producer) 1998, In Too Deep 1999, America's Sweethearts 2001, Road to Perdition 2002, The Life and Death of Peter Sellers 2004, The Terminal 2004, The Devil Wears Prada 2006, The Hoax 2007, Julie & Julia 2009, The Lovely Bones 2009, Easy A 2010, Burlesque 2010, Margin Call 2011, Captain America: The First Avenger 2011, The Hunger Games 2012. *Television:* Miami Vice 1986–88, Lifestories 1990, Conspiracy 2001, Frasier 2004, ER 2007–08. *Address:* CAA, 2000 Avenue of the Stars, Los Angeles, CA 90067, USA (office). *Telephone:* (424) 288-2000 (office).

TUCKER, Mark, ACA; British business executive; fmr tax consultant, Price Waterhouse UK; joined Prudential 1986, sr positions in UK and USA, Chief Exec. Prudential Corpn Asia 1993–2003, Exec. Dir Prudential 1999–2003, Exec. Dir and Group Chief Exec. Prudential plc 2005–09; Group Finance Dir HBOS plc and Dir

Halifax plc 2004–05. *Address:* c/o Prudential plc, Laurence Pountney Hill, London, EC4R 0HH, England (office).

TUCKER, Sir Paul, Kt; British fmr central banker; ed Trinity Coll., Cambridge; several pvt. banking positions 1980–89, including working as banking supervisor, corp. financier at merchant bank and on projects to reform Hong Kong securities markets and regulatory system following the 1987 crash; Prin. Pvt. Sec. to Bank of England Gov. Leigh-Pemberton 1989–93, Head, Gilt-Edged and Money Markets Div. 1994–97, Head, Monetary Assessment and Strategy Div. 1997–98, Deputy Dir Financial Stability 1999–2002, Exec. Dir Markets and mem. Monetary Policy Cttee 2002–09, Deputy Gov. 2009–13, mem. Secr. of Monetary Policy Cttee 1997–2002. *Address:* c/o Bank of England, Threadneedle Street, London, EC2R 8AH, England (office).

TUCKWELL, Barry Emmanuel, AC, OBE, FRCM, FRSA; Australian horn player, conductor and academic; b. 5 March 1931, Melbourne; s. of Charles Tuckwell and Elizabeth Hill; m. 1st Sally E. Newton 1958; one s. one d.; m. 2nd Hilary J. Warburton 1971; one s.; m. 3rd Susan T. Levitan 1992; ed Sydney Conservatorium; French horn player with Melbourne Symphony Orchestra 1947, Sydney Symphony Orchestra 1947–50, Hallé Orchestra 1951–53, Scottish Nat. Orchestra 1954–55, Bournemouth Symphony Orchestra, London Symphony Orchestra 1955–68; Horn Prof., RAM 1963–74; f. Tuckwell Wind Quintet 1968; int. soloist and recording artist; Conductor of Tasmanian Symphony Orchestra 1980–83; Music Dir and Conductor Md Symphony Orchestra 1982–98; Pres. Int. Horn Soc. 1969–76, 1993–95; Guest Conductor Northern Sinfonia 1993–; joined Faculty of Music, Univ. of Melbourne as Prin. Fellow 2005, currently Hon. Professorial Fellow; mem. Bd of Dirs London Symphony Orchestra 1957–68, Chair. 1961–68; mem. Chamber Music Soc. of Lincoln Center 1974–81; hon. degrees from RAM, Guildhall School of Music and Drama, Sydney Univ.; Harriet Cohen Int. Award for Solo Instruments 1968, George Peabody Medal for outstanding contribs to music in America. *Publications:* Playing the Horn, 50 1st Exercises 1978, The Horn (Yehudi Menuhin Music Guides) 1981, entire horn repertoire of G. Schirmer Inc. (Ed). *Address:* Faculty of Music, University of Melbourne, Melbourne, Vic. 3010, Australia. *Website:* www.music.unimelb.edu.au.

TUDOR, Corneliu Vadim, PhD; Romanian author, journalist and politician; *President, România Mare (Greater Romania Party);* b. 28 Nov. 1949, Bucharest; m.; two d.; ed Univs of Bucharest and Craiova; fmr court poet for Ceauşescu family; Senator 1992–2008, Sec. of the Senate 1992–96, Vice-Pres. 2004–08; Full mem. Romanian Del. to the Council of Europe Parl. Ass. 2001–02; Non-attached mem. European Parl. 2009–, mem. Cttee on Culture and Educ., Del. for relations with Switzerland, Iceland and Norway and to European Econ. Area Jt Parl. Cttee, Substitute mem. Cttee on Foreign Affairs, Del. to EU-Turkey Jt Parl. Cttee; Pres. România Mare (Greater Romania Party) 1991–; runner-up in presidential elections 2000; Kt of the Steaua României (Star of Romania) Order 2004; Herder Scholarship, Faculty of Letters, Vienna, Austria 1978–79, Bronze Medal of the Vatican, awarded by Pope Benedict XVI 2007. *Publications:* more than 20 books (current affairs, poetry, plays); writings on topical issues in numerous major Romanian publs 1968–. *Address:* Greater Romania Party (Partidul România Mare), 010296 Bucharest, Str. G. Clemenceau 8–10, Romania (office); European Parliament, 60 Rue Wiertz, WIB 05M121, 1047 Brussels, Belgium (office). *Telephone:* (21) 3130967 (Bucharest) (office); (2) 284-58-47 (Brussels) (office). *Fax:* (21) 3126182 (Bucharest) (office); (2) 284-98-47 (Brussels) (office). *E-mail:* prm@prm.org.ro (office); tudorcorneliu.vadim@europarl.europa.eu (office). *Website:* www.prm.org.ro (office).

TUGENDHAT, Baron (Life Peer), cr. 1993, of Widdington in the County of Essex; **Christopher Samuel Tugendhat,** MA; British business executive, politician and fmr international organization official; b. 23 Feb. 1937, London; s. of the late Dr Georg Tugendhat; m. Julia Lissant Dobson 1967; two s.; ed Ampleforth Coll., Gonville and Caius Coll., Cambridge; Pres. Cambridge Union; Mil. Service, commissioned in The Essex Regt 1955–57; leader and feature writer, The Financial Times 1960–70; Consultant to Wood Mackenzie & Co. Ltd, stockbrokers 1968–77; Conservative MP for Cities of London and Westminster 1970–74, for City of London and Westminster South 1974–76; Dir Sunningdale Oils 1971–77, Phillips Petroleum Int. (UK) Ltd 1972–77, Nat. Westminster Bank PLC 1985–91 (Deputy Chair. 1990–91), BOC Group PLC 1985–96, Commercial Union PLC 1988–91, LWT (Holdings) PLC 1991–94; Dir (non-exec.), Eurotunnel PLC 1991–2003, Rio Tinto PLC 1997–2004; Chair. Civil Aviation Authority 1986–91, Abbey Nat. PLC 1991–2002, Blue Circle Industries PLC 1996–2001; Chair. (non-exec.) Lehman Brothers Europe 2002–07; Chair. Imperial Coll. Healthcare NHS Trust 2007–12; mem. Comm. of EEC with responsibility for Budget and Financial Control, Financial Institutions, Personnel and Admin. 1977–81, Vice-Pres. with responsibility for Budget and Financial Control, Financial Institutions and Taxation 1981–85; Chancellor Univ. of Bath 1998–; Chair. Royal Inst. of Int. Affairs (now Chatham House) 1986–95; Gov. and mem. Council of Man., Ditchley Foundation; Patron and Vice-Pres. British Lung Foundation; Chair. Gonville & Caius Devt Campaign Cttee, Cambridge Univ.; Freeman City of London; Hon. Fellow, Gonville and Caius Coll., Cambridge; Hon. LLD (Bath) 1998; Hon. DLitt (UMIST) 2002; McKinsey Foundation Book Award 1971. *Publications:* Oil: the Biggest Business 1968, The Multinationals 1971, Making Sense of Europe 1986, Options for British Foreign Policy in the 1990s (with William Wallace) 1988; numerous articles. *Leisure interests:* reading, family, conversation. *Address:* House of Lords, London, SW1A 0PW Tel.: 35 Westbourne Park Road, London, W2 5QD, England (home). *Telephone:* (20) 7219-5353 (House of Lords). *E-mail:* tugendhatc@parliament.uk.

TUGWELL, Very Rev. Simon Charles ffoster, OP, STM, DD, STD; British ecclesiastic and historian; *Fellow, Istituto Storico Domenicano;* b. 4 May 1943, Brighton, Sussex; s. of Maj. Herbert Tugwell and Mary Brigit Tugwell (née Hutchinson); ed Lancing Coll. and Corpus Christi Coll., Oxford; received into Roman Catholic Church 1964; joined Dominican Order 1965; ordained priest 1971; Lecturer and Tutor, Blackfriars, Oxford 1972–92, Regent of Studies 1976–90; mem. Faculty of Theology, Univ. of Oxford 1982–92; Fellow, Istituto Storico Domenicano 1987– (Pres. 1992–97); Ed., Monumenta Ordinis Praedicatorum Historica 1992–; Visiting Lecturer, Pontifical Univ. of St Thomas, Rome 1977–93; Flannery Prof. of Theology, Gonzaga Univ., Spokane, Wash., USA 1982–83; Read-Tuckwell Lecturer on Human Immortality, Univ. of Bristol 1988; Consultor to

Congregation for Causes of Saints 1994–97; has lectured in many countries around the world. *Publications include:* The Way of the Preacher 1979, Early Dominicans 1982, Ways of Imperfection 1984, Albert and Thomas 1988, The Apostolic Fathers 1989, Letters of Bede Jarrett (ed.) 1989, Human Immortality and the Redemption of Death 1990, Saint Dominic 1995, Miracula S. Dominici. . . Petri Calo legendae S. Dominici (ed.) 1997, Bernardi Guidonis: Scripta de Sancto Dominico (ed.) 1998, Humberti de Romanis, Legendae Sancti Dominici (ed) 2008, Pelagius Parvus and his 'Summa' 2012; articles on aspects of theology and Dominican history, especially sources for the life of St Dominic. *Leisure interests:* music, science fiction. *Address:* Istituto Storico Domenicano, Largo Angelicum 1, 00184 Rome, Italy (office).

TUHEITIA, Te Arikinui; New Zealand Maori king; b. 21 April 1955; eldest son of the late Whatumoana Paki and Te Arikinui Dame Te Atairangikaahu (previous monarch); m. Atawhai; three c.; ed Rakaumanga School, Huntly, St Stephen's Coll., Bombay (now Mumbai), India; fmr univ. man. and Tainui cultural adviser to Te Wananga o Aotearoa, Huntly; chosen as king at secret meeting and crowned following his mother's funeral 21 Aug. 2006. *Address:* Tūrongo House, Tūranga-waewae marae, Ngaruawahia, Waikato, New Zealand.

TUITA, Baron Siosaia Aleamotu'a Laufilitonga Tuita, CBE; Tongan government official and civil servant; b. 29 Aug. 1920, Lapaha, Tongatapu; s. of 'Isileli Tupou Tuita and Luseane Halaevalu Fotofili; m. Fatafehi Lapaha Tupou 1949; two s. two d.; ed Tupou Coll., Wesley Coll., Auckland, New Zealand, Univ. of Oxford, UK; Lt Officer, Tonga Defence Service 1942–43; Court Interpreter and Registrar, Supreme Court 1945; Asst Sec. Prime Minister's Office 1954; Acting Gov. of Vava'u 1956, Gov. 1957; Acting Minister of Lands 1962, of Police 1964–65; Chair. Niuafo'ou evacuation 1965; Minister of Lands and Survey and Minister of Health 1965; assumed title of Tuita 1972, awarded title of Baron Tuita of 'Utungake 1980; Deputy Prime Minister and Minister of Lands, Survey and Natural Resources 1972–89; mem. Privy Council; Chair. Town Planning Cttee, Energy Standing Cttee, Royal Land Comm., Tonga Broadcasting Comm.; mem. numerous socs. *Leisure interests:* rugby, cricket, driving, fishing. *Address:* Mahinafekite, Nuku'alofa, Tonga (home). *Telephone:* 22451 (home).

TUITT, Roland S., BSc, MBA, CPA; St Maarten accountant and politician; b. Aruba; m. Italia Tuitt-Soon; ed Andrews Univ., USA; began career as Asst Accountant, Advent Hosp., Curaçao; worked as accountant for numerous orgs including Eilands Accountant Dienst, Aruba, Price Waterhouse, Curaçao, GEBE NV, St Maarten, Coopers & Lybrand, Amsterdam and St Maarten; Owner Tuitt CPA (financial services consultancy) 2010–12; Chair. Audit Chamber of St Maarten 2010–12; fmr Commr of Finance, Island Territory of St Maarten (whilst still part of Netherlands Antilles); fmr Senator, Parl. of Netherlands Antilles; Minister of Finance 2012–13. *Address:* c/o Ministry of Finance, Philipsburg, St Maarten (office).

TUIVAGA, Hon. Sir Timoci (Uluiburotu), Kt, BA; Fijian judge; b. 21 Oct. 1931; s. of Isimeili Siga Tuivaga and Jessie Hill; m. Vilimaina Leba Parrott Tuivaga 1958; three s. one d.; ed Univ. of Auckland, New Zealand; native magistrate 1958–61, called to the Bar, Gray's Inn, London 1964, NSW 1968; Crown Counsel 1965–68, Prin. Legal Officer 1968–70, Puisne Judge 1972, Acting Chief Justice 1974, Chief Justice of Fiji 1980–87, 1988–2002; Acting Gov.-Gen. 1983–87. *Leisure interests:* golf, gardening. *Address:* 228 Ratu Sukuna Road, Suva, Fiji. *Telephone:* 301-782.

TU'IVAKANO, Lord, BSc; Tongan politician; *Prime Minister and Minister of Foreign Affairs, Defence, Information and Communication;* b. (Siale 'Ataongo Kaho), 15 Jan. 1952, Niutoua, Hahake; s. of Siaosi Kiu Ngalumoetutulu Kaho (16th Tu'ivakano) and Fatafehi-'o-Lapaha Liku; m. Joyce Robyn Kaho (née Sanft); six c.; ed Wesley Coll., Ardmore Teacher's Coll., NZ, Flinders Univ., Australia; Asst Teacher, Tonga High School 1975–80; Head, Physical Educ. Div., Ministry of Educ. 1974, Sr Educ. Officer for Youth, Sport and Culture 1992–96; mem. Legis. Ass. as Rep. of Nobles of Tonga 1996–, Speaker 2002–04; Minister of Works 2005, of Training, Employment, Youth and Sport 2006–10, Prime Minister Dec. 2010– (first prime minister to be elected by parl. rather than being installed by king), also Minister of Foreign Affairs, Defence, Information and Communication; succeeded to hereditary title of Tu'ivakano after death of father Jan. 1986. *Address:* Office of the Prime Minister, POB 62, Nuku'alofa, Tonga (office). *Telephone:* 24644 (office). *Fax:* 23888 (office). *E-mail:* pmomail@pmo.gov.to (office). *Website:* www.pmo.gov.to (office).

TUJU, Hon. Raphael, MA; Kenyan politician, film producer, film director, broadcaster and business executive; b. 30 March 1959, Ndori, Bondo district; m.; three c.; ed Starehe Boys' Centre and School, Univ. of Leicester; producer-dir of numerous films, and radio and TV programmes principally concerned with promotion of health awareness 1992–97; chief public relations consultant Population Services Int. Social Marketing of Condoms Project 1994–95; writer of newspaper column and leader of project to promote AIDS awareness 1995–96; chief communications consultant, STI electronic media intervention in Kenya, The World Bank 1998; communications consultant UNICEF and Ministry of Health 1998; lead public relations consultant, Kenya Re-Insurance Corporation 1998–2000 (resgnd); lead consultant and communications advisor, Int. AIDS Vaccine Initiative (IAVI) 1999–2002; lead consultant, IEC component of DFID funded HIV/AIDS Prevention and Care Project (HAPAC) in Nyanza province 1999–2003; lead consultant, Poverty Reduction Strategy Paper (PRSP) 2000–01; mem. of Parliament for Rarieda; Minister for Tourism and Information 2003–04; Minister for Information and Communications 2004–05; Minister of Foreign Affairs 2005–08; team leader of first African winner of Int. Emmy Awards; Dir Ace Communications Md, USA and Nairobi, Kenya; Chair. Kenya AIDS NGOs Consortium (KANCO); Chair. Development Communications Inst.; Dir BITC; mem. Public Relations Soc. of Kenya (PRSK), Int. Mass Communication Soc. (IMCS), African Council for Communication Educ. (ACCE). *Publications:* AIDS: Understanding the Challenge. *Address:* c/o Ministry of Foreign Affairs, Old Treasury Building, Harmbee Avenue, POB 30551, Nairobi, Kenya (office).

TUKI, Nabam; Indian politician; *Chief Minister of Arunachal Pradesh;* b. 7 July 1964, Sagalee; s. of Nabam Takeh; m.; two s. five d.; Pres., Nat. Students' Union of India (NSUI), Arunachal Pradesh 1983–86, Chair. North East NSUI Coordination Cttee 1984–86, Gen. Sec. All India NSUI 1986–88; Pres. Youth Congress, Arunachal Pradesh 1989–95; Vice-Chair. North Eastern Youth Congress

Coordination Cttee 1988–93, Working Pres. 1993–95; apptd Vice-Chair. A P Cooperative Apex Bank Ltd 1992; elected to State Legis. Ass. 1995; apptd Deputy Minister of Agriculture 1995, of Transport and Civil Aviation 1998, of Environment and Forest 1999, of Public Works Dept and Urban Devt; Gen.-Sec. Arunachal Pradesh Congress Cttee (APCC) 1995–96, Vice-Pres. 1999–2004, Working Pres. 2004–08, Pres. 2008–; Chief Minister of Arunachal Pradesh 2011–; Sitting Pres. Arunachal Cricket Asscn 2008–. *Leisure interest:* sports. *Address:* Office of the Chief Minister of Arunachal Pradesh, Itanagar 791 111, India (office). *Telephone:* (360) 2212456 (office). *Fax:* (360) 2212439 (office). *E-mail:* arunachalpradeshcm@gmail.com (office). *Website:* www.arunachalpradeshcm.in (office); www.apcc.in (office).

TULAFONO, Togiola Talalelei A.; American Samoa lawyer and government official; b. 28 Feb. 1947, Aunu'u Island; m. Mary Ann Taufa'asau Mauga; six c.; ed Samoana High School, Chadron State Coll., Neb., Washburn Univ. School of Law, Topeka, Kan., National Judicial Coll., Reno, Nev., USA; lawyer in pvt. practice for 20 years; fmr policeman; fmr Admin. Asst to Sec. of Samoan Affairs; fmr Samoan Asst to Attorney Gen.; fmr Dist Court Judge; fmr Senator for Saole Co. for four years, for Sua Co. for eight years; mem. Democratic Party; Lt Gov. of American Samoa 1997–2003, Gov. 2003–13; fmr Chair. Bd of Dirs American Samoa Power Authority; fmr first Chair. Bd of High Educ.; Chair. South Pacific Mini-Games Cttee 1997, American Samoa Centennial Cttee 2000; Deacon of Congregational Christian Church of American Samoa (CCCAS), Sailele for more than 25 years, Vice-Chair. CCCAS during its Ass. 2003, 2006–08, Chair. CCCAS 2004–06, 2008–10; Dist Pres. for the American Samoa Dist, Boy Scouts of America; mem. Lions Club of Pago Pago. *Address:* c/o Office of the Governor, A.P. Lutali Executive Office Building, Pago Pago, AS 96799, American Samoa. *E-mail:* tupitosoliai@americansamoa.gov.

TULEYEV, Aman-Geldy Moldagazyevich, (Aman Gumirovich), DPolSc; Kazakhstani politician; *Governor, Kemerovo Region;* b. 13 May 1944, Krasnovodsk, Turkmenistan; s. of the late Moldagazy Kaldybayevich Tuleyev and Munira Fayzovna Vlasova (née Nasyrova); m. Elvira Fedorovna; two s. (one deceased); ed Tikhoretsk Railway Tech. School, Novosibirsk Inst. of Railway Eng, Acad. of Social Sciences at Cen. Cttee CPSU; worked on Krasnodar railway station 1961, Head Mundybash railway station 1969, Mezhdurechensk railway station 1973, Head Novokuznetsk Dept Kemerovo Railway 1978–85; Head Div. of Transport and Communications Regional Cttee CPSU 1985–88; Head Kemerovo Railway 1988; Peoples' Deputy of Russian Fed. for Kemerovo region 1990–93; Chair. Kemerovo Regional Soviet 1991; presidential cand. 1991, 1996, 2000; mem. CP of Russian Fed. 1993–2003, Yedinaya Rossiya party 2003– (mem. Supreme Council); Deputy, Fed. Council of Russia 1993–95, 1997–2001; Chair. Legis. Ass. Kemerovo Region 1994–96; Minister of Co-operation with CIS 1996–97; Gov. Kemerovo Region 1997–; Order of Honour 1999, Order of Mongolia 'Polar Star' 2000, Order of Russian Orthodox Church, Rev. Sergey Radonezhsky II degree 2001, Order for Outstanding Country Service (Fourth Degree) 2003, (Third Degree) 2008, (Second Degree) 2012, Dostyk Order (Kazakhstan) 2003, Order of Jaroslav the Wise (Ukraine) 2004; Peter the Great Int. Award 2002, Int. Millennium Award for Service to Humanity 2003, Andrey Pervozvanny Int. Award for Faith and Loyalty 2003 and more then 20 others. *Publications:* more than 20 books and several hundred publns in Russian and foreign mass media. *Leisure:* mushroom gathering, langlaufing, snow-tractor driving, taking Russian baths. *Address:* Office of the Governor, Sovetsky prosp. 62, 650000 Kemerovo, Russia (office). *Telephone:* (3842) 36-43-33 (office); (3842) 36-34-09 (office). *Fax:* (3842) 36-34-09 (office). *E-mail:* postmaster@ako.ru (office). *Website:* www.mediakuzbass.ru/tuleev (office); www.ako.ru (office).

TULIN, Dmitri Vladislavovich, MBA, PhD; Russian economist; b. 26 March 1956, Moscow; s. of the late Vladislav Tulin and of Emma S. Tulin; m. Vera Nerod 1977; two s.; ed Moscow Financial Inst. and USSR Inst. of Econs and Finance; economist, Int. Monetary and Econ. Dept USSR State Bank (Gosbank) 1978, Sr Economist 1980, Chief Economist 1985, Man. 1989, Man. Dir, mem. Bd Securities Dept 1990; Deputy Chair. Cen. Bank of Russian Fed. 1991–94; Exec. Dir for Russian Fed. IMF 1994–96; Chair. Bd Vneshtorgbank (Bank for Foreign Trade) 1996–98; Sr Adviser EBRD 1999–2004; Deputy Chair. Cen. Bank of Russian Fed. 2004. *Publications:* articles on monetary econs and banking in Russian professional journals. *Leisure interests:* gardening, chess. *Address:* c/o Central Bank of the Russian Federation, 12 Neglinnaya Street, Moscow, 107016, Russia (office).

TULLOCK, Gordon, JD; American economist and academic (retd); *Professor Emeritus of Law and Economics, George Mason University;* b. 13 Feb. 1922, Rockford, Ill.; s. of George Tullock and Helen Tullock; ed Univ. of Chicago; held State Dept postings in Tianjin, China, Hong Kong and Korea 1947–56; Postdoctoral Fellow, Univ. of Virginia 1958–59, Assoc. Prof. 1962–67; Asst Prof., Univ. of South Carolina 1959–60, Assoc. Prof. 1960–62; Prof. of Econs and Political Science, Rice Univ. 1967–68; Prof. of Econs, Virginia Polytechnic Inst. and State Univ. 1968–72; Univ. Distinguished Prof. of Econs 1972–83; Univ. Distinguished Prof. of Econs, George Mason Univ. 1983–87, Prof. of Law and Econs 1999–2008, Prof. Emer. 2008–; Editorial Dir Center for Study of Public Choice 1968–90; Prof., Univ. of Arizona 1987–99; Visiting Distinguished Scholar, Baruch Univ., New York City 1987; fmr mem. editorial bd Journal of Social and Biological Structure, International Journal of Law and Economics, Atlantic Economic Journal; Fellow, American Economic Asscn, Distinguished Fellow 1998; mem. American Acad. of Arts and Sciences, Southern Economic Asscn (fmr Pres.), Western Economic Asscn (fmr Pres.), American Political Science Asscn, Public Choice Soc. (Sec. 1965–), Asscn for Asian Studies, Inst. of Economic Affairs (mem. council), Mont Pelerin Soc., Bioecons Soc. (Hon. Chair.); Dr hc (Univ. of Chicago) 1994. *Publications:* 23 books including The Calculus of Consent (with J.M. Buchanan) 1962, Private Wants, Public Means 1970, The Logic of the Law 1971, The Social Dilemma 1974, The Vote Motive 1976; more than 150 papers. *Address:* George Mason University, Rm 433A, 3401 North Fairfax Drive, Arlington, VA 22201-4498, USA (office). *E-mail:* gtulloc1@gmu.edu (office). *Website:* www.law.gmu.edu (office).

TULLY, Daniel Patrick; American finance industry executive (retd); *Chairman Emeritus, Merrill Lynch & Co., Inc.;* b. 2 Jan. 1932, New York; m. Grace Tully; four c.; ed St John's Univ. New York and Harvard Business School; army service 1953–55; joined Merrill Lynch & Co., Inc. 1955; Account Exec., Stamford Office 1959, Man. 1970, Vice-Pres. 1971; Individual Sales Dir, New York HQ 1976; mem.

Bd Dirs Merrill Lynch, Pierce, Fenner & Smith 1977, Chair. and CEO 1985; Exec. Vice-Pres. Marketing 1979; Pres. Individual Services Group 1982 and Exec. Vice-Pres. Merrill Lynch & Co. Inc. 1982, Pres. and COO 1985–92, Chair. Bd and CEO 1992–96, Chair., CEO, Pres. 1993–97, now Chair. Emer.; Vice-Chair. American Stock Exchange 1984–86, Securities Industry Asscn 1985–86; fmr Dir New York Stock Exchange. *Address:* 398 South Beach Road, Hobe Sound, FL 33455-2609, USA.

TULLY, James Hamilton, BA, PhD, FRSC; Canadian political scientist and academic; *Distinguished Professor of Political Science, Law, Indigenous Governance and Philosophy, University of Victoria;* ed Univ. of British Columbia, Univ. of Cambridge, UK; Tutor, Depts of Philosophy and Political Science, McGill Univ. 1977–96; Prof. and Chair. Dept of Political Science, Univ. of Victoria, BC 1996–2001, Distinguished Prof. of Political Science, Law, Indigenous Governance and Philosophy 2003–; Inaugural Henry N.R. Jackman Distinguished Prof. in Philosophical Studies, Univ. of Toronto in Depts of Philosophy and Political Science and Faculty of Law 2001–03; Fellow, Trudeau Foundation; Killam Prize in the Humanities, Canada Council for the Arts 2010. *Publications:* A Discourse on Property: John Locke and his Adversaries 1980, John Locke, A Letter Concerning Toleration (ed. and Introduction) 1982, Meaning and Context: Quentin Skinner and His Critics, (ed., Introduction, and contrib.) 1988, Samuel Pufendorf, On the Duty of Man and Citizen According to Natural Law, trans. Michael Silverthorne (ed. and Introduction) 1991, An Approach to Political Philosophy: Locke in Contexts 1993, Philosophy in an Age of Pluralism: The Philosophy of Charles Taylor in Question (ed., with assistance of Daniel M. Weinstock) 1994, Strange Multiplicity: Constitutionalism in an Age of Diversity 1995, Multinational Democracies (co-ed. with Alain-G. Gagnon) 2001, Rethinking the Foundations of Modern Political Thought (co-ed. with Annabel Brett) 2006, Democracy and Civic Freedom, Vol. I of Public Philosophy in a New Key 2008, Imperialism and Civic Freedom, Vol. II of Public Philosophy in a New Key 2008; numerous papers in professional journals on contemporary political and legal philosophy (or theory) and its history, and on Canadian political and legal philosophy. *Address:* SSM A350, Department of Political Science, University of Victoria, PO Box 3060 STN CSC, Victoria, BC V8W 3R4, Canada (office). *Telephone:* (250) 721-7494 (office). *Fax:* (250) 721-7485 (office). *E-mail:* jtully@uvic.ca (office). *Website:* web.uvic.ca/~polisci (office).

TULLY, Sir (William) Mark, Kt, KBE, MA; British journalist; b. 24 Oct. 1935, Calcutta, India; s. of William S. C. Tully and Patience T. Tully; m. Frances M. Butler 1960; two s. two d.; ed Marlborough Coll., Trinity Hall, Cambridge; Regional Dir Abbeyfield Soc. 1960–64; Personnel Officer BBC 1964–65, Asst Rep. then Rep. (a.i.), BBC, Delhi 1965–69, Hindi Programme Organizer BBC External Services, London 1969–70, Chief Talks Writer 1970–71, Chief of Bureau BBC, Delhi 1971–93, BBC South Asia Corresp. 1993–94; freelance writer, broadcaster, journalist 1994–; Hon. Fellow, Trinity Hall, Cambridge 1994; Hon. DLitt (Strathclyde) 1997, Dr hc (Bradford Univ.) 2001, (York Univ.) 2008, (Open Univ.) 2009, (Queen's Univ., Belfast) 2011; Dimbleby Award (BAFTA) 1984, Padma Shri (India) 1992, Padma Bhushan (India) 2005. *Radio:* series: Raj to Rajiv BBC 1987, Something Understood BBC 1995–, Indian Army in World War II 2007. *Television:* series: Lives of Jesus BBC 1996. *Publications:* Amritsar: Mrs Gandhi's Last Battle (jtly) 1985, Raj to Rajiv (jtly) 1988, No Full Stops in India 1991, The Heart of India 1995, The Lives of Jesus 1996, India in Slow Motion (with Gillian Wright) 2002, India's Unending Journey 2007, India: The Road Ahead 2011. *Leisure interests:* bird watching, reading, railways, theology. *Address:* B.26 Nizamuddin West, New Delhi 110 013, India (office). *Telephone:* (11) 41033839 (office). *E-mail:* markandgilly@gmail.com (office).

TULYAGANOV, Kozim N.; Uzbekistani politician; fmr Mayor of Tashkent; First Deputy Prime Minister of Uzbekistan 2001; Khokim (Gov.) Tashkent Province 2004–05; sentenced to 20 years' imprisonment 2006.

TŮMA, Zdeněk, CSc, MCom; Czech economist and fmr central banker; b. 19 Oct. 1960, České Budějovice; m.; two s. one d.; ed Univ. of Econs, Prague, London School of Econs, UK, studies in the Netherlands and USA; researcher, Inst. for Forecasting, Prague 1986–90; Lecturer, School of Econs, Prague, Faculty of Social Sciences Charles Univ., Prague 1990–98, mem. Scientific Council 2003–06, mem. Graduation Council, Centre for Econ. Research and Grad. Educ.; Adviser to Minister of Trade and Industry 1993–95; Chief Economist, Patria Finance 1995–98; Exec. Dir EBRD 1998–99; Vice-Gov. Czech Nat. Bank 1999–2000, Gov. 2000–10; TOP 09 party nominee for office of Mayor of Prague in local elections Oct. 2010; Pres. Czech Econs Soc. 1999–2001; mem. Bd of Eds Finance a úvěr (Czech Journal of Economics and Finance); mem. Bd of Trustees, Jan and Meda Mládek Foundation, Univ. of Econs, Prague; mem. Bd of Govs English Coll., Prague; mem. Scientific Council, Czech Tech. Univ. 2006–10; mem. Supervisory Bd, Econs Inst., Acad. of Sciences of the Czech Repub. 2007–12; Hon. mem. Bd of Trustees, US Business School, Prague. *Publications:* articles and chapters on econ. transition. *Leisure interests:* skiing, squash, tennis, cycling. *Address:* c/o Czech National Bank, Na Příkopě 28, 115 03 Prague 1, Czech Republic. *Telephone:* (2) 24411111.

TUMEWU, Paulus; Indonesian retail executive; *President Commissioner, PT Ramayana Lestari Sentosa;* b. 1952, Ujung Pandang (now Makassar), Sulawesi; m.; three c.; began career helping out in parents' shop, Ujung Pandang; f. Ramayana 1978, opened first store on Jl Sabang, Central Jakarta 1978, inc. into PT Ramayana Lestari Sentosa Tbk 1983, currently Pres. Commr. *Address:* PT Ramayana Lestari Sentosa, Jl. K.H. Wahid Hasyim No. 220, A-B Jakarta Pusat, Jakarta 10250, Indonesia (office). *Telephone:* (21) 3106653 (office). *Fax:* (21) 3920484 (office). *E-mail:* corporate@ramayana.co.id (office). *Website:* www.ramayana.co.id (office).

TUMI, HE Cardinal Christian Wiyghan; Cameroonian ecclesiastic; b. 15 Oct. 1930, Kikaikelaki; ordained priest 1966, Bishop of Yagoua 1979–82, consecrated Bishop 1980, Coadjutor Bishop of Garoua 1982–84, Archbishop of Garoua 1984–91; cr. Cardinal-Priest of Ss. Martiri dell'Uganda a Poggio Ameno 1988; Archbishop of Douala a1991–2009 (retd). *Address:* Archdiocese of Douala, Archevêché, BP 179, Douala, Cameroon. *E-mail:* christiantumi@camnet.com (office).

TUMLINSON, James H., BS, MS, PhD; American entomologist and academic; *Ralph O. Mumma Professor of Entomology and Director, Center for Chemical Ecology, Pennsylvania State University;* ed Virginia Mil. Inst., Mississippi State

Univ.; Chemist, Boll Weevil Research Lab., US Dept of Agric. (USDA)/Agric. Research Service (ARS) 1964–69, Research Chemist, Insect Attractants, Behavior, and Basic Biology Research Lab. 1970–72, Research Leader, Center for Medical, Agricultural, and Veterinary Entomology 1972–2003; Postdoctoral Researcher, New York State Coll. of Forestry 1969–70; Adjunct Asst Prof., Univ. of Florida Inst. of Food and Agric. 1970–75, Adjunct Assoc. Prof. 1975–82, Adjunct Prof. 1982–; Ralph O. Mumma Prof. of Entomology and Dir Center for Chemical Ecology, Pennsylvania State Univ. 2003–; mem. NAS, Int. Soc. of Chemical Ecology (Vice-Pres. 1997, Pres. 1998); Fellow, Entomological Soc. of America 1996; numerous awards, including USDA Superior Service Awards 1975, 1983, ARS Distinguished Research Scientist of the Year 1984, Jean-Marie Delwart Foundation Prize 2003, Wolf Prize in Agric. (co-recipient) 2008. *Address:* Department of Entomology, 111 Chemical Ecology Lab, Pennsylvania State University, University Park, PA 16802, USA (office). *Telephone:* (814) 863-1770 (office). *E-mail:* jht2@psu.edu (office). *Website:* ento.psu.edu/directory/jht2 (office); www.huck.psu.edu/people/jht2 (office).

TUMUSIIME-MUTEBILE, Emmanuel, BA; Ugandan economist, government official and central banker; *Governor, Bank of Uganda;* b. 27 Jan. 1949; ed Balliol Coll., Oxford, Durham Univ., UK; Visiting Lecturer, Centre for Int. Briefing, Farnham, UK 1977; Lecturer in Industrial Econs, Univ. of Dar es Salaam, Tanzania 1977–79; Deputy Prin. Pvt. Sec. to the Pres. of Uganda 1979–80; Acting Under-Sec., Ministry of Planning and Econ. Devt 1981, Chief Govt Planning Economist 1982, Perm. Sec. and Chair. Agricultural Policy Cttee 1986–92; Perm. Sec. in charge of Econ. Affairs, Prime Minister's Office 1985; Sec. to the Treasury, Ministry of Finance 1992–98; Perm. Sec. to the Treasury and Chair. Agricultural Policy Cttee and Steering Cttee for Agricultural Modernization Plan, Ministry of Finance, Planning and Econ. Devt 1998–2000; mem. Bd of Dirs Bank of Uganda 1992–, Gov. 2001–; has served as consultant to IMF, OECD, World Bank, Macroeconomic and Financial Man. Inst. of Eastern and Cen. Africa, North-South Inst., Canada and the govts of Rwanda, Tanzania, Eritrea, Kenya, Nepal; Fellow, Econ. Devt Inst. of the World Bank; Hon. Prof., Makerere Univ. 2006. *Publications:* numerous articles in professional journals. *Address:* Bank of Uganda, 37–43 Kampala Road, POB 7120, Kampala, Uganda (office). *Telephone:* (41) 2258441 (office). *Fax:* (41) 2255983 (office). *E-mail:* info@bou.or.ug (office). *Website:* www.bou.or.ug (office).

TUNE, Thomas (Tommy) James, BFA; American theatrical performer, director and choreographer; b. 28 Feb. 1939, Witchita Falls, Tex.; s. of Jim Tune and Eva Tune; ed Lamar High School, Houston, Lon Morris Junior Coll., Univ. of Tex. at Austin and Univ. of Houston; began professional career as chorus dancer on Broadway 1963; appeared in films Hello, Dolly! and The Boyfriend; appeared on Broadway in Seesaw (Tony Award, Best Supporting Actor); Off-Broadway Dir The Club, Cloud 9 (Obie and Drama Desk Awards), Stepping Out 1987; Choreographer, A Day in Hollywood/A Night in the Ukraine (Tony Award); Dir The Best Little Whorehouse in Texas, Nine (Tony Award 1982); actor and choreographer, My One and Only (Tony Award 1983), Grand Hotel 1989 (London 1992), The Will Rogers Follies, Bye, Bye Birdie 1991–92; performed musical revue Steps in Time: A Broadway Biography in Song and Dance 2008–; nine Tony Awards, Nat. Medal of Arts, Helen Hayes Tribute Award 2011. *Publication:* Footnotes: A Memoir 1997. *Leisure interests:* cooking, yoga, painting. *Address:* Tommy Tune Inc., 50 East 89th Street, New York, NY 10128, USA (office). *Telephone:* (212) 695-7400. *Website:* www.tommytune.com.

TUNG, Chee-hwa, BSc; Hong Kong business executive and politician; b. 29 May 1937, Shanghai, China; m. Betty Chiu Hung Ping 1961; two s. one d.; ed Univ. of Liverpool, UK; with Gen. Electric, USA –1969; Chair. Island Navigation Corpn Ltd, fmr Chair. Orient Overseas (Holdings) Ltd; Dir Sing Tao Newspapers Ltd, Sun Hung Kai Bank Ltd, Hsin Chong Properties Ltd, Mass Transit Railway Corpn; Vice-Chair. Preparatory Cttee for Hong Kong Special Admin. Region; mem. Exec. Council, Hong Kong Govt 1992–96; Chief Exec. of Hong Kong Special Admin. Region 1997–2005 (resgnd); mem. 8th CPPCC Nat. Cttee 1993, Vice-Chair. 10th CPPCC Nat. Cttee 2005–08, 11th CPPCC Nat. Cttee 2008–13, 12th CPPCC Nat. Cttee 2013–; Hon. Consul of Monaco in Hong Kong 1982–96; Int. Councillor, Centre for Strategic and Int. Studies, Washington, DC 1983–97; mem. Advisory Council Inst. for Int. Studies, Stanford Univ. 1995–97, Int. Advisory Bd, Council on Foreign Relations, New York 1995–97. *Leisure interests:* reading, hiking, watching sport, Tai Chi, swimming. *Address:* Chinese People's Political Consultative Conference, No.23, Taipingqiao Street, Beijing 100811, People's Republic of China.

TUNG, T. H., MA; Taiwanese business executive; *Chairman, Pegatron Corporation;* ed Nat. Taipei Univ. of Tech.; joined computer maker Acer Inc. after graduation; Co-founder ASUSTeK Computer Inc. 1989, Vice-Chair. –2008; Chair. Pegatron Corpn 2008–; Chair. Unihan, Kinsus, Lumens. *Address:* Pegatron Corporation, 96 Ligong Street, Beitou, Taipei 112, Taiwan (office). *Telephone:* (2) 8143-9001 (office). *Fax:* (2) 8143-7984 (office). *E-mail:* pegatronhr@pegatroncorp.com (office). *Website:* www.pegatroncorp.com (office).

TUNLEY, David Evatt, AM, MMus, DLitt, FAHA; Australian musicologist and academic; *Professor Emeritus and Honorary Senior Research Fellow, Department of Music, University of Western Australia;* b. 3 May 1930, Sydney; s. of Leslie Tunley and Marjorie Tunley; m. Paula Patricia Laurantus 1959; one s. two d.; ed The Scots Coll., Sydney, State Conservatorium of Music, Sydney; music master, Fort Street Boys' High School, Sydney 1952–57; joined staff of Dept of Music, Univ. of Western Australia 1958, Personal Chair. of Music 1980–, now Emer., Head Dept of Music 1985–90, Hon. Sr Research Fellow in Music 1994–; studied under Nadia Boulanger with French Govt Scholarship 1964–65; Scholar-in-residence, Rockefeller Foundation, Bellagio, Italy 1987; Fowler Hamilton Visiting Research Fellow, Christ Church, Oxford 1993; Visiting Scholar, Wolfson Coll. Oxford 1996; Founder/Conductor Univ. Collegium Musicum, 1976–83; Founder/Chair. York Winter Music Festival, 1982–; Founder/Dir The Terrace Proms, Perth; Nat. Pres. Musicological Soc. of Australia 1980–81; Chair. Music Bd, Australia Council 1984–85; Hon. FMusA; Chevalier, Ordre des Palmes académiques, Australian Centenary Medal; Hon. DMus (Western Australia). *Compositions include:* Two Preludes for Piano 1962, Concerto for Clarinet and Strings 1966 (revised 2000), A Wedding Masque 1970, Two Carols (words by Gerard Manley Hopkins) 1995, Immortal Fire 1999. *Publications:* The 18th-Century French Cantata 1974, Couperin 1982, Harmony in Action 1984, The French Cantata in Facsimile, 17

Vols 1990, Romantic French Song in Facsimile (6 Vols) 1994, The Bel Canto Violin: the life and times of Alfredo Campoli 1906–1991 1999, Salons, Singers and Songs: A Background to Romantic French Song 1830–70 2002, François Couperin and The Perfection of Music 2004, William James and the Beginnings of Modern Musical Australia; contribs to the New Grove Dictionary of Music and Musicians, the New Grove Dictionary of Opera, the New Oxford History of Music, European Music 1520–1640; numerous articles in major musicological journals. *Leisure interests:* reading, travel, theatre. *Address:* School of Music, University of Western Australia, Nedlands 6009, Western Australia (office); 100 Dalkeith Road, Nedlands 6009, Western Australia, Australia (home). *Telephone:* (8) 9386-1934 (home). *E-mail:* dtunley@westnet.com.au (office).

TUNON DE LARA, (José) Manuel, MD, PhD; French physician, university administrator and academic; *President, University of Bordeaux;* b. 13 Feb. 1958; s. of the late Spanish historian Manuel Tuñón de Lara; ed Lycée Louis-Barthou de Pau, medical studies in Bordeaux, Pasteur Inst., Paris, Univ. of Southampton, UK; intern in several hosps while specializing in treatment of respiratory diseases 1983; Asst Chef de Clinique, Centre Hospitalier Universitaire (CHU) de Bordeaux 1989–94, Univ. Hosp. Practitioner, Respiratory Diseases 1994–96; Prof. of Pneumology, Univ. Victor Segalen Bordeaux 2 1996–2003; conducted research on asthma and respiratory allergies; Vice-Pres. in charge of Int. Relations, Univ. of Bordeaux 2003–08, Pres. Univ. of Bordeaux II 2008–, Pres. Univ. of Bordeaux 2010–. *Publications:* numerous scientific works and articles in professional journals. *Address:* Office of the President, Université de Bordeaux, 166 Cours de l'Argonne, 33000 Bordeaux, France (office). *Telephone:* (5) 56-33-80-80 (office). *Fax:* (5) 56-33-80-89 (office). *E-mail:* affaires.generales@univ-bordeaux.fr (office); secretaire.general@univ-bordeaux.fr (office). *Website:* www.univ-bordeaux.fr (office).

TUOMIOJA, Erkki Sakari, MA, MBA, PhD; Finnish journalist and politician; *Minister of Foreign Affairs;* b. 1 July 1946, Helsinki; s. of Sakari Tuomioja and Vappu Wuolijoki; m. Marja-Helena Rajala 1978; ed Univ. of Helsinki; reporter 1967–69; mem. Parl. (SDP) 1970–79, 1991–, Vice-Chair. SDP Parl. Group 1991–96, Chair. 1996–99, Chair. Parl. Grand Cttee (EU Affairs) 1995–99, 2007–11; mem. Helsinki City Council 1969–79, Deputy Mayor of Helsinki 1979–91; Minister of Trade and Industry 1999–2000, of Foreign Affairs 2000–07, 2011–; Pres. European Council July–Dec. 2006; Chief Ed. Ydin magazine 1977–91; Lecturer, Helsinki Univ. 1997–; Pres. Nordic Council 2008; Non-Fiction Finlandia Prize 2006. *Publications:* 20 books on history, politics and int. affairs. *Leisure interests:* history, literature, running. *Address:* Ministry of Foreign Affairs, Merikasarmi, Laivastokatu 22, PO Box 176, 00023 Helsinki, Finland (office). *Telephone:* (9) 16005 (office). *Fax:* (9) 629840 (office). *E-mail:* erkki.tuomioja@formin.fi (office); erkkituomioja@hotmail.com. *Website:* formin.finland.fi (office); www.tuomioja.org.

TUPOU VI, HM The King of Tonga, MA; Tongan politician, army officer and fmr diplomatist; b. 12 July 1959, Nuku'alofa; s. of HM the late King Taufa'ahau Tupou IV; brother of HM the late King George Tupou V; m. Nanasipau'u Vaea 1982; three c.; ed in New Zealand, Britannia Royal Naval Coll., Dartmouth, Univ. of New South Wales, Australian Jt Services Staff Coll., US Naval War Coll., Bond Univ., Australia; fmrly known as Aho'eitu' Unuaki'otonga Tuku'aho, then HRH Prince 'Ulukalala-Lavaka-Ata; joined Tonga Defence Services 1981, Second-in-Command 1995; CO, Navy 1993; Minister of Foreign Affairs and Defence 1998–06; Prime Minister of Tonga 2000–06, also Minister of Civil Aviation and Telecommunications; proclaimed Crown Prince 11 Sept. 2006; High Commr to Australia 2008–12; succeeded to the throne 18 March 2012 on death of elder brother.

TURABI, Hassan at-; Sudanese politician; Leader, Nat. Islamic Front 1986; est. Popular Arab Islamic Conference in Khartoum 1990; Pres. Nat. Ass. 1996–2000; Founder Congress Party 2000; arrested and imprisoned 2001, released Oct. 2003, arrested April 2004 in connection with alleged plot to overthrow Pres. Omar al-Bashir, released 2005. *Address:* Popular Congress Party, Khartoum, Sudan.

TURAJONZODA, Haji Akbar; Tajikistani ecclesiastic and politician; b. 16 Feb. 1954, Kafarnikhon; s. of Ishan-e Tourajon; two s. four d.; ed Tashkent Islam Inst., Uzbek SSR, Amman Univ., Jordan, Mir-e Arab School, Buxora; teacher, Tashkent Islam Inst. 1987–88; Head of Office of Qaziate of Tajikistan 1988–90; apptd Chief Qazi of Tajikistan 1990, Qaziate position abolished 1993; elected mem. Supreme Soviet Tajik SSR 1990; participant in democratic movt against Islamic fundamentalists, forced to emigrate to Iran, in hiding 1993; First Deputy Chair. Islamic Renaissance Movt of Tajikistan 1993–99; headed United Tajik Opposition in negotiations with the Govt leading to peace settlement 1995–97; fmr First Deputy Chair. of Tajikistan; currently Senator in Majlisi Milliy (Nat. Ass.); Ismael Somoni Medal of Honour, World Islamic Centre Prize for Peace 1999. *Publication:* Between Water and Fire: The Peace Plan. *Leisure interests:* reading, sports. *Address:* Majlisi Milliy (National Assembly), 734051 Dushanbe, Xiyoboni Rudaki 42, Tajikistan (office). *Telephone:* (372) 23-19-33 (office). *Fax:* (372) 21-51-10 (office). *E-mail:* mejparl@parliament.tojikiston.com (office). *Website:* www.majlisimilli.tj (office).

TURANSKAYA, Tatyana Mikhailovna; Moldovan (Ukrainian) fmr civil servant and politician; *Chairman of Government of 'Transnistrian Moldovan Republic';* b. 20 Nov. 1972, Bilhorod-Dnistrovskyi, Odesa Oblast, Ukrainian SSR, USSR; m.; ed Odesa State Econs Univ.; worked at tax inspectorate, Ribniţa 1999–2012; Deputy Head of Ribniţa dist admin on econ. issues 2012, then First Deputy Head, Acting Head June–Aug. 2012, Head Aug. 2012–13; Deputy Prime Minister for Regional Devt, 'Transnistrian Moldovan Repub.' June–July 2013; Chair. of Govt of 'Transnistrian Moldovan Repub.' July 2013–. *Address:* Office of the Chairman of the Government, 3300 Tiraspol, ul. 25 Oktyabrya 45, Moldova (office). *Telephone:* (533) 8-05-02 (office). *Fax:* (533) 8-05-02 (office). *E-mail:* psp .pmr@mail.ru (office). *Website:* president.gospmr.ru (office).

TURCHYNOV, Oleksandr Valentynovych, PhD; Ukrainian politician, economist and screenwriter; *Acting President;* b. 31 March 1964, Dnipropetrovsk; m. Hanna Volodymyrivna Turchynova; one s.; ed Dnipropetrovsk Metallurgic Inst., Dept of Technology; began career working at Kryvorizhstal complex then moved into Komsomol and CP apparatus; worked in Dnipropetrovsk regional admin; Co-founder and mem. All-Ukrainian Hromada Asscn 1993–99; apptd Adviser on Econ. Issues to Prime Minister Leonid Kuchma 1993, then apptd Vice-Pres. Ukrainian Union of Industrialist and Entrepreneurs; Dir Econ. Reforms Inst., Kyiv 1994–98,

also Head of Ukrainian Nat. Acad. of Science's Lab. of Shadow Econ. Research; mem. Verkhovna Rada (Parl.) 1998–, Chair. (Speaker) 22 Feb. 2014–; joined Yuliya Tymoshenko's Fatherland (Batkivshchyna) party 1999, currently First Deputy Leader; Chief of Security Service of Ukraine (SBU) 2004–05; Vice-Chair. Yuliya Tymoshenko Bloc (BYuT) in charge of election campaign HQ 2006–07; First Deputy Prime Minister 2007–10, Acting Prime Minister 3–11 March 2010; apptd Acting Pres. of Ukraine 23 Feb. 2014 (following impeachment of Viktor Yanukovych); pastor, or perhaps elder or lay preacher, Baptist church, Kyiv. *Publications:* Illusion of Fear 2004, script for the same-name film based on the book 2005 (film released in Ukraine 2008). *Address:* Office of the President, 01220 Kyiv, vul. Bankova 11, Ukraine (office). *Telephone:* (44) 255-73-33 (office). *Fax:* (44) 255-78-44 (office). *E-mail:* president@apu.gov.ua (office). *Website:* www.president .gov.ua (office).

TURCOTTE, HE Cardinal Jean-Claude; Canadian ecclesiastic; *Archbishop Emeritus of Montreal;* b. 26 June 1936, Montréal; ed André-Grasset School, Major Seminary, Montreal, Catholic Faculty, Lille, France; ordained priest 1959; vicar to Parish of St Mathias 1959–61, subsequently Diocesan Asst Chaplain for Christian Working Youth 1961–64; pastoral work, Montreal 1959–64, 1965–81; Diocesan Counsellor of JOC, JICF and Christian Workers' Movt 1965–67; held various posts, including Sec. Comm. des Traitemens, (responsible for studies and perm. formation of clergy), Diocesan Director for Parochial Pastoral, Diocesan Procurator and Cathedral Canon 1967–74; Vicar Gen. and Gen. Coordinator of Diocesan Pastoral Programmes 1981; Titular Bishop of Suas and Auxiliary Bishop of Montreal 1982–90; Archbishop of Montreal 1990–2012, Archbishop Emer. 2012–; attended Ninth Ordinary Ass. of World Synod of Bishops, Vatican City 1994; cr. Cardinal (Cardinal-Priest of Nostra Signora del Santissimo Sacramento e Santi Martiri Canadesi) 1994; participated in Papal Conclave 2005, 2013; mem. Council of Cardinals for Study of Organizational and Econ. Problems of Holy See 1995; attended Special Ass. for America of World Synod of Bishops, Vatican City 1997; Pres. Canadian Conf. of Catholic Bishops 1997–2000; Dr hc (Univ. of Montréal) 2007. *Address:* Archdiocese of Montreal, 2000 Rue Sherbrooke Ouest, Montréal, PQ H3H 1G4, Canada (office). *Telephone:* (514) 931-7311 (office). *Fax:* (514) 931-3432 (office). *Website:* www.diocesemontreal.org (office).

TÜRK, Danilo, PhD; Slovenian academic, diplomatist, lawyer, politician and fmr head of state; b. 19 Feb. 1952, Maribor; m. Barbara Miklič; one d.; ed Univ. of Ljubljana, Univ. of Belgrade; Lecturer in Public Int. Law, Univ. of Ljubljana 1978–88, Prof. of Int. Law 1988–, Head Inst. of Int. Law and Int. Relations 1983–95; mem. UN Sub-comm. on Prevention of Discrimination and Protection of Minorities 1984–92; Special Rapporteur 1989–92, Chair. 1990; Perm. Rep. of Slovenia to the UN 1992–2000; mem. UN Security Council 1998–99, Pres. Aug. 1998, Nov. 1999; mem. Security Council Mission to Jakarta and East Timor, Indonesia Sept. 1999, Asst Sec.-Gen. of UN for Political Affairs 2000–05; active in the field of human rights with several NGOs; apptd Chair. Int. Law Asscn, Slovenia 1990; Pres. of Slovenia 2007–12; Hon. Prof., Acad. of Public Admin, Astana, Kazakhstan 2009; Grand Cross with Diamonds, Order of the Sun (Peru) 2008; Hon. GCB 2008; Commdr, First Class, Order of the White Rose of Finland 2010; Kt Grand Cross, Order of Saint-Charles (Monaco) 2011; Kt Grand Cross with Cordon, Order of the italian Repub. 2011; Grand Star, Decoration on Honour for Services to the Repub. of Austria 2011; Grand Cross, Royal Norwegian Order of St Olav 2011; Kt Grand Cross, Order of the Falcon (Iceland) 2011; Dr hc (Univ. of Szeged, Hungary) 2010, (V.N. Karazin Kharkiv Nat. Univ., Ukraine) 2011; Gold medal, Széchenyi Scientific Soc. Hungary 2008, Arthur J. Goldberg Award, Touro Law Coll., USA 2008, Ilyas Afandiyev Int. Prize 2010. *Publications:* book on the principle of non-intervention in int. relations and int. law and over 100 articles in legal journals and other publs. *Leisure interests:* hiking, cross-country skiing, reading books, classical music. *Address:* Office of the Former President, 1000 Ljubljana, Slovenia; Železna cesta 14 (office); Faculty of Law, University of Ljubljana, 1000 Ljubljana, Kongresni trg 12, Slovenia. *Telephone:* (1) 478-1221 (office); (1) 241-8500. *Fax:* (1) 478-1191 (office); (1) 241-8660. *E-mail:* danilo.turk@up-rs.si (office); rektorat@uni-lj.si. *Website:* www2.gov.si/up-rs/bp-dt.nsf (office); www.uni-lj.si.

TURK, Žiga, BSc, MSc, PhD; Slovenian academic and politician; *Professor and Chair in Construction Informatics, Faculty of Civil and Geodetic Engineering, University of Ljubljana;* b. 1962, Ljubljana; ed Univ. of Ljubljana; Founding Ed. Moj mikro (magazine on microcomputers) 1984–87; Asst Research Engineer, Inst. of Structural Eng and Earthquake and Building Informatics, Univ. of Ljubljana 1986–89, Asst in Computer Science, Dept of Architecture 1989–93, Asst Prof. 1993–98, Assoc. Prof. of Information Tech. and Documentation, Faculty of Civil and Geodetic Eng 1998–2004, Prof. 2004–07, currently Prof. and Chair in Construction Informatics; Visiting Lecturer, Royal Inst. of Tech., Stockholm, Sweden 1997–99; Visiting Prof., Istanbul Tech. Univ. 2001–07; Minister without Portfolio, responsible for Growth 2007–08, Minister of Educ., Science, Culture and Sport 2012–13; fmr mem. Scientific Council, Slovenia Research Agency; fmr Vice-Pres. Strategic Council for Culture, Educ. and Science; Co-founder and Co-ed. ITcon (int. science magazine); fmr Chair. Supervisory Bd Telecom Slovenia, Mobitel. *Address:* Faculty of Civil and Geodetic Engineering, University of Ljubljana, Jamova cesta 2, p.p 3422, 1001 Ljubljana, Slovenia (office). *Telephone:* (1) 4768500 (office). *Fax:* (1) 4250681 (office). *E-mail:* tajnistvo@fgg.uni-lj.si (office). *Website:* www3.fgg.uni-lj.si/en; www.zturk.com.

TURKI, Abdul Aziz al-Abdullah at-, BA; Saudi Arabian international organization official; b. 12 Aug. 1936, Jeddah; m.; two d.; ed Univ. of Cairo; with US Embassy, Jeddah 1953–54, ARAMCO 1954–66; Dir Office of Minister of Petroleum and Mineral Resources 1966–68; Dir of Gen. Affairs, Directorate of Mineral Resources 1968–70; Asst Sec.-Gen. OAPEC 1970–75, Sec.-Gen. 1990–2008; Sec.-Gen. Supreme Advisory Council for Petroleum and Mineral Affairs, Saudi Arabia 1975–90; Saudi Gov. for OPEC 1975–90; Deputy Minister, Ministry of Petroleum and Mineral Resources 1975; Chair. Arab Maritime Petroleum Transport Co., Kuwait 1981–87, Pemref 1982–89; mem. Bd of Dirs Petromin 1975–89, ARAMCO 1980–89. *Leisure interests:* tennis, swimming. *Address:* c/o Organization of Arab Petroleum Exporting Countries, PO Box 20501, Safat 13066, Kuwait (office).

TURKSON, HE Cardinal Peter Kodwo Appiah, MTh, MDiv; Ghanaian ecclesiastic; *President, Pontifical Council for Justice and Peace;* b. 11 Oct. 1948, Wassaw Nsuta; ed St Teresa's Minor Seminary, Amisano, St Peter's Regional Seminary, Pedu, Seminary of St Anthony-on-Hudson, Rensaleer, New York, USA,

Pontifical Biblical Inst., Rome, Italy; ordained priest of Cape Coast 1975; staff mem., St Teresa's Minor Seminary 1975–76, 1980–81; staff mem. and lecturer of Sacred Scripture, St Peter's Major Seminary; visiting lecturer, Major Seminary, Anyama, Cote d'Ivoire 1983–86; part time lecturer and Chaplain, Univ. of Cape Coast 1984–86; promoted to episcopate while studying in Rome; Archbishop of Cape Coast 1992–2009; attended Special Ass. for Africa of World Synod of Bishops, Vatican City 1994, Ninth Ordinary Ass. of World Synod of Bishops, Vatican City 1994; cr. Cardinal (Cardinal Priest of San Liborio) 2003; participated in Papal Conclave 2005, 2013; Pres. Ghana Catholic Bishop's Conf. 1997–2004; Chancellor Catholic Univ. College of Ghana, Legon 2002–; Vice-Pres. Asscn of Episcopal Confs of Anglophone West Africa 2004–07 (merged with Conférence Episcopale de l'Afrique de l'Ouest), Pres. 2007–; Chair. Ghana Chapter of The Conf. of Religions for Peace 2003–07, Ghana Nat. Peace Council 2006–, Int. Sec. of the Pontifical Mission Socs 2006–; Treas. Symposium of Episcopal Confs of Africa and Madagascar 2007–; mem. Governing Council of Univ. of Ghana 2001–06, Bd of Dirs, Pontifical Council for Christian Unity 2002–, Pontifical Comm. for the Cultural Patrimony of the Church 2002–, Pontifical Congregation for Divine Worship 2005–, Supreme Cttee of the Pontifical Missions Soc. 2006–, Pontifical Council for Justice and Peace 2007– (Pres. 2009–13, 2013–); mem. Bd of Dirs CEDECOM 2002–, Cen. Regional Devt Cttee, Asscn of Ghana Biblical Exegetes; Trustee, Komenda-Edina-Eguafo-Abrem Educational Fund; Hon. Pres. World Conf. of Religions for Peace; Order of the Star, Order of the Rock, Ghana; Dr hc (Univ. of Ghana, Legon), (Univ. of Educ., Winneba, Ghana), (Holy Cross Coll., Notre Dame, USA). *Publications:* several articles. *Address:* Pontifical Council for Justice and Peace, Piazza San Calisto 16, 00153 Rome, Italy (office). *Telephone:* (06) 69879911 (office); (42) 32593 (home). *Fax:* (06) 69887205 (office); (42) 32593 (home). *E-mail:* pcjustpax@justpeace.va (office). *Website:* www.justpax.va (office).

TURLINGTON, Christy, BA; American fashion model; b. (Christy Nicole Turlington), 2 Jan. 1969, Walnut Creek, Calif.; d. of Dwain Turlington and María Elizabeth Turlington (née Parker); m. Edward Burns 2003; one s. one d.; ed Monte Vista High School, Fla, Gallatin School of Individualized Study, New York Univ.; discovered aged 14; moved to New York City to model full-time 1987; with Ford Models Inc. 1985; model for Calvin Klein 1987–2007, face of Calvin Klein's Eternity Fragrance; model for Revlon, Maybelline 1993; promoted advertisement campaigns for Michael Kors, Camay Soap, Special K Cereal; Spokesperson, Centers for Disease Control (CDC), American Cancer Soc. (ACS); f. Every Mother Counts campaign 2010. *Films include:* Catwalk 1996, appeared in George Michael's video Freedom, No Woman, No Cry (documentary, dir, as Christy Turlington Burns) 2010. *Publication:* Living Yoga: Creating A Life Practice 2003. *Address:* c/o United Talent Agency, 9560 Wilshire Boulevard, Suite 500, Beverly Hills, CA 90212-2401, USA (office); 344 East 59th Street, New York, NY 10022 (office); Every Mother Counts, 805 15th Street NW, Suite 700, Washington, DC 20005, USA. *Telephone:* (310) 273-6700 (office); (202) 617-3899. *Fax:* (310) 247-1111 (office). *Website:* www.unitedtalent.com (office); www.everymothercounts.org . *E-mail:* info@everymothercounts.org.

TURNAGE, Mark-Anthony; British composer; b. 10 June 1960, Corringham, Essex; s. of Roy Turnage and Patricia Knowles; m. 1st Susan Shaw 1989 (divorced 1990); m. 2nd Helen Reed 1992; two s.; ed Hassenbrook Comprehensive School, Palmers Sixth Form, Grays, Royal Coll. of Music with Oliver Knussen and John Lambert and Tanglewood, USA with Hans Werner Henze and Gunther Schuller; first opera, Greek, premiered at first Munich Biennale 1988; Composer-in-Asscn with City of Birmingham Symphony Orchestra, composing three major works 1989–93; Composer-in-Asscn with ENO 1995–99; Assoc. Composer in Asscn with BBC Symphony Orchestra 2000–03; Momentum, BBC 3 composer weekend dedicated to his music, Barbican Hall, London 2003; Composer-in-Residence London Philharmonic Orchestra 2005–, Chicago Symphony Orchestra 2006–08; one of 20 composers commissioned to write a piece of music for the 2012 Cultural Olympiad;; Guinness Prize for Composition 1982, Benjamin Britten Young Composers' Prize 1983, BMW Music Theatre Prize 1988, Laurence Olivier Award 2001. *Compositions include:* Night Dances for orchestra 1980, Lament for a Hanging Man for soprano and ensemble 1983, Sarabande for soprano saxophone and piano 1985, On All Fours for chamber ensemble 1985, Greek (opera) 1987, Three Screaming Popes for orchestra 1988, Greek Suite for mezzo soprano, baritone and ensemble 1989, Kai for solo cello and ensemble 1989, Some Days 1989, Killing Time (television scena) 1991, Drowned Out 1992, Your Rockaby saxophone concerto 1992, Blood on the Floor for large ensemble 1994, Dispelling the Fears 1994, Twice Through the Heart for mezzo and 16 players 1997, Country of the Blind 1997, The Silver Tassie (opera) 1997, Silent Cities for orchestra 1998, About Time for two orchestras 1999, Evening Songs for orchestra 2000, Another Set To for trombone and orchestra 2000, Scorched for jazz trio and orchestra (with John Scofield) 2000, On Opened Ground concerto for viola and orchestra 2000, Bass Inventions for double bass and ensemble 2001, The Torn Fields for orchestra 2001, Dark Crossing 2001, A Quick Blast 2001, The Game is Over for orchestra 2002, Scherzoid for orchestra 2003–04, From the Wreckage for trumpet and orchestra 2004, Riffs and Refrains 2005, Ceres for orchestra 2005, Lullaby for Hans for orchestra 2005, From all Sides for orchestra 2005–06, Chicago Remains for orchestra 2007, Milo 2009, Texan Tenebrae for orchestra 2010, Hammered Out 2010, Anna Nicole (opera) 2011, Beyond This 2012, Frieze (commissioned for bicentenary of Royal Philharmonic Soc.) 2012. *Leisure interests:* football, films, theatre. *Address:* Boosey and Hawkes Music Publishers, Aldwych House, 71–91 Aldwych, London, WC2B 4HN, England (office). *Telephone:* (20) 7054-7200 (office). *E-mail:* composers@boosey.com (office). *Website:* www.boosey.com (office).

TURNBERG, Baron (Life Peer), cr. 2000, of Cheadle in the County of Cheshire; **Leslie Arnold Turnberg,** Kt, MB, ChB, MD, FRCP, FMedSci; British professor of medicine; b. 22 March 1934, Manchester; s. of Hyman Turnberg and Dora Bloomfield; m. Edna Barme 1968; one s. one d.; ed Stand Grammar School, Whitefield and Univ. of Manchester; Lecturer, then Sr Lecturer in Gastroenterology, Univ. of Manchester, Manchester Royal Infirmary 1968–73; Prof. of Medicine Univ. of Manchester 1973–97, Dean Faculty of Medicine 1986–89; Hon. Consultant Physician, Hope Hosp. 1973–97; Pres. Royal Coll. of Physicians 1992–97, Asscn of Physicians of GB and Ireland 1996–97; Chair. Conf. of Medical Royal Colls 1993–95, Strategic Review of London's Health Services 1997; Pres. Medical Protection Soc. 1997–2004, Medical Council on Alcoholism 1997–2002; Chair. Bd of Public Health Lab. Service 1997–2002; Scientific Adviser Asscn of

Medical Research Charities 1997–; Pres. British Soc. of Gastroenterology 1999–2000; Chair. Bd of Health Quality Service 2000–04; Chair. UK Forum on Genetics and Insurance 2000–02; Vice-Pres. Acad. of Medical Sciences 1998–2004; Hon. FRCP (Edin.), FRCP (Glasgow), FRCPI, FRCOG; Hon. Fellow, Royal Colls of Ophthalmologists, Psychiatrists, Surgeons of England, Royal Australian Coll. of Physicians, S African Coll. of Medicine, Pakistan Coll. of Physicians, Acad. of Medicine of Hong Kong and of Singapore and several others; Hon. DSc (Salford) 1996, (Manchester) 1998, (Imperial Coll. London) 2000. *Publications include:* Intestinal Secretion 1982, Mechanisms of Mucosal Protection in the Upper Gastro-Intestinal Tract 1983, Clinical Gastroenterology 1989. *Leisure interests:* reading, antiquarian books, walking, talking, Chinese ceramics. *Address:* House of Lords, Westminster, London, SW1A 0PW, England. *Telephone:* (20) 7435-8223. *Fax:* (20) 7435-9262 (office).

TURNBULL, Baron (Life Peer), cr. 2005, of Enfield in the London Borough of Enfield; **Andrew Turnbull,** KCB, CVO; British fmr civil servant; b. 21 Jan. 1945, Enfield, Middx, England; s. of Anthony Turnbull and Mary Turnbull; m. Diane Clarke 1967; two s.; ed Enfield Grammar School, Christ's Coll., Cambridge; Overseas Devt Inst. Fellow working as economist to Govt of Zambia 1968–70; Asst Prin., HM Treasury 1970, Prin. 1972, seconded to IMF 1976–78, Asst Sec. 1978, Head of Gen. Expenditure Policy Group 1985–88, Deputy Sec. (Public Finance) 1992, Second Perm. Sec. (Public Spending) 1993–94; Pvt. Sec. to Prime Minister 1983–85, Prin. Pvt. Sec. to Prime Minister 1988–92; Perm. Sec. Dept of Environment 1994–97, Dept of Environment, Transport and the Regions 1997–98, Perm. Sec. HM Treasury 1998–2002; Cabinet Sec. and Head of Home Civil Service 2002–05 (retd); mem. (Crossbench) House of Lords 2005–; Dir (non-exec.) Prudential plc, British Land plc, Frontier Economics Ltd; Chair. Bd Govs Dulwich Coll., Zambia Orphans of Aids (UK); Trustee, Global Warming Policy Foundation; Hon. Fellow, Christ's Coll., Cambridge; hon. degrees (Middlesex, Cranfield). *Leisure interests:* walking, opera, golf, sailing. *Address:* House of Lords, Westminster, London, SW1A 0PW, England (office). *Telephone:* (20) 7219-5353 (office). *Fax:* (20) 7219-5979 (office). *Website:* www.parliament.uk/biographies/lords/lord-turnbull/3758 (office).

TURNBULL, Lucinda Mary (Lucy), LLB, MBA; Australian lawyer and politician; b. 30 March 1958, Sydney; d. of Thomas Eyre Forrest Hughes and Joanna Fitzgerald; m. Malcolm Bligh Turnbull 1980; one s. one d.; ed Univ. of Sydney, Univ. of New South Wales; Pnr, Turnbull McWilliam (solicitors) 1988–99, Turnbull & Pnrs Ltd 1988–92, Turnbull & Co. 1992–95, Dir Turnbull & Pnrs Pty Ltd 1990–; Dir FTR Holdings Ltd 1997– (Chair. 1997–2001), Melbourne IT Ltd 2006–; Deputy Lord Mayor of Sydney 1999–2003, Lord Mayor (first woman) 2003–04; Deputy Chair. Sydney Cancer Centre Foundation 2002–, Cttee for Sydney; Dir Museum of Contemporary Art 2002–, Centre for Ind. Studies, Nat. Portrait Gallery; Chair. NSW Ministerial Advisory Council on Biotechnology 2001–, WebCentral Group Ltd; mem. Australian Museum Trust 1995–99, Deputy Pres. 1995–99; Pres. Sydney Children's Hosp. Appeal, Sydney Children's Hosp. Foundation Ltd 1996–2000; Commr Australian Pavilion at Venice Architecture Biennale 2006, 2008; Gov. Woolcock Inst. of Medical Research; mem. Commonwealth of Nations Comm. on Respect and Understanding, NSW Cancer Council 1997–99. *Publications include:* Sydney: Biography of a City 1999. *Leisure interests:* history, politics, contemporary culture, visual arts, urban design, architecture. *Address:* Turnbull & Partners Pty Ltd, Level 38/264 George Street, Sydney, NSW 2000, Australia (office). *Telephone:* (2) 8248-3900 (office).

TURNBULL, Malcolm Bligh, BA, LLB, BCL; Australian banker, lawyer and politician; *Minister of Communications;* b. 24 Oct. 1954, Sydney, NSW; s. of Bruce B. Turnbull and Coral Lansbury; m. Lucinda M. F. Hughes 1980; one s. one d.; ed Sydney Grammar School, Univ. of Sydney and Univ. of Oxford (Rhodes Scholar); State Parl. Corresp. for Nation Review 1976; journalist, The Bulletin 1977–78; Exec. Asst to Chair. Consolidated Press Holdings Ltd 1978; journalist, The Sunday Times, London 1978–79; barrister, Sydney 1980–82; Gen. Counsel and Sec. Consolidated Press Holdings Ltd 1983–85; solicitor in pvt. practice, Turnbull McWilliam, Sydney 1986–87; Prin. Turnbull and Co. (solicitors) 1987; Man. Dir Turnbull & Pnrs Pty Ltd (investment bankers), Sydney 1987–97; Chair. Axiom Forest Resources Ltd (HK) 1991–92; Dir Perseverance Corpn Ltd 1993–94, Star Mining Corpn NL 1993–95, FTR Holdings Ltd 1995–2004; Chair. Oz Email Ltd 1994–99; Dir Australian Republican Movt 1991–93, Chair. 1993–2000; Chair. cttee to advise on changing Australia to Repub.; Chair. and Man. Dir Goldman Sachs Australia 1997–2001, Pnr, Goldman Sachs (US) 1998–2001; Chair. Menzies Research Centre 2001–04; Hon. Fed. Treas., Liberal Party 2002–03, Treasury Spokesman 2007–08, Leader 2008–09; mem. NSW State Exec. 2002–03, mem. Fed. Finance Cttee 2002–03, mem. Fed. Exec. 2002–03; MP for Wentworth, NSW 2004–, Parl. Sec. to Prime Minister 2006–07; Minister for the Environment and Heritage 2007; Shadow Treas. 2007–08, Leader of the Opposition 2008–09; Shadow Minister for Communications and Broadband 2010–13; Minister for Communications 2013–; Henry Lawson Prize for Poetry 1975, Centenary Medal 2003. *Publications:* The Spycatcher Trial 1988, The Reluctant Republic 1993, Fighting for the Republic 1999. *Leisure interests:* reading, walking, riding, gardening. *Address:* Department of Broadband, Communications and the Digital Economy, GPOB 2154, Canberra, ACT 2601 (office); PO Box 545, Edgecliff, NSW 2027, Australia (office). *Telephone:* (2) 6271-1000 (office). *Fax:* (2) 6271-1901 (office). *E-mail:* media@dbcde.gov.au (office). *Website:* www.dbcde.gov.au (office); www.malcolmturnbull.com.au.

TURNBULL, Rt Rev. Michael, CBE, DL, MA, DipTheol, DLitt, DD; British ecclesiastic; *Honorary Assistant Bishop in the Diocese of Canterbury, Rochester and Europe;* b. 27 Dec. 1935, Yorks., England; s. of George Turnbull and Adeline Awty; m. Brenda Merchant 1963; one s. two d.; ed Ilkley Grammar School, Keble Coll. Oxford and St John's Coll. Durham; ordained deacon 1960, priest 1961; curate, Middleton 1960–61, Luton 1961–65; Domestic Chaplain to Archbishop of York 1965–69; Rector of Heslington and Chaplain, York Univ. 1969–76; Chief Sec. Church Army 1976–84; Archdeacon of Rochester 1984–88; Bishop of Rochester 1988–94, of Durham 1994–2003; Hon. Asst Bishop, Diocese of Canterbury, Rochester and Europe 2003–; mem. Gen. Synod of Church of England 1970–75, 1987–2003; mem. Archbishops' Council 1999–2001, Chair. Ministry Div. 1999–2001; Chair. Archbishops' Comm. on Org. of Church of England; mem. House of Lords 1994–2003; Chair. Foundation for Church Leadership 2002–05;

DL, Co. of Kent; Hon. DLitt 1994; Hon. DD 2003. *Publications:* Unity: The Next Step? (contrib.) 1972, God's Front Line 1979, Parish Evangelism 1980, Learning to Pray 1981, 100 Minute Bible Reflections (ed) 2007, The State of the Church and the Church of the State 2012; numerous articles in journals. *Leisure interests:* cricket, family life, lecturer with Swan Hellenic Cruises, leader Holy Land Pilgrimages. *Address:* 67 Strand Street, Sandwich, Kent, CT13 9HN, England. *Telephone:* (1304) 611389. *E-mail:* bstmt@btopenworld.com. *Website:* www.bishopmichaelturnbull.com.

TURNER, David J.; British banker and company director; *Chairman, Commonwealth Bank of Australia;* Finance Dir GKN plc –2001; Chief Financial Officer Brambles 2001–03, CEO 2003–07 (retd); Chair. Cobham plc 2008–10; mem. Bd of Dirs Commonwealth Bank of Australia 2006–, Chair. 2010–, Chair. Bd Performance and Renewal Cttee, mem. People & Remuneration Cttee; fmr mem. Bd of Dirs Whitbread plc, Chair. Audit Cttee 2000–06; Fellow, Inst. of Chartered Accountants in England and Wales. *Address:* Commonwealth Bank of Australia, Ground Floor, Tower 1, 201 Sussex Street, Sydney, NSW 2000, Australia (office). *Telephone:* (2) 9378-2000 (office). *Fax:* (2) 9118-7192 (office). *E-mail:* info@commbank.com.au (office). *Website:* www.commbank.com.au (office).

TURNER, Grenville, MA, DPhil, FRS; British geochemist and academic; *Professor Emeritus, University of Manchester;* b. 1 Nov. 1936, Todmorden, Lancs., England; s. of Arnold Turner and Florence Turner; m. Kathleen Morris 1961; one s. one d.; ed St John's Coll., Cambridge and Balliol Coll., Oxford; Asst Prof., Univ. of California, Berkeley 1962–64; Lecturer, Univ. of Sheffield 1964–74, Sr Lecturer 1974–79, Reader 1979–80, Prof. of Physics 1980–88; Prof. of Isotope Geochemistry, Univ. of Manchester 1988–2002, Research Prof. 2002–12, Prof. Emer. 2012–; Visiting Assoc. in Nuclear Geophysics, Calif. Inst. of Tech. 1970–71; Fellow, Royal Soc. 1980, Council mem. 1990–92; Fellow, Meteoritical Soc. 1980, European Asscn of Geochemistry 1996, American Geophysical Union 1998; Rumford Medal, Royal Soc. 1996, Leonard Medal, Meteoritical Soc. 1999, Urey Medal European Asscn of Geochemistry 2002, Gold Medal Royal Astronomical Soc. 2004. *Achievements:* developed Ar-Ar method for rock dating, used it to determine first ages of Apollo lunar samples and a chronology of lunar evolution; discovered early isotopic evidence leading to discovery of pre-solar material in primitive meteorites; developed ultra-sensitive isotopic analysis by resonance ionisation mass spectrometry. *Publications:* scientific papers on the application of naturally occurring isotopes to earth science and the evolution of the solar system. *Leisure interests:* photography, walking, theatre. *Address:* School of Earth, Atmospheric and Environmental Sciences, University of Manchester, M13 9PL, England (office). *Telephone:* (161) 275-0401 (office). *Fax:* (161) 275-3947 (office). *E-mail:* grenville.turner@manchester.ac.uk (office). *Website:* www.seaes.manchester.ac.uk (office).

TURNER, Rt Hon. John Napier, PC, CC, QC, MA, BCL; Canadian lawyer and politician; b. 7 June 1929, Richmond, Surrey, England; s. of Leonard Turner and Phyllis Turner (née Gregory); m. Geills McCrae Kilgour 1963; three s. one d.; ed schools in Ottawa and Univs of British Columbia, Oxford and Paris; MP 1962–76, 1984–93; Minister without Portfolio 1965; Registrar-Gen. 1967–68; Minister of Consumer and Corp. Affairs Jan.–July 1968; Solicitor-Gen. April–July 1968; Minister of Justice and Attorney-Gen. 1968–72; Minister of Finance 1972–75; Leader Liberal Party of Canada 1984–90; Prime Minister of Canada June–Sept. 1984, Leader of Opposition 1984–90; Partner, McMillan, Binch (law firm), Toronto 1976–84; Partner, Miller Thomson LLP (law firm), Toronto 1990–2013; mem. Bd of Dirs Q9 Networks Inc. 2004–, E-L Financial Corpn Ltd, Loewen Group Inc., Noranda Forest Inc., Purolator Canada Ltd, Triple Crown Electronics Ltd, Iroquois Falls Power Corpn, Hockey Hall of Fame, Mount Sinai Hosp., Canadian Club of Toronto, World Wildlife Fund–Canada Ltd. *Publications include:* The Senate of Canada 1961, Politics of Purpose 1968. *Leisure interests:* tennis, canoeing, skiing. *Address:* 59 Oriole Road, Toronto, ON M4V 2E9, Canada (home). *E-mail:* JohnNTurner@rogers.com.

TURNER, Kathleen, BFA; American actress; b. 19 June 1954, Springfield, Mo.; m. Jay Weiss 1984 (divorced); one d.; ed Cen. School of Speech and Drama, UK, Southwest Missouri State Univ., Univ. of Maryland. *Plays include:* various theatre roles including Broadway debut, Gemini 1978, The Graduate, London 2000, Who's Afraid of Virginia Woolf? (London Evening Standard Award for Best Actress 2006, London Critics' Circle Best Actress 2006) 2006, Crimes of the Heart, New York (Dir) 2007–08, The Third Story, New York 2009. *Television series include:* The Doctors 1977, Leslie's Folly (also dir 1994, Friends at Last (also producer) 1995, Style and Substance 1996, Legalese 1998, Love and Action in Chicago 1999. *Films include:* Body Heat 1981, The Man With Two Brains 1983, Crimes of Passion 1984, Romancing the Stone 1984, Prizzi's Honour 1985, The Jewel of the Nile 1985, Peggy Sue Got Married 1986, Julia and Julia 1988, Switching Channels 1988, The Accidental Tourist 1989, The War of the Roses 1990, V.I. Warzhawski 1991, House of Cards, Undercover Blues 1993, Serial Mom 1994, Naked in New York 1994, Moonlight and Valentino 1995, A Simple Wish 1997, The Real Blonde 1997, The Virgin Suicides 1999, Baby Geniuses 1999, Prince of Central Park 2000, Beautiful 2000, Without Love 2004, Monster House 2006, The Perfect Family 2011; producer Hard Boiled 1990. *Publication:* Send Yourself Roses (auto-biog.) 2008. *Address:* c/o Phil Gersh, The Gersh Agency, 232 North Canon Drive, Suite 202, Beverly Hills, CA 90210, USA. *Website:* www.kathleen-turner.com.

TURNER, Michael John, CBE, BA, ACIS, FRAeS; British business executive; *Chairman, Babcock International Group PLC;* b. 5 Aug. 1948, Manchester; m.; four c.; ed Didsbury Tech. High School, Manchester and Manchester Polytechnic; joined Hawker Siddeley Aviation as undergraduate commercial apprentice 1966, later Contracts Officer; Contracts Man. (Mil.) British Aerospace (BAe) Aircraft Group, Manchester Div. 1978, Admin. Man. 1980, Exec. Dir of Admin. 1981, Divisional Admin. Dir 1982 (led Advanced Turboprop Project Team 1982–84), Divisional Dir and Gen. Man., Kingston 1984, Dir Divisional Man. Cttee and Gen. Man. Mil. Aircraft Div. 1986, Dir Marketing and Product Support, Mil. Aircraft Div. 1987, Exec. Vice-Pres. Defence Marketing, BAe PLC 1988; Chair. and Man. Dir BAe Regional Aircraft Ltd and Chair. Jetstream Aircraft 1992; Chair. Commercial Aerospace 1994 (mem. Main Bd BAe PLC), assumed responsibility for all BAe's defence export business 1996, mem. Airbus Supervisory Bd (renamed AIC) 1998, mem. Shareholders' Cttee AIC, COO BAE Systems (following merger of BAe PLC and Marconi Electronic Systems) 1999, CEO 2002–08; Chair. Defence

Industries Council 2007–10; Jt Chair. Nat. Defence Industries Council 2007–10; Vice-Pres. Soc. of British Aerospace Cos 1995, Pres. 1996–97; Dir (non-exec.) Babcock International Group PLC 1996–2005, Chair. 2008–; Dir (non-exec.) Lazard Ltd 2006–; Sr Ind. Dir (non-exec.) GKN plc 2009–; Hon. Doctor of Admin (Manchester Metropolitan Univ.). *Leisure interests:* Manchester United Football Club, golf, cricket, rugby. *Address:* Babcock International Group PLC, 33 Wigmore Street, London, W1U 1QX, England (office). *Telephone:* (20) 7355-5300 (office). *Fax:* (20) 7355-5360 (office). *E-mail:* mike.turner@babcock.co.uk (office). *Website:* www.babcock.co.uk (office).

TURNER, Adm. (retd) Stansfield, MA; American naval officer (retd), lecturer and author; b. 1 Dec. 1923, Chicago, Ill.; s. of Oliver Stansfield Turner and Wilhelmina Josephine Turner (née Wagner); m. 1st Eli Karin Gilbert 1985 (died 2000); m. 2nd Marion Weiss 2002; ed Amherst Coll., US Naval Acad., Annapolis, Univ. of Oxford, UK (Rhodes Scholar); active duty, USN, serving minesweeper, destroyers, USS Horne (guided missile cruiser in action in Vietnamese conflict); served in Office of Chief of Naval Operations, then in Office of Asst Sec. of Defense for Systems Analysis; Advanced Man. Program, Harvard Business School; Exec. Asst and Naval Aide to Sec. of the Navy 1968–70; Rear Adm. 1970; CO Carrier Task Group in USS Independence, US Sixth Fleet 1970; Dir Systems Analysis Div. of Office of Chief of Naval Operations, Dept of the Navy 1971–72; Vice-Adm. 1972; Pres. US Naval War Coll., Newport, RI 1972–74; Commdr US Second Fleet and NATO Striking Fleet Atlantic 1974–75; Adm. 1975; C-in-C Allied Forces Southern Europe, NATO 1975–77; Dir Cen. Intelligence (CIA) 1977–81; Sr Research Scholar, Center for Int. and Security Studies, Univ. of Maryland 1991–2007; Hon. Fellow, Exeter Coll., Oxford 1981–; Nat. Security Medal, Legion of Merit, Bronze Star. *Publications:* Secrecy and Democracy: The CIA in Transition 1985, Terrorism and Democracy 1991, Caging the Nuclear Genie: An American Challenge for Global Security 1997, Caging the Genies: A Workable Plan for Nuclear, Chemical and Biological Weapons 1998, Burning Before Reading 2005. *Leisure interests:* tennis, reading. *Address:* 488 River Bend Road, Great Falls, VA 22066, USA (home). *E-mail:* admturner@aol.com.

TURNER, Robert (Ted) Edward, III; American broadcasting executive and yachtsman; b. 19 Nov. 1938; s. of Robert Turner and Frances Rooney; m. 1st Judy Nye (divorced); one s. one d.; m. 2nd Jane S. Smith 1965 (divorced 1988); one s. two d.; m. 3rd Jane Fonda (q.v.) 1991 (divorced 2001); ed McCallie School, Brown Univ.; Gen. Man. Turner Advertising, Macon, Ga 1960–63; Pres. and CEO various Turner cos., Atlanta 1963–70; Chair. Bd and Pres. Turner Broadcasting System (TBS) Inc. 1970–96, est. Cable News Network (CNN) 1980, Headline News Network 1992, CNN Int. 1985, acquired MGM library of film and TV properties 1986, launched Cartoon Network 1992; TBS merged with New Line Cinema 1994; Vice-Chair. Time Warner Inc. (after TBS merger with Time Warner Inc.) 1996–2001, Vice-Chair. AOL Time Warner (after Time Warner Inc. merger with AOL) 2001–03, mem. Bd of Dirs –2006; f. Ted Turner Pictures and Ted Turner Documentaries (film production cos) 2001; f. Ted's Montana Grill restuarant chain 2002; fmr owner and Pres. Atlanta Braves professional baseball team, fmr owner and Chair. Bd Atlanta Hawks professional basketball team; Chair. Better World Soc., Wash., DC 1985–90; f. Turner Foundation, Inc. 1991, UN Foundation 1997, Nuclear Threat Initiative 2001; Dir Martin Luther King Center, Atlanta; sponsor, creator, The Goodwill Games 1985; Man of the Year, Time Magazine 1991, Cable and Broadcasting's Man of the Century 1999, Cable TV Hall of Fame 1999, U Thant Peace Award 1999, World Ecology Award (Univ. of Missouri) 2000, named Yachtsman of Year four times, Fastnet Trophy 1979, Delta Air Lines Prize for Global Understanding (administered by Univ. of Georgia) 2006, Bower Award for Business Leadership, Franklin Inst. 2006. *Yachting achievements include:* successful defense of 1977 America's Cup in yacht Courageous. *Publication:* The Racing Edge 1979. *Leisure interests:* fishing, sailing. *Address:* c/o Ted's Montana Grill, 133 Luckie Street NW, Atlanta, GA 30303, USA (office). *Telephone:* (404) 266-1344 (office). *Fax:* (404) 233-6717 (office). *Website:* www.tedturner.com (office).

TURNER, Tina; American singer and songwriter; b. (Annie Mae Bullock), 26 Nov. 1939, Brownsville, Tenn.; m. Ike Turner 1956 (divorced 1978); four s.; singer with Ike Turner Kings of Rhythm, Ike and Tina Turner Revue 1958–78; numerous concert tours worldwide; solo artist 1978–; Chevalier, Ordre des Arts et des Lettres; Grammy Awards include for Record of the Year, Song of the Year, Best Female Vocal Performance, Best Female Rock Vocal, MTV Music Video Award 1985, American Music Awards for Favorite Soul/R&B Female Artist, for Best Video Artist 1985, for Best Female Pop/Rock Artist 1986, World Music Award for Outstanding Contribution to the Music Industry 1993, Kennedy Center Honor 2005. *Films include:* Gimme Shelter 1970, Soul to Soul 1971, Tommy 1975, Mad Max: Beyond Thunderdome 1985, What's Love Got to Do with It (vocals) 1993, Last Action Hero 1993. *Recordings include:* albums: with Ike Turner: River Deep, Mountain High 1966, Outa Season 1969, The Hunter 1969, Proud Mary 1970, Come Together 1970, Workin' Together 1971, 'Nuff Said 1971, Blues Roots 1972, Feel Good 1972, Nutbush City Limits 1974, The Gospel According to Ike and Tina 1974; solo: Let Me Touch Your Mind 1972, Tina Turns the Country On 1974, Acid Queen 1975, Rough 1978, Private Dancer 1984, Break Every Rule 1986, Foreign Affair 1989, Wildest Dreams 1996, Dues Paid 1999, Twenty Four Seven 1999. *Publication:* I, Tina (autobiography) 1985. *Address:* RD Worldwide Management, 1158 26th Street, Suite 564, Santa Monica, CA 90403, USA (office). *Website:* www.bestoftinaturner.com; www.tinaturnerblog.com.

TURNER OF ECCHINSWELL, Baron (Life Peer), cr. 2005, of Ecchinswell in the County of Hampshire; **(Jonathan) Adair Turner,** MA; British business executive, financial administrator and academic; *Senior Research Fellow, Institute for New Economic Thinking;* b. 5 Oct. 1955, Ipswich, Suffolk; s. of Geoffrey Vincent Turner and Kathleen Margaret Turner; m. Orna Ní Chionna 1985; two d.; ed Hutcheson's Grammar School, Glasgow, Glenalmond School, Gonville & Caius Coll., Cambridge; grew up in Crawley and East Kilbride; Pres. Cambridge Union 1977, also Chair. Univ.'s Conservative Asscn; Coll. Supervisor in Econs, Gonville & Caius Coll. 1979–82, taught part time in parallel with business career; began career with BP (British Petroleum) PLC 1979; with Chase Manhattan Bank 1979–82; joined Social Democratic Party 1981; McKinsey & Co. 1982–95, Dir 1994–95; Dir-Gen. CBI 1995–99; Vice-Chair. Merrill Lynch Europe 2000–06; Strategic Adviser to British Prime Minister 2001–02; Chair. Policy Cttee, Centre for Econ. Performance 1999–2008, Low Pay Comm. 2002–06, Pensions Comm.

2003–06, Overseas Devt Inst.'s Council 2007, Cttee on Climate Change 2008–13, Financial Services Authority 2008–13 (FSA abolished and role split between Financial Conduct Authority and Prudential Regulation Authority); Sr Research Fellow, Inst. for New Econ. Thinking (think tank co-f. by George Soros), London 2013–; Dir (non-exec.) United News and Media 2000–, Netscalibur Ltd 2000–01, Standard Chartered Bank –2008; mem. British Overseas Trade Bd 1995–99, Econ. and Social Research Council (Chair. 2007), Group of Thirty Consultative Group on Int. Econ. and Monetary Affairs, Inc. (G-30), Washington, DC; Visiting Prof., LSE 1999–, City Univ. 2004–; Trustee, Save the Children UK –2008, Worldwide Fund for Nature UK 2002–08; mem. House of Lords 2005–. *Publication:* Just Capital: The Liberal Economy 2001. *Leisure interests:* skiing, opera, theatre, gardening. *Address:* c/o Institute for New Economic Thinking, 570 Lexington Avenue, 39th Floor New York, NY 10022, USA. *Telephone:* (212) 444-9612. *E-mail:* info@ineteconomics.org. *Website:* ineteconomics.org.

TURNER-WARWICK, Dame Margaret, DBE, BCh, MA, DM, PhD, FRCP, FMedSci, FRCPE, FRACP, FFPHM, FACP, FRSM, FRCS; British consultant physician; b. 19 Nov. 1924, London; d. of William Harvey Moore, QC and Maude Baden-Powell; m. Richard Turner-Warwick 1950; two d.; ed Maynard School, Exeter, St Paul's School for Girls, Univ. of Oxford and Univ. Coll. Hosp.; consultant physician, Royal Brompton Hosp., London Chest Hosp. 1965–72; Prof. of Medicine, Cardiothoracic Inst. 1972–87, Dean 1984–87; Pres. Royal Coll. of Physicians 1989–92; Emer. Prof. of Medicine, London Univ.; Chair. Royal Devon & Exeter Health Care NHS Trust; Fellow Univ. Coll. London 1991; Fellow Royal Coll. of General Practitioners, Faculty of Occupational Medicine, Royal Coll. of Physicians Canada, Royal Coll. of Pathologists, Royal Coll. of Physicians Ireland, Royal Coll. of Physicians and Surgeons (Canada) and others; Founder-mem. Nuffield Bioethics Council, Round Table on Sustainable Devt; Hon. Bencher, Middle Temple; Hon. Fellow Lady Margaret Hall, Oxford, Green Coll., Oxford, Girton Coll., Cambridge, Imperial Coll., London, Univ. Coll., London; Hon. DSc (New York, Sussex, Hull, Exeter, London, Oxford, Cambridge, Leicester); numerous other honours including Osler Medal, Oxford Univ. and President's Medal, British Thoracic Soc. and European Respiratory Soc. *Publications:* Immunology of the Lung 1978, Occupational Lung Disease (jtly) 1981; chapters in textbooks and articles in medical journals on asthma, fibrosing connective tissue disorders and occupational lung diseases. *Leisure interests:* gardening, watercolour painting, violin playing, country life and family. *Address:* Pynes House, Thorverton, Exeter, EX5 5LT, Devon, England (home). *Telephone:* (1392) 861173 (home). *Fax:* (1392) 860940 (home).

TURNQUEST, Orville A. T. (Tommy); Bahamian politician; b. 16 Nov. 1959, Nassau; s. of Sir Orville Turnquist (fmr Gov.-Gen.) and Lady Edith Turnquist; m. Shawn Carey; two s. one d.; ed St Anne's School, Nassau, Malvern Coll., UK and Univ. of Western Ontario, Canada; began career with Canadian Imperial Bank of Commerce; mem. Free Nat. Movt (FNM) 1985–, fmr Vice-Pres., Leader 2002–05; mem. Parl. 1992–2002, 2007–12; Parl. Sec., Office of the Prime Minister 1992–95; Minister of State for Public Service and Labour 1995–96, for Public Works 1996–97; Minister of Works 1997–98, of Public Service, Immigration and Nat. Insurance 1998–2000, of Tourism 2000–02, of Nat. Security and Immigration 2007–12. *Address:* c/o Ministry of National Security and Immigration, Churchill Building, 3rd Floor, PO Box N-3217, Nassau, The Bahamas (office). *E-mail:* tommyt@tommyturnquest.org. *Website:* www.tommyturnquest.org.

TURNQUEST, Sir Orville (Alton), GCMG, QC, LLB, JP; Bahamian lawyer, politician and judge; b. 19 July 1929, Grants Town, New Providence; s. of the late Robert Turnquest and Gwendolyn Turnquest; m. Edith Louise Thompson 1955; one s. two d.; ed Govt High School, Univ. of London, Lincoln's Inn, London; articled in chambers of Hon. A. F. Adderley 1947–53; called to The Bahamas Bar 1953, to English Bar (Lincoln's Inn) 1960; in pvt. practice 1953–92; stipendiary and circuit magistrate and coroner 1959; law tutor and mem. Examining Bd, The Bahamas Bar 1965–92; Sec.-Gen. Progressive Liberal Party 1960–62; MP for S Cen. Nassau 1962–67, for Montagu 1982–94; Opposition Leader in Senate 1972–79; Deputy Leader Free Nat. Movt 1987–94; Attorney-Gen. 1992–94, Minister of Justice 1992–93, of Foreign Affairs 1992–94, Deputy Prime Minister 1993–94, currently Leader; Gov.-Gen. The Bahamas 1995–2001; mem. Del. to first Bahamas Constitutional Conf., London 1963, Bahamas Independence Conf., London 1972; fmr Pres. Bahamas Bar Asscn; Chair. Bahamas Bar Council 1970–72; Pres. Commonwealth Parl. Asscn 1992–93; Patron The Bahamas Games; Chancellor of Diocese of Nassau and The Bahamas 1965–2002; mem. Anglican Can. Educational Authority, Nat. Cttee of United World Colls, Bd of Govs St John's Coll., St Anne's High School; fmr mem. Prov. Synod, Anglican Church of West Indies; Life mem. Rotary Int., Salvation Army Advisory Bd; Hon. LLD (Elmira Coll. NY, USA) 1998, (Univ. of West Indies) 2000; Hon. LHD (Sojourner-Douglass Coll., USA) 2002; Hon. Bencher, Lincoln's Inn; President's Assocs (Nova Southeastern Univ. Fla USA). *Leisure interests:* tennis, swimming, music, reading. *Address:* Kalamalka, Skyline Drive, POB N-682, Nassau, Bahamas (home). *Telephone:* (242) 3277951 (home). *Fax:* (242) 3274994 (home).

TUROK, Neil Geoffrey, PhD; South African/British physicist and academic; *Director, Perimeter Institute for Theoretical Physics;* b. 1958, Johannesburg, S Africa; s. of Ben Turock and Mary Turok; ed Churchill Coll., Univ. of Cambridge, Imperial Coll., London; fmr Assoc. Scientist, Fermilab, Chicago; Prof. of Physics, Princeton Univ. 1994–97; Chair. of Math. Physics, Univ. of Cambridge 1997–2008; f. African Inst. for Math. Sciences, Muizenberg 2003; Dir Perimeter Inst. for Theoretical Physics (ind. research inst.), Canada 2008–, also Ophelia Lazaridis Niels Bohr Chair in Theoretical Physics 2013–; Maxwell Medal, Inst. of Physics 1992, Most Innovative People Award for Social Innovation, World Summit on Innovation and Entrepreneurship 2008, TED (Tech., Entertainment, Design Conf.) Prize 2008. *Publications:* Global Texture 1999, Structure Formation in the Universe (co-author) 2001, Endless Universe: Beyond the Big Bang (co-author) 2007. *Address:* Perimeter Institute for Theoretical Physics, 31 Caroline Street, North Waterloo, ON N2L 2Y5, Canada (office). *Telephone:* (519) 569-7000 (office). *Fax:* (519) 569-7611 (office). *Website:* www.perimeterinstitute.ca (office).

TUROW, Scott F., JD; American writer and lawyer; b. 12 April 1949; s. of David Turow and Rita Pastron; ed Amherst Coll. and Stanford and Harvard Univs; mem. Bar, Ill. 1978, US Dist Court. Ill. 1978, US Court of Appeals (7th Circuit) 1979; Assoc., Suffolk Co. Dist Attorney, Boston 1977–78; Asst US Attorney, US Dist Court, Ill., Chicago 1978–86; Partner, Sonnenschein, Nath & Rosenthal (now Dentons), Chicago 1986–; mem. Chicago Council of Lawyers. *Publications include:* One L: An Inside Account of Life in the First Year at Harvard Law School 1977, Presumed Innocent 1987, The Burden of Proof 1990, Pleading Guilty 1993, The Laws of Our Fathers 1996, Personal Injuries 1999, Reversible Errors 2002, Ultimate Punishment: A Lawyer's Reflections on Dealing with the Death Penalty 2003, Ordinary Heroes 2006, The Best American Mystery Stories (ed.) 2006, Limitations 2007, Innocent 2010, Identical 2013; contribs to professional journals. *Address:* Dentons, 233 South Wacker Drive, Suite 7800, Chicago, IL 60606-6404, USA (office). *Telephone:* (312) 876-8163 (office). *E-mail:* scott.turow@dentons.com (office). *Website:* www.dentons.com (office); www.scottturow.com.

TURSUNKULOV, Nurlan Janyshevich; Kyrgyzstani lawyer and politician; b. 11 Aug. 1968, Bishkek; ed Kyrgyz State Univ.; served in Soviet Army 1986–88; Legal Consultant, Chui Oblast 1992–93; legal practise in Bishkek 1993–94; Asst Public Prosecutor, Bishkek 1994, Procurator Gen. 1994–96, Deputy Public Prosecutor, Naryn Oblast 1996–98, Chui Oblast 1999–2000, Public Prosecutor, Kara Suu Dist 2000–05, Talas Oblast 2005–06, Asst Mil. Prosecutor, Repub. of Kyrgyzstan 2006–08, Minister of Justice 2008–10; Prosecutor-Gen. 2009–10. *Address:* c/o Ministry of Justice, 720040 Bishkek, M. Gandi 32, Kyrgyzstan (office).

TURTELBOOM, Annemie, Licenciée en économie; Belgian politician; *Minister of Justice;* b. 22 Nov. 1967, Ninove; m.; two c.; ed Catholic Univ. of Leuven, Katholieke Hogeschool, Leuven; fmr Chair. Christian Democratic Students; mem. Town Council, Puurs 2001–07, Leader of Council 2007; Lector and Head of Dept, KHLeuven –2003; began political career with Christian People's Party (CVP) which later formed alliance with NCD (New Christian Democrats), NCD later joined Vlaamse Liberalen en Demokraten (Open VLD—Flemish Liberals and Democrats-Flemish-speaking wing); Fed. mem. Parl. (VLD) for Antwerp 2003–07, specializing in Social Affairs, Work and Pensions; Minister for Immigration and Asylum Policy 2008–09, Minister of Home Affairs (first woman) 2009–11, of Justice 2011–. *Address:* Federal Public Service of Justice, 115 blvd de Waterloo, 1000 Brussels, Belgium (office). *Telephone:* (2) 542-65-11 (office). *Fax:* (2) 542-70-39 (office). *E-mail:* info@just.fgov.be (office). *Website:* www.just.fgov.be (office); www.annemieturtelboom.be.

TURTURRO, John; American actor and film director; b. 28 Feb. 1957, Brooklyn; s. of Nicholas Turturro and Katherine Turturro; m. Katherine Borowitz; one s.; ed State Univ. of New York at New Paltz and Yale Drama School; fmr labourer; Best Actor Award, Cannes Film Festival, for role in Barton Fink 1991; Obie Award for stage appearance in Danny and the Deep Blue Sea. *Films include:* Raging Bull, Desperately Seeking Susan, Exterminator III, The Flamingo Kid, To Live and Die in LA, Hannah and Her Sisters, Gung Ho, Offbeat, The Color of Money, The Italian Five Corners, Do the Right Thing, Miller's Crossing, Men of Respect, Mo' Better Blues, Jungle Fever, Barton Fink, Brain Doctors, Mac (co-author, dir and actor), Being Human, Quiz Show, Fearless, Clockers, Search and Destroy, Unstrung Heroes, Sugartime (dir), Grace of My Heart (dir), Box of Moonlight (dir), The Truce (dir), The Big Lebowski 1997, Animals 1997, Lesser Prophets 1998, Rounders 1998, Illuminata (dir) 1998, The Source 1999, The Cradle Will Rock 1999, Company Man 1999, Two Thousand and None 1999, Oh Brother, Where Art Thou? 1999, The Man Who Cried 1999, The Luzhin Defense 1999, Thirteen Conversations About One Thing (dir) 2000, Collateral Damage (dir) 2001, Mr Deeds 2002, Fear X 2003, Anger Management 2003, 2BPerfectlyHonest 2004, Secret Passage 2004, Secret Window 2004, She Hate Me 2004, Romance and Cigarettes (dir) 2005, Quelques jours en septembre 2006, The Good Shepherd 2006, Slipstream 2007, Transformers 2007, Margot at the Wedding 2007, You Don't Mess with the Zohan 2008, What Just Happened? 2008, Miracle at St. Anna 2008, The Taking of Pelham 1 2 3 2009, Transformers: Revenge of the Fallen 2009, Transformers: Dark of the Moon 2011. *Television includes:* The Bronx Is Burning 2007. *Address:* c/o Bart Walker, Creative Artists Agency LLC, 162 5th Avenue, 6th Floor, New York, NY 10010; 16 North Oak Street, 2A Ventura, CA 93001, USA. *Telephone:* (212) 277-9000 (CAA).

TURUNEN, Antti; Finnish diplomatist and UN official; *Representative of the Secretary-General for Georgia, United Nations;* joined Foreign Service 1985, served in Washington, DC and Moscow, and as Adviser to EU High Rep. Javier Solana, Head of Unit for Eastern Europe and Cen. Asia, Ministry of Foreign Affairs 2004–07, led EU fact-finding mission to Tashkent, Uzbekistan Aug. 2006, Head of Perm. Mission to OSCE, Vienna 2007–10, chaired Perm. Council of OSCE during the Finnish Chairmanship 2008, was involved, among others, in settlement of Georgian-Ossetian conflict; Rep. of UN Sec.-Gen. for Georgia (Jt Incident Prevention and Response Mechanism) 2010–. *Address:* United Nations Observer Mission in Georgia (UNOMIG), 38 Krtsanisi Street, 380060 Tbilisi, Georgia (office); Office of the Secretary-General, United Nations, New York, NY 10017, USA (office). *Telephone:* (32) 926700 (Tbilisi) (office); (212) 963-1234 (New York) (office). *Fax:* (212) 963-4879 (New York) (office). *E-mail:* info@unomig.org (office). *Website:* www.unomig.org (office).

TUSA, Sir John, Kt, MA; British broadcaster and administrator; *Chairman, University of the Arts, London;* b. 2 March 1936, Zlín, Czechoslovakia (now Czech Repub.); s. of Jan Tusa and Lydie Sklenarova; m. Ann Hilary Dowson 1960; two s.; ed Gresham's School, Holt, Trinity Coll., Cambridge; joined BBC as general trainee 1960; Producer, Talks and Features, BBC World Service 1964–66; Ed., Forum World Features 1966–67; Presenter, The World Tonight, Radio 4 1970–78, 24 Hours, BBC World Service 1972–78, Newsweek, BBC2 1978–79, Newsnight, BBC2 1979–86, Timewatch, BBC2 1982–84, One O'Clock News BBC 1993–95; Chair. London News Radio 1993–94; Pres. Wolfson Coll., Cambridge Feb.–Oct. 1993; Man. Dir BBC World Service 1986–92; Man. Dir Barbican Centre 1995–2007; Chair. Advisory Cttee, Govt Art Collection 1993–2003, BBC Marshall Plan of the Mind Trust 1992–99; Chair. Clore Leadership Programme 2009–; mem. Bd ENO 1994–2005; Freeman, City of London 1997; Trustee, Nat. Portrait Gallery 1988–2000, Design Museum 1998–2000, Journalism Foundation 2012–; Vice-Chair. British Museum 2000–08; Chair. Wigmore Hall Trust 1999–2011, Univ. of the Arts, London 2007–, Architecture Club 2007–; Visiting Prof., Dept of Arts Policy and Man., City Univ.; Hon. Chair. theartsdesk.com 2010; Hon. mem. RAM 1999, Guildhall School of Music and Drama 1999; Order of the White Rose (Finland) 1998; Dr hc (Heriot-Watt) 1993, (Kingston) 2007, Hon. LLD (London) 1993, Hon. DLitt (City Univ.) 1997, (Essex) 2006, (Kent) 2007; Royal TV Soc. (RTS)

TV Journalist of the Year 1984, BAFTA Richard Dimbleby Award 1984, Broadcasting Press Guild Award 1991, RTS Presenter of the Year 1995, Broadcasting Press Guild Radio Programme of the Year (for 20/20 – A View of the Century) 1995. *Publications:* The Nuremberg Trial (with Ann Tusa) 1983, The Berlin Blockade (with Ann Tusa) 1988, Conversations with the World 1990, A World in Your Ear 1992, Art Matters 1999, On Creativity 2003, The Janus Aspect: Artists in the 21st Century 2005, Engaged with the Arts: Writings from the Frontline 2007. *Leisure interests:* tennis, string quartets, listening. *Address:* University of the Arts London, 272 High Holborn, London, WC1V 7EY (office); 16 Canonbury Place, London, N1 2NN, England (home). *Telephone:* (20) 7514-2319 (office); (20) 7704-2451 (home). *E-mail:* jtusa@arts.ac.uk (office); john.tusa@hotmail.co.uk (home). *Website:* www.arts.ac.uk (office).

TUSCHL, Thomas, PhD; German biochemist, molecular biologist and academic; *Professor and Head of Laboratory, The Rockefeller University;* b. 1 June 1966, Altdorf bei Nürnberg; ed Univ. of Regensburg, Max Planck Inst. for Experimental Medicine, Göttingen; Jr Investigator, Max Planck Inst. for Biophysical Chem. 1999–2003; fmr Researcher, Biology Dept, Whitehead Inst. for Biomedical Research, MIT 1995–99; Assoc. Prof. and Head of Lab., The Rockefeller Univ. 2003–09, Prof. 2009–; Howard Hughes Medical Inst. Investigator; mem. German Nat. Acad. of Sciences Leopoldina; Fellow, New York Acad. of Sciences 2005; Biofuture Award, German Govt 1999, Young Investigator Award, European Molecular Biology Org. 2001, Otto Klung Weberbank Prize for Chem. and Physics, Berlin 2002, Eppendorf Young Investigator Award, Hamburg 2002, Wiley Prize in Biomedical Sciences 2003, Mayor's Award for Excellence in Science and Tech. 2003, AAAS Newcomb Cleveland Prize 2003, Ernst Schering Prize (for basic scientific research) 2005, Meyenburg Prize 2005, Irma T. Hirschl Career Scientist Award 2005, Dr Albert Wander Gedenk Prize, Bern 2005, Molecular Bioanalytics Prize 2006, Max Delbrück Medal, Berlin 2007, Ernst Jung Prize 2008, NIH Director's Transformative Research Project Award 2012. *Publications:* numerous scientific papers in professional journals on studies of RNA interference. *Address:* Howard Hughes Medical Institute Laboratory of RNA, Molecular Biology, The Rockefeller University, 1230 York Avenue, Box 186, New York, NY 10065, USA (office). *Telephone:* (212) 327-7651 (ext. 7651) (office). *Fax:* (212) 327-7652 (office). *E-mail:* thomas.tuschl@rockefeller.edu (office); ttuschl@rockefeller.edu (office). *Website:* www.rockefeller.edu/labheads/tuschl (office); www.rockefeller.edu/research/faculty/labheads/ThomasTuschl (office).

TUSK, Donald Franciszek; Polish politician; *Prime Minister;* b. 22 April 1957, Gdańsk; s. of the late Donald Tusk and Ewa Tusk; m. Małgorzata Tusk; one s. one d.; ed Gdańsk Univ.; journalist Maritime Publishing House, with magazines Pomerania and Samorządność; with Gdańsk Height Services Guild Work Co-operative; Deputy ed. Gazeta Gdańska 1989; mem. Liquidation Cttee RSW Press-Books-Ruch; assoc. Free Trade Unions by the Coast; co.-f. Independent Students Union (NZS); mem. Solidarity Trade Union 1980–89; Founder and Ed. underground Publ Przegląd Polityczny; Leader Programme Council for Liberals Foundation; Leader Congress of Liberals 1989, later the Liberal-Democratic Congress (KLD), Chair. 1991–94; Vice-Chair. Freedom Union (Unia Wolnosci—UW) 1994 following the merger with Democratic Union (UD); Deputy to Sejm (Parl.) (Gdynia/Słupsk constituency) 1991–93, 2001–, Deputy Marshal of Sejm 2001–05, mem. Civic Platform Parl. Caucus 2001–; Chair. Parl. Liberal-Democratic Caucus and Special Cttee for Consideration of Constitutional Acts 1991–93; Senator (Gdańsk Voivodship) and Vice-Marshal of Senate 1997–2001; Co-founder Civic Platform (Platforma Obywatelska—PO) 2001, Leader 2005–; unsuccessful cand. in presidential elections 2006; Prime Minister 2007–; Grand Cross, Order of the Sun (Peru) 2008, Grand Cross, Royal Norwegian Order of Merit 2012; Silver Mouth Award, Radio Three (Sweden) 2004, Karlspreis of the City of Aachen, Germany 2010. *Publications:* Kashubian Lake District 1985, Once There Was Gdańsk 1996, Gdańsk 1945, 1998, Old Sopot 1998, Ideas of Gdańsk's Liberalism 1998. *Leisure interests:* football, old photography. *Address:* Chancellery of the Prime Minister, 00-583 Warsaw, Al. Ujazdowskie 1/3 (office); Civic Platform (Platforma Obywatelska), 00-159 Warsaw, ul. Andersa 21, Poland (office). *Telephone:* (22) 6946000 (Prime Minister's Office) (office); (22) 6357879 (Civic Platform) (office). *Fax:* (22) 6252637 (Prime Minister's Office) (office); (22) 6357641 (Civic Platform) (office). *E-mail:* sprm@kprm.gov.pl (office); poczta@platforma.org (office). *Website:* www.kprm.gov.pl (office); www.premier.gov.pl (office); www.platforma.org (office).

TUSQUETS BLANCA, Oscar; Spanish architect and designer; b. 14 June 1941, Barcelona; m. Eva Blanch; one s. one d.; ed Arts & Crafts School, Barcelona, School of Architecture, Barcelona; with Luis Clotet, Studio Per 1964–84; Co-Founder BD Ediciones de Diseño 1972; Prof., School of Architecture, Barcelona 1975–76, 1979–80; f. Tusquets, Diaz & Assoc. Architects' Office, with Carlos Diaz 1987; Chevalier des Arts et des Lettres; FAD Architecture Prize (five times), FAD Design prize (six times), Sant Jordi Cross 1987, Ciutat de Barcelona Prize 1988, 1989, Nat. Prize for Design 1988, Fukuoka Beautification Award 1994, Medalla de Oro 1998. *Work includes:* Casa Fullá, Barcelona, Belvedere Regas, Girona, Casa Vittoria, Sala Mae West, Dali Museum, Figueras, remodelling of Music Palace, Barcelona, Pavilion, Parc de la Villette, Paris, Chandon Vinery, Barcelona, dwellings in Kashii, Fukuoka and in Olympic Village, Barcelona, La Coupole, Montpellier, music auditorium, Canary Islands, public square, shopping mall and dwellings, Den Bosch, Netherlands; design of furniture and objects for various producers, bus stop for Hanover, Germany. *Leisure interest:* painting. *Address:* Arquitecturas Oscar Tusquets Blanca, Cavallers 50, 08034 Barcelona, Spain (office). *Telephone:* (93) 2065580 (office). *Fax:* (93) 2804071 (office). *E-mail:* tusquets@tda.es (office). *Website:* www.tusquets.com (office).

TUTKUS, Lt Gen. Valdas; Lithuanian military officer; *Chief of Defence, Armed Forces;* b. 27 Dec. 1960, Vilnius; m.; one s.; ed Frunze Mil. Acad., NATO Defence Coll., Rome; Second Lt Motorised Infantry Battalion 1982; served in Afghanistan 1983–85; promoted to First Lt 1984; Founding mem. Lithuanian Armed Forces 1991; Chief of Jt Staff, Ministry of Defence 1992–94; First Deputy Commdr, Armed Forces 1994–96, Deputy Commdr 1996–99; Mil. Rep. to NATO, Brussels, to EU, to WEU 1999–2001; Commdr Land Forces 2001–04; Chief of Defence 2004–; Officer Order of Vytautas the Great; Commemorative Badge to mark Russian Troops Withdrawal from Lithuania, Honour Award for Merits to Nat. Defence System, Honour Award Iron Wolf, Nat. Defence System Level Medal of Merit, Nat. Defence Minister's Letters of Merit. *Address:* Ministry of National Defence, Totorių 25/3,

Vilnius 01121, Lithuania (office). *Telephone:* (5) 278-50001 (office). *Fax:* (5) 212-6082 (office). *E-mail:* vis@kam.lt (office). *Website:* www.kam.lt (office).

TUTTLE, Robert Holmes, MBA; American business executive and fmr diplomatist; *Co-Chairman, Pacific Council on International Policy;* b. 4 Aug. 1943, Calif.; m. Maria Denise Hummer; two d. from previous m.; ed Stanford Univ., Univ. of Southern Calif.; Asst to Pres. Reagan 1982–85, Dir of Presidential Personnel 1985–89; Co-Man. Pnr Tuttle-Click Automotive Group; Amb. to UK 2005–09; Co-Chair. Pacific Council on Int. Policy; fmr mem. Bd Woodrow Wilson Int. Center for Scholars, Ronald Reagan Presidential Library Foundation, Annenberg School of Communication, Univ. of Southern Calif., Los Angeles Museum of Contemporary Art (Chair. 2001–04); mem. Advisory Bd Center on Communication Leadership and Policy, Univ. of Southern Calif. Annenberg School for Communication and Journalism. *Address:* Pacific Council on International Policy, 801 South Figueroa Street, Suite 1130, Los Angeles, CA 90017, USA (office). *Telephone:* (213) 221-2000 (office). *Fax:* (213) 221-2050 (office). *E-mail:* info@pacificcouncil.org (office). *Website:* www.pacificcouncil.org (office).

TUTU, Most Rev. Desmond Mpilo, MTh; South African ecclesiastic (retd) and academic; b. 7 Oct. 1931, Klerksdorp; s. of Zachariah Tutu and Aletta Tutu; m. Leah Nomalizo Tutu 1955; one s. three d.; ed Bantu High School, Bantu Normal Coll., Univ. of South Africa, St Peter's Theological Coll., Rosettenville, King's Coll., Univ. of London; schoolmaster 1954–57; parish priest 1960; Theological Seminary Lecturer 1967–69; Univ. Lecturer 1970–71; Assoc. Dir Theological Educ. Fund, World Council of Churches 1972–75; Dean of Johannesburg 1975–76; Bishop of Lesotho 1977–78, of Johannesburg 1984–86; Archbishop of Cape Town, Metropolitan of the Church of the Prov. of Southern Africa 1986–95, Archbishop Emer. 1995–; Chancellor Univ. of Western Cape 1988–; Chair. Truth and Reconciliation Comm. 1995–99; Pres. All Africa Conf. of Churches 1987–97; Sec.-Gen. South African Council of Churches 1979–84; Visiting Prof. of Anglican Studies, New York Gen. Theological Seminary 1984; elected to Harvard Univ. Bd of Overseers 1989; Dir Coca-Cola 1986–; Visiting Prof., Emory Univ., Atlanta 1998–2000; Visiting Prof. in Post-Conflict Studies, King's Coll., London 2004–; f. Desmond Tutu Peace Centre, Cape Town, supported by Desmond Tutu Peace Trust; Chair., The Elders (independent group of eminent global leaders) 2007–; mem. Third Order of the Soc. of St Francis; Freedom of Borough of Merthyr Tydfil (Wales), Durham, Hull, Borough of Lewisham (UK), Florence, Lecco (Italy), Kinshasa (Democratic Repub. of Congo), Krugersdorp, Cape Town (SA); Order of Jamaica; Hon. DD, DCL, LLD, ThD (Gen. Theol. Sem. New York, Kent Univ., Harvard Univ., Ruhr Bochum Univ.); Hon. DDiv (Aberdeen) 1981; Hon. STD (Columbia) 1982; Dr hc (Mount Allison Univ., Sackville, NB, Strasbourg) 1988, (Oxford) 1990; Hon. LLD (South Bank Univ.) 1994; Hon. DD (Exeter) 1997; FKC (Fellow of King's Coll. London); numerous awards including Onassis Award, Family of Man Gold Medal 1983, Nobel Peace Prize 1984, Carter-Menil Human Rights Prize 1986, Martin Luther King Jr Humanitarian Award 1986, Third World Prize (jt recipient) 1989, Grand Cross of Merit, Germany 1996, Bill of Rights Award, American Civil Liberation Union Fund 1997, Henry W. Edgerton Civil Liberties Award, American Civil Liberties Union 1997, One Hundred Black Men Award, USA 1997, Peace Prize, Int. Community of UNESCO, Athens 1997, Gandhi Peace Prize 2007, Presidential Medal of Freedom 2009, Templeton Prize 2013. *Publications include:* Crying in the Wilderness 1982, Hope and Suffering 1983 (both collections of sermons and addresses), The Rainbow People of God 1994, An African Prayer Book 1996, No Future Without Forgiveness 1999, Made for Goodness: And Why this Makes all the Difference (with Mpho Tutu) 2010. *Leisure interests* reading, music, jogging. *Address:* c/o Desmond Tutu Peace Trust, PO Box 8428, Roggebaai, 8012 Cape Town, South Africa (office). *Telephone:* (21) 4257002 (office). *Fax:* (21) 4189468 (office). *E-mail:* info@tutu.org (office). *Website:* www.tutu.org (office).

TUWAIJRI, Abdulrahman at-, PhD; Saudi Arabian economist; *Chairman and Chief Executive, Capital Market Authority of the Kingdom of Saudi Arabia;* b. 23 Feb. 1955, Almajmaah; s. of Abdulaziz Al-Tuwaijri and Hussah Al-Tuwaijri; m. Norah Alabdulatif 1982; three s. two d.; ed King Saud Univ. and Iowa State Univ., USA; grad. asst Dept of Econs, King Saud Univ. 1978–84, Asst Prof. 1985–88; Econ. Adviser Gen. Secr. Cooperation Council for the Arab States of the Gulf 1988–90; Alt. Exec. Dir IMF 1991–95, Exec. Dir 1995–2001; Sec.-Gen., Supreme Econ. Council 2002–08; Chair and CEO Capital Market Authority of the Kingdom of Saudi Arabia 2008–. *Leisure interests:* reading, swimming. *Address:* Capital Market Authority, Faisaliah Tower, King Fahd Rd, POB 220022, Riyadh 11311, Saudi Arabia (office). *Fax:* (1) 279-7770 (office). *E-mail:* info@cma.org.sa (office). *Website:* www.cma.org.sa (office).

TUYAKBAY, Col-Gen. Jarmakhan Aitbaiuly, CandJur; Kazakhstani politician and jurist; *Leader, Freedom National Social-Democratic Party ('Azat' Jalpyulttyk Sotsial Demokratiyalyk Partiyasy);* b. 22 Nov. 1947, South Kazakhstan Prov., Kazakh SSR, USSR; m. Bagilya Aptayeva; two s. one d.; ed Kirov Kazakh State Univ.; worked in prosecutors' bureau in S Kazakhstan –1978; Deputy Prosecutor-Gen. Kazakh SSR 1981; Prosecutor, Mangyshlak region, then Guryev region 1987–90; mem. Supreme Soviet, Repub. of Kazakhstan 1990; Prosecutor-Gen. Repub. of Kazakhstan 1990–95, Deputy Prosecutor-Gen., Chief Mil. Prosecutor 1997–99; Chair. State Investigation Comm. 1995–97; elected mem. Majlis (Parl.) 1999, Chair. 1999–2004; Leader, For a Just Kazakhstan Movt (Social Democrats) 2005–; Leader, Nat. Social Democratic Party, announced intention to merge with Real Bright Road—Democratic Party of Kazakhstan (Naghyz Ak Jol—Kazakstanyn Demokratiyalyk Partiyasy) 2007, merged with Freedom party to form Freedom Nat. Social Democratic Party ('Azat' Jalpyulttyk Sotsial Demokratiyalyk Partiyasy—Azat JSDP) 2009–; unsuccessful presidential cand. 2005; Order of Barys 2001, Council of the Inter-Parliamentary Ass. of the CIS Order of Sodruzhestvo 2002. *Publications:* Development Prosecution in Kazakhstan in the Period of Reforms 1997; numerous articles. *Leisure Interests:* golf, reading. *Address:* Freedom National Social-Democratic Party ('Azat' Jalpyulttyk Sotsial Demokratiyalyk Partiyasy), 050000 Almaty, Kabanbai batyr kosh. 58, Kazakhstan (office). *Telephone:* (727) 663-64-06 (office). *Fax:* (727) 266-36-43 (office). *E-mail:* ocdp@mail.ru (office). *Website:* www.osdp.kz (office).

TUYMANS, Luc; Belgian artist; b. 14 July 1958, Mortsel. *Address:* c/o Zeno X Gallery, Leopold de Waelplaats 16, 2000 Antwerp, Belgium. *E-mail:* info@zeno-x.com. *Website:* www.zeno-x.com.

TVEIT, Olav Fykse, DTheol; Norwegian theologian, ecclesiastic and international organization official; *General Secretary, World Council of Churches;* b. 24 Nov. 1960; ed Norwegian School of Theology/Menighetsfakultetet, Oslo; ordained as pastor in Church of Norway, served as parish priest in Haram, Møre Diocese 1988–91 and as army chaplain during compulsory year of nat. service 1987–88; Sec. Church of Norway Doctrinal Comm. 1999–2000, Church–State Relations 2001–02; Gen. Sec. Church of Norway Council on Ecumenical and Int. Relations 2002–09; mem. Faith and Order Plenary Comm. and Co-Chair. Palestine Israel Ecumenical Forum core group, WCC, Gen. Sec. WCC 2010–; mem. Bd of Dirs and Exec. Cttee Christian Council of Norway; Moderator of Church of Norway-Islamic Council of Norway contact group, Jewish Congregation contact group; fmr mem. Inter-Faith Council of Norway, Bd of Trustees, Norwegian Church Aid. *Publications include:* Evangeliet i vår kultur (The Gospel in our Culture; co-ed.) 1995, Mutual Accountability as Ecumenical Attitude. A Study in Ecumenical Ecclesiology Based on Faith and Order Texts 1948–1998 (thesis) 2001, Ei vedkjennande kyrkje. Hovudforedrag på Kyrkjemøtet 2004 2004, Christian Solidarity in the Cross of Christ 2012; several articles on ecumenism. *Address:* World Council of Churches, 150 route de Ferney. PO Box 2100, 1211 Geneva 2, Switzerland (office). *Telephone:* (22) 791-6111 (office). *Fax:* (22) 791-0361 (office). *E-mail:* info@oikoumene.org (office). *Website:* www.oikoumene.org (office).

TVIRCUN, Victor, PhD; Moldovan diplomatist and international organization executive; *Secretary-General, Organization of the Black Sea Economic Cooperation;* b. 18 Oct. 1955, Chisinau; m.; two c.; ed State Univ. of Moldova; Lab. Asst, Pedagogical State Univ. 1980–93, Prof. 2010–12; Counsellor, Embassy in Ankara 1995–98, Deputy Dir, Main Div. of Europe and North America, Ministry of Foreign Affairs 1993–95, Dir 1998–99, Chargé d'Affaires, Embassy in Budapest Hungary 1999–2001, Amb. to Turkey (also accred to UAE, Egypt, Kuwait, Qatar, Lebanon, Saudi Arabia, Oman, Org. of the Black Sea Econ. Cooperation) 2001–05; Minister of Educ. and Youth 2005–08; Dir Inst. of European Integration and Political Science, Chisinau 2009–10; Sec.-Gen. Black Sea Econ. Cooperation 2012–; mem. Acad. of Pedagogical and Sociological Science, Moscow, International Acad. of the Hi Educational School, Scientific Asscn of Genealogists, Moldova, Scientific Asscn of Genealogists (Russia); Honourable Citizen, Kars, Turkey, Honourable Citizen, Gagauz Yeri, Honourable Pres. Nat. Fed. of Karate-Do; Order of Honour, Order of Gloria Muncii, First Degree, Order of Orthodox Church of Chisinau and Moldova 'Cuviosul Paisii Velicicovschi', Order of the Moldavian Orthodox Church 'Stefan ccl Marc', Second Degree, Order of the Russian Orthodox Patriarchate 'St. Vladimir', Third Degree, Order of 'United Europe', Gold Medal 'Suleyman Demirel', Turkey; Dr hc (State Univ., South Korea); Man of the Year Award, Europe Liberty, Czech Republic 2007. *Address:* Organization of the Black Sea Economic Cooperation, Sakip Sabanci Caddesi, Müşir Fuad Paşa Yalisi, Eski Tersane, 34467 Emirgan, Istanbul, Turkey (office). *Telephone:* (212) 2296330 (office). *Fax:* (212) 2296336 (office). *E-mail:* info@bsec-organization.org (office). *Website:* www.bsec-organization.org (office).

TVRDÍK, Lt-Col Jaroslav, MSc(Econ); Czech politician and army officer; *Chairman and President, Czech Airlines (CSA);* b. 11 Sept. 1968, Prague; m. Blanka Tvrdíková; one d.; ed Mil. School, Vyškov; Head of Financial Services, Schooling and Training Centre, Ministry of Defence 1990–91, Commanding Sr Officer, Foreign Relations Section 1991–92, Head of Dept 1993–95, Dir Interior Admin. 1996, Deputy Minister of Defence 2000–01, Minister of Defence 2001–03; Dir Mil. Spa and recreations facilities 1996–2000; Chief, Financial Services, Czechoslovak contingent, UNPROFOR 1993–95; mem. Parl. 2002–03; Chair. Bd of Dirs and Pres. CSA (Ceske Aerolinie a.s.) 2003–; UN Medal for Activity in UNPROFOR 1992–93, Anniversary Medal of Honour, NATO 2002. *Publication:* Transformation of the Army 2001. *Leisure interests:* squash, swimming, historical literature. *Address:* c/o Dana Dvorakova, Ceske Aerolinie a.s., Prague Ruzyni Airport, 160 08 Prague 6, Czech Republic (office). *Telephone:* (2) 20116220 (office). *Fax:* (2) 20115397 (office). *E-mail:* dana.dvorakova@csa.cz (office). *Website:* www.csa.cz (office).

TWAIN, Shania; Canadian country singer and songwriter; b. (Eileen Regina Edwards), 28 Aug. 1965, Windsor, Ont.; d. of Gerry Twain and Sharon Twain; m. 1st Robert John Lange 1993 (divorced); one s.; m. 2nd Frederic Thiebaud 2011; fmr cabaret singer; Country Music Television Europe Rising Video Star of the Year 1993, Female Artist of the Year 1996, Canadian Country Music Award for Female Vocalist 1995, American Music Awards for Favorite New Country Artist 1995, Favorite Female Pop/Rock Artist 2000, Favorite Female Country Artist 2000, Grammy Awards for Best Female Country Vocal Performance, Best Country Song 2000, Juno Award for Songwriter of the Year 2000, Best Country Female Artist 2000, Billboard Award for Top Country Artist 2003. *Recordings:* albums: Shania Twain 1993, The Woman in Me (Grammy Award for Best Country Album 1996) 1995, Come On Over 1997, On The Way 1999, Beginnings 1989–1990 1999, Wild and Wicked 2000, Complete Limelight Sessions 2001, Up! (Billboard Award for Top Country Album 2003) 2002, Greatest Hits 2004; singles: What Made You Say That 1993, Dance With The One That Brought You 1993, You Lay A Whole Lotta Love On Me 1993, Whose Bed Have Your Boots Been Under 1995, Any Man of Mine 1995, Woman In Me 1995, You Win My Love 1996, God Bless The Child 1996, I'm Outta Here 1996, Love Gets Me Every Time 1997, Don't Be Stupid 1997, You're Still The One 1998, From This Moment On 1998, When 1998, That Don't Impress Me Much 1998, Man I Feel Like A Woman 1999, You've Got A Way 1999, Don't Be Stupid (You Know I Love You) 2000, I'm Gonna Getcha Good 2002, Ka-Ching 2003, Up 2003, Forever & Always 2003, Thank You Baby For Making Someday Come So Soon 2003, When You Kiss Me 2003, Party For Two 2005. *Address:* Georgette Pascale, Shore Fire Media, 32 Court Street, Floor 16, Brooklyn, NY 11201, USA (office); c/o Mercury Nashville, 54 Music Square E, Nashville, TN 37203, USA. *Website:* www.shaniatwain.com.

TWEEDIE, Sir David Philip, Kt, BCom, PhD, CA, FRSE; British chartered accountant; *Chairman, International Accounting Standards Board;* b. 7 July 1944; s. of Aidrian Ian Tweedie and Marie Patricia Tweedie (née Phillips); m. Janice Christine Brown 1970; two s.; ed Grangemouth High School, Univ. of Edin.; accountancy training Mann, Judd, Gordon (Glasgow) 1969–72; Lecturer in Accounting, Univ. of Edin. 1973–78; Tech. Dir Inst. of Chartered Accountants, Scotland 1978–81; Pnr, KMG Thomson McLintock 1982–87, KPMG Peat Marwick McLintock 1987–90; Chair. Accounting Standards Bd 1990–2000, Int. Accounting

Standards Bd 2001–; Hon. FIA 1999, Hon. FSIP 2004, Hon. FCCA 2005; Hon. DSc (Econ.) (Hull) 1993, Hon. LLD (Lancaster) 1993, (Exeter) 1997, (Dundee) 1998), Hon. DLitt (Heriot-Watt) 1996, Hon. DBA (Napier) 1999, (Oxford Brookes) 2004, Hon. DSc (SocSci) (Edinburgh) 2001; Founding Socs Award, Inst. of Chartered Accountants in England and Wales 1997, Chartered Inst. of Man. Accounting Award 1998. *Publications:* Financial Reporting, Inflation & The Capital Maintenance Concept 1979; co-author of three other books and contribs. to professional and academic journals. *Leisure interests:* athletics, watching rugby, walking, gardening. *Address:* International Accounting Standards Board, 30 Cannon Street, London, EC4M 6XH, England (office). *Telephone:* (20) 7246-6480 (office). *Fax:* (20) 7246-6411 (office). *E-mail:* info@ifrs.org (office). *Website:* www.ifrs.org (office).

TWEGRI, Muhammad Ibrahim at-, PhD; Egyptian academic and international organization executive; *Assistant General Secretary for Economic Affairs, League of Arab States;* Dir-Gen. Arab Admin. Devt Org. (ARADO) –2007; Asst Gen. Sec. for Econ. Affairs, League of Arab States (Arab League) 2007–; Mem.-at-Large Int. Fed. of Training and Devt Orgs; mem. Preparatory Cttee Int. Conf. of Cyberlaw (ICCY) 2005. *Publications:* numerous papers in professional journals. *Address:* League of Arab States, PO Box 11642, Arab League Bldg, Tahrir Square, Cairo, Egypt (office). *Telephone:* (2) 575-0511 (office). *Fax:* (2) 574-0331 (office). *E-mail:* info@arableagueonline.org (office). *Website:* www.arableagueonline.org (office).

TWIGGY (see LAWSON, Lesley).

TWIN, Peter John, OBE, PhD, FRS; British physicist and academic; *Professor Emeritus of Experimental Physics, University of Liverpool;* b. 26 July 1939, London; s. of Arthur James Twin and Hilda Ethel Twin; m. Jean Leatherland 1963; one s. one d.; ed Sir George Monoux Grammar School, Walthamstow, London and Univ. of Liverpool; Lecturer, Univ. of Liverpool 1964, Sr Lecturer 1973, Sir James Chadwick Prof. of Experimental Physics 1987–96, Lyon Jones Prof. of Physics 1997–2001, Sr Fellow and Prof. Emer. 2001–; Head, Nuclear Structure Facility, Daresbury Lab. Cheshire 1983–87; Weatherill Medal, Franklin Inst. USA 1991, Bonner Prize, Americal Physical Soc. 1991, Lisa Meitner Prize, European Physical Soc. 2004. *Publications:* articles in professional journals. *Address:* Room 213C, Oliver Lodge Laboratory, Department of Physics, University of Liverpool, Liverpool, L69 7ZE, England. *Telephone:* (151) 794-3378 (office). *Fax:* (151) 794-3348 (office). *E-mail:* twin@ns.ph.liv.ac.uk (office). *Website:* ns.ph.liv.ac.uk (office).

TWOMEY, Paul, MA, PhD; Australian international organization executive; b. 18 July 1961; ed Univ. of Queensland, Pennsylvania State Univ., USA, Univ. of Cambridge, UK; consultant, McKinsey & Co. –1994; Exec. Gen. Man. for Europe, Austrade-the Australian Trade Comm. 1994–97; Founding CEO Nat. Office for Information Economy 1997; Australian Fed. Govt's Special Adviser for Information Economy and Tech. 1997; Australia's Rep. at int. forums, including WTO, OECD, APEC and Internet Corpn for Assigned Names and Numbers (ICANN); Founder Argo P@cific (int. advisory and investment firm); Chair. Govt Advisory Cttee, ICANN 1999–2002, Pres. and CEO ICANN 2003–09, Sr Pres. –Jan. 2010; mem. Green Source Energy LLC Strategic Advisory Group 2010–; mem. Bd of Dir Atlantic Council of the US; Founding Chair. World Econ. Forum's Global Agenda Council on the Future of the Internet; mem. Advisory Bd UN Digital He@lth Initiative. *Address:* c/o Strategic Advisory Group, Green Source Energy LLC, 1100 Nueces Street, Austin, TX 78701, USA.

TY, George S. K. (Siao Kian); Philippine business executive; *Chairman, Metrobank Foundation Inc.;* b. 1933, China; s. of Norberto Ty; m. Mary Ty; two s. three d.; moved with family aged six from China to Philippines; co-f. Metropolitan Bank and Trust Co., Binondo 1962, becoming Dir and Chair. Metrobank Group; f. Metrobank Foundation Inc. (charitable foundation) 1979, currently Chair.; business interests include Toyota Motor Philippines, Federal Land Inc., Marco Polo Hotel, Cebu; fmr owner GT International Tower, Makati; Hon. Chair. Manila Doctors Coll.; Management Man of the Year, Man. Asscn of the Philippines 2006. *Leisure interests:* swimming, collecting Chinese paintings. *Address:* Metrobank Foundation Inc, 4th Floor, Metrobank Plaza, Sen. Gil J. Puyat Ave, 1200 Makati City, Philippines (office). *Telephone:* (2) 8575918 (office). *Fax:* (2) 8185656 (office). *E-mail:* foundation@metrobank.com.ph (office). *Website:* www.mbfoundation.org (office).

TYABJI, Hatim A., BS, MS, MBA; American (b. Indian) business executive; *Chairman, Best Buy Company Inc.;* b. 1945, Bombay, India; ed Coll. of Eng, Poona, India, State Univ. of NY, Buffalo and Syracuse Univ., USA; Unisys Pres., Information Systems Products and Technologies Group, Sperry Rand 1973–86; Pres. and CEO VeriFone 1986–98, Chair. 1992–98; CEO Saraide, Inc. 1998–2000; Exec. Chair. Bytemobile, Inc. 2001–; chairman of Jasper Wireless; mem. Bd of Dirs Best Buy Co. Inc. 1998–, Chair. 2012–; mem. Bd of Dirs Merchant eSolutions, Inc., Sierra Atlantic, Inc., Touch Networks (Australia), Missile Defense Advocacy Alliance; fmr mem. Bd of Dirs Ariba Inc., Bank of America Merchant Services, Deluxe Corpn, eFunds Corpn, Novatel Wireless, Inc., PubliCard Inc., SmartDisk Corpn, Datacard Group, Depotpoint, Inc., Impresse Corpn, Norand Corpn; Amb. at Large for Benchmark Capital; mem. Bd Carnegie Inst., Dean's Council of the Leavey School of Business at Santa Clara Univ., Dean's Council of School of Eng at State Univ. of NY, Buffalo. *Publication:* Husband, Wife & Company: An Honest Perspective on Success in Life and Work 2007. *Address:* Best Buy Company Inc., 7601 Penn Avenue South, Richfield, MN 55423, USA (office). *Telephone:* (612) 291-1000 (office). *Fax:* (612) 292-4001 (office). *E-mail:* info@bestbuy.com (office). *Website:* www.bestbuy.com (office).

TYAGACHEV, Leonid Vassilyevich; Russian sports administrator and ski coach; b. 1946, Dedenevo, Moscow region; m.; two d.; ed Moscow Pedagogical Inst., Mountain Ski School Kirschberg, Austria; participated in All-Union and int. ski competitions –1971; fmr USSR Ski Champion; Sr Ski Coach, Moscow region 1971–76; Chief Coach USSR Ski team, has coached numerous skiers, including Zhirov, Zelenskaya, Tsyganov, Makeyev, Gladyshev 1976–81; took part in organizing World Cup competitions in Saalbach, Schladming, Saint Anton 1981–95; Minister of Sport and Tourism 1995–99; First Vice-Pres. Russian Olympic Cttee 1991–2001, Pres. 2001–10, also Pres. Russian Alpine Ski and Snowboard Fed.; numerous medals. *Address:* c/o Olympic Committee of Russian Federation, 119992 Moscow, Luzhnetskaya nab. 8, Russia.

TYAHNYBOK, Oleh Yaroslavovych; Ukrainian surgeon and politician; *Leader, Freedom (Svoboda)*; b. 7 Nov. 1968, Lviv, Ukrainian SSR, USSR; s. of Yaroslav Tyahnibok; m. Olha Demchyschyn; one s. two d.; ed Lviv Medical Inst., Lviv Franko Univ.; part-time medical jobs at Lviv Medical Inst. as an orderly and nurse, later drafted into the army; returned to the Inst. and initiated creation of Med Inst. Student Brotherhood; qualified as surgeon, majoring in urology 1993; mem. Social-Nat. Party of Ukraine 1991; mem. Lviv Oblast Council 1994–98; mem. Verkhovna Rada (Parl.) 1998–, became mem. of People's Movt of Ukraine faction, re-elected as mem. of Victor Yushchenko's Our Ukraine bloc 2002–04 (expelled from bloc); Leader Freedom (Svoboda) 2004–; cand. for Mayor of Kyiv in local election 2008; unsuccessful cand. in presidential election 2010; criminal case launched by Russian Govt against him for "organizing an armed gang" that had allegedly fought against the Russian 76th Guards Air Assault Div. in the First Chechen War March 2014; voted Person of the Year by readers of Korrespondent magazine 2012, ranked 43rd by Korrespondent in list of Top 100 Most Influential Ukrainians 2012. *Address:* Freedom (Svoboda), 02140 Kyiv, vul. Vyshnyakivska 6A /70, Ukraine (office). *E-mail:* vo@svoboda.org.ua (office). *Website:* www.svoboda.org.ua (office); www.tyahnybok.info.

TYGART, Travis Thompson, BA, JD; American lawyer; *CEO, US Anti-Doping Agency;* b. 1971; ed Univ. of North Carolina, Southern Methodist Univ.; Assoc., Holme Roberts & Owen LLP 2000–02; Dir of Legal Affairs, US Anti-Doping Agency (USADA) 2002–04, Sr Man. Dir and Gen. Counsel 2004–07, CEO 2007–. *Address:* US Anti-Doping Agency, 5555 Technical Center Suite 200, Colorado Springs, CO 80919, USA (office). *Telephone:* (719) 785-2000 (office). *Fax:* (719) 785-2001 (office). *E-mail:* tt@usada.org (office). *Website:* www.usada.org (office).

TYLER, Anne, BA; American writer; b. 25 Oct. 1941, Minneapolis, Minn.; d. of Lloyd Parry Tyler and Phyllis (Mahon) Tyler; m. Taghi M. Modarressi 1963 (died 1997); two c.; ed Duke Univ., Columbia Univ.; mem. American Acad. of Arts and Letters, American Acad. of Arts and Sciences. *Publications include:* If Morning Ever Comes 1964, The Tin Can Tree 1965, A Slipping-Down Life 1970, The Clock Winder 1972, Celestial Navigation 1974, Searching for Caleb 1976, Earthly Possessions 1977, Morgan's Passing 1980, Dinner at the Homesick Restaurant 1982, The Best American Short Stories (ed. with Shannon Ravenel) 1983, The Accidental Tourist (Nat. Book Critics Circle Award for Fiction) 1985, Breathing Lessons (Pulitzer Prize for Fiction 1989) 1988, Saint Maybe 1991, Tumble Tower (juvenile) 1993, Ladder of Years 1995, A Patchwork Planet 1998, Back When We Were Grown-ups 2001, The Amateur Marriage 2004, Digging to America 2006, Noah's Compass 2010, The Beginner's Goodbye 2012; short stories in magazines. *Address:* 222 Tunbridge Road, Baltimore, MD 21212, USA (home). *E-mail:* atmBaltimore@aol.com (home).

TYLER, David, MA; British business executive; *Chairman, J Sainsbury plc;* ed Univ. of Cambridge; held sr financial and gen. man. positions with Unilever PLC 1974–86, County NatWest Ltd 1986–89, Christie's International plc 1989–96, Group Finance Dir GUS plc 1997–2006; Chair. 3i Quoted Private Equity plc 2007–09; Chair. Logica plc 2007–12; mem. Bd of Dirs J Sainsbury plc Oct. 2009–, Chair. Nov. 2009–; Dir (non-exec.) Burberry Group plc 2002–12 (Chair. Remuneration Cttee), Experian plc 2006–12, Reckitt Benckiser Group plc 2007–09, Hammerson plc 2013–; Chair. Hampstead Theatre 2012–. *Address:* J Sainsbury plc, 33 Holborn, London, EC1N 2HT, England (office). *Telephone:* (20) 7695-6000 (office). *E-mail:* info@j-sainsbury.co.uk (office). *Website:* www.j-sainsbury.co.uk (office).

TYLER, Liv; American actress; b. 1 July 1977, Portland, Me; d. of Steve Tyler and Bebe Buell; m. Royston Langdon 2003 (divorced); one s.; fmr model, Eileen Ford Agency; UNICEF Goodwill Amb. 2003–. *Film appearances include:* Silent Fall 1994, Empire Records 1995, Heavy 1995, Stealing Beauty 1996, That Thing You Do! 1996, Inventing the Abbotts 1997, Plunkett and Macleane 1999, Armageddon 1998, Cookie's Fortune 1999, Onegin 1999, The Little Black Book 1999, Dr T and the Women 2000, The Lord of the Rings: The Fellowship of the Ring 2001, One Night at McCool's 2001, The Lord of the Rings: The Two Towers 2002, The Lord of the Rings: The Return of the King 2003, Jersey Girl 2004, Lonesome Jim 2005, Reign Over Me 2007, The Strangers 2008, The Incredible Hulk 2008, Super 2010, The Ledge 2011, Robot & Frank 2012. *Address:* c/o United Talent Agency, 9560 Wilshire Blvd, Suite 500, Beverly Hills, CA 90212-2401, USA (office).

TYLER OF ENFIELD, Baroness (Life Peer), cr. 2011, of Enfield in the London Borough of Enfield; **Claire Tyler**; British organization executive; *Chief Executive, Relate;* Deputy Chief Exec. Nat. Connexions Unit (responsible for cutting number of young people not in educ. or employment) –2002; Head of Govt's Social Exclusion Unit 2002–06; Dir Vulnerable Children's Group, Dept for Educ. and Skills 2006–07; Chief Exec. Relate (relationship support charity) 2007–. *Address:* Relate, Premier House, Carolina Court, Lakeside, Doncaster, DN4 5RA (office); Relate, 24–32 Stephenson Way, London, NW1 2HD (office); House of Lords, Westminster, London, SW1A 0PW, England. *Telephone:* (300) 100-1234 (office); (20) 7219-5353. *Fax:* (20) 7219-5979. *E-mail:* enquiries@relate.org.uk (office). *Website:* www.relate .org.uk (office); www.relateforparents.org.uk (office).

TYMOSHENKO, Yuliya Volodymyrivna, CandEcon; Ukrainian business executive and politician; *Leader, Fatherland United Opposition (Batkivshchyna Obyednana Opozytsiya);* b. (Yulia Grigyan), 27 Nov. 1960, Dnipropetrovsk; d. of Vladimir Abramovich Grigyan and Ludmila Nikolaevna Telegina (née Nelepova); m. Oleksandr Hennadyovych Tymoshenko; one d.; ed Dnipropetrovsk State Univ.; planning engineer, Dnipropetrovsk Machine-Construction Plant 1984–89; Commercial Dir Dnipropetrovsk Youth Centre Terminal 1989–91; Dir-Gen. Ukraine Benzine Corpn 1991–95; Pres. Union Unified Energy Systems of Ukraine, First Deputy Chair. and Head, Cttee on Budgetary Issues 1995–97; elected to Verkhovna Rada (Parl.) 1996, joined political union Community (Hromada) with Pavlo Lazarenko, left Hromada to form and lead All-Ukrainian Union 'Fatherland' (Vseukrayinske Obyednannya Batkivshchyna) faction 1999–, merged with Conservative Republican Party 2002, with Yabluko party 2004, absorbed the Front of Changes and the Reforms and Order Party to become Fatherland United Opposition (Batkivshchyna Obyednana Opozytsiya) 2013; Deputy Prime Minister of Ukraine responsible for energy issues 1999–2001 (resgnd); joined opposition Nat. Salvation Forum 2001; arrested on charge of corruption March 2001, released due to pressure of opposition; Leader Yuliya Tymoshenko Bloc 2001–, led bloc in

2002 and 2006 elections; Prime Minister of Ukraine Jan.–Sept. 2005, 2007–10; unsuccessful cand. in presidential elections 2010; arrested for "repeated violations of court rules" during her trial (charged in May 2011) for abuse of office over a natural gas imports contract signed in 2009 with Russia Aug. 2011; charged with misusing $425m received by her govt in 2009 for the sale of carbon credits Dec. 2010; held at Lukyanivska Prison; sentenced to seven years' imprisonment Oct. 2011, appealed unsuccessfully Dec. 2011; verdict against her upheld by Supreme Court of Ukraine 29 Aug. 2012; went on hunger strike to protest against vote rigging in Oct. parl. election 29 Oct.–16 Nov. 2012; nominated by Fatherland All-Ukrainian Union as its cand. for 2015 presidential elections Dec. 2012; released from prison following removal of Pres. Viktor Yanukovych and Kyivsky Dist Court of Kharkiv closed the criminal case on financial abuse Feb. 2014; Higher Order of Orthodox Church St Barbara Great Martyr 1997; ranked by Forbes magazine amongst The World's 100 Most Powerful Women (third) 2005, (17th) 2008, (47th) 2009. *Publications:* about 50 papers on econs. *Address:* Fatherland United Opposition (Batkivshchyna Obyednana Opozytsiya), 01133 Kyiv, bulv. Lesi Ukrainky 26/615, Ukraine (office). *Telephone:* (44) 527-70-64 (office). *Fax:* (44) 285-69-07 (office). *E-mail:* pr@byut.com.ua (office). *Website:* byut.com.ua (office); www.tymoshenko.ua.

TYNDALE-BISCOE, Cecil Hugh, MSc, PhD, FAA; Australian research scientist and university teacher (retd); b. 16 Oct. 1929, Kashmir, India; s. of Eric Dallas Tyndale-Biscoe and Phyllis Mary Tyndale-Biscoe (née Long); m. Marina Szokoloczi 1960; two s. one d.; ed Wycliffe Coll., UK, Canterbury Univ., NZ, Univ. of Western Australia and Washington Univ., St Louis, USA; Animal Ecology, Dept of Scientific and Industrial Research, NZ 1951–55; Lecturer, Edwardes Coll., Peshawar, Pakistan 1955–58, Univ. of Western Australia, Perth 1961; Deputy Leader, Biologist, NZ Alpine Club Antarctic Expedition 1959–60; Lecturer, Sr Lecturer, Reader in Zoology, ANU, Canberra 1962–75, Adjunct Prof. 1996–2002; Sr Prin. Research Scientist, Div. of Wildlife Research, CSIRO, Canberra 1976–78, Chief Research Scientist, Div. of Wildlife and Ecology 1978–91; Dir Co-operative Research Centre for Biological Control of Vertebrate Pest Populations 1992–95; Hayward Fellow, Manaaki Whenua Landcare Research, NZ 1996–97; mountaineering in NZ, including first north-south traverse of Mt Cook, first ascent of Torres from the Balfour; in the Karakorum, including first ascents of Falak Sar, Barteen and Buni Zom; Fellow, Australian Inst. of Biologists; Fellow and Life mem. Australian Mammal Soc.; Hon. Fellow, Royal Soc. of NZ; Clarke Medal, Royal Soc. of NSW 1974, Troughton Medal, Australian Mammal Soc. 1982, Aitken Medal, Museum of S Australia 1986, CSIRO Medal 1987, Whitely Medal, Royal Zoological Soc. of NSW 2005. *Publications include:* Life of Marsupials 1973 (second edn 2005), Reproduction and Evolution (ed.) 1977, Reproductive Physiology of Marsupials (with M. B. Renfree) 1987, Developing Marsupials (co-ed.) 1988; about 120 papers in scientific journals of reproduction, ecology and endocrinology. *Leisure interests:* mountaineering, agroforestry, earth houses, woodwork, history of N India. *Address:* 114 Grayson Street, Hackett, ACT 2602, Australia. *Telephone:* (2) 6249-8612. *E-mail:* hughtb@bigpond.com.

TYSON, John H., BBA; American food industry executive; *Chairman, Tyson Foods, Inc.;* b. 5 Sept. 1953, Springdale, Ark.; s. of Donald John Tyson and Twilla Jean Womochil; grandson of John Tyson; m. Kimberly McCoy; one s. one d.; ed Springdale High School, Southern Methodist Univ., Dallas, Tex.; began career with Tyson Foods Inc. (family-owned business est. by grandfather John Tyson), various positions including Retail Sales Man. for NE states, Purchasing Man., Complex Man. NC Region, Pres. Beef and Pork Div., Vice-Chair. –1998, Chair. Tyson Foods 1998–2000, Chair., Pres. and CEO 2000–01, Chair. and CEO 2001–06, Chair. 2006–; fmr Pres. Ark. Poultry Fed.; mem. Bd of Dirs Nat. Council on Alcoholism and Drug Dependence, Steering Cttee Campaign for 21st Century, Univ. of Ark.; Chair. Corpn and Foundation Relations Cttee, Univ. of Ark.; mem. Walden Woods (non-profit org.), Bridge School Project; Man of the Year, Arkansas Poultry Fed. 1994, Citizen of the Year, March of Dimes, Little Rock, Ark. 2000. *Leisure interests:* golf, deep sea fishing, music, travel, culture, philanthropy. *Address:* Tyson Foods Inc., 2200 Don Tyson Parkway, Springdale, AR 72762, USA (office). *Telephone:* (479) 290-4000 (office). *Fax:* (479) 290-4061 (office). *E-mail:* info@tysonfoods.com (office). *Website:* www.tysonfoods.com (office).

TYSON, Keith, MA; British artist; b. Ulverston, Cumbria; s. of David Tyson and Audrey Rigby; ed Dowdales School, Dalton-in-Furness, Barrow-in-Furness Coll. of Eng., Carlisle Coll. of Art and Univ. of Brighton; studied mechanical eng before taking up art studies; worked as metal turner and draftsman at Vickers shipyard; has exhibited across Europe and N America; fmr Artist-in-Residence Astrophysics and Cosmology Dept, Univ. of Oxford; Dr hc (Univ. of Brighton) 2005; ICA Arts and Innovation Award 1996, Turner Prize 2002. *Group exhibitions include:* Pandemonium Show, Inst. of Contemporary Arts 1996, Venice Biennale 2001, São Paulo Bienal 2002. *Solo exhibitions include:* From The Artmachine, Anthony Reynolds Gallery 1995. *E-mail:* info@ktprojects.co.uk. *Website:* www.keithtyson.com.

TYSON, Laura D'Andrea, PhD; American economist, academic, fmr government official and fmr university administrator; *Professor, Haas School of Business, University of California, Berkeley;* b. 28 June 1947, New Jersey; m. Erik Tarloff; one s.; ed Smith Coll., Massachusetts Inst. of Tech.; Asst Prof., Princeton Univ. 1974–77; Prof., Dept of Econs and Business Admin. and Dir Inst. of Int. Studies, Univ. of California, Berkeley 1978–98, Dean, Haas School of Business 1998–2001, Prof. 2006–; Dean, London Business School 2001–06; Visiting Prof., Harvard Business School 1989–90; Chair. Council of Econ. Advisers to Pres. Clinton 1993–95, Nat. Econ. Adviser to Pres. US Nat. Econ. Council 1995–97; Visiting Scholar, Inst. of Int. Econs; mem. Bd of Economists, Los Angeles Times; mem. Council on Foreign Relations, numerous other professional and public appointments; mem. Bd of Dirs Eastman Kodak Co., Morgan Stanley, AT&T, Peter G. Peterson Inst. of Int. Econs, New America Foundation, CB Richard Ellis, Silver Spring Networks; mem. Econ. Recovery Advisory Bd (PERAB); Sr Advisor, McKinsey Global Inst. 2007–, Center for American Progress 2007–; Special Advisor, Berkeley Research Group, LLC 2010–; Nat. Fellows Program Fellowship, Hoover Inst. 1978–79; consultant to IBRD 1980–86, Pres.'s Comm. on Industrial Competitiveness 1983–84, Hambrecht & Quist 1984–86, Plan-Econ 1984–86, Western Govs Asscn 1986, Council on Competitiveness 1986–89, Electronics Industry Asscn 1989, Motorola 1989–90; columnist, Business Week magazine. *Publications:* The Yugoslav Economic System and its Performance in the 1970s

1980, Economic Adjustment in Eastern Europe 1984, Who's Bashing Whom?, Trade Conflict in High Technology Industries 1992; articles in professional journals. *Address:* Haas School of Business, S545, Haas, #1900, 2220 Piedmont Avenue, University of California, Berkeley, CA 94720-1900, USA (office). *Telephone:* (510) 643-2027 (office). *E-mail:* tyson@haas.berkeley.edu (office). *Website:* www.haas.berkeley.edu (office).

TYSON, Michael (Mike) Gerard; American professional boxer; b. 30 June 1966, New York City; s. of the late John Kilpatrick Tyson and Lorna Tyson; m. 1st Robin Givens 1988 (divorced 1989); 2nd Monica Turner 1997 (divorced 2003); two c.; m. 3rd Lakiha Spicer 2009; career record of 50 wins, five losses, two no contest; defeated Trevor Berbick to win WBC heavyweight title 1986; winner WBA heavyweight title March 1987, IBF heavyweight title Aug. 1987; fmr undefeated world champion, lost to James Buster Douglas 1990, defeated Donovan Ruddock 1991; Hon. Chair. Cystic Fibrosis Asscn 1987; sentenced to six years' imprisonment for rape and two counts of deviant sexual practice March 1992, appealed against March sentence, appeal rejected by US Supreme Court March 1994, released March 1995; regained title of heavyweight world champion after defeating Frank Bruno (q.v.) March 1996; lost to Evander Holyfield Dec. 1996; licence revoked by Nevada State Athletics Comm. after disqualification from rematch against Holyfield 1996, reinstated on appeal Oct. 1998; sentenced to a year's imprisonment for assault Feb. 1999; released on probation May 1999; fought Lennox Lewis (q.v.) June 2002 for WBC and IBF titles, knocked out in eighth round; defeated Clifford Etienne Feb. 2003; lost to Danny Williams 2004; f. Mike Tyson Collection (clothing co.), Tyrannic Productions (film production co.); BBC Sports Overseas Personality of the Year 1989, 2011 inducted into Boxing Hall of Fame 2011. *Film appearances include:* Rocky Balboa 2006, The Hangover 2009, The Hangover 2 2011. *Website:* miketyson.com.

TZABAN, Yair, BA; Israeli journalist and politician; *Chairman, Association for Modern Jewish Culture;* b. 1930, Jerusalem; one s. one d.; ed Bar-Ilan and Te-Aviv Univs; Chair. political bureau of Maki (Israeli CP) 1972–75; Co-Founder of Moked 1972–1977, Co-Founder of Sheli Coalition 1977; Political Sec. Mapam (United Workers' Party) 1981–, Chair. Mapam's faction in the Histadrut; Minister of Immigrant Absorption 1992–96; mem. Knesset 1981– (Meretz), served on numerous cttees 1981–92, Lecturer, School for Political Studies, Univ. of Tel-Aviv 1996–2002; fmr Chair. The College of Judaism as Culture (Meitar), mem. Exec. Bd; Founder and Chair. Asscn for Modern Jewish Culture; Dir-Gen. New Encyclopedia on Jewish Culture in the Era of Modernisation and Secularisation project 2000–07; Dr hc (Hebrew Union Coll.) 1996; Itamar Ben-Avi Shield 1984. *Publications:* New Jewish Time 2007; various articles on political, social and econ. topics and on Judaism and Zionism. *Address:* 1A Tarad Street, Ramat-Gan 52503, Israel (home). *Telephone:* 3-6735160 (office); 3-6121495 (home). *Fax:* 3-6727364 (office); 3-6121497 (home). *E-mail:* zabany@netvision.net.il (home).

UBAIDULLOYEV, Mahmadsaid; Tajikistani politician and electrical engineer; *Mayor of Dushanbe;* b. 1 Feb. 1952, Khatlon Oblast; s. of the late Ubaidullo Mahmudov and Sabagul Nazirova; m. R. Karimova; two s. one d.; ed Tajik Polytechnical Inst., Kharkiv Polytechnical Inst., Ukrainian SSR, Tashkent Higher CPSU School, Uzbek SSR; Sr Engineer, Kulob Regional Dept of Statistics 1974–75, Main Engineer 1975–76, Dir Computation Centre 1976–79; Instructor, Organizing Dept, CP Cttee of Kulob 1979–81, Head of Organizing Dept 1981–83; Deputy Head of Cen. Dept of Statistics, Dushanbe 1985–86; Head of Dept of Industry, Transport and People's Food Products, CP Cttee of Kulob 1986–88; Head of Khatlon Regional Dept of Statistics, Qurghonteppa 1988–90; Deputy Chair. Exec. Cttee, Kulob Regional People's Deputy Council 1990–92; Deputy Chair. Council of Ministers 1992–94; First Deputy Prime Minister 1994–96; Mayor of Dushanbe 1996–; mem. People's Democratic Party; Chair. Majlisi Milliy (Nat. Ass.) 2000–, Interparliamentary Ass. of Eurasian Econ. Community (EURASEC) 2007–09; Order of Dustlik (Friendship) 1998, Order of the Ismoili Somoni 1999, Order of the Ismoili Somoni, First Degree 2006; 21st Century Achievement Award 2001, Int. Honour Diploma and Prize, Medal in respect of IBC Leading Engineers of the World 2006, Diploma of UN-HABITAT and World Org. of United Cities and Local Govts 2006. *Publications:* The Foundation of Newest Statehood (ed.) 2002, History of Dushanbe City (from ancient times till our days) (ed.) 2004, Dushanbe: City of Peace (co-author) 2004. *Leisure interests:* politics, logic, dialectics and philosophy. *Address:* Majlisi Milliy, 734051 Dushanbe, Xiyoboni Rudaki 42 (office); Dushanbe City Administration (Khukumat), 734001 Dushanbe, Xiyoboni Rudaki 48, Tajikistan (office). *Telephone:* (372) 21-27-04 (office). *Fax:* (372) 21-85-09 (office); (372) 21-94-38 (office). *E-mail:* majmilli@netrt.org (office); mejparl@parliament .tojikiston.com (office). *Website:* www.majlisimilli.tj (office); www.dushanbe.tj (office).

UCHIDA, Dame Mitsuko; Japanese/British pianist; b. 20 Dec. 1948, Tokyo; d. of Fujio Uchida and Yasuko Uchida; partner Sir Robert Cooper; ed Vienna Acad. of Music with Prof. R. Hauser; debut Vienna 1963; recitals and concerto performances with all major London orchestras, Chicago Symphony, Boston Symphony, Cleveland Orchestra, Berlin Philharmonic, Vienna Philharmonic, New York Philharmonic, Los Angeles Philharmonic and others; played and directed the cycle of 21 Mozart piano concertos with the English Chamber Orchestra, London 1985–86; gave US premiere of piano concerto Antiphonies by Harrison Birtwistle 1996; Perspectives recital series at Carnegie Hall 2003; Co-Dir Marlboro Music Festival; Artist-in-Residence, Cleveland Orchestra 2002–07, Berlin Philharmonic Orchestra 2008–09, Vienna Konzerthaus 2008–09; Trustee, Borletti-Buitoni Trust; Hon. CBE 2001; Hon. DBE 2009; First Prize Beethoven Competition Vienna 1969, Second Prize Chopin Competition Warsaw 1970, Second Prize Leeds Competition 1975, Gramophone Award (Mozart Piano Sonatas) 1989, Gramophone Award (Schoenberg Piano Concerto) 2001, Royal Philharmonic Soc.'s Instrumentalist Award 2004, Royal Philharmonic Soc. Gold Medal 2012. *Recordings include:* Mozart Complete Piano Sonatas and 24 Piano Concertos (English Chamber Orchestra and Jeffrey Tate), Mozart Piano Concertos (Cleveland Orchestra), Chopin Piano Sonatas, Debussy 12 Etudes, Schubert Piano Sonatas, Beethoven Piano Concertos, Schoenberg Piano Concerto, Beethoven Piano Sonatas Op. 109, 110 and 111, Beethoven: Sonatas Op. 101 and 106, Schumann: Kreisleriana Carnaval Davidsbündlertänze Fantasie, Berg: Chamber Concerto, Mozart Piano Concertos Nos 23 & 24 (Grammy Award for Best Instrumental Soloist Performance) 2011. *Address:* c/o Victoria Rowsell Artist Management Ltd, 34 Addington Square, London, SE5 7LB, England (office). *Telephone:* (20) 7701-3219 (office). *Fax:* (20) 7701-3219 (office). *E-mail:* management@victoriarowsell.co .uk (office). *Website:* www.victoriarowsell.co.uk (office); www.mitsukouchida.com.

UCHIDA, Tsuneji; Japanese electronics industry executive; *President and Chief Operating Officer, Canon Inc.;* has worked with Canon Inc. for over 40 years business 1999–2000, in charge of promotion of digital photo home business 2000–01, Group Exec. Lens Products Group 1995–2001, Deputy Chief Exec. Camera Operations HQ 1995–97, Group Exec. Photo Products Group 1997–99, Chief Exec. Camera Operations HQ April–July 1999, in charge of promotion of digital photo, Man. Dir 2001–03, Sr Man. Dir 2003–06, Vice-Pres. 2006, mem. Bd of Dirs, Pres. and COO 2006–. *Address:* Canon Inc., 30-2, Shimomaruko 3-chome, Ohta-ku, Tokyo 146-8501, Japan (office). *Telephone:* (3) 3758-2111 (office). *Fax:* (3) 5482-5135 (office). *E-mail:* info@canon.com (office). *Website:* www.canon.com (office).

UCHINAGA, Yukako; Japanese business executive; *Chairman and CEO, Berlitz International, Inc.;* ed Univ. of Tokyo; joined IBM Japan in 1971, several man. positions in devt and marketing, Dir Asia Pacific Products 1989, Gen. Man. AP Cross Industry 1995, mem. Bd of Dirs 1995–, Gen. Man. Services Offerings 1998, Vice-Pres. Multi-industry Solutions, IBM Asia Pacific –1999, Vice-Pres. Software Devt Lab., Yamato 1999–2007, Tech. Advisor 2007; Vice-Chair. Benesse Holdings Corpn and Chair. and CEO Berlitz International, Inc. 2008–; mem. Bd of Dirs Sony Corpn 2008–; Visiting Prof., Coll. of Business, Rikkyo Univ. 2008–; Founder and Chair. Japan Women's Creative Network (J-WIN) 2007–; Pres. Global Workforce Diversity Council; mem. Council for Gender Equality, Japan Prime Minister's Office; mem. Council for Education, Japanese Ministry of Educ. and Science 2001–; Women in Tech. Int. Hall of Fame (first woman inducted from outside the USA) 1999–, ranked by Fortune magazine amongst 50 Most Powerful Women in Business outside the US (33rd) 2002, Upward Mobility Award, Soc. of Women Engineers 2006. *Address:* Berlitz International, Inc., 400 Alexander Park, Princeton, NJ 08540-6306, USA (office). *Telephone:* (609) 514-3400 (office). *Fax:* (609) 514-3405 (office). *Website:* www.berlitz.com (office).

UCHITEL, Aleksei Yefimovich; Russian film director; *Founder and Director-General, Rock Studio;* b. 31 Aug. 1931, Leningrad; s. of Yefim Uchitel; ed All Union State Inst. of Cinematography; with Leningrad Studio of Documentary Films, St Petersburg 1975–90; Founder and Dir-Gen. Rock Studio 1989–; Merited Worker of Arts. *Documentaries:* Its Name is Novgorod 1974, Leningrad: Years of Achievement 1975, Leningrad – Hero City 1975, Ten Thousand I's (Molodost-78 Int. Festival Prize) 1976, Irina Kolpakova, Snow Fantasy 1977, October and Youth

1977, Starting Up: Portrait of An Event (Leipzig Film Festival Prize) 1978, How many faces does the disco have? (Leningrad Komsomol Prize) 1980, Who is for? (Krasnoyarsk All-Union Film Festival Prize) 1982, The Earth is Entrusted to You (Almaty All-Union Film Festival Prize) 1983, Aktsiya (Krakow Int. Film Festival Prize) 1983, Planet Natasha 1986, Rock 1988, Obvodny Kanal (First Prize, Int. Cinema Festival, Bornholm, Denmark) 1990, Butterfly (First Prize, Best Dir, Open Russian Festival of Documentary Cinema, Ekaterinburg) 1993, Elite 1997. *Feature films:* Mania Giseli (Mania of Giselle) (Honfleur Film Festival Prize) 1996, Elite 1997, His Wife's Diary (Grand Prix, Kinotavr Open Russian Cinema Festival) 2000, The Stroll (First Prize, Cleveland Int. Film Festival, Syracuse Int. Film Festival, Special Jury Prize for Outstanding Artistic Concept, FIPRESSI prize and Boulder Prize, 13th Int. Festival of Eastern European Cinema, Kottbus, Best Direction Prize, Window onto Europe Film Festival, Vyborg) 2003, Dreaming of Space 2005, Captive 2008. *Address:* Rock Studio, 12 Krukov Canal, 190068 St Petersburg (office); 4th Krasnokararmennaya str. 6–5, Apt 4, 198052 St Petersburg, Russia (home). *Telephone:* (812) 114-2056 (office); (812) 292-59-45 (home). *E-mail:* rockfilmstudio@mail.ru (office). *Website:* www.rockfilm.ru (office); eng.uchitel.info.

UCHIYAMADA, Takeshi; Japanese motor industry executive; *Chairman and Representative Director, Toyota Motor Corporation;* joined Toyota in 1969, mem. Bd of Dirs Toyota Motor Corpn 1998–, Chief Vehicle Eng Officer 2003–04, Sr Man. Dir 2003–05, Chief Production Control and Logistics Officer 2004–06, Exec. Vice-Pres., Toyota Motor Corpn 2005–12, Vice-Chair. and Rep. Dir 2012–13, Chair. and Rep. Dir 2013–, fmr Corp. Auditor, Toyota Industries Corpn; Dir, Toyota Boshoku Corpn, JTEKT Corpn (fmrly Koyo Seiko Co. Ltd), Aisin AW Co. Ltd; Vice-Chair. Japan Automobile Mfrs Asscn Inc. 2012–, also Vice-Pres. *Address:* Toyota Motor Corpn, 1 Toyota-Cho, Toyota City, Aichi Prefecture 471-8571, Japan (office). *Telephone:* (5) 6528-2121 (office). *Fax:* (5) 6523-5800 (office). *Website:* www.toyota -global.com (office); www.toyota.co.jp (office).

UCISIK, Ahmet Hikmet, PhD; Turkish engineer and academic; *Professor of Materials Science, Boğaziçi University;* ed Istanbul Univ.; Assoc. Prof., Istanbul Tech. Univ.; Dir Marmara Scientific and Industrial Research Inst., Turkish Scientific and Tech. Research Council; instructor Metallurgical Eng Dept, Istanbul Tech. Univ.; currently Prof. of Materials Science, Bogazici Univ.; mem. American and Japanese Socs for Dental Materials and Devices; Fellow, Islamic Acad. of Sciences. *Address:* Boğaziçi University, 80815 Bebek, Istanbul, Turkey (office). *Telephone:* (212) 263-15-00 (office). *Fax:* (212) 265-63-57 (office). *E-mail:* halkilis@ boun.edu.tr (office). *Website:* www.boun.edu.tr (office).

UDALL, Mark Emery, BA; American politician; *Senator from Colorado;* b. 18 July 1950, Tucson, Ariz.; s. of the late Morris 'Mo' Udall and Patricia Emery Udall; nephew of Stewart Udall; m. Maggie Fox; one s. one d.; ed Williams Coll.; Field Organizer, Morris K. Udall for Pres. 1974–75; Course Dir and Educator, Colo Outward Bound School 1975–85, Exec. Dir 1985–95; mem. Colo State House of Reps 1997–98; mem. US House of Reps from 2nd Colo Dist 1999–2009; Senator from Colorado 2009–, mem. Cttee on Armed Services, Cttee on Energy and Natural Resources, Select Cttee on Intelligence, Special Cttee on Aging; mem. American Alpine Club, Parkinson's Action Network; mem. Bd of Dirs Berger Foundation; Democrat. *Leisure interest:* mountaineering. *Address:* 328 Hart Senate Office Building, Washington, DC 20510, USA (office). *Telephone:* (202) 224-5941 (office). *Fax:* (202) 224-6471 (office). *Website:* markudall.senate.gov (office).

UDALL, Thomas (Tom) S., BA, LLB, JD; American lawyer and politician; *Senator from New Mexico;* b. 18 May 1948, Tucson, Ariz.; s. of Stewart Udall and Lee Udall; m. Jill Cooper; one d.; ed Prescott Coll., Univ. of Cambridge, UK, Univ. of New Mexico School of Law; Legis. Asst, staff of US Senator Joe Biden 1973; clerk to Chief Justice Oliver Seth, US Tenth Circuit Court of Appeals, Santa Fe, New Mexico 1977–78; Asst US Attorney 1978–81; attorney in pvt. practice, Santa Fe 1981–83; Chief Counsel, New Mexico Health and Environment Dept 1983–84; attorney, Miller, Stratvert, Torgerson and Schlenker, Albuquerque 1985–90; State Attorney, New Mexico 1991–99; mem. US House of Reps from 3rd New Mexico Dist 1999–2009, mem. Cttees on Appropriations, Educ. and Related Agencies, Sub-cttees on Interior, Environment and Related Agencies, on Labor, Health and Human Services, on Legis. Branch; Senator from New Mexico 2009–, mem. Cttee on Foreign Relations, Cttee on Commerce, Science, and Transportation, Cttee on Environment and Public Works, Cttee on Indian Affairs, Cttee on Rules and Admin, Comm. on Security and Cooperation in Europe, Int. Narcotics Control Caucus; Pres. Nat. Asscn of Attorney Gens 1996; mem. New Mexico Environmental Improvement Bd 1986–87; mem. Kiwanis Club of Albuquerque Inc., Santa Fe Chamber Music Festival, LAW FUND, Regional Environmental Public Interest Law Firm; Democrat. *Leisure interests:* tennis, fly-fishing, mountain climbing, staying involved in his community. *Address:* 110 Hart Senate Office Building, Washington, DC 20510, USA (office). *Telephone:* (202) 224-6621 (office). *Website:* tomudall.senate.gov (office).

UDALTSOV, Sergei Stanislavovich; Russian lawyer and political activist; *Chairman, Left Front;* b. 16 Feb. 1977, Moscow, Russian SFSR, USSR; m. Anastasiya Udaltsova; two s.; Chair. Vanguard of Red Youth 1999–; Chair. Left Front 2008–; Chair. Russian United Labour Front 2010–; one of the leaders of protests against Vladimir Putin 2011–12; arrested along with Aleksei Navalnyi following anti-Putin rallies and given jail sentences Dec. 2011 and May 2012; arrested and charged with plotting riots Oct. 2012, arrested again Dec. 2012; campaign manager for CP of the Russian Fed. cand. Gennady Zyuganov during presidential election 2012; placed under house arrest Feb. 2013. *E-mail:* leftfront77@gmail.com (office). *Website:* www.leftfront.ru (office); www.akm1917 .org (office).

UDUGOV, Brig.-Gen. Movladi; Russian/Chechen economist and politician; b. 9 Feb. 1962, Grozny; m. 1st; m. 2nd; four s.; ed Chechen-Ingush State Univ.; Co-founder Soc. Kavkaz, Co-founder political org. Bart and newspaper Bart 1987; Founder and Ed. Orientir (newspaper banned by Soviet regime) 1988; organizer Mil. Patriotic Union Mansur 1990; participant in Congress of Chechen People

1990; Sec. all sessions of Chechen Nat. Congress; Leader, Formation Cttee of Nat. Congress of Chechen People, anti-Russian resistance group Nov. 1991; participant in overthrow of Communist leadership of Chechen-Ingushetia 1991; Minister of Information and Press, Dudayev Govt 1991; head of propaganda service of Chechen separatists 1994–; took part in negotiations resulting in resolution of that conflict; First Vice-Minister Coalition Govt Chechen Repub. Ichkeria 1996–97, First Deputy Prime Minister 1997–98, Foreign Minister 1998–99; fmr Pres. Kavkaz–Center News Agency; fmr Chief, External Sub-Cttee of Informational Council, State Defence Council; currently Dir Information-Analytical Service of Caucasus Emirate.

UEBBER, Bodo; German business executive; *Chairman, European Aeronautic Defence and Space Company (EADS) NV;* b. 18 Aug. 1959, Solingen; ed Tech. Univ. of Karlsruhe; joined Messerschmitt-Bölkow-Blohm GmbH 1985; held various financial positions within DASA AG, Dornier Luftfahrt and MTU Aero Engines GmbH; mem. Bd of Man. and Chief Financial Officer, Daimler Services AG 2001–03, Chair. 2003–, Deputy mem. Bd of Man., Daimler AG 2003–, responsible for finance, controlling, Corp. procurement and Daimler Financial Services, Chair. Supervisory Bd Daimler Financial Services AG, Daimler France Holding SAS, mem. Supervisory Bd Daimler España Holding SA, mem. Advisory Bd Daimler Unterstützungskasse GmbH; Chair. European Aeronautic Defence and Space Co. (EADS) NV 2009–, mem. Bd of Dirs and Chair. EADS Participations BV; Chair. Supervisory Bd Daimler Financial Services AG; mem. Supervisory Bd Mercedes-Benz Bank AG, Stiftung Deutsche Sporthilfe, Talanx AG; mem. Advisory Bd Daimler Unterstützungskasse GmbH, Deutsche Bank AG, Munich, Landesbank Baden-Württemberg; mem. Bd of Dirs Freightliner LLC; mem. Investment Council of Stifterverband der Deutschen Wissenschaft; mem. Donor's Circle of the Jewish Museum, Berlin; mem. Bd of Trustees Museumsinsel, Berlin, Stuttgarter Galerieverein. *Address:* European Aeronautic Defence and Space Co., Mendelweg 30, 2333 CS Leiden, The Netherlands (office). *Telephone:* (20) 71-524-56-00 (office). *E-mail:* info@eads.com (office). *Website:* www.eads.com (office); www.eads.net (office).

UEBERROTH, Peter Victor; American sports administrator and business executive; b. 2 Sept. 1937, Evanston, Ill.; s. of Victor Ueberroth and Laura Larson; m. Ginny Nicolaus 1959; one s. three d.; ed Freemont High School, San Jose State Univ.; Operations Man., Trans Int. Airlines 1959, later part owner; f. Transportation Consultants, later First Travel Corpn 1962, sold in 1980; Head, LA Olympic Games Organizing Cttee 1980–84; Maj. League Baseball Commr 1984–89; Head, Rebuild LA 1992–93; Co-Chair. Doubletree Hotels Corpn 1993–97 Chair. and Man. Dir Contrarian Group Inc. (investment co.) 1989–, Pres. Contrarian Center; Owner and Co-Chair. Pebble Beach Co. 1999–; Chair. US Olympic Cttee –2008; mem. Bd of Dirs Coca-Cola Co., Aircastle LTD (AYR), Easton Bell Sports; Chair. Bd Ambassadors International 1995–; mem. Young Pres.'s Org.; 12 honorary degrees; Legion déHonneur (France), Time magazine's Man of the Year 1984, Scopus Award 1985, Olympic Order-Gold (Int. Olympic Cttee, Youthlinks Indiana's Nat. Pathfinder Award 2005, John Wooden Global Leadership Award, Andersen School of Man., UCLA 2011. *Publication:* Made in America (autobiog.) 1985. *Leisure interests:* reading (especially historical non-fiction), golf. *Address:* Contrarian Group, Inc., 1071 Camelback Street, Suite 111, Newport Beach, CA 92660-3228, USA (office). *Telephone:* (949) 720-9646 (office). *Website:* www.thecontrariangroup.com (office).

UEHARA, Haruya; Japanese banking executive; *Chairman, Mitsubishi UFJ Trust and Banking Corporation;* b. 1946; Dir Mitsubishi Trust Bank 1996–98, Man.-Dir 1998–2001, Sr Man.-Dir 2001–02, Deputy Pres. 2002–04, Pres. 2004–; Dir Mitsubishi Tokyo Financial Group Inc. 2003–, Chair. and Co-CEO 2004–05, Deputy Chair. and Pres. Mitsubishi UFJ Trust and Banking Corpn 2005–08, Chair. 2008–; mem. Bd Dirs Japanese Bankers Asscn 2004–. *Address:* Mitsubishi UFJ Trust and Banking Corpn, 4-1 Marunouchi 2-chome, Chiyoda-ku, Tokyo 100-6326, Japan (office). *Telephone:* (3) 3240-8111 (office). *Fax:* (3) 3240-8203 (office). *E-mail:* info@mufg.jp (office). *Website:* www.mufg.jp (office).

UEMURA, Hiroyuki; Japanese insurance industry executive; b. 1942; Pres. Sumitomo Marine & Fire Insurance Co. Ltd 1999–2001, Pres. Mitsui Sumitomo Insurance Co. Ltd (cr. from merger between Mitsui Marine & Fire Insurance and Sumitomo Marine & Fire Insurance Cos 2001) 2001–03, Pres. and Co-CEO 2003–06, led negotiations with CitiInsurance Int. Holdings Inc. to establish jt venture Mitsui Sumitomo CitiInsurance Co. (variable annuities life insurance business) 2002; mem. Bd of Dirs Japan Telework Asscn, Yamaha Music Foundation, Japan Earthquake Reinsurance Co. Ltd; apptd Chair. Marine and Fire Insurance Asscn of Japan 2001. *Address:* c/o Mitsui Sumitomo Insurance Co. Ltd, 27-2 Shinkawa 2-chome, Chuo-ku, Tokyo 104-8252, Japan.

UENO, Chizuko, BA, MA; Japanese sociologist and academic; *Professor, Ritsumeikan University;* b. 12 July 1948, Toyama; ed Kyoto Univ.; Assoc. Prof., Heian Women's Coll. 1980–89; Prof., Kyoto Seika Univ. 1989–93; Prof., Grad. School of Humanities and Sociology, Tokyo Univ. 1993–2011; Prof., Ritsumeikan Univ. 2011–; Visiting Prof., El Collegio de Mexico 1996, Barnard Coll., Columbia Univ. 1996–97, Univ. of Bonn; Mori Hamada and Matsumoto Visiting Fellow, Cornell Univ. Law School, USA 2003–04; Suntory Prize for Social Sciences and Humanities 1994, Asahi Prize for lifetime contrib. to feminism and gender studies 2012. *Publications:* Sekushi Gyaru no Daikenkyu (A Study of Sexy Girls) 1982, Explorations in Structuralism 1986, Pleasure of Womanhood 1986, Patriarchy and Capitalism 1990, The Rise and Fall of the Modern Japanese Family 1994, Nationalism and Gender 2003, Tojishashuken 2003, Miwa Yanagi (co-author) 2004, Sociology of Care 2011. *Address:* 1-11-16-2701, Nakamachi, Musashinoshi, Tokyo, Japan (office). *Telephone:* (422) 38-9770 (office). *Fax:* (422) 38-9862 (office). *E-mail:* ueno@l.u-tokyo.ac.jp (office). *Website:* wan.or.jp (office).

UGEUX, Georges, BA (Econ), DrIur; Belgian/American investment banker, lawyer, economist and financier; *Chairman and CEO, Galileo Global Advisors LLC;* b. 20 April 1945, Brussels; m. Francine Godet 1970; two s. two d.; ed Catholic Univ. of Louvain; Lecturer in Econs, Faculty of Law, Univ. of Louvain 1970–72; fmr Gen. Man. Investment Banking & Trust Div., Générale Bank; Man. Dir Morgan Stanley 1985–88; Group Finance Dir Société Générale de Belgique 1988–92; Pres. Kidder Peabody-Europe 1992–95; Chair. Belgian Privatization Comm. 1995–96; Pres. European Investment Fund 1995–96; Group Exec. Vice-

Pres., Int., New York Stock Exchange 1996–2003; Chair. and CEO Galileo Global Advisors LLC 2003–; Adjunct Prof., European Banking and Finance, Columbia Law School; Officer of the Order of Leopold; Scientific Prize, Jean Bastien Foundation. *Publications:* Floating Rate Notes 1985, The Betrayal of Finance 2011; blog at Huffington Post and Le Monde.fr. *Leisure interests:* music, arts, philosophy, int. politics. *Address:* Galileo Global Advisors LLC, Ten Rockefeller Plaza, Suite 1001, New York, NY 10020, USA (office). *Telephone:* (212) 332-6055 (office). *Fax:* (212) 332-6033 (office). *E-mail:* gugeux@galileoadvisors.com (office). *Website:* www.galileoadvisors.com (office).

UGGLAS, Baroness Margaretha af, BA; Swedish foundation executive and fmr politician; b. 5 Jan. 1939; d. of Hugo Stenbeck; ed Harvard-Radcliffe Program in Business Admin., USA, Stockholm School of Econs; leader-writer Svenska Dagbladet 1968–74; mem. Stockholm Co. Council 1971–73; mem. Parl. 1974–95; fmr Moderate Party Spokesman on Foreign Affairs; Chair. Swedish Section, European Union of Women 1981; mem. Parl. Standing Cttee on Foreign Affairs 1982, Advisory Council on Foreign Affairs, Swedish Del. to Council of Europe; Observer, European Parl.; Minister for Foreign Affairs 1991–94; Vice-Pres. European People's Party (EPP) 1996; Chair. Save the Children Fed., Stockholm 1970–76; fmr Chair. Jarl Hjalmarson Foundation (Swedish Moderate Party); mem. Bd of Dirs Karolinska Inst., Becton, Dickinson and Co. 1997–2007; Robert Schuman Medal 1995. *Leisure interests:* art, walking, sailing, mountains, countryside. *Address:* c/o Jarl Hjalmarson Foundation, PO Box 2080, 103 12 Stockholm, Sweden. *E-mail:* stiftelsen@moderat.se.

UGOLINI, Giovanni Francesco; San Marino politician; b. 28 Feb. 1953, Borgo Maggiore; m. Loredana Mularoni; one d.; industrial chemical expert, technician in state hosp. 1974–81; with family hotel business 1981–; joined Partito Democratico Cristiano Sammarinese (PDCS) 1973–, mem. Cen. Council 1993–, Sec. Borgo Maggiore Br. 1989–93; mem. Consiglio Grande e Generale (parl.) 1998–2001; elected Mem. of Govt 2001; Jt Head of State (Capt. Regent) April–Oct. 2002, Oct. 2010–April 2011; Pres., San Marino Union of Tourist Hospitality (USOT) 1990–; mem. Foreign Policy Advisory Comm., Council of the XXII. *Address:* Partito Democratico Cristiano Sammarinese (PDCS), Via delle Scalette 6, 47890 San Marino (office). *Telephone:* (549) 991193 (office). *Fax:* (549) 992694 (office). *E-mail:* pdcs@omniway.sm (office). *Website:* www.pdcs.sm (office).

UHDE, Milan, PhDr; Czech politician, journalist and playwright; b. 28 July 1936, Brno; m. Jitka Uhdeová; two c.; ed Masaryk Univ., Brno; Ed. of literary monthly A Guest Is Coming 1958–70; signed Charter 77; published essays in unofficial periodicals and abroad; Reader, Faculty of Philosophy, Masaryk Univ., Brno Dec. 1989–; Ed.-in-chief, Atlantis Publishing House, Brno March–June 1990; Minister of Culture, Czech Repub. 1990–92; Pres. of Foundation for Preservation of Cultural Monuments 1991–; mem. Civic Democratic Party (ODS) 1991–98, Unie Svobody 1998; Deputy to Czech Nat. Council June 1992–; mem. Presidium; Pres. of Parl., Czech Repub. 1992–96; Chair. Civic Democratic Party in Parl. 1996–97; mem. State Radio Council 1999–; Medal for Merit 2000; Czechoslovak Radio Prize 1966. *Plays include:* in trans.: King Vávra 1964, The Tax-Collector 1965, Witnesses 1966, The Tart from the Town of Thebes 1967, The Gang 1969, Ballad for a Bandit 1975, Professional Woman 1975, A May Fairy Tale 1976, A Dentist's Temptation 1976, Lord of the Flames 1977, The Hour of Defence 1978, The Blue Angel 1979, Ave Maria played Softly 1981, The Annunciation 1986, The Bartered and the Bought 1987, Miracle in the Dark House (Alfred Radok Prize 2008) 2004, Depart in Peace 2004, Nana 2005. *Publications:* novels: Like Water off a Duck's Back 1961, A Mysterious Tower in B. 1967. *Address:* c/o Aura-Pont Agency, Radlická 99, 150 00 Prague, Czech Republic (office). Barvičova 59, 60200, Brno, Czech Republic (home). *Telephone:* 251554938 (office); 602366040 (home). *Fax:* 251550207 (office). *E-mail:* aura-pont@aura-pont.cz (office); milan.uhde@seznam.cz (home). *Website:* www.aura-pont.cz (office).

UHL, Petr; Czech human rights activist and journalist; *Editor, Právo;* b. 8 Oct. 1941, Prague; s. of Bedřich Uhl and Marie Kohoutová; m. Anna Šabatová 1974; three s. one d.; ed Czech. Univ. of Tech., Prague; designer and patent clerk 1964–66; teacher, Coll. of Tech. Prague 1966–69; imprisoned for political activities 1969–73; designer 1974–78; Co-Founder Charter 77; Co-Founder Cttee for Protection of the Unjustly Prosecuted 1978; imprisoned for political activities 1979–84; stoker 1984–89; ed. of East European Information Agency 1988–90; leading rep. of Civic Forum, Prague 1989–90; Dir-Gen., Czechoslovak News Agency 1990–92, Ed. 1992–94; Ed.-in-Chief Listy (magazine) 1994–96; Ed. Právo (daily) 1996–98, 2001–; Commr of Govt of Czech Repub. for Human Rights 1998–2001; Deputy to House of the Nations, Fed. Ass. 1990–92; Chair., Control and Auditing Comm. of Prison Staff Corps, Czech Repub. 1990; mem. Working Group on Arbitrary Detention of UN Comm. on Human Rights 1991–2001, Chair., Cttee for Prevention of Torture of Human Rights Council of Czech Govt 2002–07, mem. Council of Czech TV 2003–09, mem. Monitoring Centre for Racism and Xenophobia 2004–07; State Honours of Czech Repub. 1998, of Poland 2000, of Germany 2001; Chevalier, Ordre nat. du Mérite 2002, Légion d'honneur 2006; Press Freedom Award, Reporter without Borders, Austria 2002. *Publications:* The Programme of Social Self-government 1982, On Czechoslovak Prison System (co-author) 1998, Justice and Injustice in the Eyes of Petr Uhl 1999, and numerous articles in Czech and foreign press. *Address:* Londýnská 7, 120 00 Prague 2, Czech Republic (home). *Telephone:* 72-5103775 (mobile) (home). *E-mail:* uhl@seznam.cz (home).

UHLIG, Harald Friedrich Hans Volker Sigmar, PhD; German economist and academic; *Professor of Economics, University of Chicago;* b. 26 April 1961, Bonn; s. of Dr Sigmar Uhlig and Elfriede Uhlig; ed Technische Univ., Berlin, Univ. of Minnesota; Teaching Asst, Technical Univ., Berlin 1982–85; Research Asst, Fed. Reserve Bank of Minneapolis and Inst. for Empirical Macroeconomics 1986–89; Teaching Asst, Univ. of Minn. 1987; Asst Prof., Dept of Econs, Princeton Univ. 1990–94; Research Prof. for Macroeconomics, Centre for Econ. Research, Tilburg Univ., Netherlands 1994–2000; Visiting Prof., Dept of Econs, Stanford Univ. 1999–2000; Prof. of Macroeconomics and Econ. Policy, Humboldt Univ. 2000–07; Prof. of Econs, Univ. of Chicago 2007–, Chair. of Dept 2009–12; Guest Researcher, German Inst. for Econ. Research, Berlin 2002; Visiting Asst Prof., Univ. of Chicago 1992–93; Guest Lecturer, Univ. of Bonn 1993, 1994; Jt Ed. European Economic Review 1997–2001, Econometrica 2006–10, Journal of Political Economy 2012–; Fellow, Econometric Soc. 2003; Research Fellow, Centre for Econ. Research

(CEPR); Fulbright Scholarship 1985–86; consultant to Bundesbank 2004, Fed. Reserve Bank of Chicago; mem. German Scholarship Foundation 1981–85, CEPR European Business Cycle Dating Cttee (currently Chair.) 2003–12, Econometric Soc., American Econ. Asscn, European Econ. Asscn; Dissertation Support Award, Nat. Bureau of Econ. Research 1989–90, Gossenpreis, Verein für Socialpolitik 2003, Frank P. Ramsey Prize 2005. *Publications:* numerous articles in econ. journals. *Address:* Department of Economics, University of Chicago, 1126 East 59th Street, Chicago, IL 60637 (office); 5454 South Hyde Park Boulevard, Chicago, IL 60615, USA (home). *Telephone:* (773) 702-3702 (office). *Fax:* (773) 702-8490 (office). *E-mail:* huhlig@uchicago.edu (office). *Website:* economics.uchicago.edu (office).

UHRIG, John Allan, AC; Australian business executive (retd); b. 24 Oct. 1928, Newcastle, NSW; s. of L. J. Uhrig; m. Shirley Attwood 1956; two s. two d.; ed Newcastle Tech. High School, Univ. of New South Wales; Man. Dir Simpson Ltd 1975–85; Dir CRA Ltd (now Rio Tinto Australia Ltd) 1983–98, Chair. (non-exec.) 1987–98; Chair. Codan Pty Ltd 1986–2007 (retd); Chair. Australian Mineral Devt Laboratories Ltd (Amdel) 1989, Australian Minerals and Energy Environment Foundation 1991; fmr Chair. Australian Mfg Council; Dir Westpac Banking Corpn 1989, Chair. 1992–2000; Deputy Chair. Santos Ltd 1992–94, apptd Chair. 1994 (Dir 1991); Deputy Chair. RTZ 1995–; mem. Remuneration Tribunal of South Australia 1985–89; Dr hc (Univ. of Queensland) 1997. *Achievements include:* commissioned by Prime Minister John Howard to review the corp. governance of statutory authorities 2002 (called Uhrig Review), report released 2004. *Address:* c/o Codan Ltd, 81 Graves Street, Newton, SA 5074, Australia.

UJIIE, Junichi, BA, MEcons, MBA; Japanese business executive; *Senior Advisor to the Board, Nomura Holdings Inc.;* ed Univ. of Tokyo, Univ. of Chicago and Univ. of Illinois, USA; joined Nomura Securities as an analyst 1975, Pres. Nomura Bank, Switzerland 1984–87, Gen. Man. Int. Planning Dept 1987–90, Pres. Nomura Securities Int., USA 1990–92, mem. Bd of Dirs Nomura Holdings 1990–2011, Head US Div. 1992–95, Co-Chair. Nomura Securities Int., USA 1995–97, CEO and Pres. Nomura Securities Co. 1997–2003, Chair. Nomura Holdings Inc. 2003–11, Sr Advisor to the Bd 2011–; Vice-Chair. Japan Asscn of Corp. Execs (Keizai Doyukai); Chair. Bd of Govs Tokyo Stock Exchange 2000–; Co-Chair. World Econ. Forum on East Asia. *Address:* Nomura Holdings Inc., 1-9-1, Nihonbashi, Chuo-ku, Tokyo 103-8645, Japan (office). *Telephone:* (3) 3211-1811 (office). *Fax:* (3) 3278-0420 (office). *E-mail:* info@nomuraholdings.com (office). *Website:* www.nomuraholdings.com (office).

ULAAN, Chultemiin, MSc; Mongolian economist and politician; *Minister of Finance;* b. 22 April 1954, Baruun, Sukhbaatar Prov.; m. Baldan-Osor Bud; three c.; ed Irkutsk Inst. of Nat. Economy, Irkutsk, Acad. of Social Sciences, Moscow, Russia, Acad. of Social Sciences, Sofia, Bulgaria; Officer State Planning Dept 1977–82, Head of Div. 1982–85; Instructor, Cen. Cttee, Mongolian People's Revolutionary Party (MPRP) 1985–89, Deputy Dir 1989–90, Adviser to Sec.-Gen. 1990; Cabinet mem. and Minister, Nat. Devt Bd 1992–96; mem. Parl. 1996–; Minister of Finance and Economy 2000–04; Deputy Prime Minister 2004–06; Minister of Finance 2007–08, 2012–. *Address:* Ministry of Finance, Government Building 2, Negsden Ündestnii Gudmaj 5/1, Chingeltei District, Ulan Bator, Mongolia (office). *Telephone:* (11) 264891 (also fax) (office). *E-mail:* support@mof.gov.mn (office). *Website:* www.mof.gov.mn (office).

ULLMAN, Myron (Mike) Edward, III, BS; American retail executive; *Chairman and CEO, J. C. Penney Company Inc.;* b. 26 Nov. 1946, Youngstown, OH; s. of Myron Edward Ullman Jr and June Cunningham; m. Cathy Emmons 1969; six c.; ed Univ. of Cincinnati, Harvard Univ.; Int. Account Man. IBM Corpn 1969–76; Vice-Pres. for Business Affairs Univ. of Cincinnati 1976–81; White House Fellow, The White House 1981–82; Exec. Vice-Pres. Sanger Harris Div., Federated Stores 1982–86; Man. Dir and COO Wharf Holdings Ltd, Hong Kong 1986–88; Man. Dir Lane Crawford Ltd, Hong Kong 1986–88; Chair. and CEO R. H. Macy & Co. 1988–95; Deputy Chair. and Dir Federated Dept Stores Inc.; Chair. and CEO DFS Group Ltd 1995–98, Group Chair. 1999–2000; Dir-Gen. and Group Man. Dir Louis Vuitton Möet Hennessy, Paris 1999–2002; Chair. De Beers LV 2000–02; Co-Chair. Global Crossing Ltd 2002–04; Chair. and CEO J. C. Penney Co. Inc. 2004–11, 2013–; Chair. Bd of Dirs Mercy Ships Int. 1992–; mem. Bd of Dirs Starbucks Coffee, Segway LLC, Polo Ralph Lauren, Nat. Multiple Sclerosis Soc., Brunswick School, Univ. of Cincinnati Foundation, Fed. Reserve Bank of Dallas, Retail Industry Leaders Asscn, FIRST (charity); Chair. Exec. Council Univ. of California Medical Center Foundation 2002–, Nat. Retail Fed., Mercy Ships International; Int. Vice-Pres. Univ. of Cincinnati Alumni Asscn. *Address:* J. C. Penney Company Inc., 6501 Legacy Drive, Plano, TX 75024-3698, USA (office). *Telephone:* (972) 431-1000 (office). *Fax:* (972) 431-1362 (office). *E-mail:* info@jcpenney.net (office). *Website:* www.jcpenney.net (office).

ULLMAN, Tracey; British actress and singer; b. 30 Dec. 1959, Slough; d. of the late Anthony John Ullman and of Dorin Cleaver; m. Allan McKeown 1984; one s. one d.; ed Italia Conti Stage School, London; British Acad. Award 1983, Rudolph Valentino Cinema Lifetime Achievement Award 1992, Charlie Chaplin Lifetime Achievement Award, BAFTA 2009. *Films include:* The Rocky Horror Picture Show, Give My Regards to Broad Street, Plenty 1985, Jumpin' Jack Flash 1986, I Love You To Death 1990, Robin Hood: Men in Tights 1993, Household Saints, Bullets over Broadway 1994, Pret-a-Porter 1995, Everybody Says I Love You 1996, C-Scam 2000, Panic 2000, Small Town Crooks 2000, A Dirty Shame 2004, The Cat That Looked at a King (voice) 2004, Corpse Bride (voice) 2005, Kronk's New Groove (voice) 2005, I Could Never Be Your Woman 2007, The Tale of Despereaux (voice) 2008. *Stage appearances include:* Gigi, Elvis, Grease, Four in a Million (London Theatre Critics' Award 1981). *Recordings:* album: You Broke My Heart in Seventeen Places 1983. *Television appearances include:* The Tracey Ullman Show 1987–90, The Best of the Tracey Ullman Show 1990, Tracey Takes On 1996, Ally McBeal 1998–99, Visible Panty Lines (series) 2001, Tracey Ullman in the Trailer Tales 2003, Once Upon a Mattress 2005, State of the Union (series) 2008–09. *Leisure interests:* hiking, riding. *Address:* 13555 D Este Drive, Pacific Palisades, CA 90272; IFA Talent Agency, 8730 W Sunset Boulevard, Suite 490, Los Angeles, CA 90069, USA; c/o ICM, Oxford House, 76 Oxford Street, London, W1N 0AX, England. *Telephone:* (20) 7636-6565 (London). *Fax:* (20) 7323-0101 (London).

ULLMANN, Linn; Norwegian author, journalist and literary critic; b. (Karin Beate Ullmann), 9 Aug. 1966, Oslo; d. of the late Ingmar Bergman and of Liv Ullmann; m. Niels Fredrik Dahl; ed New York Univ., USA; columnist for Aftenposten newspaper; Co-founder and fmr Artistic Dir The Bergman Estate on Fårö (int. artist residency foundation) 2009; mem. jury for main competition, Cannes Film Festival 2011; Amalie Skram Award 2007, Gullpennen (Golden Pen) for her journalism, Aftenposten 2007. *Publications:* Before You Sleep (Før du sovner) 1998, Stella Descending (Når jeg er hos deg) 2001, Grace (Nåde) (Norwegian Reader's Prize 2002, named one of the top ten novels by Week-endavisen newspaper, Denmark 2002, adapted for theatre and performed at Riksteatret 2007) 2002, A Blessed Child (Et Velsignet Barn) (named Best Translated novel by The Independent newspaper, UK 2008) 2005; novels translated into 30 languages. *Address:* c/o The Wylie Agency (UK) Ltd, 17 Bedford Square, London, WC1B 3JA, England (office); c/o Forlaget Oktober AS, Postboks 6848, St Olavs plass, 0130 Oslo, Norway. *Telephone:* (20) 7908-5900 (office); 23-35-46-20. *Fax:* (20) 7908-5901 (office); 23-35-46-21. *E-mail:* mail@wylieagency.co.uk (office); oktober@oktober.no. *Website:* www.wylieagency.co.uk (office); www.oktober.no; www.linnullmann.net.

ULLMANN, Liv Johanne; Norwegian actress; b. 16 Dec. 1938, Tokyo, Japan; d. of the late Viggo Ullmann and of Janna (née Lund) Ullmann; m. 1st Dr. Gappe Stang 1960 (divorced 1965); one d.; m. 2nd Donald Saunders 1985 (divorced 1995); worked in repertory co., Stavanger 1956–59; has appeared at Nat. Theatre and Norwegian State Theatre, Oslo; work for UNICEF as Goodwill Amb.; Vice-Chair. Int. Rescue Cttee; Pres. Fed. of European Film Dirs; Commdr of Olav 1994, Commdr with Star of the Order of St Olav 2005; 12 hon. doctorates; Best Actress of the Year, Nat. Soc. of Critics in America 1969, 1970, 1974, NY Film Critics Award 1973, 1974, Hollywood Foreign Press Asscn's Golden Globe 1973, Best Actress of the Year, Swedish TV 1973, 1974, Donatello Award (Italy) 1975, Bambi Award (Fed. Repub. of Germany) 1975, nominated for Tony Award as Best Stage Actress, debut on Broadway in A Doll's House 1975, LA Film Critics' Award (Face to Face) 1976, New York Film Critics' Award (Face to Face) 1977, Nat. Bd of Review of Motion Pictures Award (Face to Face) 1977, Peer Gynt Award (Norway), Eleanor Roosevelt Award 1982, Roosevelt Freedom Medal 1984, Dag Hammarskjöld Award 1986. *Films include:* Pan 1965, Persona 1966, The Hour of the Wolf 1968, Shame 1968, The Passion of Anna 1969, The Night Visitor 1971, The Emigrants 1972, Cries and Whispers 1972, Pope Joan 1972, Lost Horizon 1973, 40 Carats 1973, The New Land 1973, Zandy's Bride 1973, Scenes from a Marriage 1974, The Abdication 1974, Face to Face 1975, The Serpent's Egg 1978, Sonate d'automne 1978, Richard's Things 1980, The Wild Duck 1983, Love Streams 1983, Let's Hope It's a Girl 1985, Baby Boy 1984, Dangerous Moves 1985, Gaby Brimmer 1986, Moscow Adieu 1986, Time of Indifference 1987, La Amiga 1987, Mindwalk, The Ox, The Long Shadow; Dir: Sophie 1993, Kristin Lavrandsdatter (wrote screenplay also), Faithless (Dir) 2000, Saraband (TV) 2003, The Danish Poet (voice) 2006, I et speil, i en gåte 2008, Zwei Leben 2012. *Plays include:* Brand 1973, A Doll's House 1975, Anna Christie 1977, I Remember Mama 1979, Ghosts 1982, Old Times 1985, The Six Faces of Women (TV), Mother Courage. *Publications include:* Changing (autobiog.) 1976, Choices (autobiog.) 1984. *Leisure interest:* reading. *Address:* c/o Jean Diamond, Diamond Management, 31 Percy Street, London, W1T 2DD, England (office). *Telephone:* (20) 7631-0400 (office). *Fax:* (20) 7631-0500 (office). *E-mail:* agents@diman.co.uk (office). *Website:* www.diamondmanagement.co.uk (office).

ULLRICH, Axel, PhD; German biochemist and academic; *Director, Department of Molecular Biology, Max Planck Institute of Biochemistry;* b. 19 Oct. 1943, Lauban; ed Univs of Tübingen, Münster and Heidelberg; Asst Biochemist, Institute of Biochemistry, Univ. of Münster 1971–72; Postdoctoral Fellow, Dept of Biochemistry and Biophysics, Univ. of California, San Francisco, USA 1975–77, Asst Research Biochemist 1977–78; Sr Scientist, Genentech, Inc., South San Francisco 1979–84, Staff Scientist 1984–88; Dir Dept of Molecular Biology, Max Planck Inst. of Biochemistry, Martinsried 1988–, Man. Dir Max Planck Inst. of Biochemistry 1999, 2007; Visiting Prof., Acad. de Paris, Sorbonne, Paris, France 1996–98; Visiting Scientist and Research Dir of Singapore Oncogenome (SOG) Project, Centre for Molecular Medicine (CMM), Agency for Science, Tech. and Research (A*STAR), Singapore 2004–, Scientific Advisor and Program Dir 2007–, mem. Int. Advisory Council 2000–04; Co-founder SUGEN, Inc., South San Francisco 1991, mem. Bd of Dirs and Science Advisory Bd 1991–99, Co-Chair. Clinical Science Advisory Bd 1999, mem. Science Advisory Bd SUGEN/Pharmacia 1999–2003; Co-founder Virgene/Axxima Pharmaceuticals AG, Martinsried 1998, mem. Bd of Dirs Axxima Pharmaceuticals AG 1998–2004; Co-founder Kinaxo Biotechnologies GmbH, Martinsried 2005; Founder U3 Pharma AG, Martinsried 2001, Chair. 2001–08; Founder and Vice-Chair. Academic Bd Cooperation Lab. for Biological Signal Transduction Research, Second Mil. Medical Univ., Shanghai, People's Repub. of China 1996–2002; mem. Science Advisory Bd, Hagedorn Research Inst., Denmark 1991–95, Receptor BioLogix, Inc., San Francisco 2006–, Centenary Inst., Newtown, Australia 2007–, The Wistar Inst., Philadelphia, USA 1995–2002, RZPD (German Resource Centre for Genome Research), Berlin 2001–03, Biomedicum, Helsinki, Finland 2001–, Univ. of Montreal, Groupe de Recherche Universitaire sur le Médicament (GRUM), Canada 2005–; mem. Advisory Bd, Max Planck Innovation GmbH, Munich 1992–, Chair. Advisory Bd 1996–2004; Vice-Chair. Advisory Bd, Hans Knöll Institut, Jena 1992–2000, Boehringer-Ingelheim, Ingelheim 2003–06, Fondazione Piemontese per la Ricerca sul Cancro, Candiolo, Italy 2008–, Nat. Center for Tumor Diseases (NCT), Heidelberg 2008–; mem. Supervisory Bd BioM AG, Martinsried 1997–2007; mem. One-North Resource Advisory Panel, JTC Corpn and Ministry for Environment, Singapore 2003–, Int. Panel for the Planning of a Research-Intensive Univ., Ministry of Educ., Singapore 2003–04; mem. Bd of Trustees, Max Delbrück Centre for Molecular Medicine, Berlin 2003–06; mem. Scientific Cttee Genoma España, Madrid, Spain 2003, Academic Research Council of Nat. Research Foundation, Singapore 2006–; Co-Ed.-in-Chief Current Signal Transduction Therapy; mem. Editorial Bd, Cancer Research, Growth Factors, Molecular Brain Research, Receptors and Channels, Journal of Cellular Physiology, Cancer Genomics & Proteomics, Molecules and Cells, Molecular Cancer Research, EMBO Molecular Medicine; mem. Academia Europaea, American Soc. for Cell Biology, European Molecular Biology Org. (EMBO) 1990, Gesellschaft für Biochemie und Moleku-larbiologie e.V., American Asscn for Cancer Research, Int. Union Against Cancer

(UICC), Deutsche Krebsgesellschaft, Int. Life Science Forum, AAAS, Deutsche Akad. der Naturforscher Leopoldina 2000, American Acad. of Arts and Sciences 2005; Hon. Prof., Second Mil. Medical Univ., Shanghai 1996, Univ. of Tübingen 2000; Hon. mem. The World Innovation Foundation 2003; Bundesverdienstkreuz 1. Klasse 2009; Laurea hc in Medicine and Surgery, Univ. of Chieti, Italy 2009; numerous awards including Paul Langerhans Medal, German Diabetes Soc. 1987, John W. Cline Memorial Lecturer (sponsored by the American Cancer Soc.), UCLA 1987, first Annual Ray A. and Robert L. Kroc Lecture, Univ. of Massachusetts 1987, Berthold Medal, German Soc. for Endocrinology 1988, Prix Antoine Lacassagne, La Ligue Nationale Française Contre le Cancer, Paris, France 1991, 11th Annual Ray A. and Robert L. Kroc Lecturer, Joslin Diabetes Center, Boston, USA 1996, Gold Medal and 'XXII Lorenzini' Annual Lecturer, Fondazione Giovanni Lorenzini, Medical Science Foundation, Bari, Italy 1997, German Cancer Prize, German Cancer Soc., Frankfurt 1998, Bruce F. Cain Memorial Award, American Asscn for Cancer Research 2000, Robert Koch Prize, Robert Koch Foundation 2001, Int. Fellow, Garvan Inst. of Cancer Research, Sydney, Australia 2001, Virchow Lecturer, Univ. of Würzburg 2002, King Faisal Int. Prize for Medicine, Saudi Arabia 2003, Meyer-Schwickerath Lecture, Soc. of Medical Science, Essen 2003, Warburg Medal, Soc. of Biochemistry and Molecular Biology (GBM) 2005, European BioBusiness Leadership Award, Univ. of Southern California Marshall School of Business 2005, Clifford Prize for Cancer Research (Shiraz Prize), Inst. of Medical and Veterinary Science, Adelaide, Australia 2005, Deutsche Krebshilfe Preis 2005, Deutsche Krebshilfe (German Cancer Aid) e.V. 2006, ASMR Medal, Australian Soc. for Medical Research 2007, Warren Alpert Prize, Harvard Medical School, Cambridge, USA (jtly) 2007, Karl Heinz Beckurts-Preis, Karl Heinz Beckurts-Stiftung, Garching 2007, Prince Mahidol Award of Medicine, Prince Mahidol Foundation, Bangkok, Thailand 2007, Hamdan Award for Medical Research Excellence, Dubai, UAE 2008, Emanuel Merck Lectureship Award, Merck KgaA and Univ. of Tech., Darmstadt 2009, Sergio Lombroso Award in Cancer Research, Weizmann Inst. of Science, Israel 2009, Debrecen Award for Molecular Medicine, Univ. of Debrecen, Hungary 2009, Wolf Foundation Prize in Medicine 2010, MTTC Lifetime Achievement Award, ESMO, Madrid, Spain 2010, GIST 2010 Hall of Fame Award, Life Raft Group, Wayne, NJ, USA 2010, Ismar Boas Medaille, DGVS, Stuttgart 2010. *Publications:* numerous papers in professional journals. *Address:* Department of Molecular Biology, Max Planck Institute of Biochemistry, Am Klopferspitz 18, 82152 Martinsried, Germany (office). *Telephone:* (89) 8578-2512 (office). *Fax:* (89) 8578-2454 (office). *E-mail:* ullrich@biochem.mpg.de (office). *Website:* www.biochem.mpg.de/en/rd/ullrich (office).

ULLRICH, Jan; German professional cyclist; b. 2 Dec. 1973, Rostock; s. of Werner Ullrich and Marianne Kaatz; m. Sara Ullrich; one s. one d.; ed S.C. Dynamo sports school, Berlin; wins as an amateur include: World Championships (Road) 1993, South Africa Tour (three stage wins) 1994, Lower Saxony Tour (two stage wins); turned professional 1995; wins as a professional include: German Time Trial Champion (50km) 1995, Regio Tour (one stage win) 1996, Tour de France 1997, German Road Championships 1997, silver and gold Olympic medals, Sydney 2000; runner-up Tour de France 1996, 1998, 2000, 2001, 2003, fourth 2004, third 2005; seven stage wins, Tour de France; in 2002 tested positive in dope test and given 6-month suspension by German Cycling Fed.; now lives in Switzerland; German Sportsman of the Year 1997, 2003, World Cyclist of the Year 1997. *Leisure interests:* cars, cinema, music. *E-mail:* jan@janullrich.de. *Website:* www.janullrich.de.

ULLSTEN, Ola; Swedish international organization official, diplomatist and fmr politician; b. 23 June 1931, Umeå; s. of C. A. Ullsten and Ştina Ullsten; graduated in social sciences 1956; Sec. Parl. Group Liberal Party 1957–61; journalist Dagens Nyheter 1962–64; mem. Riksdag (Parl.) 1965–84; Chair. Liberal Party Stockholm County 1972–76; Minister of Int. Devt Co-operation 1976–78; Deputy Prime Minister March–Oct. 1978, Prime Minister 1978–79; Minister for Foreign Affairs 1979–82, Deputy Prime Minister 1980–82; Chair. Liberal Party 1978–83; Amb. to Canada 1983–89, to Italy 1989–95; mem. Interaction Council of Former Heads of Govt; Co-Chair World Comm. on Forests and Sustainable Devt 1995–99; Chair. Int. Advisory Council, Ontario Agricultural Coll., Univ. of Guelph 2002–; fmr Sr Fellow, Int. Inst. for Sustainable Devt; currently Global Jury Chairman, Golden Peacock Awards; mem. Bd of Dirs Woods Hole Research Center, MA; hon. degree (Univ. of Guelph) 1999. *Address:* Smiss, Grotlingbo, 620 11 Havdhem, Sweden; 1941 Kerns Road, Burlington, ON L7P 3J1, Canada; ; c/o Golden Peacock Global Awards Secretariat, 1 Northumberland Avenue, Trafalgar Square, London, WC2N 5BW, England. *Telephone:* (498) 48-60-02 (Sweden); (905) 331-9972 (Canada). *Fax:* (905) 331-8336 (Canada). *E-mail:* olaullsten2@aol.com.

ULMANIS, Guntis, BEcon; Latvian fmr head of state; b. 13 Sept. 1939, Rīga; m. Aina Ulmane (née Stelce); one s. one d.; ed Univ. of Latvia; as a child was exiled to Russia together with his parents, returned to Latvia in 1946; mil. service 1963–65; Economist, bldg industry and Rīga Public Transport Bd; Man. Rīga Municipal Community Services 1965–92; fmr Lecturer in Construction Econs, Rīga Polytechnic Inst. and Econ. Planning, Latvian State Univ.; mem. CPSU 1965–89; mem. Bd of Cen. Bank of Latvia 1992–93, Deputy to Parl. (Saeima) June–July 1993; Pres. of Latvia 1993–99; Hon. Chair. Union of Farmers Party 1993–; numerous decorations, including Order of St Michael and St George (UK) 1996, Légion d'honneur 1997, Order of Merit (Germany) 1999; Dr hc (Charleston Univ., USA) 1996; Award of US Inst. for East-West Studies 1996, Cen. and E European Law Initiative Award, American Bar Asscn 1997, Distinguished Statesman Award, Anti-Defamation League 1998. *Publications:* Autobiography 1995, My Time as President 1999. *Leisure interests:* hunting, reading, playing with grandchildren. *Address:* Brīvības iela 38, Apt 5, 1050 Rīga, Latvia (home). *Telephone:* 709 2112 (office); 927 8758. *Fax:* 732 5800. *E-mail:* eva@president.lv (office).

ULOUM, Ibrahim Muhammad Bahr al-, PhD; Iraqi politician; b. 1954; s. of Muhammad Bahr al-Uloum; ed New Mexico Inst. of Mining and Tech., USA; worked for Kuwaiti Oil Ministry and Petroleum Recovery Research Center, New Mexico –1992; ind. consultant, London, UK 1992–2003; Minister of Oil of Iraq 2003–04, 2005; survived assassination attempts in 2003 and 2005; *Telephone:* (1) 7901 913315 (home).

ULRICH, Jing, BA, MA; Chinese investment manager and business executive; *Managing Director and Chairman, Global Markets, China, JPMorgan Chase;* b. (Li Jing), 1967, Beijing; m. Paul Ulrich; ed Harvard and Stanford Univs, USA;

worked as fund man. for Greater China at Emerging Markets, Washington, DC, USA 1990–96; led top-ranked team covering China market, Credit Lyonnais Securities Asia 1996–2003; Man. Dir Greater China Equities, Deutsche Bank 2003–05; Man. Dir and Chair. Global Markets, China, JPMorgan Chase 2005–; serves as adviser to Chinese insts making investments overseas; chosen by Asiamoney magazine as Best China Strategist, ranked by Institutional Investor magazine as head of the top China team world-wide 2003, 2004, 2005, 2006, 2007, chosen by The South China Morning Post and the American Chamber of Commerce in Hong Kong as Hong Kong's Young Achiever of the Year 2006, ranked by Forbes magazine amongst The World's 100 Most Powerful Women (95th) 2008, (81st) 2010, ranked by Fortune magazine amongst the 50 Most Powerful Women in Business outside the US (49th) 2009, (47th) 2010, (46th) 2011, named by Business Watch Magazine as one of the country's top female business elite April 2009, March 2010, and also by China Entrepreneur March 2010, named by Contemporary Manager journal as one of the top ten business leaders in China May 2009, included by Forbes magazine amongs the world's "20 youngest power women", featured by Vogue China as one of 15 globally influential Asian women Aug. 2010. *Address:* JF Investment Centre, Walkway Level, Jardine House, 1 Connaught Place, Central, Hong Kong Special Administrative Region, People's Republic of China (office). *Telephone:* 22651133 (office). *Fax:* 28685013 (office). *E-mail:* investor.services@jpmorgan.com (office). *Website:* www.jpmorganam.com.hk/wps/portal (office).

ULRICH, Robert (Bob) J., BA; American retail executive; *Chairman Emeritus, Target Corporation;* b. 1943, Minneapolis, Minn.; ed Univ. of Minnesota; began career as merchandising trainee, Dayton Hudson 1967, Pres. and CEO Diamond Dept Stores 1981–82, Pres. Dayton Hudson Dept Store Co. 1982–84, Pres. Target Div. 1984–87, Chair. and CEO Target 1987–94, Chair. and CEO Dayton Hudson Corpn (renamed Target Corpn 2000) 1994–2008, Chair. Target Corpn 2008–09, Chair. Emer. 2009–; mem. Bd of Dirs Yum! Brands, Inc. 1997–; Life Trustee, Minneapolis Inst. of Arts; Discounter of the Year, Discount Store News SPARC (Supplier Performance Award by Retail Category) Award 1992. *Address:* Target Corporation, 1000 Nicollet Mall, Minneapolis, MN 55403, USA (office). *Telephone:* (612) 304-6073 (office). *Fax:* (612) 696-3731 (office). *E-mail:* info@target.com (office). *Website:* www.target.com (office).

'ULUKALALA LAVAKA ATA, HRH Prince; s. of HRH King Taufa'ahau Tupou IV; m. HRH Princess Nanasipau'u Tuku; Cadet Officer, Tonga Defence Services 1981, Commdg Officer of the Navy 1991–95; Prime Minister of Tonga 2000–06 (resigned); held ministerial posts including Minister for Foreign Affairs and Defence 1999–2000, for Agric. and Forestry, Fisheries, Marine and Ports, Civil Aviation 2001–06, for Communications 2001–06, for Works and Disaster Relief Activities 2004–06; fmr Pres. ACP Council of Ministers. *Address:* POB 901, Nuku'alofa, Tonga (office). *Telephone:* 23565 (office). *Fax:* 24626 (office). *E-mail:* webmaster@parliament.gov.to (office). *Website:* parliament.gov.to (office).

ULUSU, Adm. (retd) Bülent; Turkish politician and naval officer (retd); b. 7 May 1923, Istanbul; s. of M. Salih Ulusu and Seniye Ulusu; m. Mizat Erensoy 1951; one d.; ed Naval Acad.; various command posts in navy; rank of Rear-Adm. 1967, Vice-Adm. 1970, Adm. 1974; fmr Commdr of War Fleet; Commdr of Turkish Naval Forces –1980; fmr Under-Sec., Ministry of Defence; Prime Minister of Turkey 1980–83; mem. Parl. 1983–87. *Address:* Ciftehavuzlar Yesilbahar 50K. 8/27, Kadikoy Istanbul, Turkey.

ULVÆUS, Björn Kristian; Swedish songwriter, musician (guitar), singer and producer; b. 25 April 1945, Gothenburg; m. Agnetha Fältskog 1971 (divorced 1979); songwriter with Benny Andersson 1966–; duo with Andersson as The Hootennanny Singers; partner in production with Andersson at Polar Music 1971; mem. pop group ABBA 1973–82; winner Eurovision Song Contest 1974; world-wide tours; concerts include Royal Performance, Stockholm 1976, Royal Albert Hall, London 1977, UNICEF concert, New York 1979, Wembley Arena 1979; reunion with ABBA, Swedish TV This Is Your Life 1986; continued writing and producing with Andersson 1982–; produced musical Mamma Mia! with Andersson, West End, London 1999; World Music Award for Best Selling Swedish Artist 1993, Ivor Novello Special International Award (with Benny Andersson) 2002. *Film:* ABBA: The Movie 1977. *Compositions include:* ABBA songs (with Benny Andersson); musicals: Chess (with lyrics by Tim Rice) 1983, The Immigrants 1994, Mamma Mia! (with Andersson) 1999. *Recordings include:* albums: with Andersson: Happiness 1971; with ABBA: Waterloo 1974, ABBA 1976, Greatest Hits 1976, Arrival 1977, The Album 1978, Voulez-Vous 1979, Greatest Hits Vol. 2 1979, Super Trouper 1980, The Visitors 1981, The Singles: The First Ten Years 1982, Thank You For The Music 1983, Absolute ABBA 1988, ABBA Gold 1992, More ABBA Gold 1993, Forever Gold 1998, The Definitive Collection 2001; singles include: with ABBA: Ring Ring 1973, Waterloo 1974, Mamma Mia 1975, Dancing Queen 1976, Fernando 1976, Money Money Money 1976, Knowing Me Knowing You 1977, The Name Of The Game 1977, Take A Chance On Me 1978, Summer Night City 1978, Chiquitita 1979, Does Your Mother Know? 1979, Angel Eyes/Voulez-Vous 1979, Gimme Gimme Gimme (A Man After Midnight) 1979, I Have A Dream 1979, The Winner Takes It All 1980, Super Trouper 1980, On And On And On 1981, Lay All Your Love On Me 1981, One Of Us 1981, When All Is Said And Done 1982, Head Over Heels 1982, The Day Before You Came 1982, Under Attack 1982, Thank You For The Music 1983. *Publication:* Mamma Mia! How Can I Resist You? (with Benny Andersson and Judy Craymer) 2006. *Address:* Södra Brobänken 41A, 111 49 Stockholm, Sweden. *Website:* www.abbasite.com.

ULYUKAYEV, Alexey Valentinovich, Dr Econ; Russian politician, economist and banker; *First Deputy Chairman, Central Bank of the Russian Federation;* b. 23 March 1956, Russia; m.; two s. one d.; ed Moscow State Univ.; Asst, then Assoc. Prof., Moscow Inst. of Construction Eng 1982–88; Consultant, Head of Div., Communist (journal) 1988–91; political analyst, Moskovskiye Novosti (weekly) 1991; econ. adviser to Russian Govt 1991–92; Head f Group of Advisers to Chair. of Govt, Russian Fed. 1992–93; Asst to First Deputy Chair. of Govt, Russian Fed. 1993–94; Deputy Dir Inst. of Econ. Problems of the Transition Period 1994–96, 1998–2000; Deputy, Moscow City Duma 1996–98; First Deputy Minister of Finance 2000–04; First Deputy Chair. Central Bank of the Russian Fed. 2004–, Dir Moscow Interbank Currency Exchange 2008–11. *Leisure interests:* tourism, swimming, literature. *Address:* Bank Rossii (Central Bank of the Russian Federation), 107016 Moscow, ul. Neglinnaya 12, Russia (office). *Telephone:* (495)

771-40-46 (office). *Fax:* (495) 921-91-47 (office). *E-mail:* webmaster@www.cbr.ru (office). *Website:* www.cbr.ru (office).

UMAR, Asad, MBA; Pakistani business executive; *Chairman and CEO, Engro Chemical Pakistan Ltd;* m.; two s.; ed Inst. of Business Admin, Pakistan; joined Exxon Chemical Pakistan (later renamed Engro Pakistan Ltd) 1985, worked in Karachi, Daharki and Edmonton, Canada in Finance, Manufacturing, Marketing and New Ventures Div., later Sr Vice-Pres. Engro Chemical Pakistan Ltd, Chair. and CEO 2004–, Dir Engro Chemical Pakistan Ltd, Engro Vopak Terminal Ltd, Engro Asahi Polymer & Chemicals Ltd (fmr first Pres.), Port Qasim Authority 2000–01; mem. Bd of Man. Pakistan State Oil; Chapter Chair. Young Presidents' Org. (Pakistan Chapter); mem. Overseas Investors' Chamber of Commerce and Industry's Standing Sub-cttee for Commercial and Industrial Matters 1998–2000, Man. Asscn Pakistan's Corp. Excellence Award Sub-cttee 1998–2000; mem. Bd of Dirs Pakistan Business Council, Karachi Educ. Initiative, Pakistan Inst. of Corp. Governance, State Bank of Pakistan; Trustee, Lahore Univ. of Man. Sciences,.Pakistan Centre for Philanthropy. *Address:* Engro Chemical Pakistan Ltd, 8th Floor, PNSC Building, M. T. Khan Road, Karachi, Pakistan (office). *Telephone:* (21) 5611060-69 (office). *Fax:* (21) 5611249 (office). *E-mail:* aumar@engro.com (office).

UMBELINA NETO, Natália Pedro da Costa, PhD; São Tomé and Príncipe politician; *Minister of Foreign Affairs, Co-operation and Communities;* b. Príncipe; ed Univ. Nova de Lisboa, Portugal, Univ. Aix-Marseille I, France; served two years as Sec.-Gen., São Tomé and Príncipe Comm. for UNESCO; fmr Inspector of Educ.; Sec. for Social Affairs, Regional Govt of Príncipe –2012; Minister of Foreign Affairs, Co-operation and Communities 2012–. *Address:* Ministry of Foreign Affairs, Co-operation and Communities, Av. 12 de Julho, CP 111, São Tomé, São Tomé and Príncipe (office). *Telephone:* 222309 (office). *Fax:* 223237 (office). *E-mail:* minecoop@cstome.net (office). *Website:* www.mnecc.gov.st (office).

UMEDA, Sadao; Japanese business executive; *Chairman and Representative Director, Kajima Corporation;* Pres. Kajima Corpn (building construction co. providing design, eng, building and real estate devt services) 1996–2005, Chair. and Rep. Dir 2005–; mem. Keidanren Japan-Hong Kong Business Cooperation Cttee 2000–, Chair. 2002; mem. Bd of Dirs Japan Telework Asscn 2003, Japan Fashion Asscn, Japan Water Forum Advisory Council; Pres. Ethiopian Asscn of Japan, Japanese-Turkish Econ. Council; mem. Japan Cttee, Pacific Basic Econ. Council. *Address:* Kajima Corpn, 3-1 Motoakasaka 1-chome, Minatu-ku, Tokyo 107-8388, Japan (office). *Telephone:* (3) 3403-3311 (office). *Fax:* (3) 3470-1444 (office). *E-mail:* info@kajima.co.jp (office). *Website:* www.kajima.co.jp (office).

UNAKITAN, Kemal; Turkish politician; b. 1946, Edirne; m.; three c.; ed Ankara Econ. and Commerical Sciences Acad.; fmr Financial Comptroller Ministry of Finance, Minister of Finance 2002–09; fmr mem. Exec. Bd SEKA Directorate Gen., Albaraka Türk and Family Finance. *Address:* c/o Ministry of Finance, Maliye Bakanlığı, Dikmen Cad., Ankara, Turkey (office).

UNANUE, Emil Raphael, MD; Cuban immunologist and academic; *Paul and Ellen Lacy Professor, Pathology and Immunology, Department of Pathology and Immunology, School of Medicine, Washington University in St Louis;* b. 13 Sept. 1934, Havana; ed Inst. of Secondary Educ., Havana, Univ. of Havana School of Medicine; Intern in Pathology, Presbyterian Univ. Hosp., Pittsburgh, Pa 1961–62; Research Fellow, Dept of Experimental Pathology, Scripps Clinic and Research Foundation, La Jolla, Calif. 1962–66, Assoc. 1968–70; Research Fellow, Immunology Div., Nat. Inst. for Medical Research, London, UK 1966–68; Asst Prof. of Pathology, Harvard Medical School, Boston, Mass 1970–71, Assoc. Prof. 1972–74, Mallinckrodt Prof. of Immunopathology 1974–84, Consultant in Pathology, Dept of Pathology, Brigham and Women's Hosp. 1977–84; Visiting Prof., Kuwait Univ. School of Medicine, Kuwait 1982, Royal Postgraduate Medical School, London 1983; Pathologist-in-Chief, Barnes-Jewish Hosp., St Louis, Mo. 1985–; Mallinckrodt Prof. and Chair. Dept of Pathology and Immunology, Washington Univ. School of Medicine, St Louis 1985, then Paul and Ellen Lacy Professor; Burroughs Wellcome Visiting Prof. in the Basic Medical Sciences, Tulane Univ., New Orleans, La 2000; Pres. American Asscn of Pathologists 1988–89; Assoc. Ed. Journal of Immunology 1972–77, Clinical Immunology and Immunopathology 1972–89, International Archives of Allergy and Applied Immunology 1973–91, Journal of the Reticuloendothelial Society 1974–77, Laboratory Investigation 1975–90, Immunity 1994–96 (Ed. 1996–2000); Contributing Ed. Sanguinis 1976–77; Transmitting Ed. International Immunology 1992–; mem. Editorial Bd Modern Pathology 1988–97, Molecular Medicine 1994–, Immunological Reviews 1996–; mem. American Soc. of Investigative Pathology 1966, American Asscn of Immunologists 1966, Reticuloendothelial Soc. 1977, American Soc. for Cell Biology 1984, Asscn of Pathology Chairmen 1986, US and Canadian Acad. of Pathology 1986, NAS 1987 (Chair. Section 43—Microbiology and Immunology 1998–), Alpha Omgea Alpha Hon. Medical Soc. 1988, Pew Nat. Advisory Council 1994–98, Inst. of Medicine 1995; Sr Fellow, American Cancer Soc. (Calif. Div.) 1969–70, American Acad. of Arts and Sciences 1989; Hon. mem. Venezuelan Soc. of Allergy and Immunology 1981; Hon. MA (Harvard) 1974; Dr hc (Barcelona) 1999; Helen Hay Whitney Fellowship and T. Ducket Jones Award 1966–69, NIH Research Career Development Award 1971, Parke Davis Award, American Soc. for Experimental Pathology 1973, Guggenheim Fellowship 1980–81, Marie T. Bonzainga Annual Research Award, Reticuloendothelial Soc. 1986, William B. Coley Award, Cancer Research Inst. 1989, Albert Lasker Award for Basic Medical Research 1995, Rous-Whipple Award, American Soc. for Investigative Pathology 1998, Kenneth W. Sell Memorial Lecturer, Emory Univ. 1999, Gairdner Foundation Int. Award 2000. *Publications:* more than 210 articles in scientific journals. *Address:* Room 1751, 1st Floor, West Building, Department of Pathology and Immunology, School of Medicine, Washington University in St, 660 S Euclid Avenue, St Louis, MO 63110, USA (office). *Telephone:* (314) 362-7440 (office); (314) 362-8752 (Lab). *Fax:* (314) 362-4096 (office). *E-mail:* unanue@wustl.edu (office). *Website:* pathology.wustl.edu (office).

UNGARO, Emanuel Mattéotti; French fashion designer; b. 13 Feb. 1933, Aix-en-Provence; s. of Cosimo Ungaro and Concetta Casalino; m. Laura Bernabei; one d.; ed Lycée d'Aix-en-Provence; worked as tailor at Aix-en-Provence, then with Camps, Paris, Balenciaga, Paris and Madrid 1958–64, Courrèges, Paris 1964; Couturier, Paris 1965–2004; sold Ungaro label to Asim Abdullah 2005; Chevalier, Légion d'honneur. *Leisure interests:* music, reading, skiing. *Address:* 2 avenue

Montaigne, 75008 Paris, France. *Telephone:* 1-53-57-00-00 (office). *Fax:* 1-47-23-82-31 (office). *E-mail:* info@ungaro.fr. *Website:* www.ungaro.com.

UNGER, Felix, DrMed; Austrian surgeon; *Head of Heart Surgery, University Clinic for Cardiac Surgery, Salzburg;* b. 2 March 1946, Klagenfurt; s. of Carl Unger and Maria Unger; m. Monika von Fioreschy 1971; two s.; Lecturer, Univ. of Vienna 1978–83; Prof., Univ. of Innsbruck 1983–; Head of Heart Surgery, Univ. Clinic for Cardiac Surgery, Salzburg 1984–; Founder and Pres. European Acad. of Sciences and Arts; Hon. Prof., Bundesverdienstkreuz 1992; Dr hc (Timisoara, Budapest, Tokyo, Maribor, Riga, Belgrade, Athens) 1990–2009; Dr Karl Renner Prize 1975, Sandoz Prize 1980, Plannsee Prize 1982, Österreichischer Ehrenkreuz für Wissenschaft und Kunst I. Klasse 2006, Paul-Stradins-Preis, Riga 2009. *Publications:* 15 books and more than 500 articles in specialist journals. *Leisure interest:* arts. *Address:* European Academy of Sciences and Arts, St-Peter-Bezirk 10, 5020 Salzburg (office); Schwimmschulstrasse 31, 5020 Salzburg, Austria (home). *Telephone:* (662) 841345 (office); (662) 824741 (home). *Fax:* (662) 841343 (office); (662) 8247414 (home). *E-mail:* felix.unger@euro-acad.eu (office); f.unger@salk.at (office). *Website:* www.euro-acad.eu (office); www.euinhe.eu (office); www.salk.at.

UNGER, Pierre-François, MD; Swiss physician and politician; b. 21 Aug. 1951; m.; two c.; following medical training spent several years abroad, including a long period in Paris; Head of Emergency Dept, Hôpitaux universitaires de Genève 1986–, Prof. of Medicine 1999–; mem. Grand Conseil, Geneva 1993–99; mem. Council of State of Geneva 2001–13, State Councillor in charge of Dept of Social Welfare and Health 2001–05, of Economy and Health 2005–09, Pres. Council of State 2005–06, 2011–12 mem. Parti démocrate-chrétien. *Address:* c/o Council of State of Geneva, 14, rue de l'Hôtel-de-Ville, CP 3984, 1211 Geneva 3, Switzerland (office).

UNGUREANU, Mihai-Răzvan, MA, PhD; Romanian academic, politician and government official; b. 22 Sept. 1968, Iași; m.; one s.; ed C. Negruzzi High School of Math.-Physics, Iași, Al.I. Cuza Univ., Iași, St Cross Coll., Oxford, UK; Jr Fellow, New Europe Coll. for Advanced Studies, Bucharest, mem. Admin. Bd 2002; teacher, Mihai Eminescu Philology-History High School, Iași 1992; Univ. Tutor, Faculty of History, Al.I. Cuza Univ., Iași 1992–96, Univ. Asst 1996–98, Univ. Lecturer 1998, Dir Centre for Jewish Studies 2004, mem. Senate Al.I. Cuza Univ. 1990–92; Guest Scientist, Dept for European History, Albert Ludwig Univ., Freiburg im Breisgau, Germany 1993–97; Dir Centre for Romanian Studies, Romanian Cultural Foundation, Iași 1996–99; Assoc. Prof., School of Slavonic and East European Studies, Univ. of London, UK 1996–98; Sr Fellow, Oxford Centre for Jewish and Hebrew Studies, St Cross Coll. Oxford 1998; Sec. of State, Ministry of Foreign Affairs 1998–2001, Regional Emissary, Stability Pact for South-Eastern Europe 2001–03, Deputy Coordinator SE European Cooperation Initiative (SECI), Vienna 2003, Minister-Counselor 2003, Minister of Foreign Affairs 2004–07 (resgnd); Dir Serviciului de Informații Externe—SIE (Foreign Intelligence Service) 2007–12; Prime Minister Feb.–May 2012; Acting Minister of Environment and Forests 5–10 April 2012; mem. Senate (Right Romania Alliance party list) Dec. 2012–; Sr Reader, NATO School (SHAPE), Oberammergau, Germany 2001; Assoc. Univ. Prof., SNSPA, Bucharest 2002; Sr Reader, George C. Marshall Centre for Security Studies, Garmisch-Partenkirchen, Germany 2003; Coordinator Historia Collection, Polirom Publishing House, Iași 1998; Ed.-in-Chief Revista de Istorie Sociala 1996; Ed. Dialog Magazine 1988–92, Arhiva Genealogica 1993, Revue des Etudes Roumains 1994, Nat. Council for Educ. Reform, Nat. of National Educ. 1998–2000, Scientific Council, Sever Zotta Inst. for Genealogical and Heraldic Studies, Iași 1998; Sec. Exec. Int. Students in History Asscn, Budapest-Brussels 1990–93; mem. Scientific Bd Soros Foundation for an Open Society, Iași 1996–98; Pres. Romanian Inst. for Strategic Studies, Bucharest 2001; mem. Romanian Soc. for Heraldry, Sigillography and Genealogy of the Romanian Acad. (Iași Br.) 1993, European Asscn for Jewish Studies, Oxford 1997, Scientific Bd Centre for Security Policies, Szeged, Hungary 2003; Commdr (First Rank), Royal Order of the Dannebrog (Denmark) 2000, Grand Officer of Nat. Order for Merits (Romania) 2000, Kt of Star of Romania Nat. Order 2008; Republican Praiseworthy Scholarship, Al.I. Cuza Univ. 1991, Royal Soc. Mark Rich Scholarship, St Cross Coll., Oxford 1992, Studies and Research Scholarship, Albert Ludwig Univ., Freiburg im Breisgau, Germany 1994–98, NEC Fellowship, New Europe Coll., Bucharest 1996, REX Fellowship IREX, State Dept, USA 1996, Chevening-FCO Fellowship SEEES, Univ. of London 1997, Relink Fellowship, New Europe Coll. 1998, Felix Posen Fellowship, Hebrew Univ., Jerusalem, Israel 1998–99, Andrew Mellon Fellowship, Wissenschaftskolleg zu Berlin 1998, Nat. Prize of 22 Magazine, Bucharest 1992, Felix Posen Prize, Hebrew Univ. 1996–97, 1997–98, Vasile Pogor Prize, Iași City Hall 1998, Corneliu Coposu Prize, Youth Org. of PNT-cd 1999, Dimitrie Onciul Prize, Magazin Istoric Cultural Foundation for the publication of the work Relatiile Romano-sovietice, Documente, 1917–1934, I, Bucharest, 1999 (in collaboration with the Ministry of Foreign Affairs of the Russian Federation). *Publications include:* Statistical Documents Regarding the City of Iași (1755–1828), Vols I–II (co-author) 1996–97, Marea Arhondologie a boierilor Moldovei 1998, The Comprehensive Catalogue of Moldavian Boyars 1829–1856 1997, Convertire și integrare în societatea românească la începutul epocii moderne 2004; more than 50 scientific articles and more than 60 publs in magazines and learned reviews including Dialog, Cronica, Timpul, Convorbiri literare, Astra, România Literară, 22, Dilema, Tinerama, Contrapunct, Polis, Revue des Etudes Roumaines, The Genealogic Archives, The Romanian Review of Social History, Népszabadság 1991–2004. *Address:* Senate of Romania, 050711 Bucharest, Calea 13 Septembrie nr 1–3, sector 5, Romania (office). *Telephone:* (21) 4141111 (office). *Fax:* (21) 3160300 (office). *E-mail:* infopub@senat.ro (office). *Website:* www.senat.ro (office).

UNO, Ikuo; Japanese insurance executive; *Executive Advisor to the Board, Nippon Life Insurance Company;* Pres. Nippon Life Insurance Co. 1997–2005, Chair. 2005–11, Exec. Advisor to the Bd 2011–; Vice-Chair. Kansai Econ. Fed. (Kankeiren); mem. Bd of Auditors Odakyu Electric Railway Co. Ltd 2002; Corp. Auditor Tanabe Seiyaku Co. Ltd; Chair. Life Insurance Asscn of Japan 2001–05; mem. Bd of Dirs Int. Insurance Soc. Inc., New York 2003–, Japan Investor Relations Asscn 2003–, Obayashi Foundation 2006–. *Address:* Nippon Life Insurance Co., 3-5-12 Imabashi, Chuo-ku, Osaka 541-8501, Japan (office).

Telephone: (6) 6209-5525 (office). *Fax:* (3) 5510-7340 (office). *E-mail:* info@nissay.co
.jp (office). *Website:* www.nissay.co.jp (office).

UNO, Sandiaga (Sandi) S., BBA, MBA; Indonesian business executive;
Managing Director, Saratoga Capital; b. 28 June 1969; m.; two c.; ed Wichita
State Univ., George Washington Univ., USA; fmr analyst; co-f. Saratoga Capital
(pvt. equity firm) 1998, currently Man. Dir; Finance and Accounting Officer,
Summa Group Companies, Indonesia 1990–93; Chief Financial Officer, NTI
Resources Ltd, Calgary, Canada 1995–98; co-f. PT Recapital Advisors (investment
bank), currently Pres. Commr; mem. Bd of Dirs PT Adaro Indonesia, PT Indonesia
Bulk Terminal, PT Mitra Global Telekomunikasi Indonesia, Interra Resources
Ltd; Chair. Indonesian Young Entrepreneurs Asscn 2005–08. *Address:* Saratoga
Capital, 3 Phillip Street, #15-01 Commerce Point, Singapore 048693, Singapore
(office). *Telephone:* 65368661 (office). *Fax:* 65368161 (office). *E-mail:* info@saratoga
-asia.com (office). *Website:* www.saratoga-asia.com (office).

UNOURA, Hiroo; Japanese business executive; *President and CEO, Nippon
Telegraph and Telephone Corporation (NTT);* b. 13 Jan. 1949; joined Nippon
Telegraph and Telephone Public Corpn (NTT) 1973, Sr Vice-Pres. and Dir of Dept I
2002–05, Sr Vice-Pres. and Dir of Dept V 2005–07, Exec. Vice-Pres., Dir of Corp.
Strategy Planning Dept and Exec. Man. Corp. Business Strategy Div. 2007–08,
Exec. Vice-Pres. and Dir of Strategic Business Devt Div. 2008–11, Pres. and CEO
NTT 2011–. *Address:* Nippon Telegraph and Telephone Corporation, 3-1,
Otemachi 2-chome, Chiyoda-ku, Tokyo 100-8116 Japan (office). *Telephone:* (3)
5205-5581 (office). *Fax:* (3) 5205-5589 (office). *E-mail:* info@ntt.co.jp (office).
Website: www.ntt.co.jp (office).

UNTERMANN, Jürgen, DPhil; German professor of linguistics; *Professor
Emeritus, University of Cologne;* b. 24 Oct. 1928, Rheinfelden; ed Univs of
Frankfurt and Tübingen; Asst Prof., Univ. of Tübingen 1953–58; pvt. tutor
1962–65; project on Pre-Roman inscriptions in the Iberian Peninsula 1958–62;
Full Prof. of Comparative Linguistics, Univ. of Cologne 1965–94, Dean, Faculty of
Letters 1971–72, Prof. Emer. 1994–; Dr hc (Salamanca) 1993, (Santiago de
Compostela) 2003; Premio Príncipe de Viana de la Cultura 2010. *Publications:* Die
Venetischen Personennamen 1961, Monumenta Linguarum Hispanicarum, Vol. I
1975, Vol. II 1980, Vol. III 1990, Vol. IV 1997, Einführung in die Sprache Homers
1987, Oskisch-Umbrisches Wörterbuch 2000. *Address:* Pfalzgrafenstrasse 11,
50259 Pulheim, Germany (home). *Telephone:* (2234) 82274 (home). *E-mail:*
juergen@untermannonline.de (home).

UNTERMEYER, Charles Graves (Chase); American international business
consultant and fmr diplomatist; *Managing Director, Qatus Advisors;* b. 7 March
1946, Long Branch, NJ; s. of Dewitt Edward Untermeyer and Marguerite Alonza
Graves Untermeyer; m. Diana Cumming Kendrick; one d.; ed Harvard Coll.;
served in USN during Vietnam War as destroyer officer in Pacific and as aide to
Commdr of US naval forces in the Philippines; early career as political reporter for
Houston Chronicle newspaper; mem. Tex. House of Reps for Dist in Houston
1977–81; Exec. Asst to Vice-Pres. George Bush 1981–83; Asst Sec. of the Navy for
Manpower and Reserve Affairs 1984–88; Dir Presidential Personnel, The White
House 1988–91; Dir Voice of America 1991–93; fmr mem. and Chair. Bd of Visitors,
US Naval Acad.; fmr mem. Bd Nat. Public Radio; fmr mem. Houston Port Comm.;
mem. Tex. State Bd of Educ. 1999–2003, Chair. 1999–2001; Prof. of Public Policy
and Vice-Pres. for Govt Affairs, Univ. of Texas Health Science Center, Houston
2002–04; Amb. to Qatar 2004–07; US Vice-Chair. Strategic Real Estate Advisors
Ltd 2007–09; ind. business consultant 2007–; Man. Dir Qatus Advisors 2012–;
Chair. St Luke's Episcopal Health Charities 2013–; Pres. Houston READ Comm.
1998–2001; mem. Defense Health Bd 2008–09, Texas Ethics Comm. 2010–,
Council on Foreign Relations; fmr mem. Bd Conservation Trust of Puerto Rico.
Address: 10000 Memorial Drive, Suite 920, Houston, TX 77024, USA (office).
Telephone: (713) 683-9888 (office); (713) 542-8904 (mobile). *Fax:* (713) 683-9896
(office). *E-mail:* chase@untermeyer.com. *Website:* www.untermeyer.com.

UNWIN, Eric Geoffrey (Geoff), BSc; British business executive; *Chairman,
Halma plc;* b. 9 Aug. 1942, Radcliffe-on-Trent, Notts., England; s. of Maurice
Doughty Unwin and Olive Milburn (née Watson); m. Margaret Bronia Element
1967; one s. one d.; ed Heaton Grammar School, Newcastle upon Tyne, King's Coll.,
Durham Univ.; with Cadbury Bros 1963–68; joined John Hoskyns & Co. 1968,
Man. Dir Hoskyns Systems Devt 1978, Dir Hoskyns Group 1982, Man. Dir 1984,
Exec. Chair. 1988; COO Cap Gemini 1993–2000, CEO and Vice-Chair. Exec. Bd
1996–2000, Chair. Cap Programmator AB 1993–2000, CEO, mem. Bd Cap Gemini
Ernst & Young (fmrly Cap Gemini) 2000–02; Chair. Cloud Networks Ltd 2005–06,
Omnibus Systems Ltd 2005–10, 3G Lab 2002–05, Taptu 2007–12, Alliance Medical
2008–10, OpenCloud 2011–, Xchanging 2011–, RD Card Holdings 2011–; Deputy
Chair. (now Chair.) Halma plc 2002–, Liberata PLC 2003–11; Dir (non-exec.)
Volmac Software Group NV 1990, Gemini Consulting Holding SA 1994–2000, NED
United News & Media (now United Business Media) PLC 1995–2007 (Chair.
2002–07); Dir (non-voting) CGEY 2002–12; Pres. Computing Services Asscn
1987–88; mem. Information Tech. Advisory Bd 1988–91, Palamon Capital Pnrs
and its Advisory Bd 2002–; Freeman of the City of London 1987. *Leisure interests:*
golf, riding, skiing, gardening. *Address:* 17 Park Village West, London, NW1 4AE,
England (home). *Telephone:* (1494) 789179 (High Wycombe) (office). *E-mail:* geoff
.unwin@gunwin.co.uk (office).

UNWIN, Sir (James) Brian, Kt, KCB, MA (Oxon), MA (Yale); British banker and
fmr government official; *Chairman, Assettrust Housing Association Limited;* b. 21
Sept. 1935, Chesterfield, Derbyshire, England; s. of Reginald Unwin and Winifred
Walthall; m. Diana Scott 1964; three s.; ed Chesterfield School, New Coll. Oxford
and Yale Univ., USA; Asst Prin., Commonwealth Relations Office 1960; Pvt. Sec. to
British High Commr, Salisbury, Rhodesia 1961–64; First Sec., British High
Comm. Accra 1964–65; with FCO 1965–68, transferred to HM Treasury 1968; Pvt.
Sec. to Chief Sec. Treasury 1970–72, Asst Sec. 1972, Under-Sec. 1976, Deputy Sec.
1983–85; seconded to Cabinet Office 1981–83; Dir EIB 1983–85, Pres. 1993–2000,
Hon. Pres. 2000–; Deputy Sec., Cabinet Office 1985–87; Chair. Bd HM Customs &
Excise 1987–93; Gov. EBRD 1993–2000; Chair. Supervisory Bd European
Investment Fund 1994–2000; mem. Advisory Bd IMPACT 1990–93; mem. Bd of
Dirs ENO 1993–94, 2000–08, Fondation Pierre Werner, Centre d'Etudes
Prospectives (CEPROS) 1996–2000, Dexia Bank 2000–10, European Centre for
Nature Conservation 2000– (Pres. 2001–13, Hon. Pres. 2013–), 'Britain in Europe'

Council 2002–05; Chair. Assettrust Housing 2003–12, Assettrust Housing Asscn
Ltd 2012–; Dir Fed. Trust for Educ. and Research 2003–; Pres. New College
(Oxford) Soc. 2004–08; Hon. Pres. Euronem (Athens) 2000–08; Hon. Fellow, New
Coll., Oxford 1996, Inst. of Indirect Taxation 2002; Commdr du Wissam Alloui
(Morocco) 1999, Grand Officier, Ordre de la Couronne (Belgium) 2000, Grand
Croix Ordre Grand Ducal de la Couronne de Chêne (Luxembourg) 2001; Gold
Medal, Fondation du Mérite Européen. *Publication:* Corporate Social Responsi-
bility and Socially Responsible Investing (co-author) 2002, Britain's Future and
the Euro (co-author) 2004, Terrible Exile: The Last Days of Napoleon on St Helena
2010, Financial Regulation: Britain's Next European Challenge (co-author) 2010,
A Tale in Two Cities: Fanny Burney and Adele, Comtesse de Boigne 2014. *Leisure
interests:* opera, bird-watching, Wellingtoniana and Napoleonic history, cricket.
Address: c/o Reform Club, 104 Pall Mall, London, SW1Y 5EW, England.

UOSUKAINEN, Riitta Maria, MA, PhD, LicPhil; Finnish fmr politician and
teacher; b. 18 June 1942, Jääski; d. of Reino Vainikka and Aune Vainikka; m. Toivo
Uosukainen 1968; one s.; ed Univ. of Helsinki; teacher, Imatrankoski Upper
Second School 1969–; Prov. Instructor in Finnish Language, Kymi Prov. 1976–83;
mem. Imatra Town Council 1977–92, Vice-Chair. 1980–86; mem. Eduskunta
(Parl.) 1983–2003, Minister of Educ. 1991–94, Speaker of Parl. 1994–2003;
presidential cand. 2000; Commdr Order of White Rose 1992, Commdr Italian
Repub. 1993, Order of First Class of White Star (Estonia) 1995, Grand Cross First
Class, Order of Merit (Germany) 1996, Grand Cross, Order of the Crown (Belgium)
1996, Commdr Grand Cross, Royal Order of Polar Star (Sweden) 1996, Grand
Cross, Order of Honour (Greece) 1996, Commdr Cross, Order of Falcon (Iceland)
1997, Valtioneuvos (Councillor of State) 2004; Dr hc (Finlandia Univ., USA) 1997,
(Lappeenranta Inst. of Tech.) 1999; Speaker of the Year Award 1985. *Publications
include:* (as co-author): Clues for Mother Tongue Teaching 1979, Link Exercises in
Mother Tongue 1981, Mother Tongue Fountain 1984, Liehuva Liekinvarsi
(speeches and letters) 1996, Nuijanisku pöytään (writings about politics, power
and passion) 2004. *Leisure interest:* literature. *Address:* Olkinuorankatu 11, 55910
Imatra, Finland (home). *Telephone:* (5) 4337766 (home). *Fax:* (5) 4337700 (home).
E-mail: riitta@uosukainen.com (home).

UPADHAYA, Kedar Nath; Nepalese judge (retd); *Chairman, National Human
Rights Commission;* b. Feb. 1939, Jaleshwor, Mahottari Dist; ed Tribhuwan Univ.,
Inst. of World Affairs, London, UK; served in numerous positions in the state
judiciary including Judge in the various regional courts and zonal courts, Sr Govt
Advocate in Office of Attorney Gen., Under-Sec. in Ministry of Law and Justice;
Justice, Supreme Court of Nepal 2000–04, Chief Justice 2003–04 (retd); Chair.
Nat. Human Rights Comm. 2007–; fmr Chair. Administrative Court; fmr mem.
Royal Comm. on Judicial Reform; fmr mem. Bd of Dirs Rastriya Banijya Bank.
Address: Office of the Chairman, National Human Rights Commission, GPO Box
9182, Kathmandu, Nepal. *Telephone:* (1) 5010015. *Fax:* (1) 5547973. *E-mail:* nhrc@
nhrcnepal.org. *Website:* www.nhrcnepal.org.

UPRETY, Neel Kantha, MS; Nepalese government official; *Chief Election
Commissioner;* Project Man. and Sr Electoral Adviser to Election Comm. of Nepal
1999–2004; Sr Election Coordinator, Afghanistan 2004–05; Chief Election Commr
2009–. *Address:* Election Commission, Kantipath, Kathmandu, Nepal (office).
Telephone: (1) 4228663 (office). *Fax:* (1) 4229227 (office). *E-mail:* info@election.gov
.np (office). *Website:* www.election.gov.np (office).

URBAIN, Robert; Belgian politician; b. 24 Nov. 1930, Hornu; three s.; ed Ecole
Normale, Mons; math. teacher 1950–58; Deputy for Mons 1971–95; Sec. of State
for Planning and Housing 1973, for Econ. Affairs (French region) 1977–78;
Minister of Posts and Telephones 1979, of Foreign Trade 1980–81, of Health and
Educ. (French sector) 1981–85, of Social Affairs and Health Feb.–May 1988, of
Foreign Trade 1988–92, of Foreign Trade and European Affairs 1992–95; mem.
Senate 1995–99; Minister of State 1998–; Prés. du Conseil d'Admin. de la Faculté
Polytechnique de Mons; Grand-Croix Ordre de Léopold II, Croix civique (1st
Class), Officier, Ordre de la Pléiade, Grand-Croix Ordre de la Couronne, Minister
of State 1998. *Leisure interests:* cycling, swimming. *Address:* Rue Guerin 7, 7300
Boussu (office); Rue de Bavay 42, 7301 Hornu, Belgium (home). *Telephone:* (65) 76-
59-40 (office); (65) 63-07-38 (home). *Fax:* (65) 76-59-49 (office); (65) 79-36-14
(home). *E-mail:* secretariat_r_urbain@yahoo.fr (office).

URBAN, Jerzy; Polish journalist; *President, URMA Company Ltd;* b. 3 Aug. 1933,
Łódź; s. of Jan Urban and Maria Urban; m. 1st 1957; one d.; m. 3rd Małgorzata
Daniszewska 1986; ed Warsaw Univ.; staff writer, weekly Po Prostu, Warsaw
1955–57; head of home section, weekly Polityka, Warsaw 1960–63, 1968–81;
columnist of satirical weekly Szpilki, articles written under pen-names including
Jan Rem and Jerzy Kibic; Govt Press Spokesman 1981–89; Minister without
portfolio, Head Cttee for Radio and Television April–Sept. 1989; Dir and Ed.-in-
Chief, Nat. Workers' Agency Nov. 1989–90; Dir and Ed.-in-Chief Unia-Press Feb.–
May 1990; Pres. Kier Co. Ltd 1990–; Pres. URMA Co. Ltd, Warsaw 1991–; Ed.-in-
Chief, political weekly Nie Oct. 1990–; participant Round Table debates, mem.
group for mass media Feb.–April 1990; mem. Journalists' Asscn of Polish People's
Repub. 1982–, Polish Writers' Union; Złoty KrzyżZastTugi, KrzyżKomandorski
Polonia Restituta; Victor Prize (TV) 1987. *Screenplays include:* Sekret, Otello.
Publications: Kolekcja Jerzego Kibica 1972, Impertynencje: Felietony z lat
1969–72 1974, Wszystkie nasze ciemne sprawy 1974, Grzechy chodzą po ludziach
1975, Gorączka 1981, Romanse 1981, Robak w jabłku 1982, Na odlew 1983,
Samosądy 1 1984, Felietony dla cudzych zon 1984, Samosądy 2 1984, Z pieprzem i
solą 1986, Jakim prawem 1988, Rozkosze podgłądania 1988, Cały Urban 1989,
Alfabet Urbana 1990, Jajakobyły 1991, Prima aprilis towarzysze 1992, Klątwa
Urbana 1995, Druga Klątwa Urbana 2000. *Leisure interest:* social life. *Address:*
URMA Co. Ltd, ul. Słoneczna 25, 00 789 Warsaw, Poland (office). *Telephone:* (22)
8485290 (office). *Fax:* (22) 8497258 (office). *E-mail:* nie@redakcja.nie.com.pl
(office). *Website:* www.nie.com.pl (office).

URBAN, Knut W., PhD; German physicist and fmr research institute director;
Director, Institute of Microstructure Research, Forschungszentrum Jülich; b. 25
June 1941, Stuttgart; m.; three d.; ed Technical Univ. of Stuttgart; Research
Assoc., Max Planck Inst. of Metals Research, Stuttgart 1972–86; Prof., Dept of
Materials Science and Eng, Univ. of Erlangen-Nuremberg 1986–; Chair of
Experimental Physics, RWTH Univ. Aachen 1987–, also Dir, Inst. of Micro-
structure Research, Forschungszentrum Jülich 1987–; Visiting Prof., Inst. for

Advanced Materials Processing, Tohoku Univ., Sendai, Japan 1996–97; Dir Ernst Ruska Centre for Microscopy and Spectroscopy with Electrons 2004–11, Dir Emer. 2011–; Scientific Co-ordinator, EC Network of Excellence 'Complex Metallic Alloys' 2005–09; Scientific Co-ordinator of a nat. programme of the German Science Foundation (DFG) on 'Physical Properties of Complex Metallic Alloys' 2006–12; Lecturer, Xi'an Jiaotong Univ., mem. Bd Int. Dielectrics Centre, Advisor on the construction of High-Resolution Electron Microscopy Lab. 2009–11; Chair. Scientific Council, Inst. for Solid-State and Materials Research (IFW), Dresden 2004–08; Vice-Chair. Asscn of German Scientific and Tech. Socs (DVT) 2006–08; Prin. Auditor, DFG 2007–; Senator of Leibniz Soc. 2007–; mem. Bd of Trustees, Research Asscn Berlin 2004–08; mem. Scientific Council, Physics Dept, Univ. of Vienna 2007–, Siemens Award for Industrial Entrepreneurship 2009–; mem. German Physical Soc. (Pres. 2004–06, Vice-Pres. 2006–08), Acad. of Arts and Sciences of North-Rhine Westphalia 2009; Hon. mem. Materials Research Soc. of India 2000, US Materials Research Soc. 2006; Hon. (Guest) Prof., Wuhan Univ., China 2001, Tsinghua Univ., Beijing 2009; Hon. Prof., Jiaotong Univ., Xi'an, China 2009; scholarship, Max Planck Soc. 1969–72, Acta Metallurgica Award 1986, Carl Wagner Award, Univ. of Göttingen 1986, Research Award, Japanese Soc. for the Promotion of Science 1996, Heyn Medal, Deutsche Gesellschaft für Materialkunde 1999, Medal for Scientific Publishing, German Physical Soc. 2000, Philip Morris Distinguished Lecturer in Materials Science and Eng, Rensselaer Polytechnic Inst., New York 2004, Von-Hippel Award, US Materials Research Soc. 2006, Karl Heinz Beckurts Award for Scientific and Tech. Innovation (jtly) 2006, Honda Award for Ecotechnology (jtly) 2008, 25th Global Vision Lecture, Tsinghua Univ., Beijing 2008, Wolf Prize in Physics (jtly) 2011. *Publications:* Co-ordinator and author of the series of the Frankfurter Allgemeine Zeitung on modern topics in physics 1999 and of the book Physik im Wandel (Changing Physics) 2000; about 400 original papers in peer-reviewed journals; ed. of proceedings and special vols of journals. *Address:* Forschungszentrum Jülich GmbH, Wilhelm-Johnen-Strasse, 52428 Jülich, Germany (office). *Telephone:* (2461) 614274 (office); (2461) 613153 (office). *Fax:* (2461) 616444 (office). *E-mail:* k.urban@fz-juelich.de (office). *Website:* www.fz-juelich.de (office).

URBAN, Wolfgang; German business executive; b. 1945, Oberbaumgarten, Schleisen; pnr Isabelle Werth; one s.; commercial exec. Kaufhof AG, Cologne 1973–83, Dir Accounts Dept and Finance Dept 1983–85, Gen. Man. 1985–87, mem. Finance, Accounts and Tax Cttees 1987–95; Speaker Exec. Bd Kaufhof Holding AG, Cologne 1995–96; mem. Exec. Bd Schickedanz Holding-Stiftung & Co. KG, Fürth 1998–99; mem. Exec. Bd Karstadt Quelle AG, Essen 1999–, Chair. Karstadt Warenhaus AG Jan.–Oct. 2000, Chair. Karstadt Quelle AG 2000–04 (resgnd).

URBANOVÁ, Eva; Czech singer (soprano); b. 20 April 1961, Slaný; ed Acad. of Musical Arts; opera debut at Plzeň Josef Kajetan Tyl Theatre 1987; soloist, Plzeň Opera 1988–90; Chief of Opera Singer section, Conservatory Plzeň 1989; soloist, Nat. Theatre Opera, Prague 1990–, Metropolitan Opera, New York 1996–; charity concert tours with Karel Gott, Czech Repub. 1998; concert tours and opera performances in Canada, France, Italy, USA (Dvořák operas), Hong Kong (Janáček operas) and Germany (Verdi opera); charity concerts after floods in Czech Repub. 2002–; Classic Prize for propagation of Czech music in the world 1999. *Recordings:* Duets (with Karel Gott) 1998, Czech Opera Airs 1998, Czech Christmas Carols 2000. *Leisure interests:* cooking, piano. *Address:* Národní divadlo, National Theatre, Ostrovní 1, 110 30 Prague 1, Czech Republic (office). *Telephone:* (2) 24910312 (office). *Fax:* (2) 24911524 (office). *E-mail:* herzeru .jaroslava@quick.cz. *Website:* www.evaurbanova.com/en.

URE, Sir John Burns, Kt, KCMG, LVO, MA, FRGS; British diplomatist, author and company director; b. 5 July 1931, London; s. of the late Tam Ure; m. Caroline Allan 1972; one s. one d.; ed Uppingham School, Magdalene Coll., Cambridge, Harvard Business School, USA; active service as 2nd Lt, Cameronians (Scottish Rifles), Malaya 1950–51; appointments in British Embassies in Moscow, Léopoldville, Santiago and Lisbon and at Foreign Office, London 1956–79, Asst Under-Sec. of State (Americas), FCO 1981–83; Amb. to Cuba 1979–81, to Brazil 1984–87, to Sweden 1987–91; UK Commr-Gen. for Expo '92, Seville; Dir, Thomas Cook Group 1991–99, CSE Aviation Ltd 1992–94; consultant, Sotheby's Scandinavia Advisory Bd, Robert Fleming (merchant bankers) 1995–98, Ecosse Films 1996–99; Chair., Anglo-Swedish Soc. 1992–96, Brazilian Chamber of Commerce 1994–96, Panel of judges for Travel Book of the Year Award 1991–99; Trustee, Leeds Castle Foundation 1995–2006; Pres., Weald of Kent Protection Soc. 2005–11; Commdr, Mil. Order of Christ (Portugal) 1973. *Publications:* Cucumber Sandwiches in the Andes 1973, Prince Henry the Navigator 1977, The Trail of Tamerlane 1980, The Quest for Captain Morgan 1983, Trespassers on the Amazon 1986, Royal Geographical Soc. History of World Exploration (contrib. section on Cen. and S. America) 1991, A Bird on the Wing 1992, Diplomatic Bag 1994, The Cossacks 1999, In Search of Nomads 2003, Pilgrimage: The Great Adventure of the Middle Ages 2006, The Seventy Great Journeys in History (contrib.) 2006, Shooting Leave 2009, The Great Explorers (contrib.) 2010, Sabres on the Steppes 2012; regular book reviews in Times Literary Supplement, Country Life; travel articles for Daily Telegraph and Sunday Telegraph; numerous entries in The New Dictionary of National Biography. *Leisure interests:* travel, writing. *Address:* Netters Hall, Hawkhurst, Kent, TN18 5AS, England (home). *Telephone:* (1580) 752191 (home).

URECHEAN, Serafim, DEcon; Moldovan politician; *Chairman, Alianţa Moldova Noastră (Our Moldova Alliance);* b. 2 Feb. 1950, Larga, Briceni dist; m. Tatiana Marcenco; two c.; ed Chişinău Polytechnic Inst., Inst. of Political Studies, Leningrad (now St Petersburg), Russia; Engineer, Briceni Construction Enterprise 1976–78, later Head of Dept for Industrial Devt; Second Sec., Briceni CP Cttee 1978–83; Chair. Anenii Noi CP Exec. Cttee 1985–87; Deputy Chair., First Deputy Chair., then Chair. Fed. of Ind. Trade Unions 1987–94; mem. Parl. 1990–94, 2005–, mem. Standing Bureau of Parl., Cttee for Social Policy, Healthcare and Family, Democratic Moldova electoral bloc; Acting Prime Minister of Moldova 5–17 Feb. 1999; Mayor of Chişinău 1994–2005; Chair. Alianţa Moldova Noastră (Our Moldova Alliance) 2003–; fmr Chair. Fed. of Local and Regional Authorities; Corresp. mem. Inst. for Int. Affairs, Int. Informatization Acad., Int. Acad. of Man.; Hon. mem. Int. Acad. of Eng; Order of the Repub. (USSR), Medal for Public Order Protection (Moldova), St Dumitru Order (Second Class), Sergii Radonejsky Order (Second Class), St Stanislav Order. *Address:* Alianţa Moldova Noastră, 2012 Chişinău, str. M. Eminescu 68A, Moldova (office). *Telephone:* (22)

26-00-07 (office). *Fax:* (22) 21-13-94 (office). *E-mail:* alianta@amn.md (office). *Website:* www.amn.md (office).

UREN, Thomas, AO; Australian politician (retd); b. 28 May 1921, Balmain, NSW; s. of Thomas Uren and Agnes Uren; m. 1st Patricia Uren 1947 (died 1981); one s. one d.; m. 2nd Christine Anne Logan 1992; one d.; served with Royal Australian Artillery 1939, 2nd Australian Imperial Force 1941, in Japanese prisoner-of-war camp 1942–45 (Burma–Siam Railway); Labor MP for Reid 1958–90; mem. Opposition cabinet 1969–72; mem. Fed. Parl. Labor Party Exec. 1969–72, Deputy Leader 1975–77; First Minister of Urban and Regional Devt 1972–75; Fed. Labor Spokesman, Urban and Regional Devt 1976–77, on Urban and Regional Affairs, Decentralization, Local Govt, Housing and Construction 1977–80, on Urban and Regional Affairs 1980–83; Minister for the Territories and Local Govt and Minister assisting Prime Minister for Community Devt and Regional Affairs 1983–84, Minister for Local Govt and Admin Services 1984–87; del. to Australasian Area Conf. of Commonwealth Parl. Asscn, Darwin 1968, to Australian Parl. Mission to Europe 1968, to Commonwealth Parl. Asscn Conf., Canberra 1970; Australian Rep. at Lord Mountbatten's Funeral, Westminster Abbey 1979; del. to IPU 1965, Leader Australian del. to IPU 1987–90, Chair. Asian-Pacific Group 1989–90; brought back Australian hostages from Baghdad 1990; Chair. Australia-Vietnam Soc., Parramatta Park Trust; Pres. H. V. Evatt Foundation; Patron Defenders of Sydney Harbour Foreshores; Life Mem. Australian Labor Party 1993, Australian Nat. Trust 2004; Hon. DUniv (Charles Sturt Univ.) 1997, Hon. DSciArch (Sydney) 2002. *Publication:* Tom Uren Straight Left 1994. *Leisure interests:* gardening, theatre, opera, music, art, environmental issues, photography. *Address:* 8 Gilchrist Place, Balmain, NSW 2041, Australia.

URIBE ESCOBAR, José Darío, PhD; Colombian economist and central banker; *Governor, Banco de la República;* b. 22 Dec. 1958, Medellín, Antioquia; ed Universidad EAFIT, Medellín, Universidad de los Andes, Bogotá, Univ. of Illinois at Urbana-Champaign, USA; fmr Prof., Univ. Pontificia Universidad Javeriana and Universidad de Los Andes; Head of Global Programming Unit, Nat. Planning Dept, Bogotá 1986–87; Econ. Adviser, Federación Nacional de Cafeteros (Nat. Fed. of Coffee Growers) 1992–93; Deputy Dir of Econ. Studies, Banco de la República (central bank) 1993–98, Technical Man. 1998–2004, Gov. 2005–. *Address:* Office of the Governor, Banco de la República, Carrera 7a, No 14-78, 5°, Apdo Aéreo 3551, Bogotá DC, Colombia (office). *Telephone:* (1) 343-1111 (office). *Fax:* (1) 286-1686 (office). *E-mail:* wbanco@banrep.gov.co (office). *Website:* www.banrep.gov.co (office).

URIBE VÉLEZ, Alvaro, LLB; Colombian politician and fmr head of state; b. 4 July 1952, Medellín; m. Lina Moreno; two s.; ed Univ. of Antioquia, Harvard Univ., USA, Univ. of Oxford, UK; Sec.-Gen. Ministry of Labour 1977–78; Dir of Civil Aviation 1980–82; Mayor of Medellín 1982, Councillor 1984–86, Senator of Antioquia Prov. 1986–90, 1990–94; Gov. of Antioquia 1995–97; Presidential cand. for Movimiento Primero Colombia 2002, Pres. of Colombia 2002–10; Light Unto The Nations Award 2007, US Presidential Medal of Freedom 2009. *Address:* c/o Office of the President, Palacio de Nariño, Carrera 8A, No. 7–26, Bogotá, Colombia.

URIN, Vladimir; Russian theatre director; *General Director, Bolshoi Theatre;* ed Russian Acad. of Theatre; began career as Dir Theatre for Youth, Kirov (now Vyatka) 1973–81; moved to Moscow 1981; apptd Head of Youth and Puppet Theatres Dept, All-Union Theatre Soc. (now Theatre Union of Russia) 1981; took active part in org. and promotion of World Congress ASSITEJ, Moscow, mem. Organizing Cttee and Dir Children's Theatre Festival; twice elected Sec. of the Bd, Theatre Union of Russia 1987–96, Deputy Pres. Theatre Union 1987–96, First Deputy Pres. Theatre Union 1991–96; produced Int. Festival of Theatre schools 'Podium' 1989, 1991, 1993, 1995, Russian-American Theatre Festival 'Baikal – Michigan' (first ever Russian-American festival held in Russia), Annual Drama Workshop 'Shelykovo – The Author's Stage'; conceived idea of The Golden Mask Nat. Theatre Award est. 1994; Gen. Dir Stanislavsky and Nemirovich-Danchenko Moscow Academic Music Theatre 1995–2013, Gen. Dir Int. Contemporary Dance Festivals, held by Stanislavsky and Nemirovich-Danchenko Music Theatre and Cultural Centres and Embassies of Europe, Canada and USA 1997–; Gen. Dir Bolshoi Theatre 2013–. *Address:* The State Academic Bolshoi Theatre of Russia, 125009, Moscow, Teatralnaya Square 1, Russia (office). *Telephone:* (495) 692-32-00 (office). *E-mail:* pr@bolshoi.ru (office). *Website:* www.bolshoi.ru (office).

URINSON, Yakov Moiseyevich, DEcon; Russian economist, academic, business executive and fmr government official; b. 12 Sept. 1944; m.; one s. one d.; ed Moscow Plekhanov Inst. of Nat. Econs; Researcher, Centre Inst. of Econ. and Math., USSR Acad. of Sciences 1968–72; Deputy Head of Div., Deputy Dir Computation Centre, USSR State Planning Cttee 1972–91; Dir Centre of Econ. Conjuncture and Prognosis, Russian Govt 1992–94; First Deputy Minister of Econs 1993–97; Deputy Chair. Russian Govt, Minister of Econs 1997–98; mem. Defence Council 1997–98; Chief Expert on econ. and financial problems United Power Grids of Russia Jan.–Sept. 1999, Deputy Chair. Sept. 1999; Deputy Chair. Man. Bd Unified Energy System (UES) of Russia, also Head Corp. Center, UES of Russia, Chair. Bd of Dirs Russian Communal Systems (RCS) 2005–; Chair. Bd of Pvt. Pensions Fund of Energy Industry 2001–; Prof., Faculty of Business Informatics, Dept of Business Analytics, Higher School of Economics, Moscow. *Publications:* over 50 papers and articles in specialized periodicals. *Leisure interest:* football. *Address:* Department of Business Analytics, Faculty of Business Informatics, Higher School of Economics, 101000 Moscow, 33 Kirpichnaya Str.; RAO UES of Russia, 119526 Moscow, 101-3 Vernadskogo Prosp., Russia (office). *Telephone:* (495) 771-32-38 (Higher School of Economics); (495) 710-40-01 (office). *Fax:* (495) 927-30-07 (office). *E-mail:* uym@rao.elektra.ru (office). *Website:* www .rao-ees.ru (office); bi.hse.ru.

URNOV, Mark Yuryevich, PhD, DSc; Russian academic and politician; *Academic Supervisor, Faculty of Politics, Higher School of Economics;* b. 12 May 1947, Moscow; m.; one d.; ed Moscow State Inst. of Int. Relations; on staff Inst. of Conjuncture USSR Ministry of Foreign Trade 1970–76; researcher Inst. of World Econs and Int. Relations USSR Acad. of Sciences 1976–79; sr researcher Inst. of Culture, Ministry of Culture RSFSR 1979–82; sr researcher Leningrad Inst. of Information and Automatization 1982–86; sr researcher Inst. of Int. Workers' Movt USSR Acad. of Sciences 1986–89; leading researcher USSR Acad. of Nat.

Econ. 1989–90; Dir of programmes Foundation of Social Econ. and Political Studies Gorbachev Foundation 1990–94; Head of Div., Deputy Head, Dir Analytical Centre, Russian Presidency 1994–96; mem. Political Council, Russian Presidency 1994–98; Dir Research Centre Ekspertiza 1996–98, 2000–04; First Deputy Head, Centre for Econ. Reforms 1998–2000; Dean, Faculty of Politics, Nat. Research Univ., Higher School of Econs, Moscow 2004–10, Academic Supervisor, Faculty of Politics 2010–. *Leisure interest:* cycling. *Address:* Higher School of Economics, National Research University, 3 Kochnovsky proezd, Moscow 125319, Russia (office). *Telephone:* (499) 152-12-81 (office). *Fax:* (499) 152-03-01 (office). *E-mail:* murnov@hse.ru (office). *Website:* www.hse.ru/eng (office).

UROSA SAVINO, HE Cardinal Jorge Liberato, PhD; Venezuelan ecclesiastic and academic; *Archbishop of Caracas;* b. 28 Aug. 1942, Caracas; s. of Luis Manuel Urosa Joud and Ligia Savino del Castillo de Urosa; ed Colegio De La Salle Tienda Honda, Interdiocesan Seminary of Caracas, St Augustine's Seminary, Toronto, Canada, Pontifical Gregorian Univ., Rome, Pius Latin American Pontifical Coll.; ordained priest, Archdiocese of Caracas, Santiago de Venezuela 1967; served as Prof. and Rector, Seminary San José, Caracas; later served as Rector of Interdiocesan Seminary, Caracas; later Vicar Gen. Archdiocese of Caracas; apptd Titular Bishop of Vegesela in Byzacena 1982; Auxiliary Bishop of Caracas 1982–90; Archbishop of Valencia en Venezuela 1990–2005; Archbishop of Caracas 2005–; cr. Cardinal (Cardinal-Priest of Santa Maria ai Monti) 2006; fmr Pres. Org. of Latin American Seminaries; f. a parochial vicariate in a chabolas neighbourhood of Caracas; second Vice-Pres. Venezuelan Episcopal Conf. 2006–11, Pres. 'Ad Honorem' 2011–. *Address:* Arzobispado, Apartado 954, Monjas a Gradillas, Plaza Bolivar, Caracas 1010, Venezuela (office). *Telephone:* (212) 5421611 (office); (212) 5421715 (office). *Fax:* (212) 5420297 (office). *E-mail:* infoiglesiaccs@gmail.com (office). *Website:* www.arquidiocesisdecaracas.com (office).

URPILAINEN, Jutta, MEd; Finnish politician; *Minister of Finance;* b. 4 Aug. 1975, Lapua; d. of Kari Urpilainen and Pirjo Urpilainen; m. Juha Mustonen 2006; ed Univ. of Jyväskylä, Helsinki Univ.; began career as schoolteacher in Helsinki 2001–02, Kokkola 2002–03; mem. Kokkola City Council 2001–; Asst to MP Säde Tahvanainen 2001–03; mem. Suomen Eduskunta (Parl.) for Vaasa constituency 2003–; Minister of Finance 2011–; mem. Social Democratic Party (SDP), Chair. 2008–; Vice-Chair. UN Youth and Students' Asscn of Finland 1996–97; Vice-Chair. Finnish UN Asscn 2003–05, Chair. 2008–09; Chair. Regional Council of Central Ostrobothnia Ass. 2007–08; Vice-Chair. Central Ostrobothnia Hosp. Dist Bd of Dirs 2005–10; mem. Finnish Nat. Comm. for UNESCO 1999–2011. *Leisure interests:* music, sports. *Address:* Ministry of Finance, Snellmaninkatu 1A, Helsinki, Finland (office). *Telephone:* (9) 16001 (office). *Fax:* (9) 16033123 (office). *E-mail:* valtiovarainministerio@vm.fi (office). *Website:* www.vm.fi (office); www .juttaurpilainen.fi.

URQUHART, Sir Brian, KCMG, MBE; British international official (retd); b. 28 Feb. 1919, Bridport, Dorset; s. of Murray Urquhart and Bertha Urquhart (née Rendall); m. 1st Alfreda Huntington 1944 (dissolved 1963); two s. one d.; m. 2nd Sidney Howard 1963; one s. one d.; ed Westminster School and Christ Church, Oxford; Army service 1939–45; Personal Asst to Gladwyn Jebb, Exec. Sec. of Preparatory Comm. of UN London 1945–46; Personal Asst to Trygve Lie, First Sec.-Gen. of UN 1946–49; served in various capacities relating to peace-keeping operations in Office of UN Under-Sec.-Gen for Special Political Affairs 1954–71; Exec. Sec. 1st and 2nd UN Int. Confs on Peaceful Uses of Atomic Energy 1955, 1958; Deputy Exec. Sec. Preparatory Comm. of IAEA 1957; Asst to Sec.-Gen.'s Special Rep. in the Congo July–Oct. 1960; UN Rep. in Katanga, Congo, 1961–62; Asst Sec.-Gen. UN 1972–74; Under-Sec.-Gen. for Special Political Affairs UN 1974–86; Scholar-in-residence, Ford Foundation 1986–95; Hon. LLD (Yale Univ.) 1981, (Tufts Univ.) 1985; Dr hc (Essex Univ.) 1981, (Westminster) 1993; Hon. DCL (Oxford Univ.) 1986, (Cambridge) 2005; hon. degrees (City Univ. of New York, Grinnell Coll., State Univ. of New York at Binghamton) 1986, (Univ. of Colorado, Keele) 1987, (Hobart Coll., William Smith Coll.) 1988, (Warwick Univ.) 1989, (Williams Coll.) 1992, (Lafayette Coll.) 1993, (Ohio State Univ.) 2000, (Hamilton Coll.) 2000, (Brown Univ.) 2003, (Amherst Coll.) 2008; Roosevelt Freedom Medal 1984, Int. Peace Acad. Prize 1985. *Publications:* Hammarskjöld 1973, A Life in Peace and War 1987, Decolonization and World Peace 1989, A World in Need of Leadership: Tomorrow's United Nations (with Erskine Childers) 1990, Ralph Bunche: An American Life 1993, Renewing the United Nations System (with Erskine Childers) 1994, A World in Need of Leadership: A Fresh Appraisal (with Erskine Childers) 1996. *Address:* 50 West 29th Street, New York, NY 10001 (home); Jerusalem Road, Tyringham, MA 01264, USA (home). *Telephone:* (212) 679-6358 (New York) (home); (413) 243-0542 (Tyringham) (home). *E-mail:* brianurquhart1@yahoo.com (home).

URQUIZO MAGGIA, José Antonio; Peruvian academic and politician; *Minister of Defence;* b. 13 Feb. 1967, Ayacucho; ed Universidad Nacional Federico Villarreal, Lima, Universidad Nacional de Educación a Distancia de España; Lecturer, Universidad Nacional Federico Villarreal 1991–; Dir Monsignor Victor Alvarez Huapaya Higher Technological Inst. 1995–98; Regional Vice Pres. of Ayacucho 2003–06; mem. Congreso (Parl.) for Ayacucho 2006–; Minister of Production 2011–12, of Defence 2012–. *Address:* Ministry of Defence, Edif. Quiñones, Avda de la Peruanidad s/n, Jesús María, Lima 1, Peru (office). *Telephone:* (1) 6255959 (office). *E-mail:* webmaster@mindef.gob.pe (office). *Website:* www.mindef.gob.pe (office).

URRUTIA FERNÁNDEZ, Paulina; Chilean actress and politician; b. 1969, Santiago; ed Pontificia Univ. Católica; Pres. Sindicato de Actores de Chile (Sidarte) 2001–04; mem. Nat. Council of Culture 2004–08; Minister of the Nat. Comm. for Culture and the Arts 2006–10. *Films:* Johnny cien pesos 1993 (APES Prize for Best Actress), El Encierro 1996, No tan lejos de Andrómeda 1999, Piel canela 2001, Carga vital 2003, Cachimba 2004, Tendida, mirando las estrellas 2004, Fuga 2006. *Television includes:* Sor Teresa de los Andes 1989, El Milagro de vivir 1990, Volver a empezar 1991, Trampas y caretas 1992, Jaque mate 1993, Champaña 1994, El Amor esta de moda 1995, Marrón Glacé, el regreso 1996, Eclipse de luna 1997, Amandote 1998, Fuera de control 1999, Sabor a ti 2000, Puertas adentro 2003, Cuentos de mujeres 2003, Tentación 2004, Casados 2005, Gatas & tuercas 2005–06. *Address:* c/o National Commission for Culture and the Arts, San Camilo 262, Santiago, Chile.

URRUTIA MONTOYA, Miguel, PhD; Colombian economist and banker; *Professor of Economics, Universidad de los Andes;* b. 20 April 1939, Bogotá; s. of Francisco Urrutia and Genoveva Montoya; m. Elsa Pombo 1963; three c.; ed Univ. de los Andes, Bogotá, Univs of Harvard and Calif., Berkeley, USA; Gen. Sec. Ministry of Finance 1967–68, Adviser to Monetary Bd 1969; Deputy Tech. Man. Banco de la República 1970–74; Dir Nat. Planning Dept 1974–76; Minister of Mines and Energy 1977; Vice-Rector Univ. of the UN, Tokyo 1981–85; Man. Econ. and Social Devt Dept, IDB 1985–89; Exec. Dir Fedesarrollo 1978–81, 1989–91; mem. Bd Dirs Banco de la República (Cen. Bank of Colombia) 1991–93, Gov. Banco de la República 1993–2005; has taught various courses at Univ. de los Andes at various times, currently Prof. of Econs; fmr weekly columnist for El Tiempo newspaper; decoration from the Ministry of Culture; Dr hc (Universidad de los Andes). *Publications:* Empleo y Desempleo en Colombia 1968, The Development of the Colombia Labor Movement 1969, Income Distribution in Colombia 1975, Winners and Losers in Colombia's Economic Growth of the 1970s 1985, Development Planning in Mixed Economies (with Setsuko Yukawa) 1988, Financial Liberalization and the Internal Structure of Capital Markets in Asia and Latin America 1988, Economic Development Policies in Resource Rich Countries (with Setsuko Yukawa) 1988, The Political Economy of Fiscal Policy (with Shinichi Ichimura and Setsuko Yukawa) 1989. *Leisure interests:* golf, reading. *Address:* Facultad de Economia, Universidad de los Andes, Carrera 1 N° 18A-70, Bloque W, Bogotá, Colombia (office). *Telephone:* (1) 349-4949 (ext. 2056) (office). *Fax:* (1) 332-4492 (office). *E-mail:* murrutia@uniandes.edu.co (office). *Website:* economia .uniandes.edu.co (office).

URUSEMAL, Joseph J., BA; Micronesian politician and fmr head of state; b. 19 March 1952, Woleai, Yap State; m. Olania Latileilam; three s. one d.; ed Xavier High School, Chuuk State, Rockhurst Coll., Kansas City, MO, USA; worked for Jackson Co., Mo., Dept of Correction, USA 1976–82; returned to Micronesia 1982; worked with State Dept of Educ., Yap as teacher and counsellor to Outer Islands High School and mem. Educ. Steering Cttee; elected Yap State's Rep. to Fifth Congress of Federated States of Micronesia (FSM) and mem. Standing Cttees on Health Educ. and Social Affairs, Resources and Devt and External Affairs; mem. Congress, Federated States of Micronesia 1987–2003, Floor Leader 1991–2003, mem. Standing Cttees on Health Educ. and Social Affairs, Resources and Devt, Transportation and Communication, and Judiciary and Governmental Operations 1991–2003; Pres. of Micronesia 2003–07; fmr Sec. Gen. FSM Nat. Group to Asia-Pacific Parliamentarians' Union. *Address:* c/o Office of the President, POB PS-53, Palikir, Pohnpei, FM 96941, Federated States of Micronesia (office).

URWICK, Sir Alan (Bedford), KCVO, CMG, MA; British fmr parliamentary official and diplomatist (retd); b. 2 May 1930, London; s. of the late Lyndall Fownes Urwick and Joan Saunders; m. Marta Yolanda (née Montagne) 1960; three s.; ed Dragon School, Oxford, Rugby School, New Coll. Oxford; joined Foreign Service 1952; served in embassies in Belgium 1954–56, USSR 1958–59, Iraq 1960–61, Jordan 1965–67, USA 1967–70, Egypt 1971–73; seconded to Cabinet Office as Asst Sec., Cen. Policy Review Staff 1973–75; Head of Near East and North Africa Dept, Foreign and Commonwealth Office 1975–76; Minister, British Embassy in Madrid 1977–79; Amb. to Jordan 1979–84, to Egypt 1984–87; High Commr in Canada 1987–89; Serjeant at Arms, House of Commons 1989–95; Chair. Anglo-Jordanian Soc. 1997–2001. *Leisure interests:* reading, gardening. *Address:* The Moat House, Slaugham Place, nr Haywards Heath, W Sussex, RH17 6AL, England (home). *Fax:* (1444) 400458 (home).

UŠACKA, Anita, DrIur; Latvian professor of law and judge; *Judge, International Criminal Court;* b. 26 April 1952, Rīga; m. Peter Wilkitzki; ed Moscow State Univ., Univ. of Latvia; Asst, Dept for Fundamental Legal Studies, Univ. of Latvia 1975–76, Prin. Lecturer 1980–82, Docent 1982–99, Head of Dept 1989–96, Assoc. Prof. 1999–, Prof. Dept for State Law 2002–; Assoc. Prof. Rīga Grad. School of Law 1999–2001; Exec. Dir Latvian Br., UNICEF 1994–96; Judge, Constitutional Court of Repub. of Latvia 1996–2004; Judge, Int. Criminal Court, The Hague 2003–, Pres. Appeals Div. 2011–12; mem. Editorial Bd Law and the Rights journal; mem. Bd Lawyers Training Centre of Latvia, Sub-comm. on Constitutional Legal Procedure, Council of Europe, Int. Women Lawyers Asscn 1997–; Hon. LLD (Lewis and Clark Law School, Portland, Oregon). *Publications:* numerous articles in professional journals, reports to int. scientific confs. *Address:* International Criminal Court, PO Box 19519, 2500 CM The Hague, The Netherlands (office). *Telephone:* (70) 5158212 (office). *Fax:* (70) 5158789 (office). *E-mail:* pio@icc-cpi.int (office). *Website:* www.icc-cpi.int (office).

UŠACKAS, Vygaudas, LLB; Lithuanian diplomatist and politician; *Ambassador of the European Union to the Russian Federation;* b. 16 Dec. 1964, Skuodas; m. Loreta Ušackienė-Bilkstytė; one s. one d.; ed Vilnius Univ., Univ. of Oslo, Norway, Århus Univ., Denmark; Counsellor, Lithuanian Mission to EU, Brussels 1992–94, Rep. for Relations with NATO 1994–96, mem. Del. to WEU 1995–96; Political Dir, Ministry of Foreign Affairs 1996–99, Deputy Minister of Foreign Affairs 1999–2000, also served as Chief Negotiator for Lithuania's accession to EU; Amb. to USA (also accred to Mexico) 2001–06, to UK 2006–08; Minister of Foreign Affairs 2008–10; EU Special Rep. and Head of EU Mission for Afghanistan 2010–13, Amb. of the EU to the Russia Fed. 2013–. *Address:* European External Action Service, 1046 Brussels, Belgium (office). *Telephone:* (2) 584-11-11 (office). *E-mail:* vygaudas.usackas@eeas.europa.eu (office). *Website:* www.eeas.europa.eu (office).

UŠAKOVS, Nils, BEcons, MSc; Russian editor, television producer and politician; *Chairman, Rīga City Council;* b. 8 June 1976, Rīga; ed Univ. of Latvia, Univ. of Southern Denmark; producer, Baltic Div., Russian NTV 1998–99; News Service Corresp., Latvian Public TV 1999–2000; News and Politics Section Ed., Respublika newspaper 2000–01; News and Policy Ed. Telegraf newspaper 2001–02; Ed. 'Theme of the Week' weekly programme, TV5 channel 2001–04, also 'The Russian Question', later Ed. and Head of TV5; First Baltic Channel News Service Ed. 2004–05, Evening News Ed. for Lithuania and Estonia 2005–06; mem. Saskaņas Centrs/Tsentr soglasiya (Harmony Centre) party, Chair. 2005–; Deputy for Rīga Constituency, 9th Saeima (Parl.) 2006–, mem. Foreign Affairs Cttee, European Affairs Cttee, Substitute mem. Latvian del. to NATO Parl. Ass.; mem. Bd of Dirs Baltic Forum 2002–; Chair. Rīga City Council (Mayor) 2009–; collapsed during Rīga half-marathon and was taken to hospital, later transported to Berlin in an induced coma for further treatment May 2011, made a full recovery; Cicerona

Award, Latvian Journalists' Union and Univ. of Latvia 2004. *Leisure interests:* sports, especially running and cycling. *Address:* Rīga City Council, Rātslaukums, Room 220, Rīga 1539 (office); Harmony Centre (Saskaņas Centrs/Tsentr soglasiya), Jūra Alunana 8/3, Rīga 1010, Latvia. *Telephone:* 6702-6100 (office). *Fax:* 6702-6389 (office). *E-mail:* nils.usakovs@riga.lv (office); sekretariats@riga.lv (office); office@saskanascentrs.lv. *Website:* www.riga.lv (office); www .saskanascentrs.lv; www.ushakov.lv.

USENOV, Daniyar Toktogulovich; Kyrgyzstani mining engineer, politician and banker; b. 1960, Frunze (now Bishkek); m.; two s.; ed Frunze Polytechnic Inst.; served in USSR Armed Forces 1982–84; Engineer, Mechanization and Automation Section, Kara-Balta Ore-Processing Plant 1984–90; First Deputy Chair. Kara-Balta City Exec. Council 1990–92; Deputy in Kara-Balta City Council and Chui Duban Council 1990–95; Asst Head of Chui Duban State Admin 1992–93; Gen. Dir Eridan Corpn 1994–95; Deputy in Legis. Ass. 1995–2000; banned from Parl. elections 2000; Leader of Poor and Unprotected People's Party; First Deputy Prime Minister, responsible for Econ. Issues 2005–06 (resgnd), reappointed 2007–09, Prime Minister 2009–10 (resgnd following overthrow of Pres. Bakiyev April 2010); Mayor of Bishkek 2007; Exec. Dir Kyrgyz-British Investment Co. 1992–93; Chair. Kyrgyz bank Inexitnbank 2007. *Address:* c/o Office of the Prime Minister, 720003 Bishkek, Dom Pravitelstva, Kyrgyzstan.

USHAKOV, Yuri Viktorovich, PhD; Russian diplomatist and government official; *Assistant to President of the Russian Federation;* b. 13 March 1947, Moscow; m.; one d.; ed Moscow State Inst. of Int. Relations, Diplomatic Acad.; joined diplomatic service 1970; trans., expert, attaché USSR Embassy in Denmark 1970–75, Second then First Sec. 1978–82, Minister-Counsellor 1986–92; adviser Gen. Secr. USSR Ministry of Foreign Affairs (MFA) 1982–86; Head Dept of All-Europe Co-operation, MFA 1992–96; Perm. Rep. of Russia to Org. for Security and Co-operation in Europe (OSCE) 1996–98; Deputy Minister of Foreign Affairs 1998; Amb. to USA 1999–2008; Deputy Chief of the Govt Office and Foreign Policy Asst to the Prime Minister 2008–12; Asst to Pres. of the Russian Fed. 2012–; Hon. Meritorious Diplomat of Russia; several medals and decorations. *Leisure interests:* tennis, alpine skiing. *Address:* Office of the Government of the Russian Federation, Krasnopresnenskaya nab. 2, 103274 Moscow, Russia (office). *Telephone:* (495) 605-51-45 (office). *Fax:* (495) 605-54-21 (office). *E-mail:* ushakov_yv@aprf.gov.ru (office). *Website:* www.government.ru (office).

USHER, Thomas J., PhD; American business executive; *Non-Executive Chairman, Marathon Petroleum Corporation;* b. 11 Sept. 1942, Reading, Pa; s. of Paul T. Usher and Mary Leonard; m. Sandra L. Mort 1965; three c.; ed Univ. of Pittsburgh; with Industrial Eng Dept, US Steel Corpn 1965–75, Asst to Gen. Superintendent, Superintendent of Transportation and Gen. Services, South Works 1975, Asst Div. Superintendent, Gary Works 1978–79, Dir Corp. Strategic Planning, Pittsburgh 1979–81, Asst to Pres. 1981, Man. Dir for Facility Planning, Eng, Research and Industrial Eng 1981–82, Vice-Pres. Eng and Research US Steel Mining Co. 1982–83, Pres. 1983–84, Vice-Pres. Eng, Steel 1984, Sr Vice-Pres. Operations, Steel 1984–86, Exec. Vice-Pres. Heavy Products 1986–90, Pres. Steel Div. 1990, mem. Corp. Policy Cttee, USX Corpn 1990, Bd of Dirs 1991, Pres. US Steel Corpn 1991, Pres. and COO USX Corpn 1994, Chair. and CEO 1995–2001, Chair. US Steel Corpn 2001–06 (retd), CEO 2001–04, Pres. 2001–03; mem. Bd of Dirs Marathon Oil Corpn 1991–2011, Chair. (non-exec.) 1995–2011, mem. Bd of Dirs and Chair. (non-exec.) Marathon Petroleum Corpn 2011–; mem. Bd of Dirs H.J. Heinz Co., PPG Industries, PNC Financial Services Group, Boy Scouts of America, Extra Mile Educ. Foundation; mem. The Business Council; mem. Bd of Trustees, Univ. of Pittsburgh; Iron and Steel Soc. Steelmaker of the Year 2002. *Leisure interests:* golf, tennis, racquetball, scuba diving, swimming. *Address:* Marathon Petroleum Corporation, Corporate Headquarters, 539 South Main Street, Findlay, OH 45840, USA (office). *Telephone:* (419) 422-2121 (office). *Fax:* (419) 425-7040 (office). *E-mail:* info@marathonpetroleum.com (office). *Website:* www .marathonpetroleum.com (office).

USHERWOOD, Nicholas John, BA; British curator and art critic; *Features Editor, Galleries Magazine;* b. 4 June 1943, Bucks.; s. of Stephen Usherwood and Hazel Usherwood (née Weston); m. 1st Henrietta Mahaffy (dissolved 1990); one s. one d.; m. 2nd Jilly Szaybo 1991; ed Westminster School, Courtauld Inst. of Art, Univ. of London; lecturer in art history, Portsmouth Coll. of Art, Wimbledon Coll. of Art 1965–68; researcher, Pelican History of Art 1966–68; Admin., Press Officer RA 1969–74, Exhbns Sec. 1974–77; Deputy Keeper in charge of exhbns and public relations, British Museum 1977–78; freelance exhbn curator and organizer, art-critic, lecturer, writer 1978–; Features Ed., Galleries Magazine 1998–; Curator, Topolski C Sections 2001–02; Pres. UK Chapter, Int. Asscn of Art Critics (AICA) 2000–03; mem., Critics' Circle 2004–; Trustee, Evelyn Williams Trust 1994–; Chevalier, Order of Léopold II of Belgium. *Publications include:* exhbn catalogues for Algernon Newton 1980, Tristram Hillier 1983, Alfred Munnings 1986, Richard Eurich 1991, 1994, Nolan's Nolans 1997, Julian Trevelyan 1998, Joash Woodrow 2003, Norman Adams 2007, Evelyn Williams 2008. *Leisure interests:* new maps, reading poetry, talking to artists, contemporary music. *Address:* 82 High Street, Hampton Wick, Surrey, KT1 4DQ, England (office). *Telephone:* (20) 8973-0921 (office). *E-mail:* njusherwood@hotmail.co.uk (office).

USMAN, Nenadi E., BSc; Nigerian politician; b. 12 Nov. 1966, Jere, Kaduna State; ed Ahmadu Bello Univ., Univ. of Jos; served as Commr of Health, for Environment and Natural Resources, for Women's Affairs, Youth and Social Devt; fmr Exec. Adviser for Youth, for Information, Home Affairs and Culture; Minister of State for Finance 2003–06, Minister of Finance 2006–07; Chair. Fed. Accounts Allocation Cttee 2003–06; mem. Govt Econ. Man. Team 2003–06; mem. House of Reps for Kachia/Kagarko Fed. Constituency; mem. Kaduna State Caucus, Defunct Nat. Republican Convention; f. Educ. and Empowerment for Women in Kaduna State; Peoples Democratic Party Senator for Kaduna South 2011–. *Address:* Peoples Democratic Party, Plot 1970, Michael Okpara Street, Wadata Plaza, Abuja 23409, Nigeria (office). *Telephone:* (9) 7822781 (office). *E-mail:* info@ nigeriansenate.org (office). *Website:* www.peoplesdemocraticparty.net (office).

USMAN, Shamsudeen, BSc, MSc, PhD; Nigerian economist and government official; m. Nenadi Usman; ed Ahmadu Bello Univ., London School of Econs, UK; Planning Officer, Kano State Ministry of Econ. Planning 1974–76; Lecturer, Ahmadu Bello Univ., Zaria 1976–81; Controller, Nigerian Industrial Devt Bank

1981–85; Gen. Man. Corp. Banking, NAL Merchant Bank 1985–98; Dir-Gen. Tech. Cttee on Privatization and Commercialization (TCPC) 1989–91; Exec. Dir, United Bank of Africa Plc and later Union Bank of Nigeria 1992–94; Deputy Gov. Cen. Bank of Nigeria 1999–2007; Minister of Finance 2007–08; Minister, Chair. of the Nat. Planning Comm. 2009–13; Pres. Nigerian Econ. Soc. 1986–87, Fellow 1995; Officer of the Order of the Fed. Repub. *Address:* c/o National Planning Commission, Old Central Bank Building, 4th Floor, Garki, PMB 234, Abuja, Nigeria (office).

USMANOV, Alisher Burkhanovich; Russian steel industry executive; *Co-Founder and Majority Shareholder, Metalloinvest Management Company LLC;* b. 9 Sept. 1953, Chust, Namangan Prov., Uzbek SSR, USSR; m. Irina Viner; two c.; ed Moscow State Inst. of Int. Relations; Owner Gallagher Holdings, Ural steel industrial complex, Ormeto-YUMZ mechanical eng corpn; Co-owner Oskol steel plant, Lebedinsky iron-ore mine, Mikhalovsky GOK iron ore mining and processing plant; has major stakes in Nosta steel co., Moldavia Metal, Olenegorsk iron-ore co., Australian Medusa mining, Tulachermet stock co.; Co-founder (with Vasiliy Anisimov) and majority shareholder Metalloinvest Man. Co. LLC; Co-owner Gazmetall steel and mining empire; Owner Kommersant newspaper, Muz TV; acquired large share-holding in Arsenal Football Club, UK through Red and White Holdings 2007; mem. Bd of Dirs Gazprominvestholding; mem. Bd Russian Union of Industrialists and Entrepreneurs, Chair. Cttee on Regulatory Activity Improvement and Removal of Admin. Barriers; Co-founder Arts and Sports Charity Foundation; Guarantor of Charity project 'One Thousand Russian Cities'; Pres. Int. Fencing Fed. (FIE) 2008–; mem. Councils of the 2014 Sochi XXII Olympic Winter Games and XI Paralympic Winter Games, Bd of Trustees of the Russian Olympian Sportsmen Support Fund; fmr Pres. Russian and European fencing asscns; Medal of Honour of Russia 2004, Order of Friendship (Kazakhstan) 2011, Order for Service to the Fatherland, IV Class 2013; ranked by Forbes magazine amongst The World's Most Powerful People (70th) 2011, (67th) 2012, (63rd) 2013, Medal 'For contribution to international cooperation', Foreign Ministry of Russia 2013. *Address:* Metalloinvest Management Co. LLC, 3 Lesnaya Street, Moscow 125047, Russia (office). *Telephone:* (495) 981-55-55 (office). *Fax:* (495) 981-99-92 (office). *Website:* www.metinvest.com (office).

USPASKICH, Viktor; Lithuanian (b. Russian) business executive and politician; b. 24 July 1959, Urdoma, Russia; one s. one d. from 1st m.; m. 2nd Jolanta Blazyte; two d.; mil. service 1977; welder, Northern Lights Co., worked on projects across USSR including Lithuania 1979–90; attained Lithuanian citizenship 1991; f. Efektas Co. 1990, became component of Vikonda Co. 1993, Pres. Vikonda Co. 1996; non-party mem. New Union 2000–03; Founder and Chair. Labour Party 2003–06 (resgnd), 2007–; mem. Seimas (Parl.) 2000–05, 2008–09, mem. Cttee on Econs 2004–05, Labour Party Parl. Group 2004–05; Minister of the Economy 2004–05 (resgnd following allegations of violating law on combining public and private interests); mem. European Parl. 2009–; Chair. Asscn of Lithuanian Employers 1997–2003; Order of Daniil Moskovsky 1999. *Address:* Ankštoji g. 3, Vilnius, Lithuania (office). *Telephone:* (5) 210-7152 (office). *Fax:* (5) 210-7153 (office). *E-mail:* info@uspaskich.eu (office). *Website:* www.europarl.europa.eu/meps/en/ 96698/VIKTOR_USPASKICH.html (office); www.uspaskich.eu.

USPENSKIJ, Boris, PhD, DLitt; Russian/Italian linguist, philologist, critic, semiotician and historian and academic; *Professor, Higher School of Economics, National Research University;* b. 1 March 1937, Moscow; s. of Andrej Uspenskij and Gustava Mekler; m. 1st Galina Korshunova 1963 (died 1978); two s.; m. 2nd Tatiana Vladyshevskaya 1985; ed Moscow Univ.; dissertation on structural typology of languages published 1965 and partly translated into English 1968; dissertation on history of Russian church pronunciation partly published 1968; studied under Hjelmslev at Univ. of Copenhagen 1961; expedition to Siberia to study Ket language 1962; research at USSR Acad. of Sciences Inst. of African Languages 1963–65; research mem. Lab. of Language Typology and Computational Linguistics, Moscow Univ. 1965–77, Prof., Moscow Univ. 1977–92; Fellow, Inst. for Advanced Studies, Russian State Univ. for the Humanities 1992–93, Prof. 2006–; Visiting Prof. Vienna Univ. 1988, Harvard Univ. 1990–91, Graz Univ. 1992, Cornell Univ. 1993, Univ. of Italian Switzerland 1997–2009; Fellow, Wissenschaftskolleg (Berlin) 1992–93; Prof., Oriental Univ. of Naples 1993–2009, Prof. Emer. 2009–; currently Prof., Higher School of Econs, Nat. Research Univ., also Dir Lab. of Linguistics and Semiotics; major publs 1962–; Foreign Corresp. mem. Austrian Acad. of Science 1987; Foreign mem. Norwegian Acad. of Science and Letters 1999, Polish Acad. of Arts and Sciences 2011; mem. Academia Europaea 1990, Russian PEN Centre 1994, Soc. Royale des Lettres de Lund 1996, Società Filologica Romana 2001; Hon. mem. Slavonic and E European Medieval Studies Group 1987, Asscn Int. de sémiologie de l'image 1990, Hon. Cttee, American Friends of the Warburg Inst. 1993; Dr hc (Russian State Univ. for the Humanities) 2001, (Konstantin Preslavsky Univ., Bulgaria) 2003, (Belgrade Univ.) 2010; Annual Distinguished Scholarship Award, Early Slavic Studies Asscn 2007. *Publications include:* Principles of Structural Typology 1962, Structural Typology of Languages 1965, The Archaic System of Church Slavonic Pronunciation 1968, The History of Church-Slavonic Proper Names in Russia 1969, A Poetics of Composition 1970, The First Russian Grammar in the Native Language 1975, The Semiotics of the Russian Icon 1976, Tipologia della cultura (with Yu. M. Lotman) 1975, Philological Investigations in the Field of Slavic Antiquities 1982, The Semiotics of Russian Culture (with Yu. M. Lotman) 1984, The Semiotics of Russian Cultural History (with Yu. M. Lotman and L. Ja. Ginsburg) 1985, The History of the Russian Literary Language of XVIII to early XIX centuries 1985, The History of the Russian Literary Language XI–XVII centuries 1987, Storia e Semiotica 1988, Sémiotique de la culture russe (with Yu. M. Lotman) 1990, Semiotik der Geschichte 1991, Storia della lingua letteraria russa: Dall'antica Rus' a Puškin 1993, Semiotics of Art 1995, Linguistica, semiotica, storia della cultura 1996, Selected Works (three vols) 1996–97, Tsar and Patriarch 1998, Boris and Gleb: The Perception of History in the Old Rus' 2000, "In regem unxit…" 2001, La pala d'altare di Jan Van Eyck a Gand 2001, Studies in the Russian History 2002, Part and Whole in Russian Grammar 2004, Essays in History and Philology 2004, Il segno della croce e lo spazio sacro 2005, Cross and Circle: From the History of Christian Symbolism 2006, Ego Loquens: Language and Communicational Space 2007, Works on Trediakovskij 2008, The Ghent Altarpiece of Jan van Eyck: The Composition (Divine and Human Perspective) 2009, Prospettiva divina e prospettiva umana: La pala di van Eyck a Gand 2010, "Tsar and God" and Other Essays in Russian Cultural Semiotics (with V. M. Živov) 2012; numerous articles. *Leisure interest:* travelling. *Address:* Higher School of Economics, National Research University, Xitrovskij per. 2/8, korp. 5, Moscow 109028, Russia (office); Via Principe Eugenio 15, Rome 00185, Italy (home); Serebrianicheskij per. 9 Apartment 21, Moscow 109028, Russia (home). *Telephone:* (06) 4468157 (Rome) (home); (495) 917-40-67 (Moscow) (home). *E-mail:* borisusp@gmail.com. *Website:* www.hse.ru/en (office).

USPENSKY, Vladislav Aleksandrovich; Russian composer and academic; *Professor of Composition, Leningrad State Conservatory;* b. 7 Sept. 1937, Omsk; s. of Alexander Grigoryevich Kolodkin and Vera Pavlovna Uspenskaya; m. Irina Yevgenyevna Taimanova 1963; ed Leningrad State Conservatory; postgraduate studies under Dmitri Shostakovich; teacher of music theory, Leningrad State Conservatory 1965–67, Dean of Musicology 1967–72, Prof. of Composition 1988–; Guest Composer-in-Residence, Seoul Univ., Korea 1995, Lima Univ., Peru 1997, Boston Univ. USA; Chair. Music Council of Cultural Cttee, St Petersburg Govt 1996–; Vice-Pres. Union of Composers of St Petersburg 1972–; Gen. Dir Int. Musical Children's Festival 1995–; Order of Merit of Homeland 1998, Order of Catherine the Great 2002; People's Artist of Russia, D. Shostakovich Prize 1997. *Compositions:* Phantasmagoria, Vepres, Requiem, Liturgie, Temperaments, Toccata, Sonata-Phantasia, States, Sonata for the Violin and Piano, Anna Karenina (musical), Trombone Concertino 1963, Double Piano Concerto 1965, Music for Strings and Percussion 1967, The War Against Salamanders (opera) 1967, To the Memory of a Hero (ballet) 1969, Intervention (opera) 1970, A Road to the Day (ballet) 1974, Symphonic Frescoes 1977, For You to the Sea (ballet) 1978, Nocturne for low voice and orchestra 1980, Expectation 1982, With You and Without You (oratorio) 1984, Cranes Flying (ballet) 1984, Towards the Light (symphony) 1985, Dedication (symphony) 1988, The Mushroom's Alarm (ballet) 1990, All Night Vigil 1990, The Departure of the Soul (funeral service) 1992, A Dithyramb of Love for two pianos and orchestra 1995, Trombone Concerto 1995, Concerto for low voice and orchestra 1997, Casanova in Russia (musical) 1998, Temptation of Jeanna (musical) 1999; music for plays, including Revizor, over 100 songs, music for films, theatre and TV productions. *Publication:* D. Shostakovich in My Life. *Leisure interest:* love. *Address:* Composers' Union, B. Morskaia 45, St Petersburg (office); Admiralteysky canal 5 Apt. 26, St Petersburg, Russia (home). *Telephone:* (812) 117-35-48 (office); (812) 117-74-35 (home). *Fax:* (812) 117-35-48 (office).

USTINOV, Vladimir Vassilyevich; Russian lawyer and government official; *Presidential Representative to the Southern Federal Okrug (District);* b. 25 Feb. 1953, Nikolayevsk-on-Amur, Khabarovsk Krai; m.; one s. one d.; ed Kharkiv Inst. of Law, Ukrainian SSR; prosecutor, Krasnodar Krai 1978–92, Sochi 1992–97; concurrently First Deputy Prosecutor Krasnodar Krai and Deputy Prosecutor-Gen. Russian Fed. 1997–2000; also Head, Dept Office of Prosecutor-Gen., N Caucasus 1998–99; Acting Prosecutor-Gen. Russian Fed. 1999–2000, Prosecutor-Gen. 2000–06; Minister of Justice 2006–08; Presidential Rep. to Southern Fed. Okrug (Dist) 2008–; Merited Jurist of Russian Fed. *Publication:* Indictment of Terror 2003. *Address:* Office of the Presidential Representative, 344006 Rostov-on-Don, ul. B. Sadovaya 73, Russia (office). *Telephone:* (863) 249-99-43 (office). *Fax:* (863) 249-99-47 (office). *E-mail:* pppufo@ufo.gov.ru (office). *Website:* www.ufo.gov .ru (office).

USUBOV, Col-Gen. Ramil Idris oğlu; Azerbaijani politician and government official; *Minister of Internal Affairs;* b. 22 Dec. 1948, Xocalı, Nagornyi Karabakh; m.; three c.; ed N. Rzayev Police School, Acad. of the Ministry of Internal Affairs of the USSR; joined Ministry of Internal Affairs 1970; Head, Criminal Investigation Div., Şuşa dist Police Dept 1975–80; Deputy Head, Internal Affairs Dept, Nagornyi Karabakh Autonomous Oblast 1980–84; Head, Ali-Bayramlı Region Police Dept 1984–87; Minister of Internal Affairs, Autonomous Repub. of Naxçıvan 1987–89, 1993–94; Head, Criminal Investigation Dept, then Passport, Visa and Registration Dept, then Human Resources Div., Ministry of Internal Affairs 1989–93; Minister of Internal Affairs 1994–; promoted to Maj.-Gen. 1994, Lt-Gen. 1995, Col-Gen. 2002; Azerbaijani Banner Order. *Address:* Ministry of Internal Affairs, 1005 Baku, 7 Azerbaijan Avenue, Azerbaijan (office). *Telephone:* (12) 590-91-03 (office). *Fax:* (12) 492-45-90 (office). *E-mail:* info@mia.gov.az (office). *Website:* mia.gov.az (office).

USUPASHVILI, Davit, LLB, MA; Georgian lawyer and politician; *Chairman, Sakartvelos Parlamenti (Parliament);* b. 5 March 1968, Magharo; m. Tinatin Khidasheli; ed Tbilisi State Univ., Duke Univ., USA; legal adviser with State Council of Georgia, involved in drafting Constitution of Georgia 1993–95; Founding mem. Georgian Young Lawyers' Asscn 1994, Chair. 1994–97, active in its organized protests during Rose Revolution that brought Mikheil Saakashvili to become Pres. of Georgia 2003; later distanced himself from alliance and withdrew into opposition; Chair. Republican Party of Georgia 2005–13; allied with Bidzina Ivanishvili to become a leader of Ivanishvili's Georgian Dream coalition, of which the Republican Party was part 2011; Chair. Sakartvelos Parlamenti (Parl.) 2012–. *Address:* Sakartvelos Parlamenti, Tbilisi, Kutaisi, Abashidze 26, Georgia (office). *Telephone:* (32) 228-91-57 (office). *Fax:* (32) 299-93-86 (office). *E-mail:* dusupashvili@parliament.ge (office). *Website:* www.parliament.ge (office).

UTEEM, Cassam, LèsL; Mauritian politician and fmr head of state; b. 22 March 1941, Plaine Verte; m. 1967; two s. one d.; ed Univs of Mauritius and Paris VII; fmr supervisor, Cable & Wireless Ltd; Personnel Man. Currimjee Jeewanjee & Co., Ltd; Sec.-Gen. Mauritius Nat. Youth Council 1971–72; Treas. Mauritius Council of Social Service 1971–73; Rep. of World Ass. of Youth to UNESCO 1974–76; municipal councillor, Port Louis 1969, 1977–79, 1986–88; Lord Mayor of City of Port Louis 1986; mem. Legis. Ass. 1976–92, Chair. Public Accounts Cttee 1988–90; Minister of Employment, Social Security and Nat. Solidarity 1982–83; Opposition Whip 1983–87; Deputy Leader, Mouvement Militant Mauricien 1988; Deputy Prime Minister and Minister of Industry and Industrial Tech. 1990–92; Pres. Repub. of Mauritius 1992–2002; mem. Bd Int. Inst. for Democracy and Electoral Assistance; mem. Club of Madrid, Africa Forum, Global Leadership Foundation; mem. Advisory Bd Global Peace and Unity Foundation; Hon. mem. Acad. Nationale Malgache 1995; Grand Commander of the Order of the Star and Key of the Indian Ocean; Hon. DCL (Univ. of Mauritius) 1994; Dr hc (Univ. of Marseille III) 1994, (Academie Nationale Malgache, Madagascar), (Univ. of Buckingham, UK), (Univ. of Jamia Millia Islamia, New Delhi, India). *Address:* c/o Global Leadership Foundation, 25 Knightsbridge, London, SW1X 7LY, England.

UTOIKAMANU, Siosiua Tu'italukua Tupou, MCA, MScS; Tongan politician and economist; b. 1 July 1956; ed Wellington Univ. of Victoria, New Zealand, Univ. of Birmingham, UK; trainee economist, Ministry of Finance 1981, Economist 1981, Deputy Sec. 1984, Acting Dir of Planning, Cen. Planning Dept 1987, Minister of Finance 2001–08 (resgnd); Acting Finance Man. Tonga Commodities Bd 1989; Deputy Gov. Nat. Reserve Bank of Tonga 1989–91, Gov. 1991–2001. *Address:* c/o Ministry of Finance, Treasury Building, POB 87, Vuna Road, Kolofo'ou, Nuku'alofa, Tonga (office).

UTSUDA, Shoei, BS; Japanese business executive; *Chairman, Mitsui & Company Ltd;* b. 1943; ed Univ. of Tokyo; joined Mitsui & Co. Ltd (general trading co.) 1967, mem. Bd Dirs (Dir, Gen. Man. Machinery, Information Industries Admin. Div.) 1997–, Rep. Dir, Exec. Man. Dir, Gen. Man. Corp. Planning Div. 2000–02, Rep. Dir, Sr Exec. Man. Officer, Chief Strategic Officer (responsible for Admin. Div.), COO Business Process Re-Eng Project April–Oct. 2002, Rep. Dir, Pres. and Oct. CEO 2002–09, Chair. 2009–; Chair. Keizai Doyukai Cttee on Asia-Japan Relations 2004–. *Address:* Mitsui & Co. Ltd, 2-1 Ohtemachi 1-chome, Chiyoda-ku, Tokyo 100-0004, Japan (office). *Telephone:* (3) 3285-1111 (office). *Fax:* (3) 3285-9819 (office). *E-mail:* info@mitsui.com (office). *Website:* www.mitsui.com (office).

UTSUMI, Akio; Japanese financial services industry executive; *Senior Adviser, Mitsubishi Tokyo Financial Group;* b. 7 Sept. 1942; Man. Dir Mitsubishi Trust Bank 1993–95, Sr Man.-Dir 1995–98, Deputy Pres. 1998–99, Pres. 1999–2004; Dir, Chair. and Co-CEO Mitsubishi Tokyo Financial Group Inc. (cr. following merger between Bank of Tokyo-Mitsubishi and Mitsubishi Trust & Banking Corpn 2001) 2001–04, now Sr Adviser; Corp. Auditor, Mitsubishi Materials Corpn. *Address:* Mitsubishi Tokyo Financial Group Inc., 10-1 Yurakucho 1-chome, Chiyoda-ku, Tokyo 100-0006, Japan (office). *Telephone:* (3) 3240-8111 (office). *Fax:* (3) 3240-8203 (office). *Website:* www.mtfg.co.jp (office).

UTSUMI, Yoshio, LLB, MA; Japanese civil servant and international organization official (retd); b. 14 Aug. 1942; m. Masako Utsumi 1970; one s. one d.; ed Univ. of Tokyo, Univ. of Chicago, USA; joined Ministry of Posts and Telecommunications 1966, Head of Investment Postal Life Insurance Bureau 1986–88, Head Gen. Affairs Div., Broadcasting Bureau 1988, with Communications Policy Bureau, Deputy Minister, Asst Vice-Minister, Dir-Gen. MPT 1988–98; First Sec. Perm. Mission of Japan, Int. Telecommunications Union (ITU), Geneva 1978–81, Chair. ITU Plenipotentiary Conf. 1994, Sec.-Gen. ITU 1998–2006; Prof. of Public Admin., MPT Postal Coll. 1972. *Address:* c/o Office of the Secretary-General, International Telecommunications Union, Place des Nations, 1211 Geneva 20, Switzerland.

UTTLEY-MOORE, William James, CBE, BSc, FREng, FRAeS; British electrical engineer; b. 19 July 1944, Crayford, Kent, England; s. of the late William Uttley-Moore and of Louisa Clara Dixon; m. Jennifer Benger 1966; one s.; ed Erith Tech. School, Univ. of London; student apprentice and devt engineer, Cintel Ltd 1960–68; project leader, Molins Machine Co. Ltd 1968–69; Chief Engineer, Computing Devices Co. Ltd 1969–75, Tech. Dir 1979–85, Chair. and Man. Dir 1985; Founder Dir Southern FM 1989–92, Conqueror Broadcasting Ltd 1996–; Chair. E Sussex Econ. Partnership 1998–; mem. Bd, Defence Scientific Advisory Council 1994–; Fellow Royal Acad. of Eng 1993–. *Publications:* numerous tech. papers on reconnaissance, avionics and digital battlefield. *Leisure interests:* practical eng, farming, running, classical music. *E-mail:* bill.uttleymoore@ btinternet.com (office).

UTZERATH, Hansjörg; German theatre director and author; b. 20 March 1926, Tübingen; m. Renate Ziegfeld 1957; one s. two d.; ed Kepler Oberschule, Tübingen; began as actor, later in theatre man. in Düsseldorf and then in production; Chief Stage Man., Düsseldorfer Kammerspiele 1955–59; Dir 1959–66; Intendant, Freie Volksbühne, Berlin 1967–73; Dir Städtische Bühnen, Nuremberg 1977–92; freelance dir 1993–; guest producer at Staatstheater Stuttgart, Municher Kammerspiele, Schauspielhaus Düsseldorf and Schiller-Theater, Berlin 1959–; Visiting Prof. Universitat Mozarteum, Salzburg. *Productions include:* Tango 1971, Der Vater 1972, Viele heissen Kain (TV), Waiting for Godot 1980, Mother Courage 1981, King Lear 1982, Der Hauptmann von Köpenick 1986, Liebeskonzil 1988, Richard III 1990, Lila 1990, Check-Point-Charly 1996, Besuch der Alten Dame 1998, Nathan der Weise 2002, Der Kaufmann von Venedig 2003, Purpurstaub 2005. *Publications:* Die Grossväter (novel) 2005, Fluchtlinien (novel) 2010. *Address:* Knesebeckstr. 98A, 10623 Berlin, Germany (home).

UVAROV, Andrei Ivanovich; Russian ballet dancer; *Principal Dancer, Bolshoi Ballet;* b. 28 Sept. 1971, Moscow; m. Filippova Svetlana; one d.; ed Moscow School of Choreography; soloist Bolshoi Ballet 1989–; Benoit de la Danse Int. Prize 1993, 1st Prize Int. Ballet Competition, Japan 1995, Merited Artist of Russia 1996, People's Artist of Russia 2001, Spirit of Dance Prize, Ballet magazine 2003. *Ballets:* has danced leading roles with Bolshoi Theatre including Swan Lake, Chopiniana, Ivan the Terrible, Romeo and Juliet, Giselle, La Bayadère, Sleeping Beauty. *Address:* State Academic Bolshoi Theatre, Ballet, Teatralnaya pl. 1, 103009 Moscow, Russia (office). *Telephone:* (495) 292-99-86 (office). *Website:* www.bolshoi .ru (office).

UYEDA, Seiya, DSc; Japanese geophysicist and academic; b. 28 Nov. 1929, Tokyo; s. of the late Seiichi Uyeda and of Hatsuo Uyeda; m. Mutsuko Kosaka 1952; one s. two d.; ed Univ. of Tokyo; Research Fellow, Earthquake Research Inst., Univ. of Tokyo 1955–63, Assoc. Prof., Geophysical Inst. 1963–69, Prof., Earthquake Research Inst. 1969–89; Prof., School of Marine Science and Tech., Tokai Univ. 1990–95; Harris Prof. of Geophysics, Texas A&M Univ. 1990–2008; Dir RIKEN Int. Frontier Program on Earthquake Research 1996–2002; mem. Japan Acad. 1996; Foreign Assoc. NAS 1976; Foreign mem. Russian Acad. of Sciences 1994; Hon. Foreign mem. American Acad. of Arts and Sciences 1981; Tanakadate Prize, Soc. of Terrestrial Electricity and Magnetism 1955, Okada Prize, Oceanographical Soc. of Japan 1968, Alexander Agassiz Medal, Nat. Acad. of Sciences 1972, Japan Acad. Prize 1987, George P. Woollard Award, Geological Soc. of America 1989, Walter H. Bucher Medal, American Geophysical Union 1991. *Publications include:* Debate About the Earth 1967, Island Arcs 1973, The New View of the Earth 1977; 350 scientific papers. *Leisure interest:* playing violin. *Address:* 2-39-6 Daizawa, Setagaya-ku, Tokyo 155-0032, Japan (home). *Telephone:* (3) 3412-0237 (home). *Fax:* (3) 3412-0237 (home). *E-mail:* suyeda@st.rim.or.jp (office). *Website:* www.u -tokai.ac.jp (office).

UYS, Pieter-Dirk, BA; South African playwright, performer and producer; b. 28 Sept. 1945, Cape Town; s. of Helga Bassel and Hannes Uys; ed Univ. of Cape Town, London Film School, UK; joined Space Theatre, Cape Town 1973; f. Syrkel Theatre Co.; Dir P. D. Uys Productions, Bapetikosweti Marketing Enterprises; produced and performed 30 plays in revues throughout SA and in UK, USA, Australia, Canada, Netherlands; several videos and TV films and documentaries; Hon. DLitt (Rhodes Univ.) 1997, (Univ. of Cape Town) 2003, (Univ. of the Witwatersrand) 2004; Hon. DEdu (Univ. of the Western Cape) 2003; Truth and Reconciliation Award 2001. *Theatre:* cr. Mrs Evita Bezuidenhout – the most famous white woman in South Africa. *Television:* Evita Live and Dangerous, weekly talk/satire show 1999. *Publications:* Die van Aardes van Grootoor 1979, Paradise is Closing Down 1980, God's Forgotten 1981, Karnaval 1982, Selle ou storie 1983, Farce about Uys 1984, Appassionata 1985, Skote! 1986, Paradise is Closing Down and Other Plays 1989, No one's Died Laughing 1986, P.W. Botha: In His Own Words 1987, A Part Hate, A Part Love 1990, Funigalore 1995, Elections and Erections 2002, Between the Devil and the Deep 2005. *Leisure interests:* films, music, people, South African politics. *Address:* Evita SE Perron Theatre/Cafe/Bar Darling Station, Darling 7345 (office); 17 Station Road, Darling 7345, South Africa (home). *Telephone:* (22) 4922831 (office); (22) 4923208 (home). *Fax:* (22) 4923208 (home). *E-mail:* evita@ evita.co.za (office). *Website:* www.pdu.co.za.

UYTENGSU, Wilfred Steven, Jr, BS; Philippine business executive; *President and CEO, Alaska Milk Corporation;* b. 1962; s. of Wilfred Uytengsu, Sr; m.; ed Univ. of Southern California, USA; fmr Dir General Milling Corpn, later Chief Finance Officer; Exec. Vice-Pres. and Chief Financial Officer, Alaska Milk Corpn 1994–98, Dir 1994–, COO 1998–2007, Pres. 1998–, CEO 2007–; Pres. GenOSI Inc.; fmr Chair. Young Pres.' Org.; mem. Bd of Govs Philippine Basketball Asscn; Ernst & Young Philippines Entrepreneur of the Year 2007. *Address:* Alaska Milk Corporation, 6th Floor, Corinthian Plaza Building, 121 Paseo De Roxas, Legaspi Village, Makati 1229, Philippines (office). *Telephone:* (2) 8404500 (office). *Fax:* (2) 8944929 (office). *Website:* www.alaskamilk.com.ph (office).

UZAWA, Hirofumi, PhD; Japanese economist and academic; *Professor Emeritus of Economics, University of Tokyo;* b. 21 July 1928, Tottori Province; s. of Tokio Uzawa and Toshiko Uzawa; m. Hiroko Aoyoshi 1957; two s. one d.; ed Univ. of Tokyo; Research Assoc., Lecturer, Asst Prof., Dept of Econs, Stanford Univ., Calif. 1956–60, Assoc. Prof. of Econs and Statistics 1961–64; Asst Prof. of Econs and Math., Univ. of Calif., Berkeley 1960–61; Prof. of Econs, Univ. of Chicago 1964–68, Univ. of Tokyo 1969–89, Prof. Emer. 1989–; Prof. of Econs, Niigata Univ. 1989–94; Foreign Assoc., NAS; mem., Japan Acad. 1989–; Matsunaga Memorial Prize 1969, Yoshino Prize 1971, Mainichi Prize 1974, desig. as Person of Cultural Merits 1983, Order of Culture 1997. *Publications:* in English: Studies in Linear and Nonlinear Programming (co-author) 1958; in Japanese: Economic Development and Fluctuations (co-author) 1972, Social Costs of the Automobile 1974, A Re-examination of Modern Economic Theory 1977, Transformation of Modern Economics 1986, A Critique of Japanese Economy 1987, Towards a Theory of Public Economics 1987, Preference, Production and Capital 1988, Optimality, Equilibrium and Growth 1988, A History of Economic Thought (in Japanese) 1989, Poverty Amid Economic Prosperity (in Japanese) 1989, Economic Analysis (in Japanese) 1990, Collected Papers of Hirofumi Uzawa (12 vols) 1994–95, Introduction to Mathematics (six vols) 1997–2000, Economic Theory and Global Warming 2003, Economic Analysis of Social Common Capital 2005. *Leisure interest:* walking. *Address:* Kamiyama-cho 20-23, Shibuya-ku, Tokyo, Japan (home).

UZELAC, Slobodan, PhD; Croatian psychologist, academic and politician; b. 9 Aug. 1947, Kakma; m.; two c.; ed Univ. of Zagreb, Univ. of Belgrade; Asst, Faculty of Special Educ., Univ. of Zagreb 1973–82, Asst Prof. 1982–87, Head of Dept of Behavioural Disorders 1982–86, Assoc. Prof., Faculty of Educ. and Rehabilitation 1987–99, Prof. 1999–; State Sec., Ministry of Science, Educ. and Sport 2004–08; Deputy Prime Minister for Regional Devt, Reconstruction and Return 2008–09, for Social Issues and Human Rights 2009–11; External Assoc. Zagreb Center for Social Care 1976–86; Visiting Lecturer, Pennsylvania State Univ. 1991, Univ. of Pittsburgh 1991; mem. Ind. Democratic Serb Party (Samostalna demokratska srpska stranka); mem. Advisory Bd Vukovar Inst. for Peace Research and Educ. 2000. *Leisure interests:* reading, travel. *Address:* c/o Office of the Prime Minister, 10000 Zagreb, trg sv. Marka 2, Croatia.

ÜZÜMCÜ, Ahmet, BA; Turkish diplomatist; *Director-General, Organisation for the Prohibition of Chemical Weapons;* b. 30 Aug. 1951, Armutlu; m.; one d.; ed Ankara Univ.; Attaché, Protocol Dept, Ministry of Foreign Affairs 1976; mil. service 1976–78; Attaché, then Second Sec., Bilateral Cultural Relations Dept 1978–79; Second, then First Sec., Embassy in Vienna, Austria 1979–82; Consul, Consulate-Gen. in Aleppo, Syria 1982–84; Chief of Section, Personnel Dept, Ministry of Foreign Affairs 1984–86; Counsellor, Del. to NATO, Brussels 1986–89, mem. Int. Staff 1989–94; Head of NATO Dept, Ministry of Foreign Affairs 1994–96; Minister, Head of Personnel Dept 1996–99; Amb. to Israel 1999–2002; Amb. and Perm. Rep. to NATO 2002–04; Deputy Under-Sec., Ministry of Foreign Affairs for Bilateral Political Affairs 2004–06; Amb. and Perm. Rep. to UN, Geneva 2006–09; Pres. UN Disarmament Conf. 2008; Dir-Gen. OPCW, The Hague 2010–; Dr hc (Geneva School of Diplomacy) 2010. *Address:* OPCW Headquarters, Johan de Wittlaan 32, 2517 JR The Hague, The Netherlands (office). *Telephone:* (70) 416-3300 (office). *Fax:* (70) 306-3535 (office). *E-mail:* info@opcw.org (office); media@ opcw.org (office). *Website:* www.opcw.org (office).

UZUN, Ahmet, BSc; Turkish-Cypriot civil servant and politician; b. 1950, Lefkoşa (Nicosia); m.; two c.; ed Ankara Univ.; held various political roles since 1975, including Under-Sec. to Deputy Prime Minister; Minister of Finance, 'Turkish Repub. of Northern Cyprus' 2004–09; fmr Pres. Public Officers' Union (KTAMS); mem. Cen. Admin. Council Republican Turkish Party (Cumhuriyetci Turk Partisi). *Leisure interest:* playing the trumpet. *Address:* c/o Ministry of Finance, Lefkoşa (Nicosia), Mersin 10, Turkey (office). *Telephone:* 2283116 (office). *Fax:* 2278230 (office). *E-mail:* bim@kktcmaliye.com (office). *Website:* www.kktcmaliye .com (office).

V

VAAHTORANTA, Tapani, CandPolit, MA, PhD; Finnish institute director; *Programme Director, Institute of African Leadership for Sustainable Development;* b. 6 Jan. 1955, Merikarvia; ed Univ. of Turku, Princeton Univ., USA; Asst Prof., Univ. of Turku 1986–89; Sr Research Fellow, Finnish Inst. of Int. Affairs 1989–90, Research Dir 1990–91, Dir 1991–2007, Programme Dir 2007–10; mem. Faculty, Geneva Centre for Security Policy 1998–2001; Programme Dir, Inst. of African Leadership for Sustainable Devt, Tanzania 2010–. *Publication:* How Energy and Climate Change May Pose a Threat to Sustainable Security (in, Great Powers and Strategic Stability in the 21st Century, ed. Graeme P. Herd) 2010. *Address:* Institute of African Leadership for Sustainable Development, Dar es Salaam, Tanzania (office). *Telephone:* (22) 260-2917 (office). *E-mail:* tvaahtoranta@uongozi .or.tz (office).

VACANTI, Joseph Philip, BS, MS, MD; American physician, medical scientist and academic; *John Homans Professor of Surgery, Harvard Medical School; Surgeon-in-Chief and Chief of Pediatric Surgery and Director of Pediatric Transplant Program and Co-Director of Center for Regenerative Medicine, Massachusetts General Hospital;* ed Creighton Univ., Omaha, Neb., Univ. of Nebraska Coll. of Medicine, Harvard Medical School; trained in Gen. Surgery at Massachusetts Gen. Hosp., Boston, in Paediatric Surgery at Children's Hosp., Boston, in Transplantation at Univ. of Pittsburgh; has held academic appointments at Harvard; Surgeon-in-Chief and Chief of Pediatric Surgery at MassGeneral Hosp. for Children, also Dir Pediatric Transplant Program and Co-Dir Center for Regenerative Medicine, Massachusetts Gen. Hosp.; mem. Inst. of Medicine of NAS; Thomas G. Sheen Award, New Jersey Chapter of American Coll. of Surgeons, recognized by American Acad. of Anti-Aging Medicine for contribs in the area of tissue replacement, James Bartlett Brown Award, Soc. of Plastic and Reconstructive Surgery, Clemson Award, Soc. for Biomaterials, John Scott Medal, City of Philadelphia, Flance-Karl Award, American Surgical Asscn. *Achievements include:* created artificial organs using a biodegradable polymer scaffold to develop and shape tissue. *Publications:* more than 270 reports and papers in professional journals and more than 65 book chapters; more than 80 patents or patents-pending in USA, Canada, Europe and Japan. *Address:* Pediatric Surgery, Massachusetts General Hospital, 55 Fruit Street, WRN 1151, Boston, MA 02114-2696 (office); Harvard Stem Cell Institute, Holyoke Center, Suite 727W, 1350 Massachusetts Avenue, Cambridge, MA 02138, USA (office). *Telephone:* (617) 724-1725 (Boston) (office); (617) 496-4050 (Cambridge) (office). *Fax:* (617) 726-7593 (Boston) (office). *E-mail:* jvacanti@partners.org (office). *Website:* www.massgeneral.org (office); www.hsci.harvard.edu/people/joseph-vacanti-md (office).

VĂCĂROIU, Nicolae; Romanian politician and economist; b. 5 Dec. 1943, Bolgrad, Bessarabia; m. Marilena Văcăroiu; one s.; ed Bucharest Acad. of Econ. Studies; Economist, Ilfov Co. Inst. of Design and Systemization; then with State Planning Cttee, promoted to Dir Econ.-Financial Synthesis Dept; apptd Deputy Minister of Nat. Economy 1990; subsequently Head of Price Dept, Ministry of Finance, Sec. of State and Head of Tax Dept, Chair. Interministerial Cttee for Foreign Trade Guarantees and Credits; Prime Minister 1992–96; Senator 1996–, Vice-Pres. of Senate 1999–2000, Pres. 2000–08, Chair. Privatization Cttee 1997–99, Vice-Pres. Parl. Group of Social Democratic Party (Partidul Social Democrat—PSD) 1996–2000; Pres. Court of Accounts 2008–; Chair. Romania–Brazil Friendship Asscn 1997–. *Publications:* numerous articles on econ. and financial matters. *Address:* Senatul (The Senate), 050711 Bucharest 5, Calea 13 Septembrie 1–3 (office); B-dul Gh. Prezan, nr. 4, 2nd Floor, Apt 3, Sector 1, Bucharest, Romania (home). *Telephone:* (21) 4021111 (office). *Fax:* (21) 3121184 (office). *E-mail:* csava@senat.ro (office). *Website:* www.senat.ro (office).

VACEK, Gen. (retd) Miroslav; Czech politician and army officer (retd); b. 29 Aug. 1935, Kolín; m. Helena Vacek 1958; one s.; ed A. Zápotocký Mil. Acad., Brno and Mil. Acad. of USSR; Commdr Western Mil. Dist 1985; Chief of Gen. Staff of Czechoslovak Army and First Deputy of Minister of Nat. Defence 1987; Minister of Nat. Defence 1989–90; Adviser to Ministry of Defence 1990–91; Pres. Victoria (business) 1992–; mem. Parl. of Czech Repub. 1996–98, mem. Comm. for Defence and Security 1996–98; mem. Communist Party of Bohemia and Moravia (KSČM). *Publications:* Why Should I Keep Silent? 1991, In Fairness 1994, Úsměvy v barvě (Smiles in Khaki) 2002; articles on mil. problems published in mil. press. *Address:* c/o Communist Party of Bohemia and Moravia, Politických vězňů 9, 110 00 Prague 1, Czech Republic.

VACHON, Louis; Canadian banker; *President and CEO, National Bank of Canada;* b. 1962; m.; two c.; ed Fletcher School, USA; Vice-Pres. Capital Markets Levesque Beaubien (later Nat. Bank Financial) 1986–90; with Bankers Trust 1990–96; joined Nat. Bank of Canada 1996, Pres. and CEO Innocap Investment Man. and Sr Vice-Pres. Treasury and Financial Markets, Nat. Bank of Canada 1997, Chair. Nat. Bank Financial Group and Natcan Investment Man. 2004–05, Chair. and CEO Nat. Bank Financial Group 2005–06, COO Nat. Bank of Canada 2006–07, mem. Bd of Dirs 2006–, Pres. and CEO 2007–; fmr Pres. and CEO BT Bank Canada, Innocap; mem. Bd of Dirs Montreal Exchange, Boston Option Exchange, Nat. Bank Discount Brokerage. *Address:* National Bank of Canada, 600 rue de la Gauchetière ouest, Montreal, PQ H3B 4L2, Canada (office). *Telephone:* (514) 394-5000 (office). *Fax:* (514) 394-8434 (office). *Website:* www.nbc.ca (office).

VADERA, Baroness (Life Peer), cr. 2007, of Holland Park in the Royal Borough of Kensington and Chelsea; **Shriti Vadera,** PC; British investment banker, international organization official and fmr government official; b. 1962, Uganda; ed Northwood Coll., Somerville Coll., Oxford; investment banker, UBS Warburg 1985–99; mem. Council of Econ. Advisers 2000–07, fmr Adviser to Chancellor Gordon Brown; Parl. Under-Sec. of State, Dept for Int. Devt 2007–08, Parl. Under-Sec. of State for Business and Competitiveness Jan.–Oct. 2008, Minister for Econ. Competitiveness, Small Business and Enterprise 2008–09; Sr Adviser to Chair. of Group of Twenty (G-20) Finance Ministers and Cen. Bank Govs 2009–, Adviser to Temasek Holdings, to govt of Dubai, UAE 2010–; mem. Bd of Dirs BHP Billiton 2011–, AstraZeneca 2011–; Trustee, Oxfam 2000–05. *Address:* Group of Twenty (G-20) Finance Ministers and Central Bank Governors, c/o HM Treasury, 1 Horse Guards Rd, London, SW1A 2HQ, England (office). *E-mail:* g20uk.publicenquiries@ hm-treasury.gov.uk (office). *Website:* www.g20.org (office).

VAGELOS, Pindaros Roy, MD; American biochemist, academic and pharmaceutical industry executive; *Chairman, Regeneron Pharmaceuticals Inc.;* b. 8 Oct. 1929, Westfield, NJ; s. of Roy John Vagelos and Marianthi Lambrinides; m. Diana Touliatos 1955; two s. two d.; ed Univ. of Pennsylvania and Columbia Univ. Coll. of Physicians and Surgeons; Intern in Medicine, Mass. Gen. Hosp. 1954–55, Asst Resident in Medicine 1955–56; Surgeon, Lab. of Cellular Physiology, NIH 1956–59, Surgeon, Lab. of Biochemistry 1959–64, Head of Section on Comparative Biochemistry 1964–66; Prof. of Biochemistry and Chair. Dept of Biological Chem., Washington Univ. School of Medicine, St Louis 1966–75, Dir Div. of Biology and Biomedical Sciences 1973–75; Sr Vice-Pres. Research, Merck Sharp & Dohme Research Labs, Rahway, NJ 1975–76, Pres. 1976–84, Corporate Sr Vice-Pres. Merck & Co., Inc. 1982–84, Exec. Vice-Pres. 1984–85, CEO 1985–86, Chair. and CEO 1986–95; Chair. Regeneron Pharmaceuticals Inc. 1995–, also mem. Scientific Advisory Bd; Trustee Rockefeller Univ. 1976–94, Univ. of Pa 1988– (Chair. Bd 1994–), Danforth Foundation 1978–; mem. Bd of Dirs Prudential Insurance Co. of America 1989–, Theravance, Inc 1996–2010 (Chair. –2010); fmr mem. Bd of Dirs TRW Inc., PepsiCo Inc.; mem. NAS, American Acad. of Arts and Sciences; ACS Enzyme Chem. Award 1967, NJ Science/Tech. Medal 1983, Pupin Medal 1995. *Achievements include:* discoverer of acyl-carrier protein. *Leisure interests:* jogging, tennis. *Address:* Regeneron Pharmaceuticals Inc., 777 Old Saw Mill River Road, Tarrytown, NY 10591-6707 (office); 82 Mosle Road, Far Hills, NJ 07931, USA (home). *Telephone:* (914) 347-7000 (office). *Fax:* (914) 347-2113 (office). *Website:* www.regeneron.com (office).

VAGHUL, Narayanan, BCom; Indian banker; *Non-Executive Chairman, ICICI Bank;* b. 1936, South India; ed Ramakrishna School, Chennai, Loyola Coll., Madras Univ.; mem. of staff, State Bank of India 1957–1974; fmr Dir Nat. Inst. of Bank Man.; Exec. Dir Cen. Bank of India 1978–1981; Chair., Man. Dir Bank of India 1981–84; Chair. (non-exec.) Industrial Credit and Investment Corpn of India Ltd (now known as ICICI Bank) 1985–, fmrly also Man. Dir; Dir, Wipro 1997–, Mahindra & Mahindra, Apollo Hospitals, Mittal Steel; Chair. Give India; fmr Visiting Prof. of Econs and Int. Business, Stern Business School, New York Univ.; Business Man of the Year, Business India 1991, Padma Bhushan (Trade and Industry category) 2010, Lifetime Achievement Award by the Times publs 2012. *Address:* ICICI Bank, PO Box 18712, Andheri East, Mumbai 400 069, India (office). *E-mail:* info@icicibank.com (office).

VAGNORIUS, Gediminas, DEconSc; Lithuanian politician; *Chairman, Christian-Conservative Social Union;* b. 10 June 1957, Plunge Dist; m. Nijole Vagnorenė; one s. one d.; ed Inst. of Eng and Construction, Vilnius; engineer-economist, jr researcher, then researcher, Inst. of Econs, Lithuanian Acad. of Sciences 1980–90; Deputy to Lithuanian Supreme Soviet, mem. Presidium 1990–91; Chair. Council of Ministers (Prime Minister) of Lithuania 1991–92, 1996–99; mem. Seimas (Parl.) 1992–2004; Chair. Bd Homeland Union/Lithuanian Conservative Party 1993–2000; Chair. Krikščionių Konservatorių Socialinė Sąjunga (Christian-Conservative Social Union) 2000–. *Leisure interest:* jogging. *Address:* Krikščionių Konservatorių Socialinė Sąjunga, Odminių g. 5, 01122 Vilnius, Lithuania (office). *Telephone:* (5) 212-6874 (office). *Fax:* (5) 212-6874 (office). *E-mail:* sekretoriatas@nks.lt (office). *Website:* www.nks.lt (office).

VAHANVATI, Goolam E., LLB; Indian lawyer and government official; *Attorney General;* ed St Xavier's Coll., Mumbai, Bombay Univ.; Advocate Gen., Maharashtra Govt 1999–2004, handled cases for state govt in three benches of Bombay High Court at Bombay, Aurangabad and Nagpur; Sr Advocate, Supreme Court of India; Solicitor Gen. 2004–09; Attorney Gen. of India 2009–; apptd along with Zimbabwe High Court Judge Steven Majiedt by Int. Cricket Council to hold inquiry into allegations of racism in Zimbabwe 2004, later, as single-mem. panel, inquired into allegations of racial abuse against S African cricketers during S African tour of Australia in Dec. 2005. *Address:* Office of the Attorney General, Supreme Court of India, Tilak Marg, New Delhi 110 001, India (office). *Telephone:* (11) 3383254 (office). *Fax:* (11) 3782101 (office). *E-mail:* supremecourt@nic.in (office). *Website:* www.supremecourtofindia.nic.in (office).

VAHER, Ken-Marti; Estonian politician; *Minister of the Interior;* b. 5 Sept. 1974, Tallinn; m.; one s.; ed Tallinn Secondary School No. 7, Univ. of Tartu; Adviser, Riigikogu (Parl.) Constitutional Cttee 1995–98; Adviser to Auditor Gen. on personnel and training issues 1998–99, Dir State Audit Office 1999–2001; Sec. Gen. Res Publica party 2001–02, now mem. Union of Pro Patria and Res Publica party (following merger of two parties 2006); mem. Tallinn City Council 2002–03; mem. Riigikogu (Parl.) 2003, 2005–; Minister of Justice 2003–05, of the Interior 2011–; Chair. Tallinn House Owners Asscn, Estonian Foundation for Helping the Repressed; mem. Academic Unit of Estonian Defence League. *Publications:* articles in the nat. press. *Leisure interests:* philosophy, physical education, music. *Address:* Ministry of the Interior, Pikk 61, 15065 Tallinn, Estonia (office). *Telephone:* 612-5001 (office); 631-6452 (Riigikogu) (office). *Fax:* 612-5087 (office). *E-mail:* ken-marti.vaher@siseministeerium.ee (office); ken-marti.vaher@riigikogu .ee (office). *Website:* www.siseministeerium.ee (office); www.vaher.ee.

VÄHI, Tiit; Estonian engineer, business executive and fmr politician; *Commercial Director, Silmet AS;* b. 10 Jan. 1947, Valgamaa; m.; two c.; ed Tallinn Polytechnic Inst.; fmr Production Man. Valga Motor Depot, later Deputy Dir, Chief Engineer, Dir, Chair. Transport Cttee; helped organize Estonian Popular Front, led its regional committee in Valga Co.; Minister of Transport and Communications 1989–92; Govt's Special Rep. to NE Estonia 1991; Acting Prime Minister of Estonia Jan.–Oct. 1992, Prime Minister 1995–97; mem. Bd Coalition Party, Chair. 1993–99; Chair. Tallinn City Council 1993–95; fmr Owner and CEO Silmet AS, Commercial Dir 2010–. *Address:* Silmet AS, Kesk 2, Sillamäe 40231, Estonia (office). *Telephone:* 392-9100 (office). *Fax:* 392-9111 (office). *E-mail:* sekretar@ silmet.ee (office). *Website:* www.silmet.ee (office).

VAHIDI, Gen. Ahmad, MEng, PhD; Iranian army officer and politician; b. Shiraz; ed Shiraz Univ., Imam Sadegh Univ.; joined Revolutionary Cttees and

Islamic Revolutionary Guard Corps (IRGC) 1979, becoming Commdr, Qods Force, IRGC; responsible for security affairs, Armed Forces Gen. Command HQ during Iran–Iraq war 1980–88; fmr Deputy Head of Ministry of Defence Armed Forces Logistics; fmr Head of Political, Defence and Security Cttee of State Expediency Council; Deputy Minister of Defence 2005–09, Minister of Defence and Armed Forces Logistics 2009–13. *Address:* c/o Ministry of Defence and Armed Forces Logistics, Shahid Yousuf Kaboli St, Sayed Khandan Area, Tehran, Iran.

VAIL, Peter R., PhD; American oceanographer and academic; *W. Maurice Ewing Professor Emeritus of Oceanography, Rice University;* b. 1930, New York; m. Carolyn Vail; three c.; ed Dartmouth Coll. and Northwestern Univ.; Research Geologist, Exxon Corpn 1956; Research Geologist, Esso Production Research Co. 1965, Sr Research Scientist 1980–86; W. Maurice Ewing Prof. of Oceanography, Rice Univ. 1986–2001, Prof. Emer. 2001–; Founder and Pres. Peter R. Vail Oil and Gas Consulting and Investing Co. 2001–; FGS (US) 1993–, FGS (UK) 1995–; Fellow, AAAS; mem. Sigma Xi (American Geophysical Union), American Geophysical Inst.; Hon. mem. Gulf Coast Section of the Soc. for Sedimentary Geology, Soc. of Exploration Geologists, Houston Geophysical Soc.; Penrose Medal Award, Geological Soc. of America 2003, Legendary Geoscientist Award, American Geological Inst. 2004, Hollis D. Hedbers Award in Energy, Inst. for the Study of Earth and Man 2005, Benjamin Franklin Medal in Earth Science, The Franklin Inst. 2005. *Publications:* numerous articles in scientific publications. *Address:* Keith-Weiss Geological Laboratories, Room 201, Department of Earth Science, 6100 Main Street, Houston, TX 77005 (office). *Telephone:* (713) 348-4888 (office). *E-mail:* vail@rice.edu (office). *Website:* cohesion.rice.edu/naturalsciences/earthscience (office).

VAILE, Hon. Mark Anthony James; Australian consultant and fmr politician; *Director, Vaile and Associates;* b. 18 April 1956, Sydney; s. of George Strafford Vaile and Suzanne Elizabeth Vaile; m. Wendy Jean Vaile 1976; three d.; worked as jackaroo 1973–76; farm machinery retailer 1976–79; Real Estate and Stock and Station Agent 1979–92; Chair., Wingham Chamber of Commerce 1980–85; mem. House of Reps for Lyne (Nat. Party), NSW 1993–, fmr Deputy Speaker, then Chair. House of Reps Standing Cttee on Communications, Transport and Micro-Econ. Reform, Nat. Party Whip 1994; Minister for Transport and Regional Devt 1997–98, for Agric., Fisheries and Forestry 1998–99, for Trade 1999–2006, for Transport and Regional Services 2006–07; Deputy Leader Nat. Party of Australia 1999–2005, Fed. Parl. Leader 2005–07 (resgnd); Deputy Prime Minister 2005–07; currently Dir Vaile and Associates (business consultancy); mem. Bd of Dirs Virgin Blue Holdings Ltd 2008–. *Leisure interests:* squash, tennis, water skiing, golf. *Address:* Vaile and Associates, Suite 2, Level 2, 53 Cross Street, Double Bay, NSW 2028, Australia (office). *Telephone:* (2) 9363-2422 (office). *Fax:* (2) 9363-9955 (office). *Website:* www.vaileassoc.com (office).

VAILLANT, Daniel; French politician; b. 19 July 1949, Lormes (Nièvre); s. of Raymond Vaillant and Germaine Andre; three c.; ed Ecole supérieure de biologie et biochimie; joined Convention des Institutions Républicaines 1966; Parti Socialiste (PS) official, 18th arrondissement Paris 1971–95; Special Asst to François Mitterrand, presidential election campaign 1981; Asst Nat. Sec. for PS Feds 1986, Nat. Sec. for PS Feds 1988–94, Nat. Sec. without specific assignment 1994–95; Campaign Dir, Lionel Jospin's parl. and regional election campaigns 1986, Organizer and Co-ordinator of Lionel Jospin's gen. election campaign 1997; City Councillor 18th arrondissement Paris 1977–95, Mayor of 18th arrondissement 1995–2001, 2003– (First Deputy Mayor 2001–03); Ile-de-France Regional Councillor 1986–89; Nat. Ass. Deputy for 19th Paris constituency 1988–93, 1994–97, 2002–07, 2007–; Minister for Relations with Parl. 1997–2000, of the Interior 2000–02. *Publications:* C'est ça ma gauche 2000, Sécurité, priorité à gauche 2003, PS: 40 ans d'histoire(s) 2011. *Address:* Mairie, 1 place Jules Joffrin, 75877 Paris cedex 18, France. *E-mail:* daniel.vaillant@paris.fr.

VAILLAUD, Pierre; French fmr oil industry executive; b. 15 Feb. 1935, Paris; s. of Marcel Vaillaud and Rose Larrat; m. Geneviève Dreyfus 1960; two s.; ed Lycée Janson-de-Sailly, Paris, Ecole Polytechnique, Ecole des Mines, Ecole Nat. Supérieure du Pétrole et des Moteurs; engineer, Ministry of Industry 1959–63; project man. Technip 1964–68, Dir, Vice-Pres. Eng and Construction Atochem (affiliate of Total) 1968–72; Vice-Pres. Natural Gas Div., Total 1972–74, Vice-Pres. Devt and Construction Div., Vice-Pres. Exploration and Production Operations then Pres., Total Exploration Production 1974–89, Exec. Vice-Pres. Total, Pres. and COO Total Chimie 1989–92, Chair. and CEO Technip 1992–99, Elf Aquitaine SA 1999–2000; Dir Oddo & Cie; Pres. Asscn des techniciens du pétrole 1985–87; Commdr, Ordre nat. du Mérite, Officier, Légion d'honneur. *Leisure interests:* tennis, sailing, golf. *Address:* 5 villa Madrid, 92200 Neuilly-sur-Seine, France (home). *Telephone:* (6) 03-03-00-70 (mobile) (home). *E-mail:* pierrevaillaud@gmail.com.

VAINIO, Vesa Veikko, LLM; Finnish business executive; b. 2 Dec. 1942, Helsinki; s. of Veikko Vainio and Aune Vainio; m. Marja-Liisa Harjunen 1968; two s.; ed Univ. of Helsinki; Circuit Court Notary, Rovaniemi Circuit Court 1966–67; Counsellor, Union of Finnish Lawyers 1968; Sec. Finnish Employers' Confed. 1969, Counsellor and Asst Head of Dept 1969–72; Admin. Dir Aaltonen Footwear Factory 1972, Deputy Man. Dir 1974–76; Man. Dir Aaltonen Factories Oy 1976–77; Dir Confed. of Finnish Industries 1977–83, Deputy Man. Dir 1983–85; Exec. Vice-Pres. Kymmene Corpn 1985–91, Pres. 1991–92, mem. Bd of Dirs 1996–, Chair. UPM-Kymmene Corpn 2001–08; Pres. and CEO Unitas Ltd 1992–94; Chair. and CEO Union Bank of Finland 1992–94 (after merger with Kansallis-Osake-Pankki into Merita Bank Ltd) Merita Bank Ltd 1995–97, Pres. and CEO Merita Ltd 1995–97, Pres. Merita PLC 1998–2000, Chair. MeritaNordbanken PLC 1998, Vice-Chair. Nordbanken Holding PLC 1998–2000, Vice-Chair. MeritaNordbanken PLC 1999, Chair. Nordea AB (publ» 2000–02; mem. Bd of Dirs Nokia Corpn ADS 1993–2008; fmr Vice-Chair. Wärtsilä NSD Oy Ab; Chair. Finnish Cen. Chamber of Commerce 1996–2003; Kt, Order of Finnish Lion; Commdr of Finnish White Rose. *Leisure interests:* hunting, fishing. *Address:* c/o Board of Directors, Nokia Corporation, Keilalahdentie 2–4, Espoo 02150, Finland.

VAINSHTOK, Semyon Mikhailovich; Russian business executive; b. 5 Oct. 1947, Klimatsy, Moldova; m.; one d.; ed Kiev Inst. of Construction and Eng, Acad. of KGB; engineer in Chernovtsy, Ukraine 1969–74; Head, Chernovtsy regional Dept of Provision and Trade 1974–82; Deputy Head, Povkhneft 1982–86; Deputy

Dir-Gen. Bashneft, W Siberia 1986–88; Deputy Head, Kolymneftgas 1988–93; Dir-Gen. LukOil–Kolymneftgas 1993–95, LukOil, W Siberia 1995, Vice-Pres., mem. Bd of Dirs LukOil co. 1995; Pres. Transneft 1999–2007 (retd); head of Olympstroi (state corpn overseeing preparations for 2014 Winter Olympics in Sochi) 2007–08 (resgnd); mem. Acad. of Mining Sciences; Order for Service to Motherland.

VAISEY, David George, CBE, MA, FSA, FRHistS; British librarian and archivist; *Fellow Emeritus, Exeter College, Oxford;* b. 15 March 1935; s. of William Thomas Vaisey and Minnie Vaisey (née Payne); m. Maureen Anne Mansell 1965; two d.; ed Rendcomb Coll., Glos., Exeter Coll., Oxford; archivist, Staffordshire Co. Council 1960–63; Asst, then Sr Librarian, Bodleian Library 1963–75, Keeper of Western Manuscripts 1975–86, Bodley's Librarian 1986–96, Bodley's Librarian Emer. 1997–; Deputy Keeper, Oxford Univ. Archives 1966–75, Keeper 1995–2000; Professorial Fellow, Exeter Coll., Oxford 1975–96, Fellow by Special Election 1997–2000, Fellow Emer. 2000–; Visiting Prof. of Library Studies, UCLA 1985; Chair. Nat. Council on Archives 1988–91; mem. Royal Comm. on Historical Manuscripts 1986–98, Advisory Council on Public Records 1989–94; Vice-Pres. British Records Asscn 1999–; Pres. Soc. of Archivists 1999–2002, Expert Panel on Museums, Libraries and Archives, Heritage Lottery Fund 1999–2004; Hon. Fellow, Kellogg Coll. Oxford 1996–; Hon. Research Fellow, Dept of Library, Archive and Information Studies, Univ. Coll. London 1987–; Encomienda, Order of Isabel La Catolica (Spain) 1989. *Publications:* Staffordshire and the Great Rebellion (co-author) 1964, Probate Inventories of Lichfield and District 1568–1680 1969, Victorian and Edwardian Oxford from Old Photographs (co-author) 1971, Oxford Shops and Shopping 1972, Art for Commerce (co-author) 1973, Oxfordshire: A Handbook for Students of Local History 1973, The Diary of Thomas Turner 1754–65 1984; numerous articles in learned journals. *Address:* Bodleian Library, Oxford, OX1 3BG, England (office). *E-mail:* david.vaisey@bodleian.ox.ac.uk (office).

VAITHILINGAM, Thiru V.; Indian politician; b. 5 Oct. 1950, Cuddalore, Tamil Nadu; s. of V. Venkatasubba Reddiar; m. Sasikala Sambasivam 1969; ed Loyola Coll., Chennai; raised in rural Maducarai, Pondicherry, later went to Maducarai to take care of family farms; fmr Chair. Land Devt Bank of Pondicherry State; cand. for Legis. Ass. 1980; Minister of Public Works and Power 1985; Leader Congress Legis. Party 1991–2000, 2008–; Chief Minister of Puducherry 1991–96, 2008–11, Leader of Opposition 1996–2000, 2011–. *Address:* 27 Kamatham Street, Maducarai, Puducherry 605 105, India (home). *Telephone:* (413) 2227622 (home); 94432-60363 (mobile).

VAJDA, György, DSc, FIEEE; Hungarian engineer; *President, Science Committee, Hungarian Atomic Energy Authority;* b. 18 June 1927, Budapest; s. of László Vajda and Mária Daróczi; m. 1st Magdolna Krasznai 1969 (died 1987); one s. one d.; m. 2nd Dr Klára Berei 1988; ed Tech. Univ., Budapest; Asst Lecturer 1949–50; on staff of Hungarian Acad. of Sciences 1950–52; Research Inst. of Electric Energetics 1952–57, Deputy Section Leader, Ministry of Heavy Industry 1963–70; Dir Inst. for Electrical Power Research 1970–93, Prof. 1993–97; Dir Gen. Hungarian Atomic Energy Authority 1994–99 (Vice-Pres. 1979–97), currently Pres. Science Cttee; Pres. European Atomic Energy Soc.; mem. Hungarian Nat. Comm. for Tech. Devt, Hungarian Acad. of Eng; mem. Admin. Comm. Conf. Int. des Grands Reseaux Electriques, Paris; Chair. ECE Electric Power Comm. 1972–76; Corresp. mem. Hungarian Acad. of Sciences 1976–81, mem. 1982, Section Pres. 1985–92; mem. New York Acad. of Sciences, Hungarian Acad. of Engineers; Fellow, Wireless Interconnection Forum; Hon. Prof.; Hon. Pres. Hungarian Electrotechnical Soc.; Hon. mem. Sigma Kszi; Distinguished Mem. CIGRE (Int. Council on Large Electric Systems); Hungarian Order; State Prize 1975, Szilárd Prize 1999, Széchenyi Award 2000, Renovanda Kult. Hung Grand Award 2002, Helios Award 2004, Prize of Labor (five times), Hazám Award 2008. *Publications:* A szigetelések romlása (Deterioration of Insulations) 1964, Szigetelések villamos erőterei (Electric Power Fields of Insulation) 1970, Energia és Társadalom (Energy and Society) 1975, Energetika (Energetics), Vols I–II 1984, Risk and Safety 1998, Energy Policy 2001, Energy Today and Tomorrow 2003, Utilization of Energy 2005; more than 150 papers in int. journals. *Leisure interest:* gardening. *Address:* Országos Atomenergia Hivatal, Fényes Adolf utca 4, 1036 Budapest (office); Bem rkp. 32, 1027 Budapest, Hungary (home). *Telephone:* (1) 436-4809 (office). *Fax:* (1) 436-4804 (office). *E-mail:* vajda@haea.gov.hu (office). *Website:* www.haea.gov.hu (office).

VAJPAYEE, Atal Bihari, MA; Indian politician; b. 25 Dec. 1924, Gwalior, MP; s. of Krishna Bihari Vajpayee; ed Victoria (now Laxmibai) Coll., Gwalior, D.A.V. Coll., Kanpur; mem. Rashtriya Swayamsewak Sangh 1941, Indian Nat. Congress 1942–46; mem. Lok Sabha 1957–62, 1967–84 (for New Delhi 1977–84), 1991–, Rajya Sabha 1962–67, 1986; Founder-mem. Bharatiya Jana Sangh 1951, Parl. Leader 1957–77; Chair. Cttee on Govt Assurance 1966–67, Public Accounts Cttee, Lok Sabha 1967–70, 1991–93; detained during Emergency 1975–77; Founder-mem. Janata Party 1977, Pres. Bharatiya Janata Party 1980–86, Parl. Leader 1980–84, 1986; Minister of External Affairs 1977–79; Leader of Opposition, Lok Sabha 1993–98, Chair. Standing Cttee on External Affairs 1993–96; Minister of External Affairs 1998; Prime Minister of India 15–28 May 1996, 1998–2004, also Minister of Health and Family Welfare, Atomic Energy and Agric. 1998–2004; Chair. Nat. Security Council 1998–2004; mem. Nat. Integration Council 1961–; fmr Ed. Rastradharma (monthly), Panchjanya (weekly), Swadesh and Veer Arjun (dailies); Dr hc (Kanpur Univ.) 1993; Bharat Ratna Pte Govind Ballabh Pant Award 1994, Padma Vibhushan 1992, Lokmanya Tilak Puruskar. *Publications:* New Dimensions of India's Foreign Policy, Jan Sangh Aur Musalmans, Three Decades in Parliament; collections of poems and numerous articles. *Leisure interests:* reading, writing, travelling, cooking. *Address:* c/o Bharatiya Janata Party (BJP) (Indian People's Party), 11 Ashok Rd, New Delhi 110 001 (office); 7 Race Course Rd, New Delhi 110 011, India (home). *Telephone:* (11) 23018939 (home). *Fax:* (11) 23019545 (home).

VAKHROMEYEV, Kyril Varfolomeyevich (see Philaret).

VAKSBERG, Arkady Iosifovich, DJur; Russian writer, journalist and lawyer; b. 11 Nov. 1933, Novosibirsk; m.; one d.; ed Moscow State Univ.; barrister, Moscow City Bd of Bar –1973; political observer in Paris, Literaturnaya Gazeta; Vice-Pres. Russian PEN Centre; mem. Russian Writer's Union, Journalist's Union, Union of Cinematography Workers, Int. Cttee of Writers in Prison; Grand-Prix, the

Eurasian Teleforum (Moscow). *Screenplays for films:* The Storm Warning, The Provincial Romance, In Broad Daylight. *Plays:* A Shot in the Dark, The Supreme Court, The Alarm. *TV work includes:* The Special Reporter (serial), A Dangerous Zone (actor and scriptwriter), Reprise (Grand-Prix and Best Screenplay, International Telefilm Festival), L'Asture et l'Amour (scriptwriter), Ils ont emporté avec eux la Russie (Grand-Prix, Int. Felices Documenteure 2009, Russie). *Publications include:* three books and numerous articles on copyright law; over 40 works of fiction, collections of essays, biogs. and memoirs. *Leisure interest:* collecting reference books and encyclopaedias. *Address:* Krasnoarmeiskaya str. 23, Apt 65, 125319 Moscow, Russia (home); 17 blvd Garibaldi, 75015 Paris, France (home). *Telephone:* (499) 151-33-69 (Moscow) (home); 1-45-66-45-31 (Paris) (home). *E-mail:* varkadi@yandex.ru (office).

VALCOURT, (Joseph) Bernard, PC, DHC, BA, LLB, QC; Canadian politician and lawyer; *Minister of Aboriginal Affairs and Northern Development;* b. 18 Feb. 1952, St Quentin de Restigouche, NB; s. of Bertin Valcourt and Geraldine Allain; m. (divorced); two d.; ed Académie St Joseph, Collège St Louis—Maillet, Univ. of New Brunswick; practised law, mem. Canadian Bar Asscn and New Brunswick Lawyers Asscn; MP 1984–93, Parl. Sec. to Minister of State for Science and Tech., Parl. Sec. to Minister of Revenue 1985–86; Minister of State for Small Business and Tourism 1986–89, Minister of State for Indian Affairs (renamed Aboriginal Affairs May 2011) and Northern Devt 1987–89; Minister for Consumer and Corp. Affairs Jan.–Aug. 1989, of Fisheries and Oceans 1990–91, of Employment and Immigration 1991–93; Leader Progressive Conservative Party of New Brunswick 1995; Minister of Aboriginal Affairs and Northern Devt 2013–; mem. New Brunswick Legis. Ass. 1995–99, Leader of Opposition 1995–97. *Address:* Department of Aboriginal Affairs and Northern Development, Ottawa, ON K1A 0H4, Canada (office). *Telephone:* (819) 997-0811 (office). *Fax:* (866) 817-3977 (office). *E-mail:* InfoPubs@aadnc-aandc.gc.ca (office); www.aadnc-aandc.gc.ca (office).

VALDÉS, Juan Gabriel, PhD; Chilean politician and diplomatist; b. June 1947; m. Antonia Echenique Celis; four c.; ed Catholic Univ. of Chile, Santiago, Univ. of Essex, UK, Princeton Univ., USA; Researcher, Political Science Inst. of Catholic Univ. of Chile, Inst. for Policy Studies, Washington, DC 1972–76; Officer, Latin American Inst. for Transnational Studies, Prof. of Int. Relations, Econ. Research and Devt Centre, Mexico City, Mexico 1976–1984; Research Fellow, Kellogg Inst. of Int. Studies, Notre Dame Univ., USA, Center for Latin American Studies, Princeton Univ. 1984, 1987; Consultant, Econ. Comm. for Latin America 1985; Amb. to Spain 1990–94; Dir Int. Div. and Co-ordinator NAFTA Negotiating Team, Ministry of Finance 1994–96, Lead Negotiator Chile–Canada Free Trade Agreement 1996; Consultant, UN Programme for Devt, Santiago 1994; mem. Nat. TV Council 1995; Vice-Minister Int. Econ. Affairs, Ministry of Foreign Affairs 1996–99, Minister 1999–2000; Perm. Rep. to UN, New York 2000–03, concurrently Amb. to Iran 2001; Amb. to Argentina 2003–04; Sec.-Gen.'s Special Rep., UN Stabilization Mission in Haiti (MINUSTAH) 2004–06; Dir Public Diplomacy Program, Ministry of Foreign Affairs 2006–. *Publications include:* Movimiento Sindical Y Empresas Transnacionales 1979, Chile 2000: Encuentro En Caceres De Politicos E Intelectuales Chilenos 1994, Pinochet's Economists: The Chicago School of Economics in Chile 1995; numerous articles on int. relations. *Address:* Ministry of Foreign Affairs, Catedral 1158, Santiago, Chile (office). *Telephone:* (2) 679-4200 (office). *Fax:* (2) 699-4202 (office). *Website:* www.minrel.gov.cl (office).

VALDES DANCUART, Gen. Oscar Eduardo; Peruvian politician and fmr army officer; b. 3 April 1949, Lima; ed Chorrillos Mil. School, US Army Command and Gen. Staff Coll., Fort Leavenworth; army service 1972–91, roles included Instructor, Chorrillos Mil. School, Army Technical School, School of Artillery, Chief of Artillery Group Armoured Unit No 211, Lima, Head of Artillery Group No 1, Tumbes, Head, Bureau of Foreign Acquisitions, Army Logistics Command, Chief, Office of Man. of Army Officers; Dir Chamber of Commerce, Industry and Production, Tacna 1992; Minister of the Interior July–Dec. 2011, Pres., Council of Ministers (Prime Minister) 2011–12; fmr Man. Dir SAC ADC Corpn; Pres. Regional Council, SENATI Tacna-Moquegua. *Address:* c/o Office of the President of the Council of Ministers, Jirón Carabaya, cuadra 1 s/n, Anexo 1105-1107, Lima, Peru (office).

VALDÉS MENÉNDEZ, Ramiro (Ramirito); Cuban government official; *Vice-President;* b. 28 April 1932, Artemisa, Havana Prov.; father of Cuban composer Ramiro Valdés Puentes; fmr revolutionary and one of only four so-called 'Revolutionary Commanders'; joined Fidel Castro in failed assault on Moncada Barracks 1953, jailed for two years on Isla de los Pifios; granted political asylum by Govt of Fulgencio Batista May 1955, left prison and travelled to Mexico to join in preparations, led by Fidel Castro, for Granma expedition which sailed from Mexico for Cuba Dec. 1956; took part in Sierra Maestra uprising alongside Castro, second in command of second column, led by Che Guevara, invaded cen. Prov. of Las Villas 1958; Minister of the Interior 1960–61; apptd Founder and Chief of Departamento de Investigaciones del Ejercito Rebelde; removed from Interior Ministry by Politburo 1969, reinstalled as Interior Minister 1978, removed again as Interior Minister at Third Communist Party Congress and as mem. of Politburo 1986; Dir Nat. Electronics Group (Copextel) late 1980s; Head of newly established Industrial Group for Electronics attached to Ministry of Iron and Steel and Mechanical Industry (SIME) 1990s, subsequently absorbed by Ministry of Information Tech. and Communications; Minister of Information Tech. and Communications 2006–11; re-admitted to Politburo 2008; apptd one of seven Vice-Pres. in Council of Ministers and Council of State 2009–; appointed Coordinator of the 'Battle of Ideas' 2009–; CEO of the Electronics Group 2009–. *Address:* c/o Ministry of Information Technology and Communications, Avenida Independencia No. 2, entre 19 de Mayo y Aranguren, Plaza de la Revolución, Havana, Cuba (office). *Telephone:* (7) 882-8000 (office). *Fax:* (7) 885-4048 (office). *E-mail:* dircom@mic.cu (office). *Website:* www.mic.gov.cu (office).

VÁLDEZ ALBIZÚ, Héctor, BEconSc; Dominican Republic economist and central banker; *Governor, Banco Central de la República Dominicana;* b. 10 Nov. 1947; s. of Hector Manuel Valdez Albizu and Ana Rita Valdez Albizu; m. Fior d'Aliza Martinez 1971; one s.; Tech. Asst (Publs), Cen. Bank of Dominican Repub. (Banco Central de la República Dominicana) 1970–75, Head of Banking and Monetary Div., Tech. Co-ordinator of Econ. Studies 1975–82, Econ. Asst to Gov. 1982–84, Dir Econ. Studies Dept 1984–86, Asst Man., Monetary and Exchange Policy 1986–90, Adviser to Monetary Bd 1987–89, Rep. of Cen. Bank at Banco de Reservas (state

commercial bank) 1991–92, Asst Gen. Man. and Gen. Admin. Banco de Reservas 1992–94, Gov. Cen. Bank and Pres. Monetary Bd 1994–2000, 2004–; mem. Bd of Dirs Consejo Estatal del Azucar (State Sugar Council) 1993–94; Prof., Universidad Cen. del Este and Instituto de Estudios Superiores 1975–89. *Publications:* Financial Programs for the Dominican Republic 1976–1990, Dimensions of the National Banking System and its Enhancement 1976, Exchange Emergency Regime 1985. *Address:* Banco Central de la República Dominicana, Calle Pedro Henriquez Ureña, Esq. Leopoldo Navarro, Apdo 1347, Santo Domingo, DN, Dominican Republic (office). *Telephone:* 221-9111 (office). *Fax:* 687-7488 (office). *E-mail:* info@bancentral.gov.do (office). *Website:* www.bancentral.gov.do (office).

VALDIVIESO MONTANO, Luis Miguel, BA, MA, PhD; Peruvian economist, politician and diplomatist; s. of Juan 'El Mago' Valdivieso; ed Pontificia Univ. Católica del Perú, Boston Univ., USA; fmr Sr Researcher, Centre for Latin American Monetary Studies; fmr adviser to Bank and Securities Market Directorate, Ministry of Finance and Public Credit in Mexico and adviser to the Superintendence of Banks of Ecuador; also taught Introductory Econs and Advanced Macroeconomics at Boston Univ. and was an Econometrics Instructor at the Catholic Univ. of Peru; joined IMF 1980, held several exec. positions over 28-year period, including Sr Economist positions in Western Hemisphere Dept 1980–87 and Policy Devt and Review Dept 1997–99, Chief of Mission to Cambodia and Laos and Dir Asia-Pacific Region, Advisor and Div. Chief positions in European Dept 1991–99, in Asia and Pacific Dept 1999–2008; adviser to Pres. Alberto Fujimori 1990–2000; Special Tech. Adviser to Ministry of Economy and Finance 1991; Minister of Economy and Finance July 2008–Jan. 2009 (resgnd), also Gov. for Peru in Bd Govs of World Bank and IDB, Chair. Andean Finance Corpn (CAF), Nat. Fund for the Financing of the Public Sector Entrepreneurial Activity (FONAFE), mem. Bd Peruvian Nat. Retirement Investment Fund (ONP), Pvt. Investment Promotion Agency (PROINVERSION), Inter-ministerial Cttee of Social Affairs (CIAS); Amb. to USA 2009–11. *Address:* Ministry of Foreign Affairs, Jirón Lampa 535, Lima 1, Peru (office). *Telephone:* (1) 2042400 (office). *E-mail:* informes@rree.gob.pe (office). *Website:* www.rree.gob.pe (office).

VALDIVIESO SARMIENTO, Alfonso, LLD; Colombian politician and diplomatist; b. Oct. 1949, Bucaramanga; m.; two s.; ed Javerian Univ., Bogotá, Boston Univ., USA, Univ. of Toronto, Canada, Stanford Univ., USA; Admin. Vice-Rector and Dir of Planning, Autonomous Univ. of Bucaramanga 1978–86; mem. House of Reps 1982–86; mem. Council, Bucaramanga 1988–89, Pres. 1989; Senator 1986–90, 1990–94, 2008–; Minister for Nat. Educ. 1990–91; Amb. to Israel 1992–93; Attorney-Gen. in charge of criminal investigations 1994–97; unsuccessful presidential cand. 1998; Perm. Rep. to UN 1998–2002; mem. Cambio Radical. *Address:* c/o Cambio Radical, Carrera 7, No 26-20, 26°, Bogotá, DC, Colombia. *Website:* www.alfonsovaldivieso.com.

VALE, Ronald David, BA, PhD; American biologist and academic; *Professor and Vice-Chairman, Department of Cellular and Molecular Pharmacology, University of California, San Francisco;* b. Hollywood, Calif.; ed Univ. of California, Santa Barbara, Stanford Univ., NIH Marine Biological Lab.; mem. Faculty, Univ. of California, San Francisco 1986–, currently Prof. and Vice-Chair. Dept of Cellular and Molecular Pharmacology, Investigator, Howard Hughes Medical Inst. 1995–, W.K. Hamilton Distinguished Prof., Dept of Anesthesia; Pres. American Soc. for Cell Biology 2012; mem. NAS 2001; Fellow, American Acad. of Arts and Sciences 2002; Biophysical Soc. Award for Young Investigators 1993, Keith R. Porter Lecturer 2009, Wiley Prize 2012, Albert Lasker Basic Medical Research Award (co-recipient) 2012. *Publications:* numerous papers in professional journals. *Address:* Genentech Hall, University of California, San Francisco, 600 16th Street, MC 2200, Room N312A, San Francisco, CA 94158-2517, USA (office). *Telephone:* (415) 476-6380 (office). *Fax:* (415) 476-5233 (office). *E-mail:* ron.vale@ucsf.edu (office); vale@cmp.ucsf.edu (office). *Website:* valelab.ucsf.edu (office).

VALE DE ALMEIDA, João; Portuguese diplomatist and European Union official; *Ambassador and Head of the European Union Delegation to USA;* b. 1957, Lisbon; m.; two c.; ed Univ. of Lisbon, journalism training in France, USA and Japan, attended man. schools in UK and France; EC official since 1982, began career at representation in Lisbon, becoming mem. Spokesperson's Service in Brussels 1989, under Pres. Jacques Delors, Spokesman for Energy Policy and for External Relations with the Middle East, the Mediterranean, Latin America and Asia, Head of Unit at Econ. and Social Cttee of the European Communities 1992–94, Deputy Chief Spokesman of EC under Pres. Jacques Santer 1995–97, in charge of coordinating official positions on EU's external relations, among other issues, Dir in Directorate Gen. for Information, Communication, Culture and Audiovisual 1998–2000, Dir in Directorate Gen. for Educ. and Culture 2000–04, Head of Cabinet to EC Pres. José Manuel Barroso 2004–09, Personal Rep. ('Sherpa') for G8 and G20 Summits 2004–10, Dir-Gen. for External Relations of the EU 2009–10, Amb. and Head of EU Del. to USA 2010–. *Address:* Delegation of the European Union to the United States, 2175 K Street NW, Washington, DC 20037, USA (office). *Telephone:* (202) 862-9500 (office). *Fax:* (202) 429-1766 (office). *E-mail:* delegation-usa-info@eeas.europa.eu (office); Relex-delusw-help@ec.europa.eu (office). *Website:* www.eurunion.org/eu (office).

VÁLEK, Vladimír; Czech conductor; *Chief Conductor, Prague Radio Symphony Orchestra;* b. 2 Sept. 1935, Nový Jičín; m. 1st Jana Adamová; m. 2nd Hana Patočková 1986; two s. one d.; ed Acad. of Musical Arts, Bratislava, Acad. of Performing Arts, Prague; conductor with several Czech orchestras 1962–75; Conductor FOK Prague Symphony Orchestra 1975–87; Chief Conductor Prague Radio Symphony Orchestra 1985–; Conductor Czech Philharmonic 1996–2006; Prin. Guest Conductor Orchestra Osaka Symphoniker 2003–; Chief Conductor, Slovakian Philharmonic Orchestra 2004–07; Guest Conductor with many orchestras world-wide including The Big Radio Orchestra Leipzig, Tonkuenstler and ORF (Vienna), Israeli and Japan Philharmonics; Music Critics' Award, MIDEM Classic Cannes (for recording of piano concertos by Ervin Schulhoff) 1996. *Performances:* concert tours include Japan, France, Spain, USA and Singapore; has appeared as guest conductor with numerous symphony orchestras in many countries. *Recordings:* more than 100 classical music recordings and more than 1,000 recordings for radio. *Leisure interest:* aviation. *Address:* Ceský rozhlas, Vinohradská 12, 120 00 Prague 2 (office); Nad údolím 24, 140 00 Prague 4, Czech Republic (home). *Telephone:* (2) 2155-1400 (office); (2) 4177-1463 (home). *Fax:* (2)

2155-1413 (office). *E-mail:* info@rozhlas.cz (office). *Website:* www.cro.cz/socr (office).

VALENCIA COSSIO, Fabio, LLB; Colombian politician and diplomatist; *Minister of Interior and Justice;* b. 23 March 1948, Medellín; ed Univ. de Antioquia; worked at Land Credit Inst., Bogotá 1974–81; Sec. Gen. Conservative Party 1981–84, Vice-Pres. 1984–96, Pres. Nat. Bd 1996–; mem. House of Reps 1982–91; Senator 1991–99, Pres. of Congress 1998–99; apptd negotiator in peace discussions with FARC guerilla movt 1999–2001; Amb. to Italy 2001–05; High Commr for Competitiveness 2005–08; Minister of Interior and Justice 2008–. *Address:* Ministry of the Interior and Justice, Palacio Echeverry, Carrera 8a, No 8-09, Bogotá, Colombia (office). *Telephone:* (1) 334-0630 (office). *Fax:* (1) 341-9583 (office). *Website:* www.mij.gov.co (office).

VALENCIA RODRÍGUEZ, Luis, LLD; Ecuadorean diplomatist, lawyer and academic; *Professor of Private International Law, Universidad Internacional del Ecuador;* b. 5 March 1926, Quito; s. of Pedro Valencia and María Rodríguez; m. Cleopatra Moreno 1952; two s. three d.; ed Central Univ., Quito; entered Ecuadorean Foreign Service 1944; Counsellor, Buenos Aires 1957–59; Minister-Counsellor, UN, New York 1959–64; Minister of Foreign Affairs 1965-66, 1981–84; legal adviser on foreign affairs 1964–65, 1966–69, 1980–81, 1990–94, 2001–03; Amb. to Bolivia 1969–71, to Brazil 1971–74, to Peru 1974–78, to Venezuela 1978–79, to Argentina 1988–91, to Peru 2005–06; Perm. Rep. to UN 1994–99; Prof. Cen. Univ., Quito 1984–86, Int. Univ., Quito 2001–; mem. UN Cttee on the Elimination of Racial Discrimination 1974–86, 1992–96; special citation of Ecuadorean Nat. Ass. 1966 and decorations from Ecuador, Italy, Nicaragua, Bolivia, Brazil, Peru, Venezuela, Colombia, Argentina, El Salvador, Dominican Republic and Korea. *Publications:* books on legal matters, foreign affairs etc. *Leisure interests:* swimming, reading. *Address:* Calle Agustin Mentoso 273, N47–153, Quito, Ecuador (home). *Telephone:* (2) 245-8765 (home); (2) 330-1410 (office). *Fax:* (2) 292-2668 (home). *E-mail:* luisvalro@hotmail.com (office); lvalencia@mmrree.gob.ec (office). *Website:* www.mmrree.gov.ec (office).

VALENSISE, Michele; Italian diplomatist; *Secretary-General, Ministry of Foreign Affairs;* b. 3 April 1952, Polistena; m. Elena Di Giovanni; two d.; ed Univ. La Sapienza, Rome; completed Italian State Exam in Law; joined Diplomatic Service 1975, foreign postings in Brasilia 1978, Bonn 1981–84, Beirut 1984–87, First Counsellor, Perm. Rep. to EU, Brussels 1991–97, Amb. to Bosnia–Herzegovina 1997–99, Head, Press and Information Section and Spokesman for Minister of Foreign Affairs (MFA) 2001–04, Amb. to Brazil 2004–09, to Germany 2009–12, Sec.-Gen. MFA 2012–. *Address:* Ministry of Foreign Affairs, Piazzale della Farnesina 1, 00194 Rome, Italy (office). *Telephone:* (06) 36911 (office). *Fax:* (06) 36918899 (office). *E-mail:* relazioni.pubblico@esteri.it (office). *Website:* www .esteri.it (office).

VALENTIĆ, Nikica; Croatian lawyer, business executive and fmr politician; *President, Niva Ltd;* b. 24 Nov. 1950, Gospić; m. Antoneta Valentić; one s. one d.; ed Law School, Zagreb Univ.; journalist for Radio Zagreb 1969–71; Ed. Pravnik (magazine) 1972–74; legal adviser in Zeljko Jurkovič office; Founder and Gen. Man. S2 Stanograd and Stanogradinvest (consultancy) 1978–83; f. law firm 1984–90; Gen. Man. INA Industria Nafte 1990–93; Prime Minister of Croatia 1993–95; mem. Parl. 1995–2003; Founder and Pres. Niva Ltd (eng. and design firm), Zagreb 1995–. *Leisure interests:* painting, music. *Address:* Jordanovac 71, 10000, Zagreb (home); Niva Ltd, Vlaška 83/1, 10000, Zagreb, Croatia (office). *Telephone:* (1) 4664751 (office); (1) 4664752 (office). *Fax:* (1) 4664753 (office). *E-mail:* niva-holding@niva.htnet.hr (office).

VALENTINE, Jean, BA; American poet and teacher; b. 27 April 1934, Chicago; m. James Chace 1957 (divorced 1968); two d.; ed Radcliffe Coll.; teacher, Swarthmore Coll. 1968–70, Barnard Coll. 1968, 1970, Yale Univ. 1970, 1973–74, Hunter Coll., CUNY 1970–75, Sarah Lawrence Coll. 1974–; 92nd Street Y; Guggenheim Fellowship 1976; State Poet of New York 2008–10; Nat. Endowment for the Arts grant 1972, Maurice English Prize, Teasdale Poetry Prize, Poetry Soc. of America Shelley Memorial Prize 2000, Wallace Stevens Award 2009. *Publications:* Dream Barker and Other Poems (Yale Series of Younger Poets Award) 1965, Pilgrims 1969, Ordinary Things 1974, The Messenger 1979, Home Deep Blue: New and Selected Poems 1989, The River at Wolf 1992, The Under Voice: Selected Poems 1995, Growing Darkness, Growing Light 1997, The Cradle of the Real Life 2000, The Lighthouse Keeper: Essays on the Poetry of Eleanor Ross Taylor (ed.) 2001, Door in the Mountain: New and Collected Poems 1965–2003 (Nat. Book Award for Poetry) 2004, Little Boat 2007, Break the Glass 2010. *Address:* 527 West 110th Street, Suite 81, New York, NY 10025, USA (office). *E-mail:* jeanvalentine@ mygait.com (office). *Website:* www.jeanvalentine.com.

VALENTINI, Pasquale; San Marino politician; *Secretary of State for Foreign and Political Affairs;* b. 19 July 1953; m.; three c.; ed Università degli Studi di Bologna; various trade union posts with Democratic Confed. of San Marino Workers mid-1970s to –mid 1980s; taught math., chemistry, physics and natural science 1977–93, Chair of Math., Upper Secondary School 1993; Dir, first and third Insts, Junior High School 2004–07; mem. Consiglio Grande e Generale (Parl.) 1988–, Pres. Parl. Perm. Cttee for Justice, Educ., Culture, Univ. and Scientific Research, Sport and Tourism, Pres. Cttee for Criminal Procedure Code; Sec. of State for Educ., Univ. and Cultural Insts 2001–02, 2002–03, for Finance and Budget and Relations with the Philatelic and Numismatic Autonomous State Corpn 2010–12, for Foreign and Political Affairs 2012–; mem. Council of Twelve (judicial body); mem. Partito Democratico Cristiano Sammarinese, Political Sec. 2007–10. *Address:* Secretariat of State for Foreign and Political Affairs, Palazzo Begni, Contrada Omerelli, 47890, San Marino (office). *Telephone:* 0549 882431 (office). *Fax:* 0549 882422 (office). *E-mail:* dipartimentoaffariesteri@pa.sm (office). *Website:* ww.esteri.sm (office).

VALENTINO (see Garavani, Valentino).

VALENZUELA, Luisa; Argentine writer and journalist; b. 26 Nov. 1938, Buenos Aires; d. of Luisa Mercedes Levinson and Pablo F. Valenzuela; m. Théodore Marjak 1958 (divorced); one d.; ed Belgrano Girls' School, Colegio Nacional Vicente Lopez, Buenos Aires; lived in Paris, writing for Argentinian newspapers and for the RTF 1958–61; Asst Ed. La Nación Sunday Supplement, Buenos Aires 1964–69; writer, lecturer, freelance journalist in USA, Mexico, France, Spain 1970–73, Buenos

Aires 1973–79; taught in Writing Div., Columbia Univ., New York 1980–83; conducted writers' workshops, English Dept, New York Univ. and seminars, Writing Div. 1984–89; returned to Buenos Aires 1989; mem. Acad. of Arts and Sciences, Puerto Rico; Fellow, New York Inst. for the Humanities; Foreign Hon. mem. American Acad. of Arts and Sciences 2011; lllustrious Citizen of Buenos Aires 2014; Dr hc (Knox Coll., Ill.) 1991; Fulbright Grant 1969–70, Guggenheim Fellow 1983, Machado de Assis Medal, Brazilian Acad. of Letters 1997, Instituto Literario Hispanoamericano 2004, Premio Astralba, Univ. of Puerto Rico 2004, Premio Esteban Echeverría Gente de Letras 2008, Premio cultura 400 años, Universidad de Córdoba 2012. *Publications:* novels: Hay que sonreír 1966, El gato eficaz 1972, Como en la guerra 1977, Cola de lagartija 1983, Realidad nacional desde la cama 1990, Novela negra con argentinos 1990, La travesía 2001, El mañana 2010, Cuidado con el tigre 2011, La máscara sarda, el profundo secreto de Perón 2012; short stories collections: Los heréticos 1967, Aquí pasan cosas raras 1975, Libro que no muerde 1980, Cambio de armas 1982, Donde viven las águilas 1983, Simetrías 1993, Cuentos completos y uno más 1999, Brevs. Microrrelatos completos hasta hoy 2004, Generosos inconvenientes 2008, Juego de villanos 2008, Tres por cinco 2008, ABC de las micrófabulas 2009; essays: Peligrosas palabras. Reflexiones de una escritora 2002, Escritura y secreto 2002, Los deseos oscuros y los otros (cuadernos de New York) 2002, Cortázar/Fuentes Entrecruzamientos 2014. *Leisure interests:* masks, anthropology, ceremonies. *Address:* c/o Gaspar Correa Marjak, Córdoba 2623 13A, 1187 Ciudad Autónoma de Buenos Aires, Argentina (office). *E-mail:* gasparmarjak@gmail.com (office). *Website:* www .luisavalenzuela.com.

VALIANT, Leslie Gabriel, DIC, PhD, FRS; British computer scientist and academic; *T. Jefferson Coolidge Professor of Computer Science and Applied Mathematics, School of Engineering and Applied Sciences, Harvard University;* b. 28 March 1949; ed King's Coll., Cambridge, Imperial Coll., London, Univ. of Warwick; taught at Univ. of Leeds, Univ. of Edinburgh and Carnegie-Mellon Univ., Pittsburgh, Pa, USA; fmr Gordon McKay Prof. of Computer Science and Applied Math., School of Eng and Applied Sciences, Harvard Univ. 1982–2002, T. Jefferson Coolidge Prof. of Computer Science and Applied Math. 2002–; has served on numerous editorial bds and program cttees, including Soc. for Industrial and Applied Math. Journal on Computing, Machine Learning Computational Complexity, Neural Computation, Neural Networks, International Journal of Foundations of Computer Science, Symposium on Theory of Computing, Conf. on Computational Learning Theory, EuroColt, Symposium on Parallel Algorithms and Architectures, and others; Fellow, American Asscn for Artificial Intelligence; mem. NAS; Nevanlinna Prize, Int. Congress of Mathematicians 1986, Knuth Prize 1997, European Asscn for Theoretical Computer Science (EATCS) Award 2008, A.M. Turing Award, Asscn for Computing Machinery 2010. *Achievements include:* together with Vijay Vazirani, proved the Valiant-Vazirani Theorem 1986. *Publications:* Circuits of the Mind 1994, 2000, Probably Approximately Correct: Natures Algorithms for Learning and Prospering in a Complex World 2013; more than 80 articles in scientific journals on parallel computing, computational complexity theory (and physics), computational learning and cognitive computation, neural computation, large computer systems and data centres. *Address:* School of Engineering and Applied Sciences, Harvard University, 351 Maxwell Dworkin, 33 Oxford Street, Cambridge MA 02138, USA (office). *Telephone:* (617) 495-5817 (office). *Fax:* (617) 496-6404 (office). *E-mail:* valiant@seas.harvard.edu (office). *Website:* people.seas.harvard.edu/~valiant (office).

VALINSKAS, Arūnas, MA; Lithuanian television producer and politician; b. 28 Nov. 1966, Lazdijai; m. Ingrida Valinskas; two s.; ed Vilnius Secondary School No. 12, Faculty of Law, Vilnius Univ.; 22-year career on stage and TV, host and moderator of radio and TV programmes, shows and concerts; writer and producer of popular TV shows, including TV games and quizzes: Taip ir Ne, Šeši nuliai – milijonas, and Žodžių mūšis, as well as TV entertainment show Vakarėlis jums, and music reality show Kelias į žvaigždes; co-writer TV series daily show Dviračio šou; Organizer Lithuanian Music Festival Nida; initiator and organizer of first ever beauty contest Miss Captivity at women's prison; gave more than 1,000 concerts as mem. of comic show team Dviratis; Founder Tautos prisikėlimo partija (Nat. Revival Party) 2008–; mem. Seimas (Parl.) 2008–, Speaker and Chair. Bd of the Seimas 2008–09, mem. Ass. of Elders, Group for Inter-parl. Relations with Iraq, Group for Inter-parl. Relations with USA, Del. of Seimas to Ass. of Seimas of Repub. of Lithuania, of Sejm and Senate of Repub. of Poland and of Supreme Rada of Ukraine; first Golden Medal Award, Vilnius Secondary School No. 12. *Address:* Seimas (Parliament), Gedimino pr. 53, Vilnius 01109 (office); National Revival Party (Tautos prisikėlimo partija), Prasiškony g. 4A Vilnius 01133, Lithuania. *Telephone:* (5) 239-6663 (office); (5) 239-6001. *Fax:* (5) 239-6330 (office). *E-mail:* arunas.valinskas@lrs.lt (office); bustine@prisikelimopartija.lt. *Website:* www.lrs.lt (office); www.prisikelimopartija.lt.

VALIONIS, Antanas, PhD; Lithuanian engineer, politician and diplomatist; b. 21 Sept. 1950, Kedainiai Dist; s. of Antanas Valionis and Stanislova Valioniene; m. Romualda Valionis; two s.; ed Kaunas Polytechnic Inst., Warsaw Univ., Poland; foreman, Kaunas Meat Processing Plant 1974–76, Man. Compressor House, Taurage Meat Processing Plant 1976–80; Chief Instructor, Taurage Regional Cttee, Industry and Transport Dept of Cen. Cttee, Lituanian CP 1980–85, Instructor, Agric. and Food Industry Dept 1985–90; Head of Div. of Perspective Planning and Foreign Relations, Food Industry Dept, Ministry of Agric. 1990–94; Amb. to Poland 1994–2000, to Romania (also accred to Bulgaria) 1996–2000; mem. Seimas (New Union party) 2004–08, mem. Cttee on State Admin and Local Authorities 2004–08, Cttee on European Affairs 2006–08; Minister of Foreign Affairs 2000–06; Amb. to Latvia 2008–11; Hon. Chair. North Atlantic Council 2005–06; Commdr's Cross of Order of Lithuanian Grand Duke Gediminas, Three-star Order of Repub. of Latvia, Chevalier de la Légion d'honeur, Grand Cross of Infante Dom Henriques (Portugal), Commdr's Cross with Star of Order of Merit (Poland), Commemorative Badge for Personal Input in the Development of Trans-Atlantic Relations and on the Occasion of Invitation of Lithuania to join NATO. *Publications:* numerous articles in nat and int press. *Leisure interests:* literature, traditional jazz, swing, rock 'n' roll 1950s–70s, classical music. *Address:* c/o Embassy of Lithuania, Rūpniecibas iela 24, Rīga 1010, Latvia (office).

VALIYEV, Kamil Akhmedovich; Russian/Tatar physicist; b. 15 Jan. 1931, Verkhny Shendar, Tatarstan; m.; two c.; ed Kazan State Univ.; Sr Teacher, then

Head of Lab. Kazan State Pedagogical Inst.; Dir Research Inst. of Molecular Physics; Head of Sector Ledebev Inst. of Physics 1977–83; Dir Inst. of Physics and Tech. (FTIAN), Russian Acad. of Sciences 1988–2005; mem. Russian Acad. of Sciences 1984, Presidium Tatarstan Acad. of Sciences; Ed.-in-Chief Russian Microelectronics (Mikroelektronika); Order of October Revolution, Order of Labour Red Banner; Lenin Prize, State Prize of Azerbaijan. *Publications include:* Microelectronics: Achievements and Ways of Development 1986, Physics of Submicronic Lithography 1990. *Leisure interests:* chess, photography. *Address:* c/o Institute of Physics and Technology, Russian Academy of Sciences, 117218 Moscow, 36/1 Nakhimovskii pr., Russia (office).

VALL, Col Ely Ould Mohamed; Mauritanian government official; b. 1952, Nouakchott; ed coll. and lycée in Aix-en-Provence and Le Mans, France, Mil. Acad. of Meknès; served in mil. campaign on border with Western Sahara 1970s, Commdr mil. stations of Bir-Mogreïn, Ouadane and Aïn-Benteli, Compagnie du Quartier Général, l'Etat-Major Nat. 1979–81, Seventh Mil. Area of Rosso 1982–83, Sixth Mil. Area of Nouakchott 1983–85; Dir Sûreté Nationale (nat. police force) 1985–2005; proclaimed as Pres. Mil. Council for Justice and Democracy (i.e. Pres. of Mauritania) following overthrow of Pres. Maaouya Ould Taya in a coup 2005–07; numerous decorations. *Address:* c/o Office of the President of the Military Council for Justice and Democracy, BP 184, Nouakchott, Mauritania (office).

VALLANCE OF TUMMEL, Baron (Life Peer), cr. 2004, of Tummel in Perth and Kinross; **Iain David Thomas Vallance,** BA, MSc; British business executive; *Chairman, Royal Conservatoire of Scotland;* b. 20 May 1943, London, England; s. of Edmund Thomas Vallance and Janet Wright Bell Ross Davidson; m. Elizabeth Mary McGonnigill 1967; one s. one d.; ed Edinburgh Acad., Dulwich Coll., Glasgow Acad., Brasenose Coll. Oxford, London Grad. School of Business Studies; Asst Postal Controller, Post Office 1966, Personal Asst to Chair. 1973–75, Head of Finance Planning Div. 1975–76, Dir Cen. Finance 1976–78, Telecommunications Finance 1978–79, Materials Dept 1979–81; mem. Bd for Org. and Business Systems, British Telecommunications (BT) 1981–83, Man. Dir, Local Communications Services Div. 1983–85, Chief of Operations 1985–86, Chief Exec. 1986–95, Chair. 1987–2001, Pres. Emer. 2001–02; Vice-Chair. Royal Bank of Scotland 1994–2005; Liberal Democrat Spokesperson for Trade and Industry/Business, Enterprise and Regulatory Reform, House of Lords 2005–, mem. Select Cttee on Econ. Affairs 2005–08 (Chair. 2008–10), Select Cttee on European Union (Sub-Cttee A) 2010–; Chair. Royal Conservatoire of Scotland (fmrly Royal Scottish Acad. of Music and Drama) 2006–; Founding mem. Pres.'s Cttee of European Foundation for Quality Man. 1988; mem. CBI Pres.'s Cttee, Pres. CBI 2000–02; mem. Advisory Council of Business in the Community, Allianz Int. Advisory Bd, Advisory Council of Prince's Youth Business Trust 1988–2001, Advisory Bd British-American Chamber of Commerce 1991–2001, Supervisory Bd Siemens AG 2002–; Chair. European Services Forum 2002–08; Vice-Chair. European Advisory Cttee to New York Stock Exchange, Chair. 2000–02; Vice-Pres. The Princess Royal Trust for Carers; fmr mem. Bd Scottish Enterprise, Mobil Corpn; Trustee Monteverdi Trust; Fellow, London Business School 1989, Chartered Inst. of Bankers in Scotland; Liveryman of Worshipful Co. of Wheelwrights; Freeman of the City of London; Hon. Fellow, Brasenose Coll.; Hon. Gov. Glasgow Acad. 1993–; Hon. DSc (Ulster) 1992, (Napier) 1994; Hon. DTech (Loughborough) 1992, (Robert Gordon) 1994; Hon. DBA (Kingston) 1993; Hon. DEng (Heriot-Watt) 1995; Hon. DSc (City Univ.) 1996. *Leisure interests:* walking, playing the piano, listening to music. *Address:* House of Lords, Westminster, London, SW1A 0PW, England (office); Royal Conservatoire of Scotland, 100 Renfrew Street, Glasgow, G2 3DB, Scotland. *Telephone:* (20) 7219-2715 (Westminster) (office). *Website:* www.parliament.uk/biographies/lords/iain-vallance/32277 (office); www.rcs.ac.uk.

VALLARINO BARTUANO, Arturo Ulises, BSc, DJurSc; Panamanian lawyer and politician; b. 15 Dec. 1943, Capiro Dist, Panamá; s. of Ismael Vallarino and María Concepción Bartuano; m. Elka Aparicio de Vallarino; five c.; ed Univ. of Panama, Universidad Nacional Autónoma de México, Univ. of Costa Rica; Legal Adviser, Ministry of Foreign Affairs 1966; elected Councillor for Panamá Dist 1968; lawyer, Carillo, Villalaz & Muñoz (law firm); Sr Pnr, Bufete, Vallarino y Asociados –1999; fmr Prof. of Political Science and Commercial Law Univ. of Panama; fmr Chargé d'affaires for Business, Argentina; fmr Legal Adviser Ministry of Planning and Econ. Politics, Nat. Banking Comm.; fmr Pres. Legis. Ass.; mem. Partido Movimiento Liberal Republicano Nacionalista (MOLIRENA), Sec.-Gen. –2003; First Vice-Pres. of Panama 1999–2003 (retd). *Address:* Movimiento Liberal Republicano Nacionalista, Calle 66 (Calle Belén), Casa Duplex 46-A, Corregimiento de San Francisco, Panamá, Panama. *Telephone:* 399-5280. *Fax:* 399-5288.

VALLARINO CLEMENT, Alberto, BS, MBA; Panamanian business executive and fmr politician; *President, Grupo Verdeazul SA;* b. 2 April 1951, Panamá City; s. of Alberto Vallarino Céspedes and Marta Estela Clement Linares; m. Adriana Lewis Morgan 1981; one s. two d.; ed Colegio La Salle, Cornell Univ., USA; began career at Citibank NA 1974; Man. Dir Industria Nacional de Plásticos SA 1975–88; Exec. Vice-Pres. Metalforma SA 1979–88; Exec. Vice-Pres. Banco del Istmo 1988, later becoming CEO; fmr mem. Partido Arnulfista; unsuccessful cand. in presidential election 1999; Minister of Economy and Finance 2009–11 (resgnd); Pres. Grupo Verdeazul, SA 2011–; Pres. Fundación por un Mejor Panamá; Founder Vitalicio del Instituto de Competitividad Juvenil de COSPAE; mem. Bd of Dirs Panama Canal Authority 2013–, Asociación Nacional de la Naturaleza; mem. Sindicato de Industriales de Panamá (Pres. 1981–82), Asociación de Industriales Latinoamericanos, Venezuela (Pres. 1981), Asociación Panameña de Exportadores (Pres. 1983);*Website:* www.grupoverdeazul.com (office).

VALLAUD-BELKACEM, Najat; French politician; *Minister of Women's Rights, Youth and Sports;* b. (Najat Belkacem), 4 Oct. 1977, Bni Chiker village, nr Nador, Morocco; m. Boris Vallaud 2005; ed Institut d'études politiques de Paris; grew up in suburbs of Amiens from 1982; mem. Socialist Party (Parti solocaliste—PS) 2002–, joined team of Gérard Collomb, Senator/Mayor of Lyon 2003; elected to Regional Council of Rhône-Alpes 2004, presides over Culture Comm.; adviser to the PS 2005–; columnist for cultural programme C'est tout vu on Télé Lyon Municipale alongside Stéphane Cayrol 2005, 2006; joined Ségolène Royal's campaign team as a spokesperson during the 2007 French Gen. Election 2007; Conseillère Générale for Rhône 2008–; Deputy Mayor of Lyon, responsible for major events, youth and community life 2008–; Minister of Women's Rights and Spokesperson for the Govt

2012–14, Minister of Women's Rights, Youth and Sports 2014–. *Address:* Department for Women's Rights, Ministry for Social Affairs and Health, 72 rue de Varenne, 75007 Paris (office); Mairie de Lyon, 1 place de la Comédie, 69205 Lyon Cedex 01, France. *Telephone:* (4) 72-10-30-30 (Lyon). *E-mail:* info@solidarite .gouv.fr (office). *Website:* www.solidarite.gouv.fr/espaces,770/droits-des -femmes,772 (office); lyon.fr.

VALLEE, Rodolphe M. (Skip), BS, MBA; American business executive, politician and fmr diplomatist; *Chairman and CEO, R. L. Vallee, Inc.;* b. 1960, St Albans, Vt; s. of Rod Vallee and Betty Vallee; m. Denise Vallee; two s.; ed Williams Coll., Massachusetts, Wharton School, Univ. of Pennsylvania; worked in exec. positions for several cos involved in devt and operation of refuse, biomass, hydro and other renewable energy facilities; Devt Prin., Catalyst Energy Corpn 1986–87, Vice-Pres. Catalyst Waste-to-Energy Corpn 1987–88; f. R. L. Vallee Inc. 1989, Chair. and CEO 1992–2005, 2007–; Lead Dir MSCI Inc. 2008–; mem. Bd Dirs MSCI, Inc. 2008–; began his political career in 1982 as regional campaign man. for US Senator Robert T. Stafford and later served as staff asst of Senate Sub-cttee on Educ.; apptd to Advisory Cttee for Trade Policy and Negotiation 2001; mem. Republican Nat. Cttee 1999–2004; Chair. Vt Del. to Republican Nat. Convention 2004; Amb. to Slovakia 2005–07; fmr Dir Mater Christi School; fmr Trustee, Nature Conservancy of Vt. *Leisure interests:* skiing, hunting, fishing, soccer. *Address:* R. L. Vallee, Inc., 280 South Main Street, Saint Albans, VT 05478-1866, USA (office). *Telephone:* (802) 524-8710 (office). *Fax:* (802) 524-8714 (office). *E-mail:* SkipV@rlvallee.com (office); contactus@rlvallee.com (office). *Website:* www .rlvallee.com (office).

VALLEE, Roy A.; American business executive; *Deputy Chairman, Federal Reserve Bank of San Francisco;* joined Avnet 1977, Pres. Hamilton/Avnet Computer 1989–90, Sr Vice-Pres. and Dir Worldwide Electronics Operations for Avnet 1990, mem. Bd of Dirs 1991–2012, Pres. and COO 1992–98, Chair. and CEO 1998–2011, Exec. Chair. 2011–12; Founding mem. Gov. of Arizona's Council on Innovation and Tech. 2008–; mem. Bd Arizona Econ. Resource Org.; mem. Exec. Cttee Arizona Commerce Authority 2009–11; named to Twelfth Dist Econ. Advisory Council for Federal Reserve Bank of San Francisco 2010–12, Deputy Chair. Federal Reserve Bank of San Francisco 2013–; mem. Bd of Dirs Teradyne, Synopsys, Inc.; mem. Greater Phoenix Leadership; inducted into CRN Industry Hall of Fame, Gail S. Carter Award, Nat. Electronic Distributors Asscn 2008, Lifetime Achievement Award, Phoenix Business Journal 2011, OneNeck IT Services People's Choice Lifetime Achievement Award 2011. *Leisure interests:* spending time with family, golf, tennis, hiking. *Address:* Federal Reserve Bank of San Francisco, PO Box 7702, San Francisco, CA 94120-7702 (office); Federal Reserve Bank of San Francisco, 101 Market Street, San Francisco, CA 94105, USA (office). *Telephone:* (415) 974-2000 (office). *E-mail:* info@frbsf.org (office). *Website:* ww.frbsf.org (office).

VALLINI, HE Cardinal Agostino, LTh, DCL, DCL; Italian ecclesiastic and academic; *Vicar General of Rome;* b. 17 April 1940, Poli; ed Major Archiepiscopal Seminary of Naples, Theological Faculty of Southern Italy (San Tommaso d'Aquino campus), Pontifical Lateran Univ., Rome; moved with family to Barra, nr Naples, as a child; ordained priest, Archdiocese of Naples 1964; taught canon law at Theological Faculty of Southern Italy; taught ecclesiastical law at Pontifical Lateran Univ. 1971–78; also served as adviser for Italian Catholic Univ. Fed., the movement Seguimi and Union of Major Religious Superiors of Italy; later became Rector of Major Archiepiscopal Seminary of Naples and Regional Counsellor of Catholic Action; Rector Major Archiepiscopal Seminary of Naples 1978–87; Dean of San Tommaso d'Aquino campus, Theological Faculty of Southern Italy 1987–89; apptd Titular Bishop of Tortibulum 1989; Auxiliary Bishop of Naples 1989–99; Bishop of Albano 1999–2004; Prefect of the Apostolic Signatura 2004–05, 2005–08; cr. Cardinal (Cardinal-Deacon of San Pier Damiani ai Monti di San Paolo) 2006, (Cardinal-Priest of San Pier Damiani ai Monti di San Paolo) 2009; Vicar Gen. of His Holiness for Diocese of Rome 2008–; Archpriest of Arcibasilica di San Giovanni in Laterano (St John Lateran Basilica) 2008–; Grand Chancellor, Pontifical Lateran Univ. 2008–; mem. Congregation for Causes of Saints, Congregation for Bishops, Congregation for Insts of Consecrated Life and Socs of Apostolic Life, Congregation for Evangelization of Peoples, Pontifical Council for Legis. Texts, Admin of the Patrimony of Apostolic See, Council of Cardinals for Study of Organizational and Econ. Affairs of the Holy See; named as a Synod Father of 13th Ordinary Gen. Ass. of the Synod of Bishops on New Evangelization 2012; Cavaliere di Gran Croce, Ordine al Merito della Repubblica Italiana 2008. *Address:* Diocese di Roma, Piazza San Giovanni in Laterano 6/A, 00184 Rome, Italy (office). *Telephone:* (06) 69886207 (office); (06) 69886330 (office). *Fax:* (06) 69886528 (office). *E-mail:* SegreteriaGenerale@VicariatusUrbis.org (office). *Website:* www .vicariatusurbis.org (office).

VALLS, Manuel; French politician and author; *Prime Minister;* b. 13 Aug. 1962, Barcelona, Spain; s. of Xavier Valls and Luisangela Galfetti; m. Anne Gravoin; four c.; ed Univ. of Paris I; joined Parti Socialiste (Socialist Party) 1980; fmr Moderator, Unef-ID (French student union); naturalized French citizen 1982; Parl. Attaché to Deputy Robert Chapuis 1983–86; elected to local council of Ile-de-France 1986, First Vice-Pres. 1998–2002; apptd consultant for student affairs to Prime Minister Michel Rocard 1988–91; Deputy Interdepartmental Asst, Winter Olympics, Albertville 1991–93; Nat. Sec. Socialist Party, in charge of press and communication in cabinet of Lionel Jospin 1995–97; unsuccessful cand. for Nat. Ass. 1997–2001; Mayor of Évry, Essonne 2001–12; Deputy (PS) to Nat. Ass. from 1st Dist of Essonne 2002–, mem. Comm. des affaires culturelles; Minister of the Interior 2012–14; Prime Minister 2014–; apptd Pres. Community of Agglomeration of Évry-Centre-Essonne 2008. *Publications include:* Les habits neufs de la gauche 2006, La laïcité en face, a dialog with Virginie Malabard 2005, Pour en finir avec le vieux socialisme. . . et être enfin de gauche, a dialog with Claude Askolovitch 2008, Pouvoir 2010. *Leisure interest:* supporter of FC Barcelona. *Address:* Office of the Prime Minister, Hôtel de Matignon, 57 rue de Varenne, 75700 Paris SP 07 (office); Assemblée nationale, 126 rue de l'Université, 75355 Paris 07 SP, France (office). *Telephone:* 1-42-75-80-00 (office). *Fax:* 1-42-75-78-31 (office). *E-mail:* webmestre@ assemblee-nationale.fr (office). *Website:* www.gouvernement.fr (office); www .assemblee-nationale.fr/12/tribun/fiches_id/267622.asp (office); www.valls.fr; www .evry.fr (office).

VALTINOS, Thanassis; Greek writer; b. 16 Dec. 1932, Karatoula Kynourias; m.; one d.; ed Athens Univ.; Visiting Prof., War Research Inst., Frankfurt 1993–; Pres. Hellenic Authors Soc. 1990–94, 2005–09; mem. European Acad. of Sciences and Arts, Int. Inst. of Theatre, Greek Soc. of Playwrights; mem. Greek Acad. 2008; Scenario Award Cannes Festival 1984, Cavafy Prize 2001, Acad. of Athens Petros Haris Prize for lifetime achievement 2002, Gold Cross of Honour of the Pres. of the Greek Democracy 2003. *Publications include:* The Descent of the Nine 1963, The Book of Andreas Kordopatis 1964, Voyage to Kythira (film script) 1984, Data from the Decade of the Sixties (Nat. Book Award for Best Novel 1990) 2000, Accoutumance à la nicotine 2008. *Address:* Hellenic Authors Society, Kodrigtonos 8, 112 57 Athens (office); 66 Astidamantos Street, 116 34 Athens, Greece (home). *Telephone:* (210) 8231890 (office); (210) 7218793 (home). *Fax:* (210) 8232543 (office). *E-mail:* gwrisoc@otenet.gr (office). *Website:* www.dedalus.gr (office).

VALZANIA, Sergio; Italian television journalist, author and broadcasting executive; *Deputy Director, Radio Rai, Radiotelevisione Italiana SpA (RAI);* b. 2 April 1951, Florence; ed Univ. of Florence; Dir Radio 2, Radiotelevisione Italiana SpA (RAI) 1999–2002, Dir RAI 2 and RAI 3 2002–09, Deputy Dir, Radio Rai 2009–13. *Television productions include:* Dadaumpa 1984–86, La clessidra, filosofi a confronto 1985, La macchina del tempo 1985–86, La TV delle ragazze 1988–89, Bambini 1989–90 (all for RAI 3), Viva Radio 2 2001–08, Alle 8 della Sera 2004–13, radio pilgrimages (La Via Lattea 2004, La Via Francigena 2005, La Via di Paolo e Giovanni 2006, La Via di Sigerico 2007, Il Cammino 2008, La Serenissima 2009, La Via di Olaf 2010, La via della Plata 2011, Da Roma a Gerusalemme 2012). *Publications:* Brodo nero. Sparta pacifica, il suo esercito, le sue guerre 1999, Napoleone 2001, Retorica della guerra. Quando la violenza sostituisce la parola 2002, Una radio strutturalista. Consigli per ascoltare e trasmettere 2002, Tre tartarughe greche 2002, Jutland. 31 maggio 1916: la più grande battaglia navale della storia 2006, Sparta e Atene. Il racconto di una guerra 2006, Austerlitz. La più grande vittoria di Napoleone 2006, Wallenstein. La tragedia di un generale nella guerra dei Trent'anni 2007, La morte dei dinosauri 2007, Le La città degli uomini. Cinque riflessioni in un mondo che cambia (with Fausto Bertinotti) 2007, Le radici perdute dell'Europa. Da Carlo V ai conflitti mondiali (with Franco Cardini) 2007, Amare il vino. Arte natura tecnica estetica (with Luca Maroni) 2007, La Via Lattea (with Piergiorgio Odifreddi) 2008, La Via Maestra (with Lorenzo Sganzini) 2009, Dal profondo. Posso scrivere di Cristo solo narrando la mia esperienza) 2010, U-Boot. Storie di uomini e di sommergibili nella seconda guerra mondiale) 2011 Napoleone 2011, Fare la pace. Vincitori e vinti in Europa 2011, La bolla d'oro 2012, I dieci errori di Napoleone. Sconfitte, cadute e illusioni dell'uomo che voleva cambiare la storia 2012, Invano veglia la sentinella 2013, U-Boot. Storie di uomini e di sommergibili nella seconda guerra mondiale 2014. *Address:* Direction Radio Rai, Radiotelevisione Italiana SpA, Via Asiago 10, 00195 Rome, Italy (office). *Telephone:* (06) 37352741 (office). *Fax:* (06) 3219215 (office). *E-mail:* valzania@rai .it (office). *Website:* www.rai.it (office).

VÁMOS, Éva, PhD Habil.; Hungarian museologist; *Senior Researcher, Hungarian Museum for Science, Technology and Transport (Magyar Műszaki és Közlekedési Múzeum);* b. 22 May 1950, Budapest; d. of Endre Vámos and Lilly Vámos (née Vigyázó); ed Eötvös Loránd Univ. of Budapest, Tech. Univ. of Budapest; affiliated to Hungarian Museum for Science, Tech. and Transport (Magyar Műszaki és Közlekedési Múzeum) 1973–, Curator 1973–78, Scientific Co-worker 1978–86, Head, Ind. Group of History of Science, Scientific Sec. in charge of Public Relations 1986–87, Sr Scientific Co-worker 1987–89, Head of Dept 1989–91, Scientific Deputy Dir-Gen. 1991–93, Dir-Gen. 1994–2004, Sr Researcher 2004–; Memorial Medal, Fed. of Scientific and Tech. Asscns 1997, Justus von Liebig Memorial Medal 2000. *Publications:* Chapters from the History of Communication 1979, History of Writing and Writing Utensils 1980–82, Creative Hungarians 1988, German-Hungarian Relations in the Fields of Science with Special Regard to Chemistry, Chemical Industry and Food Industry 1876–1914 1995, László József Bíró 1996, Women's Opportunities of Studying and Practising Engineering in Hungary 1998, Justus von Liebigs Hungarian Connections by Correspondence 2003, Memorial Sights of Chemistry at Budapest Universities 2007. *Leisure interests:* univ. women's movt, gardening, classical music. *Address:* Hungarian Museum for Science, Technology and Transport, 1114 Budapest, Városligeti Krt 14 (office); 1015 Budapest, Batthyány u. 3. VI. 32, Hungary (home). *Telephone:* (1) 338-06-22 (family, speaks English) (office); (1) 204-40-95 (office); (1) 541-26-74 (office); (1) 201-73-17 (home). *Fax:* (1) 204-40-88 (office). *E-mail:* vamos.endrene@ chello.hu (office); evamos@mkmm.hu (office); vamos.eva@chello.hu (home). *Website:* www.omm.hu (office); mtesz.hu.

VÁMOS, Tibor, PhD, DSc; Hungarian research professor; *Chairman, Computer and Automation Research Institute, Hungarian Academy of Sciences;* b. 1 June 1926, Budapest; s. of Miklós Vámos and Ilona Rausnitz; m. Noémi Stenczer; one s.; ed Tech. Univ. Budapest; started in process control automation of power plants and systems, worked later in computer control of processes, robot vision, artificial intelligence; Chief Engineer, Research Inst. of Power System Eng Co. 1950–54, Automation Dept Head 1954–64; Dir Computer and Automation Research Inst., Hungarian Acad. of Sciences 1964–85, Chair. 1986–; Prof. Budapest Tech. Univ. 1969–; Distinguished Visiting Prof., George Mason Univ. 1992–93, Distinguished Affiliate Prof. 1993–94; Corresp. mem. Hungarian Acad. of Sciences 1973, mem. 1979, mem. Governing Bd 1980–; Pres. Int. Fed. of Automatic Control (IFAC) 1981–84, IFAC Lifetime Advisor 1987–; mem. Editorial Bd four int. scientific journals; mem. European Coordinating Cttee for Artificial Intelligence 2004–, Fellow 2006–; chair. and bd mem. of philanthropic foundations; Fellow, IEEE Inc. 1986–, IFAC 2006–; Hon. mem. Austrian Computer Soc. 1992, Austrian Soc. for Cybernetic Studies 1994; Hon. Pres. John v. Neumann Soc. of Computer Science 1986–; Order of Hungarian Repub. 1996; Dr hc (Tallinn Univ.); State Prize 1983, Chorafas Prize, Swiss Acads 1994, World Automation Congress Dedication 2006, Széchenyi Prize, Govt of Hungary 2008. *Publications:* Nagy ipari folyamatok irányítása (Control of Large-Scale Processes) 1970, Computer Epistemology 1991; co-author: Applications of Syntactic Pattern Recognition 1977, Progress in Pattern Recognition 1981, Hand Book of Applied Expert Systems 1997, Handbook of Automation 2009, Knowledge and Computing – A Course on Computer Epistemology 2010; co-ed.: The Neumann Compendium 1995; 130 contribs to scientific journals and 170 to other publs. *Leisure interests:* fine arts, mountaineering. *Address:* Lágymányosi u. 11, 1111 Budapest, Hungary (office). *Telephone:*

(1) 209-5274 (office); (1) 320-3657 (home). *Fax:* (1) 209-5275 (office). *E-mail:* vamos@sztaki.hu (office). *Website:* www.sztaki.hu/~vamos (office).

VAN AARTSEN, Jozias Johannes, LLB; Dutch politician; *Mayor, The Hague;* b. 25 Dec. 1947, The Hague; m. Henriëtte Warsen; three c.; ed Amsterdam Free Univ.; Supervisory Dir Govt Computer Centre and Printing Office; Ed. Liberal Reveille; worked for Parl. People's Party for Freedom and Democracy (VVD) 1970–74, Dir VVD Research Org. 1974–79; staff mem. Sec.-Gen.'s Office, Minister of the Interior 1979–83, Deputy Sec.-Gen. 1983–85, Sec.-Gen. 1985–94, Chair. Council of Bd of Sec.-Gens 1994; Minister of Agric., Nature Man. and Fisheries 1994–98, of Foreign Affairs 1998–2002; Leader VVD Parl. Group 2003–06; worked with EC as coordinator of EU project to lay gas pipeline from Turkey to Austria 2006; Mayor, The Hague 2008–; fmr mem. Bd Expertise Centre for Employment among Minorities; fmr Chair. Bd Nat. Inst. for Arts Educ. *Address:* City Hall (Atrium), Spui 70, 2500 DP, The Hague, Netherlands (office). *Telephone:* (70) 3535043 (office). *Website:* www.denhaag.com (office).

VAN AGT, Andries (Dries) A. M.; Dutch international organization official and fmr politician; *Prime Counsellor, International Forum for Justice and Peace;* b. 2 Feb. 1931, Geldrop; s. of Frans van Agt and Anna Frencken; m. Eugenie Krekelberg 1958; one s. two d.; ed Catholic Univ., Nijmegen; worked at Ministry of Agric. and Fisheries, then Ministry of Justice 1958–68; Prof. of Penal Law, Univ. of Nijmegen 1968–; Minister of Justice 1971–77; Deputy Prime Minister 1973–77; Prime Minister and Minister of Gen. Affairs 1977–82; Minister of Foreign Affairs 1982; mem. Parl. 1983; Gov. Prov. of Noord-Brabant 1983–87; Amb., Head Del. of European Communities, Tokyo 1987, later Washington, DC –1995; currently Prime Counselor, Int. Forum for Justice and Peace. *Address:* International Forum for Justice and Peace, PO Box 225, Hoevelaken 3870 CE, Netherlands (office). *Telephone:* (33) 2580355 (office). *Fax:* (33) 2580874 (office).

VAN ASSCHE, Kris; Belgian fashion designer; *Artistic Director, Dior Homme;* b. 1976; ed Antwerp Royal Acad. of Fine Arts; moved to Paris in 1998; worked with Hedi Slimane at Yves Saint Laurent and then for Dior Homme; began to show original creations in 2005; f. own label, Kris Van Assche; Artistic Dir, Dior Homme 2007–. *Address:* August H, Hôtel de Retz, 9 rue Charlot, 75003 Paris, France (office). *Telephone:* 1-48-04-52-42 (office). *Fax:* 1-48-04-03-65 (office). *E-mail:* info@ krisvanassche.com (office). *Website:* www.krisvanassche.com (office); www .diorhomme.com (office).

VAN BASTEN, Marcel (Marco); Dutch professional football manager and fmr professional footballer; b. 31 Oct. 1964, Utrecht; m. Elizabeth Van Basten 1992; one s. two d.; striker; youth player, Ajax 1981–82; sr player, Ajax 1982–97 (133 appearances, 128 goals, won UEFA Cup Winners' Cup 1987, Dutch Championship 1981/82, 1982/83, 1984/85, Dutch Cup 1983, 1986, 1987), AC Milan 1987–93 (147 appearances, 90 goals, won European Cup 1989, 1990, Intercontinental Cup 1989, 1990, European Supercup 1989, 1990, Serie A 1987/88, 1991/92, 1992/93, Italian Super Cup 1988, 1992, 1993); mem. Netherlands U-21 team 1981, Netherlands nat. team 1983–92 (58 caps, 24 goals, won UEFA European Championship 1988, Nasazzi's Baton 1985); Coach Jong Ajax 2003–04, AFC Ajax 2008–09; Head Coach of Dutch nat. team 2004–08; European Silver Boot 1983–84, Dutch League Top Scorer 1983–84, 1984–85, 1985–86, 1986–87, Dutch Footballer of the Year 1984–85, European Golden Boot 1985–86, World Golden Boot 1985–86, Bravo Award 1987, Onze d'Argent 1987, 1992, Serie A Silver Top Scorer 1988–89, Ballon d'Or (European Footballer of the Year) 1988, 1989, 1992, UEFA European Championship Top Scorer and Best Player with 5 goals 1988, World Soccer Player of the Year 1988, 1992, Onze d'Or 1988, 1989, IFFHS Best Player of the Year 1988, 1989, 1990, Serie A Top Scorer 1989–90, 1991–92, UEFA Best Player of the Year 1989, 1990, 1992, European Cup Top Scorer 1989, FIFA World Player of the Year 1992, European Cup Silver Top Scorer 1993, named in FIFA 100 (list of greatest living footballers picked by Pelé) 2004. *Leisure interest:* golf. *Address:* c/o AFC Ajax, Arena Boulevard 29, 1101 AX Amsterdam, The Netherlands. *Telephone:* (20) 311-14-44. *Fax:* (20) 311-16-75. *E-mail:* info@ajax.nl. *Website:* www.ajax.nl.

VAN BENTHEM, Johannes F. A. K., MA, PhD; Dutch logician and academic; *University Professor of Logic, University of Amsterdam;* b. (Johan van Benthem), 12 June 1949, Rijswijk; s. of A. K. van Benthem and J. M. G. Eggermont; m. Lida Blom 1977; two s.; ed Gravenhaags Christelijk Gymnasium and Univ. of Amsterdam; Asst Prof. of Philosophical Logic, Univ. of Amsterdam 1972–77, Chair. Dept of Philosophy 1974–75; Assoc. Prof. of Philosophical Logic, Univ. of Groningen 1977–86, Chair. Dept of Philosophy 1979–81; Prof. of Mathematical Logic, Univ. of Amsterdam 1986–2003, Univ. Prof. of Logic 2003–, Chair. Dept of Math. and Computer Science 1987–89, Scientific Dir Research Inst. for Logic, Language and Computation 1991–98; Chair. European Asscn of Logic, Language and Information 1991–96; Sr Researcher, Center for Study of Language and Information, Stanford Univ., USA 1991–, Bonsall Visiting Chair in the Humanities 1991–2003, Henry Waldgrave Stuart Prof. of Philosophy 2003–; Distinguished Foreign Expert, Chinese Ministry of Educ. 2010–12; Changjiang Nat. Prof., Tsinghua Univ., Beijing 2013–; Vice-Pres. Int. Fed. of Computational Logic 1999–; Chair. Netherlands Nat. Cognitive Science Programme 2001–03, Vienna Circle Foundation 1997–; Man. Ed. Logic and Computation, and other journals; Chair. Advisory Bd Synthese; mem. Academia Europaea, Royal Dutch Acad. of Sciences, Institut Int. de Philosophie, Hollandse Maatschappij van Wetenschappen; First Hon. Mem. European Asscn of Logic, Language and Information; Dr hc (Liège Univ.) 1998; Spinoza Prize, Netherlands Org. for Scientific Research 1996. *Publications:* The Logic of Time 1983, Modal Logic and Classical Logic 1985, Essays in Logical Semantics 1986, A Manual of Intensional Logic 1988, Language in Action, Categories, Lambdas and Dynamic Logic 1991, Exploring Logical Dynamics 1996, Modal Logic for Open Minds 2010, Logical Dynamics of Information and Interaction 2011, Logic in Games 2014; co-author of various textbooks in logic; (ed.) Handbook of Logic and Language 1997, Handbook of Modal Logic 2006, Handbook of Spatial Logics 2007, Handbook of the Philosophy of Information 2007; more than 350 articles in scientific journals. *Address:* Institute for Logic, Language and Computation, University of Amsterdam, PO Box 94242, 1090 GE Amsterdam, Netherlands (office). *Telephone:* (20) 5256051 (office). *Fax:* (20) 5255206 (office). *E-mail:* johan.vanbenthem@uva.nl (office); johan@stanford .edu (office). *Website:* staff.science.uva.nl/~johan (office).

VAN BERKEL, Ben (Bernard Franciscus), FRIBA; Dutch architect; *Principal Architect, UNStudio*; b. 25 Jan. 1957, Utrecht; s. of Magchiel van Berkel and Maria Therese Mattaar; m. Caroline Bos; one d.; ed Rietved Acad., Amsterdam, Architectural Asscn, London; graphic designer 1977–82; Co-founder and Prin. Architect, Van Berkel & Bos 1988–99, UNStudio 1999–; projects include: switching substation, Amersfoort 1989–93, Erasmus Bridge, Rotterdam 1990–96, Villa Wilbrink, Amersfoort 1992–94, Möbius House, 't Gooi 1993–98, Museum Het Valkhof, Nijmegen 1995–99, Masterplan station area, Arnhem 1996–, City Hall and Theatre, Ijsselstein 1996–2000, switching station, Innsbruck 1998–2001, Music Faculty, Graz 1998–, WTC 2001, Mercedes Benz Museum, Stuttgart; Eileen Gray Award 1983, British Council Fellowship 1986, Charlotte Köhler Prize 1991, winning entry for Police HQ, Berlin 1995, Museum Het Valkhof 1995, music theatre, Graz, Austria 1998, Kunstpreis, Frankfurt, Red Dot Award, Charles Jencks Award 2007, German Design Prize 2008, Red Dot Best of The Best, MYchair 2009, Hugo Haring Award 2009. *Address:* UNstudio, Stadhouderskade 113, 1073 AX Amsterdam, The Netherlands (office). *Telephone:* (20) 570-20-40 (office). *Fax:* (20) 570-20-41 (office). *E-mail:* info@unstudio.com (office). *Website:* www.unstudio.com (office).

VAN BOXMEER, Jean-François, MEcons; Belgian business executive; *Chairman of the Executive Board and CEO, Heineken NV*; b. 12 Sept. 1961, Elsene; ed Facultés Universitaires Notre Dame de la Paix S.J., Namur, Belgium; traineeship in production, sales and admin areas, Heineken Nederland, assignment in Cameroon 1984–87, Sales and Marketing Man., Heineken Bralima, Rwanda 1987–90, Democratic Repub. of Congo 1990–93, Gen. Man. 1993–96, Pres. and Gen. Man. Zywiec SA, Poland 1996–99, Vice-Pres. and Gen. Man. Grupa Zywiec SA, Poland 1999–2000, Gen. Man. Heineken Italia 2000–01, mem. Exec. Bd Heineken NV, The Netherlands 2001–, Chair. Exec. Bd and CEO 2005–; mem. Bd of Dirs Kraft Foods; mem. Advisory Bd Louvain School of Man., Louvain-la-Neuve; mem. Bd of Govs De Nederlandse Opera (The Dutch Opera). *Address:* Heineken NV, PO Box 28, 1000 AA Amsterdam (office); Heineken NV, Tweede Weteringplantsoen 21, 1017 ZD Amsterdam, The Netherlands (office). *Telephone:* (20) 523-92-39 (office). *Fax:* (20) 660-35-03 (office). *E-mail:* info@heinekeninternational.com (office). *Website:* www.heinekeninternational.com (office).

VAN BROECKHOVEN, Christine, BSc, MSc, PhD, DSc; Belgian research scientist and academic; *Professor, Director of the Department of Molecular Genetics and Group Leader of the Neurodegenerative Brain Diseases Group, University of Antwerp*; b. 9 April 1953, Antwerp; ed Univ. of Antwerp; competitive PhD Fellowship, IWT 1975–78; Post-doctoral Researcher, Prov. Inst. of Hygiene, Antwerp 1978–81; Research Assoc., Univ. of Antwerp 1983–89; Research Fellow, Nat. Research Foundation (NFWO) 1989–90; Research Dir, Lab. of Neurogenetics, Inst. Born-Bunge 1990–96; Assoc. Prof., Univ. of Antwerp 1995–96, Scientific Dir, Dept of Molecular Genetics, VIB 1996–2007, Group Leader, Neurogenetics, VIB 1996–97, Prof., Univ. of Antwerp 1997–99, Full Prof. 1999–, Sr Group Leader, Neurodegenerative Brain Diseases, VIB 2005–07, Dept Dir, Dept of Molecular Genetics, VIB 2007–; Distinguished Alzheimer Prof., Univ. of Leiden, The Netherlands 1996; Guest Scientist, Scripps Research Inst., USA 2001; Royal Grand Officer, Order of Léopold 2006; Chevalier, Légion d'honneur 2009; Divry Prize, Belgian Soc. of Neurology 1991, Potamkin Prize, American Acad. of Neurology (co-recipient) 1993, Joseph Maisin Scientific Prize, Nat. Fund for Scientific Research 1995, Marie-Thérèse De Lava Prize, King Boudewijn Foundation 1995, Upjohn Inc. Scientific Prize, NFSR (co-recipient) 1995, Belgian Coll. of Neuropsychopharmacology and Biological Psychiatry Lundbeck Prize (co-recipient) 1997, L'Oréal/UNESCO Special Honour Award for Women in Science 2002, 55th Ark Prize, Belgian Ark Cttee of the Free Word 2005, Zenith Award, Alzheimer Asscn (USA) 2005, L'Oréal-UNESCO Int. Award for Women in Science (Europe) 2006, Award Lecture in the Frontiers in Clinical Neuroscience, Plenary Session of American Acad. of Neurology Annual Meeting, Boston 2007. *Publications:* more than 560 articles in peer-reviewed int. scientific journals. *Telephone:* (476) 29-88-27 (office); (3) 265-11-02 (office). *Address:* VIB Department of Molecular Genetics, University of Antwerp – CDE, Universiteitsplein 1, Building V, Antwerp 2610, Belgium (office). *Fax:* (3) 265-11-12 (office). *E-mail:* christine.vanbroeckhoven@molgen.vib-ua.be (office). *Website:* www.molgen.ua.ac.be (office).

VAN CAENEGEM, Baron Raoul Charles; Belgian academic; *Professor Emeritus, University of Ghent*; b. 14 July 1927, Ghent; s. of Jozef Van Caenegem and Irma Barbaix; m. Patricia Carson 1954; two s. one d.; ed Univs of Ghent, Paris and London; Ordinary Prof., Univ. of Ghent 1964, Prof. Emer. 1992–; Visiting Fellow, Univ. Coll. Cambridge 1968; Goodhart Prof. of Legal Science, Univ. of Cambridge 1984–85; Visiting Fellow, Peterhouse, Cambridge 1984–85; Sir Henry Savile Fellow, Merton Coll. Oxford 1989; Fiftieth Anniversary Fellow, Univ. of Queensland, Australia 1990; Erasmus Lecturer on History and Civilization of the Netherlands, Harvard Univ. 1991; Dr hc (Tübingen) 1977, (Louvain) 1984, (Paris) 1988; Francqui Prize 1974; Solvay Prize, Nat. Fund for Scientific Research, Brussels 1990. *Publications include:* Royal Writs in England from the Conquest to Glanvill. Studies in the Early History of the Common Law 1959, The Birth of the English Common Law 1973, Guide to the Sources of Medieval History 1978, English Lawsuits from William I to Richard I (two vols) 1990–91, An Historical Introduction to Private Law 1992, Judges, Legislators and Professors: Chapters in European Legal History 1993, An Historical Introduction to Western Constitutional Law 1995, Introduction aux sources de l'histoire médiévale 1997, European Law in the Past and the Future: Unity and Diversity over Two Millennia 2002. *Leisure interests:* bridge, swimming, wine. *Address:* Veurestraat 47, 9051 Afsnee, Belgium (home). *Telephone:* (9) 264-68-53 (office); (9) 222-62-11 (home). *Fax:* (9) 264-67-07 (office). *E-mail:* karin.pensaert@ugent.be (office). *Website:* www.law.ugent.be (office). *Website:* www.rechtsgeschiedenis.be (office).

VAN CITTERS, Robert L., MD; American physiologist, cardiologist and academic; *Dean Emeritus, School of Medicine, University of Washington*; b. 20 Jan. 1926, Alton, Ia; s. of Charles J. Van Citters and Wilhelmina T. Van Citters; m. Mary E. Barker 1949; two s. two d.; ed Univ. of Kansas; Intern, Univ. of Kansas Medical Center 1953–54; Medical Officer, Air Research and Devt Command, Kirtland AFB, NM 1954–55; Resident, Internal Medicine, Univ. of Kansas Medical Center 1957–58; Research Fellow Cardiovascular Physiology, Univ. of Washington 1958–62; Research Assoc. Cardiopulmonary Inst., Scripps Clinic and Research Foundation, La Jolla, Calif. 1962; Exchange Scientist, Jt US–USSR Scientific Exchange Agreement 1962; Robert L. King Chair. of Cardiovascular Research 1963–; Asst Prof. of Physiology and Biophysics School of Medicine, Univ. of Washington 1963–65, Assoc. Prof. 1965–68, Assoc. Dean for Research and Grad. Programs 1968–70, Chair. Bd of Health Sciences 1970, Dean, School of Medicine 1970–81, Dean Emer. 1981–, Prof. of Medicine (Cardiology), Prof. of Physiology and Biophysics 1981–; mem. Inst. of Medicine, NAS; Hon. DSc (Northwestern Coll.) 1978. *Publications:* 150 publs in scientific journals. *Leisure interests:* fishing, gardening. *Address:* School of Medicine, University of Washington, Seattle, WA 98195, USA (office). *Telephone:* (425) 774-1770 (office). *Fax:* (206) 543-3639 (office). *E-mail:* vancitters@comcast.com (home). *Website:* www.uwmedicine.org (office).

VAN CREVELD, Martin L.; Israeli academic; *Professor of History, Hebrew University of Jerusalem*; b. 5 March 1946, Rotterdam; s. of L. van Creveld and M. van Creveld (née Wyler); two step c.; ed Hebrew Univ., London School of Econs; Lecturer, later Prof. in History, Hebrew Univ. of Jerusalem 1971–; Fellow, War Studies Dept, King's Coll. London 1975–76, von Humboldt Foundation, Freiburg 1980–81; Faculty mem. Nat. Defense Univ., Washington DC 1986–87; Prof., Marine Corps Univ., Quantico, Va 1991–92; Sr Fellow, Humboldt Foundation, Postdam 1999–2000; Fellow, Inst. for Contemporary Historical Research, Potsdam 2005–06; Best Book Award, Mil. History Inst. USA 1990. *Publications:* Supplying War 1977, Fighting Power 1987, Command in War 1985, Technology and War 1988, The Transformation of War 1991, The Rise and Decline of the State 1999, The Changing Face of War 2007, The Culture of War 2008, The Land of Blood and Honey: The Rise of Modern Israel 2010. *Leisure interests:* reading, walking. *Address:* Hebrew University of Jerusalem, Mount Scopus, 91 905 Jerusalem, Israel (office). *Telephone:* (2) 5883769 (office); (2) 5344923 (home). *Fax:* (2) 5881118 (office). *E-mail:* msmartin@tms.huji.ac.il.

VAN-CULIN, Rev. Canon Samuel, OBE, AB, DD; American ecclesiastic; *Canon Ecumenist, Washington National Cathedral*; b. 20 Sept. 1930, Honolulu, Hawaii; s. of Samuel Van-Culin and Susie Mossman; ed Princeton Univ. and Virginia Theological Seminary; Curate, St Andrew's Cathedral, Honolulu 1955–56; Canon Precentor and Rector Hawaiian Congregation, Honolulu 1956–58; Asst Rector St John's, Washington DC 1958–60; Gen. Sec. Lyman Int., Washington, DC 1960–61; Asst Sec., Overseas Dept, Exec. Council of the Episcopal Church USA 1962–68, Sec. for Africa and Middle East 1968–76, Exec. for World Mission 1976–83; Sec. Gen. Anglican Consultative Council 1983–94, Sec. to Lambeth Conf. 1988; Asst Priest, All Hallows Church, London 1995–; Canon Ecumenist, Washington Nat. Cathedral 2004–; Hon. Canon, Canterbury, Jerusalem, Honolulu, Ibadan and Cape Town; Hon. DD (Virginia Theological Seminary). *Leisure interests:* music and travel. *Address:* 3900 Watson Place, NW, 5D-B, Washington, DC 20016, USA (home). *Website:* www.cathedral.org.

VAN DAELE, Gen. August; Belgian army officer (retd); b. 25 Feb. 1944, Sint-Niklaas; ed Royal Cadet Training School, Royal Mil. Acad., Defence Coll.; tech. officer, Proficiency Training Centre, Brustem 1967–69; with Mobile Training Unit 1969–71; assigned as line man. Inspection and Tech. Acceptance Testing Service 1971; CO Air Maintenance Squadron, 10th Fighter-Bomber Wing, Kleine-Brogel 1980–83, CO Maintenance Group 1985–87; Deputy CO of Inspection and Tech. Acceptance Testing Service 1983–84, Head of Service 1987–88; Head of Equipment Inspection Service 1988–89, Inspection Service 1989–92, Aviation Equipment Section 1992–94; apptd Deputy Chief of Staff, Logistics, Air Force HQ 1994; Dir-Gen. for Material Resources, Defence Staff 2000–02; Chief of Defence Staff 2003–09; mem. NATO Mil. Cttee; Aide to the King of Belgium. *Address:* c/o Ministry of Defence, 8 rue Lambermont, 1000 Brussels, Belgium (office).

VAN DAM, José; Luxembourg singer (bass-baritone); b. 25 Aug. 1940, Brussels, Belgium; m.; ed Acad. de Musique, Brussels, Conservatoire Royal, Brussels; operatic debut as Don Basilio in The Barber of Seville, Liège; debut in Paris in Carmen (Escamillo) 1961, with Grand Théâtre, Geneva 1965–67, Deutsche Oper, Berlin 1967–, Salzburg Festival, opera and concerts 1966–, Festival d'Aix en Provence 1966–, operatic repertoire includes title roles in St-François d'Assise, Wozzeck, Simon Boccanegra, Elijah, Boris Gudunov, Falstaff, Don Giovanni, The Flying Dutchman, Gianni Schicchi, the Speaker in Die Zauberflöte, Fra Melitone in La Forza del Destino, Germont in La Traviata, the Father in Louise, Claudius in Hamlet, Sachs in Die Meistersinger von Nürnberg, Amfortas in Parsifal, Jochanaan in Salome, Mephisto in Faust, Scarpia in Tosca; recital repertoire includes Verdi's Requiem, La Damnation de Faust; winner, Bel Canto Competition, Liège, Concours Ecole des Vedettes, Paris, Concours de la Chanson, Toulouse, Int. Music Competition, Geneva, Grand Prix de l'Acad. Française du Disque 1979, Orphée d'Or, Académie Lyrique Française 1980, Prix Européen des Critiques 1985, Diapason d'Or, two Grammy Awards. *Address:* Colbert Artists Management, 111 West 57th Street, New York, NY 10019, USA (office). *Telephone:* (212) 757-0782 (office). *Fax:* (212) 541-5179 (office). *E-mail:* nycolbert@colbertartists.com (office). *Website:* www.colbertartists.com (office).

VAN DAMME, Jean-Claude; Belgian actor; b. 18 Oct. 1961, Brussels; m. 1st Gladys Portugues; m. 2nd Darcy LaPier 1994; one s. one d.; fmr European Professional Karate Asscn Middleweight Champion. *Films include:* Monaco Forever 1984, Rue barbare 1984, Breakin' 1984, No Retreat, No Surrender 1986, Bloodsport 1988, Black Eagle 1988, Cyborg 1989, Kickboxer 1989, Lionheart 1990, Death Warrant 1990, Double Impact 1991, Universal Soldier 1992, Nowhere to Run 1993, Hard Target 1993, Timecop 1994, Street Fighter 1994, Sudden Death 1995, The Quest 1996, Maximum Risk 1996, Double Team 1997, Knock Off 1998, Legionnaire 1998, Universal Soldier: The Return 1999, Coyote Moon 1999, The Order 2001, Replicant 2001, Derailed 2002, The Savage 2003, Narco 2004, Wake of Death 2004, Second in Command 2006, Sinav 2006, Until Death 2007, JCVD 2008, Universal Soldier: Regeneration 2009, The Eagle Path (also producer, dir and writer) 2010, Assassination Games 2012, The Expendables 2 2012, Univeral Soldier: Day of Reckoning 2012, 6 Bullets 2012. *Address:* United Talent Agency, Suite 500, 9560 Wilshire Boulevard, Beverly Hills, CA 90212, USA.

VAN DE KAA, Dirk Jan, PhD; Dutch demographer and academic; *Honorary Fellow, Netherlands Interdisciplinary Demographic Institute*; b. 5 Jan. 1933, Scherpenzeel; m. Anna Jacomina van Teunenbroek 1961; one s. one d.; ed Univ. of Utrecht, Australian Nat. Univ.; Dept Dir, Demographic Research Project, Western New Guinea 1961–66; Research Fellow, Dept of Demography, Research School of Social Sciences, Inst. for Advanced Studies, ANU, Canberra 1966–71; Dir

Netherlands Interdisciplinary Demographic Inst., The Hague 1971–87, Hon. Fellow 2003–; Project Dir World Fertility Survey, London 1981–82; Dir Int. Statistical Research Centre, The Hague 1982–84; Prof. of Demography, Univ. of Amsterdam 1977–98, currently Prof. Emer.; Dir Netherlands Inst. for Advanced Study, Wassenaar 1987–95; Vice-Pres. Netherlands Org. for Scientific Research, The Hague 1988–98; mem. Royal Netherlands Acad. of Arts and Sciences (Vice-Pres. 1984–87); Pres. European Asscn for Population Studies 1983–87, Hon. Pres. 1987–; Kt, Order of the Netherlands Lion 1991; Dr hc (Instytut Statystyki i Demografii, Warsaw School of Econs) 2003; Laureate, Int. Union for Scientific Study of Population 2001. *Publications include:* (author, co-author or ed.) Results of the Demographic Research Project Western New Guinea 1964–67, The Demography of Papua and New Guinea's Indigenous Population 1971, Science for Better and for Worse 1984, Population: Growth and Decline 1986, Europe's Second Demographic Transition 1987. *Address:* Netherlands Interdisciplinary Demographic Institute, PO Box 11650, 2502 AR The Hague (office); Van Hogenhoucklaan 63, 2596 TB The Hague, The Netherlands (home). *Telephone:* (70) 356-52-00 (office). *Fax:* (70) 364-71-87 (office). *E-mail:* vandekaa@nidi.nl (office). *Website:* www.nidi.nl (office).

VAN DE WALLE, Leslie; French business executive; *Chairman, Robert Walters;* b. 27 March 1956, Paris; s. of Philippe Van de Walle and Marie Lucette Van de Walle; m. Domitille Noel 1982; two d.; ed Hautes Etudes Commerciales; started career with Danone Group; Man. Dir Schweppes Benelux 1990–92, France and Benelux 1992–93, Spain and Portugal 1993–94; Snacks Div., United Biscuits Continental Europe 1994–95 (CEO 1996–97), CEO McVities Group 1998, United Biscuits Group 1999–2000; Pres. Shell Latin America and Africa 2000–03, Shell Europe Oil Products 2003–04, Exec. Vice-Pres. of Global Retail, Royal Dutch Shell Group 2004–06; CEO Rexam plc 2007–10 (retd); Chair. Robert Walters (recruitment consultancy) 2012–; mem. Bd of Dirs DCC plc 2010–, SIG plc 2010– (Chair. 2011–), Cape plc 2012–. *Leisure interests:* golf, travel. *Address:* Robert Walters, 11 Slingsby Place, St Martin's Courtyard, London, WC2E 9AB (office); 34 Rose Square, Fulham Road, London, SW3 6RS, England (home). *Telephone:* (20) 7584-1218 (home). *Fax:* (20) 7584-9339 (home). *Website:* www.robertwalters.com (office).

VAN DEN BERG, Dirk Jan; Dutch economist, diplomatist and university administrator; *President of the Executive Board, Delft University of Technology;* b. 1953; m. Frederike Mijnlieff; two c.; ed Univ. of Groningen, Ecole Nat. d'Admin, Paris, France; Policy Planner, Ministry of Econ. Affairs 1980–84; Head of Industrial Policy and Budget Div., Directorate-Gen. for Industry and Regional Policy 1987–88; Deputy Dir-Gen. for Foreign Econ. Relations, Head of Trade Policy Div., Directorate-Gen. for Foreign Econ. Relations 1989–92; Deputy Dir-Gen., Directorate-Gen. for Industry and Regional Policy 1992; Dir Public Finance Programme, Erasmus Univ., Rotterdam 1988–88; Sec.-Gen. Ministry of Foreign Affairs 1992–2001; Perm. Rep. to UN, New York 2001–05; Amb. to People's Repub. of China 2005–07; Pres. Exec. Bd Delft Univ. of Tech. 2008–; Pres. IDEA League 2008–09, Vice-Pres. for European Affairs 2010–; Govt Rep., Zuidas Amsterdam 2009–10, Chair. Consultative Cttee of Commissioning Parties 2010–12; mem. Advisory Bd Int. Visitors' Programme, Ministry of Foreign Affairs; Commr of Ziggo; mem. Peace and Justice Cttee, The Hague 2009, Int. Academic Advisory Panel, Ministry of Educ. in Singapore, Advisory Cttee, Wuhan (China), PolyU Int. Advisory Bd. *Leisure interests:* photography, computers, history, sailing, horse riding. *Address:* Executive Board, Delft University of Technology, Postbus 5, 2600 AA Delft, Netherlands (office). *Telephone:* (15) 2783786 (office). *E-mail:* d.j .vandenberg@tudelft.nl (office). *Website:* www.tudelft.nl/en/about-tu-delft/ organisation/executive-board (office).

VAN DEN BERGH, Maarten Albert; Dutch business executive; b. 19 April 1942, New York, USA; s. of Sidney James van den Bergh and Maria Mijers; m. Marjan Désirée; two d.; ed Univ. of Groningen; joined the Shell Group 1968, held various man. positions in the Far East and UK, Group Man. Dir Royal Dutch/Shell Group 1992, Dir of Finance 1994–98, Vice-Chair. Cttee of Man. Dirs and Pres. Royal Dutch Petroleum Co. 1998–2000, Dir Royal Dutch Shell 2000–09; Dir BT Group plc 2001–09, Deputy Chair. 2006–09; Deputy Chair. Lloyds TSB Group plc 2000–01, Chair. 2001–06; Chair. Akzo Nobel NV 2006–09; Dir British Airways PLC 2002–; mem. Steering Bd and Dutch Co-Chair. Apeldoorn Conf. 2003–09; Adviser to Chief Exec. of Hong Kong Special Admin. Region 1998–2002; mem. Int. Bd of Advisers to Pres. of Philippines 2001–05, Advisory Council Amsterdam Inst. of Finance 2001–05; Fellow and Vice-Pres. Inst. of Financial Services 2001–06; mem. Guild of Int. Bankers 2001–06; Companion Chartered Man. Inst. 2001. *Leisure interests:* European history.

VAN DEN BERGH, Sidney, OC, MSc, Dr rer. nat, FRS; Canadian (b. Dutch) astronomer; b. 20 May 1929, Wassenaar, The Netherlands; s. of Sidney J. van den Bergh and S. M. van den Bergh; m. 2nd (wife deceased); one s. two d.; m. 3rd Paulette Brown; ed Leiden Univ., The Netherlands, Princeton Univ. and Ohio State Univ., USA, Univ. of Göttingen, FRG; Asst Prof., Ohio State Univ. 1956–58; Prof., Univ. of Toronto, Canada 1958–77; Dir Dominion Astrophysical Observatory, Victoria 1977–86, Astronomer 1986–98, Researcher Emer. 1998–2011; Adjunct Prof., Univ. of Victoria 1978–2011; Pres. Canadian Astronomy Soc. 1990–92; Assoc. Royal Astronomical Soc.; Hon. DSc 1998, 2001; Killam Laureate 1990, NRC Pres.'s Medal, Henry Norris Russell Lecturer 1990, Bruce Gold Medal 2009, inducted into Canadian Science and Tech. Hall of Fame 2011. *Publications include:* about 820 scientific publs, including Galaxy Morphology and Classification 1998, The Galaxies of the Local Group 2000. *Leisure interests:* archaeology, history. *Address:* Dominion Astrophysical Observatory, 5071 West Saanich Road, Victoria, BC V9E 2E7 (office); 418 Lands End Road, Sidney, BC V8L 5L9, Canada (home). *Telephone:* (250) 363-0006 (office); (250) 656-6020 (home). *Fax:* (250) 363-0045 (office); (250) 363-0045 (office). *E-mail:* sidney.vandenbergh@nrc.ca (office); sidney.vandenbergh@nrc-cnrc.gc.ca (office). *Website:* www.nrc.ca (office).

VAN DEN BROEK, Hans; Dutch institution administrator and fmr politician; b. 11 Dec. 1936, Paris, France; m.; two d.; ed Alberdingk Thym Grammar School, Hilversum, Univ. of Utrecht; attended Sr Man. training, De Baak, Noordwijk; solicitor in Rotterdam 1965–68; Sec. Man. Bd ENKA BV, Arnhem 1969–73, Commercial Man., 1973–76; City Councillor, Rheden 1970–74; mem. Second Chamber, States-Gen. (Parl.) 1976–81; served on Standing Cttees on Foreign Affairs, Devt Co-operation and Justice; Sec. of State for Foreign Affairs 1981–82, Minister 1982–93; Commr for External Relations, Foreign and Security Policy

Enlargement Negotiations, Comm. of EC (now European Comm.) 1993–95, for External Relations with Cen. and Eastern Europe, fmr Soviet Union and others for Common Foreign and Security Policy and External Service 1995–99; fmr Pres. Netherlands Inst. of Int. Relations; Chair. Bd of Govs Radio Netherlands (Radio Nederland Wereldomroep); mem. Advisory Bd Global Panel Foundation. *Address:* c/o Radio Nederland Wereldomroep, Witte Kruislaan 55, Postbus 222, 1200 JG Hilversum, Netherlands (office). *E-mail:* letters@rnw.nl (office). *Website:* www .radionetherlands.nl (office).

VAN DEN HOOGENBAND, Pieter; Dutch swimmer; b. 14 March 1978, Maastricht; s. of Astrid van den Hoogenband; mem. PSV Eindhoven club; competed at Olympic Games 1996, 2000, 2004 winning seven medals (three gold, two silver and two bronze) including gold medals at 100m. freestyle, 2000, 2004 and 200m. freestyle (world record); 12 medals at World Championships (one gold, eight silver and three bronze); 28 medals at European Championships (16 gold, eight silver, four bronze). *Address:* House of Sports, Kerkstraat 45, 1191 JD Ouderkerk aan de Amstel, Netherlands. *Website:* www.pietervandenhoogenband .nl.

VAN DEN HOUT, Tjaco T., MA (Hons); Dutch lawyer, fmr diplomatist and international organization executive; b. 23 Jan. 1949, The Hague; m. Baiba Brae; ed Leiden Univ.; joined Foreign Service 1975; postings in Africa, Asia, New York; fmr Consul-Gen., Perm. Mission to UN; Deputy Sec.-Gen., Ministry of Foreign Affairs 1996–99; Sec.-Gen. Perm. Court of Arbitration, The Hague 1999–2008; Amb. to Thailand, Myanmar, Cambodia and Laos 2008–10; Kt Grand Cross (First Class), Order of the White Elephant (Thailand). *Address:* Rupniecibas iela 15/2, 2517 Riga 1010, Latvia (office). *E-mail:* tvandenhout@gmail.com (office). *Website:* www.tjacovandenhout.com (office).

VAN DEN WYNGAERT, Christine, PhD; Belgian judge and fmr singer; *Judge, Trial Division, International Criminal Court;* b. 2 April 1952, Antwerp; ed Free Univ., Brussels; alternative career as singer-songwriter, performing with (among others) Ferre Grignard and Wannes Van de Velde, and resulting in Long Play recording 1970s; Prof. of Criminal Law, Univ. of Antwerp 1985–; Visiting Fellow, Centre for European Legal Studies 1994–96, Research Centre for Int. Law, Univ. of Cambridge, UK 1996–97; Visiting Prof., Univ. of Stellenbosch, S Africa 2001; Judge, Int. Court of Justice in the Yerodia case 2000–02; Judge, Int. Criminal Tribunal for the Fmr Yugoslavia 2003–05, Perm. Judge 2005–09; Judge, Trial Div., ICC, The Hague 2009–; Dr hc (Uppsala) 2001, (Brussels) 2010; Henri Rolin Prize for PhD thesis 1980, Human Rights Prize, Liga voor Mensenrechten 2006. *Publications include:* Political Offence Exception to Extradition: The Delicate Problem of Balancing the Rights of the Individual and the International Public Order 1980, Strafrecht en strafprocesrecht in hoofdlijnen 1991 (revised sixth edn: Strafrecht, strafprocesrecht en internationaal strafrecht in hoofdlijnen 2006); co-ed.: Criminal Procedure Systems in the European Community 1993, International Criminal Law and Procedure 1996, International Criminal Law: A Collection of International and European Instruments, and other titles. *Address:* International Criminal Court, PO Box 19519, 2500 CM The Hague, The Netherlands (office); Faculty of Law, University of Antwerp, Universiteitsplein 1, 2610 Antwerp, Belgium. *Telephone:* (70) 515-85-15 (office); (3) 820-29-23. *Fax:* (70) 515-85-55 (office); (3) 820-29-40. *E-mail:* chris.vandenwyngaert@ua.ac.be (office); otp .informationdesk@icc-cpi.int (office). *Website:* www.icc-cpi.int (office); www.ua.ac .be.

VAN DER AVOIRD, Ad, PhD; Dutch scientist and academic; *Professor, Institute of Theoretical Chemistry, University of Nijmegen;* b. 19 April 1943, Eindhoven; s. of H. J. van der Avoird and M. A. van der Avoird (née Kerkhofs); m. T. G. M. Lange 1964; two s.; ed Tech. Univ., Eindhoven; Research Fellow, Inst. Battelle, Geneva, Switzerland 1965–67; Section Man. Unilever Research Lab., Vlaardingen 1967–71; Assoc. Prof., Univ. of Nijmegen, Nijmegen 1968–71, Prof. Inst. of Theoretical Chemistry 1971–; mem. Netherlands Acad. of Sciences 1979–, Int. Acad. of Quantum Molecular Sciences 1997–. *Publications:* Interacties tussen moleculen 1989; articles in scientific journals. *Address:* Institute for Molecules and Materials, Theoretical Chemistry, Radboud University Nymegen, Heyendaalseweg 135, 6525 AJ Nymegen, Netherlands (office). *Telephone:* (24) 365-30-37 (office). *E-mail:* a.vanderavoird@theochem.ru.nl (office). *Website:* www.theochem .ru.nl (office).

VAN DER EB, Alex Jan, PhD; Dutch fmr professor of molecular carcinogenesis; *Senior Adviser, Crucell;* b. 16 Jan. 1934, Bandung, Java; s. of Wijnand Jan van der Eb and Gertrude Leonie van der Eb-Blekkink; m. Titia Brongersma 1961; two s. one d.; ed Univ. of Leiden; mil. service 1962–63; Assoc. Prof. of Tumor Virology, Univ. of Leiden 1974–80, Prof. of Molecular Carcinogenesis 1980–99, Prof. Emer. 1999–; Postdoctoral Fellow, Calif. Inst. of Tech., Pasadena, USA 1968–69; Visiting Prof. Nagasaki Univ., Japan 2002–06; Sr Adviser Crucell, Leiden (Netherlands) 2002–; mem. Royal Acad. of Sciences and Letters 1987–, European Molecular Biology Org. 1981–, Academia Europaea, Royal Holland Science Asscn (Koninklijke Hollandsche Maatschappij van Wetenschappen) 1987–; Ridder in de Orde van de Nederlandse Leeuw 1998; AKZO Prize 1975, Korteweg Overwater Fund Award 1977, Beijerinck Virology Medal 1978, Robert Koch Prize 1989, Japan Org. for Promotion Cander Research Award 1989, Hyclone Award 1993, Fedora Award 1996, Inst. of Radiation Pathology IRS Prize 1997. *Publications:* more than 250 publs on molecular carcinogenesis and radiation biology. *Leisure interests:* bird watching, photography, travelling, camping. *Address:* Crucell, POB 2048, 2301 CA Leiden (office); Prinses Beatrixlaan 63, 2341 TW Oegstgeest, Netherlands (home). *Telephone:* (71) 5199162 (office); (71) 5172178 (home). *Fax:* (71) 5199800 (office). *E-mail:* lex.vandereb@crucell.com (office); lvandereb@kpnplanet.nl (home); tvandereb@hotmail.com (home). *Website:* www.crucell.com (office).

VAN DER GEEST, Willem, MPhil; Dutch economist and international organization official; *Lead Economist, International Trade Centre;* b. 8 June 1954, Leiden; ed Univ. of Leiden, Univ. of Stockholm, Sweden, Univ. of Cambridge, UK; Research Asst Nat. Inst. of Econ. Research, Sweden 1979; Research Officer Inst. of Social Studies, The Hague 1980–82; part-time lecturer, Univ. of Leiden 1981–82; tutor in Econs, Univ. of Cambridge, UK 1983–84; Economist, Ministry of Finance, Bangladesh 1984–86; Sr Research Economist, Univ. of Oxford 1987–91, Research Assoc. 1992–95; Sr Consultant, Pakistan Inst. of Devt Econs 1992–95; Sr Economist, ILO, Geneva 1995–97; Visiting Prof., Univ. Libre de Bruxelles

2001–; Sr Adviser, Bangladesh Inst. of Devt Studies 2002–03; fmr Dir European Inst. for Asian Studies, Brussels; Consultant and Team Leader, Trade Sustainability Impact Assessment of Europe-China Partnership and Cooperation Agreement, EC –2009; Lead Economist, Int. Trade Centre 2009–, also Acting Dir, Div. of Market Devt; mem. Royal Econ. Soc.; Vice-Pres. EU-Japan Asscn, Brussels; also worked as Macronomic Planner for UN, Bangladesh; fmr Sr Economist, UNCTAD. *Publications:* Negotiating Structural Adjustment in Africa (ed) 1994, Adjustment, Employment and Missing Institutions in Sub-Saharan Africa (co-ed) 1999, Economic Reform and Trade Performance in South Asia (co-ed) 2004, numerous chapters and articles in books and journals. *Address:* International Trade Centre, Palais des Nations 1211, Geneva 10, Switzerland (office). *Telephone:* 227300111 (office). *Fax:* 227334439 (office). *Website:* www.intracen.org (office).

VAN DER HEIJDEN, Paul F., LLM, PhD; Dutch lawyer, academic and fmr university administrator; b. 18 Sept. 1949, Utrecht; m.; three c.; ed Univs of Amsterdam and Leiden; Lecturer, Dept of Law, Univ. of Leiden 1978–85, Univ. of Groningen 1987–90; lawyer, Court of Law, Amsterdam 1985–89; Prof. of Employment Law, Univ. of Amsterdam 1990–2007, Rector Magnificus 2002–07; Rector Magnificus and Pres. Univ. of Leiden 2007–13; Ed.-in-Chief Jurisprudentie Arbeidsrecht; chaired Dutch Del. at Int. Labour Conf. of ILO 1995–2001, Geneva, currently Chair. ILO Governing Body Cttee on Freedom of Asscn; Crown-apptd mem. Social and Econ. Council (SER); Chair. Supervisory Bd Amsterdam Univ. Press; mem. Supervisory Bd NUON NV, Buhrmann Nederland NV, ING Group NV, Dutch Cancer Inst./Antoni van Leeuwenhoek Hosp., AMC-UvA; Chair. De Volkskrant Foundation; mem. Royal Netherlands Acad. of Arts and Sciences. *Publications:* Beyond Employment: Changes in Work and the Future of Labour Law in Europe 2001; numerous articles in professional journals. *Address:* c/o Office of the Rektor, Leiden University, Rapenburg 70, PO Box 9500, 2300 Leiden, Netherlands.

VAN DER HOEVEN, Maria Josephina Arnoldina; Dutch politician and international organization official; *Executive Director, International Energy Agency;* b. 13 Sept. 1949, Meerssen; m. Lou Buytendijk; teacher 1969, school counsellor 1971; Head Adult Commercial Vocational Training Centre, Maastricht –1987; Head Limburg Tech. Centre 1987–91; mem. (Christian Democratic Alliance) House of Reps, States Gen. 1991–2002; Minister of Educ., Culture and Science 2002–07, of Economic Affairs 2007–10; Exec. Dir IEA 2011–; Chair. Supervisory Bd, Alzheimer Netherlands; fmr Chair. St Nicholas Catholic Asscn of Bargees; fmr mem. Bd of Govs, Maastricht Coll. of Higher Professional Educ., Southern Dutch Opera Asscn; Officer, Order of Orange-Nassau 2010. *Address:* International Energy Agency, 9 rue de la Fédération, 75739 Paris Cedex 15, France (office). *Telephone:* 1-40-57-65-00 (office). *Fax:* 1-40-57-65-09 (office). *E-mail:* info@iea.org (office). *Website:* www.iea.org (office).

VAN DER MEER, Jan, MD; Dutch physician; b. 30 Aug. 1935, Leeuwarden; s. of L. van der Meer and G. Bakker; m. Joan Alkema 1962; one d.; ed Univ. of Amsterdam; intern 1968; Sr Registrar in Internal Medicine, Binnengasthuis, Amsterdam 1970–76; Head of Coagulation Lab., Cen. Lab. of Bloodtransfusion Service of Dutch Red Cross 1969–76; Prof. of Internal Medicine, Chair. of Dept, Acad. Hosp. of Free Univ. Amsterdam 1976–2000; Chair. Govs, Cen. Lab. of Blood Transfusion Service, Netherlands Red Cross 1994–98; Chair. Landsteiner Foundation for Blood Transfusion Research 1998–2009. *Publication:* Meting van de plasma renine-activiteit met behulp van een radioimmunologische bepaling van angiotensine I 1969. *Address:* De Wijde Blik 19, 1189 WJ Amstelveen, Netherlands. *Telephone:* (297) 582553.

VAN DER MEER MOHR, Pauline F. M., LLM; Dutch lawyer and university administrator; *President, Erasmus University Rotterdam;* b. 1960; ed Erasmus Univ. Rotterdam, European Univ. Inst., Italy; began career in advocacy; worked at Royal Dutch Shell, TNT and ABN Amro; Chair. Exec. Bd and Pres. Erasmus Univ. Rotterdam 2010–. *Address:* Office of the President, PO Box 1738, 3000 DR Rotterdam (office); Office of the President, Campus Woudestein, Burgemeester Oudlaan 50, 3062 PA Rotterdam, The Netherlands (office). *Telephone:* (10) 4081751 (office). *Fax:* (10) 4089073 (office). *E-mail:* ender@abd.eur.nl (office); vallejoandres@abd.eur.nl (office). *Website:* www.eur.nl (office).

VAN DER MEULEN, Robert Paul, LLM, MCL; Dutch fmr diplomatist; b. 25 May 1950, Eindhoven; m. Majida Mouasher; two d.; ed Univ. of Leyden; Asst, European Inst., Univ. of Leyden 1974–76; with Directorate for European Integration, Foreign Econ. Relations Dept, Ministry of Econ. Affairs 1976, Head of Bureau, Accession of Greece, Spain and Portugal, Co-operation with Mediterranean Countries and EFTA 1979; with Perm. Representation of The Netherlands to EC, Brussels 1981–82; First Sec., Embassy in Washington, DC 1982–84, Counsellor 1984–85; Deputy Head, Office of Vice-Pres. of EC 1985–88; Amb. of European Comm. to Brunei, Indonesia and Singapore 1989–94, to Tunisia 1994–98; Head of Maghreb Div. (DG RELEX-F3), European Comm. 1998–2001, Dir Mediterranean and Middle East 2001–02; Amb. to Jordan (also accred to Yemen) 2002–06, to Nigeria and Perm. Rep. to Econ. Community of West African States (ECOWAS) 2006–09; Grand Officier, Ordre de la République Tunisienne. *Leisure interest:* 19th century paintings, especially works by the orientalist Marius A. J. Bauer. *Address:* Manoir de Fourneux, 49400 Saumur, France; Groot Haesebroekseweg 37A, 2243 ED Wassenaar, The Netherlands. *Telephone:* 6-78-12-83-52 (France, mobile); 64-4789387 (Netherlands, mobile). *E-mail:* robertvandermeulen@hotmail.com. *Website:* mariusbauerzijnetswerk.web .officelive.com.

VAN DER VEER, Jeroen; Dutch business executive; *Chairman of the Supervisory Board, ING Groep NV;* b. 27 Oct. 1947, Utrecht; m. Mariette van der Veer; three d.; ed Delft and Rotterdam Univs; joined Royal Dutch Petroleum Co. 1971, Area Co-ordinator Sub-Saharan Africa 1990–92, Man. Dir Shell Nederland 1992–95, Pres. and CEO Shell Chemical Co. USA 1995–97, Group Man. Dir Royal Dutch 1997–2000, Pres. 2000–04, Chair. Cttee of Man. Dirs Royal Dutch/Shell Group 2004–09, CEO Royal Dutch Shell plc 2004–09, Dir (non-exec.) 2009–; mem. Supervisory Bd ING Groep NV 2009–, Vice-Chair. 2009–11, Chair. 2011–; mem. Supervisory Bd Koninklijke Philips Electronics NV 2009–, Chair. 2011–; Vice-Chair. and Sr Ind. Dir Unilever NV 2009–11; mem. Supervisory Bd Het Concertgebouw NV; Chair. Supervisory Council Nederlands Openluchtmuseum; Chair. Platform Bètatechniek; World Pres. Soc. of Chemical Industry 2002–04;

mem. Bd Nationale Toneel (theatre); Hon. Citizen of Singapore 2010; Commdr, Order of Orange-Nassau 2009; Dr hc (Univ. of Port Harcourt, Nigeria) 2005. *Leisure interests:* visiting museums, playing golf (16 handicap), has twice skated the 200 kilometres 'Elfstedentocht' – 11 cities marathon – in the Netherlands. *Address:* ING Groep NV, PO Box 1800, 1000 BV Amsterdam, The Netherlands (office). *Telephone:* (20) 563-91-11 (office). *E-mail:* info@ing.com (office). *Website:* www.ing.com (office).

VAN DER WEE, Baron Herman Frans Anna, LLD, PhD; Belgian historian (retd) and academic; *Professor Emeritus of Economic History, Katholieke Universiteit Leuven;* b. 10 July 1928, Lier; s. of Jos Van der Wee and Martha Planckaert; m. Monique Verbreyt 1954; one s. one d.; ed Leuven Univ., Sorbonne, Paris, London School of Econs, UK; Fellow Nat. Foundation for Scientific Research of Belgium 1953–55; lecturer, Leuven Univ. 1955, Assoc. Prof. 1966, Prof. of Econ. History 1969–93, Prof. Emer. 1993–, Sec., Dept of Econs 1970–72, Chair. 1972–74, Chair. Bd of Trustees, Leuven Univ. Press 1971–93; Visiting Prof., St Aloysius Univ., Brussels 1972–76, Dean, Faculty of Econ., Political and Social Sciences 1972–75; Visiting Prof., Université Catholique de Louvain, Louvain-la-Neuve 1972–80, 1991–92; Research Fellow, Woodrow Wilson Int. Center for Scholars, Washington, DC 1975–76; Francqui Chair, Univ. of Brussels 1980–81; Visiting Fellow, Inst. for Advanced Study, School of Historical Studies, Princeton, NJ, USA 1981–82, 1991, All Souls Coll., Oxford 1985, Inst. for Advanced Study, Indiana Univ. 1986; J. Tinbergen Chair, Erasmus Univ. 1987; Chair of Econ. History, Univ. of Paris IV-Sorbonne 1987–88; Ellen MacArthur Chair., Univ. of Cambridge, UK 1989; P.P. Rubens Chair., Univ. of Calif., Berkeley 1994; Visiting Fellow, Inst. for Advanced Study (RSSC), Canberra, Australia 1994; Erasmus Chair, Harvard Univ. 1997; Chair. of Banking History, Univ. of St.-Gallen 1999; Guest of the Rector, Netherlands Inst. for Advanced Study, Wassenaar 2000; Guest of the Rector Wissenschaftskolleg Berlin, Germany 2004; Visiting Fellow, Wissenschaftszentrum fur Sozialforschung, Germany 2004; Anthony van Dyck Chair, UCLA 2010; Pres. Int. Econ. History Asscn 1986–90 (Hon. Pres. 1990–); Chair. Leuven Univ. Press 1972–85, Royal Acad. of Belgium (Class of Letters) 1987, Leuven Inst. of Cen. and E European Studies (LICOS) 1990–93, Advisory Council of W European Program at Wilson Int. Center for Scholars, Washington, DC 1986–91, Academic Advisory Council of European Asscn for Banking History 1991–99; mem. Research Council, European Univ. Inst., Florence 1985–94, 1999–2006, Bd of Trustees Cité Int. Universitaire, Paris 1993–2008; mem. Int. Comm. for accred research MA Programme in the Humanities at Dutch Univ.; mem. Royal Acad. of Belgium 1977–2003, Hon. mem. 2003–; Corresp. Foreign mem. Royal Acad. of Netherlands 1983–; Foundation mem. Academia Europaea 1987–; Corresp. Fellow, British Acad. 1987, Royal Historical Soc. 1995; Foreign Hon. mem. American Acad. of Arts and Sciences 1993–; Fellow, European Econ. Asscn 2004; Dr hc (Brussels) 1994, (Leicester) 1995; Order of Leopold Belgium, Order of the Crown Belgium, knighted by King Albert II of Belgium (title of Baron) 1994; De Stassart Prize for Nat. History, Royal Acad. of Belgium 1961–67, 1968, Eugène Baie Prize 1966, Fulbright-Hayes Award 1975, 1981, Quinquennial Solvay Prize for the Social Sciences, Nat. Foundation of Scientific Research of Belgium 1976–80, 1981, Amsterdam Biannual Prize for Historical Sciences 1992, Golden Medal for Special Merits, Flemish Parl. 1995. *Publications:* Prix et salaires: Manuel Méthodologique 1956, The Growth of the Antwerp Market and the European Economy (14th–16th centuries), 3 vols 1963, The Great Depression Revisited (ed) 1972, The Rise of Managerial Capitalism (ed) 1974, La Banque Nationale de Belgique et la politique monétaire entre les deux guerres 1975, Monetary, Credit and Banking Systems in Western Europe, 1400–1750, in The Cambridge Economic History of Europe (Part V) 1977, Productivity of Land and Agricultural Innovation in the Low Countries 1250–1800 (ed) 1978, Mint Statistics of Flanders and Brabant 1300–1506 (two vols) 1980, 1985, Prosperity and Upheaval, the World Economy, 1945–1980 1983 (trans. in several languages), The Rise and Decline of Urban Industries in Italy and in the Low Countries (Late Middle Ages–Early Modern Times) (ed) 1988, Histoire économique mondiale (trans. in several languages) 1945–1990 1990, History of European Banking (trans. in several languages) 1991, Winkler Prins. History of the Low Countries, 1500–1800 (ed.) 1992, The Economic Development of Europe, 950–1950 (13 edns) 1982–97, Constructing the World Economy 1750–1990 1992, The Low Countries in the Early Modern World 1993, The General Bank 1822–1997: A Continuing Challenge 1997, Economic Development in Belgium Since 1870 (ed.) 1997, Urban Achievement in Early Modern Europe: Golden Ages in Antwerp, Amsterdam and London (ed.) 2001, A Century of Banking Consolidation in Europe: The History and Archives of Mergers and Acquisitions (ed.) 2001, Cera 1892–1997: The Power of Cooperative Solidarity (ed.) 2002, The Woollen Industries (Cambridge History of Western Textiles) 2003, War and Monetary Policy: The National Bank of Belgium, the Bank of Issue at Brussels and the Belgian Government (1939–1945) 2005, A Small Nation in the Turmoil of the Second World War – Money, Finance and Occupation (Belgium, its Enemies, its Friends, 1939–1945) 2009. *Leisure interests:* literature, music, tennis, skiing. *Address:* Katholieke Universiteit Leuven, Centrum voor Economische Studiën, Naamsestraat 69, 3000 Leuven (office); Ettingestraat 10, 9170 Sint-Pauwels, Belgium (home). *Telephone:* (3) 776-03-33 (home). *Fax:* (3) 765-90-28 (home). *E-mail:* ces@econ.kuleuven.ac.be (office); Herman.VanDerWee@econ.kuleuven.be (home). *Website:* www.econ.kuleuven.ac .be/ew/academic/econhist/default.htm.

VAN DIJK, Petrus, LLM, SJD; Dutch state councillor and fmr professor of international law; *President, Administrative Jurisdiction Division, Council of State;* b. 21 Feb. 1943, De Lier; s. of A. A. M. van Dijk and J. H. van Straelen; m. Francisca G. M. Lammerts 1969; one s. one d.; ed Utrecht and Leyden Univs; Lecturer in Int. Law, Utrecht Univ. 1967–76, Prof. 1976–90; State Councillor 1990–, Pres. Admin. Jurisdiction Div., Council of State 2000–03, 2006–; Judge, European Court of Human Rights 1996–98, Deputy Pres. Admin. Tribunal of Council of Europe 2001–; Fullbright-Hays Scholar, Univ. of Mich. Law School 1970–71; Visiting Prof., Wayne State Univ. Law School 1978; Chair. Netherlands Inst. of Human Rights 1982–97, Netherlands Inst. of Social and Econ. Law 1986–90; Deputy Judge, Court of Appeal of The Hague 1986, Court of Appeal for Business and Industry 1992–, Cen. Appeal Bd Social Affairs 2006–; mem. Perm. Court of Arbitration 2002–; mem. Bd Trustees Inst. of Social Sciences 1992–98, Anne Frank Foundation 1994–; mem. various advisory cttees; mem. Royal Netherlands Acad. of Arts and Sciences; mem. Netherlands Del. to UN Gen. Ass.

1981, 1983, 1986; Kt, Order of the Netherlands Lion. *Publications include:* Theory and Practice of the European Convention on Human Rights (with G. J. H. van Hoof) 1979, The Final Act of Helsinki: Basis for a Pan-European System? 1980, Contents and Function of the Principle of Equity in International Economic Law 1987, Normative Force and Effectiveness of International Economic Law 1988, Access to Court 1993, Universality of Human Rights 1994; book chapters and ed. of numerous legal publs. *Address:* Council of State, PO Box 20019, 2500 EA The Hague, Netherlands (office). *Telephone:* (70) 4264645 (office). *Fax:* 3563217 (office). *E-mail:* pvandijk@raadvanstate.nl (office). *Website:* www.raadvanstate.nl (office).

VAN DÚNEM, Fernando José França, PhD; Angolan politician; ed Univ. Aix-en-Provence, France; Minister of Justice 1986–90, of Planning 1990–91; fmr Minister of External Affairs; Prime Minister of Angola 1991–98; mem. Assembléia Nacional (parl.) 1999, 2008–; First Vice-Pres. Pan-African Parl. 2004–09; mem. Marxist-Leninist Popular Movt for the Liberation of Angola Workers' Party (MPLA). *Address:* Assembléia Nacional, CP 1204, Luanda, Angola (office). *Website:* www.parlamento.ao (office).

VAN EEKELEN, Willem Frederik, D.LL.; Dutch politician and diplomatist; b. 5 Feb. 1931, Utrecht; s. of Dr. Marie van Eekelen and Anna Maria van Eekelen; m. Johanna Wentink; two c.; ed Utrecht Univ. and Princeton Univ., USA; diplomatic service 1957–77; mem. Consultative Ass. Council of Europe and WEU 1981–82; Sec. Gen. WEU 1989–94; Sec. of State for Defence 1978–81, for Foreign Affairs 1982–86; Minister of Defence 1986–88; Senator 1995–2003; Chair. European Movt in the Netherlands 1995; mem. Governing Bd Stockholm Int. Peace Research Inst. (SIPRI) 1999–; mem. Advisory Bd Geneva Centre for Democratic Control of Armed Forces (DCAF); Grand Officer Légion d'honneur, Grand Cross of Germany, Belgium, Luxembourg. *Publications:* The Security Agenda for 1996, Debating European Security 1948–1998, From Words to Deeds 2006. *Leisure interests:* old maps, trekking, sailing. *Address:* Else Mauhslaan 187, 2595 HE The Hague, Netherlands. *Telephone:* (70) 3241103. *Fax:* (70) 3241103. *E-mail:* derotte@wanadoo.nl (home).

VAN FRAASSEN, Bastiaan Cornelis, PhD; American/Canadian academic; *Distinguished Professor of Philosophy, San Francisco State University;* b. 5 April 1941, Goes, The Netherlands; s. of Jan Bastiaan van Fraassen and Dina Landman; m. Isabelle Peschard 2005; two s.; ed Univ. of Alberta, Canada, Univ. of Pittsburgh, USA; Asst Prof., Yale Univ. 1966–68, Assoc. Prof. 1969; Assoc. Prof., Univ. of Toronto 1969–73, Prof. 1973–82; Prof., Univ. of Southern Calif. 1976–81; McCosh Prof. of Philosophy, Princeton Univ. 1982–2008, Prof. Emer. 2008–; Distinguished Prof. of Philosophy, San Francisco State Univ. 2008–11; John Simon Guggenheim Fellowship 1970–71; Fellow, American Acad. of Arts and Sciences; Corresp. Fellow, British Acad.; Foreign mem. Royal Netherlands Acad. of Arts and Sciences; Titular mem. Acad. Int. de Philosophie des Sciences; Hon. DLett (Univ. of Lethbridge), Hon. LLD (Univ. of Notre Dame), Hon. PhD (Catholic Univ. of Leuven); Franklin Matchette Award (co-recipient) 1982, Imre Lakatos Award (co-recipient) 1986, Int. Giulio Preti Prize 2009, Inaugural Hempel Award 2012. *Publications:* Introduction to the Philosophy of Time and Space 1970, Formal Semantics and Logic 1971, The Scientific Image 1980, Laws and Symmetry 1989, Quantum Mechanics: An Empiricist View 1991, The Empirical Stance 2002, Scientific Representation: Paradoxes of Perspective 2008. *Leisure interests:* rock climbing, flying trapeze. *Address:* Department of Philosophy, San Francisco State University, 1600 Holloway Avenue, San Francisco, CA 94132 (office); 1347 Curtis Street, Berkeley, CA 94702, USA (home). *Telephone:* (415) 338-1596 (office). *E-mail:* fraassen@princeton.edu (office). *Website:* www.sfsu.edu/~phlsphr/?page=bas_van_fraassen (office); www.princeton.edu/~fraassen (office); philosophy.princeton.edu (office).

VAN GERVEN, Baron; Walter M., DJur, Lic.not, AgrHE; Belgian lawyer and academic; *Professor Emeritus, Catholic University of Louvain;* b. 11 May 1935, St Niklaas; s. of Willy van Gerven and Germaine van Bel; m. Frieda Sintobin 1959; four s.; ed Catholic Univ. of Louvain; Teaching Fellow, Univ. of Chicago Law School 1959–60; Assoc. Prof. of Law, Catholic Univ. of Louvain 1962–67, Prof. of Law 1967–82, Extraordinary Prof. 1982–, Vice-Rector 1970–76, now Prof. Emer.; Extraordinary Prof., Univ. of Amsterdam 1981–86; mem. Brussels Bar 1970–80; Pres. Banking Comm. of Belgium 1982–88; mem. Bd of Dirs of several commercial cos; Advocate-Gen. Court of Justice of European Communities 1988–95; mem. Ind. Expert Comm. of Investment, EU Comm. 1999, Ind. Review Panel, World Bank 2007; Visiting Prof., Univ. of Chicago 1968–69; Distinguished Arthur & Mark Payne Lecturer, Stanford Univ., USA 2003–04; Distinguished Prof., Tilburg Univ. 2005–; Distinguished Prof., Michigan Univ., USA 2006–07; mem. Royal Belgian Acad., Royal Netherlands Acad., Academia Europaea; Hon. Bencher, Gray's Inn 2003; Commdr, Order of Leopold; Dr hc (Ghent) 2005. *Publications:* Principles of Belgian Private Law 1968, Commercial and Economic Law (three vols) 1973–86, The Policy of the Judge 1973, In Law and Equity 1987, The European Union – A Polity of States and Peoples 2005. *Leisure interests:* modern art, music, golf. *Address:* Demarsinstraat 42, 3012 Wilsele, Belgium (home). *Telephone:* (16) 22-91-54 (home). *E-mail:* walter.vangerven@law.kuleuven.ac.be (home).

VAN GINKEL, Hans J. A., MSc, PhD; Dutch university administrator and academic; *Rector, United Nations University;* b. 22 June 1940, Kota-Radjah, Indonesia; m. Bep Teepen; one s. one d.; ed Utrecht Univ.; Teacher of Geography and History, Thomas à Kempis Coll., Arnhem 1965–68; joined Faculty of Geographical Sciences, Utrecht Univ. 1968, apptd Prof. of Human Geography and Planning 1980, Dean of Faculty 1981–85, mem. Exec. Bd 1985, Rector Magnificus 1986; Treas. Netherlands Foundation for Int. Co-operation in Educ. 1986–97; mem., then Chair. Bd Netherlands Interdisciplinary Demographic Inst. 1986–2000; Ind. Chair. Regional Council of Utrecht 1988–93; Pres. Governing Bd Int. Training Centre for Aerial Survey and Earth Sciences, Enschedé 1990–98; mem. Governing Bd UN Univ. 1992–97, Vice-Pres. 1995–97, Rector 1997–2007 (retd); Vice-Pres. Bd European Asscn of Univs 1994–98; mem. European Science and Tech. Ass., Brussels, Belgium 1994–98; Vice-Pres. Bd Int. Asscn of Univs 1995–2000, Pres. 2000–; mem. Nat. Council, Chair. Organizing Cttee, 28th Int. Geographical Congress, The Hague 1996; Vice-Chair. Bd of Trustees, Asian Inst. of Tech., Bangkok, Thailand 1997–; mem. Steering Cttee, UNESCO World Conf. on Higher Educ. 1998; mem. Academia Europaea; mem. Comm. on Educ. and Communication, World Conservation Union; fmr mem. UNESCO Advisory Group for Higher Educ.; fmr Chair. Co-ordinating Cttee of Advisory Councils on Science

Policy; fmr Bd mem. Utrecht Network for Innovation and Economy; fmr mem. Nat. Foresight Cttee on Science Policy; Hon. Fellow, Inst. for Aerospace Survey and Earth Sciences; Hon. mem. Comm. on the History of Geographical Thought, Int. Geographical Union; Kt Netherlands Order of the Lion 1994, Order of the Rising Sun, Grand Cordon (Japan) 2007; Dr hc (Universitatea Babes-Bolyai, Romania) 1997, (Calif. State Univ.–Sacramento) 2003, (Univ. of Ghana) 2005, (Tech. Univ. of Zvolen, Slovakia) 2006. *Publications:* more than 100 publs in academic journals. *Address:* c/o United Nations University, 53–70 Jingumae 5-chrome, Shibuya-ku, Tokyo 150-8925, Japan (office).

VAN HAMEL, Martine; Dutch/American ballerina, choreographer and teacher; *Co-founder, Kaatsbaan International Dance Center;* b. 16 Nov. 1945, Brussels, Belgium; d. of D. A. van Hamel and Manette van Hamel-Cramer; partner Kevin Mckenzie; ed Nat. Ballet School of Canada; began ballet training aged four; debut with Nat. Ballet of Venezuela aged 11; following graduation, joined Nat. Ballet of Canada as soloist 1963; moved to New York and danced with Joffrey Ballet 1969–70; joined American Ballet Theatre 1970, Prin. Ballerina 1973–91, danced classic roles, including Swan Lake, Sleeping Beauty, Raimonda, as well as contemporary works choreographed by Balanchine, Glen Tetley, Anthony Tudor, Kenneth MacMillan, Jiri Kylian, Mark Morris, Twyla Tharp, Alvin Ailey; danced with Nederlands Dans Theater III 1993–98; Artistic Dir New Amsterdam Ballet (f. 1986); Co-founder Kaatsbaan Int. Dance Center; Chorus mem. New York Choral Soc.; Teacher, The Jacqueline Kennedy Onassis School at American Ballet Theatre; Gold Medal, Varna Competition 1966, Prix de Varna 1966, Dance Magazine Award, Cue Magazine Award, Award for Excellence, Washington Coll., Dance Educators of America Award. *Films:* Turning Point, Little Nikita. *Choreography:* Amnon V'Tamar for American Ballet Theatre 1984 and creator of works for Milwaukee Ballet, Washington Ballet, Royal Winnipeg Ballet and New Amsterdam Ballet. *Leisure interest:* singing. *Address:* Kaatsbaan International Dance Center, PO Box 482, Tivoli, NY 12583 (office); 290 Riverside Drive, 6A, New York, NY 10025, USA. *Telephone:* (845) 757-5106 (office). *Fax:* (845) 757-5040 (office); (212) 600-1365 (home). *E-mail:* martinevh@rcn.com (home). *Website:* www .kaatsbaan.org (office).

VAN HEERDEN, Neil Peter, BA; South African diplomatist; b. 30 July 1939, East London; s. of J. van Heerden and C. Nel; m. Evelin Nowack 1961; one s. one d.; ed Wonderbom High School, Pretoria and Univ. of S Africa, Pretoria; joined Dept of Foreign Affairs 1959, Vice-Consul, Tokyo 1963, opened S Africa's first mission in Taipei 1967–68, opened first S African mission in Tehran 1970–71, First Sec., Embassy in Washington, DC 1971–75, Amb. to FRG 1980, Deputy Dir Gen., Dept of Foreign Affairs 1985–87, Dir-Gen. of Foreign Affairs 1987–92, Amb. to EC (now EU) 1992–96; Exec. Dir S Africa Foundation (now Business Leadership South Africa) 1996; mem. Bd of Dirs Naspers 1996–, BMW (SA); Trustee, Univ. of the Western Cape; Councillor, Business Unity South Africa; Hon. DLitt et Phil (Rand Afrikaans Univ.) 2000; Paul Harris Award. *Publications include:* articles in journals dealing with foreign affairs. *Leisure interests:* music, hiking, sailing, golf. *Address:* PO Box 7006, Johannesburg 2000, (home); 19 Raed-na-Gael Street, Hermanus 7200, South Africa (office). *Telephone:* (28) 3131792 (office). *E-mail:* neilve@iafrica.com (office).

VAN HOOFF, Jan A. R. A. M.; Dutch fmr professor of comparative physiology and ethology; b. 15 May 1936, Arnhem; s. of R. A. Th. van Hooff and L. E. Burgers; m. Anna C. M. Bluemink 1964; two s. one d.; ed Canisius Coll., Nijmegen, Univ. of Utrecht; scientific collaborator, Faculty of Biology, Univ. of Utrecht 1963–73, Lecturer in Comparative Physiology 1973–80, Prof. of Comparative Physiology and Ethology 1980–2001, Dean, Faculty of Biology 1993–96; Dir Science Bd, Burgers Zoo, Arnhem 1969–; Pres. Research Council of Ethology, Netherlands Foundation for Biological Research 1972–78, Dir 1978–83; Pres. Soc. pour l'Etude et la Protection des Mammifères 1985–89, Royal Netherlands Zoological Soc. 1996–2001, Jane Goodall Inst. 1997–2001; Sec.-Gen. Int. Primatological Soc. 2000–04; Sec. Lucie Burgers Foundation for Comparative Behaviour Research 1980–; Bd mem. Foundation Prince Bernhard Chair for Int. Nature Conservation; mem. numerous scientific foundations and socs; Fellow, Royal Netherlands Acad. of Arts and Sciences; Hon. Prof., Universitas Nasional, Jakarta, Indonesia, Hon. mem. Assoziazione Primatologica Italiana; Officer, Royal Order of Orange-Nassau 2000; Socio Onorario, La Società di Medicina e Scienze Naturali dell'Università di Parma. *Publications include:* Facial Expressions in Higher Primates 1962, The Comparison of Facial Expressions in Man and Higher Primates 1976, Categories and Sequences of Behavior: Methods of Description and Analysis 1982, Oorlog 1990, Relationships Among Nonhuman Primate Males 2000, Economics in Nature 2001, Laughter and Smiling: the intertwining of nature and culture 2003. *Address:* Vermeerlaan 24, 3723 Bilthoven, Netherlands (home). *Telephone:* (30) 228-76-39 (home). *E-mail:* jaramvanhooff@gmail.com.

VAN HOUTEN, Frans, MA; Dutch business executive; *Chairman of the Board of Management and CEO, Royal Philips Electronics NV;* b. 1960; ed Erasmus Univ., Rotterdam; began career in marketing and sales at Philips Data Systems 1986, held several leadership positions, CEO Airvision (in-flight entertainment co. in USA) 1992–93, Vice-Pres. Int. Sales and Operations, Philips Kommunikations Industrie, Germany 1993–96, joined Consumer Electronics Div. 1996, led region Asia Pacific, Middle East and Africa, based in Singapore, Co-CEO Consumer Electronics Div. 2002–03, mem. Group Man. Cttee 2003–06, CEO Philips Semiconductors 2004, mem. Bd of Man. 2006 until creation of NXP Semiconductors Sept. 2006 (CEO NXP Semiconductors 2006–10), rejoined Philips Bd of Man. 2010–, CEO-designate Royal Philips Electronics NV 2010–11, COO Jan.–April 2011, Chair. Bd of Man. and CEO April 2011–, Chair. Exec. Cttee July 2011–, Acting CEO Philips Lighting; led project to separate ING Group's banking and insurance operations as an ind. adviser to Man. Bd 2006–10; fmr Exec. Advisor and Interim Man., FVH Interventions BV; mem. European Round Table of Industrialists 2010–. *Address:* Royal Philips Electronics NV, Breitner Center, HBT 14.12, Amstelplein 2, 1096 BC Amsterdam, Netherlands (office). *Telephone:* (20) 597-71-22 (office). *Fax:* (20) 597-71-20 (office). *E-mail:* info@philips.com (office). *Website:* www.philips.com (office).

VAN INWAGEN, Peter Jan, PhD; American philosopher and academic; *John Cardinal O'Hara Professor of Philosophy, University of Notre Dame;* b. 21 Sept. 1942, Rochester, NY; s. of George Butler van Inwagen and Mildred Gloria Knudsen; m. 1st Margery Naylor 1967 (divorced 1988); one d.; m. 2nd Elisabeth

Bolduc 1989; ed Rensselaer Polytechnic Inst., Univ. of Rochester; served in US Army 1969–70; Visiting Asst Prof. of Philosophy, Univ. of Rochester 1970–71; Asst Prof., Assoc. Prof., then Prof. of Philosophy, Syracuse Univ. 1971–95; John Cardinal O'Hara Prof. of Philosophy, Univ. of Notre Dame, South Bend, Ind. 1995–; Visiting Prof., Univ. of Ariz. 1981, Rutgers Univ. 1987; research grants, Nat. Endowment for the Humanities 1983–84, 1990–91; delivered the Maurice Lectures, Kings Coll., London1999, the Wilde Lectures, Oxford 2000, the Stewart Lectures, Princeton 2002, the Gifford Lectures, St Andrews 2003; currently Pres. Central Div., American Philosophical Asscn; mem. American Acad. of Arts and Sciences 2005–. *Publications:* An Essay on Free Will 1983, Material Beings 1990, Metaphysics 1993, God, Knowledge and Mystery (essays) 1995, The Possibility of Resurrection and Other Essays in Christian Apologetics 1997, Ontology, Identity and Modality: Essays in Metaphysics 2001, The Problem of Evil 2006. *Address:* Department of Philosophy, 100 Malloy Hall, University of Notre Dame, Notre Dame, IN 46556-4619, USA (office). *Telephone:* (219) 631-5910 (office). *Fax:* (219) 631-0588 (office). *E-mail:* peter.vaninwagen.1@nd.edu (office). *Website:* www.nd.edu/~ndphilo (office).

VAN ITTERSUM, Baron Boudewijn F.; Dutch financial services industry executive; b. 7 June 1939; s. of Paul A. L. A. Van Ittersum and Henriette F. Van Lennep; m. Karin R. W. Van der Ven 1967; three c.; ed Univ. of Amsterdam; joined Ministry of Finance; seconded to IMF, IBRD, Washington, DC 1970–72; Dir of Int. Affairs, Ministry of Finance; Chair. Amsterdam Stock Exchange 1981–96, Dir 1996–2000 (merged with Paris Bourse and Brussels Exchanges to form Euronext Amsterdam 2000); Chair. Amsterdam Capital 2009–. *Address:* c/o Euronext Amsterdam, Beursplein 5, 1012 JW Amsterdam, Netherlands.

VAN KRALINGEN, Bridget; American business executive; *Senior Vice-President, IBM Global Business Services, International Business Machines (IBM) Corporation;* Man. Partner, Deloitte Consulting 1989–2004, led GBS Financial Services Sector, later served in Financial Services practice in USA and Strategy and Organizational Devt practice in SA; Gen. Man., Global Business Services, Northeast Europe, Middle East and Africa, London, UK, International Business Machines (IBM) Corpn 2007–10, Gen. Man. IBM North America 2010–12, Sr Vice-Pres., IBM Global Business Services 2012–; mem. Bd of Advisors, Catalyst, Inc.; mem. Bd of Dirs Royal Bank of Canada 2011–; ranked by Fortune magazine amongst the 50 Most Powerful Women in Business in the US (39th) 2011, (23rd) 2012. *Address:* International Business Machines Corporation, 1 New Orchard Road, Armonk, NY 10504-1722, USA (office). *Telephone:* (914) 499-1900 (office). *Fax:* (914) 765-7382 (office). *E-mail:* info@ibm.com (office). *Website:* www.ibm.com (office).

VAN LEDE, Cornelis Josephus Antonius (Cees), MBA; Dutch business executive; *Chairman of Supervisory Board, Royal Imtech NV;* b. 1942; ed Univ. of Leiden, Institut Européen d'Admin des Affaires (INSEAD), Fontainebleau, France; joined Akzo Nobel NV as mem. Bd of Man. 1991–2003, Vice-Chair. Bd of Man. 1992–94, Chair. and CEO 1994–2003, mem. Supervisory Bd 2003–09; mem. Supervisory Bd Heineken NV 2002–13, Chair. 2002–13; Chair. Supervisory Bd Dutch Cen. Bank, Royal Imtech NV 2013–; Chair. INSEAD (also Unit Bd mem. and mem. Supervisory Bd); Exec. Officer, mem. Supervisory Bd and mem. Remuneration Cttee Koninklijke Philips Electronics NV 2003–; mem. Bd of Dirs Air France KLM 2004–, (its subsidiary) Air France 2004–, Sara Lee Corpn 2002–, Air Liquide Tunisie 2003–, L'Air Liquide SA (also mem. Supervisory Bd) 2005–; Dir (non-exec.) Reed Elsevier plc 2003–07, Reed Elsevier Group plc 2003–, Reed Elsevier NV 2001– (also mem. Supervisory Bd 2003–); mem. Supervisory Bd Philips Lighting Co. 2003–, Stork NV 2007–, Philips Electronics N America Corpn 2003–, Philips Electronics Singapore Pte Ltd 2003–, Sara Lee (USA)/DE NV, Scania AB (Sweden); fmr mem. Bd of Man. Dirs HBG; served as Proposed mem. Supervisory Bd KLM Royal Dutch Airlines; mem. European Advisory Council JPMorgan Chase & Co. 2005–, Int. Council of JPMorgan Chase; Chair. Confed. of Netherlands Industry and Employers (VNO) 1984–91; Vice-Pres. Union of Industrial and Employers' Confeds of Europe (UNICE) 1991–94; mem. European Round Table of Industrialists, Bd of Trustees of The Conference Bd, Netherlands Pensions and Insurance Supervisory Authority. *Address:* Royal Imtech NV, Quinterium Offices I, Kampeningweg 45A, 2803 PE Gouda, The Netherlands (office). *Telephone:* (182) 54-35-43 (office). *E-mail:* info@imtech.com (office). *Website:* www.imtech.com (office).

VAN LOAN, Peter, MA, MSc, JD; Canadian lawyer and politician; *Leader of the Government in the House of Commons;* b. 18 April 1963, Niagara Falls; ed Univ. of Toronto, Osgoode Hall Law School; fmr Pnr and Chair Planning and Devt Law Group, Fraser Milner Casgrain LLP (law firm), Toronto; fmr Adjunct Prof. of Planning, Univ. of Toronto; Pres. Progressive Conservative Party of Ont. then Progressive Conservative Party of Canada –2000 (resgnd); MP (Conservative) for York–Simcoe 2004–, Critic for Human Resources and Skills Devt 2004–06, Parl. Sec. to Minister of Foreign Affairs –Nov. 2006, Pres. of the Queen's Privy Council for Canada, Minister of Intergovernmental Affairs and Minister for Sport Nov. 2006–Jan. 2007, Leader of the Govt in the House of Commons and Minister for Democratic Reform Jan. 2007–08, Minister of Public Safety 2008–10, of Int. Trade 2010–11, Leader of the Govt in the House of Commons 2011–. *Address:* Parliament of Canada, Ottawa, ON K1A 0A9, Canada (office). *Website:* www.parl.gc.ca (office).

VAN MIDDELKOOP, Eimert; Dutch politician; b. 14 Feb. 1949, Berkel en Rodenrijs; m.; three s. one d.; ed Netherlands School of Econs, Rotterdam; Lecturer, Reformed School of Social Work, Zwolle 1971–72; Asst, Calvinist Political Union (GPV) 1973–89; mem. House of Reps (GPV) 1989–2001, for Christian Union 2001–02; mem. Senate 2003–07; Minister of Defence 2007–10, also Acting Minister of Housing, Communities and Integration 2010; fmr mem. Supervisory Cttee, Social and Cultural Planning Office; fmr Chair. Policy Review Cttee European Defence; fmr Sec. Centre for Parl. History, Nijmegen; fmr mem. Advisory Board, East-West Parl. Practice Project, Royal Netherlands Air Force, Netherlands Inst. of Int. Relations, Inst. for Multiparty Democracy. *Address:* c/o Ministry of Defence, Plein 4, POB 20701, 2500 ES The Hague, Netherlands (office).

VAN MONTAGU, Baron; Marc Charles Ernest, MSc, PhD; Belgian plant geneticist; *Professor Emeritus, Ghent University;* b. 10 Nov. 1933, Ghent; s. of Jean Van Montagu and Irene Van Beveren; m. Nora Podgaetchi 1957; ed Ghent Univ.; Dir Bureau d'Étude, Tech. School for the Nuclear Industry 1956–60; Prof. (part-

time), Free Univ. of Brussels –1989; Full Prof. ('Gewoon Hoogleraar') of Molecular Genetics, Ghent Univ. –1999, Founder and Chair. Inst. for Plant Biotechnology Outreach, Prof. Emer. 1999–; Dir Dept of Genetics, Flanders Inst. for Biotechnology –1999; Scientific Dir and mem. Bd of Dirs Plant Genetic Systems NV 1982–96; Founder and mem. Bd of Dirs CropDesign (Belgium) 1998–2004; Chair. Scientific Advisory Cttee, Danforth Center, St Louis, Mo., USA 1999–; Scientific Advisor, Tibotech (Belgium), Extracta (Brazil); mem. Science Bd of Alellyx, São Paulo, Brazil 2003–09; Biotechnology Advisor, Int. Centre for Agric. Research in Dry and Arid Areas, Aleppo, Syria; Scientific Advisor, CIB-CSIC (Centro de Investigaciones Biologicas), Madrid, Spain; mem. Bd of Govs and Scientific Advisory Bd, Weizmann Inst. of Science, Rehovot, Israel; mem. Science Advisory Cttee, Inst. of Molecular Biology and Biotechnology, Heraklion, Crete; mem. Int. Advisory Bd, King Abdulaziz Univ., Jeddah, Saudi Arabia; mem. Bd of Dirs Avesthagen, Bangalore, India 1999–2010; Chair. Cobiotech/ACOGEB, ICSU Bodies for Biotech Research 1996–2003; mem. Bd of Trustees, IITA, Ibadan, Nigeria 1991–96; mem. Selection Cttee, King Baudouin Int. Devt Prize 1990–98; mem. Advisory Bd (EGLS) of EU Commr Ph. Busquin, Directorate Gen.– Science and Tech., EC, Brussels 2000–04; Advisor to Flemish Inst. for Biotechnology, Ghent; mem. Council of Scientific Advisors, Int. Centre for Genetic Eng and Biotechnology, Trieste, Italy; mem. Agric. Food Security and Climate Change Jt Programming (FACCE-JPI) Stakeholder Advisory Bd, EU Chair. of the Scientific Advisory Panel of Futuragene; Pres. European Fed. of Biotechnology (Central Office), Barcelona, Spain, Black Sea Biotechnology Asscn, Public Research and Regulation Initiative, Delft, the Netherlands and Brussels, Belgium; Belgian Rep. in the Biosciences Steering Panel of European Academies Scientific Advisory Council, Leopoldina Acad., Halle, Germany; mem. Selection Cttee, L'Oréal-UNESCO 'For Women in Science' Prize, Paris, Balzan Prizes, Int. Balzan Foundation, Milan, Italy; mem. Belgian Royal Acad. of Sciences 1987, Academia Europea 1989, Agricultural Academy of Russia 1991, Acad. of Eng of Sweden 1992, Agricultural Acad. of France 1992, Royal Acad. of Overseas Sciences (Belgium) 1997, Italian Acad. of Sciences dei XL 1998, American Acad. of Microbiology 1999, TWAS, The World Acad. of Sciences 2001; Foreign Assoc. NAS 1986; title of Baron granted by King Baudoin I 1990; Francqui Chair, Faculty of Medicine, Catholic Univ. of Louvain 1971–72, Faculty of Medicine, Free Univ. of Brussels 1986–87, Faculty of Sciences, Catholic Univ. of Louvain 1994–95; Hon. DPhil (Helsinki) 1990; Dr hc (Helsinki) 1990, (Compiègne, France) 1995, (Rio de Janeiro) 1997, (Liège) 1997, (Free Univ. of Brussels) 1997, (Havana) 1999, (Sofia) 2004; Rank Prize for Nutrition (UK) 1987, IBM-Europe Prize (France) 1988, Charles Leopold Mayer Prize, Acad. of Sciences, Paris 1990, Dr A. De Leeuw-Damry-Bourlart Prize 1990, Japan Prize 1998, Theodor Bücher Medal, Fed. of European Biochemical Socs 1999, ranked as the most cited scientist in the field of Plant and Animal Science until 2004, Genome Valley Excellence Award, BioAsia (India) 2009, listed amongst the top 100 living contributors to Biotechnology (The Scientist, magazine of life sciences), World Food Prize (co-recipient) 2013. *Achievements:* discovery of the gene transfer mechanism between *Agrobacterium tumefaciens* and plants; pioneering contribs on plant gene discovery and regulation; major contribs in the studies of plant molecular mechanisms of response to abiotic stresses (light, ozone, cold, salt and drought); major contribs in the identification of *Arabidopsis* genes involved in growth, development and flowering (cell cycle); Applied Research Development of methods to alter *Agrobacterium* into an efficient delivery system for gene engineering in plants; construction of first plants producing the *Bacillus thuringensis* insecticide; construction of first herbicide tolerant plants; engineering of poplar trees with improved pulping qualities (altered lignin composition). *Publications:* 253 book chapters and reviewed conf. proceedings, 614 papers in peer-reviewed journals, 248 other journal articles. *Leisure interest:* travel. *Address:* VIB/IPBO/Ghent University Institute of Plant Biotechnology Outreach (IPBO), IIC/UGent Technologiepark 3, 9052 Zwijnaarde, Belgium (office). *Telephone:* (9) 264-87-27 (office); (2) 511-25-57 (home). *Fax:* (9) 264-87-95 (office). *E-mail:* marc.vanmontagu@vib-ugent.be (office); mamon@psb.ugent.be (office). *Website:* www.ipbo.ugent.be (office).

VAN MUNSTER, Hans, DPhil; Dutch ecclesiastic; b. 17 Nov. 1925, Gouda; s. of J. M. van Munster and A. C. B. Faay; ed Univ. of Louvain; entered Order of St Francis of Assisi 1944; ordained priest 1951; Lecturer in Logic and Methodology, Philosophical Inst., Venray 1955–67; Regent, RC Lycee, Venray 1963–67; Prof. of Philosophy, Catholic Theological Faculty of Utrecht 1967–71, Rector 1968–71; Vicar-Gen. of Archdiocese of Utrecht 1970–81; Sec.-Gen. Dutch Bishops' Conf. 1981–91; Pres. Cttee on Justice and Peace 1991–99; Pres. European Conf. of Justice and Peace Comms 1996–99; Pres. Catholic Bible Soc. 1992–98, Franciscan Asscn 1992–98; Officer Order of Oranje-Nassau 1976, Kt of Netherlands Lion 1991. *Publications include:* Kierkegaard een keuze uit zijn dagboeken 1957, De filosofische gedachten van de jonge Kierkegaard 1958, Kierkegaards redevoeringen 1959, Over de vertwijfeling 1963, Sören Aabye Kierkegaard 1963, Naar woorden moet je luisteren 1981, Vanwaar? Waarheen? 1982, Drie prioriteiten voor de kerk van Europa 1983, Kantelt de Koets wel? 1989, Een steen in de vijver, vrede en gerechtigheid na de dood van Marx 1993, Te Doen gerechtigheid 1993, De ware vrede 1993, 't is een vreemdeling zeker 1994, Een ryke heeft het moeilijk 1997, De mystiek van Franciscus 2002, Een mens te zýn op aarde 2004, Wýsheid van Kierkegaard 2006. *Leisure interests:* cycling, literature. *Address:* Jan van Scorelstraat 75, 3583 CL Utrecht, Netherlands (home). *Telephone:* (30) 2510153 (home). *Fax:* (30) 2523326 (home).

VAN NIEKERK, André Isak (Kraai), PhD; South African politician and agricultural scientist; *Chairman, Democratic Alliance Parliamentary Caucus;* b. 7 Oct. 1938, Eshowe, Natal; m. Theresa Claassens 1964; three s.; ed Univ. of Stellenbosch; taught Science and Agric. Eshowe Bantu Training Coll. 1962; specialist officer, Dept of Agric. Tech. Services, Univ. of Stellenbosch 1964–67; Research at Rowett Inst., Aberdeen, UK 1968, Wageningen Agricultural Univ., Netherlands 1969; farmer, Kenhardt Dist 1971–81; elected MP for Prieska 1981; Deputy Minister of Agric. 1986, of Agric. and Water Supply in Ministers' Council 1989, of Agricultural Devt 1989; Minister of Agric. in Cabinet, of Agricultural Devt in Ministers' Council 1991–94, of Agric., Govt of Nat. Unity 1994–96; apptd Leader Nat. Party for the Northern Cape 1994; mem. Senate (for Northern Cape) 1994, Deputy Leader 1994; currently Deputy Chair. Fed. Council, Democratic Alliance and Chair. Parl. Caucus; Hon. Award of S African Agricultural Union 1996, Service to Agric. Prestigious Award, Agricultural Writers' Asscn 1996, Agricul-

2240

tural Leader of the Year, Rand Show Soc. 1996, Golden Ram Award, Nat. Woolgrowers Asscn 1997. *Leisure interest:* bee-farming. *Address:* Democratic Alliance, POB 1475, Cape Town 8000, South Africa (office). *Telephone:* (83) 2616468 (Mobile); (21) 8872596 (also fax) (home). *Fax:* (21) 4032134 (office). *E-mail:* headoffice@da.org.za (office); kraaines@mweb.co.za (home). *Website:* www .da.org.za (office).

VAN PEEBLES, Mario, BEcons; American actor and film director; b. 15 Jan. 1957, Mexico City; s. of Melvin Van Peebles and Maria Marx; ed Columbia Univ.; film debut aged 11; worked as budget analyst in New York Mayor's office; studied acting and script interpretation with Stella Adler. *Theatre:* Champion, Jungle Fever, Midnight, Friday The 13th, Deadwood Dick, Bodybags (also co-dir). *Films include:* Sweet Sweetback's Baadasssss Song 1971, Exterminator 2 1984, Cotton Club 1984, Rappin 1985, Delivery Boys 1985, South Bronx Heroes 1985, 3:15 1986, Last Resort 1986, Heartbreak Ridge 1986, Hotshot 1987, Jaws: The Revenge 1987, Identity Crisis 1989, New Jack City (also dir) 1991, Posse (also dir) 1993, Letter to Dad 1994, Gunmen (also dir) 1994, Highlander III: The Sorcerer 1994, Panther (also dir, producer) 1995, Gang in Blue 1996, Solo 1996, Los Locos (also dir and screenplay) 1997, Stag 1997, Love Kills (also dir, producer) 1998, Crazy Six 1998, Judgment Day 1999, Raw Nerve 1999, Blowback 2000, Guardian 2000, Ali 2001, The Hebrew Hammer 2003, How to Get the Man's Foot Outta Your Ass 2003 (also dir, producer and screenplay), Gang of Roses 2003, Hard Luck 2006 (also dir), Confessionsofa Ex-Doofus-Itchy Footed Mutha 2008, A Letter to Dad 2009, Tied to a Chair 2009, Multiple Sarcasms 2010. *Television includes:* Children of the Night 1985, D.C. Cops 1986, LA Law 1986, The Facts of Life Down Under 1987, The Child Saver 1988, Blue Bayou 1990, Malcolm Takes a Shot 1990, A Triumph of the Heart: The Ricky Bell Story 1991, Stompin' at the Savoy 1992, In the Line of Duty: Street War 1992, Full Eclipse 1993, Mama Flora's Family 1998, Killers in the House 1998, Sally Hemings: An American Scandal 2000, Rude Awakening (series) 2000–01, 10,000 Black Men Named George 2002, The Street Lawyer 2003, 44 Minutes: The North Hollywood Shoot-Out 2003, Crown Heights 2004, Sharp-shooter 2007, All My Children (series) 2008, Damages (series) 2009, Mario's Green House (series) 2009, Way Black When 2010. *Address:* Vincent Cirrincione Associates, 8721 Sunset Blvd., Suite 205, Los Angeles, CA 90069; United Talent Agency, c/o Steven Small, 9560 Wilshire Blvd., Beverly Hills, CA 90212, USA. *Telephone:* (310) 854-0533. *Fax:* (310) 854-0558. *E-mail:* info@vincentcirrincione .com.

VAN ROMPUY, Herman, BA, MA; Belgian politician and European Union official; *President, European Council;* b. 31 Oct. 1947, Etterbeek, Brussels; s. of Prof. Vic Van Rompuy and Germaine Geens; m. Geertrui Windels; two s. two d.; ed Sint-Jan Berchmans Coll., Brussels, Catholic Univ. of Leuven; attaché study service, Nat. Bank of Belgium 1972–75; Nat. Vice-Pres. CVP (Christian Democrat Party, now CD&V—Christen-Democratisch en Vlaams) Youth, 1973–75, mem. Nat. CVP 1978, Nat. Pres. CVP 1988–93; adviser to Cabinet of Prime Minister Leo Tindemans 1975–78, to Minister of Finance 1978–80; Lecturer, Handelshoge-school Antwerpen 1980–87, Vlaamse Economische Hogeschool Brussel (VLEKHO) 1982–; Dir Centre for Political, Econ. and Social Studies 1980–88; Senator 1988–95; Sec. of State for Finance and Small and Medium-Sized Enterprises 1988–93; Deputy Prime Minister and Minister of Budget 1993–99; mem. Chamber of Reps 1995–2009, Pres. 2007–08; Minister of State 2004; Prime Minister of Belgium 2008–09; Pres. European Council 2009–; Grand Ribbon, Order of Leopold 2009; Collier du Mérite européen, European Merit Foundation (Luxembourg) 2010, Hon. Citizen of De Haan 2012, of Olen 2013. *Publications:* De kentering der tijden 1979, Hopen na 1984, Het christendom. Een moderne gedachte 1990, Vernieuwing in hoofd en hart. Een tegendraadse visie 1998, De binnenkant op een kier. Avonden zonder politiek 2000, Dagboek van een vijftiger 2004, Op zoek naar wijsheid 2007, Haiku 2010, In de wereld van Herman Van Rompuy (with Kathleen Cools) 2010. *Address:* Office of the President of the European Council, Justus Lipsius Building, 175 rue de la Loi, 1048 Brussels, Belgium (office). *Telephone:* (2) 281-97-29 (office). *Fax:* (2) 281-67-37 (office). *E-mail:* ec.president@european -council.europa.eu (office). *Website:* www.european-council.europa.eu (office).

VAN ROOY, Yvonne Catharina Maria Theresia; Dutch politician and fmr university administrator; *President, Netherlands Organisation of Hospitals;* b. 4 June 1951, Eindhoven; ed Jeanne d'Arc Lyceum, Maastricht, Utrecht Univ.; trainee at EC, Brussels 1977; staff mem. Dutch Christian Employers' Union 1978–84; mem. European Parl. (Christian Democrats) 1984–86, 1989–90, 1994–97; Minister for Foreign Trade 1986–89, 1990–94; Pres. Exec. Bd Catholic University Brabant (renamed Tilburg Univ. 2002) 1997–2004; Pres. Exec. Bd Utrecht Univ. 2004–13; currently Pres. Netherlands Organisation of Hospitals; Chair. Bd of Foundation for Promotion of Exports; Crown mem. Social and Econ. Council of the Netherlands; mem. Advisory Bd Deloitte, Selection Cttee for the Judiciary; mem. Supervisory Bd Bank Nederlandse Gemeenten; mem. Bd of Dirs Radboud Foundation; mem. Royal Concertgebouw Orchestra; Kt, Order of the Netherlands Lion, Commdr, Order of Orange-Nassau. *Address:* c/o Utrecht University, Heidelberglaan 8, PO Box 80125, 3508 Utrecht TC, Netherlands.

VAN ROSSUM, Anton, MBA; Belgian business executive; *Chairman of the Supervisory Board, Vopak NV;* b. 1945; ed Erasmus Univ. Rotterdam; various consultancy positions in banking and insurance sectors; with McKinsey & Co. 1972–2000, co-f. McKinsey & Co. Brussels Office; CEO Fortis 2000–04; mem. Supervisory Bd Vopak NV, Rotterdam 2007–Chair. 2008–; mem. Bd of Dirs Credit Suisse Group AG 2005–, Solvay SA, Brussels 2006–, Rodamco Europe 2007–, Munich Re 2009–; Chair. Supervisory Bd Erasmus Univ. Rotterdam; mem. Bd of Dirs Credit Suisse Group AG, Solvay SA; mem. Supervisory Bd Münchener Rückversicherungs-Gesellschaft, Rodamco Europe NV; mem. Bd of Trustees, Conference Bd; Chair. Netherlands Econ. Inst.; Int. Pres. European League for Econ. Co-operation; mem. Int. Advisory Council, American EC Asscn; mem. Consultative Council, Solvay Business School, Brussels. *Address:* Office of the Chairman of the Supervisory Board, Vopak NV, PO Box 863, 3000 AW Rotterdam, Netherlands (office). *Telephone:* (10) 4002911 (office). *Fax:* (10) 4139829 (office). *E-mail:* info@vopak.com (office). *Website:* www.vopak.com (office).

VAN SANT, Gus, Jr, BA; American film director and screenwriter; b. 24 July 1952, Louisville, Ky; ed Rhode Island School of Design; fmr production asst to Ken Shapiro; Nat. Soc. of Film Critics Awards for Best Dir and Screenplay 1990, New York Film Critics and LA Film Critics Award for Best Screenplay 1989, PEN

Literary Award for Best Screenplay Adaptation (jtly) 1989; American Civil Liberties Union (ACLU) of Ore. Freedom of Expression Award 1992, Visionary Award, Stockholm Film Festival 2010. *Albums:* Gus Van Sant 1997, 18 Songs About Golf 1997. *Films include:* Mala Noche (dir, writer), Drugstore Cowboy 1989 (dir, writer, with Daniel Yost), My Own Private Idaho (dir, writer) 1991, Even Cowgirls Get the Blues (dir, writer) 1993, To Die For (dir)1995, Kids (producer) 1995, Ballad of the Skeletons (dir) 1996, Good Will Hunting (dir) 1997, Psycho (dir) 1998, Finding Forrester 2000, Gerry 2002, Elephant (documentary dir, Palme d'Or and Best Dir, Cannes Film Festival) 2003, Last Days 2005, Paris, je t'aime (segment) 2006, Paranoid Park (60th Anniversary Award, Cannes Film Festival 2007) 2007, Milk 2008, Promised Land 2012. *Publications:* 108 Portraits (collection of photgraphs) 1995, Pink 1997. *Address:* William Morris Agency, One William Morris Place, Beverly Hills, CA 90212, USA (office). *Telephone:* (310) 859-4000 (office). *Fax:* (310) 859-4462 (office). *Website:* www.wma.com (office).

VAN SCHAIK, Gerard, PhD, FCIS; Dutch business executive (retd); b. 29 March 1930, Haarlem; s. of Gerard Van Schaik and Maria Mulder; m. Moyra Colijn 1963 (deceased); two s. one d.; ed Free Univ. of Amsterdam, IMEDE, Switzerland; officer Royal Netherlands Air Force 1956–58; joined Heineken's Bierbrouwerij Maatschappij N.V. 1959, mem. Exec. Bd Heineken NV 1974, Deputy Chair. 1983, Chair. 1989–93; Pres. Supervisory Bd Aegon NV 1993–2000; Dir of numerous cos; Vice Chair. CEIBS China European Business School, Shanghai; Hon. Pres. European Foundation of Man. Devt, Brussels; Hon. Fellow, London Business School; Kt, Order of the Dutch Lion; Dr hc (State Acad. for Man., Moscow) 1997. *Leisure interests:* golf, music. *Address:* Duinvoetlaan 7, 2243 GK Wassenaar, The Netherlands. *Telephone:* (70) 5179008. *Fax:* (70) 5179008. *E-mail:* gvschaik@ ziggo.nl (home).

VAN SCHALKWYK, Marthinus Christoffel Johannes, MA; South African politician; *Minister of Environmental Affairs and Tourism;* b. 10 Nov. 1959, Pietersburg; m. Suzette van Schalkwyk; one s. one d.; ed Pietersburg High School, Rand Afrikaans Univ.; Nat. Pres. Afrikaanse Studentbond, Chair. Youth for S Africa, Fed. Youth Leader, Nat. Party; mil. service 1978–79; Lecturer in Political Science, Rand Afrikaans Univ., Univ. of Stellenbosch; MP for Randburg 1990–94; mem. Nat. Ass. 1994–, mem. Parl. Portfolio Cttee on Communications, Nat. Party Rep. at Int. Democratic Union and African Dialogue Group; apptd Exec. Dir Nat. Party 1997, Leader New Nat. Party 1997–2005 (party disbanded); Premier of the Western Cape 2002–04; Minister of Environmental Affairs and Tourism 2004–; mem. African Nat. Congress (ANC) 2005–; Pres. African Ministerial Conf. on the Environment 2008–; Abe Bailey Bursary to GB and Europe, Award for Academic Achievement, Transvaal Lawyers' Asscn. *Address:* Private Bag X9154, Cape Town 8000 (office); Private Bag X447, Pretoria 0001, South Africa (office). *Telephone:* (21) 4657240 (Cape Town) (office); (12) 3103611 (Pretoria) (office). *Fax:* (21) 4653216 (Cape Town) (office); (12) 3220082 (Pretoria) (office). *E-mail:* strugel@deat.gov.za (office). *Website:* www.environment.gov.za (office).

VAN SLINGELANDT, Diederik (Rik) Johannes Maximilianus Govert Baron, BBA; Dutch banking executive (retd); b. 17 July 1946, Delft; m.; two c.; ed Dutch High School A, Rotterdam, Univ. of Groningen; staff mem. Nationale Investeringsbank NV 1972–80; Head of Finance Dept, Rijn Schelde Verolme 1980–82; Dir of Finance, Treasury, Admin and Information Tech., Verolme Estaleiros Reunidos do Brasil ste, Rio de Janeiro 1982–85; Financial Dir Rodamco Groep 1985–89, also mem. Investment Cttee; Dir of Int. Operations, Rabobank Nederland 1989–96, mem. Bd Dirs 1996–2006, Chair. Rabobank Int. 1996–2006, Acting CEO of Exec. Bd Rabobank Group 2004, fmr Chair. Supervisory Bd Rabo Australia Ltd, Rabobank Int. Advisory Services (RIAS) BV, Interpolis NV, fmr Chair. Bd Dirs Rabobank Pension Fund; Chair. Exec. Cttee Centrale Bank Bedrijf 1989–96Vice-Chair. Supervisory Bd Bank Sarasin & Cie; apptd mem. Supervisory Bd KAS Bank NV 2007, Vice-Chair. then Chair. –2010 (retd); mem. Supervisory Bd IHC Merwede Holland B.V., Redevco Europe Services B.V, Robeco Groep NV, SNP Groep NV; mem. Advisory Cttee Issuing Insts (Euronext), Unico Steering Cttee, Bd Dirs Ubbo Emmius Fund, Univ. of Groningen; Officer, Order of Orange-Nassau 2006. *Address:* c/o Supervisory Board, KAS Bank NV, Spuistraat 172, Amsterdam 1012 VT, Netherlands (office).

VAN SWAAIJ, Willibrordus Petrus Maria, PhD; Dutch chemical engineer and academic; *Professor, University of Twente;* b. 18 Jan. 1942, Nijmegen; s. of Christian van Swaaij and C. Bosman; m. J. J. T. van den Berk 1966; one s. four d.; ed Tech. Univ. of Eindhoven, Univ. of Nancy, France; joined Shell Research 1965, worked in lab. Shell Research BV (KSLA), Amsterdam 1966–72, Section Chief, Gasification 1971–72; Prof. of Chemical Eng Science, Twente Univ. 1972–, mem. of staff Thermo-Chemical Conversion of Biomass Group 1999–; Consultant to DSM, AKZO, Unilever, Netherlands Govt, EEC; mem. Royal Netherlands Acad. of Sciences 1986; Kt Order of the Lion (Netherlands) 1997; Dr hc (Inst. Nat. Polytechnique de Lorraine, France) 1996; Australian European Fellowship Award 1984, Dow Energy Prize 1985, Grand Prix du Génie des Procédés, Inst. de France 1996, Golden Tesla Medal 1999, Golden Hoogewerff Medal for Lifetime Achievement 2000. *Publications:* Chemical Reactor Design and Operation (with Wester-terp and Beenackers); about 340 scientific papers, contribs to books etc. *Leisure interests:* sailing, surfing, photography, gardening, history. *Address:* University of Twente, TNW Meander, PO 217, 7500 AE Enschede (office); Sportlaan 60, 7581 BZ Losser, Netherlands (home). *Telephone:* (53) 4892880 (office); (53) 5382677 (home). *Fax:* (53) 4894738 (office); (53) 5384368 (home). *E-mail:* w.p.m.vanswaaij@utwente .nl (office).

VAN VLISSINGEN, Annemiek M. Fentener, MSc, AM; Dutch business executive; *Chairman of the Supervisory Board, SHV Holdings NV;* b. 14 April 1961; d. of Frits Fentener; ed Univ. of Groningen and postgraduate studies in USA; Man. of Strategy and Business Devt, SHV Holdings NV, mem. Supervisory Bd 2003–, currently Chair.; Deputy Chair. Supervisory Bd, Draka Holding NV 2001–06; mem. Supervisory Bd, Univ. Medical Centre, Utrecht, Heineken International BV, Heineken NV 2006–, Heineken Holding NV, Flint Holding NV, De Nederlandsche Bank; mem. NPM Capital NV; Commr for Heineken, Draka Holding NV, NV Buco. *Address:* SHV Holdings NV, Rijnkade 1, 3511 LC Utrecht, Netherlands (office). *Telephone:* (30) 233-88-33 (office). *Fax:* (30) 233-83-04 (office). *E-mail:* info@shv.nl (office). *Website:* www.shv.nl (office).

VAN WACHEM, Lodewijk Christiaan; Dutch business executive and mechanical engineer; b. 31 July 1931, Pangkalan Brandan, now Indonesia; m. Elisabeth G. Cristofoli 1958; two s. one d.; ed Delft Univ. of Technology; joined Bataafsche Petroleum Maatschappij, The Hague 1953; Mechanical Engineer, Cía Shell de Venezuela 1954–63; Chief Engineer, Shell-BP Petroleum Devt Co. of Nigeria 1963–66, Eng Man. 1966–67, Chair. and Man. Dir 1972–76; Head Tech. Admin. Brunei Shell Petroleum Co. Ltd 1967–69, Tech. Dir 1969–71; Head of Production Div. Shell Int. Petroleum Maatschappij, The Hague 1971–72, Co-ordinator Exploration and Production 1976–79; Man. Dir Royal Dutch Petroleum Co. 1976–82, Pres. 1982–92; mem. Presidium of Bd of Dirs, Shell Petroleum NV 1976–92; Man. Dir Shell Petroleum Co. Ltd 1976–92, Chair. Jt Cttee of Man. Dirs of the Royal Dutch/Shell Group 1985–92, Chair. Supervisory Bd Royal Dutch Petroleum Co. 1992–2002; mem. Bd of Dirs Crédit Suisse Holding 1992–96, Zurich Insurance Group (now Zurich Financial Services) 1993–2005 (Vice-Chair. 2001–02, Chair. 2002–05); mem. Supervisory Bd Akzo-Nobel NV 1992–2002, Royal Philips Electronics NV 1993 (Chair. 1999), BMW (Munich) 1994–2002, Bayer AG 1997–2002, RAND Europe (mem. Exec. Bd 2005–); Chair. Global Crossing 2003–07; Dir (non-exec.) IBM Corpn 1992–2002, ATCO Ltd 1993–, AAB Brown Boveri Ltd 1996–99; Hon. Citizen of Singapore 2004; Hon. Commdr and KBE 1989, Kt Order of Netherlands Lion 1981, Commdr, Order of Oranje Nassau 1990, Public Service Star, Singapore 1998.

VAN WALSUM, (Arnold) Peter, LLB; Dutch diplomatist; b. 25 June 1934, Rotterdam; m.; four c.; ed Univ. of Utrecht; served in Dutch mil. 1960–62; with Civil Emergency Planning Section, Ministry of Gen. Affairs 1962–63; First Sec., Perm. Mission to UN, New York 1970–74, First Sec., Embassy in New Delhi 1974–79, Counsellor, Embassy in London 1975–79, Counsellor, Perm. Mission to EC, Brussels 1979–81, Head of Western Hemisphere Dept, Ministry of Foreign Affairs 1981–85, Amb. to Thailand 1985–89, Dir-Gen. Political Affairs, Ministry of Foreign Affairs 1989–93, Amb. to Germany 1993–98, Perm. Rep. to UN, New York 1998–2001, Chair. Iran Sanctions Cttee 1999–2000; UN Sec.-Gen.'s Personal Envoy for Western Sahara 2005–08. *Address:* c/o Ministry of Foreign Affairs, Bezuidenhoutseweg 67, POB 20061, 2500 EB The Hague, Netherlands.

VAN WIJNGAARDEN, Leendert, PhD; Dutch scientist and academic; *Professor Emeritus of Fluid Mechanics, University of Twente;* b. 16 March 1932, Delft; s. of Cornelis M. van Wijngaarden and Jeanne Severijn; m. Willy F. de Goede 1962; two s.; ed Gymnasium B, Delft and Technological Univ. of Delft; Netherlands Ship Model Basin, Wageningen 1962–66, latterly Head of Hydrodynamics Dept; Prof. of Fluid Mechanics, Twente Univ. 1966–97, Prof. Emer. 1997–; mem. of Bureau and Treasurer Int. Union of Theoretical and Applied Mechanics 1984–88, Pres. 1992–96, Vice-Pres. 1996–2000; mem. Royal Netherlands Acad. of Science 1988–; Kt in the Order of the Dutch Lion 1995. *Publications:* about 70 publs in professional journals. *Leisure interests:* tennis, chess, literature, music. *Address:* University of Twente, Faculty of Science and Technology, PO Box 217, 7500 AE Enschede (office); van Weberlaan 7, 7522 KB Enschede, Netherlands (home). *Telephone:* (53) 893086 (office); (53) 352078 (home). *Fax:* (53) 4898068 (office). *E-mail:* L.vanWijngaarden@utwente.nl (office). *Website:* www.tnw.utwente.nl/pof (office).

VAN WINDEN, Jacobus Cornelis Maria; Dutch ecclesiastic and professor of Greek; *Professor Emeritus, University of Leiden;* b. 10 Oct. 1922, Schipluiden; ed in Franciscan convents and Leiden Univ.; mem. Franciscan Order (OFM) 1941; ordained priest 1948; Asst to J. H. Waszink, Prof. of Latin, Leiden 1954–56; teacher of Greek and Latin, Rotterdam 1956–66; Reader, Leiden Univ. 1966–80, Prof. of Greek of Late Antiquity 1980–87, Prof. Emer. 1987–; Ed.-in-Chief Vigiliae Christianae (review of Early Christian Life and Language) 1977–; mem. Royal Netherlands Acad. *Publications:* Calcidius on Matter: His Doctrine and Sources 1959, An Early Christian Philosopher: Justin Martyr's Dialogue with Trypho (Chapters 1–9) 1971, Tertullianus, De idolatria (critical text, trans. and commentary with J. H. Waszink) 1987, De weg eigenlijk: Wegen van vroeg-christelijk denken 1992, Bonaventura, Itinerarium. De Weg die de geest naar God voert 1996, Arche. A Collection of Patristic Studies 1997, Bonaventura, Breviloquium, De theologie in kort bestek 2000. *Address:* Haarlemmerstraat 106, 2312 GD Leiden, Netherlands. *Telephone:* (71) 5120401.

VAN WYK, Andreas Herculas, BA, LLD; South African professor of law and university rector (retd); b. 17 Sept. 1941, Pretoria; s. of Andries Hercules du Preez van Wyk and Hendrina Louise van Wyk (née Kruger); m. Magdalena Krüger 1967; two d.; ed Helpmekaar Boys' High School, Johannesburg, Univs of Stellenbosch and Leiden; Lecturer, then Prof., then Dean, Faculty of Law, Univ. of Stellenbosch 1966–84, Dir Gen. Dept of Constitutional Devt 1984–87, Prof. Faculty of Law 1987–91, Vice-Rector Operations 1991–93, Rector and Vice-Chancellor 1993–2000; Chair. South African Univs Vice-Chancellors Asscn 2001; mem. Bd of Dirs Old Mutual Life Assurance Co. (South Africa) Ltd, Chair. 2008–09; Guest, USA/SA Leadership Exchange Programme 1978; Alexander von Humboldt Foundation Fellowship 1981; mem. SA Akad. vir wetenskap en kuns; Hon. LLD (Leuven); William of Orange Medal (Leiden) 1995. *Publications:* The Power to Dispose of the Assets of the Universal Matrimonial Community of Property 1976, Die Suid-Afrikaanse Kontraktereg en Handelsreg (co-author) 1992, Family, Property and Succession 1983 and numerous articles in academic journals; has drafted various pieces of legislation. *Address:* c/o Board of Directors, Old Mutual Life Assurance Company (South Africa) Ltd, Mutualpark, Jan Smuts Drive, Pinelands, 7405, South Africa.

VAN ZYL SLABBERT, Dr F. (see Slabbert, F. Van Zyl).

VANACKERE, Steven, LenD; Belgian politician; b. 4 Feb. 1964, Wevelgem, W Flanders; s. of Leo Vanackere; m.; ed Catholic Univ. of Leuven; started career with Kredietbank SA 1987–88; adviser to Herman Van Rompuy (Chair. Christian Democratic Party) 1990–91; chief aide to Jos Chabert (Minister of Brussels-Capital Region) 1991–93; Dir-Gen. Port of Brussels 1993–95, Deputy Dir-Gen. STIB/MIVB (Brussels Public Transport Co.) 2000–05; mem. Flemish regional parl. 2004–07, Flemish Minister for Welfare, Public Health and Family Affairs 2007–08; Deputy Prime Minister and Minister for Institutional Reforms 2008–11, also Minister of Foreign Affairs 2009–11, Deputy Prime Minister and Minister for Finance and Sustainable Devt, in charge of Public Affairs 2011–13; mem. Christen-Democratisch en Vlaams. *Address:* Christen-Democratisch en Vlaams, Wetstraat

89, 1040 Brussels, Belgium (office). *Telephone:* (2) 238-38-11 (office). *Fax:* (2) 230-43-60. *Website:* www.cdenv.be (office); www.stevenvanackere.be.

VANDENBROUCKE, Frank, DPhil; Belgian politician; *Vice-Minister-President of the Flemish Government and Flemish Minister for Work, Education and Training;* b. 21 Oct. 1955, Louvain; ed Catholic Univ. of Louvain, Univs of Cambridge and Oxford, UK; Research Asst, Centrum voor Economische Studiën, Catholic Univ. of Louvain 1978–80; staff mem. SEVI (Research Dept of Socialist Party of Flemish Region) 1982–85; MP 1985–94; Leader Socialist Party 1989–94; Leader Parl. Group of Socialist Party 1995–96; Deputy Prime Minister and Minister of Foreign Affairs 1994–95; Minister of Social Affairs and Pensions July 1999–2003; Minister of Employment and Pensions 2003–04; Vice-Minister-Pres. Flemish Govt and Flemish Minister for Work, Educ. and Training 2004–. *Address:* Koning Albert II-Laan 15, 1210 Brussels, Belgium (office). *Telephone:* (2) 552-68-00 (office). *Fax:* (2) 552-68-01 (office). *E-mail:* kabinet.vandenbroucke@vlaanderen .be (office). *Website:* www.ministerfrankvandenbroucke.be (office).

VANDER ZALM, William N.; Canadian (b. Dutch) politician and business executive; *President, Van's International Projects Inc.;* b. (Wilhelmus Theodorus Nicholaas Maria Vander Zalm), 29 May 1934, Noordwykerhout, Netherlands; s. of Wilhelmus Nicholaas van der Zalm and Agatha C. Warmerdam; m. Lillian B. Mihalick 1956; two s. two d.; ed Phillip Sheffield High School, Abbotsford, BC, Canada; emigrated to Canada 1947, became Canadian citizen; purchased Art Knapp Nurseries Ltd, became Co. Pres. 1956; elected to Surrey Municipal Council as Alderman 1965, as Mayor 1969–75; elected to Prov. Legis. for Social Credit Party, Minister of Human Resources 1975; Minister of Municipal Affairs and Minister responsible for Urban Transit Authority (now BC Transit) 1978; Minister of Educ. and Minister responsible for BC Transit 1982; est. Fantasy Garden World, major tourist attraction in Richmond 1983; Leader BC Social Credit Party 1986–; Premier of BC 1986–91; Pres. Van's International Projects Inc. 1991–, Mitsch Nursery Inc., Oregon, USA 1994–; Leader Reform BC Party 1996–2001; Dir EnvirEau; Leader of "Fight HST" (first successful tax referendum in Canada) 2009; Hon. LLD (Univ. of N. British Columbia) 2004. *Publications:* Northwest's Gardener's Almanac, Vander Zalm For the People. *Leisure interests:* fishing, swimming. *Address:* 3553 Arthur Drive, Ladner, BC V4K 3N2, Canada (home). *Telephone:* (604) 946-1774. *Fax:* (604) 946-1981. *E-mail:* billvanderzalm@dccnet .com (home). *Website:* www.billvanderzalm.com; www.fighthst.com.

VANDERHAEGHE, Guy Clarence, OC, BA, BEd, MA, FRSC; Canadian writer, playwright and academic; *Assistant Professor, Department of English, St Thomas More College;* b. 5 April 1951, Esterhazy, Sask.; s. of Clarence Earl Vanderhaeghe and Alma Beth Allen; m. Margaret Nagel 1972; ed Univ. of Saskatchewan, Univ. of Regina; St Thomas More Scholar, St Thomas More Coll., Univ. of Saskatchewan 1993–, currently also Asst Prof., Dept of English; Fellow, Pierre Eliott Trudeau Foundation 2007; Saskatchewan Order of Merit 2004; Hon. DLitt (Saskatchewan) 1997; Gov.-Gen.'s Awards 1982, 1996, Canadian Authors' Asscn Award for Drama 1996, Saskatchewan Book Award 1996. *Publications include:* novels: Man Descending (Gov. Gen. Literary Award for Fiction 1982, Geoffrey Faber Memorial Prize 1987) 1982, The Trouble With Heroes 1983, My Present Age 1984, Homesick (City of Toronto Book Award 1990) 1989, Things As They Are? 1992, The Englishman's Boy (Gov. Gen. Literary Award for Fiction) 1996, The Last Crossing 2004, A Good Man 2011; plays: I Had a Job I Liked, Once (Canadian Authors Asscn Award for Drama 1993) 1991, Dancock's Dance 1995. *Address:* Department of English, St Thomas More College, 1437 College Drive, Saskatoon, SK S7N 0W6, Canada (office). *Telephone:* (306) 966-8900 (office). *Fax:* (306) 966-8904 (office). *E-mail:* gvanderhaeghe@stmcollege.ca (office). *Website:* stmcollege.ca (office).

VANDERHOEF, Larry N., BS, MS, PhD; American biochemist, academic and fmr university administrator; *Chancellor Emeritus and Professor, College of Biological Sciences, University of California, Davis;* b. 1941, Minn.; m. Rosalie Slifka Vanderhoef, two c.; ed Univ. of Wis., Purdue Univ.; Asst Prof. of Biology, Univ. of Ill. 1970–77, Prof. and Head of Dept 1977–80; Provost Univ. of Md, College Park 1980–84; Exec. Vice-Chancellor Univ. of Calif., Davis 1984–94, Provost 1991–94, Chancellor 1994–2009, Chancellor Emer. 2009–, Prof., Coll. of Biological Sciences 2009–; Dr hc (Purdue) 2000, (Inje Univ., Korea) 2002; Distinguished Community Service Award, Anti-Defamation League 1999, Outstanding Contribution Award, Arts and Business Council of Sacramento 2004, Sacramentan of the Year 2005. *Address:* 1002 Life Sciences Building, College of Biological Sciences, University of California, Davis, CA 95616, USA (office). *Telephone:* (530) 752-0617 (office). *E-mail:* lnvanderhoef@ucdavis.edu (office). *Website:* biosci.ucdavis.edu (office).

VANDEVELDE, Luc; Belgian business executive; *Founder and Executive Chairman, Change Capital Partners;* b. 1951; joined Kraft Gen. Foods Ltd 1971, later apptd CEO Kraft Jacobs Suchard France and Italy –1995, Pres., COO 1995–99, Chair., CEO 1999–2000; participated in merger of Promodès and Carrefour 1999 (apptd Exec. Vice-Chair. new group); Exec. Chair. Marks & Spencer PLC 2000–04, CEO 2000–02; Founder and Exec. Chair. Change Capital Pnrs (pvt. equity firm) 2003–; mem. Bd of Dirs Carrefour SA 2004–07, Chair. 2005–07; mem. Bd of Dirs Société Générale, Vodafone Group plc 2003–, Sr Ind. Dir 2012–. *Address:* Change Capital Partners, 2nd Floor, College House, 272 Kings Road, London, SW3 5AW, England (office). *Telephone:* (20) 7808-9110 (office). *Fax:* (20) 7808-9111 (office). *E-mail:* lvandevelde@changecapitalpartners.com (office). *Website:* www.changecapitalpartners.com (office).

VANGELIS; Greek composer, musician (keyboards) and conductor; b. (Evangelos Papathanassiou), 29 March 1943, Volos; ed Acad. of Fine Arts, Athens and private tuition with Aristotelis Coudourof; began performing own compositions aged six; moved to Paris in late 1960s; composed and recorded symphonic poem Faire que ton rêve soit plus long que la nuit; returned to Greece, after period in London 1989; formed band Formynx in Greece 1960s; mem. Aphrodite's Child (with Demis Roussos) 1966–71; composer 1972–, in Paris, France, then established Nemo recording studio, London 1974; partnership with Jon Anderson as Jon & Vangelis 1980–84. *Composition for film:* O Adelfos mou o trohonomos 1963, To prosopo tis medusas 1966, 5000 pseumata 1966, Sex Power 1970, scores for French wildlife films 1972, Salut, Jerusalem 1972, L'Apocalypse des animaux 1972, Amore 1973, Le Cantique des créatures: Georges Mathieu ou La fureur d'être 1974, Le Cantique des créatures: Georges Braque ou Le temps différent 1975, Ignacio 1975, Ace Up

My Sleeve 1976, La Fête sauvage 1976, Prkosna delta 1980, Die Todesgöttin des Liebescamps 1981, Chariots of Fire (Acad. Award for Best Original Score 1982) 1981, Missing 1982, Le Cantique des créature: Pablo Picasso pintor 1982, Blade Runner 1982, Nankyoku monogatari 1983, Wonders of Life 1983, The Bounty 1984, Sauvage et beau 1984, Nosferatu a Venezia 1988, Le Dîner des bustes 1988, Russicum - I giorni del diavolo 1989, Francesco 1989, Terminator II 1990, La Peste 1992, Bitter Moon 1992, 1492: Conquest of Paradise 1992, De Nuremberg à Nuremberg 1994, Rangeela 1995, Kavafis 1996, I Hope 2001, Alexander 2004, El Greco 2007. *Composition for television:* L'Opera sauvage (series) 1977, Cosmos (series, BBC 1) 1980. *Recordings include:* albums: with Aphrodite's Child: Aphrodite's Child 1968, Rain & Tears 1968, End Of The World 1969, It's Five O'Clock 1970, 666 1972; solo: Terra, Dragon 1971, L'Apocalypse des animaux 1972, Earth 1973, Heaven and Hell 1975, Albedo 0.39 1976, The Vangelis Radio Special 1976, Spiral 1977, Beauborg 1978, Hypothesis 1978, China 1979, Odes 1979, See You Later 1980, To The Unknown Man 1981, Soil Festivities 1984, Invisible Connections 1985, Magic Moments 1985, Mask 1985, Direct 1988, The City 1990, Themes 1989, Voices 1995, El Greco 1995, Oceanic 1996, Reprise 1990–1999 2000, Mythodea: Music for the NASA Mission – 2001 Mars Odyssey 2001; as Jon & Vangelis: Short Stories 1980, The Friends of Mr Cairo 1981, Private Collection 1983, Page of Life 1991. *Address:* c/o Sony Classical, 550 Madison Avenue, New York, NY 10022-3211, USA (office). *Website:* www.vangelisworld.com.

VANHANEN, Matti Taneli, MScS; Finnish politician; b. 4 Nov. 1955, Jyväskylä; two c.; journalist, Kehäsanomat (local newspaper) 1985–88, Ed.-in-Chief 1988–91; mem. Centre Party 1976–, mem. Bd and Chair. Youth League 1980–83, Vice-Chair. Party 2000–2003, Chair. 2003–10 (resgnd); mem. Espoo City Council 1981–84; mem. Bd Helskinki Metropolitan Area Council YTV 1983–84; mem. Nurmijärvi Municipal Council 1989–; mem. Bd Uusimaa Regional Council 1997–2000; mem. Parl. 1991–; Vice-Chair. Centre Party Parl. Group 1994–2001, Parl. Environment Cttee 1991–95; Chair. Parl. Grand Cttee 2000–01; Rep. of Parl. to European Convention on the Future of the EU 2002–03; Minister of Defence April–June 2003; Prime Minister 2003–10 (resgnd); Vice-Chair. Housing Foundation for the Young 1981–97, Chair. 1998–2003; Chair. State Youth Council 1987–90; Vice-Chair. Housing Council 1991–2003; Chair. Union for Rural Educ. 1998–2003; Vice-Chair. Pro Medi-Heli Asscn 1995–2003; mem. Supervisory Bd Neste/Fortum 1991–2003, Helsingin Osuuskauppa (Cooperative) 2002–03. *Address:* c/o Suomen Keskusta (Kesk) (Finnish Centre Party), Apollonkatu 11a, 00100 Helsinki, Finland.

VANHEVEL, Jan; Belgian banking executive; joined Legal Dept, Kredietbank 1971, Head of Litigation Dept 1974–81, Head of Credit Dept 1981–84, Br. Man., Kredietbank, Antwerp 1984–86, Deputy Commercial Man., Antwerp Regional Office 1986–90, Man. Antwerp Corp. Office, Kredietbank 1990–94, Gen. Man., Processing and Automation Directorate 1994–96, Man. Dir and mem. Exec. Cttee Kredietbank 1996–98; Man. Dir KBC Bank and mem. Exec. Cttee KBC Group 1998–2006, CEO Cen. and Eastern Europe and Russia Business Unit, KBC Group 2006–09, CEO KBC Group and CEO Corp. Banking Activities of Merchant Banking Business Unit 2009–12. *Address:* c/o KBC Group, Havenlaan 2, 1080 Brussels, Belgium. *E-mail:* info@kbc.com.

VANNI, Carla, LLD; Italian journalist, editor and publishing executive; b. 18 Feb. 1936, Leghorn (Livorno); m. Vincenzo Nisivoccia; two c.; ed Univ. of Milan; joined Mondadori Publrs, working on fashion desk of Grazia magazine 1959, Head fashion desk 1964, Jt Ed.-in-Chief 1974, Ed.-in-Chief 1978–, responsible for launch of Marie Claire magazine in Italy 1987, Publishing Dir Marie Claire until 2002 and Cento Cose-Energy 1987–99, Donna Moderna 1995–, Flair 2003–, Easy Shop 2004–; has created several new supplements of Grazia: Grazia Bricolage, Grazia Blu and Grazia Int., Grazia Accessori and Grazia Uomo, Grazia Profumi e Balocchi and introduced coverage of social problems; also Ed.-in-Chief Grazia Casa; Head, Grazia Int. Network 2005–; mem. juries of several nat. and int. literary awards and many beauty competitions; Montenapoleone d'Oro (Best Journalist) 1970, The Oner (Journalist of the Year) 1987, Gullace (for coverage of women's interest issues) 1995, Letterario Castigioncello costa degli Etruschi Award 2001, Milan Fashion Award 2003, Fondazione Marisa Bellisario Award 2003, Forte dei Marmi 'Dietro la bellezza' Award 2003, Premio Milano per la Moda 2003, Premio 'Dietro la bellezza', Ponte dei Nariù 2003, Premio Narisa Bellsario 2003. *Address:* Grazia, Arnoldi Mondadori Editore, Via Arnoldo Mondadori 1, 20090 Segrate, Milan, Italy (office). *Telephone:* (02) 754212390 (office). *Fax:* (02) 75422515 (office). *E-mail:* vanni@mondadori.it (office).

VANNI D'ARCHIRAFI, Raniero; Italian fmr diplomatist and business executive; entered diplomatic service 1956; attached to office of Italy's Perm. Rep. to EC, Brussels 1961–66; with Ministry of Foreign Affairs 1966–73; First Counsellor, Madrid 1973; Minister Plenipotentiary 1980; Prin. Pvt. Sec. to Minister of Foreign Affairs 1980; Amb. to Spain 1984–87, 1995–99, to Germany 1987–90; Dir-Gen. for Econ. Affairs 1990, for Political Affairs 1991; mem. Comm. for Institutional Questions, The Internal Market, Financial Services, Enterprise Policy, Small and Medium-sized Enterprises, Trade Services, Crafts and Tourism, EC 1993–95; Pres. RCS Iberica 2002; Dir Telepizza, Finmeccanica. *Address:* c/o Ministry of Foreign Affairs, Piazzale della Farnesina 1, 00194 Rome, Italy (office).

VANRIET, Jan; Belgian painter; b. 21 Feb. 1948, Antwerp; m. Simone Lenaerts 1971; two s. one d.; ed Royal Acad. of Fine Arts, Antwerp; Dir Antwerp Acad. of Fine Arts, Hoboken 1980–2000; works in several museums in Europe, USA and Asia; Special Prize, Art Festival, Seoul 1990, Prize, Van Acker Foundation 2001. *Achievements:* monumental works for KCB-Bank, Brussels, Metro, Brussels, Roularta, Brussels, Bourla-Theatre Antwerp, Univ. of Antwerp. *Publications:* poetry: Staat van Beleg 1982, Geen Hond die Brood Lust 1984, Stormwoiud 2009, Many Catalogs, among Café Aurora 2000, De Reiziger is Blind 2001, Transport 2002, Closing Time 2010. *Address:* Louizastraat 22, 2000 Antwerp 1, Belgium. *Telephone:* (3) 232-47-76. *E-mail:* jan@janvanriet.com. *Website:* www.janvanriet.com.

VAQUINA, Alberto Clementino António, MD; Mozambican doctor and politician; *Prime Minister;* ed Inst. of Biomedical Sciences at Universidade do Porto and Inst. of Hygiene and Tropical Medicine, Universidade Nova de Lisboa, Portugal, Université Bordeaux II, France; worked as intern and then as doctor in Hosp. Geral de Santo António, Porto; later worked at Hosp. de S. José, Lisbon and Clínica

de Socorros Médicos 'The Vigilante', Amadora; studies in Lisbon 1994–95; returned to Mozambique 1996; medical practice in Dist of Monapo, prov. of Nampula; successively Dir of local hosp., then Dist Dir of Health; Dir of Health, prov. of Cabo Delgado 1998–2000; Dir of Health, prov. of Nampula 2001–05; Gov. prov. of Sofala 2005–10, prov. of Tete 2010–12; obtained Diplôme d'études supérieures spécialisées in France for work on health projects in developing countries 2011; Prime Minister of Mozambique 2012–; mem. FRELIMO (Frente de Libertação de Moçambique). *Address:* Office of the Prime Minister, Praça da Marinha Popular, Maputo, Mozambique (office). *Telephone:* (21) 426861 (office). *Fax:* (21) 426881 (office). *E-mail:* portaldogoverno@govnet.gov.mz (office). *Website:* www.portaldogoverno.gov.mz (office).

VARADHAN, Srinivasa S. R., MA, PhD, FRS, FAAS; American (b. Indian) mathematician and academic; *Professor, Department of Mathematics, Courant Institute of Mathematical Sciences, New York University;* b. 2 Jan. 1940, Chennai, India; s. of S. V. Rangaiyengar and S. R. Janaki; m. Vasundara Narayanan; two s.; ed Madras Univ., Indian Statistical Inst.; Visiting Mem., Courant Inst., New York Univ. 1963–66, Asst Prof. 1966–68, Assoc. Prof. 1968–72, Dir 1980–84, 1992–94, Prof. of Math. 1972–; Assoc. Fellow, Third World Acad. of Sciences 1988; mem. NAS; hon. degrees from Univ. of Paris, Indian Statistical Inst. and Chennai Inst. of Math.; Birkhoff Prize 1994, Steele Prize 1996, Abel Prize 2007. *Publications:* Multi-dimensional Diffusion Processes 1979, On Diffusion Problems and Partial Differentiation Equations 1980; Large Deviations and Applications 1984. *Leisure interests:* squash, bridge, travel. *Address:* Courant Institute, New York University, 251 Mercer Street, New York, NY 10012, USA (office). *Telephone:* (212) 998-3334 (office). *Fax:* (212) 995-4121 (home). *E-mail:* varadhan@cims.nyu.edu (office). *Website:* www.math.nyu.edu (office).

VARDA, Agnès; French film writer, film director and photographer; b. 30 May 1928, Ixelles, Belgium; d. of Eugène Jean Varda and Christiane Pasquet; m. Jacques Demy 1962 (died 1990); one s. one d.; ed Sète, Hérault, Univ. of the Sorbonne, Paris, Ecole du Louvre, Paris; Official Photographer, Avignon Festival/ Théâtre Nat. Populaire 1951–61; film-maker 1954–; plastician artist, video and installation artist 2003–; Commdr des Arts et des Lettres; Officier, Légion d'honneur, Grand Officier, Ordre nat. du Mérite 2007; César d'honneur 2001. *Full-length films:* La Pointe Courte 1954, Cleo de 5 à 7 (Prix Méliès 1962) 1961, Salut les Cubains (Bronze Lion, Venice Festival 1964) 1962, Le Bonheur (Prix Louis Delluc 1965, David Selznick Award 1965, Silver Bear, Berlin Festival 1965) 1964, Les Créatures 1965, Black Panthers (First Prize, Oberhausen) 1968, Lions Love (...and Lies) (Popular Univs Jury 1970) 1969, Nausicaa 1970, Daguerreotypes 1975, L'une chante l'autre pas (Grand Prix, Taormina, Sicily 1977) 1976, Mur Murs (Grand Prix, Firenze 1981) 1980, Documenteur (An Emotion Picture) 1981, Ulysse (César Award 1984) 1983, 7P. cuis. sdb... 1984, Sans toit ni loi (Vagabond) (Golden Lion, Best Film Venice Film Festival 1985, Prix Méliès 1985, LA Critics Best Foreign Film 1985) 1985, Jane B par Agnés V 1987, Kung Fu Master 1987, Jacquot de Nantes 1990, Les Demoiselles ont eu 25 ans 1992, L'Univers de Jacques Demy 1993, Les Cent et Une nuits 1994, Les Glaneurs et La Glaneuse 2000 (Acad. of European Cinema Award, Prix du Meilleur Film Française), Deux Ans après 2002, Le Lion Volatil 2003, Ydessa, the Bears and etc... 2004, Quelques Veuves de Noirmoutier 2006, Les Plages d'Agnès 2008. *Short-length films:* O saisons, O châteaux 1957, L'opéra-Mouffe 1958, Du côté de la côte 1958, Salut les cubains 1963, Elsa la rose 1965, Uncle Yanco 1967, Black Panthers 1968, Réponse de femmes 1975, Plaisir d'amour en Iran 1975, Ulysse 1982, Les dites Cariatides 1984, T'as de beaux escaliers... tu sais 1986, Le lion volatil 2003. *Video installations:* Patatutopia 2003, L'Ile et elle 2006, Homage aux Justes de France 2007. *Publication:* Varda par Agnès 1994, L'Ile et Elle 2006. *Address:* c/o Ciné-Tamaris, 86–88 rue Daguerre, 75014 Paris, France. *Telephone:* 1-43-22-66-00 (office). *Fax:* 1-43-21-75-00 (office). *E-mail:* cine-tamaris@wanadoo.fr (office). *Website:* www.cine-tamaris.com (office).

VARDANIAN, Ruben, MA; Russian business executive; b. Armenia; ed Faculty of Econs, Moscow State Univ.; intern, Merrill Lynch, New York 1992; Co-founder Troika Dialog (investment bank) 1991, COO 1992–96, Pres. 1996–2012, CEO 1997–, also Chair. Bd of Dirs Troika Dialog Group 2001–2012, CEO Rosgosstrakh (insurance co. acquired by Troika) 2002–04, Chair. 2004–05, Troika Dialog acquired by Sberbank CIB 2012, Advisor to Pres. of Sberbank of Russia and Man. Dir ZAO Sberbank CIB 2012–; mem. Russian Union of Industrialists and Entrepreneurs, Head Cttee on Corp. Governance, Arbitrator, Corp. Ethics Cttee; Pres. Skolkovo School of Management 2006–11; mem. Bd of Dirs OAO NOVATEK 2005–, AK Bars Bank 2006–, Joule Unlimited 2010–, OAO AvtoVAZ, OAO KAMAZ, Sibur Holding 2011; mem. mem. Nat. Council for Corp. Governance; Trustee Moscow State Univ.; Businessman of the Year, US Chamber of Commerce 1999, One of the World's 25 Leaders of the New Generation, Fortune magazine 2001, Russian National Entrepreneur Of The Year 2004. *Website:* www.sberbank-cib.ru.

VAREBERG, Terje, MSc; Norwegian business executive; *Chairman, Norsk Hydro ASA;* b. 1948; ed Norwegian School of Econs and Business Admin (NHH); worked for Ministry of Trade and Industry and Ministry of Petroleum –1979; joined Statoil 1979, with Refining and Marketing Div. 1979–83, Exec. Vice-Pres. and mem. Corp. Man. 1989–99, currently Chair. Norsk Hydro ASA (acquired by Statoil 2007); Man. Dir Agro Fellesslakteri 1983–89; mem. Bd of Dirs and Man. Dir Sparebank 1 SR-Bank 1999–; has held several bd positions in Norwegian industry; Chair. Norwegian Savings Bank Asscn. *Address:* Norsk Hydro ASA, Drammensveien 264, 0283 Oslo, Norway (office). *Telephone:* 22-53-81-00 (office). *Fax:* 22-53-27-25 (office). *E-mail:* info@hydro.com (office). *Website:* www.hydro.com (office).

VARELA RODRÍGUEZ, Juan Carlos; Panamanian politician; b. 12 Dec. 1963, Panamá City; m. Lorena I. Castillo; three c.; ed Georgia Inst. of Tech., USA; Dir Varela Hermanos Group 1985–, Exec. Vice-Pres. –2008; mem. Partido Panameñista (PP), Pres. 2006–, selected as PP presidential cand. 2008, formed Alliance for Change coalition with Cambio Democrático party 2008; Vice-Pres. and Minister of Foreign Affairs 2009–11. *Address:* c/o Ministry of Foreign Affairs, Altos de Ancón, Complejo Narciso Garay, Panamá 4, Panama (office).

VARFIS, Grigorios; Greek politician; b. 2 Jan. 1927, Athens; ed Univs of Athens and Paris; journalist in Paris, 1952–58; on staff of OECD 1953–62; Econ. Adviser to Perm. Greek Del. to the EEC, Brussels 1963–74; Gen. Dir, Co-ordination Ministry, with jurisdiction over Directorate of Relations with the European Communities 1974–77 (resgnd 1977; contrib. to econ. programme of Panhellenic Socialist Movt (PASOK); Co-ordination Under-Sec. and Under-Sec. at Foreign Affairs Ministry, responsible for EEC Affairs 1981–83; mem. European Parl. 1984; mem. Comm. of the European Communities (responsible for Regional Policy and Relations with European Parl.) 1985–86, for Structural Funds and Consumer Protection 1986–89. *Address:* Spefsipou 35, 10676 Athens, Greece.

VARGA, Imre; Hungarian sculptor; b. 1 Nov. 1923, Budapest; s. of Mátyás Varga and Margit Csepeli; m. Ildikó Szabó 1944; two s.; ed Budapest Coll. of Visual Arts; Pres. FESZEK Artists Club; mem. American Acad. of Arts and Sciences, Acad. Européenne des Arts et des Sciences, Paris; Hon. Citizen of Budapest 2004; Order of the Flag 1983, Commdr, Ordre des Arts et Lettres (France), Cavaliere dell'Ordine al Merito (Italy), Verdienstkreuz, First Class (Germany) 2004, Officer de l'Ordre Leopold (Belgium) 2004; Munkácsy Prize 1969, Kossuth Prize 1973, Merited Artist 1975, Eminent Artist 1980, Herder Prize 1981. *Works:* Prometheus 1965 and The Professor 1969 in Middelheim, Belgium, Madách Memorial 1968, Radnóti Memorial 1970, Partisans Memorial 1971, Lenin Memorial, Heroes Monument, Oslo 1974, plurifigural St Stephen composition, St Peter's Basilica, Vatican 1980, Bartók Memorial, Paris 1983, Béla Kun Memorial, Budapest 1986, Raoul Wallenberg Memorial 1987; perm. collection of work in Budapest; smaller sculptures: Erölltetett menet (Forced March), A la Recherche, Baudelaire kedvese (Baudelaire's Sweetheart), Páholy (Theatre box), statue of St Stephen in Aachen Cathedral, Germany 1993, Bartók Memorial, Carrefour de l'Europe Square, Brussels 1995, Ferenc Rákóczi II, commemorative statue, Bad Kissingen, Germany 1992, Memorial to Konrad Adenauer and Charles de Gaulle, Rhöndorf 2004, Memorial to Béla Bartók, London 2004. *Address:* 1126 Budapest XII, Bartha-utca 1, Hungary. *Telephone:* (1) 2500-274 (Museum) (office); (1) 3951-983 (home). *Fax:* (1) 3951-983 (home).

VARGA, Mihály; Hungarian economist and politician; *Minister of National Economy;* b. 1965, Karcag; m.; one s. two d.; ed Budapest Univ. of Econ. Sciences; econ. adviser, Water Man. Inst. of East Hungary, Szolnok 1989–90; mem. Fidesz – Alliance of Young Democrats 1988, Vice-Pres. 1994, Deputy Head of Parl. Faction 1995–98; mem. Parl. 1990, mem. Parl. Cttee of State Budget and Finances 1990–98, of State Audit; Political State Sec., Ministry of Finance 1998–2001, Minister of Finance 2001–02, Head of Prime Minister's Office 2010–12, Minister without portfolio for liaising with int. financial orgs 2012–13, Minister of Nat. Economy 2013–; mem. Inter-parl. Union 1995, Chair. Parl. Advisory Cttee for Debtors and Banking Consolidation 1995–97; Visiting Prof., Szolnok Business School 1995–97; elder presbyter, Reformed Church Community of Karcag and Kt of St John. *Address:* Ministry of National Economy, 1051 Budapest, József Nádor tér 2–4, Hungary (office). *Telephone:* (1) 795-1400 (office). *Fax:* (1) 318-2570 (office). *E-mail:* ugyfelszolgalat@ngm.gov.hu (office). *Website:* www.kormany.hu/hu/ nemzetgazdasagi-miniszterium (office).

VARGAS DÍAZ, Marco; Costa Rican politician; *Minister of the Presidency;* Minister of Inter-Institutional Co-ordination 2006–07, of Agric. and Livestock 2007–08, of Economy, Industry and Commerce 2008–10, of the Presidency 2010–. *Address:* Office of the Presidency, 520-2010 Zapote, San José, Costa Rica (office). *Website:* www.casapres.go.cr (office).

VARGAS LLOSA, (Jorge) Mario Pedro, PhD; Peruvian/Spanish writer and journalist; b. 28 March 1936, Arequipa, Peru; s. of Ernesto Vargas Maldonado and Dora Llosa de Vargas; m. 1st Julia Urquidi 1955 (divorced 1964); m. 2nd Patricia Llosa Urquidi 1965; two s. one d.; ed Colegio La Salle, Lima, Peru, Leoncio Prado Military Acad., Lima, Colegio Nacional San Miguel, Piura, Universidad Nacional Mayor de San Marcos, Lima and Universidad Complutense de Madrid, Spain; journalist on local newspapers, Piura, Peru 1951, for magazines Turismo and Cultura Peruana and for Sunday supplement of El Comercio 1955; News Ed. Radio Panamericana, Lima 1955; Spanish teacher, Berlitz School 1959; journalist, Agence-France Presse 1959; broadcaster, Latin American services of Radio-diffusion Télévision Française 1959; Lecturer in Latin American Literature, Queen Mary Coll., Univ. of London, UK 1967, Prof. King's Coll. 1969; trans. UNESCO 1967; Visiting Prof., Washington State Univ., USA 1968, Univ. de Puerto Rico 1969, Columbia Univ., USA 1975; Prof., Univ. of Cambridge, UK 1977, Harvard Univ., USA 1992, Princeton Univ., USA 1993, Georgetown Univ., USA 1994, 1999; Writer-in-Residence, Woodrow Wilson Int. Center for Scholars, Smithsonian Inst., Washington, DC, USA 1980; Prof. and Chair., Dept of Ibero-American Literature and Culture, Georgetown Univ., Washington, DC 2001–06, Distinguished Writer-in-Residence 2003–06; Mentor, Literature Program of the Rolex Mentor and Protégé Arts Initative, Second Cycle 2004–05; Weidenfeld Visiting Prof. of European Comparative Literature, St Anne's Coll., Oxford, UK 2004; Distinguished Visitor, Program in Latin American Studies, Princeton Univ. 2010; f. Movimiento Libertad political party and co-f. Frente Democrático (FREDEMO) coalition 1988; cand. for Pres. of Peru 1990; Pres. Jury, Iberoamer-ican Film Festival, Huelva, Spain 1995, San Sebastian Int. Film Festival 2004; mem. Jury, ECHO Television and Radio Awards 1998, Miguel de Cervantes Prize 1998; Pres. PEN Club Int. 1976–79; mem. Acad. Peruana de la Lengua 1975, Real Acad. Española 1994 (incorporation 1996), Int. Acad. of Humanism 1996, Cervantes Inst. Foundation 1998; Neil Gunn Int. Fellow, Scottish Arts Council 1986; Fellow, Wissenschaftskolleg, Berlin 1991–92, Deutscher Akademischer Austauschdienst, Berlin 1997–98; Hon. Fellow, Hebrew Univ., Israel 1976, Modern Language Asscn of America 1986, American Acad. and Inst. of Arts and Letters 1986; Hon. Prof., Universidad de Ciencias Aplicadas, Lima 2001; Chevalier, Légion d'honneur, Commdr Ordre des Arts et des Lettres 1993, Medal Orden El Sol del Perú (Great Cross of Diamonds) 2001, Medalla de Honor en el Grado de Gran Cruz, Peru 2003; Hon. DHumLitt (Connecticut Coll.) 1991; Hon. DLitt (Warwick) 2004; Dr hc (Florida Int. Univ. of Miami) 1990, (Boston) 1992, (Geneva) 1992, (Dowling College) 1993, (Universidad Francisco Marroquin, Guatemala) 1993, (Georgetown) 1994, (Yale) 1994, (Rennes II) 1994, (Murcia) 1995, (Valladolid) 1995, (Lima) 1997, (Universidad Nacional de San Agustin, Peru) 1997, (Ben Gurion) 1998, (Univ. Coll. London) 1998, (Harvard) 1999, (Universidad Nacional Mayor de San Marcos, Lima) 2001, (Rome Tor Vergata) 2001, (Pau) 2001, (Universidad Nacional San Antonio Abad del Cusco) 2002, (Univ. of French Polynesia) 2002, (La Trobe Univ., Melbourne) 2002, (Skidmore Coll.) 2002, (Universidad Nacional de Piura) 2002, (Universidad Nacional Pedro Ruiz Gallo)

2002, (Catholic Univ. of Louvain) 2003, (Universidad Nacional de Ingenieria, Lima) 2003, (Oxford) 2003, (Universidad Pedagogica Nacional Francisco Morazan, Tegucigalpa, Honduras) 2003, (Universidad Católica Santa María, Arequipa) 2004; Diploma de Honor, Universidad Nacional Mayor de San Marcos 2000; Crítica Española Prize 1966, Premio de la Crítica, Argentina 1981, Ritz Paris Hemingway Prize 1985, Príncipe de Asturias Prize, Spain 1986, Castiglione de Sicilia Prize, Italy 1990, Miguel de Cervantes Prize, Spain 1994, Jerusalem Prize, Israel 1995, Congressional Medal of Honour, Peru 1982, T.S. Eliot Prize, Ingersoll Foundation of The Rockford Institute, USA 1991, Golden Palm Award, INTAR Hispanic American Arts Center, New York 1992, Miguel de Cervantes Prize, Ministry of Culture (Spain) 1994, Jerusalem Prize 1995, Peace Prize, German Publishers, Frankfurt Book Fair 1996, Pluma de Oro Award, Spain 1997, Medal and Diploma of Honour, Univ. Católica de Santa María, Arequipa, Peru 1997, Medal of the Univ. of Calif. 1999, Jorge Isaacs Award, Int. Festival of Art, Cali, Colombia 1999, Medal "Patrimonio Cultural de la Humanidad", Municipalidad de Arequipa 2000, Certificate of Recognition, Colegio de Abogados 2001, Crystal Award, World Econ. Forum, Davos, Switzerland 2001, Americas Award, Americas Foundation 2001, Son Latinos Festival Prize, Tenerife, Spain 2001, Caonabo de Oro Prize, Dominican Asscn of Journalsits and Writers, 2002, Golden Medal, City of Genoa (Italy) 2002, PEN Nabokov Award 2002, Int. Prize of Letters, Cristobal Gabarron Foundation 2002, Premio Ateneo Americano, on Xth Anniversary of Casa de America 2002, Medal of Honour, City of Trujillo, Peru 2003, Roger-Caillois PEN Club Prize 2003, Budapest Prize 2003, Presidential Medal of Hofstra Univ., New York 2003, Grinzane Cavour Prize: "A Life for Literature International Prize", Turin 2004, Konex Foundation Prize 2004, Medal of the Centenary of Pablo Neruda, Govt of Chile 2004, Medal of Honor of Peruvian Culture, Nat. Inst. of Culture 2004, Nobel Prize in Literature 2010. *Films:* Co-Dir of film version of his novel Pantaléon y las visitadoras. *Television:* Dir La torre de Babel 1981. *Publications:* novels: La cuidad y los perros (Biblioteca Breve Prize) 1963, La casa verde (Premio Nacional de Novela, Peru 1967) 1966, Conversación en la catedral 1969, Pantaléon y las visitadoras 1973, La tía Julia y el escribidor (ILLA Prize, Italy 1982) 1977, La guerra del fin del mundo (Pablo Iglesias Literature Prize 1982) 1981, Historia de Mayta 1984, ¿Quién mató a Palomino Molero? 1986, El hablador 1987, Elogio de la madrastra 1988, Lituma en los Andes (Planeta Prize, Spain 1993, Archbishop Juan de San Clemente de Santiago de Compostella Literary Prize, Spain 1994, Int. Literary Prize, Chianti Ruffino Antico Fattore, Italy 1995) 1993, Los cuadernos de Don Rigoberto 1997, La fiesta del Chivo (first Book of the Year Prize, Union of Booksellers of Spain 2001, Readers of Crisol Libraries Prize, Spain 2001) 2000, El paraíso en la otra esquina (chosen for inclusion in "Books to Remember 2003" by cttee of librarians from The New York Public Library 2004) 2003, Travesuras de la niña mala 2006, El Sueño del Celta (The Dream of the Celt) 2010; short stories: El desafio (Revue Française Prize) 1957, Los jefes (Leopoldo Alas Prize) 1959, Los cachorros 1967; anthologies: Contra viento y marea Vol. I (1962–72) 1986, Vol. II (1972–83) 1986, Vol. III (1983–90) 1990, Desafíos a la libertad 1994, Making Waves (Nat. Book Critics' Circle Award, New York 1998) 1996; plays: La huída del Inca 1952, La señorita de Tacna 1981, Kathie y el hipopótamo 1983, La Chunga 1986, El loco de los balcones 1993, Ojos bonitos, cuadros feos 1994, La verdad de las mentiras (II Bartolome March Prize for revised edn 2002) 1990; non-fiction: El pez en el agua (autobiog.) 1993, La orgía perpetua (criticism) 1975, La utopía arcaica 1978, Cartas a un joven novelista (literary essay) 1997, Nationalismus als neue Bedrohung (in German) 2000, El lenguaje de la pasión (selection of articles) 2001, L'Herne. Mario Vargas Llosa (essays etc.) 2003, Diario de Irak (essays) 2003, La tentación de lo imposible (essay on Les Misérables de Victor Hugo) 2004, Mario Vargas Llosa. Obras Completas, Vol. I Narraciones y novelas (1959–1967) and Vol. II, Novelas (1969–1977) 2004, Un demi-siècle avec Borges (interview and essays on Borges written between 1964 and 1999, in French) 2004; contrib. to El País (series Piedra de Toque), Letras Libres, Mexico (series Extemporaneos). *Address:* Las Magnolias 295, 6° Piso, Barranco, Lima 4, Peru. *Telephone:* (1) 477-3868. *Fax:* (1) 477-3518. *Website:* www .mvargasllosa.com.

VARIN, Philippe; French business executive; *Chairman of the Managing Board, PSA Peugeot Citröen SA;* b. 8 Aug. 1952; m.; four c.; ed Ecole Polytechnique and Ecole des Mines, Paris; joined Pechiney Group 1978, various positions including researcher, Head of Strategic Studies, Aluminium Br., Vice-Pres. Eng and Research, Project Dir for construction of Dunkirk aluminium smelter 1989–90, Man.-Dir Aluminium Dunkirk 1990–92, Group Financial Controller, Paris and Chicago, 1993–94, Vice-Pres. Rhenlau Div. 1995–99, apptd Sr Exec. Vice-Pres. Aluminium Sector and mem. Exec. Cttee Pechiney Group 1999; CEO Corus Group PLC, London, UK 2003–09; Chair. Man. Bd PSA Peugeot Citröen SA 2009–. *Leisure interests include:* tennis, sailing, clarinet. *Address:* PSA Peugeot Citröen SA, 75 avenue de la Grande-Armée, 75116 Paris, France (office). *Telephone:* 1-40-66-55-11 (office). *Fax:* 1-40-66-54-14 (office). *Website:* www.psa-peugeot-citroen .com (office).

VÁRKONYI, Ágnes R., PhD; Hungarian historian and academic; *Professor Emerita, Department of Medieval and Early Modern Hungarian History, Eötvös Lóránd University of Budapest;* b. 9 Feb. 1928, Salgótarján, Nógrád Co.; d. of József Várkonyi and Mária Bérczy; m. Kálmán Ruttkay; two d.; ed Eötvös Lóránd Univ. of Budapest; Asst Prof. Inst. for Historical Research of Hungarian Acad. of Sciences 1951–83; Prof., Head of Dept of Medieval and Early Modern Hungarian History in Eötvös Lóránd Univ. of Budapest 1983–98, Prof. Emer. 1998–; Corresp. Fellow, Royal Historical Soc.; mem. Hungarian-Turkish Friendship Asscn; several awards including Széchenyi Prize. *Publications:* 31 books, including Europica varietas, Hungarica varietas, 1526–1762: Selected Studies 2000; numerous articles. *Leisure interests:* gardening, travelling. *Address:* c/o Hungarian-Turkish Friendship Association (Macar-Turk Dostluk Dernegi), 1062 Budapest, Bajza u. 54 (office); 1021 Budapest, Széher út 24, Hungary (home). *Telephone:* (1) 267-0966 (office); (1) 200-9093 (home). *Fax:* (1) 266-5699 (office). *E-mail:* h7621var@ella.hu (office).

VARKULEVICIUS, Rimas; Lithuanian engineer and business executive; b. 10 March 1956, Vilnius; m. Auksuole Varkuleviciene; one s. one d.; ed Kaunas Tech. Univ., Moscow Food Industry Tech. Univ., Georgetown Univ., USA; Chief Engineer, Tauras State Brewery 1979–83; Adviser and Chief Engineer, Food Processing Co., Erdenet, Mongolia 1983–85; Exec. Officer, Food Industry Bd of Lithuania 1986; Head of Food Industry Devt Div., Ministry of Agric. 1989–91, Dir Dept of Int. Relations 1991–95, Dir Dept of Int. Integration 1995–97; Chief

Consultant, Inst. for Nat. and Int. Meat and Food Industry IFW Heidelberg GmbH 1997–98; fmr Dir-Gen. Asscn of Lithuanian Chambers of Commerce, Industry and Crafts; Marketing Dir, Achemos Group, Vilnius –2012; Council Chair. Mykolas Romeris Univ. 2009–; fmr Dir Northtown Technology Park; has represented the Lithuanian Ministry of Agric. at numerous int. orgs and confs, adviser to the Econ. Cttee of Seimas (Parl.). *Leisure interest:* yachting. *Address:* Laisves pr. 78-5, Vilnius, Lithuania.

VARLEY, John S., MA; British banking executive; *Group Chief Executive, Barclays PLC;* b. 1 April 1956; m. Carolyn Thorn Pease 1981; two c.; ed Coll. of Law, London; fmr Deputy CEO BZW Equity Div., fmr Head of BZW SE Asia; Chair. Barclays Asset Man. Div. 1995–98, mem. Group Exec. Cttee 1996–, Exec. Dir 1998–, Chief Exec. Retail Financial Services 1998–2000, Finance Dir 2000–03, Group Deputy Chief Exec. Barclays PLC and Barclays Bank PLC Jan.–Sept. 2004, Group Chief Exec. Sept. 2004–(11), Sr Advisor on Regulatory Matters (March– Sept. 2011); Dir (non-exec.) AstraZeneca PLC; Chair. Business Action on Homelessness; Pres. Employers' Forum on Disability, UK Drug Policy Comm.; mem. Int. Advisory Panel, Monetary Authority of Singapore. *Address:* Barclays PLC, One Churchill Place, Canary Wharf, London, E14 5HP, England (office). *Telephone:* (20) 7116-3000 (office). *Fax:* (20) 7116-7780 (office). *E-mail:* info@ barclays.com (office). *Website:* www.barclays.com (office).

VARLOOT, Denis; French museum administrator and engineer; *Chairman, Musée des télécommunications de Pleumeur Bodou;* b. 25 Oct. 1937, Lille; s. of Jean Varloot and Madeleine (née Boutron) Varloot; m. Marie J. Kennel 1963; two s.; ed Lycées in Paris, Ecole Polytechnique and Ecole Nat. Supérieure des Télécommunications; Centre Nat. d'Etudes des Télécommunications 1962–68; with Direction Général des Télécommunications, Service des Programmes et des Etudes Economiques 1968–73, deputized for head of service 1973–75; Dir of Telecommunications, Orléans 1975–76; Head of Telecommunications Personnel 1976–81; Dir of Scientific and Tech. Information, Ministry of Educ. 1981–82; Dir Libraries, Museums and Scientific and Tech. Information, Ministry of Educ. 1982–87; Special Adviser to Pres. of France-Télécom 1987, Adviser 1992–98; Chair. and CEO Télésystemes 1988–92; Chair. Admin. Bd Palais de la découverte 1996–2003; Chair. Musée des télécommunications de Pleumeur Bodou 1994–; Chair. Asscn des musées et centres pour le développement de la culture scientifique, technique et industrielle 2001–; mem. Haut Conseil des musées de France 2003–; Chevalier des Arts et Lettres,Officier, Légion d'honneur Ordre nat. du Mérite, Ordre des Palmes Académiques. *Leisure interest:* sailing. *Address:* Musée des télécommunications de Pleumeur Bodou, 86 rue de Lournel, 75015 Paris (office); 14 rue Campagne Première, 75014 Paris, France (home). *Telephone:* 1-43-22-31-31 (home); 1-44-37-06-72 (office). *Fax:* 1-44-37-06-80 (office). *E-mail:* mustel.dv@leradome.com (office); varloot.denis@wanadoo.fr (home). *Website:* www .leradome.com (office).

VARMA, Pavan Kumar, BA; Indian writer and diplomatist; b. 5 Nov. 1953; m. Renuka Varma; ed St Stephen's Coll., New Delhi; joined Foreign Service 1976; fmr Press Sec. to Pres. of India, Spokesman, Ministry of External Affairs, Jt Sec. for Africa, High Commr to Cyprus, Dir, Nehru Centre, London, Dir-Gen. Indian Council for Cultural Relations, New Delhi; Amb. to Bhutan 2009–12. *Publications include:* Ghalib: The Man, The Times 1989, The Havelis of Old Delhi 1992, Krishna: The Playful Divine 1993, Yudhishtar and Draupadi 1993, The Great Indian Middle Class 1998, Widows of Vrindavan 2002, Being Indian: The Truth About Why the 21st Century will be India's 2004, Kama Sutra: The Art of Making Love to a Woman 2007, Becoming Indian: The Unfinished Revolution of Culture and Identity 2010. *Address:* c/o Ministry of External Affairs, South Blk, New Delhi 110 011, India. *E-mail:* pavankvarma@hotmail.com.

VARMUS, Harold Eliot, MA, MD; American microbiologist and academic; *Director, National Cancer Institute;* b. 18 Dec. 1939, Oceanside, NY; s. of Frank Varmus and Beatrice Varmus (née Barasch); m. Constance Louise Casey 1969; two s.; ed Amherst Coll., Harvard Univ., Columbia Univ.; physician, Presbyterian Hosp., New York 1966–68; Clinical Assoc., NIH, Bethesda, Md 1968–70; lecturer, Dept of Microbiology, Univ. of Calif. at San Francisco 1970–72, Asst Prof. 1972–74, Assoc. Prof. 1974–79, Prof. 1979–83, American Cancer Soc. Research Prof. 1984–93; Dir NIH 1993–99; Pres. and CEO Memorial Sloan-Kettering Cancer Center 2000–10; Dir National Cancer Institute 2010–; Co-Chair. Council of Advisors on Science and Technology, The White House; Co-founder and Chair. Public Library of Science (publisher of open-access journals in the biomedical sciences); Chair. Scientific Bd of Grand Challenges in Global Health, Bill and Melinda Gates Foundation 2003–08, now Chair. Global Health Advisory Cttee; Consultant, Chiron Corp., Emoryville, Calif.; Assoc. Ed. Cell Journal; mem. Editorial Bd Cancer Surveys; mem. American Soc. of Virology, American Soc. of Microbiology, AAAS, Council on Foreign Relations; Calif. Acad. of Sciences Scientist of the Year 1982, Lasker Foundation Award 1982 (co-recipient), Passano Foundation Award 1983, Armand Hammer Cancer Prize 1984, Gen. Motors Alfred Sloan Award, Shubitz Cancer Prize, NAS 1984, Nobel Prize (co-recipient) 1989, Nat. Medal of Science 2001, Rave Award, Wired Magazine 2004. *Publications:* Molecular Biology of Tumor Viruses (ed.) 1982, 1985, Readings in Tumor Virology (ed.) 1983, The Art and Politics of Science 2009. *Address:* Memorial Sloan-Kettering Cancer Center, 1275 York Avenue, New York, NY 10065, USA (office). *Telephone:* (212) 639-7317 (office); (212) 639-7227 (office). *Fax:* (212) 717-3125 (office). *E-mail:* varmus@mskcc.org (office). *Website:* www.mskcc.org (office).

VARNEY, Sir David Robert, Kt, BSc, MBA; British telecommunications industry executive and government official; b. 11 May 1946, London, England; s. of Robert Varney and Winifred Varney; m. Patricia Varney; one s. one d.; ed Univs of Surrey and Manchester; fmrly with Shell, Man. Dir AB Svenska Shell, Sweden, Dir Shell Int.; CEO BG Group (fmrly British Gas) 1996–2000; Chair. mmO2 2001–2004; Exec. Chair. HM Revenue and Customs from 2004–06 (resgnd); Sr Adviser to Gordon Brown on Transformational Govt Strategy (initiative to use information tech. to overhaul UK public services) 2006–09, conducted govt review of tax policy in NI 2007, conducted Varney Review of the Competitiveness of NI 2007–08; Chair. Business in the Community 2002–04. *Address:* River Thatch, The Abbotsbrook, Bourne End, Bucks., SL8 5QU, England. *Telephone:* (1628) 521077. *E-mail:* david@varney.uk.com.

VARSHALOMIDZE, Levan, LLM, LLD; Georgian lawyer, business executive and fmr government official; *Managing Partner, LV & Partners;* b. 17 Jan. 1972, Batumi; ed Kiev Univ., Ukraine; Head, Bilateral Relations Office, Ministry of Foreign Affairs 1998–2000; Chair. Exec. Dept, Ministry of Justice 2000–02; Scientific-researcher, Int. Private Law Dept State and Law Inst. of Georgia 2002; Dir Law Dept, Ministry of Finance 2002; partner, Damenia, Varshalomidze, Nogaideli and Kavtaradze (law firm) 2002–04; Dir-Gen. Georgian Railways Ltd Jan.–May 2004; Presidential Envoy to the Autonomous Republic of Ajara May– June 2004; Chair. Govt of Autonomous Repub. of Ajara 2004–12; Man. Partner, LV & Partners 2012–; Presidential Order of Excellence 2012. *Publications:* numerous articles on int. law. *Address:* 6010 Batumi, 60 Gogebashvili Street, Mersin Business Center, Office 5, Georgia. *Telephone:* (422) 21-24-24 (office). *E-mail:* lvarshalomidze@lv.ge (office). *Website:* www.lv.ge (office).

VARSHAVSKY, Alexander Jacob, BS, PhD; American (b. Russian) biologist and academic; *Howard and Gwen Laurie Smits Professor of Cell Biology, California Institute of Technology;* b. 8 Nov. 1946, Moscow, USSR; s. of Jacob Varshavsky and Mary Zeitlin; m. Vera Bingham; one s. two d.; ed Dept of Chem., Moscow Univ., Inst. of Molecular Biology, Moscow; Research Fellow, Inst. of Molecular Biology, Moscow 1973–76; Asst Prof. of Biology, Dept of Biology, MIT, Cambridge, Mass. 1977–80, Assoc. Prof. 1980–86, Prof. 1986–92; Howard and Gwen Laurie Smits Prof. of Cell Biology, Div. of Biology, Calif. Inst. of Tech., Pasadena 1992–; Visiting Fellow, Int. Inst. for Advanced Studies, Japan 2001; Foreign Assoc. European Molecular Biology Org. 2001; Bd mem. Encyclopedia of Molecular Cell Biology and Molecular Medicine 2002–05; mem. Molecular Cytology Study Section, NIH 1983–87, NAS 1995, American Philosophical Soc. 2001, Academia Europaea 2005, Medical Advisory Bd, Gairdner Foundation, Canada 2002–06, O'Connor Advisory Cttee, March of Dimes Foundation 2007–12; mem. NAS 1995, American Philosophical Soc. 2001; Foreign Assoc., European Molecular Biology Org. 2001; Foreign mem. Academia Europaea 2005; Fellow, American Acad. of Arts and Sciences 1987, American Acad. of Microbiology 2000, AAAS 2002; NIH Merit Award 1998, Novartis-Drew Award 1998, Gairdner Int. Award (Canada) 1999, Shubitz Prize in Cancer Research, Univ. of Chicago 2000, Hoppe-Seyler Award, Soc. for Biochemistry and Molecular Biology (Germany) 2000, Sloan Prize 2000, Merck Award, American Soc. for Biochemistry and Molecular Biology 2001, Wolf Prize in Medicine (Israel) 2001, Pasarow Award in Cancer Research 2001, Massry Prize 2001, Horwitz Prize 2001, Max Planck Research Prize (Germany) 2001, Wilson Medal, American Soc. for Cell Biology 2002, Stein and Moore Award, Protein Soc. 2005, March of Dimes Prize in Developmental Biology, March of Dimes Foundation 2006, Griffuel Prize in Cancer Research, Asscn pour la Recherche sur le Cancer, France 2006, Gagna and Van Heck Prize, Fonds Nat. de la Recherche Scientifique (Belgium) 2006, Schleiden Medal, Deutsche Akad. der Naturforscher Leopoldina 2007, Gotham Prize for Cancer Research, Gotham Foundation 2008, Vilcek Prize in Biomedical Sciences 2010, BBVA Foundation Award in Biomedicine (Spain) 2011, Otto Warburg Prize, Soc. for Biochemistry & Molecular Biology (Germany) 2012, King Faisal Int. Prize for Science 2012. *Achievements include:* discoveries in fields of DNA replication, chromosome structure and segregation, ubiquitin system and regulated protein degradation; inventions of several widely used methods including the chromatin immunoprecipitation (CHIP) assay, the ubiquitin fusion technique, and the split-ubiquitin sensor of protein–protein interactions; more than 15 patents. *Publications:* more than 200 articles in professional journals in the fields of genetics and biochemistry; 16 US patents. *Address:* Division of Biology, MC 145-75, 271 Braun Laboratory, California Institute of Technology, 1200 East California Boulevard, Pasadena, CA 91125, USA (office). *Telephone:* (626) 395-3785 (office); (818) 606-1908 (mobile). *Fax:* (626) 449-0756 (office); (818) 248-5245 (home). *E-mail:* avarsh@ caltech.edu (office). *Website:* www.bbe.caltech.edu/content/alexander-j -varshavsky (office); www.its.caltech.edu/~biochem/faculty/varshavsky.html (office).

VÁSÁRY, Tamás; Hungarian concert pianist and conductor; *Lifetime Honorary Chief Musical Director, Budapest Symphony Orchestra (Symphony Orchestra of the Hungarian Radio and Television);* b. 11 Aug. 1933, Debrecen; s. of Jozsef Vasary and Elizabeth (née Baltazàr) Vasary; m. Henriette Tunyogi 2000; ed Ferenc Liszt Acad. of Music, Budapest under Lajos Hernádi, József Gát and Zoltán Kodály, also studied with Ernő Dohnányi; first solo performance aged eight; studied with Ernst von Dohnányi at Ferenc Liszt Acad. of Music –1954; remained at Ferenc Liszt Acad. as Asst Prof. to Zoltán Kodály; recitals in Leningrad (now St Petersburg), Moscow and Warsaw; settled in Switzerland 1958; London debut 1961, New York 1962; debut as conductor in Menton Festival of Music 1971; has since appeared in Europe, S Africa, S America, USA, Canada, India, Thailand, Hong Kong, Australia, Japan and Mexico; Jt Music Dir Northern Sinfonia, Newcastle, UK 1979–82; Musical Dir Bournemouth Sinfonietta 1988–96; Chief Musical Dir and Prin. Conductor Budapest Symphony Orchestra (Symphony Orchestra of the Hungarian Radio and Television) 1993–2004, Lifetime Hon. Chief Musical Dir 2004–; f. Zoltán Kodály World Youth Orchestra 2006–; Guest Conductor, London Philharmonic, Royal Philharmonic, Philharmonia, New York Philharmonic, Dallas and Houston Symphonies, Detroit Symphony; performances at Salzburg, Edin. and Merano Music Festivals; winner, Marguerite Longue Competition 1955; Int. Competition, Warsaw 1955, Queen Elisabeth Competition, Belgium 1956, Int. Competition, Brazil 1957; Bach and Paderewski Medals (London), Kossuth Prize, Presidential Gold Medal 1998, Hungarian Heritage Prize. *Principal recordings:* three records of works of Liszt; eight of works of Chopin and various recordings of works of Rachmaninoff, Dohnányi, Debussy and Mozart; all symphonies and overtures of Beethoven, Schubert and Schumann 1997–98; further records for Hungaroton. *Publications:* A zenén túl 2003. *Leisure interest:* writing fiction. *Address:* c/o Zoltán Kodály World Youth Orchestra, 6000 Kecskemét, Kápolna street 24. P.O.Box 312, Hungary (office). *E-mail:* csipero@t -online.hu (office). *Website:* www.worldyouthorchestra.eu; www.tamas-vasary .com.

VÁSÁRYOVÁ, Magdaléna; Slovak actress, writer, politician and diplomatist; b. 26 Aug. 1948, Banská Štiavnica; d. of Jozef Vášáry and Hermína Vášáry (née Schmidt); m. Milan Lasica; two d.; ed Comenius Univ., Bratislava; actress with Nová Scéna, Bratislava 1971–83, Slovak Nat. Theatre 1984–90; fmr Amb. to Austria, to Poland; State Sec., Ministry of Foreign Affairs 2005–06; mem. Nat. Council (Parl.) 2006–; mem. Slovak Democratic and Christian Union-Democratic

Party (Slovenská demokratická a kresťanská únia-Demokratická strana); Artist of Merit 1988, Prize for Dramatic Performance in …a pozdravuji vlaštovky, Italy 1972, Gold Crocodile for Za frountou 1974, Andrea 1993, Silver Medal 2000. *Films include:* Senzi mama 1964, Markéta Lazarová 1967, Sladký cas Kalimagdory 1968, Zbehovia a pútnici 1968, Královská polovacka 1969, Na komete 1970, Radúz a Mahulena 1970, Princ Bajaja 1971, …a pozdravuji vlaštovky 1972, Rusalka 1977, Postriiny 1980. *Plays include:* Ubohý moj Marat 1970, Woyzeck 1971, Three Sisters 1972, Hamlet 1074, Clavio 1976, Výnosné miesto 1984, Sleena Júlia 1986, Samovrah 1989. *Publications include:* Short Sheets to One City 1988, Diskrétní pruvodce – co moná nevíte o polecenském chování, Budme poriadni, Polnocný sused, Hlavička štátu. *Leisure interests:* literature, charity fundraising. *Address:* c/o Slovenská demokratická a kresťanská únia-Demokratická strana, Ruinovská 28, 827 35 Bratislava, Slovakia. *Telephone:* (2) 4341-4102. *Fax:* (2) 4341-4106. *E-mail:* sdku@sdkuonline.sk. *Website:* www.sdkuonline.sk.

VASELLA, Daniel L., MD; Swiss pharmaceutical industry executive; *Chairman, Novartis AG;* b. 1953; m.; three c.; ed Univ. of Berne; began career as hosp. physician; Head of Corp. Marketing, Sandoz Group 1993, Sr Vice-Pres. and Head of Worldwide Devt, Sandoz Pharma Ltd, COO –1995, mem. Exec. Cttee, then CEO 1995–96, CEO and Exec. mem. Bd of Dirs Novartis AG (following merger of Sandoz and Ciba-Geigy) 1996–2010, Chair. 1999–; mem. Bd of Dirs Crédit Suisse 2000–, PepsiCo Inc., Alcon; mem. Chair.'s Council DaimlerChrysler; mem. Supervisory Bd, Siemens AG, Munich; Pres. Int. Fed. of Pharmaceutical Mfrs and Asscns (IFPMA) 2004–06; mem. Int. Business Leaders Advisory Council for the Mayor of Shanghai, Global Health Program Advisory Panel of the Bill & Melinda Gates Foundation, Bd Inst. Européen d'Admin. des Affaires (INSEAD), Int. Inst. of Man. Devt, Bd of Dean's Advisors at Harvard Business School, Global Leaders for Tomorrow Group, World Econ. Forum, Davos, Switzerland, Int. Bd of Govs Peres Center for Peace, Tel-Aviv, Israel; Foreign Hon. mem. American Acad. of Arts and Sciences; Ordem Nacional do Cruzeiro do Sul (Brazil), Chevalier de la Légion d'honneur; Dr hc (Univ. of Basel Faculty of Medicine) 2002; Harvard Business School's Alumni Achievement Award, Appeal of Conscience Award, AJ Congress Humanitarian Award, numerous other awards. *Leisure interests:* skiing, motorcycles, collecting rare books. *Address:* Novartis AG, Lichtstrasse 35, 4056 Basel, Switzerland (office). *Telephone:* (61) 324-11-11 (office). *Fax:* (61) 324-80-01 (office). *E-mail:* info@novartis.com. *Website:* www.novartis.com (office).

VASHADZE, Grigol; Georgian business executive and politician; b. 19 July 1958, Tbilisi; s. of Nodar Vashadze and Elene Bakradze; m. Nina Ananiashvili; two c.; ed Moscow State Inst. of Int. Relations; worked in Dept of Int. Orgs, USSR Ministry of Foreign Affairs 1981–88, also worked in Dept of Cosmos and Nuclear Weapons; postgraduate student, Diplomatic Acad. 1988–90; Founder and Dir Georgia Arts Man. and Gregory Vashadze and BR 1990–2008; Deputy Minister of Foreign Affairs Feb.–Nov. 2008; Minister for Culture, Heritage Preservation and Sport Nov. 2008, of Foreign Affairs Dec. 2008–12. *Address:* c/o Ministry of Foreign Affairs, 0108 Tbilisi, Sh. Chitadze 4, Georgia. *E-mail:* inform@mfa.gov.ge.

VASILEV, Iliyan D.; Bulgarian business executive and fmr diplomatist; Chair. Foreign Investment Agency –1999; Amb. to Russia 2000–06; currently Chair. Deloitte Bulgaria; Co-founder and Hon. Chair. Bulgarian Econ. Forum and Southeast Europe Econ. Forum; fmr Pres. Bulgarian Int. Business Asscn; Int. Cyril and Methodius Award 2005. *Address:* Deloitte Bulgaria 103, Al. Stamboliiski Blvd, Sofia Tower, 1303 Sofia, Bulgaria (office). *Telephone:* (2) 80-23-300 (office). *Fax:* (2) 80-23-350 (office). *E-mail:* idvassilev@gmail.com (office). *Website:* www .deloitte.com/dtt (office); idvassilev.blog.bg.

VASILIAUSKAS, Vitas, PhD; Lithuanian lawyer and central banker; *Chairman, Bank of Lithuania;* b. 15 Oct. 1973, Kaunas; m. Rasa Vasiliauskienė; three c.; ed Vilnius Univ.; Sr Tax Inspector, Lithuanian State Tax Inspectorate 1995–97; Dir Dept of Taxation, Treasury 1998–2001; Deputy Minister of Finance 2001–04; lawyer with Lideika, Petrauskas, Valiūnas and Pnrs (law firm) 2004–11; Chief of Staff, campaign office of Dalia Grybauskaitė during presidential election 2009; Chair. Bank of Lithuania 2011–. *Address:* Office of the Chairman, Bank of Lithuania, Gedimino pr. 6, Vilnius 01103, Lithuania (office). *Telephone:* (5) 268-0029 (office). *Fax:* (5) 262-8124 (office). *E-mail:* info@lb.lt (office). *Website:* www.lb .lt (office).

VASILIEV, Vladimir Viktorovich; Russian ballet dancer, choreographer, theatre director, film director and teacher and artist; *President, Galina Ulanova Foundation;* b. 18 April 1940, Moscow; s. of Viktor Vasiliev and Tatiana Kuzmicheva; m. Ekaterina Maximova (died 2009); ed Bolshoi Theatre Ballet School, State Inst. of Theatrical Arts; with Bolshoi Theatre Ballet Co. 1958–88; toured widely 1988–94, including guest appearances with Ballet of Maurice Béjart, Ballet de Marseille of Roland Petit, Teatro di San Carlo di Napoli, La Scala, Milan, Arena di Verona, Opera di Roma, Polish Nat. Ballet, Kirov (Mariinsky) Ballet, American Ballet Theatre, Tokyo Ballet, Cuban Ballet, Co. of Teatro Colón (Argentina), Kremlin, ind. tours of 'Ekaterina Maximova & Vladimir Vasiliev – Superstars of the Bolshoi and Co.'; Head of Choreographic Dept, State Inst. of Theatrical Arts 1986–95; Artistic and Gen. Dir Bolshoi Theatre 1995–2000; Artistic Dir Open Ballet Competition 'Arabesque' 1998–; Pres. Galina Ulanova Foundation 2000–; freelance choreographer and dir 2000–; Founder and Trustee, Bolshoi School in Brazil; Prof. and Hon. Prof., Moscow State Univ.; Hon. Citizen, Buenos Aires, Argentina 1983, Tusona, USA 1989; People's Artist of USSR 1973, People's Artist of Russian Fed. 1993, Order of Lenin 1976, Order of People's Friendship 1981, Order of Red Banner of Labour 1986, Chevalier, Ordre nat. du Mérit 1999, State Order of Merit of Russian Fed. 2000, 2008, State Order of Lithuania 2002, State Order of Brazil 'Rio Branco' 2004; Hon. DHumLitt (Centre Coll., Danville, Ky, USA); First Prize and Gold Medal, Vienna Int. Youth Festival 1959, Nijinsky Prize, Paris Dance Acad. 1964, Grand Prix, Varna Int. Competition 1964, USSR State Lenin Komsomol Prize 1968, USSR State Lenin Prize 1970, Maruis Petipa Prize, Paris Dance Acad. 1972, USSR State Prize 1977, Jino Tagni Int. Prize, Rome 1989, Together for Peace Prize, Rome 1989, UNESCO Pablo Picasso Medal 1990, 2000, Diagilev Prize 1990, State Prize of Russian Fed. 1991, Moscow Mayor's Office Prize 1997, Crystal Turandot Prize – For Honor and Dignity (Russia) 2001, Premio alla carriera 'Una Vita per la Danza' (Italy) 2001, A Life for Dance Prize (USA) 2003, 2004, Ludwig Nobel Prize (Russia) 2006, 2008, State Award 'Gratitude of Voronezh Land' 2010, Stanislavsky Prize (Russia) 2010. *Principal ballet roles:* Pan (Valpurgis Night), The Poet (Chopiniana), Danila

(Stone Flower), Prince Charming/Step Mother (Cinderella), Batyr (Shurale), Andrei (A Page of Life), Basil (Don Quixote), Albert (Giselle), Frondoso (Laurencia), Nutcracker/Prince (Nutcracker), Medjnun (Leili and Medjnun), Ivanushka (The Little Humpbacked Horse), Spartacus (Spartacus), Petrushka (Petrushka) and Icarus (Icarus), Macbeth (Macbeth), Narcissus (Narcissus), Lukash (Song of the Woods), Paganini (Paganini), Romeo (Romeo and Juliet), Prince Desire (Sleeping Beauty), Ivan the Terrible (Ivan the Terrible), Sergey (Angara), Baron (Gaîté Parisienne), Zorba (Greek Zorba) Nijinsky (Nijinsky), Balda (Balda), Pyotr Leontyevich (Anyuta), Professor Unrat (The Blue Angel), Tchaikovsky (Lungo Viaggio Nella Notte de Natale), Diaghilev-Nizhinsky (Diaghilev Musaget); ballet miniatures: Narcissus, Fantasie, Melody, Football Player, Match, Mugam, Elegia, Ouverture on Jewish Themes, Diaghilev-Nizhinsky (Diaghilev-Musaget), Old Lonely Man (The Ballade). *Ballets choreographed:* cr. Anyuta, Macbeth, Icarus, These Charming Sounds, Swan Lake, Cinderella, Paganini, new version of Giselle, Balda, Nostalgie, Bolshoi Theatre, Takhir and Zukhra, Uzbek Opera; Macbeth, Novosibisk Opera, Staats Oper Berlin, Budapest Opera, Kremlin Ballet; Anyuta, Teatro di San Carlo Naples, Latvian Opera, Cheliabinsk Opera, Tatar Opera, Perm Opera, Omsk Opera, Voronezh Opera, Krasnoyarsk Opera; Romeo and Juliet, Moscow Musical Theatre of K. Stanislavsky and V. Nemirovich-Danchenko, Lithuanian Opera, Latvian Opera, Teatro Municipal of Rio de Janeiro; Don Quixote, Teatro di San Carlo, Naples, American Ballet Theatre, Kremlin Ballet, Lithuanian Ballet, Tokyo Ballet, Belgrade Ballet; Giselle, Opera di Roma, Bolshoi Ballet School in Brazil; pas de quatre in Giselle, Tokyo Ballet; Paganini, Teatro Argentino, Dresden Opera Theatre, Maggio Fiorentino: Balda, Perm Opera, Moscow Musical Theatre for Children; Cinderella, Kremlin Ballet; Cheliabinsk Opera, Voronezh Opera; Red Poppy, Krasnoyarsk Opera; Nutcracker Suite and Don Quixote Suite, Giselle, Bolshoi Ballet School in Brazil; Ballade, New York City Centre, Pushkin Fine Arts Museum, Perm Opera; House at Roadside, Altai State Dance Ensemble, Russia 2012, Triptych 'Ballet Chez d'Oeuvres in Opera Classics', Voronezh Opera 2012. *Plays:* choreographer: The Princess and Woodcutter, Sovremennik Drama Theatre, Moscow; Yunona and Avosj (rock opera), Lenkom Drama Theatre, Moscow; F. Zeffirelli's productions of Aida, Opera di Roma 1990, Arena di Verona 2002, La Scala 2006, Teatro Massimo 2008, La Traviata, Bolshoi Theatre, Khovanschina, Bolshoi Theatre, Aida (dir F.Zeffirelli). *Operas staged:* La Traviata, Bolshoi Theatre 1996, Oh, Mozart, Mozart…, Novaya Opera of Moscow 1999. *Films:* directed, choreographed and starred in Trapezium, Anyuta, House by the Roadside, Adam and Eva, Icarus, Gospel for the Sly, Gigolo and Gigolette, These Charming Sounds, Fouete, Fragments of One's Biography, I Want to Dance; choreographed Andersen – Life Without Love (Russia); appeared in Franco Zeffirelli's La Traviata. *Radio:* I. Turgenev Spring Waters (radio play). *Television:* starred in USSR with Open Heart, Road to the Bolshoi Ballet, Parade of Numbers, Moscow in Musical Notes, Recollecting Ninjinsky, Glory of the Bolshoi Ballet, Randez-vous with the Bolshoi, Creation of Dance, Choreographic Novellas, Choreographic Symphony, World of Dance, Pages of Modern Dance, The Bolshoi Ballet in Japan, Classical Duets, Grand Pas in the White Night, The World of Ulanova, Ulanova Forever, Commemorating Ulanova, Asaf Messerer, Anna Pavlova, Choreographic Images of Kasyan Goleizovsky, Magic of Giselle, Golden Age of Asaf Messerer, Katya, Ekaterina Maximova, When Dance becomes Life; Olga Lepeshinskaya, Dialogue with a Legend, Vladimir Vasiliev – Dance and Time, The Bolshoi Ballet, E. Maximova and V. Vasiliev – Dance of Fate. *Publications:* poems: The Chain of Days 2000; catalogues of paintings of V. Vasiliev 2004, 2005, 2007, Declaration d'Amour à Vladimir Vasiliev 2010, Pictures from My Memory 2010. *Leisure interests:* painting, writing poetry. *Address:* c/o Vorotnikovsky per., 7-4-26, 127006 Moscow, Russia (office); Smolenskaya naberezhnaya 5/13 62, 121099 Moscow, Russia (home). *Telephone:* (495) 699-21-51 (home). *Fax:* (495) 699-21-51 (home). *E-mail:* info@vasiliev.com (office). *Website:* www.vasiliev.com.

VASILYEV, Anatoli Aleksandrovich; Russian theatre director; b. 4 May 1942, Danilovka, Penza Region; m. Nadezhda Kalinina; one d.; ed Rostov State Univ., State Inst. of Dramatic Art, Moscow; Founder and Dir Theatre Co. School of Dramatic Art, Moscow 1988–2006; staged all works by Pirandello; numerous tours in Europe 1985–2002; Chevalier, Ordre des Arts et des Lettres 1989, Honoured Art Worker of Russia 1993; Nuova Realtà Europea Prize, Taormina, Italy 1990, Pirandello Prize, Agrigento, Italy 1992, Stanislavsky Fund Prize 1995, Stanislavsky Prize of Russian Fed. 1998, Golden Mask Prize of Russian Fed. for The Lamentation of Jeremiah (Martynov) 1997, Nat. State Prize of Russian Fed. for creation of School of Dramatic Art 1999, Triumph Prize 2001. *Productions include:* Vassa Zheleznova 1978, Grown-up Daughter of a Young Man (V. Slavkin) 1979, Cerceau (V. Slavkin) 1985, Six Characters in Search of an Author (Pirandello) 1987, Masquerade (Lermontov) at Comédie Française 1992, Uncle's Dream (Dostoyevsky), Budapest 1994, The Lamentation of Jeremiah (Martynov) 1996, The Queen of Spades (Tchaikovsky), German Nat. Theatre, Weimar 1996, Don Juan (Pushkin) 1998, Mozart and Salieri (Pushkin) 2000, Requiem (Martynov) 2000, Medee Materiaux (Heiner Muller) 2001. *Publications:* A propos de bal masqué de Mikhail Lermontov 1997, Szinházi Fuga 1998, Sept ou huit leçons de théâtre 1999, Ione e Menone di Platone 1999, A un unico lettore 2000.

VASILYEV, Sergei Aleksandrovich, PhD; Russian politician; *Chief Executive of the Federal Service for Government Registration, Cadastre, and Cartography and Chief State Registrar of the Russian Federation;* b. 8 June 1957, Leningrad; m.; two d.; ed Inst. of Economy and Finance, Leningrad; Head, Research Lab., Inst. of Finance and Economy, Leningrad 1985–90, now Prof.; took part in activities of Moscow-Leningrad group of young economists; mem. Leningrad Political Club Perestroika 1986; Chair. Cttee for Econ. Reform, Leningrad City Soviet 1990–91; Head, Working Centre for Econ. Reform under Russian Govt 1991–94; Deputy Minister of the Economy, Russian Fed. 1994–97; Deputy Head, Office of Russian Govt 1997–98; Chair. Bd Int. Investment Bank, Moscow 1998–99; Pres. Int. Centre for Social and Econ. Research (Leontief Centre), St Petersburg 1999–2001; Rep. of Leningrad Regional Govt to Council of Fed. 2001–08, Chair. Cttee on Financial Markets; Chief Executive of the Federal Service for Government Registration, Cadastre, and Cartography and Chief State Registrar of the Russian Federation 2008–. *Publications:* Economics and Power 1998, Ten Years of Russian Economic Reform 1999, Comparative Analysis of Stabilization Programs of the '90s 2003, Economic Development of the Leningrad Region 2005. *Leisure interest:* travel.

Address: Federal Service for Government Registration, Cadastre, and Cartography, c/o Office of the Government, 103274 Moscow, Krasnopresnenskaya nab. 2, Russia.

VASILYEV, Gen.-Col Vladimir A., Cand.Jur; Russian politician; *Chairman, State Duma Committee for Security;* b. 11 Aug. 1949, Klin, Moscow region; one d.; m.; ed School of Militia, Acad of USSR Ministry of Internal Affairs; held several positions in Bauman dist. Div. of Internal Affairs 1972–83, including investigator, inspector, sr inspector, deputy head; Head of Div. than Deputy Head of Dept of Property Security, Moscow Dept of Internal Affairs 1983–87; held several positions at Ministry of Internal Affairs, Moscow 1992–98, including Chief Inspector, Head of Operations Dept, Deputy Head, Head of Gen. Staff, First Deputy Minister of Internal Affairs; Deputy Sec., Security Council of Russian Fed. 1999–2001; apptd Deputy Minister of Internal Affairs 2001; currently mem. State Duma (United Russia) for Tversk Dist. 173, Chair. Cttee for Security. *Address:* State Duma Committee for Security, Okhotny Ryad 1, Moscow 103265, Russia (office). *Telephone:* (office). *Fax:* (495) 692-95-75 (office). *E-mail:* vasiliev-site@yandex.ru (office). *Website:* www.duma.gov.ru (office).

VASILYEVA, Tatyana Grigoryevna; Russian actress; b. 28 Feb. 1947, Leningrad; two s. one d.; ed Studio-School of Moscow Art Theatre; with Moscow Satire Theatre –1984; actress, Moscow Mayakovsky Theatre 1984–93; People's Artist of Russia, Nika Prize 1992. *Theatre roles include:* Ordinary Miracle, Pippi Longstocking, Run, Inspector, The Threepenny Opera, A Place Like the Heavens. *Films include:* Poedinok v tayge (The Fight in the Taiga) 1977, Prezhde chem rasstatsya (Before We Part) 1984, Salon krasoty (Beauty Salon) 1985, Bluzhdayushchiye zvyozdy (Wandering Stars) 1991, Hello, I'm Your Auntie, Uvidet Parizh i umeret (To See Paris and Die) 1992, Zhenikh iz Mayami (The Fiancé from Miami) 1994, Chyornaya vual (The Black Veil) 1995, Tsirk sgorel i klouny razbezhalis 1998, Popsa 2005, Tarif novogodniy 2008, Neporoshchennye 2009. *Address:* 121248 Moscow, Goncharny proyezd 8/40, Apt. 62, Russia.

VASPÁL, Vilmos, BEng; Hungarian business executive; *Chairman, FreeSoft Nyrt.;* m.; two c.; software developer, Videoton 1980s; fmr Chief Information Officer, SZÚV; Founding mem. FreeSoft Nyrt., Chair. 2004–; mem. Bd Asscn of IT Cos 2003–. *Address:* FreeSoft Nyrt., Neumann Janos u. 1/C, Infopark, Budapest 1117, Hungary (office). *Telephone:* (1) 371-2910 (office). *Fax:* (1) 371-2911 (office). *E-mail:* fs.inf@freesoft.hu (office). *Website:* www.freesoft.hu (office).

VASQUEZ, Gaddi Holguin; American business executive and diplomatist; *Vice-President of Public Affairs, Southern California Edison;* b. 22 Jan. 1955, Carrizo Springs, Tex.; ed Univ. of Redlands; fmr Trustee Prof., Chapman Univ.; early career as police officer in Orange, California; served as appointee of three fmr California Govs; Div. Vice-Pres. of Public Affairs, Southern California Edison 1995–2002, Vice-Pres. of Public Affairs 2009–; apptd by fmr Pres. George H. W. Bush to several fed. comms; Dir US Peace Corps 2002–06; Amb. and Perm. Rep. to UN, Rome 2006–09; three hon. doctorates; numerous awards for leadership and community service, including Outstanding Alumni Award, American Asscn of Community Colls, Coro Foundation Crystal Eagle Award, Marine Corps Scholarship Fund Globe and Anchor Award, Jewish Nat. Fund Tree of Life Award, Salvation Army's William H. Booth Award for Service, Orange County Black Chamber of Commerce Award for Community Leadership, B'nai Brith Award for Leadership and Community Service. *Address:* Southern California Edison, PO Box 800, Rosemead, CA 91770, USA (office). *E-mail:* info@sce.com (office). *Website:* www.sce.com (office).

VÁSQUEZ MORALES, Ricaurte, PhD; Panamanian government official, economist and business executive; *Vice-President, Government Affairs & Public Policy, GE Latin America;* ed Villanova Univ., Pa, N Carolina State Univ., Rensselaer Polytechnic Inst., NY, USA; Minister of Planning and Econ. Policy 1984–88; Pres. Sigma Man. Corpn 1988–96; Vice-Pres. Asesores y Gestores Bursátiles 1992–94; Dir Panama Holdings Inc. 1994–96; fmr econ. analyst Chase Manhattan Bank, econ. consultant Cámara Panameña de la Construcción, economist Corporación de Cobre de Cerro Colorado; Dir Office of Financial Admin, Panama Canal Comm. 1996; Vice-Admin. Panama Canal Authority –2004; Minister of Finance and the Treasury and Chair. Panama Canal Authority 2004–07; Pres. & CEO, GE Central America & Caribbean 2008–11, Vice-Pres. Govt Affairs & Public Policy, GE Latin America 2011–; has taught econs, econometrics and finance at Universidad Santa María La Antigua, Florida State Univ. Panamá, Universidad del Istmo;*Website:* www.ge.com (office).

VASSALLI, Jean-Dominique, PhD, MD; Swiss physician, academic and university administrator; *Rector, University of Geneva;* b. 12 Aug. 1946, Genève et Meride (Tessin); m.; two c.; ed Univ. of Geneva, The Rockefeller Univ., USA; Asst Prof., The Rockefeller Univ. 1977–81; Researcher, Dept of Morphology, Univ. of Geneva 1981–86, Assoc. Prof. 1986–90, Prof., Dept of Morphology 2004–, Prof., Dept of Genetic Medicine and Devt 1990, Vice-Dean, Faculty of Medicine 1991–99, Vice-Rector Univ. of Geneva 1999–2003 Pres., Section of Fundamental Medicine, Faculty of Medicine 2004, Rector Univ. of Geneva 2004–; mem. Exec. Cttee Union suisse des socs de biologie expérimentale 1990–93, Devt and Planning Comm., Univ. of Geneva 1991–95, Scientific Comm., ISREC 1992–2002 (Pres. 1994–2002), Audit of Insts of Anatomy, Histology, Embryology, Univ. of Lausanne 1993–94, Review Cttee Int. Human Frontier Science Program 1995–97, Friedrich Miescher Prize Cttee, Soc. suisse de biochimie 1996, Scientific Council, Fed. Research Inst., Montpellier 1997–98, Patronage Cttee Gen Suisse 1998, Prize Comm. Dr Josef Steiner Krebsstiftung 1999, Fondation Ernest et Lucie Schmidheiny 2004, Scientific Cttee Fondation Eagle 2005; Consulting Ed., The Journal of Clinical Investigation 1998–2002; Pres. Organizing Cttee VIIth Int. Workshop on Molecular and Cellular Biology of Plasminogen Activation (Les Diablerets) 1999; Jt Organizer EMBO Conf. on Extracellular Proteases and Their Inhibitors in Development, Plasticity and Pathology of the Nervous System (Ascona) 2003; mem. Swiss Acad. of Natural Sciences, Genetic Research Forum 2004; mem. ad personam Swiss Acad. of Medical Sciences 2001; Prix de la Fondation Prof. Dr Max Cloëtta 1988, Prize of Int. Soc. for Fibrinolysis and Thrombolysis 1994. *Publications:* numerous papers in professional journals. *Address:* Rectorat de l'Université de Genève, Uni Dufour, 24 rue du Général-Dufour, 1211 Geneva 4 (office); Département de médecine génétique et développement, Faculté de médecine, Centre médical universitaire, Université de Genève, 1 rue Michel-Servet, 1211

Geneva 4, Switzerland (office). *Telephone:* (22) 3797525 (office). *Fax:* (22) 3791180 (office). *E-mail:* webmaster@unige.ch (office). *Website:* www.unige.ch/rectorat/home/vassallibio.html (office).

VASSANJI, M. G., CM, BS, PhD; Canadian writer; b. 30 May 1950, Nairobi, Kenya; m. Nurjehan Vassanji (née Aziz) 1979; two s.; ed Massachusetts Inst. of Tech. and Univ. of Pennsylvania, USA; grew up in Nairobi, Kenya, and Dar es Salaam, Tanzania; Post-doctoral Fellow, Atomic Energy of Canada Ltd 1978–80; Research Assoc., Univ. of Toronto 1980–89; first novel published 1989, full-time writer 1989–; Writer-in-Residence, Int. Writing Program, Univ. of Iowa 1989; Fellow, Indian Inst. of Advanced Study 1996; Hon. DLitt (York) 2005, (McMaster) 2006, (Old Dominion) 2007, (Toronto) 2009, (Carleton, Ottawa) 2013; Harbourfront Festival Prize 1994, Giller Prize 1994, 2003, Gov. Gen.'s Prize 2009. *Publications include:* The Gunny Sack (novel) (Commonwealth First Novel Award, Africa Region 1990) 1989, No New Land (novel) 1991, Uhuru Street (short stories) 1991, The Book of Secrets (novel) (Giller Prize for Best Novel 1994, F. G. Bressani Literary Prize 1994) 1994, Amriika (novel) 1999, The In-Between World of Vikram Lall (novel) (Giller Prize for Best Novel 2003) 2003, When She Was Queen (short stories) 2005, The Assassin's Song (novel) 2007, A Place Within: Rediscovering India (travel memoir) (Gov. Gen.'s Literary Award for Best Non-fiction 2009) 2008, Mordecai Richler (biog.) 2009, The Magic of Saida (novel) 2012. *Leisure interests:* squash, tennis, films. *Address:* c/o Doubleday Canada Ltd, 5900 Finch Avenue East, Scarborough, ON M1B 0A2 (office); c/o The Wylie Agency, 17 Bedford Square, London, ON WC1B 3JA, England (office). *Telephone:* (416) 364-4449 (Toronto) (office); (20) 7908-5900 (London) (office). *E-mail:* tbohan@wylieagency.co.uk (office). *Website:* tbohan@wylieagency.co.uk (office); www.mgvassanji.com.

VASSILIKOS, Vassilis; Greek writer; b. 18 Nov. 1934, Kavala; s. of Nikolaos Aikaterini; m. Vasso Papantoniou; one d.; ed Anatolia High School of Thessaloniki, Thessaloniki Law School, Yale Drama School, USA, School of Radio and Television, USA; Dir-Gen. of Greek TV (public) 1981–85; Amb. to UNESCO 1996–2004; Pres. Hellenic Authors' Soc. 1999–2005; presenter of weekly TV show on books; mem. Int. Parl. of Writers, Athens Union of Daily Newspaper Journalists; Dr hc (Univ. of Patra, Univ. of Thessaly); Commdr des Arts et des Lettres 1999; Prize of 'The Twelve' 1961, Mediterraneo Prize 1971. *Publications include:* (in English trans.): The Plant, The Well, The Angel 1963, Z 1968, The Harpoon Gun 1972, Outside the Walls 1973, The Photographs 1974, The Monarch 1976, The Coroner's Assistant 1986, …And Dreams Are Dreams 1996, The Few Things I Know About Glafkos Thrassakis 2003. *Address:* 5 Ambrosiou Moshonision, 17123 Athens, Greece (office). *Telephone:* (210) 363-4868 (office). *Fax:* (210) 362-0844 (office). *E-mail:* newopera@otenet.gr (office).

VASSILIOU, Androulla, MIA; Cypriot lawyer, organization executive, politician and international organization official; *Commissioner for Education, Culture, Multilingualism and Youth, European Commission;* b. 30 Nov. 1943, Paphos; d. of Mr Georgiades; m. George Vassiliou 1966 (Pres. of Cyprus 1988–93); two d. one s; ed Pancyprian Gymnasium, Nicosia, Middle Temple Inn of Court, London, Inst. of World Affairs, London; called to the Bar, Middle Temple Inn of Court, London 1964; practised law, specializing in corpn and banking law 1968–88; Legal Adviser, Standard Chartered Bank, Bank of Cyprus and others 1969–88; mem. Cypriot House of Reps 1996–, mem. Cttee of European Affairs, of Educ. and Culture, Environment Cttee; Commr for Educ., Culture, Multilingualism and Youth, EC, Brussels 2010–; Vice-Pres. European Liberal Democrat and Reform Party, Pres. European Liberal Women Network; mem. Bd of Dirs of numerous cos; Hon. Pres. Bureau of Women's Affairs, Ministry of Justice 1988; Gen. Sec., then Hon. Pres. UN Asscn of Cyprus; mem. Exec. Cttee World Fed. of UN Asscns (WFUNA), later Pres. (first woman) 1991–95, now Hon. Pres.; Co-founder and Pres. Cyprus Asscn of Univ. Women, Cttee for Restoration of Human Rights Throughout Cyprus; Hon. Pres. Perm. Agency on Womens' Rights in Cyprus 1988; Founder and Pres. Cyprus Fund for Music and Other Fine Arts; Pres. Pancyprian Welfare Council 1988–93, Cyprus Fed. of Business and Professional Women 1996–2001; Alternate Mem. Convention for Future of Europe 2001–03; mem. Bd of Trustees, Pharos Trust 2001–; Pres. Bd of Trustees Oncology Centre of Bank of Cyprus 2003–; Hon. Pres. Cttee for Restoration of Human Rights; Patron, Muscular Dystrophy Research Trust, Cyprus Family Planning Asscn, Anti-rheumatism Soc., Asscn of Friends of Cancer Patients, Asscn of Friends of Children with Speech Problems; Grand Cross of Order of Beneficence from Pres. of Greece 1989. *Leisure interests:* walking, swimming, music. *Address:* European Commission, rue de la Loi 200, 1049 Brussels, Belgium (office); Orpheus str. 9A, 1583 Nicosia, Cyprus (home). *Telephone:* (2) 299-11-11 (office); 22765456 (home). *Fax:* (2) 295-01-38 (office); 22377896 (home). *Website:* ec.europa.eu/commission_barroso/vassiliou/index_en.htm (office).

VASSILIOU, Georghios Vassos, DEcon; Cypriot politician and economist; b. 20 May 1931, Famagusta; s. of Vasos Vassiliou and Sophia Othonos Vassiliou (née Yiavopoulou); m. Androulla Georgiadou 1966; one s. two d.; ed Univ. of Budapest, Hungary; Market Researcher, Reed Paper Group, London 1960–62; Founder Middle East Marketing Research Bureau (now MEMRB Int.) and Ledra Advertising Co. 1962; f. Inst. of Dirs (Cyprus Br.); mem. Exec. Cttee Cyprus Chamber of Commerce 1970–86; mem. Bd and Exec. Cttee Bank of Cyprus 1981–88; mem. Econ. Advisory Council Church of Cyprus 1982–88, Educational Advisory Council 1983–88; Pres. of Cyprus 1988–93; Founder United Democrats Movt, Pres. 1995–2005; Chair. World Inst. for Devt Econ. Research, UN Univ., Helsinki 1995–2000; mem. Parl. 1996–99; Chief Negotiator for the Accession of Cyprus to the EU 1998–2003; Visiting Prof., Cranfield School of Man., UK; mem. InterAction Council 1998–, Trilateral Comm. 2000–; Hon. Prof., Cyprus Int. Inst. of Man.; Dr hc (Univs of Cyprus, Athens, Salonica, Budapest, Belgrade); Grand Cross, Order of Merit (Cyprus), Grand Cross, Légion d'honneur, Grand Cross of the Saviour (Greece), Grand Cross of the Order of the Repub. of Italy, Grand Star (Austria), Grand Collar, Order of Infante D. Henrique (Portugal), Grand Collar of the Nile (Egypt), Standard (Flag) Order decorated with diamonds (Hungary), and other distinctions, awards and decorations. *Publications:* Marketing in the Middle East 1976, The Middle East Markets Up to 1980 1977, Moyen Orient: Le Consommateur des années '80 1980, Towards the Solution of the Cyprus Problem 1992, Modernisation of the Civil Service 1992, Overcoming Indifference 1994, Tourism and Sustainable Development 1995, Towards a Larger, Yet More Effective European Union 1999, Cyprus-European Union: From the First Steps to Accession

2004; numerous articles in various int. publs. *Leisure interests:* listening to music, reading, swimming, body exercise. *Address:* PO Box 22098, 1583 Nicosia (office); 9A Orpheos Street, 1070 Cyprus (home). *Telephone:* (2) 2336142 (office); (2) 2374888 (home). *Fax:* (2) 2336301 (office). *E-mail:* gvassiliou@memrb.com.cy (office).

VASSILYEV, Alexey Mikhailovich, DrHist; Russian scientist; *Director, Institute for African Studies, Russian Academy of Sciences;* b. 26 April 1939, Leningrad; m.; two d.; ed Moscow State Inst. of Int. Relations; with Pravda, political columnist, corresp. in Viet Nam, Turkey, Egypt 1962–83; Deputy Dir Inst. of Africa (now Inst. for African Studies), USSR (now Russian) Acad. of Sciences 1983–92, Dir 1992–, Chair. Scientific Council for the Problems of Africa; Ed.-in-Chief Asia and Africa Today (magazine) 1998–; Pres. Asscn of Cultural and Business Co-operation with African Cos; Pres. Centre of Regional and Civilisation Studies; Special Rep. of Pres. of Russian Fed. for Relations with African Leaders 2006–11; mem. Council on Foreign Policy, Ministry of Foreign Affairs, Russian Fed.; Visiting Prof. at univs in USA, UK, France, Egypt, Saudi Arabia; Medals for Labour Merit, for Labour Heroism, Merited Scholar of the Russian Fed. 1999; Russian Acad. of Sciences E. V. Tarle Prize for Best Studies in History and Int. Relations 2003. *Publications:* 36 monographs, numerous scientific works and more than 900 articles published in Russia and abroad on Middle East, Central Asia, Africa, Arab-Israeli conflict, Islam including History of Saudi Arabia, Russian Policy in the Middle East, Egypt and the Egyptians, Post-Soviet Central Asia. *Leisure interest:* Russian literature, skiing. *Address:* Institute for African Studies, Russian Academy of Sciences, Spiridonovka str. 30/1, 123001 Moscow (office); 11/13-103 Pravda str., 125040 Moscow, Russia (home). *Telephone:* (495) 690-63-85 (office); (495) 614-47-28 (home). *Fax:* (495) 697-19-54 (office). *E-mail:* dir@inafr.ru (office). *Website:* www .inafran.ru (office).

VASTAGH, Pál, PhD; Hungarian politician, jurist and diplomatist; b. 23 Sept. 1946; m. Erzsébet Fenyvesi; one s. two d.; ed József Attila Univ. of Arts and Sciences, Szeged; Asst Lecturer, later Lecturer, then Sr Lecturer, Dept of Theory of State and Law, József Attila Univ. of Arts and Sciences 1988–89, Dean 1989; mem. of Presidium HSP 1989; mem. Parl. 1990–2006, Parl.'s Cttee on Constitutional Affairs, Chair. 2002; mem. Codification and Justice Cttee on European Integration Affairs; Minister of Justice 1994–98; Deputy Leader of Socialist faction 1998–2002; Prof., Budapest School of Man. 1999–; mem. Convention on the Future of Europe 2002; Observer and mem. European Parl. 2003–04; Chief Adviser to Prime Minister 2004; Dir Gen. Coll. of Man., Budapest 2004–07; Amb. to Canada 2007–11. *Publications:* articles in nat. newspapers and professional periodicals. *Leisure interests:* reading, hiking, travelling, soccer. *Address:* Ministry of Foreign Affairs, 1027 Budapest, Bem rakpart 47, Hungary (office). *Telephone:* (1) 458-1000 (office). *Fax:* (1) 212-5918 (office). *E-mail:* kozkapcsolat@kum.gov.hu (office). *Website:* www.kormany.hu/hu/kulugyminiszterium (office).

VASUDEV, C(hander) M(ohan); Indian business executive; *Non-Executive Chairman, Housing Development Financial Corporation Bank Limited;* ed Univ. Coll. of Swansea, UK, Punjab Univ., Chandigarh; with Administrative Services 1966–2003; fmr Sec., Ministry of Finance, Jt Sec., Ministry of Commerce; Ind. Dir Housing Devt Financial Corpn (HDFC) 2006–10, Chair. (non-exec.) 2010–; mem. Bd of Dirs World Bank, Reserve Bank of India, State Bank of India, Industrial Devt of India, Industrial Credit and Investment Corpn of India, Infrastructure Development Finance Company, Nat. Bank for Agriculture and Rural Devt, Nat. Housing Bank, ICRA Man. Consultancy Services Ltd, Uttarakhand Jal Vidyut Nigam Ltd, Bombay Stock Exchange Ltd 2006–07, Cen. Depository Services India Ltd –2007, Star Paper Mills Ltd 2009–, Tourism Finance Corpn of India Ltd 2010–, Power Exchange India Ltd, ASA Int. India Microfinance Pvt. Ltd, Insync Advisory Services Pvt. Ltd, NSDL Database Man. Ltd, Centennial Development Advisory Services Pvt. Ltd. *Address:* Housing Development Financial Corporation Bank House, Senapati Bapat Marg, Lower Parel, Mumbai 400 013, India (office). *Telephone:* (22) 56521000 (office). *Fax:* (22) 24960739 (office). *Website:* www .hdfcbank.com (office).

VASUDEVA, Sudhir, BE, MBA; Indian engineer and business executive; *Chairman and Managing Director, Oil and Natural Gas Corporation;* m.; two d.; ed Nat. Inst. of Technology, Raipur, Indira Gandhi Nat. Open Univ.; joined Oil and Natural Gas Corpn as Exec. Trainee 1976, Exec. Dir 2004–09, Dir (Offshore) 2009–11, Chair. and Man. Dir 2011–; Chair. and Man. Dir Mangalore Refinery and Petrochemicals 2011–; Chair. Bd of Dirs Nat. Inst. of Tech., Raipur 2012–; apptd Chair. Soc. Petroleum Engineers (SPE) Mumbai Section 2012, Chair. SPE India Council; mem. Bd UN Global Compact 2012–; Hon. Fellow, Centre for Excellence in Project Man.-Project Man. Assocs 2012; Distinguished Service Award, Soc. Petroleum Engineers, Middle East, Outstanding Achievement in Exploration and Production Award. *Leisure interests:* reading, listening to music. *Address:* Oil and Natural Gas Corporation, Tel Bhavan, Dehradun 248 003, India (office). *Telephone:* (13) 52759561 (office). *E-mail:* ongcdelhicc@ongc.co.in (office); ongcdelhicc@gmail.com (office). *Website:* www.ongcindia.com (office).

VATOLIN, Nikolay Anatolyevich; Russian metallurgist and academic; *Professor, Institute of Metallurgy, Urals Branch of Russian Academy of Sciences;* b. 13 Nov. 1926, Yekaterinburg; m.; one s.; ed Urals Polytechnical Inst., Sverdlovsk; scientific researcher, scientific sec., Head of Lab., Dir Inst. of Metallurgy, USSR (now Russian) Acad. of Sciences (Urals Br.) 1950–98, Prof. 1973–, Adviser, Russian Acad. of Sciences 1998–; mem. CPSU 1952–91; Corresp. mem. of USSR (now Russian) Acad. of Sciences 1970–81, mem. 1981; USSR State Prize 1982, 1991, Kurnakow Gold Medal, Russian Acad. of Sciences 1995, Govt Prize, Russian Fed. 1997, Demidov's Prize 1997, Russian Fed. State Prize 2000, Bardin's Prize, Russian Acad. of Sciences 2007. *Publications:* co-author: Physico-chemical Foundations of Steel Hot Leading 1977, Oxidation of Vanadium Slags 1978, Interparticle Interaction in Molten Metals 1979, Diffraction Studies of High Temperature Melts 1980, Computerization of Thermodynamic Calculations of Metallurgical Processes 1982, Electrical Properties of Oxide Melts 1984, Hydrometallurgy of Ferropowders 1984, Computer Simulation of Amorphous Metals 1985, Vanadium Slags 1988, Thermodynamic Modelling in High Temperature Inorganic Systems 1994, Temperature Dependences of Gibbs Reduced Energy of Some Inorganic Substances 1997, Fire Processing of Integrated Ores 1997, Some Regularities of Changes of Thermochemical Properties of Inorganic Compounds and Computational Methods for these Properties 2001, Lead Wastes Recylcing in

Ionic Salt Melts 2002, Diffraction Studies of a Structure of High-Temperature Melts 2003, Nonferrous Metals Recycling in Ionic Melts 2005, Modelling of Disordered and Nano-structured Phases 2011. *Address:* Institute of Metallurgy, Ural Branch of Russian Academy of Sciences, 101 Amundsen Street, 620016 Yekaterinburg (office); 17 Polyanka Street, 620016 Yekaterinburg, Russia (home). *Telephone:* (343) 267-94-21 (office); (343) 267-89-01 (home). *Fax:* (343) 267-91-86 (office). *E-mail:* vatolin@imet.mplik.ru (home).

VAUGHAN, David Arthur John, CBE, QC, FRSA; British barrister and academic; *Visiting Professor of Law, Durham University;* b. 24 Aug. 1938; s. of the late Capt. F. H. M. Vaughan and J. M. Vaughan; m. 1st 1967 (divorced); m. 2nd Leslie A. F. Irwin 1985; one s. one d.; ed Eton Coll. and Trinity Coll. Cambridge; called to Bar, Inner Temple 1962, Bencher 1988; mem. Bar Council 1968–72, 1984–86, Bar Cttee 1987–88; mem. Int. Relations Cttee of Bar Council 1968–86, Bar/Law Soc. Working Party on EEC (now EU) Competition Law 1977– (Chair. 1978–88), UK Del. to Consultative Cttee of Bars and Law Socs of the EC 1978–81 and other cttees etc.; Chair. EC Section, Union Int. des Advocats 1987–91; a Recorder 1994–2001; Chair. Editorial Bd European Law Reports 1997–; a Deputy High Court Judge 1997–2002; Judge of the Courts of Appeal of Jersey and Guernsey 2000–09; Visiting Prof. of Law, Univ. of Durham 1989–; mem. Advisory Bd, Centre for European Legal Studies, Cambridge Univ. 1991–; mem. Council of Man., British Inst. of Int. and Comparative Law 1992–2005; mem. Editorial Advisory Bd European Business Law Review 1998–; Fellow, Soc. for Advanced Legal Studies 1998; Bronze Medal, Bar of Bordeaux 1985. *Publications:* Gen. Ed. Encyclopaedia of EU Law, Vaughan and Robertson; Co-ordinating Ed. Halsbury's Laws of England 1986; Vaughan on the Law of the European Communities (ed.) 1986–97; Consultant Ed., European Court Practice 1993, Current EC Legal Development series. *Leisure interests:* fishing, tennis. *Address:* Brick Court Chambers, 7–8 Essex Street, London, WC2R 3LD, England (office). *Telephone:* (20) 7379-3550 (office). *Fax:* (20) 7379-3558 (office). *E-mail:* vaughan@brickcourt.co .uk (office).

VAUGHAN, Michael Paul, OBE; British fmr professional cricketer; b. 29 Oct. 1974, Eccles, City of Salford, Greater Manchester, England; s. of Graham Vaughan and Deirdre Vaughan (née Greenhaugh); m. Nichola Shannon; ed St Marks, Worsley, Dore Junior School, Sheffield, Silverdale Comprehensive School, Sheffield; right-hand opening batsmen, occasional right-arm off-break bowler; teams: Yorks. 1993–2009, England Under-19, England A (Capt. 1998–99), England 1999–2008 (Capt. 2003–08, retd from One-Day Int. (ODI) team 2007), MCC; First-class debut: 1993; Test debut: South Africa v England, Johannesburg 25–28 Nov. 1999; ODI debut: Sri Lanka v England, Dambulla 23 March 2001; T20I debut: England v Australia, Southampton 13 June 2005; played in 82 Tests (23 as Capt.), scored 5,719 runs (average 41.44, highest score 197 against India 2002) with 18 hundreds and took six wickets; ODIs: 86 matches, scored 1,982 runs (average 27.15, highest score 90 not out); First-class matches: scored 16,295 runs (average 36.95, highest score 197) with 42 hundreds and took 114 wickets; first batsman for 32 years to score 600 runs in a test series in Australia 2002/03; ranked World No. 1 Batsman 2003; announced retirement from first-class cricket 30 June 2009; joined Test Match Special (BBC) as an expert summarizer during England v Australia ODI series 2009; Freeman of the City of Sheffield 2005; Professional Cricketer's Asscn Player of the Year 2002, Player of the Series Australia vs England 2002/03, Wisden Cricketer of the Year 2003, BBC Sports Personality of the Year Team Award (mem.) 2005, named in Test Team of the Year, ICC (Int. Cricket Council) Awards 2007. *Radio:* appeared on BBC Radio 5 Live's Fighting Talk. *Publications:* Michael Vaughan: A Year in the Sun 2003, Calling the Shots: The Captain's Story 2005. *Leisure interests:* golf, football (Sheffield Wednesday). *Address:* c/o International Sports Management Ltd, Cherry Tree Farm, Cherry Tree Lane, Rostherne, Cheshire, WA14 3RZ, England (office); c/o Yorkshire County Cricket Club, Headingley Cricket Ground, Leeds, LS6 7QE. *Telephone:* (1565) 832100 (office); (870) 4296774. *Fax:* (1565) 832200 (office); (113) 2784099. *E-mail:* ism@golfism.net (office); ism@sportism.net (office); cricket@yorkshireccc .org.uk. *Website:* www.sportism.net (office); www.yorkshireccc.org.uk; www .michaelvaughan.net.

VAUGHN, Vincent (Vince) Anthony; American actor; b. 28 March 1970, Minneapolis, Minn.; s. of Vernon Lindsay Vaughn and Sharon Eileen DePalmo; m. Kyla Weber 2010; ed Lake Forest High School; began acting career 1989; ShoWest Convention Comedy Star of the Year 2006. *Films include:* Swingers 1996, The Locusts 1997, The Lost World: Jurassic Park 1997, Psycho 1998, Clay Pigeons 1998, Return to Paradise 1998, A Cool, Dry Place 1998, The Cell 2000, The Prime Gig 2000, Made (also producer) 2001, Domestic Disturbance 2001, Starsky & Hutch 2004, Dodgeball: A True Underdog Story 2004, Be Cool 2005, Mr & Mrs Smith 2005, Thumbsucker 2005, Wedding Crashers 2005, The Break-Up 2006, Into the Wild 2007, Wild West Comedy Show 2008, Couples Retreat 2009, The Dilemma 2011, The Watch 2012. *Address:* United Talent Agency, 9560 Wilshire Blvd, Suite 500, Beverly Hills, CA 90212-2401, USA (office). *Telephone:* (310) 273-6700 (office). *Fax:* (310) 247-1111 (office). *Website:* www.unitedtalent.com; www.vince-vaughn.com (office).

VAUTRIN, Jean, (Jean Herman); French novelist, film director and photographer; b. 17 May 1933, Pagny sur-Moselle, Meurthe-et-Moselle; s. of Raymond Herman and Maria Schneider; m. 2nd Anne Doat; two s. one d. (and one s. from first m.); ed Lycée Jacques-Amyot, Auxerre, Institut des hautes études cinématographiques; Lecturer in French Literature, Univ. of Bombay 1955; Asst to Roberto Rossellini 1955–57, to Jacques Rivette 1958, to Vincente Minelli 1958; Asst at ORTF, Dir, Armed Forces film div. 1959–61; Asst to Jean Cayrol, then made advertising films and shorts 1958–63, full-length films 1963–; Dir Juilliard 1990–; began writing career 1973; films made under name Jean Herman, including several films for TV; Ed. Atelier Juilliard series; Conseiller, Régional d'Aquitaine; Chevalier, Légion d'honneur; Officier, Order nat. du Mérite; Commdr des Arts et descLettres; Prix Louis Guilloux pour l'ensemble de l'oeuvre 1999, Feuilles d'or de la ville de Nancy 2010. *Films include:* Actua-Tilt (Grand Prix, Festival Int. de Tours, Critics' Prize, Oberhausen) 1960, La quille (Jury's Special Prize, Venice Festival) 1961, Voyage en Boscavie (Prix Emile Cohl) 1958, Le chemin de la mauvaise route, Le Dimanche de la vie d'après Queneau (Marilyn Monroe Prize) 1965, Adieu l'ami (with Alain Delon and Charles Bronson) 1968, Jeff (with Alain Delon), L'oeuf (with Guy Bedos), Popsy Pop (with Claudia Cardinale); as scriptwriter (with Michel Audiard): L'incorrigible, Garde à vue (Prix de l'Académie française, César du meilleur scénario) 1981, Flic ou Voyou, Le Guignolo, Le Marginal, L'Entourloupe, Le Grand Escogriffe, Nos intentions sont pacifiques, Bleu comme l'Enfer, Canicule, Billy-ze-Kick, Rue Barbare, Urgence, Charlie Dingo. *Plays:* Groom, Festival d'Avignon 1991, Baby Boom avec Anémone, Théâtre de L'Atelier. *Television:* Les Grands détectives, Rendez-vous dans les ténèbres, Les Bourbons d'Espagne, Les peupliers de la Prétentaine, La Conquête de l'Angleterre par les Normands, Le comte Yoster a bien l'honneur (series), La Pêche miraculeuse, Banlieue Sud-est, Le Locataire du haut, Les Insulaires, Jean sans Terre, L'Eté des Lip. *Publications:* (under name of Jean Vautrin) include: A bulletins rouges 1973, Billy-Ze-Kick 1974, Bloody Mary (Prix Mystère de la Critique), Canicule 1982, Patchwork (Prix des Deux-Magots) 1984, Baby Boom (Prix Goncourt de la Nouvelle 1986) 1985, La Vie Ripolin (Grand Prix du Roman de la Société des gens de lettres) 1986, Un grand pas vers le Bon Dieu (Prix Goncourt des Lycéens) 1989, 18 Tentatives pour devenir un saint 1989, Courage, chacun 1992, Symphonie-Grabuge (Prix Populiste) 1994, Le Roi des ordures 1997, Un Monsieur bien mis 1997, Histoires déglinguées 1998, Le cri du peuple 1999, L'Homme qui assassinait sa vie 2001, Le Journal de Louise B. 2002, Adieu la vie, adieu l'amour 2004, La femme au gant rouge 2004, New York, 100ème rue Est 2004, Si on s'aimait (short stories) 2005, La grande Zigouille 2006, En attendant l'eau chaude 2007, La vie badaboum 2009, Docteur Herman and Mister Vautrin (conversations) 2010, Les Années Faribole 2012; (with Dan Franck): La Dame de Berlin 1988, Le Temps des cerises 1991, Les Noces de Guernica 1994, Mademoiselle Chat 1996, Boro s'en va-t-en guerre 2000, Mais elle devrait en compter 10 au total, La dame de Jérusalem 2011; Jamais comme avant (with Robert Doisneau) 1996; comic strips: Bloody Mary (primé à Angoulème) 1979, Tardi en banlieue 1990, Le cri du peuple (four vols): Les canons du 18 mars (Prix Alpha Art du dessin) 2001, L'espoir assassiné (Prix Alpha Art du public) 2002, Les Heures sanglantes 2003, Le Testament des Ruines 2004; La Dame de Berlin 2010, Le Temps des cerises 2011, Le Pogo aux yeux rouges 2013, Canicule 2013, L'Homme qui assassinait sa vie 2013. *Leisure interest:* drawing cartoons, painting. *Address:* 6 Allée des oliviers, 33170 Gradignan (home); c/o Éditions Grasset, 61 rue des Sts Pères, 75006 Paris; c/o Éditions Robert-Laffont, 24 avenue Marceau, 76008 Paris, France. *Telephone:* (5) 56-85-33-87 (home). *Fax:* (5) 56-85-15-23 (home). *E-mail:* j -vautrin@orange.fr (home).

VAUZELLE, Michel Marie; French politician and lawyer; *President, Regional Council Provence-Alpes-Côte d'Azur;* b. 15 Aug. 1944, Montelimar, Drome; s. of Fernand Vauzelle and Marine Faure; m. Sylvie Fauvet 1980; two s. one d.; ed Collège St-Joseph, Lyon, Faculty of Law, Paris, Inst. of Political Studies, Paris; barrister 1968; Chargé de mission Prime Minister's Office 1969–72; mem. Finance Section Econ. and Social Council 1972–73; town councillor, Arles 1983–95, Deputy Mayor of Arles 1977–83, 1998–2001, Mayor of Arles 1995–98; Nat. Del. of Socialist Party Council of Civil Liberties 1978–81; Spokesman for the President of the Republic 1981–86; Préfet hors cadre 1985; Socialist Deputy for Bouches-du-Rhône 1986–92, 1997–2002, 2007–; Chair. Comm. for Foreign Affairs Nat. Ass. 1989–92; Minister of Justice and Keeper of the Seals 1992–93; Vice-Pres. Gen. Council Bouches du Rhône 1992–97; Pres. Regional Council Provence-Alpes-Côte d'Azur 1998–; Vice-Pres. ARF (Association des régions de France) 2004–; Pres. Commission Interméditerranéenne, Conférence des Régions Périphériques Maritimes 2007–; Pres. Nat. School of Photography 1982–86. *Publication:* Éloge de Daniel Manin, avocat venitien 1978, La France déroutée. *Leisure interest:* riding. *Address:* Hôtel de la Région, 27 place Jules Guesde, 13481 Marseille cedex 20, (office); 20 Place de la République, BP 196, 13637 Arles Cedex (office); Assemblée nationale, 126 rue de l'Université, 75355 Paris 07 SP, France (office). *Telephone:* 4-91-57-50-57 (office); 4-90-49-67-20 (office); 1-40-63-53-16 (office). *Fax:* 4-91-57-51-51 (office). *E-mail:* mvauzelle@assemblee-nationale.fr (office). *Website:* www.cr-paca.fr (office); www.michel-vauzelle.fr; michelvauzelle.regionpaca.fr.

VAVAKIN, Leonid Vassilyevich; Russian architect; b. 6 April 1932, Moscow; ed Moscow State Inst. of Architecture; Chief Architect and Chair. Moscow Cttee on Architecture and City Construction 1987–96; Prof., Moscow Inst. of Architecture; Corresp. mem. Russian Acad. of Arts, Full mem. 1995–; mem. Int. Acad. of Architecture; mem. Russ. Acad. of Architecture; USSR Council of Ministers Prize, RSFSR Merited Architect. *Address:* c/o Russian Academy of Architecture, 103874 Moscow, Dmitrova str. 24, Russia. *Telephone:* (495) 229-65-26.

VAVILOV, Andrei Petrovich; Russian economist, business executive and politician; b. 10 Jan. 1961, Perm; m. Marina Tsaregradskaya; one d.; ed Moscow Inst. of Man., Cen. Econs and Math. Inst, of the Russian Acad. of Sciences; Eng Programmer, Computation Centre, USSR Ministry of Public Health 1982–85; Jr Researcher, Cen. Inst. of Econs and Math., USSR Acad. of Sciences 1985–88, Head of Lab., Inst. of Marketing Problems 1991–92; Sr Researcher, Inst. of Econ. Prognosis of Tech. Progress 1988–91; Head of Dept of Macroeconomic Policy, Ministry of Econs and Finance 1992; First Deputy Minister of Finance 1992–97; Pres. Int. Financial Initiative Bank 1997; mem. Bd of Dirs RAO Gazprom (Counsellor to Chair.) 1998–99; Co-founder and CEO Inst. of Financial Studies 1998–2002, Research Council Chair 2002–; Owner and Chair. Severnaya Neft (oil co.), 2000–02 (sold co. 2002); mem. Fed. Council of Russia representing Penza Region Legis. Ass. 2002–10 (resgnd); f. IFS Hedge Fund 2007; Chair. SuperOx (research and production co.) 2010–; mem. Intergovernmental Cttee for Public Debt and Property of the Russian Fed. 1992–97, Comm. for Modernisation and Technological Devt of Russia's Economy 2010–. *Publications:* The Russian Public Debt and Financial Meltdowns 2010; over 20 papers. *Leisure interests:* hunting, skiing, tennis. *Address:* Time Warner Center, 10 Columbus Circle, New York, NY 10019-1158, USA. *Telephone:* (495) 710-78-10 (office). *Fax:* (495) 710-78-11 (office). *E-mail:* info@superox.ru. *Website:* www.avavilov.ru/en; www.ifs.ru; www.superox .ru/en.

VÄYRYNEN, Paavo Matti, DPolSc; Finnish politician; b. 2 Sept. 1946, Keminmaa; s. of Juho Eemeli Väyrynen and Anna Liisa (née Kaijankoski) Väyrynen; m. Vuokko Kaarina Tervonen 1968; one s. two d.; mem. Parl. 1970–; Political Sec. to Prime Minister 1970–71; Vice-Chair. Centre Party 1972–80, Chair. 1980; mem. Nordic Council 1972–75; Minister of Educ. 1975–76, of Labour 1976–77; Minister for Foreign Affairs 1977–82, 1991–93, of Foreign Trade and Devt 2007–11; mem. European Parl. 1995–2007, mem. Cttee on Foreign Affairs,

Human Rights, Common Security and Defence Policy, Cttee on Regional Devt 2004–07; unsuccessful cand. in presidential election 2012; mem. Suomen Keskusta (Finnish Centre Party). *Publications:* Köyhän asialla (Speaking for the Poor) 1971, On muutoksen aika (This is a Time of Change) 1974, Kansallisia kysymyksiä 1981, Kansakunta – ihmiskunta 1987, Finlands utrikes politik 1988, Suomen ulkopolitiikka 1989, Yhteinen tehtävämme 1989, Igenom brytningstid 1993, On muutoksen aika II 1993, On totuuden aika I 1993, On totuuden aika II 1993, Suomen puolueettomuus uudessa Euroopassa 1996, Paneurooppa ja uusidealismi 1997, Itsenäisen Suomen puolesta 1999, Samankeskisten kehien Eurooppa 2000, Etiäisiä vai kaukoviisautta 2004, Pohjanranta 2005, Eameli Väyrysen Vuosisata 2009. *Address:* c/o Ministry of Foreign Affairs, Merikasarmi, PO Box 176, 00023 Helsinki, Finland. *Website:* www.vayrynen.com.

VAZ, José Mário; Guinea-Bissau politician; fmr Pres. Assembléia Nacional Popular (Parl.); Minister of Finance 2009–12. *Address:* c/o Ministry of Finance, Rua Justino Lopes 74a, CP 67, Bissau, Guinea-Bissau.

VAZ DE ALMEIDA, Hélio Silva, BEcons; São Tomé and Príncipe economist and politician; *Minister of Planning and Finance;* fmrly economist with Banco Central de São Tomé e Príncipe; Minister of Planning and Finance 2012–; mem. Movimento de Libertação de São Tomé e Príncipe—Partido Social Democrata. *Address:* Ministry of Planning and Finance, São Tomé, São Tomé and Príncipe (office).

VAZ RAMELA, Pedro Humberto, LLD; Uruguayan lawyer, diplomatist and politician; b. 2 Dec. 1963, Rocha; ed Univ. de la República, Montevideo; began career as French teacher 1987–89; joined Ministry of Foreign Affairs 1989, Third Sec. 1990, later Sec., W Europe Div., later Counsellor, Embassy in México City, later Minister Counsellor to Int. Orgs, Geneva, Sec., later Sec., Treaty Div., Dir of Bilateral Econ. Relations, then Deputy Dir Gen., Int. Econ. Affairs Div.; Amb. to Brazil 2005–08; Deputy Minister of Foreign Affairs 2008–09, Minister of Foreign Affairs 2009–10; mem. Frente Amplio. *Address:* c/o Ministry of Foreign Affairs, Avda 18 de Julio 1205, 11100 Montevideo, Uruguay (office).

VÁŽNY, Ľubomír; Slovak politician and business executive; *Deputy Prime Minister, responsible for Investment;* b. 15 July 1957, Žilina; ed Faculty of Civil Eng, Slovak Tech. Univ., Bratislava; worked as construction foreman, construction man., tech. devt worker, State Enterprise, Trnava 1981–85; Head of Prices and Types, Head of Unit Typing and Design, Tech. Asst and Dir Stavoinveste, Banská Bystrica 1985–94, Dir and Man. Dir Stavoinvesta sro 1994–2002; mem. Direction (Direction—Social Democracy from 2005), served as Shadow Minister for Transport and Construction, mem. Nat. Council 2002–; mem. Parl., Vice-Chair. Cttee for Economy, Privatization and Entrepreneurship and mem. Mandate and Immunity Cttee; Minister of Transport, Posts and Telecommunications 2006–10; unsuccessful cand. for Mayor of Banská Bystrica in electoral coalition of Direction—Social Democracy, Slovak Nat. Party and People's Party – Movement for a Democratic Slovakia 2010; Deputy Prime Minister, responsible for Investment 2012–. *Address:* Office of the Government, nám. Slobody 1, 813 70 Bratislava (office); Direction—Social Democracy (Smer—Sociálna demokracia), Súmračná 25, 821 02 Bratislava, Slovakia. *Telephone:* (2) 5729-5111 (office). *Fax:* (2) 5249-7595 (office). *E-mail:* vicepremier@vlada.gov.sk (office); generalny.manager@strana-smer.sk. *Website:* www.vlada.gov.sk (office); www.strana-smer.sk.

VÁZQUEZ MOTA, Josefina Eugenia; Mexican politician; b. 1961, Mexico City; m. Sergio Ocampo Muñoz; three d.; ed Universidad Iberoamerican, Panamerican Inst. for Exec. Business Admin (IPADE); fmr Head of Women's Secr., Asociación Política Nacional; adviser to Confed. of Nat. Chambers of Commerce and Tourism (Concanaco); fmr adviser to Mexican Patronal Confed. (Coparmex); elected to as mem. Congress (Nat. Action Party, PAN) 2000–11, Minister of Social Devt 2000–05 (resgnd); man. of successful presidential campaign of Filipe Calderon Hinojosa 2006, then head of transition team; Sec. of Public Educ. 2006–09; unsuccessful cand. (PAN) in 2012 presidential election; fmr Deputy Chair., Econ. Policy Cttee; participant, Latin American Social Ministers Forum; Head of Mexican Del., Gen. Conf. of UN Org. for Food and Agric., Rome, Italy; Diploma on Ideas and Insts, Autonomous Technological Inst. of Mexico (ITAM). *Publications:* Dios Mio, Hazme Viuda Por Favor 2001, Nuestra oportunidad. Un México para todos; numerous articles in newspapers including Novedades and El Economista. *Address:* Partido Acción Nacional, Avda Coyoacán 1546, Col. del Valle, Del. Benito Juárez, 03100 México, DF, Mexico (office). *Telephone:* (55) 5200-4000 (office). *E-mail:* correo@cen .pan.org.mx (office). *Website:* www.pan.org.mx (office).

VÁZQUEZ RAÑA, Mario; Mexican business executive and sports administrator; *President and Director-General, Organizacion Editorial Mexicana;* b. 7 June 1932, Mexico City; m. Paquita Ramos de Vázquez Raña; five c.; ed degree in business admin; participated in shooting competitions at nat. and int. level 1960–72; Pres. Bd Dirs Hermanos Vazquez Co. 1960–80; Pres. and Dir-Gen. Organizacion Editorial Mexicana (largest newspaper co. in Latin America) 1975–, Cartones Ponderosa 2001, Ecofibras Ponderosa 2001, Ponderosa Group 2002, Productora Nacional de Papel 2004; Owner United Press International 1986–88; Pres. Mexican Shooting Fed. 1969–74, American Shooting Confed. 1973–79; Vice-Pres. Mexican Sports Confed. 1973–76; mem. Nat. Olympic Cttee (NOC) 1972–, Pres. 1974–2001; Pres. Pan American Games Org. Cttee 1975, Pan American Sports Org. (PASO) 1975–, Asscn of Nat. Olympic Cttees 1979–; Chair. Int. Olympic Solidarity Comm. for the American Continent 1975–, Vice-Chair. Olympic Solidarity Comm. 1979–96; mem. Exec. Bd IOC as rep. of NOCs 2000–, Deputy Chair. 1997–2001, Chair. 2002–, mem. the following Comms: Olympic Movt 1990–99, Preparation of the XII Olympic Congress 1990–94, Apartheid and Olympism 1990–92, 'IOC 2000' (Exec. Cttee 1999), Marketing 2000, IOC 2000 Reform Follow-up 2002; Orden del Quetzal (Guatemala) 1980, Ordine al Merito (Italy) 1981, Orden Diego del Lozada (Venezuela) 1983, Orden Francisco Miranda (Venezuela) 1983, Ordre du Grand Lion (Senegal) 1983, Orden del Merito (Paraguay) 1999, Ordine al Merito (San Marino) 2001, Orden Heráldica de Cristóbal Colón (Dominican Repub.) 2003, Légion d'Honneur (France) 2006, Order of Merit (Lithuania) 2008, Order of Friendship (Russia) 2008, Ordem de Rio Branco (Brazil) 2008, Order of Brilliant Star (China) 2008, Orden del Merito Civil (Spain) 2008; Dr hc (Nat. Sport Univ., Seoul) 2006; Silver Olympic Order 1978, Gold Olympic Order 1988, Athina Award, Int. Olympic Acad. 2007. *Publications:* Dialogues with History, eight vols 1991–2007. *Address:* Organizacion Editorial

Mexicana, S A De C V, Guillermo Prieto No 7, Ciudad De Mexico, Distrito Federal Mexico, Mexíco, Mexico (home); Association of National Olympic Committees, 54 avenue Hoche, 75008 Paris, France (office). *Telephone:* (55) 5566-2866 (Mexico) (office); 1-56-60-52-80 (office). *Fax:* 1-56-60-55-55 (office). *E-mail:* info@acnolympic .org (office). *Website:* www.acnolympic.org (office).

VÁZQUEZ ROMERO, Antonio, BSc; Spanish business executive; *Chairman, International Airlines Group;* b. 23 Nov. 1951, Cordoba; ed Univ. of Malaga; Dir of Subsidiaries and Man. Dir, Osborne Group, Mexico 1978–83; Dir of Subsidiaries, Domecq Mexico and Man. Dir Domecq International 1983–93; Deputy Dir Int. Dept, Tabacalera 1993–96, Dir Cigar Div. 1996–2000, COO Cigar Div., Altadis (tobacco co. cr. out of merger of Seita and Tabacalera) 2000–05, CEO and Chair. Exec. Cttee 2005–08; Chair. and CEO Iberia Lineas Aereas de Espana SA 2009–13, Chair. International Airlines Group (holding co. which owns Iberia) 2013–; mem. Bd of Dirs Telefónica Internacional 2008–. *Address:* International Airlines Group, Calle Velazquez 130, Madrid 28006, Spain (office). *Website:* www.iairgroup.com (office).

VÁZQUEZ ROMERO, Antonio, BSc; Spanish business executive; *Chairman, International Airlines Group;* b. 1951, Córdoba; ed Málaga Univ.; worked for Arthur Andersen & Co. 1974–78; worked in foreign trade at various cos in consumer goods industry, including Osborne and Domecq Groups (held various exec. posts) 1978–93; Head of Devt of Int. Business, Tabacalera 1993–96, Gen. Man. Cigar Div. 1996–2005; Chair. Bd and Chair. Exec. Cttee and CEO Altadis Group 2005–08; Chair. Logista and mem. Bd of Dirs Iberia 2005–, Chair. 2009–, CEO Iberia Airlines 2009–11, Chair. International Airlines Group 2011–; mem. Bd of Dirs Telefónica Internacional 2008–; Dir (non-exec.) Transtlantic Business Dialogue Bd; Manager of the Year, AED 2010. *Address:* Iberia, Líneas Aéreas de España SA, Velázquez 130, 28006 Madrid, Spain (office). *Telephone:* (91) 587-87-87 (office). *Fax:* (91) 587-74-69 (office). *E-mail:* media@iberia.es (office). *Website:* grupo .iberia.es (office); www.iairgroup.com (office).

VÁZQUEZ ROSAS, Tabaré Ramón, PhD; Uruguayan politician, physician and fmr head of state; b. 17 Jan. 1940, Montevideo; m. Maria Auxiliadora Delgado; three c.; ed Universidad de la Republica, Gustave Roussy Inst., Paris; Prof. Faculty of Medicine, Universidad de la Republica 1987–; Mayor of Montevideo 1990–95; Leader, Encuentro Progresista-Frente Amplio (Broad Front) coalition 2001–; unsuccessful presidential cand. 2000; Pres. of Uruguay 2005–10; WHO Dir-Gen's Award for coordinating tobacco control in Uruguay 2006. *Address:* Encuentro Progresista-Frente Amplio, Colonia 1367, 2° Montevideo, Uruguay (office).

VEASEY, Josephine, CBE; British singer (mezzo-soprano) (retd) and vocal consultant; b. 10 July 1930, Peckham, London, England; m. Ande Anderson 1951 (divorced 1969); one s. one d.; ed studied with Audrey Langford; mem. chorus Covent Garden Opera Company 1948–50, returned as soloist 1955; prin. mezzo-soprano, Royal Opera House, Covent Garden; has sung every major mezzo-soprano role in repertory; many foreign engagements have included Salzburg Festival, La Scala, Milan, Metropolitan Opera House, New York and Paris Opera; Prof., RAM 1982–83; vocal consultant, ENO 1985–94; Hon. RAM. *Recordings:* has made recordings with Karajan, Solti, Bernstein and Colin Davis. *Address:* 99 Micheldever Road, Whitchurch, Hants., RG28 7JH, England (home). *Telephone:* (1256) 892930 (home).

VEBER, Francis Paul; French screenwriter and director; b. 28 July 1937, Neuilly; s. of Pierre Gilles Veber and Catherine Veber (née Agadjaniantz); m. Françoise Marie Ehrenpreis 1964; two s.; ed Paris Univ. of Science, Paris Medical School; began career as journalist, also wrote short stories, stand-up comedy material and theatre plays; wrote first film screenplay 1969; Pres. EFVE Films 1976, Escape Film Production Co. 1988; Chevalier, Légion d'honneur, Commdr des Arts et Lettres, Officier de l'Ordre Nat. du Mérite. *Films directed:* first film, Le Jouet, 1976; first American film, Three Fugitives 1989, Le Dîner de Cons 1997 (based on his stage play), Le Placard 2001, Tais-Toi 2003, La Doublure 2006, A Pain in the Ass 2008. *Publications:* Le Grand Blond avec une Chaussure Noire 1972, L'Emmerdeur 1973, Le Magnifique 1973, Le Jouet 1976, La Cage aux Folles (adaptation) 1978, La Chèvre 1981, Les Compères 1983, Les Fugitifs 1986, Le Jaguar 1996, Le Dîner de Cons 1998, Le Placard 2001, Tais-Toi 2003. *Leisure interests:* tennis, swimming. *Address:* c/o Artmédia, 20 avenue Rapp, 75007 Paris, France (office); Creative Artists Agency, 9830 Wilshire Boulevard, Beverly Hills, CA 90210, USA (office). *Telephone:* (310) 288-4545 (USA) (office).

VEBER, Janko; Slovenian politician; *President, Državni zbor (National Assembly);* b. 30 May 1960, Ljubljana; ed Secondary School of Civil Eng and Tech., Ljubljana, Univ. of Ljubljana; moved to Kočevje, worked in spatial planning and inspection services at Municipality of Kočevje 1989–90; Dir Hydrovod Kočevje-Ribnica (water supply co.) 1990–96; Mayor of Municipality of Kočevje 1994–2010; Deputy (Social Democrats) of Državni zbor (Nat. Ass.) for IV Kočevje 1 1996–, Pres. 2013–; Pres. Women's Handball Club, Kočevje 1997–2011, Asscn of Professional Drivers and Mechanics of Slovenia 2011–. *Address:* Office of the President, Državni zbor (National Assembly), 1102 Ljubljana, Šubičeva ulica 4, Slovenia (office). *Telephone:* (1) 4789400 (office). *Fax:* (1) 4789845 (office). *E-mail:* gp@dz-rs .si (office). *Website:* www.dz-rs.si (office).

VEDERNIKOV, Alexander Aleksandrovich; Russian conductor; *Chief Conductor and Artistic Adviser, Odense Symphony Orchestra;* b. 11 Jan. 1964, Moscow; s. of Aleksander F. Vedernikov and Natalya Guryeva; m. Olga Aleksandrovna Vedernikova; ed Moscow P. I. Tchaikovsky State Conservatory; Music Dir Stanislavsky Music Theatre, Moscow 1988–90; Asst, then Conductor Prin. Symphony Orchestra of Russian TV and Radio 1989–95; Founder and Chief Conductor Russian Philharmonia Symphony Orchestra 1995–98, 2000–04; Musical Dir and Chief Conductor Bolshoi Theatre of Russia 2001–09; mem. conductor's collegium, Russian Nat. Orchestra 2003–; Chief Conductor and Artistic Adviser, Odense Symphony Orchestra 2009–; conducted opera and ballet productions in European theatres including Covent Garden, London, La Scala, Milan and symphony orchestras in Russia. *Address:* c/o Bridget Canniere, IMG Artists, The Light Box, 111 Power Road, London, W4 5PY, England (office); Pyryeva str. 4, korp. 1, apt. 24, 119285 Moscow, Russia (home). *Telephone:* (20) 7957-5800 (office); (495) 147-52-17 (home). *Fax:* (20) 7957-5801 (office). *E-mail:* artistseurope@imgartists.com (office). *Website:* www.imgartists.com (office).

VÉDRINE, Hubert; French politician and civil servant; *Managing Director, Hubert Védrine Conseil;* b. 31 July 1947, Saint-Silvain-Bellegarde; s. of Jean Védrine and Suzanne Védrine; m. Michèle Froment; two s.; ed Lycée Albert Camus, Univ. of Nanterre, Institut d'Etudes Politiques, Paris, Ecole Nat. d'Admin.; Sr Civil Servant, Ministry of Culture 1974–78, Ministry for Capital Works 1978–79; Co-ordinator for Cultural Relations, Near and Middle East, Ministry of Foreign Affairs 1979–81; Technical Adviser External Affairs, Office of the Sec.-Gen. of the Pres. 1981–86, Legal Adviser, Conseil d'Etat 1986, 1995–96; Spokesman for Presidency of Repub. 1988–91, Sec.-Gen. 1991–95; Minister of Foreign Affairs 1997–2002; Man. Dir Hubert Védrine Conseil 2003–; Pnr, Jeantet et Associés (law firm) 1996–97. *Publications:* Mieux aménager sa ville 1979, Les Mondes de François Mitterrand, A l'Elysée 1981–95 1996, Dialogue avec Dominique Moïsi: Les Cartes de la France à l'heure de la mondialisation 2000, Face à l'Hyperpuissance 2003, Multilateralisme – une reforme possible 2004, François Mitterand – un dessein, un destin 2006. *Address:* Hubert Védrine Conseil, 21 rue Jean Goujon, 75008 Paris (office); 6 rue de Luynes, 75007 Paris, France (home). *Telephone:* 1-45-63-32-82 (office). *Fax:* 1-45-63-38-29 (office). *E-mail:* bureau.hv@hvconseil.com (office). *Website:* www.hvconseil.com (office); www.hubertvedrine.net.

VEGA DE SEOANE AZPILICUETA, Javier; Spanish mining engineer and business executive; *Co-Founder and President, Gestlink;* b. 13 Sept. 1947, San Sebastián; s. of Joaquín Vega de Seoane and Rosa Azpilicueta; m. Mercedes Pérez de Villaamil Lapiedra 1970; two s. one d.; ed Escuela Técnica Superior de Ingenieros de Minas, Madrid and Glasgow Business School, UK; Asst Production Dir, Fundiciones del Estanda SA 1972–75; Asst to CEO, Leyland Ibérica SA 1975–77; Gen. Man. SKF Española SA 1977–83, Pres. and CEO 1983–84; Gen. Man. Instituto Nacional de Industria 1984–86; Pnr TASA AG 1986; Co-Founder Gestlink (consultancy) 1987, Pres. 1991–; Sr Adviser in Spain, Wasserstein Perella & Co. 1992; Pres. Explosivos Río Tinto, S.A. Cros 1988, Chair. Bd Ercros (following merger) –1991; Pres. Fujitsu España; currently Pres. DKV Seguros; mem. Bd of Dirs Solvay Iberica YDILO Voice Solutions, Ecoralia, Tavex Cotton SA, MASmovil; mem. Exec. Bd Circulo de Empresarios; mem. Advisory Bd AON Gil y Carvajal. *Leisure interests:* golf, squash, scuba diving. *Address:* Gestlink, Fortuny 39, Bajo Izqda, 28010 Madrid, Spain (office). *Telephone:* (913) 91-59-10 (office). *Fax:* (913) 19-67-92 (office).

VEGA GARCÍA, Gen. Gerardo Clemente Ricardo; Mexican politician and army officer; b. 28 March 1940, Puebla City; ed War Coll., Nat. Defence Coll.; joined army 1957; nat. security studies in USA and Panama and fmr Dir of Mil. Educ.; fmr Rector Army and Air Force Univ.; fmr Deputy Chief of Mil. Doctrine, Estado Mayor of SEDENA; fmr Mil. Attaché, embassies in USSR, Poland, and Germany; fmr Deputy Dir and Dir Nat. Defence Coll.; promoted to Div. Gen. with command of Mil. Zone 2000; Sec. of Nat. Defence 2000–06; Legion of Honour and Merit and numerous other decorations. *Address:* c/o Secretariat of State for National Defence, Blvd Manuel Avila Camacho, esq. Avda Industria Militar, 3°, Col. Lomas de Sotelo, Del. Miguel Hidalgo, 11640 México, DF, Mexico (office).

VEGLIÒ, HE Cardinal Antonio Maria; Italian ecclesiastic and diplomatist; *President, Pontifical Council for Pastoral Care of Migrants and Itinerant People;* b. 3 Feb. 1938, Macerata Feltria; ordained priest, Archdiocese of Pesaro 1962; apptd Titular Archbishop of Aeclanum 1985; Apostolic Pro-Nuncio to Papua New Guinea (also accred to the Solomon Islands) 1985–89, to Senegal (also accred to Guinea-Bissau, Cape Verde and Mali) 1989–94 Apostolic Nuncio to Senegal (also accred to Guinea-Bissau, Cape Verde and Mali) 1994–97, to Lebanon (also accred to Kuwait) 1997–99; Sec. Congregation for the Oriental Churches 2001–09; Pres. Pontifical Council for Pastoral Care of Migrants and Itinerant People 2009–13, 2013–; cr. Cardinal (Cardinal-Deacon of San Cesareo in Palatio) 2012; participated in Papal Conclave 2013. *Address:* Pontifical Council for Pastoral Care of Migrants and Itinerant People, Piazza San Calisto 16, 00120 Città del Vaticano, Rome, Italy (office). *Telephone:* (06) 69887131 (office); (06) 69887193 (office); (06) 69887242 (office). *Fax:* (06) 69887295 (office); (06) 69887111 (office). *E-mail:* office@migrants .va (office). *Website:* www.vatican.va/roman_curia/pontifical_councils/migrants/ index.htm (office); www.pcmigrants.org (office).

VEIGA, Carlos Alberto Wahnon de Carvalho, PhD; Cape Verde politician and lawyer; b. 21 Oct. 1949, Mindelo; Prime Minister of Interim Govt Jan. 1991, Prime Minister of Cape Verde 1991–2000, also with responsibility for Defence; Presidential cand. 2001; fmr Chair. Movimento para a Democracia (MPD). *Address:* WV Consultores LDA, CP43-A Praia, Santiago, Cape Verde (office). *Telephone:* 60-36-70 (office); 62-12-10 (home). *Fax:* 61-95-69 (office); 62-12-20 (home). *E-mail:* wvjtv@ cvtelecom.cv (office); carlos.veiga@cvtelecom.cv (home).

VEIL, Simone, LenD; French politician and fmr lawyer; b. 13 July 1927, Nice; d. of André Jacob and Yvonne Steinmetz; m. Antoine Veil 1946 (died 2013); three s. (one deceased); ed Inst. d'Etudes Politiques de Paris; Attaché Ministry of Justice 1957–59; Tech. Adviser to Office of René Pleven, Keeper of the Seals 1969; Sec.-Gen. Conseil Supérieur de la Magistrature 1970–74; mem. ORTF Admin. Council 1971–74; Minister of Health 1974–76, of Health and Social Security 1976–79, of Social Affairs, Health and Urban Devt 1993–95; mem. European Parl. 1979–93, (Pres. 1979–82, Chair. of Legal Affairs Cttee 1982–84), Chair. Liberal and Democratic Group 1984–89; mem. Conseil Constitutionnel 1998–; Leader Centre-Right List for European elections 1989; Pres. Fondation pour la Mémoire de la Shoah 2001–, Bd Dirs for Victims Trust, Fund of Int. Criminal Court 2003–, Fondation Gustave Roussy pour la Recherche Médicale 2005; mem. Acad. Française 2008–; Grand Officier, Légion d'honneur 2009, numerous foreign decorations, including Hon. DBE (UK) 1997, Chevalier, Ordre nat. du Mérite, Grand Officier, Nat. Order of the Lion (Senegal), Order of Merit of the Repub. (Ivory Coast), Isabel la Católica (Spain), Grand Cross Order of Merit (FRG), Order of Rio Branco (Brazil), Order of Merit (Luxembourg), Order of the Phoenix (Greece); Hon. LLD (Glasgow) 1995; Dr hc (Princeton) 1975, (Weizmann Inst.) 1976, (Bar Ilan) 1980, (Yale) 1980, (Cambridge) 1980, (Edin.) 1980, (Georgetown) 1981, (Urbino) 1981, (Yeshiva) 1982, (Sussex) 1984, (Free Univ., Brussels) 1984, (Brandeis) 1989, (Pennsylvania) 1997; Onassis Foundation Prize 1980, Charlemagne Prize 1981, Louise Weiss Foundation Prize 1981, Louise Michel Prize 1983, European Merit Prize 1983, Jabotinsky Prize (USA) 1983, Prize for Everyday Courage 1984, Special Freedom Prize 1984, Fiera di Messina 1984, Thomas Dehler Prize 1988, Klein Foundation Prize, Phila 1991, Truman Prize for Peace, Jerusalem 1991,

Giulietta Prize, Verona 1991, Atlantide Prize, Barcelona 1991, Prix Grand Siècle 2005, Prix Prince des Asturies 2005 and other prizes, Médaille pénitentiaire, Médaille de l'Education surveillée. *Publications:* Les données psycho-sociologiques de l'adoption (with Prof. Launay and Dr Soule) 1969, Les hommes aussi s'en souviennent 2004, Une Vie (auto-biog.) 2007. *Address:* 10 rue de Rome, 75008 Paris (office); Conseil constitutionnel, 2 rue Montpensier, 75001 Paris; 11 Place Vauban, 75007 Paris, France (home). *Telephone:* 1-42-93-00-60 (office). *Fax:* 1-40-08-03-62 (office). *E-mail:* corinne.adamrix@wanadoo.fr (office).

VEITIA, Diego; American business executive; *Non-Executive Chairman, International Assets Holding Corporation;* launched Americas All Season Fund (global flexible fund) 1988, later Chief Investment Officer; est. International Assets Holding Corpn (INTL) 1990, currently Chair. (non-exec.); fmr Chair. Rollins Coll. Hamilton Holt School; mem. Pres.'s Council, American Grad. School of Int. Man.; appearances on CNBC, CNN and Financial News Network. *Publications:* Global Trends, The Best 50 Investments for the 21st Century. *Address:* International Assets Holding Corporation, 708 Third Avenue, Suite 1500, New York, NY 10017, USA (office). *Telephone:* (212) 485-3500 (office). *Fax:* (212) 485-3505 (office). *E-mail:* info@intlassets.com (office). *Website:* www.intlassets.com (office).

VĒJONIS, Raimonds, MA; Latvian politician; *Minister of Defence;* b. 15 June 1966, Pleskava (Pskov), Russia; m. Iveta Vējone; ed Univ. of Latvia, Tampere Univ. of Tech., Finland, Tallinn Univ. of Tech., Estonia; began career as teacher, Madona 1st High School 1987–89; mem. Madona City Council 1990–93; Deputy Dir Madona Regional Environmental Bd 1989–96; mem. Bd Skulte port 1997–98, 2000–02; Dir Lielrigas Regional Environmental Bd 1996–2002; State Rep. Getlini EKO (public authority) 1997–2002; Nat. Coordinator, EU Associated States Environmental Legislation Control 1998–2002; Minister of Environment 2002–11; mem. 11th Saeima (Parl.) 2011–14, Chair. Baltic Affairs Sub-Cttee 2011–14, mem. Public Admin and Local Govt Cttee 2011–14, Nat. Security Cttee 2011–14; Head, Latvian Del. to Baltic Assembly 2011–; mem. Strategic Devt Comm. (under the auspices of Pres. of Latvia) 2012–14; Minister of Defence 2014–; mem. Union of Greens and Farmers (ZZS). *Address:* Ministry of Defence, K. Valdemāra iela 10–12, Rīga 1473, Latvia (office). *Telephone:* 6733-5114 (office). *Fax:* 6721-2307 (office). *E-mail:* kanceleja@mod.gov.lv (office). *Website:* www.mod.gov.lv (office).

VEKARIC, Vatroslav, MA, PhD; Croatian research institute director; b. 4 March 1944, Dubrovnik; ed Univ. of Belgrade; began career as journalist with Radio Zagreb 1967–68; Research Fellow, Inst. for Int. Politics and Econs (IIPE) 1968–77, Dir Centre for Regional Studies 1977–80, Deputy Dir IIPE (Dir of Research) 1980–85, Dir IIPE 2000; Dir Centre for Strategic Studies, Belgrade 1985–2000; conducted UN research projects 1981–83; Lecturer, Univ. of Belgrade 1982–84, Centre for Post-Grad. Studies, Dubrovnik 1985–, Univ. of Bari, Italy 1997, 1999, Univ. of Sant Angelo, Rome 1998, Univ. of Florence 1998; Ed.-in-Chief Review of International Affairs 2001–; mem. Bd of Dirs Diplomatic Acad., Serbia and Montenegro 2001–; mem. Int. Advisory Bd Journal of International Relations; mem Int. Studies Asscn, USA 1986–, Cttee for Mediterranean Studies, Sassari, Italy 1983– (Deputy Sec.-Gen. 1984–87), Contemplating Group for Scenarios of Devt of the Mediterranean (UN-UNEP), Cannes, France 1983–87, Governing Bd AIRI, Rome 1989–, Int. Law Asscn 1993–, Editorial Bd Nuova Fase review, Edizioni Democrazia Domani, Rome 1994–, Scientific Council Inst. for the Study of the Greek Economy, Athens 1994–, Programme Cttee Centre for Euro-Mediterranean Studies, Rome 1999–99. *Publications:* seven books and more than 130 essays and articles. *Address:* c/o Institute for International Politics and Economics, Makedonska 25, 11000 Belgrade, Serbia (office).

VEKSELBERG, Viktor Felixovich, MA, PhD; Russian (b. Ukrainian) business executive; *Chairman, Renova Group;* b. 14 April 1957, Drogobych, Ukrainian SSR, USSR; m. Marina Vekselberg; one s. one d.; ed Moscow Inst. of Railroad Eng, Computing Center of USSR Acad. of Sciences; co-f. Renova (now Renova Group) 1990, Gen. Dir 1990–, currently Chair. Supervising Cttee for Renova group of cos; acquired Vlaimir Tractor Factory 1994; merged Siberian Irkutsk Aluminium with Ural Aluminium to form Siberial-Urals Aluminium (SUAL) Co. 1996, Pres. SUAL Group 1996–2003, Chair. 2003–12 (resgnd); Deputy Chair. TNK (Tyumen Oil Co.) Man. Bd 1998–2000, Chair. 2000–02, Chair. Man. Bd (merged with BP Russia to form TNK-BP 2003) 2002–03, Exec. Dir 2003–13; Head of Russian section of coordination council of Innovation Center Project in Skolkovo 2010–; mem. Exec. Bd of Dirs Russian Union of Industrialists and Entrepreneurs 2003–; mem. Bd of Dirs Russian Industrialists Asscn (mining and metallurgy); Co-Chair. Coordinating Council on Social Partnership; mem. Bd of Trustees Bolshoi Theatre, Moscow, State Univ. Higher School of Econs. *Address:* Office of the Chairman, Renova Group, 115184 Moscow, Malaya Ordynka 40, Russia (office). *Telephone:* (495) 777-77-07 (office). *Fax:* (495) 787-96-68 (office). *Website:* www.renova.ru (office).

VELA CHIRIBOGA, HE Cardinal Raúl Eduardo; Ecuadorean ecclesiastic; *Archbishop Emeritus of Quito;* b. 1 Jan. 1934, Riobamba; ordained priest, Diocese of Riobamba 1957; Auxiliary Bishop of Guayaquil 1972–75; Titular Bishop of Ausafa 1972–89; Bishop of Azogues 1975–89; Bishop of Ecuador, Mil. 1989–2003; Titular Bishop of Pauzera 1989–98; Archbishop of Quito 2003–10, Archbishop Emer. 2010–; cr. Cardinal (Cardinal-Priest of Santa Maria in Via) 2010; participated in Papal Conclave 2013. *Address:* Archdiocese of Quito, Apartado 17-01-00106, Calle Chile 1440, Quito, Ecuador (office). *Telephone:* (2) 524002 (office). *Fax:* (2) 580973 (office). *Website:* www.arquidiocesisdequito.org (office).

VELARDE FLORES, Julio Emilio, BEcons, MA (Econs), PhD; Peruvian economist, academic and central banker; *Governor, Banco Central de Reserva del Perú;* b. 1 July 1952, Lima; ed Univ. del Pacífico, Lima, Inst. for World Econs, Kiel, Germany, Brown Univ., USA; Sr Researcher and Prof., Dept of Econs, Univ. del Pacífico 1986–2003, Dean, Faculty of Econs 2003; Dir, Banco Central de Reserva del Perú (central bank) 1990–92, 2001–03, Gov. 2006–; CEO Latin American Reserve Fund 2004–06; fmr consultant to numerous int. orgs including IDB, World Bank, USAID, ILO, Int. Devt Research Centre, Canada. *Address:* Office of the Governor, Banco Central de Reserva del Perú, Jirón Antonio Miró Quesada 441-445, Lima 1, Peru (office). *Telephone:* (1) 4267041 (office). *Fax:* (1) 4273091 (office). *E-mail:* webmaster@bcrp.gob.pe (office). *Website:* www.bcrp.gob.pe (office).

VELASCO BARAONA, Belisario; Chilean politician; b. 5 Feb. 1935, Santiago de Chile; began career at Empresa de Comercio Agrícola (Agricultural Trade Co.) 1953, Man. Dir 1964–70; joined Partido Demócratia Cristiano (Christian Democratic Party) 1957; Man. Dir Radio Presidente Balmaceda 1973–76; co-f. agricultural export co. 1974; Chair. Análisis magazine 1980–86; Deputy Minister of the Interior 1990–99, served as acting Minister of Defence on several occasions; Amb. to Portugal 1999–2003; Minister of the Interior 2006–08. *Address:* c/o Ministry of the Interior, La Moneda Palace, Santiago de Chile, Chile (office).

VELASCO BRANES, Andrés, PhD; Chilean government official and economist; ed Yale and Columbia Univs, USA; Chief of Staff to Minister of Finance 1990–92, later Dir of Int. Finance; Postdoctoral Fellow in Political Economy, Harvard Univ. and MIT 1994–95; Chief Economist and Deputy Lead Negotiator NAFTA accession team, Chile 1995; fmr adviser to govts of Ecuador and El Salvador; fmr consultant World Bank, IMF, Inter-American Devt Bank, UN Econ. Comm. for Latin America, Fed. Research Bank of Atlanta; fmr Dir Center for Latin American and Caribbean Studies, New York Univ.; Sumitomo-FASID Prof. of Int. Finance and Devt, Harvard Univ. 2000–06; Minister of Finance 2006–10. *Publications:* Trade, Development and the World Economy: Selected Essays of Carlos Díaz-Alejandro (ed.) 1988, Vox Populi (novel) 1995, Lugares Comunes (novel) 2003, Free Trade and Beyond: Prospects for Integration in the Americas (co-ed.) 2004. *Address:* c/o Ministry of Finance, Teatinos 120, 12°, Santiago, Chile (office). *Website:* ksghome.harvard.edu/~avelasco.

VELASQUEZ QUESQUÉN, Angel Javier, LLM; Peruvian lawyer and politician; b. 12 March 1960; m. Maritza Suclupe; two s.; pnr Jenny Obando Popuche; one s. one d.; ed Univ. Nacional Pedro Ruiz Gallo de Lambayeque, Pontificia Univ. Católica del Perú; fmr Prof. of Law, Univ. San Martín de Porres; mem. Congress representing Lambayeque 1995–, mem. Congress Exec. Council 2002–03, mem. Budget and Control Comm. 2002–03 (Pres. 2003–05), Pres. of Congress 2008–09; Pres. Council of Ministers (Prime Minister) 2009–10 (resgnd); mem. Partido Aprista Peruano (PAP), Vice-Pres. Exec. Cttee 1999, mem. PAP Nat. Strategic Comm. 2002–04, mem. PAP Nat. Exec. 2004–08. *Address:* c/o Office of the President of the Council of Ministers, Avda 28 de Julio 878, Miraflores, Lima, Peru (office).

VELAYATI, Ali Akbar, MD; Iranian politician, medical scientist and academic; *Professor, Shahid Beheshti University of Medical Sciences and Health Education;* b. 1945, Tehran; s. of Ali Asghar and Zobeideh Asgah; m. Skina Khoshnevisan; four c.; ed Tehran Univ., Johns Hopkins Univ., USA; joined Nat. Front (of Mossadegh) 1961; f. Islamic Asscn of Faculty of Medicine, Tehran Univ. 1963; took part in underground political activities in support of Ayatollah Khomeini 1979; Vice-Minister, Ministry of Health 1979–80; proposed for Prime Minister by Ayatollah Khomeini Oct. 1981 (candidature rejected by the Majlis); Minister of Foreign Affairs 1981–97; Adviser to Supreme Leader in int. affairs; unsuccessful cand. in presidential election 2013; currently Prof., Shahid Beheshti Univ. of Medical Sciences and Health Educ.; Head, Islamic And Traditional Medicine Dept, Iranian Acad. of Medical Sciences; Pres. Iranian Journal of Infectious Diseases and Tropical Medicine, Iranian Soc. for Support of Patients with Infectious Diseases; mem. Int. Soc. for History of Medicine; Zmaj Od Bosne Gold Medal for Services to Peace in the Balkans 1995; Dr hc (Al-Farabi, Kazakhstan) 1992, (Teflis, Georgia) 1993, (Avecina, Tajikistan) 1995. *Publications:* several books including Infectious Diseases (3 vols) 1979; numerous articles in professional journals. *Address:* Shahid Beheshti University of Medical Sciences and Health Services, Shahid Chamran Highway, Evin, POB 4139-19395, Tehran (office); Iranian Academy of Medical Sciences, PO Box 19395/4655, Pasdaran Avenue, Tehran, Iran. *Telephone:* (21) 220109555 (office). *Fax:* (21) 220109484 (office). *E-mail:* icrd@sbmu.ac.ir (office); vlayati@ams.ac.ir (office); aavelayati@nritld.ac.ir (office). *Website:* www.sbmu.ac.ir (office); www.velayati.ir.

VELDHUIS, Johannes (Jan) G. F.; Dutch university president (retd); b. 4 Oct. 1938, Hengelo; m. Monica M. H. Thier 1969; three s.; ed Univs of Utrecht and Minnesota; Ministry of Foreign Affairs 1968–70; Sec. Univ. Bd Univ. of Leiden 1970–74; Deputy Sec.-Gen. Ministry of Educ. and Science 1974–79, Dir-Gen. and Insp.-Gen. of Educ. and Science 1979–86; Pres. Utrecht Univ. 1986–2003; Chair. Netherlands del. OECD Educ. Cttee 1984–86; Chair. Bd Netherlands-America Comm. for Educational Exchange (Fulbright Comm.) 1984–2001, Netherlands Inst. for Art History, Florence, Fondation Descartes Amsterdam, Museum Catharÿneconvent Utrecht, Stichting Carmelcollege Hengelo; mem. Bd Netherlands History Inst., Rome, Netherlands Archaeological Inst., Cairo, Japan-Netherlands Inst., Tokyo; mem. bds of several hosps in The Hague area; Chevalier, Légion d'Honneur 1997, Officer Order Orange Nassau 1998, Commdr Order Isabel la Católica (Spain) 2001; Dr hc (Florida Gainesville); Univ. of Minn. Distinguished Leadership Award for Ints 2005. *Publications:* various publs in the field of educ. and public admin. *Leisure interests:* comparative educ., literature, botany, tennis, skiing, bridge. *Address:* Roucooppark 12, 2251 AV Voorschoten, Netherlands (home). *Telephone:* (71) 5617696 (home). *Fax:* (71) 5620029 (home). *E-mail:* monica.jan.veldhuis@planet.nl (home).

VELDRE, Vinets; Latvian veterinarian and fmr politician; b. 26 March 1971; m.; one s. one d.; ed Latvian Univ. of Agriculture, Faculty of Veterinary Medicine, Uppsala Univ., Sweden, Free Univ. of Berlin, Danish Meat Trade Coll., A & G Univ., Tex., USA, Massey Univ., New Zealand; Lab Asst, Latvian Univ. of Agriculture, Faculty of Veterinary Medicine, Dept of Epizootics 1993–95; Sr Inspector State Veterinary Service, Rīga Dist Veterinary Authority 1995–97, Head, Control Div. for Food of Animal Origin 1997–99, Dir and State Chief Veterinary Inspector 1999–2001, Dir-Gen. Food and Veterinary Service 2001–07; Minister for Health Jan.–Dec. 2007, for Defence Dec. 2007–09; currently working as consultant, Baltijas Marka (Baltic Trademark) SIA; mem. fmr People's Party (TP) (Tautas partija); Ministry of Agriculture Diligence Award 2005. *Address:* c/o Baltijas Marka SIA, Rīga 1050, Pils iela 16-1, Latvia (office).

VELIKHOV, Yevgeniy Pavlovich; Russian physicist; b. 2 Feb. 1935, Moscow; s. of Pavel Pavlovich Velikhov and Natalia Vsevolodoma Velikhova; m. Natalia Alekseevna Arseniyeva 1959; two s. one d.; mem. of staff, Kurchatov Inst. of Atomic Energy 1958–, Head of Lab. 1962–70, Deputy Dir, then Dir of br. of Inst. 1971–89; Dir Russian Scientific Centre, Kurchatov Inst. 1989–; Founder and Dir Inst. for Security Problems of Nuclear Energy Devt 1988–91; Prof., Moscow Univ.

1973–; mem. CPSU Cen. Cttee 1989–90; mem. USSR (now Russian) Acad. of Sciences 1974, Presidium, Vice-Pres. 1978–96, 2002–, Academician-Sec. Dept of Information Technology, Cybernetics and Automatic Systems 1985–92; mem. Supreme Soviet of USSR; People's Deputy of the USSR 1989–91; mem. Pres. Council 1992–93; Chair. Cttee of Soviet Scientists for Peace against Nuclear Threat; Co-founder Int. Foundation for Survival and Devt of Humanity; del. to numerous scientific and peace confs; Chair. Soviet Nuclear Soc. 1989–; Co-Chair. Jr Achievement of Russia 1991–; Chair. Council, Int. Thermonuclear Experimental Reactor 1992–; mem. Presidential Council of Science and Tech. 1995–; Pres. Shelf-Developing Co. Rosshelf 1992–; mem. American Geophysical Soc. 1981; Foreign mem. Swedish Royal Acad. of Eng Sciences 1989; Dr hc (Notre Dame, Susquachana, Tufts, London); USSR State Prize 1977, Lenin Prize 1984, Hero of Socialist Labour 1985, Science for Peace Prize, Italy, Szillard Award, American Physical Soc.; Order of Lenin (three times). *Publications:* numerous, related both to science and the problems of prevention of nuclear war. *Leisure interests:* skiing, underwater swimming, windsurfing. *Address:* Kurchatov Institute, 123182 Moscow, pl. Academician Kurchatov, d. 1, Russia. *Telephone:* (495) 196-92-41. *E-mail:* presscentr@kiae.ru. *Website:* www.kiae.ru.

VELJANOSKI, Trajko; Macedonian lawyer and politician; *President, Sobranie (Assembly);* b. 2 Nov. 1962, Skopje; m.; two c.; ed Law Faculty, SS Cyril and Methodius Univ.; passed Bar examination 1988, est. ind. law office and worked as lawyer 1988–99; began political career by joining Internal Macedonian Revolutionary Organization—Democratic Party for Macedonian National Unity (VMRO-DPMNE) 1993, Head of Legal Affairs Cttee for several years, mem. Political System Cttee, also headed VMRO-DPMNE Forum on Legal and Political Affairs and Judicial System; elected Under-Sec., Ministry of Justice 1999, later Deputy Minister; fmr mem. Pres.'s Cttee of Appeals, Man. Bd Centre for European Integration, State Election Comm.; mem. Sobranie (Ass.) 2006–, Chair. Cttee on Election and Appointment Issues 2006–08, Pres. of Sobranie 2008–, Chair. Cttee on Constitutional Issues, Chair. Del. of Ass. to Inter-Parl. Union. *Address:* Office of the President of the Sobranie (Assembly), 1000 Skopje, 11 Oktomvri bb, Former Yugoslav Republic of Macedonia (office). *Telephone:* (2) 3113268 (office); (2) 3112255 (ext. 353) (office). *Fax:* (2) 3237947 (office). *E-mail:* pretsedatel@sobranie .mk (office). *Website:* www.sobranie.mk (office).

VELLA, George William, MD; Maltese physician and politician; *Minister of Foreign Affairs;* b. 24 April 1942, Zejtun; m. Miriam Grima; three c.; ed De La Salle Coll., Univ. of Malta; Medical Officer, Malta Drydocks 1966–73; Demonstrator in Physiology and Biochemistry, Univ. of Malta 1966–73; Aviation Medicine Consultant with Air Malta and Dept of Civil Aviation 1976–90; mem. House of Reps (Parl.) 1987–87, 1992–; Deputy Prime Minister and Minister for Foreign Affairs and Environment 1996–98, Minister of Foreign Affairs 2013–; mem. Partit Laburista. *Address:* Ministry of Foreign Affairs, Palazzo Parisio, Merchants Street, Valletta VLT 1171, Malta (office). *Telephone:* 21242191 (office). *Fax:* 21236604 (office). *E-mail:* info.mfa@gov.mt (office). *Website:* www.mfa.gov.mt (office).

VELTCHEV, Milen, MA, MBA; Bulgarian politician; *Vice-Chairman, National Movement for Stability and Progress (Natsionalno dvizhenie za stabilnost i vazhod);* b. 24 April 1966; ed Univ. of Nat. and World Economy, Sofia, Univ. of Rochester, Mass Inst. of Tech., USA; attaché, Ministry of Foreign Affairs, Bulgaria 1990–92; Assoc., Chemical Bank USA 1994, Merrill Lynch & Co., UK 1995–99, Vice-Pres. Emerging Markets 1999–2001; mem. Parl. 2001–; Minister of Finance 2001–05, Gov. for Bulgaria, World Bank, EBRD; currently Vice-Chair. Nat. Movt for Stability and Progress (Natsionalno dvizhenie za stabilnost i vazhod); fmr Chair. Monetary Council, Council for Internal Financial Control, Tax Policy Advisory Council; Euromoney Finance Minister of the Year 2002. *Address:* National Movement for Stability and Progress (Natsionalno dvizhenie za stabilnost i vazhod), 1000 Sofia, ul. Vrabcha 23, Bulgaria (office). *Telephone:* (2) 921-81-63 (office). *Fax:* (2) 921-81-65 (office). *E-mail:* ndsv@ndsv.bg (office). *Website:* www.ndsv.bg (office).

VELTMAN, Martinus J. G., PhD; Dutch physicist and academic; *John D. MacArthur Professor Emeritus of Physics, University of Michigan;* b. 1931; ed Univ. of Utrecht; Prof. of Physics, Univ. of Utrecht 1966–81, Univ. of Mich. 1981–, now Prof. Emer.; mem. Dutch Acad. of Sciences; High Energy and Particle Physics Prize, European Physical Soc. 1993, Nobel Prize for Physics (jtly) 1999. *Achievement:* one of the developers of gauge theories. *Publications include:* Facts and Mysteries in Particle Physics. *Address:* Physics Department, University of Michigan, 450 Church Street, Ann Arbor, MI 48109-1040, USA (office). *E-mail:* veltman@umich.edu. *Website:* www.lsa.umich.edu/physics/directory/ emeritus/ci.veltmanmartinus_ci.detail (office).

VELTRONI, Walter; Italian politician; b. 3 July 1955, Rome; m.; two c.; ed Film Inst., Rome; fmr journalist and TV Asst Dir; Sec. Rome Br. Fed. of Young Italian Communists 1975, also mem. Nat. Exec.; mem. Rome City Council 1976–81; Deputy in Nat. Ass. 1987–; mem. Nat. Secr. PCI–PDS 1988–1992; Founder mem. Democratici di Sinistra (PDS—Democratic Left) 1991, apptd to Political Co-ordination Bureau 1991, Political Sec. 1998; Ed. L'Unità daily newspaper 1992–96, now Dir; Deputy Prime Minister, Minister for Cultural Heritage, Performing Arts and Sport 1996–98; mem. European Parl. (Party of European Socialists Group) 1999–; Mayor of Rome 2001–08; Exec. Vice-Pres. Council of European Municipalities and Regions 2003–; Vice-Pres. Socialist Int. 1999–; Leader Partito Democratico (formed following the merger of the left wing Socialist Democrats and Margherita parties) 2007–09 (resgnd); Chevalier, Légion d'Honneur 2000. *Publications include:* several books including Il sogno spezzato (on Robert Kennedy), La sfida interrotta (on the ideas of Enrico Berlinguer), Forse Dio è malato (travel book on Africa) and Il disco del mondo – Vita breve di Luca Flores, musicista. *Address:* Partito Democratico, Piazza Sant'Anastasia 7, 00186 Rome, Italy (office); European Parliament, Bâtiment Altiero Spinelli 15G210, 60 rue Wiertz, 1047 Brussels, Belgium (office). *Telephone:* (6) 675471 (office). *Fax:* (6) 67547319 (office); (2) 284-93-45 (Belgium) (office). *E-mail:* wveltroni@europarl.eu .int (office); info@partitodemocratico.it (office). *Website:* www.partitodemocratico .it (office).

VENABLES, Terence Frederick (Terry); British professional football manager, fmr footballer and commentator; b. 6 Jan. 1943, Dagenham, London,

England; m. Yvette Venables; two d.; ed Dagenham High School; youth player, Chelsea 1958–60; sr player, Chelsea 1960–66 (Capt. 1962, 202 appearances, 26 goals, won Football League Cup 1964/65), England nat. team 1964, Tottenham Hotspur 1966–69 (115 appearances, 19 goals, won FA Cup 1967), Queens Park Rangers 1969–73 (179 appearances, 19 goals), Crystal Palace 1974–76 (14 appearances), St Patrick's Athletic 1976 (two appearances); Man. Crystal Palace 1976–80, Queens Park Rangers 1980–84, Barcelona 1984–87 (won La Liga 1985); Man. Tottenham Hotspur 1987–91 (won FA Cup 1991), Chief Exec. Tottenham Hotspur PLC 1991–93; Coach, England nat. team 1994–96, Asst Coach 2006–07; Dir of Football, Portsmouth FC 1996–98; Coach, Australian nat. team 1997–98; Head Coach, Crystal Palace 1998–99; Coach, Middlesbrough (jt role with Bryan Robson) 2000–01; Man. Leeds United 2002–03; football analyst, BBC mid-1980s–1994, ITV 1994–; only player to have represented England at all levels (schoolboy, youth, amateur, U-23 and for full int. team); co-devised board game, Terry Venables invites you to be. . . The Manager 1990; guided England Legends and Celebrities squad to victory in charity Soccer Aid programme 2006; Hon. Fellow, Univ. of Wolverhampton; Don Balón Award for Coach of the Year in La Liga 1985. *Recording:* recorded England Crazy single for World Cup together with band Rider (reached No. 46 in UK charts) 2002. *Television:* co-creator Hazell (ITV detective series). *Publications:* They Used to Play on Grass (co-author) 1973; co-authored (as P. B. Yuill) four novels with Gordon Williams: The Bornless Keeper 1974, Hazell Plays Solomon 1974, Hazell and the Three Card Trick 1975, Hazell and the Menacing Jester 1976; Terry Venables: The Autobiography (with N. Hanson) 1994, Venables' England – The Making of the Team 1996, The Best Game in the World 1997. *Address:* Terance Venables Holdings Ltd, Palladium House, 1–4 Argyll Street, London, W1F 7LD, England.

VENDLER, Helen Hennessy, AB, PhD; American academic and literary critic; *A. Kingsley Porter University Professor, Department of English, Harvard University;* b. (Helen Marie Hennessy), 30 April 1933, Boston, Mass; d. of George Hennessy and Helen Conway; m. Zeno Vendler (deceased); one s.; ed Emmanuel Coll. and Harvard Univ.; Instructor, Cornell Univ. 1960–63; Lecturer, Swarthmore Coll., Pa and Haverford Coll., Pa 1963–64; Asst Prof., Smith Coll. Northampton, Mass 1964–66; Assoc. Prof., Boston Univ. 1966–68, Prof. 1968–85; Visiting Prof., Harvard Univ. 1981–85, Kenan Prof. 1985–, Assoc. Acad. Dean 1987–92, A. Kingsley Porter Univ. Prof. 1990–; Sr Fellow, Harvard Soc. of Fellows 1981–92; poetry critic, New Yorker 1978–90; mem. Educ. Advisory Bd, Guggenheim Foundation, Pulitzer Prize Bd 1990–99; Fulbright Lecturer, Univ. of Bordeaux 1968–69; Overseas Fellow, Churchill Coll. Cambridge 1980; Parnell Fellow, Magdalene Coll., Cambridge 1986, Hon. Fellow 1996–; mem. American Acad. of Arts and Sciences, Norwegian Acad., American Philosophical Soc., American Acad. of Arts and Letters (Bd mem. 2006–09); 24 hon. degrees; Fulbright Fellow 1954, A.A.U.W. Fellow 1959, Lowell Prize 1969, Explicator Prize 1969, Guggenheim Fellow 1971–72, American Council of Learned Socs Fellow 1971–72, Nat. Inst. of Arts and Letters Award 1975, Nat. Book Critics Award 1980, Nat. Endowment for the Humanities (NEH) Fellow 1980, 1985, 1994, 2006, Wilson Fellow 1994, Newton Arvin Award, Jefferson Medal, Jefferson Lecturer, NEH, A.W. Mellon Lecturer in Fine Arts, Nat. Gallery of Art 2007, Siemens Fellow 2009. *Publications include:* Yeats's Vision and the Later Plays 1963, On Extended Wings: Wallace Stevens' Longer Poems 1969, The Poetry of George Herbert 1975, Part of Nature, Part of Us 1980, The Odes of John Keats 1983, Wallace Stevens: Words Chosen Out of Desire 1985, Harvard Book of Contemporary American Poetry 1985, The Music of What Happens 1988, The Given and the Made 1995, The Breaking of Style 1995, Soul Says 1995, Poems, Poets, Poetry 1996, The Art of Shakespeare's Sonnets 1997, Seamus Heaney 1998, Coming of Age as a Poet: Milton, Keats, Eliot, Plath 2003, Poets Thinking: Pope, Whitman, Dickinson, Yeats 2005, Invisible Listeners: Lyric Intimacy in Herbert, Whitman, and Ashbery 2005, Our Secret Discipline 2007, Dickinson, Selected Poems with Commentaries 2010. *Leisure interests:* travel, music, grandchildren. *Address:* Harvard University, Department of English, Barker Center 205, 12 Quincey Street, Cambridge, MA 02138 (office); 54 Trowbridge Street, Apt B, Cambridge, MA 02138, USA. *Telephone:* (617) 496-6028 (office). *Fax:* (617) 496-8737 (office). *E-mail:* vendler@fas .harvard.edu (office). *Website:* www.fas.harvard.edu/~english (office).

VENEMAN, Ann Margaret, MA, JD; American lawyer, government official and international organization official; b. 29 June 1949, Modesto, Calif.; d. of John Veneman (fmr US Under-Sec. of Health, Educ. and Welfare and mem. Calif. State Ass.); ed Univ. of California, Davis, Univ. of California, Berkeley and Hastings Coll. of Law; staff attorney, Gen. Counsel's Office, Bay Area Rapid Transit Dist, Oakland, Calif. 1976–78; Deputy Public Defender, Modesto 1978–80; Assoc., later Pnr, Damrell, Damrell & Nelson (law firm), Modesto 1980; Assoc. Admin., Foreign Agric. Service, US Dept of Agric. 1986–89, Deputy Under-Sec. of Agric. for Int. Affairs and Commodity Programs 1989–91, Deputy Sec. of Dept 1991–93, with Patton, Boggs & Blow (law firm), Washington, DC 1993–95; Sec., Calif. Dept of Food and Agric. 1995–99; Partner, Nossaman, Guthner, Knox & Elliott (law firm) 1999–2001; US Sec. of Agric. 2001–05 (resgnd); Exec. Dir UNICEF 2005–10; currently Co-Chair. Nutrition and Physical Activity Initiative, Bipartisan Policy Center; mem. Bd of Dirs Alexion; fmr mem. Bd of Dirs Calgene (first co. to market genetically engineered food); mem. Council on Foreign Relations, Trilateral Comm.; Hon. mem. US Afghan Women's Council, US State Dept 2004, Modesto Rotary Club 2008; Dr hc (California Polytechnic State Univ., San Luis Obispo) 2001, (Lincoln Univ. of Mo.) 2003, (Delaware State Univ.) 2004, (Middlebury Coll.) 2006; Outstanding Woman in Int. Trade Award 2001, Outstanding Alumna of the Year Award, Univ. of California, Davis 2001, Food Research and Action Center Award 2001, Nat. 4-H Alumni Recognition Award 2002, Dutch American Heritage Award 2002, Statesman of the Year Award, Jr Statesman Foundation 2002, Alumnus of the Year Award, Goldman School of Public Policy 2003, American PVO Partners Award for Service to People in Need 2004, Richard E. Lyng Award for Public Service 2005, Sesame Workshop's Leadership Award for Children 2006, ranked by Forbes magazine amongst 100 Most Powerful Women (46th) 2009. *Address:* Bipartisan Policy Center 1225 Eye Street, NW, Suite 1000, Washington, DC 20005, USA (office). *Website:* bipartisanpolicy.org/projects/nutrition-and -physical-activity-initiative (office).

VENESS, Sir David, CBE, MA, LLM; British police officer and fmr UN official; m.; three c.; ed Raynes Park Co. Grammar School, London, Trinity Coll. Cambridge, Royal Coll. of Defence Studies; joined London Metropolitan Police

Cadet Corps 1964, Metropolitan Police 1966; apptd Officer, Criminal Investigation Dept (CID) 1969, served as detective in N, E and Cen. London, various specialist depts in Scotland Yard; served as Detective Chief Superintendent in Fraud Squad (5O6) and Crime Operations Group (5O15); trained as hostage negotiator 1979, mem. negotiating team, London Iranian Embassy siege 1980; led negotiations at Libyan Peoples Bureau incident 1984; Instructor, then Dir Scotland Yard Negotiators Course 1980–87; apptd Commdr 1987; served with Royalty and Diplomatic Protection 1987–90; Commdr Public Order, Territorial Security and Operational Support 1990–91; Deputy Asst Commr, Specialist Operations, Crime 1991–94, Asst Commr 1994–2005; Under-Sec.-Gen. for Safety and Security, UN 2005–08 (resgnd); fmr mem. Service Authorities, Nat. Criminal Intelligence Service, Nat. Crime Squad; HM Queen's Police Medal 2000. *Leisure interests:* rugby, reading. *Address:* c/o Office of the Under-Secretary-General for Safety and Security, United Nations, New York, NY 10017, USA.

VENETIAAN, Runaldo Ronald; Suriname mathematician and fmr head of state; b. 1936, Paramaribo; ed Leiden Univ.; moved to Netherlands to further educ.; early career as math. lecturer; fmr Minister of Educ.; fmr mem. Exec. Bd UNESCO; Leader Suriname Nat. Party; Pres. of Suriname 1991–96, 2000–10. *Address:* c/o Office of the President, Kleine Combéweg 2–4, Centrum, Paramaribo, Suriname.

VENGEROV, Maxim; Israeli (b. Russian) violinist and conductor; *Menuhin Professor, Royal Academy of Music;* b. 1974, Novosibirsk, Western Siberia, USSR; s. of Alexander Vengerov and Larissa Vengerov; m. Olga Gringolts 2011; two d.; has performed with the world's leading orchestras and conductors and has given solo recitals in every major city; began career as a solo violinist aged five; won the Wieniawski and Carl Flesch int. competitions aged ten 10 and 15, respectively; made first recording aged ten; also inspired by many different styles of music, including Baroque, jazz and rock; turned his attention to conducting 2007, studying with Vag Papian in St Petersburg and with Yuri Simonov, an exponent of the Russian-German conducting school; Carnegie Hall conducting debut during the Verbier Festival Orchestra's tour 2007; has since conducted major orchestras, including the Toronto and Montreal Symphony orchestras, Enescu, Israel, London and Russian Nat. Philharmonic orchestras, as well as the English and Paris Chamber orchestras; first Chief Conductor Gstaad Festival Orchestra 2010; returned to the violin in 2011, now divides his time equally between violin performance, conducting and teaching; annual Vengerov Festival in Tokyo launched 2013; season 2013–14 highlights include Barbican residency, tour in China with Long Yu and numerous recitals world-wide devoted to the Romantic virtuoso repertoire; Prof. of Violin, RAM, London 2005–; Menuhin Prof. 2012–; Amb. and Visiting Prof. of the Menuhin Acad. in Switzerland; Artist- in-Residence, Oxford Philomusica 2013–; regularly serves on competition juries, including the Yehudi Menuhin Int. Violin Competition, Donatella Flick Conducting Competition, appeared at Montreal Int. Violin Competition as conductor of the competition finals 2013; Chair. Wieniawski Violin Competition 2011, auditioned live more than 200 musicians in nine world capitals to select the finalists, re-elected to return as Chair. in 2016; UNICEF Goodwill Amb. (first classical musician) 1997–; future plans include the launch of his own recording label VMV (Vengerov Music Vision); plays the ex-Kreutzer Stradivari (1727); fellowships and honours from several insts, including RAM; First Prize, Jr Wieniawski Competition, Poland 1984, Winner Carl Flesch Int. Violin Competition 1990, Gramophone Young Artist of the Year 1994, Ritmo Artist of the Year 1994, Gramophone Record of the Year 1996, Edison Award 1997, Gramophone Artist of the Year 2002. *Recordings include:* Sonatas by Beethoven and Brahms and Paganini 1st Concerto 1992, Sonatas by Mozart, Beethoven and Mendelssohn 1992, Virtuoso Violin Pieces, Bruch and Mendelssohn Violin Concertos, Britten Violin Concerto and Walton Viola Concerto with Mstislav Rostropovich and London Symphony Orchestra (Grammy Award 2004, Classical BRIT Critics' Award 2004) 2002, Best of Maxim Vengerov 2006, Phenomenal Vengerov 2011. *Address:* c/o Nicola-Fee Bahl, NFBM Ltd, 3rd Floor Offices, 24 Endell Street, London, WC2H 9HQ, England (office). *Telephone:* (20) 7359-4771 (office). *Fax:* (20) 3292-1913 (office). *E-mail:* nicola-fee@nfbm.com (office). *Website:* www.nfbm.com (office).

VENIAMIN, Christodoulos; Cypriot government official; b. Sept. 1922; ed in Nicosia and Middle Temple, London; jr officer in govt service 1942, admin. officer 1949; served as Asst Sec. in Depts of Local Govt and Admin, Personnel, Finance, Commerce and Industry, Social Services, Communications and Works, Agric. and Natural Resources; Asst Dist Commr, Larnaca; Asst Sec. Ministry of Interior during transitional period; Dist Officer, Limassol Dist 1960–68; Dir-Gen. Ministry of Foreign Affairs 1968; Minister of Interior and Defence 1975–84, of Interior 1988–93; mem. House of Reps 1997–2001; Grosse Verdienstkreuz mit Stern und Schulterband (Germany), Onorifiecenza di Grande Ufficiale (Italy), Order of the Cedar (Lebanon). *Publications:* Ta dyskola chronia: hoi anamnēseis mias zōēs. *Leisure interests:* reading and walking. *Address:* Kleanthi Ierodiaconou No. 5, 2411 Engomi, Nicosia, Cyprus. *Telephone:* (22) 680339 (office); (22) 352400 (home). *Fax:* (22) 671821.

VENIZELOS, Evangelos, PhD; Greek lawyer and politician; *Deputy Prime Minister and Minister of Foreign Affairs;* b. 1 Jan. 1957, Thessaloníki; m. Lila A. Bakatselou; one d.; ed Aristotle Univ. of Thessaloníki, Univ. of Paris II; Asst Prof., then Prof. of Constitutional Law, Aristotle Univ. of Thessaloniki 1984–87; Attorney at Law for Council of State and Supreme Court 1984–87; apptd mem. Bd Nat. Centre of Public Admin 1987; apptd mem. Bd Nat. Bank of Greece 1988; mem. Local Radio Cttee; elected to Cen. Cttee of the Panhellenic Socialist Movt (PASOK) 1990, unsuccessful cand. for leadership of the party 2007, Chair. PASOK 2012–; mem. Vouli (Parl.) for Thessaloníki A 1993–; Deputy Minister to the Prime Minister's Office, responsible for Press Affairs 1993–94; Minister for Press and Media Affairs 1994–95, of Transportation and Communications 1995–96, of Justice Jan.–Aug. 1996, of Culture and Sport 1996–99, 2000–04, of Devt 1999–2000, of Nat. Defence 2009–11, Deputy Chair. of the Govt and Minister of Finance 2011–12; Deputy Prime Minister and Minister of Foreign Affairs 2013–. *Address:* Ministry of Foreign Affairs, Odos Sofias 1, 106 71, Athens (office); Panhellenic Socialist Movement (PASOK), Odos Hippocrates 22, 106 80 Athens (office); Odos Danaidon 4, 546 26 Thessaloníki, Greece (home). *Telephone:* (210) 3681000 (Ministry) (office); (210) 3665000 (PASOK) (office); (2310) 548600 (home). *Fax:* (210) 3681717 (Ministry) (office); (210) 3665209 (PASOK) (office). *E-mail:*

mfa@mfa.gr (office); pasok@pasok.gr (office). *Website:* www.mfa.gr (office); www .pasok.gr (office); www.evenizelos.gr.

VENNER, Sir K. Dwight, Kt, CBE, BSc, MSc; economist and central banker; *Governor and Chairman, East Caribbean Central Bank;* m. Lynda Arnolde Winville Venner (née St Rose); seven c.; ed Univ. of the West Indies, Mona; fmr Research Asst, Univ. of the W Indies, Jr Research Fellow, Inst. of Social and Econ. Reseach, Lecturer, Dept of Econs; Dir Finance and Planning, Govt of St Lucia 1981–89;; Chair. Air and Seaports Authority, St Lucia 1981–89, Nat. Insurance Investment Cttee 1981–89, Caricom Cen. Bank Govs, Eastern Caribbean Home Mortgage Bank; Gov. and Chair. Eastern Caribbean Cen. Bank 1989–; Chair. Tech. Restructuring Cttee, Org. of Eastern Caribbean States; Dir St Lucia Devt Bank, Nat. Commercial Bank, St Lucia; mem. Chancellor's Governance Cttee, Univ. of the W Indies; mem. Univ. Strategy Cttee; Dr hc (Univ. of the W Indies) 2003. *Address:* East Caribbean Central Bank, Headquarters Bldg, Bird Rock, PO Box 89, Basseterre, St Kitts (office). *Telephone:* 465-2537 (office). *Fax:* 465-9562 (office). *E-mail:* info@eccb-centralbank.org (office). *Website:* www.eccb-centralbank .org (office).

VENTER, J(ohn) Craig, PhD; American scientist; *President, J. Craig Venter Institute;* b. 14 Oct. 1946, Salt Lake City, UT; m. Claire Fraser; ed Univ. of California, San Diego; served in USN, served in Viet Nam 1967; Prof., State Univ. of NY, Buffalo –1984; Section and Lab. Chief, NIH, Bethesda, Md 1984–92; Founder, Chair. and Chief Scientist, The Inst. for Genomic Research 1992–; Founder, Pres. and Chief Scientific Officer, Celera Genomics Corpn, Rockville, Md 1998–2002, Chair. Scientific Advisory Bd 2002–; Pres. J. Craig Venter Inst. 2004–; Founder, Chair., CEO and Co-Chief Scientific Officer, Synthetic Genomics, Inc. 2005–; mem. NAS, American Acad. of Arts and Sciences, American Soc. for Microbiology; numerous hon. degrees; Beckman Award 1999, Chiron Corpn Biotechnology Research Award 1999, King Faisal Int. Prize for Science 2000, Taylor Prize 2001, Paul Ehrlich and Ludwig Darmstaedter Prize 2001, Gairdner Foundation Int. Award 2002, listed on TIME 100 list of the most influential people in the world 2007, 2008. *Achievements include:* one of the first scientists to sequence the human genome; led team of scientists who were first to successfully create a cell with a synthetic genome May 2010. *Publications:* A Life Decoded (autobiog.) 2007; more than 200 articles in scientific journals. *Leisure interest:* sailing. *Address:* J. Craig Venter Institute, 9704 Medical Center Drive, Rockville, MD 20850 (office); Synthetic Genomics, Inc., 11149 North Torrey Pines Road, La Jolla, CA 92037, USA (office). *Telephone:* (301) 795-7000 (Venter Inst.) (office); (858) 754-2900 (Synthetic Genomics) (office). *Fax:* (858) 754-2988 (office). *E-mail:* info@jcvi.org (office); info@syntheticgenomics.com (office). *Website:* www.jcvi.org (office); www.syntheticgenomics.com (office).

VENTURA, Jesse; American radio presenter, actor, fmr professional wrestler and fmr politician; b. (James George Janos), 15 July 1951, Minneapolis, Minn.; s. of George Janos and Bernice Janos; m. Terry Ventura; two c.; ed North Hennepin Community Coll.; served in USN 1969–73, USNR 1973–75; fmr bodyguard for The Rolling Stones; professional wrestler 1973–84; TV commentator, actor 1984–97; Mayor of Brooklyn Park, Minn. 1991–95; radio talk show host 1995–98; Gov. of Minn. 1998–2002; fmr mem. Reform Party; host, Jesse Ventura's America (TV program) 2003, Conspiracy Theory with Jesse Ventura 2009–13, Off the Grid 2014–; mem. Advisory Bd Operation Truth (addresses issues of US Nat. Guard in Iraq) 2004; Spokesman for BetUS.com 2005. *Films include:* Predator 1987, Running Man 1987, Abraxas, Guardian of the Universe 1991, Demolition Man 1993, Batman & Robin 1997. *Publication:* I Ain't Got Time to Bleed 2000, Don't Start the Revolution Without Me 2008, American Conspiracies (co-author) 2010. *Website:* www.ora.tv/offthegrid.

VENTURI, Robert, AB, MFA, FAIA, Int. FRIBA; American architect; b. 25 June 1925, Philadelphia, Pa; s. of Robert C. Venturi and Vanna Lanzetta; m. Denise Scott Brown (née Lakofski) 1967; one s.; ed Princeton Univ.; Designer, Oskar Stonorov 1950, Eero Saarinen & Assoc. 1950–53; Rome Prize Fellow, American Acad. in Rome 1954–56; Designer, Louis I. Kahn 1957; Assoc. Prof., School of Fine Arts, Univ. of Pennsylvania 1957–65; Charlotte Shepherd Davenport Prof., Yale Univ. 1966–70; Prin., Venturi, Cope & Lippincott 1958–61, Venturi and Short 1961–64, Venturi and Rauch 1964–80, Venturi, Rauch and Scott Brown (architects and planners) 1980–89; Venturi, Scott Brown and Assocs June 1989–; Fellow, Accademia Nazionale di San Luca, American Acad. of Arts and Sciences; mem. Advisory Bd of Dirs Sir John Soane's Museum Foundation; mem. American Philosophical Soc. of Philadelphia, European Acad. of Sciences and Arts, Pennsylvania Soc. of Architects, American Acad. of Arts and Letters, Royal Soc. for the Encouragement of Arts, Manufacture & Commerce; mem. Bd of Overseers, School of Fine Arts, Univ. of Pennsylvania, 1985–2002; Hon. Fellow, Royal Incorporation of Architects in Scotland, American Acad. and Inst. of Arts and Letters; Hon. Prof., Xi'an Acad. of Fine Arts; Hon. mem. Bund Deutscher Architekten; Commandeur, Ordre des Arts et Lettres 2000; Hon. DFA (Oberlin, Yale, Penn., Princeton, Phila Coll of Art); Hon. LHD (NJ Inst. of Tech.); Laurea hc (Univ. of Rome La Sapienza) 1994; Dr hc (Zhejiang Univ., Hangzhou, China) 2005; Wyck-Strickland Award, 1989, Pritzker Prize 1991, Nat. Medal of Arts 1992, Centennial Medal of American Acad. in Rome 1998, Vincent J. Scully Prize (jtly) 2002, Nat. Design Mind Award, Cooper-Hewitt, Nat. Design Museum (jtly),2007, The International Award, Soc. of American Registered Architects 2010, Anne d'Harnoncourt Award for Artistic Excellence, Arts and Business Council of Greater Philadelphia (jtly) 2010, and numerous other awards. *Works include:* Vanna Venturi House, Phila, Pa 1961, Guild House, Phila 1961, Franklin Court, Phila 1972, Allen Memorial Art Museum Addition, Oberlin, Ohio 1973, Inst. for Scientific Information Corpn HQ, Phila 1978, Gordon Wu Hall, Princeton Univ., NJ 1980, Seattle Art Museum, Seattle, Wash. 1984, Clinical Research Bldg, Univ. of Pa 1985 (with Payette Assocs.), Nat. Gallery, Sainsbury Wing, London, UK 1986, Fisher-Bendheim Hall, Princeton Univ. 1986, Charles P. Stevenson Library, Bard Coll. 1989, Regional Govt Bldg, Toulouse, France 1992, Kirifuri Resort facilities, Nikko, Japan 1992, Univ. of Del. Student Center, Newark, Del. 1992, Memorial Hall Restoration and Addition, Harvard Univ. 1992, The Barnes Foundation Restoration and Renovation, Merion, Pa 1993, Disney Celebration Bank, Celebration, Fla 1993, Irvine Auditorium, Perelman Quadrangle, Univ. of Pa 1995, Princeton Campus Center, Princeton Univ. 1996, Congress Avenue Building, Yale Univ. School of Medicine 1998, Master Plan and Bldgs for Univ. of

Michigan 1997–. *Publications:* Complexity and Contradiction in Architecture 1966, Learning from Las Vegas (with Denise Scott Brown and Steven Izenour) 1972, A View from the Campidoglio: Selected Essays, 1953–1984 (with Denise Scott Brown) 1984, Iconography and Electronics upon a Generic Architecture 1996, Architecture as Signs and Systems: for a Mannerist Time 2004; numerous articles in professional journals. *Leisure interest:* travel. *Address:* Venturi, Scott Brown and Associates, 4236 Main Street, Philadelphia, PA 19127-1696, USA (office). *Telephone:* (215) 487-0400 (office). *Fax:* (215) 487-2520 (office). *E-mail:* info@vsba.com (office). *Website:* www.vsba.com (office).

VENTURONI, Adm. Guido; Italian naval officer and international organization official; *President, Marconi Selenia Communications SpA;* b. 10 April 1934, Teramo; m. Giuliana Marinozzi; two s. one d.; ed Naval Acad. 1952–56; Navigator, Communications Officer, maritime patrol pilot and tactical instructor; Head of Naval Helicopter Studies and Projects Office; Exec. Asst to Chief of Navy Staff, to Chief of Defence at Naval Personnel Directorate; Head of Plans and Operation Dept at Navy Gen. Staff, at Defence Gen. Staff 1982–86; Commdr, First Naval Div. 1986–87; Head Financial Planning Bureau, Naval Gen. Staff 1987–89; Deputy Chief of Staff of Navy 1989–90; Vice-Adm. 1990–91; C-in-C of Fleet and NATO Commdr of Cen. Mediterranean 1991–92; Chief of Staff of Navy 1992–93, Chief of Defence Gen. Staff 1994–99; Over Commdr, Int. Security Mission to Albania 1997; Chair. Mil. Cttee, NATO 1999–2002; Pres. Marconi Selenia Communications SpA 2002–; Kt of Grand Cross of Order of Merit, Silver Medal for sea-duty service, Gold Medal for air service; Medal for Merit (Mauritius); Officer Légion d'honneur; Grand Cross of Orden de Mayo al Mérito Naval (Argentina); First Class Cross of Order of Mérito Naval (Spain); Second Class Decoration of Order of Mérito Naval (Venezuela). *Address:* Marconi Selenia Communications, Pomezia, Via dell'Industria 4, 00040 Pomezia RM, Italy (office). *Telephone:* (06) 910911 (office). *Fax:* (06) 91091339 (office). *Website:* www.seleniacomms.com (office).

VERA BEJARANO, Candido, Lic.; Paraguayan politician; b. 16 July 1957, San Pedro de Yeuamandyzú; s. of Candido Vera and Florencia Bezarano; m.; two s. two d.; ed Escuela Agricola Carlos Pfannl, Universidad del Norte, Asunción, Degree in Farm Man.; elected mem. Nat. Congress (Liberal Party) 1993, re-elected 1998; Pres. Nat. Congress 2000–; Senator 2003–08; Minister of Agric. and Livestock 2008–11. *Publications include:* Proyecto de Modificacion del Estatuto Agraiio 2002, Proyecto de ley que creo el Instituto de Desarollo Rural y de la Tierra 2003. *Address:* c/o Ministry of Agriculture and Livestock, Presidente Franco 472, Asunción (office); Pedro Ciancio 1075, Concordia, Asunción, Paraguay (home). *Telephone:* (21) 21-4612 (home). *Fax:* (21) 21-4612 (home).

VERA CRUZ, Tomé; São Tomé and Príncipe politician; ed in Romania; fmr Head, Water and Electricity Co.; Minister of Natural Resources 2003–04; Prime Minister and Minister of Information and Regional Integration 2006–08 (resgnd); fmr Sec. Gen. Movimento Democrático Força da Mudança (MDFM) 2001–. *Address:* Movimento Democrático Força da Mudança (MDFM), São Tomé, São Tomé and Príncipe (office).

VERANNEMAN DE WATERVLIET, Jonkheer Jean-Michel, Licencié ULB, Licentiaat VUB; Belgian diplomatist; *Ambassador to Portugal;* b. 11 July 1947, Bruges; s. of Jonkheer Raymond Veranneman de Watervliet and Baroness Manuela van Bogaerde de Terbrugge; m. Maria do Carmo Neves da Silveira; three s.; ed Institut d'Etudes Politiques, Paris, Université Libre de Bruxelles, Vrije Universiteit Brussel; six months as trainee European Comm., Brussels; mil. service with Chasseurs Ardennais Regt (Reserve Officer); joined Diplomatic Corps 1976, postings include Bonn, Brasilia, La Paz, UN, New York, EU, Brussels, Amb. to Mozambique 1983–86, Consul Gen., São Paulo 1991–94, Minister Plenipotentiary, London 1994–97, Amb. to Brazil 2000–03, to Israel 2004–06, to UK 2006–10, to Portugal 2010–; Grand Officier, Ordre de Léopold II; Commdr, Ordre de Léopold, Ordre de la Couronne; Médaille Civique de Ière Classe (Belgium); Grand Cross, Order of the Southern Cross (Brazil). *Publications:* The Portuguese Immigrant Workers, History of Africa, Is the Sovereign Nation State Obsolete?. *Leisure interests:* model ships, archery, hiking, boating, reading history books. *Address:* Belgian Embassy, Praça Marquês de Pombal, n° 14 - 6°, 1269-024 Lisbon, Portugal (office). *Telephone:* (21) 3170517 (office). *Fax:* (231) 561556 (office). *E-mail:* lisbon@diplobel.fed.be (office). *Website:* www.diplomatie.be/lisbon (office).

VERBA, Sidney, PhD; American academic; b. 26 May 1932, Brooklyn, New York; s. of Morris Verba and Recci Salman; m. E. Cynthia Winston 1955; three d.; ed Harvard and Princeton Univs; Asst, then Assoc. Prof. of Politics Princeton Univ. 1960–64; Prof. of Political Science, Stanford Univ. 1964–68; Sr Study Dir Nat. Opinion Research Center 1968–72; Prof. of Political Science, Univ. of Chicago 1968–72; Prof. of Govt, Harvard Univ. 1972–2006, Clarence Dillon Prof. of Int. Affairs 1983–84, Carl H. Pforzheimer Prof. 1984–2006, Assoc. Dean for Undergraduate Educ., Faculty of Arts and Sciences 1981–84, Dir Harvard Univ. Library 1984–2006; Chair. Bd of Dirs Harvard Univ. Press 1991–2006; Pres. American Political Science Asscn 1994–95; mem. NAS, American Acad. of Arts and Sciences; Guggenheim Fellow; Woodrow Wilson and Kammerer Book Awards, James Madison Award (American Political Science Asscn). *Publications:* Small Groups and Political Behavior 1961, The Civic Culture 1963, Participation in America 1972, Participation and Political Equality 1978, The Changing American Voter 1979, Injury to Insult 1979, Equality in America 1985, Elites and the Idea of Equality 1987, Designing Social Inquiry 1994, Voice and Equality 1995. *Address:* Harvard University, Department of Government, Littauer Center (North Yard), Room M–18, 1875 Cambridge Street, Cambridge, MA 02138 (office); 142 Summit Avenue, Brookline, MA 02138, USA (home). *Telephone:* (617) 495-4421 (office); (617) 232-4987 (home). *Fax:* (617) 495-0438 (office). *E-mail:* sverba@harvard.edu (office). *Website:* www.gov.harvard.edu (office).

VERBERG, George H. B., PhD; Dutch business executive; *Chairman of the Supervisory Board, Berenschot Groep B.V.;* b. 2 Sept. 1942, Batavia, Dutch E Indies; ed Netherlands School of Econs, Erasmus Univ., Rotterdam, MIT and Univ. of Calif. at Berkeley; joined Ministry of Educ. and Science 1971, Ministry of Econ. Affairs 1974, positions include Gen. Econ. Policy Dir, Dir-Gen. for Trade, Industry and Services, Dir-Gen. for Energy –1988; joined NV Nederlandse Gasunie 1988, Commercial Man.-Dir 1989–92, CEO 1992–2004; currently Chair. Supervisory Bd Berenschot Groep B.V., UCN NV; fmr Vice-Pres. Int. Gas Union; fmr Vice-Chair. Eurogas Asscn; Vice-Chair. Supervisory Bd Univ. of Groningen;

mem. Bd Advisory Council ING-Group; mem. Supervisory Bd IKN (Integrated Cancer Centre for N Netherlands); Chair. Advisory Bd Sogeo Co.; fmr Chair. Advisory Bd UN-Gas Centre. *Address:* Berenschot Groep B.V., Europalaan 40, 3526 KS Utrecht, Netherlands (office). *Telephone:* (30) 2916916 (office). *Fax:* (30) 2947090 (office). *Website:* www.berenschot.com (office).

VERBITSKAYA, Ludmila Alekseyevna, PhD; Russian philologist and university administrator; *President, St Petersburg State University;* b. 17 June 1936, Leningrad (now St Petersburg); m. (deceased); two d.; ed Leningrad State Univ.; lab. asst, then jr researcher, Docent, Chair. of Philology, Leningrad (now St Petersburg) State Univ. –1979, Prof. Chair. of Phonetics 1979–85, Head Chair. of Gen. Linguistics 1985–, Pro-Rector on scientific work, First Pro-Rector 1989, Acting Rector 1993–94, Rector 1994–2008, Pres. 2008–; Vice-Pres. UNESCO Comm. on Problems of Women's Educ.; Rep. to Exec. Council of Int. Asscn of Univs; mem. Russian Acad. of Humanitarian Sciences, Acad. of Sciences of Higher School, Presidium Int. Asscn of Russian Language and Literature Teachers, Presidium Conf. of Rectors of European Univs; mem. of Council Our Home Russia Movt 1996–99; Verbitskaya planet named after her 2000; Hon. Employee of Higher Educ. in Russia, Hon. Citizen of St Petersburg 2006; Order of Friendship, Order for Nat. Service Third Degree and Fourth Degree, Commdr Academic Palm (France), Knight's Cross for Service (Poland), Chevalier, Légion d'Honneur 2005; Dr hc (Bologna Univ., New York Univ., St Petersburg State Tech. Univ., St Petersburg State Medical Univ., Novgorod State Univ. Yaroslav Mudry); Medal of Honour of Saint Grand Duchess Olga III of the Russian Orthodox Church, Medal of Honour of Grand Duchess Olga III (Ukraine), Medal of Merit in Nat. Healthcare, Queen's Anniversary Prize for Higher and Further Educ. (UK) 1997, Woodrow Wilson Award for Public Service 2008. *Publications:* over 300 publs. *Address:* St Petersburg State University, Universitetskaya nab. 7/9, 199034 St Petersburg, Russia (office). *Telephone:* (812) 3200717 (office). *Fax:* (812) 3241250 (office). *E-mail:* president@pu.ru (office). *Website:* www.spbu.ru (office).

VERDONCK, Ferdinand, BEcons, MA, LLD; Belgian business executive; *Chairman of the Supervisory Board, Amsterdam Molecular Therapeutics BV;* b. 1942; ed Catholic Univ. of Leuven, Univ. of Chicago; began financial services career at Continental Ill. Bank of Chicago; with Lazard Frères and Co., New York –1984; Head of Operational and Admin Affairs, Bekaert 1984–92; Man.-Dir and mem. Exec. Cttee Almanij NV 1992–2003 (retd; fmr Chair. Banco Urquijo; Chair. Supervisory Bd Amsterdam Molecular Therapeutics BV 2007–; mem. Bd of Dirs Galapagos NV 2005–, Movetis NV 2008–, JP Morgan European Investment Trust, Phoenix Funds, Groupe SNEF, Laco Information Services. *Address:* Amsterdam Molecular Therapeutics BV, Meibergdreef 61, 1105 BA Amsterdam Zuidoost, Netherlands (office). *Telephone:* (20) 5667394 (office).

VERE-JONES, David, MSc, DPhil, FRSNZ; British mathematician, academic and statistical seismologist; *Professor Emeritus, Victoria University of Wellington;* b. 17 April 1936, London; s. of Noel W. Vere-Jones and Isabel M. I. Wyllie; m. Mary To Kei Chung 1965 (died 2000); two s. one d.; ed Cheadle Hulme School, Cheshire, Hutt Valley High School, New Zealand, Victoria Univ. of Wellington and Univ. of Oxford; emigrated to New Zealand 1949; Rhodes Scholar 1958–61; Scientific Officer, Applied Math. Div. Dept of Scientific and Industrial Research, New Zealand 1962–63, Sr Scientific Officer 1963–64; Fellow, Dept of Statistics, ANU 1965–67, Sr Fellow 1967–69; Prof. of Math. with special responsibility for statistics, Victoria Univ. of Wellington 1970–2000, Prof. Emer. 2000–; Dir Statistical Research Asscn (New Zealand) Ltd 1999–2009, Assoc. 2009–; Distinguished Assoc. Statistics Research Associates Ltd 2009–; Founding Pres. New Zealand Math Soc. 1975; Pres. New Zealand Statistical Asscn 1981–83; Chair. International Statistical Inst. (ISI) Educ. Comm. 1987–91; Pres. of Interim Exec., International Asscn for Statistical Educ. 1991–92; Sr Researcher and Bd mem. New Zealand Inst. of Math. and its Applications 2002; Visiting Prof., Inst. Statistical Mathematics, Tokyo 1976, Imperial Coll., London, Univ. of Oxford 1986, Tokyo Inst. of Tech. 1995; Hon. mem. ISI, New Zealand Math. Soc. 2000, Life mem. New Zealand Statistical Asscn; Henri Willem Methorst Medal 1995, Royal Soc. of New Zealand Rutherford Medal 1999, New Zealand Science and Tech. Medal 2000, NZSA Campbell Award 2009. *Publications include:* An Introduction to the Theory of Point Processes (with D. J. Daley) 1988; about 150 papers on probability theory, seismology, mathematical educ. *Leisure interests:* table tennis, walking, languages. *Address:* Statistics Research Associates Ltd, PO Box 12-649, Thorndon, Wellington (office); 4 Forest Walk, Waikanae, New Zealand (home). *Telephone:* (4) 293-3342 (office). *E-mail:* dvj@statsresearch.co.nz (office); dvj@paradise.com.nz (office). *Website:* www.statsresearch.co.nz (office).

VEREKER, Sir John (Michael Medlicott), KCB, KStJ, BA, CIMgt, FRSA; British business executive and fmr public servant; b. 9 Aug. 1944; s. of the late Charles W. M. Vereker and Marjorie Vereker (née Whatley); m. Judith Diane Rowen 1971; one s. one d.; ed Marlborough Coll., Keele Univ.; Asst Prin., Overseas Devt Ministry 1967–69, Adviser, World Bank, Washington, DC 1970–72, Prin., Overseas Devt Ministry 1972, Pvt. Sec. to Minister of Overseas Devt 1977–78, Asst Sec. 1978; Asst Sec., Prime Minister's Office 1980–83, Under-Sec. 1983–88; Prin. Finance Officer Overseas Devt Admin., FCO 1986–88; Deputy Sec. Dept of Educ. and Science, then Dept for Educ. 1988–93; Perm. Sec. Dept for Int. Devt 1994–2002; Gov. and C-in-C of Bermuda 2002–07; Ind. Dir, XL Group plc 2007–, MWH Global 2009–; mem. Bd of Dirs XL Insurance Co. Ltd 2010–; Chair. Students Loans Co. Ltd 1989–91; Vice-Pres. Raleigh Int. 2002–; mem. Council, Inst. of Manpower Studies 1989–92, Bd British Council 1994–2002, IDS 1994–2001, VSO 1994–2002, Advisory Bd for British Consultants Bureau 1998–2002; Trustee, Ditchley Foundation 2007–; Hon. DLitt (Keele) 1997.

VERES, János, PhD; Hungarian politician; b. 5 Feb. 1957, Nyírbátor; m. Éva Szabó; two c.; ed Univ. of Agriculture, Debrecen and Karl Marx Univ. of Econs; began career in business sector 1981–2002; mem. Nyírbátor local govt 1990–94; mem. Parl. 1994–; Chair., Chamber of Commerce and Trade, Szabolcs-Szatmár-Bereg County 1997–2002; Mayor of Nyírbátor 2002–03; mem. Exec. Cttee, Socialist Party of Hungary 2004–; Sec. of State for Political Affairs, Ministry of Finance 2003–04; Chief of Staff, Office of the Prime Minister 2004–05; Minister of Finance 2005–09. *Address:* c/o Ministry of Finance, 1051 Budapest, József Nádor tér 2–4, Hungary.

VERESHCHETIN, Vladlen Stepanovich, DJur; Russian international lawyer and judge; b. 8 Jan. 1932, Briansk; m.; one d.; ed Moscow Inst. of Int. Relations; mem. staff, Presidium of USSR Acad. of Sciences 1958–67; First Vice-Chair. and Legal Counsel, Intercosmos, USSR Acad. of Sciences 1967–81; Prof. of Int. Law, Univ. of Friendship of Peoples 1979–82; Deputy Dir and Head, Dept of Int. Law, Inst. of State and Law, Russian Acad. of Sciences 1981–95; mem. Perm. Court of Arbitration, The Hague 1984–95; judge, Int. Court of Justice, The Hague 1995–2006; Vice-Pres. Russian (fmrly Soviet) UN Asscn 1984–97; Vice-Pres. Russian (fmrly Soviet) Asscn of Int. Law 1985–97; mem. UN Int. Law Comm. 1992–95; Foreign mem. Bulgarian Acad. of Sciences 2006; Hon. Dir Int. Inst. of Space Law 1995–; Order of Friendship of Peoples 1975, October Revolution Order 1981; Hon. Master of Sciences, Russian Fed. 1995; Hon. Awards from German Acad. of Sciences 1978, Bulgarian Acad. of Sciences 1979, Int. Acad. of Astronautics 1987, 1994, Hugo Grotius Award 2001, Int. Inst. of Space Law Lifetime Achievement Award 2009. *Publications:* books and more than 150 articles on int. law, law of the sea, space law, state responsibility, int. criminal law. *Address:* 117420 Moscow, Profsouyaznaya str. 43, Bldg 1, Apt 255, Russia. *E-mail:* vsvereshchetin@ziggo.nl.

VERGARA, Sofía; Colombian actress, comedienne, television hostess, model and entrpreneur; b. (Sofia Margarita Vergara Vergara), 10 July 1972, Barranquilla, Atlántico; d. of Julio Enrique Vergara Robayo and Margarita Vergara Dávila de Vergara; m. Joe Gonzalez 1991 (divorced 1993); one s.; ed Marymount School, Barranquilla, studied pre-dentistry at a univ. in Colombia for three years; moved to Miami, USA with members of her family 1990s; pursued modelling career; known for co-hosting two TV shows for Univision late 1990s; first important acting role in Chasing Papi 2003; named the new face of CoverGirl 2011; appeared in a Diet Pepsi commercial with David Beckham 2011; designed a clothing line for K-Mart 2011; ranked by Forbes magazine amongst The World's 100 Most Powerful Women (75th) 2012, (38th) 2013. *Films include:* Big Trouble 2002, Chasing Papi 2003, The 24th Day 2004, Soul Plane 2004, Lords of Dogtown 2005, Four Brothers 2005, Grilled 2006, Meet the Browns 2008, Madea Goes to Jail 2009, The Smurfs 2011, Happy Feet Two (voice) 2011, New Year's Eve 2011, The Three Stooges 2012, Machete Kills 2013, The Smurfs 2 2013. *Television includes:* Acapulco, cuerpo y alma (series) 1995, My Wife and Kids (series) 2002, Eve (series) 2004, El escándalo del mediodía (series) 2004, Rodney (series) 2004, Hot Properties (series) 2005, Entourage (series) 2007, Amas de casa desesperadas (series) 2007, The Knights of Prosperity (series) 2007, Dirty Sexy Money (series) 2007, Fuego en la sangre (series) 2008, Men in Trees (series) 2008, Dancing with the Stars 2009, Modern Family (series) 2009–, The Cleveland Show (series) (voice) 2011, Plaza Sésamo 2011. *Address:* c/o Latin World Entertainment Agency, 4770 Biscayne Boulevard, Suite 1100, Miami, FL 33137, USA (office). *Telephone:* (305) 572-1515 (office). *Website:* www.sofiavergara.com.

VERGE, Pierre, MA, LLD, FRSC; Canadian lawyer, legal scholar and academic; *Professor Emeritus, Faculty of Law, Université Laval;* b. 9 Jan. 1936, Québec City; m. Colette Habel 1963; two s. one d.; ed Université Laval, McGill Univ. and Univ. of Toronto; called to the Québec Bar 1961; QC 1976; Prof. of Law, Université Laval 1967, now Prof. Emer., Dean, Faculty of Law 1973–77; currently mem. Centre de recherche interuniversitaire sur la mondialisation et le travail (CRIMT); Commonwealth Fellowship, St John's Coll., Cambridge 1977; mem. Canadian Asscn of Law Teachers (Pres. 1972–73); Bora Laskin Award 2004. *Publications:* Le droit de grève, fondement et limites, Le droit et les syndicats (co-author) 1991, Un droit du travail? (co-author) 1997, La représentation syndicale: vision juridique actuelle et future (co-author) 1999, Configuration juridique de l'entreprise et droit du travail (co-author) 2003. *Address:* Faculté de droit, Université Laval, Bureau 2107, Pavillon Charles-De Koninck, Québec, PQ G1K 7P4 (office); 2542 de la Falaise, Sillery, Québec, PQ G1T 1W3, Canada (home). *Telephone:* (418) 656-5009 (office); (418) 651-4829 (home). *Fax:* (418) 656-7230 (office). *E-mail:* pierre.verge@fd.ulaval .ca (office). *Website:* www.fd.ulaval.ca (office).

VERHAEGEN, Georges, PhD; Belgian scientist and academic (retd); *Professor and Honorary Rector, Université Libre de Bruxelles;* b. 26 March 1937, Brussels; s. of Col J. Verhaegen and L. Neufcoeur; m. M. Van de Keere 1965; two s.; ed Ashbury Coll., Ottawa, Canada, Univ. Libre, Brussels, CNRS, France; Pres. Dept of Chem., Univ. Libre de Bruxelles 1973–75, Dean Faculty of Sciences 1978–81, Prof. 1979–, mem. Governing Body 1975–84, 1986–, Rector 1986–90, Pro-Rector 1990, now Hon. Rector; Pres. Belgian Conf. of Rectors (French speaking) 1986–90, Belgian NSF 1990, Network of Univs of Capital Cities of Europe (UNICA) 1989–97; Expert for Univ. Man. (European Univ. Asscn, IBRD, European Comm.) 1993–; winner of three Belgian scientific prizes. *Publications:* more than 60 scientific publs. *Leisure interests:* reading, tennis, handicrafts, travelling. *Address:* C.P. 160/09, Université Libre de Bruxelles, 50 avenue F.D. Roosevelt, 1050 Brussels (office); 2 rue des Aulnes, 7090 Braine le Comte, Belgium (home). *Telephone:* (2) 650-24-24 (office); (67) 63-82-86 (home). *E-mail:* gverhaeg@ulb.ac.be (office). *Website:* www .ulb.ac.be (office).

VERHAGEN, Maxime Jacques Marcel; Dutch historian, politician and entrepreneur; *President, Bouwend Nederland;* b. 14 Sept. 1956, Maastricht; m.; two s. one d.; ed Leiden Univ.; began career as Asst at Christian Democratic Alliance (CDA) 1984–87, Head of European Affairs, Devt Co-operation and Trade Policy 1987–89; mem. Oegstgeest Municipal Council 1986–89; MEP 1989–94; mem. House of Reps 1996–2010, Chair. Christian Democratic Appeal (CDA) 2002–12; Minister of Foreign Affairs 2007–10; Deputy Prime Minister, Minister of Econ. Affairs, Agric. and Innovation 2010–12; Advisor, VOPAK 2012–, VDL 2012–, Chemelot 2012–, Prov. of Limburg 2012–; mem. Bd VNO-NCW (gen. employers' org.) 2013–; Pres. Bouwend Nederland (employers' org. of building and construction cos) 2013–; Special Envoy for the Dutch participation in the F-35 programme 2014–; fmr Vice-Chair. ACP-EU Joint Ass., Parl. Cttee on Foreign Affairs; fmr Bd mem. Eduardo Frei Foundation, Netherlands Atlantic Asscn, European Movt, Univ. of Nijmegen Parl. History Foundation, Free Voice. *Leisure interests:* skiing, motorcycling, travelling, sailing. *Address:* Bouwend Nederland, Zilverstraat 69, 2718 RP Zoetermeer, The Netherlands (office). *Telephone:* (79) 3252252 (office). *E-mail:* m.verhagen@bouwendnederland.nl (office). *Website:* www .bouwendnederland.nl (office).

VERHEUGEN, Günter; German politician; b. 28 April 1944, Bad Kreuznach; s. of Leo Verheugen and Leni Verheugen (née Holzhäuser); m. Gabriele Verheugen (née Schäfer; ed in Cologne and Bonn; trainee, Neue Rhein-Neue Ruhr-Zeitung 1963–65; Head of Public Relations Div., Fed. Ministry of the Interior 1969–74; Head of Analysis and Information Task Force, Fed. Foreign Office 1974–76; Fed. Party Man., Free Democratic Party (FDP) 1977–78; Gen. Sec. FDP 1978–82; joined Sozialdemokratische Partei Deutschlands (SPD) 1982; mem. Bundestag 1983–99, Chair. EU Special Cttee 1992, mem. Foreign Affairs Cttee 1983–98; Spokesman, SPD Nat. Exec. 1986–87; Ed.-in-Chief Vorwärts (SPD newspaper) 1987–89; Chair. Radio Broadcasting Council, Deutsche Welle 1990–99; Fed. Party Man. SPD 1993–95; Deputy Chair. SPD Parl. Group for Foreign, Security and Devt Policy 1994–97; Chair. Socialist Int. Peace, Security and Disarmament Council 1997–; mem. SPD Nat. Exec.; Minister of State, Fed. Foreign Office 1998–99; EU Commr for Enlargement 1999–2004, for Enterprise and Industry 2004–, Vice-Pres EU Comm. 2004–10; Commdr Distinguished Service Cross (Italy). *Publications:* Eine Zukunft für Deutschland 1980, Das Programm der Liberalen Baden-Baden 1980, Der Ausverkauf-Macht und Verfall der FDP 1984, Apartheid-Südafrika und der Deutschen Interessen am Kap 1986.

VERHOEVEN, Michael; German screenwriter, director and producer; *Head, Sentana Filmprodukten GmbH;* b. 13 July 1938, Berlin; s. of the late Paul Verhoeven and Doris Kiesow; m. Senta Berger 1966; two s.; actor stage, TV and cinema 1953–; Co-founder (with wife) and Head of Sentana Filmproduktion GmbH, Munich 1965–; medical studies Munich, Berlin and Worcester, Mass., LA, Calif., USA; worked as doctor Munich –1973; taught at Film Acad. Baden-Württemberg; Cross of Merit; New York Critics Circle Award, BAFTA Award, Joseph Neuberger-Medaille 1996, Award, Festival Int. de Programmes Audiovisuels, Biarritz 2001, Visionary Award, Washington Jewish Film Festival 2009; several other awards for writing, directing and producing. *Films:* Dance of Death 1967, O.K. 1970, Great Escape 1973, Sunday Children 1979, The White Rose 1981, Killing Cars 1985, The Nasty Girl 1989, My Mother's Courage 1995, The Legend of Mrs. Goldman and the Almighty God 1996, Der unbekannte Soldat 2006, Menschliches Versagen 2008. *Plays (director and producer):* The Guns of Mrs Carrar, Believe Love Hope, The Tribades Night, Volpone. *Television (director and producer):* The Challenge 1974, The Reason 1978, Dear Melanie 1983, Gunda's Father 1986, Semmelweis MD 1987, The Fast Gerdi 1989, Land of Milk and Honey 1991, Unholy Love 1993, Tabori – Theatre is Life (documentary) 1998, Room to Let 1999, Metamorphosis 2000, The Fast Gerdi in Berlin 2002, Pictures of an Exhibition (docu-essay) 2004. *Publications:* Liebe Melanie 1974, Sonntagskinder 1979, Die Weisse Rose 1980. *Address:* Sentana Filmproduktion GmbH, Gebsatelstr. 30, 81541 Munich (office); Robert-Koch-Str. 10, 82031 Grünwald, Germany (home). *Telephone:* (89) 4485266 (office). *Fax:* (89) 4801968 (office). *E-mail:* sentana@sentana.de (office). *Website:* www.sentana.de (office).

VERHOEVEN, Paul, PhD; Dutch film director; b. 18 July 1938, Amsterdam; ed Leiden Univ.; worked as a documentary filmmaker for Dutch navy and then for TV. *Films include:* directed: (shorts) A Lizard Too Much 1960, Let's Have a Party 1963, The Wrestler 1971; (feature length) Wat zien ik (Business is Business/Any Special Way) 1971, Turks fruit (Turkish Delight) 1973, Keetje Tippel 1975, Soldaat van Oranje 1940–45 (Soldier of Orange/Survival Run) 1978, Spetters 1980, De vierde man (The Fourth Man) 1984, Flesh and Blood 1985, RoboCop 1987, Total Recall 1989, Basic Instinct 1992, Showgirls 1995, Starship Troopers 1997, Hollow Man 2000, Black Book 2006, The Winter Queen (producer) 2010. *Address:* c/o Beth Swofford, 9830 Wilshire Boulevard, Beverly Hills, CA 90212, USA (office).

VERHOFSTADT, Guy, LLB; Belgian politician; b. 11 April 1953, Dendermonde; s. of the late Marcel Verhofstadt and of Gaby Stockmans; m. Dominique Verkinderen 1981; one s. one d.; ed Koninklijk Atheneum, Ghent and Univ. of Ghent; began career as attorney-at-law Ghent Bar; Councillor Ghent 1976–82; Political Sec. to Willy De Clercq, Nat. Pres. Party for Freedom and Progress (PVV) 1977–81; mem. House of Reps Ghent-Eeklo Dist 1978–84; Nat. Pres. PVV Youth Div. 1979–81, Nat. Pres. PVV 1982–85; Deputy Prime Minister and Minister for the Budget, Scientific Research and the Nat. Plan 1985–88; Pres. of Shadow Cabinet 1988–91; Nat. Pres. of PVV 1989–92, of Flemish Liberals and Democrats (VLD) 1992–95, 1997–99; Minister of State 1995–99; Senator VLD 1995–99, Vice-Pres. of Senate 1995–99; Prime Minister of Belgium 1999–2007 (resgnd), reappointed Dec. 2007, resgnd March 2008; mem. European Parl. (Group of the Alliance of Liberals and Democrats for Europe) 2009–. *Publications:* Het Radicaal Manifest: Handvest voor een nieuwe liberale omwenteling 1979, Burgermanifest 1991, De Weg naar politieke vernieuwing: Het tweede burgermanifest 1992, Angst, afgunst en het algemeen belang 1994, De Belgische ziekte: Diagnose en remedies 1997, In goede banen: VLD-plan voor meer tewerks telling 1999; De vierde golf – een liberaal project voor de nieuwe eeuw 2002, De verenigde staten van Europa, 2007 (Awarded Best European Book of the Year 2007), Een new age of empires 2009; contribs to books and articles in periodicals. *Leisure interests:* cycling, literature, Italy. *Address:* Vlaamse Liberalen en Demokraten (VLD, Flemish Liberals and Democrats—Liberal Party), Melsensstraat 34, 1000 Brussels, Belgium (office). *Telephone:* (2) 549-00-20 (office). *Fax:* (2) 512-60-25 (office). *E-mail:* contact@openvld.be (office). *Website:* www.openvld.be (office); www .guyverhofstadt.be (home).

VERMA, Adm. (retd) Nirmal Kumar, ADC; Indian diplomatist and fmr naval officer; *High Commissioner to Canada;* b. 14 Nov. 1950; m. Madhulika Verma; two s.; ed Royal Naval Staff Coll., UK, Naval War Coll., USA; joined Indian Navy 1970; crew mem. for first Kashin Class Destroyer inducted into Indian Navy 1980 (trained in fmr Soviet Union); specialist in communication and electronic warfare; sea tenures have included commands of INS Udaygiri (Leander Class Frigate), INS Ranvir (Kashin Class Destroyer), INS Viraat (Aircraft Carrier); commanded Indian Naval Acad. at Goa, fmr Head of Naval Training Team at Defence Services Staff Coll., Wellington and Sr Directing Staff (Navy), Nat. Defence Coll., New Delhi; promoted to Flag Rank as Rear Adm., Chief of Staff of Eastern Naval Command, later Flag Officer Commdg Maharashtra Naval Area, later Flag Officer Commdg-in-Chief (FOC-in-C) Eastern Naval Command; rank of Vice-Adm. and Chief of Personnel 2005; Asst Chief of Naval Staff (Policy & Plans) –2009, apptd Chair. Chiefs of Staff Cttee 2011; Chief of Naval Staff 2009–12, High Commr to Canada 2012–; Hon. ADC to Pres. of India; Param Vishist Seva Medal, Ati Vishist Seva Medal. *Address:* High Commission of India, 10 Springfield Road, Ottawa, ON K1M 1C9, Canada (office). *Telephone:* (613) 744-3751. *Fax:* (613) 744-0913. *E-mail:* hicomind@hciottawa.ca. *Website:* www.hciottawa.ca.

VERMA, Om Prakash, LLB; Indian judge; b. 20 March 1937, Garh Mukteshwar, Hapur Dist, UP; ed Delhi Univ.; Civil Judge (Jr Div.), UP Civil Judicial Service 1961; Deputy Sec., Deputy Legal Adviser, Ministry of Law, Govt of India 1971–75; Judge, Allahabad High Court 1984–1997; Chief Justice, Kerala High Court 1997–99; Lokayukta and Chair. State Human Rights Comm., Himachal Pradesh; Gov. of Punjab 2003–04; Admin. Union Territory of Chandigarh 2003–04. *Address:* R 8/49 Raj Nagar, Ghaziabad, Uttar Pradesh, India. *Telephone:* (120) 2822500. *Fax:* (120) 2822500. *E-mail:* justiceopverma@yahoo.com.

VERMA, Rajani Kant; Indian government official; b. 23 April 1959; joined Indian Admin. Service; fmr Commr of Sales Tax, Govt of India, New Delhi; fmr Man. Dir Delhi State Industrial Devt Corpn; fmr High Commr in Canada; Admin. Union Territories of Dadra and Nagar Haveli and Daman and Diu 2006–08. *Address:* c/o Office of the Administrator, Silvassa, Dadra and Nagar Haveli, India. *Telephone:* 2642777 (Dadra and Nagar Haveli); 2230700 (Daman and Diu); 2251977 (home). *Fax:* 2642702. *E-mail:* vermark@ias.nic.in (office).

VERNER, Josée; Canadian politician; b. 30 Dec. 1959, Gatineau, Québec; m.; three c.; began career as admin. officer and political adviser, Université du Québec; worked for fmr pres. Robert Bourassa, Deputy Speaker of Ass., Ministry of Health; unsuccessful Conservative Party cand in Fed. election 2004, apptd Opposition Spokesperson on Econ. Devt Agency 2004, on Official Languages 2005, MP for Louis-Saint-Laurent, Québec 2006–11; Minister of Int. Co-operation and Minister for La Francophonie and Official Languages 2006–07, for Canadian Heritage 2007–08, for Intergovernmental Affairs and Francophonie 2008–11; mem. Senate for Montarville 2011–; also currently Chair. Québec Caucus of Conservative Party. *Address:* The Senate of Canada, Ottawa, ON K1A 0A4, Canada (office). *Website:* www.joseeverner.ca (home).

VERNIER, Jacques; French politician and environmentalist; *Mayor of Douai;* b. 3 July 1944, Paris; s. of Charles Vernier and Georgette Mangin; m. Bertille Janssen 1968; two s. two d.; ed Ecole Polytechnique and Ecole des Mines, Paris; engineer, Service des Mines, Strasbourg 1968–72; Sec.-Gen. Agence de l'eau Seine-Normandie 1972–74; Dir Agence de l'Eau Artois-Picardie 1974–83, Pres. Comité de Bassin Artois-Picardie (Agence de l'Eau) 1992–2004; Founder and Pres. Asscn Douai-Consommateurs 1976–83; Pres. PACT de Douai 1976–83; Mayor of Douai 1983–; Councillor, Régional du Nord – Pas-de-Calais 1983–90, 1998–, Pres. Communauté d'agglomération du Douaisis 2002–05, Vice-Pres. 2005–; mem. European Parl. 1984–93; Deputy (RPR) to Nat. Ass. 1993–97; Pres. Agence de l'Environnement 1994–97, Syndicat Mixte pour l'Aménagement et l'Equipement des Zones Industrielles du Douaisis 1995–2001, Comm. interministérielle du transport des matières dangereuses 1998–, Council of Admin Institut nat. de l'environnement industriel et des risques (INERIS) 2003–, Comité départemental de l'UMP du Nord 2003–, Conseil supérieur des installations classées 2004–; Nat. Sec. then Gen. Del., Environnement au sein du RPR 1989–95, mem. Political Bureau RPR 1993–98, Departmental Sec. RPR du Nord 1992–94; Chef de la mission du transport des matières dangereuses 1997–; Officier des Palmes académiques 2001, Chevalier, Légion d'honneur 2002, Commdr, Ordre nat. du Mérite 2005. *Publications:* La bataille de l'environnement 1971, Guide Pratique pour les habitants de Douai 1981–, L'environnement (eighth edn) 2007, Les énergies renouvelables (fourth edn) 2007; several publs on environmental matters. *Leisure interests:* tennis, flying aircraft. *Address:* Hôtel de ville, 59508 Douai (office); 162 quai du Petit Bail, 59500 Douai, France (home). *Telephone:* (3) 27-93-58-00 (office). *Fax:* (3) 27-96-58-22 (office). *E-mail:* cabinet@ville-douai.fr (office); *Website:* www.ville-douai.fr (office); www.jacques-vernier.fr.

VERNON, Sir (William) Michael, Kt, MA, CCMI; British business executive (retd); b. 17 April 1926, Cheshire; s. of the late Sir Wilfred Vernon; m. 1st Rosheen O'Meara 1952 (divorced 1977); one s.; m. 2nd Jane Kilham-Roberts 1977 (died 1998); m. 3rd Penelope Cuddeford 2001; ed Marlborough Coll. and Trinity Coll. Cambridge; joined Spillers (millers and animal food mfrs) as trainee 1948, Dir 1960–80, Joint Man. Dir 1962–67, Deputy Chair. 1967–68, Chair. 1968–80; Chair. Famous Names Ltd 1981–85, Granville Meat Co. Ltd 1981–94; Dir Electrical and Musical Industries (later EMI) Ltd 1973–80, Strong and Fisher (Holdings) PLC 1980–91; Pres. British Food Export Council 1977–79; Vice-Pres. Royal Nat. Lifeboat Inst. 1975–2001, Deputy Chair. 1980–89, Chair. 1989–96, Chair. Emer. 2006–; Bronze Medal, Royal Humane Soc. 1956. *Leisure interests:* travel, shooting. *Address:* Fyfield Manor, Andover, Hants., SP11 8EL, England (home).

VERPLAETSE, Baron Alphonse Remi Emiel; Belgian fmr central banker; *Honorary Governor, National Bank of Belgium;* b. 19 Feb. 1930, Zulte; m. Odette Vanhee 1954; three s. two d.; ed Katholieke Universiteit Leuven; Nat. Bank of Belgium 1953–81, Dir 1988–, Deputy Gov. 1988–89, Gov. 1989–99, Hon. Gov. 1999–; Office of the Prime Minister 1981–88; Hon. Gov. and Vice-Pres. Higher Finance Council, Admin. BIS, Basle; Gov. IMF 1989–99; Deputy Gov. IBRD 1989–99, IFC 1989–99; Grand Officier, Ordre de la Couronne 1991; Grande Ufficiale, Ordine al Merito (Italy) 1986; Officier, Légion d'honneur 1994. *Address:* c/o National Bank of Belgium, Boulevard de Berlaimont 14, 1000 Brussels (office); Schaveyslaan 25, 1650 Beersel, Belgium (home). *Telephone:* (2) 221-30-21 (office). *E-mail:* kristof.smeyers@nbb.be (office). *Website:* www.nbb.be (office).

VERSACE, Donatella; Italian designer; b. 2 May 1955, Reggio di Calabria; d. of Antonio Versace and Francesca Versace; sister of the late Gianni Versace; m. Paul Beck (divorced); one s. one d.; ed Univ. of Florence; joined Versace 1978, fmrly overseer of advertising and public relations, accessories designer, children's collection designer (Versace Young) 1993, Head Designer for Versus and Isante lines; Style and Image Dir and Vice-Chair. Gianni Versace Group 1997–; solo debut for mainline collection 1998; first couture show for Versace Atelier in Paris Ritz 1998; launched her own fragrance Versace Woman 2001; ranked 43rd by Fortune magazine amongst 50 Most Powerful Women in Business outside the US 2002. *Address:* c/o Keeble Cavaco and Duka Inc., 450 West 15th Street, Suite 604, New York, NY 10011, USA (office); Versace SpA Headquarters, Via Manzoni 38, 20121 Milan, Italy (office). *Telephone:* (02) 760931 (Milan) (office). *Fax:* (02) 76004122 (Milan) (office). *Website:* www.versace.com (office).

VERSALDI, HE Cardinal Giuseppe, DCL; Italian ecclesiastic; *President, Prefecture for the Economic Affairs of the Holy See;* b. 30 July 1943, Villarboit (Vercelli); ed Pontifical Gregorian Univ., Rome, Sacred Roman Rota; ordained priest, Archdiocese of Vercelli 1967; est. diocesan Family Counselling centre,

Vercelli 1976; entrusted with care of parish of Larizza in diocese 1977; taught canon law and psychology at Pontifical Gregorian Univ. 1980–85; apptd to Supreme Tribunal of the Apostolic Signatura 1985–94; Vicar Gen. of Vercelli 1994–2007; Bishop of Alessandria (della Paglia) 2007–11; apptd Archbishop ad personam 2011; Pres. Pref. for Econ. Affairs of Holy See 2011–13, 2013–; cr. Cardinal (Cardinal-Deacon of Sacro Cuore di Gesù a Castro Pretorio) 2012; participated in Papal Conclave 2013. *Address:* Prefecture for the Economic Affairs of the Holy See, Palazzo della Congregazioni, Largo del Colonnato 3, 00193 Rome, Italy (office). *Telephone:* (06) 69884263 (office). *Fax:* (06) 69885011 (office). *E-mail:* info@www.vatican.va (office). *Website:* www.vatican.va/roman_curia/uffici/prefettura/index_en.htm (office).

VERSHBOW, Alexander R., BA, MA; American diplomatist; *Assistant Secretary of Defense for International Security Affairs;* b. 3 July 1952, Boston, Mass; s. of Arthur E. Vershbow and Charlotte Z. Vershbow; m. Lisa K. Vershbow 1976; two s.; ed Yale Coll. and School of Int. Affairs, Columbia Univ.; joined Foreign Service 1977, Bureau of Politico-Military Affairs 1977–79, US Embassy, Moscow 1979–81, Office of Soviet Union Affairs 1981–85, US Embassy, London 1985–88; adviser US Del. to SALT II and START negotiations; Dir State Dept's Office of Soviet Union Affairs 1988–91; US Deputy Perm Rep. to NATO and Chargé d'affaires US Mission 1991–93; Prin. Deputy Asst Sec. of State for European and Canadian Affairs (responsibilities covered the Balkan conflict) 1993–94; Special Asst to the Pres. and Sr Dir for European Affairs at Nat. Security Council 1994–97 (worked on US policy which laid foundations of the Dayton Peace Agreement, adaptation and enlargement of NATO and its new relationship with Russia); Perm. Rep. to NATO 1998–2001; Amb. to Russian Fed. 2001–05, to S Korea 2005–08; Asst Sec. of Defense for Int. Security Affairs 2009–; Anatoly Sharansky Freedom Award, Union of Councils of Soviet Jews 1990, first Joseph J. Kruzel Award for contribs to the cause of peace, US Dept of Defense 1997, Distinguished Service Award for Work at NATO, US State Dept 2001, ABA Amb.'s Award 2004, Cordell Hull Award for Economic Achievement, US State Dept 2007. *Publications:* articles on arms control, speeches on Russia and NATO issues. *Leisure interests:* music, theatre. *Address:* Office of the Assistant Secretary of Defense for International Security Affairs, Department of Defense, 1400 Defense Pentagon, Washington, DC 20301-1400, USA (office). *Telephone:* 703-571-3343 (office). *Website:* www.defense.gov (office).

VERSTRAETE, Baron Marc, MD, PhD, FRCP, FACP; Belgian medical scientist and academic; *Director, Centre for Molecular and Vascular Biology, University of Leuven;* b. 1 April 1925, Bruges; s. of Louis Verstraete and Jeanne Coppin; m. Bernadette Moyersoen 1955; one s. four d.; ed Leuven and Oxford Univs and Cornell Univ. Medical Coll., New York; Lecturer, Univ. of Leuven 1957, Asst Prof. 1961, Assoc. Prof. 1963, Prof. 1968–; Dir Centre for Molecular and Vascular Biology; Visiting Prof., Harvard Medical School, Boston, USA; Past-Pres. Royal Acad. of Medicine of Belgium; mem. Acad. of Medicine of South Africa and of Argentina; Dr hc (Edinburgh, Córdoba (Argentina), Bologna, Bordeaux, London). *Publications:* Arterial Hypertension 1966, 1972, Haemostatic Drugs 1977, Methods in Angiology 1980, Haemostasis 1980, Thrombosis 1982, Thrombolysis 1985, Thrombosis and Haemostasis 1987, Thrombosis in Cardiovascular Disorders 1992; numerous articles in scientific journals. *Leisure interests:* reading, skiing, swimming, tennis. *Address:* Centre for Molecular and Vascular Biology, Campus Gasthuisberg, University of Leuven, Herestraat 29, 3000 Leuven (office); Fac. Geneeskunde, Minderbroedersstraat 17, 3000 Leuven (office); Minderbroedersstraat 29, 3000 Leuven, Belgium (home). *Telephone:* (16) 34-57-75 (office); (16) 22-66-74 (home). *Fax:* (16) 34-59-90 (office); (16) 22-66-74 (home). *E-mail:* marc.verstraete@med.kuleuven.ac.be (office). *Website:* www.med.kuleuven.ac.be (office).

VÉRTES, Attila, EngChem, MEconSc, Dr rer. techn., DChemSci; Hungarian nuclear chemist and academic; *Professor Emeritus of Chemistry, Eötvös Loránd University;* b. 10 Oct. 1934, Türje; s. of György Vértes and Erzsébet Nagy; m. Irén Vértes 1959; two s.; ed Tech. Univ. of Budapest, Univ. of Econs, Budapest, Lomonosov Univ., Moscow; Prof. of Chem., Eötvös Loránd Univ., Budapest; Visiting Scientist, Univ. of Newcastle, UK 1969; Humboldt Fellow, Tech. Univ., Munich, Germany 1970; Visiting Prof., Lehigh Univ., Bethlehem, Pa USA 1976–77, 1982, 1986, Johannes Gutenberg Univ., Mainz, Germany 1991, 1992, 1993, various univs in Japan 1987, in People's Repub. of China 1989; Chair. Cttee of Radiochemistry, Hungarian Acad. of Sciences 1993–2002; Assoc. mem. IUPAC Comm. on Radiochemistry and Nuclear Techniques, Analytical Chem. Div. 1999–; mem. Int. Bd of Applied Mössbauer Effect 1988–98; mem. Editorial Bd Journal of Radioanalytical and Nuclear Chemistry 1980–2009, Structural Chemistry 1990–2009; Corresp. mem., Hungarian Acad. of Sciences 1993–98, Ordinary mem. 1998–; Hon. DSc (Glasgow Caledonian Univ.)1996; Széchenyi Prize 2001, Hevesy Medal 2004. *Publications:* eight textbooks and ten scientific monographs, including Mössbauer Spectroscopy 1979, Nuclear Chemistry 1987, Nuclear Methods in Mineralogy and Geology: Techniques and Applications (co-ed.) 1998, Handbook of Nuclear Chemistry (Ed.-in-Chief) 2003; more than 610 papers in scientific journals. *Address:* Eötvös Loránd University, Department of Nuclear Chemistry, PO Box 32, 1518 Budapest 112, Hungary (office). *Telephone:* (1) 372-2543 (office). *Fax:* (1) 372-2592 (office). *E-mail:* vertesa@chem.elte.hu (office). *Website:* www.chem.elte.hu (office).

VERWAAYEN, Bernardus (Ben) J., LLM; Dutch telecommunications industry executive; *CEO, Alcatel-Lucent;* b. Feb. 1952, Utrecht; m.; two c.; ed State Univ. of Utrecht; various man. posts with ITT Nederland BV 1975–88, rising to Gen. Man.; joined Koninklijke PTT Nederland (KPN) 1996, Chair. Unisource European Venture 1996–97, Pres. and Man. Dir PTT Telecom 1997–98; Exec. Vice-Pres. of Int. Div., Lucent Technologies Inc. Sept.–Oct. 1997, Exec. Vice-Pres. and COO 1997–99, Vice-Chair. Man. Bd 1999–2002, CEO Alcatel-Lucent (following acquisition of Lucent by Alcatel) 2008–; CEO British Telecommunications PLC (now BT Group plc) 2002–08 (Chair. Operating Cttee); Chair. CBI Climate Change Bd; mem. World Econ. Forum's Foundation Bd 2010–; mem. Advisory Council ING; mem. Bd Astro All Asia Networks (ASTRO), Health Center Internet Services Inc.; Officer, Order of Orange-Nassau, Chevalier, Légion d'honneur 2006, Hon. KBE 2007. *Leisure interest:* Arsenal football club. *Address:* Alcatel-Lucent, 3 avenue Octave Gréard, 75007 Paris, France (office). *Telephone:* 1-40-76-10-10 (office).

E-mail: ben.verwaayen@alcatel-lucent.com (office); execoffice@alcatel-lucent.com (office). *Website:* www.alcatel-lucent.com (office).

VERWILGHEN, Marc, BL; Belgian politician and lawyer; b. 21 Sept. 1952, Dendermonde; ed Free Univ. of Brussels; practising lawyer 1975–; Deputy 1991–99; Senator 1999–2010; Chair. Comms of Inquiry on Dutroux-Nihoul and on Missing and Murdered Children 1996–98; Chair. Chamber Comm. on Justice; mem. Vlaamse Liberalen en Demokraten-Partij van de Burger (PVV-VLD); Minister of Justice 1999–2003, of Devt Co-operation 2003–04, of Economy 2004–07; Dr hc (Univ. of Ghent) 1999. *Publications:* Het V-Plan 1999, Over bruggen bouwen 1999. *Address:* Open Vld, Melsensstraat 34, 1000 Brussels, Belgium (office). *Telephone:* (2) 549-00-20 (office). *E-mail:* contact@openvld.be (office). *Website:* www.openvld.be (office).

VESHNYAKOV, Aleksander Albertovich, CandJurSc; Russian lawyer, government official and diplomatist; *Ambassador to Latvia;* b. 24 Nov. 1952, Baikalovo, Arkhangelsk Region; m.; two c.; ed Arkhangelsk Navigational School, Leningrad Higher School of Marine Eng, Leningrad Higher CP School, Diplomatic Acad., Russian Ministry of Foreign Affairs; worked for Arkhangelsk (Northern Sea steamship line) 1973–87; Sec., Arkhangelsk City CP Cttee 1987–90; Deputy Chair. Council of Repub. Supreme Soviet Russian Fed. 1990–91; Chair. Sub-comm. of Comm. for Transportation, Communications, Information Science and Space, Council of Repub. 1991–93; Econs Adviser, Marine Transport Dept, Ministry of Transportation 1993–97; Consultant, Information and Analysis Dept, Cen. Election Comm. 1994, Sec. 1995–99, Chair. 1999–2007; Amb. to Latvia 2008–; Defender of Free Russia Medal 1997, Medal in Commemoration of 850th Anniversary of Moscow 1997, Class IV Order for Service to the Fatherland 2009, Class II 2007. *Address:* Russian Embassy, Antonijas iela 2, Rīga 1010, Latvia (office). *Telephone:* 6733-2151 (home). *Fax:* 6783-0209 (office). *E-mail:* rusembas@delfi.lv (office). *Website:* (office).

VESKIMÄGI, Taavi, BEng; Estonian business executive and fmr politician; *Managing Director, Elering OÜ;* b. 28 Nov. 1974, Rapla; m.; one d.; ed Tallinn Tech. Univ. Tallinn Pedagogical Univ.; Head of State Admin Dept and Adviser, Ministry of Finance 1996–2001; mem. Parl. 2003, 2005–06, Vice-Speaker of Parl. 2005–06; Minister of Finance 2003–05; mem. Res Publica Party, Treas. 2001–02, Chair. Parl. Group 2003, Vice-Chair. Res Publica (later Isamaa ja Res Publica Liit–Union of Pro Patria and Res Publica, after merger with Pro Patria Union in 2006) 2003–05, Co-Chair. 2006–07; Lecturer and Consultant in Public Admin and Financial Man. 1998–2003; mem. Rapla City Council and Head of Econ. Cttee 1999–2002; Man. Dir Elering OÜ (transmission grid operator) 2009–; fmr Dir Eesti Post, Tallinn Olympic Sport Centre, Tallinn Harbour, Narva Electricity, Estonian Air Navigation Services. *Leisure interest:* football, restoration of motorbikes. *Address:* Elering OÜ, Kadaka tee 42, Tallinn 12915, Estonia (office). *Telephone:* 715-1222 (office). *Fax:* 715-1200 (office). *E-mail:* info@elering.ee (office). *Website:* www.elering.ee (office).

VESSEY, Gen. John William, Jr, DSC, DSM, BS, MS; American army officer; *Emeritus Chairman, Advisory Committee, Center for Preventive Action, Council on Foreign Relations;* b. 22 June 1922, Minneapolis, Minn.; s. of John William Vessey and Emily Vessey (née Roche); m. Avis C. Funk; two s. one d.; ed Univ. of Maryland, George Washington Univ.; enlisted in Minnesota Nat. Guard 1939; commissioned 2nd Lt, Field Artillery, Anzio May 1944; served successively with 34th Infantry Div., N Africa and Italy, 4th Infantry and 3rd Armoured Div., Germany, 25th Infantry Div., S Viet Nam; promoted Gen. 1976; Commdr US Forces, S Korea 1976–79; Army Vice-Chief of Staff 1979–82; Chair. Joint Chiefs of Staff 1982–85; Presidential Emissary to Hanoi 1987–93; Co-founder and Chair. Bd Center for Preventive Action, Council on Foreign Relations 1995, now Emer. Chair. Advisory Cttee; mem. Defense Science Bd 1987–90, 1992–2000, Defense Policy Bd 1990–93, Bd of Dirs Martin Marietta, Illinois Tool Works, Nat. Computer Systems, United Services Life Insurance, Nat. Flag Day Foundation, Youth Services USA, Advisory Bd Gen. Atomics; Trustee AAL Mutual Funds; Distinguished Service Cross, Defense Distinguished Service Medal, Army, Navy and Air Force Distinguished Service Medals, Legion of Merit, Bronze Star, Air Medal, Jt Services Commendation Medal, Purple Heart, Presidential Medal of Freedom 1992, Excellence in Diplomacy Award American Acad. of Diplomacy 1994, and other decorations. *Address:* 27650 Little Whitefish Road, Garrison, MN 56450, USA. *Telephone:* (320) 692-4488. *Fax:* (320) 692-4939. *E-mail:* vjack@frontiernet.net.

VESTBERG, Hans, BBA; Swedish business executive; *President and CEO, Telefonaktiebolaget L.M. Ericsson;* b. 1965, Hudiksvall; ed Univ. of Uppsala; joined Telefonaktiebolaget L. M. Ericsson 1991, held various managerial positions in China, Sweden, Chile and Brazil 1991–98, Chief Financial Officer (CFO), Brazil 1998–2000, CFO, N America, and Controller for the Americas 2000–02, Vice-Pres. and Head of Market Unit Mexico 2002–03, Sr Vice-Pres. and Head of Business Unit Global Services 2003–07, Exec. Vice-Pres. 2005–07, CFO and Head of Group Function Finance 2007–09, First Exec. Vice-Pres. –2009, mem. Bd of Dirs, Pres. and CEO 2010–; mem. Bd of Dirs Sony Ericsson Mobile Communications AB, Svenska Handbollsförbundet (Chair.). *Address:* Telefonaktiebolaget L.M. Ericsson, Telefonvägen 30, 126 25 Stockholm, Sweden (office). *Telephone:* (8) 719000 (office). *Fax:* (8) 184085 (office). *E-mail:* info@ericsson.com (office). *Website:* www.ericsson.com (office).

VESTERDORF, Bo, LLM; Danish fmr judge, international official and legal consultant; b. 11 Oct. 1945; ed Copenhagen Univ.; fmr Jurist-Linguist Court of Justice; fmr Admin. Ministry of Justice, later Head Constitutional and Admin. Law Dept, then apptd Dir Ministry of Justice; fmr Legal Attaché with Perm. Rep. of Denmark to EC; fmr temporary judge Eastern Regional Court; fmr mem. Human Rights Steering Cttee, then Bureau, Council of Europe; Judge, Court of First Instance of the European Communities 1989–2007, Pres. 1998–2007; Sr Legal Consultant, Plesner (Law Firm), Copenhagen 2007–.

VETTEL, Sebastian; German professional racing driver; b. 3 July 1987, Heppenheim, Bergstraße dist, Hesse; began racing karts in 1995, won various titles, including Jr Monaco Kart Cup 2001; upgraded to open-wheel cars 2003; won German Formula BMW Championship with 18 victories from 20 races 2004; drove for ASL Mucke Motorsport in Formula Three Euroseries 2005; was brought to Formula One by BMW Sauber; finished as runner-up in the F3 Euroseries 2006;

took part in Friday practice for the 2006 Turkish Grand Prix and became youngest Formula One driver to drive at a Grand Prix meeting, aged 19 years and 53 days; went on to become sixth youngest Formula One driver to start a Grand Prix at US Grand Prix 2007; moved to Toro Rosso 2007, youngest driver to lead a race at Japanese Grand Prix 2007; youngest Formula One driver to secure pole position, Italian Grand Prix 2008, went on to win; joined Red Bull Racing 2009, finished season as youngest ever runner-up (behind Jenson Button); winner Formula One Driver's Championship 2010 (youngest driver ever to win the championship), 2011 (youngest double champion in history), 2012 (third driver to win three consecutive championships and youngest triple champion in history), 2013 (youngest quadruple champion in history), helped Red Bull win World Constructors' Championship, along with team-mate Mark Webber 2010, 2011, 2012, 2013; DMV Jr Driver of the Award Year 2001, ADAC Jr Driver of the Year Award 2004, 2009, DMSB-Jr Award 2006, Autosport Rookie Of The Year Award 2008, DMV Driver of the Year Award 2008, Lorenzo Bandini Trophy 2009, BRDC Johnny Wakefield Trophy 2009, DHL Fastest Lap Award 2009, Motorsport Total Fahrer des Jahres Award 2010, German Athlete of the Year Award 2010, Autosport Int. Driver of the Year Award 2010, SPEED Performance Award 2011, Silver Bay Laurel Leaf Award 2012, Sports Acad. Grand Prix Prize 2012. *Leisure interests:* snowboarding, mountain biking, swimming, fitness, Eintracht Frankfurt football team. *Address:* Red Bull Racing, Bradbourne Drive, Tilbrook, Milton Keynes, MK7 8BJ, England (office); Postfach 1479, 64632 Heppenheim, Germany. *E-mail:* info@redbullracing.com (office). *Website:* www.redbullracing.com (office); www.sebastianvettel.de.

VETTER, Hans-Jörg; German business executive; *Chairman of the Board of Managing Directors, Landesbank Baden-Württemberg;* b. 22 Aug. 1952, Göppingen; m.; three c.; with Deutsche Bank AG, Göppingen Br. 1969–76, Head of Commercial Property Financing, Export – Special Financing, Municipal Loan Business, Frankfurter Hypothekenbank (Group Deutsche Bank AG) 1976–84, Dir Cen. Construction Financing and Real Estate, Deutsche Bank AG, Frankfurt 1987–90; Dir, Head of Leasing Div. Man. of Deutsche Anlagen-Leasing (DAL), Westdeutsche Landesbank, Düsseldorf, Mainz 1985–87; mem. Bd of Man. Dirs, responsible for the Real Estate Business, Bank für Gemeinwirtschaft AG (BfG Bank), Frankfurt 1990–95, Co-mem. Bd of Man. Dirs, Corp. Customers and Pvt. Customers 1995, also mem. responsible for Treasury/Sales and Security Trading; Personally liable Pnr, M.M. Warburg & Co. KG a. A., Hamburg, responsible for Corp. Customers, Foreign Operations, Corp. Finance 1995–97; Vice-Chair. Bd of Man. Dirs, Landesbank Hessen-Thüringen (Helaba), Frankfurt 1997–2000; Vice-Chair. Bd of Man. Dirs, Bankgesellschaft Berlin AG (renamed Landesbank Berlin Holding AG 2006), Berlin Nov.–Dec. 2001, Chair. Dec. 2001–, Chair. Bd of Man. Dirs, Landesbank Berlin (renamed Landesbank Berlin AG 2006) 2002–; Chair. Bd of Man. Dirs, Landesbank Baden-Württemberg (LBBW), Stuttgart 2009–. *Address:* Landesbank Baden-Württemberg, Am Hauptbahnhof 2, Stuttgart 70173, Germany (office). *Telephone:* (711) 127-0 (office). *Fax:* (711) 12743544 (office). *E-mail:* kontakt@lbbw.de (office). *Website:* www.lbbw.de (office).

VETTIER, Jean-Paul; French business executive; *CEO, Petroplus Holdings;* b. 1945; m.; two c.; ed Univ. of Paris; various staff and line positions with Rhône-Poulenc 1970–86, including Exec. Vice-Pres. Chemical Br.; Gen. Man. Petrochemical Div. and mem. Exec. Cttee, Orkem 1987–89; Exec. Vice-Pres., Refining and Marketing, Total 1990–93, Chair. (non-exec.) Total Petroleum N America 1992–96, Chair. and CEO Total Refining and Marketing and mem. Exec. Cttee 1993–2000, Chair. and CEO TotalFinaElf Refining and Marketing and mem. Exec. Cttee 2000–06; CEO Petroplus Holdings 2009–; Pres. Europia (European oil industry asscn) for two terms; Sr Advisor, First Reserve Corpn (pvt. equity firm), Roland Berger Strategy Consultants; mem. Bd Dirs SNC-Lavalin Group, Inc., Overseas Shipholding Group, Inc., Dresser-Rand Group, Inc., Eiffage SA; mem. Bd Institut Francais du Petrole; Chevalier, Légion d'honneur, Ordre nat. du Mérite. *Address:* Petroplus Holdings, Industriestrasse 24, 6300 Zug, Switzerland (office). *Telephone:* (58) 580-11-00 (office). *E-mail:* info@petroplus.biz (office). *Website:* www.petroplusholdings.com (office).

VETTORI, Daniel Luca, ONZM; New Zealand professional cricketer; b. 27 Jan. 1979, Auckland; m. Mary O'Connel; two c.; ed Marian School, St Paul's Collegiate School; all-rounder; slow left-arm orthodox spin bowler; left-handed batsman; plays for Northern Districts Cricket, youngest player to represent NZ in Tests and One-Day Ints (ODIs) aged 18, occasional Capt. ODI side 2005–06, overall Capt. 2007–11), Notts. 2003, Warwicks. 2006, Delhi Daredevils 2008–10, Queensland 2010, Royal Challengers Bangalore (Capt.) 2011–, Brisbane Heat 2011–, has also played for Hamilton in the Hawke Cup; First-class debut: 1996/97; Test debut: NZ v England, Wellington 6–10 Feb. 19979; One-Day Int. (ODI) debut: NZ v Sri Lanka, Christchurch 25 March 1997; T20I debut: Kenya v NZ, Durban 12 Sept. 2007; has played in 112 Tests, taken 360 wickets and scored 4,516 runs (6 centuries, 23 half-centuries), highest score 140, average 30.10, best bowling (innings) 7/87, (match) 12/149; ODIs: 275 matches, took 284 wickets and scored 2,110 runs, highest score 83, average 17.29, best bowling 5/7, average 31.50; T20Is: 33 matches, scored 205 runs, highest score 38, average 13.66, took 37 wickets, best bowling 4/20, average 19.45; only New Zealander to have taken 12 wickets in a Test on two occasions; eighth player in Test history to take 300 wickets and score 3000 runs 26 Aug. 2009; youngest player to have represented NZ in Test cricket; ranked first on ICC Player Rankings for One Day Bowlers, ranked 2nd and 10th for Test and One Day all-rounders, respectively 20 March 2008; currently NZ's leading ODI wicket-taker; stood down from the captaincy and retired from ODIs and T20Is after the ICC World Cup 2011; Officer, NZ Order of Merit. *Address:* c/o Northern District Cricket, PO Box 1347, Hamilton, New Zealand. *Telephone:* (7) 839-3783. *Fax:* (7) 839-5542. *E-mail:* info@ndcricket.co.nz. *Website:* www.ndcricket.co.nz.

VETTRIANO, Jack, OBE; British artist; b. (Jack Hoggan), 1951, Methil, Fife, Scotland; s. of William Hoggan; m. Gail Cormack 1981 (divorced); one adopted d.; fmr mining engineer; self-taught, full-time painter 1989–, adopting pseudonym from his mother's maiden name, Vettrino; Dr hc (Univ. of St Andrews) 2003, (Open Univ.) 2004. *Publications include:* Fallen Angels 1999, Lovers and Other Strangers 2000, Vettriano: A Life 2004. *Address:* c/o Heartbreak Publishing Ltd, 17 Bulstrode Street, London, W1U 2JH, England (office). *Telephone:* (20) 3219-5710 (office). *Fax:* (84) 5508-4629 (office). *E-mail:* info@heartbreakpublishing.com (office). *Website:* www.heart-break.co.uk (office); www.jackvettriano.com (office).

VEVERS, Stuart; British fashion designer; *Creative Director, Loewe;* b. 17 Nov. 1973; ed Univ. of Westminster, London; has worked as an accessories designer for Louis Vuitton, Calvin Klein, Givenchy and Bottega Veneta; also collaborates with Luella Bartley and Giles Deacon; Creative Dir, Mulberry, London 2005–08; Creative Dir, Loewe, Madrid 2008–; Accessory Designer of the Year Award, British Fashion Awards 2006. *Address:* Loewe, Carrera de San Jerónimo 15, 28014 Madrid, Spain (office). *Telephone:* (913) 606100 (office). *E-mail:* info@loewe.com (office). *Website:* www.loewe.com (office).

VEYRAT, Marc; French chef and restaurant owner; *Owner and Chef, L'Auberge de l'Eridan;* b. 1950; worked as shepherd before opening first restaurant aged 29; Owner and Chef, restaurants L'Auberge de l'Eridan, Annecy 1987–, La Ferme de Mon Père Megève 1999–2006 (both received three stars from Michelin and Gault Millau magazine 2003), Le Roland Garros 2005–. *Publications include:* Fou de saveurs 1994, Herbier gourmand 1997, La cuisine paysanne 1998, Quatre saisons (à la carte) 2000, L'herbier des montagnes: Tout savoir sur les plantes et les fleurs d'altitude 2000, Déguster les plantes sauvages 2003, L'encyclopédie culinaire du XXIe siècle 2003, L'herbier à croquer 2004, Le gibier en 80 recettes 2004. *Address:* La Maison de Marc Veyrat, 13 Vieille Route des Pensières, 74290 Veyrier du Lac, France (office). *Telephone:* 4-50-60-24-00 (office). *Fax:* 4-50-60-23-63 (office). *E-mail:* contact@marcveyrat.fr (office). *Website:* www.marcveyrat.fr (office).

VEZZAZ, Abderrahmane Ould Hamma, MBA; Mauritanian politician; b. 1956, Tidjikja; m.; six c.; ed Institut Supérieur de Commerce et d'Administration des Entreprises, Casablanca, Morocco and Univ. of Paris IX, France; Dir Overseas Trade Dept, Ministry of Trade 1992–97; Adviser on Public Sector, Office of the Prime Minister 1997–98; Minister of Rural Devt and the Environment Jan.–July 1998; also worked with Arab Bank for Econ. Devt in Africa (BADEA), Tech. Adviser to Prime Minister of Niger 2002–06; Exec. Dir private credit business 2006–07; Minister of the Economy and Finance 2007–08. *Address:* c/o Ministry of the Economy and Finance, BP 181, Nouakchott, Mauritania (office).

VIAL, Martin Marie-Charles François; French civil servant and economist; *Director-General, Europ'Assistance;* b. 8 Feb. 1954, Lyon; s. of René Vial and Thérèse Giuliani; m. Nelly Waldmann 1978; two s. two d.; ed Lycée Ampère, Inst. of Political Studies Paris; Prof. of Econ. and Reform Inst. of Tech. of Commerce Algiers 1977–78, Prof. of Finance Higher School of Applied Commercial Sciences 1978–82; with Office of Gen. Compatibility and Budget for External Services 1982–84, also Head; Head of Office of the Treasury and Financial Man. 1984–86; with Office of Banks and Nat. Financial Cos. 1986–88, tech. adviser Postal Sector 1988–89, charged with reform of Post, Telecommunications and Broadcasting (PTT) 1989–91; Jt Dir office of Minister for Post, Telecommunications and Space 1991, Dir Ministry of Post and Telecommunications 1992–93, Jt Dir for Space Equipment, Accommodation and Transport 1991, Dir 1991–92; Pres. Aéropostale 1993–97; Dir La Poste 1997–2000, Pres. 2000–02; mem. Cen. Cttee Union of Air Transport and Nat. Fed. of Aviation Trade 1994–96, Pres. 1996–; mem. Supervisory Bd Caisse Nat. de Prévoyance (CNP) 1998–, Vice-Pres. 2002–; Conseiller-Maître, Cour des Comptes 2002–; Dir-Gen. Europ'Assistance 2003–; Chevalier, Légion d'Honneur, Ordre National du Mérite. *Publication:* La Lettre et la toile 2000. *Leisure interests:* tennis, skiing. *Address:* Europ'Assistance Holding, 1 boulevard Haussmann, 75309 Paris Cedex 09, France (office). *E-mail:* webmaster@ europ-assistance.com (office). *Website:* www.europ-assistance.com (office).

VIAN, Dominique, Maitrise de Droit; French government official; *Special Advisor to President of Senat;* b. 25 Dec. 1944, Valence; m., three s.; ed Institut d'Etudes Politiques; Prefect of French Guyana 1997–99, Ardeche 1999–2002, Guadeloupe 2002–04, Alpes-Maritimes 2006–08; Deputy Special Rep. to UN Gen. Sec. in Kosovo 1999; Special Advisor to Pres. of Senat 2008–; Officier de la Légion d'honneur, Officier de l'Ordre National du Mérite, Officier du Mérite Maritime, Chevalier de l'Ordre des Palmes académiques, Chevalier du Mérite Agricole, Médaille d'honneur pour Actes de Courage et de Dévouement, Commdr de la Croise du Sud (Brazil), Chevalier de l'Ordre de Saint Charles (Monaco). *Address:* Senat Petit Luxembourg, 17 rue de Vaugirard, 75006 Paris Cedex 6 (office); Chemin du Sourcier, 83600 Fréjus, France (home). *Telephone:* 1-42-34-37-81 (office). *Fax:* 1-42-34-36-47 (office). *E-mail:* dominique.vian@senat.fr (office). *Website:* www.senat.fr (office).

VIAN, Giovanni Maria; Italian professor of patristic philology, journalist and editor; *Editor-in-Chief, L'Osservatore Romano;* s. of Nello Vian; m. Margarita Vian 1984 (died 2000); ed Virgilio Classical High School, Rome, Univ. of Rome 'La Sapienza', Inst. for Religious Sciences of Bologna; began to write for Catholic daily newspaper 1973; ed. and scientific adviser with Inst. of the Italian Encyclopedia 1976–; currently Univ. Prof. of Patristic Philology, Univ. of Rome 'La Sapienza'; part-time Prof., Vita-Salute San Raffaele Univ. of Milan; teaches History of Christian Tradition and Identity; mem. Papal Cttee of Historical Sciences 1999–; editorial writer for Avvenire and Giornale di Brescia; has written for various daily papers and periodicals, including L'Osservatore Romano 1977–87 and the fortnightly of the Catholic Univ. of the Sacred Heart Vita e Pensiero; Ed.-in-Chief L'Osservatore Romano 2007–; scholarship from Nat. Research Council 1976. *Publications:* more than 90 specialist studies, including Bibliotheca divina. Filologia e storia dei testi cristiani 2001, La donazione di Costantino 2004; ed. of anthology of writings by Montini with the title Carità intellettuale 2005. *Address:* L'Osservatore Romano, Tipografia Vaticana, Via del Pellegrino, 00120 Città del Vaticano, Rome, Italy (office). *Telephone:* (06) 69899390 (office). *Fax:* (06) 69883252 (office). *E-mail:* ornet@ossrom.va (office). *Website:* www.vatican.va/news_services/ or/home_ita.html (office).

VIANA, Marcelo, PhD; Brazilian mathematician and academic; *Professor of Mathematics and Deputy Director, Instituto de Matemática Pura e Aplicada (IMPA);* b. 4 March 1962, Rio de Janeiro; ed Univ. of Porto, Inst. of Pure and Applied Math.; Research Asst, Univ. of Porto 1984–91, Asst Prof. 1991–93; Research Asst, Instituto de Matemática Pura e Aplicada 1987–91, Asst Prof. 1991–92, Assoc. Prof. 1992–97, Prof. of Math. 1997–, Deputy Dir 2004–, Chair. for Scientific Activities 1996–2004; Chair. Cttee for Math. and Statistics, CAPES 2005–07; Forum for Research and Grad. Studies in Brazil 2008–09, Regional Office for Latin America and the Caribbean, Acad. of Sciences for the Developing World (TWAS) 2009–10; Scientific Coordinator, Math. Union of Latin America and the Caribbean 2001–; mem. Brazilian Math. Soc. 1987– (Vice-Pres. 2009–11), Ameri-

can Math. Soc. 1994–, Brazilian Acad. of Sciences 1997–, Third World Acad. of Sciences 2000–, Portuguese Acad. of Sciences and Letters 2006–; Elected Mem. Exec. Cttee Int. Math. Union, 2007–10; Corresp. mem. Portuguese Acad. of Sciences 2006–, Chilean Acad. of Sciences 2009–; mem. Editorial Bd Dynamics and Stability of Systems 1995–99, Nonlinearity 1996–2003, Ergodic Theory & Dynamical Systems 1998–, Dynamical Systems: An International Journal 1999–, Portugaliae Mathematica 1999–, Discrete and Continuous Dynamical Systems 1999–, Journal of Stochastics and Dynamics 2000–, Nonlinear Differential Equations and Applications 2001–08, Dynamics of Partial Differential Equations 2004–; mem. Advisory Bd Universidade do Minho 2009–11; Calouste Gulbenkian Foundation Fellowship 1988–90, Guggenheim Foundation Fellowship 1993–94; Invited Prof. Coll. de France, Paris 2002; Santaló Distinguished Lecturer, Univ. Complutense, Madrid 2005; Grand Cross of the Order of Scientific Merit 2000; Best Undergraduate in Science, António José de Almeida Foundation, Porto 1984, Third World Acad. of Sciences Award 1998, Math. Union of Latin America and the Caribbean Award 2000, Ramanujan Prize, Int. Centre for Theoretical Physics 2005, Prize Univ. of Coimbra 2007. *Publications include:* numerous articles in professional journals. *Address:* Instituto de Matemática Pura e Aplicada, Estrada Dona Castorina, 110, Jardim Botânico, 22460-320 Rio de Janeiro, Brazil (office). *Telephone:* (21) 2529-5114 (office). *Fax:* (21) 2529-5019 (office). *E-mail:* viana@impa.br (office). *Website:* www.impa.br/~viana (office).

VIAR OLLOQUI, Javier, BPharm; Spanish arts administrator; *Director, Bilbao Fine Arts Museum;* b. 1946, Bilbao; poet, novelist, art critic and historian; mem. Bd Bilbao Fine Arts Museum late 1980s–, Dir 2002–; tenured academic at Bilbao, Royal Acad. of Fine Arts of St Isabel of Hungary, Seville 2010–; fmr mem. Acquisitions Advisory Bd, Guggenheim Bilbao; fmr mem. Dept of Culture, Basque Govt; organizer of numerous int. and nat. exhbns; Chevalier des Arts et des Lettres 2008; Euskadi Literature Award, City of Irun Short Story Prize 1992. *Address:* Museo de Bellas Artes de Bilbao, Museo Plaza 2, 48009 Bilbao, Spain (office). *Telephone:* (94) 4396060 (office). *Fax:* (94) 4396145 (office). *E-mail:* info@ museobilbao.com (office). *Website:* www.museobilbao.com (office).

VIARDO, Vladimir Vladimirovich, DJur; Russian/American concert pianist and academic; *Professor and Artist-in-Residence, College of Music, University of North Texas;* b. 14 Nov. 1949; ed Moscow State Conservatory; Asst Prof., later Prof., Moscow State Conservatory 1975–; resident in USA 1988–; Prof. and Artist-in-Residence, Coll. of Music, Univ. of N Texas 1988–; Visiting Prof., Moscow State Conservatory 1998–2000; Grand Prix, Marguerite Long Int. Competition, Gold Medal and 1st Prize, Van Clibern Int. Competition, USA 1973. *Performances:* played with conductors Mehta, Kitayenko, Maazel, Spivakov, Comissiona, Penderecki; toured in major European, N American and Canadian cities, Asia and S Africa, Israel, Cen. and S America. *Address:* UNT College of Music, PO Box 311367, Denton, TX 76203-1367, USA (office); c/o Concerts de Valmalete, 7 rue Hoche, 92300 Levallois Perret, France (office). *Telephone:* (940) 565-4653 (office); 1-47-59-87-59 (office). *Fax:* (940) 565-2002 (office); 1-47-59-87-50 (office). *E-mail:* vladimir.viardo@unt.edu (office). *Website:* www.music.unt.edu/bio/viardo.shtml (office); www.valmalete.com (office).

VICARI, Andrew; British artist; b. 20 April 1938, Port Talbot, Wales; s. of Cav. Vittorio Vicari and Itala Bertani; ed Slade School of Art and Univ. Coll., London; works held in many perm. and pvt. collections, including Dallas Museum of Fine Arts, Nat. Library of Wales, Museum of Tel-Aviv, Contemporary Arts Soc. of GB, Columbus Museum of Fine Arts, USA, Pezzo Pozzoli Museum, Milan, Petit Palais Museum of Modern Art, Geneva; official painter of King and Govt of Saudi Arabia; Fellow, London Zoological Soc.; Freedom of the City of London 2002, Liveryman of Wales 2002, Liveryman of the Guilds of London 2002; Chevalier, Order of Merit (Monaco), Brig. d'honneur, Compagnie Républicaine de Sécurité (France); European Beaux Arts Prize 1995. *Publications:* Triumph of the Bedouin 1984, The Truth is Not Enough (autobiog.) 2003. *Leisure interests:* squash, salsa, food and wine. *Address:* c/o The East India Club, 16 St James's Square, London, SW1Y 4LH, England. *Telephone:* 7976-310352 (mobile) (office). *Fax:* 7092-006234 (office). *E-mail:* reception@eastindiaclub.co.uk (office). *Website:* www.andrew-vicari.com.

VICKERS, Sir John Stuart, Kt, FBA, MA, DPhil; British economist; *Warden, All Souls College, Oxford;* b. 7 July 1958, Eastbourne, Sussex, England; s. of Aubrey Vickers and Kay Vickers; m. Maureen Freed 1991; one s. two d.; ed Eastbourne Grammar School and Oriel Coll., Oxford; Fellow, All Souls Coll. Oxford 1979–84, 1991–2008, Warden 2008–; Shell UK Oil 1979–81; Roy Harrod Fellow, Nuffield Coll. Oxford 1984–90; Drummond Prof. of Political Economy, Univ. of Oxford 1991–2008; Chief Economist, Bank of England 1998–2000; Dir Gen./Chair. Office of Fair Trading 2000–05; Pres. Royal Econ. Soc. 2007–10; Chair. Ind. Comm. on Banking 2010–11; Visiting Lecturer, Princeton Univ., USA 1988, Harvard Univ., USA 1989, 1990; Visiting Prof., London Business School 1996; Fellow, Econometric Soc. 1998–; Hon. DLitt (Univ. of East Anglia) 2001; Pres.'s Medal, British Acad. 2012. *Publications:* Privatization: An Economic Analysis (co-author) 1988, Regulatory Reform (co-author) 1994; articles on competition, regulation etc. *Address:* Office of the Warden, All Souls College, Oxford, OX1 4AL, England (office). *Website:* www.all-souls.ox.ac.uk (office).

VICKERS, Jon, CC, RA; Canadian singer (tenor); b. 29 Oct. 1926, Prince Albert, Saskatchewan; s. of William Vickers and Myrle Mossip; m. 1st Henrietta Outerbridge 1953 (died 1991); three s. two d.; m. 2nd Judith Stewart 1993; began career as concert and opera singer in Canada; joined Royal Opera House, Covent Garden (London) 1957; sang at Bayreuth Festival, Vienna State Opera, San Francisco, Chicago Lyric Opera, Metropolitan Opera, La Scala, Milan, Paris Opera, Boston, Buenos Aires, Athens, Ottawa, Houston, Dallas, Hamburg, Berlin, Munich, Athens Festival, Salzburg Festival, Festival of Orange, Tanglewood Festival, Rio de Janeiro; Hon. LLD (Sask.); Hon. CLD (Bishop's Univ.); Hon. MusD (Brandon, Univ. of Western Ont.); Hon. LLD (Guelph); Hon. Civ. LD (Laval); Hon. DMus (Univ. of Ill.); Critics Award, London 1978, Grammy Award 1979. *Films include:* Carmen, Pagliacci, Norma, Otello. *Recordings:* Messiah, Otello, Aida, Die Walküre, Samson and Delilah, Fidelio, Italian Arias, Verdi Requiem, Peter Grimes, Das Lied von der Erde, Les Troyens, Tristan und Isolde; Enoch Arden (poem by Alfred Lord Tennyson, piano played by Mark Ammelain). *Address:* PO Box 290 WKBX, Warwick, WK 03, Bermuda (home).

VICTOR, Edward (Ed), MLitt; British literary agent; b. 9 Sept. 1939, New York, USA; s. of the late Jack Victor and the late Lydia Victor; m. 1st Michelene Dinah Samuels 1963 (divorced); two s.; m. 2nd Carol Lois Ryan; one s.; ed Dartmouth Coll., USA, Pembroke Coll., Cambridge; Arts Book Ed., then Editorial Dir Weidenfeld & Nicolson 1964–67; Editorial Dir Jonathan Cape Ltd 1967–71; Sr Ed. Alfred A. Knopf Inc., New York 1972–73, literary agent and Dir John Farquharson Ltd 1974–76; Founding Ed. Victor Agency 1977; mem. Council Aids Crisis Trust 1986–98; Vice-Chair. Almeida Theatre 1994–2002 (Dir 1993–2002); Trustee, The Arts Foundation 1991–2004. *Publications include:* The Obvious Diet 2001. *Leisure interests:* golf, tennis, travel, opera. *Address:* Ed Victor Ltd, 6 Bayley Street, Bedford Square, London, WC1B 3HE (office); 10 Cambridge Gate, Regents Park, London, NW1 4JX, England (home). *Telephone:* (20) 7304-4100 (office); (20) 7224-3030 (home). *Fax:* (20) 7304-4111 (office); (20) 7935-3096 (home). *E-mail:* ed@edvictor.com. *Website:* www.edvictor.com (office).

VICTORIA INGRID ALICE DÉSIRÉE, HRH Crown Princess (Duchess of Västergötland); Swedish; b. 14 July 1977, Stockholm; d. of HM King Carl XVI Gustaf and HM Queen Silvia of Sweden; m. Daniel Westling (HRH Prince Daniel, Duke of Västergötland) 2010; one d., Princess Estelle Silvia Ewa Mary, Duchess of Östergötland; ed Enskilda Gymnasiet, Stockholm, Université Catholique de l'Ouest, Angers, France, Yale Univ., USA and Nat. Defence Coll., Stockholm; internships at Embassy in Washington, DC 1999, UN, New York 2002, Swedish Trade Council, Berlin and Paris 2002; has completed study programmes at Offices of the Swedish Govt and the Swedish Int. Devt Co-operation Agency; participated in state visits to study int. aid efforts; Mem. with Collar, Royal Order of the Seraphim 1995, Royal Family Order of King Carl XVI Gustaf of Sweden, HM King Carl XVI Gustaf 50th Anniversary Medal 1996, Commemorative Ruby Jubilee Medal of HM The King 2013; more than 20 foreign decorations. *Leisure interests:* nature and outdoor pursuits. *Address:* c/o Information and Press Department, Kungliga Slottet, Stockholm 111 30, Sweden. *E-mail:* info@royalcourt.se. *Website:* www.royalcourt.se.

VIDAL, HE Cardinal Ricardo; Philippine ecclesiastic; b. 6 Feb. 1931, Mogpog, Marinduque; s. of Fructuoso Vidal and Natividad Jamin; ordained priest 1956; consecrated Bishop (Titular Church of Claterna) 1971; Archbishop of Lipa 1973–82, of Cebu 1982–2010 (retd); cr. Cardinal 1985, apptd Cardinal-Priest of Ss. Pietro e Paolo a Via Ostiense; Chair. Episcopal Comm. on Clergy; mem. Congregation for the Evangelization of Peoples, Congregation for Catholic Educ., Pontifical Council for Pastoral Assistance to Health Care Workers; Pres. Pontificio Collegio Filippino 2000; Bailiff Grand Cross of Honour and Devotion of the Sovereign Order of Malta 2002; Dr hc (Univ. of Santo Tomas) 1985, (San Carlos Univ.) 1995, Hon. DHumLitt (Manuel S. Enverga Foundation Univ.) 1990, (Ateneo de Manila Univ.) 1993; Univ. of Southern Philippines Rizal Peace Award 2002. *Leisure interests:* walking, classical music, gardening. *Address:* Chancery, PO Box 52, Cardinal Rosales Pastoral Center, Corner P Gomez and P. Burgos Streets, Cebu City 6000, Philippines. *Telephone:* (32) 2533382. *Fax:* (32) 2544458. *E-mail:* rcv@cebu.pworld.net.ph (office).

VIDAL SALINAS, Francisco; Chilean politician; b. 20 Sept. 1953; ed Univ. of Chile; Prof. of History and Geography, Univ. of Chile; Sec., Faculty of Econ. Sciences, Univ. Central de Chile 1993–99, Dean, Faculty of Econ. and Admin. Sciences 1998–99; Exec. Dir Fundación Chile 21 1994–2000; mem. Partido por la Democracia 1987–; consultant to Higher Educ. Council and Higher Educ. Div., Ministry of Educ. 1993; Councillor Metropolitan Regional Govt 1993–2000; Under-Sec. for Regional and Admin. Devt, Ministry of the Interior 2000–03; Minister, Sec.-Gen. of the Govt 2003–05, 2007–09; Minister of the Interior 2005–06, of Nat. Defence 2009–10; Pres. Directorate, Televisión Nacional de Chile 2006–07; Dir School of Govt, Univ. Alberto Hurtado 2006–. *Address:* c/o Ministry of National Defence, Villavicencio 364, 22°, Edif. Diego Portales, Santiago, Chile (office).

VIDEANU, Adrian; Romanian business executive and politician; *Vice-President, Democratic Liberal Party (Partidul Democrat-Liberal);* b. 1 June 1962, Crevenicu, Teleorman Co.; m. Moriţa Videanu; one s. one d.; ed Faculty of Transport, Bucharest Polytechnic Inst.; business exec. in marble and granite industry; Head of Section, SUT Ploieşti 1987–90; Chair. CA Titan Mar SA 2003–04; Deputy (Democratic Liberal Party (Partidul Democrat-Liberal—PD-L)) for Teleorman Co. 1990–2003, Vice-Pres. Budget Cttee (Finance-Banks) 2000; Chair. Nat. Youth, PD-L 1992–96, Exec. Sec. PD-L 1996–2000, Vice-Pres. and Spokesman for PD-L, responsible for matters of image and media relations 2001–03, currently a Vice-Pres.; Minister of State and Deputy Prime Minister 2004–05; Mayor of Bucharest 2005–08; Minister of the Economy, Trade and the Business Environment 2008–10. *Address:* Partidul Democrat Liberal, 011825 Bucharest, Sector 1, Al. Modrogan 1, Romania (office). *Telephone:* (21) 2303701 (office); (21) 2302202 (office). *Fax:* (21) 2301625 (office). *E-mail:* contact@videanu.ro; office@pd.ro (office). *Website:* www.pd-l.ro (office); www.videanu.ro.

VIDEGARAY CASO, Luis, BA, PhD; Mexican economist and politician; *Secretary of Finance and Public Credit;* b. 10 Aug. 1968, México City; ed Instituto Tecnológico Autónomo de México (ITAM), Massachusetts Inst. of Tech., USA; fmr Lecturer, ITAM and Ibero-American Univ., Mexico City; mem. Partido Revolucionario Institucional (PRI) 1987–; Adviser to Sec. of Finance 1992–94, to Sec. of Energy 1996; Dir of Public Finance, Protego Asesores (bank) 1998–2005; Regional Sec. of Finance, Planning and Admin, State of Mexico 2005–09; Nat. Co-ordinator, Secr. of State for Finance 2008–09; mem. Cámara Federal de Diputados (Parl.) 2009–11, Pres. Budget and Public Accounts Debt Comm. 2009–11; PRI Pres., State of Mexico 2011–12; Gen. Co-ordinator of political campaign of Eruviel Avila Villegas (Gov., State of Mexico) 2011, of presidential campaign of Enrique Peña Nieto (Pres. of Mexico) 2012; Co-ordinator of Public Policy and Gen. Co-ordinator of Govt Transition Team 2012; Sec. (Minister) of Finance and Public Credit 2012–; Hon. Mention from ITAM, Nat. Econs Award, Banco Nacional de México 1995. *Address:* Secretariat of State for Finance and Public Credit, Palacio Nacional, Plaza de la Constitución, Col. Centro, Del. Cuauhtémoc, 06000 México DF, Mexico (office). *Telephone:* (55) 3688-2000 (office). *E-mail:* secretario@hacienda.gob.mx (office). *Website:* www.hacienda.gob.mx (office).

VIDOKLE, Anton; Russian artist and editor; *Founding Director, e-flux;* b. 1965, Moscow; arrived in USA with parents 1981; Founding Dir e-flux (int. network reaching more than 50,000 visual art professionals daily through website, e-mail list and special projects), Organizer, with Julieta Aranda, e-flux video rental (travelled to numerous insts. including Portikus, Frankfurt, KunstWerk, Berlin, Extra City, Antwerp, Carpenter Center, Harvard Univ., Cambridge, Mass, and others); has produced projects such as Next Documenta Should Be Curated By An Artist, Do it, Utopia Station poster project, and organized An Image Bank for Everyday Revolutionary Life and Martha Rosler Library; set up ind. project in Berlin called Unitednationsplaza (12-month project involving more than 100 artists, writers, philosophers and diverse audiences); co-f., with Julieta Aranda, a time bank for artists, curators, writers and others in the arts to exchange their time and skills 2008, has nearly 4,000 members and operates branches in The Hague, Moscow, Berlin, Frankfurt and other cities; co-f. imprint, with the Sternberg Press, Berlin, that publishes a series of paperback readers consisting of monographic publs and thematic compilations of essays 2008. *Films and videos on contemporary art:* A Crime Against Art (directed by Hila Peleg) 2008, A Guiding Light (with Liam Gillick) 2010, New York Conversations 2011. *Publications:* essays and texts in various publications including October, Frieze and Aprior, as well as numerous books and catalogues. *Address:* e-flux, 311 East Broadway, New York, NY 10002, USA (office). *E-mail:* info@e-flux.com (office). *Website:* www.e-flux.com (office); www.unitednationsplaza.org.

VIEGAS FILHO, José; Brazilian diplomatist and politician; b. 14 Oct. 1942, Campo Grande; s. of José Viegas and Dirce Bastos Viegas; m. Erika Stockholm de Viegas; one s. two d.; ed Diplomatic Acad. Instituto Rio Branco; joined Instituto Rio Branco 1964; Deputy Consul, New York 1969–73; Embassy Sec., Santiago 1973–78; mem. Policy Planning Unit, Ministry of External Relations 1979–84; Chargé d'affaires a.i. in Rome 1984–85, Minister-Counsellor and Chargé d'affaires a.i. in Paris 1985–86, in Havana 1986–91; Head of Multilateral Dept 1992, of Policy Planning Unit 1992–93, Undersecretary-Gen. for Policy Planning 1993–94; Amb. to Denmark 1995–98, to Peru 1998–2001, to Russia 2001–02, to Spain 2005–09, to Italy 2009–12; Minister of Defence 2003–04 (resgnd); Prof. of Brazilian Foreign Policy, Instituto Rio Branco 1982–83, mem. Examination Bd, High Studies for Diplomats 1992–94, Pres. Examination Bd, Master's Degree for Diplomats 2005–07, mem. Comm. for Examination of the Course of High Studies, Instituto Rio Branco 1992–94, Pres. Comm. for Examination of Masters' Theses 2005–07; Grand Cross of Rio Branco, Grand Cross for Merit in Defence, Grand Cross for Mil. Merit, Grand Cross for Naval Merit, Grand Cross for Aeronautical Merit, Grand Cross for Mil. Judicial Merit, Grand Cross of the Order of the Sun (Peru), Grand Cross, Order of the Dannebrog (Denmark). *Leisure interests:* cosmology, translation. *Address:* c/o Embassy of Brazil, Piazza Navona 14, 00186 Rome, Italy (office).

VIEHBACHER, Christopher A.; Canadian/German business executive; *CEO, Sanofi SA;* b. 26 March 1960, Ottawa; m.; three c.; ed Queens Univ., Ottawa; began career at PriceWaterhouseCoopers; Chief Financial Accountant, Wellcome GmbH, Germany 1988, Finance Dir 1989–93, Pres. and CEO Burroughs Wellcome Inc., Canada 1993–95, Vice-Pres. Glaxo Wellcome France 1995–96, Gen. Man. 1996–97, Chair. and Man. Dir 1997–2003, Pres. US Pharmaceuticals, GlaxoSmithKline 2003–08, Pres. North American Pharmaceuticals May–Dec. 2008, mem. Bd of Dirs GlaxoSmithKline Jan.–Sept. 2008; CEO Sanofi SA 2008– (name changed to Sanofi May 2011); Chair. Genzyme 2011–; mem. Bd of Dirs The Pharmaceutical Research and Mfrs of America (PhRMA), Chair. 2010–12; Chair. CEO Roundtable on Cancer 2011–; Chevalier, Légion d'honneur 2008. *Address:* Sanofi SA, 174 avenue de France, 75013 Paris Cedex 13, France (office). *Telephone:* 1-53-77-42-23 (office). *Fax:* 1-53-77-42-65 (office). *E-mail:* info@sanofi.com (office). *Website:* www.sanofi.com (office).

VIEIRA, Meredith Louise; American television broadcaster and journalist; b. 30 Dec. 1953, East Providence, RI; d. of Edwin Vieira and Mary Elsie Vieira; m. Prof. Richard M. Cohen 1986; two s. one d.; ed Tufts Univ.; began career as news announcer for WORC Radio, Worcester, Mass 1975; started in TV working as local reporter and anchor at WJAR-TV Providence; later worked in newsroom at WCBS-TV, New York City; first came to nat. recognition as CBS reporter based in Chicago Bureau, later became a corresp. for CBS news-magazine shows including West 57th and 60 Minutes, then Co-anchor of CBS Morning News; corresp. for ABC news-magazine show Turning Point; Moderator and Co-host, The View 1997–2006; Host Lifetime's Intimate Portrait 1999–; Host, Who Wants to Be a Millionaire? 2002–13; Co-anchor, The Today Show (NBC) 2006–11, now contrib. to NBC News shows; seven Emmy Awards for her work on West 57th, 60 Minutes, Turning Point and Daytime Emmy for Outstanding Game Show Host 2005, P.T. Barnum Award, Tufts Univ. 2006, ranked by Forbes magazine amongst The World's 100 Most Powerful Women (69th) 2006, (55th) 2007, (61st) 2008, (40th) 2010. *Address:* NBC News, 30 Rockefeller Plaza, New York, NY 10112, USA (office).

VIÉNOT, Marc, LèsL; French banker; *Honorary Chairman, Société Générale, Paris;* b. 1 Nov. 1928, Paris; s. of the late Jacques Viénot and of Henriette Brunet; m. Christiane Regnault 1953; two s. two d.; ed Nat. Inst. of Political Studies and Ecole Nat. d'Admin.; Inspector of Finance 1955; special envoy to Cabinet of Minister of Econ. and Finance April–June 1957, to Cabinet of Minister of Finance, Econ. and Planning June–Nov. 1957; special envoy to cabinet of Pres. of French Parl. 1957–58; special envoy to Treasury Div. July 1958; Chair. Study Cttee OECD 1961–65; Sec. to Bd of Econ. and Social Devt Fund 1963–65; Under-Sec. Treasury Div. 1965; Head, Financial Activities Service, Treasury Div. 1967; Minister (Financial Counsellor), French Embassies in USA and Canada and Dir IBRD and IMF 1970–73; Deputy Gen. Man. Société Générale, Paris 1973, Gen. Man. 1977–86, Chair. and CEO 1986–97, now Hon. Chair, mem. Bd of Dirs –2007; Interim Pres. Alcatel Alsthom April–July 1995; Pres. Paris Europlace 1998–; Chair. Bd Aventis; Dir Alcatel, Ciments Français, Chemin de fer franco-éthiopien, Electricité de France, Canal Plus, SNECMA, Vivendi Universal; mem. Supervisory Bd Compagnie bancaire, Carnaud Metalbox; mem. and fmr Vice-Pres. French Banks Asscn; Officier, Légion d'honneur; Commdr, Ordre nat. du Mérite. *Address:* 4 avenue Raymond Poincaré, 75116 Paris, France.

VIERA GALLO QUESNEY, José Antonio; Chilean politician; b. 2 Dec. 1943, Santiago; m. María Teresa Chadwick; three c.; ed Univ. Católica de Chile; fmr Prof. of Political Theory, Univ. Católica de Chile; Under-Sec. for Justice during Presidency of Salvador Allende; exiled in Italy following mil. coup 1973; f. Chileamerica magazine (published in Rome during exile); fmr adviser to UNESCO, FAO and World Council of Churches; fmr Deputy Sec.-Gen. Institutional

Documentation Service, Rome; Dir Centro de Estudios Sociales 1983–2001; returned to Chile 1985; mem. Chamber of Deputies 1990–98, Pres. 1990–93, mem. Internal Order, Constitutional, Legislation and Justice Perm. Comms, Defence Comm; Senator for Octava 1998–2004, currently Pres. Senate Human Rights, Nationality and Citizenship Comm; Sec.-Gen. of the Presidency 2007–10; mem. Cen. Cttee Partido Socialista. *Address:* c/o Office of the Minister, Secretary-General of the Presidency, Palacio de la Moneda, Santiago, Chile (office).

VIERMETZ, Kurt F.; German banker and stock exchange official; b. 27 April 1939, Augsburg; m. Felicity Viermetz; began career as foreign exchange trader with Deutsche Bank AG, Frankfurt 1960–65; Asst Treasurer, JP Morgan & Co. Inc., Frankfurt 1965–70, Vice-Pres. Paris Br. 1970–75, involved in est. of Saudi Int. Bank Ltd, London 1975–77, Vice-Pres. JP Morgan, New York, responsible for foreign exchange and Euro treasury world-wide 1977–80, Sr Vice-Pres. JP Morgan, Frankfurt, responsible for German and Continental European business 1980–85, Treas. JP Morgan & Co. Inc., New York 1985–90, Vice-Chair. Man. Bd and Supervisory Bd, New York 1990–2000, mem. Bd Dirs 1998–2000; Chair. Supervisory Bd Bayerische Hypo- und Vereinsbank AG, Munich 1999–2002, Vice-Chair. Jan.–Dec. 2003; Chair. Supervisory Bd Hypo Real Estate Holding AG, Munich 2003–09 (resgnd); Chair. Supervisory Bd, Deutsche Börse AG 2005–08 (resgnd); mem. Supervisory Bd Hoechst AG, Frankfurt 1990–98 (also Chair. Bd Finance Cttee), Advisory Bd Metro Co., Zug, Switzerland 1990–98, Supervisory Bd Veba AG, Düsseldorf 1993–2003, Supervisory Bd E.ON AG, Düsseldorf 1993–2003, Supervisory Bd ERGO Versicherungs AG, Düsseldorf 2003–, Supervisory Bd E.ON-Ruhrgas AG, Essen 2003–05, KfW IPEX-Bank GmbH 2008–; Dir (non-exec.) Grosvenor Estate Holdings Ltd, London, UK 1996–2004; Chair. Int. Capital Markets Advisory Bd Cttee, New York Stock Exchange 1995–2004; Chair. Bd of Overseers, Univ. of Augsburg 2002–; Founder and mem. Man. Bd, Förderkreis Schaezlerpalais e.V.; mem. Bd Int. Advisory Cttee Fed. Reserve Bank of New York 1995–, American Council of Germany, New York 1987–; Trustee New York Philharmonic Soc. 1988–2002, Haniel Foundation, Duisberg 1998–, Vereins Atlantik-Brücke, American Acad. in Berlin, Berlin and New York; Hon. Citizen of City of Augsburg; Order of Merit, Fed. Repub. of Germany 2006, Bavarian Order of Merit 2007. *Address:* c/o Deutsche Börse AG, Neue Börsenstrasse 1, 60485 Frankfurt, Germany.

VIGENIN, Kristian; Bulgarian politician; *Minister of Foreign Affairs;* b. 12 June 1975, Sofia; m.; two c.; ed Univ. of Nat. and World Economy, Sofia, courses in Belgium, Sweden and USA; worked at Ministry of Finance 1999–2001; elected to Nat. Council of Bulgarian Socialist Party (BSP) 2000–, began at Foreign Policy and Int. Relations Dept of Supreme Council of Bulgarian Socialist Party (BSP) 2001, Head 2003–10, mem. Exec. Bureau responsible for Int. Relations from 2001, later mem. Exec. Bureau and Sec. Supreme Council for Foreign Affairs and Int. Relations, Chair. Foreign Affairs and Int. Relations Cttee, Nat. Council of BSP 2005–08, took part in PES Presidium and coordinated work of PES network for Southeastern Europe from 2006, Chair. Council on Foreign Affairs, Nat. Council of BSP 2010–; mem. Parl. 2005–07, mem. leadership of Parl. Group of Coalition for Bulgaria as Sec. for Int. Affairs, participated in work of Parl. Cttees on Foreign Affairs and on European Integration; observer in European Parl. 2005–07, leader of six-mem. del. of Coalition for Bulgaria, mem. European Parl. 2007–13, Vice-Pres. Party of European Socialists Group 2007–13, Co-Chair. Parl. Ass. Euronest platform for inter-parl. co-operation with Eastern Partnership countries 2009–13, mem. Conf. of Presidents of Del., mem. numerous dels and cttees, Coordinator Group of Progressive Alliance of Socialists & Democrats Foreign Affairs Cttee 2009–12; Minister of Foreign Affairs 2013–. *Address:* Ministry of Foreign Affairs, 1040 Sofia, ul. Al. Zhendov 2, Bulgaria (office). *Telephone:* (2) 948-29-99 (office). *Fax:* (2) 971-36-20 (office). *E-mail:* info@mfa.bg (office). *Website:* www.mfa .government.bg (office).

VIGNERON, Luc; French business executive; *Chairman and CEO, Thales SA;* b. 11 Oct. 1954, Senegal; m. Annie Hainneville 1976; three c.; ed Ecole Polytechnique, Ecole Nationale des Ponts et Chaussées; began career with Harbour and Shore Authority for Boulogne-sur-Mer and Calais, Ministry of Infrastructure and Territorial Devt 1978–82; Adviser, Budget Dept, Ministry of Economy, Finance and Budget 1982–84; Special Adviser, Finance Dept, Compagnie Générale d'Electricité (now Alcatel-Lucent) 1984–86, Head of Operations, Alcatel Telspace 1986, Dir, Alcatel CIT Distribution Product Lines, Dir of Strategy and New Businesses, Alcatel RSD 1990–91, Man. Dir, Alcatel Radiotéléphone 1991–94, Exec. Vice Pres., Alcatel Mobile Communication Group 1994–95, Dir of Strategy, Alcatel Alsthom 1995–98; CEO Giat Industries (renamed Nexter 2006) 1998–2001, Chair. and CEO 2001–09; Chair. and CEO Thales SA 2009–; Chair. GICAT 2002–06, CIDEF (advisory council) 2004–06. *Address:* Thales SA, 45 rue de Villiers, 92526 Neuilly-sur-Seine Cedex, France (office). *Telephone:* 1-57-77-80-00 (office). *Fax:* 1-57-77-86-59 (office). *E-mail:* info@thalesgroup.com (office). *Website:* www.thalesgroup.com (office).

VIGNOLI, Ana María; Uruguayan politician and fmr social worker; *Minister of Social Development;* b. 27 July 1945, Montevideo; two c.; lived in exile in Sweden 1973–84; worked for Comisión por El Reencuentro de los Uruguayos 1984–89; social worker, Instituto Nacional del Menor (child protection agency) 1989; joined Montevideo Municipal Authority 1990, becoming Dir Personnel Man. Div. 2005–09; Minister of Social Devt 2010–; mem. Frente Amplio. *Address:* Ministry of Social Development, Avda 18 de Julio 1453, esq. Dr Javier Barrios Amorín, 2°, 11200 Montevideo, Uruguay (office). *Telephone:* (2) 4000302 (office). *Fax:* (2) 4000302 (office). *E-mail:* ministra@mides.gub.uy (office). *Website:* www.mides.gub .uy (office).

VĪĶE-FREIBERGA, Vaira, MA, PhD; Latvian psychologist and fmr head of state; *Chairman, High Level Group on Media Freedom and Pluralism, European Commission;* b. (Vaira Vīķe) 1 Dec. 1937, Rīga; m. Imants Freibergs 1960; one s. one d.; ed Univ. of Toronto, McGill Univ., Canada; Prof. of Psychology, Univ. of Montreal, Canada 1965–98, Prof. Emer. 1998–; Vice-Chair. Science Council of Canada 1984–89; Dir Latvian Inst., Rīga 1998–99; Pres. of Latvia 1999–2007; fmr Pres. Canadian Psychological Asscn; Pres. Social Science Fed. of Canada; Pres. Asscn for Advancement of Baltic Studies, USA; Pres. Acad. des Lettres et des Sciences Humaines, RSC; mem. Latvian Acad. of Sciences, Royal Belgian Acad., Council of Women Leaders 1999–; mem. Bd of Dirs Club de Madrid 2010–, Bibliotheca Alexandrina 2010–; cand. for UN Sec.-Gen. 2006, for Presidency of EC

2009; Vice-Chair. Reflection Group on the Future of Europe 2020–30, European Council, Chair. High Level Group on Media Freedom and Pluralism, EC 2011–; Chair. Review Panel, European Research Council 2009; lectures and seminars on democracy, truth and reconciliation, woman's rights, future of Europe in USA, Canada, Latvia and numerous countries; Prof. Emer., Univ. of Montreal 1998, Latvia Univ. 2010; thirty four Orders of Merit including Three Star Order of Latvia 1995, Legion of Honour, France 2001, Dame of GCB 2006, Officer of the National Order of Québec, Canada 2006; Hon. LLD (Queen's Univ., Canada) 1991, Hon. DLitt (Victoria Univ., Toronto) 2000, Hon. DSci (McGill Univ.) 2002, Dr hc (Latvia) 2000, (Vytautas Magnus Univ., Lithuania) 2002, (Astana, Kazakhstan) 2004, (Baku, Azerbaijan) 2005, (Tbilisi) 2005, (Yerevan) 2005, (Ottawa) 2006, (Liège, Belgium) 2006, (Odense, Denmark) 2007, (Dalhousie, Halifax) 2007, (Dublin) 2007, (Toronto) 2008, (York, Toronto) 2008, (Georgia) 2011; numerous prizes include Marcel-Vincent Prize 1992, Pierre Chauveau Medal 1995, American Acad. of Achievement Gold Plate 2000, awards from Georgetown Univ., USA 2002, Free Univ. of Berlin 2003, Grand Prize of Folklore, Ministry of Culture, Latvia 2003, Forbes Executive Women's Forum Trailblazer Award 2005, Medal of the American Jewish Cttee 2005, Baltic Freedom Award 2005, Hannah Arendt Prize for Political Thought 2005, Coudenhove-Kalergi Foundation Europa Prize, Pan-Europa Union 2006, Baltic Statesmanship Award of the US-Baltic Foundation 2006, J.W. Goethe Univ. Medal and Walter Hallstein Prize 2006, UN FAO Ceres Medal 2007, Von Hayek Medal 2009, Konrad Adenauer Prize 2010, Ladies First Int. Prize 2011. *Publications include:* La Frequence Lexicale des Mots au Québec 1974, Latvian Sun-Songs (co-author) 1988, Linguistic and Poetics of Latvian Folk Songs 1989, On the Amber Mountain 1993, Against the Current 1993, The Cosmological Sun 1997, The Chronological Sun 1999, The Warm Sun 2002, The Luminous Sun 2011, Latvian Sun Song Melodies 2005, Logique de la Poésie 2007, Latvian Culture and Identity 2010, The Meteorological Sun 2011; contrib. of more than 400 articles and papers. *Leisure interests:* reading, crosswords, nature walks, gardening, swimming, and needlework. *Address:* Chancery of the President, Pils lauk. 3, Rīga 1900, Latvia (office). *Telephone:* 6709-2191 (office). *Fax:* 6709-2157 (office). *E-mail:* vvf@ president.lv (office); daina.lasmane@president.lv (office). *Website:* www.vvf.lv (office).

VIKTYUK, Roman Grigoryevich; Russian/Ukrainian theatre director; b. 28 Oct. 1936, Lvov; ed A. Lunacharcky State Inst. of Theatre Art; Chief Dir Kalinin Theatre of Lenin Komsomol 1968–71; Dir Russian Drama Theatre in Vilnius 1971–77; Artistic Dir Students' Theatre of Moscow Univ. 1977–91; Founder and Artistic Dir Roman Viktyuk Theatre 1991–; directed productions in Swedish Theatre Helsinki, theatres of Brescia, Rome, San Diego; USA tour 1998; several TV productions; Prof., Acad. of the Performing Arts (GITIS); People's Artist of Ukraine 2006, Honoured Artist of Russia. *Address:* Roman Viktyuk Theatre, Stromynka str. 6, 107014 Moscow (office); Tverskaya 4, Apt 87, 103009 Moscow, Russia (office); (499) 268-06-69 (office). *Telephone:* (495) 292-68-95 (home).

VILA-MATAS, Enrique; Spanish writer; b. 1948, Barcelona; fmr journalist for Fotogramas magazine, Paris; Chevalier, Légion d'honneur 2006; Premio Ciudad de Barcelona 2000, Prix au meilleur livre étranger 2000, Premio de la Crítica 2002, Premio Herralde 2002, Prix Médicis 2003. *Publications include:* non-fiction: Al sur de los párpados 1980, Nunca voy al cine 1982, El viajero más lento 1992, Veneno en la boca, conversaciones con 18 escritores: Antón Castro 1994, Recuerdos inventados: primera antología personal 1994, El traje de los domingos 1995, Para acabar con los números redondos 1997, Desde la ciudad nerviosa 2000; fiction: La asesina ilustrada 1977, Impostura 1984, Historia abreviada de la literatura portátil 1985, Una casa para siempre 1988, Suicidios ejemplares 1991, Hijos sin hijos 1993, Lejos de Veracruz 1995, Extraña forma de vida 1997, El viaje vertical (Premio Rómulo Gallegos 2001) 1999, Bartleby y compañía 2000, El mal de Montano (trans. as Montano's Malady) 2002, París no se acaba nunca 2003, Doctor Pasavento (Premio de la Real Academia Española 2006, Internazionale Mondello Prize 2009) 2005, Exploradores del abismo 2007, Dietario voluble 2008, Dublinesca (trans. as Dublinesque) (Bottari Lattes Grinzane Prize, Prix Jean Carriere, Leteo Award) 2010, Chet Baker pense à son art 2011, Aire de Dylan 2012. *Address:* c/o Editorial Anagrama SA, Pedró de la Creu 58, 08034 Barcelona, Spain (office). *E-mail:* anagrama@anagrama-ed.es (office). *Website:* www.enriquevilamatas.com.

VILADECANS, Joan-Pere; Spanish artist; b. 1948, Barcelona; s. of Joan-Pere Viladecans and Carme Viladecans; Chevalier, Ordre des Arts et Lettres. *Address:* c/o Galería Joan Gaspar, Plaza Dr. Letamendi 1, 08007 Barcelona (office); Córcega 589, 08025 Barcelona, Spain. *Telephone:* (93) 323-07-48 (office); (93) 455-93-85. *Fax:* (93) 451-13-43 (office). *E-mail:* joangaspar@galgasparjoan.com (office).

VILÁGOSI, Gábor, DJur; Hungarian lawyer and politician; *Deputy Speaker, Országgyülés (National Assembly);* b. 12 Jan. 1956, Devecser; m.; four c.; ed Univ. of Pécs; legal affairs official, Cen. Transdanubia Water Man. Directorate 1980–83; legal adviser to Alkotmány Agricultural Co-operative, then to Fehérvár Dept Store 1983–89; among first members of Alliance of Free Democrats (SZDSZ) 1989, mem. SZDSZ governing cttee for Székesfehérvár 1989–90, Chair., SZDSZ Fejér County 1999–, mem. Nat. Exec. 2007–; practised law in Székesfehérvár 1990–94; mem., Hungarian Olympic Cttee 1994–98; co-Chair., Lake Velence Regional Council 1995–98; Mem. Országgyülés (Nat. Ass., parl.) 1990–, Keeper of the Minutes of the Országgyülés 1998–2004, Deputy Speaker 2004–, mem., Cttee on Sport and Tourism 2006–; State Sec. for Policy, Ministry of Interior 1994–98; mem., Fejér County Ass. 1998–2002; mem. Székesfehérvár Municipal Ass. 2002–06. *Address:* Országgyülés, 1357 Budapest, Kossuth tér 1–3, Hungary (office). *Telephone:* (1) 441-4000 (office); (1) 441-4809 (office). *Fax:* (1) 441-4072 (office). *E-mail:* gabor .vilagosi@parlament.hu (office). *Website:* www.parlament.hu (office).

VILARDELL, Francisco, MD, DSc (Med); Spanish physician and gastroenterologist; b. 1 April 1926, Barcelona; s. of Jacinto Vilardell and Mercedes Viñas; m. Leonor Vilardell 1958; one s. two d.; ed Univs of Barcelona and Pennsylvania; Dir Gastroenterology Service, Hosp. Santa Cruz y San Pablo, Barcelona 1963–; Dir Postgraduate School of Gastroenterology, Autonomous Univ. of Barcelona 1969–; Pres. European Soc. for Digestive Endoscopy 1970–74, European Asscn for Study of the Liver 1975–76; Pres. World Org. of Gastroenterology 1982–90 (Sec.-Gen. 1974–82), now Hon. Pres.; Pres. Council of Int. Orgs in Medical Science 1987–93, Perm. Adviser 1994–; Dir-Gen. Health Planning, Ministry of Health 1981–82, mem. Advisory Council 1997–; f. Fundación Privada de Gastroenterología Dr. Francisco Vilardell 1992; Hon. Pres. World Gastroenterology Org.; Chevalier,

Légion d'honneur; Gold Medal, Barcelona Acad. of Medicine, Gold Medal, Spanish Soc. of Gastroenterology. *Publications:* ed. of six books; 170 papers in medical journals. *Leisure interests:* music, philology. *Address:* Fundación Privada de Gastroenterología Dr. Francisco Vilardell, C./ Virgen de la Salud, 78, Planta 5 Puerta F, 08024 Barcelona; Juan Sebastian Bach 11, 08021 Barcelona, Spain (home). *Telephone:* (93) 2197343; (93) 2014511 (home). *Fax:* (93) 2010191 (home). *Website:* www.fvilardell.org.

VILARIÑO PINTOS, Daría; Spanish librarian (retd); b. 26 Jan. 1928, Santiago de Compostela; d. of José Vilariño de Andrés and Daría Pintos Castro; mem. staff, state library, museum and archives depts 1957–70; Deputy Dir, Library of Univ. of Santiago 1970–73, Dir 1973–93; Insignia de Oro de la Univ. de Santiago 1993; Medalla de Bronce de Galicia 1993. *Publications:* O Libro Galego onte e hoxe (with Virtudes Pardo) 1981, Hechos de D. Berenguel de Landoria (co-author) 1983, Vasco de Aponte: Recuento de las Casas Antiguas del Reino de Galicia. Edición crítica (co-author) 1986, Ordoño de Celanova: Vida y Milagros de San Rosendo. Edición crítica (co-author) 1990, Guía do Fondo Antigo de Monografías da Biblioteca Xeral da USC: Literaturas Hispánicas Séculos XV–XVIII (co-author) 2000; articles in professional journals, bibliographical catalogues. *Leisure interest:* reading. *Address:* Calle San Miguel No. 5, 2°, 15704 Santiago de Compostela, La Coruña, Spain. *Telephone:* (981) 583658.

VILELA SAMPAIO, Suely, BSc, MSc, DSc; Brazilian toxicologist and university administrator; b. 22 Feb. 1954, Ilicínea, Minas Gerais; divorced; one s.; ed Univ. of Ribeirão Preto; Assoc. Prof., Clinical Analysis, Toxicology and Bromatology Dept, Univ. of Ribeirão Preto 1991, Full Prof. of Pharmaceutical Sciences 1996, Pro-Rector of Post-Graduation 2002; fmr Asst Rector, Univ. of São Paulo, Rector 2005–10; Visiting Prof., Univ. of Nice, France 1993, Univ. of Chile 1996, Univ. of Costa Rica 1997, Univ. of London, UK 1999, Univ. of Parma, Italy 2004, Univ. of Havana, Cuba 2004, Rutgers Univ., USA 2004, Univ. of Barcelona, Spain 2004, Ohio Univ., USA 2004; Dir Int. Asscn of Univs. *Address:* c/o Office of the Rector, Universidade de São Paulo, Rua da Reitoria 109, 05508-900 São Paulo, Brazil (office).

VILHJALMSSON, Thor, Cand. juris; Icelandic judge (retd) and professor of law; b. 9 June 1930, Reykjavik; s. of Vilhjalmur Th. Gislason and Inga Arnadóttir Gislason; m. Ragnhildur Helgadóttir 1950; one s. three d.; ed Reykjavik Grammar School, St Andrews Univ., Scotland, Univ. of Iceland, New York Univ. and Univ. of Copenhagen; Asst Lecturer, Univ. of Iceland 1959–62, part-time Lecturer 1962–67, Prof. 1967–76 and Dean, Faculty of Law 1968–70, Dir Inst. of Law 1974–76; Deputy Judge Reykjavik Civil Court 1960–62, Judge 1962–67; Judge, European Court of Human Rights 1971–98, Vice-Pres. 1998; Assoc. Justice of the Supreme Court of Iceland 1976–93, Pres. 1983–84, 1993; Judge, EFTA Court, Geneva 1994–96, Luxembourg 1996–2002 (Pres. 2000–02); mem. Icelandic Del. to UN Gen. Ass. 1963, UN Sea-Bed Cttee 1972, 1973 to Law of the Sea Conf. 1974, 1975 and other int. confs; Pres. Asscn of Icelandic Lawyers 1971–74; Ed. Icelandic Law Review 1973–83; Commdr, Order of the Icelandic Falcon. *Publications:* Civil Procedure I–IV and several studies and articles on constitutional law, human rights and legal history. *Address:* Midleiti 10, 1S 103 Reykjavik, Iceland (home). *Telephone:* 5535330 (home). *Fax:* 5535330 (home). *E-mail:* thorhv@vortex.is (home).

VILI, Valerie; New Zealand athlete; b. (Valerie Adams), 6 Oct. 1984, Rotorua; d. of a Scottish father and Tongan mother; m. Bertrand Vili (discus thrower from New Caledonia); shot putter; Olympic Champion, World Champion and Commonwealth record-holder, having thrown a distance of 20.56m; won World Youth Championships 2001 (with a throw of 16.87m); World Jr Champion 2002 (throw of 17.73m); Silver Medal, Commonwealth Games, Manchester 2002 (throw of 17.45m); finished fifth at World Championships, Paris 2003, eighth at Athens Olympics 2004; Bronze Medal, World Championships, Helsinki 2005 (personal best throw of 19.87m); finished second at World Athletics Final; Gold Medal, Commonwealth Games, Melbourne 2006 (broke 20-year-old Commonwealth Games record with a throw of 19.66m); Gold Medal, World Championships, Osaka 2007 (Commonwealth record throw of 20.54m); one of the few female athletes ever to take Int. Asscn of Athletics Feds (IAAF) World Titles at youth, jr and sr levels; broke the Oceania record in winning her first World Indoor Title in Valencia 2008 (throw of 20.19m); Gold Medal, Olympic Games, Beijing 2008 (throw of 20.56m, personal best, first Olympic gold medal in track and field for New Zealand since John Walker in 1976); New Zealand Sports Award of the Year 2008. *Address:* c/o Athletics New Zealand, PO Box 741, Wellington 6140, New Zealand. *Telephone:* (4) 384-6021. *Fax:* (4) 385-1758. *E-mail:* info@athletics.org.nz. *Website:* www.athletics .org.nz.

VILINBAKHOV, Georgy Vadimovich, D.Hist.SC; Russian historian; b. 13 April 1949; ed Leningrad (now St Petersburg) State Univ.; researcher, later Prof., State Hermitage Museum 1969–, Treas., collection of mil. banners and graphic works 1970–92, Deputy, then First Deputy Dir 1991–; Head, State Heraldic Council 1992–, Head of State Heraldry 1994, then Chair. Herald Council, State Heraldmeister 1999–; mem. Exec. Cttee Int. Asscn of Mil. Museums and Museum of Arms; Order Sign of Honour 1997, Order for Service to Motherland 1999. *Publications:* over 150 articles and publs on Russian history and heraldry. *Leisure interests:* collecting tin soldiers, mil. music. *Address:* State Hermitage Museum, Dvortsovaya nab. 34, St Petersburg, Russia (office). *Telephone:* (812) 710-96-02 (office). *Fax:* (812) 571-90-09 (office). *E-mail:* vilinbakhov@hermitage.ru (office). *Website:* www.hermitagemuseum.org (office).

VILJOEN, Hendrik Christo, PhD (Eng); South African academic and electronics engineer; *Chairman, Huguenot Society of South Africa;* b. 31 Aug. 1937, Graaff-Reinet; s. of Hendrik Christoffel Viljoen and Anna Pienaar; m. Hana Stehlik 1965; one s. two d.; ed Univ. of Stellenbosch; engineer, Dept of Posts and Telecommunications, Pretoria 1961–65; Sr Lecturer, Stellenbosch Univ. 1966–70, apptd Prof. 1970, Dean of Eng 1979–93, Vice-Rector of Operations 1993–98, Man. Dir Unistel Group Holdings (Pty) Ltd 2000–08; Chair. SABC 1989–93; Visiting Prof., Georgia Inst. of Tech., Atlanta, USA 1975–76, Nat. Chiao Tung Univ., Hsinchu, Taiwan 1981; est. Office for Intellectual Property, Dir –2002; Chair. Task Group on Broadcasting in SA 1987–91, Huguenot Soc. of SA; Deputy Chair. Genealogical Inst. of SA; mem. Council, Univ. Stellenbosch of 2006–09; Sr mem. IEEE, USA 1978–; Fellow, S African Acad. for Arts & Science; Order for Meritorious Service

1991; Sir Ernest Oppenheimer Memorial Trust Fellowship, Engineer of the Year, S African Asscn for Professional Engineers 1991, Merit Medal, S African Acad. for Arts and Science 2000. *Publications include:* Viljoen Family Register 1968 Viljoen Family Memorial Book 1968, Elektronika 1971, Cyber Dictionary 2007; 18 articles in scientific journals. *Leisure interests:* genealogy, writing, scuba diving. *Address:* 6 Hof Avenue, Stellenbosch 7600, South Africa. *Telephone:* (21) 8833754. *Fax:* (21) 866162234. *E-mail:* hcv@sun.ac.za (home); viljoen@mail.com (home). *Website:* www.hugenoot.org.za/Viljoen (home).

VILKAS, Eduardas, DPhys-MathSc, DrHabil; Lithuanian mathematician and economist; *Director, Ekonomikos Institutas, Lithuanian Academy of Sciences;* b. 3 Oct. 1935, Gargzdai; m. Stefa Vilkienė; two s. one d.; ed Vilnius Univ.; researcher, Inst. of Physics and Math., Lithuanian Acad. of Sciences 1958–77, researcher, Inst. of Math. and Cybernetics 1977–79, Deputy Dir 1979–85, Dir Inst. of Econs 1985–; teacher, Vilnius Univ. 1958–78, Prof. 1976; Prof., Vytautas Magnus Univ.; Chair. Parl. Privatization Comm. 1996–2001; mem. Lithuanian Acad. of Sciences, Vice-Pres. 1991–99; Lithuanian Grand Duke Gediminas Order. *Publications:* What is the Theory of Games? 1976, Mathematical Methods in the Economy 1980, Solutions: Theory, Information, Modelling (together with E. Maiminas) 1981, Optimality in Games and Decisions 1991, Lithuanian White Paper for Science and Technology (co-author) 2001, Decision-Making Theory 2003; numerous articles in scientific periodicals on probability theory, game theory, math. econs and their application in nat. econs and the strategy for long-term devt of the Lituanian economy. *Leisure interest:* tennis. *Address:* Ekonomikos Institutas, A. Goštanto 12, 01108 Vilnius (office); Zirgo 20, 10007 Vilnius, Lithuania (home). *Telephone:* (5) 2623502 (office); (5) 2700404 (home). *Fax:* (5) 2127506 (office). *E-mail:* ei@ktl.mii.lt (office); evilkas@takas.lt (home).

VILKS, Andris; Latvian economist and politician; *Minister of Finance;* b. 15 June 1963, Jaunpiebalga; m. Diāna Vilka; ed Univ. of Latvia, Nordisk Landboskole, Odense, Denmark; worked with various state-owned cos and public orgs 1986–94; Analyst, Credit Dept, Latvijas Unibanka 1995–97, Strategy and Analysis Dept 1997–99, Head of Equity Market Analysis Div. 2000–02; Analyst, SEB Merchant Banking, Stockholm 2002, Head of Market and Sector Analysis Dept, SEB Unibanka 2002–07, Chief Economist, SEB Banka 2007–09; mem. Saeima (Parl.) 2010–; Minister of Finance 2010–; mem. of the party union 'Unity' 2010–; Best Minister of Finance in the European Region, The Banker 2012. *Address:* Ministry of Finance, Smilšu iela 1, Riga 1919, Latvia (office). *Telephone:* 6709-5405 (office). *Fax:* 6709-5503 (office). *E-mail:* info@fm.gov.lv (office). *Website:* www.fm.gov.lv (office).

VILKUL, Oleksander Yuriyovych; Ukrainian mining engineer and politician; *Deputy Prime Minister;* b. 24 May 1974, Kryvyi Rih, Dnipropetrovsk Region; m.; one d.; ed Kryvyi Rih Technical Univ., Dnipropetrovsk Regional Inst. of Public Admin; started career as asst excavator driver, ore enrichment works, later becoming Head of Commercial Financial Dept, Deputy Dir-Gen. and Deputy Chair. JSC Southern Ore Enrichment Works, Kryvyi Rih 1997–2003, Chair. 2003–04, also Dir of Mining Div. JSC Metinvest Holding 2004–06; mem. Verkhovna Rada (Supreme Council, Parl.) 2006–10, Deputy Chair. Regulatory Policy and Entrepreneurship Cttee 2006–10; Gov. Dnipropetrovsk Oblast (Regional State Admin) 2010–12; Deputy Prime Minister 2012–; Companion of the Order of Merit, Third Class 2008, Second Class 2011, Honoured Worker of Industry of Ukraine 2005. *Leisure interests:* history and books. *Address:* Office of the Cabinet of Ministers, 01008 Kyiv, vul. M. Hrushevskoho 12/2, Ukraine (office). *Telephone:* (44) 254-05-84 (office). *Fax:* (44) 254-05-84 (office). *E-mail:* web@kmu .gov.ua (office). *Website:* www.kmu.gov.ua (office).

VILLA-VICENCIO, Rev. Charles, BA, STM, PhD; South African theologian and academic; b. 7 Nov. 1942, Johannesburg; s. of Charles Villa-Vicencio and Paula Villa-Vicencio; m. Eileen van Sittert 1968; two d.; ed Rhodes Univ., Natal Univ. and Yale Univ. and Drew Univ., USA; with Standard Bank of SA 1961–64; Probationer Minister, Methodist Church of Southern Africa 1965–70; ordained Minister 1970; Minister of various congregations in S Africa and USA; Teaching Fellow, Drew Univ. 1974–75; part-time lecturer, Univ. of Cape Town 1976–77; Sr Lecturer, Univ. of S Africa 1978–81, Assoc. Prof. 1981–82; Sr Lecturer, Univ. of Cape Town 1982, Assoc. Prof. 1984–88, Head of Dept of Religious Studies 1986–97, Prof. of Religion and Society 1988–97; mem. S African Theological Soc., Nat. Research Dir Truth and Reconciliation Comm., Exec. Dir Inst. for Justice and Reconciliation 2000–07; Fellow, Univ. of Cape Town 1996; Claude Ake Visiting Chair, Dept of Peace and Conflict Research, Uppsala Univ. and Nordic Africa Inst., Sweden 2007; Visiting Research Fellow, Berkley Center for Religion, Peace, and World Affairs, Georgetown Univ., USA 2008; mem. Council, Stellenbosch Univ.; Hon. DHumLitt (Elmhurst Coll., Chicago) 1998; Abraham Kuyper Prize, Princeton Theological Seminary 2005. *Publications include:* Between Christ and Caesar: Classical and Contemporary Texts 1986, Trapped in Apartheid 1988, Civil Disobedience and Beyond 1990, A Theology of Reconstruction 1992, A Spirit of Hope: Conversations on Politics, Religion and Values 1993; ed. or co-ed. of and contrib. to several vols of essays; numerous articles including many on the church and politics in S Africa. *Address:* 14 Annerley Road, Rosebank, Cape Town 7700 (home); c/o Institute for Justice and Reconciliation, POB 205, Rondebosch, Cape Town 7700, South Africa (office). *Telephone:* (21) 6868643 (home). *Fax:* (21) 6592721. *E-mail:* ijr@grove.uct.ac.za (office). *Website:* www.ijr.org.za (office).

VILLAIN, Claude Edouard Louis Etienne, LenD; French civil servant and business executive; *President, Ardo Violaines;* b. 4 Jan. 1935, Paris; s. of Etienne Villain and Marie Louise (née Caudron) Villain; m. Bernadette Olivier 1962 (deceased); two s.; ed Lycée Voltaire, Lycée Louis-le-Grand, Univ. of Paris, Ecole Nat. de la FOM; trainee in French Overseas Admin 1956–59, Officer in Dept of Algerian Affairs 1959–61; Officer for Econ. Studies in Agricultural Devt Bureau 1962–64; Officer in Ministry of Econ. and Finance 1964, Head of Dept 1969, Deputy Dir of Ministry 1973; Tech. Adviser in Office of Valéry Giscard d'Estaing (then Minister of Econ. and Finance) 1973–74; Dir-Gen. of Competition and Prices in Ministry of Econ. and Finance 1974–78; Admin. Soc. Nat. des Chemins de fer Français (SNCF) 1974–78; Admin. Soc. Nat. Elf Aquitaine 1974–79; Dir-Gen. of Agric., Comm. of EEC 1979–85; Dir-Gen. Socopa Int., Vice-Pres. Socopa France 1985–86; Special Adviser to Minister of Econ. and Finance 1986–88; Inspector-Gen. of Finances 1987–2003; Del. Interministerial Mission for Cen. and Eastern Europe (MICECO) 1992–93, for Euro-Disneyland 1993–2003; Chair. Admin. Bd

Comilog SA 1996–; mem. Intergovernmental Comm. of the Channel Tunnel 1990–2000, of the Lyon-Turin rail project 1996–2001; Admin. Soc. Nat. RATP 1998–2004; Pres. Ardo Violaines (frozen food enterprise) 2005–; Officier, Légion d'honneur, Commdr, Ordre nat. du Mérite, du Mérite Agricole, Croix de Valeur Mil. *Leisure interests:* tennis, skiing. *Address:* Ardo Violaines, 62138 chemin de la cochiette, 62138 Violaines, France (office); 103 avenue Félix Faure, 75015 Paris, France (home). *Telephone:* 3-20-29-30-30 (office); 1-44-26-01-67 (home). *Fax:* 3-20-29-36-10 (office).

VILLANI, Cédric, PhD; French mathematician, academic and research institute director; *Director, Institut Henri Poincaré;* b. 5 Oct. 1973, Brive-la-Gaillarde (Corrèze); two c.; ed Lycée Louis-le-Grand, École Normale Supérieure, Paris Dauphine Univ.; agrégé-préparateur (tutor), École Normale Supérieure –2000; Prof., École Normale Supérieure de Lyon 2000–10; Dir Institut Henri Poincaré, Paris 2009–; Prof., Univ. of Lyon 2010–; Visiting Asst Prof., Georgia Tech Inst., USA 1999; Visiting Research Miller Prof., Univ. of California, Berkeley, USA 2004; Invited mem. Inst. for Advanced Study, Princeton, USA 2009; Admin. for several asscns, including EuropaNova (pro-European think-tank); Pres. Scientific Bd AIMS-Senegal; mem. Editorial Bd, Inventiones Mathematicae, Journal of Functional Analysis, Journal of Mathematical Physics, Journal of Statistical Physics; mem. Institut Universitaire de France 2006; Chevalier, Ordre nat. du Mérite 2009, Légion d'honneur 2011; Louis Armand Prize, Acad. des sciences 2001, Peccot-Vimont Prize and Cours Peccot, Collège de France 2003, Plenary Lecturer, Int. Congress of Math. Physics, Lisbon 2003, Harold Grad Lecturer 2004, Invited Lecturer, Int. Congress of Mathematicians, Madrid 2006, Jacques Herbrand Prize, Acad. des sciences 2007, Prize of European Math. Soc. 2008, Fermat Prize 2009, Henri Poincaré Prize, Int. Asscn of Math. Physics 2009, Fields Medal (co-recipient) 2010. *Publications:* A Review of Mathematical Topics in Collisional Kinetic Theory 2002, Topics in Optimal Transportation 2003, Optimal Transport, Old and New 2005; more than 50 papers in professional journals on kinetic theory (Boltzmann and Vlasov equations and their variants) and optimal transport and its applications. *Leisure interests:* walking, music (piano). *Address:* Institut Henri Poincaré (UPMC/CNRS), 11 rue Pierre et Marie Curie, 75230 Paris Cedex 05, France (office). *Telephone:* 1-44-27-67-92 (office); 1-44-27-64-18 (office). *Fax:* 1-46-34-04-56 (office). *E-mail:* villani@ihp.fr (office); villani@math.univ-lyon1.fr (office). *Website:* math.univ-lyon1.fr/~villani (office); cedricvillani.org.

VILLANUEVA ARÉVALO, César; Peruvian politician; b. 5 Aug. 1946, Tarapoto, San Martín; ed Univ. Nacional Federico Villarreal; Pres., Regional Govt of San Martin 2007–13; Pres., Council of Ministers (Prime Minister) 2013–14; fmr mem. High Level Corruption Comm.; Chair. Agency for the Promotion of Private Investment in the Amazon; Chair. Interregional Amazon; mem. Movimiento Independiente Regional Nueva Amazonía. *Address:* c/o Office of the President of the Council of Ministers, Jirón Carabaya, cuadra 1 s/n, Anexo 1105-1107, Lima, Peru.

VILLAPALOS-SALAS, Gustavo; Spanish academic and university administrator; b. 15 Oct. 1949, Madrid; s. of Gustavo Villapalos-Salas and Juana Villapalos-Salas; Prof., Faculty of Law, Universidad Complutense de Madrid 1970–75, Prof. of Law 1976, Dir Dept of History of Law 1980–84, Dean, Faculty of Law 1984–87, Rector, Universidad Complutense de Madrid 1987–2000; Head, Ministry of Educ., Culture and Sports, Community of Madrid 1995–2001; Research Fellow, Instituto de Estudios Jurídicos 1972–74, Centro de Investigaciones Jurídicas, Económicas y Sociales 1975; Visiting Prof., Univ. of Calif., Berkeley 1976, Univ. of Freiburg 1976–77; mem. Real Academia de Jurisprudencia y Legislación; Gran Cruz de la Orden de Alfonso X el Sabio, Gran Cruz del Mérito Civil, Hon. CBE; Dr hc (Paris-Sud, St Louis, USA, Guanajuato, Mexico, La Plata, Argentina). *Publications:* Colección Diplomática del Archivo Municipal de Santander: Documentos Reales II (1525–1599) 1982, Los Regímenes Económicos Matrimoniales en la Historia del Derecho Español: Prelección 1983, El Fuero de León: Comentarios 1984, Cortes de Castilla en el siglo XV 1986, La Baja Edad Media, Vol. IV, Historia General de Cantabria 1986, La Alta Edad Media, Vol. III 1987. *Leisure interests:* astronomy, cinema, classical music, reading. *Address:* c/o Real Academia de Jurisprudencia y Legislación, C/ Marqués de Cubas, 13, 28014 Madrid, Spain (home).

VILLAR, Manuel Bamba; Philippine politician and business executive; *President, Nacionalista Party;* b. 13 Dec. 1949, Tondo; s. of Manuel Montalban Villar and Curita Bamba; m. Cynthia Aguilar; two s. one d.; ed Univ. of the Philippines; began professional career as accountant with Sycip, Gorres, Velayo & Co.; fmr financial analyst, Private Devt Corpn of the Philippines; f. a construction business 1975, eventually becoming biggest housebuilder in SE Asia with firms Vista Land & Lifescapes and Polar Property Holdings; elected mem. House of Reps for Las Piñas-Muntinlupa constituency 1992, Speaker 1998–2000; Senator 2001–, Pres. of Senate 2006–08; mem. Nacionalista Party (NP) 2003–, Pres. 2004–; unsuccessful NP cand. in 2010 presidential election; numerous hon. degrees. *Address:* Nacionalista Party, 2nd Floor, Starmall EDSA, cnr Shaw Blvd, Mandaluyong City, 1552 Metro Manila, Philippines (office). *Telephone:* (2) 7224727 (office). *Fax:* (2) 7274223 (office). *Website:* www.nacionalistaparty.com (office); www.mannyvillar.com.ph.

VILLARAIGOSA, Antonio, BA; American politician; b. (Antonio Villar), 23 Jan. 1953, Los Angeles; m. Corina Raigosa (divorced); one s. one d. (and two c. from previous relationship); ed Univ. of California, Los Angeles; mem. Calif. State Ass. 1994, Speaker 1999; unsuccessful cand. for Mayor of Los Angeles 2001; Distinguished Fellow, UCLA, Univ. of Southern Calif. 2001–03; mem. LA City Council 2003; Chair. Transportation Cttee, mem. Bd Metropolitan Transportation Authority 2003; Mayor of LA 2005–13; Chair. Democratic Nat. Convention 2012. *Address:* c/o City Hall, 200 North Spring Street, Room 303, Los Angeles, CA 90012, USA.

VILLARROEL LANDER, Mario Enrique; Venezuelan lawyer, academic and international organization official; *President, Venezuelan Red Cross;* b. 20 Sept. 1947, Caracas; m. Norka Sierraalta 1969; three s. one d.; ed Cen. Univ. of Venezuela, Santa María Univ., Caracas; joined Venezuelan Red Cross as a volunteer 1967, Nat. Pres. 1978–, Pres. Int. Fed. of Red Cross and Red Crescent Socs 1987–98; Pres. Mirandino Historical Studies Inst., Henry Dunant Inst. 1992–93; Prof. of Penal Law, Chair. of Criminal Law Santa María Univ.; lawyer in pvt. legal practice, Caracas; fmr Dir La Voz del Derecho (legal review); numerous distinctions from Red Cross orgs. *Publications:* El Cuerpo Técnico de Policía

Judicial en el Proceso Penal Venezolano, Habeas Corpus y antejuicio de Mérito; legal articles in Venezuelan and foreign periodicals. *Leisure interest:* journalism. *Address:* Venezuelan Red Cross, Apartado 3185, 1010 Caracas, Venezuela (office). *Telephone:* (212) 571-4380 (office). *Fax:* (212) 576-1042 (office). *E-mail:* mariovillarroel@cantv.net (office). *Website:* www.cruzroja.org.ve (office); www.ifrc.org (office); www.mariovillarroel.com.

VILLAS-BOAS, José Manuel P. de; Portuguese academic and fmr diplomatist; *Professor, Department of Political Science and International Relations, Universidade do Minho;* b. 23 Feb. 1931, Oporto; s. of João de Villas-Boas and Maria Margarida de Villas-Boas; m. Maria do Patrocinio de Almeida Braga 1956; ed Lisbon Univ.; Attaché, Ministry of Foreign Affairs 1954, served in Embassies in Pretoria 1959, London 1963, Counsellor 1969, Head of African Dept, Ministry of Foreign Affairs 1970–72, Consul-Gen., Milan 1972–74, Minister Plenipotentiary and Asst Dir-Gen. of Political Affairs, Ministry of Foreign Affairs 1974–77, Dir-Gen. of Political Affairs 1977–79, Amb. and Perm. Rep. to NATO, Brussels 1979–84, Amb. to South Africa 1984–89, to People's Repub. of China 1989–93, to Russia 1993–97; Prof., Dept of Political Science and Int. Relations, Univ. of Minho, Braga 1997–; mem. Strategic Council 2003–; Grand Cross Order of Merit (Portugal), Hon. KCMG (UK), Grand Cross of St Olav (Norway), of Merit (Spain), Cruzeiro do Sul (Brazil), of Rio Branco (Brazil), of Good Hope (S Africa), Grand Officer of the Order of Merit (FRG), of the Lion (Senegal), Commdr, Légion d'honneur (France), Order of Merit (Italy), and others. *Publications include:* Orthodoxy and Political Power in Russia 1999, Caderno de Memórias 2003. *Leisure interests:* music, travelling. *Address:* Casa de Esteiro, Vilarelho 4910 Caminha (home); Department of Political Science and International Relations, Universidade do Minho, Campus de Gualtar, 4710-057 Braga, Portugal (office). *Telephone:* (258) 721333 (home); (253) 604518 (office). *Fax:* (258) 921356 (home). *E-mail:* casaesteiro@iol.pt (home). *Website:* www.eeg.uminho.pt (office).

VILLASECA MARCO, Rafael, MBA; Spanish business executive; *CEO, Gas Natural Fenosa;* b. 30 April 1951, Barcelona; ed Tech. Univ. of Barcelona (UPC), Univ. of Navarra's IESE Business School; fmr Gen. Man. Dir Grupo Panrico; fmr Man. Dir Nueva Montaña Quijano, SA; CEO and Exec. Advisor, Unión Fenosa, SA; CEO Gas Natural SDG SA (renamed Gas Natural Fenosa following acquisition of Unión Fenosa 2008) 2005–, Man. Dir and CEO Gas Natural SA ESP (subsidiary) 2005–; Chair. Gas Natural Aprovisio; fmr Chair. Túneles y Accesos de Barcelona SA (TABASA), Túnel de Cádiz SAC (affiliate of la Caixa), Gestión de Infraestructuras, SA, Grupo INISEL (now Grupo INDRA); Vice-Chair. Repsol-Gas Natural LNG, S.L.; mem. Bd of Dirs Unión Fenosa, SA, Indra Sistemas, SA, Amper SA, Enagas SA 2002–09; fmr Chair. IESE's Alumni Asscn. *Address:* Gas Natural Fenosa, Plaça del Gas 1, 08003 Barcelona, Spain (office). *Telephone:* (902) 199199 (office); (93) 4025897 (office). *Fax:* (93) 4025870 (office). *E-mail:* info@gasnaturalfenosa.com (office). *Website:* www.gasnaturalfenosa.com (office).

VILLEGAS QUIROGA, Carlos; Bolivian economist and government official; *President, Yacimientos Petrolíferos Fiscales Bolivianos;* fmr Dir of Postgraduate Devt Studies, Univ. of San Andres, La Paz; Econ. Adviser to presidential cand. Evo Morales 2005; Minister of Sustainable Devt and Planning –2006, also Gov. IDB and Inter-American Investment Corpn; Minister of Hydrocarbons and Energy 2006–09; Pres. Yacimientos Petrolíferos Fiscales Bolivianos (state-owned petrol co.) 2009–. *Address:* Yacimientos Petrolíferos Fiscales Bolivianos Calle Bueno 185, 6°, Casilla 401, La Paz, Bolivia (office). *Telephone:* (2) 237-0210 (office). *E-mail:* webmaster@ypfb.gov.bo (home). *Website:* www.ypfb.gob.bo (office).

VILLELA FILHO, Alfredo Egydio Arruda, MBA; Brazilian engineer and business executive; *President and CEO, Itaúsa-Investimentos Itaú SA;* ed Escola de Engenharia Mauá, Instituto Mauá de Tecnologia, Fundação Getúlio Vargas; mem. Admin. Council Itaúsa-Investimentos Itaú SA 1995–, mem. Disclosure and Procedure on Insider Trading Cttees, mem. Admin. Council Itautec Philco SA 1997–, mem. Bd of Dirs Itautec SA 1997–, Vice-Chair. Itaú Unibanco SA 2001–03, Vice-Chair. Itaú Unibanco Holding SA 2003–, mem. Disclosure and Procedure on Insider Trading Cttees, Banco Itaú SA 2005–, mem. Accounting Policy and Investment Policy Cttees 2008–, Pres. and CEO Itaúsa-Investimentos Itaú SA 2008–, mem. Promotion and Remuneration and Disclosure and Insider Trading Cttees 2005–09, Vice-Chair. Itautec SA 2007–09, 2010–, Chair. 2009–10; Vice-Chair. Elekeiroz SA 2004–09, Chair. 2009–; Vice-Chair. Duratex SA 2009–. *Address:* Itaúsa-Investimentos Itaú SA, Praça Alfredo Edydio de Souza Aranha 100, Torre Itaúsa, São Paulo 04344-902, SP, Brazil (office). *Telephone:* (11) 5019-1677 (office). *Fax:* (11) 5019-1114 (office). *E-mail:* info@itausa.com.br (office). *Website:* www.itausa.com.br (office).

VILLELLA, Edward, BS; American ballet dancer; *Artistic Director, Miami City Ballet;* b. 1 Oct. 1936, New York; s. of Joseph Villella and Mildred Villella (née De Giovanni); m. 1st Janet Greschler 1962 (divorced 1980); one s.; m. 2nd Linda Carbonetta 1981; two d.; ed New York State Maritime Coll.; joined New York City Ballet 1957, becoming soloist within a year, now Premier Dancer; originated leading roles in George Balanchine's Bugaku, Tarantella, Stars and Stripes, Harlequinade, Jewels, Glinkaiana, A Midsummer Night's Dream; first danced his famous role of Prodigal Son 1960; has also danced leading roles in Allegro Brillante, Jeux, Pas de Deux, Raymonda Variations, Scotch Symphony, Swan Lake; choreographed Narkissos; has appeared at Bolshoi Theatre, with Royal Danish Ballet and in London and made numerous guest appearances; choreographed and starred in revivals of Brigadoon, Carousel; Chair. New York City Comm. of Cultural Affairs 1978; Artistic Co-ordinator Eglersky Ballet Co. (now André Eglersky State Ballet of New York) 1979–84, Choreographer 1980–84; Choreographer NJ Ballet 1980; Artistic Dir Ballet Okla 1983–86, Miami City Ballet 1985–; Heritage Chair in Arts and Cultural Criticism, George Mason Univ. 1992–93, 1993–94; mem. Nat. Council on the Arts 1968–74; Artist-in-Residence, Dorothy F. Schmidt Coll. of Arts and Letters 2000–01; Robert Kiphuth Fellow, Yale Univ. 2001; Fellow, American Acad. of Arts and Sciences 2009–; Hon. DFA (State Univ. of New York Maritime Coll.) 1998; Dance Magazine Award 1965, Golden Plate Award, American Acad. of Achievement 1971, Emmy Award 1975, Gold Medal Award, Nat. Soc. of Arts and Letters 1990, Nat. Medal of Arts Award 1997, other awards. *Publication:* Prodigal Son (co-author) 1992. *Address:* Miami City Ballet, Ophelia and Juan Js Roca Center, 2200 Liberty Avenue, Miami Beach, FL 33139, USA (office). *Telephone:* (305) 929-7000 (office). *Website:* www.miamicityballet.org (office).

VILLENEUVE, Jacques, OQ; Canadian racing driver; b. 9 April 1971, Saint-Jean-sur-Richelieu, Québec; s. of the late Gilles Villeneuve and of Joanne Barthe; m. Johanna Martinez 2006; ed Beau-Soleil School, Villars, Switzerland, Jim Russell Formula Ford School, Mont-Tremblant, Formula 2000 Racing School, Shannonville; first raced in three Alfa Italian touring car races; raced Italian Formula 3 series 1989–91; second place in Japanese F3 series for Team Tom's Toyota with three wins 1992; third place in Macao F3 Grand Prix 1992; Formula Atlantic debut and third place in Player's Grand Prix de Trois-Rivières; Forsythe-Green racing team Formula Atlantic: five wins and three second places in 15 races and third in championship 1993; named Formula Atlantic Rookie-of-the-Year 1993; IndyCar debut with team Players Forsythe-Green, three podiums, finished sixth in championship 1994; finished second in Indianapolis 500 race behind Al Unser Jt 1994; won his first IndyCar race at Elkhart Lake 1994; named IndyCar Rookie-of-the-Year 1994; sole driver for team Players Forsythe-Green 1995; named IndyCar Champion 1995 with seven podium finishes, four wins, one second place, two third places and six poles; first Canadian and youngest driver (aged 24) to win the Indianapolis 500 race 1995; moved to Williams/Renault Fl team 1996; pole position in his first Formula One race at Australian Grand Prix; second in Formula One World Championship 1996 with 78 points, three pole positions, four wins (Europe, GB, Hungary and Portugal), five second places and two third places; named Fl Rookie-of-the-Year 1996; driver for Williams/Renault Fl team 1997; Formula One World Champion 1997 with 81 points, seven wins (Brazil, Argentina, Spain, GB, Hungary, Austria and Luxembourg) and 10 pole positions; driver for Williams/Mecachrome Fl team 1998; fifth in Formula One World Championship with two third places (Germany and Hungary) 1998; driver for B.A.R. Fl team 1999–2003; two third places (Spain and Germany) 2001; moved to Renault Formula One team for last three races of 2004; moved to Sauber Petronas Formula One team in 2005; driver with BMW-Sauber 2006; 150 Formula One Grand Prix races (as at Belgium Grand Prix 2005); Team Peugeot Le Mans 24-h 2007; Bill Davis Racing NASCAR Team (Truck Series) 2007, (Sprint Cup) 2008; Owner, Newtown restaurant/club, Montreal; Founder and Patron Formula Charity; inductee into Canada's Walk of Fame 1998. *Recording:* first album as singer/songwriter: Private Paradise 2007. *Leisure interests:* reading, music, skiing, ice hockey, computers/gaming. *Address:* c/o Claymore SA, CP 195, 1884 Villars-sur-Ollon, Switzerland (office). *Telephone:* (24) 496-30-40 (office). *Fax:* (24) 496-30-41 (office). *E-mail:* jvmgt@claymore.ch (office). *Website:* www.jv-world.com; www.myspace.com/jvofficial; www.bcv24hvillars.com

VILLEPIN, Dominique Marie François René Galouzeau de, LenD; French diplomatist, civil servant and lawyer; b. 14 Nov. 1953, Rabat, Morocco; s. of Xavier Galouzeau de Villepin and Yvonne Hétier; m. Marie-Laure Le Guay 1985; one s. two d.; ed Paris Inst. of Political Sciences, Ecole Nationale d'Administration; responsible for Horn of Africa, Office of African Affairs 1980–81, Head of Mission attached to Dir's Office 1981–84, Asst Dir 1992–93; with Centre d'Analyse et de Prévision 1981–84; First Sec. Washington 1984–1987, Embassy Press and Information Dir, Washington 1987–89, Ministerial Councillor, India 1989–92; Deputy Head of African Affairs, Ministry of Foreign Affairs 1992–93, Dir de Cabinet to Alain Juppé (q.v.), Minister of Foreign Affairs 1993–95; Sec. Gen. to Presidency 1995–2002; Minister of Foreign Affairs, Cooperation and Francophony 2002–2004, Minister of the Interior, Internal Security and Local Rights 2004–05, Prime Minister 2005–07; Chair. Admin. Council Nat. Forests Office (ONF) 1996–99; Rep. Convention on the Future of Europe 2002; f République solidaire (political party) 2010; Chevalier de la Légion d'honneur. *Publications:* Parole d'Exil 1986 (poetry), Le Droit d'Aînesse 1988 (poetry), Elégies barbares (poetry) 1996, Secession (poetry) 1996, Les Cent-Jours ou l'Esprit de sacrifice (Amb.'s Prize) 2001, Le Cri de la Gargouille 2002, In Praise of Those Who Stole the Fire (poetry) 2003, Un Autre Monde – Cahiers de l'Herne 2003, Le Requin et la Mouette 2004. L'Homme Européen 2005, Le Soleil Noir de la Puissance 2007, Hôtel de L'Insomnie 2008, La Chute ou L'Empire de la Solitude 2008, La Cite des Hommes 2009, Le Dernier Temoin 2009, De L'Esprit de Cour une Malediction Française 2010, Notre Vieux Pays 2011, Seul le Devoir Nous Rendra Libres 2012. *Leisure interest:* marathon running. *Address:* République Solidaire, 91 bis rue du Cherche-Midi, 75006 Paris, France (office). *Telephone:* 1-84-16-10-47 (office). *Website:* www.dominiquedevillepin.fr (office).

VILLIERS, Rt Hon. Theresa Anne, PC, LLB (Hons), BCL; British politician, barrister and lecturer; *Secretary of State for Northern Ireland;* b. 5 March 1968, London, England; d. of George Edward Villiers and Anne Virginia Villiers (née Threlfall); m. Sean Wilken 1997 (divorced); ed Francis Holland School, Univ. of Bristol, Jesus Coll., Oxford; worked as Barrister and lecturer at King's Coll. London; MEP for London constituency 1999–2005; Deputy Leader, Conservatives in Europe 2001–02; MP for Chipping Barnet 2005–10, for Chipping Barnet (revised boundary) 2010–, mem. Environmental Audit Select Cttee 2005–06; Shadow Chief Sec. to the Treasury 2005–07, Shadow Sec. of State for Transport 2007–10, Minister of State, Dept for Transport 2010–12, Sec. of State for Northern Ireland 2012–; Vice-Pres. Conservative Future, Asscn of Conservative Cands. *Publication:* Law of Estoppel, Variation and Waiver (with Sean Wilken) 1998. *Address:* Northern Ireland Office, 11 Millbank, London, SW1P 4PN, England (office); Northern Ireland Office, Stormont House, Belfast, BT4 3ST, Northern Ireland (office). *Telephone:* (20) 7210-6460 (NI Office, London) (office); (28) 9052-7021 (NI Office, Belfast) (office). *Fax:* (20) 7210-6449 (NI Office, London) (office); (28) 9052-7040 (NI Office, Belfast) (office). *E-mail:* theresa.villiers@nio.x.gsi.gov.uk (office); theresa@theresavilliers.co.uk (office). *Website:* www.nio.gov.uk (office); www.theresavilliers.com

VILLIERS de SAINTIGNON, Philippe le Jolis de; French politician; b. 25 March 1949, Boulogne; s. of Jacques le Jolis de Villiers de Saintignon and Hedwige d'Arexy; m. Dominique de Buor de Villeneuve 1973; four s. three d.; ed Saint-Joseph Inst., Ecole Nat. d'Admin.; civil servant Ministry of Interior 1978; Prin. Pvt. Sec. to Prefect of La Rochelle 1978; Deputy Prefect Vendôme 1979; f. Alouette FM (regional radio station) 1981; Fondation pour les Arts et les Sciences de la Communication, Nantes 1984; Jr Minister of Culture and Communications 1986–87; mem. Conseil Gen. de la Vendée 1987–, Pres. 1988–; Deputy to Nat. Ass. from Vendée 1988–94 (UDF), 1997– (Ind.); MEP 1994–97, 1999, 2004–; Nat. Del. of UDF in charge of youth and liaising with cultural groups 1988; Founder and Pres. Mouvement pour la France 1994–; Co-Founder Rassemblement pour la France 1999, Vice-Pres. 1999–2000. *Publications:* Lettre Ouverte aux Coupeurs de

Têtes et aux Menteurs du Bicentenaire 1989, La Chienne qui Miaule 1990, Notre Europe sans Maastricht 1992, Avant qu'il ne soit trop tard 1993, La Société de connivence 1994, Dictionnaire du politiquement correct à la française 1996, La machination d'Amsterdam 1998. *Address:* Conseil Général de la Vendée, 40 rue Foch, 85923 La Roche-sur-Yon cedex 9, France (office); European Parliament, Bât. Altiero Spinelli 07H154, 60, rue Wiertz, 1047 Brussels, Belgium (office). *Telephone:* 1-40-63-82-05 (Paris) (office); (2) 284-58-95 (Brussels) (office). *Fax:* 1-40-63-82-80 (Paris) (office). *E-mail:* philippe.devilliers@europarl.europa.eu (office).

VILLIGER, Kaspar; Swiss business executive and fmr head of state; b. 5 Feb. 1941, Pfeffikon, Lucerne; m.; two d.; ed Swiss Fed. Inst. of Tech. (ETH), Zurich; Man. of cigar factory Villiger Söhne AG, Pfeffikon 1966–89; subsequently bought bicycle factory in Buttisholz; fmr Vice-Pres. Chamber of Commerce of Cen. Switzerland and mem. Cttee Swiss Employers' Cen. Asscn; mem. Lucerne Cantonal Parl. 1972–82; mem. Nat. Council, Liberal Party of Switzerland (FDP) 1982; mem. Council of States 1987; Swiss Fed. Councillor 1989–2003; Head, Fed. Mil. (Defence) Dept 1989–95, Dept of Finance 1996–2001, 2003; Vice-Pres. of Swiss Confed. 1994, 2001, Pres. 1995, 2002; Chair. UBS AG 2009–12, Chair. Governance and Nominating Cttee, Strategy Cttee, Corp. Responsibility Cttee; Dir Nestlé 2004–, Swiss Re 2004–, Neue Zürcher Zeitung; mem. Global Leadership Foundation. *Address:* c/o UBS AG, Bahnhofstrasse 45, 8021 Zurich, Switzerland. *E-mail:* info@ubs.com.

VILLIS, Hans-Peter; German business executive; b. 1958, Castrop-Rauxel; Commercial Dir Bergbau AG 1987–89; Man. Planning and Control, VEBA Kraftwerke Ruhr AG 1989–92, Project Man. E Germany VEBA AG 1992–93; Man. Dir Städtische Werke Magdeburg GmbH 1993–99; mem. Bd Gelsenwasser AG 2000–02; Man. Dir Elektrizitätswerk Wesertal GmbH Jan.–Sept. 2003, Chair. Bd of Man. E.ON Westfalen Weser AG 2003–06, Chief Financial Officer and Deputy Chair. Bd of Man. E.ON Nordic AB 2006–07, Chair. Bd of Man. and CEO Energie Baden-Württemberg AG 2007–12. *Address:* c/o Energie Baden-Württemberg AG, Durlacher Allee 93, 76131 Karlsruhe, Germany. *E-mail:* info@enbw.com.

VILSACK, Thomas (Tom), BA, JD; American lawyer, government official and fmr politician; *Secretary of Agriculture;* b. 13 Dec. 1950, Pittsburgh, Pa; s. of Bud Vilsack and Dolly Vilsack; m. Christine Bell 1973; two s.; ed Hamilton Coll., NY, Albany Law School; in pvt. law practice, Mt Pleasant, Iowa 1975–98; Mayor of Mt Pleasant 1987–92; elected Iowa Senate 1993–98; Gov. of Iowa 1998–2007; Chair. Democratic Leadership Council 2005-07; Of Counsel, Dorsey & Whitney LLP, Des Moines 2007–08; US Sec. of Agric., Washington, DC 2009–; Distinguished Visiting Prof. of Law, Drake Univ. Law School; mem. Democratic Govs Asscn 1999–2007; Distinguished Fellow, Biosafety Inst. for Genetically Modified Agricultural Products, Iowa State Univ.; mem. Bd of Dirs United Way, Mt Pleasant; unsuccessful cand. for 2008 Democratic party nomination for Pres. of US; Nat. Co-Chair. for Sen. Hillary Clinton's presidential nomination campaign 2007–08; Fellow, Iowa Acad. of Trial Lawyers; mem. ABA, Iowa State Bar Asscn, Iowa Trial Lawyers Asscn (Pres. 1985), Council on Foreign Relations; Democrat. *Address:* Department of Agriculture, 1400 Independence Ave, SW, Washington, DC 20250, USA (office). *Telephone:* (202) 720-5539 (office). *Fax:* (202) 720-9997 (office). *Website:* www.usda.gov.

VIMONT, Pierre, LenD; French diplomatist; *Executive Secretary-General, European External Action Service;* b. 15 June 1949; ed Institut d'Etudes Politiques and Ecole Nationale d'Admin, Paris; Sec., Ministry of Foreign Affairs 1977, Second Sec., Embassy in London 1977–78, First Sec. 1978–81, with Press and Information Office, Ministry of Foreign Affairs 1981–85; seconded to Inst. for East-West Security Studies, New York 1985–86; Second Counsellor, French Perm. Representation to European Communities, Brussels 1986–90; Head of Pvt. Office, Minister of European Affairs 1990–93; Dir for Devt and Scientific, Tech. and Educational Cooperation 1993–97; Dir for European Cooperation 1997–99, Ministry of Foreign Affairs; Amb. and Perm. Rep. to EU 1999–2002; Prin. Pvt. Sec., Minister of Foreign Affairs 2002–07; Amb. to USA 2007–10; Exec. Sec.-Gen. European External Action Service 2010–; fmr Pres. Group of Personal Reps to Intergovernmental Conf.; Chevalier, Ordre nat. du Mérite 1993. *Address:* European External Action Service, Triangle Building, 1046 Brussels, Belgium (office). *Telephone:* (2) 584-11-11 (office). *E-mail:* info@eeas.europa.eu (office). *Website:* eeas.europa.eu (office).

VINCENT, Jean-Pierre, LèsL; French theatre director; b. 26 Aug. 1942, Juvisy-sur-Orge, Essonne; s. of André Vincent and Paulette Loyot; one s.; ed Lycées Montaigne, Louis-le-Grand, Paris, Univ. de Paris (Sorbonne); amateur actor Univ. Theatre, Lycée Louis-le-Grand 1958–64; mem. Patrice Chéreau theatre co. 1965–68, Dir 1968–72; Dir, Admin. Dir Espérance Theatre 1972–74; Dir at Théâtre Nat. and École Supérieure d'art dramatique, Strasbourg 1975–83; Gen. Admin. Comédie-Française 1983–86; Dir Théâtre de Nanterre-Amandiers 1990–2001; Co-Founder Studio Libre 2002; Lecturer Inst. d'études théâtrales de Paris 1969–70; Studio Dir Conservatoire Nat. Supérieur d'art dramatique 1969–70, Prof. 1986–89; Pres. Syndicat nat. de directeurs d'entreprises artistiques et culturelles (Syndeac) 1978–82, Vice-Pres. 1992; mem. Bd of Dirs Festival d'Avignon; numerous critics' prizes, including Molière Prize for Best Dir 1987, Prix de la Critique 1988. *Plays include:* La noce chez les petits-bourgeois 1968, Tambours et Trompettes 1969, Les acteurs de bonne foi 1970, Le marquis de Montefosco 1970, La Cagnotte 1971, Capitaine Ecço 1971, Dans la jungle des villes 1972, La suicide 1984, Six personnages en quête de l'auteur 1986, Le Mariage de Figaro 1987, Fantasio, Les caprices de Mariane 1991, Woyzeck 1973, 1993, Violences à Vichy 1995, Tartuffe 1998, Pièces de guerre 1999, Homme pour homme, Lorenzaccio 2000, Les Prétendants 2003, Derniers remords avant l'oubli 2003–04, Onze Débardeurs 2004–05, La mort de Danton 2005, Les Antilopes 2006, Le silence des communistes 2007. *Opera include:* Les Noces de Figaro 1994, Mitridate 2000, Le drame et la vie 2001. *Address:* Bureau du Festival d'Avignon, Cloître Saint-Louis, 20 rue du Portail Bouqier, 84000 Avignon, France (office). *E-mail:* infodoc@festival-avignon.com (office). *Website:* www.festival-avignon.com (office).

VINCENT, Rev. John James, DTheol; British theologian, broadcaster and writer; b. 29 Dec. 1929, Sunderland; s. of David Vincent and Beatrice Ethel Vincent (née Gadd); m. Grace Johnston Stafford 1958; two s. one d.; ed Manchester

Grammar School, Richmond Coll., London Univ., Drew Univ., USA, Basel Univ., Switzerland; ordained in Methodist Church 1956; Minister, Manchester and Salford Mission 1956–62; Supt Minister, Rochdale Mission 1962–69, Sheffield Inner City Ecumenical Mission 1970–77; Dir, Urban Theology Unit, Sheffield 1969–97, Dir Emer. and Doctoral Supervisor 1997–; Pres., Methodist Conf. 1989–90; Visiting Prof. of Theology, Boston School of Theology, USA 1969, New York Theological Seminary 1970, Theological School, Drew Univ. 1977; elected mem., Studiorum Novi Testamenti Societas 1961; Sec. Regional Working Party, WCC Faith and Order 1958–63; mem., British Council of Churches Comm. on Defence and Disarmament 1963–65, 1969–72; NW Vice-Pres., Campaign for Nuclear Disarmament 1957–69; Founding mem., Methodist Renewal Group 1961–70; Founding mem. and Leader, Ashram Community 1967–; Chair., Alliance of Radical Methodists 1971–74, Urban Mission Training Asscn of GB 1976–77, 1985–90; Co-ordinator, British Liberation Theology Project 1990–; mem. Bd, Int. Urban Ministry Network 1991–; presented Petition of Distress from the Cities to HM the Queen 1993; mem., Ind. Human Rights Del. to Colombia 1994; Partnership Bd Burngreave New Deal for Communities 2001–11; Chaplain to the Lord Mayor of Sheffield 2006–07; Chair., Methodist Report on The Cities 1997; Hon. Lecturer, Biblical Studies Dept, Univ. of Sheffield 1990–2011, Theology Dept, Univ. of Birmingham 2003–; Fellow, St Deiniol's Library 2003; Centenary Achievement Award, Univ. of Sheffield 2005. *Publications:* Christ in a Nuclear World 1962, Christ and Methodism 1964, Here I Stand 1967, Secular Christ 1968, The Race Race 1970, The Jesus Thing 1973, Stirrings, Essays Christian and Radical 1975, Alternative Church 1976, Disciple and Lord 1976, Starting All Over Again 1981, Into the City 1982, O.K. Let's Be Methodists 1984, Radical Jesus 1986, Mark at Work 1986, Britain in the 90s 1989, Discipleship in the 90s 1991, Liberation Theology from the Inner City 1992, A Petition of Distress from the Cities 1993, Liberation Theology UK (ed.) 1995, The Cities: A Methodist Report 1997, Gospel from the City (ed.) 1997, Hope from the City 2000, Journey: Explorations in Discipleship 2001, Bible and Practice (ed.) 2001, Faithfulness in the City (ed.) 2003, Methodist and Radical (ed.) 2003, Outworkings: Gospel Practice and Interpretation 2005, Mark: Gospel of Action (ed.) 2006, A Lifestyle of Sharing 2009, The City in Biblical Perspective (jtly) 2009, The Drama of Mark (jtly) 2010, Christian Communities (ed.) 2011, Stilling the Storm (ed.) 2011, Acts in Practice (ed.) 2012, British Liberation Theology – For Church and Nation (ed.) 2013, Christ in the City 2013. *Leisure interests:* jogging, writing. *Address:* 178 Abbeyfield Road, Sheffield, S4 7AY, England (home). *Telephone:* (114) 270-9907 (office); (114) 243-6688 (home). *Fax:* (114) 243-5356 (office). *E-mail:* john@utusheffield.org.uk.

VINCENT, John Russell, PhD; British historian and academic; *Emeritus Professor, University of Bristol;* b. 20 Dec. 1937, Cheshire; s. of J.J. Vincent; m. Nicolette Kenworthy 1972; two s. (one deceased); ed Bedales School, Christ's Coll., Cambridge; Fellow of Peterhouse, Cambridge 1962–70, Lecturer in History, Univ. of Cambridge 1967–70; Prof. of Modern History, Univ. of Bristol 1970–84, Prof. of History 1984–2002, currently Emer. Prof.; Visiting Prof., Univ. of East Anglia, Norwich 2003–08. *Publications:* The Formation of the Liberal Party 1966, The Governing Passion 1974, The Crawford Papers 1984, Disraeli 1990, An Intelligent Person's Guide to History 1995, Derby Diaries, 1869–1878 1995, Derby Diaries 1878–93 2003; various works on political history. *Address:* Senate House, University of Bristol, Bristol, BS8 1TH, England (office).

VINCENT, Olatunde Olabode, BA, CFR, FCIB; Nigerian banker; b. 16 May 1925, Lagos; s. of Josiah O. Vincent and Comfort A. Vincent; m. Edith Adenike Gooding 1958; three s. one d.; ed CMS. Grammar School, Lagos, Chartered Inst. of Secs, London, Univ. of Manchester and Admin. Staff Coll., Henley, England; Nigerian Army 1942–46; Financial Sec.'s Office 1947–56; Fed. Ministry of Finance 1956–61; Asst Gen. Man. Cen. Bank of Nigeria 1961–62, Deputy Gen. Man. 1962, Gen. Man. 1963–66, Adviser 1973–75, Deputy Gov. 1975–77, Gov. 1977–82; co-f., then Vice-Pres. African Devt Bank, Abidjan, Ivory Coast 1966–73; part-time Lecturer in Econs, Extra-Mural Dept, Univ. Coll. of Ibadan 1957–60; mem. Lagos Exec. Devt Bd 1960–61; Dir Nigerian Industrial Devt Bank 1964–66, Nigerian Security Printing and Minting Co. Ltd, Lagos, 1975–77; Chair. Sona Dairies Ltd 1985–90, City Business Computers Ltd 1985–, Equity and Trust Ltd 1986–; Chair. Capital Issues Comm., Lagos, 1975–77, Southern Africa Relief Fund 1977–82, Cttee on Motor Vehicle Advances and Basic Allowance 1978; Chair. Visitation Panel, Lagos State Univ. (LASU) 1993–, Governing Bd, Centre for Environment and Science Educ., LASU 1996–2005; Chair. Bd of Trustees, Nigerian Lions Charity Foundation 1993–; Life mem. Soc. for Int. Devt; Fellow Nigerian Inst. of Bankers, Inst. of Dirs, Nigerian Inst. of Man.; mem. Nat. Econ. Council 1979–82, Life mem. Nigerian Econ. Soc., Nigeria-Britain Assoc., Cancer Aid Foundation, Soc. for Prevention of Cruelty to Animals, Nigerian Red Cross Soc., Order of Int. Fellowship; Charter mem. Int. Honour Soc. and World Peace and Diplomacy Forum; Grand Patron, Lagos Diocese of African Church 2000; mem. Nat. Exec. Council Nigerian Conservation Foundation; mem. Nigeria Soc. for the Blind; mem. Nigeria mem. Bd of Dirs Industrial and Gen. Insurance PLC; Patron Lagos State Chapter, Spinal Cord Injuries Assoc of Nigeria, African Church, Eye Bank of Nigeria, Skylark Sports Club of Nigeria for the Disabled; Grand Patron African Church Coll. of Theology; Commdr Order of Fed. Repub. 1982, Kt Commdr Order of the Peacock (Island Club, Lagos); Hon. DSc (Lagos State Univ.) 2000; African Church Primatial Honours Award 1981, Distinguished Nigerian Community Leader Award 1983. *Publication:* Ola Vincent's Speeches, Writings and Presentations 2005. *Leisure interests:* reading, listening to African and light classical music, gardening. *Address:* 8 Balarabe Musa Crescent, Victoria Island, PO Box 8780, Lagos, Nigeria (home). *Telephone:* 4617699 (home).

VINCENT OF COLESHILL, Baron (Life Peer), cr. 1996, of Coleshill in the County of Oxfordshire; **Field Marshal The Lord Richard (Frederick) Vincent,** GBE, KCB, DSO, FIMechE, FRAeS, FIC; British fmr army officer; b. 23 Aug. 1931, London; s. of the late Frederick Vincent and Frances Elizabeth Vincent (née Coleshill); m. Jean Paterson (née Stewart) 1955; two s. (one deceased) one d.; ed Aldenham School, Royal Mil. Coll. of Science; Nat. Service 1950; Germany 1951–55, Gunnery Staff 1959, Radar Research Establishment, Malvern 1960–61, BAOR 1962, Tech. Staff Training, Royal Mil. Coll. of Science 1963–64; Staff Coll. 1965, Commonwealth Brigade, Malaysia 1966–68, Ministry of Defence 1968–70; Commdr, 12th Light Air Defence Regt, Germany, England and NI 1970–72; Instructor, Staff Coll. 1972–73; Mil. Dir of Studies, RMCS 1974–75;

Commdr, 19 Airportable Brigade 1975–77; RCDS 1978; Deputy Mil. Sec. 1979–80; Commandant, Royal Mil. Coll. of Science 1980–83; Master Gen. of Ordnance, Ministry of Defence 1983–87; Vice-Chief, Defence Staff 1987–91, Chief 1991–92; Chair., Mil. Cttee of NATO 1993–96; Chair., MoDeM Consortium 1997–99; Chancellor, Cranfield Univ. 1998–2010, Sr Fellow 2010; Col Commandant, REME 1981–87, RA 1983–2000; Hon. Col, 100 (Yeomanry) Field Regt RA, TA 1982–91, 12th Air Defence Regt 1987–91; Chair. (non-exec.), Hunting Defence Ltd 1996–2003; Dir (non-exec.), Hunting Eng Ltd 1996–2001 (Chair. 1998–2001), Vickers Defence Systems 1996–2002, R.A. Museums Ltd 1996–2000, INSYS Ltd 2001–05; Pres., Cranfield Trust 1999–2011, Old Aldenhamian Soc. 1999–2003; Vice-Pres., The Defence Mfrs Assoc 1996–2000, Pres. 2000–05; Vice-Pres., Officers' Pension Soc. 1997–2006; Dir, Hunting-BRAE 1997–2003 (Chair. 1998); Kermit Roosevelt Lecturer 1988; mem. Court, Cranfield Inst. of Tech. 1981–83, Greenwich Univ. 1997–2000; mem. Guild of Freemen of the City of London 1992–, Comm. on Britain and Europe (Royal Inst. for Int. Affairs) 1996–97, Advisory Council, RMCS 1983–91; Fellow, Imperial Coll. London 1996, City and Guilds, London Inst. 1999–; Gov., Aldenham School 1987–2009, Ditchley Foundation 1992–2007, Imperial Coll. London 1995– (Chair. Bd Govs 1996–2004); Master Gunner, St James's Park 1996–2000; Patron, Inspire Foundation 1999–2011; Freeman City of London 1992, Worshipful Co. of Wheelwrights 1997, Fellow, City and Guilds of London Inst.; Jordanian Order of Merit (First Class), USA Legion of Merit (Degree of Cdre); Hon. DSc (Cranfield) 1985. *Publications:* contrib. to journals and publs. *Leisure interests:* seven grandchildren. *Address:* House of Lords, Westminster, London, SW1A 0PW, England (office).

VINCENT-ROSTOWSKI, Jan (Jacek), BSc, MSc, MA; Polish/British economist, politician and academic; b. (Jan Rostowski), 30 April 1951, London, England; s. of Roman Rostowski; m.; two c.; ed Westminster School, London, Univ. Coll., London, UK, School of Slavonic and East European Studies, Univ. of London, London School of Econs and Political Science; born into Polish immigrant family in London, spent much of his childhood in Kenya, Mauritius and the Seychelles where his father was posted, grew up and educated in UK; Lecturer, Kingston Polytechnic –1988; Lecturer, School of Slavonic and East European Studies 1988–95; Adviser to Deputy Prime Minister and Minister of Finance of Poland 1989–91; worked at Centre for Econ. Performance, LSE 1992–95; Prof. of Economy, Cen. European Univ., Budapest 1995–, Dean of Faculty of Economy 1995–2000, 2005–06; Chair. Macro-econ. Policy Cttee, Ministry of Finance 1997–2001; Adviser to Pres. Nat. Bank of Poland 2002–04, to Bd of Bank PEKAO SA 2004–; Minister of Finance 2007–13; Deputy Prime Minister 25 Feb.–27 Nov. 2013; fmr Adviser to Govt of Russian Fed. on macro-econ. policy; Co-founder Centre for Social and Econ. Analysis (CASE), Warsaw, mem. Supervisory Council 1991–2007; mem. Supervisory Bd Polish Privatization Soc.– Kleinwort Benson, Polski Bank Rozwoju SA 1994–95; mem. Platforma Obywatelska (Civic Platform) party 2010–; mem. Sejm (Parl.) (Platforma Obywatelska) 2011–; Trustee, CASE Foundation; named European Finance Minister of the Year by The Banker magazine 2009, cited by the Financial Times as the third best Finance Minister in Europe 2012. *Publications include:* author or ed. of several books, book chapters and numerous articles in professional journals on an enlarged EU, monetary policy, exchange rate policy and transformations of post-communist economies. *Address:* c/o Chancellery of the Prime Minister, 00-583 Warsaw, Al. Ujazdowskie 1/3, Poland. *E-mail:* sprm@kprm.gov.pl.

VINDE, Pierre L. V., JurCand, FilCand; Swedish fmr civil servant, fmr international civil servant and consultant; *Project Director, International Development and Strategies France;* b. 15 Aug. 1931, Paris, France; s. of Victor Vinde and Rita Wilson; m. Lise Le Coeur; ed schools in France, Sweden and UK, Univs. of Uppsala and Stockholm; in Prime Minister's Office 1957–58; Ministry of Trade 1958–60; Ministry of Finance 1961–76, Budget Dir 1970–74, Under-Sec. 1974–76; mem. Bd Devt Assistance Agency 1962–65, Inst. of Defence Org. and Man. 1968–70, Nat. Audit Office 1969–74, Agency for Admin. Devt 1974–76; Deputy Group of Ten 1974–76; Chair. Bd of Dirs Bank of Sweden 1974–76; mem. Police Comm. 1962–64, Defence Comm. 1965–68; Chair. Relocation of Gov. Admin. Comm. 1970–72; Sr Vice-Pres. PKbanken 1977–80; Asst Admin. (Finance and Admin), UNDP 1980–85, Deputy Sec.-Gen. OECD 1985–96; Adviser, Ministry of Finance 1996–97; consultant to OECD 1998, to UNDP 1999–2000, 2003–, to Swedish Ministry of Trade 2002; currently Project Dir, International Development & Strategies France. *Publications:* Frankr av i dag o i morgon 1960, Hur Sverige styres (The Government of Sweden) 1968, Den sv. statsförvaltningen 1969, Swedish Government Administration 1971. *Address:* International Development & Strategies, 22 boulevard Pereire, 75017 Paris, France (office). *Telephone:* 1-53-81-13-35 (office). *Fax:* 1-53-81-01-78 (office). *E-mail:* pierre.vinde@id-strategies.com (office). *Website:* www.id-strategies.fr (office).

VINE, Barbara (see Rendell of Babergh, Ruth Barbara).

VINE, Jeremy, BA; British broadcaster; b. 17 May 1965, Epsom, Surrey; s. of Guy Vine and Diana Vine; m. Rachel Vine; ed Epsom Coll. and Durham Univ.; journalist, Coventry Evening Telegraph 1986–87; joined BBC 1987, News Trainee 1987–89, Programme Reporter, Today 1989–93, Political Corresp. 1993–97, Africa Corresp. 1997–99, Presenter, Newsnight 1996–2002 (full-time 1999–2002), The Politics Show 2003–05, Panorama 2007–10, Eggheads 2008–, Points of View 2008–; Presenter, The Jeremy Vine Show, BBC Radio 2 2003–; Sony Radio Acad. Awards Speech Broadcaster of the Year 2005, 2011. *Publications:* It's All News to Me (autobiography) 2012. *Leisure interest:* Chelsea Football Club, films of Alfred Hitchcock, poems of W. H. Auden. *Address:* c/o Noel Gay, 19 Denmark Street, London, WC2H 8NA, England. *E-mail:* info@noelgay.com; vine@bbc.co.uk (office). *Website:* www.bbc.co.uk/radio2/shows/vine (office).

VINEN, William Frank, PhD, FRS; British physicist and academic; *Professor Emeritus of Physics, University of Birmingham;* b. 15 Feb. 1930, England; s. of Gilbert Vinen and Olive Maud Vinen; ed Clare Coll., Cambridge; fmr Prof. of Physics, Univ. of Birmingham, now Emer.; mem. Academia Europaea (Physics, Astrophysics and Eng Section); The Simon Memorial Prize, Inst. of Physics (co-recipient) 1963, Holweck Medal and Prize, Inst. of Physics and the French Physical Soc. 1978, Rumford Medal, Royal Soc. 1980, Guthrie Medal and Prize, Inst. of Physics 2005. *Achievements include:* the observation and measurement of quantized vortices in superfluid helium, the first direct confirmation of the application of quantum mechanics to a macroscopic body. *Publications:* numerous scientific papers in professional journals on superfluids and superconductors. *Address:* School of Physics and Astronomy, University of Birmingham, Birmingham, B15 2TT, England (office). *Telephone:* (121) 414-4667 (office). *E-mail:* w.f .vinen@bham.ac.uk (office). *Website:* www.ph.bham.ac.uk (office).

VINES, David Anthony, PhD; British/Australian economist and academic; *Professor of Economics, University of Oxford;* b. 8 May 1949, Oxford, England; s. of Robert Vines and Vera Vines; m. 1st Susannah Lucy Robinson 1979 (divorced 1992); three s.; m. 2nd Jane E. Bingham 1995; two step-s.; ed Scotch Coll., Melbourne, Australia and Univs of Melbourne and Cambridge; Fellow, Pembroke Coll. Cambridge 1976–85; Research Officer, Sr Research Officer, Dept of Applied Econs, Univ. of Cambridge 1979–85; Adam Smith Prof. of Political Econ. Univ of Glasgow 1985–92; Fellow and Tutor in Econs Balliol Coll. Oxford 1992–, Prof. of Econs, Univ. of Oxford 2000–; Adjunct Prof. of Econs, Inst. of Advanced Studies, ANU 1991–; Dir ESRC Research Programme on Global Econ. Insts 1993–2000; mem. Bd Channel 4 TV 1986–92, Glasgow Devt Agency 1990–92, Analysis, Scottish Early Music Asscn 1988–95; econ. consultant to Sec. of State for Scotland 1988–92; consultant to IMF 1988, 1989; mem. Acad. Panel, HM Treasury 1986–; mem. Research Programmes Bd, ESRC 1990–92; mem. Int. Policy Forum, HM Treasury 1999–; Houblon Norman Fellow, Bank of England 2001–02. *Publications:* Stagflation, Vol. II: Demand Management (with J. E. Meade and J. M. Maciejowski) 1983, Macroeconomic Interactions Between North and South (with D. A. Currie) 1988, Macroeconomic Policy: inflation, wealth and the exchange rate (jtly) 1989, Deregulation and the Future of Commercial Television (with G. Hughes) 1989, Information, Strategy and Public Policy (with A. Stevenson) 1991, North South Macroeconomic Interactions and Global Macroeconomic Policy (co-ed. with D. A. Currie) 1995, Europe, East Asia and APEC: a Shared Global Agenda (with P. Drysdale) 1998, The Asian Financial Crisis: Causes Contagion and Consequences (co-ed. with P. Agenor, M. Miller and A. Weber) 1999, Integrity in the Public and Private Domains (ed. with A. Montefiore) 1999, The World Bank: Structure and Policies (co-ed. with C. L. Gilbert) 2000, The IMF and its Critics: Reform of Global Financial Architecture (co-ed. with C. L. Gilbert) 2004; numerous papers in professional journals. *Leisure interests:* hillwalking, music. *Address:* Balliol College, Oxford, OX1 3BJ (office); Department of Economics, Manor Road, Oxford, OX1 3UQ, England (office). *Telephone:* (1865) 271067 (Coll.) (office); (1865) 242621 (Dept) (office). *Fax:* (1865) 277803 (Coll.) (office); (1865) 271094 (Dept) (office). *E-mail:* david.vines@economics.ox.ac.uk (office). *Website:* www.economics .ox.ac.uk (office).

VINGT-TROIS, HE Cardinal André Armand; French ecclesiastic; *Archbishop of Paris;* b. 7 Nov. 1942, Paris; ed Catholic Inst., Paris; ordained priest in Paris 1969; after five years in a parish, began teaching at Issy-les-Moulineaux seminary; Vicar Gen. of Paris Archdiocese and Dir of Vocations 1981–88; Auxiliary Bishop of Paris and Titular Bishop of Thibilis 1988–99; Archbishop of Tours 1999–2005, of Paris 2005–; Ordinary of France and Faithful of Eastern Rites 2005–; cr. Cardinal (Cardinal-Priest of S. Luigi dei Francesi) 2007; mem. Congregation for Bishops and the Pontifical Council for the Family 2008–, Congregation for the Clergy 2010–, Congregation for the Oriental Churches 2012–; apptd by Pope Benedict XVI to serve as a Synod Father for the Ordinary Gen. Ass. of the Synod of Bishops on the New Evangelization 2012; participated in Papal Conclave 2013; apptd by Pope Francis as Pres. of the 3rd Extraordinary Gen. Ass. of the Synod of Bishops 2014; Ordre nat. du Mérite 2007, Grand Croix de l'Ordre nat. du Bénin 2010, Officier, Légion d'honneur 2012, Chevalier Grand Croix de l'Ordre Equestre du St Sépulcre 2012. *Publications include:* Évêques, prêtres et diacres (Bishops, Priests and Deacons) 2009, Médiaspaul, Une mission de liberté (A Mission for Liberty) 2010, Prier. Pourquoi? Comment? (Prayer. Why? How?) 2010, La Famille: un bonheur à construire (Family Life: Building Happiness) 2011, Parole et Silence, Quelle société voulons-nous? (What Kind of Society Do We Want?) 2012. *Address:* Archdiocese of Paris, 10 rue du Cloître Notre-Dame, 75004 Paris, France (office). *Telephone:* 1-78-91-91-91 (office). *Fax:* 1-78-91-92-73 (office). *E-mail:* communication@diocese-paris.net (office). *Website:* paris.catholique.fr (office).

VINNICHENKO, Nikolai Alexandrovich; Russian lawyer and politician; b. 10 April 1965, Oktyabrskoye Village, Shemonaikha Dist, Kazakhstan SSR; Chief Prosecutor, St Petersburg 2003–04; Chief Bailiff and Dir Russian Federal Bailiffs Service 2004–08; Plenipotentiary Rep. of Russian Pres. to Urals Fed. Okrug (Dist) 2008–11, to North-Western Federal Okrug 2011–13; First Class Councillor in Justice. *Address:* c/o Office of the Plenipotentiary Representative of the President, 199004 St Petersburg, Vasilyevskii ostrov, 3-ya liniya 12, Russia (office).

VINOGRADOV, Oleg Mikhailovich; Russian ballet master; *Principal Guest Choreographer, Mikhailovsky Theatre;* b. 1 Aug. 1937; ed Vaganov Choreographic School, Leningrad; danced with Novosibirsk Acad. Theatre and Dir Cinderella 1964, Romeo and Juliet 1965; ballet master at Kirov Ballet, Leningrad 1968–72; Chief Ballet Master of Maly Theatre Dance Co. 1973–77; Chief Ballet Master of Kirov (now Mariinsky) Theatre 1977–99; works in USA and S Korea; Artistic Dir Universal Ballet 1998–2008; Prin. Guest Choreographer, Mikhailovsky Theatre, St Peterburg 2008–; People's Artist of USSR 1983; RSFSR State Prize for Kazhlaev's Goryanka 1970, Marius Petipa Prize, Paris 1978, Pablo Picasso Prize 1987. *Productions include:* Useless Precaution (Hérold) 1971, Coppélia 1973, Yaroslavna (B. Tishchenko) 1974, The Hussar's Ballad (Khrennikov), The Government Inspector, The Battleship Potemkin (A. Chaikovsky), Behests of the Past 1983 and numerous others. *Address:* Mikhailovsky Theatre, 191186 St Petersburg, Arts Square, 1, Russia (office). *Website:* www.mikhailovsky.ru (office).

VINOGRADOV, Vladimir Alekseyevich; Russian information specialist and economist; b. 2 July 1921, Kazan; s. of Aleksei Alexandrovich and Maria Alexandrovna; m. Marianna B. Antsuta 1943; one s.; ed Inst. of Int. Relations, Moscow; served in Soviet Army 1939–41; mem. staff Presidium of USSR (now Russian) Acad. of Sciences 1948–60, Deputy Chief Scientific Sec. 1961–71, Dir Inst. of Scientific Information on Social Sciences 1972–98, mem. Acad. 1984–; Counsellor 1998–; Lecturer Dept of Political Economy, Moscow Univ. 1954–60; Chair. Cttee on Russian and World Econ. History, Russian Acad. of Sciences 1983–; mem. Soviet Cttee of UNESCO 1965–91; Vice-Pres. Int. Asscn for Econ. History 1968–78, Int. Social Sciences Council 1978–81; Hon. Vice-Pres. Vienna Centre 1981–93; USSR State Prize 1982, Chernishevskii Prize (Presidium of Acad. of Sciences) and other awards and prizes. *Publications:* numerous books and articles on the genesis of property in Russian and West European countries and on

problems of information in the social sciences and the humanities, including Social Sciences and Information 1978, Workers' Control over Production: Theory, History and Contemporaneity 1983, What Type of Privatization Do We Need? 1991, State Property and Privatization in France 1998, Privatization: Global Trends and National Peculiarities 2006, My 20th Century: Memoirs 2008. *Leisure interest:* poetry. *Address:* Institute of Scientific Information in Social Sciences, Moscow 117997, Nakhimovski prosp. 51/21 (office); Moscow 111480, Profsokinojastr. 43-1-102, Russia. *Telephone:* (499) 128-15-51 (office); (495) 331-32-16 (home). *Fax:* (499) 128-88-81 (office).

VINOKOUROV, Alexandr; Kazakhstani cyclist; b. 16 Sept. 1973, Pavlodar; s. of Nikolay Vinokourov; three c.; started cycling at the age of 11, initially competed within fmr Soviet Union, undertook initial training at a sports school in Almaty 1986–91, also trained as part of Soviet Union nat. team, participated in Tour of Ecuador 1995, Tour of Slovenia 1996, Olympic Games, Atlanta 1996, moved to France 1997; silver medal, road race, Olympic Games, Sydney 2000; found guilty of blood-doping during Tour de France 2007, banned for one year, returned to cycling 2009; gold medal, time trial, silver medal, road race, Asian Cycling Championships 2009; gold medal, road race, Olympic Games, London 2012; winner Four Days of Dunkirk 1998, Tour de l'Oise, Tour de Picardie 1998, Circuit de Lorraine 1998, Critérium du Dauphiné 1999, Volta a la Comunitat Valenciana 1999, Deutschland Tour 2001, Paris-Nice 2002, 2003, Amstel Gold Race 2003, Tour de Suisse 2003, Regio-Tour 2004, Liège-Bastogne-Liège 2005, 2010, Nat. Road Race Championship 2005, Vuelta a Castilla y León 2006, Chrono des Nations 2009, Giro del Trentino 2010; teams: Casino-Ag2r 1998–99, Team Telekom 2000–05, Liberty Seguros-Würth 2006, Astana 2007–; candidate for parl. elections 2011; Hon. Col, Kazakh Army 2009; People's Hero First Class Medal. *Address:* Astana Pro Team, Abacanto SA, 48bd Grande Duchesse Charlotte, 1330, Luxembourg. *E-mail:* info@astana.lu. *Website:* www.proteam-astana.com.

VIOT, Pierre, LèsL, LenD; French barrister; b. 9 April 1925, Bordeaux; s. of Edmund Viot and Irma Viot; m. Monique Fruchier 1952 (deceased); two s. two d.; ed Faculté de droit de Bordeaux, Inst. d'études politiques de Paris, Ecole Nat. d'Admin.; Jr Official, Cour des Comptes 1953, Chief Counsel; Asst, Bureau des Commissaires aux Comptes, NATO 1957–61; Regional and Urban Dept Head, Gen. Planning Office 1961; Spokesman, Nat. and Regional Devt Cttee 1961; Sec.-Gen., Conseil des Impôts 1971; Dir-Gen., Centre nat. de la Cinématographie 1973–84; Pres., Cannes Film Festival 1984–2000, Cinefondation Cannes Film Festival 2000–; Pres. Bd of Dirs, Etablissement public de l'Opéra de la Bastille 1985–89; Commdr, Légion d'honneur, Croix de guerre, Grand Croix, Ordre nat. du Mérite, Commdr Arts et Lettres, Commdr, Ordine al Merito della Repubblica Italiana, Officier, Verdienstorden der Bundesrepublik Deutschland. *Leisure interests:* tennis, gardening. *Address:* 38 avenue Emile Zola, 75015 Paris, France (home).

VIRANT, Gregor; Slovenian lawyer, politician and public servant; *Deputy Prime Minister and Minister of the Interior;* b. 4 Dec. 1969, Ljubljana; m.; two s.; ed Univ. of Ljubljana, Glasgow Caledonian Univ., UK; worked as legal adviser to Constitutional Court of Slovenia 1995–99; Sec.-Gen., Ministry of the Interior 2000–04, one of the authors of the reform of public admin; cand. for Državni zbor (Nat. Ass.) on list of Slovenian Democratic Party (though never joined) 2004; Head of newly created Ministry of Public Admin 2004–08; Chair. Rally for the Republic (Zbor za republiko) 2008–11; mem. Council of Experts, Slovenian Democratic Party 2009–11; Leader of Gregor Virant's Civic List (renamed Civic List April 2012) 2011–; elected to Nat. Ass. as an ind. 2011, Chair. 2011–13; Deputy Prime Minister and Minister of the Interior 2013–. *Address:* Ministry of the Interior, 1501 Ljubljana, Štefanova 2, Slovenia (office). *Telephone:* (1) 4284721 (office). *Fax:* (1) 4284972 (office). *E-mail:* gp.mnz@gov.si (office). *Website:* www.mnz.gov.si (office).

VIRATA, Cesar Enrique, BS (MechEng), MBA; Philippine politician and banker; *Chairman and President, C. Virata & Associates Inc.;* b. 12 Dec. 1930, Manila; s. of Enrique Virata and Leonor Aguinaldo; m. Joy Gamboa 1956; two s. one d.; ed Univ. of Pennsylvania, USA and Univ. of the Philippines; Dean, Coll. of Business Admin., Univ. of the Philippines 1961–69; Chair. and Dir Philippine Nat. Bank 1967–69; Deputy Dir-Gen. Presidential Econ. Staff 1967–68; Under-Sec. of Industry 1967–69; Chair. Bd of Investments 1968–70; Minister of Finance 1970–86; Prime Minister of the Philippines 1981–86; Chair. Land Bank of the Philippines 1973–86; mem. Nat. Ass. 1978–86, Monetary Bd, Nat. Econ. and Devt Authority 1972–86, Comm. on the Future of the Bretton Woods Insts 1992–; Adviser to the Co-ordinating Council for the Philippines Aid Plan 1989–90; Chair. IMF and IBRD Devt Cttee 1976–80; Chair. and Pres. C. Virata & Assocs Inc. (Man. Consultants) 1986–; Chair. Bd of Govs, Asian Devt Bank 1979–80; Dir Philippine Stock Exchange, Inc. 1992; Dir and Corp. Vice-Chair. Rizal Commercial Banking Corpn 1995–; Hon. LHD, Hon. DPA, Dr hc (Philippines). *Leisure interests:* tennis, reading. *Address:* C. Virata & Associates Inc., Development Academy of the Philippines Building, San Miguel Avenue, Pasig City, Metro Manila 1600 (office); Rizal Commercial Banking Corporation, 46th Floor, Yuchengco Tower, RCBC Plaza, 6819 Ayala Avenue, Makati City 0727 (office); 63 East Maya Drive, Quezon City, Philippines (home). *Telephone:* (2) 631-2161 (office); (2) 844-8889 (office). *Fax:* (2) 631-2161 (office); (2) 878-3400 (office). *E-mail:* cvirata@pacific.net.ph (office); ceavirata@rcbc.com (office).

VIREN, Lasse; Finnish politician and fmr athlete; b. 22 July 1949, Myrskylä; m. Päivi Kajander 1976; three s.; competed in Olympic Games, Munich 1972, won gold medal at 5,000m and 10,000m; Montréal 1976, won gold medal at 5,000m and 10,000m, 5th in marathon; Moscow 1980, 5th in 10,000m; only athlete to retain 5,000m and 10,000m titles at successive Olympics; held world records at two miles, 5,000m and 10,000m; sports promoter in schools at the Union Bank of Finland; elected pres. of his local town council while running own transport business; MP (Conservative Party) 1999–2007. *Publication:* The Golden Seconds. *Address:* Suomen Urheilulitto ry, Box 25202, 00250, Helsinki 25, Finland.

VIRILIO, Paul; French writer, artist and academic; b. 1932, Paris; ed Ecole des Métiers d'Art, Paris, Univ. of Paris (Sorbonne); worked as artist in stained glass alongside Matisse in various churches in Paris; untrained architect; Chair. and Dir Ecole Spéciale d'Architecture, Paris 1968–98, Prof. Emer. 1998–; Ed. Espace Critique, Editions Galilee, Paris 1973; Co-Founder and Programme Dir Collège Int. de Philosophie 1990; Prof. of Philosophy, European Graduate School, Saas-Fee, Switzerland; mem. French Comm. concerned with housing for the poor

(HCLD) 1992–; fmr mem. Editorial Bds Esprit, Cause Commune, Critiques, Traverses; has worked with Fondation Cartier pour l'art contemporain on several exhbns including Bunker Archeology, Pompidou Centre 1975, Speed, Jouy-en-Josas 1991, Unknown Quantity, Paris 2002; Grand Prix Nat. de la Critique 1987. *Publications include:* Bunker Archéologie 1975, L'Insecurité du territoire 1976, Speed and Politics 1977, Popular Defense and Ecological Struggles 1978, L'Esthetique de la disparition 1980, Pure War (with Sylvère Lotringer) 1983, War and Cinema: The Logistics of Perception 1984, L'Espace critique 1984, Polar Inertia 1990, The Art of the Motor 1995, Politics of the Very Worst 1996, Open Sky 1997, The Information Bomb 1998, The Strategy of Deception 1999, A Landscape of Events 2000, Ground Zero 2002, Negative Horizon 2005, The Accident of Art 2005, City of Panic 2005, The Original Accident 2007, Art as Far as the Eye Can See 2007, Strategy of Deception 2007, The University of Disaster 2009; numerous technical works. *Address:* c/o European Graduate School, Media and Communication Division, Alter Kehr 20, 3953 Leuk-Stadt, Switzerland (office). *Website:* www.egs.edu/faculty/paul-virilio/biography.

VIRSALADZE, Elisso Konstantinovna; Georgian pianist; b. 14 Sept. 1942, Tbilisi; studied under grandmother, Prof. Anastasia Virsaladze, then at Tbilisi Conservatory; teacher, Moscow Conservatory 1962; Prof., Musikhochschule, Munich; played as soloist world-wide; f. Telavi Music Festival, Georgia; First Prize, All-Union Competition of Performing Musicians, Moscow 1961, Bronze Medal, Tchaikovsky Competition 1962, Prize at Schumann Competition, Georgian State Prize 1983, USSR People's Artist 1989. *Telephone:* (89) 26024335 (office). *Fax:* (89) 26024344 (office). *E-mail:* hahn@augstein.info (office). *Website:* www.augstein.info (office).

VIRZÌ, Paolo; Italian screenwriter, director and producer; b. 4 March 1964, Livorno, Tuscany; m. Micaela Ramazzotti; ed Univ. of Pisa, studied at Centro sperimentale di cinematografia, Rome under Gianni Amelio and Furio Scarpelli; formed artistic asscn with fmr fellow student Francesco Bruni that became important in later years; later, Furio Scarpelli became his teacher and mentor; f. Motorino Amaranto s.r.l. production house 2007. *Films:* Turnè (writer) 1990, Condominio (Condominium) (story; writer) 1991, Tempo di uccidere (Time to Kill; aka The Short Cut) (writer) 1991, Donne sottotetto (aka Centro storico) (writer) 1992, La bella vita (Living It Up) (writer and dir) (Ciak d'Oro, Nastro d'Argento and David di Donatello Award for Best New Dir 1995, Silver Ribbon for Best New Dir, Italian Nat. Syndicate of Film Journalists 1995) 1994, Ferie d'agosto (story, screenplay) (David di Donatello for Best Film of the Year 1996) 1995, Intolerance (dir segment Roma Ovest 143) 1996, Ferie d'agosto (dir) 1996, Cuba libre – velocipedi ai tropici (writer) 1997, Ovosodo (Hardboiled Egg) (story, screenplay and dir) (Grand Special Jury Prize and Little Golden Lion, Venice Film Festival 1997, Youth Audience Award, Montpellier Mediterranean Film Festival 1997) 1997, Baci e abbracci (Kisses and Hugs) (dir) 1999, Provino d'ammissione (writer and dir) 1999, My Name is Tanino (writer and dir) 2002, Caterina va in città (Caterina in the Big City) (writer, dir and co-producer) (Future Film Festival Digital Award – Special Mention, Venice Film Festival 2002) 2002, 4-4-2 – Il gioco più bello del mondo (all segments) 2006, L'estate del mio primo bacio (writer) 2006, N (Io e Napoleone) (Napoleon and Me) (screenplay and dir) 2006, Il caimano (The Caiman) (actor) 2006, Tutta la vita davanti (writer, dir and producer) 2008. *Television:* Une questione privata (A Private Affair) (writer) 1991. *Address:* Motorino Amaranto s.r.l., Via Miani 40, 00154 Rome, Italy (office). *Telephone:* (06) 5747488 (office). *E-mail:* info@motorinoamaranto.it (office). *Website:* www.motorinoamaranto.it (office).

VISCHER, Ulrich, lic. iur., Dr. iur., PhD; Swiss lawyer and university administrator; *President of the University Council, University of Basel;* b. 1951; m.; two s.; ed Univ. of Basel; began career with Basler Volkswirtschaftsbund (Basel Econ. Fed.); with Schweizerischer Bankverein (Swiss Bank Corpn) 1977–78; fmrly with Baloise Insurance Co.; mem. Basel City Parl. 1980–92 (Pres. 1989); mem. Govt of Canton Basel-Stadt and Minister of Finance 1992–2005; Pnr, Vischer & Assocs (law firm) Basel 2005–; Pres. Univ. Council, Univ. of Basel 2005–; Chair. MCH Swiss Exhibition (Holding) Ltd; Dir Warteck Invest AG 2007–; mem. Soc. of Trust and Estate Practitioners, Basel. *Address:* Office of the President, University of Basel, Leimenstrasse 1, 4001 Basel (office); Vischer, Aeschenvorstadt 4, 4010 Basel, Switzerland (office). *Telephone:* (61) 267-84-05 (office). *Fax:* (61) 267-84-34 (office). *E-mail:* uvischer@vischer.com (office). *Website:* www.unibas.ch (office); www.vischer.com (office).

VISCO, Ignazio, MA, PhD; Italian economist and central banker; *Governor, Banca d'Italia;* b. 21 Nov. 1949, Naples; m.; three d.; ed La Sapienza Univ., Rome, Univ. of Pennsylvania, USA; Lecturer in Econometrics, La Sapienza Univ., Rome 1983–85, in Econ. Policy 1989; joined Research Dept, Banca d'Italia 1974, Head of Dept 1990, Deputy Dir-Gen. 2007–11, Gov. 2011–; Chief Economist and Dir Dept of Econs, OECD 1997–2002; Pres. European System of Central Banks Int. Relations Cttee 2009–10; Assoc. Ed. European Economic Review 1986–91; mem. Società Italiana degli Economisti, Società Italiana di Statistica, American Econ. Asscn; Cavaliere, Ordine al merito della Repubblica italiana 1991, Ufficiale 1993, Commendatore 2002, Grande Ufficiale 2007, Cavaliere di Gran Croce al merito 2011. *Publications include:* Le aspettative nell'analisi economica 1985, Inflazione, concorrenza e sviluppo (with S. Micossi) 1993, Saving and the Accumulation of Wealth (with A. Ando and L. Guiso) 1994, L'economia italiana (with L. F. Signorini) 2002, Investire in conoscenza 2009. *Address:* Banca d'Italia, Via Nazionale 91, 00184 Rome, Italy (office). *Telephone:* (06) 47921 (office). *E-mail:* email@bancaditalia.it (office). *Website:* www.bancaditalia.it/bancaditalia/direttorio/visco (office).

VISHNEVA, Diana Viktorovna; Russian ballerina; *Principal Dancer, Mariinsky Theatre;* b. 13 July 1976, Leningrad; d. of Victor Vishnev and Guzel Vishneva; ed Vaganova Acad. of Russian Ballet; with Mariinsky Theatre 1995–, Prin. Dancer 1996–; Guest Artist, Teatro alla Scala, Milan 2001, Staatsoper Unter den Linden, Berlin 2002–, Grand d'Opera 2002; f. Diana Vishneva Foundation for the Development of Ballet; Prix de Lausanne 1994, Divine Isadora Prize, Benois de la danse prize 1995, Golden Sophit St Petersburg Theatre Prize 1996, State Prize of Russia, Baltika Prize 1998, Golden Mask 2001, Dance of Europe Prize 2002, Ballet Magazine Prize 2003, People's Artist of Russia 2007. *Main roles include:* Masha (Nutcracker), Kitri (Don Quixote), Aurore (Sleeping Beauty), Henriette and Raymonda (Raymonda), Gulnary (Corsaire), Giselle (Giselle), Nikia (La Bayadere),

Odette/Odile (Swan Lake), Juliet (Romeo and Juliet), Manon (Manon), Carmen (Carmen), Rubies (Jewels). *Address:* c/o Diana Vishneva Foundation, 199106 St Petersburg, 80 Bolshoi Prospekt V.O.; Mariinsky Theatre, 190000 St Petersburg, Teatralnaya pl. 1, Russia (office). *Telephone:* (812) 326-4141 (office); (812) 303-0607 (home). *Fax:* (812) 314-1744 (office); (812) 570-2331 (office). *E-mail:* info@vishneva.ru (office). *Website:* www.vishneva.ru.

VISHNEVSKY, Yuri Georgyevich; Russian geophysicist and civil servant; b. 13 May 1943, Orlovorozka, Kemerovo region; m.; one s.; ed Tomsk Polytech. Inst.; engineer, then sr engineer, Tomsk-7 (chemical co.), Siberia for Ministry of Machine Construction 1966–85; Head of Volzhsk br., then Cen. Br. State Inspection of Atomic and Energy Safety (Balakovo Nuclear Station) 1985–91; Chair. State Cttee for Inspection of Radiation Safety 1991, Chair. RSFSR State Cttee for Inspection of Nuclear and Radiation Safety at Russian Presidency 1991–92; Dir Fed. Inspectorate of Nuclear and Radiation Safety (Gosatomnadzor) 1992–2003. *Address:* c/o Federal Inspection of Nuclear and Radiation Safety of Russian Federation, Taganskaya str. 34, 109147 Moscow, Russia (office).

VISHWANATHAN, Anand, BComm; Indian chess player; b. 11 Dec. 1969, Chennai, Tamil Nadu; s. of K. Viswanathan and Susila Viswanathan; m. Aruna Anand; ed Loyola Coll., Chennai; winner of 72 int. chess tournaments; Nat. Sub-Jr Chess Champion 1983; Int. Master (aged 15) 1984; Indian Nat. Champion 1985; first Indian Int. Grandmaster 1987; World Jr Champion 1987; beat fmr world champions Mikhail Tal and Boris Spassky at Fourth Int. Games Festival 1989; Asian Champion 1990; captained Indian team at Chess Olympiad, Manila 1992; placed second in PCA ranking 1995; World Chess Champion 2000; FIDE World Cup Champion 2002, 2007, 2008; Jameo de Oro, Govt of Spain 2001; Doctorate hc (Jawaharlal Nehru Technological Univ., Hyderabad) 1988; Arjuna Award 1985, Padma Shri 1987, Soviet Land Nehru Award 1987, Nat. Citizens' Award 1987, Shri Rajiv Gandhi Award 1988, Rajiv Gandhi Khel Ratna Award 1991–92, K Birla Award 1995, Sportstar Millenium Award 1998, Oscar Best Chess Player 1997, 1998, 2003, 2004, 2007, Padma Bhushan 2000, CNN IBN Sportsperson of the Year 2007, Padma Vibhushan 2007, NDTV Indian Sportsperson of the Year 2008. *Publication:* My Best Games of Chess (Book of the Year Award, British Chess Fed. 1998). *Leisure interests:* reading, swimming, listening to music. *Address:* 7 (old No. 4) II Cross Street, Customs Colony, Besant Nagar, Chennai 600 090, India (home).

VITA, Giuseppe, DrMed; Italian business executive; *Chairman, UniCredit Group;* b. 28 April 1935, Sicily; m.; two c.; ed in Catania and at Univ. La Sapienza, Rome and Univ. of Rome; qualified as specialist in radiology; Asst Röntgeninstitut, Univ. of Mainz 1962; joined Schering AG as asst in clinical research 1964, Gen. Dir Schering SpA Milan 1965, Deputy mem. Man. Bd Schering AG 1987, mem. 1988, Chair. 1989–2001, Chair. Supervisory Bd 2001–06; Chair. Deutsche Bank SpA 1998–2002, Hon. Chair. 2002–; Chair. Supervisory Bd Hugo Boss AG 2000–08, Axel Springer AG 2002–, Deutz (Germany) 2006–09; Chair. RAS (Italy) 2001–06; Chair. UniCredit Group 2012–; Chair. Allianz SpA 2007–09, 2011–12, Vice-Pres. 2009–11; Chair. Gruppo Banca Leonardo 2007–12; mem. Supervisory Cttee Vattenfall Europe 1990–2008, Continental 1991–2002, Allianz Versicherung 1996–2003, Allianz Lebensvericherung (Assicurazione Vita) 1997–2004, Degussa 2000–04, Medical Park AG 2001–12, Dussmann Stiftung (Germany) 2006–12; mem. Bd of Dirs Marzotto di Agenzia Nazionale per Attrazione Investimenti e Sviluppo d'Impresa 1995–98, Marzotto (Italy) 2003–05, Barilla SpA 2003–12, Humanitas Istituto Clinico 2003–12, Istituto Europeo di Oncologia 2007–12, Fondazione IEO (Italy) 2007–12, Fondazione Cerba (Italy) 2007–12, Fondazione Feltrinelli (Italy) 2007–12, Consiglio per le relazioni fra Italia e Stati Uniti (Italy) 2007–12, Pirelli & C. (Italy) March–May 2012, RCS MediaGroup SpA 2012–13, ABI (Italian Banking Asscn) 2012–, Associazione Italiana per la Ricerca sul Cancro 2012–; Advisory Bd mem. Lazard (Italy) 2002–06; Advisor to Bd Dirs Ikonisys 2004–; mem. Gen. Council Institue Italia 2012–, Trilateral Comm. (Italian Group) 2012–; Cavaliere del Lavoro, Verdienstorden des Landes Berlin, Verdienstkreuz am Bande des Verdienstordens der Bundesrepublik Deutschland. *Address:* UniCredit Group, Piazza Cordusia, 20123 Milan, Italy (office). *Telephone:* (02) 88621 (office). *Fax:* (02) 88628503 (office). *E-mail:* info@unicreditgroup.eu (office). *Website:* www.unicreditgroup.eu (office).

VITAL, Brig. Gen. Albert Camille; Malagasy civil engineer, army officer and politician; b. 18 July 1952, Toliara; m.; five c.; ed Ecole Spéciale Militaire de Saint-Cyr, France, Ecole Supérieure Militaire, Paris; Chief of Tech. Office, State Forces Staff Devt 1987–91, Instructor, Army Staff Coll. 1993–96, Corps Commdr, 1st Regt, Mil. Region No. 5, Toliara 1998–2001; Prime Minister of Madagascar 2009–11 (resgnd), also Minister of the Armed Forces 2010; unsuccessful cand. for Mayor of Toliara; f. Toliara (security firm); fmr Pres. Toliara Chamber of Commerce and Industry. *Address:* c/o Office of the Prime Minister, BP 248, Palais d'Etat Mahazoarivo, 101 Antananarivo, Madagascar.

VITALE, Alberto; American publishing executive; b. 22 Dec. 1933, Vercelli, Piedmont, Italy; s. of Sergio Vitale and Elena Segre; m. Gemma G. Calori 1961; two s.; ed Turin Univ., IPSOA Business School and Wharton School, Univ. of Pennsylvania; joined Olivetti 1958; moved to USA to assist in Olivetti's acquisition of Underwood 1959; Exec. IFI (Agnelli family holding co.) 1971; Exec. Vice-Pres. for Admin Bantam Books, New York 1975, Co-CEO 1985, sole CEO 1986; Pres. and CEO Bantam-Doubleday-Dell 1987; Chair., Pres. and CEO Random House 1989–96, Chair., CEO 1996–98, Chair. Supervisory Bd Random House Inc., New York 1998; mem. Bd of Dirs Transworld Publrs; mem. Bd of Trustees Mercy Coll. NY; mem. Nat. Advisory Council, Reading is Fundamental; Chevalier, Ordre des Arts et des Lettres 1996. *Address:* 135 Grace Trail, Palm Beach, FL 33480, USA (home). *E-mail:* aavitale1@aol.com (home).

VITERBI, Andrew J., BS, MS, PhD, FIEEE; American (b. Italian) telecommunications engineer, business executive and academic; *President, The Viterbi Group, LLC; Presidential Chair and Professor of Electrical Engineering, University of Southern California;* b. 9 March 1935, Bergamo, Italy; m. Erna Viterbi; two s. one d.; ed Massachusetts Inst. of Tech., Univ. of Southern California; family moved to USA in 1939; began career at Jet Propulsion Lab., Calif. Inst. of Tech. 1968; Prof., School of Eng and Applied Science, UCLA 1963–73; Adjunct Prof. of Electrical Eng and Computer Science, Univ. of California, San Diego 1975, now Prof. Emer.; currently Presidential Chair. and Prof. of Electrical Eng, Andrew and Erna Viterbi School of Eng, Univ. of Southern California, Los Angeles; Co-founder

Linkabit Corpn, Exec. Vice-Pres. 1974–82, Pres. M/A-COM Linkabit, Inc. 1982–; Co-founder Qualcomm, Inc. 1985, Vice-Chair. and Chief Tech. Officer –2000; currently Pres. The Viterbi Group, LLC (advises and invests in startup cos in communication, network and imaging technologies); fmr Chair. US Commission C, Int. Radio Scientific Union (URSI), Visiting Cttee, Electrical Eng Dept, Technion, Israel Inst. of Tech.; apptd mem. Presidential Advisory Cttee on Information Tech. 1997–2001; mem. MIT Corpn Visiting Cttee for Electrical Eng and Computer Science; fmr mem. Army Science Bd; fmr mem. or Chair. Bd Govs IEEE Information Theory Group (Transactions Assoc. Ed. for Coding); mem. Nat. Acad. of Eng 1978, NAS 1996, American Acad. of Arts and Sciences 2001; fmr Chair. NAS Computer and Information Sciences Section; developed Viterbi Algorithm, used in wide-ranging applications including mobile phones, DNA analysis and speech recognition; Grande Ufficiale della Repubblica (Italy) 2001; Dr hc (Waterloo, Rome, Technion, Notre Dame); IEEE Information Theory Group Outstanding Paper Award 1968, Christopher Columbus Int. Award, Italian Nat. Research Council 1975, AIAA Aerospace Communications Award (co-recipient) 1980, IEEE Alexander Graham Bell Medal 1984, Marconi Int. Fellowship Award 1990, Claude Shannon Award 1990, Benjamin Franklin Medal in Electrical Eng 2005, James Clerk Maxwell Medal, IEEE and Royal Soc. of Edinburgh (co-recipient) 2007, Robert Noyes Award, Semiconductor Industry Asscn (co-recipient) 2007, Nat. Medal of Science 2007. *Publications:* Principles of Coherent Communication 1966, Principles of Digital Communication and Coding (co-author) 1979, CDMA: Principles of Spread Spectrum Communication 1995; numerous scientific papers in professional journals. *Address:* Andrew and Erna Viterbi School of Engineering, University of Southern California, Los Angeles, CA 90089, USA (office). *Telephone:* (213) 740-4750 (office). *E-mail:* viterbi.communications@usc .edu (office). *Website:* viterbi.usc.edu (office).

VITERI ACAITURRI, Maria Elsa; Ecuadorean economist and politician; *Minister of Finance;* b. 25 Feb. 1965; ed Univ. Católica de Santiago de Guayaquil, Iowa State Univ., USA; Head of Research, Centre for Econ. Research, Univ. Católica de Santiago de Guayaquil 1989–90, Dir 1992–95, Prof. of Econs 1990–96; Dir of Admin and Finance, Grupo SUPAN 1995–2000; Under-Sec. for the Budget, Ministry of Finance 2007, Vice Minister of Finance 2007–08, Minister of Finance 2008–; Premio Benemérita 1971, 1973, 1987. *Address:* Ministry of the Economy and Finance, Avda 10 de Agosto 1661 y Jorge Washington, Quito, Ecuador (office). *Telephone:* (2) 254-4500 (office). *Fax:* (2) 253-0703 (office). *Website:* minfinanzas.ec -gov.net (office).

VITORGAN, Emmanuil; Russian actor and film and theatre director; b. 27 Dec. 1939, Baku, Azerbaijan; m. 1st Alla Balter (deceased), m. 2nd Irina Mlodek-Vitorgan; one s. one d.; ed Leningrad State Inst. of Theatre Arts; with Leningrad Theatre of Drama and Comedy 1961–63, Leningrad Theatre of Leninsky Komsomol 1964–71, Moscow Stanislavsky Drama Theatre 1971–82, Moscow Taganka Theatre 1982–84, Moscow Academic Mayakovsky Theatre 1984–; f. Vitorgan Foundation 2003–; Merited Artist of Russia 1990, People's Artist of Russia 1998. *Films include:* King Lear 1972, And This is All About Him 1974, Fortress 1978, Two People in a New House 1979, Profession – Investigator 1982, Devout Marta 1983, The Grown-up Daughter of a Young Man 1990, When Saints are Marching 1990, The Scam 2001, Lady in Spectacles with a Gun in a Car 2002, Tyazhyolyy pesok 2008,. *Plays include:* Westside Story, Humiliated and Insulted, Rain Seller, Shadows, Grown-Up Daughter of a Young Man, Sirano de Berjerac, Circle, The Doll's House. *Address:* Moscow Academic Mayakovsky Theatre, Bolshaya Nikitskaya str. 19, 103009 Moscow (office); Maly Kislovsky per.7, apt 26, 103009 Moscow, Russia (home). *Telephone:* (495) 290-30-31 (office); (495) 291-89-89 (office). *Website:* www.mayakovsky.ru (office).

VITORINO, António, LLM; Portuguese politician and lawyer; b. 12 Jan. 1957, Lisbon; m.; two c.; ed Lisbon Law School; fmr Prof., Lisbon Autonomous Univ.; mem. Parl. (Partido Socialista) 1981, 2005; Sec. of State for Parl. Affairs 1984–85, for Admin and Justice of Macao Govt 1986–87; Judge, Portuguese Constitutional Court 1989–94; Minister for Defence and the Presidency 1995–97; Vice-Pres. Portugal Telecom Internacional 1998–99; EU Commr for Freedom, Security and Justice 1999–2004; Assoc., Cuatrecasas, Gonçalves Pereira & Associates (law firm) 2005–; Pres., Gen. Ass., Santander Totta 2005–; Visiting Prof., Law Faculty, Universidade Nova de Lisboa. *Address:* Cuatrecasas, Gonçalves Pereira & Associates, Marquess of Pombal Square 2, 1250-160 Lisbon, Portugal (office). *Website:* www.gpcb.pt.

VITRENKO, Natalia Mikhailovna, DEcon; Ukrainian politician; *Chairman, Progressive Socialist Party of Ukraine;* b. 28 Dec. 1951, Kiev; m.; one s. two d.; ed Kiev State Inst. of Nat. Econs; Sr Economist Cen. Dept of Statistics 1973–76; Sr Researcher Research Inst. of Information, State Planning Comm. 1979–89; Docent Kiev Inst. of Nat. Econs 1979–89; Sr Researcher Council on Production Forces, Ukrainian Acad. of Sciences 1989–94; presidential cand. 1994, 2004; People's Deputy 1994–2002; Counsellor on Socio-econ. Problems, Verkhovna Rada; mem. Socialist Party of Ukraine 1991; mem. Progressive Socialist Party of Ukraine (Prohresyvna Sotsialistychna Partiya Ukrainy) 1996–, currently Chair.; mem. Presidium of Political Council 1993–, Acad. of Construction, Acad. of Econ. Cybernetics 1997, Int. Acad. of Social Technologies (Russian Fed.); Corresp. mem. Peter's Acad. of Arts and Sciences (Russian Fed.); Chair. 'Gift of Life' (public women's org.) 2000–, Cathedral Orthodox Women in Ukraine 2010–, Eurasian People's Union 2011–. *Leisure interests:* fishing, camping. *Address:* Progressive Socialist Party of Ukraine (Prohresyvna Sotsialistychna Partiya Ukrainy), 01011 Kyiv, vul. P. Miroho 27/51 (office); Podgornaya/Tatarskaya str., 3/7, 98 office, 04107 Kyiv, Ukraine (office). *Telephone:* (44) 483-32-57 (office). *Fax:* (44) 483-32-57 (office). *E-mail:* n-vitrenko@yandex.ru (office). *Website:* www.vitrenko.org (office).

VITRUK, Nikolai Vasilievich, LLD; Russian lawyer and judge (retd); b. 4 Nov. 1937, Zharovka, Tomsk Region; m. (divorced 1988); one d.; ed Tomsk State Univ.; Man. Legal Advice Bureau, Tomsk Regional Lawyers' Bd 1959; Asst Chair. of Theory and History of State and Law, Tomsk Univ. 1960–63; Asst, Sr Teacher, Asst Prof. Chair. of Theory of State and Law, T. G. Shevchenko Kiev State Univ. 1966–71; Sr Scientific Researcher, Inst. of State and Law, USSR Acad. of Sciences 1971–81; Prof. Chair. of Theory of State and Law and Constitutional Law, Acad. of Ministry of Internal Affairs of USSR 1981–84; Chief, Chair of State and Law Discipline, High Correspondence Law Coll., Ministry of Internal Affairs of USSR 1984–91; Justice, Constitutional Court of Russian Fed. 1991–2003 (retd), Deputy

Chair. 1991–96, Acting Chair. 1993–95; mem. Venice Comm., Strasbourg, France 1992; Rep. of Russian Fed., European Comm. for Democracy Through Law; Labour Veteran Medal, Medal for Irreproachable Service, Honoured Scientist of Russian Fed. *Publications:* about 300 legal works. *Leisure interests:* theatre, modern realistic painting, poetry, art, culture of Russia during the 'Silver Age'. *Address:* c/o Constitutional Court, 103132 Moscow, 21 Ilyinka Street, Russia.

VITRYANSKY, Vassily Vladimirovich, DJur; Russian lawyer and academic; b. 8 May 1956, Gomel, Belarus; m.; one s. two d.; ed Moscow State Univ.; mem. staff RSFSR State Court of Arbitration 1978–86; Sr Asst Admin. RSFSR Council of Ministers 1986–89, consultant, Dept of Law 1989–90; Deputy Chief State Arbiter of RSFSR 1990–92; Deputy Chair. Higher Court of Arbitration of Russian Fed. 1992–; teacher, Moscow State Univ., participated in devt of civil law in Russian Fed. *Publications include:* Protection of Property Rights of Businessmen, Protection of Property Rights of Stock Companies and Shareholders, Law and Bankruptcy; numerous publications on protection of civil rights, civil and legal responsibility, bankruptcy. *Address:* Higher Court of Arbitration, M. Kharitonyevsky per. 12, 111001 Moscow, Russia (office). *Telephone:* (495) 208-12-81 (office).

VITTER, David, BA, LLB; American lawyer and politician; *Senator from Louisiana;* m. Wendy Vitter; four c.; ed Tulane Univ, Univ of Oxford, UK, Harvard Univ; served as mem. Louisiana House of Reps 1992–99, concurrently Adjunct Law Prof., Tulane and Loyola Univs and pvt. business attorney; mem. US House of Reps, Washington, DC 1999–2004, served on House Appropriations Cttee, House Republican Policy Cttee; Senator from Louisiana 2005–, mem. Cttee on Environment and Public Works, Cttee on Banking, Housing and Urban Affairs, Cttee on Armed Services, Cttee on Small Business and Entrepreneurship; Republican; Alliance for Good Govt Legislator of the Year, Victims and Citizens Against Crime Outstanding Legislator Award and Lifetime Achievement Award. *Address:* 516 Hart Senate Office Building, Washington, DC 20510, USA (office). *Telephone:* (202) 224-4623 (office). *Fax:* (202) 228-5061 (office). *Website:* vitter.senate.gov (office).

VIVANCO CASAMADRID, Antonio, BA (Econs), MBA, MA; Mexican government official and business executive; ed Instituto Tecnológico Autónomo de México, Harvard Univ., USA; worked in Finance and Public Credit Ministry (Hacienda) and Fed. Mortgage Soc. (SHF); Chief of Staff, Office of Pres. Felipe Calderón 2008–11; Asst Dir Gen. Comisión Fed. de Electricidad Feb.–March 2011, Dir Gen. 2011–12; Substitute Bd mem. Petroleos Mexicanos. *Address:* c/o Comisión Federal de Electricidad, Rio Rodano 14, Col. Cuauhtemoc, México DF 06598, Mexico.

VIVARELLI, Roberto; Italian historian and academic; *Professor Emeritus of History, Scuola Normale Superiore;* b. 8 Dec. 1929, Siena; s. of Lavinio Vivarelli and Margherita Cosci; m. Ann Sheldon West 1960 (died 1999); two s. one d.; ed Univs of Siena, Florence and Pennsylvania, USA and Istituto Italiano di Studi Storici; Research Fellow, St Antony's Coll. Oxford, UK 1961–62; Asst Prof., Univ. of Siena 1962–70, Full Prof. 1972–75; Assoc. Prof., Univ. of Florence 1970–72, Full Prof. 1975–86; Prof. of History, Scuola Normale Superiore, Pisa 1986–2005, Prof. Emer. 2005–; Visiting Prof., Inst. for Advanced Study, Princeton, USA 1969–70, 1980–81, Harvard Univ. 1976; Visiting Fellow, All Souls Coll. Oxford 1993–94; mem. Editorial Bd, Rivista Storica Italiana; mem. Academia Europaea. *Publications:* Gaetano Salvemini's Scritti sul Fascismo (ed.) 1961, 1974, Georges Sorel's Scritti politici (ed.) 1963, Il dopoguerra in Italia e l'avvento del fascismo 1967, Il fallimento del liberalismo 1981, Storia delle origini del fascismo (two vols) 1991, vol. 3 2012, Profilo di storia (three vols) 1996, La fine di una stagione: Memoria 1943–1945 2000, Storia e storiografia 2004, I caratteri della contemporanea 2005, Fascismo e storia d'Italia 2008, Italia 1861 2013. *Address:* Via Dante da Castiglione 1, 50125 Florence, Italy (home). *Telephone:* (055) 223190 (home).

VIVES, Xavier, MA, PhD; Spanish economist; *Professor of Economics and Finance, Institut Européen d'Administration des Affaires (INSEAD);* b. 23 Jan. 1955, Barcelona; m. Aurora Bastida; two s.; ed Autonomous Univ. of Barcelona, Univ. of California, Berkeley, USA; Sr Researcher, Fundación de Estudios de Economía Aplicada (FEDEA); Programme Dir Applied Microecons. and Industrial Org. Programmes, Centre for Econ. Policy Research, London; Dir Institut d'Analisi Económica, Barcelona 1991–2001; Prof. of Econs and Finance, Institut Européen d'Admin des Affaires (INSEAD) 2001–; Visiting Prof., Harvard Univ., Univs of Pa, Calif., Berkeley and New York Univ.; Fellow, Econometric Soc. 1992; Premio Extraordinario de Licenciatura, Autonomous Univ. of Barcelona 1978, King Juan Carlos I Prize for Research in Social Science 1988, Societat Catalana d'Economía Prize 1996. *Publications:* Monitoring European Integration: The Future of European Banking (co-author) 1999, Oligopoly Pricing: Old Ideas and New Tools 2000, Corporate Governance: Theoretical and Empirical Perspectives (ed.) 2000, Politicas Publicas y Equilibrio Territorial en el Stado Autonomico. *Address:* INSEAD, boulevard de Constance, 77305 Fontainebleau Cedex (office); Bat. C, Royal Paic, Appt 138, 39, Rue Royal, 77300 Fontainebleau France (home). *Telephone:* 1-60-72-42-79 (office); 1-60-72-83-01 (home). *Fax:* 1-60-74-67-19 (office). *E-mail:* xavier.vives@insead.edu (office). *Website:* faculty.insead.edu/vives (office).

VIVES SICÍLIA, Mgr Joan-Enric, PhD; Spanish/Andorran ecclesiastic; *Archbishop of Urgell and Episcopal Co-Prince of Andorra;* b. 24 July 1949, Barcelona, Spain; s. of the late Francesc Vives Pons and of Cornèlia Sicília Ibáñez; ed Escola 'Pere Vila', Institut 'Jaume Balmes', Barcelona, Conciliary Seminary of Barcelona, Faculty of Theology of Barcelona, Univ. of Barcelona; ordained priest 1974; apptd Prof. of Catalan, Univ. of Barcelona; apptd Prof. of Theology and Philosophy, Univ. 'Ramon Llull' and Faculty of Theology of Catalonia 1979; Auxiliary Bishop of Barcelona and Titular Bishop of Nona 1993–2001; Co-Adjutor Bishop of Urgell 2001–03; Bishop of Urgell and Episcopal Co-Prince of Andorra 2003–, Archbishop ad personam 2010–; Order of Cross of Christ (Portugal) 2010; Medal of Honour of the City of Barcelona 1999. *Address:* Pati Palau 1-5, 25700 La Seu d'Urgell, Lleida, Spain (home). *Telephone:* (973) 350054 (office). *Fax:* (973) 352230 (home). *E-mail:* jevs@bisbaturgell.org (office); secretaricoprincep@bisbaturgell.org (office). *Website:* www.bisbaturgell.org (office).

VIVIAN, Young; Niuean politician; b. 1935; Leader Niue People's Party (disbanded 2003); Premier Dec. 1992–March 1993, 2002–08, also Minister responsible for Legis. Ass., Premier's Dept and Cabinet, Civil Aviation, Crown Law Office, Econ. Devt Planning and Statistics, External Affairs and Niueans

Abroad, Niue Public Service Comm., Niue Broadcasting Corpn, Finance, Customs and Revenue, Police, Prison and Nat. Security, Environment, Niue Tourism, Public Works (Civil and Quarry, Outside Services and Heavy Plant) and Recovery Task Force. *Address:* c/o Fono Ekepule (Parliament), Alofi, Niue (office).

VIZJAK, Andrej, MEng; Slovenian politician and engineer; b. 6 Aug. 1964, Brežice; ed Brežice Gymnasium, Faculty of Electrical Eng and Computing, Univ. of Ljubljana; began career as electrical engineer, Litostroj, Ljubljana; researcher in computer automatisation of industrial processes, Jožef Stefan Inst. –1994; Labour Insp., Krško Unit, Nat. Labour Inspectorate 1994–2000; State Sec., Ministry of Labour, Family and Social Affairs 2000; elected to Nat. Ass. 2000–04, 2004–; Minister of Economy 2004–08, of Labour, Family and Social Affairs 2012–13; Leader of Slovenska demokratska stranka (SDS) Parl. Group 2000–04, currently mem.; elected Mayor of Brežice 2002. *Address:* Slovenska demokratska stranka (SDS), 1000 Ljubljana, Trstenjakova 8, Slovenia (office). *Telephone:* (1) 4345450 (office). *Fax:* (1) 4345452 (office). *E-mail:* tajnistvo@sds.si (office). *Website:* www .sds.si (office).

VIZZINI, Carlo; Italian politician and academic; b. 28 April 1947, Palermo, Sicily; elected Social Democrat mem. Parl. for Palermo-Trapani-Agrigento-Caltanisetta 1976, now Senator; Nat. Deputy Sec. Italian Social Democrat Party and Head of Econ. Dept 1980–88; Under-Sec. of State in Ministry of Budget and Econ. Planning; Minister for Regional Affairs 1986–87, of Cultural Heritage 1987–88, of the Merchant Navy 1989–91, of Posts and Telecommunications 1991–92; Sec. Partido Socialista Democratica Italiano (PSDI); Pres. Bicameral Comm. for Regional Questions; mem. Parliamentary Comm. of Inquiry into Organized Crime and the Mafia; Prof. of History of Econs, Univ. of Palermo. *Address:* Segretaria Politica, Centro Studi – Laboratorio Politico, Via di Stefano 19, Palermo, Italy (office). *Telephone:* (91) 332697 (office). *Fax:* (91) 321038 (office). *E-mail:* carlovizzini@carlovizzini.it (office).

VLĂDESCU, Sebastian; Romanian politician and business executive; b. 3 April 1958; ed Inst. Acad. of Econ. Studies, Bucharest, Merrill Lynch Inst., USA; economist, COS 1983, IRVMR Co. 1983–90; Shareholder and Dir Gas Prod Com LLC 1990–92, Banc Comp LLC 1992–94, Medist SA 1994–97 (Shareholder and Financial Dir 1998–99, Financial Dir 2001–05); Sec. of State, Ministry of Industry and Commerce Jan.–June 1997 (Adviser to the Minister July–Dec. 1997), Ministry of Finance Jan.–Dec. 2000 (Advisor to the Minister Jan.–April 1998, Oct.–Dec. 1999); mem. Guarantees for External Credits Inter-ministerial Comm., Eximbank Feb.–Aug. 1997, 2000; Chair. Trust Bd Company Bank Assets Recovery Agency 2000, Co. Chamber of Auditors 2000, Supervisory Bd Romanian Commercial Bank 2005– (mem. Privatization Comm. 2000–01); mem. Bd of Dirs CEC Savings House 2000–01, Petrom Service 2002–03, Upetrom 2002–05, Romanian Centre for Econ. Policies (CEROPE) 2003–05, Petrom SA 2005; Minister of Public Finance 2005–07, 2009–10; Sec. of State on Treasury Issues, Ministry of the Economy and Finance 2007. *Address:* c/o Ministry of Public Finance, 050741 Bucharest 5, Str. Apolodor 17, Romania (office).

VLADIMIR, Metropolitan (Victor Markianovich Sabodan), MTheol; Ukrainian ecclesiastic; *Metropolitan of Kiev and All Ukraine;* b. 23 Nov. 1935, Khmelnitsky Region; ed Leningrad and Moscow Theological Acads.; ordained as deacon, then priest 1962–66; Bishop, Archbishop 1966–82; Metropolitan 1982; taught in Odessa Seminary, then Rector; Deputy Chief Russian Orthodox Mission in Jerusalem 1966–68; Bishop of Pereslavl-Zalessky; Archbishop of Dmitrov, Rector Moscow Theological Acad., Prof. 1973–82; Metropolitan of Rostov and Novocherkassk 1982–86; Patriarch Rep. in West Europe 1986–87; Man. Moscow Patriarchy, Perm. mem. Holy Synod 1987–; Metropolitan of Kiev and All Ukraine 1992–; Dr hc (Christian Theological Acad., Warsaw) 2008. *Publications:* 10 volumes including Ecclesiology in Russian Theology, Paul the Called Apostle, Christ the Saviour, Principle of the World. *Address:* Ukrainian Orthodox Church, Pechensk Monastery, Sichnevoho Povstannia 25, Kiev, Ukraine. *Telephone:* (44) 280-15-08. *E-mail:* metropolia@svitonline.net (office). *Website:* www.orthodox.org .ua.

VLADISLAVLEV, Alexander Pavlovich, DTechSc; Russian politician; b. 21 May 1936, Moscow; m. Karina Lisitsian; one s.; ed Gubkin Petroleum Inst., Moscow, Oil and Gas Inst., Bucharest; mem. CPSU 1959–91; researcher, sr teacher, Docent, Pro-Rector Gubkin Moscow Inst. 1959–74; Vice-Pres. All-Union Soc. Znanie 1974–86; First Vice-Chair. USSR Council of Scientific and Eng Socs 1988–90; Chair. Exec. Cttee, First Vice-Pres. USSR (now Russian) Scientific-Industrial Union 1990–92; Chair. Council of Business of USSR, Pres. 1991; First Deputy Minister of Foreign Econ. Relations of USSR Nov.–Dec. 1991; First Vice-Pres. Russian Union of Industrialists and Entrepreneurs 1990; USSR People's Deputy 1989–91; Founder and Co-Chair. Democratic Reform Movt 1991–92; a leader of Civic Union 1992–93; mem. State Duma (Parl.) 2000–, Chair. Sub-Cttee on Investment Policy 2002–03; Chair. ZIL motor co. 1994–95; mem. Bd of Dirs Moscow CableCom Corpn 2004–; Pres. Ind. Fund for Realism in Politics 1994–; mem. Presidium of Eng Acad., founder and mem. of admin of non-govt foundations and socs; mem. Advisory Council of UNO on Science and Tech.; mem. faction Otechestvo. *Publications:* six books; over 200 articles and papers; 15 patents. *Address:* Gosudarstvennaya Duma (State Duma), 103265 Moscow, Okhotnyi ryad 1 (home); Novy Arbat prosp. 15, Suite 2424, Moscow, Russia (office). *Telephone:* (495) 202-26-25 (office); (495) 203-55-15 (home). *E-mail:* stateduma@duma.ru (home). *Website:* www.duma.ru (office).

VLAHOVIĆ, Miodrag; Montenegrin politician and diplomatist; b. 1961, Djakovica; m.; three d.; ed Univ. of Montenegro, Podgorica, Univ. of Belgrade, Luxembourg Int. Univ.; f. STUDEKS Cultural Centre, Podgorica 1985; mem. Fed. Presidency and Int. Sec., Socialist Youth Union of Yugoslavia 1986–88; Sec. for Montenegro Asscn for Yugoslav Democratic Unity 1989; co-f. Citizens Cttee for Peace 1991–92, organized first peace rally in Montenegro 1991; mem. Parl., Repub. of Montenegro, mem. Parl. Cttee for Int. Relations, Cttee for Political System, Cttee for Legal and Admin. Matters 1992–94 (resgnd); Liberal Party of Montenegro Int. Sec. 1992–93; columnist for ind. weekly 'Monitor' 1991–93, 1999–2000; Founder-mem. Montenegrin Centre for Democracy and Human Rights (CEDEM) 1998; co-author of new Montenegrin law on NGOs; Dir Centre for Regional and Security Studies (CeRS) 1999–; Minister of Foreign Affairs, Repub. of Montenegro 2004–06; Amb. to USA 2006–10 (also accred to Canada and Iceland 2007–10); Owner MConsult LLC 1990–; mem. Socialiat Democratic Party of Montenegro; mem. Bd Open Society Inst. Montenegro 2002–04. *Address:* Ministry of Foreign Affairs and European Integration, 81000 Podgorica, Stanka Dragojevića 2, Montenegro (office). *Telephone:* (20) 246357 (office). *Fax:* (20) 224670 (office). *E-mail:* milan.rocen@gov.me (office). *Website:* www.mip.gov.me (office).

VLČEK, Miloslav; Czech politician; b. 1 Feb. 1961, Konice; m.; two s. two d.; ed Univ. of Brno; fmr tractor mechanic; mem. Czech SDP (Česká strana sociálně demokratická—ČSSD); mem. Poslanecká sněmovna (Chamber of Deputies) 1996–2010, Chair. 2006–10 (resgnd), Chair. Steering Cttee 2006–10. *Address:* c/o Office of the Chairman, 1 Poslanecká sněmovna, Sněmovní 4, 118 26 Prague 1, Czech Republic. *E-mail:* info@miloslavvlcek.cz. *Website:* www.miloslavvlcek.cz.

VLK, HE Cardinal Miloslav, BSc; Czech ecclesiastic; b. 17 May 1932, Sepekov-Líšnice, Písek Dist of Southern Bohemia; ed Faculty of Philosophy, Charles Univ. Prague, Faculty of Theology, Litoměřice; archivist Třeboň and Jindřichův Hradec 1960–61, Czech Budějovice 1961–64; ordained priest 1968; sec. to Roman Catholic Bishop of České Budějovice 1968–71; parish priest Laiště and Zablatí Romitál pod Třemšínem 1971–78; denied permission to work as priest 1978; window cleaner, Prague 1978–1986; archivist, Czechoslovak State Bank, Prague 1986–88; parish priest, parishes in Šumava Mountains 1989–90; cr. Bishop of České Budějovice 1990, Archbishop of Prague 1991–2010, Archbishop Emer. 2010–; cr. Cardinal-Priest of S. Croce in Gerusalemme 1994; mem. Consilium Conferentiarum Episcopalium Europae 1990–2001 (Pres. 1993–2001), Pontificum Consilium de Communicationibus Socialibus 1994–2007, Congregatio pro Ecclesiis Orientalibus 1994; Hon. Citizen, Romál pod Třemšínem 1992, Cedar Rapids, USA 1992, Baltimore, USA 1992, Kłodzko, Poland 1996, Třeboň 1996, Roudnice nad Labem 1997, Mníšek pod Brdy 1998, Brandýs nad Labem – Stará Boleslav 2010; Grosses Verdienstkreuz 1999, TGM Order 2002; Hon. LHD (Ill. Benedictine Coll., USA, Univ. of St Thomas, Minn., USA) 1992; Hon. DTheol (Univ. Passau, Germany) 1993, (Pontificia Academia Theologica Cracoviensys, Poland) 2001, (Univ. Opole, Poland) 2002; Görlitz Brückepreis 2001, European St Ulirchs Prize 2007. *Publications:* Reifezeit 1996, Wird Europa neidisch? 1999, Avanti! 1999; numerous ecclesiastical articles. *Leisure interests:* classical and oriental languages, classical music, mountain tourism, skiing, cycling. *Address:* c/o Arcibiskupství praské, Hradčanské nám. 16/56, 119 02 Prague 1, Czech Republic. *Telephone:* (2) 20392202. *E-mail:* sekretar.vlk@apha.cz. *Website:* www.kardinal.cz.

VLOK, Adriaan; South African politician; b. 11 Dec. 1937, Sutherland; m. Cornelia Burger; two s. one d.; joined Dept of Justice 1957, became Prosecutor and Sr Magistrate; Asst Pvt. Sec. to Prime Minister John Vorster 1967; subsequently entered pvt. business; later Deputy Sheriff, E Pretoria; MP 1974–94; fmr Deputy Speaker of House of Ass., Leader House of Ass. 1992–94; Deputy Minister of Defence and Deputy Minister of Law and Order 1985–86, Minister of Law and Order 1986–91, of Correctional Services and the Budget 1991–92, of Correctional Services and of Housing and Works 1992, of Correctional Services 1992–94; mem. Truth and Reconciliation Comm. for amnesty for criminal acts 1998; received suspended ten year sentence for involvement in plot to kill anti-apartheid activist Frank Chikane July 2007. *Leisure interests:* rugby (referee in Northern Transvaal), military history, chewing biltong.

VO, Trong Nghia, PhD; Vietnamese architect; b. 1976, Quang Binh Prov.; ed Hanoi Architectural Univ., Ishikawa Coll. of Tech., Japan, Tokyo Univ. *Projects include:* Wind and Water (wNw) Café, Binh Duong (Asian Architects' Asscn Gold Arcasia Award 2007–08, Int. Acad. of Architecture—IAA Special Award 2009), Trung Nguyen Coffee Culture Centre, Hanoi (IAA Special Award 2009), Can Tho Univ. Campus, Mekong Delta (co-designer) (Silver Global Holcim Award 2009), Bamboo Wings (culture centre), Vinh Phuc Prov. *Address:* Vo Trong Nghia Co. Ltd, 85 Bis Phan Ke Binh, DaKao, District 1, Ho Chi Minh City, Viet Nam (office). *Telephone:* (8) 38297763 (office). *Fax:* (8) 39110103 (office). *E-mail:* info@votrongnghia.com (office). *Website:* www.votrongnghia.com (office).

VODIČKA, Jindřich, Czech politician; b. 22 July 1952, Prague; m.; two s.; ed Univ. of Maritime Studies, Odessa; sailed as deck engineer, later First Officer in merchant navy 1977–90; First Deputy Dir Office for Protection of Constitutional Officials –1990; Dir Job Centre, Prague-West Dist 1990–92; mem. Civic Democratic Party (CDP) 1991–97, 1998–, Unie Svobody Jan.–March 1998; Deputy to House of Nations (Fed. Ass. of ČSFR) June–Dec. 1992; Minister of Labour and Social Affairs of Czech Repub. 1992–97; Minister of Interior 1997–98; Dir-Gen. České přístavy (Czech Ports Ltd). *Address:* c/o Civic Democratic Party, Sněmovní 3, 110 00 Prague 1, Czech Republic.

VOEVODSKY, Vladimir, PhD; Russian mathematician and academic; *Professor, School of Mathematics, Institute for Advanced Study;* b. 4 June 1966, Moscow, USSR; ed Moscow State Univ., Harvard Univ., USA; held visiting posts at Inst. for Advanced Study and Harvard Univ., USA and Max-Planck-Institut für Mathematik, Germany; mem. Faculty, Northwestern Univ., Evanston, Ill., USA 1996–98; mem. School of Math., Inst. for Advanced Study, Princeton, NJ, USA 1998–2002, Prof. 2002–; Fields Medals, Int. Congress of Mathematicians, Beijing (co-recipient) 2002. *Publications:* Cycles, Transfers and Motivic Homology Theories 2000; numerous articles in math. journals on algebraic geometry and K-theory. *Address:* School of Mathematics, Institute for Advanced Study, Fuld 116, Einstein Drive, Princeton, NJ 08540, USA (office). *Telephone:* (609) 734-8117 (office). *Fax:* (609) 951-4459 (office). *E-mail:* vladimir@ias.edu (office). *Website:* www.math.ias .edu/~vladimir (office).

VOGEL, Bernhard, DPhil; German politician; b. 19 Dec. 1932, Göttingen; s. of Prof. Dr Hermann Vogel and Caroline Vogel (née Brinz); ed Univs of Heidelberg and Munich; Lecturer, Inst. for Political Sciences, Heidelberg 1961–67; mem. Bundestag (Parl.) 1965–67, Speaker of Bundesrat (Upper House) 1976–77, 1987–88; Minister of Educ. and Culture, Rhineland-Palatinate 1967–76; Chairman / Deputy Chairman of the Joint Commission of the Federal and State Governments for Education Planning and Research Development 1970–1976; mem. Rhineland-Palatinate State Parl. 1971–88, Thuringia State Parl. 1994–2004; Chair. CDU, Rhineland-Palatinate 1974–88, mem. Fed. Exec. Cttee of CDU 1975–, Chair. CDU, Thuringia 1993–2000; Minister-Pres., Rhineland-Palatinate 1976–88, Thuringia 1992–2003, Chair. Conf. of State Prime Ministers 1981–82, 1996–97; Rep. for Cultural Affairs of FRG within framework of Agreement on German-French Co-operation 1979–82; Chair. Advisory Bd of

German TV Broadcasting/Second Channel (ZDF) 1979–92, Deputy Chair. 1992–2007; Chair. Konrad Adenauer Foundation 1989–95, 2001–09; Pres. Cen. Cttee of German Catholics 1972–76; Hon. Prof., award from State of Baden-Wurttemberg; Hon. Chair. Konrad Adenauer Foundation 2010–; Grosses Bundes-verdienstkreuz; decorations from France, Luxembourg, Poland, UK, and the Vatican; Grosskreuz St Gregorius; Gold Medal of Strasbourg; Dr hc (Catholic Univ. of America, Catholic Univ. of Lublin, German Coll. for Admin. Sciences, Speyer, Ben-Gurion Univ. of the Negev). *Publications:* Die Unabhangigen in den Kommunalwahlen westdeutscher Lander 1960, Wahlen und Wahlsysteme 1961, Kontrolliert der Bundestag die Regierung? 1964, Wahlkampf und Wählertradi-tion. Eine Studie zur Bundestagswahl von 1961 1965, Wahlen in Deutschland 1848–1970 (co-author), Schule am Scheideweg 1974, Die Wahl der Parlamente und anderer Staatsorgane 1969–1978 (co-ed.), Neue Bildungspolitik (ed.) 1975, Foderalismus in der Bewahrung (ed.) 1992, Sorge tragen fur die Zukunft 2002, Religion und Politik (ed.) 2003, Im Zentrum: Menschenwürde. Politisches Handeln aus christlicher Verantwortung, christliche Ethik als Orientierungshilfe (ed.) 2006, Deutschland aus der Vogel Perspektive. Eine kleine Geschichte der Bundesrepublik Deutschland (zusammen mit Hans-Jochen Vogel) 2007, Mutige Bürger braucht das Land. Chancen der Politik in unübersichtlichen Zeiten (co-ed.) 2012; Ed. Politische Meinung; numerous essays and speeches. *Leisure interests:* mountaineering, literature, swimming. *Address:* c/o Konrad-Adenauer-Stiftung e.V., Der Vorsitzende, Rathausallee 12, 53757 Sankt Augustin, Germany.

VOGEL, Dieter H., DrIng; German business executive; *Chairman of the Supervisory Board, Bertelsmann AG;* b. 14 Nov. 1941; m. Ursula Gross 1970; two c.; ed Tech. Univ. of Darmstadt, Tech. Univ. of Munich; Asst Prof., Thermic Turbo Engines, Tech. Univ. of Munich 1967–69; Vice-Pres. Printing Div., Bertelsmann AG 1970–74, Pegulan AG 1975–85 (Chair. 1978), Chair. Supervisory Bd Bertelsmann AG 2003–, Chair. Bd of Trustees Bertelsmann Stiftung 2007–; Vice-Chair. Man. Bd Batig (BAT Industries) 1978–85; joined Thyssen Group 1986, Chair. Thyssen Handelsunion AG 1986–96, mem. Exec. Bd 1986–91, Deputy Chair. Thyssen AG 1991–96, Chair. 1996–98; f. Bessemer Vogel & Treichl (consultancy), Dusseldorf 1998; Man. Pnr, Lindsay Goldberg Vogel GmbH, Düsseldorf 2004–; Chair. Supervisory Bd Klöckner & Co. AG, Deutsche Bahn AG 1999–2001. *Leisure interest:* skiing. *Address:* Bertelsmann AG, Carl-Bertelsmann-Strasse 270, 33311 Gütersloh, Germany. *Telephone:* 5241-80-0 (office). *Fax:* 5241-80-9662 (office). *Website:* www.bertelsmann.de (office).

VOGEL, Hans-Jochen, DJur; German politician; b. 3 Feb. 1926, Göttingen; m. 1st Ilse Leisnering 1951 (divorced 1972); one s. two d.; m. 2nd Liselotte Sonnenholzer (née Biersack) 1972; ed Univs of Munich and Marburg; asst, Bavarian Justice Ministry 1952–54; judge, Traunstein Dist Court 1954–55; Bavarian State Chancellery 1955–58; professional mem. Munich City Council 1958–60; Chief Burgomaster of Munich 1960–72; mem. Bundestag 1972–81, 1983–94; Minister for Regional Planning, Building and Urban Devt 1972–74, of Justice 1974–81; Mayor, West Berlin Jan.–June 1981; Chair. SPD Parl. Party 1984–91; Deputy Chair. SPD 1984–87, Chair. 1987–91; Vice-Pres. Org. Cttee for Munich Olympic Games 1972; apptd Chair. Gegen Vergessen (Against Forgetting) Project 1993; mem. Nationalen Ethikrat 2001–05; numerous decorations including Grosses Bundesverdienstkreuz, Bayerischer Verdienstorden, Hon. CBE and honours from France, Italy, etc.; Leo Baeck Prize 2001. *Publications:* Die Amtskette: Meine zwölf Münchner Jahre 1972, Nachsichten: Meine Bonner und Berliner Jahre 1996, Politik und Anstand: Warum wir ohne Werte nicht leben können 2005, Deutschland aus der Vogel Perspektive (with Bernhard Vogel) 2007. *Leisure interests:* mountain walking, history. *Address:* c/o Gegen Vergessen - Für Demokratie e.V., Stauffenbergstraße 13-14, 10785 Berlin (office); Stiftsbogen 74, 81375 Munich, Germany (home). *Telephone:* (30) 2639783 (office). *Fax:* (30) 26397840 (office); (89) 70962211 (home). *E-mail:* info@gegen-vergessen.de (office).

VOGEL, Viola, PhD; German scientist and academic; *Professor, Department of Materials, Swiss Federal Institute of Technology, Zürich (ETH);* ed Max-Planck Inst. for Biophysical Chemistry, Göttingen, Frankfurt am Main Univ.; Post-doctoral Fellow, Univ. of California, Berkeley 1988–90; joined faculty Dept of Bioengineering, Univ. of Washington, Seattle 1990, also adjunct appointment in Physics, Founding Dir Center for Nanotechnology 1997–2003; Prof., Dept of Materials, ETH 2004–, also serves as Head, Lab. for Biologically Oriented Materials; Fellow, American Inst. for Medical and Biological Eng, mem. Gordon Research Conf. Selection and Scheduling Cttee; mem. Selection Cttee British Marshall Fund Fellowships 1993–95, German Ministry of Science and Educ. (BMBF) 1998; mem. numerous advisor bds including Wyss Institute at Harvard Univ., Max-Planck Institute for Colloids and Interfaces (Golm), Institute of Bioengineering and Nanotechnology (Biopolis Singapore); mem. Bd of Regents, Ludwig-Maximilians-Universität München; Dr hc (Univ. of Tampere, Finland) 2012; Max-Planck Soc. Otto-Hahn Medal 1988, NIH First Award 1993, Philip Morris Foundation Research Award 2005, Julius Springer Award for Applied Physics 2006. *Address:* Biologisch-Orientierte Materialwissens, Wolfgang-Pauli-Str. 10, ETH-Hönggerberg, 8093 Zürich, Switzerland (office). *Telephone:* (44) 6320887 (office). *Fax:* (44) 6321073 (office). *E-mail:* viola.vogel@hest.ethz.ch (office). *Website:* www.nanomat.mat.ethz.ch (office).

VOGELSTEIN, Bert E., BA, MD; American oncologist, pathologist and academic; *Clayton Professor of Oncology and Professor of Pathology, School of Medicine and Director of the Ludwig Center for Cancer Genetics and Therapeutics, Johns Hopkins University;* b. 1949; ed Univ. of Pennsylvania, Johns Hopkins Univ. School of Medicine, Baltimore, Md; Pediatric Intern, Johns Hopkins Hosp., Baltimore 1974–75, Pediatric Resident 1975–76; Postdoctoral research at Nat. Cancer Inst. 1976–78; Asst Prof. of Oncology, Johns Hopkins Univ. School of Medicine 1978–83, Assoc. Prof. 1983–89, Clayton Prof. of Oncology 1989–, Jt Appointment in Molecular Biology and Genetics 1992–, Prof. of Pathology 1998–, currently Dir Ludwig Center for Cancer Genetics and Therapeutics; Investigator, Howard Hughes Medical Inst., Chevy Chase, Md 1995–; Assoc. Ed. Cancer Research 1988–90, Genes, Chromosomes, and Cancer 1988–; mem. Bd of Reviewing Eds Science 1988–; mem. Editorial Bd Cancer and Metastasis 1993–, New England Journal of Medicine 1994–; mem. American Acad. of Arts and Sciences 1992, NAS 1992, American Philosophical Soc. 1995, Inst. of Medicine 2001, European Molecular Biology Org. 2005; Bristol Myers Squibb Award for Distinguished Achievement in Cancer Research 1990, Young Investigator Award,

American Fed. for Clinical Research 1992, Gairdner Foundation Int. Award in Science 1992, Medal of Honor, American Cancer Soc. 1992, Shacknai Memorial Prize, Hebrew Univ. of Jerusalem 1993, Dickson Prize, Univ. of Pittsburgh 1994, Pezcoller Foundation Award 1993, NAS Richard Lounsbery Award 1993, Baxter Award, Asscn of American Medical Colls 1993, Ernst Schering Prize 1994, Passano Award 1994, David A. Karnofsky Memorial Award, American Soc. for Clinical Oncology 1995, William Beaumont Prize in Gastroenterology, American Gastro-enterological Asscn 1997, Louisa Gross Horwitz Prize 1998, Paul Ehrlich and Ludwig Darmstaedter Prize, Paul Ehrlich Foundation 1998, William Allan Award, American Soc. of Human Genetics 1998, Charles S. Mott Prize, General Motors Cancer Research Foundation 2000, John Scott Award, John Scott Trust 2003, Prince of Asturias Awards in Science 2004, Charles Rodolphe Brupbacher Prize for Cancer Research 2011, Howard Taylor Ricketts Award, Univ. of Chicago, Clowes Memorial Award, American Asscn for Cancer Research, Karnofsky Memorial Award, American Soc. for Clinical Oncology, Harvey Prize in Human Health, Technion, Israel, New York Acad. of Medicine Medal for Distinguished Contribs to Biomedical Science, Pasarow Award for Medical Research, Pioneer in Science Award, American Research Forum, Breakthrough Prize in Life Sciences (co-recipient) 2013. *Publications:* more than 450 articles in medical and scientific journals on molecular genetics of human cancer. *Address:* Johns Hopkins Oncology Center/HHMI, 1650 Orleans Street, Room 589, Baltimore, MD 21231-1001, USA (office). *Telephone:* (410) 955-8878 (office). *Fax:* (410) 955-0548 (office). *E-mail:* vogelbe@welch.jhu.edu (office). *Website:* www.hopkinsmedicine.org (office).

VOGT, Margaret, BA, MA, PhD; Nigerian academic and UN official; b. 1950; m.; six c.; ed Barnard Coll., Columbia Univ., USA; held numerous academic positions, including Dir of Studies, Command and Staff Coll. Jaji, Nigeria, Lecturer, Nigerian War Coll. and Inst. for Strategic Studies, Kuru, Nigeria, Dir Africa Programme, Int. Peace Acad., Assoc. Research Prof., Nigerian Inst. of Int. Affairs; served in African Union as Dir Office of the African Union Comm. Chair.; Acting Deputy Special Rep. of Sec.-Gen., UN Political Office for Somalia, then Deputy Dir Africa I Div., Dept of Political Affairs, UN Secr. –2011; Special Rep. of the Sec.-Gen. and Head, UN Integrated Peacebuilding Office in Cen. African Repub. (BINUCA) 2011–13; mem. Bd of Trustees Centre for Peace Initiatives in Africa. *Publications include:* The Liberian Crisis and ECOMOG: A Bold Attempt at Regional Peace Keeping 1992, Nigerian Defence Policy: Issues and Problems, International Peacekeeping (co-ed.). *Address:* c/o United Nations Integrated Peacebuilding Office in Central African Republic (BINUCA), Department of Political Affairs, United Nations, New York, NY 10017, USA (office).

VOGT, Peter K., PhD; American professor of molecular and experimental medicine; *Professor and Head, Division of Oncovirology, Scripps Research Institute;* b. 3 Oct. 1932; s. of Josef Vogt and Else Vogt; m. Hiroko Ishino 1993; ed Univ. of Tubingen; Asst Prof. of Pathology, Univ. of Colorado 1962–66, Assoc. Prof. 1966–67; Assoc. Prof. of Microbiology, Univ. of Washington 1967–69, Prof. 1969–71; Hastings Prof. of Microbiology, Univ. of Southern California 1971–78, Hastings Distinguished Prof. of Microbiology 1978–80, Chair. Dept of Microbiology 1980–; Chair. Div. of Oncovirology and Prof., Dept of Molecular and Experimental Medicine, The Scripps Research Inst. 1993–; Calif. Scientist of the Year 1975, NAS Award 1980, Alexander von Humboldt Prize 1983, Ernst Jung Prize for Medicine 1985, Howard Taylor Ricketts Award 1991, Charles S. Mott Prize 1991. *Publications:* Genetics of RNA Tumor Viruses 1977, The Genetic Structure of RNA Tumor Viruses 1977 and numerous articles in scientific journals. *Leisure interest:* painting. *Address:* The Vogt Laboratory, Division of Oncovirology, Department of Molecular and Experimental Medicine, The Scripps Research Institute, 10550 North Torrey Pines Road, BCC–239, La Jolla, CA 92037, USA (office). *Telephone:* (858) 784-8079 (office). *Fax:* (858) 784-2070 (office). *E-mail:* pkvogt@scripps.edu (office). *Website:* www.scripps.edu/mem/vogt (office).

VÖGTLE, Fritz, PhD Habil.; German chemist and academic; *Professor Emeritus, Kekulé Institute for Organic Chemistry and Biochemistry, University of Bonn (Rheinische Friedrich-Wilhelms-Universität Bonn);* ed Univs of Freiburg and Heidelberg; Asst, then Assoc. Prof., Univ. of Würzburg 1970–75; Assoc. and Dir Kekulé-Institut for Organic Chem. and Biochemistry, Univ. of Bonn (Rheinische Friedrich-Wilhelms-Universität Bonn) 1975–, Prof. Emer. 2006–; Guest Prof., Univ. of Barcelona, Spain, 1986; Fellow, Japanese Soc. for the Promotion of Science 1987; Hon. DrPhil (Jyväskylä Univ., Finland) 2000; Dozenten Prize, Fonds der Chemischen Industrie 1973, Lise Meitner-Alexander von Humboldt Prize (Israel) 1993, Lilly Lecture, Ohio State Univ., Columbus, USA 1993, Thomas Lecture, Univ. of Missouri, Columbia, USA 1996, MIT and HMR Special Lecture (USA) 1999, Int. Izatt-Bradshaw-Christensen Award for Macrocyclic Chem. (USA) 1999, A.V. Baeyer Medal of GdCh 2003. *Achievements include:* jtly invented and developed dendritic polymers. *Publications:* Supramolecular Chemistry (Litera-ture Prize, Fonds der Chemischen Industrie) 1990; numerous papers in profes-sional journals. *Address:* Kekulé-Institut für Organische Chemie und Biochemie, Gerhard-Domagk-Str.1, 53121 Bonn, Germany (office). *Telephone:* (228) 733496 (office). *Fax:* (228) 735662 (office). *E-mail:* voegtle@uni-bonn.de (office). *Website:* organik.chemie.uni-bonn.de/ak_vo (office).

VOHOR, Serge Rialuth; Ni-Vanuatu politician; *Minister of Health;* b. 23 April 1955; began career as medical dresser/nurse/technician 1980–83; mem. Parl. (UMP) for Santo rural 1983–; Minister for Foreign Affairs 1991–93, Minister for Econ. Affairs 1993–95, Prime Minister 1995–96, July–Dec. 2004, April–May 2011; Minister for Trade 2001, for Foreign Affairs and External Trade 2002, Deputy Prime Minister 2001–02; Leader of Opposition 2003, 2004–07, Minister for Infrastructure and Public Utilities June 2007, Minister of Health 2013–; Pres. Union of Moderate Parties. *Address:* Ministry of Health, PMB 9042, Port Vila (office); Union of Moderate Parties, POB 698, Port Vila, Vanuatu (office). *Telephone:* 22413 (office). *Fax:* 26301 (office).

VOHRA, Narinder Nath; Indian politician; *Governor of Jammu and Kashmir;* ed Punjab Univ., Univ. of Oxford; served in Indian Admin. Service 1959–94, positions included Home Sec., Punjab, Additional Sec., Defence, Sec., Defence Production, Home Sec. and Prin. Sec. to Prime Minister, Special Services Bureau in Western Tibet border areas 1962–64; with WHO, Geneva 1982–84; mem. Nat. Security Advisory Bd 1998–2001; Co-Chair. India-European Union Round Table 2001–08; Special Rep. of Govt of India, Jammu and Kashmir Dialogue 2003–08; Gov. of Jammu and Kashmir 2008–; fmr Dir India Int. Centre; fmr Chair. Nat. Task Force on Internal Security, IDSA Review Cttee, Cttee on Review of Mil. Histories; mem. Indian Inst. of Public Admin, United Services Inst., Inst. of Defence Studies and Analysis and Int. House of Japan; Padma Vibhushan 2007. *Address:* Raj Bhawan, Guwahati, India (office). *Telephone:* (361) 540500 (office). *Fax:* (361) 540310 (office). *E-mail:* rakesh.jamwal@nic.in (office). *Website:* jkrajbhawan.nic.in (office).

VOIGHT, Jon; American actor; b. 29 Dec. 1938, Yonkers, New York; s. of Elmer Voight and Barbara Voight (née Kamp); m. 1st Lauri Peters 1962 (divorced 1967); m. 2nd Marcheline Bertrand 1971 (divorced); one s. one d.; ed Catholic Univ.; f. Jon Voight Entertainment (production co.). *Theatre includes:* A View From the Bridge (New York); That Summer That Fall (New York) 1966; played Romeo at the San Diego Shakespeare Festival; Stanley Kowalski in A Streetcar Named Desire, Los Angeles 1973, Hamlet 1975. *Films include:* Hour of the Gun 1967, Fearless Frank 1968, Out of It 1969, Midnight Cowboy 1969, The Revolutionary 1970, The All-American Boy 1970, Catch 22 1970, Deliverance 1972, Conrack 1974, The Odessa File 1974, Coming Home (Acad. Award for Best Actor) 1979, Golden Globe Award for Best Actor) 1978, The Champ 1979, Lookin' to Get Out (also wrote screenplay) 1982, Table for Five 1983, Runaway Train 1985, Desert Bloom 1986, Eternity, Heat, Rosewood, Mission Impossible 1996, U-Turn 1997, The Rainmaker 1997, Varsity Blues 1998, The General 1998, Enemy of the State 1998, Dog of Flanders 1999, Lara Croft: Tomb Raider 2001, Pearl Harbor 2001, Ali 2001, Zoolander 2002, Holes 2003, Superbabies 2003, Karate Dog 2003, The Manchurian Candidate 2004, National Treasure 2004, Superbabies: Baby Geniuses 2 2004, Glory Road 2006, The Legend of Simon Conjurer 2006, Transformers 2007, Bratz 2007, National Treasure Book of Secrets 2007, Pride and Glory 2008, An American Carol 2008, Four Christmases 2008, Dracula: The Dark Prince 2013. *Television includes:* End of the Game 1976, Gunsmoke and Cimarron Strip, Chernobyl: The Final Warning 1991, The Last of His Tribe 1992, The Tin Soldier (also dir), Convict Cowboy 1995, The Fixer 1998, Noah's Ark 1999, Second String 2000, Jasper Texas 2003, The Five People You Meet in Heaven 2004, Pope John Paul II 2005, 24 2009, Lonestar 2010, Ray Donovan (Golden Globe Award for Best Supporting Actor in a Series, Mini-Series, or TV Movie 2014) 2013. *Address:* c/o Martin Baum and Patrick Whitesell, CAA, 9830 Wilshire Boulevard, Beverly Hills, CA 90212,; Jon Voight Entertainment, 10203 Santa Monica Blvd, Los Angeles, CA 90067, USA. *Telephone:* (310) 288-4545; (310) 843-0223 (Jon Voight Entertainment). *Fax:* (310) 553-9895 (Jon Voight Entertainment).

VOINOVICH, George Victor, BA, JD; American lawyer and politician; b. 15 July 1936, Cleveland, Ohio; m. Janet Allen 1962; two s. two d. (one deceased); ed Collinwood High School, Ohio Univ., Moritz Coll. of Law at Ohio State Univ.; called to the Ohio Bar 1961, US Supreme Court 1968; Asst Attorney Gen., Ohio 1963–64; mem. Ohio House of Reps 1967–71; Auditor, Cuyahoga Co., Ohio 1971–76, Commr 1977–78; Lt-Gov. of Ohio 1979; Mayor of Cleveland 1980–89; Gov. of Ohio 1991–98; Senator from Ohio 1999–2011 (retd), mem. Foreign Relations Cttee, Senate Appropriations Cttee 2009–11, Chair. Ethics Cttee 2003–07; fmr mem. Nat. Govs Asscn (Chair. 1997–98), Chair. Educ. Action Team on School Readiness 1991, Child Support Enforcement Work Group 1991–92, Co-Chair. Task Force on Educ. 1992–93, mem. Exec. Cttee 1993; Pres. Nat. League of Cities 1984–85; Trustee, US Conf. of Mayors; Chair. Midwestern Govs Conf. 1991–92, Council of Great Lakes Govs 1992–94, Jobs for America's Grads Program (Nat. Leadership Award 1993); Co-Lead Gov. on Fed. Mandates 1993; Hon. LLD (Ohio Univ.) 1981; named as one of The Outstanding Young Men in Ohio, Ohio Jaycees 1970, Tree of Life Award, Jewish Nat. Foundation 1981, Certificate of Merit Award, Ohio Univ., Humanitarian Award, Nat. Conf. of Christians and Jews 1986, Distinguished Urban Mayor Award, Nat. Urban Coalition 1987, One of Outstanding Young Men in Greater Cleveland, Cleveland Jaycees, Ohio Univ. Humanitarian Award, Nat. Conf. for Community and Justice 1986, named to The All-Pro City Management Team, City & State Magazine 1987, Certificate of Merit Award, Dist Urban Mayor Award, Nat. Urban Coalition 1987, Nat. Public Service Award, Students Against Destructive Decisions 1991, Educ. Reform Pioneer Award, Nat. Business Roundtable 1994, George Falcon Golden Spike Award, Nat. Asscn of Railroad Passengers 2000. *Address:* c/o 317 Hart Senate Office Building, Washington, DC, 20510-0001, USA.

VOITOVICH, Aleksander Pavlavich, DrPhys-MathSci; Belarusian physicist and politician; b. 5 Jan. 1938, Rachkevich, Minsk region; s. of Pavel Voitovich and Nadezhda Voitovich; m.; one s.; ed Belarus State Univ.; mem. research staff, Inst. of Physics, Belarus Acad. of Sciences (BAS) 1962–84, Deputy Research Dir 1984–92, Deputy Research Dir then Dir Inst. of Molecular and Atomic Physics, BAS 1992–97; Chair. Nat. Ass. of Repub. of Belarus Council of Repub. 2000–03; Head of Lab., Inst. of Molecular and Atomic Physics 2003–; Academician, Nat. Acad. of Sciences of Belarus 1996–, Pres. 1997–2000; Order of Francisk Skaryna 1998; Badge of Honour 1981, State Prize 1996. *Achievements include:* creator of 24 scientific inventions. *Publications:* Magneto-Optics of Gas Lasers 1984, Lasers with Anisotropic Resonators (with V. Severikov) 1990; some 200 research papers. *Leisure interests:* fishing, carpentry. *Address:* Storojevskaia Str. 8-436, 220002, Minsk (home); Nezavisimosti Pr. 70, 220072 Minsk, Belarus. *Telephone:* (17) 2841732 (office); (17) 2840879. *E-mail:* avoitovich@gmail.com (home). *Website:* www.voitovich.org.

VOLCHEK, Galina Borisovna; Russian stage director and actress; b. 19 Dec. 1933, Moscow; d. of Boris Volchek and Vera Maimyna; m. 1st Yevgeniy Yevstigneyev 1957 (divorced 1964); m. 2nd Mark Abelev 1966 (divorced 1976); one s.; ed Studio-School of Moscow Art Theatre; Co-founder, actress and Stage Dir Theatre Sovremennik 1956–72, Artistic Dir 1972–; Deputy to State Duma (Parl.) 1995–99; stage productions in numerous countries including USA (first Soviet stage dir to work in USA, Alley Theatre, Houston, Echelone by M. Roshchin), Ireland (Abbey Theatre), Hungary, Finland, Bulgaria, Germany, Czechoslovakia; masterclasses in Tisch School, New York Univ.; USSR People's Artist, State Prize, State Orders of USSR, Hungary, Bulgaria and Russia, GA Tovstonogov Prize 2006. *Dramatic roles include:* Martha (Who's Afraid of Virginia Woolf?), Miss Amelia (The Ballad of the Sad Café by Albee), Wife of Governor (Inspector by Gogol). *Films:* roles in films by directors Kozintsev (King Lear), Yutkevich, Danelia and others. *Leisure interest:* designing clothes. *Address:* 101000 Moscow, Chistoprudny blvd 19A, (theatre); Povarskaya str. 26, Apt 43, Moscow, Russia (home). *Telephone:* (495) 921-25-43 (theatre). *Fax:* (495) 921-66-29 (office). *E-mail:* teatr@sovremennik .ru (office). *Website:* www.sovremennik.ru (office).

VOLCKER, Paul A., MA; American economist, banker, academic and government official; b. 5 Sept. 1927, Cape May, NJ; s. of Paul A. Volcker and Alma Klippel Volcker; m. Barbara Marie Bahnson 1954 (died 1998); one s. one d.; m. Anke Dening 2010; ed Princeton Univ., Harvard Univ. Grad. School of Public Admin. and London School of Econs, UK; Economist and Special Asst, Securities Dept, Fed. Reserve Bank of New York 1953–57; Financial Economist, Chase Manhattan Bank, New York 1957–62, Dir of Forward Planning 1965–69; Dir Office of Financial Analysis, US Treasury Dept 1962–63, Deputy Under-Sec. for Monetary Affairs 1963–65, Under-Sec. Monetary Affairs 1969–74; Sr Fellow, Woodrow Wilson School of Public and Int. Affairs, Princeton Univ. 1974–75; Pres. NY Fed. Reserve Bank 1975–79; Chair. Bd of Govs, Fed. Reserve System 1979–87; Frederick H. Schultz Prof. of Int. Econ. Policy, Princeton Univ. 1988–95, Prof. Emer. 1995–; Chair. James D. Wolfensohn Inc. 1988–96, CEO 1995–96; Henry Kaufman Visiting Prof., Stern School of Business, New York Univ. 1998; Chair. Int. Accounting Standards Cttee Foundation 2000–05; Chair. UN comm. investigating Iraq Oil for Food Program 2004–05; Chair. Bd of Trustees, Group of Thirty Consultative Group on Int. Econ. and Monetary Affairs, Inc., Washington, DC; first Chair. Pres.'s Econ. Recovery Advisory Bd, The White House, Washington, DC 2009–11; apptd by World Bank to lead ind. investigation of its Dept of Institutional Integrity 2007; mem. Bd of Dirs (non-exec.) ICI 1988–93, Nestlé 1988–2000, Prudential Insurance 1988–2002; consultant, Arthur Anderson 2002; Dr hc (Harvard, Yale, Princeton, and other univs); Admin. Fellowship, Harvard, Rotary Foundation Fellow, LSE, Arthur S. Fleming Award, Fed. Govt, US Treasury Dept Exceptional Service Award, Alexander Hamilton Award, Fred Hirsch Memorial Lecture 1978, Public Service Award, Tax Foundation 1981, Courage Award 1989. *Publications:* Changing Fortunes (with Toyoo Gyohten) 1992, Forbes Great Minds Of Business (co-author) 1997, Good Intentions Corrupted: The Oil for Food Scandal And the Threat to the U.N. (co-author) 2006. *Leisure interest:* avid fly-fisherman. *Address:* 610 Fifth Avenue, New York, NY 10020, USA (office). *Telephone:* (212) 218-7878 (office). *Fax:* (212) 218-7875 (office).

VOLK, Igor Petrovich; Russian cosmonaut; b. 12 April 1937; m.; two d.; ed Kirovograd Mil. Pilot School, School of Pilot Testers, Moscow Aviation Inst.; army service 1956–63; made a cosmonaut in 1978, first space flight 1984; leading test pilot for Buran aircraft 1984–95; Dir V. Chkalov Test Flights Centre, Gromov Flight Research Centre, M. Gromov Research Flight Inst. (GNC RFLII) 1995–2002; Deputy Zhykovsky City Council 1984–87; Pres. Council of USSR Tennis Fed. 1986–90; Pres. Amateur Pilots Fed. 1988; Exec. Pres. Russian Cosmonauts Fed. 2003–05; Order of Merit for the Fatherland, class 4 1997, Order of Lenin 1984, Order of the Red Banner of Labour, Order of Friendship of Peoples; Hero of USSR 1984. *Leisure interests:* flying, football, skiing, tennis. *Address:* c/o GNC RFLII, Zhukovskiy-2, Moscow 140160, Russia (office).

VOLKOV, Vladimir Konstantinovich, DHist; Russian historian; b. 15 Dec. 1930, Voronezh; m.; two d.; ed Moscow State Univ.; started career as journalist; broadcasting for Bulgaria and Albania 1954–56; researcher, Prof. and Head of Div., Deputy Dir Inst. of Slavonic Studies, USSR (now Russian) Acad. of Sciences 1956–87, Dir 1987–; mem. Council Pres. Boris Yeltsin 1993–98; Vice Pres. Nat. Cttee of Historians, mem. several scientific socs. *Publications:* over 160 works on problems of culture and history of Slavic peoples. *Address:* Institute of Slavonic Studies, Leningradsky pr. 7, 125040 Moscow, Russia. *Telephone:* (495) 250-77-08 (office).

VOLLEBAEK, Knut, MSc; Norwegian diplomatist; *High Commissioner on National Minorities, Organization for Security and Co-operation in Europe;* b. 11 Feb. 1946, Oslo; m. Ellen Sofie Aadland Vollebaek; one s.; ed Inst. Catholique de Paris, Univ of Oslo, Univ of California, Santa Barbara, USA, Universidad Complutense, Madrid, Norwegian School of Econs and Business Admin, Bergen; joined Foreign Service 1973; Second Sec. Embassy in Delhi 1975–78, First Sec. Embassy in Madrid 1978–81; Exec. Officer, then Sr Exec. Officer, Ministry of Foreign Affairs 1981–84; Counsellor, Embassy in Harare, Zimbabwe 1984–86; Head of First Political Affairs Div., Ministry of Foreign Affairs 1986–89, State Sec. and Deputy Minister of Foreign Affairs 1989–90; Amb. to Costa Rica 1991–93; Dir Gen. Dept of Bilateral Devt Cooperation, Ministry of Foreign Affairs 1993–94; Gov. IDB, Asian Devt Bank and African Devt Bank 1994–97; Deputy Co-Chair. Int. Conf. on the Fmr Yugoslavia, Geneva 1993; Asst Sec. Gen. for Devt Cooperation 1994–97; Minister of Foreign Affairs 1997–2000; Chair. Barents Euro-Arctic Council 1997–98, Council of Baltic Sea States 1999–2000; Chair.-in-Office OSCE 1999; Amb. to USA 2001–07; High Commr on Nat. Minorities, OSCE 2007–; Commdr, Royal Norwegian Order of St Olav 2001; Hon. DJur (St Olaf Coll., Minn., USA) 2003; Hon. DHumLitt (Concordia Coll., Minn., USA) 2003. *Address:* High Commissioner on National Minorities, Prinsessegracht 22, 2514 AP The Hague, Netherlands (office). *Telephone:* (70) 3125500 (office). *Fax:* (70) 3635910 (office). *E-mail:* hcnm@hcnm.org (office). *Website:* www.osce.org/hcnm (office).

VOLLHARDT, Dieter, Dr rer. nat (habil.); German theoretical physicist and academic; *Professor of Theoretical Physics and Dean, Faculty of Mathematical and Natural Science, University of Augsburg;* b. 8 Sept. 1951, ; ed Univ. of Hamburg, Univ. of Southern California, USA; Postdoctoral Research Assoc., Max Planck Inst. for Physics and Astrophysics, Werner Heisenberg Inst., Munich 1979–84, Heisenberg Fellow, Deutsche Forschungs Gemeinschaft 1984–87; Prof. of Physics, Dir Inst. for Theoretical Physics, Rheinisch-Westfälische Technische Hochschule, Aachen 1987–96; Prof. of Theoretical Physics, Chair in Theoretical Physics, Centre for Electronic Correlations and Magnetism, Inst. for Physics, Univ. of Augsburg 1996–, mem. Exec. Bd, Augsburg Centre for Innovative Technologies 2007–, Man. Dir Inst. of Physics 2010–11, Vice-Dean, Faculty of Math. and Natural Sciences 2011–13, Dean 2013–; Visiting Scientist, Inst. for Theoretical Physics, Santa Barbara, Calif., USA 1983, Bell Laboratories, Murray Hill, NJ, USA 1983; Chair. Prize Cttee for Max Planck Medal of Deutsche Physikalische Gesellschaft 2013–; mem. Bavarian Acad. of Sciences and Humanities 2011 (Chair. Comm. for Low Temperature Research 2012–); scholarships from Studienstiftung des Deutschen Volkes 1969–79, Ehrenfest Colloquium, Univ. of Leiden 2001, Europhysics Prize, European Physical Soc. 2006, Max Planck Medal, Deutsche Physikalische Gesellschaft 2010, Ernst Mach Hon. Medal, Acad. of Sciences of Czech Repub. 2011, Dvorak Lecturer, Acad. of Sciences of Czech Repub. 2011, Einstein Lecturer, Annalen der Physik 2012. *Publications:* numerous papers in professional journals.

Address: Room 4A 408, EKM-Building, Centre for Electronic Correlations and Magnetism, Theoretical Physics III, Institute of Physics, University of Augsburg, 86135 Augsburg, Germany (office). *Telephone:* (821) 5983700 (office). *E-mail:* dieter.vollhardt@physik.uni-augsburg.de (office). *Website:* www.physik.uni-augsburg.de (office).

VOLLMER, Dana; American swimmer; b. 13 Nov. 1987, Syracuse, New York; m. Andy Grant 2011; ed Univ. of Florida, Univ. of California, Berkeley; raised in Granbury, Tex.; swam for coach Ron Forrest at Fort Worth Area Swim Team (FAST) as a child; initially swam for Univ. of Florida before transferring to Univ. of California, Berkeley; youngest swimmer competing at US Olympic Trials 2000 aged 12; Goodwill Games, Brisbane 2001: bronze medal, 4×100m medley; Pan American Games, Santo Domingo 2003: gold medal, 200m freestyle, 4×200m freestyle, 4×100m medley 2003; Olympic Games, Athens 2004: gold medal, 4×200m freestyle; World Championships (short course), Indianapolis 2004: gold medal, 4×100m freestyle, 4×200m freestyle, bronze medal, 200m freestyle, Dubai 2010: silver medal, 4×100m freestyle, 4×100m medley, bronze medal, 100m butterfly; Summer Universiade, Izmir 2005: gold medal, 4×100m freestyle, silver medal, 50m butterfly; Pan Pacific Championships, Victoria 2006: gold medal, 4×200m freestyle, Irvine 2010: gold medal, 100m butterfly, 4×100m freestyle, 4×200m freestyle, 4×100m medley, silver medal, 100m freestyle; World Championships (long course), Melbourne 2007: gold medal, 4×200m freestyle, silver medal, 4×100m freestyle, 4×100m medley, Rome 2009: silver medal, 4×200m freestyle, bronze medal, 200m freestyle, Shanghai 2011: gold medal, 100m butterfly, 4×100m medley, silver medal, 4×100m freestyle, Barcelona 2013: gold medal, 4×100m medley, bronze medal, 100m butterfly; Olympic Games, London 2012: gold medal, 100m. butterfly, 4×100m medley relay (with Missy Franklin, Rebecca Soni and Allison Schmitt), 4×200m freestyle relay; swims for California Aquatics and Univ. of California, Berkeley. *Address:* c/o Wasserman Media Group, 10960 Wilshire Blvd, Suite 2200, Los Angeles, CA 90024, USA (office); c/o Cal Aquatics Athletic Department, Office 195, Haas Pavilion Berkeley, CA 94720-4422, USA. *Telephone:* (310) 407-0200 (office). *E-mail:* info@wmgllc.com (office). *Website:* www.wmgllc.com (office); www.danavollmer.com.

VOLOCHKOVA, Anastasiya; Russian ballet dancer; b. 20 Jan. 1976, St Petersburg; ed Russian Vaganova Acad. of Ballet; soloist, Maryinsky Theatre, St Petersburg 1994–98; with Bolshoi Theatre 1998–2003; Gold Medal, 2nd Ballet Contest, Kiev. *Roles include:* Odyllia and Swan Princess in Swan Lake, Gisele in Gisele, Raimonda in Raimonda, Niknya in Bayder, Aurora and Lilac Fairy in Sleeping Beauty, Zarema in Fountain of Bakhchisarai, Girl in Spirit of Rose, Medora in Corsair, Carmen in Carmen-Suite. *Leisure interests:* walking, reading, classical and modern music. *Telephone:* (495) 126-17-53 (home). *E-mail:* office@volochkova.ru. *Website:* www.volochkova.ru.

VOLODIN, Vyacheslav Viktorovich, DJur; Russian politician; *First Deputy Chief of Staff of the Presidential Executive Office;* b. 4 Feb. 1964, Alekseyevka, Saratov Oblast; m.; one d.; ed Saratov Inst. of Agric. Mechanisation, Acad. of Civil Service; teacher, Docent, Saratov Inst. of Agric. Mechanisation 1987–92; Deputy Head Admin. of Saratov 1992–93; Prof., Head of Chair., Pro-Rector Povolzhye Personnel Centre 1993–94; mem., Deputy Chair. Saratov Oblast Duma 1994–, Vice-Gov., First Deputy Chair. Saratov Oblast Govt 1996–99; Prof. Povolzhye Acad. of Civil Service until 1999; mem. State Duma (Parl.) 1999–, mem. Homeland–All Russia faction, Deputy Sec. Political Council 1999, mem. Unity and Fatherland 2001–03, re-elected to State Duma as mem. of United Russia faction 2003, 2007, Deputy Chair. State Duma 2004–10, First Sec., United Russia 2005–10; Deputy Prime Minister and Chief of Staff of the Prime Minister 2010–11; Deputy Head of Kremlin Modernization Comm. 2010–; First Deputy Chief of Staff of the Presidential Exec. Office 2011–. *Leisure interests:* painting, sports. *Address:* Presidential Executive Office, 103132 Moscow, Staraya Square 4 (office). *Telephone:* (495) 925-35-81 (office). *Fax:* (495) 206-07-66 (office). *E-mail:* president@gov.ru (office). *Website:* www.kremlin.ru (office); www.state.kremlin.ru (office).

VOLONTIR, Mikhail; Moldovan actor; b. 9 March 1934; s. of Ermolae Volontir and Feodosia Volontir; m. Eufrosinia Volontir 1961; one d.; ed Actors' Training School; actor and producer with Alecsandri Moldavian Music and Drama Theatre in Beltsy 1957–; work in TV and films 1968–; mem. Pres. Council 1997–2001; Dr hc (Acad. of Sciences) 2009; USSR People's Artist 1984. *Theatre includes:* Misfortune (producer), The Twilight (actor, producer), Alecsandri's Agaki Flutur, Bayescu's Preshul (actor, producer), Drutsa's Beautiful and Saint (producer), Tanev's The Last Night of Socrates (actor, producer). *Films include:* A Movement of Answer, The Only Man, The Hunting of Deer, Am I Guilty?, Traces of a Wolf, We Shall Remain Faithful, One-Sided Love. *Leisure interest:* protection of animals. *Address:* Str. Independentsei 34, Apt. 4, 3100 Beltsy, Moldova. *Telephone:* (31) 2-80-52.

VOLOSHIN, Alexander Stalyevich; Russian government official; b. 3 March 1956, Moscow; m.; three s.; ed Moscow Inst. of Transport Eng, Ail-Union Acad. of Foreign Trade; Head of Lab. of Scientific Org. of Labour; Sec. Comsomol Org.; Moskva-Sortirovochnaya railway station 1973–83; Researcher, then Sr Researcher, Head of Sector, Deputy Head of Section Ail-Union Research Inst. of Conjuncture 1986–92; Exec. Dir Analysis, Consultations and Marketing 1992–; Pres. ESTA Corpn 1993–96; Pres. Fed. Funds Corpn 1996–97; apptd Asst to Head of Admin. of Presidency (for Econ. Problems) 1997, Deputy Head 1998–99, Head 1999–2003 (resgnd); Chair. Bd of Dirs RAO EES 1999–; Chair. Supervisory Bd Unified Energy Systems (EES) 2004–; Chair. Collegium of Reps, State Bd of Public Radio and TV. *Address:* RAO Unified Energy System of Russia, Bld. 3, 101 Vernadsky Ave., Moscow, 119526, Russia (office). *Telephone:* (495) 220-4001 (office). *Fax:* (495) 927-3007 (office). *Website:* www.rao-ees.ru (office).

VOLPINARI, Antonio Lazzaro, III; San Marino politician; b. 2 Oct. 1943, Domagnano; m. Claudia Berti; one d.; joined Partito Socialista Sammarinese (PSS) 1959, elected to Cen. Cttee 1963–, with Secr. Youth Movt, Vice-Sec. PSS 1980–82, Gen.-Sec. before and after Conf. Socialist Unification 1991, mem. Secr., Pres. of Group of Advisers; elected mem. of Govt 1969–, Mayor of Govt 1974–76, Deputy to Agric., Communications and Transport 1976–78, to Agric. and Commerce 1978–83, to the Territory and Atmosphere 1983–86, Sec. of State for Internal Affairs 1992–2000; Supreme Magistracy of Captain Regent 1973–74, April–Sept. 1977; Head of State (Capt. Regent) 2002; mem. Advisory Comm. on Internal Affairs; Del. to the Council of Europe; Pres. San Marino Equestrian Fed. 2013–.

Address: c/o Partito Socialista Sammarinese (PSS), Via G. Ordelaffi 46, 47890 San Marino (office).

VOLTEN, Peter M.E., MA, PhD; Dutch research institute director; *Director, Centre for European Security Studies;* m. Karin Deen; four c.; ed Free Univ. of Amsterdam; Visiting Scholar, Stanford Univ., USA 1975–77; Sr Staff mem. Dutch Ministry of Defence 1977–85, Dir of Studies and Strategic Planning 1987–89; Prof. of History, Univ. of Utrecht 1984–89; Sr Research Fellow, Netherlands Inst. of Int. Relations 1985–87; Dir of Research, Inst. for East-West Security Studies 1989–92, Sr Vice-Pres. and Dir Netherlands Centre 1992–93; Prof. of Int. Relations and Orgs, Univ. of Groningen 1994–, Dir Centre for European Security Studies 1994–; mem. Bd Dirs Free Univ. of Amsterdam. *Publications include:* Brezhnev's Peace Program: a Study of Soviet Domestic Political Process and Power 1982, Uncertain Futures: Eastern Europe and Democracy (ed.) 1990, The Guns Fall Silent: the End of the Cold War and the Future of Conventional Disarmament (co-ed.) 1990, Bound to Change: Consolidating Democracy in East Central Europe (ed.) 1992; numerous articles on security and defence policy in learned journals. *Address:* Centre for European Security Studies, Lutkenieuwstraat 31a, 9712 AW, Groningen, Netherlands (office). *Telephone:* (50) 3132520 (office). *Fax:* (50) 3132506 (office). *E-mail:* p.m.e.volten@let.rug.nl (office). *Website:* www.cess.org (office).

VON BOMHARD, Nikolaus, DrJur; German insurance industry executive; *Chairman of the Board of Management, Münchener Rückversicherungs-Gesellschaft AG (Munich Re);* b. 28 July 1956, Gunzenhausen; m. Charlotte von Bomhard; two c.; ed Univs of Munich and Regensburg; joined grad. trainee programme, Münchener Rückversicherungs-Gesellschaft AG (Munich Reinsurance Co.) 1985–87, later worked as underwriter in Operational Div.: Fire/Treat, Deputy Head of Operational Div.: Germany 1992–97, Head, Brazil Office, São Paulo 1997–2000, mem. Bd of Man. 2000–, responsible for Europe 2/Latin America Div. 2001–04, Chair. Bd of Man. Munich Re 2004–; Chair. Supervisory Bd ERGO Versicherungsgruppe AG, Düsseldorf; Chair. Munich Health Holding AG, ERGO Versicherungsgruppe AG; mem. Bd of Dirs AIEEA of Geneva ('Geneva Asscn'), Fed. Financial Supervisory Authority (BaFin), Berlin, Freunde des Münchener Bach-Chores e.V., Freundeskreis der Münchener Assekuranz (Juniorenkreis); mem. Presiding Cttee and Gen. Cttee Gesamtverband der Deutschen Versicherungswirtschaft e.V; mem. Supervisory Bd Commerzbank AG 2009–; Dir UniCredit SpA (Unicredito Italiano) 2005–; mem. Bd of Trustees Gesellschaft Freunde der Hochschule für Musik und Theater München e.V., Munich, Pinakotheks-Verein Verein zur Förderung der Alten und Neuen Pinakothek München e.V., Munich, Verein der Freunde und Förderer der Glyptothek und der Antikensammlungen München e.V., Munich; mem. Univ. Council Ludwig-Maximilian Univ., Munich; mem. Foundation Bd Munich Re Foundation. *Address:* Münchener Rückversicherungs-Gesellschaft AG, Königinstrasse 107, 80802 Munich, Germany (office). *Telephone:* (89) 38910 (office). *Fax:* (89) 399056 (office). *E-mail:* info@munichre.com (office). *Website:* www.munichre.com (office).

VON BRAUN, Joachim, PhD; German agricultural economist, research institute director and academic; *Director, Department of Economic and Technological Change, Centre for Development Research, University of Bonn;* b. 10 July 1950, Brakel; m. Dr Barbara von Braun; three d.; ed Univ. of Göttingen; Dir Food Consumption and Nutrition Div., Int. Food Policy Research Inst. (IFPRI), Washington, DC 1990–93, Dir-Gen. IFPRI 2002–09; Prof. and Dir Inst. for Food Econs and Consumer Analyses, Univ. of Kiel 1993–97; Dir Dept of Econ. and Technological Change, Centre for Devt Research, Univ. of Bonn 1997–2002, 2009–; Pres. Int. Asscn of Agricultural Economists 2000–03; mem. Hunger Task Force, UN Millennium Devt Project 2003–05; Fellow, German Econs Asscn 1996, AAAS 2006; Hon. Prof., Int. Research Center for Food and Agric. Econs, Nanjing Agricultural Univ., China 2004–; Dr hc (Stuttgart-Hohenheim) 2005; Josef G. Knoll Science Prize 1988. *Publications:* Famine in Africa: Causes, Responses and Prevention (co-author) 1999, Russia's Agro-Food Sector: Towards Truly Functioning Markets (co-ed.) 2000, Agricultural Biotechnology in Developing Countries: Towards Optimizing the Benefits for the Poor (co-author) 2000, Villages in the Future: Crops, Jobs and Livelihood (co-ed.) 2001, Information and Communication Technologies for Development and Poverty Reduction – The Potential of Telecommunications (co-ed.) 2005, Globalization of Food and Agriculture and the Poor (co-ed.) 2008. *Address:* Centre for Development Research, University of Bonn, Walter-Flex-Str. 3, 53113 Bonn, Germany (office). *Telephone:* (228) 731800 (office). *Fax:* (228) 731869 (office). *E-mail:* jvonbraun@uni-bonn.de (office). *Website:* www.zef.de (office).

VON BÜLOW, Andreas, DJur; German politician and lawyer; b. 17 July 1937, Dresden; s. of Georg-Ulrich Bülow and Susanne von Bülow (née Haym); m. Anna Barbara Duden 1961; two s. two d.; law studies in Heidelberg, Berlin and Munich, studied in France and USA; entered higher admin. service of State of Baden-Württemberg 1966, on staff of Rural Dist Offices of Heidelberg and Balingen, Pres. Admin. Dist of Süd-Württemberg Hohenzollern at Tübingen; mem. Bundestag (Parl.) 1969–94; Parl. State Sec. Fed. Ministry of Defence 1976–80; Fed. Minister for Research and Tech. 1980–82; mem. Social Democratic Party 1960–, Public Services and Transport Workers' Union. *Publications:* Die Überwachung der Erdgasindustrie durch die Federal Power Commission als Beispiel der Funktionen der unabhängigen Wirtschaftsüberwachungskommissionen der amerikanischen Bundesverwaltung 1967 (dissertation), Gedanken zur Weiterentwicklung der Verteidigungsstrategien in West und Ost 1984, Alpträume West gegen Alpträume Ost—ein Beitrag zur Bedrohungsanalyse 1984, Skizzen einer Bundeswehrstruktur der 90er Jahre 1985, Die eingebildete Unterlegenheit—das Kräfteverhältnis West-Ost, wie es wirklich ist 1985, The Conventional Defense of Europe, New Technologies and New Strategies 1986, Im Namen des Staates, CIA, BND und die Kriminellen Machenschaften der Geheimdienste 1998, Die CIA und der 11 September 2003. *Leisure interests:* music, geology, history, swimming, hiking, skiing. *Address:* c/o Sozialdemokratische Partei Deutschlands (SPD), Wilhelmstr. 141, 10963 Berlin, Germany (office).

VON DASSANOWSKY, Robert, (Robert Dassanowsky), BA, MA, PhD, FRHistS, FRSA; American/Austrian writer, academic and film producer; *Professor of German and Film and Director of Film Studies, University of Colorado, Colorado Springs;* b. 28 Jan. 1960, New York, NY; s. of the late Elfi von Dassanowsky; ed American Acad. of Dramatic Arts, American Film Inst. Conservatory Program, Univ. of California, Los Angeles; Founding Ed. Rohwedder: InternationalMagazine of Literature and Art 1986–93; writer/researcher, Stone-Stanley TV Productions/Disney Channnel 1990–92; Corresp. Ed. Rampike 1991–; consultant/trans., J. Paul Getty Conservation Inst., Los Angeles 1991–92; Visiting Asst Prof. of German, UCLA 1992–93, Visiting Prof. of German 2007–08; Asst Prof. of German, Univ. of Colorado, Colorado Springs 1993–99, Dir of Film Studies 1997–, Assoc. Prof. of German and Film Studies 1999–2006, Prof. of German and Film Studies 2006–, Chair., Dept of Languages and Cultures 2001–07, Chair. Dept of Visual and Performing Arts 2001–02, 2010–11; Adjunct Faculty, Media Communication and Film, Webster Univ. Vienna 2013–; Producer and CEO Belvedere Film, LLC 1999–; mem. Editorial Bd Osiris 1991–, Modern Austrian Literature/Journal of Austrian Studies 1997–2000, 2011–14, Ariadne Press 1999–, Poetry Salzburg Review 2002–; Dir, Elfi von Dassanowsky Foundation 2009–; mem. Bd Los Angeles Flickapalooza Film Festival 2001–03, TIE The Int. Experimental Cinema Exposition 2002–10; Co-founder and mem. Bd Int. Alexander Lernet-Holenia Soc. 1997–; Co-founder and Vice-Pres. Austrian American Film Asscn 1998–2009, Exec. Council, Modern Austrian Literature and Culture Asscn (MALCA) 2006–09, 2010–11 (Vice-Pres. Austrian Studies Asscn (fmrly MALCA) 2011–13, Pres. 2012–14); External Reviewer, Fund for the Improvement of Postsecondary Educ. (FIPSE)/EC Directorate Gen. for Educ. and Culture Atlantis Project 2010–14; mem. Modern Language Asscn, PEN/USA, Austrian PEN, Poets and Writers, Asscn of Austrian Film Producers, Film Independent Los Angeles, Soc. for Cinema and Media Studies, Screen Actors Guild, German Studies Asscn, PEN Colorado (Founding Pres. 1994–99, 2001–02), Acad. of Austrian Film, European Film Acad., European Acad. of Sciences and Arts (Cen. US Del. 20; mem. Bd European Soc. Coudenhove-Kalergi 2013; Constantinian Order of St George, Order of Vitez (Hungary), Decoration of Honour in Silver (Austria); Academico hc (Academia Culturale d'Europa, Italy) 1989; Pres.'s Fund for the Humanities grants, Univ. of Colorado 1996, 2001, Outstanding Teaching Award, Univ. of Colorado at Colorado Springs 2001, Faculty Research Award, Coll. of Letters, Arts and Sciences, Univ. of Colorado at Colorado Springs 2002, US Prof. of the Year for Colorado, Carnegie Foundation/CASE 2004, Chancellor's Award, Univ. of Colorado at Colorado Springs 2006, Taft Center Lecturer, Univ. of Cincinnati 2011, Faculty Award for Excellence in Research, Univ. of Colorado, Colorado Springs 2013. *Films include:* as producer, assoc. producer or exec. producer: Semmelweis 2001, Epicure 2001, The Nightmare Stumbles Past 2002, Believe 2002, Wilson Chance 2005, The Last Bogatyr 2009, The Retreat 2010, Vidas ambulante/The Troubadours 2011, Waking Eyes 2011, Deadline 2012, Menschen 2012, Dog Eat Dog 2012, Felix Austria! (aka The Archduke and Herbert Hinkel) 2013, Styria 2013, Chariot 2013, Future Present Past 2013, Never Kissed by the Queen (The Black Countess from Bain Street) 2014, Creep! 2014; audio commentary: Leni Riefenstahl's Tag der Freiheit 2000, Self, Be Natural: The Untold Story of Alice Guy-Blaché 2014; historical adviser, Paul Henreid: Beyond Victor Laszlo Documentary 2014. *Television:* writer and script supervisor, Teen Win, Lose or Draw (Disney Channel) 1989–90, Self, Porträt von Elfi von Dassanowsky, Wilkommen Österreich (ORF) 1998, Co-producer, De Expressione Humanitatis Von Schauspiel und Musik (Austria) 2014. *Publications include:* Phantom Empires: The Novels of Alexander Lernet-Holenia and the Question of Postimperial Austrian Identity 1996, Hans Raimund: Verses of a Marriage (trans.) 1996, Telegrams from the Metropole: Selected Poetry 1999, Alexander Lernet-Holenia: Mars in Aries (trans.) 2003, Austrian Cinema: A History 2005, Soft Mayhem: Poetry 2010, New Austrian Cinema (co-ed.) 2011, The Nameable and the Unnameable: Hofmannsthal's 'Der Schwierige' Revisited (ed. and contrib.) 2011, Tarantino's Inglourious Basterds: Manipulations of Metacinema (ed.) 2012, World Film Locations: Vienna 2012, Screening Transcendence: Film under Austrofascism and the Hollywood Hope 1933–38 2014; other: several plays, film and TV scripts; contribs: Contributing Ed., Gale Encyclopedia of Multicultural America 1999; mem. Editorial Bd and contrib. to International Dictionary of Films and Filmmakers 2000, Guest Co-Ed., Filmkunst 154, Special Issue: Austria's Hollywood/Hollywood's Austria 1997, Literatur der inneren Emigration in Österreich 1998, Thunder Rumbling at My Heels: Tracing Ingeborg Bachmann 1998, Alexander Lernet-Holenia: Poesie auf dem Boulevard 1999, Der BergFilm 1920–1940 2002, Harvard's Notable American Women, Vol. 5 2005, Landvermessung: Eine österreichische Bibliothek nach 1945, 2005, Greenwood Encyclopedia of World Popular Culture 2007, Cinema and the Swastika: The International Expansion of Third Reich Cinema 2007, Crime and Madness in Modern Austria: Myth, Metaphor and Cultural Realities 2008, Österreich 1918 und die Folgen 2008, European Academy of Sciences and Arts Twentieth Anniversary Festschrift 2009, Guest Ed., Modern Austrian Literature Special Issue: Michael Haneke, 43.2 2010, Women Film Pioneers Sourcebook, Vol. II 2011–12, selected poems in French trans., 12×2, ed. Teric Boucebci, Sexuality, Eroticism and Gender in Austrian Literature and Culture 2011, Zeitenwende: Österreichische Literatur seit dem Millennium 2011, Nazisploitation! The History, Aesthetics, and Politics of the Nazi Image in Low-Brow Cinema 2011, A New History of German Cinema 2012, Auf dem Weg in die Moderne, 2013, Tarantino's Django Unchained: A Continuation of Metacinema 2014, Austro-Italian Encounters: Modern Austrian-Italian Cultural Relationships 2014, Poetics and Politics of the Danube River 2014, The Women of James Bond: Critical Perspectives on Feminism and Femininity in the Bond Franchise 2014; Women Screenwriters: An International Guide 2014; numerous additional book chapters, poetry and articles in periodicals and anthologies. *Leisure interests:* art collecting, travel, fencing. *Address:* Department of Languages and Cultures, University of Colorado, 1420 Austin Bluffs Parkway, Colorado Springs, CO 80918, USA (office). *E-mail:* rvondass@uccs.edu (office). *Website:* www.belvederefilm.com (office); www .elfivondassanowsky.org.

VON DER DUNK, Hermann Walther; Dutch historian and academic; *Professor Emeritus, University of Utrecht;* b. 9 Oct. 1928, Bonn, Germany; s. of Heinrich M. von der Dunk and Ilse Löb; m. Goverdina Schuurmans Stekhoven 1958; two s. one d.; ed Univ. of Utrecht and Inst. für Europäische Geschichte, Mainz; Asst, Mainz Institut für Europäische Geschichte; school teacher, Bilthoven 1961–63; Asst Prof., Dept of History, Univ. of Utrecht 1963–67, Prof. of Contemporary History and Head of Dept 1967–88, Prof. and Head, Dept of Cultural History 1988–90, now Prof. Emer.; Visiting Prof., Univ. of Nijmegen 1993–94; mem. Royal Netherlands Acad., Academia Europaea, Dutch Soc. of Science; Grosses Bundesverdienstkreuz 1989, Ridder, Nederlandse Leeuw 1991, Vondel Prize 1994, Goethe-Medaille 1995. *Publications:* Der deutsche Vormärz u. Belgien (thesis) 1966, Kleio heeft 1000 ogen (essays) 1974, Conservatisme 1976, De organisatie van het verleden 1982, Voorbij

de verboden drempel: de Shoah 1990, Cultuur & Geschiedenis (articles) 1990, Sprekend over identiteit en geschiedenis 1992, Twee buren, twee culturen (essays) 1994, Elke tijd is overgangstijd (essays) 1996, De verdwijnende hemel. Over de Cultuur van Europa in de twintigste eeuw (two vols) 2000, Mensen, Machten, Mogelijkheden (essays) 2002, In het huis van de herinnering, een cultuurhistorische verkenning 2007, Op schuivende planken.Nederlands perikelen in het licht van zijn verleden.Een essay 2007, Terugblik bij strijklicht. Jeugdherinneringen 2008, De glimlachende Sfinx Kernvragen in de geschiedenis 2011, Voordat de voegen kraakten. Student in de jaren vijftig 2013; essays, articles and contribs to textbooks, journals and newspapers. *Leisure interests:* music (playing piano), drawing and painting, literature. *Address:* Nicolailaan 20, 3723 HS Bilthoven, Netherlands. *Telephone:* (30) 2285401. *E-mail:* dunk001@kpnmail.nl.

VON DER LEYEN, Ursula, BSc, MPH; German gynaecologist and politician; *Federal Minister of Defence;* b. 8 Oct. 1958, Brussels, Belgium; m. Heiko E. von der Leyen; seven c.; ed European School, Brussels, Lehrte Gymnasium, Medizinische Hochschule Hannover (MHH), London School of Econs, UK; Asst Physician, Women's Clinic, MHH 1988–92; Residence at Stanford Univ., USA 1992–96, Auditing Guest, Grad. School of Business 1993, Market Analyst, Stanford Health Services Hosp. Admin 1995; Scientific Researcher, Epidemiology Dept, MHH 1998–2002; joined CDU 1990, mem. Physicians Team, Lower Saxony CDU 1999, mem. Parl. Group in Lower Saxony State Parl. (Landtag) 2003–, mem. Exec. German CDU 2004–, Chair. Parents, Child and Profession Cttee, Family Comm., German CDU 2005–; Lower Saxony Minister for Social Affairs, Women, the Family and Health 2003; Fed. Minister of Family Affairs, Sr Citizens, Women and Youth 2005–09, of Labour and Social Affairs 2009–13, of Defence 2013–. *Address:* Federal Ministry of Defence, Stauffenbergstr, 18, 10785 Berlin, Germany (office). *Telephone:* (30) 182400 (office). *Fax:* (30) 18245357 (office). *E-mail:* poststelle@bmvg.bund.de (office). *Website:* www.bmvg.de (office).

VON DOHNÁNYI, Christoph; German conductor; b. 8 Sept. 1929, Berlin; s. of Hans von Dohnányi and Christine (née Bonhoeffer) von Dohnányi; brother of Klaus von Dohnányi; m. 1st Renate Zillessen; one s. one d.; m. 2nd Anja Silja (q.v.) 1979; one s. two d.; m. 3rd Barbara Koller; ed Munich Musikhochschule; abandoned legal training to study music 1948; studied in USA under grandfather, Ernst von Dohnányi 1951; répétiteur and conductor under Georg Solti, Frankfurt Oper 1952–56; Gen. Music Dir Lübeck 1957–63, Kassel 1963–66; London debut with London Philharmonic Orchestra 1965; Chief Conductor of Cologne Radio Symphony Orchestra 1964–69; Gen. Music Dir and Opera Dir, Frankfurt 1968–77; Chief Conductor and Intendant, Hamburg State Opera 1977–84; Music Dir (desig.) Cleveland Orchestra 1982–84, Music Dir 1984–2002, Music Dir Laureate 2002–; Prin. Guest Conductor Philharmonia Orchestra 1994, Prin. Conductor 1997–08, Hon. Conductor for Life 2008–; Chief Conductor, NDR Sinfonieorchester Hamburg 2004–11; numerous guest appearances; numerous recordings of symphonies with Cleveland Orchestra and opera recordings; Commdr des Arts et des Lettres; Commdr's Cross, Order of Merit; Commdr's Cross (Austria); Dr hc (Kent State Univ.), (Case Western Univ.), (Oberlin Coll.), (Eastman School of Music), (Cleveland Inst. of Music); Richard Strauss Prize, Bartok Prize, Goethe Medal, Frankfurt, Arts and Science Prize, City of Hamburg, Abraham Lincoln Award. *Address:* c/o Harrison Parrott, 5–6 Albion Court, London, W6 0QT, England (office). *Telephone:* (20) 7229-9166 (office). *Fax:* (20) 7221-5042 (office). *E-mail:* info@harrisonparrott.co.uk (office). *Website:* www.harrisonparrott.com (office).

VON DOHNÁNYI, Klaus, DJur, LLB; German politician and political publicist; b. 23 June 1928, Hamburg; s. of Johann-Georg von Dohnányi and Christine (née Bonhoeffer) von Dohnányi; brother of Christoph von Dohnányi; m. Ulla Ahla 1997; two s. one d.; ed Munich, Columbia, Stanford and Yale Univs; fmrly with Ford Motor Co., Detroit, Mich. and Cologne; Dir Planning Div. Ford-Werke, Cologne 1956-60; Dir Inst. für Marktforschung und Unternehmensberatung, Munich 1960–68; Sec. of State, Fed. Ministry of Economy 1968–69; mem. Bundestag 1969–81; Parl. Sec. of State, Ministry of Educ. and Science 1969–72; Minister of Educ. and Science 1972–74; Minister of State and Parl. Sec. of State, Fed. Foreign Office 1976–81, First Burgomaster and Pres. Senate, Hamburg 1981–88; Chair. Bd, TAKRAF AG, Leipzig 1990–94; fmr Co-Chair., Comm. 'Restructuring East Germany'; Chair. Bd Kirow AG Leipzig; mem. Club of Rome 1996–, Konvent für Deutschland; mem. SPD; Heuss Medal Theodor Heuss Foundation 1988; Gold Medal for Distinguished Leadership and Service to Humanity, B'nai B'rith 1988, Stolten Medal, Hamburg,. *Publications:* Japanese Strategies 1969, Brief an den Deutschen Demokratischen Revolutionäre 1990, Das Deutsche Wagnis 1990, Im Joch des Profits? (The German Model) 1996, Dichter, Denker, Schulversager: Gute Schulen sind machbar – Wege aus der Bildungskrise (with Jorg Dräger) 2011. *Leisure interests:* writing, reading. *Address:* Heilwigstrasse 5, 20249 Hamburg, Germany. *Telephone:* (40) 4505789 (office). *Fax:* (40) 4505790 (office).

VON ESCHENBACH, Andrew C., BS, MD; American surgeon and fmr government official; b. Philadelphia, Pa; ed St Joseph's Univ., Phila and Georgetown Univ. School of Medicine, Washington, DC; completed residencies in gen. surgery and urology at Pa Hosp., Phila; fmr Instructor in Urology, Univ. of Pa School of Medicine; served as Lt Commdr in USN Medical Corps; Urologic Oncology Fellow, Univ. of Tex. M. D. Anderson Cancer Center, Houston 1976, mem. Faculty 1977, Chair. Dept of Urology 1983, later Consulting Prof. of Cell Biology and Prof. of Urology, Roy M. and Phyllis Gough Huffington Clinical Research Distinguished Prof. of Urologic Oncology, Vice-Pres. for Academic Affairs and Exec. Vice-Pres. and Chief Academic Officer Univ. of Tex. M. D. Anderson Cancer Center –2002, Founding Dir Prostate Cancer Research Program and Dir Genitourinary Cancer Center; Dir Nat. Cancer Inst., NIH 2002–06; Commr US Food and Drug Admin 2006–09; Pres. Samaritan Health Initiatives Inc.; currently Sr Fellow, Milken Inst.; Founding mem. C-Change; Pres. American Cancer Soc.; mem. editorial bds several leading journals and on several organizational bds; awards from American Medical Writers' Asscn, American Urological Asscn, Uniformed Services Univ. of Health Sciences, included in The Best Doctors in America publs, Medical Award of Excellence, Cancer Counseling, Achievement Awards from 100 Black Men of Metropolitan Houston and Partners in Courage, Julie Rogers 'Spirit of Love' Award. *Publications:* more than 200 articles, books, and book chapters. *Address:* Milken Institute, 1250 Fourth Street, Santa Monica, CA 90401, USA (office). *Telephone:* (310) 570-4600 (office). *Fax:* (310) 570-4601

(office). *E-mail:* info@milkeninstitute.org (office). *Website:* www.milkeninstitute
.org (office).

VON FIGURA, Kurt, DrMed; German microbiologist, academic and university administrator; *President, Georg-August-Universität Göttingen;* b. 16 May 1944, Heiningen, Baden-Württemberg; m.; four c.; ed Tübingen Univ., Univ. of Vienna; Medical Asst, Bad Wildungen, Tübingen und Munich 1969–70; Scientific Asst, Univ. of Münster Physiologisch-Chemisches Institut 1972–76, Sr Asst 1976–77, Prof. 1977–86; Prof. of Biochemistry, Faculty of Medicine, Georg-August-Universität Göttingen 1986–2004, Pres. 2005–; mem. Deutsche Akademie der Naturforscher Leopoldina 2004–, Max-Planck-Gesellschaft; Dr hc (Namur) 2002; Hoechst AG Prize 1978, Otto-Warburg-Medaille 2002. *Address:* Office of the President, Georg-August-Universität, Göttingen, Germany (office). *Telephone:* (551) 39-4311 (office). *Fax:* (551) 39-4135 (office). *E-mail:* praesident@uni-goettingen.de (office). *Website:* www.uni-goettingen.de (office).

VON GERKAN, Meinhard, PhD, Dipl-Ing; German architect; *CEO, gmp – von Gerkan, Marg and Partners Architects;* b. 3 Jan. 1935, Riga, USSR (now Latvia); m. Sabine von Gerkan; six c.; freelance architect in collaboration with Volkwin Marg 1965– (four partners, one partner for China); with Freie Akad. der Künste Hamburg 1972–; Prof., Inst. für Baugestaltung A, Technische Univ. Brunswick 1974–2002; with Kuratorium Jürgen-Ponto-Stiftung Frankfurt 1982; Guest Prof., Nihon Univ., Tokyo 1988, Univ. of Pretoria 1993; Visiting Prof., Dalian Univ. of Tech., Architecture and Art Coll., People's Repub. of China 2007; Founder and CEO gmp Foundation to enhance architectural educ. 2007–; work includes airport bldgs, cultural insts, railway stations, hotels, offices, public bldgs, housing, master plans and interior design and housing throughout Germany and in Italy, Latvia, Turkey, China, Viet Nam, Algeria, Saudi Arabia, South Africa, UAE, Poland, Ukraine, Romania, Brazil; mem. Convent Chairmanship of Bundesstiftung Baukultur, Berlin 2003; Pres. Acad. for Architectural Culture 2007–; Hon. FAIA 1995, Inst. of Mexican Architects 1995; Hon. mem. Berlin-Brandenburg Acad. of Sciences 2000; Bundesverdienstkreuz 2009; Dr hc (Philipps-Univ., Marburg) 2002; Hon Dr in Design (Christian Univ., Chung li, Taiwan) 2005; Dr hc (East China Normal Univ. Coll. of Design, Shanghai) 2007; more than 270 first prizes at nat. and int. architecture competitions, including Fritz Schumacher Award 2000, Romanian Nat. Award 2002, Plakette of Freie Akad. der Künste, Hamburg 2005, Grand Award, Asscn of German Architects (BDA) 2005; more than 150 awards for outstanding architecture. *Publications:* Architektur 1966–78 1978, Die Verantwortung des Architekten 1982, Architektur 1978–83 1983, Alltagsarchitektur, Gestalt und Ungestalt 1987, Architektur 1983–88 1988, Architektur 1988–91 1992, von Gerkan, Marg and Partners 1993, Idea and Model: 30 years of architectural models 1994, Architektur im Dialog 1994, Culture Bridge 1995, Architecture 1991–95 1995, Architecture for Transportation 1997, Architecture 1995–97 1998, Möbel Furniture 1998, Architecture 1997–99: Vol. 1 Selected Projects 2000, Modell Virtuell 2000, Architecture 1999–2000 2002, Vol. 2 Erlebnisräume – Spaces Design Construction 2002, Geometrie der Stille 2002, Luchao – Born from a Drop: Architecture for China 2003, Architecture 2000–01 2003, Vol. 3 Berliner Bauten und Projekte, 1965–2005 2005, Ideal City – Real Projects in China 2005, Architecture 2001–03 2005, Vol. 4 Private Houses 2006, Vol. 5 Möbel Furniture 2007, Bauten Buildings 2007, Architecture 2003–07 2009, From Cape Town to Brasília New Stadiums by gmp 2010. *Address:* Elbchaussee 139, 22763 Hamburg, Germany (office). *Telephone:* (40) 881510 (office). *Fax:* (40) 88151177 (office). *E-mail:* hamburg-e@gmp-architekten.de (office). *Website:* www.gmp-architekten.de (office).

VON GRÜNBERG, Hubertus, DSc; German business executive; *Chairman, ABB Ltd;* b. 20 July 1942; ed Univ. of Cologne; began his career with Alfred Teves GmbH (ITT), Frankfurt am Main, various posts in Germany, Brazil and USA 1971–82, Head of Devt and Tech., Frankfurt am Main 1982–84, Chair. Man. Bd 1984–89, Vice-Pres. ITT Corpn, New York, USA 1987–89, Pres. and CEO ITT Automotive Inc., Auburn Hills, Mich., USA 1989–91, Sr Vice-Pres. ITT Corpn; CEO Continental AG 1991–99, Chair. Supervisory Bd of Dirs 1999–2009; Chair. ABB Ltd, Zurich 2007–; Chair. Advisory Bd Sapinda Holding BV (Netherlands); mem. Bd of Dirs, Schindler Holding AG (Switzerland); mem. Supervisory Bd Deutsche Telekom AG 2000–, Allianz Versicherung AG. *Address:* ABB Ltd, Affolternstrasse 44, 8050 Zurich, Switzerland (office). *Telephone:* (43) 317-71-11 (office). *Fax:* (43) 317-44-20 (office). *E-mail:* info@abb.com (office). *Website:* www.abb.com (office).

VON HEBEL, Herman, LLM; Dutch lawyer and international organization official; *Registrar International Criminal Court;* b. 22 Nov. 1961, Coevorden; m.; two c.; ed Univ. of Groningen; Legal Researcher, Univ. of Utrecht 1987–89; Legislation Expert, Ministry of Justice 1990–91; Asst Legal Adviser, Sr Legal Counsel, Ministry of Foreign Affairs 1991–2000; Sr Legal Officer of Trial Chamber II, Int. Criminal Tribunal for the fmr Yugoslavia 2001–06; Deputy Registrar, then Acting Registrar and Registrar, Special Court for Sierra Leone 2006–09; Deputy Registrar, then Acting Registrar and Registrar, Special Tribunal for Lebanon 2009–13; Registrar, Int. Criminal Court 2013–; Chair. Int. Comm. of Jurists (Dutch section) 1988–90. *Address:* International Criminal Court, PO Box 19519, 2500 The Hague, The Netherlands (office). *Website:* www.icc-cpi.int (office).

VON KLITZING, Klaus; German physicist; *Director, Max Planck Institute for Solid State Research;* b. 28 June 1943, Schroda; s. of Bogislav von Klitzing and Anny von Klitzing (née Ulbrich); m. Renate Falkenberg 1971; two s. one d.; ed Tech. Univ. Brunswick, Univ. Würzburg; Prof., Tech. Univ., Munich 1980–84; Dir Max-Planck Inst. for Solid State Research, Stuttgart 1985–; Foreign mem. NAS, Russian Acad. of Sciences, Royal Soc. of London, Chinese Acad. of Science, Pontifical Acad. of Sciences, Österreichische Akad. der Wissenschaften, Deutsche Akad. der Naturforscher Leopoldina; Hon. mem. German Physical Soc.; numerous hon. doctorates; Nobel Prize for Physics 1985. *Achievements include:* discovered quantum Hall effect. *Address:* Max-Planck Institut für Festkörperforschung, Heisenbergstr. 1, Postfach 800665, 70569 Stuttgart, Germany (office). *Telephone:* (711) 6891570 (office). *Fax:* (711) 6891572 (office). *E-mail:* k.klitzing@fkf.mpg.de (office). *Website:* www.fkf.mpg.de/klitzing (office).

VON LUCIUS, Wulf D., Dr rer. pol; German scientific publisher; *Publisher and President, Lucius & Lucius Verlag;* b. 29 Nov. 1938, Jena; s. of the late Tankred R. von Lucius and of Annelise Fischer; m. Akka Achelis 1967; three s.; ed Heidelberg,

Berlin and Freiburg, Univ. of Hohenheim, Stuttgart; mil. service 1958–60; Asst Inst. of Econometrics, Freiburg 1965–66; worked in several publishing houses and as public accountant 1966–69; Partner and Man. Dir Gustav Fischer Verlag 1969–95; mem. Bd of Exec. Officers, German Publrs Asscn (Börsenverein) 1976–86; mem. Bd C. Hanser Verlag 1984–2013; Publr and Pres. Lucius & Lucius Verlag, Stuttgart 1996–; Chair. Int. Publishers Copyright Council 1995–98, Asscn of Scientific Publrs in Germany 1994–2001, Wüstenrot Stiftung 2009–; mem. Exec. Cttee Int. Publrs Asscn Geneva 1996–2004; Bd German Nat. Library 1981–; Hon. Prof., Univ. of Hohenheim, Stuttgart; Friedrich-Perthes-Medaille 1999, Antiquaria Preis 2001, Ludwig Erhard Preis 2004. *Publications:* Bücherlust–Vom Sammeln 2000, Verlagswirtschaft 2005 (third edn 2014), Das Glück der Bücher 2012; numerous articles on publishing, copyright and book history. *Leisure interests:* collecting fine prints and artists' books. *Address:* Gerokstrasse 51, 70184 Stuttgart, Germany (office). *Telephone:* (711) 242060 (office). *Fax:* (711) 242088 (office). *E-mail:* lucius@luciusverlag.com (office). *Website:* luciusverlag.com (office).

VON MOLTKE, Gebhardt, LLB; German diplomatist; *Chairman, German-British Society;* b. 28 June 1938, Wernersdorf, Silesia; m. Dorothea von Moltke 1965; one s. one d.; ed Univs of Heidelberg, Grenoble, Berlin, Freiburg im Breisgau; practical legal training 1963–67; with Fed. Foreign Office, Bonn 1968–71, Personnel Admin. 1977–82, Head of US Dept 1986–91; served in Embassy in Moscow 1971–75, in Yaoundé 1975–77, in Washington, DC 1982–86; Asst Sec.-Gen. for Political Affairs NATO 1991–97; Amb. to UK 1997–99; Perm. Rep. to NATO 1999–2003; Chair. German-British Soc. 2003–; Hon. GCVO, Great Cross (Hungary), Grand Cross (Germany), Commdr Cross (Poland), Grand Decoration in Gold with Star (Austria); Hon. DrJur (Birmingham) 2000; US Army Commdr's Award. *Leisure interests:* tennis, music, drawings (old masters).

VON OTTER, Anne-Sofie; Swedish singer (mezzo-soprano); b. 9 May 1955, Stockholm; ed Stockholm Conservatory, Guildhall School of Music and Drama, London, studied interpretation with Erik Werba (Vienna) and Geoffrey Parsons (London), vocal studies with Vera Rozsa; mem. Basel Opera, Switzerland 1982–85; French debut at Opéra de Marseille (Nozze di Figaro—Cherubino) and Aix-en-Provence Festival (La Finta Giardiniera) 1984, Rome, Accad. di Santa Cecilia 1984, Geneva (Così fan tutte—Dorabella) 1985, Berlin (Così fan tutte) 1985, USA in Chicago (Mozart's C minor Mass) and Philadelphia (Bach's B minor Mass) 1985, London at Royal Opera, Covent Garden (Le Nozze di Figaro) 1985, Lyon (La Finta Giardiniera) 1986, La Scala, Milan (Alceste) 1987, Munich (Le Nozze di Figaro) 1987, Stockholm (Der Rosenkavalier) 1988, The Metropolitan Opera, New York (Le Nozze di Figaro) 1988, The Royal Albert Hall, London (Faust) 1989, Handel's Ariodante 1997; Glyndebourne (Carmen) 2002, Théâtre des Champs Elysées (Handel's Serse) 2003, Metropolitan Opera, New York (Mélisande) 2005, Santa Fe (Carmen) 2006; Waltraute in Götterdammerung for Aix-en-Provence Festival 2009 and Salzburg Easter Festival 2010; appeared in Lulu at the Met 2010; Irene in Tamerlano, Liceu Barcelona 2011; 2012 roles included Geneviève in Pelleas et Melisande, Opéra de Paris and Cornelia in Giulio Cesare at Salzburg; repertoire extends from baroque music, German lieder through opera to 20th century music; recorded For the Stars with Elvis Costello 2001; has given recitals in New York, Paris, Brussels, Geneva, Stockholm, Vienna, London, Verbier, Toulouse and many others; Hon. DSc (Bath) 1992. *Address:* c/o Shirley Thomson, Harrison Parrott Ltd, 5-6 Albion Court, Albion Place, London, W6 0QT, England (office). *E-mail:* shirley.thomson@harrisonparrott.co.uk (office). *Website:* www.annesofievonotter.com.

VON PIERER, Heinrich, DrIur, DipEng; German business executive; b. 26 Jan. 1941, Erlangen; m. Annette von Pierer; three c.; ed Univ. of Erlangen–Nuremberg; Asst, Faculty of Law, Univ. of Erlangen–Nuremberg 1965–69; joined legal dept, Corp. Finance Div., Siemens AG 1969, various commercial assignments in sales and marketing at Kraftwerk Union AG div. and in various corp. depts 1977–1987, apptd Commercial Head of Kraftwerk Union AG 1988, Group Pres. Kraftwerk Union AG, mem. Man. Bd Siemens AG 1989, mem. Corp. Exec. Cttee 1990, Deputy Chair. Man. Bd 1991, Chair. Man. Bd, Pres. and CEO 1992–2005, Chair. Supervisory Bd 2005–07; mem. Supervisory Bd Bayer AG 2000–, Hochtief AG 2000–10, Münchener Rückversicherungs-Gesellschaft AG (Munich Re) 2000–, Volkswagen AG 2000–, Deutsche Bank AG –2008; mem. Econ. Cttee RWE AG; Chair. Asien-Pazifik-Ausschuss der Deutschen Wirtschaft (Asia-Pacific Cttee of the German Economy); mem. Bd Bundesverbandes der Deutschen Industrie (Fed. Asscn of German Industry); Chair. Int. Advisory Bd Allianz AG Holding; mem. Senate Max Planck Soc.; Founding mem. UNESCO–Children in Need; Hon. Prof., Friedrich-Alexander Univ. of Erlangen–Nuremberg 2006; Hon. Citizen Award (Singapore) 2007; Großes Bundesverdienstkreuz des Verdienstordens der Bundesrepublik Deutschland 2001, Bayerischer Verdienstorden 2005,; Dr hc (Technischen Universität München) 1997, (Katholieke Universiteit Leuven) 1998, (Tongji Univ., Shanghai) 2004, (Technischen Universität Berlin) 2004, (Technischen Universität Graz) 2005; Global Leadership Award, American Inst. for Contemporary German Studies 2002, Scopus Award, Hebrew Univ. of Jerusalem 2002, World Business Award 2003. *Address:* c/o Siemens AG, Wittelsbacherplatz 2, 80333, Munich, Germany (office).

VON ROHR, Hans Christoph (see ROHR, Hans Christoph von).

VON SCHIMMELMANN, Wulf, DBA; German business executive; *Chairman of the Supervisory Board, Deutsche Post DHL;* b. 19 Feb. 1947, Steinhöring; ed Univ. of Hamburg, Univ. of Zurich, Switzerland; Pnr, McKinsey & Co. 1972–78, worked in offices in Zurich, Cleveland, OH, USA, Kuwait and Dusseldorf; mem. Bd of Dirs Landesgirokasse-Bank, Stuttgart 1978–84; mem. Man. Bd DG Bank, Frankfurt am Main 1984–91; CEO and Head of Financial Services, Deutsche Postbank AG (also Head of Financial Services, Deutsche Post AG) 1999–2007, Interim Chief Financial Officer 2004–06, Deputy Chair. Deutsche Postbank Financial Services GmbH, also served as its Head of Corp. Devt, Investor Relations and Research Corp. Communications; Chair. Supervisory Bd Deutsche Post DHL 2009–; Chair. PB (USA) Holdings Inc., Wilmington, Del., USA, PB Capital Corpn; Chair. Supervisory Bd PB Versicherung AG, PB Lebensversicherung AG, Hilden, Postbank Filialvertrieb AG, Bonn, Postbank Finanzberatung AG, Hameln, Bawag P.S.K., BHW Bausparkasse AG; Man. Pnr, Regius investment co. 1991–, responsible for investment banking, payment transactions, int. business cooperation and corp. customers, Regius GmbH & Co. KG 1997–; mem. Bd of Dirs Accenture UK Ltd 2001– (Gen. Pnr, Accenture SCA 2001–), Tchibo Holding AG, Hamburg, BHW Holding AG, Berlin/Hameln, Western Union Co. 2009–; fmr mem.

Bd of Man. Dirs BHF-Bank, Frankfurt am Main; mem. Supervisory Bd Deutsche Telekom AG 2006–, Maxingvest AG; Ind. Dir Altadis SA 2004–; Hon. Prof., Univ. of Constance 2006; Dr hc (Univ. of Constance) 2006. *Address:* Deutsche Post DHL, Charles-de-Gaulle-Strasse 20, 53113 Bonn, Germany (office). *Telephone:* (228) 182-63001 (office). *Fax:* (228) 182-63099 (office). *E-mail:* info@dp-dhl.com (office). *Website:* www.dp-dhl.com (office).

VON SCHLABRENDORFF, Fabian Gotthard Herbert, MA, DrIur; German lawyer; *Of Counsel, Clifford Chance LLP;* b. 23 Dec. 1944, Berlin; s. of Fabian von Schlabrendorff and Luitgarde von Schlabrendorff (née von Bismarck); m. Maria de la Cruz Caballero Palomero 1977; one s. one d.; ed Univs of Tübingen and Berlin, Univ. of Geneva, Switzerland, Univ. of Frankfurt, Univ. of Chicago, USA; service in Bundeswehr 1964–68; Research Co-ordinator, Inst. of Int. and Foreign Trade and Business Law, Frankfurt 1975–82; joined Clifford Chance LLP Frankfurt 1983, Pnr 1986–2009, Of Counsel 2010–; CEPES Award 1987. *Publications: Mining Ventures in Developing Countries* (Parts 1 and 2) (co-author) 1979/81, The Legal Structure of Transnational Forest-Based Investments in Developing Countries (co-author) 1987, Substantive Law in International Long-term Infrastructure Contracts, ADRLJ 3-18 2000, Article 6 of the European Convention on Human Rights and its Bearing upon International Arbitratio, in Liber Amicorum Karl-Heinz Böckstiegel (co-author) 2001, Mehrparteiensituationen und Inter-Omnes-Wirkung, in DIS-Materialien VIII 2001, El Régimen Jurídico del Arbitraje en Alemania, in Anuario de Justicia Alternativa 2003, Geldwäsche in internationalen Schiedsverfahren, in Festschrift Peter Schlosser 2005, Conflict of Legal Privileges in International Arbitration (co-author) in Liber Amicorum Robert Briner 2005, SchiedsVZ (German Arbitration Journal), Parallele Verfahren, Aufnahme von Dritten, Verbindung von Verfahren: Erfahrungen aus der Praxis in der ICC, in Schriftreihe der Deutschen Institution für Schiedsgerichtsbarkeit, Band 16, Die Beteiligung Dritter an Schiedsverfahren (co-ed.) 2005, Legal Privilege and Confidentiality in Arbitration (co-author) in Privilege and Confidentiality: An International Handbook 2006. *Leisure interest:* classical music. *Address:* Clifford Chance LLP, Mainzer Landstrasse 46, 60325 Frankfurt am Main, Germany (office). *Telephone:* (69) 7199-1441 (office). *Fax:* (69) 7199-4000 (office). *E-mail:* fabian.schlabrendorff@cliffordchance.com (office). *Website:* www.cliffordchance.com (office).

VON STADE, Frederica; American mezzo-soprano; b. 1 June 1945, Somerville, NJ; m. 1st Peter Elkus 1973 (divorced); two d.; m. 2nd Michael G. Gorman 1991; ed Mannes Coll. of Music, New York; opera début with Metropolitan Opera, New York (in Le Nozze di Figaro) 1970; has also sung with Paris Opera, San Francisco Opera, Lyric Opera of Chicago, LA Opera, Salzburg Festival, Covent Garden, London, Spoleto Festival, Boston Opera Co., Santa Fe Opera, Houston Grand Opera, La Scala, Milan, Vienna State Opera; appearances with Lyric Opera of Chicago in 2010 included Madeline in Three Decembers and Despina in Cose fan tutte; recital and concert artist; mem. American Acad. of Arts and Sciences 2012; Officier, Ordre des Arts et des Lettres 1998; Dr hc (Yale Univ.), (Boston Univ.), (Georgetown Univ. School of Medicine), (Mannes School of Music), (San Francisco Conservatory of Music), (Cleveland Institute of Music); two Grand Prix du Disc awards, Deutsche Schallplattenpreis, Premio della Critica Discografica and many other awards and prizes. *Recordings:* over 70 albums include Frederica von Stade Sings Mozart and Rossini Opera Arias, French Opera Arias 1998, Songs of the Cat (with Garrison Keillor) 2010, Fauré: Mélodies 2011. *Website:* www.fredericavonstade.com.

VON SYDOW, Björn, MS, PhD; Swedish politician, political scientist and academic; b. 26 Nov. 1945, Stockholm; s. of Bengt Sköldenberg and Tullia von Sydow; m. Madeleine von Sydow; three s. one d.; ed Stockholm and Linköping Univs; worked as librarian for fmr Prime Minister Tage Erlander 1970–74; Lecturer in Political Science, Linköping Univ. 1974–78; Assoc. Prof. of Political Science, Stockholm Univ. 1978–83, 1992–2012; Prin. School of Social Work and Public Admin 1983–88; work on study of gen. election of Bd Dirs Nat. Pension Insurance Fund 1984–86; Visiting Research Scientist, Case Western Reserve Univ., Ohio 1986, Pomona and Scripps Colls Clairmont, Calif. 1992; active in municipal politics in Solna 1979–96, Chair. Swedish Social Democratic Party (SAP), Solna 1983–2000, in Sigtuna 2013–; mem. Editorial Cttee Tiden (political journal) 1983–89; mem. SAP programme comm. 1987–2001; mem. Riksdag (Parl.) (Social Democrat) 1994–, Speaker 2002–06, mem. Parl. Cttee on Constitutional Affairs 1994–96, 2012–, SI Cttee on Econ. Policy, Devt and Environment 1995–96, Alt. Parl. Cttee on Educ. 2010–12, Chair. SAP Cttee on EU Affairs, mem. IGC and EU Enlargement Cttee of Party of European Socialists, Chair. EU Cttee of Nordic Labour Movt (SAMAK) 1996–98; Head of Political Planning responsible for Research and Devt, Econ. Growth and Environment, Office of Prime Minister 1988–91; mem. Cttee on Civil Rights, Ministry of Justice 1993–94; Chair. Cttee on Environmental Protection, Ministry of Environment 1994–96, Parl. Cttee preparing EU Treaty revision, Ministry for Foreign Affairs 1995–96; Minister of Trade at Ministry for Industry and Commerce 1996–97; Minister of Defence 1997–2002; Chair. Univ. Centre for Physics and Astronomy, Stockholm 1992–95, Swedish Research Council 2007–09, Swedish Secr. for Environmental Earth System Sciences 2011–; mem. Swedish Del. to Parl. Ass. of Council of Europe 2007–, Rapporteur on Kosovo and Council of Europe 2010–14, Chair. Political Affairs Cttee 2010–12, 2013. *Publications:* Can We Rely on Politicians? – Public and Private Politics in the Leadership of the Swedish Social Democratic Party 1955–1960 1978, Parliamentarism in Sweden: Development and Forms up to 1945 1997, Sweden's Security in the 21st Century 1999, The Constitutional Developments of Sweden Since 1809 2009, The Swedish Social Democratic Party – Programmes 2009, Therefore a Defence – Philosophy, Defence and Constitution 2012. *Leisure interests* horse riding, railway enthusiast. *Address:* Riddarhustorget 7–9, Sveriges Riksdag, 100 12 Stockholm (office). Stora Malmgatan 27, 193 35 Sigtuna, Sweden (home). *Telephone:* (8) 786-42-10 (office); (8) 27-66-80 (home); 70-576-17-29 (mobile); (8) 592-500-71 (home). *E-mail:* bjorn.von.sydow@riksdagen.se (office). *Website:* www.riksdagen.se (office).

VON TRIER, Lars; Danish film director; b. 30 April 1956; s. of Ulf Trier and Inger Trier; m. 1st Cæcilia Holbek Trier (divorced); two c.; m. 2nd Bente Frøge 1997; ed Danish Film School; Co-founder and Head, Dogme School of Film 1995–. *Films include:* Orchidégartneren (The Orchid Gardener) 1977, Menthe - la bienheureuse 1979, Nocturne 1980, Den Sidste Detalje (The Last Detail) 1981, Befrielsesbilleder 1982, Forbrydelsens element (The Element of Crime; Cannes Film Festival

Technical Grand Prize) 1984, Europa (aka Zentropa) 1991, Epidemic 1988, The Kingdom 1994, Breaking the Waves (Cannes Film Festival Grand Prix) 1996, The Idiots 1998, Dancer in the Dark (Cannes Film Festival Palme d'Or) 2000, Dogville 2003, Dear Wendy (script) 2005, Manderlay 2005, Direktøren for det hele (The Boss Of It All) 2006, De unge år: Erik Nietzsche sagaen del 1 2007, Antichrist 2009, Melancholia 2011, Nymphomaniac: Volume I 2013, Nymphomaniac: Volume II 2013. *Publication:* Trier on Von Trier 2004. *Address:* Zentropa, Filmbyen 22, 2650 Hvidovre, Denmark (home). *Telephone:* 36868788 (office). *Fax:* 36868789 (office). *E-mail:* zentropa@filmbyen.com (office). *Website:* www.dogme95.dk.

VON TROTTA, Margarethe; German film director and actress; b. 21 Feb. 1942, Berlin; has written scripts for The Sudden Wealth of the Poor People of Kombach 1971, Summer Lightning 1972, Fangschuss 1974, Unerreichbare Nahe 1984. *Films include:* Die Verlorene Ehre der Katharina Blum (The Lost Honour of Katharina Blum) 1975, Das zweite Erwachen der Christa Klages (The Second Awakening of Christa Klages) 1978, Schwestern, oder die Balance des Glücks (Sisters, or the Balance of Happiness) 1979, Die Bleierne Zeit (The German Sisters) 1981, Heller Wahn (Friends and Husbands) 1983, Rosa Luxemburg 1985, Felix 1987, Paura e amore (Love and Fear) 1988, L'Africana 1990, Il lungo silenzio 1992, Das Versprechen (The Promise) 1994, Rosenstrasse 2003, Ich bin die Andere 2006, Vision 2009, Hannah Arendt 2012. *Television include:* Winterkind (film) 1996, Dunkle Tage (film) 1999, Jahrestage (mini-series) 2000, Die Andere Frau (The Other Woman) (film) 2004.

VONA, Gábor; Hungarian politician; *Chairman, Jobbik – Movement for a Better Hungary;* b. (Gábor Zázrivecz), 20 Aug. 1978, Gyöngyös; m.; one s.; ed Eötvös Loránd Univ., Budapest; worked briefly as teacher; Co-founder Jobbik Youth Movt 1999, Founding mem. and Deputy Chair. Jobbik –Movt for a Better Hungary 2003–06, Chair. 2006–; Chair. Hungarian Guard (uniformed paramilitary group) 2007–08 (org. banned Dec. 2008); mem. Országgyűlés (Parl.) 2010–, Jobbik's cand. for Prime Minister in parl. elections 2010; extreme nationalist. *Address:* Jobbik – Movement for a Better Hungary, 1113 Budapest, Villányi u. 20A, Hungary (office). *Telephone:* (1) 3651488. *E-mail:* vona.gabor@parlament.hu (office); jobbik@jobbik .hu (office). *Website:* www.jobbik.hu (office); www.vonagabor.hu.

VONDRA, Alexandr; Czech diplomatist, politician, academic and consultant; b. 17 Aug. 1961, Prague; m. Martina Vondrova; three c.; ed Charles Univ.; worked at Náprstek Museum of Asian, African and American Cultures, Prague 1985–87; also active in Czechoslovakia's democratic opposition mid-1980s; fmr man. rock band Národni třída; Spokesperson for Charter 77 1989; Co-founder Civic Forum Movt 1989; Foreign Policy Adviser to Pres. Václav Havel 1990–92; First Deputy Minister of International Affairs 1992, First Deputy Minister of Foreign Affairs 1993–97, Chief negotiator in process of preparing Czech-German Declaration 1995–96; Amb. to USA 1997–2001; Czech Govt Commr to Prague NATO Summit (coordinated Prague NATO Summit 2002) 2001–02; Deputy Minister of Foreign Affairs 2003; Asst Lecturer, German Marshall Fund 2003–04; Man. Dir Dutko Worldwide (consulting firm), Prague 2004–06; Minister of Foreign Affairs 2006–07; mem. Civic Democratic Party (ODS) 2006–, currently a Deputy Chair.; elected Senator (ODS) for Litoměřice, Roudnice and Slaný regions 2006–; Deputy Prime Minister, responsible for European Affairs 2007–09; Minister of Defence 2010–12 (resgnd); Adjunct Prof., New York Univ. in Prague; Pres. Czech Euro-Atlantic Council; mem. Bd of Dirs Program of Atlantic Security Studies, Prague; Hon. Chair. Czech Euro-Atlantic Council 2004–06; Gold Plaque (Slovakia) 2001, Cross of Merit (Czech Repub.) 2002, Cross of Order of Merit (Poland) 2004, Commdr of the Three Stars (Latvia) 2005; US Nat. Endowment for Democracy Medal 1999, NATO Meritorious Service Medal 2005, Award for Human Understanding, Tolerance and Peace 2006. *Address:* Civic Democratic Party, Polygon House, Doudlebská 1699/5, 140 00 Prague 4, Czech Republic (office). *Telephone:* 234707111 (office). *Fax:* 234707103 (office). *E-mail:* hk@ods.cz (office). *Website:* www.ods.cz (office); www.alexandrvondra.cz.

VONDRAN, Ruprecht, DrIur; German business executive and politician (retd); *Honorary Chairman, German-Japanese Industrial Co-operation Committee, and President, Association of German-Japanese Societies;* b. 31 Dec. 1935, Göttingen; s. of Rudolf Vondran and Anneliese Unterberg; m. Jutta Paul 1970; two s. two d.; ed Univs. of Göttingen, Bonn and Würzburg; mem. Bundestag 1987–94; Pres., Wirtschaftsvereinigung Stahl (Steel Industry Asscn) 1988–2000, Verband Deutsch–Japanischer Gesellschaften (Asscn of German-Japanese Socs); Hon. Chair., Deutsch-Japanischer Wirtschaftskreis (German-Japanese Industrial Co-operation Cttee); Chair., Poensgen-Stiftung; Order of the Rising Sun (Gold and Silver stars), Japan; Hon. DEng. *Publication:* Der politische Auftrag der Nato und seine Verwirklichung 1966, Wie bewältigt die japanische Wirtschaft ihre Anpassungsprobleme? 1996, Stahl ist Zukunft 1999, Warum Japan? 2005, Ewiger Friede und Bestandige Freundschaft 2005, Deutschland in Japan 2005/2006: was hat es gebracht? 2006, Für ein weltoffenes Deutschland, Japan und China: Auf der Suche nad einer neuen Ordnung, Chancen und Grenzen der Electromobilität 2010, Und Alle Fluten Leben 2010, Tobi Ishi Springsteine 2010, Ferne Gefährten 2011, Schwerkraft der Wissenschaft 2012. *Leisure interests:* modern graphics, Japanese porcelain. *Address:* Urdenbacher Allee 63, 40593 Düsseldorf, Germany (home). *Telephone:* (211) 7182231 (office). *Fax:* (211) 7118734 (office).

VONGKUSOLKIT, Isara, BA; Thai business executive; *Chairman, Mitr Phol Sugar Corporation Ltd;* b. 1946, Ratchaburi; m.; four c.; ed Univ. of North Carolina, USA; Pres. Mitr Phol Sugar Corpn Ltd –2008, Chair. 2008–; Dir and Chair. Exec. Cttee, United Standard Terminal (UST) Public Co. Ltd; Chair. Thai Chamber of Commerce 2013–; Chair. Board of Trade of Thailand 2013–; Dir Fed. of Thai Industries; Trustee, Kenan Inst. Asia 2009. *Address:* 88 Moo 2 Tiwanont Road, Muang, Pathumtani 12000; Mitr Phol Sugar Corpn, Ltd, 3rd Floor, Ploenchit Center, Building 2, Sukhumvit Road, Klongtoey, Bangkok 10110, Thailand (office). *Telephone:* (2) 656-8488 (office). *Fax:* (2) 656-8494 (office). *E-mail:* info@mitrphol.com (office). *Website:* www.mitrphol.com (office).

VONN, Lindsey Caroline; American skier; b. (Lindsey Caroline Kildow), 18 Oct. 1984, St Paul, Minn.; d. of Alan Kildow; m. Thomas Vonn 2007 (divorced); ed Univ. of Missouri High School; won three consecutive overall World Cup championships 2008–11 and six downhill championships 2008–13; Gold Medal, Downhill, World Championships, Val d'Isère 2009, Super-G 2009; Silver Medal, Downhill, World Championships, Åre 2007, Super-G 2007; Gold Medal, Downhill, Winter Olympics,

Vancouver 2010 (first ever for an American woman), Bronze Medal, Super-G 2010; also won consecutive World Cup season titles in Super G (first American woman), and a title in the combined; 59 wins in four disciplines (downhill, Super G, slalom, and super combined) as of Jan. 2013; most successful American female in ski racing history; US Olympic Cttee Sportswoman of the Year for 2010, Laureus World Sports Awards Sportswoman of the Year for 2010. *Leisure interests:* cycling, tennis, reading, listening to hip hop music. *Address:* c/o Sue Dorf, IMG, 767 5th Avenue, New York, NY 10153, USA (office). *Telephone:* (212) 489-8300 (office). *Fax:* (212) 759-9059 (office). *E-mail:* sue.dorf@imgworld.com (office). *Website:* www .imgworld.com (office); www.lindseyvonn.com.

VORA, Motilal; Indian politician; b. 29 Dec. 1928, Nagor, Rajasthan; s. of Mohanlal Vora; m. Shanti Vora; two s. four d.; fmr journalist; elected Councillor, Durg Municipality 1968, Congress Party mem. Madhya Pradesh Vidhan Sabha 1972–90; Minister of State for Educ. and Minister for Local Govt 1981–82; Minister of Transport, Science and Tech. 1982–83, of Higher Educ. 1983–84, of Health and Family Welfare and Civil Aviation 1988–89; Pres. Madhya Pradesh Congress (I) Cttee 1984–85; elected Leader Congress (I) Legis. Party 1985; Chief Minister Madhya Pradesh 1985–88, Jan.–Dec. 1989; Gov. of UP 1993–96; mem. Lok Sabha 1998–99, mem. Cttee on Home Affairs; mem. Rajya Sabha 2002–. *Address:* 33, Mohan Nagar, Durg, Chhattisgarh; 33 Lodhi Estate, New Delhi 110011, India (office). *Telephone:* (11) 24651313 (office). *E-mail:* vora@sansad.nic.in (office). *Website:* rajyasabha.nic.in (office).

VOROBYEV, Andrei Ivanovich, DrMed; Russian haematologist; *Director, Haematological Scientific Centre, Russian Academy of Medical Sciences;* b. 1 Oct. 1928; m.; two s.; ed First Inst. of Medicine; worked as house painter 1941–44; practitioner, Head of Polyclinics Volokolamsk Moscow Region 1953–54; Prof., Cen. Inst. of Advanced Medical Studies 1956–66; Head of Div., Inst. of Biophysics 1966–84; mem. Acad. of Medical Sciences 1986–; Dir All-Union (now All-Russian) Scientific Cen. of Haematology 1987–91; Minister of Health of Russia 1991–92; Dir Haematological Scientific Centre, Russian Acad. of Medical Sciences 1993–; Ed.-in-Chief Gematologiya i Transfuziologiya; USSR State Prize. *Leisure interest:* history of Russian Acad. of Science. *Address:* Haematological Scientific Centre, 125167 Moscow, Novy Zhukovsky pr. 4A, Russia (office). *Telephone:* (495) 212-21-23 (office). *Fax:* (495) 438-18-00 (office). *E-mail:* tt@blood.ru (office).

VOROBYEV, Yuri Leonidovich; Russian politician and engineer; b. 2 Feb. 1948, Krasnoyarsk; m.: two s.; ed Krasnoyarsk Inst. of Non-Ferrous Metals; mem. staff Krasnoyarsk plant; Sec. Sosnovoborsk dist. CPSU Cttee, Krasnoyarsk 1971–88, instructor Krasnoyarsk regional CPSU Cttee 1988–90; Dir-Gen. Foundation for Protection of Small Business and Devt of Econ. Reforms 1990–91; Deputy Chair. Russian Rescue Corps 1991–92; First Deputy Chair. Russian Fed. State Cttee on Problems of Civil Defence and Emergency Situations 1992–94; First Deputy Minister of Civil Defence and Emergency Situations 1994, now Asst. Dir; Head of Internal Anti-Corruption Comm. 2004; mem. Tech. Comm. at Russian Presidency 1993–; Order for Personal Courage. *Leisure interests:* sports, tourism. *Address:* c/o Ministry of Civil Defence and Emergency Situations, Teatralny pr. 3, 103012 Moscow, Russia (office).

VORONIN, Vladimir Nikolayevich; Moldovan economist, engineer and politician; *First Secretary, Party of Communists of the Republic of Moldova;* b. 25 May 1941, Corjova, Chişinău Dist; m. Taisia Mihailovna 1962; one s. one d.; ed Tech. Coll., Chişinău, Union Inst. of the Alimentary Industry, Acad. of Social Sciences, Cen. CPSU Cttee, Acad. of Ministry of Internal Affairs; bakery man., Criuleni 1961–66, Dubăsari 1966–71; fmr Deputy to Supreme Council, Moldovan SSR, First Sec., Party Cttee, Bender (Tighina) 1985–89, Minister of Internal Affairs, Moldovan SSR 1989–90; mem. Police Reserve, Russian Fed. 1989–93; Co-Pres. Organizational Cttee for Consolidation of CP 1993; revived CP Party of Moldova as Party of Communists of the Repub. of Moldova 1994, First Sec. 1994–; presidential cand. (placed third) 1996; Deputy in Parl. Repub. of Moldova 1998; Pres. of Moldova 2001–09; rank of Maj. Gen. from fmr Ministry of Internal Affairs, USSR; Kt Grand Cross, Grand Order of King Tomislav (Croatia) 2007. *Address:* Party of Communists of the Republic of Moldova (Partidul Comuniştilor din Republica Moldova), 2012 Chişinău, str. N. Iorga 11, Moldova (office). *Telephone:* (22) 23-46-14 (office). *Fax:* (22) 23-36-73 (office). *E-mail:* pcrmcc@gmail.com (office). *Website:* www.pcrm.md (office).

VORONKOV, Mikhail Grigorievich, DrChemSc; Russian chemist; *Head of Department, Institute of Silicate Chemistry, St Petersburg;* b. 6 Dec. 1921, Orel; s. of Grigorii Vasilievich and Raisa Mikhailovna Voronkov; m. Lilia Iliinichna Makhnina 1943; one s. one d.; ed Leningrad Univ.; Sr Scientist, Chemical Dept, Leningrad Univ. 1944–54; Head of Lab., Inst. of Chem. of Silicates, USSR Acad. of Sciences 1954–61; Head of Lab. Inst. of Organic Synthesis, Latvian Acad. of Sciences 1961–70; Dir Inst. of Organic Chem., Siberian Br. of USSR (now Russian) Acad. of Sciences, Irkutsk 1970–94; Scientific Adviser 1994–; Head of Dept, Inst. of Silicate Chem., St Petersburg 2002–; Corresp. mem. USSR (now Russian) Acad. of Sciences 1970, mem. 1990; Corresp. mem. Latvian Acad. of Sciences 1966–91, Foreign mem. 1991–; mem. Braunschweig Scientific Soc., FRG 1976, Asia-Pacific Acad. of Advanced Materials 1992; Prof. Emer., Ulan Bator Univ., Mongolia; mem. Emer. Florida Center of Heterocyclic Chem., USA 1998; Hon. Chemist of the USSR 1983; Honoured Mem. Mongolian Acad. of Sciences; five orders and 20 medals for services to the motherland; Dr hc (Gdansk Tech. Univ., Poland); Laureate, State Prize of Ukrainian SSR 1981, Prize of the USSR Council of Ministers 1991, Laureate, State Prize of Russia 1997, Laureate, A.N. Nesmeyanov Prize of Russian Acad. of Sciences 2003, A.N. Kost Medal for outstanding achievements in the chem. of heterocyclic compounds. *Publications:* more than 3,800 scientific papers, including 45 monographs and 50 patents. *Leisure interests:* numismatics, humour in chemistry. *Address:* A.E. Favorsky Irkutsk Institute of Chemistry, 1 Favorsky Street, 664033 Irkutsk (office); Lermontova Street, 297B-196, 664033 Irkutsk, Russian Federation (home). *Telephone:* (3952) 42-64-00 (office); (3952) 42-85-81 (home). *Fax:* (3952) 51-19-26 (office); (3952) 41-93-46 (office). *E-mail:* voronkov@ irioch.irk.ru (office).

VOROSHILO, Aleksander Stepanovich; Russian singer (baritone), theatre manager and business executive; b. 15 Dec. 1944, Dniepropetrovsk region, Ukraine; m. Svetlana Voroshilo; one d.; ed Odessa State Conservatory; served in the army; began vocal studies 1969; soloist Odessa Opera Theatre 1972–75,

Bolshoi Theatre, Moscow 1975–91; ended singing career 1991; employee at sausage production cos 1992–; owner of two meat processing, sausage production plants 1997–; Exec. Dir Bolshoi Theatre 2000–02; Gen. Dir Moscow Int. House of Music 2002–2003; USSR State Prize, USSR Peoples' Artist. *Opera:* leading roles in Bolshoi Theatre include Onegin in Eugene Onegin, Chichikov in Dead Souls, Iago in Othello and Rigoletto in Rigoletto. *Address:* c/o Moscow Int. House of Music, 115054 Moscow, Kosmodamianskaya Naberezhnaya 52, Bldg 8, Russia.

VORRES, Ian, CM, MA; Canadian/Greek art museum president; *President, Vorres Museum;* b. 19 Sept. 1924, Athens, Greece; s. of Andrew Vorres and Stephanie Vorres; one adopted c.; ed Queen's Univ. and Univ. of Toronto; Founder and Pres. Bd Vorres Museum 1983–; Mayor of Paiania 1991–98; decorations from the govts of Portugal, Austria and Finland; Hon. DFA (American Coll. of Greece). *Publication:* The Last Grand Duchess (biog. of Grand Duchess Olga of Russia) 1964. *Leisure interests:* collection of antiques, collection of contemporary Greek art, writing, architecture, gardening. *Address:* Vorres Museum, 190 02 Paiania, Attica, Greece. *Telephone:* (210) 6642520; (210) 6644771. *Fax:* (210) 6645775. *E-mail:* mvorres@otenet.gr. *Website:* www.vorresmuseum.gr.

VOS, Marianne; Dutch cyclist; b. 13 May 1987, 's-Hertogenbosch; took up cycling aged six, initially trained with brother's cycling team, also participated in speed skating, inline speed skating, later also took to mountain biking; won (at junior level) Nat. Mountain Biking Championships 2002, Nat. Road Race Championships 2002, Nat. Mountain Biking Championships 2003; started participating in senior level events 2006; competes in cyclo-cross, road bicycle racing, track racing; bronze medal, Union Cycliste Internationale (UCI) Cyclo-cross European Championships 2006; gold medal, points race, Olympic Games, Beijing 2008; gold medal, road race, Olympic Games, London 2012; winner: Nat. Road Race Championships 2006, 2008, 2009, 2011, World Road Race Championship 2006, 2012, 2013, UCI Cyclo-cross World Championships 2006, 2009, 2010, 2011, 2012, Rund um die Nürnberger Altstadt 2007, La Flêche Wallonne Féminine 2007, 2008, 2009, 2011, 2013, UCI Women's Road World Cup 2007, 2009, 2010, 2012, 2013, Emakumeen Bira 2008, 2011, Tour de l'Aude Cycliste Féminin 2009, Holland Ladies Tour 2009, 2010, 2011, 2012, Trofeo Alfredo Binda-Comune di Cittiglio 2009, 2010, 2012, Open de Suède Vårgårda 2009, 2013, Nat. Time Trial Championship 2010, 2011, UCI Track Cycling World Championships (scratch race) 2011, GP Ciudad de Valladolid 2011, Giro d'Italia Femminile 2011, 2012, Ronde van Drenthe 2011, 2012, 2013, Nat. Cyclo-cross Championships 2011, 2012, GP de Plouay 2012, Tour of Flanders for Women 2013; rides for Rabobank Women Cycling Team (fmrly DSB-Ballast Nedam) 2006–; Amb. for Youth United for Sri Lanka; Sport FM Sportswoman of the Year 2004, 2005, Dutch Sports Talent of the Year 2006, Dutch Athlete of the Year 2008, 2009. *Leisure interests:* sports, internet. *Address:* c/o Zeloo, PO Box 223, 5100 AE Dongen, Netherlands (office). *Telephone:* (162) 387387 (office). *Fax:* (162) 370264 (office). *Website:* mariannevosofficial.com.

VOSCHERAU, Eggert; German business executive; *Chairman of the Supervisory Board, BASF SE;* b. 1943, Hamburg; began career as man. trainee in business admin at Unilever; joined BASF 1969, man. position, BASF Brasileira SA 1981–84, Exec. Pres. BASF Brasileira SA 1984–87, Pres. Crop Protection Div., BASF, Ludwigshafen, Germany 1987–91, Exec. Vice-Pres. BASF Corpn, USA and Pres. North American Consumer Products Div. (Pharmaceuticals, Crop Protection and Fine Chemicals) 1991–98, Pres. Latin America North Div. 1994–98, mem. Bd of Exec. Dirs BASF AG 1996–2008, Chair. and CEO BASF Corpn, USA, responsible on Bd of Exec. Dirs for company's regional activities in the Americas (N and S America) as well as Fibre Products Div. 1997–98, responsible for the units Crop Protection, Pharmaceuticals, Fine Chemicals, Main Lab. and Europe region 1998–2001, Industrial Relations Dir, BASF, Head of Ludwigshafen Site and Verbund Site Man. Europe 2001–08, Vice-Chair. Bd of Exec. Dirs 2003–08 (retd), Chair. Supervisory Bd BASF SE 2009–; mem. Supervisory Bd ZEW, Mannheim 2007–, Zentrum für Europäische Wirtschaftsforschung (Centre for European Econ. Research) 2007–, Carl-Zeiss-Stiftung 2008– (Chair. Bd of Trustees), Carl Zeiss AG 2008– (Chair.), Schott AG 2008– (Chair.); Pres. BAVC (German Fed. of Chemical Employers' Asscns) 2005–; Vice-Pres. BDA (Fed. of German Employers' Asscns) 2005–; mem. Bd of Trustees Foundation Wittenberg Centre for Global Ethics 2009–; Bundesverdienstkreuz 2008; Hon. DBA (Univ. of Mannheim) 2006. *Address:* BASF SE, Carl-Bosch Strasse 38, 67056 Ludwigshafen, Germany (office). *Telephone:* (621) 60-0 (office); (621) 60-20916 (Corporate Media Relations) (office). *Fax:* (621) 60-92693 (office); (621) 60-42525 (office). *E-mail:* presse.kontakt@basf .com (office); info@basf.de (office). *Website:* www.basf.com (office); www.basf.de (office).

VOSCHERAU, Henning, LLD; German fmr politician; b. 13 Aug. 1941, Hamburg; m.; three c.; qualified as notary public; joined SPD 1966; mem. Borough of Wandsbek Dist Ass. 1970–74, Chief Whip SPD Parl. Group 1971–74; mem. Hamburg City Parl., mem. SPD Parl. Exec. Cttee 1974–, Deputy Chair. 1976–82, Chair. 1982–87, Chair. City Parl. Cttee on Home Affairs 1974–82, Deputy Party Chair. SPD, Hamburg 1981–89; First Mayor and Pres. of Senate, City of Hamburg 1988–97; Pres. Bundesrat 1990–91; Chair. Jt Comm. for Reform of the Fed. Constitution 1992–93; SPD Speaker on Financial Policy 1995–97; Chair. Mediation Cttee 1996–97; currently notary, Notariat am Alstertor. *Address:* Notariat am Alstertor, Alstertor 14, 20095 Hamburg, Germany (office). *E-mail:* voscherau@ alstertor.de (office). *Website:* www.alstertor.de (office).

VOSER, Peter Robert, BBA; Swiss business executive; *Chairman, St Gallen Foundation for International Studies;* b. 29 Aug. 1958; m. Daniela Voser; three c.; ed Univ. of Applied Sciences, Zurich; employed by Royal Dutch/Shell Group of Cos in a variety of finance and business roles 1982–2002, worked in Switzerland for five years, in UK for eight years, in Argentina for five years and in Chile for two years, Group Chief Internal Auditor, London 1997–99, Chief Financial Officer (CFO), Shell Europe Oil Products 1999–2001, CFO Global Oil Products Business and mem. Oil Products Exec. Cttee 2001–02, CFO Royal Dutch/Shell Group of Cos 2004–05, CFO and Exec. Dir Royal Dutch Shell plc 2004–09, CEO 2009–14; CFO and mem. Group Exec. Cttee Asea Brown Boveri (ABB) Group of Cos, Switzerland 2002–04, also responsible on Exec. Cttee for Group IT and the Oil, Gas and Petrochemicals business (upstream and downstream); mem. Supervisory Bd Aegon NV 2004–06; mem. Bd of Dirs UBS AG 2005–10, Catalyst (non-profit org.) 2010–, Roche 2011–; Chair. St Gallen Foundation for Int. Studies 2013–; mem.

Swiss Fed. Auditor Oversight Authority 2006–10, European Round Table of Industrialists, The Business Council; awarded title of Dato Seri Laila Jasa by the Sultan of Brunei 2011. *Address:* c/o St Gallen Foundation for International Studies, St Gallen Symposium, Dufourstrasse 83, PO Box 1045, 9001 St Gallen, Switzerland (office). *Website:* www.symposium.org (office).

VOSGANIAN, Varujan, PhD; Romanian politician; b. 25 July 1958, Craiova; m. Mihaela Vosganian; one d.; ed Acad. of Econ. Sciences, Bucharest and Bucharest Univ.; Assoc. Prof., Acad. of Econ. Sciences, Bucharest; Sr Researcher, Nat. Inst. of Economy; Deputy, Romanian Parl. 1990–96, Senator 1996–2000, 2004–, Chair. Cttee on Budget, Finances, Banking Activity and Capital Markets 1996–98, 2004–06, Pres. Econ. Comm., Industry and Services 2008–12; mem. Romanian Del. to Parl. Ass. of the Council of Europe (APCE) 2004–06, 2012, mem. Political and Econ. Comms 2004–; Minister of the Economy and Commerce 2006–07, of the Economy and Finance 2007–08, of the Economy, Trade and Business Environment 2012–14; mem. Nat. Liberal Party (PNL), Vice-Pres. 2007–; Founding mem. Romanian Soc. of the Economy (SOREC); Vice-Pres. Romanian Writers Union 2005–; Hon. mem. Scientific Council, Nat. Inst. of Prognosis, Romania; St Andrew's Cross, Romanian Patriarchate, Order Italiana della solidarità (Italy) 2008; Dr hc (Vasile Goldis Univ.) 2006, (Leibniz Univ., Milan) 2006; Special Prize for Poetry, Nichita Stanescu Int. Poem Festival 2006, Prize for Excellency for Contrib. to the Devt of Capital Markets in Romania, Bucharest Stock Exchange 2006, Prize for Contrib. to Devt of Romanian Science and Culture, Romanian Acad. 2006, Gold Medal for Culture, Govt of Armenia, Academy Award for Literature 2009. *Publications include:* The Book of Whispers (novel) (Sadoveanu Prize for fiction) 2010; more then 500 econ., political and literary articles, studies, essays and poems. *Address:* c/o Ministry of the Economy, 010096 Bucharest 1, Calea Victoriei 152, Romania. *E-mail:* birou_presa@minind.ro. *Website:* vosganian.ro.

VOTRON, Jean-Paul, MA; Belgian banking executive; b. 1951; m.; two c.; ed Institut Catholique des Hautes Etudes Commerciale, Brussels; began career at Unilever 1975, various man. positions in sales, marketing and gen. man. 1975–91; joined Citibank 1991, served as Pres. Citibank Belgium, Marketing Dir for Europe, Dir for Marketing and Tech. US and European Consumer Bank, Dir of Insurance for USA, Head of US Investment Business, Chair. and CEO Citibank FSB (br. network in USA) –1997; Sr Exec. Vice-Pres. Int. Consumer Banking and E-Commerce, ABN-AMRO 1997–2001; apptd mem. Man. Cttee Citigroup 2002, CEO Citigroup Retail Bank for Western Europe, Cen. Europe, Russia, Middle E and Africa 2002–04; CEO Fortis NV and Chair. Fortis Bank and Fortis Insurance 2004–08 (resgnd); The Business Leader of the Year, European Business Awards Conf. and Ceremony 2007. *Address:* c/o Fortis NV, Archimedeslaan 6, 3584 Utrecht, Belgium. *Telephone:* (30) 2576576. *Website:* www.fortis.com.

VOURLOUMIS, Panagis; Greek business executive and banker; b. 1937; ed London School of Econs, UK; Head, SE Asia Div., International Finance Corpn 1966–73; Head, Commercial Bank of Greece Group 1979–81; fmr Dir Panagis Vourloumis & Assocs, Financial Advisors; fmr Chair. Askbali.com travel group; Chair. and CEO Alpha Finance, Alpha Mutual Funds and Alpha Bank Romania 1988–2000, Exec. Dir Alpha Bank 1988–2000; Chair. Frigoglass 2000–04, Aegean Baltic Bank 2000–04; Chair. and CEO Hellenic Telecommunications Org. SA 2004–10, Cosmote Mobile Telecommunications SA; mem. Trilateral Comm. 1998–. *Address:* c/o Hellenic Telecommunications Organization SA, 99 Kifissias Avenue, Amaroussion, 15181 Athens, Greece.

VOUTILAINEN, Pertti Juhani, MSc; Finnish banker and business executive; b. 22 June 1940, Kuusjärvi; s. of Otto Voutilainen and Martta Voutilainen; m. Raili Juvonen 1963; two s.; ed Helsinki Univ. of Tech., Helsinki School of Econs, Pennsylvania State Univ., USA; joined Outokumpu Oy as mining engineer 1964, Production Man. 1971–73, Corp. Planning Dir 1973–77, Corp. Planning 1976–78, mem. Exec. Bd 1977–91, Pres. 1980–91, Chair. Exec. Bd 1983–91; Chair. and CEO Kansallis-Osake-Pankki (merged with Unitas Ltd) 1992–95; Chair. and CEO Merita Bank plc 1995–2000; Pres. Merita Nordbanken 2000–02; Chair. Viola Systems Ltd. 2002; Chair. Riddarhyttan Resources Ltd 2004–05; Vice-Chair. Technopolis plc 2003–05, Chair. 2006–07; mem. Bd of Dirs Agnico-Eagle Mines 2005–, HIM Specialty Furniture Ltd 2005–; Commdr Order of Lion of Finland. *Leisure interests:* hunting, fishing. *Address:* c/o Board of Directors, Agnico-Eagle Mines Ltd, 145 King Street East, Suite 400, Toronto, ON M5C 2Y7, Canada.

VOYNET, Dominique; French physician and politician; *Mayor of Montreuil;* b. 4 Nov. 1958, Montbéliard, Doubs; d. of Jean Voynet and Monique Richard; two d.; ed Faculty of Medicine, Besançon; anaesthetist and intensive care specialist, Dole (Jura) public hosp. 1985–89; activist in several ecological and other orgs, Belfort and Besançon 1976–; Co-Founder Les Verts ('Green' Movt) 1984, Gen. Sec. Green Group in European Parl. 1989–91, Nat. Spokesperson 1991–02, Nat. Sec. 2001–02; Municipal Councillor, Dole 1989–2004; mem. regional council Franche-Comté 1992–94 (resgnd); cand. in presidential election 1995, 2007; elected Deputy (Les Verts and Parti Socialiste) for Dole-Arbois, Nat. Ass. 1997, Minister for Town and Country Planning and the Environment 1997–2001; Councillor-Gen. Jura 1998–2004; Senator for Seine-Saint Denis 2004–11; Mayor of Montreuil 2008–. *Address:* Hôtel de Ville, 93105 Montreuil Cedex, France (office). *Telephone:* 1-48-70-63-78 (office). *Website:* www.montreuil.fr (office).

VOYNOVICH, Vladimir Nikolayevich; Russian author, playwright and film scriptwriter; b. 26 Sept. 1932, Stalinabad (now Dushanbe), Tajikistan; s. of Nikolai Pavlovich Voinovich and Rosa Voinovich (née Goikhman); m. 1st Valentina Voinovich; one s. one d.; m. 2nd Irina Braude 1970; one d.; served in Soviet Army 1951–55; worked as carpenter 1956–57; studied Moscow Pedagogical Inst. 1958–59; started literary activity (and song writing for Moscow Radio) 1960; various dissident activities 1966–80; expelled from USSR Writers' Union 1974; elected mem. French PEN Centre 1974; emigrated from USSR 1980; USSR citizenship restored 1990; mem. Bavarian Acad. of Fine Arts. *Publications include:* The Life and Unusual Adventures of Private Ivan Chonkin (samizdat 1967) 1975 (English trans. 1977), Ivankiada 1976, By Way of Mutual Correspondence 1979, Pretender to the Throne 1981, Moscow–2042 1987, The Fur Hut 1989, The Zero Decision 1990, Case N3484 1992, The Conception 1994, Tales for Adults 1996, By Means of Mutual Correspondence 1998, Monumental Propaganda 2000, A Portrait Against the Background of a Myth 2002. *E-mail:* webmaster@voinovich.ru (office). *Website:* www.voinovich.ru.

VRAALSEN, Tom Eric, MEcon; Norwegian diplomatist; *Special Adviser, Ministry of Foreign Affairs;* b. 26 Jan. 1936, Oslo; m. Viebecke Vraalsen; five c.; ed Århus School of Econs and Business Admin., Denmark; joined Foreign Service 1960, various diplomatic positions in Embassies in Beijing 1962–64, 1969–70, Cairo 1964–67, Manila 1970–71, Jakarta 1971, in charge of Norwegian relations with Africa, Asia and Latin America, Political Dept, Ministry of Foreign Affairs 1971–73, in charge of UN and int. org. affairs 1973–75, Deputy Perm. Rep. to UN, New York 1975–79, Perm. Rep. 1982–89, Dir-Gen. Political Dept, Ministry of Foreign Affairs 1981–82, Minister for Devt Co-operation, for Nordic Co-operation 1989–90; Sr Vice-Pres. Saga Petroleum 1991–92; Asst Sec.-Gen. Ministry of Foreign Affairs 1992–94, Amb. to UK 1994–96, to USA 1996–2001, to Finland 2001–03; UN Special Envoy for Humanitarian Affairs for the Sudan 1998–2006; Special Adviser, Ministry of Foreign Affairs 2008–; Chair. Task Force for Int. Co-operation on Holocaust Educ., Remembrance and Research 2009–10; Dr hc (Augustana Coll.) 2000. *Publications:* UN in Focus (co-author) 1975, The UN: Dream and Reality 1984. *Address:* Ministry of Foreign Affairs, 7 juni pl., POB 8114 Dep., 0032 Oslo, Norway (office). *Telephone:* 22-24-36-00 (office). *Fax:* 22-24-95-80 (office). *E-mail:* post@mfa.no (office). *Website:* www.regjeringen.no/ud (office).

VRABIE, Vitalie; Moldovan politician; b. 2 Oct. 1964, Costuleni Village, Ungheni Dist; m.; two c.; ed Agricultural Inst., Chişinău, Acad. of Public Admin, Moscow; began career as Sr Agronomist, Prut Farm; Dir JSV Garant-impex, Ungheni 1994–99; mem. Ungheni City Council 1995–99, fmr Dir Office of Chamber of Commerce and Industry; elected Mayor of Ungheni 1999, re-elected 2003; Chair. Asscn of Mayors and Local Communities 2003–06; fmr mem. Council of Europe Congress of Local and Regional Authorities, fmr Head Nat. Del.; Minister of Local Public Admin 2006–07; Minister of Defence 2007–09; mem Democratic Party of Moldova. *Address:* c/o Ministry of Defence, 2021 Chişinău, şos. Hânceşti 84, Moldova (office).

VRANITZKY, Franz, DComm; Austrian politician, banker and business executive; *Chairman, Magic Life der Club International Hotelbetriebs GmbH;* b. 4 Oct. 1937, Vienna; s. of Franz Vranitsky and Rosa Vernitsky; m. Christine Kristen; one s. one d.; ed Vienna XVII High School, Coll. (now Univ.) of Commerce, Vienna; joined Siemens-Schuckert GmbH, Vienna 1961; Dept of Nat. Econs, Austrian Nat. Bank 1961–69, seconded to the Office of the First Vice-Pres. 1969–70; Adviser on Econ. and Financial Policy to Minister of Finance 1970–76; Deputy-Chair. Bd of Dirs Creditanstalt-Bankverein 1976–81, Österreichische Länderbank 1981, Chair. Bd of Dirs 1981–84; Fed. Minister of Finance 1984–86; Fed. Chancellor 1986–96; fmr Chair. Austrian Socialist Party (now Social Democratic Party of Austria); Pres. Vienna Inst. for Devt and Co-operation 1990; mem. Bd of Dirs Magna International Inc. 1997, Touristik Union International, Magic Life der Club International Hotelbetriebs GmbH (currently Chair.); Hon. KCMG 1995; J. William Fulbright Prize For International Understanding 1995. *Address:* Office of the Chairman, Magic Life der Club International Hotelbetriebs GmbH, Landstraßer Hauptstraße 153-155, 1030 Vienna, Austria (office).

VRANKIĆ, Dragan; Bosnia and Herzegovina politician; b. 23 Jan. 1955, Capljina; m.; three c.; ed Faculty of Tourism and Foreign Trade, Univ. of Dubrovnik; began career in Energoinvest; later Head of Dept of Econs and Deputy Mayor for Financial and Econ. Affairs in Municipality of Capljina; fmr Gov. of Herzegovina-Neretva canton; twice elected mem. Parl., Fed. of Bosnia and Herzegovina; Deputy Prime Minister and Minister of Finance, Fed. of Bosnia and Herzegovina 2003–07; Minister of Finance and the Treasury, Bosnia and Herzegovina 2007–12; participated in establishment of Indirect Taxation Authority, now mem. Governing Bd; mem. of the Presidency Hravstke Democratic Union of Bosnia and Herzegovina. *Address:* c/o Ministry of Finance and the Treasury, 71000 Sarajevo, trg Bosne i Hercegovine 1, Bosnia and Herzegovina.

VRDOLJAK, Ivan; Croatian electrical engineer and politician; *Minister of the Economy;* b. 22 June 1972, Osijek; m. Ivana Vrdoljak; one c.; ed Braća Ribar Secondary School and Faculty of Electrical Eng, Osijek; AutoCad designer, RPM Engeharia, Porto Alerge, Brazil 1996; automation eng intern commissioning the Plomin 2 thermoelectric power plant, NOVA LIVANA d.o.o, Osijek 1999; Project Man. in automation and control systems of Puris Pazin, Moste Ljubljana, thermoelectric power plant of Šoštanj Velenje – Simatic S7, WinCC SCADA, PCS7 WinCC OS, FIX Intelution; Co-founder and mem. Bd of Dirs ATO Inženjering d.o.o., Osijek; with Dept for Electrical and IT Eng, transferred to Neo Inženjering d.o.o., Osijek 2000–08; mem. Croatian People's Party-Liberal Democrats 2000–, Chair. Cen. Bd 2008–; Deputy Mayor of Osijek, responsible for social services and the economy 2008–11; Minister of Construction and Physical Planning 2011–12, of the Economy 2012–. *Leisure interests:* soccer, tennis, squash, mem. Croatian Hunting Asscn, Mursa Hunting Soc., Osijek. *Address:* Ministry of the Economy, 10000 Zagreb, ul. grada Vukovara 78, Croatia (office). *Telephone:* (1) 6106111 (office). *Fax:* (1) 6109110 (office). *E-mail:* ministar@mingo.hr (office). *Website:* www.mingorp.hr (office).

VU, Van Ninh, MBA; Vietnamese government official; b. 23 Feb. 1955, Nam Dinh Prov.; ed Hanoi Univ. of Finance and Accountancy; mem. staff, Ministry of Finance 1977–82, Head of Economy Div. 1982–90, Deputy Dir of State Budget Dept 1990–93, Dir 1993–99; Vice-Minister of Finance 1999–2003, Minister of Finance 2006–11; Vice-Chair. Hanoi People's Cttee 2003–06; mem. CP of Viet Nam Cen. Cttee. *Address:* c/o Ministry of Finance, 28 Tran Hung Dao, Hoan Kiem District, Hanoi, Viet Nam (office).

VUČIĆ, Aleksandar; Serbian politician; *Prime Minister;* b. 5 March 1970, Belgrade; s. of Andjelko Vučić and Angelina Milovanov; m. Ksenija Janković; one s. one d.; ed Belgrade Univ.; reporter, Channel S (TV channel), Pale, Repub. of Serbia 1992–93; mem. Serbian Radical Party (SRS) 1993–2008, Gen. Sec. 1995–2008; Dir Pinki Sports and Business Centre, Zemun 1996; mem. Nat. Ass. (Parl. of Repub. of Serbia) 1993, 2004–08, May–July 2012, fmr Deputy Chair. SRS parl. group, mem. Admin. Cttee, Cttee on Constitutional Affairs, Deputy Chair. Cttee on Kosovo-Metohija and Cttee on Culture and Information; Minister of Information (Govt of Nat. Unity) 1998–2000; First Deputy Prime Minister, responsible for Defence, Security, the Fight against Corruption and Crime 2012–14, Minister of Defence 2012–13, Prime Minister 2014–; unsuccessful cand. for Mayor of Belgrade 2004, 2008; mem. Serbian Progressive Party (SNS) 2008–, Vice-Pres. 2008–12, Acting Pres. May–Sept. 2012, Pres. Sept. 2012–. *Leisure interests:* chess, basketball, soccer, wine. *Address:* Office of the Prime Minister, 11000 Belgrade, Nemanjina 11, Serbia (office). *Telephone:* (11) 3617586 (office). *Fax:* (11) 3617586 (office). *E-mail:* kabinetpremijera@gov.rs (office). *Website:* www.mod.gov.rs (office); www.srbija.gov.rs (office).

VUČINIĆ, Boro, PhD; Montenegrin politician; b. 1 Sept. 1954, Podgorica; m.; four c.; ed Faculty of Law, Montenegrin State Univ.; started career at Titograd Civil Eng Org.; Dir Social Fund for Building Land, Business Premises and Roads; Deputy Municipal Ass. of Podgorica; mem. Parl. (Democratic Socialist Party), mem. Constitutional Affairs Cttee, Cttee for Drafting of Constitutional Charter of State Union of Serbia and Montenegro; Minister of Environmental Protection and Urban Planning 2004–06, of Defence 2006–12; fmr Chair. Nat. Rifle Ass. of Yugoslavia; fmr Vice-Chair. Yugoslav Olympic Cttee; Head, Yugoslav Sports Del., Mediterranean Games 1997; Chair. Montenegrin Olympic Cttee. *Address:* c/o Ministry of Defence, Jovana Tomaševića 29, 81000 Podgorica, Montenegro (office).

VUJANOVIĆ, Filip; Montenegrin politician, lawyer and head of state; *President;* b. 1 Sept. 1954, Belgrade, Serbia; m. Svetlana Vujanović 1985; one s. two d.; ed Univ. of Belgrade; began career with First Municipal Court; Official Assoc., Dist Attorney's Office, Belgrade 1978–80; Sec. to Dist Court, Titograd (now Podgorica) 1980–81, mem. Attorney's Chamber, Chair. Chamber 1989; lawyer, pvt. legal practice 1982–93; Minister of Justice, Repub. of Montenegro 1992–95, of the Interior 1995–98; Prime Minister of Montenegro 1998–2002, with responsibility for Religious Affairs 2001–02; Pres. Parl. Ass. (Acting Pres. of Montenegro) 2002–03; Pres. of Montenegro 2003–; mem. Democratic Party of Socialists of Montenegro, currently Deputy Chair. *Address:* Office of the President, 81000 Podgorica, Sveti Petar Cetinjski 3, Montenegro (office). *Telephone:* (20) 241410 (office). *Fax:* (20) 245849 (office). *E-mail:* filip.vujanovic@predsjednik.me (office); predsjednik@predsjednik.me (office). *Website:* www.predsjednik.me (office).

VUKELIĆ, Branko, Dipl Ing; Croatian politician; b. 9 March 1958, Karlovac; m. Đurđica Vukelić; one c.; ed Faculty of Electrical Eng, Univ. of Zagreb; project engineer, Chief of Preparation and Installation, EAB, Karlovac 1982–90; Man. INA Br. Office, Karlovac 1991–97; Pres. Karlovac City Croatian Democratic Union (Hrvatska demokratska zajednica—HDZ) Cttee 1993–; mem. Karlovac City Council 1993–97, 2001–, Mayor of Karlovac 1997–2001; Pres. Karlovac Co. HDZ Cttee March 2002; Gen. Sec. HDZ June 2002; Minister of Economy, Labour and Entrepreneurship 2003–08, of Defence 2008–10. *Leisure interests:* football, horticulture, music. *Address:* c/o Ministry of Defence, 10000 Zagreb, trg kralja Petra Krešimira IV 1, Croatia.

VULF, Vitaly Yakovlevich, DHist; Russian broadcaster and writer; b. 23 May 1930, Baku, Azerbaijan; s. of Yakov Vulf; ed Moscow State Univ.; barrister, Baku and Moscow 1961–67; Sr, then Leading Researcher, Inst. of Int. Workers' Movt (now Inst. of Comparative Politology), USSR (now Russian) Acad. of Sciences 1967–97; Broadcaster, VID TV Co. 1997; currently Vice-Pres. Rossiya Kultura TV; creator of Silver Ball TV programme; mem. editorial Bd Ballet (magazine); mem. Union of Theatre Workers. *Publications:* Theatre of the USA of the Seventies and Political Reality, A Little Aside from Broadway, A. Stepanova – Actress of Moscow Art Theatre, Idols, Stars, People, Stars of Difficult Destiny, Theatre Rain and numerous other works on Russian and foreign theatre. *Address:* Telekanal Kultura, 123995 Moscow, ul. M. Nikitskaya 24, Russia (office). *E-mail:* kultura@tvkultura.ru (office). *Website:* www.tvkultura.ru (office).

VUNIBOBO, Berenado, CBE, BAgrSc; Fijian government official, diplomatist and agronomist; b. 24 Sept. 1932, Nukutubu, Rewa; s. of Mateo Vunibobo and Maria Kelekeletabua; m. Luisa Marama Tabumoce 1953; two s. three d.; ed St Joseph's Catholic Mission School, Rewa, Marist Brothers High School, Suva, Queensland State Agric. Coll., Queensland Univ. Imperial Coll. of Tropical Agric., Trinidad; Govt Service 1951–, Dist Agric. Officer 1962–67, Sr Agric. Officer and later Chief Agric. Officer 1968–69; Deputy Dir of Agric. 1969–70, Dir of Agric. 1970–71; Perm. Sec. for Agric., Fisheries and Forests 1971–72, for Works 1973–76; Amb. and Perm. Rep. to UN, New York, Amb. to USA and High Commr to Canada 1976–80; Perm. Sec. for Tourism, Transport and Civil Aviation 1980–81; Resident Rep. UNDP, Repub. of Korea 1981–86; Resident Rep. UNDP, Pakistan 1986–87; Minister of Trade and Commerce 1987–92, for Home Affairs, Immigration, Employment, Youth and Sports 1994, of Finance and Econ. Devt 1994–97, for Foreign Affairs and External Trade 1997–99; Special Envoy of Prime Minister on special mission 2001; Amb. and Perm. Rep. to UN, New York 2008–10; Chair. UN Visiting Mission to Cayman Islands and US Virgin Islands 1978; fmr Vice-Pres.

UN Gen. Ass.; Pres. UN Pledging Conf., Governing Council, UNDP; Chair. UN Observer Mission to New Hebrides (now Vanuatu); Chair. Coconut Pests and Diseases Bd, Banana Marketing Bd, Nat. Marketing Authority 1970–72; Chair. Civil Aviation Authority, Fiji, Air Terminal Services, Fiji; Chair. Preparatory Cttee for Celebration of Catholic Evangelisation of Fiji 1995–97; Chair. Building Cttee of Completion and Refurbishing of Sacred Heart Cathedral 1995–97; mem. Papal Mission led by HE Cardinal Josef Tomko, Special Envoy of His Holiness Pope John Paul II; mem. Constitutional Cttee appointed by Qarase Govt 2003–04; mem. and Chair. Advisory Cttee on Fijian Educ. 2005–08; mem. Bd, Fiji Devt Bank 1970–72; mem. Native Lands Trust Bd 1968–75, Fijian Affairs Bd 1968–76, Great Council of Chiefs 1968–76, Cen. Whitley Council 1970–76, Jt Industrial Council 1970–76, Fiji Electricity Authority 1975–76; Gold Medal, Queensland Agric. Coll. 1986. *Leisure interests:* reading, debating, walking, gardening, swimming, golf. *Address:* Lot 82, Maivurevure, Tamavua, Suva, Fiji (office). *Telephone:* 3323706 (office). *Fax:* 3320352 (office). *E-mail:* info@foreignaffairs.gov.fj (office). *Website:* www.foreignaffairs.gov.fj (office).

VUONG, Dinh Hue, PhD; Vietnamese economist, academic and politician; b. 15 March 1957, Nghi Xuan, Nghi Loc, Nghe An Prov.; ed Univ. of Econs, Bratislava, Slovakia; Lecturer in Econs, Hanoi Univ. of Finance and Accounting 1979–85, 1991–92, Assoc. Dir Dept of Accounting 1992–93, Univ. Vice-Chancellor 1999–2001; Auditor-Gen. (Chair.), State Audit Office of Viet Nam 2006–10; Minister of Finance 2011–13; mem. Dang Cong San Viet Nam (Communist Party of Viet Nam), mem. Cen. Cttee; Hon. mem. ACCA 2011. *Address:* Dang Cong San Viet Nam, 1A Hung Vuong, Hanoi, Viet Nam (office). *E-mail:* dangcongsan@cpv.org.vn. *Website:* www.cpv.org.vn.

VURAL, Volkan, MA; Turkish journalist, business executive and fmr diplomatist; *Counselor to the Chairman, Doğan Şirketler Grubu Holding A.Ş.;* b. 29 Dec. 1941, Istanbul; m.; ed Ankara Coll. and Univ.; early career as journalist; joined Foreign Ministry 1964, Third Sec., Econ. Affairs Dept 1964–65; mil. service 1965–67; Third Sec., Dept of Bilateral and Regional Econ. Affairs 1967–68, Second then First Sec., Embassy in Seoul 1968–71, Consul, then Deputy Consul Gen. Consulate in Munich 1971–73, Acting Head of Dept of Int. Econ. Insts, Foreign Ministry 1973–76, Int. Officer, Political Dept, NATO HQ 1976–82, Deputy Dir Gen. for Bilateral Econ. Affairs, Foreign Ministry 1982–87, Amb. to Iran 1987–88, to USSR 1988–93, Spokesman Foreign Ministry 1993, Chief Adviser to the Prime Minister 1993–95, Amb. to Germany 1995–98, Perm. Rep. to UN, New York 1998–2000, Amb. to Spain 2003–06; Counselor to Chair., Doğan Şirketler Grubu Holding A.Ş. 2006–; University Presidential Medal, La Salle Univ., Philadelphia 1999. *Address:* Office of the Chairman, Doğan Şirketler Grubu Holding A.Ş., Oymacı Sok. No:51 Altunizade 34662, Üsküdar İstanbul, Turkey (office). *Telephone:* (216) 5569000 (office). *Fax:* (216) 5569398 (office). *Website:* www.doganholding.com.tr (office).

VYACHORKA, Vintsuk; Belarusian linguist and politician; b. 7 July 1961, Bieraście; s. of Ryhor Viačorka and Alaucina Viačorka; m. 1980; two s. one d.; ed Belarus State Univ., Acad. of Sciences; Lecturer, Minsk Pedagogical Univ. 1986–; Co-founder and fmr Chair. Belarusian Popular Front (now Revival—Belarusian National Front), currently Deputy Chair.; Deputy Ed.-in-Chief bi-monthly Spadčyna. *Publication:* Orthography: An Attempt at Comprehensive Standardization 1994. *Leisure interest:* ethno-music. *Address:* Revival—Belarusian National Front (Belaruski Narodny Front 'Adradzhenniye'), 220005 Minsk, pr. Masherova 8, Belarus. *Telephone:* (17) 284-50-12. *E-mail:* pbnf@pbnf.org. *Website:* www.pbnf.org.

VYUGIN, Oleg Vyacheslavovich, CandPhys-MathSc; Russian economist, banker and fmr government official; *Chairman, MDM Bank;* b. 29 July 1952, Ufa, Bashkortostan; m. Irina; one d.; ed Moscow State Univ.; Researcher, then Sr Researcher and Head of Lab., Inst. of Prognosis of Nat. Econ., Russian Acad. of Sciences 1989–92; Head of Dept of Macroeconomic Policy, Ministry of Finance 1993–96, Deputy Minister of Finance 1996–99, First Deputy 1999–2000; mem. Bd, Exec. Vice-Pres. and Chief Economist Troyka-Dialog (investment co.) 2000–2002; First Deputy Chair. Bank Rossii—Central Bank of the Russian Fed. 2002–04; Chair. Fed. Financial Markets Service 2004–07; Chair. MDM-Bank 2007–; Chair. Nat. Assc of Securities Market Participants (NAUFOR) 2010–. *Address:* Office of the Chairman, MDM Bank, 18 Ul. Lenina, Novosibirsk 630004, Russia (office). *Telephone:* (495) 777-95-00 (office). *Fax:* (495) 797-95-01 (office). *Website:* mdmbank.com (office).

WA THIONG'O, Ngugi, (James Thiong'o Ngugi), BA; Kenyan writer, dramatist, critic and academic; *Distinguished Professor of English and Comparative Literature, University of California, Irvine;* b. 5 Jan. 1938, Limuru; m. 1st Nyambura 1961 (divorced 1982); m. 2nd Njeeri 1992; four s. two d.; ed Makerere Univ. Coll., Uganda and Univ. of Leeds, UK; Lecturer in Literature, Univ. Nairobi 1967–69, Sr Lecturer, Assoc. Prof. and Chair Dept of Literature 1972–77; Fellow in Creative Writing, Makerere Univ. 1969–70; Visiting Assoc. Prof., Northwestern Univ., USA 1970–71; arrested and detained Dec. 1977, released Dec. 1978; in exile in London 1982–; Lecturer in Politics and Literature, Yale Univ.; currently Distinguished Prof. of English and Comparative Literature, Univ. of California, Irvine, fmr Dir Int. Center for Writing and Translation; Foreign Hon. mem. American Academy of Arts and Letters; Hon. Life Mem. Council for the Devt of Social Sciences Research in Africa 2003; Dr hc (Univ. of Leeds), (Univ. of Transkei); Fonlon-Nicholas Award 1996, Medal of the Presidency of the Italian Cabinet, Fourth Memorial Steve Biko Lecture 2003, Grinzane for Africa Heritage Prize 2008. *Publications include:* The Black Hermit (play) 1962, Weep Not, Child (novel) 1964, The River Between (novel) 1965, A Grain of Wheat (novel) 1967, This Time Tomorrow: Three Plays 1970, Homecoming: Essays on African and Caribbean Literature, Culture and Politics 1972, Secret Lives and Other Stories 1973, The Trial of Dedan Kimathi (with Micere Githae-Mugo) 1976, Petals of Blood (novel) 1977, Mtawa Mweusi 1978, Caitaani mutharaba-ini (trans. as Devil on the Cross) 1980, Writers in Politics: Essays 1981, Detained: A Writer's Prison Diary 1981, Njamba Nene na mbaathi i mathagu (trans. as Njamba Nene and the Flying Bus) 1982, Ngaahika Ndeena: Ithaako ria Ngerekano (play, with Ngugi wa Mirii), (trans. as I Will Marry When I Want) 1982, Barrel of a Pen: Resistance to Repression in Neo-Colonial Kenya 1983, Bathitoora va Njamba Nene, 1984, English trans. as Njamba Nene's Pistol 1986, Decolonising the Mind: The Politics of Language in African Literature 1986, Writing Against Neo-colonialism 1986, Matigari ma Ngirũũngi (trans. as Matigari) 1986, Njambas Nene no Chiubu King'ang'i 1986, Moving the Centre: The Struggle for Cultural Freedoms 1992, Wizard of the Crow 2006, Dreams in a Time of War 2010. *Address:* 279 Humanities Instruction Building, University of California, Irvine, CA 92697-2651, USA (office). *E-mail:* ngugi@uci.edu (office). *Website:* www.humanities.uci.edu/complit (office); www.ngugiwathiongo.com.

WAAGSTEIN, Finn, MD, PhD; Danish cardiologist and academic; *Professor Emeritus in Cardiology, Institute of Internal Medicine, Sahlgrenska Academy, Gothenburg University;* b. 27 Feb. 1938, Copenhagen; s. of Peter Hans Dahl Waagstein and Elisabeth Waagstein (née Kongstad Rasmussen); m. Lisbeth Marika Ekstrand; three s. one d.; ed Sorö Academi Boarding School, Aarhus Univ.; Surgery resident, Torsby Hosp., Sweden 1964–65; Internal Medicine resident, Gävle Hosp. 1965–70; Cardiology resident, Sahlgrenska Univ. Hosp. 1970–76; Prof. of Cardiology, Inst. of Heart and Lung Diseases, Gothenberg Univ., Prof. Emer. in Cardiology, Inst. of Internal Medicine, Sahlgrenska Acad.; Hon. mem. Japanese Circulation Soc. 2012, Swedish Soc. of Cardiology 2012; Werköpriset Award, Swedish Heart & Lung Foundation 2001, King Faisal Int. Prize for Medicine 2002 (jt recipient), Silver Medal, European Soc. if Cardiology 2002. *Achievements include:* pioneered treatment of heart failure with beta-blockers 1973, first publ. 1975, mandatory treatment in patients with systolic heart failure not finally approved in Europe and USA until 2001. *Publications:* 183 peer-reviewed mainly on cardiovascular topics 1970–2012. *Leisure interests:* music (playing guitar and piano), sailing, hiking, gardening, reading (mainly science and history). *Address:* Wallenberg Laboratory, Bruna stråket 16, SU/Sahlgrenska, 413 45 Gothenberg, Sweden (office); Stallviksvägen 11, 428 43 Saro, Sweden (office). *Telephone:* (31) 342-30-14 (Gothenberg); (31) 93-64-96 (Saro) (office); 76-1387477 (mobile). *E-mail:* finn.waagstein@wlab.gu.se (office).

WACHS, Joel, BA, MA, JD; American lawyer and arts administrator; *President, Andy Warhol Foundation for the Visual Arts;* b. 1 March 1939, Scranton, Pa; ed Univ. of California, Los Angeles, Harvard Law School, New York Univ.; began career as corp. tax lawyer, Los Angeles; mem. Los Angeles City Council 1971–2001, Pres. 1981; Lecturer, Univ. of Southern California Law Center 1999; Pres. Andy Warhol Foundation for the Visual Arts, New York 2001–; mem. Calif. Bar Asscn. *Address:* Andy Warhol Foundation for the Visual Arts, 65 Bleecker Street, Seventh Floor, New York, NY 10012, USA (office). *Telephone:* (212) 387-7555 (office). *Fax:* (212) 387-7560 (office). *E-mail:* info@warholfoundation.org (office). *Website:* www.warholfoundation.org (office).

WACKERNAGEL, Mathis, BEng, PhD; Swiss engineer and environmental organization administrator; *President, Global Footprint Network;* b. 10 Nov. 1962, Basel; ed Swiss Fed. Inst. of Tech., Univ. of British Columbia, Canada; Dir Centro de Estudios para la Sustentabilidad, Anáhuac Univ., Mexico 1995–2001; Dir Sustainability Program at Redefining Progress, Oakland, Calif. 1999–2003; Co-creator Ecological Footprint and Pres. Global Footprint Network (think-tank) 2003–; mem. Adjunct Faculty, SAGE of Univ. of Wisconsin 2004; Frank H.T. Rhodes Class of 1956 Visiting Prof., Cornell Univ. 2011–13; Dr hc (Berne) 2007; Herman Daly Award, US Soc. for Ecological Econs 2005, WWF Award for Conservation Merit 2006, Skoll Award for Social Entrepreneurship (co-recipient) 2007, Int. Prize Calouste Gulbenkian (shared with Global Footprint Network) 2008, Zayed Int. Prize for Environment (co-recipient) 2011, Kenneth E. Boulding Memorial Award, Int. Soc. for Ecological Econs (co-recipient) 2012, Binding Prize for Environmental Conservation 2012, Blue Planet Prize, Asahi Foundation (co-recipient) 2012, Prix Nature Swisscanto 2013. *Publications:* Our Ecological Footprint: Reducing Human Impact on the Earth (co-author) 1995, Sharing Nature's Interest (co-author) 2001, The Winners and Losers in Global Competition: Why Eco-Efficiency Reinforces Competitiveness: A Study of 44 Nations (co-author) 2003, Der Ecological Footprint. Die Welt neu vermessen (co-author) 2010, WWF International's Living Planet Report; more than 50 peer-reviewed papers in professional journals, numerous articles and reports and various books on sustainability. *Address:* Global Footprint Network Headquarters, 312 Clay Street, Suite 300, Oakland, CA 94607-3510, USA (office). *Telephone:* (510) 839-8879 (office). *Fax:* (510) 251-2410 (office). *E-mail:* info@footprintnetwork.org (office). *Website:* www.footprintnetwork.org (office).

WADA, Akihiro; Japanese motor industry executive; b. 1934, Aichi Pref.; m.; one d. two s.; ed Nagoya Univ.; trained as mechanical engineer; joined Toyota 1956, specialised in automotive design, Gen. Man. Product Planning Div. 1978–86, apptd Dir 1986, Man.-Dir 1990–92, Sr Man.-Dir 1992–94, Exec. Vice-Pres. 1994–2001; Chair. Aisin Seiki Co. Ltd 2001–09; mem. Hon. Cttee FISITA. *Leisure interest:* golf. *Address:* c/o Aisin Seiki Company Ltd, 2-1 Asahi-machi, Kariya, Aichi 448-8650, Japan. *Telephone:* (5) 6624-8411. *Fax:* (5) 6624-8003. *E-mail:* info@aisin.co.jp. *Website:* www.aisin.co.jp.

WADA, Akiyoshi, PhD; Japanese research director and academic; b. 28 June 1929, Tokyo; s. of Koroku Wada and Haruko Kikkawa; m. Sachiko Naito 1958; two s.; ed Gakushūin High School and Univ. of Tokyo; Prof. of Physics, Univ. of Tokyo 1971–90, Prof. Emer. 1990–, Dean Faculty of Science 1989–90; Dir Sagami Chemical Research Center 1991–2001; Vice-Pres. Advanced Tech. Inst. 1988–; Dir Kazusa DNA Research Inst. 1991–; mem. Science Council of Japan 1991–2000; Pres. Nestlé Science Foundation (Japan) 1992–2004; Dir Genomic Sciences Centre (RIKEN) 1998–2004, Adviser 2004–; Dir Yokohama Science Centre 2004–12; Dir Ohanomizu Univ. 2005–09; Second Order of the Sacred Treasure 2002; Matsunaga Prize 1971, Shimadu Prize 1983, Polymer Soc. Prize 1995, Purple Ribbon Medal 1995, 10th Anniversary Award, Human Frontier Science Program 1998, Yokohama Prize of Cultural Merit 2003. *Publications:* Macrodipole of α-helix 1976, Molten Globule State of Proteins 1980, Automated DNA Sequencing 1987, Stability Distribution of DNA Double Helix 1987. *Leisure interests:* orchid cultivation, stamp collection. *Address:* 11-1-311, Akasaka 8, Minato-ku, Tokyo 107, Japan. *Telephone:* (3) 3408-2932.

WADA, Hiroko; Japanese business executive and consultant; *CEO, Office Wada;* b. 4 May 1952; joined Procter & Gamble Sun Home K.K. (currently Procter & Gamble Far East, Inc.) 1977, Vice-Pres. Corp. New Ventures, Asia, Procter & Gamble 1998–2001; Pres. Dyson 2001–02; Pres. and COO Toys "R" Us (Japan) Ltd 2004; Founder, CEO and Rep. Dir Office Wada (man. consultancy) 2004–; Guest Prof., Momoyama Gakuin Univ. 2009–; mem. Bd of Dirs Aderans Holdings Co. Ltd 2009–; ranked by Fortune magazine amongst 50 Most Powerful Women in Business outside the US (41st) 2004. *Address:* c/o Board of Directors, Aderans Holdings Company Ltd, 1-6-3 Shinjuku Shinjuku-ku, 160-8429, Tokyo, Japan. *E-mail:* info@wadahiroko01.com (office). *Website:* www.wadahiroko.com (office).

WADA, Isami; Japanese real estate industry executive; *Chairman, CEO and Representative Director, Sekisui House Group;* began career in sales; joined Sekisui House Ltd (property devt firm) 1965, has held several exec. positions, Chair., CEO and Rep. Dir Sekisui House Group 2008–; Pres. Japan Fed. of Housing Orgs. *Address:* Sekisui House Group, 1-1-88 Oyodonaka, Kita-ku, Osaka 531-0076, Japan (office). *Telephone:* (6) 6440-3111 (office). *Fax:* (6) 6440-3331 (office). *E-mail:* info-ir@qz.sekisuihouse.co.jp (office). *Website:* www.sekisuihouse.co.jp (office); www.judanren.or.jp.

WADA, Norio, BEcons; Japanese telecommunications executive; b. 16 Aug. 1940; ed Kyoto Univ.; joined Nippon Telegraph and Telephone (NTT) Public Corpn 1964, Sr Vice-Pres. and Gen.-Man. Tohoku Regional Communications Sector 1992–96, Exec. Vice-Pres. and Sr Exec. Man. of Affiliated Business HQ 1997–98, In June 1998, he became an Exec. Vice-Pres. and Sr Exec. Man. of Affiliated Business HQ and Exec. Man. of NTT-Holding Organizational Office 1998–99, Exec. Vice-Pres. and Sr Exec. Man. of NTT-Holding Provisional HQ 1999–2002, Sr Exec. Vice-Pres. NTT 1999–2002, Pres. NTT 2002–07, Chair. NTT 2007–12. *Address:* c/o Nippon Telegraph and Telephone Corporation, 3-1 Otemachi 2-chome, Chiyoda-ku, Tokyo 100-8116, Japan. *E-mail:* info@ntt.co.jp.

WADDELL, (John) Rankin; British photographer; *Director, Rankin Photography;* b. 1966, Glasgow, Scotland; m. Kate Hardie (divorced); one s.; ed Brighton Polytechnic, London Coll. of Printing; co-f. Dazed and Confused magazine; co-f. Vision On Publishing; photographed Golden Queen's Jubilee 2002; Dir Rankin Photography. *Films:* Perfect (short), The Lives of the Saints 2006. *Television:* Germany's Next Top Model 2009, 2010, BBC 4's Seven Photographs that Changed Fashion 2009, BBC 2 Culture Show Review of Irving Penn Exhbn 2010, interview with Rankin (GMTV) 2010, CBS feature televised in USA 2010. *Publications include:* Nudes, Male Nudes 2000, Fashion Stories 2004, Portraits 2004. *Publications:* Hello Sexy 1998, Rankin Photographs 1998, Female Nudes 1999, Rankin Works 2000, Snog 2000, Celebritation 2000, Male Nudes 2001, Sofasosexy 2002, Breeding 2002, Rankin Bailey 2003, This is the Work of Rankin 2003, Rankin Portraits 2004, Fashion Stories 2004, Surface Seduction 2005, Hard Sell 2005, The Lives of the Saints (production hardback) 2005–06, Breast Friends 2006, Tuulitastic 2006, Beautyfull 2007, Visually Hungry 2007, Sold Out 2009, Surface Attraction 2009, Rankin's Cheeky 2009, Heidilicious 2009, Destroy 2009, Macallan 2009, We Are Congo 2010, Portraits 2010, Painting Pretty Pictures 2010, RANKINJOZI 2010, Ten Times Rosie 2010. *Address:* Rankin Photography, 112–114 Grafton Road, London, NW5 4BA, England (office). *Telephone:* (20) 7284-7320 (office). *Fax:* (20) 7284-7330 (office). *E-mail:* info@rankin.co.uk (office). *Website:* www.rankin.co.uk (office).

WADDINGTON, Baron (Life Peer), cr. 1990, of Read in the County of Lancashire; **David Waddington,** GCVO, PC, QC, DL; British politician; b. 2 Aug. 1929, Burnley, Lancs., England; s. of Charles Waddington and Minnie Hughan Waddington; m. Gillian Rosemary Green 1958; three s. two d.; ed Sedbergh and Hertford Coll., Oxford; Pres. Oxford Union Conservative Asscn 1950; called to the Bar, Gray's Inn 1951, Recorder of the Crown Court 1972; MP for Nelson and Colne 1968–74, for Clitheroe (Ribble Valley constituency from 1983) March 1979–91; Parl. Pvt. Sec. to Attorney-Gen. 1970–72; Lord Commr of the Treasury 1979–81, Parl. Under-Sec. of State for Employment 1981–83; Minister of State at the Home Office 1983–87, Parl. Sec. to HM Treasury and Govt Chief Whip 1987–89, Home Sec. 1989–90, Lord Privy Seal and Leader of the House of Lords 1990–92; Gov. and C-in-C of Bermuda 1992–97. *Leisure interests:* golf, sailing. *Address:* House of Lords, Westminster, London, SW1A 0PW (office); Old Bailiffs, South Cheriton, nr Templecombe, Somerset, BA8 0BH, England (home). *Telephone:* (20) 7219-6448 (office); (1963) 371662 (home). *Fax:* (20) 7219-6807 (office). *E-mail:* waddingtond@parliament.uk (office).

WADDINGTON, Leslie; British art dealer; *Chairman, Waddington Custot Galleries;* b. 9 Feb. 1934, Dublin, Ireland; s. of Victor Waddington and Zelda Waddington; m. 2nd Clodagh F. Waddington 1985; two d. by first marriage; ed Portora Royal School, Enniskillen and Ecole du Louvre, Paris; Dir Waddington Galleries (now Waddington Custot Galleries) 1957–, Man. Dir 1966–, now Chair.; Chair. Modern Painting Section Maastricht Art Fair 1994–2004, Pictura Section 1996–2000; Sr Fellow, RCA 1993; Dr hc (RCA) 1993; European Fed. of Art Gallery Asscns Award 2013. *Leisure interests:* reading. *Address:* Waddington Custot Galleries, 11 Cork Street, London, W1S 3LT, England (office). *Telephone:* (20) 7851-2200 (office). *E-mail:* mail@waddingtoncustot.com (office). *Website:* www.waddingtoncustot.com (office).

WADE, Abdoulaye; Senegalese lawyer, politician and fmr head of state; *Secretary-General, Parti Démocratique Sénégalais;* b. 29 May 1926, Kebemer; m.; two c.; ed Univs of Besançon and Dijon, France, Univ. of Dakar; fmr univ. teacher of law in Senegal and abroad; barrister, Court of Appeal, Senegal; Founder and Pres. Parti Démocratique Sénégalais (Senegalese Democratic Party) 1974, now Sec.-Gen.; mem. Parl. 1974–2012; Minister of State 1991–92, 1995–97; Pres. of Senegal 2000–12; mem. Int. Acad. of Trial Lawyers; Commdr, Order of Merit, Grand Officer, Légion d'honneur; UNESCO Félix Houphouët-Boigny Peace Prize 2005. *Publications:* author of several books and essays on law, economics and political science. *Address:* Parti Démocratique Sénégalais, blvd Dial Diop, Immeuble Serigne Mourtada Mbacké, Dakar, Senegal (office). *Telephone:* 33-823-5027 (office). *Fax:* 33-823-1702 (office). *E-mail:* cedobe@aol.com (office).

WADE, (Sarah) Virginia, OBE, BSc; British broadcaster and fmr tennis player; b. 10 July 1945, Bournemouth, Hants. (now Dorset); d. of Canon Eustace Wade (fmr Archdeacon of Durban, SA) and Joan Barbara Wade; ed Univ. of Sussex; amateur tennis player 1962–68, professional 1968–87; British Hard Court Champion 1967, 1968, 1973, 1974; USA Champion 1968 (singles), 1973, 1975 (doubles); Italian Champion 1971; Australian Champion 1972; Wimbledon Ladies Champion 1977; played Wightman Cup for GB 1965–85, Capt. 1973–80; played Fed. Cup for GB 1967–83 (a record), Capt. 1973–81; won 55 singles titles; commentator BBC 1980–; mem. Cttee All England Lawn Tennis Club 1983–91 (first woman to be elected); Hon. LLD (Sussex) 1985; Int. Tennis Hall of Fame 1989; Fed. Cup Award of Excellence 2002. *Publications:* Courting Triumph (with Mary Lou Mellace) 1978, Ladies of the Court 1984. *Leisure interest:* reading. *Address:* Red Baron Enterprises Ltd, c/o ET Global Group, 35 Britannia Row, London, N1 8QH, UK (office). *Telephone:* (20) 7288-7693 (office). *Fax:* (20) 8863-6908 (office). *E-mail:* dm@redbaronenterprises.co.uk (office). *Website:* www.virginia-wade.com (office).

WADE-GERY, Sir Robert (Lucian), KCMG, KCVO, MA; British fmr diplomatist and banker; *Fellow, All Souls College, Oxford;* b. 22 April 1929, Oxford; s. of Prof. H. T. Wade-Gery and V. Wade-Gery; m. Sarah Marris 1962; one s. one d.; ed Winchester Coll. and New Coll., Oxford; Fellow, All Souls Coll. Oxford 1951–73, 1987–89, 1997–; joined Foreign (now Diplomatic) Service 1951; in Foreign Office (FO) Econ. Relations Dept 1951–54; at Embassy in Bonn 1954–57, Tel-Aviv 1961–64, Saigon (now Ho Chi Min City) 1967–68; FO 1957–60, 1964–67; Cabinet Office 1968–69; Counsellor 1969; on loan to Bank of England 1969; Head of Financial Policy and Aid Dept, FCO 1970; Under-Sec., Cen. Policy Review Staff, Cabinet Office 1971–73; Minister at Embassy, Madrid 1973–77, Moscow 1977–79; Deputy Sec. of Cabinet 1979–82; High Commr in India 1982–87; Vice-Chair. Barclays de Zoete Wedd 1994–98 (Exec. Dir 1987–93), Vice-Chair. Barclays Capital 1998–99; Sr Consultant to Int. Financial Services London 1991–2001 and to Barclays Private Bank 1999–2002; Chair. SOAS 1990–98; Chair. Anglo-Spanish Soc. 1995–98. *Leisure interests:* walking, sailing, travel, history. *Address:* 14 Hill View, 2 Primrose Hill Road, London, NW3 3AX (home); The Old Vicarage, Cold Aston, Cheltenham, Glos., GL54 3BW, England (home). *Telephone:* (20) 7722-4754 (home); (1451) 821115 (home). *Fax:* (20) 7586-5966 (home); (1451) 822496 (home).

WADHWANI, Sushil Baldev, CBE, BSc, MSc, PhD; British economist and investment manager; *CEO, Wadhwani Asset Management;* b. 7 Dec. 1959, Kenya; s. of Baldev Wadhwani and Meena Wadhwani; m. Renu Wadhwani; one s. one d.; ed London School of Econs; Reader in Econs, LSE 1984–91, Visiting Prof. 2000–; Visiting Prof., Sir John Cass Business School, City of London 2000–; Dir of Equity Strategy, Goldman Sachs Int. 1991–95; Dir of Research, Tudor Proprietary Trading LLC 1995–99; mem. Bank of England Monetary Policy Cttee 1999–2002; CEO Wadhwani Asset Man./Wadhwani Capital 2002–; Partner, Caxton Assocs 2012–; Gov. LSE 2004–; Allyn Young Prize, C.S. McTaggart Scholarship, Clothworkers' Co. Exhbn, Gonner Prize, Raynes Undergraduate Prize, Sir Edward Stern Scholarship, Ely Devons Prize, Sayers Prize. *Publications:* numerous articles in academic journals. *Leisure interest:* cricket. *Address:* Wadhwani Asset Management LLP, 40 Berkeley Square, London, W1J 5AL, England (office). *Telephone:* (20) 7663-3420 (office). *Fax:* (20) 7663-3410 (office). *E-mail:* sushilw@waniasset.com (office).

WADIA, Jamshed (Jim), FCA, FRSA; British chartered accountant; b. 12 April 1948; m. Joelle Garnier 1972; one s. one d.; ed Le Rosey, Rolle, Switzerland, Inns of Court School of Law; called to Bar, Inner Temple 1969; Pnr, Arthur Andersen 1982–2000, Man. Pnr UK 1993–97, Worldwide Man. Pnr and CEO 1997–2000 (resgnd); COO Linklaters & Alliance (law firm) 2001–04; Dir (non-exec.) Wragge & Co LLP 2005–. *Leisure interests:* tennis, theatre. *Address:* c/o Board of Directors, Wragge & Co LLP, 55 Colmore Row, Birmingham, B3 2AS, England.

WADIA, Nusli; Indian business executive; *Chairman, Bombay Dyeing & Manufacturing Company Ltd;* grandson of Muhammad Ali Jinnah; m. Maureen Wadia; two s.; Chair. Bombay Dyeing & Manufacturing Co. Ltd, Gherzi Eastern Ltd, Bombay Burmah Trading Corpn Ltd, BRT Ltd, NW Exports Ltd, Britannia Industries Ltd, National Peroxide Ltd, Citurgia Biochemicals Ltd, Wadia BSN India Ltd; Chair. and Man. Dir Nowrosjee Wadia & Sons Ltd; Dir Anil Starch Products Ltd, Tata Chemicals Ltd, Atul Products Ltd, Naira Holdings Ltd, Radley Cotton Mills Ltd, ABI Holdings Ltd, Associated Biscuits International Ltd; mem. Bd of Dirs Oberoi Group. *Address:* Bombay Dyeing, Neville House, J. N. Heredia Marg, Ballard Estate, Mumbai 400 038, India (office). *Telephone:* (22) 22618071 (office). *Fax:* (22) 22614520 (office). *Website:* www.bombaydyeing.com (office).

WAENA, Sir Nathaniel Rahumaea, GCMG; Solomon Islands politician and government official; Minister of Prov. Govt and Rural Devt c. 2001; Minister for Nat. Unity, Reconciliation and Peace –2004; Gov.-Gen. Solomon Islands 2004–09; Patron St Martins, Tenar 2004, Stuyvenberg Rural Training Centre, Nana 2006, Pawa Prov. Secondary School Fund Raising Drive 2007; Solomon Island Cross (CSI), KStJ. *Address:* c/o Office of the Governor-General, Honiara, Solomon Islands (office).

WAGENER, Hans; German business executive and accountant; *Chairman of the Supervisory Board, Landesbank Baden-Württemberg;* b. 6 Feb. 1950, Rosdorf; ed Univ. of Göttingen; began career as bank clerk at Commerzbank; later accounting asst with Treuarbeit AG (predecessor of PricewaterhouseCoopers (PwC) Germany) 1977, passed exams for both tax adviser and Certified Public Accountant in early 1980s, left co. 1985; moved to Auditing Asscn of German Banks 1985; returned to Germany 1987; mem. PwC Financial Services Bd 1992, assumed responsibility for various int. activities, CEO PwC Germany 2003–10; Chair. Supervisory Bd Landesbank Baden-Wuerttemberg 2010–; fmr Lecturer, Dept of Accounting, Johann Wolfgang Goethe Univ., Frankfurt; mem. Bd Inst. of Chartered Accountants. *Address:* Landesbank Baden-Württemberg, Am Hauptbahnhof 2, 70173 Stuttgart, Germany (office). *Telephone:* (711) 127-0 (office). *Fax:* (711) 127-43544 (office). *E-mail:* kontakt@lbbw.de (office). *Website:* www.lbbw.de (office).

WAGGONER, Paul Edward, PhD, FAAS; American horticultural scientist; *Distinguished Scientist, Department of Forestry and Horticulture, Connecticut Agricultural Experiment Station;* b. 29 March 1923, Appanoose Co., Ia; s. of Walter Loyal Waggoner and Kathryn Maring Waggoner; m. Barbara Ann Lockerbie 1945; two s.; ed Univ. of Chicago and Iowa State Univ.; Asst, then Assoc. Plant Pathologist, Connecticut Agricultural Experiment Station, Dept of Forestry and Horticulture, New Haven, 1951–56, Chief Scientist, Soils, Climatology, Ecology 1951–71, Vice-Dir 1969–71, Dir 1972–87, Distinguished Scientist 1987–; Lecturer, Yale Forestry School, New Haven 1962–; Guggenheim Fellow 1963; mem. NAS; Fellow, American Soc. of Agronomy, American Phytopathological Soc.; Anton-de Bary Medal 1996. *Publications:* Agricultural Meteorology (ed.) 1965, Climate Change and US Water Resources 1990, How Much Land Can 10 Billion People Spare for Nature? 1994 and articles on phytopathology. *Leisure interests:* gardening, bicycling. *Address:* Connecticut Agricultural Experiment Station, Box 1106, New Haven, CT 06504 (office); 314 Vineyard Point Road, Guilford, CT 06437, USA (home). *Telephone:* (203) 974-8494 (office); (203) 453-2816 (home). *E-mail:* paul.waggoner@po.state.ct.us. *Website:* www.caes.state.ct.us/Departments/forestry.htm (office).

WAGNER, Heinz Georg, Dr rer. nat; German scientist and academic; *Professor Emeritus, Institut für Physikalische Chemie, University of Göttingen;* b. 20 Sept. 1928, Hof, Bavaria; s. of Georg Wagner and Frieda Spiess; m. Renate C. Heuer 1974; ed Tech. Hochschule, Darmstadt and Univ. of Göttingen; Lecturer, Univ. of Göttingen 1960–65, Prof. of Physical Chem. 1971–97, now Prof. Emer.; Prof. Ruhr Univ. Bochum 1965–70; Dir Max-Planck-Inst. für Strömungsforschung, Göttingen 1971–97; Vice-Pres. Deutsche Forschungsgemeinschaft 1983–89; mem. Exec. Council ESF; Scientific mem. Max-Planck-Gesellschaft; mem. Göttingen Acad., Acad. Leopoldina, Int. Acad. of Astronautics, Heidelberg Acad., Acad. of Natural Sciences of Russia, Academia Europaea, American Physical Soc., Royal Soc. of Chem. etc.; Hon. mem. Bunsen-Gesellschaft; Grosses Bundesverdienstkreuz; several hon. doctorates; Fritz-Haber Prize, Bernard Lewis Gold Medal, Achema Medal, Numa Manson Medal, Dionizy Smoleński Medal, Walther-Nernst-Denkmünze, Dechema Medal. *Publications:* articles on combustion, reaction kinetics, thermodynamics of liquid mixtures. *Address:* Institut für Physikalische Chemie, Universität Göttingen, Tammannstr. 6, 37077 Göttingen, Germany (office). *Telephone:* (551) 3933100 (office). *Fax:* (551) 3933117 (office). *E-mail:* jkupfer@gwdg.de (office). *Website:* www.uni-goettingen.de/de/sh/28451.html (office).

WAGNER, Robert; American actor; b. 10 Feb. 1930, Detroit, Mich.; m. 1st Natalie Wood 1957 (divorced 1962, re-married 1972, died 1981); one d. one step-d.; m. 2nd Marion Marshall Donen; one d. *Films include:* Halls of Montezuma 1951, The Frogmen 1951, Let's Make It Legal 1951, With a Song in My Heart 1952, What Price Glory? 1952, Stars and Stripes Forever 1952, The Silver Whip 1953, Titanic 1953, Star of Tomorrow, Beneath the 12-Mile Reef 1953, Prince Valiant 1954, Broken Lance 1954, White Feather 1955, A Kiss Before Dying 1956, The Mountain 1956, The True Story of Jesse James 1957, Stopover Tokyo 1957, The Hunters 1958, In Love and War 1958, Mardi Gras 1958, Say One For Me 1959, Between Heaven and Hell, All the Fine Young Cannibals 1960, Sail a Crooked Ship 1961, The Longest Day 1962, The War Lover 1962, The Condemned of Altona 1962, The Pink Panther 1963, Harper 1966, Banning 1967, The Biggest Bundle of Them All 1968, Don't Just Stand There! 1968, Winning 1969, Madame Sin 1972, Journey Through Rosebud 1972, The Towering Inferno 1974, Midway 1976, The Concorde: Airport '79 1979, Curse of the Pink Panther 1983, I Am the Cheese 1983, Delirious (uncredited) 1991, Dragon: The Bruce Lee Story 1993, Overdrive 1997, Austin Powers: International Man of Mystery 1997, Wild Things 1998, Something to Believe In 1998, The Kidnapping of Chris Burden 1999, Dill Scallion 1999, Crazy in Alabama 1999, No Vacancy 1999, Love and Fear, Austin Powers: The Spy Who Shagged Me 1999, Play It to the Bone 1999, Forever Fabulous 2000, The Mercury Project 2000, The Retrievers 2001, Sol Goode 2001, Jungle Juice 2001, Nancy and Frank – A Manhattan Love Story 2002, Austin Powers in Goldmember 2002, The Calling 2002, El Padrino 2004, The Fallen Ones 2005, The Wild Stallion 2006, Hoot 2006, Man in the Chair 2007, Netherbeast Incorporated 2007,. *Television series include:* How I Spent My Summer Vacation 1967, Hart to Hart 1979–84, It Takes a Thief (series) 1967–70, City Beneath the Sea 1971, Crosscurrent 1971, Killer by Night 1972, The Streets of San Francisco 1972, Colditz (series) 1972, The Affair 1973, The Abduction of Saint Anne 1975, Switch (series) 1975, Death at Love House 1976, Cat on a Hot Tin Roof 1976, The Critical List 1978, Pearl (mini-series) 1978, Hart to Hart (series) 1979, To Catch a King 1984, Lime Street (series) 1985, There Must Be a Pony 1986, Love Among Thieves 1987, Windmills of the Gods 1988, Indiscreet 1988, Around the World in 80 Days (mini-series) 1989, This Gun for Hire 1991, False Arrest 1991, Jewels (mini-series) 1992, The Trials of Rosie O'Neill (series) 1992, Les audacieux 1993, Hart to Hart: Hart to Hart Returns 1993, Hart to Hart: Home Is Where the Hart Is 1994, Heaven & Hell: North & South, Book III (mini-series) 1994, Hart to Hart: Crimes of the Hart 1994, Hart to

Hart: Old Friends Never Die 1994, Parallel Lives 1994, Hart to Hart: Secrets of the Hart 1995, Dancing in the Dark 1995, Hart to Hart: Two Harts in Three-Quarters Time 1995, Hart to Hart: Harts in High Season 1996,Hart to Hart: Till Death Do Us Hart 1996, Camino de Santiago (mini-series) 1999, Fatal Error 1999, Die Abzocker – Eine eiskalte Affäre (aka A Sordid Affair, and The Hustle) 2000, Rocket's Red Glare 2000, Becoming Dick 2000, The Retrievers 2001, Mystery Woman 2003, Hope & Faith 2003–06, Boston Legal 2006, Two and a Half Men 2007; numerous other TV appearances. *Address:* c/o William Morris Agency, One William Morris Place, Beverly Hills, CA 90212, USA (office). *Telephone:* (310) 859-4000 (office). *Fax:* (310) 859-4462 (office). *Website:* www.robert-wagner.com (office); www.wma.com (office).

WAGNER, Susan L., BA, MBA; American business executive; *Vice-Chairman, BlackRock, Inc.;* ed Wellesley Coll., Univ. of Chicago; Vice-Pres., Mortgage and Savings Insts Group, Lehman Brothers –1988; joined BlackRock, Inc. 1988, Man. Dir and Head of Strategy and Product Devt –2005, COO 2005–10, Co-Chair. Corp. Council and mem. Office of Chair., Operating Cttee, Corp. Risk Cttee and Leadership Cttee. BlackRock, Inc. 2006–, mem. Global Exec. Cttee; mem. Business Leadership Council of Wellesley Coll., Bd of Trustees of Hackley School; ranked by Fortune magazine amongst the 50 Most Powerful Women in Business in the US (19th) 2011. *Publications:* assisted in writing and editing Conversations with Economists (named one of the ten best business and economics books published in 1984) 1984; author of several articles for Lehman Brothers. *Address:* Corporate Communications Department, BlackRock, Inc., 55 East 52nd Street, New York, NY 10055, USA (office). *Telephone:* (212) 810-5300 (office). *Fax:* (212) 810-8760 (home). *E-mail:* blackrockbod@blackrock.com (office). *Website:* www2.blackrock.com (office).

WAGNER TIZÓN, Allan; Peruvian politician and diplomatist; *Ambassador to the Netherlands;* b. 7 Feb. 1942, Lima; s. of Carlos Wagner Vizcarra and Antonieta Tizón Ponce; m. Julia de la Guerra Urquiaga; five d.; ed Nat. Univs of Trujillo and of Engineering, Lima, Universidad Católica and Universidad de San Marcos; joined Ministry of Foreign Affairs 1963; joined Diplomatic Service 1968; Chief of Econ. Dept, Embassy in Washington, DC 1972–74, Deputy Chief of Mission and Chargé d'affaires 1983–85; Chief of Political Dept, Embassy in Chile 1978–79; Minister of Foreign Affairs 1985–88, 2002–03; Amb. to Spain 1988–90, to Venezuela 1991–92 (resgnd); Prof. Diplomatic Acad. 1991; Dir of Devt and Adviser to Latin American Econ. System (SELA) 1992–98; Founder-mem. Peruvian Centre of Int. Studies (CEPEI), Pres. 1999–; Founder-mem. Inst. of European–Latin American Relations (IRELA); Amb. to USA 2001–02; Adviser to Sec.-Gen. of Andean Community of Nations –2002, Sec.-Gen. 2004–06; Minister of Defence 2006–07; Del. of Peru, Int. Court of Justice trying land and maritime boundary dispute with Chile 2007–; Amb. to the Netherlands 2008–; Gran Cruz de la Orden El Sol del Perú, Orden al Mérito por Servicios Distinguidos, seven other decorations from Peru and 26 decorations from foreign countries. *Address:* Embassy of Peru, Nassauplein 4, 2585 The Hague, Netherlands (office). *Telephone:* (70) 3653500 (office). *Fax:* (70) 3651929 (office). *E-mail:* info@embassyofperu.nl (office). *Website:* www.embassyofperu.nl (office).

WAGONER, Dan; American dancer, choreographer, dance company director and academic; b. 1932, West Virginia; studied pharmacy; joined Martha Graham co. 1957; danced with Merce Cunningham's and Paul Taylor's cos; f. Dan Wagoner and Dancers (dance co.) 1969, fmr Dir; has choreographed about 40 works; Artistic Dir London Contemporary Dance Theatre 1989–90; Distinguished Guest Artist, Connecticut Coll. 1999–2003; mem. Faculty, School of Dance, Florida State Univ. 2003–. *Address:* Florida State University School of Dance, 130 Collegiate Loop, PO Box 3062120, Tallahassee, FL 32306-2120, USA (office). *E-mail:* dwagoner@fsu.edu (office). *Website:* dance.fsu.edu (office).

WAGONER, David Russell, MA; American writer and academic; *Professor Emeritus of English, University of Washington;* b. 5 June 1926, Massillon, Ohio; m. 1st Patricia Parrott 1961 (divorced 1982); m. 2nd Robin H. Seyfried 1982; two d.; ed Pennsylvania State Univ., Indiana Univ.; served in USN 1944–46; Instructor, DePauw Univ., Greencastle, Ind. 1949–50, Pennsylvania State Univ. 1950–54; Assoc. Prof., Univ. of Washington, Seattle 1954–66, Prof. of English 1966–2000, Prof. Emer. 2000–; Elliston Lecturer, Univ. of Cincinnati 1968; Ed. Poetry Northwest, Seattle 1966–2002, Ed. Princeton Univ. Press Contemporary Poetry Series 1977–81; Poetry Ed. Missouri Press 1983–2000; Guggenheim Fellowship 1956, Ford Fellowship 1964, American Acad. Grant 1967, Nat. Endowment for the Arts Grant 1969; Morton Dauwen Zabel Prize (Poetry, Chicago) 1967, Ruth Lilly Prize 1991, Levinson Prize (Poetry, Chicago) 1994, Union League Prize (Poetry, Chicago) 1997, Pacific NW Booksellers Award 2000. *Short Stories:* Afternoon on the Ground 1978, Wild Goose Chase 1978, Mr. Wallender's Romance 1979, Cornet Solo 1979, The Water Strider 1979, Fly Boy 1980, The Bird Watcher 1980, Snake Hunt 1980. *Play:* An Eye for an Eye for an Eye 1973. *Verse:* Dry Sun, Dry Wind 1953, A Place to Stand 1958, Poems 1959, The Nesting Ground 1963, Five Poets of the Pacific Northwest (with others) 1964, Staying Alive 1966, New and Selected Poems 1969, Working Against Time 1970, Riverbed 1972, Sleeping in the Woods 1974, A Guide to Dungeness Spit 1975, Travelling Light 1976, Who Shall Be the Sun? Poems Based on the Lore, Legends and Myths of Northwest Coast and Plateau Indians 1978, In Broken Country 1979, Landfall 1981, First Light 1983, Through the Forest 1987, Walt Whitman Bathing 1996, Traveling Light: Collected and New Poems 1999, The House of Song 2002, Good Morning and Good Night 2005, A Map of the Night 2008, After the Point of No Return 2012. *Novels:* The Man in the Middle 1955, Money, Money, Money 1955, Rock 1958, The Escape Artist 1965, Baby, Come On Inside 1968, Where is My Wandering Boy Tonight? 1970, The Road to Many a Wonder 1974, Tracker 1975, Whole Hog 1976, The Hanging Garden 1980. *Address:* 5416 154th Place, SW, Edmonds, WA 98026-4348, USA (home). *Telephone:* (425) 745-6964 (home). *E-mail:* renogawd@aol.com (home).

WAGONER, G. Richard, Jr, BEcons, MBA; American automobile industry executive; b. 9 Feb. 1953, Wilmington, Del.; s. of the late George Wagoner and Martha Wagoner; m. Kathy Wagoner (née Kaylor) 1979; three s.; ed Duke and Harvard Univs; joined General Motors (GM) 1977, analyst, Office of the Treas., New York 1977, Treas. of GM do Brasil (GMB), São Paulo 1981–84, Exec. Dir of Finance, GMB 1984–87, Vice-Pres. and Finance Man. GM Canada Ltd 1987–88, Group Dir (Strategic Business Planning) Chevrolet-Pontiac-GM, Canada 1988–89, Vice-Pres. Finance, GM Europe, Zürich, Switzerland 1989–90, Pres. and Man.

GMB 1991–92, Exec. Vice-Pres. and Chief Financial Officer 1992–94, Head of Worldwide Purchasing 1993–94, Exec. Vice-Pres. and Pres. N American Operations 1994–98, Pres. and COO 1998–2000, Chair. Automotive Strategy Bd, Pres. and CEO 2000–03, Chair. and CEO May 2003–09 (resgnd); Chair. A World in Motion Exec. Cttee, Soc. of Automotive Engineers; mem. Business Council, Business Roundtable; mem. Bd Trustees Duke Univ., Detroit Country Day School; mem. Bd Dean's Advisers, Harvard Business School. *Address:* c/o General Motors Corporation, 300 Renaissance Center, Detroit, MI 48265-3000, USA (office).

WAHEED HASSAN MANIK, Mohamed, MA, PhD; Maldivian politician and fmr UN official and fmr head of state; m. Ilham Hussain; three c.; ed American Univ. of Beirut, Stanford Univ., USA; fmr Lecturer, Michigan State Univ., USA; fmr Programme Man. HSQ Technology Inc., San Francisco, USA; began political career by running first Western-style election campaign in Maldives in 1998, elected mem. Parl. for Malé 1998; served as Sec. of Educ., in Office of the Pres. and as mem. Atolls Devt Advisory Bd, Maldives Youth Council and Council for Dhivehi Language and Literature; worked with UNDP and UNESCO in Swaziland, Lesotho, Mozambique, Bangladesh, Fiji and Western Samoa 1991–92; joined UNICEF as Chief of Educ. for UNICEF in Tanzania 1992, served UNICEF as its Rep. and Head of Mission in several countries, including Acting Regional Dir UNICEF Regional Office for S Asia, Interim Rep. of Afghanistan, Yemen and Montenegro, and Acting Rep. in FYR Macedonia, Special Rep. in Afghanistan 2002–05, advised Govt of Pres. Hamid Karzai and assisted in co-ordination and rehabilitation of educ. sector on behalf of UN Assistance Mission for Afghanistan, apptd Assoc. Dir UN Devt Group (UNDG) Office, New York 2005, served as Sec. UNDG Man. Group, exercised oversight responsibilities for setting up of first UN Jt Office pilot and led HQ support to UN Resident Co-ordinator system for Europe and Middle East, UNICEF Country Rep. in Turkmenistan –2008; fmr mem. Maldivian Democratic Party (MDP), cand. for presidency at second party congress; est. Nat. Alliance party; Leader Gaumee Itthihaad Party, formed alliance with MDP Sept. 2008; Vice-Pres. of Maldives (first elected vice-pres.) 2008–12, Pres. 2012–13. *Address:* c/o The President's Office, Boduthakurufaanu Magu, Malé 20-05, Maldives (office).

WAHL, Jacques Henri; French fmr civil servant; b. 18 Jan. 1932, Lille; s. of Abraham Wahl and Simone Kornbluth; m. Inna Cytrin 1969; two s. one d.; ed Inst. d'Etudes Politiques, Paris, Univs of Lille and Paris, Ecole Nat. d'Admin; Insp. des Finances 1961–; Treasury Dept 1965–68; Special Asst to Ministers of Econ. and Finance, François Ortoli 1968–69, Valéry Giscard d'Estaing 1969–71; Asst Dir of the Treasury for Int. Affairs 1971–73; Chair. Invisible Transactions Cttee, OECD 1971–73; Lecturer Inst. d'Etudes Politiques and Ecole Nat. d'Admin., Paris 1969–73; Financial Minister, French Embassies, USA and Canada 1973–78; Exec. Dir IMF, IBRD 1973–78; Sec.-Gen. to the Presidency of the French Repub. 1978–81; Insp.-Gen. des Finances 1981; Dir-Gen. Banque Nat. de Paris 1982 (known as BNP Paribas 2000–), Vice-Chair. 1993–97, Adviser to Chair. 1994–2001, Chair. Bd of Dirs BNP Paribas Canada 2010, mem. Bd of Dirs BancWest (subsidiary of BNP Paribas) 1998–2012; Chair. Banque Nat. de Paris Intercontinentale 1993–97, mem. Bd 1994–; Officier, Légion d'honneur, Officier Ordre nat. du Mérite, Commdr Ordre Nat. de Côte d'Ivoire, Officier Ordre du Mérite de la République Centrafricaine, Chevalier Ordre du Mérite de Haute Volta, also honours from Portugal, Brazil, Venezuela, Greece, Sweden and Germany. *Address:* BNP Paribas, 19 boulevard des Italiens, 75009 Paris (office); 15 avenue de la Bourdonnais, 75007 Paris, France (home).

WAHL, Philippe, MA; French business executive; *Chairman, President and CEO, La Poste;* ed Sciences-Po Paris, École Nationale d'Admin; began career as auditor and maître des requêtes at Council of State, Special Adviser to Chair. of Bd 1986; Tech. Adviser for Econ., Financial and Tax Affairs, Office of Prime Minister Michel Rocard 1989; CEO Caisse Nationale des Caisses d'Epargne (CNCE) and mem. Man. Bd CNCE at CE Participations; Adviser to Chair. of Compagnie Bancaire 1991–94, Sr Vice-Pres. 1994–97, apptd CEO Groupe Caisse d'Epargne, SA 1999, Adviser to Global Banking and Markets Board in London and Man. Dir for France, Belgium and Luxembourg 2008–11; Specialist Financial Services, BNP Paribas 1997–2002; Chair. Ecureuil Assurances Iard –2002, Ecureuil Gestion –2002, Ecureuil Vie –2002; Vice-Chair. Supervisory Bd Crédit Foncier de France; Vice-Chair. Bolloré group 2006–; Man. Dir Royal Bank of Scotland, France at Royal Bank of Scotland Group plc 2007–08; Group Sr Vice-Pres. La Poste SA –2013, Chair. Man. Bd, La Banque Postale SA and Sr Vice-Pres. La Poste Group 2011–13, Chair., Pres. and CEO La Poste 2013–; Chair. and CEO Holassure, Sopassure; CEO Havas Group 2005–06; Dir, Cie Financière Eulia, Caisse d'Epargne Financement; mem. Supervisory Bd CNP Assurances SA 2001–, CDC IXIS (Perm. Rep. of CNCEP on Supervisory Bd of CDC IXIS Capital Markets, CDC IXIS Asset Management, CDC IXIS Private Capital Management); Perm. Rep. of Ecureuil Participations on Bd of Dirs of Alliance Entreprendre, of CNCEP on Bd of Dirs of Mutuelle du Mans Assurances IARD (MMA IARD) and Mutuelle du Mans Assurances Vie; Dir, CNP Assurances SA 2011–. *Address:* La Poste, 44 boulevard de Vaugirard, 75757 Paris Cedex 15, France (office). *Telephone:* 1-55-44-01-01 (office). *Fax:* 1-55-44-01-25 (office). *E-mail:* jean-paul.bailly@laposte.fr (office). *Website:* www.laposte.fr (office).

WAHLBERG, Mark Robert; American actor and musician; b. 5 June 1971, Dorchester, Boston, Mass; s. of the late Donal E. Wahlberg and of Alma Wahlberg; m. Rhea Durham; three c. *Films:* Renaissance Man 1994, The Basketball Diaries 1995, Fear 1996, Traveller 1997, Boogie Nights 1997, The Big Hit 1998, The Corruptor 1999, Three Kings 1999, The Yards 2000, The Perfect Storm 2000, Metal God 2000, Planet of the Apes 2001, Rock Star 2001, The Truth About Charlie 2003, The Italian Job 2003, I Heart Huckabees 2004, Four Brothers 2005, Invincible 2006, The Departed (Best Supporting Actor Nat. Soc. of Film Critics 2007) 2006, Shooter 2007, We Own the Night 2007, The Happening 2008, Max Payne 2008, The Lovely Bones 2009, Date Night 2010, The Other Guys 2010, The Fighter 2010, Contraband 2012, Ted 2012, Pain & Gain 2013. *Television:* Teen Vid II (Video) 1991, The Substitute 1993; exec. producer Entourage (series). *Recordings include:* albums: Music For the People 1991, You Gotta Believe 1992 (as Marky Mark and the Funky Bunch). *Address:* William Morris Endeavor Entertainment, 9601 Wilshire Blvd., Beverly Hills, CA 90210, USA. *Website:* www.markwahlberg.com (office).

WAHLROOS, Björn Arne Christer, MSc, DSc; Finnish economist, academic and banking executive; *Chairman, Nordea Bank AB*; b. 10 Oct. 1952, Helsinki; s. of Bror Wahlroos and Marita Wahlroos; m. Saara Wahlroos; one s. one d.; ed Hanken School of Econs; Acting Lecturer and Asst Prof. of Finance, Swedish School of Econs 1974–79, Prof. and Acting Prof. of Econs 1979–85; Visiting Asst Prof. of Econs, Brown Univ., USA 1980–81; Visiting Assoc. Prof. of Managerial Econs and Decision Sciences, Kellogg Grad. School of Man., Northwestern Univ., USA 1983–84; various positions with Union Bank of Finland, including Exec. Vice-Pres. and mem. Exec. Cttee 1985–92; Pres. Mandatum & Co. Ltd 1992–97; Chair. Mandatum Bank Plc 1998–2000; Pres. and Group CEO Sampo Plc 2001–09, Chair. 2009–, Chair. Sampo Bank Plc 2005–07; Chair. Nordea Bank AB 2011–; Chair. UPM-Kymmene; rank of Capt. in Reserves, Finnish Defence Forces. *Address:* Nordea Bank AB, Smålandsgatan 17, 105 71 Stockholm, Sweden (office). *Telephone:* (8) 614-7000 (office). *Fax:* (8) 105-069 (office). *E-mail:* info@nordea .com (office). *Website:* www.nordea.com (office).

WAHLSTRÖM, Margareta, BA; Swedish international organization official and UN official; *Assistant Secretary-General for Disaster Risk Reduction and Special Representative of the Secretary-General for the Implementation of the Hyogo Framework for Action in the Secretariat for the International Strategy for Disaster Reduction, United Nations;* b. 30 March 1950; ed Univ. of Stockholm; has held numerous positions with non-governmental orgs and pvt. cos in SE Asia, Latin America and Africa; several sr positions with Int. Fed. of the Red Cross and Red Crescent Socs, Geneva 1989–2000, including Under-Sec.-Gen. for the Response and Operations Coordination Div.; ind. consultant 2000–02; fmr Chief of Staff of the Special Rep. of the Sec.-Gen., UN Assistance Mission in Afghanistan (UNAMA), Deputy Special Rep. responsible for relief, reconstruction and devt –2004, Asst Sec.-Gen. for Humanitarian Affairs and Deputy Emergency Relief Coordinator, UN 2004–08, concurrently Special Coordinator of the Sec.-Gen. for Humanitarian Assistance to Tsunami-Affected Countries, Asst Sec.-Gen. for Disaster Risk Reduction and Special Rep. of the Sec.-Gen. for Implementation of Hyogo Framework for Action in Secr. for Int. Strategy for Disaster Reduction, Geneva 2008–; mem. Comm. on Climate Change and Devt. *Address:* UN International Strategy for Disaster Reduction, Palais des Nations, Geneva 10, Switzerland (office). *E-mail:* isdr@un.org (office). *Website:* www.unisdr.org (office).

WAIGEL, Theodor, DJur; German politician; b. 22 April 1939, Oberrohr; s. of August Waigel and Genoveva Konrad; m. 1st Karin Hönig 1966 (divorced 1994); m. 2nd Irene Epple 1994; two s. one d.; ed Univs of Munich and Würzburg; with Bavarian Ministries of Finance and of Econ. and Transport 1969–72; mem. Bundestag 1972–2002; Chair. CSU Land (Bavarian) Group in Bundestag 1982–89; Chair. of CSU 1988–98; Minister of Finance 1989–98; Bayerischer Verdienstorden, Dr hc (Univ. of S Carolina) 1997. *Leisure interests:* climbing, theatre. *Address:* c/o Bundestag, 11011 Berlin, Germany.

WAIHEE, John David, III, BA, JD; American lawyer, fmr politician and fmr state governor; *Partner, Waihee & Nip LLC;* b. 19 May 1946, Honakaa, Hawaii; m. Lynne Kobashigawa; one s. one d.; ed Andrews Univ., Cen. Michigan Univ. and Univ. of Hawaii; admitted to Hawaii Bar 1976; Community Educ. Co-ordinator, Benton Harbor, Mich. area schools 1968–70; Asst Dir Community Educ. 1970–71; Program Evaluator, Admin. Asst to Dirs, Planner, Honolulu Model Cities Program 1971–73; Sr Planner, Office of Human Resources, City and Co. of Honolulu 1973–74, Program Man. 1974–75; Assoc. Shim, Sigal, Tam & Naito (law firm), Honolulu 1975–79; Pnr, Waihee, Manuia, Yap, Pablo & Hoe (law firm), Honolulu 1979–82; mem. Hawaiian State House of Reps 1980–82; Lt Gov. of Hawaii 1982–86, Gov. of Hawaii 1986–95; Head of Hawaii office of Verner, Liipfert, Bernhard, McPherson and Handwith (law firm), Honolulu 1995–2001; Waihee & Nip LLC (law firm), Honolulu 2002–; Sr Advisor, Dubin Financial LLC (finance co.), also Of Counsel, Dubin Law LLC; mem. Advisory Bd World Wide Real Estate & Development Corpn; Democrat. *Address:* Waihee & Nip LLC, 333 Queen Street, Suite 608, Honolulu, HI 96613-4716, USA (office). *Fax:* (808) 566-0999 (office).

WAINBERG, Mark A., OC, BSc, PhD, FRSC; Canadian medical researcher and academic; *Professor of Molecular Biology and Virology, McGill University;* b. 21 April 1945, Montreal; ed McGill Univ., Columbia Univ., USA; post-doctoral research at Hadassah Medical School of the Hebrew Univ. of Jerusalem, Israel; currently Prof. of Molecular Biology and Virology, McGill Univ., Dir McGill AIDS Centre, Montreal Jewish Gen. Hosp.; Pres. Int. AIDS Soc. 1998–2000; Co-Chair. XVI Int. AIDS Conf., Toronto 2006; Past Pres. Canadian Asscn for HIV Research; Ed.-in Chief Journal of the International AIDS Society; Ed. Retrovirology; Ed. or fmr Ed. Journal of Human Virology, Journal of Leukocyte Biology, International Antiviral News, AIDS Patient Care and STDs, Brazilian Journal of Infectious Diseases, AIDS Research and Human Retroviruses; Officer, Nat. Order of Quebec 2005; Chevalier, Légion d'honneur 2008; Killam Prize (co-recipient), Canada Council for the Arts 2012. *Achievements include:* credited, with his collaborators, with developing the antiretroviral drug 3TC (Lamivudine) to fight HIV/AIDS 1989. *Publications:* numerous papers in professional journals on studies of HIV reverse transcriptase and the molecular basis for drug resistance. *Address:* McGill AIDS Centre, Lady Davis Institute, Jewish General Hospital, 3755 Côte-Ste-Catherine Road, Montreal, QC H3T 1E2, Canada (office). *Telephone:* (514) 340-8307 (office). *Fax:* (514) 340-7537 (office). *E-mail:* mark.wainberg@mcgill.ca (office). *Website:* www.mcgill.ca/microimm/members/professors/wainberg (office).

WAINWRIGHT, Geoffrey, MA, DD (Cantab.), DrThéol; British ecclesiastic and academic; *Robert Earl Cushman Professor of Christian Theology, Divinity School, Duke University;* b. 16 July 1939, Yorks., England; s. of Willie Wainwright and Martha Burgess; m. Margaret H. Wiles 1965; one s. two d.; ed Gonville & Caius Coll. Cambridge and Univ. of Geneva; Prof. of Dogmatics, Protestant Faculty of Theology, Yaoundé, Cameroon 1967–73; Lecturer in Bible and Systematic Theology, Queen's Coll. Birmingham 1973–79; Roosevelt Prof. of Systematic Theology, Union Theological Seminary, New York 1979–83; Robert Earl Cushman Prof. of Christian Theology, Duke Univ. 1983–; mem. Faith and Order Comm. WCC 1977–91; Pres. Soc. Liturgica 1985–87; Co-Chair. Jt Comm. between World Methodist Council and Roman Catholic Church 1986–2011; Sec. American Theological Soc. 1988–95, Pres. 1996–97; Leverhulme European Fellow 1966–67; Pew Evangelical Fellow 1996–97; Hon. DD (North Park Univ.) 2001; Berakah Award, N American Acad. of Liturgy 1999, Festschrift: 'Ecumenical Theology in Worship, Doctrine and Life: Essays Presented to Geoffrey Wainwright on his

Sixtieth Birthday' (ed. David Cunningham and others), Oxford Univ. Press 1999, Outstanding Ecumenist Award, Washington Theological Consortium 2003, Johannes Quasten Medal for excellence in theological scholarship, The Catholic University of America 2006. *Publications include:* Christian Initiation 1969, Eucharist and Eschatology 1971, Doxology 1980, The Ecumenical Moment 1983, On Wesley and Calvin 1987, Methodists in Dialogue 1995, Worship With One Accord 1997, For Our Salvation: Two Approaches to the Work of Christ 1997, Is the Reformation Over? Protestants and Catholics at the Turn of the Millennia 2000, Lesslie Newbigin: A Theological Life 2000, Oxford History of Christian Worship 2006, Embracing Purpose: Essays on God, the World and the Church 2007, Faith, Hope and Love: The Ecumenical Trio of Virtues 2014. *Leisure interests:* music, art, cricket, tennis, travel. *Address:* The Divinity School, Box 90967, Duke University, Durham, NC 27708-0967 (office); 4011 W Cornwallis Road, Durham, NC 27705, USA (home). *Telephone:* (919) 660-3460 (office); (919) 489-2795 (home). *Fax:* (919) 660-3473 (office). *Website:* www.divinity.duke.edu/academics/faculty/geoffrey -wainwright (office).

WAISMAN RJAVINSTHI, David; Peruvian politician and business executive; b. 4 May 1937, Chiclayo (Lambayeque); fmr Chair. Cttee for Small Industries and mem. Bd of Dirs Nat. Soc. of Industries in Peru; nat. spokesman Bd of Co-ordination, Corpn of Small and Micro Enterprises; Man. Dir Industrial Gameda; Founder-mem. and Chair. COPEI 1997–2000; mem. and Congressman Perú Posible (PP) party; elected mem. Congreso (Parl.) 2000; Second Vice-Pres. of Peru and Minister of Defence 2000–02. *Address:* c/o Ministry of Defence, Avda Arequipa 291, Lima 14, Peru (office).

WAITE, Terence Hardy, CBE; British fmr religious adviser, author and broadcaster; b. 31 May 1939, Bollington, Cheshire; s. of Thomas William Waite and Lena Waite (née Hardy); m. Helen Frances Watters 1964; one s. three d.; ed Wilmslow School, Stockton Heath, Cheshire, Church Army Coll., London; Lay Training Adviser to Bishop and Diocese of Bristol 1964–69; Prov. Training Adviser to Archbishop of Uganda, Rwanda and Burundi 1969–71; int. consultant working with Roman Catholic Church 1972–79; Adviser to Archbishop of Canterbury on Anglican Communion Affairs 1980–92, Iranian hostages mission 1981, Libyan hostages mission 1985; kidnapped in Beirut Jan. 1987, held for four years in solitary confinement, released 19 Nov. 1991 after 1,763 days; mem. Church of England Nat. Asscn 1966–68; Founder and Co-ordinator Southern Sudan Project 1969–71; fmr mem. Royal Inst. of Int. Affairs; Trustee Butler Trust (Prison Officers Award Project) 1986–; Founder-Pres. Y-Care Int. (YMCA Int. Devt Cttee) 1998–; Pres. Emmaus UK 1998–, Suffolk Br. of Far East Prisoners of War Asscn; Founder-Chair. Hostage UK 2005–; Chair. Prisons' Video Trust 1998–; Amb. for WWF-UK; Vice-Pres. Suffolk Asscn of Local Councils 1999–, East Cheshire Hospice 2001–; mem. Advisory Bd Gorton Monastery 2003–; Patron The Abbeyfield (Ipswich) Soc. 1996–, Canterbury Oast Trust, COFEPOW (Children (and families) of the Far East Prisoners of War), Friends of the Samaritans (Bury St Edmunds Br.), One World Broadcasting Trust 1987–, Strode Park Foundation for the Disabled, Hearne, Kent 1988–, Bury St Edmunds Volunteer Centre 1994–, Warrington Male Voice Choir 1996–, The Romany Soc. 1997–, West Suffolk Voluntary Asscn for the Blind 1998–, The Bridge Project Sudbury Appeal 1999–, Save Our Parsonages 1999–, The British Friends of Neve Shalom, Wahat al-Salam 2003–, Underpriv-ileged Children's Charity, Bristol 2003–, Children with Aids Charity 2004–, Habitat for Humanity 2004–, Rapid UK 2004–, Sunderland Counselling Services 2004–, and many other orgs; Fellow Commoner, Trinity Hall, Cambridge 1992–; Visiting Fellow, Magdalen Coll., Oxford 2006; Freeman, City of Canterbury 1992, Borough of Lewisham 1992; Hon. DCL (Kent) 1986, (City of London) 1992, (Sussex) 1992, (Robert Gordon Univ.) 2007; Hon. LLD (Durham) 1992, (Liverpool) 1992; Hon. LHD (Wittenberg) 1992; Hon. DHumLitt (Southern Florida) 1992, (Virginia Commonwealth) 1996; Hon. DPhil (Anglia Polytechnic) 2001, (Anglia Ruskin) 2005; Hon. DLitt (Nottingham Trent) 2001, (De Montfort) 2005, (Chester) 2008; Dr hc (Yale Univ. Divinity School) 1992, (Open Univ.) 2009; Templeton UK Award 1985, Roosevelt Four Freedoms Medal 1992. *Publications:* Taken on Trust 1993, Footfalls in Memory 1995, Travels with a Primate 2000; numerous contribs to journals and periodicals. *Leisure interests:* music, walking, travel, Jungian studies, int. affairs and politics. *Address:* Trinity Hall, Cambridge, CB2 1TJ, England.

WAITS, Tom; American singer, songwriter, musician (piano, guitar, percussion) and actor; b. 7 Dec. 1949, Pomona, Calif.; m. Kathleen Brennan 1980; two s. one d.; recording artist 1971–; Grammy Award for Best Alternative Album 1992, for Best Contemporary Folk Album 2000, inducted into Rock N Roll Hall of Fame 2011. *Theatre:* Frank's Wild Years (co-writer, play and music) 1986, The Black Rider 1989, Alice 1992, Woyzeck 2002. *Films:* Paradise Alley 1978, Wolfen 1981, One From the Heart 1982, The Outsiders 1983, Rumblefish 1983, The Cotton Club 1984, Down By Law 1986, Ironweed 1987, Candy Mountain 1988, Cold Feet 1989, Mystery Train 1989, Bearskin: An Urban Fairytale 1989, The Two Jakes 1990, Queen's Logic 1991, The Fisher King 1991, At Play in the Fields of the Lord 1991, Bram Stoker's Dracula 1992, Short Cuts 1993, Mystery Men 1999, Coffee and Cigarettes 2003, Domino 2005, Wristcutters: A Love Story 2006, Seven Psycho-paths 2012. *Compositions include:* Ol' 55, The Eagles 1974, Angel Wings, Rickie Lee Jones 1983, Downtown Train, Rod Stewart 1990, The Long Way Home, Norah Jones 2004, Temptation, Diana Krall 2004, Jersey Girl, Bruce Springsteen, Domino 2005. *Recordings include:* albums: Closing Time 1973, The Heart of Saturday Night 1974, Nighthawks at the Diner 1975, Small Change 1976, Foreign Affairs 1977, Blue Valentine 1978, Heartattack and Vine 1980, Bounced Checks 1981, One from the Heart 1982, Swordfishtrombones 1983, Anthology 1983, Asylum Years 1984, Rain Dogs 1985, Frank's Wild Years 1987, Big Time 1988, The Early Years 1991, The Early Years Vol. 2 1992, Night on Earth (with Kathleen Brennan) 1992, Bone Machine (Grammy Award for Best Alternative Music 1993) 1992, The Black Rider 1993, Beautiful Maladies 1998, Mule Variations 2000, Used Songs 1973–80 2001, Alice 2002, Blood Money 2002, Real Gone 2004, Orphans: Brawlers, Bawlers & Bastards 2006, Bad As Me 2011. *Address:* c/o Anti-Inc, 2798 Sunset Blvd, Los Angeles, CA 90026, USA (office). *Website:* www.anti.com (office). www.tomwaits.com (office).

WAITT, Theodore (Ted) W.; American computer industry executive; *Founder, Waitt Family Foundation;* b. 18 Jan. 1963, Sioux City, Iowa; m. Joan Waitt; four c.; ed Univ. of Iowa; f. Gateway (with Mike Hammond) 1985, Pres. 1985–96, CEO

1993–99, Chair. 1993–2005, relected Pres. and CEO 2001–04; f. Waitt Family Foundation 1993, Waitt Inst. Institute for Violence Prevention 2005, Waitt Inst. for Discovery 2005; Founder, Avalon Capital Group (pvt. investment co.); Vice Chair. Jonas Salk Inst. for Biological Studies; mem. Advisory Council Nat. Geographic Soc.; fmr Chair. Founding Fathers campaign of Family Violence Prevention Fund; Hon. DSc (Univ. of S Dakota); US Small Business Asscn Young Entrepreneur of the Year, US Jr Chamber of Commerce Ten Outstanding Young Americans Award, Nat. Alliance of Business Henry Ford II Award. *Address:* c/o Waitt Family Foundation, PO Box 1948, La Jolla, CA 92038-1948, USA. *Telephone:* (858) 551-4400. *Fax:* (858) 551-6871. *Website:* waittfoundation.org; avalon.com.

WAJDA, Andrzej; Polish film and theatrical director; b. 6 March 1926, Suwałki; s. of Jakub Wajda and Aniela Wajda; m. 1st Beata Tyszkiewicz 1967 (divorced); one d.; m. 2nd Krystyna Zachwatowicz 1975; ed Acad. of Fine Arts, Kraków and Higher Film School, Łódź; Film Dir 1954–; Theatre Dir Teatr Stary, Kraków 1962–98; Man. Dir Teatr Powszechny, Warsaw 1989–90; Senator of Repub. of Poland 1989–91; Pres. Polish Film Asscn 1978–83, Solidarity Lech Wałęsa Council 1981–89, Presidential Council for Culture 1992–94; Founder Manggha Centre of Japanese Art and Technology, Kraków 1987; mem. Inst. de France 1997–, Acad. des Beaux Arts, France 1997–; Hon. mem. Union of Polish Artists and Designers (ZPAP) 1977; Order of the Banner of Labour (Second Class) 1975, Officer's Cross of Polonia Restituta Order, Order of Kirill and Methodius (First Class), Bulgaria 1978, Order of Rising Sun, Japan 1995, Commdr Légion d'honneur 2001, Grosses Verdienstkreuz des Verdienstordens der Bundesrepublik Deutschland 2001; Dr hc (American Univ. Washington) 1981, (Bologna) 1988, (Jagiellonian Univ., Kraków) 1989, (Lyon Univ.) 1995, (Univ. Libre, Brussels) 1995 (Acad. of Fine Arts, Warsaw) 2000, (Polish. Nat. Films, TV and Theatre School, Łódź) 2000; numerous prizes including State First Class Prize 1974, Konrad Swinarski Prize 1976, Premio David di Donatello 'Luchino Visconti' 1978, Prize of Cttee for Polish Radio and TV 1980, Onassis Prize, Greece 1982, Kyoto Prize, Japan 1987, Praemium Imperiale, Japan 1997, BAFTA Fellowship 1982, César Award, France 1983, Pirandello Artistic Award, Italy 1986, 'Felix' European Film Awards (Lifetime Achievement Award) 1990, Golden Lion, Venice 1998, Acad. Award (Oscar) 2000 (donated his Oscar statuette to Museum of Jagiellonian Univ., Kraków 2006). *Films:* Pokolenie (A Generation) (Polish State Prize) 1955, Idę do słońca (I'm Going to the Sun) 1955, Kanal (Jury Special Silver Palm Award, Cannes 1957) 1957, Popiół i diament (Ashes and Diamonds) (Fipresci Prize, Venice 1959, David O. Selznick's 'Silver Laurel' Award 1962) 1957, Lotna 1959, Niewinni czarodzieje (Innocent Sorcerers) 1960, Samson 1961, Sibirska Ledi Makbet (Siberian Lady Macbeth) 1962, L'Amour à Vingt Ans (Love at Twenty) 1962, Popioły (Ashes) 1965, Gates to Paradise 1968, Wszystko na sprzedaż (Everything for Sale) 1969, Polowanie na muchy (Hunting Flies) 1969, Krajobraz po bitwie (Landscape After Battle) (Golden Globe, Milan 1971) 1970, Brzezina (The Birch Wood) (Fipresci Prize, Milan 1970, Golden Medal, Moscow 1971) 1970, Wesele (The Wedding) (Silver Shell, San Sebastián 1973) 1973, Ziemia obiecana (The Promised Land) (Gdańsk Golden Lions 1975, Golden Medal, Moscow 1975) 1975, Człowiek z marmuru (Man of Marble) (Fipresci Prize, Cannes 1978, Jury Special Prize, Cartagena 1980) 1977, Bez znieczulenia (Without Anaesthetic) (OCIC Prize, Cannes 1979) 1978, Panny z Wilka (The Maids of Wilko) 1979, Dyrygent (The Orchestral Conductor) 1980, Człowiek z żelaza (Man of Iron) (Palme d'Or, Cannes 1981) 1981, Danton (Prix Luis Delluc 1982) 1982, Eine Liebe in Deutschland (A Love in Germany) 1983, Kronika wypadków miłosnych (Chronicle of Love Affairs) 1986, Les Possédés (The Possessed) 1987, Korczak 1990, Pierścionek z orłem w koronie (The Crowned-Eagle Ring) 1992, Nastasya 1994, Wielki Tydzień (The Holy Week) (Silver Bear, Berlin 1996) 1995, Panna Nikt (Miss Nobody) 1996, Pan Tadeusz (The Last Foray in Lithuania) 1999, Zemsta (Revenge) 2002, Lekcja polskiego kina (Lesson of Polish Cinema, document) 2002, Katyn 2007, Tatarak 2009. *Television:* Przekładaniec (Roly-Poly) 1968, Macbeth 1969, Pilatus und Andere (for German TV ZDF) (Bambi Award 1972) 1971, Noc listopadowa (November Night) 1975, The Shadow Line (for Thames TV, London) 1976, Z biegiem lat z beiegiem dni (Gone with the Years, Gone with the Days) 1978–79, Zbrodnia i kara (Schuld und Suhne) 1985, Wieczernik (The Last Supper) 1985, Hamlet IV 1989, Silniejsza (The Stronger One) 1990, Mishima 1995, Bigda idzie (Bigda Comes) 1999, Wyrok na Franciszka Kłosa (Judgment on Franciszek Kłos) 2000, Noc czerwcowa (June Night) 2002. *Plays:* Kapelusz pełen deszczu (Hatful of Rain) 1959, Hamlet 1960, 1980, 1989, Dwoje na huśtawce (Two on the Seesaw) 1960, 1990, Demons 1963, Wesele (The Wedding) 1962, 1991, Play Strindberg 1970, Sticks and Bones (Moscow) 1972, Noc listopadowa (November Night) 1974, Sprawa Dantona (The Danton Case) 1975, 1980, Kiedy rozum śpi (When Reason is Asleep) 1976, Emigranci (Emigrés) 1976, Nastasya Filipowna (improvisation based on Dostoyevsky's The Idiot) 1977, Rozmowy z Katem (Conversation with the Executioner) 1977, White Marriage (Yale Repertory) 1977, Z biegiem lat z biegiem dni (Gone with the Years, Gone with the Days) 1978, Antygona 1984, Zbrodnia i kara (Crime and Punishment) 1984, Wieczernik (The Last Supper) 1985, Zemsta (Revenge) 1986, Panna Julia (Miss Julia) 1988, Dybuk 1988, Lekcja polskiego (Lesson of Polish Language) 1988, Romeo and Juliet 1990, The Ghost Sonata (Stockholm) 1994, Mishima 1994, Klątwa (The Curse) 1997, Słomkowy kapelusz (The Straw Hat) 1998. *Publications:* Powtórka z całości) 1986, My Life in Film 1989, Wajada mówi o sobie (Wajda Talks about Himself) 1991, Wajda o polityce, o srtuce, o sobie (Wajda about Politics, Arts and Himself) 2000, Podwojne spojnenie (Double Take), Kino i reszta świata (Cinema and the Rest of the World) 2000. *Address:* Manggha Centre of Japanese Art and Technology, ul. M. Konopnickiej 26, 30-302 Kraków, Poland (office). *Telephone:* (12) 2672703 (office); (12) 2673753 (office). *Fax:* (12) 2674079 (office). *Website:* www.manggha.krakow.pl (office); www.wajda.pl.

WAJED, Sheikh Hasina, BA; Bangladeshi politician; *Prime Minister;* b. 28 Sept. 1947, Tungipara, Gopalganj dist; d. of Bangabandhu Sheikh Mujibur Rahman and Begum Fazilatunnesa; m. Dr M. A. Wazed Miah 1968 (died 2009); one s. one d.; ed Dhaka Univ.; Gen. Sec., Student League, Bodrunnessa Girl's Coll., Dhaka, 1965, Pres. 1966; Sec., Student League, Rokeya Hall br., Dhaka Univ. 1968–69, Founding mem. Abahani Krira Chakra (sports club) 1969; Pres. Bangladesh Awami League 1981–, Leader of Opposition, Bangladesh Jatiya Sangsad (Parl.) 1986–87, 1991–95, 2001–09, Prime Minister 1996–2001, 2009–, also Minister of the Armed Forces Div., the Cabinet Div., Defence, Power, Energy and Mineral Resources, Establishment, Housing and Public Works, Religious Affairs, and Women and Children's Affairs 2009–, also of Home Affairs 2013–, of Foreign

Affairs 2014–; Chair. Bangabandhu Memorial Trust 1994–; mem. Council of Women World Leaders; Dr hc (Boston Univ.) 1997, (Waseda Univ., Japan) 1997, (Univ. of Abertay, Dundee, UK) 1997, (Visva-Bharati Univ., Shantiniketan, India) 1999, (ANU) 1999, (Bridgeport Univ., Conn.) 2000, (Catholic Univ. of Brussels) 2000, (Barry Univ., Fla) 2004; Head of State Medal, Int. Asscn of Lions Clubs 1996, 1998, Medal of Distinction, Int. Asscn of Lions Clubs 1997, Netaji Subhas Chandra Bosh Memorial Medal, West Bengal Cttee of All India Congress 1997, Mother Teresa Award, All India Peace Council 1998, UNESCO Houphouet-Boigny Peace Prize 1998, CERES Medal, FAO 1999, Asia Personality of 2000, Afro-Asian Lawyers Fed. for Human Rights 2000, Pearl S. Buck Award, Randolph-Macon Women's Coll. 2000; ranked by Forbes magazine amongst 100 Most Powerful Women (79th) 2009. *Publications include:* Oraᶄ ᶄokai kêno? (Why Are They Street Children?) 1987, Bangladeshe shoirotôntrer jônmo (Birth of Autocracy in Bangladesh) 1993, Daridro bimochon, kichhu bhabna (Thoughts on Eradication of Poverty) 1993, Amar shôpno, amar shônggram (My Dream, My Struggle) 1996, People and Democracy 1997, Amra jônogoner kôtha bolte eshechhi (We Want to Speak for the People) 1998, Brihot jônogoshᶄhir jonno unnôeon (Development for the Large Masses) 1999, Development of the Masses 1999, Shamorik tôntro bônam gônotôntro (Military Rule versus Democracy) 1999, Antorjatik shômporko unnôeon (Improvement of International Relations) 2001, Bipônno gônotôntro, lanchhito manobota 2002, Democracy in Distress, Demeaned Humanity 2003, (Against Degradation of Humanity) 2003, Living with Tears 2004. *Address:* Office of the Prime Minister, Old Sangsad Bhaban, Tejgaon, Dhaka 1215 (office); Sudha Sudan, Road #5, House #54, Dhanmondi, Dhaka, Bangladesh. *Telephone:* (2) 8151159 (office). *Fax:* (2) 8113244 (office). *E-mail:* info@pmo.gov.bd (office). *Website:* www.pmo.gov.bd (office); www.albd.org.

WAJIH, Sakhr Ahmad al-; Yemeni politician; *Minister of Finance;* Minister of Finance 2011–; mem. Gen. People's Congress –2011, now ind. MP; mem. Yemen Parliamentarians Against Corruption. *Address:* Ministry of Finance, POB 190, San'a, Yemen (office). *Telephone:* (1) 260365 (office). *Fax:* (1) 263040 (office). *E-mail:* support@mofyemen.net (office). *Website:* www.mof.gov.ye (office).

WAKABAYASHI, Masatoshi; Japanese politician; b. 4 July 1934; ed Tokyo Univ.; joined Ministry of Agric. and Forestry 1957, Dir Agricultural Policy Planning Div., Agricultural Structure Improvement Bureau 1978–81; Dir Gen. Affairs Div., Agricultural Structure Improvement Bureau, Ministry of Agric., Forestry and Fisheries 1981–83; Dir Gen. Affairs Div., Dir-Gen.'s Secr., Nat. Land Agency 1981; elected to House of Reps 1983, re-elected 1986, 1993, served as Parl. Vice-Minister, Man. and Coordination Agency 1989–90, Dir Cttee on Transport, LDP 1994; elected to House of Councillors 1998, re-elected 2004, Chair. Cttee on Agric., Forestry and Fisheries 1999; Parl. Vice-Minister, Ministry of Finance 1999–2001, Sr Vice-Minister of Finance 2001, Dir Cttee on Financial Affairs 2001, Research Comm. on the Constitution 2002, Special Cttee on Financial Issues and Revitalization of the Economy 2002, Special Cttee on Protection of Personal Information 2003, Chair. Special Cttee on Prevention of Int. Terrorism 2003, Cttee on Discipline 2004, Dir Cttee on the Budget 2004, Chair. Special Cttee on Mountain Villages 2004; Chair. LDP Policy Bd 2005, Acting Chair. LDP Research Comms on the Constitution and Election System 2005; Minister of the Environment 2006–07, Minister in Charge of Global Environmental Problems 2006–07, Minister of Agric., Forestry and Fisheries 2007–08. *Address:* Liberal-Democratic Party (LDP), 1-11-23, Nagata-cho, Chiyoda-ku, Tokyo 100-8910, Japan (office). *Telephone:* (3) 3581-6211 (office). *Website:* koho@ldp.jimin.or.jp (office); www.jimin.jp (office).

WAKEFIELD, Mary Katherine, BSN, MSN, PhD; American nurse, academic and government official; *Administrator, Health Resources and Services Administration, Department of Health and Human Services;* b. 12 Aug. 1954, Devils Lake, ND; m. Charles Christianson; ed Univ. of Mary, Bismarck, Univ. of Texas; practising nurse and nursing instructor 1975–87; Admin. and Legislative Asst to US Senator Quentin Burdick, Washington, DC 1987–92; Chief of Staff to Senator Kent Conrad 1993–96; Dir Center for Health Policy, Research and Ethics, George Mason Univ., Fairfax, Va 1996–2001; Assoc. Dean for Rural Health, School of Medicine and Health Sciences, Univ. of North Dakota 2001–09, also tenured Prof. and Dir; Admin. Health Resources and Services Admin (HRSA), US Dept of Health and Human Services, Rockville, Md 2009–; fmr Consultant to WHO's Global Programme on AIDS, Geneva; Chair., Nat. Advisory Council for Agency for Healthcare Research and Quality; mem. Pres. Clinton's Advisory Comm. on Consumer Protection and Quality in the Health Care Industry; fmr mem. Medicare Payment Advisory Comm., Nat. Advisory Cttee to HRSA Office of Rural Health Policy; mem. Inst. of Medicine Cttee; Fellow, American Acad. of Nursing. *Address:* Office of the Administrator, Health Resources and Services Administration, Department of Health and Human Services, 5600 Fishers Lane, Rockville, MD 20857, USA (office). *Telephone:* (888) 275-4772 (office). *E-mail:* ask@hrsa.gov (office). *Website:* www.hrsa.gov (office).

WAKEHAM, Baron (Life Peer), cr. 1992, of Maldon in the County of Essex; **John Wakeham,** JP, FCA, PC, DL; British politician and chartered accountant; b. 22 June 1932, Godalming, Surrey; s. of the late Maj. W. J. Wakeham and Mrs E. R. Wakeham; m. 1st Anne Roberta Bailey 1965 (died 1984); two s.; m. 2nd Alison Bridget Ward 1985; one s.; ed Charterhouse; JP Inner London 1972–; MP for Maldon 1974–83, for Colchester S and Maldon 1983–92; Asst Govt Whip 1979–81, Govt Chief Whip 1983–87; Lord Commr of HM Treasury 1981, Minister of State 1982–83; Parl. Under-Sec. of State, Dept of Industry 1981–82; Lord Privy Seal 1987–88; Leader of House of Commons 1987–89, Sec. of State for Energy 1989–92; Lord Privy Seal and Leader of the House of Lords 1992–94; Chair. House of Lords Econ. Affairs Cttee 2005–08; Lord Pres. of Council 1988–89; Chair. Carlton Club 1992–98, Press Complaints Comm. 1995–2002, British Horseracing Bd 1996–98 (mem. 1995–98); Chair. Genner Holdings Ltd 1994–, Alexandra Rose Day 1998–2010; Chair. Royal Comm. on Lords Reform 1999–2000; Chancellor Brunel Univ. 1998–2012; Trustee HMS Warrior 1860 1997–. *Leisure interests:* sailing, reading. *Address:* House of Lords, Westminster, London, SW1A 0PW, England (office). *Telephone:* (20) 7219-3162 (office). *Fax:* (20) 8672-8839 (office). *E-mail:* wakehamj@parliament.uk (office).

WAKEHAM, Sir William Arnot, Kt, PhD, CEng, CPhys, FREng, FIChemE, FIEE, FInstP; British chemical engineer, academic and university vice-chancellor; *Senior Vice-President, Royal Academy of Engineering;* b. 25 Sept. 1944, Bristol,

England; s. of Stanley William Wakeham and Winifred Wakeham; m. Sylvia Frances Wakeham; two s.; ed Univ. of Exeter; fmr Research Assoc., Brown Univ., USA; Lecturer, Dept of Chemical Eng and Chemical Tech., Imperial Coll. London 1971–79, Reader 1979–85, Prof. of Chemical Physics 1985–96, Head of Dept of Chemical Eng 1988, Pro-Rector (Research) and subsequently also Deputy Rector and Pro-Rector (Resources), Imperial Coll. 1997–2001; Vice-Chancellor Univ. of Southampton 2001–09; Visiting Prof., Imperial Coll. London, Univ. of Exeter, Instituto Superior Tecnico, Lisbon; UK Chair. British-Italian Partnership Programme; Chair. SEPnet (South East Physics Network) 2009–; Sr Vice-Pres., Royal Acad. of Eng 2011–; mem. Eng and Physical Science Research Council 2005–11, Chair. Resource Audit Cttee; mem. SE England Devt Agency 2004–09, Bd EU Expert Panel on Philanthropy and Univs; Treas. European Council of Academies of Eng and Technological Sciences, Inc. 2009–; Chair. Exeter Sceince Park Ltd; Dir (non-exec.) Ilika plc 2009–; Fellow, Imperial Coll. London, Portuguese Acad. of Eng 2012; hon. degrees from Univs of Lisbon, Exeter, Loughborough, Portsmouth, Southampton, Southampton Solent and Nova de Lisboa; Touloukian Medal, ASME 1997, Rossini Lecturer, Int. Conf. on Chemical Thermodynamics, Halifax, NS 2000, Ared Cezairliyan Lecturer, Int. Thermal Conductivity Conf. 2001. *Publications:* author, co-author or ed. of nine books; more than 4000 scientific and eng papers on thermophysical properties of fluids, intermolecular forces and thermodynamics. *Address:* Royal Academy of Engineering, 3 Carlton House Terrace, London, SW1Y 5DG, England (office). *Telephone:* (20) 7766-0600 (London) (office); (1392) 861390 (Exeter) (office). *Fax:* (20) 7930-1549 (office). *E-mail:* w.a.wakeham@soton.ac.uk (office). *Website:* www.raeng.org.uk (office).

WAKELEY, Amanda, OBE; British fashion designer; *Creative Director, Amanda Wakeley;* b. 15 Sept. 1962, Chester, England; d. of Sir John Wakeley; ed Cheltenham Ladies' Coll.; launched eponymous label 1990; operation includes retail, wholesale world-wide, bridal and corporatewear consultancy, diffusion range and fine jewellery collection; Co-Chair. Fashion Targets Breast Cancer Campaign 1996–; Glamour Award, British Fashion Awards 1992, 1993, 1996. *Achievements:* raised over £10 million for 'Breakthrough' as Co-Chair. of Fashion Targets Breast Cancer Campaign. *Leisure interests:* travel, sailing, waterskiing, snowskiing. *Address:* Amanda Wakeley, 175–177 Fulham Road, London, SW3 6JW, England (office); c/o Hugh Morrison (office). *Telephone:* (20) 7590-9105 (office); 7739-655492 (mobile) (office). *E-mail:* customercare@amandawakeley.com (office); morrison@mcomgroup.com (office). *Website:* www.amandawakeley.com (office).

WAKUI, Yoji; Japanese business executive and fmr politician; b. 5 Feb. 1942; began career at Ministry of Finance 1964, Deputy Vice-Minister of Finance 1995–97, Dir-Gen. Budget Bureau 1997–99; Vice-Chair. General Insurance Asscn of Japan 1999–2004; Chair. and Rep. Dir Japan Tobacco Inc. 2004–12 (retd); Auditor Nipponkoa Insurance Co. 2006, now Outside Dir; mem. Ind. Cttee, Kewpie Corpn. *Address:* c/o Japan Tobacco Inc., 2-1, Toranomon 2-chome, Minato-ku, Tokyo, 105-8422, Japan. *E-mail:* info@jti.com.

WALA, Adolf; Austrian fmr banker; *Co-Chairman, Finanzmarktbeteiligung Aktiengesellschaft des Bundes (FIMBAG);* b. 18 May 1937, Dürnholz; m.; three c.; ed Commercial School of Vienna Merchants' Asscn; Deputy Supervisor, later Supervisor, Foreign Exchange Dept, Creditanstalt-Bankverein 1957–65; joined Credit and Loans Dept, Austrian Nat. Bank (OeNB) 1965, Head of Office of First Deputy Gov. 1973–80, Deputy Exec. Dir Credit and Loans Dept 1980–88, Gen. Man. 1988–98, Pres. of OeNB 1998–2003; fmr mem. Supervisory Bd Casinos Austria AG 1999, Burgtheater GmbH 1999; currently co-Chair. Finanzmarktbeteiligung AG des Bundes (FIMBAG); currently Pres. Vereins der Freunde der Wiener Polizei (Asscn of Friends of the Vienna Police); Order of Merit, Order of Kts of Malta 1998, Grand Decoration of Honour in Gold with Star for Services to Repub. of Austria 1999; Gold Medal for Outstanding Services to State of Vienna 1994, Arthur von Rosthon Medal 2000. *Address:* FIMBAG, Finanzmarktbeteiligung Aktiengesellschaft des Bundes, Frankhplatz 3, 1090 Vienna, Austria (office). *E-mail:* fimbag@fmarktbet.at (office). *Website:* www.fmarktbet.at (office).

WALCH, Ernest Joseph, M.J., DR.IUR.; Liechtenstein lawyer and politician; *Partner, Walch & Schurti;* b. 1956; ed Univ. of Innsbruck, Austria, New York Univ. School of Law., USA; admitted to Bar, USA 1983, Liechtenstein 1984; Rep. of Progressive Citizens' Party (FBP) to Steering Cttee. of European Democratic Union 1983–93, Pres. FBP 2000–01; mem. Parl. 1989–96, FPB Parl. Spokesman 1992–93, Pres. of Parl. 1993; Minister of Foreign Affairs 2001–05; Co-founder and Pnr, Walch & Schurti (law firm) 1991–; mem. New York State Bar Asscn., Liechtenstein Bar Asscn, Europäische Anwaltsvereinigung e.V., Int. Acad. of Estate and Trust Law, Liechtenstein Asscn of Professional Trustees. *Publications include:* numerous works on int. legal issues. *Address:* Walch & Schurti, Zollstrasse 9, 9490 Vaduz, Liechtenstein (office). *Telephone:* 2372000 (office). *Fax:* 2372100 (office). *Website:* www.walchschurti.net (office).

WALCOTT, Derek, OBE, BA, FRSL; Saint Lucia poet and playwright; b. 23 Jan. 1930, Castries; s. of Warwick Walcott and Alix Walcott; m. 1st Fay Moston 1954 (divorced 1959); one s.; m. 2nd Margaret R. Maillard 1962 (divorced); two d.; m. 3rd Norline Metivier 1982 (divorced 1993); ed St Mary's Coll., Castries, Univ. of the West Indies, Jamaica; teacher, St Mary's Coll., Castries 1947–50, 1954, Grenada Boys' Secondary School, St George's 1953–54, Jamaica Coll., Kingston 1955; feature writer, Public Opinion, Kingston 1956–57; Founder-Dir, Little Carib Theatre Workshop, later Trinidad Theatre Workshop 1959–76; feature writer, Trinidad Guardian, Port-of-Spain 1960–62, drama critic 1963–68; Visiting Prof., Columbia Univ., USA 1981, Harvard Univ. 1982, 1987; Asst Prof. of Creative Writing, Brown Univ. 1981; Prof. of Creative Writing and Playwriting, Boston Univ. 1982–2008; Distinguished Scholar-in-Residence, Univ. of Alberta 2009–11; hon. mem. American Acad. of Arts and Letters; mem. Poetry Soc. (vice-pres.); Rockefeller Foundation grants 1957, 1966, and Fellowship 1958, Ingram Merrill Foundation grant 1962, Eugene O'Neill Foundation Fellowship 1969, Guggenheim Fellowship 1977, John D. and Catherine T. MacArthur Foundation Fellowship 1981; Commdr des Arts et des Lettres 2007; Arts Advisory Council of Jamaica Prize 1960, Guinness Award 1961, Borestone Mountain Awards 1964, 1977, RSL Heinemann Awards 1966, 1983, Cholmondeley Award 1969, Gold Hummingbird Medal, Trinidad 1969, Obie Award 1971, Welsh Arts Council Int. Writers Prize 1980, Los Angeles Times Book Prize 1986, Queen's Gold Medal for Poetry 1988, Nobel Prize for Literature 1992, T.S. Eliot Prize 2011, Eugenio Montale Prize 2011,

BOCA Prize 2011. *Plays:* Cry for a Leader 1950, Henri Christophe: A Chronicle 1950, Robin and Andrea 1950, Senza Alcun Sospetto 1950, The Price of Mercy 1951, Three Assassins 1951, Harry Dernier 1952, The Charlatan 1954, Crossroads 1954, The Sea at Dauphin 1954, The Golden Lions 1956, The Wine of the Country 1956, Ione: A Play with Music 1957, Ti-Jear and his Brothers 1957, Drums and Colours 1958, Jourmard 1959, Malcochon 1959, Batai 1965, Dream on Monkey Mountain 1967, Franklin: A Tale of the Islands 1969, In a Fine Castle 1970, The Joker of Seville (with G. Mcdermott) 1974, O Babylon! 1976, Remembrance 1977, The Snow Queen 1977, Pantomime 1978, Marie Leveau (with G. Mcdermott) 1979, The Isle is Full of Noises 1982, Beef, No Chicken 1985, The Odyssey 1993, The Capeman (musical, jtly) 1997. *Publications:* poetry: 25 Poems 1948, Epitaph for the Young: XII Cantos 1949, Poems 1951, In a Green Night, Poems 1948–60 1962, Selected Poems 1964, The Castaway and Other Poems 1965, The Gulf and Other Poems 1969, Another Life 1973, Sea Grapes 1976, The Star-Apple Kingdom 1979, Selected Poetry 1981, The Fortunate Traveller 1981, The Caribbean Poetry of Derek Walcott, and the Art of Romare Bearden 1983, Midsummer 1984, Collected Poems 1948–1984 1986, The Arkansas Testament 1987, Omeros (epic poem) (WHSmith Literary Award 1991) 1989, Poems 1965–1980 1992, The Bounty 1997, Tiepolo's Hounds 2000, The Prodigal: A Poem 2005, Selected Poems 2007, White Egrets (TS Eliot prize 2010) 2010; non-fiction: The Antilles, Fragments of Epic Memory: The Nobel Lecture 1993, What the Twilight Says (essays) 1998, Homage to Robert Frost (jtly) 1998. *Address:* PO Box GM 926, Becune Point, Castries, Saint Lucia (home). *Telephone:* (758) 450-0559 (home). *Fax:* (758) 450-0935 (home).

WALD, Sir Nicholas John, Kt, MBBS, DSc (Med), FRS, FRCP, FFPH, FRCOG, FMedSci, CBiol. FIBiol; British medical scientist and academic; *Director, Wolfson Institute of Preventive Medicine, Barts and The London, Queen Mary's School of Medicine and Dentistry;* b. 31 May 1944; s. of Adolf Max Wald and Frieda Shatsow; m. Nancy Evelyn Miller 1966; three s. one d.; ed Univ. Coll. London, Univ. Coll. Hosp. Medical School; mem. science staff MRC 1971–; mem. science staff Imperial Cancer Research Fund (ICRF) Cancer Epidemiology and Clinical Trials Unit, Oxford 1972–82, Deputy Dir 1982–83, Prof. and Head, Centre for Environmental and Preventive Medicine, Barts and The London, Queen Mary's School of Medicine and Dentistry 1983–, Hon. Consultant 1983–, Dir Wolfson Inst. of Preventive Medicine 1991–95, 1997–; Hon. Dir Cancer Research Campaign Screening Group 1986–2000; Chair. Study Monitoring Cttee of MRC Randomised Clinical Trial of Colo-Rectal Cancer Screening 1986–, Steering Cttee for Multicentre Aneurysm Screening Study 1997–; mem. Scientific Cttee on Tobacco and Health, Dept of Health 1993–2002, Medicines Control Agency Expert Advisory Panel 1996–; mem. Cttee on Ethical Issues in Medicine, Royal Coll. of Physicians 1988–, HPV/LBC Pilots Screening Group 2000–, National Radiological Protection Bd Advisory Group on Nuclear Test Veterans 2000–; mem. Wellcome Trust Physiology and Pharmaceutical Panel 1995–2000; mem. Information Sub-Cttee, Faculty of Public Health 2001–; mem. Council of Trustees, Foundation for Study of Infant Deaths 2001; mem. Council, Action on Smoking and Health 2002–; Ed.-in-Chief Journal of Medical Screening 1994–; Hon. DSc (Med) (London) 2005; Kennedy Foundation Int. Award in Scientific Research 2000, Foundation for Blood Research Award 2000, Obstetrical Soc. of Philadelphia Int. Speakers' Award 2001, BMA Medical Book Competition Award 2001, US Public Health Service and Centers for Disease Control Award 2002, Harvard School of Public Health Award 2004. *Publications:* Alpha-Fetoprotein Screening – The Current Issues (co-ed.) 1981, Antenatal and Neonatal Screening 1984 (2nd edn co-ed. 2000), Nicotine Smoking and the Low Tar Programme (co-ed.) 1989, Passive Smoking: A Health Hazard (co-ed.) 1991, International Smoking Statistics (co-author) 1993 (2nd edn, co-ed.) 2004, Epidemiological Approach 2004. *Leisure interests:* economics, boating. *Address:* Barts and The London, Queen Mary's School of Medicine and Dentistry, Charterhouse Square, London, EC1M 6BQ (office); Centre for Environmental and Preventive Medicine, Wolfson Institute of Preventive Medicine, Barts and The London, Queen Mary's School of Medicine and Dentistry, Charterhouse Square, London, EC1M 6BQ; 9 Park Crescent Mews East, London, W1W 5AF, England (home). *Telephone:* (20) 7882-6269 (office); (20) 7636-2721 (home). *Fax:* (20) 7882-6270 (office). *E-mail:* n.j.wald@qmul.ac.uk (office). *Website:* www.smd.Qmul.ac.uk/wolfson (office).

WALD, Patricia McGowan, LLB; American lawyer and judge; b. 16 Sept. 1928, Torrington, Conn.; d. of Joseph McGowan and Margaret McGowan (née O'Keefe); m. Robert L. Wald 1952; two s. three d.; ed Connecticut Coll. for Women, Yale Law School; Law Clerk, US Court of Appeals for the Second Circuit 1951–52; Assoc., Arnold, Fortas and Porter (law firm), Washington, DC 1952–53; mem. Nat. Conf. on Bail and Criminal Justice 1963–64; Consultant, Nat. Conf. on Law and Poverty 1965; mem. President's Comm. on Crime in the Dist of Columbia 1965–66, on Law Enforcement and Admin. of Criminal Justice 1966–67; Attorney, Office of Criminal Justice, US Dept of Justice 1967–68, Neighborhood Legal Services Program 1968–70; Co-Dir Ford Foundation Drug Abuse Research Project 1970; Attorney, Center for Law and Social Policy 1971–72, Mental Health Law Project 1972–77; Asst Attorney for Legis. Affairs, Dept of Justice 1977–79; Circuit Judge, US Court of Appeals for the DC Circuit 1979–99, Chief Judge 1986–91; First Vice-Pres. American Law Inst. 1993–98; mem. Exec. Bd CEELI (ABA) 1994–97; Judge Int. Criminal Tribunal for Fmr Yugoslavia, The Hague, Netherlands 1999–2001; Chair. Open Soc. Inst. Justice Initiative 2002–04, now mem. Bd of Dirs; Commr, Pres.'s Comm. on Intelligence Capabilities of US Regarding Weapons of Mass Destruction 2004–05; numerous hon. degrees including Hon. LLD (Yale) 2001; August Voelmer Award, American Soc. of Criminology 1976, Woman Lawyer of the Year, Women's Bar Asscn 1984; Sandra Day O'Connor Medal of Honor (Seton Hall Law School) 1993; Margaret Brent Award for Distinguished Women in the Legal Profession 1994, American Inns of Court Award for Ethics 2003, American Lawyer Lifetime Achievement Award 2004. *Publications:* Bail in the United States (with Daniel J. Freed) 1964, Law and Poverty: Report to the Nat. Conf. on Law and Poverty 1965, Bail Reform: A Decade of Promise Without Fulfillment, Vol. 1 1972, Dealing with Drug Abuse: A Report to the Ford Foundation (with Peter Barton Hutt) 1972, Juvenile Detention in 'Pursuing Justice for the Child' 1977, The Rights of Children and the Rites of Passage in 'Child Psychiatry and the Law' 1980, Provisional Release at the ICTY: A Work in Progress in Essays on ICTY, Procedure and Evidence 2001; and numerous learned articles and contribs to journals. *Address:* 2101 Connecticut Avenue, NW, Apartment 38, Washington, DC 20008-1728, USA (home). *Telephone:* (202) 232-1158 (home). *Fax:* (202) 232-2360 (home). *E-mail:* patwald2@cs.com (home).

WALD, Richard C., BA, MA, AB; American journalist, news executive and academic; *Fred W. Friendly Professor of Media and Society, Graduate School of Journalism, Columbia University;* b. New York City; s. of Joseph S. Wald and Lily Wald (née Forstate); m. Edith May Leslie; two s. one d.; ed Columbia Univ. and Clare Coll., Cambridge, UK; reporter, later Man. Ed. New York Herald Tribune 1955–66; Asst Man. Ed. Washington Post 1967; Exec. Vice-Pres. Whitney Communications Corpn New York 1968; Pres. NBC News, 1968–77; asst to Chair. Bd Times-Mirror Co. LA 1977; Sr Vice-Pres. ABC News 1978–2000; Fred W. Friendly Prof. of Media and Society Columbia Univ. 2000–; Chair. of Bd Columbia Spectator (Columbia Coll. daily newspaper); Chair. Worldwide TV News; mem. Advisory Bd Knight Fellowships Stanford Univ.; mem. Bd of Dirs Correspondents Fund, Center for Communication; mem. Bd of Visitors, School of Communication, Univ. of Colo. *Leisure interests:* reading, running. *Address:* School of Journalism, Columbia University, Mail Code 3801, 701 Journalism, 2950 Broadway, New York, NY 10027, USA (office). *Telephone:* (212) 854-0116 (office). *Fax:* (212) 854-7837 (office). *E-mail:* rcw25@columbia.edu (office). *Website:* www.journalism.columbia.edu (office).

WALD, Robert M., AB, PhD; American physicist and academic; *Charles H. Swift Distinguished Service Professor, Department of Physics, Enrico Fermi Institute, University of Chicago;* b. 29 June 1947, New York City; ed Columbia Univ., Princeton Univ.; Research Assoc., Univ. of Maryland 1972–74, Asst Prof. 1976–80, Assoc. Prof. 1980–85, Prof. 1985–2003; Charles H. Swift Distinguished Service Prof., Dept of Physics, Enrico Fermi Inst. 2002–, Chair. Dept of Physics, Univ. of Chicago 2003–; mem. NAS, American Acad. of Arts and Sciences. *Publications:* Space, Time, and Gravity: The Theory of the Big Bang and Black Holes 1977, 1992, General Relativity (widely used graduate textbook) 1984, Quantum Field Theory in Curved Spacetime and Black Hole Thermodynamics 1994, Black Holes and Relativistic Stars (ed.) 1999; more than 100 papers in professional journals. *Address:* Department of Physics, Enrico Fermi Institute, EFI Box 34 - RI 388-C KPTC, University of Chicago, 5801 South Ellis Avenue, Chicago, IL 60637, USA (office). *Telephone:* (773) 702-7765 (office); (773) 702-7006 (office). *Fax:* (773) 702-2045 (office). *E-mail:* rmwa@uchicago.edu (office); rmwa@midway.uchicago.edu (office); physics-chair@listhost.uchicago.edu (office). *Website:* physics.uchicago.edu (office).

WALDEGRAVE OF NORTH HILL, Baron (Life Peer), cr. 1999, of Chewton Mendip in the County of Somerset; **William Waldegrave,** PC, JP; British banker and fmr politician; *Provost, Eton College;* b. 15 Aug. 1946; s. of the late Earl Waldegrave, KG, GCVO and Mary Hermione Waldegrave (née Grenfell); m. Caroline Burrows 1977; one s. three d.; ed Eton Coll., Corpus Christi Coll., Oxford, Harvard Univ., USA; fmr Pres. Oxford Union; Fellow, All Souls Coll., Oxford 1971–86, 1999–; attached to Cabinet Office as mem. Cen. Policy Review Staff 1971–73; mem. staff political office of Rt Hon. Sir Edward Heath 1973–76; worked for GEC PLC 1975–81; MP for Bristol W 1979–97; Parl. Under-Sec. of State, Dept of Educ. and Science 1981–83, Dept of Environment and Spokesman for the Arts 1983–85; Minister of State, Dept of the Environment (Minister for the Environment, Countryside and Local Govt, subsequently Minister for Housing and Planning) 1985–88; Minister of State, FCO 1988–90; Sec. of State for Health 1990–92, Chancellor of the Duchy of Lancaster 1992–94; Sec. of State for Agric., Fisheries and Food 1994–95; Chief Sec. to Treasury 1995–97; Man. Dir Dresdner Kleinwort Wasserstein 1998–2003; Man. Dir and Vice-Chair. UBS 2003–08, Consultant 2008–; Provost, Eton Coll. 2008–; Dir Waldegrave Farms Ltd 1975–; Bristol and West PLC 1997–2006, Henry Sotheran Ltd 1998– (Chair 2007–), Biotech Growth Trust PLC 1998– (Chair. 2012–), Corp. Finance, Dresdner Kleinwort Benson 1998–; Bank of Ireland Financial Services (UK) PLC 2002–06, Fleming Family and Partners Ltd 2008–; Chair. Rhodes Trust 2002–, Nat. Museum of Science and Industry 2002–10, Royal Mint Advisory Cttee 2011–; Pres. Royal Bath and West Soc. 2006; mem. IBA Advisory Council 1980–81, Int. Advisory Bd, Teijin Ltd 2006–08, Remuneration and Nomination Cttee, Bergesen Worldwide Gas ASA 2006–08; Founder Trustee and Chair., Bristol Cathedral Trust 1989–2002; Trustee, Rhodes Trust 1992–2002 (Chair. 2002–11), Beit Meml Fellowships for Medical Research 1998–2006, Mandela Rhodes Foundation 2003–11, Dyson School of Design Innovation 2007–08, Strawberry Hill Trust 2008–, Cumberland Lodge, Windsor 2009, Bd of Lewis Walpole Library, Yale Univ., USA 2008–; Hon. Fellow, Corpus Christi Coll., Oxford 1991. *Publication:* The Binding of Leviathan – Conservatism and the Future 1977. *Address:* House of Lords, London, SW1A 0PW; Provost's Lodge, Eton College, Windsor, Berkshire, SL4 6DH (office); 62 Hornton Street, London, W8 4NU, England (home). *Telephone:* (1753) 671234. *Fax:* (1753) 671283. *E-mail:* provostsecretary@etoncollege.org.uk.

WALDEN, (Alastair) Brian; British broadcaster, journalist and university lecturer; b. 8 July 1932; s. of W. F. Walden; m. Hazel Downes; one s. (and three s. from fmr marriages); ed West Bromwich Grammar School, Queen's Coll. and Nuffield Coll., Oxford; MP (Labour) for Birmingham All Saints 1964–74, Birmingham Ladywood 1974–77; TV presenter, Weekend World (London Weekend TV) 1977–86; mem. W Midland Bd, Cen. Ind. TV 1982–84; columnist London Standard 1983–86, Thomson Regional Newspapers 1983–86, The Sunday Times; presenter, The Walden Interview (London Weekend TV for ITV network) 1988, 1989, 1990–94, Walden on Labour Leaders (BBC) 1997, Walden on Heroes (BBC) 1998, Walden on Villains 1999, A Point of View (BBC Radio 4) 2005–; Chair. Paragon 1994–, Ten Alps 2002–, Capital 2006–; Shell Int. Award 1982, BAFTA Richard Dimbleby Award 1985; Aims of Industry Special Free Enterprise Award 1990; ITV Personality of the Year 1991. *Publication:* The Walden Interviews 1990. *Leisure interests:* chess, reading. *Address:* Landfall, Fort Road, St Peter Port, Guernsey, GY1 1ZU, United Kingdom. *Telephone:* (1481) 722860. *E-mail:* walden@guernsey.net.

WALES, HRH The Prince of; (Prince Charles Philip Arthur George), (Earl of Chester (cr.1958), Duke of Cornwall, Duke of Rothesay, Earl of Carrick, Baron Renfrew, Lord of the Isles and Great Steward of Scotland (cr.1952), KG, KT, GCB, OM, PC, MA; b. 14 Nov. 1948, London, England; eldest s. of HM Queen Elizabeth II q.v.) and Prince Philip, Duke of Edinburgh (q.v.); m. 1st Lady Diana Spencer (subsequently Diana, Princess of Wales) 29 July 1981 (divorced 28 Aug. 1996, died 31 Aug. 1997); two s., HRH Prince William Arthur Philip Louis, b. 21 June 1982, HRH Prince Henry Charles Albert David, b. 15 Sept. 1984; m. 2nd Camilla Parker

Bowles (subsequently The Duchess of Cornwall) 9 April 2005; ed Cheam School, Gordonstoun School, Geelong Grammar School, Trinity Coll. Cambridge and Univ. Coll. of Wales, Aberystwyth; mem. Gray's Inn 1974, Hon. Bencher 1975; Personal ADC to HM the Queen 1973–; Capt. RN 1988, Rear Adm. 1998–, Vice-Adm. 2002–; Maj.-Gen. Army 1998–, Lt-Gen. 2002–; Group Capt. RAF 1988–, Air Vice-Marshal 1998–, Air Marshal 2002–; Col-in-Chief The Royal Regt of Wales (24th/41st Foot) 1969–; Col Welsh Guards 1975–; Col-in-Chief The Cheshire Regt 1977–, Lord Strathcona's Horse (Royal Canadian) Regt 1977–, The Parachute Regt 1977–, The Royal Australian Armoured Corps 1977–, The Royal Regt of Canada 1977–, The Royal Winnipeg Rifles 1977–, Royal Pacific Islands Regt, Papua New Guinea 1984–, Royal Canadian Dragoons 1985–, Army Air Corps 1992–, Royal Dragoon Guards 1992–, Royal Gurkha Rifles 1994–; Deputy Col-in-Chief The Highlanders (Seaforth, Gordons, Camerons) 1994–; Air Cdre-in-Chief RNZAF 1977–; Col-in-Chief Air Reserve 1977–; Pres. Soc. of St George's and Descendants of Knights of the Garter 1975–; Adm. Royal Thames Yacht Club 1974–; High Steward, Royal Borough of Windsor and Maidenhead 1974–; Chair. The Mountbatten Memorial Trust 1979–, The King's Fund 1986; Pres. The Prince's Trust 1976–, The Prince's Scottish Youth Business Trust, Business in the Community 1985, Prince of Wales's Foundation for Architecture and the Urban Enviroment 1992–, Prince of Wales's Business Leaders Forum 1990–; Chancellor, Univ. of Wales 1976–; mem. Bd Commonwealth Devt Corpn 1979–89; Hon. Pres. Royal Acad. Trust 1993–; Trustee Gurkha Welfare Trust 1989; Patron Royal Opera, Oxford Centre for Islamic Studies 1993–, British Orthopaedic Asscn 1993–, Royal Coll. of Music 1993–, Nat. Gallery 1993–, ActionAid 1995–, Help the Aged 1997–, Welsh Nat. Opera 1997–, Guinness Trust 1997–; represented HM the Queen at Independence Celebrations in Fiji 1970, at Requiem Mass for Gen. Charles de Gaulle 1970, at Bahamas Independence Celebrations 1973, at Papua New Guinea Independence Celebrations 1975, at Coronation of King of Nepal 1975, at funeral of Sir Robert Menzies 1978, at funeral of Jomo Kenyatta 1978, at funeral of Rajiv Gandhi 1990, at funeral of King Olav of Norway 1991; Pres. Royal Ballet, Birmingham Royal Ballet 2003–; Hon. FRCS 1978; Hon. FRAeS 1978; Hon. FIMechE 1978; Royal Fellowship of the Australian Acad. of Science 1977; Hon. Fellow, Trinity Coll. Cambridge 1989; Hon. mem. Hon. Company of Master Mariners 1977 (Master 1988), Company of Merchants of City of Edinburgh 1979; Hon. Life mem. Incorporation of Gardeners of Glasgow 1987; Hon. Air Cdre RAF Valley 1993–; received Freedom of City of Cardiff 1969, of Royal Borough of New Windsor 1970, of City of London 1971, of Chester 1973, of City of Canterbury 1978, of City of Portsmouth 1979, of City of Lancaster 1993, of City of Swansea 1994; Liveryman of Fishmongers' Co. 1971; Freeman of Drapers' Co. 1971; Freeman of Shipwrights' Co. 1978; Hon. Freeman and Liveryman of Goldsmiths Co. 1979, Liveryman of Farmers' Co. 1980, of Pewterers' Co. 1982, of Fruiterers' Co. 1989; Hon. Liveryman of Worshipful Co. of Carpenters 1992; Grand Cross of The Southern Cross of Brazil 1978, Grand Cross of The White Rose of Finland 1969, Grand Cordon of the Supreme Order of the Chrysanthemum of Japan 1971, Grand Cross of The House of Orange of the Netherlands 1972, Grand Cross Order of Oak Crown of Luxembourg 1972, Kt of The Order of Elephant of Denmark 1974, Grand Cross of The Order of Ojasvi Rajanya of Nepal 1975, Order of the Repub. of Egypt (First Class) 1981; Grande Croix, Légion d'honneur 1984; Order of Mubarak the Great of Kuwait 1993; cr. Prince of Wales and Earl of Chester (invested July 1969); KG 1958 (invested and installed 1968), KT 1977, PC 1977, GCB and Great Master of Order of the Bath 1975; Dr hc (Royal Coll. of Music) 1981; Hon. DCL (Durham) 1998; Spoleto Prize 1989, Author of the Year 1989, Premio Fregene 1990, Coronation Medal 1953, The Queen's Silver Jubilee Medal 1977, Global Environmental Citizen Prize 2007. *Publications:* The Old Man of Lochnagar 1980, A Vision of Britain 1989, HRH The Prince of Wales Watercolours 1990, Urban Villages 1992, Highgrove: Portrait of an Estate 1993, Prince's Choice: A Selection from Shakespeare by the Prince of Wales 1995, Travels with the Prince 1998, The Garden at Highgrove (with Candida Lycett Green) 2000, The Elements of Organic Gardening (with Stephanie Donaldson) 2007, Harmony: A New Way of Looking at the World (with Tony Juniper and Ian Skelly) 2010. *Address:* Clarence House, London, SW1A 1BA; Highgrove House, Doughton, Nr Tetbury, Gloucestershire, GL8 8TN, England. *Website:* www.princeofwales.gov.uk (office).

WAŁĘSA, Lech; Polish fmr politician and trade union official; b. 29 Sept. 1943, Popowo; s. of Bolesław Wałęsa and Feliksa Wałęsa; m. Danuta Wałęsa 1969; four s. four d.; ed primary and tech. schools; electrician, Lenin Shipyard, Gdańsk 1966–76, 1983–; Chair. Strike Cttee in Lenin Shipyard 1970; employed Zremb and Elektromontaż 1976–80; Chair. Inter-institutional Strike Cttee, Gdańsk Aug.–Sept. 1980; Co-Founder and Chair. Solidarity Ind. Trade Union 1980–90, Chair. Nat. Exec. Comm. of Solidarity 1987–90; interned 1981–82; Founder of Civic Cttee attached to Chair. of Solidarity 1988–90; participant and Co-Chair. Round Table debates 1989; Pres. of Polish Republic 1990–95, Chair. Country Defence Cttee 1990–95, Supreme Commdr of Armed Forces of Polish Republic for Wartime 1990–95; Founder of Lech Wałęsa Inst. Foundation 1995; Founder Christian Democratic Party of the Third Republic (ChDTRP) 1997, apptd Pres. 1998, Chair. –2000, Hon. Chair. 2000–; retd from politics; resgnd from Solidarity 2006; Order of the Bath 1991, Grand Cross of Légion d'honneur 1991, Grand Order of Merit (Italy) 1991, Order of Merit (FRG) 1991, Great Order of the White Lion 1999, Orden Heraldica do Cristobal Colon 2001; 100 hon. doctorates including Harvard Univ. and Univ. of Paris; Man of the Year, Financial Times 1980, The Observer 1980, Die Welt 1980, Die Zeit 1981, L'Express 1981, Le Soir 1981, Time 1981, Le Point 1981; awarded Let Us Live Peace Prize of Swedish journal Arbetet 1981, Love International Award (Athens) 1981, Freedom Medal (Philadelphia) 1981, Medal of Merit (Polish American Congress) 1981, Free World Prize (Norway) 1982, Int. Democracy Award 1982, Social Justice Award 1983, Nobel Peace Prize 1983, Humanitarian Public Service Medal 1984, Int. Integrity Award 1986, Phila Liberty Medal 1989, Human Rights Prize, Council of Europe 1989, White Eagle Order (Poland) 1989, US Medal of Freedom 1989, Meeting-90 Award (Rimini) 1990, Path for Peace Award, Apostolic Nuncio to the UN 1996, Freedom Medal of Nat. Endowment for Democracy (Washington USA) 1999, Int. Freedom Award (Memphis USA), and other awards, orders and prizes. *Publications:* autobiogs: Droga nadziei (A Path of Hope) 1987, Droga do wolności (The Road to Freedom) 1991, The Struggle and the Triumph 1992, Wszystko co robię, robię dla Polski (Everything I Do, I Do for Poland) 1995. *Leisure interests:* crossword puzzles, fishing. *Address:* Lech Wałęsa Institute Foundation, Al. Jerozolimskie 11/19, 00

508 Warsaw, Poland. *Telephone:* (22) 622 22 20 (office). *Fax:* (22) 625 14 14 (office). *E-mail:* sekretariat@ilw.org.pl (office). *Website:* www.ilw.org.pl (office).

WALEWSKA, Malgorzata; Polish singer (mezzo-soprano); b. 5 July 1965, Warsaw; one d.; ed Acad. of Music, Warsaw, Nat. Opera, Warsaw; has sung at Bremer Theater 1994, Staatsoper, Vienna 1996–98, Semperoper, Dresden 1999 and Rome (Teatro della Opera), Berlin (Deutsche Open), Düsseldorf (Deutsche Open am Rhein), Florida (Palm Bech Opera) and others; has participated in numerous festivals in Brussels, Seville, London, Bregenz, Nantes and Athens; numerous honours or prizes including 1st Prize Alfredo Kraus Int. Competition 1992, Prize for Best Mezzo-Soprano, Stanislav Moniuszko Int. Competition, Warsaw 1992, Laureate Luciano Pavarotti Vocal Competition, Phila 1992, Best Graduate, Chopin Acad. of Music, Warsaw, 1994. *Roles include:* Carmen (Carmen), Delilah (Samson and Delilah) Charlotte (Werther), Emilia (Otello), Olga (Eugene Onegin), Jocaste (Oedipus Rex). *Recordings include:* Voce di Donna (a compilation of famous mezzo-soprano arias) 2000, Mezzo (songs and arias in contemporary arrangements) 2000. *Address:* c/o Isabel Wolf, Wolf Artists International LLC, PO Box 492, Gracie Station, New York, NY 10028, USA (office). *E-mail:* bogdanwaskiewicz@wp.pl (office); info@walewska.net (office). *Website:* www.walewska.net (office).

WALI, Yousuf Amin, PhD; Egyptian politician; b. 1930; ed Faculty of Agric., Cairo Univ. and in USA; Reader, later Prof. Faculty of Agric., Cairo Univ.; consultant, Ministry of Scientific Research and Ministry of Agric. and Land Reform; fmr Agric. Planning Consultant in Libya; mem. Nat. Democratic Party, Sec.-Gen. –2002, Deputy Chair. in charge of Internal Affairs 2002; Deputy Prime Minister Sept. 1985; Minister of State for Agric. and Food Security 1982–87, Minister of Agric. and Land Reclamation 1987–2004. *Address:* c/o Ministry of Agriculture and Land Reclamation, Sharia Nadi es-Sayed, Dokki, Egypt.

WALKEN, Christopher; American actor; b. 31 March 1943, Astoria, NY; s. of Paul Walken and Rosalie Walken; m. Georgianne Thon 1969; ed Hofstra Univ. *Films include:* Me and My Brother 1969, The Anderson Tapes 1971, The Happiness Cage 1972, Next Stop Greenwich Village 1976, Roseland 1977, The Sentinel 1977, Annie Hall 1977, The Deer Hunter (New York Film Critics and Acad. Awards for Best Supporting Actor) 1978, Last Embrace 1979, Heaven's Gate 1980, Shoot the Sun Down 1981, The Dogs of War 1981, Pennies from Heaven 1981, The Dead Zone 1983, Brainstorm 1983, A View to a Kill 1984, At Close Range 1986, Deadline 1987, The Milagro Beanfield War 1988, Biloxi Blues 1988, Homeboy 1988, Communion 1989, The Comfort of Strangers 1989, King of New York 1990, McBain 1991, Mistress 1992, Batman Returns 1992, Day of Atonement 1992, True Romance 1993, Wayne's World II 199, A Business Affair 1994, Scam 1994, Pulp Fiction 1994, Wild Side 1995, Search and Destroy 1995, Things To Do In Denver When You're Dead 1995, The Prophecy 1995, The Addiction 1995, Nick of Time 1995, Celluloide 1996, Basquiat 1996, The Funeral 1996, Last Man Standing 1996, Touch 1997, Excess Baggage 1997, Suicide Kings 1997, Mousehunt 1997, Illuminata 1998, New Rose Hotel (also producer) 1998, Trance 1998, Antz (voice) 1998, Blast from the Past 1999, Sleepy Hollow 1999, Kiss Toledo Goodbye 1999, The Opportunists 2000, Jungle Juice 2001, Scotland, Pa. 2001, Joe Dirt 2001, America's Sweethearts 2001, The Affairs of the Necklace 2001, Poolhall Junkies 2002, The Country Bears 2002, Plots with a View 2002, Catch Me If You Can (BAFTA Award for Best Supporting Actor) 2003, Kangaroo Jack 2003, Gigli 2003, The Rundown 2003, Man on Fire 2004, Envy 2004, The Stepford Wives 2004, Around the Bend 2004, Romance & Cigarettes 2005, Wedding Crashers 2005, Domino 2005, Man of the Year 2006, Fade to Black 2006, Hairspray 2007, Balls of Fury 2007, Five Dollars a Day 2008, The Maiden Heist 2009, The Irishman 2011, Dark Horse 2011, Seven Psychopaths 2012, Stand Up Guys 2012; writer and dir Popcorn Shrimp 2001. *Stage appearances include:* West Side Story, Macbeth, The Lion in Winter (Clarence Derwent Award 1966), The Night Thoreau Spent in Jail (Joseph Jefferson Award 1970–71), Cinders 1984, A Bill of Divorcement 1985, The Dead 2000, The Seagull 2001, A Behanding in Spokane 2010. *Address:* ICM New York, 825 8th Avenue, New York, NY 10019, USA. *Telephone:* (212) 556-5600.

WALKER, Alan Cyril, BA, PhD, FRS; British medical scientist and academic; *Evan Pugh Professor Emeritus of Anthropology and Biology, Pennsylvania State University;* b. 23 Aug. 1938; s. of Cyril Walker and Edith Walker (née Tidd); m. 1st Patricia Dale Larwood 1963 (divorced); one s.; m. 2nd Patty Lee Shipman 1976; ed St John's Coll. Cambridge, Royal Free Hosp., London; Asst Lecturer in Anatomy, Royal Free Hosp. School of Medicine 1965; Lecturer in Anatomy, Makerere Univ. Coll., Kampala, Uganda 1965–69; Hon. Keeper of Paleontology, Uganda Museum 1967–69; Sr Lecturer in Anatomy, Univ. of Nairobi, Kenya 1969–73; Visiting Lecturer, Dept of Anatomy, Harvard Univ. 1973–74, Assoc. Prof. of Anatomy 1974–78, Assoc. Prof. of Anthropology 1974–78; Research Assoc., Peabody Museum 1974–78; Prof. of Cellular Biology and Anatomy, Johns Hopkins Univ. School of Medicine 1978–95 (part-time 1995–97); Prof. of Anthropology and Biology, Pennsylvania State Univ. 1995–96, apptd Evan Pugh Prof. 1996, currently Evan Pugh Prof. Emer. of Anthropology and Biology; Assoc. Ed. American Journal of Physical Anthropology 1974–79, Journal of Human Evolution 1994–98; John Guggenheim Memorial Foundation Fellow 1986, MacArthur Foundation Fellow 1988–93; mem. American Acad. of Arts and Sciences 1996; Foreign Assoc. NAS 2004; Rhône-Poulenc Prize 1997, Int. Foundation Fyssen Prize 1998; Hon. DSc (Univ. of Chicago) 2000. *Publications include:* Prosimian Biology (co-ed.) 1974, Structure and Function of the Human Skeleton (co-author) 1985, Nariokotome Homo Erectus Skeleton (co-ed.) 1993, The Wisdom of the Bones (co-author) 1996, numerous papers published in scientific journals. *Address:* c/o Department of Anthropology, 409 Carpenter Building, Pennsylvania State University, University Park, Pittsburgh, PA 16802, USA.

WALKER, Alice Malsenior, BA; American writer; b. 9 Feb. 1944, Eatonton, Ga; d. of Willie L. Walker and Minnie Walker (née Grant); m. Melvyn R. Leventhal 1967 (divorced 1977); one d.; ed Sarah Lawrence Coll.; Hon. PhD (Russell Sage Univ.) 1972; Hon. DHL (Univ. of Mass.) 1983; Bread Loaf Writers Conf. Scholar 1966, Ingram Merrill Foundation Fellowship 1967, McDowell Colony Fellowships 1967, 1977–78, Nat. Endowment for the Arts Grants 1969, 1977, Richard and Hinda Rosenthal Pound Award, American Acad. and Inst. of Arts and Letters 1974, Lillian Smith Award 1974, Rosenthal Award, Nat. Inst. of Arts and Letters 1973, Guggenheim Foundation Award 1979, Nat. Book Award (for The Color Purple) 1983, Pulitzer Prize (for The Color Purple) 1983, O. Henry Award 1986,

Nora Astorga Leadership Award 1989, Freedom to Write Award, PEN Center West 1990. *Publications include:* Once 1968, The Third Life of George Copeland 1970, Five Poems 1972, In Love and Trouble 1973, Langston Hughes, American Poet 1973, Revolutionary Petunias 1974, Meridian 1976, I Love Myself When I am Laughing 1979, You Can't Keep a Good Woman Down 1981, Good Night Willi Lee, I'll See You in the Morning 1979, The Color Purple 1982, In Search of Our Mothers' Gardens 1983, Horses Make a Landscape Look More Beautiful 1984, To Hell with Dying 1988, Living By the Word 1988, The Temple of My Familiar 1989, Her Blue Body Everything We Know: Earthling Poems (1965–90) 1991, Finding the Green Stone 1991, Possessing the Secret of Joy 1992, Warrior Marks (with Pratibha Parmar) 1993, Double Stitch: Black Women Write About Mothers and Daughters (jtly) 1993, Everyday Use 1994, By the Light of my Father's Smile 1998, Alice Walker Banned 1996, Everything We Love Can Be Saved 1997, The Same River Twice 1997, The Way Forward is with a Broken Heart (ed.) 2000, Absolute Trust in the Goodness of the Earth: New Poems 2003, The Third Life of Grange Copeland 2003, Now is the Time to Open Your Heart 2004, We Are the Ones We Have Been Waiting For (essays) 2007, Overcoming Speechlessness 2010, The World Has Changed: Conversations with Alice Walker 2010, Hard Times Require Furious Dancing 2010, Chicken Chronicles, A Memoir 2011. *Address:* Wendy Weil Agency Inc, 232 Madison Avenue, Suite 1300, New York, NY 10016, USA (office). *Website:* www.wendyweil.com (office); www.alicewalkersgarden.com.

WALKER, Charls Edward, MBA, PhD; American economist, academic and fmr government official; *Founder and Chairman Emeritus, American Council for Capital Formation;* b. 24 Dec. 1923, Graham, Tex.; s. of Pinkney Clay Walker and Sammye McCombs Walker; m. Harmolyn Hart 1949; one s. one d.; ed Univs of Texas and Pennsylvania; Pilot instructor, USAF World War II; Instructor in Finance and later Asst and Assoc. Prof., Univ. of Tex. 1947–54; Instructor in Finance, Wharton School 1948–50; Assoc. Economist, Fed. Reserve Bank of Philadelphia 1953–54; Economist and Special Asst to Pres. of the Repub. Nat. Bank of Dallas 1955–56; Vice-Pres. and Financial Economist, Fed. Reserve Bank of Dallas 1958–61; Asst to the Sec. of the Treasury 1959–61; Exec. Vice-Pres., American Bankers' Asscn 1961–69; Under-Sec. of the Treasury 1969–72; Deputy Sec. of the Treasury 1972–73; Adjunct Prof. for Finance and Public Affairs, LBJ School of Public Affairs, Univ. of Texas 1986, now Distinguished Adjunct Prof.; Distinguished Visiting Prof., Emory Univ.; Adjunct Prof., Texas A & M Univ. 2001; Chair. Walker and Walker LLC; Founder and Chair. Emer. American Council for Capital Formation; Co-Chair. Presidential Debates 1976; Chair., Pres. Reagan's Task Force on Tax Policy 1980; Co-Founder Cttee on the Present Danger; Founder Chair. Bretton Woods Cttee, Advisory Cttee on Nat. Issues Convention; Chair. Pres. Nixon's Advisory Cttee on Minority Enterprise; fmr Chair. Walker/Potter Associates; mem. Bd of Dirs Enron Corpn 1985–99; Hon. LLD (Ashland Coll.) 1970; Alexander Hamilton Award, US Treasury; Distinguished Alumnus Award, Univ. of Texas, Baber Award for Exemplary Service to Econ. Educ., Distinguished Service Award, Urban League Award for Contributions to Minority Enterprise and Educ. *Publications:* The Banker's Handbook 1978 (co-ed.), New Directions in Federal Tax Policy 1983 (co-ed.), The Consumption Tax: A Better Alternative (co-ed.) 1987, Intellectual Property Rights and Capital Formation in the Next Decade 1988, Saving: The Challenge for the US Economy 1990; numerous articles in newspapers, magazines and economic and other journals. *Leisure interests:* golf, music. *Address:* American Council for Capital Formation, 1750 K Street, NW, Suite 400, Washington, DC 20006 (office); 10120 Chapel Road, Potomac, MD 20854, USA (home). *Telephone:* (301) 299-5414 (home). *Fax:* (301) 299-5024 (home). *E-mail:* info@accf.org (office). *Website:* www.accf.org (office).

WALKER, Sir David Alan, Kt, MA; British banking executive; *Chairman, Barclays PLC;* b. 31 Dec. 1939; m. Isobel Cooper 1963; one s. two d.; ed Chesterfield School and Queens' Coll., Cambridge; joined HM Treasury 1961, Pvt. Sec. to Jt Perm. Sec. 1964–66, Asst Sec. 1973–77; seconded to staff IMF, Washington, DC 1970–73; joined Bank of England as Chief Adviser, then Chief Econ. Intelligence Dept 1977, Dir 1981–88 (non-exec. 1988–93); Chair. Johnson Matthey Bankers Ltd (later Minories Finance Ltd) 1985–88, Financial Markets Group, LSE 1987–95, Securities and Investments Bd 1988–92, Agric. Mortgage Corpn PLC 1993–94, Morgan Stanley (Europe) (now Morgan Stanley Dean Witter (Europe) Ltd) 1994–2000, Morgan Stanley International 1995–2000, 2004–05 (Sr Adviser 2001–04, 2005–12), Reuters Venture Capital; Dir (non-exec.) and Chair. Barclays PLC 2012–; Vice-Chair. Legal and General group; Deputy Chair. Lloyds Bank Ltd 1992–94; British Co-Chair. British-Moroccan Business Council; UK Chair. Univ. of Cambridge 800th Anniversary Campaign; Chair. London Investment Bankers' Asscn 2001–04; Dir (non-exec.) British Invisibles 1993–, Nat. Power 1990–93; part-time Bd mem. Cen. Electricity Generating Bd 1987–89; mem. Council, Lloyd's of London 1988–92; Gov. Henley Man. Coll. 1993–99, LSE 1993–; Chair. Exec. Cttee of Int. Org. of Securities Comms 1990–92, Cttee of Inquiry into Lloyd's Syndicate Participations and the LMX Spiral; mem. Group of Thirty Consultative Group on Int. Econ. and Monetary Affairs, Inc. (G-30), Washington, DC 1993–; Co-Chair. Univ. of Cambridge 800 Anniversary Appeal; St Paul's Cathedral Devt Appeal, Cicely Saunders Foundation; Amb. for Community Links (East End charity); Hon. Fellow, Queens' Coll. Cambridge 1989; Hon. LLD (Exeter) 2002. *Leisure interests:* music, long-distance walking. *Address:* Barclays PLC, One Churchill Place, Canary Wharf, London, E14 5HP, England (office). *Telephone:* (20) 7116-1000 (office). *Website:* www.barclays.com (office).

WALKER, Derek, MArch, RIBA, FRCA; British architect, town planner, university professor and designer; b. 15 June 1931, Ribchester, Lancs.; s. of the late William Walker and Ann Nicholson; m. 1st Honora Jill Messenger 1957; two s.; m. 2nd Jan Larrance 1983; one d.; m. 3rd Evelyn Claire Happold 2003; f. Derek Walker Assocs, Architects & Urban Planners 1960, Walker, Wright, Schofield, Interior Design/Furniture Design 1966; Chief Architect and Planner, New City of Milton Keynes, UK 1969–76; re-formed practices, Sr Partner Derek Walker Assocs, Walker Wright 1976–; Prof. of Architecture & Design, RCA 1984–90, Chair. Design Faculty; Architectural Design Awards, pvt. houses, urban devts, village plans (two), 1966 (two), 1967, 1968, Civic Trust Awards 1965, 1967, 1968, Financial Times Architectural Awards 1969, first prize numerous nat. and int. competitions for theatres, new towns, shopping bldgs, waterside devts and parks, RIBA Awards 1979, 1980. *Principal projects:* New City of Milton Keynes 1969–82, Sculpture Park, Milton Keynes 1972, Master Planning New City of Jubail, Saudi Arabia 1979–82, WonderWorld Themepark 1982–, StarSite

Birmingham Urban Plan 1984, Commodores Point, Jacksonville, Fla Urban Plan, USA 1985, Ski Resort, Telluride, Colo, USA 1986–88, Lijnbaan Shopping Centre, Rotterdam 1987–89, Gyosei Japanese School 1985–87, Kowloon Park, Hong Kong 1985–87, Energy World, Corby 1986, Olympic Pool and Sports Hall, Kowloon 1986–88, Happy Valley Racecourse Re devt, Hong Kong 1990–96, Ushiku New Town Plan, Japan 1991–95, Clarence Dock Master Plan, Leeds 1991, Royal Armouries Museum, Leeds 1992–96, Museum of British History, London 1996–, Newmarket Racing Museum and Stables 1996–, Xanadu Snow and Leisure Dome, Lancashire 1999–2001, Redcar Super Racecourse Devt 2000–, Nat. Museum for the US Army, Washington, DC 2000–03, Leigh Sports Village 2002–09, Calder Valley Racecourse 2002–, Second Gateway Site, Blackpool 2003–06, Earth Angel (Eco friendly global farm) 2003–, Int. Resort Kalpitiya, Sri Lanka 2006–. *Publications:* British Architects 1981, Los Angeles 1982, Architecture and Planning of Milton Keynes 1982, Animated Architecture 1995, The Royal Armouries: The Making of a Museum (with Guy Wilson) 1996, Derek Walker Associates: The View from Great Lindford 1997, New Towns 1999, Happold: The Confidence to Build (with Bill Addis) 1998; numerous articles. *Leisure interests:* fine art, classical music, jazz, literature and most sports. *Address:* Derek Walker Associates, 45 Black Lion Lane, London, W6 9BG; 4 Widcombe Terrace, Bath BA2 6AJ, England (home). *Telephone:* (20) 8563-9435 (office); (20) 8748-48302 (office); (1908) 605883 (office). *E-mail:* derekwalker@dwadesign.com (office).

WALKER, Donald J., BMechEng; Canadian automotive industry executive; *CEO, Magna International Inc.;* ed Univ. of Waterloo; began career with General Motors Corpn, served in numerous mfg and eng positions; joined Magna International Inc. 1987, served as Vice-Pres. for Product Devt and Strategic Planning, COO 1991–92, Pres. 1992–94, mem. Bd of Dirs 1994–2002, 2005–, CEO 1994–2005, Co-CEO 2005–10, CEO 2010–, also Pres. and CEO Intier Automotive Inc. (subsidiary of Magna); Co-Chair. Canadian Automotive Partnership Council; Founding mem. Yves Landry Foundation. *Address:* Magna International Inc., 337 Magna Drive, Aurora, ON L4G 7K1, Canada (office). *Telephone:* (905) 726-2462 (office). *Fax:* (905) 726-7164 (office). *E-mail:* info@magnaint.com (office). *Website:* www.magnaint.com (office); www.magna.com (office).

WALKER, Sir John Ernest, Kt, MA, DPhil, ScD, FRS; British chemist and academic; *Director, Mitochondrial Biology Unit, Medical Research Council;* b. 7 Jan. 1941, Halifax, W Yorks., England; s. of Thomas Ernest Walker and Elsie Walker (née Lawton); m. Christina Jane Westcott 1963; two d.; ed Rastrick Grammar School, W Yorks., St Catherine's Coll., Oxford; Visiting Research Fellow, Univ. of Wisconsin, USA 1969–71; NATO Research Fellow, CNRS, Gif-sur-Yvette, France 1971–72; European Molecular Biology Org. (EMBO) Research Fellow, Pasteur Inst., Paris 1972–74; Staff Scientist, MRC Lab. of Molecular Biology, Cambridge 1974–98; Dir MRC Mitochondrial Biology (fmrly MRC Dunn Human Nutrition Unit), Cambridge 1998–; Prof. of Molecular Bioenergetics, Univ. of Cambridge 2002; mem. EMBO 1983; Fellow, Sidney Sussex Coll. Cambridge 1997–; mem. Academia Europaea 1998; Foreign mem. Royal Netherlands Acad. of Arts and Science 1999, Accad. Nazionale dei Lincei, Rome 2003; Foreign Assoc. NAS 2004; Founding Fellow, Acad. of Medical Sciences, London 1998; Millennium Fellow, Royal Soc. of Chem. 2000; Fellow, Science Museum, London 2009; Lee Kong Chian Distinguished Prof., Nanyang Technological Univ. 2010; Hon. Prof., Peking Union Medical Coll., Beijing 2001, Univ. of Cambridge 2002; Hon. Fellow, St Catherine's Coll. Oxford 1998, Inst. of Biology 2002, Soc. of Biology, London 2009, FMedSci 2012; Hon. mem. Biochemical Soc. 1998, British Biophysical Soc. 2000; Hon. DSc (London) 2002, (Sussex) 2003, (Liverpool) 2004, (East Anglia) 2006, (Moscow State Univ.) 2007, (Toyo Univ., Japan) 2007; Dr hc (Bradford, Leeds, Oxford, Gröningen, Manchester, Huddersfield, Buenos Aires), (Univ. Paul Sabatier, Toulouse) 2007; A. T. Clay Gold Medal for academic distinction 1959, Johnson Foundation Prize, Univ. of Pennsylvania 1994, CIBA Medal and Prize, Biochemical Soc. 1995, Peter Mitchell Medal, European Bioenergetics Congress 1996, Nobel Prize in Chem. (co-recipient with Paul Boyer) 1997, Gaetano Quagliariello Prize for Mitochondrial Research, Univ. of Bari, Italy 1997, Soc. of Chemical Industry Messel Medal 2000, Royal Soc. of Chem. Award of Biomembrane Chem. 2003, JSPS Award for Eminent Scientists, Japanese Soc. for the Promotion of Science 2004, Lifetime Achievement Award for the topic Molecular mechanisms in mitochondrion and associated human diseases, GeneExpression Systems Inc., Waltham, Mass, USA 2008, Ahmed Zewail Medal, Wayne State Univ. 2010, The Skou Award, Århus Univ. 2011, Gold Seal, Univ. of Bari Aldo Moro 2011, Keilin Memorial Medal and Award of the Biochemical Soc. 2012, Copley Medal, Royal Soc. 2012. *Publications include:* research papers and reviews in scientific journals. *Leisure interests:* cricket, opera music, walking. *Address:* MRC Mitochondrial Biology Unit, Wellcome Trust/MRC Building, Hills Road, Cambridge, CB2 2XY, England (office). *Telephone:* (1223) 252701 (office). *Fax:* (1223) 252705 (office). *E-mail:* walker@mrc-mbu.cam.ac.uk (office); john.walker@mrc-mbu.cam.ac.uk (office). *Website:* www.mrc-mbu.cam.ac.uk/people/walker (office).

WALKER, Lucy, BA (Hons), MA, MFA; British film director; b. London; ed New Coll., Oxford, New York Univ. Tisch School of the Arts (Fulbright Scholar), USA; began directing theatre at secondary school and continued as an undergraduate; directed and produced Querm at Oxford which won the Oxford Univ. Dramatic Soc. Cuppers Awards; fmr Artistic Dir New Company (theatre group), produced outdoor musical productions of The Jungle Book and Tintin and the Broken Ear; appeared frequently at the Soundlab and all over New York City as well as in Los Angeles, San Francisco and Europe, performing mostly solo and also as mem. of experimental ensemble Byzar. *Films include:* Blue's Birthday (video short) 1998; documentaries: Devil's Playground (Best Documentary, American Film Inst. (AFI) DV Fest 2001, Grand Prize Best Film, AFI DV Fest 2001, Audience Award for Best Film, Sarasota Int. Film Festival 2002, Special Jury Prize for Best Documentary, Karlovy-Vary Int. Film Festival 2002) 2002, Blindsight (Audience Award for Best Film (tie), AFI Film Festival 2006, Audience Award Panorama Publikumspreis for Best Film, Berlin Int. Film Festival 2007, Audience Award for Best Documentary, Palm Springs Int. Film Festival 2007, Audience Award for Best Film, Ghent Film Festival 2007) 2006, Waste Land (Audience Award for Best World Cinema Documentary, Sundance Film Festival 2010, Audience Award Panorama Publikumspreis for Best Film, Berlin Int. Film Festival 2010, Amnesty International Award, Berlin Int. Film Festival 2010, Audience Award for Best Film, Full Frame Film Festival 2010, HBO Audience Choice Award for Best Documentary Feature,

Provincetown Int. Film Festival 2010, Audience Award for Best World Cinema Documentary, Maui Int. Film Festival 2010, Audience Award for Best Film, Paulinia Film Festival 2010, Best Film, Paulinia Film Festival 2010, Best Documentary Feature $25,000 Target Filmmaker Award, Dallas Int. Film Festival 2010, Best Documentary Golden Space Needle Award, Seattle Int. Film Festival 2010, Best Documentary, Durban Int. Film Festival 2010, Audience Choice Best Film, Durban Int. Film Festival 2010, Amnesty International Durban Human Rights Award, Durban Int. Film Festival 2010, Crystal Heart Best Documentary Award, Heartland Film Festival 2010, Human Spirit Award, EcoFocus Film Fest 2010, Audience Award for Best Feature Film, EcoFocus Film Fest 2010, Best Documentary, Trinidad & Tobago Film Festival 2010, Jury Award, Flagstaff Mountain Film Festival 2010, Roger's People's Choice Award, Vancouver Int. Film Festival 2010, Prêmio Itamaraty for Best Documentary Feature, São Paulo Int. Film Festival 2010, Special Jury Prize for Best Feature, Amazonas Film Festival 2010, Audience Award, Int. Documentary Film Festival, Amsterdam 2010, Audience Award, Stockholm Int. Film Festival 2010, Pare Lorentz Award, Int. Documentary Asscn Awards 2010, Best Documentary, Int. Documentary Asscn Awards 2010, Grand Prix du Festival, Int. Environmental Film Festival 2010, Jury Award, Frozen River Film Festival 2011, Best of Festival, Wild & Scenic Film Festival 2011, Best in Festival, Princeton Environmental Film Festival 2011, Best Documentary, Movies For Grownups Awards 2011, Best Documentary Feature Film Audience Choice Award, Sedona Int. Film Festival 2011, Keen Hybrid Life Filmmaker Grant, Boulder Int. Film Festival 2011) 2010. *Television includes:* Blue's Clues (series) 1998–2001, Countdown to Zero (documentary) 2010, Independent Lens (series documentary: Waste Land) 2011; acted in: Doc Talk (series) (episodes, War: Past, Present & Future 2010, Episode #2.6 2010). *Publication:* contrib., with Moby, of a chapter to 'Sound Unbound, Sampling Digital Music and Culture' (ed. Paul D. Miller aka DJ Spooky that Subliminal Kid) 2008.

WALKER, Martin, MA; British journalist, writer and broadcaster; *Senior Fellow, Global Business Policy Council, A.T. Kearney Inc.;* b. 23 Jan. 1947, Durham, England; m. Julia Watson 1978; ed Balliol Coll., Oxford, Harvard Univ., USA; mem. staff, The Guardian, Manchester 1972, Moscow Bureau Chief 1983–88, US Bureau Chief 1989–98; Ed.-in-Chief United Press International 2004–07; Sr Fellow, Global Business Policy Council, A.T. Kearney Inc. 2007–; creator and author, Bruno Courrèges crime novel series 2009–; numerous radio and TV broadcasts; many lectures; Congressional Fellow, American Political Science Asscn 1970–71; Public Policy Fellow, Woodrow Wilson Int. Center for Scholars 2000–01; Sr Fellow, World Policy Inst., New School Univ., New York; mem. Nat. Union of Journalists. *Television:* Martin Walker's Russia (BBC series) 1989. *Publications:* The National Front 1977, Daily Sketches: A History of Political Cartoons 1978, The Infiltrators (novel) 1978, A Mercenary Calling (novel) 1980, The Eastern Question (novel) 1981, Powers of the Press: A Comparative Study of the World's Leading Newspapers 1981, The Waking Giant: Gorbachev and Perestroika 1987, Martin Walker's Russia 1989, The Independent Traveller's Guide to the Soviet Union 1990, The Insight Guide to Washington, DC 1992, The Cold War: A History 1993, The President We Deserve: Bill Clinton: His Rise, Falls, and Comebacks 1996, America Reborn: A Twentieth-Century Narrative in Twenty-Six Lives 2000, The Iraq War 2003, Bruno: Chief of Police 2009 (novel), Dark Vineyard (novel) 2009, Black Diamond (novel) 2010, The Crowded Grave (novel) 2011, The Devil's Cave (novel) 2012; contrib. to anthologies and periodicals. *Leisure interests:* skiing, food, wine. *Address:* Global Business Policy Council, A.T. Kearney, Inc., 8100 Boone Blvd, Suite 400, Vienna, VA 22182, USA (office). *Telephone:* (703) 891-5500 (office). *Website:* www.atkearney.com (office).

WALKER, Baron (Life Peer), cr. 2006, of Aldringham in the County of Suffolk; **Gen. Michael John Dawson Walker,** GCB, CMG, CBE, DL; British army officer (retd); b. 7 July 1944, Salisbury, Rhodesia (now Harare, Zimbabwe); s. of William Hampden Dawson Walker and Dorothy Helena Walker (née Shiach); m. Victoria Margaret Holme 1973; two s. one d.; ed Royal Mil. Acad., Sandhurst; joined Royal Anglian Regt 1966, Regimental and Staff Duties 1966–82, with Staff Coll. 1976–77, Mil. Asst to Chief of Gen. Staff 1982–85, CO 1985–87, Col 1996–; Commdr 20th Armoured Brig. 1987–89; Chief of Staff 1 (Br.) Corps 1989–91; GOC NE Dist and Commdr 2nd Infantry Div. 1991–92; Col Commdt Queen's Div. 1991–2000, Army Air Corps 1994–2004; Col Royal Anglian Regt 1997–2002; GOC Eastern Dist 1992; Asst Chief of the Gen. Staff Ministry of Defence 1992–94; Commdr Ace Rapid Reaction Corps 1994–97; Head NATO Ground Forces, Bosnia 1995–96; C-in-C Land Command 1997–2000; ADC Gen. to the Queen 1997–2006; Chief of the Gen. Staff 2000–03; Chief of the Defence Staff 2003–06; mem. NATO Mil. Cttee 2003–06; Gov. Royal Hospital Chelsea 2006–11; Hon. LLD, Hon. DSc. *Leisure interests:* skiing, sailing, golf, shooting, motorcycling. *Address:* c/o House of Lords, Westminster, London, SW1A 0PW, England. *Telephone:* (20) 7219-3000. *E-mail:* walkermjd@parliament.uk (office).

WALKER, Sir Miles Rawstron, CBE; British fmr politician and business executive; b. 13 Nov. 1940, Isle of Man; s. of George D. Walker and Alice Rawstron; m. Mary L. Cowell 1966; one s. one d.; ed Castle Rushen High School and Shropshire Agricultural Coll.; co. dir farming and retail trade; mem. and fmr Chair. Arbory Parish Commrs 1970–76; mem. House of Keys (Ind.) 1976–; mem. Bd of Agric., Local Govt Bd, Manx Museum 1976–81; Chair. Broadcasting Comm. 1979, Local Govt Bd 1981–86; mem. Exec. Council 1981–; mem. Assessment Bd 1983–86; Vice-Chair. Post Office Authority 1984–86; Chief Minister, Isle of Man Govt 1986–96; mem. Isle of Man Treasury 1996–2000; Chair. Isle of Man Swimming Asscn 1997–2005; Pres. Rotary Club 2000–01, Southern Amateur Swimming Club, Port St Mary Rifle Club 1988–2006; Hon. LLD (Liverpool) 1994. *Publication:* Isle of Man Government Policy Documents 1987–1996. *Leisure interest:* Rotary Club, charitable fund raising. *Address:* Magher Feailley, Main Road, Colby, IM9 4AD, Isle of Man (home). *Telephone:* (1624) 833728 (home). *Fax:* (1624) 833728 (office). *E-mail:* miles.walker@manx.net.

WALKER, Neil, LLB, PhD; British academic; b. 5 July 1960; m.; three c.; ed Univ. of Strathclyde; research work and part-time lecturing at Univ. of Strathclyde 1981–86; Lecturer, Faculty of Law, Univ. of Edinburgh 1986–92, Sr Lecturer 1992–95, Prof. of Legal and Constitutional Theory 1996–2006, Hon. Tercentenary Prof. of Law 2007–; Visiting Prof., Univ. of Puerto Rico, Univ. of Tilburg 2000; Prof. of European Law European Univ. Inst. 2000–08, Dean of Studies 2003–05; Regius

Prof. of Public Law 2008–; mem. Ed. . Bds Edinburgh Law Review, European Law Journal; mem. Ed. Cttee European Law series, Cambridge Univ. Press. *Publications include:* Managing the Police: Law, Organisation and Democracy (jtly) 1986, The Scottish Community Charge (jtly) 1989, Edinburgh Essays in Public Law (co-ed) 1991, Policing the European Union (jtly) 1996, Legal Aspects of the European Single currency (co-ed) 1999, Policing in a Changing Constitutional Order 2000, Convergence and Divergence in European Public Law (co-ed) 2002, Sovereignty in Transition (ed) 2003, The Area of Freedom, Security and Justice (ed) 2004. *Address:* School of Law, Edinburgh University, Old College South Bridge, Edinburgh, EH8 9YL, England (office). *Telephone:* (131) 650-2353. *Fax:* (131) 650-2005. *E-mail:* neil.walker@ed.ac.uk. *Website:* www.law.ed.ac.uk/staff/neilwalker.

WALKER, Roger Neville, BArch, FNZIA; New Zealand architect; b. 21 Dec. 1942, Hamilton; s. of Andrew Frank Walker and Margaret Clothier; m. 1985; three s. one d.; ed Hamilton Boys' High School, Univ. of Auckland School of Architecture; with corp. architectural practice, Wellington 1968–70; own practice 1970–; designs include Rainbow Springs, Rotorua, Waitomo Visitor Centre, Whakatane Airport, Gardens Park Royal Hotel, Queenstown, City Centre Shopping Devt, New Plymouth, Marist Provincial Bldg, Ropata Medical Centre, Thorndon New World Shopping Devt, Willis Street Village, Wellington, over 120 houses and apartment devts in New Zealand, Australia and UK; lecturer Auckland School of Architecture, Wellington School of Architecture; New Zealand Order of Merit for services to architecture 1999; New Zealand Steel Award 1984, 16 NZ Inst. of Architecture Awards, five NZ Tourism Awards. *Leisure interests:* photography, travel, motor sport, basketball. *Address:* Roger Walker Architects Ltd, 1920 Egmont Street, Te Aro, Wellington, New Zealand. *Telephone:* (4) 385-9307. *Fax:* (4) 385-9348.

WALKER, Sarah Elizabeth Royle, CBE, FRCM, FGS, LRAM; British singer (mezzo-soprano); b. 11 March 1943, Cheltenham, Glos., England; d. of Elizabeth Brownrigg and Alan Royle Walker; m. Graham Allum 1972; ed Pate's Grammar School for Girls, Cheltenham and Royal Coll. of Music (RCM), London; studied violin and cello and then voice (with Ruth Packer and Cuthbert Smith) at RCM; Martin Musical Trust Scholarship to begin vocal studies with Vera Rozsa 1967; operatic debuts: Kent Opera, Ottavia in Coronation of Poppea 1969, Glyndebourne Festival, Diana/Giove in La Calisto 1970, Scottish Opera, Didon in Les Troyens 1971, ENO, Wellgunde in The Ring 1971; Prin. Singer with ENO 1972–76; debut at Royal Opera House, Covent Garden as Charlotte in Werther 1979; debut at Metropolitan Opera, New York, as Micha in Handel's Samson 1986; has sung opera in Chicago, San Francisco, Göttingen, Geneva, Vienna and Brussels; concert repertoire includes, in addition to standard works, contemporary and avant-garde works by Berio, Boulez, Cage, Ligeti, Xenakis and others; sang Rule Britannia at last night of 1985 and 1989 BBC Promenade Concerts, London; recital début, Wigmore Hall, London 1979; recital tours Australia, N America, Europe; numerous recordings including Handel's Hercules and Julius Caesar and Stravinsky's Rake's Progress; video recordings of Gloriana (title role), Julius Caesar (Cornelia) and King Priam (Andromache); Prince Consort Prof. of Singing, RCM 1993–; vocal performance consultant, Guildhall School of Music and Drama 1999–; Prof., Vocal Dept, RAM 2009–; Pres. Cheltenham Bach Choir 1986–; Liveryman, Worshipful Co. of Musicians. *Leisure interests:* interior design, gardening, battling against incipient laziness. *E-mail:* megamezzo@sarahwalker.com. *Website:* www.sarahwalker.com.

WALKER, Scott Kevin; American politician and state governor; *Governor of Wisconsin;* b. 2 Nov. 1967, Colorado Springs, Colo; s. of Llewellyn Scott Walker and Patricia Ann Walker (née Fitch); m. Tonette Marie Tarantino 1993; two s.; ed Delavan-Darien High School, Marquette Univ.; family moved to Delavan, Wis. 1977; Accountant-Admin., IBM 1988–90; Marketing and Devt position at the Red Cross 1990–93; mem. Exec. Cttee, Wisconsin State Republican Party 1991–, Chair. 5th Congressional Dist 1991–93; elected in special election to Wisconsin State Ass. for 14th Dist 1993–2002 (re-elected several times), Chair. Cttee on Elections and Constitutional Law 1995, Cttee on Corrections and the Courts 1997, mem. Cttee on Health, Cttee on Census and Redistricting, Cttee on Financial Insts, Cttee on Housing; won special election for Milwaukee Co. Exec., Wis. 2002–10; Gov. of Wisconsin 2011– (first US gov. to have successfully kept his seat in a recall election June 2012); Council mem. Milwaukee Co. Boy Scouts America; mem. Wauwatosa Area chamber of Commerce, Wauwatosa Historical Soc.; Republican. *Address:* Office of the Governor, 115 East State Capitol, Madison, WI 53702, USA (office). *Telephone:* (608) 266-1212 (office). *Fax:* (608) 267-8983 (office). *E-mail:* govgeneral@wisconsin.gov (office). *Website:* www.wisgov.state.wi.us (office); www.scottwalker.org.

WALKER PRIETO, Ignacio, PhD; Chilean lawyer, politician and diplomatist; b. 7 Jan. 1956, Santiago; m. Cecilia Echenique; ed Univ. of Chile, Princeton Univ., USA; lawyer, Vicariate of Solidarity, Archbishop of Santiago 1978–82; Research Assoc., CIEPLAN (Economic Research Corporation for Latin America) 1985–90, Exec. Dir 2003–04; Dir of Policy and Institutional Relations, General Secretariat of the Presidency 1990–93; mem. Chamber of Deputies 1994–2002; Head of Political Studies, Andrés Bello Univ. 2002–03; Amb. to Italy 2004; Minister of Foreign Affairs 2004–06; Visiting Prof. and Researcher, Princeton Univ. 2007–08; mem. Senate for Quinta, de Valparaíso (Cordillera) 2010–; Visiting Prof., Kellogg Inst. for Int. Relations, Univ. of Notre Dame 1987; mem. Advisory Council Latin America Studies Program, Princeton Univ. 1994–97; mem. Advisory Council, Kellogg Inst. for Int. Relations, Univ. of Notre Dame 2000. *Address:* Senado de la República de Chile, Avenida Pedro Montt s/n Valparaíso, Chile (office). *Telephone:* (32) 25-4688 (office). *Fax:* (32) 25-4752 (office). *E-mail:* iwalker@senado.cl (office). *Website:* www.ignaciowalker.cl (office).

WALL, Brad, BPA; Canadian politician; *Premier of Saskatchewan and President of the Executive Council;* b. 24 Nov. 1965, Swift Current, Sask.; m. Tami Wall; one s. two d.; ed Univ. of Saskatchewan, Saskatoon, Investment Funds Inst. of Canada; fmr Ministerial Asst, Prov. Govt of Sask.; fmr owner of several businesses, including The Last Stand Adventure Co.; Dir of Business Devt, City of Swift Current 1991; MLA, Sask. Legislature (Swift Current) 1999–; Leader Saskatchewan Party 2004–; Premier of Sask. and Pres. Exec. Council 2007–; Founding mem. and Western Co-Chair. Alliance for the Future of Young Canadians late 1980s; Founding Bd mem. Southwest Centre for Entrepreneurial Devt; active in community service work and on several bds spanning local events, econ. devt, and

health care recruitment and retention; Econ. Developer of the Year Award for 1998, Saskatchewan Econ. Developers Asscn 1999. *Address:* Office of the Premier, Room 226, Legislative Building, 2405 Legislative Drive, Regina, SK S4S 0B3, Canada (office). *Telephone:* (306) 787-9433 (office). *Fax:* (306) 787-9433 (office). *E-mail:* premier@gov.sk.ca (office). *Website:* www.gov.sk.ca (office); www.bradwall.com.

WALL, Brian; American sculptor and academic (retd); *Emeritus Professor, University of California, Berkeley;* b. 5 Sept. 1931, London, England; s. of Arthur F. Wall and Dorothy Seymour; m. Sylvia Brown 1973; two s.; ed Luton Coll. of Art, England; Asst Prof. of Art, Univ. of Calif. at Berkeley 1975–77, Assoc. Prof. 1977–81, Prof. 1981–94, Emer. Prof. 1994–. *Address:* 306 Lombard Street, San Francisco, CA 94133, USA. *Telephone:* (510) 652-6042.

WALL, Charles Terence Clegg (Terry), PhD, FRS; British mathematician and academic; *Professor Emeritus of Pure Mathematics, University of Liverpool;* b. 14 Dec. 1936, Bristol, England; s. of Charles Wall and Ruth Wall (née Clegg); m. Alexandra Joy Hearnshaw 1959; two s. two d.; ed Marlborough Coll. and Trinity Coll., Cambridge; Fellow of Trinity Coll. 1959–64; Harkness Fellow, Inst. for Advanced Study, Princeton, USA 1960–61; Lecturer, Univ. of Cambridge 1961–64; Reader in Math. and Fellow of St Catherine's Coll., Oxford 1964–65; Prof. of Pure Math., Univ. of Liverpool 1965–99, Prof. Emer. 1999–; Royal Soc. Leverhulme Visiting Prof., CIEA, Mexico 1967; Science and Eng Research Council Sr Research Fellow 1983–88; mem. Council of Royal Soc. 1974–76, Council of London Math. Soc. 1972–80, 1992–96, Pres. 1978–80; Treas. Wirral Area SDP 1985–88, Wirral West Liberal Democrat Party 1988–2013; Foreign mem. Royal Danish Acad. 1990; Hon. mem. Irish Math. Soc. 2001; Jr Berwick Prize 1965, Sr Whitehead Prize 1976, Polya Prize, London Math. Soc. 1988, Sylvester Medal, Royal Soc. 1988. *Publications:* Surgery on Compact Manifolds 1971, A Geometric Introduction to Topology 1971, The Geometry of Topological Stability 1995, Singular Points of Plane Curves 2004; more than 170 research publs in math. journals. *Leisure interests:* reading, walking, gardening. *Address:* Department of Mathematical Sciences, University of Liverpool, Liverpool, L69 3BX (office); 5 Kirby Park, West Kirby, Wirral, Merseyside, CH48 2HA, England (home). *Telephone:* (151) 794-4060 (office); (151) 625-5063 (home). *E-mail:* ctcw@liv.ac.uk (office). *Website:* www.liv.ac.uk/~ctcw/homepage.html (office).

WALL, Frank A., BCL, LLB, LLM; Irish public official and solicitor; *Director, Fisheries Policy, European Union;* b. 10 Oct. 1949, Limerick; s. of Frank M. Wall and Eileen Pierse; m. Margot Hourigan 1977; three s. one d.; ed Mungret Coll., Limerick, Univ. Coll., Cork, Inc. Law Soc., Dublin and Free Univ. of Brussels; Adviser Group of European Progressive Democrats, European Parl. 1974–79; Adviser to Minister for Agric., Dublin 1980; Nat. Dir of Elections 1982; Senator 1982–83; mem. Exec. Cttee, European Movt 1980–91, Chair. 1987–91; Gen. Sec. Fianna Fáil 1981–91; mem. Bd, Friends of Fianna Fáil Inc., USA 1986–91; Co-founder Inst. of Int. and European Affairs 1990, Chair. Brussels Br. 1998–2001, 2011–12; Dir Inter-Institutional Affairs, Council of the EU 1991–2004; Dir Fisheries Policy 2004–. *Publications:* European Regional Policy (with Sean Brosnan) 1978, Changing Balance between European Institutions 1999. *Leisure interests:* politics, Gaelic football, golf, rugby (Chair. Munster Rugby Supporters Club, Brussels). *Address:* Council of the European Union, Rue de la Loi 175, 1048 Brussels, Belgium (office). *Telephone:* (2) 281-80-55 (office). *Fax:* (2) 281-82-61 (office). *E-mail:* frank.wall@consilium.europa.eu (office).

WALL, Jeffrey (Jeff) D., OC, MA, FRSC; Canadian artist and academic; b. 29 Sept. 1946, Vancouver, BC; ed Univ. of British Columbia, Courtauld Inst., Univ. of London, UK; Asst Prof., Nova Scotia Coll. of Art and Design 1974–75; Assoc. Prof., Simon Fraser Univ., Vancouver 1976–87; fmr Prof. of Fine Arts, Univ. of British Columbia; mem. Faculty, European Graduate School; Int. Photography Prize, Hasselblad Foundation 2002, Audain Prize for Lifetime Achievement (BC's annual award for the visual arts) 2008. *Works include:* The Destroyed Room 1978, Picture for Women 1979, The Children's Pavilion (with Dan Graham), Woman and Her Doctor 1980, Mimic 1982, The Storyteller 1986, The Outburst 1989, The Vampires' Picnic 1991, Dead Troops Talk 1992, A Sudden Gust of Wind (after Hokusai) 1993. *Publications include:* Jeff Wall: Transparencies 1987, De Duve, Thierry and Boris Groys 1996.

WALLACE, Bruce, PhD; American geneticist and academic; *University Distinguished Professor Emeritus of Biology, Virginia Polytechnic Institution and State University;* b. 18 May 1920, McKean, Pa; s. of George E. Wallace and Rose Paterson Wallace; m. Miriam Covalla 1945; one s. one d.; ed Columbia Coll. and Columbia Univ.; Research Assoc., Dept of Genetics, Carnegie Inst. of Washington 1947–49; Geneticist, later Asst Dir, Biological Lab., Cold Spring Harbour, NY 1949–58; Assoc. Prof., Cornell Univ. 1958–61, Prof. of Genetics 1961–81; Univ. Distinguished Prof. of Biology, Virginia Polytechnic Inst. and State Univ. 1981–94, Prof. Emer. 1994–; mem. NAS, American Acad. of Arts and Sciences; Alexander von Humbolt Sr US Scientist Award 1986. *Publications:* Radiation, Genes and Man (with Th. Dobzhansky) 1959, Adaptation (with A. M. Srb) 1961, Chromosomes, Giant Molecules and Evolution 1966, Topics in Population Genetics 1968, Genetic Load 1970, Essays in Social Biology (3 vols) 1972, Basic Population Genetics 1981, Dobzhansky's Genetics of Natural Populations I–XLIII (with others) 1982, Human Culture: A Moment in Evolution (with others) 1983, Biology for Living (with G. M. Simmons, Jr) 1987, Fifty Years of Genetic Load: An Odyssey 1991, The Search for the Gene 1992, The Study of Gene Action (with J. O. Falkinham) 1997, The Environment: As I See It, Science Is Not Enough 1998, The Environment 2: As I See It, The Mold Must Be Broken 2000, The Fringes of Glory: The Cold Spring Harbor Laboratories of the 1950s. *Leisure interest:* promotion of environmental literacy. *Address:* 940 McBryde Drive, Blacksburg, VA 24060, USA. *Telephone:* (540) 951-2464. *Fax:* (540) 951-2464.

WALLACE, Sir David James, Kt, CBE, PhD, FRS, CEng, FREng, FInstP, FRSE; British theoretical physicist and fmr college principal; b. 7 Oct. 1945, Hawick, Scotland; s. of Robert Elder Wallace and Jane McConnell Wallace (née Elliot); m. Elizabeth Anne Yeats 1970; one d.; ed Hawick High School and Univ. of Edinburgh; Harkness Fellow, Princeton Univ., USA 1970–72; Lecturer in Physics, Univ. of Southampton 1972–78, Reader 1978–79; Tait Prof. of Math. Physics, Univ. of Edinburgh 1979–93, Head of Physics 1984–87; Vice-Chancellor Loughborough Univ. 1994–2005; Master of Churchill Coll. Cambridge 2006–14, N. M. Rothschild

& Sons Prof. of Math. Sciences, Univ. of Cambridge and Dir Isaac Newton Inst. 2006–11; Dir Edin. Concurrent Supercomputer 1987–89, Edinburgh Parallel Computing Centre 1990–93; mem. Science and Eng Research Council 1990–94, subsequently Eng and Physical Sciences Research Council 1994–98, Chair. Physics Cttee 1987–90, Chair. Science Bd 1990–94, Chair. Tech. Opportunities Panel 1994–98; mem. EC Physics Panel, Human Capital and Mobility Programme 1991–94, EC Large Scale Facilities Evaluation Panel 1995–97; mem. European Science and Tech. Ass. 1997–98; Chair. CVCP/SCOP Task Force on Sport in Higher Educ. 1995–97, Value for Money Steering Group, Higher Educ. Funding Council for England 1997–2003; mem. Royal Soc. Scientific and Industrial Award Cttees 1990–95, Scottish Higher Educ. Funding Council 1993–97, LINK Bd, Office of Science and Tech. 1995–98, LINK/Teaching Co. Scheme Bd 1999–2001; Chair. e-Science Steering Cttee, Office of Science and Tech. 2001–06, Teaching Co. Scheme Quinquennial Review 2001; Dir (non-exec.) The Scottish Life Assurance Co. 1999–2001, Taylor & Francis Group PLC 2000–04, UK e-Universities Ltd 2001–04; Pres. Physics Section Br. Asscn for the Advancement of Science 1994, Inst. of Physics 2002–04; mem. Council, Royal Soc. 2001–02, Treas. and Vice-Pres. 2002–07; Chair. Council for the Math. Sciences 2006–10; Vice-Pres. and mem. Council, Royal Soc. of Edinburgh 2013–; DL for Leics. 2001–06; Hon. Fellow, Inst. of Math. and Its Applications 2009; Hon. DEng (Heriot Watt) 2002; Hon. DSc (Edinburgh) 2003, (Leicester) 2005, (Loughborough) 2006, (Southampton) 2006, (East Anglia) 2009; Maxwell Medal, Inst. of Physics 1980. *Publications:* numerous publs in research and review journals on a number of areas of theoretical physics and computing. *Leisure interests:* exercise, eating well, mycophagy. *Address:* Churchill College, Cambridge, CB3 0DS, England (office). *Telephone:* (1223) 336142 (office). *E-mail:* david.wallace@chu.cam.ac.uk (office). *Website:* www.chu.cam.ac.uk/fellows/111-David-Wallace (office).

WALLACE, Dame Helen, DBE, CMG, PhD, FBA; British fmr professor of European studies; *Foreign Secretary, British Academy;* b. 25 June 1946, Manchester, England; d. of the late Edward Rushworth and Joyce Rushworth (née Robinson); m. William Wallace (now Lord Wallace of Saltaire) 1968; one s. one d.; ed Univs of Oxford, Bruges, Belgium and Manchester; Lecturer in European Studies, UMIST 1974–78, Visiting Prof., Coll. of Europe, Bruges 1976–2001; in Public Admin., Civil Service Coll. 1978–85; mem. Planning Staff, FCO 1979–80; Head W European Programme, Royal Inst. of Int. Affairs 1985–92; Prof. of Contemporary European Studies and Dir Sussex European Inst., Univ. of Sussex 1992–2001, Professorial Fellow 2001–06; Dir Robert Schuman Centre for Advanced Studies, European Univ. Inst. 2001–06; Centennial Prof., European Inst., LSE 2006–11, Prof. Emer. 2011–13; Foreign Sec., British Acad. 2013–; mem. Better Regulation Comm. 2006–07; Assoc. mem. Acad. Royale des Sciences, des Lettres et des Beaux-Arts, Belgium; Foreign Sec. and Int. Vice-Pres. British Acad. 2011–; mem. Acad. for Learned Socs for the Social Sciences 2000; Chevalier, Ordre nat. du Mérite 1996; Hon. LLD (Sussex) 2002; Hon. DLitt (Loughborough) 2004, (Aston) 2009; Dr hc (Sciences Po) 2011; Lifetime Achievement in European Studies, Univ. Asscn for Contemporary European Studies 2006. *Publications include:* French and British Foreign Policies in Transition (co-author) 1990, The Wider Western Europe (ed.) 1991, The European Community: The Challenge of Enlargement (co-author) 1992, Participation and Policy-Making (co-author) 1997, Interlocking Dimensions of European Integration (ed.) 2001, The Council of Ministers (co-author) 2006, Policy Making in the European Union (ed.) 2010. *Leisure interests:* gardening, walking. *Address:* The British Academy, 10-11 Carlton House Terrace, London, SW1Y 5AH, England (office). *E-mail:* h.s.wallace@btopenworld.com. *Website:* www.britac.ac.uk (office).

WALLACE-CRABBE, Christopher Keith, MA, FAHA; Australian poet and critic; b. 6 May 1934, Melbourne, Vic.; s. of Kenneth Eyre Inverell Wallace-Crabbe and Phyllis Vera May Wallace-Crabbe (née Cock); m. 1st Helen Margaret Wiltshire 1957; one s. one d.; m. 2nd Marianne Sophie Feil 1979; two s.; m. 3rd Kristin Headlam; ed Melbourne Univ., Yale Univ., USA; cadet metallurgist 1951–52; then journalist, clerk, schoolteacher; Lockie Fellow in Australian Literature, Univ. of Melbourne 1962; Harkness Fellow, Yale Univ., USA 1965–67; Sr Lecturer in English, Univ. of Melbourne 1967, Reader 1976, Prof. 1987–, Personal Chair 1987–97, Prof. Emer. Australian Centre 1997–; Visiting Chair in Australian Studies, Harvard Univ., USA 1987–88; Chair. Australian Poetry Centre 2007; Hon. DLitt (Melbourne) 2006; Masefield Prize for Poetry 1957, Farmer's Poetry Prize 1964, Grace Leven Prize 1986, Dublin Prize 1987, Christopher Brennan Award 1990, Age Book of the Year Prize 1995, Philip Hodgins Memorial Medal 2002, Centenary Medal 2003. *Publications:* The Music of Division 1959, Selected Poems 1974, Melbourne or the Bush 1974, The Emotions are not Skilled Workers 1980, Toil and Spin: Two Directions in Modern Poetry 1980, Splinters (novel) 1981, The Amorous Cannibal 1985, I'm Deadly Serious 1988, Sangue è l'Acqua 1989, For Crying out Loud 1990, Falling into Language 1990, Poetry and Belief 1990, From the Republic of Conscience 1992, Rungs of Time 1993, Selected Poems 1956–94 1995, Whirling 1998, By and Large 2001, The Universe Looks Down 2005, Read It Again 2005, The Thing Itself 2007, Telling a Hawk from a Handsaw 2008. *Leisure interests:* drawing, tennis, beachwalking, making artist's books. *Address:* The Australian Centre, University of Melbourne, Parkville, Vic. 3052 (office); 7 De Carle Street, Brunswick, Vic. 3056, Australia (home). *Telephone:* (3) 8344-6998 (office); (3) 9386-6938 (home). *Fax:* (3) 9347-7731 (office). *E-mail:* ckwc@unimelb.edu.au (office). *Website:* www.hlc.unimelb.edu.au/cwc (office).

WALLACE OF SALTAIRE, Baron (Life Peer) cr. 1995, of Shipley in the County of West Yorkshire; **William John Lawrence Wallace,** BA, PhD; British academic; *Emeritus Professor of International Relations, London School of Economics;* b. 12 March 1941; m. Dame Helen Wallace 1968; ed Univ. of Cambridge, Cornell Univ., USA; Dir of Studies, Royal Inst. of Int. Affairs 1978–90; Walter F. Hallstein Fellow, St Antony's Coll., Oxford 1990–95; Prof. of Int. Studies, Central European Univ., Budapest 1994–97; Prof. of Int. Relations, LSE, Prof. Emer. 2005–; nominated to House of Lords 1995, mem. European Union Cttee 1996–2001, Chair. Sub-Cttee on Justice and Home Affairs 1997–2000; Ordre pour le Mérite 1995. *Publications include:* Regional Integration: the West European Experience 1994, Integration in a Larger and More Diverse European Union (jtly) 1995, Policy-making in the European Union (jtly) 2000, Rethinking European Order: West European Responses, 1989–97 (jtly) 2001, Non-State Actors in International Relations (jtly) 2001. *Address:* House of Lords, London, SW1A 0PW, England (office).

WALLACE OF TANKERNESS, Baron (Life Peer), cr. 2007, of Tankerness in Orkney; **Rt Hon. James Robert (Jim) Wallace,** PC, QC, MA, LLB; British politician; *Advocate General for Scotland;* b. 25 Aug. 1954, Annan, Dumfries and Galloway, Scotland; s. of John F. T. Wallace and Grace Hannah Maxwell; m. Rosemary Janet Fraser 1983; two d.; ed Annan Acad., Downing Coll. Cambridge, Univ. of Edinburgh; Chair. Edinburgh Univ. Liberal Club 1976–77; called to Scots Bar 1979; advocate 1979–83; mem. Scottish Liberal Exec. 1976–85; Vice-Chair. (Policy) Scottish Liberal Party 1982–85; MP for Orkney and Shetland 1983–2001 (Liberal 1983–88, Liberal Democrat 1988–2001), MSP for Orkney 1999–2007; Hon. Pres. Scottish Young Liberals 1984–85; Liberal Spokesman on Defence 1985–87; Deputy Whip 1985–87; Chief Whip 1987–88; first Liberal Democrat Chief Whip 1988–92; Alliance Spokesman on Transport 1987; Liberal Democrat Spokesman on Employment and Training 1988–92, on Fisheries 1988–97, on Scottish Affairs 1992–2001, on Maritime Affairs 1994–97; Leader Scottish Liberal Democrats 1992–2005; Deputy First Minister of the Scottish Exec. 1999–2005, Minister for Justice 1999–2003, for Enterprise and Lifelong Learning 2003–05; Chair. Relationships Scotland 2008–10; mem. Comm. on Scottish Devolution 2008–09; Advocate Gen. for Scotland 2010–; Hon. DLitt (Heriot Watt Univ.) 2007, Hon. DUniv (Open Univ.) 2009, Dr hc (Edinburgh Univ.) 2009. *Leisure interests:* golf, music, travel. *Address:* House of Lords, Westminster, London, SW1A 0PW, England (office); Northwood House, Tankerness, Orkney, KW17 2QS, Scotland (home). *Telephone:* (20) 7219-3526 (office); (1856) 861-383 (home). *Fax:* (1856) 861-383 (home). *E-mail:* wallacej@parliament.uk (office).

WALLACH, Eli, MS (Educ); American actor; b. 7 Dec. 1915, Brooklyn, NY; s. of Abraham Wallach and Bertha Schorr; m. Anne Jackson 1948; one s. two d.; ed Univ. of Texas, City Coll. of New York, Neighborhood Playhouse School of Theatre; started theatre career 1946, film career 1955; Donaldson Award, Tony Award, British Film Acad. Award 1956, Hon. Acad. Award, Acad. of Motion Picture Arts and Sciences 2010. *Plays include:* The Rose Tattoo, The Teahouse of the August Moon 1954–55, Camino Real, Luv, Typists and Tiger 1964, Promenade All 1973, Waltz of the Toreadors 1974, The Diary of Anne Frank 1978, Opera Comique 1987, The Flowering Peach in Florida 1987, Visiting Mr. Green 1997, Down the Garden Paths 1998–99, Remembered 1999. *Films include:* Baby Doll 1956, The Line-Up 1958, Seven Thieves 1960, The Magnificent Seven 1960, The Misfits 1961, Hemingway's Adventures of a Young Man 1962, How the West Was Won 1962, The Victors 1963, Act One 1963, The Moon-Spinners 1964, Kisses for My President 1964, Lord Jim 1965, Genghis Khan 1965, Poppies Are Also Flowers 1966, How to Steal a Million 1966, The Good, the Bad and the Ugly 1967, The Tiger Makes Out (also producer, uncredited) 1967, I quattro dell'Ave Maria (aka Ace High, USA) 1968, How to Save a Marriage (And Ruin Your Life) 1968, A Lovely Way to Die 1968, Le cerveau 1969, Mackenna's Gold 1969, The Adventures of Gerard 1970, The Angel Levine 1970, The People Next Door 1970, Zigzag 1970, Romance of a Horsethief 1971, ¡Viva la muerte… tua! 1971, Cinderella Liberty 1973, Crazy Joe 1974, L'ultima chance (Last Chance) 1975, Il bianco, il giallo, il nero (White, the Yellow, and the Black) 1975, …e tanta paura 1976, Attenti al buffone (aka Eye of the Cat) 1976, Independence 1976, The Sentinel 1977, The Deep 1977, The Domino Principle 1977, Nasty Habits 1977, Squadra antimafia (aka Little Italy) 1978, Girlfriends 1978, Movie Movie 1978, Circle of Iron 1978, The Silent Flute 1978, Firepower 1979, Winter Kills 1979, The Hunter 1980, The Salamander 1981, The Wall 1982, Sam's Son 1984, Tough Guys 1986, Nuts 1987, The Rose Garden 1989, The Two Jakes 1990, The Godfather: Part III 1990, Nonesense and Lullabyes: Poems (video) 1992, The Godfather Trilogy: 1901–1980 (video) 1992, Nonesense and Lullabyes: Nursery Rhymes (video) 1992, Article 99 1992, Mistress 1992, Night and the City 1992, Caro dolce amore (Honey Sweet Love) 1994, Two Much 1995, The Associate 1996, Uninvited 1999, Keeping the Faith 2000, Advise and Dissent 2002, Merci Docteur Rey 2002, The Root 2003, Mystic River (uncredited) 2003, King of the Corner 2004, The Moon and the Son (voice) 2005, The Easter Egg Adventure (voice) 2005, A Taste of Jupiter 2005, The Hoax 2006, The Holiday 2006. *Television includes:* Where Is Thy Brother? 1958, Gift of the Magi 1958, Lullaby 1960, The Chill Factor 1973, Indict and Convict 1974, Houston, We've Got a Problem 1974, Paradise Lost 1974, Seventh Avenue (mini-series) 1977, The Pirate 1978, Fugitive Family 1980, The Pride of Jesse Hallam 1981, Skokie 1981, The Executioner's Song 1982, Anatomy of an Illness 1984, Murder: By Reason of Insanity 1985, Embassy 1985, Christopher Columbus (mini-series) 1985, Our Family Honor (series) 1985, Something in Common 1986, Rocket to the Moon 1986, The Impossible Spy 1987, A Matter of Conscience 1989, Vendetta: Secrets of a Mafia Bride 1991, Legacy of Lies 1992, Teamster Boss: The Jackie Presser Story 1992, Vendetta II: The New Mafia 1993, Naked City: Justice with a Bullet 1998, The Bookfair Murders 2000, Monday Night Mayhem 2002, Character Studies (series) 2005. *Leisure interest:* photography.

WALLBERG-HENRIKSSON, Harriet, MD, PhD; Swedish university administrator, academic and physiologist; *President, Karolinska Institutet;* two c.; ed Karolinska Institutet, Univ. Coll. of Physical Educ. and Sports; fmr Dir of Gymnastics; fmr Assoc. Prof., Karolinska Institutet, Prof. 1998–, Pres. (first female) 2004–, mem. Nobel Ass. 2002–; Dean and Chair., Bd of Research, Royal Swedish Acad. of Sciences 1999–2001, currently mem. Physiology Cttee; Asst Sec.-Gen. Scientific Council for Medicine, Swedish Research Council 1996–98, Sec.-Gen. 2001–03; Vice-Chair. European Asscn for the Study of Diabetes (EASD); has led Swedish dels to Japan and UN; rep. of Sweden on Bds of European Science Foundation, WHO Agency for Cancer Research, Heads of Int. Research Orgs (HIRO); mem. EU Expert Group, EU strategy for competitive research environments. *Publications:* approx. 140 scientific articles on diabetes and clinical physiology. *Address:* Karolinska Institutet, 171 77 Stockholm, Sweden (office). *Telephone:* (8) 524-800-00 (office). *Fax:* (8) 524-866-44 (office). *E-mail:* Rektor@ki.se (office). *Website:* www.ki.se (office).

WALLENBERG, Jacob, BS (Econ), MBA; Swedish business executive; *Chairman, Investor AB;* b. 1956, Stockholm; s. of Peter Wallenberg; m. Marie Wallenberg; three c.; ed Wharton School, Univ. of Pennsylvania, Royal Swedish Naval Acad.; officer in Royal Swedish Naval Reserve; extensive training programmes at several int. banks; joined Skandinaviska Enskilda Banken (SEB) AB 1984, held various posts, primarily in Sweden but also in Singapore, Hong

2288

Kong, London and New York, rejoined SEB 1993, CEO 1997, Chair. 1998–2005; Deputy Man. Dir Investor AB (Wallenberg family fund man. firm) 1990–92, Vice-Chair. 2005–; Vice-Chair. Atlas Copco AB, SAS AB; mem. Bd of Dirs ABB; mem. Bd Nobel Foundation, Knut and Alice Wallenberg Foundation AB, Wharton European Advisory Bd. *Leisure interests:* golf, sailing. *Address:* Investor AB, Arsenalsgatan 8C, 103 32 Stockholm, Sweden (office). *Telephone:* (8) 614-20-00 (office). *Fax:* (8) 614-21-50 (office). *E-mail:* fredrik.lindgren@investorab.com (office). *Website:* www.investorab.com (office).

WALLENBERG, Marcus, BSc; Swedish business executive and international organization official; *Honorary Chairman, International Chamber of Commerce;* b. 1956; s. of Marc Wallenberg; ed Edmund A. Walsh School of Foreign Service, Georgetown Univ., USA; fmr Dir Stora Feldmühle, Düsseldorf; Exec. Vice-Pres. Investor AB –1999, Pres. and CEO 1999–2005; Chair. Saab, Skandinaviska Enskilda Banken (SEB) AB 2005–, Electrolux; Vice-Chair. L. M. Ericsson; mem. Bd of Dirs AstraZeneca, Stora Enso Oyj, Foundation Asset Management Sweden AB, Knut and Alice Wallenberg Foundation; Chair. ICC 2005–08, Hon. Chair. 2008–; fmr mem. Advisory Council Stanford Grad. School of Business, Founder Wallenberg Global Learning Center at Stanford Univ.; mem. Royal Swedish Acad. of Eng and Sciences; European Business Leadership Award, Stanford Business School Alumni Asscn 2003. *Address:* International Chamber of Commerce, 38 cours Albert 1er, 75008 Paris, France (office). *Telephone:* 1-49-53-28-28 (office). *Fax:* 1-49-53-28-59 (office). *E-mail:* info@iccwbo.org (office). *Website:* www.iccwbo.org (office).

WALLENBERG, Peter, LLB; Swedish business executive; *Chairman, Knut and Alice Wallenberg Foundation;* b. 29 May 1926, Stockholm; s. of Dr Marcus Wallenberg and Dorothy Mackay; m. (divorced); two s. one d.; ed Univ. of Stockholm; various positions with Atlas Copco Group 1953-74; fmr Chair. Atlas Copco AB, STORA, ASEA, Hon. Chair. Atlas Copco AB; fmr Co-Chair. ASEA Brown Boveri (ABB); First Vice-Chair. Skandinaviska Enskilda Banken 1984–96; mem. Bd Dirs Investor AB 1969–82, Chair. 1982–97, Hon. Chair. 1997–; Chair. Knut and Alice Wallenberg Foundation 1982–; Hon. Kt 1989; Dr hc (Stockholm School of Econs, Augustana Coll. and Uppsala Coll., USA, Uppsala Univ., Royal Inst. of Tech., Stockholm). *Leisure interests:* hunting, tennis, sailing. *Address:* c/o Investor AB, 10332 Stockholm, Sweden. *Telephone:* 86-14-20-00. *Fax:* 86-14-28-15. *Website:* www.investorab.com.

WALLER, Rev. Ralph, PhD; British minister of religion and academic; *Principal, Harris Manchester College, University of Oxford;* b. 11 Dec. 1945; m. Carol Roberts 1968; one d.; ed John Leggott Grammar School, Scunthorpe, Richmond Coll. Divinity School, Univ. of London, Univ. of Nottingham, King's Coll. London; service in India, teaching math. and physical educ., House Master Shri Shivah Mil. School, Pune 1967–68; Math. Teacher, Riddings Comprehensive School, Scunthorpe 1968–69; Methodist Minister, Melton Mowbray 1972–75; ordained 1975; Minister Elvet Methodist Church, Durham City, Methodist Chaplain, Univ. of Durham 1975–81, Chaplain St Mary's Coll. and St Aidan's Coll. 1979–81; Chaplain, Tutor in Theology and Resident Tutor, Westminster Coll., Oxford 1981–88; Prin. and Tutor in Theology, Harris Manchester (fmrly Manchester) Coll., Univ. Oxford 1988–, Chair. Faculty of Theology, Univ. Oxford 1995–97, mem. Hebdomadal Council 1997–2000; Chair. Environmental Cttee 1997–2000; Dir Farmington Inst. 2001–; Hon. DLitt (Menlo Coll., Calif.) 1994; Hon. DHum (Ball State Univ., Ind.) 1998; Hon. DHL (St Olaf Coll., Minn.) 2001, (Christopher Newport) 2005; Hon. DTheol (Uppsala) 1999; Hon. DD (Hartwick) 2003; Templeton Prize UK 1993. *Publications:* Christian Spirituality (co-ed.) 1999, John Wesley 2003, Basic Texts in Christian Spirituality (co-ed.) 2003. *Leisure interests:* swimming, walking, browsing round second-hand bookshops. *Address:* Principal's Lodgings, Harris Manchester College, Mansfield Road, Oxford, OX1 3TD, England (home). *Telephone:* (1865) 271006 (office). *Fax:* (1865) 281474 (office). *E-mail:* principal@hmc.ox.ac.uk (office). *Website:* www.hmc.ox.ac.uk (office).

WALLER, Robert James; American writer and musician; b. 1 Aug. 1939; s. of Robert Waller Sr and Ruth Waller; m. Georgia A. Wiedemeier 1961 (divorced 1997); one d.; ed Univ. of Northern Iowa, Indiana Univ.; Prof. of Man., Univ. of Northern Iowa 1968–91, Dean of Business School 1979–86 (retd). *Album:* The Ballads of Madison County 1993. *Publications:* Just Beyond the Firelight 1988, One Good Road is Enough 1990, Iowa: Perspectives on Today and Tomorrow 1991, The Bridges of Madison County 1992, Slow Waltz at Cedar Bend 1994, Old Songs in a New Café 1994, Selected Essays 1994, Border Music 1995, Puerto-Vallarta Squeeze 1995, A Thousand Country Roads 2002, High Plains Tango 2005, The Long Night of Winchell Dear 2006. *Leisure interests:* photography, basketball.

WALLIN, Stefan Erik; Finnish politician; *Chairman, Swedish People's Party;* b. 1 June 1967, Vaasa; m. Elina Pirjatanniemi; two d.; ed Åbo Akademi Univ., Turku; summer reporter for Vasabladet newspaper 1989–93, for Åbo Underrättelser newspaper 1993–94; Special Adviser to Minister of Transport 1994–95, to Minister for Foreign Trade 1995–98, to Minister of the Interior 1998–99, to Minister of Defence 1999–2000; Deputy Ed.-in-Chief Åbo Underrättelser 2000–05; State Sec. for Minister of the Environment 2005–07; mem. Suomen Eduskunta (Parl.) 2007–; Minister of the Environment and Minister at the Ministry for Foreign Affairs Jan.–April 2007, Minister of Culture and Sport 2007–10, 2010–11, Minister at the Ministry of Social Affairs and Health 2007–10, 2010–11, Minister of Defence 2011–12; mem. Swedish People's Party (SPP), Chair. 2006–; mem. Turku City Council 2009–; mem. Ass., Regional Council of SW Finland 2009–. *Leisure interests:* cooking, reading, gym, English Premier League football. *Address:* Svenska Folkpartiet, Simonkatu 8a, PO Box 430, 00101 Helsinki, Finland (office). *Telephone:* (9) 693070 (office). *E-mail:* info@sfp.fi (office). *Website:* www.sfp.fi (office); www.stefanwallin.fi.

WALLINGER, Mark; British artist; b. 1959, Chigwell, Essex; ed West Hatch High School, Chigwell, Loughton Coll., Chelsea School of Art, London, Goldsmiths Coll.; represented GB at the Venice Biennale 2001; video work, Via Dolorosa, permanently installed in a crypt in the Duomo in Milan; his sculpture Ecce Homo was the first project chosen for the vacant Fourth Plinth in Trafalgar Square; installation State Britain on display at Tate Britain 2007; curated Hayward touring exhbn, The Russian Linesman 2009; proposal for a 165ft high White Horse won the Ebbsfleet Landmark Comm.; work is represented in major museum collections in Europe, USA and the Far East; Hon. Fellow, London Inst. 2002; Dr hc (Univ. of Central England) 2003; Henry Moore Fellowship, British School, Rome 1998, DAAD Artists Programme, Berlin 2001–02, Turner Prize 2007. *Dance:* UNDANCE, Sadler's Wells 2011, Metamorphoses: Titian 2012, Royal Opera House 2012. *Publication:* Mark 2011. *Address:* c/o Anthony Reynolds Gallery, 60 Great Marlborough Street, London, W1F 7BG, England. *Telephone:* (20) 7439-2201. *Fax:* (20) 7439-1869. *E-mail:* info@anthonyreynolds.com. *Website:* www.anthonyreynolds.com.

WALLIS, Stanley (Stan) David Martin, AC, BCom, FAIM, FCPA, FCIS, FCIM; Australian financial services executive (retd); b. 23 July 1939, Melbourne; s. of S. E. Wallis; m. Judith Logan 1962; three s. two d.; ed Wesley Coll., Melbourne, Univ. of Melbourne, Stanford Univ., USA; joined AMP/Amcor 1960, Chief Accountant 1986, Financial Man. 1972, Deputy Man. Dir 1975, Man. Dir 1977–96; Chair. Amcor Ltd 1997–2000; Dir AMP Ltd 1990–2003, Chair. 2000–03; Chair. Pine-applehead Ltd 2000–02; Dir Coles Myer Ltd 1996–2002, Chair. 1997–2002; currently Chair. SANE Australia; Dir Dir Walter & Eliza Hall Inst. of Medical Research; Chair. and Dir Santos Ltd 1989–94; Dir Australian Foundation Investment Co. 1987–2009; fmr Dir Nicholas-Kiwi Australasia Ltd, NZ Forest Products Ltd, Mayne Nickless Ltd, Spicers Paper Ltd; Chair. 1997–2002; currently Chair. SANE Australia (mental health charity) Chair. Inquiry into Australian Financial System 1996–97; Pres. Business Council of Australia 1996–98; fmr Vice-Pres. Melbourne Business School, Univ. of Melbourne; Hon. LLD (Monash); Award for Outstanding Achievement in Business, Melbourne Univ. Grad. School of Man. 1990, Bulletin Deloitte Business Leader Award 1995. *Leisure interests:* tennis, skiing, sailing. *Address:* SANE Australia, PO Box 226, South Melbourne, Vic. 3205, Australia. *Telephone:* (3) 9682-5933. *Fax:* (3) 9682-5944. *E-mail:* info@sane.org. *Website:* www.sane.org.

WALLNER, Nicolai; Danish gallery owner; f. Galleri Nicolai Wallner in Copenhagen 1993, moved to Islands Brygge 1999, opening second kunsthal in Charlottenborg 2011; represents artists including Gitte Villesen, Michael Elm-green & Ingar Dragset, Jens Haaning, Mari Eastman, Joachim Koester, Jakob Kolding, Peter Land, Jonathan Monk, David Shrigley, Christian Schmidt-Rasmussen, Glenn Sorensen, Clare Rojas, Jeppe Hein, Daniel Buren, Christoph Ruckhäberle, Douglas Gordon, Chris Johanson, Dan Graham, Richard Tuttle and Alexander Tovborg. *Address:* Ny Carlsbergvej 68, 1760 Copenhagen, Denmark (office). *Telephone:* 32570970 (office). *Fax:* 32570971 (office). *E-mail:* nw@nicolaiwallner.com (office). *Website:* www.nicolaiwallner.com (office).

WALLSTRÖM, Margot; Swedish politician and UN official; b. 28 Sept. 1954, Kåge, Västerbotten Co.; m. Håkan Wallström; two s.; Organizing Sec. Värmland br., Social Democratic Youth League; Accountant, Alfa Savings Bank, Karlstad 1977–79, Sr Accountant 1986–88; mem. Parl. 1979–85; fmr mem. Värmland Co. Council, Directorate of Bd of Civil Aviation, Directorate of Nat. Environment Protection Bd; Minister with responsibility for Ecclesiastical, Consumers, Equality and Youth Affairs, Ministry of Public Admin 1988–92; Minister of Cultural Affairs 1994–96, of Health and Social Affairs 1996–98; Exec. Vice-Pres. Worldview Global Media, Sri Lanka 1998–99; EC Commr for the Environment 1999–2004, Vice-Pres. and Commr for Institutional Relations and Communication Strategy 2004–10; Special Rep. of the UN Sec.-Gen. on Sexual Violence in Conflict 2010–12 (resgnd); Chair. of Ministerial Initiative, Council of World Women Leaders 2007; Dr hc (Chalmers Univ.) 2001, (Mälardalen Univ.) 2004, (Univ. of Massachusetts, Howell) 2005; IAIA Global Environmental Award 2004. *Publications include:* The People's Europe or Why is It so Hard to Love the EU? (with Göran Färm) 2004, EU Elite Project? No! The People's Europe (with Göran Färm) 2008. *Address:* c/o Ministry for Foreign Affairs, Gustav Adolfs torg 1, 103 39 Stockholm, Sweden (office).

WALMSLEY, David George, PhD, DSc, FInstP, MRIA; British physicist and academic; *Professor Emeritus of Physics, Queen's University Belfast;* b. 3 Feb. 1938, Newtownstewart, Northern Ireland; s. of Robert Gwynne Walmsley and Elizabeth Johnston; m. Margaret Heather Edmonstone 1965; two s.; ed Royal School, Armagh, Queen's Univ. Belfast and McMaster Univ., Hamilton, Ont.; NRC Canada Post-doctoral Fellow, MacMaster Univ. 1965; Scientific Officer, Sr Scientific Officer, AERE Harwell 1966–70; Lecturer, Sr Lecturer, Reader in Physics, New Univ. of Ulster 1970–84; Prof. of Physics, Univ. of Ulster 1984–88; Prof. of Physics, Queen's Univ. Belfast 1988–2003, Prof. Emer. 2003–, Dir School of Math. and Physics 1993–98, Dean Faculty of Science and Agric. 1998–2002; Chair. Northern Ireland Regional Medical Physics Agency 2001–09; Fellow, American Physical Soc. 2001. *Publications:* numerous articles on superconductivity and the electron tunnel effect in scientific journals. *Address:* Department of Physics and Astronomy, Queen's University, Belfast, BT7 1NN (office); 5 Newforge Grange, Belfast, BT9 5QB (home); 29 Swilly Road, Portstewart, BT55 7DJ, Northern Ireland (home). *Telephone:* (28) 9097-3531 (office); (28) 9066-4141 (home); (28) 7083-3257 (home). *Fax:* (28) 9027-3110 (office). *E-mail:* dg.walmsley@qub.ac.uk (office). *Website:* www.qub.ac.uk/mp (office).

WALPORT, Sir Mark Jeremy, Kt, MB, BChir, MA, PhD, FRCP, FRCPath, FMedSci; British physician, academic and trust executive; *Director, The Wellcome Trust;* b. 25 Jan. 1953; s. of Samuel Walport and Doreen Walport (née Music); m. Julia Elizabeth Neild 1986; one s. three d.; ed St Paul's School, London, Clare Coll. Cambridge, Middx Hosp. Medical School; House Officer, Middx Hosp. and Queen Elizabeth II Hosp., Welwyn 1977–78, House Officer 1978–80; Hon. Registrar, Brompton Hosp. 1980; Registrar, Hammersmith Hosp. 1980–82, Hon. Consultant Physician 1985–, Dir Research and Devt 1994–98; MRC Training Fellow, MRC Mechanisms in Tumour Immunity Unit, Cambridge 1982–85; Harrison–Watson Student, Clare Coll. Cambridge 1982–85; Sr Lecturer in Rheumatology, Imperial Coll. School of Medicine 1985–90, Reader Rheumatological Medicine 1990–91, Prof. of Medicine 1991–2003, Head of Div. of Medicine 1997–2003, Fellow, Imperial Coll. 2006–; Gov. Wellcome Trust 2000–03, Dir 2003–; mem. Scientific Advisory Bd, Cantab Pharmaceuticals, Cambridge 1989–2000, Research and Devt Advisory Bd, Smithkline Beecham 1998–2000; mem. Council, British Soc. for Rheumatology 1989–95, British Soc. for Immunology 1998–2000; Asst Ed. British Journal of Rheumatology 1990–97; Ed. Clinical and Experimental Immunology 1990–97; Series Ed. British Medical Bulletin 1998–; Hon. DSc (Univ. of Sheffield, King's Coll. London); Roche Prize for Rheumatology 1991, Graham Bull Prize in Clinical Science 1996. *Publications:* Immunobiology (co-author); Clinical Aspects of Immunology (co-ed.); numerous papers published in scientific journals on immunology and rheumatology. *Leisure interest:* natural history. *Address:* The Wellcome Trust, 215 Euston Road, London, NW1 2BE, England (office). *Telephone:* (20) 7611-8888 (office). *Fax:* (20) 7611-8545 (office). *Website:* www.wellcome.ac.uk (office).

WALSER, Martin, DPhil; German writer, playwright and poet; b. 24 March 1927, Wasserburg, Bodensee; s. of Martin Walser and Augusta Schmid; m. Käthe Jehle 1950; four d.; ed Theologisch-Philosophische Hochschule, Regensburg and Univ. of Tübingen; writer 1951–; Grosses Bundesverdienstkreuz mit Stern 1997, Officier, L'Ordre des Arts et des Lettres; Group 47 Prize 1955, Hermann-Hesse Prize 1957, Gerhart-Hauptmann Prize 1962, Schiller Prize 1980, Büchner Prize 1981, Orden pour le mérite 1994, Friedenspreis des Deutschen Buchhandels 1998. *Publications include:* novels include: Ehen in Philippsburg 1957, Halbzeit 1960, Das Einhorn 1966, Fiction 1970, Die Gallistlische Krankheit 1972, Der Sturz 1973, Jenseits der Liebe 1976, Ein fliehendes Pferd 1978, Seelenarbeit 1979, Das Schwanenhaus 1980, Brief an Lord Liszt 1982, Brandung 1985, Dorle und Wolf 1987, Jagd 1988, Die Verteidigung der Kindheit 1991, Ohne einander 1993, Finks Krieg 1996, Ein springender Brunnen 1998, Der Lebenslauf der Liebe 2001, Tod eines Kritikers 2002, Der Augenblick der Liebe 2004, Die Verwaltung des Nichts 2004, Leben und Schreiben 2005, Angstblüte 2006, Der Lebensroman des Andreas Beck 2006, Das geschundene Tier 2007, Ein Liebender Mann 2008; short stories: Ein Flugzeug über dem Haus 1955, Lügengeschichten 1964; plays: Der Abstecher 1961, Eiche und Angora 1962, Überlebensgross Herr Krott 1963, Der schwarze Schwan 1964, Die Zimmerschlacht 1967, Ein Kinderspiel 1970, Das Sauspiel 1975, In Goethe's Hand 1982, Die Ohrfeige 1986, Das Sofa 1992, Kaschmir in Parching 1995; essays: Beschreibung einer Form, Versuch über Franz Kafka 1961, Erfahrungen und Leseerfahrungen 1965, Heimatkunde 1968, Wie und wovon handelt Literatur 1973, Wer ist ein Schriftsteller 1978, Selbstbewusstsein und Ironie 1981, Messmers Gedanken 1985, Über Deutschland reden 1988, Vormittag eines Schriftstellers 1994, Messmers Reisen 2003; poetry: Der Grund zur Freude 1978, Die Verwaltung des Nichts 2004. *Address:* Zum Hecht 36, 88662 Überlingen-Nussdorf, Germany (home). *Telephone:* (7551) 4131 (home). *Fax:* (7551) 68494 (home). *E-mail:* nussdorf@t-online.de (home).

WALSH, Arthur Stephen, CBE, MA, FEng, FIEE; British business executive; b. 16 Aug. 1926, Wigan, Greater Manchester, England; s. of Wilfrid Walsh and Doris Walsh; m. 1st. Gwendoline Mary Walsh (divorced 1983); m. 2nd Judith Martha Westenborg 1985; one s. one d.; ed Selwyn Coll. Cambridge; joined GEC 1952, various sr appointments, including Tech. Dir of GEC/AEL 1952–79; Man. Dir Marconi Space and Defence Systems 1979–82; Man. Dir The Marconi Co. 1982–85; Chief Exec. STC PLC (now Northern Telecom Europe Ltd) 1985–91; Chair. Telemetrix PLC 1991–97, Simoco Int. Ltd 1997–2001; Dir FKI PLC 1991–99, Deputy Chair. 1993–; Hon. DSc (Ulster) 1988, (Southampton) 1993. *Leisure interests:* sailing, skiing, golf. *Address:* Aiglemont, Trout Rise, Loudwater, Rickmansworth, Herts., WD3 4JS, England (home). *Telephone:* (1923) 770883 (office). *E-mail:* alvecote@aol.com (office).

WALSH, Christopher T., AB, PhD; American biochemist and academic; *Hamilton Kuhn Professor, Harvard Medical School;* ed Harvard Univ., The Rockefeller Univ.; Postdoctoral Fellow, Brandeis Univ. 1970–72, Helen Hay Whitney Foundation Fellow, Grad. Dept of Biochemistry 1970-72; Asst, Assoc. and Full Prof. of Chemistry and Biology, MIT 1972–87, Uncas and Helen Whitaker Prof. 1980–85, Chair. Dept of Chem. 1982–87, Karl Taylor Compton Prof. 1985–87; Chair. Dept of Biological Chem. and Molecular Pharmacology, Harvard Medical School 1987–95, Hamilton Kuhn Prof. of Biological Chem. and Molecular Pharmacology 1991–; Pres. Dana-Farber Cancer Inst. 1992–95; Panel mem. NSF Research Grants Study 1977–79, NIH Study Section in Biochemistry 1978–82 (Chair. 1982); mem. NIH Gen. Medical Sciences Advisory Council 1996–99; Biology Section Ed. Annual Reports in Medicinal Chemistry 1978–80; Assoc. Ed. Protein Science 1991–92, Annual Review of Biochemistry 1990–95; mem. Editorial Bd Journal of Biological Chemistry 1978–80, Journal of the American Chemical Society 1991–94, Chemistry and Biology 1993–; Co-Chair. Gordon Research Conf. on Conference on Enzymes, Coenzymes and Molecular Biology 1978, Conf. on Methanogenesis 1984; mem. Bd of Dirs, Whitehead Inst., Versicor, Kosan Biosciences, Transform Pharmaceuticals; mem. Structural Biology Review Group, Howard Hughes Medical Inst.; mem. Scientific Advisory Bd, Epix Medical, KOSAN Biosciences, Caliper Technologies, Dyax, Millenium Pharmaceuticals, MPM Asset Management; mem. American Acad. of Arts and Sciences 1988, Inst. of Medicine 1989, NAS 1989; Alfred P. Sloan Foundation Fellow 1975–77, Camille & Henry Dreyfus Teacher-Scholar Grant Recipient 1976–80, Eli Lilly Award in Biochemistry 1979, ACS Arthur C. Cope Scholar Award 1998, ACS Repligen Award 1999, Welch Award in Chem. (co-recipient) 2010. *Publications:* Enzymatic Reaction Mechanisms 1978, Antibiotics: Actions, Origins, Resistance 2003, Post-translation Modification of Proteins: Expanding Nature's Inventory 2006; numerous papers in professional journals. *Address:* Department of Biological Chemistry and Molecular Pharmacology, Armenise Building, Room 616, 200 Longwood Avenue, Boston, MA 02215, USA (office). *Telephone:* (617) 432-1715 (office). *Fax:* (617) 432-0438 (office). *E-mail:* christopher_walsh@hms.harvard.edu (office). *Website:* walsh.med.harvard.edu (office); bcmp.med.harvard.edu/faculty/walsh (office).

WALSH, Courtney Andrew, OJ; Jamaican fmr cricketer; b. 30 Oct. 1962, Kingston; s. of Joan Woollaston; right-hand batsman, right-arm fast bowler; player for Jamaica 1981–2001, Glos. 1984–98, West Indies 1984–2001 (Capt. 1993/94–97/98); Test debut with West Indies against Australia at Perth 9–12 Nov. 1984; played in 132 Tests, took 519 wickets (average 24.44), best bowling (innings) 7/37, (match) 13/55, scored 936 runs (average 7.54, highest score 30 not out); played in 132 One-Day Ints, took 227 wickets (average 30.47), best bowling 5/1, scored 321 runs (average 6.97, highest score 30); played in 429 First-class matches, took 1,807 wickets (average 21.71), best bowling 9/72, scored 4,530 runs (average 11.32, highest score 66); world record 519 Test wickets (average 24.44) at time of his retirement in April 2001 and 1,807 first-class wickets (average 21.71); currently a regular feature of the Lashings World XI; Owner Cuddy'z Sports Bar, Kingston; Wisden Cricketer of the Year 1987, Jamaica Sportsman of the Year 1998–2000. *Leisure interests:* cooking, dancing, music, cars. *Address:* Cuddy'z Sports Bar, The New Kingston Shopping Centre, Dominica Drive, Kingston, Jamaica (office).

Telephone: 920-8019 (office). *Fax:* 968-0495 (office). *E-mail:* contact@cuddyzsportsbar.com (office). *Website:* www.cuddyzsportsbar.com (office).

WALSH, Capt. Don, BS, MA, MS, PhD; American business executive, fmr university administrator and fmr naval officer; *President and CEO, International Maritime, Inc.;* b. 2 Nov. 1931, Berkeley, Calif.; s. of J. Don Walsh and Marta G. Walsh; m. Joan A. Betzmer 1962; one s. one d.; ed San Diego State Coll., Texas A&M Univ., US Naval Acad.; entered USN 1950, submarine service 1956–64; became Officer-in-Charge Submersible Test Group and Bathyscaph Trieste 1959, made record dive to 35,840 ft Jan. 1960, designated USN submersible pilot No. 1 1960; at Dept of Oceanography, Texas A&M Univ. 1965–68; commanded submarine Bashaw 1968–69; Scientific Liaison Officer Submarine Devt Group One 1969–70; Special Asst (submarines) to Asst Sec. of the Navy for Research and Devt, Washington, DC 1970–73; Resident Fellow, Woodrow Wilson Int. Center for Scholars 1973–74; Deputy Dir Naval Labs. 1974–75; retd from navy with rank of Capt. 1975; Dir Inst. for Marine and Coastal Studies and Prof. of Ocean Eng, Univ. of Southern Calif. 1975–83; Pres. and CEO International Maritime, Inc. 1976–; Vice-Pres. Parker Diving Service 1985–94; mem. Marine Bd, Nat. Research Council 1990–93, Ocean Studies Bd 2010–; Exec. Dir Deep Ocean Eng 1990–2000; mem. Bd of Dirs Explorers Club 1994–2000; mem. US Naval Inst., Nat. Advisory Cttee on Oceans and Atmosphere 1979–86, Law of the Sea Advisory Cttee (US State Dept) 1979–83, Soc. of Naval Architects and Marine Engineers, American Soc. for Naval Engineers, Bd of Govs, Calif. Maritime Acad. 1985–94; Ed. Marine Technical Society Journal 1976–80; mem. Nat. Acad. of Eng 2001–, Ocean Elders 2011–; Fellow, Marine Tech. Soc. 1980; Hon. Life mem. Explorers' Club (Hon. Pres. 2008–), Adventurers' Club, American Geographical Soc. 2000; Legion of Merit (two awards), Meritorious Service Medal (two awards), Antarctic Service Medal, USN Dept Distinguished Civilian Service Medal, US Coast Guard Meritorious Service Medal, Admin.'s Award (Medal), Nat. Oceanic and Atmospheric Admin; The Walsh Spur (ridge) in the Antarctic, NSF 1973, Gold Medals from City of Trieste and Chicago Geographic Socs, US Coast Guard Meritorious Public Service Medal 1980, Meritorious Service Medal (two awards), Lowell Thomas Award, Explorers' Club 1987, Compass Distinguished Achievement Award, Marine Tech. Soc. 1996, Explorers' Medal, Explorers' Club 2001, L'Etoile Polaire, Jules Verne Aventures 2001, Hubbard Medal, Nat. Geographic Soc., NOGI Award, Acad. of Underwater Arts and Sciences, Peter Benchley Award, Blue Frontier Foundation, Ralph White Memorial Award, Los Angeles Chapter of the Explorers Club, Distinguished Public Service Award, USN, NOAA Administrators Award, Lifetime Achievement Award, BLUE Underwater Film Festival, Distinguished Achievement Award, Nat. Maritime Historical Soc. *Achievements:* made 57 expeditions to the Arctic and Antarctic from 1955, including five to the North Pole. *Publications:* author of more than 200 papers, articles, etc. on marine subjects; ed. and contrib. Law of the Sea: Issues in Ocean Resources Management; Energy and Resource Development of the Continental Margins (co-ed.) 1980, Energy from the Sea: Challenge for the Decade (ed.) 1982, Waste Disposal in the Oceans: Minimum Impact, Maximize Benefits (co-ed.) 1983, Twenty Thousand Jobs Under the Sea: A History of Diving. *Leisure interests:* writing, travel, sailing, flying his aeroplane. *Address:* International Maritime Inc., 14758 Sitkum Lane, Myrtle Point, OR 97458, USA (office). *Telephone:* (541) 572-2313. *Fax:* (541) 572-4041. *E-mail:* imiwalsh@mac.com (office).

WALSH, Edward (Ed) M., BEng, MSc, PhD, FIEE, FRSA, MRIA; Irish chartered engineer, fmr university administrator and consultant; *Founding President and President Emeritus, University of Limerick;* b. 3 Dec. 1939, Cork; s. of Michael Walsh and Margaret Walsh (née Leonard); m. Stephanie Barrett 1965; three s. one d.; ed Nat. Univ. of Ireland, Iowa State Univ., USA; Assoc., US Atomic Energy Comm. Lab., Ames, Ia 1963–65; Assoc. Prof., Virginai Polytechic Inst. and State Univ. 1965–69; Dir Energy Research Group Programme, Va 1966–69; Founding Pres. Nat. Inst. for Higher Educ., Limerick 1970–98, Univ. of Limerick 1989–98, Pres. Emer. 1998–, mem. Bd Univ. of Limerick Foundation 2006–; Prin. of Oakhampton Consultants 1999–; Dir, Wind Energy Direct 2008–; Founding Chair. Nat. Self-Portrait Collection of Ireland 1979–2002, Nat. Technological Park 1983–88, Nat. Council for Curriculum and Assessment 1984–90; Chair. Advisory Bd, Barrington's Hosp., Shannon Development 1987, Cttee of Heads of Irish Univs 1991–92 Birr Historic Science Foundation 1994–99, IAUP Int. Comm. on Educational Tech. 1996–2002, Irish Council for Science, Tech. and Innovation 1997–2004, Citywest Growcorp 1998–2011, Project Biostart 2000–02, ECET International Group 2000–03, of the Nat. Science, Tech. and Innovation Framework 2002, Nat. Allocation Advisory Group (Carbon Trading) 2003–, Steering Group, Adare Hosp. and Clinic 2005–10, Stokes Bio 2006–10; Deputy Chair. Irish Chamber Orchestra 2002–08; Vice-Pres. Int. Asscn of Univ. Presidents 1987–99; mem. Bd Nat. Microelectronics Applications Centre 1981–84, Shannon Devt 1976– (Chair. 1987), Advisory Council, Transparency International 2004–, Legal Affairs Council, Gerson Lehrman Group, New York 2005–, Advisory Bd, Ryan Acad. for Entrepreneurship 2009–, Advisory Bd, Pontificio Ateneo S. Anselmo, Rome 2010–; mem. New York Acad. of Science 1988; Fellow, Inst. of Engineers of Ireland 1995, Irish Acad. of Eng 1998 (mem. Energy Standing Cttee 2008–), World Innovation Foundation 2001; Patron Asscn for Children and Adults with Learning Disabilities 1998–2004; Registered Silversmith, Co. of Goldsmiths of Dublin; Freeman, City of Limerick 1995; Hon. mem. Royal Hibernian Acad. of Arts 1994, Nat. Coll. of Art and Design 1997; Hon. LLD (Dublin) 1992, (Queen's Univ., Belfast) 1995, (Nat. Univ. of Ireland) 1998, (Limerick) 2010; Hon. DSc (Ulster) 1997; Paul Harris Fellow, Rotary International 1990. *Publications:* Energy Conversion: Electro-mechanical, Direct, Nuclear 1967, Fluid Dynamic Energy Conversion 1967, Vision 2020: What Future for Business? 1995, Upstart: Friends, Foes and Founding a University (memoir, with Kieran Fagan) 2011; more than 50 publs in various journals and proceedings. *Leisure interests:* sailing, skiing, walking, gardening, playing violin, piano and clarinet. *Address:* Oakhampton House, Newport, Co. Tipperary (home); University of Limerick, Limerick, Ireland (office). *Telephone:* (61) 213198 (office). *Fax:* (61) 213197 (office). *E-mail:* oakhampton@gmail.com (office). *Website:* www2.ul.ie/web/WWW/Administration/Ceremonies/Honorary_Conferrings/Honoured_by_UL/Recipients/Edward%20M%20Walsh (office); sites.google.com/site/oakhamptonconsultants; www.edwalsh.ie.

WALSH, Joe; Irish politician; b. May 1943, Ballineen, Co. Cork; m. Marie Donegan; three s. two d.; ed Univ. Coll. Cork; fmr dairy man.; mem. Irish Creamery Mans Asscn, Soc. of Dairy Tech., mem. Cork Co. Council 1974–91; mem.

Dáil 1977–81, 1982–2007 (retd); Senator 1981–82; Minister of State, Dept of Agric. and Food 1987, 1989–93; Minister for Agric., Food and Forestry 1993–94, 1997, for Agric. and Food 1997–99, for Agric., Food and Rural Devt 1999–2002, for Agric. and Food 2002–04; Chair. Irish Horse Bd 2005–, Cork Racecourse Mallow 2006–, Horse Sport Ireland 2006–, Hunger Task Force 2007; mem. Fianna Fáil. *Address:* 5 Emmet Square, Clonakilty, Co. Cork, Ireland. *Telephone:* (23) 33575. *Fax:* (23) 34267. *Website:* www.joewalsh.ie.

WALSH, Patrick Craig, AB, MD; American urologist and academic; *University Distinguished Service Professor of Urology, Johns Hopkins Medical Institutions;* b. 13 Feb. 1938, Akron, Ohio; s. of Raymond Walsh and Catherine Walsh; m. Margaret Louise Campbell 1964; three s.; ed Case Western Reserve Univ. School of Medicine; internship, Peter Bent Brigham Hosp., Boston, Mass 1964–65, Jr Asst Resident in Surgery 1965–66; Asst Resident in Pediatric Surgery, The Children's Hosp. Medical Center, Boston 1966–67; Resident in Urology, UCLA, Calif. 1967–71, Fellow in Endocrinology, UCLA School of Medicine, Harbor Gen. Hosp. Campus 1968–70; tour of mil. service as Urologist at US Naval Hosp., San Diego 1971–73; Asst Clinical Prof. of Surgery/Urology, Univ. of California, San Diego 1971–73; Visiting Asst Prof. of Medicine, Div. of Metabolism, Univ. of Texas Southwestern Medical School, Dallas 1973–74; David Hall McConnell Prof. and Dir Dept of Urology, Johns Hopkins Univ. School of Medicine, Baltimore, Md 1974, Urologist-in-Chief, The James Buchanan Brady Urological Inst. 1974–2004, Univ. Distinguished Service Prof. of Urology 2004–, fmr Vice-Chair. Exec. Cttee for Medical Institutional Campaign Fund for Johns Hopkins Univ., served on Professional Promotions Cttee, Research Space Planning Cttee, Finance Cttee of Advisory Bd; serves as consultant to US Naval Hosp., Walter Reed Hosp., Clinical Center of NIH, Advisory Bd of Nat. Inst. of Diabetes, Digestive and Kidney Diseases, as well as several local hosps; Trustee, American Bd of Urology; Ed.-in-Chief Campbell's Textbook of Urology 1980–2005 (renamed Cambell Walsh in his honour); mem. Editorial Bd Journal of Urology, New England Journal of Medicine; mem. 14 professional socs, including Inst. of Medicine of NAS, Soc. of Univ. Surgeons, Clinical Soc. of Genitourinary Surgeons (fmr Pres.), American Asscn of Genito-Urinary Surgeons (fmr Pres.), Endocrine Soc., Peripatetic Club; Fellow, American Coll. of Surgeons 1976–80; Paul Harris Fellow, Int. Rotary Foundation 1999; Hon. mem. Urological Soc. of Australasia, German Soc. of Urology, British Asscn of Urologic Surgeons 1998, Royal Coll. of Surgeons of Ireland 2003, Royal Coll. of Surgeons of England 2004, American Urological Asscn 2007; Hon. Dr of Medical Sciences (Masaryk Univ., Brno, Czech Repub.) 2007; prizes for lab. research, American Urological Asscn 1970, 1974, Gold Cystoscope Award, American Urological Asscn 1978, Eugene Fuller Award, American Urological Asscn 1978, Grand Prize, William R. Smart Film Award, American Urological Asscn 1985 and Golden Eagle Award, Council on Nontheatrical Events 1985 for two teaching films, Charles F. Kettering Medal, General Motors Cancer Research Foundation 1996, Robert V. Day Lecturer, Bruce Stewart Lecturer, Southern Lecturer, King Faisal Int. Prize in Medicine, King Faisal Foundation (co-recipient) 2007, Nat. Physician of the Year for Clinical Excellence 2007. *Films:* The Art of Retropubic Prostatectomy 1969, Visits in Urology – Renal Revascularization for Hypertension 1984, Radical Retropubic Prostatectomy and Cystoprostatectomy: Surgical Technique for Preservation of Sexual Function 1985, Radical Cystectomy with Preservation of Sexual Function 'Neuroanatomical Considerations and Surgical Technique' 1987, Radical Retropubic Prostatectomy with Preservation of Sexual Function – An Update after 500 Cases 1987, Radical Retropubic Prostatectomy: Evolution of the Surgical Technique 1993, Radical Prostatectomy, Simultaneous Demonstration by Patrick C. Walsh, M.D. and Fritz H. Schroder, M.D 1993, Alpha Omega Alpha Leaders in American Medicine, Radical Retropubic Prostatectomy: A Detailed Description of the Surgical Technique 2004. *Publications:* Male Infertility (co-ed.) 1977, The Prostate: A Guide for Men and the Women Who Love Them (with Janet F. Worthington) 1995, Campbell's Urology, Seventh Edn (co-ed.) 1997, Dr. Patrick Walsh's Guide to Surviving Prostate Cancer (with Janet F. Worthington) 2001; more than 500 scientific papers in professional journals. *Leisure interests:* sailing, swimming, cycling. *Address:* James Buchanan Brady Urological Institute, Johns Hopkins Medical Institutions, 600 North Wolfe Street, Baltimore, MD 21287, USA (office). *Fax:* (410) 614-3695 (office). *E-mail:* webmaster@urology.jhu.edu (office). *Website:* urology.jhu.edu (office).

WALSH, Paul S.; British business executive; *CEO, Diageo plc;* joined GrandMet's brewing div., Watney Mann and Truman Brewers 1982, Finance Dir 1986, Chief Financial Officer Inter-Continental Hotels 1987, GrandMet's Food Div. 1989, CEO Pillsbury 1992, mem. Bd 1995; mem. Bd Diageo plc (f. after merger of GrandMet and Guinness) 1997–, CEO 2000–; Chair. Scottish Whisky Asscn 2008–11; 0; mem. Bd of Dirs (non-exec.) Federal Express Corpn, Unilever plc, Unilever NV, Avanti Communications Group PLC 2012–; Gov. Henley Management Coll. 2003–1. *Address:* Diageo PLC, Lakeside Drive Park Royal, London, NW107HQ, England (office). *Telephone:* (20) 8978-6000 (office). *Website:* www.diageo.com (office).

WALSH, Sam Maurice Cossart, AO, BCom, FAIM; Australian business executive; *Chief Executive, Rio Tinto Group;* b. 27 Dec. 1949, Middle Brighton, Vic.; s. of Maurice John Walsh and Winifred Margaret Lois Cossart; m. Leanne Roki; two s. one d.; ed Brighton Grammar School, Melbourne, Univ. of Melbourne, Kettering Univ., USA (Fellowship Program); spent 20 years in sr positions in automotive industry at General Motors and Nissan Australia; joined Rio Tinto 1991, Vice-Pres. Rio Tinto Iron Ore 2000–01, Chief Exec. Aluminium Group of Rio Tinto Ltd 2001–04, Chief Exec. Rio Tinto Australia –2009, mem. Bd of Dirs Rio Tino Group 2009–, Chief Exec. Iron Ore Group 2009–13, Chief Exec. Rio Tinto Group 2013–; Man. Dir Hamersley Sales and Marketing 1994–97, Hamersley Operations 1997–2000; Dir, North Ltd 1997–2000, Australian Chamber of Commerce and Industry 2003–05, Western Australian Chamber of Commerce and Industry 2005–13; Dir (non-exec.), Seven West Media 2008–13; Chair. WA chapter of Australian Business Arts Foundation 2008; Past Pres. Western Australia Br. of Scouts Australia; Patron State Library of Western Australia, Univ. of Western Australia's Hackett Foundation; Fellow, Australasian Inst. of Mining and Metallurgy, Chartered Inst. of Purchasing and Supply Man., Australian Inst. of Company Dirs; Hon. Dr of Commerce (Edith Cowan Univ.) 2010; Western Australian Citizen of the Year, Industry and Commerce and an Australian Export Hero 2007, Richard Pratt Business Arts Leadership Award, Australia Business Arts Foundation 2011, Gold Medal, Australian Inst. of Company Dirs 2012. *Address:* Rio Tinto plc, 2 Eastbourne Terrace, London, W2

6LG, England (office); Rio Tinto Ltd, 120 Collins Street, Melbourne, Vic. 3000, Australia (office). *Telephone:* (20) 7781-2000 (London) (office); (3) 9283-3333 (Melbourne) (office). *Fax:* (20) 7781-1800 (London) (office); (3) 9283-3707 (Melbourne) (office). *E-mail:* info@riotinto.com (office). *Website:* www.riotinto.com (office).

WALSH, William (Willie) M., MSc, FRAeS; Irish airline executive; *Chief Executive, International Airlines Group;* b. 1961, Dublin; m.; one d.; ed Trinity Coll. Dublin; Cadet Pilot, Aer Lingus 1979, later Capt., CEO Futura (Aer Lingus Spanish charter operation) 1998–2000, COO Aer Lingus 2000–01, CEO 2001–05, mem. Bd 2001–; mem. Exec. Bd and Chief Exec.-Designate British Airways plc May–Oct. 2005, Chief Exec. Oct. 2005–11, Chief Exec. International Airlines Group (following merger with Iberia) 2011–; mem. Bd of Dirs Fyffes plc 2004–; Pres. Heathrow Br. of Royal Aeronautical Soc.; mem. Chartered Inst. of Logistics and Transport (UK); Hon. Bd mem. Flight Safety International; Hon. mem. The Aviation Club. *Leisure interests:* all sports, especially soccer, rugby and motor sports. *Address:* International Airlines Group, 2 World Business Centre, Heathrow, Newall Road, London Heathrow Airport, Hounslow, TW6 2SF, England (office); Company Secretary, IAG Registered Office, Calle Velázquez 130, Madrid 28006, Spain (office). *Telephone:* (20) 8564-2800 (Hounslow) (office). *E-mail:* media.relations@iairgroup.com (office). *Website:* www.iairgroup.com (office).

WALTER, Andrew, DPhil; Australian academic; ed Univ. of Western Australia, Univ. of Oxford, UK; Tutor in Int. Relations, Univ. of Oxford 1985–86, Lecturer in Int. Relations, Lady Margaret Hall, Oxford 1987–88, Univ. Lecturer in Int. Relations and Fellow, St Anthony's Coll. Oxford 1990–97, European Studies Centre Fellow, Lecturer in Int. Trade and Finance, Univ. of Oxford Foreign Service Programme 1990–97; Assoc., European Mergers and Acquisitions Group, Leveraged Finance Group, JP Morgan, London 1987–90, JP Morgan Finance Program, New York, USA 1989; Sr Lecturer in Int. Relations and Dir MSc Politics of the World Economy Programme, LSE 1997–2012, Reader in Int. Political Economy 2009–12, London Academic Dir TRIUM EMBA Programme; Sr Visiting Fellow, Inst. of Defence and Strategic Studies, Nat. Technological Univ., Singapore 2001–02; other visiting fellowships include Univ. of British Columbia 1994, Int. Univ. of Japan 1994, Pacific Council on Int. Policy and Center for Int. Studies (Univ. of Southern California, Los Angeles) 1996, Univ. of Melbourne Business School 2008; mem. Chatham House Council 2009–. *Publications include:* World Power and World Money; The Role of Hegemony and International Monetary Order (revised edn) 1993; numerous articles on political economy of int. finance and investment and history of thought. *Leisure interests:* . *E-mail:* c.easom@lse.ac.uk.

WALTER, Bernhard; German banker; *Chairman of the Supervisory Board, Bilfinger Berger AG;* joined Dresdner Bank on leaving school; fmr responsibilities include operations in the fmr GDR, corp. finance, Eastern European operations, CEO, mem. Bd 1987–2000, Chair. 1998–2000 (resgnd); currently Chair. Supervisory Bd Bilfinger Berger AG; Chair. Advisory Bd Frauenkirche Dresden Foundation –2005. *Leisure interests:* golf, jogging, music. *Address:* Bilfinger Berger AG, Carl-Reiss-Platz 1-5, 68165 Mannheim, Germany (office). *Telephone:* (621) 4590 (office). *Fax:* (621) 4592366 (office). *Website:* www.bilfingerberger.de (office).

WALTER, Robert D., MBA; American health care industry executive; *Chairman, Cardinal Health Inc.;* m. Peggy McGreevey 1967; three s.; ed Ohio Univ., Harvard Business School; Engineer, North American Rockwell 1968; Founder Cardinal Foods Inc., Dublin, Ohio 1971–88 (acquired by Roundy's Inc. 1988); Founder and CEO Cardinal Distribution Inc. (wholesale drug and health care products distributor, renamed Cardinal Health Inc. 1994) 1979–2006, Chair. 2006–; mem. Bd of Dirs Bank One Corpn, Viacom Inc., Westinghouse Electric; mem. Bd of Trustees Battelle Memorial Inst., Ohio Univ.; fmr mem. Bd of Trustees Ohio Univ. Foundation. *Address:* Cardinal Health Inc., 7000 Cardinal Place, Dublin, OH 43017, USA (office). *Telephone:* (614) 757-5000 (office). *Fax:* (614) 757-8871 (office). *Website:* www.cardinal-health.com (office).

WALTERS, Barbara, BA; American broadcast journalist and producer; b. 25 Sept. 1929, Brookline, Mass.; d. of Lou Walters and Dena Walters (née Selett); m. 1st Robert Henry Katz (m. annulled); m. 2nd Lee Guber 1963 (divorced 1976); one adopted d.; m. 3rd Merv Adelson 1986 (divorced 1992); ed Sarah Lawrence Coll., Bronxville, NY; fmr writer and producer with WNBC–TV, then with Station WPIX and CBS TV morning broadcasts; Producer, NBC TV; joined Today programme, NBC TV 1961 as a writer, then gen. reporter, regular panel mem. 1963–74, Co-Host 1974–76; moderator, Not for Women Only (syndicated TV programme) for five years; Corresp., ABC News, Co-Anchor of evening news programme 1976–78, Co-Host 20/20 1979–2004; Host Barbara Walters Specials 1976–, Ten Most Fascinating People 1994–; Co.-Exec. Producer and Co-Host The View (ABC), NY 1997–; Hon. LHD (Ohio State Univ., Marymount Coll., New York Temple Univ., Wheaton Coll., Hofstra Univ.); Broadcaster of the Year, Int. Radio and TV Soc. 1975, Emmy Award of Nat. Acad. of TV Arts and Sciences 1975, 1983, Silver Satellite Award, American Women in Radio and TV 1985, named one of the 100 Most Important Women of the Century, Good Housekeeping 1985, Pres.'s Award, Overseas Press Club 1988, Lowell Thomas Award for Journalism 1990, 1994, Lifetime Achievement Award, Int. Women's Media Foundation 1992, Lifetime Achievement Award, Daytime Emmy Awards 2000, ranked by Forbes magazine amongst 100 Most Powerful Women (25th) 2004, (63rd) 2008, and several other awards. *Publications:* How to Talk with Practically Anybody about Practically Anything 1970, Audition: A Memoir 2008; contribs to Good Housekeeping, Family Weekly, Reader's Digest, and other periodicals. *Address:* Barwall Productions, 320 West 66th Street, New York, NY 10023 (office); c/o 20/20, 147 Columbus Avenue, 10th Floor, New York, NY 10023, USA. *Website:* abc.go.com/daytime/theview.

WALTERS, Carl John, BSc, MSc, PhD, FRSC; American marine biologist and academic; *Professor, Fisheries Centre, University of British Columbia;* b. 14 Sept. 1944, New Mexico; s. of Carl H. Walters and Eleanor Jonathan; m. Sandra Buckingham; two s.; ed Humboldt State Univ., Colorado State Univ.; currently Prof., Fisheries Centre, Univ. of British Columbia; mem. several NSERC grant cttees 1970–; has done extensive fisheries advisory work for public agencies and industrial groups; has conducted more than 20 workshops for Int. Canadian Fisheries Service, US Fish and Wildlife Service and Int. Inst. for Applied Systems

Analysis 1997–2007; Grand Canyon Sr Scientist 2008–; Ed. Open Fish Science Journal; mem. Editorial Bd Coastal and Estuarine Fisheries, Canadian Journal of Fisheries and Aquatic Sciences; keynote speaker, American Fisheries Soc. 1992, Award of Excellence, American Fisheries Soc. 2006, Volvo Environment Prize, Volvo Environment Foundation (co-recipient) 2006, Timothy Parsons Medal for Oceanography. *Publications:* numerous scientific papers in professional journals on fish population dynamics, fisheries assessment and sustainable man. *Address:* Fisheries Centre, University of British Columbia, 2202 Main Mall, Vancouver, BC V6T 1Z4, Canada (office). *Telephone:* (604) 822-6320 (office). *Fax:* (604) 822-2416 (office). *E-mail:* c.walters@fisheries.ubc.ca (office). *Website:* www.fisheries.ubc.ca/members/cwalters (office).

WALTERS, John P., BA, MA; American fmr government official; ed Michigan State Univ., Univ. of Toronto, Canada; Lecturer, Michigan State Univ. and Boston Coll.; acting Asst Dir and Programme Officer, Educ. Programmes Div., Nat. Endowment for the Humanities 1982–85; Asst to US Sec. of Educ., Dept of Educ., Washington, DC 1985–88; Chief of Staff, White House Office of Nat. Drug Control Policy (ONDCP) 1989–91, Deputy Dir Supply Reduction 1991–93, Dir ONDCP 2001–09; Visiting Fellow, Hudson Inst. 1993, COO and Exec. Vice-Pres. 2009–; Pres. New Citizenship Project –1996; Pres. Philanthropy Round Table 1996–2001. *Publications include:* Body Count: Moral Poverty and How to Win America's War Against Crime and Drugs (with William J. Bennett and John J. Di Iulio Jr). *Address:* Hudson Institute, Washington, 1015 15th Street, NW, 6th Floor, Washington DC, 20005, USA (office). *Telephone:* (202) 974-2400 (office). *Fax:* (202) 974-2410 (office). *E-mail:* info@hudson.org (office). *Website:* www.hudson.org (office).

WALTERS, Julie, CBE; British actress; b. 22 Feb. 1950, Birmingham; d. of the late Thomas Walters and Mary Bridget O'Brien; m. Grant Roffey 1998; one d.; ed St Pauls Prep. School, Edgbaston, Holly Lodge Grammar School for Girls, Smethwick, Manchester Polytechnic; Variety Club Best Newcomer Award 1980, Best Actress Award 1984, British Acad. Award for Best Actress 1984, Golden Globe Award 1984, Show Business Personality of the Year Variety Club Award 2001, Richard Harris Award for Outstanding Contribution by an Actor 2013. *Stage appearances include:* Educating Rita 1980, Fool for Love 1984-85, When I was a Girl I used to Scream and Shout 1986-87, Frankie and Johnny in the Clair de Lune 1989, The Rose Tattoo 1991, All My Sons (Olivier Award 2001) 2000, Acorn Antiques 2005, The Last of the Haussmans 2012. *Films include:* Educating Rita 1983, She'll be Wearing Pink Pyjamas 1984, Personal Services 1986, Prick Up Your Ears 1986, Buster 1987, Mack the Knife 1988, Killing Dad 1989, Stepping Out (Variety Club Award for Best Actress 1991) 1991, Just Like a Woman 1992, Sister My Sister 1994, Intimate Relations 1996, Titanic Town 1997, Girls Night 1997, All Forgotten 1999, Dancer 1999, Billy Elliot (Evening Standard Award, BAFTA Award) 2000, Harry Potter and the Philosopher's Stone 2001, Before You Go 2002, Harry Potter and the Chamber of Secrets 2002, Calendar Girls 2003, Harry Potter and the Prisoner of Azkaban 2004, Mickybo and Me 2005, Wah-Wah 2005, Driving Lessons 2006, Becoming Jane 2007, Harry Potter and the Order of the Phoenix 2007, Mamma Mia! 2008, Harry Potter and the Half-Blood Prince 2009, Harry Potter and the Deathly Hallows, Part I 2010, Gnomeo and Juliet 2010, Harry Potter and the Deathly Hallows, Part II 2011, Brave (voice) 2012, Effie 2013, Justin and the Knights of Valour (voice) 2013, One Chance 2013. *Television includes:* Talent 1980, Wood and Walters (with (Victoria Wood) 1981–82, Boys from the Blackstuff 1982, Say Something Happened 1982, As Seen On TV 1984, 1986, 1987, The Birthday Party 1986, Her Big Chance 1987, GBH 1991, Stepping Out 1991, Julie Walters and Friends 1991, Clothes in the Wardrobe 1992, Wide Eyed and Legless 1993, Bambino Mio 1993, Pat and Margaret 1994, Jake's Progress 1995, Little Red Riding Hood 1995, Intimate Relations 1996, Julie Walters is an Alien 1997, Dinnerladies 1998–99, Jack and the Beanstalk 1998, Oliver Twist 1999, My Beautiful Son (BAFTA Award) 2001, Murder (BAFTA and Royal TV Soc. Awards for Best Actress 2003) 2002, The Canterbury Tales (mini-series, The Wife of Bath) 2003, The Return 2003, Ahead of the Class 2005, The Ruby in the Smoke 2006, Filth! The Mary Whitehouse Story 2007, A Short Stay in Switzerland 2009, Victoria Wood's Midlife Christmas 2009, Mo (BAFTA Award for Best Actress, Int. Emmy Award for Best Actress 2011) 2010, The Jury 2011, The Hollow Crown: Henry V 2012. *Publications include:* Baby Talk 1990, Maggie's Tree (novel) 2006, That's Another Story (autobiography) 2008. *Leisure interests:* reading, travel. *Address:* c/o Independent Talent Group, 76 Oxford Street, London, W1D 1BS, England (office). *Telephone:* (20) 7636-6565 (office).

WALTERS, Sir Peter Ingram, Kt, BCom; British business executive; b. 11 March 1931, Birmingham, England; s. of the late Stephen Walters and of Edna F. Walters (née Redgate); m. 1st Patricia Anne Tulloch 1960 (divorced 1991); two s. one. d.; m. 2nd Meryl Marshall 1992; ed King Edward's School, Birmingham and Univ. of Birmingham; served in Royal Army Service Corps 1952–54; joined BP 1954, Vice-Pres. BP North America 1965–67, Gen. Man. Supply and Devt 1969–70, Regional Dir Western Hemisphere 1971–72; Dir BP Trading Ltd 1971–73, BP Chemicals International 1972, Chair. 1978–90; Deputy Chair. The British Petroleum Co. Ltd 1980–81, Chair. 1981–90; Vice-Pres. Gen. Council of British Shipping 1974–76, Pres. 1977–78; Pres. Soc. of Chemical Industry 1978–79, Inst. of Manpower Studies 1980–86; Dir Post Office 1978–79, Nat. Westminster Bank 1981– (Deputy Chair. 1988–89); Dir Thorn EMI (now EMI) 1989, Deputy Chair. 1990–99; Dir SmithKline Beecham PLC 1989–2000, apptd Deputy Chair. GlaxoSmithKline PLC 2000, Deputy Chair. 1990–94, Chair. 1994–2000; Chair. Blue Circle Industries Ltd 1990–96, Midland Bank PLC 1992; Deputy Chair. HSBC Holdings 1992–2001; Adviser Union Bank of Switzerland 1990–92; Dir (non-exec.) Nomura Int. plc, Saatchi and Saatchi 1993–2000; Pres. Police Foundation; Pres. Advisory Council, Inst. of Business Ethics 2004–08; Chair. Advisory Bd TNK International 2002–06; mem. of Council, Industrial Soc.; Gov. London Business School 1981–91; Pres. Inst. of Directors 1986–92; Trustee, mem. Foundation Bd, Nat. Maritime Museum 1982–89; Chair. Int. Man. Inst., Geneva 1984–86; Trustee Inst. of Econ. Affairs; Hon. DUniv (Birmingham) 1986, (Stirling) 1987; Commdr, Order of Léopold (Belgium). *Leisure interests:* golf, gardening, sailing. *Address:* 1 St James's Square, London, SW1Y 4PD, England (office). *Telephone:* (20) 7496-5821 (office). *Fax:* (20) 7496-4436 (office). *E-mail:* sjs1@bp .com (office).

WALTON, Jim; American broadcasting news executive; b. 1958; m.; two s.; ed Univ. of Maryland; joined Cable News Network (CNN) 1980, various positions including video journalist, tape editor, exec. producer, launched CNN/Sports Illustrated (all-sports TV channel), served as Pres. 1996–2000, Deputy Pres., Pres. CNN Domestic Networks 2001, Pres. and COO 2001–03, Pres. CNN News Group 2003–12; Emmy Award for coverage of 1996 Olympic Park bombing, Atlanta, several Cable Ace awards. *Leisure interests:* Nebraska football, Allman brothers. *Address:* c/o CNN Center, 1 CNN Center, Marietta Street NW, Atlanta, GA 30303, USA.

WALTON, Samuel Robson (Rob), BA, JD; American retail executive; *Chairman, Walmart;* b. 1944, Tulsa, Okla; s. of the late Sam Moore Walton (founder of Wal-Mart; died 1992); m. Carolyn F. Walton (divorced); one c.; ed The Coll. of Wooster, Ohio, Univ. of Arkansas, Columbia Univ., New York; fmrly with Conner, Winters, Ballaine, Barry & McGowen (law firm), Tulsa –1969; joined Wal-Mart Stores Inc. (now called Walmart), Bentonville, Ark. 1969–, Sr Vice-Pres., Sec. and Gen. Counsel 1978–82, Dir and Vice-Chair. Bd 1982–92, Chair. 1992–; currently involved with several non-profit and educational orgs, including Conservation International (Chair. Exec. Cttee); Emer. Life Trustee, Coll. of Wooster. *Address:* Walmart, 702 SW 8th Street, Bentonville, AR 72716-8611, USA (office). *Telephone:* (479) 273-4000 (office). *Fax:* (479) 277-1830 (home). *Website:* www.walmart.com (office); corporate.walmart.com (office).

WALTON OF DETCHANT, Baron (Life Peer), cr. 1989, of Detchant in the County of Northumberland; **John Nicholas Walton,** Kt, TD, MA, MD, DSc, FRCP, FMedSci; British neurologist; b. 16 Sept. 1922, Rowlands Gill, Co. Durham; s. of Herbert Walton and Eleanor Watson Walton (née Ward); m. Mary Elizabeth Harrison 1946 (died 2003); one s. two d.; ed Alderman Wraith Grammar School, Spennymoor, Co. Durham, King's Coll., Medical School, Univ. of Durham; served RAMC 1947–49, Col L/RAMC OC 1(N) Gen. Hosp. (TA) 1963–66 (Hon. Col 1968–73); Medical Registrar, Royal Victoria Infirmary, Newcastle-upon-Tyne 1949–51; Nuffield Foundation Travelling Fellow, Mass. Gen. Hosp., Harvard Medical School, Boston, USA, King's Coll. Travelling Fellow, MRC Neurology Unit, Nat. Hosp., Queen Sq., London 1954–55; First Asst in Neurology, Univ. of Durham (Newcastle-upon-Tyne) 1955–58; Consultant Neurologist, Newcastle Hosps 1958–83; Prof. of Neurology, Univ. of Newcastle-upon-Tyne 1968–83, Dean of Medicine 1971–81; Warden, Green Coll. Oxford 1983–89; mem. MRC 1974–78, Gen. Medical Council (Chair. Educ. Cttee) 1971–89, Pres. 1982–89; Chair. Muscular Dystrophy Group of GB 1971–95, Hamlyn Foundation Nat. Comm. on Educ. 1990–96, House of Lords Select Cttee on Medical Ethics 1992–93; Pres. British Medical Asscn 1980–82; Pres. Royal Soc. of Medicine 1984–86; First Vice-Pres. World Fed. of Neurology 1981–89, Pres. 1989–97; Hon. Freeman of Newcastle upon Tyne 1980, of Worshipful Soc. of Apothecaries 2013; Hon. FACP; Hon. FRCP (Edin.); Hon. FRCP (Canada); Hon. FRCPath; Hon. FRCPsych; Hon. FRCPCH; Hon. Fellow Inst. of Educ. (London) 1995; Hon. mem. Norwegian Acad. of Arts and Sciences 1992; Hon. Dr de l'Université (Aix-Marseille) 1975; Hon. DSc (Leeds) 1979, (Leicester) 1980, (Hull) 1988, (Oxford Brookes) 1994, (Durham) 2002; Hon. MD (Sheffield) 1987, (Mahidol Univ., Thailand) 1998; Hon. DCL (Newcastle) 1988, (Northumbria) 2013; Dr hc (Genoa) 1992. *Publications:* Subarachnoid Haemorrhage 1956, Polymyositis (with R. D. Adams) 1958, Oxford Companion to Medicine (ed.) 1986, Essentials of Neurology (6th edn) 1989, Skeletal Muscle Pathology (with F. L. Mastaglia, 2nd edn) 1992, Brain's Diseases of the Nervous System (ed., 10th edn) 1993, The Spice of Life (autobiog.) 1993, Disorders of Voluntary Muscle (ed., 6th edn) 1994, Oxford Medical Companion (ed.) 1994 and numerous articles in scientific journals. *Leisure interests:* music, golf (Pres. Bamburgh Castle Golf Club), reading, cricket. *Address:* 15 Croft Way, Belford, Northumberland, NE70 7ET, England (home). *Telephone:* (1668) 219009 (home). *Fax:* (1668) 219010 (home). *E-mail:* waldetch@aol.com (office).

WALTZ, Christoph; Austrian/German actor; b. 4 Oct. 1956, Vienna, Austria; s. of Johannes Waltz and Elisabeth Urbancic; three adult c. from a prior m.; m. 2nd Judith Holste; one d.; ed Max Reinhardt Seminar, Vienna, Lee Strasberg Theatre and Film Inst., New York, USA; began as a stage actor, performing at venues including Schauspielhaus Zürich, Burgtheater, Vienna and the Salzburg Festival; numerous TV appearances; directorial debut with the German-language TV production, Wenn man sich traut 2000; Österreichisches Ehrenzeichen für Wissenschaft und Kunst (Austria) 2012. *Films include:* Kopfstand 1981, Fire and Sword 1982, Wahnfried 1986, Quicker Than the Eye 1990, Zycie za zycie 1991, St. Petri Schnee 1991, Ein Anfang von etwas 1995, Our God's Brother 1997, Sieben Monde 1998, Das merkwürdige Verhalten geschlechtsreifer Großstädter zur Paarungszeit 1998, Die Braut 1999, Ordinary Decent Criminal 2000, Falling Rocks 2000, She 2001, Queen's Messenger 2001, Death, Deceit & Destiny Aboard the Orient Express 2001, Angst 2003, Gun-shy 2003, Herr Lehmann 2003, Dorian 2004, Lapislazuli – Im Auge des Bären 2006, Inglourious Basterds (Best Actor Award, Cannes Film Festival, BAFTA, Golden Globe, Screen Actors Guild Award and Academy Award for Best Supporting Actor 2009) 2009, The Green Hornet 2011, Water for Elephants 2011, The Three Musketeers 2011, Carnage 2011, Django Unchained 2012, The Zero Theorem 2013, Epic (voice) 2013. *Television includes:* Der Einstand (film) 1977, Feuer! (film) 1979, Parole Chicago (series) 1979, Die Weltmaschine (film) 1981, Dr. Margarete Johnsohn (film) 1982, The Mysterious Stranger (film) 1982, Der Sandmann (film) 1983, A Case for Two (series) 1985, Lenz oder die Freiheit (mini-series) 1986, Derrick (series) 1986–88, The Old Fox (series) 1986–90, Das andere Leben (film) 1987, Tatort (series) 1987–2008, The Alien Years (film) 1988, Goldeneye (film) 1989, The Gravy Train (mini-series) 1990, The Gravy Train Goes East (mini-series) 1991, Die Angst wird bleiben (film) 1992, 5 Zimmer, Küche, Bad (film) 1992, König der letzten Tage (mini-series) 1993, Die Staatsanwältin (film) 1994, Tag der Abrechnung – Der Amokläufer von Euskirchen (film) 1994, Jacob (film) 1994, Man(n) sucht Frau (film) 1995, Prinz zu entsorgen (film) 1995, Die Staatsanwältin (series) 1995, The All New Alexei Sayle Show (series) 1995, Catherine the Great (film) 1996, Du bist nicht allein – Die Roy Black Story (film) 1996, Rosa Roth (series) 1996, Rex: A Cop's Best Friend (series) 1996, Der Tourist (film) 1996, Maître Da Costa (series) 1997, Faust (series) 1997, Schimanski (series) 1997, Rache für mein totes Kind (film) 1998, Mörderisches Erbe – Tausch mit einer Toten (film) 1998, Einsteins Ende (film) 1998, Vickys Alptraum (film) 1998, Schock – Eine Frau in Angst (film) 1998, Das Finale (film) 1998, Dessine-moi un jouet (film) 1999 The Beast (film) 2000, Engel sucht Flügel (film) 2001, Riekes Liebe (film) 2001, Der Tanz mit dem Teufel

– Die Entführung des Richard Oetker (film) 2001, Dienstreise – Was für eine Nacht (film) 2002, Weihnachtsmann gesucht (film) 2002, Jagd auf den Flammenmann (film) 2003, Der Fall Gehring (film) 2003, Zwei Tage Hoffnung (film) 2003, Jennerwein (film) 2003, Tigeraugen sehen besser (film) 2003, Scheidungsopfer Mann (film) 2004, Mörderische Suche (film) 2004, Schöne Witwen küssen besser (film) 2004, Die Patriarchin (mini-series) 2005, Der Elefant – Mord verjährt nie (series) 2005, Die Spezialisten: Kripo Rhein-Main (series) 2006, Polizeiruf 110 (series) 2006, Stolberg (series) 2006, Franziskas Gespür für Männer (film) 2006, Der Staatsanwalt (series) 2007, Die Verzauberung (film) 2007, Der letzte Zeuge (series) 2007, Under Suspicion (series) 2007, Die Zürcher Verlobung – Drehbuch zur Liebe (film) 2007, Die Anwälte (series) 2008, Das jüngste Gericht (film) 2008, Todsünde (film) 2008, Das Geheimnis im Wald (film) 2008, Late Night with Jimmy Fallon (series) 2012. *Address:* c/o Players Agentur Management GmbH, Sophienstrasse 21, 10178 Berlin - Mitte, Germany (office); c/o ICM, 730 Fifth Avenue, New York, NY 10019-4105, USA. *E-mail:* info@players.de (office). *Website:* www.players .de (office).

WALZER, Michael, BA, PhD; American writer, academic and editor; b. 3 March 1935, New York, NY; m. Judith Borodovko 1956; two d.; ed Brandeis and Harvard Univs, Univ. of Cambridge, UK; Asst Prof. of Politics, Princeton Univ., NJ 1962–66; Assoc. Prof., Harvard Univ. 1966–68, Prof. of Govt 1968–80; Ed. Dissent 1964–; Prof. of Social Science, School of Social Science, Inst. for Advanced Study, Princeton, NJ 1980, Prof. Emer. 2005–; Fellow, Straus Inst. for the Advanced Study of Law and Justice, New York Univ. School of Law 2010–11; mem. Conf. on the Study of Political Thought, Soc. of Ethical and Legal Philosophy; mem. Editorial Bd Political Theory; Contributing Ed. The New Republic (weekly news magazine); mem. Bd of Govs Hebrew Univ.; Dr hc (Lawrence Univ.) 1980, (Brandeis Univ.) 1981, (Georgetown Univ.) 1992, (Kalamazoo Coll.) 1994, (Tel-Aviv Univ.) 2003, (Athens) 2007, (Hebrew Univ.) 2012, Brandeis Univ. Doctorate Alumni Award 2001; Fulbright Fellow, Univ. of Cambridge 1956–57, Harbison Award 1971, Spinoza Lens 2008. *Publications include:* The Revolution of the Saints: A Study in the Origins of Radical Politics 1965, The Political Imagination in Literature (co-ed. with Philip Green) 1968, Obligations: Essays on Disobedience, War and Citizenship 1970, Political Action: A Practical Guide to Movement Politics 1971, Regicide and Revolution: Speeches at the Trial of Louis XVI (ed.) 1974, Just and Unjust Wars: A Moral Argument with Historical Illustrations 1977, Radical Principles: Reflections of an Unreconstructed Democrat 1977, Spheres of Justice: A Defense of Pluralism and Equality 1983, Exodus and Revolution 1985, Interpretation and Social Criticism 1987, The Company of Critics: Social Criticism and Political Commitment in the Twentieth Century 1988, Civil Society and American Democracy (selected essays in German) 1992, What it Means to be an American 1992, Thick and Thin: Moral Argument at Home and Abroad 1994, Pluralism, Justice and Equality (with David Miller) 1995, Toward a Global Civil Society (ed.) 1995, On Toleration 1997, Arguments from the Left (selected essays in Swedish) 1997, Pluralism and Democracy (selected essays in French) 1997, Reason, Politics and Passion (The Horkheimer Lectures, in German) 1999, The Jewish Political Tradition, Vol. 1 Authority (co-ed with Menachem Lorberbaum, Noam Zohar and Yair Lorberbaum) 2000, Exilic Politics in the Hebrew Bible 2001, War, Politics, and Morality (selected essays in Spanish) 2001, The Thread of Politics: Democracy, Social Criticism, and World Government (selected essays in Italian) 2002, Erklärte Kriege—Kriegserklärungen (selected essays in German) 2003, Arguing About War (selected essays and articles) 2004, Politics and Passion 2004, Law, Politics, and Morality in Judaism 2006, Thinking Politically 2007, In God's Shadow: Politics in the Hebrew Bible 2012; contribs to professional journals. *Address:* School of Social Science, Institute for Advanced Study, Einstein Drive, Princeton, NJ 08540, USA (office). *Telephone:* (609) 734-8253 (office). *Fax:* (609) 951-4434 (office). *E-mail:* walzer@ias.edu (office). *Website:* www.sss.ias.edu (office).

WAMALA, HE Cardinal Emmanuel, DipEd; Ugandan ecclesiastic; *Archbishop Emeritus of Kampala;* b. 15 Dec. 1926, Kamaggwa; s. of Cosma Kyamcra and Theresa Nnamayanja; ed Minor Seminary, Bukalasa, Major Seminary, Katigondo, Pontifical Urban Univ. and Pontifical Gregorian Univ., Rome, Italy, Makerere Univ., Kampala, Univ. of Notre Dame, South Bend, Ind., USA; ordained priest 1957; worked at parish of Villa Maria, acted as Diocesan School Supervisor in Diocese of Masaka 1960–62; mem. Faculty, Minor Seminary of Bukalasa 1964–68; Chaplain, faculty mem. and Rector Univ. of Makerere 1968–74; Vicar Gen. Diocese of Masaka 1974–81; Parish Priest of Nkoni 1975–77, of Kimaanya 1977–79; Chaplain of His Holiness Pope Paul VI 1977; Bishop of Kiyinda-Mityana 1981; attended Sixth Ordinary Ass. of World Synod of Bishops, Vatican City 1983; Coadjutor Archbishop of Kampala 1988–90, Archbishop of Kampala 1990–2006, Emer. 2006–; Pres. Episcopal Conf. of Uganda 1990–94; First Rector Nuova Uganda Martyrs Univ. 1993–; attended Special Ass. of World Synod of Bishops for Africa, Vatican City 1994; cr. Cardinal (Cardinal Priest of S. Ugo) 1994; Pres. Uganda Joint Christian 1990–. *Address:* Archdiocese of Kampala, PO Box 14125, Mengo-Kampala, Uganda (office). *Telephone:* (41) 270183/4 (office); (41) 342622 (office). *Fax:* (41) 345441 (office).

WAMBACH, Abby; American professional football player and coach; b. 2 June 1980, Rochester, NY; d. of Pete Wambach and Judy Wambach; ed Our Lady of Mercy High School, Rochester, Univ. of Florida, Gainesville; plays as a forward; youth career: Our Lady of Mercy High School 1994–98, Rochester Spirit (Capt.) 1995–97, Univ. of Florida 1998–2001; senior career: Washington Freedom 2002–03, 2009–10, USA 2003–, magicJack (also Coach) 2011; began playing football aged four; at high school, scored 142 goals, including 34 in 1997; mem. Olympic Devt Team (ODP) U-16 Nat. Team 1996, Nat. U-20 Pool 1997; trained and played with US Nat. Team while competing in US Soccer Festival, Blaine, Minn. 1997; travelled to Beijing, China as a mem. of the first American youth football team to compete there 1997; played for coach Becky Burleigh's Florida Gators women's football team in Nat. Collegiate Athletic Asscn (NCAA) competition 1998–2001, won an NCAA nat. championship 1998, four consecutive Southeastern Conf. (SEC) championships 1998, 1999, 2000, 2001, set school career records for goals (96), assists (49), points (242), game-winning goals (24) and hat tricks (10); second overall draft pick for the Women's United Soccer Assen (WUSA)'s second season; went on to play for the Washington Freedom 2002, won Founders Cup III (WUSA championship match) 2003; returned to the Washington Freedom for the 2010 WPS season (team relocated to Boca Raton, Fla and became magicJack 2011); named to US World Cup team 2003 (bronze medal), 2007 (bronze medal), 2011

(silver medal); gold medal, Olympic Games, Athens 2004, London 2012; named to Parade magazine's high school All-America team and voted Nat. Player of the Year by Umbro and the Nat. Soccer Coaches Assen of America (NSCAA), named All-Greater Rochester Player of the Year 1995, 1997, named NSCAA Regional Player of the Year 1997, NSCAA State of New York Player of the Year 1997, Gatorade Circle of Champions New York Player of the Year 1997, SEC Freshman of the Year 1998, a freshman All-American 1998, a first-team All-SEC selection 1998, 1999, 2000, 2001, two-time SEC Player of the Year 2000, 2001, SEC Tournament Most Valuable Player 2000, 2001, named a first-team All-American for her sophomore, junior and senior seasons 1999, 2000, 2001, WPS Rookie of the Year 2002, US Soccer Athlete of the Year Award 2003, 2004, 2007, 2010, 2011, Associated Press Female Athlete of the Year 2011, ESPN's ESPY Award for Best Play of the Year 2011, FIFA Women's World Cup Silver Ball 2011, FIFA Women's World Cup Bronze Boot 2011, inducted into Univ. of Florida Athletic Hall of Fame 2012, FIFA World Player of the Year 2012, FIFA Women's World Player of the Year 2013. *E-mail:* contact@abbywambach.com. *Website:* www.abbywambach.com.

WAMBAUGH, Joseph, MA; American writer; b. 22 Jan. 1937, East Pittsburgh, Pa; s. of Joseph A. Wambaugh and Anne Malloy; m. Dee Allsup 1955; two s. (one deceased) one d.; ed California State Coll., Los Angeles; served in US Marine Corps 1954–57; police officer in LA 1960–74; creator, TV series, Police Story 1973; Int. Asscn of Crime Writers Rodolfo Walsh Prize 1989, Mystery Writers of America Grand Master Award 2004, Strand Magazine Lifetime Achievement Award 2012. *Publications include:* The New Centurions 1971, The Blue Knight 1972, The Onion Field (Mystery Writers of America Edgar Allan Poe Award 1974) 1973, The Choirboys 1975, The Black Marble 1978, The Glitter Dome 1981, The Delta Star 1983, Lines and Shadows 1984, The Secrets of Harry Bright 1985, Echoes in the Darkness 1987, The Blooding 1989, The Golden Orange 1990, Fugitive Nights 1992, Finnegan's Week 1993, Floaters 1996, Fire Lover: A True Story 2002, Hollywood Station 2007, Hollywood Crows 2008, Hollywood Moon 2009, Hollywood Hills 2010, Harbor Nocturne 2012. *E-mail:* info@josephwambaugh.net. *Website:* www.josephwambaugh.net.

WAMMEN, Nicolai, MSc; Danish politician; *Minister of Defence;* b. 7 Feb. 1971; s. of Christian Frederik Wammen and Lotte Wammen; one s.; ed Univ. of Aarhus; Pres. Frit Forum Aarhus (social democrat student org.) 1996–97; mem. Aarhus City Council 1998–2006; mem. Folketing (Parl.) (Social Democratic Party) 2001–05; Mayor of Aarhus 2006–11; Minister for European Affairs 2011–13, Minister of Defence 2013–; mem. Bd Aarhus Festival 1997–2001 (fmr Chair.); fmr Chair. Port of Aarhus; mem. Bd Danish Ports; mem. Growth Forum Central Jutland. *Address:* Ministry of Defence, Holmens Kanal 42, 1060 Copenhagen K, Denmark (office). *Telephone:* 33-92-33-20 (office). *Fax:* 3-32-06-55 (office). *E-mail:* fmn@fmn.dk (office). *Website:* www.fmn.dk (office).

WAMYTAN, Roch, MA; New Caledonian politician; b. 13 Dec. 1950, Nouméa; s. of the late Benjamin Wamytan and Philomène Pidjot; three s. one d.; ed Grand Séminaire St Paul, Nouméa, Univ. of Lyon II and Centre d'Etudes Financières Economiques et Bancaires, Paris; fmr Head of Office for the Devt of the Interior and Islands; Attaché to Econ. Devt Sec. 1988; mem. Union Calédonienne, now Pres.; Chief, St Louis tribal village; mem. Mt Dore Town Council; mem. Southern Prov. Govt; Deputy Speaker, Congress of New Caledonia, responsible for external relations 1989–; Vice-Pres. Kanak Socialist Nat. Liberation Front (FLNKS) 1990, Pres. 1995–2001; Pres. New Caledonian Diocese Pastoral Council 1996; Chair. Melanesian Spearhead Group –2003. *Address:* BP 288, Mont-Dore, 98810 New Caledonia. *Telephone:* 26-58-83; 27-31-29. *Fax:* 26-58-88; 27-32-04.

WAN, Feng, MBA, DEcon; Chinese insurance executive; *Vice-President, China Life Insurance (Group) Company;* b. 1958; ed Open Univ. of Hong Kong, Nankai Univ.; Dir and Sr Vice-Pres. Tai Ping Life Insurance Co., Hong Kong –1977; fmr Deputy Chief, Life Insurance Div., People's Insurance Co. of China, Jilin br., becoming Gen. Man. Shenzhen br., People's Insurance Co. of China Life 1997–99; fmr Asst Pres. China Life Insurance Co. Ltd Hong Kong br., Vice-Pres. and Gen. Man. Shenzhen br. 1999, Dir China Life-CMG 1999, Vice-Pres. China Life Insurance Co. Ltd 2003–07, Exec. Dir 2006–, Acting Pres. Jan.–Oct. 2007, Pres. Oct. 2007–, Vice-Pres. China Life Insurance (Group) Co. 2007–, also Dir China Life Property and Casualty Insurance Co. Ltd 2006–, China Life Insurance Asset Management Co. Ltd 2006–, China Life Pension Insurance Co. Ltd 2007–. *Address:* China Life Insurance Co. Ltd, 23rd Floor, China Life Building, 16 Chaowai Street, Chaoyang District, Beijing, 100020, People's Republic of China (office). *Telephone:* (10) 85659999 (office). *Fax:* (10) 85252232 (office). *E-mail:* serve@e-chinalife.com (office). *Website:* www.e-chinalife.com (office).

WAN, Gang, MEng, PhD; Chinese mechanical engineer, academic and politician; *Minister of Science and Technology;* b. 1952, Shanghai; ed Northeast Forestry Univ., Tongji Univ.; mem. Faculty, Dept of Mechanics, Tongji Univ. 1981–85; Visiting Scholar, Dept of Mechanical Eng, Clausthal Univ. of Tech., Germany 1985–91, Visiting Prof. 1994; worked in R&D Dept, Audi Corpn, Germany 1991–2001; Dean, New Energy Automobile Eng Centre, Tongji Univ. 2001, Asst Pres. Tongji Univ. 2001–03, Vice-Pres. 2003–04, Pres. 2004–07; Vice-Chair. China Zhi Gong Party 2006–07, Chair. 2007–; Minister of Science and Tech. 2007–; mem. Nat. Cttee and Standing Cttee 10th CPPCC 2003, Vice-Chair. 11th CPPCC Nat. Cttee 2008–13, 12th CPPCC Nat. Cttee 2013–. *Address:* Ministry of Science and Technology, 15b Fuxing Lu, Haidian Qu, Beijing 1000862, People's Republic of China (office). *Telephone:* (10) 58881888 (office). *Fax:* (10) 68515006 (office). *E-mail:* officemail@mail.most.gov.cn (office). *Website:* www.most.gov.cn (office).

WAN, Guoquan; Chinese politician; b. March 1919, Tao'an Co., Jilin Prov.; ed Zhonghua Univ., May 7th Cadre School; worker, Taxation Bureau, Shenyang City, Liaoning Prov. 1945–47, Lizhong Acid Factory, Tianjin 1947–56; joined China Democratic Nat. Construction Assen 1950; Deputy Dir Tianjin Dyestuff Chemical Industry Co. 1956–57; Dir Tianjin Fed. of Industry and Commerce 1956–63, Sec.-Gen. 1964, Vice-Chair. 1977; Chair. Hedong Dist Industry and Commerce 1957–63; Perm. mem. Exec. Cttee All-China Fed. of Industry and Commerce 1978–83, Vice-Chair. Tianjin Municipal Cttee 1978; Vice-Chair. 4th China Democratic Nat. Construction Assen Cen. Cttee 1983–88, Dir Cen. Cttee Exec. Bureau 1985–88, Vice-Chair. 5th Cen. Cttee 1988–92, Vice-Chair. 6th Cen. Cttee 1992–97, Hon. Vice-Chair. 7th Cen. Cttee 1997–2002; mem. 5th CPPCC Nat. Cttee 1978–82, Perm. mem. 6th CPPCC Nat. Cttee 1983–87, 7th CPPCC Nat. Cttee

1988–92, 8th CPPCC Nat. Cttee 1993–98 (Vice-Chair. 1993–98), Vice-Chair. 9th CPPCC Nat. Cttee 1998–2003; Pres. China Council for the Promotion of Peaceful Reunification 1993–99; Vice-Pres. Asscn for Int. Understanding of China 1993–. *Address:* c/o National Committee of Chinese People's Political Consultative Conference, 23 Taipingqiao Street, Beijing, People's Republic of China (office).

WAN, Li; Chinese government official (retd); b. Dec. 1916, Dongping Co., Shandong Prov.; m. Bian Tao; four s. one d.; joined CCP 1936; trained as teacher; various posts in Dongping Co. CCP Cttee; served on Hebei-Shangdong CCP Cttee, Deputy Dir Financial and Econ. Cttee, Nanjing Mil. Control Comm.; Head Econ. Dept and Dir Construction Bureau 1947–49; Deputy Head, then Head Industrial Dept, Southwest China Mil. and Admin. Cttee; Vice-Minister of Bldg, Minister of Urban Construction 1949–58; subsequently Sec. Beijing Municipal CCP Cttee, Deputy Mayor of Beijing, Asst to Premier Zhou Enlai in planning and organizing work of Ten Major Projects of the Capital (including Great Hall of the People) and other important construction projects; persecuted during Cultural Revolution 1966–73; Vice-Chair. Municipal Revolutionary Cttee; fmr Minister of Railways, Head Provisional Leading Party mems' group in Ministry; closely allied with Deng Xiaoping's policies; dismissed as Minister when latter fell from favour 1976; First Vice-Minister of Light Industry 1977; First Sec. Anhui Prov. CCP Cttee, Chair. Anhui Prov. Revolutionary Cttee, First Political Commissar, Anhui Mil. Area 1977–80; Vice-Premier, State Council and Chair. State Agricultural Comm., Sec. Leading Party Group, Chair. Cen. Afforestation Comm. 1982–89, State People's Air Defence Comm. 1980; Deputy to 2nd, 3rd, 4th, 5th and 7th NPC, Chair. Standing Cttee 7th NPC 1988–93; elected mem. CCP 11th Cen. Cttee, mem. Secr. CCP 11th Cen. Cttee; elected mem. Politburo CCP Cen. Cttee and mem. Secr. 1982, 1987; mem. Presidium 14th Nat. Congress CCP 1992; Hon. Pres. Bridge Asscn 1980–, Literature Foundation 1986–, Chinese Youth Devt Foundation 1993–, Greening Foundation 1989–, China Environmental Protection Foundation 1993–. *Leisure interests:* tennis, bridge. *Address:* c/o Standing Committee, National People's Congress, Tian An Men Square, Beijing, People's Republic of China (office).

WAN, Xueyuan; Chinese administrator; *Vice-President, China Association for International Exchange of Personnel;* b. 1941; ed Jiaotong Univ., Shanghai; joined CCP 1964; Dir Gen. Office and Deputy Dir, later Deputy Sec.-Gen., later Sec.-Gen. People's Govt, Shanghai Municipality; Vice-Gov. Zhejiang Prov. 1992–93, Gov. 1993–97; Deputy Sec. CCP 9th Zhejiang Prov. Cttee 1993–97; Vice-Minister of Personnel, State Admin of Foreign Experts Affairs 1997, Dir State Admin of Foreign Experts Affairs 1997–2006; Vice-Pres. China Asscn for Int. Exchange of Personnel 1999–; Alt. mem. 13th CCP Cen. Cttee 1987–92, mem. 14th CCP Cen. Cttee 1992–97; Del., 15th CCP Nat. Congress 1992–97; Deputy, 8th NPC 1992–97, 9th NPC 1997–2002. *Address:* China Association for International Exchange of Personnel, Beijing, People's Republic of China (office). *Website:* caiep@caiep.org (office).

WAN, Zhexian; Chinese mathematician and academic; b. Nov. 1927; s. of Wan Cheggui and Zhou Weijin; m. Wang Shixiau; two d.; ed Qinghua Univ.; Prof. of Math., Division of Pure Math. and Applied Math., Inst. of Systems Science (now Chinese Acad. of Math. and System Sciences) 1978–; Ed.-in-Chief Algebra Colloquium (journal); mem. Chinese Acad. of Sciences 1992; Hua Lookeng Award for Math. 1995. *Publications:* Classical Groups 1963, Geometry of Classical Groups over Finite Fields 1993, Geometry of Matrices 1996. *Address:* Academy of Mathematics and System Science, 1A Nansi Street, Zhongguancun, Beijing 100080, People's Republic of China (office). *Telephone:* (10) 62553005 (office); (10) 62559148 (home). *Fax:* (10) 62568364 (office). *E-mail:* issb@bamboo.iss.ac.cn. *Website:* www.iss.ac.cn/laboratory/purelab (office).

WANAMAKER, Zoë, CBE; British/American actress; b. New York, USA; d. of the late Sam Wanamaker and of Charlotte Wanamaker; m. Gawn Grainger 1994; one step-s. one step-d.; ed Cen. School of Speech and Drama, London; professional debut as Hermia in A Midsummer Night's Dream, Manchester 1970; repertory at Royal Lyceum 1971–72, Oxford Playhouse 1974–75, Nottingham 1975–76; Assoc., Royal Nat. Theatre; Patron Prisoners of Conscience; Vice-Patron The Actors Centre; Hon. Pres. Shakespeare's Globe Theatre, Hon. Vice-Pres. Dignity in Dying; Hon. DLitt (South Bank Univ.) 1993; Dr hc (Richmond American Int. Univ. of London); Soc. of West End Theatres (SWET) Award (Once in a Lifetime) 1979, Gold Hugo for Narration 1998, Award for Excellence in the Arts, Theatre School, DePaul Univ., Chicago 2004. *RSC and Royal Nat. Theatre includes:* Toine in Piaf, London and New York 1980, Viola in Twelfth Night 1983, Adriana in A Comedy of Errors 1983, Kitty Duval in Time of Your Life 1983, Kattrin in Mother Courage (Drama Award 1985) 1984, Othello 1989, The Crucible 1990, The Last Yankee 1993, Battle Royal 1999, His Girl Friday 2003, The Rose Tattoo 2007, The Rose Tattoo 2007, Much Ado About Nothing 2007–08, The Cherry Orchard 2011. *Other theatre includes* Fay in Loot, Broadway 1986, Ellie in Terry Johnson's Dead Funny, London 1994, Amanda in The Glass Menagerie, London 1995/96, Sylvia 1996, Electra, Chichester and London (Olivier Award for Best Actress 1998, Variety Club Award for Best Actress 1998, Calaway Award (New York) for Best Actress 1998) 1997, Princeton and Broadway 1998, The Old Neighbourhood, Royal Court 1998, Boston Marriage, Donmar Warehouse, London 2001, New Ambassadors, London 2001–02, Awake and Sing!, Lincoln Center Production, The Belasco Theater, New York (Drama Desk Best Revival, Out of Critics Circle Best Ensemble, Tony Award for Best Revival and Joan Cullman Award for Best Revival), All My Sons, Apollo Theatre, London (Whatsonstage.com Theatre Award for Best Actress 2011) 2010, Passion Play, Duke of York's Theatre 2013, Stevie, Chichester 2014. *Films include:* The Raggedy Rawney 1987, Wilde (BAFTA Award for Best Actress) 1997, Swept by the Sea 1997, Harry Potter and The Philosopher's Stone 2001, Five Children and It 2004, It's a Wonderful Afterlife 2010, My Week with Marilyn 2011, The Man 2012, An Innocent Abroad 2013. *Video:* Fable 2, 3 & 4: Theresa (Xbox game). *Radio:* The Golden Bowl, Plenty, Bay at Nice, A February Morning, Carol, Such Rotten Luck, The Older Woman. *Television includes:* Inside the Third Reich 1982, The Tragedy of Richard the Third 1983, Edge of Darkness 1985, Paradise Postponed 1986, Poor Little Rich Girl (mini-series) 1987, Morse 1990, Prime Suspect 1990, The Blackheath Poisonings 1992, Love Hurts (series) (BAFTA Award for Best Actress) 1992–94, The Widowing of Mrs. Holroyd 1995, The English Wife 1995, Dance to the Music of Time 1997, David Copperfield 1999, Gormenghast 2000, Adrian Mole: The Cappucino Years 2000, My Family (series)

(Best Sitcom Actress, Rose d'Or Awards) 2000–11, Miss Marple: Murder is Announced 2004, A Waste of Shame 2005, Dr Who 2005, 2006, Agatha Christie: Poirot (series; Cards on the Table 2005, The Third Girl 2008, Mrs McGinty's Dead 2008, The Hallowe'en Party 2010, Elephants Can Remember 2013, Dead Man's Folly 2013), Johnny and the Bomb (series) 2006, The Old Curiosity Shop (film) 2007, Who Do You Think You Are? 2009, National Theatre Live (series) – The Cherry Orchard 2011, Playhouse Presents (series) – The Man 2012, Wodehouse in Exile (film) 2013. *Address:* c/o Conway van Gelder Grant Ltd, 3rd Floor, 8–12 Broadwick Street, London, W1F 8HW, England (office). *Telephone:* (20) 7287-0077 (office). *Fax:* (20) 7287-1940 (office). *Website:* www.zoewanamaker.com.

WANANDI, Jusuf; Chinese/Indonesian lawyer, politician and educator; *Senior Fellow, Centre for Strategic and International Studies;* b. (Liem Bian Kie), 15 Nov. 1937, Sawahlunto, West Sumatra; brother of Sofjan Wanandi; ed junior high school study, Padang, Jesuit Kanisius High School, Jakarta, Faculty of Law, Universitas Indonesia, took part in Catholic leadership course taught by Father Joop Beek; leader in Catholic Univ. Students Asscn (PMKRI) in 1960s; taught at Kanisius High School; later Asst Lecturer, Universitas Indonesia; apptd Gov. East West Centre, Hawaii 1984; political career in Golongan Karya (Golkar Party), Vice-Gen. Sec.; currently Sr Fellow, Centre for Strategic and Int. Studies (CSIS), Jakarta, Vice-Chair. Bd of Trustees, CSIS Foundation; Co-Chair. Pacific Econ. Cooperation Council, Chair. Indonesian Nat. Cttee; Chair. Council for Security Cooperation in the Asia-Pacific (CSCAP) Indonesia, Co-Chair. Steering Cttee of CSCAP; Pres. Dir Jakarta Post (national English daily); Chair. Grad. School of Man. Prasetiya Mulya, Foundation of Panca Bhakti Univ., Pontianak; mem. Int. Advisory Council of the Asia Soc., New York, Bd of Govs Pacific Forum/CSIS, HI, Council of IISS, London, Int. Advisory Bd Babson Coll., Wellesley, Mass, USA; fmr Sec. Indonesian Supreme Advisory Council; fmr Sec. Gen. Nat. Educ. Council; fmr four-term Rep. in People's Consultative Ass. *Publications:* Strategic Issues and Linkages; has edited several books, written several book chapters and published numerous articles in professional journals on political and security developments in the Asia Pacific region; articles in nat. and int. magazines and newspapers. *Address:* Centre for Strategic and International Studies, The Jakarta Post Building, Third Floor, Jl. Palmerah Barat 142–143, Jakarta 10270, Indonesia (office). *Telephone:* (21) 5365-4601 (office). *Fax:* (21) 5365-4607 (office). *E-mail:* info@csis.or.id (office). *Website:* www.csis.or.id (office); www.pecc.org (office).

WANASUNDERA, Shanthi Eva, LLM, PC; Sri Lankan lawyer, judge and fmr government official; b. Kurunegala; d. of Hector Jayasena and Sumana Jayasena; m. Indrajith Wanasundera; one s. one d.; ed Canyon del Oro High School Tucson, Ariz., USA, Sri Lanka Law School, Univ. of Leicester, UK, Dharmapala Vidyalaya, Pannipitiya; early career as Attorney-at-Law, Gangodawila Magistrate Court (Nugegoda), Dist Courts in Mount Lavinia and Colombo; apptd State Counsel, Attorney-Gen.'s Dept 1979, also served as Sr State Counsel, Deputy Solicitor-Gen., Additional Solicitor-Gen., Solicitor-Gen., Attorney-Gen. 2011–; Judge, Supreme Court 2012–. *Leisure interests:* meditation, speaking with strangers as and when I meet them. *Address:* Supreme Court, Superior Court Complex, POB 01200, Colombo 12 (office); 237/6 3rd Lane, Bankhill Gardens, Pahalawela Road, Pelawatta, Battaramulla, Sri Lanka (home). *Telephone:* (11) 2327852 (office); (11)2787244 (home). *Fax:* (11) 2327852 (office). *E-mail:* wshanthieva@yahoo.com (office); iwanasundera@yahoo.com (home). *Website:* www.supremecourt.lk (office).

WANCER, Józef, MA; Polish banker and economist; *President, Bank BPH SA;* b. 26 May 1942, Komi, Russia; s. of Jakub Wancer and Edwarda Wancer; m. Krystyna Antoniak; one s. one d.; ed City Univ. of New York City, Webster Univ., Saint Louis, Mo., USA; Vice-Pres. Citibank of New York, managerial posts at Citibank units, including Japan, Austria, UK, France; Vice-Pres., then Pres. Raiffeisen Centrobank, Warsaw 1995–2000; Pres. Man. Bd Przemyslowo-Handlowy Bank (BPH) 2000–01, Pres. BPH PBK (following merger with HVB, now Bank BPH SA) 2001–. *Leisure interests:* cycling, logotherapy, history. *Address:* Bank BPH SA, Al. Pokoju 1, 31-548 Kraków, Poland (office). *Telephone:* (22) 5319230 (office). *Fax:* (22) 5319286 (office). *E-mail:* jozef.wancer@bph.pl (office). *Website:* www.bph.pl (office).

WANDREY, Christian, MSc, PhD (Habil.); German chemist and academic; b. 12 April 1943, Plauen; m.; three c.; ed Univ. of Hanover, Univ. of Bristol, UK; mil. service 1962–64; Asst Prof., Univ. of Hanover 1976, Habilitation, venia legendi Privat-Dozent (Lecturer) in Chemical Eng 1977; Assoc. Prof. of Chemical Eng, Univ. Clausthal Zellerfeld Yield 1977–79; Prof. of Biotechnology, Univ. of Bonn and Dir Inst. of Biotechnology at Research Centre, Jülich 1979–2008; Visiting Prof., Inst. for Physical and Chemical Research (RIKEN), Wako-Shi, Saitama, Japan 1983; mem. Editorial Bd Chemie Ingenieur Technik, Weinheim Advances in Biochemical Engineering, Journal of Molecular Catalysis B: Enzymatic, Biocatalysis and Biotransformation, The Chemical Record; consultant on biochemical eng and process econs, Degussa AG, DSM Research, Netherlands, Novartis, Basel; mem. Bd of Dirs ScheBo, Biotech AG, Dahlem Biomed AG; Co-initiator of four start-up cos, DSM Biotech GmbH, Jülich, Papaspyrou biotechnologie GmbH, Jülich, Jülich Fine Chemicals, AC Biotec GmbH Jülich 1995–; mem. Working Party on Biochemical Eng, Gesellschaft Verfahrenstechnik und Chemieingenieurwesen, Working Party on Biotechnology, DECHEMA, Germany Working Party on Catalysis, DECHEMA; Corresp. mem., Braunschweigische Wissenschaftlichen Gesellschaft (Div. of Math. and Natural Science), Sächsische Akad. der Wissenschaften zu Leipzig (Div. of Tech. Science), Schweizerische Akad. der Technischen Wissenschaften; undergraduate scholarship, Konrad-Adenauer-Stiftung, Bonn 1965–70, Karmarsch-Stipendium, City of Hannover 1967, graduate scholarship, Konrad-Adenauer-Stiftung, Bonn 1971–73, Christian-Kuhlemann-Stipendium, Univ. of Hanover for best PhD thesis in natural science 1973, Tech. Transfer Prize, Minister for Research and Tech. (FRG) 1983, Philip Morris Research Award for development of a biogas high performance process for treatment of highly polluted waste waters 1987, Enzyme Eng Award, Eng Foundation, New York 1995, Carl Friedrich Gauss Medal, Braunschweigische Wissenschaftliche Gesellschaft 1999, Friedrich Wöhler Award, German Chemical Soc. (Gesellschaft Deutscher Chemiker) 2002, Wilhelm Exner Medal, Austrian Asscn for SME (Oesterreichischer Gewerbeverein—OGV) (jtly) 2009. *Achievements include:* development of the Enzyme Membrane Reactor (in cooperation with Degussa AG, Hanau) for the production of L-amino acids 1977–. *Publications:* editor of three books, including Biotechnology 1989, Industrial Biotransformations (co-ed.) 2000; more than 330 scientific publs on enzyme and fermentation technology, cell culture technology, waste water and bioorganic chemistry; about 100 patents and patent applications. *Address:* Forschungszentrum Jülich, Wilhelm-Johnen-Strasse, 52425 Jülich, Germany (office). *Telephone:* (2461) 61-3955 (office). *Fax:* (2461) 61-3870 (office). *E-mail:* c.wandrey@fz-juelich.de (office). *Website:* www.fz-juelich.de (office).

WANG, Alexander; American fashion designer; *Creative Director, Alexander Wang, Inc. and Balenciaga;* b. 1983, San Francisco, Calif.; ed Parsons Design School, New York; moved to New York City aged 18; several internships; launched first full collection of women's wear for spring 2007; launched full accessories collection 2008; designs sold to more than 500 boutiques and retail stores worldwide; labels include Alexander Wang, T by Alexander Wang; Creative Dir Balenciaga 2012–; Vogue/CFDA Fashion Fund Award 2008, CFDA Swarowski Women's Wear Designer of the Year 2009, CFDA Swarovski Accessories Designer of the Year 2010, GQ Menswear Designer of the Year 2011. *Address:* Alexander Wang, Inc., 386 Broadway, 3rd Floor, New York, NY 10013, USA (office). *Telephone:* (212) 532-3103 (office). *Fax:* (212) 532-3110 (office). *E-mail:* corporate@alexanderwang.com (office). *Website:* www.alexanderwang.com (office).

WANG, Anshun; Chinese government official; *Mayor of Beijing;* b. 1957, Henan Prov.; ed Nankai Univ., Tianjin; began career working in oil exploration, Jilin Prov.; held positions with North China Petroleum Geology Bureau, Ministry of Geology and Mineral Resources; joined CCP 1984; Sec. CCP Standing Cttee, Gansu Prov. 1999–2001; Sec., CCP Municipal State-Owned Assets Supervision and Admin Comm., Shanghai Municipality 2003–07; Deputy Sec., Shanghai Municipal CCP Cttee 2003–07; Deputy Sec., Beijing Municipal CCP Cttee 2007–; Alt. mem. 17th CCP Cen. Cttee 2007–; Deputy, 11th NPC 2008–; Chair. Beijing CPPCC Municipal Cttee 2011–; Acting Mayor of Beijing 2012–13, Mayor 2013–. *Address:* Office of the Mayor, 2 Zhengyi Lu, Beijing, People's Republic of China (office). *Telephone:* 6512-8080 (office). *Website:* www.ebeijing.gov.cn/Government/Mayor_office (office).

WANG, Anyi; Chinese writer and academic; *Professor, Department of Chinese Language and Literature, Fudan University;* b. 1954, Tong'an, Fujian Prov.; d. of Ru Zhijuan; ed Xiangming Middle School; joined as musician, Xuzhou Pref. Song and Dance Ensemble 1972; Ed. Children's Time 1978; currently Prof., Dept of Chinese Language and Literature, Fudan Univ., Shanghai; Vice-Chair. Shanghai Writers Asscn, Chair. 2001–; Vice-Pres. Writers' Asscn of China; Outstanding Writer Award, Chinese Language Literary Media Awards 2008. *Publications:* Song of Eternal Hatred (Mao Dun Prize for Literature), Xiaobao Village, The Love of a Small Town, The Story of a School Principal, Self-selected Works of Wang Anyi (six vols), Lapse of Time, The Song of Everlasting Sorrow 2008. *Address:* Department of Chinese Language and Literature, Fudan University, 220 Handan Road, Shanghai 200433, People's Republic of China (office).

WANG, Bingqian; Chinese politician; b. 1925, Li Co., Hebei Prov.; Deputy Section Chief, Auditing Div., Dept of Finance 1948–49; Section Chief, later Dir, Vice-Minister, Minister of Finance, Cen. Govt; Dir Budget Dept 1963; Deputy Minister of Finance 1973–80, Minister of Finance 1980–92; mem. 12th Cen. Cttee CCP 1982, 13th Cen. Cttee 1987–92; Pres. Accounting Soc. 1980–; Hon. Chair. Bd of Dirs China Investment Bank 1981–; State Councillor 1983–93; Chair. Cen. Treasury Bond Sales Promotion Cttee 1984–; Vice-Chair. Standing Cttee of 8th NPC 1993–98; mem. State Planning Comm. 1988–92; NPC Deputy Hebei Prov.; Hon. Pres. Auditing Soc. 1984–, China Scientific Research Soc. for Policy Study. *Address:* c/o Standing Committee of National People's Congress, Beijing, People's Republic of China (office).

WANG, Bingzhang, MD; Chinese political activist; b. 30 Dec. 1947; one d.; ed Beijing Medical Univ., McGill Univ., Canada; jailed twice by Chinese authorities during Cultural Revolution; moved to USA 1979; f. China Spring magazine 1980s; Founder and Leader Chinese Alliance for Democracy, New York 1980s; attempted to return to China, but expelled 1998; entered Viet Nam to hold meetings with activists 2002; allegedly abducted by Chinese security forces and held at secret location July 2002; arrested in Fanchenggang City, S China Dec. 2002; convicted of espionage and leading terrorist group (sentenced to life imprisonment), Guang-dong Prov. Court, S China Jan. 2003; imprisoned in Shaoguan Prison, Guangdong Prov.

WANG, Chang-Ching, MSc; Taiwanese politician; b. 22 Sept. 1920, Chingshan Co., Hupeh; s. of C. S. Wang and late Si Teng; m. Hsueh Chen L. Wang; one s. one d.; ed Nat. Chiaotung Univ. and Johns Hopkins Univ., USA; Sr Eng and concurrently Div. Chief, Dept of Communications, Taiwan Provincial Govt 1949–58; Dir Public Works Bureau, Taiwan Provincial Govt 1958–69; Dir Dept of Public Works, Taipei City Govt 1967–69; Vice-Chair. Ministry of Communications 1969–77; Vice-Chair. Council for Econ. Planning and Devt 1977–84; Sec.-Gen. Exec. Yuan 1984–88; Chair. China External Trade Devt Council 1988–; Vice-Chair. Straits Exchange Foundation 1993–. *Leisure interest:* golf. *Address:* 7th Floor, 333 Keelung Road, Sec. 1, Taipei 10548, Taiwan. *Telephone:* (2) 7576293. *Fax:* (2) 7576653.

WANG, Chaowen; Chinese politician; b. 1930, Huangping, Guizhou Prov.; joined CCP 1951; Sec. Guizhou Communist Youth League 1973; Vice-Chair. Prov. Revolutionary Cttee, Guizhou 1977–79; Sec. CCP Guizhou Prov. Cttee 1980–81, Deputy Sec. 1981; Vice-Gov. of Guizhou 1977–83, Gov. 1983–93; Chair. Guizhou Prov. 8th People's Congress 1994–98; mem. 12th CCP Cen. Cttee 1982–87, 13th CCP Cen. Cttee 1987–92, 14th CCP Cen. Cttee 1992–97; mem. 8th Standing Cttee of NPC 1993–98, 9th Standing Cttee of NPC 1998–2003, Chair. Nationalities Cttee 1998–2003; Del., 15th CCP Nat. Congress 1997–2002. *Address:* c/o Standing Committee of the National People's Congress, 19 Xi-Jiaoming Xiang Road, Xicheng District, Beijing 100805, People's Republic of China (office).

WANG, Charles B., BS; Chinese computer executive and philanthropist; *Chairman Emeritus, Computer Associates;* b. 19 Aug. 1944, Shanghai; s. of Kenneth Wang and Mary Wang; m. 2nd Nancy Li; ed Queen's Coll.; programming trainee, Riverside Research Inst., Columbia Univ., USA 1976; Founder, Chair., CEO Computer Assocs 1976–2002, Chair. Emer. 2002–; Co-owner New York Islanders professional ice hockey team 1999–; f. Charles B. Wang Foundation 1999; Co-founder and Chair. Smile Train (charity) 1999. *Publications:* Techno

Vision 1994, Techno Vision II: Every Executive's Guide to Understanding and Mastering Technology and the Internet 1997. *Leisure interests:* basketball, cooking. *Address:* c/o New York Islanders Hockey Club, L.P., 1535 Old Country Road. Plainview, NY 11803, USA.

WANG, Chen, MScS; Chinese journalist, editor and government official; *Director, State Internet Information Office;* b. 1950, Beijing; ed School of Postgraduate Studies, Chinese Acad. of Social Sciences, Beijing; joined CCP 1969; reporter, CCP Yijun Co. Cttee 1970–73, CCP Yan'an Municipal Cttee, Shaanxi Prov.; reporter, Guangming Daily 1974, then successively Ed., Dir Chief Ed.'s Office, Assoc. Chief Ed. 1982–95, Chief Ed. 1995–2000; Deputy Dir Dept of Propaganda, CCP Cen. Cttee 2000–01; Ed.-in-Chief Renmin Ribao (People's Daily) 2001–02, Pres. 2002–08; Deputy Dir CCP Cen. Cttee Publicity Dept 2008–; Dir State Council Information Office 2008–11; Dir State Internet Information Office 2011–; mem. CPPCC Nat. Cttee 1998–2003; mem. 16th CCP Cen. Cttee 2002–07, 17th CCP Cen. Cttee 2007–12, 18th CCP Cen. Cttee 2012–; Sec.-Gen. NPC Standing Cttee 2013–. *Address:* State Internet Information Office, c/o State Council Information Office, Beijing, People's Republic of China (office).

WANG, Cher, MA (Econs); Taiwanese computer industry executive; *Chairperson, HTC Corporation;* b. 14 Sept. 1958; d. of Wang Yung-ching and Liao Chiao; m. Wenchi Chen; two c.; ed Univ. of California, Berkeley, USA; Gen. Man. PC Div., First International Computer 1982–87; Co-founder and Chair. VIA Technologies 1987–, High Tech Computer (HTC) Corpn 1997–; selected by Business Week as an Innovator in the 2005 Stars of Asia: 25 Leaders on the Forefront of Change and one of the 10 executives to watch in Asia 2005, ranked by Forbes magazine amongst The World's 100 Most Powerful Women (20th) 2011, (56th) 2012, (46th) 2013, ranked by Fortune magazine amongst the 50 Most Powerful Women in Business outside the US (20th) 2011, (47th) 2012. *Address:* HTC Headquarters, 23 Xinghua Road, Taoyuan 330, Taiwan. *Telephone:* (3) 3753252 (office). *Fax:* (3) 3753251 (office). *E-mail:* info@htc.com (office). *Website:* www.htc.com (office).

WANG, Chien-shien, BA, MA; Taiwanese politician and government official; *President, The Control Yuan;* b. 7 Aug. 1938, Hefei, Anhwei; m. Fa-jau Su; ed Nat. Cheng Kung Univ., Nat. Chengchi Univ., Harvard Univ., USA; Sr Specialist, Taxation & Tariff Comm., Ministry of Finance 1971–73; Dir First Div., Dept of Taxation 1973–76, Fourth Dept, Exec. Yuan 1976–80; Dir-Gen. Dept of Customs Admin, Ministry of Finance 1980–82, Public Finance Training Inst. 1982–84; Admin. Vice-Minister of Econ. Affairs 1984–89, Political Vice-Minister 1989–90, Minister of Finance 1990–92; mem. Legis. Yuan 1993–; Founder and Sec.-Gen. New Party 1994; Chair. Chinese Man. Asscn 1990–; Pres. The Control Yuan 2008–; Asian Finance Minister of the Year 1992. *Publications:* several works on income tax and business. *Address:* The Control Yuan, No. 2, Sec. 1, Zhongxiao East Road, Taipei 10051, Taiwan. *Telephone:* (2) 2341-3183. *Fax:* (2) 2341-0324. *E-mail:* csw@cy.gov.tw. *Website:* www.cy.gov.tw.

WANG, Dazhong, DSc; Chinese professor of nuclear engineering; b. 1935, Changli, Hebei Prov.; ed Nankai Middle School, Tianjin, Tsinghua Univ., Beijing; Visiting Scholar, Nuclear Research Centre, Juelich (KFA Juelich), FRG 1980–82; fmr Chief Scientist, First Expert Cttee on Energy, Nat. High Tech. Devt Programme; Assoc. Prof., Prof., Research Fellow, Dir of Nuclear Energy Research Inst., Tsinghua Univ. 1958–99, Vice-Chair. Univ. Council, Pres. Tsinghua Univ. 1999–2003; Pres. Beijing Nuclear Soc.; Vice-Pres. China Nuclear Soc.; mem. Chinese Acad. of Sciences 1993–, 4th Presidium of Depts Chinese Acad. of Sciences 2000–; Hon. Dr rer. nat (Aachen Univ. of Tech.) 1982; Nat. Advanced Scientist 1989, Nat. Award of Science & Technology Progress 1992, 2002, Ho Leung Ho Lee Foundation Science & Technology Achievement Award 1994. *Address:* c/o Tsinghua University, 1 Qinghuayuan, Beijing 100084, People's Republic of China (office). *Telephone:* (10) 62561144 (office). *Website:* www.tsinghua.edu.cn/eng/faculties/wdz.htm (office).

WANG, Dazong, MEng, PhD; Chinese business executive; *President and CEO, Beijing Automotive Industry Holding Company Limited (Beijing Automotive Group);* ed Huazhong Univ. of Science and Tech., Cornell Univ., USA; Sr Research Engineer, Research Labs, General Motors (GM) 1985; Country Man. and Chief Engineer, Delphi Energy and Engine Management Systems, China 1994–97; Director of Eng, GM North America Technical Center 1997–2006; Vice-Pres., Shanghai Automotive Industry (GM's Chinese production partner) 2006–08; joined Beijing Automotive Group 2008, Pres. and CEO 2011–; Founding Pres. and Adviser, Chinese Asscn of Greater Detroit 1992, Council for Asian Pacific Americans. *Address:* Beijing Automotive Industry Holding Co. Ltd, Zhangxinz-huang Village, Liqiao Town, Shunyi District, Beijing 101300, People's Republic of China (office). *Telephone:* (10) 67699888 (office). *Fax:* (10) 87664048 (office). *E-mail:* info@baihc.com (office). *Website:* www.baihc.com (office).

WANG, Demin; Chinese petroleum engineer; b. 9 Feb. 1937, Tangshan, Hebei Prov.; ed Beijing Petroleum Inst.; technician, engineer, Chief Engineer, Daqing Petroleum Admin Bureau, currently Vice Pres.; Prof. Daqing Petroleum Inst.; Fellow, Chinese Acad. of Eng 1994; 10 nat. level and 26 ministerial level awards. *Address:* Daqing Petroleum Administration, Daqing 163453, Heilongjiang Province, People's Republic of China (office).

WANG, Deshun; Chinese mime artist; b. 1938; m. Zhao Aijun; one s. one d.; fmr street performer; with army drama co. 1960–70; joined state-run Changchun Theatre Troupe, NE China 1970; since 1984 has been appearing in 'modelling pantomime' show in which he adopts series of sculpture-like poses to develop a theme; has taken his show to France, Germany and Macao and China's first int. mime festival, Shanghai 1994.

WANG, Deyan; Chinese banker; b. 1931; ed Tsinghua Univ., Cen. Inst. of Finance and Econ., Beijing Foreign Languages Inst.; joined Bank of China 1953, served as Sec., Asst Man., Deputy Gen. Man. 1953–84, Vice-Pres. 1984–85, Pres. 1985–93, Chair. Bd Dirs 1986–93; Dir Council's Office of People's Bank of China, Welfare Fund for Chinese Disabled Persons; Guest Adviser, China Council for Promotion of Int. Trade; Adviser to Coordination Group for Sino-Japanese Econ. and Trade Affairs; Vice-Chair. China Int. Finance Soc.; mem. Leading Group for Introduction of Foreign Capital under State Council; mem. Nat. Geographic Soc., USA; Asian Banker of 1987, Asian Finance; Hon. Dir Research Fund for Prevention of AIDS in

China. *Address:* c/o Bank of China, 410 Fuchengmennei Dajie, Beijing, People's Republic of China (office).

WANG, Dianzuo; Chinese metallurgist and academic; b. 23 March 1934, Linghai, Liaoning Prov.; ed Central-South Univ.; currently Prof. and Hon. Pres. Gen. Research Inst. for Nonferrous Metals; Chair. Int. Mineral Processing Congress Beijing 2008; Dir (non-exec.) Aluminum Corpn of China Ltd 2001–; Foreign Assoc. mem. Nat. Acad. of Eng, USA 1990–; Fellow, Chinese Acad. of Sciences 1991, Chinese Acad. of Eng 1994 (Vice-Pres. 1998–2006); made pioneering contribs in flotation theory for mineral processing; many nat., provincial and ministerial awards including He Liang and He Li Prizes 1994. *Publications:* eight monographs and over 300 research papers. *Address:* General Research Institute for Nonferrous Metals, 2 Xinjiekou Wai Street, Beijing 100088, People's Republic of China (office). *Telephone:* (10) 62055356 (office). *Fax:* (10) 62055345 (office). *E-mail:* wangdz@grinm.com (office). *Website:* http://en.grinm.com (office).

WANG, Enge, BS, MS, PhD, FInstP; Chinese physicist, academic and university administrator; *President, Peking University;* b. 1957, Shenyang; ed Liaoning Univ., Peking Univ.; post-doctoral fellow and research scientist, Chinese Acad. of Sciences (CAS), Institut d'Electronique, de Microelectronique et de Nanotechnologie, France, Univ. of Houston, USA; Prof., Inst. of Physics, CAS 1995, Dir 1999–2007; Founding Dir Int. Centre for Quantum Structures 2000; Dir Beijing Nat. Lab. for Condensed Matter Physics 2004–09; Deputy Sec.-Gen. CAS 2008–09, Exec. Pres. CAS Grad. Univ. 2008–09; Chair Prof. of Physics, Peking Univ. 2009–, Dean, School of Physics and Grad. School 2009–11, Provost and Vice-Pres. Peking Univ. 2011–12, Provost and Exec. Vice-Pres. 2012–13, Pres. 2013–; Academician, CAS, Acad. of Sciences for the Developing World (TWAS); Fellow, American Physical Soc.; JSPS Prof., Tohoku Univ., Japan; AvH Scholar, Fritz-Haber Inst. der MPG, Germany; GCEP Scholar, Stanford Univ., USA; KITP Visiting Prof., Univ. of California, Santa Barbara, USA; Visiting Prof., Univ. of California, Berkeley, USA, Int. Centre for Theoretical Physics, Italy; several nat. and int. academic awards. *Publications:* more than 280 papers in peer-reviewed journals on kinetics of formation and decay of surface-based nanostructures, development of chemical vapour deposition of light-element nanomaterials, and studies of behaviour of water in confined systems. *Address:* Office of the President, Administrative Building, Peking University, 5 Yiheyuan Road, Haidian District, Beijing 100871, People's Republic of China (office). *Telephone:* (10) 62751201 (office); (10) 62751301 (office). *Fax:* (10) 62751207 (office). *E-mail:* webmaster@pku.edu.cn (office). *Website:* www.office.pku.edu.cn (office).

WANG, Fengying, MA (Econs); Chinese automotive industry executive; *General Manager and President, Great Wall Motor Company Ltd;* ed Tianjin Inst. of Finance; joined Great Wall Group 1991, Exec. Dir 2001–, Gen. Man. Great Wall Automobile Sales Network Co. Ltd and Great Wall Bus Sales Co., currently Pres. and Gen. Man. Great Wall Motor Co. Ltd (fmrly Great Wall Automobile Holding Co. Ltd), mem. Strategic Cttee, also Gen. Man. Baoding Great Wall Automobile Sales Co. Ltd; accredited as Fifth Anniversary Ten Outstanding Young Persons of Baoding 1999, Fifth Anniversary Hebei Outstanding Young Entrepreneur, Chinese Marketing Professional Golden Tripod Outstanding Marketing Gen. Man. Award 2000, 8th of March Red Signal Soldier of Hebei Province 2004, Model Staff of Hebei Province 2004, Luding Award for PRC Marketing Gen. Man. 2008, Top 100 female news-makers in the 30 years since PRC's economic reform 2008, Top Marketing Professional of the Year 2009, ranked by Fortune magazine amongst the 50 Most Powerful Women in Business outside the US (29th) 2011, (36th) 2012. *Address:* Great Wall Motor Co. Ltd, 2266 Chaoyang South Avenue, Baoding City, Hebei Province, People's Republic of China (office). *Telephone:* (312) 2197688 (office). *Fax:* (312) 2197680 (office). *E-mail:* gwmomd@gwm.cn (office). *Website:* www.gwm.com.cn (office).

WANG, Fosong; Chinese chemist; b. 1933, Xingning Co., Guangdong Prov.; ed Wuhan Univ.; Researcher and Vice-Pres. Chinese Acad. of Sciences 1988, Fellow 1999–, mem. 4th Presidium of Depts Chinese Acad. of Sciences 2000–; Deputy Chair. China Petroleum Asscn; mem. 8th NPC 1993–98; second class Nat. Prize in Nature Science 1982, 1986, third class Nat. Prize in Nature Science 1991, Japanese Soc. of Polymer Science Int. Award 2002. *Publications:* more than 300 scientific papers. *Address:* Chinese Academy of Sciences, 52 San Li He Road, Beijing 100864, People's Republic of China (office).

WANG, Fuzhou; Chinese mountaineer and sports administrator; b. 1931, Xihua, Henan Province; s. of Wang Daikuang and Shen Xiozhen; m. Lia Aihua; one d.; mem. of Chinese mountaineering team that conquered Mt Everest for first time from north 1960; Sec.-Gen. Chinese Mountaineering Asscn 1980–93, Pres. 1993–; Gen. Man. of China Int. Sports Travel Co. 1983–. *Address:* State Physical Culture and Sports Commission, 9 Tiyuguang Road, Beijing (office); Chinese Mountaineering Association, 10 Zuoanmen Nei Street, Beijing, People's Republic of China (office). *Telephone:* 7017810 (office). *Fax:* 5114859 (office).

WANG, Gang; Chinese archivist and party official; *Vice-Chairman, 11th CPPCC National Committee;* b. Oct. 1942, Fuyu Co., Jilin Prov.; ed Jilin Univ.; clerk, Publicity Section, No. 8 Company, 7th Bureau, Ministry of Construction 1968–69, Publicity Div., Political Dept, 7th Bureau 1969–77; joined CCP 1971; Sec. Gen. Office of CCP Xinjiang Autonomous Region Cttee 1977–81; Sec. (rank of Div. Dir) Taiwan Affairs Office of CCP Cen. Cttee 1981–85; Deputy Dir-Gen. Petition Letters Bureau, Gen. Office of CCP Cen. Cttee and Gen. Office of the State Council 1985–87, Exec. Deputy Dir-Gen. 1987–90; Exec. Deputy Dir CCP Cen. Cttee Cen. Archives 1990–93, Sec. Head Office 1990–93, Dir Cen. Archives 1993–99, Dir State Archives Bureau 1993–94, Dir-Gen. 1994–99; Deputy Dir-Gen. Office CCP Cen. Cttee 1994–99, Dir 1999–2007; Chair. Int. Archives Council 1996–; Alt. mem. 15th CCP Cen. Cttee 1997–2002 (Sec. Work Cttee of Dept CCP Cen. Cttee 1999–), mem. 16th CCP Cen. Cttee 2002–07 (Alt. mem. Politburo, mem. Politburo Secr.), mem. 17th CCP Cen. Cttee 2007–12 (mem. Politburo 2007–12); Vice-Chair. 11th CPPCC Nat. Cttee 2008–. *Address:* CPPCC National Committee, No. 23, Taipingqiao Street, Beijing 100811, People's Republic of China (office). *Website:* www.cppcc.gov.cn (office).

WANG, Guangtao, MEng; Chinese politician; b. 1943, Shanghai; ed Tongji Univ., Shanghai; technician, Urban Construction Bureau, Xuzhou City, Jiangsu Prov. 1965; engineer, Technique Section, Urban and Rural Construction Cttee, Xuzhou City 1980–81, Chief 1981, Deputy Chief Engineer and Deputy Dir Urban and Rural Construction Cttee 1981–82; joined CCP 1983; Vice-Mayor of Xuzhou City 1988; Dir and Chief Engineer, Urban Construction Dept, Ministry of Construction 1989–95, Minister of Construction 2001–; Deputy Sec. Harbin Municipal Cttee 1995; Acting Mayor, then Mayor of Harbin, Helongjiang Prov. 1995–98; Vice-Mayor of Beijing 1998–2001; mem. CCP Leading Party Group, Ministry of Construction 2001–07; mem. 16th CCP Cen. Cttee 2002–07; Chair. 11th NPC Environmental and Resources Protection Cttee 2008–13; Hon. Prof., Dept of Architecture, Chinese Univ. of Hong Kong 2005. *Address:* c/o Ministry of Construction, 9 Sanlihe Dajie, Xicheng Qu, Beijing 100835, People's Republic of China (office).

WANG, Guangying; Chinese business executive; b. 1919, Beijing; s. of Wang Huaiqing; m. 1943; ed Furen Univ., Beijing; Co-founder Xiandai Chemical Factory in Tianjin 1943; f. Lisheng Knitwear Factory, Tianjin 1949; Vice-Chair. China Democratic Nat. Construction Asscn 1954; Man. Knit Goods Manufacturing Co., Tianjin 1956; mem. Standing Cttee All-China Fed. of Industry and Commerce 1956, Vice-Chair. All-China Fed. of Industry and Commerce 1982–93, Hon. Chair. 1993–97; Chair. Tianjin Fed. of Industry and Commerce 1956; jailed for eight years during cultural revolution 1967–75; Vice-Mayor Tianjin Municipality 1980; Founder, Chair. and Pres. China Everbright Co. (China's first trans-nat. corpn), Hong Kong 1983–90; mem. Bd China Int. Trust and Investment Corpn 1983; Exec. Chair. Presidium CPPCC 1983–; Vice-Chair. 6th CPPCC 1983–88, 7th CPPCC 1988–93, Standing Cttee of 8th NPC 1993–98, of 9th NPC 1998–2003; NPC Deputy Tianjin Municipality; Pres. China Council for Promotion of Peaceful Reunification 1990–98; Hon. Vice-Chair. Red Cross Soc. of China 1994–99, Hon. Vice-Pres. 1999; Hon. Chair. China Overseas Friendship Asscn 1997. *Address:* All China Federation of Industry and Commerce, 93 Beiheyan Dajie, Beijing, People's Republic of China (office).

WANG, Gungwu, CBE, PhD, FAHA; Australian historian, academic and university vice-chancellor; *University Professor, National University of Singapore;* b. 9 Oct. 1930, Indonesia; s. of Wang Fo Wen and Ting Yien; m. Margaret Lim Ping-Ting 1955; one s. two d.; ed Nat. Cen. Univ., Nanjing, Univ. of Malaya and Univ. of London; Asst Lecturer Univ. of Malaya, Singapore 1957–59, lecturer 1959; lecturer, Univ. of Malaya, Kuala Lumpur 1959–61, Sr Lecturer 1961–63, Dean of Arts 1962–63, Prof. of History 1963–68; Rockefeller Fellow, Univ. of London 1961–62, Sr Visiting Fellow 1972; Prof. of Far Eastern History, ANU 1968–86, Prof. Emer. 1986–, Dir Research School of Pacific Studies 1975–80; Visiting Fellow, All Souls Coll. Oxford 1974–75; Vice-Chancellor, Univ. of Hong Kong 1986–95; Chair. Inst. of E Asian Political Economy, Nat. Univ. of Singapore 1996–97, Dir East Asian Inst. 1997–, Univ. Prof. 2007–; Distinguished Sr Fellow Inst. of Southeast Asian Studies, Singapore 1996–99, Distinguished Professorial Fellow 1999–2003; Univ. Fellow and Hon. Corresp. mem. for Hong Kong of Royal Soc. of Arts 1987–95; Pres. Australian Acad. of the Humanities 1980–83, Asian Studies Asscn of Australia 1978–80; Chair. Australia-China Council 1984–86, Asia-Pacific Council, Griffith Univ. 1997–2001; mem. Exec. Council, Hong Kong 1990–92; Adviser Chinese Heritage Centre, Nanyang Tech. Univ. 1995–2000 (Vice-Chair.) 2000–, Southeast Asian Studies, Academia Sinica, Taipei 1994–; mem. Council Int. Inst. for Strategic Studies, London 1992–2001; mem. Nat. Arts Council, Singapore 1996–2000, Nat. Heritage Bd 1997–99 (Adviser 2000–), Nat. Library Bd 1997–2003; mem. Academia Sinica, Taipei, DD Social Science Research Council, NY 1999–; Foreign Hon. mem. American Acad. of Arts and Science; Hon. Fellow SOAS, London; Hon. Sr Fellow Chinese Acad. of Social Sciences, Beijing;; Hon. Prof. Beijing Univ., Fudan Univ., Hong Kong Univ., Nanjing Univ., Tsinghua Univ.; Hon. DLitt (Sydney, Hull, Hong Kong); Hon. LLD (Monash, ANU, Melbourne); Hon. DUniv (Griffith, Soka). *Publications:* 21 books, including The Chineseness of China 1991, China and the Chinese Overseas 1991, Community and Nation: China, South-East Asia and Australia 1992, Zhongguo yu Haiwai Huaren 1994, The Chinese Way: China's Position in International Relations 1995; Hong Kong's Transition: A Decade after the Deal (ed.) 1995, Global History and Migrations (ed.) 1997, The Nanhai Trade 1998, The Chinese Overseas: From Earthbound China to the Quest for Autonomy 2000, Joining the Modern World: Inside and Outside China 2000, Don't Leave Home: Migration and the Chinese 2001, To Act is to Know: Chinese Dilemmas 2002, Bind Us in Time: Nation and Civilisation in Asia 2002, Anglo-Chinese Encounters since 1800: War, Trade, Science and Governance 2003, Ideas Won't Keep: the Struggle for China's Future 2003, Reform, Legitimacy and Dilemmas: China's politics and Society (ed.) 2003, Damage Control: the Chinese Communist Party in the era of Jiang Zeming (ed.) 2004, Diasporic Chinese Ventures 2004; also numerous articles on Chinese and South-East Asian history; Gen. Ed. East Asian Historical Monographs series. *Leisure interests:* music, reading, walking. *Address:* National University of Singapore, Kent Ridge, Singapore 117571. *Telephone:* 7752033. *Fax:* 7793409. *E-mail:* eaiwgw@nus.edu.sg (office). *Website:* nus.edu.sg/nusinfo/eai (office).

WANG, Gen. Hai; Chinese army officer (retd); b. 1925, Weihai City, Shandong Prov.; ed China's North-East Aviation Acad.; joined PLA 1945; Group Commdr, air force brigade and sent to Korean battlefield 1950; promoted Col PLA 1964; Commdr, Air Force of Guangzhou Mil. Region 1975–83; Deputy Commdr PLA Air Force 1983–85, Commdr 1985; mem. CCP 12th Cen. Cttee 1982–87, 13th CCP Cen. Cttee 1987–92, 14th CCP Cen. Cttee 1992–97; promoted Gen. PLA 1988. *Address:* c/o Ministry of Defence, Beijing, People's Republic of China (office).

WANG, Hanbin; Chinese state official and party official; b. 28 Aug. 1925, Fujian Prov.; m. Peng Peiyun; two s. two d.; joined CCP in Burma 1941; Deputy Sec.-Gen. NPC Legal Comm. 1979–80; Vice-Chair. and Sec.-Gen. NPC Legal Comm. 1980–83; Deputy Sec.-Gen., Political and Legal Comm. of CCP Cen. Cttee 1980–82, Constitution Revision Cttee of People's Repub. of China 1980–82; Vice-Pres. Chinese Law Soc. 1982–91, Hon. Pres. 1991–; Chair. Legis. Affairs Comm. 1983–87; Vice-Chair. Cttee for Drafting Basic Law of Hong Kong Special Admin. Zone of People's Repub. of China 1985–90, for Drafting Basic Law of Macau Special Admin. Region of People's Republic of China 1988–, Preparatory Cttee, Hong Kong Special Admin. Region 1995–97; mem. 12th CCP Cen. Cttee 1982–87, 13th Cen. Cttee 1987–92, 14th Cen. Cttee 1992–97; Sec.-Gen. NPC Standing Cttee 1983–87, Vice-Chair. NPC 7th Standing Cttee 1988–93; Alt. mem. Politburo CCP 1992–97; Vice-Chair. Standing Cttee 8th NPC 1993–98. *Leisure interest:* bridge. *Address:* c/o National People's Congress Standing Committee, Beijing, People's Republic of China (office).

WANG, Hongzhang, BA, MA; Chinese economist, certified accountant and business executive; *Chairman and Executive Director, China Construction Bank;* ed Liaoning Inst. of Finance and Econs (now Dongbei Univ. of Finance and Econs); worked successively in Credit Bureau, Savings Dept and Industrial and Commercial Credit Dept, People's Bank of China 1978–84, worked successively in Industrial and Commercial Credit Dept and Gen. Admin Office of Industrial & Commercial Bank of China 1984–89, Asst Pres. Qingdao City Br. 1989–91, served in various positions including Deputy Dir of Gen. Admin Office, Deputy Dir of Finance Planning Dept and Gen. Man. of Operations Office, Industrial & Commercial Bank of China 1991–96, Deputy Dir-Gen. Supervision Bureau and Dir-Gen. Internal Auditing Dept, People's Bank of China 1996–2000, Pres. Chengdu Br. and Admin. of Sichuan Br. of State Admin of Foreign Exchange 2000–03, Party Cttee mem. and Chief Disciplinary Officer, People's Bank of China 2003–12; Chair. and Exec. Dir, China Construction Bank 2012–. *Address:* China Construction Bank, 25 Finance Street, Xicheng District, Beijing 100032, People's Republic of China (office). *Telephone:* (10) 6759-7114 (office). *Fax:* (10) 6360-3194 (office). *E-mail:* info@ccb.com (office). *Website:* www.ccb.com (office).

WANG, Huning; Chinese academic and party official; *Director, CCP Central Policy Research Centre;* b. 1955, Laizhou City, Shandong Prov.; ed Shanghai Normal Univ., Fudan Univ.; began career as Cadre, Municipal Publication Admin, Shanghai 1977–78; Prof., Dept of Int. Politics, Fudan Univ., Shanghai 1981–89, Dean, Dept of Int. Politics 1989–94, Dean, Law School 1994–95; joined CCP 1984; Dir CCP Cen. Cttee Policy Research Office, Policy Div. 1995–98, Deputy Dir, Policy Research Office 1998–2002, Dir Central Policy Research Centre 2002–; mem. 16th CCP Cen. Cttee 2002–07, 17th CCP Cen. Cttee 2007–12, also mem. 17th CCP Cen. Cttee Politburo Secr. 2007–12, mem. 18th CCP Cen. Cttee 2012– and 18th CCP Cen. Cttee Politburo 2012–; Visiting Prof., Univ. of Iowa and Univ. of California, Berkeley, USA 1988–89. *Publications include:* Logic of Politics: The Principal of Marxist Politics, America against America 1991, General Introduction to New Politics, Analysis of Modern Western Politics, Analysis of Comparative Politics, Debate Contest in Lion City, New Authoritarianism. *Address:* Central Committee Central Policy Research Centre, Chinese Communist Party, Quanguo Renmin Diabiao Dahui, Zhongguo Gongchan Dang, 1 Zhongnanhai, Beijing, People's Republic of China (office). *Website:* www.cppcc.gov.cn (office).

WANG, J. T., BEng, MBA; Taiwanese computer industry executive; *Chairman and CEO, Acer Inc.;* *CEO, Acer Group;* m.; two d.; ed Nat. Taiwan Univ., Nat. Cheng-Chi Univ.; sales engineer, Multitech (forerunner of Acer) 1981, held increasingly sr posts until Pres. Acer Sertek 1990–2000, Pres. Acer Inc. 2000–05, Chair. Acer Inc. 2005–, CEO 2005–08, 2011–, CEO Acer Group 2008–; Pres. Taipei Computer Assen (Taiwan) 2008–. *Address:* Acer Inc., 9F, 88 Hsin Tai Wu Road, Sec 1, Hsichih, Taipei 221, Taiwan (office). *Telephone:* (2) 696-1234 (office). *Fax:* (2) 696-3535 (office). *Website:* www.acer-group.com (office); www.acer.com (office).

WANG, Jianzhou, DBA; Chinese telecommunications executive; b. Dec. 1948, Wenzhou, Changxing Co., Zhejiang; ed Zhejiang Univ., Hong Kong Polytechnic Univ.; professor-level sr engineer with experience in telecommunications industry since 1970s; served as Dir-Gen. Posts and Telecommunications Bureau, Hangzhou; Dir-Gen. Planning and Construction Dept, Ministry of Posts and Telecommunications 1996–99; Dir-Gen. Gen. Planning Dept, Ministry of Information Industry 1996–99; Dir China Unicom 1999–2001, Exec. Vice-Pres. 2001–02, Pres. 2002–04, Exec. Dir, Chair. and CEO China Mobile Communications Corpn 2004–10, Exec. Dir and Chair. 2010–12 (retd). *Address:* c/o China Mobile Communications Corpn, 29 Financial Street, Xicheng District, Beijing 100032, People's Republic of China. *E-mail:* info@chinamobile.com.

WANG, Jida; Chinese sculptor; b. 27 Oct. 1935, Beijing; s. of Wang Sho Yi and Chiu Chen Shin; m. Jin Gao 1971; one s. one d.; ed Cen. Inst. of Fine Arts, Beijing; worked in Nei Monggol 1966, 1976–84; moved to USA 1984; Asst Dir Standing Council, Nei Monggol Sculptors' Assen; mem., Chinese Artist's Assen, American Nat. Sculpture Soc. 1988–; Honour Prize, China 1977. *Works include:* The Struggle (commissioned by Exec. Council on Foreign Diplomats) 1987, Natural Beauty (a collection of 18 pieces portraying women and animals) 1987, Statue of Liberty (commissioned by Statue of Liberty/Ellis Island Foundation), several monumental sculptures in Chairman Mao's image, in China. *Leisure interests:* athletics, music, literature. *Address:* Inner Mongolia Artist's Association, 33 West Street, Hohhot, Inner Mongolia, People's Republic of China (office); 76-12 35th Avenue, Apartment 3E, Jackson Heights, NY 11372, USA. *Telephone:* 25775 (China); (718) 651-3944 (USA).

WANG, Jin, PhD; Chinese physicist and academic; *Adjunct Professor of Chemistry, Changchun Institute of Applied Chemistry, Chinese Academy of Sciences;* ed Jilin Univ., Univ. of Illinois, USA; Post-doctoral Research Assoc. (Chem. and Biophysics), Univ. of Illinois 1991–96; Guest Scientist, NIH 1996–97; Adjunct Prof. of Physics, Jilin Univ. 1997–; Adjunct Prof. of Chem., State Univ. of New York at Stony Brook 1999–2004, Adjunct Prof., Dept of Applied Math. and Statistics 2006–, also Adjunct Prof., Harriman School of Man. 2008–; Adjunct Prof., Changchun Inst. of Applied Chem., Chinese Acad. of Sciences 2002–; Nat. Science Foundation Career Award 2005. *Publications:* more than 40 articles in scientific journals on mechanism of biomolecular folding and recognition, especially protein folding and protein-protein/protein-DNA interactions. *Address:* Department of Chemistry, State University of New York, Stony Brook NY 11794, USA (office). *E-mail:* jin .wang.1@stonybrook.edu (office). *Website:* www.sunysb.edu/chemistry/index.html (office).

WANG, Jin-Pyng, BS; Taiwanese politician; *President of the Li-Fa Yuan (Legislative Yuan);* b. 17 March 1941, Kaohsiung Co.; m. Chen Tsai-Lien; one s. two d.; ed Nat. Taiwan Normal Univ.; teacher, Chin-Teh High School, Changhwa 1965; Chair. Kaohsiung Co. Industrial 1975–81; elected mem. (Kuomintang—KMT), Legis. Yuan 1976–, Co-Chair. Finance Cttee 1981–88, Vice-Chair. KMT Cen. Policy Cttee 1990–91, Chair. Finance Cttee, Cen. Policy Cttee 1990, Vice-Pres. (Deputy Speaker) 2nd and 3rd Legis. Yuan 1993–99, Pres. 4th Legis. Yuan 1999–2002, 5th Legis. Yuan 2002–05, 6th Legis. Yuan 2005–08, 7th Legis. Yuan 2008–12, 8th Legis. Yuan 2012–; Pres. Taiwan-Japan Interparliamentary Friendship Assen 1992–99; Dir KMT Party and Govt Coordination Cttee in Legislature and KMT Caucus Whip in Legis. Yuan 1992–93; mem. KMT Cen. Standing Cttee 1992–2000, Vice-Chair. KMT 2000–05, Chair. KMT Cen. Advisory Cttee 2005–;

Chair. Assen of Members of the Legis. Yuan 2001–09, Repub. of China (ROC) Legislators' Assen 2009–; Chair. Formosa Cancer Foundation 1997–, Inst. for Biotechnology & Medical Industry 2001–09, Ten Outstanding Young Persons' Foundation 2002–, Taiwan Foundation for Democracy 2003–, ROC Volunteer Fire-Fighter Council 2004–, ROC Volunteer Police Council 2006–, Research Centre for Biotechnology and Medicine Policy 2009–; Pres. Taiwan Major League (professional baseball) 1997–2002, ROC Volunteer Fire-Fighter Assen 1997–2006, Union Against Cancer (Taiwan) 2003–, Chinese Taipei Gateball Assen 2008–; SKKU Distinguished Fellow, Sungkyunkwan Univ. 2012; Hon. PhD (Nat. Taiwan Normal Univ.) 2007; Highest Recognition Award, European Parl. 2009. *Address:* Legislative Yuan, 1 Chuanshan South Road, Taipei, Taiwan (office). *Telephone:* (2) 23586011 (office). (2) 23586015 (office). *Fax:* (2) 23955317 (office). *Website:* www.ly .gov.tw (office).

WANG, Jiong; Chinese business executive; *Vice-Chairman and President, CITIC Group;* fmr Chair. and Dir, CITIC Heavy Industries Co. Ltd (alternative name CITIC HIC), fmr Chair. Citic Heavy Machinery Co. Ltd, Man. Dir and Vice-Pres. Citic Group Co. –2013, Vice-Chair. and Pres. 2013–, Exec. Dir CITIC Group Corpn. *Address:* CITIC Group, Capital Mansion, 6 Xinuan Nanlu, Beijing 10004, People's Republic of China (office). *Telephone:* (10) 64660088 (office). *Fax:* (10) 64661186 (office). *Website:* www.citic.com (office); www.citic.com.cn (office).

WANG, Joseph, BSc, MSc, DSc, FRSC; American electrochemist and academic; *Distinguished Professor, Department of Nanoengineering, University California, San Diego;* b. 1948; ed Technion – Israel Inst. of Tech.; Research Assoc., Univ. of Wisconsin-Madison 1978–80; Asst Prof., later Assoc. Prof. of Chem., New Mexico State Univ. (NMSU) 1980–88, Prof. of Chem. 1988–2004, Regents Prof. and Manasse Chair 2002–04; Prof. of Chemical Eng and Chem., Arizona State Univ. and Dir Center for Bioelectronics and Biosensors, Biodesign Inst. 2004–08; Distinguished Prof. of Nanoengineering, Univ. of California, San Diego 2008–; NAS Visiting Scientist Fellowship to People's Repub. of China 1986; Founder and Chief Ed. Electroanalysis 1988–; Assoc. Ed. Wiley Encyclopedia of Analytical Chemistry 2007–; mem. Editorial Advisory Bd Analyst 1989–95, Talanta 1990–, Analytical Instrumentation 1991–, Encyclopedia of Analytical Sciences 1991–, Analytica Chimica Acta 1992–2007, Croatian Chemica Acta 1992–, Analytical Letters 1991–95, Analysis Europa 1994–98, Analytical Communications 1995–2000, Current Topics in Analytical Chemistry 1996–, Quimica Analitica 1997–, Electrochemistry Communications 1998–, General Physiolgy and Biophysics 1998–, Sensors 2001–, Sensors Letters 2003–, Journal of Microfluidics and Nanofluidics 2005–, International Journal of Electrochemical Science 2006–, Wiley Nanoscience and Nanotechnology Series 2007–, International Journal for Analytical Chemistry 2008–, Medical Devices 2008–, Reviews in Environmental Science and Bio/Technology 2008–, Sensors and Actuators B 2008–, Journal of Chinese Clinical Medicine International 2009–, Current Nanoscience 2010–, Nano-Bio-Analysis 2010–, Nanoscience & Nanotechnology-ASIA 2010–, Current Nanoscience 2011–, Research and Reports in Transdermal Drug Delivery 2011–, Theranostics 2011–, Advanced Carbon Materials 2012–, ChemElectroChem 2013–; served as instructor ACS Short Course 'Electrochemical Sensors'; mem. IUPAC Comm. for Electroanalytical Chem.; Fellow, Japan Soc. for Promotion of Science 2000, American Inst. for Medical and Biological Eng 2009; more than 50 plenary lectures and keynote addresses at int. meetings (among over 300 presentations) in 40 countries; Hon. Prof., Nat. Univ., Cordoba, Argentina 2003, Univ. of Science and Tech., Beijing 2011; Nanyang Prof., Nanyang Technological Univ., Singapore 2007–; Hon. mem. Nat. Inst. of Chem. (Slovenia) 2007; Dr hc (Nat. Univ., Cordoba) 2003, (Complutense Univ., Madrid) 2007, (Univ. of Alcalá, Spain) 2011, (Central Michigan Univ.) 2012; Young Faculty Award, Soc. of Analytical Chemists, Pittsburgh 1981, Heyrovsky Memorial Medal (Czech Repub.) 1994, ACS Award for Chemical Instrumentation 1999, ISI 'Citation Laureate' Award as Most Cited Scientist in Eng in the World 1991–2001, Westhafer Award for Research, NMSU 1990, most-cited electrochemist in the world 1995, 1997, ranked the Most Cited Researcher in Eng 1997–2007, ranked the Most Cited Chemist in ISI's list of Most Cited Researchers in Chem. 1997–2007, ACS Nat. Award for Electrochemistry 2006, B. Breyer Medal, Royal Australian Chemical Inst. 2012, Kapp Lecturer, Univ. of Virginia, Richmond 2012, Best Teacher Award, UCSD Dept of Nanoengineering 2012, RSC Spiers Memorial Award 2013, listed in the World Analytical Power List (100 most influential people in the analytical sciences) 2013. *Publications:* 11 books, including Stripping Analysis, Electroanalytical Techniques in Clinical Chemistry and Laboratory Medicine, Biosensors and Chemical Sensors, Analytical Electrochemistry (third edn) 2006, Biosensors and Chemical Sensors, Biosensors for Direct Monitoring of Environmental Pollutants in Field, Electrochemistry of Nucleic Acids and Proteins, Electrochemical Techniques in Clinical Chemistry and Laboratory Medicine, Stripping Analysis: Principles, Instrumentation, and Applications, Electrochemical Sensors, Biosensors and their Biomedical Applications, NanoBiosensing, Nanomachines: Fundamentals and Applications 2013; 15 patents, 35 chapters and more than 900 articles in scientific journals on nanobioelectronics and electroanalytical techniques. *Address:* Room 245E, SME Building, Department of Nanoengineering, University California San Diego, La Jolla, CA 92093-0448, USA (office). *Telephone:* (858) 246-0128 (office); (858) 822-1588 (Lab.) (office). *Fax:* (858) 534-9553 (office). *E-mail:* josephwang@ucsd.edu (office). *Website:* www.joewang.ucsd.edu (office).

WANG, Jun; Chinese business executive; *Chairman and Executive Director, Goldbond Group Holdings Ltd;* b. 11 April 1941, Munan, Human; s. of the late Wang Zhen; joined China Int. Trust and Investment Corpn (CITIC) 1979, served as Deputy Gen. Man. then Gen. Man. Business Dept, Vice-Pres., Vice-Chair. and Pres. CITIC Hong Kong (Holdings), Vice-Pres. CITIC 1986–93, Pres. 1993–95, Chair. of Bd 1995–2006; Chair. Bd of Dirs Poly Group 1991–2007; Chair. Planning Comm. Gansu Prov. People's Govt; Chief Procurator Guangdong Prov. People's Procuratorate; Chair. and Exec. Dir Goldbond Group Holdings 2007–; Chair. China Professional Golfers' Assen; mem. 10th CPPCC Nat. Cttee. *Leisure interests:* golf, go. *Address:* Goldbond Group Holdings Ltd, 1901-06, Tower 1, Lippo Centre, 89 Queensway, Hong Kong Special Administrative Region, People's Republic of China (office). *Telephone:* 21115666 (office). *E-mail:* kellyli@goldbondgroup.com (office). *Website:* (office).

WANG, Gen. Ke; Chinese army officer; b. Aug. 1931, Xiaoxian Co., Jiangsu Prov.; ed Mil. Acad. of the Chinese PLA; joined CCP-led armed work team 1944; joined

CCP 1947; Asst Literacy Teacher, E China Field Army, PLA Services and Arms 1947–48; Deputy Political Instructor, Field Army, Regimental Training Team, PLA Services and Arms 1949; took part in Jiaozhou Counterattack Battle 1949, Huaihai Campaign 1949; Regimental Staff Officer, Jiangsu Mil. Dist, PLA Nanjing Mil. Region 1949–51; Bn Commdr, PLA, Korea War 1953–56; Deputy Regimental Commdr, later Chief of Staff, Artillery Force, PLA Services and Arms, Korea 1956–61; Section Chief, Training Dept, PLA Artillery School, Beijing 1961–62; Deputy Dir Training Dept, PLA Wuwei Artillery School 1962–64; Deputy Commdr Garrison Div., PLA Lanzhou Mil. Region 1970–72, Political Commissar 1972–78; Div. Commdr PLA 1980–83, Army Commdr 1983–85; Commdr Xinjiang Mil. Dist, Xinjiang Mil. Region 1986–90, Commdr Lanzhou Mil. Region 1990–92; Commdr Shenyang Mil. Region 1992–95; Dir PLA Gen. Logistics Dept 1995–2002; rank of Lt-Gen. 1988, Gen. 1994; mem. 14th CCP Cen. Cttee 1992–97, 15th CCP Cen. Cttee 1997–2002; mem. CCP Cen. Cttee Cen. Mil. Comm. 1992–97; mem. Cen. Mil. Comm. of People's Repub. of China 1995–. *Address:* c/o People's Liberation Army General Logistics Department, Beijing, People's Republic of China (office).

WANG, Kefen; Chinese dance historian; b. 1 April 1927, Yunyang, Chongqing; d. of Wang Baifan and Liao Huiqing; m. Zhang Wengang 1949; one s. one d.; choreographer and dancer Cen. Nat. Song and Dance Co. 1952–58; Research Fellow Chinese Nat. Dance Asscn 1956–66, Inst. of Dance, China Nat. Arts Acad. (CNAA) 1977–; Academic Prize, Arts Acad. of China 1989, Award for Special Contrib., State Council of China, Award for Outstanding Contribs of Culture and Educ. Exchange, Columbus, USA. *Publications:* The History of Chinese Dance 1980, The Stories of Ancient Chinese Dancers 1983, The History of Chinese Dance: Ming Dynasty, Qing Dynasty 1984, Sui Dynasty and Tang Dynasty 1987 (CNAA Research Excellence Award 1989), The History of Chinese Dance Development (CNAA Research Excellence Award 1994, Chinese Ministry of Culture Art Research Award 1999); Dictionary of Chinese Dance (Chief Ed.) (Nat. Award for Best Dictionary 1995); Chief Ed. on subject of dance in 10-vol. History of Chinese Civilization (Nat. Award for Best Book 1994); Sui and Tang Culture (Co-Ed. and contrib.) 1990 (Social Science Book Award 1992), Chinese Dance of the 20th Century 1991 (Nat. Best Book Award 1993), Buddhism and Chinese Dance 1991, Chinese Ancient Dance History (co-author), The Chinese Contemporary History of Dance 1840–1996 (Ed.-in-Chief), The Music and Dance of the Tang Dynasty recorded in Japanese History 1999, The Culture of the Wei Dynasty, Jin Dynasty, Northern Dynasty and Southern Dynasty (jtly) 2000, The Complete Works of Dunhuang Caves – Dance Vol. 2001, Chinese Dance: An Illustrated History (First Prize, Chinese Ministry of Culture Art Research Awards 2006) 2002, On the Development and Far-reaching Significance of the Chinese Palace Dance 2004, Dance from Heaven to Earth (Dunhuang Myth series) 2007, and other works on Chinese Dance. *Leisure interests:* choreography, writing and dance.

WANG, Kui; Chinese chemist; *Director, National Laboratory of Natural Medicine and Bionic Medicine, Beijing Medical University;* b. 7 May 1928, Tianjin; ed Yanjing Univ.; teaching asst, Beijing Medical Univ., Instructor, Assoc. Prof., Prof., Chair. of Dept, Dean Pharmaceutics School, Dean Coll. of Pharmaceutics, now Dir Nat. Laboratory of Natural Medicine and Bionic Medicine 1950–; Chair. Chem. Dept of Nat. Natural Science Foundation; Fellow, Chinese Acad. of Science 1991–; mem. 4th Presidium, Chinese Acad. of Sciences 2000–; Chinese Acad. of Sciences Award for Advancement in Science and Tech. (2nd Class), State Educ. Comm. Award for Advancement in Science and Tech. (2nd Class). *Publications:* over 100 research papers. *Address:* Beijing Medical University, 38 Xue Yuan Ju, Beijing 100083, People's Republic of China (office). *Telephone:* (10) 62091334 (office). *Fax:* (10) 62015681 (office). *E-mail:* dxb@mail.bjmu.edu.cn (office). *Website:* www.bjmu .edu.cn (office).

WANG, Lequan; Chinese politician; b. Dec. 1944, Shouguang Co., Shandong Prov.; sent to do manual labour, Jiaonan Co., Shandong Prov. 1965–66; joined CCP 1966; Deputy Head, Houzhen Commune, Shouguang Co. 1966–75, mem. Standing Cttee CCP Revolutionary Cttee and Standing Cttee CCP Party Cttee 1966–75, Deputy Sec. CCP Shouguang Co. Cttee and Vice-Chair. CCP Revolutionary Cttee 1975–82; Deputy Sec. CCP Party Cttee, Chengguan Commune 1966–75; Deputy Sec. CCP Communist Youth League of China Shandong Prov. Cttee 1982–86; Deputy Sec. CCP Liaocheng Prefectural Cttee 1986–88, Sec. 1988–89; Vice-Gov. Shandong Prov. 1989–91; Vice-Chair. Xinjiang Uygur Autonomous Regional People's Congress 1991–95; Deputy Sec. CCP Xinjiang Uygur Autonomous Regional Cttee 1992–94, Acting Sec. 1994–95, Sec. 1995–2010; First Political Commissar, Production and Construction Corps, Xinjiang Uygur Autonomous Region 1995–2010; Alt. mem. 14th CCP Cen. Cttee 1992–97, mem. 15th CCP Cen. Cttee 1997–2002, 16th CCP Cen. Cttee 2002–07 (mem. Politburo 2002–07), 17th CCP Cen. Cttee 2007–12 (mem. Politburo 2007–12). *Address:* c/o Chinese Communist Party Xinjiang Uygur Autonomous Regional Committee, Urumqi City, Xinjiang Uygur Autonomous Region, People's Republic of China (office).

WANG, Lianzheng, MTAA, PhD; Chinese agronomist and administrator; *Honorary Chair of Academy Committee, Academy of Agricultural Sciences;* b. 15 Oct. 1930, Haicheng, Liaoning Prov.; s. of Wang Dianche and Wang Youzhen; m. Li Shuzhen 1959; two d.; ed Northeast Agricultural Coll., Harbin and Moscow Timiryazeev Agricultural Acad.; Asst Prof., Heilongjiang Acad. of Agricultural Sciences (HAAS) 1964–78, Assoc. Prof. 1979–82, Prof. 1983–; Dir Soybean and Crop Breeding Inst. HAAS 1970–78; Vice-Pres. HAAS 1978–82, Pres. 1983–86, Vice-Gov. Heilongjiang Prov. (in charge of Agricultural Production, Science and Tech.) 1983–87; Vice-Minister of Agric. 1988–91; mem. Agricultural Devt Group at State Council 1988–93; mem. and Convenor Plant Genetics, Breeding, Cultivation Academic Degree Cttee at State Council 1991–96; Pres. Chinese Acad. of Agricultural Sciences (CAAS) 1987–94, Pres. and Prof. Grad. School CAAS 1988–95, Hon. Chair. Acad. Cttee of CAAS 1995–; Vice-Chair. Chinese Crop Science Soc. 1988–94, Chair. 1994–2002; Vice-Chair. Scientific Tech. Cttee (Ministry of Agric.) 1988–96, Chinese Cttee for Release of New Crop Varieties 1989–96, Vice-Pres. China Asscn for Science and Tech. 1991–2001, Heilongjiang Asscn of Science and Tech., Chinese Asscn of Agricultural Science Socs; Chair. China Int. Exchange Asscn of Agricultural Science and Tech. 1992–96; mem. Bd IFAD 1988–91, Centre for Agric. and Biosciences (CABI) 1994–97; Co-Chair. Advisory Cttee China-EC Centre for Agricultural Tech. 1992–97; Pres. China Seed Asscn 1998–2006, China Agricultural Tech. Soc. 2000–06; mem. Chinese dels to numerous int. confs; Deputy to NPC; mem. Agricultural and Rural Affairs Cttee of

Congress 1998–2003; has developed 34 soya bean cultivars; Foreign mem. Russian Acad. of Agricultural Sciences 1988–; Foreign Fellow Indian Nat. Acad. of Agricultural Sciences 1994–; Second Class Chinese State Prize for Invention, for new soyabean cultivar 'Heinong 26', Second Class Chinese State Prize for Invention, for new potato cultivar 'Kexin No. 1', First Class Prize for Scientific Progress, Ministry of Agric., for collection and investigation of wild soya bean; Second Class Heilongjiang Prov. Prize for Tech. Progress, for high-yielding high-protein soyabean cultivar 'Heinong 35' 1994, Winner of Timiryazeev Award for Science and Education in Agriculture, Moscow 2009, First Class Beijing Science and Technology Award (for soyabean cultivar 'Zhonghuang 13' with high yield and broad adaptability) 2010, First Class Chinese State Science and Technology Award (for 'Zhonghuang 13') 2012, Winner of Award for Agronomy, Ho Leung Ho Lee Foundation Prize for Scientific and Technological Progress, Hong Kong, China 2012. *Publications:* Feeding a Billion (co-author) 1987, Soyabean Breeding and Genetics (Ed.-in-Chief) 1992, Agriculture in Modern China (co-ed.) 1992, Soyabean Cultivation for High Yielding (Ed.-in-Chief) 1994, Soybean in Mordesa China (co-ed.) 2007, Seed Industry of Field Crops in China 2007, Soybean Research for 50 Years (Ed.-in-Chief) 2010, and more than 164 papers. *Leisure interest:* classical music. *Address:* Chinese Academy of Agricultural Sciences, 12 Zhongguancun Nan (Southern) Street, Haidian District, Beijing 100081 (office); Cui wei xili 14-12-2, Haidian District, Beijing, 100036, People's Republic of China (home). *Telephone:* (10) 82103007 (office); (10) 68258061 (home). *Fax:* (10) 82105805 (office). *E-mail:* wanglz@mail.caas.net.cn (office).

WANG, Liheng; Chinese astronomer, space scientist and academic; *Director and Researcher, Scientific and Technical Committee;* b. 1938, Zhen Jiang, Jiangsu Prov.; ed Shanghai Jiao Tong Univ.; led and organized project approval and implementation of several major aerospace projects, including as adviser to SZ-3 project; fmr Chief Engineer and Vice-Minister, Dept of Aeronautics and Astronautics; fmr Gen. Man. China Aerospace Science and Tech. Corpn (CASC); Dir and Researcher, Scientific and Tech. Cttee 2002–; Academician, Chinese Acad. of Eng (Assoc. Dir Dept of Eng Man.), Int. Acad. of Astronautics; Mykhailo Yangei Medal. *Address:* c/o Ministry of Science and Technology, 15B Fuxing Lu, Haidian Qu, Beijing 100862, People's Republic of China (office). *Telephone:* (10) 58881888 (office). *Fax:* (10) 68515006 (office). *E-mail:* officemail@mail.most.gov.cn (office). *Website:* www.most.gov.cn (office).

WANG, Linxiang; Chinese business executive; *President and Chairman, Erdos Group;* b. 1951, Baotou, Nei Monggol Autonomous Region; joined CCP 1974; Dir Erdos Cashmere Sweater Mill 1983–89; Pres. and Chair. Bd Erdos Group 1989–; Standing Dir Asscn of Inner Mongolia Import and Export Firms 1997; Vice-Chair. CPPCC Yih Ju Autonomous League Cttee, Inner Mongolia Autonomous Region; Deputy to NPC; mem. All-China Youth Fed.; Hon. Chair. Asscn of Friendship Liaison of Yih Ju League 1999; numerous awards including Sr Economist, Silver Medal of Nat. Frontier Talents, State Econ. and Trade Comm., named Inner Mongolia Most Outstanding Entrepreneur, Model Worker in China's Textile Circle, Nat. Model Worker, Nat. Most Outstanding Young Entrepreneur, Most Outstanding Member of CCP. *Address:* Erdos Group, Baotou, Nei Monggol, People's Republic of China (office). *Website:* (office).

WANG, Liqin; Chinese table tennis player; b. 18 June 1978, Shanghai; began playing aged six and was picked for Chinese men's nat. squad aged 15 in 1993; numerous titles; winner men's singles: Asian Youth Championships 1994, Pro Tour Grand Finals 1998, 2000, Asian Championships 1998, World Championships, Osaka 2001, Asian Games, Busan 2002, World Championships, Shanghai 2005, World Championships, Zagreb 2007; winner men's doubles: Pro Tour Grand Finals 1996, 1998, 2000, 2007, Olympic Games, Sydney 2000 (gold medal), World Championships 2001, 2003; winner mixed doubles: Asian Championships 1998, Asian Games 1998; winner team events: Asian Championships 1998, 2000, Asian Games 1998, 2000, World Championships, Osaka 2001, World Championships 2006, Olympic Games, Beijing 2008 (gold medal); men's singles, Olympic Games, Athens 2004, Beijing 2008 (bronze medal); has won highest number of pro tours, winning more than 20; ranked No. 1 (Int. Table Tennis Fed.—ITTF) in the world 2005, No. 3 2007, No. 4 July 2008, No. 8 Oct. 2011, No. 12 Nov. 2013; plays for Shanghai city team. *Address:* c/o Chinese Table Tennis Federation, C3 Longtan Road, Chongwen District, Beijing 100061, People's Republic of China.

WANG, Luolin; Chinese economist; b. June 1938, Wuchang City, Hunan Prov.; ed Beijing Univ.; joined CCP 1978; Asst Lecturer, Lecturer, Assoc. Prof., Amoy Univ. 1961–84; fmr Dean, Zhejiang Univ. Coll. of Econs, currently Hon. Dean; Deputy Dean, later Vice-Pres. Amoy Univ. 1984; Vice-Pres. Chinese Acad. of Social Sciences 1993–2005, now Special Adviser and Prof.; Vice-Chair. State Academic Degrees Cttee 1999; Alt. mem. 13th CCP Cen. Cttee 1987–92, 14th CCP Cen. Cttee 1992–97, mem. 15th CCP Cen. Cttee 1997–2002, Alt. mem. 16th CCP Cen. Cttee 2002–07; Vice-Chair. CPPCC Econ. Sub-Cttee 2005–; Hon. PhD (Hong Kong Lingnan Univ.). *Publications:* Blue Book of China's Economy (co-ed. annually). *Address:* Chinese Academy of Social Sciences, Jianguomennei Dajie 5 Hao, Beijing 100732, People's Republic of China (office). *Telephone:* (10) 65137744 (office). *Fax:* (10) 65138154 (office). *E-mail:* wangll@cass.net.cn (office). *Website:* www.cass.net .cn (office).

WANG, Maolin; Chinese party and government official; b. 1934, Qidong, Jiangsu Prov.; ed Shanghai Financial and Econ. Coll.; joined CCP 1956; Vice-Chair. Shanxi Prov. Revolutionary Cttee 1977–78; Mayor Taiyuan City, Shanxi Prov. 1979–83; Vice-Gov. Shanxi Prov. 1979–83; Vice-Chair. Shanxi Prov. People's Congress 1981–88; Deputy Sec. Shanxi Prov. Cttee 1988–91, Sec. 1991; Chair. 7th CPPCC Shanxi Prov. Cttee 1993; Sec. 7th CCP Hunan Prov. Cttee 1993–98; mem. 13th CCP Cen. Cttee 1987–92, 14th CCP Cen. Cttee 1992–97, 15th CCP Cen. Cttee 1997–2002; Vice-Chair. 10th NPC Law Cttee 2003–; Prin. Adviser China Int. Council for the Promotion of Multinational Corpns. *Address:* China International Council for the Promotion of Multinational Corporations, 82, Donganmen Street, Beijing, People's Republic of China (office). *Website:* www.cicpmc.org.

WANG, Gen. Maorun; Chinese army officer; b. May 1936, Rongcheng, Shandong Prov.; ed Mil. Acad. of the Chinese PLA; joined PLA 1951, CCP 1956; staff officer, Qingdao Garrison 1962; various posts in a corps political dept 1969–73; Deputy Sec.-Gen. Political dept Jinan Mil. Region 1973–76; Dir of a corps political dept 1976–83; corps deputy political commissar 1983–85; Dir Political Dept PLA

Lanzhou Mil. Region 1985–90; Deputy Political Commissar and Sec. CCP Comm. for Inspecting Discipline, Lanzhou Mil. Region 1990; Political Commissar, Nat. Defence Univ. 1990–; rank of Maj.-Gen. 1988, Lt-Gen. 1993, Gen. 1998; mem. 15th CCP Cen. Cttee 1997–2002; Del., 11th CCP Nat. Congress 1977–82. *Address:* c/o National Defence University, Beijing, People's Republic of China (office).

WANG, Meng; Chinese politician and writer; b. 15 Oct. 1934, Beijing; s. of Wang Jindi and Tong Min; m. Cui Ruifang 1957 (died 2012); two s. one d.; joined CCP 1948; criticized 1957–76; rehabilitated 1979; Minister of Culture 1986–89; mem. Secr. Chinese Writers' Asscn 1981–86, Vice-Pres. 1986–89, Vice-Chair. 2001; Vice-Pres. China PEN Centre 1982–; Vice-Pres. Asscn for Int. Understanding 1985–; Chief Ed. People's Literature 1983–86; Alt. mem. 12th Cen. Cttee CCP 1982–85, mem. 12th Cen. Cttee CCP 1985–87, 13th Cen. Cttee 1987–92; mem. Standing Cttee 8th CPPCC Nat. Cttee 1993–98, Standing Cttee 9th CPPCC Nat. Cttee 1998–2003; Award for Excellent Chinese Biographic Works 2013. *Publications include:* The Young Newcomer in the Organization Department 1956, Long Live the Youth 1957, Bolshevik State: A Modernist Chinese Novel 1979, The Barber's Tale 1979, A Night in the City 1979, A Spate of Visitors 1980, The Butterfly 1980, The Metamorphosis of Human Nature 1986, Selected Works (Vols I–IV) 1986, Adventures of a Soccer Star 1990, You Can Come into My Dream Again 1991, Revelation from The Dream of Red Mansion 1991, Notes on Styles (collection of literary criticisms) 1991, The Seasons for Love 1992, Hard Gruel (short stories) 1992, The Season for Losing Self-Control 1995, The Season for Hesitation 1997, The Season for Carnivals 2000. *Leisure interests:* swimming, drinking. *Address:* China PEN, Shatan Beijie 2, Beijing, People's Republic of China (office).

WANG, Mengkui; Chinese academic; b. April 1938, Wenxian Co., Henan Prov.; ed Beijing Univ.; joined CCP 1956; Ed. Red Flag Magazine 1964–69; Assoc. Research Fellow then Research Fellow, Research Dept of Secr. CCP Cen. Cttee 1981–87; Exec. Vice-Dir Econs Research Centre of State Planning Comm. 1987; Deputy Dir Research Office of State Council 1990–95, Dir 1995–98, Dir Devt Research Centre of the State Council 1998–2007; Alt. mem. 14th CCP Cen. Cttee 1992–97, mem. 15th CCP Cen. Cttee 1997–2002; Dir (non-exec.) Aluminum Corpn of China 2008–. *Publications:* China's Economic Transformation over 20 Years 2000, China in the Wake of Asia's Financial Crisis 2008, Good Governance in China - A Way Towards Social Harmony 2008. *Address:* Development Research Centre of the State Council, No 225, Chaoyangmen Nei Dajie, Beijing 100010, People's Republic of China (office). *E-mail:* drc@drc.gov.cn (office). *Website:* (office).

WANG, Nan; Chinese table tennis player; b. 23 Oct. 1978, Fushun City, Liaoning Prov.; started playing aged seven; joined Liaoning prov. table tennis team in 1989 and nat. team in 1993; numerous titles; winner women's singles: Swedish Open 1994, Asian Youth Championships 1994, World Cup 1997, 1998, 2003, Pro Tour Grand Finals 1998, 2001, Asian Games, Bangkok 1998, World Championships 1999, 2001, 2003, Olympic Games, Sydney 2000 (gold medal); winner women's doubles: Asian Championships 1996, Pro Tour Grand Finals 1997, 1998, 1999, Asian Games 1998, World Championships 1999, 2001, 2003, Olympic Games, Sydney 2000 (gold medal), Athens 2004 (gold medal); winner mixed doubles: Asian Games 1998, Asian Championships 1998, World Championships 2003; winner women's team events: Asian Youth Championships 1994, Asian Championships 1996, 1998, World Championships 1997, 2000, 2001, Asian Games 1998, Olympic Games, Beijing 2008 (gold medal); runner-up in women's singles and women's team events, Asian Games, Busan 2002; women's singles, Olympic Games, Beijing 2008 (silver medal); ranked World No. 1 1999–2001; has led Chinese women's table-tennis team following retirement of Deng Yaping. *Leisure interests:* listening to music, watching television, reading, playing tennis. *Address:* c/o Chinese Table Tennis Federation, C3 Longtan Road, Chongwen District, Beijing 100061, People's Republic of China.

WANG, Pinxian; Chinese marine geologist; *Professor of Marine Geology, Tongji University;* b. 14 Nov. 1936, Suzhou, Jiangsu Prov.; ed Moscow State Univ., USSR; joined Geology and Geography Dept, East China Normal Univ., Shanghai 1960; moved to Tongji Univ. 1972, later Prof. of Marine Geology, Head of Marine Geology Dept 1982–90; mem. Chinese Acad. of Science 1991–, Vice-Chair. Earth Sciences Div. 1997–2002; mem. NPC (legislature) 1986–92; Co-Chief Scientist, ODP Leg 184 (first scientific deep-sea drilling operation in China Seas) 1999; Pres. Chinese Cttee on Ocean Research 1994–2002; Vice-Pres. Int. Scientific Cttee for Ocean Research 1994–98, Oceanological and Limnological Soc. of China; von Homboldt Research Fellow, Kiel Univ., Germany 1981–82; Vice-Chair. Chinese Cttee for Quaternary Research, PAGES (Past Global Changes) Scientific Steering Cttee 2004–07; Hon. Fellow, Geological Soc., London 1991; Ho Leung Ho Li Earth Sciences Prize 2006, European Geosciences Union Milutin Milankovic Medal for long-term climatic research 2007. *Achievements include:* first to study paleoceanography in China early 1980s. *Publications:* book: Marine Micropaleontology of China 1985, Proceeding, Ocean Drilling Program, Initial Reports, 184 2000, The South China Sea – Paleoceanography and Sedimentology 2009; research: Distribution of Calcareous Microfossils in the China Seas and its Paleoenvironmental Significance (State Educ. Comm. first prize for Advancement of Science and Tech.), Dynamic Progression and Development Trend of the Evolution of Environment in the last 150,000 years in Drought and Semi-drought Areas (Chinese Acad. of Science first prize for Advancement of Science and Tech.) 1998. *Address:* School of Ocean and Earth Science, Tongji University, 1239 Siping Road, Shanghai, People's Republic of China (office). *Telephone:* (21) 65983207 (office). *Fax:* (21) 65988808 (office). *E-mail:* pxwang@tongji.edu.cn (office). *Website:* tongji.edu.cn (office).

WANG, Qimin; Chinese petroleum executive; *President, Daqing Research Institute of Oilfield Exploration and Development;* b. 1937; ed Beijing Petroleum Inst.; joined CCP 1978; technician, Vice-Chief Geologist, Sr Engineer and then Vice-Pres. Daqing Research Inst. of Oilfield Exploration and Devt 1961–96, Pres. 1996–; took part in torch-bearer in Olympic Flame Relay, Daqing July 2008; China Gen. Co. of Oil and Natural Gas Iron Man Achievement Prize. *Address:* Daqing Research Institute of Oilfield Exploration and Development, Daqing 163000, Heilongjiang Province, People's Republic of China (office).

WANG, Qinghai; Chinese business executive; Gen. Man. and Vice-Chair. Shougang Corpn –2012, concurrently Chair. Beijing Shougang Flourish Coil Coating Co. Ltd, Vice-Chair. Beijing Shougang Co. Ltd 2006–12, Shougang Gen. Co., Shougang Jingtang Iron & Steel United Co. Ltd; Dir, Beijing Shougang Co.

Ltd. *Address:* c/o Shougang Corporation, Shijingshan Road, Beijing 100041, People's Republic of China. *E-mail:* info@shougang.com.cn.

WANG, Qishan; Chinese economist and politician; *Secretary, Central Commission for Discipline Inspection;* b. July 1948, Tianzhen, Shanxi Prov.; ed Northwest China Univ.; Researcher, Modern History Inst., Chinese Acad. of Social Sciences 1982, Researcher, Secr. (Rural Policies Dept) CCP Cen. Cttee Politboro 1982; joined CCP 1983; Div. Head, Rural Devt Research Centre of State Council, Acting Dir then Dir Rural Devt Inst. 1982–87; Gen. Man. China Rural Trust and Investment Corpn 1988–89; Vice-Pres. Construction Bank of China 1989–93, Pres. 1994–97; Vice-Gov. People's Bank of China 1993–94, Gov. 1994 (Sec. CCP Party Cttee); Chair. of China Investment Bank 1994–97; Chair. China International Capital Corpn Ltd 1995–97; mem. CCP Standing Cttee Guangdong Prov. Cttee 1997–2000; Exec. Vice-Gov. Guangdong Prov. 1998–2000; Dir Econ. Restructuring Office of the State Council 2000–; Sec. Econ. System Reform Scheme Office, CCP Party Cttee 2000–02; Sec. CCP Hainan Prov. Cttee 2002–03; Chair. Standing Cttee Hainan Prov. People's Congress 2003; Acting Mayor of Beijing 2003–04, Mayor 2004–07; Exec. Chair. Beijing Organizing Cttee for XXIX Olympiad and Deputy Sec. Leading Party Mem.'s Group 2004–07; Vice-Premier State Council and mem. CCP Leading Party Group 2008–13; Sec. CCP Cen. Comm. for Discipline Inspection 2012–; Alt. mem. 15th CCP Cen. Cttee 1997–2002; mem. 16th CCP Cen. Cttee 2002–07, 17th CCP Cen. Cttee 2007–12; mem. Standing Cttee CCP Beijing Municipal Cttee 2003–, Deputy Sec. CCP Beijing Municipal Cttee 2003–; mem. 18th CCP Cen. Cttee 2012–, Politburo 2012–, Politburo Standing Cttee 2012–. *Address:* Great Hall of the People, West Edge, Tiananmen Square, Beijing, People's Republic of China (office). *Telephone:* (10) 88050813 (office). *Fax:* (10) 63070900 (office). *Website:* english.gov.cn/2008-03/16/content_921792.htm (office).

WANG, Gen. Ruilin; Chinese army officer and party official; b. Dec. 1929, Zhaoyuan Co., Shandong Prov.; joined PLA 1946, CCP 1947; copy clerk, Shandong Mil. Dist (Co. Ind. Bn) PLA Jinan Mil. Region 1946–47; decoder and staff officer, Confidential Div., PLA Northeast Mil. Dist 1947–49; Deputy Section Chief, Confidential Div., Govt Admin. Council 1949–52; Sec. Office of Vice-Premier Deng Xiaoping 1973–76; Dir Vice-Chair.'s Office of CCP Cen. Cttee Mil. Comm., then Chair.'s Office; Deputy Dir of Gen. Office, CCP Cen. Cttee 1983–97, Vice-Dir PLA Gen. Political Dept 1992– (concurrently Dir Office of Deng Xiaoping –1997); mem. 13th CCP Cen. Cttee 1987–92 (Sec. Comm. for Discipline Inspection CCP Cen. Cttee Mil. Comm. 1990–93), 14th CCP Cen. Cttee 1992–97 (mem. Cen. Mil. Comm. 1995–97), 15th CCP Cen. Cttee 1997–2002; rank of Lt-Gen. 1988, Gen. 1994. *Address:* Central Office, Chinese Communist Party Central Committee, Beijing, People's Republic of China (office).

WANG, Senhao; Chinese government official; b. 1933, Cixi, Zhejiang Prov.; two s.; joined CCP 1955; Dir Mining Admin, Shanxi Prov. 1970–82; Sec. CCP Party Cttee, Shanxi Prov. 1970–82; Deputy Sec. CCP Party Cttee, Shaanxi Prov. 1983–93; Gov. of Shanxi Prov. 1983–92; Minister of Coal Industry 1993–98; mem. CCP 12th Cen. Cttee 1982–87, 13th Cen. Cttee 1987–92, 14th Cen. Cttee 1992–97; mem. Standing Cttee 9th CPPCC Nat. Cttee 1998–2003, Chair. Society and the Rule of Law Cttee. *Address:* National Committee of Chinese People's Political Consultative Conference, 23 Taipingqiao Street, Beijing, People's Republic of China (office).

WANG, Shenghong; Chinese fmr university administrator; b. 1942, Shanghai; ed Shanghai Univ. of Science and Tech., Purdue Univ. and Univ. of Texas, USA; fmr Dir and Party Sec., Higher Educ. Bureau, Shanghai, fmr Chair. Shanghai Educ. Asscn for Int. Exchange; fmr Pres. Shanghai Univ. of Science and Tech.; apptd Head, CCP Municipal Cttee, United Front Work Dept, Shanghai 1984, Vice-Chair., CPPCC Municipal Cttee, Shanghai 1995–; Assoc. Dir, China Electro-Mechanical Eng Asscn 1980–90; del. to 15th Nat. CCP Congress, 9th CPPCC 1998–2003, 6th and 7th CCP Congress of Shanghai, 7th and 10th People's Congress of Shanghai; Pres. Fudan Univ. 1998–2009; mem. Univ. Grants Cttee of Hong Kong, Int. Academic Advisory Panel, Ministry of Educ., Singapore; Dr hc (Univ. of Manchester, UK, Nat. Univ. of Ireland, Waseda Univ., Japan, Chonnam Nat. Univ., South Korea); Chinese Acad. of Sciences Award for Scientific and Technological Breakthroughs 1986, First Prize, Nat. Awards for Scientific and Technological Advancement 1987, First Prize, Shanghai Awards for Scientific and Technological Advancement 1990, Outstanding Worker in the Frontline of Science and Tech. of Shanghai, Outstanding Worker in the Frontline of Educ. of Shanghai, Shanghai Model Worker, Pres.'s Medal, George Washington Univ., USA. *Publications:* Structural Design of Electronic Apparatus, Finite Element Method and Its Application; over 40 papers in scientific journals. *Address:* c/o Office of the President, Fudan University, 220 Handan Road, Shanghai 200433, People's Republic of China.

WANG, Sheping; Chinese business executive; *Chairman and President, Jizhong Energy Group Company Limited;* Chair. Jizhong Energy Resources Co. Ltd, currently Chair. and Pres. Jizhong Energy Group Co. Ltd, also Chair. and Gen. Man. Jizhou Energy Resources Group; Dir, HeBei Jinniu Chemical Industry Co. Ltd (Chair. 2008–), fmr Chair. Hebei Jinniu Energy Group Co. Ltd, Heibei Jinniu Energy Resources Co. Ltd; fmr Chair. Xingtai-based mining co., of a Handan-based mining co. *Address:* Jizhong Energy Group Company Ltd, 191 West Zhongxing Avenue, Xingtai 054000, People's Republic of China (office). *Telephone:* (319) 2098828 (office). *Fax:* (319) 2068666 (office). *E-mail:* info@hbjnjt.com (office). *Website:* www.jznyjt.com (office); www.hbjnjt.com (office); www.jnny.com.cn (office).

WANG, Shi; Chinese business executive; *Chairman, China Vanke Co. Ltd;* b. Jan. 1951, Liuzhou, Guanxi Prov.; ed Lanzhou Railway Inst.; worker, Railway Bureau, Guangzhou City (Shenzhen Econ. Special Zone), Guangdong Prov.; f. Modern Scientific and Educational Instrument Exhbn Centre, Shenzhen City, Guangdong Prov., Gen. Man. Shenzhen Vanke Co. Ltd Exhbn Centre 1984, Corp. Rep., Shenzhen Vanke Co. Ltd 1988, Gen. Man. 1988–99, Chair. and CEO China Vanke Co. Ltd 1988–99, Chair. 1999–; Vice-Chair. Shenzhen Real Estate Asscn, Shenzhen Gen. Chamber of Commerce; Standing Dir China Real Estate Asscn (Vice-Dean City House Devt Cttee); initiated and organized 'New Residence Forum' Shanghai Conf. and promoted New Residence Campaign 2000; visiting scholar, Harvard Univ. 2011–13; elected one of the Top Ten Econ. Figures in China 2000. *Leisure interest:* mountaineering (succeeded in reaching the highest summits of seven continents, including two ascents of Mount Everest). *Address:*

China Vanke Company Ltd, 27 Shuibei 2 Rd, Luohu Dist, Shenzhen 266101, Guangdong Province, People's Republic of China (office).

WANG, Shouguan; Chinese astronomer and university professor; b. 15 Jan. 1923, Fuzhou; s. of B. L. Wang and S. Y. Gao; m. Lin Zhihuan 1955; one s. one d.; Deputy Head, Div. of Math. and Physics, Chinese Acad. of Sciences 1981–; Prof., Beijing Normal Univ. 1987–, Univ. of Science and Tech. of China 1991–; Chief Ed. Vol. Astronomy, Chinese Encyclopaedia 1980; Chief Ed. Astrophysics Sinica; mem. Chinese Acad. of Sciences 1981; Hon. Dir Beijing Astronomical Observatory 1987–; Hon. Pres. Chinese Astronomical Soc. 1988–; Nat. Science Congress Award 1978, Nat. Science and Tech. Progress Award 1985. *Leisure interest:* poetry. *Address:* Beijing Normal University, Xinyiekouwai Street 19, Beijing 100875 (office); No. 404, Block 808, Zhong-Guan-Cun, Beijing 100080, People's Republic of China. *Telephone:* (10) 62207960 (office). *Fax:* (10) 62200074 (office). *E-mail:* ipo@bnu.edu .cn (office). *Website:* www.bnu.edu.cn (office).

WANG, Shu, PhD; Chinese architect; *Dean, School of Architecture, China Academy of Art;* b. 4 Nov. 1963, Ürümqi, Xinjiang Uyghur Autonomous Region; m. Lu Wenyu; ed Nanjing Inst of Tech., Tongji Univ.; co-f. (with Lu Wenyu) Amateur Architecture Studio, Hangzhou 1997; Prof., China Acad. of Art 2000–, Head, Architecture Dept 2003–, Dean, School of Architecture 2007–; Kenzo Tange Visiting Prof. (first Chinese) Harvard Grad. School of Design 2011; Schelling Architecture Prize 2010, French Acad. of Architecture Gold Medal 2011, Pritzker Architecture Prize 2012. *Address:* School of Architecture, China Academy of Art, 18 Nanshan Road, Shangcheng, Hangzhou, Zhejiang Province, People's Republic of China (office). *Telephone:* (571) 8716-4630 (office). *Website:* eng.caa.edu.cn (office).

WANG, Shucheng; Chinese politician; b. Dec. 1941, Liyang, Jiangsu Prov.; ed Tsinghua Univ., Beijing; joined CCP 1965; technician, then Deputy Sec. Eng Bureau No. 6, Ministry of Water Resources and Power Industry 1968–84; Deputy Chief, 1st Eng Section, 6th Eng Bureau, Ministry of Power Industry 1980; Deputy Gen. Man. Water Conservancy and Hydroelectric Power Construction Co. 1984–86, Deputy Dir 1986–87, Dir 1987–88; Dir Dept of Hydroelectric Devt, Ministry of Energy 1988–93; Vice-Minister of Power Industry 1993–97; Deputy Gen. Man. State Power Corpn 1997–98; Minister of Water Resources 1998–2007; mem. 16th CCP Cen. Cttee 2002–07. *Address:* c/o Ministry of Water Resources, 2 Baiguang Lu, Ertiao, Xuanwu Qu, Beijing 100053, People's Republic of China (office).

WANG, Shuguo, DEng; Chinese engineer and university administrator; *President, Harbin Institute of Technology;* b. 1958, Hebei Prov.; ed Harbin Inst. of Tech.; joined CCP 1976, Sec., CCP Prov. Cttee, Heilongjiang Prov. Science and Tech. Comm. 1993–2003; Visiting Scholar, Univ. of Paris VI, Pierre et Marie Curie, France 1987–89; Prof. of Mechanical Design, Harbin Inst. of Tech., becoming Deputy Dean, Inst. of Robotics Research 1989–93, Dean, Mechanical and Electrical Eng Coll. 1993–98, Vice-Pres., Harbin Inst. of Tech. 1998–99, Pres. 2003–; Deputy Dir State 863 Project, Intelligent Robot Research Programme 1993–2003; Deputy 10th NPC 2003–08; seven consecutive awards of Advanced Prize in Science and Tech. from Heilongjiang Prov. Govt. *Publications:* over 70 academic papers. *Address:* Office of the President, Harbin Institute of Technology, 92 West Dazhi Street, Nan Gang District, Harbin 150001, People's Republic of China (office). *Telephone:* (451) 86413925 (office). *Website:* en.hit.edu.cn (office).

WANG, Shuo; Chinese writer; b. 1958, Nanjing; spent four years in navy, then worked at various jobs before becoming a full-time writer 1983; first novel Air Stewardesses published 1984; collected works banned by authorities in China 1996; has written over 20 novels with 10 million copies in print, has written scripts for TV and films including work for American Zeotrope, USA. *Film screenplays include:* The Trouble-Shooters 1989, I Love You 2002, Little Red Flowers 2006, Dreams May Come 2006. *Publications include:* Playing for Thrills (translated into English 1997), Please Don't Call Me Human (translated into English 1998), A Sigh 2000, A Conversation with Our Daughter 2008. *Address:* c/o No Exit Press, Oldcastle Books, PO Box 394, Harpenden, AL5 1XJ, England (office).

WANG, Sung; Chinese zoologist and conservationist; b. 1933, Jiangsu; ed Fudan Univ., Shanghai; researcher, Inst. of Zoology, Chinese Acad. of Science, Beijing, later Pres.; was part of first team to catalogue flora and fauna in some of remotest parts of China; work interrupted during Cultural Revolution late 1960s; scientific adviser to Cities Treaty early 1980s; mem. China Council for Int. Cooperation on Environment and Devt; reintroduced Père David deer, extinct in China since 1901, from captive stock in UK; highlighted importance of indigenous domestic stock such as yak of high Tibetan plateau; brought in outside conservation expertise from countries such as UK, Japan and USA; involved with Eco Security Task Force, set up to control 'alien invasive species' in China; Joseph Grinnell Award 1998, Edinburgh Medal 2003. *Publications:* numerous articles in scientific journals. *Address:* c/o Institute of Zoology, Chinese Academy of Sciences, 25 Beisihuanxi Road, Haidan, Beijing 100080, People's Republic of China (office). *Telephone:* (10) 6254-7675 (office). *Fax:* (10) 6256-5689 (office). *E-mail:* wangs@ panda.ioz.ac.cn (office). *Website:* www.oiz.ac.cn (office).

WANG, Taihua; Chinese politician; b. Oct. 1945, Xingguo, Jiangxi Prov.; ed Jiangxi Teachers' Coll., CCP Cen. Cttee Cen. Party School; worker, No. 9 Regiment, Jiangxi Production and Construction Corps, Jiangxi Prov. 1968–70; joined CCP 1973; Vice-Principal No. 3 Secondary School, Ganzhou City, Jiangxi Prov. 1978; Vice-Pres. Ganzhou City Educ. School 1979; mem. Standing Cttee CCP Ganzhou City Cttee and Head, Publicity Dept 1980; Deputy Commr Ganzhou Prefectural Admin. Office 1983; mem. Standing Cttee CCP Jiangxi Prov. Cttee and Head, Publicity Dept 1985; Vice-Sec. CCP Anhui Prov. Cttee 1992–2000, Sec. 2000–04; Sec. CCP Hefei City Cttee 1992–98; Vice-Gov. Anhui Prov. 1998–99, Gov. 1999–2001; Chair. Standing Cttee Anhui Prov. People's Congress 2003–04; Dir State Admin for Radio, Film and TV 2004–11; Alt. mem. 14th CCP Cen. Cttee 1992–97, 15th CCP Cen. Cttee 1997–2002, mem. 16th CCP Cen. Cttee 2002–07, 17th CCP Cen. Cttee 2007–12; Deputy 8th NPC 1983–88; Del., 13th CCP Nat. Congress 1987–92, 14th CCP Nat. Congress 1992–97, 15th CCP Nat. Congress 1997–2002, 16th CCP Nat. Congress 2002–07. *Address:* c/o State Administration for Radio, Film and Television, 2 Fu Xing Men Wai Dajie, Beijing 100866, People's Republic of China.

WANG, Tao; Chinese geologist; *Honorary Chairman, Sino Union Petroleum & Chemical International Ltd;* b. 1931, Leting, Hebei Prov.; joined CCP 1948; Chief Geologist, Dagang Oil Field; Chief Geologist, Liaohe Petroleum Prospecting Bureau; Gen. Man., South China Sea Eastern Br. of China Nat. Offshore Oil Corpn; Minister of Petroleum Industry 1985–88; Pres. China Nat. Petroleum Corpn 1988–97; Exec. Dir Sino Union Petroleum & Chemical International Ltd, currently Hon. Chair.; Prof. China Univ. of Petroleum; Chair. Chinese Nat. Cttee for World Petroleum Council; Vice-Chair. Chinese-Arab Friendship Asscn, Chair. Chinese-Saudi Arabia Friendship Asscn; mem. CCP 12th Cen. Cttee 1982–87, 13th Cen. Cttee 1987–92, 14th Cen. Cttee 1992–97; mem. Standing Cttee 9th NPC 1998–2003, Vice-Chair. Environment and Resources Protection Cttee 1998–2003; Foreign Academician, Russian Acad. of Natural Sciences; World Petroleum Congress Outstanding Contribution Award 2005. *Address:* Sino Union Petroleum & Chemical International Ltd, Unit 1909A–1912, China Merchants Tower, Shun Tak Centre, 168–200 Connaught Road Central, Hong Kong Special Administrative Region, People's Republic of China. *Website:* www.sunpec.com/english/rel_info .htm (office).

WANG, Tian-Ren; Chinese sculptor, artist and calligrapher; b. 26 July 1939, Henan; s. of Zheng-gang Wang and Shu-zheng Ren; m. Zhang Pei 1969; one s.; ed Xian Acad. of Fine Arts; worked as art designer and sculptor at Shaanxi Exhbn Hall 1963–79, worked on construction 1964–65; cr. sculptures for Yanan Revolution Memorial Hall 1968–71; Dir group sculptures for Shaanxi Exhbn Hall 1972–75; participated in group sculptures for Chairman Mao Memorial Hall 1976–78; calligraphy works exhibited in Chinese and Japanese cities; Pres. Shaanxi Sculpture Inst. 1996–2000; Vice-Dir of Sculpture Art Cttee, Shaanxi Br. Nat. Asscn of Artists; Art Dir, Dir of Creation Office, Shaanxi Sculpture Inst.; mem. Nat. Calligraphers Asscn, Shaanxi Folk Art Inst., Shaanxi Industrial Artists Asscn. *Works include:* Hou Ji 1980–81, Flower, The Morning Rooster, Qin Ox, Zebra, Tang Dynasty Musicians in Nishang and Yuyi (Copper Medal, Nat. City Sculptures Designing Exhbn 1983), Letter Carrier Goose (Copper Medal, Nat. City Sculptures Designing Exhbn 1983), Biaoqi General of Han Dynasty Huo Qu-bing (Excellent Prize, 6th Nat. Art Works Exhbn 1984, First Prize, Shaanxi Art Works Exhbn 1984), Rising to the Sky (for Urumuqi, Xinjing; Prize for Excellence, Nat. Ministry of Urban Construction, Nat. Asscn of Artists 1987) 1985, Qin Unification 1992, Unification of Qin Dynasty (selected for 2nd Nat. City Sculpture, Nat. Prize from Nat. Construction Ministry, Ministry of Culture and Asscn of Nat Artists) 1994, Yu Youren (selected for 8th Nat. Arts Exhbn) 1994, sign sculpture for Xijiang Chemical Fertilizer Factory 1995, civic scenery sculpture for Hejin, Shaanxi Prov. 1995, Soar Aloft (sign sculpture for Xian Yanliang city) 1996, Zhao Hongzhang (granite-sculpture) 1996, Hou Ji (stone sculpture for Shaanxi) 1996, large city sign sculpture for Shanxi 1996, Flying Phoenix 1997, Wang Ding 1997, Surpass 1998, Flying 1998, Fountain 1999, Unlimited 1999, Phoenix Sing 1999, Unrestrained and Far-Ranging 2000, Liang Sicheng 2001, Yu Hua Long 2001, Space Navigation 2001, Li Xiaolong 2002, Happy Fish 2002, Shi Qingyun 2002, Doctor Bethune 2002, A group of little girls and boys 2003, Soul of poetry 2004, Canyon of poetry 2004, A group of figures 2004, Yellow Emperor 2010. *Leisure interests:* Chinese classical literature, poetry, music. *Address:* 9 Wenyibeilu, Wenhua Guangxia 14–1, Xian, Shaanxi 710054, People's Republic of China (home); Shaanxi Sculpture Institute, Longshoucun, Xian, Shaanxi 710016, People's Republic of China (office). *Telephone:* (29) 87855551; (29) 6261002 (office); (29) 6253551 (home). *Fax:* (29) 87855551; (29) 3237768.

WANG, Tianpu, MBA, PhD; Chinese oil industry executive; *President, China Petrochemical Corporation (Sinopec Group);* ed Qingdao Chemical Inst., Dalian Polytechnic Univ., Zhejiang Univ.; Vice-Pres. Qilu Petrochemical Co., China Petrochemical Corpn (Sinopec Group) 1999–2000, Vice-Pres. Qilu Co., Sinopec Group 2000, Pres. Qilu Co., Sinopec Group 2000–01, Vice-Pres. Sinopec Group 2000–03, Sr Vice-Pres. 2003–11, Pres. 2011–, Dir 2006–, mem. Party Cttee 2001–. *Address:* Sinopec Group, 22 Chaoyangmen North Street, Chaoyang District, Beijing 100728, People's Republic of China (office). *Telephone:* (10) 64990060 (office). *Fax:* (10) 64990022 (office). *E-mail:* info@sinopec.com (office). *Website:* www.sinopecgroup.com (office); www.sinopec.com (office).

WANG, Vera; American fashion designer; *Chairman and CEO, Vera Wang Bridal House Limited;* b. 27 June 1949, New York, NY; d. of Cheng Ching and Florence Wu; m. Arthur Becker; two d.; ed Chapin School, NY, Sarah Lawrence Coll. and Sorbonne Univ., France; trained as figure skater before moving into fashion; Fashion Ed., Vogue USA 1971–87; Design Dir, Ralph Lauren 1987–89; Founder, Chair. and CEO Vera Wang Bridal House Ltd 1990–, opened flagship salon at Carlyle Hotel, New York; best known for her chic bridal collections; began selling bath, bedding and house wares 2002; has also produced a mass-market line, Simply Vera By Vera Wang, for chain store Kohls 2007–; Womenswear Designer of the Year, Council of Fashion Designers of America 2005, André Leon Talley Lifetime Achievement Award, Savannah Coll. of Art and Design 2006, ranked by Forbes magazine amongst The World's 100 Most Powerful Women (91st) 2010, Geoffrey Beene Lifetime Achievement Award, Council of Fashion Designers of America 2013. *Publication:* Vera Wang on Weddings 2001. *Address:* Vera Wang Bridal House Ltd, 225 West 39th Street, 9th Floor, New York 10018, USA (office). *Telephone:* (212) 575-6400 (office). *Fax:* (212) 354-2548 (office). *E-mail:* prassistant@verawang.com (office); webcustomercare@verawang.com (office). *Website:* www.verawang.com (office).

WANG, Wayne; Chinese/American film director; b. 1949, Hong Kong; m. Cora Miao; ed Coll. of Arts and Crafts, Oakland, Calif. *Films directed:* Chan is Mission, Dim Sum, Slamdance, Eat a Bowl of Tea, Life is Cheap... But Toilet Paper is Expensive, The Joy Luck Club 1993, Smoke 1995, Blue in the Face 1995, Chinese Box, Anywhere But Here, The Centre of the World 2001, Maid in Manhattan 2002, Because of Winn-Dixie 2005, Last Holiday 2006, A Thousand Years of Good Prayers (Golden Shell for Best Film, San Sebastian Film Festival 2007) 2007, The Princess of Nebraska 2007. *Address:* 916 Kearny Street, San Francisco, CA 94133, USA (office).

WANG, Weicheng; Chinese party official; b. 1929, Tonglu Co., Zhejiang Prov.; joined CCP 1948; Dir Research Office of the State Council 1977–83; Deputy Head of Propaganda Dept, CCP Cen. Cttee 1987; Dir Cen. Policy Research Center 1989–; Vice-Pres. China Asscn for Int. Exchange of Personnel, Soc. for study of Workers' Political and Ideological Work; mem. 14th CCP Cen. Cttee 1992–97; mem. 9th

Standing Cttee of Cttee 1998–2003, Chair. Legal Affairs Cttee 1998–2003. *Address:* c/o Standing Committee of National People's Congress, Beijing, People's Republic of China (office).

WANG, Weimin; Chinese business executive; b. 1961; ed Acad. of Armoured Force Eng; fmrly with Cadre, Training Dept of Acad. of Armoured Force Eng, Armoured Force Political Section of Gen. Staff Dept of PLA, Gen. Office of Economy and Trade Office under State Council, Personnel Dept of State Econ. and Trade Comm. (SETC); fmr Deputy Dir, later Dir, later Deputy Dir-Gen. of Tech. Progress Dept and Arms and Equipment Dept of SETC; fmr Deputy Dir-Gen. High-tech Industry Dept of Nat. Devt and Reform Comm.; fmr Deputy Insp., Gen. Office of State-owned Assets Supervision and Admin Comm. under State Council, Sec. of Party Cttee (Directorate Grade) 2006–07; Vice-Chair. and Sec. of Party Cttee, China Metallurgical Group Corpn 2009–12. *Address:* c/o China Metallurgical Group Corporation, 11 Gaoliangqiao Xiejie, Haidian, Beijing 100081, People's Republic of China. *E-mail:* mcc@mcc.com.cn.

WANG, Wenyin; Chinese business executive; *Chairman, Amer International Group;* b. Anqing, Anhui Prov.; Pres. Anhui Chamber of Commerce in Guangdong Prov., Shenzhen-Anhui Enterprise Asscn; Vice-Pres. China Enterprise Dirs Asscn, Anhui Enterprise Confed.; Vice-Chair. Anhui Fed. of Industry and Commerce; Econ. Adviser to Hefei City; Chair. Confed. of Top 500 Chinese Companies 2010–11, 2012; Founder and Chair. Amer International Group Co. Ltd; mem. Anhui CPPCC; honoured as The Most Creative Chinese Business Leader and Outstanding Chinese Entrepreneur Venture Influential Man of Shenzhen's new generation. *Address:* East Pacific International Center, 7888th Shennan Boulevard, Shenzhen 518040, People's Republic of China (office). *Telephone:* (755) 82785868 (office). *Fax:* (755) 27118899 (office). *E-mail:* webmaster@amer.com.cn (office). *Website:* www.amer.com.cn (office).

WANG, Wenyuan; Chinese politician and economist; b. Feb. 1931, Huangpi, Hubei Prov.; ed Northeast China Inst. of Finance and Econs; teaching asst, Lecturer, Assoc. Prof., Prof. and Pres. Econs Coll., Liaoning Univ. 1958–88; Deputy Sec.-Gen. CPPCC, Shenyang City Cttee, Liaoning Prov., 1982–88; mem. Standing Cttee CPPCC Liaoning Prov. Cttee 1982–92; Vice-Chair. Shenyang City Cttee Jiusan Soc. 1982–88, Liaoning Prov. Cttee Jiusan Soc. 1988–92, Cen. Cttee Jiusan Soc. 1988–; Vice-Gov. of Liaoning Prov. 1988–92; Deputy Procurator Gen. Supreme People's Procuratorate 1992–98; Vice-Pres. China Sr Procurators' Training Centre 1992–98; mem. 7th CPPCC Nat. Cttee 1988–93, 8th CPPCC Nat. Cttee 1993–98, 9th CPPCC Nat. Cttee 1998–2003 (Vice-Chair. 1998); Pres. 6th Council of China Council for the Promotion of Peaceful Reunification 1999. *Address:* c/o National Committee of Chinese People's Political Consultative Conference, 23 Taipingqiao Street, Beijing, People's Republic of China (office).

WANG, Wilfred, BEng; Taiwanese business executive; *Executive Director, Formosa Petrochemical Corporation;* ed Univ. of London, UK; Exec. Vice-Pres. Formosa Petrochemical Corpn 1998–2003, Pres. 2003–09, Chair. 2006–11, Exec. Dir 2011–; Chair. Mailiao Harbor Admin Corpn, Formosa Plastics Marine Corpn, Nan Ya Photonics Inc.; Exec. Dir Formosa Plastics Corpn, Nan Ya Plastics Corpn. *Address:* Formosa Petrochemical Corpn, 1-1, Formosa Plastics Group Industrial Zone, Mailiao, Yunlin, Taiwan (office). *Telephone:* (2) 27122211 (office). *Fax:* (2) 87128050 (office). *E-mail:* fpccpre@fpcc.com.tw (office). *Website:* www.fpcc.com.tw (office); www.fpg.com.tw (office).

WANG, Xianjin; Chinese politician; b. 1930, Haiyang, Shandong; fmr Vice-Sec. Jilin, concurrently Dir State Bureau of Land Admin; Pres. Asscn of Land Valuers of China 1994–. *Address:* Association of Land Valuers of China, Beijing, People's Republic of China (office).

WANG, Xianzhang; Chinese insurance executive; b. May 1942, Hebei Prov.; ed Liaoning Finance & Econ. Inst. (now Northeastern Univ. of Finance and Econs); began career in insurance industry 1965, held positions successively as Gen.-Man. People's Insurance Co. of China, Liaoning Br., Vice-Pres. People's Insurance Co. of China, Vice-Pres. People's Insurance (Group) Co. of China, Pres. China Insurance H.K. (Holding) Co. Ltd, Chair. and Pres. China Life Insurance Co. Ltd 2000–05; Vice-Pres. Insurance Inst. of China; mem. China Enterprise Confed. & China Enterprise Dirs Asscn (CEC-CED); mem. CCP, Del. to CCP Nat. and mem. CPPCC. *Publications include:* China Insurance Dictionary, Insurance Marketing Psychology, An Insurance Specialist's Comments of Insurance. *Address:* c/o China Life Insurance Company Ltd, 16 Chaowai Avenue, Chaoyang District, Beijing 100020, People's Republic of China.

WANG, Xiaochu, DBA; Chinese telecommunications industry executive; *Chairman and CEO, China Telecommunications Corporation (China Telecom);* b. 1953, Beijing; ed Beijing Inst. of Posts and Telecommunications, Hong Kong Polytechnic Univ.; fmr Deputy Dir and Dir Hangzhou Telecommunications Bureau, Zhejiang Prov.; fmr Dir-Gen. Tianjin Posts and Telecommunications Admin; Dir China Mobile (Hong Kong) Ltd 1999–, also fmr CEO and Chair.; fmr Vice-Pres. China Mobile Communications Corpn; Gen. Man. China Telecommunications Corpn 2004, Exec. Dir 2005–, Chair. and CEO 2004–, Hon. Chair. China Communications Services Corpn Ltd, Sec. Party Leadership Group; Alt. mem. 17th CCP Cen. Cttee 2007–12, 18th CCP Cen. Cttee 2012–; Class Three Nat. Science and Tech. Advancement Award, Ministry of Posts and Telecommunications, Class One Science and Tech. Advancement Award. *Address:* China Telecommunications Corporation, 31 Jinrong Street, Xicheng District, Beijing 100032, People's Republic of China (office). *Telephone:* (10) 6602-7217 (office). *Fax:* (10) 6602-1147 (office). *E-mail:* info@chinatelecom.com.cn (office). *Website:* www.chinatelecom.com.cn (office); www.chinatelecom-h.com/en/global/home.php (office).

WANG, Xiaodong, BS, PhD; American (b. Chinese) biochemist and academic; *George L. MacGregor Distinguished Chair Professor in Biomedical Science, University of Texas Southwestern Medical Center;* b. 1963, Wuhan, People's Repub. of China; ed Beijing Normal Univ., Univ. of Texas Southwestern Medical Center, Dallas; grew up in Xingxiang, Henan Prov.; Post-doctoral researcher, Univ. of Texas Southwestern Medical Center 1991–95, apptd Asst Prof., Dept of Biochemistry 1996, currently George L. MacGregor Distinguished Chair Prof. in Biomedical Science; at Emory Univ. 1995–96; Asst Investigator, Howard Hughes Medical Inst. 1997, currently Investigator; Co-Dir Nat. Inst. of Biological Sciences, Beijing 2003–; mem. American Asscn of Cancer Research, American Soc. of

Biochemistry and Molecular Biology, American Soc. of Cell Biology, NAS, Soc. of Chinese Biomedical Scientists in America; Damon Runyon-Walter Winchell Cancer Research Fund Postdoctoral Fellowship 1991–94, ACS Eli Lilly Award 2000, Paul Marks Prize, Memorial Sloan-Kettering Cancer Center 2001, Hackerman Award, The Welch Foundation 2002, Shaw Prize in Life Science and Medicine, The Shaw Foundation 2006, NAS Molecular Biology Award 2006, NAS Richard Lounsbery Award 2007. *Publications:* numerous scientific papers in professional journals on biochemical mechanism of programmed cell death, or apoptosis, in human cells. *Address:* Department of Biochemistry, University of Texas Southwestern Medical Center at Dallas, 5323 Harry Hines Blvd, Dallas, TX 75390-9038, USA (office). *Telephone:* (214) 648-6713 (office). *Fax:* (214) 648-8856 (office). *E-mail:* wwwbio@utsouthwestern.edu (office). *Website:* www8 .utsouthwestern.edu (office).

WANG, Xiaofeng; Chinese politician; b. Oct. 1944, Cili Co., Hunan Prov.; ed Beijing Mining Inst.; technician, later Deputy Dir, later Dir Changde July 1st Machinery Plant, Hunan Prov. 1970–83; joined CCP 1973; Deputy Sec. CCP Changde Prefectural Cttee 1983–86, Commr Changde Prefectural Admin. Office 1983–86; Dir Hunan Provincial Planning Cttee 1986–90; Vice-Gov. Hunan Prov. 1990–93, Exec. Vice-Gov. 1993–98; Deputy Sec. CCP Hunan Prov. Cttee 1992–93; Deputy Sec. CCP Hainan Prov. Cttee 1993–98, Sec. 2004–06; Vice-Gov. Hainan Prov. 1993–98, Gov. 1998–2003; Pres. Hainan Prov. Entrepreneurs Asscn 1993; Chair. Standing Cttee Hainan Prov. People's Congress 2004–06; Alt. mem. 14th CCP Cen. Cttee 1992–97, mem. 15th CCP Cen. Cttee 1997–2002, 16th CCP Cen. Cttee 2002–07. *Address:* c/o Hainan Provincial People's Congress, Haikou City, Hainan Province, People's Republic of China (office).

WANG, Xiaoguang; Chinese jurist; b. 1924, Anguo, Hebei; Deputy Procurator-Gen. 1983; mem. CCP Discipline Inspection Comm. 1982; Sec. Party Cttee Beijing Univ. 1985; Deputy Procurator Gen., Supreme People's Procuratorate, Pres. Soc. of Procuratorial Work; NPC Deputy Hebei Prov.; mem. 8th NPC 1993–98, Internal and Judicial Affairs Cttee. *Address:* Supreme People's Procuratorate, Beijing, People's Republic of China (office).

WANG, Xiaoshuai; Chinese film director and screenwriter; b. 22 May 1966, Shanghai; ed Beijing Film Acad.; mem. jury BigScreen Italia Film Festival 2006; Chevalier, Ordre des Arts et des Lettres (France) 2010. *Films include:* Dongchun de rizi (The Days) 1993, Da youxi 1994, Jidu hanleng (Frozen) 1996, Biandan, guniang (So Close to Paradise) 1998, The House 1999, Beijing Bicycle (Silver Bear for Best Dir, Berlin Film Festival 2001) 2001, After War (segment) 2002, Drifters 2003, Shanghai Dreams (Jury Prize, Cannes Film Festival 2005) 2005, In Love We Trust (Silver Bear Best Script) 2008, Chongqing Blues 2010, 11 Flowers 2011.

WANG, Xiji, BEng, MS; Chinese engineer; b. 1921, Dali, Yun'nan Prov.; ed Southwest China United Univ., Virginia Polytechnic Inst., USA; returned to China 1950; fmrly Assoc. Prof. Dalian Polytechnic; Prof., Shanghai Jiaotong Univ. and Shanghai Univ. of Science and Tech.; Chief Engineer, Shanghai Mechanical and Electrical Designing Inst., Chinese Acad. of Sciences; Chief Engineer, Ministry of Aerospace Industry; Vice-Pres. Research Inst. No. 5, Ministry of Aerospace Industry; researcher and adviser, China Aerospace Science and Tech. Corpn, China Space Tech. Research Inst.; Fellow, Chinese Acad. of Sciences 1993–; was in charge of the research and devt of 12 types of sounding rockets and the technical design of China's first launch vehicle Long March I in the 1960s; was first chief designer of China recoverable satellites (CRSAT) and successfully conducted China's micro-gravity space experiments on CRSAT; Special Prize of Nat. Science and Tech. Advancement Award 1985, Meritorious Service Medal for the devt of China's Atomic and Hydrogen Bombs and Satellites by the CCP Cen. Cttee, the State Council and the Cen. Mil. Comm. 1999. *Address:* c/o Chinese Academy of Sciences, 52 Sanlihe Road, Beijing 100864, People's Republic of China (office).

WANG, Xudong; Chinese politician; b. Jan. 1946, Yancheng, Jiangsu Prov.; ed Tianjin Coll. for Advanced Studies in Science and Tech.; joined CCP 1972; fmrly Sec. of Chinese Communist Youth League Cttee; Vice-Sec. CCP Cttee PLA 1418 Research Inst.; Dir Research Inst. No. 18, Ministry of Electronics Industry; Dir Org. Dept, CCP Tianjin Municipal Cttee, also Deputy Sec.; Vice-Dir Org. Dept, CCP Cen. Cttee 1993–2000; mem. Standing Cttee CCP Hebei Prov. Cttee 2000–02, Sec. Prov. Cttee 2000–02; Minister of Information Industry 2003–08; Chair. State Electricity Regulatory Comm. 2008–11; Vice-Chair. CPPCC Nat. Cttee, Cttee for Social and Legal Affairs 2011–; Alt. mem. 15th CCP Cen. Cttee 1997–2002, mem. 16th CCP Cen. Cttee 2002–07, 17th CCP Cen. Cttee 2007–12. *Address:* c/o State Electricity Regulatory Commission, 86 Xichangan Jie, Beijing 100031, People's Republic of China (office).

WANG, Xuebing; Chinese banker; ed Univ. of Int. Business and Econs, Beijing; Adviser Steering Group, Gold and Exchange Rate Man. of State Council; Gen. Man. US Operations, Bank of China 1988–93; Chair. and Pres. Bank of China 1993–2000; Pres. and CEO China Construction Bank 2000–02 (dismissed following alleged financial irregularities at Bank of China); expelled from CCP 2002; sentenced to 12 years in prison for taking bribes 2003; Alt. mem. 15th CCP Cen. Cttee 1997–2002.

WANG, Yang; Chinese politician; *Vice-Premier;* b. 1955, Suzhou City, Anhui Prov.; ed CCP Cen. Cttee Central Party School; joined CCP 1975; began career working in food processing factory, becoming supervisor 1972–76; teacher, CCP Party School, Suxian, Anhui Prov. 1980–81; Deputy Dir, later Dir Anhui Provincial Sports Bureau 1984–88; Mayor, Tongling City, Anhui Prov. 1988–98; Vice-Gov. Anhui Prov. 1993–99; Vice-Minister, Nat. Devt and Reform Comm. 1999–2003; Deputy Sec.-Gen., State Council 2003–05; Sec., Chongqing Municipality CCP Cttee 2005–07, Chair., Standing Cttee, Chongqing Municipality Municipal People's Congress 2006–08; Sec., CCP Provincial Cttee, Guangdong Prov. 2007–12, also mem. Standing Cttee, CCP Provincial Cttee, Guangdong Prov. 2007–12; Vice-Premier 2013–; mem. State Council CCP Leading Party Group 2013–; Dir Nat. Afforestation Cttee 2013–; alt. mem. 16th CCP Cen. Cttee 2002–07; mem. 17th CCP Cen. Cttee 2007–12, also mem. 17th CCP Cen. Cttee Politburo 2007–12, 18th CCP Cen. Cttee 2012–, also mem. 18th CCP Cen. Cttee Politburo 2012–. *Address:* Chinese Communist Party Politburo, Quanguo Renmin Diabiao Dahui, Zhongguo Gongchan Dang, 1 Zhongnanhai, Beijing, People's Republic of China. *Website:* cpc.people.com.cn (office).

WANG, Yi, MEconSc; Chinese diplomatist and government official; *Minister of Foreign Affairs;* b. 1953, Beijing; clerk, Asian Affairs Dept, Ministry of Foreign Affairs, subsequently served as Deputy Chief and Chief 1982–89; Counsellor, Embassy in Japan 1989–94; returned to Asian Affairs Dept as Deputy Chief 1994–95, Chief 1995–98, Asst to Minister for Foreign Affairs 1998–2001, Vice-Minister for Foreign Affairs 2001–04, 2007, Minister 2013–; Amb. to Japan 2004–07; Dir Taiwan Affairs Office 2008–13; mem. 17th CCP Cen. Cttee 2007–12, 18th CCP Cen. Cttee 2012–. *Address:* Ministry of Foreign Affairs, 225 Chaoyangmen Nan Dajie, Chaoyang Qu, Beijing 100701, People's Republic of China (office). *Telephone:* (10) 65961114 (office). *Fax:* (10) 65962146 (office). *E-mail:* webmaster@mfa.gov.cn (office). *Website:* www.fmprc.gov.cn (office).

WANG, Yifang, MSc; Chinese engineer and steel industry executive; *Chairman and General Manager, Hebei Iron & Steel Group;* b. 1948, Pingxiang, Hebei Prov.; ed Wuhan Steel and Iron Coll., Beijing Steel and Iron Coll.; joined CCP 1948; Dir and Deputy Gen. Man. Handan Steel and Iron Co. Ltd (Hangang Group), Hebei Prov. 2000–08, Gen. Man. 2003–08; Chair., Gen. Man. and Deputy Party Sec., Hebei Iron and Steel Group Co. Ltd (formed from merger of Tangsteel and Hansteel) 2008–; Hebei Prov. Award for Excellent Science and Tech. 2000, State Award for Top Worker 2000, State Award for Excellent Promoter. *Address:* Hebei Iron & Steel Group Co. Ltd, 81 Jianshe Road, Tangshan 063016, Hebei Province, People's Republic of China (office). *Telephone:* (315) 2793048 (office). *E-mail:* info@hebgtjt.com (office). *Website:* www.hebgtjt.com (office).

WANG, Yilin, PhD; Chinese oil industry executive; *Chairman, China National Offshore Oil Corporation (CNOOC) Limited;* ed China Univ. of Petroleum; Deputy Dir and Chief Exploration Geologist, Xinjiang Petroleum Admin Bureau 1996–99; Gen. Man. Xinjiang Oilfield Co. 1999–2003; Asst Pres. China Nat. Petroleum Corpn (CNPC) July–Dec. 2003, Vice-Pres. Dec. 2003–11, Safety Dir of CNPC 2004–07; Chair. and Party Leadership Group Sec. China Nat. Offshore Oil Corpn (CNOOC) Ltd 2011–. *Address:* China National Offshore Oil Corpn, Box 4705, 25 Chao Yangmen North Street, Dongcheng District, Beijing 100010, People's Republic of China (office). *Telephone:* (10) 84521010 (office). *Fax:* (10) 64602600 (office). *E-mail:* webmaster@cnooc.com.cn (office). *Website:* www.cnooc.com.cn (office).

WANG, Yingfan, BA; Chinese diplomatist and politician; m.; one d.; ed Beijing Univ.; on staff, Office of Chargé d'affaires of People's Repub. of China, London 1964; joined Dept of Translation and Interpreting, Ministry of Foreign Affairs 1967; attaché, Embassies in Ghana and Philippines; Deputy Div. Dir, Dept of Asian Affairs, Foreign Ministry 1978, Deputy Dir-Gen. 1988; Amb. to the Philippines 1988–90; Dir-Gen. Dept of Asian Affairs, Foreign Ministry 1990–94, Asst Foreign Minister 1994–95, Vice-Minister for Foreign Affairs 1995–2000; Perm. Rep. to UN 2000–03; Vice-Chair. 10th NPC Foreign Affairs Cttee 2003–08. *Address:* c/o Foreign Affairs Committee, National People's Congress, Great Hall of the People, Beijing, People's Republic of China (office).

WANG, Yong, MEng; Chinese government official; *State Councillor and Director, National Committee for Disaster Reduction;* b. 1955, Gaizhou City, Liaoning Prov.; ed Harbin Inst. of Tech.; began working 1969; joined CCP 1974; worked in Heilongjiang Construction Corps, Seventh Ministry of Mechanical Industry, Ministry of Aerospace, No. 230 Factory under China Aerospace Corpn, held successive posts of Asst to the Dir, Deputy Chief Economist, Deputy Dir, Exec. Deputy Dir, Dir and Deputy Party Sec. (Dir-Gen. level); transferred to China Astronautics Corpn, Deputy Dir and Head of Personnel Dept 1997–98; Deputy Gen. Man. China Aerospace Mechanic and Electronic Corpn 1999–2000; Dir Org. Dept, Enterprise Cadre Office, CCP Cen. Cttee 2000–01, Dir 5th Dept 2001–03; Deputy Dir State-owned Assets Supervision and Admin Comm. (SASAC) 2003–05, Dir 2010–13, also mem. CCP Party Cttee 2003–05, Deputy Sec. 2005–08, Sec. 2010–; State Councillor 2013–; Dir Gen. Admin of Quality Supervision, Inspection and Quarantine 2008–10, Sec. CCP Leading Party Group 2008–10; Dir, Nat. Cttee for Disaster Reduction 2013–; mem. Cen. Comm. for Discipline Inspection, 16th CCP Cen. Cttee 2003–07, 17th CCP Cen. Cttee 2007–12, 18th CCP Cen. Cttee 2012–; ranked by Forbes magazine amongst The World's Most Powerful People (62nd) 2010. *Address:* National Committee for Disaster Reduction, Department of Foreign Affairs, 147 Beiheyan Street, Beijing 100721, People's Republic of China (office). *Telephone:* (10) 65235511 (office). *Fax:* (10) 65121882 (office). *E-mail:* kp@mca.gov.cn (office). *Website:* www.mca.gov.cn (office).

WANG, Yongyan; Chinese doctor; b. Sept. 1938, Tianjin; ed Beijing Chinese Medical Coll.; Assoc. Prof., Prof., Chief Doctor, Pres. Beijing Chinese Medical Univ. 1962; Dir Chinese Acad. of Traditional Chinese Medicine; Fellow, Chinese Acad. of Sciences; Vice-Chair. Chinese Medical Soc. of China; Fellow Chinese Acad. of Engineering 1997–. *Address:* Institute of Basic Research in Clinical Medicine, 16 Nanxiaojie, Dongzhimennei Street, Dongcheng District, Beijing 100700, People's Republic of China (office). *E-mail:* wangyyan@public.bta.net.cn.

WANG, Yongzhi; Chinese aerospace scientist; b. Nov. 1932, Changtu, Liaoning Prov.; ed Moscow Aeronautics Inst.; Dir Research Section, Dir Design Dept, Pres. No. 1 Research Inst. of Ministry of Aerospace Industry; Gen. Designer of Rockets 1961–91; Vice-Dir Science and Tech. Cttee, Ministry of Aerospace Industry 1991–98; designer of rocket launcher series 1991–; Sr Consulting Engineer for manned space programme, including launch of Shenzhou VII spacecraft Sept. 2008; Academician, Int. Astronautical Acad., Foreign Academician Konstantin Eduardovich Ziolkowski Acad., Russia 1992–; Academician Chinese Acad. of Engineering 1994–; mem. 11th CPPCC Nat. Cttee 2008–13; Prize of Nat. Scientific Conf., Scientific Advancement Prize, State Pre-eminent Science and Technology Award 2003, Meritorious Scientist of Manned Spaceflight 2005, HoLeung Ho Lee Foundation Technological Science Prize. *Address:* The People's Liberation Army General Equipment Department, 4 Beisanhuan Middle Road, Beijing 100720, People's Republic of China (office). *Telephone:* (10) 66350660 (office). *Fax:* (10) 66061566 (office). *E-mail:* engach@mail.cae.ac.cn (office).

WANG, You-Tsao, MSc, PhD; Taiwanese politician and agricultural adviser; b. 2 July 1925, Chinchiang Co., Fukien; s. of Wang Hsiao-kwei and Wang-Huang Pei-feng; m. Jean Eng-ling 1954; two s. one d.; ed Nat. Taiwan Univ., Iowa State Univ., USA; Asst, Instructor, Assoc. Prof., Dept of Agric. Econs, Nat. Taiwan Univ. 1954–60, Prof. 1960–73; Specialist, Rural Econs Div., Jt Comm. on Rural Reconstruction (JCRR) 1960–63, Sr Specialist 1965–66, Chief, Rural Econs Div.

1966–71, Chief, Office of Planning and Programming 1971–72, Deputy Sec.-Gen. JCRR 1972–73, Sec.-Gen. 1973–79; Sec.-Gen. Council for Agric. Planning and Devt, Exec. Yuan 1979, Vice-Chair. 1979–84, Chair. 1984, Chair. and Chief Operating Admin. 1984–88, Adviser 1990–2004; Minister without Portfolio, Exec. Yuan 1988–90; Nat. Policy Adviser to Pres. 1990–96; Dir Asian Agric. Tech. Service Center 1993–95; Pres. Rural Devt Foundation 1995–98 (Chair. 1998); Chair. Bd of Dirs Harvest (farm magazine) 1995–2002; mem. Agric. Asscn of China, Rural Econs Asscn of China. *Publications:* Statistical Analysis of Resources Productivity in Shihmen Reservoir Area of Taiwan 1963, Technological Changes and Agricultural Development of Taiwan 1946–65 1966. *Address:* Rural Development Foundation, 5F, No. 7, Section 1, Roosvelt Road, Taipei 100 (office); 7F, No. 2, Alley 8, Lane 216, Sect. 4, Chung Hsiao East Road, Taipei, Taiwan (home).

WANG, Yuan; Chinese mathematician; b. 30 April 1930; Dir Inst. of Math., Acad. Sinica March–Oct. 1985; mem. Dept of Math. and Physics, Acad. Sinica 1985–; mem. Nat. Cttee 6th CPPCC 1986; Pres. Chinese Math. Soc. 1989–92; mem. Presidium Chinese Acad. of Sciences 1996–; numerous awards including Hua Loo-Keng Math. Prize. *Leisure interest:* calligraphy. *Address:* Institute of Mathematics, Academia Sinica, Zhong Guan Cun, Beijing 100080, People's Republic of China (office). *Telephone:* (10) 62541846 (office). *Website:* http://infolab.stanford.edu/~wangy/home/link/wangy/.

WANG, Yunkun; Chinese politician; *Chairman, Standing Committee, Jilin Provincial People's Congress Standing Committee;* b. Dec. 1942, Liyang Co., Jiangsu Prov.; ed Tianjin Univ.; joined CCP 1966; Chief, Publicity Section, Chemical Machinery Plant, Jilin Chemical Industry Co., Deputy Dir, later Dir Political Dept, engineer, Refinery, Research Inst. and Organic Synthesis Plant; Vice-Mayor Jilin City 1982–83, Mayor 1983–86; Dir Dept of Electronic Industry, Jilin Prov. 1986–88; Chair. Comm. for Restructuring the Economy, Jilin Prov. 1988; Sec.-Gen. People's Govt, Jilin Prov. 1988–89; Vice-Gov. Jilin Prov. 1989–92, Acting Gov. 1995, Gov. 1996–98; Sec. CCP Changchun City Cttee 1992–95; Deputy Sec. Jilin Prov. Cttee 1995–98, Sec. 1998–2006; Chair. Standing Cttee Jilin Prov. People's Congress 1999–; mem. 15th CCP Cen. Cttee 1997–2002, 16th CCP Cen. Cttee 2002–07. *Address:* c/o Jilin Provincial Government, Changchun City, Jilin Province, People's Republic of China (office).

WANG, Zhaoguo; Chinese party official; *Chairman, All-China Federation of Trade Unions;* b. 1941, Fengrun, Hebei Prov.; ed Harbin Technological Univ.; joined CCP 1965; technician, later Deputy Dir Axle Plant, Second Automotive Works 1968–79 (mem. Standing Cttee, later First Sec. CCP Party Cttee 1968–79), Dir Second Automotive Works 1979–82 (Sec. CCP Party Cttee 1979–82); mem. Standing Cttee CCP Shiyan Municipal Cttee, Hubei Prov. 1968–79; First Sec. CCP Communist Youth League of China and Pres. Party School 1982–84; Deputy for Hubei to 6th NPC 1983; Dir-Gen. Office Cen. Cttee CCP 1984–86; Chief Rep. 21st Century Cttee for Chinese-Japanese Friendship 1984–89; Vice-Gov. and Acting Gov. of Fujian 1987–88, Gov. 1988–90; Dir Taiwan Affairs Office, State Council 1990–96; Chair. All-China Fed. of Trade Unions 2002–; mem. 12th CCP Cen. Cttee 1982–87, 13th CCP Cen. Cttee 1987–92, 14th CCP Cen. Cttee 1992–97, 15th CCP Cen. Cttee 1997–2002, 16th CCP Cen. Cttee 2002–07 (mem. Politburo 2002–07), 17th CCP Cen. Cttee 2007–12 (mem. Politburo 2007–12); mem. Secr., CCP Cen. Cttee 1985–87; mem. Presidium 6th NPC 1983–88, Standing Cttee 6th NPC 1983–88, Vice-Chair. Standing Cttee 10th NPC 2003–08, Standing Cttee 11th NPC 2008–; Head, United Front Work Dept 1992–2007; Vice-Chair. 8th CPPCC Nat. Cttee 1993–98, 9th CPPCC Nat. Cttee 1998–2003; Pres. China Overseas Friendship Asscn 1997–. *Address:* All-China Federation of Trade Unions, 10 Fu Xing Men Wai Jie, Beijing 100865, People's Republic of China (office).

WANG, Zhengwei; Chinese government official; *Minister of State Ethnic Affairs Commission;* b. June 1957, Ningxia Hui Autonomous Region; ed Ningxia Univ., Central Univ. for Nationalities; joined CCP 1981; Sec., Gen. Office, CCP Autonomous Regional Cttee, Ningxia Hui Autonomous Region 1984–89, Deputy Dir, Policy Research Office 1989–97, Dir, Publicity Dept 1997–2001; Acting Chair., Autonomous Region People's Govt, Ningxia Hui Autonomous Region 2007–08, Chair. 2008–13; Minister of State Ethnic Affairs Comm. 2013–; Vice-Chair., 12th CPPCC Nat. Cttee 2013–; mem. 16th CCP Cen. Cttee 2002–07, 17th CCP Cen. Cttee 2007–12, 18th CCP Cen. Cttee 2012–. *Address:* State Ethnic Affairs Commission, 252 Taipingqiao Dajie, Xicheng Qu, Beijing 100800, People's Republic of China (office). *Telephone:* (10) 66080952 (office). *Fax:* (10) 66057719 (office). *E-mail:* webmaster@seac.gov.cn (office). *Website:* www.seac.gov.cn (office).

WANG, Zhenyi, DMed; Chinese haematologist; *Honorary Director, Shanghai Institute of Haematology;* b. 30 Nov. 1924, Shanghai; m. Xie Jin-xiong; three s.; ed Aurora Univ. Medical Coll.; Pres. Shanghai Second Medical Univ. 1984–88; currently Prof. Emer. of Medicine and Pathophysiology, School of Medicine, Shanghai Jiao Tong Univ.; Foreign Corresp., French Acad. of Sciences 1992–; mem. Chinese Acad. of Eng 1994–; Hon. Dir Shanghai Inst. of Haematology; Chevalier, Légion d'honneur (France) 1993; numerous awards, including Kettering Prize 1994, Charles Rodolphe Brupbacher Prize 1997, Prix mondial Cino Del Duca 1998, State Supreme Science and Tech. Award 2011. *Publications:* chief ed. of five books and author of more than 320 scientific papers. *Leisure interest:* listening to classical music. *Address:* Shanghai Institute of Haematology, Rui-jin Hospital, 197 Rui-jin Er Road, Shanghai 200025, People's Republic of China (office). *Telephone:* (21) 6437-0045 (ext. 610701) (office). *Fax:* (21) 6474-3206 (office). *E-mail:* xiejx@sh163.net (office).

WANG, Zhibao; Chinese administrator; *Chairman, China Green Foundation;* b. July 1938, Zhaoyuan, Shandong Prov.; ed Northeast Electric Power Inst.; joined CCP 1965; Deputy Chief, Machinery and Electrical Div., Yikeshi Forestry Admin 1975; Dir Planning Dept, Ministry of Forestry 1986; Vice-Minister of Forestry 1992–98; Dir State Forestry Bureau 1998–2000; Pres. China Wildlife Conservation Asscn 1998; currently Chair. China Green Foundation; mem. 9th CPPCC Nat. Cttee 1998–2003. *Address:* China Green Foundation, 18 Hepingli Dongjie Street, Dongcheng District, Beijing 100714, People's Republic of China (office). *Telephone:* (10) 84238200 (office). *E-mail:* cgf@cgf.org.cn (office). *Website:* www.cgf.org.cn/en (office).

WANG, Zhixin, PhD; Chinese biophysicist; *Professor of Biological Sciences and Biotechnology, Tsinghua University;* b. 10 Aug. 1953, Beijing; ed Tsinghua Univ., Beijing; Research Fellow, Vice-Dir Biophysics Research Inst. of Chinese Acad. of

Sciences 1993–; Prof., Dept of Biological Sciences and Biotechnology, Tsinghua Univ. 2003–; Dir Nat. Biomolecular Lab.; Dir SinoBiomed Inc. 2007–; mem. Chinese Acad. of Sciences 1997–; Chair. Chinese Soc. of Biochemistry and Molecular Biology; mem. Chinese Soc. of Biophysics; Hon. DSc (Biophysics Research Inst. of Chinese Acad. of Sciences) 1988. *Address:* Department of Biological Sciences and Biotechnology, Tsinghua University, Haidan District, Beijing 100084, People's Republic of China (office). *Telephone:* (10) 62785474 (office). *E-mail:* zhixinwang@mail.tsinghua.edu.cn (office). *Website:* www.biosci .tsinghua.edu.cn (office).

WANG, Zhizhong; Chinese business executive; *President, Tianjin Material and Equipment Group Corporation (Teewo Group Company Limited);* joined Tianjin Enterprise Group (Teewo) 1999, currently Pres. Tianjin Materials and Equipments Group Corpn (fmrly Bureau of Materials, f. 1993), Teewo Metals International Trade Co. Ltd. *Address:* Teewo Group Co. Ltd, 4 Yingkoudao Road, Heping District, Tianjin 300041, People's Republic of China (office). *Telephone:* (22) 23030779 (office). *E-mail:* info@tewoo.com (office). *Website:* www .tewoo.com (office).

WANG, Zhongshu; Chinese archaeologist and academic; *Professor, Institute of Archaeology, Chinese Academy of Social Sciences;* b. 15 Oct. 1925, Ningbo; s. of Wang Xuanbing and Ling Sujuan; m. Chen Kai 1960; one s.; ed Univ. of Bejing; Sr Fellow Inst. of Archaeology, Chinese Acad. of Social Sciences 1979–, Dir 1982–88; Prof. and Tutor for Doctoral Studies, Grad. School Chinese Acad. of Social Sciences 1982–; mem. Nat. Council of Cultural Relics 1983–; Corresp. Fellow, German Archaeological Inst. 1988–; Hon. Prof., Nat. Univ. of San Antonio Abad (Cuzco, Peru) 1973; 7th Fukuoka Grand Asian Cultural Prize, Fukuoka, Japan 1996. *Publications:* Han Civilization 1982, An Outline of Archaeology of the Han Period 1984, Triangular-rimmed Bronze Mirrors with Mythical Figure and Animal Designs unearthed from Japan 1992, Ancient Japan seen from China 1992. *Leisure interests:* Chinese and Japanese classical literature. *Address:* Institute of Archaeology, Chinese Academy of Social Sciences, 27 Wangfujing Dajie, Beijing 100710 (office); 1-2-602 Chang Yun Gong, Zi Zhu Yuan, Beijing 100044, People's Republic of China (home). *Telephone:* (10) 65234003 (office); (10) 68411820 (home). *Fax:* (10) 65135532 (office). *E-mail:* liu.jg@history.cass.net.cn (office); yidan@pku.edu.cn (home).

WANG, Zhongyu; Chinese politician; *Vice-Chairman, 10th National Committee, Chinese People's Political Consultative Conference;* b. Feb. 1933, Changchun, Jilin Prov.; two s. one d.; ed Light Industry Sr Vocational School, Shenyang City, Liaoning Prov., CCP Cen. Cttee Party School; technician, Deputy Workshop Dir, engineer, Deputy Planning Section Chief, Jilin Paper Mill 1953–67, Deputy Head of Production Man. Group, Deputy Dir, Dir Office of CCP 1970–75, Deputy Dir and Chief Engineer 1975–80; joined CCP 1956; Deputy Dir Light Industry Bureau, Jilin Prov. 1980–81, Dir CCP Leading Party Group, 1982–83; mem. Standing Cttee, Dir Research Office and Sec.-Gen. CCP Jilin Prov. Cttee 1983–85, Deputy Sec. 1985–92; Vice-Gov. Jilin Prov. 1983–85, Acting Gov. 1985–92; Deputy, Jilin Prov., 7th NPC 1988–93; Vice-Gov. Jilin Prov. 1988–89, Gov. 1989–93; Deputy Dir Production Office of the State Council 1992–93 (also Deputy Sec. CCP Party Cttee); Minister in charge of State Econ. and Trade Comm. 1993–98; State Councillor and Sec.-Gen. State Council 1998–2003; Pres. Nat. School of Admin 1998–2003; Head, 5th Nat. Census Leading Group 1998; mem. Govt Del., Macao Hand-Over Ceremony, Macao Special Admin. Region Preparatory Cttee 1999; Alt. mem. 13th Cen. Cttee CCP 1987–92, mem. 14th Cen. Cttee 1992–97, mem. 15th CCP Cen. Cttee 1997–2002, 16th CCP Cen. Cttee 2002–07; Vice-Chair. 10th CPPCC Nat. Cttee 2003–. *Address:* Chinese People's Political Consultative Conference, Beijing, People's Republic of China (office).

WANG, Zikun, DSc; Chinese professor and university administrator; b. 30 April 1929, Jiangxi Prov.; s. of Wang Zhao-ji and Guo Xiang-e; m. Tian Der-Lin 1958; two s.; ed Wuhan Univ., Moscow Univ., USSR; Asst Prof., then Prof., Nankai Univ. 1952–84; Prof. and Pres. Beijing Normal Univ. 1984; Prof., Shantou Univ. 1993–; Dir China Math. Soc.; mem. Standing Bd China Probilistical-Statistics Soc., China Higher Educational Soc.; mem. Editorial Bd Soc., Scientia Sinica, Science Bulletin of China; mem. Chinese Acad. of Sciences 1991–; Hon. DSc (Macquarie Univ., Australia) 1988; China Science Conf. Award 1978, China Natural Science Prize 1982, China Excellent Popular Science Works Award 1981, Ho Leung Ho Lee Foundation Math. and Mechanics Prize, and numerous other awards. *Publications:* Foundations of Probability Theory and Their Applications 1976, Theory of Stochastic Processes 1965, Brownian Motion and Potentials 1982, Probability Theory and Statistical Prediction 1978, Talks on Scientific Discovery 1978, Birth-Death Processes and Markov Chains 1992 and many other math. articles and popular scientific publs. *Leisure interest:* literature. *Address:* Shantou University, Shantou, Guangdong Province, People's Republic of China (office). *E-mail:* web@ stu.edu.cn (office). *Website:* www.stu.edu.cn (office).

WANG, Gen. Zuxun; Chinese army officer; b. May 1936, Qujing, Yunnan Prov.; joined PLA 1951; Vice-Commdr, then Commdr Yunnan Mil. Command 1984–89; Commdr Army Group 1989–93; Vice-Pres. PLA Acad. of Mil. Science 1993–99, Pres. 1999; rank of Gen. 2000. *Address:* c/o Xianghongqi, Beijing 100091, People's Republic of China (office).

WANGCHUCK, HM Dasho Jigme Khesar Namgyel, (The Druk Gyalpo — 'Dragon King'— of Bhutan), MPhil; b. 21 Feb. 1980; s. of King Jigme Singye Wangchuck and Queen Ashi Tshering Yandon Wangchuck; m. Jetsun Pema 13 Oct. 2011; ed Cushing Acad. and Wheaton Coll., USA, Magdalen Coll., Oxford, UK; proclaimed Crown Prince Oct. 2004; succeeded to throne 14 Dec. 2006, on the abdication of his father; participated in official visits; officially crowned 6 Nov. 2008; Chair. Bhutan Trust Fund for Environmental Conservation; Pres. Bhutan-India Friendship Asscn; Chancellor Royal Univ. of Bhutan; Chief Patron Scouts Asscn of Bhutan; Patron Royal Soc. for the Protection of Nature, Bhutan Chamber of Commerce and Industry, India-Bhutan Foundation, European Convention of Bhutan Socs, Oxford Centre for Buddhist Studies, Bhutan Shooting Fed.; Hon. Royal Bencher, Hon. Soc. of the Inner Temple, UK; Red Scarf 2002, Grand Master, Order of the Dragon King 2008, Grand Master, Royal Order of Bhutan 2008, Grand Master, Nat. Order of Merit 2008, Grand Master, Order of Great Victory of the Thunder Dragon 2008, Medal of the Great Victory of the Thunder Dragon 2008, Kt Grand Cross, Order of Queen Sālote Tupou III (Tonga) 2010; Hon. LLD

(Univ. of New Brunswick, Canada) 2005, (Univ. of Calcutta) 2010; Hon. Dr of Philosophy, Politics and Econs (Rangsit Univ., Thailand); Hon. DEcon (Keio Univ., Japan). *Address:* Royal Palace, Thimphu, Bhutan. *Website:* www.bhutan.gov.bt.

WANGCHUCK, HM Jigme Singye; Bhutanese fmr ruler; b. 11 Nov. 1955, Thimphu; s. of the late Druk Gyalpo Jigme Dorji Wangchuk and of Queen Ashi Kesang; m.; ten c. (including HM King Dasho Jigme Khesar Namgyal Wangchuck); ed North Point, Darjeeling, Ugyuen Wangchuk Acad., Paro, also in UK; Crown Prince March 1972; succeeded to throne 24 July 1972, crowned 2 June 1974, abdicated 14 Dec. 2006; Chair. Planning Comm. of Bhutan 1972–; C-in-C of Armed Forces; Chair. Council of Ministers 1972–98. *Address:* Royal Palace, Thimphu, Bhutan (office). *Website:* www.bhutan.gov.bt.

WANGCHUCK, Lyonpo Khandu, BA; Bhutanese politician; b. 24 Nov. 1950; ed St Stephen's Coll., India; Asst Sec., Ministry of Trade, Industry and Forests 1974, Deputy Dir 1976, Man. Dir Industrial Devt Corpn 1978, Dir of Trade and Commerce 1980–84; Dir of Agric. 1986, Dir Gen. 1987–89, Sec. 1989–1991; Sec. Royal Civil Service Comm. 1991–94; Prime Minister and Chair. 2001–02, 2006–07 (resgnd); Minister of Trade and Industry 1998–2003, of Foreign Affairs 2003–07 (resgnd), of Econ. Affairs 2008–13; mem. Nat. Ass. for Lamgong-Wangchang constituency; mem. Druk Phuensum Tshogpa party; fmr Chair. Bhutan Nat. Bank; Red Scarf 1987, Orange Scarf 1998, Coronation Medal 1999. *Address:* c/o Ministry of Economic Affairs, Tashichhodzong, PO Box 141, Thimphu; Jangsa, Shari Geog, Paro, Bhutan (home). *E-mail:* kdorjee@druknet.bt.

WANGCHUK, Dasho Lhatu; Bhutanese diplomatist, government official and airline industry executive; b. 15 Dec. 1951, Rongthung, Trashigang; Accountant, Foreign Affairs Dept 1972–74, Attaché 1974–75, Under-Sec. 1975–76; Third Sec., Perm. Mission to UN, New York 1976–79; Second Sec., Embassy in New Delhi 1979–81; Deputy Sec. 1981–83; Sec. Nat. Urban Devt Corpn 1983–88; Promotions Officer, Marketing and Promotions Div.; Chief of Protocol, Ministry of Foreign Affairs –1994, also Acting Foreign Sec.; Amb. to Bangladesh 1998–2001; apptd Admin. Officer, Admin. and Finance Section of then Ministry of Trade and Industry 1998; Dir-Gen. Dept of Tourism, Ministry of Econ. Affairs 2004–08; Chair. Druk Air (Royal Bhutan Airlines) 2007–08; Amb. and Perm. Rep. to UN, New York (also accred as Amb. to Canada) 2009–14; Bd mem. Bhutan Foundation. *Address:* Ministry of Foreign Affairs, Gyalyong Tshokhang, PO Box 103, Thimphu, Bhutan (office). *Telephone:* (2) 322459 (office). *Fax:* (2) 331465 (office). *E-mail:* ugyen@mofa.gov.bt (office). *Website:* www.mfa.gov.bt (office).

WANGCHUK, Dasho Penden; Bhutanese government official; *Secretary, Ministry of Home and Cultural Affairs;* currently Sec., Ministry of Home and Cultural Affairs; mem. Royal Civil Service Comm.; Patron Asian Art Museum; mem. Advisory Council, Friends of Bhutan's Culture. *Address:* Ministry of Home and Cultural Affairs, Tashichhodzong, POB 133, Thimphu, Bhutan (office). *Telephone:* (2) 322301 (office). *Fax:* (2) 335905 (office). *E-mail:* lmd@mohca.gov.bt (office). *Website:* www.mohca.gov.bt (office).

WANGDI, Kesang; Bhutanese diplomatist and airline industry executive; joined Ministry of Foreign Affairs 1982, served in various positions including Head of Chancery and Head of Econ. Section, Embassy in Delhi, Head of Finance and Admin Div., Ministry of Foreign Affairs, represented Bhutan at UN, New York including at Security Council, Non-Aligned Group, Asian Group and Forum of Small States, served as Consul Gen. in USA, Chief of Protocol and Head of Protocol Dept, Ministry of Foreign Affairs, served as Dir of SAARC at SAARC in Kathmandu and Head of SAARC and Others Div. Ministry of Foreign Affairs, fmr Planning Officer, Policy and Planning Div., Ministry of Trade and Industry; Dir Dept of Bilateral Affairs, Ministry of Foreign Affairs –2008; Dir Gen. Tourism Council of Bhutan 2008–; Chair. Druk Air Corpn Ltd (nat. airline) 2008–11. *Address:* c/o Druk Air Corpn Ltd (Head Office), Royal Bhutan Airlines, Nemeyzampa, Paro, Bhutan.

WANGDI, Dasho Kunzang, BA, MPA; Bhutanese government official; *Chief Election Commissioner;* b. 17 July 1953, Ura, Bumthang; s. of the late Sithar Norbhu and Mrs Choki; m. Pem Tandi; ed Delhi Univ., India, Pennsylvania State Univ., USA, London School of Econs, UK; worked in various capacities in govt ministries for more than 28 years; Auditor-Gen. 1999–2005; Chief Election Commr 2006–, in charge of two rounds of trial parl. elections in 2007 and first-ever parl. elections in 2008; Druk Thuksey Medal from the Fifth King of Bhutan. *Publications:* drafted Royal Charters, Audit Act, Anti-Corruption Act, Election Acts. *Leisure interests:* reading, photography, cinema. *Address:* Election Commission of Bhutan, Thimphu, Bhutan (office). *Telephone:* (2) 334761 (office). *Fax:* (2) 334763 (office). *E-mail:* kwangdi@druknet.bt (office). *Website:* www.election -bhutan.org.bt (office).

WANGDI, Phuntsho, BL; Bhutanese government official; *Attorney-General;* ed Sherubtse Coll., Royal Inst. of Man., Univ. of Mumbai, India, Univ. of Adelaide, Australia; began career as Judicial Officer, High Court; Chief Prosecutor and Head, Prosecution and Litigation Div., Office of Attorney-Gen. –2010, Attorney-Gen. 2010–. *Address:* Office of the Attorney General, Post Box No. 1045, Thori Lam, Lower Motithang, Thimphu, Bhutan (office). *Telephone:* (2) 326889 (office). *Fax:* (2) 324606 (office). *E-mail:* oag@oag.gov.bt (office). *Website:* www.oag.gov.bt (office).

WANIEK, Danuta, DJur; Polish politician and political scientist; b. 26 Oct. 1946, Włocławek; d. of Jerzy Waniek and Jozefina Wisniewski; m. (husband deceased); two s.; ed Warsaw Univ., Institut für Höhere Studien und Wissenschaft, Vienna; with Inst. of Political Studies, Polish Acad. of Sciences (PAN) 1989–; mem. Polish United Workers' Party (PZPR) 1967–90; mem. Social Democracy of Polish Repub. (SDRP) 1990–; Deputy to Sejm (Parl.) 1991–2001, mem. Parl. Cttee of Nat. Defence; Chair. Women's Democratic Union 1990–; Deputy Minister of Nat. Defence 1994–95; Minister of State and Head of Chancellery of Pres. of Poland 1995–97; mem. Nat. Broadcasting Council 2001–, Pres. 2003–05; with Instytut Problemów Strategicznych 2007–; Krzyz Zaslugi (Cross of Merit). *Publications:* Compromise within the Political System of Germany: Partnership or Struggle? 1988, Constitution and Political Reality 1989, Debate over 'Little Constitution' (ed.) 1992, Creating New Constitutional Order in Poland (ed.) 1993. *Leisure interests:* opera, reading newspapers, embroidering, painting, music (listening and playing). *Address:* Instytut Problemów strategicznych, Al. Ujazdowskie 20/6, 00-

478 Warsaw, (office); ul. Protazego 61, 03-606, Warsaw, Poland (home). *Telephone:* (22) 622-07-35 (office). *E-mail:* zarzad@ips.org.pl (office).

WANKA, Johanna, DrRerNat; German academic and politician; *Federal Minister for Education and Research;* b. (Johanna Müller), 1 April 1951, Rosenfeld, Saxony; m. Gert Wanka; two c.; ed Univ. of Leipzig; Academic Assoc., Technical Univ. Merseburg 1974–85, Sr Academic Assoc. 1985–93, Prof. of Eng Math., Merseburg Univ. of Applied Sciences 1993–, Rector 1994–2000; Founding mem. Neues Forum (citizens' movt in former GDR), Merseburg 1989; Vice-Pres. Saxony-Anhalt Rectors Conf. 1994–98; Deputy Chair. Saxony-Anhalt Advisory Council for Science and Research 1995–98; mem. Bd of Trustees, Körber Foundation Hamburg's German Study Award 1996–2004; mem. Standing Cttee for Planning and Org. of German Rectors Conf. (HRK) 1998–2000, mem. HRK Senate 1999–; mem. Brandenburg Higher Educ. Council 1999–2000; Brandenburg Regional Minister of Science, Research and Culture 2000–09; Lower Saxony Regional Minister of Science and Culture 2012–13; Fed. Minister for Educ. and Research 2013–; mem. CDU 2001–, CDU Party Chair. in Brandenburg Land Parl. 2009–10, mem. Brandenburg CDU Land Exec. Cttee 2003–10, Chair. Brandenburg CDU 2009–10; Deputy Chair. Konrad Adenauer Foundation 2010–11. *Address:* Federal Ministry of Education and Research, Heinemannstr. 2, 53175 Bonn, Germany (office). *Telephone:* (228) 99570 (office). *Fax:* (228) 995783601 (office). *E-mail:* information@bmbf.bund.de (office). *Website:* www.bmbf.de (office).

WANSIRU, Samuel Kamau, (Samuel Wanjiru); Kenyan athlete; b. 10 Nov. 1986, Nyahururu; ed Sendai Ikuei Gakuen High School; long-distance runner; began running aged 15; moved to Japan 2002; joined Toyota Kyushu athletics team, coached by 1992 Olympic marathon silver medallist Koichi Morishita; set 5,000m best time of 13:12.40 in Hiroshima, Japan April 2004; broke half marathon world record in Rotterdam Half Marathon with time of 59:16 minutes Sept. 2005; broke 10,000m World Jr Record at Int. Asscn of Athletics Feds (IAAF) Golden League Van Damme Memorial Race Aug. 2005; broke half marathon world record again in a time of 58:53 minutes in Ras al Khaimah Feb. 2007, and again (58:33) in The Hague March 2007; broke 20km world record with a time of 55:31 2007; made marathon debut at Fukuoka Marathon in course record time of 2:06:39 Dec. 2007; finished second in London Marathon, breaking 2:06:00 for first time April 2008; Gold Medal, marathon, Olympic Games 2008 (Olympic record time of 2:06:32; first male runner from Kenya to win gold in this event); Kenyan Most Promising Sportsman of the Year Award 2005. *Address:* c/o Kenya Athletics Federation, PO Box 46722, Aerodrome Road, Riadha House, 00100 Nairobi West, Kenya. *Telephone:* (2) 605021. *Fax:* (2) 605020. *E-mail:* athleticskenya@gt.co.ke. *Website:* www.athleticskenya.org.

WAQA, Baron Divavesi; Nauruan politician and head of state; *President;* b. 31 Dec. 1959; mem. Parl. for Boe constituency 2003–; held various portfolios including Health, Repub. of Nauru Telecommunications Corpn and Public Works, Minister of the Interior and of Educ. 2004–07; Pres. of Nauru 2013–. *Address:* Office of the President, Yaren, Nauru (office). *Telephone:* 557-3133 (office). *Fax:* 444-3776 (office). *E-mail:* andromeda.amram@naurugov.nr (office).

WAQAR YOUNIS; Pakistani sports commentator, cricket coach and fmr professional cricketer; b. (Waqar Younis Maitla), 16 Nov. 1971, Vehari; m.; one s. two d.; ed Sadiq Public School, Bahawalpur, Pakistani Coll. Sharjah, Govt Coll., Vehari; right-hand lower-order batsman, right-arm fast bowler; played for Multan 1987/88–97/98, United Bank Ltd 1988–97, Pakistan 1989–2003 (Capt. 2001–03), Surrey 1990–91, 1993, Glamorgan 1997–98 (took career-best 8 for 17 against Sussex), Karachi 1998–99, Rawalpindi 1998–99, REDCO Pakistan Ltd 1999–2000, Lahore Blues 2000–01, Nat. Bank of Pakistan 2001–03, Warwickshire 2003, Allied Bank Ltd 2003–04; Test debut: Pakistan v India, Karachi 15–20 Nov. 1989; played in 87 Tests for Pakistan (17 as Capt.) taking 373 wickets (average 23.56), best bowling (innings) 7/76, (match) 13/135, scored 1,101 runs (average 10.20, highest score 45); played in 262 One-Day Ints (ODIs), 56 as Capt., took 416 wickets (average 23.84), best bowling 7/36, scored 969 runs (average 10.30, highest score 37); played in 228 First-class matches, took 956 wickets (average 22.33), best bowling 8/17, scored 2,972 runs (average 13.38, highest score 64); only bowler to have taken five-wicket hauls in three consecutive ODIs; has taken the fastest 50, 300, 350 and 400 wickets in ODI matches and fastest 150, 200, 250, 300 and 350 wickets in Test matches; only batsman to pass 1,000 run mark without ever scoring a 50; has best strike rate for any bowler with more than 200 Test wickets; first player to be banned for ball tampering, fined 50% of match fee July 2000; retd April 2004; bowling coach for Pakistan 2006–07 (resgnd); lives in Kellyville, North-Western Sydney, Australia, coach at local cricket club; TV cricket commentator for Australia's Nine Network; Wisden Cricketer of the Year 1992. *Leisure interests:* football, badminton, squash. *Address:* c/o Pakistan Cricket Board, Gaddafi Stadium, Ferozepur Road, Lahore 54600, Pakistan. *Telephone:* (42) 571-7231. *Website:* www.pcboard.com.pk.

WARBURTON, Dame Anne Marion, DCVO, CMG, MA; British diplomatist; b. 8 June 1927, London; d. of Capt. Eliot Warburton and Mary Louise Warburton (née Thompson); ed Barnard Coll., Columbia Univ. USA, Somerville Coll. Oxford; with Econ. Co-operation Admin., London 1949–52; NATO Secr., Paris 1952–54; Lazard Bros, London 1955–57; entered Diplomatic Service 1957; Second Sec., Foreign Office 1957–59; Second, then First Sec., UK Mission to UN, New York 1959–62; First Sec., Bonn 1962–65; Diplomatic Service Admin Office, London 1965–67; Foreign Office, then FCO 1967–70; Counsellor, UK Mission to UN, Geneva 1970–75; Head of Guidance and Information Policy Dept, FCO 1975–76; Amb. to Denmark 1976–83, to UN at Geneva 1983–85; Pres. Lucy Cavendish Coll. Cambridge 1985–94; Equal Opportunities Commr 1986–87; Leader EU Investigative Mission on the Abuse of Bosnian Muslim Women 1992–93; mem. British Library Bd 1989–95, Council of Univ. of East Anglia 1991–97, Cttee on Standards in Public Life (Nolan Cttee) 1994–97; Hon. Fellow Somerville Coll. Oxford 1977–, Lucy Cavendish Coll. 1994–; Verdienstkreuz (First Class), FRG 1965; Grand Cross, Order of Dannebrog, Denmark 1979; Order of Isabel la Católica, Spain 1988; Dr hc (Arkansas) 1994. *Leisure interests:* the arts, travel. *Address:* Ansted, Thornham Magna, Eye, Suffolk, IP23 8HB, England (home).

WARBURTON, Sam; Welsh rugby union player; *Captain, Wales National Rugby Union Team;* b. (Sam Kennedy-Warburton), 5 Oct. 1988, Cardiff, Wales; ed Whitchurch High School; openside flanker; played for Glamorgan Wanderers 2007–09, Cardiff Blues 2009–, Wales (Capt. 2011–) 2009– British and Irish Lions

(Capt.) 2013. *Address:* Welsh Rugby Union, Millennium Stadium, Westgate Street, Cardiff, CF10 1NS, Wales (office). *E-mail:* info@wru.co.uk (office). *Website:* www .wru.co.uk (office).

WARCHUS, Matthew, BA; British theatre director; b. 24 Oct. 1966, Rochester; ed Univ. of Bristol; Dir Nat. Youth Theatre 1989, 1990, Bristol Old Vic 1991; Asst Dir RSC 1991–92; Assoc. Dir West Yorkshire Playhouse 1993; freelance dir; Shakespeare's Globe Award 1994, Sydney Edwards Award 1995, Evening Standard Award 1995. *Films directed include:* Simpático (feature film) 1999. *Plays directed include:* (for RSC) Henry V 1995, The Devil is an Ass 1995, Hamlet 1997; (for West Yorkshire Playhouse) Life is a Dream, Who's Afraid of Virginia Woolf?, The Plough and the Stars, Death of a Salesman, Betrayal, True West; other productions The Stuff of Life (Donmar Warehouse) 1994, Volpone (Royal Nat. Theatre) 1995, Art (Wyndhams) 1996, The Unexpected Man (Duchess) 1998, Life x 3 (West End) 2001, Art, True West, Follies (all Broadway), The Lord of the Rings 2007, Boeing Boeing 2008, The Norman Conquests 2008. *Opera:* Troilus and Cressida (Opera North), The Rake's Progress, Falstaff, Cosí fan tutte (ENO). *Address:* c/o Hamilton Asper Management, 24 Hanway Street, London, W1T 1OH, England (office). *Telephone:* (20) 7636-1221.

WARD, Ian Macmillan, MA, DPhil, FRS; British physicist and academic; *Research Professor Emeritus, University of Leeds;* b. 9 April 1928, Stockton-on-Tees, Cleveland, England; s. of Harry Ward and Joan Ward; m. Margaret Linley 1960; two s. one d.; ed Royal Grammar School, Newcastle upon Tyne and Magdalen Coll. Oxford; Tech. Officer, ICI Fibres 1954–61; seconded to Div. of Applied Math., Brown Univ., USA 1961–62; Head, Basic Physics Section, ICI Fibres 1962–65; Sr Lecturer in Physics of Materials, Univ. of Bristol 1965–69; Prof. of Physics, Univ. of Leeds 1970–93, Cavendish Prof. 1987–94 (Chair. of Dept 1975–78, 1987–89), Research Prof. Emer. 1994–, Dir IRC in Polymer Science and Tech. 1989–94; Pres. British Soc. of Rheology 1984–86; Hon. DSc (Bradford) 1993; A.A. Griffith Medal 1982, S.G. Smith Memorial Medal 1984, Swinburne Award 1988, Charles Vernon Boys Medal 1993, Glazebrook Medal 2004, Netlon Medal 2004. *Publications:* Mechanical Properties of Solid Polymers 1971, 1983, Structure and Properties of Oriented Polymers (ed.) 1975, 1997, Ultra High Modulus Polymers (ed.) 1979, An Introduction to Mechanical Properties of Solid Polymers (with D. W. Hadley) 1993, (second edn with J. Sweeney) 2004, Solid Phase Processing of Polymers (ed.) 2000. *Leisure interests:* music, walking. *Address:* School of Physics and Astronomy, University of Leeds, Leeds, Yorks., LS2 9JT, England (office). *Telephone:* (113) 343-3808 (office); (113) 267-3637 (home). *Fax:* ((113) 343-3846 (office). *E-mail:* i.m .ward@leeds.ac.uk (office).

WARD, Jacqueline (Jackie) M., LLD; American business executive; *Senior Director of Human Resources, Digg Inc.;* ed Georgia State Coll. for Women, Univ. of Georgia Extension Center, London School of Business, UK, Mercer Univ.; co-f. Computer Generation Inc. 1968, Pres. and CEO 1968–2000, Chair. May–Dec. 2000; Outside Man. Dir Intec Telecom Systems 2000–06; Dir, Anthem Southeast, Inc. (fmrly Trigon Healthcare Inc.) 1993–2002, Anthem Insurance (subsidiary of WellPoint Inc. 2002–03, Dir WellPoint Inc. 2002–13, Lead Ind. Dir, Chair. (non-exec.) 2012–13; Senior Director of Human Resources, Digg Inc. 2013–; mem. Bd of Dirs Sanmina, Inc. (fmrly SCI Systems Inc.) 1992–2002, Bank of America Corpn 1994–2009, PRG-Schultz International Inc. 1999–2004, PRGX Global Inc. (fmrly Profit Recovery Group International Inc.) 1999–, Flowers Industries, Inc. (renamed Keebler Holdings Corpn) 1999–, Sysco Corpn 2001–, Equifax Inc., Matria Healthcare Inc., Premier Technologies Inc., PTEK Holdings Inc.; Ind. Dir, Flowers Foods Inc. 2001–, Sanmina-SCI Corpn 2001–; Sr Dir Human Resources, Digg Inc.; mem. Bd of Govs The Ravinia Club, Inc.; ind. licensee, Blue Cross and Blue Shield Asscn. *Address:* Digg Inc., 135 Mississippi Street, 3rd Floor, San Francisco, CA 94107-2536, USA (office). *Telephone:* (415) 436-9638 (office). *Fax:* (415) 621-6461 (office). *E-mail:* info@digg.com (office). *Website:* www.digg.com (office).

WARD, Richard, PhD, FRSA; British insurance company executive; *CEO, Lloyd's of London;* m.; two s.; ed Exeter Univ.; Sr Physicist, Science and Eng Council 1982–88; Sr Man., Research, BP plc 1988–91, Head, Business Devt and Marketing, BP Oil Trading Int. 1991–94; Head, Marketing and Business Devt, Tradition Financial Services 1994–95; Dir Product Devt and Research, Int. Petroleum Exchange (ICE) 1995–96, Exec. Vice-Pres. 1996–99, CEO 1999–2005, Vice-Chair. ICE Futures 2005; CEO Lloyd's of London 2006–; mem. Bd of Dirs LCH Clearnet; mem. Royal Inst., Inst. of Dirs. *Address:* Society of Lloyd's, 1 Lime Street, London EC3M 7HA, England (office). *Telephone:* (20) 7327-1000 (office). *Fax:* (20) 7327-5599 (office). *Website:* www.lloyds.com (office).

WARD, Vincent; New Zealand film director, screenwriter and artist; b. 16 Feb. 1956, Greytown; ONZM; ed St Patrick's Coll., Silverstream, Ilam School of Fine Arts at the Univ. of Canterbury, Christchurch; while still at art school, began writing and directing films; named by the Boston Globe as "one of the world's great image-makers". *Films include:* A State of Siege (Miami Film Festival Special Jury Prize, Chicago Film Festival Golden Hugo) 1978, Sons for the Return Home (art dir) 1979, In Spring one Plants Alone (documentary) (Silver Hugo at Chicago Film Festival 1980, Grand Prix Co-Winner Cinéma du Réel 1982) 1980, Vigil (also co-writer) (Grand Prix Prades and Madrid Film Festivals) 1984, The Navigator: A Medieval Odyssey (Grand Prix Film Festivals in Rome, Munich, Sitges 1988, Oporto Film Festival 1989, Best Film and Best Director Australian Film Inst. and New Zealand Listener Awards 1989) 1988, Alien[3] (writer) 1991, Map of the Human Heart (also story and co-writer, producer) (Most Significant Artistic Achievement Tokyo Film Festival 1993) 1992, Leaving Las Vegas (actor) 1995, The Shot (actor) 1996, One Night Stand (actor) 1997, What Dreams May Come (Acad. Award for Best Visual Effects, Best Renting Drama Video Australian Video Ezy Prestige Awards 1999) 1998, The Last Samurai (exec. producer) 2003, Spooked (actor) 2004, River Queen (also story and co-writer) 2005, Rain of the Children (documentary) (also writer and producer) 2008. *Publications:* The Navigator, A Medieval Odyssey 1989, Edge of the Earth: Stories and Images from the Antipodes 1990, The Past Awaits, people, images, film (large format, full colour photographic book of images and stories) 2010, Inhale | Exhale (large format, full colour reproductions of his artwork from his 2011–12 exhbns) 2013. *Address:* PO Box 78-078, Grey Lynn, Auckland 1245, New Zealand. *E-mail:* info@vincentwardfilms.com. *Website:* vincentwardfilms.com.

WARDAK, Gen. Abdul Rahim; Afghan government official and military officer; b. 1945, Wardak Prov.; s. of Abdul Ghani; ed Habibia High School, Ali Naser Acad. of Cairo, Egypt; previous positions include Lecturer Cadet Univ., Asst of Protocol, Ministry of Defence, Mil. Attaché, India, Dir Mil. Officers Soc., Educ. Comm., Disarmament Program; apptd Chief of Army Staff 1992; fmr Deputy Minister of Defence, Minister of Defence 2004–12. *Address:* c/o Ministry of Defence, Shash Darak, Kabul, Afghanistan.

WARDAK, Capt. Moin Khan; Afghan airline industry executive; *President and CEO, Ariana Afghan Airlines;* pilot and Capt. with Ariana Afghan Airlines since 1984, Pres. and CEO 2009–. *Address:* Ariana Afghan Airlines, PO Box 76, Ansari Watt, Kabul, Afghanistan (office). *Telephone:* (75) 2041013 (office); (20) 2100351. *Fax:* (873) 762523846 (office). *E-mail:* afghanairlines@yahoo.com (office); flyariana@mail.com (office); info@flyariana.com (office). *Website:* www.flyariana.com (office).

WARDAK, Taj Mohammad; Afghan politician; Gov. of Badakshan Prov. c. 1970s; apptd Gov. of Paktia Prov. 2002; Minister of Interior Affairs 2002–03; govt adviser on tribal matters 2003–; mem. Nat. Security Comm. 2003–.

WARDLE, Len; British business executive; following graduation, worked for PriceWaterhouse in North East England then spent five years teaching in the Midlands; entered local govt in East Sussex, spent two years with Eastbourne Borough Council before moving to East Sussex Co. Council and holding several man. positions, culminating in Head of Resources; later Fellow, Univ. of Surrey in School of Man.; first elected to Co-operative Group 1992, Chair. 2007–13 (resgnd); held appointments in Co-operative Financial Services, The Co-operative Bank, Co-operative Insurance Soc. Ltd, CIS General Insurance Ltd, ICA (ex officio), Mutuo, PACE Trustees Ltd, CIS Pension Scheme Nominee Ltd. *Address:* c/o The Co-operative Group Ltd, New Century House, Manchester, M60 4ES, England.

WARINER, Jeremy; American athlete; b. 31 Jan. 1984, Irving, Tex.; s. of Danny Wariner and Linda Wariner; ed Lamar High School, Arlington, Tex. and Baylor Univ.; coached by Clyde Hart; volunteer asst coach; mem. USA World Jr Team; three-time Jr All-American in 400m 2002; Nat. Collegiate Athletic Asscn (NCAA) Outdoor Champion, 400m 2004, 4×400m relay 2004; NCAA Indoor Champion, 400m 2004, 4×400m relay 2004; US Olympic Trials 400m Champion 2004; Gold Medal, 400m, Olympic Games, Athens 2004, 4×400m relay 2004; first athlete in history to win both collegiate titles, US Championship and Olympic Gold Medal in 400m; turned professional 2004; USA Outdoor Champion 2005; Gold Medal, 400m, World Outdoor Championships, Helsinki, Finland 2005, 4×400m relay 2005; Silver Medal, 400m, Olympic Games, Beijing 2008; Gold Medal, 4×400m relay, Olympic Games, Beijing 2008; current coach Michael Ford; Jesse Owens Award 2004, named by ESPN.com Top Rookie of 2004, named Mondo Track Athlete of the Year 2004. *Address:* c/o USA Track and Field, 1 RCA Dome, Suite 140, Indianapolis, IN 46225, USA. *E-mail:* Sariyu.Suggs@usatf.org. *Website:* www.usatf.org.

WARLOW, Charles Picton, MD, FRCP, FRSE, FMedSci; British neurologist, epidemiologist and academic; *Professor of Medical Neurology, University of Edinburgh;* b. 29 Sept. 1943, Nottingham; s. of Charles Edward Picton Warlow and Nancy Mary Maclennan Hine; partner Cathie Sudlow; two s. two d.; ed Univ. of Cambridge and St George's Hosp. Medical School, London; Lecturer in Medicine, Aberdeen 1971–74; specialist training in neurology, London and Oxford 1974–77; Clinical Reader in Neurology and Hon. Consultant Neurologist, Oxford 1977–87; Prof. of Medical Neurology, Univ. of Edin. 1987–; Pres. Asscn of British Neurologists 2001–03; Ed. Practical Neurology; Tenovus-Scotland Margaret MacLellan Award 1989–90, Soc. of Authors and Royal Soc. of Medicine Medical Book Award, Advanced Author Book Category 1997, Osler Oration, Royal Coll. of Physicians 1998, Willis Lecturer, American Heart Asscn 2003, Asscn of British Neurologists Medal 2005. *Publications include:* Handbook of Clinical Neurology 1991, Transient Ischaemic Attacks of the Brain and Eye (with G.J. Hankey) 1994, Stroke: A Practical Guide to Management (co-author) (2nd edn) 2001, Lancet Handbook of Treatment in Neurology (ed.) 2006. *Leisure interests:* sailing, photography, mountains. *Address:* Department of Clinical Neurosciences, Western General Hospital, Crewe Road, Edinburgh, EH4 2XU (office); 6 South Gray Street, Edinburgh, EH9 1TE, Scotland (home). *Telephone:* (131) 537-2082 (office). *Fax:* (131) 332-5150 (office). *E-mail:* cpw@skull.dcn.ed.ac.uk (office). *Website:* www.dcn.ed.ac.uk (office).

WARNE, Shane Keith; Australian sports commentator, cricket coach and fmr professional cricketer; b. 13 Sept. 1969, Upper Ferntree Gully, Melbourne, Vic.; s. of Keith Warne and Bridgette Warne; m. Simone Callahan 1995 (divorced 2005); one s. two d.; ed Hampton High School, Mentone Grammar School; right arm leg break bowler; right-hand lower-order batsman; played for Victoria 1990–2007 (Capt. 1996–99), Australia 1992–2007 (Capt. ODI side 1997–99), Hants. 2000–07 (Capt. 2004–07), ICC (Int. Cricket Council) World XI, Rajasthan Royals (Coach and Capt.) 2008–11, Melbourne Stars (Capt.) 2011–; First-class début: Feb. 1991; Test debut (cap 350): Australia v India, Sydney 2–6 Jan. 1992; One-Day Int. (ODI) debut: NZ v Australia, Wellington 24 Mar 1993; played in 145 Tests, took 708 wickets and scored 3,154 runs, bowling average 25.41, best bowling (innings) 8/71, (match) 12/128, economy rate 2.65, highest batting score 99, batting average 17.32, 12 fifties; took hat-trick against England, Melbourne 1994; ODIs (11 as Capt.): 194 matches, took 293 wickets and scored 1,018 runs; First-class cricket: 301 matches, took 1,319 wickets and scored 6,919 runs; toured England 1993, 1997, 2001, 2005; received 12-month ban for testing positive for a banned substance Feb. 2003; announced retirement from limited-overs ints 2004, from int. cricket 2007, from First-class cricket 2008, from IPL (Indian Premier League) cricket 2011; leading wicket-taker in test cricket; has scored the most Test runs (3,154) without making a century; works for Shane Warne Foundation; Wisden Cricketer of the Year 1994, One-Day Int. Player of the Year 2000, selected as one of five Wisden Cricketers of the Century 2000, Wisden Leading Cricketer in the World 2005, Overseas Personality of the Year, BBC Sports Personality of the Year Awards 2005, Test Player of the Year 2006, inducted into ICC Hall of Fame 2013. *Publication:* Shane Warne: The Autobiography 2001, My Illustrated Career 2006, Shane Warne's Century – My Top 100 Cricketers 2008. *Leisure interest:* collecting cars. *Address:* c/o Melbourne Stars, PO Box 327, East Melbourne, Vic. 8002, Australia. *Fax:* (3)

9653-1196. *E-mail:* info@melbournestars.com.au; info@shanewarne.com. *Website:* www.melbournestars.com.au; www.shanewarne.com.

WARNER, Bishop Bennie Dee, MSc, ThM, DD; Liberian ecclesiastic and politician; b. 30 April 1935, Caresburg Dist; ed Monrovia Gbarnga United Methodist Mission School, Booker Washington Inst., Kakata, Cuttington Univ. Coll., Suakoto, Syracuse Univ. and Boston Univ. School of Theology, USA; ordained deacon 1961; Acting Dir Pastors' Inst. of the United Methodist Church 1961; educ. counsellor and maths and social studies teacher, W.V.S. Tubman Elementary School 1962–68; fmr Chair. Nat. Student Christian Council of Liberia; later ordained Elder; fmr Pastor, St John's United Methodist Church, Gbarnga and Reeves Memorial United Methodist Church, Crozierville; fmr Chair. Interim Cttee for the Admin of the Coll. of West Africa (later Chair. Bd of Trustees), Bd of Ministry, Liberia Annual Conf. of United Methodist Church; ordained Bishop 1973; Vice-Pres. of Liberia 1977–80; mem. Bd of Trustees, Cuttington Coll. and Divinity School, Bd of the Booker Washington Inst., Nat. Disaster Comm., Council of Bishops, World Methodist Council; in exile in USA; Interim Pastor, Wesley United Methodist Church, Oklahoma City, USA 2007; Grand Band, Order of the Star of Africa. *Address:* c/o Wesley United Methodist Church, 1401 NW 25th Street, Oklahoma City, OK 73106, USA. *E-mail:* wesleyokc@coxinet.net.

WARNER, Brian, BSc, MA, PhD, DSc; British astronomer and academic; *Distinguished Professor Emeritus of Natural Philosophy and Senior Scholar, University of Cape Town;* b. 25 May 1939, Crawley Down, Sussex, England; s. of Leslie Warner and Edith M. Warner (née Bashford); m. 1st Carole Christian 1965 (divorced 1973); one s. one d.; m. 2nd Nancy Russell 1976 (divorced 1987); ed Univs of London and Oxford; Research Asst, Univ. of London Observatory 1964–65; Radcliffe-Henry Skynner Sr Research Fellow, Balliol Coll. Oxford 1965–67; Asst Prof., Univ. of Texas at Austin 1967–69, Assoc. Prof. 1969–72; Prof. and Head, Dept of Astronomy, Univ. of Cape Town 1972–99, Distinguished Prof. of Natural Philosophy 1999–2004, Distinguished Prof. Emer. 2005–, Fellow 1978–, Sr Scholar 2011–; Alfred P. Sloan Fellow 1969–71; Visiting Fellow, Univ. of Colorado 1977; Visiting Sr Fellow, Dept of Astrophysics, Univ. of Oxford 1985; Visiting Prof., Dartmouth Coll. and Univ. of Texas 1986–87, Univ. of Sussex 1997, Univ. of Southampton 2007, 2008, 2009, 2010, 2011, 2012; Visiting Fellow, Univ. of California, Santa Cruz 1990, ANU 1989, 1993, 1996, 1998, 2000, 2003; Visiting Scientist, European Southern Observatory 1996; Sr Fellow, Copernicus Centre, Warsaw 2003; Adjunct Prof., James Cook Univ., Townsville 2006–09; Fellow, Stellenbosch Inst. of Advanced Study 2013; Pres. Royal Soc. of S Africa 1981–83, Foreign Sec. 1996–2001, Hon. Fellow 2009–; mem. Acad. of Sciences of S Africa 1994–; Pres. Comm. 41 of Int. Astronomical Union (IAU) 1978–82 (Vice-Pres. IAU 2003–09), Astronomical Soc. of Southern Africa 1977–78, The Owl Club 1985–86; mem. Bd of Trustees, S African Museum 1981–99, Deputy Chair. 1988–91, Chair. 1991–99; mem. Council S Africa Library 1991–99; Ernest Oppenheimer Travelling Fellowship 1990; Fellow, TWAS, acad. of sciences for the developing world 2009; Hon. Fellow, Royal Astronomical Soc. 1994; Hon. mem. Royal Astronomical Soc. of NZ 1995; Hon. Fellow, Univ. Coll. London 2009; Hon. DSc (Univ. of Cape Town) 2009; Boyden Premium, Franklin Inst. 1980; McIntyre Award, Astronomical Soc. of Southern Africa 1983, John F.W. Herschel Medal, Royal Soc. of South Africa 1988, South African Medal, South African Asscn for the Advancement of Science 1989, Gill Medal, Astronomical Soc. of Southern Africa 1992, Univ. of Cape Town Book Award 1997, Science for Society Gold Medal, Acad. of Sciences of South Africa 2004. *Publications:* Astronomers at the Royal Observatory, Cape of Good Hope 1979, Charles Piazzi Smyth 1983, Maclear and Herschel 1984, The Journal of Lady Jane Franklin 1985, High Speed Astronomical Photometry 1988, William Mann 1989, Lady Herschel 1991, Cataclysmic Variable Stars 1995, Dinosaurs' End 1996, Flora Herscheliana 1998, Cape Landscapes 2006, Scatological Verse 2007; more than 400 scientific research papers. *Leisure interests:* 19th-century science and exploration, baroque music. *Address:* Department of Astronomy, University of Cape Town, Rondebosch, 7700 Cape (office); 401 Blenheim, Marlborough Park, Claremont, 7700 Cape, South Africa (home). *Telephone:* (21) 650-2391 (office); (21) 671-1850 (home). *Fax:* (21) 650-4547 (office). *E-mail:* warner@physci.uct.ac.za (office). *Website:* mensa.ast.uct.ac.za/Staff (office).

WARNER, David; British actor; b. 29 July 1941, Manchester; s. of Herbert Simon Warner; ed Feldon School, Leamington Spa and Royal Acad. of Dramatic Art; worked as bookseller; stage début as Snout in A Midsummer Night's Dream, Royal Court 1962; film début in Tom Jones 1963; joined RSC 1963 and appeared as Trinculo in The Tempest, title role in Henry VI, Edward IV in adaptation of Henry VI (Parts I, II and III) comprising first two parts of trilogy The Wars of the Roses (Stratford). *Other roles include:* Henry VI in The Wars of the Roses, Aldwych 1964; Richard II, Mouldy in Henry IV (Part II) and Henry VI in The Wars of the Roses, RSC, Stratford 1964; Valentine Brose in Eh?, Aldwych 1964, Hamlet, Stratford and Aldwych 1965; the Postmaster in The Government Inspector, Aldwych 1965; Hamlet, Sir Andrew Aguecheek in Twelfth Night, Stratford 1966; Claudius in I, Claudius, Hampstead 1972. *Films include:* Morgan – A Suitable Case for Treatment 1966, Work is a Four Letter Word 1967, The Bofors Gun, The Fixer, The Seagull 1968–69, The Ballad of Cable Hogue 1970, Straw Dogs 1971, A Doll's House 1972, The Omen 1975, Cross of Iron, Providence, Silver Bears 1976, The Disappearance 1977, The Thirty Nine Steps 1978, Nightwing, Time After Time 1979, The Island 1980, Hanna's War 1988, The Secret Life of Ian Fleming 1990, Dark at Noon, Mortal Passions, In the Mouth of Madness, Titanic 1997, Scream 2 1997, Money Talks 1997, Shergar 2000, In the Beginning 2000, Horatio Hornblower 2001. *Television includes:* Clouds of Glory 1977, Holocaust 1977, Charlie 1984, The Choir 1995. *Address:* c/o Julian Belfrage Associates, 3rd Floor, 9 Argyll Street, London, W1F 7TG, England (office). *E-mail:* davidwarnerfilm@hotmail.co.uk. *Website:* www.davidwarnerfilm.co.uk.

WARNER, Deborah, CBE; British theatre and opera director; b. 12 May 1959, Oxford; d. of Ruth Warner and Roger Warner; ed Sidcot School, Avon, St Clare's, Oxford, Cen. School of Speech and Drama, London; Founder and Artistic Dir Kick Theatre Co 1980–86; Resident Dir RSC 1987–89; Assoc. Dir Royal Nat. Theatre 1989–98; Assoc. Dir Abbey Theatre, Dublin 2000; has also staged productions at ENO (Bach's St John Passion, Janacek's Diary of One Who Vanished and Britten's Death in Venice), Glyndebourne Festival Opera (Don Giovanni 1994, Fidelio 2001, 2006), Royal Opera House (Turn of the Screw), Opera North (Wozzeck, La Voix Humaine), London Proms (concert of Honegger's Jeanne d'Arc au Bûcher), and has staged productions for Fitzroy Productions, Odeon Theatre, Chaillot and Bobigny Theatre, Paris, Salzburg Festival (Coriolan), LIFT and Perth Int. Arts Festival, Lincoln Center Festival, New York, Venice Festival (Dido and Aeneas), Bavarian State Opera (The Rape of Lucretia) 2004; Dir Fitzroy Productions; Chevalier, Ordre des Arts et des Lettres 2000; Evening Standard Award 1988, 1998, 2002, Laurence Olivier Award 1989, 1992, New York Drama Desk Award 1997, South Bank Arts Award 1998, OBIE Award 2003. *Productions include:* Titus Andronicus (RSC), King John (RSC), Electra (RSC), Hedda Gabler (Abbey Theatre, Dublin/West End), The Good Person of Sichuan (Royal Nat. Theatre), King Lear (Royal Nat. Theatre), Richard II (Royal Nat. Theatre), The Powerbook (Royal Nat. Theatre), The Waste Land (Fitzroy Productions), Medea (Abbey Theatre/West End/Broadway), The St Pancras Project (LIFT), The Tower Project (LIFT)The Angel Project (Perth Int. Arts Festival and Lincoln Center Festival), Readings (Fitzroy Productions). *Films:* The Waste Land 1996, The Last September 1999. *Television includes:* Richard II (BBC), Hedda Gabler (BBC), Don Giovanni (Channel 4). *Leisure interest:* travelling. *Address:* c/o Leah Schmidt, The Agency, 24 Pottery Lane, London, W11 4LZ, England (office). *Telephone:* (20) 7727-1346 (office). *Fax:* (20) 7727-9037 (office). *E-mail:* info@theagency.co.uk (office). *Website:* www.theagency.co.uk (office).

WARNER, Douglas Alexander III, BA; American banker; b. 9 June 1946, Cincinnati; s. of Douglas Alexander Warner Jr and Eleanor Warner (née Wright); m. Patricia Grant 1977; two s. one d.; ed Yale Univ.; Officer's Asst, Morgan Guaranty Trust Co., New York 1968–70, Asst Treas. 1970–72, Asst Vice-Pres. 1972–75, Vice-Pres. 1975–85, Sr Vice-Pres. Morgan Guaranty Trust Co., London 1983–87, Exec. Vice-Pres. Morgan Guaranty Trust Co., New York 1987–89, Man. Dir 1989–90, Pres. 1990–95, Chair. and CEO 1995–2000; Chair. J.P. Morgan Chase & Co. 2000–01; mem. Bd of Dirs General Electric Co., Anheuser-Busch Cos Inc., Motorola Inc.; Chair. Bd of Man. Overseers Memorial Sloan-Kettering Cancer Center, New York; Trustee Pierpont Morgan Library, Cold Spring Harbor Lab. *Leisure interests:* golf, tennis, shooting. *Address:* PO Box 914, New York, NY 10268, USA (home).

WARNER, H. Ty; American business executive and philanthropist; *Chairman and CEO, Ty Inc.;* b. 3 Sept. 1944, Chicago, Ill.; s. of Harold Warner and Georgia Warner; ed St. John's Military Academy, Wis., Kalamazoo Coll., Mich.; early career selling toys for Dakin LLC, San Francisco; f. Ty Inc. 1986, currently Chair. and CEO; creator of Beanie Babies; significant investments in hotels, property and golf courses, Ty Warner Hotels and Resorts include the Four Seasons Hotel, New York, Sandpiper golf course, Four Seasons Resort, Santa Barbara, Calif., San Ysidro Ranch, Montecito, Calif., Kona Village resort, Hawaii, Montecito Country Club and Las Ventanas al Paraiso Resort, Los Cabos, Mexico; bought the beachfront Miramar resort and Rancho San Marcos golf course 2005; sentenced to two years' probation plus community service for tax evasion 2014; Children's Champion Award, Children's Hunger Fund 2006. *Address:* Ty Inc., 280 Chestnut Avenue, Westmont, IL 60559, USA (office). *Telephone:* (630) 920-1515 (office). *Fax:* (630) 920-1980 (office). *E-mail:* info@ty.com (office). *Website:* www.ty.com (office). www.tywarnerhotelsandresorts.com (office).

WARNER, Jack Austin, BA; Trinidad and Tobago fmr football executive and politician; b. 26 Jan. 1943, Rio Claro, South Trinidad; ed Coll. of St Phillip and St James (now Presentation Coll.), Chaguanas, Mausica Teacher Training Coll., Univ. of the West Indies; teacher, Polytechnic Inst., Port of Spain 1970–93; Gen. Sec. Trinidad and Tobago Football Fed. 1973–90, Special Adviser 1990; Gen. Sec. Caribbean Football Union 1978–83, Pres. 1983; mem. FIFA Exec. Cttee 1983–2011, Vice-Pres. FIFA 1997; Pres. Confed. of North, Central American and Caribbean Asscn Football 1990–2011; mem. House of Reps (Parl.) for Chaguanas West 2007–; Minister of Works and Transport 2010, of Nat. Security 2012–13 (resgnd); Founding Chair. Joe Public Football Club 1996–; mem. United Nat. Congress. *Address:* c/o Ministry of National Security, Temple Court, 31–33 Abercromby Street, Port of Spain, Trinidad and Tobago.

WARNER, John W., BS, LLB; American lawyer and fmr politician; *Senior Advisor, Hogan Lovells US LLP;* b. 18 Feb. 1927, Washington, DC; s. of the late Dr John W. Warner and of Martha Warner (née Budd); m. 1st Catherine Conover Mellon (divorced 1973); one s. two d.; m. 2nd the late Elizabeth Taylor 1976 (divorced 1982, died 2011); m. 3rd Jeanne van der Myde 2003; ed public schools in Washington, DC, school of Naval Research Lab., Washington, DC, Washington and Lee Univ. and Univ. of Virginia Law School; served in USN, attained rank of Electronic Technician 3rd Class 1944–46; subsequently enlisted in US Marine Corps Reserve, active duty as Communications Officer 1950–52, Capt. in US Marine Corps Reserve 1952–61; admitted to the Bar 1954; pvt. practice 1954–56; served in US Attorney's office as Special Asst 1956, Asst 1957; joined campaign staff of then Vice-Pres. Richard Nixon 1960; Assoc. Hogan & Hartson (now Hogan Lovells US LLP) 1960, Gen. Pnr 1964–69, Sr Advisor 2009–; Dir of Ocean Affairs as rep. of US Dept of Defense 1971; Under-Sec. of US Navy 1969–72, Sec. 1972–74; Dir American Revolution Bicentennial Admin. 1974–76; Senator from Virginia 1979–2009 (retd), Chair. Armed Services Cttee; fmr Head of US Del. to Moscow on Naval Affairs; Hon. KBE 2009; Nat. Intelligence Distinguished Public Service Medal, Office of the Dir of Nat. Intelligence (first ever awarded) 2008. *Address:* Hogan Lovells US LLP, Columbia Square, 555 Thirteenth Street, NW, Washington, DC 20004, USA (office). *Telephone:* (202) 637-8875 (office). *Fax:* (202) 637-5910 (office). *E-mail:* john.warner@hoganlovells.com (office). *Website:* www.hoganlovells.com/john-warner (office).

WARNER, Marina Sarah, CBE, MA, FBA, FRSL; British writer and academic; *Professor of Literature, Film and Theatre Studies, University of Essex;* b. 9 Nov. 1946, London, England; d. of Esmond Warner and Emilia Terzulli; m. 1st William Shawcross 1971; one s.; m. 2nd John Dewe Mathews 1981; pnr Graeme Segal FRS; ed St Mary's Convent, Ascot and Lady Margaret Hall, Univ. of Oxford; Getty Scholar, Getty Centre for the History of Art and the Humanities 1987–88; Tinbergen Prof., Erasmus Univ., Rotterdam 1990–91; Visiting Prof., Queen Mary and Westfield Coll., Univ. of London 1994, Univ. of Ulster 1994, Univ. of York 1996–2000, Birkbeck Coll., London; Tanner Lecturer, Yale Univ. 1999; Clarendon Lecturer, Oxford 2001; Prof. of Literature, Film and Theatre Studies, Univ. of Essex 2004–; Visiting Prof., RCA 2008–12; Distinguished Visiting Prof., Queen Mary, Univ. of London 2009–12, New York Univ., Abu Dhabi 2012–; Fellow, Commonership, Trinity Coll. Cambridge 1998; Visiting Fellow, All Souls Coll.,

Oxford 2001; Univ. Paris XIII 2003; Fellow, Italian Acad., Columbia Univ., New York, 2003; Sr Fellow, Remarque Inst., New York Univ. 2006; Fellow, All Souls Coll., Oxford 2013–15; Pres. Virgil Soc. 2004; Vice-Pres. Inst. of Greece, Rome, and Classical Studies, Univ. of Bristol 2004; mem. Exec. Cttee Charter 88 –1997, Literature Panel Arts Council of England –1997, Advisory Council British Library –1997, Man. Cttee Nat. Council for One-Parent Families, Bd Artangel, Cttee London Library, Cttee PEN, Council of the British School at Rome 2009–, Judge, The Man Booker Int. Prize 2015; Trustee, Nat. Portrait Gallery; Hon. Fellow, Queen Mary and Westfield Coll., London 1994, Lady Margaret Hall, Oxford 2000, London Inst. of Pataphysics 2007, Mansfield Coll., Oxford 2013, St Cross Coll., Oxford 2013; Chevalier des Arts et des Lettres 2000, Commendatore dell'Ordine della Stella di Solidarietà (Italy) 2005; Hon. DLitt (Exeter) 1995, 1997, (York) 1997, (St Andrews) 1998, (Leicester) 2006, (Oxford) 2006; Dr hc (Sheffield Hallam) 1995, (Univ. of North London) 1997, (Tavistock Inst., Univ. of East London) 1999, (RCA) 2004, (Kent) 2005, (Leicester) 2006, (King's Coll., London) 2009; Runner Up, W.H. Smith Children's Poetry Prize 1964, Young Writer of the Year (Daily Telegraph Award) 1971, Daily Express Award 1972, Fawcett Prize 1986, PEN Silver Pen Award 1988, Commonwealth Writer's Prize (Eurasia) 1989, Mythopoeic Scholarship Award 1996, Katharine Briggs Memorial Prize 1999, Harvey Darton Prize 1996, Rose Mary Crawshay Prize, British Acad. 2000, Aby Warburg Prize 2004, Nat. Book Critics Circle Award for Criticism 2012, Truman Capote Award for Literary Criticism 2013, Sheikh Zayed Book Award for Arab Culture in Non-Arabic Languages 2013. *Radio:* short stories, criticism. *Publications:* The Dragon Empress 1972, Alone of All Her Sex: The Myth and the Cult of the Virgin Mary 1976, Joan of Arc 1981, Monuments and Maidens: The Allegory of the Female Form 1985, The Lost Father 1988, Indigo 1992, Mermaids in the Basement (short stories) 1993, Wonder Tales (ed.) 1994, Six Myths of Our Time – The 1994 Reith Lectures, From the Beast to the Blonde: On Fairy Tales and Their Tellers 1994, The Inner Eye: Art Beyond the Visible 1996, No Go the Bogeyman: On Scaring, Lulling and Making Mock 1998, The Leto Bundle 2001, Fantastic Metamorphoses, Other Worlds: The Clarendon Lectures 2002, Murderers I Have Known (short stories) 2002, Signs and Wonders: Essays on Literature and Culture 2003, Phantasmagoria: Spirit Visions, Metaphors, and Media 2006, Stranger Magic: Charmed States and the Arabian Nights 2011, Scheherazade's Children: Global Encounters with the Arabian Nights (co-ed.) 2013. *Leisure interests:* travel, friendship. *Address:* c/o Rogers, Coleridge & White Literary Agency, 20 Powis Mews, London, W11 1JN, England (office); LIFTS, University of Essex, Wivenhoe Park, Colchester, CO4 3SQ, England (office). *Telephone:* (20) 7221-3717 (office); (1206) 873073 (office). *Fax:* (20) 7229-9084 (office). *E-mail:* info@rcwlitagency.co.uk (office); mswarner@essex.ac.uk (office). *Website:* www.rcwlitagency.co.uk (office); www.marinawarner.com.

WARNER, Mark Robert, BA, JD; American lawyer and politician; *Senator from Virginia;* b. 15 Dec. 1954, Indianapolis, Ind.; m. Lisa Collis; three d.; ed Rockville High School, Conn., George Washington Univ., Harvard Law School; Founding Pnr, Columbia Capital Corp; Gov. of Virginia 2002–06; Senator from Virginia 2009–, mem. Cttee on Banking, Housing, and Urban Affairs, Cttee on the Budget, Cttee on Commerce, Science and Transportation, Cttee on Rules and Admin, Select Cttee on Intelligence, Jt Econ. Cttee; organized the Senate's bipartisan Gang of Six 2011; Chair. Nat. Govs' Asscn 2004–05; involved in farming and winemaking at his Rappahannock Bend farm; Democrat; fmr Hon. Chair. Forward Together Political Action Cttee. *Address:* 475 Russell Senate Office Building, Washington, DC 20510 (office); c/o Friends of Mark Warner, 1029 North Royal Street, Alexandria, VA 22314, USA. *Telephone:* (202) 224-2023 (office). *Fax:* (202) 224-6295 (office). *Website:* warner.senate.gov (office).

WARNOCK, John Edward, MS, PhD; American computer industry executive; *Co-Chairman, Adobe Systems Inc.;* b. 6 Oct. 1940, Salt Lake City, Utah; ed Univ. of Utah; fmrly with Evans & Sutherland Computer Corpn, Computer Sciences Corpn, IBM and Univ. of Utah; Prin. Scientist, Xerox Palo Alto Research Centre (PARC) –1982; Co-founder, with Charles Geschke, Adobe Systems Inc. 1982, Pres. 1982–84, Co-Chair. and CEO 1984–2000, Co-Chair. 2000–, Chief Tech. Officer –2001; mem. Bd of Dirs Octavo Corpn, mem. Bd, fmr Chair. Tech. Museum of Innovation; mem. Entrepreneurial Bd Advisory Cttee, American Film Inst.; mem. Nat. Acad. of Eng, Utah Information Tech. Asscn 2000, American Acad. of Arts and Sciences, American Philosophical Soc.; Fellow, Asscn for Computing Machinery (ACM) 1999, Computer History Museum 2002; hon. degrees from Univ. of Utah, American Film Inst., Univ. of Nottingham, UK; numerous awards, including Distinguished Service to Art and Design Int. Award and Corp. Outstanding Achievement Award, Rhode Island School of Design 1998, Award for Tech. Excellence, Nat. Graphics Asscn, Lifetime Achievement Award for Tech. Excellence, PC Magazine, Cary Award, Rochester Inst. of Tech., Software Systems Award, ACM 1989, Distinguished Alumnus Award, Univ. of Utah 1995, Edwin H. Land Medal, Optical Soc. of America 2000, Bodley Medal, Bodleian Library, Univ. of Oxford 2003, Lovelace Medal, British Computer Soc. 2004, Medal of Achievement, American Electronics Asscn (with Charles Geschke) 2006, Computer Entrepreneur Award, IEEE Computer Soc. (with Charles Geschke) 2008, Nat. Medal of Tech. and Innovation (with Charles Geschke) 2009, Marconi Prize (with Charles Geschke) 2010. *Publications:* numerous articles in technical journals and industry magazines. *Address:* Adobe Systems Inc., 345 Park Avenue, San Jose, CA 95110-2704, USA (office). *Telephone:* (408) 536-6000 (office). *Fax:* (408) 537-6000 (office). *Website:* www.adobe.com (office).

WARNOCK, Baroness (Life Peer), cr. 1985, of Weeke in the City of Winchester; **(Helen) Mary Warnock,** DBE, FCP, FRSM; British philosopher and university administrator (retd); b. 14 April 1924, Winchester; d. of the late Archibald Edward Wilson and Ethel Schuster; m. Sir Geoffrey J. Warnock 1949 (died 1995); two s. three d. (one deceased); ed St Swithun's, Winchester and Lady Margaret Hall, Oxford; Tutor in Philosophy, St Hugh's Coll. Oxford 1949–66; Headmistress, Oxford High School 1966–72; Talbot Research Fellow, Lady Margaret Hall 1972–76; Sr Research Fellow, St Hugh's Coll. 1976–84; Mistress of Girton Coll. Cambridge 1985–91; Chair. Cttee of Inquiry into Special Educ. 1974–78, Advisory Cttee on Animal Experiments 1979–86, Cttee of Inquiry into Human Fertilization 1982–84, Educ. Cttee Girls' Day School Trust 1994–2001; mem. IBA 1973–81, Royal Comm. on Environmental Pollution 1979–84, Social Science Research Council 1981–85, UK Nat. Comm. for UNESCO 1981–85, Archbishop of Canterbury's Advisory Group on Medical Ethics 1992–2002; Fellow, Coll. of

Teachers (fmrly Coll. of Preceptors); Hon. Master of the Bench, Gray's Inn 1986; Hon. Fellow, Imperial Coll. London 1986, Hertford Coll. Oxford 1997, Lady Margaret Hall Oxford, St Hugh's Coll. Oxford; Hon. FRCM; Hon. Fellow, Royal Soc. of Physicians, Scotland; Hon. FBA 2000; Hon. FRCP 2002; Hon. DUniv (Open Univ.) 1980, (St Andrews) 1992; Hon. LLD (Manchester) 1987, (Liverpool) 1991, (London) 1991; Hon. DLitt (Glasgow) 1988; Dr hc (Univ. of York) 1989; RSA Albert Medal 1998. *Publications:* Ethics since 1900 1960, J.-P. Sartre 1963, Existentialist Ethics 1966, Existentialism 1970, Imagination 1976, Schools of Thought 1977, What Must We Teach? (with T. Devlin) 1977, Education: A Way Forward 1979, A Question of Life 1985, Teacher Teach Thyself (Dimbleby Lecture) 1985, Memory 1987, A Common Policy for Education 1989, Universities: Knowing Our Minds 1989, The Uses of Philosophy 1992, Imagination and Time 1994; Women Philosophers (ed.) 1996, An Intelligent Person's Guide to Ethics 1998, A Memoir: People and Places 2000, Making Babies 2002, Nature and Mortality 2003, Utilitariansim (ed.) 2003, Special Education: A New Look 2005, Easeful Death (with Elisabeth MacDonald) 2008, Dishonest to God 2010. *Leisure interests:* music, gardening. *Address:* House of Lords, Westminster, London, SW1A 0PW (office); 2 Longdown Road, London, SE6 3SN, England (home). *Telephone:* (20) 7219-8619 (office); (20) 8461-3214 (home). *E-mail:* warnock@parliament.uk.

WARRELL, David Alan, MA, DM, DSc, FRCP, FRCPE, FMedSci, FRGS; British specialist in tropical medicine and venoms; *Professor Emeritus of Tropical Medicine, University of Oxford;* b. 6 Oct. 1939, Singapore; s. of the late Mr & Mrs A. T. Warrell; m. Dr Mary J. Prentice 1975; two d.; ed Portsmouth Grammar School, Christ Church, Oxford and St Thomas's Hosp. Medical School, London; Oxford Univ. Radcliffe Travelling Fellow, Univ. of Calif. at San Diego 1969; Sr Lecturer, Ahmadu Bello Univ., Nigeria and Lecturer and Consultant Physician, Royal Postgrad. Medical School, London and Hammersmith Hosp. 1970–75; Founding Dir Wellcome-Mahidol Univ., Oxford Tropical Medicine Research Programme, Bangkok and Wellcome Reader in Tropical Medicine, Univ. of Oxford 1979–86; Prof. of Tropical Medicine and Infectious Diseases and Dir Emer. (fmrly Dir) Centre for Tropical Medicine, Univ. of Oxford 1987–2001, Head Nuffield Dept Clinical Medicine 2002–04, Deputy Head 2004–06, Prof. Emer. of Tropical Medicine 2006–; sr adviser to MRC on tropical medicine 2001–; Hon. Consultant in Malariology to British Army 1989–; Hon. Medical Adviser, Royal Geographical Soc. 1993–, Earthwatch Int. 2007–, Foreign and Commonwealth Office 2002–; WHO Consultant 1979–; mem. WHO Expert Advisory Panel on Malaria 1989–; Fellow, St Cross Coll. 1975–2007, Hon. Fellow 2007–; Chair. AIDS Therapeutic Trials Cttee, MRC; Trustee, Tropical Health and Education Trust; Pres. British Venom Group 1992–, Int. Fed. for Tropical Medicine 1996–2000, Royal Soc. of Tropical Medicine and Hygiene 1997–99; Del., Oxford University Press 1999–2006; Adjunct Prof., Univ Xi'an, People's Repub. of China 2009–; Visiting Prof., Capital Medical Univ., Beijing 2011–; Hon. mem. Assem of Physicians GB and NI 2003, American Soc. of Tropical Medicine and Hygiene 2003, Instituto de Medicina Tropical 'Alexander von Humboldt', Universidad Peruana Cayetano Heredia, Lima, Peru 2010; Hon. Fellow, Ceylon Coll. of Physicians, Hon. FZS; Profesor Honorario, Universidad Nacional Mayor de San Marcos, Lima, Peru 2005; Kt Commdr, Order of the White Elephant (Thailand) 2004; Chalmer's Medal, Royal Soc. of Tropical Medicine and Hygiene 1981, Ambuj Nath Bose Prize, Royal Coll. of Physicians 1994, Runme Shaw Lecturer, Acad. of Medicine, Singapore 1997, Queen's Award for Higher and Further Educ. 2000, Marc Daniels, Bradshaw, Croonian and Coll. Lecturer and Harveian Orator, Royal Coll. of Physicians 2001, Guthrie Medal, Royal Army Medical Corps (RAMC) 2004, Mary Kingsley Medal, Liverpool School of Tropical Medicine 2005, Lloyd-Roberts Lecturer, Royal Soc. of Medicine 2008, Osler Memorial Medal, Univ. of Oxford 2010, Redi Award, Int. Soc. on Toxinology 2012. *Publications include:* scientific papers and book chapters; Ed.: Oxford Textbook of Medicine, Essential Malariology, Oxford Handbook Expedition and Wilderness Medicine. *Leisure interests:* book-collecting, music, bird-watching, hill-walking. *Address:* Nuffield Dept of Clinical Medicine, University of Oxford, John Radcliffe Hospital, Headley Way, Oxford, OX3 9DU, England (office). *Telephone:* (1865) 234664 (office); (1865) 766865 (office). *Fax:* (1865) 760683 (office). *E-mail:* david.warrell@ndm.ox.ac.uk (office). *Website:* www.ndm.ox.ac.uk (office).

WARREN, Christopher (Chris), BA (Hons), MBA; Australian fmr journalist and international organization executive; *Federal Secretary, Media, Entertainment & Arts Alliance;* ed Univ. of Sydney, Australian Grad. School of Man.; completed journalist cadetship at The Sydney Morning Herald and worked as a staff and freelance journalist for various employers 1976–86; Fed. Sec., Australian Journalists Assen 1986–92, Media Entertainment & Arts Alliance 1992–; Pres. Int. Fed. of Journalists 1998–2007. *Address:* Media, Entertainment & Arts Alliance, PO Box 723, Strawberry Hills, NSW 2012, Australia (office). *Telephone:* (1300) 656513 (office). *Fax:* (1300) 730543 (office). *E-mail:* christopher.warren@alliance.org.au (office). *Website:* www.alliance.org.au (office).

WARREN, Sir David Alexander, Kt, KCMG, CMG, MA (Oxon.); British diplomatist (retd); *Chairman, The Japan Society;* b. 11 Aug. 1952, London, England; s. of the late Alister Warren and Celia Warren; m. Pamela Warren; ed Epsom Coll., Exeter Coll., Oxford; began FCO career at S East Asian Dept 1975–76, Second, later First Sec., Embassy in Tokyo 1977–81, Head of Recruitment Section, Personnel Policy Dept, FCO 1981–83, EC Dept (External) 1983–86, First Sec. and Head of Chancery, High Comm. in Nairobi 1987–90, Asst Head of Far East Dept 1990–91, Dir Int. Div. Office of Science and Tech., Cabinet Office 1991–93, Commercial Counsellor, Embassy in Tokyo 1993–98, Head of China Hong Kong Dept, FCO 1998–2000, Dir UK Trade and Investment 2000–04, Dir Human Resources, FCO 2004–07, Amb. to Japan 2008–12 (retd); Chair. The Japan Soc., London 2013–; mem. Council Univ. of Kent; mem. Advisory Council, London Symphony Orchestra, Advisory Bd Migration Matters Trust; Bd mem. Sainsbury Inst. for the Study of Japanese Arts and Culture; Hon. Fellow, Exeter Coll., Oxford; Hon. DLitt (Sheffield), (De Montfort). *Address:* The Japan Society, 13/14 Cornwall Terrace, London, NW1 4QP, England (office). *Telephone:* (20) 7935-0475 (office). *Fax:* (20) 7828-6331 (office). *E-mail:* david.warren@japansociety.org.uk (office). *Website:* www.japansociety.org.uk (office).

WARREN, Sir Frederick Miles, Kt, KBE, CBE, ONZ, FNZIA, ARIBA, DipArch; New Zealand architect; b. 10 May 1929, Christchurch; s. of M. B. Warren and J. Warren (née Hay); ed Christ's Coll., Auckland Univ. School of Architecture;

worked for the late C. W. Wood, 1946–47, for the late R. C. Munroe, ANZIA 1948; joined partnership with the late G. T. Lucas 1956; started firm Warren & Mahoney 1958, Sr Partner 1958–95 (retd); Pres. Canterbury Soc. of Arts 1972–76; Warren & Mahoney awarded New Zealand Inst. of Architects (NZIA) Gold Medal for Dental Nurses' Training School 1959, for Christchurch Memorial Garden Crematorium 1964, for Christchurch Coll. Halls of Residence 1969, for Christchurch Town Hall and Civic Centre 1973; won Architectural Competition for design of Condominium Offices, New Hebrides 1966; gifted his house and garden to the people of NZ through the Ohinetahi Charitable Trust 2012; Dr hc (Auckland) 2001; AIA Pan Pacific Citation 1966, NZIA Gold Medal 1980, 1981, 1983, 1984, 1985, 1986, 1988–91, 2000 (individual), Icon Award, Arts Foundation of NZ 2003, commemorated as one of the Twelve Local Heroes and a bronze bust of him unveiled outside Christchurch Arts Centre 2009. *Works include:* Dorset Street Flats 1956–57, Dental Nurses Training School 1958–59, Carlton Mill Road Flats 1960, MB Warren House 1961, Architect's Office and Flat 1962–79, Harewood Memorial Gardens and Crematorium 1962–63, Christchurch Wool Exchange 1962–64, Christchurch Coll., Univ. of Canterbury 1964–70, I. Munro House 1968, Christchurch Town Hall 1966–72, NZ Chancery, Washington, DC 1975–81, Canterbury Public Library, Christchurch 1982, The Oaks Complex, Wellington 1982, Michael Fowler Centre, Wellington 1983, Rotorua Civic Offices 1985–86, Clarendon Tower 1986–87, AXA New Zealand Wellington Office 1987–89, Compudigm House, Wellington 1989, TVNZ Centre, Auckland 1990. *Television:* profiled on Artsville (TVNZ arts documentary series) 2011. *Publications:* Warren & Mahoney Architects 1990, Miles Warren: An Autobiography 2008. *Leisure interests:* yachting, water-colouring, sketching. *Address:* 65 Cambridge Terrace, Christchurch 1, New Zealand. *Telephone:* 799640. *Website:* www.warrenandmahoney.com.

WARREN, John Robin, AC, MB, BS, MD, FAA, FRCPA; Australian pathologist; b. 11 June 1937, Adelaide, S Australia; s. of Roger Warren and Helen Warren (née Verco); m. Winifred Teresa Williams; four s. two d.; ed Univ. of Adelaide and Royal Melbourne Hosp.; Jr Resident Medical Officer, Queen Elizabeth Hosp., Woodville, S Australia 1961; Registrar in Haematology and Clinical Pathology, Inst. of Medical and Veterinary Science, Adelaide 1962; Registrar in Clinical Pathology, Royal Melbourne Hosp. 1964–66, Registrar in Pathology 1966–68; Sr Pathologist, Royal Perth Hosp., Western Australia 1968–99; demonstrated, with Barry J. Marshall, the association of *Helicobacter pylori* and peptic ulcers, particularly duodenal ulcers; Fellow, Royal Coll. of Pathologists of Australasia 1967; Hon. Fellow, Royal Australian Coll. of Physicians 2006; Hon. Mem. Polish Soc. of Gastroenterology, German Soc. of Pathology 2007; Hon. MD (Univ. of Western Australia) 1997; Dr hc (Univ. of Adelaide) 2006, (Univ. of Toyama, Japan) 2007, (Otto-von-Guericke Universität, Magdeburg) 2007; Guest of Honour, Sixth Int. Workshop on Campylobacter, Helicobacter and Related Organisms 1991, Distinguished Fellows Award, Coll. of Pathologists 1995, Inaugural Award, First Western Pacific Helicobacter Congress 1996, Medal of Univ. of Hiroshima 1996, Australian Medical Assen (WA) Award 1995; jtly with Prof. Barry Marshall: Warren Alpert Foundation Prize, Harvard Medical School 1995, Paul Ehrlich and Ludwig Darmstaedter Award, Goethe-Universität, Frankfurt, Germany 1997, Inaugural Florey Medal Award 1998, Nobel Prize in Physiology or Medicine 2005, Australian Medical Assen Gold Medal 2006, Western Australian of the Year 2007, Medal of the Hirosaki Univ. School of Medicine 2007, Special Recognition Award for Distinguished Service to Surgical Pathology, American Soc. for Clinical Pathology 2007, Govt of Western Australia Premier's Science Awards, Western Australian Science Hall of Fame 2007. *Publications:* numerous articles in scientific journals. *Leisure interest:* photography. *Address:* PO Box 3041, Broadway, Nedlands, WA 6009, Australia (office). *Telephone:* (8) 6488-4658 (office). *E-mail:* klaurie@helicobacter.com (office).

WARREN-GASH, Haydon Boyd, MA (Cantab.); British consultant and fmr diplomatist; b. 8 Aug. 1949, Nairobi, Kenya; m. Caroline Emma Bowring; one s. one d.; joined FCO 1971, Latin America Dept 1971–72, Third Sec., Chancery, Ankara 1973–76, Rhodesia Dept 1976–77, Second Sec., Chancery, Madrid 1977–81, Perm. Under-Sec.'s Dept 1981–82, Pvt. Sec., Minister of State's Office 1982–85, Asst Head, Southern European Dept 1989–90, Deputy High Commr, Nairobi 1991–94, Head of Southern European Dept 1994–97, Amb. to Côte d'Ivoire (also accred to Liberia, Niger and Burkina Faso) 1997–2001, HIV/AIDS Special Project Coordinator 2001–02, Amb. to Morocco (also accred to Mauritania) 2002–05, to Colombia 2005–08; mem. Bd of Dirs Foro Consulting 2010–. *Address:* 98 Overstrand Mansions, Prince of Wales Drive, London, SW11 4EU, England (home). *Telephone:* (20) 8246-5798 (office). *E-mail:* h.warrengash@foroconsulting.com (office). *Website:* www.foroconsulting.com (office).

WARRINGTON, Elizabeth Kerr, PhD, DSc, FRS; British academic; *Professor Emerita of Clinical Neuropsychology, National Hospital for Neurology and Neurosurgery;* d. of the late Prof. John A. V. Butler, FRS and Margaret L. Butler; m.; one d.; ed Univ. Coll. London; Research Fellow, Inst. of Neurology 1956; Sr Clinical Psychologist, Nat. Hosp. for Neurology and Neurosurgery 1960, Prin. Psychologist 1962, Top Grade Clinical Psychologist 1972–82, Prof. of Clinical Neuropsychology 1982–96, Hon. Consultant Neuropsychologist to Dementia Research Centre 1996–, Prof. Emer. of Clinical Neuropsychology, Univ. of London 1996–; Fellow, Univ. Coll. London; Dr hc (Bologna) 1998, (York) 1999, (Univ. Louis Pasteur) 2006; Ipsen Foundation Prize 2008. *Publications:* Cognitive Neuropsychology (co-author) 1990; numerous papers in professional journals. *Leisure interests:* entertaining granddaughters. *Address:* Dementia Research Centre, Box 16, National Hospital for Neurology and Neurosurgery, Queen Square, London, WC1N 3BG, England (office). *Telephone:* (20) 3448-3291 (office). *E-mail:* e.warrington@ucl.ac.uk (office). *Website:* www.uclh.org/about/nhnn.shtml (office).

WARRIOR, Padmasree, BS, MS; Indian/American engineer and business executive; *Chief Technology and Strategy Officer, Cisco Systems Inc.;* b. Vijayawada, AP, India; m.; ed Maris Stella Coll., Vijayawada, Indian Inst. of Tech. (IIT), New Delhi, Cornell Univ., Ithaca, NY; Vice-Pres. Motorola, Inc. 1999, Motorola's Liaison Exec. for Cornell Univ. 2001, Exec. Vice-Pres. and Chief Tech. Officer, Motorola, Inc. 2003–07; Chief Tech. Officer, Cisco Systems Inc. 2007–12, Chief Tech. and Strategy Officer 2012–; mem. Bd of Dirs Corning Corpn 2005–08; mem. Bd Joffrey Ballet, Chicago, Museum of Science and Industry, Chicago, Singapore Agency for Science, Tech. and Research (ASTAR), Chicago Mayor's

Tech. Council, Cornell Univ. Eng Council, IIT Advisory Council; mem. Selection Bd for White House Fellows 2001; fmr mem. Texas Gov.'s Council for Digital Economy, Tech. Advisory Council Fed. Communications Comm., Advisory Cttee NSF Computing and Information Science and Eng; Dr hc (New York Polytechnic) 2007; Women Elevating Science and Tech. Award, Working Woman Magazine (co-recipient) 2001, achievements recognized by American Immigration Law Foundation 2003, Nat. Medal of Tech. 2004, ranked by The Economic Times as 11th Most Influential Global Indian 2006, IIT Distinguished Alumni Award 2006, ranked by Forbes magazine amongst The World's Most Powerful Women (58th) 2012, (57th) 2013. *Leisure interests:* novels of P. G. Wodehouse, arts and crafts, exercising, meditation. *Address:* Cisco Systems Inc., 170 West Tasman Drive, Building 10, San Jose, CA 95134-1706, USA (office). *Telephone:* (408) 526-4000 (office). *Fax:* (408) 526-4100 (office). *E-mail:* info@cisco.com (office). *Website:* www.cisco.com (office).

WARSHEL, Ariel, BS, MS, PhD, FRSC; American/Israeli chemist and academic; *Distinguished Professor of Chemistry and Biochemistry, University of Southern California;* b. 20 Nov. 1940, Kibbutz Sde Nahum, Beit She'an Valley; m. Tamar Warshel; two c.; ed Israel Inst. of Tech., Weizmann Inst. of Science; served in Israel Defense Forces (attained rank of capt.); Research Fellow, Dept of Chemistry, Harvard Univ. 1970–72; Research Assoc., Weizmann Inst. of Science 1972–73, Sr Scientist 1973–77, Assoc. Prof. 1977–78; Visiting Scientist, MRC Lab. of Molecular Biology, Cambridge, UK 1974–76; Asst Prof. of Chemistry, Univ. of Southern Calif. 1976–78, Assoc. Prof. 1979–84, Prof. 1984, Prof. of Chemistry and Biochemistry 1991, Distinguished Prof. of Chemistry and Biochemistry 2011–; Fellow, Biophysical Soc.; mem. NAS 2009; several awards including Tolman Medal 2003, Royal Soc. of Chemistry Soft Matter and Biophysical Chemistry Award 2012, Nobel Prize in Chemistry (jtly with Martin Karplus and Michael Levitt) 2013. *Address:* University of Southern California, Department of Chemistry, SGM 406, Los Angeles, CA 90089, USA (office). *Telephone:* 213) 740-4114 (office). *Fax:* (213) 740-2701 (office). *E-mail:* warshel@usc.edu (office). *Website:* chem.usc.edu (office).

WARSI, Baroness (Life Peer), cr. 2007, of Dewsbury in the County of West Yorkshire; **Rt Hon. Sayeeda Hussain Warsi,** LLB, PC; British lawyer and politician; *Senior Minister of State and Government Spokesperson, Foreign and Commonwealth Office and Minister for Faith and Communities;* b. 1971, Dewsbury, Yorks., England; ed Birkdale High School, Dewsbury Coll., Univ. of Leeds, York Coll. of Law; completed Legal Practice Course and trained with Crown Prosecution Service and Home Office Immigration Dept; worked for John Whitfield (last Conservative MP for Dewsbury) at Whitfield Hallam Goodall Solicitors; later est. specialist practice, George Warsi Solicitors, Dewsbury; also worked overseas for Ministry of Law in Pakistan and in Kashmir as Chair. Savayra Foundation (women's empowerment charity); Conservative Party parl. cand. for Dewsbury at Gen. Election (first Muslim woman to be selected by Tories) 2005; has served as special adviser to Michael Howard on Community Relations; apptd by David Cameron as Vice-Chair. Conservative Party with specific responsibility for cities 2005–07; mem. (Conservative) House of Lords 2007; Shadow Minister for Community Cohesion and Social Action 2007–10; Minister without Portfolio (Minister of State) 2010–12; Govt Spokesperson, Cabinet Office 2011–12; Sr Minister of State and Govt Spokesperson, FCO 2012–; Minister for Faith and Communities 2012–; Co-Chair. Conservative and Unionist Party 2010–12; Dir, Shire Bed Co. (family business), Azam Associates Ltd (food consultancy, owned jtly with husband); Trustee, Savayra Foundation UK. *Address:* House of Lords, Westminster, London, SW1A 0PW, England (office). *Telephone:* (20) 7219-6097 (office). *E-mail:* sayeeda.warsi@conservatives.com (office). *Website:* www.parliament.uk/biographies/lords/sayeeda-warsi/35329 (office); www.sayeedawarsi.com.

WARWICK, Dionne; American singer; b. (Marie Dionne), 12 Dec. 1941, East Orange, NJ; m. Bill Elliott (divorced 1975); two s.; pnr Bruce Garrick; ed Hartt Coll. of Music, Hartford, Conn.; as teenager formed Gospelaires; later sang background for recording studio 1966; début, Philharmonic Hall, Lincoln Center, New York 1966; appearances at London Palladium, Olympia, Paris, Lincoln Center; co-host, Solid Gold (TV show); host, A Gift of Music (TV show) 1981; star, Dionne Warwick Special (TV show); appeared in Sisters in the Name of Love on TV 1986; named UN FAO Amb. 2002; Co-founder Carr/Todd/Warwick Production, Inc., Dionne Warwick Design Group Inc.; five Grammy Awards, Luminary Award, American Soc. of Young Musicians 1997, Chairman's Award for Sustained Creative Achievement, Nat. Asscn of Record Merchandisers 1998, History Maker, History Makers Org. of Chicago 2001, Heroes Award, New York Chapter of Recording Acad. 2002, Lifetime Achievement Award, R&B Foundation 2003, named one of Top Faces of Black History 2003. *Films:* The Slaves 1969, No Night, So Long, Hot! Live and Otherwise. *Singles include:* I'll Never Love this Way Again, That's What Friends are For. *Albums include:* Valley of the Dolls and Others 1968, Promises, Promises 1975, Dionne 1979, Then Came You, Friends 1986, Reservations for Two 1987, Greatest Hits 1990, Dionne Warwick Sings Cole Porter 1990, Hidden Gems: The Best of Dionne Warwick (Vol. 2) 1992, Friends Can Be Lovers (with Whitney Houston) 1993, Dionne Warwick and Placido Domingo 1994, Aquarela do Brasil 1994, From the Vaults 1995, Dionne Sings Dionne 1998, I Say a Little Prayer For You 2000. *Publications:* My Point of View 2003, My Life, As I See It 2010. *Address:* c/o Entertainment1 Productions, 6033 West Century Blvd., Suite 610, Los Angeles, CA 90045, USA (office). *E-mail:* Ent1pro@gmail.com (office). *Website:* www.dionnewarwick.net.

WARWICK OF UNDERCLIFFE, Baroness (Life Peer), cr. 1999, of Undercliffe in the County of West Yorkshire; **Diana Warwick,** BA; British academic; b. 16 July 1945, Bradford; d. of Jack Warwick and Olive Warwick; m. Sean Young 1969; ed Bedford Coll., Univ. of London; Gen. Sec. Asscn of Univ. Teachers 1983–92; mem. RIIA, Inter-Parl. Union, Commonwealth Parl. Asscn, British American Parl. Group, Employment Appeals Tribunal 1984–99; mem. Bd British Council 1985–95, Commonwealth Inst. 1988–95; Chief Exec. Westminster Foundation for Democracy 1992–95; Chair. VSO 1994–2005; Chair. Human Tissue Authority 2009–, NED Pension Protection Fund 2011–; mem. Standing Cttee on Standards in Public Life (Nolan/Neill Cttee) 1994–99, OST Tech. Foresight Steering Group 1997–2000; Chief Exec. Universities UK (fmrly Cttee of Vice-Chancellors and Prins) 1995–2009; Trustee St Catharine's Foundation, Windsor 1996–2008; Hon. DLitt (Bradford) 1993, (Open Univ.) 1998, (Royal Holloway Coll., Univ. of London)

2007, (London Metropolitan) 2008, (Brunel) 2009,. *Address:* House of Lords, London, SW1A 0PW, England. *Telephone:* (20) 7269-1900 (office).

WARWICK-THOMPSON, Paul, PhD; British museum director and university rector; *Rector, Royal College of Art;* b. 9 Aug. 1959, Oxford; s. of Sir Michael Thompson; m. Adline Finlay 1984; one s. one d.; ed Bryanston School, Univ. of Bristol, Univ. of East Anglia; Curator Design Museum, London 1989–92, Dir 1992–2000; Dir Cooper-Hewitt Nat. Design Museum, New York 2001–09; Rector RCA 2009–; Hon. Fellow, RCA 2000. *Leisure interests:* theatre, cinema, gardening. *Address:* Royal College of Art, Kensington Gore, London SW7, England (office). *Telephone:* (20) 7590-4444 (office). *E-mail:* press@rca.ac.uk (office).

WASACZ, Emil; Polish economist, business executive and fmr government official; b. 1 Aug. 1945, Zabratówka, Rzeszów Prov.; m.; three c.; ed Łódź Tech. Univ., Main School of Commerce (SGH), Warsaw; employee, Katowice Steelworks 1976–94, Supreme Dir then Chair. Katowice Steelworks SA 1991–94; adviser to Chair. Bank Śląski SA, Bank PeKaO SA and enterprise Stalexport SA; Chair. Szczecin Steelworks SA 1995–97; Vice-Leader Supervisory Bd, later Chair. Progress Nat. Investment Fund 1995–97; Minister of the Treasury 1997–2001; CEO Stalexport Serwis-Centrum S.A. (steel products co.) 2001, then Chair. Man. Bd, suspended from position 2006; mem. Solidarity Trade Union, Leader Plant Cttee in the Katowice Steelworks 1989–90; voluntary worker, Catholic Family Clinic, Sosnowiec 1983–90. *Leisure interests:* tourism, history, astronomy, literature, romantic poetry. *Address:* c/o Management Board, Stalexport Serwis-Centrum S.A, 40-780 Katowice, ul.Owsiana 60a, Poland. *Website:* www .stalexport.katowice.pl.

WASE, Brenson S.; Marshall Islands politician; b. 28 May 1952; m. Antonia U. Wase; five c.; ed Univ. of Hawaii-Hil; Senator from Arno 1988–99, from Majuro Atoll 1999–; Minister of Social Service 1984–87, of Resources and Devt 1988–91, of Interior and Outer Islands Affairs 1991–95, of Internal Affairs 1995–99, of Transportation and Communications 2000–02, of Finance 2002–08, of Justice 2009–; Gov. of the Marshall Islands to ADB 2000–, Vice-Chair. Bd of Dirs 2004–; Acting Pres. of Repub. of Marshall Islands 2003; Minister of Justice 2009–12. *Address:* Ministry of Justice, c/o Office of the Attorney General, Majuro, MH 96960, Marshall Islands (office). *Telephone:* (625) 3244 (office). *Fax:* (625) 5218 (office). *E-mail:* agoffice@ntamar.net (office).

WASHIDA, Kiyokazu; Japanese philosopher, academic and fmr university administrator; *Professor, Otani University;* b. 2 Sept. 1949, Kyoto; ed Kyoto Univ.; fmr Prof., School of Letters and Dean, Grad. School of Letters, Kyoto Univ., later Vice-Pres. in charge of Educ. and Information; Asst Prof., Faculty of Literature, Osaka Univ. Grad. School 2005, becoming Univ. Vice-Pres., then Pres. 2007–11; Prof., Otani Univ. 2011–; mem. Kyoto Nat. Festival Planning Cttee; Assoc. mem. Science Council of Japan; Dir Japan Asscn of Nat. Univs; mem. Cabinet Office Council for Science and Tech. Policy Expert Panel on Bioethics; Medal of Honour with Purple Ribbon 2004; Suntory Prize for Social Sciences and Humanities 1989, Kuwabara Takeo Prize 2000. *Publications:* Bunsansuru risei: Genshogaku no shisen 1989, Modo no meikyu 1989, Kimochi no ii hanashi 2001, Talking to Myself (co-author) 2002. *Address:* Otani University, Koyama-Kamifusacho, Kita-ku, Kyoto 603-814, Japan (office). *Telephone:* (75) 411-8161 (office). *Fax:* (75) 411-8162 (office). *Website:* www.otani.ac.jp (office).

WASHINGTON, Denzel Hayes, Jr, BA; American film actor, film director and film producer; b. 28 Dec. 1954, Mt Vernon, New York City; s. of Rev. Denzel Hayes Washington, Sr and Lennis 'Lynne' Washington; m. Pauletta Pearson 1983; two s. two d.; ed Mainland High School, Daytona Beach, Fla, Fordham Univ. and American Conservatory Theater, San Francisco; worked at New York Shakespeare Festival and American Place Theater; off-Broadway appearances include: Ceremonies in Dark Old Men, When the Chickens Come Home to Roost and A Soldier's Play (Negro Ensemble Co.), Public Theater's production of Shakespeare's Richard III 1990, as Marcus Brutus in Julius Caesar on Broadway 2005; played young doctor in TV series St Elsewhere; Harvard Foundation Award 1996. *Films include:* A Soldier's Story 1984, The Mighty Quinn, Cry Freedom 1987, Heart Condition 1989, Glory (Acad. Award for Best Supporting Actor) 1990, Love Supreme 1990, Mo' Better Blues 1990, Ricochet 1991, Mississippi Masala 1991, Much Ado About Nothing, Malcolm X 1992, The Pelican Brief 1993, Philadelphia 1993, Hank Aaron: Chasing the Dream (documentary) (exec. producer) 1995, Devil in a Blue Dress 1995, Courage Under Fire 1996, The Preacher's Wife 1996, Fallen 1997, He Got Game 1998, The Siege 1998, The Bone Collector 1999, The Hurricane 1999, Remember the Titans 2001, Training Day (Acad. Award for Best Actor 2002) 2001, John Q (Award for Best Actor, Nat. Asscn for the Advancement of Colored People (NAACP) Awards 2003) 2002, Antwone Fisher (also producer and dir) 2002; Awards for Best Supporting Actor and Best Dir, NAACP Awards 2003) 2002, Out of Time 2003, Man on Fire 2004, The Manchurian Candidate 2004, Inside Man 2006, Deja Vu 2006, American Gangster 2007, The Great Debaters (also dir) 2007, The Taking of Pelham 1 2 3 2009, The Book of Eli (also producer) 2010, Unstoppable 2010, Safe House (also exec. producer) 2012, Flight 2012, 2 Guns 2013. *Television includes:* Half Past Autumn: The Life and Works of Gordon Parks (documentary) (producer) 2000. *Leisure interests:* cooking, reading, basketball. *Address:* c/o WME Entertainment, 9601 Wilshire Boulevard, Beverley Hills, CA 90210-5213, USA (office). *Website:* www.wma.com.

WASIM AKRAM; Pakistani sports commentator and fmr professional cricketer; b. 3 June 1966, Lahore, Punjab; m. Huma Akram (died 2009); two s.; ed Islamia Coll., Lahore; left-hand middle-order batsman, left-arm fast bowler; played for Pakistan Automobile Corpn 1984/85–85/86, Lahore City Whites 1985–86, Pakistan 1985–2002 (Capt. 1999–2000), Lahore City 1986–87, 1997–98, Lancashire 1988–98 (Capt. 1998), Pakistan International Airlines 1992/93–2001/02, Lahore Blues 2000–01, Hampshire 2003; regarded as one of the greatest fast bowlers ever, holds world records for the most wickets taken in List A cricket (881), and is second only to Muttiah Muralitharan in terms of One-Day Int. (ODI) wickets (502); considered to be a pioneer of reverse swing bowling; only bowler to have captured more than 400 wickets both in Test and ODI cricket; Test debut: NZ v Pakistan, Auckland 25 Jan. 1985; played in 104 Tests (25 as Capt.), scoring 2,898 runs (average 22.64, highest score 257 not out) including three hundreds and taking 414 wickets (average 23.62), best bowling (innings) 7/119, (match) 11/110; achieved highest score by a No. 8 batsman in Test cricket: 257 not out from 363 balls against

Zimbabwe at Sheikhupura, innings contained 12 sixes which is also a world record for Test cricket; played in 350 ODIs (109 as Capt.), scoring 3,717 runs (average 16.52, highest score 86) and taking 502 wickets (average 23.52), best bowling 5/15; played in 257 First-class matches, scoring 7,161 runs (average 22.73) and taking 1,042 wickets (average 21.64), best bowling 8/30; retd 2003; currently sportscaster for ESPN Star network and ARY Digital; commentated on Int. Cricket Council (ICC) Women's Cricket World Cup in Australia 2009, ICC World Twenty20 in England 2009, Champion's Trophy in S Africa 2009; Wisden Cricketer of the Year 1993, one of five new members inducted into ICC Cricket Hall of Fame 2009. *Publication:* Wasim (autobiography). *Leisure interest:* Manchester United Football Club. *Address:* c/o Pakistan Cricket Board, Gaddafi Stadium, Ferozepur Road, Lahore 54600, Pakistan. *Telephone:* (42) 571-7231. *Website:* www.pcboard.com.pk; www.espnstar.com.

WASMOSY, Juan Carlos, DCE; Paraguayan civil engineer, politician and fmr head of state; b. 15 Dec. 1938, Asunción; s. of Dr Juan Bautista Wasmosy and María Clotilde Monti Paoli; m. Maria Teresa Carrasco Dos Santos; five s. (one deceased) one d.; ed San José School, Asunción and Nat. Univ. of Asunción; fmr Asst Prof. Univ. of Asunción; sometime Pres. ECOMIPA, CONEMPA, COCEP, GOYA (pvt. construction and industrial cos); other business affiliations; mem. construction holding which built Itaipú Hydroelectric Power Station; currently engaged in construction of Yacyretá power station; Pres. Int. Fed. of Zebu Cattle Breeders; mem. Colorado Party 1973–; Minister of Integration 1993; Pres. of Paraguay 1993–98, Senator for Life 1998–; Orden de Solidaridad de Brasil; other medals and awards. *Address:* The Senate, Asunción, Paraguay.

WASS, Sir Douglas William Gretton, GCB, MA; British fmr civil servant and business executive; b. 15 April 1923, Wallasey, Cheshire, England; s. of the late Arthur W. Wass and Elsie W. Wass; m. Dr Milica Pavičić Wass; one s. one d.; ed Nottingham High School, St John's Coll. Cambridge; Scientific Research with Admiralty 1943–46; Asst Prin., Treasury 1946, Prin. 1951; Commonwealth Fund Fellow, USA 1958–59; Fellow, Brookings Inst., Washington 1959; Pvt. Sec. to Chancellor 1959–61; Pvt. Sec. to Chief Sec. 1961–62; Alt. Exec. Dir to IMF and Financial Counsellor, British Embassy, Washington, DC 1965–67; Under-Sec. of Treasury 1968, Deputy Sec. 1970, Second Perm. Sec. 1973, Perm. Sec. 1974–83; Jt Head, Home Civil Service 1981–83; Chair. Econ. Policy Cttee, OECD 1982; Reith Lecturer, BBC 1983; Chair. British Selection Cttee, Harkness Fellowships 1981–84, Governing Body of the Ditchley Foundation, Council of the Policy Studies Inst.; Chair. Nomura Int. PLC 1986–98 (Sr Adviser 1998–2002), Axa Equity and Law Life Assurance Soc. PLC 1986–95, N.C.M. (Credit Insurance) Ltd 1991–95; Gov. Centre for Econ. Policy Research 1983–90; Adviser to Campaign for Freedom of Information; Dir De La Rue Co. PLC 1983–93, Coopers and Lybrand 1984–86, Barclays Bank PLC 1984–87, African Capacity Bldg Foundation, Harare 1991–98, Equitable Cos Inc. New York 1992–95; Administrateur, Cie du Midi SA (now Axa SA) 1987–95; Vice-Pres. Constitutional Reform Centre 1984–92; mem. Council of Univ. of Bath 1985–91; Pres. Market Research Soc. 1987–91; mem. Overseas Devt Council 1990–96; mem. Council British Heart Foundation 1990–96; Dir Soho Theatre Co. 1996–2000; Hon. Fellow, St John's Coll. Cambridge; Hon. DLitt (Bath). *Publications:* The Changing Problems of Economic Management 1978, The Public Service in Modern Society 1982, Government and the Governed 1984, The Civil Service at the Crossroads 1985, What Sort of Industrial Policy? 1986, Checks and Balances in Public Policy Making 1987, Decline to Fall 2008. *Leisure interests:* swimming, reading, listening to music. *Address:* 6 Dora Road, Wimbledon, London, SW19 7HH, England (home). *E-mail:* douglas.wass@ blueyonder.co.uk (home).

WASSENER, Albert; German cultural institute director; b. 25 April 1936, Essen; s. of Albert Wassener and Gertrud Wassener (née Forstbauer); m. Renate Wassener 1962; one s. one d.; ed Univs of Bonn and Munich; Dir Goethe Inst., Tripoli, Libya 1965–66, Officer, Cultural Programmes, Goethe Inst., Rome 1966–74, Head, Teachers' Training Dept, Goethe Inst. Head Office, Munich 1974–78, Dir Goethe Inst., Tel-Aviv 1978–84, Copenhagen 1984–89, Istanbul 1989–90, Head, Talks Dept, Goethe Inst. Head Office, Munich 1990–95, Dir Goethe Inst., London and Regional Dir, GB and NI 1995–2000. *Publication:* German Foreign Cultural Politics: Principles, Perspectives and the Future (Discussion Papers in German Studies) 1998. *Address:* c/o Goethe-Institut Berlin, Neue Schönhauser Str. 20, Berlin 10178, Germany. *Telephone:* (30) 259063. *Fax:* (30) 25906400. *E-mail:* berlin@goethe.org. *Website:* www.goethe.de.

WASSERBURG, Gerald Joseph, BSc, MSc, PhD; American geologist, geophysicist, astrophysicist and academic; *John D. MacArthur Professor Emeritus of Geology and Geophysics, California Institute of Technology;* b. 25 March 1927, New Brunswick; s. of Charles Wasserburg and Sarah Levine Wasserburg; m. Naomi Z. Orlick 1951; two s.; ed Univ. of Chicago; served in US Army as rifleman, Second Infantry Div. 1943–46; with Resurrection Mining Co. 1947; Juneau Ice Field Research Project, Alaska 1950; Consultant, Argonne Nat. Laboratory, Lamont, Ill. 1952–55; Research Assoc., Inst. for Nuclear Studies, Chicago 1954–55; Asst Prof. of Geology, Calif. Inst. of Tech. 1955–59, Assoc. Prof. of Geology 1959–62, Prof. of Geology and Geophysics 1962–82, John D. MacArthur Prof. of Geology and Geophysics 1982–2002, Prof. Emer. 2002–, Chair. Div. of Geological and Planetary Sciences 1987–89; Adviser to NASA 1968–88; mem. Lunar Sample Analysis Planning Team, MSC, NASA 1968–71 (Chair. 1970), Lunar Sample Review Bd 1970–72, Johnson Space Center Facilities Working Group (FAG) 1972–82, Science Working Panel 1971–73, Physical Sciences Cttee 1971–75; Ed. Earth and Planetary Science Letters 1967–74; Chair. Comm. for Planetary and Lunar Exploration, NAS, Space Science Bd 1975–78; Vinton Hayes Sr Fellow, Harvard 1980; Jaeger-Hales Lecture, ANU 1980; Harold Jeffreys Lecture, Royal Astronomical Soc. 1981; Distinguished Visiting Scholar, Harvard Univ. 2001; Pres. Meteoritical Soc. 1987–88; mem. NAS; Fellow, American Acad. of Arts and Sciences, American Geophysical Union, Geological Soc. of America; Regents Fellow, Smithsonian Inst. 1982; Geochemistry Fellow, Geochemical Soc. and European Asscn for Geochemistry 1996; mem. American Philosophical Soc.; Foreign mem. Norwegian Acad. of Science and Letters 1988; Hon. Fellow, Geological Soc. London, Hon. Foreign Fellow, European Union of Geosciences 1983; Dr hc (Brussels) 1985, (Paris) 1986, (Chicago) 1992, (Rennes) 1998, (Torino) 2000; Hon. DSc (Ariz.) 1987; Combat Infantryman's Badge 1945, Exceptional Scientific Achievement Medal, NASA 1970, Arthur L. Day Medal, Geological Soc.

of America 1970, Distinguished Public Service Medal, NASA 1972 and with cluster 1978, James Furman Kemp Medal, Columbia Univ. 1973, Leonard Medal, Meteoritical Soc. 1975, V. M. Goldschmidt Medal, Geochemical Soc. 1978, Univ. of Chicago Alumni Asscn Professional Achievement Award 1978, Arthur L. Day Prize, NAS 1981, J. Lawrence Smith Medal, NAS 1985, Wollaston Medal, Geological Soc. of London 1985, Sr US Scientist Award, Alexander von Humboldt-Stiftung 1985, Harry H. Hess Medal, American Geophysical Union, Crafoord Prize, Swedish Royal Acad. 1986, Holmes Medal, EUG 1987, Gold Medal (Royal Astronomical Soc.) 1991, Bowie Medal, American Geophysical Union 2008. *Publications* include: research papers in several scientific journals, in the fields of geochemistry, geophysics and astrophysics, cosmology and the application of the methods of chemical physics to problems in the earth and planetary sciences; major researches: determination of the time scale of the solar system, chronology of the moon, establishment of dating methods using long-lived natural radio-activities, study of geological processes using nuclear and isotopic effects as a tracer in nature, nuclear astrophysics and stellar evolution and the application of thermodynamic methods to geological systems. *Leisure interests:* hiking, music, art. *Address:* California Institute of Technology, Division of Geological and Planetary Sciences, Pasadena, CA 91125 (office); PO Box 2959, Florence, OR 97439, USA (home). *Telephone:* (541) 997-9224 (home). *E-mail:* gjw@gps.caltech .edu (office). *Website:* www.gps.caltech.edu/people/gjw/profile (office).

WASSERMAN, Baron (Life Peer), cr. 2011, of Pimlico in the City of Westminster; **Gordon Wasserman;** Canadian/British civil servant and consultant; *Senior Adviser and Chief of Staff to Philadelphia Police Commissioner;* b. Montreal, Quebec; ed McGill Univ., Montreal, Univ. of Oxford, UK (Rhodes Scholar); ind. consultant specializing in public sector man.; began service to UK Govt as Econ. Adviser to the Home Office 1967–73, Head of Urban Deprivation Unit 1973–81, apptd Asst Under-Sec. of State and Dir of Social Policy in Cabinet of Margaret Thatcher 1981, later Asst Under-Sec. of State for Police Science and Tech.; spent a year working at Nat. Asscn for the Advancement of Colored People (NAACP) Legal Defense Fund, Inc., New York City while on sabbatical from UK Govt; Special Adviser on Science and Tech. to Police Commissioner, New York City 1996–98; Sr Adviser and Chief of Staff to Philadelphia Police Commr 1998–; CEO The Gordon Wasserman Group, LLC 2003–; fmr Chair. (non-exec.) Ion Track Inc. (developer of trace detection tech. for explosives and narcotics); mem. Bd of Dirs Orchid BioSciences, Inc. 2004–; Chair. Advisory Bd Center for Criminal Justice Science and Tech., Georgia Tech. Inst.; mem. Council of Advisors, Inst. for Int. Criminal Investigations. *Address:* The Gordon Wasserman Group, LLC, 225 S 18th Street, Unit 1207, Philadelphia, PA 19103, USA (office); House of Lords, Westminster, London, SW1A 0PW, England. *Telephone:* (20) 7219-5353. *Fax:* (20) 7219-5979.

WASSERMAN, Robert Harold, PhD; American biologist and academic; *James Law Professor Emeritus of Physiology, College of Veterinary Medicine, Cornell University;* b. 11 Feb. 1926, Schenectady, NY; s. of Joseph Wasserman and Sylvia Rosenburg; m. Marilyn Mintz 1950; three d.; ed Mount Pleasant High School, NY, Cornell Univ., Michigan State Univ.; Research Assoc. and Assoc. Prof. of Biochemistry, Univ. of Tenn. Atomic Energy Comm. Agricultural Research Program, Oak Ridge 1953–55; Sr Scientist, Medical Div., Oak Ridge Inst. of Nuclear Studies 1955–57; Research Assoc. in Radiation Biology NY State Veterinary Coll., Cornell Univ. 1957–59; Assoc. Prof. of Radiation Biology, Dept of Physical Biology 1959–63, Prof. of Radiation Biology 1963–80, Prof. of Physiology, Coll. of Veterinary Medicine 1980–89, Prof. and Chair. of Dept and Section 1983–87, James Law Prof. of Physiology 1989–97, Prof. Emer. 1998–; Chair. Cttee Meat and Poultry Inspection, Nat. Research Council 1983–85, mem. Food and Nutrition Bd 1984–87; Visiting Scientist Inst. of Biological Chem., Copenhagen, Denmark 1964–65; Guggenheim Fellowship 1964, 1972; mem. NAS 1980; Fellow, American Inst. of Nutrition 1992; Mead-Johnson Award in Nutrition 1969, Wise and Helen Burroughs Lectureship 1974, 1987, A. Lichtwitz Prize, Institut nat. de la santé et de la recherche médicale 1982, Merit Status, NIH 1989, Newman Award, American Soc. Bone and Mineral Research 1990, Career Recognition Award, Vitamin D Workshop 1994. *Publications:* Cellular Mechanisms for Calcium Transfer and Homeostasis (co-author) 1972, Calcium Binding Proteins and Calcium Function (co-ed.) 1977; numerous articles in specialist journals. *Leisure interests:* reading, sports, computers, cards, writing. *Address:* Department of Biomedical Sciences, Room 08-017, Vet Research Tower, College of Veterinary Medicine, Cornell University, Ithaca, NY 14853 (office); 207 Texas Lane, Ithaca, NY 14850, USA (home). *Telephone:* (607) 253-3437 (office). *E-mail:* rhw2@cornell.edu (office). *Website:* www.vet.cornell.edu (office).

WASSON, Gregory (Greg) D.; American business executive; *President and CEO, Walgreen Company;* ed Purdue Univ.; joined Walgreen as pharmacy intern, Houston, Tex. 1980, managed several drugstores then promoted to dist man. 1986, Regional Vice-Pres. Walgreens store operations 1999–2001, Vice-Pres. and Exec. Vice-Pres. Walgreens Health Initiatives 2001–02, Pres. 2002–04, Sr Vice-Pres. 2004–05, Exec. Vice-Pres. 2005–07, Pres. and COO Walgreen Co. 2007–09, Pres. and CEO 2009–. *Address:* Walgreen Co., 200 Wilmot Road, Deerfield, IL 60015, USA (office). *Telephone:* (847) 914-2500 (office). *Fax:* (847) 914-2804 (office). *E-mail:* info@walgreens.com (office). *Website:* www.walgreens.com (office).

WÄSTBERG, Olof (Olle), BA; Swedish politician, writer and diplomatist; *Director-General, Swedish Institute;* b. 6 May 1945, Stockholm; s. of Erik Wästberg and Greta Hirsch; m. Inger Claesson 1968; two s.; ed Univ. of Stockholm; Vice-Pres. Liberal Youth Sweden 1968–71; mem. Bd Liberal Party 1972–93, 1997–, Pres. Exec. Cttee 1982–83; teacher of political science, Univ. of Stockholm 1967–68; journalist, political Dept Expressen 1968–71, Ed. 1994–95; Research Fellow, Business and Social Research Centre 1971–76; Pres. Akieframjandet 1976–82; mem. Parl. 1976–82; Pres. Swedish Newspaper Promotion Asscn 1983–91; Under-Sec. of State, Ministry of Finance 1991–93; Ed.-in-Chief Expressen 1993–95; Consul Gen. of Sweden, New York 1999–2004; Dir-Gen. Swedish Inst., Stockholm 2005–; Dir Stockholm Stock Exchange 1977–82, 1988–94; Pres. Nordic Investment Bank 1992–94; Chair. Bd Swedish Broadcasting Corpn 1996–99, Stockholm City Theatre 1998–99; Pres. Hirsch Foundation 2004–; mem. Bd Swedish American Foundation 2009–; mem. Govt comms on S African consumer politics, stock market, globalization and media; Gold Medal, Swedish Marketing Group 1982, Bertil Ohlin Medal 1996, Man of the Year, Swedish-American Community of New York 2003. *Publications:* books on African problems, immigration policies and economic topics; articles in professional journals. *Address:* Swedish Institute, Slottsbacken 10, Box 7434, 103 91 Stockholm (office); Bellmangatan 6, 11820 Stockholm, Sweden (home). *Telephone:* (8) 453-78-00 (office). *Fax:* (8) 20-72-48 (office). *E-mail:* olle@wastberg.se (office). *Website:* www.si.se (office); www.wastberg.se.

WATANABE, Arata; Japanese business executive; *Representative Director and Corporate Advisor, Alfresa Holdings Corporation;* with Takeda Pharmaceutical Co. Ltd –2003; joined Alfresa Holdings Corpn 2003, held several sr man. positions, including Sr Man. Dir, Vice-Pres. and Pres. –2009, Rep. Dir and Chair. Alfresa Holdings Corpn 2009–12, Rep. Dir and Corporate Advisor 2012–. *Address:* Alfresa Holdings Corpn, 1-1-3 Otemachi, Chiyoda-ku, Tokyo 100-0004, Japan (office). *Telephone:* (3) 5219-5102 (office). *Fax:* (3) 5219-5103 (office). *E-mail:* info@alfresa.com (office). *Website:* www.alfresa.com (office).

WATANABE, Katsuaki; Japanese automotive industry executive; *Vice-Chairman, Toyota Motor Corporation;* b. 14 Feb. 1942, Mie Pref.; m.; three d.; ed Keio Univ.; joined Toyota Motor Corpn 1964, Man. Dir and mem. Bd 1997–99, Sr Man. Dir 1999–2001, Exec. Vice-Pres. 2002–05, Pres. and Rep. Dir 2005–09, Vice-Chair. 2009–. *Address:* Toyota Motor Corporation, 1 Toyota-cho, Toyota, Aichi 471-8571, Japan (office). *Telephone:* (565) 28-2121 (office). *Fax:* (565) 23-5800 (office). *Website:* www.toyota.co.jp (office).

WATANABE, Kazuhide; Japanese automobile executive; b. 1941; Man.-Dir in charge of Personnel and Human Affairs, Mazda Motor Corpn 1998, Chair. and Rep. Dir 2001–06; mem. Council Japan Productivity Centre for Socio-Econ. Devt (JPC-SED); mem. Bd of Dirs The Energy Conservation Center Japan (ECCJ) 2001–03, also Trustee. *Address:* c/o Mazda Motor Corpn, 3-1 Shinchi, Fuchu-cho, Aki-gun, Hiroshima 730-8670, Japan. *Telephone:* (82) 282-1111. *Fax:* (82) 287-5190. *E-mail:* info@mazda.com. *Website:* www.mazda.com.

WATANABE, Ken; Japanese actor; b. 21 Oct. 1959, Koide, Niigata; m. 1st Yumiko Watanabe (divorced 2004); two c.; m. 2nd Kaho Minami 2005. *Films include:* Setouchi shonen yakyu dan 1984, Kekkon annai mystery 1985, Tampopo 1985, Umi to dokuyaku (The Sea and Poison) 1986, Bakumatsu jyunjyoden 1991, Kimitachi ga ite boku ga iru 1992, Rajio no jikan 1997, Kizuna 1998, Oboreru sakana 2000, Supêsutoraberâzu (Space Travelers) 2000, Zawa-zawa Shimokita-sawa 2000, Sennen no koi – Hikaru Genji monogatari 2001, Hi wa mata noboru 2002, T. R. Y. 2003, The Last Samurai 2003, Kita no zeronen 2005, Batman Begins 2005, Memoirs of a Geisha 2005, Ashita no kioku (also producer) 2006, Letters from Iwo Jima 2006. *Television includes:* Sanga moyu 1984, Dokugan-ryu Masamune 1987, Takeda Shingen 1990, Ikebukuro West Gate Park 2000, Hojo Tokimune 2001, Suna no utsuwa 2004. *Address:* c/o The Endeavor Agency, 9601 Wilshire Boulevard, 10th Floor, Beverly Hills, CA 90212, USA (office). *Telephone:* (310) 248-2000 (office). *Fax:* (310) 248-2020 (office).

WATANABE, Koichiro, BEcons; Japanese insurance industry executive; *President and Representative Director, Dai-ichi Life Insurance Company Limited;* ed Tohoku Univ.; joined Dai-ichi Life Insurance Co. Ltd 1976, served as Sr Man. Exec. Officer, Dir of Research, Chief Dir of Planning and Research, Dir of First Planning, Man. Dir and Man. Exec. Officer –2010, Pres. and Rep. Dir 2010–. *Leisure interests:* karate, kendo. *Address:* Dai-ichi Life Insurance Co. Ltd, 13-1, Yurakucho 1-chome, Chiyoda-ku, Tokyo 100-8411, Japan (office). *Telephone:* (3) 3216-1211 (office). *E-mail:* info@dai-ichi-life.co.jp (office). *Website:* www.dai-ichi-life.co.jp (office).

WATANABE, Shigeo, BS; Japanese business executive; *Member of the Board and Adviser, Bridgestone Corporation;* b. 10 April 1942; ed Keio Univ.; joined Bridgestone Tire Co. Ltd (renamed Bridgestone Corpn) 1965, Tech. Adviser Bridgestone Tire Mfg USA Inc., Gen.-Man. Truck and Bus Devt Dept 1988, Tech. Adviser Firestone Tire and Rubber Co. Int. Tech. Centre 1988–90, Gen. Man. Mfg and Tech. 1990–93, Dir Quality Assurance Div. 1993–94, Dir Tire Devt Div. 1994–97, mem. Bd 1994–, Vice-Pres. and Dir Tire Devt Div. 1997, Vice-Pres. and Dir Commercial Tire Devt and Tire Tech. Admin 1997–98, Sr Vice-Pres. Tire Devt 1998–2000, Sr Vice-Pres. Tire Devt and Quality Assurance 2000–01, Chair., Pres. and CEO 2001–06, Mem. Bd and Adviser 2006–. *Address:* Bridgestone Corporation, 10-1 Kyobashi 1-chome, Chuo-ku, Tokyo 104-8340, Japan (office). *Telephone:* (3) 3567-0111 (office). *Fax:* (3) 3535-2553 (office). *E-mail:* bfspr@bfusa.com (office). *Website:* www.bridgestone.co.jp (office).

WATANABE, Shuichi; Japanese health care industry executive; *Representative Director, President and CEO, Medipal Holdings Corporation;* apptd Dir Kuraya Sanseido Inc. 2001, Pres. and Rep. Dir Kuraya Sanseido Inc. (following separation of pharmaceutical distribution from purchasing businesses to form new Kuraya Sanseido Inc., took over prescription pharmaceutical wholesale business of Medipal Holdings Corpn, merged with Senshu Yakuhin Co. Ltd, Ushioda Kuraya Sanseido Inc., Yamahiro Kuraya Sanseido Inc., Heisei Yakuhin Co. Ltd and Izutsu Kuraya Sanseido Inc. and changed its corp. name to Mediceo Corpn) 2004–12, Rep. Dir, Pres. and CEO Medipal Holdings Corpn 2012–, Rep. Dir and Chair. Mediceo Corpn 2012–. *Address:* Medipal Holdings Corporation, 2-7-15, Yaesu, Chuo-ku, Tokyo 104-8461, Japan (office). *Telephone:* (3) 3517-5800 (office). *Fax:* (3) 3517-5011 (office). *E-mail:* info@medipal.co.jp (office). *Website:* www.medipal.co.jp (office).

WATANABE, Tsuneo; Japanese newspaper executive; *President, CEO and Editor-in-Chief, Yomiuri Shimbun;* b. 1926; began career with Yomiuri Shimbum newspaper as reporter 1950, fmr Washington, DC corresp., chief editorial writer, Pres. 1991–, currently Pres., CEO and Ed.-in-Chief, also Chair. Yomiuri Group; Man. Exec. Officer, Tanker Div. and Dir Mitsui OSK Lines Ltd; Owner, Yomiuri Giants Co., Ltd. 2002–; mem. Bd of Dirs Nippon Television Network Corpn. *Publications:* Memoirs of Tsuneo Watanabe 2000. *Address:* Yomiuri Shimbun, 1-7-1, Otemachi, Chiyoda-ku, Tokyo 100-8055, Japan (office). *Telephone:* (3) 3242-1111 (office). *E-mail:* webmaster@yomiuri.com (office). *Website:* www.yomiuri.co.jp (office).

WATANABE, Yoshimi, LLB; Japanese politician; b. 17 March 1952, Nasu Dist, Tochigi; s. of Michio Watanabe; ed Waseda and Chuo Univs; served as pvt. sec. to Minister of Int. Trade and Industry 1986–92, Minister of Foreign Affairs 1992–96; elected to House of Reps 1996, representing Tochigi Pref. Third Dist, re-elected 2000, 2003, 2005, parl. posts have included Chief Sec., Research Comm. on Finance

and Banking; Sr Vice-Minister of Cabinet Office 2006, Minister of State for Regulatory Reform 2006–07, Minister of State for Financial Services and Admin. Reform 2007–08 (resgnd); mem. LDP (Liberal Democratic Party), Acting Chair., Public Relations HQ 2004, Acting Dir-Gen., Int. Bureau 2004, Man., Research Comm. on Tax System 2005, resigned from party 2009. *Television:* appears in Takeshi-no-TV-tackle, a humorous political discussion show hosted by comedian Takeshi Kitano. *Address:* c/o Liberal-Democratic Party (LDP), 1-11-23, Nagata-cho, Chiyoda-ku, Tokyo 100-8910, Japan (office).

WATARI, Fumiaki, BA; Japanese oil industry executive; *Chairman, Nippon Oil Corporation;* ed Keio Univ.; joined Nippon Oil 1960, numerous positions in Marketing Dept 1960–95, Marketing Dir 1995–98, Vice-Pres. 1998–99, Vice-Pres. Nippon Mitsubishi Oil 1999–2000, Pres. Nippon Oil Corpn 2000–05, Chair. and Rep. Dir 2005–; Pres. Petroleum Asscn of Japan; Dir Japan Cooperation Center for the Middle East. *Address:* Nippon Oil Corpn, 3-12 Nishi Shimbashi 1-chome, Minato-ku, Tokyo 105-8412, Japan (office). *Telephone:* (3) 3502-1131 (office). *Fax:* (3) 3502-9352 (office). *E-mail:* info@eneos.co.jp (office). *Website:* www.eneos.co.jp (office).

WATERMAN, Ewen Leith, BEcons; Australian civil servant; b. 2 Dec. 1943, Adelaide, S Australia; s. of Gordon Waterman and Elsie Waterman (née Batty); m. Barbara Prideaux 1966; two s. one d.; ed Pulteney Grammar School, Adelaide, Univ. of Adelaide; Gen. Financial and Econ. Policy Div., Australian Treasury 1967–72, Overseas Econ. Relations Div., 1973–75, Asst Sec. State and Local Govt Finances Br. 1982–84, Prin. Adviser, Gen. Financial and Econ. Policy Div., 1984–85, First Asst Sec., Revenue Loans and Investment Div. 1985–87, Capital Markets Div. 1987–89, Deputy Sec. (Financial) 1989–93; Prime Minister's Dept 1972; Counsellor (Financial), Australian Embassy, Washington, DC 1976–79; Sec. Australian Loan Council 1986–87, Australian Nat. Debt Comm. 1986–87; Exec. Dir IMF, Washington, DC 1993–97; Exec. Dir Access Economics 1997–2001; Man. Dir Export Finance and Insurance Corpn (EFIC) 2001–03. *Leisure interests:* tennis, golf. *Address:* Export Finance and Insurance Corporation, 22 Pitt Street, Sydney, NSW 2000, Australia. *Telephone:* (2) 9201-2111. *Fax:* (2) 9201-5222. *E-mail:* info@efic.gov.au. *Website:* www.efic.gov.au.

WATERS, John; American film director, actor, producer and screenwriter; b. 22 April 1946, Baltimore, Md; given an 8 mm camera aged 17; formed repertory troupe Dreamland Players to produce films. *Films include:* dir, producer, actor, writer, ed. and cinematographer: Hag in a Black Leather Jacket 1964, Roman Candles 1966, Eat Your Makeup 1968, The Diane Linkletter Story 1969, Mondo Trasho 1969, Pink Flamingos 1972, Hairspray (co-producer) 1988; producer, dir and writer: Multiple Maniacs 1970, Female Trouble 1974, Desperate Living 1977, Polyester 1981; dir, actor and writer: Cry-Baby 1990, Serial Mom 1994, Pecker 1998, Cecil B. DeMented 2000; dir and writer: A Dirty Shame 2004, This Filthy World 2006; actor: Sweet and Lowdown 1999, Blood Feast 2: All U Can Eat 2002, Seed of Chucky 2004. *Television includes:* Family Album (actor) 1994. *Publications include:* Shock Value: A Tasteful Book About Bad Taste 1981, Crackpot: The Obsession of John Waters 1986, Role Models 2010; articles for National Lampoon. *Address:* c/o Creative Artists Agency, 9830 Wilshire Blvd, Beverly Hills, CA 90212-1825, USA. *Telephone:* (310) 288-4545. *Fax:* (310) 288-4800. *Website:* www.caa.com.

WATERS, Ralph Graham, CPEng, FIEAust, MBus; Australian engineer and business executive; *Chairman, Woolworths Limited;* ed Curtin Univ. of Technology; has eng and man. experience in London and the Middle East; fmr Man. Dir Email Ltd; fmr Chief Exec. Fletcher Building Ltd, mem. Bd of Dirs 2001–, currently Chair.; Dir and Chair. Fisher & Paykel Appliances Holdings Ltd 2001–11; mem. Bd of Dirs Woolworths Ltd 2011–, Chair. 2012–, mem. People Policy Cttee (Chair. 2011–12), Audit, Risk Man. and Compliance Cttee, Nomination Cttee; Dir, Fonterra Co-operative Group Ltd 2006–13, Westpac New Zealand Ltd 2006–12, Asciano Ltd 2012–; Chair. Cricket World Cup 2015 Ltd; Fellow, Inst. of Engineers Australia. *Address:* Woolworths Ltd, PO Box 8000, Baulkham Hills, NSW 2153 (office); Woolworths Ltd, 1 Woolworths Way, Bella Vista, NSW 2153, Australia (office). *Telephone:* (2) 8885-0000 (office). *E-mail:* info@woolworthslimited.com.au (office). *Website:* www.woolworthslimited.com.au (office).

WATERS, Sarah, PhD; British author; b. 1966, Neyland, Wales; ed Univs of Kent, Lancaster and London; fmr Assoc. Lecturer, Open Univ.; Betty Trask Award 1999, Mail on Sunday/John Llewellyn Rhys Prize 1999, CWA Ellis Peters Historical Dagger 2002, British Book Award for Author of the Year 2002. *Publications include:* Tipping the Velvet 1998, Affinity (Sunday Times Young Writer of the Year 2000, Somerset Maugham Award 2000) 1999, Fingersmith 2002, The Night Watch 2006, The Little Stranger 2009. *Leisure interests:* cinema, theatre. *Address:* c/o Greene & Heaton (Authors' Agents) Ltd, 37 Goldhawk Road, London, W12 8QQ, England (office). *Telephone:* (20) 8749-0315 (office). *Website:* www.sarahwaters.com.

WATERSTON, Robert Hugh, BSE, MD, PhD; American geneticist and academic; *William H. Gates III Endowed Chair in Biomedical Sciences and Chairman of the Department of Genome Sciences, University of Washington, Seattle;* b. 17 Sept. 1943, Detroit; ed Princeton Univ., courses in biology in Germany, Univ. of Chicago; NIH Predoctoral Trainee 1968–71; American Cancer Soc. Postdoctoral Fellowship 1972–74; Muscular Dystrophy Asscn Postdoctoral Fellowship 1975–76; Postdoctoral Researcher, MRC Lab. of Molecular Biology, Cambridge, UK 1972–74, 1975–76, Sabbatical Visitor, Dir's Div. 1985–86; Postdoctoral Researcher, Children's Hosp. Medical Center, Boston, Mass 1974–75; Asst Prof., Dept of Anatomy and Neurobiology, Washington Univ., St Louis, Mo. 1976–80, Asst Prof. of Genetics, Washington Univ. School of Medicine 1980–81, Assoc. Prof. of Genetics 1981–87, Prof. of Genetics 1987–91, Prof. and Acting Head, Dept of Genetics 1991–93, James S. McDonnell Prof. and Chair. Dept of Genetics 1993–2002; William H. Gates III Endowed Chair in Biomedical Sciences and Chair. Dept of Genome Sciences, Univ. of Washington, Seattle, Wash. 2003–; American Heart Asscn Established Investigator 1980–85; John Simon Guggenheim Fellowship 1985–86; City of Medicine Award, Dan David Prize, The Dan David Foundation, Gairdner Award (co-recipient), The Gairdner Foundation, General Motors Prize (co-recipient), George W. Beadle Medal, Genetics Soc. of America, Gruber Genetics Prize, The Peter and Patricia Gruber Foundation 2005.

Publications: numerous scientific papers in professional journals. *Address:* Department of Genome Sciences, Foege S-350D, Box 355065, University of Washington School of Medicine, 1705 NE Pacific Street, Seattle, WA 98195-5065, USA (office). *Telephone:* (206) 685-7347 (office). *Fax:* (206) 685-7301 (office). *E-mail:* waterston@gs.washington.edu (office). *Website:* waterston.gs.washington.edu (office).

WATERSTONE, Timothy John Stuart, MA; British business executive; b. 30 May 1939; s. of Malcolm Waterstone and Sylvia Sawday; m. 1st Patricia Harcourt-Poole (divorced); two s. one d.; m. 2nd Clare Perkins (divorced); one s. two d.; m. 3rd Mary Rose (Rosie) Alison; two d.; ed Tonbridge School and St Catharine's Coll., Cambridge; Carritt Moran, Calcutta 1962–64; Allied Breweries 1964–73; W. H. Smith 1973–81; Founder, Chair. and Chief Exec. Waterstone's Booksellers Ltd 1982–93; Chair. Priory Investments Ltd 1990–95, Golden Rose Radio (London Jazz FM) 1992–93; Founder and Chair. Chelsea Stores Ltd children's stores 1996–; Chair. HMV Media Group PLC 1998–2001; Deputy Chair. Sinclair-Stevenson Ltd 1989–92; mem. Bd Yale Univ. Press 1992–, Futurestart 1992–, Virago Press 1995–96, Hill Samuel UK Emerging Cos Investment Trust PLC 1996–2000, Downing Classic VCT 1998–; Chair. Dept of Trade and Industry Working Group on Smaller Quoted Cos and Pvt. Investors 1999, Shelter 25th Anniversary Appeal Cttee 1991–92; mem. Bd London Philharmonic Orchestra 1990–97 (Trustee 1995–98), Portman House Trust 1994–96; Chair. Acad. of Ancient Music 1990–95, London Int. Festival of Theatre 1991–92, Elgar Foundation 1992–98, King's Coll. Library Bd 2000–; Co-Founder BOOKAID 1992–93; Advisory mem. Booker Prize Man. Cttee 1986–93; Chair. of Judges Prince's Youth Business Trust Awards 1990. *Publications:* Lilley and Chase 1994, An Imperfect Marriage 1995, A Passage of Lives 1996, Swimming Against the Stream: Ten Rules for Creating Your Business and Making your Life 2006, In for a Penny, In for a Pound 2010. *Leisure interest:* being with Rosie Alison. *Address:* c/o Ed Victor Ltd, 6 Bayley Street, London, WC1B 3HB, England (office).

WATKINS, Alan Keith, PhD; British business executive; b. 9 Oct. 1938, Birmingham, England; s. of the late Wilfred Watkins and of Dorothy Watkins; m. Diana E. Wynne 1963; two s.; ed Moseley Grammar School and Univ. of Birmingham; Mfg Process Research, Lucas Group Research 1962–69, Mfg and Production Eng, Lucas Batteries Ltd 1969–75, Div. Dir, Electrical Div., Lucas Aerospace Ltd 1975–82, Man. Dir Lucas Aerospace Ltd 1982–87, Man. Dir Aerospace, Lucas Industries PLC 1987–89; Man. Dir and Chief Exec. Hawker Siddeley Group PLC 1989–91; CEO London Transport 1992–94, Vice-Chair. 1992–93, Deputy Chair. 1993–94, Dir Senior Engineering Group (now Senior PLC) 1994–2001, Deputy Chair. 1995–96, Chair. 1996–2001; Chair. High Duty Alloys Ltd 1997–2000; Dir (non-exec.), Dobson Park Industries PLC 1992–95, Hepworth PLC 1995–98, Carey Holdings Ltd 1997, Eyres Forgemaster Ltd; mem. Review Bd for Govt Contracts from 1993. *Leisure interests:* tennis, photography, golf, hot-air ballooning, vintage cars. *Address:* c/o Senior PLC, The Dower House, Grove Lane, Lapworth, Solihull, West Midlands, B94 6AR, England.

WATKINS, David John, BA, FRSA; British jewellery artist, sculptor and academic; *Head of Department and Professor of Goldsmithing, Silversmithing, Metalwork and Jewellery, Royal College of Art;* b. 14 Nov. 1940, Wolverhampton; m. Wendy Ann Jopling Ramshaw 1962; one s. one d.; ed Wolverhampton Grammar School and Univ. of Reading; sculptor, musician, special effects model maker (including for film 2001: A Space Odyssey) and jewellery designer 1963–71; co-f. with Wendy Ramshaw the fashion jewellery co. Something Special 1965; Visiting Lecturer, Berkshire Coll. of Art, Guildford School of Art 1964–66; own studios for jewellery and sculpture 1971–; est. second studio/workshop for large-scale forged and fabricated steel, utilising combination of eng and hot metal processes for sculpture and public art projects 1980s; mem. Membership Cttee, Crafts Council 1976–78; Artist-in-Residence, Western Australian Inst. for Tech. 1978 Collection Cttee, Crafts Council 1983–84; Visiting Prof., Bezalel Acad., Jerusalem, Israel 1984; mem. Bd of Trustees Haystack Mountain School of Crafts, Me, USA 1999–; Head of Dept and Prof. of Goldsmithing, Silversmithing, Metalwork and Jewellery, Royal Coll. of Art, London 1984–; works in major collections, including American Craft Museum, Australian Nat. Gallery, Birmingham City Museum and Art Gallery, Crafts Council, London, Die Neue Sammlung, Munich, Kunstgewerbe Museum, Berlin, Kunstindustrimuseet, Oslo, Musée des Arts Decoratifs, Paris, Museum für Angewandte Kunst, Cologne, Museum für Kunst und Gewerbe, Hamburg, Nat. Gallery of Victoria, Nat. Museum of Modern Art, Tokyo, Nat. Museums of Scotland, Schmuckmuseum, Pforzheim, Science Museum, London, Stedelijk Museum, Amsterdam, Victoria & Albert Museum, London; Fellow, Chartered Society of Designers 1984; Freeman, Goldsmiths' Co. 1988, Liveryman 1989; De Beers Diamonds Today 1974, Crafts Advisory Cttee Bursary 1976, Japan Foundation Travel Award 1978, Art for Architecture Award, Royal Soc. of Arts 1995. *Publications include:* The Best in Contemporary Jewellery 1994, A Design Sourcebook: Jewellery 1999, The Paper Jewellery Collection 2000; subject of biog., David Watkins—Wendy Ramshaw: A Life's Partnership 2009. *Leisure interest:* listening to jazz and classical music. *Address:* Royal College of Art, Kensington Gore, London, SW7 2EU, England (office). *Telephone:* (20) 7590-4261 (office). *E-mail:* david.watkins@rca.ac.uk (office). *Website:* www.rca.ac.uk (office).

WATSON, Emily; British actress; b. 14 Jan. 1967, London, England; m. Jack Waters; one s. one d.; ed London Drama Studio, Univ. of Bristol. *Theatre includes:* Uncle Vanya, Twelfth Night (both at Donmar Warehouse, London 2002, at Brooklyn Acad. of Music, New York 2003). *Films include:* Breaking the Waves (New York Soc. of Film Critics Award, Nat. Soc. of Film Critics Award, European Film Award, Evening Standard Film Award) 1996, Mill on the Floss 1997, Metroland 1997, The Boxer 1997, Hilary and Jackie (British Independent Film Award) 1998, Angela's Ashes 1999, Trixie 2000, The Luzhin Defense 2000, In Search of the Assassin 2001, Gosford Park 2001, Red Dragon 2002, Punch-Drunk Love 2002, Equilibrium 2002, Boo, Zino and the Snurks (voice) 2004, The Life and Death of Peter Sellers 2004, The Proposition 2004, Separate Lies 2005, Corpse Bride (voice) 2005, Wah Wah 2005, Crusade in Jeans 2005, Miss Potter 2006, The Waterhorse 2007, Fireflies in the Garden 2008, Synecdoche, New York 2008, Within the Whirlwind 2008, Cold Souls 2009, Oranges and Sunshine 2010, Cemetery Junction 2010, War Horse 2011, Little Boy 2012, Anna Karenina 2012, Some Girl(s) 2013, Molly Moon 2013, Belle 2013, The Book Thief 2013. *Television includes:* The Memory Keeper's Daughter 2008, Appropriate Adult (BAFTA Award

for Best Leading Actress 2012) 2011, The Politician's Husband 2013. *Address:* c/o Independent Talent Group, Oxford House, 76 Oxford Street, London, W1D 1BS, England (office). *E-mail:* info@independenttalent.com (office). *Website:* www.independenttalent.com (office).

WATSON, Emma Charlotte Duerre; British actress; b. 15 April 1990, Paris, France; d. of Chris Watson and Jacqueline Luesby; ed Dragon School, Headington School, Oxford; learned acting, singing and dancing at Stagecoach Theatre Arts, Oxford; performed in several school plays including Arthur: The Young Years and The Happy Prince; model representing Burberry. *Films include:* Harry Potter and the Philosopher's Stone (Young Artist Award for Best Performance in a Feature Film – Leading Young Actress 2002) 2001, Harry Potter and the Chamber of Secrets 2002, Harry Potter and the Prisoner of Azkaban 2004, Harry Potter and the Goblet of Fire 2005, Harry Potter and the Order of the Phoenix 2007, December Boys 2007, The Tale of Despereaux (voice) 2008, Harry Potter and the Half-Blood Prince 2009, Harry Potter and the Deathly Hallows: Part 1 2010, Harry Potter and the Deathly Hallows: Part 2 2011, My Week with Marilyn 2011, The Perks of Being a Wallflower 2012. *Television includes:* Ballet Shoes 2007. *Address:* Special Artists Agency Inc, 9465 Wilshire Blvd, Suite 470, Beverly Hills, CA 90210, USA (office). *Telephone:* (310) 859-9688 (office). *E-mail:* info@specialartists.com (office). *Website:* www.specialartists.com (office).

WATSON, James Dewey, BS, PhD; American biologist and academic; *Chancellor Emeritus, Cold Spring Harbor Laboratory;* b. 6 April 1928, Chicago, Ill.; s. of James D. Watson and Jean Mitchell Watson; m. Elizabeth Lewis 1968; two s.; ed Univs of Chicago and Indiana; Research Fellow, US Nat. Research Council, Univ. of Copenhagen, Denmark 1950–51; Fellow, US Nat. Foundation, Cavendish Lab., Univ. of Cambridge, England 1951–53, 1955–56; Sr Research Fellow in Biology, Calif. Inst. of Tech. 1953–55; Asst Prof. of Biology, Harvard Univ. 1956–58, Assoc. Prof. 1958–61, Prof. 1961–76; Dir Cold Spring Harbor Lab. 1968–93, Pres. 1994–2003, Chancellor 2003–07, Chancellor Emer. 2007–; Assoc. Dir NIH, USA 1988–89, Dir Nat. Center for Human Genome Research, NIH 1989–92; Newton-Abraham Visiting Prof., Univ. of Oxford, UK 1994; mem. NAS, Danish Acad. of Arts and Sciences, American Acad. of Arts and Sciences, American Soc. of Biological Chemists; Sr Fellow, Soc. of Fellows, Harvard Univ. 1964–70; mem. American Philosophical Soc. 1978; Foreign mem. Royal Soc. 1981, USSR (now Russian) Acad. of Sciences 1989; Hon. Fellow, Clare Coll., Cambridge 1967; Hon. KBE 2002; Hon. DSc (Chicago, Indiana, Long Island, Adelphi, Brandeis, Hofstra, Harvard, Rockefeller, State Univ. of New York, Albert Einstein Coll. of Medicine, Clarkson Coll., Stellenbosch, Fairfield, Cambridge, Oxford, Charleston Medical Coll., Washington Coll., Univ. of Judaism, Univ. Coll. London, Wesleyan, Widener, Dartmouth, Trinity Coll. Dublin); Hon. LLD (Notre Dame) 1965; Hon. MD (Buenos Aires) 1986, (Charles Univ., Prague) 1998; Hon. DSc (Rutgers Univ.) 1988, (Bard Coll.) 1991, (Melbourne) 1997; Dr hc (Barcelona) 2005, (Royal Irish Acad.) 2002, (Int. Acad. of Humanism) 2005; Eli Lilly Award in Biochemistry 1959, Lasker Prize (American Public Health Asscn) 1960, Nobel Prize for Medicine (with F. H. C. Crick and M. F. H. Wilkins) 1962, John J. Carty Gold Medal (Nat. Acad. of Sciences) 1971, Medal of Freedom 1977, Gold Medal Award, Nat. Inst. of Social Sciences 1984, Kaul Foundation Award for Excellence 1992, Copley Medal of Royal Soc. 1993, Nat. Biotechnology Award 1993; Lomosonov Medal 1994, Nat. Medal of Science 1997, Liberty Medal Award 2000, Benjamin Franklin Medal 2001, Gairdner Award 2002, Lotos Club Medal of Merit 2004, Othmer Gold Medal, Chemical Heritage Foundation 2005. *Achievements include:* discovered structure of DNA (with Francis Crick) 1953. *Publications:* Molecular Biology of the Gene 1965, The Double Helix 1968, The DNA Story (with John Tooze) 1981, Recombinant DNA– A Short Course 1983 (co-author), The Molecular Biology of the Cell (co-author) 1986, Recombinant DNA (2nd edn) (co-author) 1992, A Passion for DNA 2000, Genes, Girls and Gamow 2001, DNA– The Secret of Life 2003, Avoid Boring People: And Other Lessons from a Life in Science (auto-biog.) 2007, Darwin: The Indelible Stamp (Ed.) 2007; papers on structure of deoxyribonucleic acid (DNA), on protein synthesis and on the induction of cancer by viruses. *Address:* c/o Bungtown Road, Cold Spring Harbor, New York, NY 11724, USA (office). *Telephone:* (516) 367-8311 (office).

WATSON, James Kay Graham, BSc, PhD, FRS, FRSC; British/Canadian research scientist; *Researcher Emeritus, National Research Council of Canada;* b. 20 April 1936, Denny, Scotland; s. of Thomas Watson and Mary C. Miller; m. Carolyn M. L. Kerr 1981; ed Denny High School, High School of Stirling and Univ. of Glasgow; Carnegie Sr Scholar, Dept of Chem., Univ. Coll. London 1961–63; Postdoctoral Fellow, Nat. Research Council, Ottawa, Canada 1963–65; ICI Research Fellow, Univ. of Reading 1965–66, Lecturer in Chemical Physics 1966–71; Visiting Assoc. Prof. in Physics, Ohio State Univ. 1971–75; SRC Sr Research Fellow in Chem., Univ. of Southampton 1975–79, 1980–82; Visiting Scientist, Nat. Research Council, Ottawa, Canada 1979–80, Sr Research Officer 1982–87, Prin. 1987–2007, Researcher Emer. 2008–; Fellow, American Physical Soc. 1990; Chem. Soc. Award 1974, Plyler Prize, American Physical Soc. 1986, RSC Henry Marshall Tory Medal 1999, ACS E.B.Wilson Award 2004. *Publications:* more than 160 articles on molecular physics in learned journals. *Leisure interests:* music, golf, tree-watching. *Address:* Steacie Institute for Molecular Sciences, National Research Council of Canada, Ottawa, ON K1A 0R6 (office); 183 Stanley Avenue, Ottawa, ON K1M 1P2, Canada (home). *Telephone:* (613) 990-0739 (office); (613) 745-7928 (home). *Fax:* (613) 991-2648 (office). *E-mail:* james.watson@nrc-cnrc.gc.ca (office).

WATSON, Jim, BA; Canadian politician; *Mayor of Ottawa;* b. 1961; ed Carleton Univ.; mem. Ottawa City Council for Capital Ward 1992–98; Mayor of Ottawa 1997–2000, 2010–; Pres. and CEO Canadian Tourism Comm. 2000–03; host The New RO@Noon, CHRO-TV's 2003; regular contributor to CFRA (radio station) and Ottawa Citizen (daily newpaper); mem. Ont. Prov. Parl. for Ottawa West-Nepean 2003–10, Minister of Consumer and Business Services 2003–05, of Health Promotion 2005–07, of Municipal Affairs and Housing 2007–10; mem. bd of several community orgs including Riverside Hospital, Nat. Arts Centre, Christmas Exchange of Ottawa, Forum for Young Canadians; Chair. United Way 2002 campaign; several awards including Maclean's magazine's 100 Young Canadians To Watch, Carleton Univ. Honours Award, City of Ottawa Key to the City, Queen's Golden Jubilee Medal, Ontario Pharmacists' Asscn Visionary Award, Canadian Council for Tobacco Control Nat. Leadership Award. *Address:* 110 Laurier Avenue

West, Ottawa, ON K1P 1J1, Canada (office). *Telephone:* (613) 580-2496 (office). *Fax:* (613) 580-2509 (office). *E-mail:* Jim.Watson@ottawa.ca (office). *Website:* www .ottawa.ca/city_hall/mayor_council/mayor/index_en.html (office).

WATSON, John S., BA, MBA; American business executive; *Chairman and CEO, Chevron Corporation;* b. 1956, Calif.; ed Univ. of California, Davis, Univ. of Chicago; joined Chevron Corpn as financial analyst 1980, held financial, analytical and supervisory positions before being elected Pres. Chevron Canada Ltd 1996, named Vice-Pres. Chevron Corpn, with responsibility for strategic planning and mergers and acquisitions 1998, led co.'s integration effort following Chevron-Texaco merger, Chief Financial Officer 2001–05, Pres. Chevron Int. Exploration and Production 2005–07, Exec. Vice-Pres. for Strategy and Devt 2008–09, Vice-Chair. Chevron Corpn 2009–10, Chair. and CEO 2010–; Chair. Bd of Dirs and Exec. Cttee, American Petroleum Inst.; mem. Nat. Petroleum Council, The Business Council, Business Roundtable, J.P. Morgan Int. Council, American Soc. of Corp. Execs, Univ. of California, Davis Chancellor's Bd of Advisors. *Address:* Chevron Corporation, 6001 Bollinger Canyon Road, San Ramon, CA 94583, USA (office). *Telephone:* (925) 842-1000 (office). *Fax:* (925) 842-3530 (office). *E-mail:* comment@chevron.com (office). *Website:* www.chevron.com (office).

WATSON, Sir Robert Tony, Kt, CMG, PhD, FRS; British environmental scientist and academic; *Chief Scientific Adviser, Department for Environment, Food and Rural Affairs;* ed Queen Mary Coll., London; fmr Dir Science Div. and Chief Scientist for the Office of Mission to Planet Earth, NASA; fmr Assoc. Dir for Environment, Office of the President, The White House, Washington, DC, USA; joined the World Bank as Sr Scientific Adviser in Environment Dept 1996, apptd Dir of Environment Dept and Head of Environment Sector Bd 1997, later Chief Scientist and Dir for Environmentally and Socially Sustainable Devt; Prof. of Environmental Sciences and Dir of Strategic Devt, Tyndall Centre, Univ. of East Anglia 2007–; Chief Scientific Adviser, Dept for Environment, Food and Rural Affairs 2007–; Chair. Global Environment Facility's Scientific and Tech. Advisory Panel 1991–94, Intergovernmental Panel on Climate Change (IPCC) 1997–2002; Co-Chair. Millennium Ecosystem Assessment 2000–05, Int. Scientific Assessment of Stratospheric Ozone; Dir Int. Assessment of Agricultural Science and Tech. for Devt; fmr Chair. or Co-Chair. of other int. scientific assessments, including the IPCC Working Group II, UNEP/WMO, UNEP Global Biodiversity Assessment; NAS Award for Scientific Reviewing 1992, AAAS Award for Scientific Freedom and Responsibility 1993. *Publications:* numerous papers in professional journals. *Address:* Room ZICER 1.22, School of Environmental Sciences, University of East Anglia, Norwich Research Park, Norwich, NR4 7TJ, England (office). *Telephone:* (1603) 593118 (office). *Fax:* (1603) 593901 (office). *E-mail:* robert .watson@uea.ac.uk (office). *Website:* www.uea.ac.uk/env (office).

WATSON, Shane Robert; Australian professional cricketer; b. 17 June 1981, Ipswich, Queensland; m. Lee Furlong 2010; all-rounder; right-handed batsman; right-arm fast-medium bowler; plays for Tasmania 2001–04, Australia 2002– (Vice-Capt. Test, ODI and T20I teams 2011–13), Queensland 2004–09, Hants. 2005, Rajasthan Royals 2008–, NSW 2009–, Sydney Sixers 2011–12, Brisbane Heat 2012–; First-class debut: 2000/01; Test debut: Australia v Pakistan, Sydney 2–5 Jan. 2005; One-Day Int. (ODI) debut: S Africa v Australia, at Centurion 25 March 2002; T20I debut: S Africa v Australia, Johannesburg 24 Feb. 2006; has played in 51 Tests, taken 68 wickets, average 31.83 and scored 3,343 runs (4 centuries, 22 half-centuries), highest score 176, average 36.33, best bowling (innings) 6/33, (match) 6/51; ODIs: 173 matches, scored 5,256 runs, average 41.06, highest score 185 not out, took 163 wickets, average 30.26, best bowling 4/36; First-class: 124 matches, 8,822 runs, average 43.67, highest score 203 not out, took 202 wickets, average 28.77, best bowling 7/69; mem. winning Australian ODI team, ICC (Int. Cricket Council) Cricket World Cup 2003, 2007; made 185 not out off 96 balls against Bangladesh 11 April 2011, hitting 15 sixes and breaking record held by Xavier Marshall, also highest ODI score by an Australian batsman, passing Matthew Hayden's score of 181 not out set in 2007; mem. Ashes-winning team against England 2013–14; Allan Border Medal 2010, 2011, Test Player of the Year 2011, One Day Int. Player of the Year 2011, named Player of the Tournament, ICC World Twenty20 2012. *Address:* c/o Cricket NSW, PO Box 333, Paddington, NSW 2021; c/o Cricket NSW, Driver Avenue, Moore Park, NSW 2021 Australia. *Telephone:* (2) 8302-6000. *Fax:* (2) 8302-6080. *E-mail:* info@cricketnsw.com. *Website:* www.cricketnsw.com.

WATSON, Thomas Sturges (Tom), BS; American professional golfer; b. 4 Sept. 1949, Kansas City, Mo.; s. of Raymond Etheridge Watson and Sarah Elizabeth Ridge; m. 1st Linda Tova Rubin 1972; one s. one d.; m. 2nd Hilary Watson 1999; three step-c.; ed Stanford Univ.; turned professional 1971; The Open Champion 1975, 1977, 1980, 1982, 1983; record low aggregate for The Open Championship of 268, record two single round scores of 65, lowest final 36-hole score of 130, Turnberry 1977; won US Masters title 1977, 1981; won US Open 1982; won World Series 1975, 1977, 1980; winner of numerous other open championships; top money winner on US Professional Golf Asscn (PGA) circuit 1977, 1978, 1979, 1980; first player ever to win in excess of $500,000 in prize money in one season 1980; Ryder Cup Player 1977, 1981, 1983, 1989 (Capt. at The Belfry 1993 (won), Gleneagles 2014); Sr Tour victories: Bank One Championship 1999, IR Sr Tour Championship 2000, Sr PGA Championship 2001, Sr Tour Championship 2002, Sr British Open 2003, 2005, 2007; joined European Seniors Tour 2011; 71 professional wins; became involved with golf course design early 1990s, has designed courses through his co. Tom Watson Design, Kan. in USA, Ireland and Japan; visited US troops in Iraq with Corey Pavin and Tim Simpson 2007, 2009; active in Kansas City-area charitable endeavours, including Children's Mercy Hosp. and devt of golf courses for junior players; Hon. mem. Royal and Ancient Golf Club of St Andrews 1999; US PGA Player of the Year 1977, 1978, 1979, 1980, 1982, 1984, PGA Tour leading money winner 1977, 1978, 1979, 1980, 1984, Vardon Trophy 1977, 1978, 1979, Bob Jones Award 1987, PGA World Golf Hall of Fame 1988, Old Tom Morris Award 1992, ranked by Golf Digest magazine as the 10th greatest golfer of all time 2000, Payne Stewart Award 2003, Charles Schwab Cup 2003, 2005, Card Walker Award 2003. *Publications:* Getting Back into Basics (co-author) 1992, Tom Watson's Strategic Golf 1995, The Timeless Swing 2011; has written a golf instruction column in Golf Digest magazine since the mid-1970s. *Leisure interests:* current affairs, outdoor life, baseball (Kansas City Royals fan). *Address:* c/o PGA Tour, 100 PGA TOUR Boulevard, Ponte Vedra Beach, FL 32082; 1901 West 47th

Place, Suite 200, Shawnee Mission, KS 66205, USA. *Website:* www.pgatour.com/ players/player.02256.tom-watson.html; www.tomwatson.com.

WATT, James Gaius, BS, JD; American lawyer and fmr politician; b. 31 Jan. 1938, Lusk, Wyo.; s. of William G. Watt and Lois M. Watt (née Williams); m. Leilani Bomgardner 1957; one s. one d.; ed Univ. of Wyoming; Instructor, Coll. of Commerce and Industry, Univ. of Wyo. 1960–62; admitted to Wyo. Bar 1962, US Supreme Court Bar 1966; Legis. Asst, Counsel to Senator Simpson of Wyo. 1962–66; Sec. Natural Resources Comm. and Environmental Pollution Advisory Panel, US Chamber of Commerce 1966–69; Deputy Asst Sec. for Water and Power, Dept of the Interior 1969–72; Dir Bureau of Outdoor Recreation, US Dept of the Interior 1972–75; Vice-Chair. Fed. Power Comm. 1975–77; Founding Pres., Chief Legal Officer, Mountain States Legal Foundation, Denver 1977–80; US Sec. of the Interior 1981–83; practised law, Washington, DC 1983–86, Jackson Hole, Wyo. 1986–; Chair. of Bd Environmental Diagnostics Inc. 1984–87, Disease Detection Int. 1987–90. *Publication:* The Courage of a Conservative (with Doug Wead) 1985. *Address:* P.O. Box 3705, 755 East Paintbrush Drive, Box 3705, Jackson, WY 83001, USA.

WATTS, Charles (Charlie) Robert; British musician (drums); b. 2 June 1941, London, England; m. Shirley Anne Shepherd 1964; one d.; fmr mem. Blues Incorporated; mem. The Rolling Stones 1963–, numerous tours world-wide; toured with Charlie Watts Orchestra 1985–86; Nordoff-Robbins Silver Clef 1982, Grammy Lifetime Achievement Award 1986, Ivor Novello Award for Outstanding Contribution to British Music 1991. *Recordings include:* albums: with The Rolling Stones: The Rolling Stones 1964, The Rolling Stones No. 2 1965, Out Of Our Heads 1965, Aftermath 1966, Between The Buttons 1967, Their Satanic Majesties Request 1967, Beggar's Banquet 1968, Let It Bleed 1969, Get Yer Ya-Ya's Out 1969, Sticky Fingers 1971, Exile On Main Street 1972, Goat's Head Soup 1973, It's Only Rock And Roll 1974, Black And Blue 1976, Some Girls 1978, Emotional Rescue 1980, Tattoo You 1981, Still Life 1982, Undercover 1983, Dirty Work 1986, Steel Wheels 1989, Flashpoint 1991, Voodoo Lounge 1994, Stripped 1995, Bridges to Babylon 1997, Forty Licks 2002, Live Licks 2004, A Bigger Bang 2005; solo: Live at Fulham Town Hall 1986, From One Charlie 1992, Tribute To Charlie Parker With Strings 1991, Warm & Tender 1993, Long Ago and Far Away 1996, Charlie Watts/Jim Keltner Project 2000, Watts At Scott's 2004, The Magic of Boogie Woogie 2010, The ABC&D of Boogie Woogie Live In Paris 2012. *Films include:* Sympathy For The Devil 1969, Gimme Shelter 1970, Ladies and Gentlemen, The Rolling Stones 1977, Let's Spend the Night Together 1983, Flashpoint 1991, Shine a Light 2007. *Publications include:* Ode to a High Flying Bird 1965, According to the Rolling Stones (autobiog., jtly) 2003. *Leisure interest:* jazz music. *Address:* c/o Rosebud Agency, PO Box 170429, San Francisco, CA 94117, USA (office). *Telephone:* (415) 386-3456 (office). *Website:* www.rollingstones.com.

WATTS, Donald Walter, AM, PhD, FACE; Australian business executive and academic administrator; *Senior Policy Advisor, University of Notre Dame, Australia;* b. 1 April 1934, Western Australia; s. of Horace Frederick Watts and Esme Anne White; m. Michelle Rose Yeomans 1960; two s.; ed Hale School, Perth, Univ. of Western Australia, Univ. Coll. London, UK; CSIRO Postdoctoral Fellow 1959; Dept of Scientific and Industrial Research Postdoctoral Fellow 1961; Personal Chair. in Physical and Inorganic Chem., Univ. of Western Australia 1977–79; Dir Western Australian Inst. of Technology 1980–86; Japan Foundation Visiting Fellow 1984; Vice-Chancellor Curtin Univ. of Tech. 1987; Pres. and Vice-Chancellor Bond Univ. 1987–90, Prof. Emer. 1990–; CEO Trade Devt Zone Authority, Darwin 1990–91; Chair. NT Employment & Training Authority 1991–93; Prof. of Science and Educ. and Dean Coll. of Arts and Sciences, Univ. of Notre Dame, Western Australia 1995–97, Dean of Research 1998–2004, Sr Policy Adviser (part-time) 2004–; Dir Advanced Energy Systems 1995–96 (Chair. 1997–2003); Chair. and Dir Tech. Training Inst. Pty Ltd 2001–03; Councillor Australian Acad. of Technological Sciences and Eng 2001–; mem. ACS, Chemical Educ. Sub-cttee, Australian Acad. of Science; Fellow, Royal Australian Chemical Inst., Australian Acad. of Tech. Sciences and Eng; Hon. Fellow, Marketing Inst. of Singapore; Hon. DTech (Curtin Univ. of Tech.) 1987, Hon. DUniv (Bond Univ.) 2009, Dr hc (Univ. of Western Australia) 2001; Hackett Scholar 1953, Gledden Fellow 1957, Fulbright Scholar 1967, Rennie Medal 1967, Leighton Medal, Royal Australian Chemical Inst. 1987, Australian and New Zealand Asscn for the Advancement of Science (ANZAAS) Medal 1998. *Publications include:* The School Chemistry Project – A Secondary School Chemistry Syllabus for Comment (with N. S. Bayliss) 1978, Chemical Properties and Reactions (with A. R. H. Cole and R. B. Bucat) 1978, Chemistry for Australian Secondary School Students (with N. S. Bayliss) 1979, Elements of Chemistry: Earth, Air, Fire and Water 1984, Higher Education in Australia: A Way Forward, Policy Paper No. 8 1986, The Private Potential of Australian Higher Education 1987, A Private Approach to Higher Education 1987; numerous scientific publs and articles on education and policy. *Leisure interests:* golf, tennis, reading. *Address:* University of Notre Dame Australia, Mouat Street, PO Box 1225, Fremantle, WA 6959 (office); 87 Evans Street, Shenton Park, WA 6008, Australia (home). *Telephone:* (8) 9433-0862 (office); (8) 9381-1667 (home). *E-mail:* dwatts@nd.edu.au (office); don9chel@ bigpond.com. *Website:* www.nd.edu.au (office).

WATTS, Sir Philip Beverley, Kt, KCMG, BA, BSc, MSc, FInstP, FEI, FRGS, FGS, FRSA; British oil company executive (retd); *Assistant Curate, Binfield Parish, Oxford Diocese;* b. 25 June 1945, Leicester, England; s. of Samuel Watts and Philippa Watts (née Wale); m. Janet Edna Watts (née Lockwood) 1966; one s. one d.; ed Wyggeston Grammar School, Leicester and Univ. of Leeds, Open Univ., Oxford Brookes Univ.; science teacher, Methodist Boys High School, Freetown, Sierra Leone 1966–68; joined Shell Int. 1969; held various posts: seismologist, Indonesia 1970–74, geophysicist UK/Europe 1974–77, Exploration Man., Norway 1978–81, Div. Head, Malaysia, Brunei, Singapore, London 1981–83, Exploration Dir, UK 1983–85; Head EP Liaison—Europe, The Hague 1986–88, Head EP Econs and Planning, The Hague 1989–91, Man. Dir, Nigeria 1991–94, Regional Co-ordinator, Europe, The Hague 1994–95; Dir Planning, Environment and External Affairs, London 1996–97; Chair. Royal Dutch/Shell Group 2001–04 (Group Man. Dir 1997–2004); Chair. Shell Transport and Trading 2001 (Man. Dir 1997–2004); Chair. World Business Council for Sustainable Devt 2001–03 (mem. Exec. Cttee 1998–2004); Chair. ICC-UK 1998–2004 (mem. Governing Body 1997–2004), Worldwide ICC, Exec. Bd 1997–2000; Asst Curate, Binfield Parish, Oxford

Diocese. *Leisure interests:* travel, gardening, reading. *Address:* Sunnyridge, Hill Farm Lane, Binfield, Berks., RG42 5NR, England (home). *E-mail:* philbwatts@googlemail.com (home).

WAU, Guma; Papua New Guinea politician; mem. Nat. Parl. for Kerowagi constituency; Minister for Tourism, Arts and Culture 2010, Minister of Defence 2011–12; mem. United Resource Party. *Address:* c/o Department of Defence, Murray Barracks, Free Mail Bag, Boroko 111, Port Moresby, NCD, Papua New Guinea.

WAUGH, John Stewart, AB, PhD; American chemist and academic; *Institute Professor Emeritus, Massachusetts Institute of Technology;* b. 25 April 1929, Willimantic, Conn.; s. of Albert E. Waugh and Edith S. Waugh; m. Susan M. Walsh 1983; one s. one d.; ed Windham High School, Dartmouth Coll., California Inst. of Tech.; mem. Faculty, MIT 1953–, A.A. Noyes Prof. of Chem. 1973–88, Inst. Prof. 1989–96, Inst. Prof. Emer. 1996–; Visiting Scientist, USSR Acad. of Sciences 1962, Univ. of Calif. 1963, Harvard Univ. 1975; Visiting Prof. Max Planck Inst. for Medical Research 1971, East China Normal Univ., Shanghai 1984, Texas A & M Univ. 1986; Joliot-Curie Prof. Ecole Supérieure de Physique et Chimie, Paris 1985, 1997; Fairchild Scholar, California Inst. of Tech. 1989; Chair. Div. of Chem. Physics, American Physical Soc. 1984–85; Vice-Pres. Int. Soc. of Magnetic Resonance 1996–98, Pres. 1998–2001; mem. NAS, American Acad. of Arts and Sciences 1962–96, Slovenian Acad. of Sciences and Arts; Hon. ScD (Dartmouth Coll.) 1989; Von Humboldt Award 1971, Langmuir Award 1974, Pittsburgh Spectroscopy Award 1978, Wolf Foundation Prize in Chem. 1984, Pauling Medal 1985, Richards Medal 1992, Welch Award in Chem. 2011. *Publications:* numerous scientific research papers mainly on computational studies of spin systems; author of ANTIOPE (freeware general purpose Windows-based simulator of NMR spectra and dynamics). *Leisure interests:* sailing, harpsichord. *Address:* Department of Chemistry, Room 6-231, Massachusetts Institute of Technology, 77 Massachusetts Avenue, Cambridge, MA 02139 (office); 60 Conant Road, Lincoln, MA 01773, USA (home). *Telephone:* (617) 253-1901 (office). *Fax:* (617) 253-7030 (office). *E-mail:* jswaugh@mit.edu (office). *Website:* chemistry.mit.edu/people/waugh-john (office).

WAUGH, Richard (Rick) E., BComm (Hons), MBA; Canadian banking executive; m. Lynne Waugh; three s.; ed Univ. of Manitoba, York Univ.; began career with The Bank of Nova Scotia (Scotiabank), Winnipeg 1970, served in investment, corp., int. and retail banking areas, Sr Exec. of US Operations, New York 1985–93, Sr Exec. Vice-Pres. of Corp. Banking, responsible for Global Corp. Banking, Toronto 1993–95, Vice-Chair. of Corp. Banking 1995–98, Vice-Chair. of Int. Banking and Wealth Man. 1998–2003, mem. Bd of Dirs, Pres. and CEO 2003–13; Co-Chair. Canada-Brazil CEO Forum 2011; mem. Bd of Dirs Catalyst Inc. (Chair. Catalyst Canada Advisory Bd), Inst. of Int. Finance (IIF), Int. Monetary Conf.; Trustee, IIF's Principles for Stable Capital Flows in Emerging Markets; mem. Council of the Americas, Chair.'s Int. Advisory Council for the Americas Soc., Advisory Council of the Schulich School of Business at York Univ., Guanghua School of Man. at Peking Univ., Canadian Museum of Human Rights, amongst others; Campaign Chair. United Way of Greater Toronto 2006; has worked extensively with the MS Society, both as Hon. Chair. endMS Capital Campaign and as mem. Bd Scientific Research Foundation; Dir St Michael's Hosp., Co-Chair. Hosp.'s Campaign to build the Li Ka Shing Knowledge Inst.; Fellow, Inst. of Canadian Bankers; Order of Merit (Dominican Repub.) 2010; Hon. LLD (York Univ., Assumption Univ.); Merit of Honor, Council of the Americas, Award of Merit, B'nai Brith Canada 2008, Corp. Social Responsibility Award, Foreign Policy Asscn, New York 2009, Int. Award, Horatio Alger Asscn of Distinguished Americans 2011. *Address:* c/o The Bank of Nova Scotia (Scotiabank), 44 King Street West, Toronto, ON M5H 1H1, Canada.

WAUGH, Scott L., BA, PhD; American historian, academic and university administrator; *Executive Vice-Chancellor and Provost, University of California, Los Angeles;* ed Univ. of California, Los Angeles, Univ. of London, UK; taught in Dept of History, UCLA from 1975, Dean of Div. of Social Sciences 1992–2006, Acting Exec. Vice-Chancellor and Provost, UCLA 2006–08, Exec. Vice-Chancellor and Provost 2008–; honours, fellowships and grants from Nat. Endowment for the Humanities, American Philosophical Soc., and others, UCLA Distinguished Teaching Award, Harvey L. Eby Award for Art of Teaching, Univ. of California Pres.'s Fellowship in Humanities, UCLA Faculty Devt Award. *Publications:* two books and co-ed. of a third; numerous articles in scholarly journals. *Address:* Office of the Chancellor, University of California, Los Angeles, 2147 Murphy Hall, 405 Hilgard Avenue, Los Angeles, CA 90095-1405, USA (office). *Telephone:* (310) 825-2052 (office). *Fax:* (310) 206-6030 (office). *E-mail:* evc@conet.ucla.edu (office). *Website:* evc.ucla.edu/biography (office).

WAUGH, Stephen Rodger (Steve), AO; Australian foundation director and fmr professional cricketer; b. 2 June 1965, Canterbury, Sydney, NSW; s. of Rodger Waugh and Beverley Waugh; elder twin of Mark Edward; m. Lynette Waugh; one s. two d.; ed East Hills High School; right-hand batsman and right-arm medium-fast bowler; teams: New South Wales 1984/85–2003/04, Australia 1985–2004 (Capt. 1999–2004), Somerset 1987–88, Ireland 1998, Kent 2002; Test debut: Australia v India, Melbourne 26–30 Dec. 1985; played in 168 Tests (most capped Test player in history), scoring 10,927 runs (average 51.06, highest score 200) including 32 hundreds, taking 92 wickets (average 37.44), best bowling (innings) 5/28, (match) 8/169; played in 325 One-Day Ints (106 as Capt.), scoring 7,569 runs (average 32.90, highest score 120 not out) including three hundreds, taking 195 wickets (average 34.67), best bowling 4/33; played in 356 First-class matches, scoring 24,052 runs (average 51.94, highest score 216 not out) including 79 hundreds, taking 249 wickets (average 32.75), best bowling 6.51; shared world record 5th wicket stand of 464 (unbroken) with brother M. E. Waugh for NSW vs Western Australia, Perth 1990–91; retd Jan. 2004; Patron Camp Quality, Cerebral Palsy Asscn, Udayan Home for Girls, India; Chair. Steve Waugh Foundation; Wisden Cricketer of the Year 1989, Australian Sports Medal 2000, Australian Cricketer of the Year 2000–01, Allan Border Medal 2001, Laureus Sports Award (World's Best Team) 2001, Australian of the Year 2004, an Australian Living Treasure, one of five new members inducted into ICC (Int. Cricket Council) Cricket Hall of Fame 2009. *Publications:* South African Tour Diary 1995, Steve Waugh's West Indies Tour Diary 1996, Steve Waugh's World Cup Diary 1997, Images of Waugh, Never Satisfied, Ashes Summer (co-author), Ashes Diary 1997, 2001, Out of My Comfort Zone: Captain's Diary 2002, Never Say Die 2003. *Leisure interests:*

golf, photography, reading, writing. *Address:* c/o Team-Duet, 3 Winnie Street, Cremorne, NSW 2090, Australia (office); The Steve Waugh Foundation, GPO Box 3331, Sydney, NSW 2001, Australia. *Telephone:* (2) 9909-2188 (office); (1300) 669935. *Fax:* (2) 9909-2157 (office); (2) 9964-6255. *E-mail:* admin@duetgroup.com (office); info@stevewaughfoundation.com.au. *Website:* www.stevewaughfoundation.com.au.

WAWRINKA, Stanislas (Stan); Swiss/German professional tennis player; b. 28 March 1985, Lausanne; s. of Wolfram Wawrinka and Isabelle Wawrinka; m. Ilham Vuilloud 2009; one d.; ed distance educ. with Centre nat. d'enseignement à distance, France; right-handed (one-handed backhand); began playing int. junior events aged 14, entered the satellite circuit 2000, turned professional 2002; won French Open Junior championships 2003; gold medal for Switzerland, Men's Doubles, Summer Olympics, Beijing partnering Roger Federer 2008; won Croatia Open Umag 2006, Grand Prix Hassan II, Casablanca, Morocco 2010, Aircel Chennai Open, India 2011, 2014, Portugal Open 2014, Monte Carlo Rolex Masters 2014; won doubles, with Benoît Paire, Chennai Open 2013; Grand Slam Singles results: fourth round, Wimbledon 2008, 2009, fourth round, US Open 2008, quarterfinalist, French Open 2013, semifinalist, US Open 2013, winner, Australian Open 2014; other tournaments: semifinalist, ATP World Tour Finals, London 2013; ranked World No. 3 27 Jan. 2014; coached by Dimitri Zavialoff 1993–2010, Peter Lundgren 2010–11, Magnus Norman 2013–; Flagbearer for Switzerland, Summer Olympic Games, London 2012; mem. Admin. Council Lausanne HC ice hockey club 2011–; Swiss Team of the Year Award 2008. *Address:* c/o Nicolas Lamperin, IMG, 5 bis rue Mahias, 92100 Boulogne-Billancourt, France.

WEAH, George Tawlon Manneh Oppong Ousman; Liberian politician and fmr professional footballer; b. 1 Oct. 1966, Clara Town, Monrovia; s. of William T. Weah, Sr and Anna Quayeweah; raised by his paternal grandmother, Emma Klonjlaleh Brown; m. Clar Weah; four c.; ed Wells Hairston High School, univ. in Fla, USA; forward; worked for Liberia Telecommunications Corpn as a switchboard technician; played for Liberian and Cameroonian clubs, Young Survivors Clareton 1981–84, Bongrange Company 1984–85, Mighty Barolle 1985–86, Invincible Eleven 1986–87, Africa Sports 1987, Tonnerre Yaoundé 1987–88 (won LFA Championship 1987, Cameroon Championship 1988); player, AC Monaco 1988–92 (102 games, 47 goals), Paris Saint-Germain 1992–95 (96 games, 32 goals, won French Championship 1994, French Cup, 1991, 1993, 1995, French League Cup 1995), AC Milan 1995–2000 (114 games, 46 goals, won Serie A 1995, 1999), Chelsea (on loan) 2000 (11 games, four goals, won FA Cup 2000), Manchester City 2000 (seven games, one goal), Olympique Marseille 2000–01 (19 games, five goals), Al Jazira, UAE 2001–03 (eight games, 13 goals); player, Cameroon nat. team 1988–92 (93 games, 47 goals), Liberia nat. team 1988–2002 (60 games, 22 goals), also Tech. Dir until retd after African Nations Cup Jan. 2002; UNICEF Goodwill Amb. 1997–; Amb. for SOS Children's Villages; unsuccessful cand. for Pres. of Liberia 2005; remained active in Liberian politics, returning from USA to campaign for Congress for Democratic Change cand. in Montserrado Co. senatorial by-election 2009; African Player of the Year 1989, 1994, 1995, European Player of the Year 1995, FIFA Football Player of the Year 1995, FIFA Fair Play Award 1996, African Footballer of the Century 1998. *Address:* Liberian National Congress, c/o CDC Headquarters, Bernard Beach Compound, Sinkor, Liberia.

WEAIRE, Denis Lawrence, PhD, FRS, MRIA, MAE; British/Irish physicist and academic; *Erasmus Smith's Professor of Natural and Experimental Philosophy and Head, Physics Department, Trinity College Dublin;* b. 17 Oct. 1942, Dalhousie, India; s. of Allen M. Weaire and Janet E. Rea; m. Colette O'Regan 1969; one s.; ed Belfast Royal Acad. and Cambridge Univ.; Harkness Fellowship 1964–66; Fellow, Clare Coll. Cambridge 1967–69; Instructor, Assoc. Prof. Yale Univ. 1970–74; Sr Lecturer, Prof. Heriot-Watt Univ. 1974–79; Chair. of Experimental Physics, Univ. Coll. Dublin 1980–84; Erasmus Smith's Prof. of Natural and Experimental Philosophy, Trinity Coll. Dublin 1984–, Dean of Science 1989; mem. Academia Europaea, Vice-Pres. 2005–08; Hon. Sec. European Asscn of Deans of Science 1991–93; Vice-Pres. European Physical Soc. 1995–96, 1999–2000, Pres. 1997–99; Vice-Pres. Inst. of Physics 2008–; Dr hc (Tech. Univ., Lisbon) 2001; Cecil Powell Medal 2002, RIA Cunningham Medal 2006, IOP/French Phys Soc Holweck Medal 2008. *Publications:* Introduction to Physical Mathematics (co-author) 1985, The Physics of Foams (co-author) 2000, The Pursuit of Perfect Packing (co-author) 2000; co-ed. of several other vols. *Leisure interests:* sport, sea-fishing, theatre, humorous writing, book collecting. *Address:* School of Physics, Trinity College, Dublin 2; 26 Greenmount Road, Terenure, Dublin, Ireland (home). *Telephone:* (1) 8961675 (office); (1) 4902063 (home). *Fax:* (1) 6711759 (office). *E-mail:* dweaire@tcd.ie (office). *Website:* www.tcd.ie/Physics (office).

WEALE, Martin Robert, CBE, MA, ScD; British economist; *External Member, Monetary Policy Committee, Bank of England;* b. 4 Dec. 1955, Barnet, Herts., England; s. of R. A. Weale and M. E. Weale; ed Clare Coll., Cambridge; Overseas Devt Inst. Fellow, Nat. Statistical Office, Malawi 1977–79; Researcher and Lecturer, Faculty of Econs and Politics, Univ. of Cambridge 1979–95, Econs Fellow, Clare Coll. 1981–95; Dir Nat. Inst. of Econ. and Social Research 1995–2010, mem. Statistics Commr 2000–07; mem. Bd for Actuarial Standards 2006–11; External mem. Monetary Policy Cttee, Bank of England 2010–; Hon. Fellow, Inst. of Actuaries 2001; Hon. DSc (City Univ.) 2007. *Publications include:* Macroeconomic Policy: Inflation, Wealth and the Exchange Rate (co-author) 1989, Reconciliation of National Income and Expenditure (co-author) 1995, Econometric Modelling: Techniques and Applications (co-ed.) 2000; numerous journal articles. *Leisure interests:* bridge, walking, art exhbns, music. *Address:* Bank of England, Threadneedle Street, London, EC2R 8AH (office); 63 Noel Road, London, N1 8HE, England (home). *Telephone:* (20) 7601-4271 (office); (20) 7359-8210 (home). *Fax:* (20) 7601-5460 (office). *E-mail:* martin.weale@bankofengland.co.uk (office). *Website:* www.bankofengland.co.uk (office).

WEARING, Gillian, OBE, BA, RA; British artist; b. 1963, Birmingham, England; ed Chelsea School of Art, Goldsmiths Coll., London; first solo exhbn City Racing, London 1993, numerous exhbns around the world; concentrates on video and photography; BT Young Contemporaries 1993, Turner Prize 1997, Prize of Ministry of Employment, Social Affairs and Urban Devt, Culture and Sport, Oberhausen Short Film Festival 1998, British Television Advertising Award, Public Service: Gold 2002, Grazia o2 X Award for Art 2007. *Film:* Self Made 2010. *Publications include:* Gillian Wearing City Projects Prague 1996, Signs that say what you want them to say and not Signs that say what someone else wants you to say 1997, Gillian Wearing 1997, A Woman Called Theresa 1999, Gillian Wearing 1999, 2000, 2001, Broad Street 2001, Unspoken 2001, Sous Influence 2001, Mass Observation 2002, A Trilogy 2002, Living Proof 2006, Family History 2007. *Address:* c/o Maureen Paley, 21 Herald Street, London, E2 6JT, England (office). *Telephone:* (20) 7729-4112 (office). *Fax:* (20) 7729-4113 (office). *E-mail:* info@maureenpaley.com (office). *Website:* www.maureenpaley.com (office).

WEATHERALL, Sir David John, Kt, MD, FRCP, FRS; British medical specialist and academic; *Regius Professor of Medicine Emeritus, University of Oxford;* b. 9 March 1933, Liverpool; s. of the late Harry Weatherall and Gwendoline Weatherall; m. Stella Nestler 1962; one s.; ed Calday Grammar School and Univ. of Liverpool; various resident posts in medicine 1956–58; Jr medical specialist, Royal Army Medical Corps, Singapore 1959–60; Research Fellow, Johns Hopkins Hosp. 1961–65; Reader in Haematology, Univ. of Liverpool 1969–71, Prof. 1971–74; consultant to WHO 1967–82; Nuffield Prof. of Clinical Medicine, Univ. of Oxford 1974–92, Regius Prof. of Medicine 1992–2000, Regius Prof. Emer. 2000–; Chancellor Univ. of Keele 2002–; Fellow, Magdalen Coll. 1974–92, Emer. Fellow 1992, Student, Christ Church 1992–2000; Hon. Dir MRC Molecular Haematology Unit 1979–2000, Inst. of Molecular Medicine 1988–2000; Trustee Wellcome Trust 1990–2000; Pres. British Asscn for the Advancement of Science 1993, Int. Soc. of Haematology 1993; Pres. Kennedy Foundation 2000–02; Trustee Wolfson Trust 2000–, Imperial Cancer Research Fund 2000–02; mem. American Acad. of Arts and Sciences; Watson-Smith Lecture 1974, Croonian Lecture 1984, Foundation Lecture (FRCPath) 1979, Darwin Lecture (Eugenics Soc.) 1979; Sims Visiting Prof. 1982; Fellow Imperial Coll. 1984; Foreign Assoc. NAS 1990, Inst. of Medicine 1991, Founder Fellow Acad. Med. Sci. 1998; Hon. FRCOG; Hon. FACP; Hon. FRCPCH; Hon. MD (Leeds) 1988, (Sheffield) 1989, (Nottingham) 1993; Hon. DSc (Manchester) 1989, (Edin.) 1989, (Aberdeen) 1991, (Leicester) 1991, (London) 1992, (Keele) 1993, (Mahidol Univ., Thailand) 1997, (Exeter) 1999, (McGill Univ., Canada) 1999, (Cambridge) 2004; Hon. DHumLitt (Johns Hopkins Univ.) 1990; Hon. DSc (Oxford Brookes) 1995, (South Bank) 1995, (Exeter) 1998; Hon. LLD (Liverpool) 1992, (Bristol) 1994, (Dundee) 2009; Stratton Award and Medal (Int. Soc. of Haematology) 1982, Ballantyne Prize (Royal Coll. of Physicians, Edin.) 1983, Feldberg Foundation Award 1984, Royal Medal (Royal Soc.) 1989, Conway Evans Prize (Royal Soc. and Royal Coll. Physicians) 1991, Gold Medal, Royal Soc. of Medicine 1992, Buchanan Medal (Royal Soc.) 1994, Helmut Horten Int. Prize in Biomedical Science 1995, Manson Medal, Royal Soc. of Tropical Medicine 1998, Prince Mahidol Award, Thailand 2001, Allen Award (American Soc. of Human Genetics) 2003, Genetics Soc. Mendel Medal 2006, Lasker-Koshland Award 2010, Karl Landsteiner Memorial Award, AABB 2011. *Publications:* The New Genetics and Clinical Practice 1982, The Thalassaemia Syndromes (with J.B. Clegg) 1982, 2001, Oxford Textbook of Medicine (with others) 1983, Science and the Quiet Art 1995, Genomics and World Health (co-author) 2002, Thalassaemia: The Biography 2010; over 600 reviews and papers on human genetic disease. *Leisure interest:* music. *Address:* Weatherall Institute of Molecular Medicine, John Radcliffe Hospital, Headington, Oxford, OX3 9DU (office); 8 Cumnor Rise Road, Cumnor Hill, Oxford, OX2 9HD, England (home). *Telephone:* (1865) 222398 (office). *Fax:* (1865) 222424 (office). *E-mail:* liz.rose@imm.ox.ac.uk (office). *Website:* www.imm.ox.ac.uk (office).

WEATHERALL, Vice-Adm. Sir James (Lamb), KCVO, KBE; British naval officer; b. 28 Feb. 1936, Newton Mearns, Renfrewshire, Scotland; s. of Lt Commdr Alwyne Weatherall and Joan Cuthbert; m. Hon. Jean Stewart Macpherson 1962; two s. three d.; ed Glasgow Acad., Gordonstoun School; commanded HM Ships Soberton 1966–67, Ulster 1970–72, Tartar 1975–76, Andromeda 1982–84 (in Falklands Conflict), Ark Royal 1 985–87; on staff of Supreme Allied Commander Europe (NATO) as Rear-Adm. 1987–89; Deputy Supreme Allied Commdr Atlantic 1989–91; HM Marshal of the Diplomatic Corps 1992–2001; Extra Equerry to HM The Queen 2001; DL for Hampshire 2004; one of HM The Queen's Commrs of the Lieutenancy for the City of London 2001; Liveryman Worshipful Co. of Shipwrights 1985, Asst to Court 1989, Prime Warden 2001–02; Younger Brother Trinity House 1986; Trustee Marwell Zoological Preservation Trust 1992 (Chair. 1999–2007); Gov. Box Hill School 1992–2003 (Chair. 1994–2003, Warden 2003–), Gordonstoun School 1994–2003 (Chair. 1996–2003, Warden 2004–11); Pres. Int. Social Service 1996–2001; Chair. Lord Mayor of London's Appeal 1997–98; Chair. Sea Cadet Asscn 1992–98, Vice-Pres. 2009–; Trustee, World Wildlife Fund UK 2001–07; Patron Marwell Wildlife; Sea Cadet Medal 1998. *Leisure interests:* fishing, stamp collecting. *Address:* Craig House, Street End, Bishop's Waltham, Hants., SO32 1FS, England. *Telephone:* (1489) 892483. *E-mail:* jimweatherall@btinternet.com.

WEAVER, Jacqueline (Jacki) Ruth; Australian actress; b. 25 May 1947, Sydney; d. of Arthur Weaver and Edith Weaver (née Simpson). *Television includes:* Homicide 1967–77, Trial by Marriage 1980, The Challenge 1986, Hammer Bay 2007, Satisfaction 2009. *Films include:* Stork (Australian Film Inst. Award for Best Actress in a Leading Role) 1971, Picnic at Hanging Rock 1975, The Removalists 1975, Caddie (Australian Film Inst. Award for Best Actress in a Supporting Role) 1976, The Perfectionist 1987, Animal Kingdom (Australian Film Inst. Award for Best Actress in a Leading Role, Nat. Bd of Review Award for Best Supporting Actress, Los Angeles Film Critics Asscn Award for Best Supporting Actress, San Francisco Film Critics Circle Award for Best Supporting Actress, Satellite Award for Best Supporting Actress – Motion Picture, Utah Film Critics Asscn Award for Best Supporting Actress) 2010, Summer Coda 2010, The Five-Year Engagement 2012, Silver Linings Playbook 2012. *Address:* c/o International Casting Service & Associates Pty Ltd, 2/218 Crown Street, Darlinghurst, Sydney, NSW 2010, Australia (office).

WEAVER, Sigourney, BA, MFA; American actress and environmentalist; b. (Susan Alexandra Weaver), 8 Oct. 1949, Manhattan, New York; d. of 'Pat' Laflin Weaver and Elizabeth Inglis (née Desiree Mary Lucy Hawkins); m. James Simpson 1984; one d.; ed Stanford Univ., Yale Univ.; f. Goat Cay Productions (film production co.); Hon. Chair. The Dian Fossey Gorilla Fund International. *Films include:* Annie Hall 1977, Tribute to a Madman 1977, Camp 708 1978, Alien 1979, Eyewitness 1981, The Year of Living Dangerously 1982, Deal of the Century 1983, Ghostbusters 1984, Une Femme ou Deux 1985, Half Moon Street 1986, Aliens 1986, Gorillas in the Mist (Golden Globe Best Actress Award) 1988, Working Girl

(Best Supporting Actress Award Golden Globe) 1988, Ghostbusters II 1989, Aliens 3 1992, 1492: Conquest of Paradise 1993, Dave 1993, Death and the Maiden 1994, Jeffrey 1995, Copycat 1996, Snow White in the Black Forest 1996, Ice Storm 1996, Alien Resurrection 1997, A Map of the World 1999, Galaxy Quest 1999, Get Bruce 1999, Company Man 1999, Airframe 1999, Heartbreakers 2001, Tadpole 2002, The Guys 2002, Holes 2003, The Village 2004, Imaginary Heroes 2004, Snow Cake 2006, The TV Set 2006, Infamous 2006, Happily N'Ever After (voice) 2006, The Girl in the Park 2007, Be Kind Rewind 2008, Vantage Point 2008, Baby Mama 2008, Wall-E (voice) 2008, The Tale of Despereaux (narrator) 2008, Avatar 2009, Crazy on the Outside 2010, You Again 2010, Cedar Rapids 2011, The Cold Light of Day 2012, Red Lights 2012. *Television includes:* Somerset (series) 1970, The Best of Families (mini-series) 1977, 3 by Cheever: The Sorrows of Gin 1979, 3 by Cheever: O Youth and Beauty! 1979, Snow White: A Tale of Terror 1997, Late Night with Conan O'Brien (one episode) 1997, Futurama – Planet Express Ship 2002, Love and Rocket 2002, The TV Set 2006, narrated US version of BBC/Discovery Channel documentary Planet Earth 2006, Eli Stone – The Path 2008, Prayers for Bobby 2009. *Address:* c/o William Morris Agency, One William Morris Place, Beverly Hills, CA 90212, USA (office); Goat Cay Productions, PO Box 38, New York, NY 10150, USA. *Telephone:* (310) 859-4000 (office); (212) 421-8293. *Fax:* (310) 859-4462 (office); (212) 421-8294. *Website:* www.wma.com (office).

WEBB, Sir Adrian Leonard, Kt, BSocSci, MSc, DLitt, FRSA, FCGI; British academic and university administrator; b. 19 July 1943, Newport, Wales; s. of Leonard Webb and Rosina Webb; m. 1st Caroline Williams 1966 (divorced 1995); two s.; m. 2nd Monjulee Dass 1996; ed St Julian's High School, Newport, Gwent, Univ. of Birmingham, London School of Econs, Loughborough Univ.; Lecturer, LSE 1966–74; Research Dir Personal Social Services Council 1974–76; Prof. of Social Policy, Loughborough Univ. 1976–93; Dir Centre for Research in Social Policy 1983–90, Dean, later Pro-Vice-Chancellor, 1986–93; Vice-Chancellor, Univ. of Glamorgan 1993–2005; Visiting Prof., Cardiff Business School; Chair. Bd Govs, Volunteer Centre 1978–84, Cttee on Workforce Planning and Training in Social Services 1987–88, Dept of Health Task Force on Nursing Research 1992–93, Heads of Higher Educ. in Wales 2000–03, Pontypridd and Rhondda NHS Trust 2005–08, Enquiry into Further Educ. Wales 2006–07, Wales Employment and Skills Bd 2008–11, Tenovus (cancer charity) 2008–11, Enquiry into Higher Educ. in NE Wales 2012–13, Review of Post 14 Educ. in Wales (published as Promise and Performance); Wales Commr, UK Comm. for Employment and Skills –2012; mem. DHSS Research Liaison Groups 1975–90 (science adviser, Chief Scientist's Departmental Research Cttee, DHSS 1987–90), Sociology and Social Admin Cttee, SSRC 1976–80, Council on Tribunals 1985–91, English Nat. Bd on Nursing Midwifery and Health Visiting 1988–93, CBI Council Wales 1993–98, Nat. Cttee of Inquiry into Higher Educ. (Dearing Cttee) 1996–97, BBC Broadcasting Council for Wales 1998, Public Services Productivity Panel, HM Treasury 2000–06, Admin. Justice and Tribunals Council 2008– (also Chair. Welsh Cttee), Big Lottery Fund 2012– (also Chair. Wales Cttee), Beecham Review of the Delivery of Public Services in Wales (published as Beyond Boundaries), Wales Cttee Royal Soc. for the Protection of Birds; Dir (non-exec.), East Glamorgan NHS Trust 1997–, Nat. Council Educ. and Learning Wales (ELWa) 2001–06, Nat. Ass. for Wales 2003–08, Bd Inst. of Welsh Affairs 2008–, Bd Wales Govt 2012–; adviser on social policy and social work, Univ. Funding Council 1989–92, Leics. DHA 1992–93, NHS Wales R&D Forum 1993–96; Vice-Pres. Leics. Regional Council Guideposts Trust Ltd 1988–93; Chair. Social Admin Asscn 1977–80; mem. Social Policy Asscn, British Sociological Asscn, Political Studies Asscn; Founding Trustee, Bevan Foundation. *Publications:* Change, Choice and Conflict in Social Policy 1975; Planning Need and Scarcity 1986; The Economic Approach to Social Policy 1986; Social Work, Social Care and Social Planning 1987; Joint Approaches to Social Policy 1988. *Leisure interests:* walking, painting (water colour), ornithology. *Address:* Welsh Government, Cathays Park, Cardiff, CF10 3NQ, Wales (office). *Telephone:* (1443) 845500 (office). *E-mail:* wag-en@mailuk.custhelp.com (office). *Website:* wales.gov.uk (office).

WEBB, James (Jim) H., Jr, JD; American writer and politician; b. 9 Feb. 1946, Arlington, Va; m. Hong Le Webb; one s. three d. one step-d.; ed US Naval Acad. and Georgetown Univ.; Asst Minority Counsel, House Cttee on Veterans Affairs, Washington, DC 1977–78, Chief Minority Counsel 1979–81; Visiting Writer, US Naval Acad. 1979; Asst Sec. for Reserve Affairs, Dept of Defense 1984–87; Sec. of the Navy 1987–88 (resgnd); Senator from Virginia 2007–13 (retd), mem. Cttee on Foreign Relations (Chair. East Asian and Pacific Affairs Subcommittee), Cttee on Armed Services (Chair. Key Personnel Subcommittee), Veterans' Affairs Cttee, Jt Econ. Cttee; Fellow, Harvard Inst. of Politics 1992; Democrat; Distinguished Public Service Medal, Dept of Defense, Patriot Award, Medal of Honor Soc., Public Service Award, American Legion Nat. Commdr, VFW Media Service Award, Mil. Order of the Iron Mike Award, Marine Corps League, John Russell Leadership Award, Robert L. Denig Distinguished Service Award, Emmy Award for 1983 PBS coverage of US Marines in Beirut. *Film:* Rules of Engagement (wrote story and exec. producer) 2000. *Publications:* Fields of Fire 1978, A Sense of Honor 1981, A Country Such as This 1983, Something to Die For 1991, A Sense of Honor 1995, The Emperor's General 1999, Lost Soldiers 2001, Born Fighting 2004. *Address:* c/o 248 Russell Senate Office Building, Washington, DC 20510, USA.

WEBB, Leslie Roy, AO, BCom, PhD; Australian university vice-chancellor (retd); b. 18 July 1935, Melbourne, Vic.; s. of Leslie Hugh Charles Webb and Alice Myra Webb; m. Heather Brown 1966; one s. one d.; ed Wesley Coll., Melbourne, Univ. of Melbourne, London School of Econs; Sr Lecturer in Econs, Univ. of Melbourne 1964–68, Truby Williams Prof. of Econs 1973–84, Prof. Emer. 1985–; Pro-Vice-Chancellor 1982–84, Chair. Academic Bd 1983–84; Reader in Econs, La Trobe Univ. 1969–72; Vice-Chancellor Griffith Univ. 1985–2002; Chair. Queensland Non-State Schools Accreditation Bd 2001–09; Visiting Prof. Cornell Univ., USA 1967–68; Consultant, UNCTAD 1974–75; Jt Ed. The Economic Record 1973–77; Chair. Cttee of Inquiry into S Australian Dairy Industry 1977, Library Bd of Queensland 2002–08; Assoc. mem. Prices Justification Tribunal 1978–79, 1980–81; mem. Council of Advice, Bureau of Industry Econs 1982–84; Chair. Australian-American Educational Foundation (Fulbright Program) 1986–90; mem. Bd of Govs Foundation for Devt Co-operation 1990–2007; Dir and mem. Australian Vice-Chancellors' Cttee Bd of Dirs 1991–94; Pres. Victorian Br., Econ. Soc. of Australia and NZ 1976; Cavaliere, Ordine al Merito (Italy) 1995, Officer of the Order of Australia 2003; Hon. DUniv (Queensland Univ. of Tech.) 2002,

(Griffith Univ.) 2002, Hon. DLitt (Univ. of South Queensland) 2002; Award for Outstanding Achievement, US Information Agency 1987. *Publications include:* Industrial Economics: Australian Studies (co-ed.) 1982; articles in learned journals. *Leisure interests:* music, art, gardening. *Address:* 3 Davrod Street, Robertson, Queensland 4109, Australia (home). *Telephone:* (7) 3345-7141 (home). *E-mail:* lroywebb@optusnet.com.au.

WEBBER, Tristan, BA, MA; British fashion designer; b. 1973; ed SE Essex Coll. of Arts and Tech., Cordwainers Coll., London and St Martin's School of Art and Design; work exhibited at Colette, Paris and Powerhouse Exhbn, London 1998; third collection shown at London Fashion Week 1998 and MTV Fashionably Loud event, Miami 1998; fmr Visiting Lecturer, Royal Coll. of Art, currently Senior Tutor, Fashion Womenswear Programme, School of Material. *Address:* c/o Royal College of Art, Kensington Gore, London, SW7 2EU, England (office). *Website:* www.tristanwebber.com.

WEBER, Axel A., MA, PhD Habil.; German economist, academic and banking executive; *Chairman, UBS AG;* b. 8 March 1957, Kusel, Rhineland-Palatinate; ed Univs of Siegen and Konstanz; Prof. for Monetary Econs, Sr Research Fellow and Dir Centre for Financial Studies, Goethe Univ., Frankfurt am Main 1998–2001; Prof. for Int. Econs and Dir Centre for Financial Research, Univ. of Cologne 2001–04, on leave of absence; Visiting Prof., Booth School of Business, Univ. of Chicago 2011–12; Research Fellow, Centre for Econ. Policy Research, London, UK, Centre for Financial Research, Cologne; Pres. Bundesbank 2004–11, mem. Governing Council, European Cen. Bank 2004–11, mem. Bd of Dirs BIS 2004–11, Gov. for Germany, IMF 2004–11, mem. G7 and G20 Ministers and Govs 2004–11; mem. Bd of Dirs and Chair. UBS AG 2012–, Chair. Governance and Nominating Cttee, mem. Corp. Responsibility Cttee 2012–, Chair. 2013–; mem. Financial Stability Bd 2010–11, Steering Cttee, European Systemic Risk Bd 2011; mem. German Council of Econ. Experts 2002–04; mem. Group of Thirty, Washington, DC; mem. Bd Int. Inst. of Finance; mem. Monetary Econs Council and Int. Econs Council Verein für Socialpolitik, Advisory Bd German Market Economy Foundation, Advisory Council (Hochschulrat) Goethe Univ.; Dr hc (Duisburg-Essen), (Konstanz). *Address:* UBS AG, Bahnhofstrasse 45, 8021 Zurich, Switzerland (office). *Telephone:* (44) 234-11-11 (office). *Fax:* (44) 239-91-11 (office). *E-mail:* info@ubs.com (office). *Website:* www.ubs.com (office).

WEBER, Bruce; American photographer, film director and producer; b. 29 March 1946, Greensburg, Pa; ed Hun School at Princeton, Denison Univ., Ohio, New York Univ. Art and Film Schools, New School for Social Research, New York; numerous exhbns in New York, Los Angeles, Chicago, Dallas, San Francisco, Atlanta, New Orleans, St Louis, Paris, London, Dortmund, Basel, Lausanne, Tokyo, Frankfurt etc. 1973–; photographs in perm. collections of Victoria and Albert Museum, London and Photography Div., City of Paris; numerous commercials 1988–; numerous awards, including Council of Fashion Designers of America for Achievement in Photography 1984, 1985, American Soc. of Magazine Photographers Fashion Photographer of the Year 1984, Int. Film and TV Festival of New York Silver Medal 1985, Cannes Int. Advertising Film Festival Silver Lion for Beauty Brothers (commercial) 1988, Int. Center of Photography Award for use of Photography in Advertising 1994, Best Advertising in Print and TV, Fragrance Foundation 1997, First Alfred Eisenstaedt Award for Portrait Photography, Life magazine 1998. *Films produced and directed include:* Broken Noses (Int. Documentary Asscn Award 1988) 1987, Let's Get Lost (Critics' Award, Venice Film Festival 1988, Int. Documentary Asscn Award 1989) 1988, Backyard Movie 1991, Gentle Giants 1994, The Teddy Boys of the Edwardian Drape Society 1996, Chop Suey 1999; music videos: Being Boring, The Pet Shop Boys (Video of the Year Award, Music Week 1990) 1990, Blue Spanish Sky, Chris Isaak 1991, Se A Vida E, The Pet Shop Boys 1996. *Film directed:* A Letter to True 2003. *Publications:* Sam Shepard 1990, Bear Pond 1990, Hotel Room with a View (photographs) 1992, Gentle Giants: A Book of Newfoundland 1994, A House is Not a Home 1996, Branded Youth and other stories 1997, The Chop Suey Club 1999. *Address:* c/o Little Bear Inc., 135th Watts Street, 5th Floor, New York, NY 10013, USA (office). *Telephone:* (212) 226-0814 (office). *Fax:* (212) 334-5180 (office). *Website:* www.bruceweber.com.

WEBER, Christophe, MFin, MPM, DPharm; French pharmaceutical industry executive; *President and COO, Takeda Pharmaceutical Company Limited;* ed Univ. of Lyon; began career in Australia, working for Rhône-Poulenc-Rorer Pharmaceuticals; joined GlaxoSmithKline 1993, positions included Gen. Man. Swiss subsidiary, Chair. and CEO GSK France 2003–08, Sr Vice-Pres. and Regional Director, Asia Pacific 2008–11, mem. Corp. Exec. Team and Pres. GlaxoSmithKline Vaccines (GSK Biologicals SA) 2012–13; COO Takeda Pharmaceutical Co. Ltd April 2014–, Pres. June 2014–. *Address:* Takeda Pharmaceutical Co. Ltd, 1-1, Doshomachi 4-chome, Chuo-ku, Osaka 540-8645, Japan (office). *Telephone:* (6) 6204-2111 (office). *Fax:* (6) 6204-2880 (office). *E-mail:* info@www .takeda.com (office). *Website:* www.takeda.com (office).

WEBER, George Brian, MA; Canadian national organization official and fmr Red Cross official; *President and CEO, Royal Ottawa Health Care Group;* b. 18 April 1946, Montreal; s. of Harry Weber and Johanna Alexopoulos; m. Mary Morris 1976; ed McGill Univ., Harvard Univ., USA; voluntary instructor/examiner, Canadian Red Cross 1963–73, Field Del. Viet Nam, Int. Red Cross 1973–74, Disaster Relief Officer, Chief Del., League of Red Cross Socs 1974–76, Nat. Dir of Int. Affairs, Canadian Red Cross 1976–81, Nat. Dir of Programmes 1981–83, Sec. Gen. Canadian Red Cross 1983–92, Hon. Vice-Pres. 1993–, Sec. Gen. and CEO Int. Fed. of Red Cross and Red Crescent Socs 1992–2000, Sec. Gen. Emer. 2000–11; Chair. Canadian Soc. Assoc. Execs; Exec. Dir/CEO Canadian Dental Asscn 2000–07; Pres. and CEO Royal Ottawa Health Care Group 2007–; CEO Continovation Services Inc.; mem., Dir numerous bodies, including Canadian Inst. of Int. Affairs, Amundsen Foundation, Earth Foundation, American Coll. of Sports Medicine; Vanier Award 1984. *Leisure interests:* diving, tennis, squash, skiing. *Address:* Royal Ottawa Mental Health Centre, 1145 Carling Avenue, Ottawa, ON K1Z 7K4, Canada (office). *Telephone:* (613) 722-6521 (office). *E-mail:* info@theroyal.ca (office). *Website:* www.theroyal.ca (office).

WEBER, Jonathan N., FMedSci, FRCP, FRCPath; British clinical professor; *Jefferiss Professor of Communicable Diseases and GU Medicine, Imperial College London;* Wellcome Clinical Training Fellow, St Mary's Hosp. Medical School

1982–85; Wellcome Trust Lecturer in Cell and Molecular Biology, Inst. for Cancer Research Chester Beatty Labs 1985–88; Sr Lecturer in Infectious Diseases, Royal Postgraduate Medical School, Hammersmith Hosp. 1988–91; Jefferiss Prof. of Communicable Diseases and GU Medicine, Faculty of Medicine, Imperial Coll. London 1990–, also Head of Div. of Medicine; Founding Ed. AIDS (journal) 1987–92; co-f. WHO Network for HIV Characterisation 1992; Adviser on HIV to numerous orgs including WHO, UNAIDS, EC, Elton John Foundation, Wellcome Trust, Dept for Int. Devt, Russian Fed. AIDS Centre, Ivanovsky Inst. of Virology; Collaborator, European Vaccine Effort Against HIV/AIDS, Int. AIDS Vaccine Initiative; Dir Weber Investments 1996–. *Publications:* over 200 scientific papers on HIV and other STIs. *Address:* Faculty of Medicine, Imperial College, St Mary's Hospital, Norfolk Place, London, W2 1PG, England (office). *Telephone:* (20) 7594-3905 (office). *E-mail:* j.weber@imperial.ac.uk (office). *Website:* www1.imperial.ac .uk/medicine/people/j.weber (office).

WEBER, Jürgen, Dipl-Ing, FRAeS; German business executive; *Honorary Chairman of the Supervisory Board, Deutsche Lufthansa AG;* b. 17 Oct. 1941; m. Sabine Rossberg 1965; one s. one d.; ed Stuttgart Tech. Univ., Massachusetts Inst. of Tech., USA; with Lufthansa Eng Div. 1967–74, Dir Line Maintenance Dept 1974–78, with Aircraft Eng Sub-div. 1978–87, COO (Tech.) 1987–89, deputy mem. Exec. Bd 1989–90, CEO (Tech.) 1990–91, Chair. Exec. Bd Deutsche Lufthansa AG 1991–2003, CEO 1998–2003, mem. Supervisory Bd 2001–, Chair. –2013, Hon. Chair. 2013–; Chair. Supervisory Bd Deutsche Post AG 2006–; Chair. Supervisory Bd Thomas Cook AG; mem. Supervisory Bd Allianz-Lebensversicherungs AG, Bayer AG, Deutsche Bank AG, Voith AG, Loyalty Partner GmbH, Tetra Laval Group (Switzerland); Hon. DEng (Stuttgart) 1998; Bambi Award for Industry 1994, Anti-Defamation League Champion of Liberty Award, Man. Magazin Man. of the Year 1999, Wirtschaftswoche Best Man. 2002, L. Welch Pogue Award, Airline Business Award 2003. *Leisure interests:* jogging, skiing. *Address:* Deutsche Lufthansa AG, Von-Gablenz-Strasse 2–6, 50679 Cologne, Germany (office). *Telephone:* (69) 6960 (office). *Fax:* (69) 6966818 (office). *Website:* www.lufthansa .com (office).

WEBER, Manfred, Dr rer. pol; German banking official; *CEO, Association of German Banks;* b. 18 Dec. 1950, Altenkofen, Landshut; ed Johann Wolfgang Goethe Univ., Frankfurt am Main; Research Asst, Research Dept, Deutsche Bundesbank 1980, Head, Office of Deputy Gov. 1986–91; Monetary and Econ. Dept B.I.S., Basle 1991–92; CEO and mem. Bd of Dirs Bundesverband deutscher Banken, Berlin 1992–; Hon. Prof., Univ. of Potsdam 2004. *Address:* Bundesverband deutscher Banken, Burgstrasse 28, 10178 Berlin, Germany. *Telephone:* (30) 16631000 (office). *Fax:* (30) 16631399 (office). *Website:* www.germanbanks.org (office).

WEBSTER, Peter; Irish business executive; joined Jefferson Smurfit Group 1978, fmr Regional Operations Dir, Chair. and Chief Exec. Smurfit Ireland Group 1996, now Dir Smurfit Group Ireland; Pres. Dublin Chamber of Commerce 2002, now mem. Council; Chair. RMI. *Address:* c/o Dublin Chamber of Commerce, 7 Clare Street, Dublin 2, Ireland.

WEBSTER, Toby; British gallery owner; *Director, The Modern Institute;* held first show in flat in Glasgow entitled The World of Ponce; worked for Transmission Gallery; co-f. (with Will Bradley) the Modern Institute; artists represented include Dirk Bell, Martin Boyce, Jeremy Deller, Alex Dordoy, Urs Fischer, Kim Fisher, Luke Fowler, Henrik Håkansson, Mark Handforth, Thomas Houseago, Richard Hughes, Chris Johanson, Andrew Kerr, Jim Lambie, Duncan MacQuarrie, Victoria Morton, Scott Myles, Nicolas Party, Toby Paterson, Simon Periton, Manfred Pernice, Mary Redmond, Anselm Reyle, Eva Rothschild, Monika Sosnowska, Simon Starling, Katja Strunz, Tony Swain, Spencer Sweeney, Joanne Tatham & Tom O'Sullivan, Padraig Timoney, Hayley Tompkins, Sue Tompkins, Cathy Wilkes, Michael Wilkinson, Gregor Wright and Richard Wright; curated My Head is on Fire, but My Heart is Full of Love, in Copenhagen; guest curator at numerous venues; co-opened, with New York gallerist Gavin Brown, a space in Rome called Roma Roma Roma 2009. *Address:* The Modern Institute, 14–20 Osborne Street, Glasgow, G1 5QN, Scotland (office). *Telephone:* (141) 248-3711 (office). *Fax:* (141) 552-5988 (office). *E-mail:* mail@themoderninstitute.com (office). *Website:* www.themoderninstitute.com (office).

WEBSTER, William Hedgcock, LLB, JD; American fmr government official, judge and lawyer; *Chairperson, Homeland Security Advisory Council;* b. 6 March 1924, St Louis, Mo.; s. of Thomas M. Webster and Katherine Webster (née Hedgcock); m. 1st Drusilla Lane 1950 (died 1984); one s. two d.; m. 2nd Lynda Clugston 1990; ed Amherst Coll., Mass, Washington Univ. in St Louis Law School; served as Lt USNR 1943–46, 1951–52; admitted to Missouri Bar 1949; attorney with Armstrong, Teasdale, Kramer & Vaughan and predecessors, St Louis 1949–50, 1952–59, Partner 1956–59, 1961–70; US Attorney, Eastern Dist, Mo. 1960–61; Judge, US Dist Court, Eastern Mo. 1971–73, US Court of Appeals 1973–78; Dir FBI 1978–87; Dir CIA 1987–91; apptd Sr Partner, Millbank, Tweed, Hadley & McCloy LLP 1991 (now retd); Chair. Homeland Security Advisory Council 2002–; head of investigation into police response to LA Riots 1992; head of ind. investigation of the FBI's actions surrounding the Fort Hood shooting 2009; Trustee, Washington Univ. 1974–; mem. ABA, Fed., Mo. and St Louis Bar Asscns, American Law Inst., Council 1978–, Inst. of Judicial Admin Inc.; Fellow, American Bar Foundation; Hon. Chair. The OSS Soc.; Hon. Fellow, American Coll. of Trial Lawyers; Order of the Coif; Hon. LLD (Amherst Coll.) 1975, (DePauw Univ.) 1978, (Washington Univ.) 1978, (William Woods Coll.) 1979, (Inst. of World Politics) 2008 and numerous others; Washington Univ. Distinguished Alumnus Award 1977, American Legion Distinguished Service Award 1979, St Louis Globe-Democrat Man of the Year 1980, Washington Univ. William Greenleaf Elliot Award 1981, Riot Relief Fund of New York Award 1981, Young Lawyers of the ABA Award 1982, Fordham-Stein Award 1982, William Moss Inst.-American Univ. Award 1983, Freedoms Foundation Medal 1985, Presidential Medal of Freedom 1991, Nat. Security Medal 1991, Justice Award, American Judicature Soc. 2001, ABA Medal 2002, Distinguished Public Service Medal from NASA, William J. Donovan Award, The OSS Soc. 2005. *Leisure interest:* tennis. *Address:* Homeland Security Advisory Council, Washington, DC 20528, USA (office). *Telephone:* (202) 282-8000 (office). *Website:* www.dhs.gov/homeland-security-advisory-council-members (office).

WEDER, Hans, PhD, DHabil; Swiss theologian, university rector and academic; *Rector, University of Zurich;* b. 1946, Diepoldsau; ed Gymnasium, St Gallen, Univ. of Zürich, Univ. of St Andrews, UK; Prof. of New Testament Science, Univ. of Zürich 1980–, Dean Theological Faculty 1986–88, Rector, Univ. of Zürich 2000–; mem. Cttee of Reform UNI2000; Pres. Rectors' Conf. of Swiss Univs 2006–. *Publications:* numerous articles in professional journals on hermeneutics and philosophy. *Address:* Office of the Rector, University of Zurich, Stockargut, Künstlergasse 15, Office 205, 8001 Zürich, Switzerland (office). *Telephone:* (44) 634-22-11 (office). *E-mail:* rektor@uzh.ch (office). *Website:* www.uzh.ch (office).

WEDGEWORTH, Robert, AB, MS, LHD; American university librarian, academic and association executive; b. 31 July 1937; m. Chung-Kyun Wedgeworth; one d.; ed Wabash Coll., Univ. of Illinois; Exec. Dir American Library Asscn (ALA) 1972–85; Dean School of Library Service, Columbia Univ. 1985–92; Librarian, Prof. of Library Admin, Univ. of Ill. at Urbana-Champaign 1993–99; Pres. Int. Fed. of Library Asscns and Insts (IFLA) 1991–97, Hon. Pres. 1997–; fmr interim Pres. Laubach Literacy Int. (LLI), fmr Vice Chair., Bd of Trustees, Pres. and CEO ProLiteracy Worldwide (formed by merger of Laubach Literacy Int.and Literacy Volunteers of America, Inc.) 2000–07; Chair. Advisory Cttee ALA Office of Information Tech. Policy 1995–97; mem. Cttee to Visit Harvard Coll. Library 1994–97; mem. Nat. Comm. on Adult Literacy 2006–; Trustee Newberry Library, Chicago; mem. Bd of Trustees Poetry Foundation; ALA Joseph Lippincott Award 1989, Medal of Honor, Int. Co-operation Admin. 1996, Melvil Dewey Award 1997. *Publications:* World Encyclopaedia of Library and Information Services (ed.) 1993, Issues Affecting the Development of Digital Libraries in Science and Technology (UNESCO) 1996, Courtship, Marriage and Librarianship: A Vision of a 21st Century Profession (IFLA) 1996, Beyond Unification 1997, Reaffirming Professional Values 1997. *Address:* 2626 North Lakeview #3603, Chicago, IL 60614, USA (home). *Telephone:* (773) 525-6609 (home). *E-mail:* rwedge@uiuc.edu (home).

WEE, Cho Yaw; Singaporean banker; *Chairman, United Overseas Bank Group;* s. of Wee Kheng Chiang, founder of United Chinese Bank; m.; five c.; ed high school in China; joined Bd of Dirs of then United Chinese Bank (now United Overseas Bank) 1958, Man. Dir 1960–74, Chair. and CEO United Overseas Bank Group 1974–2007, Chair. 2007–; Pres. Singapore Fed. of Chinese Clan Asscns; Public Service Star, Singapore Govt 1971, named Businessman of the Year 1990, inaugural Credit Suisse-Ernst & Young Lifetime Achievement Award 2006, Distinguished Service Order 2011. *Address:* United Overseas Bank, 80 Raffles Place, UOB Plaza, 048624 Singapore (office). *Telephone:* 6533-9898 (office). *Fax:* 6534-2334 (office). *E-mail:* info@uobgroup.com (office). *Website:* www.uobgroup .com (office), www.uob.com.sg (office).

WEEKES, Sir Everton de Courcy, KCMG, GCM, OBE; Barbadian fmr cricketer; b. 26 Feb. 1925, Pickwick Gap, Westbury, St Michael; ed St Leonard's School, Bridgetown; right-hand batsman; teams: Barbados 1944–64, West Indies 1948–58; played in 48 Tests, scoring 4,445 runs (average 58.61, highest score 207) including 15 hundreds, took one wicket for eight runs (average 77.00); played in 152 First-class matches, scoring 12,010 runs (average 55.34, highest score 304 not out) including 36 hundreds, took 17 wickets (average 43.00), best bowling 4/38; Umpire, Int. Cricket Council (ICC) (four Tests, three One-Day Ints); Wisden Cricketer of the Year 1951, one of 55 players inducted into ICC Cricket Hall of Fame 2009. *Leisure interest:* int. bridge player. *Address:* c/o West Indies Cricket Board Inc., PO Box 616 W, St John's, Antigua, West Indies. *Telephone:* 481-2450. *Fax:* 268-481-2498. *E-mail:* wicb@windiescricket.com. *Website:* www .windiescricket.com.

WEERAMANTRY, Christopher Gregory, BA, LLD; Sri Lankan judge and academic; *Professor Emeritus of Law, Monash University;* b. 17 Nov. 1926, Colombo; ed Univ. of London, UK; advocate, Supreme Court of Sri Lanka 1948–65, Commr of Assize 1965–67, Justice of Supreme Court 1967–72; Sir Hayden Starke Prof. of Law, Monash Univ., Melbourne, Australia 1972–91, Prof. Emer. of Law 1991–; Judge, Int. Court of Justice 1991–2000, Vice-Pres. 1997–99; Lecturer and Examiner, Council of Legal Educ. 1951–56; mem. Council of Legal Educ. 1967–72; Visiting Prof., Univs of Tokyo 1978, Stellenbosch 1979, Papua New Guinea 1981, Florida 1984, Lafayette Coll., Pa 1985, Hong Kong 1989, Harvard Univ. 2002; Chair. Comm. of Inquiry into Int. Responsibility for Phosphate Mining on Nauru 1987–88; mem. Editorial Bd Sri Lankan Journal of International Law, Human Rights Quarterly (Johns Hopkins Univ.), Interdisciplinary Peace Research (La Trobe Univ.), Journal of Ceylon Law; mem. Advisory Bd China Law Reports; Vice-Chair. UN Centre against Apartheid/Govt of Nigeria Conf. on Legal Status of Apartheid Regime, Lagos 1984; Co-ordinator UN Univ./Netherlands Inst. of Human Rights Workshop on Science, Tech. and Human Rights, Utrecht 1989; Vice-Pres. Int. Comm. of Jurists, Vic.; Past Pres. World Fed. of Overseas Sri Lankan Orgs; Pres. Int. Asscn of Lawyers against Nuclear Arms; Chair. Judicial Integrity Group of Chief Justices; mem. Int. Law Inst., Europa Mundi (UNESCO project), Club of Rome (Australia), Commonwealth Lawyers' Asscn and other professional bodies; Academician, Int. Acad. of Comparative Law, Paris; Patron, Centre for Int. Sustainable Devt Law, McGill Univ., Canada; Hon. Visiting Prof., Univ. of Colombo 1984–; Hon. Life mem. Bar Asscn of Sri Lanka; Order of Deshamanya; Hon. LLD (Colombo), (Monash Univ.) 2000, (Nat. Law School of India), Hon. DLit (London); Mohamed Sahabdeen Award for Int. Understanding in the SAARC Region 1993, UNESCO Prize for Peace Educ. 2006, Sri Lankabhimanya (Pride of Sri Lanka) Award 2007, Right Livelihood Award (Alternative Noble Prize) 2007, Lifetime Achievement Award, Nuclear Age Peace Foundation 2008. *Publications:* numerous books on law, human rights and related topics; numerous articles in law journals world-wide and published lectures. *Leisure interests:* enjoys playing the piano. *Address:* 5/2 Roland Towers, Dharmaraja Mawatha, off Alfred House Avenue, Colombo 3 (office); 5/1 Roland Towers, Dharmaraja Mawatha, off Alfred House Avenue, Colombo 3, Sri Lanka (home). *Telephone:* (11) 2500229 (office); (11) 2555028 (home). *Fax:* (11) 4720480 (office). *E-mail:* cweeramantry@gmail.com (home); info@wicper.org (office). *Website:* www.wicper .org (office); www.judgechristopherweeramantry.com.

WEERASETHAKUL, Apichatpong (Joe), MFA; Thai artist and film director; b. 1970, Bangkok; ed Khon Kaen Univ., Art Inst. of Chicago, USA; began career as architect and multi-media artist before becoming filmmaker; f. Kick the Machine (production co.) 1999; mem. jury, Cannes Film Festival 2008; commissioned by UN to make short film (Mobile Men) to mark 60th anniversary of the Universal

Declaration of Human Rights 2008; Chevalier, Ordre des arts et des lettres 2008; Thai Office of Contemporary Culture Silpathorn Award 2005. *Feature films:* Blissfully Yours (Un Certain Regard prize, Cannes Film Festival) 2002, Tropical Malady (Jury Prize, Cannes Film Festival, Tokyo FilmEx first prize) 2004, Syndromes and a Century 2006, A Letter to Uncle Boonmee (Grand Prize of the City of Oberhausen, Germany, Prize of the Jury of the Minister Pres. of N Rhine-Westphalia, Best Film, Prize of the Jury of the Pernambuco Asscn of Filmmakers, Janela Internacional de Cinema do Recife, Brazil) 2009, Uncle Boonmee Who Can Recall His Past Lives 2010. *Address:* Kick The Machine, 44/17 Ladprao 15, Jatujak, Bangkok 10900, Thailand (office). *Website:* www.kickthemachine.com (office).

WEERASOORIYA, Gen. C. S.; Sri Lankan army officer (retd) and diplomatist; m. Dilhani Weerasooriya; ed St Thomas Coll., Pakistan Mil. Acad., Nat. Defence Coll., India; commanded Operation Jayasikurui to regain the Liberation Tigers of Tamil Eelam-held Wanni and Mullaitivu areas and subsequently to open a land route through Wanni and Kilinochchi dists to link up with Jaffna Peninsula 1997; Commdr of the Army (rank of Lt-Gen.) 1998–2000; High Commr to Pakistan 2001–07; Rana Wickrama Padakkama, Rana Sura Padakkama, Vishista Seva Vibhushanaya, Uttama Seva Padakkama. *Address:* c/o Ministry of External Affairs, Republic Building, Colombo 1, Sri Lanka.

WĘGLEŃSKI, Piotr, Dr habil.; Polish molecular geneticist; b. 29 June 1939, Swidniki; m. Teresa Juszczyk; two d.; ed Univ. of Warsaw; academic, Univ. of Warsaw 1961–, Pro-Rector 1985–88, 1990–96, Ordinary Prof. 1989–, Rector 1999–2002, 2002–05; Visiting Prof., MIT, USA 1987–88, Univ. of Paris-Sud 1991; mem. Programme Bd of Polish Radio 2010–; mem. Polish Genetic Soc., Warsaw Scientific Soc., Corresp. mem. Polish Acad. of Sciences 1994; Officier des Palmes académiques 2002, Commdr's Cross, Order of Polonia Restituta Polish 2005; Dr hc (Prikarpatsky State Univ.) 2002. *Publications:* Genetic Engineering (co-author) 1980, Molecular Genetics (co-author and ed.) 1996; numerous scientific articles. *Leisure interests:* tennis, travel, volleyball. *Address:* Uniwersytet Warszawski, ul. Krakowskie Przedmieście 26/28, 00-927 Warsaw, Poland (office). *Telephone:* (22) 5922243 (office). *Fax:* (22) 5540808 (office). *E-mail:* piotr.weglenski@adm.uw.edu .pl (office). *Website:* www.uw.edu.pl (office).

WEHNER, Rüdiger, BA, PhD; German zoologist, neurobiologist and academic; *Professor, Institute of Molecular Life Sciences, University of Zurich;* b. 6 Feb. 1940, Nuremberg; m. Sibylle Segesser Brunegg; ed Univs of Frankfurt and Munich; Research Asst, Univ. of Frankfurt 1966–70; Asst, Inst. of Zoology, Univ. of Zurich 1967–70, Asst Prof. of Animal Physiology 1970–72, Assoc. Prof. 1972–73, Prof. 1974–2005, Research Prof. Emer. 2005–08, Dir Inst. 1986–2005; Sr Research Fellow, Dept of Biology, Yale Univ., USA 1973–74; Andrew Dixon White Prof. (at Large), Cornell Univ., USA 1988–94; Non-Resident Perm. Fellow, Wissenschafts-kolleg (Inst. for Advanced Study) 1991–2008; Visiting Prof., Biozentrum, Univ. of Würzburg 2007–10; mem. Advisory Bd Inst. for Integrative Life Sciences, Humboldt Univ., Berlin 2007; Assoc., Neurosciences Research Program (USA) 2010; mem. Academic Foundation of German People 1960–67; mem. Acad. of Natural Scientists Leopoldina, Halle (Saale) 1985, Academia Europaea 1989, Berlin-Brandenburg Acad. of Sciences 1995, Royal Swedish Physiographic Soc. 2000; Corresp. mem. Acad. of Sciences and Literature, Mainz 1977, Acad. of Sciences, Göttingen 1996, Bavarian Acad. of Sciences 1987; Corresp. mem. (abroad), Austrian Acad. of Sciences 1998; Chair. Section of Organismic and Evolutionary Biology, German Nat. Acad. of Sciences Leopoldina 2004–05; Senator for Leopoldina Adjunktenkreis Switzerland 2005; Fellow, Int. Soc. for Neuroethology 2012; Hon. mem. German Zoological Soc. 2006; Foreign Hon. mem. American Acad. of Arts and Sciences 2005; Hon. Dr rer. nat (Carl von Ossietzky Univ., Oldenburg) 2002, (Humboldt Univ., Berlin) 2005; Carus Medal, Leopoldina and Carus Award, City of Schweinfurt 1993, Karl-von-Frisch Medal, German Zoological Soc. 1994, Distinguished Scientist Award, UCLA 1996, Marcel Benoist Prize 2002, Humboldt Research Award 2007, King Faisal Int. Prize for Science 2008, Univ. Medal in Silver, Univ. of Tübingen 2009. *Publications:* numerous papers in professional journals. *Address:* Institute of Molecular Life Sciences, University of Zurich, Winterthurerstrasse 190, 8057 Zurich, Switzerland (office). *Telephone:* (44) 6354831 (office). *Fax:* (44) 6355716 (office). *E-mail:* rwehner@zool .uzh.ch (office). *Website:* www.neuroscience.ethz.ch (office); www.imls.uzh.ch (office).

WEI, Ing-chou; Taiwanese business executive; *Chairman and CEO, Tingyi (Cayman Islands) Holdings Corpn;* m.; three c.; more than 30 years' experience in factory construction, production man. and research in relation to food production; joined Tingyi (Cayman Islands) Holdings Corpn (China's largest instant noodle producer) 1991, currently Chair. and CEO, introduced Master Kong instant noodles to Chinese consumers 1990s. *Address:* Tingyi (Cayman Islands) Holdings Corpn, No. 15 The 3rd Street, Tianjin Economic-Technological Development Area, Tianjin 300457 (office); Tingyi (Cayman Islands) Holdings Corpn, Suite 5607, 56/F, Central Plaza, 18 Harbour Road, Wanchai, Hong Kong Special Administrative Region, People's Republic of China (office). *Telephone:* 2511-1911 (Hong Kong) (office). *Fax:* 2511-7911 (Hong Kong) (office). *E-mail:* info@tingyi.com (office). *Website:* www.tingyi.com (office).

WEI, Jiafu, MEng, PhD; Chinese shipping industry executive; b. 1950, Jiangsu; ed Wuhan Marine Coll., Dalian Maritime Univ., Tianjin Univ.; with Guangzhou Ocean Shipping Co. 1967–92; Gen. Man. Chinese-Tanzanian Jt Shipping Co., Tanzania 1992–93; Pres. COSCO Holdings Pte Ltd, Singapore 1993–95; Gen. Man. and CEO Tianjin Ocean Shipping Co. 1995–97, COSCO Bulk Carriers Co. Ltd 1997–98, Exec. Pres. and CEO China Ocean Shipping (Group) Co. (COSCO) Group 1998–2011, Chair. 2011–13, Sec. CCP Party Cttee; Chair. China Shipowners' Asscn, China Shipowners Mutual Assurance Asscn, China Fed. of Industrial Econs, China Group Cos Promotion Asscn; apptd Vice-Chair. China Merchants Bank 2001; mem. Panama Canal Authority Advisory Bd, Harvard Business School Asia-Pacific Advisory Bd; mem. 17th CCP Cen. Cttee Cen. Comm. for Discipline Inspection 2007–12; mem. Hong Kong Man. Asscn 2006; Hon. Dean, Shanghai Maritime Univ. School of Econs and Man., Hon. Chief Commdr with Four Star rank of Massport Police, AAPA Security Cttee and Massachusetts Port Authority 2011; Commdr. Order of Leopold II (Belgium) 2005; Hall of the Fame, Lloyd's List and Maritime Asia 2003, Port Authority of Long Beach Port Pilot Award 2004, Int. Who's Who Professional, Int. Who's Who Historical Soc. 2004, Valuable Manager of the Year, China's leading media 2004, Economic Booster Award, Massachusetts Alliance for Econ. Devt 2004, Port Pilot Award, Port Authority of Long Beach 2004, Int. Maritime Achievement Award 2005, CCTV Annual Econ. Leaders 2005, Leader in Global Shipping and Logistics, US Journal of Commerce 2006, Outstanding Dir's Award, Hong Kong Dirs Asscn 2008, named by People's Daily amongst the 30 Most Influential People in China's Economy 1978–2008 2008, CMA Commodore Award 2009, named China Charity Amb. by China Charity Asscn 2009, Personality Award, Sea Trade 2009, CCTV Outstanding Contrib. Award of Chinese Brands 2009, commended by US House of Reps as a People's Amb. 2009, named by US Business Week amongst the 40 Most Influential People in China 2009, Third Place, top 500 Chinese business leaders roll by CEIBS 2009, CCTV Outstanding Business Leaders in Ten Years 2009, Guardian of American Workers Award, Int. Longshoremen Asscn (USA) 2011. *Address:* c/o China Ocean Shipping (Group) Company (COSCO), Ocean Plaza, 158 Fuxingmennei Street, Beijing 100031, People's Republic of China.

WEI, Jianxing; Chinese state official; b. Jan. 1931, Xinchang Co., Zhejiang Prov.; ed Dalian Eng Inst., CCP Cen. Cttee Cen. Party School and in USSR; joined CCP 1949; section chief, Northeast China Light Alloy Processing Factory 1961–64, Dir 1977–81; Deputy Sec. Harbin Municipality CCP Cttee 1981–83; Mayor of Harbin City 1981–83; Sec. and mem. Exec. Cttee All-China Fed. of Trade Unions 1983, Vice-Pres. 1983–84, Pres. 1993–2002; Deputy Dir CCP Cen. Cttee Org. Dept 1984–85, Dir 1985–87; Minister of Supervision 1987–93; Sec. CCP Beijing Municipal Cttee 1995–97; Alt. mem. 12th CCP Cen. Cttee 1982–87, mem. 13th CCP Cen. Cttee 1987–92, 14th CCP Cen. Cttee 1992–97, 15th CCP Cen. Cttee 1997–2002; mem. CCP Cen. Cttee Politburo, Cttee and Secr. for Inspecting Discipline 1992–2002; Head Cen. Leading Group for Party Bldg Work; Sec. Secr. CCP Cen. Cttee; mem. CCP Standing Cttee Politburo 1997–2002. *Address:* c/o All-China Federation of Trade Unions, 10 Fu Xing Men Wai Jie, Beijing 100865, People's Republic of China (office).

WEI, Jingsheng; Chinese dissident; fmr mem. Red Guards and PLA; active in pro-democracy movt, contrib. to underground magazine Exploration 1978; sentenced to 15 years' imprisonment for allegedly leaking mil. secrets to a foreign journalist and for counter-revolutionary activities Spring 1979, released Sept. 1993; held incommunicado and without charge April 1994; sentenced to 14 years' imprisonment for alleged subversive activities 1995; deported March 1998; f. Wei Jingsheng Foundation, New York City 1998; f. Overseas Chinese Democracy Coalition 1998; Olof Palme Memorial Prize 1994, Sakharov Prize for Freedom of Thought 1996, Robert F. Kennedy Human Rights Award 1996, Nat. Endowment for Democracy Award 1997. *Publication:* The Courage to Stand Alone. *Address:* Wei Jingsheng Foundation, PO Box 15449, Washington, DC 20003, USA. *Telephone:* (1) 202-270-6980. *Website:* weijingsheng.org.

WEI, Wei; Chinese singer; b. Hohhot, Inner Mongolia; m. Michael J. Smith (divorced 2004); three s.; singer at 11th Asian Games, Beijing 1990, performed a duet with Julio Iglesias at East Asian Games, Shanghai 1993; represented Asia at the ceremony of the Olympic Games, Atlanta, USA 1996; performed at closing ceremony, Beijing 2008 Summer Olympics; winner Nat. Young Singers' contest on Chinese TV 1986, Sopot Int. Music Festival 1987. *Film appearance:* The Singer's Story. *Recordings include:* albums: Twilight, I Believe In China. *Address:* Wei Wei International Management, Jing Da International 4E, Chao Yang Park West Road 11, 100026 Beijing, People's Republic of China (office). *E-mail:* info@weiweiint.com (office). *Website:* www.weiweiint.com.

WEI, Yang, BS, MS, PhD; Chinese engineer and academic; *President, National Natural Sciences Foundation;* b. 16 Feb. 1954, Beijing; ed Tsinghua Univ., Brown Univ., USA; Prof. of Solid Mechanics and Chair., Dept of Eng Mechanics, Tsinghua Univ. 1989–2006; Pres. Zhejiang Univ. 2006–13; Visiting Scientist, Univ. of Sheffield, UK 1987–88, Univ. of Calif., Santa Barbara, USA 1993, 1995, Taiwan Univ. 1996–97, Princeton Univ., USA 1998; Visiting Prof. Inst. of Mechanics, Grenoble, France 1988, Brown Univ., USA 1990, Tokyo Inst. of Tech., Japan 2000–01, Univ. of Illinois, Urbana-Champaign, USA 2002; Pres. Far East and Oceanic Fracture Soc. 2004–08; Pres. Nat. Natural Sciences Foundation 2013–; Vice Pres., Chinese Soc. of Theoretical and Applied Mechanics; Council Mem. China Asscn of Science and Tech.; mem. Scientific Cttee, Ministry of Educ.; mem. Gen. Ass., Int. Union of Theoretical and Applied Mechanics; Regional Ed. International Journal of Fracture; mem. Editorial Bds International Journal of Damage Mechanics, Fatigue and Fracture of Engineering Materials and Structures, International Journal of Solids and Structures, Archive in Applied Mechanics; mem. Chinese Acad. of Sciences; Hon. DS (Brown Univ.) 2012; three Scientific Achievement Awards, State Educ. Comm., Young Scientists Award 1994, Nat. Natural Science Award 1995, Scientific Achievement Award, Ministry of Educ. 2002. *Publications:* Mesoplasticity and its Applications (jtly) 1993, Macroscopic and Microscopic Fracture Mechanics 1995, Mechatronic Reliability 2001, Interfacial and Nanoscale Failure (co-ed.) 2003; over 240 technical papers. *Address:* National Natural Sciences Foundation, 83 Shuangqing Rd, Haidian, Beijing , People's Republic of China (office). *Telephone:* (10) 62327001 (office). *E-mail:* Bic@nsfc.gov.cn (office). *Website:* www.nsfc.gov.cn (office).

WEICKER, Lowell Palmer, Jr, LLB; American fmr politician; b. 16 May 1931, Paris, France; s. of Lowell Palmer Weicker and Mary Paulsen Weicker (née Bickford); m. 1st Camille Di Lorenzo Butler; eight c.; m. 2nd Claudia Testa Ingram 1984; ed Lawrenceville School, Yale Univ. and Univ. of Virginia; State Rep. in Conn. Gen. Ass. 1963–69; US Rep., Fourth Congressional Dist, Conn. 1969–71; Senator from Conn. 1971–89; Gov. of Conn. 1991–95; 1st Selectman of Greenwich 1964–68; mem. Select Cttee for Investigation of the Watergate Case 1973; fmr mem. Senate Appropriations Cttee, Senate Labor and Human Resources Cttee, fmr Chair. Senate Small Business Cttee, Sub-cttee on State, Justice, Commerce, the Judiciary and related agencies, Senate Energy and Natural Resources Cttee; fmr Republican, then Ind.; Pres. Bd of Dirs, Trust for America's Health 2001–11; mem. Bd of Dirs Compuware Co. 1996–, World Wrestling Entertainment 1996–2011, Medallion Financial Corpn 2003–, Phoenix, Duff & Phelps Mutual Funds; Chair. Pew Foundation Environmental Health Comm. 2000, Century Fund Comm. 2001; fmr mem. Bd of Dirs United States Tobacco. *Publication:* Maverick: My Life in Politics 1995. *Leisure interests:* tennis, scuba, history.

WEIDENFELD, Baron (Life Peer), cr. 1976, of Chelsea in Greater London; **Arthur George Weidenfeld,** Kt, GBE; British publisher; *Chairman, Weidenfeld & Nicholson Limited;* b. 13 Sept. 1919, Vienna, Austria; s. of the late Max Weidenfeld and Rosa Weidenfeld; m. 1st Jane Sieff 1952; one d.; m. 2nd Barbara Skelton Connolly 1956 (divorced 1961); m. 3rd Sandra Payson Meyer 1966 (divorced 1976); m. 4th Annabelle Whitestone 1992; ed Piaristengymnasium, Vienna, Univ. of Vienna and Konsular Akad.; came to UK 1938; BBC Monitoring Service 1939–42; BBC News Commentator on European Affairs on BBC Empire and N American service 1942–46; Foreign Affairs columnist, News Chronicle 1943–44; Political Adviser and Chief of Cabinet of Pres. Weizmann of Israel 1949–50; Founder, Contact Magazine 1945, George Weidenfeld & Nicolson Ltd 1948–; Chair. George Weidenfeld & Nicolson Ltd 1948–, Wheatland Corpn, New York 1985–90, Grove Press, New York 1985–90, Wheatland Foundation, San Francisco and New York 1985–92; Dir (non-exec.) Orion 1991–; Consultant, Bertelsmann Foundation 1991–, Axel Springer AG Germany; Hon. Chair. Bd of Govs, Ben Gurion Univ. of the Negev 1996–; Gov. of Tel-Aviv Univ. 1980–, Weizmann Inst. of Science 1964–; Columnist Die Welt, Die Welt am Sonntag, Bild am Sonntag; mem., South Bank Bd 1986–99; mem. Bd ENO 1988–98, Herbert Quandt Foundation 1999–2008; Trustee, Royal Opera House 1974–87, Nat. Portrait Gallery 1988–95, Potsdam Einstein Forum, Jerusalem Foundation; Chair. Cheyne Capital 2000–10, Trialogue Educational Trust 1996–; mem. Governing Council, Inst. of Human Science, Vienna; Vice-Chair. Oxford Univ. Devt Programme 1994–99; Pres., Inst. for Strategic Dialogue 2006–; Freeman of the City of London; Honour of City of Vienna 2003; Hon. Senator, Bonn Univ. 1996; Hon. Fellow, St Peter's Coll. Oxford 1992, St Anne's Coll. Oxford 1993; Golden Kt's Cross of Order of Merit (Austria) 1989, Chevalier, Légion d'honneur 1990, Kt Commdr's Cross (Badge and Star) of Order of Merit (Germany) 1991, Cross of Honour First Class for Arts and Science (Austrian) 2003, Grand Officer, Order of Merit (Italy) 2005, Order of Merit of Baden-Württemberg 2008, Bene Merito (Poland) 2011; Hon. MA (Oxon.) 1992; Hon. PhD (Ben Gurion Univ.); Hon. DLitt (Exeter) 2001, (Oxford) 2010; Charlemagne Medal 2000, London Book Fair/Trilogy Lifetime Achievement Award 2007, Teddy Kollek Lifetime Achievement Award 2009. *Publications include:* The Goebbels Experiment 1943, Remembering My Good Friends 1994. *Leisure interests:* opera, travel. *Address:* Orion House, 5 Upper St Martin's Lane, London, WC2H 9EA (office); 9 Chelsea Embankment, London, SW3 4LE, England (home). *Telephone:* (20) 7520-4411 (office); (20) 7351-0042 (home). *Fax:* (20) 7379-1604 (office). *E-mail:* george.weidenfeld@orionbooks.co.uk (office).

WEIDENFELD, Werner, DPhil; German political scientist and academic; *Professor of Political Science and Director, Center for Applied Policy Research, Geschwister Scholl Institute for Political Science, Ludwig-Maximilians-Universität München;* b. 2 July 1947, Cochem; s. of Dr Josef Weidenfeld and Maria Weidenfeld (née Walther); m. Gabriele Kokott-Weidenfeld 1976; ed Univ. of Bonn; Prof. of Political Science, Univ. of Mainz 1976–95; Assoc. Prof., Sorbonne, Paris 1986–88; Co-ordinator for German-American Co-operation 1987–99; Prof. of Political Science, Ludwig-Maximilians-Universität München 1995–, Dir Centre for Applied Policy Research; Perm. Guest Prof., Remnim Univ., Beijing, People's Repub. of China 2000–; mem. Exec. Bd Bertelsmann Foundation, Gütersloh 1992–2007; Bundesverdienstkreuz (First Class) 1998, Commdr, Ordinul serviciul Credincios of the Repub. of Romania; Dr hc; Columbus Medal, German-American Soc., Munich 1991, Europe Medal (Bavaria) 1996, Bavarian Europe-Schoolbook Award 1997, Gen. Lucius D. Clay Medal, Asscn of German-American Clubs 1998, World of Difference Award, Anti-Defamation League 1999, European Cultural Award, European Cultural Foundation 2001. *Publications:* Die Englandpolitik Gustav Stresemanns 1972, Konrad Adenauer und Europa 1976, Europa 2000 1980, Die Frage nach der Einheit der deutschen Nation 1981, Die Identität der Deutschen 1983, Die Bilanz der Europäischen Integration 1984, Nachdenken über Deutschland 1985, 30 Jahre EG 1987, Geschichtsbewusstsein der Deutschen 1987, Der deutsche Weg 1990, Jahrbuch der Europäischen Integration (ed.) 1980ff, Die Deutschen – Profil einer Nation 1991, Europa von A bis Z, Taschenbuch der Europäischen Integration (co-ed. with Wolfgang Wessels) 1991ff, Handwörterbuch zur deutschen Einheit 1992, Osteuropa: Herausforderungen-Probleme-Strategien 1992, Technopoly, Europa im globalen Wettbewerb 1993, Maastricht in der Analyse, Materialien zur Europäischen Union (ed.) 1994, Europa '96: Reformprogramm für die Europäische Union (ed.) 1994, Reform der Europäischen Union 1995, Kulturbruch mit Amerika? 1996, Handbuch zur deutschen Einheit 1996, Demokratie am Wendepunkt? (ed.) 1996, Europa öffnen–Anforderungen an die Erweiterung (ed.) 1997, Aussenpolitik für die deutsche Einheit: Die Entscheidigungsjahre 1989/90 1998, Amsterdam in der Analyse: Strategien für Europa (ed.) 1998, Handbuch zur deutschen Einheit 1949–1989–1999 (ed.) 1999, Deutschland-Trendbuch (ed.) 2001, Herausforderung Terrorismus 2004, Wie Zukunft entsteht 2002, Europa-Handbuch (ed.) 2004, Die Europäische Verfassung in der Analyse (ed.) 2005, Managing Integration (ed.) 2005, Rivalität der Partner (ed.) 2005, Die Europäische Verfassung verstehen 2006, Partners at Odds 2006, Werte 2006, Understanding the European Constitution 2007, Europa leicht gemacht 2007, Reformen kommunizieren (ed.) 2007, Europäische Identität: Voraussetzungen und Strategien (co-ed. with Nida Rümelin) 2007, Lissabon in der Analyse – Der Reformvertrag der Europäischen Union (ed.) 2008, Die Europäische Union – Politisches System und Politikbereiche (ed.) 2008, Die Staatenwelt Europas (ed.) 2009, Die Europäische Union 2010, Deutsche Kontraste (co-ed. with Manuela Glaab and Michael Weigl) 2010. *Address:* Center for Applied Policy Research, Geschwister Scholl Institute for Political Science, Ludwig-Maximilians-Universität München, Maria-Theresia-Str. 21, 81675 Munich (office); Oettingenstr. 67, 80538 Munich, Germany (home). *Telephone:* (89) 21801300 (office). *Fax:* (89) 21809042 (office). *E-mail:* cap.office@lrz.uni-muenchen.de (office). *Website:* www.cap-lmu.de/english/index.php (office).

WEIDINGER, Christine, BA; American singer (soprano); b. 31 March 1946, Springville, NY; m. Kenneth Smith 1976; ed Grand Canyon Coll., Phoenix, studied singing with Marlene Delavan in Phoenix, Adrian de Peyer in Wuppertal, Dean Verhines in Los Angeles; debut as Musetta in La Bohème at Metropolitan 1972, sang at Metropolitan Opera 1972–76, at Stuttgart and Bielefeld Operas, Germany 1979–; roles include Malvina in Heinrich Marschner's Der Vampyr, Anina in Bellini's La Sonnambula, Berthe in Meyerbeer's Le Prophète, Elizabeth I in Donizetti's Roberto Devereux, Inez in L'Africaine, Lucia and Juliet in I Capuleti e i

Montecchi, Pamira in Rossini's Siege of Corinth, Eupaforice in Heinrich Graun's Spanish Conquest, Constanze in Abduction from the Seraglio, Electra in Idomeneo, Leonora in Trovatore, Adèle in Le Comte Ory, Vitellia in La Clemenza di Tito, Tancredi, Violetta, Gilda, Donna Anna, Mimi, Liu, and the title roles in Thea Musgrave's Mary, Queen of Scots, Donizetti's Lucia di Lammermoor, Bellini's Norma, Bellini's Beatrice di Tenda; Nat. first prize Metropolitan Opera Auditions 1972. *Recordings:* Handel's Rinaldo with Marilyn Horne, L'Africaine with Caballé and Domingo, Die Freunde von Salamanka by Schubert, Médée with Caballé and Lima, Mitridate by Mozart. *Leisure interests:* yoga, jogging, electric trains. *Address:* Robert Lombardo Associates, 61 W 62nd Street, Suite 6F, New York, NY 10023, USA (office).

WEIDMANN, Jens, PhD; German economist and central banker; *President, Deutsche Bundesbank;* b. 20 April 1968, Solingen; m. Anja Weidmann; one s., one d.; ed Université de Droit, d'Economie et des Sciences, Aix-Marseille III, France, Rheinische Friedrich-Wilhelms Univ., Bonn; internship at Banque de France; Research Asst, Inst. for Int. Econ. Policy, Univ. of Bonn 1994–97; Economist with IMF, Washington, DC 1997–99; Sec.-Gen. German Council of Econ. Experts 1999–2003; Head of Monetary Policy and Analysis Div. and Deputy Head of Econs Dept, Deutsche Bundesbank 2003–06; Head, Dept of Econ. and Financial Policy, Fed. Chancellor's Office 2006–11, also personal rep. of Chancellor Angela Merkel charged with preparations for world econ. summits of G8 and G20 countries; Pres. Deutsche Bundesbank 2011–; mem. Governing Council, European Cen. Bank 2011–. *Address:* Deutsche Bundesbank, Wilhelm-Epstein-Strasse 14, 60431 Frankfurt am Main, Germany (office). *Telephone:* (69) 95663511 (office). *Fax:* (69) 95663077 (office). *E-mail:* info@bundesbank.de (office). *Website:* www .bundesbank.de (office).

WEIKL, Bernd; Austrian singer (baritone); b. 29 July 1942, Vienna; ed Mainz Conservatoire and Hochschule für Musik, Hanover; mem. Hamburg State Opera 1973–, Deutsche Oper Berlin 1974–; guest artist, Bayreuth Festivals 1973–75; Covent Garden debut 1975 as Rossini's Figaro; Metropolitan Opera debut 1977 as Wolfram; guest engagements at La Scala Milan, Bavarian State Opera, Salzburg Festival; performed Iago at Stuttgart 1990, Boccanegra at Hamburg 1991, Dutchman at Bayreuth 1990, Sachs at the Metropolitan 1993, Jochanaan at San Francisco 1997, Kurwenal in Tristan und Isolde at Munich 1998.

WEILL, Sanford I., BA; American banker; *Chairman Emeritus, Citigroup Inc.;* b. 16 March 1933, New York; s. of Max Weill and Etta (née Kalika) Weill; m. Joan Mosher 1955; one s., one d.; ed Peekskill Mil. Acad., Cornell Univ., School Business and Public Admin.; CEO Carter, Berlind and Weill (now Shearson/American Express Inc.) New York 1960–, Pres. and CEO 1978–85; Chair., Pres., CEO Commercial Credit Co., Baltimore 1986–; Chair., CEO Primerica Corpn 1989–, Pres. 1989–92; Chair., CEO Travelers Group 1996–98; apptd Co-Chair. Citigroup (merger between Citicorp and Travelers Group) 1999, CEO –2003, Chair. –2006, now Chair. Emer.; f. Acad. of Finance; Dir Terra Nova Insurance Co. 1984–; Chair. Carnegie Hall 1991–; mem. Midwest Stock Exchange Bd; Assoc. mem. New York Stock Exchange, Bd of Overseers Cornell Medical Coll., Business Cttee Museum of Modern Art, NY. *Address:* Citigroup, 153 East 53rd Street, New York, NY 10043 (office); Citigroup Inc., 399 Park Avenue, New York, NY 10013, USA. *Telephone:* (212) 559-1000 (office). *Fax:* (212) 793-3946 (office). *Website:* www.citigroup.com (office).

WEINBACH, Lawrence A., BS (Hons), CPA; American business executive; *Managing Director, Yankee Hill Capital Management LLC;* b. 8 Jan. 1940, Brooklyn, New York; s. of Max Weinbach and Winnefred Weinbach; m. Patricia Lieter 1961; two s. one d.; ed Wharton School, Univ. of Pennsylvania; joined Arthur Andersen 1961, Man. Pnr, Stamford, Conn. office 1974–83, Man. Pnr, New York office 1983–87, COO 1987–89, Man. Pnr and CEO 1989–97; Chair., Pres. and CEO Unisys Corpn 1997–2004, Exec. Chair. 2005–06; Man. Dir Yankee Hill Capital Management LLC 2006–; Chair. Great Western Products Holdings LLC 2009–; mem. Bd of Dirs Avon Products 1999–2013, UBS AG 2001–08, Quadra Realty Trust Inc. 2007–, Discover Bank 2009–; Outside Ind. Dir, Discover Financial Services LLC 2007–, Lead Dir 2009–; Trustee, Univ. of Pennsylvania, Carnegie Hall, Wharton School; fmr Trustee, The Carnegie Hall Corpn; mem. Bd Nat. Security Telecommunications Advisory Cttee. *Leisure interests:* reading, golf. *Address:* Yankee Hill Capital Management LLC, 300 East 42nd Street, Suite 1400, New York, NY 10017, USA (office). *Telephone:* (646) 356-8450 (office). *Fax:* (212) 661-2601 (office). *E-mail:* lawrence.weinbach@yankeehillcapital.com (office). *Website:* www.yankeehillcapital.com (office).

WEINBERG, Adam D., BA, MFA; American museum director; *Director, Whitney Museum of American Art;* ed Brandeis Univ., State Univ. of NY at Buffalo; Dir of Educ. and Asst Curator, Walker Art Center, Minneapolis 1981–89; Artistic and Program Dir, American Center in Paris 1989–93; Sr Curator of Perm. Collection, Whitney Museum of American Art, NY 1993–99, Alice Pratt Brown Dir of Museum 2003–, also a Trustee; Mary Stripp and R. Crosby Kemper Dir Addison Gallery of American Art at Phillips Acad., Andover 1999–2003, also Curator of Temporary Exhbns. *Address:* Whitney Museum of Modern Art, 945 Madison Avenue at 75th Street, New York, NY 10021, USA (office). *Telephone:* (212) 570-3633 (office). *Fax:* (212) 570-4169 (office). *E-mail:* info@whitney.org (office). *Website:* www.whitney .org (office).

WEINBERG, Robert A., PhD; American biochemist and academic; *Member, Whitehead Institute and Daniel K. Ludwig Professor for Cancer Research, Massachusetts Institute of Technology;* b. 11 Nov. 1942, Pittsburgh, Pa; s. of Dr Fritz E. Weinberg and Lore W. Weinberg (née Reichhardt); m. Amy Shulman 1976; one s. one d.; ed Massachusetts Inst. of Tech.; Instructor in Biology, Stillman Coll., Ala 1965–66; Fellow, Weizmann Inst., Israel 1969–70; Fellow, Salk Inst., Calif. 1970–72; Research Assoc. Fellow, MIT 1972–73, Asst Prof., Dept of Biology and Center for Cancer Research 1973–76, Assoc. Prof. 1976–82, Founding mem. and Prof., Whitehead Inst. for Biomedical Research 1982–, currently Daniel K. Ludwig Prof. for Cancer Research; mem. NAS; Hon. ScD (Northwestern Univ.) 1984; numerous awards, including 'Scientist of the Year', Discover magazine 1982, Bristol-Myers Award for Distinguished Achievement in Cancer Research 1984, Nat. Medal of Science 1997, Wolf Prize in Medicine 2004, Landon-AACR Award for Cancer Research 2006, Otto Warburg Medal 2007, Breakthrough Prize in Life Sciences (co-recipient) 2013. *Achievements include:* identified and characterized both the first oncogene and the first tumour suppressor gene. *Leisure interests:* house building, gardening, genealogy. *Address:* Whitehead Institute, 9 Cambridge Center, Cambridge, MA 02142 (office); Department of Biology, Massachusetts Institute of Technology, Cambridge, MA 02139, USA (office). *Telephone:* (617) 258-5159 (office). *Fax:* (617) 258-5213 (office). *E-mail:* weinberg@wi.mit.edu (office). *Website:* www.wi.mit.edu/research/faculty/weinberg.html (office); weinberglab.wi .mit.edu (office); biology.mit.edu/people/robert_weinberg (office); wi.mit.edu/ people/faculty/weinberg (office).

WEINBERG, Serge, LenD; French business executive; *Chairman, Sanofi SA;* b. 10 Feb. 1951; ed Univ. of Paris, Institut d'Etudes Politiques de Paris, Ecole Nationale d'Admin, Strasbourg; Pvt. Prin. Sec. to Budget Minister 1981–82; Deputy Dir-Gen. FR3 1982–83; Chair. Havas Tourisme 1983–87; Dir-Gen. Pallas Finances 1987–90; Chair. Rexel (affiliate of Pinault) 1991–95, mem. Man. Bd Pinault Printemps-Redoute (PPR) 1993–2005, Chair. and CEO 1995–2005, mem. Supervisory Bd PPR Interactive; Founder and Chair. Weinberg Capital Partners 2005–; Chair. (non-exec.) Accor 2006–09; mem. Bd of Dirs Sanofi-Aventis 2009–, Chair. 2010– (name changed to Sanofi May 2011); Chair. Supervisory Bd Conforama Holding, France-Printemps, Guilbert SA, Redcats; Vice-Chair. Supervisory Bd Schneider Electric; mem. Supervisory Bd Boucheron Holding, Gucci Group NV (Netherlands), Yves Saint Laurent Perfumes; Dir, Fnac SA, Artémis, Gucci, French Asscn of Pvt. Enterprises, Soc. des Amis du Musée d'Orsay); mem. Growth Release Cttee (Attali Cttee) 2007–08; Founding mem. and Treas. Institut du Cerveau et de la Moelle Épinière (ICM—Brain and Spinal Cord Inst.); mem. Nat. Econ. Comm. *Address:* Weinberg Capital Partners, 40 rue La Boétie, 75008 Paris (office); Sanofi SA, 174 avenue de France, 75013 Paris Cedex 13, France (office). *Telephone:* 1-53-53-55-00 (Weinberg Capital Partners) (office); 1-53-77-42-23 (Sanofi) (office). *Fax:* 1-53-53-55-19 (Weinberg Capital Partners) (office); 1-53-77-42-65 (Sanofi) (office). *E-mail:* serge.weinberg@weinbergcapital.com (office); info@sanofi.com (office). *Website:* www.weinbergcapital.com (office); www.sanofi .com (office).

WEINBERG, Steven, PhD; American physicist and academic; *Jack S. Josey-Welch Foundation Chair in Science and Regental Professor and Director, Theory Research Group, Department of Physics, University of Texas;* b. 3 May 1933, New York; s. of Fred Weinberg and Eva Weinberg; m. Louise Goldwasser 1954; one d.; ed Cornell Univ., Univ. of Copenhagen and Princeton Univ.; Columbia Univ. 1957–59; Lawrence Radiation Lab. 1959–60; Univ. of Calif. at Berkeley 1960–69; Prof. of Physics, MIT 1969–73; Higgins Prof. of Physics, Harvard Univ. 1973–83; Sr Scientist, Smithsonian Astrophysical Observatory 1973–83, Sr Consultant 1983–; Josey Chair and Regental Prof. of Science, Univ. of Texas, Austin 1982–, also Dir Theory Research Group; Co-Ed. Cambridge Univ. Press Monographs on Mathematical Physics 1978; Dir Jerusalem Winter School of Theoretical Physics 1983–, Headliners Foundation 1993–; mem. A.P. Sloan Foundation Science Book Cttee 1985–90, Einstein Archives Int. Advisory Bd 1988–, Scientific Policy Cttee, Supercollider Lab. 1989–93, American Acad. of Arts and Sciences 1968–, NAS 1972–, Council for Foreign Relations, President's Cttee on the Nat. Medal of Science 1979–80, Royal Soc. 1982–, American Philosophical Soc. 1983–; fmr mem. Council, American Physical Soc., Int. Astronomical Union, Philosophical Soc. of Tex. (Pres. 1994); Loeb Lecturer, Harvard Univ. and Visiting Prof. MIT 1966–69, Richtmeyer Lecturer of American Asscn of Physics Teachers 1974, Scott Lecturer, Cavendish Lab. 1975, Silliman Lecturer, Yale Univ. 1977, Lauritsen Lecturer, Calif. Inst. of Tech. 1979, Bethe Lecturer, Cornell Univ. 1979, Harris Lecturer, Northwestern Univ. 1982, Cherwell-Simon Lecturer, Oxford Univ. 1983, Bampton Lecturer, Columbia Univ. 1983, Hilldale Lecturer, Univ. of Wisconsin 1985, Brickweede Lecturer, Johns Hopkins Univ. 1986, Dirac Lecturer, Univ. of Cambridge 1986, Klein Lecturer, Univ. of Stockholm 1989, Sackler Lecturer, Univ. of Copenhagen 1994, Brittin Lecturer, Univ. of Colorado 1994, Gibbs Lecturer, American Math. Soc. 1996, Bochner Lecturer, Rice Univ. 1997, Sanchez Lecturer, Witherspoon Lecturer, Washington Univ. 2001.; Hon. DSc (Knox Coll.) 1978, (Chicago, Yale, Rochester) 1979, (City Univ., New York) 1980, (Clark Univ.) 1982, (Dartmouth) 1984, (Weizmann Inst.) 1985, (Columbia) 1990, (Salamanca) 1992, (Padua) 1992, (Barcelona) 1996, (Bates Coll.) 2002, (McGill Univ.) 2003; Hon. DLitt (Washington Coll.) 1985; J. R. Oppenheimer Prize 1973, Dannie Heinemann Mathematical Physics Prize 1977, American Inst. of Physics-U.S. Steel Foundation Science Writing Award 1977, Elliott Cresson Medal, Franklin Inst. 1979, Joint Winner, Nobel Prize for Physics 1979, James Madison Medal (Princeton) 1991, Nat. Medal of Science 1991, Andrew Gemant Award 1997, Piazzi Prize 1998, Lewis Thomas Prize Honoring the Scientist as Poet 1999, Benjamin Franklin Medal, American Philosophical Soc. 2004. *Publications:* Gravitation and Cosmology 1972, The First Three Minutes 1977, The Discovery of Subatomic Particles 1982, Elementary Particles and the Laws of Physics (with R. P. Feynman) 1987, Dreams of a Final Theory 1993, The Quantum Theory of Fields (Vol. I) 1995, (Vol. II) 1996, (Vol. III) 2000, Facing Up 2001, Lake Views: This World and the Universe 2010, Lectures on Quantum Mechanics 2012; and over 250 articles. *Leisure interest:* medieval history. *Address:* Department of Physics, University of Texas, Theory Group, RLM 5.208 C1608, Austin, TX 78712-1081, USA. *Telephone:* (512) 471-4394 (office). *Fax:* (512) 471-4888 (office). *E-mail:* weinberg@physics.utexas.edu (office). *Website:* www.ph.utexas.edu/~weintech/weinberg.html (office).

WEINER, Matthew, MFA; American television producer and writer; b. 29 June 1965, Baltimore; m. Linda Brettler; four s.; ed Wesleyan Univ., Univ. of Southern California. *Television* includes The Naked Truth (writer) 1995, Becker (producer and writer) 1999–2002, Andy Richter Controls the Universe (producer) 2002–03, The Sopranos (writer and exec. producer) 2004–07 (Emmy for Outstanding Drama Series 2004, 2007, TV Producer of Year awards in Episodic, Producers' Guild of America 2005, 2008, Best Dramatic Series award, Writers' Guild of America 2007), Mad Men (creator and exec. producer) 2007– (Best New Series award, Writers' Guild of America 2008, Emmy for Outstanding Writing for a Drama Series 2008, 2010, Emmy for Outstanding Drama Series 2008, 2010, 2011, Best TV Series - Drama, Golden Globe award, Hollywood Foreign Press Asscn 2009, 2010, Norman Felton Producer of Year award in TV - Drama, Producers' Guild of America 2009, 2010, Best Dramatic Series, Writers' Guild of America 2009). *Address:* c/o AMC, 11 Penn Plaza, 15th Floor, New York, NY 1001, USA (office).

WEINGARTEN, David Michael, BA, MArch; American architect; *Principal, Ace Architects;* b. 22 Jan. 1952, Fort Ord, Calif.; s. of Saul M. Weingarten and Miriam

E. Moore; one s.; ed Monterey High School, Yale Univ. and Univ. of California, Berkeley; Partner, Ace Architects 1979–, now Prin.; Lecturer, Univ. of California, Berkeley 1980–81; Graham Foundation for Advances Studies Award 1987, Interiors Magazine '40 under 40' Award 1990, Architectural Digest 'AD 100' Award 1994, 1996. *Publications:* Souvenir Buildings/Miniature Monuments 1996, Monumental Miniatures 1997, Bay Area Style: San Francisco Bay Region Houses 2004, Ten Houses: Ace Architects 2000, California Ranch Houses (co-author) 2009; articles for several design and other periodicals. *Address:* Ace Architects, 330 Second Street #1, Oakland, CA 94607, USA (office). *Telephone:* (510) 452-0775 (office). *Fax:* (510) 452-1175 (office). *E-mail:* ace@aceland.com (office). *Website:* www.aceland.com (office).

WEINGARTNER, Paul Andreas, DPhil; Austrian academic; *Professor Emeritus of Philosophy, Institut für Philosophie, Universität Salzburg;* b. 8 June 1931, Innsbruck; s. of Karl Weingartner and Maria Weingartner; five s. one d.; ed Univ. of Innsbruck; Research Fellow, Univ. of London 1961–62; Research Asst Inst. für Wissenschaftstheorie, Int. Research Centre, Salzburg 1962–67, Chair. Dept I (Philosophy of Natural Science) 1967–72; Assoc. Prof. of Philosophy, Univ. of Salzburg 1970, Prof. of Philosophy 1971–, now Prof. Emer., Chair. Inst. für Philosophie 1971–79, 1988–90, 1994–98, Chair. Inst. für Wissenschaftstheorie 1972–; mem. Acad. Internationale de Philosophie des Sciences 1975–; New York Acad. of Sciences 1997–; Dr hc (M. Curie Univ., Poland) 1995. *Publications:* Wissenschaftstheorie (two vols) 1976, 1978, Logisch-philosophische Untersuchungen zu Werten und Normen 1996, Zu philosophie-historischen Themen 1996, Basic Questions on Truth 2000; Evil, Different Kinds, In the Light of a Modern Theodicy 2003; Laws of Nature (with P. Mittelstaedt) 2005, Omniscience: From a Logical Point of View 2008; ed of 36 vols; about 150 research articles. *Leisure interests:* sport (climbing, skiing), photography. *Address:* Department of Philosophy, University of Salzburg, Franziskanergasse 1, 5020 Salzburg, Austria (office). *Telephone:* (662) 8044-4070 (office). *Fax:* (662) 8044-4074 (office). *E-mail:* paul .weingartner@sbg.ac.at (office). *Website:* www.uni-salzburg.at/phs (office).

WEINRIB, Ernest J., BA, LLD, PhD, FRSC; Canadian professor of law; *Cecil A. Wright Professor of Law, University of Toronto;* b. 1943, Toronto; m. Lorraine Eistenstat; one s. two d.; ed Univ. of Toronto, Harvard Univ., USA; Asst Prof. of Classics, Univ. of Toronto 1968–72, Asst Prof. of Law 1972–75, Assoc. Prof. of Law 1975–81, Prof. of Law 1981, Univ. Prof. 1999–, Cecil A. Wright Prof. of Law 2000–; Visiting Prof. of Law, Univ. of Tel-Aviv, Israel 1979, Yale Law School, USA 1984; Book Review Ed. Univ. of Toronto Law Journal; mem. Editorial Cttee Ratio Juris, Law and Philosophy Library; mem. Advisory Bd Israel Law Review; Fellow, Royal Soc. of Canada; Foreign Hon. mem. American Acad. of Arts and Sciences 2008; Canada Council for the Arts Killam Prize 2009. *Publications:* The Idea of Private Law 1995, Tort Law: Cases and Materials 1997; numerous essays and articles. *Address:* Faculty of Law, University of Toronto, 78 Queen's Park, Toronto, ON M5S 2C5, Canada (office). *Telephone:* (416) 978-8581 (office). *E-mail:* e.weinrib@ utoronto.ca (office). *Website:* www.law.utoronto.ca (office).

WEINSTEIN, Alan, BSc, MA, PhD; American mathematician and academic; *Professor of the Graduate School, Department of Mathematics, University of California, Berkeley;* b. 1943, New York; m. Margo Weinstein; ed Massachusetts Inst. of Tech., Univ. of California, Berkeley; conducted postdoctoral research at Institut des Hautes Etudes Scientifiques, France and Univ. of Bonn, Germany; joined Faculty of Dept of Math., Univ. of California, Berkeley 1969, Full Prof. 1976–2009, Prof. of the Grad. School 2009–; Visiting Prof., Univ. of Paris, France 2009; mem. American Acad. of Arts and Sciences 1992–; Dr hc (Utrecht) 2003; Guggenheim Fellowship, Sloan Fellowship. *Address:* Department of Mathematics, University of California, 825 Evans Hall, Berkeley, CA 94720-3840, USA (office). *Telephone:* (510) 642-6550 (office). *Fax:* (510) 642-8204 (office). *E-mail:* alanw@ math.berkeley.edu (office). *Website:* math.berkeley.edu/~alanw (office).

WEINSTEIN, Allen; American historian, academic and archivist; *Archivist of the United States; Prof.* of History, Smith Coll., Chair. American Studies Program 1966–81; Univ. Prof., Georgetown Univ., Washington, DC 1981–84, Exec. Ed. The Washington Quarterly, Center for Strategic and Int. Studies 1981–83; mem. editorial staff, The Washington Post 1981; Univ. Prof. and Prof. of History, Boston Univ. 1985–89; directed research study that led to creation of Nat. Endowment for Democracy, Acting Pres. Endowment 1982–84; founding mem. Bd of Dirs US Inst. of Peace 1985, Dir 1985–2001; founder, Pres. and CEO Center for Democracy 1985–2003; Sr Advisor, Int. Foundation for Election Systems 2003–05; ninth Archivist of the USA, Nat. Archives and Records Admin 2005–; Fellow, Woodrow Wilson Int. Center for Scholars, American Council of Learned Socs; held two Sr Fulbright Lectureships, Commonwealth Fund Lecturer, Univ. of London, UK, among other awards and fellowships; UN Peace Medal 1986, Bicentennial Fourth of July Orator, Faneuil Hall, Boston 1987, Council of Europe Silver Medal 1990, 1996, awards from Presidents of Nicaragua and Romania. *Publications:* The Story of America 2002, The Haunted Wood: Soviet Espionage in America–The Stalin Era 1999, Perjury: The Hiss-Chambers Case (revised edn) 1997, Freedom and Crisis: An American History, Prelude to Populism: Origins of the Silver Issue; eight ed collections; articles and essays have appeared in numerous scholarly and popular publs. *Address:* The National Archives and Records Administration, 8601 Adelphi Road, College Park, MD 20740-6001, USA (office). *Telephone:* 301-837-1600 (office). *Fax:* 301-837-3218 (office). *Website:* www.archives.gov (office).

WEINSTEIN, Harvey; American film industry executive; b. 1952, Buffalo, NY; s. of Mira Weinstein and Max Weinstein; brother of Robert Weinstein (q.v.); Co-Chair. Miramax Films Corpn, New York with brother Robert 1979–2005; co-founder with brother The Weinstein Co. 2005. *Films produced include:* Playing for Keeps 1986, Scandal 1989, Strike it Rich 1990, Hardware 1990, A Rage in Harlem 1991, The Crying Game 1992, The Night We Never Met 1993, Benefit of the Doubt 1993, True Romance 1993, Mother's Boys 1994, Like Water for Chocolate 1994, Pulp Fiction 1994, Pret-A-Porter 1994, Smoke 1995, A Month by the Lake 1995, The Crossing Guard 1995, The Journey of August King 1995, Things To Do In Denver When You're Dead 1995, The Englishman Who Went Up A Hill But Came Down a Mountain 1995, Blue in the Face 1995, Restoration 1995, Scream 1996, The Pallbearer 1996, The Last of the High Kings 1996, Jane Eyre 1996, Flirting with Disaster 1996, The English Patient 1996, Emma 1996, The Crow: City of Angels 1996, Beautiful Girls 1996, Addicted to Love 1997, Shakespeare in Love 1998, Allied Forces, She's All That 1999, My Life So Far 1999, The Yards 1999,

Bounce 2000, Scary Movie 2000, Boys and Girls 2000, Love's Labour's Lost 2000, Scream 3 2000, About Adam 2000, Highlander: Endgame 2000, Chocolat 2000, Dracula 2000, Spy Kids 2001, Texas Rangers 2001, Daddy and Them 2001, Scary Movie 2 2001, The Others 2001, Jay and Silent Bob Strike Back 2001, Lord of the Rings: Fellowship of the Ring 2001, Iris 2001, Shipping News 2001, Kate and Leopold 2001, Imposter 2002, Only the Strong Survive 2002, Heaven 2002, Halloween: Resurrection 2002, Full Frontal 2002, Spy Kids 2 2002, Below 2002, Equilibrium 2002, Waking Up in Reno 2002, Lord of the Rings; Two Towers 2002, Gangs of New York 2002, Chicago 2002, Confessions of a Dangerous Mind 2002, Spy Kids 3–D 2003, Human Stain 2003, Duplex 2003, Kill Bill: Vol. 1 2003, Scary Movie 3 2003, Bad Santa 2003, Lord of the Rings: Return of the King 2003, Cold Mountain 2003, The I Inside 2003, Mindhunters 2004, Jersey Girl 2004, Ella Enchanted 2004, Kill Bill: Vol. 2 2004, Paper Clips 2004, Fahrenheit 9/11 2004, Shall We Dance 2004, Cursed 2004, Aviator 2004, Derailed 2005. *Address:* The Weinstein Company, 345 Hudson Street, 13th Floor, New York, NY 10014, USA (office). *Website:* www.weinsteinco.com.

WEINSTEIN, Robert (Bob); American film industry executive; b. 1954, Flushing, NY; s. of Max Weinstein and Mira Weinstein; brother of Harvey Weinstein (q.v.); m. 1st; two d.; m. 2nd Anne Clancy 2000; one s. one d.; produced rock concerts with brother Harvey as Harvey & Corky Productions, Buffalo 1970s; Co-founder and Co-Chair. Miramax Film Corpn with brother Harvey 1979–2005; Co-founder with brother The Weinstein Co. 2005; Founder and Head of Dimension Films. *Broadway productions:* co-producer: The Real Thing (revival) (Tony Award for Best Revival of a Play, Drama Desk Award for Outstanding Revival of a Play) 2000, The Producers (musical) (Tony Award for Best Musical, Drama Desk Award for Outstanding New Musical) 2001, Sweet Smell of Success (musical) 2002, La bohème (revival) 2003, All Shook Up (musical) 2005, The Color Purple (musical) 2005. *Screenplay:* The Burning 1981. *Films produced include:* (all with Harvey Weinstein q.v.) Playing for Keeps (with Alan Brewer) (also writer and dir) 1986, Scandal (with Joe Boyd and Nik Powell) 1989, Strike it Rich 1990, Hardware (with Nik Powell, Stephen Woolley and Trix Worrell) 1990, A Rage in Harlem (with Terry Glinwood, William Horberg and Nik Powell) 1991, The Night We Never Met (with Sidney Kimmel) 1993, Benefit of the Doubt 1993, True Romance (with Gary Barber, Stanley Margolis and James G. Robinson) 1993, Clerks 1994, Mother's Boys (with Randall Poster) 1994, Pulp Fiction (with Richard N. Gladstein) 1994, Pret-A-Porter (with Ian Jessel) 1994, Smoke (with Satoru Iseki) 1995, A Month By the Lake (with Donna Gigliotti) 1995, The Crossing Guard (with Richard N. Gladstein) 1995, The Journey of August King 1995, Things To Do In Denver When You're Dead (with Marie Cantin) 1995, The Englishman Who Went Up a Hill But Came Down a Mountain (with Sally Hibbin and Robert Jones) 1995, Blue in the Face (with Harvey Keitel) 1995, Restoration (with Donna Gigliotti) 1995, Flirting with Disaster 1996, The English Patient 1996, Scream 1996, The Faculty 1998, Halloween H20: 20 Years Later 1998, Good Will Hunting 1998, Velvet Goldmine 1998, Jackie Brown 1998, Shakespeare in Love 1998, Allied Forces 1999, My Life So Far 1999, The Yards 1999, Music of the Heart 1999, The Cider House Rules 1999, She's All That 1999, Down To You 2000, Committed 2000, The Crow: Salvation 2000, The Prophecy 3: The Ascent 2000, Boys and Girls 2000, Scream 3 2000, Love's Labour's Lost 2000, Scary Movie 2000, Highlander: Endgame 2000, Backstage 2000, Malena 2000, Bounce 2000, Chocolat 2000, Dracula 2000 2000, Serendipity 2001, Spy Kids 2001, Texas Rangers 2001, Daddy and Them 2001, Scary Movie 2 2001, The Others 2001, Legend of Zu 2001, Jay and Silent Bob Strike Back 2001, Lord of the Rings: Fellowship of the Ring 2001, Shipping News 2001, Kate and Leopold 2002, Ritual 2001, Imposter 2002, Only the Strong Survive 2002, Halloween: Resurrection 2002, Full Frontal 2002, Spy Kids 2 2002, Darkness 2002, Below 2002, Waking Up in Reno 2002, Lord of the Rings: Two Towers 2002, Equilibrium 2002, Gangs of New York 2002, Chicago 2002, Confessions of a Dangerous Mind 2002, Spy Kids 3-D: Game Over 2003, My Boss's Daughter 2003, Human Stain 2003, Duplex 2003, Kill Bill: Vol. 1 2003, Scary Movie 3 2003, Bad Santa 2003, Lord of the Rings: Return of the King 2003, Cold Mountain 2003, The I Inside 2003, Mindhunters 2004, Jersey Girl 2004, Ella Enchanted 2004, Kill Bill: Vol. 2 2004, Paper Clips 2004, The Great Raid 2004, Fahrenheit 9/11 2004, Finding Neverland 2004, Shall We Dance 2004, Cursed 2004, The Aviator 2004, Derailed 2005, Sin City 2005, Breaking and Entering 2006, Clerks 2 2006, Pulse 2006, Halloween 2007, The Mist 2007, Rogue 2007, Sicko 2007, The Great Debaters 2007, Fanboys 2008, The Reader 2008, Zack and Miri Make a Porno 2008, Capitalism: A Love Story 2009, Youth in Revolt 2009, Janky Promoters 2009, Inglourious Basterds 2009, Nine 2009, Hurricane Season 2009, Shanghai 2010, Piranha 3-D 2010, The King's Speech 2010, My Week with Marilyn 2011, Scream 4 2011, Hoodwinked Too! Hood vs. Evil 2011, The Artist 2011, Spy Kids: All the Time in the World in 4D 2011, Apollo 18 2011, Butter 2011, I Don't Know How She Does It 2011, My Week with Marilyn 2011, Piranha 3DD 2012, The Sapphires 2012, Silver Linings Playbook 2012, Song for Marion 2012, Django Unchained 2012, Ain't Them Bodies Saints 2013, Escape from Planet Earth 2013, Dark Skies 2013, Scary Movie 5 2013, Beyond Memories (short) 2013, A Better Tomorrow (short) 2013, uwantme2killhim? 2013, The Butler 2013, August: Osage County 2013, The Art of the Steal 2013, Philomena 2013, Vampire Academy 2014, Sin City: A Dame to Kill For 2014, Big Eyes 2014, The Amityville Horror: The Lost Tapes 2015. *Television includes:* Project Runway (series) 2004–13, After the Runway (series) 2011, Project Accessory (series) 2011, Supermarket Superstar (series) 2012, Mob Wives: The Sit Down (series) 2012, Mob Wives Chicago (series) 2012, Big Ang (series) 2012, Code Name: Geronimo (film) 2012, Project Runway All Stars (series) 2012–14, Under the Gunn (series) 2014. *Address:* The Weinstein Company, 345 Hudson Street, 13th Floor, New York, NY 10014, USA. *E-mail:* info@weinsteinco .com. *Website:* www.weinsteinco.com.

WEIR, Dame Gillian Constance, DBE, LRAM, LTCL, FRCM; British concert organist, harpsichordist, broadcaster and lecturer; *Prince Consort Professor of Organ, Royal College of Music;* b. 17 Jan. 1941, Martinborough, New Zealand; d. of Cecil Alexander Weir and Clarice Mildred Foy Weir (née Bignell); m. 1st Clive Rowland Webster 1967 (divorced 1971); m. 2nd Lawrence Irving Phelps 1972 (died 1999); ed Wanganui Girls' Coll., NZ and Royal Coll. of Music, London with Cyril Smith (piano) and Ralph Downes (organ), pvt. studies in London and Paris with Anton Heiller, Marie-Claire Alain and Nadia Boulanger; Winner, St Albans Int. Organ Festival Competition 1964; debuts at Royal Festival Hall and Royal Albert Hall, London 1965; worldwide career since 1965 as concert organist, comprising some 2,000 appearances in major concert halls etc., including 50 at South Bank Centre, London; has appeared with all leading British orchestras and many abroad, including Vienna Symphony, Boston Symphony, San Francisco Symphony, ORF, under leading conductors; many radio and TV appearances; adjudicator in int. competitions and artist-in-residence at major univs including Yale; gives lectures and master classes in many countries; organ consultant, Birmingham Symphony Hall; Visiting Prof. of Organ, RAM, London 1997–98; Prince Consort Prof. of Organ, Royal Coll. of Music, London 1999–; Int. Chair. in Organ, Royal Northern Coll. of Music, Manchester 2006–07; Distinguished Visiting Artist, Peabody Conservatory of Music, Baltimore, USA 2006–12; Visiting Tutor Curtis Inst., Philadelphia 2006–09; many premières including first British performance of Messiaen's Meditations of 1972; many works written for her including concertos by William Mathias and Peter Racine Fricker; many recordings including complete organ works of Olivier Messiaen 1995 and complete works of César Franck 1997; recognized world-wide as authority on and pre-eminent performer of Messiaen; Concerto soloist First Night of the Proms 1967 and Last Night of the Proms 1999, many other Proms appearances; Pres. Inc. Asscn of Organists (first woman Pres.) 1981–83, Inc. Soc. of Musicians 1992–93, Soloists' Ensemble 1998–2000; mem. Exec. Council, Royal Coll. of Organists (first woman mem.) 1981–85, Council (first woman mem.) 1977–, Pres. (first woman Pres.) 1994–96; mem. Council of Royal Philharmonic Soc. 1995–2001; mem. Royal Soc. of Musicians of GB 1996–; Trustee, Eric Thompson Charitable Trust 1993–; Patron Friends of Young Artists' Platform 1991–, Oundle Int. Festival 1998–, Cirencester Early Music Festival 1999, Northern Ireland Int. Organ Competition 2011–, various organ socs in UK and abroad; Hon. FRCO 1975; Hon. Fellow, Royal Canadian Coll. of Organists 1983; Hon. RAM 1989; Hon. Bencher of the Middle Temple, London 2012; Hon. DMus (Victoria Univ. of Wellington, NZ) 1983, (Hull) 1999, (Exeter) 2001, (Leicester) 2003, (Aberdeen) 2004, (London) 2008, (Durham) 2012; Hon. DLitt (Huddersfield) 1997; Hon. DUniv (Univ. of Central England) 2001; Countess of Munster Award 1965, Int. Performer of the Year Award, American Guild of Organists 1981, Musician of the Year, Int. Music Guide 1982, Turnovsky Foundation Award for Outstanding Contrib. to the Arts (first musician) 1985, Silver Medal, Albert Schweitzer Asscn (Sweden) 1998, Evening Standard Award for Outstanding Solo Performance 1999, Lifetime Achievement Award, The Link Foundation 2005. *Television:* presenter and performer, The King of Instruments (six-part series, BBC) 2000, A Year in the Life of Gillian Weir (NZTV), appearances on Omnibus (BBC), South Bank Show (ITV) 2000, and numerous other programmes. *Publications include:* contrib. to Grove's Dictionary of Music and Musicians 1980, Faber's The Messiaen Companion 1995; articles in professional journals. *Leisure interests:* theatre, reading. *E-mail:* gillianweir@onetel.com (home). *Website:* gillianweir.com.

WEIR, Judith, CBE, MA; British composer; b. 11 May 1954, Cambridge, England; ed North London Collegiate School, King's Coll., Cambridge; Composer-in-Residence, Southern Arts Asscn 1976–79; Fellow in Composition, Univ. of Glasgow 1979–82, Creative Arts Fellowship, Trinity Coll. Cambridge 1983–85, Composer-in-Residence, Royal Scottish Acad. of Music and Drama (RSAMD) 1988–91; Fairbairn Composer in Asscn with City of Birmingham Symphony Orchestra 1995–98; Artistic Dir Spitalfields Festival 1995–2000; Hambro Visiting Prof. in Opera Studies, Univ. of Oxford 1999–2000; Visiting Prof., Princeton Univ., USA 2001; Fromm Foundation Visiting Prof., Harvard Univ. 2004; Distinguished Visiting Research Prof. in Composition, School of Music, Cardiff Univ. 2006–13; Trustee, Royal Opera House 2002–11; Hon. Fellow, St Hilda's Coll. Oxford 2000, King's Coll. Cambridge 2003; Hon. RAM 1997; Hon. FRCM 2006; Dr hc (Aberdeen) 1995, (Univ. of Central England) 1999, (RSAMD) 2001, (Queen's Univ. Belfast) 2001, (Glasgow) 2005, (King's Coll. London) 2007, (Glasgow Caledonian) 2008; Critics' Circle Award 1994, Elise L Stoeger Prize 1997, South Bank Award 2000, Queen's Medal for Music 2007, Distinguished Musician Award, Incorporated Soc. of Musicians 2010. *Compositions include:* King Harald's Saga 1979, The Consolations of Scholarship 1985, The Black Spider 1985, A Night At The Chinese Opera 1987, Missa Del Cid 1988, Heaven Ablaze In His Breast 1989, The Vanishing Bridegroom 1990, Music Untangled 1991–92, Heroic Strokes of the Bow 1992, Blond Eckbert 1993, Musicians Wrestle Everywhere 1994, Moon and Star 1995, Forest 1995, Storm 1997, Piano Concerto 1997, Piano Trio 1998, Natural History 1999, We Are Shadows (South Bank Show Award 2001) 2000, Piano Quartet 2000, The Welcome Arrival of Rain 2001, Tiger under the Table 2002, The Voice of Desire 2004, Piano Trio No. 2 2004, Armida 2005, Blond Eckbert Pocket Version 2006, Winter Song 2007, Concrete 2008, Miss Fortune 2009–11, I give you the end of a golden string 2011–13. *Address:* c/o Promotion Department, Chester Music, 14–15 Berners Street, London, W1T 3LJ, England (office). *Telephone:* (20) 7612-7400 (office). *Fax:* (20) 7612-7549 (office). *E-mail:* promotion@musicsales.co.uk (office). *Website:* www.musicsalesclassical.com (office).

WEIR, Peter Lindsay; Australian film director; b. 21 Aug. 1944, Sydney; s. of Lindsay Weir and Peggy Barnsley; m. Wendy Stites 1966; one s. one d.; ed Scots Coll., Sydney, Vaucluse Boys' High School, Sydney Univ.; worked in real estate until 1965; worked as stagehand in television, Sydney 1967; dir film sequences in variety show 1968; Dir amateur univ. reviews 1967–69; dir for Film Australia 1969–73; made own short films 1969–73, independent feature-film dir and writer 1973–; Broadcast Film Critics Asscn Passion in Film Award 2004. *Films:* Cars that Ate Paris 1973, Picnic at Hanging Rock 1975, The Last Wave 1977, The Plumber (television) 1978, Gallipoli 1980, The Year of Living Dangerously 1982, Witness 1985, The Mosquito Coast 1986, Dead Poets Society 1989, Green Card 1991, Fearless 1994, The Truman Show (BAFTA Award for Best Dir) 1997, Master and Commander: The Far Side of the World (BAFTA Award for Best Dir) 2003, The Way Back 2010. *Address:* c/o International Creative Management, 10250 Constellation Boulevard, Los Angeles, CA 90067, USA (office).

WEIR, Stuart Peter, BA; British journalist and academic; *Director, Democratic Audit, Human Rights Center and Visiting Professor, Government Department, University of Essex;* b. 13 Oct. 1938, Frimley, Surrey; s. of Robert H. Weir and Edna F. Lewis; m. 1st Doffy Burnham 1963; two s.; m. 2nd Elizabeth E. Bisset 1987; one s. two d.; ed Peter Symonds School, Winchester and Brasenose Coll. Oxford; Feature Writer, Oxford Mail 1964–67; Diarist, The Times 1967–71; Dir Citizens Rights Office 1971–75; Founding Ed. Roof Magazine (Shelter) 1975–77; Deputy Ed. New Society 1977–84; Ed. New Socialist 1984–87; Political Columnist, London Daily News 1987; Ed. New Statesman 1987–88, New Statesman and Society

1988–90; Founder Charter 88 1988; Dir Democratic Audit and Prof. and Sr Research Fellow Human Rights Centre, Univ. of Essex 1991–, Visiting Prof. 1999–; Series Consultant, The People's Parl. (Channel 4 TV) 1994–97; Consultant, State of Democracy Project, Int. IDEA, Stockholm 1997–2003; Assoc. Consultant (Governance) British Council 1997–; Consultant on Governance Dept for Int. Devt 1999–2002; Sr Int. Facilitator Namibian Govt and Democracy Project 1994–95; UK Facilitator Zimbabwe Parl. Democracy Project; Chair. Parl. Assessment Team, Zimbabwe 2002–03; Lecturer on Politics and the Media, LSE 1994. *Publications:* Manifesto 1981; contributor to: The Other Britain 1982, Consuming Secrets 1982, Defining and Measuring Democracy 1995; Ego Trip (ed.) 1995, Behind Closed Doors 1995, The Three Pillars of Liberty 1996, Making Votes Count 1997, Political Power and Democratic Control in Britain 1998, Voices of the People (jtly.) 2001, The IDEA Handbook on Democracy Assessments (jtly.) 2001, The State of Democracy (jtly) 2002, Democracy Under Blair 2003. *Leisure interests:* children, cooking, walking, football. *Address:* Butts Orchard, Butts Batch, Wrington, Bristol, BS40 5LN, England. *Telephone:* (1934) 863668. *E-mail:* stuart@democraticaudit.demon.co.uk (office). *Website:* www.essex.ac.uk (office).

WEIR, Viscount; William Kenneth James Weir, FRSA, BA; British business executive; b. 9 Nov. 1933, Glasgow, Scotland; s. of Lord Weir and Lady Weir (née Crowdy); m. 1st Diana Lucy MacDougall 1964 (divorced 1972); one s. one d.; m. 2nd Jacqueline Mary Marr 1976 (divorced); m. 3rd Marina Sevastopoulo 1988; one s.; ed Eton Coll., Trinity Coll. Cambridge; served Royal Navy 1955–56; Chair. Weir Group PLC 1972–99, Balfour Beatty PLC (fmrly BICC PLC) 1996–2003, CP Ships Ltd 2001–04; Dir Bank of England 1972–84, British Steel Corpn 1972–76, British Bank of Middle East 1977–79, Canadian Pacific Ltd 1989–2001, St James Place Capital 1990, Canadian Pacific Railway Co. 2001; Pres. British Electrotechnical Mfrs Asscn 1988-89, 1993–95; mem. London Advisory Cttee, Hong Kong Shanghai Bank 1980–92, Export Credit Advisory Cttee 1991–98; Chair. British Water 1999–2000; Hon. FREng; Hon. DEng (Glasgow). *Publication:* The Weir Group 2008. *Leisure interests:* shooting, golf. *Address:* Rodinghead, Mauchline, Ayrshire, KA5 5TR, Scotland (home). *Telephone:* (1563) 884233 (home).

WEISBROD-WEBER, Wolfgang; German UN official; *Special Representative of the Secretary-General for Western Sahara and Head, United Nations Mission for the Referendum in Western Sahara (MINURSO);* b. 1955, Hanau; m.; three c.; ed Freie Universität, Berlin; various appointments within UN Secr. and in UN field operations, including Dir Europe and Latin American Div., UN Dept of Peacekeeping Operations 2004–06, Chief of Staff, UN Integrated Mission in Timor-Leste 2006–08, Dir of Asia and Middle East Div., UN Dept of Peacekeeping Operations 2008–12, Deputy Special Rep. of Sec.-Gen. ad interim for UN Assistance Mission in Afghanistan 2009, 2010, Special Rep. of Sec.-Gen. for Western Sahara and Head of UN Mission for Referendum in Western Sahara 2012–. *Address:* United Nations Mission for the Referendum in Western Sahara (MINURSO) Headquarters, PO Box 80,000, Laâyoune, Western Sahara (office); Office of the Secretary-General, United Nations, New York, NY 10017, USA (office). *Telephone:* (528) 986-000 (Laâyoune) (office); (212) 963-1234 (New York) (office). *Fax:* (212) 963-4879 (New York) (office). *E-mail:* minursoinformationofficer@un.org (office). *Website:* minurso.unmissions.org (office); www.un.org (office).

WEISFELDT, Myron Lee, BA, MD; American cardiologist and academic; *Director, Department of Medicine, School of Medicine, Johns Hopkins University;* b. 25 April 1940, Milwaukee, Wis.; m. Linda Weisfeldt 1963; three c.; ed Johns Hopkins Univ.; intern then resident, Columbia-Presbyterian Medical Center, New York 1965–67; Fellow in Cardiology, Mass Gen. Hosp., Boston 1970–72; Asst Prof. of Medicine, Johns Hopkins Univ., Baltimore 1972–78, Prof. of Medicine 1978–91, Robert L. Levy Prof. of Cardiology 1979–91, Dir, Cardiology Div., Johns Hopkins Univ. School of Medicine 1975–91, William Osler Prof. of Medicine and Physician-in-Chief, Johns Hopkins Hosp. 2001–, also Dir, Dept of Medicine; Samuel Bard Prof. of Medicine and Chair. Dept of Medicine, Columbia-Presbyterian Medical Center 1991–2001; Pres. American Heart Asscn 1989–90; Fellow, AAAS, American Coll. of Physicians, American Coll. of Cardiology; mem. NAS Inst of Medicine, American Soc. for Clinical Investigation, Asscn of American Physicians, Asscn of Profs of Medicine, Nat. Inst. on Aging Nat. Advisory Council; mem. Bd of Advisers KBL Healthcare Acquisition Corpn; numerous awards including American Heart Asscn Golden Heart Award 1998, Phillips Award in Clinical Medicine, American Coll. of Physicians 2006, Diversity Award, Asscn of Profs of Medicine 2008. *Address:* Office of the Director, Department of Medicine, Johns Hopkins University School of Medicine, 733 N. Broadway, Suite G49, Baltimore, MD 21205-2196, USA (office). *Telephone:* (410) 955-3182 (office). *Website:* www.hopkinsmedicine.org/som (office).

WEISKRANTZ, Lawrence, PhD, FRS; American/British psychologist and academic; *Fellow Emeritus of Magdalen College and Professor Emeritus of Psychology, University of Oxford;* b. 28 March 1926, Philadelphia, Pa, USA; s. of Benjamin Weiskrantz and Rose Weiskrantz (née Rifkin); m. Barbara Collins 1954; one s. one d.; ed Girard Coll. of Philadelphia, Swarthmore and Univs of Oxford and Harvard; part-time Lecturer, Tufts Univ. 1952; Research Assoc., Inst. of Living 1952–55; Sr Postdoctoral Fellow, NAS 1955–56; Research Assoc., Cambridge Univ., England 1956–61, Asst Dir of Research 1961–46, Fellow, Churchill Coll. 1964–67, Reader in Physiological Psychology 1966–67; Prof. of Psychology and Head of Dept of Experimental Psychology, Oxford Univ. 1967–93, Prof. Emer. 1993–; Fellow of Magdalen Coll., Oxford, now Fellow Emer.; Kenneth Craik Research Award, St John's Coll., Cambridge 1975–76; Sir Frederick Bartlett Memorial Lecturer 1980; Ferrier Lecturer, Royal Soc. 1989; Hughlings Jackson Lecturer/Medallist (Royal Soc. of Medicine) 1990; Harry Camp Memorial Lecturer, Stamford Univ. 1997; Werner Heisenburg Lecturer, Bavarian Acad. of Science 1998; John P. McGovern Award Lecture, AAAS 2002; Deputy Ed. Brain 1981–91; mem. NAS. *Publications:* Analysis of Behavioral Change (ed.) 1967, Animal Intelligence (ed.) 1985, Neuropsychology of Cognitive Function (ed.) 1986, Blindsight 1986, Thought Without Language (ed.) 1988, Consciousness Lost and Found 1997 and articles in Science, Nature, Quarterly Journal of Experimental Psychology, Journal of Comparative Physiological Psychology, Animal Behaviour and Brain. *Leisure interests:* music, walking. *Address:* Department of Experimental Psychology, University of Oxford, South Parks Road, Oxford, OX1 3UD,

England (office). *Telephone:* (1865) 271444 (office). *E-mail:* larry.weiskrantz@psy .ox.ac.uk (office). *Website:* www.psych.ox.ac.uk (office).

WEISS, Ulrich, DBA; German banker; b. 3 June 1936; ed Univ. of Hamburg; fmr mem. Bd of Man. Dirs, Deutsche Bank AG, Frankfurt, Chair. Admin. Council, Deutsche Bank SAE, Barcelona/Madrid, Deutsche Bank de Investimento SA, Lisbon, Deutsche Bank Luxembourg SA, Chair. Admin. Council, Deutsche Bank SpA, Milan 1979–88; fmr Chair. O&K Orenstein & Koppel AG, Heidelberg; fmr Deputy Chair. Südzuker AG, Mannhei and Deputy Chair. Supervisory Bd; Chair. Supervisory Bd Continental AG –2005, Hanover; Dir, Ducati Motor Holding SpA from 1998, Bego Medical AG, Bremen, Edizione Holding SpA, Mittel SpA, Mittel Private Equity SpA; Ind. Dir, Benetton Group SpA 1997–2007; mem. Supervisory Bd HeidelbergCement AG (fmrly Heidelberger Zement AG) –2004, Asea Brown Boveri AG –2005, Mannheim, BASF AG, Ludwigshafen, Heidelberger Zement AG, Klein, Schanzlin & Becker AG, Frankenthal, Rheinelektra AG, Mannheim; mem. Admin. Council Fiat SpA, Turin; mem. Advisory Bd Deutsche Bahn AG, EPCI Srl, ECPI Group SpA, Bausparkasse Schwaebisch Hall AG; Co-founder and mem. Bd Stiftung Marktwirtschaft, Berlin (think tank). *Address:* c/o Deutsche Bank AG, 60325 Frankfurt am Main, Germany.

WEISSER, Alberto, BBA; American business executive; *Executive Chairman, Bunge Ltd;* b. 26 June 1955, Argentina; ed Universidade de São Paulo, Harvard Business School, Institut Européen d'Admin des Affaires (INSEAD), France; began career with BASF Group, worked in Brazil, Germany, USA and Mexico 1978–93; joined Bunge Ltd as Chief Financial Officer 1993–99, mem. Bd of Dirs 1997–, CEO 1999–2013, Chair. 2001–13, Exec. Chair. 2013–; mem. Int. Paper Co. 2006–; mem. North American Agribusiness Advisory Bd of Rabobank; mem. Council on Foreign Relations, Council of the Americas. *Address:* Bunge Ltd, 50 Main Street, 6th Floor, White Plains, NY 10606, USA (office). *Telephone:* (914) 684-2800 (office). *Fax:* (914) 684-3499 (office). *E-mail:* info@bunge.com (office). *Website:* www.bunge.com (office).

WEISSER, Hellmuth; German business executive; *Chairman of the Supervisory Board, Marquard & Bahls AG;* CEO Marquard & Bahls AG 1981–2003, Chair. Supervisory Bd 2003–; Pres. Union Pétrolière Européenne Indépendante, Paris, AFM+E (Aussenhandelsverband für Mineralöl und Energie e.V.), Hamburg; mem. EC Energy Consultative Cttee. *Address:* Marquard & Bahls AG, Admiralitaetstr. 55, 20459 Hamburg, Germany (office). *Telephone:* (40) 37004-0 (office). *Fax:* (40) 37004-225 (office). *E-mail:* office@mbholding.de (office). *Website:* www.mbholding .com (office).

WEISSLEDER, Ralph, MD, PhD; German radiologist and academic; *Professor of Radiology, Harvard Medical School;* ed Univ. of Heidelberg; currently Prof. of Radiology, Harvard Medical School, Boston, Mass, USA, Dir Center for Molecular Imaging Research and Attending Interventional Radiologist, Massachusetts Gen. Hosp., Charlestown; Researcher, The Breast Cancer Research Foundation, New York; Founding-mem. Soc. for Molecular Imaging Research, Pres. 2002; J. Allyn Taylor Int. Prize in Medicine 2004; Acad. of Molecular Imaging Distinguished Basic Scientist Award 2006, RSNA Outstanding Researcher Award 2008, European Soc. of Radiology Gold Medal 2011. *Publications:* Primer of Diagnostic Imaging (co-author) 2002; 10 US and int. patents and more than 300 articles in medical journals on molecular imaging research in living organisms. *Address:* Center for Systems Biology, Simches Research Bldg, 185 Cambridge Street, 5th Floor, Boston, MA 02114, USA (office). *Telephone:* (617) 726-8226 (office); (617) 726-8396 (Clinic) (office). *Fax:* (617) 643-6133 (office); (617) 726-4891 (Clinic) (office). *E-mail:* rweissleder@mgh.harvard.edu (office); rweissleder@partners.org (office). *Website:* https://csb.mgh.harvard.edu/ (office); www.massgeneralimaging .org (office).

WEISSMAN, Irving L., BS, MD, FAAS; American biologist and academic; *Karel and Avice Beekhuis Professor of Cancer Biology, Professor of Pathology and of Developmental Biology, Professor (By Courtesy) of Neurosurgery and of Biological Sciences, Director, Institute for Stem Cell Biology and Regenerative Medicine and Director, Stanford Ludwig Center for Cancer Stem Cell Research and Medicine, Stanford University School of Medicine;* b. 21 Oct. 1939, Great Falls, Mont.; ed Dartmouth Coll., Montana State Coll., Univ. of Oxford, UK, Stanford Univ.; Montana Cancer Soc. Student Research Fellow, Lab. for Experimental Medicine, Montana Deaconess Hosp., Great Falls 1961; Medical Student Research Fellow, Dept of Genetics, Stanford Univ. School of Medicine 1961, NIH Student Traineeship, Dept of Radiology 1961–64, NIH Postdoctoral Fellowship 1965–67, Research Asscn 1967–68, Asst Prof., Dept of Pathology 1969–74, Assoc. Prof. 1974–81, Prof. 1981–, Chair. Stanford Univ. Immunology Program 1986–, Karel and Avice Beekhuis Prof. of Cancer Biology 1987–, Prof. of Developmental Biology 1989–, Investigator, Howard Hughes Medical Inst., Stanford Univ. 1990–92, Prof. (By Courtesy) of Neurosurgery and of Biological Sciences, Dir Inst. of Stem Cell Biology and Regenerative Medicine, School of Medicine 2003–; NIH Student Traineeship, Cellular Immunology Research Unit, Sir William Dunn School of Pathology, MRC, Oxford 1964; Sr Dernham Fellow, American Cancer Soc. (Calif. Div.) 1969–73; Josiah Macy Foundation Scholar 1974–75; Co-Founder and mem. Bd of Dirs SyStemix, Palo Alto, Calif. 1988, Chair. Scientific Advisory Bd 1988–97; Founder Stem Cells, Inc., Palo Alto 1998; mem. Scientific Advisory Bd Amgen, Calif. 1981–89, DNAX, Germany 1981–92, T Cell Sciences, Inc., Mass 1988–92; Pres. American Asscn of Immunologists 1994–95; mem. Nat. Bd of Govs Project Inform; Assoc. Ed. Molecular Therapy 1999–; mem. Editorial Bd Journal of Cellular Biochemistry 1980–, Molecular Marine Biology and Biotechnology 1991–, Biology of Blood and Marrow Transplantation 1995–, Experimental Hematology 1996–, Journal of Clinical Investigation 1998–; mem. NAS 1987 (mem. Council 2011)), American Acad. of Arts and Sciences 1990, American Acad. of Microbiology 1997, American Asscn of Immunologists, American Asscn of Univ. Pathologists (PLUTO), American Asscn of Pathologists, American Soc. for Microbiology, American Asscn of Cancer Research, American Acad. of Microbiology, Clinical Immunology Soc., American Soc. of Hematology, Int. Soc. of Experimental Hematology, American Soc. for Blood and Marrow Transplantation, Int. Cytokine Soc., Molecular Medicine Soc.; Hon. mem. Israel Immunological Soc. 1995; Hon. Dir Centre for Biotech/BioMedicine and Shenzhen Key Lab. of Gene and Antibody Therapy, Grad. School of Shenzhen, Tsinghau Univ., People's Repub. of China; Hon. Investigator, State Key Lab. of Experimental Hematology, Chinese Acad. of Medical Sciences and Peking Union Medical Coll. 2010; Hon. Prof., Peking Union

Medical Coll. 2010; Hon. DSc (Montana State Univ.) 1992; Faculty Research Award, American Cancer Soc. 1974–78, NIH Outstanding Investigator Award 1986, Kaiser Award for Excellence in Pre-clinical Teaching 1987, Harvey Lecturer 1989, Pasarow Award for Outstanding Contrib. to Cancer Biology 1989, Selected Top 100, Alumni, Montana State Univ. 1993, de Villier's Int. Achievement Award, Leukemia Soc. of America 1999, E. Donnall Thomas Prize to Recognize Pioneering Research Achievements in Hematology, American Soc. of Hematology 1999, J. Allyn Taylor Prize in Medicine 2003, The Cockrell Foundation Award in Clinical or Translational Research, The Methodist Hospital Research Inst. 2009, Simon M. Shubitz Award for Excellence in the Field of Cancer Research, Univ. of Chicago 2010. *Publications:* more than 410 articles in scientific journals on hematopoietic stem cells, lymphocyte differentiation, lymphocyte homing receptors, normal and neoplastic hematolymphoid devt, phylogeny of stem cells and alloreactivity in protochordates. *Address:* Stanford University School of Medicine, Mail Code 5501-0, 265 Campus Drive, Room 3167, Stanford, CA 94305-5461, USA (office). *Telephone:* (650) 723-6520 (office). *Fax:* (650) 723-4034 (office). *E-mail:* irv@ stanford.edu (office). *Website:* biology.stanford.edu (office); med.stanford.edu/ profiles/faculty/Irving_Weissman (office).

WEISSMAN, Myrna M., PhD; American epidemiologists and academic; *Professor of Psychiatry and Epidemiology, College of Physicians and Surgeons and Mailman School of Public Health, Columbia University;* b. (Myrna Milgram), Boston, Mass; d. of Samuel Milgram and Jeanette Milgram; m. Dr Marshall Nirenberg; one s. three d.; ed Yale Univ. Medical School Dept of Epidemiology; Prof. of Psychiatry and Epidemiology, Yale Univ. School of Medicine, Dir Depression Research Unit –1987; Prof. of Psychiatry and Epidemiology, Coll. of Physicians and Surgeons and Mailman School of Public Health, Columbia Univ. 1987–; Chief of Dept, Clinical-Genetic Epidemiology, NY State Psychiatric Inst. 1987–; Visiting Sr Scholar, Inst. of Medicine, NAS, Washington, DC 1979–80 (mem. 1996–); mem. editorial bd of several journals including Archives of General Psychiatry; mem. Nat. Advisory Mental Health Council, Inst. of Medicine, NAS 1998–, Nat. Inst. of Mental Health 1999–2000, Council, American Coll. of Neuropsychopharmacology 1999–2002; Pres. American Psychopathological Asscn, New York 1998–99; Fellow, Royal Soc. of Psychiatrists (UK) 1998–, New York Acad. of Sciences; American Psychiatric Asscn Foundation's Fund Prize 1978, Rema Lapouse Mental Health Epidemiology Award, American Public Health Asscn 1985, Research Award, American Suicide Foundation 1990, Joseph Zubin Award, American Psychopathological Asscn 1996 and other prizes and awards. *Publications:* author or co-author of over 500 scientific articles and book chapters and seven books including The Depressed Woman: A Study of Social Relationships 1974, Interpersonal Psychotherapy of Depression 1984, A Comprehensive Guide to Interpersonal Psychotherapy 2000. *Leisure interests:* running, hiking, family. *Address:* College of Physicians and Surgeons, Nyspi-Unit 24, 1051 Riverside Drive, Columbia University, New York, NY 10032, USA (office). *Telephone:* (212) 543-5880 (office). *Fax:* (212) 568-3534 (office). *E-mail:* mmw3@columbia.edu (office). *Website:* www.mailman.columbia .edu (office); www.mailmanschool.org/sphdir/Pers.asp?ID=544 (office).

WEISSMANN, Charles, MD, PhD, FMedSci; Swiss (b. Hungarian) molecular biologist and academic; *Professor Emeritus, Department of Infectious Diseases, The Scripps Research Institute;* b. 14 Oct. 1931, Budapest, Hungary; ed Univ. of Zurich; Prof. and Dir Inst. of Molecular Biology, Zurich –1999, Prof. Emer. 1999–; fmr Sr Researcher, Neurogenetics Unit, Imperial Coll. School of Medicine, London, UK; Sr Research Scientist, Dept of Neurodegenerative Diseases, Inst. for Neurology, Univ. Coll., London 1999–2004; Prof. and Chair. Dept of Infectious Diseases, The Scripps Research Inst., Palm Beach Co., Fla 2004–12, Prof. Emer. 2012–, mem. Scripps Bd of Scientific Govs 2004–; Distinguished Research Prof., Dept of Biological Sciences, Florida Atlantic Univ. 2004; Co-founder Biogen (first European biotechnology co.); Pres. Roche Research Foundation; co-publr several journals; mem. Bd of Dirs F. Hoffmann-La Roche –2001, Speedel 2003–, several startup firms in Switzerland and Germany; mem. Bd Govs Tel-Aviv Univ. 1997–; mem. Editorial Bd Proceedings of the Royal Soc. 1999–; mem. Akad. der Naturforscher Leopoldina, American Soc. of Biological Chem.; Foreign mem. Royal Soc.; Foreign Assoc. NAS; Fellow, American Acad. of Microbiology 1999; first to genetically engineer Interferon-Alpha; Hon. Sr Fellow, Inst. of Neurology, Univ. Coll. London 2004; Orden Pour le Mérite (Germany); seven hon. doctorate degrees; many leading scientific prizes including Dr H.P. Heineken Prize for Biochemistry and Biophysics 1982, Betty and David Koetser Award, Zürich 2001, Friedrich-Bauer-Prize for Medical Research, Univ. of Munich 2001, Warren Alpert Foundation Prize, Harvard Medical School 2004, Betty and David Koetser Award, Zurich 2001, Friedrich-Bauer-Prize for Medical Research, Univ. of Munich 2001, Warren Alpert Foundation Prize, Harvard Medical School, Boston 2004, Fifth Annual Dart/NYU Biotechnology award (New York University, April 2006. *Publications:* numerous articles in scientific journals on RNA phages, terferon and prion diseases. *Leisure interest:* art collection. *Address:* Department of Infectious Diseases, The Scripps Research Institute, 5353 Parkside Drive, Jupiter, FL 33458, USA (office). *Telephone:* (561) 543-2500 (office). *Fax:* (561) 297-0329 (office). *E-mail:* charlesw@scripps.edu (office). *Website:* www.scripps.edu/florida/ research/faculty/weissmann (office).

WEISSMANN, Mariana, PhD; Argentine physicist and academic; *Senior Researcher, Argentine National Research Council;* ed Univ. of Buenos Aires; Practical Work Asst, Dept of Physics, Univ. of Buenos Aires 1957–61, Chief of Practical Works, Dept of Meteorology 1963–65, Assoc. Prof., Dept of Meteorology 1965–66, Assoc. Prof., Dept of Physical Chem. 1973–74, Contracted Lecturer, Dept 1989; Visiting Prof., Univ. of Oregon, USA 1966–67; Research Assoc., Syracuse Univ. 1967; Research Officer, Univ. of Chile 1968–71; Assoc. Prof., Dept of Physics, Univ. Simon Bolivar, Venezuela 1979–81; Sr Assoc., Int. Centre for Theoretical Physics, Trieste, Italy 1985–94; Prof. on Sabbatical, Dept of Condensed Matter Physics, Univ. Autonoma de Madrid, Spain 1990–91; Career Investigator, CONICET 1972–; Senior Researcher, Dept of Physics, Nat. Comm. Atomic Energy; currently Sr Researcher, Argentine Nat. Research Council, Buenos Aires; mem. Nat. Acad. of Exact, Physical and Natural Sciences of Argentina (first woman); UNESCO-L'Oréal Award for Women in Science (Latin America) 2003. *Publications include:* numerous papers in scientific journals on condensed matter and solid-state physics. *Address:* c/o Sección de Matemática, Física y Astronomía, Academia Nacional de Ciencias Exactas, Físicas y Naturales, Avda. Alvear 1711, 4° piso, 1014 Buenos Aires, Argentina (office). *Telephone:* (11) 4811-2998 (office).

(11) 4815-9451 (office). *Fax:* (11) 4811-6951 (office). *E-mail:* acad@ancefn.org.ar (office). *Website:* www.ancefn.org.ar (office).

WEISZ, Rachel; British actress; b. 7 March 1971, London; one s.; ed Univ. of Cambridge; London Critics Circle Theatre Award for Most Promising Newcomer 1994. *Films include:* Seventeen, Chain Reaction, Stealing Beauty, Going All the Way, Amy Foster, Bent, I Want You 1998, Land Girls 1998, The Mummy 1999, Sunshine 2000, Beautiful Creatures 2001, Enemy at the Gates 2001, The Mummy Returns 2001, About a Boy 2002, Confidence 2003, Runaway Jury 2003, Envy 2004, Constantine 2005, The Constant Gardener 2005 (Golden Globe Award for Best Supporting Actress, Screen Actors Guild Award for Best Supporting Actress, Acad. Award for Best Supporting Actress 2006), The Fountain 2006, Eragon (voice) 2006, My Blueberry Nights 2007, Fred Claus 2007, Definitely, Maybe 2007, The Lovely Bones 2009, The Whistleblower 2010, The Deep Blue Sea 2011, The Bourne Legacy 2012, Oz the Great and Powerful 2013. *Plays include:* Design for Living 1994, Suddenly Last Summer 1999, The Shape of Things, A Streetcar Named Desire 2009. *Address:* c/o ICM Ltd., Oxford House, 76 Oxford Street, London, W1N 0AX, England (office). *Telephone:* (20) 7636-6565 (office). *Fax:* (20) 7323-0101 (office).

WEITZMANN, Horst, Dipl.-Ing; German business executive; b. 1941, Riesa, Saxony; m. Marlis Weitzmann 1967; two d.; Man. Dir Vereinigten Schraubenwerke Thyssen/Otto Wolff 1972–77; Man. Dir American Airfilter Co., Düsseldorf 1978–80; Jt Owner, Badische Stahlwerke (following man. buyout 1982); Man. Partner, NDW Beteiligungsgesellschaft mbH; Chair. Supervisory Bd Südweststahl AG, BCT Technology AG; Chair. Bd of Trustees Albert-Ludwigs-Universität Freiburg, also Hon. Senator and Chair. Univ. Council; fmr Pres. European Steel Works Asscn; mem. International Advisory Board, IEDC (fmrly International Executive Development Center) Bled School of Management. *Leisure interest:* collecting contemporary art. *Address:* NDW Beteiligungsgesellschaft mbH, Friedrichstr. 16, Eberbach 69412, Germany (office).

WEIZSÄCKER, Richard von, DJur; German lawyer, politician and fmr head of state; b. 15 April 1920, Stuttgart; s. of the late Baron Ernst von Weizsäcker; m. Marianne von Kretschmann 1953; three s. one d.; ed Berlin, law studies at Oxford, Grenoble, Göttingen; army service 1938–45; prof. lawyer 1955–; fmr mem. Bd Allianz Lebensversicherung-AG, Stuttgart, Robeco-Gruppe, Amsterdam; mem. Robert Bosch Foundation, Stuttgart; mem. Synod and Council of German Protestant Church 1969–84, Pres. Protestant Church Congress 1964–70; mem. Fed. Bd CDU, Deputy Chair. CDU/CSU Party 1972–79; mem. Bundestag 1969–81, Vice-Pres. 1979–81; Governing Mayor of West Berlin 1981–84; Pres. FRG 1984–94; Co-Chair. Ind. Working Group on the Future of the UN 1994–95; Chair. Comm. Common Security and the Future of the German Fed. Army 1999–2000; mem. Nomination Cttee Praemium Imperiale 1998–2006, 'Three Wise Men' Comm. on Institutional Reforms of the EU 1999; mem. Eminent Persons Group requested by UN Sec.-Gen. Kofi Annan to write report Crossing the Divide – Dialogue Among Civilizations 2001; Hon. Pres. Int. Council of Christians and Jews 1994–, Hon. Senator Max Planck Soc.; Hon. DCL (Oxford) 1988; Dr hc (Cambridge) 1994; Theodor Heuss Prize 1983, Leopold Lucas Prize 2000, Franklin D. Roosevelt Four Freedoms Award 2008. *Publications:* Die deutsche Geschichte geht weiter 1983, Von Deutschland aus 1985, Die politische Kraft der Kultur 1987, Von Deutschland nach Europa 1991, Vier Zeiten 1997, Drei Mal Stunde Null? 2001, Was für eine Welt wollen wir? 2005, Der Weg zur Einheit 2009. *Address:* Am Kupfergraben 7, 10117 Berlin, Germany (office).

WEK, Alek; Sudanese fashion model; b. 1977, Wau, southern Sudan; fled with younger sister to UK to escape civil war between Muslim north and Christian south of Sudan 1991; discovered at an outdoor market in Crystal Palace, south London by Fiona Ellis (scout for Models 1) 1995; first appeared on catwalks 1995; later moved to USA; has modelled for fashion designers John Galliano, Donna Karan, Calvin Klein and Ermanno Scervino; also designs range of designer handbags called Wek 1933; mem. US Cttee for Refugees' Advisory Council; named Model of the Year by MTV 1997, ranked 14th in Channel 5's World's Greatest Supermodel, Venus de la Mode Award, honoured by Clutch magazine as one of 21 International Women of Power 2008. *Publication:* Alek (autobiography) 2007. *Address:* c/o Storm Models, 1st Floor, 5 Jubilee Place, Chelsea, London, SW3 3TD, England (office). *E-mail:* info@alekwek.com. *Website:* alek-wek.com.

WELBY, Most Rev. and Rt Hon. Justin Portal, PC, BA, DipMin; British ecclesiastic, writer, theologian and fmr oil industry executive; *Archbishop of Canterbury;* b. 6 Jan. 1956, London; s. of the late Gavin Bramhall James Welby (b. Bernard Gavin Weiler) and of Jane Gillian (née Portal), later Baroness Williams of Elvel; m. Caroline Eaton; two s. four d. (one deceased); ed Eton Coll., Trinity Coll., Cambridge, St John's Coll., Durham; worked in the oil industry for 11 years, including with Société Nationale Elf Aquitaine, Paris 1978–83, Elf UK plc, London 1983–84; Treas. Enterprise Oil PLC, London 1984–89; studied theology and trained for the priesthood 1989–92; Deacon 1992, Priest 1993; Asst Curate, All Saints, Chilvers Coton and St Mary the Virgin, Astley, Nuneaton 1992–95; Rector St James, Southam, later Vicar of St Michael and All Angels, Ufton, Diocese of Coventry 1995–2002; Canon Residentiary, Coventry Cathedral and Co-Dir for Int. Ministry, Int. Centre for Reconciliation 2002–05; Canon Residentiary and Sub-Dean, Coventry Cathedral 2005–07; Priest-in-Charge, Holy Trinity, Coventry 2007; Dean of Liverpool Cathedral 2007–11; Bishop of Durham 2011–12; Archbishop of Canterbury 2013–; mem. House of Lords 2012–, mem. Parl. Comm. on Banking Standards 2012; Chair. an NHS hosp. trust in S Warwicks. 2000–02. *Publications:* Managing the Church?: Order and Organisation in a Secular Age, Explorations in Financial Ethics, Can Companies Sin?: 'Whether', 'How' and 'Who' in Company Accountability 1992; articles on ethics, international finance and reconciliation. *Leisure interests:* French culture, sailing, politics. *Address:* Lambeth Palace, London, SE1 7JU, England (office). *Telephone:* (20) 7898-1200 (office). *Fax:* (20) 7261-9836 (office). *E-mail:* contact@lambethpalace.org .uk (office). *Website:* www.archbishopofcanterbury.org (office).

WELCH, C. David, MA; American business executive and fmr diplomatist; *President of Europe, Africa, Middle East Region, Bechtel Ltd;* b. 1953, Munich, Germany; m. Gretchen Gerwe Welch; three d.; ed London School of Econs, UK, Georgetown Univ., Washington, DC, Fletcher School of Law and Diplomacy, Tufts Univ., Medford, Mass; Officer responsible for Syria, Bureau of Near Eastern Affairs and South Asian Affairs, Dept of State, Washington, DC 1981–82, for Lebanon 1982–83, Chief of Political Section, US Embassy, Damascus, Syria 1984–86, Political Counselor, US Embassy, Amman, Jordan 1986–88, mem. staff, Nat. Security Council, White House, Washington, DC 1989–91, Exec. Asst to Under-Sec. of State for Political Affairs 1991–92, Chargé d'Affaires, US Embassy, Riyadh, Saudi Arabia 1992–94, Deputy Chief of Mission 1994–95, Prin. Deputy Asst Sec., Bureau of Near Eastern Affairs 1995–98, Asst Sec. of State for Int. Org. Affairs 1998–2001, Amb. to Egypt 2001–05, Asst Sec., Bureau of Near Eastern Affairs 2005–08; Pres. of Europe, Africa, Middle East Region, Bechtel Ltd, London 2008–, also Man. of Civil Strategy and Business Devt in civil business unit; mem. Council on Foreign Relations, American Foreign Service Asscn, American Acad. of Diplomacy; mem. Europe Advisory Group for the Fletcher School; several Awards for exceptional service to US Govt. *Address:* Bechtel Ltd, 11 Pilgrim Street, London, EC4V 6RN, England (office). *Telephone:* (20) 7651-7777 (office). *Fax:* (20) 7651-7972 (office). *Website:* www.bechtel.com (office).

WELCH, John Francis (Jack), Jr, PhD; American business executive; *Special Partner, Clayton, Dubilier & Rice Inc.;* b. 19 Nov. 1935, Peabody, Mass; s. of John Francis Welch and Grace Welch (née Andrews); m. 1st Carolyn B. Osburn 1959 (divorced 1987); two s. two d.; m. 2nd Jane Beasely 1989 (divorced 2002); m. 3rd Suzy Wetlaufer 2004; ed Univs of Massachusetts and Illinois; joined Gen. Electric Co., Fairfield, Conn. 1960, Vice-Pres. 1972, Vice-Pres. Exec. Components and Materials Group 1973–77, Sr Vice-Pres. Sector Exec., Consumer Products and Services Sector 1977–79, Vice-Chair and CEO 1979–81, Chair. and CEO 1981–2001, Pres. and CEO Nat. Broadcasting Co. 1986–2000; mem. Bd of Dirs Fiat 2002-03, Idealab 2000; Special Pnr, Clayton, Dubilier & Rice Inc. 2001–. *Publications:* Jack Welch and the GE Way 1998, Jack: Straight from the Gut 2000, Winning (with Suzy Welch) 2005. *Address:* Clayton, Dubilier & Rice, Inc., 375 Park Avenue, 18th Floor, New York, NY 10152, USA (office). *Telephone:* (212) 407-5200 (office). *Fax:* (212) 407-5252 (office). *Website:* www.cdr-inc.com (office).

WELCH, Raquel; American actress; b. (Jo Raquel Tejada) 5 Sept. 1940, Chicago, Ill.; d. of Armand Tejada and Josepha Tejada (née Hall); m. 1st James Westley Welch 1959 (divorced); one s. one d.; m. 2nd Patrick Curtis (divorced); m. 3rd Andre Weinfeld 1980 (divorced); m. 4th Richard Palmer 1999 (divorced 2003). *Films include:* Fantastic Voyage 1966, One Million Years BC 1967, Fathom 1967, The Biggest Bundle of Them All 1968, Magic Christian 1970, Myra Breckinridge 1970, Fuzz 1972, Bluebeard 1972, Hannie Caulder 1972, Kansas City Bomber 1972, The Last of Sheila 1973, The Three Musketeers 1974, The Wild Party 1975, The Four Musketeers 1975, Mother, Jugs and Speed 1976, Crossed Swords 1978, L'Animal 1979, Right to Die 1987, Scandal in a Small Town 1988, Trouble in Paradise 1989, Naked Gun 33$^{1/3}$1993, Folle d'Elle 1998, Chairman of the Board 1998, The Complete Musketeers 1999, Tortilla Soup 2001, Legally Blonde 2001, Forget About It 2006. *Television includes:* Central Park West (series) 1996, American Family (series) 2002, The Captain (series) 2008. *Plays include:* Woman of the Year (Broadway) 1982, Torch Song 1993. *Videos:* Raquel: Total Beauty and Fitness 1984, A Week with Raquel 1987, Raquel: Lose 10lbs in 3 Weeks 1989. *Publications:* The Raquel Welch Total Beauty and Fitness Program 1984, Raquel: Beyond the Cleavage 2010. *Address:* Innovative Artists, 1999 Avenue of the Stars, Suite 2850, Los Angeles, CA 90067, USA.

WELD, Tuesday Ker; American actress; b. (Susan Ker Weld), 27 Aug. 1943, New York City; d. of Lathrop M. Weld and Aileen Ker; m. 1st Claude Harz 1965 (divorced 1971); one d.; m. 2nd Dudley Moore 1975 (divorced); one s.; m. 3rd Pinchas Zukerman (q.v.) 1985; ed Hollywood Professional School; fashion and catalogue model aged three; regular appearances as magazine cover-girl and in child roles on TV by age twelve; appears in numerous TV programmes and TV films including The Many Loves of Dobie Gillis 1959 and numerous guest roles. *Films include:* Rock Rock (debut) 1956, Serial, Rally Round the Flag Boys, The Five Pennies, The Private Lives of Adam and Eve, Return to Peyton Place, Wild in the Country, Bachelor Flat, Lord Love a Duck, Pretty Poison, I Walk the Line, A Safe Place, Play it as it Lays, Because They're Young, High Time, Sex Kittens Go to College, The Cincinnati Kid, Soldier in the Rain, Looking for Mr Goodbar, Thief, Author!, Once Upon a Time In America 1984, Heartbreak Hotel 1988, Falling Down 1993, Feeling Minnesota 1996, Chelsea Walls 2001, Investigating Sex 2002.

WELD, William Floyd, AB, JD; American business executive and fmr politician; b. 31 July 1945, Smithtown, NY; s. of the late David Weld and Mary Weld (née Nichols); m. 1st Susan Roosevelt 1975 (divorced 2002); two s. three d.; m. 2nd Leslie Marshall; ed Middlesex School, Mass, Harvard Coll., Univ. Coll., Oxford, UK, Harvard Univ.; admitted Mass Bar 1970; law clerk, Supreme Judicial Court, Mass 1970–71; Partner, Hill & Barlow, Boston 1971–81; Assoc. Minority Counsel, US House of Reps Judiciary Comm. Impeachment Inquiry 1973–74; US Attorney for Dist of Mass 1981–86; Asst Attorney-Gen. Criminal Div. US Justice Dept, Washington, DC 1986–88; Gov. of Massachusetts 1991–97; nominated as Amb. to Mexico but was never confirmed; Prin., Leeds Weld & Co. (pvt. equity firm) –2005; CEO Decker Coll., Louisville, Ky (after acquisition by Leeds Weld) Jan.–Oct. 2005; announced candidacy for Gov. of NY Aug. 2005; admitted to practise law in NY State 2008; Co-Chair. for Mitt Romney's presidential campaign in NY State 2007–08; co-chaired Ind. Task Force on North America under the Council on Foreign Relations, which studied the integration of the USA, Canada and Mexico; mem. ABA, American Law Inst., Boston Bar Asscn; Republican. *Film:* Traffic (as himself) 2000. *Publications:* novels: Mackerel By Moonlight 1988, Big Ugly 1999, Stillwater 2002. *Address:* c/o Leeds Equity Partners, 350 Park Avenue, 23rd Floor, New York, NY 10022, USA. *E-mail:* info@leedsequity.com

WELDON, Fay, CBE, MA, FRSA; British author and academic; *Professor of Creative Writing, Brunel University;* b. 22 Sept. 1931, Alvechurch, Worcs., England; d. of Frank T. Birkinshaw and Margaret J. Birkinshaw; m. 1st Ronald Weldon 1960 (divorced 1994); four s.; m. 2nd Nicholas Fox 1995; ed Girls' High School, Christchurch, New Zealand, South Hampstead School for Girls and Univ. of St Andrews; Chair. of Judges, Booker McConnell Prize 1983; Writer-in-Residence Savoy Hotel, London Oct.-Dec. 2002; Prof. of Creative Writing, Brunel Univ. 2006–; fmr mem. Arts Council Literary Panel; mem. Video Censorship Appeals Cttee; Fellow, City of Bath Coll. 1999; Hon. DLitt (Bath) 1989, (St Andrews) 1992, (Birmingham), (Univ. of Connecticut); Women in Publishing Pandora Award 1997. *Theatre plays:* Words of Advice 1974, Friends 1975, Moving House 1976, Mr Director 1977, Action Replay 1979, I Love My Love 1981,

Woodworm 1981, Jane Eyre 1986, The Hole in the Top of the World 1987, Jane Eyre (adaptation), Playhouse Theatre, London 1995, The Four Alice Bakers, Birmingham Repertory 1999, Breakfast with Emma, Lyric Hammersmith 2003; more than 30 television plays, dramatizations and radio plays. *Television:* Big Women (series), Channel 4 1999. *Publications:* novels: The Fat Woman's Joke (aka And the Wife Ran Away) 1967, Down Among the Women 1972, Female Friends 1975, Remember Me 1976, Little Sisters (aka Words of Advice) 1977, Praxis 1978, Puffball 1980, The President's Child 1982, The Life and Loves of a She-Devil 1984, The Shrapnel Academy 1986, The Heart of the Country 1987, The Hearts and Lives of Men 1987, The Rules of Life (novella) 1987, Leader of the Band 1988, The Cloning of Joanna May 1989, Darcy's Utopia 1990, Growing Rich 1992, Life Force 1992, Affliction (aka Trouble) 1994, Splitting 1995, Worst Fears 1996, Big Women 1997, Rhode Island Blues 2000, Bulgari Connection 2001, She May Not Leave 2005, The Spa Decameron 2007, The Stepmother's Diary 2008, Chalcot Crescent 2009, Kehua 2010; children's books: Wolf the Mechanical Dog 1988, Party Puddle 1989, Nobody Likes Me! 1997; short story collections: Watching Me Watching You 1981, Polaris 1985, Moon Over Minneapolis 1991, Wicked Women 1995, Angel All Innocence and Other Stories 1995, A Hard Time to be a Father 1998, Nothing to Wear, Nowhere to Hide 2002; other: Letters to Alice 1984, Rebecca West 1985, Godless in Eden (essays) 2000, Auto da Fay (autobiography) 2002, Mantrapped (autobiography) 2004, What Makes Women Happy 2006. *Address:* c/o Capel Land, 29 Wardour Street, London, W1V 6HB, England (office); Brunel University, School of Arts, Uxbridge, Middx, UB8 3PH, England (office). *Telephone:* (20) 7734-2414 (office). *E-mail:* fay.weldon@brunel.ac.uk (office). *Website:* www.brunel.ac.uk/about/acad/sa (office).

WELDON, William C., BS; American pharmaceutical industry executive; *Chairman, Johnson & Johnson;* b. 26 Nov. 1948, Brooklyn, NY; m. Barbara Weldon; one s. one d.; ed Quinnipiac Univ., Hamden, Conn.; joined Johnson & Johnson 1971, served in sales and marketing positions with McNeil Pharmaceuticals affiliate 1971–82, led pharmaceutical orgs for Johnson & Johnson in SE Asia and UK 1982–89, Vice-Pres. Sales and Marketing Janssen Pharmaceutica 1989–92, Pres. Ethicon Endo-Surgery 1992–95, Group Chair. 1995–98, mem. Exec. Cttee and Worldwide Chair. Pharmaceuticals Group 1998–2001, mem. Bd of Dirs Johnson & Johnson 2001–, Vice-Chair. 2001–02, Chair. and CEO 2002–12, Chair. 2012–; mem. Bd of Dirs JPMorgan Chase & Co. 2005–; Chair. CEO Roundtable on Cancer; Vice-Chair. The Business Council; mem. The Sullivan Comm. on Diversity in the Health Professions Workforce, Liberty Science Center Chair.'s Advisory Council; fmr Chair. Pharmaceutical Research and Mfrs of America; Trustee, Quinnipiac Univ. *Address:* Johnson & Johnson, 1 Johnson & Johnson Plaza, New Brunswick, NJ 08933, USA (office). *Telephone:* (732) 524-0400 (office). *Fax:* (732) 524-3300 (office). *E-mail:* info@jnj.com (office). *Website:* www.jnj.com (office).

WELLAND, Colin; British playwright and actor; b. (Colin Williams), 4 July 1934, Liverpool; s. of John Arthur Williams and Norah Williams; m. Patricia Sweeney 1962; one s. three d.; ed Newton-le-Willows Grammar School, Bretton Hall, Goldsmiths' Coll., London; art teacher 1958–62; entered theatre 1962, Library Theatre, Manchester 1962–64; Fellow, Goldsmiths Coll., Univ. of London 2001. *Stage roles:* Waiting for Godot 1987, The Churchill Play, Man of Magic, Say Goodnight to Grandma, Ubu Roi. *Plays written:* Roomful of Holes 1972, Say Goodnight to Grandma 1973, Roll on Four O'Clock 1981. *Film roles:* Kes (BAFTA Award for Best Supporting Actor), Villain, Straw Dogs, Sweeney, The Secret Life of Ian Fleming, Dancing through the Dark. *Screenplays:* Yanks 1978, Chariots of Fire 1980 (Acad. Award), Twice in a Lifetime 1986, A Dry White Season, War of the Buttons 1994. *Television appearances:* Blue Remembered Hills, The Fix, United Kingdom. *Television plays include:* Kisses at 50, Leeds United, Your Man from Six Counties, Bambino Mio, Slattery's Mounted Foot, Jack Point, The Hallelujah Handshake, Roll on Four O'Clock (BAFTA Award for Best TV Screenplay). *Leisure interests:* sport (particularly Rugby League), films, dining out, politics, travel. *Address:* United Agents, 12–26 Lexington Street, London, W1F 0LE, England (office). *Telephone:* (20) 3214-0800 (office). *Fax:* (20) 3214-0801 (office). *E-mail:* info@unitedagents.co.uk (office). *Website:* unitedagents.co.uk (office).

WELLER, Malcolm Philip Isadore, MB BS, MA; British medical practitioner; *Honorary Research Professor, Middlesex University;* b. 29 May 1935, Manchester, England; s. of Solomon George Weller and Esther Weller; m. Davina Reisler 1966; two s.; ed Perse School, Cambridge, Cambridge and Newcastle Univs; Consultant Neuropsychiatrist Emer., Barnet Enfield & Haringey Mental Health NHS Trust, Chartered Psychologist (Neuropsychology Section); Hon. Sr Lecturer, Mental Health Sciences, School of Medicine, Univ. of London –1997; Hon. Research Prof., Middlesex Univ. 1997–; Chair. N Thames Region Psychiatric Cttee 1997, London Region Psychiatric Cttee 1995–2000; Vice-Chair. NE Thames Regional Cttee for Hosp. Medical Services 1984–96; Hon. Medical Adviser, Nat. Alliance of Relatives of the Mentally Ill, Jewish Asscn of the Mentally Ill, Nat. Schizophrenia Fellowship and Founder-mem. Parl. Cttee; Chair. CONCERN 1992–99; co-opted mem. Bd of Studies in Psychology, London Univ. and Higher Degrees Sub-cttee 1976–; Royal Coll. of Psychiatry Examiner for Master in Medicine (Psychiatry) Degree, Nat. Univ. of Singapore 1988, 1989; External Examiner, Univ. of Manchester PhD degree 1990; mem. Standing Cttee, Bd of Studies in Medicine, Univ. of London 1981–84, Cen. Cttee of BMA 1994–96, Gen. Psychiatry Exec. Cttee of Royal Coll. of Psychiatry, also of Pharmacology and Social, Community and Rehabilitation Cttees; previously Royal Coll. Rep. to Asscn of the British Pharmaceutical Industry; Exec. mem. Neuropsychiatry Section, Royal Coll. of Psychiatrists; Council mem. Psychiatry Section, Royal Soc. of Medicine (RSM), RSM Rep. to Nat. Inst. for Clinical Excellence, also RSM Prize Adjudicator; Concert organizer, Newcastle Festival 1970–71; co-opted mem. Laing Art Gallery Cttee 1972–73; Chair. Govs Gosforth Middle School 1971–74; Fellow, British Psychological Soc., Royal Coll. of Psychiatrists, Collegium Internationale Neuro-Psychopharmacology; initiated and ran courses for British Postgraduate Fed. and prepared teaching videos and a rating scale for WHO; Hon. Lifetime Achievement Fellow, CINP; Scholarship Mental Health Research Fund, Ver Heyden de Lancey Prize, Univ. of Cambridge, Wilfred Kingdom Prize, Univ. of Newcastle, Brit Council Travel Award, Invited Fellow, Royal Soc. of Arts. *Radio:* adviser and participant in BBC radio feature: Breakdown (Italia Prize). *Publications include:* Founder, Ed.-in-Chief Baillière's Clinical Psychiatry series (11 vols); Progress in Clinical Psychiatry 1997, Genetics of Mental Disorder, Vols I and II,

Epidemiological Psychiatry, Hypnotics and Anxiolytics, Pharmacological Management of Chronic Psychiatric Disorders, Post Traumatic Stress Disorder, Drugs of Abuse, Psychiatric Issues in Women, Sexual Dysfunction, Eating Disorders, Psychosocial Aspects of Chronic Fatigue Syndrome; editor: Scientific Basis of Psychology 1983, 1992, International Perspectives in Schizophrenia 1989, Dimensions of Community Care 1993; about 200 editorials and papers in learned journals, mainly on psychosis, depression, head injury, psychological medicine and medico-legal matters; about 100 publs on music in various music journals. *Leisure interests:* fine art, music. *Address:* 30 Arkwright Road, Hampstead, London, NW3 6BH, England (home). *Telephone:* (20) 7794-5804 (home). *Fax:* (20) 7431-1589 (office). *E-mail:* malcolm@weller.tv (home); office@malcolmweller.com (office). *Website:* malcolmweller.com.

WELLER, Paul; British musician (guitar, piano), singer and songwriter; b. 25 May 1958, Woking, Surrey; founder mem. and lead singer, The Jam 1972–82, The Style Council 1983–89, The Paul Weller Movement and solo artist 1990–; own record label Freedom High; Ivor Novello Award, BRIT Awards for Best Male Artist 1995, 1996, 2009, Mojo Award for Best Songwriter 2005, Q Award for Outstanding Contribution to Music 2005, BRIT Award for Outstanding Contribution 2006, Silver Clef Award 2007, Ivor Novello Award for Lifetime Achievement 2010. *Recordings include:* albums: with The Jam: In the City 1977, This is the Modern World 1977, All Mod Cons 1978, Setting Sons 1979, Sound Affects 1980, The Gift 1982; with The Style Council: Introducing The Style Council 1983, Café Bleu 1984, Our Favourite Shop 1985, Home and Abroad 1986, The Cost of Loving 1987, Confessions of a Pop Group 1988, Singular Adventures of the Style Council 1989, Here's Some That Got Away 1993; solo: Paul Weller 1992, Wild Wood 1993, Live Wood 1994, Stanley Road 1995, Heavy Soul 1997, Modern Classics 1998, Heliocentric 2000, Days Of Speed 2001, Illumination 2002, Fly on the Wall: B-Sides and Rarities 2003, Studio 150 2004, As Is Now 2005, Catch-Flame! 2006, Hit Parade 2006, 22 Dreams 2008, Wake Up the Nation 2010. *Film:* JerUSAlem 1987. *Address:* c/o William Morris Agency, Centrepoint, 103 Oxford Street, London, WC1A 1DD, England. *Website:* www.paulweller.com.

WELLER, Walter; Austrian conductor; *Music Director, Orchestre National de Belgique;* b. 30 Nov. 1939; s. of Walter Weller and Anna Weller; m. Elisabeth Samohyl 1966; one s.; ed Realgymnasium, Vienna, Akad. für Musik, Vienna; f. Weller Quartet 1958–69; mem. Vienna Philharmonic 1958–60, First Leader 1960–69; Conductor, Vienna State Opera 1969–75; guest conductor with all main European, American and Japanese Broadcasting Corpn orchestras 1973–; Chief Conductor, Tonkünstler Orchestra, Vienna 1974–77; Prin. Conductor and Artistic Adviser Royal Liverpool Philharmonic Orchestra 1977–80, Guest Conductor Laureate 1980; Prin. Conductor, Royal Philharmonic Orchestra 1980–85, Chief Guest Conductor 1985–; Chief Guest Conductor, Nat. Orchestra of Spain 1987–; Prin. Conductor and Music Dir Royal Scottish Nat. Orchestra 1992–97, now Conductor Emer.; Artistic Dir Allgemeine Musikgesellschaft Basel, Gen. Dir Basel Theatre and Chief Conductor, Sinfonieorchester Basel 1994–97; Music Dir Orchestre Nat. de Belgique 2007–12, Hon. Music Dir 2012–; Great Silver Cross of Honour 1998; Medal of Arts and Sciences 1968, Grand Prix du Disque Charles Cros (for Duke's Symphony in C). *Leisure interests:* magic, model railways, sailing, swimming, stamp-collecting, skiing. *Address:* c/o Harrison Turner Artists Management, 53 Ticknell Piece Road, Charlbury, Oxon., OX7 3TN, England (office). *Telephone:* (1608) 810330 (office). *Fax:* (1608) 811331 (office). *E-mail:* artists@harrisonturner.co.uk (office). *Website:* www.harrisonturner.co.uk (office); www.music.at/walter-weller.

WELLERSHOFF, Dieter, DPhil; German writer; b. 3 Nov. 1925, Neuss/Rhein; s. of Walter Wellershoff and Kläre Weber; m. Dr Maria von Thadden 1952; one s. two d.; ed Gymnasium in Grevenbroich and Univ. Bonn; Ed. 1952–55; freelance writer 1956–59, 1981–; Reader, Kiepenheuer and Witsch Publishing House, Cologne 1959–81; author of 11 radio plays and 10 TV plays; Hörspielpreis der Kriegsblinden 1961; Literaturpreis Verband der deutschen Kritiker 1970, Heinrich-Böll-Preis, Köln 1988, Hölderlin-Preis 2001, Breitbach-Preis 2001, Niederrhein-Preis, Krefeld 2002, E. R. Curtius-Preis, Bonn 2005, Rheinischer Kulturpreis, Köln 2007. *Publications:* Gottfried Benn, Phänotyp dieser Stunde 1958, Der Gleichgültige 1963, Ein schöner Tag 1966, F Die Schattengrenze 1969, Literatur und Veränderung 1969, Einladung an alle 1972, Die Schönheit des Schimpansen 1977, Die Sirene 1980, Der Sieger nimmt alles 1983, Die Arbeit des Lebens 1985, Die Körper und die Träume 1986, Der Roman und die Erfahrbarkeit der Welt 1988, Pan und die Engel. Ansichten von Köln 1990, Blick auf einen fernen Berg 1991, Das geordnete Chaos 1992, Angesichts der Gegenwart 1993, Der Ernstfall. Innenansichten des Krieges 1995, Zikadengeschrei 1995, Werke in 6 Bänden 1996–97, Der Liebeswunsch 2000, Der verstörte Eros 2001, Das normale Leben 2005, Der lange Weg zum Anfang 2007, Zwischenreich 2008, Der Himmel ist kein Ort 2009; (ed.) Gottfried Benn, Gesammelte Werke 1958; works translated into 15 languages. *Address:* Mainzer Strasse 45, 50678 Cologne, Germany. *Telephone:* (221) 388565 (home). *Fax:* (221) 3406127 (office).

WELLINK, Arnout (Nout) H. E. M., PhD; Dutch international banking executive and fmr central banker; b. 1943; m. M. V. Volmer; five c.; ed Leyden Univ., Univ. of Rotterdam; teacher, Leyden Univ. 1965–70; staff mem. Ministry of Finance 1970–75, Head of Directorate-Gen. Financial and Econ. Policy 1975–77, Treas.-Gen. 1977–81; Exec. Dir De Nederlandsche Bank NV 1982–2011, Pres. 1997–2011; mem. Bd Bank of China 2012–; Chair. of Bd and Pres. Bank for Int. Settlements (BIS) 2002–05; mem. Council, European Cen. Bank 1999–2012; mem. Bd of Trustees Museum Mauritshuis, Supervisory Bd Openlucht Museum; Kt, Order of the Netherlands. *Address:* c/o De Nederlandsche Bank NV, Westeinde 1, PO Box 98, 1000 AB Amsterdam, Netherlands (office).

WELLS, George Andre; Ni-Vanuatu politician; worked for Sofrana Line (shipping co.) 1980–85; Minister of Internal Affairs 2004, 2007, 2011–13; fmr Minister of Nat. Defence; Minister of Foreign Affairs, External Trade and Telecommunications 2007, 2010–11; mem. Parl. for Luganville (suspended 2013), Leader of Govt Business 2002–03, Speaker of Parl. 2010–13; fmr mem. Vanuaaku Pati and Nat. United Party; currently mem. Nat. Community Asscn Party (NCAP). *Address:* c/o Ministry of Internal Affairs, PMB 9036, Port Vila, Port Vila, Vanuata (office).

WELLS, Peter N. T., CBE, PhD, DSc, CEng, CPhys, CSci, CClinSci, FRS, FRSM, FREng, FMedSci, FIET, FInstP FLSW; British medical physicist and academic; *Distinguished Research Professor, Institute of Medical Engineering and Medical Physics, Cardiff University;* b. 1936, Bristol, England; ed Clifton Coll., Birmingham Coll. of Advanced Tech. (now Univ. of Aston), Univ. of Bristol; Research Asst (MRC grants), United Bristol Hosps 1960–71; Prof. of Medical Physics, Welsh Nat. School of Medicine (now Cardiff Univ. School of Medicine) 1972–74; Chief Physicist, United Bristol Healthcare NHS Trust (fmrly Avon Area Health Authority (Teaching), Bristol Health Dist (Teaching), Bristol and Weston Health Authority) 1975–2000; Gen. Man., Medical Sciences (Depts of Medical Physics, Pathology, Pharmacy and Radiology), Bristol and Weston Health Authority 1985–89; Gen. Man., Dental Hosp., Eye, Medical Physics, Oncology Centre, Bristol and Weston Health Authority 1989; Clinical Dir, Speciality Services, United Bristol Healthcare NHS Trust (fmrly Bristol and Weston Health Authority) 1990–2000; Assoc. Medical Dir for Research and Devt, United Bristol Healthcare NHS Trust 1996–99; Hon. Prof. in Clinical Radiology, Univ. of Bristol 1986–2000, Dir Centre for Physics and Eng Research in Medicine 1996–2001, Prof. of Physics and Eng in Medicine 2000–01, Prof. Emer. 2001–; Dir (non-exec.), Weston Area Health NHS Trust 2001–04; Consultant, Cen. Lab. of Research Councils 2001–05; Visiting Prof., Imperial Coll. London 2002–; Distinguished Research Prof. and Sr Scientific Dir, Inst. of Medical Eng and Medical Physics, School of Eng, Cardiff Univ. 2004–; Visiting Prof., Dept of Medical Physics and Bioengineering, Univ. Coll. London 2011–; Founding Fellow, Learned Soc. of Wales; Fellow, Royal Acad. of Eng, Inst. of Eng and Tech., Int. Acad. for Medical and Biological Eng, American Inst. for Medical and Biological Eng; Hon. Fellow, British Inst. of Radiology, Inst. of Physics and Eng in Medicine, Royal Coll. of Radiologists, American Inst. of Ultrasound in Medicine, Australasian Coll. of Physical Scientists and Engineers in Medicine, Int. Soc. for Therapeutic Ultrasound; Hon. Life mem. World Fed. for Ultrasound in Medicine and Biology; Hon. mem. British Medical Ultrasound Soc., Australasian Soc. for Ultrasound in Medicine, Korean Soc. of Ultrasound in Medicine; Hon. DTech (Lund) 1997; Hon. MD (Erasmus, Rotterdam) 1998; Hon. DSc (Aston) 2010; IEE (now Inst. of Eng and Tech.) Silvanus Thompson Scholar 1959–60, Founders' Prize, Hosp. Physicists' Asscn 1971, Achievement Medal, IEE 1993, Ian Donald Medal for Tech. Merit, Int. Soc. of Ultrasound in Obstetrics and Gynecology 1998, EFOMP Medal, European Fed. of Orgs for Medical Physics 2001, Duddell Medal and Prize, Inst. of Physics 2006, NHS Lifetime Achievement Award 2007, Royal Medal, Royal Soc. 2013. *Publications:* numerous papers in professional journals. *Address:* Institute of Medical Engineering and Medical Physics, Cardiff University, Room W/2.40, 30–36 Newport Road, Cardiff, CF24 0DE, Wales (office). *Telephone:* (29) 2087-4154 (office). *E-mail:* wellspn@cardiff.ac.uk (office). *Website:* www.engin.cf.ac.uk (office).

WELLS, Rufus Michael Grant, PhD, DSc, FRSNZ; New Zealand marine biologist and academic; *Professor, Marine Biology Group, University of Auckland;* b. 3 July 1947, Cardiff, Wales; s. of Peter F. Wells and Jean Chiles; m. Jane Nelson 1969; one s. one d.; ed Hamilton Boys' High School, Univ. of Auckland, Bedford Coll., Univ. of London, UK; researcher in molecular physiology of haemoglobin and respiration (medical, animal and fisheries science), Antarctic biology; Asst Lecturer in Statistics, Univ. of Auckland 1970–71; Research Asst and PhD student Bedford Coll., London 1971–74; Biochemist and MRC Fellow, Univ. Coll. Hosp., London 1974–75; Lecturer, then Sr Lecturer in Zoology, then Prof., Univ. of Auckland 1975–; biological and editorial consultant, specializing in Antarctic Science and Science Educ.; fmr mem. Nat. Comm. for Antarctic Research; Physiological Soc. of NZ Medal 1983, Royal Soc. of NZ Hutton Medal 1989. *Publications:* more than 220 scientific papers. *Address:* School of Biological Sciences, Marine Biology Group, Thomas Building, Level 1, Room 138, 3 Symonds Street, City Campus, University of Auckland, Auckland 1, New Zealand (office). *Telephone:* (9) 373-7999 (ext. 87206) (office). *Fax:* (9) 373-7668 (office). *E-mail:* r.wells@auckland.ac.nz (home). *Website:* www.sbs.auckland.ac.nz (office).

WELSER-MÖST, Franz; Austrian/Liechtenstein conductor; *Music Director, Cleveland Orchestra, Vienna Staatsoper;* b. 16 Aug. 1960, Linz; m.; ed Musikgymnasium, Linz and Staatliche Musikhochschule, Munich; Chief Conductor, Jeunesse Orchestra, Linz 1982–85, Norrköping Symphony Orchestra 1985, Musikkollegium Winterthur, Switzerland 1986; Music Dir London Philharmonic Orchestra 1990–96; Music Dir Zürich Opera 1995–2002, Principal Conductor 2002–05, Music Dir Cleveland Orchestra 2002–; Gen. Music Dir Vienna Staatsoper 2010–; has also appeared at Deutsche Oper Berlin, Glyndebourne festival; regularly works with Berlin Philharmonic, Vienna Philharmonic, Bavarian Radio Symphony and Gustav Mahler Youth Orchestra; has conducted all major US orchestras; Outstanding Achievement Award from Western Law Centre, LA, for work for people with disabilities, Musical America's Conductor of the Year 2003, Diasapon d'Or, Japanese Record Acad. Award. *Recordings include:* Mendelssohn Symphonies Nos 3 and 4, Schumann Symphonies Nos 2 and 3, Bruckner Symphony No. 7, Strauss Waltzes, Carl Orff's Carmina Burana, Stravinsky's Oedipus Rex, Bartók's Miraculous Mandarin, Kodaly's Peacock Variations, Kancheli's Symphony No. 3, Pärt's Symphony No. 3, Fratres, Schmidt's Symphony No. 4 (Gramophone Award 1996) (all with LPO), world premiere recording of Johann Straus Jr's Simplicius with Zurich Opera Orchestra, Beethoven's Symphony No. 9 (with The Cleveland Orchestra), the Welser-Möst Edition, New Year's Day Concert (Vienna Musikverein) on CD and DVD 2011, 2013. *Publication:* Kadenzen: Notizen und Gespräche 2007. *Leisure interests:* literature, mountain hiking, marathons. *Address:* c/o IMG Artists, The Light Box, 111 Power Road, London, W4 5PY, England (office); The Cleveland Orchestra, Severance Hall, 11001 Euclid Avenue, Cleveland, OH 44106-1796, USA (office). *Telephone:* (20) 7957-5800 (office); (20) 7957-5801 (office); (216) 231-7300 (office). *E-mail:* twalton@imgartists.com (office); sweatherstone@imgartists.com (office); info@clevelandorchestra.com (office). *Website:* www.imgartists.com (office); www.clevelandorchestra.com (office).

WELSH, Irvine, MBA; British writer; b. 1958, Edinburgh, Scotland; ed Heriot-Watt Univ.; Co-owner, 4 Way Productions film studio; Amb. for Unicef. *Publications include:* Trainspotting (novel) 1993, The Acid House (short stories) 1994, Marabou Stork Nightmares: A Novel 1995, Ecstasy: Three Chemical Romances 1996, The Wedding (with Nick Waplington) 1996, You'll Have Had Your Hole (play) 1997, Filth: A Novel 1998, Glue (novel) 2000, Porno (novel) 2002, Soul Crew (screenplay, also dir) 2003, Meat Trade (screenplay) 2004, The Bedroom Secrets of the Master Chefs (novel) 2006, Babylon Heights (with Dean Cavanagh) 2006, If You Liked School, You'll Love Work (short stories) 2007, Crime (novel) 2008, Reheated Cabbage (short stories) 2009, Skagboys 2012; contrib. to newspapers; contrib. to anthologies, including Children of Albion Rovers 1996, Disco Biscuits 1996, Ahead of its Time 1997, The Weekenders 2002, One City 2006; contrib. to Loaded, Guardian, Daily Telegraph. *Address:* c/o Jonathan Cape, 20 Vauxhall Bridge Road, London, SW1V 2SA, England. *Website:* www.irvinewelsh.net.

WELSH, Moray Meston, BA, LRAM, ARCM, GradDip; British cellist; *Member, Cropper-Welsh-Roscoe Trio;* b. 1 March 1947, Haddington, Scotland; s. of D. A. Welsh and C. Welsh (née Meston); partner, Jonathan Papp; ed York Univ. and Moscow Conservatoire; debut, Wigmore Hall 1972; cello solo appearances in UK, USA, USSR, Europe and Scandinavia; appeared with major UK orchestras, including London Symphony Orchestra, Royal Philharmonic Orchestra, BBC Symphony; festivals at Bath, Edinburgh, Aldeburgh, Bergen and Helsinki; appeared as soloist internationally under Colin Davis, André Previn, Rafael Frühbeck de Burgos, Bernard Haitink; chamber music performances with Previn, Bashmet, Midori, Galway and Chung; Prin. Cellist, London Symphony Orchestra 1992–2005; mem. Cropper-Welsh-Roscoe Trio; recitals with Jonathan Papp; teaches privately and in masterclasses; British Council Scholarship 1969, Gulbenkian Fellowship 1970. *Recordings include:* concertos by Boccherini, Vivaldi, Alexander Goehr, Hoddinott, Hugh Wood (Sunday Times record of the year); recorded with James Galway, Kyung-Wha Chung, Allegri Quartet, Alberni Quartet; cello and orchestra music by Herbert Howells with LSO; Rachmaninov Complete Works for Cello and Piano. *Radio:* frequent broadcasts on BBC Radio 3. *Leisure interests:* art, gardening, skiing, writing. *Address:* 32 Dartmouth Road, London, NW2 4EX, England (home). *Telephone:* (20) 8933-3032 (home). *E-mail:* moraywelsh@thecello.net (office). *Website:* www.moraywelsh.com (home).

WELTEKE, Ernst; German economist; b. 21 Aug. 1942, Korbach; ed Univ. Marburg, Univ. Frankfurt am Main; Chair. Parl. Group of Social Democratic Party in Hessen Land Parl. 1984–87, 1988–91; Minister for the Economy, Transport and Tech. in Hessen 1991–94, for Finance 1994–95; Pres. Land Cen. Bank, Hessen 1995–99; Pres. Deutsche Bundesbank Sept. 1999–2004 (resgnd); mem. Governing Council European Central Bank 1999–2004. *Address:* Westerbachstraße 23E, 61476 Kronberg im Taunus, Germany (office).

WELTY, John D., MA, EdD; American university administrator; *President, California State University, Fresno;* b. 24 Aug. 1944, Amboy, Ill.; s. of John D. Welty and Doris E. Donnelly; m. Sharon Brown 1996; three d. two s.; ed Western Illinois, Michigan State and Indiana Univs; Admissions Counsellor, Michigan State Univ. 1966–67; Asst Vice-Pres. for Student Affairs, Southwest Minnesota State Univ. 1967–74; Dir of Residences and Asst Prof., State Univ. of NY, Albany 1974–77, Assoc. Dean of Students and Dir of Residences 1977–80; Vice-Pres. for Student and Univ. Affairs, Ind. Univ. of Pennsylvania 1980–84, Pres. 1984–91; Pres. California State Univ., Fresno 1991–; several distinguished service awards. *Publication:* Alcohol and Other Drugs: A Guide for College Presidents and Governing Boards. *Leisure interests:* golf, jogging, reading, racquetball. *Address:* Office of the President, California State University, 5200 N Barton Avenue, Henry Madden Library, Fresno, CA 93704 (office); 4411 N Van Ness Boulevard, Fresno, CA 93704, USA (home). *Telephone:* (559) 278-2324 (office); (559) 222-2920 (home). *Fax:* (559) 278-4715 (office). *E-mail:* johnw@csufresno.edu (office). *Website:* www.csufresno.edu (office).

WEN, Carson, BA, BA, MA, JP (Hong Kong); Hong Kong lawyer; *Chairman, Sancus Capital Limited;* b. 16 April 1953, Hong Kong; s. of Sir Yung Wen and Tsi Fung Chu; m. Julia Fung Yuet Shan 1983; one c.; ed Diocesan Boys' School, Hong Kong, Nat. Jr Coll. Singapore, Columbia Univ., USA and Univ. of Oxford, UK; Singapore Govt Scholar 1971–72; Partner, Siao, Wen and Leung (Solicitors and Notaries), Hong Kong 1982–, Jones Day; Dir and Sec.-Gen. Hong Kong Kwun Tong Industries and Commerce Asscn 1982–, Pres. Emer. 1989–; mem. Kwun Tong Dist Bd 1983–85; Dir Banco Delta Asia SARL, Macau 1992–; Hon. Pres. Hong Kong Industrial Dists., Industry and Commerce Asscn Ltd 1993–; Attesting Officer apptd. by Ministry of Justice of China 1992–; Special Adviser to China Sr Prosecutors Educ. Foundation under the auspices of the Supreme People's Procurate of People's Repub. of China 1993–; Hong Kong Affairs Adviser to Govt of China 1993–; mem. Selection Cttee for First Govt of Hong Kong Special Admin. Region 1996; Vice-Chair. The Hong Kong Progressive Alliance 1994–; Deputy, Nat. People's Congress, People's Repub. of China for three terms from 1998; Partner, Hong Kong Office, Heller Ehrman (pvt. law practice) as Head, China Practice Group 2003–07; Chair. Sancus Capital Ltd 2007–; Founding Exec. Cttee mem. China M&A Asscn; mem. Bd China Africa Business Council (Hong Kong), Pacific Basin Econ. Council, California Asscn of Hong Kong and China; mem. Business Advisory Council of the UN Econ. and Social Comm. for Asia Pacific (UNESCAP); fmr Vice-Chair. Democratic Alliance for the Betterment and Progress of Hong Kong; Guest Prof., Law School of Sun Yat-Sen Univ. (Zhongshan Univ.), Guangzhou, China; Hon. Life Pres. Hong Kong Sze Yap Industry and Commerce Asscn 1983–; Bronze Bauhinia Star. *Publications:* contribs to 13 lectures on Hong Kong Law; articles in journals, magazines and newspapers. *Leisure interests:* reading, golf. *Address:* Sancus Group, Level 18, Wheelock House, 20 Pedder Street, Central, Hong Kong Special Administrative Region, People's Republic of China (office). *E-mail:* info@sancusgroup.com (office). *Website:* sancuscapital.com (office).

WEN, Jiabao; Chinese party and state official and geologist; b. 15 Sept. 1942, Tianjin; m. Zhang Peili; one s. one d.; ed Beijing Inst. of Geology; joined CCP 1965; technician and political instructor, Geomechanics Survey Team, Gansu Prov. Geological Bureau, Ministry of Land and Resources 1968–1978, Deputy Head 1978–79; Engineer and Deputy Section Head, Gansu Prov. Geological Bureau 1979–81, Deputy Dir-Gen. 1981–82; Dir Reform Research Office of the Geological and Mining Bureau of the State Council 1982–83; Deputy Minister of Geology and Mining 1983–85; Deputy Dir, Gen. Office of 12th CCP Cen. Cttee 1985–86, Dir, Gen. Office of 13th and 14th CCP Cen. Cttee 1986–93; Alt. mem. Secr. of Cen. Cttee 1987; Sec. CCP Cen. Organs Working Cttee 1988; mem. 13th CCP Cen. Cttee 1987–92, 14th CCP Cen. Cttee 1992–97, Alt. mem. CCP Politburo 1992–97, mem. 1997–2012; Sec. Secr. of Cen. Cttee 1992; mem. 15th CCP Cen. Cttee 1997–2002, 16th CCP Cen. Cttee 2002–07 (mem. Standing Cttee of the Politburo 2002–07), 17th CCP Cen. Cttee 2007–12 (mem. Standing Cttee of the Politburo 2007–12); Sec. Financial Work Cttee of Cen. Cttee 1998–2002; Vice-Premier State Council

1998–2003, Premier State Council (Prime Minister) 2003–13; Chair. State Comm. for Public Sector Reform 2003, Nat. Defence Mobilization Comm. 2003; Leader of the Leading Group for Financial and Econ. Affairs 2003; ranked by Forbes magazine amongst The World's Most Powerful People (14th) 2011. *Address:* c/o Office of the Premier, Great Hall of the People, West Edge, Tiananmen Square, Beijing, People's Republic of China (office). *Website:* www.gov.cn (office).

WEN, Shizhen; Chinese party official; b. 1940, Haicheng Co., Liaoning Prov.; ed Faculty of Mechanical Eng, Dalian Inst. of Tech.; Deputy Dir, later Dir Dalian Oil Pump Nozzle Plant, Liaoning Prov. 1965–82; joined CCP 1979; Deputy Dir Dalian City Machinery Bureau 1982–83, Machine Building Industry Dept 1983–85; Asst Gov. Liaoning Prov. 1985–86, Deputy Gov. 1986–93, Vice-Gov. 1993–95, Gov. 1995; Deputy Sec. CCP Liaoning Prov. Cttee 1986–97, Sec. 1997–2004, mem. Standing Cttee 2001–; Chair. Standing Cttee Liaoning Prov. People's Congress 2003–04; Alt. mem. 13th CCP Cen. Cttee 1987–91, mem. 14th CCP Cen. Cttee 1992, 15th CCP Cen. Cttee 1997–2002, 16th CCP Cen. Cttee 2002–07; Deputy, 8th NPC 1993–98, 9th NPC 1998–2003. *Address:* c/o Liaoning Provincial People's Congress, Shengyang City, Liaoning Province, People's Republic of China (office).

WEN, Gen. Zongren; Chinese army officer; b. Nov. 1940, Chaoxian Co., Anhui Prov.; ed PLA Tank School, PLA Political Acad., PLA Mil. Acad.; joined PLA 1959, CCP 1961; platoon leader, Tank Regt, PLA Services and Arms, Beijing 1962–67 (also Sec. Political Dept); clerk, Org. Section (Political Dept), Tank Div. and Armoured Force, PLA Services and Arms, Nanjing City Jiangsu Prov. 1967–73; Political Commissar, Tank Regt, PLA Services and Arms 1973–79; Dir 2nd Tank Div. Political Dept 1980–83; Div. Political Commissar 1980–83; Dir 12th Group Army Political Dept 1983–85; 12th Group Army Political Commissar 1985–94; rank of Maj.-Gen. 1988, Lt-Gen. 1996, Gen. 2002; Dir Political Dept of Nanjing Mil. Area Command 1994–96; Political Commissar, Lanzhou Mil. Area Command 1996–2000; Political Commissar, PLA Mil. Acad. of Sciences 2000–05; Alt. mem. 14th CCP Cen. Cttee 1992–97, mem. 15th CCP Cen. Cttee 1997–2002, 16th CCP Cen. Cttee 2002–07. *Address:* c/o PLA Military Academy of Sciences, Beijing, People's Republic of China (office).

WENDERS, Wim; German film director and writer; b. 14 Aug. 1945, Düsseldorf; m. Donata Schmidt 1993; ed Filmhochschule, Munich; film critic, Die Suddeutsche Zeitung, Filmkritik 1968–70; Chair. European Film Acad. 1991–96, Pres. 1996–; mem. Akad. der Künste; Hon. Prof., HFF (Acad. of Film and Television), Munich 1993; Dr hc (Sorbonne, Paris) 1989, (Univ. of Freiburg, Switzerland) 1995; Friedrich Wilhelm Murnau Award 1991. *Films include:* Summer in the City 1970, The Goalie's Anxiety at the Penalty Kick 1972, The Scarlet Letter 1973, Alice in the Cities 1974, The Wrong Move 1975, Kings of the Road 1976, The American Friend 1977, Lightning Over Water 1980, The State of Things (Golden Lion, Venice Film Festival) 1982, Hammett 1982, Paris, Texas 1984, Wings of Desire 1987 (Cannes Film Festival Award), Aufzeichnungen zu Kleidern und Städten 1989, Until the End of the World 1991, Faraway, So Close! 1993, Lisbon Story, The Million Dollar Hotel 1999, Buena Vista Social Club 1999, Vill Passiert 2002, Soul of a Man 2003, Land of Plenty 2004, Don't Come Knockin' 2004, Palermo Shooting 2008, Pina 2011. *Publications include:* Emotion Pictures 1986, Written in the West 1987, Die Logik der Bilder 1988, The Act of Seeing 1992. *Address:* c/o Paul Kohner, 9300 Wilshire Boulevard, #555, Beverly Hills, CA 90212, USA. *E-mail:* office@neueroadmovies.com. *Website:* www.wim-wenders.com.

WENDT, Albert, CNZM; Samoan/New Zealand author and academic; *Professor Emeritus, Department of English, University of Auckland;* b. 1939, Apia; three c.; ed Ardmore Teachers Coll., Victoria Univ.; fmr Prin., Samoa Coll.; Prof. of Pacific Literature and Pro-Vice Chancellor, Univ. of the South Pacific 1974–88; Prof. of New Zealand Literature, Auckland Univ. 1988, now Prof. Emer.; Distinguished Writer-in-Residence, Univ. of Hawaii at Manoa 2004–08; Order of Merit (Western Samoa), Companion, Order of Merit (New Zealand) 2000; Hon. PhD (Univ. de Bourgogne, France) 1993, Hon. DLit (Victoria Univ.) 2005; Hon. DHumLitt (Hawaii) 2009; Sr Pacific Islands Artist's Award 2003, Nikkei Asia Prize 2004, Prime Minister's Award for Literary Achievement for Fiction 2012. *Play:* The Songmaker's Chair 2004. *Publications include:* novels: Sons for the Return Home 1973, Pouliuli 1977, Leaves of the Banyan Tree 1979, Ola 1991, Black Rainbow 1992, Mango's Kiss 2003, The Adventures of Vela (Commonwealth Writers Prize for Best Book, South East Asia and Pacific Region 2010) 2009; short stories: Flying Fox in a Freedom Tree 1974, The Birth and Death of the Miracle Man 1986, Ancestry 2012; poetry: Inside us the Dead: Poems 1961–1974 1976, Shaman of Visions 1984, Photographs 1995, The Book of the Black Star 2002. *Address:* c/o Huia Publishers, PO Box 17-335, Karori 6147, Wellington; c/o Department of English, University of Auckland, Arts 1 Building, 14a Symonds Street, Level 4, Auckland 1, New Zealand (office).

WENDT, Henry, III, AB; American business executive; *Co-Founder, Healthcare Investment Partners;* b. 19 July 1933, Neptune City, NJ; s. of Henry Wendt and Rachel Lindsey Wendt; m. Holly Ann Peterson 1956; one s. one d.; ed Hackley School, Tarrytown, NY and Princeton Univ., NJ; joined SmithKline and French Labs 1955; Pres. SmithKline Corpn 1976–89, CEO 1982–89, Chair. SmithKline Beckman Corpn Feb.–July 1989, Chair. SmithKline Beecham PLC 1989–94; Founder and Chair. Global Health Care Partners 1995–2001; Chair. DLJ Merchant Banking 1997–, Computerized Medical Systems, Inc.; Co-founder Healthcare Investment Partners 2004–; Dir West Marine Inc. 1997–2001; Chair. Computerized Medical Systems Inc., Arrail Dental (China) Ltd; Dir, Bio Partners SA 2000–, Cambridge Laboratories, PLC, Wilson Greatbatch Technologies Ltd, Focus Technologies Inc., Seven Hills Group LLC, Prometheus Laboratories Inc.; Propr Quivira Estate Vineyards and Winery 1983–; mem. Advisory Bd CTPartners Board Consultants; Chair. Community Foundation of Sonoma Co.; Dir The Pacific Basin Inst., Pomona Coll.; Trustee Emer., American Enterprise Inst.; Order of the Rising Sun with Gold and Silver Star (Japan) 1994; Hon. CBE 1995. *Publications:* Global Embrace 1993 Mapping the Pacific Coast 2004; various articles. *Leisure interests:* viticulture, oenology, 16th and 18th century cartography, fly fishing, sailing. *Address:* Healthcare Investment Partners, 111 Monte Vista Avenue, Suite A, Healdsburg, CA 95448, USA (office).

WÉNÉZOUI, Charles; Central African Republic politician; fmr Sec. of State for Foreign Affairs, ., Minister of Foreign and Francophone Affairs and Regional

Integration 2003–06. *Address:* c/o Ministry of Foreign and Francophone Affairs and Regional Integration, Bangui, Central African Republic (office).

WENG, Yueh-Sheng, LLB, DrJur; Taiwanese judge and academic; *Professor, National Chengchi University;* b. 1 July 1932, Chia-yi; m. Chuan Shu-Chen; three d.; ed Nat. Taiwan Univ., Heidelberg Univ., Germany; Assoc. Prof., Nat. Taiwan Univ. 1966–70, Prof. 1970–72; Commr Legal Comm., Exec. Yuan 1971–72, Commr Research, Devt and Evaluation Comm. 1972, Commr and Convenor Admin. Procedure Act Research Comm., Judicial Yuan 1981–92; Grand Justice, Judicial Yuan 1972–99, Presiding Justice, Constitutional Court 1992–99, Pres. Judicial Yuan 1999–2007, Chief Justice of Constitutional Court 2003–07; currently Prof., Nat. Chengchi Univ., Nat. Taiwan Univ.; mem. Council of Academic Review Evaluation, Ministry of Educ. 1998–99; Visiting Prof., School of Law, Univ. of Washington, USA 1991; Commr Academic Consultation Comm., Sun Yat-Sen Inst. of Social Sciences and Philosophy, Academia Sinica 1991–2001, Convenor 1998–2001; mem. Bd of Dirs Chiang Ching-kuo Foundation for Int. Scholarly Exchange 2004–13; Pres. Taiwan Admin. Law Asscn 1998–2004 (Hon. Pres. 2004–), Chinese Soc. of Constitutional Law 1999–2004 (Hon. Pres. 2004–); Chair. Nat. Taiwan Univ. Law Foundation 2010–(16); Hon. Fellow, Soc. for Advanced Legal Studies (UK) 2002; Hon. Pres. Taiwan Jurist Asscn 2003–06; Order of Propitious Clouds with Special Grand Cordon by Pres. of Taiwan 2000; Judicial Medal of the First Grade, Merit and Achievement Medal of the First Grade, Judicial Yuan of Taiwan 1994, Golden Medal of the Distinguished Justice, Supreme Court of the Repub. of Guatemala 2000, Chung-Cheng Medal of Honour, Pres. of Taiwan 2007. *Publications include:* Die Stellung der Justiz im Verfassungsrecht der Republik China 1970, Administrative Law and Rule of Law 1976, Administrative Law and Judiciary in a State Under the Principle of the Rule of Law 1994, Administrative Law I and II (co-author and co-ed.) 1998, 2000, Annotation of Administrative Procedure Act (co-author and ed.) 2003. *Leisure interests:* reading, hiking. *Address:* 19 Alley 9, Lane 143, Jiung Gong Road, Taipei 116, Taiwan (home). *Telephone:* (2) 2230-6339 (home). *Fax:* (2) 2230-6339 (home). *E-mail:* weng.ys21@msa.hinet.net (home). *Website:* www.cckf.org.tw (office).

WENNEMER, Manfred, BSc, MBA; German business executive; *Chairman of the Supervisory Board, Hochtief AG;* b. 19 Sept. 1947, Ottmarsbocholt, Münster-land; ed Univ. of Münster, Institut Europée d'Admin des Affaires (INSEAD), Fountainebleau, France; Project Man. Procter & Gamble, Schwalbach 1974–77, Arthur D. Little, Wiesbaden 1978–80; Head of Planning and Controlling Non-Woven Fabrics Div. Freudenberg & Co., Weinheim 1980–82, Gen.-Man. Lady Esther, Weinheim 1982–84, Man.-Dir Freudenberg Nonwovens, Capetown, SA 1984–87, Pres. and CEO Nonwovens N America USA 1987–92, Head of Special Nonwoven Fabrics Business Unit for Europe, Weinheim 1992–93, Head of Spunbounded Fabrics Operations, Kaiserlautern 1993–94; Head Exec. Bd Benecke-Kaliko AG, Hannover 1994–98; joined Continental Aktiengesellschaft (Continental AG) 1998, mem. Exec. Bd ContiTech Group 1998–2001, Chair. Exec. Bd and CEO Continental AG 2001–08; Chair. Supervisory Bd Hochtief AG 2011–; Ind. Dir Bekaert 2009–. *Address:* Hochtief AG, Opernplatz 2, 45128 Essen, Germany (office). *Telephone:* (201) 824-0 (office). *Fax:* (201) 824-2777 (office). *E-mail:* info@conti-online.com (office). *Website:* www.hochtief.com (office).

WENNER, Jann S.; American publisher; *Editor and Publisher, Rolling Stone;* b. 7 Jan. 1946, New York, NY; m. Jane Schindelheim (divorced); six c.; Founder, Ed and Publisher, Rolling Stone magazine 1967–; TV appearances include Crime Story 1987–88; currently oversees Us and Men's Journal magazines; Chair., Wenner Media Inc.. *Film appearances:* Up Your Legs Forever 1970, Perfect 1985, Jerry Maguire 1996, Almost Famous 2000. *Publications include:* Lennon Remembers (ed.) 1972, 20 Years of Rolling Stone: What a Long Strange Trip It's Been 1987, Rolling Stone Environmental Reader 1992, Gonzo: The Life of Hunter S. Thompson (with Corey Seymour) 2007, Fear and Loathing at Rolling Stone: The Essential Writing of Hunter S. Thompson (ed.) 2011. *Address:* Rolling Stone, Wenner Media Inc., 1290 Avenue of the Americas, New York, NY 10104-0298, USA (office). *Telephone:* (212) 484-1616 (office). *E-mail:* editors@rollingstone.com (office). *Website:* www.rollingstone.com (office).

WENNING, Werner; German business executive; *Chairman of the Supervisory Board, E.ON SE;* b. 21 Oct. 1946, Leverkusen-Opladen; m.; two d.; joined Bayer AG, Leverkusen 1966, Commercial Trainee, mem. staff Corp. Auditing Dept, Man. Finance and Accounting Dept Bayer Industrial SA, Lima, Peru 1970–75, Man. Dir and Admin. Head 1978–83, Head of Staff Dept Health Care Sector, Leverkusen 1983–86, Head Marketing Thermoplastics, Plastics Business Group 1986, Head Worldwide Marketing Operations 1987–91, seconded to Treuhandanstalt privatization agency, Berlin 1991–92, Man. Dir Bayer Hispania Industrial SA, Sr Bayer Rep. Spain 1992–96, Head Corp. Planning and Controlling, Leverkusen 1996–97, mem. Bd of Man. Bayer AG 1997–2010, Chair. 2002–10, Chair. Supervisory Bd 2012–; mem. Shareholders' Cttee Henkel AG & Co. KGaA; mem. Supervisory Bd E.ON SE (Chair. 2011–), Deutsche Bank AG; Pres. German Chemical Industry Asscn (VCI) 2005–07, Vice-Pres. 2007–. *Address:* E.ON SE, E.ON-Platz 1, 40479 Düsseldorf, Germany (office). *Telephone:* (211) 45790 (office). *Fax:* (211) 4579501 (office). *E-mail:* info@eon.com (office). *Website:* www.eon.com (office).

WENSLEY, Penelope Anne, AC, BA; Australian diplomatist and government official; *Governor of Queensland;* b. 18 Oct. 1946, Toowoomba, Qld; m. Dr Stuart McCosker 1974; two d.; ed Univ. of Queensland; diplomatic service 1968–, Paris 1969–72, Mexico City 1975–77, Wellington, NZ 1982–85, Consul Gen. Hong Kong 1986–88; Head Int. Orgs Div., Dept of Foreign Affairs and Trade 1991–92, Perm. Rep. to UN, Geneva 1993–95, also Amb. for Environment, UN 1992–95, Head of N Asia Div. 1996–97; Amb. and Perm. Rep. to UN, New York 1997–2002; High Commr to India 2002–04; Amb. to Bhutan 2002–04, to France (also accred to Algeria, Mauritania, Morocco, Monaco) 2005–08; Gov. of Queensland 2008–; Sr Adviser, Australian del. to UN Conf. on Environment and Devt 1992; Vice-Pres. World Conf. on Human Rights, Vienna 1993; Vice-Chair. UN Climate Change Convention Negotiations 1993–96; Coordinator Western Group Negotiations on UN Conventions on Biodiversity and Desertification 1994–96; Chair. Preparatory Process UN Conf. for the Sustainable Devt of Small Island Developing States 1993–94; Chair. Int. Coral Reef Initiative Conf. 1995; Vice-Chair. UN Inst. for Training and Research; mem. WHO High Level Advisory Council on Health and the Environment; Chair. UN Gen. Ass. Fifth Cttee (Admin. and Budgetary) 1999; Co-Chair. Preparatory Process for UN Gen. Ass. Special Session on HIV/AIDS

2001; Adjunct Prof., Univ. of Queensland 2000; Patron UN Youth Asscn of Australia; Fellow, Women's Coll., Univ. of Queensland; Hon. PhD and Alumnus of the Year (Univ. of Queensland) 1994; Hon. PhD (Griffith Univ.) 2008, (Queensland Univ. of Tech.) 2011. *Leisure interests:* music, theatre, reading, tennis, bushwalking. *Address:* Government House, GPO Box 434, Brisbane, Qld 4001, Australia (office). *Telephone:* (7) 3858-5700 (office). *Fax:* (7) 3858-5701 (office). *E-mail:* govhouse@govhouse.qld.gov.au (office). *Website:* (office).

WENT, David, BA, LLB, BL; Irish barrister, banker and business executive; b. 25 March 1947, Dublin; s. of Arthur Went and Phyllis Went (née Howell); m. Mary Christine Milligan 1972; one s. one d.; ed Trinity Coll. Dublin; Barrister-at-Law, King's Inns, Dublin; grad. trainee, Citibank, Dublin 1970, Gen. Man. 1975, Gen. Man., Jeddah 1975–76; Dir Ulster Investment Bank 1976, Chief Exec. 1982, Deputy Chief Exec. Ulster Bank Belfast 1987, Chief Exec. 1988–94; CEO Coutts & Co. Group 1994–97; CEO Irish Life Assurance PLC 1998–; Group CEO Irish Life and Permanent PLC 1999–2007; Gov., The Irish Times Trust 2002–07, Chair. The Irish Times Ltd 2007–13; Chair. Trinity Foundation; fmr Chair. Financial Services Consultative Industry Panel; mem. Bd of Dirs Allianz (Ireland); Dir (non-exec.), Goldman Sachs Bank (Europe) Ltd; fmr Dir (non-exec.), VHI Healthcare; Paul Prize, Trinity Coll. 1969, Brook Scholar, King's Inns 1970. *Leisure interests:* tennis, reading. *Address:* c/o The Irish Times, PO Box 74, 24–28 Tara Street, Dublin 2, Ireland. *E-mail:* services@irishtimes.com.

WERGER, Marinus Johannes Antonius, PhD; Dutch academic; *Professor of Plant Ecology and Vegetation Science, Utrecht University;* b. 3 May 1944, Enschede; s. of Johannes G. Werger and Gezina M. Zwerink; m. Karin E. Klein 1968; one d.; ed Jacobus Coll. Enschede and Utrecht, Groningen and Nijmegen Univs; professional research officer, Botanical Research Inst. Pretoria, S Africa 1968–73; Asst Prof., later Assoc. Prof., Nijmegen Univ. 1974–79; Prof. of Plant Ecology and Vegetation Science, Utrecht Univ. 1979–, Dean Faculty of Biology 1990–93; Consultant Prof., SW China Univ., Beibei 1984–; Visiting Prof., Univ. of Tokyo 1985; mem. Royal Netherlands Acad.; Mid-America State Univs Asscn Award 1986. *Publications:* Biogeography and Ecology of Southern Africa (two vols) 1978, The Study of Vegetation 1979, Man's Impact on Vegetation 1983, Plant Form and Vegetation Structure 1988, Tropical Rain Forest Ecosystems 1989. *Leisure interests:* history, travel, cooking. *Address:* Department of Plant Ecology and Biodiversity, Went Building, Room Z425, PO Box 800.84, 3508 TB Utrecht (office); Nieuwe Gracht 145, 3512 LL Utrecht, Netherlands (home). *Telephone:* (30) 2536843 (office); (30) 311969 (home). *E-mail:* m.j.a.werger@bio.uu.nl (office); m.j.a .werger@uu.nl (office). *Website:* www3.bio.uu.nl/peb (office).

WERLEIGH, Claudette Antoine; Haitian politician, educator, lawyer and organization official; b. 26 Sept. 1946, Cap-Haitien; m. Georges Werleigh; two d.; worked for Caritas (Catholic aid org.) 1976–87; Minister of Social Affairs March–Aug. 1990, of Foreign Affairs 1993–95; Prime Minister of Haiti 1995–96; Rep. to OAS summit 1998; Dir of Conflict Transformation Programmes, Life and Peace Inst., Uppsala, Sweden 1999–2007; Sec.-Gen. Pax Christi International 2007–12; fmr Vice-Pres. Pax Christi Int.; fmr Bd mem. Forum on Early Warning and Early Response (FEWER), London, UK, Bd mem. Life and Peace Inst., Uppsala, Sweden. *Address:* c/o Pax Christi International, 21 rue Vieux Marche aux Grains, 1000 Brussels, Belgium (office).

WERNER, Hans-Joachim, DipChem; German chemist and academic; *Professor and Director, Institute of Theoretical Chemistry, University of Stuttgart;* b. 16 April 1950, Hamburg; ed Univ. of Mainz, Univ. of Göttingen, Univ. of Frankfurt; Visiting Prof., Los Alamos Nat. Lab., Los Alamos, NM, USA 1983–84; Fellow, Churchill Coll., Cambridge, UK 1984–85; Heisenberg Fellowship, Deutsche Forschungsgemeinschaft, Univ. of Frankfurt 1985–87; Prof., Univ. of Bielefeld 1987; Prof. and Dir Inst. for Theoretical Chem., Univ. of Stuttgart 1994–, Dean (Dekan), Faculty of Chem. 2006–12, Vice-Rector for Organisation and Research 2012–; mem. Editorial Bd Zeitschrift für Physikalische Chemie, International Reviews in Physical Chemistry, Theoretical Chemistry Accounts, Physical Chemistry/Chemical Physics; Ed. Molecular Physics; mem. Int. Acad. of Quantum Molecular Science, Akad. der Wissenschaften zu Göttingen, Deutsche Bunsengesellschaft; City of Mainz Gutenbergpreis 1972, Max-Planck Research Award for Int. Collaboration 1996, Akad. der Wissenschaften zu Göttingen Jost Medal 1999, Deutsche Forschungsgemeinschaft Gottfried Wilhelm Leibniz Award 2000, Gay-Lussac-Humboldt Award 2008, ERC Advanced Grant 2013. *Address:* Institute of Theoretical Chemistry, University of Stuttgart, Pfaffenwaldring 55, 70569 Stuttgart, Germany (office). *Telephone:* (711) 685-64401 (office). *Fax:* (711) 685-64442 (office). *E-mail:* werner@theochem.uni-stuttgart.de (office). *Website:* www.theochem.uni -stuttgart.de/~werner (office).

WERNER, Helmut, Dr rer. nat; German chemist and academic; *Professor Emeritus of Inorganic Chemistry, University of Würzburg;* b. 19 April 1934, Mühlhausen; ed Univ. of Jena, Technische Hochschule, Munich, Calif. Inst. of Tech. (Caltech), Pasadena, Calif., USA; Lecturer in Inorganic Chem., Technische Hochschule, Munich, 1967–68; Asst Prof., Univ. of Zürich, Switzerland 1968–70, Prof. of Inorganic Chem. 1970–75; Prof. of Inorganic Chem. and Head, Inorganic Dept, Univ. of Würzburg 1975–2002, Prof. Emer. 2002–, Dean, Faculty of Chem. and Pharmacy 1987–89; Visiting Prof., Chemical Lab., Univ. of Cambridge, UK 1983; Visiting Prof., Chem. Dept, Universidad Catolica de Chile 1984; Visiting Prof., Research Unit, CNRS, Toulouse, France 1990, Univ. of Zaragoza, Spain 2003; mem. Editorial Advisory Bd Journal of Organometallic Chem. 1988–, Gazzetta Chimica Italiana 1990–97, Comments on Inorganic Chem. 1990–, Monatsheft für Chemie 1993–96, Journal of the Chemical Society 1994–96; mem. German Chemical Soc., ACS, Royal Soc. of Chem. (Fellow 1987–), Swiss Chemical Soc., Nat. Acad. of Science, Leopoldina 1988–, New York Acad. of Sciences 1997–; Dr hc (Zaragoza) 2001, (Jena) 2006; Lessing Medal 1952, German Chemical Soc. Alfred Stock Memorial Prize 1988, Max-Planck Research Award 1994, Royal Soc. of Chem. Centenary Medal 1994, Spanish Ministry of Science Mutis Award 1995, Paolo Chini Memorial Lecturer 1995, Gordon Stone Lecturer 2004. *Address:* Institut für Anorganische Chemie, Universität Würzburg, Am Hubland, 97074 Würzburg (office); Georg-Sittig-str. 1, 97074 Würzburg, Germany (home). *Telephone:* (931) 31-85270 (office). *Fax:* (931) 31-84623 (office). *E-mail:* helmut.werner@mail.uni-wuerzburg.de (office). *Website:* www-anorganik.chemie .uni-wuerzburg.de/werner/eng-index.html (office).

WERNER, Patrick; French banking executive; *Chairman of the Management Board, La Banque Postale;* ed Institut d'Études Politiques de Paris, École Nat. d'Admin; began career as Chief of Service of Internal Audit, Caisse des Dépôts 1980–83; mem. Bd then Man. Dir C3D (holding co. of subsidiaries of Caisse des Dépôts) 1983–91; Man. Dir groupe d'assurances Victoire 1991–95; joined Fédération Française des Socs d'Assurances 1996, Acting Man. Dir then Acting Vice-Pres. 1997; Dir-Gen. La Poste, in charge of Financial Affairs 1999–, Chair. Man. Bd La Banque Postale (subsidiary of La Poste) 2006–; Pres. SF2 (holding co. of subsidiaries of La Banque Postale related to financial activities), Assurposte, Supervisory Bd of La Banque Postale Asset Management, man. co. of OPCVM of La Banque Postale, BMS Exploitation, BMS Développement, SFPMEI (Soc. Financière du Porte-Monnaie Electronique Interbancaire). *Address:* La Banque Postale, 115 rue de Sèvres, 75275 Paris Cedex 06, France (office). *Telephone:* 1-45-45-36-39 (office). *E-mail:* legroupe@laposte.fr (office). *Website:* www .labanquepostale.fr (office); www.laposte.fr/legroupe (office).

WERNER, Wendelin, PhD; French (b. German) mathematician; *Professor of Mathematics, Université Paris-Sud;* b. Sept. 1968; ed École Normale Supérieure, Université Paris VI; Research Officer, CNRS 1991–97; Postdoctoral work Univ. of Cambridge, UK 1993–95; Prof. of Math., Université Paris-Sud 1997–, École Normale Supérieure (part time) 2005–; Rollo Davidson Prize 1998, Doisteau-Blutet Prize (Academie des Sciences) 1999, EMS Prize 2000, Fermat Prize 2001, Jacques Herbrand Prize (Academie des Sciences) 2003, Loeve Prize 2005, Soc. for Industrial and Applied Math. Polya Prize (co–winner) 2006, Fields Medal 2006. *Address:* Laboratoire de Mathématiques, Université Paris-Sud, Bâtiment 425, Orsay 91405, France (office). *Telephone:* 8-70-44-70-88 (office). *Fax:* 1-69-15-72-34 (office). *Website:* www.math.u-psud.fr/~werner (office).

WERTENBAKER, Timberlake, FRSL; British playwright; *Artistic Director, Natural Perspective Theatre Company;* m. John Man; one d.; Resident Playwright, Royal Court Theatre 1984–85; Dir English Stage Co. 1991–99; mem. Exec. Cttee PEN 1999–2002; Royden B. Davis Visiting Prof. of Theatre, Georgetown Univ., Washington, DC 2005–06; Artistic Dir Natural Perspective Theatre Co. 2007–; Leverhulme Artist-in-Residence, Freud Museum, London 2011–; UNESCO City of Literature Visiting Prof. of Creative Writing, Univ. of East Anglia 2012; mem. Artistic Advisory Panel, Royal Acad. of Dramatic Art 2008–, Council of the Royal Soc. of Literature 2011–; Dr hc (Open Univ.); Plays and Players Most Promising Playwright (for The Grace of Mary Traverse) 1985, Evening Standard Most Promising Playwright, Olivier Play of the Year (for Our Country's Good) 1988, Eileen Anderson Drama Award (for The Love of the Nightingale) 1989, Critics' Circle Best West End Play 1991, Writers' Guild Best West End Play, Susan Smith Blackburn Award (for Three Birds Alighting on a Field) 1992, Mrs Giles Whiting Award (for gen. body of work) 1989, Guggenheim Fellowship 2004. *Plays include:* (for the Soho-Poly): Case to Answer 1980; (for the Women's Theatre Group): New Anatomies 1982; (for the Royal Court): Abel's Sister 1984, The Grace of Mary Traverse 1985, Our Country's Good 1988, Three Birds Alighting on a Field 1991, Credible Witness 2001; (for Out of Joint): The Break of Day 1995; (for RSC): The Love of the Nightingale 1988; (for Hampstead Theatre): After Darwin 1998; (for Birmingham Rep.): The Ash Girl 2000; (for Theatre Royal, Bath): Galileo's Daughter 2004; (for Arcola Theatre, London) The Line 2009; (for RSC): trans. Arianne Mnouchkine's Mephisto, trans. Sophocles' Thebans; (for San Francisco ACT): trans. Euripides' Hecuba; (for Peter Hall Co.): trans. Eduardo de Filippo's Filumena (Piccadilly Theatre) 1998, (for Chichester) Jean Anouilh's Wild Orchards 2002, trans. Gabriela Preissová's Jenufa (for Arcola Theatre, London) 2008; trans. Euripides' Hippolytus (Riverside Studios, London) 2009; trans. Racine's Phèdre (Stratford, Ontario) 2009, (ACT, San Francisco) 2010, Sophocles' Elektra (Getty, Los Angeles) 2010; trans. Racine's Britannicus (Wilton's Music Hall) 2011; other trans. include Successful Strategies, False Admissions, La Dispute (Marivaux), Come tu mi vuoi (Pirandello), Pelléas and Mélisande (Maeterlinck). *Libretto:* The Love of the Nightingale (music by Richard Mills, Sydney Opera House) 2011. *Films:* The Children (Channel 4), Do Not Disturb (BBC TV). *Radio includes:* Credible Witness, Dianeira, Hecuba (trans. and adaptation), The H. File (adaptation of novel by Ismail Kadaré), Scenes of Seduction 2005, Divine Intervention 2006, What is the Custom of Your Grief? 2009, adaptation of A. S. Byatt's Possession 2011. *Television:* Belle and the Beast (BBC). *Publications:* Timberlake Wertenbaker: Plays 1 1996, The Break of Day 1996, After Darwin 1999, Filumena 1999, The Ash Girl 2000, Credible Witness 2001, Timberlake Wertenbaker: Plays 2 2002, Jenufa (Adaption) 2007, Hippolytus 2009, The Line 2009, Britannicus (trans.) 2011, Timberlake Wertenbaker: Teatro: Dopo Darwin, Testimone Credibile, Le Leggi del Moto 2011. *Leisure interest:* mountains. *Address:* c/o The Agency, 24 Pottery Lane, Holland Park, London, W11 4LZ, England (office).

WERTMULLER, Lina; Italian film director; b. (Arcangela Felice Assunta Wertmuller von Elgg), 14 Aug. 1928, Rome; m. Enrico Job; ed Rome Theatre Acad.; toured Europe with a puppet show after graduating; worked in theatre for ten years as actress, director and playwright; First Asst to Federico Fellini in Ottoemezzo; Commendatore Repubblica Italiana. *Plays:* Amore e magia nella cucina di mamma, Storia d'amore e d'anarchia, Lasciami andare madre, La vedova Scaltra. *Films as director and screenwriter:* I Basilischi (The Lizards) 1963, Questa Volta parliamo di Uomini (Let's Talk About Men) 1965, Rita la zanzara (Rita the Mosquito) 1966, Non stuzzicate la zanzara (Don't Sting the Mosquito) 1967, Mimi Metallurgio Ferito nell'Onore (The Seduction of Mimi) 1972, Film d'amore e d'anarchia (Love and Anarchy) 1973, Tutto a Posto e Niente in Ordine (All Screwed Up), Travolti da un Insolito Destino nell'Azzurro Mare d'Agosto (Swept Away) 1974, Pasqualino Settebellezze (Seven Beauties) 1976, The End of the World in our Usual Bed in a Night Full of Rain, Shimmy Lagano Tarantelle e Vino 1978, Revenge 1979, Summer Night, On a Moonlit Night, Saturday, Sunday, Monday, Ciao, Professore! 1993, The Nymph 1996, Ferdinando e Carolina 1999, Francesca e Nunziata 2001, Il giornalino di Gianburrasca. *Music:* La Pappa con il pomodoro. *Radio:* Sceicchi e femministe. *Television:* Peperoni ripieni e pesci in faccia (dir) 2004, Canzonissima, Studio Uno. *Address:* Via P. Clotilde 5, 00196 Rome, Italy.

WESCOT-WILLIAMS, Sarah; St Maarten politician; *Prime Minister;* m. Louis E. Wescot (deceased); fmr Commr of Finance, of Educ., of Constitutional Affairs, fmr Leader of Govt; Prime Minister of St Maarten 2010– (first Prime Minister following dissolution of Netherlands Antilles); currently also Minister of Gen.

Affairs and Acting Minister of Tourism, Econ. Affairs, Transport and Telecommunication; Leader, Democratic Party; Person of the Year Award, Paul Harris Fellow Award, Woman of Great Esteem Award. *Leisure interests:* music, reading, volleyball. *Address:* Office of the Prime Minister, PO Box 943, Clem Labega Square, Philipsburg, Sint Maarten (office). *E-mail:* Sarah.Wescot-Williams@sintmaartengov.org (office). *Website:* www.sintmaartengov.org (office).

WESKER, Sir Arnold, Kt, FRSL; British playwright and director; b. 24 May 1932, Stepney, London, England; s. of Joseph Wesker and Leah Wesker (née Perlmutter); m. Doreen (Dusty) Cecile Bicker 1958; two s. one d.; ed mixed elementary schools and Upton House Central School, Hackney, London, London School of Film Technique; left school 1948, worked as furniture maker's apprentice, carpenter's mate, bookseller's asst; RAF 1950–52 (ran drama group); plumber's mate, road labourer, farm labourer, seed sorter, kitchen porter and pastry-cook; Dir Centre 42 1961–70; Chair. British Centre of Int. Theatre Inst. 1978–82; Pres. Int. Cttee of Playwrights 1979–83; Arts Council Bursary 1959; Hon. Fellow, Queen Mary Coll. London 1995; Hon. DLitt (Univ. of E Anglia) 1989, Hon. DHumLitt (Denison Univ., Ohio) 1997; Evening Standard Award for Most Promising Playwright (for Roots) 1959, third prize Encyclopaedia Britannica Competition (for The Kitchen) 1961, Premio Marzotto Drama Prize (for Their Very Own and Golden City) 1964, Gold Medal, Premios el Espectador y la Critica (for The Kitchen) 1973, (for Chicken Soup with Barley) 1979, The Goldie Award (for Roots) 1986, Last Frontier Award for Lifetime Achievement, Valdez, Alaska 1999, Royal Literary Fund annual pension and award for lifetime achievement 2003. *Film scripts:* The Master (free adaptation of An Unfortunate Insider by F. Dostoevsky) 1966, Madam Solario (from anonymous novel of same title) 1969, The Wesker Trilogy 1979, Lady Othello 1980, Homage to Catalonia (from George Orwell's autobiography) 1991, Maudie (from Doris Lessing's novel Diary of a Good Neighbour) 1995, The Kitchen (for Italian film co.). *Opera libretttos:* Caritas (music by Robert Saxton) 1988, Grief (one-woman opera commissioned by Japanese composer Shigeaki Saegusa) 2004. *Plays:* The Kitchen, Royal Court Theatre 1959, 1961, 1994, Chicken Soup with Barley, Roots, I'm Talking about Jerusalem (The Wesker Trilogy), Belgrade Theatre, Coventry 1958–60, Royal Court Theatre 1960, Chips with Everything, Royal Court 1962, Vaudeville 1962, Broadway 1963, The Four Seasons, Belgrade Theatre then The Saville Theatre 1965, Their Very Own and Golden City, Brussels and Royal Court 1966, The Friends (Stockholm and London) 1970, The Old Ones, Royal Court 1972, The Wedding Feast, Stockholm 1974, Leeds 1977, The Journalists, Coventry 1977, Germany 1981, The Merchant (later entitled Shylock), Stockholm and Arthus 1976, Broadway 1977, Birmingham 1978, Love Letters on Blue Paper, Nat. Theatre 1978, Fatlips 1978, Caritas, Nat. Theatre 1981, Sullied Hand 1981, Edinburgh Festival and Finnish TV 1984, Four Portraits, Tokyo 1982, Edin. Festival 1984, Annie Wobbler, Birmingham 1983, Fortune Theatre 1984, New York 1986, One More Ride on the Merry-Go-Round, Leicester 1985, Yardsale, Edinburgh Festival and Stratford-on-Avon 1985, When God Wanted a Son, New End Theatre, London 1986, Whatever Happened to Betty Lemon, Yardsale, Lyric Studio, London 1987, Little Old Lady, Sweden 1988, The Mistress 1988, Beorhtel's Hill, Towngate, Basildon 1989, Three Women Talking (now Men Die Women Survive) 1990, Chicago 1992, Letter to a Daughter 1990, Blood Libel 1991, Wild Spring 1992, Tokyo 1994, Denial, Bristol Old Vic 2000, Groupie 2001 (based on radio play), Longitude 2002 (freely adapted from book by Dava Sobel), Letter To Myself 2004; 45-minute adaptations for Schools Shakespeare Festival of Much Ado About Nothing and Henry V 2006, Phoenix Phoenix Burning Bright 2006, The Rocking Horse Kid (adapted from radio play) 2008, Joy and Tyranny 2010. *Own plays directed:* The Four Seasons, Cuba 1968, world première of The Friends at Stadsteatern, Stockholm 1970, London 1970, The Old Ones, Munich, Their Very Own and Golden City, Arhus 1974, Love Letters on Blue Paper, Nat. Theatre 1978, Oslo 1980, Annie Wobbler, Birmingham 1983, London 1984, Yardsale and Whatever Happened to Betty Lemon, London 1987, Shylock (workshop production), London 1989, The Kitchen, Univ. of Wis. 1990, The Mistress, Rome 1991, The Wedding Feast, Denison Univ., Ohio 1995, Letter to a Daughter, Edin. Festival 1998; also Dir Osborne's The Entertainer, Theatre Clwyd 1983, The Merry Wives of Windsor, Oslo 1989. *Radio includes:* Bluey (Cologne Radio) 1985, (BBC) 1985, Groupie (commissioned by BBC) 2001, adaptation of Shylock (commissioned by BBC Radio 3) 2006, The Rocking Horse (commissioned by BBC World Service) 2006. *Adaptations for TV:* Menace 1961, Thieves in the Night (after Arthur Koestler) 1984–85, Diary of a Good Neighbour (Doris Lessing) 1989, Phoenix Phoenix Burning Bright (from own story, The Visit) 1992, Barabbas 2000. *Publications include:* plays: The Kitchen 1957, Chicken Soup with Barley 1958, Roots 1959, I'm Talking About Jerusalem 1960, Chips with Everything 1962, The Four Seasons 1965, Their Very Own and Golden City 1966, The Old Ones 1970, The Friends 1970, The Journalists 1972, The Wedding Feast 1974, Shylock (previously The Merchant) 1976, Love Letters on Blue Paper (TV play) 1976, (stage play) 1977, Words – As Definitions of Experience 1976, One More Ride on the Merry-Go-Round 1978, Fatlips 1980, Caritas 1980, Annie Wobbler 1982, Four Portraits – of Mothers 1982, Yardsale 1983, Cinders 1983, Bluey 1984, Whatever Happened to Betty Lemon 1986, When God Wanted a Son 1986, Badenheim 1939 1987, Shoeshine & Little Old Lady 1987, Lady Othello 1987, Beorhtel's Hill 1988, The Mistress 1988, Three Women Talking 1990, Letter to a Daughter 1990, Blood Libel 1991, Wild Spring 1992, Circles of Perception 1996, Break My Heart 1997, Denial 1997; essays, stories, etc.: Fears of Fragmentation 1971, Six Sundays in January 1971, Love Letters on Blue Paper 1974, Journey into Journalism 1977, Said the Old Man to the Young Man 1978, Distinctions 1985, As Much As I Dare (autobiog.) 1994, The Birth of Shylock and the Death of Zero Mostel (non-fiction) 1997, The King's Daughters 1998, The Wesker Trilogy 2001, One Woman Plays 2001; novels: Honey 2005, Longitude 2006; poetry: All Things Tire of Themselves 2009. *Leisure interest:* listening to music. *Address:* Hay on Wye, Hereford, Herefords., HR3 5RJ, England. *Telephone:* (1497) 820473. *E-mail:* wesker@compuserve.com. *Website:* www.arnoldwesker.com.

WESSELS, Wolfgang, Dr rer. pol; German academic; *Professor of European Politics, University of Cologne;* b. 19 Jan. 1948, Cologne; s. of Theodor Wessels and Emma Wessels; m. Aysin Wessels 1973; two d.; Dir Institut für Europäische Politik, Bonn 1974–94; Dir Admin. Studies and Prof., Coll. of Europe, Bruges, Belgium 1980–96; Jean Monnet Prof., Univ. of Cologne 1994–; Jean Monnet – European Studies GOLD Lifelong Learning Award, European Comm. 2007.

Publications include: The European Council, Decision-Making in European Politics (with Simon Bulmer) 1987; Co-Ed.: Die Europäische Politische Zusammenarbeit in den achtziger Jahren—Eine gemeinsame Aussenpolitik für Westeuropa? 1989, Jahrbuch der Europäischen Integration 1980–, Europa vom A-Z. Taschenbuch der Europäischen Integration 1991–, Foreign Policy of the European Union. From EPC to CFSP and Beyond 1997, Die Öffnung des Staates. Modelle und Wirklichkeit grenzüberschreitender Verwaltungspraxis 2000, Das politische System der Europäischen Union. Die institutionelle Architektur des EU-Systems 2008; papers and articles on European integration. *Address:* Forschungsinstitut für Politische Wissenschaft und Europäische Fragen, University of Cologne, Gottfried-Keller-Strasse 6, 50931 Cologne, Germany (office). *Telephone:* (221) 4704131 (office). *Fax:* (221) 9402542 (office). *E-mail:* wessels@uni-koeln.de (office). *Website:* www.wessels.uni-koeln.de (office).

WESSEX, HRH The Earl of; (Prince Edward Antony Richard Louis), (Viscount Severn), KCVO, ADC, KG, MA; British; b. 10 March 1964; s. of Queen Elizabeth II (q.v.) and Prince Philip, The Duke of Edinburgh; m. Sophie Rhys-Jones (now HRH The Countess of Wessex) 1999; one s. one d.; ed Heatherdown Prep. School, Gordonstoun School, Jesus Coll. Cambridge; fmrly Second Lt Royal Marines; worked in theatre production with Really Useful Group, Theatre Div.; f. Ardent Productions Ltd 1993; opened Commonwealth Games, Auckland 1990 and Malaysia 1998, Pres. Nat. Youth Music Theatre, Commonwealth Games Fed.; UK and Int. Trustee, The Duke of Edinburgh's Award; Chair. Int. Council and Trustee, The Duke of Edinburgh's Award Int. Asscn; Patron ADC Theatre Appeal Cambridge, BADMINTONscotland, British Paralympic Asscn, British Ski and Snowboard Fed., Cen. Caribbean Marine Inst., Chetham's School of Music, Manchester, The Church Army 121 Club, City of Birmingham Symphony Orchestra, Glassworks Theatre, Cambridge, Globe Theatre, Saskatchewan, Canada, Gordon's School Stepping Forward Appeal, Haddo Arts Trust, Aberdeen Haddo House Choral and Operatic Soc. (Royal Patron), Headway Dorset, His Majesty's Theatre Aberdeen, The Stage Man. Asscn, UNITEC, Auckland, Nat. Youth Orchestras of Scotland, Nat. Youth Theatre of Great Britain, Northern Ballet Theatre, The Orpheus Trust, Queen Victoria School, Auckland, Real Tennis Professionals Asscn, Royal Exchange Theatre Co., Royal Fleet Auxiliary Asscn, Manchester, Royal Wanganui Opera House, The London Gardens Soc., London Mozart Players, Royal Wolverhampton School; Patron of Appeal, St Thomas Church Appeal, Newport; Col-in-Chief Hastings and Prince Edward Regt, Saskatchewan Dragoons; Royal Hon. Col Royal Wessex Yeomanry; Hon. Chair. The Duke of Edinburgh's Award, Young Canadian's Challenge Charter for Business. *Publication:* Crown and Country 1999. *Leisure interests:* the arts, horse-riding, sailing, skiing, badminton, Real Tennis. *Address:* Buckingham Palace, London, SW1A 1AA; Bagshot Park, Bagshot, Surrey, GU19 5PL, England. *Website:* www.royal.gov.uk.

WEST, Martin Litchfield, OM, DPhil, DLitt, FBA; British classicist and academic; *Emeritus Fellow, All Souls College, Oxford;* b. 23 Sept. 1937, London, England; s. of Maurice Charles West and Catherine Baker West (née Stainthorpe); m. Stephanie Roberta Pickard 1960; one s. one d.; ed St Paul's School, London and Balliol Coll., Oxford; Woodhouse Jr Research Fellow, St John's Coll., Oxford 1960–63; Fellow and Praelector in Classics, Univ. Coll., Oxford 1963–74; Prof. of Greek, Univ. of London (Bedford Coll., then Royal Holloway and Bedford New Coll.) 1974–91; Sr Research Fellow, All Souls Coll., Oxford 1991–2004, Fellow Emer. 2004–; mem. Academia Europaea, London; Corresp. mem. Akad. der Wissenschaften, Göttingen, Accad. dei Lincei; Int. mem. American Philosophical Soc.; Fellow, Acad. of Athens; Hon. Fellow, Univ. Coll. Oxford 2001, Balliol Coll. Oxford 2004, St John's Coll. Oxford 2007; Dr hc (Univ. of Cyprus) 2008, (Univ. of Urbino) 2011; Balzan Prize for Classical Antiquity 2000, British Acad. Kenyon Medal for Classical Studies 2002. *Publications:* Hesiod, Theogony (ed.) 1966, Fragmenta Hesiodea (co-ed. with R. Merkelbach) 1967, Early Greek Philosophy and the Orient 1971, Sing Me, Goddess 1971, Iambi et Elegi Graeci (ed.) 1971–72, revised edn 1989–92, Textual Criticism and Editorial Technique 1973, Studies in Greek Elegy and Iambus 1974, Hesiod, Works and Days (ed.) 1978, Theognidis et Phocylidis fragmenta 1978, Delectus ex Iambis et Elegis Graecis 1980, Greek Metre 1982, The Orphic Poems 1983, Carmina Anacreontea 1984, The Hesiodic Catalogue of Women 1985, Introduction to Greek Metre 1987, Euripides Orestes (ed.) 1987, Hesiod (trans.) 1988, Aeschyli Tragoediae 1990, Studies in Aeschylus 1990, Ancient Greek Music 1992, Greek Lyric Poetry (trans.) 1993, The East Face of Helicon 1997 (Runciman Prize 1998), Homeri Ilias (ed.) Vol. I 1998, Vol. II 2000, Studies in the Text and Transmission of the Iliad 2001, Documents of Ancient Greek Music (with E. Pöhlmann) 2001, Homeric Hymns, Homeric Apocrypha, Lives of Homer 2003, Greek Epic Fragments 2003, Indo-European Poetry and Myth 2007, The Hymns of Zoroaster 2010, The Making of the Iliad 2011, Old Avestan Syntax and Stylistics 2011, Hellenica Vol. I 2011, Vol. II 2013, The Epic Cycle 2013. *Leisure interest:* music. *Address:* All Souls College, Oxford, OX1 4AL (office); 42 Portland Road, Oxford, OX2 7EY, England (home).

WEST, Paul, MA; American (b. British) author; b. 23 Feb. 1930, Eckington, Derbyshire, England; s. of Alfred West and Mildred Noden; ed Univ. of Oxford, UK and Columbia Univ.; served with RAF 1954–57; Asst Prof. of English, Memorial Univ., Newfoundland 1957–58, Assoc. Prof. 1958–60; arrived in USA 1961, became naturalized 1971; contrib., Washington Post, New York Times 1962–95, also contributes to Harper's and GQ magazines, Paris Review; mem. of staff, Pennsylvania State Univ. 1962, Prof. of English and Comparative Literature 1968–1995, Prof. Emer. 1995–; Crawshaw Prof., Colgate Univ. 1972; Melvin Hill Distinguished Visiting Prof., Hobart and William Smith Colls 1973; Distinguished Writer-in-Residence, Wichita State Univ. 1982; Writer-in-Residence, Univ. of Arizona 1984; Visiting Prof. of English, Cornell Univ. 1986, Brown Univ. 1992; Guggenheim Fellow 1962–63; Nat. Endowment for Arts Creative Writing Fellow 1979, 1984; mem. Author's Guild; Chevalier, Ordre Arts et Lettres; Aga Khan Fiction Prize 1973, Hazlett Memorial Award for Excellence in Arts (Literature) 1981, Literature Award, American Acad. and Inst. of Arts and Letters 1985, Pushcart Prize 1987, 1991, Best American Essays Award 1990, Grand Prix Halpérine Kaminsky Award 1992, Lannan Fiction Award 1993, Teaching Award NE Asscn of Grad. Schools 1994, Art of Fact Prize, State Univ. of NY 2000; Outstanding Achievement Medal, Pa State Univ. 1991. *Publications include:* Byron and the Spoiler's Art 1960, I, Said the Sparrow 1963, The Snow Leopard 1965, Tenement of Clay 1965, The Wine of Absurdity 1966, I'm Expecting to Live

Quite Soon 1970, Words for a Deaf Daughter 1970, Caliban's Filibuster 1971, Bela Lugosi's White Christmas 1972, Colonel Mint 1973, Gala 1976, The Very Rich Hours of Count von Stauffenberg 1980, Out of My Depths: A Swimmer in the Universe and Other Fictions 1988, The Place in Flowers Where Pollen Rests 1988, Lord Byron's Doctor 1989, Portable People, The Women of Whitechapel and Jack the Ripper 1991, James Ensor 1991, Love's Mansion 1992, A Stroke of Genius 1995, Sporting with Amaryllis 1996, Terrestrials 1997, Life with Swan 1999, O.K.: The Corral 2000, The Earps 2000, Doc Holliday 2000, The Dry Danube: A Hitler Forgery 2000, The Secret Lives of Words 2000, A Fifth of November 2001, Master Class 2001, Portable People 2001, Oxford Days 2002, Cheops: A Cupboard for the Sun 2002, The Immensity of the Here and Now: A Novel of 9.11 2003, My Father's War 2005, Tea with Osiris (poems) 2006, The Shadow Factory 2008. *Leisure interests:* swimming, astronomy, classical music, cricket, films. *Address:* c/o Lumen Books, 40 Camino Cielo, Santa Fe, NM 87506, USA.

WEST, Richard G., MA, ScD, FRS; British botanist and academic; b. 31 May 1926, Hendon, Middx; m. 1st Janet Abram 1958; one s.; m. 2nd Hazel Gristwood 1973 (died 1997); two d.; ed King's School, Canterbury and Univ. of Cambridge; Fellow, Clare Coll., Cambridge 1954–; Lecturer in Botany, Univ. of Cambridge 1960–68, Reader in Quaternary Research 1968–74, Prof. of Palaeoecology 1974–77, Prof. of Botany and Head, Dept of Botany 1977–91, Dir Sub-Dept of Quaternary Research 1966–87; Hon. mem. Royal Belgian Acad.; Foreign mem. Finnish Acad. of Sciences and Letters 1999; Hon. MRIA; Bigsby Medal, Geological Soc. 1968, Lyell Medal, Geological Soc. 1988, Albrecht Penck Medal, Deutsche Quartärvereinigung 1988. *Publications:* Pleistocene Geology and Biology 1968, The Ice Age in Britain (jtly) 1972, The Pre-glacial Pleistocene of the Norfolk and Suffolk Coasts 1980, Pleistocene Palaeoecology of Central Norfolk 1991, Plant Life in the Quaternary Cold Stages 2000, Brandon to Bungay 2009. *Leisure interest:* sailing. *Address:* Clare College, Cambridge (office); 3A Woollards Lane, Great Shelford, Cambridge, CB22 5LZ, England (home). *Telephone:* (1223) 842578 (home).

WEST, Stephen Craig, PhD, FRS, FMedSci; British scientist; *Senior Group Leader, Cancer Research UK;* b. 11 April 1952, Hull, England; s. of Joseph West and Louisa West; m. Phyllis Fraenza 1985; ed Univ. of Newcastle and Yale Univ., USA; Research Scientist, Yale Univ. 1983–85; Sr Scientist, Imperial Cancer Research Fund (now Cancer Research UK) 1985–89, Prin. Scientist 1989–, now Sr Group Leader; mem. European Molecular Biology Org. 1994–; Hon. Prof., Univ. Coll. London 1997–; Swiss Bridge Prize 2001, 2009, Louis-Jeantet Prize for Medicine 2007, Novartis Prize 2008, GSK Prize 2010, Genetics Soc. Medal 2012. *Publications:* more than 200 research articles. *Leisure interests:* sport, music. *Address:* Cancer Research UK, London Research Institute, Clare Hall Laboratories, South Mimms, Herts., EN6 3LD (office); Meadowbank, Riverside Avenue, Broxbourne, Herts., EN10 6RA, England (home). *Telephone:* (1707) 625868 (office); (1992) 470147 (home). *Fax:* (1707) 625801 (office). *E-mail:* stephen.west@cancer .org.uk (office). *Website:* www.cancerresearchuk.org (office).

WEST, Timothy Lancaster, CBE, FRSA; British actor and director; b. 20 Oct. 1934, Bradford, Yorks.; s. of the late H. Lockwood West and Olive Carleton-Crowe; m. 1st Jacqueline Boyer 1956 (dissolved); one d.; m. 2nd Prunella Scales (q.v.) 1963; two s.; ed John Lyon School, Harrow and Regent Street Polytechnic; repertory seasons, Wimbledon, Hull, Salisbury, Northampton 1956–60; mem. Royal Shakespeare and Prospect Theatre Cos. 1962–79; Artistic Dir, Old Vic 1980–81; Dir-in-Residence Univ. of WA 1982; Assoc. Dir Bristol Old Vic. –1991; Pres. London Acad. of Music and Dramatic Art, Soc. for Theatre Research; Hon. DLitt (E Anglia, W of England) (London), (Hull); Hon. DUniv (Bradford); Hon. LLD (Westminster); Hon. Dr Drama, Royal Scottish Acad. of Music and Drama (RSAMD). *Stage appearances include:* (in London): Caught Napping 1959, Galileo 1960, Gentle Jack 1963, The Tango 1963, The Italian Girl 1968, Abelard and Heloise 1970, Exiles 1970, The Critic as Artist 1971, The Houseboy 1973, A Month in the Country 1974, A Room with a View 1975, Laughter 1978, The Homecoming 1978, Beecham 1980, Master Class 1984, The War at Home 1984, When We are Married 1986, The Sneeze 1988, Long Day's Journey into Night 1991, It's Ralph 1991, Twelve Angry Men 1996, Henry IV Parts 1 and 2 1996, King Lear 1997, The Birthday Party 1999, Luther 2001, King Lear 2003, HMS Pinafore 2003, National Hero 2005, Galileo 2006, The Old Country 2006, A Number 2006, Coriolanus 2007, The Collection 2007, The Lover/ The Collection 2008; numerous appearances with Prospect Theatre Co., Royal Shakespeare Co. and regional theatres. *Film appearances include:* The Looking Glass War 1969, Nicholas and Alexandra 1971, The Day of the Jackal 1973, The Devil's Advocate 1978, The Thirty-Nine Steps 1978, Agatha 1979, Rough Cut 1980, Cry Freedom 1987, Consuming Passions 1988, The Tempest (voice) 1992, Ever After 1998, The Messenger: The Story of Joan of Arc 1999, 102 Dalmatians 2000, The Fourth Angel 2001, Iris 2001, Shrink 2002, Villa des Roses 2002, Sinbad: Legend of the Seven Seas (voice) 2003, Beyond Borders 2003, Endgame 2009. *Television appearances include:* Persuasion (mini-series) 1960, Witch Hunt (mini-series) 1967, Feet Foremost 1968, Big Breadwinner Hog (series) 1969, The Tragedy of King Richard II 1970, Edward II 1970, The Edwardians (mini-series) 1972, Horatio Bottomley 1972, Edward the King (mini-series) 1975, Hard Times (series) 1977, Henry VIII 1979, Churchill and the Generals 1979, Crime and Punishment (mini-series) 1979, Masada (mini-series) 1981, Murder Is Easy 1982, Oliver Twist 1982, Brass (series) 1983, The Last Bastion (mini-series) 1984, A Pocket Full of Rye 1985, Florence Nightingale 1985, Tender Is the Night (mini-series) 1985, The Good Doctor Bodkin-Adams 1986, The Monocled Mutineer (series) 1986, When We are Married 1987, What the Butler Saw 1987, Harry's Kingdom 1987, Breakthrough at Reykjavik 1987, Strife, Beryl Markham: A Shadow on the Sun 1988, The Contractor, Blore M.P. 1989, Lenin: The Train 1990, The Tragedy of Flight 103: The Inside Story (aka Why Lockerbie?) 1990, Bye Bye Columbus 1991, Shakespeare: The Animated Tales (mini-series) (voice) 1992, Framed 1992, Survival of the Fittest, Smokescreen (mini-series) 1994, Reith to the Nation, Eleven Men Against Eleven 1995, Hiroshima 1995, The Place of the Dead 1996, Over Here 1996, Cuts 1996, Rebecca 1997, Animated Epics: Beowulf (voice) 1998, Bramwell: Our Brave Boys 1998, King Lear 1998, The Big Knights (series) (voice) 1999, Midsomer Murders 2000, Bedtime (series) 2001, Murder in Mind 2001, Station Jim 2001, Martin Luther 2002, Dickens 2002, The Alan Clark Diaries 2004, The Inspector Lynley Mysteries: In Pursuit of the Proper Sinner 2004, London 2004, Essential Poems for Christmas 2004, Waking the Dead 2004, Colditz 2005, Bleak House (mini-series) 2005, A Room With a View 2007,

Terry Pratchett's Going Postal 2010. *Radio:* has appeared in more than 500 programmes since 1960. *Concerts:* with London Philharmonic Orchestra, Royal Philharmonic Orchestra, Britten Ensemble, Sinfonia 21 etc. *Publications:* I'm Here I Think, Where Are You? 1997, A Moment Towards the End of the Play 2001, So You Want To Be an Actor (with Prunella Scales) 2005. *Leisure interests:* music, travel, inland waterways, old railways. *Address:* c/o Gavin Barker Associates, 2D Wimpole Street, London, W1M 7AA, England.

WESTDAL, Christopher, BA, MBA; Canadian fmr diplomatist; ed St John's Coll., Univ. of Manitoba; previous positions beginning 1973 with Canadian Int. Devt Agency (CIDA); Amb. to Bangladesh and Burma 1982–85, to South Africa 1991–93, to Ukraine 1995–98, to UN, Geneva 1999–2003, to Russian Fed. 2003–06; currently mem. Bd of Dirs Silver Bear Resources Inc. *Address:* c/o Board of Directors, Silver Bear Resources, 65 Queen Street West, Suite 800, PO Box 71, Toronto, ON M5H 2M5, Canada (office).

WESTERBERG, Bengt, MedKand, FilKand; Swedish politician and banker; *Chairman, Financial Supervision Authority;* b. 23 Aug. 1943, Solna; s. of the late Carl-Eric and of Barbro Westerberg; m. 2nd Marie Ehrling; one s., two d. from a previous marriage; ed Karolinska Inst., Univ. of Stockholm; joined Liberal Youth League 1965, held elected office at all levels, Chair. Exec. Cttee 1970–71; joined Liberal Party 1965, Pres. 1993–95; Deputy Sec. to Commr for Greater Stockholm 1969, Sec. to Commr for Municipal Services 1970, Sec. to Stockholm County Council Traffic Commr 1971, Research Dir Traffic Cttee 1972, Adviser Govt Comm. on Traffic Policy 1975, Adviser Ministry of Labour 1976, Liberal Party's Coordination Office 1978; State Sec., Ministry of Industry 1978, Ministry of the Budget 1979–82; f. Foundation for Market-Economy Alternative for Sweden 1983; mem. Parl. 1984–94; Minister of Social Affairs and Deputy Prime Minister 1991–94; Research and Devt Leader, Centre of Gender Studies, Univ. of Karlstad 1995–2000; Chair. Telia AB 1995–98, BTJ 1995–98, Swedish Petrol Inst., Financial Supervision Authority, Swedish Inst. of Disabilty Research, Cirkus Cirkor, Bonus-Presskopia, Swedish Author's Foundation, Inst. of Future Studies, Univ. of Linkoping; Vice-Chair. Riksbank (Cen. Bank of Sweden) 1994–98, mem. Bd 2002–06; Pres. Swedish Athletics Asscn 1995–2004, Swedish Foundation of Dyslexia 1995–2005, Swedish Red Cross; Vice-Pres. Int. Fed. of Red Cross and Red Crescent Socs; mem. Bd Swedish Sports Confed. 1999–2005; Dr hc (Univ. of Karlstad) 2008. *Address:* Financial Supervision Authority, Box 7821, 103 97 Stockholm, Sweden (office). *Telephone:* (8) 787-80-00 (office). *Fax:* (8) 24-13-35 (office). *E-mail:* finansinspektionen@fi.se (office). *Website:* www.fi.se (office).

WESTERBERG, Lars, MSc; Swedish business executive; *Chairman, Vattenfall AB;* b. 1948; ed Univ. of Stockholm, Royal Inst. of Tech.; began career with ASEA 1972, later Sales Man., ASEA Robotics –1984; joined Esab 1984, Pres. and CEO 1991–94; Pres. and CEO Gränges AB 1994–99; Pres. and CEO Autoliv AB 1999–2007, Chair. 2007–; Ind. Chair. Vattenfall AB 2008–; Chair. Husqvarna AB; mem. Bd of Dirs SSAB Svenskt Stål AB, AB Volvo 2007–, Plastal AB. *Address:* Vattenfall AB, Jamtlandsgaten 99, 162 87 Stockholm, Sweden (office). *Telephone:* (8) 739-50-00 (office). *Fax:* (8) 37-01-70 (office). *E-mail:* info@vattenfall.com (office). *Website:* www.vattenfall.com (office).

WESTERFIELD, Putney, BA; American business executive; b. 9 Feb. 1930, New Haven, Conn.; s. of Ray Bert Westerfield and Beatrice Putney; m. Anne Montgomery 1954; two s. one d.; ed Choate School and Yale Univ.; Vice-Pres. and Co-Founder, Careers Inc. 1950–52; Man. SE Asia Operations, Swen Publs; service with Dept of State in Korea, Washington, Saigon 1953–59; Asst to Publr of Time 1957–59, Asst to Circulation Dir 1959–61, Circulation Dir 1961–66, Asst Publr 1966–68; Asst Publr of Life 1968–69; Publr of Fortune 1969–73; Pres. Chase World Information Corpn 1973–75; Vice-Pres. Boyden Assocs Int. 1976–80, Sr Vice-Pres., Western Man. 1980–84, Pres. and CEO 1984–90, Man. Dir 1990, now Chair. Emer.; Dir East Meets West Foundation 1991; Chair. Bd Dirs Upside Media Inc. *Leisure interests:* reading, music, tennis, swimming. *Address:* c/o Boyden International, 275 Battery Street, Suite 420, San Francisco, CA 94111 (office); 10 Green View Lane, Hillsborough, CA 94010, USA (home).

WESTERWELLE, Guido; German lawyer and politician; b. 27 Dec. 1961, Bad Honnef; pnr, Michael Mronz; ed Gymnasium, Univs of Bonn and Hagen; passed First and Second State Law Examinations 1987, 1991 respectively, began practising as attorney in Bonn 1991; joined Freie Demokratische Partei (Free Democratic Party—FDP) 1980, founding mem. Junge Liberale (youth org. of FDP, Chair. 1983–88), mem. Exec. Bd of FDP 1988–, Sec.-Gen. 1994–2001, Chair. 2001–; elected to Bundestag (Parl.) 1996–, Leader of Parl. Group and Leader of Opposition 2006–; FDP cand. in elections for Chancellor 2002; Vice-Chancellor 2009–11; Federal Minister of Foreign Affairs 2009–13. *Address:* Freie Demokratische Partei, Reinhardtstr. 14, 10117 Berlin, Germany (office). *Telephone:* (30) 2849580 (office). *Fax:* (30) 28495822 (office). *Website:* www.fdp.de (office); www.guido -westerwelle.de.

WESTMACOTT, Sir Peter John, Kt, KCMG, LVO; British diplomatist; *Ambassador to USA;* b. 23 Dec. 1950, Edington, Somerset; m. Susan Nemazee; two s. two d.; ed New Coll., Oxford; joined FCO in 1972, in Middle East Dept and Persian language training 1973–74, Second Sec., Embassy in Tehran 1974–78, Perm. Mission to EU, Brussels 1978–80, First Sec. for Econs, Embassy in Paris 1980–84, with FCO 1984–87, Head of Chancery, Embassy in Ankara 1987–90, Deputy Pvt. Sec. to HRH Prince of Wales 1990–93, Counsellor for Political and Public Affairs, Embassy in Washington, DC 1993–97, Dir for Americas, later Deputy Under-Sec., FCO 1997–2002, Amb. to Turkey 2002–07, to France 2007–11, to USA 2012–. *Address:* British Embassy, 3100 Massachusetts Avenue, NW, Washington, DC 20008, USA (office). *Telephone:* (202) 588-6500 (office). *Fax:* (202) 588-7850 (office). *E-mail:* britishembassyenquiries@gmail.com (office). *Website:* www.gov.uk/government/world/usa (office); www.gov.uk/government/world/ organisations/british-embassy-washington (office).

WESTMINSTER, Archbishop of (see HE Cardinal Cormac Murphy-O'Connor).

WESTON, (Willard Gordon) Galen, OC, OOnt, BA, LLD; Canadian business executive; *Executive Chairman, George Weston Ltd;* b. 29 Oct. 1940, grandson of George Weston; m. Hilary Weston; one s. one d.; ed Univ. of Western Ontario; Chair. and Pres. George Weston Ltd (family business est. by grandfather) –2011, Exec. Chair. 2011–; Chair. Holt Renfrew & Co. Ltd, Brown Thomas Group Ltd,

Selfridges & Co. Ltd, De Bijenkorf BV 2011–; fmr Chair. Loblaw Companies Ltd; Pres. Garfield Weston Foundation (majority owner of Wittington Investments Ltd, owner of Associated British Foods, Fortnum & Mason, Heal's); Hon. LLD (Univ. of Western Ontario). *Leisure interest:* art collecting. *Address:* George Weston Ltd, 22 St Clair Avenue East, Suite 1901, Toronto, ON M4T 2S7, Canada (office). *Telephone:* (416) 922-2500 (office). *Fax:* (416) 922-4395 (office). *E-mail:* info@weston.ca (office). *Website:* www.weston.ca (office).

WESTON, John Pix, CBE, BA, MA, FRAeS, FRSA, FREng; British business executive; *Chairman, International Advisory Board, ASPIDE;* b. 16 Aug. 1951, Kendal, Cumbria, England; s. of John Pix Weston and Ivy Weston (née Glover); m. Susan West 1974; one s. one d.; ed Kings School, Worcester and Trinity Hall, Cambridge; under-grad. apprentice, British Aircraft Corpn 1970–75; various sales appointments, Panavia Aircraft GmbH 1975–82, seconded to Ministry of Defence as Project Officer P110 and Tornado, Defence Sales Org. 1982–84; Middle East Sales Man., British Aerospace Mil. Aircraft 1984–85, Exec. Project Dir, Al-Yamamah Programme 1985–87, Dir in Charge, Saudi Arabia 1987–90, Man. Dir Mil. Aircraft Div. 1990–92, Group Man. Dir and Chair. British Aerospace Defence Businesses 1992–98, mem. Bd 1993–2002, Chief Exec. BAe (later BAE Systems following merger with Marconi Electric Systems) 1998–2002; Chair. (non-exec.) Spirent plc 2002–06, Acra Controls Ltd 2003–, Inbis PLC 2004–05, University for Industry (Learn-Direct) 2004–, ISOFT PLC 2005–07, MB Aerospace 2006–, Insensys PLC 2007–08, AWS PLC 2008–; currently Chair. Int. Advisory Bd, ASPIDE; mem. CBI Pres.'s and Chair.'s Cttees 2000–09, Chair. CBI European Group 2000–09; Vice-Pres. Royal United Services Inst. 1992–; Dir, The German/British Forum 2002–, Assystem-Brime, Paris 2005–06; mem. Council Royal Acad. of Eng 2003–06; Patron Combined Services Winter Sports Asscn 2003–; Fellow, Royal Acad. of Eng; Freeman, City of London; Commdr, Order of the Pole Star (Sweden); Gold Medal, Royal United Services Inst. *Leisure interests:* skiing, photography, mountain walking. *Address:* ASPIDE, Pariser Platz 4A 10117 Berlin, Germany (office). *Telephone:* (30) 2067356-0 (office). *Fax:* (30) 2067356-10 (office). *E-mail:* mail@ASPIDEpartners.com (office). *Website:* www.aspidepartners.com (office).

WESTON, Sir Michael Charles Swift, Kt, KCMG, CVO, MA; British diplomatist (retd); b. 4 Aug. 1937, Crowborough, Sussex, England; s. of Edward C. S. Weston and Kathleen M. Mockett; m. 1st Veronica A. Tickner 1959 (divorced 1990); two s. one d.; m. 2nd Christine J. Ferguson 1990; one s. one d.; ed Dover Coll. and St Catharine's Coll., Cambridge (Exhibitioner); joined HM Diplomatic Service 1961; Third Sec. Kuwait 1962; First Sec. Tehran 1968; UK mission, New York 1970; Counsellor Jeddah 1977; Royal Coll. of Defence Studies 1980; Counsellor Paris 1981, Cairo 1984; Head S European Dept, FCO 1987–90; Amb. to Kuwait 1990–92; Leader UK Del. to Conf. on Disarmament, Geneva 1992–97; mem. Special Immigration Appeals Comm. 1999–2007, Advisory Group of the Comprehensive Nuclear Test Ban Treaty Org. 2006– (Chair. 2009–). *Leisure interests:* squash, tennis, walking. *Address:* Beech Farm House, Beech Lane, Matfield, Kent, TN12 7HG, England (home). *Telephone:* (1892) 824666 (home). *E-mail:* michael.c.s.weston@talk21.com (office).

WESTON, Sir (Philip) John, Kt, KCMG; British diplomatist, company director and poet; b. 13 April 1938; s. of Philip G. Weston and Edith Ansell; m. Sally Ehlers 1967; two s. one d.; ed Sherborne School and Worcester Coll. Oxford; served Royal Marines 1956–58; entered HM Diplomatic Service 1962; Treasury Centre for Admin. Studies 1964; Chinese language student, Hong Kong 1964–66; Beijing 1967–68; Office of UK Perm. Rep. to EEC 1972–74; Asst Pvt. Sec. to Sec. of State for Foreign and Commonwealth Affairs 1974–76; Counsellor, Head of EEC Presidency Secr., FCO 1976–77; Visiting Fellow, All Souls Coll. Oxford 1977–78; Counsellor, Washington, DC 1978–81; Head, Defence Dept FCO 1981–84, Asst Under-Sec. of State 1984–85; Minister, Paris 1985–88; Deputy Sec. to Cabinet, Cabinet Office 1988–89; Deputy Under-Sec. of State, FCO 1989–90, Political Dir 1990–91; Amb. and Perm. Rep. to N Atlantic Council (NATO) 1992–95; Amb. and Perm. Rep. to UN 1995–98; Dir (non-exec.) British Telecommunications 1998–2002, Rolls Royce Group 1998–2005, Hakluyt & Co. 2001–07; mem. Council IISS 2001–05; Pres. Community Foundation Network (UK) 1998–2008, Worcester Coll. Soc. 2003–12; Gov. Ditchley Foundation 2000–11; Chair. Govs Sherborne School 2002–07; Chair. of Trustees The Poetry School 2004–08; mem. Council and Trustee, The Poetry Soc. 2005–08; Trustee, Nat. Portrait Gallery 1999–2008; Hon. Pres. Community Foundation Network (UK) 1998–2008, Hon. Fellow, Worcester Coll. Oxford 2003; Order of Merit (with Star) (FRG). *Publications:* Take Five – 04 (poetry anthology) 2004, Chasing the Hoopoe (first poetry collection) 2005, Echo Soundings (second poetry collection) 2012; poems published by The Guardian, The Spectator, The London Magazine and many other literary magazines. *Leisure interests:* poetry, beekeeping, fly-fishing, running, birds. *Address:* 139 Queens Road, Richmond, Surrey, TW10 6HF, England. *E-mail:* john.weston-pjweston@btinternet.com.

WESTPHAL, Cheyenne, BA (Hons), MA; British art dealer; *Co-Worldwide Head, Contemporary Art, Sotheby's;* ed St Andrews Univ., Univ. of California, Berkeley, USA; joined Sotheby's, London 1990, joined Contemporary Art Dept 1992, Head of European div. 1999–2006, mem. Bd of Dirs 2002, Chair. Contemporary Art, Sotheby's Europe 2006–13, Co-Worldwide Head, Contemporary Art 2013–. *Address:* Sotheby's, 34–35 New Bond Street, London, W1A 2AA, England (office). *Telephone:* (20) 7293-5390 (office); (20) 7293-5000 (office). *Fax:* (20) 7293-5989 (office). *E-mail:* cheyenne.westphal@sothebys.com (office). *Website:* www.sothebys.com (office).

WESTWOOD, Lee John, OBE; British professional golfer; b. 24 April 1973, Worksop, Notts., England; s. of John Westwood and Trish Westwood; m. Laurae Coltart 1999; one s. one d.; began to play golf aged 13; England Boys, Youths and Srs amateur teams 1989–93, won Peter McEvoy Trophy 1990, Lagonda Trophy 1992, British Youths Championships 1993; turned professional 1993, won Volvo Scandinavian Masters 1996, 2000, Sumitomo VISA Taiheiyo Masters 1996, 1997, 1998, Benson and Hedges Malaysian Open 1997, Volvo Masters Andalucia 1997, Holden Australian Open 1997, McDermott-Freeport Classic 1998, Deutsche Bank SAP Open TPC of Europe 1998, 2000, Nat. Car Rental English Open 1998, The Standard Life Loch Lomond 1998, Belgacom Open 1998, 2000, Dunlop Phoenix Tournament 1998, Macau Open 1999, TNT Dutch Open 1999, Smurfit European Open 1999, 2000, Cannon European Masters 1999, Dimension Data Pro Am 2000, Compaq European Grand Prix 2000, Cisco World Match Play Championship 2000,

BMW Int. Open 2003, Dunhill Links Championship 2003, Nelson Mandela Invitational (with Simon Hobday) 2003, Valle Romano Open de Andalucia 2007, Quinn Direct British Masters 2007, Portugal Masters 2009, Dubai World Championship 2009, Nedbank Golf Challenge (South Africa) 2010, Indonesian Masters (Asian Tour) 2011, Ballantines Championship 2011, Thailand Golf Championship 2011, Nordea Masters 2012; PGA Tour wins: Freeport-McDermott Classic 1998, St Jude Classic 2010; won renamed Race to Dubai 2009; best results in major championships: The Masters: tied for sixth place 1999, second 2010, tied for third 2012, US Open: tied for seventh place 1998, tied for fifth place 2000, third 2008, tied for third place 2011, tied for tenth place 2012, The Open Championship: tied for tenth place 1997, fourth 2004, tied for third place 2009, second 2010, PGA Championship: tied for third place 2009, tied for eighth place 2011; results in World Golf Championship events: CA Championship tied for fourth place 1999, second 2000, Bridgestone Invitational: tied for ninth place 2004, tied for second place 2008, ninth 2009, HSBC Champions: tied for eighth place 2009, second 2010; Team appearances: Ryder Cup (representing Europe): 1997 (winners), 1999, 2002 (winners), 2004 (winners), 2006 (winners), 2008, 2010 (winners), 2012 (winners), Alfred Dunhill Cup (representing England): 1996, 1997, 1998, 1999, Seve Trophy (representing GB & Ireland): 2000, 2002 (winners), 2003 (winners), Royal Trophy (representing Europe): 2007 (winners); spent over 180 weeks in top 10 of Official World Golf Rankings 1998–2001, returned to top 10 at end of the 2008 season and again after 2009 PGA Championship; ranked World No. 1 31 Oct. 2010–26 Feb. 2011, 25 April–28 May 2011; announced creation of Lee Westwood Acad. (set of three-day acads across nine venues in England) 2009; opened his first golf school 2010; Hon. DSc (Nottingham Trent Univ.) 2007; named Player of the Year 1998, 2000, 2009, European Tour Order of Merit 2000, Volvo Order of Merit 2000, 'Spirit of Golf' Award, Golf Foundation 2010, Nottingham Trent Univ. named its sports hall after him 2010, named by Golf Club Managers' Asscn's Golf Club Management magazine as the ninth most powerful person in British golf 2012. *Leisure interests:* snooker, horse racing (racehorse owner), sports cars, Nottingham Forest Football Club, cinema, shows. *Address:* c/o International Sports Management Ltd, Cherry Tree Farm, Cherry Tree Lane, Rostherne, Cheshire, WA14 3RZ, England (office). *E-mail:* ism@golfism.net (office). *Website:* www.leewestwood.com.

WESTWOOD, Dame Vivienne Isabel, OBE, DBE; British fashion designer; b. (Vivienne Isabel Swire), 8 April 1941, Tintwistle, Derbyshire; d. of Gordon Swire and Dora Swire; m. 1st Derek Westwood 1962, one s.; one s. with Malcolm McLaren; m. 2nd Andreas Kronthaler 1993; worked with Malcolm McLaren 1970–83, developing 'punk' look, and her clothes were sold at McLaren's shop on King's Road, London; designed for the Sex Pistols, Boy George and Bananarama; created first catwalk collection, Pirate (adopted by Adam Ant and Bow Wow Wow) 1981; showed in Paris 1983, in Tokyo 1984; moved to Italy with new business pnr Carlo D'Amario 1984; opened first Vivienne Westwood shop, London 1990; launch of signature fragrance, Boudoir 1998, further fragrances Libertine 2000, Boudoir Sin City 2007, Let it Rock 2007; Prof. of Fashion Acad. of Applied Arts 1989–91, Hochschule der Künste, Berlin 1993–; trustee Civil Liberties Trust 2007–; Hon. Sr Fellow, Royal Coll. of Art) 1992; Dr hc (Heriot-Watt) 1995, (Acad. of Art Univ. School of Fashion) 2006; Designer of the Year 1990, 1991, Queen's Award for Export 1998, Moet & Chandon Red Carpet Dresser 2006, Outstanding Achievement in Fashion Award, British Fashion Awards 2007. *Television:* South Bank Show: Vivienne Westwood 1990. *Address:* Vivienne Westwood Ltd, Westwood Studios, 9–15 Elcho Street, London, SW11 4AU, England (office). *Telephone:* (20) 7924-4747 (office). *Fax:* (20) 7738-9655. *E-mail:* info@viviennewestwood.co.uk. *Website:* www.viviennewestwood.com.

WETANG'ULA, Moses Masika, LLB; Kenyan lawyer and politician; *Minister of Trade;* b. 13 Sept. 1956, Western Kenya; m.; c.; ed Univ. of Nairobi, Kenya School of Law; Professional Dist. Magistrate, Chief Magistrate's Court, Nakuru 1982, Dist. Magistrate's Court, Rongo, South Nyanza 1983; Sole Practitioner, M. M Wetang'ula Advocate Chambers, Nairobi 1983–85, currently Proprietor, Wetang'ula & Co. Advocates; mem. Parl. (FORD–Kenya) for Sirisia constituency 1993–97, 2002–07, fmr mem. Parl. Cttee on Legal and Constitutional Affairs, Foreign Affairs and Standing Orders, Chair Electricity Regulatory Bd 1998–2001; fmr mem. Jt Ass. of African Caribbean and Pacific/EU, Pres. Jt Ass Working Group on Regional Cooperation; Asst Minister for Int. Affairs –2008, Minister of Foreign Affairs 2008–12, of Trade 2012–; mem. Law Soc. of Kenya, Commonwealth Parl. Asscn, Int. Bar Asscn, Int. Comm. of Jurists, Kenya Chapter; Parliamentarians for Global Action, Inter-Parl. Union. *Leisure interests:* reading, swimming and other health activities, farming, traveling, intellectual debates and politics. *Address:* Ministry of Trade, Teleposta Towers, Kenyatta Ave, POB 30430, 00100, Nairobi, Kenya (office). *Telephone:* (20) 315001 (office). *Fax:* (20) 252896 (office). *E-mail:* info@trade.go.ke (office). *Website:* www.trade.go.ke (office).

WETHINGTON, Charles T., Jr, PhD; American fmr university president; b. 2 Jan. 1936, Merrimac, Ky; m. Judy Woodrow 1962; two c.; ed Brescia Coll., Eastern Kentucky Univ., Syracuse Univ., Univ. of Kentucky; Instructor, Univ. of Kentucky 1965–66; Dir Maysville Community Coll. 1967–71; Asst Vice-Pres. for the Community Coll. System, Univ. of Kentucky 1971–81, Vice-Pres. 1981–82, Chancellor 1982–88, Chancellor for the Community Coll. System and Univ. Relations 1988–89, Interim Pres. Univ. of Kentucky 1989–90, Pres. 1990–2001, then Fund Raiser; Bd mem. Nat. Coll. Athletic Asscn Foundation 1999–2002. *Address:* c/o University of Kentucky, 5-52 Wm. T. Young Library, Lexington, KY 40506 (office); 2926 Four Pines Drive, Lexington, KY 40502, USA (home). *Telephone:* (606) 257-5646 (office). *Fax:* (859) 323-3777 (office).

WETTER, HE Cardinal Friedrich; German ecclesiastic; *Archbishop of Munich and Freising;* b. 20 Feb. 1928, Landau, Speyer; s. of Peter Wetter and Hedwig Böttinger; ed Univ. Gregoriana Rom; ordained priest 1953; Bishop of Speyer 1968–82; Archbishop of Munich and Freising 1982–; Cardinal-Priest of S. Stefano al Monte Celio 1985; Hon. Prof., Univ. of Mainz 1967–; Grosses Bundesverdienstkreuz mit Stern, Bayerischer Verdienstorden. *Publications:* Zeit-Worte 1993, Er allein trägt 1996, Mit Euch auf dem Weg 1998. *Address:* Postfach 330360, 80063 Munich, Germany. *Telephone:* (89) 21370. *Fax:* (89) 21371585. *Website:* www.erzbistum-muenchen-und-freising.de.

WETTSTEIN, Diter von, Dr rer. nat; Danish geneticist and academic; *R.A. Nilan Distinguished Professor, Department of Crop and Soil Sciences, Washington State*

University; b. (Dietrich von Wettstein), 20 Sept. 1929, Göttingen, Germany; s. of Fritz von Wettstein and Elsa Jesser; m. Penny von Wettstein-Knowles 1967; two d.; ed school in Innsbruck, Austria, Univ. of Tübingen, Germany, Univ. of Stockholm, Sweden; Research Asst, Genetics Dept, Forest Research Inst., Stockholm 1951–54; Asst and Assoc. Prof. in Genetics, Univ. of Stockholm 1954–62; Prof. of Genetics and Head, Inst. of Genetics, Univ. of Copenhagen, Denmark 1962–75; Acting Head, Dept of Physiology, Carlsberg Lab., Copenhagen 1972–75, Prof. of Physiology and Head of Dept 1975–96; R.A. Nilan Distinguished Prof., Washington State Univ., USA 1994–; Rockefeller Fellow 1958; Visiting Prof., Univ. of California, Davis 1966, 1972, 1973, 1974, Washington State Univ., USA 1969; Hon. DrAgr. *Publications include:* 300 scientific papers on mutation research, developmental physiology and cell research. *Leisure interests:* skiing, mountaineering. *Address:* Department of Crop and Soil Sciences, Washington State University, Pullman, WA 99164, USA (office); Aasevej 13, 3500 Vaerløse, Denmark (home). *Telephone:* (509) 335-3635 (office); 44-48-19-98 (home). *Fax:* (509) 335-8674 (office). *E-mail:* diter@wsu.edu (office). *Website:* css.wsu.edu (office).

WEXLER, Haskell; American cinematographer, film producer and director; b. 6 Feb. 1922, Chicago, Ill.; s. of Simon Wexler and Lottie Wexler; m. 1st Nancy Ashenhurst (divorced); two c.; m. 2nd Marian Witt (divorced); one c.; m. 3rd Rita Taggart 1989; ed Francis Parker School, Univ. of California, Berkeley; tour in US Merchant Marine during World War II; briefly made industrial films in Chicago before becoming an asst cameraman 1947; worked on documentary features and shorts and low-budget docu-dramas; Lifetime Achievement Award, American Soc. of Cinematographers 1993, awarded a star on the Hollywood Walk of Fame 1996, subject of a documentary, Tell Them Who You Are, directed by his son, Mark Wexler 2004, Lifetime Achievement Award, Ind. Documentary Asscn 2007, Lifetime Achievement Award, Soc. of Operating Cameramen 2007, adjudged one of the ten most influential cinematographers in film history according to an Int. Cinematographers Guild survey of its membership. *Cinematography:* The Living City (documentary short) (also producer) 1953, Stakeout on Dope Street 1958, T Is for Tumbleweed (short) 1958, The Savage Eye 1960, Five Bold Women 1960, Studs Lonigan (uncredited) 1960, The Runaway 1961, The Fisherman and His Soul 1961, Hoodlum Priest 1961, Angel Baby 1961, Lonnie 1963, America, America 1963, Face in the Rain 1963, The Best Man 1964, The Bus (documentary) 1965, The Loved One (also producer) 1965, Who's Afraid of Virginia Woolf? (director of photography) (Academy Award for Best Cinematography in Black-and-White 1967) 1966, One (short) 1966, In the Heat of the Night 1967, Faces (uncredited) 1968, The Thomas Crown Affair 1968, Medium Cool 1969, Interviews with My Lai Veterans 1971, The Trial of the Catonsville Nine 1972, The Conversation (uncredited) 1974, Introduction to the Enemy (documentary) 1974, One Flew Over the Cuckoo's Nest 1975, Underground (documentary) 1976, Bound for Glory (Academy Award) 1976, Coming Home (also actor) 1978, War Without Winners (documentary short) 1978, Paul Jacobs and the Nuclear Gang 1978, No Nukes (documentary) 1980, Second-Hand Hearts 1981, Richard Pryor Live on the Sunset Strip 1982, Lookin' to Get Out 1982, Hail Columbia! (short documentary) 1982, The Man Who Loved Women 1983, Matewan 1987, Uncle Meat 1987, Colors 1988, Three Fugitives 1989, Bruce Springsteen: Video Anthology 1978–1988 (video documentary) 1989, Blaze 1989, Other People's Money 1991, The Babe 1992, The Secret of Roan Inish 1994, Canadian Bacon 1995, The Sixth Sun: Mayan Uprising in Chiapas 1995, Mulholland Falls 1996, The Rich Man's Wife 1996, Limbo 1999, Good KurdsBad Kurds: No Friends But the Mountains (documentary) 2000, Bus Rider's Union (documentary) 1999, The Man On Lincoln's Nose (documentary) 2000, Mexico (documentary short) 2000, Bruce Springsteen: The Complete Video Anthology 1978–2000 (video documentary) 2001, SOA: Guns and Greed (documentary short) (co-cinematographer) 2001, Bridge to Havana (video documentary) 2004, Silver City 2004, Bastards of the Party (documentary) 2005, Who Needs Sleep? (documentary) 2006, From Wharf Rats to the Lords of the Docks 2007, A Sense of Wonder (video) 2008, In the Name of Democracy: America's Conscience, a Soldier's Sacrifice (documentary) 2009, Something's Gonna Live (documentary) 2010, Will the Real Terrorist Please Stand Up? (documentary) 2010, Bringing King to China (documentary) 2011, Occupy Los Angeles (documentary) 2012, Medium Cool Revisited (documentary short) 2013, Four Days in Chicago (documentary) 2013; miscellaneous: Wild River (additional photographer, uncredited) 1960, Medium Cool (camera operator) 1969, Gimme Shelter (thanks) 1970, THX 1138 (special thanks) (director's cut) 1971, American Graffiti (visual consultant) 1973, Days of Heaven (additional cinematographer) 1978, The Rose (additional photographer: concert scenes) 1979, The Kid from Nowhere (TV) (photographer: Special Olympics) 1982, Blade Runner (additional photographer, uncredited) 1982, To the Moon Alice (TV) (camera operator: second unit) 1990, At the Max (camera consultant, camera operator) 1991, Visions of Light (special thanks from afi) 1992, A Few Good Men (thanks) 1992, Steal Big Steal Little (additional photographer) 1995, Bread and Roses (second camera operator) 2000, Tell Them Who You Are (additional camera operator) 2004. *Films directed:* The Bus (also producer and writer) 1965, Medium Cool (also actor, producer and writer) 1969, Brazil: A Report on Torture 1971, Introduction to the Enemy 1974, Underground (documentary) 1976, War Without Winners (documentary short) 1978, Bus II 1983, Latino (also writer) 1985, Bus Rider's Union (also producer) 2000, Who Needs Sleep? (documentary) 2006, From Wharf Rats to the Lords of the Docks 2007, Medium Cool Revisited (documentary short) 2013, Four Days in Chicago (documentary) (also writer and producer) 2013. *Film roles:* Out of These Rooms 2002, The Big Empty (short) 2005, Battle in Seattle 2007, The Moving Picture Co. 1914 (short) 2014. *Television:* Sandra Bernhard: I'm Still Here... Damn It! (film) 1999, 61* (film) 2001, Big Love (series) 2007. *Address:* c/o ASC, PO Box 2230, Hollywood, CA 90078, USA.

WEXLER, Nancy Sabin, AB, PhD, FRCP; American neurologist and academic; *Higgins Professor of Neuropsychology, Departments of Neurology and Psychiatry, College of Physicians and Surgeons, Columbia University;* b. 19 July 1945, Washington, DC; ed Radcliffe Coll., Univ. of the West Indies, Jamaica (Fulbright Scholarship), Hampstead Clinic Child Psychoanalytic Training Inst., UK, Univ. of Michigan; Psychological Intern and Teaching Fellow, Univ. of Michigan 1968–74; Licensed Psychologist, New York State 1974–; Asst Prof. of Psychology, New School of Social Research, Grad. Faculty, New York City 1974–76; pvt. practice, psychologist, New York City 1974–76; Exec. Dir Congressional Comm. for Control

of Huntington's Disease and Its Consequences, based in Nat. Inst. of Neurological, Communicative Disorders and Stroke, NIH, Bethesda, Md 1976–78; Co-organizer Public Forum on Nat. Genetic Diseases Act 1977; Health Science Admin. Demyelinating, Atrophic and Degenerative Diseases Program, Nat. Inst. of Neurological, Communicative Disorders and Stroke, NIH 1978–83; Pres. Hereditary Disease Foundation 1983–; Assoc. Prof. of Clinical Neuropsychology, Depts of Neurology and Psychiatry, Coll. of Physicians and Surgeons, Columbia Univ. 1985–92, mem. Center for Brain and Behavior 1985, Prof. of Clinical Neuropsychology 1992–93, Higgins Prof. of Neuropsychology 1993–; Chair. Jt NIH/DOE Ethical, Legal and Social Issues Working Group of Nat. Center for Human Genome Research, Human Genome Org. (HUGO); Councillor, Soc. for Neuroscience 2000–; mem. Inst. of Medicine, NAS 1997– (mem. Council 2007–); mem. Bd Dirs AAAS, Advisory Cttee on Research on Women's Health, NIH; mem. American Psychological Asscn, American Psychological Soc., American Soc. for Human Genetics, Soc. for Neuroscience, World Fed. of Neurology, Research Group on Huntington's Disease, American Neurological Asscn, American Soc. of Law and Medicine, Inst. of Medicine, NAS, European Acad. of Sciences and Arts 2001, American Acad. of Arts and Sciences 2005; Fellow, New York Acad. of Sciences 1998, AAAS 2002; Order of Merit in Work First Class (Venezuela) 1990; Hon. DHumLitt (New York Medical Coll.) 1991; Hon. DSc (Univ. of Michigan) 1991, (Bard Coll.) 1998; Hon. Doctor of Medical Sciences (Yale Univ.) 2006; PHS-NIMH Fellowship 1969–70, Univ. Fellowship 1973–74, PHS Certificate of Merit 1980, NIH Director's Award 1980, Hon. Declaration, Community of San Luis, Venezuela 1982, 1987, Award for Research, Nat. Huntington's Disease Soc. 1984, Landacre Day Award, Ohio State Univ. 1986, Maracaibo Rotary Club Award (Venezuela) 1986, Award for Research, Huntington's Disease Soc. of America 1986, The SOMA Distinguished Prof. Lecture Series, Univ. of California, San Diego School of Medicine 1987, First Robert J. and Claire Pasarow Foundation Award 1987, Living Legacy Award, Women's Int. Soc. 1988, Esquire Magazine Register 1988, Alumnae Athena Award, Alumnae Council, Univ. of Michigan 1989, Award from Gov.'s Office, State of Zulia, Venezuela 1989, Huntington's Disease Benefit Dinner Honoree 1989, Legislative Resolution of Commendation, New York State 1990, 21st Annual Louis B. Flexner Lecturer, Univ. of Pennsylvania 1992, Dean's Distinguished Lecture in the Clinical Sciences, Columbia Univ. 1992, Distinguished Service Award for Enhancing Educ. Through Biological Research, Nat. Asscn of Biology Teachers 1993, Foster Elting Bennett Memorial Lecturer, 118th Annual Meeting of American Neurological Asscn, Boston 1993, Nat. Health Council Nat. Medical Research Award to Huntington's Disease Collaborative Research Group 1993, Albert Lasker Public Service Award 1993, American Captains of Achievement Golden Plate Award, American Acad. of Achievement 1994, J. Allyn Taylor Int. Prize in Medicine 1994, Asscn of Neuroscience Depts and Programs' Educ. Award 1997, Venezuela Award, Casa Hogar 1999, Soc. for Neuroscience Public Advocacy Award 2003, Distinguished Investigator Award, NARSAD 2006, NARSAD Lieber Investigator 2006, Benjamin Franklin Medal in Life Science 2007. *Achievements include:* important scientific contrib. on Huntington's disease; 20-year study of world's largest family with Huntington's disease, in Venezuela, developing pedigree of more than 18,000 individuals and collecting more than 4,000 blood samples helped lead to identification of Huntington's disease gene on human chromosome 4. *Publications:* numerous scientific papers in professional journals. *Address:* College of Physicians and Surgeons, Columbia University, 1051 Riverside Drive, Unit 6, PI Annex 371, New York, NY 10032 (office); Hereditary Disease Foundation, 3960 Broadway, 6th Floor, New York, NY 10032, USA (office). *Telephone:* (212) 543-5667 (Coll. of Physicians) (office); (212) 928-2121 (Hereditary Disease Foundation) (office). *Fax:* (212) 543-6002 (Coll. of Physicians) (office); (212) 928-2172 (Hereditary Disease Foundation) (office). *E-mail:* wexlern@pi.cpmc .columbia.edu (office); cures@hdfoundation.org (office). *Website:* pi.cpmc.columbia .edu (office); www.hdfoundation.org (office).

WEXNER, Leslie (Les) Herbert; American retail executive and philanthropist; *Chairman and CEO, L Brands, Inc.;* b. 8 Sept. 1937, New Albany, Ohio; s. of Bella Wexner; m. Abigail S. Koppel 1993; two s. two d.; ed Ohio State Univ.; Founder, Chair. and CEO Limited Inc. fashion chain (now L Brands, Inc.), Columbus, OH 1963–; est. the Wexner Foundation 1984; Dir and mem. Exec. Comm. Banc One Corpn, Sotheby's Holdings Inc.; mem. Business Admin Advisory Council, Ohio State Univ.; Chair. Retail Industry Trade Action Coalition, Columbus Urban League 1982–84, Hebrew Immigrant Aid Soc. 1982–; Co-Chair. Int. United Jewish Appeal Cttee; Nat. Vice-Chair. and Treas. United Jewish Appeal; mem. Bd Dirs and Exec. Cttee American Jewish Jt Distribution Cttee Inc.; Founding mem. and first Chair. The Ohio State Univ. Foundation; mem. Exec. Cttee American Israel Public Affairs Cttee; fmr mem. Governing Cttee Columbus Foundation; Trustee, Columbus Jewish Fed. 1972–, Columbus Jewish Foundation, Aspen Inst., Ohio State Univ. 1988–97, 2005–12 (Chair. 2009–12), Columbus Capital Corpn for Civic Improvement; fmr Trustee, Columbus Museum of Art, Columbus Symphony Orchestra, Whitney Museum of American Art, Capitol South Community Urban Redevelopment Corpn; mem. Young Presidents Org.; considered to have one of the 50 largest art collections in the world; Hon. Vice-Chair. Congregation Agudas Achim, Bexley; Hon. mem. 104th Class of SPHINX Sr Class Hon., Ohio State Univ. 2010; Cavaliere of Repub. of Italy; Hon. HHD 1986; Hon. LLD (Hofstra Univ.) 1987; Hon. LHD (Brandeis Univ.) 1990; Hon. PhD (Jewish Theological Seminary) 1990; American Marketing Asscn Man of the Year 1974, Woodrow Wilson Award for Corporate Citizenship 2004, The Medical Center at Ohio State Univ. officially changed its name to the Wexner Medical Center at The Ohio State Univ. 2012, Women's Wear Daily Beauty Inc. Visionary Award 2013. *Address:* L Brands, Inc., 3 Limited Way Parkway, Columbus, OH 43230, USA (office). *Telephone:* (614) 415-7000 (office). *Fax:* (614) 415-7440 (office). *E-mail:* info@lb.com (office). *Website:* www.lb.com (office).

WEYERGANS, François; Belgian writer and critic; b. 9 Dec. 1941, Etterbeek; ed Jesuit school, Brussels and Institut des Hautes Etudes Cinématographiques, Paris; fmr film dir; literary and film critic, contributing to Cahiers du cinéma; mem. Académie Française 2009–. *Films:* Béjart (writer, dir) 1962, Hieronymus Bosch (writer, dir) 1963, Cinéma de notre temps: Robert Bresson - Ni vu, ni connu (TV film; dir) 1965, Beaudelaire est mort en été (dir) 1967, Aline (writer, dir) 1967, Un film sur quelqu'un (dir) 1972, Maladie mortelle (dir) 1977, Je t'aime, tu danses (writer, dir) 1977, Couleur chair (writer, dir) 1979, Une femme en Afrique (writer) 1985. *Publications:* novels: Le Pitre (Prix Roger Nimier) 1973, Berlin, mercredi

1979, Les Figurants (Prix de la Société des Gens de Lettres, Académie Royale de Langue et de Littérature françaises de Belgique Prix Sander Pierron) 1980, Macaire le Copte (Prix Rossel, Belgium, Prix des Deux Magots) 1981, Le Radeau de la méduse (Prix méridien des quatre jurys) 1983, La Vie d'un bébé 1986, Françaises, français 1988, Je suis écrivain 1989, Rire et pleurer 1990, La Démence du boxeur (Prix Renaudot) 1992, Franz et François (Grand prix de la langue Française) 1997, Salomé 2005, Trois jours chez ma mère (Prix Goncourt) 2005, La Démence du Boxeur 2008. *Address:* c/o Editions Gallimard, Folio, 5, rue Sébastian-Bottin, 75328 Paris, France (office). *Website:* www.folio-lesite.fr (office).

WEYMOUTH, Katharine Bouchage, BA, JD; American lawyer and publishing executive; *Publisher, The Washington Post and CEO, Washington Post Media;* b. 1966; d. of Yann R. Weymouth and Lally Weymouth; grand-d. of the late Katharine Graham (Chair. Washington Post and publr; died 2001); niece of Tina Weymouth; m. Richard Alan Scully 1998 (divorced 2004); one s. two d.; ed Harvard Coll., Univ. of Oxford, UK, Stanford Univ. Law School; mother's family has owned The Washington Post newspaper since 1933; Assoc., Williams & Connolly (law firm), Washington, DC 1993–96; Asst Counsel, The Washington Post 1996–98, Advertising Liason 2000–02, Dir Advertising Jobs Unit 2002–04, Dir Advertising Sales 2004–05, Vice-Pres. Advertising 2005–08, Publr The Washington Post and CEO Washington Post Media 2008–; mem. Bd of Dirs Online Publrs Assocn. *Address:* The Washington Post, 1150 15th Street, NW, Washington, DC 20071, USA (office). *Telephone:* (202) 334-6000 (office). *E-mail:* info@washingtonpost.com (office). *Website:* www.washingtonpost.com (office).

WHALLEY, Joanne; British actress; b. 25 Aug. 1964, Salford; m. Val Kilmer 1988 (divorced 1996); one s. one d.; stage career began during teens and has included season of Edward Bond plays at Royal Court Theatre, London and appearances in The Three Sisters, What the Butler Saw (NW Manhattan Theatre Club), Lulu (Almeida, London). *Films include:* Pink Floyd: The Wall 1982, Dance With a Stranger 1985, No Surrender 1985, The Good Father 1985, Will You Love Me Tomorrow 1987, Willow 1988, To Kill a Priest 1988, Scandal 1989, Kill Me Again 1989, The Big Man 1990, Navy Seals 1990, Miss Helen, Shattered 1991, Crossing the Line, Storyville 1992, The Secret Rapture 1993, Mother's Boys 1994, A Good Man in Africa 1994, Trial By Jury 1994, The Man Who Knew Too Little 1997, A Texas Funeral 1999, Run the Wild Fields 2000, The Guilty 2000, Breathtaking 2000, Virginia's Run 2001, Before You Go 2002, The Californians 2005, Played 2006, 44 Inch Chest 2009, Diverted 2009, Golf in the Kingdom 2010. *Television includes:* Coronation Street (series) 1974, Emmerdale Farm (series) 1977, A Kind of Loving (series) 1982, Reilly: Ace of Spies (mini-series) 1983, Edge of Darkness (mini-series) 1985, The Singing Detective (mini-series) 1986, A TV Dante (mini-series) 1989, Scarlett (mini-series) 1994, Jackie Bouvier Kennedy Onassis (mini-series) 2000, 40 2003, Child of Mine 2005, Life Line 2007, Flood 2007, Diverted 2009. *Address:* Creative Artists Agency, 2000 Avenue of the Stars, Los Angeles, CA 90067, USA.

WHALLEY, John, BA (Hons), MA, MA, MPhil, PhD, FRSC; British/Canadian economist and academic; *Professor of Economics, University of Warwick and University of Western Ontario;* ed grammar school, Lancs., Univ. of Essex, Yale Univ., USA; Teaching Assistant, Univ. of Essex 1968–69, Yale Univ. 1970-73; Lecturer in Econs, LSE 1973–76; Assoc. Prof. of Econs, Univ. of Western Ontario, Canada 1976–78, Prof. of Econs 1978–, Dir Centre for the Study of Int. Econ. Relations 1979–, William G. Davis Prof. of Int. Trade 1986–90, 2004–09; Research Assoc., Nat. Bureau of Econ. Research, Cambridge, Mass 1985–; Sr Advisor, Tax Policy Br., Dept of Finance, Govt of Canada 1985–86; Visiting Fellow, Inst. for Int. Econs, Washington, DC 1990–91; Sr Research Fellow, Inst. for Policy Reform, Washington, DC 1992–93; Prof. of Int. and Devt Econs, Univ. of Warwick 1994–98, 2010–, Assoc. Dir Centre for the Study of Globalisation and Regionalisation; Guest Prof., Univ. of Peking, People's Repub. of China 2003–04; Co-ordinator, Global Economy Research Group, Univ. of Munich, Germany 2003–; Distinguished Fellow, Centre for Int. Governance Innovation, Waterloo, Ont. 2006–; Co-Investigator, Centre for Competitive Advantage in the Global Economy (CAGE); has served on a Canada-US trade dispute panel; fmr Research Dir for the MacDonald Royal Comms in Canada; Co-Ed. CESifo Econ. Studies; fmr Jt Man. Ed. The World Economy; Foreign mem. Russian Acad. of Natural Sciences; Fellow, Econometric Soc.; Hellmuth Prize for Achievement in Research 2009, Killam Prize (co-recipient), Canada Council for the Arts 2012. *Publications:* The International Taxation of Multinational Enterprises in Developed Countries (with John Adams) 1977, Tax Policy Options in the 1980's (co-ed.) 1982, Federalism and the Canadian Economic Union (co-ed.) 1983, Trade Liberalization Among Major World Trading Areas 1985, A General Equilibrium Model for Tax Policy Evaluation (with John Shoven, Charles Ballard and Don Fullerton) 1985, UK Tax Policy and Applied General Equilibrium Analysis (with John Piggott) 1985, New Developments in Applied General Equilibrium Analysis (with John Piggott) 1985, Canada/United States Trade and Investment Issues (co-ed.) 1985, Canadian Trade Policies and the World Economy (with Colleen Hamilton and Rod Hill), Vol. 9 of the Research Studies for the Royal Commission on the Economic Union and Development Prospects for Canada 1985, Canada and the Multilateral Trading System, Vol. 10 of the Research Studies for the Royal Commission on the Economic Union and Development Prospects for Canada 1985, Canada-United States Free Trade (co-ed.), Vol. 11 of the Research Studies for the Royal Commission on the Economic Union and Development Prospects for Canada 1985, Domestic Policies and the International Economic Environment (co-ed. with Rod Hill), Vol. 12 of the Research Studies for the Royal Commission on the Economic Union and Development Prospects for Canada 1985, Canada's Resource Industries (ed.), Vol. 14 of the Research Studies for the Royal Commission on the Economic Union and Development Prospects for Canada 1986, Regional Aspects of Confederation (with Irene Trela), Vol. 68 of the Research Papers for the Royal Commission on the Economic Union and Development Prospects for Canada 1986, General Equilibrium Trade Policy Modeling (co-ed.) 1986, Dealing with the North: Developing Countries and the Global Trading System (ed. CSIER Research Monograph) 1987, Perspectives on a US-Canadian Free Trade Agreement (co-ed.) 1987, Developing Countries and the Global Trading System, Vol. I, Thematic Studies From a Ford Foundation Project 1989, Developing Countries and the Global Trading System, Vol. II, Country Studies From a Ford Foundation Project 1989, The Uruguay Round and Beyond, Final Report From the Ford Foundation Supported Project on Developing Countries and the Global Trading System 1989, Economic Impacts of

Tax Reform (co-ed. 1989, The Economics of the Goods and Services Tax (with Deborah Fretz), Canadian Tax Paper No. 88 1990, Applied General Equilibrium, Studies in Empirical Economics (co-ed.) 1991, Applying General Equilibrium (with John Shoven) 1992, Canada-U.S. Tax Comparisons (co-ed.) 1992, Applying General Equilibrium (with John Shoven) 1993, The Trading System After the Uruguay Round (with Colleen Hamilton) 1996, Environmental Issues in the New World Trading System (with Peter Uimonen) 1997, Uruguay Round Results and the Emerging Trade Agenda: Quantitative-Based Analyses from the Developmental Perspective (co-ed.) 1998, 30, Fiscal Reform and Structural Change in the Developing Countries, Vols 1 and 2 (co-ed.) 2000, The WTO, Trade and the Environment (co-ed.) 2005, Frontiers in Applied General Equilibrium Modeling (co-ed.) 2005, Privatization Experiences in the European Union (co-ed.) 2006, Globalisation and the Labour Market: Trade, Technology and Less-Skilled Workers in Europe and the United States (co-ed.) 2006, China's Integration Into The World Economy (ed.) 2011, Puzzles over International Taxation of Cross-Border Flows of Capital Income, Chapter 17 in International Handbook on the Economics of Integration, Vol. II 2011, Global General Equilibrium Modelling (ed.) 2012; numerous papers in professional journals. *Address:* Department of Economics, University of Warwick, Coventry, CV4 7AL, England (office); Department of Economics, Faculty of Social Science, University of Western Ontario, London, ON N6A 5C2, Canada. *Telephone:* (519) 661-3509 (Western Ontario) (office). *Fax:* (24) 7652-3032 (Warwick) (office). (519) 661-3064 (Western Ontario) (office). *E-mail:* jwhalley@uwo.ca (office). *Website:* www2.warwick.ac.uk/fac/soc/csgr/people/staff/jwhalley (office); economics.uwo.ca/faculty/whalley (office).

WHARTON, Clifton R., Jr., PhD; American academic, university administrator, financial services executive and government official; b. 13 Sept. 1926, Boston, Mass.; s. of Hon. Clifton R. Wharton Sr and Harriette B. Wharton; m. Dolores Duncan 1950; one s.; ed Boston Latin School, Harvard Univ., Johns Hopkins Univ. School of Advanced Int. Studies and Univ. of Chicago; Head of Reports and Analysis Dept, American Int. Assocn for Econ. and Social Devt 1948–53; Research Assoc., Univ. of Chicago 1953–57; Assoc., Agricultural Devt Council 1957–58, stationed in SE Asia 1958–64; Dir of the Council's American Univs. Research Program 1964–66, Vice-Pres. 1967–69, mem. Bd of Dirs 1973–80; Pres. Mich. State Univ. and Prof. of Econs 1970–78; Chancellor, State Univ. of NY System 1978–87; Chair. and CEO TIAA-CREF 1987–93; Deputy Sec. of State, US Dept of State 1993; Visiting Prof., Univ. of Malaya 1958–64, Stanford Univ. 1964–65; fmr Chair. Bd for Int. Food and Agric. Devt (AID), US Dept of State; mem. Presidential Comm. on World Hunger, Presidential Mission to Latin America, Presidential Mission to S Viet Nam; Chair. Bd Rockefeller Foundation 1982–87; mem. Knight Foundation Comm. on Intercollegiate Athletics 1989– (fmr Co-Vice Chair.); dir of numerous cos and orgs including Ford Motor Co. 1973–93, 1994–97, Tenneco Inc. 1994–99, NY Stock Exchange 1991–93, 1994–2000, Harcourt Gen. 1994–2001, Equitable Life 1969–82, Overseas Devt Council 1969–79, 1994–2000, Aspen Inst. 1980–93, Time Inc. 1982–89, Federated Dept Stores 1985–88, Rockefeller Foundation 1970–87; Comm. for Econ. Devt 1980–93, 1994–; Deputy Chair. Fed. Reserve Bank, New York 1985–86; mem. Knight Foundation Comm. on Inter-collegiate Athletics 1990–93, Council on Foreign Relations 1983–93, Advisory Comm. on Trade Policy and Negotiations 1990–93; 62 hon. degrees. *Publications:* Subsistence Agriculture and Economic Development (ed.) 1969, Patterns for Lifelong Learning (co-author) 1973. *Address:* c/o Knight Foundation Commission on Intercollegiate Athletics, One Biscayne Tower, Suite 3800, 2 South Biscayne Blvd., Miami, FL 33131-1803, USA (office). *Website:* www.knightcommission.org (office).

WHEATCROFT, Baroness (Life Peer), cr. 2010, of Blackheath in the London Borough of Greenwich; **Patience Wheatcroft,** LLB; British journalist; b. 28 Sept. 1951, Chesterfield, Derbyshire, England; m. Tony Salter; three c.; ed Univ. of Birmingham; launched, with her husband, Retail Week 1988, Ed. 1988–92; has worked on financial sections of The Daily Mail, The Sunday Times and The Daily Telegraph; Deputy City Ed. Mail on Sunday –1997; Business and City Ed. The Times 1997–2006; Ed. The Sunday Telegraph 2006–07; Ed.-in-Chief The Wall Street Journal Europe 2009–10; mem. (Conservative) House of Lords 2010–; Dir (non-exec.) Barclays Bank 2007–09, Shaftesbury plc 2008–09; Head of Mayor of London's newly created Forensic Audit Panel 2008; mem. UK-India Round Table, Bd British Museum 2010–, Council of the Royal Albert Hall 2011–, Advisory Bd, British Olympic Assocn, Advisory Bd, Reuters Inst. for Study of Journalism; mem. (Conservative) House of Lords 2010–; Hon. Dr of Arts (City Univ.) 2011; Wincott Sr Journalist of the Year Award 2001, London Press Club Business Journalist of the Year 2003. *Leisure interests:* opera, theatre. *Address:* House of Lords, Westminster, London, SW1A 0PW, England (office). *Telephone:* (20) 7219-3107 (office); (20) 7219-1570 (office).

WHEATLEY, Martin; British business executive and banking regulator; *Chief Executive, Financial Conduct Authority;* worked for London Stock Exchange for 18 years, including six years on its bd, later Deputy Chief Exec. –2003; fmr Chair. FTSE International; mem. Listing Authority Advisory Cttee, Financial Services Authority (FSA); Exec. Dir for Market Supervision, Securities and Futures Comm., Hong Kong 2004–05, Chair. 2005–06, CEO 2006–11; Man. Dir FSA Conduct Business Unit 2011–13, mem. Bd of Dirs and Chief Exec. Financial Conduct Authority (successor of FSA, along with Prudential Regulatory Authority) 2013–; mem. Financial Stability Bd Standing Cttee on Standards Implementation, Int. Org. of Securities Comms (IOSCO) Tech. Cttee, Chair. IOSCO Tech. Cttee Task Force on Short Selling. *Address:* Financial Conduct Authority, 25 The North Colonnade, Canary Wharf, London, E14 5HS, England (office). *Telephone:* (20) 7066-1000 (office). *E-mail:* info@fca.org.uk (office). *Website:* www.fca.org.uk (office).

WHEELDON, Christopher; British ballet dancer and choreographer; b. 22 March 1973, Yeovil, Somerset; ed Royal Ballet School, London; began training to be ballet dancer aged eight; joined Royal Ballet 1991; moved to USA to join New York City Ballet (NYCB) 1993, Soloist 1998, began choreographing for NYCB 1997, retd as dancer to focus on choreography 2000, Resident Choreographer and first Resident Artist 2001–08; dances commissioned by several other ballet cos, including San Francisco Ballet, Bolshoi Ballet, Royal Ballet, London; Co-founder and Artistic Dir Morphoses/The Wheeldon Company (transatlantic co. with a US base at City Center, New York and in UK at Sadler's Wells Theatre, London) 2007–10; has collaborated with composers James MacMillan, Bright Sheng and

Michael Nyman, with artists Ian Falconer, James Buckhouse and Jean Marc Puissant, with designers Adrianne Lobel and Narciso Rodriguez, with author and actor John Lithgow, and with dir Nicholas Hytner; Gold Medal Prix de Lausanne competition 1991, Mae L. Wien Award, School of American Ballet, Martin E. Segal Award, Lincoln Center, New York City, London Critics' Circle Award for Best New Ballet for Polyphonia 2005, American Choreography Award, Dance Magazine Award for Best New Ballet for Polyphonia 2005, Olivier Award 2006, South Bank Show Award 2007, featured in The Advocate magazine amongst artists who made the "Forty Under 40" list 2009. *Ballets choreographed include:* Slavonic Dances for Diamond Project, NYCB 1997, cr., in collaboration with artist Ian Falconer, Scènes de Ballet for School of American Ballets Workshop Performances 1999 and NYCB's 50th anniversary season, Mercurial Manoeuvers for NYCB's Spring Diamond Project 2000, Polyphonia, set to piano music by Györgi Ligeti 2000, Variations Sérieuses, set to a score by Felix Mendelssohn 2001, Morphoses and Carousel (A Dance) 2002, Carnival of the Animals and Liturgy 2003, After the Rain 2005, An American in Paris 2005, Klavier 2006, The Nightingale and the Rose 2007; for other cos: Continuum, for San Francisco Ballet 2002, Tryst and DGV (Danse à Grande Vitesse), for The Royal Ballet 2002, 2006 (respectively), Swan Lake, for Pennsylvania Ballet 2004, Dance of the Hours, for The Metropolitan Opera's production of Ponchielli's La Gioconda 2006, Misericors, for the Bolshoi Ballet 2007, ballet based on Lewis Carroll's Alice's Adventures in Wonderland, for The Royal Ballet 2011; ballet sequences for feature film Center Stage 2000, stage version of Broadway's Sweet Smell of Success 2002. *Address:* c/o Morphoses Ltd, The Wheeldon Company, 800 Fifth Avenue, Suite 18F, New York, NY 10065, USA (office).

WHEELER, Fraser William; British diplomatist (retd) and business executive; *CEO, Sambora Communications Inc.;* b. 23 March 1957; m. Sarah Wheeler; one s. one d.; Finance Dept, FCO 1980–81, Defence Dept 1981–82, Entry Clearance/ Consular Officer, Accra 1982–84, Third Sec., UK Mission to UN, Geneva 1984–87, Soviet Dept, FCO 1987–91, Second Sec. (Trade), Moscow 1991–94, Deputy Consul Gen., Vancouver 1994–98; Vice-Pres. Nat. Communications plc (Canada) 1998–2000; Strategic Policy Adviser, Directorate for Strategy and Innovation, FCO 2000–02, Head of Partnerships and Networks Devt Unit, Directorate for Strategy and Innovation 2002–04, Deputy Head of Mission, Basra 2004–06, High Commr to Guyana (also accred as Amb. to Suriname) 2006–10; UK Rep., Handsome Hero 2010–11; CEO Sambora Communications Inc. 2011–. *Address:* Sambora Communications Inc., 2 Avenue of the Republic, Georgetown, Guyana (office). *E-mail:* business@samboracommunications.com (office). *Website:* samboracommunications.com (office).

WHEELER, Graeme; New Zealand international organization official and central banker; *Governor and Chief Executive, Reserve Bank of New Zealand;* ed Univ. of Auckland; Adviser, later Sr Adviser, NZ Treasury 1973–84, Dir of Macroeconomic Policy and Strategy 1990–93, Treas., NZ Debt Man. Office and Deputy Sec. NZ Treasury 1993–97; Econ. and Financial Counsellor to NZ Del. to OECD, Paris 1984–90; Dir Financial Products and Services Dept, World Bank (IBRD) 1997–2001, Vice-Pres. and Treas. 2001–05, Acting Man. Dir, then Man. Dir 2005–10; Dir (non-exec.) Thyssen-Bornemisza Group 2010–12; Gov. and Chief Exec., Reserve Bank of New Zealand (central bank) 2012–. *Address:* Office of the, 2 The Terrace, POB 2498, Wellington, New Zealand (office). *Telephone:* (4) 472-2029 (office). *Fax:* (4) 473-8554 (office). *E-mail:* rbnz-info@rbnz.govt.nz (office). *Website:* www.rbnz.govt.nz (office).

WHEELER, Gen. Sir Roger Neil; GCB, CBE, MA, FRGS; British army officer; *President, Forces Pension Society;* b. 16 Dec. 1941, Fulmer, Bucks.; s. of Maj.-Gen. T.N.S. Wheeler, C.B., CBE; m. Felicity Hares 1980; three s. one d. (from previous marriage); ed All Hallows School, Devon and Hertford Coll. Oxford; commissioned Royal Ulster Rifles 1964; early service in Borneo, Middle East and Cyprus; Chief of Staff, Falkland Islands June–Dec. 1982; Command, 11th Armoured Brig. 1985–87; Dir Army Plans 1987–89; Command, 1st Armoured Div. 1989–90; Asst Chief of Gen. Staff, Ministry of Defence 1990–92; GOC Northern Ireland 1993–96; C-in-C Land Command 1996–97; Chief of Gen. Staff 1997–2000; ADC Gen. to Queen 1996–2000; Constable HM Tower of London 2001–09; Pres. Army Rugby Football Union 1995–99, Army Rifle Assoc. 1995–2000; Col The Royal Irish Regt 1996–2001; Col Commdt Intelligence Corps 1996–2001; Pres. Combat Stress 2001–09, Forces Pension Soc. 2007–; Dir Thales UK Plc 2001–, Aegis Specialist Risk Man. 2005–, Serious and Organised Crime Agency 2005–09; Patron Police Foundation 2001–; Hon. Fellow, Hertford Coll. Oxford. *Leisure interests:* fly fishing, ornithology, cricket, shooting. *Address:* Forces Pension Society, 68 South Lambeth Road, London, SW8 1RL, England (office). *Telephone:* (20) 7820-9988 (office). *Fax:* (20) 7820-7583 (office). *E-mail:* roger_wheeler@btinternet.com. *Website:* www.forcespensionsociety.org (office).

WHELAN, Máire, BA, LLB, LLM, SC; Irish politician and barrister; *Attorney General;* b. 1962, Kinvara, Co. Galway; m. Bernard McCabe; one c.; ed Univ. Coll., Galway, King's Coll., London; called to the Bar 1985, apptd Sr Counsel 2005; fmr Financial Sec., Labour Party; Attorney General 2011–; fmr Rep. of Bar Council, Property Registration Authority; Vice-Chair. Inc. Council of Law Reporting for Ireland; fmr Chair. Free Legal Advice Centres; fmr Advisor to Irish Comm. for Prisoners Overseas. *Publication:* National Asset Management Agency Act 2009: A Reference Guide (co-author) 2011. *Address:* Attorney General's Office, Upper Merrion Street, Dublin 2 (office); 5 Arran Square, Lincoln Lane, Dublin 7, Ireland. *Telephone:* (1) 6314000 (office). *Fax:* (1) 6761806 (office). *E-mail:* mwhelan@ lawlibrary.ie (office). *Website:* www.attorneygeneral.ie/index_en.html (office).

WHELAN, Michael John, MA, PhD, FRS, FInstP; British scientist and academic; *Professor Emeritus and Fellow, Linacre College, University of Oxford;* b. 2 Nov. 1931, Leeds; s. of William Whelan and Ellen Whelan (née Pound); ed Gonville and Caius Coll., Cambridge; Royal Soc. Mr and Mrs John Jaffé Donation Research Fellow 1959–61; Demonstrator in Physics, Univ. of Cambridge 1961–65, Asst Dir of Research 1965–66, Fellow of Gonville and Caius Coll. 1958–66; Reader, Dept of Materials, Univ. of Oxford 1966–92, Prof. 1992–97, Prof. Emer. 1997–; Fellow, Linacre Coll., Univ. of Oxford 1968–; Hon. Prof., Univ. of Science and Tech., Beijing 1995; Hon. Fellow, Royal Microscopical Soc. 2001, Japanese Soc. of Microscopy 2003, Microscopy Soc. of America 2009; C.V. Boys Prize, Inst. of Physics 1965, Hughes Medal, Royal Soc. 1988, Distinguished Scientist Award, Microscopy Soc. of America 1998, Gjønnes Medal in Electron Crystallography, Int.

Union of Crystallography 2011. *Publications:* Electron Microscopy of Thin Crystals (co-author) 1965, Worked Examples in Dislocations 1990, High-Energy Electron Diffraction and Microscopy (co-author) 2004, numerous papers and articles in scientific journals. *Leisure interests:* gardening, tinkering, Japanese language. *Address:* Department of Materials, Engineering and Technology Buildling, Room 50.14, Parks Road, Oxford, OX1 3PH (office); 18 Salford Road, Old Marston, Oxford, OX3 0RX, England (home). *Telephone:* (1865) 273742 (office); (1865) 244556 (home). *Fax:* (1865) 273789 (office); (1865) 244556 (home). *E-mail:* michael .whelan@materials.ox.ac.uk (office). *Website:* www.materials.ox.ac.uk/ peoplepages/whelan.html (office).

WHELAN, Noel, BComm, MEconSc, PhD, DPA; Irish civil servant, international public servant, academic and banker; *Vice-President, Dean and Professor Emeritus, University of Limerick;* b. 28 Dec. 1940, Cork; s. of Richard Whelan and Ann Whelan (née Crowley); m. Joan Gaughan 1970; two s. two d.; ed Sacred Heart Coll., Buttevant, Univ. Coll., Dublin; Exec. Officer, Irish Civil Service 1960–62; Sr Admin. Officer and Head of Research Evaluation, an Foras Taluntais (Agricultural Research Inst. of Ireland) 1962–69; Asst Gen. Man. Córas Iompair Éireann (Irish Transport Authority) 1969–74; Deputy Sec. Dept of Public Service and Dept of Finance 1974–77; Special Consultant, OECD (part-time) 1975–80; Sec. Dept of Econ. Planning and Devt 1977–80; Sec. Dept of the Taoiseach (Prime Minister) 1979–82, 1988–; Chair. Sectoral Devt Cttee, Irish Govt 1980–82; Vice-Pres. and Vice-Chair. Bd of Dirs European Investment Bank, Luxembourg 1982–88, Hon. Vice-Pres. 1988–; Vice-Pres. External Univ. of Limerick, Dean, Coll. of Business 1989–, Prof. of Business and Man. 1989–2005; Chair. Sectoral Devt Cttee 1989–97; Special Consultant, UN and World Bank 1989–; Chair./Dir Corp. Bds 1989–; Chair. Nat. Econ. and Social Council of Ireland 1978–84; Adviser to Irish Ministry of Foreign Affairs on Ireland's Foreign Aid Programme 1999–; Chair. Telephone Users' Advisory Council 1993–98; Chair. Caritas Consultative Forum (Health Sector) 1998–, Nat. Adult Learning Council of Ireland 2000–, St Vincent's Healthcare Group 2002–, Dublin Area Teaching Hosps' Group 1998–2009, State Claims Agency 2002–; Pres. European Univ. Foundation 2002–07, Pres. Emer. 2008–, mem. Strategic Evaluation Panel, European Univ. Asscn; Dir (non-exec.) on various pvt. sector corp. bds; Pres. and Chair. Inst. of Public Admin. (part-time); Council mem. and mem. Exec. Cttee, Econ. and Social Research Inst.; Council mem. Statistical and Social Enquiry Soc.; Council mem. and Fellow, Irish Man. Inst. 1984–; mem. Chartered Accountants Regulatory Bd of Ireland 2008–. *Publications:* miscellaneous papers and reports in various academic and research journals. *Leisure interests:* reading, photography, music. *Address:* Office of the Chairman, St Vincent's Healthcare Group Ltd, Elm Park, Dublin 4 (office); 93 Burleigh Court, Burlington Road, Dublin 4, Ireland (home). *Telephone:* 87-2530565 (mobile) (office). *E-mail:* noel.whelan@ul.ie (office); noelwhelan2@gmail .com. *Website:* www.ul.ie (office).

WHELAN, Peter, BA; British playwright; b. 3 Oct. 1931, Newcastle-under-Lyme, Staffs.; s. of Thomas Whelan and Bertha Whelan; two s. one d.; ed Univ. of Keele; advertising copywriter and dir 1959–90; Hon. Assoc., RSC 1995; Lloyds Private Banking Playwright of the Year 1996, TMA Regional Theatre Award for Best New Play 1996. *Plays:* Double Edge (with Leslie Darbon, Vaudeville Theatre) 1975, Captain Swing (RSC) 1978, The Accrington Pals (RSC) 1981, Clay (RSC) 1982, The Bright and Bold Design (RSC) 1991, The School of Night (RSC) 1992, Shakespeare Country (Amateur Estival) 1993, Worlds Apart (RSC) 1993, The Tinderbox (New Vic) 1994, Divine Right (Birmingham Rep.) 1996, The Herbal Bed (RSC, West End and Broadway) 1996, Nativity (co-author, Birmingham Rep.) 1999, A Russian in the Woods (RSC) 2001, The Earthly Paradise (Almeida, London) 2004. *Television:* In Suspicious Circumstances (Granada) 1992, The Trial of Lord Lucan (Granada) 1994. *Leisure interests:* cricket, politics, theatre and film, TV (especially The Wire). *Address:* c/o The Agency, 24 Pottery Lane, Holland Park, London, W11 4LZ, England (office). *Telephone:* (20) 7727-1346 (office). *E-mail:* info@theagency.co.uk (office). *Website:* www.theagency.co.uk (office).

WHISHAW, Anthony Popham Law, RA, ARCA; British painter; b. 22 May 1930, London; s. of Robert Whishaw and Joyce Wheeler; m. Jean Gibson 1957; two d.; ed Chelsea School of Art, Royal Coll. of Art; work for BBC Monitor; work in collections including Arts Council of GB, Royal Acad., London, Tate Gallery, London, Christchurch, Kensington, London, Nat. Gallery of Wales, Royal West of England Acad., Bristol, Bolton Art Gallery, Chantrey Bequest, City Art Galleries, Sheffield, Coventry Art Gallery, Dept of the Environment, Huddersfield Museum and Art Gallery, Leicester City Art Gallery, European Parl., Strasbourg, Museu de Arte da Bahia, Brazil, Museo de Murcia, Spain, Nat. Gallery of Victoria, Melbourne, Australia, Power Art Gallery Sydney, Australia, Museum of Contemporary Art, Helsinki, Seattle Museum of Art, USA, Western Australia Gallery and several pvt. and corp. collections; Hon. mem. Royal West of England Acad.; Royal Coll. of Art Travelling Scholarship 1952, Royal Coll. of Art Drawing Prize 1953, Abbey Minor Scholarship 1954, Spanish Govt Scholarship 1954, Spanish Govt Scholarship 1955, Perth Int. Drawing Biennale Prize 1973, Byer Int. Painting Prize 1973, South East Arts Asscn Painting Prize 1975, Greater London Arts Council Award 1978, Greater London Council Painting Prize 1981, Abbey Premier Scholarship 1982, Lorne Scholarship 1982, Jt Winner, Hunting Group Nat. Art Competition 1986, Korn Ferry Carre Oban Int. Picture of the Year 1996. *Address:* 7A Albert Place, Victoria Road, London, W8 5PD, England. *Telephone:* (20) 8981-2139 (Studio); (20) 7937-5197. *Fax:* (20) 7937-5197. *E-mail:* anthony.whishaw@ btinternet.com. *Website:* www.anthonywhishaw.com.

WHITACRE, Edward E., Jr, BEng; American business executive; *Chairman, General Motors Corporation;* b. 4 Nov. 1941, Ennis, Tex.; ed Texas Tech. Univ.; joined Southwestern Bell Telephone Co., Dallas, Tex. 1963, subsequently facility engineer, Lubbock and various posts in operational depts, Tex., Ark. and Kan.; Pres. Kan. Div. 1982–85; Group Pres., subsequently Vice-Pres. (Revenues and Public Affairs), Vice-Chair. and Chief Financial Officer, Southwestern Bell Corpn 1986–88, Pres. and COO 1988–90, Chair. and CEO (subsequently called SBC Communications Inc.) 1990–2005, Chair. and CEO AT&T Inc. (after merger of SBC Communications and AT&T) 2005–07 (retd); Chair. General Motors Corpn, Detroit July 2009–, CEO Dec. 2009–Aug. 2010); mem. Bd of Dirs Anheuser-Busch Cos Inc., May Department Stores Co., Emerson Electric Co., Burlington Northern Inc.; mem. Bd of Regents, Tex. Tech. Univ. and Tex. Tech. Univ. Health Sciences Center; mem. Bd of Govs, Southwest Foundation for Biomedical Research;

Trustee, Southwest Research Inst.; actively involved with Boy Scouts of America; Int. Citizen of the Year Award, World Affairs Council, San Antonio 1997, Spirit of Achievement Award, Nat. Jewish Medical and Research Center 1998, Freeman Award, San Antonio Chamber of Commerce 1998, named one of the Top 25 Executives of the Year by BusinessWeek, several awards for contribs to business and civic affairs, including Corp. Leadership Award from Nat. Minority Supplier Devt Council and Obelisk Leadership Award. *Address:* General Motors Corporation, 300 Renaissance Center, Detroit, MI 48265-3000, USA (office). *Telephone:* (313) 556-5000 (office). *Website:* www.gm.com (office).

WHITAKER, Forest; American actor and film director; b. 15 July 1961, Longview, Tex.; m. Keisha Nash; two c.; ed School of Theater, Univ. of Southern California; f. Spirit Dance Entertainment (production co.); BET Award for Best Actor 2007. *Films include:* Tag: The Assassination Game 1982, Fast Times at Ridgemont High 1982, Vision Quest 1985, The Color of Money 1986, Platoon 1986, Stakeout 1987, Good Morning, Vietnam 1987, Bloodsport 1988, Bird 1988, Johnny Handsome 1989, Downtown 1990, A Rage in Harlem 1991, Diary of a Hitman 1991, Article 99 1992, The Crying Game 1992, Consenting Adults 1992, Body Snatchers 1993, Bank Robber 1993, Blown Away 1994, Jason's Lyric 1994, Prêt-à-Porter 1994, Waiting to Exhale (dir) 1995, Smoke 1995, Species 1995, Phenomenon 1996, Body Count 1998, Hope Floats (dir) 1998, Ghost Dog: The Way of the Samurai 1999, Light It Up 1999, Battlefield Earth 2000, Four Dogs Playing Poker 2000, Green Dragon 2001, The Fourth Angel 2001, Panic Room 2002, Phone Booth 2002, First Daughter (dir, producer and voice) 2004, Mary 2005, A Little Trip to Heaven 2005, American Gun 2005, The Marsh 2006, Even Money 2006, The Last King of Scotland (Best Actor, Nat. Bd of Review 2006, Best Actor, Los Angeles Film Critics Asscn 2006, Nat. Soc. of Film Critics 2007, Golden Globe for Best Actor (drama) 2007, Screen Actors' Guild Award for Outstanding Performance by an Actor in a Leading Role 2007, Best Actor, London Film Critics' Circle Awards 2007, BAFTA Award for Best Actor 2007, Acad. Award for Best Actor 2007) 2006, Everyone's Hero (voice) 2006, The Air I Breathe 2007, Ripple Effect 2007, The Great Debaters 2007, Vantage Point 2008, Street Kings 2008, Winged Creatures 2009, Where the Wild Things Are (voice) 2009, Repo Men 2010, My Own Love Song 2010, Catch .44 2011, Crossfire 2012, A Dark Truth 2012, The Last Stand 2013, Repentance 2013, Pawn 2013, Zulu 2013, The Butler 2013, Out of the Furnace 2013, Black Nativity 2013, Two Men in Town 2014. *Television includes:* North and South (mini-series) 1985, Strapped (dir) 1993, North and South, Book II (mini-series) 1986, Black Jaq (dir) 1998, Witness Protection 1999, Twilight Zone (series) 2002–03, Deacons for Defense 2003, The Shield (series) 2006, Criminal Minds 2010, Criminal Minds: Suspect Behavior 2011., *Address:* Spirit Dance Entertainment, 1023 North Orange Drive, Los Angeles, CA 90038-2317; William Morris Endeavor, 9601 Wilshire Blvd, Beverly Hills, CA 90210, USA. *Telephone:* (323) 512-7988 (Spirit Dance).

WHITAKER, Mark Theis, BA, LLD; American journalist, editor and media executive; *Executive Vice-President and Managing Editor,, CNN Worldwide;* b. 7 Sept. 1957, Lower Merion, Pa; m. Alexis Lynn Gelber; one s. one d.; ed Harvard Univ., Univ. of Oxford, UK, Wheaton Coll.; Marshall Scholar, Balliol Coll., Oxford 1979–81; Assoc. Ed. Newsweek 1981–83, Gen. Ed. 1983, Sr Writer 1984–86, Sr Ed., Business Ed. 1987–91, Asst Man. Ed. 1991–95, Man. Ed. 1996–98, Ed. 1998–2006; Vice-Pres. and Ed.-in-Chief of New Ventures, Digital Division, Washington Post 2006–07 Sr Vice-Pres. for News, NBC 2007–11, Washington bureau chief, NBC News 2008–11; Exec. Vice-Pres. and Man. Ed., CNN Worldwide 2011–; mem. Nat. Asscn of Black Journalists, Bd Dirs American Soc. of Magazine Eds 1999– (Pres. 2004–06), Council on Foreign Relations, Century Asscn. *Publications:* My Long Trip Home (autobiography) 2011. *Address:* CNN Worldwide, One Time Warner Center, New York, NY 10019, USA (office). *Website:* edition.cnn.com/WORLD (office).

WHITBREAD, Sir Samuel Charles, Kt, KCVO; British business executive; b. 22 Feb. 1937, London; s. of Maj. Simon Whitbread and H. B. M. Trefusis; m. Jane M. Hayter 1961; three s. one d.; ed Eton Coll.; served in Beds. and Herts. Regt 1955–57; Dir Whitbread & Co. 1972, Deputy Chair. 1984, Chair. Whitbread & Co. (Whitbread PLC from 1991) 1984–92, Dir 1972–2001; Chair. Herts. Timber Supplies 2000–; Vice-Pres. East Anglia TA and VRA 1991–; Lord-Lt of Beds. 1991–2012; Hon. LLB (Bedfordshire). *Publications include:* Southill and the Whitbreads 1995, Straws in the Wind 1997, Plain Mr Whitbread 2007. *Leisure interests:* shooting, travel, painting, music. *Address:* Glebe House, Southill, Biggleswade, Beds., SG18 9LL, England (home). *Telephone:* (1462) 813272 (home).

WHITE, B. Joseph, DBA; American academic and university administrator; *President, University of Illinois;* b. Detroit; m. Mary White; two c.; ed Georgetown Univ. School of Foreign Service, Washington, DC, Harvard Univ., Univ. of Mich.; Asst Prof. of Organizational Behavior and Industrial Relations, Univ. of Mich. 1975, Assoc. Prof. 1978–80, Assoc. Dean Business School 1987–90, Interim Dean 1990–91, Dean 1991–2001, Pres. William Davidson Inst. 1993–2001, Interim Pres. Univ. of Mich. 2002, Wilbur K. Pierpont Collegiate Prof., Prof. of Business Admin, Research Prof., Life Sciences Inst. and Head, Project for a Positive Healthcare Future 2002–05; Pres. Univ. of Illinois 2005–; Vice-Pres. for Man. Devt, later Vice-Pres. for Personnel and Public Affairs, Cummins Engine Co., Inc. 1981–87; ind. dir or trustee of several cos including Equity Residential, Chicago, Gordon Food Service, Kaydon Corpn, Kelly Services; mem. Bd of Dirs W. E. Upjohn Inst. for Employment Research; fmr chair. several large healthcare orgs including Univ. of Mich. Health System, St Joseph Hosp., Ann Arbor, Catherine McAuley Health System; hon. degree (Wabash Coll.) 2003. *Publications:* numerous articles on leadership, man. and organizational matters. *Address:* President's Office, 349 Henry Administration Building, m/c 346, 506 South Wright Street, Urbana, IL 61801, USA (office). *Telephone:* (217) 333-3070 (office). *Fax:* (217) 333-3072 (office). *E-mail:* bjwhite@uillinois.edu (office). *Website:* www.uillinois.edu (office); www .uiuc.edu.

WHITE, Sir Christopher John, CVO, PhD, FBA; British fmr arts administrator; b. 19 Sept. 1930; s. of Gabriel Ernest E. F. White; m. Rosemary Katharine Desages 1957; one s. two d.; ed Downside School, Courtauld Inst. of Art, Univ. of London; army service 1949–50; Asst Keeper, Dept of Prints and Drawings, British Museum 1954–65; Dir P. and D. Colnaghi 1965–71; Curator of Graphic Arts, Nat. Gallery of Art, Washington, DC 1971–73; Dir of Studies, Paul Mellon Centre for Studies in British Art 1973–85; Assoc. Dir Yale Centre for British Art, New Haven 1976–85; Adjunct Prof. of History of Art, Yale Univ. 1977–85; Dir Ashmolean

Museum, Oxford 1985–97; Prof. of the Art of the Netherlands, Oxford 1992–97; Hermione Lecturer, Alexandra Coll., Dublin 1959; Adjunct Prof., Inst. of Fine Arts, New York Univ. 1973, 1976; Visiting Prof., Yale Univ. 1976; Conf. Dir, European-American Ass. on Art Museums 1975; Reviews Ed., Master Drawings 1967–80; Gov. British Inst. of Florence 1994–2002; mem. Exec. Cttee NACF 1998, Raad van Toezicht, Mauritshuis, The Hague 1999; Dir Burlington Magazine 1981– (Chair. 1995–2001); Fellow, Worcester Coll., Oxford 1985–97; Trustee, Victoria and Albert Museum 1997–2004; Visiting Curator, Courtauld Inst. Gallery, London 2011. *Publications include:* Rembrandt and His World 1964, The Flower Drawings of Jan van Huysum 1965, Rubens and His World 1968, Rembrandt's Etchings: a catalogue raisonné (co-author) 1970, Dürer: the Artist and His Drawings 1972, English Landscape 1630–1850 1977, The Dutch Paintings in the Collection of HM The Queen 1982, Rembrandt in Eighteenth Century England (ed.) 1983, Peter Paul Rubens: Man and Artist 1987, Drawing in England from Hilliard to Hogarth (co-author) 1987, Rubens in Oxford (co-author) 1988, One Hundred Old Master Drawings from the Ashmolean Museum (co-author) 1991, Dutch and Flemish Drawings at Windsor Castle (co-author) 1994, Anthony van Dyck: Thomas Howard, the Earl of Arundel 1995, Rembrandt by Himself (co-author) 1999, Ashmolean Museum Catalogue of the Dutch, Flemish and German Paintings 1999, Rembrandt as an Etcher (second edn) 1999, The Later Flemish Paintings in the Collection of HM The Queen 2007. *Address:* 34 Kelly Street, London, NW1 8PH, England (home). *Telephone:* (20) 7485-9148.

WHITE, Sir David Harry, Kt, DL; British business executive; b. 12 Oct. 1929, Nottingham, England; s. of Harry White and Kathleen White; m. Valerie White 1971; one s. four d. (one deceased); ed Nottingham High School and Master Mariner, Liverpool; Master Mariner's Certificate, HMS Conway; apprentice, Shell Co. 1946–56; Terminal Man., Texaco (UK) Ltd 1956–64; Operations Man., Gulf Oil (GB) 1964–68; Asst Man. Dir Samuel Williams, Dagenham 1968–70; Man. Dir Eastern British Road Services 1970–76; Group Man. Dir British Road Services 1976–82, Pickfords 1982–84; Deputy Chair. Nat. Freight Corpn 1984–89; Group Man. Dir Nat. Freight Consortium Property Group 1984–87; Chair. Pension Fund, Nat. Freight Co. 1985–99; Chair. Nottingham Devt Enterprise 1987–93; Dir (non-exec.) British Coal 1993–94; Chair. Nottingham Health Authority 1986–98, Bd of Govs Nottingham Trent Univ. 1988–99, Mansfield Brewery PLC 1993–99, The Coal Authority 1994–99, EPS Ltd 1997–2000; Dir Hilda Hanson 1997–2010, James Bell 1998–2010, Nottingham Forest 1999–2002, Coutts & Co. 1999–2010, Alkane Ltd 2000–02; DL 1989; Hon. DBA (Nottingham Trent) 1999; Hon. LLD (Nottingham) 2011. *Leisure interests:* football, walking. *Address:* Whitehaven, 6 Croft Road, Edwalton, NG12 4BW, England. *Telephone:* (115) 923-4199. *E-mail:* sdw@pobox.com.

WHITE, Edmund Valentine, III, BA; American writer and academic; *Professor of Creative Writing, Princeton University;* b. 13 Jan. 1940, Cincinnati, OH; s. of E. V. White and Delilah Teddlie; ed Univ. of Michigan; writer, Time-Life Books, New York 1962–70; Sr Ed. Saturday Review, New York 1972–73; Asst Prof. of Writing Seminars, Johns Hopkins Univ. 1977–79; Adjunct Prof., Columbia Univ. School of the Arts 1981–83; Exec. Dir New York Inst. for the Humanities 1982–83; Prof. of English, Brown Univ., Providence, RI 1990–92; Prof. of Humanities, Princeton Univ. 1999, now Prof. of Creative Writing in the Lewis Center for the Arts; Guggenheim Fellowship; mem. Acad. of Arts and Letters 1998; Officier, Ordre des Arts et des Lettres 1999. *Play:* Terre Haute. *Publications:* fiction: Forgetting Elena 1973, Nocturnes for the King of Naples 1978, A Boy's Own Story 1982, Aphrodisiac (with others) 1984, Caracole 1985, The Darker Proof: Stories from a Crisis (with Adam Mars-Jones) 1987, The Beautiful Room is Empty 1988, Skinned Alive 1995, The Farewell Symphony 1997, The Married Man 2000, Fanny: A Fiction 2003, Chaos 2007, Hotel de Dream 2007; non-fiction: The Joy of Gay Sex: An Intimate Guide for Gay Men to the Pleasures of a Gay Lifestyle (with Charles Silverstein) 1977, States of Desire: Travels in Gay America 1980, The Faber Book of Gay Short Fiction (ed.) 1991, Genet: A Biography (Nat. Book Critics' Circle Award 1994) 1993, The Selected Writings of Jean Genet (ed.) 1993, The Burning Library (essays) 1994, Sketches from Memory 1994, Our Paris 1995, Proust 1998, The Flâneur 2001, My Lives (autobiog.) 2005, Rimbaud: The Double Life of a Rebel 2008, City Boy: My Life in New York During the 1960s and '70s 2009, Chaos 2010, Jack Holmes and His Friend 2013. *Address:* c/o Amanda Urban, ICM, 825 8th Avenue, New York, NY 10019, USA (office); New South Building, Floor 6, Lewis Center for the Arts, Princeton, NJ 08544, USA (office). *Telephone:* (212) 556-5764 (office); (609) 258-8561 (office). *E-mail:* ewhite@princeton.edu (office). *Website:* www .princeton.edu/~visarts/cwr (office); www.edmundwhite.com.

WHITE, Guy Kendall, AM, MSc, DPhil, FAA; Australian fmr physicist; b. 31 May 1925, Sydney; s. of Perceval George White and Eugenie White (née Kendall); m. 1st Judith Kelly McAuliffe 1955 (divorced); one s. two d.; m. 2nd Belinda Dawson 2005; ed The Scots Coll., Sydney, Univ. of Sydney, Magdalen Coll., Oxford, UK; Research Officer, CSIRO Div. of Physics 1950–54, Prin. Research Scientist 1958–62, Sr Prin. Research Scientist 1962–69, Chief Research Scientist 1969–90, Hon. Fellow 1990–2008; Assoc. Research Officer, Nat. Research Council of Canada 1955–58; Visiting Fellow, ANU 2000–01; Hon. DSc (Wollongong) 1994; Syme Medal (Melbourne Univ.) 1966, Armco Iron Award, USA 1983, Touloukian Award, USA 1994. *Publications include:* Experimental Techniques in Low Temperature Physics 1958, 4th edn jtly 2002, Heat Capacity and Thermal Expansion (co-author) 1999; 200 research papers and review articles. *Leisure interests:* golf, tennis, swimming. *Address:* 6 Abbott Street, Bellerive, Tasmania 7018, Australia (home). *Telephone:* (3) 6244-8256 (home); 417-407696 (mobile). *E-mail:* guy .white1@gmail.com (office).

WHITE, Adm. Sir Hugo (Moresby), GCB, CBE, DL; British naval officer (retd); b. 22 Oct. 1939, Torquay; s. of the late Hugh F. M. White, CMG and Betty White; m. Josephine Pedler 1966; two s.; ed Dragon School, Nautical Coll. Pangbourne and Britannia Royal Naval Coll. (BRNC), Dartmouth; served on HMS Blackpool 1960; submarine training 1961; served on HMS Submarines Tabard, Tiptoe, Odin 1961–65; navigation course 1966; Navigator, HMS Warspite 1967; First Lt HMS Osiris 1968–69; CO HMS Oracle 1969–70; staff, BRNC, Dartmouth 1971–72; submarine sea training 1973–74; CO HMS Salisbury (cod war) 1975–76; with Naval Sec.'s Dept 1976–78; Asst Dir Naval Plans 1978–80; CO HMS Avenger (Falklands) and 4th Frigate Squadron 1980–82; Prin. Staff Officer to Chief of Defence Staff 1982–85; CO HMS Bristol and Flag Capt. 1985–87; Flag Officer,

Third Flotilla and Commdr Anti-Submarine Warfare Striking Force Atlantic 1987–88; Asst Chief of Naval Staff 1988–89; Flag Officer, Scotland and N Ireland 1991–92; C-in-C Fleet, Allied C-in-C Channel and E Atlantic 1992–94; C-in-C Fleet, Allied C-in-C Atlantic and Naval Commdr NW Europe 1994–95; Gov. and C-in-C Gibraltar 1995–97; DL Devon 1999. *Leisure interests:* sailing, travelling, gardening, reading, biography. *Address:* c/o Naval Secretary, Victory Building, HM Naval Base, Portsmouth, PO1 3AS, England (office).

WHITE, Jack; American singer and musician (guitar, drums); b. (John Anthony Gillis), 9 July 1975, Detroit, Mich.; m. 1st Meg White 1996 (divorced 2000); m. 2nd Karen Elson 2005 (divorced 2013); one s. one d.; fmrly played in a number of Detroit-based bands; Founder-mem. The White Stripes 1997–2011; Founder-mem. The Raconteurs 2006–, The Dead Weather 2009–; f. Third Man Records 2001; MTV Europe Music Award for Best Rock Act 2003, BRIT Award for Best Int. Group 2004, Grammy Awards for Best Rock Song (for Seven Nation Army) 2004, for Best Rock Performance by a Duo or Group with Vocals (for Icky Thump) 2008, Music City Amb. Award, City of Nashville 2011. *Film appearances:* Cold Mountain 2003, Coffee and Cigarettes 2003. *Recordings include:* albums: with The White Stripes: White Stripes 1999, De Stijl 2000, White Blood Cells 2001, Elephant (Grammy Award for Best Alternative Album) 2003, Get Behind Me Satan (Grammy Award for Best Alternative Music Album 2006) 2005, Icky Thump (Grammy Award for Best Alternative Music Album 2008) 2007, Under Great White Northern Lights 2010; with The Raconteurs: Broken Boy Soldiers 2006, Consolers of the Lonely 2008; with The Dead Weather: Horehound 2009, Sea of Cowards 2010; solo: Blunderbuss 2012. *Address:* Third Man Records, 623 7th Avenue South, Nashville, TN 37203 (office); Monotone Management, 820 Seward Street, Hollywood, CA 90038, USA (office). *Telephone:* (615) 891-4393 (Nashville) (office); (323) 308-1818 (office). *Fax:* (323) 308-1819 (office). *Website:* www.thirdmanrecords.com (office); www.whitestripes.com (office); www.thedeadweather.com (office); www.theraconteurs.com (office).

WHITE, Jake; South African rugby union coach; b. (Jacob Westerduin), 19 March 1963, Johannesburg; ed Jeppe High School for Boys,; played as hooker in First XV for Jeppe High School for Boys and for Jeppe Old Boys Under 20, also for Johannesburg Coll. of Educ. First XV; began coaching career as high school rugby coach at Parktown Boys High School's First XV 1982–85; worked as physical educ. teacher 1986–94; coached 14a, 15a 1986–88; returned to his old school as teacher and as coach of First XV 1989–94; Dir of Coaching, Transvaal Rugby Union 1995–97; Fitness Coach and Tech. Adviser for Gauteng Lions in Super 12; Nat. Coaching Congress 1997; Asst Coach to Natal Sharks 2000; Asst Coach to South African Nat. Rugby Union Team (Springboks) 2000–01, Head Coach 2004–07; coached various Under 19 and Under 21 sides, including Under 21 Springbok side that won U-21 Rugby Union World Cup 2002; guided Springboks to victory in a two-Test home series against Ireland and against Wales during their opponents' tours of Southern Hemisphere 2004; won Tri Nations trophy 2004; won Rugby World Cup, Paris 2007; Int. Rugby Bd (IRB) Int. Coach of the Year 2004, 2007. *Address:* c/o South African Rugby Union, PO Box 99, Newlands 7725, South Africa. *Telephone:* (21) 6596700. *Fax:* (21) 6863907. *E-mail:* yourview@sarugby.co.za. *Website:* www.sarugby.co.za; jakewhiterugby.blogspot.com.

WHITE, James Boyd, AM, LLB; American academic; *L. Hart Wright Professor of Law, University of Michigan;* b. 28 July 1938, Boston, Mass.; s. of Benjamin White and Charlotte Green White; m. 1st Constance Southworth 1959; m. 2nd Mary Fitch 1978; two s. two d.; ed Groton School, Amherst Coll. and Harvard Univ.; pvt. practice of law, Foley Hoag & Eliot 1964–67; Prof. of Law, Univ. of Colorado 1967–75, Univ. of Chicago 1975–82; Hart Wright Prof. of Law, Prof. of English Language and Literature and Adjunct Prof. of Classics, Univ. of Mich. 1982–. *Publications:* The Legal Imagination 1973, When Words Lose Their Meaning 1984, Heracles' Bow: Essays on the Rhetoric and Poetics of the Law 1986, Justice as Translation: An Essay in Cultural and Legal Criticism 1990, This Book of Starres: Learning to Read George Herbert 1994, Acts of Hope: Creating Authority in Literature, Law and Politics 1994, From Expectation to Experience: Essays in Law and Legal Education 1999, The Edge of Meaning 2001, Living Speech 2006. *Leisure interests:* reading, walking, swimming. *Address:* University of Michigan Law School, 332 Hutchins Hall, Ann Arbor, MI 48109 (office); 1606 Morton, Ann Arbor, MI 48104, USA (home). *Telephone:* (734) 936-2989 (office); (734) 662-6464 (home). *Fax:* (734) 763-9375 (office). *E-mail:* jbwhite@umich.edu (office). *Website:* www.law.umich.edu (office).

WHITE, Marco Pierre; British chef and restaurateur; b. 11 Dec. 1961, Leeds; s. of the late Frank White and Maria Rosa Gallina; m. 1st Alexandra McArthur 1988 (divorced 1990); one d.; m. 2nd Lisa Butcher 1992 (divorced 1994); m. 3rd Matilda Conejero-Caldera 2000; two s. one d.; ed Allerton High School, Leeds; Commis Chef Hotel St George, Harrogate 1978, Box Tree, Ilkley 1979; Chef de Partie Le Gavroche 1981, Tante Claire 1983; Sous Chef Manoir aux Quat' Saisons 1984–85; Propr and Chef Harveys 1986–93, The Canteen Restaurant, Chelsea Harbour (co-owner Michael Caine) 1992–96, Restaurant Marco Pierre White 1993–, Criterion Marco Pierre White (co-owner Sir Rocco Forte) 1995–, Quo Vadis 1996–, Oak Room, Le Meridien 1997–99, MPW Canary Wharf 1997–, Café Royal Grill Room 1997–, Mirabelle Restaurant, Curzon Street 1998–, L'Escargot, Belvedere 1999, Wheelers of St James 2002, Frankie's Bar and Grill; Catey Award for Newcomer of the Year 1987, Chef of the Year, Egon Ronay 1992, youngest and first British chef to win 3 Michelin stars 1995, Restaurant of the Year, Egon Ronay (for The Restaurant) 1997. *Television includes:* Hell's Kitchen (presenter) 2007. *Publications include:* White Heat 1990, White Heat II 1994, Wild Food from Land and Sea 1994, Canteen Cuisine 1995, Glorious Puddings 1998, The Mirabelle Cookbook 1999, White Slave (autobiography) 2006, The Devil in the Kitchen 2007, Frankie's: Recipes from an Italian Family (with Frankie Dettori) 2007. *Leisure interests:* fishing, shooting, bird-watching. *Website:* www.mpwrestaurants.co.uk; www.marcopierrewhite.org.

WHITE, Mary Jo, BA, MA, JD; American lawyer and government official; *Chairman, Securities and Exchange Commission;* b. 27 Dec. 1947, Kansas City, Mo.; d. of Carl Monk and Ruth King Monk; m. John White 1970; ed Coll. of William and Mary, New School for Social Research, New York, Columbia Univ.; called to the Bar, New York 1975; clerk to Marvin E. Frankel, US Dist Court (Southern Dist), New York 1976–77; Assoc., Debevoise & Plimpton LLP 1976–78, Litigation Partner 1983–90, Partner and Chair., Litigation Dept 2002–13; Asst US Attorney,

Chief Appellate Attorney, Criminal Div., US Dept of Justice (Southern Dist), New York 1978–81, Chief Asst and Acting US Attorney (Eastern Dist), Brooklyn 1990–93, US Attorney (Southern Dist), New York (first woman) 1993–2002; Chair. SEC, Washington, DC 2013–; Dir Nasdaq Stock Exchange and mem. Exec., Audit and Policy Cttees 2002–06; Lecturer in Professional Responsibility and Ethics, Columbia Law School 1981–; mem. ABA, New York State Bar Asscn, New York City Bar Asscn; Fellow, American Coll. of Trial Lawyers; included among 100 Most Influential Lawyers in America 2006, 50 Most Influential Women Lawyers in America 2007, Sandra Day O'Connor Award for Distinction in Public Service 2002, FBI Jefferson Cup Award 2002, George W. Bush Award for Excellence in Counter-terrorism 2002, CIA Agency Seal Medallion 2002, ranked by Forbes magazine amongst The World's 100 Most Powerful Women (72nd) 2013. *Address:* Securities and Exchange Commission, Station Place, 100 F Street NE, Washington, DC 20549, USA (office). *Telephone:* (202) 942-8088 (office). *E-mail:* publicinfo@sec.gov (office). *Website:* www.sec.gov (office).

WHITE, Michael D.; American business executive; *Chairman, President and CEO, The DIRECTV Group;* joined Frito-Lay as Vice-Pres. of Planning 1990, later Exec. Vice-Pres. and Chief Financial Officer (CFO) PepsiCo Foods International and CFO Frito-Lay North America, later Sr Vice-Pres. and CFO PepsiCo 1998–2000, Pres. and CEO Frito-Lay's Europe/Africa/Middle East div. 2000–03, Chair. and CEO PepsiCo International 2003–09, mem. Bd of Dirs and Vice-Chair. PepsiCo 2006–09; mem. Bd of Dirs, Chair., Pres. and CEO The DIRECTV Group 2009–; mem. Bd of Dirs Whirlpool Corpn. *Address:* The DIRECTV Group, Inc. 2230 East Imperial Highway, El Segundo, CA 90245, USA (office). *E-mail:* info@directv.com (office). *Website:* www.directv.com (office).

WHITE, Michael Simon; British theatrical and film producer and impresario; b. 16 Jan. 1936; s. of Victor White and Doris White; m. 1st Sarah Hillsdon 1965 (divorced 1973); two s. one d.; m. 2nd Louise Moores 1985; one s.; ed Lyceum Alpinum, Zuoz, Switzerland, Pisa Univ. and Sorbonne, Paris; began career by bringing Cambridge Footlights to London's West End; Asst to Sir Peter Daubeny 1956–61. *Stage productions include:* Rocky Horror Show, Jabberwocky, Sleuth, America Hurrah, Oh, Calcutta!, The Connection, Joseph and the Amazing Technicolour Dreamcoat, Loot, The Blood Knot, A Chorus Line, Deathtrap, Annie, Pirates of Penzance, On Your Toes, The Mystery of Edwin Drood, Metropolis, Bus Stop, Crazy for You, Looking Through a Glass Onion, Me and Mamie O'Rourke, She Loves Me, Fame, Voyeurz 1996, Notre Dame de Paris 2000–01, Contact 2002. *Films include:* Monty Python and the Holy Grail, Rocky Horror Picture Show, My Dinner with André, Ploughman's Lunch, Moonlighting, Strangers' Kiss, The Comic Strip Presents, The Supergrass, High Season, Eat the Rich, White Mischief, The Deceivers, Nuns on the Run 1989, Robert's Movie, The Pope Must Die, Widow's Peak, Enigma 2000. *Publication:* Empty Seats 1984. *Leisure interests:* art, skiing, racing. *Address:* 48 Dean Street, London, W1V 5HL, England. *Telephone:* (20) 7734-7707.

WHITE, Miles D., BA, MBA; American pharmaceutical industry executive; *Chairman and CEO, Abbott Laboratories;* b. 1955, Minneapolis, Minn.; m.; ed Stanford Univ.; began career as Man. Consultant with McKinsey & Co.; Man. Nat. Account Sales and later other Sr Man. posts, Diagnostics Div., Abbott Laboratories 1984–93, Vice-Pres. Diagnostics Systems and Operations 1993–94, Sr Vice-Pres. 1994–98, Exec. Vice-Pres. 1998–99, mem. Bd of Dirs 1998–, CEO Jan. 1999–, Chair. April 1999–; mem. Bd of Dirs Fed. Reserve Bank of Chicago 2002–04, Chair. 2005–07; mem. Bd of Dirs Caterpillar Inc., McDonald's Corpn, Northwestern Memorial Hosp.; Chair. Civic Cttee of the Commercial Club of Chicago, Dean's Advisory Bd at Kellogg School of Man., The Culver Educational Foundation; mem. Bd of Trustees Northwestern Univ., Museum of Science and Industry, The Field Museum in Chicago (fmr Chair.); fmr Chair. Fed. Reserve Bank of Chicago, The Econ. Club of Chicago, Pharmaceutical Research and Mfrs of America (PhRMA); Distinguished Executive Award, Lake Forest Grad. School of Man. 2004. *Address:* Abbott Laboratories, 100 Abbott Park Road, Abbott Park, IL 60064-6400, USA (office). *Telephone:* (847) 937-6100 (office). *Fax:* (847) 937-1511 (home). *E-mail:* info@abbott.com (office). *Website:* www.abbott.com (office).

WHITE, Norman A., PhD, FIMechE, FRSA; British business executive, academic and international consultant; *Chairman, Board of Trustees, Spacelink Learning Foundation;* b. 11 April 1922, Hetton-le-Hole, Durham; s. of Charles Brewster White and Lilian Sarah White (née Finch); m. 1st Joyce Marjorie Rogers 1944 (died 1982); one s. one d.; m. 2nd Marjorie Iris Rushton 1983; ed Univs of Manchester and London, Univ. of Philippines, London Polytechnic (now Univ. of Westminster), Harvard Business School, London School of Econs; apprenticeship with George Kent Ltd and D. Napier and Sons Ltd 1936–43; Flight Test Engineer, Mil. Aircraft Devt 1943–45; with Royal Dutch Shell Group 1945–72, numerous posts, including Chair. and Dir of Royal Dutch/Shell Oil and int. mining cos 1963–72; f. Norman White Assocs 1972, Pres. Exec. 1972–92, Chair. 1992–95; tech. consultant to numerous cos 1972–96; Chair. and Dir numerous eng and oil cos 1972–97; Chair. Millennium Satellite Centre 1995–2000, Spacelink Learning Foundation 2000 (currently Chair. Bd of Trustees); mem. Council and Chair. Eng-Man. Div., IMechE 1980–85, 1987–91; mem. Council and Vice-Pres. Inst. of Petroleum 1975–81; Founder, Chair. Jt Bd for Engineering Man., IMechE, ICE, IEE, Inst. of Chemical Engineers 1990–94, Chair. Academic Bd 1994–97; Visiting Prof., Univ. of Manchester, Henley Man. Coll., City Univ. 1971–96; mem. numerous academic and educational cttees including Senate and Advisory Bd in Eng, Univ. of London; mem., Bd of Govs Royal Grammar School, Guildford, Surrey 1976–2004; Chair. Transnational Satellite Educ. Centre, Univ. of Surrey 1991–94; mem. House of Commons Parl. and Scientific Cttee 1977–83, 1987–92; Chair. British Nat. Cttee of World Petroleum Congresses (WPC) 1987–95 (Deputy Chair. 1977–87), UK Rep. WPC Int. Exec. Bd and Perm. Council 1979–97, Treas. 1983–91, 1994–97, Vice-Pres. 1991–94; mem. Conservation Comm. for World Energy 1979–87; Chair. Int. Task Force on Oil Substitution 1979–84; mem. int. energy/petroleum dels to USSR, People's Repub. of China, Romania, GDR, Japan, Korea, India, Mexico, Argentina, Brazil, Venezuela, Nepal, Indonesia, Southern Africa, Iran 1979–97; Founding mem. British Inst. of Energy Econs; Fellow, Inst. of Man., British Interplanetary Soc.; mem. American Soc. of Petroleum Engineers, Canadian Inst. of Mining and Metallurgy; Liveryman, Worshipful Co. of Engineers, Worshipful Co. of Spectacle Makers, Worshipful Co. of World Traders; mem. numerous professional eng insts; Freeman, City of London; Hon. Calgarian, Alberta, Canada; Hon. DipEM 1998;

numerous other honours and awards. *Publications:* Financing the International Petroleum Industry 1978, The International Outlook for Oil Substitution to 2020 1983, Handbook of Engineering Management 1989, articles in professional journals in UK, USA and Canada. *Leisure interests:* family, walking, international affairs, comparative religions, odd-jobbing. *Address:* Spacelink Learning Foundation, PO Box 415, Guildford, Surrey, GU5 7WZ (office); Green Ridges, Downside Road, Guildford, Surrey, GU4 8PH, England (home). *Telephone:* (1483) 855329 (office); (1483) 567523 (home). *Fax:* (1483) 504314 (home). *E-mail:* n.white@spacelink.org (office); normanwhite@norsco-demon.co.uk (home). *Website:* www.spacelink.org (office).

WHITE, Raymond P., DDS, PhD; American oral and maxillofacial surgeon and academic; *Dalton L. McMichael Distinguished Professor of Oral and Maxillofacial Surgery, University of North Carolina;* b. 13 Feb. 1937, New York; s. of Raymond P. White and Mabel S. White; m. Betty P. White 1961; one s. one d.; ed Medical Coll. of Virginia and Washington & Lee Univ.; Asst Prof. of Oral Surgery, Univ. of Kentucky 1967–70, Assoc. Prof. 1970–71, Chair. Oral Surgery Dept 1969–71; Prof. of Oral Surgery, Virginia Commonwealth Univ. 1971–74; Dalton L. McMichael Prof. of Oral and Maxillofacial Surgery, Univ. of N Carolina School of Dentistry 1974–, Dean 1974–81; Assoc. Dean. Univ. of N Carolina School of Medicine 1981–93; Research Assoc., Univ. of N Carolina Health Services Research Center 1982–98; mem. Inst. of Medicine, NAS; William Gies Award, American Asscn of Oral and Maxillofacial Surgeons 2000, Distinguished Service Award, American Asscn of Oral and Maxillofacial Surgeons 2003, Torch Distinguished Service Award, Oral and Maxillofacial Surgery Foundation 2006. *Publications:* co-author: Fundamentals of Oral Surgery 1971, Surgical Correction of Dentofacial Deformities 1980, Surgical Orthodontic Treatment 1990, Rigid Fixation for Maxillofacial Surgery 1991, Contemporary Treatment of Dentofacial Deformity 2002. *Leisure interests:* tennis, sailing. *Address:* Department of Oral and Maxillofacial Surgery, CB 7450, University of North Carolina, Chapel Hill, NC 27599-7450 (office); 1506 Velma Road, Chapel Hill, NC 27514, USA (home). *Telephone:* (919) 966-1126 (office); (919) 967-4064 (home). *Fax:* (919) 966-6019 (office). *E-mail:* ray_white@dentistry.unc.edu (office). *Website:* www.dent.unc.edu/depts/academic/oms (office).

WHITE, Robert James, AO; Australian banker; b. 18 Oct. 1923, Deniliquin, NSW; s. of A. W. White and S. J. White; m. 1st Molly McKinnon 1950 (died 1994); m. 2nd Janice Anne White 1996; ed War Memorial High School, Hay, NSW; joined Bank of NSW 1940, Asst Chief Man., NZ 1965–66, Deputy Chief Accountant 1967–69, Man., Sydney 1970–71, Chief Man., UK and Europe 1972–74, Gen. Man. 1974–77, Dir and CEO Bank of NSW 1977–82, Man. Dir Westpac Banking Corpn (merger of Bank of NSW with Commercial Bank of Australia) 1982–87, Dir 1977–90; Dir ICI Australia Ltd 1987–93, IBM Australia Ltd 1988–95, Atlas Copco Australia Pty Ltd 1989–94; Commr Electricity Comm. of NSW 1989–95; Pres. Australian Inst. of Bankers 1980–86; Chair. Australian Bankers' Asscn 1978–79, 1983–84, 1987; Dir Int. Monetary Conf. 1982–85; Pres. Asian Pacific Bankers' Club 1983–84, Business Council of Australia 1984–86, Australian Coalition of Service Industries 1988–94, Australian Inst. for Int. Affairs 1988–91, German-Australian Chamber of Industry and Commerce 1988–91, Council for Int. Business Affairs 1992–95; mem. Trade Devt Council 1981–84, Australian Pacific Econ. Co-operation Cttee 1984–91; mem. Exec. Bd ICC 1987–90; Fellow, Austrinlian Inst. of Bankers, Australian Inst. of Co. Dirs; Commdr's Cross, Order of Merit (Germany); Storey Medal, Australian Inst. of Man. 1987. *Publication:* Cheques and Balances (memoir) 1995. *Address:* PO Box 616, Lindfield, NSW 2070, Australia. *Telephone:* (2) 9417-4989.

WHITE, Robert Mayer, BA, MS, ScD; American meteorologist; *Director, The Washington Advisory Group;* b. 13 Feb. 1923, Boston, Mass; s. of David White and Mary White (née Winkeller); m. Mavis Seagle 1948; one s. one d.; ed Harvard Univ., Massachusetts Inst. of Tech.; war service with USAF, exec. at Atmospheric Analysis Lab., Geophysics Research Directorate, Air Force Cambridge Research Center 1952–58, Chief of Meteorological Devt Lab. 1958; Research Assoc., MIT 1959, Karl T. Compton Lecturer 1995–96; Travelers Insurance Cos 1959–60, Pres. Travelers Research Center, Hartford 1960–63; Chief of Weather Bureau, US Dept of Commerce 1963–65; Admin. Environmental Science Services Admin., US Dept of Commerce 1965–70; Perm. Rep. and mem. Exec. Cttee of World Meteorological Org. 1963–77; Admin. Nat. Oceanic and Atmospheric Admin. 1971–77; Chair. Joint Oceanographic Insts., Inc. 1977–79; Chair. Climate Research Bd of NAS 1977–79; Admin. Nat. Research Council, Exec. Officer 1979–80; Pres. Univ. Corpn for Atmospheric Research 1979–83, Sr Fellow 1995–; Pres. Washington Advisory Group 1996–98, now Dir; mem. Exec. Cttee American Geophysical Union, Council Nat. Acad. of Eng, (Pres. 1983–), Marine Tech. Soc., Royal Meteorological Soc., Nat. Advisory Cttee on Oceans and Atmosphere 1979–84, Nat. Advisory Cttee on Govt and Public Affairs, Univ. of Ill. 1987–; Bd of Overseers Harvard Univ. 1977–79; mem. of numerous weather research cttees; Commr Int. Whaling Comm. 1973–77; Hon. DEng (Drexel Univ.) 1985; Cleveland Abbe Award, American Meteorological Soc. 1969, Rockefeller Public Service award 1974, David B. Stone Award, New England Aquarium 1975, Matthew Fontaine Maury Medal, Smithsonian Inst. 1976, Int. Conservation Award Nat. Wildlife Fed. 1976, Neptune Award American Oceanic Org. 1977, Charles Franklin Brooks Award 1978, Int. Meteorological Asscn Prize 1980, Fahrney Award, Franklin Inst. 1983, Tyler Prize, Univ. of California 1992, Vannevar Bush Award 1998, Australian Centenary Medal 2003. *Leisure interests:* gardening, reading. *Address:* The Washington Advisory Group, 1275 K Street, NW, Suite 1025, Washington, DC 20005 (office); Somerset House II, 5610 Wisconsin Avenue, Apt 1506, Bethesda, MD 20815, USA (home). *Telephone:* (202) 682-0164 (office); (301) 652-2901 (home). *Fax:* (202) 682-9335 (office); (301) 052-2901 (home). *E-mail:* qmw@theadvisorygroup.com (office). *Website:* www.theadvisorygroup.com (office).

WHITE, Simon David Manton, BA, MSc, PhD, FRS; British astrophysicist, academic and research institute director; *Director, Max Planck Institute for Astrophysics;* b. 30 Sept. 1951, Ashford, Kent, England; ed Jesus Coll., Cambridge, Univ. of Toronto, Canada; Lindemann Fellow, Dept of Astronomy, Univ. of California, Berkeley 1977–78; Visiting Research Astronomer, Nat. Radio Astronomy Observatory, Charlottesville, Va Sept.–Dec. 1978; Research Fellow, Churchill Coll., Cambridge 1979–80; Attaché au CNRS, Institut d'Astrophysique de Paris Jan.–June 1980; Sr Fellow, Space Sciences Lab., Univ. of California, Berkeley 1980–84, Adjunct Asst Prof., Astronomy Dept 1981–84; mem. Inst. for Advanced Study, Princeton, NJ, USA 1982, Inst. for Theoretical Physics, Santa Barbara, Calif. 1984, Inst. for Advanced Study, Jerusalem 1990; Assoc. Prof./Astronomer, Steward Observatory, Univ. of Arizona 1984–87, Prof./Astronomer 1987–91, Research Prof. 1992–; Sheepshanks Reader in Astronomy, Univ. of Cambridge 1991–94; Dir European Asscn for Research in Astronomy 1992–94; Scientific mem. Max Planck Soc. 1994–, Dir Max Planck Inst. for Astrophysics, Garching, Germany 1994–; Visiting Prof., Durham Univ. 1994–; mem. Academia Europaea 2009, European Physical Soc. 2011; Foreign Assoc., NAS 2007; Fellow, Leopoldina, Nationale Akad. der Wissenschaften 2005; Hon. Prof., Ludwig Maximilians Univ., Munich 1995–, Shanghai Astronomical Observatory 1999–, Nat. Observatory, Beijing 2001–; Hon. Citizen of City of Padua 2010; Hon. DSc (Durham) 2007; NSF Presidential Young Investigator 1984–89, Helen B. Warner Prize, American Astronomical Soc. (AAS) 1986, Grubb Parsons Lecturer, Durham Univ. 1996, George Darwin Lecturer, Royal Astronomical Soc. 1998, Lansdowne Lecturer, Univ. of Victoria, BC 1999, Max-Planck-Forschungspreis, Internationale Kooperation 2000, Sackler Lecturer, Physics Dept, Princeton Univ. 2003, Blaauw Lecturer, Groningen Univ. 2005, Dannie Heineman Prize, American Inst. of Physics/AAS 2005 Gold Medal, Royal Astronomical Soc. 2005, Gold Medal, Royal Astronomical Soc. 2006, Dirk Brouwer Award, Dynamical Div. of AAS 2008, Oort Professorship 2008, European Latsis Prize, Leiden Univ., European Science Foundation 2008, Max Born Prize, Inst. of Physics and German Physical Soc. 2010, Cosmology Prize, Peter Gruber Foundation 2011, Marsilius-Vorlesung, Univ. of Heidelberg 2012. *Publications:* numerous papers in professional journals on the structure, formation, evolution and clustering of galaxies; dark matter and dark energy; gravitational dynamics, simulation of cosmic structure formation; cosmology. *Address:* Max-Planck-Institut für Astrophysik, Karl-Schwarzschild-Str. 1, Postfach 1523, 85740 Garching, Germany (office). *Telephone:* (89) 30000-2211 (office). *Fax:* (89) 30000-2899 (office). *E-mail:* swhite@mpa-garching.mpg.de (office); *Website:* www.mpa-garching.mpg.de (office); www.mpg.de/379074/astrophysik_wissM2 (office).

WHITE, Terrence Harold, PhD; Canadian academic and fmr university president; *Professor of Management and President Emeritus, University of Calgary;* b. 31 March 1943, Ottawa; s. of William H. White and Shirley M. Ballantine; m. Susan E. Hornaday 1968; two d.; ed Univ. of Toronto; Head, Dept of Sociology and Anthropology, Univ. of Windsor 1973–75; Chair. Dept of Sociology, Univ. of Alberta 1975–80, Dean, Faculty of Arts 1980–88; Pres. and Vice-Chancellor Brock Univ. 1988–96, Univ. of Calgary 1996–2001, Prof. of Man. and Pres. Emer. 2001–; Rotary Int. Paul Harris Fellow, Canada 125 Commemorative Medal 1999, Queen's Jubilee Medal 2004. *Publications:* Power or Pawns: Boards of Directors in Canadian Corporations 1978, Quality of Working Life 1984. *Leisure interests:* hockey, skiing, squash, tennis, painting. *Address:* Haskayne School of Business, 452 Scurfield Hall, The University of Calgary, 2500 University Drive NW, Calgary, Alberta, T2N 1N4, Canada (office). *E-mail:* twhite@ucalgary.ca (office). *Website:* www.haskayne.ucalgary.ca (office).

WHITE, Tony L; American business executive; b. 1947; ed Western Carolina Univ.; Exec. Vice-Pres. Baxter Int. Inc., Group Vice-Pres. 1986–92; Dir and Chair., Pres. and Chief Exec. PE Corpn (called Applera Corpn since 2000) 1995–2008; co-f. Celera Genomics Group 1998, Pres. (acting) 2002; mem. Bd of Dirs CVS Caremark Corpn, C.R. Bard Inc., Ingersoll-Rand Co.; mem. Advisory Bd Kellogg Center for Biotechnology, Northwestern Univ.; Trustee, North Carolina Univ., Centenary Coll.

WHITE, Sir Willard Wentworth, Kt, OM, CBE, BA; Jamaican/British singer (bass); *President, Royal Northern College of Music;* b. 10 Oct. 1946, Ewarton, St Catherine, Jamaica; s. of Egbert White and Gertrude White; m. Gillian Jackson 1972; three s. one d.; ed Excelsior School, Kingston and Juilliard School of Music, NY; debut with New York City Opera as Colline in La Bohème 1974–75; European debut as Osmin with Welsh Nat. Opera 1976; has performed in most int. opera houses, including Royal Opera House, La Scala, Glyndebourne; roles include: Porgy, Orestes, Banquo, King Henry (Lohengrin), Pizarro, Wotan, Mephistopheles, Boris Godunov, Golau, Leporello, Prince Kovansky, Napoleon; extensive concert appearances; appeared as Othello, RSC, Stratford-upon-Avon; Falstaff at Aix Festival 2001, Klingsor in Parsifal, Covent Garden 2001, Bartok's Bluebeard 2002, Messiaen's St Francis, San Francisco 2002, Wotan in the Ring, Aix and Salzburg 2005; Méphistophélès in LaDamnation de Faust, Geneva 2008; appeared in Janáček's From the House of the Dead at the Met, New York 2009, La Scala 2010 and Unter den Linden, Berlin 2011; Bottom in A Midsummer Night's Dream for ENO 2011; Pres. Royal Northern Coll. of Music 2008–; Patron, London Southbank Scheme for Young Singers; Prime Minister of Jamaica's Medal of Appreciation 1987. *Recordings include:* Porgy and Bess 1991, Mozart Requiem, Orfeo, Die Aegyptische Helena, Acis and Galatea, Willard White Sings: Copland; American Spirituals; Folk Songs 1999, Willard White in Concert 2004, The Paul Robeson Legacy 2007. *Address:* IMG Artists, The Light Box, 111 Power Road, London, W4 5PY, England (office); Royal Northern College of Music, 124 Oxford Road, Manchester, M13 9RD, England. *Telephone:* (20) 7957-5800 (office); (161) 907-5200. *Fax:* (20) 7957-5801 (office). *E-mail:* bsegal@imgartists.com (office). *Website:* www.imgartists.com (office); /www.rncm.ac.uk.

WHITE, William James, BS, MBA; American business executive (retd); b. 30 May 1938, Kenosha, Wis.; s. of William H. White and Dorothy Caroline White; m. Jane Schulte 1960; two s. two d.; ed Northwestern and Harvard Univs; Mechanical Planning Engineer, Procter & Gamble Corpn 1961–62; Corp. Vice-Pres. Hartmarx Corpn, Chicago 1963–74; Group Vice-Pres. Mead Corp, Dayton, Ohio 1974–81; Pres., COO and Dir Masonite Corpn, Chicago 1981–85; Exec. Vice-Pres. and Dir USG Corpn 1985–88; Pres., CEO Whitestar Enterprises Inc. 1989–90; Chair., Pres., CEO Bell & Howell Co. 1990–95, Chair. CEO Bell and Howell Holdings Co. 1995; Chair. ContextMedia Company; Prof., Northwestern Univ. 1998–; Visiting Prof., Univ. of Virginia Darden School of Business 2000–01, Univ. of Chicago Business School 2000–04; fmr Dir Midwest Stock Exchange, Evanston Hosp., Ill. Math. and Science Foundation, Business Advisory Council, Univ. of Ill.; mem. The Chicago Cttee, Advisory Council Tech. Inst., Northwestern Univ.; Trustee Northwestern Univ. *Publication:* Creative Collective Bargaining (co-author) 1965, From Day One: CEO Advice to Launch an Extraordinary Career 2005. *E-mail:* white@iems.northwestern.edu. *Website:* www.williamjwhite.com.

WHITEHOUSE, Sheldon; American lawyer and politician; *Senator from Rhode Island;* b. 20 Oct. 1955, New York, NY; s. of Charles Whitehouse; m. Dr Sandra Thornton; one s. one d.; ed St Paul's School, Concord, NH, Yale Univ., Univ. of Virginia School of Law; worked as clerk for Judge Richard F. Neely, Supreme Court of Appeals of W Va 1982–83; Special Asst Attorney Gen., RI Attorney Gen.'s Office 1985–90, Chief of Regulatory Unit 1988–90, Asst Attorney Gen. 1989–90; Exec. Counsel for Gov. Bruce Sundlun of RI 1991–94, later Dir of Policy, Dir of Business Regulation 1992–94; US Attorney for RI 1994–98; State Attorney Gen. 1998–2006; cand. for Gov. 2002; Senator from Rhode Island 2007–; mem. Budget Cttee, Environment and Public Works Cttee, Judiciary Cttee, Health, Educ., Labor, and Pensions Cttee, Special Cttee on Aging; f. Rhode Island Quality Inst.; Democrat. *Address:* 717 Hart Senate Office Building, Washington, DC 20510, USA (office). *Telephone:* (202) 224-2921 (office). *Fax:* (202) 228-6362 (office). *Website:* whitehouse.senate.gov (office).

WHITELAW, Billie, CBE; British actress; b. 6 June 1932, Coventry; d. of Perceval Whitelaw and Frances Whitelaw; m. 1st Peter Vaughan (divorced); m. 2nd Robert Muller; one s.; ed Thornton Grammar School, Bradford; Annenberg-Beckett Fellow, Univ. of Reading 1993; Hon. DLitt (Bradford) 1981, (Birmingham, St Andrew's) 1997; Variety Club Silver Heart Award 1961, TV Actress of Year 1961, 1972, British Acad. Award 1968, US Film Critics' Award 1977, Evening News Film Award as Best Actress 1977, Sony Best Radio Actress Award 1987, Evening Standard Best Film Actress Award 1988. *Plays include:* Hotel Paradiso, Winter Garden 1954 and Oxford Playhouse 1956, Progress to the Park, Theatre Workshop and Saville 1961, England our England, Prince's 1962, Touch of the Poet, Venice and Dublin 1962; with Nat. Theatre 1963–65, Othello, London and Moscow, Hobson's Choice, Play (Beckett), Trelawny of the Wells, The Dutch Courtesan, After Haggerty, Criterion 1971, Not I, Royal Court 1973 and 1975, Alphabetical Order, Mayfair 1975, Footfalls, Royal Court 1976, Molly, Comedy 1978, Happy Days, Royal Court 1979, The Greeks, Aldwych 1980, Passion Play, Aldwych 1981, Rockaby, Nat. Theatre 1982, New York 1982, 1984, Riverside Studios 1986, world tour 1985/86, Tales from Hollywood, Nat. Theatre 1983, Who's Afraid of Virginia Woolf?, Young Vic 1987. *Films include:* No Love For Johnnie 1961, Charlie Bubbles 1968, Twisted Nerve 1968, The Adding Machine 1968, Start the Revolution Without Me, Leo the Last, Eagle in a Cage 1969, Gumshoe 1971, Frenzy 1972, Night Watch 1973, The Omen 1976, Leopard in the Snow, The Water Babies 1977, An Unsuitable Job for a Woman 1981, Slayground 1983, The Chain 1984, Shadey 1985, Maurice 1986, The Dressmaker 1988, Joyriders 1989, The Krays 1990, Deadly Advice 1993, Jane Eyre 1994, Canterbury Tales (animated film), Quills 2000, Hot Fuzz 2007. *Television includes:* No Trams to Lime Street, Lena Oh My Lena, Resurrection, The Skin Game, Beyond the Horizon, Anna Christie, Lady of the Camelias, The Pity of It All, Love on the Dole, A World of Time, You and I, Poet Game, Sextet (8 plays), Napoleon and Love (9 plays, as Josephine), The Fifty Pound Note (Ten From the Twenties), The Withered Arm (Wessex Tales), The Werewolf Reunion (2 plays), Shades by Samuel Beckett, Not I, Eustace and Hilda (2 plays), The Serpent Son, Happy Days (Dir by Beckett), A Tale of Two Cities, Jamaica Inn, Private Schultz, Camille, Old Girlfriends, The Picnic, The Secret Garden, Imaginary Friends, The Entertainer, The 15 Streets, Footfalls, Rockaby, Eh Joe, Duel of Love, Lorna Doone, Murder of Quality, The Cloning of Joanna May, Firm Friends, Born to Run, Shooting the Past, A Dinner of Herbs (miniseries), Last of the Blonde Bombshells 2000. *Plays for radio:* The Master Builder, Hindle Wakes, Jane Eyre, The Female Messiah, Alpha Beta, Marching Song, The Cherry Orchard, Vassa, Beckett's All that Fall, Embers, Beckett Evening (one-woman) 1997. *Publication:* Billie Whitelaw – Who He? (memoirs) 1995. *Leisure interest:* pottering about the house. *Address:* c/o Michael Foster, ICM, Oxford House, 76 Oxford Street, London, W1N 0AX, England.

WHITEREAD, Rachel, CBE; British artist and sculptor; b. 20 April 1963, London, England; d. of Thomas Whiteread and Patricia Whiteread; partner Marcus Taylor; two s.; ed Brighton Polytechnic, Slade School of Art, Univ. Coll. London; some works use casts of sinks, baths, beds, mattresses, floors and mortuary slabs; work includes 'Ghost', a white plaster cast of an entire room shown at Chisenhale Gallery, London 1990 and 'House', a cast of an entire London terraced house on show in Bow, East London 1993–94; Hon. DLitt (Brighton Polytechnic) 1998, (Univ. of East London) 1998; Turner Prize 1993, Venice Biennale Award for Best Young Artist 1997. *Publication:* Whiteread 2007. *Address:* c/o Gagosian Gallery, 6–24 Britannia Street, London, WC1X 9JD, England. *Telephone:* (20) 7841-9960. *Fax:* (20) 7841-9961. *E-mail:* info@gagosian.com (office). *Website:* www.gagosian.com.

WHITESIDES, George M., PhD, FInstP; American chemist and academic; *Mallinckrodt Professor of Chemistry, Harvard University;* b. 3 Aug. 1939, Louisville, Ky; ed Harvard Univ. and Calif. Inst. of Tech.; mem. Faculty, MIT 1963–82; mem. Faculty, Dept of Chem., Harvard Univ. 1982–86, Chair. 1986–89, Mallinckrodt Prof. of Chem. 1989–; mem. Defense Advanced Research Projects Agency, Defense Science Research Council, US Dept of Defense 1984–, Defense Science Bd 1993–, Threat Reduction Advisory Cttee to Defense Threat Reduction Agency 1998–; Chair. NSF Chem. Advisory Cttee 1986, Nat. Research Council Bd of Chemical Sciences and Tech. 1986–99, NSF Materials Research Advisory Cttee 1993; mem. Scientific Advisory Cttee, Scripps Research Inst. 1993–; mem. NSF Sr Assessment Panel: Int. Assessment of US Math. Sciences 1997; mem. Nat. Research Council Bd on Physics and Astronomy 1997–; Ed. Science Reviewing; mem. Editorial Bd Journal of Applied Biochemistry and Biotechnology, BioOrganic Chemistry, BioOrganic and Medicinal Chemistry Letters, Chemistry of Materials, Journal of Physical Chemistry, Angewandte Chemie, Chemistry and Biology, Langmuir, Nanotechnology, Colloids and Surfaces B: Biointerfaces; mem. American Acad. of Arts and Sciences, NAS, Nat. Acad. of Eng, American Philosophical Soc., World Tech. Network, Royal Netherlands Acad. of Arts and Sciences, Institut de France-Acad. des sciences 2010; Fellow, AAAS, New York Acad. of Science; Foreign Fellow, Indian Nat. Science Acad. 2000; Hon. mem. Materials Research Soc. of India; Hon. Fellow, Chemical Research Soc. of India 2000; Hon. FRSC; Wallac Oy Innovation Award in High Throughput Screening, Soc. for Biomolecular Screening, ACS (Sierra Nevada Section) Distinguished Chemist Award, Alfred P. Sloan Fellowship 1968, ACS Award in Pure Chem. 1975, ACS (Rochester Section) Harrison Howe Award 1979, Alumni Distinguished Service Award, Calif. Inst. of Tech. 1980, ACS (Maryland Section) Remsen Award 1983, ACS Arthur C. Cope Scholar Award 1989, 1995, ACS (New England Section)

James Flack Norris Award 1994, ACS Madison Marshall Award 1996, Award for Significant Tech. Achievement, Defense Advanced Research Projects Agency 1996, Nat. Medal of Science, Nat. Science Bd 1998, Award for Excellence in Surface Science, Surfaces in Biomaterials Foundation 1999, Von Hippel Award, Materials Research Soc. 2000, Dan David Prize 2005, ACS Priestley Medal 2007, Scientist of the Year, R&D Magazine 2007, August Wilhelm von Hofmann Lecture, German Chemical Soc. 2007, Gold Medal, American Inst. of Chemists 2007, Wheland Medal, Univ. of Chicago 2008, Outstanding Achievement Award in Nanotechnology, Ohio State Univ. 2008, Nanoscience Prize, Int. Soc. for Nanoscale Science, Computation and Eng 2008, Prince of Asturias Award in Science and Tech. (Spain) 2008, Benjamin Franklin Medal in Chem., Franklin Foundation 2009, Popular Mechanics Breakthrough Award 2009, 100 Most Creative People, FAST Company 2009, Dreyfus Prize in the Chemical Sciences 2009, IKCOC Prize, Int. Kyoto Conf. on Organic Chem. 2009, Othmer Gold Medal, Chemical Heritage Foundation 2010, King Faisal Int. Prize for Science (co-recipient) 2011. *Publications:* more than 630 articles in scientific journals on materials science, biophysics, surface science, polyvalency, microfluidics, optics, self-assembly, microfabrication, nanotechnology and cell surface biochemistry. *Address:* Department of Chemistry and Chemical Biology, Harvard University, Mallinckrodt 232, 12 Oxford Street, Cambridge, MA 02138, USA (office). *Telephone:* (617) 495-9430 (office). *Fax:* (617) 495-9857 (office). *E-mail:* gwhitesides@gmwgroup.harvard.edu (office). *Website:* gmwgroup.harvard .edu (office).

WHITLAM, (Edward) Gough, AC, QC, BA, LLB, FAHA; Australian politician and diplomatist; b. 11 July 1916, Melbourne, Vic.; s. of the late H. F. E. Whitlam and Martha Whitlam (née Maddocks); m. Margaret Dovey 1942 (died 2012); three s. one d.; ed Knox Grammar School, Sydney, Canberra High School, Canberra Grammar School and Univ. of Sydney; RAAF 1941–45; admitted to NSW Bar 1947; mem. House of Reps. 1952–78; mem. Parl. Cttee on Constitutional Review 1956–59; mem. Federal Parl. Exec. of Australian Labor Party 1959–77; Deputy Leader of Australian Labor Party in Fed. Parl. 1960–67, Leader 1967–77; Leader of the Opposition 1967–72, 1975–77; Prime Minister 1972–75, concurrently Minister of Foreign Affairs 1972–73; Rep. to UNESCO, Paris 1983–86, mem. Exec. Bd 1985–89; mem. Australian Constitutional Convention 1973–76, Independent Comm. on Int. Humanitarian Issues 1983–86, Constitutional Comm. 1986–88; Chair. Australia-China Council 1986–91, Australian Nat. Gallery 1987–90; Vice-Pres. Socialist Int. 1976–77, Hon. Pres. 1983–; Visiting Fellow (lecturing in Political Science and Int. Relations) Australian Nat. Univ. 1978–80, Nat. Fellow 1980–81; Fellow Univ. of Sydney Senate 1981–83, 1986–89; Pres. Int. Comm. of Jurists (Australian Section) 1982–83; Visiting Prof., Harvard Univ., USA 1979; f. Hanoi Architectural Heritage Foundation 1993; mem. Sydney Olympics 2000 del. to Africa 1993; Corresp. mem. Acad. of Athens 1992; Hon. Pres. Australian Nat. Council for the Celebration of the Bicentenary of the French Revolution 1989; Grand Cross, Order of Makarios III (Cyprus) 1983, Grand Commdr, Order of Honour (Greece) 1996, Grand Cross of the Order of the Phoenix (Greece) 1998, Grande Ufficiale nell' Ordine Al Merito (Italy) 1999, Grand Cross of the Apostle Andrew (Greek Orthodox Archdiocese of Australia) 2002, Grand Companion of the Order of Logohu (Papua New Guinea) 2005, Grand Cordon, Order of the Rising Sun (Japan) 2006; Hon. LLD (The Philippines) 1974; Hon. DLitt (Sydney) 1981, (Wollongong) 1989, (La Trobe, Wodonga) 1992, (Univ. of Tech., Sydney) 1995, (Univ. of Western Sydney) 2002; Socialist Int. Silver Plate of Honour 1976, Mem. of Honour Int. Union for Nature Conservation (now World Conservation Union) 1988, Australian Library and Information Assoc Redmond Barry Award 1994. *Publications:* On Australia's Constitution (articles and lectures 1957–77) 1977, The Truth of the Matter 1979, A Pacific Community (Harvard lectures) 1981, The Whitlam Government 1985, Living with the United States: British Dominions and New Pacific States 1990, Hellenism in the Antipodes 1993, Abiding Interests 1997, My Italian Notebook 2002. *Address:* Level 14, 100 William Street, Sydney, NSW 2011, Australia (home). *Telephone:* (2) 9358-2022 (home). *Fax:* (2) 358-2753 (home).

WHITMAN, Christine Todd, BA; American consultant and fmr politician; *President, Whitman Strategy Group;* b. 26 Sept. 1946, New York, NY; d. of Webster Bray Todd and Eleanor Schley Todd; m. John R. Whitman 1974; two c.; ed Wheaton Coll.; fmr freeholder, Somerset Co., NJ; fmr Pres. State Bd of Public Utilities; Gov. of New Jersey 1994–2001; Admin. US Environmental Protection Agency, Washington, DC 2001–03; Pres. Whitman Strategy Group (consulting firm), Washington, DC 2006–; Co-Chair. Republican Leadership Council 2007–11, Clean and Safe mem. Bd of Dirs S.C. Johnson & Son, Inc., Texas Instruments Inc., United Technologies Corpn, American Security Project, Center for Sustainable Shale Devt, 2014 NY/NJ Super Bowl Host Cttee, Council on Foreign Relations; Trustee, Eisenhower Fellowships; adviser, Aspen Rodel Fellowship Program; mem. Advisory Bd, Corporate Eco Forum; Republican. *Publication:* It's My Party Too 2005. *Address:* Whitman Strategy Group, 116 Village Boulevard, Suite 200, Princeton, NJ 08540 (office); Whitman Strategy Group, 888 16th Street NW, Suite 800, Washington, DC 20006, USA (office). *Telephone:* (609) 524-4068 (Princeton) (office); (202) 355-1374 (Washington, DC) (office); (646) 330-4850 (NY) (office). *E-mail:* christie@christiewhitman.com (office). *Website:* www.whitmanstrategygroup.com (office); www.christiewhitman.com.

WHITMAN, Margaret (Meg) Cushing, AB, MBA; American business executive and fmr politician; *President and CEO, Hewlett-Packard Company;* b. 4 Aug. 1956, Cold Spring Harbor, Long Island, NY; d. of Hendricks Hallett Whitman and Margaret Whitman (née Goodhue); m. Griffith R. Harsh IV; two s.; ed Cold Spring Harbor High School, Princeton Univ., Harvard Business School; Brand Asst, Procter & Gamble, Cincinnati, Ohio 1979–81; with Bain & Co., San Francisco, Calif. 1982–89, becoming Vice-Pres.; Sr Vice-Pres. Marketing in Consumer Products Div., Walt Disney Co. 1989–92; Pres. Stride Rite Div., Stride Rite Corpn 1993–95, Exec. Vice-Pres. Keds Div.; Pres. and CEO Florists Transworld Delivery 1995–97, leading launch of co.'s internet strategy; Gen. Man. Hasbro Inc.'s Preschool Div., Brand Man. responsible for global marketing of Playskool and Mr Potato Head brands 1997–98; mem. Bd of Dirs, Pres. and CEO eBay Inc. 1998–2008, mem. Bd of Dirs eBay Foundation –2009; co-f., with her husband, Griffith R. Harsh IV and Margaret C Whitman Charitable Foundation 2006; unsuccessful Republican cand. for Gov. of Calif. 2010; mem. Bd of Dirs Hewlett-Packard Co. Jan. 2011–, Pres. and CEO Sept. 2011–; Strategic Advisor (part-time), Kleiner Perkins Caufield & Byers March–Sept. 2011; mem. Bd of Dirs Goldman

Sachs 2001–02, Gap Inc. 2003–06, Procter & Gamble 2003–09, DreamWorks Animation SKG, Inc. 2005–09; Co-Trustee, Princeton Univ.; named by Business Week magazine amongst 25 Most Powerful Business Managers annually 2000–, ranked number one by Worth magazine on its list of Best CEOs 2002, ranked by Fortune magazine amongst the 50 Most Powerful Women in Business in the US (third) 2002, (second) 2003, (first) 2004–05, (third) 2006–07, (ninth) 2011, (third) 2012, also ranked by Fortune magazine amongst 25 Most Powerful People in Business 2004, ranked by Forbes magazine amongst The World's 100 Most Powerful Women (51st) 2004, (fifth) 2005, (22nd) 2006, (22nd) 2007, (47th) 2010, (18th) 2012, (15th) 2013, named by TIME magazine as one of the World's 100 Most Influential People 2004, 2005, named by The Wall Street Journal as one of the 50 Women to Watch 2005. *Publication:* The Power of Many: Values for Success in Business and in Life 2010. *Address:* Hewlett-Packard Company, 3000 Hanover Street, MS 1050, Palo Alto, CA 94304-1185, USA (office). *Telephone:* (650) 857-1501 (office). *Fax:* (650) 857-5518 (office). *E-mail:* bod@hp.com (office). *Website:* www.hp.com (office).

WHITMAN, Marina von Neumann, BS, MA, PhD; American economist and academic; *Professor of Business Administration and Public Policy, Stephen M. Ross School of Business Administration and Professor of Public Policy, Gerald R. Ford School of Public Policy, University of Michigan;* b. (Marina von Neumann), 6 March 1935, New York, NY; d. of John von Neumann and Mariette Kovesi (Mrs J. B. H. Kuper); m. Robert F. Whitman 1956; one s. one d.; ed Radcliffe Coll., Cambridge, Mass, Columbia Univ., New York; Lecturer in Econs, Univ. of Pittsburgh 1962–64, Asst Prof. 1964–66, Assoc. Prof. 1966–71, Prof. of Econs 1971–73, Distinguished Public Service Prof. 1973–79; Sr Staff Economist, Council of Econ. Advisers 1970–71; mem. President's Price Comm. 1971–72; mem. Pres.'s Council of Econ. Advisers (with special responsibility for int. monetary and trade problems) 1972–73; Vice-Pres. and Chief Economist, Gen. Motors Corpn, New York 1979–85, Group Exec. Vice-Pres. for Public Affairs 1985–92; Distinguished Visiting Prof. of Business Admin. and Public Policy, Univ. of Michigan 1992–94, Prof. 1994–, currently Prof. of Business Admin. and Public Policy, Stephen M. Ross School of Business Admin. and Prof. of Public Policy, Gerald R. Ford School of Public Policy; mem. Trilateral Comm. 1973, Bd of Dirs Council on Foreign Relations 1977–87, Peterson Inst.; mem. Bd of Dirs J. P. Morgan Chase Corpn 1973–2002, Procter and Gamble Co. 1976–2003, Alcoa 1993–2002, Unocal 1993–2005; mem. Bd of Overseers Harvard Univ. 1972–78, Bd of Trustees, Princeton Univ. 1980–90; mem. Group of Thirty Consultative Group on Int. Econ. and Monetary Affairs, Inc. (G-30), Washington, DC 1979–; more than 20 hon. degrees. *Publications:* New World, New Rules: The Changing Role of the American Corporation 1999, The Martian's Daughter: A Memoir 2012; numerous books and articles on econ. topics. *Address:* Gerald R. Ford School of Public Policy, University of Michigan, Weill Hall, 735 South State Street #3228, Ann Arbor, MI 48109-3091, USA (office). *Telephone:* (734) 763-4173 (office). *Fax:* (734) 763-9181 (office). *E-mail:* marinaw@umich.edu (office). *Website:* www.fordschool.umich.edu (office).

WHITNEY, John Norton Braithwaite, CBE, FRSA; British broadcasting executive; b. 20 Dec. 1930, Gerrards Cross, Bucks., England; s. of Willis Bevan Whitney and Dorothy Anne Whitney; m. Roma Elizabeth Hodgson 1956; one s. one d.; ed Leighton Park Friends' School, Reading; radio producer 1951–64; set up Ross Radio Productions Ltd 1951, Autocue Ltd 1955; f. Radio Antilles 1963; Man. Dir Capital Radio 1973–82; Dir-Gen. Ind. Broadcasting Authority 1982–89; Man. Dir The Really Useful Group 1989–90, Chair. 1990–95, Dir 1990–97; Dir VCI PLC 1995–98; Chair. The Radio Partnership Ltd 1996–99; Chair. Caspian Publishing Ltd 1996–2002; Dir Galaxy Media Corp PLC 1997–2000, Bird and Co. International 1999–2001, Friends Provident PLC 2001–02; wrote, edited and devised numerous TV series 1956–82; mem. Bd Royal Nat. Theatre 1992–94, City of London Sinfonia 1994–2001; Founder-Dir Sagitta Productions 1968–82; Dir Duke of York's Theatre 1979–82, Consolidated Productions (UK) Ltd 1980–82, Friends' Provident Life Office 1982–2001 (Chair. Friends' Provident Stewardship Cttee of Reference 1985–2000); Chair. Theatre Investment Fund 1990–2001, Trans-World Communications PLC 1992–94, Sony Music Pace Partnership (Nat. Bowl) 1992–95, Rajar Ltd 1992–2002, Friends' Provident Ethical Investment Trust PLC 1992–2001; Trustee Pension and Life Assurance Plan RNT 1994–2003; Chair. and co-f. Local Radio Asscn 1964; Chair. Asscn of Ind. Local Radio Contractors 1973–75, 1980; f. Recidivists Anonymous Fellowship Trust 1962; mem. Films, TV & Video Advisory Cttee, British Council 1983–89, Royal Coll. of Music Centenary Devt Fund 1982–84 (Chair. Media & Events Cttee 1982–94), Royal Jubilee Trusts Industry & Commerce Liaison Cttee 1986–88 (mem. Admin. Council of Trusts 1981–85); mem. Council Royal London Aid Soc. 1966–90, Fairbridge Drake Soc. 1981–96, Intermediate Tech. Group 1982–85, Council for Charitable Support 1989–92; Pres. TV & Radio Industries Club 1985–86, London Marriage Guidance Council 1983–90; Vice-Pres. Commonwealth Youth Exchange Council 1982–85, RNID 1981–2003; Chair. Trustees, Soundaround 1981–2000, Artsline 1983–2000; Chair. Festival Media Cttee 1991–92, British American Arts Asscn 1992–95, Sony Radio Awards 1992–98, Friends Provident Charitable Foundation 2002–06, RADA 2003–07; mem. Bd Open Coll. 1987–89; Gov. English Nat. Ballet 1989–91, Performing Arts and Tech. School; Fellow and Vice-Pres. Royal Television Soc. 1986–89; Trustee, Venture Trust 1982–86, Japan Festival Educ. Trust 1992–2003; Patron Music Space Trust 1990–; Hon. FRCM; Hon. mem. BAFTA. *Publication:* To Serve the People 2013. *Leisure interests:* chess, photography, sculpture. *Address:* The Long Barn, 5 Church Close, Todber, Dorset, DT10 1JH, England. *E-mail:* john@johnwhitney.co.uk (office).

WHITNEY, Meredith Ann, BA; American business analyst; *CEO, Meredith Whitney Advisory Group LLC;* b. 20 Nov. 1969; m. John 'Bradshaw' Layfield 2005; ed Brown Univ., Providence, RI; joined Oppenheimer & Co. Inc. as a research analyst 1993, with Specialty Finance Group 1995–98, returned to Oppenheimer & Co. Inc. 2004, Man. Dir and Sr Financial Analyst 2008–09; Head of Financial Insts Research, Wachovia Securities 1998–2001; Analyst, FrontPoint Partners 2001–04; Sr Financial Insts Analyst, CIBC World Markets 2004–07; Founder and CEO Meredith Whitney Advisory Group LLC 2009–; frequent contrib. to CNBC, Fox Business and Bloomberg News programs; listed as the second best stock picker in the capital markets industry on Forbes.com's list of The Best Analysts: Stock Pickers 2007, named one of NY Post's 50 Most Powerful Women in NYC 2007, ranked by Fortune magazine amongst the 50 Most Powerful Women in Business in the US (38th) 2008, (39th) 2009, (38th) 2010, (48th) 2011, Power Player of the Year, CNBC 2008. *Address:* Meredith Whitney Advisory Group LLC, 50 West 57th Street, 2nd Floor, New York, NY 10019, USA (office). *Telephone:* (212) 542-4320 (office). *E-mail:* info@meredithwhitneyllc.com (office). *Website:* www.meredithwhitneyllc.com (office).

WHITTAM SMITH, Andreas, CBE; British journalist; b. 13 June 1937; s. of Canon J. E. Smith; m. Valerie Catherine Sherry 1964; two s.; ed Keble Coll., Oxford; with N. M. Rothschild 1960–62, Stock Exchange Gazette 1962–63, Financial Times 1963–64, The Times 1964–66; Deputy City Ed. The Telegraph 1966–69; City Ed. The Guardian 1969–70; Ed. Investors Chronicle, Stock Exchange Gazette and Dir Throgmorton Pubs 1970–77; City Ed. Daily Telegraph 1977–85; Ed. The Independent 1986–94, Ed.-in-Chief Independent on Sunday 1991–94, Dir Newspaper Publishing PLC 1986–, CEO 1987–93, Chair. 1994–95; f. Democracy 2015 movement 2012; Chair., Publr Notting Hill 1995–, Sir Winston Churchill Archive Trust 1995–2000, Financial Ombudsman Service Ltd. 1999–2003; Pres. British Bd of Film Classification 1998–2002; First Church Estates Commr; Vice-Pres. Nat. Council for One Parent Families 1982–86, 1991–; currently commentator, The Independent; Hon. Fellow, Keble Coll., Oxford, UMIST 1989, Liverpool John Moores 2001; Dr hc (Bath) 1988; Hon. DLitt (St Andrew's, Salford) 1989; Wincott Award 1975, Journalist of the Year 1987. *Leisure interests:* music, history, walking. *Address:* c/o The Independent, 2 Derry Street, London W8 5HF, England (office). *Website:* www.democracy2015.co.uk (office).

WHITTLE, Peter, PhD, FRS; New Zealand mathematician and academic; *Professor Emeritus, Statistical Laboratory, University of Cambridge;* b. 27 Feb. 1927, Wellington; s. of Percy Whittle and Elsie (née Tregurtha) Whittle; m. Kathe Hildegard Blomquist 1951; three s. three d.; ed Wellington Boys' Coll., Victoria Univ. Coll., NZ, Uppsala Univ., Sweden; NZ Sr Prin. Scientific Officer 1953–59; Lecturer in Math. Univ. of Cambridge 1959–61, Churchill Prof. of the Math. of Operational Research 1967–94, Prof. Emer. 1994–; Prof. of Math. Statistics, Univ. of Manchester 1961–67; Sr Fellow, Science and Eng Research Council 1988–91; mem. Royal Soc. of NZ 1981; Hon. DSc (Victoria Univ. of Wellington) 1987; Lanchester Prize, Operational Research Soc. of America 1987, Sylvester Medal (Royal Soc.) 1994, Guy Medal in Gold, Royal Statistical Soc. 1996, J. von Neumann Theory Medal, Inst. of Operational Research Man. Science 1997. *Publications:* Hypothesis Testing in Time Series Analysis 1951, Prediction and Regulation 1963, Probability 1970, Optimisation under Constraints 1971, Optimisation over Time 1982, Systems in Stochastic Equilibrium 1986, Risk-sensitive Optimal Control 1990, Probability via Expectation 1992, Optimal Control; Basics and Beyond 1995, Neural Nets and Chaotic Carriers 1998. *Leisure interests:* variable. *Address:* Statistical Laboratory, Pavilion D, Centre for Mathematical Studies, Wilberforce Road, Cambridge, CB3 0WB (office); 268 Queen Edith's Way, Cambridge, CB1 8NL, England (home). *Telephone:* (1223) 245422 (home). *Fax:* (1223) 337956. *E-mail:* whittle@statslab.cam.ac.uk (office). *Website:* www.statslab.cam.ac.uk (office).

WHITTLE, Stephen Charles, OBE, LLB, FRSA; British broadcasting executive; b. 26 July 1945, London, England; s. of Charles William Whittle and Vera Lillian Whittle (née Moss); m. 1st Claire Walmsley 1988 (divorced 1999); m. 2nd Eve Salomon 2004; ed St Ignatius Coll., Stamford Hill, Univ. Coll., London; Asst Ed. New Christian 1968–70; Communications Officer, World Council of Churches, Geneva 1970–73; Ed. One World 1973–77, Asst Head Communications Dept 1975–77; Sr Producer BBC Religious Programmes, Manchester 1977–82, Producer Newsnight 1982, Ed. Songs of Praise and Worship 1983–89, Head of Religious Programmes 1989–93, Chief Adviser, Editorial Policy 1993–96; Dir Broadcasting Standards Council 1996–97, Broadcasting Standards Comm. 1997–2001; Controller of Editorial Policy, BBC 2001–05; Chair. Broadcast Equality and Training Regulator 2007–11; Gov. European Inst. for the Media, Düsseldorf 1997–2002; Visiting Fellow, Reuters Inst. for the Study of Journalism, Oxford 2007–; mem. Solicitors Regulation Authority 2005–12, Gen. Medical Council 2009–12; Expert for Council of Europe; Freeman, City of London 1990; Personal Award, Sandford St Martin Trust 1993. *Publication:* Privacy, Probity and Public Interest 2009. *Leisure interests:* cinema, theatre, music, reading, walking. *Address:* 4 Carmarthen Place, London, SE1 3TS, England (home). *Telephone:* (20) 7407-2016 (home). *E-mail:* stephen_whittle@btopenworld.com (office).

WHITWAM, David R., BS; American business executive; b. Madison, Wis.; ed Univ. of Wisconsin; joined Whirlpool Corpn 1968, various sr and marketing positions including Vice-Pres. Whirlpool brand business 1983–85, mem. Bd of Dirs 1985–, Vice-Chair. and Chief Marketing Officer 1985–87, Pres. 1987–92, Chair. and CEO 1987–2004 (retd); mem. Bd of Dirs PPG Industries Inc., Business Roundtable Policy Cttee and Educ. Task Force; Chair. Mich. Business Leaders for Educational Excellence Org.; Trustee Univ. of Wis. Alumni Research Foundation. *Address:* c/o Whirlpool Corporation, 2000 North M-63, Benton Harbor, MI 49022-2692, USA (office).

WHITWORTH, Ralph Victor, BA, JD; American business executive and philanthropist; *Principal, Relational Investors LLC;* b. 1955, Nev.; ed Univ. of Nevada, Reno, Georgetown Univ. Law Center; Supt of Parks and Recreation, Winnemucca, Nev. 1974–78; began career serving on US Senate Judiciary Cttee Staff of Senator Paul Laxalt 1981–84; Asst to Gen. Partner, Mesa Ltd Partnership under T. Boone Pickens 1985–88; Pres. of Devt, United Thermal Corpn 1989–92, mem. Bd of Dirs 1989–93, chaired special cttee to represent minority shareholders during its sale to Trigen Energy Corpn; Pres. (pro bono) United Shareholders Asscn 1986–94; Chair. Apria Healthcare Group 1998–2005; Chair. Waste Management Inc. 1999, mem. Bd of Dirs and Chair. Nominating and Governance Cttee –2004; mem. or fmr mem. Bd of Dirs Mattel, Sirius Satellite Radio, Tektronix, Inc., Sprint Nextel, Wilshire Technologies, Inc., United Thermal Corpn, Sovereign Bancorp, Genzyme Corpn, Hewlett-Packard Co. 2011– (Interim Chair. 2013–); Co-founder and Prin. Relational Investors LLC, San Diego, Calif. 1996–; mem. Bd of Trustees, Georgetown Univ. Law Center, The Bishop's School, La Jolla, Calif.; Dir of the Year, Corp. Dirs Forum 2004. *Address:* Relational Investors LLC, 12400 High Bluff Drive, Suite 600, San Diego, CA 92130, USA (office). *Telephone:* (858) 704-3333 (office). *Fax:* (858) 704-3344 (office). *E-mail:* info@rillc.com (office). *Website:* www.rillc.com (office).

WHITWORTH-JONES, Anthony, CA; British arts administrator; b. 1 Sept. 1945, Bucks., England; s. of Henry Whitworth-Jones and Patience Martin; m.

Camilla Barlow 1974; one d.; ed Wellington Coll.; Admin. Dir London Sinfonietta 1972–81; Admin. Glyndebourne Touring Opera 1981–89, Opera Man. Glyndebourne Festival Opera 1981–89, Gen. Dir Glyndebourne 1989–98; Chair. Michael Tippett Musical Foundation 1998–; Gen. Dir The Dallas Opera 2000–02; Artistic Dir Casa da Musica, Oporto, Portugal 2004–05, Artistic Consultant 2007–08; Gen. Dir Garsington Opera 2005–12; mem. Bd Spitalfields Festival 2003–06 (Hon. Advisor 2006–), Young Concert Artists Trust 2006–, ENO 2012–; Trustee, Leonard Ingrams Foundation 2006–. *Leisure interests:* the arts, jazz, golf, mountains. *Address:* 81 St Augustine's Road, London, NW1 9RR, England (home). *Telephone:* (20) 7267-3154 (home). *Fax:* (20) 7482-7017 (home). *E-mail:* awjones@onetel.com (office).

WHYBROW, John W., BSc, MBA; British business executive; *Chairman, Wolseley PLC;* b. 11 March 1947; m.; two c.; ed Imperial Coll. London, Manchester Business School; joined Philips 1970, apptd Man.-Dir Philips Power Semiconductors and Microwave business 1987, Chair. and Man.-Dir Philips Electronics UK –1995, Pres. and CEO Philips Lighting Holding BV, The Netherlands 1995–2001, Exec. Vice-Pres. Royal Philips Electronics and mem. Bd of Man. 1998–2002; Dir (non-exec.) Wolseley PLC 1997, Chair. Remuneration Cttee 1998–2002, Deputy Chair. April–Dec. 2002, Chair. 2002–, Chair. Nominations Cttee; Chair. CSR PLC 2004–07; Dir (non-exec.) DSG International PLC 2003–; Chair. Petworth Cottage Nursing Home; Order of Merit for Services to Econ. Devt of Poland (Poland) 2002. *Leisure interests:* sailing, shooting. *Address:* Wolseley PLC, Parkview 1220, Arlington Business Park, Theale, West Berks., RG7 4GA, England (office). *Telephone:* (118) 9298700 (office). *Fax:* (118) 9298701 (office). *E-mail:* info@wolseley.com (office). *Website:* www.wolseley.com (office).

WIATR, Jerzy Józef, MPh, PhD; Polish politician and sociologist; *Rector, European School of Law and Administration;* b. 17 Sept. 1931, Warsaw; s. of Wilhelm Wiatr and Zofia Wiatr; m. Ewa Żurowska-Wiatr; one s.; ed Warsaw Univ.; Asst Warsaw Univ. 1951–59; Mil. Political Acad. 1959–65; Polish Acad. of Sciences (PAN) 1965–69; Prof., Warsaw Univ. 1969–2001, Dean of Social Sciences 1977–80; participant Round Table debates 1989; Deputy to Sejm (Parl.) 1991–2001; mem. Cttee for Nat. Defence and Cttee for Constitutional Responsibility 1991–97; Minister of Educ. 1996–97; Dir Inst. for Social and International Studies, Keller-Krauz Foundation 1998–; Pres. Cen. European Political Science Asscn 2000–03; Vice-Pres. International Political Science Asscn 1979–82; Vice-Pres. International Studies Asscn 1980–81; mem. Polish United Workers Party (PZPR) 1949–90; mem. Social Democracy of Polish Repub. (SdRP) 1990–99; mem. Democratic Left Alliance 1999–; Rector, European School of Law and Admin, Warsaw 2007–; Hon. Senator Univ. of Ljubljana 2006, Hon. Pres. Cen. European Political Science Asscn 2009; Commdr's Cross with Star of Polonia Restituta Order 1996. *Publications include:* over 30 books including Education For and In the 21st Century 1997; numerous articles on sociology and political science. *Leisure interests:* tourism, books, chess. *Address:* European School of Law and Administration, Grudzienska 21/29, 03 750 Warsaw (office); ul. Komisji Edukacji Narodowej 98/49, 02 777 Warsaw, Poland (home). *Telephone:* (22) 619-90-11 (office); (22) 643-54-41 (home). *Fax:* (22) 643-54-41 (home). *E-mail:* jwiatr@ewspa.edu.pl (office). *Website:* www .ewspa.edu.pl (office).

WIBERG, Kenneth Berle, PhD; American academic; *Professor Emeritus of Chemistry, Yale University;* b. 22 Sept. 1927, New York, NY; s. of Halfdan Wiberg and Solveig Berle; m. Marguerite Louise Koch 1951; two s. one d.; ed Mass Inst. of Tech. and Columbia Univ., New York; Instructor, Univ. of Washington 1950–52, Asst Prof. 1952–55, Assoc. Prof. 1955–57, Prof. 1958–62; Prof., Yale Univ. 1962–68, Chair. Dept of Chem. 1968–71, Whitehead Prof. of Chem. 1968–90, Eugene Higgins Prof. 1990–97, Prof. Emer. 1997–; Visiting Prof., Harvard Univ. 1957–58; mem. NAS, AAAS; Sloan Foundation Fellow 1958–62, Guggenheim Fellow 1961–62, ACS California Section Award 1962, ACS J.F. Norris Award 1973, ACS Arthur C. Cope Award 1988, Linus Pauling Award 1992. *Publications:* Laboratory Technique in Organic Chemistry 1960, Interpretation of NMR Spectra 1964, Physical Organic Chemistry 1964, Oxidation in Organic Chemistry (ed.) 1965, Computer Programming for Chemists 1966, Sigma Molecular Orbital Theory (with Sinanoglu) 1970; approx. 400 articles in scientific journals. *Address:* 865 Central Avenue, Apt A404, Needham, MA 02492, USA. *Telephone:* (781) 400-5039. *E-mail:* kenneth.wiberg@yale.edu.

WICKER, Roger Frederick, BA, JD; American lawyer and politician; *Senator from Mississippi;* b. 5 July 1951, Pontotoc, Miss.; m. Gayle Long; one s. two d.; ed Univ. of Mississippi; Judge Advocate and Capt. in USAF 1976–80, Lt-Col in USAF Reserve 1980–2004; Pnr, Sparks, Wicker & Colburn (law firm) 1982–94; public defender, Lee Co., Miss. 1984–87; judge pro tempore, Tupelo, Miss. 1986–87; mem. Mississippi State Senate 1987–94; mem. US House of Reps from 1st Miss. Dist 1995–2007, Deputy Majority Whip; Senator from Mississippi 2007–, mem. Armed Services Cttee, Commerce, Science, and Transportation Cttee, Veterans' Affairs Cttee; Republican, mem. Republican Policy Cttee 2001–. *Address:* 555 Dirksen Senate Office Building, Washington, DC 20510, USA (office). *Telephone:* (202) 224-6253 (office). *Fax:* (202) 228-0378 (office). *Website:* wicker.senate.gov (office).

WICKER-MIURIN, Fields, OBE, BA, MA, FRSA, FKC; American/British company director; *Co-founder and Partner, Leaders' Quest Limited;* b. (Jane Fields Wicker), 30 July 1958, USA; d. of Warren Jake Wicker and Marie Peachee Wicker; m. Paolo Miurin; ed Univ. of Virginia, l'Institut d'Etudes Politiques, Paris, Johns Hopkins School of Advanced International Studies, Bologna, Italy and Washington, DC; Chief Financial Officer and Dir of Finance and Strategy, London Stock Exchange 1994–97; fmr Vice-Pres. A.T. Kearney (strategy consultancy), London; fmr Sr Partner, Mercer Man. Consulting London; fmr Man. Dir Vesta Capital Advisors (venture capital firm); Co-founder and Partner, Leaders' Quest Ltd 2002–; Dir (non-exec.) CDC Group 2004–, BNP Paribas 2011–, BILT Industries 2011–, SCOR SE 2013–, UK Ministry of Justice 2013–; fmr Dir (non-exec.) Bd of UK Dept of Trade and Industry (DTI), fmr Chair. DTI Investment Cttee, mem. DTI Tech. Strategy Bd 2002–08; fmr Dir (non-exec.) D. Carnegie & Co. AB, Royal London Insurance, United Business Media plc, Savills plc; mem. Advisory Council, Univ. of Virginia Batten School of Leadership; fmr mem. Nasdaq Tech. Advisory Cttee, Panel of Experts to advise EU Parl. on harmonization of financial services; fmr Fellow, World Econ. Forum; Gov. and Fellow, King's Coll. London; Global Leader for Tomorrow, World Econ. Forum. *Publications:* monthly column, The Earth Times; numerous articles in the financial press. *Leisure*

interests: horses, nature, music, ideas and the world. *Address:* Leaders' Quest Ltd, 11–13 Worple Way, Richmond-upon-Thames, Surrey, TW10 6DG, England (office). *Telephone:* (20) 8948-5200 (office). *Fax:* (20) 8332-6423 (office). *E-mail:* info@ leadersquest.org (office). *Website:* www.leadersquest.org (office).

WICKRAMANAYAKA, Hon. Ratnasiri; Sri Lankan politician; b. 5 May 1933; ed Dharmapala Vidyalaya, Pannipitiya, Ananda Coll., Colombo, Lincoln's Inn, London, UK; Pres. Ceylon Students' Asscn, UK 1955; elected mem. Mahajana Eksath Peramuna for Horana 1960; apptd Deputy Minister of Justice 1970; Gen. Sec. Sri Lankan Freedom Party 1977; won Kalutara Dist seat 1994; apptd Minister of Public Admin, Home Affairs and Plantation and Leader of the House 1994; Prime Minister of Sri Lanka 2000–01; Minister of Buddha Sasana and Religious Affairs 2000–02; Chair. United People's Freedom Alliance; Prime Minister and Minister of Internal Admin 2005–10; ex-officio Chair. Bd of Govs Cen. Cultural Fund. *Address:* c/o Prime Minister's Office, 58 Sir Ernest de Silva Mawatha, Colombo 7, Sri Lanka. *Telephone:* (11) 2575317. *E-mail:* pmo@pmoffice.gov.lk.

WICKRAMASINGHE, Nalin Chandra, BSc, MA, PhD, ScD (Cantab.), FIMA, FRAS, FRSA; British mathematician, astronomer, astrobiologist and academic; *Honorary Professor and Director, Buckingham Centre for Astrobiology, University of Buckingham;* b. 20 Jan. 1939, Colombo, Sri Lanka; s. of Percival H. Wickramasinghe and Theresa E. Wickramasinghe; m. Nelum Priyadarshini Pereira 1966; one s. two d.; ed Royal Coll., Colombo and Univs of Colombo and Cambridge; Research Fellow, Jesus Coll., Cambridge 1963–66, Fellow 1967–73, Tutor 1970–73; Staff mem. Inst. of Theoretical Astronomy, Univ. of Cambridge 1968–73; Prof. and Head of Dept of Applied Math. and Astronomy, Univ. Coll., Cardiff 1973–88; Prof. of Applied Math. and Astronomy, Univ. of Wales Coll. of Cardiff (now Cardiff Univ.) 1988–2006, Dir Cardiff Centre for Astrobiology 2000–10; Dir Buckingham Centre for Astrobiology, Univ. of Buckingham 2010–; Adjunct Prof., Ruhuna Univ., Sri Lanka; Dir Inst. of Fundamental Studies, Sri Lanka 1982–83; UNDP Consultant and Scientific Adviser to Pres. of Sri Lanka 1970–81; Visiting Prof., Univs of Ceylon, Maryland, Arizona and Kyoto 1966–70, Univ. of Western Ontario 1974–76, Inst. of Space and Astronomical Science, Japan 1993, Univ. of the West Indies, Mona, Kingston, Jamaica 1994; Fellow, Inst. of Math. and Its Applications; Hon. Prof., Univ. of Buckingham; Vidya Jyothi (Sri Lanka Nat. Honour) 1992; Hon. DLitt (Tokyo, Soka Univ.) 1996; Hon. DSc (Ruhuna Univ.); Dag Hammarskjöld Laureate in Science 1986, Scholarly Achievement Award of Inst. of Oriental Philosophy, Japan 1989, Sahabdeen Award for Science 1996. *Publications:* Interstellar Grains 1967, Light Scattering Functions for Small Particles with Applications in Astronomy 1973, The Cosmic Laboratory 1975; with Sir Fred Hoyle: Life Cloud: The Origin of Life in the Universe 1978, Diseases from Space 1979, The Origin of Life 1980, Evolution from Space 1981, Space Travellers, The Bringers of Life, Is Life an Astronomical Phenomenon? 1982, Why Neo-Darwinism Doesn't Work 1982, Proofs That Life Is Cosmic 1982, Fundamental Studies and the Future of Science 1984, From Grains to Bacteria 1984, Living Comets 1985, Archaeopteryx, the Primordial Bird: a case of fossil forgery 1986, Cosmic Life Force 1987, The Theory of Cosmic Grains 1991, Our Place in the Cosmos: the Unfinished Revolution 1993, Life on Mars? The Case for a Cosmic Heritage 1996; with F. D. Kahn and P. G. Mezger: Interstellar Matter 1972; with D. J. Morgan: Solid State Astrophysics 1976; with Daisaku Ikeda: 2000 A.D. – Emergent Perspectives 1992, Glimpses of Life, Time and Space 1994, Space and Eternal Life 1997, Cosmic Dragons 2001, A Journey with Fred Hoyle 2004, Comets and the Origin of Life (with J. Wickramasinghe and W. M. Napier) 2010, A Destiny of Cosmic Life: Chapters in the Life of an Astrobiologist 2014. *Leisure interests:* photography, poetry. *Address:* Buckingham Centre for Astrobiology, University of Buckingham, Buckingham, Bucks., MK18 1EG England (office); 24 Llwynypia Road, Lisvane, Cardiff, CF14 0SY, Wales (home). *Telephone:* (29) 2075-2146 (home); 7778-389243 (mobile). *E-mail:* chandra.wickramasinghe@ buckingham.ac.uk (office); ncwick@gmail.com (home). *Website:* www.buckingham .ac.uk/directory/professor-chandra-wickramasinghe (office); drchandra.org.

WICKREMASINGHE, Nishanta; Sri Lankan business executive; *Chairman, SriLankan Airlines Ltd;* brother-in-law of Mahinda Rajapaksa; m.; ed St Thomas Coll.; fmr Gen. Man. James Finlay Plantation Holdings Ltd; mem. Bd of Dirs SriLankan Airlines Ltd 2006–, Exec. Dir 2008–09, Acting Chair. 2008–09, Chair. 2009–; fmr mem. Volunteer Army. *Address:* SriLankan Airlines Ltd., Airline Centre, Bandaranaike International Airport, Katunayake, Sri Lanka (office). *Telephone:* (19) 7335555 (office). *Fax:* (19) 7335122 (office). *Website:* www .srilankan.lk (office).

WICKREMASINGHE, Ranil, LLB; Sri Lankan politician and lawyer; *Leader, United National Party;* b. 24 March 1949, Colombo; s. of Esmond Wickremasinghe; m. Maithree Wickremasinghe 1995; ed Royal Coll. of Colombo, Univ. of Colombo and Sri Lanka Law Coll.; attorney-at-law, Supreme Court; elected mem. Parl. 1977, 1989; Leader of House 1989–93; Deputy Minister of Foreign Affairs 1977–79; Minister of Youth Affairs and Employment 1978–89, of Educ. 1980–89, of Industries 1989–90, of Industries, Science and Tech. 1990–94; Prime Minister of Sri Lanka 1992, 2001–04, also Minister of Policy Devt and Implementation 2001–04; Leader, United Nat. Party 1994–, Leader of the Opposition 1994–2001, 2006–; cand. in presidential elections 1999, 2005. *Address:* United National Party (UNP), 30 Sir Marcu Fernando Mawatha, Colombo 7, Sri Lanka (office). *Telephone:* (11) 5636551 (office). *Fax:* (11) 2682905 (office). *E-mail:* info@unp.lk (office). *Website:* www.unp.lk (office).

WICKS, Sir Nigel Leonard, Kt, GCB, CVO, CBE, MA (London), MA (Cantab.); British business executive and civil servant (retd); *Chairman, British Bankers Association;* b. 16 June 1940; s. of the late Leonard Charles Wicks and Beatrice Irene Wicks; m. Jennifer Mary Coveney 1969; three s.; ed Beckenham and Penge Grammar School, Portsmouth Coll. of Tech., Univ. of Cambridge, Univ. of London; British Petroleum 1958–68; served HM Treasury 1968–75, 1978–83, Second Perm Sec. (Finance) 1989–2000; Pvt. Sec. to Prime Minister 1975–78; mem. Bd BNOC 1980–82; Econ. Minister Embassy, Washington and UK; Exec. Dir IMF and IBRD 1983–85; Prin. Pvt. Sec. to Prime Minister 1985–88; Pres. Monetary Cttee of EC 1993–98; Chair. Cttee on Standards in Public Life 2001–04, panel appointing initial members of the then-new Judicial Appointments Comm. 2005; Commr Jersey Financial Services Comm. 2007–12; Chair. CRESTCo (settlement system for UK and Irish securities) 2001–02, Deputy Chair. (following merger with Euroclear plc) 2002–06, Chair. 2007–13; Chair. British Bankers Asscn 2012–; Dir (non-exec.), Morgan Stanley 2004–06, The Edinburgh Investment Trust 2005–; mem. EU Cttee of 'Wise Men' on European Securities Regulation (the Lamfalussy group) 2000–01; Gov., King's Coll. School, Wimbledon; Grand Officier, Ordre grand-ducal de la Couronne de Chêne (Luxembourg); Hon. LLD (Bath) 1999, (Portsmouth). *Address:* British Bankers Association, Pinners Hall, 105–108 Old Broad Street, London, EC2N 1EX (office); Steeple Ashton, Lime Grove, West Clandon, Guildford, Surrey, GU4 7UT, England (home). *Telephone:* (20) 7216-8800 (office). *Fax:* (20) 7216-8811 (office). *E-mail:* info@bba.org.uk (office); nigel.wicks@ bigfoot.com (home). *Website:* www.bba.org.uk (office).

WIDDECOMBE, Rt Hon. Ann Noreen, PC, MA; British writer and fmr politician; b. 4 Oct. 1947, Bath, Somerset; d. of the late James Murray Widdecombe and of Rita Noreen Plummer; ed La Sainte Union Convent, Bath, Univ. of Birmingham, Lady Margaret Hall, Oxford; with Marketing Dept Unilever 1973–75; Sr Admin. Univ. of London 1975–87; contested Burnley 1979, Plymouth Devonport 1983; MP (Conservative) for Maidstone 1987–97, Maidstone and The Weald 1997–2010; Parl. Pvt. Sec. to Tristan Garel-Jones, MP 1990; Parl. Under-Sec. State Dept of Social Security 1990–93, Dept of Employment 1993–94; Minister for Employment 1994–95, Home Office 1995–97; Shadow Health Minister 1998–99, Shadow Home Sec. 1999–2001; columnist, Daily Express newspaper; Spectator/Highland Park Minister of the Year 1996, Despatch Box Best Front Bencher 1998, Talk Radio Straight Talker of the Year 1998. *Publications:* Layman's Guide to Defence 1984, Inspired and Outspoken 1999, The Clematis Tree (novel) 2000, An Act of Treachery 2001, An Act of Peace 2005, Father Figure 2005, Strictly Ann: The Autobiography 2013. *Leisure interests:* reading, researching Charles II's escape. *Address:* c/o United Agents, 12-26 Lexington St, London, W1F 0LE, England (office). *Website:* www.annwiddecombemp.com (office).

WIDJAJA, Eka Tjipta, (Oei Ek Tjhong); Indonesian (b. Chinese) business executive (retd); b. 1924, Fujian Prov., China; started business career as biscuit salesman, before moving into pulp, paper and palm oil industries; f. Sinar Mas Group (conglomerate), associated cos include Asian Pulp and Paper Co. Ltd, Golden Agri-Resources Ltd, Asia Food & Properties Ltd; numerous business concerns in People's Repub. of China; f. Eka Tjipta Foundation. *Address:* Eka Tjipta Foundation, Plaza BII, Tower 2, 33rd Floor, Jalan M.H. Thamrin, 51 Jakarta Pusat, 10350, Indonesia (office).

WIDMER-SCHLUMPF, Eveline, LLB, JD; Swiss lawyer and politician; *Head of Federal Department of Finance;* b. 16 March 1956, Felsberg, Graubünden; d. of Leon Schlumpf and Trudi Rupp; m.; three c.; ed Univ. of Zürich; admitted to the bar, Graubünden, pvt. practice as lawyer and notary public 1987–98; elected to Dist Court, Trin 1985, Pres. 1991–97; mem. Grosser Rat (Great Council), Graubünden 1994–98; elected to Regierungsrat 1998, Head, Cantonal Dept of Finance 1999–2007, Pres. Cantonal Council 2001, 2005; mem. Fed. Council 2008–, Head, Fed. Dept of Justice and Police 2008–10, Head, Fed. Dept of Finance 2010–, Vice-Pres. 2011, Pres. Jan.–Dec. 2012; fmr mem. Swiss People's Party; mem. Conservative Democratic Party 2008–. *Address:* Federal Department of Finance, Bernerhof, Bundesgasse 3, 3003 Bern, Switzerland (office). *Telephone:* 313226033 (office). *Fax:* 313233852 (office). *E-mail:* info@gs-efd.admin.ch (office). *Website:* www.efd.admin.ch (office).

WIDNALL, Sheila Evans, BSc, MS, PhD, FAAS; American astrophysicist and academic; *Institute Professor and Professor of Aeronautics and Astronautics, Massachusetts Institute of Technology;* b. 13 July 1938, Tacoma, Wash.; d. of Rolland Evans and Genevieve Krause; m. William Widnall 1960; one s. one d.; ed Massachusetts Inst. of Technology; Research Staff Engineer, MIT 1961–62, Research Asst 1962–64, Asst Prof. 1964–70, Assoc. Prof. 1970–74, Prof. 1974–86, Abby Rockefeller Mauze Prof. of Aeronautics and Astronautics 1986–93, Assoc. Provost 1992–93, Inst. Prof. 1998–; Dir Fluid Dynamics Research Lab. 1979–90, Chair. of Faculty 1979–80, Assoc. Provost 1992–93; Dir Univ. Research, US Dept of Transportation, Washington, DC 1974–75; Sec. of US Air Force 1993–98, Co-Chair. Dept of Defense Task Force on Sexual Harassment and Discrimination; fmr Dir Aerospace Corpn, Draper Laboratories, ANSER Corp., Chemical Fabrics Inc.; fmr Pres. AAAS; Dir GenCorp Inc.; Vice-Pres. Nat. Acad. of Eng 1998; Fellow, American Inst. of Aeronautics and Astronautics (AIAA), mem. Bd of Dirs 1975–77, Pres. 2000–01; mem. Nat. Research Council Governing Bd 1999; Fellow, APS, American Acad. of Arts and Sciences, Royal Aeronautical Soc.; fmr mem. Carnegie Comm. on Science, Council of Smithsonian Inst. of Washington; mem. Exec. Cttee, Nat. Research Council of the Nat. Acads; mem. Int. Acad. of Astronautics, Seattle Mountaineers, Appalachian Mountain Club, Eastern Yacht Club, Charles River Wheelman, Potomac Peddlers; fmr consultant, Macarthur Foundation; fmr Trustee, Carnegie Corpn (also Vice-Chair.), Boston Museum of Science; Trustee, Sloan Foundation, Inst. for Defense Analysis; Hon. DSc (Princeton) 1994; American Inst. of Aeronautics Lawrence Sperry Achievement Award 1972, Soc. of Women Engineers Outstanding Achievement Award 1975, Boston Museum of Science Washburn Award 1987, Nat. Acad. of Eng Distinguished Service Award 1993, Barnard Coll. Medal of Distinction 1994, Air Force Asscn W. Stuart Symington Award 1995, Air Force Asscn Maxwell A. Kriendler Memorial Award 1995, Boston USO Mil. Award 1995, ASME Applied Mechanics Award 1996, New England Council New Englander of the Year 1996, Women's Int. Center Living Legacy Award 1998, Nat. Space Club Goddard Award 1998, NDIA Hartinger Award 1999, AIAA Reed Aeronautics Award 2000, ASME Spirit of St Louis Medal 2001, Arthur M. Bueche Award, Nat. Acad. of Eng 2009. *Publications:* contrib. articles to professional journals. *Address:* Room 33-411, Department of Aeronautics and Astronautics, Massachusetts Institute of Technology, 77 Massachusetts Avenue, Cambridge, MA 02139-4307, USA (office). *Telephone:* (617) 253-3595 (office). *E-mail:* sheila@mit.edu (office). *Website:* web.mit.edu/aeroastro/www (office).

WIDOM, Benjamin, PhD; American chemist and academic; *Goldwin Smith Professor Emeritus of Chemistry, Cornell University;* b. 13 Oct. 1927, Newark, New Jersey; s. of Morris Widom and Rebecca Hertz Widom; m. Joanne McCurdy 1953; two s. one d.; ed Stuyvesant High School, New York and Columbia and Cornell Univs; Research Assoc., Univ. of NC 1952–54; Instructor in Chem., Cornell Univ. 1954–55, Asst Prof. 1955–59, Assoc. Prof. 1959–63, Prof. 1963–, Goldwin Smith Prof. Emer. 1983–; van der Waals Prof., Univ. of Amsterdam 1972; Visiting Prof. of Chem., Harvard Univ. 1975; IBM Visiting Prof. of Theoretical Chem., Univ. of Oxford 1978; Lorentz Prof., Leiden Univ. 1985; Visiting Prof., Katholieke Univ.,

Leuven 1988, Université d'Aix Marseille III 1995; Kramers/Debye Prof., Univ. of Utrecht 1999; Fellow, American Acad. of Arts and Sciences, New York Acad. of Sciences; mem. NAS, American Philosophical Soc.; Hon. DSc (Chicago), Dr hc (Utrecht); Boris Pregel Award, New York Acad. of Sciences, ACS Langmuir Award, Dickson Prize for Science, Carnegie-Mellon Univ., ACS Hildebrand Award, Hirschfelder Prize in Theoretical Chem., Univ. of Wisconsin, Bakhuis Roozeboom Medal, Royal Netherlands Acad. of Arts and Sciences, Onsager Medal, Univ. of Trondheim, Boltzmann Medal, IUPAP Comm. on Statistical Physics, ACS Award in Theoretical Chem. *Publications include:* Molecular Theory of Capillarity (with J. S. Rowlinson) 1982, Statistical Mechanics: A Concise Introduction for Chemists 2002. *Address:* Department of Chemistry, 220 Baker Laboratory, Cornell University, Ithaca, NY 14853, USA (office). *Telephone:* (607) 255-3363 (office). *Fax:* (607) 255-4137 (office). *E-mail:* bw24@cornell.edu (office). *Website:* www.chem.cornell .edu (office).

WIEANDT, Axel, MBA, Dr rer. pol; German banker and business executive; *Chairman of the Management Board and CEO, Hypo Real Estate Holding AG;* b. 19 Sept. 1966, Bochum; s. of Paul Wieandt; ed Kellogg School of Man., Northwestern Univ., Evanston, Ill., USA, Koblenz School of Corp. Man. (WHU), Vallendar, Germany; began career as Man. Consultant in Financial Services and Media Industry at McKinsey & Co., Inc., Düsseldorf, followed by one year at Morgan Stanley Ltd & Co., London, UK; Deputy Global Head of Corp. Strategy, Deutsche Bank Group, Frankfurt am Main 1998–99, Man. Dir Deutsche Asset Man. Europe GmbH/Deutsche Asset Man. International GmbH, Frankfurt am Main 1999–2000, Global Head of Corp. Devt (AfK), Deutsche Bank Group 2000–08, Global Head of Corp. Investments, Deutsche Bank Group 2003–08; Chair. Man. Bd and CEO Hypo Real Estate Holding AG 2008–; mem. Supervisory mem. Atradius NV, Amsterdam 2003–; Lecturer, Koblenz School of Corp. Man. (WHU); mem. Advisory mem. Kellogg School of mem., Northwestern Univ.; Hon. Prof. (Koblenz School of Corp. Man.—WHU) 2005–. *Address:* Hypo Real Estate Holding AG, Unsöldstrasse 2, 80538 Munich, Germany (office). *Telephone:* (89) 2030-070 (office). *Fax:* (89) 2030-077-72 (office). *E-mail:* info@hyporealestate.com (office). *Website:* www.hyporealestate.com (office).

WIEBE, Rudy Henry, OC, BA, MA, ThB; Canadian writer and academic; *Professor Emeritus of English and Creative Writing, University of Alberta;* b. 4 Oct. 1934, Fairholme, Sask.; m. Tena F. Isaak 1958, two s. one d.; ed Univ. of Alberta, Univ. of Tübingen, Mennonite Brethren Bible Coll., Univ. of Manitoba, Univ. of Iowa; Asst and Assoc. Prof. of English, Goshen College, Ind. 1963–67; Asst Prof., Univ. of Alberta 1967–71, Assoc. Prof. 1971–77, Prof. of English and Creative Writing 1977–92, Prof. Emer. 1992–; mem. Writers Guild of Alberta (Founding Pres. 1980), Writers Union of Canada (Pres. 1986–87); Hon. DLitt Univ. of Winnipeg 1986, Wilfred Laurier Univ. 1991, Brock Univ. 1991; Dr hc (Alberta) 2009; Gov.-General's Awards for Fiction 1973, 1994, Lorne Pierce Medal, Royal Soc. of Canada 1987, Charles Taylor Prize for Literary Non-fiction 2007, Lt-Gov. of Alberta Distinguished Artist Award 2009. *Publications:* fiction: Peace Shall Destroy Many 1962, First and Vital Candle 1966, The Blue Mountains of China 1970, The Temptations of Big Bear 1973, Where is the Voice Coming From? 1974, The Scorched-Wood People 1977, Alberta: A Celebration 1979, The Mad Trapper 1980, The Angel of the Tar Sands and Other Stories 1982, My Lovely Enemy 1983, A Chinook Christmas 1992, A Discovery of Strangers 1994, River of Stone: Fictions and Memories 1995, Sweeter Than All the World 2001; non-fiction (memoir): Of This Earth: A Mennonite Boyhood in the Boreal Forest 2006, Extraordinary Canadians: Big Bear 2008; play: Far as the Eye Can See 1977; essays: A Voice in the Land 1981, Playing Dead: A Contemplation Concerning the Arctic 1989, Place 2003; editor: The Story-Makers: A Selection of Modern Short Stories 1970, Stories from Western Canada 1971, Stories from Pacific and Arctic Canada (with Andreas Schroeder) 1974, Double Vision: Twentieth Century Stories in English 1976, Getting Here 1977, More Stories from Western Canada (with Aritha van Herk) 1980, West of Fiction (with Aritha van Herk and Leah Flater) 1983; numerous contribs to anthologies and periodicals. *Address:* c/o Penguin Group (Canada), 90 Eglinton Avenue East, Suite 700, Toronto, ON M4P 2Y3, Canada (office).

WIEDEKING, Wendelin, Diplom Ingenieur; German automotive industry executive; b. 28 Aug. 1952, Ahlen; m.; ed Aachen Univ. of Tech.; studied mechanical eng and worked as scientific asst Machine Tool Lab. Rhine-Westphalian Coll. of Advanced Tech. Aachen; Dir's Asst Production and Materials Man. Porsche AG 1983–88; Div. Man. Glyco Metall-Werke KG 1988, advanced to CEO and Chair. Bd of Man. 1990; Production Dir Porsche 1991, CEO 1992–2009, Chair. of Exec. Bd 1993–2009, also Pres.; mem. Bd of Dirs Novartis AG, Eagle Picher Inc. *Publications:* Das Davidprinzip, Anders ist Besser. *Address:* c/o Porsche AG, Porscheplatz 1, Stuttgart, Germany (office).

WIEGHARDT, Karl Ernst, DipChem, PhD; German chemist and academic; *Director, Max-Planck-Institut für Bioanorganische Chemie;* b. 25 July 1942, Göttingen; ed Univ. of Heidelberg; Postdoctoral Fellow, Univ. Heidelberg 1969–72, Asst Prof. of Inorganic Chem., 1974–75; Postdoctoral Fellow, Univ. of Leeds, UK 1972; Assoc. Prof. of Inorganic Chem., Univ. of Hanover 1975–81; Prof. of Inorganic Chem., Ruhr-Univ. Bochum 1981–94, Hon. Prof. 1994–; Dir Max-Planck-Institut für Bioanorganische Chemie, Mulheim 1994–; Alexander von Humboldt Research Award 1995, Univ. of Ill. John Bailar Medal 2000, German Chemical Soc. Wilhelm-Klemm-Medal 2000, Royal Soc. of Chem. Centenary Medal 2002. *Address:* Max-Planck-Institut für Bioanorganische Chemie, Stiftstrasse 34-36, Postfach 10 13 65, 45413 Mülheim an der Ruhr, Germany (office). *Telephone:* (208) 306-3609 (office). *Fax:* (208) 306-3952 (office). *E-mail:* wieghardt@mpi -muelheim.mpg.de (office). *Website:* www.mpi-muelheim.mpg.de/strneu/staff/ wieghardt/wieghardt_home_e.html (office).

WIEKER, Gen. Volker; German army officer; *Chief of the Defence Staff, Federal Armed Forces (Bundeswehr);* b. 1 March 1954, Delmenhorst, Lower Saxony; m. Sabine Wieker; two c.; ed Fed. Armed Forces Univ., Munich, Command and Gen. Staff Coll. (Führungsakademie), Hamburg, US Army Command and Gen. Staff Coll., Fort Leavenworth, Kan., USA; graduate engineer; joined Bundeswehr (Fed. Armed Forces) 1974, trained as artillery officer, 315 Armoured Artillery Bn, Wildeshausen, posts held include platoon leader, battery officer, battery commdr, later Asst Br. Chief, Personnel Div., Fed. Ministry of Defence, Bonn 1989, becoming G3 Staff Officer, 21 Armoured Brigade, Augustdorf, Commdr, 215 Armoured Artillery Bn 1993–96, Staff Officer for Training and Operations and

Chief of Operations Centre, German Army Contingent, IFOR Multinational Force, Bosnia-Herzegovina 1993–96, Exec. Asst. Admin. Control, Fed. Ministry of Defence, Mil. Asst to Fed. Minister of Defence 1997–99, Commdr, Armoured Infantry Brigade 40 Mecklenburg, Schwerin 1999–2001, Commdr, Multinational Brigade S and Nat. Commdr in Theatre, 3rd KFOR Contingent, Kosovo May–Dec. 2001, Chief of Staff, Army Office in Cologne 2002–04, Chief of Staff in the Army Staff 2004–07, Deputy Commanding Gen., 1 German–Netherlands Corps, Münster 2007–08, Commanding Gen. 2008–09, Chief of Staff, Int. Security Assistance Force (ISAF), Afghanistan Oct.–Dec. 2009, Chief of the Defence Staff, Fed. Armed Forces (Bundeswehr) 2010–; Bundeswehr Foreign Duty Medal (IFOR) 1996, NATO Service Medal 1996, Gold Cross of Honour of the Bundeswehr 1999, Bundeswehr Foreign Duty Medal (KFOR) 2001, Order of Merit of Bulgaria 2001, Bundeswehr Foreign Duty Medal (ISAF) 2010, Officer, Degree of the Legion of Merit (USA) 2010, Medal of Merit in Gold (Netherlands) 2011. *Address:* Office of the Chief of the Defence Staff, Bundeswehr, Federal Ministry of Defence, Stauffenbergstr. 18, 10785 Berlin, Germany (office). *Telephone:* (30) 18240 (office). *Fax:* (30) 18245357 (office). *E-mail:* poststelle@bmvg.bund.de (office). *Website:* www.bmvg.de (office).

WIELGUS, Archbishop Stanisław Wojciech; Polish ecclesiastic and professor of history of philosophy; b. 23 April 1939, Wierzchowiska; ed Catholic Univ. of Lublin, Univ. of Munich; ordained priest 1962; curate and parish catechist 1962–69; Prof., Catholic Univ. of Lublin 1969–, Pro-Rector 1988–92, Rector 1989–98; Bishop of Płock 1999–2006; apptd Archbishop of Warsaw Jan. 2007 (resgnd Jan. 2007), Archbishop Emer. 2007–; Head, Dept of the History of Philosophy in Poland, Head, Interdisciplinary Centre of the History of Medieval Culture; Head, Catholic Univ. of Lublin (KUL) Catholic Encyclopaedia Editing Offices; Vice-Pres. Conf. of Polish Univ. of Rectors 1990–93; del. Extraordinary Synod of European Bishops, Rome 1991; canon Lublin Cathedral Chapter; leader Coll. of Rectors, Lublin Region 1992–93; mem. Ethical Team of Scientific Research attached to Minister of Educ. 1998–; Chair. Educ. Council of the Nat. Conf. of Bishops in Poland 2001–; Chair. Council of the Polish Rectors Foundation 2001; mem. KUL Science Soc. (Gen. Sec. 1985–88), Acad. Council of the John Paul Second Inst., mem. numerous socs; Officer's Cross, Order of Polonia Restituta 1993; Award of the Minister of Nat. Educ., Catholic Soc. Civitas Christiana Award 1998, Honour of the Societas Scientiarum Lublinensis Resolutio Pro Laude 1999. *Publications:* Quaestiones Nicolai Peripatetici 1973, Benedykta Hessego Quaestiones super octo libros Physicorum Aristotelis 1983, Bible Research in Ancient Times and in the Middle Ages 1990, Foreign Biblical Literature in Medieval Poland 1990, Mediaeval Biblical Literature in the Polish Language 1991, Mediaeval Polish Bible Studies in the Latin Language 1992, From Research into the Middle Ages 1995, The Medieval Polish Doctrine of the Law of Nations: Jus Gentium 1998, Deo et Patriae, vol. 1 1996, vol. II 1999, Dobra jest więcej 2001, Na Skale budujmy nasz świat 2002, Z obszarów średniowiecznej mysli islamskiej, żydowskiej i chrzescijańskiej 2002, Filozofie w Rzeczypospolitej 2002, Ducha nie gaście 2004, Zachodnia i polska nauka średniowieczna 2005, Mocni w wierze 2005, Moja umilowana Ojczyzna 2010, Zyc prawdziwie 2010, Chrzéscijaństwo zobowiązuje 2011, Stanąć po stronie Dobra 2013. *Leisure interests:* factual literature, memoirs, film. *Address:* ul. Jana Pawla II, 11, 20-585 Lublin, Poland (home).

WIELICKI, Krzysztof; Polish mountaineer and business executive; b. 5 Jan. 1950, Szklarka Przygodzka; m.; one s. two d.; ed Tech. Univ. of Wrocław; owner of four commercial cos (distribution of alpine and outdoor equipment and garments) and mountain agencies; began climbing 1970; joined 27 high mountain expeditions including Dolomites, Alps, Caucasus, Pamir, Hindukush, Karakoram and Himalayas; leader of 12 expeditions; the fifth man in the world to climb all 14 8,000m peaks; first person to climb in winter: Mount Everest (with partner Leszek Cichy) 1980, Kanchenjunga 1986, Lhotse (solo) 1988; leader climbing expedition on K-2 (Karakoram); mem. The Explorers' Club 1997, Group de Haute Montagne (France) 2001–; Pres. Jury, Piolet d'Or 2004. *Publications:* Talks about Everest (co-author) 1980, The Crown of the Himalayas 1997. *Leisure interest:* travelling. *Address:* ul. A. Frycza Modrzewskiego 21, 443-100 Tychy, Poland (home). *Telephone:* (32) 227-15-00 (home).

WIELOWIEYSKI, Andrzej Jan, LLM; Polish politician, economist and publicist; b. 16 Dec. 1927, Warsaw; m. Zofia Wielowieyska; one s. six d.; ed Jagiellonian Univ., Kraków; trainee, Radomsko Forest Inspectorate 1942–44; Head, Foreign Dept Bratnia Pomoc students' org. Jagiellonian Univ., Kraków 1945–48; mem. Wici Rural Youth Union (ZMW Wici) 1945–48; subsequently councillor and inspector in Ministry of Finance 1948–52; Ed., Słowo Powszechne, Warsaw 1948; inspector, Head Office of Workers' Housing Estates Enterprise Warsaw-South, subsequently Warsaw-Śródmieście 1952–55; inspector, Head Urban Devt Dept, Municipal Comm. of Econ. Planning, Warsaw 1956–62; Head of Section Więź, Warsaw 1961–80; Lecturer, Doświadczenie i Przyszłość (Experience and the Future) Conversatorium, Warsaw 1978–82; Ed. Królowa Apostołów, Warsaw 1982–84, Gość Niedzielny, Katowice 1982–90; mem. Solidarity Ind. Self-governing Trade Union 1980–, adviser to Nat. Comm. of Solidarity 1980–81; Head of Social and Labour Study Centre attached to Nat. Comm. of Solidarity, Warsaw 1981; adviser to Nat. Executive Comm. of Solidarity 1987–89; mem. Civic Cttee attached to Lech Wałęsa (q.v.), Chair. of Solidarity 1988–90; participant Round Table plenary debates, Co-Chair. group for economy and social policy Feb.–April 1989; Senator 1989–91, 2001–05 (Pres. Freedom Union Group), Vice-Marshal of the Senate 1989–91, Deputy Speaker 2001–05; mem. European Parl. 2008–09; Chair. Civic Parl. Caucus of Senate 1989–90; Deputy to Sejm (Parl.) 1991–, mem. Parl. Comm. Foreign Affairs 1991–, 2001–; Polish del. and Vice-Pres. Council of Europe Parl. Ass. 1992–; mem. Democratic Action of Civic Movement (ROAD) 1990, Democratic Union 1991–94, Freedom Union 1994–; mem. Pax Romana Catholic Intelligentsia Int. Fed., mem. of Council 1979–83; mem. of European Council 1987–89; co-f. Int. Fed. of Family Life Promotion 1979–; Silver Cross of Merit with Swords, Cross of Valour, Partisan Cross, Cross of Home Army (AK), Victory and Freedom Medal, Commdr's Cross, Order of Polonia Restituta 2006, Kt, Order of the White Eagle 2011. *Publications:* Przed trzecim przyśpieszeniem 1969, Przed nami małżeństwo 1972, over 300 articles on politics, religion, educ. and history. *Leisure interests:* gardening, skiing, yachting, historical and detective stories. *Address:* c/o Senate, ul. Wiejska 4/6/8, 00-902 Warsaw; Biuro Senatora UW, Andrzeja Wielowiejskiego, ul. Marsza łkowska 77/79, 00-683 Warsaw, Poland (home). *E-mail:* biuro@unia-wolnosci.pl (office). *Website:* www.uw.org.pl (office).

WIEMAN, Carl Edwin, BS, PhD; American physicist and academic; *Professor of Physics and of the Graduate School of Education, Stanford University;* b. 26 March 1951, Corvallis, Ore.; s. of N. Orr and Alison Wieman; ed Massachusetts Inst. of Tech., Stanford Univ.; Asst Research Scientist, Dept of Physics, Univ. of Michigan 1977–79, Asst Prof. 1979–84; Assoc. Prof. of Physics, Univ. of Colorado, Boulder 1984–87, Prof. 1987–97, Distinguished Prof. 1997–2013, Fellow, Jt Inst. for Lab. Astrophysics 1985–2007, Chair. 1993–95, Presidential Teaching Scholar 2004–13, Dir Science Educ. Initiative 2006–13, Founder and Chair. of PhET; Prof. of Physics, Univ. of British Columbia 2007–13, Dir Carl Wieman Science Educ. Initiative 2007–13; Prof. of Physics and of Grad. School of Educ., Stanford Univ. 2013–; Assoc. Dir of Science, White House Office of Science and Tech. Policy 2010–12; mem. Advisory Bd USA Science and Eng Festival; mem. Optical Soc. of America, American Asscn of Physics Teachers, Nat. Acad. of Educ. 2008; Fellow, American Physical Soc. 1990, NAS 1995, American Acad. of Arts and Sciences 1998; Hon. DS (Univ. of Chicago) 1997; numerous awards, including Sloan Research Fellowship 1984, Guggenheim Fellowship 1990–91, E.O. Lawrence Award in Physics 1993, Fritz London Award 1996, King Faisal Int. Prize for Science 1997, Lorentz Medal 1998, Schawlow Prize for Laser Science 1999, Benjamin Franklin Medal in Physics 2000, Nobel Prize in Physics (shared with Eric Allin Cornell and Wolfgang Ketterle) 2001, named US Prof. of the Year, Carnegie Foundation for the Advancement of Teaching and Council for Advancement and Support of Educ. 2004 Oersted Medal, American Asscn of Physics Teachers 2007, Vollum Award for Distinguished Accomplishment in Science and Tech., Reed Coll. 2009, Science Educ. Research Award, Council of Scientific Socs 2011, Presidential Citation for Lifetime Achievement, Nat. Science Teachers Asscn 2012. *Address:* Department of Physics, Stanford University, 382 Via Pueblo Mall, Stanford, CA 94305-4060, USA (office). *Telephone:* (650) 497-3491 (office). *E-mail:* cwieman@stanford.edu (office). *Website:* physics.stanford.edu/people/faculty/carl -wieman (office).

WIESCHAUS, Eric Francis, BS, PhD; American molecular biologist and academic; *Squibb Professor in Molecular Biology, Princeton University;* b. 8 June 1947, South Bend, Ind.; s. of Leroy Joseph Wieschaus and Marcella Carner Wieschaus; m. Gertrud (Trudi) Schüpbach 1982; three d.; ed John Carroll Catholic High School, Birmingham, Ala, Univ. of Notre Dame, Yale Univ.; Research Fellow, Zoological Inst., Univ. of Zurich 1975–78; Group Leader European Molecular Biology Lab., Germany 1978–81; Asst Prof. then Assoc. Prof., Princeton Univ. 1981–87, Prof. of Biology 1987–, Squibb Prof. in Molecular Biology 2005–; Adjunct Prof. of Biochemistry, Robert Wood Johnson Medical School, Univ. of Medicine and Dentistry of New Jersey 2005–; Prof. of Molecular Biology, Lewis-Sigler Inst. for Integrative Genomics; Visiting Researcher, Center for Pathobiology, Univ. of California, Irvine 1977; Fellow, Laboratoire de Génétique Moléculaire, France; mem. Damon Runyon-Walter Winchell Cancer Fund 1987–92; mem. NAS; Fellow, AAAS; Nobel Prize for Medicine and Physiology (shared with Edward B. Lewis and Christiane Nüsslein-Volhard) 1995. *Publications:* numerous articles. *Address:* Moffett Lab-435, Department of Molecular Biology, Princeton University, Princeton, NJ 08544, USA (office). *Telephone:* (609) 258-5383 (office), (609) 258-5401 (Lab.) (office). *E-mail:* efw@princeton.edu (office). *Website:* molbio.princeton .edu/faculty/molbio-faculty/140-wieschaus (office); www.molbio1.princeton.edu/ wieschaus (office).

WIESE, Christoffel Hendrik, BA, LLB, CA; South African business executive; *Chairman, Shoprite Holdings Ltd;* b. 10 Sept. 1941; m.; three c.; ed Univs of Cape Town, Stellenbosch; Exec. Dir Pep Stores 1967–73; Dir (non-exec.) Shoprite Holdings Ltd 1979–, Chair. 1991–; Chair. and Dir (non-exec.) Pepkor Ltd 1981–; Chair. Instore plc 1994–2008, African Dawn Capital Ltd 2011–, Tradehold Ltd, Orion Selections Holdings Ltd, Industrial Devt Corpn of South Africa Ltd, Smart Centre Holdings, BoE (Pty) Ltd, Brown and Jackson plc, Pepgro Ltd; mem. Bd of Dirs Invicta Holdings Ltd 2004–, Chair. (non-exec.) 2006–; mem. Bd of Dirs KWV Holdings Ltd –2009, Brait SA Ltd 2011–, Primedia (Pty) Ltd, PSG Financial Services Ltd 2007–12, Metropolitan Life Ltd, Monex Group of Cos, Titan Financial Services, Co-Operative Winegrowers of South Africa, Lenco Holdings Ltd, Luna Group (Pty) Ltd; Owner, Lanzerac Manor and Winery, Stellenbosch, Lourensford Estate (wine producer); also owns pvt. game reserve in Kalahari Desert; Dr hc (Univ. of Stellenbosch); Diagonal Strategic Communicator of the Year, Marketing Man. of the Year, Inst. of Marketing Man., Business Leader of the Year, Cape Town Sakekamer, Pioneer of the 20th Century Award, South African Council of Shopping Centres, MS Louw Award for Exceptional Business Achievements. *Address:* Shoprite Holdings Ltd, PO Box 215, Brackenfell, Cape Town 7561, South Africa (office). *Telephone:* (21) 9804000 (office). *Fax:* (21) 9804050 (office). *Website:* www.shopriteholdings.co.za (office).

WIESEL, Elie(zer); American author and academic; *University Professor, Andrew W. Mellon Professor in the Humanities and Professor of Philosophy and Religion, Boston University;* b. 30 Sept. 1928, Sighet, Romania; s. of Shlomo Wiesel and Sarah Wiesel (née Feig); m. Marion E. Wiesel 1969; one s. one step d.; ed Univ. of Paris (Sorbonne); naturalized US citizen 1963; Distinguished Prof., Coll. of City of New York 1972–76; Andrew Mellon Prof. in Humanities, Boston Univ. 1976–, Prof. of Philosophy and Religion 1988–; Founder The Elie Wiesel Foundation for Humanity 1986; mem. Bd Fund for the Holocaust 1997–; Founding Pres. Universal Acad. of Cultures, Paris 1993; mem. numerous bds of dirs, trustees, govs and advisers including Int. Rescue Cttee, American Jewish World Service, Yad Vashem, Mutual of America, AmeriCares, US Cttee for Refugees; mem. PEN, The Authors' Guild, Foreign Press Asscn, Writers and Artists for Peace in the Middle East, Council of Foreign Relations, American Acad. of Arts and Sciences, American Acad. of Arts and Letters (Dept of Literature), Jewish Acad. of Arts and Sciences, European Acad. of Arts, Sciences and Humanities, Royal Norwegian Soc. of Sciences and Letters; Hon. KBE 2006; Grand Officer, Légion d'honneur, Grand Cross of the Order of the Southern Cross, Brazil 1987, Grand Cross of the Order of Rio Branco, Brazil 2001, Grand Officer, The Order of the Star of Romania 2002, Commander's Cross, Order of Merit of Hungary 2004, King Hussein Award, Jordan 2005; recipient of over 110 hon. degrees; Prix Rivarol 1964, Jewish Heritage Award 1965, Remembrance Award 1965, Prix Médicis 1968, Prix Bordin (Acad. Française) 1972, Eleanor Roosevelt Memorial Award 1972, American Liberties Medallion, American Jewish Comm. 1972, Martin Luther King Jr Award (Coll. of City of New York) 1973, Faculty Distinguished Scholar Award, Hofstra Univ. 1973–74, Congressional Gold Medal of Achievement 1985, Nobel Peace Prize

1986, Medal of Liberty Award 1986, Ellis Island Medal of Honor 1992, Presidential Medal of Freedom 1993, Nat. Humanities Medal 2009, Norman Mailer Prize for Lifetime Achievement 2011, Florida Holocaust Museum Loebenberg Humanitarian Award 2012, Chicago Tribune Literary Prize 2012, and numerous other awards. *Publications:* Night 1960, Dawn 1961, The Accident 1962, The Town Beyond the Wall 1964, The Gates of the Forest 1966, The Jews of Silence 1966, Legends of Our Time 1968, A Beggar in Jerusalem 1970, One Generation After 1971, Souls on Fire 1972, The Oath 1973, Ani Maamin, Cantata 1973, Zalmen or the Madness of God (play) 1975, Messengers of God 1976, A Jew Today 1978, Four Hasidic Masters 1978, The Trial of God 1979, One Generation After 1979, Le testament d'un poète juif assassiné 1980 (Prix Livre-Inter 1980, Prix des Bibliothéquaires 1981), The Testament 1980, Images from the Bible 1980, Five Biblical Portraits 1981, Somewhere a Master: Further Tales of the Hasidic Master 1982, Paroles d'étranger 1982, The Golem 1983, The Fifth Son (Grand Prix de la Littérature, Paris) 1985, Signes d'exode 1985, Against Silence 1985, A Song for Hope 1987, Job ou Dieu dans la tempête (with Josy Eisenberg) 1987, A Nobel Address 1987, Twilight (novel) 1988, The Six Days of Destruction (with Albert Friedlander) 1988, L'oublie 1989, Silences et mémoire d'hommes 1989, From the Kingdom of Memory, Reminiscences (essays) 1990, Evil and Exile 1990, A Journey of Faith 1990, Sages and Dreamers 1991, Célébration Talmudique 1991, The Forgotten 1992, A Passover Haggadah 1993, Se taire est impossible 1995, All Rivers Run to the Sea (Memoirs, Vol.I) 1995, Et la mer n'est pas remplie (Memoirs, Vol.II) 1996 (trans. as And the Sea Is Never Full 1999), Célébration prophétique 1998, King Solomon and His Magic Ring 2000, D'où viens-tu? 2001, The Judges 2002, After the Darkness 2002, Wise Men and Their Tales 2003, Et où vas-tu? 2004, The Time of the Uprooted 2005, Un Désir fou de Danser (trans. as A Mad Desire to Dance) 2006, Confronting Anti-Semitism (with Kofi Annan) 2006, Sonderberg 2008, Rashi 2009, Otage 2010, Hostage 2012. *Address:* Department of Philosophy, Boston University, 745 Commonwealth Avenue, Room 516, Boston, MA 02215, USA (office). *E-mail:* mcintyre@bu.edu (office). *Website:* www.bu.edu/philo (office).

WIESEL, Torsten Nils, MD; Swedish neurobiologist, university administrator and academic; *President Emeritus and Vincent and Brooke Astor Professor Emeritus, The Rockefeller University;* b. 3 June 1924, Uppsala, Sweden; ed Karolinska Inst. Stockholm; Instructor, Karolinska Inst. 1954–55; Asst, Karolinska Hosp. 1954–55; Fellow in Ophthalmology, Johns Hopkins Univ. Medical School, Baltimore, Md, USA 1955–58, Asst Prof. of Ophthalmic Physiology 1958–59; Assoc. in Neurophysiology/Neuropharmacology, Harvard Medical School, Boston 1959–60, Asst Prof. 1960–64, Asst Prof. Dept of Psychiatry 1964–67, Prof. of Physiology 1967–68, Prof. of Neurobiology 1968–74, Chair. Dept of Neurobiology 1973–82, Robert Winthrop Prof. of Neurobiology 1974–83; Vincent & Brooke Astor Prof. and Head, Lab. of Neurobiology, The Rockefeller Univ. New York 1983–2001, Gen. Sec. Human Frontier Science Program 2000–09, Pres. The Rockefeller Univ. 1991–98, Pres. Emer. 1998–; Pres. Int. Brain Research Org. 1999–2005; Dir Shelby White & Leon Levy Center for Mind, Brain and Behavior 1999–; Chair. Borderline Personality Disorder Research Foundation 2001–02, New York Acad. of Sciences 2001–; Co-Chair. Bd Govs, Okinawa Inst. of Science and Tech. 2002–; mem. American Physiology Soc., American Acad. of Arts and Sciences, AAAS, NAS etc.; Foreign mem. Royal Soc.; Nobel Prize in Physiology or Medicine 1981; numerous honours and awards. *Publications:* more than 80 articles in medical journals. *Address:* The Rockefeller University, 1230 York Avenue, New York, NY 10065, USA (office). *Telephone:* (212) 327-7093 (office). *Fax:* (212) 327-8988 (office). *E-mail:* wiesel@rockefeller.edu (office). *Website:* www.rockefeller.edu/research/faculty/labheads/TorstenWiesel (office); www.nobelprize.org/nobel_prizes/medicine/laureates/1981/wiesel-autobio.html (office).

WIGDERSON, Avi, BSc, MSE, MA, PhD; Israeli computer scientist and academic; *Herbert H. Maass Professor, School of Mathematics, Institute for Advanced Study;* b. 9 Sept. 1956; m.; three c.; ed Technion-Israel Inst. of Tech., Princeton Univ., NJ, USA; Visiting Asst Prof., Prof., Dept of Computer Science, Univ. of California, Berkeley 1983–84; Visiting Scientist, IBM Research, San José, Calif. 1984–85; Fellow, Math. Sciences Research Inst., Berkeley 1985–86; Sr Lecturer, Dept of Computer Science, Hebrew Univ. of Jerusalem 1986–87, Assoc. Prof. (with tenure) 1987–92, Prof., Computer Science Inst. 1991–2003, Chair. Computer Science Inst. 1993–95; Visiting Assoc. Prof., Dept of Computer Science 1990–92, Prof., Computer Science Inst. 1991–2003; Visiting Prof., Inst. for Advanced Study (IAS), Princeton and Dept of Computer Science, Princeton Univ. 1995–96, Prof., School of Math., IAS 1999–2003, Herbert H. Maass Prof. 2003–; Rothschild Visiting Fellow, Isaac Newton Inst. 2011; mem. Editorial Bd Society for Industrial and Applied Mathematics (SIAM) Journal on Discrete Mathematics, Information and Computation, Complexity Theory; mem. American Acad. of Arts and Sciences 2011, NAS 2013; Pres.'s List of Excellence, The Technion 1977–80, IBM Grad. Fellowship, Princeton Univ. 1982–83, Alon Fellowship 1986–89, Bergman Fellowship 1989, Invited Speaker, Int. Congress of Mathematicians, Kyoto 1990, Zurich 1994, Nevanlinna Prize 1994, Yoram Ben-Porat Presidential Prize for Outstanding Research, ICM Plenary Lecturer, Madrid 2006, Gibbs Lecturer, San Diego 2008, Conant Prize 2008, Gödel Prize 2009, Fields Inst. Distinguished Lecture Series 2010. *Publications:* more than 150 articles in math. journals on complexity theory, parallel computation, combinatorics and graph theory, combinatorial optimization algorithms, randomness and cryptography, distributed and neural networks. *Address:* Simonyi Hall 013, School of Mathematics, Institute for Advanced Study, Einstein Drive, Princeton, NJ 08540, USA (office). *Telephone:* (609) 734-8115 (office). *E-mail:* avi@math.ias.edu (office). *Website:* www.math.ias.edu/avi (office); www.ias.edu/people/faculty-and-emeriti/wigderson (office).

WIGGINS, Sir Bradley Marc, Kt, CBE, OBE; British cyclist; b. 28 April 1980, Ghent, Belgium; s. of the late Gary Wiggins and of Linda Wiggins; m. Cath Wiggins; one s. one d.; ed St Augustine's Church of England High School; began racing at South London's Herne Hill Velodrome aged 12, represented Camden in London Youth Games; began career as track cyclist (specialized in pursuit and madison events), later took to road cycling; turned professional with Francaise des Jeux team 2002; silver medal, team pursuit, 100m, Commonwealth Games, Kuala Lumpur 1998; bronze medal, team pursuit, Olympics Games, Sydney 2000; silver medal, team pursuit, Union Cycliste Internationale (UCI) World Championships (track cycling), Manchester 2000; silver medal, team pursuit, UCI World Championships (track cycling), Antwerp 2001; silver medal, 4km individual pursuit, team pursuit, 100m, Commonwealth Games, Manchester 2002; bronze medal, team pursuit, UCI World Championships (track cycling), Copenhagen 2002; gold medal, 4km individual pursuit, silver medal, team pursuit, UCI World Championships (track cycling), Stuttgart 2003; gold medal, 4km individual pursuit, silver medal, team pursuit, bronze medal, madison, Olympics Games, Athens 2004; gold medal, 4km individual pursuit, gold medal, team pursuit, UCI World Championships (track cycling), Palma de Mallorca 2007; gold medal, 4km individual pursuit, team pursuit, Olympics Games, Beijing 2008; gold medal, 4km individual pursuit, team pursuit, Madison, UCI World Championships (track cycling), Manchester 2008; UCI World Championships (road cycling): silver medal, individual time trial, UCI Road World Championships 2011, 2013; gold medal, road time trial, Olympics Games, London 2012; winner: British Nat. Time Trial Championships 2009, Herald Sun Tour 2009, Nat. Time Trial Champion 2009, 2010, British Nat. Road Race Championships 2011, Critérium du Dauphiné 2011, 2012, Paris–Nice 2012, Tour de Romandie 2012, Olympic Time Trial Champion 2012, Tour de France (first British cyclist, also two individual stages) 2012, Tour of Britain 2013; only cyclist to have won Tour de France and an Olympic gold medal in the same year; teams: Linda McCartney Racing Team 2001, Française des Jeux 2002–03, Crédit Agricole 2004–05, Cofidis 2006–07, Team High Road 2008, Garmin-Slipstream 2009, Team Sky 2010–; Bradley Wiggins X Fred Perry Collaboration clothing range launched 2012; f. Bradley Wiggins Foundation 2012; coached by Rod Ellingworth; inducted into London Youth Games Hall of Fame 2010, BBC Sports Personality of the Year 2012. *Publication:* In Pursuit of Glory (autobiog.) 2008. *Leisure interests:* owns a collection of classic motor scooters and guitars from the 1960s and 1970s, supports Liverpool Football Club and Wigan Warriors rugby league club, spending time with family. *Address:* Bradley Wiggins Foundation, Suite 19, Hattersley House, Hattersley Court, Ormskirk, L39 2AY, England (office). *Website:* www.bradleywigginsfoundation.org (office).

WIGGINS, David, MA, FBA; British academic; *Professor Emeritus, University of Oxford;* b. 8 March 1933, London; s. of Norman Wiggins and Diana Wiggins (née Priestley); m. 1st Hideko Ishiguro 1969 (separated 1973); m. 2nd Jennifer Hornsby 1980 (separated 1987); one s.; m. 3rd Phillida Gili (née Stone) 2010; ed St Paul's School and Brasenose Coll., Oxford; Asst Prin. Colonial Office 1957–58; Jane Eliza Procter Visiting Fellow, Princeton Univ. 1958–59; Lecturer, New Coll., Oxford 1959, Fellow and Lecturer 1960–67; Prof. of Philosophy, Bedford Coll., London 1967–78; Fellow and Praelector in Philosophy, Univ. Coll., Oxford 1981–89; Prof. of Philosophy, Birkbeck Coll., London 1989–94, Visiting Prof. 2008–10; Wykeham Prof. of Logic, New Coll., Oxford Univ. 1993–94, now Prof. Emer.; visiting appointments at Stanford Univ. 1964, 1965, Harvard Univ. 1968, 1972, All Souls Coll., Oxford 1973, Princeton Univ. 1980, Univ. Coll., Oxford 1989–; Findlay Visiting Prof., Boston Univ. 2001; Fellow, Center for Advanced Study in Behavioral Sciences, Stanford 1985–86; mem. Independent Comm. on Transport 1973–74, Cen. Transport Consultative Cttee; Chair. Transport Users' Consultative Cttee for South-East 1977–79; Foreign Hon. mem. American Acad. of Arts and Sciences 1992, Hon. Fellow, Brasenose Coll. 2010; Dr hc (York) 2005. *Publications:* Identity and Spatio Temporal Continuity 1967, Truth, Invention and the Meaning of Life 1978, Sameness and Substance 1980, Needs, Values, Truth 1987, Sameness and Substance Renewed 2001, Ethics: Twelve Lectures on the Philosophy of Morality 2006, Univ. of Kansas Lindley Lecture: Solidarity at the Root of the Ethical 2008; articles in learned journals. *Address:* New College, Oxford, OX1 3BN, England. *Telephone:* (20) 7584-9009.

WIGLEY OF CAERNARFON, Baron (Life Peer), cr. 2011, of Caernarfon in the County of Gwynedd; **Dafydd Wigley,** PC, BSc; Welsh politician; b. (David Wigley), 1 April 1943, Derby, England; s. of Elfyn Edward Wigley and Myfanwy Wigley (née Batterbee); m. Elinor Bennett Owen 1967; three s. (two deceased) one d.; ed Sir Hugh Owen School, Caernarfon, Rydal School, Colwyn Bay, Victoria Univ. of Manchester; Econ. Analyst, Ford Motor Co. 1964–67; Chief Cost Accountant, Mars Ltd 1967–71; Financial Controller, Hoover Ltd 1971–74; Pres. S Caernarfon Creamery 1987–2002; Co. Borough Councillor, Merthyr Tydfil 1972–74; Vice-Chair. Plaid Cymru 1972–74, Pres. (Party Leader) 1981–84, 1991–2000, Hon. Pres. 2001–; MP for Caernarfon 1974–2001, Assn. Mem. 1999–2003; Chair. All Party House of Commons Reform Group 1983, Vice-Chair. All-Party Disablement Group 1992–2001; Vice-Chair. Parl. Social Services Group 1985–88; mem. Nat. Ass. for Wales 1999, Leader of the Opposition 1999–2000, Chair. Audit Cttee of Nat. Ass. 2002; Chair. Ymddiriedolaeth Hybu Gwydoniaeth 2002, now retd; Pres. Spastic Soc. of Wales 1985–90, Mencap Wales 1991–; Pres. Nat. Library of Wales 2007–11; Vice-Pres. Welsh Asscn of Community Councils 1978–2001, Nat. Fed. of Industrial Devt Authorities 1981–2001; Sponsor, Disabled Persons Act 1981; Chair. Alpha Dyffryn Cyf/Ltd 1980–91; Dir (non-exec.) Gwernafalau Cyf/Ltd 2001–; Pro-Chancellor Univ. of Wales 2003–06; mem. (Plaid Cymru) House of Lords 2011–; Freeman of the Borough of Arfon 1994, Royal Town of Caernarfon 2001; Hon. mem. Gorsedd of Welsh Bards; Hon. Fellow, Univ. of N Wales Bangor 1995; Hon. LLD (Univ. of Wales) 2002; Grimshaw Memorial Award, Nat. Fed. of the Blind 1982. *Publications:* An Economic Plan for Wales 1970, O Ddifri 1992, Dal Ati 1993, A Democratic Wales in a United Europe 1995, A Real Choice for Wales 1996, Maen i'r Wal 2001, Be Nesa! (autobiog.) 2013. *Leisure interests:* football, tennis, chess, hill walking, writing. *Address:* c/o Rhian Medi Roberts (PA), Room 4/1, Norman Shaw North, House of Lords, Victoria Embankment, London, SW1A 1AA, England (office); Hen Efail, Bontnewydd, Caernarfon, Gwynedd, LL54 7YH, Wales (home). *Telephone:* (20) 7219-5021 (office); (1286) 830010 (home). *E-mail:* wigleyd@parliament.uk (office); dafydd.wigley@hotmail.com (home).

WIGZELL, Hans Lennart Rudolf, MD, PhD; Swedish physician, immunologist, academic and company director; *Professor Emeritus of Immunology, Karolinska Institute;* b. 28 Oct. 1938, Stockholm; m. Kerstin Largell 1964; one s. three d.; ed Karolinska Inst., Stockholm; Prof. of Immunology, Uppsala Univ. 1972–82; Prof. of Immunology, Karolinska Inst. 1982–2003, Prof. Emer. 2003–, Pres. 1995–2003, fmr Dir Centre for Medical Innovation; Dir Nat. Bacteriological Lab. Stockholm 1988–; Chair. Nobel Cttee, Karolinska Inst. 1990–92; Chair. Nobel Cttee 1990–92, Nobel Ass. 2000, Stockholm School of Entrepreneurship; scientific adviser to Govt of Sweden 1999–; one of 11 appointed Advisors to the EU Commr for research on life science issues; Chair. Karolinska Development AB 2006–13; fmr Chair. WHO-UNAIDS Vaccine Advisory Cttee 2002–; fmr Sec.-Gen. Swedish Inst. for Infectious

Disease Control; fmr Dir Gen. Nat. Bacteriological Lab., Stockholm; mem. Council of Trustees, TuBerculosis Vaccine Initiative; mem. Bd of Dirs Sobi AB, Biovitrum AB, uMabs (Switzerland), RaySearch Laboratories AB 2004–, Apogee Technology, Inc. 2005–, Intercell AG 2006–, Mertiva AB 2006–, Probi AB 2007–10, Sarepta Therapeutics Inc. 2010–; mem. editorial bds of several int. journals; mem. Royal Acad. of Sciences, Royal Swedish Acad. of Eng Sciences, Finnish Soc. of Sciences and Letters, Danish Acad. of Sciences and Letters, European Molecular Biology Org., Academia Europaea, American Acad. of Arts and Sciences; Hon. mem. American Asscn of Immunologists; Dr hc (Univ. Tor Vergata, Rome), (Univ. of Turku, Finland); Anders Jahres Medical Prize, Oslo 1975, Erik Fernström Prize for Young Scientists, Uppsala 1979, Russel Weiser Lecturer Prize, Smith Lecture Award. *Play:* The Gene Scene 1989. *Publications:* more than 700 scientific articles, textbooks and popular science books. *Leisure interests:* music, nature, tropical plants, Japanese carp. *Address:* Karolinska Institute, Department of Microbiology, Tumor and Cell Biology, C1, Martin Rottenberg group, Box 280, Nobels Väg 16, 171 77 Stockholm, Sweden (office). *Telephone:* (8) 52486680 (office). *Fax:* (8) 31-11-01 (office). *E-mail:* hans.wigzell@ki.se (office); hans.wigzell@mtc.ki.se (office). *Website:* ki.se/mtc (office).

WIIG, Ole, BArch, MArch; Norwegian architect; *Senior Partner, Narud-Stokke-Wiig AS;* b. 22 Oct. 1946, Trondheim; s. of Thorvald Wiig and Esther-Marie Wiig; m. 1st Alison Wiig 1972; two d.; m. 2nd Cathrine Lerche 2002; ed Harvard Univ., USA, Manchester Univ., Dundee Univ.; joined Kallmann, McKinnel & Wood, Boston 1973; Community Design Services, Boston 1974; City Architects Dept, Edin. 1974–80; lecturer and studio critic, Univ. of Edin. Dept of Architecture 1979–80, Visiting Lecturer and studio critic 1999–2000; External Examiner, Dublin Inst. of Tech. Dept of Architecture 2000–04; Founding Partner Narud-Stokke-Wiig AS 1979–, now Sr Partner; Pres. Nat. Asscn of Norwegian Architects 1990–94, Council Colletta di Castelbianco, Italy; lecturer at univs and confs in Europe and USA; initiated Ligurian Int. Workshop for architecture students; British Tourist Authority Certificate of Distinction, Museum of the Year Award, Edin. Civic Trust Award 1981, RIBA Award, Civic Trust Award, Disabled Design Award 1983, Homansbyen Environmental Award 1991, Nordic Copper Award 1994, First Prize Int. Competition for Scottish Architecture and Design Centre 1995; several first prizes in Norwegian and int. architecture competitions. *Publications:* numerous articles on architecture and planning topics in books, newspapers and magazines. *Leisure interest:* introducing modern architecture and design into medieval Italian villages. *Address:* c/o Narud-Stokke-Wiig AS, Rådhusgaten 27, 0158, Oslo (office); Bryggegaten 16, 0250 Oslo, Norway (home). *Telephone:* 22-40-37-40 (office); 22-83-41-01 (home). *Fax:* 22-40-37-41 (office); 22-83-21-86 (home). *E-mail:* ow@nsw.no. *Website:* www.nsw.no (office); www.olewiig.no (home).

WIJDENBOSCH, Jules Albert, PhD; Suriname fmr head of state; b. 2 May 1941, Paramaribo; one d.; customs officer 1962–66; civil servant, Municipality of Amsterdam 1966–81; mem. State Cttee on Remigration of Surinamese est. by Dutch Govt 1978–81; sr civil servant, Ministry of Dist Admin. and Decentralization 1981, Under-Dir in charge of Bureau for Decentralization of Admin. 1983, Dir of Dist Admin, Ministry of Dist Admin and Decentralization and Nat. Mobilization 1985; Minister of Home Affairs, Dist Admin and Nat. Mobilization and Minister of Justice and Police 1986–87; Prime Minister, Minister of Gen. Affairs and Minister of Foreign Affairs 1987–88; sr civil servant, Ministry of Regional Devt 1988–91; Vice-Pres. Repub. of Suriname and Minister of Finance Jan.–Sept. 1991, Pres. 1996–2000; sr civil servant, Ministry of Regional Devt 1991–; Co-ordinator Jongerengroep (Youth Section) of Suriname Nat. Party 1962–63; Co-ordinator Verenigung van Bestuurskundigen 1982–; mem. and Acting Chair. Political Advisory Group 25th Feb. Movt 1983; mem. Higher Political Council on the Political and Admin. Future of Suriname 1985–87; first Chair. Nationale Democratische Partij (NDP) 1987–91, Deputy Chair. 1992–96; mem. Nat. Ass. and Floor Leader NDP 1991; Deputy Chair. Foundation for the Promotion of Remigration of Surinamese; Chair. Amsterdam Welfare Foundation; Chair. Union of Customs Officers 1962–66; co-f. Algemene Jongeren Organisatie (Youth Org.) 1962, Dir 1963; Chair. Surinamese Basketball Fed., Deputy Chair. Surinamese Football Fed.; mem. Editorial Bd Lanti; Grand Master, Order of the Yellow Star, Order of the Palm. *Publications:* Schets voor de Republiek Suriname eigen stijl (A Personal View of the Republic of Suriname) 1974, Bestuurlijke organisatie in een leefgemeenschap (Administrative Organisation in Surinamese Society) 1980, Politieke orde en legitimiteit (Political Order and Legitimacy) 1981, Statuut van het Koninkrijk der Nederlanden (Charter for the Kingdom of the Netherlands) 1979, Participatie in een waarachtige democratie (Participating in a Modern Democracy) 1983. *Address:* c/o Office of the President, Kleine Combeweg 1, Paramaribo, Suriname.

WIJERS, G(erardus) J(ohannes) (Hans), MA, PhD; Dutch business executive; *Chairman of the Supervisory Board, Heineken NV;* b. 11 Jan. 1951, Oostburg; ed Univ. of Groningen, Erasmus Univ. of Rotterdam; Asst Prof. of Econs, Erasmus Univ. of Rotterdam 1976–82; participation in two think-tanks for govt ministers 1982–84; sr consultant and partner for various consulting firms 1984–86; Man.-Partner Horringa and De Koning 1986–93; Man.-Partner Amsterdam Office, Boston Consulting Group (BCG) 1993–94; Minister for Econ. Affairs 1994–98; Sr Vice-Pres. BCG and Chair. Dutch Office 1999–2002; adviser to Man. Bd AkzoNobel NV 2002, mem. Bd 2002–12, Chair. Man. Bd and CEO AkzoNobel NV 2003–12; Chair. Supervisory Bd Heineken NV 2013–; Chair. Oranje Fonds, Ubbo Emmius Fund Foundation at Univ. of Groningen; Dir (non-exec.) Royal Dutch Shell plc 2009–; Vice-Pres. Young Pianist Foundation; mem. Bd of Dirs Concertgebouw; mem. European Roundtable of Industrialists. *Address:* Heineken NV, PO Box 28, 1000 AA Amsterdam (office); Heineken NV, Tweede Weteringplantsoen 21, 1017 ZD Amsterdam, The Netherlands (office). *Telephone:* (20) 523-92-39 (office). *Fax:* (20) 626-35-03 (office). *E-mail:* info@heinekeninternational.com (office). *Website:* www.heinekeninternational.com (office).

WIJN, Joop, PhD; Dutch politician; b. 20 May 1969, Haarlem; ed Univ. of Amsterdam; taught course for entrepreneurs Schoevers Acad., Amsterdam 1989–94, also taught course in marketing at Netherlands Marketing Inst. and course in business econs at sr secondary vocational level 1991–94; owned and operated personnel recruitment agency, Amsterdam 1992–94; trainee then Investment Man., ABN AMRO Bank 1994–98; mem. House of Reps of the States

Gen. 1998–2002; Sec. of State for Econ. Affairs 2002–03, Sec. of State for Finance 2003–July 2006, Minister for Econ. Affairs 2006–07. *Address:* c/o Ministry of Economic Affairs, Bezuidenhoutseweg 30, POB 20101, 2594 AV The Hague, Netherlands (office).

WIJNHOLDS, Johannes de Beaufort (Onno), MA, PhD; Dutch banker, international civil servant and economist; b. 24 Oct. 1943, Amsterdam; s. of Heiko W. de Beaufort Wijnholds and Benudina M. de Beaufort Wijnholds; m. Jolanthe de Graaf 1968; one s. one d.; ed Univ. of Amsterdam; economist, De Nederlandsche Bank, Amsterdam 1968, various positions in bank 1974–84, Deputy Exec. Dir 1987–94; Asst to Exec. Dir IBRD and IMF, Washington, DC 1972–74, Alt. Exec. Dir IMF 1985–87, Exec. Dir 1994–2003; Perm. Rep. of European Cen. Bank, Washington, DC and its Observer at the IMF –2008; Alt. mem. Social Econ. Council of the Netherlands 1987–94; Prof. of Money and Banking, Univ. of Groningen 1992–95; Order of the Duke of Branimir (Croatia) 2003. *Publications:* The Need for International Reserves and Credit Facilities 1977, The International Banking System (in Dutch) 1985, A Framework for Monetary Stability (co-ed.) 1994, The Dollar's Last Days? 2009; numerous articles on int. financial subjects. *Address:* c/o International Monetary Fund, 700 19th Street, NW, Washington, DC 20431, USA. *Telephone:* (202) 623-8350. *E-mail:* jwijnholds@imf.org.

WIJNSCHENK, Harry; Dutch politician; b. 1964; fmr motorcycle and watch magazine publisher; fmr mem. Liberal Party; fmr State Gen. Lijst Pim Fortuyn, Leader Aug.–Oct. 2002.

WIKTORIN, Gen. Owe Erik Axel; Swedish air force general; b. 7 May 1940, Motala; s. of Erik Wiktorin and Ester Wiktorin (née Johnsson); m. Cajs Gårding 1965; two s.; ed AF Flying Training School, AF Acad., Armed Forces Staff and War Coll., USAF Air Command and Staff Coll.; fighter pilot, Skaraborg Wing 1964–69, CO squadron 1969–71; staff officer, Swedish Defence Staff 1973–79, Head of Planning Section 1980–83, Dir of Plans and Policy and Deputy Chief 1986–91, Chief 1991–92; Deputy CO Jämtland (Sector) Wing 1983–84; Head of Planning Section AF Staff 1984–86; CO Southern Jt Command Swedish Armed Forces 1992–94, Supreme Commdr 1994–2000; Fellow, Royal Swedish Acad. of War Sciences 1985; Kt Commdr of White Rose of Finland; Chevalier, Légion d'honneur; Gold Medal for Merit, Southern Skåne Regt, Swedish Home Guard; Gold Medal for Merit, Nat. Fed. of AF Asscns. *Leisure interests:* sailing, skiing, cooking, sky-diving, hunting. *Address:* c/o The Swedish Armed Forces, 107 85 Stockholm, Sweden (office).

WILANDER, Mats Arne Olof; Swedish fmr professional tennis player and sports commentator; *Tennis Instructor, WilanderOnWheels, LLC;* b. 22 Aug. 1964, Vaxjo; s. of Einar Wilander and Karin Wilander; m. Sonya Mulholland 1987; turned professional 1981; Australian Open Champion 1983, 1984, 1988 (finalist 1985), French Open Champion 1982, 1985, 1988 (finalist 1983, 1987), US Open Champion 1988 (finalist 1987); winner Wimbledon Men's Doubles Championship (with Joakim Nystrom) 1986; mem. victorious Swedish Davis Cup Team 1984, 1987, 1988; ranked world No. 1 1988; voted official World Champion 1988; won 33 singles and six doubles titles (including seven Grand Slam titles); coach of Russian player Marat Safin 2001; Capt. Swedish Davis Cup Team 2002–; mem. Sr Tour; International Tennis Hall of Fame 2003. *Music:* released CD 1991. *Leisure interests:* art, music, skiing, golf. *Address:* c/o Tennis HOF, 194 Bellevue Avenue, Newport, RI, 02840-3515, USA. *Fax:* (208) 748-4796 (office). *E-mail:* wilanderonwheels@gmail.com (office). *Website:* www.wilanderonwheels.com (office).

WILBUR, Richard Purdy, MA; American poet and academic; b. 1 March 1921, New York City; s. of Lawrence L. Wilbur and Helen Purdy Wilbur; m. Charlotte Ward 1942; three s. one d.; ed Amherst Coll. and Harvard Univ.; Asst Prof. of English, Harvard Univ. 1950–54; Assoc. Prof., Wellesley Coll. 1954–57; Prof., Wesleyan Univ. 1957–77; Writer in Residence, Smith Coll., Northampton, Mass. 1977–86; mem. American Acad. of Arts and Sciences, Soc. of Fellows of Harvard Univ. 1947–50; Guggenheim Fellow 1952–53, 1963, Ford Fellow 1961; Chancellor, Acad. of American Poets 1961; Poet Laureate of USA 1987–88; mem. PEN; Pres. American Acad. of Arts and Letters 1974–76, Chancellor 1977–78; mem. Dramatists Guild; Hon. Fellow, Modern Language Asscn 1986; Chevalier, Ordre des Palmes Académiques 1984; Dr hc (Yale) 2012; Harriet Monroe Prize 1948, Oscar Blumenthal Prize 1950, Prix de Rome from American Acad. of Arts and Letters 1954–55, Edna St Vincent Millay Memorial Award 1956, Nat. Book Award, Pulitzer Prize 1957, co-recipient Bollingen Translation Prize 1963, co-recipient Bollingen Prize in Poetry 1971, Prix Henri Desfeuilles 1971, Brandeis Creative Arts Award 1971, Shelley Memorial Prize 1973, Harriet Monroe Poetry Award 1978, Drama Desk Award 1983, PEN Translation Prize 1983, St Botolph's Foundation Award 1983, Aiken Taylor Award 1988, L.A. Times Book Award 1988, Pulitzer Prize 1989, Gold Medal for Poetry, American Acad. of Arts and Letters 1991, MacDowell Medal 1992, Nat. Arts Club Medal of Honour for Literature 1994, PEN/Manheim Medal for Translation 1994, Nat. Medal of Arts 1994, Milton Center Prize 1995, Robert Frost Medal, Poetry Soc. of America 1996, T. S. Eliot Award 1996, Wallace Stevens Award 2003, Theater Hall of Fame 2003, Ruth Lilly Prize for Poetry 2006, National Translation Award (for translation of The Theatre of Illusion by Pierre Corneille) 2010. *Publications include:* The Beautiful Changes and Other Poems 1947, Ceremony and Other Poems 1950, A Bestiary (anthology, with Alexander Calder) 1955, The Misanthrope (trans. from Molière) 1955, Things of This World (poems) 1956, Poems 1943–1956 1957, Candide (comic opera, with Lillian Hellman and others) 1957, (edition of his poems with introduction and notes) 1959, Advice to a Prophet (poems) 1961, Tartuffe (trans. from Molière) 1963, The Poems of Richard Wilbur 1963, Loudmouse (for children) 1963, Poems of Shakespeare (with Alfred Harbage) 1966, Walking to Sleep (new poems and translations) 1969, School for Wives (trans. from Molière) 1971, Opposites (children's verse, illustrated by the author) 1973, The Mind-Reader 1976, Responses: Prose Pieces 1953–1976 1976, The Learned Ladies (trans. from Molière) 1978, Selected Poems of Witter Bynner (editor) 1978, Seven Poems 1981, Andromache (trans. from Racine) 1982, The Whale (translations) 1982, Molière: Four Comedies (contains 4 plays translated previously listed) 1982, Phaedra (trans. from Racine) 1986, Lying and Other Poems 1987, New and Collected Poems 1988, More Opposites 1991, School for Husbands (trans. from Molière) 1992, The Imaginary Cuckold (trans. from Molière) 1993, A Game of Catch 1994, Amphitryon (trans. from Molière) 1995, The Catbird's Song (prose pieces) 1997, The

Disappearing Alphabet (for children and others) 1998, Bone Key and Other Poems 1998, Mayflies (poems) 2000, Don Juan (trans. from Molière) 2000, The Bungler (trans. from Molière) 2000, Opposites, More Opposites and Some Differences (for children) 2000, The Pig in the Spigot (for children) 2000, Collected Poems 1953–2004 2004, Anterooms: New Poems and Translations 2010, The Nutcracker 2012. *Leisure interests:* tennis, walking, herb gardening. *Address:* 87 Dodwells Road, Cummington, MA 01026, USA (home).

WILBUR, Hon. Richard Sloan, MD, JD; American physician and association executive; *Chairman, American Medical Foundation for Peer Review and Education;* b. 8 April 1924, Boston, Mass; s. of Blake Colburn Wilbur and Mary Caldwell Sloan; m. Betty Lou Fannin 1951; three s.; ed John Marshall Law School, Stanford Univ. Medical School; Intern, San Francisco County Hosp. 1946–47; Resident, Stanford Hosp. 1949–51, Univ. of Pennsylvania Hosp. 1951–52; mem. of Staff, Palo Alto Medical Clinic, Calif. 1952–69; Deputy Exec. Vice-Pres., American Medical Asscn, Chicago 1969–71, 1973–74; Asst Sec., Health and Environment Defense Dept 1971–73; Sr Vice-Pres., Baxter Labs Inc., Deerfield, Ill. 1974–76; Exec. Vice-Pres. Council Medical Speciality Socs 1976–91, Emer. 1992–; Sec., Accreditation Council for Continuing Medical Educ. 1979–91; Assoc. Prof. of Medicine, Stanford Medical School 1952–69, Georgetown Univ. Medical School 1971–77; Vice-Pres. Nat. Resident Matching Plan 1990–91, Pres. 1991–92; Chair. Bd Calif. Medical Asscn 1968–69; Chair. Calif. Blue Shield 1966–68; Chair. American Medical Foundation 1987–, Professional Advisory Bd, Royal Soc. of Medicine Foundation 1995–; Pres. American Coll. of Physician Executives 1988–89; Pres. American Bd Medical Man. 1992–93; Pres. MedicAlert Foundation Int. 1992–94, MedicAlert Foundation, USA 1992–94, Dir MedicAlert Germany 1992–94, Iberica 1992–94, Europe (UK) 1992–95; Chair. Bd and CEO Inst. for Clinical Information 1994–; Sr Vice-Pres. Healthcare, Buckeye Corpn Pte. Ltd 1997–2000; Chair. Medical Advisory Bd, Medical City, Bangalore 1997–2000; Pres. Royal Soc. of Medicine Foundation 1998–, American Coll. of Legal Medicine 2006–07; Ed. World Association Medical Law Bulletin 2009–; mem. numerous other medical asscns; Distinguished Service Medal, Dept of Defense 1973. *Publications:* contribs to medical journals. *Address:* APT Management Inc., 736 North Western Road, Suite 222, Lake Forest, IL 60045 (office); 985 North Hawthorne Place, Lake Forest, IL 60045, USA (home). *Telephone:* (847) 234-6337 (office). *Fax:* (847) 234-5294 (office). *E-mail:* aptmgmnt@aol.com (office). *Website:* www.medicalfoundation.org (office).

WILBY, James; British actor; b. 20 Feb. 1958, Rangoon, Burma; s. of Geoffrey Wilby and Shirley Wilby; m. Shana Louise Magraw 1988; three s. one d.; ed Sedbergh School, Durham Univ., Royal Acad. of Dramatic Art, London; Outstanding Performance by a Cast, Screen Actors' Guild 2001. *Stage appearances:* Another Country (West End début), Who's Afraid of Virginia Woolf (Belgrade Theatre, Coventry), Chips With Everything (Leeds Playhouse), As You Like It (Royal Exchange Theatre, Manchester and tour), Jane Eyre (Chichester), A Patriot for Me (Barbican), Helping Harry (Jermyn Street), Don Juan (Lyric Hammersmith). *Films:* Dreamchild, Maurice (Best Actor, Venice Film Festival 1988), A Handful of Dust (Best Actor, Bari Film Festival 1989), A Summer Story, Howards End 1991, Immaculate Conception 1992, Une partie d'echec, Regeneration, An Ideal Husband, Tom's Midnight Garden, Cotton Mary, Jump Tomorrow, Gosford Park, C'est Gradiva qui vous appelle 2006, The Wreck 2007. *Television:* Sherlock Holmes, The Crooked Man, Dutch Girls, A Tale of Two Cities, Mother Love, Tell Me That You Love Me, Adam Bede, You, Me And It, Lady Chatterley, Crocodile Shoes, Woman in White 1997, The Dark Room, Trial and Retribution IV, Bertie and Elizabeth, Island at War, Jericho 2005, Marple: The Sittaford Mystery 2005, Little Devil 2006, Nero 2006, Lewis 2006, The Last Days of the Raj 2007, Clapham Junction 2007, Impact Earth 2008, A Risk Worth Taking 2008, Shadows in the Sun 2009. *Leisure interests:* playing piano, tennis, sailing. *Address:* c/o Sue Latimer, A.R.G., 4 Great Portland Street, London, W1W 8PA, England. *Telephone:* (20) 7436-6400. *Fax:* (20) 7436-6700.

WILBY, Peter, BA (Hons); British journalist; *Columnist, New Statesman and Guardian;* b. 7 Nov. 1944, Leicester, England; m. Sandra James; two s.; ed Univ. of Sussex; reporter, The Observer 1968–72, Educ. Corresp. 1972–75; Educ. Corresp. The New Statesman 1975–77, Ed. 1998–2005, now writes weekly column; Educ. Corresp., The Sunday Times 1977–86; Educ. Ed., The Independent 1986–89, Home Ed., Independent on Sunday 1989–91, Deputy Ed. 1991–95, Ed. 1995–96; Press Commentator, The Guardian newspaper 2007–09; columnist; Hon. LLD (Leicester). *Publication:* Anthony Eden 2006. *Address:* 51 Queens Road, Loughton, Essex, IG10 1RR, England. *E-mail:* peter.wilby@gmail.com.

WILCZEK, Frank, BS, MA, PhD; American physicist and academic; *Herman Feshbach Professor of Physics, Massachusetts Institute of Technology;* b. 15 May 1951, New York; s. of Frank Wilczek and Mary Cona; m. Elizabeth Devine 1973; two d.; ed Univ. of Chicago, Princeton Univ.; Instructor, Princeton Univ. 1974, Asst Prof. 1974–76, 1977–78, Visiting Fellow, Inst. for Advanced Study 1976–77, Assoc. Prof. 1978–80, Prof. 1980–81, R. J. Oppenheimer Prof., Inst. for Advanced Study, School of Natural Sciences 1989–2000; mem. Inst. for Theoretical Physics, Univ. of Calif., Santa Barbara 1980–88, Robert Huttenback Prof. of Physics 1980–88; Visiting Prof., Harvard Univ. 1987–88; Herman Feshbach Prof. of Physics, MIT 2000–; Adjunct Prof., Centros Estudios Cientificos, 2002–; Schrödinger Prof., Vienna 2002; Rudolf Peiriels Visiting Prof., Univ. of Oxford 2008; mem. Editorial Bd, Zeitschrift für Physik C 1981–87, Annual Reviews of Nuclear & Particle Science 1985–89; mem. Scientific Advisory Cttee, CERN 2002–, Perimeter Inst. for Theoretical Physics 2003–; Ed.-in-Chief Annals of Physics 2001–; Editorial Adviser Daedalus 2002–; mem. American Acad. of Arts and Sciences 1993–, NAS 1990–; foreign mem. Royal Netherlands Acad. of Arts and Sciences 2000–; Fellow AAAS 2000–, American Physical Soc. 2004–, American Philosophical Soc. 2005–, Polish Acad. of Arts and Sciences 2007–; hon. lecturerships at numerous int. univs; numerous hon. doctorates; Sakurai Prize, American Physical Soc. 1986, Lorentz Medal, Royal Netherlands Acad. of Arts and Sciences 2002, Michelson-Morley Prize, Case Western Reserve Univ. 2002, Lillienfeld Prize, American Physical Soc. 2003, High Energy and Particle Physics Prize, European Physical Soc. 2003, Nobel Prize in Physics (jt recipient) 2004, King Faisal Prize 2005, Julius Wess Award 2008, Casimir Funk Award 2008. *Publications include:* Longing for the Harmonies 1989, Fantastic Realities: 49 Mind Journeys and A Trip to Stockholm 2006, The Lightness of Being: Mass, Ether and the Unification of Forces 2008; more than 200 contribs to academic journals and books. *Leisure interests:* music, learning things,

solving puzzles. *Address:* Department of Physics, Massachusetts Institute of Technology, 77 Massachusetts Avenue, 6-301, Cambridge, MA 02139 (office); 4 Wyman Road, Cambridge, MA 02138, USA (home). *Telephone:* (617) 253-0284 (office). *Fax:* (617) 253-8674 (office). *E-mail:* wilczek@mit.edu (office). *Website:* frankwilczek.com.

WILD, Christopher, PhD; British medical scientist and academic; *Director, International Agency for Research on Cancer;* ed Univ. of Manchester; postdoctoral fellow, Int. Agency for Research on Cancer (IARC), Lyon, France 1984–85, staff scientist 1987, later Chief of Unit of Environmental Carcinogenesis, Dir IARC 2009–; Royal Soc. European Exchange Fellowship, Netherlands Cancer Inst., Amsterdam 1986–87; apptd Prof. of Molecular Epidemiology, Univ. of Leeds and Head of Centre for Epidemiology and Biostatistics 1996, later Dir Leeds Inst. of Genetics, Health and Therapeutics 2005–08, Hon. Prof. of Molecular Epidemiology 2008–; Chair. UK Molecular Epidemiology Group 2001–05; Founding mem. Ethics and Governance Council of the UK Biobank; UK Molecular Epidemiology Group 10th Anniversary Medal 2006. *Publications:* more than 170 peer-reviewed scientific papers in professional journals on the interplay between environmental and genetic risk factors in the causation of human disease. *Address:* IARC, 150 Cours Albert Thomas, 69372 Lyon CEDEX 08, France (office). *Telephone:* (4) 72-73-84-85 (office). *Fax:* (4) 72-73-85-75 (office). *E-mail:* www@iarc.fr (office). *Website:* www.iarc.fr (office).

WILDENTHAL, Kern, MD, PhD; American university administrator and physician; *Professor of Internal Medicine and Physiology, University of Texas Southwestern Medical Center;* b. 1 July 1941, San Marcos, Tex.; m. Margaret Wildenthal (née Dehlinger) 1964; two d.; ed Sul Ross Coll., Univ. of Tex. Southwestern Medical Center, Univ. of Cambridge, UK; Intern, Bellvue Hosp., NY 1964–65; Resident, Parkland Hospital, Dallas 1965–67; Asst Prof. then Prof. of Internal Medicine and Physiology, Univ. of Tex. Southwestern Medical School, Dallas 1970–76, Prof. and Dean of Grad. School 1976–80, Prof. and Dean Southwestern Medical School 1980–86, Pres. Univ. of Tex. Southwestern Medical Center 1986–2008, also Prof. of Internal Medicine and Physiology; fmr Chair. American Section, Int. Soc. for Heart Research, Science Policy Cttee, Asscn of Academic Heart Centers, Basic Science Council, Science Advisory Cttee, American Heart Asscn, Program Project Research Review Cttee, Nat. Heart, Lung and Blood Inst.; mem. NAS Inst. of Medicine, American Soc. for Clinical Investigation, Asscn of American Physicians; mem. Bd of Dirs Dallas Center for the Performing Arts, Dallas Museum of Art, Dallas Symphony Asscn, Dallas Opera, Greater Dallas Chamber of Commerce, Dallas Citizens Council, Southwestern Medical Foundation, Hoblitzelle Foundation, Wendy and Emery Reves Foundation; Hon. Fellow, Hughes Hall, Univ. of Cambridge. *Publications:* 130 scientific papers in basic research and clinical cardiology, numerous articles on health and educ. policy issues. *E-mail:* priscilla.alderman@utsouthwestern.edu (office). *Address:* University of Texas Southwestern Medical Center, 5323 Harry Hines Blvd, Dallas, TX 75390-9002, USA (office). *Telephone:* (214) 648-2508 (office). *Fax:* (214) 648-8690 (office). *Website:* www.utsouthwestern.edu (office).

WILDER, C. John, BS, MBA; American energy industry executive; *Chairman, Bluescape Resources;* b. Missouri; ed SE Missouri State Univ., Univ. of Tex.; joined Royal Dutch/Shell Group 1980, various man. positions including CEO Shell Capital, London, UK –1998; Exec. Vice-Pres. and Chief Financial Officer Entergy Corpn 1998–2004; Pres., CEO and Dir TXU Corpn 2004–07; currently Chair. Bluescape Resources; served as dir of more than 65 Entergy-related cos and 75 Shell-related cos; mem. Bd of Dirs Univ. of Tex. and Tulane Univ. Business Schools; mem. Financial Execs Inst., Edison Electric Inst., United Methodist Church Admin. Bd. *Address:* Bluescape Resources, 200 Crescent Court, Suite 200, Dallas, TX 75201, USA (office). *Telephone:* (214) 855-2260 (office). *Fax:* (214) 855-2265 (office). *Website:* www.bluescaperesources.com (office).

WILDER, Gene, BA; American film actor, director and producer; b. (Jerry Silberman), 11 June 1933, Milwaukee, Wis.; s. of William J. Silberman and Jeanne Silberman (née Baer); m. 1st Mary Joan Schutz 1967 (divorced 1974); one d.; m. 2nd Gilda Radner 1984 (deceased); m. 3rd Karen Boyer 1991; ed Univ. of Iowa, Bristol Old Vic Theatre School, London; served with US Army 1956–58; Broadway play: The Complaisant Lover 1962, West End play Laughter on the 23rd Floor 1996. *Films include:* Bonnie and Clyde 1966, The Producers 1968, Start the Revolution Without Me 1970, Quacksor Fortune Has a Cousin in the Bronx 1970, Willy Wonka and the Chocolate Factory 1971, Everything You Always Wanted to Know About Sex, But Were Afraid to Ask 1972, Young Frankenstein 1974, The Little Prince 1974, Young Frankenstein 1974, Rhinoceros 1974, Blazing Saddles 1974, Thursday's Game 1974, The Adventure of Sherlock Holmes's Smarter Brother (also writer and dir) 1975, Silver Streak 1976, The World's Greatest Lover (also writer, producer and dir) 1977, The Frisco Kid 1979, Stir Crazy 1980, Sunday Lovers (also writer and dir) 1980, Hanky Panky 1982, The Woman in Red (also writer and dir) 1984, Hanky Panky 1982, Haunted Honeymoon (also writer and dir) 1986, See No Evil, Hear No Evil 1989, Funny About Love 1990, Another You 1991, Stuart Little (voice) 1999, Instant Karma 2005. *Television includes:* Death of a Salesman 1966, The Scarecrow 1972, The Electric Company (series) (voice) 1972–77, The Trouble With People 1973, Marlo Thomas Special 1973, Thursday's Games 19741974, Annie and the Hoods, Something Wilder (series) 1994, Murder in a Small Town (film) 1999, Alice in Wonderland (film) 1999, The Lady in Question (film) 1999. *Publications include:* My French Whore (novel) 2007, The Woman Who Wouldn't 2008, What is This Thing Called Love? 2010.

WILDEROTTER, Maggie, BA; American business executive; *Chairman and CEO, Frontier Communications Corporation;* b. (Mary Agnes Sullivan), 9 Feb. 1955, Neptune, NJ; ed Holy Cross Coll., Worcester, Mass; with CableData for 12 years following graduation; later Sr Vice-Pres. McCaw Cellular Communications Inc., a Regional Pres. managing the co.'s Calif., Nev. and Hawaii Region, remained with AT&T following its acquisition of McCaw, later Exec. Vice-Pres. Nat. Operations for AT&T Wireless Services Inc. and CEO AT&T's Aviation Communications Div. (Claircom) –1997; fmr Pres. and CEO Wink Communications Inc. (acquired by Liberty Media) 1997–2002; Sr Vice-Pres. Worldwide Public Sector, Microsoft Corpn 2002–04; mem. Bd of Dirs, Pres. and CEO Citizens Communications (renamed Frontier Communications 2008) 2004–06, Chair. and CEO 2006–; mem. Bd of Dirs Xerox Corpn, Procter & Gamble Co.; Vice-Chair. Pres. Obama's Nat. Security Telecommunications Advisory Cttee 2010–12, Chair.

2012–; mem. Directorship 100 (list compiled by Nat. Asscn of Corp. Dirs), Bd of Advisors of BoardroomIQ, WomenCorporateDirectors Global CEO Task Force; mem. Exec. Cttee Business Roundtable 2012–; fmr mem. Bd of Trustees, Holy Cross Coll.; ranked by Fortune magazine amongst the 50 Most Powerful Women in Business in the US (50th) 2009, (40th) 2010, (37th) 2011, (35th) 2012, November 2011, named by The Financial Times her as one of The Top 50 Women in World Business 2011, The Business Media Award, Women's Media Center 2011, Distinguished Achievement Award, B'nai B'rith International 2012. *Address:* Frontier Communications Corporation, 3 High Ridge Park, Stamford, CT 06905-1390, USA (office). *Telephone:* (203) 614-5600 (office). *Fax:* (203) 614-4602 (office). *E-mail:* frontier@frontiercorp.com (office). *Website:* www.frontier.com (office).

WILDERS, Geert; Dutch politician; *Leader, Partij voor de Vrijheid;* b. 6 Sept. 1963, Venlo; m. Krisztina Wilders 1992; ed Open Univ.; lived in Israel 1981–83; began career working for health insurance co., Utrecht; mem. Volkspartij voor Vrijheid en Democratie (VVD) 1998–2004, becoming speech-writer and public spokesman 2002; VVD mem. Utrecht city council 1998; Parl. Asst to VVD leader Frits Bolkestein, specializing in foreign policy 1990–98; mem. House of Reps 1998–2002, 2002–; f. Groep Wilders 2004 (renamed Partij voor de Vrijheid, Freedom Party 2006). *Films:* Fitna (short film about Islam) 2008. *Publication:* Marked for Death: Islam's War Against the West and Me 2012. *Address:* Partij voor de Vrijheid, POB 20018, 2500 EA The Hague, Netherlands (office). *E-mail:* g.wilders@tweedekamer.nl (office). *Website:* www.pvv.nl (office); www.geertwilders.nl (home).

WILDHABER, Luzius, DrIur, LLM, JSD; Swiss judge and professor of law; b. 18 Jan. 1937, Basle; m. 1st Simone Wildhaber-Creux 1963 (died 1994); m. 2nd Gill Reilly 1998 (divorced 2004); two d.; ed Univ. of Basle, Univ. of Paris, France, Univ. of Heidelberg, Germany, Univ. of London, UK, Yale Univ., USA; Int. Law Div. Fed. Dept of External Affairs 1968–71; Prof. of Int. Constitutional and Admin. Law, Univ. of Fribourg 1971–77; Prof. of Int. and Constitutional Law, Univ. of Basle 1977–98, Rector (desig.) 1990–92, Rector 1992–94, Pro-Rector 1994–96; Judge, Supreme Court of Liechtenstein 1975–88, Admin. Tribunal, IDB 1989–94, European Court of Human Rights 1991–2007; Pres. European Court of Human Rights 1998–2007; Pres. Admin Tribunal, Council of Europe 2009–11; Pres. Advisory Panel of Experts on Cands for Election as Judge to European Court of Human Rights 2011–13; Hon. Bencher, Inner Temple 2002, King's Inns Soc. Dublin 2005, Hon. mem. Int. Comm. of Jurists 2008; Star of Romania 2000, Order of Merit of Lithuania 2003, Order of St Agata (San Marino), Great Gold Badge of Honour with Sash (Austria) 2006, Commdr, Order of Orange-Nassau (Netherlands) 2007; Dr hc (Charles Univ., Prague) 1999, (Sofia Univ.) 1999, (American Univ., Bulgaria) 1999, (Bratislava) 2000, (State Univ. of Moldova) 2000, (Bucharest) 2000, (Russian Acad. of Sciences) 2000, (Law Univ. of Lithuania) 2000, (Tbilisi) 2001, (Nat. Law Acad. of Ukraine) 2001, (Neuchâtel) 2004, Hon. LLD (McGill Univ., Montreal) 2002, (Augsburg) 2009; Marcel Benoist Prize 1999, Anna Göldi Prize 2009, Award of Merit, Yale Law School Asscn 2011. *Publications:* Advisory Opinions – Rechtsgutachten höchster Gerichte 1962, Treaty-making Power and Constitution 1971, Erfahrungen mit der Europäischen Menschenrechtskonvention 1979, Wechselspiel zwischen Innen und Aussen 1996, Praxis des Völkerrechts (with J. P. Müller, 3rd edn) 2001, The European Court of Human Rights: History, Achievements, Reform 2006; more than 200 articles. *Leisure interests:* travel, skiing, hiking, mountaineering. *Address:* Auf der Wacht 21, 4104 Oberwil, Switzerland. *Telephone:* (61) 401-25-21. *Fax:* (61) 401-25-75. *E-mail:* luzius.wildhaber@unibas.ch (office).

WILES, Sir Andrew John, KBE, PhD, FRS; British mathematician and academic; *Royal Society 2010 Anniversary Research Professor, University of Oxford;* b. 11 April 1953, Cambridge, England; s. of the late Rev. Prof. Maurice Frank Wiles and of Patricia Wiles (née Mowll); m.; two d.; ed King's Coll. School, Cambridge, The Leys School, Cambridge, Merton Coll., Oxford and Clare Coll., Cambridge; fmr Fellow, Clare Coll., Cambridge; mem. Inst. for Advanced Study, Priceton, NJ, USA 1981; Prof. of Math., Princeton Univ. 1982–88, 1990–2011; Royal Soc. Research Prof. in Math. and Professorial Fellow, Merton Coll., Oxford 1988–90, Royal Soc. 2010 Anniversary Research Prof. in Math. and Professorial Fellow in Math., Merton Coll. 2011–; Foreign mem. NAS 1996; Hon. DSc (Oxford) 1999; Guggenheim Fellow, Institut des Hautes Études Scientifiques, Paris and École Normale Supérieure 1985–86, Jr Whitehead Prize, London Math. Soc. (co-recipient) 1988, Wolf Prize 1995–96, Wolfskehl Prize (for proving Fermat's Last Theorem), Göttingen 1997, Silver Plaque, Berlin Int. Congress of Mathematicians 1998, King Faisal Prize 1998, asteroid 9999 Wiles named for him 1999, Clay Research Award 1999, Pythagoras Award 2004, Shaw Prize 2005, Math. Inst. building at Oxford named the Andrew Wiles Building in his honour 2013. *Address:* Mathematical Institute, University of Oxford, Andrew Wiles Building, Radcliffe Observatory Quarter, Woodstock Road, Oxford, OX2 6GG (office); Merton College, Merton Street, Oxford, OX1 4JD, England. *Telephone:* (1865) 273525 (office); (1865) 276310. *Fax:* (1865) 276361. *E-mail:* andrew.wiles@merton.ox.ac.uk (office). *Website:* www.maths.ox.ac.uk (office).

WILEY, John D., BS, MS, PhD; American physicist, university administrator and academic; *Chancellor, University of Wisconsin-Madison;* ed Indiana Univ., Grad. School, Univ. of Wisconsin-Madison (NSF Fellow); mem. tech. staff, Bell Telephone Labs, Murray Hill, NJ 1968–74; at Max Planck Inst., Stuttgart, Germany (awardee of Alexander von Humboldt Sr US Service Award for Research and Training) 1974–75; mem. faculty, Dept of Electrical and Computer Eng, Univ. of Wisconsin-Madison 1975–, Assoc. Dean for Research, Coll. of Eng 1986–89, Dean Grad. School and Sr Research Officer 1989–94, Provost and Vice-Chancellor for Academic Affairs 1994–2000, Chancellor 2001–; Co-founder several research centres, including Center for X-ray Lithography, Eng Research Center for Plasma-Aided Manufacturing; Chair. Materials Science Program 1982–86, Big Ten Council of Pres and Chancellors, Bd for the Council on Higher Educ. Accreditation; mem. Nat. Security Higher Educ. Advisory Cttee; also serves on several local and community bds, including William T. Evjue Foundation, Greater Madison Chamber of Commerce. *Address:* Office of the Chancellor, University of Wisconsin-Madison, 161 Bascom Hall, 500 Lincoln Drive, Madison, WI 53706, USA (office). *Telephone:* (608) 262-9946 (office). *E-mail:* chancellor@news.wisc.edu (office). *Website:* www.wisc.edu (office).

WILHELM, Ivan, CSc; Czech physicist, academic and university administrator; *Government Plenipotentiary, Ministry of Education, Youth and Sports;* b. 1 May 1942, Trnava, Slovakia; m.; one d.; ed Czech Tech. Univ. (CVUT), Prague; Asst, Dept of Nuclear Physics, CVUT 1964–67; study attachment to Neutron Physics Lab., United Inst. for Nuclear Research, Dubna, USSR 1967–71; Sr Research Officer, Faculty of Math. and Physics, Charles Univ. 1971–89, Chief Research Officer 1989–91, Dir Nuclear Centre 1990–94, Vice-Rector for Devt 1994–2000, Rector of Charles Univ. 2000–06; Pres. Czech Rectors' Conf. 2000–06; mem. Exec. Council European Univ. Asscn 2000–06, Admin. Council Int. Asscn of Univs 2000–; Govt Plenipotentiary, Ministry of Educ., Youth and Sports 2006–; Ordre des Palmes académiques, St Gregory Order of the Holy Sea; Dr hc (Univ. of Lyon 1-Claude Bernard) 2003, (Comenius Univ., Bratislava) 2006. *Publications include:* more than 100 research papers on nuclear and neutron physics. *Leisure interests:* cycling, walking, skiing. *Address:* Ministry of Education, Youth and Sports, Karmelitska 8, 11812 Prague 1, Czech Republic (office). *Telephone:* (2) 34811749 (office). *E-mail:* ivan.wilhelm@msmt.cz (office); ivan.wilhelm@ruk.cuni.cz. *Website:* www.msmt.cz (office).

WILHELMSSON, Hans K. B., DTech; Swedish physicist and academic; *Professor Emeritus, Fondation de France, Ecole Polytechnique, Palaiseau;* b. 4 Oct. 1929, Göteborg; s. of Wilhelm Petterson and Clara M. Johansson; m. 1st Birgitta Fredrikson 1960 (divorced 1995); one s. one d.; m. 2nd Julie Baudin 1995; ed Chalmers Univ. of Tech.; Prof. and Dir Inst. for Electromagnetic Field Theory, Chalmers Univ. of Tech. Göteborg 1971; Prof. of Plasma Physics, Fondation de France, Ecole Polytechnique, Palaiseau 1987–93, Prof. Emer. 1994–; mem. Royal Swedish Acad. of Science, Royal Swedish Acad. of Eng Science, Acad. Nationale des Sciences, Belles-Lettres et Arts de Bordeaux; John Ericson Medal (Chalmers Univ.) 1952, Montesquieu Medal (Bordeaux Acad.) 1999, Hon. Medal of the City of Nantes 2004. *Publications:* Fusion: A Voyage Through the Plasma Universe 2000; more than 200 scientific articles in theoretical and plasma physics. *Leisure interests:* art, travel. *Address:* 2 rue Marcellin Berthelot, 33200 Bordeaux, France. *Telephone:* (5) 56-02-19-80. *Fax:* (5) 56-02-19-80. *E-mail:* lotus15@free.fr.

WILKINS, David Horton, BA, JD; American lawyer, politician and diplomatist; *Partner, Nelson Mullins Riley & Scarborough LLP;* b. 12 Oct. 1946, Greenville; s. of the late William Walter Wilkins and Evelyn Wilkins; m. Susan Clary; two s.; ed Greenville High School, Clemson Univ., Univ. of S Carolina; served in US Army as a First Lt; practised law for 30 years while serving in S Carolina House of Reps for 25 of those years; Chair. Greenville Co. Legis. Del. 1985–86, 1989–94; Chair. Judicial Comm. 1986–92; Chair. Southern Legis. Conf. 1998; Pres. Nat. Speakers Conf. 2001; Speaker Pro Tempore S Carolina Legislature 1992–94, Speaker 1994–2005; State Chair. Bush-Cheney Re-election Campaign; Amb. to Canada 2005–09; Pnr, Nelson Mullins Riley & Scarborough LLP 2009–; Chair. Clemson Univ. 2009–; Chair. Public Policy and Int. Law practice group; mem. Bd of Dirs Porter Airlines 2009–; Dr hc (Clemson Univ.) 2003; William M. Bulger Excellence in State Legis. Leadership Award 2004. *Address:* Nelson Mullins Riley & Scarborough LLP, Poinsett Plaza, Suite 900, 104 South Main Street, Greenville, SC 29601-2122, USA (office). *Telephone:* (864) 250-2231 (office). *Fax:* (864) 250-2925 (office). *Website:* www.nelsonmullins.com (office).

WILKINSON, Sir Denys Haigh, Kt, PhD, DSc, ScD, FRS; British physicist, academic and academic administrator; *Professor Emeritus, Sussex University;* b. 5 Sept. 1922, Leeds; s. of Charles Wilkinson and Hilda Wilkinson; m. 1st Christiane Clavier 1947; three d.; m. 2nd Helen Sellschop 1967; ed Jesus Coll., Cambridge; worked on British Atomic Energy Project 1943–46, on Canadian Atomic Energy Project 1945–46; Demonstrator Cavendish Lab., Univ. of Cambridge 1947–51, Lecturer 1951–56 and Reader 1950–57, Fellow, Jesus Coll., Cambridge 1944–59, Hon. Fellow 1961–; Student of Christ Church, Oxford 1957–76, Emer. 1976–79, Hon. 1979–; Prof. of Nuclear Physics, Clarendon Laboratory, Univ. of Oxford 1957–59, Prof. of Experimental Physics 1959–76, Head of Dept of Nuclear Physics 1962–76; Vice-Chancellor Univ. of Sussex 1976–87, Prof. Emer. 1987–; Pres. Inst. of Physics 1980–82, Hon. Fellow 2002–; Rutherford Memorial Lecturer of British Physical Soc. 1962; mem. Governing Bd Nat. Inst. for Research in Nuclear Science 1958–64; Queen's Lecturer, Berlin 1966, Cherwell-Simon Memorial Lecturer, Oxford 1970, Tizard Memorial Lecturer 1975, Lauritsen Memorial Lecturer, Calif. Inst. of Tech. 1976, Schiff Memorial Lecturer, Stanford Univ. 1977, Racah Memorial Lecturer, Univ. of Jerusalem 1977, Solly Cohen Memorial Lecturer, Hebrew Univ. of Jerusalem 1985, Axel Memorial Lecturer, Univ. of Ill. 1985, Breit Memorial Lecturer, Yale Univ. 1987, W. B. Lewis Memorial Lecturer, Chalk River 1989, Humphry Davy Lecturer, Acad. of Science (Paris) 1990, Rutherford Memorial Lecturer, NZ 1991, W. V. Houston Memorial Lecturer, Rice Univ., Houston, Tex. 1994, Hudspeth Lecturer, Univ. of Tex. Austin 1994, McPherson Memorial Lecturer, McGill Univ., Montreal 1995, Pickavance Memorial Lecturer, Rutherford Lab., Oxford 1997, Sargent Memorial Lecturer, Queen's Univ., Kingston, Ont. 1998, Saha Memorial Lecturer, Kolkata 2001; mem. Science Research Council 1967–70; Chair. SRC Nuclear Physics Bd 1968–70, Physics III Cttee CERN, Geneva 1971–75, Radioactive Waste Man. Advisory Cttee 1978–83; Vice-Pres. IUPAP 1975–93; mem. Council of the Asscn of Commonwealth Univs 1981–87; mem. Academia Europaea; Foreign mem. Royal Swedish Acad. of Sciences; Battelle Distinguished Prof., Univ. of Washington 1970; Hon. DSc (Univ. of Saskatchewan, Utah State Univ., Univ. of Guelph, Queen's Univ., Ont.); Hon. FilDr (Univ. of Uppsala); Hon. LLD (Sussex); Hon. DSc (Coll. of William and Mary, Williamsburg); Holweck Medallist of French and British Physical Socs 1957, Hughes Medal of the Royal Soc. 1965, Bruce-Preller Prize of Royal Soc. of Edinburgh 1969, Tom W. Bonner Prize of American Physical Soc. 1974, Royal Medal, Royal Soc. 1980, Guthrie Medal of Inst. of Physics 1986, CCSEM Gold Medal 1988. *Publications:* Ionization Chambers and Counters 1950, Our Universes 1991; Ed.: Isospin in Nuclear Physics 1969, Progress in Particle and Nuclear Physics 1977–84; Mesons in Nuclei (jt ed.) 1979; many articles in learned journals. *Leisure interests:* early music and art, ornithology. *Address:* Gayles Orchard, Friston, Eastbourne, BN20 0BA, England (home). *Telephone:* (1323) 423333 (home).

WILKINSON, Jonathan Peter (Jonny), OBE; British professional rugby football player (rugby union); b. 25 May 1979, Frimley, Surrey, England; s. of Philip Wilkinson and Philippa Wilkinson; ed Lord Wandsworth Coll., Hants., Durham Univ.; fly-half; player for Farnham, Newcastle Falcons 1997–2009 (mem.

winning squad, Allied Dunbar Premiership 1997/98, Powergen Cup 2001, 2004), England Under-18s, England 1998–2011 (debut vs Ireland, second youngest England int. at 18 years and 314 days, apptd Capt. Nov. 2004), Rugby Club Toulonnais (France) 2009– (mem. Heineken Cup winning squad 2013); 91 Test caps for England (won 67 of them), 1,179 points, has also scored 67 Test points for British and Irish Lions, total of 1,246 points (second only to Dan Carter's 1,385); mem. Grand Slam winning squad 2003, Five Nations Championship winners 1999, Six Nations Championship winners 2000, 2001, World Cup winning squad 2003, 2nd place 2007, 4th place 1995, 1999; mem. British Lions' team Australia 2001 (three test caps), New Zealand 2005 (two Test caps); scored most points at World Cup 2003 (113), all-time highest points scorer in history of World Cup with 277; announced retirement from int. rugby union 2011; Co-founder Fineside Ltd (clothing co.) 2010–; Freeman, City of Greater London, Newcastle-upon-Tyne 2004; Hon. DCL (Northumbria) 2005; Dr hc (Surrey) 2009; Int. Rugby Board Player of the Year 2003. *Publications:* Lions and Falcons: My Diary of a Remarkable Year 2001, My World 2004, Jonny's Hotshots: How to Play Rugby My Way 2005, Tackling Life 2008, Jonny – My Autobiography 2011. *Leisure interests:* tennis, swimming, basketball, cricket, playing guitar and piano, travelling, speaking and reading French and Spanish. *Address:* Rugby Club Toulonnais SASP, 53 rue Melpomène, 83100 Toulon, France (office); Fineside, Unit B4, Benfield Business Park, Newcastle upon Tyne, NE6 4NQ, England (office). *Telephone:* (8) 92-68-06-80 (Toulon) (office); (191) 265-9446 (Newcastle upon Tyne) (office). *Fax:* (4) 94-41-92-16 (office). *E-mail:* info@fineside.com (office); rctoulon-sasp@rctoulon.com (office). *Website:* www.rctoulon.com (office); www.fineside.com (office); www.jonnywilkinson.com.

WILKINSON, Tom, OBE; British actor; b. (Thomas Geoffrey Wilkinson), 12 Dec. 1948, Leeds, Yorks., England; m. Diana Hardcastle; two d.; ed Univ. of Kent, Royal Acad. of Dramatic Arts; London Critics Circle Theatre Award Best Supporting Actor (for Ghosts) 1986, Best Actor (for An Enemy of the People) 1988; Dr hc (Univ. of Kent) 2001. *Plays:* plays with Royal Nat. Theatre, RSC and Oxford Playhouse include Peer Gynt, Brand, Henry V, Three Sisters, Uncle Vanya, Julius Caesar, Hamlet, The Merchant of Venice, The Crucible, As You Like It. *Films include* Sylvia 1985, Wetherby 1985, Sharma and Beyond 1986, Paper Mask 1990, In the Name of the Father 1993, All Things Bright and Beautiful 1994, Priest 1994, A Business Affair 1994, Sense and Sensibility 1995, The Ghost and the Darkness 1996, Oscar and Lucinda 1997, Smilla's Sense of Snow 1997, Wilde 1997, The Full Monty 1997, Jilting Joe 1997, The Governess 1998, Shakespeare in Love 1998, Rush Hour 1998, Father Damien 1999, Ride with the Devil 2000, Chain of Fools 2000, Black Knight 2001, The Importance of Being Earnest 2002, The Gathering Storm 2002, Girl with a Pearl Earring 2003, If Only 2004, Eternal Sunshine of the Spotless Mind 2004, Stage Beauty 2004, Piccadilly Jim 2004, Ripley Under Ground 2005, Batman Begins 2005, The Exorcism of Emily Rose 2005, A Good Woman 2005, Separate Lies 2005, The Night of the White Pants 2006, The Last Kiss 2006, Dedication 2007, Michael Clayton 2007, Cassandra's Dream 2007, RocknRolla 2008, Valkyrie 2008, Duplicity 2009, 44 Inch Chest 2009, The Ghost 2010, Jackboots on Whitehall (voice) 2010, The Debt 2010, The Conspirator 2010, Burke and Hare 2010, The Green Hornet 2010, The Best Exotic Marigold Hotel 2011, Mission: Impossible – Ghost Protocol (voice) 2011, The Samaritan 2012, Belle 2013, The Grand Budapest Hotel 2014. *Television includes:* Prime Suspect 1991, Martin Chuzzlewit 1994, Crossing the Floor 1996, Eskimo Day 1996, Cold Enough for Snow 1997, David Copperfield 1999, The Gathering Storm 2002, An Angel for May 2002, Normal 2003, John Adams (series, HBO) (Golden Globe Award for Best Supporting Actor in a Series 2009) 2008–, Recount 2008, A Number 2008, The Gruffalo (film) (voice) 2009, The Kennedys (mini-series) 2011, The Gruffalo's Child (film) (voice) 2011. *Address:* c/o The Gersh Agency, 232 North Canon Drive, Suite 201, Beverly Hills, CA 90210, USA (office). *Telephone:* (310) 274-6611 (office). *Fax:* (310) 278-6232 (office). *Website:* www.gershcomedy.com (office).

WIŁKOMIRSKA, Wanda, MMus; Polish violinist; b. 11 Jan. 1929, Warsaw; d. of Alfred Wiłkomirski and Dorota Temkin; divorced since 1976; two s.; ed Higher State of Music, Łódź, Franz Liszt Acad. of Music, Budapest and pvt. studies with Henryk Szeryng, Paris; public debut playing a Mozart Sonata aged seven; first appearance with orchestra aged 15, in Kraków; numerous recordings; concerts in 50 countries with most of the major orchestras throughout the world; toured as soloist with, amongst others, Nat. Philharmonic, Warsaw and Minnesota Symphony; has given world premiere performances of numerous contemporary works including works by Baird and Penderecki; has toured with her sister and brother as the Wiłkomirska Trio and has performed with Martha Argerich, Gidon Kremer, Daniel Barenboim, Misha Maisky and others; defected whilst on tour of FRG March 1982; Prof., Hochschule für Musik, Heidelberg-Mannheim 1983–98; Guest Prof. now part-time staff mem. Sydney Conservatorium of Music, Australia 1999–; has also worked with Australian Nat. Acad. of Music, Melbourne 2001–; master classes in Melbourne and Sydney; adjudicator, Hannover Int. Violin Competition 1997, 2000, Kendall Nat. Violin Competition (Australia); Officer's Cross Order of Polonia Restituta 1953, Commdr's Cross with Star 2001, Order of Banner of Labour 2nd Class 1959, (1st Class) 1964; Polish State Prize 1952, 1964; several foreign prizes, including Second Prize, Leipzig 1950, Bach Competition Award of Democratic German Radio, Culture and Arts Prize (1st Class) 1975, Orpheus Prize, Polish Musicians' Asscn 1979. *Leisure interests:* films, literature, sports. *Address:* Sydney Conservatorium of Music, Building C41, The University of Sydney, Sydney, NSW 2006, Australia (office). *Telephone:* (2) 9351-1222 (office). *Fax:* (2) 9351-1287 (office). *E-mail:* info@greenway.usyd.edu.au (office). *Website:* www.music.usyd.edu.au (office).

WILLATS, Stephan; British artist; b. 17 Aug. 1943, London, England; m. Stephanie Craven 1983; three s.; ed Drayton School and Ealing School of Art; Ed. and Publr Control magazine 1965–; Lecturer, Ipswich School of Art 1965–67; Lecturer, Nottingham Coll. of Art 1968–72; Organiser, Centre for Behavioural Art, Gallery House, London 1972–73; numerous group exhbns in the UK, Netherlands, Italy, FRG, Switzerland, Belgium, Australia; numerous project works, including Inside an Ocean, Mile End, London 1979, Two Worlds Apart, Hayes 1981 and Blocks, Avondale Estate, London 1982, Brentford Towers, W London 1985, White Towers, Helsinki 1989, Private Network, Oxford 1990; DAAD Fellowship, Berlin 1979–81. *Publications include:* several books, including The Artist as an Instigator of Changes in Social Cognition and Behaviour 1973, Art and Social Function 1976, The Lurky Place 1978, Doppelgänger 1985, Intervention and Audience 1986, The

House that Habitat Built 1989, Between Buildings and People 1996, The Art Museum in Society – Collected Writings 1997, Through Symbolic Worlds 2002, The Speculative Diagram 2008, Street Talk 2011, Artwork as Social Process 2012; numerous articles in art magazines. *Address:* c/o Victoria Miro Gallery, 16 Wharf Road, London, N1 7RW, England. *E-mail:* info@victoria-miro.com. *Website:* stephenwillats.com.

WILLCOX, Peter John, MA; Australian business executive; ed Univ. of Cambridge, UK; began career in oil industry 1975; CEO BHP Petroleum Ltd 1986–94; apptd Dir AMP Ltd 2002, Chair. 2003–05; Chair. Mayne Group Ltd 2002–05, Mayne Pharma Ltd 2005–07; Chair. Telstra Corpn Ltd 2006–09; Chair. and Dir, CSIRO 2006–07; mem. Bd of Dirs F.H. Faulding & Co. Ltd, Woodside Petroleum Ltd 1986–93, Hamilton Oil Corpn (USA) 1987–91, Tejas Gas Corpn (USA) 1987–94, BHP Ltd 1988–94, James Hardie Industries Ltd (now James Hardie Industries SE) 1992–2001, Schroders Holdings Australia Ltd 1994–99, Lend Lease Corpn Ltd 1994–2000, North Ltd 1994–2000, Energy Developments Ltd 1994–2002; fmr Dir, The Broken Hill Pty Co. Ltd, MLC Ltd; mem. Advisory Bd CVC Asia Pacific (Australia) Ltd; non-exec.), F.H Faulding & Co Ltd 1996–2000; Fellow, Australian Inst. of Co. Dirs. *Address:* c/o Telstra Corpn Ltd, 363 Oxford Street, Paddington, Sydney, NSW 2021, Australia. *E-mail:* info@telstraglobal.com.

WILLEM-ALEXANDER, HM King of The Netherlands Willem-Alexander Claus George Ferdinand, MA; Dutch; b. 27 April 1967, Utrecht; s. of HRH Princess Beatrix and Prince Claus; m. Máxima Zorreguieta (now Queen Maxima of The Netherlands) 2002; three d.; ed Baarns Lyceum, Eerste Vrijzinnig Christelijk Lyceum, The Hague, Atlantic Coll. Llantwit Major, Wales, Leiden Univ.; succeeded to the throne 30 April 2013, on the abdication of his mother HM Queen Beatrix (now HRH Princess Beatrix); mil. service in Royal Netherlands Navy 1985–87, gained Mil. Pilot's Licence 1993, attended Netherlands Defence Coll. 1994, currently holds ranks of Commodore Navy Reserve and Air Force Reserve, Brig.-Gen. Army Reserve and Royal Mil. Constabulary Reserve, ADC Extraordinary to HM The Queen; Patron Global Water Partnership 1998; fully-qualified pvt, commercial and airline pilot, volunteer pilot African Medical Research and Educ. Foundation 1989, Kenya Wildlife Service 1991; mem. founding cttee World Water Vision 1999–2000; Chair. Second World Water Forum, The Hague 2000; mem. Panel of Eminent Persons, UN conf. on sustainable devt, Johannesburg 2002; Chair. Integrated Water Man. Comm. 2002–04; Chair. Water Advisory Cttee 2004–; mem. IOC 1999–; Patron Orange Fund; Hon. mem. Royal Naval Yacht Club, Royal Dutch Yachting and Rowing Asscn; Officers' Long Service Decoration 2001. *Address:* Noordeinde Palace, Postbus 30412, The Hague 2500 GK, The Netherlands (office). *Website:* www.koninklijkhuis.nl (office).

WILLEMS, Lodewijk, MA; Belgian diplomatist; *Adviser to the CEO, BNP Paribas Fortis;* b. 6 April 1948, Etterbeek; m. Lindsay Edwards; four c.; ed Vrije Universiteit, Brussels, Yale Univ.; began career at IAEA 1977; adviser to Deputy Prime Minister and Minister for Econ. Affairs 1977–81; Deputy Sec. Gen. Benelux Econ. Union 1981–85; Political Counselor, Embassy in Kinshasa 1985–88; Advisor to Deputy Prime Minister and Minister for Econ. Affairs 1988–91; Deputy Perm. Rep. to EC 1991–92; Chief of Cabinet to Minister of Foreign Affairs 1992–94, Perm. Rep. to UN, Geneva 1994–97, Amb. to UK 1997–2002, to Germany 2002–06; fmr Chair. ECE; Dir of External and Governmental Affairs, BNP Paribas Fortis 2006–12; currently Adviser to the CEO; mem. Advisory Bd, LSE Alumni Asscn, Belgium. *Leisure interests:* opera. *Address:* BNP Paribas Fortis, Montagne du Parc 3, 1000 Brussels, Belgium (office). *Telephone:* (2) 565-52-16 (office). *Fax:* (2) 565-27-39 (office). *Website:* www.bnpparibasfortis.com (office).

WILLES, Mark Hinckley, PhD; American economist and media executive (retd); b. 16 July 1941, Salt Lake City, Utah; s. of Joseph Simmons Willes and Ruth Willes (née Hinckley); m. Laura Fayone 1961; three s. two d.; ed Columbia Univ., New York; with Banking and Currency Cttee House of Reps 1966–67; Asst Prof. of Finance, Univ. of Pennsylvania, Phila 1967–69; economist, Fed. Reserve Bank 1967, Sr Economist 1969–70, Dir Research 1970–71, Vice-Pres. 1971, First Vice-Pres. 1971–77; Pres. Fed. Reserve Bank of Minneapolis 1977–80; Exec. Vice-Pres., Chief Finance Officer Gen. Mills Inc. 1980–85, Pres., COO 1985–92, Vice-Chair. 1992–95; Chair., Pres., CEO Times Mirror Co. 1995–2000; Pres. and CEO Deseret Man. Corpn 2009–12; Publr LA Times 1997–99; Pres. Hawaii Honolulu Mission, Church of the Latter Day Saints 2001. *E-mail:* willesmh@deseretmgmt.com. *Website:* www.deseretmanagement.com.

WILLIAMS, (Elizabeth) Betty; Irish campaigner for children's rights, peace and justice; *Founder and President, World Centers of Compassion for Children International;* b. 22 May 1942, Belfast, Northern Ireland; ed Queen's Univ., Belfast; worked as office receptionist; jt winner of Nobel Peace Prize for launching the Northern Ireland Peace Movt (later renamed Community of the Peace People) 1976, Jt Leader 1976–78; fmr Visiting Prof., Sam Houston State Univ.; Founder and Head, The Global Children's Studies Center 1992; Founder and Pres. World Centers of Compassion for Children International 1997–; Co-f. Nobel Women's Initiative 2006; Chair. Inst. for Asian Democracy, Washington DC; Distinguished Visiting Prof., Nova Southeastern Univ.; mem. Bd of Dirs Adoption Options, Inc.; Founding mem. Alliance for the New Humanity; mem. Advisory Bd Dalai Lama Center for Peace and Educ., Camfed Int., Mahatma Gandhi Center for Global Nonviolence, Vermont Peace Acad., Int. Cttee of Artists for Peace Council, The Pangaea Project; mem. Council of Honour UN Univ. for Peace, Costa Rica; mem. Bd of Trustees Pax Natura; Patron, Int. Peace Foundation, Vienna; Hon. mem. Club of Budapest, World Wisdom Acad., Global Vision for Peace; Hon. DHumLitt (Coll. of Siena Heights, Mich.) 1977, (The Monmouth Coll.), Hon. LLD (Yale Univ.), Beloit Coll., St Norbert Coll., Williams Woods Univ.), Hon. Dr of Humanities (Mount Merry Coll.), Laurea hc (Università degli Studi Della Basilicata, Potenza, Italy); Nobel Peace Prize (jtly) 1976, People's Peace Prize of Norway 1976, Carl von Ossietzky Medal for Courage (Berlin Section, Int. League of Human Rights), Schweitzer Medallion for Courage, Eleanor Roosevelt Award 1984, Frank Foundation Child Assistance Int. Oliver Award, Together for Peace Foundation Peace Building Award 1995, Gandhi, King, Ikeda Community Builders Prize 2003, Ischia Peace Award (Italy) 2003, Soka Gakkai Int. Peace and Culture Award 2004, The Martin Luther King, Jr Award, Paul Harris Fellowship, Rotary Club International, The Raoul Wallenberg Humanitarian Award, Old Dominion Univ., The Max and Betty Walker Distinguished Speaker Series Certificate of Honor, Fed. of World Peace and Love Humanity in the Arts Founders Award, Int. Cttee of Artists for Peace, Premio Mediterraneo Award, Eleanor Roosevelt Global Women's Rights Award. *Leisure interest:* gardening. *Address:* World Centers of Compassion for Children International, Knock Inverin, Co. Galway, Ireland (office). *Telephone:* (91) 593304 (office). *E-mail:* bwccc@eircom.net (office). *Website:* www.wccco.org (office).

WILLIAMS, Brian; American television journalist; *Anchor and Managing Editor, NBC Nightly News;* b. 5 May 1959, Elmira, NY; m. Jane Stoddart Williams; one s. one d.; ed George Washington Univ, Catholic Univ of America; intern, The White House; TV reporter KOAM-TV, with WTTG-TV, WCAU-TV; joined WCBS-TV 1993; joined NBC 1993, Chief White House Corresp. 1994–96; anchor, Man. Ed. The News With Brian Williams MSNBC 1996–2004, Anchor and Man. Ed. NBC Nightly News 2004–; mem. Council on Foreign Relations; Emmy Awards for reporting 1987, 1989, 1993. *Address:* NBC News, 30 Rockefeller Plaza, 3rd Floor, New York, NY 10112-0002, USA (office). *Telephone:* (212) 664-4444 (office). *Fax:* (212) 664-4426 (office). *E-mail:* nightly@nbc.com (office). *Website:* www.nbc.com/nbc/NBC_News (office).

WILLIAMS, C(harles) K(enneth), BA; American poet and academic; *Lecturer, Creative Writing, Department of Comparative Literature, Princeton University;* b. 4 Nov. 1936, Newark, NJ; s. of Paul Bernard Williams and Dossie Williams (née Kasdin); m. 1st Sarah Dean Jones 1966 (divorced 1975); one d.; m. 2nd Catherine Justine Mauger 1975; one s.; ed Univ. of Pennsylvania; Visiting Prof. of Literature, Beaver Coll., Jenkintown, Pa 1975, Drexel Univ., Philadelphia 1976, Franklin and Marshall Coll., Pa 1977, Univ. of Calif., Irvine 1978, Boston Univ. 1979–80, Brooklyn Coll., CUNY 1982–83; Prof. of Writing, Columbia Univ. 1981–85; Prof. of Literature, George Mason Univ., Fairfax Va 1982–95; Halloway Lecturer, Univ. of Calif., Berkeley 1986; Lecturer, Creative Writing, Dept of Comparative Literature, Princeton Univ. 1995–; contributing Ed. American Poetry Review 1972–; mem. PEN, American Acad. of Arts and Sciences, American Acad. of Arts and Letters; Fellow, Guggenheim Foundation 1975–, Nat. Endowment for Arts 1985, 1993; Pushcart Press Prizes 1982, 1983, 1987, Nat. Book Critics Circle Award for Poetry 1987, Morton Dauwen Zabel Prize, American Acad. of Arts and Letters 1989, Lila Wallace Writers Award 1993, Harriet Monroe Prize 1993, Berlin Prize, American Acad. in Berlin 1998, Voelcker Career Achievement Award, PEN 1998, Pulitzer Prize for Poetry 2000, Los Angeles Times Book Award 2000, Weathertop Prize 2000, Nat. Book Award 2003, Ruth Lilly Prize for Poetry 2005. *Publications include:* A Day for Anne Frank 1968, Lies 1969, The Sensuous President 1972, I am the Bitter Name 1972, With Ignorance 1977, The Women of Trachis (co-trans.) 1978, The Lark, The Thrush, The Starling 1983, Tar 1983, Flesh and Blood 1987, Poems 1963–1983, 1988, The Bacchae of Euripides (trans.) 1990, Helen 1991, A Dream of Mind 1992, Selected Poems 1994, The Vigil 1997, Poetry and Consciousness (selected essays) 1998, Repair (poems) 1999, Misgivings: A Memoir 2000, Love About Love 2001, The Singing 2004, Pétain (1856–1951) 2005, Collected Poems 2006, Wait 2010, On Whitman 2010, Writers Writing Dying 2012, In Time: Poets, Poetry and the Rest 2012; contrib. to Akzent, American Poetry Review, Atlantic, Carleton Miscellany, Crazyhorse, Grand Street, Iowa Review, Madison Review, New England Review, New Yorker, Poetry, Seneca Review, Transpacific Review, TLS, TriQuarterly, Yale Review, Threepenny Review. *Leisure interest:* piano. *Address:* Lewis Center for the Arts, Princeton University, 6 New South, Princeton, NJ 08544, USA (office). *Telephone:* (609) 258-3176 (office). *E-mail:* ckwms@princeton.edu (office). *Website:* www.princeton.edu/arts (office); www.ckwilliams.com.

WILLIAMS, Sir Daniel Charles, GCMG, QC, LLB; Grenadian lawyer, consultant and fmr government official; *Lawyer and Business and Legal Consultant, Law Office of Danny Williams & Company;* b. 4 Nov. 1935, Grenada; s. of Adolphus D. Williams and Clare Stanislaus; m. Cecilia Patricia Gloria Modeste 1970; two s. four d.; ed Holborn Coll. of Law, Languages and Commerce, Univ. of London, UK Council of Legal Educ.; called to the Bar, Lincoln's Inn, London 1968; barrister 1969–70, 1974–84, 1990–96; Magistrate, St Lucia 1970–74; mem. Parl. (New Nat. Party) 1984–89; Minister of Health, Housing and Environment 1984–89, of Legal Affairs and Attorney-Gen. 1988–89; Acting Prime Minister July 1988; Gov.-Gen. of Grenada 1996–2008; currently lawyer and business and legal consultant, Law Office of Danny Williams & Co.; fmrly several lay positions in RC Church; Chief Scout; Founder-mem. Grenada Foundation for Needy Students Inc. 1996; sole sponsor of cricket competition of the six primary schools in parish of St David's, Grenada 1985–. *Publications:* Index of Laws of Grenada 1959–79, The Office and Duties of the Governor-General of Grenada 1998, A Synoptic View of the Public Service of Grenada 1999, Prescription of a Model Grenada 2000, God Speaks 2001, The Layman's Lawbook 2002, The Love of God 2003, Government of the Global Village 2007; contrib. to Modern Legal Systems Cyclopedia: Central America and the Caribbean, Vol. 7 1985. *Leisure interests:* lawn tennis, gardening. *Address:* PO Box 346, St George's, Grenada (office).

WILLIAMS, Hon. Danny, QC, JD; Canadian politician; b. 4 Aug. 1949, St John's; m. Maureen Williams; four c.; ed Memorial Univ. of Newfoundland, Univ. of Oxford, UK, Dalhousie Univ.; practised law in Newfoundland and Labrador 1972; led Cable Atlantic (cable TV co.) in series of acquisitions 1975; Pres. OIS Fisher (offshore oil and gas supply and services co.); apptd QC 1984; MLA for Humber West, Newfoundland 2001–; Leader Progressive Conservative Party 2001–, also Opposition Leader; Premier of Newfoundland and Labrador 2003–10 (resgnd); Founder and Pres. St John's Jr Hockey League; fmr Chair. Canadian Parl. Channel, Newfoundland and Labrador Film Devt Corpn, Provincial Govt Offshore Oil Impact Advisory Council; fmr mem. Bd of Govs Canadian Sports Hall of Fame; fmr mem. Terry Fox Marathon of Hope, Big Brothers/Big Sisters, Iris Kirby House, Arthritis Soc. *Address:* Progressive Conservative Party, 20 Hallett Crescent, PO Box 8551, St John's, Newfoundland A1B 3P2, Canada (office). *Telephone:* (709) 753-6043 (office). *Fax:* (709) 753-6059 (office). *E-mail:* pcparty@nf.aibn.com (office). *Website:* www.pcparty.nf.net (office).

WILLIAMS, David J., PhD, DIC; British chemist and academic; *Senior Research Fellow and Professor Emeritus, Imperial College London;* Sr Research Fellow, Computational, Theoretical and Structural Chem. Section, Dept of Chem., Imperial Coll., London, now Prof. Emer. *Publications:* numerous articles in scientific journals. *Address:* c/o Department of Chemistry, Imperial College, London, SW7 2AY, England (office). *Telephone:* (20) 7589-5111 (office). *Website:* www.imperial.ac.uk/chemistry (office).

WILLIAMS, Sir Denys Ambrose, Kt, KCMG, BCL, MA; Barbadian attorney-at-law; b. 12 Oct. 1929; s. of George Cuthbert Williams and Violet Irene Gilkes; m. Carmel Mary Coleman 1954; two s. four d.; ed Combermere School and Harrison Coll., Barbados, Worcester Coll., Oxford and Middle Temple, London, UK; Asst Legal Draftsman, Asst to Attorney Gen., Barbados; Asst Legal Draftsman, Fed. of West Indies; Sr Parl. Counsel, Barbados 1963–67, Supreme Court Judge 1967–86, Chief Justice 1987–2001; Acting Gov.-Gen. 1995–96; Gold Crown of Merit. *Leisure interests:* horse-racing, tennis, gardening, walking. *Address:* 9 Garrison, St Michael, Barbados. *Telephone:* 4271164.

WILLIAMS, Eliud Thaddeus, BSc, MBA; Dominican accountant, politician and fmr head of state; *Management Consultant, WHITCO Inc.;* b. 21 Aug. 1948, St Joseph, Dominica; m. Cornelia Henry; two s.; ed Univ. of the West Indies, ICTC, Loughborough, UK, Manitoba Inst. of Management, Canada, Univ. of Florida, USA; Financial Controller, Dominica Banana Growers Asscn 1978–79; Licensed Public Accountant, Inland Revenue, Dominica 1985–; Commr of Cooperatives 1985–87; Perm. Sec., Ministry of Agric. and Environment 1987–92, 1996–2000, Ministry of Health and Social Security 1992–96, Ministry of Communications, Works and Housing 2000–04; Man. Dir Eastern Caribbean Telecommunications Authority (ECTEL) 2004–08; Management Consultant, WHITCO Inc. 2008–, also mem. Bd of Dirs; Pres. of Dominica 2012–13; Chair. Independent Regulatory Comm. 2010–12; fmr Dir Caribbean Agricultural Research & Devt Inst., Caribbean Food Corpn, Org. of Caribbean Utility Regulators; Pres. Roseau Coop Credit Union 1997–99; Dir Cooperative Societies League 1999–2002; fmr Chair. and mem. Bd of Govs Dominica State Coll.; fmr Vice-Pres. Helping Hands Inc.; mem. Inst. of Financial Accountants (UK) 1985, Fellow 1995, Fellow, Chartered Management Inst. (UK) 2004; mem. Manitoba Inst. of Management 1990; Dominica Award of Honour 2012. *Leisure interests:* walking, wimming. *Address:* Whitco Inc., PO Box 2130, 37 Kennedy Avenue, Roseau, Dominica (office). *Telephone:* 4499800 (office). *Fax:* 4499777 (office). *E-mail:* info@whitco-inc.com (office). *Website:* www.whitco-inc.com (office).

WILLIAMS, Sir Francis Owen Garbatt, Kt, CBE; British motor racing team owner; *Team Principal, Williams F1 racing team;* b. 16 April 1942, South Shields, Tyne and Wear; ed St Joseph's Coll., Dumfries, Scotland; worked as travelling grocery salesman; brief career as driver and mechanic; f. Frank Williams Racing Cars 1966; hired drivers including Piers Courage and Tony Trimmer for several years in Formula Two and Formula Three; bought Brabham Formula One chassis for 1969 Formula One season, two second place finishes; brief partnership with Alessandro de Tomaso 1970; raced Henri Pescarolo with chassis bought from March Engineering 1971; first F1 car built by Williams works, Politoys FX3 designed by Len Bailey 1972, crashed by Pescarolo and destroyed in first race; sought sponsorship from Marlboro and Iso Rivolta (Italian car co.); partnership with oil magnate Walter Wolf 1976; left team along with fmr employee, engineer Patrick Head, and acquired empty carpet warehouse in Didcot, Oxon. 1977, announced formation of Williams Grand Prix Engineering 1977, now known as Williams F1, Team Principal 2012–; first win with Clay Regazzoni 1979, first title with Alan Jones 1980, second championship with Keke Rosberg 1982; six further drivers' championships and eight constructors' championships 1981–97; Chevalier, Légion d'honneur; Wheatcroft Trophy 2008, BBC Sports Personality of the Year Helen Rollason Award for "outstanding achievement in the face of adversity" 2010. *Address:* Williams F1, Grove, Wantage, Oxon., OX12 0DQ, England (office). *Telephone:* (1235) 777700 (office). *Fax:* (1235) 764705 (office). *E-mail:* enquiries@williamsf1.com (office). *Website:* www.williamsf1.com (office).

WILLIAMS, Jody, BA, MA; American international organization official, campaigner, academic and writer; *Chairwoman, Nobel Women's Initiative;* b. 9 Oct. 1950, Poultney, Vt; d. of John C. Williams and Ruth C. Williams; m. Stephen D. Goose 2001; ed Univ. of Vermont, School for Int. Training, Vt, Johns Hopkins School of Advanced Int. Studies; English teacher, Mexico, UK and Washington, DC 1978–81; campaigned to spread awareness of US policy in Cen. America 1981–92; Co-ordinator Nicaragua-Honduras Educ. Project 1984–86; Deputy Dir Medical Aid for El Salvador, Los Angeles 1986–92; Founding Co-ordinator Int. Campaign to Ban Landmines (ICBL) 1992–98, ICBL Campaign Amb. 1998–; Tech. Adviser, UN Study on Impact of Armed Conflict on Children 1996; Distinguished Visiting Prof. of Social Work, Grad. Coll. of Social Work, Univ. of Houston 2003–14, Sam and Cele Keeper Endowed Prof. in Peace and Social Justice 2007–; Founding Chair. Nobel Women's Initiative 2006–; Head, UN Human Rights Council High-Level Mission to Darfur 2007; more than 15 hon. degrees in USA and Canada, including from the Royal Mil. Coll. of Canada, Smith Coll., Wesleyan Univ., Penn State Univ.; Nobel Peace Prize (jt recipient with ICBL) 1997, Distinguished Peace Leadership Award, Nuclear Age Peace Foundation 1998, Olender Foundation Peacemaker of the Year 1999, Eleanor Roosevelt Global Women's Rights Award 2004, ranked 100th by Forbes magazine amongst 100 Most Powerful Women in the World 2004. *Publications:* After the Guns Fall Silent: The Enduring Legacy of Landmines (with Shawn Roberts) 1995, Banning Landmines: Disarmament, Citizen Diplomacy and Human Security 2008; more than 24 chapters and articles for books and journals; numerous articles for newspapers around the world, including The Wall Street Journal, The Independent (UK), the Economist. *Address:* Nobel Women's Initiative, 430-1 Nicholas Street, Ottawa, ON K1N 7B7, Canada (office). *Telephone:* (613) 569-8400 (office). *Fax:* (613) 563-0682 (office). *E-mail:* jwilliams@nobelwomensinitiative.org (office). *Website:* www.nobelwomensinitiative.org (office); www.icbl.org.

WILLIAMS, John, AO, OBE; Australian classical guitarist; b. 24 April 1941, Melbourne; s. of Len Williams and Melaan Ket; m. 1st Linda Susan Kendall 1964 (divorced); one d.; m. 2nd Sue Cook 1981 (divorced); one s.; m. 3rd Kathleen Panama 2000; ed Friern Barnet Grammar School and Royal Coll. of Music, London; studied guitar with father, Segovia and at Accad. Chigiana, Siena; has toured widely and appears frequently on TV and radio; numerous transcriptions and gramophone recordings as solo guitarist and with leading orchestras; f. The Height Below (ensemble) with Brian Gascoigne, John Williams and Friends (ensemble) and founder-mem. groups, SKY and John Williams' Attacca; current ensembles include John Williams and Richard Harvey's World Tour and 'Together and Solo' with John Etheridge, as well as solo recitals worldwide; other collaborations with Julian Bream, Itzhak Perlman, Andre Previn, Cleo Lane and John Dankworth, Nat. Youth Jazz Orchestra, Paco Pena and Inti Illimani; Artistic

Dir South Bank Summer Music Festival 1984–85, Melbourne Arts Festival 1987; Hon. FRCM, FRAM, FRNCM; Dr hc (Melbourne); Edison Award for Lifetime Achievement 2007. *Films:* composed and played music for film Emma's War. *Recordings:* include Takemitsu Played by John Williams (music by Toru Takemitsu, with the London Sinfonietta) 1991, several of Rodrigo's Conciertos de Aranjuez, Vivaldi Concertos 1991, The Seville Concert/The Film Profile of John Williams (also on laserdisc and VHS) 1993, From Australia (featuring music by Peter Sculthorpe and Nigel Westlake) 1994, The Great Paraguayan 1995, concerti by Richard Harvey and Steve Gray 1996, John Williams Plays the Movies 1997, The Black Decameron (music by Leo Brouwer) 1997, The Guitarist 1998, Schubert and Giuliani 1999, The Magic Box 2002, El Diablo Suelto 2003, The Ultimate Guitar Collection 2004, Places Between (with John Etheridge) 2006, From a Bird 2008, The Guitarist (3 CD set) 2011. *Leisure interests:* tennis, badminton, chess, table tennis. *Website:* www.JohnWilliamsGuitarNotes.com.

WILLIAMS, (John) Gwynn, CBE, MA; British historian and academic; b. 19 June 1924, Wales; s. of the late John Ellis Williams and Annie Maude Rowlands; m. Beryl Stafford Thomas 1954; three s.; ed Holywell Grammar School, Univ. Coll. of North Wales; with RN 1943–46; staff tutor Dept of Extra Mural Studies Univ. of Liverpool 1951–54; Asst lecturer Univ. of North Wales 1955, Prof. of Welsh History 1963–83, Dean Faculty of Arts 1972–74, Vice-Prin. 1974–79, Vice-Pres. 1993–98; Chair. Press Bd Univ. of Wales 1979–91; Dir Gregynog Press 1979–2002; Vice-Pres. Nat. Library of Wales 1984–86, Pres. 1986–96; Pres. Cambrian Archaeological Asscn 1987–88; Vice-Pres. Hon. Soc. of Cymmrodorion 1988–; mem. Royal Comm. on Ancient and Historical Monuments in Wales 1967–91; Hon. mem. Gorsedd of Bards 1983, Hon. Fellow Bangor Univ. 2007; Hon. DLitt (Univ. of Wales) 1999; Prince Llywelyn Medal 1952. *Publications include:* The Founding of the University College of North Wales, Bangor 1985, The University College of North Wales: Foundations 1985, University and Nation 1893–1939 (The Thomas Jones Pierce Memorial Lecture) 1992, The Report on the Proposed University of Wales (ed.) 1993, The University Movement in Wales 1993, The University of Wales 1893–1939 1997; numerous articles on 17th-century Wales for learned journals. *Leisure interests:* travelling, walking. *Address:* Llywenan, Siliwen, Bangor, Gwynedd, LL57 2BS, Wales (home). *Telephone:* (1248) 353065 (home).

WILLIAMS, John Peter Rhys (J.P.R.), MBE, MB, BS, LRCP, MRCS, FRCSE; British orthopaedic surgeon (retd) and fmr rugby union player; b. 2 March 1949, Cardiff; s. of Peter Williams and Margaret Williams; m. Priscilla Parkin 1973; one s. three d.; ed Bridgend Grammar School, Millfield, St Mary's Hosp. Medical School; British Jr Tennis Champion, Wimbledon 1966; Welsh int. rugby player 1969–79, 1980–81; 55 caps for Wales; Capt. of Welsh rugby team 1978–79; on tour with British Lions to New Zealand 1971, South Africa 1974; eight test matches for British Lions, winning both series; qualified as medical doctor 1973; surgical Registrar, Cardiff Hosp. 1977–80, Orthopaedic Registrar 1980–82; Orthopaedic Sr Registrar, St Mary's Hosp., London 1982–85; Consultant Orthopaedic Surgeon, Princess of Wales Hosp., Bridgend 1986–2005; Primary FRCS 1976; inducted into Int. Rugby Hall of Fame 1997. *Publications:* Irish Conference on Sporting Injuries, Dublin (ed.) 1975, JPR (autobiog.) 1979, Cervical Neck Injuries in Rugby Football, British Medical Journal 1978, Trans-Oral Fusion of the Cervical Spine, Journal of Bone and Joint Surgery 1985. *Leisure interests:* sport, music. *Address:* Llansannor Lodge, Llansannor, nr Cowbridge, Vale of Glamorgan, CF71 7RX, Wales (home). *Telephone:* (1446) 772590 (home). *E-mail:* jprw15@aol.com (home).

WILLIAMS, John Towner; American composer, conductor and pianist; b. 8 Feb. 1932, Flushing, NY; ed Juilliard School, New York, Univ. of California, Los Angeles; pianist, Columbia Pictures; jazz pianist working with Henry Mancini on television scores; Conductor Boston Pops Orchestra 1980–98; numerous hon. degrees; five Academy Awards, seven BAFTA Awards, three Emmy Awards, four Golden Globes, 21 Grammy Awards, recipient of Kennedy Center Honors 2004, Classical BRIT Award for Soundtrack Composer of the Year 2005, Grammy Awards for Best Instrumental Composition (for A Prayer for Peace, from Munich) 2007, (for The Adventures of Mutt, from Indiana Jones and the Kingdom of the Crystal Skull) 2009, Nat. Medal of Arts 2009. *Film scores:* The Secret Ways 1961, Diamond Head 1962, None But the Brave 1965, How to Steal a Million 1966, Valley of the Dolls 1967, The Cowboys 1972, The Poseidon Adventure 1972, Tom Sawyer 1973, Earthquake 1974, The Towering Inferno 1974, Jaws (Acad. Award) 1975, The Eiger Sanction 1975, Family Plot 1976, Midway 1976, The Missouri Breaks 1976, Raggedy Ann and Andy 1977, Black Sunday 1977, Star Wars (Acad. Award) 1977, Close Encounters of the Third Kind 1977, The Fury 1978, Jaws II 1976, Superman 1978, Dracula 1979, 1941 1979, The Empire Strikes Back 1980, Raiders of the Lost Ark 1981, E.T.: The Extra Terrestrial (Acad. Award) 1982, Return of the Jedi 1983, Indiana Jones and the Temple of Doom 1984, The River 1985, Space Camp 1986, The Witches of Eastwick 1987, Empire of the Sun (BAFTA Award for Best Score) 1988, Always 1989, Born on the Fourth of July 1989, Indiana Jones and the Last Crusade 1989, Stanley and Iris 1990, Presumed Innocent 1990, Home Alone 1990, Hook 1991, JFK 1993, Far and Away 1993, Home Alone 2: Lost in New York 1993, Jurassic Park 1993, Schindler's List (Acad. Award) 1993, Sabrina 1995, The Reivers 1995, Nixon 1995, Sleepers 1996, Rosewood 1996, Land of the Giants 1997, Seven Years in Tibet 1997, The Lost World: Jurassic Park 1997, Amistad 1997, Lost in Space 1997, Time Tunnel 1997, Saving Private Ryan 1998, Star Wars: Episode I – The Phantom Menace 1999, Angela's Ashes 1999, Harry Potter and the Sorcerer's Stone 2001, Star Wars: Episode II – Attack of the Clones 2001, Minority Report 2002, Harry Potter and the Chamber of Secrets 2002, Catch Me if You Can 2002, Harry Potter and the Prisoner of Azkaban 2004, The Terminal 2004, Star Wars: Episode III – Revenge of the Sith 2005, War of the Worlds 2005, Harry Potter and the Goblet of Fire 2005, Memoirs of a Geisha (Golden Globe for Best Original Score in a Motion Picture 2006, BAFTA Anthony Asquith Award for Achievement in Film Music 2006, Grammy Award for Best Score Soundtrack Album for Motion Picture 2007) 2005, Munich 2005, Superman Returns 2006, Harry Potter and the Order of the Phoenix 2007, Indiana Jones and the Kingdom of the Crystal Skull 2008, Harry Potter and the Half-Blood Prince 2009, Lincoln (Critics Choice Award 2013) 2012, The Book Thief 2013. *Recordings include:* John Williams Plays the Movies 1996, Music From The Star Wars Saga 1999, Jane Eyre 1999, Themes From Academy Award Winners, Over The Rainbow: Songs From The Movies 1992, John Williams Conducting The Boston Pops 1996, The Hollywood Sound 1997, From Sousa To Spielberg, Best Of John Williams 1998, Treesong 2001, Call Of The Champions (official theme of 2002 Winter Olympics,

Salt Lake City) 2001, John Williams Trumpet Concerto 2002, American Journey 2002; recordings of film scores. *Address:* c/o Michael Gorfaine, Gorfaine & Schwartz, 4111 West Alameda Avenue, Suite 509, Burbank, CA 91505, USA (office). *Website:* www.johnwilliams.org.

WILLIAMS, Keith, BA (Hons); British chartered accountant and business executive; *Chief Executive, British Airways plc;* ed Univ. of Liverpool; worked for Apple, Arthur Andersen and Boots plc; joined British Airways as Head of Taxation 1998, Group Treas. 2000–06, mem. Exec. Bd and Chief Financial Officer British Airways 2006–11, Chief Exec. 2011– (following merger with Iberia), mem. Bd of Dirs Iberia Lineas Aéreas de España SA 2009–, International Airlines Group (parent co.) 2011–; Dir (non-exec.) Transport for London; Accountancy Age Award for Blue Chip Finance Dir of the Year 2010. *Address:* British Airways plc, PO Box 365, Waterside, Harmondsworth, London, UB7 0GB, England (office). *Telephone:* (20) 8738-5100 (press office) (office). *Fax:* (20) 8759-4314 (office). *E-mail:* info@britishairways.com (office). *Website:* www.britishairways.com (office).

WILLIAMS, Marion V., PhD, FCIB, CMA, GCM; Barbadian economist and fmr central banker; ed Univ. of Surrey, UK, Univ. of the West Indies; fmr Deputy Man. Research Dept, East Caribbean Currency Authority; joined Cen. Bank of Barbados 1973–, Adviser, Sr Adviser, Deputy Gov. 1993–99, Gov. 1999–2009; numerous articles for professional journals; consultant, USAID, Commonwealth Secr., ILO; Pres. Barbados Inst. of Banking and Finance; mem. Barbados Econs Soc., Asscn of Caribbean Econs. *Publications:* Liberalising a Regulated Banking System: The Caribbean Case 1996, Managing Public Finances in a Small Developing Economy—the Case of Barbados 2001, Strategic Repositioning: A Caribbean Perspective on Economic Policy Making 2005. *Address:* c/o Central Bank of Barbados, Tom Adams Financial Centre, Spry Street, POB 1016, Bridgetown, Barbados (office).

WILLIAMS, Mark James, MBE; British professional snooker player; b. 21 March 1975, Cwm, Ebbw Vale, Wales; s. of Dilwyn Williams; m. Joanne Dent; two s.; won first junior event aged 11; made first century break aged 13; turned professional 1992; winner of 23 titles (18 ranking, 1 minor-ranking, 4 non-ranking); ranking titles: Welsh Open 1996, 1999, Grand Prix 1996, 2000, British Open 1997, Irish Open 1998, Thailand Masters 1999, 2000, 2002, UK Championship 1999, 2002, Embassy World Snooker Championship 2000 (first left-handed player), 2003, China Open 2002, 2006, 2010, LG Cup 2003, German Masters 2011; minor-ranking event title: Players Tour Championship – Event 1 2010; non-ranking titles: Benson & Hedges Championship 1994, Masters 1998, Masters 2003, Pot Black 2006; Pro-am event title: Finnish Snooker Challenge 2010; winner Nations Cup (with team Wales) 1999; became second player to hold all four major titles at one time 2003; ranked World No. 1 2000–01, 2003, 2011; 284 competitive century breaks, including two maximum (147) breaks; Owner, Tredegar Snooker Club, Wales. *Leisure interests:* golf, badminton, poker, cars, fmr amateur boxer. *Address:* Tredegar Snooker Club, Park Place, Tredegar, NP22 4LD, Wales.

WILLIAMS, Mark R., PhD; American business executive; *Non-Executive Chairman, Hess Corporation;* ed Stanford Univ.; joined Royal Dutch Shell plc's upstream oil business in USA 1979, held several upstream and downstream positions in Shell's upstream business, including Exec. Vice-Pres. of Supply and Distribution in Oil Products at Shell's upstream business, Downstream Dir 2009–12; Chair. (non-exec.) Hess Corpn 2013–; Dir (non-exec.), Intertek Group Plc 2013–; Chair. Exec. Cttee of Athabasca Oil Sands Project, Downstream Cttee of American Petroleum Inst. *Address:* Hess Corporation, 1185 Avenue of the Americas, New York, NY 10036, USA (office). *Telephone:* (212) 997-8500 (office). *Fax:* (212) 536-8390 (office). *E-mail:* info@hess.com (office). *Website:* www.hess.com (office).

WILLIAMS, Martin John, CVO, OBE, BA; British consultant and diplomatist (retd); b. 3 Nov. 1941; s. of John Henry Stroud Williams and Barbara Williams (née Benington); m. Susan Dent 1964; two s.; ed Manchester Grammar School, Corpus Christi Coll. Oxford; joined Commonwealth Relations Office 1963; various posts including service at Embassy in Manila 1966–69, Consulate-Gen. in Milan 1970–72, Embassy in Tehran 1977–80, High Comm. in New Delhi 1982–86, Embassy in Rome 1986–90; Head of S. Asian Dept, FCO 1990–92; seconded to NI Office, Belfast as Asst Under-Sec. (Political Affairs) 1993–95; High Commr in Zimbabwe 1995–98, in NZ (also accred to Samoa and Gov. Pitcairn Island) 1998–2001; UK Consultant to New Zealand Antarctic Heritage Trust 2002–12; Chair. Link Foundation for UK–NZ Relations 2004–09. *Leisure interests:* music, gardening, woodwork, theatre. *Address:* Russet House, Lughorse Lane, Yalding, Kent, ME18 6EG, England (home). *Telephone:* (1622) 815403 (home).

WILLIAMS OF BAGLAN, Baron (Life Peer), cr. 2010, of Baglan in the County of Neath Port Talbot; **Michael C. Williams,** BSc, MSc, PhD; British diplomatist, international organization official and UN official; b. 11 June 1949, Bridgend, Wales; m. Isobelle Jaques; two c.; ed Univ. Coll., London, School of Oriental and African Studies, Univ. of London; worked for several years with Amnesty International as Head of Asia Research; Ed., later Sr Ed. for Asia, BBC World Service 1984–91; held several sr positions with UN in 1990s, including Dir of Human Rights in UN Transitional Admin in Cambodia (UNTAC) and Dir of Information in UN Protection Force in Fmr Yugoslavia (UNPROFOR); Sr Fellow, IISS, London 1996–98; Special Adviser to UK Foreign Sec. Robin Cook 1999–2001 and Jack Straw 2001–05; fmr Dir for Asia and Pacific Div., Dept of Political Affairs, later Sec.-Gen.'s Special Adviser on Situation in Middle East, Special Co-ordinator for Middle East Peace Process and Personal Rep. to Palestine Liberation Org. and Palestinian Authority 2007–08 (also served as Sec.-Gen.'s Envoy to Quartet), UN Special Co-ordinator for Lebanon (UNSCOL) 2008–12; mem. House of Lords 2011–; mem. Exec. Cttee and Council of Royal Inst. for Int. Affairs (now Chatham House); currently Distinguished Visiting Fellow and Acting Head, Asia Programme, Chatham House. *Publications include:* Vietnam at the Crossroads 1992, Civil Military Relations and Peacekeeping 1998; has written widely on Asian politics, int. security and peacekeeping. *Address:* House of Lords, London, SW1A 0PW, England (office). *Telephone:* (20) 7219-5353 (office). *Fax:* (20) 7219-5979 (office). *E-mail:* contactholmember@parliament.uk (office). *Website:* www.parliament.uk/biographies/lords/lord-williams-of-baglan/4185 (office).

WILLIAMS, Michael J., BS, MBA; American business executive; ed Drexel Univ.; began career with DuPont Co.; Sr Man., Strategic Systems Practice, KPMG Peat Marwick's information tech. consulting group –1991; joined Fannie Mae (Fed.

Nat. Mortgage Asscn) 1991, served in several areas of co., developed tech. tools, Sr Vice-Pres., e-Commerce 1999–2000, Pres. Fannie Mae eBusiness 2000–05, Exec. Vice-Pres., Regulatory Agreements and Restatement Feb.–Nov. 2005, Exec. Vice-Pres. and COO Fannie Mae, responsible for Tech., Enterprise Operations, Human Resources, Community and Charitable Giving, Compliance and Ethics, Corp. Facilities and Security, and Corp. Procurement 2005–09, mem. Bd of Dirs, Pres. and CEO Fannie Mae 2009–12. *Address:* c/o Fannie Mae, 3900 Wisconsin Avenue NW, Washington, DC 20016-2892, USA. *E-mail:* headquarters@fanniemae.com.

WILLIAMS, Michelle Ingrid; American actress; b. 9 Sept. 1980, Kalispell, Mont.; d. of Larry Williams and Carla Williams (née Swenson); one d. with Heath Ledger (died 2008); began career with appearances in several 1990s TV series, including Baywatch, Step by Step, Home Improvement; mem. Acad. of Motion Picture Arts and Sciences 2009. *Films include:* Lassie 1994, Species 1995, Timemaster 1995, A Thousand Acres 1997, Halloween H20: 20 Years Later 1998, Dick 1999, But I'm a Cheerleader 1999, Perfume 2001, Me Without You 2001, Prozac Nation 2001, The United States of Leland 2003, The Station Agent 2003, A Hole in One 2004, Imaginary Heroes 2004, Land of Plenty 2004, The Baxter 2005, Brokeback Mountain (Broadcast Film Critics Asscn Award for Best Supporting Actress, Phoenix Film Critics Soc. Award for Best Supporting Actress) 2005, The Hawk Is Dying 2006, The Hottest State 2006, I'm Not There 2007, Incendiary 2008, Deception 2008, Wendy and Lucy (Online Film Critics Soc. Award for Best Actress, Toronto Film Critics Asscn Award for Best Actress) 2008, Synecdoche, New York 2008, Mammoth 2009, Blue Valentine (San Francisco Film Critics Circle Award for Best Actress) 2010, Shutter Island 2010, Meek's Cutoff 2010, Take This Waltz 2011, My Week with Marilyn (Golden Globe Award for Best Performance by an Actress in a Motion Picture – Comedy or Musical 2012) 2011, Tar 2012, Oz the Great and Powerful 2013. *Television includes:* Baywatch (series) 1993, Step by Step (series) 1994, Raising Caines (series) 1995, Home Improvement (series) 1995, My Son is Innocent (film) 1996, Killing Mr. Griffin (film) 1997, If These Walls Could Talk 2 (film) 2000, Dawson's Creek (six seasons) 1998–2003. *Address:* c/o Creative Artists Agency, 2000 Avenue of the Stars, Los Angeles, CA 90067, USA (office). *Telephone:* (424) 288-2000 (office). *Fax:* (424) 288-2900 (office). *Website:* www.caa.com (office).

WILLIAMS, Nigel, MA; British writer and television producer; b. 20 Jan. 1948, Cheadle, Cheshire, England; s. of the late David Ffrancon Williams; m. Suzan Harrison 1973; three s.; ed Highgate School, Oriel Coll., Oxford; trainee, BBC 1969–73, Producer/Dir Arts Dept 1973–85, Ed. Bookmark 1985–92, Omnibus 1992–96, writer and presenter 1997–2000. *Stage plays include:* Class Enemy (Plays and Players Award for Most Promising Playwright) 1978, Trial Run 1980, Line 'Em 1980, Sugar & Spice 1980, My Brother's Keeper 1985, Country Dancing 1986, Nativity 1989, Harry & Me 1995, The Last Romantics 1997, Lord of the Flies (adapted from William Golding's novel). *Radio:* HR Series 1–5 (BBC) 2009–14. *Television includes:* Double Talk, Talking Blues, Real Live Audience 1977, Baby Love 1981, Breaking Up 1986, The Last Romantics 1992, Skallagrig (BAFTA Award) 1994, Elizabeth 1 (Emmy Award, Golden Globe Award) 2006, Wodehouse at War 2013. *Publications:* novels: My Life Closed Twice (jt winner Somerset Maugham Award) 1977, Jack Be Nimble 1980, Star Turn 1985, Witchcraft 1987, The Wimbledon Poisoner 1990, They Came from SW19 1992, East of Wimbledon 1994, Scenes from a Poisoner's Life 1994, Stalking Fiona 1997, Fortysomething 1999, Hatchett and Lycett 2002; travel: Wimbledon to Waco 1995, Unfaithfully Yours 2013. *Leisure interests:* dogs, drinking, talking, family, swimming, walking. *Address:* 18 Holmbush Road, Putney, London, SW15 3LE, England. *Telephone:* (20) 8964-8811. *Fax:* (20) 8964-8966.

WILLIAMS, Sir Peter, Kt, CBE, MA, PhD, FRS; British physicist, academic and university administrator; *Chairman, Daiwa Anglo Japanese Foundation;* m. 1970; one s.; ed Hymers Coll., Hull, Trinity Coll., Cambridge; Research Fellow, Univ. of Cambridge –1970; Lecturer, Dept of Chemical Eng and Chemical Tech., Imperial Coll., London 1970–75; joined VG Instruments 1975, later Deputy Group Man. Dir; joined Oxford Instruments (first spin-off co. of Univ. of Oxford) 1982, Chief Exec. 1985–91, Chair. 1991–99 (retd); Master, St Catherine's Coll., Oxford 2000–2002; Chancellor, Univ. of Leicester 2005–10; Chair. Bd of Trustees, Nat. Museum of Science and Industry 1996–2002; Chair. Particle Physics and Astronomy Research Council 1990s, Eng and Tech. Bd 2001–06, Nat. Physical Lab. 2002–; Pres. Inst. of Physics 2000–02, BAAS 2003; Dir (non-exec.) GKN plc (Sr Ind. Dir) 2001–10, W.S. Atkins plc 2004–11; Vice-Pres. and Treas. The Royal Soc. 2006–12; Chair. Daiwa Anglo Japanese Foundation 2012–; Fellow, Imperial Coll. London 1996; Hon. Fellow, Univ. Coll., London 1997, Selwyn Coll., Cambridge 1997, St Catherine's Coll., Oxford 2002, City & Guilds 2002; Hon. FICE 2004; Hon. FIEE 2004; Hon. Fellow, Inst. of Measurement and Control 2006; Hon. FIMechE 2008; Hon. DSc (Leicester) 1995, (Nottingham Trent) 1995, (Loughborough) 1996, (Brunel) 1997, (Univ. of Wales, Swansea) 1997, (Univ. of Wales, Cardiff) 1999, (Sheffield) 1999, (Warwick) 1999, (Staffordshire) 2004, (City) 2007, (Hull) 2010, (Bedford) 2010; Guardian Young Business Man of the Year 1986, Glazebrook Medal, Inst. of Physics 2005. *Leisure interests:* travelling, hiking, skiing, music, collecting wine. *Address:* Daiwa Foundation, Japan House, 13–14 Cornwall Terrace, London, NW1 4QP, England (office). *Telephone:* (20) 7486-4348 (office). *Fax:* (20) 7486-2914 (office). *E-mail:* office@dajf.org.uk (office). *Website:* www.dajf.org.uk (office).

WILLIAMS, R. Stanley (Stan), BA, PhD; American physicist, academic and industrial researcher; *HP Senior Fellow and Founding Director, HP Quantum Science Research Group, Hewlett-Packard Laboratories;* b. 1951, Kodiak, Alaska; s. of Bobby L. Williams and Shirley A. Williams; ed Rice Univ., Univ. of California, Berkeley; mem. Tech. Staff, AT&T Bell Labs 1978–80; Asst Prof., Dept of Chem., UCLA 1980–84, Assoc. Prof. 1984–86, Prof. 1986–95, now Adjunct Prof. of Chem.; Adjunct Prof. of Computer Science, Univ. of N Carolina; joined Hewlett-Packard Labs 1995, HP Sr Fellow and Founding Dir HP Quantum Science Research Group 1995–; consultant to several corpns and law firms; mem. Defense Science Study Group; Advisor, Defense Science Bd, Frontier Research Program, Inst. for Physics and Chem. Research (RIKEN), Japan, Nat. Inst. for Materials Science, Japan; Julius Springer Award for Applied Physics 2000, Feynman Prize in Nanotechnology 2000, Dreyfus Teacher-Scholar Award, Sloan Foundation Fellowship, Scientific American Top 50 Technology Leaders 2002, Peter Debye Lecturer, Cornell Univ. 2004, Herman Block Lecturer, Univ. of Chicago 2004, Joel Birnbaum Award 2005, EETimes Innovator of the Year 2009, HP CEO Innovation Award 2010.

Achievements: holder of 34 US patents. *Publications:* more than 290 papers in peer-reviewed scientific journals and more than 130 patents world-wide. *Leisure interests:* cookery, long beach walks with wife and dogs. *Address:* Hewlett-Packard Company, 1501 Page Mill Road, MS 1123, Palo Alto, CA 94304-1185, USA (office). *Telephone:* (650) 857-1501 (office). *Website:* (office).

WILLIAMS, Richard Edmund; Canadian animated film producer, director and writer; b. 19 March 1933, Toronto, Ont.; s. of Kenneth D. C. Williams and Kathleen (née Bell) Williams; m. 2nd Margaret French 1976; four c. (including two from a previous m.); ed Royal Ontario Coll. of Art; f. Richard Williams Animation Ltd 1962; produced and directed: The Little Island (British Acad. Award, 1st Prize Venice Film Festival) 1958, Love Me, Love Me, Love Me 1962, The Dermis Probe 1965, A Christmas Carol (Oscar for Best Animated Short Subject) 1971, Ziggy's Gift 1982; designed film sequences and titles for: What's New Pussycat 1965, A Funny Thing Happened on the Way to the Forum 1966, The Spy with a Cold Nose 1966, Casino Royale 1967, The Charge of the Light Brigade 1968, Prudence and the Pill 1968, Murder on the Orient Express (uncredited) 1974, The Return of the Pink Panther 1975, The Pink Panther Strikes Again 1976; animation for Raggedy Ann & Andy: A Musical Adventure 1977, Who Framed Roger Rabbit (Special Achievement Oscar) 1988, Arabian Knight (produced and directed) 1995; mem. Acad. of Motion Picture Arts and Sciences; est. Richard Williams Animation Masterclasses for professionals and students worldwide 1995–; mem. Asscn of Cinematographers and TV Technicians. *Publication:* The Animator's Survival Kit 2000.

WILLIAMS, Robert (Robbie) Peter; British singer; b. 13 Feb. 1974, Stoke-on-Trent, Staffs., England; s. of Pete Williams and Theresa Janette Williams; m. Ayda Field 2010; one d.; played the Artful Dodger in Oliver 1982; mem. group Take That 1991–95, 2010–; solo artist 1995–; tours: The Show Off Must Go On 1997, The Ego Has Landed 1998, One More for the Rogue Tour/For a Few Dollars More... Tour 1998–99, Robbie Williams North American Tours 1999, The Sermon on the Mount Tour 2000–01, Weddings, Barmitzvahs & Stadiums Tour/Sing When You're Pacific Rimming Tour 2001, Weekends of Mass Distraction Tour/Cock of Justice/Aussie Typo Tour 2003, Close Encounters Tour 2006, Take the Crown Stadium Tour 2013; recording collaborators as soloist include: Kylie Minogue, Nicole Kidman, Maxi Jazz, Pet Shop Boys, Dean Martin, Gary Barlow, Thalia; mem. Equity, Musicians' Union, Mechanical-Copyright Protection Soc., Performing Right Soc., ADAMI, GVC, AURA; numerous including: nine Smash Hits Awards 1992–98, 16 BRIT Awards (13 solo), Levi's Nordoff-Robbins Music Therapy Original Talent Award 1998, MTV Award for Best Male 1998, Echo Award for Best Int. Male Rock and Pop Artist, Germany 2005, 2006, MTV Europe Music Award for Best Male 2005, MTV Latin America Music Award for Best Int. Pop Artist 2006, Q Idol Awards (with Take That) 2006, (solo) 2013, BRIT Award for Outstanding Contrib. to Music 2010, Echo Award for Best Int. Male 2010, NRJ Music Award for Best Int. Male Artist 2010, Virgin Media Award for Best Male Artist 2010, BRIT Award (with Take That) for Best British Group 2011. *Films:* Nobody Someday 2002, De-Lovely 2004, The Magic Roundabout (voice) 2005. *Recordings include:* albums: with Take That: Take That And Party 1992, Everything Changes 1993, Nobody Else 1995, Greatest Hits 1996, Progress 2010; solo: Life Thru' a Lens 1997, I've Been Expecting You 1998, The Ego Has Landed 1999, Sing When You're Winning 2000, Swing When You're Winning 2001, Escapology 2002, Live At Knebworth 2004, Intensive Care 2005, Rudebox 2006, Reality Killed the Video Star 2009, Take the Crown 2012, Swings Both Ways 2013. *Publications:* F for English 2000, Robbie Williams: Performance (with Mark McCrun) 2001, Robbie Williams: Somebody Someday 2001, Feel (with Chris Heath) 2004, You Know Me (with Chris Heath) 2010. *Leisure interests:* golf, rollerblading. *Address:* IE Music Ltd, 111 Frithville Gardens, London, W12 7JG, England (office). *Telephone:* (20) 8600-3400 (office). *Fax:* (20) 8600-3401 (office). *E-mail:* info@iemusic.co.uk (office). *Website:* www .iemusic.co.uk (office); www.takethat.com; www.robbiewilliams.com.

WILLIAMS, Robert Joseph Paton (Bob), MBE, DPhil, FRS, FRCS; British chemist and academic; *Professor Emeritus of Chemistry and Fellow Emeritus, Wadham College, University of Oxford;* b. 25 Feb. 1926, Wallasey; s. of Ernest Ivor Williams and Alice Roberts; m. Jelly Klara Buchli 1952; two s.; ed Univ. of Oxford; Rotary Int. Fellow 1951–52; Research Fellow, Merton Coll., Oxford Univ. 1952–55; Tutor and Lecturer (Fellow), Wadham Coll., Oxford 1955–74, Professorial Fellow 1974–93, Prof. Emer. 1991–, Fellow Emer. 1993–; Lecturer, Oxford Univ. 1955–70, Reader 1970–72, Royal Soc. Napier Research Prof. 1974–91; Pres. Dalton Div. Royal Soc. of Chemistry 1991–93; Foreign mem. Royal Swedish Acad. of Science, Lisbon Acad. of Science, Czechoslovak Acad. of Science, Royal Soc. of Science, Liège; Hon. Fellow, Merton Coll., Oxford 1991; Hon. DSc (Louvain, Leicester, East Anglia, Keele, Lisbon); Tilden Medal (Chem. Soc. of England), Liversidge Medal (Chem. Soc. of England), Keilen Medal (Biochem. Soc.), Hughes Medal (Royal Soc.), Sir Hans Krebs Medal (European Biochemical Soc.), Linderstrøm-Lang Medal (Denmark), Sigillum Magna (Univ. of Bologna), Heyrovsky Medal (Int. Union of Biochemistry), Sir Frederick Gowland Hopkins Medal (Biochemical Soc.), Royal Medal (Royal Soc.), Longstaff Medal (Chem. Soc. of England), Lord Goodman Lecturer 1992, J.D. Bernal Lecturer 1993, Canada Lecturer, Royal Soc. 1996, J.D. Birchall Lecturer 1999, Huxley Lecturer 2000, Certificate of Honour for Charity Work, City of Oxford 2003. *Publications:* Inorganic Chemistry (with C. S. G. Phillips), NMR in Biology, Recent Trends in Bioinorganic Chemistry, The Natural Selection of the Chemical Elements (with J.J.R. Frausto da Silva) 1996, Bringing Chemistry to Life (with J.J.R. Frausto da Silva) 1999, The Biological Chemistry of the Elements (with J.J.R. Frausto da Silva) (2nd edn) 2001, The Chemistry of Evolution (with J.J.R. Frausto da Silva) 2005. *Leisure interests:* walking in the country, local planning. *Address:* Wadham College, Oxford, OX1 3QR (office); Corner House, 1A Water Eaton Road, Oxford, OX2 7QQ, England (home). *Telephone:* (1865) 272600 (office); (1865) 558926 (home). *Fax:* (1865) 272690 (office); (1865) 558926 (home). *E-mail:* bob.williams@chem.ox.ac.uk (office). *Website:* www.chem.ox.ac.uk (office).

WILLIAMS, Robin; American actor and comedian; b. 21 July 1951, Chicago, Ill.; s. of Robert Williams and Laurie Williams; m. 1st Valerie Velardi 1978 (divorced); one s.; m. 2nd Marsha Garces 1989 (divorced); one s. one d.; m. 3rd Susan Schneider 2011; ed Detroit Country Day, Mich., Claremont Men's Coll., Marin Coll., Kentfield, Calif., Juilliard School, New York; f. Blue Wolf Productions Inc. (film production co.); Cecil B. DeMille Award, Golden Globe Awards 2005.

Television appearances include: Laugh-In 1977, The Richard Pryor Show (also writer) 1977, America 2-Night 1978, Happy Days 1978, Mork and Mindy 1978–82, Carol and Carl and Whoopi and Robin (Emmy Award), Royal Gala: Prince's Trust (Emmy Award); Homicide: Life on the Streets 1994, LA Doctors 1999, Law & Order: Special Victims Unit 2008, What Up with That 2010, The Crazy Ones (series) 2013–14. *Stage appearances include:* Waiting for Godot 1988, Bengal Tiger at the Baghdad Zoo, Broadway 2011. *Films include:* Popeye 1980, The World According to Garp 1982, The Survivors 1983, Moscow on the Hudson 1984, Club Paradise 1986, Good Morning Vietnam 1987 (Golden Globe Award 1988), Dead Poets' Society 1989, Awakenings 1990 (Best Actor, Nat. Bd of Review), The Fisher King 1991 (Golden Globe Award), Hook 1991, Dead Again 1991, Toys 1992, Being Human 1993, Aladdin (voice) 1993, Mrs Doubtfire (also producer) 1993, Jumanji 1996, The Birdcage 1996, Jack 1996, Hamlet 1996, Joseph Conrad's The Secret Agent 1996, Fathers' Day 1997, Deconstructing Harry 1997, Good Will Hunting 1997 (Acad. Award), Flubber 1997, What Dreams May Come 1998, Patch Adams 1998, Jakob the Liar 1999, Bicentennial Man 1999, One Hour Photo 2002, Insomnia 2002, Death to Smoochy 2002, The Final Cut 2004, House of D 2004, Robots (voice) 2005, The Big White 2005, The Night Listener 2006, RV 2006, Everyone's Hero 2006, Man of the Year 2006, Happy Feet (voice) 2006, Night at the Museum 2006, License to Wed 2007, August Rush 2007, Shrink 2009, World's Greatest Dad 2009, Night at the Museum: Battle of the Smithsonian 2009, Old Dogs 2009, Happy Feet 2 (voice) 2011, The Big Wedding 2013, The Butler 2013, The Face of Love 2013, Boulevard 2014, The Angriest Man in Brooklyn 2014. *Recordings:* Reality, What a Concept 1979 (Grammy Award), Throbbing Python of Love, A Night at the Met. *Address:* Blue Wolf Productions, Inc. 725 Arizona Avenue, Suite 202, Santa Monica, CA 90401; c/o Creative Artists Agency, 9830 Wilshire Boulevard, Beverly Hills, CA 90212; PO Box 480909, Los Angeles, CA 90048, USA. *Telephone:* (310) 451-8890 (Blue Wolf).

WILLIAMS, Roger Stanley, CBE, MD, FRCP, FRCS, FRCPE, FRACP, FRCPI, FMedSci; British consultant physician; *Director, Institute of Hepatology, Foundation for Liver Research;* b. 28 Aug. 1931; s. of Stanley George Williams and Doris Dagmar Clatworthy; m. 1st Lindsay Mary Elliott 1954 (divorced 1977); two s. three d.; m. 2nd Stephanie Gay de Laszlo 1978; one s. two d.; ed St Mary's Coll., Southampton, London Hosp. Medical School, Univ. of London; House Doctor, London Hosp. 1953–56; Jr Medical Specialist, Queen Alexandra Hosp. 1956–58; Medical Registrar and Tutor, Royal Postgraduate Medical School 1958–59; Lecturer in Medicine Royal Free Hosp. 1959–65; Consultant Physician Royal S. Hants. and Southampton Gen. Hosp. 1965–66; Consultant Physician and Dir, Inst. of Liver Studies, King's Coll. Hosp. (now King's Coll. School of Medicine and Dentistry), London 1966–96, Prof. of Hepatology; Dir Inst. of Hepatology, Foundation for Liver Research, Hon. Consultant Physician, Univ. Coll. London Hosps NHS Trust 1996–; mem. WHO Scientific Group on Viral Hepatitis, Geneva 1972, Transplant Advisory Panel DHSS 1974–83, Advisory Group on Hepatitis DHSS 1980–, European Asscn for the Study of the Liver (Pres. 1983) 1966–, Harveian Soc. of London (Pres. 1974–75), British Asscn for the Study of the Liver (Pres. 1984), Royal Soc. of Medicine, British Soc. of Gastroenterology (Pres. 1989); Vice-Pres. Royal Coll. of Physicians 1991; Hon. Consultant in Medicine to the Army 1988–98; Rep. to Select Cttee of Experts on Organizational Aspects of Co-operation in Organ Transplantation, Congress of Europe; Sir Ernest Finch Visiting Prof., Univ. of Sheffield 1974; Hon. FACP; Hon. FRCPI. *Publications:* Fifth Symposium on Advanced Medicine (ed.) 1969, Immunology of the Liver 1971, Artificial Liver Support 1975, Immune Reactions in Liver Disease 1978, Drug Reactions and the Liver 1981, Clinics in Critical Care Medicine – Liver Failure 1986, Liver Tumours (Baillière's Clinical Gastroenterology) 1987, The Practice of Liver Transplantation 1995, International Developments in Health Care. A review of Health Systems in the 1990s 1995, Acute Liver Failure 1997; more than 2,500 papers, reviews and book chapters. *Leisure interests:* tennis, sailing, opera. *Address:* Institute of Hepatology, Harold Samuel House, 69–75 Chenies Mews, Harold Samuel House, 69–75 Chenies Mews, London, WC1E 6HX (office); 30 Devonshire Place, London, W1G 7BE, England (home). *Telephone:* (20) 7255-9830 (office); (20) 7637-2844 (home). *Fax:* (20) 7380-0405 (office). *E-mail:* r.williams@researchinliver.org.uk (office). *Website:* www.liver-research.org.uk (office).

WILLIAMS, Ronald Allen, MS; American business executive; b. 11 Nov. 1949, Chicago, Ill.; ed Roosevelt Univ., Sloan School of Management, Massachusetts Inst. of Tech.; Sr Vice-Pres. of Marketing Blue Cross of California 1987–95, Pres. 1995–99; Co-founder and fmr Sr Vice-Pres. Vista Health Corpn; fmr Group Marketing Exec. Control Data Corpn; Co-founder and fmr Pres. Integrative Systems; Group Pres., Large Group Div. WellPoint Health Networks Inc. 1999–2001; Exec. Vice-Pres. and Chief of Health Operations, Aetna Inc. 2001–02, Pres. 2002–07, mem. Bd of Dirs 2002–11, Chair. and CEO 2006–10, Chair. 2010–11 (retd); mem. Bd of Dirs American Express Co. 2007–, The Boeing Co.; mem. or fmr MIT Sloan Dean's Advisory Council, MIT North America Exec. Bd 2002–10, Alfred P. Sloan Man. Soc., Business Council (Vice-Chair. 2008–10), Business Roundtable, Council for Affordable Quality Healthcare (Chair. 2007–10), Int. Fed. of Health Plans, Healthcare Leadership Council, GE Healthymagination Advisory Cttee, The Wall Street Journal CEO Council; Co-Chair. World Econ. Forum's Annual Meeting, Davos, Switzerland Jan. 2010; mem. Pres. Obama's Man. Advisory Bd 2011–; Trustee, Connecticut Science Center. *Publications:* author or co-author of op-ed articles in The Wall Street Journal, Washington Post, The Financial Times and the Seattle Post-Intelligencer. *Address:* c/o Aetna Inc., 151 Farmington Avenue, Hartford, CT 06156, USA.

WILLIAMS, Most Rev., Rt Hon. Rowan Douglas, PC, MA, DPhil, DD, FRSL, FBA; British ecclesiastic, academic and college principal; *Master, Magdalene College, Cambridge;* b. 14 June 1950, Ystradgynlais, Swansea, Wales; s. of Aneurin Williams and Delphine (Del, Nancy) Morris; m. Jane Paul 1981; one s. one d.; ed Dynevor School, Swansea, Christ's Coll., Cambridge, Wadham Coll., Oxford; lectured at Coll. of the Resurrection, Mirfield, W Yorks. 1975–77; deacon, Ely Cathedral 1977; priest 1978; tutor, Westcott House, Univ. of Cambridge 1977–80, Lecturer in Divinity 1980–1986, Dean and Chaplain, Clare Coll. 1984–86; Canon Theologian Leicester Cathedral 1981–82; Canon Residentiary, Christ Church, Oxford 1986–92; Lady Margaret Prof. of Theology, Oxford Univ. 1986–92; consecrated Bishop of Monmouth in the Church in Wales 1992–2002; Archbishop of Wales 2000–02; Archbishop of Canterbury, Metropolitan of the Prov. of Canterbury and Primate of All England 2002–12; Master of Magdalene Coll.,

Cambridge 2013–; inaugurated as first Chancellor of Canterbury Christ Church Univ. 2005; Visitor at King's Coll., London, Univ. of Kent, Keble Coll., Oxford; Gov. of Charterhouse School; Patron Peace Mala Youth Project for World Peace 2002–, Canterbury Open Centre run by Catching Lives; Founding Fellow, Learned Soc. of Wales 2010; Hon. Student of Christ Church, Oxford; Hon. Curate, St George's, Chesterton, Cambridge 1980–83, Hon. Fellow, Univ. of Wales, Bangor 2003, Univ. of Wales, Swansea, Newport, Aberystwyth, Cardiff, Clare Coll., Cambridge, Christ Church, Oxford, Wadham Coll., Oxford, Christ's Coll., Cambridge; Order of Friendship (Russia) 2010; Hon. DD (Kent) 2003, (Univ. of Wales) 2003, (Cambridge) 2006, (Trinity Coll., Univ. of Toronto) 2007, (Wycliffe Coll., Univ. of Toronto) 2007, (Durham) 2007, (St Vladimir's Orthodox Theological Seminary) 2010, (Catholic Univ. of Louvain) 2011, (King's Coll., London) 2011; Hon. DrTheol (Evangelisch-Theologische Fakultät, Univ. of Bonn) 2004; Hon. DCL (Oxford) 2005; Dr hc (Erlangen, Nashoteh House, Exeter, Aberdeen, Open Univ., Roehampton). *Television:* Conversations with Rowan Williams 2003. *Publications include:* The Wound of Knowledge 1979, Resurrection 1982, The Truce of God 1983, Arius: Heresy and Tradition 1987, Teresa of Avila 1991, Open to Judgement: Sermons and Addresses 1994, Sergei Bulgakov: towards a Russian political theory 1999, Christ on Trial: How the Gospel Unsettles our Judgement 2000, Lost Icons: Reflection on Cultural Bereavement 2000, On Christian Theology 2000, Love's Redeeming Work (ed.) 2001, Ponder These Things: Praying With Icons of the Virgin 2002, Writing in the Dust: Reflections on 11th September and its Aftermath 2002, Silence and Honey Cakes 2003, The Dwelling of the Light 2003, Anglican Identities 2004, Why Study the Past? 2005, Grace and Necessity 2006, Tokens of Trust: An Introduction to Christian Belief 2007, Wrestling with Angels: Conversations in Modern Theology 2007, Dostoevsky: Language, Faith and Fiction 2008; poetry: After Silent Centuries 1994, Remembering Jerusalem 2001, The Poems of Rowan Williams 2002, Headwaters 2008, Uncommon Gratitude (with Joan Chittister) 2010, Crisis and Recovery (with Larry Elliot) 2010. *Leisure interests:* music, fiction, languages. *Address:* Magdalene College, Cambridge, CB3 0AG, England (office). *Telephone:* (1223) 332100 (office). *E-mail:* enquiries@magd.cam.ac.uk (office). *Website:* www.magd.cam.ac.uk (office).

WILLIAMS, Serena Jameka; American professional tennis player; b. 26 Sept. 1981, Saginaw, Mich.; d. of Richard Williams and Oracene Williams; sister of Venus Williams (q.v.); began playing tennis aged five; turned professional 1995; coached by her father Richard Williams; singles semi-finalist, Sydney Open 1997, Chicago 1998; won mixed doubles (with Max Mirnyi) at Wimbledon 1998, US Open 1998; doubles winner (with Venus Williams) Oklahoma City 1998, French Open 1999, 2010, Hanover 1999, US Open 1999, 2009, Wimbledon 2000, 2002, 2008, 2009, 2012, Australian Open 2001, 2003, 2009, 2010, Olympic Games, London 2012; winner (singles) US Open 1999, 2002, 2008, 2012, 2013, Paris Indoors 1999, 2003, Indian Wells 1999, 2001, LA 1999, 2000, Grand Slam Cup 1999, Hanover 2000, Tokyo 2000, Canadian Open 2001, French Open 2002, 2013, Wimbledon 2002, 2003, 2009, 2010, 2012, Australian Open 2003, 2005, 2007, 2009, 2010, Miami 2002, 2003, 2004, 2007, 2008, 2013, 2014, Madrid 2012, Olympic Games, London 2012, Brisbane International 2013, Family Circle Cup, Charleston 2013, Mutua Madrid 2013 China Open 2013; singles finalist, Wimbledon 2004, 2008, US Open 2011; US Fed. Cup Team 1999; winner WTA Tour Championships, Munich 2001, Doha 2009, Istanbul 2012, 2013; doubles gold medal with sister, Venus, Olympic Games, Sydney 2000, Beijing 2008; singles quarter-finalist, Olympic Games, Beijing 2008; 585 career singles wins, 110 defeats, 169 career doubles wins, 22 defeats; 30 Grand Slam titles: 15 in singles, 13 in women's doubles and two in mixed doubles; ranked World No. 1 (singles) 8 July 2002, 8 Sept. 2008, 2 Feb. 2009, 2 Nov. 2009, 5 April 2010, 13 May 2013; debuted The Serena Williams Collection by Nike, an apparel and footwear collection 2005; f. clothing label Aneres; numerous appearances as actress on TV programmes; f. Serena Williams Foundation (education foundation); Sanex WTA Tour Most Impressive Newcomer Award 1998, WTA Most Improved Player 1999, Tennis Magazine Player of the Year 1999, Teen Awards Achievement Award (shared with sister, Venus) 2000, WTA Doubles Team of the Year Award (with Venus Williams) 2000, WTA Player of the Year 2002, 2008, 2009, ITF Women's Singles World Champion 2002, Associated Press Female Athlete of the Year 2002, World Sportswoman of the Year 2002, 34th NAACP Image Awards Pres.'s Award 2003, ESPY Award for Best Female Athlete 2003, ESPY Award for Best Female Tennis Player 2003, 2004, 2009, 2010, 2011, Laureus World Sportswoman of the Year 2003, 2010, Avon Foundation Celebrity Role Model Award 2003, BET's Best Female Athlete of the Year 2003, 2004, 2005, 2009, 2010, 2011, Family Circle/Prudential Financial Player Who Makes a Difference Award 2004, WTA Comeback Player of the Year 2004, Laureus World Comeback of the Year 2007, Harris Poll Most Favorite Female Sports Star 2009, Glamour Magazine Women of the Year Award 2009, SI.com Best Female Athlete of the Decade 2009, AP Female Athlete of the Year Award 2009, ITF Women's Singles World Champion 2009, ITF Women's Doubles World Champion (with Venus Williams) 2009, named Second Best Tennis Player of the Decade by ESPN (with Roger Federer at No. 1) 2009, ranked by Forbes magazine amongst The World's 100 Most Powerful Women (55th) 2010, WTA Fan Favorite Doubles Team of the Year Award (with Venus Williams) 2009, 2010, Doha 21st Century Leaders Awards – Outstanding Leadership 2009, Forbes The Celebrity 100 (No. 67) 2009, (No. 61), (No. 84) 2011, 2010, TIME magazine The World's 100 Most Influential People 2010, BET Award for Female Athlete of the Year 2010, Harris Poll Top 10 Favorite Female Sports Star (No. 1) 2010, Forbes 30 Utterly Inspiring Role Models 2010, Teen Choice Awards – Female Athlete Award 2010, TIME magazine 30 Legends of Women's Tennis 2011, Forbes Most Powerful Black Women in the US (No. 10) 2011, ranked 41st by The Root 100 2011: Influencers and Iconoclasts 2011. *Publication:* On the Line (autobiog.) 2009. *Leisure interests:* watching movies, playing football and basketball, reading, acting, music, designing clothing. *Address:* c/o William Morris Endeavor Entertainment, 9601 Wilshire Blvd. 3rd Floor, Beverly Hills, CA 90210, USA (office). *Website:* www.serenawilliams.com.

WILLIAMS, Stephen, MA, PhD; American anthropologist, archaeologist, academic and museum curator; *Peabody Professor Emeritus of North American Archaeology and Ethnography, Harvard University;* b. 28 Aug. 1926, Minneapolis, Minn.; s. of Clyde G. Williams and Lois M. Williams (née Simmons); m. Eunice Ford 1962; two s.; ed Yale Univ. and Univ. of Michigan; Historical and Archaeological Research on Caddo Indians for U.S. Dept of Justice 1954–55;

Research Fellow in N American Archaeology, Peabody Museum of Archaeology and Ethnology, Harvard Univ. 1955–58; Lecturer in Anthropology, Harvard Univ. 1956–58, Asst Prof. of Anthropology 1958–62, Assoc. Prof. 1962–67, Prof. of Anthropology 1967–72, Peabody Prof. of North American Archaeology and Ethnography 1972–93, Prof. Emer. 1993–, Chair. Dept of Anthropology 1967–69, mem. Bd of Freshmen Advisers, Harvard Univ. 1959–60, 1961–65; Asst Curator of N American Archaeology, Peabody Museum 1957–58, Curator of N American Archaeology 1962–93; Dir Peabody Museum, Harvard Univ. 1967–77, Dir Lower Mississippi Survey 1958–93, Hon. Curator N American Archaeology, 1993–; mem. Bd Dirs Archaeological Conservancy 1984–88; Distinguished Fellow School of American Research, Santa Fe 1977–78; Hon. MA (Harvard Univ.); Distinguished Service Award, Southeast Archaeological Conf. 1992, Dean's Distinguished Service Award, Harvard Extension Program 1993. *Publications:* six books and monographs including Excavations at the Lake George Site, Yazoo County, Miss. 1958–60 (with Jeffrey P. Brain), Fantastic Archaeology: The Wild Side of North American Prehistory 1991; numerous articles in journals and magazines. *Leisure interest:* bird watching. *Address:* PO Box 22354, Santa Fe, NM 87502 (office); 1017 Foothills Trail, Santa Fe, NM 87505, USA (home). *Telephone:* (505) 983-8836 (office). *E-mail:* williamsstephen@msn.com (home).

WILLIAMS, Steven (Steve) W., BSc (ChemEng), FIChemE; British oil industry executive; *President and CEO, Suncor Energy Inc.;* ed Univ. of Exeter, Harvard Business School, Univ. of Oxford; was responsible for Octel Corpn's global operation; also managed operation of largest refinery in UK for Esso; joined Suncor 2002, Exec. Vice-Pres., Corp. Devt and Chief Financial Officer 2002–07, also served as Exec. Vice-Pres., Oil Sands, COO Suncor Energy 2007–11, mem. Bd of Dirs Suncor Energy 2011–, Pres. 2011–, CEO 2012–; Chair. Suncor United Way campaign, Fort McMurray 2003–07, Suncor United Way campaign 2011; Co-Chair. Oil Sands Leadership Initiative 2009–; mem. Alberta Govt Oil and Gas Econs Advisory Council 2010, Canadian Asscn of Petroleum Producers Bd Govs 2009–10, Nat. Roundtable on the Environment and the Economy 2007–09, CEO Cttee of Syncrude Canada Ltd 2009–, Business Advisory Council, School of Business, Univ. of Alberta 2004–, Alberta Carbon Capture and Storage Devt Council 2008–10, Bd Alberta Chamber of Resources 2003–07, Bd Northern Lights Regional Hosp. Foundation 2003–07; Founding Bd mem. Oil Sands Safety Asscn 2003, Chair. 2005; Founding mem. COSIA 2012; mem. Inst. of Dirs. *Address:* Suncor Energy Inc., PO Box 2844, 150 – 6 Avenue SW, Calgary, Alberta, T2P 3E3, Canada (office). *Telephone:* (403) 296-8000 (office). *Fax:* (403) 296-3030 (office). *E-mail:* info@suncor.com (office). *Website:* www.suncor.com (office).

WILLIAMS, HE Cardinal Thomas Stafford, ONZ, STL, BSocSc; New Zealand ecclesiastic (retd); *Archbishop Emeritus of Wellington;* b. 20 March 1930, Wellington; s. of Thomas S. Williams and Lillian M. Williams (née Kelly); ed St Patrick's Coll., Wellington, Victoria Univ., Wellington, St Kevin's Coll., Oamaru, Holy Cross Coll., Mosgiel, Pontifical Urban Coll. de Propaganda Fide, Rome and Univ. Coll., Dublin; ordained priest, Rome 1959; Asst St Patrick's Parish, Palmerston North 1963; Dir of Studies, Catholic Enquiry Centre, Wellington 1965; parish priest, St Anne's, Leulumoega, Western Samoa 1971, Holy Family Parish, Porirua East, Wellington 1976; Archbishop of Wellington and Metropolitan of NZ 1979–2005, Archbishop Emer. 2005–; Bishop of New Zealand, Mil. 1995–2005; cr. Cardinal (Cardinal-Priest of Gesù Divin Maestro alla Pineta Sacchetti) 1983. *Address:* 40 Walton Avenue, Waikanae Park, Kapiti 5036, New Zealand. *Telephone:* (4) 293-4684. *E-mail:* t.williams@wn.catholic.org.nz.

WILLIAMS, Venus Ebone Starr; American professional tennis player; b. 17 June 1980, Lynwood, Calif.; d. of Richard Williams and Oracene Williams; sister of Serena Williams (q.v.); ed Art Inst. of Fort Lauderdale; made professional debut Bank of West Classic, Oakland, Calif. 1994; Bausch & Lomb Championships 1996; winner numerous singles titles (WTA Tour) including Oklahoma City 1998, Lipton 1998, 1999, Hamburg 1999, Italian Open 1999, Grand Slam Cup 1998; seven Grand Slam singles titles: Wimbledon 2000, 2001, 2005, 2007, 2008, US Open 2000, 2001; 13 Grand Slam doubles titles (with Serena Williams): French Open 1999, 2010, US Open 1999, 2009, Wimbledon 2000, 2002, 2008, 2009, 2012, Australian Open 2001, 2003, 2009, 2010; two Grand Slam mixed doubles titles: Australian Open 1998, French Open 1998; singles finalist, Wimbledon 2002, 2003, 2009, French Open 2002, Australian Open 2003; mixed doubles finalist, Wimbledon 2006; with Serena Williams, first sisters in tennis history to have each won a Grand Slam singles title; singles Gold Medal, Olympic Games, Sydney 2000; doubles Gold Medal (with sister Serena), Olympic Games, Sydney 2000, Beijing 2008, doubles Gold Medal (with sister Serena) London 2012; only sisters in 20th century to win a Grand Slam doubles title together; US Fed. Cup Team 1995, 1999; 610 career singles wins, 152 defeats, 150 career doubles wins, 23 defeats, 26 career mixed doubles wins, six defeats; 43 career singles titles, 21 doubles titles, two mixed doubles titles; highest ranking (singles): No. 1 25 Feb. 2002, (doubles): No. 3 14 Sept. 2009; awarded largest-ever endorsement contract for a female athlete by Reebok 2002; Founder and CEO V Starr Interiors (design firm), Jupiter, Fla 2002–; Global Amb. for UNESCO to address worldwide gender issues 2006; teamed up with retailer Steve & Barry's to launch own fashion line EleVen 2007; Sports Image Foundation Award 1995, WTA Newcomer of the Year 1997, September's Olympic Cttee Female Athlete 1997, Tennis Magazine's Most Impressive Player 1998, WTA Player of the Year 2000, Sports Illustrated for Women's Sportswoman of the Year 2000, Teen Awards Achievement Award 2000, Sanex WTA Tour Player of the Year and Doubles Team of the Year (with sister, Serena) 2000, Women's Sports Foundation Athlete of the Year 2000, WTA Most Improved Player of the Year 2001, ESPY Awards for Best Female Athlete and Best Female Tennis Player of 2001, 2002, Certificate of Achievement Howard Univ. 2002, 34th NAACP Image Awards' Pres.'s Award 2003, Harris Poll Most Favorite Female Sports Star 2004, 2006, Glamour Magazine's Woman of the Year Award 2005, ESPY Award for Best Female Tennis Player 2006, BET's Best Female Athlete of the Year 2006, Whirlpool 6th Sense Player of the Year Awar 2008, 2009, Anti-Defamation League Americanism Award 2009, ITF Women's Doubles World Champion (with sister Serena Williams) 2009, Caesars Tennis Classic Achievement Award 2010, ranked 83rd in Forbes The Celebrity 100 2010, YWCA GLA Phenomenal Woman of the Year Award 2010, WTA Fan Favorite Doubles Team of the Year Award (with Serena Williams) 2010, Forbes 30 Utterly Inspiring Role Models 2010, ranked by Forbes magazine amongst The World's 100 Most Powerful Women (60th) 2010, Harris Poll Top 10 Favorite Female Sports Star (second) 2010,

ranked 86th in Forbes The Celebrity 100 2011, TIME Magazine 30 Legends of Women's Tennis 2011, ranked tenth in Forbes Most Powerful Black Women in the US 2011. *Leisure interests:* sumo wrestling, surfing, reading, languages, antique furniture, writing poetry. *Address:* c/o IMG Tennis, IMG Center, 1360 East 9th Street, Suite 100, Cleveland, OH 44114-1782, USA (office); V Starr Interiors, 1102 West Indiantown Road, Suite 11, Jupiter, FL 33458, USA (office). *Telephone:* (216) 522-1200 (office). *Fax:* (216) 436-3477 (office). *E-mail:* cleresumes@imgworld.com (office). *Website:* www.imgworld.com (office); www.vstarrinteriors.com; www .venuswilliams.com.

WILLIAMS-JONES, Michael Robert; British/South African film executive; *President, Miramax Film Corporation;* b. 3 June 1947, Sussex, England, UK; s. of Hugh E. Williams-Jones and Valerie Lyons; m. 1st Lynne Williams-Jones 1969 (deceased); m. 2nd Eve Foreman 1994; two s. one step-s. one step-d.; ed Selborne Coll., East London, S Africa; trainee, United Artists, Southern Africa region 1967, Man. Dir 1969, Brazil 1971, UK 1975; Sr Vice-Pres., United Artists International 1978; Pres. United International Pictures Film Group 1981; Pres. and CEO United International Pictures Corpn 1984–96; Owner/Co-founder Merlin Anglesey UK, Ltd 1996–; currently Pres. Miramax Film Corpn; City of Rio de Janeiro Honour 1974, Golden Horse Lifetime Achievement Award, Taiwan 1986, Lifetime Achievement Award, Locarno 1989, Int. Distributor of the Year 1995. *Leisure interests:* movies, theatre, reading, opera, walking, snorkelling. *Address:* Miramax Film Corporation, 161 Avenue Of The Americas, 15th Floor, New York, NY 10013-1205, USA (office). *Telephone:* (212) 941-3800 (office). *Fax:* (212) 941-2098 (office). *E-mail:* info@miramax.com (office). *Website:* www.miramax.com (office).

WILLIAMS OF CROSBY, Baroness (Life Peer), cr. 1993, of Stevenage in the County of Hertfordshire; **Rt Hon. Shirley Williams**, PC, MA; British politician and academic; *Public Service Professor of Electoral Politics, Emerita, John F. Kennedy School of Government, Harvard University;* b. 27 July 1930, London; d. of the late Sir George Catlin and Vera Brittain; m. 1st Bernard Williams 1955 (divorced 1974, died 2003); one d.; m. 2nd Prof. Richard Neustadt 1987 (died 2003); ed Summit School, Minn., USA, St Paul's Girls' School, Somerville Coll., Oxford and Columbia Univ., New York; Gen. Sec. Fabian Soc. 1960–64; Labour MP for Hitchin 1964–74, for Hertford and Stevenage 1974–79; SDP MP for Crosby 1981–83; Parl. Pvt. Sec., Minister of Health 1964–66; Parl. Sec. Minister of Labour 1966–67; Minister of State, Dept of Educ. and Science 1967–69; Minister of State, Home Office 1969–70; Opposition Spokesman on Health and Social Security 1970–71, on Home Affairs 1971–73, on Prices and Consumer Affairs 1973–74; Sec. of State for Prices and Consumer Protection 1974–76, for Educ. and Science 1976–79; Paymaster-Gen. 1976–79; Sr Research Fellow (part-time), Policy Research Inst. 1979–85; mem. Labour Party Nat. Exec. Cttee 1970–81; mem. Council for Social Democracy Jan.–March 1981; left Labour Party March 1981; Co-Founder SDP March 1981, Pres. 1982–88; Public Service Prof. of Elective Politics, John F. Kennedy School of Govt, Harvard Univ. 1988–2000, Prof. Emer. 2000–, Dir Inst. of Politics 1988–89; mem. Social and Liberal Democratic Party 1988–; Deputy Leader Liberal Democrat Party, House of Lords 1999–2001, Leader Nov. 2001–; Visiting Fellow, Nuffield Coll., Oxford 1967–75; Fellow, Inst. of Politics, Harvard 1979–80 (mem. Sr Advisory Council 1986–); Regents Lecturer and Fellow, Inst. of Politics, Univ. of Calif., Berkeley; Dir Turing Inst., Glasgow 1985–90, Learning by Experience Trust 1986–94, Project Liberty 1990–98; Janeway Lecturer, Princeton Univ., NJ; Pick Lecturer, Univ. of Chicago; Godkin Lecturer, Harvard Univ.; Montgomery Lecturer, Dartmouth Coll.; Heath Fellow, Grinell Coll.; Rede Lecturer and Darwin Lecturer, Univ. of Cambridge; Hoover Lecturer, Strathclyde Univ.; Dainton Lecturer, British Library; Gresham Lecturer, Mansion House; mem. EC Comité des Sages 1996–97, Council Int. Crisis Group 1996–, Int. Advisory Council, Council on Foreign Relations (US); Chair. EC Job Creation Competition 1997–98; Trustee, The Century Foundation, New York, Inst. for Public Policy Research, London, RAND Europe UK; Gov. The Ditchley Foundation; mem. Bd Moscow School of Political Studies; Hon. Fellow, Somerville Coll., Oxford, Newnham Coll., Cambridge; Grand Cross (FRG); Hon. DEd, CNAA; Hon. DrPolEcon (Univ. of Leuven, Belgium, Radcliffe Coll., Harvard, USA); Hon. LLD (Leeds) 1979, (Southampton) 1981, (Ulster) 1997; Dr hc (Aston, Bath, Essex, Heriot-Watt, Napier, Sheffield, Washington Coll. (USA)); RSA Silver Medal. *Radio:* Snakes and Ladders – A Political Diary (BBC Radio 4) 1996, Women in the House (BBC Radio 4) 1998. *Television:* Shirley Williams in Conversation (BBC series) 1979. *Publications:* Youth Without Work (OECD Study) 1981, Politics is for People 1981, A Job to Live 1985, 'Human Rights in Europe' for Human Rights: What Work? (ed. Power and Alison) 2000, Making Globalisation Good (Chapter 15: Global Social Justice – The Moral Responsibilities of the Rich to the Poor) (ed. John Dunning) 2003, God and Caesar 2003, Climbing the Bookshelves: The Autobiography 2009; pamphlets on EC and economics of Central Africa; articles for The Times, Guardian, Independent, Int. Herald Tribune, Political Quarterly, Prospect etc. *Leisure interests:* riding, rough walking, music. *Address:* House of Lords, Westminster, London, SW1A 0PW, England (office). *Telephone:* (20) 7219-5850 (office); (20) 7219-3242 (office); (617) 495-8866 (Harvard, USA). *Fax:* (20) 7219-1174 (office). *E-mail:* williamss@parliament.uk (office); shirley_williams@ksg .harvard.edu. *Website:* hks.harvard.edu/about/faculty-staff-directory/shirley -williams.

WILLIAMS OF ELVEL, Baron (Life Peer), cr. 1985, of Llansantffraed in Elvel in the County of Powys; **Charles Cuthbert Powell Williams**, PC, CBE, MA; British business executive, author and politician; b. 9 Feb. 1933, Oxford; s. of the late Dr Norman P. Williams and Muriel Cazenove; m. Jane G. Portal 1975; one step-s.; ed Westminster School, Christ Church, Oxford and London School of Econs; British Petroleum Co. Ltd 1958–64; Bank of London and Montreal 1964–66; Eurofinance SA, Paris 1966–70; Baring Brothers & Co. Ltd 1970–77, Man. Dir 1971–77; Chair. Price Comm. 1977–79; Man. Dir Henry Ansbacher & Co. Ltd 1980–82, Chair. 1982–85; Chief Exec. Henry Ansbacher Holdings PLC 1982–85; Chair. Acoustiguide UK Ltd 1989–95; Pres. Campaign for the Protection of Rural Wales 1989–95, Pres. Radnor Br. 1995–; Pres. Fed. of Econ. Devt Authorities 1990–96; parl. cand. (Labour) 1964; Opposition Spokesman for Trade and Industry, House of Lords 1986–92, for Defence 1990–, for Environment 1992–; Deputy Leader of Opposition in House of Lords 1989–92; Chair. Acad. of St Martin in the Fields 1989–91, Mid Wales Chamber Orchestra 1991–93; Patron Llandrindod Wells Spa Town Trust 1991–. *Publications:* The Last Great Frenchman: A Life of General de Gaulle 1993, Bradman: An Australian Hero 1996, Adenauer: The Father of the New

Germany 2000, Pétain 2005, Harold Macmillan 2009, Gentlemen and Players 2012. *Leisure interests:* cricket, music. *Address:* 48 Thurloe Square, London, SW7 2SX, England.

WILLIAMSON, David Keith, AO, BE; Australian playwright and screenwriter; b. 24 Feb. 1942, Melbourne, Vic.; s. of Edwin Keith David Williamson and Elvie May Williamson (née Armstrong); m. Kristin Ingrid Lofven 1974; two s. one d.; ed Monash Univ., Univ. of Melbourne; Design Engineer, Gen. Motors-Holden's 1965; Lecturer, Swinbourne Tech. Coll. 1966–72; freelance writer 1972–; Hon. DLitt (Sydney), (Monash), (Swinburne); numerous writing, TV and cinema awards including JC Williamson Award for Lifetime Achievement, Live Performance Australia 2005. *Plays:* The Removalists 1972, Don's Party 1973, Three Plays 1974, The Department 1975, A Handful of Friends 1976, The Club 1977, Travelling North 1979, The Perfectionist 1981, Sons of Cain 1985, Emerald City 1987, Top Silk 1989, Siren 1990, Money and Friends 1992, Brilliant Lies 1993, Sanctuary 1994, Dead White Males 1995, Corporate Vibes 1999, Face to Face 1999, The Great Man 2000, Up for Grabs 2001, A Conversation 2001, Charitable Intent 2001, Soulmates 2002, Amigos 2004, Influence 2005, Scarlett O'Hara at the Crimson Parrot 2008, Let The Sunshine 2009, Rhinestone Rex & Miss Monica 2010, Don Parties On 2011, At Any Cost? 2011, Nothing Personal 2011, When Dad Married Fury 2011, Nothing Personal 2011, Happiness 2012, Rupert 2012, Managing Carmen 2012. *Screenplays:* Gallipoli 1981, Phar Lap 1983, The Year of Living Dangerously 1983, Travelling North 1986, Emerald City 1988, The Four Minute Mile (two-part TV series) 1988, A Dangerous Life (six-hour TV series) 1988, Top Silk 1989, Siren 1990, Money and Friends 1992, Dead White Males 1995, Heretic 1996, Third World Blues 1997, After the Ball 1997, Brilliant Lies 1996, On the Beach 2000, Balibo 2008, Face to Face 2010. *Address:* c/o Cameron Cresswell Management, Level 7, 61 Marlborough Street, Surry Hills, NSW 2010, Australia (office). *Telephone:* (2) 9319-7199 (office). *E-mail:* info@cameronsmanagement.com .au (office). *Website:* www.cameronsmanagement.com.au (office).

WILLIAMSON, Sir (George) Malcolm, Kt, FCIB; British banker; *Chairman, National Australia Group Europe Ltd;* b. 27 Feb. 1939, Oldham; s. of George Williamson and Margery Williamson; m. Hang Thi Ngo; one s. one d.; one s. one d. by previous marriage; local dir, Barclays Bank PLC, N London 1978–79; Asst Gen. Man. Barclays Bank PLC 1979–82, Treas. UK 1982–83, Regional Man. 1983–85; Man. Dir Girobank PLC and mem. Bd The Post Office 1985–89; Group Exec. Dir Banking (Eastern Hemisphere), Standard Chartered Bank 1989–90, Group Exec. Dir Banking 1990–91, Group Man. Dir 1991–93, Group Chief Exec. 1993–98; Dir Nat. Grid Group 1995–99; UK Chair. Thai-British Group 1997–; Pres. and Chief Exec. Visa Int. 1998–2004; Chair. Britannic Group 2004–05; Chair. CDC Group PLC 2004–; Dir Group 4 Securicor plc (now G4S PLC) 2004–08; mem. Bd of Dirs Nat. Australia Bank 2004–, Chair. Nat. Australia Group Europe Ltd 2004–, Clydesdale Bank 2004–, (all mems Nat. Australia Bank Group); Deputy Chair. Resolution plc 2005–08; Dir JP Morgan Cazenove Holdings 2005–; Chair. Signet Group plc 2006–; Chair. Advisory Bd Youth Business Int. (now Princes Youth Business Int.) 2005–08; Dir The Prince of Wales Int. Business Leaders Forum 2006–. *Leisure interests:* mountaineering, walking, chess, bridge. *Address:* National Australia Group Europe Ltd, 88 Wood Street, London, EC2V 7QQ, England (office). *Telephone:* (20) 7710-1784 (office). *Website:* www.nabgroup.com (office).

WILLIAMSON, John, PhD; British economist and academic; *Senior Fellow, Peterson Institute for International Economics;* b. 7 June 1937, Hereford; s. of A. H. Williamson and Eileen Williamson; m. Denise R. de Souza 1974; two s. one d.; ed London School of Econs and Princeton Univ.; Lecturer, Reader, Univ. of York 1963–68; HM Treasury 1968–70; Prof., Univ. of Warwick 1970–77; adviser, IMF 1972–74; Prof., Catholic Univ. of Rio de Janeiro 1978–81; Sr Fellow, Inst. for Int. Econs (now Peterson Inst. for Int. Econs) 1981–; Chief Economist South Asia, World Bank 1996–99; Project Dir UN High-Level Panel on Financing for Devt 2001. *Publications:* The Crawling Peg 1965, The Failure of World Monetary Reform 1977, The Exchange Rate System 1983, Targets and Indicators (with M. H. Miller) 1987, Latin American Adjustment: How Much Has Happened? 1990, The Political Economy of Policy Reform 1993, The Crawling Band as an Exchange Rate Regime 1996, A Survey of Financial Liberalization (co-author) 1998, Exchange Rate Regimes for Emerging Markets 2000, After the Washington Consensus: Restarting Growth and Reform in Latin America (co-ed.) 2003, Dollar Adjustment: How Far? Against What? (co-ed.) 2004. *Leisure interest:* birding. *Address:* Institute for International Economics, 1750 Massachusetts Avenue, NW, Washington, DC 20036-1903 (office); 3919 Oliver Street, Chevy Chase, MD 20815, USA. *Telephone:* (202) 454-1340 (office); (301) 654-5312 (home). *Fax:* (202) 328-5432 (office). *E-mail:* jwilliamson@iie.com (office). *Website:* www.iie.com/jwilliamson.htm (office).

WILLIAMSON, Kevin; American screenwriter and producer; b. 14 March 1965, New Bern, NC; ed East Carolina Univ., UCLA; fmr actor, asst dir, music videos; f. Outerbanks Entertainment 1995; Entertainer of the Year, Entertainment Weekly 1997, mem. Power 100 List, Premiere Magazine 1998. *Films include:* Scream (writer) 1996, Scream 2 1997, I Know What You Did Last Summer (writer) 1997, Halloween: H20 (producer) 1998, The Faculty (writer) 1998, Teaching Mrs. Tingle (writer, dir) 1999, Her Leading Man (dir), Cursed (writer, producer) 2005, Venom 2005, Retribution 2006. *TV series include:* Dawson's Creek (creator) 1998–2003, Wasteland (writer, producer) 1998, Glory Days (creator) 2002. *Address:* c/o William Morris Agency, 151 El Camino Drive, Beverly Hills, CA 90212, USA (office).

WILLIAMSON, Matthew, BA; British fashion designer; b. 23 Oct. 1971, Chorlton, Manchester; ed St Martin's School of Art and Design; worked as freelance designer for two years; travelled frequently to India for Marni, Georgina von Ertzdorf and Monsoon fashion retailers; f. and Creative Dir Matthew Williamson (with Joseph Velosa) 1997–; Creative Dir Emilio Pucci 2005–; trademark details are embroidery, beading and sequins; *Address:* Matthew Williamson Ltd, 46 Hertford Street, London, W1J 7DP, England (office). *Telephone:* (20) 7491-6220 (office). *Fax:* (20) 7491-6252 (office). *E-mail:* press@ matthewwilliamson.co.uk (office). *Website:* www.matthewwilliamson.com.

WILLIAMSON, Oliver E., SB, MBA, PhD; American economist and academic; *Edgar F. Kaiser Professor Emeritus of Business, Economics, and Law, University of California, Berkeley;* b. 27 Sept. 1932; m. Dolores Celeni 1957; three s. two d.; ed Massachusetts Inst. of Tech., Stanford Univ., Carnegie Mellon Univ.; Project Engineer with US Govt 1955–58; Asst Prof. of Econs, Univ. of California, Berkeley 1963–65, Prof. of Business, Econs and Law 1988–94, Edgar F. Kaiser Prof. of Business Admin and Prof. of Econs and Law 1994–2008, Prof. Emer. 2008–; Assoc. Prof., Pennsylvania State Univ. 1965–68, Prof. 1968–83, Charles and William L. Day Prof. of Econs and Social Science 1977–83; Gordon B. Tweedy Prof. of Econs of Law and Org., Yale Univ. 1983–88; visiting prof. at numerous int. univs; Special Econ. Asst to Asst Attorney-Gen. for Antitrust, US Dept of Justice 1966–67, consultant to US Dept of Justice 1967–69; consultant, NSF 1976–77; consultant to US Fed. Trade Comm. 1978–80; Fellow, American Acad. of Arts and Sciences 1983, Econometrics Soc. 1977, American Acad. of Political and Social Science 1997; mem. NAS 1994–, American Econ. Asscn 1960–, Western Econs Asscn 1995– (Pres. 1999–2000), American Law and Econs Asscn (Pres. 1997–98), Int. Soc. for New Institutional Econs 1997– (Pres. 1999–2001); mem. numerous advisory and editorial bds; Distinguished Fellow, Industrial Org. Soc. 2005, American Econ. Soc. 2007; several hon. degrees; Alexander Henderson Award for Excellence in Econ. Theory 1962, Irwin Award for Scholarly Contributions to Man. 1988, John von Neumann Award, Laszlo Rajk Coll. for Advanced Studies, Budapest 1999, Horst Claus Recktenwald Prize in Econs 2004, Nobel Prize in Econs (with Elinor Ostrom) 2009. *Publications include:* The Economics of Discretionary Behavior: Managerial Objectives in a Theory of the Firm 1964, Corporate Control and Business Behavior: An Inquiry into the Effects of Organization Form on Enterprise Behavior 1970, Markets and Hierarchies: Analysis and Antitrust Implications 1975, The Economic Institutions of Capitalism: Firms, Markets, Relational Contracting 1985. *Address:* Walter A. Haas School of Business, S545 Student Services Bldg, #1900, Berkeley, CA 94720-1900, USA (office). *Telephone:* (510) 642-8697 (office). *Fax:* (510) 642-4700 (office). *E-mail:* owilliam@haas .berkeley.edu (office). *Website:* groups.haas.berkeley.edu/bpp/oew (office).

WILLIAMSON, Sir (Robert) Brian, Kt, CBE, MA, FRSA; British business executive; b. 16 Feb. 1945; m. Diane Marie Christine de Jacquier de Rosée 1986; ed Trinity Coll., Dublin; Personal Asst to Maurice Macmillan (later Viscount Macmillan) 1967–71; Ed. Int. Currency Review 1971; Man. Dir Gerrard & Nat. Holdings (later Gerrard Group PLC) 1978–89, Chair. 1989–98; Dir London Int. Financial Futures and Options Exchange (LIFFE) 1982–89, Chair. 1985–88, 1998–2003; Chair. GNI Ltd 1985–89; Dir Fleming Int. High Income Investment Trust PLC 1990–96, Deputy Chair. Fleming Worldwide Investment Trust PLC 1996; Dir Bank of Ireland 1990–98 (mem. Bd Bank of Ireland Britain Holdings 1986–90); Chair. MT Fund Management Ltd, Armed Forces Charities Advisory Co., Electra Partners LLP; Group Chair. Resolution Life Group Ltd –2005; Chair. London Int. Financial Futures and Options Exchange (alternative name, LIFFE (Holdings) plc) 1985–88, 1998–2003; Chair. Gerrard Group PLC 1989–98; Chair. Electra Private Equity PLC (fmrly Electra Investment Trust PLC) 2009–10, Electra Private Equity Investments PLC –2010; Chair. NASDAQ's Int. Markets Advisory Bd of Army Common Investment Fund UK 1995–98; Chair. Macmillan Trustees Fund Management Ltd; fmr Chair. Fleming Worldwide Investment Trust plc; Dir, Politeia, Live-Ex Ltd, Barlows PLC 1986–98, Electra Partners LLP, Electra Private Equity PLC 1994–2010, Templeton Emerging Markets Investment Trust PLC 2002–03, Pearl Group Holdings (No. 1) Ltd from 2005, AMP Holdings Plc, Winston Churchill Memorial Trust, Edenberg Ltd Partnership, Liv-Ex Ltd; Ind. Dir, Climate Exchange Plc 2007–11; Dir (non-exec.), MT Fund Management Ltd 1995–, Resolution PLC 2004–08, NYSE Euronext, Inc. 2007–13, Waverton Investment Management Ltd 2010–; Ind. Dir (non-exec.), HSBC Holdings Plc 2002–12; mem. Supervisory Bd Euronext NV 2002–07; mem. Dean and Canons Advisory Cttee on Finance of the Coll. of St George's Chapel, Windsor Castle, Finance Cttee of St George's House Trust, Windsor Castle; Pres. St Moritz Toboganning Club; Hon. Bencher of the Inner Temple; HM Lt for the City of London. *Leisure interests:* tobogganing, hot air ballooning. *Address:* Waverton Investment Management Ltd, 21 St James's Square, London, SW1Y 4HB, England (office); MT Fund Management Ltd, Calton Square, 1 Greenside Row, Edinburgh, EH1 3AN, Scotland (office); 8 Canada Square, London, E14 5EQ, England. *Telephone:* (20) 7484-7484 (Waverton) (office). *Fax:* (20) 7484-7400 (Waverton) (office). *E-mail:* info@waverton.co.uk (office). *Website:* www.waverton.co.uk (office).

WILLIAMSON OF HORTON, Baron (Life Peer), cr. 1999, of Horton in the County of Somerset; **David Francis Williamson,** GCMG, CB, MA, DCL, DEconSc; British government official (retd); *Convenor, Independent Cross-bench Peers, House of Lords;* b. 8 May 1934; m. Patricia M. Smith 1961; two s.; ed Tonbridge School and Exeter Coll. Oxford; army service 1956–58; entered Ministry of Agric., Fisheries and Food 1958; seconded to HM Diplomatic Service as First Sec. (Agric. and Food), Geneva, for Kennedy Round Trade Negotiation 1965–67; Prin. Pvt. Sec. to successive Ministers, Ministry of Agric., Fisheries and Food 1967–70; Head of Milk and Milk Products Div. 1970–74; Under-Sec. 1974; Deputy Dir-Gen. (Agric.), Comm. of European Communities 1977–83; Deputy Sec. and Head of European Secr. Cabinet Office 1983–87; Sec.-Gen. Comm. of European Communities (now EC) 1987–97; mem. EU Cttee, House of Lords 2000–04; Convenor, Ind. Cross-bench Peers, House of Lords 2004–; Visiting Prof., Univ. of Bath 1997–2001; Dir (non-exec.) Whitbread PLC 1998–2005; Trustee, Thomson Foundation; Kt Commdr's Cross of the Order of Merit (Germany); Commdr, Légion d'honneur; Commdr, Grand Cross of the Royal Order of the Polar Star (Sweden). *Address:* House of Lords, Westminster, London, SW1A 0PW, England (office). *Telephone:* (20) 7219-3583 (office). *E-mail:* williamsond@parliament.uk (office). *Website:* www.parliament.uk/about_lords/about_lords.cfm (office).

WILLIS, Bruce Walter; American actor; b. 19 March 1955, Idar-Oberstein, Germany; s. of David Willis and Marlene Willis; m. 1st Demi Moore (q.v.) 1987 (divorced 2000); three d.; m. 2nd Emma Heming 2009; one d.; ed Montclair State Coll.; moved to USA 1957; studied with Stella Adler; mem. First Amendment Comedy Theatre; Officier, Ordre des Arts et des Lettres. *Stage appearances:* (off-Broadway): Heaven and Earth 1977, Fool for Love 1984, The Bullpen, The Bayside Boys, The Ballad of Railroad William. *Films:* Blind Date 1987, Sunset 1988, Die Hard 1988, In Country 1989, Die Hard 2, Die Harder 1990, Bonfire of the Vanities 1990, Hudson Hawk 1991, The Last Boy Scout 1991, Billy Bathgate 1991, Death Becomes Her 1992, Striking Distance 1993, Color of Night 1994, North 1994, Nobody's Fool 1994, Pulp Fiction 1994, Die Hard with a Vengeance 1995, 12 Monkeys 1995, Four Rooms, Last Man Standing 1996, The Jackal 1997, The Fifth

Element 1997, Mercury Rising 1998, Armageddon 1998, Breakfast of Champions 1998, The Story of US 1999, The Sixth Sense 1999, Unbreakable 2000, Disney's the Kid 2000, Bandits 2001, Hart's War 2002, Tears of the Sun 2003, The Whole Ten Yards 2004, Hostage 2005, Sin City 2005, Alpha Dog 2006, Lucky Number Slevin 2006, 16 Blocks 2006, Over the Hedge (voice) 2006, Hammy's Boomerang Adventure (voice) 2006, Fast Food Nation 2006, The Hip Hop Project 2006, The Astronaut Farmer 2007, Perfect Stranger 2007, Grindhouse 2007, Live Free or Die Hard (also producer) 2007, Planet Terror 2007, Assassination of a High School President 2008, What Just Happened? 2008, Surrogates 2009, Red 2010, Catch 44 2010, Setup 2011, Lay the Favorite 2012, Moonrise Kingdom 2012, G.I.Joe: Retaliation 2012, The Expendables 2 2012, Looper 2012, The Cold Light of Day 2012. *Television includes:* Moonlighting 1985–89 (series; People's Choice award 1986, Emmy award 1987, Golden Globe award 1987), Friends 2000. *Recordings:* The Return of Bruno 1987, If It Don't Kill You, It Just Makes You Stronger 1989. *Address:* 22470 Pacific Coast Highway, Malibu, CA 90265, USA.

WILLIS, Norman David, MA, DipEconPolSc; British trade union official; b. 21 Jan. 1933; s. of Victor J. M. Willis and Kate E. Willis; m. Maureen Kenning 1963; one s. one d.; ed Ashford Co. Grammar School, Ruskin and Oriel Colls, Oxford; Personal Research Asst to Gen. Sec. Transport & General Workers' Union (TGWU) 1959–70; Nat. Sec. Research and Educ. TGWU 1970–74; Asst Gen. Sec. Trades Union Congress 1974–77, Deputy Gen. Sec. 1977–84, Gen. Sec. 1984–93; Councillor (Labour), Staines Urban Dist Council 1971–74; Chair. Nat. Pensioners Convention Steering Cttee 1979–93; Vice-Pres. European TUC 1984–91, Pres. 1991–93; ICFTU 1984–93, Inst. of Manpower Studies 1985–93; Trustee Anglo-German Foundation for Study of Industrial Soc. 1986–95, Duke of Edinburgh's Commonwealth Study Conf. 1986–93; Patron West Indian Welfare (UK) Trust 1986; mem. NEDC 1984, Council, Overseas Devt Inst. 1985–93, Council, Motability 1985–93, Exec. Bd UNICEF 1986–90, Trade Union Advisory Cttee to OECD 1986–93, Council of Prince of Wales Youth Business Trust 1986–93, Employment Appeal Tribunal 1995–2003; Pres. The Arthur Ransome Soc.; Vice-Pres. West Indian Welfare Trust (UK) 1986–93; Patron Docklands Sinfonietta 1986–93; Trustee, Royal School of Needlework 1995–2007; Trustee and Black Bin Bag Operative (grade two), Sunbury Millenium Embroidery Gallery; Hon. Fellow, Oriel Coll., Oxford; Hon. mem. Poetry Soc., Writers Guild of Great Britain. *Leisure interests:* embroidery, poetry, natural history, architecture, canals, snooker, birding. *Address:* c/o Trades Union Congress, Congress House, Great Russell Street, London, WC1B 3LS, England.

WILLIS, Ralph, AO, BCom; Australian politician; b. 14 April 1938, Melbourne, Vic.; s. of Stanley Willis and Doris Willis; m. Carol Joyce Dawson 1970; one s. two d.; ed Univ. High School and Univ. of Melbourne; research officer, Australian Council of Trade Unions 1960, industrial advocate 1970; mem. (Australian Labor Party) Fed. Parl. for Gellibrand 1972–98; Minister for Employment and Industrial Relations and Minister assisting Prime Minister in Public Service Industrial Matters 1983–87, Minister for Industrial Relations and Minister assisting Prime Minister in Public Service Matters 1987–88, for Transport and Communications 1988–90, for Finance 1990–91, Treas. 1991, Minister for Finance 1991–93, Treas. 1993–96; Vice-Pres. Exec. Council 1992; Chair. Western Health Bd 2004, Construction and Building Industry Superannuation Fund (C+BUS), Melbourne City Opera, LeadWest 2008–11; Dir, Australian Super Developments; Chair. and Treas., Mietta Foundation; mem. Australian Council of Superannuation Investors, UN Sec.-Gen.'s High Level Panel on Youth Employment, Bd Westgate Community Initiatives Group, Bd Stan Willis Trust; Centenary Medal 2001; Hon. DUniv (Victoria Univ.) 2009. *Leisure interests:* tennis, reading, watching football. *Address:* 24 Gellibrand Street, Williamstown, Vic. 3016, Australia.

WILLMOTT, Peter S., BA, MBA; American business executive; *Chairman and CEO, Willmott Services Inc.;* ed Williams Coll., Harvard Univ.; began career as sr financial analyst American Airlines; fmr Man. Consultant Booz, Allen & Hamilton; fmr Vice-Pres. ITT Continental Banking Co.; fmr Chief Financial Officer, then Pres. and COO Federal Express Corpn; fmr Chair. and Pres. Carson Pirie Scott, Zenith Electronics Corpn; currently Chair. and CEO Willmott Services (consultancy), Chicago; mem. Bd Fleming Cos Inc. 2002–, interim CEO and Pres. March-Aug. 2003; apptd Man.-Partner Berkshires Capital Investors (BCI) 2001; mem. Bd Dirs Federal Express, Security Capital Group; mem. bd several civic orgs in Chicago and Berkshires; fmr Chair. Bd Trustees Williams Coll. *Address:* Willmott Services Inc., 333 North Michigan Avenue, Chicago, IL 60601, USA.

WILLOCH, Kåre Isaachsen, Cand Oecon; Norwegian politician (retd); b. 3 Oct. 1928, Oslo; s. of Haakon Willoch and Agnes Saure; m. Anne-Marie Jørgensen 1954; one s. two d.; ed Ullern Gymnasium and Univ. of Oslo; Sec. Fed. of Norwegian Shipowners 1951–53, Counsellor Fed. of Norwegian Industries 1954–63; mem. Storting 1958–89; mem. Nat. Cttee Conservative Party 1961–89, Sec.-Gen. Conservative Party 1963–65, Chair. 1970–74, Chair. Conservative Party Parl. Group 1970–81; Minister of Trade and Shipping 1963, 1965–70; Chair. World Bank Group 1967; mem. Nordic Council 1970–86, Pres. 1973; Prime Minister 1981–86; Chair. Int. Democratic Union 1987–89; Chair. Foreign Affairs Cttee of Parl. 1986–89; Co-Gov. of Oslo and Akershus 1989–98; Chair. Norwegian Defence Comm. 1990–92; Chair. Supervisory Bd, Norwegian Bank 1990–96; Chair. Bd of Norwegian Broadcasting Corpn 1998–2000; Chair. Norwegian Comm. on the Vulnerability of Soc. 1999–2000; Dir Fridtjof Nansen Inst. 1999–2001; Commdr with Star, Royal Norwegian Order of St Olav; Dr hc (St Olav's Coll. Minn., USA); Fritt Ords Pris, Norwegian Inst. for Free Speech 1997, Opinion Maker of the Year, Asscn of Norwegian Eds 1996, C.J. Hambro's Prize 2000. *Publications include:* Personal Savings 1955, Price Policy in Norway (with L. B. Bachke) 1958, Memoirs (Vol. I) 1988, (Vol. II) 1990, Krisetid 1992, A New Policy for the Environment 1996, Ideas (Tanker i Tiden) 1999, Myths and Realities ((Myter og virkelighet) (memoirs) 2002, Alvorlig talt (Seriously Speaking) (with fmr Prime Minister Odvaar Nordli) 2008, Erfaringer for fremtiden (Experience for the Future) 2010. *Leisure interests:* skiing, touring. *Address:* Blokkaveien 6B, 0282 Oslo, Norway. *Telephone:* 22-50-72-89.

WILLOTT, (William) Brian, CB, PhD; British public official; *Visiting Professor, University of Glamorgan;* b. 14 May 1940, Swansea; s. of William Harford and Beryl P. M. Willott; m. Alison Leyland Pyke-Lees 1970; two s. two d.; ed Trinity Coll., Cambridge; Research Assoc., Univ. of Md 1965–67; Asst Prin. Bd of Trade 1967–69, Prin. 1969–73; HM Treasury 1973–75; Asst Sec. Dept of Industry

1975–78, Sec. Ind. Devt Unit 1978–80; Sec. Nat. Enterprise Bd 1980–81; CEO British Tech. Group (Nat. Enterprise Bd and Nat. Research and Devt Corpn) 1981–84; Head, Information Tech. Div., Dept of Trade and Industry 1984–87, Head, Financial Services Div. 1987–91; Chief Exec. Export Credit Guarantee Dept 1992–97; CEO Welsh Devt Agency 1997–2000; Chair. Gwent NHS Healthcare Trust 2003–08; Dir Dragon Int. Studios Ltd; mem. Council Nat. Museums and Galleries of Wales 2001–09; Visiting Prof. Univ. of Glamorgan 2000–. *Leisure interests:* music, reading, ancient history, gardening. *Address:* Coed Cefn, Tregare, Monmouth, NP25 4DT, Wales (home).

WILLOUGHBY, Christopher R., MA; British economist; b. 24 Feb. 1938, Guildford; s. of Ronald James Edward Willoughby and Constance Louisa (née Sherbrooke) Willoughby; m. Marie-Anne Isabelle Normand 1972; ed Lambroke School, Marlborough Coll., Univ. of Grenoble, Jt Services School for Linguists, Balliol Coll., Oxford, Univ. of California, Berkeley; served in RN 1956–58, Lt, RNR 1958; New York Times Wash. Bureau 1962–63; economist, World Bank 1963, Dir Operations Evaluation Dept 1973–76, Transport, Water and Telecommunications Dept 1976–83, Econ. Devt Inst. 1983–90, Chief, World Bank Mission in Bangladesh 1990–94, in Belarus 1994–97, Infrastructure Lead Adviser Europe and Cen. Asia Region 1997, Lead Specialist Infrastructure Dept 1999, now retd; Assoc. Consultant, Oxford Policy Man. *Leisure interests:* running, swimming, house re-modelling. *Address:* c/o Oxford Policy Management, 6 St Aldates Courtyard, 38 St Aldates, Oxford, OX1 1BN, England.

WILLS, Dean Robert, AO; Australian business executive; b. 10 July 1933, Australia; s. of the late Walter W. Wills and Violet J. Dryburgh; m. Margaret F. Williams 1955; one s. two d.; ed Sacred Heart Coll., S. Australia and S. Australian Inst. of Tech.; Dir W. D. & H. O. Wills (Australia) 1974–, Man. Dir 1977–83, Chair. 1983–86; Dir AMATIL Ltd 1975–, Deputy Chair. 1983–84, Man. Dir Coca-Cola AMATIL Ltd 1984–94, Chair. 1984–99; mem. Business Council of Australia 1984–94, Vice-Pres. 1987–88, Pres. 1988–90; mem. Bd Australian Grad. School of Man. (Univ. of NSW) 1985–92; Gov. Medical Foundation (Univ. of Sydney) 1990–94; mem. Corps. and Securities Panel 1991–94; Vice-Chair. Nat. Mutual Life 1992–97, Chair. 1997–2000; Deputy Chair. Nat. Mutual Holdings 1995–97, Chair. 1997–2000; Chair. Transfield Services Ltd 2001–05, Coca-Cola Australia Foundation Ltd 2002–05; Dir Microsurgery Foundation, Melbourne 1992–, John Fairfax Holdings Ltd 1994–2005 (Chair. 2002–05), Westfield Holdings Ltd 1994–; Gov. Australian Naval Aviation Museum; Deputy Chair. Australian Grand Prix Corpn 1994–2002; Trustee Museum of Applied Arts and Sciences 1986–90. *Leisure interests:* tennis, performance cars. *Address:* 71 Circular Quay East, Sydney, NSW 2000, Australia. *Telephone:* (2) 9259-6420 (office). *Fax:* (2) 9259-6628 (office).

WILLS, Garry, BA, MA, PhD; American writer, journalist and academic; *Professor of History Emeritus, Northwestern University;* b. 22 May 1934, Atlanta, Ga; m. Natalie Cavallo 1959; two s. one d.; ed St Louis Univ., Xavier Univ., Univ. of Cincinnati and Yale Univ.; Fellow, Center for Hellenic Studies 1961–62; Assoc. Prof. of Classics 1962–67, Adjunct Prof. 1968–80, Johns Hopkins Univ.; newspaper columnist, Universal Press Syndicate 1970–; Henry R. Luce Prof. of American Culture and Public Policy, Northwestern Univ. 1980–88, Adjunct Prof., later Prof. of History Emer. 1988–; mem. American Philosophical Soc., American Acad. of Arts and Letters, American Acad. of Arts and Sciences; Dr hc (Coll. of the Holy Cross) 1982, (Bates Coll.) 1995; Nat. Humanities Medal 1998, St Louis Literary Award, St Louis Univ. Library Associates 2004. *Publications include:* Chesterton 1961, Politics and Catholic Freedom 1964, Roman Culture 1966, Jack Ruby 1967, Second Civil War 1968, Nixon Agonistes 1970, Bare Ruined Choirs 1972, Inventing America 1978, At Button's 1979, Confessions of a Conservative 1979, Explaining America 1980, The Kennedy Imprisonment 1982, Lead Time 1983, Cincinnatus 1984, Reagan's America 1987, Under God 1990, Lincoln at Gettysburg (Nat. Book Critics Circle Award 1993, Pulitzer Prize for General Non-Fiction 1993) 1992, Certain Trumpets: The Call of Leaders 1994, Witches and Jesuits: Shakespeare's Macbeth 1994, John Wayne's America 1997, Saint Augustine 1999, A Necessary Evil: A History of American Distrust of Government 1999, Papal Sin: Structures of Deceit 2000, Saint Augustine's Childhood 2001, Why I Am a Catholic 2002, President 2003, Saint Augustine's Sin 2004, Saint Augustine's Conversion 2004, Bush's Fringe Government 2006, Head and Heart: American Christianities 2007, What the Gospels Meant 2008, Martial's Epigrams (trans.) 2008, Bomb Power 2010, Outside Looking In: Adventures of an Observer 2010, Augustine's 'Confessions': A Biography 2011, Verdi's Shakespeare: Men of the Theater 2011, Rome and Rhetoric: Shakespeare's Julius Caesar 2011, Font of Life: Ambrose, Augustine, and the Mystery of Baptism 2012, Why Priests? 2013. *Address:* Department of History, Northwestern University, Harris Hall 202, 1881 Sheridan Road, Evanston, IL 60208, USA (office). *Telephone:* (847) 491-3406 (office). *Fax:* (847) 467-1393 (office). *E-mail:* g-wills@northwestern.edu (office). *Website:* www.history.northwestern.edu (office).

WILLSON, C. Grant, BS, MS, PhD; American chemist and academic; *Professor of Chemical Engineering Rashid Engineering Regents Chair, University of Texas;* b. 30 March 1939; ed Univ. of California, Berkeley, San Diego State Univ.; Asst Prof., California State Univ., Long Beach 1973–74; Asst Prof., Univ. of California, San Diego 1974–78; IBM Fellow and Man. of Polymer Science and Tech., IBM San Jose Research Center 1978–93; Prof. of Chem. and Chemical Eng and Rashid Eng Regent's Chair, Dept of Chem. and Biochemistry, McKetta Dept of Chemical Eng, Univ. of Texas 1993–; affiliated with Beckman Center for Design and Fabrication of Sensor Arrays, Microelectronics Research Center, Center for Nano- and Molecular Science and Tech., Environmental Science Inst., Texas Materials Inst.; Fellow, Int. Soc. for Optics and Photonics (SPIE) 2007, Materials Research Soc. 2012; Inaugural Fellow, ACS 2009; SPIE Frits Zernike Award 2005, ACS Heroes of Chem. Award 2005, AIChE Arthur Dehon Little Award for Chemical Eng Innovation 2005, Teaching Excellence Award in Chemical Eng 2006, SEMI North America Award 2007, Nat. Medal of Tech. and Innovation 2007, Gordon E. Moore Medal 2009, ACS Award in Applied Polymer Science 2004, Inventor of the Year, Univ. of Texas 2012, Japan Prize (co-recipient) 2013. *Publications:* numerous papers in professional journals. *Address:* Department of Chemistry and Biochemistry, University of Texas, 1 University Station A5300, Welch 5.240, Austin, TX 78712-0165, USA (office). *Telephone:* (512) 471-4342 (office); (512) 471-3975 (office). *Fax:* (512) 471-7222 (office). *E-mail:* willson@che.utexas.edu (office). *Website:* www.cm.utexas.edu/grant_willson (office); willson.cm.utexas.edu (office).

WILLSON, Francis Michael Glenn, BA, MA, DPhil; British university administrator and academic; *Professor Emeritus, Murdoch University;* b. 29 Sept. 1924, Carlisle; s. of the late Christopher Glenn Willson and Elsie Katrine Mattick; m. Jean Carlyle 1945; two d.; ed Carlisle Grammar School, Univ. of Manchester, Balliol and Nuffield Colls., Oxford; war service in Merchant Navy 1941–42 and RAF 1943–47; seconded to BOAC 1946–47; Research Officer, Royal Inst. of Public Admin. 1953–60; Research Fellow, Nuffield Coll., Oxford 1955–60; Lecturer in Politics, St Edmund Hall, Oxford 1958–60; Prof. of Govt, Univ. Coll. of Rhodesia and Nyasaland 1961–64, Dean of Social Studies 1962–64; Prof. of Govt and Politics, Univ. of California, Santa Cruz 1965–74, Provost Stevenson Coll. 1967–74, Vice-Chancellor Coll. and Student Affairs 1973–74, Visiting Prof. 1985–92; Warden of Goldsmiths Coll., London 1974–75; Prin. Univ. of London 1975–78; Vice-Chancellor Murdoch Univ., Western Australia 1978–84, Prof. Emer. 1985–. *Publications:* Organization of British Central Government 1914–1956 (with D. N. Chester) 1957, 2nd edn 1914–1964 1968, Administrators in Action 1961, A Strong Supporting Cast – The Shaw Lefevres 1789–1936 1993, Our Minerva – The Men and Politics of the University of London 1836–1858 1995, In Just Order Move – The Progress of the Laban Centre for Movement and Dance 1946–96 1997, The University of London – The Politics of Senate and Convocation 1858–1900 2004. *Leisure interests:* listening to music, reading. *Address:* Galsworthy House, 177 Kingston Hill, Kingston-upon-Thames, Surrey, KT2 7LX, England (home). *Telephone:* (20) 8741-1247.

WILLUMSTAD, Robert B.; American insurance executive; *Senior Adviser, Brysam Global Partners;* b. Brooklyn, New York; m. Carol Willumstad; two c.; ed Adelphi Univ.; worked in various positions in operations, retail banking and computer systems, Chemical Bank 1967–87; joined Commercial Credit, Baltimore (later CitiFinancial div. of Citigroup) 1987, Chair. and CEO Consumer Financial Services, Travelers Group –1998, Vice-Chair. Global Consumer Group and Chair. Global Consumer Lending, Citigroup Inc. (following merger of Citicorp and Travelers Group in 1998) 1998–2002, Chair. and CEO Citigroup Global Consumer Group 2000–03, Pres. Citigroup Inc. 2002–05, COO 2003–05, also CEO and Pres. Citibank NA 2003–05; mem. Bd of Dirs AIG 2006–08, Chair. 2006–08, CEO June–Sept. 2008; Co-founder and Sr Adviser, Brysam Global Pnrs 2007–; Dir S.C. Johnson & Son Inc., Habitat for Humanity, MasterCard International; mem. Adelphi Univ. Bd of Trustees 2005–; Hon. LLD (Adelphi) 2005; New York City Urban League Frederick Douglass Award 2002. *Address:* Brysam Global Partners, 277 Park Avenue, 35th Floor, New York NY 10172, USA (office). *Telephone:* (212) 622-4378 (office). *E-mail:* marge.magner@brysam.com (office). *Website:* www .brysam.com (office).

WILMOTT, Peter Graham, CMG, MA; British consultant and fmr civil servant; *Director, GlobalLink Border Solutions Ltd;* b. 6 Jan. 1947, Cuckfield, West Sussex, England; s. of John Wilmott and Violet Wilmott; m. Jennifer Plummer 1969; two d.; ed Hove Grammar School and Trinity Coll., Cambridge; Asst Prin., HM Customs & Excise 1968, Prin. 1973, Asst Sec. 1983, Commr 1988; seconded to UK Perm. Rep. to EC 1971–73, 1977–79, to EC Court of Auditors 1980–82; Dir-Gen. Customs and Indirect Taxation, EC Comm. 1990–96; partner with Prisma Consulting Group 1996–2000; Chair. Int. Value Added Tax Asscn 1998–2000; Pres. Office du Développement par l'Automatisation et la Simplification du Commerce Extérieur (ODASCE), Paris 2000–04, First Vice-Pres. 2004–08; Dir Ad Valorem International Ltd 2002–08, GlobalLink Border Solutions Ltd 2006–; Dir (non-exec.) SITPRO 2001–07. *Address:* GlobalLink Border Solutions Ltd, 1 Tunsgate, Jarvis Lane, Steyning, West Sussex, BN44 3EZ, England (office).

WILMUT, Sir Ian, Kt, OBE, PhD, FRS, FRSE; British geneticist; *Director, Centre for Regenerative Medicine, University of Edinburgh;* b. 7 July 1944, Hampton Lucy, Warwicks., England; s. of Leonard (Jack) Wilmut and Mary Wilmut; m. Vivienne Mary Craven 1967; two d. one adopted s.; ed Univ. of Nottingham and Darwin Coll., Cambridge; Post-doctoral Fellow, Unit of Reproductive Physiology and Biochemistry, Cambridge 1971–73; various research posts, Animal Breeding Research Org. (ARC, now BBSRC Roslin Inst.) 1973–2006, Head of Div. Gene Expression and Devt, jtly responsible (with Keith Campbell) for cloning of Dolly (a sheep, first animal produced from an adult cell) 1996; Prof. Emer., Univ. of Edin. 1998–, Chair. Scottish Centre for Regenerative Medicine 2005–; Foreign Assoc. NAS 2004; Hon. DSc (Nottingham) 1998, (North Eastern Univ., Boston) 1999, (Edin.) 2002; Shaw Prize (co-recipient) 2008. *Publications:* The Second Creation (co-author) 2000, After Dolly: The Uses and Misuses of Human Cloning 2006; and contribs to numerous papers on cloning of Dolly the sheep. *Leisure interests:* curling, photography, walking in the countryside. *Address:* MRC Centre for Regenerative Medicine, SCRM Building, University of Edinburgh, Edinburgh bioQuarter, 5 Little France Drive, Edinburgh, EH16 4UU, Scotland (office). *Telephone:* (131) 651-9500 (office). *Fax:* (131) 651-9501 (office). *E-mail:* ian .wilmut@ed.ac.uk (office). *Website:* www.crm.ed.ac.uk/research/group/redirecting -cell-fate (office).

WILSEY, Gen. Sir John, GCB, CBE, DL; British former army officer and business executive; *Chairman, Western Provident Association;* b. 18 Feb. 1939, Frimley, Hants.; s. of the late Maj.-Gen. J. H. O. Wilsey and B. S. F. Wilsey; m. Elizabeth P. Nottingham 1975; one s. one d.; ed Sherborne School and Royal Mil. Acad., Sandhurst; commissioned 1959; served in Cyprus, North Africa, Guyana, USA, Malta, Germany, UK (mem. Blue Nile Expedition 1968), Staff Coll. 1973; Commdg 1st Bn, The Devonshire & Dorset Regt 1979–82, Col 1990–97; Chief of Staff, HQ, NI 1982–84; Commdg 1st Infantry Brigade and UK Mobile Force 1985–86; Royal Coll. of Defence Studies 1987; Chief of Staff, HQ UK Land Forces 1988–90; GOC and Dir Mil. Operations, NI 1990–93; C-in-C Land Command 1993–96; ADC Gen. to the Queen 1994–96; Chair. Western Provident Asscn 1996–; Hon. Col Royal Jersey Militia, Royal Engineers 1993–; Vice-Chair. Sherborne School 1996–; mem. Council Royal Bath & West 1996–, Commonwealth War Graves Comm. 1998– (Vice-Chair. 2001–); Commr Royal Hosp., Chelsea 1996–; Gov. Suttons Hosp. in Charterhouse 1996–2001, Sherborne School for Girls 1996–2001. *Publications:* Service for the Nation 1987, H. Jones, VC 2002. *Leisure interests:* skiing, fishing, sailing, breeding alpacas. *Address:* Western Provident Association, Rivergate House, Blackbrook Park, Taunton, Somerset, TA1 2PE, England (office). *Telephone:* (1823) 623502 (office).

WILSON, Sir Alan Geoffrey, Kt, MA, DSc, DUniv, LLD, DEd, FRS, FBA, FCGI, AcSS; British geographer, mathematician, academic and fmr university vice-chancellor; *Professor of Urban and Regional Systems, Centre for Advanced Spatial Analysis, University College London;* b. 8 Jan. 1939, Bradford, Yorks.; s. of Harry Wilson and Gladys Naylor; m. Sarah Fildes 1987; ed Queen Elizabeth Grammar School, Darlington, Corpus Christi Coll., Cambridge; Chartered Geographer; Scientific Officer, Rutherford High Energy Lab. 1961–64; Research Officer, Inst. of Econs and Statistics, Univ. of Oxford 1964–66; Math. Adviser to Ministry of Transport 1966–68; Asst Dir Centre for Environmental Studies, London 1968–70; Prof. of Urban and Regional Geography, Univ. of Leeds 1970–2004, Pro-Vice-Chancellor 1989–91, Vice-Chancellor 1991–2004; Dir-Gen. for Higher Educ., Dept for Education and Skills 2004–06; Prof. of Urban and Regional Systems, Centre for Advanced Spatial Analysis, Univ. Coll. London 2007–; Chair. Arts and Humanities Research Council; Ed. Environment and Planning 1969–91; Dir GMAP 1991–2001; mem. Academia Europaea 1991–, Acad. of Learned Socs for the Social Sciences; Dr hc (Univ. of Leeds) 2004; Hon. Fellow, Univ. Coll. London 2003, Corpus Christi Coll. Cambridge 2004; Gill Memorial Award, Royal Geographical Soc. 1978, Hons Award, Asscn of American Geographers 1987, Founder's Medal, Royal Geographical Soc. 1992. *Publications:* Entropy in Urban and Regional Modelling 1970, Urban and Regional Models in Geography and Planning 1974, Spatial Population Analysis (with P. H. Rees) 1977, Mathematics for Geographers and Planners (with M. J. Kirkby) 1980, Models of Cities and Regions (co-ed.) 1977, Catastrophe Theory and Bifurcation: applications to urban and regional systems 1981, Geography and the Environment: Systems Analytical Methods 1981, Mathematical Methods in Geography and Planning (with R. J. Bennett) 1985, Urban Systems (co-ed.) 1987, Urban Dynamics (co-ed.) 1990, Modelling the City: Performance, Policy and Planning (with Bertuglia, Clarke and others) 1994, Intelligent Geographical Information Systems (with Birkin, Clarke and Clarke) 1996, Complex Spatial Systems 2000. *Leisure interests:* writing, miscellaneous fads. *Address:* UCL Centre for Advanced Spatial Analysis, 1st Floor, 90 Tottenham Court Road, London, W1T 4TJ, England. *Telephone:* (20) 3108-3877 (office). *Fax:* (20) 3108-3258 (office). *E-mail:* casa@ucl.ac.uk (office). *Website:* www.casa.ucl.ac .uk (office).

WILSON, Alexander (Sandy) Galbraith; British writer and composer; b. 19 May 1924, Sale, Cheshire; s. of George Wilson and Caroline Humphrey; ed Harrow School, Univ. of Oxford and Old Vic Theatre School; contributed to revues Slings and Arrows, Oranges and Lemons 1948; wrote revues for Watergate Theatre, London, See You Later, See You Again 1951–52; wrote musical The Boy Friend for Players Club Theatre 1953, transferred to Wyndhams Theatre and on Broadway 1954 (London revival 1984), The Buccaneer 1955, Valmouth London 1958, USA 1960, Chichester 1982, Divorce me Darling! 1965 (revival Chichester 1997); Dir London revival of The Boy Friend 1967; Composed music for As Dorothy Parker Once Said, London 1969; songs for BBC TV's Charley's Aunt 1969; wrote and performed Sandy Wilson Thanks the Ladies (one-man show) London 1971; wrote His Monkey Wife London 1971, The Clapham Wonder 1978, Aladdin (London) 1979. *Publications:* This is Sylvia 1954, The Poodle from Rome 1962, I Could be Happy (autobiog.) 1975, Ivor 1975, The Roaring Twenties 1977. *Leisure interests:* cinema, cookery, travel. *Address:* Flat 4, 2 Southwell Gardens, London, SW7 4SB, England (home). *Telephone:* (20) 7373-6172 (home).

WILSON, A(ndrew) N(orman), MA, FRSL; British writer; b. 27 Oct. 1950; s. of the late N. Wilson and of Jean Dorothy Wilson (née Crowder); m. 1st Katherine Dorothea Duncan-Jones 1971 (divorced 1989); two d.; m. 2nd Ruth Guilding 1991; one d.; ed Rugby School and New Coll., Oxford; Asst Master Merchant Taylors' School 1975–76; Lecturer, St Hugh's Coll. and New Coll., Oxford 1976–81; Literary Ed. Spectator 1981–83, Evening Standard 1990–97; columnist, The Daily Mail; Hon. mem. American Acad. of Arts and Letters 1984; Chancellor's Essay Prize 1975, Ellerton Theological Prize 1975. *Publications include:* fiction: The Sweets of Pimlico 1977, Unguarded Hours 1978, Kindly Light 1979, The Healing Art (Somerset Maugham Award) 1980, Who Was Oswald Fish? 1981, Wise Virgin (WHSmith Award) 1982, Scandal 1983, Gentleman in England 1985, Love Unknown 1986, Stray 1987, Incline Our Hearts 1988, A Bottle in the Smoke 1990, Daughters of Albion 1991, The Vicar of Sorrows 1993, Hearing Voices 1995, A Watch in the Night 1996, Hazel the Guinea-pig (for children) 1997, Dream Children 1998, My Name is Legion 2004, A Jealous Ghost 2005, Winnie and Wolf 2007, The Potter's Hand 2012; non-fiction: The Laird of Abbotsford 1980, A Life of John Milton 1983, Hilaire Belloc 1984, How Can We Know? An Essay on the Christian Religion 1985, The Church in Crisis (jtly) 1986, Landscape in France 1987, The Lion and the Honeycomb 1987, Penfriends from Porlock: Essays and Reviews 1977–86 1988, Tolstoy (Whitbread Award for Biography and Autobiography) 1988, Eminent Victorians 1989, John Henry Newman: prayers, poems, meditations (ed.) 1989, C.S. Lewis: A Biography 1990, Against Religion 1991, Jesus 1992, The Faber Book of Church and Clergy (ed.) 1992, The Rise and Fall of the House of Windsor 1993, The Faber Book of London (ed.) 1993, Paul: The Mind of the Apostle 1997, God's Funeral 1999, The Victorians 2003, Beautiful Shadow: A Life of Patricia Highsmith 2003, Iris Murdoch as I Knew Her 2004, London: A Short History 2004, After the Victorians 2005, Betjeman (biog.) 2006, Harold Robbins: The Man Who Invented Sex 2007, Our Times: The Age of Elizabeth II 2008, Dante in Love 2011, The Elizabethans 2011, Hitler: A Short Biography 2011. *Address:* c/o Daily Mail, Northcliffe House, 2 Derry Street, London, W8 5TT; 5 Regent's Park Terrace, London, NW1 7EE, England.

WILSON, Blake S., PhD; American medical scientist, electrical engineer and academic; *Adjunct Professor of Surgery, of Biomedical Engineering, of Electrical and Computer Engineering and Co-Director, Duke Hearing Center, Duke University;* worked full time at Research Triangle Inst. (now RTI International) 1974–2007; Adjunct Prof. of Surgery, of Biomedical Eng, of Electrical and Computer Eng and Co-Dir Duke Hearing Center, Duke Univ. 2007–, helped establish the Duke Cochlear Implant Program 1984; Distinguished Alumnus Award, Pratt School of Eng, Duke Univ. 2007, Lasker–DeBakey Clinical Medical Research Award (co-recipient) 2013. *Publications:* numerous papers in professional journals. *Address:* Biomedical Engineering Department, Room 136, Hudson Hall, Box 90281, Durham, NC 27708-0281, USA (office). *Telephone:* (919) 660-5131 (office). *Fax:* (919) 684-4488 (office). *E-mail:* blake.wilson@duke.edu (office). *Website:* www.ee.duke.edu/faculty/blake-s-wilson (office).

WILSON, Brian; American musician (bass, keyboards), singer, songwriter and producer; b. 20 June 1942, Inglewood, Calif.; m. 2nd Melinda Ledbetter 1995; two d.; Founder-mem., The Beach Boys 1961–; retired from live performance to concentrate on composing and recording 1964; numerous live appearances, tours; band est. Brother Records label 1967–; simultaneous solo artist 1988–; American Music Awards Special Award of Merit 1988, Grammy Lifetime Achievement Award 2001, US Recording Acad. Musicares Award 2004, Kennedy Center Honor 2007. *Recordings include:* albums: with The Beach Boys: Surfin' Safari 1962, Surfer Girl 1963, Little Deuce Coupe 1963, Shut Down Vol. 2; All Summer Long 1964, Christmas Album 1964, The Beach Boys Today! 1965, Summer Days (and Summer Nights) 1965, Beach Boys Party 1966, Pet Sounds 1966, Smiley Smile 1967, Wild Honey 1968, Friends 1968, 20/20 1969, Sunflower 1970, Surf's Up 1971, Carl and the Passions – So Tough 1972, Holland 1973, The Beach Boys in Concert 1973, Endless Summer 1974, 15 Big Ones 1976, The Beach Boys Love You 1977, M.I.U. 1978, LA (Light Album) 1979, Keepin' The Summer Alive 1980, The Beach Boys 1985, Still Cruisin' 1989, Two Rooms 1991, Summer in Paradise 1992, The Sounds of Summer – The Very Best of The Beach Boys 2003, Smile Sessions (Grammy Award for Best Historical Album 2013) 2011, That's Why God Made the Radio 2012; solo: Brian Wilson 1988, I Just Wasn't Made For These Times 1995, Imagination 1998, Pet Projects: The Brian Wilson Productions 2003, Smile 2004, What I Really Want For Christmas 2005, That Lucky Old Sun 2008, Brian Wilson Reimagines Gershwin 2010. *Compositions for stage:* Shine 2002, That Lucky Old Sun (a Narrative) 2007. *Address:* c/o Elliott Lott, Boulder Creek Entertainment Corporation, 4860 San Jacinto Circle West, Fallbrook, CA 92028, USA (office). *Website:* www.thebeachboys.com; www.brianwilson.com.

WILSON, Brian G., AO, BSc, PhD; Australian/British physicist and university administrator (retd); b. 9 April 1930, Belfast, NI; s. of Charles W. Wilson and Isobel C. Wilson (née Ferguson); m. 1st Barbara Wilkie 1959 (divorced 1975); two s. one d.; m. 2nd Jeanne Henry 1978 (divorced 1988); m. 3rd Joan Opdebeeck 1988; three s.; ed Methodist Coll., Belfast, Queen's Univ. Belfast and Nat. Univ. of Ireland; Postdoctoral Fellow, Nat. Research Council of Canada 1955–57; Officer-in-charge, Sulphur Mount Lab., Banff, Alberta 1957–60; Assoc. Prof. of Physics, Univ. of Calgary 1960–65, Prof. 1965–70, Dean of Arts and Science 1967–70; Vice-Pres. Simon Fraser Univ., Burnaby, BC 1970–78; Vice-Chancellor Univ. of Queensland 1979–95; Deputy Chair. Australian Vice-Chancellors' Cttee 1987–88, Chair. 1989–90; mem. Council, Northern Territory Univ. 1988–93, Univ. of the South Pacific 1991–95; Pres. Int. Devt Program of Australian Univs and Colls 1991–92; Chair. Australian Cttee for Quality Assurance in Higher Educ. 1993–95; Founder-Chair. Uniquest Pty Ltd (Australia), UQ Tech. Transfer Co. 1984–95; Fellow, Acad. of Technological Sciences and Eng (Australia); Hon. LLD (Calgary) 1984; Hon. DUniv (Queensland Univ. of Tech.) 1995; Hon. DSc (Queensland) 1995. *Publications:* one book and more than 50 scientific articles in int. journals. *Leisure interest:* golf. *Address:* Les Grezes, 11400 Montauriol, France. *Telephone:* (4) 68-23-14-06. *E-mail:* opdebeeck.wilson2@aliceadsl.fr.

WILSON, Charles; British journalist; b. 18 Aug. 1935, Glasgow, Scotland; s. of Adam Wilson and Ruth Wilson; m. 1st Anne Robinson 1968 (divorced 1973); one d.; m. 2nd Sally O'Sullivan 1980 (divorced 2001); one s. one d.; m. 3rd Rachel Pitkeathley 2001; ed Eastbank Acad., Glasgow; copy boy, The People 1951; later reporter with Bristol Evening World, News Chronicle and Daily Mail; Deputy Ed. Daily Mail (Manchester) 1971–74; Asst Ed. London Evening News 1974–76; Ed., Evening Times, Glasgow 1976; later Ed., Glasgow Herald; Ed. Sunday Standard, Glasgow 1981–82; Exec. Ed., The Times 1982, Jt Deputy Ed. 1984–85, Ed. 1985–90; Int. Devt Dir News Int. 1990–91; Ed.-in-Chief, Man. Dir The Sporting Life 1990–98; Editorial Dir Mirror Group Newspapers 1991–92, Group Man. Dir Mirror Group 1992–98; Acting Ed. The Independent 1995–96; Dir (non-exec.) Chelsea and Westminster Hosp. 1999–; mem. Newspaper Panel, Competition Comm. 1999–2007; mem. Jockey Club 1993–, Youth Justice Bd 1998–2004; Trustee World Wildlife Fund-UK 1997–2004, Royal Naval Museum 1999–. *Leisure interests:* current affairs, National Hunt racing, hunting, reading. *Address:* Chairman's Office, Chelsea and Westminster Trust, 369 Fulham Road, London, SW10 9NH (office); 23 Campden Hill Square, London, W8 7JY, England. *Telephone:* (20) 7727-3366 (home). *E-mail:* wcampden@aol.com (home).

WILSON, Sir David Mackenzie, Kt, LittD, FBA, FSA; British fmr museum director; b. 30 Oct. 1931, Dacre Banks, N Yorks., England; s. of Rev. J. Wilson; m. Eva Sjögren 1955; one s. one d.; ed Kingswood School, St John's Coll., Cambridge, Lund Univ., Sweden; Asst Keeper, The British Museum 1955–64; Reader in Archaeology, Univ. of London 1964–71, Prof. of Medieval Archaeology 1971–76; Dir British Museum 1977–92; Commr English Heritage 1990–97; mem. Royal Swedish Acad. of Science, Norwegian Acad. of Science and Letters; Hon. Fellow, Univ. Coll. London; numerous other honours and awards. *Publications:* The Anglo-Saxons 1960, Catalogue of Anglo-Saxon Metalwork 700–1100 in the British Museum 1964, Anglo-Saxon Art 1964, The Bayeux Tapestry 1965, Viking Art (with O. Klindt-Jensen) 1966, Three Viking Graves in the Isle of Man (with G. Bersu) 1966, The Vikings and their Origins 1970, The Viking Achievement (with P. Foote) 1970, St Ninian's Isle and its Treasure (with A. Small and A. C. Thomas) 1973, The Viking Age in the Isle of Man 1974; editor: The Archaeology of the Anglo-Saxons 1976, The Northern World 1980, The Art of the Anglo-Saxons 1984, The Bayeux Tapestry 1985, The British Museum: Purpose and Politics 1989, Awful Ends 1992, Showing the Flag 1992, Vikingetidens Konst 1995, Vikings and Gods in European Art 1997, The British Museum – A History 2002, The Vikings in the Isle of Man 2008; numerous articles and pamphlets. *Address:* The Lifeboat House, Castletown, IM9 1LD, Isle of Man (home). *Telephone:* (1624) 822800 (home). *E-mail:* dmw@mcb.net (office).

WILSON, Edward Osborne, Jr, BS, MS, PhD; American biologist, academic and writer; *University Professor Emeritus and Honorary Curator of Entomology, Museum of Comparative Zoology, Harvard University;* b. 10 June 1929, Birmingham, Ala; s. of the late Edward Osborne Wilson, Sr and Linnette Freeman Huddleston; m. Irene Kelley 1955; one d.; ed Univ. of Alabama and Harvard Univ.; Jr Fellow, Soc. of Fellows, Harvard Univ. 1953–56, Prof. of Zoology 1964–76, F.B. Baird Prof. of Science 1976–94, Pellegrino Univ. Prof. 1994–97, Univ. Research Prof. 1997–2002, Prof. Emer. 2002–, Curator of Entomology, Museum of Comparative Zoology 1974–97, Hon. Curator of Entomology 1997–; Lecturer, Duke Univ. 2014–; Fellow, Guggenheim Foundation 1977–78, Advisory Bd 1979–90, mem. Selection Cttee 1982–90; mem. Bd of Dirs World Wildlife Fund 1983–94, Org. for Tropical Studies 1984–91, American Museum of Natural History

1992–, American Acad. of Liberal Educ. 1993–2004, Nature Conservancy 1994–, Conservation Int. 1997–; Foreign mem. Royal Soc. 1990, Finnish Acad. of Science and Letters 1990, Russian Acad. of Natural Sciences 1994; Founding mem. Int. Centre of Insect Physiology and Ecology, Org. for Tropical Studies, Ecosystems Center of Marine Biological Lab.; mem. NAS 1969; Fellow, American Acad. of Arts and Sciences 1959, American Philosophical Soc. 1976, Animal Behavior Soc. 1976, Deutsche Akad. der Naturforscher Leopoldina 1977, Royal Soc. of Sciences of Uppsala 1989, World Econ. Forum 2000; Hon. Life mem. American Genetic Asscn 1981, British Ecological Soc. 1983, Entomological Soc. of America 1987, Darwin Soc., Univ. of Bergen 1987, American Humanist Asscn 1989, Zoological Soc. of London 1992, Linnean Soc. of London 1994, Netherlands Entomological Soc. 1995, Asscn for Tropical Biology 1999, European Sociobiological Soc. 2000, Royal Entomological Soc. 2001; mem. Hon. Bd World Knowledge Dialogue and Scientist in Residence for symposium organized in Crans-Montana, Switzerland 2008; Silver Cross of Columbus (Dominican Repub.) 2003, Commdr (First Class), Royal Order of the Polar Star (Sweden) 2009; Hon. DHC (Univ. of Madrid Complutense) 1995; Hon. DPhil (Uppsala University) 1987; Hon. Dr rer. nat (Univ. of Wurzburg) 2000; Hon. DSc (Duke Univ.) 1978, (Grinnell Coll.) 1978, (Univ. of West Florida) 1979, (Muhlenberg Coll.) 1998, (Yale Univ.) 1998, (Cedar Crest Coll.) 1999, (State Univ. of NY, Albany) 1999; Hon. LHD (Univ. of Alabama) 1980, (Hofstra Univ.) 1986, (Pennsylvania State Univ.), (Lawrence Univ.) 1979, (Fitchburg State Coll.) 1989, (Macalester Coll.) 1990, (Univ. of Massachusetts) 1993, (Univ. of Oxford) 1993, (Ripon Coll.) 1994, (Univ. of Connecticut) 1995, (Bates Coll.) 1996, (Ohio Univ.) 1996, (Coll. of Wooster) 1997, (Univ. of Guelph) 1997, (Univ. of Portland) 1997, (Bradford Coll.) 1997; Hon. LLD (Simon Fraser Univ.) 1982; Nat. Medal of Science 1976, Tyler Prize for Environmental Achievement 1983, Ingersoll Foundation Weaver Award for Scholarly Letters 1989, Crafoord Prize, Royal Swedish Acad. of Sciences 1990, Int. Prize for Biology, Govt of Japan 1993, Carl Sagan Award for Public Understanding of Science 1994, Audubon Soc. Medal 1995, Los Angeles Times Book Prize for Science 1995, Time Magazine's 25 Most Influential People in America 1995, Schubert Prize (Germany) 1996, German Ecological Foundation Book Award 1998, Franklin Prize for Science, American Philosophical Soc. 1999, Humanist of the Year, American Humanist Asscn 1999, Nonino Prize (Italy) 2000, Lewis Thomas Prize for Writing about Science 2000, King Faisal Int. Prize for Science (Saudi Arabia) 2000, Foundation for the Future Kistler Prize 2000, Nierenberg Prize 2001, Addison Emery Verrill Medal, Peabody Museum of Natural History 2007, TED (Tech. Entertainment Design) Prize (co-recipient) 2007, XIX Premi Internacional Catalunya 2007, EarthSky Science Communicator of the Year 2010, and others. *Achievements include:* coined the term 'sociobiology'. *Publications include:* The Theory of Island Biogeography (with R. H. MacArthur) 1967, The Insect Societies 1971, Sociobiology: The New Synthesis 1975, On Human Nature (Pulitzer Prize for Gen. Non-Fiction 1979) 1978, Caste and Ecology in the Social Insects (with G. F. Oster) 1978, Genes, Mind and Culture (with C. J. Lumsden) 1981, Promethean Fire (with C. J. Lumsden) 1983, Biophilia 1984, Biodiversity (ed.) 1988, The Ants (with Bert Hölldobler) (Pulitzer Prize for Gen. Non-Fiction 1991) 1990, Success and Dominance in Ecosystems 1990, The Diversity of Life 1991, In Search of Nature (with Laura Simonds Southworth) 1996, Journey to the Ants (with Bert Hölldobler) 1994, Pheidole in the New World: A Dominant, Hyperdiverse Ant Genus 2002, From So Simple a Beginning: Darwin's Four Great Books 2005, The Creation: An Appeal to Save Life on Earth 2006, Nature Revealed: Selected Writings 1949–2006 2006, The Superorganism: The Beauty, Elegance, and Strangeness of Insect Societies (with Bert Hölldobler) 2009, Anthill: A Novel (Heartland Prize 2010) 2010, The Social Conquest of Earth 2012, Letters to a Young Scientist 2013; numerous articles on evolutionary biology, entomology and conservation. *Address:* Museum of Comparative Zoology, Harvard University, 26 Oxford Street, Cambridge, MA 02138-2902 (office); 1010 Waltham Street, A-208, Lexington, MA 02421-8062, USA (home). *Telephone:* (617) 495-2315 (office). *Fax:* (617) 495-1224 (office). *E-mail:* ewilson@oeb.harvard.edu (office). *Website:* www.mcz.harvard.edu/Departments/Entomology (office).

WILSON, Jacqueline, DBE, OBE, FRSL; British writer, academic and university administrator; *Pro-Chancellor, Roehampton University;* b. 17 Dec. 1945, Bath, England; d. of the late Harry Aitken and of Margaret Aitken (née Clibbons); m. William Millar Wilson 1965 (divorced 2004); one d.; ed Coombe Girls' School; journalist, D.C. Thomsons 1963–65; teenage magazine Jackie named after her; Amb. Reading is Fundamental, UK 1998–; mem. Cttee Children's Writers and Illustrators Group, Soc. of Authors 1997–; Advisory mem. Panel Costa (fmrly Whitbread) Book Awards 1997–; Judge, Rhône-Poulenc Prizes for Jr Science Books 1999, Orange Prize for Fiction 2006, Prince Maurice Award 2006; mem. Bd Children's Film and TV Foundation 2000–; Children's Laureate 2005–07; Visiting Prof. of Children's Literature, Roehampton Univ. 2010–, Pro-Chancellor, Roehampton Univ. 2011–; Hon. DLitt (Winchester) 2005, (Bath) 2005, (Roehampton) 2007; Hon. DEd (Kingston Univ.) 2006; Hon. LLD (Dundee) 2007; Oak Tree Award 1992, Sheffield Children's Book Award, WHSmith Children's Book of the Year 2002, BT Childline Award 2004, British Book Award for Services to Bookselling 2004. *Plays:* books adapted for the stage include Lottie Project 1999, Double Act 2003, Bad Girls 2004, Midnight 2005, Tracy Beaker Gets Real 2006, Suitcase Kid 2007, Secrets 2008. *Television:* novels Girls in Love, Girls Under Pressure, Girls Out Late and Girls in Tears adapted into 13-part TV series, Granada 2003; The Story of Tracy Beaker adapted into five series on BBC children's TV; The Illustrated Mum adapted for Channel 4 children's TV (two BAFTA Awards, one Emmy Award). *Publications include:* fiction: Hide and Seek 1972, Truth or Dare 1973, Snap 1974, Let's Pretend 1975, Making Hate 1977; juvenile fiction: Nobody's Perfect 1982, Waiting for the Sky to Fall 1983, The Other Side 1984, Amber 1986, The Power of the Shade 1987, Stevie Day Series 1987, This Girl 1988, Is There Anybody There? 1990, Deep Blue 1993, Take a Good Look 1990, The Story of Tracy Beaker 1991, The Suitcase Kid (Children's Book of the Year Award 1993) 1992, Video Rose 1992, The Mum-minder 1993, The Werepuppy 1993, The Bed and the Breakfast Star (The Young Telegraph/Fully Booked Award 1995) 1994, Mark Spark in the Dark 1994, Twin Trouble 1995, Glubbslyme 1995, Jimmy Jelly 1995, The Dinosaur's Packed Lunch 1995, Cliffhanger 1995, Double Act (Children's Book of the Year Award, Smarties Prize) 1995, My Brother Bernadette 1995, Werepuppy on Holiday 1995, Bad Girls 1996, Mr Cool 1996, Monster Story-teller 1997, The Lottie Project 1997, Girls in Love 1997, Connie and the Water Babies 1997, Buried Alive! 1998, Girls Under Pressure 1998, How to Survive Summer

Camp 1998, The Illustrated Mum (Guardian Children's Book of the Year Award, Children's Book of the Year Award 1999) 1999, Girls Out Late 1999, Lizzie Zipmouth 1999, The Dare Game 2000, Vicky Angel 2000, The Cat Mummy 2001, Sleepovers 2001, Dustbin Baby 2001, Secrets 2002, Girls in Tears 2002, The Worry Website 2002, Lola Rose 2003, Midnight 2004, The Diamond Girls 2004, Clean Break 2005, Love Lessons 2005, Best Friends (Red House Children's Book Award) 2005, Candyfloss 2006, Starring Tracy Beaker 2006, Kiss 2007, My Sister Jodie 2008, Cookie 2008, Hetty Feather 2009, Little Darlings 2010, The Longest Whale Song 2010, Lily Alone 2011, Sapphire Battersea: Hetty Feather 2 2011, Lily Alone 2011, Green Glass Beads 2011, The Worst Thing About My Sister 2012, Big Day Out 2012, Four Children and It 2012, Emerald Star 2012, Queenie 2013; other: Jacky Daydream (autobiog.) 2007, My Secret Diary (autobiog.) 2009. *Leisure interests:* reading, swimming, going to art galleries and films, shopping, dancing. *Address:* c/o David Higham Associates, 5–8 Lower John Street, Golden Square, London, W1F 9HA, England (office). *Telephone:* (20) 7434-5900 (office). *Website:* www.jacquelinewilson.co.uk.

WILSON, Jean Donald, MD, FRCP; American endocrinologist and academic; *Professor of Internal Medicine and Charles Cameron Sprague Distinguished Chair in Biomedical Science, University of Texas Southwestern Medical School;* b. 26 Aug. 1932, Wellington, Tex.; s. of J. D. Wilson and Maggie E. Wilson (née Hill); ed Hillsboro Coll., Univ. of Texas at Austin and Univ. of Texas Southwestern Medical School, Dallas; Medical Intern and Asst Resident in Internal Medicine, Parkland Memorial Hosp. Dallas 1955–58; Clinical Assoc. Nat. Heart Inst. Bethesda, Md 1958–60; Instructor, Univ. of Texas Health Science Center 1960–, Prof. of Internal Medicine 1968–, Charles Cameron Sprague Distinguished Chair in Biomedical Science, Southwestern Medical School, Dallas; Established Investigator, American Heart Assoc 1960–65; Travelling Fellow, Royal Soc. of Medicine, Strangeways Research Lab. Cambridge 1970; mem. NAS, Inst. of Medicine of NAS, American Philosophical Soc., American Acad. of Arts and Sciences, Royal Coll. of Physicians; Amory Prize, American Acad. of Arts and Sciences 1977, Henry Dale Medal, Soc. for Endocrinology 1991, Gregory Pincus Award, Worcester Foundation for Experimental Biology 1992, Fred Conrad Koch Award, The Endocrine Soc. 1993, Kober Medal, Assocn of American Physicians 1999. *Publications:* more than 300 scientific articles in various medical journals. *Leisure interests:* birding, opera. *Address:* Division of Endocrinology and Metabolism, Department of Internal Medicine, University of Texas Southwestern Medical Center at Dallas, 5323 Harry Hines Boulevard, Dallas, TX 75390-8857, USA (office). *Telephone:* (214) 648-3469 (office). *Fax:* (214) 648-8917 (office). *E-mail:* jean.wilson@utsouthwestern.edu (office). *Website:* www.swmed.edu (office).

WILSON, Linda S., PhD, FAAS; American chemist and fmr university administrator; *President Emerita, Radcliffe College;* b. (Linda Lee Smith), 10 Nov. 1936, Washington DC; d. of Fred M. Smith and Virginia T. Smith; m. 1st Malcolm C. Whatley 1957 (divorced); one d.; m. 2nd Paul A. Wilson 1970; one step-d.; ed Tulane Univ. and Univ. of Wisconsin; Asst Vice-Chancellor for Research, Washington Univ., St Louis, Mo. 1968–74, Assoc. Vice-Chancellor 1974–75; Assoc. Vice-Chancellor for Research, Univ. of Illinois, Urbana 1975–85, Assoc. Dean, Grad. Coll. 1978–85; Vice-Pres. for Research, Univ. of Michigan, Ann Arbor 1985–89; Pres. Radcliffe Coll., Cambridge, Mass. 1989–99, Pres. Emer. 1999–; Chair. Advisory Cttee Office of Science and Eng Personnel, Nat. Research Council 1990–96; mem. Council on Govt Relations 1971–77, Nat. Inst. of Health Advisory Council on Research Resources 1978–82, Nat. Comm. on Research 1978–80, NSF Dirs Advisory Council 1980–89, Govt-Univ.-Industry Research Roundtable (NAS) 1984–88, Inst. of Medicine Council 1986–89, Inst. of Medicine Cttee on Govt-Industry Collaboration in Research and Educ. 1988–89, Inst. of Medicine Cttee on NIH Priority-Setting 1998–99; mem. Bd of Dirs AAAS 1984–88, Mich. Materials Processing Inst. 1986–89, Mich. Biotechnology Inst. 1986–89, Inst. of Medicine, ACS, AAAS; mem. Bd of Overseers Museum of Science, Boston 1992–2001; Trustee Mass. Gen. Hosp. 1992–99 (Hon. Trustee 1999–2002), Cttee on Econ. Devt 1995–; mem. Bd of Dirs Citizens Financial Group 1996–99, Inacom Corpn 1997–2003, ValueLine Inc. 1998–2000, Myriad Genetics Inc. 1999–2010, Internet Corpn for Assigned Names and Numbers (ICANN) 1998–2003; Friends of DaPonte String Quartet 2002–07; mem. Bd of Admins (Trustee) Tulane Univ. 2002–; elected to Inst. of Medicine 1983; Dr hc (Tulane Univ.), (Univ. of Maryland); Distinguished Contribution to Research Admin. Award, Soc. of Research Admins, Distinguished Service Award, Univ. of Illinois Coll. of Medicine, Centennial Award for Outstanding Accomplishments, Newcomb Coll., Distinguished Alumni Award, Univ. of Wisconsin 1997, Endowed Chair. for Dir of Radcliffe Public Policy Center 1999, Radcliffe Medal 1999. *Publications:* seven book chapters, 10 journal articles, six maj. reports, four commissioned studies, 12 papers on chem., science policy and research policy. *Leisure interests:* cello, reading, music. *Address:* 26 Honey Locust Drive, Topsham, ME, 04086, USA (office). *Telephone:* (207) 729-9129 (office).

WILSON, Lynton Ronald, OC, BA, MA; Canadian business executive; b. 3 April 1940, Port Colborne, Ont.; s. of Ronald Alfred Wilson and Blanche Evelyn Matthews; m. Brenda Jean Black; two d. one s.; ed Port Colborne High School, McMaster Univ., Cornell Univ., USA; Foreign Service Officer, Dept of Trade and Commerce 1962; Asst Commercial Sec., Embassy in Vienna 1963–65; Second Sec., Embassy in Tokyo 1967–68; Corp. Economist and Dir of Econ. Research, John Labatt Ltd 1969–71; Coordinator, Industrial R & D Policy, Ministry of State, Science and Tech. 1972; Strategic Planning and Devt Officer, MacMillan Bloedel Ltd 1973–74, Vice-Pres. and Dir, MacMillan Bloedel Enterprises Inc. 1974–77; Exec. Dir, Policy and Priorities, Ministry of Industry and Tourism, Govt of Ont. 1977–78, Deputy Minister 1978–81; Pres. and CEO Redpath Industries Ltd, Toronto 1981–88, Chair. Bd 1988–89; Man. Dir N America, Tate & Lyle PLC 1986–89; Vice-Chair. Bank of Nova Scotia, Toronto 1989–90; Pres. and COO BCE Inc., Montreal 1990–92, Pres. and CEO 1992–93, Chair., Pres. and CEO 1993–96, Chair. and CEO 1996–98, Chair. Bd Dirs 1998–2000; Chair. Bell Canada, CAE Inc. 1999–2013, Nortel Networks Corpn 2000–05; Chair. Govt's Competition Policy Review Panel 2007–08; Chancellor McMaster Univ. 2007–13; Founding Chair. Historica Foundation of Canada; Dir BCE Mobile Communications Inc., Bell Canada Int. Inc., Northern Telecom Ltd, Bell-Northern Research Ltd, Teleglobe Inc., Chrysler Canada Ltd, Chrysler Corpn, Tate & Lyle PLC, UK, Stelco Inc., CD Howe Inst., Canadian Inst. for Advanced Research; mem. Business Council on Nat. Issues (Policy Cttee), Trilateral Comm., Int. Council JP Morgan & Co., New York, Bd of Trustees Montreal Museum of Fine Arts Foundation; Gov. Olympic Trust of

Canada, McGill Univ.; six hon. degrees including Dr hc (Montreal) 1995, Hon. LLD (McMaster) 1995, (Cape Breton) 1998, (Mount Allison) 2000. *Address:* c/o CAE Inc., 8585 Côte de Liesse, Saint-Laurent, Montreal, Quebec H4T 1G6 (office); 2038 Lakeshore Road East, Oakville, Ont. L6J 1M3, Canada (home).

WILSON, Hon. Margaret, DCNZM, LLB (Hons), M.jur; New Zealand lawyer, politician and academic; *Professor of Law and Public Policy, University of Waikato;* b. 20 May 1947, Gisborne; ed St Dominic's Coll., Northcote, Morrinsville Coll., Univ. of Auckland; sec. for Legal Employers Union 1970–1971; law clerk and solicitor, Peter Jenkins, barrister and solicitor in Auckland 1970–72; taught at Univ. of Auckland; Founder-mem. Industrial Relations Soc. 1973; Acting Ed. Recent Law 1974; Founding Ed. New Zealand Journal of Industrial Relations 1976–77, mem. Editorial Bd 1994–; Exec. mem., Vice-Chair. and Chair. Auckland Br., Asscn of Univ. Teachers 1976–84; Founder-mem. and Vice-Pres. Auckland Women Lawyers' Asscn 1984, Life mem. 1985–; Convenor, Govt Working Party on Equal Pay and Equal Opportunities 1988; Dir Reserve Bank of New Zealand 1985–89; Chief Political Adviser and Head of Prime Minister's Office 1987–89; Chair. Nat. Advisory Council on Employment of Women 1987–91; Chair. TV3 News Ltd 1988–89; Law Commr of the Law Comm. 1988–89; apptd Foundation Dean and Prof. of Law, Univ. of Waikato 1990; mem. Advisory Cttee to establish the Ministry of Women's Affairs 1985, Advisory Group on restructuring of the Ministry of Justice 1995, team to review the Crown Forestry Rental Trust 1995, Judicial Working Group on Gender Equality 1995–97; Chief Govt Law Officer; Attorney-Gen. 1999–2005; Minister of Labour 1999–2004; Minister in Charge of Treaty of Waitangi Negotiations 1999–2005; Assoc. Minister of Justice 1999–2004, Assoc. Minister of State Services 2000–02; Minister responsible for the Law Comm. 2001–02; Minister for Courts 2002–03, Assoc. Minister 2003–04; Minister of Commerce 2004; Speaker of House of Reps 2005–08; Prof. of Law and Public Policy, Univ. of Waikato 2008–; Pres. NZ Labour Party 1984–87; Hon. LLD (Waikato) 2004. *Address:* School of Law, University of Waikato, Private Bag 3105, Hamilton, New Zealand (office). *Telephone:* (7) 856-2889 (office). *E-mail:* mwilson@waikato.ac.nz (office). *Website:* www.waikato.ac.nz/law (office).

WILSON, Mark, BMS; New Zealand business executive; *Group CEO, Aviva plc;* b. Sept. 1966; ed Univ. of Waikato; held several sr man. positions at National Mutual in New Zealand –2001; CEO AXA South East Asia (insurance) 2001–03, CEO AXA China (insurance) 2003–06, Pres. and CEO AIA Group (insurance), Hong Kong 2006–10, mem. Bd of Dirs Aviva plc (as Group CEO-designate) Dec. 2012–, Group CEO Jan. 2013–. *Address:* Aviva plc, St Helen's, 1 Undershaft, London, EC3P 3DQ, England (office). *Telephone:* (20) 7283-2000 (office). *E-mail:* aviva.info@aviva .com (office). *Website:* www.aviva.com (office).

WILSON, Hon. Michael, PC, OC, BA; Canadian business executive, diplomatist and fmr politician; b. 4 Nov. 1937, Toronto, Ont.; ed Univ. of Toronto, London School of Econs, UK; MP for Etobicoke Centre 1979–93; Minister of Finance 1984–91, of Industry, Science and Tech. and Minister for Int. Trade –1993, represented Canada at IMF, IBRD, OECD, GATT and G-7 Ministers' meetings; Vice-Chair. RBC Dominion Securities and institutional asset management business 1993; Chair. UBS Canada 2001–06; Amb. to USA 2006–09; mem. Bd of Dirs BP plc 1998–2006; Chair. Council for Public-Private Partnerships 2001–06, Canadian Coalition for Good Governance; Chancellor Trinity Coll., Univ. of Toronto 2003–06; Dr hc (Univ. of Toronto), (York Univ.). *Address:* c/o Foreign Affairs and International Trade Canada, 125 Sussex Drive, Ottawa, ON K1A 0G2, Canada.

WILSON, Nigel, PhD; British business executive; *Group Chief Executive, Legal and General Group Plc;* m.; five d.; ed Massachusetts Inst. of Tech. (Kennedy Scholar), USA; fmr consultant, McKinsey & Co.; fmr Man. Dir Stanhope Properties Plc; fmr Chief Exec., Corp., Guinness Peat Aviation; fmr Group Commercial Dir Dixons Group Plc; Deputy Chief Exec. and Chief Financial Officer (CFO) United Business Media plc –2009; Group CFO Legal & General 2009–12, Group Chief Exec. 2012–; Sr Ind. Dir, The Capita Group plc 2010–; Sr Ind. Dir/Chair. Halfords Group Plc –2011. *Achievements include:* current 800m British Masters Athletics Champion. *Address:* Legal & General Group Plc, One Coleman Street, London, EC2R 5AA, England (office). *Telephone:* (20) 3124-2000 (office). *Fax:* (20) 7528-6222 (office). *E-mail:* info@legalandgeneralgroup.com (office). *Website:* www .legalandgeneralgroup.com (office).

WILSON, Nigel Guy, MA, FBA; British academic; b. 23 July 1935, London; s. of Noel Wilson and Joan L. Wilson; m. Hanneke Marion Wirtjes 1996; ed Univ. Coll. School and Corpus Christi Coll., Oxford; Lecturer, Merton Coll., Oxford 1957–62; Fellow and Tutor in Classics, Lincoln Coll., Oxford 1962–2002; James P. R. Lyell Reader in Bibliography 2003; Hon. LittD (Uppsala) 2001, (Cyprus) 2013; Gordon Duff Prize 1968, Premio Anassilaos 1999. *Publications:* Scribes and Scholars (with L. D. Reynolds) (fourth edn) 2013, An Anthology of Byzantine Prose 1971, Medieval Greek Bookhands 1973, St Basil on the Value of Greek Literature 1975, Scholia in Aristophanis Acharnenses 1975, Menander Rhetor (with D. A. Russell) 1981, Scholars of Byzantium 1983, Oxford Classical Text of Sophocles (with Sir Hugh Lloyd-Jones) 1990, From Byzantium to Italy 1992, Photius: the Bibliotheca 1994, Aelian: Historical Miscellany 1997, Pietro Bembo: Oratio pro litteris graecis 2003, Oxford Classical Text of Aristophanes 2007, Aristophanea 2007, A Descriptive Catalogue of the Greek Manuscripts of Corpus Christi College, Oxford 2011, The Archimedes Palimpsest (with R. Netz, W. Noel and Natalie Tchernetska) 2011. *Leisure interests:* bridge, real tennis, wine. *Address:* Lincoln College, Oxford, OX1 3DR, England (office). *Fax:* (1865) 279802 (office).

WILSON, Owen; American actor; b. 18 Nov. 1968, Dallas, Tex.; s. of Robert Andrew Wilson and Laura Cunningham Wilson; one s. with Jade Duell. *Films include:* The Cable Guy 1996, Armageddon 1998, The Haunting 1999, Meet the Parents 2000, Shanghai Noon 2000, The Royal Tenenbaums (also writer and exec. producer) 2001, Zoolander 2001, Shanghai Knights 2003, The Life Aquatic with Steve Zissou 2004, Meet the Fockers 2004, Around the World in 80 Days 2004, Starsky & Hutch 2004, Wedding Crashers 2005, You, Me and Dupree (also producer) 2006, Cars (voice) 2006, The Darjeeling Limited 2007, Marley & Me 2008, Fantastic Mr Fox (voice) 2009, How Do You Know 2010, Little Fockers 2010, Midnight in Paris 2011. *Address:* c/o United Talent Agency, 9560 Wilshire Blvd, Suite 500, Beverly Hills, CA 90212-2410, USA (office).

WILSON, Peter Barton (Pete), LLB, JD; American fmr politician and lawyer; *Distinguished Visiting Fellow, Hoover Institution, Stanford University;* b. 23 Aug. 1933, Lake Forest, Ill.; s. of James Boone Wilson and Margaret (née Callahan) Wilson; m. 1st Betty Robertson (divorced); m. 2nd Gayle Edlund Graham 1983; ed Yale Univ., Univ. of Calif., Berkeley; admitted to Calif. Bar; Asst Exec. Dir Republican Asscn, San Diego Co. 1963–64; Exec. Dir San Diego Co. Republican Cen. Comm. 1964–65; legal service officer, Calif. State Republican Cen. Comm. 1965; mem. Calif. Ass. 1967–71; Mayor of San Diego 1971–83; Senator from Calif. 1983–91; Gov. of Calif. 1991–99; Nat. Dir Pacific Capital Group, Calif. 1999–; Distinguished Visiting Fellow, Hoover Inst., Stanford Univ. 1999–; Chair. campaign for Republican Gov. Arnold Schwarzenegger 2003; mem. Presidential Advisory Cttee on Environmental Quality, Task Force Land Use and Urban Growth Policy. *Address:* c/o Hoover Institution, Stanford University, Stanford, CA 94305-6010, USA. *Telephone:* (650) 723-1754. *Fax:* (650) 723-1687. *Website:* www .hoover.org.

WILSON, Peter L., A.A. Diploma; Australian architect; b. 27 Sept. 1950, Melbourne; s. of the late Jack Wilson and of Betty Wilson; m. Julia B. Bolles; one s. one d.; ed Univ. of Melbourne, Architectural Asscn School of Architecture, London; Asst Teacher, Architectural Asscn School of Architecture, London 1974–75, Intermediate Unit Master 1976–79, Diploma Unit Master 1980–88; f. Wilson Partnership, London (with Julia Bolles-Wilson) 1980, Architekturbüro Bolles + Wilson (now Bolles+Wilson GmbH & Co) Münster 1988; Visiting Prof. Kunsthochschule Weisensee, Berlin 1996–98, Accademia di Architettura, Mendrisio, Switzerland 2006–07; winner of more than 20 int. architectural competitions. *Buildings include:* Suzuki House, Tokyo 1993, New City Library, Münster 1993, WLV Office Bldg, Münster 1993, Quay Landscape, Rotterdam 1998, New Luxor Theatre, Rotterdam 2001, BEIC Library and Media Centre, Milan 2001–06, Nord LB Bank, Cathedral Square, Magdeburg, Germany 2002, National Library, Luxembourg 2003–04, Falkenried Urban Quartier, Hamburg 1999–2004. *Publications:* El Croquis No 105 – Bolles and Wilson 1995–2001, Bolles and Wilson Monograph Electra 2008. *Address:* Bolles+Wilson GmbH & Co., KG, Hafenweg 16, 48155 Münster, Germany (office). *Telephone:* (251) 482720 (office); (251) 43888 (home). *Fax:* (251) 4827224 (office). *E-mail:* info@bolles-wilson.com (office). *Website:* www.bolles-wilson.com (office).

WILSON, (Robert) Gordon, BL, LLD; Scottish politician and solicitor (retd); b. 16 April 1938, Glasgow, Scotland; s. of Robert George Wilson and Robina Wilson; m. Edith Hassall 1965; two d.; ed Douglas High School and Univ. of Edinburgh; Asst Nat. Sec. Scottish Nat. Party 1963–64, Nat. Sec. 1964–71, Exec. Vice-Chair. 1972–73, Sr Vice-Chair. 1973–74, Chair. 1979–90, Vice-Pres. 1992–; MP for Dundee E 1974–87; Party Spokesman on Oil and Energy 1974–87, on Energy 1992–93, on Treasury 1993–94; Jt Spokesman on Devolution 1976–79; Rector, Univ. of Dundee 1983–86; Chair. Marriage Counselling (Tayside) 1989–92; Gov. Dundee Inst. of Tech.; Court mem. Univ. of Abertay Dundee 1991–96; mem. Church and Nation Cttee of Church of Scotland 2000–03, Bd Dundee Age Concern 2001–05; Clerk, St Aidan's Church Congregational Bd 2003–05, (now New Kirk 2005–06); Chair. Solas (Centre for Public Christianity), Dundee Citizens Advice Bureau 2011. *Publications:* SNP: The Turbulent Years 1960–1990, Pirates of the Air – The Story of Radio Free Scotland 2012. *Leisure interests:* reading, writing. *Address:* 48 Monifieth Road, Dundee, DD5 2RX, Scotland. *E-mail:* gordonwilson10@blueyonder.co.uk.

WILSON, Robert M.; American theatre and opera director and artist; b. 4 Oct. 1941, Waco, Tex.; s. of D. M. Wilson and Velma Loree Wilson (née Hamilton); ed Univ. of Tex., Pratt Inst.; began creating innovative theatre in New York in the 1960s; worked mainly in Europe in the 1980s and 1990s, directing original works as well as traditional opera and theatre; Guggenheim Fellow 1971, 1980; Trustee Nat. Inst. of Music Theatre; mem. Dramatists Guild, Soc. des Auteurs et Compositeurs Dramatiques, Soc. of Stage Dirs. and Choreographers, PEN American Center, American Acad. of Arts and Letters; hon. Dir American Repertory Theatre; has given lectures and workshops at numerous insts.; Dr. hc Calif. Coll. of Arts and Letters, Pratt Inst. New York City; numerous awards and decorations including the Maharam Award for Best Set Design 1975, Lumen Award 1977, First Prize San Sebastian Film and Video Festival 1984, Picasso Award 1986, Inst. Skowhegan Medal for drawing 1987, Grand Prix Biennale, Barcelona Festival of Cinema Art 1989, Germna Theatre Critics Award 1990, Brandeis Univ. Poses Creative Arts Award 1991, Venice Biennale Golden Lion Award for Sculpture 1993, Dorothy and Lillian Gish Prize 1996, Tadeusz Kantor Prize 1997, Harvard Excellence in Design Award 1998, Pushkin Prize 1999; Most Outstanding Theater Designer of the Seventies, U.S. Inst. of Theater Tech. 1977. *Dance created and choreographed:* Snow on the Mesa (for Martha Graham Dance Co.) 1995. *Stage appearances include:* Deafman Glance 1970, The Life and Times of Joseph Stalin (Dir) 1974, A Letter for Queen Victoria 1974, Einstein on the Beach 1976, 1984, Death, Destruction and Detroit 1979, The Golden Windows 1982, 1985, The Civil Wars 1983–85, Hamletmachine 1986, Doktor Faustus 1989, The Black Rider 1990, King Lear 1990, The Magic Flute 1991, Alice 1993, Der Mond in Gras 1994, The Death of Molière 1994, Hamlet: A Monologue 1995, Prometeo 1997, Saints and Singing 1997, Monsters of Grace 1998, Dream Play 1998, Scourge of Hyacinths 1999, The Days Before 1999, Hot Waters 2000, Relative Light 2000. *Plays directed and designed include:* Deafman Glance 1970, Einstein on the Beach 1976, Death, Destruction and Detroit 1979, The Golden Windows 1982, the CIVIL warS 1983–85, Hamletmachine 1986, Doktor Faustus 1989, The Black Rider 1990, The Magic Flute 1991, Doktor Faustus Lights the Lights 1992, Alice 1992, Madame Butterfly 1993, Hanjo 1994, Hamlet: A Monologue 1995, Time Rocker 1996, Lady from the Sea 1998, Das Rheingold 2000, POEtry 2000, Woyzeck 2001, Three Penny Opera, Spoleto Festival, Italy 2008. *Films include:* Overture for a Deafman, Monsters of Grace 1998. *Videos include:* The Spaceman 1976, 1984, Video 50 1978, Stations 1982, La Femme à la Cafétière 1989, Mr. Bojangles' Memory 1991, La Mort de Molière 1994. *Publications include:* The King of Spain 1970, Einstein on the Beach: An Opera in Four Acts (with Philip Glass q.v.) 1976, A Letter for Queen Victoria 1977, Death, Destruction and Detroit 1979, the CIVIL warS 1985, Mr. Bojangles' Memory 1991, RW Notebook 1999. *Leisure interest:* collecting fine art and design. *Address:* RW Work Ltd, 155 Wooster Street, Suite 4F, New York, NY 10012, USA. *Telephone:* (212) 253-7484. *Fax:* (212) 253-7485 (office). *Website:* www.robertwilson.com (office).

WILSON, Sir Robert Peter, KCMG, FRSA, CIMgt; British business executive; *Chairman, BG Group plc;* b. 2 Sept. 1943, Carshalton, Surrey, England; s. of the late Alfred Wilson and Dorothy Wilson (née Mathews); m. Shirley Elisabeth Robson 1975; one s. one d.; ed Epsom Coll., Univ. of Sussex, Harvard Business School, USA; Asst Economist, Dunlop Ltd 1966–67; Economist, Mobil Oil Co. Ltd 1967–70; with Rio Tinto PLC (fmrly RTZ Corpn PLC) starting 1970, Man. Dir AM & S Europe 1979–82, Project Dir RTZ Devt Enterprise 1982–83, Head of Planning and Devt RTZ Corpn PLC 1984–86, Dir 1987–2003, Chief Exec. 1991–97, Chair. 1997–2003; Dir Rio Tinto Ltd (fmrly CRA Ltd) 1990–2003, Deputy Chair. 1995–98, Chair. 1999–2003; Chair. BG Group plc 2004–; fmr Dir (non-exec.) BP PLC, The Boots Co. PLC 1991–98, Diageo PLC; Dir (non-exec.) GlaxoSmithKline plc 2003–, Sr Ind. Dir 2009–; mem. Bd of Dirs The Economist Group Ltd 2002–09, Chair. 2003–09; Trustee, Camborne School of Mines 1993–99; Hon. DSc (Exeter) 1993, (Birmingham) 2002, (Sussex) 2004; Hon. LLD (Dundee) 2001. *Leisure interests:* theatre, opera. *Address:* BG Group plc, Eagle House, 108–110 Jermyn Street, London, SW1Y 6RP, England (office). *Telephone:* (20) 7707-4878 (office). *Fax:* (20) 7707-4858 (office). *Website:* www.bg-group.com (office).

WILSON, Robert Woodrow, PhD; American radio astronomer; *Senior Scientist, Harvard-Smithsonian Center for Astrophysics;* b. 10 Jan. 1936, Houston, Tex.; s. of Ralph Woodrow Wilson and Fannie May Wilson (née Willis); m. Elizabeth Rhoads Sawin 1958; two s. one d.; ed Rice Univ., California Inst. of Tech.; mem. Tech. Staff, AT&T Bell Labs, Holmdel, NJ 1963–76, Head of Radio Physics Research Dept 1976–94; Sr Scientist, Harvard-Smithsonian Center for Astrophysics 1994–; mem. NAS, American Astronomical Soc., American Physical Soc., Int. Astronomical Union; Henry Draper Award 1977, Herschel Award 1977, Nobel Prize for Physics (shared with Arno Allan Penzias for their discovery of the cosmic microwave background) 1978. *Publications:* numerous articles in scientific journals. *Address:* Harvard-Smithsonian Center for Astrophysics, 60 Garden Street, #42, Cambridge, MA 02138 (office); 9 Valley Point Drive, Holmdel, NJ 07733, USA (home). *Telephone:* (617) 496-7744 (office); (201) 671-7807 (home). *Fax:* (617) 496-7554 (office). *E-mail:* rwilson@cfa.harvard.edu (office). *Website:* cfa-www.harvard.edu (office).

WILSON, Sandy (see Wilson, Alexander Galbraith).

WILSON, Thomas Joseph, BBA, MBA; American business executive; *Chairman, President and CEO, The Allstate Corporation;* b. St Clair Shores, Mich.; m. Jill Wilson (née Garling); three c.; ed Univ. of Michigan, J.L. Kellogg Grad. School of Man., Northwestern Univ.; held various financial positions at Amoco Corpn 1980–86; Man. Dir Mergers and Acquisitions, Dean Witter Reynolds 1986–93; Vice-Pres., Strategy and Analysis, Sears, Roebuck and Co. 1993–95; Chief Financial Officer Allstate Corpn 1995–98, Chair. and Pres. Allstate Financial 1999–2002, Pres. Allstate Protection 2002–06, Pres. and COO 2005–06, Pres. and CEO 2007–, Chair. 2008–; Vice-Chair. Fed. Reserve Bank of Chicago; mem. Bd Rush Univ. Medical Center, Museum of Science and Industry, Financial Services Roundtable, Catalyst; mem. World Presidents' Org., Financial Services Forum, The Business Roundtable, Civic Cttee of Commercial Club of Chicago; CFO Magazine's Excellence Award 1998. *Address:* The Allstate Corporation, 2775 Sanders Road, Suite F7, Northbrook, IL 60062-6127, USA (office). *Telephone:* (847) 402-5000 (office). *Fax:* (847) 326-7519 (office). *E-mail:* directors@allstate.com (office). *Website:* www.allstate.com (office).

WILSON, Trevor Gordon, AM, MA, DPhil, FRHistS, FAHA; New Zealand military historian and academic; *Professor Emeritus and Honorary Visiting Research Fellow, School of History and Politics, University of Adelaide;* b. 24 Dec. 1928, Auckland; s. of the late Gordon Wilson and Winifred Wilson; m. Jane Verney 1957; two d.; ed Mount Albert Grammar School, Univs. of Auckland and Oxford; Asst Lecturer in History Canterbury Univ. 1952, Auckland Univ. 1953–55; Research Asst in Govt, Univ. of Manchester 1957–59; Lecturer then Sr Lecturer in History, Univ. of Adelaide 1960–67, Prof. 1968–, now Prof. Emer. and Hon. Visiting Research Fellow; Commonwealth Fellow, St John's Coll., Cambridge 1972; Visiting Fellow, Magdalen Coll., Oxford 1987; Drinko Distinguished Visiting Prof., Marshall Univ. 1989; Nuffield Dominion Travelling Fellowship 1964–65; Univ. of NZ Overseas Travelling Scholarship 1953; Gilbert Campion Prize (jt winner) 1960, Higby Prize 1965, Adelaide Festival of Arts Literature Award 1988. *Publications:* The Downfall of the Liberal Party (1914–35) 1966, The Political Diaries of C. P. Scott 1911–28 1970, The Myriad Faces of War: Britain and the Great War 1914–18 1986, Command on the Western Front: The Military Career of Sir Henry Rawlinson 1914–1918 (with Robin Prior) 1992, Passchendaele: the Untold Story (with Robin Prior) 1996, The First World War (Cassell History of Warfare) (with Robin Prior) 1999, The Somme (with Robin Prior) 2005. *Leisure interests:* listening to jazz, watching musical movies, ten-pin bowling. *Address:* Department of History and Politics, Room 314, Napier Building, University of Adelaide, North Terrace, South Australia 5005, Australia. *Telephone:* (8) 8303-5633 (office). *Fax:* (8) 8303-3443 (office). *E-mail:* tjwilson@senet.com.au (home). *Website:* www.arts.adelaide.edu.au/historypolitics (office).

WILSON-JOHNSON, David Robert, BA, FRAM; British baritone; b. 16 Nov. 1950, Northampton; s. of Harry K. Johnson and Sylvia C. Wilson; ed Wellingborough School, Northants., British Inst. of Florence, St Catharine's Coll., Cambridge and Royal Acad. of Music; debut at Royal Opera House, Covent Garden in We Come to the River 1976; regular appearances for over 20 years including in Billy Budd, L'Enfant et les Sortilèges, Le Rossignol, Les Noces, Boris Godunov, Die Zauberflöte, Turandot, Werther, Madame Butterfly, Così fan tutte; Wigmore Hall recital debut 1977; BBC Promenade Concert debut 1981; debut at Edin. Festival 1976, Glyndebourne Festival 1980 and at festivals in Bath, Bergen, Berlin, Geneva, Graz, Netherlands, Hong Kong, Jerusalem, Orange, Paris, Salzburg, Tanglewood and Vienna; Paris Opera debut in Die Meistersinger 1989; American debut in Paulus (title role) 1990; ENO debut (in Billy Budd) 1991; Netherlands Opera debut in Birtwistle's Punch and Judy 1993; Founder Dir Ferrandou Summer Singing School 1985–; many concert tours with David Owen Norris (voice and piano duo for 40 years), Pierre Boulez/ Ensemble Intercontemporain, Gennadi Rozhdestvensky /BBCSO, David Atherton/London Sinfonietta/Hong Kong Symphony, Charles Dutoit Philadelphia Orchestra/Tonhalle Orchestra/ NHK Symphony, Frans Bruggen/Orchestra of the 18th Century, Robert King/The King's Consort; Prof. of Voice, Amsterdam Conservatorium 2005–10; Gulbenkian Fellowship 1978–81; Nat. Fed. of Music Soc. Award 1977, Evening Standard

Award for Opera 1989. *Films include:* Give my Regards to Broad Street (The Beatles), A Midsummer Marriage (Michael Tippett) 1988, Or Shall we die? (Michael Berkeley/Ian McEwan). *Television:* BBC Handel 250th Anniversary Celebrations from Westminster Abbey 1985, BBC TV Purcell Tercentenary Celebration from Westminster Abbey 1995, Olivier Messiaen's 80 birthday Concert from Royal Festival Hall (title role in St François d'Assise) 1988. *Recordings include:* Schubert's Winterreise with David Owen Norris, Mozart Masses from King's Coll., Cambridge, Haydn's Nelson Mass (English Concert/Trevor Pinnock), Schoenberg's Ode to Napoleon (Ensemble Intercontemporain), King Priam, Punch and Judy, The Ice Break (London Sinfonietta/ David Atherton), La Traviata, Lucrezia Borgia (Joan Sutherland, Luciano Pavarotti/Richard Bonynge), Michael Berkeley's Or Shall We Die?, Belshazzar's Feast, The Kingdom, Caractacus (LSO/ Richard Hickox), Odes (Purcell), Black Pentecost (BBCPO/Maxwell Davies), Mass in B Minor (Bavarian Radio Symphony Orchestra/Carlo Maria Giulini), Peter Grimes (ROH /Bernard Haitink), Roméo et Juliette, Damnation of Faust, Oedipus Rex (Philadelphia Orchestra/Charles Dutoit). *Leisure interests:* swimming, slimming, gardening and growing walnuts in the Dordogne. *Address:* c/o Ben Rayfield, Rayfield Artists, Southbank House, Black Prince Road, London, SE1 7SJ, England (office); Prinsengracht 455, 1016 HN Amsterdam, Netherlands (home); 28 Englefield Road, London, N1 4ET, England (home). *Telephone:* (20) 7193-1531 (office); (20) 7254-0941 (London); 5-65-10-94-11 (France); (20) 7728104 (home). *E-mail:* ben@rayfieldartists.com (office); info@ferrandou.org (office). *Website:* www .rayfieldartists.com (office); www.ferrandou.org (office); www.davidwilsonjohnson .com.

WILSON OF DINTON, Baron (Life Peer), cr. 2003, of Dinton in the County of Buckinghamshire; **Richard Thomas James Wilson,** GCB, MA, LLM; British civil servant and college principal; *Master, Emmanuel College, Cambridge;* b. 11 Oct. 1942, Cardiff, South Wales; s. of the late Richard Ridley Wilson and Frieda Bell Wilson (née Finlay); m. Caroline Margaret Lee 1972; one s. one d.; ed Radley Coll., Clare Coll., Cambridge; called to the Bar 1965; Asst Prin. Board of Trade 1966, Pvt. Sec. to Minister of State, Board of Trade 1969–71, Prin. Cabinet Office 1971–73, Dept of Energy 1974, Asst Sec. Dept of Energy 1977–82, Under-Sec. 1982, Prin. Establishment and Finance Officer 1982–86; on loan to Cabinet Office Man. and Personnel Office 1986–87, Deputy Sec. Cabinet Office 1987–90; Deputy Sec. (Industry) HM Treasury 1990–92; Perm. Sec. Dept of Environment 1992–94; Perm. Under-Sec. of State, Home Office 1994–97; Cabinet Sec. and Head of the Home Civil Service 1997–2002; Master, Emmanuel Coll., Cambridge 2002–; mem. (Crossbench) House of Lords 2003–; Chair. C Hoare & Co. 2006–; Dir (non-exec.) BSkyB 2003–; Chair. Radley Coll. Council 2004–10; Trustee, Ewing Foundation 1994–, Cicely Saunders International 2004–, Cambridge Arts Theatre 2007–11; Pres. Chartered Inst. of Personnel and Devt 2004–06. *Address:* The Master's Lodge, Emmanuel College, St Andrew's Street, Cambridge, CB2 3AP, England (office). *Telephone:* (1223) 334248 (office). *Fax:* (1223) 331867 (office). *E-mail:* master@emma.cam.ac.uk (office). *Website:* www.emma.cam.ac.uk (office).

WILSON OF TILLYORN, Baron (Life Peer), cr. 1992, of Finzean in the District of Kincardine and Deeside and of Fanling in Hong Kong; **David Clive Wilson,** KT, GCMG, PhD, FRSE; British diplomatist and public servant; b. 14 Feb. 1935, Alloa, Scotland; s. of Rev. William Skinner Wilson and Enid Wilson; m. Natasha Helen Mary Alexander 1967; two s.; ed Glenalmond and Keble Coll., Oxford; nat. service, The Black Watch 1953–55; entered Foreign Service 1958, Third Sec., Vientiane 1959–60, Second then First Sec., Peking 1963–65, FCO 1965–68 (resgnd 1968, rejoined Diplomatic Service 1972), Cabinet Office 1974–77, Political Adviser, Hong Kong 1977–81, Head S. European Dept, FCO 1981–84, Asst Under-Sec. of State 1984–87; Gov. and Commdr-in-Chief of Hong Kong 1987–92; Chancellor, Univ. of Aberdeen 1997–2013; Vice-Pres. Royal Scottish Geographical Soc. 1996–; Language Student, Hong Kong 1960–62; Ed. China Quarterly 1968–74; Visiting Scholar, Columbia Univ., New York 1972; Chair. Scottish Hydro-Electric PLC 1993–2000 (Scottish and Southern Energy PLC 1998–2000); mem. Bd of Govs. SOAS 1992–97; mem. Bd British Council 1993–2002 (Chair. Scottish Cttee 1993–2002); Chancellor's Assessor, Univ. of Aberdeen 1993–96; Chair. Council, Glenalmond Coll. 2000–05; Scottish Peers' Asscn 2000–02; Dir Martin Currie Pacific Trust 1993–2003; mem. Advisory Cttee on Business Appointments 2000–09 (Chair. 2008–09); Pres. Bhutan Soc. of the UK 1993–2008, Hong Kong Asscn 1994–, Hong Kong Soc. 1994–2013; Fellow, Royal Soc. of Edinburgh 2000–, Pres. 2008–11; Registrar of the Most Distinguished Order of St Michael and St George 2001–10; Chair. Trustees Nat. Museums of Scotland 2002–06; Chair., St Paul's Cathedral Advisory Council 2009–; Lord High Commr to Gen. Ass., Church of Scotland 2010, 2011; Hon. Fellow, Keble Coll. Oxford; Hon. Burger of Guild of City of Aberdeen 2003; Hon. LLD (Aberdeen) 1990, (Chinese Univ., Hong Kong) 1996; Hon. DLitt (Sydney) 1991, (Abertay Dundee) 1994, (Univ. of Hong Kong) 2006; Dr hc (Edinburgh) 2011. *Leisure interests:* mountaineering, reading, theatre. *Address:* c/o House of Lords, Parliament Square, London, SW1A 0PW, England (office). *Telephone:* (20) 7219-3107 (office). *E-mail:* wilsondc@parliament.uk (office).

WILUAN, Kris Taenar, BSc; Indonesian business executive; *Chairman, Citramas Group;* b. 1948; s. of Henk Wiluan; m.; three c.; ed Univ. of London, UK; began career as computer programmer, Guest, Keen and Nettlefold, England; moved to Singapore 1973; Gen. Man. United Motor Works 1973–77; f. own business as logistics contractor for oil cos, Indonesia 1977; f. PT Citra Bonang 1979 (currently Chair.) PT Citra Bonindo 1983, PT Citra Tubindo Tbk 1983 (currently Pres. and CEO), Chair. Citramas Group (holding co. with interests in oil, tourism, real estate, logistics and transportation); Chair. and CEO KS Energy 2006–; Chair. and CEO Aqua-Terra Supply Co. Ltd; Exec. Chair. and CEO SSH Corpn Ltd; Pres. Asean Taekwondo Fed., Vice-Chair. World Taekwondo Federation; Pres. Riau Porlasi (sailing asscn); Ernst and Young Indonesian Entrepreneur of the Year Award 2009. *Address:* PT Citramasjaya Teknikmandiri, Jl Diponegoro No. 108, Tambun, Bekasi 17510, Indonesia (office). *Telephone:* (21) 8822149 (office). *Fax:* (21) 8807335 (office). *E-mail:* cti@citramas.co.id (office). *Website:* www.citramas.co .id (office).

WINBERG, (Sven) Håkan, LLB; Swedish politician and lawyer; b. 30 July 1931, Ange; s. of Sven Winberg and Sally Angman; m. Ulla Greta Petersson 1957; Justice, Court of Appeal; mem. Parl. 1971–82; mem. Exec. Swedish Moderate Party 1972–; mem. Steering Cttee 1975–; mem. Press Assistance Bd 1971–79, Bd

of Council for Prevention of Crime 1974–79, Co. Boundaries Cttee 1970–74, Cttee of Inquiry into the Press 1972–75, New Labour Laws Cttee 1976–78, Nat. Police Bd 1977–79, Nordic Council 1977–82; County Councillor 1974–79; Minister of Justice 1979–81; Pres. Court of Appeal, Sundsvall from 1982; mem. Election Review Cttee of the Riksdag from 1983; mem. Parl. Comm. for Investigation into the murder of Prime Minister Olof Palme 1987–88, new Comm. for same investigation 1994; mem. Security Police Cttee from 1989, Court of Law Cttee from 1990. *Leisure interest:* skiing.

WINBLAD, Ann L., BA, MA, PhD; American investment company executive; *Managing Director, Hummer Winblad Venture Partners;* b. Minn.; ed Univ. of St Thomas, St Paul, Minn.; began career as systems programmer with San Francisco Fed. Reserve Bank; co-f. Open Systems Inc. 1976, sold co. 1983; Co-founder and Man. Dir Hummer Winblad Venture Partners 1989–; Co-Chair. SDForum; serves as adviser to many entrepreneurial orgs; mem. Bd of Trustees Univ. of St Thomas; Hon. LLD (Univ. of St Thomas). *Publication:* Object-Oriented Software (co-author) 1990; numerous articles in industry journals. *Address:* Hummer Winblad Venture Partners, One Lombard Street, Suite 300, San Francisco, CA 94111, USA (office). *Telephone:* (415) 979-9600 (office). *Fax:* (415) 979-9601 (office). *E-mail:* awinblad@ humwin.com (office). *Website:* www.humwin.com (office).

WINCH, Donald Norman, BSc (Econ), PhD; British academic; *Research Professor Emeritus, University of Sussex;* b. 15 April 1935, London, England; s. of Sidney Winch and Iris Winch; m. Doreen Lidster 1983; ed Sutton Grammar School, London School of Econs, Princeton Univ.; Visiting Lecturer, Univ. of California 1959–60; Lecturer in Econs, Univ. of Edin. 1960–63; Univ. of Sussex 1963–66, Reader 1966–69, Prof. History of Econs 1969–, now Research Prof. Emer., Dean School of Social Studies 1968–74, Pro-Vice-Chancellor (Arts and Social Studies) 1986–89; Vice-Pres. British Acad. 1993–94; Visiting Fellow, School of Social Science, Inst. of Advanced Study, Princeton 1974–75, King's Coll., Cambridge 1983, History of Ideas Unit, ANU 1983, St Catharine's Coll., Cambridge 1989, All Souls Coll., Oxford 1994; Visiting Prof., Tulane Univ. 1984; Carlyle Lecturer, Univ. of Oxford 1995, Publr Sec., Royal Econ. Soc. 1971–; Review Ed. The Economic Journal 1976–83; Hon. DLit (Sussex) 2005. *Publications:* Classical Political Economy & Colonies 1965, James Mill, Selected Economic Writings 1966, Economics and Policy 1969, The Economic Advisory Council 1930–39 (with S. K. Howson) 1976, Adam Smith's Politics 1978, That Noble Science of Politics (with S. Collini and J. W. Burrow) 1983, Malthus 1987, Riches and Poverty 1996, Wealth and Life 2009. *Leisure interest:* gardening. *Address:* Arts B, University of Sussex, Brighton, East Sussex, BN1 9QN, England (office). *Telephone:* (1273) 678634 (office); (1273) 400635 (home). *E-mail:* d.winch@sussex .ac.uk (office). *Website:* www.economistpapers.org.uk (office).

WINCHESTER, Robert J., MD; American paediatrician, pathologist and academic; *Professor of Pediatrics, Pathology, and Medicine, Division of Rheumatology, Department of Medicine, Columbia University;* ed Cornell Univ.; Internship and Residency, Cornell Medical Center, New York Hosp.; currently Prof. of Pediatrics, Pathology, and Medicine, Div. of Rheumatology, Dept of Medicine, Columbia Univ.; mem. NIH Study Section: Gen. Medicine A 1980–84, AIDS-Related Research-2 1995–97; Assoc. Ed., Journal of Clinical and Experimental Immunology 1995–97; mem. American Soc. for Clinical Investigation, American Fed. for Clinical Research, Asscn of American Physicians, American Coll. of Rheumatology, American Asscn of Immunologists; Fellow, AAAS 1992; Councillor, Int. Workshop on Human Leukocyte Differentiation Antigens 1989–96, Lee C. Howley, Sr Prize for Arthritis Research, Arthritis Foundation 1990, Craoford Prize, Royal Swedish Acad. of Sciences (co-recipient) 2013. *Publications:* numerous papers in professional journals. *Address:* New York-Presbyterian Hospital/CUMC, 630 West 168th Street, P&S Building, 10th Floor, Room 10-432, New York, NY 10032, USA (office). *Telephone:* (212) 305-7226 (office). *Fax:* (212) 305-9078 (office). *E-mail:* rjw8@columbia.edu (office). *Website:* www.rheumatologyatcolumbia.org/ rwinchester.html (office); nyp.org/physician/rjwinchester (office).

WINCKLER, Georg; Austrian university rector and academic; *President, ERSTE Foundation;* b. 27 Sept. 1943, Ostrava, Czechoslovakia; m.; two d.; ed Princeton Univ., USA, Univ. of Vienna; with Austrian Inst. of Econ. Research, Vienna 1967; Univ. Asst, Dept of Econs, Univ. of Vienna 1968–75, Docent 1976–78, Prof. 1978–, Head 1980–82, Dir Centre for Int. and Interdisciplinary Studies 1994–99, mem. Senate 1997–99, Univ. Rector 1999–2011; Visiting Prof., Univ. of Graz, Université Fribourg, Switzerland 1977–78, Univ. of Linz 1985–86, Georgetown Univ., USA 1995, Comenius Univ. of Bratislava, Slovakia 1998; with Research Dept IMF 1990–91; Rector Univ. of Vienna 1999–2011; Pres. Austrian Rectors Conf. 2000–05; Vice-Pres. European Univ. Asscn 2001–05, Pres. 2005–09; Gen. Sec. Austrian Econ. Asscn 1978–85, Vice-Pres. 1985–99; apptd Lecturer, Diplomatic Acad., Vienna 1974, Bd mem. 1985–2011; mem. cadre, Pont-à-Mousson SA, France 1971–72; mem. Council of Scientists, INTAS-Int. Asscn for Promotion of Cooperation with Scientists from New Ind. States of fmr Soviet Union, EC, Brussels 1993–96, TRM Panel 1995–99; Speaker, Chair. Confs of IMF 1992–94, EFTA, Bulgaria 1994, OECD 1996, Euromoney, England, Centre for Econ. Policy Research 1997–99; mem. European Research Advisory Bd 2004–07, European Research Area Board, EC, Brussels 2008–12, People Advisory Group 2009–12; Pres. ERSTE Foundation 2011–; Vice-Chair. Supervisory Bd UNIQA AG 2009–, ERSTE Group AG. *Publications include:* as co-author or co-ed.: Handbook of Austrian Economic Policy 1982, Financial Liberalisation and Tax Harmonisation in Europe 1992, Central and Eastern Europe: Roads to Growth 1992, International Trade and Restructuring in Eastern Europe 1994, Output Decline in Eastern Europe: Unavoidable, External Influence or Homemade? 1995, Macroeconomic Policy Games 1995, Central Banks and Seigniorage: A Study of Three Economies in Transition (European Econ. Review) 1996, Grundzüge der Wirtschaftspolitik Österreichs (third edn) 2001. *Leisure interests:* mountaineering, skiing, reading. *Address:* ERSTE Stiftung Graben 21, 3rd floor, 1010 Vienna, Austria (office). *Telephone:* (43) 50100-11584 (office); (1) 328-12-72 (home). *E-mail:* georg.winckler@erstestiftung.org (office). *Website:* www.erstestiftung.org (office).

WINDLE, Alan Hardwick, PhD, FRS, FIM, FInstP; British scientist and academic; *Professor of Materials Science, University of Cambridge;* b. 20 June 1942, Croydon, Surrey, England; s. of Stuart George Windle and Myrtle Lillian Windle (née Povey); m. Janet Susan Carr 1968; one s. three d.; ed Whitgift School,

Imperial Coll. London, Trinity Coll., Cambridge; ICI Research Fellow, Imperial Coll., London 1966–67, Lecturer in Metallurgy 1967–75; Lecturer in Metallurgy and Materials Science, Univ. of Cambridge 1975–92, Fellow, Trinity Coll. 1978–, Lecturer and Dir of Studies in Natural Sciences, Trinity Coll. 1978–92, Tutor 1983–91, Prof. of Materials Science 1992–, Head of Dept of Materials Science, Univ. of Cambridge 1996–2001; Visiting Prof., N Carolina State Univ., USA 1980; Exec. Dir Cambridge-MIT Inst. 2000–03; Vice-Pres. Inst. of Materials 2001–; Dir Pfizer Inst. for Pharmaceutical Materials Science 2005–; Commr Royal Comm. for Exhbn of 1851 2001–11; mem. Indian Acad. of Science; Fellow, American Physical Soc.; Bessemer Medal, Imperial Coll. 1963, RSA Silver Medal 1963, Rosenhain Medal & Prize 1987, Swinburne Medal & Prize, Plastics and Rubber Inst. 1992, Founders' Medal and Prize, Polymer Physics Group, Inst. of Physics and Royal Soc. of Chem. 2007, Royal Soc. Armourers and Braziers Medal and Prize 2007. *Publications:* A First Course in Crystallography 1978, Liquid Crystalline Polymers (with A. M. Donald) 1992 (second edn with A. M. Donald and S. Hanna 2005). *Leisure interest:* flying light aircraft. *Address:* Department of Materials Science and Metallurgy, New Museums Site, Pembroke Street, Cambridge, CB2 3QZ, England (office). *Telephone:* (1223) 334321 (office). *Fax:* (1223) 334366 (office). *E-mail:* ahw1@cam.ac.uk (office).

WINDSOR, Colin, DPhil, FRS, FInstP; British physicist and academic; *Consultant, Culham Centre for Fusion Energy;* b. 28 June 1938, Beckenham, Kent, England; s. of George Thomas and Mabel Rayment; m. 1st Margaret Lee 1963; one s. two d.; m. 2nd Maureen Watkins 2005; ed Magdalen Coll., Oxford, Clarendon Lab., Oxford; Research Assoc., Yale Univ., USA 1963–64; scientist, UKAEA 1964–96, Programme Area Man. UKAEA Fusion 1996–98; Visiting Fellow, Japanese Asscn for the Advancement of Science, Sendai 1980; Consultant, UKAEA Fusion (now the Culham Centre for Fusion Energy) 1998–; Sr Consultant, PenOp UK 1998–2000; Hon. Prof. of Physics, Univ. of Birmingham 1990–; Duddell Medal, Inst. of Physics 1986. *Publications include:* Pulsed Neutron Scattering 1981, Four Computer Models 1983, Solid State Science, Past, Present and Predicted (ed.) 1987. *Leisure interests:* singing, playing piano and recorder, composing, cycling to work, naturism. *Address:* D3, Culham Centre for Fusion Energy, Culham Science Centre, Oxford, OX14 3DB (office); 116 New Road, East Hagbourne, Oxon., OX11 9LD, England (home). *Telephone:* (1235) 466676 (office); (1235) 812083 (home). *Fax:* (1235) 463414 (office). *E-mail:* colin.windsor@ccfe.org .uk (office). *Website:* www.ccfe.ac.uk (office); freespace.virgin.net/colin.windsor (home).

WINELAND, David Jeffrey, BS, MS, PhD; American physicist; *Professor and Group Leader, Time and Frequency Division, National Institute of Standards and Technology (NIST);* b. 24 Feb. 1944, Milwaukee, Wis.; m. Sedna Helen Quimby; two s.; ed Univ. of California, Berkeley, Harvard Univ.; Group Leader, Time and Frequency Div., Nat. Inst. of Standards and Tech. (NIST), Boulder, Colo, also NIST Fellow; Prof. Adjoint, Univ. of Colorado; mem. NAS 1992; Fellow, American Physical Soc., American Optical Soc.; Davisson-Germer Prize in Atomic or Surface Physics 1990, William F. Meggers Award, Optical Soc. of America (OSA) 1990, Einstein Prize for Laser Science, Soc. of Optical and Quantum Electronics 1996, IEEE Rabi Award 1998, Arthur L. Schawlow Prize in Laser Science 2001, OSA Ives Medal 2004, Nat. Medal of Science 2007, OSA Herbert Walther Award 2009, Benjamin Franklin Medal, Franklin Inst. (with Juan Ignacio Cirac and Peter Zoller) 2010, Nobel Prize in Physics (shared with Serge Haroche) 2012. *Address:* National Institute of Standards and Technology, 325 Broadway, Mailcode 847.10, Boulder, CO 80305-3328, USA (office). *Telephone:* (303) 497-5286 (office). *E-mail:* david.wineland@nist.gov (office). *Website:* www.nist.gov/pml/div688/index.cfm (office).

WINFREY, Oprah, BA; American broadcaster, actress and producer; *Chairman, Harpo Inc.;* b. (Orpah Gail Winfrey), 29 Jan. 1954, Kosciusko, Miss.; d. of Vernon Winfrey and Vernita Lee; ed Tennessee State Univ.; worked for WVOL radio, Nashville, Tenn. while still at school, subsequently as reporter/anchor, WTVF-TV, Nashville; joined WJZ-TV news, Baltimore, as co-anchor 1976, became co-host, People Are Talking 1978; joined WLS-TV, Chicago as host, AM Chicago, subsequently renamed The Oprah Winfrey Show 1985–2011; f. Harpo Productions Inc. 1986, Owner and Producer 1986–; Founder and Editorial Dir O, The Oprah Magazine 2000–, O at Home 2004–; f. The Oprah Winfrey Foundation; Partner, Oxygen Media 2000–; launched Oprah & Friends (XM Satellite Radio network) 2006; f. OWN: The Oprah Winfrey Network 2011; est. Leadership Acad. for Girls, S Africa 2007–; Hon. LLD (Harvard) 2013; numerous awards, including Int. Radio and TV Soc.'s Broadcaster of the Year Award 1988, 1995 Individual Achievement Award, George Foster Peabody Awards 1996, Int. Radio and TV Society's Foundation Gold Medal Award 1996, TV Guide Television Performer of the Year 1997, named by Newsweek as the Most Important Person in Books and Media 1997, Nat. Acad. of TV Arts and Sciences Lifetime Achievement Award 1998 (in 1999 Oprah removed herself from future Emmy consideration and the show followed suit in 2000), Oprah and The Oprah Winfrey Show received more than 40 Daytime Emmy Awards: seven for Outstanding Host, nine for Outstanding Talk Show, more than 20 in the Creative Arts categories, and one for Oprah's work as supervising producer of the ABC After School Special Shades of Single Protein), named by Time Magazine amongst 100 Most Influential People of the 20th Century 1998 and amongst 100 Most Influential People in the World 2004, 2005, 2006, ranked by Fortune magazine amongst the 50 Most Powerful Women in Business in the US 1998–2001, (tenth) 2002, (seventh) 2003, (sixth) 2004, (fourth) 2005, (eighth) 2006–08, (sixth) 2009–10, (16th) 2011, (50th) 2012, Nat. Book Foundation 50th Anniversary Gold Medal 1999, Broadcasting & Cable Hall of Fame 2002, Bob Hope Humanitarian Award, 54th Annual Primetime Emmy Awards 2002, named the Greatest Pop Culture Icon of All Time by VH1 2003, elected to Nat. Women's Hall of Fame, Seneca, NY, Asscn of American Publrs AAP Honors Award 2003, ranked by Forbes magazine amongst The World's 100 Most Powerful Women (62nd) 2004, (ninth) 2005, (14th) 2006, (21st) 2007, (36th) 2008, (41st) 2009, (third) 2010, (14th) 2011, (11th) 2012, (13th) 2013, Nat. Asscn of Broadcasters Distinguished Service Award 2004, UNA of the USA Global Humanitarian Action Award 2004, Int. Acad. of TV Arts and Sciences Int. Emmy Founders Award 2005, Nat. Asscn for the Advancement of Colored People Hall of Fame 2005, Nat. Civil Rights Museum Nat. Freedom Award 2005, ranked by Forbes magazine amongst The World's Most Powerful People (45th) 2009, (64th) 2010, Kennedy Center Honor 2010. *Achievements include:* helped initiate

US Nat. Child Protection Act 1991, signed by Pres. Clinton ('Oprah's Law') 1993. *Theatre:* Broadway debut as a producer of The Color Purple 2005. *Films include:* acting roles: Sofia in The Color Purple 1985, Mrs Thomas in Native Son 1986, Throw Momma From The Train 1988, Mattie Michael in The Women of Brewster Place (TV) 1989, Listen Up: The Lives of Quincy Jones 1990, LaJoe Rivers in There Are No Children Here (TV) 1993, Sethe in Beloved 1998, Coretta Scott King (voice) in Our Friend, Martin (video) 1999, Charlotte's Web (voice) 2006, Bee Movie (voice) 2007, The Butler 2013; producer and/or exec. producer of several TV films, including Nine 1992, Overexposed 1992, Beloved 1998, Their Eyes Were Watching God 2005, Legends Ball 2006. *Publications:* Oprah (autobiog.) 1993, In the Kitchen with Rosie 1996, Make the Connection (with Bob Greene) 1996. *Address:* Harpo Inc., 110 North Carpenter Street, Chicago, IL 60607, USA (office). *Telephone:* (312) 633-1000 (office). *Fax:* (312) 633-1976 (office). *Website:* www.oprah.com (home).

WINGER, Debra; American actress; b. 16 May 1955, Cleveland, Ohio; d. of Robert Winger and Ruth Winger; m. 1st Timothy Hutton 1986 (divorced); one s.; m. 2nd Arliss Howard 1996; one c.; ed California State Univ., Northridge; first professional appearance in Wonder Woman TV series 1976–77. *Films include:* Thank God It's Friday 1978, French Postcards 1979, Urban Cowboy 1980, Cannery Row 1982, An Officer and a Gentleman 1982, Terms of Endearment (Nat. Soc. of Film Critics Award for Best Actress 1983) 1983, Mike's Murder 1984, Legal Eagles 1986, Black Widow 1987, Made in Heaven 1987, Betrayed 1988, The Sheltering Sky, Everybody Wins 1990, Leap of Faith 1992, Shadowlands 1993, A Dangerous Woman (Tokyo Int. Film Festival Award for Best Actress) 1993, Forget Paris 1995, Big Bad Love (also producer) 2001, Radio 2003, Eulogy 2004, Dawn Anna (TV) 2005, Sometimes in April (TV) 2005, Rachel Getting Married 2008, Lola Versus 2012. *Television includes:* In Treatment (series) 2010. *Publication:* Undiscovered 2008. *Address:* c/o CAA, 2000 Avenue of the Stars, Los Angeles, CA 90067, USA (office).

WINGTI, Rt Hon. Paias, CMG, PC; Papua New Guinea politician; b. 2 Feb. 1951, Moika Village; five s.; ed Univ. of Papua New Guinea; MP 1977–97; apptd. Asst Speaker and mem. Public Accounts Cttee; elected Govt Whip; Minister for Transport and Civil Aviation 1978–80; Deputy Prime Minister and Minister for Nat. Planning and Devt 1982–84, for Educ. 1984–85; resgnd from Govt, co-f. People's Democratic Movt 1985; Leader of Opposition March–Nov. 1985, 1988–92, 1994; Prime Minister 1985–88, 1992–94; Gov. Western Highlands Prov. *Leisure interests:* playing golf and watching Rugby League. *Address:* People's Democratic Movement, P.O. Box 972, Boroko, Papua New Guinea. *Telephone:* 277631. *Fax:* 277611.

WINIGER, Matthias; Swiss geographer, academic and fmr university administrator; b. 1943, Berne; ed Univ. of Berne; Prof. of Geography, Univ. of Berne 1978–88; Prof. of Geography, Rheinische Friedrich-Wilhelms-Universität, Bonn 1988–, Dean, Faculty of Math. and Natural Sciences 2002–04, Rector 2004–09; mem. Acad. Science and Literature, Mainz. *Address:* Department of Geography, Rheinische Friedrich-Wilhelms-Universität, Meckenheimer Allee 166, 53115 Bonn, Germany (office). *Telephone:* (228) 73-7293 (office). *Fax:* (228) 73-7506 (office). *E-mail:* winiger@uni-bonn.de (office). *Website:* www.uni-bonn.de (office).

WINKLER, Hans Günter; German show jumper and company executive; b. 24 July 1926, Barmen; s. of Paul Winkler; m. 4th Debby Malloy 1994; mem. Exec., German Olympic Riding Cttee 1981–; winner of about 1,000 events, including over 500 int. events, up to 1964; world's most successful Olympic show jumping rider, took part in 3 Olympiads 1956–76, winning a still (2010) record haul of five gold medals, one bronze medal (Mexico City) 1968, one silver medal (Montreal) 1976; World Champion, Madrid 1954, Aachen 1955 (record of two wins he shares with Raimondo d'Inzeo); European Champion, Rotterdam 1957; Winner, King George V Cup 1965, 1968; currently Sports Dir, Riders Tour; Hon. Citizen of Warendorf; Hon. mem. Riding Clubs of Warendorf, Ludwigsburg, Herborn, Darmstadt, Bayreuth, Salzburg, Frankfurt am Main, Mitterfels, Kassel, Hünfeld, Deutsche Reiterliche Vereinigung, Aachen-Laurensberger Rennverein; Grand Cross of Honour of FRG 1974; German Rider's Cross in Gold 1950, Best Sportsman of the Decade 1950, 1960, Needle of Honour, Senate of West Berlin 1954, Sportsman of the Year 1955, 1956, Gold Band, German Sports Press Asscn 1956, Needle of Honour, Int. Riding Asscn 1964, FN Award in Gold with Olympic Rings, Laurel Wreath and Diamonds 1976, Media Prize 'Bambi' 1990, Prize of Honour of Spoga 1990, Westfälischer Friedensreiterpreis 1997, Golden Sports Pyramid for Lifetime Work in Sport 2000, Silver Horse 2002, German Rider's Cross in Gold with Brilliants 2006, FELIX of Honour LandsSportBund, North Rhine-Westphalia 2009. *Publications:* Meine Pferde und ich (My Horses and I), Pferde und Reiter in aller Welt (Horses and Riders of the World) 1956, Die Geschichte ihrer Laufbahn (A History of Her Career) 1961, Springreiten (Jumping) 1979, Die Olympiadiva, Olympiareiter in Warendorf 1981. *Leisure interests:* skiing, hunting, tennis. *Address:* Dr. Rau Allee 48, 48231 Warendorf, Germany. *Telephone:* (2581) 2361. *Fax:* (2581) 62772. *E-mail:* info@hgwinkler.de (office). *Website:* www.hgwinkler.de (office).

WINKLER, Josef; Austrian writer; b. 3 March 1953, Kamering, Kärnten; ed Handelsakademie, Klagenfurt; administrator, Univ. of Klagenfurt 1973–82, now teacher; Publisher, literary magazine Schreibarbeiten 1979; freelance writer and novelist 1982–; Writer-in-Residence, Bergen 1994–95; Anton Wildgans Prize 1980, Theodor Körner Foundation Funds literary grant 1990, Robert Musil Scholarship 1990, German Literary Fund's Kranich mit dem Stein Prize 1990, Bettina von Arnim Prize 1994, Berlin Literature Prize 1996, Otto Stoessl Prize 2000, André-Gide Prize 2000, Alfred Döblin Prize 2001, George Saiko travel grant 2004, Franz Nabl Prize 2005, Georg Büchner Preis 2008. *Publications include:* Das wilde Kärnten (trilogy): Menschenkind 1979, Der Ackermann aus Kärnten 1980, Muttersprache 1982, Die Verschleppung 1983, Der Leibeigene (trans. as The Serf) (novel) 1987, Friedhof der bitteren Orangen (novel) 1990, Das Zöglingsheft des Jean Genet (trans. as Flowers for Jean Genet) (essay) 1992, Das Wilde Kärnten 1995, Domra 1996, Wern es soweit ist 1998, Natura morta (novella) 2001, Leichnam, seine Familie belauernd 2003, Requiem für einen Vater 2004, Roppongi 2007, Ich eiss mir eine Wimper aus und stech dich damit tot 2008. *Address:* c/o Suhrkamp Verlag, Postfach 101945, 60019 Frankfurt, Germany (office). *E-mail:* geschaeftsleitung@suhrkamp.de (office). *Website:* www.suhrkamp.de (office).

WINOCK, Michel, LèsL, DèsL; French historian, academic, writer and publisher; *Professor Emeritus, Institut d'Etudes politiques;* b. 19 March 1937, Paris; s. of Gaston Winock and Jeanne Winock (née Dussaule); m. Françoise Werner 1961; two s.; ed Sorbonne; teacher, Lycée Joffre, Montpellier 1961–63, Lycée Hoche, Versailles 1963–66, Lycée Lakanal, Sceaux 1966–68; Lecturer, Sr Lecturer Univ. of Paris VIII-Vincennes à St-Denis 1968–78; Sr Lecturer, Institut d'Etudes politiques (Sciences-Po), Paris 1978–90, Prof. 1990, now Prof. Emer.; Publr Editions du Seuil, Paris 1960–; radio producer, France-Inter 1983–85; Ed.-in-Chief L'Histoire magazine 1978–81, Editorial Adviser 1981–. *Publications include:* Histoire politique de la revue esprit 1930–1950 1975, La république se meurt 1978, Les grandes crises politiques 1971–1968 1986, La Fièrе hexagonale 1986, Nationalisme, antisemitisme et fascisme en France 1990, Le socialisme en France et en Europe XIXe–XXe siècle 1992, Le siècle des intellectuels (essays) 1997, La guerre de 1914–1918 racontée aux enfants 1998, La France politique XIXe–XXe siècle 1999, Les Voix de la liberté 2001, Les écrivains engagés au XIXe siècle 2001, La France et les juifs (Prix Montaigne de Bordeaux 2005) 2004, Pierre Mendès France 2005, Victor Hugo dans l'arène politique 2005, La Gauche au pouvoir: L'héritage du Front populaire 2006, La France antijuive de 1936: L'agression de Léon Blum à la Chambre des députés 2006, L'Agonie de la IVe République 2006, La Gauche en France 2006, La Mêlée présidentielle 2007, Clemenceau 2007, Madame De Stael (Prix Goncourt de la Biographie 2010) 2010. *Leisure interest:* tennis. *Address:* Institut d'Etudes politiques, 25 Rue Gaston De Saporta, Aix En Provence, 13100 Paris, France (office). *Telephone:* 4-42-17-01-91 (office). *Fax:* 4-42-96-36-99 (office). *E-mail:* wimi@cybercable.fr; wimi@noos.fr.

WINSER, Kim, OBE; British business executive; *President and CEO, Aquascutum Limited;* b. 1959, Helensburgh, Scotland; one s.; ed Purbrook Grammar School, Hampshire; man. trainee Marks & Spencer 1977, various positions including Exec. for Menswear Buying, Div. Dir for Ladies Casualwear Group, est. Corp. Marketing Group 1999, Dir Marks & Spencer (first female in position) –2000; Chief Exec. Pringle of Scotland 2000–06; Pres. and CEO Aquascutum Ltd 2006–; Chair. Charity Events and Exec. mem. Co-operation Ireland 1996–; Hon. DLitt (Heriot-Watt) 2002. *Leisure interests:* being with her family, entertaining, sports, fashion. *Address:* Aquascutum Flagship Store, 100 Regent Street, London, W1B 5SR, England. *Telephone:* (20) 7675-9113 (office). *Website:* www.aquascutum.com (office).

WINSLET, Kate Elizabeth, CBE; British actress; b. 5 Oct. 1975, Reading, Berks.; d. of Roger Winslet and Sally Winslet; m. 1st Jim Threapleton 1998 (divorced 2001), one d.; m. 2nd Sam Mendes (q.v.) 2003 (divorced 2010); one s.; m. 3rd Ned Rocknroll 2012; one s.; ed Theatre School, Maidenhead; Grammy Award for Best Spoken Word Album for Children 2000, Film Critics' Annual Achievements Award for Best Supporting Actress 2002. *Stage appearances include:* Peter Pan, What the Butler Saw (Manchester Evening News Award for Best Supporting Actress), A Game of Soldiers, Adrian Mole. *Films include:* Heavenly Creatures (New Zealand Film and TV Award for Best Foreign Actress, London Film Critics Circle Award for Best British Actress, Empire Magazine Award for Best British Actress 1995) 1994, A Kid in King Arthur's Court 1995, Sense and Sensibility (BAFTA Award for Best Supporting Actress 1996, Screen Actors' Guild Award for Best Supporting Actress 1996, Evening Standard British Film Award for Best Actress 1997) 1995, Jude 1996, Hamlet 1996, Titanic (Variety Club of Great Britain Film Actress of the Year 1998, European Film Acad. Award for Best European Actress 1998, BAFTA Award, Empire Magazine Award for Best British Actress 1998) 1997, Hideous Kinky 1998, Holy Smoke 1998, Faeries (voice) 1999, Quills (Evening Standard British Film Award for Best Actress 2002) 2000, Enigma (Empire Magazine Award for Best British Actress 2002) 2001, A Christmas Carol: The Movie (voice) 2001, Iris (European Film Acad. Award for Best European Actress 2002) 2001, War Game 2001, The Life of David Gale 2003, Plunge: The Movie 2003, Pride (TV film, voice) 2004, Eternal Sunshine of the Spotless Mind (London Film Critics Circle Award, Empire Magazine Award for Best British Actress 2005) 2004, Finding Neverland 2004, Romance & Cigarettes 2005, All the King's Men 2006, Little Children (Desert Palm Achievement for Acting, Palm Springs Int. Film Festival 2007) 2006, The Holiday 2006, Flushed Away (voice) 2006, The Fox & the Child (voice) 2007, The Reader (Golden Globe Award for Best Supporting Actress 2009, BAFTA Award for Leading Actress 2009, Acad. Award for Best Actress 2009) 2008, Revolutionary Road (Golden Globe Award for Best Actress 2009) 2008, Carnage 2011, Contagion 2011, Movie 43 2012, Labor Day 2013, Divergent 2014. *Television includes:* Shrinks (series) 1991, Dark Season (series) 1991, Anglo Saxon Attitudes (mini-series) 1992, Get Back (series) 1992, Casualty (series) 1993, Pride (film) 2004, Mildred Pierce (mini-series) (Emmy Award for Outstanding Lead Actress in a Miniseries or Movie 2011, Golden Globe Award for Best Actress in a Mini-series or Motion Picture Made for Television 2012) 2011. *Address:* c/o Dallas Smith, United Agents, 12–26 Lexington Street, London, W1F 0LE, England (office); c/o Hylda Queally, CAA, 2000 Avenue of the Stars, Los Angeles, CA 90067, USA (office). *E-mail:* info@unitedagents.co.uk (office). *Website:* unitedagents.co.uk (office); www.caa.com (office).

WINSTON, Baron (Life Peer) cr. 1995, of Hammersmith in the London Borough of Hammersmith and Fulham; **Robert Maurice Lipson Winston,** MB, BS, DSc, FRCP, FRCOG, FRCPE, FRCPS, FMedSci, FIBiol, FRSA; British medical researcher; *Professor Emeritus of Reproductive Medicine, Imperial College London;* b. 15 July 1940, London, England; s. of the late Laurence Winston and of Ruth Winston-Fox; m. Lira Feigenbaum 1973; two s. one d.; ed St Paul's School, London and London Hosp. Medical Coll., Univ. of London; Registrar and Sr Registrar, Hammersmith Hosp. 1970–74; Wellcome Research Sr Lecturer, Inst. of Obstetrics and Gynaecology 1974–78, Sr Lecturer 1978–81, Consultant Obstetrician and Gynaecologist 1978–2005; Prof. of Gynaecology, Univ. of Texas at San Antonio, USA 1980–81; Reader in Fertility Studies, Royal Postgraduate Medical School 1982–86, Prof. 1987–97; apptd Prof. of Fertility Studies, Imperial Coll. London 1997, now Prof. Emer. of Reproductive Medicine, Devt Cttee mem., Imperial Coll. London; Dir NHS Research and Devt, Hammersmith Hosps Trust 1998–2005; Chancellor Sheffield Hallam Univ. 2001–; Visiting Prof., Univ. of Leuven, Belgium 1976–77, Mount Sinai Hosp., New York, USA 1985; mem. (Labour) House of Lords 1995–, Chair. Select Cttee of Science and Tech. 1999–2002; Chair. Royal Coll. of Music 2008–; Vice-Chair. Parl. Office of Science and Tech. 2005–; Founder-mem. British Fertility Soc.; mem. Eng and Physical Sciences Research Council 2008–, Council mem. Surrey Univ. 2008–, Scottish

Scientific Advisory Council; Trustee, Genesis (scientific research); numerous other professional appointments; Hon. Fellow, Queen Mary and Westfield Coll. 1996; Hon. FRCSE; Hon. Fellow, Royal Coll. of Physicians and Surgeons (Glasg); Hon. FIBiol; 20 hon. doctorates at British univs, including: Hon. DSc (Cranfield) 2001, (UMIST) 2001, (Oxford Brookes) 2001, (St Andrews) 2003, (Exeter) 2004, (Trinity Coll. Dublin) 2005, (Univ. of Auckland) 2008; Victor Bonney Prize, Royal Coll. of Surgeons 1991–93, Chief Rabbinate Award for Contribution to Society 1992–93, Cedric Carter Medal, Clinical Genetics Soc. 1993, Gold Medal, Royal Soc. of Health 1998, Michael Faraday Award, Royal Soc. 1999, Wellcome Award for Science in the Media 2001, Edwin Stevens Medal, Royal Soc. of Medicine 2003, Gold Medal, North of England Zoological Soc. 2004, VLV Individual Award for Best contribs to UK Broadcasting 2004, Al Hammadi Medal, Royal Coll. of Surgeons, Edin. 2005. *Director:* Each in His Own Way (Pirandello), Edinburgh Festival 1969. *Radio:* Robert Winston's Musical Analysis 2009. *Television:* Presenter, Your Life In Their Hands (BBC) 1979–87, Making Babies 1996, The Human Body 1998, The Secret Life of Twins 1999, Child of our Time (BBC) 2000, Superhuman 2000, Human Instinct 2002, 2003, Threads of Life (BBC) 2003, The Human Mind (BBC) 2004, Story of God (BBC) 2005, Child Against All Odds (BBC) 2006, Superdoctors 2008. *Publications:* Reversibility of Sterilization 1978, Tubal Infertility (jtly) 1981, Infertility: A Sympathetic Approach 1987, Getting Pregnant 1989, Making Babies 1996, The IVF Revolution 1999, Superman 2000, Human Instinct 2002, The Human Mind 2003, What Makes Me, Me? (Aventis Jr Prize, Royal Soc. 2005) 2004, Human (BMA Award for Best Popular Medicine Book) 2005, The Story of God 2005, Body 2005, A Child Against All Odds 2006, It's Elementary 2007, Evolution Revolution 2009; about 300 scientific articles on reproduction. *Leisure interests:* theatre, broadcasting, music, wine, festering. *Address:* Imperial College, Exhibition Road, London, SW7 2AZ (office); House of Lords, Westminster, London, SW1A 0PW, England. *Telephone:* (20) 7594-5959 (office); (20) 7219-6020 (House of Lords). *Fax:* (20) 8458-4980 (home). *E-mail:* r.winston@imperial.ac.uk (office); info@robertwinston.org. *Website:* www.robertwinston.org.uk.

WINTER, Sir Gregory (Greg), Kt, CBE, PhD, FRS, FMedSci; British biochemist and academic; *Master, Trinity College, Cambridge;* b. 14 April 1951; ed Trinity Coll., Cambridge; fmr Postdoctoral Researcher, Lab. of Molecular Biology, Cambridge, Deputy Dir, Lab. of Molecular Biology, MRC and Head of Div. of Protein and Nucleic Acids Chem.; Fellow, Trinity Coll., Cambridge, Master of Trinity Coll. 2012–; Co-founder Cambridge Antibody Technology 1989; Founder Domantis 2000 (acquired by GlaxoSmithKline 2006), Bicycle Therapeutics Ltd; mem. Scientific Advisory Bd, Covagen; King Faisal Int. Prize for Medicine (Molecular Immunology), William B. Coley Award, Cancer Research Inst. 1999, Royal Medal, Royal Soc. 2011. *Publications:* numerous papers in professional journals. *Address:* Trinity College, Cambridge, CB2 1TQ, England (office). *Telephone:* (1223) 338595 (office). *Fax:* (1223) 338500 (office). *E-mail:* masters .secretary@trin.cam.ac.uk (office). *Website:* www.trin.cam.ac.uk (office).

WINTER, William Forrest, BA, LLB; American lawyer and politician; *Senior Partner and Shareholder, Watkins Ludlam Winter & Stennis P.A.;* b. 21 Feb. 1923, Grenada, Miss.; s. of William A. Winter and Inez P. Winter; m. Elise Varner 1950; three d.; ed Univ. of Miss.; Miss. House of Reps. 1948–56; Miss. state tax collector 1956–64; State Treas. 1964–68; Lt-Gov. of Miss. 1972–76, Gov. 1980–84; Sr Pnr, Shareholder, Watkins, Ludlam Winter & Stennis P.A. (law firm), Jackson, Miss. 1985–; Eudora Welty Prof. of Southern Studies, Millsaps Coll. 1989; Jamie Whitten Prof. of Law, Univ. of Miss. 1989; Chair. Advisory Comm. on Intergovernmental Relations 1993–97, Ole Miss Alumni Asscn 1978, Southern Growth Policies Bd 1981, Southern Regional Educ. Bd 1982, Appalachian Regional Comm. 1983, Comm. on the Future of the South 1986, Foundation for the Mid South 1990–92, Kettering Foundation 1990–93, Nat. Comm. on the State and Local Public Service; Fellow, Miss. Bar Foundation; Fellow, Inst. of Politics, Harvard Univ. 1985; mem. American Bar Asscn, DC Bar, Miss. Bar, Hinds Co. Bar Asscn, Nat. Advisory Bd on Race Relations 1997–; Pres. Bd of Trustees Miss. Dept of Archives and History; Dr hc (Univ. of North Carolina, Tougaloo Coll.) 2004; Miss. Bar Lifetime Achievement Award 1998, Martin Luther King, Jr. Memorial Award, Nat. Educ. Asscn 2001. *Address:* Watkins Ludlam Winter & Stennis P.A., 633 North State Street, PO Box 427, Jackson, MS 39202, USA (office). *Telephone:* (601) 949-4800 (office). *Fax:* (601) 949-4804 (office). *E-mail:* wwinter@watkinsludlam .com (office). *Website:* www.watkinsludlam.com (office).

WINTERBOTTOM, Michael; British film director; b. 29 March 1961, Blackburn, Lancs.; ed Univ. of Oxford; fmr ed., Thames TV. *Films include:* Butterfly Kisses 1995, Go Now, Jude 1996, Welcome to Sarajevo 1997, I Want You 1998, Resurrection Man (exec. producer) 1998, Wonderland 1999, With or Without You 1999, The Claim 2000, 24 Hour Party People 2002, In This World (Golden Bear, Berlin Film Festival 2003) 2002, Code 46 2003, 9 Songs 2004, A Cock and Bull Story 2005, The Road to Guantánamo (Silver Bear Berlin Film Festival 2006) 2005, A Mighty Heart 2007, Genova 2008, The Shock Doctrine 2009, The Killer Inside Me 2010, The Trip 2010, Trishna 2011, 2012 Everyday 2012, The Look of Love 2013. *Television includes:* Cracker Mysteries – The Mad Woman in the Attic 1993, Family 1994, Cinema Europe: The Other Hollywood (mini-series) 1996, The Trip (series) 2010, The Trip to Italy 2014. *Address:* Independent Talent Group, Oxford House, 76 Oxford Street, London, W1D 1BS, England. s.

WINTERBOTTOM, Michael, DPhil, FBA; British classicist; b. 22 Sept. 1934, Sale, Cheshire, England; s. of Allan Winterbottom and Kathleen Mary Winterbottom (née Wallis); m. 1st Helen Spencer 1963 (divorced 1983); two s.; m. 2nd Nicolette Janet Streatfeild Bergel 1986; ed Dulwich Coll., London and Pembroke Coll. Oxford; Domus Sr Scholar, Merton Coll. Oxford 1958–59; Research Lecturer, Christ Church Oxford 1959–62; Lecturer in Latin and Greek, Univ. Coll. London 1962–67; Fellow and Tutor in Classics, Worcester Coll. Oxford 1967–92, Reader in Classical Languages 1990–92; Corpus Christi Prof. of Latin, Fellow, Corpus Christi Coll., Oxford 1993–2001, Fellow Emer. 2001–; Craven Scholar 1954; Derby Scholar 1956; Dr hc (Besançon) 1985. *Publications:* Quintilian (ed.) 1970, Ancient Literary Criticism (with D. A. Russell) 1972, Three Lives of English Saints 1972, The Elder Seneca (ed. and trans.) 1974, Tacitus, Opera Minora (co-ed. with R. M. Ogilvie) 1975, Gildas (ed. and trans.) 1978, Roman Declamation 1980, The Minor Declamations Ascribed to Quintilian (ed., with commentary) 1984, Sopatros the Rhetor (with D. C. Innes) 1988, Cicero, De Officiis (ed.) 1994, William of Malmesbury, Gesta Regum Anglorum Vol. I (co-ed. and co-trans. with R. A. B.

Mynors and R. M. Thomson) 1998, William of Malmesbury, Saints' Lives (co-ed. and co-trans. with R. M. Thomson) 2002, Quintilian, Institutio Oratoria Book 2 (co-ed. with T. Reinhardt) 2006, William of Malmesbury, Gesta Pontificum Anglorum Vol. I (ed. and trans.) 2007, William of Malmesbury, Liber super explanationem Lamentationum Ieremiae prophetae (co-ed. with R. M. Thomson) 2011, William of Malmesbury, On Lamentations (trans.) 2013. *Leisure interests:* travel, geology, walking. *Address:* 53 Thorncliffe Road, Oxford, OX2 7BA, England. *Telephone:* (1865) 513066.

WINTERFELDT, Ekkehard, Dr rer. nat; German scientist and academic; *Professor Emeritus of Organic Chemistry, University of Hanover;* b. 13 May 1932, Danzig; s. of Herbert Winterfeldt and Herta Winterfeldt; m. Marianne Heinemann 1958; one s. one d.; ed Tech. Hochschule Braunschweig, Tech. Univ. of Berlin; Asst Prof., Tech. Univ. of Berlin 1959, Assoc. Prof. 1967; Prof. and Head of Dept of Organic Chem., Univ. of Hanover 1970–, now Prof. Emer.; mem. Braunschweigische Wissenschaftliche Gesellschaft, Akad. der Wissenschaften zu Göttingen, Akad. Leopoldina, Halle, Academia Europea; Hon. mem., Gesellschaft Deutscher Chemiker 2012; Dr hc (Liège) 1991; Dozentenstipendium des Fonds der Chemischen Industrie 1969, Emil Fischer Medal (German Chem. Soc.) 1990, Adolf Windaus-Medaille, Univ. of Göttingen 1993, Richard Kuhn-Medaille (Gesellschaft Deutscher Chem.) 1995, Hans Herloff-Inhoffen-Medaille 1998. *Publications:* 175 publs in scientific journals. *Leisure interests:* music, gardening, history. *Address:* Sieversdamm 34, 30916 Isernhagen, Germany (office). *Telephone:* (511) 9735293 (office). *Fax:* (511) 7623011 (office). *E-mail:* winterfeldt@ mbox.sci.uni-hannover.de (office).

WINTERKORN, Martin, Dr rer. nat; German automotive industry executive; *Chairman, Board of Management, Volkswagen AG;* b. 24 May 1947, Leonberg; m.; two c.; ed Univ. of Stuttgart, Max-Planck-Inst. for Metal Research and Metal Physics; Special Asst in Process Eng, Robert Bosch GmbH 1977, Head, Substances and Processes Group, Bosch-Siemens-Hausgeräte GmbH 1978–81; Asst to Mem. of Bd for Quality Assurance, AUDI AG 1981–83, Head, Measuring Tech./Sampling and Test Lab. 1983–88, Dept Head, Cen. Quality Assurance 1988–90, Head, Audi Quality Assurance 1990–93, Head, Group Quality Assurance, Volkswagen AG 1993, Gen. Man. Volkswagen AG 1994–96, Head, Volkswagen Group Product Man. 1995–96, mem. Brand Bd of Man. for Tech. Devt 1996–2002, mem. Group Bd of Man. for Tech. Devt 2000–02, Chair. Bd of Man. AUDI AG 2002–06, also Chair. Bd of Dirs SEAT, also responsible for AUDI AG Tech. Devt 2003–06, mem. Bd of Man. Volkswagen AG 2002–, mem. Bd of Man. with responsibility for Group Research and Devt and Chair. Bd of Man. Volkswagen AG 2007–, Chair. Supervisory Bd Audi AG 2007–, Chair. Bd of Man. Porsche Automobil Holding SE 2009–; Hon. Prof., Budapest Univ. of Tech. and Econs 2003, Dresden Univ. of Tech. 2004, Tongji Univ., Shanghai 2007; Hon. Dr-Ing (Chemnitz Univ. of Tech.) 2011; ranked by *Forbes* magazine amongst The World's Most Powerful People (49th) 2013. *Address:* Volkswagen AG, VHH 11. Floor, PO Box 1849, 38436 Wolfsburg, Germany (office). *Telephone:* (5361) 9-86622 (office). *Fax:* (5361) 9-30411 (office). *Website:* www .volkswagenag.com (office).

WINTERS, L(eonard) Alan, CB, MA, PhD; British economist and academic; *Professor of Economics, University of Sussex;* b. 8 April 1950, London, England; s. of Geoffrey Walter Horace Winters and Christine Agnes Ive; m. 1st Margaret Elizabeth Griffin 1971; m. 2nd Zhen Kun Wang 1997; one s. two d.; ed Chingford Co. High School, Univs of Bristol and Cambridge; Jr, Research Office, Dept of Applied Econs, Univ. of Cambridge 1971–80; Lecturer in Econs, Univ. of Bristol 1980–86; economist, World Bank 1983–85, Div. Chief/Research Man. 1994–99; Prof. of Econs, Univ. of Wales at Bangor 1986–90, Univ. of Birmingham 1990–94, Univ. of Sussex 1999–; Dir World Bank Devt Research Group, Washington, DC 2004–07; Chief Economist, UK Dept for Int. Devt 2008–11; fmr adviser to OECD, UK Dept for Int. Devt, Commonwealth Secr., EC, European Parl., UNCTAD, WTO, Inter-American Devt Bank; Founder-Dir and Co. Sec. Cambridge Econometrics Ltd 1978–80; Sec., Int. Econs Study Group, Univ. of Stockholm 1979–83, Visiting Research Fellow 1987–88, 1991; Visiting Prof., Swedish Nat. Univ. of Agricultural Sciences, Uppsala 1988, Univ. of Bordeaux 1 1992, Argentine Council for Int. Relations, Buenos Aires 1993; Research Fellow, Centre for Econ. Policy Research 1985–, Co-Dir Int. Trade Programme 1987–94; Vice-Pres. British Asscn for Advancement of Science, Econs Section 1989–94, Treas. 1990–94; Econs Advisory Bd, Royal Inst. for Int. Affairs 1992–94; Exec. Cttee, Royal Econ. Soc. 1992–94; Visiting Lecturer, Finnish Doctoral Programme, Helsinki 1993; mem. Advisory Bd, Vienna Inst. for Comparative Econ. Studies 1998–2006; Sr Visiting Research Fellow, Centre for Econ. Policy, LSE 1999–2004; Research Fellow, IZA Inst. for Study of Labor 2005–; mem. European Devt Network 2000–; mem. Bd Global Devt Network 2005–07, 2009–, Chair. 2011–; mem. Steering Cttee, Cttee of Heads of Univ. Depts of Econs, Royal Econs Soc. 1988–93; mem. UGC Research Assessment Panel in Econs 1989, Council of Royal Econ. Soc. 1991–94; mem. UFC Research Assessment Panel in Economics 1992. *Publications:* Econometric Model of the British Export Sector 1981, International Economics 1984, Europe's Domestic Market 1987, Eastern Europe's International Trade 1994, Sustainable Development 1995, The Uruguay Round and the Developing Countries 1996, Trade Liberalisation and Poverty 2001, Making Sense of Globalization: A Guide to the Economic Issues 2002, Regional Integration and Development 2003, Challenges to Globalization: Analyzing the Economics 2004, Poverty and the WTO: Impacts of the Doha Development Agenda 2006, Dancing with Giants: China, India, and the Global Economy 2007, Critical Perspectives on the World Trading System: The WTO and Poverty and Inequality 2007. *Leisure interests:* walking, music, cricket. *Address:* Jubilee Building 280, University of Sussex, Falmer, Brighton, BN1 8SL, England (office). *Telephone:* (1273) 678332 (office). *E-mail:* l.a .winters@sussex.ac.uk (office). *Website:* www.sussex.ac.uk/economics (office).

WINTERS, Robert Cushing, BA, MBA; American insurance company executive; *Chairman Emeritus, Prudential Insurance Company;* b. 8 Dec. 1931, Hartford, Conn.; s. of George Warren and Hazel Keith (née Cushing) Winters; m. Patricia Ann Martini 1962; two d.; ed Yale and Boston Univs; with Prudential Insurance Co. of America 1953–, Vice-Pres., Actuary 1969–75, Sr Vice-Pres. Cen. Atlantic Home Office 1975–78, Exec. Vice-Pres., Newark 1978–84, Vice-Chair. 1984–86, Chair. and CEO 1987–94, Chair. Emer. 1995–; Fellow Soc. of Actuaries; mem. and fmr Pres. American Acad. of Actuaries; mem. Business Council, Business

Roundtable. *Address:* c/o Prudential Insurance Company, 751 Broad Street, Newark, NJ 07102, USA.

WINTERSON, Jeanette, OBE, BA (Hons) (Oxon.); British writer; b. 27 Aug. 1959, Manchester; partner Susie Orbach; ed Accrington Girls' Grammar School, St Catherine's Coll., Oxford; Hon. Fellow, Royal Acad.; John Llewellyn Rhys Memorial Book Prize 1987, American Acad. of Arts and Letters E. M. Forster Award 1989, Golden Gate Award, San Francisco Int. Film Festival 1990, Best of Young British Novelists Award 1992, Int. Fiction Award, Festival Letteratura Mantua 1999. *Play:* The Power Book (Royal Nat. Theatre, London, Théâtre de Chaillot, Paris). *Screenplay:* Great Moments in Aviation 1992. *Television:* Oranges Are Not The Only Fruit (BBC) (BAFTA Award for Best Drama 1990, FIPA d'Argent Award for screenplay, Cannes Film Festival 1991) 1990, Orlando – Art That Shook the World (BBC) 2002, South Bank Show 2004, Ingenious (BBC) 2009, My Monster and Me (BBC 2) 2012. *Publications:* fiction: Oranges Are Not The Only Fruit (Whitbread Prize for Best First Novel 1985) 1985, Boating for Beginners 1985, The Passion 1987, Sexing the Cherry 1989, Written on the Body 1992, Art and Lies 1994, Gut Symmetries 1997, The World and Other Places (short stories) 1998, The Power Book 2000, The King of Capri (juvenile) 2003, Lighthousekeeping 2004, Weight: The Myth of Atlas and Heracles 2005, Tanglewreck (juvenile novel) 2006, The Stone Gods 2007, The Battle of the Sun (juvenile novel) 2009, The Lion, The Unicorn and Me (juvenile picture book) 2009, The Daylight Gate 2012; nonfiction: Fit for the Future 1986, Art Objects (essays) 1994, Why Be Happy When You Could Be Normal? (memoir) 2011; editor and contrib.: Midsummer Nights (short stories). *Leisure interests:* opera, champagne, Paris, house building. *Address:* c/o Caroline Michel, PFD, Drury House, 34–43 Russell Street, London, WC2B 5HA, England (office). *E-mail:* cmichel@pfd.co.uk (office). *Website:* www .jeanettewinterson.com.

WINTON, Timothy John; Australian writer; b. 4 Aug. 1960, nr Perth, WA; m. Denise Winton; two s. one d.; ed Western Australian Inst. of Tech.; Australian Soc. of Authors Medal 2003. *Publications include:* An Open Swimmer (Australian Vogel Nat. Literary Award 1981) 1981, Shallows (Miles Franklin Award) 1985, Scisson and Other Stories (Western Australian Council Literary Award 1985) 1985, That Eye, The Sky 1986, Minimum of Two 1987, In the Winter Dark 1988, Jesse 1988, Lockie Leonard, Human Torpedo (Western Australian Premier's Book Award for Children's Fiction 1990, American Library Asscn Best Book for Young Adults Award 1993) 1990, The Bugalugs Bum Thief 1991, Cloudstreet (Miles Franklin Award 1991, NBC Banjo Award for Fiction 1991, West Australian Fiction Award 1991, Deo Gloria Award 1992) 1991, Lockie Leonard, Scumbuster (Wilderness Soc. Environment Award 1993) 1993, Land's Edge (with Trish Ainslie and Roger Garwood) 1993, Local Colour: Travels in the Other Australia 1994, The Riders (Commonwealth Writers Prize (South East Asia and South Pacific Region), Best Book 1994) 1994, Lockie Leonard, Legend (Family Award for Children's Literature) 1997, Blueback (Wilderness Soc. Environment Award 1998, WAYRBA Hoffman Award for Young Readers 1999) 1997, The Deep 1998, Down to Earth 1999, Dirt Music (Western Australian Premier's Book Award Premier's Prize 2001, Australian Booksellers Asscn Book of the Year Award 2002, Miles Franklin Award 2002, New South Wales Premier's Literary Award, Christina Stead Prize for Fiction 2002) 2001, The Turning (Colin Roderick Award 2004, Queensland Premier's Literary Awards, Best Fiction Book 2005, New South Wales Premier's Literary Awards, Christina Stead Prize for Fiction 2005) 2004, Breath (Age Book of the Year, Fiction 2008, Miles Franklin Literary Award 2009) 2008. *Address:* c/o Jenny Darling & Associates, PO Box 413, Toorak, Vic. 3142, Australia (office). *Telephone:* (3) 9827-3883 (office). *Fax:* (3) 9827-1270 (office). *E-mail:* timwinton@jd -associates.com.au (office). *Website:* www.jd-associates.com.au (office); breath .timwinton.com.au.

WINTOUR, Anna, OBE; British editor; *Editor-in-Chief, Vogue (US);* b. 3 Nov. 1949, London, England; d. of the late Charles Wintour and of Eleanor ('Nonie') Trego Baker; m. David Shaffer 1984 (divorced); one s. one d.; ed Queen's Coll. School, London, North London Collegiate School; Deputy Fashion Ed., Harpers & Queen 1970–76; moved to New York 1976; Jr Fashion Ed., Harper's Bazaar, New York 1976–77; Fashion and Beauty Ed., Viva magazine 1977–78; contributing ed. for fashion and style, Savvy Magazine 1980–81; Sr Ed. New York Magazine 1981–83; Creative Dir US Vogue 1983–86; returned to London 1986; Ed.-in-Chief, UK Vogue 1986–87; moved back to New York 1987; Ed. House & Garden 1987–88; Ed.-in-Chief Vogue (US) 1988–, Artistic Dir Condé Nast 2013–; Co-Chair. Metropolitan Museum of Art's Costume Inst. Gala 1995; host, VH1/Vogue Fashion Awards 1999; est. CFDA/Vogue Fashion Fund 2003; produced Fashion Rocks (music supplement to Vogue) 2006; instigated first Fashion's Night Out event 2009; Trustee, Metropolitan Museum of Art 2011; Chevalier, Légion d'honneur 2011; ranked by Forbes magazine amongst The World's 100 Most Powerful Women (56th) 2010, (69th) 2011, (51st) 2012, (41st) 2013. *Address:* Vogue, 4 Times Square, 12th Floor, New York, NY 10036, USA (office). *Telephone:* (212) 286-2810 (office). *Fax:* (212) 286-8593 (office). *Website:* www.vogue.com/magazine (office).

WINWOOD, Stephen (Steve) Lawrence; British musician and composer; b. 12 May 1948, Birmingham; s. of Lawrence Samuel Winwood and Lillian Mary Winwood (née Saunders); m. Eugenia Crafton 1987; one s. three d.; singer and musician, Spencer Davis Group 1964–67, Traffic 1967–74, Blind Faith 1969; British tours with The Rolling Stones 1965, The Who 1966, The Hollies 1967; solo artist 1974–; Dir F.S. Ltd/Wincraft Music Ltd; 14 Gold Record Awards, four Platinum Record Awards. *Recordings:* albums include: three with Spencer Davis Group 1966; with Traffic: Mr Fantasy 1968, Traffic 1968, John Barleycorn Must Die 1970, The Low Spark of High Heeled Boys 1972, When the Eagle Flies 1974; with Blind Faith: Blind Faith 1969; solo: Steve Winwood 1977, Arc of a Diver 1980, Talking Back to the Night 1982, Back in the Highlife 1986, Roll With It 1988 (Grammy Award 1989), Chronicles, Refugees of the Heart 1991, Far from Home 1994, The Finer Things 1995, Junction 7 1997, About Time 2003, Nine Lives 2008; singles: with Spencer Davis Group: Keep On Running 1966, Somebody Help Me 1966, Gimme Some Lovin' 1966, I'm a Man 1967; with Traffic: Paper Sun 1967, Hole in My Shoe 1967, solo singles: While You See A Chance 1980, Freedom Overspill 1986, Higher Love (two Grammy Awards: Record of the Year and Best Pop Vocal Performance 1987) 1986, The Finer Things 1987, Valerie 1987, Roll With It 1988, Don't You Know What the Night Can Do 1988, Holding On 1989, One and Only Man 1990, I Will Be Here 1991, Reach for the Light 1995, Spy in the

House of Love 1997; other session work includes: Lou Reed, Berlin 1973, John Martyn, Inside Out 1973, Viv Stanshall, Men Opening Umbrellas Ahead 1974, Marianne Faithfull, Broken English 1979, Talk Talk, The Colour of Spring 1986, Paul Weller, Stanley Road 1995. *Address:* Wincraft Music, Ltd, PO Box 41, Cheltenham, Glos., GL54 4WA, England (office). *E-mail:* management@ wincraftmusic.com (office). *Website:* www.stevewinwood.com.

WIRAJUDA, Nur Hassan, MA, LLM, SJD; Indonesian politician; b. 9 July 1948, Tangerang; m.; four c.; ed Univ. of Indonesia, Univ. of Oxford, UK, Tufts Univ., Harvard Univ. and Univ. of Virginia, USA; practising lawyer (legal aid) and univ. lecturer, Jakarta 1972–75; Legal Council Corp. Sec., Dockyard State Enterprise, Jakarta 1972–73; Head of Section, Secr. of the Foreign Affairs Cttee of the Nat. Council for Political and Security Stabilization, Secr. Gen., Dept of Foreign Affairs 1974–75; Third Sec., then Second Sec. for Political Affairs, Indonesian Embassy, Cairo 1977–81; Head of Section, Politics-Legal Affairs, Directorate of Int. Orgs, Dept of Foreign Affairs 1981, Dir for Int. Orgs 1993–97, Deputy Dir for Territorial Treaties, Directorate of Legal and Treaty Affairs 1998, Dir Gen. for Political Affairs 2000–01; Counsellor, later Minister Counsellor for Political Affairs, Perm. Mission in Geneva 1989–93; Amb. to Egypt (also accred to Djibouti) 1997–98; Amb. and Perm. Rep. to the UN, Geneva, WTO and the Conf. on Disarmament 1998–2000; Personal Rep. of the Pres. to the Group of Fifteen Developing Countries (G-15) 1998–2000; represented the Govt in the sovereignty case concerning Pulau Ligitan and Pulau Sipadan before Int. Court of Justice, The Hague 2000; Leading Govt Negotiator in the Dialogue on Aceh with Free Aceh Movt Reps, Switzerland 2000; Minister of Foreign Affairs 2001–09. *Address:* c/o Ministry of Foreign Affairs, Jalan Taman Pejambon 6, 10th Floor, Jakarta 10110, Indonesia (office).

WIRANTO, Gen.; Indonesian politician and army officer (retd); Minister of Defence and Security and C-in-C of Armed Forces –1999; Co-ordinating Minister for Politics and Security 1999–2000; indicted by UN for crimes against humanity in E Timor in 1999 Feb. 2003; unsuccessful presidential cand. for Partai Golongan Karya (Golkar) party 2004 elections. *Address:* c/o Partai Golongan Karya (Golkar), Jalan Anggrek Nellimurni, Jakarta 11480, Indonesia (office).

WIRTH, Iwan; Swiss gallery owner and art dealer; *Director, Galerie Hauser & Wirth;* b. 1970, Zurich; m. Manuela Hauser; bought first art work aged 13; opened first gallery aged 16; f. Galerie Hauser & Wirth, Zurich (with Ursula Hauser) 1992; est. London br., Piccadilly 2003, Hauser & Wirth, New York 2009, Hauser & Wirth, London, Savile Row 2010; Co-founder and Partner, with David Zwirner, Zwirner & Wirth Gallery, New York City 2000–09. *Publications:* numerous catalogues and monographs. *Address:* Galerie Hauser & Wirth, Limmatstrasse 270, 8005 Zurich, Switzerland (office). *Telephone:* (44) 4468050 (office). *Fax:* (44) 4468055 (office). *E-mail:* zurich@hauserwirth.com (office). *Website:* www.hauserwirth.com (office). www.zwirnerandwirth.com (office).

WIRTH, Timothy Endicott, PhD; American fmr politician and international organization executive; *President, United Nations Foundation;* b. 22 Sept. 1939, Santa Fe, NM; s. of Cecil Wirth and Virginia Maude Davis; m. Wren Winslow 1965; one s. one d.; ed Harvard Coll., Stanford Univ.; served as a Harvard 'Baby Dean' after graduation; Special Asst to Sec. Dept of Health, Educ. and Welfare 1967, Deputy Asst Sec. for Educ. 1969; Asst to Chair., Nat. Urban Coalition 1968; Vice-Pres. Great Western United Corpn, Denver 1970; Man. Arthur D. Little Inc. 1971–73; mem. 94th–99th Congresses from 2nd Dist Colo; Senator from Colorado 1987–92; Counsellor Dept of State 1993–97; Pres. UN Foundation 1998–, Better World Fund 1998–; Ford Foundation Fellow 1964–66; Pres. White House Fellows Asscn 1968–69; mem. Exec. Cttee Denver Council Foreign Relations 1974–75, Harvard Bd of Overseers; mem. Bd of Visitors, USAF Acad. 1978–; Adviser, Pres. Comm. on the 80s 1979–80; Democrat; numerous awards and hon. degrees; honoured by UNEP as a Champion of the Earth 2008. *Address:* United Nations Foundation, 1800 Massachusetts Avenue, NW, Washington, DC 20036, USA (office). *Telephone:* (202) 887-9040 (office). *Fax:* (202) 887-9021 (office). *E-mail:* kmiller@unfoundation.org (office). *Website:* www.unfoundation.org (office).

WISE, Michael John, CBE, MC, PhD, FRGS, FRSA; British professor of geography; *Professor Emeritus, London School of Economics;* b. 17 Aug. 1918, Stafford; s. of Harry Cuthbert Wise and Sarah Evelyn Wise; m. Barbara Mary Hodgetts 1942 (died 2007); one s. one d.; ed Saltley Grammar School, Birmingham and Univ. of Birmingham; served with RA and Northamptonshire Regt in Middle East and Italy 1941–46; Lecturer in Geography, Univ. of Birmingham 1946–51, LSE 1951–54, Cassel Reader in Econ. Geography 1954–58, Prof. of Geography 1958–83, now Prof. Emer., Pro-Dir LSE 1983–85, (Hon. Fellow 1988); Erskine Fellow, Univ. of Canterbury, NZ 1970; Chair. Ministry of Agric. Cttee of Inquiry into Statutory Smallholdings 1963–67; Chair. Dept of Transport Landscape Advisory Cttee 1981–90; Chair. Court of Govs, Birkbeck Coll. 1983–89, Fellow 1990–; Pres. Inst. of British Geographers 1974, Int. Geographical Union 1976–80, Geographical Asscn 1976–77; Pres. Royal Geographical Soc. 1980–82; Chair. Dudley Stamp Memorial Trust 1986–2007; mem. Univ. Grants Cttee, Hong Kong 1966–73, Social Science Research Council 1976–82; Hon. mem. Geographical Soc., USSR 1975, Paris 1984, Mexico 1984, Poland 1986, Asscn Japanese Geographers 1980, Inst. of British Geographers 1989, Geographical Asscn 1990; Hon. Fellow, Landscape Inst. 1991; Hon. DUniv (Open Univ.) 1978, Hon. DSc (Birmingham) 1982; Gill Memorial Award of Royal Geographical Soc. 1958, Founder's Medal 1977, Alexander Csoma Körös Medal of Hungarian Geographical Soc. 1980, Tokyo Geographical Soc.'s Medal 1981, Lauréat d'honneur, Int. Geographical Union 1984. *Publications include:* Birmingham and its Regional Setting (Hon. Ed.) 1950, A Pictorial Geography of the West Midlands 1958, R. O. Buchanan and Economic Geography (co-ed. with E. M. Rawstron) 1973, General Consultant, An Atlas of Earth Resources 1979, The Ordnance Survey Atlas of Great Britain 1982; numerous papers on economic and urban geography. *Leisure interests:* music, gardening. *Address:* 45 Oakleigh Avenue, Whetstone, London, N20 9JE, England. *Telephone:* (20) 8445-6057.

WISE, Phyllis, BS, PhD; American physiologist, academic and university administrator; *Chancellor, University of Illinois at Urbana-Champaign;* ed Swarthmore Coll., Univ. of Michigan; mem. Faculty, Univ. of Maryland, Baltimore 1976–93, Full Prof. of Physiology 1987–93; Prof. and Chair. Dept of Physiology, Univ. of Kentucky 1993–2001; Dean of Div. of Biological Sciences, Univ. of

California, Davis 2002–05; Vice-Pres. for Academic Affairs and Provost, Univ. of Washington 2005–07, Exec. Vice-Pres. and Provost 2007–10, 2011, Interim Pres. 2010–11; Chancellor Univ. of Illinois at Urbana-Champaign 2011–; mem. American Acad. of Arts and Sciences, Inst. of Medicine of NAS 2008; Fellow, AAAS 2008; Dr hc (Swarthmore Coll.) 2008; Ford Foundation Postdoctoral Fellowship 1972–74, NIH Research Career Devt Award 1982–87, NIH MERIT Award 1986–96, 2001–10, Nathan W. Shock Award for outstanding research in aging 1991, Presidential Speaker, Soc. of Neuroscience 1997, Burroughs-Wellcome Professorship 1997, Solomon Berson Award, American Physiological Soc. 1998, Robert W. Kleemeier Award, Gerontological Soc. of America 1999, Albert D. and Elizabeth H. Kirwan Memorial Prize 2000, FASEB Excellence in Science Award 2002, Women in Endocrinology Mentor Award 2003, Roy O. Greep Award for Excellence in Endocrine Research 2004, Women of Influence Award, Puget Sound Business Journal 2008, Asscn of Chairs of Depts of Physiology Service Award 2009, Chang-Lin Tien Award for Educational Leadership 2011. *Publications:* numerous papers in professional journals on issues concerning women's health and gender-based biology. *Address:* Office of the Chancellor, Swanlund Administration Building, 601 East John Street, Champaign, IL 61820, USA (office). *Telephone:* (217) 333-6290 (office). *E-mail:* pmwise@illinois.edu (office). *Website:* oc.illinois.edu (office).

WISE, Robert E. (Bob), BA, JD; American politician and lawyer; *President, Alliance for Excellent Education;* b. 6 Jan. 1948, Washington, DC; m. Sandy Wise; one s. one d.; ed Duke Univ., Tulane Univ. Coll. of Law; pvt. law practice, Charleston, W. Va. 1975–80; attorney legis. council for judiciary comm., W. Va. House of Dels. 1977–78; elected to W. Va. State Senate 1980–82, Congress (W. Va. Second Dist.) 1983–2001, whip-at-large 1986–2001, mem. House Transportation and Infrastructure Cttee; Gov. of W. Va. 2001–05; Pres. Alliance for Excellent Education, Washington, DC 2005–; mem. ABA, W. Va. State Bar Asscn. *Leisure interests:* keeping fit, bluegrass music. *Address:* Alliance for Excellent Education, 1201 Connecticut Avenue, NW, Suite 901, Washington, DC 20036, USA (office). *Telephone:* (202) 828-0828 (office). *Fax:* (202) 828-0821 (office). *Website:* www .all4ed.org (office).

WISEMAN, Debra (Debbie), MBE, FGSM, FTCL; British composer and conductor; b. 10 May 1963, London, England; d. of Paul Wiseman and Barbara Wiseman; m. Tony Wharmby 1987; ed Trinity Coll. of Music, Kingsway Princeton/ Morley Coll., Guildhall School of Music and Drama, London; composer and conductor of music for film and TV productions 1989–; Visiting Prof. of Film Composition, Royal Coll. of Music 1995–; mem. Performing Right Soc., BAFTA, Musicians' Union, British Acad. of Composers and Songwriters, European Film Acad.; Hon. Fellow, Trinity Coll. of Music London 2006, Guildhall School of Music and Drama 2007. *Compositions include:* Inside Looking Out 1989, Squares and Roundabouts 1989, Echoes of Istria 1989, The Guilty, Lighthouse, Female Perversions, The Dying of the Light, Shrinks (Silents to Satellite Award for Best Original TV Theme Music 1991), The Good Guys (Television and Radio Industries Club Award for TV Theme Music of the Year 1993), Tom and Viv 1994, The Project, Judge John Deed, P.O.W., Wilde Stories, The Upper Hand, The Churchills, Serious and Organised, The Second Russian Revolution, Little Napoleons, Children's Hospital, Death of Yugoslavia, Haunted 1995, Wilde 1997, The Fairy Tale of the Nightingale and the Rose 1999, The Fairy Tale of the Selfish Giant 1999, It Might be You, A Week in Politics, People's Century, What Did You Do In The War, Auntie?, The Cuban Missile Crisis, Vet's School, The Missing Postman, Tom's Midnight Garden, Absolute Truth, Warriors (Royal TV Soc. Award) 2000, My Uncle Silas 2001, Othello 2001, Oscar Wilde Fairy Stories 2002, Freeze Frame 2004, He Knew He Was Right 2004, The Andrew Marr Show, The Truth About Love 2004, Arsène Lupin 2004, Johnny and the Bomb 2005, Middletown 2005, Feather Boy: The Musical 2005, Middletown (film music) 2006, Jekyll 2007, Walter's War 2008, Stephen Fry in America 2008, The Passion 2008, Lesbian Vampire Killers 2009, The Hide 2009, Land Girls 2009, 2010, 2011, Joanna Lumley's Nile 2010, Martin Clunes: Horsepower 2010, The Promise 2011, Joanna Lumley's Greek Odyssey 2011, Fry's Planet Word 2011, Lost Christmas 2011, The Whale 2013, Father Brown 2013–14, WPC 56 2013–14, A Poet in New York 2014. *Leisure interests:* swimming, snooker. *Address:* c/o Roz Colls, Music Matters International, Crest House, 102–104 Church Road, Teddington, Middx, TW11 8PY, England (office); c/o Rich Jacobellis, First Artists Management, 4764 Park Granada, Suite 210, Calabasas, CA 91302, USA (office). *Telephone:* (20) 8979-4580 (Teddington) (office). *Fax:* (20) 8979-4590 (Teddington) (office). *E-mail:* dwiseman10@aol.com (office). *Website:* www.debbiewiseman.co.uk.

WISEMAN, Frederick, BA, LLB; American documentary filmmaker and theatre director; b. 1 Jan. 1930, Boston, Mass; ed Williams Coll., Yale Univ.; fmr law professor; turned to television documentary film making 1967; Founder and Gen. Man. Zipporah Films Inc. 1971–; mem. Bd of Dirs Int. Documentary Asscn 1986–, Theater for a New Audience (also mem. Artistic Council) 1998–; mem. Advisory Bd New York Documentary Festival 1997–; mem. Advisory Cttee Learning from Performers, Harvard Univ. 1991–, Margaret Mead Film Festival, American Museum of Natural History 1992–; mem. Festival Cttee Human Rights Watch Int. Film Festival 1994–; mem. Massachusetts Bar Asscn 1955–; Fellow, American Acad. of Arts and Letters 1991–; mem. Hon. Advisory Cttee, American Repertory Theatre, Harvard Univ. 1986–; Hon. mem. Les Amis du Cinéma du Réel Association 1987–; mem. Boston Jewish Film Festival, Hon. Cttee 1994–; Fellow, American Acad. of Arts and Letters 1991–; Chevalier, Ordre des Arts et des Lettres 1987, Commdr, Ordre des Arts et des Lettres 2000; Hon. DHumLitt (Cincinnati) 1973, (Williams Coll.) 1976, (John Jay Coll. of Criminal Justice) 1994; Hon. DFA (Lake Forest Coll.) 1991, (Princeton) 1994, (Bowdoin Coll.) 2005; Peabody Award for Significant and Meritorious Achievement 1990, Rosenberger Medal, Univ. of Chicago 1999, Yale Law Asscn Award of Merit 2002, Dan David Prize Laureate 2003, American Soc. of Cinematographers Distinguished Achievement Award 2006, George Polk Career Award 2006. *Documentary films include:* Titicut Follies 1967, High School 1968, Law and Order 1969, Hospital 1969, Basic Training 1971, Essene 1972, Juvenile Court 1973, Primate 1974, Welfare 1975, Meat 1976, Canal Zone 1977, Sinai Field Mission 1978, Manoeuvre 1979, Model 1980, Seraphita's Diary 1982, The Store 1983, Racetrack 1985, Blind 1986, Deaf 1986, Adjustment & Work 1986, Multi-Handicapped 1986, Missile 1987, Near Death 1989, Central Park 1989, Aspen 1991, Zoo 1993, High School II 1994, Ballet 1995, La Comedie Francaise 1996, Public Housing 1997, Belfast, Maine 1999, Domestic Violence 2001, La Dernière lettre 2002, Domestic Violence II 2002, The Garden 2005, State

Legislature 2007, La danse 2009, Boxing Gym 2010, Crazy Horse 2011, At Berkeley 2013. *Plays include:* as dir: The Last Letter (adaptation from the novel Life and Fate by Vasily Grossman), Hate by Joshua Goldstein, Welfare: The Opera, Oh Les Beaux Jours (Happy Days) by Samuel Beckett. *Publications:* numerous articles in journals and magazines including The Threepenny Review. *Address:* Zipporah Films, One Richdale Avenue, Unit 4, Cambridge, MA 02140, USA (office). *Telephone:* (617) 576-3603 (office). *Fax:* (617) 864-8006 (office). *E-mail:* info@ zipporah.com (office). *Website:* www.zipporah.com (office).

WISNER, Frank George, BA; American business executive and fmr diplomatist; *Vice-Chairman for External Affairs, American International Group;* b. 2 July 1938, New York; s. of Frank G. Wisner and Mary E. Knowles; m. 1st Genevieve de Virel 1969 (deceased 1974); one d.; m. 2nd Christine de Ganay 1976; one s. one d. and one step-s. one step-d.; ed Woodberry Forest School, Rugby School and Princeton Univ.; joined US Foreign Service 1961; various posts 1961–75; Special Asst to Under-Sec. for Political Affairs 1975–76; Dir Office of Southern African Affairs 1976–77; Deputy Exec. Sec. 1977–79; Amb. to Zambia 1979–82; Deputy Asst Sec. for African Affairs 1982–86; Amb. to Egypt 1986–91, to Philippines 1991–92, to India 1994–97; Under-Sec. of Defence 1993–94; currently Vice-Chair. for External Affairs, American Int. Group; mem. Bd Dirs Ethan Allen Interiors, EOG Resources; Romanian Order of Merit; Presidential Meritorious Service Awards, Dept of State Honor Awards, Repub. of Vietnam Mil. Medal of Honour, Dept of Defense Service Medal. *Leisure interests:* hunting, horseback riding, golf. *Address:* American International Group Inc., 18th Floor, 70 Pine Street, New York, NY 10270 (office); 164 East 72nd Street, Apt. 5B, New York, NY 10021, USA (home). *Telephone:* (212) 770-5262 (office); (212) 517-2028 (home). *Fax:* (212) 480-5400 (office). *E-mail:* frank.wisner@aig.com (office).

WISSMANN, Matthias; German lawyer and politician; *President, German Automotive Industry Association;* b. 15 April 1949, Ludwigsburg; s. of Paul Wissmann and Margarete Kalcker; ed Univs of Tübingen and Bonn; practised as lawyer; mem. Fed. Exec. of CDU 1975–; mem. Bundestag 1976–; Pres. European Union of Young Christian Democrats 1976–82; Minister of Research and Technology Jan.–May 1993, of Transport 1993–98; Chair. Parl. Cttee of Econ. and Tech. 1998–2001, Speaker Parl. Group for Econ. and Tech. 2001–02, Chair. Cttee of European Affairs; apptd Sr Int. Counsellor, Wilmer Cutler Pickering Hale and Dorr (law firm), Berlin 1999; currently Pres. German Automotive Industry Asscn; mem. Int. Rolls-Royce Advisory Bd; Vice-Chair. Supervisory BD Seeburger AG; Grand Order of Merit (Germany), Grand Order of Merit (Austria), Grand Cross (Chile), Chevalier de Légion d'Honneur. *Publications include:* Zukunftschancen der Jugend 1979, Einsteigen statt Aussteigen 1983, Marktwirtschaft 2000 1993, Soziale Marktwirtschaft 1998. *Leisure interests:* piano, literature, hockey, tennis, skiing, golf. *Address:* VDA, Behrenstraße 35, 10117 Berlin (office); Am Zuckerberg 79, 71640 Ludwigsburg, Germany (home). *Telephone:* (30) 897842100 (office). *Fax:* (30) 8978427100 (office). *E-mail:* prokurat@vda.de (office). *Website:* www.wilmerhale.com (office); www.vda.de (office).

WISZNIEWSKI, Andrzej, PhD, DSc; Polish electrical engineer, politician and academic; *Professor, Institute of Electrical Power Engineering, Wrocław University of Technology;* b. 15 Feb. 1935, Warsaw; s. of Tadeusz Wiszniewski and Ewa Wiszniewski (née Ciechomska); m. Ewa Lutosławska; one d.; ed Wrocław Univ. of Tech.; researcher, Wrocław Univ. of Tech. 1957, Extraordinary Prof. 1972, Ordinary Prof., Inst. of Electrical Power Eng 1990–, Rector 1990–96; at Univ. of Garyounis Benghazi, Libya 1976–79; Head of Scientific Research Cttee and mem. Council of Ministers 1997–99; Minister of Science 1999–2001; mem. Speech Communication Asscn, USA, Solidarity Trade Union 1980–, Social Movt of Solidarity Election Action 1998–2001; Distinguished mem. Int. Conf. on Large Electric Systems 2000; Hon. mem. IEE 1999; Kt's Cross, Order of Polonia Restituta 1979, Officer's Cross 2004, Commdr's Cross 2009; Grand Cross, Order of St Stanisław with Star 1998; Commdr, Order of St Sylvester 1998; Grand Cross, Order of Merit (Peru) 2001; Dr hc (Cen. Conn. State Univ., USA) 1993, (Tech. Univ. of Lvov) 1999, (Wrocław Univ. of Tech.) 2001; City of Wrocław Award 1996, Council of Rectors Award 1998. *Publications include:* Measuring Transformers 1983, Algorithms of Numeral Measurements in Electroenergetic Automatics 1990, Schutztechnik in Elektroenergiesystemen (co-author) 1994, Protective Automatics in Electroenergetics Systems 1998, How to Speak and Make Speeches Convincingly 1994, Aphorisms and Quotations: for Orators, Disputants and Banqueters 1997, Measuring and Decision Making Algorithms (co-author), Art of Writing 2003; over 130 articles on electrotechnics and electroenergetics. *Leisure interests:* contemporary literature, dog walking, skiing, mountaineering, rhetoric. *Address:* Institute of Power Engineering, Wrocław University of Technology, Wybrzeze Wyspianskiego 27, 50-370 Wrocław (office); Krasickiego 18, 51-144 Wrocław, Poland (home). *Telephone:* (71) 3203487 (office); (71) 3726477 (home); (601) 381944 (home). *Fax:* (71) 3202656 (office). *E-mail:* andrzej.wiszniewski@pwr.wroc.pl (office); awiszniewski@wr.home.pl. *Website:* www.pwr.wroc.pl (office); www.wme .pwr.wroc.pl (office).

WIT, Antoni; Polish conductor and academic; *Managing and Artistic Director, National Philharmonic Orchestra of Poland;* b. 7 Feb. 1944, Kraków; m. Zofia Cwikilewicz; ed State Higher School of Music, Kraków (conducting and composition), Jagiellonian Univ., Kraków (law), Nadia Boulanger, Paris (composition); Asst Conductor Nat. Philharmonic Orchestra of Poland, 1967–70, Man. and Artistic Dir 2002–; conductor, Poznań Nat. Philharmonic 1970–72; Artistic Dir Pomeranian Philharmonic, Bydgoszcz 1974–77; Man. and Artistic Dir, Polish Radio Symphony Orchestra and Choir, Kraków 1977–83; Dir Polish Nat. Radio Symphony Orchestra, Katowice 1983–2000; Artistic Dir Orquesta Filarmonica de Gran Canaria, Las Palmas 1987–91; Prof., Fryderyk Chopin Acad. of Music, Warsaw 1997–; has conducted LPO, RPO, BBC Symphony Orchestra, Berliner Philharmoniker, Orchestre National de Belgique, Tokyo Symphony Orchestra, Montreal Symphony Orchestra, Orquesta Nacional de España, Staatskapelle Dresden, Accad. di Santa Cecilia, Rome, Tonhalle-Orchester; numerous prizes include Second Prize, Herbert von Karajan Conducting Competition, Berlin 1971; Orpheus (Warsaw Autumn Festival Critics' Award) 1984, 1996, Diapason d'Or, Grand Prix de Disque de la Nouvelle Académie du Disque 1992, Diamond Baton Award of Polish Public Radio 1998, Cannes Classical Award, Midem Classique 2002. *Compositions include:* soundtracks: Kronika wypadków miłosnych (The

Chronicle of Love Affairs) 1986, Korczak 1990, Pan Tadeusz (Last Foray in Lithuania) 1999. *Recordings include:* more than 90 recordings for EMI-HMV, CBS, Decca, Naxos, NVS Arts, Pony Canyon, Polskie Nagrania; albums include symphonies by Tchaikovsky, Górecki, Schumann, Penderecki, Lutosławski (all), Olivier Messiaen (Turangalila Symphony) (Cannes Classical Award—Midem Classique 2002), Penderecki: Fonogrammi; Horn Concerto; Partita; The Awakening Of Jacob; Anaklasis (Grammy Award for Best Classical Compendium 2013) etc. *Address:* National Philharmonic Orchestra of Poland, The National Orchestra and Choir of Poland, ul. Jasna 5, 00-950 Warsaw, Poland (office). *Telephone:* (22) 5517102 (office). *Fax:* (22) 5517200 (office). *E-mail:* sekretariat@filharmonia.pl (home). *Website:* www.filharmonia.pl (office).

WITBOOI, Hendrik; Namibian politician; b. 7 Jan. 1934, Gibeon; m. Paulina Joseph 1973; ed Rheinisch Mission School, African Methodist Episcopalian (AME) School, Gibeon, Methodist Church School, Mariental, Wilberforce Inst., S Africa, Augustineum, Okahandja; teacher, Keetmanshoop AME Pvt. School 1955–58, Prin. 1965–67; Sec. to Samuel Witbooi 1958; Prin. State School, Gibeon 1967–77; ordained Deacon in AME Church 1974, Elder Pastor 1976, Presiding Elder for Windhoek Dist 1994–; joined South West African People's Organization (SWAPO) after collapse of Namibian Nat. Convention 1976, mem. SWAPO Del. to NY to take part in talks to draft Resolution 435 1978; elected SWAPO Sec. for Educ. and Culture on Nat. Exec. Cttee; elected Chief of Witboois while in detention; f. pvt. school and initiated community devt projects in Gibeon 1979; Acting Vice-Pres. SWAPO 1983, Vice-Pres. 1991; mem. Constituent Ass. and mem. first Parl. 1989–2004; Minister of Labour and Human Resources Devt 1990–95; Deputy Prime Minister 1995; DHumLitt hc (St Augustine's Coll., NC, USA) 1990; Dr hc (Paul Quin Univ., USA) 1990, (St Augustine Univ., USA) 1990, (Morris Brown Coll., Atlanta, Ga, USA) 1998; Women's Missionary Soc. of the AME Church Award 1990, AME Church Mission Dept Award, Orlando, Fla, USA 1990, Richard Allen Award 1992. *Address:* c/o Office of the Prime Minister, Robert Mugabe Avenue, PMB 13338, Windhoek, Namibia (office).

WITHEROW, John Moore, BA (Hons); British journalist and editor; *Editor, The Times;* b. 20 Jan. 1952, Johannesburg, S. Africa; m. Sarah Linton 1985; two s. one d.; ed Bedford School, Univ. of York, Univ. of Cardiff; voluntary service in Namibia (then SW Africa) after school; posted to Madrid for Reuters; covered Falklands War for The Times 1982; joined The Sunday Times 1984, successively Defence and Diplomatic Corresp., Focus Ed., Foreign Ed., Man. Ed. (news), Ed., The Sunday Times 1994–2012, Acting Ed. The Times Jan.–Sept. 2013, Ed. Sept. 2013–. *Publications include:* The Winter War: The Falklands (with Patrick Bishop) 1982, The Gulf War 1993. *Leisure interests:* sailing, skiing, tennis. *Address:* Office of the Editor, The Times, 3 Thomas More Square, London, E98 1TT, England (office). *Website:* www.thetimes.co.uk (office).

WITHERSPOON, Reese; American actress; b. 22 March 1976, Baton Rouge, La; d. of John Witherspoon; m. 1st Ryan Phillippe 1999 (divorced 2007); one s. one d.; m. 2nd Jim Toth 2011; ed Harpeth Hall, Nashville, Stanford Univ.; f. production co. Type A Films. *Films:* The Man in The Moon 1991, Wildflower (for TV) 1991, Solomon's Choice (for TV), Return to Lonesome Dove (TV mini-series) 1993, A Far Off Place 1993, Jack the Bear, S.F.W. 1995, Fear, Freeway 1996, (Best Actress, Catalonian Int. Film Festival, Cognac Film Festival) 1996, Twilight, Overnight Delivery, Pleasantville 1998, Cruel Intentions (Best Supporting Actress in a Drama Romance, Blockbuster Entertainment Awards) 1999, Election (Best Actress, Nat. Soc. of Film Critics) 1999, Best Laid Plans 1999, American Psycho 2000, Little Nicky 2000, The Trumpet of the Swan (voice) 2001, Legally Blonde (Best Actress, Cosmo Movie Awards, Best Comedic Performance, MTV Movie Awards) 2001, Sweet Home Alabama 2002, The Importance of Being Earnest 2002, Legally Blonde 2: Red, White & Blonde 2003, Vanity Fair 2004, Just Like Heaven 2005, Walk the Line (Best Actress Critics' Choice Awards 2006, Golden Globe Award for Best Performance by an Actress in a Musical or Comedy, Screen Actors Guild Award for Best Actress 2006, BAFTA Award for Best Actress in a Leading Role 2006, Acad. Award for Best Actress 2006) 2005, Penelope 2006, Rendition 2007, Four Christmases 2008, Monsters vs. Aliens (voice) 2009, How Do You Know 2010, This Means War 2012. *Television:* Friends, King of the Hill, Saturday Night Live. *Address:* c/o CAA, 2000 Avenue of the Stars, Los Angeles, CA 90067, USA (office).

WITKIN, Joel-Peter, BFA, MA, MFA; American art photographer; b. 13 Sept. 1939, Brooklyn, New York; s. of Max Witkin and Mary Pelligrino; m. Barbara Anne Witkin 2008; one s.; ed The Cooper Union, Columbia Univ., Univ. of New Mexico; began photography at age 11; photographer, US Army 1961–64; art photographer 1970–; Commdr des Arts et des Lettres 2000; four Nat. Endowment Awards 1980, 1981, 1986, 1992, Int. Center of Photography Award, New York City 1988, The Augustus Saint Gaudens Medal, The Cooper Union 1996, New York Times Award (for The Plague Years) 2000. *Publications:* Joel-Peter Witkin (monograph) 1984, Gods of Earth and Heaven 1994, Guggenheim Museum monograph 1995, The Bone House 1996, Joel-Peter Witkin, Disciple and Master 2000; illustrated editions of William Blake's poetry: Songs of Experience 2002, Songs of Innocence 2003, Songs of Innocence and Experience 2004–05, Bourgeoisie-in-de-Nile, 2007, The Journal of Joel-Peter Witkin 2010, Maestro Witkin, Master of Photography Collection 2010, Heaven and Hell 2012. *Address:* 1707 5 Points Road, SW, Albuquerque, NM 87105, USA (home). *Telephone:* (505) 843-6682 (office); (505) 842-6511 (home). *Fax:* (505) 842-1611 (home). *E-mail:* jwitkin1@comcast.net (home).

WITSCHEL, (Johann) Georg, PhD; German diplomatist; *Ambassador to Canada;* b. May 1954; m. Sabine Jean-Guy Dumoulin; one c.; ed Coll. in Nuremberg, Univ. of Erlangen; mil. service 1973–75; legal studies in Erlangen, barrister exam, doctoral thesis, various internships, public int. law summer schools, language courses in Geneva, Lima, Salamanca, The Hague 1975–82; Diplomatic School, Foreign Office, Bonn 1983–85; Political Advisor, Fed. Chancellor's Office, Bonn 1985–86; Public Int. Law Div., Foreign Office, Bonn 1986–89; Political Counsellor, Embassy in Tel-Aviv 1989–92, Deputy Amb. and Head of Econ. Dept, Embassy in Ljubljana, Slovenia 1992–95; Deputy Dir Sr Personnel Div., Foreign Office, Bonn 1995–98; Deputy Dir Political Dept and Legal Advisor, Perm. Mission to UN, New York 1998–2001; Dir UN Policy Div., Foreign Office, Berlin 2001–02; Fed. Govt Commr for Combating Int. Terrorism, Foreign Office, Berlin 2002–06; Asst Deputy Minister, Head of Legal Dept, Foreign Office and Legal Advisor of Fed. Govt on int. law 2006–09; Amb. to Canada 2009–; Bundesverdienstkreuz. *Publications:* various publs in fields of int. law, counter-terrorism and on econ. questions relating to Slovenia. *Address:* Embassy of Germany, 1 Waverley Street, Ottawa, ON K2P 0T8, Canada (office). *Telephone:* (613) 232-1101 (office). *Fax:* (613) 594-9330 (office). *E-mail:* germanembassyottawa@on.aibn.com (office). *Website:* (office).

WITTEN, Edward, BA, MA, PhD; American physicist and academic; *Charles Simonyi Professor, School of Natural Sciences, Institute for Advanced Study;* b. 26 Aug. 1951, Baltimore, Md; s. of Louis Witten and Lorraine Wollach Witten; m. Chiara R. Nappi 1979; one s. two d.; ed Brandeis and Princeton Univs; Postdoctoral Fellow, Harvard Univ. 1976–77, Jr Fellow, Harvard Soc. of Fellows 1977–80; Prof. of Physics, Princeton Univ. 1980–87; Prof., School of Natural Sciences, Inst. for Advanced Study, Princeton, NJ 1987–, Charles Simonyi Prof. 1997–; Visiting Prof., California Inst. of Tech. 1999–2001; mem. Bd of Dirs Americans for Peace 1992–; Foreign mem. Royal Soc. 1998; Fellow, American Acad. of Arts and Sciences 1984, American Physical Soc. 1984, NAS 1988, American Philosophical Soc. 1994, American Math. Soc. 2013; Hon. Citizen of Padua, Italy 2009; Dr hc (Brandeis Univ.) 1988, (Hebrew Univ. of Jerusalem) 1993, (Columbia Univ.) 1996, (Univ. of Southern California) 2004, (Johns Hopkins Univ.) 2005, (Harvard Univ.) 2005, (Univ. of Cambridge, UK) 2006; Hon. PhD (UNESP, São Paulo) 2011; MacArthur Fellowship 1982, Einstein Medal, Einstein Soc. of Berne, Switzerland 1985, Award for Physical and Math. Sciences, New York Acad. of Sciences 1985, Dirac Medal, Int. Center for Theoretical Physics 1985, NSF Alan T. Waterman Award 1986, Fields Medal, Int. Union of Mathematicians 1990, Madison Medal, Princeton Univ. 1992, New Jersey Pride Award 1996, Award of the Golden Plate, American Acad. of Achievement 1997, Klein Medal, Stockholm Univ. 1998, Dannie Heineman Prize 1998, Nemmers Prize in Math., Northwestern Univ. 2000, Clay Research Award 2001, Shalom Award, Americans for Peace 2002, Nat. Medal of Science 2003, Harvey Prize, Technion 2006, Poincaré Prize, Int. Asscn of Math. Physics 2006, Crafoord Prize (co-recipient) 2008, Lorentz Medal, Royal Dutch Acad. of Sciences 2010, Isaac Newton Medal, Inst. of Physics 2010, Solomon Lefschetz Medal, Math. Soc. of Mexico 2011, Fundamental Physics Prize, The Milner Foundation 2012. *Publications:* Superstring Theory, Vols 1 and 2 (with M. B. Green and J. H. Schwarz) 1987; more than 300 scientific papers. *Address:* Institute for Advanced Study, School of Natural Sciences, Einstein Drive, Princeton, NJ 08540, USA (office). *Telephone:* (609) 734-8021 (office). *E-mail:* witten@ias.edu (office). *Website:* www.sns.ias.edu/~witten (office).

WITTY, Sir Andrew, Kt, BA (Econ); British business executive; *CEO, GlaxoSmithKline plc;* m.; two c.; ed Univ. of Nottingham; joined Glaxo UK 1985, held various positions in UK, including Dir of Pharmacy and Distribution, Int. Product Man. and a variety of other sales and marketing positions, later served as Man. Dir Glaxo South Africa and Area Dir for South and East Africa, then Vice-Pres. and Gen. Man. Marketing for Glaxo Wellcome Inc. (US subsidiary), Sr Vice-Pres., Asia Pacific, based in Singapore –2003, Pres. Pharmaceuticals Europe, GlaxoSmithKline 2003–08, mem. Corp. Exec. Team, CEO Designate 2007–08, CEO 2008–; served as Econ. Advisor to Gov. of Guangzhou, People's Repub. of China 2000–02; mem. Singapore Econ. Devt Bd 2000–02, Econ. Devt Bd Audit Cttee 2000–02, Singapore Land Authority Bd 2000–02; Pres. European Fed. of Pharmaceutical Industries and Asscns 2010–; Chancellor Univ. of Nottingham 2013–; mem. INSEAD UK Council, Interim Bd of Office for Strategic Coordination of Health Research, Imperial Coll. Commercialisation Advisory Bd, London Council for the Advancement of Science and Tech.; mem. Pharma Futures Working Group, Health Innovation Council (UK); Lead Non-Exec. Bd mem. Dept of Business, Innovation and Skills 2011–; Bd mem. INSEAD Business School 2011–; mem. Prime Minister's Business Advisory Group; Public Service Medal, Govt of Singapore 2003, Public Service Star 2012. *Leisure interests:* tennis, running, watching rugby and cricket. *Address:* GlaxoSmithKline plc, 980 Great West Road, Brentford, London, TW8 9GS, England (office). *Telephone:* (20) 8047-5000 (office); (20) 8990-9000 (office). *Fax:* (20) 8990-4321 (office). *E-mail:* info@gsk .com (office). *Website:* www.gsk.com (office).

WŁOSOWICZ, Zbigniew; Polish lawyer, diplomatist and UN official; b. 1955; ed Jagiellonian Univ.; First Sec., Perm. Del. of Poland to UN 1990–91, Deputy Rep 1991–93, Rep. to UN Security Council 1996–97; Special Adviser on Inter-Governmental Affairs, UNDP 1998–2000; UN Special Rep. of the Sec.-Gen. in Cyprus and Chief of Mission, UNFICYP 2000–05; Dean, Faculty of Int. Relations, School of Business Admin., Bielsko-Biala 2006–07, lecturer 2009–10; lecturer, Higher School of European Studies, Krakow 2008–; Sec. of State for Int. Affairs, Ministry of Defence 2010–12. *Address:* c/o Ministry of Foreign Affairs, 00-580 Warsaw, Al. Szucha 23, Poland.

WOELKI, HE Cardinal Rainer Maria, DTheol; German ecclesiastic; *Archbishop of Berlin;* b. 18 Aug. 1956, Köln-Mühlheim; ed Theological Faculties, Univs of Bonn and Freiburg im Breisgau, Pontifical Univ. of the Holy Cross, Rome; ordained priest, Archdiocese of Cologne 1985; Asst Priest, St Mary's Parish, Neuss 1985–89; mil. chaplain in Münster 1989; Pvt. Sec. to Archbishop of Cologne 1990–97; Dir Collegium Albertinum (residence for major seminarians of the archdiocese studying at Univ. of Bonn) 1997–2011; rank of Chaplain of His Holiness, with title of Mgr 1999; apptd Auxiliary Bishop of Cologne and Titular Bishop of Scampa 2003; Archbishop of Berlin 2011–; cr. Cardinal (Cardinal-Priest of San Giovanni Maria Vianney) 2012; participated in Papal Conclave 2013; mem. Comm. for Vocations and Ministries of the Church and for Science and Culture, German Bishops' Conf.; Consultor of the Holy See's Congregation for Catholic Educ. *Address:* Archdiocese of Berlin, Postfach 040406, 10062 Berlin (office); Archdiocese of Berlin, Niederwallstr. 8–9, 10117 Berlin, Germany (office). *E-mail:* sekretariat.erzbischof@erzbistumberlin.de (office). *Website:* www.erzbistumberlin .de (office).

WOERTH, Éric; French business executive and politician; *Mayor of Chantilly;* b. 29 Jan. 1956, Creil; m.; two c.; ed HEC School of Man., Paris; legal and tax adviser, Arthur Andersen Int. 1981–82; Head of Internal Audit and Asst Head of Service Operations and Financial Negotiations, Pechiney (aluminium producing co.) 1982–90; Dir, then Pnr Bossard Consultants 1990–97; Assoc. Dir Arthur Andersen 1997–2002; mem. Regional Council, Picardy 1986–2002, Vice-Pres. 1992–98; Mayor of Chantilly 1995–2004, 2005–, Deputy Mayor 2004–05; Adviser, Cabinet of the Prime Minister 1995–97; mem. Union pour un Mouvement Populaire (UMP),

Treas. 2002–10; Deputy for Oise, Nat. Ass. 2002–04, 2005–07; Treas., Jacques Chirac's presidential campaign 2002; Sec. of State for Reforms 2004–05; Minister of Budget, Public Accounts and Civil Service 2007–10, of Labour, Solidarity and the Civil Service March–Nov. 2010; mem. Finance Comm., Nat. Ass. 2005–07. *Address:* Conseil Municipal, 60500 Chantilly, France (office). *Telephone:* 3-44-62-42-00 (office). *E-mail:* eric.woerth@wanadoo.fr (home). *Website:* www.blog-ewoerth .com.

WOERTZ, Patricia (Pat) A., BA, CPA; American business executive; *Chairman, President and CEO, Archer Daniels Midland Company;* b. 17 March 1953, Pittsburgh, Pa; m.; three c.; ed Pennsylvania State Univ. and Columbia Univ.; joined Ernst & Young, Pittsburgh as a certified public accountant 1974; positions in refining and marketing, strategic planning and finance with Gulf Oil Corpn, Pittsburgh 1977–81, head of US upstream audit group, Houston, Tex. 1981–85, worked on asset divestitures during merger of Gulf and Chevron 1985–87, Finance Man. Chevron Information Tech. Co. 1989–91, Strategic Planning Man. Chevron Corpn 1991–93, Pres. Chevron Canada Ltd, Vancouver, BC 1993–96, Pres. Chevron Int. Oil Co. and Vice-Pres. Logistics and Trading for Chevron Products Co. 1996–98, Pres. Chevron Products Co. and Vice-Pres. Chevron Corpn 1998–2001, Exec. Vice-Pres. Global Downstream, ChevronTexaco Corpn 2001–06; Pres., CEO and mem. Bd of Dirs Archer Daniels Midland Co. (ADM) 2006–, Chair. 2007–; apptd to the President's Export Council by Pres. Obama 2010–; mem. Bd of Dirs Procter & Gamble Co., US-China Business Council, American Petroleum Inst., Bd of Visitors Pennsylvania State Univ.; Vice-Chair. Kennedy Center Corp. Fund; mem. Nat. Petroleum Council, Int. Business Council of the World Econ. Forum, US Chamber of Commerce, The Business Council, Business Roundtable; Trustee, Univ. of San Diego; mem. Bd of Visitors Pennsylvania State Univ.; ranked by Fortune magazine amongst the 50 Most Powerful Women in Business in the US (eighth) 2002, (ninth) 2003–04, (sixth) 2005, (fourth) 2006, (sixth) 2007, (third) 2008–11, (sixth) 2012, named Distinguished Alumna by Pennsylvania State Univ. 2005, ranked by Forbes magazine amongst The World's 100 Most Powerful Women (seventh) 2006, (eighth) 2007, (12th) 2008, (26th) 2009–10, (45th) 2011, (97th) 2012, (71st) 2013. *Address:* Archer Daniels Midland Company, 4666 Faries Parkway, Decatur, IL 62526, USA (office). *Telephone:* (217) 424-5200 (office). *Fax:* (217) 424-6196 (office). *E-mail:* media@adm .com (office). *Website:* www.adm.com (office).

WOESSNER, Mark Matthias, DrIng; German business executive; b. 14 Oct. 1938, Berlin; m.; two c.; ed Tech. Univ., Karlsruhe; Man. Asst Bertelsmann AG 1968–70; Production Man. Mohndruck Printing Co. 1970–72, Tech. Dir 1972–74, Man. Dir 1974–76; mem. Exec. Bd Bertelsmann AG, Pres. Printing and Mfg Div. 1976–83, Pres. and CEO 1983–98, Chair. Supervisory Bd 1998–2000; Deputy Chair. Exec. Bd Bertelsmann Foundation 1996–98, Chair. Exec. Bd 1998–2000; Chair. Supervisory Bd, Heidelberger Druckmaschinen AG, eCircle AG; Deputy Chair. Supervisory Bd, Loewe AG; mem. Supervisory Bd DaimlerChrysler AG, Dussmann AG & Co. KGaA, Douglas Holding AG; mem. Bd of Trustees, Univ. of Munich; Hon. Senator, Univ. of St Gallen, Univ. of Witten/Herdecke; Hon. Prof. of Business Admin, Univ. of Munich 2005–. *Leisure interest:* sport. *Address:* c/o Bertelsmann Stiftung, Carl-Bertelsmann-Strasse 256, 33311 Gütersloh, Germany.

WOESTE, Albrecht, Dipl-Ing; German business executive; b. 1935; ed Berlin Tech. Univ.; f. Woeste GmbH & Co. KG 1963, Man. Dir and Chair. Advisory Bd; mem. Supervisory Bd Henkel KGaA 1988–2009, Chair. Supervisory Bd and Shareholders' Cttee 1990–2009; mem. Bd of Dirs Ecolab Inc. 1991–2001; mem. Supervisory Bd Allianz Lebensversicherungs-AG, Deutsche Bank AG 1993–2006; mem. Advisory Bd IKB Deutsche Industriebank AG; mem. Int. Advisory Bd IESE Business School, Univ. of Navarra. *Address:* c/oHenkel AG & Co. KGaA, Henkelstrasse 67, Düsseldorf 40191, Germany. *Telephone:* (211) 797-0. *Fax:* (211) 7982484. *E-mail:* info@henkel.com. *Website:* www.henkel.com.

WOFFORD, Harris Llewellyn, LLB; American writer, attorney and fmr politician; b. 9 April 1926, New York, NY; s. of Harris L. Wofford and Estelle Gardner; m. Emmy Lou Clare Lindgren 1948 (died 1996); two s. one d.; ed Univ. of Chicago and Yale and Howard Univ. Law Schools; admitted to DC Bar 1954, US Supreme Court Bar 1958, Pennsylvania Bar 1978; Asst to Chester Bowles 1953–54; law assoc., Covington & Burling, Washington, DC 1954–58; legal asst to Rev. T. Hesburgh, Comm. on Civil Rights 1958–59; Assoc. Prof., Notre Dame Law School 1959–60, on leave 1961–66; Special Asst to Pres. John F. Kennedy 1961–62; Special Rep. for Africa, Dir Ethiopian Program, US Peace Corps 1962–64; Assoc. Dir Peace Corps, Washington, DC 1964–66; Pres. Coll. at Old Westbury, State Univ. of NY 1966–70, Bryn Mawr (Pa) Coll. 1970–78; Counsel, Schnader, Harrison, Segal and Lewis, Philadelphia and Washington 1979–86; Sec. Labor and Industry, Commonwealth of Pa 1987–91; Senator from Pennsylvania 1991–95; CEO Corpn for Nat. Service 1995–2001; Chair. America's Promise: The Alliance for Youth (now America's Promise Alliance) from 2002; mem. Bd of Dirs Youth Service America, Points of Light Foundation; mem. Council on Foreign Relations; mem. Bd Center for Citizen Leadership, Malaria No More, Bd of Selectors, Jefferson Awards for Public Service; nat. spokesperson for Experience Wave 2007–; Sr Fellow, Case Foundation, Washington, DC; Democrat; John W. Gardner Leadership Award 2002, Nat. Leadership Award, Nat. Center for Leadership 2003, Harris Wofford Global Citizen Award est. by the Nat. Peace Corps Asscn in his honour 2011, Presidential Citizen's Medal 2012. *Publications include:* It's Up to Us 1946, India Afire (with Clare Wofford) 1951, Of Kennedys and Kings 1980. *Address:* c/o America's Promise Alliance, 1110 Vermont Avenue NW, Suite 900, Washington, DC 20005; 955 26th Street NW, Apartment 501, Washington, DC 20037, USA. *E-mail:* info@americaspromise.org.

WOGAN, Gerald Norman, BS, MS, PhD; American chemist and academic; *Professor Emeritus of Chemistry and Underwood-Prescott Professor Emeritus of Toxicology, Massachusetts Institute of Technology;* b. 11 Jan. 1930, Altoona, Pa; s. of Thomas B. Wogan and Florence E. (Corl) Wogan; m. Henrietta E. Hoenicke 1957; one s. one d.; ed Juniata Coll., Pa and Univ. of Illinois, Urbana; Teaching Asst in Mammalian Physiology, Univ. of Illinois 1953–54, Teaching Asst in Anatomy 1954–55, Dept Fellow in Metabolic Physiology 1955–56, Instructor in Physiology 1956–57; Asst Prof. of Physiology, Rutgers Univ., NJ 1957–61; Research Assoc. in Food Toxicology, MIT 1961–62, Asst Prof. of Food Toxicology 1962–65, Assoc. Prof. of Food Toxicology 1965–69, Prof. of Toxicology 1969–2001,

Dir Environmental Health Sciences Center 1978–96, Underwood-Prescott Prof. and Head, Dept of Applied Biological Sciences 1979–88, Prof. of Chem. 1988–2001, Underwood-Prescott Prof. and Dir Div. of Toxicology, Whitaker Coll. of Health Sciences and Tech. 1988–96, Prof. of Toxicology and Prof. of Chem. 1996–2001, Prof. Emer. of Chem. 2001–, Underwood-Prescott Prof. Emer. of Toxicology 2001–; Scientific Advisor, Lab. of Human Carcinogenesis, Nat. Cancer Inst., NIH 1999–, Sr Research Fellow 2001–; Scholar-in-Residence, Fogarty Int. Center 1997–99; Visiting Prof. of Environmental Health Sciences, Johns Hopkins University 1997–; Visiting Prof., Distinguished Visitor Program, Nat. Univ. of Singapore 1999; consultant to nat. and int. govt agencies and industries; Section Ed. Journal of Environmental Pathology, Toxicology and Oncology 1992–; mem. Editorial Bd Journal of the American College of Toxicology 1987–, Methods in Toxicology 1994–; mem. Editorial Acad. International Journal of Molecular Medicine 1997–; mem. NAS 1977, Inst. of Medicine 1994, American Asscn for Cancer Research, ACS, Soc. for Free Radicals in Biology and Medicine, The Nitric Oxide Soc., Environmental Mutagen Soc., American Soc. for Preventive Oncology, Soc. of Toxicology, American Coll. of Toxicology, American Soc. for Microbiology, American Soc. of Pharmacology and Experimental Therapeutics, American Soc. for Nutrition Sciences, AAAS; Fellow, American Acad. of Microbiology 1992; Lecturer, Japan Foundation for the Promotion of Cancer Research 1988, Distinguished Alumnus Award, Univ. of Illinois 1995, Distinguished Lectureship, Republic of Singapore Cancer Society 1991, Harvard School of Public Health 1996, Founders' Award, Chemical Industry Institute of Toxicology 1999, George H. Scott Memorial Award, Toxicology Forum 2003, Award of Merit, Princess Takamatsu Cancer Research Fund (Japan) 2001. *Publications:* articles and reviews in professional journals. *Address:* Room 26-009, Biological Engineering Division, Massachusetts Institute of Technology, 77 Massachusetts Avenue, Cambridge, MA 02139, USA (office). *Telephone:* (617) 253-3188 (office). *Fax:* (617) 258-9733 (office). *E-mail:* wogan@mit .edu (office). *Website:* web.mit.edu/be/people/wogan.shtml (office); web.mit.edu/ gnwlab (office).

WOGAN, Sir Michael Terence (Terry), Kt, KBE, DL; Irish broadcaster; b. 3 Aug. 1938; s. of the late Michael Thomas Wogan and Rose Wogan; m. Helen Joyce 1965; two s. one d.; ed Crescent Coll., Limerick, Belvedere Coll., Dublin; announcer Radio Telefís Eireann (RTE) 1963, Sr Announcer 1964–66; various programmes for BBC Radio 1965–67, 1970–83, 1993–, BBC TV, ITV, Channel 5, UKTV Gold 1972–; now freelance; weekly columnist (Wogan's World), Sunday Telegraph 2005–; Freeman of the Cities of London and Limerick; DL of Buckinghamshire; Hon. DLitt (Limerick) 2004, Hon. LLD (Leicester) 2010, Dr hc (Buckinghamshire New Univ.) 2012; Pye Radio Award 1980, Radio Industries Award (Radio Personality three times, TV Personality 1982, 1984, 1985, 1987), TV Times TV Personality of the Year (10 times), Daily Express Award (twice), Carl Alan Award (three times), Variety Club of GB: Special Award 1982, Showbusiness Personality 1984, Radio Personality of Last 21 Years, Daily Mail Nat. Radio Awards 1988, Sony Radio Award, Barcelona Olympics 1993, Best Breakfast Show 1994, Sony Awards 2001, 2002, Best Broadcast Music Show 2002, Sony Gold Achievement Award 2006. *Radio programmes include:* Late Night Extra BBC Radio 1967–69; The Terry Wogan Show, BBC Radio One 1969–73, BBC Radio Two 1973–84, 1993, Wake Up to Wogan, BBC Radio Two 1995–2009, Weekend Wogan 2009–. *Television shows include:* Lunchtime with Wogan, ATV; BBC: Come Dancing, Song for Europe, The Eurovision Song Contest 1983–2008, Children in Need, Wogan's Guide to the BBC, Blankety Blank, Wogan, Terry Wogan's Friday Night, Do The Right Thing 1994–95, Auntie's Bloomers, Wogan's Web, Points of View 2000–01, 2003–, Proms in the Park 1997–, Wogan on Wodehouse 2011, Wogan's Ireland 2011; Channel 5: Terry and Gaby Show 2003–04; UKTV Gold: Wogan Now and Then 2006–. *Publications:* Banjaxed 1979, The Day Job 1981, To Horse, To Horse 1982, Wogan on Wogan 1987, Wogan's Ireland 1988, Bumper Book of Togs 1995, Is It Me? (autobiog.) 2000, Musn't Grumble (autobiog.) 2006, Wogan's Year 2007, Where Was I?! The World According to Terry Wogan 2009, Wogan's Ireland 2011. *Leisure interests:* tennis, golf, swimming, reading, writing, watching rugby. *Address:* c/o Jo Gurnett Personal Management Ltd, 12 Newburgh Street, London, W1F 7RP, England (office). *Telephone:* (20) 7440-1850 (office). *Fax:* (20) 7287-9642 (office). *E-mail:* info@jgpm.co.uk (office). *Website:* www.jgpm.co.uk (office).

WOICKE, Peter L.; German banker and international finance official; *Member, Supervisory Board, Raiffeisen International Bank-Holding AG;* with J. P. Morgan for over 30 years, in particular in Latin America and the Middle East, Head Banking Div., Beirut, Lebanon, Man. Global Gas and Petroleum Group, fmr mem. Exec. Man. Group, Chair. J.P. Morgan Securities Asia, Singapore; Man. Dir Pvt. Sector Operations, IBRD (World Bank) 1999–2005, Exec. Vice-Pres. IFC 1999–2005; mem. Supervisory Bd Raiffeisen International Bank-Holding AG (Raiffeisen International, subsidiary of RZB Group) 2005–, ProCredit Holding 2005–, Anglo American (to begin 2006); Diageo Africa Business Reporting Award 2005. *Address:* Raiffeisen International Bank-Holding AG, Am Stadtpark 9, Vienna, 1030, Austria (office). *Telephone:* (1) 71707-0 (office). *E-mail:* peter .woicke@ri.co.at (office). *Website:* www.ri.co.at (office).

WOJCICKI, Susan D., AB, MA, MBA; American business executive; *Senior Vice-President of Advertising, Google Inc.;* b. 5 July 1968, Santa Clara Co., Calif.; d. of Prof. Stanley Wojcicki and Esther Wojcicki; m. Dennis Troper; four c.; ed Harvard Univ., Univ. of California, Santa Cruz, Univ. of California, Los Angeles Anderson School of Man.; worked at Intel; man. consultant at Bain & Co. and R.B. Webber & Co.; joined Google as co.'s first marketing man. 1999, worked on initial marketing programmes and branding and then the syndication of Google search to partners, also led initial development of Google Images, Google Books and Google Video, currently Sr Vice-Pres. of Advertising, Google Inc.; ranked by Fortune magazine amongst the 50 Most Powerful Women in Business in the US (43rd) 2010, (28th) 2011, (18th) 2012, ranked by Forbes magazine amongst The World's 100 Most Powerful Women (16th) 2011, (25th) 2012, (30th) 2013. *Address:* Google Inc., 1600 Amphitheatre Parkway, Mountain View, CA 94043, USA (office). *Telephone:* (650) 253-0000 (office). *Fax:* (650) 253-0001 (office). *Website:* www.google.com (office).

WOJTYŁA, Andrzej Franciszek; Polish politician and paediatrician; b. 1 May 1955, Kalisz; s. Franciszek Wojtyła and Stanisława Wojtyła; m. Ewa Wojtyła; one s. one d.; ed Medical Acad., Poznań, George Washington, Georgetown and La Salle Univs, USA; paediatrician, Children's Ward Municipal Hosp., Pleszew 1980–89; Head, Village Health Service Centre, Jastrzębniki 1985–92; Visiting Researcher,

George Washington Univ., USA 1995, Visiting Prof., Center for Health Policy and Research 1995–96; mem. Solidarity Trade Union 1980–89, Solidarity of Individual Farmers Trade Union 1989–91; Councillor of Commune of Blizanów 1990; mem. Polish Peasant Party Solidarity (PSL Solidarność) 1990–92, Peasant Christian Party (SLCh) 1992–97; Pres. SLCh Voivodship Bd, Kalisz, mem. SLCh Nat. Political Council; mem. Conservative Peasant Party (SKL) 1997–; Deputy to Sejm (Parl.) 1991–93, 1997–2005, Vice-Chair. Parl. Health Cttee; mem. Parl. Constitutional Responsibility Cttee 1991–93; Minister of Health and Social Welfare 1992–93, Sec. of State, Ministry of Health 2005–06; Chief Sanitary Insp. 2006–10; Dir Inst. of Rural Health, Lublin from 2010; fmr Sec. Gen. World Org. of Rural Medicine; fmr mem. Scientific Cttee, International Journal of Rural Health; Gold Cross of Merit 2010. *Publication:* Third International Conference: Health Education for Children, International Conference: Health Care Reform in Poland 1995. *Leisure interests:* fitness, walking, history, health care reforms in the world. *Address:* c/o Instytut Medycyny Wsi im. Witolda Chodzki (Institute of Rural Health), Jaczewskiego 2, 20-090 Lublin, Poland. *E-mail:* imw@galen.imw.lublin.pl (home).

WOLDE-GIORGIS, Girma; Ethiopian fmr head of state; b. Dec. 1925, Addis Ababa; m.; five c.; ed School of Social Science, Netherlands, Air Traffic Man. School, Sweden, Air Traffic Control Man. School, Canada; served in Ethiopian Army, rank of Lt 1941–45; trainee, Ethiopian Air Force 1946–47; Instructor in Air Navigation and Air Traffic Control 1948–54; Head Civil Aviation Authority, Eritrean Fed. State, Asmara 1955–57; Dir-Gen. Ethiopian Civil Aviation, mem. Bd Ethiopian Airlines 1958; Dir-Gen. Ministry of Commerce, Industry and Planning 1959–60; elected mem. Parl., Pres. 1st Session 1961; Vice-Pres. 52nd Int. Parl. Ass., Belgrade 1961; mem. Bd Ethiopian Chamber of Commerce 1967, Civil Advisory Council 1973; Vice-Commr to Peace Comm. 1974; Rep. of Ministry of Transport and Communications to Northern Region of Eritrea and Tigrai 1974; mem. Int. Cttee of the Red Cross, Head of Logistics to Demobilize ex-Army Personnel 1990; mem. House of People's Reps Econ. Cttee 2000–01; Pres. of Ethiopia 2001–13; Medal of Genet, Mil. Officers' Acad. 1944, Haile Selassie Star, Cavalry 1956, Minilik Star, Cavalry 1960, Haile Selassie Gold Medal 1960, City Council Gold Medal 1971, Red Cross Silver Medal 1988. *Publication:* Air and Men (in Amharic) 1954. *Leisure interests:* farming, afforestation. *Address:* c/o Office of the President, PO Box 1362, Addis Ababa, Ethiopia.

WOLF, (Richard Anthony) Dick; American television producer; b. 20 Dec. 1946, New York, NY; s. of George Wolf and Marie G. Wolf (née Gaffney); m. 1st Susan Scranton 1970 (divorced 1981); m. 2nd Christine Marburg 1983 (divorced 2005); three c.; m. 3rd Noelle Lippman 2006; ed Saint David's School, New York, Phillips Acad., The Gunnery, Univ. of Pennsylvania; worked as advertising copywriter at Benton & Bowles; moved to Los Angeles and had three screenplays produced, including Masquerade 1988; began TV career as staff writer on Hill Street Blues; moved over to Miami Vice as supervising producer; f. Wolf Films (production co.); creator and producer of Law & Order series which equalled Gunsmoke as the longest-running dramatic show in TV history 1990–2010; several awards, including an Emmy Award. *Television includes:* exec. producer: Skateboard (producer, as Richard A. Wolf) 1978, No Man's Land (producer) 1987, Masquerade 1988, Miami Vice (series) (co-producer) 1986–87, (co-exec. producer) 1987–88, (exec. producer) 1989, The Last Plane from Coramaya (video) (producer) 1989, Gideon Oliver (series) 1989, Christine Cromwell (series) 1989, H.E.L.P. (series) 1990, Law & Order (series) 1990–2010, Mann & Machine (series) 1992, The Human Factor (series) 1992, Crime & Punishment (series) 1993, South Beach (series) 1993, New York Undercover (series) 1994–99, The Wright Verdicts (series) 1995, Swift Justice (series) 1996, Feds (series) 1997, Players (series) 1997, The Invisible Man (film) 1998, Exiled (film) 1998, Law & Order: Special Victims Unit (series) 1999–2012, D.C. (series) 2000, Arrest & Trial (series documentary) 2000, Deadline (series) 2000–01, Law & Order: Criminal Intent (series) 2001–11, Crime & Punishment (series documentary) 2002, Twin Towers (short) (producer) (Academy Award for Best Short Documentary) 2003, Dragnet (series) 2003–04, Law & Order: Trial by Jury (series) 2005–06, Conviction (series) 2006, Bury My Heart at Wounded Knee (film) 2007, Lost & Found (film) 2009, American Masters (series documentary) (producer) 2009, Home Is Where You Find It (documentary short) (producer) 2009, Law & Order: Los Angeles (series) 2010–11, Law & Order: UK (series) (exec. producer, Wolf Films) 2009–11, (exec. producer) 2010, Stars Earn Stripes (series) 2012, Chicago Fire (series) 2012. *Address:* Wolf Films, 100 Universal City Plaza Bldg, 2252, Universal City, CA 91608-1085, USA (office).

WOLF, Günter, PhD; German particle physicist and academic; *Senior Researcher, Deutsches Elektronen-Synchrotron (DESY);* b. 23 Nov. 1937, Ulm/ Donau; ed Univs of Tübingen and Hamburg; worked at Stanford Linear Accelerator Center (SLAC), Stanford Univ., Calif., USA 1960s; co-spokesman for DASP experiment at Electron-Positron Storage Ring DORIS, Deutsches Elektronen-Synchrotron (DESY), Hamburg; spokesman for TASSO experiment at Electron-Positron Storage Ring PETRA, (DESY); C-discoverer of the gluon with the TASSO experiment, Hamburg 1979; spokesman for ZEUS experiment at Electron-Proton Storage Ring HERA (DESY) 1986–94, mem. of ZEUS collaboration –2011; Prof. of Physics 1994–; European Physical Soc. High Energy and Particle Physics Prize (jtly) 1995, Stern-Gerlach Medal, German Physical Soc. 2011. *Publications:* numerous articles in scientific journals. *Address:* Deutsches Elektronen-Synchrotron DESY, ZEUS/F1, 1B/252, Notkestraße 85, 22607 Hamburg, Germany (office). *Telephone:* (40) 8998-3841 (office). *E-mail:* guenter.wolf@ desy.de (office). *Website:* www.desy.de (office).

WOLF, Martin Harry, CBE, MA; British economist and journalist; *Associate Editor and Chief Economics Commentator, Financial Times;* b. 16 Aug. 1946, London; s. of Edmund and Rebecca Wolf; m. Alison Margaret Wolf; two s. one d.; ed Univ. of Oxford; joined World Bank 1971 Sr Economist in 1974; Dir of Studies, Trade Policy Research Centre, London 1981; Chief Econs Leader Writer, Financial Times 1987–96, Assoc. Ed. 1990, Chief Econs Commentator 1996, currently Assoc. Ed. and Chief Econs Commentator; Special Prof., Univ. of Nottingham; mem. Council of Royal Econ. Soc. 1991–96; Forum Fellow, World Econ. Forum 1999–, mem. Int. Media Council 2006–; Hon. Fellow, Corpus Christi Coll., Oxford, Hon. Fellow, Oxford Inst. for Econ. Policy (Oxonia), Hon. Patron, Philosophical Soc. of Trinity Coll., Dublin 2013; Hon. DLitt (Nottingham) 2006, Hon. DSc (Econ) (LSE) 2006; Wincott Foundation Sr Prize for excellence in financial journalism (jtly)

1989, 1997, Commemoration Medal 1990, RTZ David Watt Memorial Prize 1994, Business Journalist of the Year Decade of Excellence Award 2003, Newspaper Feature of the Year Award, Workworld Media Awards 2003, First Magazine Award for Advocacy of Responsible Capitalism 2005, sixth winner, Journalism Prize, Fundacio Catalunya Oberta (Open Catalonia Foundation) 2006, Lifetime Achievement Award, AMEC 2007. *Publication:* Why Globalization Works 2004. *Address:* Financial Times Group, 1 Southwark Bridge, London, SE1 9HL, England (office). *Telephone:* (20) 7873-3673 (office). *Fax:* (20) 7873-3421 (office). *E-mail:* martin.wolf@ft.com (office). *Website:* www.ft.com (office).

WOLF, Naomi, BA; American writer and feminist; b. 15 Nov. 1962, San Francisco, Calif.; d. of Leonard Wolf and Deborah Wolf; m. David Shipley 1993 (divorced 2005); one c.; ed Yale Univ., New Coll., Univ. of Oxford, UK; Rhodes Scholar 1986; Co-founder Woodhull Inst. for Ethical Leadership 1997–, now Scholar-in-Residence and Woodhull Fellow; fmr columnist, George magazine; consultant, Al Gore Presidential campaign 2000. *Publications include:* The Beauty Myth: How Images of Beauty Are Used Against Women 1990, Fire With Fire: The New Female Power and How It Will Change in the 21st Century 1993, Promiscuities: The Secret Struggle for Womanhood 1997, Misconceptions: Truth, Lies and the Unexpected on the Journey to Motherhood 2001, The Treehouse: Eccentric Wisdom from my Father on How to Live, Love and See 2006, The End of America: A Letter of Warning to a Young Patriot 2007, Give Me Liberty: A Handbook for American Revolutionaries 2008, Vagina: A New Biography 2012. *Address:* c/o The Woodhull Institute, 770 Broadway, 2nd Floor, New York, NY 10003; c/o Royce Carlton Inc., 866 UN Plaza, New York, NY 10017, USA. *Telephone:* (646) 495-6060 (Woodhull). *Fax:* (646) 495-6059 (Woodhull). *E-mail:* info@woodhull.org. *Website:* woodhull.org.

WOLF, Siegfried; Austrian automotive industry executive; *Chairman, GAZ Group;* b. 31 Oct. 1957; trained as tool and die-maker and then as mem. of tech. staff, Quality Lab. at Philips; joined VereinigteMetallwerke Wien (VMW) as Quality Man. and Asst Dir of Quality Control; joined Hirtenberger AG, positions included Dir for Quality Control, then Gen. Man. and Vice Pres.; joined Magna Europe 1994, Pres. 1995–99, mem. Bd Dirs and Vice-Chair. Magna International Inc. 1999–, Pres. and CEO Magna Steyr 2001–02, Exec. Vice-Chair. Magna International Inc. 2002–05, Co-CEO 2005–10; Chair. GAZ Group and Glavstroy JSC 2010–; Chair. Russian Machines Corpn, Gazprom Open JSC 2011–; mem. Supervisory Bd Verbundgesellschaft (Austria Hydro Power), Österreich Industrieholding AG 2002– (Second Vice-Chair. 2006–08, First Vice-Chair. 2008–), Siemens AG Österreich, HGI Beteiligungs AG; mem. Bd Decoma International Inc. –2005, Intier Automotive Inc. –2005, Tesma International Inc. –2005; mem. Supervisory Bd Strabag SE 2007–10, Continental AG 2010–. *Address:* GAZ Group, 603004 Nizhny Novgorod, 88 Lenina Prospect, Russia (office). *Telephone:* (831) 299-09-90 (office). *Fax:* (831) 299-09-90 (office). *E-mail:* info@gazgroup.ru (office). *Website:* www.gazgroup.ru (office).

WOLF, Stephen M., BA; American business executive; *Chairman, R.R. Donnelley & Sons Company;* b. 7 Aug. 1941, Oakland, Calif.; ed San Francisco State Univ.; with American Airlines 1966–81, Vice-Pres. Western Div.; Sr Vice-Pres., Pan American World Airways 1981; Pres. and COO Continental Airlines 1982–83; Pres. and CEO Republic Airlines 1984–86; Chair., Pres. and CEO Tiger International Inc. 1986–88; Chair. and CEO UAL Corpn 1987–94, also fmr Pres.; Chair. and CEO United Airlines 1992–94; Chair. US Air Group Inc. 1996–98 (Pres. 1987–92), Chair. USAIR Inc. (later US Airways) 1998–2002; Sr Adviser, Lazard Frères 1994–2003; Man. Partner, Alpilles LLC 2003–; Dir R.R. Donnelley & Sons Co. 1995–, Chair. 2004–; Chair. Lehman Brothers Private Equity Advisory Bd 2005–08, Trilantic Capital Partners (fmrly Lehman Brothers Merchant Banking) 2009–; mem. Bd of Dirs Altria Group Inc. 1993–2008, Philip Morris International 2008–, Chrysler Group, LLC 2009–; fmr Dir Air Transport Asscn of America; Trustee, Georgetown Univ., World Wide Fund for Nature; Hon. Trustee, The Brookings Inst. *Address:* R.R. Donnelley Global Headquarters, 111 South Wacker Drive, Chicago, IL 60606-4301, USA (office). *Telephone:* (312) 326-8000 (office). *Fax:* (312) 326-8001 (office). *E-mail:* info@rrdonnelly.com (office). *Website:* www .rrdonnelly.com (office).

WOLFE, Nathan, BA, MA, DSc; American virologist and academic; *Founder, CEO and Director, Global Viral Forecasting Initiative;* b. 24 Aug. 1970, Detroit; ed Stanford Univ., Harvard Univ.; Postdoctoral fellow, Dept of Int. Health, Johns Hopkins Univ. 1999–2003, Asst Prof., Dept of Epidemiology, Dept of Molecular Microbiology & Immunology 2003–06, Adjunct Prof., Bloomberg School of Public Health 2006–; Prof., Dept of Epidemiology, UCLA 2006–08; Lorry I. Lokey Visiting Prof. of Human Biology, Stanford Univ. 2008–; Founder, CEO and Dir, Global Viral Forecasting Initiative 2008–; mem. AAAS, Int. Soc. of Ecosystem Health, Int. Primatological Soc., Ecological Soc. of America, American Soc. of Virology, American Soc. of Tropical Medicine & Hygiene, American Soc. of Microbiology. *Publications include:* The Viral Storm: The Dawn of a New Pandemic Age 2011; numerous articles in scientific journals. *Address:* Global Viral Forecasting Initiative, One Sutter, Suite 600, San Francisco, CA 94104, USA (office). *Telephone:* (415) 398-4712 (office). *Fax:* (415) 398 4716 (office). *Website:* www.gvfi .org (office).

WOLFE, Thomas (Tom) Kennerly, Jr, AB, PhD; American author and journalist; b. 2 March 1930, Richmond, Va; s. of Thomas Kennerly and Helen Hughes; m. Sheila Berger; one s. one d.; ed Washington and Lee, and Yale Univs; reporter, Springfield (Mass) Union 1956–59; reporter, Latin American Corresp., Washington Post 1959–62; reporter, magazine writer, New York Herald Tribune 1962–66; magazine writer, New York World Journal Tribune 1966–67; Contributing Ed. New York magazine 1968–76, Esquire Magazine 1977–; Contributing Artist, Harper's magazine 1978–81; exhibited one-man show of drawings, Maynard Walker Gallery, New York 1965, Tunnel Gallery, New York 1974; mem. American Acad. of Arts and Letters 1999; Hon. DFA (Minneapolis Coll. of Art) 1971; Hon. LittD (Washington and Lee) 1974; Hon. LHD (Virginia Commonwealth Univ.) 1983, (Southampton Coll., NY) 1984, (Johns Hopkins Univ.) 1990, (Boston Univ.) 2000, (Duke Univ.) 2002, Yale Univ.) 2004, (Trinity Coll.) 2007; Front Page Awards for Humour and Foreign News Reporting, Washington Newspaper Guild 1961, Award of Excellence, Soc. of Magazine Writers 1970, Frank Luther Mott Research Award 1973, Virginia Laureate for Literature 1977, Harold D. Vursell Memorial Award, American Acad. and Inst. of Arts and Letters

1980, American Book Award for Gen. Non-Fiction 1980, Columbia Journalism Award 1980, Citation for Art History, Nat. Sculpture Soc. 1980, John Dos Passos Award 1984, Gari Melchers Medal 1986, Benjamin Pierce Cheney Medal (E Washington Univ.) 1986, Washington Irving Medal (St Nicholas Soc.) 1986, Theodore Roosevelt Medal 1990, St Louis Literary Award 1990, Yale Graduate School Wilbur L. Cross Medal 1990, President's Humanities Medal 2001, Manhattan Inst. Alexander Hamilton Award 2006, Virginia Library Foundation Lifetime Achievement Award 2007, Nat. Book Awards Medal for Distinguished Contrib. to American Letters 2010. *Publications:* The Kandy-Kolored Tangerine-Flake Streamline Baby 1965, The Electric Kool-Aid Acid Test 1968, The Pump House Gang 1968, Radical Chic and Mau-mauing the Flak Catchers 1970, The New Journalism 1973, The Painted Word 1975, Mauve Gloves and Madmen, Clutter and Vine 1976, The Right Stuff 1979, In Our Time 1980, From Bauhaus to Our House 1981, The Purple Decades: A Reader 1982, The Bonfire of the Vanities 1987, Ambush at Fort Bragg 1998, A Man in Full 1998, Hooking Up (essays and a novella) 2000, I Am Charlotte Simmons 2005, Back to Blood 2012. *Address:* c/o Janklow & Nesbit Associates, 445 Park Avenue, New York, NY 10022-2608, USA. *E-mail:* postmaster@janklow.com. *Website:* www.tomwolfe.com.

WOLFE-SIMON, Felisa, BM, BA, PhD; American biologist; *Astrobiology Research Fellow, NASA Astrobiology Institute;* ed Oberlin Coll., Rutgers Univ.; studied oboe performance before turning to biology; Graduate Fellow, Graduate Asst/Teaching Asst, Dept of Oceanography, Rutgers Univ. 2000–06; Postdoctoral Research Fellow in Biology, NSF 2006–09; Astrobiology Research Fellow, NASA Astrobiology Inst. 2010–; mem. Soc. of Bio-inorganic Chemistry, Soc. of Molecular Biology and Evolution, Int. Soc. for the Study of the Origin of Life, American Soc. of Plant Biologists, American Soc. of Limnology and Oceanography, American Geophysical Union, ACS; NAS Kavli Fellow 2010. *Address:* PO Box 985, Berkeley, CA 94701, USA (office). *E-mail:* felisawolfesimon@gmail.com (office). *Website:* felisawolfesimon.com (office).

WOLFENDALE, Sir Arnold (Whittaker), Kt, PhD, FRS, FRAS, FInstP; British physicist and academic; *Professor Emeritus, Department of Physics, University of Durham;* b. 25 June 1927, Rugby; s. of Arnold Wolfendale and Doris Wolfendale; m. Audrey Darby 1951; twin s.; ed Univ. of Manchester; Asst Lecturer, Univ. of Manchester 1951–54, Lecturer 1954–56; Lecturer, Univ. of Durham 1956–59, Sr Lecturer 1959–63, Reader in Physics 1963–65, Prof. 1965–92, Prof. Emer. 1992–, Head of Dept 1973–77, 1980–83, 1986–89; Chair., Northern Region Action Cttee, Manpower Services Comm. Job Creation Programme 1975–78; Pres. Royal Astronomical Soc. 1981–83, Univ. of Durham Soc. of Fellows 1988–, Inst. of Physics 1994–96, European Physical Soc. 1999–; Prof. of Experimental Physics, Royal Inst. of GB 1996–; mem. Science and Eng Research Council 1988–94; Astronomer Royal 1991–95; Fellow Tata Inst. Fund 1996; mem. Academia Europaea 1998; Foreign Fellow, Nat. Acad. of Sciences of India 1990, Indian Nat. Science Acad.; Foreign Assoc. Royal Soc. of SA 1996; Pres. Antiquarian Horological Soc.; Freeman Worshipful Co. of Clockmakers, Worshipful Co. of Scientific Instrument Makers; Hon. Fellow, Lancs. Polytechnic 1991; Dr hc (Potchefstroom, Łódź, Teesside, Newcastle, Open Univ., Paisley, Lancaster, Bucharest, Durham, Neofit Rilski Southwest Univ. (Bulgaria); Silver Jubilee Medal 1977, Univ. of Turku Medal 1987, Armagh Observatory Medal 1992, Marian Smoluchowski Medal (Polish Physics Soc.) 1992, Powell Memorial Medal, European Physical Soc. 1996, Royal Soc. Bakerian Lecture and Medal 2002, Il Fiorino d'Oro, City of Florence 2004. *Publications:* Cosmic Rays 1963; Ec. Cosmic Rays at Ground Level 1973, Origin of Cosmic Rays 1974, Gamma Ray Astronomy 1981, Progress in Cosmology 1982, Gamma Ray Astronomy (with P. V. Ramana Murthy) 1986, Secular, Solar and Geomagnetic Variations in the last 1,000 years 1988; Origin of Cosmic Rays (co-ed.) 1981, Observational Tests of Cosmological Inflation (co-ed.) 1991; numerous papers on cosmic radiation. *Leisure interests:* walking, gardening, foreign travel. *Address:* Department of Physics, University of Durham, Rochester Building, Science Laboratories, South Road, Durham, DH1 3LE (office); Ansford, Potters Bank, Durham, England (home). *Telephone:* (191) 334-3580 (office); (191) 384-5642 (home). *Fax:* (191) 374-3749 (office). *E-mail:* a.w .wolfendale@durham.ac.uk (office). *Website:* www.dur.ac.uk/Physics (office).

WOLFENSOHN, James (Jim) D., KBE, AO, BA, LLB, MBA; American (b. Australian) international organization official, business executive, arts administrator and diplomatist; *Senior Advisor and Chairman, International Advisory Board, Citigroup Inc.;* b. 1 Dec. 1933, Sydney, Australia; s. of Hyman Wolfensohn and Dora Weinbaum; m. Elaine Botwinick 1961; one s. two d.; ed Univ. of Sydney, Harvard Business School; Pres. J. Henry Schroder Banking Corpn 1970–76; Chair. Salomon Brothers Int. 1977–81; Owner, Pres. James D. Wolfensohn Inc. 1981–95, fmr Chair., also CEO; Pres. World Bank 1995–2005; US Special Envoy for Gaza Disengagement 2005–April 2006 (resgnd); Sr Advisor and Chair. Int. Advisory Bd, Citigroup Inc., New York 2006–; Chair. Wolfensohn and Co. (corp. advisory and investment firm), New York 2005–; Chair. Kennedy Center for the Performing Arts 1990–95, Chair. Emer. 1995–; Chair. Advisory Group, Wolfensohn Center, Brookings Inst.; Chair. Bd Inst. for Advanced Study, Princeton, NJ; mem. Bd Carnegie Hall; Trustee Rockefeller Univ. 1985–94, Howard Hughes Medical Inst. 1987–96; mem. Global Bd of Dirs Endeavor (nonprofit org.), Conservation Int.; mem. Council on Foreign Relations; Montblanc de la Culture Award 1992; sponsor of The Elaine and Jim Wolfensohn Gift. *Achievements include:* Capt. Australian Olympic fencing team. *Publication:* Voice for the World's Poor: Selected Speeches and Writings 2005, A Global Life: My Journey among Rich and Poor, from Sydney to Wall Street to the World Bank 2010. *Leisure interest:* playing the cello. *Address:* Citigroup Inc., 399 Park Avenue, New York, NY 10043, USA (office). *Telephone:* (212) 559-1000 (office). *Fax:* (212) 793-3946 (office). *Website:* www.citigroup.com (office).

WOLFENSTEIN, Lincoln, PhD; American particle physicist and academic; *Professor Emeritus of Physics, Carnegie-Mellon University;* b. 10 Feb. 1923, Cleveland, Ohio; s. of Leo Wolfenstein and Anna Koppel; m. Wilma C. Miller 1957; one s. two d.; ed Univ. of Chicago; Physicist, Nat. Advisory Comm. for Aeronautics 1944–46; Asst Prof., Carnegie-Mellon Univ. 1948–57, Assoc. Prof. 1957–60, Prof. 1960–78, Univ. Prof. 1978–2000, Prof. Emer. 2000–; Guggenheim Fellow 1973–74, 1983–84; mem. NAS; J.J. Sakurai Prize, American Physical Soc. 1992, Bruno Pontecorvo Prize, Scientific Council of the Jt Inst. for Nuclear Research 2005. *Publications:* more than 100 papers on theoretical particle and nuclear physics, weak interactions, c.p. violation and neutrino physics. *Address:* Physics Department, Carnegie-Mellon University, Wean Hall 7418, 5000 Forbes Avenue, Pittsburgh, PA 15213, USA (office). *Telephone:* (412) 268-2752 (office). *Fax:* (412) 681-0648 (office). *E-mail:* lincolnw@andrew.cmu.edu (office). *Website:* www.cmu .edu/physics/people/emeritus-faculty/wolfenstein.html (office).

WOLFF, Hugh; American conductor; *Stanford and Norma Jean Calderwood Director of Orchestras, New England Conservatory of Music;* b. 21 Oct. 1953, Paris, France; m. Judith Kogan; three s.; ed Harvard Univ.; began career as Asst Conductor, Nat. Symphony Orchestra, with the late Mstislav Rostropovich; Musical Dir New Jersey Symphony 1985–92; Prin. Conductor, Saint Paul Chamber Orchestra 1988–92, Musical Dir 1992–2000; Prin. Conductor, Frankfurt Radio Symphony Orchestra 1997–2006; Stanford and Norma Jean Calderwood Dir of Orchestras, New England Conservatory of Music 2008–; regularly guest-conducts the major orchestras in N America and Europe; Seavor/Nat. Endowment for the Arts Conducting Prize 1985. *Address:* c/o Will Parsons, International Classical Artists, Dunstan house, 14A Street, Cross Street, London, EC1N 8XA, England (office); New England Conservatory of Music, 290 Huntingdon Avenue, Boston, MA 02115, USA (office). *Telephone:* (20) 7902-0520 (office); (617) 585-1100 (office). *Fax:* (20) 7902-0530 (office). *E-mail:* lsam@icartists.co.uk (office). *Website:* www.icartists.co.uk (office); www.newenglandconservatory.edu (office); www .hughwolff.com.

WOLFF, Tobias Jonathan Ansell, BA, MA; American writer; *The Ward W. and Priscilla B. Woods Professor, Stanford University;* b. 19 June 1945, Birmingham, Ala.; s. of Arthur S. Wolff and Rosemary Loftus; m. Catherine Dolores Spohn 1975; two s. one d.; ed The Hill School, Univ. of Oxford, UK, Stanford Univ.; served in US Army 1964–68; reporter, Washington Post 1972; Writing Fellow, Stanford Univ. 1975–78, Prof. of English and Creative Writing 1997–, currently The Ward W. and Priscilla B. Woods Prof.; Writer-in-Residence, Ariz. State Univ. 1978–80; Peck Prof. of English, Syracuse Univ. 1980–97; Wallace Stegner Fellowship 1975–76, Nat. Endowment Fellow 1978, 1984; Arizona Council on the Arts and Humanities Fellowship 1980, Guggenheim Fellow 1983; mem. PEN; Fellow, American Acad. of Arts and Sciences 2009–; Hon. Fellow, Hertford Coll., Oxford 2000; St Lawrence Award for Fiction 1982, Rea Award for Short Story 1989, Whiting Foundation Award 1989, LA Times Book Prize for Biography 1989, Amb. Book Award 1990, Lila Wallace/Reader's Digest Award 1993, Lyndhurst Foundation Award 1994, Esquire-Volvo-Waterstones Award for Non-Fiction 1994, Award of Merit, American Acad. of Arts and Letters 2001, Fairfax Award for Lifetime Achievement in Fiction 2007, The Story Prize 2009. *Publications include:* Ugly Rumours 1975, Hunters in the Snow 1981, The Barracks Thief (PEN/Faulkner Award for Fiction 1985) 1984, Back in the World 1985, A Doctor's Visit: The Short Stories of Anton Chekhov (ed.) 1987, The Stories of Tobias Wolff 1988, This Boy's Life 1989, The Picador Book of Contemporary American Stories (ed.) 1993, In Pharaoh's Army: Memories of a Lost War 1994, The Vintage Book of Contemporary American Short Stories 1994, The Best American Short Stories 1994, The Night in Question (short stories) 1996, Writers Harvest 3 (ed.) 2000, Old School 2003, Our Story Begins (short stories) 2008. *Address:* English Department, Building 460, Room 218, Stanford University, Stanford, CA 94305-2087, USA (office). *Telephone:* (650) 723-0504 (office). *Fax:* (650) 725-0755 (office). *E-mail:* twolff@stanford.edu (office). *Website:* english.stanford.edu (office).

WOLFOWITZ, Paul Dundes, BA, PhD; American academic, government official and fmr international organization official; *Visiting Scholar, American Enterprise Institute;* b. 22 Dec. 1943, Brooklyn, New York; s. of the late Jacob Wolfowitz and of Lillian Dundes; m. Clare Selgin; three c.; ed Cornell Univ., Univ. of Chicago; Man. Intern Bureau of the Budget 1966–67; Prof., Dept of Political Science, Yale Univ. 1970–73; mem. staff Arms Control and Disarmament Agency 1973–77, also Special Assst Strategic Arms Limitation Talks (SALT); Deputy Asst Sec. of Defense for Regional Programs 1977–80; Dir of Policy Planning, US Dept of State 1981–82, Asst Sec. of State for E Asia and Pacific Affairs 1982–86; Amb. to Indonesia 1986–89; Under-Sec. of Defense for Policy 1989–93, Deputy Sec. of Defense 2001–05; George F. Kennan Prof. of Nat. Security Strategy, Nat. War Coll. 1993; Visiting Prof., Paul H. Nitze School of Advanced Int. Studies (SAIS), Johns Hopkins Univ. 1980–81, Dean and Prof. of Int. Relations 1994–2001; Pres. World Bank Group 2005–07 (resgnd); Visiting Scholar, American Enterprise Inst. 2007–; mem. Advisory Bd Foreign Affairs, National Interest (journals); numerous awards including Presidential Citizen's Medal, Dept of Defense Distinguished Public Service Medal, Distinguished Honor Award, Distinguished Civilian Service Medal, Arms Control and Disarmament Agency Distinguished Honor Award. *Address:* American Enterprise Institute, 1150 Seventeenth Street, NW, Washington, DC 20036, USA (office). *Telephone:* (202) 862-5948 (office). *Fax:* (202) 862-7177 (office). *Website:* www.aei.org (office).

WOLFRAM, Herwig, DPhil; Austrian historian and academic; b. 14 Feb. 1934, Vienna; s. of Dr Fritz Wolfram and Rosa Wolfram; m. Adelheid Schoerghofer 1958; three s. one d.; ed Univ. of Vienna; Lecturer, Univ. of Vienna 1959–68, Docent 1967; Assoc. Prof., Los Angeles 1968; Assoc. Prof. of Medieval History, Vienna 1969, Prof. of Medieval History and Auxiliary Sciences 1971–2002, Dean Faculty of Arts 1981–83; Dir Institut für Österreichische Geschichtsforschung, Vienna 1983–2002; Corresp. mem. Monumenta Historica; Fellow, Austrian Acad. of Sciences 1985; Corresp. Fellow, Medieval Acad. of America 1990, Royal Historical Soc., London 1995, British Acad. 1996; Theodor-Koerner Foederungspreis 1962, 1964, Kardinal Innitzer-Foederungspreis 1964, Kardinal Innitzerpreis fuer Geisteswissenschaft 1994, Austrian Medal for Science and Art 2000, Cardinal Innitzer Prize 2011. *Television:* adviser to Sturm Ueber Europa I–IV (ZdF, ORF, Arte) 2002. *Publications include:* Splendor Imperii 1963, Intitulatio I 1967, II 1973, III 1988, History of the Goths 1988, Die Geburt Mitteleuropas 1987, Die Goten (seventh edn) 2001, Das Reich und die Germanen 1990–92, Salzburg, Bayern, Oesterreich. Die Conversio Bagoariorum et Carantanorum und die Quellen ihrer Zeit 1995, Grenzen und Räume 1995, The Roman Empire and its Germanic Peoples 1997, Konrad II (990–1039): Kaiser dreier Reiche 2000 (English trans. 2006), Die Goten und ihre Geschichte 2001, Die Germanen (seventh edn) 2002, Gotische Studien 2005, Die 101 wichtigsten Fragen. Germanen 2008, Die Germanen 2009, 99 Fragen an die Geschichte Österreichs 2009. *Leisure interests:* sport, music, theatre. *Address:* Wilhelminenstr. 173, 1160 Vienna; Sommeregg 13,

5301, Eugendorf, Austria. *Telephone:* (1) 485-63-28; (6221) 77-43. *Fax:* (1) 485-63-28; (6221) 20277. *E-mail:* herwig.wolfram@univie.ac.at.

WOLFSON, Dirk (Dik) Jacob, PhD; Dutch economist; *Professor Emeritus of Economics, Erasmus University;* b. 22 June 1933, Voorburg; s. of Dirk Wolfson and Gerdina Akkerhuys; m. Anna Maaike Hoekstra 1960; three c.; ed Univ. of Amsterdam; Teaching Asst Univ. of Amsterdam 1961–63; Economist, IMF, Washington, DC 1964–70; Dir (Chief Economist), Econ. Policy Div. Netherlands Treasury Dept 1970–75; Prof. of Public Finance, Erasmus Univ., Rotterdam 1975–86, Prof. of Econs 1992–99, Prof. Emer. 1999–; Rector, Inst. of Social Studies, The Hague 1986–90; mem. Social and Econ. Council 1982–96, Scientific Council for Govt Policy 1990–98; Royal Supervisor, Netherlands Cen. Bank and Chair. Banking Council 1990–99; mem. Senate (Social Democratic Party) 1999–2003; mem. Royal Netherlands Acad. of Arts and Sciences 1989–; Kt, Order of the Netherlands Lion, Commdr, Order of Orange Nassau. *Publications include:* Public Finance and Development Strategy 1979; numerous books and articles on econ. theory and policy. *Leisure interests:* theatre, hiking. *Address:* Aelbrechtskolk 41A, 3025 HB Rotterdam, Netherlands (home). *Telephone:* (10) 4779497 (home). *Fax:* (10) 4764667 (home). *E-mail:* dwolfson@xs4all.nl (home).

WOLINSKY, Leo C., BA; American journalist and editor; b. 9 May 1949, Los Angeles; m. Roberta Leith (née Wardle); ed Univ. of Southern California; joined Los Angeles Times newspaper in 1977, positions included staff writer South Bay Bureau 1977–79, transportation and environment corresp. Orange Co. Edn 1979–82, City Co. Bureau 1982–85, Sacramento Bureau 1985–87, Asst Bureau Chief 1987–88, Asst City Ed. 1989–90, Calif. Political Ed. 1990–91, City Ed. 1991–93, Metropolitan Ed. 1994–97, Man. Ed. of News 1997–2000, Exec. Ed. Los Angeles Times 2000–01, Deputy Man. Ed. 2001–05, Man. Ed. 2005–08; Ed. Daily Variety 2009–10; Prin., Creative Media (consultancy), Los Angeles 2009–; Pulitzer Prize 1993, 1995, 1998. *Achievements include:* directed teams that won Pulitzer Prizes for coverage of the Los Angeles Riots in 1992 and the Northridge Earthquake in 1994.

WOLMAN, M. Gordon, BA, MA, PhD; American environmental scientist and academic; *B. Howell Griswold, Jr Professor of Geography and International Affairs, The Johns Hopkins University;* s. of Abel Wolman; ed The Johns Hopkins Univ., Harvard Univ.; mil. service, USNR 1943–46; hydrologist, US Geological Survey (USGS) 1951–58; Assoc. Prof. of Geography, Johns Hopkins Univ. 1958–62, Chair. Isaiah Bowman Dept of Geography 1958–68, Prof. of Geography 1962–, B. Howell Griswold, Jr Prof. of Geography and Int. Affairs 1975–, Chair. Dept of Geography and Environmental Eng 1970–90, Interim Provost Johns Hopkins Univ. 1987, 1990–91; Fellow, American Acad. of Arts and Sciences 1981, AAAS 1984; mem. NAS 1988, American Philosophical Soc. 1999, Nat. Acad. of Eng 2002, American Geophysical Union; Award of Jt Eng and Architects Socs of Washington, DC 1957, Meritorious Contrib. Award, Asscn of American Geographers 1972, Distinguished Mentor, Nat. Council for Geographic Educ. 1989, Cullum Geographical Medal, Council of the American Geographical Soc. 1989, USGS John Wesley Powell Award 1989, Distinguished Career Award, Asscn of American Geographers Geomorphology Specialty Group 1993, D. L. Linton Award, British Geomorphological Research Group 1994, Rachel Carson Award, Chesapeake Appreciation, Inc. 1995, Medal in Memory of Ian Campbell, American Geological Inst. 1997, Penrose Medal, Geological Soc. of America 1999, Horton Medal, American Geophysical Union 2000, Nevada Medal, Desert Research Inst. 2002, Abel Wolman Award, Chesapeake Water Environment Fed. 2003, Lifetime Achievement Award, Nat. Council for Science and the Environment 2004, Benjamin Franklin Medal in Earth and Environmental Science, The Franklin Inst. 2006. *Publications:* numerous scientific papers in professional journals. *Address:* Department of Geography and Environmental Engineering, Johns Hopkins University, 3400 North Charles Street, Baltimore, MD 21218, USA (office). *Telephone:* (410) 516-7090 (office). *Fax:* (410) 516-8996 (office). *E-mail:* wolman@jhu.edu (office). *Website:* engineering.jhu.edu/~dogee (office).

WOLPERT, Lewis, CBE, DIC, PhD, FRS, FRSL; British biologist and academic; *Professor Emeritus of Biology as Applied to Medicine, University College and Middlesex School of Medicine;* b. 19 Oct. 1929, South Africa; s. of William Wolpert and Sarah Wolpert; m. Elizabeth Brownstein; two s. two d.; ed Univ. of Witwatersrand, Imperial Coll. London, King's Coll. London; civil engineer S African Council for Scientific and Industrial Research and Israel Water Planning Dept 1951–54; Reader in Zoology, King's Coll. London 1964–66; Prof. of Biology as Applied to Medicine, Dept of Anatomy and Developmental Biology, Univ. Coll. and Middlesex School of Medicine (fmrly at Middx Medical School) 1966–2005, Prof. Emer. 2005–; presenter Antenna (BBC 2) 1988–89, TV documentaries and radio interviews with scientists; Chair. MRC Cell Bd 1984–88; Chair. Comm. on the Public Understanding of Science 1994–; mem. various cttees, scientific panels etc.; Hon. DSc (Leicester) 1996, (Westminster) 1997, (Bath); Hon. DUniv (Open Univ.) 1998; Medanear Lecture, Royal Soc. 1998, Michael Faraday Medal, Royal Soc. 2000. *Publications:* A Passion for Science 1988, The Triumph of the Embryo 1991, The Unnatural Nature of Science 1992, Principles of Development 1998, Malignant Sadness: The Anatomy of Depression 1999, Six Impossible Things Before Breakfast 2006, How We Live and Why We Die 2009. *Leisure interests:* cycling, tennis. *Address:* Department of Anatomy and Developmental Biology, University College London, Gower Street, London, WC1E 6BT (office); 63A Belsize Park Gardens, London, NW3 4JN, England (home). *Telephone:* (20) 7679-1320 (office); (20) 7586-7694 (home). *E-mail:* l.wolpert@ucl.ac.uk (office); lewiswolpert@yahoo .com (home).

WOLSZCZAN, Aleksander, PhD; Polish astronomer; *Evan Pugh Professor of Astronomy and Astrophysics, Penn State University;* b. 29 April 1946, Szczecinek; m.; one d.; ed Nicolaus Copernicus Univ., Toruń; Dir Astronomy Centre, Nicolaus Copernicus Univ. 1997–2000; Evan Pugh Prof. of Astronomy and Astrophysics, Penn State Univ. 2000–; Kt's Cross, Order of Polonia Restituta 1997; Young Astronomer Prize, Polish Astronomical Society 1977, Annual Award, Foundation of Polish Science 1992, Annual Award, Alfred Jurzykowski Foundation 1993, Faculty Scholar Medal, Pa State Univ. 1994, Beatrice M. Tinsley Prize, American Astronomical Society 1996, Casimir Funk Natural Sciences Award, Polish Inst. of Arts and Sciences of America 1996, M. Smoluchowski Medal, Polish Physical Soc. *Publications include:* Interstellar Interferometry of the Pulsar PSR 1237+25 1987 (co-author), Experimental Constraints on Strong-Field Relativistic Gravity 1992 (co-author), A Planetary System Around the Millisecond Pulsar PSR 1257+12 1992 (co-author), Confirmation of Earth-Mass Planets Orbiting the Millisecond Pulsar PSR B1257+12 1994, Binary Pulsars and Relativistic Gravitation 1994. *Leisure interests:* climbing, hiking. *Address:* 501 Davey Laboratory, Department of Astronomy and Astrophysics, Penn State University, University Park, PA 16802, USA (office). *Telephone:* (814) 863-1756 (office). *Fax:* (814) 863-3399 (office). *E-mail:* alex@astro.psu.edu (office). *Website:* www.astro.psu.edu (office).

WOLTER, Frank; German international civil servant; b. 22 Nov. 1943, Seehausen, Bavaria; s. of Dr Hans Wolter and Ilse Wolter (née Henrici); m. Birgit Rein 1975; one s. one d.; ed Univs of Freiburg, Saarbrücken and Kiel; Research Fellow, Kiel Inst. of World Econs 1969–74, Head Research Groups 1974–83; Dir Research Project, German Research Foundation 1977–79; Sr Economist, Econ. Research and Analysis Unit, GATT Secr., Geneva 1983–89, Dir Trade Policies Review Div. 1989–91, Dir Agric. and Commodities 1991–. *Publications:* numerous studies and articles on structural change in industry, int. trade and econ. growth. *Leisure interests:* tennis, skiing, classical music, historical literature, golf. *Address:* 154 rue de Lausanne, 1211 Geneva 21, Switzerland (office); 38 La Clé des Champs, 01280 Moens, France (home). *E-mail:* frank.wolter@wto.org (office); wolterfrank@aol.com (home).

WONDER, Stevie; American singer, musician and composer; b. (Steveland Judkins Morris), 13 May 1950, Saginaw, Mich.; step-s. of Paul Hardaway; m. 1st Syreeta Wright 1971 (divorced 1972, died 2004); m. 2nd Yolanda Simmons; m. 3rd Kai Millard Morris; seven c.; ed Michigan School for the Blind; first appeared as solo singer at Whitestone Baptist Church, Detroit 1959; recording artist with Motown, Detroit, initially as Stephen Judkins, 1963–70; f. and Pres. Black Bull Music Inc. 1970–, Wondirection Records 1982–; owner, KJLH, LA; Edison Award 1973, Nat. Asscn of Record Merchandisers Best Selling Male Soul Artist of Year 1974, and Presidential Award 1975, Golden Globe (for I Just Called To Say I Love You) 1985, numerous American Music Awards, including Special Award of Merit 1982, Acad. Award for Best Song 1984, Soul Train Heritage Award 1987, numerous Grammy Awards, including Grammy Award (for Superstition) 1974, Grammy Award (for You are the Sunshine of My Life) 1974, Grammy Award (for Living For The City) 1975, Grammy Award (for Boogie on Reggae Woman) 1975, Grammy Award (for I Wish) 1977, Grammy Lifetime Achievement Award 1990, Nelson Mandela Courage Award 1991, IAAAM Diamond Award for Excellence 1991, National Acad. of Songwriters Lifetime Achievement Award 1992, NAACP Image Award 1992, Polar Music Prize, Swedish Acad. of Music, Grammy Award for Best Male Pop Vocal Performance (for From the Bottom of my Heart) 2006, Grammy Award for Best R&B Performance by a Duo or Group with Vocals (for So Amazing, with Beyoncé) 2006, Grammy Award for Best Pop Collaboration with Vocals (with Tony Bennett) 2007, Gershwin Prize for Popular Song, US Library of Congress 2009. *Film appearances:* Bikini Beach 1964, Muscle Beach Party 1964. *Recordings include:* albums: Little Stevie Wonder: The Twelve-Year-Old Genius 1963, Tribute To Uncle Ray, Jazz Soul, With A Song In My Heart, At The Beach, Uptight 1966, Down To Earth 1966, I Was Made To Love Her 1967, Someday At Christmas 1967, For Once In My Life 1969, My Cherie Amour 1969, Signed Sealed and Delivered 1969, Music Of My Mind 1972, Talking Book 1972, Innervisions (Grammy Award 1974) 1973, Fulfillingness' First Finale (Grammy Award 1975) 1974, Songs in the Key of Life (Grammy Award 1977) 1976, Journey Through the Secret Life of Plants 1979, Hotter than July 1980, Original Musiquarium 1982, Woman in Red (soundtrack) 1984, Love Songs 1984, In Square Circle 1985, Characters 1987, Jungle Fever (film soundtrack) 1991, Conversation Peace 1995, Motown Legends 1995, Natural Wonder 1996, Song Review 1996, At The Close Of A Century 1999, A Time To Love 2005. *Address:* Steveland Morris Music, 4616 W Magnolia Boulevard, Burbank, CA 91505 (office); c/o Motown Records, 1755 Broadway, New York, NY 10019, USA. *Website:* www.steviewonder.net.

WONG, Andrea, BS, MBA; American television and media executive; *President, International Production for Sony Pictures Television and President, International, Sony Pictures Entertainment;* ed Massachusetts Inst. of Tech., Stanford Univ. Grad. School of Business; Analyst, High Yield Investment Banking, The First Boston Corpn 1988–90; Strategic Planning Analyst, PepsiCo 1990–91; Researcher, ABC News 1993–94; Exec. Asst to the Pres. of ABC Television 1994–96, Vice-Pres. and Exec. Asst to the Pres. of ABC, Inc. 1996–98, Vice-Pres., Alternative Series, Specials & LateNight, ABC Entertainment 1998–2000, Sr Vice-Pres. 2000–04, Exec. Vice-Pres. 2004–07; Pres. and CEO Lifetime Entertainment Services 2007–10; mem. Bd Liberty Media Corpn 2010–; Pres., International Production, Sony Pictures Television and Pres., International, Sony Pictures Entertainment, London, UK 2011–; mem. Visiting Cttee, MIT Media Lab Cttee of 100, Stanford Women on Bds Initiative; Henry Crown Fellow, Aspen Inst. 2010. *Address:* Sony Pictures Entertainment, 25 Golden Square, London, W1F 9LU, England (office). *Telephone:* (20) 7533-1000 (office). *E-mail:* info@sonypictures.co .uk (office). *Website:* www.sonypictures.com (office).

WONG, Anthony Chau-Sang; Hong Kong actor; b. 2 Sept. 1961; m.; one s.; ed Acad. of Performing Arts; began acting career at ATV; film debut in Flower Street Era 1985; writer and dir films New Tenant 1995 and Top Banana Club 1996; lead singer in punk music band. *Films include:* No Risk, No Gain 1990, The Big Score 1990, Dancing Bull 1990, Angel Hunter 1991, Her Fatal Ways 1991, Lucky Encounter 1992, Lady Hunter 1992, The Untold Story (Best Actor Hong Kong Film Award, Golden Horse Award) 1992, Hard Boiled 1992, Executioners 1992, Legal Innocence 1993, The Tigers 1993, Taxi Hunter 1993, Love to Kill 1993, Full Contact 1993, Physical Weapon 1994, Rock n' Roll Cop 1994, Now You See Me, Now You Don't 1994, Highway Man 1994, Husbands and Wives 1995, Another Chinese Cop 1996, Mangkok Story 1996, Blind Romance 1996, Beyond the Cop Line 1996, Young and Dangerous 1996, Armageddon 1997, Midnight Zone 1997, Beast Cops (Best Actor Hong Kong Film Award) 1998, Ordinary Heroes 1998, Haunted Mansion 1998, The Deadly Camp 1999, A Man Called Hero 1999, The Mission 1999, When a Man Loves a Woman 2000, Violent Cop 2000, What is a Good Teacher 2000, Ransom Run 2000, Runaway 2001, U-Man 2002, Just One Look 2002, Infernal Affairs (Best Supporting Actor Hong Kong Film Award, Hong Kong Film Critics Soc. 2003) 2002, The Twins Effect 2002, Princess D (Best Supporting Actor, Taiwan Golden Horse Awards) 2002, Internal Affairs II (Hong Kong Film Award) 2003, Magic Kitchen 2004, Kung Fu Soccer 2004, House of Fury 2005, Initial D 2005, Exiled 2006, The Painted Veil 2006, On the Edge 2006, Sweet

Revenge 2007, Great Uncle 2007, Mr Cinema 2007, Simply Actors 2007, Secret 2007, The Sun also Rises 2007. *Leisure interests:* martial arts, kung fu, singing.

WONG, Chi-Huey, BS, MS, PhD; American/Taiwanese chemist, biochemist and academic; *Ernest W. Hahn Professor of Chemistry, The Scripps Research Institute;* b. 3 Aug. 1948, Chiayi Co., Taiwan; ed Nat. Taiwan Univ., Massachusetts Inst. of Tech.; Postdoctoral Fellow, Harvard Univ. 1982–83; Asst Prof. of Chem., Texas A&M Univ. 1983–86, Assoc. Prof. 1986–87, Prof. 1987–89; Prof. and Ernest W. Hahn Chair in Chem., Scripps Research Inst. 1989–; Dir Genomics Research Center, Academia Sinica, Taipei 2003–06, now Distinguished Research Fellow; jt appointment as Distinguished Prof. of Chem. and Biochemical Sciences, Nat. Taiwan and Nat. Tsing-Hua Univ.; Scientific Adviser, Max Planck Inst.; Founding Scientist and Chair. Scientific Advisory Bd, Optimer Pharmaceuticals, Inc.; Head of Frontier Research Program on Glycotechnology, RIKEN (Inst. of Physical and Chemical Research, Japan) 1991–99; mem. Bd US Nat. Research Council on Chemical Sciences and Tech. 2000–03; Ed.-in-Chief, Bioorganic & Medicinal Chemistry; mem. Exec. Bd, Tetrahedron Publications; mem. Academia Sinica 1994 (Pres. 2006–), American Acad. of Arts and Sciences 1996, NAS 2002; Searle Scholar Award in Biomedical Sciences 1985, Presidential Young Investigator in Chemistry 1986, ACS Arthur C. Cope Scholar Award 1993, IUPAC Int. Carbohydrate Award 1994, ACS Harrison Howe Award in Chem. 1998, ACS Claude S. Hudson Award in Carbohydrate Chem. 1999, Int. Enzyme Eng Award 1999, Presidential Green Chem. Award 2000, ACS Award for Creative Work in Synthetic Organic Chem. 2006, Humboldt Research Award for Sr Scientists 2008, F.A. Cotton Medal for Excellence in Chemical Research 2008, ACS Arthur C. Cope Award 2012. *Publications:* about 700 papers in professional journals; 105 patents. *Address:* The Scripps Research Institute, 10550 North Torrey Pines Road, BCC-338, La Jolla, CA 92037, USA (office). *Telephone:* (858) 784-2487 (office). *Fax:* (858) 784-2409 (office). *E-mail:* wong@scripps.edu (office). *Website:* www.scripps.edu/ research/faculty/wong (office); www.scripps.edu/wong (office).

WONG, Kam-po; Hong Kong cyclist; b. 13 March 1973, Shatin; joined Hong Kong Cycling Team 1994; wins include gold medals at Nat. Games of the People's Repub. of China 1997, 2001, 2009, Asian Games, Bangkok 1998, Doha 2006, Track World Cup Round 5, Copenhagen, 2009; winner Philippines Marlboro Tour 1997, UCI Track World Championships, Mallorca 2007; chosen as flag bearer for Hong Kong at opening ceremony of Summer Olympic Games, Beijing 2008. *Address:* c/o Hong Kong Cycling Association, Room 1015, Olympic House, 1 Stadium Path, So Kon Po, Causeway Bay, Hong Kong Special Administrative Region, People's Republic of China (office). *Telephone:* 25048176 (office).

WONG, Kan Seng, BA, MBA; Singaporean politician; b. 1946; m. Ruth Wong; two s.; ed Univ. of Singapore, London Business School, UK; began career as trainee teacher, Teacher's Training Coll. 1964–67; joined Admin. Service, Ministry of Labour 1970; called to Nat. Service, Singapore Armed Forces 1970–71; Admin. Officer, Ministry of Defence 1971; Head of Navy Personnel, Dir of Manpower Div., then Deputy Sec., Ministry of Defence 1971–81; Personnel Man., Hewlett Packard, Singapore 1981–85; MP (People's Action Party) for Kuo Chuan Constituency 1984–88, Toa Payoh Constituency 1988–91, Thomson Constituency 1981–97, Bishan-Toa Payoh Constituency 1997–2001, 2001–; Minister of State for Home Affairs, then for Community Devt 1985–86; Minister of State for Communications and Information 1985–87; Acting Minister for Community Devt 1986–87, Minister 1987–91; Leader of the House of Parl. 1987–2007; Second Minister for Foreign Affairs 1987–88, Minister 1988–94; Deputy Chair. of the People's Asscn 1992–2006; Minister for Home Affairs 1994–2010; Deputy Prime Minister 2005–11; mem. Cen. Exec. Cttee, People's Action Party 1987–, Second Asst Sec.-Gen. 1992–2004, First Asst Sec.-Gen. 2004–; Adviser to Nat. Transport Worker's Union 1985–; Chair. Chinese Devt Assistance Council 1992–2004; mem. Global Advisory Bd, London Business School 1999–; Public Admin Medal (Silver) 1976, Nat. TUC May Day Medal of Honour 1998. *Leisure interests:* working out at gym, golf. *Address:* People's Action Party, Blk 57b, PCF Building, 01-1402 New Upper Changi Road, Singapore 463057 (office). *Telephone:* 62444600 (office). *Fax:* 62430114 (office). *E-mail:* paphq@pap.org.sg (office); wongkanseng@gmail.com. *Website:* www.pap.org.sg (office).

WONG, Kar Wai, BA; Chinese film director; b. 1959, Shanghai; ed Hong Kong Polytechnic; TV drama production training programme Hong Kong TV Broadcasts Ltd 1980–82; Pres. 2006 Cannes Film Festival; has also directed numerous TV commercials and music videos; Pres. of the Jury, 63rd Berlin Int. Film Festival 2013; Foreign Hon. Fellow, American Acad. of Arts and Sciences 2009; Best Dir Award Cannes Film Festival 1997 (for Happy Together). *Films:* As Tears Go By 1988, Days of Being Wild 1990, Days of Being Wild II, Ashes of Time 1994, Chungking Express 1994, Fallen Angels 1995, Happy Together 1997, In the Mood for Love 2000, 2046 2004, My Blueberry Nights 2007, The Lady from Shanghai 2009, The Grandmaster 2013. *Television:* scriptwriter Don't Look Now 1981. *Address:* c/o Jet Tone Films, Flat E, Third Floor, Kalam Court, 9 Grampian Road, Kowloon, Hong Kong Special Administrative Region, People's Republic of China (office).

WONG, Penny, BA, LLB; Australian politician; b. 5 Nov. 1968, Kota Kinabalu, Sabah, Malaysia; ed Scotch Coll., Vic., Univ. of Adelaide; moved to Australia aged eight years; began career as industrial officer, Adelaide 1990–96, barrister and solicitor 1996–2000, legal officer 2000–02; fmr Adviser to Carr Govt, NSW; Labor Senator for S Australia 2001–, Shadow Minister for Employment and Workforce Participation and for Corp. Governance and Responsibility 2004–07, also for Public Admin and Accountability 2006–07, Minister for Climate Change and Water 2007–10, for Finance 2010–13. *Address:* Electorate Office, 81 Carrington Street, Adelaide, SA 5000, Australia. *E-mail:* info@pennywong.com.au. *Website:* www .pennywong.com.au.

WONG YICK MING, Dame Rosanna, DBE, JP, BSc, MS, MA, PhD; Hong Kong administrator and government official; b. 15 Aug. 1952, Hong Kong; ed St Stephen's Girls' School, Univ. of Hong Kong, Univ. of Toronto, Canada, London School of Econs. UK, Chinese Univ. of Hong Kong, Univ. of California, Davis, USA; Exec. Dir Hong Kong Fed. of Youth Groups 1980–; Chair. Hong Kong Housing Authority 1993–2000, Complaints Cttee of Hong Kong Ind. Comm. Against Corruption, Children's Thalassaemia Foundation, Social Welfare Advisory Cttee 1988–91, Comm. on Youth 1990–91, Police Complaints Cttee 1993; mem. Legis.

Council 1985–91, Exec. Council 1988–91, 1992–97, Exec. Council of Hong Kong Special Admin. Region 1997–2002; Chair. Educ. Comm. 2001, 2003–07; Hong Kong mem., CPPCC Nat. Cttee 2003–; mem. Judicial Officers Recommendation Comm. 2005–07; mem. Bd of Dirs Hongkong and Shanghai Banking Corpn Ltd 1996–, Cheung Kong (Holdings) Ltd 2001–; Founding Dir Dragon Foundation; Patron Mother's Choice, Children's Kidney Trust Fund; mem. Co-ordinating Cttee for Children and Youth at Risk, Exec. Cttee Hong Kong Council of Social Service; Hon. Fellow, Hong Kong Inst. of Housing 1994; Hon. mem. Chartered Inst. of Housing 1994; Dr hc (Hong Kong Univ.), (Hong Kong Polytechnic Univ.) 2002.

WONGSUWON, Gen. Prawit; Thai army officer and politician; b. 11 Aug. 1945; ed Chulachomklao Royal Mil. Acad., Army Command and Gen. Staff Coll., Nat. Defence Coll.; rifle platoon leader, 2nd Bn, 3rd combat team 1969; heavy mortar platoon leader, 21st Regt 1971; Commdr infantry co., 2nd Bn 1974; Operations and Training Officer, 2nd Infantry Bn 1976; Officer Student, Command and Gen. Staff Coll. 1977; Officer, Operations Unit 1979; Deputy Commdr 1st Infantry Bn, 21st Regt 1980; Commdr 2nd Infantry Bn, 2nd Regt 1981; Commdr 3rd Infantry Bn, 12th Regt 1984; Deputy Commdr 12th Infantry Regt 1986, Commdr 1989; Deputy Commdg Gen. 2nd Infantry Div. 1993, Commdg Gen. 1996–97; Deputy Commdg Gen. 1st Army Area 1997–98, Commdg Gen. 2002–03; Commdg Gen. 1st Corps 1998–2000; Army Specialist 2000–01; Asst Chief of Staff, Operations 2001–02; Asst C-in-C Royal Thai Army 2003–04, C-in-C 2004–06; Minister of Defence 2008–11.

WONGTSCHOWSKI, Pedro, BEng, MEng, DEng; Brazilian chemical engineer and business executive; ed Escola Politécnica da Universidade de São Paulo; with Ultrapar (chemical fertilizer co.) 1970–72, rejoined Ultrapar 1977, officer of Ultrapar 1985–2102, mem. Bd of Dirs Ultraprev 1989–2006, CEO Ultrapar Holdings 2007–12, Dir 2013–; officer of Oxiteno and Oxiteno Nordeste 1992–2006; mem. Bd Arteris SA, Brazilian Asscn for Chemical Eng, Latin American Petrochemical and Chemical Asscn (APLA, Pres. –2012); Vice-Chair. ABIQUIM –2010; Chair. Nat. Asscn for Research, Devt and Eng of Innovative Cos (ANPEI), Nat. Centre for Research in Energy and Materials (CNPEM); mem. Council of Tech. and Competitiveness of FIESP. *Publication:* Indústria Química – Riscos e Oportunidades (Chemical Industry – Risks and Opportunities) 2002. *Address:* Ultrapar Holdings, Avenida Brigadeiro Luiz Antônio 1343, São Paulo 01317-910, Brazil (office). *Telephone:* (11) 3177-7014 (office). *Fax:* (11) 3177-6107 (office). *E-mail:* info@ultra.com.br (office). *Website:* www.ultra.com.br (office).

WONOWIDJOJO, Susilo; Indonesian business executive; *President, PT Gudang Garam Tbk;* b. (Cai Daoping), spent entire career with family business PT Gudang Garam Tbk (clove cigarette mfr), Dir 1990–, Deputy Pres. Dir 2008–09, Pres. Dir Feb.–June 2009, Pres. June 2009–; Founder and Owner PT Matahari Kahuripan Indonesia (Makin Group) (plantation). *Address:* PT Gudang Garam Tbk, Jl. Semampir II/1, Kediri 64121, Indonesia (office). *Telephone:* (354) 682091 (office). *Fax:* (354) 681555 (office). *Website:* www.gudanggaramtbk.com (office).

WOO, John; Chinese film director and producer; b. (Yu Sum Woo), 23 Sept. 1946, Guangzhou; m. Annie Woo Ngau Chun-lung 1976; three c.; ed Matteo Ricci Coll., Hong Kong; family moved to Hong Kong 1951; started making experimental 16 mm films in 1967; entered film industry 1969 as Production Asst Cathay Film Co., Asst Dir 1971; later joined Shaw Bros as Asst Dir to Zhang Che; arrived in Hollywood 1992, debut with Hard Target 1993; Silver Bauhinia Star, Hong Kong 2010. *Films include:* The Young Dragons (debut) 1973, The Dragon Tamers, Countdown in Kung Fu, Princess Chang Ping, From Riches to Rags, Money Crazy, Follow the Star, Last Hurrah for Chivalry, To Hell with the Devil, Laughing Times, Sunset Warriors (Heroes Shed No Tears), The Time You Need a Friend, Run Tiger, Run, A Better Tomorrow 1986, A Better Tomorrow II, Just Heroes, The Killer 1989, Bullet in the Head, Once a Thief 1990, Hard Boiled 1992, Hard Target 1993, Broken Arrow 1996, Face/Off 1997, King's Ransom, M: I-2 2000, The Last Word (producer), Windtalkers 2002, The Hire: Hostage 2002, Bulletproof Monk (producer) 2003, Paycheck 2003, All the Invisible Children 2005, Red Cliff 2008, Red Cliff II 2009, Reign of Assassins 2010, The Killer (producer) 2012, The Crossing 2014. *Television includes:* Once a Thief 1996, Blackjack 1998, The Robinsons: Lost in Space 2004. *Address:* c/o Endeavor Agency, 9601 Wilshire Blvd., 10th Floor, Beverly Hills, CA 90212, USA (office). *Telephone:* (310) 248-2000. *Fax:* (310) 248-2020.

WOO, Peter Kwong Ching, JP, MBA, DLitt, DSC; Chinese business executive; *Chairman, Wheelock & Company Limited;* b. 1946, Shanghai; m. Bessie Pao; ed St Stephen's Coll., Hong Kong, Univ. of Cincinnati and Columbia Business School, USA; family moved to Hong Kong 1949; worked at Chase Manhattan Bank and Worldwide Shipping Group following graduation; Chair. Wheelock & Co. Ltd 1986–96, 2002–; Chair. Wharf (Holdings) Ltd 1986–94, Hon. Chair 1994–; Founding Chair. Wheelock NatWest Ltd 1995–, The Wharf (Holdings) Ltd 1992–, Chair. and Dir Wheelock Properties (Singapore) Ltd 2006–13; Hong Kong (now Hong Kong Special Admin. Region) Affairs Adviser to People's Repub. of China 1993–; non-official mem. Comm. on Strategic Devt 2007–; mem. Int. Advisory Bd Chemical Banking Corpn 1981–, Nat. Westminster Bank PLC 1992–, Gen. Electric 1994–, Elf Aquitaine 1994–; Dir Standard Chartered Bank PLC 1986–89; mem. Hong Kong (now Hong Kong Special Admin. Region)/US Econ. Co-operation Cttee 1989–95, Hong Kong Gov.'s Business Council 1993–97; Chair. Hong Kong (now Hong Kong Special Admin. Region) Environment and Conservation Fund Cttee 1994–, Hong Kong Hosp. Authority 1995–, Hong Kong Trade t Council 2000–08; Deputy Chair. Prince of Wales Business Leaders' Forum 1991–; mem. Court of Hong Kong Polytechnic Univ.; cand. for Chief Exec. of Hong Kong 1996; Officer, Order of Leopold (Belgium) 1993, Gold Bauhinia Star 1998, Grand Bauhinia Medal 2012; Leader of the Year (Hong Kong Standard) 1995. *Publication:* The Challenge of Hong Kong Plus 1991. *Leisure interests:* golf, tennis. *Address:* Penthouse, Wheelock House, 20 Pedder Street, Central, Hong Kong Special Administrative Region, People's Republic of China. *Website:* www .wheelockcompany.com.

WOO, Sir Po-shing, FCIA, FID; British solicitor; b. 19 April 1929, Hong Kong; s. of the late Seaward Woo and of Ng Chiu Man; m. Helen Woo Fong Shuet Fun (Lady Woo) 1956; four s. one d.; ed La Salle Coll., Hong Kong and King's Coll., London; admitted to practice as solicitor in England and Hong Kong 1960; Notary Public 1966; admitted to practice as barrister and solicitor, Supreme Court of Victoria,

Australia 1983; Founder Woo Kwan Lee & Lo, Solicitors and Notaries 1973; Chair. Kailey Enterprises Ltd, Kailey Devt Ltd; Dir Sun Hung Kai Properties Ltd, Henderson Devt Co. Ltd and more than 40 other cos; mem. Inst. of Admin. Man., Inst. of Trade Mark Agents; f. Woo Po Shing Medal in Law (Hong Kong Univ.) 1982, Woo Po Shing Overseas Summer School Travelling Scholarship (Hong Kong Univ.) 1983, The Po-Shing Woo Charitable Foundation 1994, Woo Po Shing Chair of Chinese and Comparative Law (City Univ.) 1995; fmr mem. Council Univ. of Hong Kong; Hon. Voting mem. Hong Kong Jockey Club, Po Leung Kuk Advisory Bd, Tung Wah Group of Hosps; Legal Adviser Chinese Gold and Silver Exchange Soc.; Hon. Pres. and Legal Adviser, South China Athletic Asscn; Patron Woo Po Shing Gallery of Chinese Bronze, Shanghai Museum, The Auckland Observatory (renamed Sir Po-Shing Woo Auckland Observatory Bldg); Patron RCA, Tsinghua Univ., Beijing; Fellow, Inst. of Man., King's Coll., London Univ., Hong Kong Man. Asscn; Hon. Prof., Nankai Univ. of Tianjin, China; Chevalier, Ordre des Arts et des Lettres 2004; Hon. LLD (City Univ. Hong Kong), Hon. LLB (King's Coll. London); World Fellowship of Duke of Edinburgh's Award. *Leisure interests:* travelling, viewing and collecting antiques including Chinese paintings, bronzes and ceramics, racehorses. *Address:* 2/F Kailey Tower, 16 Stanley Street, Central, Hong Kong Special Administrative Region, People's Republic of China (home). *Telephone:* 2522-4825 (home). *Fax:* 2537-9747 (home). *Website:* www.kailey.com .hk (office).

WOOD, Adrian John Bickersteth, CBE, MA, MPA, PhD; British economist and academic; *Professor Emeritus of International Development, University of Oxford;* b. 25 Jan. 1946, Woking, Surrey; s. of the late John H. F. Wood and of Mary E. B. Wood (née Ottley); m. Joyce M. Teitz 1971; two d.; ed Bryanston School, King's Coll., Cambridge, Harvard Univ., USA; Fellow, King's Coll. Cambridge 1969–77; Asst Lecturer, then Lecturer, Univ. of Cambridge 1973–77; Economist, Sr Economist, IBRD 1977–85; Professorial Fellow, Inst. of Devt Studies, Univ. of Sussex 1985–2000; Chief Economist, Dept for Int. Devt 2000–05; Prof. of Int. Devt, Univ. of Oxford 2005–11, Prof. Emer. 2011–; Harkness Fellowship 1967–69. *Publications include:* A Theory of Profits 1975, A Theory of Pay 1978, Poverty and Human Development (with others) 1981, China: Long-Term Development Issues and Options (with others) 1985, North-South Trade, Employment and Inequality 1994. *Leisure interests:* music, art, tennis. *Address:* Queen Elizabeth House, 3 Mansfield Road, Oxford, OX1 3TB, England (office). *Telephone:* (1865) 281711 (office). *Fax:* (1865) 281801 (office). *E-mail:* adrian.wood@qeh.ox.ac.uk (office). *Website:* www.qeh.ox.ac.uk (office).

WOOD, Anne, CBE, FRTS; British television producer; *Chairman, Ragdoll Ltd;* b. 1937, Spennymoor, Co. Durham; m. Barrie Wood; one s. one d.; teacher of English Language and Literature 1960s; f. Books For Your Children magazine; co-creator and producer TV programme The Book Tower 1979, Ragdolly Anna; Head of Children's Programmes TV AM (ITV) 1982–84; f. Ragdoll Ltd (TV production co.) 1984, Creative Dir 1984, now Chair.; creator of Pob, Rosie and Jim, Tots TV, Brum, Open a Door, Teletubbies (shown in 120 countries worldwide), Boohbah; Fellow, Royal TV Soc. 1998–; Eleanor Farjeon Award for Services to Children's Books 1969, Ronald Politzer Award 1974; for the Book Tower: BAFTA 1979, 1982, Prix Jeunesse 1980; for Tots TV: Prix Jeunesse 1996, BAFTA 1996, 1997; Baird Medal, Royal TV Soc. 1997; numerous awards for Teletubbies including Grand Prize, Winner Pre-School Educ. Category, Prize Int. Contest (Japan) 1997, Children's BAFTA for Best Pre-School Programme 1998, Indies Nickleodeon UK Children's Award 1999, five awards at Int. Licensing Industry Merchandisers' Asscn 1999, BBC Audiocall Children's Award 2000; Veuve Clicquot Award for Business Woman of the Year 1999; BAFTA Special Award for Outstanding Contrib. in Children's TV and Film 2000, Olswang Business Award, Women in Film and Television 2003, Harvey Lee Award, Broadcasting Press Guild 2007. *Leisure interests:* gardening, reading. *Address:* Ragdoll Limited, Pinewood Studios, Pinewood Road, Iver Heath, Bucks., SL0 0NH, England (office). *Telephone:* (1789) 404100 (office). *Fax:* (1789) 404136 (office). *E-mail:* annew@ragdoll.co.uk (office). *Website:* www.ragdoll.co.uk (office).

WOOD, Brian Kuan; American writer and artist; was based in Cairo 2000–05, produced publs and sound projects in collaboration with artists, and began an on-line journal with artist Iman Issa featuring artists based in Cairo and Alexandria; with Anton Vidokle and Julieta Aranda, began a set of projects related to their interests, including an art collective (e-flux), a school (unitednationsplaza; Night School), an archive (e-flux video rental; Martha Rosler Library) and an activist group (The Next Documenta Should Be Curated By an Artist) 2008; co-f., with Julieta Aranda, a time bank for artists, curators, writers and others in the arts to exchange their time and skills 2008, has nearly 4,000 members and operates branches in The Hague, Moscow, Berlin, Frankfurt and other cities; co-f. imprint, with the Sternberg Press, Berlin, that publishes a series of paperback readers consisting of monographic publs and thematic compilations of essays 2008. *Publications include:* Selected Maria Lind Writing (ed.) 2010; writing has appeared in Bidoun, CAC Interviu, Paletten, e-flux journal and various artist-initiated platforms and publs. *Address:* e-flux, 311 East Broadway, New York, NY 10002, USA (office). *E-mail:* info@e-flux.com (office). *Website:* www.e-flux.org (office). *Website:* www.unitednationsplaza.org (office).

WOOD, Charles Gerald, FRSL; British playwright and scriptwriter; b. 6 Aug. 1932, St. Peter Port, Guernsey; s. of John Edward Wood and Catherine Mae Wood (née Harris); m. Valerie Elizabeth Newman 1954; one s. one d.; ed King Charles I School, Kidderminster and Birmingham Coll. of Art; corporal, 17/21st Lancers 1950–55; factory worker 1955–57; Stage Man., scenic artist, cartoonist, advertising artist 1957–59; Bristol Evening Post 1959–62; mem. Drama Advisory Panel, South Western Arts 1972–73; consultant to Nat. Film Devt Fund 1980–82; mem. Council BAFTA 1991–93; Evening Standard Drama Award 1963 1972, Screenwriters Guild Award 1965, Royal TV Soc. Award 1988, BAFTA Award 1988, Prix Italia 1988, Humanitas Award 2002. *Plays include:* Prisoner and Escort, Spare, John Thomas 1963, Meals on Wheels 1965, Don't Make Me Laugh 1966, Fill the Stage with Happy Hours 1967, Dingo 1967, H 1969, Welfare 1971, Veterans 1972, Jingo 1975, Has 'Washington' Legs? 1978, Red Star 1984, Across from the Garden of Allah 1986; adapted Pirandello's Man, Beast and Virtue 1989, The Mountain Giants 1993, Alexandre Dumas's The Tower 1995. *TV plays include:* Prisoner and Escort, Drill Pig, A Bit of a Holiday, A Bit of an Adventure, Love Lies Bleeding, Dust to Dust. *Screenplays include:* The Knack 1965, Help! 1965, How I Won the

War 1967, The Charge of the Light Brigade 1968, The Long Day's Dying 1969, Cuba 1980, Wagner 1983, Red Monarch 1983, Puccini 1984, Tumbledown 1988, Shooting the Hero 1991, An Awfully Big Adventure 1993, England my England (with John Osborne) 1995, The Ghost Road 1996, Mary Stuart 1996, Iris (with Richard Eyre) 1999, Snow White in New York 2001, The Other Man 2008. *TV series:* Don't Forget to Write 1986, My Family and Other Animals 1987, The Settling of the Sun 1987, Sharpe's Company 1994, Sharpe's Regiment 1996, Mute of Malice (Kavanagh QC) 1997, Sharpe's Waterloo 1997, Monsignor Renard 1999. *Publications include:* (plays): Cockade 1965, Fill the Stage with Happy Hours 1967, Dingo 1967, H 1970, Veterans 1972, Has 'Washington' Legs? 1978, Tumbledown 1987, Man, Beast and Virtue 1990, The Giants of the Mountain 1994, The Tower 1995, Iris 2002. *Leisure interests:* military and theatrical studies, gardening.

WOOD, David M., BSc; British/American oil industry executive; ed Univ. of Nottingham, Advanced Man. Program, Harvard Univ.; served in various exploration capacities for oil co. 1980–94; Man. of Frontier Exploration, Murphy Oil Corpn 1994–95, Gen. Man. Frontier Exploration 1995–97, Vice-Pres. of Frontier Exploration and Production 1997–99, Sr Vice-Pres. 1999–2003, Pres. Murphy Exploration & Production Co.-International 2003–06, Exec. Vice-Pres. of Worldwide Exploration and Production Operations 2007–08, Pres. Murphy Exploration & Production Co. for Murphy Oil Corpn 2007–08, mem. Bd of Dirs, Pres. and CEO Murphy Oil Corpn 2009–12 (resgnd). *Address:* c/o Murphy Oil Corporation, PO Box 7000, El Dorado, AR 71731-7000, USA. *E-mail:* info@murphyoilcorp.com.

WOOD, Elijah; American actor; b. 28 Jan. 1981, Cedar Rapids, Iowa. *Films include:* Back to the Future Part II 1989, Internal Affairs 1990, Avalon 1990, Paradise 1991, Radio Flyer 1992, Forever Young 1992, The Adventures of Huck Finn 1993, The Good Son 1993, North 1994, The War 1994, Flipper 1996, The Ice Storm 1997, Deep Impact 1998, The Faculty 1998, Black and White 1999, The Bumblebee Flies Anyway 1999, Chain of Fools 2000, The Lord of the Rings: The Fellowship of the Ring 2001, Ash Wednesday 2002, The Adventures of Tom Thumb and Thumbelina (voice) 2002, Try Seventeen 2002, The Lord of the Rings: The Two Towers 2002, Spy Kids 3-D: Game Over 2003, The Lord of the Rings: The Return of the King 2003, Eternal Sunshine of the Spotless Mind 2004, Christmas on Mars 2005, Sin City 2005, Hooligans 2005, Everything Is Illuminated 2005, Paris, je t'aime 2006, Bobby 2006, Legend of Spyro: A New Beginning (voice) 2006, Happy Feet (voice) 2006, Day Zero 2007, The Oxford Murders 2008, 9 (voice) 2008, The Romantics 2010, The Hobbit: An Unexpected Journey 2012. *Address:* William Morris Agency, Inc., 1 William Morris Place, Beverly Hills, CA 90212, USA. *Telephone:* (310) 859-4550. *Fax:* (310) 248-5650. *E-mail:* nd@wma.com. *Website:* www.wma.com.

WOOD, Graham Charles, MA, PhD, ScD, FRS, FREng; British scientist, engineer and academic; *Professor Emeritus of Corrosion Science and Engineering, University of Manchester;* b. 6 Feb. 1934, Farnborough; s. of Cyril Wood and Doris Hilda Wood (née Strange); m. Freda Nancy Waithman 1959; one s. one d.; ed Bromley Grammar School, Kent, Christ's Coll., Cambridge; Lecturer, then Sr Lecturer, Reader in Corrosion Science UMIST 1961–72, Prof. of Corrosion Science and Eng 1972–97, now Prof. Emer., UMIST and Univ. of Manchester; Vice-Prin. for Academic Devt UMIST 1982–84, Deputy Prin. 1983, Dean of Faculty of Tech. 1987–89, Pro-Vice-Chancellor 1992–97; Chair. Int. Corrosion Council 1993–96; Pres. Inst. of Corrosion Science and Tech. 1978–80; Hon. DSc (UMIST) 2001; U.R. Evans Award, Inst. of Corrosion, C. Wagner Award of Electrochemical Soc., Beilby Medal, Griffith Medal, Inst. of Materials, Cavallaro Medal, European Fed. of Corrosion, European Corrosion Medal, European Fed. of Corrosion, Hothersall Medal, Inst. of Metal Finishing. *Publications:* more than 400 papers in various learned journals. *Leisure interests:* travel, cricket, walking, history of art, science and politics. *Address:* University of Manchester, School of Materials, Corrosion and Protection Centre, Faculty of EPS, Room E39, DMU, Manchester, M13 9PL, England (office). *Telephone:* (161) 306-4850 (office); (161) 306-4851 (office). *Fax:* (161) 306-4865 (office).

WOOD, (James) Sebastian (Lamin), CMG; British diplomatist; *Ambassador to China;* b. 6 April 1961; m.; four c.; EC Dept (External), FCO 1983, Thai language training, Thailand 1984–86, Second, later First Sec., Bangkok 1986–89, Security Policy Dept, FCO 1989–91, Mandarin language training, Taiwan 1991, First Sec. and Consul for Macao BTC, Hong Kong 1992–94, First Sec., UKREP Jt Liaison Group, Hong Kong 1994–96, Security Policy Dept then UN Dept, FCO 1996–98, Prin. Pvt. Sec. to Cabinet Sec. 1998–2000, Weatherhead Centre for Int. Affairs, Harvard Univ., USA 2000–01, Counsellor (Political), Washington, DC 2001–05, Dir Asia Pacific, FCO 2005–08; secondment to Rolls-Royce Group 2008–09; Amb. to China 2010–. *Address:* British Embassy, 11 Guang Hua Lu, Jian Guo Men Wai, Beijing 100600, People's Republic of China (office). *Telephone:* (10) 51924000 (office). *Fax:* (10) 51924239 (office). *E-mail:* consular.beijing@fco.gov.uk (office). *Website:* www.gov.uk/government/world/organisations/british-embassy-beijing (office); www.gov.uk/government/world/china (office).

WOOD, L. John, QSO, BA, MA (Oxon.); New Zealand diplomatist and academic; *Chancellor, University of Canterbury;* b. 31 March 1944, Kaikoura; s. of Lionel Wood and Margaret Wood; m. 1st Rosemary Taunt 1969 (died 1995); one s.; m. 2nd Rose Newell; ed Lincoln Country Dist High School, Christchurch Boys' High School, Univ. of Canterbury and Balliol Coll., Oxford; joined Ministry of Foreign Affairs 1969, seconded to Treasury 1971–72, Second Sec., later First Sec., Embassy in Tokyo 1973–76, seconded to Prime Minister's Dept 1976–78, First Sec., later Counsellor and Consul-Gen. Bonn 1978–82, at Ministry of Foreign Affairs 1982–83, Minister, Deputy Chief of Mission, Embassy in Washington, DC 1984–87, Amb. to Iran (also accred to Pakistan and Turkey) 1987–90, Dir N Asia Div., Ministry of External Relations and Trade 1990–91, Deputy Sec. Econ. and Trade Relations 1991–94, Amb. to USA 1994–98, 2001–06, Deputy Sec. External Econ. and Trade Policy, Ministry of Foreign Affairs and Trade 1991–94, 1998–2002; Adjunct Prof. of Political Science, Univ. of Canterbury 2006–, Trustee, Univ. of Canterbury Foundation 2006–, elected by Court of Convocation to Univ. of Canterbury Council 2007, 2010–, Pro-Chancellor 2008–10, Chancellor 2012–; mem. Advisory Bd NZ/US Council 2006–; mem. Governing Bd Econ. Research Inst. for ASEAN and East Asia (ERIA), Jakarta 2008; mem. Council, Lincoln Univ. 2013–; Chief Crown Treaty of Waitangi Negotiator 2009–; Companion of the Queen's Service Order for Public Service 2006; Hon. DLitt (Canterbury) 2006;

Consumers for World Trade Hall of Fame 2004, Paul Harris Fellow, Rotary International 2005. *Publication:* Negotiating within Washington: Thrown in at the Deep End – A New Zealand Diplomat Looks Back, In 'American Negotiating Behaviour, Wheeler-Dealers, Legal Eagles, Bullies, And Preachers' 2010. *Leisure interests:* rare books and bindings, New Zealand literature, sport, V8 cars. *Address:* 'Blue Ridge', 215 Bay Paddock Road, R.D.I. Hapuku, Kaikoura (home); Office of the Chancellor, University of Canterbury, Private Bag 4800, Christchurch, New Zealand (office). *Telephone:* (3) 319-7074 (home). *Fax:* (3) 319-7073 (home). *E-mail:* blue-duck@xtra.co.nz. *Website:* www.posc.canterbury.ac.nz (office).

WOOD, Mark William, BA (Hons), MA; British journalist and broadcasting executive; *CEO, Independent Television News (ITN);* b. 28 March 1952, Rochester, Kent; m.; one d. one s.; ed Univs of Leeds, Warwick and Oxford; joined Reuters 1976, Corresp. Vienna, East Berlin and Moscow 1977–85, Chief Corresp., W Germany 1985–87, European Ed. 1987–89, Ed.-in-Chief 1989–2000, Exec. Dir 1990–96, Chair. Visnews Reuters TV 1992–2002, Man. Dir Reuters Contents Partners 2000–02; Dir (non-Exec.) Ind. TV News (ITN) 1993–2002, Chair. 1998–, CEO 2003–; Chair. Meteor GmbH 2000–02; Dir London News Radio 1999–2002; Chair. Museums, Libraries and Archives Council 2003–08; Dir Citywire 2002–, Espresso Education 2005–. *Address:* Independent Television News, 200 Gray's Inn Road, London, WC1X 8XZ, England (office). *Telephone:* (20) 7430-4249 (office). *Fax:* (20) 7430-4868 (office). *E-mail:* mark.wood@itn.co.uk (office). *Website:* www .itn.co.uk (office).

WOOD, Sir Martin (Francis), Kt, OBE, MA, FRS, DL; British engineer and business executive; b. 19 April 1927; s. of Arthur Henry Wood and Katharine Mary Altham Wood (née Cumberlege); m. Audrey Buxton Wood (née Stanfield) 1955; one s. one d. one step-s. one step-d.; ed Gresham's, Trinity Coll., Cambridge, Imperial Coll., London, Christ Church, Oxford; with Nat. Coal Bd 1953–55; Sr Research Officer, Clarendon Lab., Oxford of Oxford 1956–69; f. Oxford Instruments PLC 1959, Chair. 1959–83, Deputy Chair. 1983–; Chair. Nat. Comm. for Superconductivity 1987–91; mem. Advisory Bd for Research Councils 1983–89, ACOST 1990–93, Central Lab. of Research Councils 1995–98; Dir Orbit Precision Machining Ltd 1965–, Oxford Seedcorn Capital Ltd 1986–, Oxford Ventures Group Ltd 1988–, ISIS Innovation Ltd 1989–, Oxford Innovation Ltd 1989–, Newport Tech. Group Ltd 1989–, FARM Africa Ltd 1985–; Tech. Consultant African Medical and Research Foundation; f. Northmoor Trust (for nature conservation), Oxford Trust (for encouragement of study and application of science and tech.); Trustee Oxon. Council for Voluntary Action 1994–; Fellow, Wolfson Coll., Oxford 1967–94, Hon. Fellow 1994; Hon. Fellow, UMIST 1989; Hon. DSc (Cranfield Inst. of Tech.) 1983; Hon. DTech (Loughborough Univ. of Tech.) 1985; Hon. DEng (Birmingham) 1997; Hon. DUniv (Open) 1999; Mullard Medal, Royal Soc. 1982.

WOOD, Maurice, MB, BS, MD, FRCGP, FAAFP, FWOFD; American physician and academic; *Physician and Academic Professor Emeritus, Department of Family Practice, Medical College of Virginia, Virginia Commonwealth University;* b. 28 June 1922, Pelton, Co. Durham, England; s. of Joseph Wood and Eugenie Wood (née Lumley); widowed; two s. one d.; ed Chester-le-Street Grammar School and Univ. of Durham; various hosp. appointments 1945–46, 1949-50; Maj., RAMC 1946–49; Sr Pnr, Medical Practice, South Shields 1950–71; Gen. Practice Teaching Group, Univ. of Newcastle-upon-Tyne 1969–71; Clinical Asst Dept of Psychological Medicine, South Shields Gen. Hosp. 1966–71; Assoc. Prof., Dir of Research, Dept of Family Practice, Medical Coll. of Virginia, Virginia Commonwealth Univ., Richmond, Va 1971–73, Prof. and Dir of Research 1973–87, Prof. Emer. 1987–, now Physician and Academic Prof. Emer.; Career Founding mem. and Pres. N American Primary Care Research Group 1972–83, Exec. Dir 1983–92, Pres. Emer. 1992–; Consultant Adviser, WHO 1979–90; other professional appointments and memberships; mem. US Nat. Comm. on Vital and Health Statistics 1976–79; mem. Inst. of Medicine, NAS; Fellow, American Acad. of Family Physicians, Royal Coll. of Gen. Practitioners, World Org. of Family Doctors 2008; Maurice Wood Award, N American Primary Care Research Group 1995 and other awards and distinctions. *Publications:* International Classification of Primary Care 1987, 2005, The International Classification of Primary Care in the European Community – with a multilanguage layer (co-ed.) 1993, Organization, Funding, Distribution 2003–05; numerous articles in professional journals and book chapters. *Leisure interests:* sailing, gliding, skiing. *Address:* Department of Family Practice, Virginia Commonwealth University, Medical College of Virginia Station, Box 980-257, Richmond, VA 23298-0251 (office); 176 Lakeside Close, Stoney Creek at Wintergreen, Nellysford, VA 22958-8093, USA (home). *Telephone:* (804) 828-9625 (office); (434) 361-1275 (home). *Fax:* (434) 361-1275 (home). *E-mail:* wood150w@earthlink .net (home); nbl4wd@verizon.net (home).

WOOD, Michael M.; American business executive and fmr diplomatist; *Chairman, Investment Committee, Redwood Investments;* b. 1947; m. Judy Wood; one s. one d.; Co-founder and CEO Hanley Wood, LLC 1976–2005, mem. Bd 2005; mem. Bd of Advisors, Veronis Suhler Stevenson 2005; f. Redwood Investments, LLC 2005, currently Chair. Investment Cttee; mem. US del. attending inauguration of Pres. Lucio Gutierrez Borbua of Ecuador 2003; organized Building the American Dream housing industry round table with Pres. Ronald Reagan 1984; fmr mem. Harvard Jt Center for Housing Studies; has served on Nat. Asscn of Home Builders Long-Range Planning Cttee; Amb. to Sweden 2006–09; Top Executive of the Year Award, Media Business magazine 2005. *Leisure interests:* mountain biking, golf. *Address:* Redwood Investments, PO Box 55327, Washington, DC 20027, USA (office). *Telephone:* (202) 333-1395 (office). *E-mail:* mail@redwoodinvestments.net (office). *Website:* www.redwoodinvestments.ne (office).

WOOD, Peter, CBE; British insurance industry executive and entrepreneur; *Chairman, Esure;* b. 1946, Surrey, England; m. (divorced); five d.; Founder and CEO Direct Line Insurance 1985–96, Chair. 1996–97; Chair. Privilege Insurance 1993–98; Vice-Chair. Plymouth Rock Co. 1994–; Founder and Chair. Esure 2000– (purchased Lloyds Banking Group's 70% stake in the co. 2010), First Alternative 2003–, also set up two insurance cos in USA, Response 1995 and Homesite 1997, involvement ended 2004; est. a women-only specialist insurance brand, Sheilas' Wheels 2005; Dir (non-exec.), The Economist Newspaper Ltd 1998–2004. *Address:* Esure at The Observatory, Reigate, Surrey, RH2 0SG, England (office). *Telephone:*

(1737) 222222 (office). *Fax:* (1737) 235000 (office). *E-mail:* info@esure.com (office). *Website:* www.esure.com (office).

WOOD, Peter (Lawrence); British theatre and television director; b. 8 Oct. 1928; s. of Frank Wood and Lucy E. Meeson; ed Taunton School and Downing Coll. Cambridge; Resident Dir Arts Theatre 1956–57; Assoc. Dir Nat. Theatre 1978–89; numerous other productions at theatres in London, Edin., New York, Stratford (Ont.), Vienna etc.; dir of plays for TV in USA and UK since 1970. *Theatre productions include:* (for Nat. Theatre) The Master Builder 1964, Love for Love 1965, 1985, Jumpers 1972, The Guardsman, The Double Dealer 1978, Undiscovered Country 1979, The Provok'd Wife 1980, On the Razzle 1981, The Rivals 1983, Rough Crossing 1984, Dalliance 1986, The Threepenny Opera 1986, The American Clock 1986, The Beaux' Stratagem 1989, The School for Scandal 1990, (for RSC) Winter's Tale 1960, The Devils 1961, Hamlet 1961, The Beggar's Opera 1963, Travesties 1974, The Strange Case of Dr. Jekyll and Mr. Hyde 1991, Indian Ink 1995, (for Chichester) The Silver King 1990, She Stoops to Conquer 1992, Arcadia 2000, On the Razzle 2001. *Opera productions include:* The Mother of Us All, Santa Fe 1976, Il Seraglio, Glyndebourne 1980, 1988, Don Giovanni, Covent Garden 1981, Macbeth, Staatsoper, Vienna 1982, Orione, Santa Fe 1983, Otello, Staatsoper, Vienna 1987. *Leisure interests:* swimming, sailing, travelling. *Address:* The Old Barn, Batcombe, Somerset, BA4 6HD, England.

WOOD, Ronald (Ronnie); British musician (guitar, bass guitar); b. 1 June 1947, Hillingdon, London, England; m. 1st; one s.; m. 2nd Jo Howard 1985 (divorced 2009); one s. one d.; guitarist with Jeff Beck Group 1968–69, The Faces 1969–75, The Rolling Stones 1976–; tours worldwide; has also played with Bo Diddley, Rod Stewart, Jerry Lee Lewis; Nordoff-Robbins Silver Clef 1982, Grammy Lifetime Achievement Award 1986, Ivor Novello Award for Outstanding Contribution to British Music 1991. *Recordings include:* albums: with Jeff Beck Group: Truth 1968, Beck-Ola 1969; with The Faces: First Step 1970, Long Player 1971, A Nod's As Good As A Wink… To A Blind Horse 1971, Ooh La La 1973, Coast To Coast Overtures and Beginners 1974; with The Rolling Stones: Black And Blue 1976, Some Girls 1978, Emotional Rescue 1980, Tattoo You 1981, Still Life 1982, Undercover 1983, Dirty Work 1986, Steel Wheels 1989, Flashpoint 1991, Voodoo Lounge 1994, Stripped 1995, Bridges to Babylon 1997, Forty Licks 2002, Live Licks 2004, A Bigger Bang 2005; solo: I've Got My Own Album To Do 1974, Now Look 1976, Mahoney's Last Stand 1976, Gimme Some Neck 1979, 1234 1981, Live At The Ritz 1988, Slide On This 1992, Slide On Live: Plugged In And Standing 1994, Live & Eclectic 2000, Not For Beginners 2002, Live At Electric Ladyland 2008, Always Wanted More 2003, Buried Alive 2006, The First Barbarians 2007, I Feel Like Playing 2010. *Film:* Shine a Light 2007. *Publications include:* According to the Rolling Stones (autobiography, jtly) 2003, Ronnie Wood: The Autobiography 2007. *Website:* www.rollingstones.com; www.ronniewood.com

WOOD, William B., III, PhD; American biologist and academic; *Distinguished Professor Emeritus, University of Colorado;* b. 19 Feb. 1938, Baltimore, Md; s. of Dr W. Barry Wood, Jr and Mary L. Hutchins; m. Renate Marie-Elisabeth Hartisch 1961; two s.; ed Harvard Coll., Stanford Univ. and Univ. of Geneva, Switzerland; NAS-Nat. Research Council Postdoctoral Fellow, Univ. of Geneva 1964; Asst Prof. of Biology, California Inst. of Tech. 1965–68, Assoc. Prof. 1968–70, Prof. 1970–77; Prof. of Molecular Biology, Univ. of Colorado, Boulder 1977–2008, Distinguished Prof. Emer. 2008–, Chair. of Dept 1978–83; Co-Chair. NRC Cttee tasked with initiating the Nat. Acads Summer Inst. on Undergraduate Educ. 2003; Ed.-in-Chief CBE-Life Sciences Education 2005–10; mem. NAS, American Acad. of Arts and Sciences, AAAS, American Soc. of Biological Chemists, Soc. for Developmental Biology; US Steel Award in Molecular Biology, NAS 1969, Bruce Alberts Award, American Soc. for Cell Biology 2004, Viktor Hamburger Outstanding Educator Prize, Soc. for Developmental Biology 2013. *Publications include:* Biochemistry, A Problems Approach (co-author) 1974, 1981, Molecular Design in Living Systems 1974, The Molecular Basis of Metabolism 1974, Molecular Biology of Eucaryotic Cells (co-author) 1975, Immunology (co-author) 1978, 1984, The Nematode Caenorhabditis Elegans (ed.) 1988, Learning and Understanding (report) 2002; articles in professional journals. *Leisure interests:* music, tennis, camping. *Address:* Molecular, Cellular and Developmental Biology, University of Colorado, PORT B345A, Boulder, CO 80309-0347 USA (office). *Telephone:* (303) 492-6680 (office); (303) 492-2272 (Lab.) (office). *E-mail:* wood@colorado.edu (office). *Website:* mcdb.colorado.edu/directory/wood_b.html (office).

WOOD OF ANFIELD, Baron (Life Peer), cr. 2011, of Tonbridge in the County of Kent; **Lord Stewart Martin Wood,** MA, PhD; British politician, political adviser and academic; *Shadow Cabinet Minister Without Portfolio;* b. 25 March 1968, Kent, England; s. of Brian Wood and Gisela Wood; m. Camilla Bustani; two c.; ed Univ. of Oxford, Harvard Univ., USA, Wissenschaftszentrum, Germany; Lecturer, Univ. of Oxford 1996–2010, Fellow in Politics, Magdalen Coll. Oxford; co-f. 'Third Way' think-tank, Nexus 1996; became Special Adviser to the Treasury under Chancellor of the Exchequer, Gordon Brown 2001; Sr Foreign Policy Adviser to Prime Minister Gordon Brown 2007–10, also advised Prime Minister on culture, media and sport; Communications Chief for Labour Party Leader, Ed Miliband 2010–11; Shadow Minister without Portfolio 2011–; Bd mem. English Stage Co., Royal Court Theatre 2006–, YouGov/Cambridge; Fulbright Scholar 1989–90. *Address:* House of Lords, Westminster, London, SW1A 0PW, England (office). *Telephone:* (20) 7219-7304 (home). *E-mail:* stewart.wood@parliament.uk (office).

WOODHEAD, Sir Christopher (Chris) Anthony, Kt, MA; British academic and educational administrator; *Professor, University of Buckingham;* b. 20 Oct. 1946, Middx; s. of Anthony Woodhead and Doris Woodhead; m. 1970 (divorced 1995); one d.; ed Wallington Co. Grammar School, Univs of Bristol and Keele; English teacher Priory School, Shrewsbury 1969–72; Deputy Head of English Newent School, Gloucester 1972–74; Head of English Gordano School, Avon 1974–76; Lecturer in English, Univ. of Oxford 1976–82; English Adviser Shropshire Local Educ. Authority 1982–84, Chief Adviser 1984–86; Deputy Chief Educ. Officer Devon Local Educ. Authority 1988–90, Cornwall Local Educ. Authority 1990–91; Deputy Chief Exec. Nat. Curriculum Council 1990, Chief Exec. 1991–93; Chief Exec. School Curriculum and Assessment Authority 1993–94; HM Chief Inspector of Schools 1994–2001; Prof., Univ. of Buckingham 2002–; Chair. Cognita Schools Ltd 2004–; mem. Advisory Council of Reform; columnist, Sunday Times. *Publication:* Class War 2002. *Leisure interests:* rock

climbing, running. *Address:* Hendre Gwenllian, Llanfrothen, Penrhyndeudraeth, Gwynedd, LL48 6DJ, Wales.

WOODLAND, Alan Donald, PhD, FASSA; Australian economist and academic; *Professor and Australian Professorial Fellow, School of Economics, Australian School of Business, University of New South Wales;* b. 4 Oct. 1943, Dorrigo, NSW; s. of C. J. Woodland and E. Shephard; m. Narelle Todd 1966; one s. two d.; ed Univ. of New England, Armidale, NSW; Lecturer, Univ. of New England 1967–69; Asst Prof., Univ. of British Columbia, Canada 1969–74, Assoc. Prof. 1974–78, Prof. of Econs 1978–81; Prof. of Econometrics and Australian Professorial Fellow, Faculty of Econs and Business, Univ. of Sydney 1982–2008; Prof. and Australian Professorial Fellow, School of Econs, Australian School of Business, Univ. of New South Wales 2008–; Jt Ed. The Economic Record 1987–92; Fellow, Reserve Bank 1981; Fellow, Econometric Soc.; Distinguished Economist Award, Econ. Soc. of Australia 2008. *Publications include:* International Trade and Resource Allocation 1982, International Trade Policy and the Pacific Rim, Institute of Economic Affairs Conference Vol. Number 120, (co-ed.) 1999, Economic Theory and International Trade: Essays in Honour of Murray C. Kemp (ed.) 2002, The Economics of Illegal Immigration (co-author) 2005. *Leisure interests:* bridge, tennis. *Address:* Room 416, School of Economics, Australian School of Business Building, University of New South Wales, Sydney, NSW 2052 (office); 5 Rosebery Road, Killara, NSW 2071, Australia (home). *Telephone:* (2) 9385-9707 (office); (2) 9416-3100 (home). *Fax:* (2) 9313-6337 (office). *E-mail:* a.woodland@unsw.edu.au (office). *Website:* www.asb.unsw.edu.au/schools/economics (office).

WOODRELL, Daniel, BA, MFA; American author; b. 4 March 1953, Springfield, Mo.; m. Katie Estill; ed Univ. of Kansas, Iowa Writers Workshop; grew up in northern Mo.; dropped out of high school to join US Marines aged 17; spent a year on a Michener Fellowship. *Publications include:* Under the Bright Lights 1986, Woe to Live On (adapted into a film Ride with the Devil by Ang Lee 1999) 1987, Muscle for the Wing 1988, The Ones You Do 1992, Give Us a Kiss: A Country Noir 1996, Tomato Red (PEN Center USA Award for Fiction 1999) 1998, The Death of Sweet Mister (Clifton Fadiman Medal, The Center for Fiction, Sponsored by Reba and Dave Williams 2011) 2001, Winter's Bone (adapted into an Oscar-nominated film of the same name 2010, Sundance Film Festival Award for top dramatic film 2010) 2006, The Outlaw Album 2011. *Address:* c/o Little Brown, 1269 Lexington Avenue, New York, NY 10028, USA.

WOODROW, William Robert (Bill), DipAD, RA; British artist and sculptor; b. 1 Nov. 1948, nr Henley-on-Thames, Oxon., England; s. of Geoffrey W. Woodrow and Doreen M. Fasken; m. Pauline Rowley 1970; one s. one d.; ed Barton Peveril Grammar School and Winchester, St Martin's and Chelsea Schools of Art; numerous solo exhbns in UK, FRG, France, Australia, Netherlands, Belgium, Italy, USA, Canada, Switzerland, Sweden, Ireland and Yugoslavia since 1979; works in many public collections in UK and abroad; Trustee, Tate Gallery 1996–2001, Imperial War Museum 2003–11, Roche Court Educational Trust 2008–; Gov. Univ. of the Arts, London 2003–08; elected to Royal Acad. of Arts 2002; finalist in Turner Prize 1986, Winner Anne Gerber Award, Seattle Museum of Art, USA 1988. *Publications include:* Bill Woodrow, Sculpture 1980–86, A Quiet Revolution – Recent British Sculpture, Bill Woodrow, Eye of the Needle, Sculptures 1987–1989, Bill Woodrow, XXI Bienal de São Paulo 1991, In Awe of the Pawnbroker 1994, Fools' Gold 1996, Lead Astray 2004, Brood 2007. *Address:* c/o Royal Academy of Arts, Piccadilly, London, W1J 0BD, England. *E-mail:* bill@billwoodrow.com (office). *Website:* www.billwoodrow.com.

WOODRUFF, Judy Carline, BA; American broadcast journalist; *Senior Correspondent and Political Editor, The Newshour with Jim Lehrer;* b. 20 Nov. 1946, Tulsa, Okla; d. of William Henry Woodruff and Anna Lee Woodruff (née Payne); m. Albert R. Hunt, Jr 1980; two s. one d.; ed Meredith Coll., Duke Univ.; News Announcer and Reporter WAGA-TV, Atlanta 1970–75; News Corresp. NBC News, Atlanta 1975–76; White House Corresp., NBC News, Washington 1977–83; Corresp., MacNeil-Lehrer News Hour, PBS, Washington 1983–93, Sr Corresp. and Political Ed. The News Hour With Jim Lehrer 2007–; Anchor and Sr Corresp. Cable News Network (CNN) 1993–2005, also anchored Judy Woodruff's Inside Politics; anchor for Frontline (PBS documentary series) 1983–90; Visiting Fellow, Joan Shorenstein Center on the Press, Politics and Public Policy, Harvard Univ. 2005–; Visiting Prof. of Media and Politics, Duke Univ. 2006; mem. Bd of Advisers Henry Grady School of Journalism, Univ. of Georgia 1979–82, Bd of Visitors Wake Forest Univ. 1982–88, Bd of Advisers Benton Fellowship in Broadcast Journalism, Univ. of Chicago 1984–90, Families and Work Inst. 1989–, Freedom Forum First Amendment Center 1992–, Comm. on Women's Health 1993–, Radio and TV News Dirs' Foundation 1994–; Co-Chair. Int. Women's Media Foundation 1991– (Founder, Dir 1989–); mem. Nat. Acad. of TV Arts and Sciences, White House Corresps Asscn; Trustee, Duke Univ. 1985–97, now Trustee Emer.; Knight Fellowship in Journalism, Stanford Univ. 1985–99, Edward Weintal Award 1987, Joan Shorenstein Barone Award 1987, Helen Bernstein Award for Excellence in Journalism, New York Public Library 1989, Pres.'s 21st Century Award, Nat. Women's Hall of Fame 1994, CableAce Award for Best Newscaster 1995, CableAce Best Anchor Team Award 1996, Allen H. Neuharth Award for Excellence in Journalism 1995, News and Documentary Emmy Award 1997, Int. Matrix Award, Asscn for Women in Communications 2003, Leonard Zeidenberg First Amendment Award, Radio-TV News Dir Asscn and Foundation 2003; elected to Georgia Asscn of Broadcasters Hall of Fame 2003. *Publication:* This is Judy Woodruff at the White House 1982. *Address:* The Newshour with Jim Lehrer, PBS, 3620 27th Street S, Arlington, VA 22206-2350, USA (office). *Telephone:* (703) 998-2481 (office). *Fax:* (703) 998-4154 (office). *E-mail:* newshour@pbs.org (office). *Website:* www.pbs.org/newshour (office).

WOODS, Eldrick Tont (Tiger); American professional golfer; b. 30 Dec. 1975, Cypress, Calif.; s. of the late Lt-Col Earl Woods and Kultida Woods; m. Elin Nordegren 2004 (divorced 2010); one s. one d.; ed Stanford Univ.; winner Int. Jr World Championship 1984–91, Nat. Youth Classic 1990, US Jr Amateur Championship 1991 (youngest winner), 1992, 1993, US Amateur Championships 1994 (youngest winner), 1995, 1996; turned professional 1996; winner, Las Vegas Invitational competition 1996, Walt Disney Classic 1996, Honda Asian Classic 1997, Mercedes Championships 1997, 2000, US Masters 1997 (youngest winner, broke records for lowest score and greatest margin of victory), 2001, 2002, 2005, Bell South Classic 1998, US PGA Championship 1999, 2000, 2006, 2007, Nat. Car

Rental Golf Classic 1999, WGC American Express Championship 1999, 2006, AT & T Pebble Beach Nat. Pro-Am 2000, Bay Hill Invitational 2000, 2001, 2002 US Open 2000, 2002, 2008, British Open 2000, 2005, 2006, PGA Tour's Arnold Palmer Invitational Golf Tournament 2012, 2013, Memorial Tournament 2012, AT&T National 2012, and numerous other titles; mem. US team World Amateur Team Championship 1994, US Walker Cup team 1995, US Ryder Cup team 1997, 1999, 2002 (postponed from 2001), 2004, 2006, 2010, 2012; first ranked World No. 1 following maiden victory at The Masters, Augusta 1997, held World No. 1 ranking Aug. 1999–Sept. 2004, June 2005–Oct. 2010, also for most consecutive weeks and for greatest total number of weeks; contract with Nike 1999 (biggest sponsorship deal in sporting history); f. Tiger Woods Foundation, Tiger Woods Learning Center; announced indefinite leave from professional golf 11 Dec. 2009, returned to competition for The Masters 8 April 2010; won Chevron World Challenge title 2011; regained World No. 1 ranking after winning Arnold Palmer Invitational 25 March 2013; co-f. with his father The Tiger Woods Foundation 1996; numerous awards, including Sports Star of the Year Award 1997, PGA Player of the Year and PGA Tour Player of the Year 1997, 1999–2003, 2005–06, 2009, Sports Illustrated Sportsman of the Year 1996, 2000, Mark H. McCormack Award 2006, Byron Nelson Award for lowest adjusted scoring average a record nine times, inducted into the California Hall of Fame 2007, named Athlete of the Decade by the Associated Press 2009, named Associated Press Male Athlete of the Year four times. *Leisure interests:* basketball, fishing, sport in general. *Address:* Tiger Woods Foundation, 4281 Katella Avenue, Suite 111, Los Alamitos, CA 90720; Tiger Woods Learning Center, One Tiger Woods Way, Anaheim, CA 92801; IMG Golf, IMG Center, 1360 East 9th Street, Suite 100, Cleveland, OH 44114, USA. *Telephone:* (714) 765-8000 (Tiger Woods Learning Center); (216) 522-1200 (IMG). *Fax:* (216) 436-3477 (IMG). *Website:* www.tigerwoodsfoundation.org; www.twlc.org; www.tigerwoods.com.

WOODS, James Howard; American actor; b. 18 April 1947, Vernal, Utah; s. of Gail Woods and Martha Woods; m. 1st Kathryn Greko 1980 (divorced 1983); m. 2nd Sarah Owen 1989 (divorced 1990); ed Univ. of California, Los Angeles and Massachusetts Inst. of Tech.; first Broadway appearance in Brendan Behan's Borstal Boy; Obie Award for appearance in Brooklyn Acad. of Music Production of Edward Bond's Saved, New York 1971; other stage appearances in 1970s include Moonchildren 1972, The Trial of the Catonsville Nine, Finishing Touches, Conduct Unbecoming; two Emmy Awards. *Films include:* The Visitors 1971, The Way We Were 1972, The Gambler 1974, Distance 1975, Alex and the Gypsy 1976, The Choirboys 1977, The Onion Field 1979, Black Marble 1980, Fast Walking 1982, Split Image 1982, Videodrome 1983, Once Upon a Time in America 1984, Against All Odds 1984, Joshua Then and Now 1985, Best Seller 1987, Cop 1987, The Boost 1989, True Believer 1989, Immediate Family 1989, Straight Talk 1992, Diggstown, Chaplin 1992, The Getaway 1994, Curse of the Starving Class 1994, Casino 1995, Nixon 1996, Killer: A Journal of Murder, Ghosts of Mississippi 1996, Hercules (voice) 1997, Contact 1997, Vampires 1998, True Crime 1999, Virgin Suicides 2000, Race to Space 2001, John Q 2001, Recess, School's Out (voice) 2001, Riding in Cars with Boys 2001, Scary Movie 2 2001, Northfork 2003, This Girl's Life 2003, Ark 2004, Pretty Persuasion 2005, Be Cool 2005, End Game 2006, Surf's Up (voice) 2007, An American Carol 2008, Jobs 2013, White House Down 2013, Jamesy Boy 2014. *Television include:* Holocaust 1978, Badge of the Assassin 1985, Promise 1986, My Name is Bill. W. 1989, Citizen Cohn 1992, Jane's House 1994, Next Door 1994, Indictment: The McMartin Trial 1995, The Summer of Ben Tyler 1996, Dirty Pictures 2000, Showtime 2000, Rudy: The Rudy Giuliani Story 2003, Shark (series) 2006–08, Too Big to Fail (film) 2011, Coma (mini-series) 2012, Mary and Martha (film) 2013, Ray Donovan (series) 2013. *Leisure interest:* poker. *Address:* c/o Guttman Associates, 118 S Beverly Drive, Suite 201, Beverly Hills, CA 90210, USA.

WOODS, Michael, PhD, DSc; Irish politician; b. 8 Dec. 1935, Bray, Co. Wicklow; m. Margaret Maher; three s. two d.; ed University Coll., Dublin and Harvard Business School, USA; Lecturer, Franciscan Coll. of Agric., Multyfarnham, Co. Westmeath 1958–59; Head of Dept and Prin. Officer, Agric. Research Inst. 1960–70; Man. Dir F11 Produce Ltd 1970–73, Associated Producer Groups Ltd 1974–79; TD (mem. Dáil) 1977–2011; Minister of State, Depts of Taoiseach and Defence 1979; Minister for Health and Social Welfare 1979–81, March–Dec. 1982, for Social Welfare 1987–91, for Agric. 1991–92, for the Marine 1992, for Social Welfare 1993–94, for Health 1994, Spokesperson on Equality and Law Reform 1994–97, Minister for Marine and Natural Resources 1997–2000, for Educ. and Science 2000–02, Chair. Jt Cttee of Foreign Affairs 2002–11; Fellow, Inst. of Public Admin; mem. Fianna Fáil. *Publications:* Research in Ireland – Key to Economic and Social Development; numerous tech. and scientific papers. *Address:* 13 Kilbarrack Grove, Raheny, Dublin 5, Ireland (home). *Telephone:* (1) 8392439 (home). *E-mail:* michaelwoods.dsc@gmail.com (office).

WOODS, Philip (Phil) Wells, BMus; American jazz musician (alto saxophone), composer and teacher; b. 2 Nov. 1931, Springfield, Mass; s. of Stanley J. Woods and Clara Markley; m. 1st Beverly Berg 1957 (divorced 1973); one s. one d.; m. 2nd Jill Goodwin 1985; two step-d.; ed studied privately with Harvey LaRose in Springfield, Lenny Tristano in New York, Manhattan School of Music and Juilliard Conservatory; numerous appearances and recordings with own bands and as featured performer; Co-founder Clark Terry Big Bad Band; mem. The European Rhythm Machine 1968–73; Leader, The Phil Woods Quartet 1955–99, The Phil Woods Quintet 1977–; Phil Woods Little Big Band 1988–; mem. Advisory Bd Delaware Water Gap Celebration of the Arts, Bd of Dirs Al Cohn Memorial Jazz Collection, American Fed. of Musicians; Hon. LLD (East Stroudsberg Univ.) 1994, Hon. DHumLitt (DePaul Univ.) 2009; Officier, Ordre des Arts et des Lettres; Grammy Awards, Beacon Jazz Award 2001, American Jazz Hall of Fame 1994, Jazz Master Fellowship, Nat. Endowment for the Arts 2007, Grammy Foundation President's Merit Award 2007, Kennedy Center Living Legends in Jazz Award 2007, Creative Community Award 2008. *Compositions include:* Three Improvisations (saxophone quartet), Sonata for alto and piano (Four Moods), Rights of Swing, The Sun Suite, I Remember, The Deer Head Suite, Fill the Woods with Light (for Parsons Dance Co.), Requiem (saxophone quartet), The Children's Suite. *Recordings include:* albums: Early Quintets 1954, New Jazz Quintet 1954, Pot Pie (with Jon Eardley) 1954, New Jazz Quartet 1955, Woodlore 1955, Pairing Off (with Gene Quill) 1956, Phil and Quill (with Gene Quill) 1956, The Young Bloods (with Donald Byrd) 1956, Young Woods 1956, New York Scene (with George Wallington

and Donald Byrd) 1957, Phil and Quill with Prestige (with Gene Quill) 1957, Bird Feathers (with Gene Quill) 1957, Four Altos (with Gene Quill) 1957, Bird's Night (with Cecil Payne) 1957, The Jazz We Heard Last Summer (with Herbie Mann and Eddie Costa) 1957, Phil Talks with Quill (with Gene Quill) 1957, Warm Woods 1957, In Paris 1961, Rights of Swing 1961, Jazz at the Liberty 1963, Directly from the Half Note 1966, What Happens? (with Art Farmer) 1968, Alto Summit (with others) 1968, Alive and Well in Paris 1968, Round Trip 1969, A Jazz Life 1970, Gravenstein (with Daniel Humair) 1971, Gargoyle Wedding 1973, New Music 1973, Phil Woods Broadcasts 1973, The New Phil Woods Album 1975, I Remember 1978, A Live Recording Vol. One 1979, More Live (Grammy Award 1982) 1979, European Tour Live 1980, The Macerata Concert 1980, Birds of a Feather 1981, Live from New York 1982, At the Vanguard 1982; with The European Rhythm Machine: 9th Int. Jazz Festival Ljubljana 1968, The Birth of the ERM 1968, Stolen Moments 1968, Freedom Jazz Dance 1969, At the Montreux Jazz Festival 1969, Woods Notes 1969, At the Frankfurt Jazz Festival 1970, Chromatic Banana 1970, Jazz Workshop 1971, Live at Montreux 1972; with The Phil Woods Quintet: Song for Sisyphus 1977, Integrity 1984, Heaven 1984, Dizzy Gillespie Meets The Phil Woods Quintet 1986, Gratitude 1986, Bop Stew 1987, Bouquet 1987, Flash 1989, All Bird's Children 1990, Full House 1991, An Affair to Remember 1993, Souvenirs 1994, Plays the Music of Jim McNeely 1995, Mile High Jazz 1996, American Songbook 2002, In Her Eyes 2005, American Songbook II 2007; with Phil Woods Little Big Band: Musique Dubois 1974, Images (with Michel Legrand) (Grammy Award 1976) 1975, Phil Woods and the Japanese Rhythm Machine 1975, Live from the Showboat 1976, Floresta Canto (with Chris Gunning Orchestra) 1976, Crazy Horse (with Chris Swansen) 1979, Three for All (with Tommy Flanagan and Red Mitchell) 1981, The New York-Montreux Connection (with others) 1981, Ole Dude & the Fundance Kid (with Budd Johnson) 1984, Piper at the Gates of Dawn (with Chris Swansen) 1984, Anything Goes (with Stéphane Grappelli) 1987, Embraceable You (with Big Bang Orchestra) 1988, Evolution 1988, Phil on Etna (with Catania City Brass Orchestra) 1989, My Man Benny My Man Phil (with Benny Carter) 1989, Here's to my Lady 1989, Real Life 1990, Phil's Mood (with Space Jazz Trio) 1990, Flowers for Hodges (with Jim McNeely) 1991, Live at the Corridonia Jazz Festival (with Space Jazz Trio) 1991, Elsa (with Enrico Pieranunzi) 1991, Ornithology: Phil Salutes Bird (with Franco d'Andrea Trio) 1994, Our Monk (with Franco d'Andrea) 1994, Alto Summit (with Vincent Herring, Antonio Hart) 1995, The Complete Concert (with Gorden Beck) 1996, Another Time Another Place (with Benny Carter) 1996, Astor & Elis 1996, The Summit (with George Robert) 1997, Celebration! (with the Festival Orchestra) 1997, Chasin' the Bird 1997, The Rev & I (with Johnny Griffin) 1998, Soul Eyes (with George Robert) 2000, Voyage (with the Bill Charlap Trio) 2000, Giants at Play (John Coates) 2001, Beyond Brooklyn (with Herbie Mann) 2002, The Thrill is Gone 2002, Big Encounter at Umbria (Vols 1–4, with Lee Konitz) 2003, Play Henry Mancini (with Carl Saunders) 2003, Bouncin' with Bud & Phil (with Bud Shank) 2003, This is How I Feel About Quincy 2003, Unheard Herd 2004, Groovin' to Marty Paich (with Los Angeles Jazz Orchestra) 2004, Swingchronicity (with DePaul Univ. Jazz Ensemble) 2007, The Children's Suite 2009, Songs for COTA 2010. *Leisure interests:* computer games, reading, public television, movies. *Address:* PO Box 278, Delaware Water Gap, PA 18327, USA (office). *Telephone:* (570) 421-3145 (home). *Website:* www.philwoods.com.

WOODWARD, Robert (Bob) Upshur, BA; American journalist and writer; *Associate Editor, The Washington Post;* b. 26 March 1943, Geneva, Ill.; s. of Alfred Woodward and Jane Upshur; m. Elsa Walsh 1989; two c.; ed Yale Univ.; reporter, Montgomery Co. (Md) Sentinel 1970–71; reporter, Washington Post 1971–78, Metropolitan Ed. 1979–81, Asst Man. Ed. 1981–2008, Assoc. Ed. 2008–. *Publications:* All the President's Men (with Carl Bernstein, Pulitzer Prize 1972) 1973, The Final Days (with Carl Bernstein) 1976, The Brethren (with Scott Armstrong) 1979, Wired 1984, Veil: The Secret Wars of the CIA 1987, The Commanders 1991, The Man Who Would Be President (with David S. Broder) 1991, The Agenda: Inside the Clinton White House 1994, The Choice 1996, Shadow: Five Presidents and the Legacy of Watergate 1999, Maestro, Greenspan's Fed and the American Boom 2000, Bush at War... Inside the Bush White House 2002, Plan of Attack 2004, The Secret Man 2005, State of Denial: Bush at War, Part III 2006, The War Within: A Secret White House History 2006–2008 2008, Obama's Wars 2010, The Price of Politics 2012. *Address:* The Washington Post, 1150 15th Street, NW, Washington, DC 20071, USA (office). *E-mail:* woodwardb@washpost.com (office).

WOODWARD, Sir Clive, Kt, OBE, BSc; British professional rugby football coach (rugby union), business executive and former rugby player; *Director of Elite Performance, British Olympic Association;* b. 6 Jan. 1956, Ely, Cambridgeshire; m. to Jayne; two s., one d.; ed degree in Physical Education and Sports Science at Loughborough Univ.; centre; player for Leicester 1979–85, Manly 1985–88, England Under-23, England 1980–84, British Lions (two tours: 1980, 1983); 21 caps for England (mem. Grand Slam winning side 1980), two caps for British Lions in 1980; coach for Henly 1993–95, London Irish 1995, Bath (assistant coach) 1996–97, England Under-21 1996–97, England 1997–2004 (winners Grand Slam 2003, World Cup 2003); coached England to record 14 consecutive victories in 2002–03; apptd Head Coach of British Lions for tour of NZ 2005, resgnd; Dir of Football, Southampton Football Club 2004–06; Dir of Elite Performance, British Olympic Asscn 2006–; freeman, City of Greater London, Royal Borough of Windsor and Maidenhead; Dr hc (Loughborough Univ.) 2004. *Publication:* Winning 2004. *Leisure interests:* golf, skiing, football. *Address:* British Olympic Association, 1 Wandsworth Plain, London SW18 1EH, England. *Telephone:* (20) 8871-2677. *Fax:* (20) 8871-9104. *E-mail:* boa@boa.org.uk. *Website:* www.olympics.org.uk.

WOODWARD, Joanne Gignilliat; American actress; b. 27 Feb. 1930, Thomasville, Ga; d. of Wade Woodward and Elinor Trimmier; m. Paul Newman 1958 (died 2008); three d.; ed Louisiana State Univ.; Trustee, Westport (Conn.) Country Playhouse; numerous awards including Foreign Press Award for Best Actress 1957, Acad. Award 1957, Nat. Bd Review Award 1957, Best Actress Award, Soc. of Film and TV Arts 1974; Franklin D. Roosevelt Four Freedoms Medal 1991, Kennedy Center Honor 1992. *Films include:* Count Three and Pray 1955, A Kiss Before Dying 1956, The Three Faces of Eve 1957, The Long Hot Summer 1958, Rally Round the Flag Boys 1958, The Sound and the Fury 1959, The Fugitive Kind 1959, From the Terrace 1960, Paris Blues 1961, The Stripper 1963, A New Kind of Love 1963, Signpost to Murder 1964, A Big Hand for the Little Lady 1966, A Fine Madness 1966, Rachel Rachel 1968, Winning 1969, W.U.S.A. 1970, They Might Be

Giants 1971, The Effects of Gamma Rays on Man-in-the-Moon Marigolds 1972, The Death of a Snow Queen 1973, Summer Wishes, Winter Dreams 1973, The Drowning Pool 1975, The End 1978, The Shadow Box 1980, Candida (Play) 1981, Harry and Son 1984, The Glass Menagerie 1987, Mr and Mrs Bridge 1990, Philadelphia 1993, My Knees Were Jumping: Remembering the Kindertransports (voice) 1998. *Television includes:* All the Way Home, See How She Runs 1978, Streets of LA 1979, Crisis at Central High 1981, Do You Remember Love? 1985, Blind Spot 1993, Breathing Lessons 1994, James Dean: A Portrait 1996, Empire Falls 2005. *Address:* 246 Post Road East, Westport, CT 06880, USA.

WOODWARD, Maj.-Gen. Margaret H., BS; American air force officer; *Commander, 17th Air Force & US Air Forces Africa (AFRICOM);* b. 1960; m. Daniel Woodward; ed Arizona State Univ., Embry-Riddle Aeronautical Univ., Nat. War Coll.; Instructor pilot, USAF, Columbus Air Force Base 1983–87, Flight Examiner and Aircraft Commdr, Plattsburgh Air Force Base 1987–90, Operations Group Exec. Officer, Laughlin Air Force Base 1990–94, Deputy Dir and Dir of Protocol, Office of Sec. of Defense, Washington, DC 1995–98, Operations Officer and Commdr 97th Air Refueling Squadron, Fairchild Air Force Base 1998–2000, Deputy Chief, Strategy, Concepts and Doctrine Div., USAF 2001–02, Commdr, 12th Operations Group, Randolph Air Force Base 2002–04, Deputy Dir, Colonel Matters, Air Force Sr Leader Man. Office, Washington, DC 2004–05, Commdr, 6th Air Mobility Wing, MacDill Air Force Base 2005–07, Commdr, 89th Airlift Wing, Andrews Air Force Base 2007–09, Vice Commdr, 18th Air Force, Scott Air Force Base 2009–10, Commdr, 17th Air Force & USAF Africa (AFRICOM), Ramstein Air Base, Germany 2010–; Defense Superior Service Medal, Legion of Merit with two oak leaf clusters, Bronze Star Medal, Meritorious Service Medal with two oak leaf clusters, Air Force Commendation Medal. *Achievements include:* commanded air operations of US involvement in no-fly zone over Libya, part of Operation Odyssey Dawn (first woman to oversee a US combat air campaign) 2011. *Address:* Ramstein Air Base Unit, 10340 APO, AE 09094-0340, Germany (office). *Website:* www .ramstein.af.mil (office).

WOODWARD, Roger Robert, OBE, AC; Australian pianist, conductor and composer; b. 20 Dec. 1942, Sydney; s. of Francis W. Woodward and Gladys A. Woodward; one s. one d.; ed Conservatorium of Music, Sydney and PWSH, Warsaw; debut at Royal Festival Hall, London 1970; subsequently appeared with the five London orchestras; has performed throughout Eastern and Western Europe, Japan and the USA; has appeared at int. festivals and with the major orchestras throughout world; extensive repertoire and is noted for interpretation of Chopin, Beethoven, Bach and Twentieth Century Music; Artistic Dir Nat. Chamber Orchestra for Contemporary Music in Australia 'Alpha Centaure' 1989 and festivals in London; performs each season at leading int. festivals works by contemporary composers; Nat. Treas. 1998; Fellow Chopin Inst., Warsaw 1976; Kt (Breffini) 1985. *Leisure interests:* cooking, chess, swimming, gardening, painting, design. *Address:* LH Productions, 2/37 Hendy Avenue, Coogee, NSW 2034, Australia. *E-mail:* woodward@metz.une.edu.au.

WOODWARD, Rt Hon. Shaun Anthony; British politician; b. 26 Oct. 1958, Bristol, England; m. Camilla Davan Sainsbury 1987; one s. three d.; ed Bristol Grammar School, Jesus Coll., Cambridge; Researcher, BBC 1981–91; Dir of Communications, Conservative Party 1991–92; Lecturer on Politics, Queen Mary and Westfield Coll. 1992–94; Fellow, Inst. of Politics, Kennedy School, Harvard Univ., USA 1994; MP (Conservative) for Witney 1997–99, MP (Labour) for St Helens S 2001–10, St Helens S and Whiston 2010–; mem. Parl. Jt Cttee on Human Rights 2001–05, fmr mem. Foreign Affairs Select Cttee, EU Scrutiny Select Cttee, Minister for Creative Industries and Tourism and Parl. Under-Sec. of State for NI 2005–06, Parl. Under-Sec., Dept for Culture, Media and Sport 2006–07, Sec. of State for NI 2007–10; Shadow Sec. of State for NI 2010–11; Dir ENO 1994–2002; fmr Trustee, Homes for Homeless People, Marine Stewardship Council; fmr Chair. Understanding Industry; mem. Advisory Council, Royal Shakespeare Co. *Address:* House of Commons, Westminster, London, SW1A 0AA (office); St Helens South and Whiston Parliamentary Office, Century House, Hardshaw Street, St Helens, WA10 1QW, England (office). *Telephone:* (20) 7219-2680 (London) (office); (1744) 24226 (St Helens) (office). *Fax:* (1744) 24306 (St Helens) (office). *E-mail:* woodwardsh@parliament.uk (office). *Website:* www.shaunwoodward.com (office).

WOOLARD, Edgar Smith, Jr, BSc; American business executive; *Advisor, Acorn Energy, Inc.;* b. 15 April 1934, Washington, NC; s. of Edgar Smith and Mamie Woolard (née Boone); m. Peggy Harrell 1956; two d.; ed North Carolina State Univ.; fmr Lt, US Army; industrial engineer, Du Pont at Kinston, NC 1957–59, various supervisory and managerial posts 1959–75, Man. Dir textile marketing div. 1975–76, Man. corp. plans dept 1976–77, Gen. Dir products and planning div. 1977–78, Gen. Man. textile fibres, Wilmington, Del. 1978–81, Vice-Pres. textile fibres 1981–83, Exec. Vice-Pres. 1983–85, Vice-Chair. 1985–87, Pres. and COO 1987–89, Chair., CEO 1989–96, Chair. 1996–98, also mem. Bd of Dirs 1996–2000; mem. Bd of Dirs Telex Communications Inc. 1998 (Chair. 2000–03); fmr mem. Bd of Dirs Citicorp, New York Stock Exchange, Council for Aid to Educ., IBM, Apple Computer Inc., Bell Atlantic, Jt Council on Econ. Educ., Raleigh, Seagram Co. (Canada); Chair. The Business Council 1995–96; mem. Bretton Woods Cttee, North Carolina Textile Foundation; Advisor, Acorn Energy, Inc. 2010–; mem. Bd of Trustees NC Textile Foundation, Christiana Care Corpn; mem. Nat. Acad. of Eng, American Philosophical Soc.; Distinguished Engineering Alumnus Award, North Carolina State Univ. 1988, Int. Palladium Medal Soc. Chimie Industrielle (American Section) 1995, The Edgar S. Woolard Chair at Univ. of Delaware is named after him. *Address:* Acorn Energy, Inc., 3903 Centerville Road, Wilmington, DE 19807, USA (office). *Telephone:* (302) 656-1708 (office). *E-mail:* acorn@acornenergy.com (office). *Website:* www.acornenergy.com (office).

WOOLCOTT, Richard, AC, AO, BA; Australian consultant, company director and fmr diplomatist; b. 11 June 1927, Sydney; s. of A. R. Woolcott; m. Birgit Christensen 1952 (deceased); two s. one d.; ed Frankston High School, Geelong Grammar School, Univ. of Melbourne and London Univ. School of Slavonic and East European Studies; joined Australian Foreign Service 1951; served in Australian missions in London, Moscow (twice), South Africa, Malaya, Singapore and Ghana; attended UN Gen. Ass. 1962; Acting Commr to Singapore 1963–64; High Commr to Ghana 1967–70; accompanied Prime Ministers Menzies 1965, Holt 1966, McMahon 1971, 1972, Whitlam 1973, 1974 and Hawke 1988–91 on visits to Asia, Europe, the Americas and the Pacific; Adviser at Commonwealth Heads of

Govt Confs London 1965, Ottawa 1973, Kuala Lumpur 1989; Pacific Forum 1972, 1973, 1988; Australia-Japan Ministerial Cttee 1972, 1973, 1988, 1989; Head, S Asia Div., Dept of Foreign Affairs 1973; Deputy Sec. Dept of Foreign Affairs 1974; Amb. to Indonesia 1975–78, to Philippines 1978–82; Perm. Rep. to UN 1982–88; Sec. of Dept of Foreign Affairs and Trade 1988–92; Prime Minister's Special Envoy to develop Asia Pacific Econ. Co-operation 1989; Australian Rep. on UN Security Council 1985–86; rep. of Australia at Non-aligned Summit meeting, Harare 1986; ASEAN Post-Ministerial Conf. 1989, 1990, 1991; Alt. Australian Gov., inaugural EBRD meeting 1991; Chair. Australia Indonesia Inst. 1992–98, Official Establishments Trust 1992–99, Nat. Cttee on Population and Devt 1993–95, Across Asia Multimedia (Hong Kong) 2000–, Cttee to review the Australian Citizenship Test 2008; Dir Auric Pacific (Singapore) 2001–02; mem. int. council of The Asia Soc.; Vice-Pres. Multiple Sclerosis Soc. of Australia 1995–2000; Founding Dir Australasia Centre, Asia Soc. 1997–; Founding Dir or consultant several firms; mem. Bd of Commrs, Lippo Bank, Indonesia 1999–2002; apptd Special Envoy to develop idea of an Asia Pacific community 2008; Life Fellow, Trinity Coll., Melbourne Univ. 1995; Bintang Mahaputra Utama (Indonesia) 2000. *Publications include:* Australian Foreign Policy 1973, The Hot Seat: Reflections on Diplomacy From Stalin's Death to the Bali Bombings 2003, Undiplomatic Activities 2006; numerous articles, including special features for The Australian, articles for International Herald Tribune, Time. *Leisure interests:* writing, cricket, photography. *Address:* Asia Society, AustralAsia Centre, Level 1, 175 Collins Street, Melbourne, Vic. 3000 (office); PO Box 3926, Manuka, Canberra, ACT 2603 (office); 19 Talbot Street, Forrest, Canberra, ACT 2603, Australia (home). *Telephone:* (2) 6295-3206 (office). *Fax:* (2) 6295-3066 (office). *E-mail:* rwoolcot@ozemail.com.au. *Website:* www.asiasociety.org (office).

WOOLDRIDGE, Hon. Michael Richard Lewis, BSc, MB BS, MBA; Australian politician and company director; *Lead Independent Director and Chairman, Nomination Committee, Australian Pharmaceuticals Industry Limited;* b. 7 Nov. 1956; m. Michele Marion Colman 1988; two s.; ed Scotch Coll., Melbourne, Univ. of Melbourne, Monash Univ.; Resident Medical Staff (Surgical), Alfred Hosp. 1982–85; MP (Liberal Party) for Chisholm, Vic. 1987–88, for Casey, Vic. 1998–2001; pvt. practice 1985–87; Shadow Minister for Aboriginal Affairs 1990–92, for Aboriginal and Torres Strait Islander Affairs 1992–93; Deputy Leader of the Opposition, Shadow Minister for Educ., Employment and Training 1993–94, for Community Services, Sr Citizens and Aged Care 1994–95, for Health and Human Services 1995–96; Minister for Health and Family Services 1996–98, for Health and Aged Care 1998–2001; Ind. Dir (non-exec.), Australian Pharmaceuticals Industry Ltd 2006–, mem. Remuneration Cttee 2007–, Lead Ind. Dir 2008–, Chair. Nomination Cttee 2012–; mem. or fmr mem. Bd Resonance Health Ltd, Dia-B Tech Ltd 2009 (resgnd, co. since de-listed), Prime Trust Ltd, CogState Ltd, Vision Eye Inst. Ltd; Chair. Neurosciences Australia, Healthsource Australia (Ministerial Advisory Cttee on AIDS, Sexual Health and Hepatitis), CRC for Mental Health, Oral Health Co-operative Research Centre; mem. Bd Waubra Foundation (anti-wind energy org.); Assoc. Prof., Univ. of Melbourne; Hon. Fellow, Australasian Faculty of Public Health Medicine; Hon. LLD. *Leisure interests:* tennis, skiing, reading. *Address:* Australian Pharmaceuticals Industry Ltd, Locked Bag 5061, Parramatta, ACT 2124, Australia (office). *Telephone:* (2) 8844-2000 (office). *Fax:* (2) 8844-2896 (office). *E-mail:* info@api.net.au (office). *Website:* www.api.net.au (office).

WOOLDRIDGE, Richard; British media executive; fmr journalist; fmr Ed. Yorkshire Evening Press; Man. Ed. York and Country Press –1992; Dir Westminster Press (regional newspaper group) 1992–96; joined International Herald Tribune 1996, various positions including consultant, Pres. and COO –2003, Chair. and CEO 2003–08. *Address:* c/o International Herald Tribune, 6 bis, rue des Graviers, 92521 Neuilly Cedex, France (office).

WOOLF, Baron (Life Peer), cr. 1992, of Barnes in the London Borough of Richmond; **Rt Hon. Harry Kenneth Woolf,** PC, LLB; British judge; b. 2 May 1933, Newcastle upon Tyne, England; s. of Alexander Woolf and Leah Woolf; m. Marguerite Sassoon 1961; three s.; ed Glasgow Acad., Fettes Coll., Univ. Coll. London; Nat. Service, 15/19th Royal Hussars 1954, Capt., Army Legal Services 1955; called to Bar, Inner Temple 1955, began practising 1956; Recorder, Crown Court 1972–79; Jr Counsel, Inland Revenue 1973–74; First Treasury Counsel (Common Law) 1974–79; Judge, High Court, Queen's Bench Div. 1979–86; Presiding Judge, S Eastern Circuit 1981–84; Lord Justice of Appeal 1986–92; Lord of Appeal in Ordinary 1992–96; Master of the Rolls 1996–2000; Lord Chief Justice of England and Wales 2000–05; mem. (Crossbench) House of Lords 1992–, fmr Chair. Parl. Standards Sub-cttee, mem. Constitution Cttee; non-perm. judge, Court of Final Appeal, Hong Kong 2003–; mediator and arbitrator, Blackstone Chambers, London 2005–; Founding Pres. Civil, Commercial and Appeal Court, Qatar Financial Centre 2006–; conducted review of working methods of the European Court of Human Rights 2005; fmr Chair. Bank of England Financial Market's Law Cttee; Visiting Prof. of Law and fmr Chair. of Council, Univ. Coll. London; mem. Bd of Man., Inst. of Advanced Legal Studies 1985–94 (Chair. 1986–94); Chair. Lord Chancellor's Advisory Cttee of Legal Educ. 1986–94, Middx Advisory Cttee on Justices of the Peace 1986–90, Magna Carta Trust 1996, Lord Chancellors' Advisory Cttee on Public Records 1996–2000, Council of Civil Justice 1997–2000, Civil Procedure Rules Cttee 1997–2000; Pro-Chancellor Univ. of London 1994–2002; Visitor, Nuffield Coll. Oxford 1996–2000, Downing Coll. Cambridge 2000–, Univ. Coll. London 1996–2000; Trustee, Butler Trust 1991–96, Chair. 1992–96, Pres. 1996–; Hon. Visiting Prof., Chinese Univ. of Hong Kong; Hon. FBA 2002; Hon. FMedSci; Hon. Fellow, Univ. Coll. London, Coll. of Trial Lawyers, USA; Hon. LLD (Buckingham) 1992, (Bristol) 1992, (London) 1993, (Anglia Poly Univ.) 1994, (Manchester Metropolitan) 1994, (Hull) 2001, (Cranfield) 2001, (Cambridge) 2002, (Exeter) 2002; Hon. DLitt (London) 2002; Hon. DSc (Cranfield) 2002; Dr hc (Oxford) 2004, (Open Univ.) 2010. *Publications:* Protection of the Public – The New Challenge 1990, Declaratory Judgement (co-ed.) 1993, Judicial Review of Administrative Action (co-ed.) (fifth edn) 1995; reports: Prisons in England and Wales 1991, Access to Justice (Interim) 1995, (Final) 1996, Principles of Judicial Review (co-author) 1999, Pursuit of Justice 2008. *Address:* House of Lords, Westminster, London, SW1A 0PW, England (office). *Telephone:* (20) 7219-1788 (office). *Fax:* (20) 7219-0785 (office).

WOOLFSON, Michael Mark, MA, PhD DSc, CPhys, FRAS, FInstP, FRS; British physicist and academic; *Professor Emeritus, University of York;* b. 9 Jan. 1927, London, England; s. of Maurice Woolfson and Rose Woolfson (née Solomons); m. Margaret Frohlich 1951; two s. one d.; ed Jesus Coll., Oxford, Univ. of Manchester Inst. of Science and Tech.; Nat. Service, Royal Engineers 1947–49; Research Asst, Cavendish Lab., Cambridge 1952–54; ICI Fellow, Univ. of Cambridge 1954–55; Lecturer, Faculty of Tech., Univ. of Manchester 1955–61, Reader 1961–65; Prof. of Theoretical Physics, Univ. of York 1965–94, Prof. Emer. 1994–; Chair. Royal Soc. Planetary Sciences Sub-cttee 1979–83, British Crystallographic Asscn 1985–90, British Nat. Cttee for Crystallography 1985–90; Pres. Yorks. Philosophical Soc. 1985–99; Hughes Medal, Royal Soc. 1986, Patterson Award, American Crystallographic Asscn 1990, Gregori Aminoff Medal and Prize, Royal Swedish Acad. of Sciences 1992, Dorothy Hodgkin Prize, British Crystallographic Asscn 1997, Ewald Prize, Int. Union of Crystallography 2002. *Publications:* Direct Methods in Crystallography 1960, The Origin of the Solar System, The Capture Theory 1989, Physical and Non-physical Methods of Solving Crystal Structures 1995, An Introduction to X-ray Crystallography 1997, An Introduction to Computer Simulation 1999, The Origins and Evolution of the Solar System 2000, Planetary Science 2002, Mathematics for Physics 2007, The Formation of the Solar System: Theories Old and New 2007, Everyday Probability and Statistics 2008, Time, Space, Stars and Man 2008, Materials, Matter and Particles 2010, On the Origin of Planets 2011, The Fundamentals of Imaging 2011. *Leisure interest:* writing. *Address:* Department of Physics, University of York, York, North Yorks., YO1 5DD (office); 24 Sandmoor Green, Leeds, South Yorks., LS17 7SB, England (home). *Telephone:* (1904) 432230 (office); (113) 266-2166 (home). *Fax:* (1904) 432214 (office). *E-mail:* mmw1@york.ac.uk (office). *Website:* www.york.ac.uk/physics/people/emeritusprof/woolfson (office).

WOOLGAR, Stephen, BA (Hons), DPhil; British sociologist and academic; *Professor of Marketing and Head, Science and Technology Studies Academic Area, Institute for Science, Innovation and Society, Saïd Business School, University of Oxford;* b. 1950; ed Emmanuel Coll., Cambridge; Visiting Lecturer, McGill Univ., Montréal, Canada 1979–81, MIT 1983–84, École Nat. Supérieure des Mines, Paris 1988–89, Univ. of California, San Diego 1995–96; Prof. of Sociology, Brunel Univ. 1996–2000, Head of Dept of Human Sciences –2000, Dir Centre for Research into Innovation, Culture and Tech. Technology 1998–2000; Dir Virtual Society Program, Econ. and Social Research Council 1997–2002; Prof. of Marketing and Head, Science and Tech. Studies Academic Area, Inst. for Science, Innovation and Society, Saïd Business School, Univ. of Oxford 2000–; mem. Man. Bd, Oxford e-Science Centre, Oxford Internet Inst.; mem. Council Consumer's Asscn; mem. Research Assessment Exercise Sociology Panel, Higher Educ. Funding Council for England 1996, 2001; fmr mem. EC (VALUE) Think Tank, Information Tech., Electronics and Communications Foresight Panel for UK Govt, Leisure and Learning Foresight Panel; fmr Adviser to Cabinet Office Better Govt Team; fmr mem. E-Commerce and Consumer Affairs Ministerial Advisory Groups; fmr Adviser to Research Councils of Denmark, Netherlands and Norway; Fulbright Scholarship, Fulbright Sr Scholarship, ESRC Sr Research Fellowship, Econ. and Social Research Council; Bernal Prize, Soc. for Social Studies of Science 2008. *Publications:* Laboratory Life: The Social Construction of Scientific Facts (co-author) 1979, Science: The Very Idea 1988, The Cognitive Turn: Sociological and Psychological Perspectives on Science (co-author) 1989, Representation in Scientific Practice (co-author) 1990, The Machine at Work: Technology, Work and Society (co-author) 1997, Virtual Society? Technology, Cyberbole, Reality (ed.) 2002. *Leisure interest:* hot air ballooning. *Address:* Saïd Business School, University of Oxford, Park End Street, Oxford, OX1 1HP, England (office). *Telephone:* (1865) 288934 (office). *E-mail:* steve.woolgar@sbs.ox.ac.uk (office). *Website:* www.sbs.ox.ac.uk (office).

WOOLLEY, Kenneth Frank, AM, BArch, LFRAIA; Australian architect; b. 29 May 1933, Sydney, NSW; s. of Frank Woolley and Doris May Woolley (née Mudear); m. 1st Cynthia Stuart (divorced 1979); m. 2nd Virginia Braden 1980; two s. one d.; ed Sydney Boys' High School, Univ. of Sydney; Design Architect, Govt Architect's Office, Sydney 1955–56, 1957–63; Asst Architect, Chamberlin, Powell and Bon, London 1956–57; Partner, Ancher, Mortlock, Murray & Woolley, Sydney 1964–69, Dir 1969–75; Dir Ancher, Mortlock & Woolley Pty Ltd, Sydney from 1975 (joined with Conrad Gargett Riddel 2013); mem. Quality Review Cttee Darling Harbour Redevelopment Authority 1985; Visiting Prof., Univ. of New South Wales School of Architecture 1983; Visiting Tutor and Critic, Visiting Prof., Univ. of Sydney, Univ. of New South Wales, NSW Inst. of Tech., Sydney; mem. NSW Bd of Architects 1960–72, NSW Bldg Regulations Advisory Cttee 1960–74, NSW Bd of Architectural Educ. 1969–72, Royal Australian Inst. of Architects Aboriginal Housing Panel 1972–76; Life FRAIA 1976; Hon. DSc in Architecture (Sydney) 2010; Sulman Award 1962, Bronze Medal 1962, Wilkinson Award 1962, 1968, 1982, 1987, Blacket Award 1964, 1967, 1969, 1987, Civic Design Award 1983, Gold Medal, Royal Australian Inst. of Architects 1993, numerous other architectural awards. *Major works include:* Australian Embassy, Bangkok, ABC Radio Bldg, Sydney, Hyatt Hotel, Campbell's Cove, Sydney, Control Tower, Sydney Airport, Sydney Town Hall renovations, The Olympics and RAS Exhbn Halls and Hockey Stadium, new offices and city square, three student union bldgs, univs in NSW, numerous urban housing devts, radio stations, Vanuatu, Solomon Islands, over 4,000 production houses, State Govt offices, Sydney, Fisher Library, Sydney Univ., State Library of Vic., Royal Agricultural Showground Dome and Exhbn Halls, Sydney. *Publications:* numerous papers and articles in architectural journals. *Leisure interests:* golf, sailing, music, drawing. *Address:* c/o Conrad Gargett Riddel Ancher Mortlock Woolley, Suite C3.18, 22–36 Mountain Street, Ultimo, NSW 2007, Australia (office). *Telephone:* (2) 8218-9100 (office). *Fax:* (2) 8218-9199 (office). *E-mail:* mail@conradgargett.com.au (office). *Website:* www.conradgargett.com.au (office).

WOOLLISCROFT, James O., BSc, MD; American physician and medical educator; *Dean of the Medical School, University of Michigan;* ed Univ. of Minnesota; Chief Resident, Univ. of Michigan Medical School 1980, Faculty mem., Dept of Internal Medicine 1980, Prof. of Internal Medicine 1993, Josiah Macy Jr Prof. of Medical Educ. 1996–2001, Lyle C. Roll Prof. of Medicine 2001–, Exec. Assoc. Dean 1999–2006, Interim Dean 2006–07, Dean 2007–; Fellow, Council of Deans, Asscn of American Medical Colls (AAMC) 2003–04; mem. Inst. of Medicine 2013; Soc. of Gen. Internal Medicine Medical Educ. Award 2004, Merril Flair

Award, AAMC, GEA 2008. *Address:* Office of the Dean, University of Michigan Medical School, 1301 Catherine Road, Ann Arbor, MI 48109, USA (office). *Telephone:* (734) 764-8175 (office). *Fax:* (734) 763-4936 (office). *E-mail:* woolli@umich.edu (office). *Website:* www.med.umich.edu/medschool/dean (office).

WOOLSEY, R. James, LLB, MA; American lawyer and fmr government official; *Vice-President, Global Assurance, Booz Allen Hamilton;* b. 1941, Tulsa, Okla; m. Suzanne Haley; three s.; ed Tulsa Cen. High School, Stanford Univ., Univ. of Oxford, UK and Yale Law School; staff mem. Nat. Security Council 1968–70; Adviser US Del. to Strategic Arms Limitation Talks 1969–70; Gen. Counsel to Senate Cttee on Armed Services 1970–73; Under-Sec. of the Navy 1977–79; del.-at-large to US–Soviet Strategic Arms Reduction Talks and space talks 1983–86; Amb. and US Rep. to negotiations on Conventional Armed Forces in Europe Treaty 1989–91; Chair. CIA task force on future of satellite spying 1991; Dir of CIA 1993–95; Pnr, Shea & Gardner 1991–93, 1995–2002; Vice-Pres. Global Assurance, Booz Allen Hamilton 2002–; Chair. Advisory Cttee, Clean Fuels Foundation; Dir USF&G 1995, Sun HealthCare Group Inc. 1995, Yurie Systems Inc. 1996; mem. Bd Govs Philadelphia Stock Exchange; mem. Pres.'s Comm. on Strategic Forces 1983, Pres.'s Blue Ribbon Comm. on Defense Man. 1985–86, Pres.'s Comm. on Fed. Ethics Law Reform 1989, Comm. to Assess the Ballistic Missile Threat to the US 1998, Nat. Comm. on Terrorism 1999–2000; Trustee Center for Strategic and Int. Studies; Rhodes Scholar 1963–65; mem. Bd Advisors BioDefense Corpn 2004–. *Address:* Booz Allen Hamilton, 8283 Greensboro Drive, McLean, VA 22102, USA (office). *Telephone:* (703) 902-5701 (office). *E-mail:* woolsey_jim@bah.com (office). *Website:* www.bah.com (office).

WOONTON, Robert Philip, PhD; Cook Islands politician; b. 1949; m. Sue Woonton; Minister of Foreign Affairs and Immigration 1999–; Prime Minister Feb. 2002–04, portfolio also included Police, Parl., House of Ariki, Tourism, Agric., Marine Resources, Transport, Airport and Ports Authorities, Nat. Disaster Man. *Address:* c/o Office of the Prime Minister, Government of the Cook Islands, Private Bag, Avarua, Rarotonga, Cook Islands (office). *E-mail:* rwoonton@oyster.net.ck (home).

WOOSNAM, Ian Harold, OBE; British (Welsh) professional golfer; b. 2 March 1958, Oswestry, Wales; s. of Harold Woosnam and Joan Woosnam; m. Glendryth Pugh 1983; one s. two d.; ed St Martin's Modern School; professional golfer 1976–; tournament victories: News of the World under-23 Matchplay 1979, Cacharel under-25 Championship 1982, Swiss Open 1982, Silk Cut Masters 1983, Scandinavian Enterprise Open 1984, Zambian Open 1985, Lawrence Batley TPC 1986, 555 Kenya Open 1986, Hong Kong Open 1987, Jersey Open 1987, Cepsa Madrid Open 1987, Bell's Scottish Open 1987, 1990, Lancome Trophy 1987, Suntory World Match-Play Championship 1987, 1990, 2001, Volvo PGA Championship 1988, 1997, Carrolls Irish Open 1988, 1989, Panasonic Euro Open 1988, Am Express Mediterranean Open 1990, Torras Monte Carlo Open 1990, Epson Grand Prix 1990, US Masters 1991, USF+G Classic 1991, Fujitsu Mediterranean Open, Torras Monte Carlo Open 1991, European Monte Carlo Open 1992, Lancôme Trophy 1993, Murphy's English Open 1993, British Masters 1994, Cannes Open 1994, Heineken Classic 1996, Scottish Open 1996, Volvo German Open 1996, Johnnie Walker Classic 1996, Parkridge Polish Seniors' Championship 2008, Russian Seniors' Open 2008, Irish Seniors' Open 2009, Professional Golfers' Asscn (PGA) Handa Cup 2009; team events: Ryder Cup 1983–97, Dunhill Cup 1985, 1986, 1988, 1989, 1990, 1991, 1993, 1995, World Cup 1980, 1982, 1983, 1984, 1985, 1987, 1990, 1991, 1992, 1993, 1994, 1996, 1997; finished top Order of Merit 1987, 1990 and Seniors' Order of Merit 2008; ranked No. 1, Sony world rankings 1991; World Cup Individual, PGA Grand Slam 1991; Pres. World Snooker Asscn 1999–2002; eighth on all-time European Tour earnings list; 29 European PGA Tour titles; Capt. European Ryder Cup Team 2006; BBC Wales Sports Personality of the Year Award 1987, 1990, 1991. *Publications:* Ian Woosnam's Golf Masterpieces (with Peter Grosvenor) 1991, Golf Made Simple: The Woosie Way 1997, Woosie: My Autobiography 2002. *Leisure interests:* snooker, water skiing, sports, fishing. *Address:* c/o Vicky Cuming, IMG, McCormack House, Hogarth Business Park, Burlington Lane, Chiswick, London, W4 2TH, England (office). *Telephone:* (20) 8233-5000 (office). *Fax:* (20) 8233-5301 (office). *E-mail:* vicky.cuming@imgworld.com (office). *Website:* www.woosie.com.

WORCESTER, Sir Robert Milton, KBE, BSc, FRSS, FMRS; British (b. American) company chairman; *Senior Adviser, Ipsos MORI;* b. 21 Dec. 1933, Kansas City, Mo., USA; s. of the late C. M. Worcester and Violet Ruth Worcester; m. 1st Joann Ransdell 1958 (deceased); m. 2nd Margaret Noel Smallbone 1982; two s.; ed Univ. of Kansas, London School of Econs; Consultant, McKinsey & Co. 1962–65; Chief Financial Officer, Opinion Research Corpn 1965–68; Man. Dir Market & Opinion Research International Ltd (MORI) 1969–94, Chair. 1973–2005; Int. Dir, Ipsos 2005–08, Sr Adviser, Ipsos MORI 2008–; Pres. World Asscn for Public Opinion Research 1983–84; Visiting Prof., City Univ. 1990–2002, LSE 1992– (Hon. Fellow 2005), Univ. of Strathclyde 1996–2001; Pres. Environmental Campaigns Ltd 2002–06; Chair. Magna Carta 2015 800th Anniversary Cttee 2009–; Vice-Pres. Int. Soc. Science Council, UNESCO 1989–94, European Atlantic Group, UNA 1999–, Royal Soc. for Wildlife Trusts 1995–; Co-Chair. Jamestown 2007 British Cttee 2004–07; mem. Pilgrims Soc. of GB (Chair. 1993–2010, Vice-Pres. 2010–); mem. Court of Govs LSE 1995–, Advisory Bd European Business Journal, Fulbright Comm. 1995–2005, Court Univ. of Middx 2001–, Council Univ. of Kent 2002–13 (also mem. Court, Chancellor 2006–13), Advisory Bd Nat. Consumer Council 2002–, Media Standards Trust 2006–, Camelot Advisory Panel for Corp. Responsibility 2006–11, GovNet 2008–, Advisory Council Inst. of Business Ethics (Pres. 2010–13); Gov. Ditchley Foundation, English-Speaking Union; Dir (sr non-exec.) Kent Messenger Group 2004–08; Chair. Maidstone Radio Ltd (CTR 105.4 fm) 2004–06; Founding Co-Ed. Int. Journal of Public Opinion Research; wrote monthly columns for Profile (magazine of C. Inst. of Public Relations) and Parliamentary Monitor; Trustee, WorldWide Fund for Nature (WWF-UK) 1988–94, Natural History Museum Devt Trust 1989–94, Magna Carta Trust 1995–, Wildfowl and Wetlands Trust 2002–08 (currently Vice-Pres.); Fellow, Market Research Soc. 1997–, King's Coll. 2007; apptd Kent Amb., Environment Champion by Kent Co. Council; Freeman of the City of London 2001, Hon. Prof. of Politics, Univ. of Kent 2002, Hon. Prof., Univ. of Warwick 2005, Hon. Fellow, LSE, King's Coll. London, Hon. DL of Kent 2006; Hon. DSc (Buckingham) 1998, Hon. DLitt (Bradford) 2001, Hon. DUniv (Middlesex)

2001, Hon. LLD (Greenwich) 2002, Hon. DCL (Kent) 2006, Distinguished Grad. (Univ. of Kansas) 2006, Hon. DLaws (Richmond American Int. Univ. in London) 2009; Helen Dinerman Award, World Assen for Public Opinion Research 1996. *Publications include:* Political Communications (with Martin Harrop) 1982, Political Opinion Polling: An International Review (ed.) 1983, Consumer Market Research Handbook (3rd edn, co-ed. with John Downham) 1986, Private Opinions, Public Polls (with Lesley Watkins) 1986, We British (with Eric Jacobs) 1990, British Public Opinion: History and Methodology of Political Opinion Polling in Great Britain 1991, Typically British (with Eric Jacobs) 1991, Dynamics of Societal Learning about Global Environmental Change (with Samuel H. Barnes) 1992, The Millennial Generation (with Madsen Pirie) 1998, The Next Leaders (with Madsen Pirie) 1999, Explaining Labour's Landslide (with Roger Mortimore) 1999, The Big Turn Off (with Madsen Pirie) 2000, How to Win the Euro Referendum: Lessons from 1975 2000, Facing the Future (with Madsen Pirie) 2000, The Wrong Package (with Madsen Pirie) 2000, Explaining Labour's Second Landslide (with Roger Mortimore) 2001, Explaining Labour's Landslip (with Roger Mortimore and Paul Baines) 2005, Explaining Cameron's Coalition: How It Came About: An Analysis of the 2012 General Election 2011. *Leisure interest:* castles, choral music, gardening. *Address:* MORI House, 79–81 Borough Road, London, SE1 1FY, England (office). *Telephone:* (20) 7347-3000 (office). *Fax:* (20) 7347-3017 (office). *E-mail:* rmworcester@yahoo.com (office). *Website:* www.ipsos-mori.com (office); www.magnacarta800th.com (office).

WORMS, Gérard Etienne; French business executive and company director; *Chairman, International Chamber of Commerce;* b. 1 Aug. 1936, Paris; s. of André Worms and Thérèse Dreyfus; m. Michèle Rousseau 1960; one s. one d.; ed Lycées Carnot and Saint-Louis, Ecole Polytechnique and Ecole Nat. Supérieure des Mines, Paris; Engineer, Org. commune des régions sahariennes 1960–62; Head of Dept, Délégation à l'Aménagement du Territoire et à l'Action Régionale 1963–67; Tech. Adviser, Office of Olivier Guichard (Minister of Industry, later of Planning) 1967–69, Office of Jacques Chaban-Delmas (Prime Minister) 1969–71; Asst Man. Dir, Librairie Hachette 1972–75, Man. Dir 1975–81, Dir 1978–81; Prof., Ecole des Hautes Etudes Commerciales 1962–69, Supervisor of complementary courses, Faculty of Letters and Human Sciences, Paris 1963–69; Prof. Ecole Polytechnique 1974–85; Vice-Pres. Syndicat nat. de l'édition 1974–81; Exec. Vice-Pres. Rhône-Poulenc SA 1981–83; Exec. Vice-Pres. Compagnie de Suez 1984–90, Chair. and CEO 1990–95; Pres. Banque Indosuez 1994–95; Pres. Supervisory Bd Rothschild, Compagnie Banque Paris 1995–99, Man. Partner Rothschild et Cie and Rothschild et Cie Banque 1999–, Vice-Chair. Rothschild Europe; Chair. Int. Chamber of Commerce (ICC) France 2006–, ICC 2011–; Pres. Centre for research into econ. expansion and business Devt 1996–, Supervisory Council for health information systems 1997–2000, History channel 1997–; Hon. Chair. Nat. Technical Research Assen, Société d'Economie Politique; mem. bd Telecom Italia 1998–2001, Publicis, Métropole Télévision; Chevalier, Ordre nat. du Mérite, Ordre du Mérite maritime, Commdr Légion d'honneur 2007. *Publications include:* Les méthodes modernes de l'économie appliquée 1965; various articles on econ. methods in specialized journals. *Address:* International Chamber of Commerce, 38 cours Albert 1er, 75008 Paris (office); 61 bis avenue de la Motte Picquet, 75015 Paris, France (home). *Telephone:* 1-49-53-28-28 (office); 1-47-83-99-43 (home). *Fax:* 1-49-53-28-59 (office). *Website:* www.iccwbo.org (office).

WORRALL, Denis John, PhD; South African business executive, politician, diplomatist and lawyer; b. 29 May 1935, Benoni; s. of Cecil John Worrall and Hazel Worrall; m. Anita Denise Ianco 1965; three s.; ed Univ. of Cape Town, Univ. of South Africa, Cornell Univ., USA; taught political science, Cornell Univ., UCLA, Univ. of Natal, Univ. of South Africa and Univ. of Witwatersrand; Cornell Research Fellow, Univ. of Ibadan, Nigeria 1962–63; Founder-Ed. New Nation 1967–74; Research Prof. and Dir Inst. for Social and Econ. Research, Rhodes Univ. –1974; Senator for Cape 1974–77; Amb. to Australia 1983–84, to UK 1984–87; Advocate, Supreme Court of SA; MP for Cape Town-Gardens 1977–83; independent cand. for Helderberg in 1987 Election; mem. Pres.'s. Council 1980–83; f. Ind. Movt 1988; Leader Ind. Party 1988–89; Co-founder Democratic Party 1989; MP for Berea, Durban 1989–94; Chair. Omega Investment Research Ltd. *Publication:* South Africa: Government and Politics. *Leisure interests:* reading, cycling. *E-mail:* denisw@omegainvest.co.za.

WORSTHORNE, Sir Peregrine Gerard, Kt, MA; British journalist, writer and broadcaster; b. 22 Dec. 1923, London; s. of Col A. Koch de Gooreynd and the late Baroness Norman; m. 1st Claudia Bertrand de Colasse 1950 (died 1990); one d. one step-s.; m. 2nd Lady Lucinda Lambton 1991; ed Stowe School, Peterhouse, Cambridge and Magdalen Coll., Oxford; mem. editorial staff, Glasgow Herald 1946–48; mem. editorial staff, The Times 1948–50, Washington corresp. 1950–52, leader writer 1952–55; leader writer, Daily Telegraph 1955–61; Deputy Ed. Sunday Telegraph 1961–76, Assoc. Ed. 1976–86, Ed. 1986–89, Ed. Comment Section 1989–91; columnist, The Spectator 1997–, The New Statesman; fmr columnist, The First Post (online news magazine); Granada TV Journalist of the Year 1981. *Publications include:* The Socialist Myth 1972, Peregrinations 1980, By The Right 1987, Tricks of Memory (memoirs) 1993, In Defence of Aristocracy 2004. *Leisure interests:* walking, tennis. *Address:* The Old Rectory, Hedgerley, Bucks., SL2 3UY, England (home). *Telephone:* (1753) 646167 (home). *Fax:* (1753) 646914 (home). *E-mail:* therectory.hedgerley@virgin.net (office).

WORTH, Richard, OBE, LLB, MJ, MBA, PhD; New Zealand politician; *Minister of Internal Affairs;* b. 3 July 1948, Auckland; ed Univ. of Auckland, Massey Univ., Royal Melbourne Inst. of Tech.; Pnr, Simpson Grierson 1972–99, Exec. Chair. 1986–99; MP for Epsom 1999–2005, mem. Select Cttees on Regulations Review 1999–2002, on Law and Order 2001–02, on Justice 2005–06, Chair. Regulations Review Cttee 2005–08; Spokesman on Defence 2002–03 on Veterans' Affairs 2002–03, Justice 2003–06; Assoc. Spokesman on Local Govt 2005–06; Minister of Internal Affairs 2008–, also Minister for Land Information, Minister Responsible for Archives New Zealand and for Nat. Library and Assoc. Minister of Justice; Fellow, NZ Inst. of Dirs, NZ Inst. of Man.; Chair. P F Olsen Ltd; Chair. Korea/NZ Business Council, Korean Parl. Group; Trustee, Royal NZ Coastguard Foundation; mem. Council of Legal Educ.; fmr Chair. Willis NZ Ltd; fmr Dir Prada America's Cup NZ Ltd; fmr mem. and Treas. NZ Law Soc. Bd; mem. and fmr Dir Auckland Rotary Club; fmr Pres. The Northern Club, Outward Bound Trust Bd of NZ; Order of St John. *Address:* Department of Internal Affairs, 46 Waring Taylor Street, POB

805, Wellington, New Zealand (office). *Telephone:* (4) 495-7200 (office). *Fax:* (4) 495-7222 (office). *E-mail:* info@dia.govt.nz (office). *Website:* www.dia.govt.nz (office).

WORTHINGTON, Baroness (Life Peer), cr. 2011, of Cambridge in the County of Cambridgeshire; **Bryony Worthington;** British organization executive; *Director, Sandbag;* climate change policy expert and campaigner; career has focused on promoting environmental and social change; fmr Head of Friends of the Earth's climate change campaign; fmr policy adviser to Scottish and Southern Electricity and its CEO Ian Marchant, seconded to Govt to take part in writing the Climate Change Bill, originator of idea nat. carbon budgets; Founder and Dir Sandbag (carbon trading think tank and campaign group); mem. Bd 10:10 campaign. *Address:* Sandbag Climate Campaign, 4 Charterhouse Square, London, EC1M 6EE (office); House of Lords, Westminster, London, SW1A 0PW, England. *Telephone:* (20) 3215-0050 (office); (20) 7219-5353. *Fax:* (20) 7219-5979. *E-mail:* info@sandbag.org.uk (office). *Website:* www.sandbag.org.uk (office).

WOUK, Herman, AB; American writer and dramatist; b. 27 May 1915, New York, NY; s. of Abraham Isaac Wouk and Esther Levine; m. Betty Sarah Brown 1945; three s. (one deceased); ed Columbia Univ.; radio scriptwriter for leading comedians, New York 1935–41; presidential consultant to US Treasury 1941; served in USNR 1942–46; Visiting Prof. of English, Yeshiva Univ., New York 1952–57; Trustee, Coll. of the Virgin Islands 1961–69; mem. Authors' Guild, USA, Authors' League, Center for Book Nat. Advisory Bd, Library of Congress, Advisory Council, Center for US–China Arts Exchange; Hon. LHD (Yeshiva Univ.); Hon. DLitt (Clark Univ.), (George Washington Univ.) 2001; Hon. DLitt (American Int. Coll.) 1979; Hon. PhD (Bar Ilan) 1990, (Hebrew Univ.) 1997; Hon. DST (Trinity Coll.) 1998; Pulitzer Prize for Fiction 1952, Columbia Univ. Medal for Excellence, Alexander Hamilton Medal, Columbia Univ. 1980, Ralph Waldo Emerson Award, Int. Platform Assen 1981, Univ. of Calif., Berkeley Medal 1984, Yad Vashem Kazetnik Award 1990, USN Memorial Foundation Lone Sailor Award 1987, Washingtonian Book Award (for Inside, Outside) 1986, American Acad. of Achievement Golden Plate Award 1986, Bar Ilan Univ. Guardian of Zion Award 1998, Univ. of California at San Diego Medal 1998, Jewish Book Council Lifetime Literary Achievement Award 2000. *Publications include:* fiction: The Man in the Trench Coat 1941, Aurora Dawn 1947, The City Boy 1948, Slattery's Hurricane 1949, The Caine Mutiny 1951, Marjorie Morningstar 1955, Slattery's Hurricane 1956, Youngblood Hawke 1961, Don't Stop the Carnival 1965, The Lomokome Papers 1968, The Winds of War (also TV screenplay) 1971, War and Remembrance (also TV screenplay) 1978, Inside, Outside 1985, The Hope 1993, The Glory 1994, A Hole in Texas 2004, The Lawgiver 2012; plays: The Traitor 1949, Modern Primitive 1951, The Caine Mutiny Court-Martial 1953, Nature's Way 1957; non-fiction: This is My God: The Jewish Way of Life 1959, The Will to Live on: The Resurgence of Jewish Heritage 2000, The Language God Talks: On Science and Religion 2010. *Leisure interests:* Hebraic studies, travel. *Address:* BSW Literary Agency, 303 Crestview Drive, Palm Springs, CA 92264, USA (office). *Website:* www.hermanwouk.net (office).

WOUTS, Bernard François Emile; French business executive; *CEO, Éditions Tallandier;* b. 22 March 1940, Roubaix; s. of Emile Wouts and Marie Vanderbauwede; m. Annick Memet 1965; two s. one d.; ed Lycée St Louis, Paris; engineer, then Deputy Dir-Gen. and Man. Bayard Presse and Pres. subsidiaries of Bayard Presse group 1966–81; Dir-Gen. Soc. de Publications et d'Editions Réunies 1980–85; Gen. Man. Le Monde 1985–90; Pres. Coopérative des quotidiens de Paris 1988–90; apptd Pres.-Dir-Gen. Le Point 1990, Chair. and CEO –2004; Pres. SPMI (Syndicat de la Presse Magazine et d'Information) 1995–99, Vice-Pres. 1999–; CEO Editions Tallendier 2001–; Pres. Diffusion Contrôle 2002–06. *Publication:* La presse entre les lignes 1990. *Leisure interest:* sailing. *Address:* Éditions Tallandier, 2 rue Routrou, 75006 Paris, France (office). *Telephone:* 1-40-46-43-88 (office). *Fax:* 1-40-46-43-98 (office). *E-mail:* atalland@tallandier.com (office). *Website:* www.tallendier.com (office).

WOWEREIT, Klaus, LLB; German politician; *Mayor of Berlin;* b. 1 Oct. 1953, Berlin; adviser to Senator for Internal Affairs, Berlin 1981–84; mem. Regional Cttee and Del. to SPD, Tempelhof Regional Council 1984–95; Chair. SPD Group, Tempelhof Dist 1981–84, Vice-Chair. 1995–99, Chair. SPD Group, Parl. of Berlin 1999–2001; Mayor of Berlin 2001–; Vice-Chair. SPD 2009–; Partner, Tempelhof Haus-, Wohnungs- und Grundstückseigentümerverein Berlin-Lichtenrade eV, European Acad.; mem. Tempelhof Art and Cultural Union (TKK); Commdr, Légion d'honneur 2004. *Address:* Senate Chancellery, 10871 Berlin, Germany (office). *E-mail:* der-regierende-buergermeister@SKZL.Verwalt-Berlin.de (office). *Website:* www.berlin.de (office); www.klaus-wowereit.de.

WOZNIACKI, Caroline; Danish professional tennis player; b. 11 July 1990, Odense; d. of Piotr Wozniacki and Anna Wozniacki; plays right-handed (two-handed backhand); won several jr tournaments in 2005, including Orange Bowl tennis championship, Fla, Osaka Mayor's Cup, Japan; debut on WTA (Women's Tennis Assn) Tour at Cincinnati's Western & Southern Financial Group Women's Open 2005; winner Girls' Singles Jr Championship, Wimbledon 2006; winner Pilot Pen, New Haven, USA 2008, Nordic Light Open, Stockholm, Sweden 2008, Mirage Cup, Las Vegas, USA 2008, Ortisei ITF, Italy 2008, Ponte Vedra Beach 2009, 2010, Eastbourne 2009, New Haven 2009, 2010, Copenhagen 2010, 2011, Montreal 2010, US Open Summer Series 2010, Tokyo 2010, Beijing 2010, Dubai 2011, Indian Wells 2011, Brussels 2011; Grand Slam results: fourth round, Wimbledon 2009, 2010, 2011, finalist, US Open 2009, quarter-finalist, French Open 2010, semi-finalist, Australian Open 2011; finalist, WTA Tour Championships, Doha 2010; also holds two WTA titles in doubles: China Open, Beijing, China 2008, Cellular South Cup, Memphis, Tenn. 2009; three-time mem. Danish Fed. Cup Team 2009; WTA Tour Most Impressive Newcomer of the Year 2008, Youngest Player in the WTA Top 10 2009, ITF Player of the Year 2010, Danish Sports Name of the Year 2010. *Leisure interests:* playing handball and football, swimming, playing the piano, Liverpool Football Club. *Address:* c/o Lagardère Unlimited, 4 rue de Presbourg, 75016 Paris, France (office). *Telephone:* 1-40-69-16-00 (office). *E-mail:* jtobias@lagardere-unlimited.com (office). *Website:* www.lagardere-unlimited.com (office); www.carolinewozniacki.dk.

WOŹNIAK, Piotr Grzegorz, MSc; Polish business executive and government official; b. 13 Feb. 1956, Warsaw; m.; five c.; ed Warsaw Univ.; Asst Prof. State

Geological Inst. 1980–84, 1986–89; head field group Geopol-Polservice in Libya 1985; adviser to Minister of Agric. and Food Economy 1989–90; adviser to Minister of Industry 1990–91; Dir TUW (mutual insurance soc.) 1991; Vice–Chair., mem. of Bd RUCH SA; Rep. of Poland UNIDO Programme; Commercial Consul Polish Embassy Ottawa and Montreal Consulate 1992–96; mem. Bd PAKTO SA 1997–98; Prime Minister's adviser on infrastructure 1998–2000; mem. Supervisory Bd EkoFundusz Foundation 1998–2001, KUKE SA 1998-2002, Polish Oil and Gas Extraction Co. (PGNiG S.A) 1999–2000, Gas Trading S.A. 2000–02, EuRoPol Gaz SA 2000–01; mem. Council for Motorways 1998–2002; Vice-Pres. of Man. Bd for Trade and Restructuring PGNiG SA 2000–02; Deputy of Warsaw Council, Vice-Chair. Econ. Development and Infrastructure Cttee 2002; econ. adviser on fuel gas trading and power industry 2002–05; Chair. Bd of Dirs Ence.Eko Ltd 2004–05; expert, Sejm Investigative Comm. investigating PKN Orlen SA 2004–05; Minister of the Economy 2005–07; mem. Catholic Intelligentsia Club.

WOZNIAK, Stephen (Steve) Gary, BS; American computer scientist and business executive; *Chief Scientist, Fusion-io;* b. 11 Aug. 1950; m. 1st Alice Robertson 1980 (divorced); m. 2nd Candice Clark Wozniak 1987 (divorced), three c.; m. 3rd Suzanne Mulkern 1990; ed Univ. of California, Berkeley; joined Hewlett Packard Co. as designer of calculator chips 1976; Co-founder (with Steve Jobs q.v.) Apple Computer Inc. 1976, co-designed world's first personal computers, the Apple I and II, Vice-Pres., Research and Devt 1976–81, Designer 1979–81, Vice-Pres., Eng 1983–85, consultant 1985–; Co-founder and Pres. CL9 Remote Control Co. 1985–89; Co-Chair. Axlon Inc. 1986–; Co-founder Wheels of Zeus (wOz) 2002, CEO and Chair. 2002–04, Pres. 2004–06; Co-founder and Exec. Vice-Pres. Acquicor Tech Inc. (now Jazz Technologies, Inc.) 2005–; mem. Bd of Dirs Fusion-io, Salt Lake City 2008–, Chief Scientist 2009–; Founder, Electronic Frontier Foundation; Founding Sponsor, Tech Museum, Silicon Valley Ballet, Children's Discovery Museum of San Jose; Hon. DSc (North Carolina State Univ.) 2004; Grace Murray Hopper Award, Asscn of Computing Machinery 1979, Nat. Medal of Tech. 1985, Inventors Hall of Fame 2000, Heinz Award for Tech. 2000. *Publications:* iWoz: Computer Geek to Cult Icon 2006. *Address:* Fusion-io, 6350 South 3000 East, 6th Floor, Salt Lake City, UT 84121 (office); Acquicor Tech Inc., 4910 Birch Street, Suite 102, Newport Beach, CA 92660, USA (office). *Website:* www.fusionio.com (office); www.woz.org (office).

WOŹNICKI, Jerzy, DSc, PhD; Polish scientist and business executive; *Chairman, Bank Pekao SA;* b. 22 May 1947, Kotuń; ed Warsaw Univ. of Tech.; Asst Prof. and later Full Prof., Faculty of Electronics and IT, Warsaw Univ. of Tech. 1973, Vice-Dir, Inst. of Microelectronics and Optoelectronics 1984–87, Head, Image Processing Div. 1987–, Dean, Faculty of Electronics and IT 1990–, Chair., Univ. Senate Cttee on Univ. Organization 1990, Rector, Warsaw Univ. of Tech. 1996–2002; Deputy Chair., Supervisory Bd, Bank Pekao SA 1999–2005, Chair. 2005–; mem., Presidential Bd, Polish Section, Int. Soc. for Optical Eng (SPIE); mem. Scientific Council, Inst. of Vacuum Tech.; fmr Polish Govt Scientific Expert, UNESCO; fmr Pres., Conf. of Rectors of Academic Schools in Poland (later Hon. Pres.); Pres., Polish Rectors Foundation; Dir, Inst. of Knowledge Soc.; Deputy Chair., Nat. Council of European Integration; mem. Cttee for Electronics and Telecommunications, Polish Acad. of Sciences; Chair. Poland in the United Europe Cttee, Polish Acad. of Sciences; Kt Cross, Order of Rebirth of Poland, Chevalier, Légion d'Honneur (France); many awards from Ministry of Nat. Educ.; Award of the Stefan Batory Foundation. *Address:* Bank Pekao SA, ul. Grzybowska 53/57 Str., 00–950 Warsaw, Poland (office). *Telephone:* (22) 6210972 (office). *Fax:* (22) 6210973 (office). *E-mail:* frpfund@mbox.pw.edu.pl (office). *Website:* www.frp.org.pl (office).

WRAGG, John, ARCA, RA; British sculptor; b. 20 Oct. 1937, York, England; s. of Arthur Wragg and Ethel Wragg; ed York School of Art and Royal Coll. of Art, London; ARA 1983, RA 1991; taught at Chelsea School of Art 1961–90; work represented in several public collections, including Tate Gallery, London, Arts Council of GB, Arts Council of NI, Contemporary Art Soc., Nat. Gallery of Modern Art, Edin., Israel Museum, Jerusalem, Wellington Art Gallery, NZ, Sainsbury Centre for Visual Arts, Univ. of East Anglia; mem. Royal Soc. of British Sculptors 1996; Sainsbury Award 1960, winner, Sainsbury Sculpture Competition, Chelsea 1966, Arts Council of GB Major Award 1977, Chantrey Bequest 1981. *Leisure interests:* walking, listening to music, reading. *Address:* 6 Castle Lane, Devizes, Wilts., SN10 1HJ, England. *Telephone:* (1380) 727087. *E-mail:* john@johnwraggra .co.uk. *Website:* www.johnwraggra.co.uk.

WREN, John D.; American advertising executive; *Co-CEO, Publicis Omnicom Group;* joined Needham Harper Worldwide as an Exec. Vice-Pres. 1984; part of team that created Omnicom 1986, CEO Omnicom's Diversified Agency Services div. 1990, grew Diversified Agency Services into Omnicom's largest operating group, comprising cos ranging from public relations to branding, Pres. Omnicom Group 1996–2013, CEO 1997–2013 (merged with Publicis Groupe to form Publicis Omnicom Group 2013), Co-CEO 2013–. *Address:* Publicis Omnicom Group, 437 Madison Avenue, New York, NY 10022, USA (office). *Telephone:* (212) 415-3600 (office). *Fax:* (212) 415-3530 (office). *Website:* www.omnicomgroup.com (office).

WRIGHT, Alexander (Alastair) Finlay, MBE, MD; British fmr medical practitioner; b. 19 March 1933, Blantyre, Scotland; s. of Alexander Finlay Wright and Mary Paterson; m. Barbara Lattimer 1957; three s. one d.; ed Hamilton Acad., Univ. of Glasgow; gen. medical practitioner, medical researcher, teacher 1961–92; Council of Europe Fellowship, France 1976; Chair. Clinical and Research Div. Royal Coll. of Gen. Practitioners 1990–91; mem. Scientific Cttee, Jt Royal Coll. 'Defeat Depression' Campaign 1991–98; Ed. British Journal of Gen. Practice 1991–99; Fellow, Royal Coll. of Gen. Practitioners; Hon. Fellow, Royal Coll. of Psychiatrists 1998; Sima/Jansson Prize for Research in Gen. Practice 1981, George Abercrombie Award, Royal Coll. of Gen. Practioners 2000. *Publications include:* Medicine and the New Towns of France 1976, Female Sterilisation: The View From General Practice 1981, Depression: Recognition and Management in General Practice 1993, Psychiatry and General Practice (co-author) 1994. *Leisure interests:* walking, spoken French, grandchildren. *Address:* 5 Alburne Crescent, Glenrothes, Fife, KY7 5RE, Scotland (home). *E-mail:* drafw@blueyonder.co.uk (home).

WRIGHT, Sir David John, Kt, GCMG, LVO, MA; British diplomatist and banker; *Vice-Chairman, Barclays Capital;* b. 16 June 1944; s. of J. F. Wright; m. Sally Ann Dodkin 1968; one s. one d.; ed Wolverhampton Grammar School,

Peterhouse, Cambridge; Third Sec., Foreign Office 1966, Third Sec., later Second Sec., Tokyo 1966–72, FCO 1972–75, Ecole Nat. d'Admin., Paris 1975–76, First Sec., Paris 1976–80, Pvt. Sec. to Sec. of Cabinet 1980–82, Counsellor (Econ.), Tokyo 1982–85, Head Personnel Services Dept FCO 1985–88; Deputy Pvt. Sec. to HRH the Prince of Wales 1988–90 (on secondment); Amb. to Repub. of Korea 1990–94, to Japan 1996–99; Deputy Under-Sec. of State, FCO 1994–96; Group Chief Exec. (Perm. Sec.) British Trade Int. 1999–2002; Vice-Chair. Barclays Capital 2002–; Hon. Fellow, Peterhouse, Cambridge 2002; Grand Cordon, Order of the Rising Sun (Japan) 1998; Hon. LLD (Wolverhampton) 1997, (Birmingham) 2000. *Leisure interests:* golf, cooking, military history. *Address:* Barclays Capital, 5 North Colonnade, Canary Wharf, London, E14 4BB, England (office). *Telephone:* (20) 7773-5599 (office). *Fax:* (20) 7773-1806 (office). *E-mail:* david.wright@barcap.com (office).

WRIGHT, James Claude (Jim), Jr; American fmr politician; b. 22 Dec. 1922, Fort Worth, Tex.; s. of James C. Wright and Marie (née Lyster) Wright; m. Betty Hay 1972; one s. three d. (by previous m.); ed Weatherford Coll. and Univ. of Texas; army service 1942–45, DFC, Legion of Merit; Partner, advertising and trade extension firm; mem. Texas Legislature 1947–49; Mayor of Weatherford, Tex. 1950–54; mem. League of Texas Municipalities, Pres. 1953; fmr Lay Minister in Presbyterian Church; mem. for Fort Worth (12th District of Tex.), US House of Reps 1954–89; Deputy Democratic Whip –1976, Majority Leader in House of Reps 1976–87; Chair. Democratic Steering and Policy Cttee in House, Vice-Chair. 1976–87, Speaker, House of Reps 1987–89 (resgnd), mem. Budget Cttee 1974–87; Sr Political Consultant, American Income Life Insurance Co. 1989–; Political Consultant, Arch Petroleum 1989–; fmr ranking mem. Public Works and Transportation Cttee; currently Prof. Tex. Christian Univ.; fmr mem. Govt Operations Cttee; fmr Chair. Comm. on Highway Beautification; cand. for US Senate 1961. *Publications:* You and Your Congressman 1965, The Coming Water Famine 1966, Of Swords and Plowshares 1968, Worth It All 1993, Balance of Power 1996; co-author: Congress and Conscience 1970, Reflections of a Public Man 1984. *Address:* c/o Department of Political Science, Texas Christian University, 2800 South University Drive, Fort Worth, TX 76129, USA. *E-mail:* J.Wright@tcu .edu.

WRIGHT, James E., PhD; American historian, academic and university administrator; *President Emeritus and Eleazar Wheelock Professor of History, Dartmouth College;* b. 1939, Madison, Wis.; m. Susan DeBevoise Wright; two s. one d.; ed Galena High School, Wisconsin State Univ. (now Univ. of Wisconsin-Platteville), Univ. of Wisconsin-Madison; enlisted in US Marine Corps, served for three years in postings that included Calif., Hawaii and Japan; Asst Prof. of History, Dartmouth Coll., Hanover, NH 1969–74, Assoc. Prof. 1974–80, Prof. of History 1980, Dean Faculty of Arts and Sciences 1989–97, Provost and Acting Pres. 1995, Chair. numerous cttees, Acting Provost, then Provost 1997, Pres. Dartmouth Coll. 1998–2009, Pres. Emer. and Eleazar Wheelock Prof. of History 2009–; Sr Historian, Univ. of Mid-America (consortium of nine Midwestern univs, Lincoln, Neb.) 1976–77; mem. Faculty Dartmouth Inst. 1981–83; Sr Historian for award-winning six-film series on history of the Great Plains 1976–78; participated in confs on 'TV and the Historian' and 'The Historian as Film-Maker' 1978; served as Chair. American Historians' Cttee on TV, Film and Media; mem. American Acad. of Arts and Sciences, Org. of American Historians, Western History Asscn; mem. Bd of Trustees Sherman Fairchild Foundation; fellowships from Danforth Foundation and IBM Corpn, Social Science Research Council Grant, Guggenheim Fellowship, Charles Warren Fellowship, Harvard Univ., American Acad. of Arts and Sciences, Marine Corps Scholarship Foundation's Semper Fidelis Award, New Englander of the Year, New England Council 2007. *Publications:* author or ed. of six books: The Galena Lead District: Federal Policy and Practices, 1824–1847 1966, The West of the American People 1970, The Politics of Populism: Dissent in Colorado 1974, The Great Plains Experience: Readings in the History of a Region 1978, The Progressive Yankees: Republican Reformers in New Hampshire 1987, Those Who Have Borne the Battle: A History of America's Wars and Those Who Fought Them 2012. *Address:* History Department, Dartmouth College, 300 Carson Hall, Hanover, NH 03755, USA (office). *Telephone:* (603) 646-0016 (office). *E-mail:* James.E.Wright@Dartmouth.edu (office). *Website:* www.dartmouth.edu/~history (office).

WRIGHT, James R., BA, MA; Canadian diplomatist; b. Montreal; m. Donna Thomson; one s. one d.; ed McGill Univ., Montreal; joined Dept of Foreign Affairs 1976, fmr Dir of Personnel, Dir-Gen. for Cen., East and S Europe Bureau 1996–2000, Political Dir and Asst Deputy Minister, Int. Security Br. 2000–06; served at Embassy in Moscow 1978–80, Embassy in Washington, DC 1983–87, Minister Political and Public Affairs, High Comm. to UK 1992–96, High Commr 2006–11; ex officio Gov. Ditchley Foundation; mem. Bd of Dirs Commonwealth War Graves Comm., Imperial War Museum; Dr hc (Univ. of Ulster) 2008. *Address:* Foreign Affairs and International Trade Canada, Lester B. Pearson Bldg, 125 Sussex Drive, Ottawa, ON K1A 0G2, Canada (office). *Telephone:* (613) 944-4000 (office). *Fax:* (613) 996-9709 (office). *E-mail:* enqserv@international.gc.ca (office). *Website:* www.international.gc.ca (office).

WRIGHT, Joe; British film and television director; b. 25 Aug. 1972, London; m. Anoushka Shankar (d. of Ravi Shankar); one s. *Films directed:* Pride & Prejudice 2005, Atonement 2007, The Soloist 2009, Hanna 2011, Anna Karenina 2012. *Films produced:* Small Gifts (short) (exec. producer) 2010, Plagium (short) (exec. producer) 2011. *Television includes:* Nature Boy (mini-series) 2000, Bob & Rose (series) 2001, Bodily Harm (mini-series) 2002, Charles II: The Power & the Passion (mini-series) 2003. *Address:* c/o Independent, Oxford House, 76 Oxford Street, London, W1D 1BS, England (office). *Telephone:* (20) 7636-6565 (office). *Fax:* (20) 7323-0101 (office). *E-mail:* info@independenttalent.com (office). *Website:* www .independenttalent.com (office).

WRIGHT, Rt Rev. N(icholas) T(homas), BA, MA, DPhil, DD; British theologian, academic and fmr Anglican bishop; *Professor of New Testament and Early Christianity, School of Divinity, St Mary's College University of St Andrews;* b. 1 Dec. 1948, Morpeth, Northumberland; s. of Nicholas Irwin Wright and Rosemary Wright (née Forman); m. Margaret Elizabeth Anne Fiske 1971; two s. two d.; ed Sedbergh School, Exeter Coll., Oxford, Wycliffe Hall, Oxford; ordained deacon 1975, priest 1976; Jr Research Fellow, Merton Coll., Oxford 1975–78, Jr Chaplain 1976–78; Fellow and Chaplain, Downing Coll., Cambridge 1978–81; Asst Prof. of

New Testament Studies, McGill Univ., Montreal and Hon. Prof., Montreal Diocesan Theological Coll., Canada 1981–86; Lecturer in Theology, Univ. of Oxford and Fellow, Tutor and Chaplain, Worcester Coll., Oxford 1986–93; Dean of Lichfield 1994–99; Canon Theologian of Coventry Cathedral 1992–99; Canon Theologian of Westminster 2000–03; Bishop of Durham 2003–10 (retd); Professor of New Testament and Early Christianity, St Mary's Coll., Univ. of St Andrews 2010–; Fellow, Inst. for Christian Studies, Toronto 1992–; mem. Doctrine Comm., Church of England 1979–81, 1989–95, Lambeth Comm. 2004; regular broadcasts on TV and radio; Hon. Fellow, Downing Coll., Cambridge 2003, Merton Coll., Oxford 2004; Hon. DD (Aberdeen) 2000, (Nashotah House) 2006, (Wycliffe Coll., Toronto) 2006, (Durham) 2007, (St Andrews) 2009, (Northumbria) 2010, (London) 2010; Hon. DHumLitt (Gordon Coll., Mass) 2003. *Publications include:* Small Faith, Great God 1978, The Work of John Frith 1983, The Epistles of Paul to the Colossians and to Philemon 1987, The Glory of Christ in the New Testament (co-ed.) 1987, The Interpretation of the New Testament 1861–1986 (co-author) 1988, The Climax of the Covenant 1991, New Tasks for a Renewed Church 1992, The Crown and the Fire 1992, The New Testament and the People of God 1992, Who Was Jesus? 1992, Following Jesus 1994, Jesus and the Victory of God 1996, The Lord and His Prayer 1996, What Saint Paul Really Said 1997, For All God's Worth 1997, Reflecting the Glory 1998, The Meaning of Jesus (co-author) 1999, The Myth of the Millennium 1999, Romans and the People of God (co-ed.) 1999, Holy Communion for Amateurs 1999, The Challenge of Jesus 2000, Twelve Months of Sundays, Year C 2000, Easter Oratorio (co-author) 2000, Twelve Months of Sundays, Year A 2001, Luke for Everyone 2001, Mark for Everyone 2001, Paul for Everyone: Galatians and Thessalonians 2002, John for Everyone 2002, Twelve Months of Sundays, Year B 2002, New Interpreter's Bible, Vol. X (contrib.) 2002, The Contemporary Quest for Jesus 2002, Paul for Everyone (The Prison Letters) 2002, Matthew for Everyone 2002, Paul for Everyone (I Corinthians 2003), Paul for Everyone (II Corinthians) 2003, Quiet Moments 2003, The Resurrection of the Son of God 2003, For All the Saints? 2003, Hebrews for Everyone 2003, Paul for Everyone (The Pastoral Letters) 2003, Paul for Everyone: Romans 2004, Scripture and the Authority of God 2005, Paul: Fresh Perspectives 2005, Simply Christian 2006, Evil and the Justice of God 2006, Judas and the Gospel of Jesus 2006, The Cross and the Colliery 2007, Surprised by Hope 2007, Acts for Everyone 2008, Jesus: the Final Days 2008, Anglican Evangelical Identity 2008, Justification 2009, For Everyone Bible Study Guides 2009, Lent for Everyone 2009, Virtue Reborn 2010, Simply Jesus: A New Vision of Who He Was, What He Did, and Why He Matters 2011, How God Became King: The Forgotten Story of the Gospels 2012, Lent for Everyone: Mark 2012, The Case for the Psalms 2013, Pauline Perspectives 2013, Paul and the Faithfulness of God 2013, Creation Power and Truth 2013. *Leisure interests:* music, hill walking, poetry, cricket, golf. *Address:* School of Divinity, St Mary's College, University of St Andrews, South Street, St Andrews, Fife, KY16 9JU, Scotland (office). *Telephone:* (1334) 462827 (office). *E-mail:* ntw2@st-andrews.ac.uk (office). *Website:* www.st-andrews.ac.uk/divinity (office); www.ntwrightpage.com.

WRIGHT, Patrick (Paddy); Irish business executive; joined Jefferson Smurfit 1976, fmrly Chief Exec. UK and Ireland, Pres. and COO 1996–2000 (retd); Chair. RTE Authority 2000–05; fmr Chair. Aon MacDonagh Boland Group; fmr Pres. Confed. of Irish Industry; Chair. Dublin City Univ. Educational Trust 1995–2006; mem. Bd of Dirs Anglo Irish Bank 2000–, Croke Park; Fellow Irish Man. Inst.; Dr hc (Dublin City Univ.) 2004; Hon. Fellow, Nat. Coll. of Ireland. *Address:* c/o Board of Directors, Anglo Irish Bank, Stephen Court, 18/21 St. Stephens Green, Dublin 2, Ireland.

WRIGHT OF RICHMOND, Baron (Life Peer), cr. 1994, of Richmond-upon-Thames in the London Borough of Richmond-upon-Thames; **Patrick Richard Henry Wright,** KStJ, GCMG, MA, FRCM; British diplomatist (retd); b. 28 June 1931, Reading, Berks., England; s. of Herbert H. S. Wright and Rachel Wright (née Green); m. Virginia Anne Gaffney 1958; two s. one d.; ed Marlborough Coll., Merton Coll., Oxford; served with RA 1950–51; joined Diplomatic Service 1955, Middle East Centre for Arabic Studies 1956–57, Third Sec., Embassy in Beirut 1958–60, Pvt. Sec. to Amb., later First Sec., Embassy in Washington, DC 1960–65, Pvt. Sec. to Perm. Under-Sec., FCO 1965–67, First Sec. and Head of Chancery, Embassy in Cairo 1967–70, Deputy Political Resident, Bahrain 1971–72, Head of Middle East Dept, FCO 1972–74; Pvt. Sec. (Overseas Affairs) to Prime Minister 1974–77; Amb. to Luxembourg 1977–79, to Syria 1979–81, to Saudi Arabia 1984–86, Deputy Under-Sec., FCO 1982–84, Chair. Jt Intelligence Cttee 1982–84, Perm. Under-Sec. of State, FCO and Head of Diplomatic Service 1986–91; Dir Barclays Bank PLC 1991–96, BP 1991–2000, De La Rue 1991–2000, Unilever 1991–99, British Airports Authority 1992–98; mem. Council, Royal Coll. of Music 1991–2001; Chair. Royal Inst. for Int. Affairs 1995–99, Home-Start Int. 2004–07, currently Hon. Pres.; mem. (Crossbench), House of Lords 1994–, Chair. Sub-cttee F (Home Affairs) 2004–07, mem. European Select Cttee 2004–07, Sub-cttee E (Law and Insts) 2008–12; Gov. Wellington Coll. 1991–2001, Fellow 2012–; Hon. Fellow, Merton Coll., Oxford; Parliamentary Speech of the Year, House Magazine 2004. *Leisure interests:* philately, piano duets. *Address:* House of Lords, Westminster, London, SW1A 0PW, England. *Telephone:* (20) 8876-4176 (home). *E-mail:* prhwright@btinternet.com (office).

WRIGHT, Sir Peter Robert, Kt, CBE; British ballet director and choreographer; *Director Laureate, Birmingham Royal Ballet;* b. 25 Nov. 1926, London, England; s. of Bernard Wright and Hilda Wright (née Foster); m. Sonya Hana 1954; one s. one d.; ed Bedales School and Leighton Park School, Reading; 1944 debut as professional dancer with Ballets Jooss; during 1950s worked with several dance cos. including Sadler's Wells Theatre Ballet; created first ballet, A Blue Rose, for Sadler's Wells 1957; Ballet Master, Sadler's Wells Opera and teacher, Royal Ballet School 1959–61; teacher and ballet master to ballet co. formed by John Cranko in Stuttgart 1961–65; choreographed several ballets in Stuttgart including The Mirror Walkers, Namouna, Designs for Dancers, Quintet and mounted his first production of Giselle; producer of TV ballets and choreographer of various London West End musicals and revues during 1960s; Asst Dir The Royal Ballet 1969, later Assoc. Dir; Dir Sadler's Wells Royal Ballet (Birmingham Royal Ballet since 1990) 1977–95, Dir Laureate, Birmingham Royal Ballet 1995–; Gov. Royal Ballet School 1976–2002, Sadler's Wells Theatre 1987–2000; Special Prof. of Performance Studies, Univ. of Birmingham 1990–; Fellow, Birmingham Conservatoire of Music 1991–; Pres. Council of Dance Educ. and Training 1994–99, Friends of Sadler's

Wells Theatre 1995–2003, Benesh Inst. of Choreology 1994–; Vice-Pres. Royal Acad. of Dancing 1993–; Hon. DMus (London) 1990, Hon. DLitt (Birmingham) 1994; Evening Standard Award for Ballet 1981, Elizabeth II Coronation Award, Royal Acad. of Dancing 1990, Digital Premier Award 1991, Critics' Award for Services to the Arts 1995, De Valois Award for Outstanding Achievement, Critics' Circle Nat. Dance Awards 2004, Critics' Circle Centenary Award 2014. *Ballets directed include:* many new productions in various countries of the full-length classics Giselle, Coppelia, Swan Lake, The Sleeping Beauty, The Nutcracker, but particularly for The Royal Ballet and the Birmingham Royal Ballet; original works for Sadlers Wells Royal Ballet include: A Blue Rose, Arpège, El Amor Brujo, Summer's Night, Summertide; for the Stuttgart Ballet: Mirror Walkers, Designs for Dancers, Quintet; for Western Theatre Ballet: Musical Chairs. *Leisure interests:* ceramics, gardens, travel, music. *Address:* Flat 5, Wedderburn House, 95 Lower Sloane Street, London, SW1W 8BZ, England (home). *Telephone:* (20) 7823-4530 (home). *E-mail:* petsoprods@aol.com (home).

WRIGHT, Robert C., LLB; American broadcasting executive; b. 23 April 1943, Hempstead, NY; m. Suzanne Wright 1967; one s. two d.; ed Chaminade High School, Holy Cross Coll. and Univ. of Virginia Law School; career in gen. man. marketing, broadcasting, strategic planning and law; fmr Pres. Cox Cable Communications; later Pres. Gen. Electric Financial Services, Vice-Chair. 2001; Pres. and CEO Nat. Broadcasting Co. (NBC) 1986–2001, Chair. and CEO 2001–2004, then Chair. and CEO NBC Universal Inc. (after NBC merger with Vivendi Universal) 2004–07. *Address:* c/o NBC Universal Inc., 30 Rockefeller Plaza, 52nd Floor, New York, NY 10112, USA (office).

WRIGHTON, Mark Stephen, BS, MS, PhD; American chemist, academic and university administrator; *Chancellor, Washington University in St Louis;* b. 1949, Jacksonville, Fla; ed Florida State Univ., California Inst. of Tech.; Asst Prof. of Chem., MIT 1972–76, Assoc. Prof. 1976–77, Prof. 1977–81, Frederick G. Keyes Chair in Chem. 1981–89, Ciba-Geigy Chair in Chem. (first holder) 1989, Head of Dept of Chem. 1987–90, Provost of MIT 1990–95; Chancellor Washington Univ. in St Louis 1995–; titular mem. IUPAC Comm. on Photochemistry 1976–83; mem. Chem. Research Evaluation Panel for Air Force Office of Scientific Research 1976–80, American Physical Soc. Study Group on Solar Photovoltaic Energy Conversion 1977–79, Nat. Materials Advisory Bd Study on Battery Materials 1979–80, Energy Research Advisory Bd Solar Panel 1982, Advisory Cttee of Chem. Div., Oak Ridge Nat. Lab. 1983–85, Advisory Cttee for NSF Chem. Div. 1984—87 (Chair. 1986–87), Basic Energy Sciences Advisory Cttee of Dept of Energy 1986–89, Energy Research Advisory Bd Panel on Cold Fusion 1989, Nat. Research Council Bd on Chemical Sciences and Tech. 1986–89, Governing Bd Council on Chemical Research 1988–91, Science Advisory Cttee of Electric Power Research Inst. 1990–92, NSF Materials Research Advisory Cttee 1990–91, Defense Sciences Research Council (fmrly the Materials Research Council) of Advanced Research Projects Agency 1981–97, NSF Advisory Cttee for Directorate for Math. and Physical Sciences 1995–96, Bd of Overseers Boston Museum of Science 1991–97, Corpn of Woods Hole Oceanographic Inst. 1991–95, Corpn of Draper Lab. 1994–96; mem.-at-large Gordon Research Council 1986–89; presidential appointee to Nat. Science Bd 2000–06, Chair. Audit and Oversight Cttee; mem. Bd Dirs Chemical Heritage Foundation 1998–2002, Nat. Asscn of Ind. Colls and Univs 2002–05; mem. Bd Dirs Brooks Automation, Inc., Cabot Corpn, Donald Danforth Plant Science Center, A.G. Edwards, Inc., Nidus Center for Scientific Enterprise, Universities Research Asscn; *ex officio* mem. Bd of Dirs St Louis Regional Chamber and Growth Asscn, Missouri Botanical Garden, Civic Progress; fmr Chair. Business-Higher Educ. Forum, Asscn of American Univs; Ed. (Physical Electro-chemistry Division) Journal of the Electrochemical Society 1980–83, two vols of ACS's Advances in Chemistry series; Consulting Ed. General Chemistry (1st, 2nd, 3rd and 4th edns); mem. Editorial Advisory Bd Inorganic Chemistry 1983–89, Chemical and Engineering News 1984–86, Journal of Molecular Electronics 1985–90, Chemtronics 1985–90, Chemistry of Materials 1989–93, Inorganica Chimica Acta 1984–93, Journal of Physical Chemistry 1994–95; Trustee Higher Learning Comm. of North Cen. Assen of Colls and Schools 1998–2002, Barnes-Jewish Hosp., BJC Healthcare, Innovate St Louis, Saint Louis Art Museum, St Louis Science Center, Saint Louis Symphony Orchestra; mem. American Philosophical Soc. 2001; Fellow, AAAS 1986, Acad. Academy of Arts and Sciences 1988; Hon. Prof., Shandong Univ., Jinan, People's Repub. of China 2002; Hon. DSc (Univ. of West Florida) 1983; Monsanto Chem. Award for outstanding research, Florida State Univ., Alfred P. Sloan Research Fellowship 1974–76, Dreyfus Teacher-Scholar Grant 1975–80, ACS Pure Chem. Award 1981, MIT Chem. Dept Grad. Teaching Award 1981, ACS Award in Inorganic Chem. 1988, MacArthur Prize Fellowship 1983, Gregory and Freda Halpern Award in Photochemistry, New York Acad. of Sciences 1983, E.O. Lawrence Award, US Dept of Energy 1983, Fresenius Award, Phi Lambda Upsilon 1984, named by Science Digest magazine as one of America's brightest scientists under age 40 1984, named by Science Digest magazine as one of America's top 100 innovators of the year 1985, MIT School of Science Teaching Prize 1987, first recipient of Herbert Newby McCoy Award, Calif. Inst. of Tech., Distinguished Alumni Award, Calif. Inst. of Tech. 1992, named by Business Week magazine as one of ten innovators in science 1989, included in Esquire magazine's Register along with 38 other men and women "who are making America a smarter, healthier, wealthier, safer, livelier, prettier, all around more interesting place to live" 1989, named by the Arthritis Foundation's Eastern Missouri Chapter Humanitarian of the Year 2000, Right Arm of St Louis Award, St Louis Regional Chamber and Growth Asscn 2010. *Publications:* Organometallic Photochemistry (co-author) 1979; 14 patents and more than 300 articles published in professional and scholarly journals on transition metal catalysis, photochemistry, surface chemistry, molecular electronics and photo-processes at electrodes. *Address:* Office of the Chancellor, Washington University in St Louis, Campus Box 1192, One Brookings Drive, St Louis, MO 63130, USA (office). *Telephone:* (314) 935-5100 (office). *Fax:* (314) 935-4744 (office). *E-mail:* wrighton@wustl.edu (office). *Website:* www.wustl.edu (office).

WRIGLEY, Sir Edward Anthony, Kt, MA, PhD, FBA; British academic; b. 17 Aug. 1931, Manchester, England; s. of Edward Wrigley and Jessie Wrigley; m. Maria Laura Spelberg 1960; one s. three d.; ed King's School, Macclesfield and Peterhouse, Cambridge; William Volker Research Fellow, Univ. of Chicago 1953–54; Fellow, Peterhouse 1958–79, Sr Bursar 1964–74, Hon. Fellow 1996–; Lecturer in Geography, Univ. of Cambridge 1958–74; Assoc. Dir Cambridge Group for the History of Population and Social Structure 1964–95; mem. Inst. of Advanced Study, Princeton 1970–71; Hinkley Visiting Prof., Johns Hopkins Univ. 1975; Tinbergen Visiting Prof., Erasmus Univ., Rotterdam 1979; Prof. of Population Studies, LSE 1979–88; Pres. Manchester Coll. Oxford 1987–96; Sr Research Fellow All Souls Coll. Oxford 1988–94, Acad. Sec. 1992–94, Fellow 2002–05; Prof. of Econ. History, Univ. of Cambridge 1994–97; Master, Corpus Christi Coll. Cambridge 1994–2000; Ed. Econ. History Review 1985–92; Treas. British Acad. 1989–95, Pres. 1997–2001; Pres. British Soc. for Population Studies 1977–79; Chair. Population Investigation Cttee 1984–90; Hon. Fellow, LSE 1997; Hon. DLitt (Manchester) 1997, (Sheffield) 1997, (Bristol) 1998, (Oxford) 1999, (Leicester) 1999, (Queen Mary) 2004; Hon. DScS (Edin.) 1998; James Ford Special Lecturer, Oxford 1986, Ellen Macarthur Lecturer, Cambridge 1987, Linacre Lecturer, Oxford 1998, Laureate of the Int. Union for the Scientific Study of Population 1993, Founder's Medal, Royal Geographical Soc. 1997, Leverhulme Medal, British Acad. 2005. *Publications:* Continuity, Chance and Change 1989, Poverty, Progress and Population 2004, several works on econ. and demographic history. *Leisure interest:* gardening. *Address:* 13 Sedley Taylor Road, Cambridge, CB2 8PW, England (home). *Telephone:* (1223) 247614 (home). *E-mail:* eaw20@cam.ac.uk (office).

WU, Aiying; Chinese politician; *Minister of Justice;* b. 1951, Changle Co., Shandong Prov.; ed Shandong Univ., Cen. Communist Party School; joined CCP 1970, began career 1973; served successively as teacher in Communist Party (CP) School of Party Cttee of Changle Co., Deputy Sec. Gen. CP Cttee of Gaoya Communist Soc. under Changle Co., Perm. mem. CP Cttee of Changle Co., Deputy Sec. Gen. Chengguan Communist Soc. under Changle Co., Deputy Sec. Gen. CP Cttee of Changle Co., Deputy Dir Revolutionary Cttee of Co. and concurrently Sec. Gen. CP Cttee and Dir Revolutionary Cttee of Chengguan Communist Soc. 1973–78; served successively as Sec. Gen. Changwei Regional Cttee of Communist Youth League and Sec. Gen. Regional Party Group 1978–82; worked successively as Deputy Sec. Gen. Shandong Prov. Cttee of Communist Youth League, Vice-Pres. and Pres. Shandong Prov. Youth Union and Dir Gen. Shandong Provincial Youth Working Cttee 1982–89; Vice-Chair. Shandong Prov. Women's Fed. 1989–90, Chair. 1990–93; Deputy Sec. Gen. Prov. Party Group 1989–93; Sec. Gen. Party Group and concurrently Pres. Shandong Br. of China Women Leaders' Training Coll. 1989–93; Vice-Gov. Shandong Prov. and mem. Shandong CP Prov. Cttee 1993–98; Deputy Sec. Gen. Shandong CP Prov. Cttee 1998–2002, Pres. Prov. Cttee of CPPCC and Sec. Gen. Party Group of Cttee 2002–04; Vice-Minister of Justice and Deputy Sec. Gen. of Party Group, Ministry of Justice (with rank of Prin. Minister) 2003–05; Minister of Justice and Sec. Gen. Party Group, Ministry of Justice 2005–; Alt. mem. 14th CCP Cen. Cttee 1992–97, 15th CCP Cen. Cttee 1997–2002, 16th CCP Cen. Cttee 2002–07, mem. 17th CCP Cen. Cttee 2007–12, 18th CCP Cen. Cttee 2012–; mem. 10th Nat. People's Political Consultative Conf. 2003–08. *Address:* Ministry of Justice, 10 Chaoyangmen, Nan Dajie, Chao Yang Qu, Beijing 100020, People's Republic of China (office). *Telephone:* (10) 65205114 (office). *Fax:* (10) 65205316 (office).

WU, Bai; Taiwanese actor and musician; b. 1968, Chaiyi Prov., Taiwan. *Films include:* Zheng hun qi shi 1998, Meili xin shijie 1999, Seunlau ngaklau 2000, San ging chaat goo si 2004. *Music:* singer, songwriter with band China Blue 1993–.

WU, Bangguo; Chinese party official and engineer; b. July 1941, Feidong Co., Anhui Prov.; m. Zhang Ruizhen; ed Tsinghua Univ., Beijing; joined CCP 1964; worked at Shanghai No. 3 Electronic Tube Factory, progressing from freight worker to Factory Dir 1967–78; Deputy Man. Shanghai Municipal Electronics Components Industry Co., Shanghai Municipal Electrical Vacuum Device Co. 1979–81; Deputy Sec. Parl. Cttee Shanghai Municipal Instruments Bureau 1981–83; mem. Standing Cttee Shanghai Municipal CCP Cttee 1983–85, Deputy Sec. 1986–89, Sec. 1991–94; a Shanghai del. to 8th NPC 1993; mem. CCP Secr. 1994–97; Vice-Premier of State Council 1995–2007; Alt. mem. 13th CCP Cen. Cttee 1987–92, mem. 14th CCP Cen. Cttee 1992–97, 15th CCP Cen. Cttee 1997–2002, 16th CCP Cen. Cttee 2002–07, 17th CCP Cen. Cttee 2007–12; mem. CCP Politburo 1992–2012, CCP Politburo Standing Cttee 2002–12; Chair. Standing Cttee 10th NPC 2003–07, Standing Cttee 11th NPC 2008–13. *Address:* c/o Quangguo Renmin Daibiao Dahui (National People's Congress), Beijing, People's Republic of China (office).

WU, Dechang; Chinese toxicologist; b. 22 Oct. 1927, Beijing; m. Lin Rhi-zhu 1951; one s. two d.; ed Peking Univ. and in USSR; Asst Lecturer, later Lecturer, Xiehe Hosp., Beijing 1949; Prof. of Toxicology, Inst. of Radiation Medicine, Beijing 1981–; Commdt Mil. Medical Science Acad. of PLA 1990–94; Del. to 14th Nat. Conf. CCP 1992–97; mem. 8th Nat. Cttee CPPCC 1993–97; Deputy Rep., UN Atomic Radiation Effectiveness Science Cttee; Pres. Chinese Soc. of Toxicology 1995–; Academician, Chinese Acad. of Eng 1994–; Nat. Science and Tech. Awards 1985, 1993, 1995, Prize for Outstanding Contributions 1991, Ho Leung Ho Lee Medical Sciences and Materia Medica Prize 2003. *Publications:* Radiation Risk and Assessment 1999, Radiation Medicine 2000. *Leisure interest:* classical music. *Address:* Military Medical Science Academy of People's Liberation Army, 27 Tai-Ping Road, Beijing 100850, People's Republic of China (office). *Telephone:* (10) 68186211 (office). *Fax:* (10) 68214653 (office). *E-mail:* wudc@nic.bmi.ac.cn (office); wudc@public.bta.net.cn (office).

WU, Den-Yih, BA; Taiwanese politician; *Vice-President;* b. 30 Jan. 1948, Tsaotun, Nantou Co.; m. Tsai Ling-yi; three s. one d.; ed Nat. Taiwan Univ.; Pres. and Ed.-in-Chief Univ. News, Nat. Taiwan Univ. 1968–69; Instructor, Military Acad. 1970–71; journalist and editorial writer, China Times newspaper 1971–73; mem. Taipei City Council 1973–83; Magistrate, Nantou Co. 1981–89; Chair. Kuomintang (KMT) Taipei Municipal Cttee 1989–90, mem. KMT Cttee. Standing Cttee 1993–2000, Vice Chair. and Sec.-Gen., KMT 2007–09; Mayor of Kaohsiung City 1990–98; Chair. (volunteer), Nantou Co. Cttee, China Youth Corps 2000–02; mem. Legis. Yuan (Parl.) 2002–09; Premier, Repub. of China (Taiwan) 2009–12; Vice-Pres. 2012–. *Address:* Office of the Vice President, 122 Chungking South Rd, Zhongzheng District, Taipei 10048, Taiwan (office).

WU, Dingfu; Chinese government official; b. July 1946, Hubei; m.; ed Hubei Univ.; joined CCP 1972; has held numerous govt positions including Magistrate, Guangji Co. 1984, Deputy Commr, Huanggang Pref., Hubei Prov. 1987–90, Auditor-Gen., Prov. Auditing Office, Hubei Prov. 1991–95; joined Nat. Audit Office 1995, Head, Comm. for Discipline Inspection 1998–2000; Vice-Chair. China

Insurance Regulatory Comm. 1998–2000, Chair. 2002–11; mem. Cen. Comm. for Discipline Inspection, CCP Cen. Cttee 2000–02, Sec.-Gen. 2001–02; Alt. Mem. 16th CCP Cen. Cttee 2002–07, 17th CCP Cen. Cttee 2007–12. *Address:* c/o China Insurance Regulatory Commission (CIRC), 15 Financial Street, Xicheng District, Beijing 100034, People's Republic of China (office).

WU, Sir Gordon Ying Sheung, Kt, KCMG, FICE, BSc; Chinese real estate executive; *Chairman, Hopewell Holdings;* b. 3 Dec. 1935, Hong Kong; s. of Wu Chung and Wu Sum (née Kang); m. Kwok San-Ping Wu 1970; two s. two d.; ed Princeton Univ., USA; Man. Dir Hopewell Holdings, Hong Kong 1972–2001, Chair. 2001–; responsible for construction of colony's tallest bldg, Hopewell Holdings HQ; projects constructed include China Hotel, Canton, China, coal-fired power station for Prov. of Guangdong, China, motorway linking Hong Kong to Shenzhen and Canton; responsible for design of many of his own bldgs; Vice-Pres. Hong Kong Real Estate Developer's Asscn 1970–; mem. CPPCC 1984–; several hon. degrees; numerous honours including Gold Bauhinia Star 2004, Officer de l'Ordre de la Couronne (Belgium) 2007, Order of Croatian Danica 2007. *Leisure interest:* classical music. *Address:* 64/F, Hopewell Centre, 183 Queen's Road East, Wan Chai, Hong Kong Special Administrative Region, People's Republic of China (office). *Telephone:* 25284975 (office). *Fax:* 28612068 (office). *E-mail:* ir@hopewellholdings.com (office). *Website:* www.hopewellholdings.com (office).

WU, Lt-Gen. Guangyu; Chinese air force officer; b. Dec. 1940, Hongze Co., Jiangsu Prov.; ed middle school and Air Force Aviation School; joined PLA 1958, CCP 1964; air force pilot and squadron leader 1962–70; various posts in Air Force Aviation 1970–85; Commdr Air Force units, PLA Shanghai Base 1985; Commdr PLA Air Force Command Post 1985–90; Deputy Commdr Nanjing Mil. Regional Air Force 1990–93; Deputy Commdr and Air Force Commdr Jinan Mil. Region 1993; Deputy Commdr PLA Air Force 1995; Deputy to 6th NPC 1983; Alt. mem. 14th CCP Cen. Cttee 1992–97, 15th CCP Cen. Cttee 1997–2002. *Address:* c/o Ministry of National Defence, Jingshanqian Jie, Beijing, People's Republic of China (office). *Telephone:* (10) 6370000 (office).

WU, Guanzheng; Chinese government official; b. 25 Aug. 1938, Yugan Co., Jiangxi Prov.; s. of Wu Enshui and Dong Gelao; m. Zhang Jinshang 1959; three s.; ed Tsinghua Univ., Beijing; joined CCP 1962; Deputy Sec. CCP Party Br., Tsinghua Univ. 1965–68; mem. CCP Cttee of Wuhan Gedian Chemical Plant, Deputy Dir Revolutionary Cttee of Wuhan Gedian Chemical Plant 1968–75; Deputy Dir Wuhan Science and Tech. Cttee, Vice-Chair. Wuhan City Assocn of Science and Tech., Deputy Commdr and Dir of Gen. Office, Wuhan City Technical Innovation Headquarters; Dir, Sec. CCP Cttee of Wuhan City Eng Science and Tech. Research Centre 1975–82; Standing mem. CCP Cttee of Wuhan City 1982–83; Sec. CCP Cttee and Mayor of Wuhan City 1983–86; Deputy Sec. Jiangxi Prov. CCP Cttee, Acting Gov., Gov. Jiangxi Prov. 1986–95; Sec. CCP Cttee Jiangxi Prov., First Sec. CCP Cttee Jiangxi Prov. Mil. Command 1995–97, Sec. CCP Cttee Shandong Prov. and Prin. of School for CCP Shandong Cttee 1997–07; Alt. mem. 12th CCP Cen. Cttee 1982–87, mem. 13th CCP Cen. Cttee 1987–92, 14th CCP Cen. Cttee 1992–97, 15th CCP Cen. Cttee 1997–2002, 16th CCP Cen. Cttee 2002–07; mem. CCP Cen. Cttee Politburo 1997–2007, Standing Cttee CCP Cen. Cttee Politburo 2002–07; Sec. 16th CCP Cen. Cttee Cen. Comm. for Discipline Inspection 2002–07. *Leisure interests:* reading, sports. *Address:* 482 Weiyi Road, Jinan City, Shandong, People's Republic of China. *Telephone:* (531) 2033333.

WU, Guoxiong, PhD; Chinese meteorologist; *Academician, Chinese Academy of Sciences;* b. March 1943, Chaoyang, Guangdong; ed Nanjing Meteorological Inst., Beijing Univ., Imperial Coll. London, UK; Visiting Scientist, ECMWF 1983–84; Research Fellow, Inst. of Atmospheric Physics, Chinese Acad. of Sciences 1985–, currently Sr Scientist; Deputy Chair. Advisory Cttee, Nat. Key Lab. of Atmospheric Sciences and Geophysical Fluid Dynamics 1993–2000; Sr Visiting Research Prof., Geophysical Fluid Dynamics Lab., Princeton Univ., USA 1989–91; Chair. Chinese Cttee for Int. Council for Science (ICSU), mem. Exec. Bd, ICSU; Academician, Chinese Acad. of Sciences 1997–; Hon. Fellow, Royal Meteorological Soc., UK 2012, Second Nat. Natural Science Prize 2007. *Publications:* Time-Mean Statistics of Global General Circulation 1987, Dynamics of the Formation and Variation of the Subtropical Anticyclones 2002. *Address:* Institute of Atmospheric Physics, Chinese Academy of Sciences, Qijiahuozi, Building 100029 (office); Room 1302, Building 801-B, Huangzhuang Dwelling, Beijing 100080, People's Republic of China (home). *Telephone:* (10) 82995266 (office). *Fax:* (10) 82995172 (office). *E-mail:* gxwu@lasg.iap.ac.cn (office). *Website:* www.lasg.ac.cn (office).

WU, Hsing-kuo; Taiwanese theatre and film actor; *Artistic Director, Contemporary Legend Theatre;* ed trained in classical Peking Opera from age of 11 in state-run Fu-Hsing Chinese Opera School, Taiwan, specialized in wu sheng (male martial) roles, Theatre Dept of Chinese Culture Univ., Taipei, trained under Chou Cheng-jung (Zhou Zheng-rong); known for his film roles and his adaptations of Western classics into traditional Peking Opera; became leading dancer of Lin Hwai-min's Cloud Gate Dance Theatre; co-f with friends, Contemporary Legend Theatre, Taipei 1986, sought to revive traditional Chinese theatre by adapting Western classical plays to the style and techniques of Peking Opera; leading actor and director of four Shakespeare adaptations, including Kingdom of Desire, an adaptation of Macbeth, and King Lear (played all the parts); currently Artistic Dir Contemporary Legend Theatre; Fulbright Scholarship to study in New York with Richard Schechner 1992, Best New Performer, Hong Kong Film Awards 1992. *Films include:* Shi ba 1993, Temptation of a Monk 1993, Green Snake 1993, The Great Conqueror's Concubine 1994, What Price Survival 1994, Rock 'n' Roll Cop 1994, Red Rose White Rose 1994, God of Gamblers Returns 1994, Shanghai Grand 1996, The Soong Sisters 1997, The Accidental Spy 2001, Master Swordsman Lu Xiaofeng 2001. *Television includes:* Metropolitan Opera: Live in HD (series) 2007. *Address:* Contemporary Legend Theatre, No. 40, 3F-1, Ting Zhou Road Section 2, Taipei 10077, Taiwan (office). *Telephone:* (2) 2369-2616 (office). *Fax:* (2) 2369-2667 (office). *E-mail:* info@cl-theatre.com (office). *Website:* clients.mingisland.com/CLT (office).

WU, Hualun; Chinese artist; b. June 1942, Tianjin; s. of Wu Bing-Zheng and Wang Yaxin; m. Zeng Wan 1985; ed Cen. Acad. of Arts and Crafts; mem. China Artists' Assocn 1982–, China Calligraphists' Assocn 1986–; Sr Art Ed., China People's Fine Art Publishing House; Prof. 1999–; works have been exhibited many times in Japan, Hong Kong and USA; First Prize, Chinese Paintings Competition

1988, Gold Medal, Japan-China Art Exchange Centre 1988. *Publication:* Chinese Paintings by Wu Hualun 1989. *Leisure interests:* travelling, playing badminton. *Address:* People's Fine Arts Publishing House, 32 Bei Zong Bu Hutong, Beijing 100735, People's Republic of China (office). *Telephone:* (10) 65244901 (office).

WU, Huatai, BA; Chinese engineer and mining industry executive; *Chairman, Shanxi Jincheng Anthracite Coal Mining Group;* b. 1959, Shanxi; fmr capt., electromechanical section chief and deputy dir, Xishan Mining Bureau Xiqu Coal Mine, Sec. of Party Cttee, Xiqu Coal Mine, Xishan Coal Electricity Group Co., mem. Party Cttee, Shanxi Coking Coal Group Tunlan Mine, Deputy Gen. Man. and mem. Party Cttee Standing Cttee, Xishan Coal Corpn (Xishan Coal Electricity Group Co.), Sec. of Party Cttee and Chair. Huajin Coking Coal Co., mem. Bd of Dirs, Chair. Shanxi Coking Coal Group Co., mem. Party Standing Cttee, Xishan Coal and Electricity (Group) Ltd and Sec. of Party Cttee, Chair. and Sec. of Party Cttee, Shanxi Jincheng Anthracite Coal Mining Group Ltd 2010–; part-time Chair. Taiyuan Coal Gasification Co. 2013–; mem. 18th CCP Nat. Congress 2012–. *Address:* Shanxi Jincheng Anthracite Coal Mining Group, Beishidian Town, Jincheng 048006, Shanxi, People's Republic of China (office). *Telephone:* (356) 3664145 (office). *E-mail:* webmaster@jccoal.com (office). *Website:* www.jccoal.com (office).

WU, Jianchang; Chinese engineer and business executive; b. June 1939, son-in-law of the late Deng Xiaoping; m. Deng Lin; ed Henyang Mining Coll.; fmr Deputy Gen. Man. China Nat. Nonferrous Metals Import and Export Corpn; Vice-Pres. China Nat. Nonferrous Metals Industry Corpn 1984–94, later Pres.; Dir (non-exec.) Jianxi Copper Co. Ltd 2008–, Shanxi Tai Gang Stainless Steel Co. 2007–, Silver Grant Int. Industries (Hong Kong), Ind. Dir (non-exec.) Aluminum Corpn of China Ltd 2013–; Consultant China Iron and Steel Asscn; Hon. Chair. China Council for the Promotion of Int. Trade. *Address:* c/o China Iron and Steel Association, No 46 Dong Si Xi Da Jie, Beijing 100711, People's Republic of China (office). *E-mail:* info-cisa@chinaisa.org.cn (office).

WU, Jichuan; Chinese fmr politician; b. 1937, Changning Co., Hunan Prov.; ed Beijing Inst. of Posts and Telecommunications; joined CCP 1960; technician, later Div. Chief, later Bureau Dir, Ministry of Posts and Telecommunications 1960–84; Vice-Minister of Posts and Telecommunications 1984–90, Minister 1993–98; Minister of Information Industry 1998–2003 (retd); Deputy Sec. Henan Prov. CCP Cttee 1990–93; Vice-Chair. State Radio Regulatory Cttee; Deputy Head, State Leading Group for Information 1996; Dir China Telecom Corpn Ltd 2007–; Alt. mem. 14th CCP Cen. Cttee 1992–97, mem. 15th CCP Cen. Cttee 1997–2002, 16th CCP Cen. Cttee 2002–07. *Address:* c/o China Telecom Corporation Ltd, 31 Jinrong Street, Xicheng District, Beijing 100032, People's Republic of China (office).

WU, Jinglian; Chinese economist; *Senior Researcher, State Council Development Research Centre (DRC);* b. Jan. 1930, Nanjing, Jiangsu Prov.; ed Fudan Univ.; Asst Research Fellow, Econs Research Inst. of Chinese Acad. of Sciences 1954–79; Assoc. Research Fellow, Econs Inst. of Chinese Acad. of Social Sciences 1979–83, Research Fellow and Prof. 1983–; Vice-Dir Office for Econ. Reform Programmes of State Council; Sr Researcher, State Council Devt Research Centre; mem. Standing Cttee 9th CPPCC Nat. Cttee 1998–2003, Vice-Chair. Econ. Cttee of CPPCC 1998–2003; Faculty mem., China Europe Int. Business School (CEIBS) 1996–, currently Baosteel Chair Prof. of Econs; Hon. Pres. Int. Econ. Assc 2011; elected one of China's Top Ten Econ. Figures 2000. *Publications:* Explorations into Problems of Economic Reform, Planned Economy or Market Economy, Fifteen Critical Issues of the Reform of SOEs 1999, Reform: Now at a Critical Point 2001, Understanding and Interpreting Chinese Economic Reform 2005. *Address:* Development Research Center of the State Council, No. 225, Chaoyangmen Nei Dajie, Dongcheng District, Beijing 100010, People's Republic of China (office). *Website:* www.drc.gov.cn/english/ (office).

WU, Liang-Yong; Chinese architect; b. 7 May 1922, Nanjing, Jiangsu Prov.; m. Yao Tong-zhen; two s.; ed Nat. Cen. Univ. China, Cranbrook Acad. of Art, USA; Assoc. Prof. of Architecture and Urban Planning, Tsinghua Univ. 1951–61, Prof. 1961–; Dir Inst. of Architectural and Urban Studies 1983–, Centre for Human Settlements 1995–; Visiting Prof. Centre of Urban Studies and Urban Planning, Univ. of Hong Kong 1983, Ecole de Hautes Etudes Sociales, Paris 1987, Univ. of California, Berkeley 1988, Sydney Univ. of Tech. 1993, Univ. of Cambridge, UK 1995; Vice-Pres. Chinese Soc. for Urban Studies 1984–, Int. Union of Architects 1987–90; Pres. Urban Planning Soc. of China 1993–; mem. Academia Sinica 1980; Fellow, Chinese Acad. of Science 1980–, Int. Acad. of Architecture 1989, Chinese Acad. of Eng 1995–; Hon. mem. Architectural Inst. of Japan 1994; Hon. Fellow, American Inst. of Architects 1990, Royal Inst. of British Architects 1998; Chevalier des Arts et Lettres 1999; numerous awards including Gold Medal in Architecture for the Ju'er Project 1992, Jean Tschumi Prize, Int. Union of Architects 1996, Architectural Soc. of China First Prize of Architecture Design Award for Research Institute of Confucius 2006, State Supreme Science and Tech. Award 2011, Nanjing Univ. Distinguished Alumnus Award 2012. *Publications include:* A Brief History of Ancient Chinese City Planning 1985, Selected Essays on Urban Planning and Design 1987, Rehabilitating the Old City of Beijing 1999, Reflections at the Turn of the Century: The Future of Architecture 1999, Buildings, Cities and Human Settlements 2003; more than 200 academic papers. *Leisure interests:* fine arts including painting and calligraphy. *Address:* School of Architecture, Tsinghua University, Beijing 100084 (office); No. 12, Apt 10, Tsinghua University, Beijing 100084, People's Republic of China (home). *Telephone:* (10) 62784567 (office); (10) 62784507 (home). *Fax:* (10) 6562768 (office); (10) 62781048 (home). *E-mail:* engach@mail.cae.ac.cn (office); wuly@public.bta.net.cn (home).

WU, Min, DMed; Chinese geneticist; b. 1925, Changzhou, Jiangsu Prov.; ed Tongji Univ. Medical Coll., USSR Acad. of Medical Science; Research Fellow and then Dir Cytobiology Section of Tumour Research Inst., Chinese Acad. of Medical Sciences 1961–; one of the initiators of nat. Human Genome project in China; Vice-Pres. Council of Chinese Genetics Soc.; mem. Standing Cttee Biology Dept Chinese Acad. of Sciences; mem. 4th Presidium, Chinese Acad. of Sciences 2000–; several awards including Golden Bull Prize for Devt of Nat. Labs 1990, 1994, China Technology Science Prize 1996, Ho Leung Ho Lee Medical Sciences Prize 1998. *Publications:* The Mitotic Caryotype of the Chinese; more than 300 scientific publications. *Address:* Chinese Academy of Sciences, 52 Sanlihe Road, Beijing

100864, People's Republic of China (office). *Telephone:* (10) 68597219 (office). *Fax:* (10) 68511095 (office).

WU, Poh-Hsiung, BSc; Taiwanese politician; *Honorary Chairman, Kuomintang (KMT);* b. 19 June 1939, Taoyuan County; m. Dai Mei-yu; two s. one d.; ed Nat. Cheng Kung Univ., Sun Yat-sen Inst. of Policy and Research and Devt; schoolteacher 1963–65; mem. Taiwan Prov. Ass. 1968–72; Assoc. Prof., Nan Ya Jr Coll. of Tech. 1972–73; Magistrate, Taoyuan Co. 1973–76; Dir Inst. of Industry for Workmen and Friends of Labour Asscn, Dir-Gen. Taiwan Tobacco and Wine Monopoly Bureau 1976–80; Dir Inst. of Industrial and Vocational Training for Workmen 1976–80; Chair. Repub. of China Amateur Boxing Asscn 1981–82; Dir Secr., Cen. Cttee, Kuomintang (KMT) 1982–84, Chair. Cen. Exec. Cttee, Vice-Chair. KMT 2000–07, Chair. 2007–09, now Hon. Chair.; Minister of Interior 1984–88, 1991–94; Mayor of Taipei 1988–90; Minister of State 1990–91; apptd Sec.-Gen. Office of the Pres. 1994; Chair. Cen. Election Comm. 1991–94, Political Party Review Cttee 1991–94. *Address:* c/o Kuomintang (KMT), 11 Chung Shan South Road, Taipei 100, Taiwan (office).

WU, Rong-i, MA, MS, PhD; Taiwanese government official and economist; *Chairman, Taiwan Brain Trust;* b. 15 Dec. 1939; m.; one d. one s.; ed Nat. Taiwan Univ., Université Catholique de Louvain, Belgium; Prof. and Dir Dept of Econs., Nat. Chung Hsing Univ. 1975–93; Visiting Scholar, Yale Univ., USA 1982–83; Vice-Pres. Taiwan Inst. of Econ. Research 1991–92, Pres. 1993–; Commr Fair Trade Comm., Exec. Yuan 1992–93, mem. Science and Tech. Advisory Group 2004–; Nat. Policy Adviser to Pres. 2000–, mem. Econ. Advisory Group to Pres. 2000–; Vice-Premier and Minister of the Consumer Protection Commission 2005; fmr Chair. Taiwan Stock Exchange; mem. Eminent Persons Group, Asia-Pacific Econ. Co-operation 1993–94; Prof. of Econ. Devt and Industrial Policy, Nat. Chung Hsing Univ.; Chair Taiwan Brain Trust (think tank). *Address:* Taiwan Brain Trust, 42 Civil Rights East Road, Taipei 10469, Taiwan (office). *E-mail:* info@braintrust.tw (office).

WU, Adm. Shengli; Chinese naval officer; *Commander, People's Liberation Army Navy;* b. 1945, Wuqiao City, Hebei Prov.; ed PLA Inst. of Surveying and Mapping; joined PLA 1964, eventually becoming Deputy Commdr, East China Sea Fleet, later Commdr, South China Sea Fleet, Deputy Commdr, Guangzhou Mil. Region, Navy Deputy Chief, HQ of Gen. Staff 2004–06, Commdr, PLA Navy 2006–; rank of Rear-Adm. 1994, Vice-Adm. 2003, Adm. 2007; Del. 17th CCP Nat. Congress 2007–12; Deputy 11th NPC 2008–13; mem. State Central Mil. Comm. 2008–; mem. 17th CCP Cen. Cttee 2007–12, also 17th CCP Cen. Cttee Cen. Mil. Comm. 2007–12; mem. 18th CCP Cen. Cttee 2012–, also 18th CCP Cen. Cttee Cen. Mil. Comm. 2012–. *Address:* Office of the Commander, People's Liberation Army Navy, c/o Ministry of National Defence, 20 Jingshanqian Jie, Beijing 10009, People's Republic of China (office). *Website:* www.mod.gov.cn (office).

WU, Lt-Gen. Shuangzhan; Chinese police officer; b. Feb. 1945, Qingfeng, Henan Prov.; ed PLA Nat. Defence Univ.; joined PLA 1963, CCP 1965; promoted to rank of Maj.-Gen. 1990, Lt-Gen. 1997; Deputy Chief of Staff of Beijing Mil. Area Command 1993; Chief of Staff of the People's Armed Police Force 1993–99, Deputy Commdr-in-Chief 1996–99, C-in-C 1999–2009; mem. 16th CCP Cen. Cttee 2002–07, 17th CCP Cen. Cttee 2007–12; Deputy Dir 11th NPC Internal and Judicial Affairs Cttee 2010–13. *Address:* c/o People's Armed Police Headquarters, Suzhou Jie, Beijing 100089, People's Republic of China (office).

WU, Shuoing; Chinese economist; b. Jiangyin, Jiangyin Prov.; ed Shanghai East-China People's Revolution Univ.; research student of political econ., Renmin Univ.; fmrly Prof., Pres. of Grad. School, Vice-Pres. Renmin Univ.; Prof., Pres. Peking Univ. 1989–96; mem. Standing Cttee 8th and 9th NPC 1993–2003. *Publications:* Shenme Shi Zhengzhi Jingyixue (What Is Political Economy?), Zhongguo Shehuizhuyi Jianshe (China's Socialist Construction), Moshi, Yunxing and Kongzhi (Model, Operation and Control). *Address:* c/o Peking University, 1 Loudouqiao, Beijing 100871, People's Republic of China (office).

WU, Weiran; Chinese surgeon (retd); *Honorary President, Beijing Hospital;* b. 14 Oct. 1920, Changzhou, Jiangsu Prov.; s. of Wu Jingyi and Zheng Zhixia; m. Huang Wuchiang 1951; three d.; ed West China Union Univ.; joined CCP 1956; Deputy Dir Surgery Soc., attached to the Medical Soc. 1972; Deputy Dir Surgery Dept, Beijing Union Medical Coll. Hosp., Chinese Acad. of Medical Sciences 1972; now Prof. of Surgery, Surgical Dept, Beijing Union Medical Coll. Hosp., Chinese Acad. of Medical Sciences; Hon. Pres. Beijing Hosp.; Alt. mem. 12th CCP Cen. Cttee 1982, mem. 1985, 13th Cen. Cttee 1987–92; Del., 14th CCP Nat. Congress 1992–97; mem. 9th CPPCC Nat. Cttee 1998–2003; Nat. Class 2 Award for Scientific and Technological Progress, Nat. Award for his special contribs to work related to health and care, Ministry of Health Class 2 Award for his research into the 'artificial gut' technique. *Publication:* Surgery (co-author). *Leisure interest:* gardening. *Address:* Surgery Department, Beijing Hospital, 1 Dahalu, Dondan, Beijing 100730, People's Republic of China. *Telephone:* 65132266. *Fax:* 65132969.

WU, Xichao; Chinese surgeon; b. Aug. 1922, Malaysia; ed Shanghai Tongji Univ. Medical Coll.; Doctor in Charge, Lecturer, Assoc. Prof., Prof., Vice-Pres. PLA Second Medical Univ. 1949; Vice-Chair. Medical Soc. of China; Fellow Chinese Acad. of Sciences; named Model Medical Expert by CCP Cen. Mil. Comm. 1996. *Address:* Chinese People's Liberation Army Second Medical University, Shanghai, People's Republic of China (office).

WU, Xiucheng, PhD; Chinese physicist; *Chief Technology Officer, D-Tech Optoelectronics, Incorporated;* held various sr eng positions with Perkin Elmer, Agere and Finisar; fmr Researcher, Centre for Electrophotonic Materials and Devices, McMaster Univ., Hamilton, Ont., Canada; mem. Man. Team AdTech Optics Inc., USA; Chief Tech. Officer D-Tech Optoelectronics Inc. 2008–. *Publications:* numerous articles in scientific journals. *Address:* D-Tech Optoelectronics Inc., 18007 Cortney Court, City of Industry, CA 91748-1203, USA (office). *Telephone:* (626)581-3755 (office). *E-mail:* xiucheng.wu@atoptics.com (office). *Website:* www.dtechopto.com (office).

WU, Maj.-Gen. Xu; Chinese army officer; b. March 1939, Changsu City, Jiangsu Prov.; ed 5th Artillery School and PLA Mil. Acad.; joined PLA 1954, CCP 1959; various posts in artillery, reconnaissance and training 1956–85; army corps political commissar and army corps commdr 1985–92; Asst Chief of Gen. Staff 1992; Deputy Chief, PLA Gen. Staff 1995–; mem. 15th CCP Cen. Cttee 1997–2002.

Address: Ministry of National Defence, Jingshanqian Jie, Beijing, People's Republic of China (office). *Telephone:* (1) 6370000 (office).

WU, Yajun, BEng; Chinese real estate executive; *Chairman and CEO, Longfor Properties Limited;* b. 1964, Hechuan, Chongqing; m. Cai Kui (divorced 2012); ed Northwestern Polytechnical Univ.; began career as engineer, Qianwei Meter Factory 1984–88; reporter and ed., China Shirong News Agency 1989–93; f. Jiacheng Econ. Devt Co., Chongqing 1993; f. Longhu Real Estate Devt Co. Ltd 1995; Exec. Dir Longfor Properties Ltd 2007–, also Chair. and CEO; mem. NPC; Vice-Chair. Fed. of Industry and Commerce of Chongqing Municipality; Vice-Chair. Real Estate Br., Chongqing Gen. Chamber of Commerce; ranked by Forbes magazine amongst The World's 100 Most Powerful Women (48th) 2013. *Address:* Longfor Properties Ltd, 7/F Tower 2, FuSheng Building, 4 Huixin East Street, Beijing, People's Republic of China (office). *Telephone:* (10) 8466-1857 (office). *Website:* www.longfor.com (office).

WU, Yan; Chinese business executive; currently Chair. and Pres. People's Insurance Co. (Group) of China Ltd. *Address:* People's Insurance Co. (Group) of China Ltd, 28 Qinghua Xi Road, Haidian District, Beijing 100084, People's Republic of China (office). *Telephone:* (10) 62616611 (office); (10) 82653062 (office). *E-mail:* bianji@picc.com.cn (office). *Website:* www.picc.com (office); www.picc.cn (office).

WU, Yigong; Chinese film director; b. 1 Dec. 1938, Chongqing, Sichuan Prov.; s. of Wu Tiesan and Yu Minhua; m. Zhang Wen Rong 1967; one s.; Dir Shanghai Film Bureau, Gen. Man. Shanghai Film Corpn, Vice-Pres. China Film Artists' Asscn 1985–; Vice-Chair. China Fed. of Literary and Art Circles 1996–; Alt. mem. 14th CCP Cen. Cttee 1992–97, 15th CCP Cen. Cttee 1997–2002. *Films include:* University in Exile, The Tribulations of a Chinese Gentleman, Bitter Sea, Evening Rain 1980, My Memories of Old Beijing (Golden Rooster Award for Best Dir 1984), A Man Aged 18 (Magnolia Prize 1988), A Confucius Family 1992. *Leisure interests:* music, sports. *Address:* 52 Yong Fu Road, Shanghai, People's Republic of China. *Telephone:* 4332558. *Fax:* 4370528.

WU, Zuqiang; Chinese musician and composer; *Vice-Chairman, China Federation of Literary and Art Circles;* b. 24 July 1927, Beijing; s. of Wu Jingzhou and Wu Qinqi (née Zhou); m. Li-qin Zheng 1953; one s. one d.; Vice-Pres. Cen. Conservatory of Music 1978–82, Pres. 1982–88, now Prof., Hon. Pres.; Vice-Pres. Chinese Musicians' Asscn 1985, now Hon. Chair.; Vice-Exec. Chair. China Fed. of Literary and Art Circles 1988–92, Vice-Chair. 1992–; Adviser to China Nat. Symphony Orchestra 1996; Alt. mem. 12th CCP Cen. Cttee 1982–87; Perm. mem. Nat. Cttee 7th, 8th and 9th CPPCC 1988–2003; artistic adviser for opening and closing ceremonies, Beijing Summer Olympic Games 2008. *Compositions include:* Sunrise at the Tu Mountains – Fighting against the Floods, Little Sisters at the Grasslands, The Moon's Reflection On ErQuan, Listening to the Pines, A Lovely Night, Revival. *Publications:* Musical Form, Analysis of Music Works. *Leisure interests:* literature, fine arts, tourism. *Address:* Central Conservatory of Music, 43 Baojiajie West District, Beijing 100031, People's Republic of China (office). *Telephone:* (10) 66414887 (office). *Fax:* (10) 66417211 (office).

WUERL, HE Cardinal Donald William, STD; American ecclesiastic and academic; *Archbishop of Washington, DC;* b. 12 Nov. 1940, Pittsburgh, Pa; s. of Francis J. Wuerl and Mary Anne Wuerl (née Schiffauer); ed Mount St Mary's Seminary, Cincinnati, Ohio, Catholic Univ. of America, Washington, DC (Basselin Scholar), Pontifical Gregorian Univ. and Pontifical Univ. of St Thomas Aquinas, Rome; ordained priest, Diocese of Pittsburgh 1966; first assignment as Asst Pastor at St Rosalia Parish, Greenfield, Pittsburgh and as Sec. to the then Bishop of Pittsburgh, John Wright; full-time Sec. to Cardinal Wright in Vatican City 1969–79; Rector St Paul Seminary, Pittsburgh 1981–85; Exec. Sec. to Bishop John Marshall for papally mandated study of US seminaries 1982; Titular Bishop of Rossmarkaeum and Auxiliary Bishop of Seattle 1985–87; Bishop of Pittsburgh 1988–2006; taught at Duquesne Univ., Pittsburgh as Distinguished Service Prof.; Chaplain for the Order of Malta, Fed. Asscn, USA (div. of Sovereign Mil. Order of Malta, commonly referred to as the Knights of Malta) 1999–; Archbishop of Washington, DC 2006–; cr. Cardinal (Cardinal-Priest of San Pietro in Vincoli) 2010; participated in Papal Conclave 2013; Chair. Nat. Catholic Educational Asscn 2005–; Chancellor Catholic Univ. of America; apptd by Congregation for the Doctrine of the Faith as Del. in USA to facilitate mass receptions of Anglicans in accord with norms of Anglicanorum Coetibus issued in Nov. 2009 2010–; heads US Bishops' ad hoc cttee in implementing the apostolic constitution. *Television:* launched and hosted programme, The Teaching of Christ 1990. *Publications include:* The Forty Martyrs: New Saints of England and Wales 1971, Fathers of the Church 1975, The Catholic Priesthood Today 1976, The Teaching of Christ: A Catholic Catechism for Adults 1976, St Christopher: A Military Martyr (unpublished) 1979, A Visit to the Vatican: For Young People 1981, The Gift of Faith: A Question and Answer Version of The Teaching of Christ 2001; has written regular columns in Columbia, the major publ. of the Knights of Columbus in USA. *Address:* Archdiocese of Washington, PO Box 29260, Washington, DC 20017-0260 (office); Archdiocese of Washington, 5001 Eastern Avenue, Hyattsville, MD 20782-3447, USA (office). *Telephone:* (301) 853-4500 (office). *Fax:* (301) 853-5346 (office). *E-mail:* info@adw.org (office). *Website:* www.adw.org (office).

WUFFLI, Peter A.; Swiss banking executive; b. 26 Oct. 1957; s. of Heinz Wuffli; m.; three c.; ed Univ. of St Gall; began career as econs journalist, Neue Zurcher Zeitung 1978–84; Man. Consultant, McKinsey & Co. 1984–90, Pnr, McKinsey Switzerland 1990–94; joined Swiss Banking Corpn 1994, Chief Financial Officer, mem. Exec. Cttee 1994–98; Chief Financial Officer UBS Group (following merger with UBS) 1998–99, Chair. and CEO UBS Asset Man. 1999–2001, Pres. and CEO UBS AG 2001–07; mem. Bd of Dirs Inst. of Int. Finance Inc., Zurich Opera House; Vice Chair. Int. Inst. for Man. Devt; Vice Chair. Swiss-American Chamber of Commerce; European Banker of the Year 2005. *Address:* c/o UBS AG, Bahnhofstrasse 45, 8098 Zürich, Switzerland (office).

WULF-MATHIES, Monika, PhD; German consultant, business executive, government official and fmr politician; b. 17 March 1942, Wernigerode; d. of Carl-Hermann Baier and Margott Baier (née Meisser); m. Dr Carsten Wulf-Mathies 1968; ed Univs of Hamburg and Freiburg; Br. Asst Fed. Ministry of Econs 1968–71; Head of Dept for Social Policy, Fed. Chancellery 1971–76; mem. ÖTV (Public Services and Transport Workers' Union) 1971–, mem. Man. Exec. Cttee

1976–95, Chair. of ÖTV (representing around 2.3 million workers) 1982–95; Pres. Public Services Int. 1989–94; Commr for Regional Policies of EU 1995–99; Adviser to the Chancellor on European Policy 2000; mem. Supervisory Bd Deutsche Lufthansa AG 1978–95 (Deputy Chair. 1988–95), VEBA 1989–95; mem. SPD 1965–; Exec. Vice-Pres. Corp. Public Policy and Sustainability, Deutsche Post AG 2001–08 (retd); Pres. Netzwerks Europäische Bewegung Deutschland 2001–06, Hon. Pres. 2006–; Founding mem. Policy Fellow, Institut zur Zukunft der Arbeit (IZA) (Inst. for the Study of Labour), Bonn; Vice-Chair. Supervisory Bd Univ. of Bonn 2008–13; mem. Senate Leibniz-Gemeinschaft 2010–; mem. EC; Chair. Beethoven Foundation, Bonn 2007–; currently consultant, Wulf-Mathies Consult; Grand Cross of the Order of Infante D. Henrique (Portugal). *Leisure interests:* gardening, cross-country skiing. *Address:* Max-Franz-Street 12, 53177 Bonn, Germany (office). *Telephone:* (228) 55547091 (office). *Fax:* (228) 3867466 (office). *E-mail:* wumconsult@t-online.de (office). *Website:* www.iza.org (office).

WULFF, Christian Wilhelm Walter; German lawyer, politician and fmr head of state; b. 19 June 1959, Osnabrück; s. of Rudolf Wulff and Dagmar Wulff; m. 1st Christiane Vogt 1988, one d.; m. 2nd Bettina Körner 2008, one s.; ed Osnabrück Univ.; mem. Christlich-Demokratische Union (CDU) 1975–2010, Chair. CDU in Lower Saxony 1994–2008, Deputy Fed. Chair. CDU 1998–2010; mem. Osnabrück city council 1986, leader of CDU group 1989–94; mem. Lower Saxony Landtag (regional parl.) 1994, Ministerpräsident (Prime Minister) of Lower Saxony 2003–10; Pres. of Germany 2010–12 (resgnd); Dr hc (Tongji Univ., Shanghai), (Univ. of Tokyo-Tsukuba); Leo Baeck Prize 2011. *Address:* Deutscher Bundestag, Platz der Republik 1, 11011 Berlin, Germany (office). *E-mail:* buerowulff@bpra.bund.de (office). *Website:* www.christianwulff.de.

WUNSCH, Carl Isaac, PhD; American oceanographer and academic; *Visiting Professor, Harvard University;* b. 5 May 1941, Brooklyn, New York; s. of Harry Wunsch and Helen Wunsch (née Gellis); m. Marjory Markel 1980; one s. one d.; ed Massachusetts Inst. of Tech.; Lecturer in Oceanography, MIT 1966–67, Asst Prof. 1967–70, Assoc. Prof. 1970–75, Prof. of Physical Oceanography 1975–76, apptd Cecil and Ida Green Prof. 1976, Sec. of Navy Research Prof. 1985–89; Sr Visiting Fellow, Dept of Applied Math. and Theoretical Physics, Univ. of Cambridge, UK 1969, 1974–75, 1981–82; currently Visiting Prof., Harvard Univ.; Fulbright Scholar 1981–82; John Simon Guggenheim Foundation Fellow 1981–82; Visiting Sr Scientist, GFDL, Princeton Univ. 1993–94; Visiting Scientist, CNES/CNRS, Toulouse, France 1994; Moore Distinguished Scholar, Calif. Inst. of Tech. 2000; Visiting Prof., Univ. Coll., London 2001; Visiting Scientist, Southampton Oceanography Centre 2001; Distinguished Visiting Scientist, Jet Propulsion Lab. 1994–2011; George Eastman Visiting Prof., Balliol Coll., Oxford, 2011–12; Chair. Ocean Studies Bd, NRC; consultant to NAS, NSF; mem. NAS, Soc. for Industrial and Applied Math.; Foreign mem. Royal Soc. 2002, American Philosophical Soc. 2003; Fellow, American Acad. of Arts and Sciences, American Geophysical Union, American Meteorological Soc., AAAS; Hon. Fellow, Royal Meteorological Soc. 2012; James R. Macelwane Award 1971, Maurice Ewing Medal 1990, American Geophysical Union, Founders Prize, Texas Instrument Foundation 1975, A.G. Huntsman Prize 1988, NASA Public Service Medal 1993, Henry Stommel Prize, American Meteorological Soc. 2000, Bowie Medal, American Geophysical Union 2006, Prince Albert 1er Medal 2007. *Publications:* Evolution of Physical Oceanography (co-ed.), Ocean Acoustic Tomography (co-author), The Ocean Circulation Inverse Problem, Discrete Inverse and State Estimation Problems; many tech. papers. *Leisure interests:* sailing, history, reading. *Address:* Geological Museum 451, Harvard University, Cambridge, MA 02138 (office); 78 Washington Avenue, Cambridge, MA 02140, USA (home). *Telephone:* (617) 496-0194 (office). *Fax:* (617) 253-4464 (office). *E-mail:* cwunsch@fas.harvard.edu (office).

WURTH, Hubert, LLB; Luxembourg diplomatist and painter; *Ambassador to Austria, Slovakia and Slovenia;* b. 15 April 1952; m. 1st Lydie Polfer (q.v.) (divorced 1998); one c.; m. 2nd Francisca Passchier; one c.; ed Univ. de Paris II Inst. d'Etudes Politiques, Paris; called to the Luxembourg Bar 1977; Attaché, Dept of Int. Econ. Relations, Ministry of Foreign Affairs 1978, Deputy Perm. Rep. to Council of Europe 1979, Chief Sec. to Vice-Pres. of the Govt and Minister for Foreign Affairs, Econ. Affairs and Justice 1981, Deputy Dir of Political Affairs 1986; Amb. to USSR (also accred to Poland, Finland and Mongolia) 1988–92, to the Netherlands 1992–98 (also served as rep. for the Pact on Stability in Europe 1993–95 and on special mission in Fmr Yugoslavia 1996), Perm. Rep. to UN, New York 1998–2003, to OECD 2003–, to UNESCO 2003–07, Amb. to France 2003–07, to UK 2007–11 (also accred to Ireland 2007–11 and Iceland 2008–11), to Austria, Slovakia and Slovenia 2011–; Perm. Rep. OSCE and int. orgs in Vienna. *Publication:* Monography on Hubert Wurth as a Painter 1998. *Address:* Embassy of Luxembourg, 81 Sternwartestrasse, 1180 Vienna, Austria (office). *Telephone:* (1) 478-2142 (office). *Fax:* (1) 478-2144 (office). *E-mail:* vienne.amb@mae.etat.lu (office). *Website:* vienne.mae.lu (office).

WÜRTH, Reinhold; German trading company executive; *Chairman, Supervisory Board, Würth Group's Family Trusts;* b. 20 April 1935, Öhringen; m. Carmen Würth; three c.; joined father's wholesale screw business as second employee, Künzelsau 1949, took over man. of business 1954–94, Chair. Advisory Bd Würth Group 1994–2006, Chair. Supervisory Bd Würth Group's Family Trusts; Head Interfacultative Inst. for Entrepreneurship, Univ. of Karlsruhe 1999–2003; Chair. Advisory Bd Entrepreneurs of the Soc. of Int. Cooperation Baden-Württemberg GmbH; Chair. Gesellschaft zur Förderung des württembergischen Landesmuseums e.V., Freunde der Burgfestspiele Jagsthausen e.V., Pro Region Heilbron-Franken; mem. Supervisory Bd IKB Deutsche Industriebank AG, Düsseldorf; mem. Bd Trustees Robert-Bosch-Foundation; made his art collection of over 15,000 items by Edvard Munch, Max Beckmann, Pablo Picasso and others accessible to the public 1991–; est. Kunsthalle Würth, Schwäbisch Hall 2001–; Hon. Senator, Univ. of Tübingen; Distinguished Service Cross (First Class) of the Order of Merit (FRG); Chevalier des Arts et des Lettres 2000, Légion d'honneur 2004; Officer, Order of Orange-Nassau (Netherlands) 2005; Dr hc (Tübingen); Medal of Econ. Merits (Baden-Württemberg); Freedom of Erstein (France) 1997, Künzelsau 2003. *Leisure interests:* flying, motor bikes, art collecting. *Address:* Adolf Würth GmbH & Co. KG, Reinhold-Würth-Str. 12–17, 74653 Künzelsau, Germany (office). *Telephone:* (7940) 15-0 (office). *Fax:* (7940) 15-1000 (office). *E-mail:* info@wuerth.de (office). *Website:* www.wuerth.com (office).

WURTZ, Robert (Bob) H., AB, PhD; American psychologist, neuroscientist and academic; *NIH Distingusihed Investigator, Laboratory of Sensorimotor Research, National Eye Institute, National Institutes of Health;* b. 1936, St Louis, Mo.; ed Oberlin Coll., Univ. of Michigan; Research Asst, Univ. of Michigan 1958–61, PHS Predoctoral Fellow 1961–62, Predoctoral Instructor 1962; Research Assoc., Cttee for Nuclear Information, St Louis, Mo. 1962–63; Postdoctoral Fellow, Dept of Physiology and Research Fellow, Dept of Neurology, Washington Univ. School of Medicine, St Louis 1964–65; Research Psychologist, Spinal Cord Section, Lab. of Neurophysiology, Nat. Inst. of Neurological Diseases and Blindness, NIH 1965–66, Physiologist, Lab. of Neurobiology, Nat. Inst. of Mental Health, NIH 1966–78, Founding Chief, Lab. of Sensorimotor Research, Nat. Eye Inst., NIH 1978–2002, Sr Investigator, Lab. of Sensorimotor Research 2002–, NIH Sr Investigator 2007, currently NIH Distinguished Investigator, apptd to Sr Exec. Service, NIH 1984, apptd to Sr Biomedical Research Service, NIH 1996; Visiting Scientist, Physiological Lab., Univ. of Cambridge, UK 1975–76, Assoc., Neuroscience Research Program 1989–94; mem. Scientific Bd McGovern Inst. for Brain Research, MIT; Pres. Soc. for Neuroscience 1990–91; mem. NAS 1988 (mem. Council 1996), Inst. of Medicine 1997; non-resident Fellow, Salk Inst.; Fellow, AAAS 1990, American Acad. of Arts and Sciences 1990; Hon. DSc (Oberlin Coll.) 2009; Grass Foundation Research Fellow, Marine Biological Lab. 1961, Gordon Holmes Lecturer, European Neuroscience Soc. 1985, James M. Sprague Lecturer, Univ. of Pennsylvania 1986, Morris B. Bender Lecturer, Mount Sinai Medical School 1986, Special Lecturer, Soc. for Neuroscience Meeting 1986, W. Alden Spencer Award, Columbia Univ. 1987, George H. Bishop Lecturer, Washington Univ. 1988, Clinton N. Woolsey Lecturer 1991, Keynote Lecturer, Neural Control of Movement Meeting 1992, Presidential Award, Soc. for Neuroscience 1993, Special Lecturer, Soc. for Neuroscience Meeting 1994, AAAS John P. McGovern Award 1995, Karl Spencer Lashley Award, American Philosophical Soc. 1995, NIH G. Burroughs Mider Lecturer 1995, Friedenwald Award, Asscn for Research in Vision and Ophthalmology 1996 Distinguished Scientific Contrib. Award, American Psychological Asscn 1997, Keynote Lecturer, Neurobiology Retreat, Washington Univ. 1999, Plenary Lecturer, Japanese Neuroscience Soc. 2000, Seventh Annual Lecturer, Center for Neural Basis of Cognition, Univ. of Pittsburgh 2001, Eighth Annual American Legion Lecturer, Univ. of Minnesota Brain Sciences 2002, Keynote Lecturer, Salk Inst. Annual Faculty Meeting 2003, Nat. Eye Inst. Dir's Award 2004, Dan David Prize for the Future Time Dimension: Brain Sciences (with William T. Newsome and Amiram Grinvald) 2004, Ralph W. Gerard Prize, Soc. for Neuroscience 2006, Albert and Ellen Grass Lecture Society for Neuroscience 2009, Gruber Neuroscience Prize 2010. *Publications:* more than 140 scientific papers in professional journals on neurobiology of vision and eye movements. *Address:* National Eye Institute, Building 49, Room 2A50, Bethesda, MD 20892-4436, USA (office). *Telephone:* (301) 496-9375 (office). *Fax:* (301) 402-0511 (office). *E-mail:* bob@lsr.nei.nih.gov (office). *Website:* www.nei.nih.gov (office).

WÜTHRICH, Kurt, PhD; Swiss scientist and academic; *Cecil H. and Ida M. Green Professor of Structural Biology, The Scripps Research Institute;* b. 4 Oct. 1938, Aarberg; s. of Hermann Wüthrich and Gertrud Bertha Wüthrich-Kuchen; m. Marianne Briner 1963; one s. one d.; ed Univs of Bern, Basel and Calif. at Berkeley, USA; mem. tech. staff Bell Telephone Labs 1967–69; Privatdozent, ETH, Zürich 1970–72, Asst Prof. 1972–76, Assoc. Prof. 1976–80, Prof. of Biophysics 1980– (Chair. Biology Dept 1995–2000); Visiting Miller Research Prof., Univ. of Calif., Berkeley 1988; Scholar-in-Residence, Johns Hopkins Univ., Baltimore, USA 1992; Sherman Fairchild Distinguished Scholar, Caltech, Pasadena, Calif. 1994, Visiting Assoc. in Biology and Chem. 1995; Guest Scientist, The Scripps Research Inst., Calif. 1994, Cecil H. and Ida M. Green Prof. of Structural Biology 2001–; Visiting Prof., Inst. of Physical and Chemical Research (RIKEN), Tokyo, Japan 1997–98, Univ. of Edinburgh, UK 1997–2000; consultant, Hoechst AG, Frankfurt, Germany 1985–92, Sandoz Pharma AG, Basel 1987–96, Hoffman-La Roche AG, Basel 1987–2004, Ciba-Geigy AG, Basel 1989–96, Tripos Inc., St Louis, USA 1992–94, Novartis AG, Basel 1997–; mem. European Molecular Biology Org. (EMBO) 1984, Deutsche Akad. der Naturforscher Leopoldina 1987, Academia Europaea 1989, Schweizerische Akad. der Technischen Wissenschaften 2001, Schweizerische Akad. der Medizinischen Wissenschaften 2002; Foreign Fellow, Indian Nat. Science Acad. 1989; Foreign Assoc. NAS 1992, Acad. des Sciences, Institut de France 2000; Fellow, AAAS 1998; mem. Schweiz Kommission für Molekularbiologie 1973–76, Pres. 1977–82; mem. Council Int. Union of Pure and Applied Biophysics (IUPAB) 1975–78, 1987–90, Sec.-Gen. 1978–84, Vice-Pres. 1984–87; mem. Gen. Cttee Int. Council of Scientific Unions (ICSU) 1980–86, Standing Cttee on the Free Circulation of Scientists 1982–90; mem. Kommission für die Wolfgang Pauli-Vorlesungen, ETH Zürich 1984–92, Pres. 1993–2001; Pres. Züricher Chemische Gesellschaft 1990–91; mem. Exec. Cttee Schweiz Gesellschaft für Biochemie 1986–92, Pres. Biophysics Section 1985–88; mem. IUPAC, Comm. on Biophysical Chem. 1969–99, Chair. 2000–01; mem. Prix Marcel Benoist, Conseil de Fondation, Berne 2001–; mem. Bds Centro Stefano Franscini, Monte Verità and ETH Zürich 1989–98, European Molecular Biology Lab., Heidelberg, Germany 1989–95, Nat. Lab. of Biomacromolecules, Academia Sinica, Beijing, China 1989–, Deutsche Forschungsgemeinschaft, Bonn, Germany: Schwerpunktsprogramm 'Protein Design' 1989–95, Comm. of the European Communities: Human Capital and Mobility Programme 1992–94, Inst. für Molekulare Biotechnologie, Jena, Germany 1993–96, Ciba Foundation, London, UK 1994–96, Institut de Biologie Structurale Jean-Pierre Ebel, Grenoble, France 1994–97, Inst. of Biotechnology, Univ. of Helsinki, Finland 1997–, Novartis Foundation, London 1997–, Triad Therapeutics Inc., San Diego, Calif. 1998–04, Genomics Sciences Centre, RIKEN, Tokyo 2000–, Syrrx Inc., San Diego 2000–04, Groupement d'Intérêt Scientifique 'Infections à Prions', France 2001–, Nat. Inst. of Chemical Physics and Biophysics, Tallinn, Estonia 2001–, Nat. High Field NMR Center (NANUC), Univ. of Alberta, Edmonton, Canada 2001–, Eidogen Inc., Pasadena, Calif. 2002–; Titular mem. European Acad. of Arts, Sciences and Humanities 2003; Foreign mem. Latvian Acad. of Sciences; Hon. Prof., Dalian Inst. of Chemical Physics, Chinese Acad. of Sciences, Dalian Inst. of Light Industry; Profesor Extraordinario con distinción de Académico Ilustre, U.N. de Mar del Plata, Argentina; Hon. Fellow, Nat. Acad. of Sciences, India 1991, Royal Soc. of Chem., UK 2003; Hon. FRSE 2003; Foreign Hon. mem., American Acad. of Arts and Sciences 1993; Hon. mem. Japanese Biochemical Soc. 1993, Nat. Magnetic Resonance Soc. of India 1998, The World Innovation Foundation 2003, Swiss Chemical Soc. 2003, Int. Soc. for Magnetic Resonance in Medicine 2003, Wallisellen Football Club 2003, Hungarian Acad. of Sciences 2004, World Acad. of Young Scientists 2004, World High Tech. Soc., Dalian, China 2004, European Acad. of Sciences and Arts 2004, Groupement Ampère 2004, The Nuclear Magnetic Resonance Soc. of Japan 2004, Indian Biophysical Soc. 2005; Hon. DPhil (Zürich) 1997; Hon. DSc (Sheffield), (King George's Medical Univ., Lucknow, India); Dr hc (Siena, Italy) 1997, (Ecole Polytechnique Fédéral de Lausanne) 2001, (Valencia); Friedrich-Miescher-Preis, Schweizerische Gesellschaft für Biochemie 1974, Shield of the Faculty of Medicine, Tokyo Univ. 1983, Médaille P. Bruylants, Université Catholique de Louvain, Belgium 1986, Stein and Moore Award of the Protein Soc., USA 1990, Louisa Gross Horwitz Prize, Columbia Univ., New York 1991, Gilbert Newton Lewis Medal, Univ. of Calif., Berkeley 1991, Marcel Benoist-Preis, Swiss Confed. 1992, Distinguished Service Award, The Miami Bio/Technology Winter Symposia, USA 1993, Prix Louis Jeantet de Médecine, Fondation Louis Jeantet, Geneva 1993, Kaj Linderstrom-Lang Prize, Carlsberg Foundation, Copenhagen, Denmark 1996, Eminent Scientist of RIKEN, Tokyo 1997, Kyoto Prize in Advanced Tech., Inamori Foundation, Kyoto 1998, Günther Laukien Prize, Experimental NMR Conf., USA 1999, Otto-Warburg-Medaille, Gesellschaft für Biochemie and Molekularbiologie, Germany 1999, Médaille d'Honneur en Argent, Soc. d'Encouragement au Progrès, Paris, France 2001, Nobel Prize in Chem. 2002, World Future Award, The World Awards, Vienna, Austria 2002, Swiss Soc. Award 2002. *Publications:* NMR in Biological Research: Peptides and Proteins 1976, NMR of Proteins and Nucleic Acids 1986, NMR in Structural Biology – A Collection of Papers by Kurt Wüthrich 1995; also published 650 papers and reviews. *Leisure interests:* sports, French literature. *Address:* Institut für Molekularbiologie & Biophysik, ETH Zürich, HPK, 8093 Zürich, Switzerland (office); The Scripps Reseach Institute, MB-44, 10550 North Torrey Pines Road, La Jolla, CA 92037, USA (office); Fliederstrasse 7, 8304 Wallisellen, Switzerland (home). *Telephone:* (44) 6332473 (Zürich) (office); (858) 784-8011 (La Jolla) (office). *Fax:* (44) 6331151 (Zürich) (office); (858) 784-8014 (La Jolla) (office). *E-mail:* wuthrich@mol.biol.ethz .ch (office); wuthrich@scripps.edu (office). *Website:* www.mol.biol.ethz.ch (office).

WYATT, Christopher Terrel, BSc, FREng, FICE, FRSA, FIStructE, DIC, CBIM; British business executive and engineer; b. 17 July 1927, Ewell, Surrey; s. of Lional H. Wyatt and Audrey Vere Wyatt; m. 1st Doreen Mary Emmerson; three s.; m. 2nd Geertruida Willer 1970; one s.; m. 3rd Patricia Perkins 1990; ed Kingston Grammar School, Battersea Polytechnic and Imperial Coll., London; Charles Brand & Son, Ltd, 1948–54; joined Richard Costain Ltd, 1955, Dir 1970–87, Group Chief Exec. 1975–80, Deputy Chair. 1979–80, Chair. Costain Group PLC 1980–87; Chair. W. S. Atkins Ltd 1987–97; Fellow Royal Acad. of Eng, Inst. of Structural Engineers. *Leisure interests:* sailing, music, painting. *Address:* Ryderwells Farm, Uckfield Road, Lewes, East Sussex, BN8 5RN, England (home). *Telephone:* (1273) 812219 (home).

WYATT, (Alan) Will, BA, CBE, FRTS; British consultant, media commentator and TV producer; b. 7 Jan. 1942, Oxford; s. of Basil Wyatt and Hettie Wyatt (née Hooper); m. Jane Bridgit Bagenal 1966; two d.; ed Magdalen Coll. School, Oxford, Emmanuel Coll. Cambridge; trainee reporter, Sheffield Telegraph 1964; Sub-Ed. BBC Radio News 1965; joined BBC TV 1968, Producer, Late Night Line-Up, In Vision, The Book Programme, B. Traven – a mystery solved, etc. 1970–77, Asst Head of Presentation (Programmes) 1977, Head Documentary Features 1981, Features and Documentaries Group 1987, Asst Man. Dir BBC Network TV 1988–91; Man. Dir BBC Network TV 1991–96; Chief Exec. BBC Broadcast 1996–99; Chair. Human Capital Ltd 2001–, Goodwill Assocs (Media) Ltd 2003–; Vice-Chair. Shadow Racing Trust 2003–; Chair. BBC Guidelines on Violence 1983, 1987; Dir Broadcasters' Audience Research Bd 1989–91, BBC Subscription TV 1990–93, BBC Enterprises 1991–93, UKTV 1997–99; Vice-Pres. Royal TV Soc. 1997, Pres. 2000–04; Vice-Pres. Euro Broadcasting Union 1998–99; Gov. Univ. of the Arts, London (fmrly London Inst.) 1990–2007, Chair. 1999–2007; Huw Wheldon Memorial Lecture 1996; Royal Inst. Discourse 1996; Dir Coral Eurobet 2000–02, Vitec Group plc 2002–11, Racing UK 2004–12 (Chair. 2008–12), Racecourse Media Services 2007–12 (Chair. 2008–12); Chair. Teaching Awards Trust 2008–13; mem. British Horseriding Bd Comm. into Stable and Stud Staff 2003–04, Welsh Nat. Opera Board 2013–; Gov. Magdalen Coll. School 2000–06; Trustee, Services Sound and Vision Corpn 2007–13. *Television:* The Fifties, Late Night Line Up, The Book Programme, Edition, All the Buildings Fit to Print, The Golden Trashery of Ogden Nashery, Robinson's Travels – The Mormon Trail, B. Traven – A Mystery Solved, Toni and Rosi (documentary film) 2012. *Publications include:* The Man Who Was B. Traven 1980, Masters of the Wired World (contrib.) 1999, The Fun Factory – A Life in the BBC 2003; articles on broadcasting in Evening Standard, The Times, Daily Telegraph etc. *Leisure interests:* fell walking, horse racing, opera, theatre. *Address:* Abbey Willows, Rayford Lane, Middle Barton, Oxon., OX7 7DD, England (home). *Telephone:* (1869) 340234 (office). *E-mail:* will.wyatt@btinternet.com (office).

WYDEN, Ronald (Ron) Lee, BA, JD; American politician; *Senator from Oregon;* b. 3 May 1949, Wichita, Kan.; s. of Peter Wyden and Edith Wyden; m. 1st Laurie Oseran 1978; one s. one d.; m. 2nd Nancy Wyden 2005; one s. one d.; ed Univ. of Santa Barbara, Stanford Univ. and Univ. of Oregon; campaign aide, Senator Wayne Morse 1972, 1974; Co-Founder, Co-Dir Oregon Gray Panthers 1974–80; Dir Oregon Legal Services for Elderly 1977–79; Instructor in Gerontology, Univ. of Oregon 1976, Portland State Univ. 1979, Univ. of Portland 1980; mem. 97th–103rd Congresses from 3rd Oregon Dist 1981–95; Senator from Oregon 1996–, mem. Energy and Natural Resources Cttee (Chair. Subcommittee on Public Lands and Forests), Finance Cttee (Chair. Subcommittee on Int. Trade, Customs and Global Competitiveness), Budget Cttee, Select Cttee on Intelligence, Special Cttee on Aging; mem. ABA; Democrat. *Address:* 221 Dirksen Senate Office Building, Washington, DC 20510, USA (office). *Telephone:* (202) 224-5244 (office). *Fax:* (202) 228-2717 (office). *Website:* wyden.senate.gov (office).

WYLIE, Andrew, BA; American literary agent; *President, The Wylie Agency;* b. 4 Nov. 1947; m. 1st Christina Meyer 1969; one s.; m. 2nd Camilla Carlini; two d.; ed St Paul's School, Harvard Coll.; Founder and Pres. The Wylie Agency, New York 1980–, London 1996–, Madrid 1999–; f. Odyssey Editions (e-book publishing co.) 2010. *Address:* The Wylie Agency, 250 West 57th Street, Suite 2114, New York, NY 10107, USA. *Telephone:* (212) 246-0069. *Fax:* (212) 586-8953. *E-mail:* mail@wylieagency.com. *Website:* www.wylieagency.com.

WYLLER, Egil A., DPhil; Norwegian professor of philosophy; *Professor Emeritus of Philosophy, University of Oslo;* b. 24 April 1925, Stavanger; s. of Trygve Wyller and Anne-Kathrine Wyller; m. Eva Middelthon 1949; three s.; ed Univs of Oslo, Tübingen and Freiburg im Breisgau; fmr Prof. of History of the Ideas of Antiquity, Dept of Philosophy, Univ. of Oslo 1969–95, currently Prof. Emer.; Commdr, Order of Phoenix (Greece), Kt First Class, Order of St Olav (Norway) 2000; Gold Medal of HM King of Norway 1958, Cultural Prize of City of Oslo 1986. *Publications include:* Platons 'Parmenides' 1960, Der späte Platon 1965–1970, Enhet og Annethet I–III 1981, Johannes' Aapenbaring 1985, Prinsesse Europa 1989, Platonismus/Henologie in der Antike und im Mittelalter I–II (textbook) 1993, Henologisk Skriftserie I–XX 1994–2002, Henologische Perspektiven I–II 1995, Platon und Platonismus Tre 1996, Henrik Ibsen I–II: 1999–2002, Gestern und Morgen Heute 2005. *Leisure interests:* music, poetry, natural life. *Address:* Institute of Philosophy, University of Oslo, Blindern, Oslo 3 (office); Kaptein Oppegaards v. 15, 1164 Oslo, Norway (home). *Telephone:* 22-84-40-97 (office). *E-mail:* egil.wyller@filosofi.uio.no (office). *Website:* www.hf.uio.no/filosofi/english (office).

WYLLIE, Peter John, BSc, PhD, FRS; American geologist and academic; *Professor Emeritus of Geology, Division of Geological and Planetary Sciences, California Institute of Technology;* b. 8 Feb. 1930, London, England; s. of George W. Wyllie and Beatrice G. Weaver; m. F. Rosemary Blair 1956; one s. one d. (and one s. and one d. deceased); ed Univ. of St Andrews, Scotland; glaciologist, British West Greenland Expedition 1950; geologist, British North Greenland Expedition 1952–54; Asst Lecturer in Geology, Univ. of St Andrews 1955–56; Research Asst to O. F. Tuttle, Pennsylvania State Univ. 1956–58, Asst Prof. of Geochemistry 1959–60; Research Fellow in Chem., Univ. of Leeds 1959–60, Lecturer in Experimental Petrology 1960–61; Assoc. Prof. of Petrology, Pennsylvania State Univ. 1961–65, Acting Head of Dept of Geochemistry and Mineralogy 1962–63; Prof. of Petrology and Geochemistry, Univ. of Chicago 1965–83, Master of Physical Sciences, Collegiate Div., Assoc. Dean Physical Sciences, Assoc. Dean of the Coll. 1972–73, Homer J. Livingston Prof. 1978–83, Chair. Dept of Geophysical Sciences 1979–82; Chair. Div. of Geological and Planetary Sciences, Calif. Inst. of Tech. 1983–87, Prof. of Geology 1983–99, Academic Officer 1994–99, Prof. Emer. 1999–; Chair. Comm. Experimental Petrology, Int. Union of Geological Sciences 1976–80; Vice-Pres. Mineralogical Soc. of America 1976–77, Pres. 1977–78; Vice-Pres. Int. Mineralogical Asscn 1978–86 (Pres. 1986–90), Int. Union of Geodesy and Geophysics 1991–95 (Pres. 1995–99); Foreign Assoc. NAS 1981; Fellow, American Acad. of Arts and Sciences 1982; Corresp. Fellow, Edin. Geological Soc. 1985–; Foreign Fellow (Corresp. mem.) Indian Geophysical Union 1987; Foreign mem. USSR (now Russian) Acad. of Sciences 1988, Academia Europaea 1996; Foreign Fellow, Indian Nat. Science Acad. 1991, Nat. Acad. of Science of India 1992, Chinese Acad. of Science 1996; Louis Murray Visiting Fellow, Univ. of Cape Town March 1987; Hon. Prof., China Univ. of Geosciences, Beijing 1996–; Hon. mem. Mineralogical Soc. of GB and Ireland 1986, German Geological Soc. 2001, Mineralogical Soc. of Russia 1987; Hon. DSc (St Andrews) 1974; Polar Medal, HM Queen Elizabeth II 1954; Mineralogical Soc. of America Award 1965, Quantrell Award 1979, Wollaston Medal, Geological Soc., London 1982, Abraham-Gottlob-Werner-Medaille, German Mineralogical Soc. 1987, Roebling Medal, Mineralogical Soc. of America 2001, Leopold von Buch Medal, German Geological Soc. 2001. *Sport:* Heavyweight Boxing Champion, RAF Scotland 1949, Pres. Athletic Union, Univ. of St Andrews 1951–52. *Publications:* Ultramafic and Related Rocks (ed.) 1967, The Dynamic Earth 1971, The Way the Earth Works 1976, Solid-Earth Sciences and Society (Chair. NAS Cttee) 1993; numerous book chapters and articles in scientific journals. *Leisure interests:* writing science. *Address:* Division of Geological and Planetary Sciences, California Institute of Technology, Pasadena, CA 91125, USA (office). *E-mail:* wyllie@gps.caltech.edu (office). *Website:* www.gps.caltech.edu/~wyllie (office).

WYMAN, Bill; British musician (bass guitar); b. (William George Perks), 24 Oct. 1936, Lewisham, London; m. 1st Diane Cory 1959 (divorced 1968); one s.; m. 2nd Mandy Smith 1989 (divorced 1991); m. 3rd Suzanne Accosta 1993; three d.; founder mem., The Rolling Stones 1962–91; numerous tours and concerts worldwide; solo artist and mem., Willie and the Poor Boys 1985, Bill Wyman's Rhythm Kings 1998–2004; owner WGW Holdings, WGW Enterprises, Wytel Music, Ripple Records, Ripple Music, Ripple Publications, Ripple Productions, KJM Nominees, Sticky Fingers Restaurant; Lord of the Manor of Gedding and Thornwoods 1968–; Nordoff-Robbins Silver Clef 1982, Grammy Lifetime Achievement Award 1986, Ivor Novello Award for Outstanding Contribution to British Music 1991, Blues Foundation Memphis Literary Award 2002. *Films:* Sympathy for the Devil 1970, Gimme Shelter 1970, Ladies and Gentlemen the Rolling Stones 1974, Let's Spend the Night Together 1982, Digital Dreams 1983. *Recordings include:* albums: with The Rolling Stones: The Rolling Stones 1964, The Rolling Stones No. 2 1965, Out Of Our Heads 1965, Aftermath 1966, Between The Buttons 1967, Their Satanic Majesties Request 1967, Beggar's Banquet 1968, Let It Bleed 1969, Get Yer Ya-Ya's Out 1969, Sticky Fingers 1971, Exile On Main Street 1972, Goat's Head Soup 1973, It's Only Rock And Roll 1974, Black And Blue 1976, Some Girls 1978, Emotional Rescue 1980, Tattoo You 1981, Still Life 1982, Undercover 1983, Dirty Work 1986, Steel Wheels 1989, Flashpoint 1991; solo: Monkey Grip 1974, Stone Alone 1976, Green Ice (film soundtrack) 1981, Bill Wyman 1981, Digital Dreams (film soundtrack) 1983, Stuff 1991, Struttin' Our Stuff 1998, Anyway the Wind Blows 1999, Groovin' 2000, Double Bill 2001, Blues Odyssey 2001, Rude Dudes 2003, Just For The Thrill 2004; singles: with The Rolling Stones: Come On 1963, I Wanna Be Your Man 1963, Not Fade Away 1964, It's All Over Now 1964, Little Red Rooster 1964, The Last Time 1965, (I Can't Get No) Satisfaction 1965, Get Off Of My Cloud 1965, 19th Nervous Breakdown 1966, Paint It Black 1966, Have You Seen Your Mother Baby, Standing In The Shadow 1966, Let's Spend The Night Together/Ruby Tuesday 1967, We Love You 1967, Jumping Jack Flash 1968, Honky Tonk Women 1969, Brown Sugar 1971, Tumbling Dice 1972, Angie 1973, It's Only Rock 'N' Roll 1974, Fool To Cry 1976, Miss You 1978, Emotional Rescue 1980, Start Me Up 1981, Waiting On A Friend 1981, Undercover Of The Night 1983, Harlem Shuffle 1986, Mixed Emotions 1989, Rock And A Hard Place 1989, Highwire 1991; solo: (Si Si) Je Suis Un Rock Star 1981, Come Back Suzanne 1981, A New Fashion 1981, Groovin' 2000. *Publications:* Stone Alone – The Story of a Rock and Roll Band (with Ray Coleman) 1990, Wyman Shoots Chagall 2000, Bill Wyman's Blues Odyssey (with Richard Havers) 2001, Rolling With The Stones (with Richard Havers) 2002, Bill Wyman's Treasure Islands 2005, The Stones: A History in Cartoons 2006. *Address:* Tony Denton Promotions Ltd, 19 South Molton Lane, Mayfair, London, W1K 5LE, England (office). *Telephone:* (20) 7629-4666 (office). *Fax:* (20) 7629-4777 (office). *E-mail:* mail@tdpromo.com (office). *Website:* www.tdpromo.com (office); www.billwyman.com.

WYNAENDTS, Alexander Rijn; Dutch business executive; *CEO and Chairman of the Executive and Management Boards, AEGON NV;* b. 1960; began career with ABN Amro, working in Amsterdam and London in bank's capital markets, asset man., corp. finance and pvt. banking operations 1985; joined AEGON NV as Sr Vice-Pres. for Group Business Devt 1997, mem. Exec. Bd 2003–, COO 2007–08, CEO and Chair. Exec. and Man. Bds 2008–. *Address:* AEGON NV, PO Box 202, 2501 The Hague, The Netherlands (office). *Telephone:* (70) 344-3210 (office). *E-mail:* info@aegon.com (office). *Website:* www.aegon.com (office).

WYNDHAM, Henry Mark; British art expert and company director; *Chairman, Sotheby's;* b. 19 Aug. 1953, London, England; s. of Hon. Mark Wyndham and Anne Wyndham; m. Rachel Pritchard 1978; three s.; ed Wellesley House, Broadstairs, Eton Coll., Sorbonne, Paris and Sotheby's Fine Art Course; joined Christie's 1974, Head, 19th Century European Picture Dept, Christie's, New York 1978–82, Vice-Pres. 1979, Dir Christie's, London 1983–87; set up Henry Wyndham Fine Art of St James's Art Group 1987–93; set up Portrait Commissions 1992; Chair. Sotheby's UK 1994–, Sotheby's Europe 1997–; Trustee, Glyndebourne Opera, Prince of Wales Drawing School. *Films:* Entrapment 1999, Tomb Raider 2001, And Now Ladies and Gentlemen 2002. *Television:* Antiques Roadshow 1980s, 1990s. *Leisure interests:* cricket, golf, fishing, shooting, travelling, soccer (Brighton & Hove Albion supporter), visiting museums and art, galleries, opera, landscape. *Address:* Sotheby's, 34 New Bond Street, London, W1S 2RT (office); The Old Rectory, Southease, nr Lewes, Sussex, BN7 3HX, England (home). *Telephone:* (20) 7293-5000 (office). *Fax:* (20) 7293-5065 (office). *E-mail:* henry.wyndham@sothebys.com (office). *Website:* www.sothebys.com (office).

WYNNE, Gen. Khalid Shamim; Pakistani fmr army officer; b. 28 Aug. 1953, Abbottabad; s. of Arshad Shameem Wynne; m.; one s. two d.; ed Command and Staff Coll., Quetta, Führungsakademie der Bundeswehr, Germany, Nat. Defence Coll., Islamabad, Quaid-i-Azam Univ.; commissioned in an infantry bn 1972, served as Brigade Maj. of two Infantry Brigades; commanded 20th Bn of Punjab Regt, two Infantry Brigades, 41st Infantry Div., Quetta, Southern Command, Quetta; Deputy Chief, Gen. Staff 2006–07, Chief of Gen. Staff April–Oct. 2010; Commdr of the Southern Command (fmrly XII Corps), Quetta 2007–10; Chair. Jt Chiefs of Staff Cttee 2010–13 (retd); has served as mem. Faculty, School of Infantry and Tactics, Quetta, Command and Staff Coll., Quetta, Pakistan Mil. Acad., Kakul; Hilal-e-Imtiaz, Nishan-e-Imtiaz. *Address:* c/o Joint Chiefs of Staff Committee, Ministry of Defence, Pakistan Secretariat, No. II, Rawalpindi 46000, Pakistan.

WYNNE, Kathleen O., BA, MA; Canadian politician; *Premier of Ontario;* b. 21 May 1953, Richmond Hill, Ont.; divorced; three c.; pnr Jane Rounthwaite; ed Univ. of Toronto, Ontario Inst. for Studies in Educ., Harvard Univ., USA; Public School Trustee, Toronto 2000–03; MPP, Legis. Ass. of Ont. for Don Valley West (Ont. Liberal Party) 2003–, Parl. Asst to Ont. Minister of Training, Colls and Univs 2003–04, to Minister of Educ. 2004–06, Ont. Minister of Educ. 2006–10, of Transportation 2010–11, of Municipal Affairs and Housing and of Aboriginal Affairs 2011–12, Premier of Ont. (first woman) 2013–; Leader, Ont. Liberal Party 2013–; fmr Chair. Liberal Women's Caucus. *Address:* Office of the Premier, Legislative Bldg, Room 281, Queen's Park, Toronto, ON M7A 1A1, Canada (office). *Telephone:* (416) 325-1941 (office). *Fax:* (416) 325-3745 (office). *Website:* www.premier.gov.on.ca (office); www.kathleenwynne.ca.

WYNNE-MORGAN, David; British public relations executive; *Founding Partner, Chairman and CEO, WMC Communications Limited;* b. 22 Feb. 1931; s. of John Wynne-Morgan and of the late Marjorie Wynne-Morgan; m. 1st Romaine Ferguson; two s.; m. 2nd Sandra Douglas-Home (divorced); m. 3rd Karin E. Stines; two s.; ed Bryanston School; reporter, Daily Mail 1952–55; Foreign Corresp., later William Hickey, Daily Express 1955–58; contracted to Sunday Times to write biographical features including ghosting autobiog. of the late Pres. Nasser of Egypt; Founder, Chair. and Man. Dir Partnerplan 1964–80; Man. Dir Extel Public Relations 1980–83, Chair. 1983–84; Chair. and Chief Exec. Hill & Knowlton (UK) Ltd 1984–90, Pres. Hill & Knowlton Europe, Middle East and Africa 1990–94; Chair. Worldwide Exec. Cttee 1994, Marketing Group of GB 1989–90; Founding Partner, Chair. and CEO WMC Communications Ltd 1997–; Dir Horsham Corpn 1995–97; Council mem. Lord's Taverners 1992–96; mem. Inst. of Public Relations. *Publications:* biogs of Pietro Annigoni, Margot Fonteyn, Sir Malcolm Sargent. *Leisure interests:* squash (fmr Welsh int.), cricket, tennis, riding, golf. *Address:* WMC Communications Ltd, 11–12 Pall Mall, London, SW1Y 5LU (office); Lowndes Flat, 136 Brompton Road, London, SW3 1HY, England. *Telephone:* (20) 7930-9030 (office). *Fax:* (20) 7930-9038 (office). *Website:* www.wmccommunications.com (office).

WYPLOSZ, Charles, PhD, DipEng; French professor of economics; *Professor of Economics, Graduate Institute, Geneva;* b. 5 Sept. 1947, Vichy; s. of Jacob Wyplosz and Félicia Zanger; m. Claire-Lise Monod 1967; one s. three d.; ed Ecole Centrale de Paris, Harvard Univ.; Asst, Assoc., then Full Prof. of Econs, Institut Européen d'Admin des Affaires (INSEAD), Fontainebleau 1978–, Assoc. Dean (Research and Devt) 1986–89; Directeur d'études, École des hautes études en sciences sociales (EHESS), Paris 1988–95; Prof. of Econs, Grad. Inst. of Int. Studies, Geneva 1995–; Man. Ed. Econ. Policy 1984–2001; mem. Council of Econ. Advisers to Prime Minister of France 1999–2006, Comm. Economique, Ministry of Finance, France 1999–2005; mem. Panel of Econ. and Monetary Experts, Cttee for Econ. and Monetary Affairs, European Parl. 2000–, Group of Econ. Analysis, EC 2001–10, Advisory Scientific Cttee of European Systemic Risk Bd 2010–, Consultative Group to the Monetary and Capital Markets Dept, IMF 2010–; European Commission Fellow 2012–; Chevalier, Légion d'honneur. *Publications:* numerous publs in professional journals; occasional contribs to press. *Leisure interests:* skiing, music, family. *Address:* Graduate Institute of International Studies, 11 avenue de la Paix, 1202 Geneva (office); 3 rue du Valais, 1202 Geneva, Switzerland (home). *Telephone:* (22) 9085946 (office). *Fax:* (22) 7333049 (office). *E-mail:* charles.wyplosz@graduateinstitute.ch (office). *Website:* www.wyplosz.eu (office).

WYZNER, Eugeniusz, LLM; Polish diplomatist; *Member, International Civil Service Commission;* b. 1931, Chełmno; s. of Henryk Wyzner and Janina Wyzner; m. Elżbieta Laudańska; one s.; ed Jagiellonian Univ., Kraków, Warsaw Univ. and Acad. of Int. Law, The Hague; Deputy Perm. Rep. to UN 1961–68; Deputy Dir of Dept at Ministry of Foreign Affairs 1968–71, Dir of Dept 1971–73; Amb., Perm. Rep. to UN, Geneva 1973–78; Dir of Dept, Ministry of Foreign Affairs 1978–81; UN Under-Sec.-Gen. 1982–94; Deputy Minister for Foreign Affairs and Parl. Sec., Ministry of Foreign Affairs 1994–97, Acting Minister for Foreign Affairs Dec. 1995; Amb. and Rep. to UN 1998–99; mem. Int. Civil Service Comm., apptd Vice-Chair. 1999; mem. Bd of Dirs Int. Inst. of Space Law, Paris, Int. Peace Acad., New York, Int. Congress Inst. 1987–; Chair. UN Steering Cttee on Status of Women 1989–91, UN Appointments and Promotion Bd 1991–94, UN Exhibits Cttee 1992–94; mem. UN Sr Bd on Services to the Public 1989–94; Vice-Pres. Jan Karski Soc. 2009–; Amb. ad personam 1999–; Gold Cross of Merit, Grand Commdr's Cross, Order of Polonia Restituta, Grand Commdr, Order of the Phoenix (Greece), Commdr, Légion d'honneur and other decorations; Testimonial from UN Sec.-Gen. for dedicated service in support of UN peacekeeping operations 2009, Citation, Int. Inst. of Space Law. *Publications:* Wybrane zagadnienia z działalności ONZ w dziedzinie kodyfikacji i postępowego rozwoju prawa międzynarodowego, Niektóre aspekty prawne finansowania operacji ONZ w Kongo i na Bliskim Wschodzie, Poland and 50 Years of the United Nations Existence 1995. *Leisure interests:* cross-country skiing, mountain walking, theatre. *Address:* International Civil Service Commission, 2 United Nations Plaza, New York, NY 10017, USA (office). *Telephone:* (212) 963-8465 (office). *Fax:* (212) 963-1717 (office). *E-mail:* wyzner@un.org (office).

XAYRULLOYEV, Col-Gen. Sherali; Tajikistani government official and army officer; b. 8 Nov. 1949, Danga City, Khatlon Prov.; m.; c.; ed Tajikistan State Univ.; conscripted to serve in USSR Ministry of Internal Affairs 1970, served in various positions including Platoon Commdr 1970–77, subsequently served in various Ministry depts; Deputy Internal Affairs Minister 1988–95; Minister of Defence 1995–2013. *Address:* c/o Ministry of Defence, 734025 Dushanbe, Bokhtar Kuchai 59, Tajikistan.

XHAFERI, Musa; Macedonian politician; *Deputy Prime Minister, responsible for the implementation of the Ohrid Framework Agreement;* b. 7 July 1959, Zajaz, Kichevo; m.; one c.; ed Priština Univ., Univ. of Zurich and Acad. for Adult Educ., Lucerne, Switzerland; teacher in Lucerne, Switzerland 1996–2001; Deputy Prime Minister, responsible for the implementation of the Ohrid Framework Agreement 2002–06, 2011–; Minister of Local Self-Govt 2008–11; Co-founder and mem. Democratic Union for Integration, Sec. Gen. 2002–03, mem. Cen. Cttee 2002–, Sec. Human Resources Secr. 2003–09, Sec. Local Self-Govt and Decentralization Secr. 2009–. *Address:* Government of the Republic of Macedonia, Bul. Ilindenska 2, 1000 Skopje (office); Democratic Union for Integration (Bashkimi Demokratik për Integrim, BDI), 1200 Tetovo, RR 170 No. 2, Reçicë e Vogël, Former Yugoslav Republic of Macedonia. *Telephone:* (2) 3118022 (office); (4) 4334398. *Fax:* (2) 3112561 (office); (4) 4334397. *E-mail:* primeminister@primeminister.gov.mk (office); bdi@bdi.org.mk. *Website:* www.vlada.mk (office); www.bdi.org.mk.

XI, Guohua, PhD; Chinese business executive; *Chairman and Executive Director, China Mobile Communications Corporation;* b. 1951; ed Hefei Univ. of Tech., Jiaotong Univ., Tongji Univ.; Chair. Shanghai Bell Co. Ltd, Shanghai 2000–01; Exec. Vice-Pres. 2000–01; Vice-Minister, Ministry of Industry and Information Tech. 2001; Gen. Man. China Network Communications Group Corpn 2002–11, Sec. CCP Leading Party Group 2002–11; Exec. Dir and Chair. China Mobile Communications Corpn 2011–; Alt. mem. 16th CCP Cen. Cttee 2002–07, mem. Cen. Comm. for Discipline Inspection, 17th CCP Cen. Cttee 2007–12; Deputy Dir State Internet Information Office 2011–. *Address:* China Mobile Communications Corpn, 29 Financial Street, Xicheng District, Beijing 100032, People's Republic of China (office). *Telephone:* (10) 3121-8888 (office). *Fax:* (10) 2511-9092 (office). *E-mail:* info@chinamobile.com (office). *Website:* www.chinamobile.com (office).

XI, Jinping, LLD; Chinese politician and head of state; *President;* b. 1953, Fuping, Shaanxi Prov.; s. of the late Xi Zhongxun (fmr Vice-Premier and a founder of Communist guerrilla movt in northern China); m. 1st Ke Lingling (divorced); m. 2nd Peng Liyuan 1987; one d.; ed Tsinghua Univ., Beijing; sent to do manual labour, Yanchuan Co., Shaanxi Prov. 1969; joined CCP 1974; served as Sec. to Geng Biao 1982; Vice-Sec., Sec. CCP Zhengding Co. Cttee 1982–85; First Political Commissar, Chinese People's Armed Police Force; Vice-Mayor of Xiamen, Fujian Prov. 1985–88; Sec. CCP Ningde Pref. Cttee 1988–90; First Sec. Fujian Mil. Dist (Ningde Mil. Sub-Area Command), PLA Nanjing Mil. Region 1988; Sec. CCP Fuzhou Municipal Cttee, Chair. Standing Cttee Fuzhou Municipal People's Congress 1990–96; Deputy Sec. CCP Fujian Prov. Cttee 1995–2002; Vice-Gov. of Fujian Prov. 1999–2000, Gov. 2000–02; Acting Gov. of Zhejiang Prov. 2002–07; Deputy Sec. CCP Zhejiang Prov. Cttee 2002, Sec. 2002–07; Chair. Standing Cttee of Zhejiang Prov. People's Congress 2003–07; Sec. CCP Shanghai Municipal Cttee 2007; First Sec., Cen. Secr., CCP 2007–12; Pres. CCP Central Party School 2007–13; Vice-Pres. People's Repub. of China 2008–13, Pres. 2013–; Gen. Sec. CCP 2012–; Chair. CCP Cen. Mil. Comm. 2012–, State Cen. Mil. Comm. 2013–; Chair., CCP, Cen. Cttee Nat. Security Comm. 2014–; Del., 14th CCP Nat. Congress 1992–97; Alt. mem. 15th CCP Cen. Cttee 1997–2002; mem. 16th CCP Cen. Cttee 2002–07; mem. 17th CCP Cen. Cttee 2007–12, also mem. 17th CCP Cen. Cttee Politburo 2007–12 and Politburo Standing Cttee 2007–12; mem. 18th CCP Cen. Cttee 2012–, also mem. 18th CCP Cen. Cttee Politburo 2012– and Politburo Standing Cttee 2012–; ranked by Forbes magazine amongst The World's Most Powerful People (69th) 2011, (ninth) 2012, (third) 2013. *Publications include:* Research on Developing Chinese Rural Market-orientated Economy, Science and Patriotism (Chief Ed.). *Leisure interests:* reading, sports. *Address:* Office of the President, Great Hall of the People, West Edge, Tiananmen Square, Beijing, People's Republic of China (office). *Website:* www.gov.cn (office).

XIAN, Dingchang; Chinese nuclear physicist; *Research Professor, Institute of High Energy Physics, Chinese Academy of Sciences;* b. 15 Aug. 1935, Guangzhou, Guangdong Prov.; s. of Xian Jiaqi and Li Zuoming; m. 1st Ren Mengmei 1966 (died 1994); two s.; m. 2nd Chu Shiuling 2001 (divorced 2005); two s.; ed Beijing Univ.; Research Prof., Inst. of High Energy Physics, Chinese Acad. of Sciences; Chair. Chinese Synchrotron Radiation Soc. 1996–; mem. Chinese Acad. of Sciences 1992–, Acad. of Sciences for the Developing World 2002–; Nat. Science Conf. Prize 1978, State Natural Science Prize 1982, Ho Leung Ho Lee Physics Prize, Supreme Prize for State Science and Tech. Progress 1989. *Publications:* Synchrotron Radiation Applications 1997, Contemporary Scientific and Technological Techniques in Ancient Ceramics Research 1999, Platform for Biomacromolecule Crystal Structure Research with Sychrotron Radiation 2004, Precambrian Fossil Research with Synchrotron Radiation 3D Non-destructive Imaging Fossil Research with Synchrotron Radiation 3D Non-destructive Imaging 2006. *Leisure interests:* literature, music. *Address:* Institute of High Energy Physics, 19 Yuquan Road, Beijing 100049, People's Republic of China (office). *Telephone:* (10) 88235988 (office); (10) 82661342 (home). *Fax:* (10) 88233201 (home). *E-mail:* xian@ihep.ac.cn (office). *Website:* www.ihep.ac.cn (office).

XIANG, Junbo, MEconD, PhD; Chinese banking executive; *Chairman, China Insurance Regulatory Commission;* b. Jan. 1957, Sichuan Prov.; ed Peking Univ., Nankai Univ., Renmin Univ. of China; Vice-Pres. Nanjing Audit Inst. 1993–96; Deputy Dir-Gen., Supervision Dept, Nat. Audit Office of China (CNAO) 1996, Special CNAO Attaché to Beijing, Tianjin and Hebei Prov. 1996–99, Dir-Gen. Personnel and Educ. Dept 1999–2000, Dir-Gen. Personnel Dept 2000–02, Deputy Auditor 2002–04; Deputy Gov. People's Bank of China (PBC) 2004–07, also Pres. PBC Shanghai Head Office 2005–07; Pres. Agricultural Bank of China Head Office 2007–09, Exec. Chair. Agricultural Bank of China 2009–11; Chair. China Insurance Regulatory Comm. 2011–; Adjunct Prof., China Europe Int. Business

School; Guest Prof., Fudan Econ. Forum 2007; mem. Expert Cttee for Devt of Shanghai as Int. Financial Centre 2007–; Alt. mem. 17th CCP Cen. Cttee 2007–12, mem. 18th CCP Cen. Cttee 2012–; Research Fellow, Peking Univ. *Address:* China Insurance Regulatory Commission, 15 Financial Street, Xicheng District, Beijing 100140, People's Republic of China (office). *Website:* www.circ.gov.cn (office).

XIAO, Gang, LLM; Chinese banker; *Chairman, Bank of China Ltd;* b. 1959; ed Hunan Inst. of Finance and Econs, Renmin Univ. of China; joined People's Bank of China (PBC) 1981, various roles including Gen. Man. China Foreign Exchange Trading Center, Dir-Gen. Policy Research Dept, Asst Gov. PBC 1996–98, Deputy Gov. 1998–2003, also mem. PBC Monetary Policy Cttee 1998–2003; Pres. Bank of China Ltd 2003–04, Chair. 2003–, mem. Bd of Dirs BOC Hong Kong Holdings (subsidiary) 2003–; Chair. China Asscn of Banks 2003–04; fmr Deputy 9th Nat. People's Congress; fmr Alt. mem. 8th Chinese CP Guangdong Prov. Cttee; Alt. mem. 17th CCP Cen. Cttee 2007–12, mem. 18th CCP Cen. Cttee 2012–. *Address:* Bank of China Ltd, 1 Fuxingmen Nei Dajie, Beijing 100818, People's Republic of China (office). *Telephone:* (10) 6659-6688 (office). *Fax:* (10) 6659-3777 (office). *E-mail:* info@boc.cn (office). *Website:* www.boc.cn (office).

XIAO, Yang; Chinese judge and party and government official; b. Aug. 1938, Heyuan Co., Guangdong Prov.; ed People's Univ. of China, Beijing; joined CCP 1966; imprisoned during Cultural Revolution 1968–71; teacher of political science and law, Heyuan Co. 1969–75; Deputy Dir Qujiang Co. CCP Cttee Office, then various party posts 1971–81; Sec. CCP Cttee of Wujiang Dist, Shaoguan City, Guangdong Prov. 1981–83; Deputy Sec. Qingyuang Prefectural CCP Cttee, Guangdong 1983; Deputy Chief, Guangdong Prov. Procurator's Office, Deputy Sec. CCP Leadership Group 1983–86; Procurator-Gen. Guangdong Prov. Procurator's Office 1986–90; Deputy Procurator-Gen. Supreme Procurator's Office, Deputy Sec. CCP Leadership Group 1990–92; teacher, China Univ. of Political Science and Law, Beijing 1990; Minister of Justice 1993–98; Pres. Supreme People's Court 1998–2008, China Asscn of Judges 1999–; Alt. mem. 14th CCP Cen. Cttee 1992–97, mem. 15th CCP Cen. Cttee 1997–2002, 16th CCP Cen. Cttee 2002–07; Vice-Chair. Cen. Cttee for Comprehensive Man. of Public Security 1998. *Address:* c/o Supreme People's Court, 27 Dongjiaominxiang, Beijing 100745, People's Republic of China (office).

XIAO, Yaqing; Chinese engineer, business executive, academic and government official; b. 1959, Beijing; ed Cen. South Univ. of Tech.; began working as engineer 1982; fmr Dept Head and Chief Engineer, Tech. Div., Northeast Light Alloy Fabrication Plant; fmr Gen. Man. Northeast High Alloy Corpn Ltd; fmr Factory Man. Southwest Aluminum Fabrication Plant (renamed Southwest Aluminum Industry Group 1999), Chair. and Gen. Man. 1999–2003; Pres. China Aluminum Corpn (CHINALCO) 2003–09; Chair. and CEO Aluminum Corpn of China (CHALCO) Ltd –2009; Deputy Sec.-Gen., State Council 2009–13; Deputy Dir, State Council Leading Group for Promoting Medium and Small Enterprise Devt 2013–; Vice-Chair. China Non-ferrous Metals Fabrication Asscn; part-time Prof., Cen. South Univ. of Tech., Chongqing Univ.; mem. CCP 1981–; Del., Nat. Congress, 16th CCP 2002–07; Alt. mem. 17th CCP Cen. Cttee 2007–12. *Address:* c/o State Council, Zhongnanhai, Beijing, People's Republic of China (office).

XIE, Duyang, PhD; Chinese business executive and fmr civil servant; *Chairman, CCB International (Holdings) Ltd;* ed Wuhan Univ.; served in several positions including as officer of Dir-Gen. level, Ministry of Org. and Nat. Econ. Gen. Affairs Bureau of State Planning Comm. 1986–92; Vice-Pres. Industrial and Commercial Bank of China 1992–2000; Chair. Bd of Supervisors, People's Insurance Co. of China and China Reinsurance Co. 2000–03; Chair. Bd of Supervisors, China Construction Bank 2004–10, Chair. CCB International (Holdings) Ltd (CCB International), Hong Kong 2010–; Research Fellow and mem. 11th Nat. Cttee of CPPCC. *Address:* CCB International, Suite 3408, 34/F, Two Pacific Place, 88 Queensway, Hong Kong Special Administrative Region, People's Republic of China (office). *Telephone:* 25326100 (office). *Fax:* 25326100 (office). *E-mail:* info@ccbintl.com (office). *Website:* www.ccbintl.com.hk (office).

XIE, Heping, DEng, PhD; Chinese mining engineer and university administrator; *President, Sichuan University;* b. Jan. 1956, Shuangfeng Co., Hunan Prov.; ed China Univ. of Mining and Tech.; joined CCP 1986; Prof., China Univ. of Mining and Tech., Beijing 1990, Dean, Postgraduate Dept 1992, Pres. China Univ. of Mining and Tech. 1998, also Deputy Sec., China Univ. of Mining and Tech. CCP Cttee 1999–2000, Sec. 2000; currently Pres. Sichuan Univ.; Alt. mem. 17th CCP Cen. Cttee 2007–; mem. Chinese Acad. of Eng 2001–; numerous awards including Award of Chinese Youth Scientists 1993, Nat. Prize of Natural Sciences 1995, Nat. Prize of Progress in Science and Tech. 1999, 2000, Ho Leung Ho Lee Prize. *Publications:* five books in English and Chinese and over 150 journal papers. *Address:* Office of the President, Sichuan University, 24 South Section 1, Yihuan Road, Chengdu 610065, Sichuan Province, People's Republic of China (office). *Telephone:* (28) 85403116 (office). *Fax:* (28) 85403260 (office). *E-mail:* wsc@scu.edu.cn (office). *Website:* www.scu.org.cn (office).

XIE, Qihua; Chinese steel industry executive; *Chairwoman, China Metallurgical Council;* b. June 1943, Shanghai; ed Tsinghua Univ., Beijing Municipality; trained as engineer; began career in steel industry 1968; joined Shanghai Baoshan Iron & Steel Group 1978, held positions successively as Planning Section Chief, Asst Commdr and Vice-Commdr of Baosteel Project HQ, Dir and Deputy Man. of Group Eng HQ, Dir of Planning and Devt Dept 1993–94, Deputy Pres. and Gen. Man. 1994–98, Vice-Chair. and Pres.; Pres. Shanghai Baosteel Group Corpn (following merger of Baoshan Iron & Steel with Shanghai Metallurgical and Meishan Steel to form new co. 1998) 1998–2004, 2005, Chair. and Pres. 2004–07 (retd); Alt. mem. 16th CCP Cen. Cttee 2002–07; Chair. China Fed. of Industrial Econs Presidium; Chair. China Metallurgical Council; Vice-Chair. China Iron & Steel Asscn (Chair. 2005–), China Women Entrepreneur Asscn, China Group Cos Promotion Asscn, China Investment Asscn, China Enterprise Confed., China Enterprise Dirs Asscn; Shanghai Excellent Entrepreneur 1995, 1995, Outstanding Entrepreneur of Shanghai Municipality, Nat. Outstanding Female Entrepreneur, ranked by Fortune magazine amongst 50 Most Powerful Women in Business outside the

US 2002–03, (second) 2004, (second) 2005, (sixth) 2006, Chinese Businesswoman of 2003, ranked by Forbes magazine amongst 100 Most Powerful Women (55th) 2004, (14th) 2005, Outstanding Contrib. to Chinese Enterprise Prize 2004. *Address:* c/o Shanghai Baosteel Group Corporation, Baosteel Tower, Pudian Road 370, Pudong New Distict, Shanghai, People's Republic of China (office).

XIE, Shijie; Chinese administrator; b. 1934, Liangping Co., Sichuan Prov.; ed South-West Agricultural Coll.; joined CCP 1954; apptd Dir Ya'an Agricultural School, Sichuan Prov. 1959; fmr Deputy Sec., later Sec. CCP Ya'an Prefectural Cttee, Sichuan Prov.; mem. Standing Cttee CCP Sichuan Prov. Cttee 1985–92, Deputy Sec. CCP Sichuan Prov. Cttee 1992–93, Sec. 1993–2000; Vice-Gov. of Sichuan Prov. 1985–1992; Deputy, 8th NPC 1993–98, 9th NPC 1998–2003; Chair. Standing Cttee of NPC, Sichuan Prov. 1998–2003; mem. 14th CCP Cen. Cttee 1992–1997, 15th CCP Cen. Cttee 1997–2002. *Address:* c/o Standing Committee of Sichuan People's Congress, Chengdu, Sichuan Province, People's Republic of China (office).

XIE, Tieli; Chinese film director; b. 1925, Huaiyin Co., Jiangsu Prov.; joined CCP 1942; film dir, Beijing Film Studio; mem. 5th Nat. Cttee Chinese Fed. of Literary and Art Circles 1988–93, CPPCC, 8th NPC 1993–98; mem. Educ., Science, Culture and Health Cttee; Vice-Chair. Chinese Film Artists Asscn 1985; leading figure in "Third Generation" of Chinese dirs; Golden Rooster Lifetime Achievement Award 2005. *Films include:* Early Spring in February (Zao Chun Er Yue) 1963, Violent Storm, Taking Tiger Mountain by Strategy 1970, Ode to the Dragon River 1972, The Azalea Mountain 1974, Haixia 1975, Zhi yin 1981, Bao shi fu zi 1983, A Dream in Red Mansions 1988. *Address:* Beijing Film Studio, 19 Beihuan Xilu Road, Beijing 100088, People's Republic of China (office).

XIE, Xuren; Chinese economist and government official; b. 1947, Ningbo City, Zhejiang Prov.; ed Zhejiang Univ.; began career as technician, Ningbo Zhenhai Machinery Factory, Ningbo City 1967, served as Section Chief and later Deputy Dir –1981; Magistrate, People's Court, Zhejiang Prov. 1984–85; Dir Investment and Planning Offices, Prov. Planning and Econ. Comm., Zhejiang Prov. 1985–88; Deputy Dir Prov. Planning and Econ. Comm. 1988–90; Deputy Dir Budget Dept, Ministry of Finance 1990–91, Deputy Dir Planning Dept 1990–93, Dir Planning Dept and Asst to Minister 1993–94, Dir Reforms Dept 1994–95, Vice-Minister 1995–98; Pres. Agricultural Devt Bank of China 1998–2000; Vice-Minister, State Econ. and Trade Comm. 2001–03; Dir State Admin of Taxation 2003–07; Minister of Finance 2007–13; joined CCP 1980, Deputy Sec., Yinxian Co. Cttee 1984–85, Deputy Sec., Work Cttee Depts, Financial Work Cttee, CCP Cen. Cttee 2000–01, Deputy Sec., Leading Party Group, CCP 2001–03, Alt. mem. 16th CCP Cen. Cttee 2002–07, mem. 17th CCP Cen. Cttee 2007–12; named by Emerging Markets Magazine as Asian Finance Minister of the Year 2009. *Address:* c/o Ministry of Finance, 3 Nansanxiang, Sanlihe, Xicheng Qu, Beijing 100820, People's Republic of China (office).

XIE, Zhenhua; Chinese civil servant; *Vice Minister, State Development and Reform Commission;* b. Oct. 1949, Tianjin; ed Tsinghua Univ., Beijing, Wuhan Univ. Environmental Law Research Inst.; joined CCP 1969; Sec. Production and Construction Corps, Heilongjiang Prov. 1979–80; teaching asst, No. 2 Subsidiary School, Tsinghua Univ. 1979–80 (Sec. CCP Revolutionary Cttee); Org. Sec. CCP Party Cttee State Construction Comm. 1980–82; various man. roles, Ministry of Urban and Rural Construction and Environmental Protection 1982–88; Deputy Dir State Environment Protection Bureau 1990–93, Dir 1993–2007; apptd Vice-Chair. and Sec.-Gen. Environmental Protection Cttee of the State Council 1993, Nat. Cttee for the Patriotic Public Health Campaign 1994; apptd Chair. Chinese Comm. for Certification of Produce Conformity and Environmental Standards 1994; apptd Dir Specialists Examination Cttee of Nuclear Environment 1994; Vice-Minister, State Devt and Reform Comm. 2007–; Del., 15th CCP Nat. Congress 1997–2002; mem. 15th CCP Cen. Cttee for Discipline Inspection 1997–2002, 16th CCP Cen. Cttee 2002–07, 17th CCP Cen. Cttee for Discipline Inspection 2007–12, mem. 18th CCP Cen. Cttee 2012–; Global Environment Facility (GEF) Leadership Award (jt winner) 2002, UNEP Sasakawa Environment Prize (jt winner) 2003. *Address:* State Development and Reform Commission, 38 Yuetannan Jie, Xicheng Qu, Beijing 100824, People's Republic of China (office).

XIMENES BELO, Mgr Carlos Filipe, SDB; Timor-Leste ecclesiastic; b. 3 Feb. 1948, Baucau, Dili; ordained priest (mem. Salesians of St John Bosco) 1980; consecrated Titular Bishop of Lorium 1988; Papal Admin., Dili; active in campaign for human rights in Timor-Leste; fmr Apostolic Admin. to Bishopric of Dili (resgnd 2002); Nobel Peace Prize (shared with José Ramos-Horta q.v.) 1996. *Address:* c/o Camara Eclesiaastica, Av. Direitos Humanos, Bidau Lecidere, Dili 88010, Timor-Leste. *Telephone:* (390) 3322850. *Fax:* (390) 3322308.

XING, Bensi; Chinese philosopher and academic; b. 7 Oct. 1929, Sheng Co., Zhejiang Prov.; s. of Xing Tinxu and Guei Yuyin; m. Zhou Bangyuan 1953; two d.; ed Special School of Russian Language of CCP Cen. Cttee; joined CCP 1950; teacher, Beijing Inst. of Russian Language 1952–56; Asst Researcher and Academic Sec. Inst. of Philosophy under Chinese Acad. of Sciences 1957–66, Deputy Dir, Dir, Vice-Chair. Academic Cttee, under Chinese Acad. of Social Sciences 1978–82, Academician 1983–85; Guest Prof., Qinghua Univ. 1984–; mem. Council for Int. Cultural Exchange 1984; Deputy Gen. Ed. Philosophy Vol. of Chinese Encyclopaedia 1983–; Vice-Pres. CCP Cen. Cttee Party School 1988–; Ed.-in-Chief Party journal Qiushi 1994–; NPC Deputy, Zhejiang Prov.; mem. NPC Law Cttee; Visiting Scholar Columbia Univ. 1981. *Publications:* The Dualism of Ludwig Feurbach's Anthropology 1963, The Social Theory and Historical Viewpoint of Saint-Simon 1964, Humanism in the History of European Philosophy 1978, Philosophy and Enlightenment 1979, The Anthropology of Ludwig Feurbach 1981, Philosophy and Time 1984, Philosophy (Introduction to Philosophy Vol. of Chinese Encyclopaedia) 1987, The Past, Present and Future of Philosophy (Introduction, Little Encyclopaedia of Philosophy) 1987 and many other essays. *Leisure interests:* music, literature, Peking Opera, Chinese calligraphy. *Address:* Institute of Philosophy, Chinese Academy of Social Sciences, Beijing, People's Republic of China (office).

XING, Gen. Shizhong; Chinese army officer; b. Sept. 1938, Licheng Co., Shandong Prov.; ed Nanjing Eng Army School; joined PLA 1953, CCP 1957; staff officer in a div. engineer section 1959, a div. operational training section 1965, commdr of corps-affiliated eng bn 1969, regt commdr 1975, chief of corps

operational training div. 1978, div. chief of staff 1978, div. commdr 1979, corps commdr 1983, Chief of Staff, Lanzhou Mil. Region 1985–88, Deputy Commdr 1988; Deputy Commdr Jinan Mil. Region 1995–96; Commandant Nat. Defence Univ. 1995–2002; mem. 15th CCP Cen. Cttee 1997–2002; mem. 10th Standing Committee of NPC 2003–; Group Leader, State Language Work Cttee 2003–; rank of Maj.-Gen. 1988, Lt-Gen. 1993, Gen. 1998. *Address:* National Defence University, Beijing, People's Republic of China (office).

XIONG, Shen; Chinese mechanical engineer and academic; b. 13 Sept. 1935, Jiangsu Prov.; s. of Shen Baozhang and Xu Shifeng; m. Xia Xuejian 1965; one d.; ed Tsinghua Univ., Beijing; Prof. Dept of Eng Mechanics, Tsinghua Univ. 1959–; several prizes including State Prize of Science Congress 1978, Prize of Science and Tech. of State Bureau of Instrumentation Industry 1981, Prizes of Science and Tech., State Educational Comm. 1986, 1988, State Prize of Invention 1992, Prize of Zhou Peiyuan Foundation 1992, State Prize of Excellent Book in Science and Tech. 1992. *Publications include:* Modern Techniques and Measurements in Fluid Flows 1989, Fluid Velocity Measurement Techniques (in Chinese) 1987, Laser Doppler Velocimetry and Its Applications (in Chinese) 2004. *Leisure interests:* music, playing piano and accordion. *Address:* Department of Engineering Mechanics, Tsinghua University, Beijing 100084, People's Republic of China (office). *Telephone:* (10) 62784476 (office). *Fax:* (10) 62785576 (office). *E-mail:* shenx@tsinghua .edu.cn (office).

XIONG, Weiping, PhD; Chinese academic and business executive; *Chairman and CEO, Aluminum Corporation of China (CHALCO); President, China Aluminum Corporation (CHINALCO);* Prof. of Mineral Eng, Cen. South Univ. of Industry; fmr Exec. Vice-Pres., Cen. South Univ. of Industry, fmr Dean of School of Man.; fmr Deputy Gen. Man. China Copper, Lead and Zinc Group Co.; fmr Deputy Gen. Man. and Vice-Pres. China Aluminum Corpn (CHINALCO), Pres. and Sec.-Gen. Exec. Cttee 2009–, joined Aluminum Corpn of China (CHALCO) 2000, served as Sr Vice-Pres., Pres. 2004–06, Chair. and CEO 2009–; Vice-Chair. and Pres. China Nat. Travel Service (HK) Group Corpn and China Travel Service (Holdings) Hong Kong Ltd as well as Vice-Chair. and Pres. China Travel International Investment Hong Kong Ltd 2006–09; PhD Supervisor, Guanghua School of Man., Beijing Univ. *Address:* Aluminum Corporation of China (CHALCO), 62 North Xizhimen Street, Haidian District, Beijing 100082, People's Republic of China (office). *Telephone:* (10) 8229-8103 (office). *Fax:* (10) 8229-8081 (office). *E-mail:* webmaster@chalco .com.cn (office). *Website:* www.chalco.com.cn (office).

XIU, Heyi; Chinese business executive; *Chairman and President, Beijing Automotive Industry Holding Company Limited (Beijing Automotive Group);* serves as a Consultant of Shunyi People's Govt; Pres. and Sec., Party Cttee, Beijing Automotive Industry Holding Co. Ltd, Vice-Chair. –2006, Chair. 2006–; Chair. Beijing Hyundai Motor Co., Beijing Benz-Daimler Chrysler Automotive Co. Ltd, Beijing Automotive Investment Co. Ltd, Beiqi Foton Motor Co. Ltd, Beijing Hyundai Mobis Automotive Parts Co. Ltd; Assoc. Pres. Beijing Asscn of Automobile Mfrs, Beijing Entrepreneurs Asscn, Beijing Consumers Asscn; Exec. Dir China Asscn of Automobile Mfrs; Deputy Dir Capital Entrepreneurs Club; mem. Standing Cttee, Beijing Asscn of Science and Tech. *Address:* Beijing Automotive Industry Holding Co. Ltd, Zhangxinzhuang Village, Liqiao Town, Shunyi District, Beijing 101300, People's Republic of China (office). *Telephone:* (10) 67699888 (office). *Fax:* (10) 87664048 (office). *E-mail:* info@baihc.com (office). *Website:* www .baihc.com (office).

XU, Bin; Chinese automotive industry executive; Pres. China South Industries Group Corpn (state-owned enterprise run by Cen. Govt and an investment inst. authorized by the State Council) –2012, owns more than 40 industrial enterprises, including Chang'an Automobile (Group) Corpn Ltd, China Jialing (Group) Corpn Ltd, Jianshe Industries (Group) Corpn Ltd, four research insts and 23 research and devt centres) 2003–, also Chair. China Chang'an Automobile Group. *Address:* c/o China South Industries Group Corpn, 10 Chedaogou, 69 Zizhuyuan Road, Haidian District, Beijing 100089, People's Republic of China. *E-mail:* info@csgc .com.cn.

XU, Bing, MFA; Taiwanese artist; b. 8 Feb. 1955, Chongqing; s. of Hua-min Xu and Shi-ying Yang; ed Cen. Acad. of Fine Arts, Beijing; Asst Prof. Printmaking Dept, Cen. Acad. of Fine Arts 1987–, Assoc. Dir 1988–; Hon. Adviser, Dept of Art, Beijing Univ. 1989–; exhbns in China, France, USA, Switzerland, UK, Italy, Japan, Germany, Turkey 1979–; one man exhbns Beijing Art Gallery 1988, Taipei 1988, Taiwan 1990; mem. Chinese Engraving Artists' Asscn 1981–, Chinese Artists' Asscn 1982–, Dir 1985–; Dir Chinese Engraving Artists' Asscn 1986–; mem. Acad. Affairs Cttee, Cen. Acad. of Fine Arts 1988–; mem. Printmaking Artists' Cttee, Chinese Fine Arts Asscn 1989–; mem. Appraisal Cttee, 7th Chinese Nat. Exhbn of Fine Arts 1989; Hon. Fellow, Art Dept, Univ. of Wisconsin at Madison 1990; prizes from Art Exhbns. of Chinese Young Artists' Works 1980, 1985, 8th Exhbn of China's Wooden Paintings 1983, Medal, 9th Chinese Engraving Exhbn 1986, Award for Excellent Prints, Taiwan 1988, Henry E. T. Kok Educ. Foundation Prize for Young Instructors at Insts of Higher Learning 1989, Artes Mundi Prize 2004. *Publications:* Wooden Painting Sketches of Xu Bing 1986, Engravings of Xu Bing; numerous articles in magazines and newspapers. *Leisure interest:* hiking.

XU, Caidong; Chinese administrator and engineer; b. 1919, Fengxin Co., Jiangxi Prov.; ed Tangshan Inst., Jiaotong Univ., Shanghai and Grenoble Inst., France; returned to China 1955; Prof., Guizhou Eng Inst. 1958–; Pres., Science Acad. of Guizhou Prov. 1978, now Hon. Pres.; Vice-Gov. Guizhou Prov. 1983; mem. Dept of Tech. Sciences, Academia Sinica 1985–; Vice-Chair. Jiu San Soc. 1983–; mem. 7th Nat. People's Congress, 8th NPC 1993–98, mem. Educ., Science, Culture and Public Health Cttee; NPC Deputy, Guizhou Prov.; Fellow, Chinese Acad. of Sciences 1980–. *Publication:* The Physical Chemistry of Zinc. *Address:* Guizhou Provincial People's Government, Guiyang, Guizhou Province, People's Republic of China (office).

XU, Gen. Caihou; Chinese army officer; *Vice-Chairman, Central Military Commission, Chinese Communist Party Central Committee;* b. 1943, Wafangdian City, Liaoning Prov.; ed Harbin Inst. of Mil. Eng and PLA Mil. Eng Acad., PLA Inst. of Political Sciences; sent to do manual labour (Farm of the 39th Army) 1968–70; joined CCP 1971; soldier, Jilin Mil. Dist (Third Regt, Second Bn), PLA Shenyang Mil. Region 1970–71; Deputy Political Instructor, Shenyang Garrison

(3rd Div., 3rd Artillery Regt, 1st Bn, 2nd Co.), PLA Shenyang Mil. Region 1971–72; Sec., later Deputy Chief, Jilin Mil. Dist (Political Dept), PLA Shenyang Mil. Region 1972–82, Chief of Personnel Div. and of Office for Retired Officers 1982–83, Deputy Dir Political Dept 1983–84, Dir 1985–90; Political Commissar, Army Group, PLA Services and Arms 1990–92; Asst Dir PLA Gen. Political Dept 1992–93, Dir-Gen. PLA Gen. Political Dept 2003–05; Dir Jiefangjun Bao (Liberation Army Daily) 1993, Vice-Dir 1993–99, Exec. Vice-Dir 1999–; Political Commissar, PLA Jinan Mil. Region 1996–99; mem. 15th CCP Cen. Cttee 1997–2002, 15th CCP Cen. Mil. Comm. 1999, 16th CCP Cen. Cttee 2002–07, 16th CCP Cen. Cttee Politburo Secr. 2002, 16th CCP Cen. Mil. Comm. 2002–04 (Vice-Chair. 2004–07), mem. 17th CCP Cen. Cttee 2007–12, also mem. Politburo 2007–12, Vice–Chair. Cen. Mil. Comm. 2007–; rank of Maj.-Gen. 1990, Lt-Gen. 1993, Gen. 1999. *Address:* People's Liberation Army General Political Department, Beijing, People's Republic of China (office).

XU, Guanhua; Chinese scientist and politician; *Wei Lun Research Professor of Space and Earth Sciences, Institute of Space and Earth Information Science, Chinese University of Hong Kong;* b. 1941, Shanghai; ed Beijing Inst. of Forestry; research intern, teacher, Asst Research Fellow, Chinese Acad. of Forestry Sciences; Researcher, Stockholm Univ., Sweden 1979–81, Research Fellow and Dir Natural Resources Information Inst.; joined CCP 1984; Asst Research Fellow, Inst. of Remote Sensing Application, Chinese Acad. of Sciences 1964–93, Fellow, Chinese Acad. of Sciences 1991, Research Prof., Dir 1993, Vice-Pres. 1994–95, Chair. Div. of Earth Sciences 1996; Vice-Chair. State Science and Tech. Comm. 1995; Vice-Minister of Science and Tech. 1998, Minister 2001–07; Wei Lun Research Prof. of Space and Earth Sciences, Inst. of Space and Earth Information Science, Chinese Univ. of Hong Kong 2009–; mem. 9th CPPCC Nat. Cttee 1998–2003; mem. 16th CCP Cen. Cttee 2002–07; mem. Third World Acad. of Sciences, Royal Swedish Acad. of Eng Sciences, Int. Acad. of Astronautics; awarded title of Outstanding Scientist. *Address:* Institute of Space and Earth Information Science, Fok Ying Tung Remote Sensing Science Building, The Chinese University of Hong Kong, Shatin, Hong Kong Special Administrative Region, People's Republic of China (office). *Telephone:* 39436538 (office). *Website:* www.iseis.cuhk.edu.hk (office).

XU, Houze; Chinese geodesist and geophysicist; b. 4 May 1934, Anhui; s. of Xu Zuoren and Jiang Xinghua; m. Yang Huiji 1967; one s. one d.; ed Tongji Univ., Shanghai; Asst Researcher, Inst. of Geodesy and Geophysics, Chinese Acad. of Sciences 1963, Assoc. Prof. 1978, Prof. 1982–, Dir 1983–, Fellow 1991–; Dir Survey and Geophysics Inst. 1992–; mem. Chinese Geophysics Soc. 1978–; Vice-Pres. Int. Gravimetry Cttee and Pres. Perm. Cttee of Earth Tides, Int. Asscn of Geodesy 1983–; Vice-Pres. Science-Tech. Soc. of Hubei Prov. 1984–, Chinese Survey and Mapping Soc. 1985–; Prof., Tongji Univ. 1985–, Wuhan Tech. Univ. of Survey and Mapping 1986–, Shandong Univ. of Tech.; NPC Deputy, Hubei Prov.; Ho Leung Ho Lee Foundation Earth Sciences Prize. *Publications:* The Approximation of Stokes' Function and the Estimation of Truncation Error 1981, The Effect of Oceanic Tides on Gravity Tide Observations 1982, The Tidal Correction in Astrometry 1982, Accuracy Estimation of Loading Correction in Gravity Observation 1984, The Effect of Different Earth Models on Load Tide Correction 1985, Representation of Gravity Field outside the Earth using Fictitious Single Layer Density 1984, Collected Papers on Earth Tides 1988, Model of Oceanic Load Tide Correction in Chinese Continent 1988. *Address:* 54 Xu Dong Road, Wuchang 430077, Hubei Province, People's Republic of China. *Telephone:* 813405.

XU, Maj.-Gen. Huaizhong; Chinese writer; b. 1929, Hebei Prov.; s. of Xu Hongchang and Xin Zhuoliang; m. Yu Zengxiang; one s. two d.; mem. Presidium and Bd of Dirs, Chinese Writers' Asscn 1983–; Deputy Cultural Dir, Gen. Political Dept of PLA 1985–88, Dir 1988–; rank of Maj.-Gen. 1988; mem. Nat. Cttee CPPCC 1993–98; Vice-Chair. Chinese Writers' Asscn 1996–; a Deputy Head Propaganda Dept, CCP 5th Fujian Prov. Cttee 1989–96. *Publications:* Rainbow over the Earth, On the Tibetan Highlands, Anecdotes from the Western Front, The Wingless Angel (collection of medium-length novels and short stories), The Selected Works of Xu Huaizhong 1989. *Leisure interests:* playing table tennis and traditional Chinese shadow boxing. *Address:* 21 North Street Andeli, East District, Beijing, People's Republic of China.

XU, Jian; Chinese business executive; *Chairman, China National Machinery Industry Corporation (Sinomach);* currently Dir and Chair. China Nat. Machinery Industry Corpn (Sinomach). *Address:* China National Machinery Industry Corporation, 3 Danling Street, Haidian District, Beijing, 100080, People's Republic of China (office). *Telephone:* (10) 82688888 (office). *Fax:* (10) 82688811 (office). *E-mail:* office@sinomach.com.cn (office). *Website:* www.sinomach.com.cn (office).

XU, Jianyi, MBA; Chinese business executive; *Chairman, China FAW Group Corporation;* Vice-Chair. FAW Car Co. Ltd –2008, Chair. 2008–, fmr Deputy Gen. Man., now Chair. China FAW Group Corpn; mem. Jilin Prov. Standing Cttee and Sec. of Jinlin City. *Address:* China FAW Group, 2259 Dongfeng Street, Changchun 130011, People's Republic of China (office). *Fax:* (431) 87614780 (office). *E-mail:* info@faw.com (office). *Website:* www.faw.com (office).

XU, Jiayin; Chinese real estate executive; *President, Evergrande Real Estate Group Ltd;* b. 1958, Henan; ed Wuhan Univ. of Science and Tech.; Founder, Guangzhou Hengda Group 1996, renamed Evergrande Real Estate Group Ltd, currently Pres. and Sec.; mem. CCP; Deputy Chair. China Enterprise Confed., China Entrepreneur Asscn, China Real Estate Asscn, Guangdong Fund for Justice and Courage, Guangdong Private Enterprise Chamber, Guangdong General Chamber of Commerce; Pres. Guangzhou Real Estate Asscn; Hon. Chair. Guangdong Charity Fed.; mem. 11th CPPCC Nat. Cttee; Deputy 12th Guangzhou NPC; numerous awards including one of the People of the Year, Guangzhou Business Circles Award 2005. *Address:* Evergrande Real Estate Group, Tianlun Building, No. 45 Tianhe Road, Guangzhou, Guangdong, People's Republic of China (office). *Website:* www.gzhengda.com.cn (office).

XU, Kuangdi; Chinese engineer, academic and politician; *President, Chinese Academy of Engineering;* b. 11 Dec. 1937, Tongxiang Co., Zhejiang Prov.; ed Beijing Metallurgy Inst.; asst, Beijing Metallurgy Inst. 1959–63; May 7th Cadre School (Fengyang) 1971–72; Asst, later Lecturer, Metallurgical Dept, Shanghai Inst. of Mechanical Eng 1972–79; Deputy Dean and Assoc. Prof., later Dean and Prof., Metallurgical Dept, Shanghai Polytechnical Univ. 1980–86, Exec. Vice-Pres.

Shanghai Polytechnical Univ. 1986–89; joined CCP 1983; Deputy Dir Educ. and Public Health Office, Shanghai 1989–91; Dir Shanghai Higher Educ. Bureau 1989–91; Dir Shanghai Planning Comm. 1991–92; Vice-Mayor of Shanghai Municipality 1992–95, Mayor 1995–2001; mem. Standing Cttee CCP Shanghai Municipal Cttee 1992, Deputy Sec. 1994–2001; Dir Labour and Wages Cttee, Shanghai Municipality 1993; Vice-Pres. Chinese Mayors' Asscn 1996; Sec. CCP Leading Party Group of Chinese Acad. of Eng 2001–, Pres. Chinese Acad. of Eng 2002–, also Chair. China Fed. of Industrial Econs (CFIE); Alt. mem. 14th CCP Cen. Cttee 1992–97, mem. 15th CCP Cen. Cttee 1997–2002, 16th CCP Cen. Cttee 2002–07; Vice-Chair. 10th CPPCC Nat. Cttee 2003–; Fellow, Chinese Acad. of Sciences (Div. of Chemical, Metallurgical and Materials Eng) 1995–; Hon. DEng (Polytechnic Inst. of New York Univ.) 2007; Hon. Pres. Red Cross Soc. of China 1996; honoured for his achievements in some key projects in 6th Five-Year Plan 1986, Royal Acad. of Eng Int. Medal 2008. *Publication:* The Refining of Stainless Steel. *Address:* Chinese Academy of Engineering, 2 Bingjiaokou Hutong, Xicheng District, Beijing 100088, People's Republic of China (office). *Fax:* (10) 59300071 (office). *E-mail:* gjd@cae.cn (office). *Website:* www.cae.cn (office).

XU, Lejiang, MBA; Chinese steel industry executive; *Chairman, Baosteel Group Corporation;* b. Feb. 1959; ed Jiangxi Metallurgy Inst., Univ. of West Virginia, USA, Fudan Univ.; mem. CCP; joined Baosteel 1982, mem. Bd of Dirs 1998–, Vice-Pres. 1998–2004, Pres. 2004–07, Chair. Baoshan Iron and Steel Co. Ltd 2006–07, 2007–10, Standing mem. CCP Cttee 2007–10, Dir and Pres. Baosteel Group Corpn 2005–07, Chair. 2007–, also Dir, CCP Sec. and Standing mem. CCP Cttee, Baosteel Group Corpn 2014–; Deputy Chair. HKU Alumni Asscn of Chinese Mainland; Alt. mem. 17th CCP Cen. Cttee 2007–12, 18th CCP Cen. Cttee 2012–. *Address:* Baosteel Group Corpn, Baosteel Tower, 370 Pudian Road, Shanghai 200122, People's Republic of China (office). *Telephone:* (21) 58350000 (office). *Fax:* (21) 68404832 (office). *E-mail:* info@baosteel.com (office). *Website:* www.baosteel.com (office).

XU, Ning; Chinese business executive; *Chairman and General Manager, Shougang Corporation;* ed Party School of Chinese Communist Party Cen. Cttee; joined Shougang Corpn (holding co. of Shougang Holding) 1970, Dir and Exec. Deputy Gen. Shougang General Co. 2002–, Chair. and Gen. Man. Shougang Corpn, Chair. Shougang Holding (Hong Kong) Ltd 2012–, Shougang Concord International Enterprises Co. Ltd 2012–; Vice-Chair. Beijing Zhongguancun Software Park Development Co. Ltd; Dir (non-exec.) Shougang Concord International Enterprises Co. Ltd 2012–, Beijing Shougang Co. Ltd, Shougang Jingtang Iron & Steel United Co. Ltd. *Address:* Shougang Corporation, Shijingshan Road, Beijing 100041, People's Republic of China (office). *Telephone:* (10) 88291381 (office). *Fax:* (10) 88294300 (office). *E-mail:* info@shougang.com.cn (office). *Website:* www.shougang.com.cn (office).

XU, Ping, BEng; Chinese automobile industry executive; *Chairman, Dongfeng Motor Company Limited;* ed Hefei Industrial Univ.; joined Dongfeng Motor Corpn 1982, fmr Pres. thermo-electricity factory, served as Sec. CCP and Deputy Gen. Man. Dongfeng Motor Corpn 2001–03, Dir and Vice-Pres. Dongfeng Motor Co. Ltd 2003–05, Gen. Man. and Sec. CCP, Dongfeng Motor Corpn 2005–, mem. Bd of Dirs Dongfeng Motor Co. Ltd 2004–, Chair. and CEO 2005–11, Chair. 2011–, Chair. Dongfeng Peugeot Citroën Automobiles Co. Ltd 2005–, Dongfeng Automobile Co. Ltd 2005–; Rep. of 11th NPC, 17th CCP Cen. Cttee. *Address:* Dongfeng Motor Co. Ltd, 29 Baiye Road, Wuhan, Hubei 430015, People's Republic of China (office). *Telephone:* (719) 8226-962 (office). *Fax:* (719) 8226-845 (office). *E-mail:* info@dfmc.com.cn (office). *Website:* www.dfmc.com.cn (office).

XU, Gen. Qiliang; Chinese air force officer; *Vice-Chairman, State Central Military Commission;* b. 1950, Shandong Prov.; ed Air Force 1st Aviation Reserve Coll., 8th Aviation School, 5th Aviation School, Univ. of Nat. Defence; joined PLA and CCP 1967; Aviator, Air Force Div. Command 1969–83, becoming Bn Chief and Deputy Div. Commdr, later Div. Commdr 1983–84, Deputy Army Commdr (Air Force) 1984–85, Chief of Staff (Air Force), Shanghai Municipality 1985–88, Chief of Staff (Air Force) 1989–93, 1994–99, Deputy Chief of Staff 1993–94, Deputy Commdr, Shenyang Mil. Region, Liaoning Prov. 2000, Commdr (Air Force), Shenyang Mil. Region 2000–07, Commdr PLA Air Force 2007–12; Vice-Chair. State Cen. . Comm. 2013–; attained rank of Maj.-Gen. 1991, Lt-Gen. 1996, Gen. 2007; Alt. mem. 14th CCP Cen. Cttee 1992–97, mem. 15th CCP Cen. Cttee 1997–2002, 16th CCP Cen. Cttee 2002–07, 17th CCP Cen. Cttee 2007–12, also mem. 17th CCP Cen. Cttee Cen. Mil. Comm. 2007–12, mem. 18th CCP Cen. Cttee 2012–, also mem. 18th CCP Cen. Cttee Politburo 2012– and Vice-Chair. 18th CCP Cen. Cttee Cen. Mil. Comm. 2012–. *Address:* Ministry of National Defence, 20 Jingshanqian Jie, Beijing 10009, People's Republic of China (office). *Website:* www .mod.gov.cn (office).

XU, Qin; Chinese politician; b. 1928, Suizhong Co., Fengtian (now Liaoning) Prov.; joined CCP 1949; Deputy for Jiangxi to 5th NPC 1978; Vice-Gov. Jiangxi 1979–83; Deputy Sec. CCP Cttee, Jiangxi Prov. 1981; Vice-Chair. Jiangxi People's Congress 1981, Chair. Feb. 1988; Alt. mem. 12th CCP Cen. Cttee 1982–87; mem. 8th NPC 1993–98; NPC Deputy, Jiangxi Prov. *Address:* Jiangxi Provincial Chinese Communist Party, Nanchang, Jiangxi, People's Republic of China (office).

XU, Rongkai; Chinese politician; b. Feb. 1942, Chongqing; ed Tsinghua Univ., Beijing; joined CCP 1960; engineer, Sichuan Dongfang Steam Turbine Factory, then Dir Sichuan Dept of Light Industry 1966–91; Vice-Minister of Light Industry 1991–93; Vice-Pres. Chinese Nat. Asscn of Light Industry 1993–95; Deputy Dir Research Centre of State Council 1995–98, Deputy Sec.-Gen. of State Council 1998–2001; Deputy Dir China Comm. of Int. Decade for Disaster Reduction 1998–2001, Nat. Leading Group Concerned With Work Supporting the Army and the People 1999–2001; apptd Vice-Chair. China Int. Cttee for Natural Disaster 2000; Deputy Sec. Yunnan Prov. Cttee 2001–02, Vice-Gov. 2001, Acting Gov. 2001–02, Gov. 2002–06; mem. CCP Yunnan Prov. Cttee 2001–, Deputy Sec. 2001–; mem. 16th CCP Cen. Cttee 2002–07. *Address:* Yunnan Provincial People's Government, Wuhuashan, Kunming 650021, Yunnan Province, People's Republic of China (office).

XU, Rongmao, (Hui Wing Mao), MBA; Chinese business executive and property developer; *Chairman, Shimao Corporation;* b. 1950, Shishi, Fujian Prov.; m. two c.; ed Univ. of South Australia; moved to Hong Kong to work as stockbroker in 1970s; returned to China to export textiles 1980s; Founder and CEO Shimao

Group 1985, currently Chair. Shimao Corpn; investor in high-end property market in Fujian Prov., Beijing and Shanghai; Chair. Shanghai Overseas Chinese Chamber of Commerce; Vice-Chair. Shanghai Business Asscn; mem. 10th Chinese People's Political Consultative Conf. (CPPCC), Sub-Cttee Social and Legal Affairs of CPPCC, Standing Cttee Nat. Business Asscn; mem. Standing Cttee All-China Fed. of Industry and Commerce, Vice-Pres. 2007–; Chair. Shanghai Overseas Chinese Chamber of Commerce, Shanghai Real Estate Chamber of Commerce, Vice-Chair. China Real Estate Chamber of Commerce, Hong Kong Chinese Cultural Asscn, Fujian Overseas Friendship Asscn, Beijing Univ. of Chemical Tech.; Life Hon. Chair. Hong Kong Fed. of Overseas Chinese Asscns, Friends of Hong Kong Asscn; Hon. Chair. Conf. on Non-Independence and Pro-Reunification of China; Hon. Vice-Chair. Council of Shanghai Charity Foundation; Vice-Pres. Chinese Red Cross Foundation; mem. Council of Chinese Overseas Friendship Asscns; Hon. JP; Hon. Prof., Tongji Univ.; Shanghai Magnolia Award, Lilac-Bauhinia Golden Award (govt of Heilongjiang) 2006, Gold Bauhinia Star 2011. *Address:* Shimao Group, Jin Mao Tower, 45th Floor, 88 Shi Ji Avenue, Shanghai, 200121 People's Republic of China (office). *Telephone:* (21) 50473399 (office). *Website:* www.shimaogroup.com (office).

XU, Shaoshi, MEcons; Chinese geologist and government official; *Head, National Development and Reform Commission;* b. Oct. 1951, Ningbo, Zhejiang Prov.; ed Changchun Univ. of Earth Sciences, CCP Central Party School, Nankai Univ., Tianjin; sent to countryside to do manual labour during Cultural Revolution, Jilin Prov. 1969–71; joined CCP 1974; Officer, Policy Office, Ministry of Geology and Mineral Resources (now Ministry of Land and Resources) 1980–86, Dir Minister's Office 1986–88, Deputy Dir Gen. Office 1988–93, Dir 1993, Minister of Land and Resources 1987–2013, also Sec., CCP Leading Party Group 2007–13; Deputy Dir, Mining Bureau, Shenzhen City 1991–93; Dir Secr., Gen. Office of State Council 1996–2000, Deputy Sec.-Gen. 2000–07; Head, Nat. Devt and Reform Comm. 2013–; mem. 17th CCP Cen. Cttee 2007–12, 18th CCP Cen. Cttee 2012–. *Address:* National Development and Reform Commission, 38 Yuetannan Jie, Xicheng Qu, Beijing 100824, People's Republic of China (office). *Telephone:* (10) 68504409 (office). *Fax:* (10) 68512929 (office). *E-mail:* ndrc@ndrc.gov.cn (office). *Website:* www.ndrc.gov.cn (office).

XU, Xianming, LLB; Chinese lawyer; b. 1957, Shandong Prov.; ed Jilin Univ., Wuhan Univ.; Vice-Pres. Shandong Univ. 1985–2001, also Head of Grad. School and Dean of Law School, Pres. Shandong Univ. 2008–13; Pres. China Univ. of Political Science and Law, Beijing 2001–08; Deputy Dir, General Office, Central Governance Cttee 2013–; Deputy, 10th NPC 2003–08; Commr, 10th NPC Law Cttee 2003–08; Vice-Chair. China Law Soc.; First Nat. Social Science Achievement Award for Young Scholars, Ministry of Educ. Social Science Achievement Award. *Address:* c/o Office of the President, Shandong University, 27 Shanda Nanlu, Jinan 250100, Shandong Province, People's Republic of China (office).

XU, Yinsheng; Chinese government official; *President, Chinese Table Tennis Association;* b. 12 June 1938, Suzhou City, Jiangsu Prov.; m. Chen Liwen; one s.; World Table Tennis Champion three times; joined CCP 1961; Vice-Minister State Physical Culture and Sport Comm. 1977–98; Vice-Dir State Gen. Admin. of Physical Culture; Pres. Chinese Table Tennis Asscn 1979–, Chinese Boxing Asscn 1987–; Exec. Vice-Chair. Preparatory Cttee for 6th Nat. Games 1985; Vice-Pres. Chinese Olympic Cttee 1986–89, 1994–, All-China Sports Fed. 1989–; Exec. Vice-Pres. XIth Asian Games Organizing Cttee 1990–; Pres. Int. Table Tennis Fed. 1995–99; Deputy, 4th NPC 1975–78, 5th NPC 1978–83, 6th NPC 1983–88, 7th NPC 1988–93, 8th NPC 1993–98. *Publication:* How to Play Table Tennis by Dialectics. *Leisure interests:* tennis, fishing. *Address:* Chinese Table Tennis Association, No. 4 Tiyuguan Road, Beijing 100061, People's Republic of China (office). *Website:* tabletennis.sport.org.cn (office).

XU, Yongyue; Chinese politician; b. July 1942, Zhenping Co., Henan Prov.; ed Beijing Municipal People's Public Security School; joined CCP 1972; served consecutively as Sec. Beijing Municipal People's Public Security School, Gen. Office of Chinese Acad. of Sciences, Gen. Office of Ministry of Educ., Gen. Office of Ministry of Culture 1960–83; Political Sec. to Chen Yun 1983–93; Deputy Sec.-Gen. CCP Cen. Cttee Cen. Advisory Comm. 1988; Deputy Sec. Hebei Prov. Cttee 1994–98; Minister of State Security 1998–2007; Alt. mem. 15th CCP Cen. Cttee 1997–2002, mem. 16th CCP Cen. Cttee 2002–07. *Address:* c/o Ministry of State Security, 14 Dongchangan Jie, Dongcheng Qu, Beijing 100741, People's Republic of China (office).

XU, Yuanhe; Chinese philosopher; b. 1942, Rugao, Jiangsu Prov.; ed Peking Univ.; Asst Research Fellow, Assoc. Research Fellow then Research Fellow Inst. of Philosophy, Chinese Acad. of Social Sciences 1980–; Dir Oriental Philosophy Research Centre, Chinese Acad. of Social Sciences; State Council Prize 1993. *Publications:* Origin and Development of Luo Studies, The School of Reason and the Yuan Society, Confucianism and Oriental Culture, Survey of Chinese Civilization. *Address:* 5 Jian guo men wai Street, Beijing (office); 502 F2, 2T Bei tai pin zhuang Road, Haichian District, Beijing (home); Institute of Philosophy, Chinese Academy of Social Sciences, Beijing, People's Republic of China. *Telephone:* (10) 65137744 (office); (10) 63240875 (home). *Fax:* (10) 63240815 (home).

XU, Zhenshi; Chinese photographer, artist and publisher; b. 18 Aug. 1937, Songjiang Co., Shanghai; s. of Xu Weiqing and Jiang Wanying, step-s. of Cheng Shi-fa; m. Zhang Fuhe 1967; one d.; ed No. 1 High School, Songjiang Co., Zhejiang Acad. of Fine Arts; moved to Beijing 1965; Ed. People's Fine Arts Publishing House 1965–86, Dir Picture Editorial Dept 1986–, Ed.-in-Chief 1992–; mem. China Artists' Asscn; Deputy Sec.-Gen. Spring Festival Pictures Research Centre, Publrs' Asscn of China; Deputy Sec.-Gen. and Assoc. Dir Photography Research Centre; mem. Selection Cttee 3rd, 4th and 5th Nat. Exhbns of Spring Festival Pictures and other exhbns; Assoc. Dir Standing Cttee Spring Festival Pictures; Sr Adviser,

Office of East China–UN TIPS Nat. Exploit Bureau 1994–; exhbns in China, Japan, Korea, Hong Kong, Thailand; Vice-Ed.-in-Chief Gouache Vol. of Anthology of Contemporary Chinese Fine Arts 1996; Vice-Pres. Chinese Fan Art Soc. 1997; organized 1st Nat. Exhbn of Calligraphy and Paintings to Help the Poor 1998; Dir Foundation for Underdeveloped Regions in China 1998–; prepared 6th Nat. Exhbn of Spring Festival Pictures 1998; union art exhib., St Petersburg, Russia 2006; numerous awards including Bronze Medal for albums of photographs, Leipzig Int. Book Exhbn 1987, Nat. Award 1993, Model Ed. Nat. Press and Publs System 1997, 1998, State Prize for Spring Festival Pictures 2001, two 6th Nat. Exhbn of Spring Festival Pictures Prizes (China) 1998, Chinese Contemporary Art Achievement Prize, Hong Kong, State Prize of Spring Festival Pictures 2001, Prize of A Brilliant Contrib. 2001, Outstanding People's Artist Award. *Publications:* China's Cultural Relics Unearthed during the Great Cultural Revolution 1973, Travel in China (four vols) 1979–80, Tibet 1981, Travel in Tibet 1981, Costumes of China's Minority Nationalities 1981, Travel in Guilin 1981, Travel Leisurely in China 1981, Travel in Yunnan 1982, China's Flowers in Four Seasons 1982, Poet Li Bai 1983, Native Places of Tang Dynasty Poems 1984, Travel along the Yangtse River 1985, Through the Moongate: A Guide to China's Famous Historical Sites 1986, Waters and Mountains in China 1986, Travel in Guangzhou 1986, China 1987, The Chinese Nation 1989, Poet Du Fu 1989, Selected Works of Xu Zhenshi 1990, 1993, Selected Paintings of Xu Zhenshi 1993, 1994, Boat on the Plateau 1998, Album of Xu Zhenshi's Sketches 1999, Love for China 2003; collection of Xu Zhenshi published in 2003, Love for China 2003; ed Olympic Games picture book 2008. *Leisure interest:* sports. *Address:* People's Fine Arts Publishing House, No. 32 Beizongbu Hutong, Beijing, People's Republic of China (office). *Telephone:* (10) 65244901 (office); (10) 65246353 (home).

XU, Zhihong; Chinese plant physiologist and academic; b. 14 Oct. 1942, Wuxi, Jiangsu Prov.; ed Peking Univ.; research student, Chinese Acad. of Sciences Shanghai Plant Physiology Research Inst. 1969; Researcher, Assoc. Research Fellow, Research Fellow, Vice-Dir Chinese Acad. of Sciences Shanghai Plant Physiology Research Inst. 1969–91, Dir 1991–94; Vice-Pres. Chinese Acad. of Sciences and Dir Shanghai Life Science Research Centre 1992–2003, mem. 4th Presidium of Depts, Chinese Acad. of Sciences 2000–; Fellow, Third World of Sciences 1995–, Acad. Chinese Acad. of Sciences 1997– (also Deputy Dean); Pres. Peking Univ. 1999–2008; Hon. Prof. Hong Kong Univ.; Hon. DrSc (De Montfort) 1994, (Nottingham) 2000, (Hong Kong City) 2001, (Wasada) 2002, (McGill) 2003; Hon. DIur (Melbourne) 2003; Natural Science First Prize, Third Prize (Chinese Acad. of Science) 1990, 1991. *Address:* c/o Peking University, 1 Loudouqiao, Beijing 100871, People's Republic of China (office). *Telephone:* (10) 62752114 (office). *Fax:* (10) 62751207 (office). *Website:* (office).

XU, Zhijun, (Eric Xu), PhD; Chinese business executive; *Deputy Chairman and Rotating CEO, Huawei Technologies Company Ltd;* b. 1967; ed Nanjing Univ. of Science and Tech.; joined Huawei 1993, served successively as Pres. of Wireless Product Line, Chief Strategy and Marketing Officer, Chief Products and Solutions Officer, Chair. Investment Review Bd, Corp. Exec. Vice-Pres., Chair. SDC, Deputy Chair. and Rotating CEO, Huawei Technologies Co. Ltd Oct. 2013–March 2014. *Address:* Huawei Technologies Co. Ltd, Bantian, Longgang District, Shenzhen 518129, People's Republic of China (office). *Telephone:* (755) 28780808 (office). *E-mail:* hwtech@huawei.com (office). *Website:* www.huawei.com (office).

XU, Zhizhan, MSc; Chinese optical scientist; b. Dec. 1938, Changzhou, Jiangsu Prov.; ed Fudan and Beijing Univs; research student of physics, Peking Univ.; Prof., Shanghai Inst. of Optics and Fine Mechanics, East China Normal Univ., Chinese Acad. of Sciences; Chief Ed. Journal of Optics; Vice-Chair. Optical Soc. of China 1992–; Fellow, Chinese Acad. of Sciences 1992–, Third World Acad. of Sciences (now TWAS) 2004–; mem. Standing Cttee 9th CPPCC Nat. Cttee 1998–2003; Nat. Award for Natural Sciences numerous times; Ho Leung Ho Lee Foundation Award. *Publications:* over 300 essays on laser and related studies. *Address:* Shanghai Institute of Optics and Fine Mechanics, Chinese Academy of Sciences, Shanghai 201800, People's Republic of China (office). *E-mail:* hxlin@siom .ac.cn (office). *Website:* www.siom.ac.cn (office).

XU, Zhonglin; Chinese politician; b. Dec. 1943, Wujin Co., Jiangsu Prov.; ed PLA Survey and Cartography Inst., Zhengzhou, CCP Cen. Acad., Beijing; teaching asst, PLA Survey and Cartography Inst. 1962; joined CCP 1964; Deputy Sec., City Instrument, Meter and Electronics Bureau, Xuzhou City, Jiangsu Prov. 1975–80; Deputy Dir Planning and Science Cttees, Xuzhou City 1975–80; Deputy Dir, CCP Revolutionary Cttee, Xuzhou City 1980; Vice Mayor of Xuzhou 1980-86, Mayor 1986–89; mem. Standing Cttee CCP Xuzhou Municipal Cttee 1984–89, Dir Org. Dept 1984–86, Deputy Sec. Xuzhou Municipal Cttee 1986–89; Deputy Dir Org. Dept, CCP Jiangsu Prov. Cttee 1989–91, Dir 1991–94 (mem. Standing Cttee 1992–99), Deputy Sec. CCP Jiangsu Prov. Cttee 1994–99; mem. Standing Cttee CCP Anhui Prov. Cttee 1999–2002, Deputy Sec. CCP Anhui Prov. Cttee 1999–2002; Gov. Anhui Prov. 2001–02; mem. Standing Cttee CCP Jiansu Prov. Cttee 2002–, Deputy Sec. CCP Jiangsu Prov. Cttee 2002–; Chair. CPPCC Jiangsu Prov. Cttee 2003–08. *Address:* c/o Jiangsu People's Government, Nanjing, Jiansu Province, People's Republic of China (office).

XUE, Wei; Chinese violinist; b. 21 Dec. 1963, Henan; s. of Xue-Ming and Shang Yi-qing; ed Shanghai Conservatory, Beijing Conservatory of Music and Guildhall School of Music, London; appears regularly with the major London orchestras; performs in solo recitals and as concert soloist at int. music festivals; guest soloist with Shanghai Symphony on tour in Japan; Prof., RAM, London 1989–; numerous prizes including Silver Medal, Tchaikovsky Int. Competition (violin), Moscow 1986; Gold Medal, Carl Flesch Int. Competition 1986; London Philharmonic Soloist of the Year 1986. *Recordings include:* Great Violin Concertos 2001, Dreamland: Xue Wei Plays Chinese Violin Pieces 2002, Xue Wei and the Romance of Cremona 2003, Jue Ban 2008. *Leisure interests:* reading, chess, poker.

Y

YAACOB, Tan Sri Nik Mohamed; Malaysian business executive; *Chairman, Kencana Petroleum Bhd;* ed Monash Univ., Asian Inst. of Man.; with Sime Darby, fmrly Regional Dir, Dir of Operations, Malaysia, mem. Bd 1990–2004, mem. Exec. Cttee, CEO 1993–2004 (retd), fmr Dir, DMIB, Sime UEP Properties, Tractors Malaysia holdings, Consolidated Plantations, Port Dickson Power, SD Holdings, Sime Malaysia Region, SIRIM; mem. Bd of Dirs Kencana Petroleum Bhd 2008–, currently Chair.; mem. Bd of Dirs Scomi Group Berhad, Perbadanan Nasional Berhad, GuocoLand (Malaysia) Berhad, Bolton Berhad, Scomi Marine Bhd. *Address:* Kencana Petroleum Bhd, 50-2-2, Level 2, Wisma UOA Damansara 50, Jalan Dungun, Damansara Heights, 50490 Kuala Lumpur, Malaysia (office). *Telephone:* (3) 20932280 (office). *Fax:* (3) 20921180 (office). *Website:* www .kencanapetroleum.com.my (office).

YA'ALON, Lt-Gen. (retd) Moshe, BA; Israeli politician and army officer (retd); *Minister of Defence;* b. (Moshe Smilansky), 24 June 1950, Kiryat Haim; m.; three c.; ed Command and Staff Coll., Camberley, UK, Univ. of Haifa; drafted into Israeli Defence Forces (IDF) 1968, served in Nahal Paratroop Regt; reserve paratrooper during Yom Kippur War 1973, participated in liberation of Suez Canal; held several command positions in IDF Paratroop Brigade, Commdr reconnaisance unit during Litani Operation 1978, later Deputy Commdr, apptd Commdr 1990; served in elite unit 1979–82, later Deputy Commdr; fought in Operation Peace for Galilee; retrained in IDF Armoured Corps 1989–90; apptd CO Judea and Samaria, promoted Brig.-Gen. 1992; Commdr of Ground Forces, Tze'elim 1993; apptd CO Intelligence, rank Maj.-Gen. 1995; apptd CO Cen. Command 1998, IDF Deputy Chief-of-Staff 2000, Chief-of-Staff 2002–05; mem. Knesset (Likud) 2009–; Vice-Prime Minister and Minister of Strategic Affairs 2009–13, Minister of Defence 2013–; Pres. Shekel: Community Services for People with Special Needs; Chair. Center for Jewish Identity and Culture; Chair. Bd of Dirs Bishvil Hamachar. *Publications include:* The Long Short Road 2008. *Address:* Ministry of Defence, Kirya, Tel-Aviv 64734, Israel (office). *Telephone:* 3-6975540 (office). *Fax:* 3-6976711 (office). *E-mail:* pniot@mod.gov.il (office). *Website:* www.mod.gov.il (office).

YABLOKOV, Alexey Vladimirovich, DSc, DBiolSc; Russian population biologist and ecologist; *Councillor, Russian Academy of Sciences;* b. 3 Oct. 1933, Moscow; s. of Vladimir Yablokov and Tatiana Sarycheva; m. 1st Eleonora Bakulina 1955 (died 1987); one s.; m. 2nd Dil'bar Klado 1989; ed Moscow Univ.; researcher, Head of Lab., Prof. N. Koltsov Inst. of Developmental Biology 1959–89; political activities since late 1980s; Chair. Ichthyological Comm. of USSR Ministry of Fishery 1989–92; USSR People's Congress 1989–91; Deputy Chair. Comm. on Ecology of USSR Supreme Soviet 1989–91; State Counsellor on Ecology and Public Health to Pres. of Russia 1991–93; Chair. Interagency Comm. on Environmental Security, Russian Security Council 1993–97, Pres. Centre of Russian Environmental Policy 1993–2005; Regional Councillor for E Europe, N and Cen. Asia 2005–08; Chair. Green Russia political party 2005–06, Green Russia faction in Yabloko political party 2006–; Corresp. mem. USSR (now Russian) Acad. of Sciences 1984, Counsellor 2003–; Pres. Moscow Soc. for Protection of Animals 1988–; mem. Exec. Cttee Stockholm Environmental Inst. 1994–98; Environmental Adviser to Pres. EBRD 1997–99; Vice-Pres. World Conservation Union 2001–04; Foreign Hon. mem. American Acad. of Arts and Sciences 1996; Severtsov Prize 1976, Pew Fellowship 1992–94, WASA Prize 1995, Busk Medal 1996, Karpinsky Prize 1997, WWF Gold Medal 2002, Nuclear-free Future World Award 2002. *Publications:* 26 books and numerous articles on population, evolution and conservation biology, zoology, ecology, including Population Biology 1987, Nuclear Mythology 1997, Pesticides – The Chemical Weapons That Kill Life 2003, Non-Invasive Study of Mammalian Populations (co-author) 2004, Russia: Health of People and Nature 2007, Environment and Public Health in Moscow 2009, Chernobyl: Consequences for People and Nature (co-author) 2011. *Leisure interests:* writing, carpentry. *Address:* Russian Academy of Sciences, Office 319, 33 Leninksy Prospect, Moscow 119071, Russia (office). *Telephone:* (495) 952-80-19 (office). *Fax:* (495) 952-30-07 (office). *E-mail:* yablokov@ecopolicy.ru (office). *Website:* www.ras.ru (office).

YABLONOVITCH, Eli, BSc, AM, PhD; American physicist and academic; *Professor and James and Katherine Lau Chair in Engineering, Department of Electrical Engineering and Computer Sciences, University of California, Berkeley;* b. 15 Dec. 1946; ed McGill Univ., Canada, Harvard Univ.; Teaching Fellow, Harvard Univ. 1971, 1972, Asst Prof. of Applied Physics 1974–76, Assoc. Prof. 1976–79, Research Assoc. and Head of Optical Sciences Group; mem. Tech. Staff, Bell Telephone Labs 1972–74; mem. Tech. Staff, Exxon Research Center 1979–84; mem. Tech. Staff Bell Communications Research 1984–90, Distinguished Mem. of Staff 1990–93, Dir Solid State Physics Research 1991–93; Northrop-Grumman Chair Prof. of Electrical Eng, UCLA 1992–2007, Adjunct Prof. of Electrical Eng 2007–; Prof. and James and Katherine Lau Chair in Eng, Dept of Electrical Eng and Computer Sciences, Univ. of California, Berkeley 2007–, Dir NSF Center for Energy Efficient Electronics Science (E³S) 2010–; Visiting Prof., Inst. for Advanced Study, Princeton, NJ 2010–, Hong Kong Univ. of Science and Tech. 2010–; Distinguished Visiting Prof., Technion, Haifa, Israel 2012–; Founder W/PECS series of Photonic Crystal Int. Workshops 1999–; mem. NAS 2003, Nat. Acad. of Eng 2003, American Acad. of Arts and Sciences 2012; Foreign mem. Royal Soc. 2013; Fellow, Optical Soc. of America 1982, American Physical Soc. 1990, IEEE 1992; Moore Distinguished Scholar, Caltech 2003–04; Dr hc (Royal Inst. of Tech., Sweden) 2004, (Hong Kong Univ. of Science and Tech.) 2011; Alfred P. Sloan Fellow 1978–79, Adolf Lomb Medal, Optical Soc. of America 1978, IEEE/LEOS W. Streifer Scientific Achievement Award 1993, R.W. Wood Prize, Optical Soc. of America 1996, Clifford Paterson Lecturer, Royal Soc. of London 2000, Julius Springer Prize in Applied Physics 2001, Edison Lecture, Notre-Dame Univ. 2004, Anson L. Clark Memorial Lecture, Univ. of Texas, Dallas 2004, Morris Loeb Lecturer, Harvard Univ. 2005, Mountbatten Medal, Inst. of Eng and Tech. (UK) 2010, IEEE Photonics Award 2012, Harvey Prize, Technion, Israel (co-recipient) 2012, Rank Prize (UK) 2014. *Publications:* more than 200 scientific papers in professional journals; 15 patents. *Address:* 267M Cory Hall, Electrical Engineering and Computer Sciences Department, University of California, Berkeley, Berkeley, CA 94720-1770, USA (office). *Telephone:* (510) 642-6821 (office). *Fax:* (510) 666-

3409 (office). *E-mail:* eliy@eecs.berkeley.edu (office). *Website:* www.eecs.berkeley .edu (office); www.e3s-center.org (office).

YACHROUTU, Mohamed Caabi El; Comoran politician; fmr Counsellor to Pres. of Repub.; fmr Amb. to France; fmrly Vice-Pres., with responsibility for Finance, the Budget, the Economy, Foreign Trade, Investments and Privatization. *Address:* c/o Ministry of Finance, the Budget and Privatization, BP 324, Moroni, The Comoros (office).

YACOUB, Sir Magdi Habib, Kt, FRCS, FRS; Egyptian cardiac surgeon and academic; *Professor of Cardiothoracic Surgery, National Heart and Lung Institute, Imperial College London;* b. 16 Nov. 1935, Cairo; m. Marianne Yacoub; one s. two d.; ed Univ. of Cairo; Consultant Cardiothoracic Surgeon, Harefield Hosp., Middx 1969–2001, Royal Brompton Hosp. 1986–2001, British Heart Foundation Prof. of Cardiothoracic Surgery 1986–2006; Prof. of Cardiothoracic Surgery, Nat. Heart and Lung Inst., Imperial Coll. London 1986–, also Founder and Dir of Research, Harefield Heart Science Centre (Magdi Yacoub Inst.); performed first live lobe lung transplant in UK 1984; pioneered techniques of repair of complex congenital heart disease, homograft valve surgery and heart, heart-lung and lung transplantation; Founder and Pres. Chain of Hope (charity) 1995–; numerous hon. degrees including Hon. MCh (Wales) 1986, Hon. DSc (Loughborough Univ. of Tech.) 1990, (Keele) 1995, (Middx) 2002; Order of Pakistan, Order of Lebanon; WHO Prize for Humanitarian Services, Int. Soc. for Heart & Lung Transplantation Lifetime Achievement Award 2004, European Soc. of Cardiology Gold Medal 2006. *Publications:* numerous medical papers. *Leisure interest:* orchid growing. *Address:* National Heart and Lung Institute, Dovehouse Street, London, SW3 6LY, England (office). *Telephone:* (0)1895828 893 (office); (20) 7351-8534. *Fax:* (20) 7351-8229. *E-mail:* m.yacoub@imperial.ac.uk (office). *Website:* www1.imperial.ac.uk/ medicine/about/divisions/nhli (office).

YADAV, Akhilesh, BEng, MEng; Indian politician; *Chief Minister of Uttar Pradesh;* b. 1 Aug. 1973, Saifai village, Etawah Dist; s. of Mulayam Singh Yadav and Malti Devi; m. Dimple Yadav 1999; three c.; ed Dholpur Mil. School, Rajasthan, Sri Jayachamarajendra Coll. of Eng, Mysore, Univ. of Sydney, Australia; mem. 13th Lok Sabha (Parl.) from Kannauj constituency 2000–04, 14th Lok Sabha 2004–09, 15th Lok Sabha 2009–; mem. Cttee on Science and Tech., Environment & Forests, Cttee on Food, Civil Supplies and Public Distribution; Chief Minister of Uttar Pradesh 2012–; mem. Samajwadi Party. *Leisure interests:* reading, music, films, football, cricket. *Address:* Office of the Chief Minister, Government of Uttar Pradesh, Secretariat, Lucknow 226 001, India (office). *Telephone:* (522) 2239296 (office). *Fax:* (522) 2230002 (office). *E-mail:* cmup@up.nic .in (office).

YADAV, Lalu Prasad; Indian politician; b. 1948; m. Rabri Devi; elected to Lok Sabha 1977; Chief Minister of Bihar 1990–97; Leader Rashtriya Janata Dal (Nat. People's Party); Minister of Railways 2004–09. *Address:* Rashtriya Janata Dal, 13 V. P. House, Rafi Marg, New Delhi 110 011 (office); 25, Tughlak Rd, New Delhi 110 011, India; Vill. Samanpura, Bihar Veterinary College, Patna 800 014, Bihar (home). *Telephone:* (11) 23012777. *Fax:* (11) 23017986. *E-mail:* rjdal@rediffmail .com (office). *Website:* www.rashtriyajanatadal.com (office).

YADAV, Mulayam Singh, MA; Indian politician; *President, Samajwadi Party (Socialist Party);* b. 22 Nov. 1939, Safayee, Etawah Dist; s. of the late Sudhar Singh; m.; one s.; Minister of Co-operative and Animal Husbandry, UP 1977; Pres. Lok Dal 1980; Leader of the Opposition, UP Legis. Council 1982–85, of UP Legis. Ass. 1985–89; Leader Janata Dal Legis. Party UP 1989; Chief Minister of Uttar Pradesh 1989, 1993–95, 2003–07; Minister of Defence 1996–98; Founder-Pres. Samajwadi Party (Socialist Party) 1992–; Convenor Rashtriya Loktantrik Morcha (Nat. Democratic Front). *Address:* Samajwadi Party, 18 Copernicus Lane, New Delhi, India (office). *E-mail:* contact@samajwadipartyindia.com (office). *Website:* www.samajwadipartyindia.com (office).

YADAV, Ram Baran, MBBS, MD; Nepalese physician, politician and head of state; *President;* b. 4 Feb. 1948, Sapahi, Dhanusa dist; s. of the late Thani Yadav and Ramrati Yadav; ed Calcutta Medical Coll., Inst. of Medical Educ. and Research, India; worked as physician for more than two decades in hospitals in south Nepal's Terai region; joined Nepali Congress Party 1987, Gen. Sec. –2008 (resgnd); elected to House of Reps 1991, 1994; Minister for Health 1991–94; Pres. of Nepal (first elected Pres.) 2008–. *Address:* Office of the President, Kathmandu, Nepal (office).

YADAV, Ram Naresh; Indian lawyer and politician; *Governor of Madhya Pradesh;* b. 1 Aug. 1928, Azamgarh, Uttar Pradesh; m. Shanti Devi Yadav; several years' practice as lawyer, Azamgarh; fmr mem. Janata Party; mem. Indian Nat. Congress Party; mem. Lok Sabha (lower house of parl.) for Azamgarh constituency 1977; Chief Minister of Uttar Pradesh 1977–79; Gov. of Madhya Pradesh 2011–. *Address:* Office of the Governor, Raj Bhavan, Bhopal 462 003, India (office). *Telephone:* (755) 2551946 (office). *Fax:* (755) 2554711 (office). *E-mail:* rajyapal@mp .nic.in (office). *Website:* www.rajbhavanmp.ind.in (office).

YADAV, Sharad, BSc, BEE; Indian politician; *President, Janata Dal (United);* b. 1 July 1947, Babai Dist, Hoshangabad, Madhya Pradesh; m. Rekha Yadav; one s. one d.; ed Jabalpur Eng Coll.; active youth leader, took part in several mass movements; detained 1969–70, 1972, 1975; mem. Lok Sabha (Parl.) 1974–; Pres. Yuva Janata 1977, Yuva Lok Dal 1979; mem. Rajya Sabha 1986–87; Minister of Textiles and Food Processing Industries 1989–90, of Civil Aviation 1999–2001, of Labour 2001–02, of Consumer Affairs, Food and Public Distribution 2002–04; Gen. Sec. Janata Dal 1989–97, Acting Pres. 1995–97, Pres. 1997– (party merged with Lok Shakti to form Janata Dal—United 1999). *Leisure interests:* reading, music, cricket. *Address:* Janata Dal (United), 7 Jantar Mantar Road, New Delhi 110 001 (office); 7 Tughlak Road, New Delhi 110 003, India (home). *Telephone:* (11) 23368833 (office); (11) 23792738 (home). *Fax:* (11) 23368138 (office); (11) 23017118 (home).

YADAV, Upendra, BA, BL, MSc; Nepalese politician; *Chairman, Madhesi Jana Adhikar Forum Nepal;* b. 1960; joined Maoists and was briefly in dist leadership; Chair. Madhesi Jana Adhikar Forum Nepal (Madhesi People's Rights Forum Nepal) 2006–; Minister of Foreign Affairs 2008–09; Deputy Prime Minister and Minister of Foreign Affairs May–Sept. 2011. *Leisure interest:* reading books. *Address:* Madhesi Jana Adhikar Forum Nepal, Kathmandu, Nepal (office). *Telephone:* (1) 4486990; 9841764990 (mobile). *E-mail:* info@mjfn.org (office). *Website:* mprfn.org (office).

YADE, Ramatoulaye (Rama); French politician and consultant; b. 13 Dec. 1976, Dakar, Senegal; m. Joseph Zimet; one d.; ed Institut d'études politiques, Paris; immigrated to France with family 1987; Admin. Sénat Local Authorities Dept 2002–07, Deputy Dir Programmes Public Sénat (Parl. TV channel), becoming Dir of Communication 2005–07; Exec. Sec. France–W Africa Friendship Group; joined UMP (Union pour un Mouvement Populaire) 2005, UMP Nat. Sec. for Francophone Affairs 2006; Minister of State, attached to Ministry of Foreign and European Affairs, responsible for Foreign Affairs and Human Rights 2007–09; Minister-Del. for Sport 2009–10; left UMP and joined Parti Radical 2012, now Vice-Pres.; Pres. Allons Enfants! (think-tank); joined Cursus Management (consultancy), Paris 2011; Regional Adviser in Ile-de-France 2010–; Amb. of France to UNESCO 2010–11; cand. for municipal elections, Colombes 2008. *Publications include:* Noirs de France 2007, Les droits de l'homme expliqués aux enfants de 7 à 77 ans 2008, Lettre à la jeunesse 2010, Plaidoyer pour une instruction publique 2011. *Address:* Cursus Management, 242 Rue de Rivoli, 75001 Paris, France (office). *Telephone:* 1-77-35-94-45 (office). *Fax:* 1-47-03-66-45 (office). *E-mail:* contact@cursus-management.com (office). *Website:* www.cursus-management.com (office); www.allons-enfants.org; www.rama-yade.fr.

YADLIN, Aharon, BA; Israeli politician and educationalist; b. 17 April 1926, Tel-Aviv; s. of Haim Yadlin and Zipora Yadlin; m. Ada Hacohen 1950; three s.; ed Hebrew Univ.; Co-founder Kibbutz Hatzerim; fmr mem. Presidium, Israel Scouts Movement; mem. Exec. Council Histadrut (Israel Fed. of Labour) 1950–52; Prin. Beit Berl (Labour Party's Centre for Educ.) 1956–58; mem. Knesset (Parl.) 1959–79; Deputy Minister of Educ. and Culture 1964–72; Gen. Sec. Israel Labour Party 1972–74; Minister of Educ. and Culture 1974–77; Chair. Educational and Cultural Cttee, Knesset 1977–79; Chair. Beit Berl Coll. of Educ. 1977–85; Chair. Bialik Inst., Books Publishing House and Acad. for Philosophy, Jewish Studies and World Literature 1990–; Sec.-Gen. United Kibbutz Movt (TAKAM) 1985–89; Chair. Beer-Sheva Theatre, Janush Korczak Asscn in Israel, Scientific Cttee Ben Gurion Research Inst. and Archives 1979–85, Yad Tabenkin (Research Centre of Kibbutz Movt), Beith Yatziv Educational Centre, Beer-Sheva, World Labour Zionist Movt 1992–; Chair. Exec. Cttee, Ben Gurion Univ. of the Negev; lecturer and researcher in EFAL (educ. centre of TAKAM); Dr hc (Ben Gurion Univ. of the Negev) 1988. *Publications:* Introduction to Sociology 1957, The Aim and The Movement 1969, articles on sociology, educ. and youth. *Leisure interests:* stamps, gardening. *Address:* World Labour Zionist Movement, Alcharizi 9, Jerusalem (office); Kibbutz Hatzerim, Mobile Post Hanegev 85420, Israel (home). *Telephone:* 2-5671184 (office); 8-6473436 (home). *Fax:* 2-5671182 (office); 8-6473199 (home). *E-mail:* wlzm@jazo.org.il (office).

YADOV, Vladimir Aleksandrovich, DPhilSc; Russian sociologist; *Director, Research Centre of Social Transformations, Institute of Sociology, Russian Academy of Sciences;* b. 25 April 1929, Leningrad; m.; one s.; ed Leningrad State Univ., Univ. of Manchester, London School of Econs; with Inst. of Sociological Studies USSR (now Russian) Acad. of Sciences, Inst. of Social and Econ. Problems USSR (now Russian) Acad. of Sciences, Leningrad br. of Inst. of History of Nat. Sciences and Tech.; Dir, Prof. Inst. of Sociology Russian Acad. of Sciences 1986–99, now Dir Research Centre of Social Transformation; Chief Scientific Researcher 1999–; Dean, Inst. of Sociological Educ. at Repub. Centre of Humanitarian Educ. in St Petersburg 1995–; Pres. Russian Sociological Soc. 1991–; mem. Int. Sociological Asscn 1990– (Vice-Pres. 1990–94); mem. European Asscn of Experimental Social Psychology 1989–, Int. Inst. of Sociology 1990–, Centre for Social Sciences and Documentation, Vienna 1991–; Dr hc (Univs of Tartu and Helsinki). *Publications:* numerous papers on theory and methods of sociology, sociology of labour, social psychology of personality and of science. *Address:* Institute of Sociology, Research Centre of Social Transformations, Krzhizhanovskogo str. 24/35, korp 5, 117218 Moscow, Russia. *Telephone:* (495) 719-09-40 (office).

YAGHI, Omar M., PhD; American chemist and academic; *Jean Stone Professor, Department of Chemistry and Biochemistry, University of California, Los Angeles;* b. 1965, Amman, Jordan; ed Univ. of Illinois-Urbana; NSF Postdoctoral Fellow, Harvard Univ. 1990–92; mem. Faculty, Arizona State Univ. 1992–98, Univ. of Michigan 1999–2006; currently Jean Stone Prof. of Chem., UCLA; Solid State Chem., ACS and Exxon Co. 1998, Sacconi Medal, Italian Chemical Soc. 1999, listed by Popular Science Magazine amongst the 'Brilliant 10' scientists and engineers in USA for his work on hydrogen storage 2006, Hydrogen Program Award for outstanding contribs to hydrogen storage, US Dept of Energy 2007, Materials Research Soc. Medal, AAAS Newcomb Cleveland Prize for the best paper published in Science 2007, ACS Chem. of Materials Award 2009; ranked by Arabian Business amongst the Power 500: The World's Most Influential Arabs (11th) 2013. *Achievements include:* widely known for inventing several extensive classes of new materials termed metal-organic frameworks, zeolitic imidazolate frameworks and covalent organic frameworks. *Publications:* more than 130 scientific papers in professional journals on the synthesis, structure and properties of inorganic compounds and the design and construction of new crystalline materials. *Address:* Yaghi Laboratory, Department of Chemistry and Biochemistry, UCLA, 607 Charles E. Young Drive East, Los Angeles, CA 90095-1569, USA (office). *Telephone:* (310) 206-0398 (office). *Fax:* (310) 206-5891 (office). *E-mail:* yaghi@chem.ucla.edu (office). *Website:* yaghi.chem.ucla.edu (office).

YAGI, Makoto; Japanese business executive; *President, Kansai Electric Power Company Inc.;* ed Kyoto Univ.; joined Kansai Electric Power Co. Inc. in 1972, has held numerous exec. positions including Deputy Chief Dir of Electric System Business and Exec. Vice-Pres., served as Man. Dir –2010, Pres. and Dir 2010–; Chair. Fed. of Electric Power Cos of Japan. *Address:* Kansai Electric Power Co. Inc., 6-16 Nakanoshima 3-chome, Kita-ku, Osaka 530-8270, Japan (office). *Telephone:* (6) 6441-8821 (office). *Fax:* (6) 6447-7174 (office). *E-mail:* finance@kepco.co.jp (office); info@kepco.co.jp (office). *Website:* www.kepco.co.jp (office).

YAGODIN, Gennadiy Alekseyevich; Russian physical chemist and academic; *First Vice-President, International University, Moscow;* b. 3 June 1927, Vyass, Penza region; s. of Alexei Yagodin and Alexandra Yagodina; m. 1949; one s. one d.; ed Mendeleyev Chemical Tech. Inst., Moscow; mem. CPSU 1948–91; Deputy Dean, Mendeleyev Chemical Tech. Inst., Moscow 1956–59, Dean, Dept of Physical Chemistry 1959–63, Prof. of Chemical Tech. 1959–63, 1966–73, Rector 1973–85; Deputy Dir-Gen. (Head of Dept of Training and Technical Information 1963–64, Head of Dept of Technical Operations 1964–66), IAEA, Vienna 1963–66; USSR Minister of Higher and Secondary Specialized Educ. 1985–89; Chair. State Cttee for Nat. Educ. 1988–91; Rector Int. Univ. in Moscow 1992–2001, First Vice-Pres. 2001–; Head Environmental Science Dept, Mendeleyev Chemical Tech. Univ. 2002–; Deputy, USSR Supreme Soviet 1986–89; mem. Cen. Cttee CPSU 1986–89; Corresp. mem. USSR (now Russian) Acad. of Sciences 1976–; mem. Russian Acad. of Educ.; Order of Lenin; D. Y. Mendeleyev Prize 1981, USSR State Prize 1985, Koptyug Prize 2003. *Leisure interest:* collecting butterflies. *Address:* International University, Leningradsky prosp. 17, 125040 Moscow, Russia. *Telephone:* (495) 250-15-43. *Fax:* (502) 221-10-60; (495) 250-15-43 (office); (495) 332-13-15 (home). *E-mail:* yagodin@interrun.ru (office).

YAHAV, Yona, LLB; Israeli politician and lawyer; *Mayor of Haifa;* b. 9 June 1944, Haifa; ed Univ. of Jerusalem, London Univ.; served as Lt-Col in Israeli Mil. Police; mem. 14th Knesset (Parl.) 1996–1999, parl. posts included Chair. Subcommittee for Banking, mem. Constitution, Law and Justice Cttee, substitute mem., Finance Cttee; fmr Deputy and Alternating Mayor of Haifa, Mayor of Haifa 2003–; Chair. Haifa Econ. Co.; fmr Chair. Petrol and Gas Resources, Govt Co., Municipal Theatre Exec., Haifa Int. Film Festival Org.; fmr Dir-Gen. Haifa Tourist Devt Org., David Ben-Gurion Foundation; fmr Sec.-Gen. World Jewish Student Union; mem. Israel Labour Party –2006, mem. Kadima party 2006–. *Publications:* The Anatomy of the Fall of the Labor Party (with Prof. Shevach Weiss) 1977, Libel and Slander 1987. *Address:* Office of the Mayor, Municipality of Haifa, Haifa, Israel (office). *Telephone:* 4-8356767 (office). *Fax:* 4-8356020 (office). *E-mail:* haifa@haifa.muni.il (office). *Website:* www.haifa.muni.il (office).

YAK, Mary Awaj Jervase, BSc, MA; South Sudanese politician; ed Univ. of Khartoum, Univ. of Sussex, UK; fmr mem. Nat. Ass., Khartoum; worked with Sudan Council of Churches and Ministries of Finance and Econ. Planning in Khartoum and Juba; Minister of Human Resources Devt 2011, fmr Deputy Minister of Finance and Economic Planning. *Address:* c/o Ministry of Finance and Economic Planning, Ministries Complex, Juba, South Sudan (office).

YAKCOP, Tan Sri Nor Mohamed; Malaysian economist and politician; b. 24 Aug. 1947, Butterworth, Penang; m.; ed St Xavier's Inst., George Town, Univ. of Malaya, Kuala Lumpur, Leuven Catholic Univ., Belgium; worked at Bank Negara Malaysia 1968–2000, positions included Deputy Man. in 1985, Man. 1986; Special Econ. Adviser to Prime Minister Tun Dr Mahathir Mohamad 1997–98; Dir Khazanah Nasional 2002–04; Minister of Finance II 2004–09, Minister in the Prime Minister's Dept 2009–; mem. Parl. for Tasek Gelugor 2008–; mem. Exec. Cttee Nat. Econ. Action Council; mem. Bd Khazanah Berhad; mem. Barisan Nasional. *Address:* Prime Minister's Office (Jabatan Perdana Menteri), Federal Government Administration Center, Bangunan Perdana Putra, 62502 Putrajaya, Malaysia (office). *Telephone:* (3) 88888000 (office). *Fax:* (3) 88883444 (office). *E-mail:* fuad@pmo.gov.my (office). *Website:* www.pmo.gov.my (office).

YAKIŞ, Yaşar; Turkish politician; b. 1938, Akçakoca; m.; one c.; ed Ankara Univ.; joined Ministry of Foreign Affairs 1962; Councillor, Turkish Embassy, Damascus, Syria 1980; est. OIC's Standing Cttee for Econ. and Commercial Co-operation 1985; Amb. to Saudi Arabia 1988–92; Deputy Under-Sec., Ministry of Foreign Affairs, responsible for Econ. Affairs 1992–95; Amb. to Egypt 1995–98; Perm. Rep. to UN, Vienna 1998–2002; Minister of Foreign Affairs 2002–03; Chair. EU Cttee in Turkish Parl. 2003–; Decoration of King Abdul Aziz, Saudi Arabia 1992. *Address:* AB Uyum Komisyonu TBMM, Ankara, Turkey (office). *Telephone:* (312) 420-54-01 (office). *Fax:* (312) 420-54-03 (office). *E-mail:* abuyum@tbmm.gov.tr (office). *Website:* www.tbmm.gov.tr (office).

YAKORO, Rémi; Central African Republic economist and government official; *Minister of Finance and the Budget;* ed Univ. Félix Houphouët-Boigny, Abidjan, Côte d'Ivoire; several years with Direction Générale des Douanes (Directorate-Gen. of Customs) including as Inspector of Taxes 2008, Dir-Gen. of Customs and Excise 2013–14; Minister of Finance and the Budget 2014–. *Address:* Ministry of Finance and the Budget, BP 696, Bangui, Central African Republic (office). *Telephone:* 21-61-38-05 (office).

YAKOVENKO, Alexander Vladimirovich, DIur, CandJurSc; Russian diplomat; *Ambassador to UK;* b. 1954, Homel, Byelorussian SSR, USSR; m.; one d.; ed Moscow State Inst. of Int. Relations; joined Foreign Services 1976, served with USSR Mission to UN, New York 1981–86, Head of Div., Dept on Security and Co-operation in Europe, Ministry of Foreign Affairs, Russian Fed. 1986–92, Deputy Dir Dept of Int. Scientific and Technological Cooperation 1993–95, Deputy Dir Dept on Problems of Security and Disarmament, Ministry of Foreign Affairs 1995–97, Perm. Rep. to Int. Orgs, Vienna 1997–2000, Dir Information and Press Dept, Ministry of Foreign Affairs 2000–04, Deputy Minister of Foreign Affairs 2005–11, Amb. to UK 2011–; Head of Russian del. to intergovernmental negotiations on Int. Space Station 1993–98; mem. Russian Acad. of Natural Sciences, Space Council of the Russian Acad. of Sciences, Int. Inst. of Space Law, Int. Acad. of Astronautics; Corresp. mem. Tatarstan Acad. of Sciences. *Publications:* several books and a manual on int. law; more than 150 publs on int. relations and Russian foreign policy, science, education and cultural issues. *Address:* Russian Embassy, 13 Kensington Palace Gardens, London, W8 4QX, England (office). *Telephone:* (20) 7229-3620 (office); (20) 7229-8625 (office). *Fax:* (20) 7229-5804 (office); (20) 7727-8625 (office). *E-mail:* info@rusemb.org.uk (office); office@rusemblon.org (office). *Website:* www.rusemb.org.uk (office).

YAKOVLEV, Aleksandr Maksimovich, DJur; Russian lawyer; *Rector, New Moscow Law Institute;* b. 30 Aug. 1927, Leningrad; s. of Maxim Yakovlev and Maria Yakovleva; m. Eugenia Yakovleva 1950; ed Moscow Inst. of Law; sr research fellow Inst. of Law, USSR Ministry of Internal Affairs, then USSR Ministry of Justice 1957–75; Head Dept of Criminal Law and Criminology USSR (now Russian) Inst. of State and Law, Prof. 1975–94, Chief Researcher 1996–; in democratic movt since late 1980s; USSR People's Deputy 1989–91; mem. Perm.

Cttee on Legis. USSR Supreme Soviet 1989–91; Plenipotentiary Rep. of Pres. of Russia at Federal Ass. 1994–96, Expert to Council of Fed. 1997–; Rector New Moscow Law Inst. 1998–; Visiting Prof. Univ. of Manitoba 1990, Rutgers Univ. 1991, Alberta Univ., New York and Toronto Univ. 1992, Emory Univ. Atlanta 1993, 1997; mem. Bd of Dirs Int. Soc. of Social Defence, Paris, UN Cttee Against Torture 1994, Inst. of Sociology of Law for Europe; Hon. LLD (Alberta Univ., Canada) 1991; Merited Lawyer of Russia. *Publications:* The Bear That Wouldn't Dance: Failed Attempts to Reform the Former Constitution of the Soviet Union (with Dale Gibson) 1992, Striving for Law in a Lawless Land 1995, Sociology of Crime 2000, The Social Structure of Society 2003; several other books and more than 100 articles on various aspects of constitutional law, publs in journals. *Leisure interest:* travelling. *Address:* Dolgorukovskaya str. 40, Apt. 153, 127030 Moscow (home); Pogonnyi pz. 78, 107504 Moscow, Russia (office). *Telephone:* (495) 978-84-97 (office). *Fax:* (495) 734-56-03 (office). *E-mail:* yakovlev.27@mail.ru (home).

YAKOVLEV, Veniamin Fedorovich, DJur; Russian politician and lawyer; b. 12 Feb. 1932, Petukhovo, Kurgan Region; s. of Fedor Kuzmich Yakovlev and Domna Pavlovna Yakovleva; m. Galina Ivanovna Yakovleva 1956; two d.; ed Sverdlovsk Inst. of Law; mem. CPSU 1956–91; teacher, then Dir Yakut School of Law 1953–56; Asst Procurator/Attorney-Gen. of Yakut Autonomous Repub. 1956–60; aspirant, teacher, docent, Dean, Pro-Rector Sverdlovsk Inst. of Law 1960–87; Dir All-Union Research Inst. of Soviet Legis. 1987–89; Deputy Chair. Public Comm. of Int. Co-operation on Humanitarian Problems and Human Rights 1988; USSR Minister of Justice 1989–90; Chair. USSR Supreme Arbitration Court 1991, Supreme Arbitration Court of Russian Fed. 1992–. *Publications:* Civil Law Method of Regulation for Social Relations and more than 150 other publs. *Leisure interests:* skiing and other sports. *Address:* Supreme Arbitration Court, Maly Kharitonyevski 12, 101000 Moscow, Russia. *Telephone:* (495) 208-11-19. *Fax:* (495) 208-44-00.

YAKOVLEV, Vladimir Anatolyevich, CandEconSc; Russian politician; b. 25 Nov. 1944, Olekminsk, Yakutia; m. Irina Ivanovna Yakovleva; one s.; ed NW Polytech. Inst.; master on construction sites, Head Repair-Construction Trust 1965–80, Deputy Man. Housing Dept, Leningrad (St Petersburg) 1980–93; First Deputy Mayor of St Petersburg, Russia. Head Cttee on Man. of Municipal Econ. 1993–96; Mayor (Gov.) of St Petersburg 1996–2003; Deputy Chair. (Deputy Prime Minister) Govt of the Russian Fed. 2003–04; Rep. of the Pres. in the S Fed. Dist 2004–05; Minister of Regional Development 2005–07; mem. Council of Fed. of Russia 1996–2001; Pres. Ass. of Heads of Regions and Repubs of NW Russia 1997; Pres. Basketball Club Spartacus; Founder and Leader of Vsya Rossiya Movt 1999; Pres. Fed. of Bicycle Sports of St Petersburg; Order of Honour 2000; Merited Constructor of Russia. *Address:* c/o Ministry of Regional Development, ul. Sadovaya-Samotechnaya, 103059 Moscow, Russia.

YAKOVLEV, Gen. Vladimir Nikolayevich, CAND.MIL.SC.; Russian army officer; b. 17 Aug. 1954, Tver; s. of Nikolai Vassilyevich Yakovlev and Erika Alexeyevna Yakovleva; m. Raisa Anatolyevna Yakovleva; two d.; ed Dzerzhinsky Mil. Acad., Mil. Acad. of Gen. Staff; served with strategic rocket forces incl. Commdr rocket regt 1985–89; Deputy Commdr rocket div. 1989–91, Commdr 1991–93; Head of Staff Rocket Army 1993–94, Commdr 1994–97; Head of Gen. Staff Rocket Troops Jan. 1999; C-in-C Rocket Strategic Forces of Russian Fed. 1997–2001; Head of Staff for Co-ordination of Mil. Co-operation within CIS 2001; Prof. Acad. of Mil. Sciences; mem. Russian Acad. of Eng; corresp. mem. Russian Acad. of Rocket and Artillery Sciences; Order of Red Star, Order for Mil. Service, Prize of Russian Pres. for Achievement in Educ. 1998. *Publications include:* Military Work: Science, Art, Vocation 1998, Organizational Activities of General Staff in Rocket Strategic Forces 1999, Rocket Shield of the Motherland 1999, co-author Mil. Encyclopaedic Dictionary of Rocket Strategic Forces. *Leisure interests:* music, reading, tennis, swimming. *Address:* c/o Ministry of Defence, Bolshaya Pirogovskaya str. 23, K-160 Moscow, Russia.

YAKUNIN, Gleb Pavlovich; Russian politician and ecclesiastic; b. 4 March 1934; m.; one s. two d.; ed Irkutsk Inst. of Agriculture, Moscow Theological Seminary; sexton, Minister in Zaraisk, Dmitrov; expelled from Moscow Theological Seminary and deprived of the right to be a minister for public protest against collaboration of church admin. with CP; Founder and Leader Christian Cttee for Protection of Believers; sentenced to five years' imprisonment and five-year term of exile for anti-Soviet propaganda 1979; then Minister in St Nicholas Church, Shchelykovo Village, Moscow Region; exonerated 1991; active participant of Movt for Democratic Russia, Co-Chair. Coordination Council; People's Deputy of Russia 1990–93; fmr mem. Supreme Soviet of Russia; Chair. Cttee for Protection of Freedom of Conscience 1996; excommunicated by Holy Synod for political activities Dec. 1993; mem. State Duma (Parl.) 1993–95; Chair. L. Tolstoy Cttee for Defence of Freedom of Conscience. *Address:* Bolshoy Golovin per. 22, 103045 Moscow, Russia. *Telephone:* (495) 207-60-69. *Fax:* (495) 207-60-69.

YAKUNIN, Vladimir I., PhD; Russian transport industry executive; *President and CEO, Russian Railways OAO (Rossiiskiye zheleznyye dorogi—RZhD);* b. 30 June 1948, Zakharovo, Vladimir prov.; m.; two s.; ed Leningrad Mechanical Inst.; Jr Research Asst, State Inst. of Applied Chem. 1972–75; mil. service 1975–77; worked for Cttee on Foreign Econ. Relations, USSR Ministerial Council 1977–82; Chief of Foreign Dept, Inst. of Physics and Technics, USSR Acad. of Sciences 1982–85; Second then First Sec., Perm. Rep. to UN, New York 1985–91; Co-founder and Chair. Cttee of Dirs CJSC Int. Center For Business Partnership 1991–97; Head North-Western Revision, Chief Control Dept of Pres. of Russian Fed. 1997–2000; Deputy Minister of Transport 2000–02; First Deputy Minister of Transport 2002–03; First Vice-Pres. Russian Railways OAO (Rossiiskiye zheleznyye dorogi—RZhD) 2003–05, Pres. and CEO 2005–; Chair. Bd Trustees, Centre of Nat. Glory, Andrew the First-Called Foundation; mem. Council of Co-Chair. World Public Forum—Dialogue of Civilizations, Vienna; Order of Saint Equal-to-the-Apostles Grand Duke Vladimir (Second Degree), Russian Orthodox Church, Order for Merit to the Fatherland of the Fourth Class, Medal for Mil. Merit and Medal for the Development of Railways, Orders of the Russian Orthodox Church: Order of St Seraphim of Sarov (Second Class), Order of Venerable Andrew Rublyov (First Class), Order of Honour of the Russian Muftis Council (First Class); Order of the Holy Sepulchre of the Jerusalem Orthodox Church, Chevalier, Légion d'honneur, Decoration of Honour for Services to the Repub. of Austria, Order of Friendship

(Order Dostyk) of the Repub. of Kazakhstan, Grande Ufficiale, Ordine al Merito della Repubblica Italiana. *Address:* Russian Railways OAO (Rossiiskiye zheleznyye dorogi—RZhD), 107174 Moscow, ul. Novobasmannaya 2, Russia (office). *Telephone:* (495) 262-10-02 (office). *Fax:* (495) 262-90-95 (office). *E-mail:* info@rzd .ru (office). *Website:* www.rzd.ru (office); v-yakunin.livejournal.com.

YAM, Joseph C. K., CBE, BSc; Hong Kong banker; b. 9 Sept. 1948, Canton, China; s. of Shun Yam and Hok-chun Shum; m. Grace Fong 1972; one s. one d.; ed Univ. of Hong Kong, Inst. of Social Studies, The Hague, Netherlands; Demonstrator in Econs, Econs Dept, Univ. of Hong Kong 1970–71; statistician, Census and Statistics Dept, Hong Kong Govt 1971–76, economist, Econ. Services Br. 1976–77, Sr Economist 1977–79, Prin. Asst Sec. (Econ. Services) 1979–82, (Monetary Affairs) 1982–85, Deputy Sec. for Monetary Affairs 1985–91; Dir Office of the Exchange Fund 1991–93; Chief Exec. Hong Kong Monetary Authority 1993–2009; Hon. DScS (Hong Kong Univ.) 2008, Hon. DBA (Hong Kong Univ. of Science and Tech.) 2009; Banker of the Year in Hong Kong 1995. *Leisure interests:* golf, horse racing, swimming, hiking. *Address:* c/o Hong Kong Monetary Authority, 30/F, 3 Garden Road, Central, Hong Kong Special Administrative Region, People's Republic of China.

YAM, Vivian Wing-Wah, BSc, PhD, CChem, FRSC; Hong Kong chemist and academic; *Chair of Chemistry and Philip Wong Wilson Wong Professor in Chemistry and Energy, University of Hong Kong;* ed Univ. of Hong Kong; mem. Faculty, City Polytechnic of Hong Kong 1988–90; joined Dept of Chem., Univ. of Hong Kong 1990, Chair of Chem. and Prof. 1999–, Head of Chem. Dept 2000–05, Philip Wong Wilson Wong Prof. in Chem. and Energy 2009–; Academician, Chinese Acad. of Sciences; Croucher Foundation Sr Research Fellow 2000–01; RSC Chartered Scientist; Fellow, TWAS, The World Acad. of Sciences; RSC Centenary Lectureship and Medal, L'Oréal-UNESCO Women in Science Award (Asia/Pacific) 2011, Lectureship Award for Asian and Oceanian Photochemist (Eikohsha Award), Japanese Photochemistry Asscn, State Natural Science Award (Second Class Prize), Prize for Scientific and Technological Progress, Ho Leung Ho Lee Foundation. *Address:* Room 504, Chong Yuet Ming Chemistry Building, University of Hong Kong, Pokfulam Road, Hong Kong Special Administrative Region, People's Republic of China (office). *Telephone:* (852) 2859-2153 (office). *E-mail:* wwyam@hku.hk (office). *Website:* www.chemistry.hku.hk (office).

YAMADA, Tadataka (Tachi), BA, MD; American physician, academic and foundation executive; *President, Global Health Program, Bill and Melinda Gates Foundation;* b. Japan; ed Stanford Univ., New York Univ. School of Medicine; emigrated to USA at age 15; started career in Dept of Gastroenterology, UCLA; Chief of Gastroenterology then Chair. Dept of Internal Medicine and Physician-in-Chief, Univ. of Mich. Medical Center 1989–99, now Adjunct Prof. of Internal Medicine, Univ. of Mich. Medical School; mem. Bd of Dirs SmithKline Beecham (now GlaxoSmithKline) 1994–2006, Pres. SmithKline Beecham Healthcare Services 1996–99, Chair. Research and Devt, Pharmaceuticals 1999–2001, Chair. of Research and Devt 2001–06; Pres. Global Health Program, Bill and Melinda Gates Foundation 2006–; mem. Bd of Dirs Research!America; Trustee Rockefeller Brothers Fund; mem. Advisory Bd Quaker BioVentures, Inc.; Sr Advisor Frazier Healthcare Ventures 2006–; mem. Pres.'s Council of Advisors on Science and Tech. 2004–; mem. Advisory Cttee to Dir NIH 2004–; fmr Pres. Asscn of American Physicians, American Gastroenterological Asscn; Master, American Coll. of Physicians; mem. Inst. of Medicine, NAS, Acad. of Medical Sciences (UK); fmr mem. American Bd of Medical Examiners; numerous awards including Distinguished Achievement Award in Gastrointestinal Physiology, American Physiological Soc., Friedenwald Medal, American Gastroenterological Asscn, Distinguished Faculty Achievement Award, Univ. of Mich. and Distinguished Medical Scientist Award, Medical Coll. of Va. *Publications:* Textbook of Gastroenterology (ed.), Yamada Textbook of Medicine (ed.). *Address:* Global Health Program, Bill and Melinda Gates Foundation, POB 23350, Seattle, WA 98102, USA (office). *Telephone:* (206) 709-3100 (office). *E-mail:* info@gatesfoundation.org (office). *Website:* www.gatesfoundation.org/GlobalHealth (office).

YAMADA, Noboru; Japanese business executive; *Representative Director, Chairperson and CEO, Yamada Denki Company Ltd;* left JVC to start own business 1976, Yamada Denki Co. Ltd f. 1983, listed on JASDAQ 1989, started business as Internet service provider 1996, promoted to first section of Tokyo Stock Exchange 2000, acquired Daikuma from Ito Yokado as subsidiary 2002, opened Tecc Land Gushikawa store in Gushikawa (now Uruma), Okinawa 2004, first city-based store, main Hiroshima store, opened 2004, invested in Kouziro Co. Ltd, Owner of Shopland PC 2004, first Japanese specialist store or consumer electronics store to record consolidated sales in excess of 1 trillion yen 2005, entered business alliance (and capital alliance) with Kyūshū-based consumer electronics retailer, Shōichi Denki 2006, moved co. HQ from Maebashi to new Takasaki store 2007, cos in group include Daikuma (discount store in the southern Kantō area), Minami Kyūshū Yamada Denki Co. Ltd, Okinawa Yamada Denki Co. Ltd, Kansai Yamada Denki Co. Ltd, Chūgoku/Shikoku Tecc Land, Cosmos Berry's. *Address:* Yamada Denki Co. Ltd, 4-40-11 Hiyoshi-cho, Maebashi 371-0017, Gunma, Japan (office). *Telephone:* (2) 7233-5522 (office). *Fax:* (2) 7233-3309 (office); (2) 7233-3568 (office). *E-mail:* info@yamada-denki.jp (office). *Website:* www.yamada-denki.jp (office).

YAMAGUCHI, Kenji, MA (Econs); Japanese government official and economist; *Representative, WELL (World Economy and Land Laboratory);* b. 19 July 1933, Yamagata; s. of Futao Yamaguchi and Yoshi Yamaguchi; m. Momoe Matsumoto 1962; one s. one d.; ed Univ. of Tokyo; entered Budget Bureau, Ministry of Finance 1956; Nat. Tax Admin. Agency 1963; Ministry of Interior 1966; Econ. Planning Agency 1968; First Sec. Okinawa Reversion Preparatory Cttee, Foreign Minister's Office and Counsellor, Okinawa Bureau, Prime Minister's Office 1969; Int. Finance Bureau, Ministry of Finance 1971; Consul for Japan, Sydney 1972; Counsellor, Personnel Bureau, Prime Minister's Office 1975; Finance Bureau, Ministry of Finance 1977; Dir-Gen. North East Japan Finance Bureau, Ministry of Finance 1981; Special Asst to Minister of Foreign Affairs 1982–87; Exec. Dir for Japan, IBRD and affiliates 1982–87, Dean IBRD Bd 1985–87; Sr Exec. Dir Water Resources Devt Public Corpn 1988–; Co-ordination Leader, Org. for Industry, Science and Cultural Advancement (OISCA) 1987–99; Exec. Adviser Mitsui Trust Bank, Tokyo 1993–97; Chair. Mitsui Trust Int. Ltd, London 1993–97, Mitsui Trust Bank Ltd, Switzerland 1993–97; Exec. Adviser Chiyoda Mutual Life Insurance

Co., Tokyo 1997–99; f. WELL (World Economy and Land Lab.) a think-tank seeking a balanced relationship between the nat. econ. and land ownership 1998; Human Life Rescue Award 1954, Zuihou Chuujushou conferred by the Emperor 2004. *Publications:* The World Bank – How Can Japan Contribute to the World? 1988, Land Policy for Prosperity – Land as Public Property 1997, Land is to be Owned by the Public 2000, A Cool Observation on the Japanese Economy 2006; and several books on financial matters, foreign affairs, etc. *Leisure interests:* reading, swimming, music. *Address:* 3-16-43 Utsukushiga-Oka, Aoba-ku, Yokohama City 225-0002, Japan. *Telephone:* (45) 901-7309. *Fax:* (45) 901-7309. *E-mail:* well@mx7.ttcn.ne.jp (office). *Website:* www2.ttcn.ne.jp/~well (office).

YAMAGUCHI, Masanori; Japanese business executive; *President and CEO, Sun Corporation;* Vice-Pres., then Pres. Kinki Nippon Railway Co. –2004, Chair. Kinki Nippon Tourist Co. Ltd (now KNT-CT Holdings Co. Ltd) 2008–; Man. Dir Kintetsu Corpn 1993–97, Sr Man. Dir 1997–98, Chief of Secr. Office 1998–99, Vice-Pres. 1999–2003, CEO and Pres. 2003–07, Chair. 2007–, Chair. Kintetsu Department Store Co. Ltd 2007–; fmr Pres. Origin Electric Shoji Co. Ltd; Dir, Sr Man. Dir Sun Corpn from 2008, Dir, Pres. and CEO 2012–; Chair. CelleBrite USA Corpn, Kintetsu World Express, Inc., Wakayama Kintetsu Department Store Co. Ltd; Adviser, KNT-CT Holdings Co. Ltd 2013–; mem. Bd of Dirs Int. Business Org. of Osaka Inc., Asahi Broadcasting Corpn 2007–, Nippon Pallet Pool Co. Ltd 2007–; External Dir, KNT-CT Holdings Co. Ltd 2002–. *Address:* Sun Corporation, 250 Asahi Konan, Aichi 483-8555, Japan (office). *Fax:* (5) 8755-3851 (office). *E-mail:* info@sun-denshi.co.jp (office). *Website:* www.sun-denshi.co.jp (office).

YAMAGUCHI, Nobuo; Japanese business executive; Chair. and Rep. Dir Asahi Kasei Corpn (changed name from Asahi Chemical Industry Co. Ltd 2000) –2010, Hon. Chair. April–Sept. 2010; Chair. Japan Chamber of Commerce and Industry 2001–, Tokyo Chamber of Commerce and Industry from 2001; Dir Asahi Breweries Ltd from 2004, Nippon Television Network Corpn; mem. Pacific Basin Econ. Council. *Address:* c/o Asahi Kasei Corporation, Hibiya-Mitsui Building, 1-1-2 Yurakucho, Chiyoda-ku, Tokyo 100-8440, Japan. *E-mail:* info@asahi-kasei.co.jp.

YAMAGUCHI, Yutaka; Japanese business executive; ed Univ. of Tokyo; joined Bank of Japan as staff economist 1964, spent most of career in policy planning and policy-related research areas, experiences at sr man. level included being Bank of Japan's Chief Rep. in New York 1989–91, Dir of Research and Statistics 1991–92, of Policy Planning 1992–96, Exec. Dir 1996–98, Deputy Gov. 1998–2003 (retd); also chaired Cttee for Global Financial System, Basel, Switzerland 1998–2003; currently advises Japanese and int. firms on econ. and policy devts; mem. Group of Thirty Consultative Group on Int. Econ. and Monetary Affairs, Inc. (G-30), Washington, DC, Keizai Doyukai (a leading business group in Japan). *Address:* c/o The Group of Thirty, 1726 M Street, NW, Suite 200, Washington, DC 20036, USA.

YAMAMOTO, Keith R., BSc, PhD; American biochemist, academic and writer; ed Iowa State Univ., Princeton Univ., Univ. of California, San Francisco; Asst Prof. of Biochemistry, Univ. of California, San Francisco 1976–79, Assoc. Prof. of Biochemistry 1979–83, Prof. of Biochemistry 1983–, Vice-Chair. 1985–94, Dept of Biochemistry and Biophysics, Dir of Biochemistry and Molecular Biology Program in Biological Sciences 1988, now Prof. of Cellular and Molecular Pharmacology, Chair. Dept of Cellular and Molecular Pharmacology 1994–2003, currently Vice Chancellor for Research, Exec. Vice Dean, School of Medicine, Prin. Investigator, Yamamoto Lab; Chair. Coalition for Life Sciences, NAS Bd on Life; Founding Ed., Molecular Biology of the Cell; Program mem., Univ. of California, San Francisco Comprehensive Cancer; mem. Univ. of California, San Francisco Biomedical Sciences Program; mem. Herbert Boyer Program in Biological Sciences. *Publications include:* co-author: Gene Wars: Military Control over the New Genetic Technologies 1988, Transcriptional Regulation: Monograph 22 1992; contrib. to numerous academic publications. *Address:* Cellular and Molecular Pharmacology, University of California, San Francisco, Mission Bay, 600 16th Street, GH-S574, San Francisco, CA 94143-2280, USA (office). *Telephone:* (415) 476-3240 (office). *Fax:* (415) 514-4112 (office). *E-mail:* yamamoto@cmp.ucsf.edu (office). *Website:* yamamotolab.ucsf.edu (office).

YAMAMOTO, Masami; Japanese business executive; *President and Representative Director, Fujitsu Ltd;* joined Fujitsu 1976, Corp. Vice-Pres. Fujitsu Ltd –2007, Corp. Sr Vice-Pres. 2007–10, Corp. Sr Exec. Vice-Pres. 2007–10, Pres. and Rep. Dir, Fujitsu Ltd 2010–, also Corp. Vice-Pres. Fujitsu Microelectronics Ltd, Dir of Fujitsu Technology Solutions (Holding) BV, Dir at Fujitsu Laboratories Ltd 2010–. *Address:* Fujitsu Headquarters, Shiodome City Centre, 1-5-2 Higashi-Shimbashi, Minato-ku, Tokyo 105-7123, Japan (office). *Telephone:* (3) 6252-2220 (office). *Fax:* (3) 6252-2783 (office). *E-mail:* info@fujitsu.com (office). *Website:* www.fujitsu.com (office).

YAMAMOTO, Yohji; Japanese fashion designer; b. 3 Oct. 1943, Tokyo; one d.; ed Keio Univ. and Bunkafukuso Gakuin School of Fashion, Tokyo; launched first collection Tokyo 1977, Paris 1981, New York 1982, first menswear collection, Paris 1984; costume designer for Opéra de Lyon's production of Madame Butterfly 1990, Wagner Opera's production of Tristan und Isolde, Bayreuth 1993, Kanagawa Art Festival Opera Susanoo 1994; launched first perfume Yohji 1996, second perfume Yohji Essential 1998; participant in 25th Anniversary of Pina Bausch Co., Wuppertal 1998; launched first perfume Yohji Homme 1999; designed costumes for the Ryuichi Sakamoto Opera 'Life' 1999; subject of Wim Wenders' film Notebook on Cities and Clothes 1989; designed costumes for Dir Takeshi Kitano's films, Dolls and Zatoichi; debut of Y-3 line 2003; designs costumes for Elton John's The Red Piano show in Las Vegas 2003; invited to curate second issue of A MAGAZINE curated by 2005; co. restructured following debts 2009–10; Yohji Yamamoto Fund for Peace est. to foster devt of China's fashion industry and to help heal China–Japan relations 2008; Chevalier des Arts et des Lettres 1994, Medal of Honour with Purple Ribbon, Chevalier, Ordre nat. du Mérite; So-en Award, Endo Award 1969, Fashion Eds Club Award, Tokyo 1982, 1991, 1997, Mainichi Fashion Award, Tokyo 1986, 1994, Night of Stars Award Fashion Group, New York 1997, Arte e Moda Award, Pitti Imagine, Florence 1998, Int. Award Council of Fashion Designers of America 1999, Royal Designer for Industry, Master of Design Award, Fashion Group International. *Publication:* Talking to Myself. *Address:* Yohji Yamamoto Inc., 133 2-2-43 Higashi-Shinagawa, Shinagawa-ku, Tokyo 140-0002, Japan (office). *E-mail:* info@yohjiyamamoto.co.jp (office). *Website:* www.yohjiyamamoto.co.jp (office).

YAMAMOTO, Yuji, BA; Japanese politician; b. 11 May 1952; ed Waseda Univ.; began career as lawyer; mem. Kochi Prefectural Ass. 1985–90; mem. House of Reps for Kochi Pref. constituency 1990–, State Sec. for Home Affairs 1996, State Sec. for Justice 1999, 2000, Chair. House of Reps Cttee on Economy, Trade and Industry 2001, Cttee on Judicial Affairs 2002, Sr Vice-Minister of Finance 2003, Minister of State for Financial Services 2006–07; Acting Dir Judicial Affairs Div., Policy Research Council, LDP 1995, mem. LDP Gen. Council 1997–, Dir Infrastructure Div., Policy Research Council 1998, Exec. Deputy Sec.-Gen., LDP 2000–. *Address:* Liberal-Democratic Party (Jiyu-Minshuto), 1-11-23, Nagata-cho, Chiyoda-ku, Tokyo 100-8910, Japan (office). *Telephone:* (3) 3581-6211 (office). *E-mail:* koho@ldp.jimin.or.jp (office). *Website:* www.jimin.jp (office).

YAMANAKA, Shinya, MD, PhD; Japanese medical scientist and academic; *Director, Center for iPS Cell Research and Application, Kyoto University;* b. 4 Sept. 1962, Higashiōsaka; ed Kobe Univ., Osaka City Univ. Grad. School; resident in orthopedic surgery, Nat. Osaka Hosp. 1987–89; postgraduate studies 1989–93; Post-doctoral Fellow, Gladstone Inst. for Cardiovascular Disease, San Francisco, USA 1993–95, Staff Research Investigator 1995–96, currently Sr Investigator and L.K. Whittier Foundation Investigator in Stem Cell Biology; Asst Prof., Osaka City Univ. Medical School 1996–99; Assoc. Prof., Nara Inst. of Science and Tech., Nara 1999–2003, Prof. 2003–05; Prof., Inst. for Frontier Medical Sciences, Kyoto Univ. 2004–10, Prof., Inst. for Integrated Cell-Material Sciences (iCeMS) 2007–12, Dir Centre for iPS Cell Research and Application (CiRA), iCeMS 2008–10, Dir Centre for iPS Cell Research and Application (CiRA) 2010–, Prof., Centre for iPS Cell Research and Application (CiRA) 2012–; Prof. of Anatomy, Univ. of California, San Francisco; Pres. Int. Soc. for Stem Cell Research 2012–13; Fellow, NAS 2012; Medal of Honour with Purple Ribbon 2008, Bunka-kunsho (Order of Culture) 2012; Hon. DSc (Mount Sinai School of Medicine) 2010; Prize of the Japan Soc. for the Promotion of Science 2007, Asahi Award 2007, Inoue Prize for Science 2007, Special Prize for Science and Tech., Minister of Educ., Culture, Sports, Science and Tech. 2008, Shaw Prize (co-recipient) 2008, Robert Koch Award 2008, Gairdner International Award 2009, Gairdner Award 2009, Albert Lasker Basic Medical Research Award 2009, Kyoto Prize for Advanced Tech. (co-recipient) 2010, March of Dimes Prize 2010, The Imperial Prize, The Japan Acad. 2010, Balzan Prize 2010, Frontiers of Knowledge Award, BBVA Foundation 2010, Wolf Prize in Medicine 2011, McEwen Award for Innovation (co-recipient) 2011, King Faisal Int. Prize in Medicine (co-recipient) 2011, Millennium Tech. Prize (co-recipient) 2012, Nobel Prize in Physiology or Medicine (with Sir John Gurdon) 2012, Breakthrough Prize in Life Sciences (co-recipient) 2013. *Achievements include:* discovered how to make induced pluripotent stem cells (iPS cells) from ordinary skin cells. *Publications:* numerous articles in professional journals. *Address:* Center for iPS Cell Research and Application (CiRA), Kyoto University, 53 Kawahara-cho, Shogoin Yoshida, Sakyo-ku, Kyoto 606-8507, Japan (office). *Telephone:* (75) 366-7000 (office). *Fax:* (75) 366-7023 (office). *E-mail:* yamanaka-g@cira.kyoto-u.ac.jp (office). *Website:* www.cira.kyoto-u.ac.jp/e/research/yamanaka_master.html (office).

YAMANI, Sheikh Ahmed Zaki; Saudi Arabian government official and oil industry executive; b. 30 June 1930, Mecca; ed Cairo Univ., New York and Harvard Univs, USA; Saudi Arabian Govt Service; pvt. law practice; Legal Adviser to Council of Ministers 1958–60; mem. Council of Ministers 1960–86; Minister of State 1960–62; Minister of Petroleum and Mineral Resources 1962–86; Dir Arabian American Oil Co. 1962–86; Chair. General Petroleum and Mineral Org. (PETROMIN) 1963–86, Coll. of Petroleum and Minerals, Dhahran 1963–86, Saudi Arabian Fertilizer Co. (SAFCO) 1966–86; f. Centre for Global Energy Studies; Sec.-Gen. OAPEC 1968–69, Chair. 1974–75; mem. several int. law asscns; state decorations from many countries; Dr hc from univs in N and S America, Europe, Asia and Africa. *Publication:* Islamic Law and Contemporary Issues. *Address:* PO Box 14850, Jeddah 21434, Saudi Arabia.

YAMANI, Hashim ibn Abdullah ibn Hashim al-, PhD; Saudi Arabian politician; b. 1945; ed Harvard Univ., USA; Prof. and later Chair. of Physics Dept, King Fahd Univ. of Petroleum and Minerals; Vice-Pres. King Abdul Aziz City for Science; Minister of Industry and Electricity 1995–2003, Minister of Commerce and Industry 2003–08; Chair. Sabic. *Address:* c/o Ministry of Commerce and Industry, POB 1774, Airport Road, Riyadh 11162, Saudi Arabia.

YAMANISHI, Kenichiro; Japanese business executive; *Representative Executive Officer, President and CEO, Mitsubishi Electric Corporation;* b. 1951, Osaka Pref.; joined Mitsubishi Electric Corpn 1975, first served as a researcher in Applied Equipment Lab., Exec. Officer and Group Pres. of Corp. Total Productivity Man. and Environmental Programs 2006–08, Sr Exec. Officer and Group Pres. of Semiconductor & Devices 2008–10, Rep. Exec. Officer, Pres. and CEO Mitsubishi Electric Corpn 2010–. *Address:* Mitsubishi Electric Corpn, Tokyo Bldg, 2-7-3, Marunouchi, Chiyoda-ku, Tokyo 100-8310, Japan (office). *Telephone:* (3) 3218-2111 (office). *E-mail:* info@mitsubishi.com (office). *Website:* global.mitsubishielectric.com (office); www.mitsubishi.com (office).

YAMANOUCHI, Takashi; Japanese automotive industry executive; *Chairman and Representative Director, Mazda Motor Corporation;* b. 10 Jan. 1945; joined Toyo Kogyo Co. Ltd (renamed Mazda Motor Corpn) 1967, Gen. Man. Corp. Planning Div. 1996, Dir 1996–97, Man. Dir 1997–99, Sr Man. Dir 1999–2002, Sr Man. Exec. Officer of Corp. Liaison, Purchasing, Human Resources, Admin, Secr. and Global Auditing 2002–07, Dir and Exec. Vice-Pres. April–June 2007, Exec. Vice-Pres. and Rep. Dir June 2007–08, Rep. Dir, Pres. and CEO 2008–13, Chair. and Rep. Dir 2010–; Order of the Aztec Eagle (Mexico) 2013. *Address:* Mazda Motor Corpn, 3-1 Shinchi, Fuchu-cho, Aki-gun, Hiroshima 730-8670, Japan (office). *Telephone:* (82) 282-1111 (office). *Fax:* (82) 287-5190 (office). *E-mail:* info@mazda.com (office). *Website:* www.mazda.com (office).

YAMASHITA, Ryuichi; Japanese automobile industry executive; ed Tohoku Univ.; joined Yamaha 1962, Sr Gen. Man. Automotive Engine operation 1983–2001, apptd Dir 1983, Exec. Vice-Pres. 2001, then Chair. Yamaha Motor Co. Ltd –2005, Dir and Corp. Adviser from 2005; Chair. Motorcycle Cttee, Japan Automobile Manufacturers Asscn, Inc. *Address:* c/o Yamaha Motor Co. Ltd, 2500 Shingai, Iwata, Shizuoka 438-8501, Japan. *E-mail:* info@yamaha-motor.co.jp.

YAMASHITA, Yasuhiro, MA; Japanese judo coach and judo player (retd) and academic; *Professor and Dean, School of Physical Education, Tokai University;* b. 1 June 1957, Yamato, Kumamoto; m. Midori Ono 1986; two s. one d.; ed Kyushu

Gakuin High School, Tokai Univ. Sagami High School and Tokai Univ.; winner nine consecutive times, All Japan Judo Tournament; four-time World Judo Champion, +95kg, Paris 1979, +95kg, Maastricht 1981, Open, Maastricht 1981, +95kg, Moscow 1983; achieved unbroken record of 203 consecutive wins from 1977 till he retd in 1985; gold medal, Summer Olympic Games, Los Angeles 1984; Prof., Dept of Sports, Tokai Univ. 1986–, now Dean, School of Physical Educ., fmr Team Man. Univ. Judo Team; Man. Japanese Nat. Judo Team 1992–; currently works as an instructor or adviser for orgs including Int. Judo Fed. (Dir of Educ. 2003–), All Japan Judo Fed.; Chair. Solidarity of Int. Judo Educ.; has trained youth Judo teams in Israel and Palestine and local children at China-Japan Friendship Judo Hall est. in Tsingtao and Nanjing; mem. Laureus World Sports Acad.; Nat. Honour Prize (Japan, first amateur sportsman to achieve award) 1984, Foreign Minister's Commendation 2011. *Film:* compiled an instructional judo video with Russian Pres. Vladimir Putin (black belt). *Publications include:* Young Days with Black Belt, Enjoyable Judo, The Moment of Fight, Osoto-Gari, Judo with Fighting Spirits. *Leisure interests:* reading, playing with my kids, karaoke (with family), dining out. *Address:* 4-1-1 Kitakaname, Hitatsuka-shi, Kanagawa 259-1292 (office); 661-104 Higashi Koiso, Oiso-machi, Naka-gun, Kanagawa -ken, Japan (home). *Telephone:* (463) 581211 (ext. 3532) (office). *Fax:* (463) 502405 (office). *E-mail:* info@yamashitayasuhiro.com (office). *Website:* www.u-tokai.ac.jp/international/undergraduate/physical_education.html (office); www.yamashitayasuhiro.com.

YAMASSOUM, Nagoum; Chadian politician; b. 1954; s. of Jean Yamassoum and Alice Titingone; m. Brigitte Boukar Belingar; two s.; ed Univ. of Bordeaux, Univ. of Paris XI, France; Prime Minister of Chad Aug. 1999–2002; Minister of State, Minister of Foreign Affairs and African Integration 2003–05; Head of AU observation mission to presidential election in Benin 2011; Nat. Order of Chad, Nat. Order of Taiwan. *Leisure interests:* tennis, soccer, gardening. *Address:* POB 4321, N'Djamena, Moursal, Chad (home). *Telephone:* 51-51-59 (home). *Fax:* 51-70-21 (home). *E-mail:* nagoumy@hotmail.com (home).

YAMAUCHI, Yasuhito; Japanese automotive industry executive; *Vice-Chairman, Aisin Seiki Company Ltd;* joined Toyota 1968, Man. Dir, also Chair. Plant Production Environmental Sub-cttee, Overseas Production Environmental Sub-Cttee 1999–2001, Sr Man. Dir 2001–03, Chair. Production Environment Cttee 2003–; Pres. Aisin Seiki Co. 2005–09, Vice-Chair. 2009–. *Address:* Aisin Seiki Co. Ltd, 2-1 Asahi-machi, Karlya, Aichi 448-8650, Japan (office). *Telephone:* (5) 6624-8239 (office). *Fax:* (5) 6624-8003 (office). *E-mail:* info@aisin.com (office). *Website:* www.aisin.com (office).

YAMEEN, Abdullah; Maldivian politician and head of state; *President;* brother of fmr Pres. Maumoon Abdul Gayoom; fmr Minister of Trade, Industries and Labour; Chair. State Trading Org., Island Aviation, Electricity Bd; fmr Minister of Higher Educ., Employment and Social Security; left govt's Dhivehi Raiyyithunge Party (Maldivian People's Party) 2007; Founder and Leader People's Alliance party 2008–; Pres. of Maldives 2013–. *Address:* The President's Office, Boduthakurufaanu Magu, Malé 20-05, Maldives (office). *Telephone:* 3320701 (office). *Fax:* 3325500 (office). *E-mail:* info@presidencymaldives.gov.mv (office). *Website:* www.presidencymaldives.gov.mv (office).

YAMEY, Basil Selig, CBE, BComm, FBA; British economist and academic; *Professor Emeritus of Economics, London School of Economics;* b. 4 May 1919, Cape Town, South Africa; s. of Solomon Yamey and Leah Yamey; m. 1st Helen Bloch 1948 (died 1980); one s. one d.; m. 2nd Demetra Georgakopoulou 1991; ed Tulbagh High School and Univ. of Cape Town; Prof. of Econs LSE 1960–84, Prof. Emer. 1984–; mem. Monopolies and Mergers Comm. 1966–78; Trustee Nat. Gallery, London 1974–81, Tate Gallery, London 1977–81, Inst. of Econ. Affairs 1987–91; Hon. Fellow LSE 1988. *Publications:* Economics of Resale Price Maintenance 1951, Economics of Underdeveloped Countries (with P. T. Bauer) 1956, Economics of Futures Trading (with B. A. Goss) 1976, Essays on the History of Accounting 1978, Art and Accounting 1989. *Address:* 27B Elsworthy Road, London, NW3 3BT, England. *Telephone:* (20) 7586-9344. *Fax:* (20) 7586-9344.

YAN, Bing; Chinese business executive; *President, China National Pharmaceutical Group Corporation (Sinopharm);* fmr Vice-Pres. and Gen. Man. of Sinopharm Foreign Trade, China Nat. Pharmaceutical Group Corpn (Sinopharm), currently mem. Bd of Dirs and Pres. *Address:* Sinopharm, 20 Zhichun Road, Beijing 100088, People's Republic of China (office). *Telephone:* (10) 82287727 (office). *E-mail:* webmaster@sinopharm.com (office). *Website:* www.sinopharm.com (office).

YAN, Haiwang; Chinese politician; b. Sept. 1939, Zhengzhou City, Henan Prov.; ed Harbin Architectural Eng Inst.; joined CCP 1966; Dir Urban and Rural Construction Cttee, Gansu Prov. 1983–87; Vice-Gov. Gansu Prov. 1987–93, Gov. 1993–97; Deputy Sec. CCP Gansu Provincial Cttee 1988–93; Sec. CCP Gansu Provincial Cttee 1993–98; Deputy Gov. People's Bank of China 1998–2000; Deputy Sec. Financial Work Committee, CCP Cen. Cttee Work Cttee Depts 1998–2003; Vice-Chair. China Banking Regulatory Comm. 2003–05; Alt. mem. 14th CCP Cen. Cttee 1992–97, mem. 15th CCP Cen. Cttee 1997–2002, 16th CCP Cen. Cttee 2002–07. *Address:* c/o General Office, China Banking Regulatory Commission, No. 33 Cheng Fang Street, West District, Beijing, People's Republic of China.

YAN, Jiehe; Chinese business executive; *Chairman and CEO, China Pacific Construction Group;* b. 1960, Huai'an, Jiangsu Prov.; taught Chinese language in middle school in Huai'an 1980s; took job as clerk at local cement factory, then apptd man.; expanded into construction materials business by taking over bankrupt state-owned collective; started construction co. in Huai'an 1992; launched his first pvt. business, Jiangsu Pacific Eng Ltd in 1995; currently Chair. and CEO China Pacific Construction Group (leading pvt. co. in building nat. expressways, urban construction and hydraulic projects); purchased ST Zongheng (Shanghai-listed machinery manufacturer based in Jiangsu Prov.) 2003; Chair. Pacific Architect Group; Chair. Huatuo CEO Forum; named by a business magazine as one of Ten Best Managers in China and the Ten Famous People in China Economic Field. *Address:* Huatuo CEO Forum, 100 Saoziying, Haidian District, Beijing 100091, J People's Republic of China (office). *Website:* en.ht-ceo.com (office).

YAN, Liangkun; Chinese orchestral conductor; b. Oct. 1923, Wuchang City, Hubei Prov.; ed Nat. Conservatory of Music, Tchaikovsky Conservatory of Music,

Moscow; Artistic Dir and Conductor, Symphony Orchestra of China Cen. Philharmonic Soc.; Vice-Pres. China Musicians' Asscn 1992–; mem. 6th CPPCC Nat. Cttee 1983–88, 7th CPPCC Nat. Cttee 1988–93, 8th CPPCC Nat. Cttee 1993–98. *Address:* Central Philharmonic Society, 11-1 Hepingjie (Peace Street), Beijing 100013, People's Republic of China (office).

YANAGIMACHI, Ryuzo, PhD; American/Japanese biologist and academic; *Professor Emeritus of Anatomy and Reproductive Biology, Institute for Biogenesis Research, John A. Burns School of Medicine, University of Hawaii-Manoa;* b. 27 Aug. 1928, Ebetsu, Hokkaido, Japan; s. of Kyuzo Yanagimachi and Hiroko Yanagimachi; ed Hokkaido Univ., Sapporo; on staff, Worcester Foundation for Experimental Biology, Shrewsbury, Mass 1960–64; returned to Japan 1964–66; Asst Prof., John A. Burns School of Medicine, Univ. of Hawaii-Manoa 1966–74, Prof. of Anatomy and Reproductive Biology 1974–2005, Prof. Emer. 2005–, Founding Dir Inst. for Biogenesis Research 1999–2004; mem. NAS 2001, mem. Editorial Bd Proceedings of the National Academy of Sciences; pioneering work on in vitro fertilization, assisted fertilization and animal cloning; Marshall Medal, Soc. of Study of Fertility 1994, Int. Prize of Biology 1996, Distinguished Andrologist Award, American Soc. of Andrology 1998, Carl G. Hartman Award, Soc. of Study of Reproduction 1999, inducted into Hall of Honor, Nat. Inst. of Child Health and Human Devt 2003. *Publications:* numerous articles in scientific journals on assisted fertilization, freeze-dried sperm tech. and cloning. *Address:* Institute for Biogenesis Research, John A. Burns School of Medicine, University of Hawaii-Manoa, 1960 East-West Road, Honolulu, HI 96822, USA (office). *Telephone:* (808) 956-8746 (office). *Fax:* (808) 956-7316 (office). *E-mail:* yana@hawaii.edu (office). *Website:* manoa.hawaii.edu (office).

YANAGISAWA, Hakuo; Japanese politician; b. 18 Aug. 1935; ed Tokyo Univ.; joined Ministry of Finance 1961; Consul in New York 1971–75; Sec. to Chief Cabinet Sec. 1978–79; mem. House of Reps for Shizuoka 3rd Dist (LDP) 1980–, Parl. Vice-Minister, Ministry of Foreign Affairs 1994–95, Chair. House of Reps Educ. Cttee 1995–96, Health and Welfare Cttee 1998, Minister of State, Dir-Gen., Nat. Land Agency 1998, Minister of State for Financial Reconstruction 1998, Minister of State and Chair., Financial Reconstruction Comm. 1998–99, 2000–2001, Minister of State for Financial Services 2001–02, Minister of Health, Labour and Welfare 2006–07; Man. Chair. LDP Admin. Reform Task Force 1995–98, Chair., LDP Research Comm. on Tax System 2005–06. *Address:* Liberal-Democratic Party (Jiyu-Minshuto), 1-11-23, Nagata-cho, Chiyoda-ku, Tokyo 100-8910, Japan (office). *Telephone:* (3) 3581-6211 (office). *E-mail:* koho@ldp.jimin.or.jp (office). *Website:* www.jimin.jp (office).

YANAI, Tadashi; Japanese retail executive; *Chairman, President and CEO, Fast Retailing Co. Ltd;* b. 7 Feb. 1949; s. of Hitoshi Yanai; m.; two c.; ed Waseda Univ.; joined Fast Retailing Co. Ltd (family retail business) 1972, Dir 1972, Sr Man. Dir 1973, Pres. and CEO 1984–, currently also Chair., Pres. and CEO Uniqlo Co. Ltd (subsidiary), Chair. Uniqlo USA Inc. 2004–, Uniqlo France SAS 2005–, Uniqlo UK Ltd 2005–; Chair. Link Theory Holdings Co. Ltd 2004–, Cabin Co. Ltd 2006–, Gov Retailing Co. Ltd 2008–; Dir Softbank Corpn 2001–, Nippon Venture Capital Co. Ltd 2009–. *Address:* Office of the Chairman, Fast Retailing Co. Ltd, 717-1 Sayama, Yamaguchi City, Yamaguchi 754-0894, Japan (office). *Website:* www.fastretailing.com (office).

YÁÑEZ-BARNUEVO, Juan Antonio, LLM; Spanish diplomatist (retd) and foundation director; *Director General, Women for Africa Foundation;* b. 15 Feb. 1942, Coria del Río, Seville; s. of the late Luis Yáñez-Barnuevo and Angeles García; m. Isabel Sampedro 1969; one s.; ed Univs of Seville and Madrid, Univ. of Cambridge, UK, School for Int. Civil Servants, Hague Acad. of Int. Law and Diplomatic School; Sec. of Embassy, Perm. Mission to UN, New York 1970–73, Deputy Head, Office of Int. Legal Affairs, Ministry of Foreign Affairs 1975–78, Deputy Perm. Rep. to Council of Europe, Strasbourg 1978–82; Dir of Int. Dept of Presidency of Govt (Foreign Policy Adviser to Prime Minister) 1982–91; Amb. and Perm. Rep., UN, New York 1991–96, Rep. in Security Council 1993–94, Deputy Dir Diplomatic School 1996–98, Amb.-at-Large 1998–2004, Head of Spanish Del. to UN negotiations on Int. Criminal Court 1998–2004, Head of Legal Dept, Ministry of Foreign Affairs 2002–04, Amb. and Perm. Rep., UN, New York 2004–10, Rep. in Security Council 2004, Chair. Sixth Cttee (Legal) of UN Gen. Ass. 2005–06, Vice-Pres. UN Gen. Ass. 2008–09, Co-Chair. consultations leading to adoption by UN Gen. Ass. Counter Terrorism Strategy 2006, Co-Chair. consultations leading to adoption of UN Gen. Ass. Resolution on UN system-wide coherence, including reform of UN gender architecture; mem. Int. Humanitarian Fact-finding Comm. 2002–06; mem. Perm. Court of Arbitration 2008–; Sec. of State for Foreign Affairs, Ministry of Foreign Affairs and Cooperation 2010–11; Grand Cross, Order of Civil Merit, Grand Cross, Order Merit (Germany), Francisco Tomás y Valiente Prize (Seville) 1998, Jurist of the Year (Madrid Law School) 1999. *Publication:* La Justicia Penal Internacional: Una perspectiva iberoamericana 2001. *Leisure interests:* reading, music, nature. *Address:* Fundacion Mujeres por Africa, Paseo de la Castellana, 144, 28046 Madrid (office); Carretera de Húmera, 1 (Aravaca), 28023 Madrid, Spain (home). *Telephone:* (914) 570945 (office); (913) 078017 (home). *E-mail:* juan.yanezb@mujeresporafrica.es (office); juanyanezb@hotmail.com (home). *Website:* www.mujeresporafrica.es (office).

YANG, Chao, MBA; Chinese insurance industry executive; b. 1950; ed Shanghai Int. Studies Univ., Univ. of Middlesex, UK; served in various man. positions with People's Insurance Co. of China 1976–96, including Deputy Gen. Man. and Asst Gen. Man. Shanghai Br., Gen. Man. Shanghai Pudong Br.; Chair. and Pres. China Insurance (Holdings) Co., Europe 1996–2000, China Insurance (Holdings) Co. 2000–05, China Insurance HK (Holding) Co. 2000–05; Pres. China Life Insurance (Group) Co. Ltd 2005–11, Chair. China Life Insurance Co. Ltd 2005–11, China Life Property and Casualty Insurance Co. Ltd; mem. Bd of Dirs Pacific Century Insurance Holdings, CITIC Int. Financial Holdings. *Address:* c/o China Life Insurance (Group) Co. Ltd, 16 Chaowai Avenue, 23rd Floor Chinalife Building, Chaoyang District, Beijing 100020, People's Republic of China.

YANG, Chen Ning (Frank), (Yang Zhenning), MSc, PhD; American (b. Chinese) physicist and academic; *Albert Einstein Professor Emeritus of Physics, State University of New York at Stony Brook;* b. 1 Oct. 1922, Hefei, Anhui Prov.; s. of Ke Chuan Yang and Meng Loh Yang; m. 1st Chih Li Tu 1950 (died 2003); two s. one d.; m. 2nd Weng Fan 2004; ed Nat. Southwest Associated Univ., Kunming, Tsinghua

Univ., Univ. of Chicago, USA; Research Student, Univ. of Chicago, USA 1946, Instructor 1948; joined Inst. for Advanced Study, Princeton, NJ 1949, Prof. 1955–66; naturalized US citizen 1964; Albert Einstein Prof. of Physics, State Univ. of NY at Stony Brook 1966–99, Prof. Emer. 1999–; Distinguished Prof.-at-Large, Chinese Univ. of Hong Kong 1986–; Prof., Tsinghua Univ., People's Repub. of China 1998–; Pres. Nat. Asscn of Chinese Americans 1977–80, Asscn of Asia Pacific Physical Socs 1989–94, Asia Pacific Center of Theoretical Physics 1996–; mem./Foreign mem. NAS, Royal Soc. (London), Chinese Acad. of Sciences, Russian Acad. of Sciences, Brazilian Acad. of Sciences, Polish Acad. of Sciences, Royal Spanish Acad. of Science, Korean Acad. of Science and Tech., Venezuelan Acad. of Sciences, Pontifical Acad. of Sciences; Fellow, American Physical Soc., Academia Sinica (Taiwan); now lives in China, granted permanent residency 2005; 18 hon. degrees, including Dr hc (Princeton) 1958, (Moscow State Univ.) 1992, (Chinese University of Hong Kong) 1997, (State Univ. of NY, Stony Brook) 1999, (Baptist Univ., Hong Kong) 1999, (Chung-Cheng Univ., Taiwan) 2000, (Hong Kong Univ. of Science and Tech.) 2002, (Ecole Normale Superieure, Paris) 2003; Nobel Prize in Physics (shared with Tsung-dao Lee) 1957, Albert Einstein Commemorative Award 1957, Rumford Prize 1980, Nat. Medal of Science 1986, Benjamin Franklin Medal 1993, Bower Award 1994, N. Bogoliubov Prize 1996, Lars Onsager Prize 1999, King Faisal Int. Prize 2001, Yang Coll. at Stony Brook Univ. named in his honour 2010. *Publications:* numerous articles in scientific journals. *Address:* Department of Physics and Astronomy, State University of New York at Stony Brook, Stony Brook, NY 11794, USA (office). *Telephone:* (631) 632-8100 (office). *Fax:* (631) 632–8176 (office). *E-mail:* yang@insti.physics.sunysb.edu (office). *Website:* insti.physics.sunysb.edu/~yang (office); www.castu.tsinghua.edu.cn/cnyang.

YANG, Cheng-Zhi, BSc; Chinese petroleum engineer; b. 8 Aug. 1938, Henan; s. of Yang Xian-zun and Hou Yang; m. Li Yan-qin 1969; one s. one d.; ed Beijing Univ. of Petroleum; Asst Prof., Beijing Univ. of Petroleum 1961–75; Asst Prof., Vice-Dir Dept of Petroleum Eng, Sheng-li Coll. of Petroleum 1976–78; Prof., Sr Research Engineer and Dir of Research for Interface Chem., Research Inst. of Petroleum Exploration and Devt of Beijing 1979–; Dir Jr Lab. for Colloid and Interface Science, Acad. Sinica and China Nat. Petroleum Co. 1990–; Visiting Sr Research Engineer, Inst. Français du Pétrole 1979–80, 1985–87, 1989–90; mem. China Petroleum Soc., Soc. of Petroleum Engineers of USA; research into enhanced oil recovery, the physical chem. of oil reservoirs, surfactant solution properties, absorption of surfactants and polymers, colloid and interface chem. etc.; Hon. Prof., Da-qing Univ. of Petroleum 1988–; Science-Tech. Award in Petroleum Eng 1991, 1996, World Lifetime Achievement Award, ABI, USA 1992 and other awards. *Publications:* Petroleum Reservoir Physics 1975, World Fine Chemical Engineering Handbook (jtly), Enhanced Oil Recovery Theory and Practice 1995, Improved Oil Recovery 1997, Enhanced Oil Recovery by Chemical Flooding 1999; more than 60 articles in professional journals. *Leisure interests:* collecting stamps and badges. *Address:* Research Institute of Petroleum Exploration and Development, PO Box 910, Beijing 100083 (office); No. 1107, West-Beido Lodging House, Zhixing Road, Beijing 100083, People's Republic of China (home). *Telephone:* (10) 62098371 (office); (10) 62397956 (home). *Fax:* (10) 62097181 (office); (10) 62397956 (home). *E-mail:* ylang@public.fhnet.cn.net (office).

YANG, Chin-tien (Timothy), BA; Taiwanese diplomatist and politician; *Secretary General, Office of the President;* b. 1 July 1942; ed Nat. Chengchi Univ., Univ. of Witwatersrand, SA; Officer, Dept of African Affairs, Ministry of Foreign Affairs (MFA) 1972–74; Third, later Second and First Sec., Embassy in Lesotho 1974–83; Sr Specialist, MFA 1986–88; Rep., Taipei Rep. Office, Ireland 1988–91; Dir-Gen. Taipei Econ. and Cultural Office, Houston, Tex., USA 1991–95; Dir-Gen., Dept of African Affairs, MFA 1995–99, Sec. Gen., MFA 1999–2000; Rep., Taipei Econ. and Cultural Office, Australia 2000–06; positions at MFA 2006–07; Rep., Taipei Econ. and Trade Office, Indonesia 2007–09; Minister of Foreign Affairs 2009–12; Sec. Gen., Office of the Pres. 2012–. *Address:* Office of the President, No. 122, Sec. 1, Chongqing South Road, Taipei 100, Taiwan (office).

YANG, Chuantang; Chinese government official; *Minister of Transport;* b. 1954, Yucheng County, Shandong Prov.; ed Shandong Normal Univ., CCP Cen. Cttee Cen. Party School, Chinese Acad. of Social Sciences; began career as worker, Shengli Petrochemical Complex, No. 2 Fertilizer Plant, Shandong Prov. 1975–78; Deputy Group Chief, Qilu Petrochemical Corpn, Ethylene Production Headquarters, Shandong Prov. 1978–81, Deputy Chief, Admin Office 1983–84, Deputy Sec. CCP Party Cttee 1984–87; Pres., Young Cadres Management Coll., Shandong Prov. 1987–92; Administrative Vice-Chair., Autonomous Region People's Govt, Tibet Autonomous Region 1993–96, 1998–2003, Chair. 2004–06; Acting Gov., Qinghai Prov. 2003–04, Gov. 2004; Vice-Chair., State Ethnic Affairs Comm. 2004–06; Minister of Transport 2013–; alt. mem. 16th CCP Cen. Cttee 2002–07, mem. 17th CCP Cen. Cttee 2007–12, 18th CCP Cen. Cttee 2012–. *Address:* Ministry of Transport, 11 Jianguomennei Dajie, Beijing 100736, People's Republic of China (office). *Telephone:* (10) 65292327 (office). *Fax:* (10) 65292345 (office). *E-mail:* jtbweb@moc.gov.cn (office). *Website:* www.mot.gov.cn (office).

YANG, Deqing; Chinese army officer and politician; b. Sept. 1942, Yingcheng, Hubei Prov.; joined PLA 1963, CCP 1964; mem. Secr., Wuhan Mil. Dist, PLA Guangzhou Mil. Region 1973–77, Political Commissar PLA Armoured Force Regt 1977–80, Dir Political Dept, Armoured Force Regt 1982–85; Dir Political Dept, 54th Group Army of Ground Force 1985–89; Dir Political Dept and Political Commissar, Acad. of Mil. Economy 1989–91; Dir PLA Gen. Logistics Dept 1991–94, Sec., later Deputy Sec. CCP Party Cttee Comm. for Discipline Inspection 1994–99; Political Commissar, PLA Chengdu Mil. Region 1999–2005; Sec. CCP Party Cttee, Chengdu City, PLA Guangzhou Mil. Region 1999–; mem. Cen. Comm. for Discipline Inspection; Mayor Zhangjiakou City, Hebei Prov.; mem. 15th CCP Cen. Cttee 1997–2002, 16th CCP Cen. Cttee 2002–07. *Address:* c/o PLA Headquarters, Chengdu Military Region, Chengdu 610000, Sichuan Province, People's Republic of China (office).

YANG, Fudong; Chinese artist; b. 1971, Beijing; ed China Acad. of Fine Arts, Hangzhou; Shanghai-based multimedia artist, works include paintings, photography and film.

YANG, Fujia, BSc; Chinese nuclear physicist and fmr university administrator; *Chancellor Emeritus, University of Nottingham;* b. June 1936, Shanghai; ed Fudan Univ.; Lecturer, Dept of Physics, Fudan Univ., later Prof. and Pres. Fudan Univ. 1993–99; Dir Shanghai Inst. of Nuclear Research 1987–2001; Chancellor, Univ. of Nottingham, UK 2001–12 (first Chinese academic to become Chancellor of a UK univ.), Chancellor Emer. 2013–; fmr Visiting Prof., Niels Bohr Inst., Copenhagen, Rutgers Univ., State Univ. of NY, Univ. of Tokyo; Chair. Shanghai Science and Tech. Union 1992–96; Vice-Chair. Chinese Asscn for Science and Tech. 2001–; Pres. Asscn of Univ. Presidents of China 1997–99; mem. Int. Asscn of Univ. Presidents, Asscn of Univ. Presidents of the Pacific Rim; Fellow, Chinese Acad. of Sciences; Dr hc (Soka Univ., Tokyo), (State Univ. of NY), (Univ. of Hong Kong), (Univ. of Nottingham), (Univ. of Connecticut). *Address:* Office of the Vice-Chancellor, University of Nottingham, University Park, Nottingham, NG7 2RD, England (office). *Telephone:* (115) 951-3001 (office). *Fax:* (115) 951-3005 (office).

YANG, Fuqing; Chinese computer scientist and academic; *Dean, Faculty of Information and Engineering Sciences and Director, National Engineering Research Center for Software Engineering, Peking University;* b. 6 Nov. 1932, Wuxi, Jiangsu Prov.; ed Tsinghua and Peking Univs; Prof., Dept of Computer Science and Tech., Peking Univ. 1983–, Dean 1983–99, Dean Faculty of Information and Eng Sciences 1999–, Dir Nat. Eng Research Center for Software Eng Research 1997–, Dir Computer Science and Tech. Dept 1983–99; mem. Chinese Acad. of Sciences 1991–, Academic Degree Cttee of the State Council; Fellow, IEEE 2003–; numerous awards and prizes including Special Prize for Advancement of Science and Tech., Electronics Industry Admin. 1996, First Class Prize of the Guang Hua Tech. Fund from the Nat. Defence Tech. Ministry 1996, Science and Tech. Progress Awards of He Liang and He Li Fund 1997, Pioneer of Software Engineering in China. *Publications:* Operating System, Compiler, The Fundamental Theory of Software Engineering, Software Engineering Environment, Software Production Industrialization Technology; more than 150 papers. *Address:* Department of Computer Science and Technology, Peking University, Beijing 100871, People's Republic of China (office). *Telephone:* (10) 62751782 (office). *Fax:* (10) 62751792 (office). *E-mail:* yang@sei.pku.edu.cn. *Website:* www.sei .pku.edu.cn/en/yangfuqing.html (office).

YANG, Gen. Guoping; Chinese army officer; b. Oct. 1934, Zhongxiang Co., Hubei Prov.; ed PLA Mil. Acad.; joined PLA 1950, fought in Korean War 1951; joined CCP 1956; Staff Officer of Combat Troops, Deputy Section Chief, Section Chief, Deputy Dept Chief, Dept Chief of Combat Troops for Shenyang Mil. Region, Deputy Chief of Staff 1987; Chief of Staff, 14th Army 1983–87; rank of Maj.-Gen. 1988; Chief of Staff, Jinan Mil. Region 1990–94, Deputy Commdr 1994–96; mil. rep. to 14th Cen Cttee CCP 1992–97; rank of Lt-Gen. 1993; Commdr People's Armed Police 1996–99; rank of Gen. 1998; mem. 15th CCP Cen. Cttee 1997–2002. *Address:* c/o People's Liberation Army Headquarters of Armed Police, Beijing, People's Republic of China (office).

YANG, Henry T. Y., BS, MS, PhD; American (b. Chinese) engineer and university administrator; *Chancellor, University of California, Santa Barbara;* b. 29 Nov. 1940, Chungking, China; m. Dilling Yang 1966; two d.; ed Nat. Taiwan Univ., West Virginia Univ., Cornell Univ.; Asst Prof., School Aeronautics and Astronautics, Purdue Univ. 1969, Assoc. Prof. 1972–76, Prof. 1976–88, Neil A. Armstrong Distinguished Prof. of Aeronautics and Astronautics 1988–94, Head, School of Aeronautics and Astronautics 1979–84, Dean of Eng and Dir, Computer Integrated Design, Mfg and Automation Center 1984–94; Chancellor and Prof., Dept of Mechanical Eng, Univ. of Calif., Santa Barbara 1994–; mem. Nat. Acad. of Eng 1991, Academia Sinica 1992; Fellow, American Inst. of Aeronautics and Astronautics 1985, American Soc. for Eng Educ. 1993, ASME 2008; has served on numerous bds and cttees including Defense Science Board, USAF Scientific Advisory Bd, Naval Research Advisory Cttee, NASA's Aeronautical Advisory Cttee, NSF Eng Advisory Cttee; Dr hc (Purdue Univ.) 1996, (Hong Kong Univ. of Science and Tech.) 2002, (Nat. Taiwan Univ.) 2004, (City Univ. Hong Kong) 2005, (Chinese Univ. of Hong Kong) 2008, (West Virginia Univ.) 2011, (Hong Kong Polytechnic Univ.) 2011; numerous awards, including USAF Meritorious Civilian Service Award 1989, Centennial Medal, American Soc. of Eng Educ. 1993, Benjamin Garver Lamme Award, American Soc. of Eng Educ. 1998, Structures, Structural Dynamics and Materials Award, AIAA 2008, 12 outstanding teaching awards, Purdue Univ. 1971–94, Hon. Distinguished Teaching Award, Univ. of Calif., Santa Barbara 2007. *Publications:* Finite Element Structural Analysis; author or co-author of more than 170 articles for scientific journals. *Address:* Office of the Chancellor, 5221 Cheadle Hall, University of California, Santa Barbara, CA 93106-2030, USA (office). *Telephone:* (805) 893-2231 (office). *Fax:* (805) 893-8717 (office). *E-mail:* henry.yang@chancellor.ucsb.edu (office). *Website:* www.chancellor .ucsb.edu (office).

YANG, Hua, BSc, MBA; Chinese oil industry executive; *President, China National Offshore Oil Corporation (CNOOC) Limited;* b. 1961; ed China Univ. of Petroleum, Sloan School of Man., Massachusetts Inst. of Tech. (Sloan Fellow), USA; joined China Nat. Offshore Oil Corpn (CNOOC) Ltd 1982, served in several positions in CNOOC Research Centre, including Man. of Reservoir Eng Dept and Dir of Field Devt Dept 1982–92, Deputy Chief Geologist and Deputy Dir for the Overseas Devt Dept of CNOOC and Vice-Pres. CNOOC Overseas Oil and Natural Gas Ltd 1993–99, Sr Vice-Pres. CNOOC Ltd 1999–2005, Exec. Vice-Pres. 2005–06, Pres. CNOOC Southeast Asia Ltd (subsidiary of CNOOC) 2002–03, Pres. CNOOC International Ltd 2004–05, Chief Financial Officer CNOOC Ltd 2005–06, Asst Pres. 2006–10, Pres. 2009–10, Vice-Pres. and Party Leadership Group mem. May–Sept. 2010, Vice-Chair. and CEO CNOOC Ltd 2010–11, Pres. and Party Leadership Group mem. 2011–. *Address:* China National Offshore Oil Corpn, Box 4705, 25 Chao Yangmen North Street, Dongcheng District, Beijing 100010, People's Republic of China (office). *Telephone:* (10) 84521010 (office). *Fax:* (10) 64602600 (office). *E-mail:* webmaster@cnooc.com.cn (office). *Website:* www.cnooc .com.cn (office).

YANG, Hyong-sop; North Korean politician; *Vice-President, Presidium of the Supreme People's Assembly;* b. 1 Oct. 1925, Hamhung; ed Kim Il Sung Univ.; Speaker, Supreme People's Ass. 1983, Chair. 1983–98, Assoc. mem. Politburo 1993–, Vice-Pres., Presidium of the Supreme People's Ass. 1998–; Vice-Chair. Peaceful Reunification of Fatherland Cttee 1984–; Chair. Korean Asscn of Social Sciences 1997–; Alt. mem. Political Bureau of Cen. Cttee of the Workers' Party; Head of Del. to China 2004, to S Africa 2005, to Venezuela 2005.

Presidium of the Supreme People's Assembly, Pyongyang, Democratic People's Republic of Korea (office).

YANG, Jerry, BS, MS; American computer industry executive; b. (Yan Chih-Yuan), 6 Nov. 1968, Taipei, Taiwan; m. Akiko Yamazaki; one c.; ed Stanford Univ.; moved to San Jose, Calif. at age 10 years; Co-Creator Yahoo! (internet navigational guide) 1994, Co-Founder, Yahoo! Inc. 1995, mem. Bd of Dirs 1995–2012, Chief Yahoo! 1995–2007, 2009–12, CEO 2007–09, mem. Bd of Dirs 1995–2012; mem. Bd of Dirs (non-exec.) Cisco Systems Inc. 2000–, Alibaba 2005–12, Asian Pacific Fund; mem. Bd of Trustees, Stanford Univ.; Co-Chair. (with wife) $1B Campaign for Undergraduate Educ., Stanford Univ. *Address:* c/o Board of Directors, Cisco Systems Inc., 170 West Tasman Drive, San Jose, CA 95134, USA.

YANG, Jian; Chinese automotive industry executive; *President, Zhejiang Geely Holding (Group) Company Limited;* ed Zhejiang Radio and Television Univ.; joined Zhejiang Geely Holding (Group) Co. Ltd 1995, involved in several different job functions within the group, including Production Man., Quality Control, Gen. Admin, Research and Devt, and Project Man., later First Vice-Pres. Zhejiang Geely Holding Group Co. Ltd and Head of Zhejiang Geely Automobile Research Inst. Ltd, responsible for overall admin of Zhejiang Geely JV, Exec. Dir 2005–, Vice-Chair. Geely Automobile Holdings Ltd 2008–, currently Pres. Zhejiang Geely Holding (Group) Co. Ltd. *Address:* Zhejiang Geely Holding Group, 1760 Jiangling Road, Hangzhou 310051, People's Republic of China (office). *Telephone:* (571) 28001111 (office). *E-mail:* info@geely.com (office). *Website:* www.geely.com (home).

YANG, Jiechi, PhD; Chinese diplomatist and government official; *Member, State Council;* b. May 1950, Shanghai; m.; one d.; ed Univ. of Bath and London School of Econs, UK; staff mem., later Second Sec. Trans. and Interpretation Dept, Ministry of Foreign Affairs 1975–84, Counsellor, later Div. Dir 1987–90, Counsellor, later Div. Dir, later Dir-Gen. North American and Oceania Affairs Dept 1990–93, Asst Minister, Ministry of Foreign Affairs 1995–98, Vice-Minister 1998–2000; Second Sec., later First Sec., later Counsellor, Chinese Embassy, Washington, DC, USA 1983–87, Minister and Deputy Chief of Mission 1993–95, Amb. to USA 2001–05; Vice-Minister of Foreign Affairs in charge of region of N America and Oceania and Latin America, foreign-related affairs involving Hong Kong, Macao and Taiwan, work of translation and interpretation 2005–07, Minister of Foreign Affairs 2007–13; Alt. mem. 16th CCP Cen. Cttee 2002–07, mem. 17th CCP Cen. Cttee 2007–12, 18th CCP Cen. Cttee 2012–; mem. State Council 2013–; Hilal-i-Pakistan (Crescent of Pakistan) 2013. *Leisure interests:* playing table tennis, listening to choral music, writing poems. *Address:* State Council, Beijing, People's Republic of China (office).

YANG, Jike; Chinese scientist and administrator; b. 6 Nov. 1921, Shanghai; m. Wang Anqi; one s. two d.; ed Ohio State Univ., USA; Prof., Chinese Univ. of Science and Tech. 1966–; Vice-Gov. of Anhui Prov. 1979–88; Vice-Pres. Energy Research Asscn 1982–90, Pres. 1990–; Vice-Chair. China Zhi Gong Dang (Party for Public Interests) 1988–97, Hon. Vice-Chair. 11th China Zhi Gong Party (Public Interest Party) Cen. Cttee; Pres. Cen. Coll. of Socialism of China (now Cen. Socialist Acad.) 1991–; Dir Nat. Council for Social Security Fund; Vice-Chair. Environmental and Resources Protection Cttee, 8th NPC 1993–98; mem. Standing Cttee 9th CPPCC Nat. Cttee 1998–2003, Vice-Chair. Population Resources and Environment Sub-cttee 1998–2003. *Address:* c/o Zhi Gong Dang, Taiping Qiao Street, Xi Cheng District, Beijing, People's Republic of China.

YANG, Jing; Chinese politician; *Secretary-General, State Council;* b. Dec. 1953, Jungar Banner, Inner Mongolia; ed Inner Mongolia Univ.; began career as worker at agricultural equipment factory, Jungar Banner, Inner Mongolia Autonomous Region 1970–74; joined CCP 1976; Sec., Communist Youth League of China Regional Cttee, Ih Ju League 1982–97; Magistrate, County (Dist) People's Court, Inner Mongolia Autonomous Region 1985–88; Deputy Dir, Statistics Bureau, Inner Mongolia Autonomous Region 1991–92; Dir, Tourism Bureau, Inner Mongolia Autonomous Region 1992–93; Deputy Sec., Inner Mongolia Autonomous Region CCP Cttee 2003–08, Acting Chair. Inner Mongolia Regional Govt 2003–04, Chair. 2004–08; Minister of State Ethnic Affairs Comm. 2008–13; Sec.-Gen., State Council (first from ethnic minority background) 2013–; Pres. Chinese Acad. of Governance 2013–; alt. mem. 16th CCP Cen. Cttee 2002–07, 17th CCP Cen. Cttee 2007–12, 18th CCP Cen. Cttee 2012–, also mem. 18th CCP Cen. Cttee Politburo Secr. 2012–. *Address:* State Council, Great Hall of the People, West Edge, Tiananmen Square, Beijing, People's Republic of China (office). *Website:* english.gov.cn (office).

YANG, Jingyu; Chinese politician; b. Sept. 1936, Xingyang, He'nan Prov.; ed Beijing Foreign Trade Inst.; joined CCP 1954, Deputy Dir Econ. Law Office, Dir Research Office, Deputy Sec.-Gen., Deputy Dir Comm. of Legis. Affairs, Standing Cttee of 5–7th NPC 1981–91; Dir Bureau of Legis. Affairs, State Council 1991–98, Deputy Sec. 1995–98, Minister, Office of Legis. Affairs 1998–2002; Del. to 14–16th CCP Nat. Congress 1992–2007; Chair. Law Cttee, 10th NPC 2003–08, Hon. Expert, Standing Cttee of 11th NPC 2008–; Visiting Prof., Renmin Univ. of China, China Univ. of Int. Business and Econs, Nat. Admin School. *Publications:* Rational Explorations in the Process of Rule of Law 2002, My Meditations 2006, Reflections on the Practice of Rule of Law 2008. *Address:* National People's Congress, Beijing, People's Republic of China (office).

YANG, Kaisheng, DEcon; Chinese banking executive; b. Nov. 1949, Hubei; ed Beijing Coll. of Chemical Tech., Wuhan Univ.; joined Industrial & Commercial Bank of China (ICBC) 1985, Head of Planning and Information Dept 1985–90, Gen. Man. Shenzhen City Br. 1990–95, Vice-Gov. ICBC 1995–99, Pres. 2005–13, also Vice-Chair. and Exec. Dir and Deputy ICBC Party Sec. and Chair. ICBC Credit Suisse Asset Man. Co. Ltd –2013; Pres. China Huarong Asset Man. Corpn 1999–; Dir (non-exec.) and Deputy Chair. Standard Bank Group (South Africa) 2008–; Adjunct Prof., Wuhan Univ.; Deputy Dir 16th Cttee, China Int. Econ. and Trade Arbitration Comm., consultant to 17th Cttee. *Address:* c/o Industrial & Commercial Bank of China Ltd, 55 Fuxingmennan Dajie, Xicheng Qu, Beijing 100140, People's Republic of China. *E-mail:* webmaster@icbc.com.cn.

YANG, Lan, BA, MA; Chinese journalist, broadcaster and media executive; *Chairperson, Sun Media Group;* b. 31 March 1968, Beijing; m. 1st Yibin Zhang (divorced); 2nd m. Bruno Wu Zheng 1995; two c.; ed Beijing Foreign Studies Univ., Columbia Univ., USA; Presenter, Zheng Da variety show, China Cen. TV Station 1990–94; Producer and Presenter, Chinese Channel Phoenix Satellite TV, Hong Kong 1997–99; Co-founder and Chair. Sun Media Investment Holdings Ltd (Sun Media Group) 1998–; Founder and Chair. Sun Cultural Foundation, Hong Kong 2005; creator Her Village website; apptd image Amb. for Beijing 2008 Olympics bid; Global Amb. for Special Olympics Movt; first UNICEF Ambassador in Amb.; Co-Chair. Lincoln Center China Advisory Council; mem. 10th CPPCC Nat. Cttee 2003–; mem. Columbia Univ. Int. Advisory Council 2005–; often referred to as "China's Oprah"; Golden Microphone Winner 1994, Chinese Women of the Year Award, Top Ten Women Entrepreneurs Award, 'She Made It' Award, The Paley Center for Media, Global Leadership Award, SIPA of Columbia Univ., Nat. Philanthropy Award, Women's Achievement Award in China, ranked by Forbes magazine amongst The World's 100 Most Powerful Women (100th) 2013. *Address:* Sun Media Investment Holdings, No. 387 Yong Jia Road, Shanghai 200031, People's Republic of China (office). *Telephone:* (21) 68419980 (office). *Website:* www .chinasunmedia.com (office).

YANG, Le, (Lo Yang); Chinese mathematician; b. Nov. 1939, Nantong, Jiangsu Prov.; m. Qieyuan Huang; two d.; ed Peking Univ. and Inst. of Math., Chinese Acad. of Sciences; Pres. Acad. of Math. and System Sciences, Chinese Acad. of Sciences 1998–; mem. 4th Presidium of Depts, Chinese Acad. of Sciences 2000–; Research Fellow and Dir Inst. of Math., Chinese Acad. of Sciences; Fellow, Chinese Acad. of Sciences; invited to deliver lectures in 60 univs abroad and to speak at over 20 int. confs; Nat. Natural Science Prize, Hua Luogeng Math. Prize, Tan Kah Kee Prize, Ho Leung Ho Lee Math. Prize. *Publication:* Value Distribution Theory 1993. *Address:* Institute of Mathematics, Chinese Academy of Sciences, 55 Zhongguan-cun, Haidian District, Beijing, People's Republic of China (office). *Telephone:* (10) 62541848 (office). *Fax:* (10) 62568356 (home). *Website:* www.mcm.ac.cn (office).

YANG, Maj.-Gen. Liwei; Chinese astronaut; *Deputy Director, China Manned Space Engineering Office;* b. June 1965, Suizhong Co., Liaoning Prov.; m.; one s.; joined PLA 1983, entered No. 8 Aviation Coll. of PLA, became fighter pilot 1987; selected to fly Project 921 (later Shenzhou) spacecraft 1988, in training Astronaut Training Base, Beijing 1988–93; became first Chinese citizen launched aboard a Chinese spacecraft (Shenzhou-5) Oct. 2003; Deputy Dir China Manned Space Eng Office 2010–; rank of Col 2003, Maj.-Gen. 2008; Alt. mem. 17th CCP Cen. Cttee 2007–12; Dr hc (Chinese Univ. of Hong Kong) awarded title Space Hero 2003. *Address:* China Manned Space Engineering Office, A8 Fucheng Road, Haidian, Beijing, People's Republic of China (office). *Website:* en.cmse.gov.cn (office).

YANG, Marjorie Mun-tak, BS, MBA; Hong Kong business executive; *Chairman and CEO, Esquel Group;* b. 1952, d. of Yang Yuan-loong; m. Dickson Poon (divorced); one d.; ed Baldwin School, Bryn Mawr, Pa, Massachusetts Inst. of Tech., Harvard Business School, USA; Assoc. in Corp. Finance, Mergers and Acquisitions, First Boston Corpn, New York 1976–77; Chair. YTT Tourism Advisor Ltd, Hong Kong 1978–87; helped her father to found Esquel Group in 1978, Chair. and CEO 1995–; mem. Bd of Dirs of Assocs, Harvard Business School 1997–; mem. Bd of Dirs Wuxi Int. Man. Services Pte Ltd 1997–, Gillette Co. 1998–, RandD Corpn Ltd, Hong Kong Univ. of Science and Tech. 2000–, Pacific Century Regional Devts 2000–, BlueDot Capital Pte Ltd 2000–, Clarke Quay Ltd 2001–, China Exploration and Research Soc. 2000–; business adviser to Chair. Sembcorp Industries Ltd; Council Chair. Hong Kong Polytechnic Univ.; Chair. HK-US Business Council, Quality Migrant Program; Yang Yuan-Loong Educ. Fund, Suzhou, People's Repub. of China 1995–; mem. mem. MIT Corpn; Vice-Pres., Exec. Dir Women Entrepreneur Asscn 1995–; mem. Govt's Strategic Devt Comm.; mem. Standing Cttee CPPCC, Xinjian Prov. 1998, Foshan, Guangdong Prov. 1998, mem. Cttee CPPCC, Gaoming, Guangdong Prov. 1998; mem. Hong Kong Exec. Council 2009–; apptd by Gov. of Hong Kong as Immigration Tribunal Adjudicator 1982–88; mem. Asia Advisory Bd of MIT/China Int. Man. Educ. Project, Dean's Council of Advisors, Sloan School of Man., MIT; Hon. Pres. Hong Kong Fed. of Women 1994–; Hon. Citizen of Foshan, Guangdong Prov. 1995, of Turpan, Xinjiang Prov. 1996; Hon. Darjah Setia Pangkuan Negeri, Penang State, Malaysia 1996; Hon. Chargé d'affaires, China Nat. Table Tennis Team 1997–; Commdr of the Star and Key of the Indian Ocean (Mauritius) 1997; Alumnae Award, Baldwin School, Bryn Mawr, Pennsylvania, USA 1996, Gold Bauhinia Star 2013, selected as one of 50 Stars of Asia by Business Week magazine 1998, Owner Operator Award, DHL/South China Morning Post Hong Kong Business Award 1999, selected by Fortune magazine as one of the Six Most Powerful Businesswomen from Asia 2000, ranked by Fortune magazine amongst the 50 Most Powerful Women in Business outside the US (48th) 2000, (36th) 2002, (36th) 2003, (44th) 2004, (41st) 2005, (39th) 2009. *Address:* Esquel Enterprises Limited, 12/F, Harbour Centre, 25 Harbour Road, Wanchai, Hong Kong Special Administrative Region, People's Republic of China (office). *Telephone:* 28118077 (office). *Fax:* 29606988 (office). *E-mail:* questions@esquel.com (office). *Website:* www.esquel.com (office).

YANG, Mianmian; Chinese business executive; *President, Haier Group;* b. 1945; joined Haier Group (fmrly Qingdao Refrigerator Plant) 1984, later Exec. Pres. –2000, Pres. 2000–05, 2006–, Exec. Dir and Chair. 2005–06, Deputy Dir Technological Centre; Vice-Pres. China Asscn of Women Entrepreneurs; ranked by Fortune magazine amongst the 50 Most Powerful Women in Business outside the US (eighth) 2004, (15th) 2005, (20th) 2006, (25th) 2007, (17th) 2008–10, (26th) 2011, ranked by Forbes magazine amongst The World's 100 Most Powerful Women (70th) 2006, (43rd) 2007, (70th) 2008. *Address:* Haier Group Company, No. 1 Haier Road, Hi-tech Zone, Qingdao 266101, People's Republic of China (office). *Telephone:* (532) 8939999 (office); (532) 8938093 (Technology Centre) (office). *Fax:* (532) 8938666 (office); (532) 8938555 (Technology Centre) (office). *E-mail:* tech@haier.com (office). *Website:* www.haier.com (office).

YANG, Mingsheng, MA; Chinese economist and banking executive; *Chairman and Executive Director, China Life Insurance (Group) Company;* b. 1955; ed Nankai Univ.; joined Agricultural Bank of China 1980, Deputy Gen. Man., Shenyang Br. 1987–90, Gen. Man., Tianjin Br. 1990–97, Exec. Vice-Pres. 1997–2003, Pres. and CEO 2003–07; Vice-Chair. China Insurance Regulatory Comm. 2007–12; Chair. and Exec. Dir China Life Insurance (Group) Co. 2012–. *Address:* China Life Insurance Co. Ltd, 23rd Floor, China Life Building, 16 Chaowai Street, Chaoyang District, Beijing, 100020, People's Republic of China (office). *Telephone:* (10) 85659999 (office). *Fax:* (10) 85252232 (office). *E-mail:* serve@e-chinalife.com (office). *Website:* www.e-chinalife.com (office).

YANG, Mu, BA, DipMus, PhD; Chinese ethnomusicologist; *Senior Lecturer, School of Humanities and Languages, University of New South Wales;* b. 16 Aug. 1949, Fuzhou; ed Central Conservatory of Music, Beijing, Univ. of Queensland, Australia; violinist, composer, conductor 1971–78; Music Editor and Programme Producer, Nat. Broadcasting Service, Beijing 1983–85; Sessional Lecturer, Project Dir, Research Fellow in Ethnomusicology, Monash Univ., Melbourne 1990–95; Visiting Fellow, ANU 1995–98; Research Fellow, Northern Territory Univ. 1999–2002; currently Sr Lecturer, Univ. of New South Wales; mem. Society for Ethnomusicology; Int. Council of Traditional Music; Musicological Society of Australia; Asscn for Chinese Music Research, USA; Jaap Kunst Prize, Society for Ethnomusicology, USA 1998. *Publications include:* Chinese Musical Instruments: An Introduction, 1993; Articles in Music Research (Beijing), Musicology Australia, Ethnomusicology, International Journal of Music Education, Yearbook for Traditional Music, Asian Music, Journal of the Central Conservatory of Music (Beijing). *Address:* School of Humanities and Languages, UNSW, Sydney, NSW 2052, Australia (office). *Telephone:* (4) 3440-3479 (office). *E-mail:* yang.mu@unsw.edu.au (office). *Website:* www.hal.arts.unsw.edu.au (office).

YANG, Pan-chyr, MD, PhD; Taiwanese physician, academic and university administrator; *President, National Taiwan University;* ed Nat. Taiwan Univ.; Attending Physician, King Fahad Hosp., Hofuf, Saudi Arabia 1984–86; Attending Physician, Dept of Internal Medicine, Nat. Taiwan Univ. Hosp. (NTUH) 1986–, Prof., Dept of Internal Medicine, Coll. of Medicine, Nat. Taiwan Univ. 1993–; Chair. Dept of Internal Medicine, NTUH 1998–2004; Jt Appointment, Inst. of Biomedical Sciences, Academia Sinica 1999–, Assoc. Dean for Academic Affairs, Coll. of Medicine, Nat. Taiwan Univ. 2001–07, Vice-Supt, NTUH 2004–07, Dir NTUH Nat. Clinical Trial and Research Centre 2005–07, Distinguished Prof. and Chair Prof., Nat. Taiwan Univ. 2006–, Dean, Coll. of Medicine 2007–13, Supt, Nat. Taiwan Univ. Cancer Centre 2011–, Pres. Nat. Taiwan Univ. 2013–; Dir Advisory Office, Ministry of Educ. 2002–05, mem. Cttee on Medical Science Educ. 2008–09, Chair. and mem. Perm. Cttee, Cttee on Medical Science Educ. 2012–; Adjunct Investigator, Nat. Health Research Inst. 2006–; Dir and Co-Prin. Investigator, Nat. Research Program for Biopharmaceuticals 2011–; Ed.-in-Chief MicroRNA 2011–, Lung Cancer: Targets and Therapy 2012–; Academic Ed. PLoS One 2010–; mem. Editorial Bd Journal of the Formosan Medical Association 2005–10, Carcinogenesis 2007–, American Journal of Respiratory Cell Molecular Biology 2007–, The International Journal of Tuberculosis and Lung Disease 2007–, Journal of Clinical Oncology 2008–, European Respiratory Journal 2012–, Journal of Thoracic Oncology 2012–; Academician, Academia Sinica 2006, Acad. of Sciences for the Developing World 2008; Ten Outstanding Youth Award 1993, Distinguished Clinical Teacher Award, NTUCMAF 1993, 1997, Outstanding Research Award, Nat. Science Council 1994–95, 1996–97, 1998–99, The 7th Annual Wang Ming-Ning Award 1997, Distinguished Teacher Award, Nat. Taiwan Univ. 1999, 2012, Outstanding Scholar Award, Foundation for the Advancement of Outstanding Scholarship 2001–06, Academic Award, Ministry of Educ. 2002, 10th TECH Tech. Award 2003, Nat. Chair Prof., Ministry of Educ. 2007–09. *Publications:* numerous papers in professional journals. *Address:* Office of the President, 1 Roosevelt Road, Section 4, Taipei 106, Taiwan (office). *Telephone:* (2) 3366-2000 (office). *Fax:* (2) 2362-1877 (office). *E-mail:* pcyang@ntu.edu.tw (office); president@ntu.edu.tw (office). *Website:* www.ntu.edu.tw (office).

YANG, Peidong, BA, PhD; American (b. Chinese) chemist and academic; *Professor of Chemistry, University of California, Berkeley;* b. 1971, Suzhou; m. Mei Wang; one d.; ed Univ. of Science and Tech. of China (USTC), Hefei, Harvard Univ., USA; Postdoctoral Fellow, Univ. of Calif., Santa Barbara 1997–99; joined Chem. Dept, Univ. of Calif., Berkeley 1999, Chevron Texaco Asst Prof. 2003–04, Assoc. Prof. 2004, now Prof. of Chemistry and S.K. and Angela Chan Distinguished Prof. of Energy; Co-Founder Nanosys Inc.; Assoc. Ed. Journal of the American Chemical Soc.; mem. ACS (Chair., Nanoscience Div. 2003–), American Physical Soc., Materials Research Soc., American Acad. of Arts and Sciences 2012; known for work in nanotechnology; USTC Guo Moruo Prize 1993, Camille and Henry Dreyfus New Faculty Award 1999, 3M Untenured Faculty Award 2000, Research Innovation Award 2001, NSF Career Award 2001, Hellman Family Faculty Award 2001, ACS ExxonMobil Solid State Chem. Award 2001, Beckman Young Investigator Award 2002, Camille Dreyfus Teacher-Scholar Award 2004, Materials Research Soc. Outstanding Young Investigator Award 2004, ACS Pure Chem. Award 2005, NSF Waterman Award 2007, Scientific American 50 Award 2008. *Address:* Department of Chemistry, University of California, Berkeley, CA 94720-1460, USA (office). *Telephone:* (510) 643-1545 (office). *Fax:* (510) 642-7301 (office). *E-mail:* p_yang@berkeley.edu (office). *Website:* www.cchem.berkeley.edu (office).

YANG, Philémon Yunji; Cameroonian lawyer, politician and fmr diplomatist; *Prime Minister;* b. 14 June 1947, Jiketum-Oku, NW Prov.; ed Univ. of Yaoundé; began career as Prosecutor, Court of Appeal, Buea 1975; Vice-Minister of Territorial Admin 1975–78, Minister of Mines and Power, Livestock and Animal Industries 1978–80, Minister of Mines and Power 1980–84; Amb. to Canada 1984–95, High Commr to Canada 1995–2004; Asst Sec. Gen. at the Presidency 2004–09; Prime Minister 2009–; mem. Rassemblement démocratique du peuple camerounais. *Address:* Office of the Prime Minister, Yaoundé, Cameroon (office). *Telephone:* 2223-8005 (office). *Fax:* 2223-5735 (office). *E-mail:* spm@spm.gov.cm (office). *Website:* (office).

YANG, Rudai; Chinese party official; b. 1926, Renshou Co., Sichuan Prov.; m. Tan Xiaoying; joined CCP 1952; Sec. CCP Renshou Co. Cttee 1952–68; mem. 4th NPC 1975–78; Sec. CCP Leshan Prefectural Cttee, Sichuan Prov. 1977–78; mem. Standing Cttee CCP Sichuan Prov. Cttee 1978–82, Sec. CCP Sichuan Prov. Cttee 1982; Vice-Gov. of Sichuan Prov. 1978–82; mem. 12th Cen. Cttee CCP 1982–87, 13th Cen. Cttee CCP 1987–92; mem. Politburo 1987–92; Political Commissar, Sichuan Mil. Dist 1983–86; First Sec. Party Cttee 1985; Sec. CCP Sichuan 1983–93; mem. Presidium 14th CCP Nat. Congress 1992; Vice-Chair. 8th CPPCC Nat. Cttee 1993–98, 9th CPPCC Nat. Cttee 1998–2003; Hon. Pres. Special Rural Tech. Asscn of China 1995. *Address:* c/o National Committee of Chinese People's Political Consultative Conference, 23 Taipingqiao Street, Beijing, People's Republic of China (office).

YANG, Tae-jin, BA; South Korean business executive; *Co-CEO and Representative Director, Trade Division, Hanwha Corporation;* ed Seoul Nat. Univ., Grad. School of Business Admin, Yonsei Univ.; joined Korea Explosives 1971, Dir in charge of Business, Golden Bell Trading Inc. 1994–97, Man. Dir Hanwha Japan 1997–2002, Officer in charge of Hanwha Corpn/Trade Div. 2002–04, Rep. Dir Hanwha Corpn/Trade Div. 2004–10, Co-CEO and Rep. Dir Trade Div., Hanwha Corpn 2010–. *Address:* Hanwha Corpn, Hanwha Building, 1 Changgyo-dong, Chung-ku, Seoul 100-797, Republic of Korea (office). *Telephone:* (2) 729-2700 (office); (2) 729-1114 (office). *Fax:* (2) 729-1762 (office). *E-mail:* hanwhacorp@hanwha.co.kr (office). *Website:* english.hanwhacorp.co.kr (office).

YANG, Taifang; Chinese politician (retd); b. 30 April 1927, Mei Co., Guangdong Prov.; s. of Yang Shukum and Wen Xinyun; m. Wu Youhong 1957; one s. two d.; ed Zhongshan Univ.; Vice-Minister of Posts and Telecommunications 1982–84, Minister 1984–92; mem. 12th Cen. Cttee CCP 1982–87, 13th Cen. Cttee 1987–92; Chair. Overseas Chinese Cttee 8th NPC 1993–98; mem. Presidium 14th CCP Nat. Congress 1992–97; NPC Deputy, Guangdong Prov.; mem. Standing Cttee 8th NPC 1993–98; Chair. All-China Fed. of Returned Overseas Chinese 1994; expert in telecommunications tech. *Leisure interests:* music, bridge, Taiji boxing. *Address:* c/o Overseas Chinese Committee of the National People's Congress, 23 Xijiao Minxiang Road, West District, Beijing 100805, People's Republic of China (office).

YANG, Hon. Sir Ti Liang, Kt, LLB, FCIA; Chinese judge (retd); b. 30 June 1929, Shanghai; s. of Shao-nan Yang and Elsie Chun; m. Eileen Barbara Tam 1954 (died 2006); two s.; ed The Comparative Law School of China, Soochow Univ., Shanghai, Univ. Coll. London, UK; called to Bar (with Hons), Gray's Inn 1954; Magistrate, Hong Kong 1956, Sr Magistrate 1963, Dist Court 1968, Judge of High Court 1975, Justice of Appeal 1980, Vice-Pres. Court of Appeal 1987, Chief Justice of Hong Kong 1988–96; mem. Exec. Council, Hong Kong Special Admin. Region 1997–2002; Pres. of Court of Appeal of Negara Brunei Darussalam 1988–92; Rockefeller Fellow, London Univ. 1963–64; Chair. Kowloon Disturbances Claims Assessment Bd 1966, Compensation Bd 1967, Comm. of Inquiry into the Rainstorm Disasters 1972, into Lelung Wing-sang Case 1976, into McLennan Case 1980; mem. Law Reform Comm. (Chair. Sub-Cttee on law relating to homosexuality 1980) 1980–96; Chair. Chief Justice Working Party on Voir Dire Procedures and Judges' Rules 1979, Univ. and Polytechnic Grants Cttee 1981–84, Hong Kong Univ. Council 1987–2001; Chair. ICAC Complaints Cttee 1999–2002, Hong Kong Red Cross 2000–; Pro-Chancellor, Hong Kong Univ. 1994–2001; Patron The Soc. for the Rehabilitation of Offenders, Hong Kong; Vice-Patron Hong Kong Scouts Asscn; Hon. Prof., Open Univ. of Hong Kong 2006; Order of Chivalry (First Class), SPMB, Negara Brunei Darus-salam 1990, Grand Bauhinia Medal 1999; Hon. LLD (Chinese Univ. of Hong Kong) 1984, (Hong Kong Polytechnic) 1992; Hon. DLitt (Hong Kong Univ.) 1991. *Publications:* (trans.) General Yue Fei (by Qian Cai) 1995, (trans.) Peach Blossom Fan (novel by Gu Shifân 1948) 1998, (trans.) Officialdom Unmasked (novel by Li Boyuan) 2001. *Leisure interests:* philately, reading, walking, oriental ceramics, travelling, music. *Address:* GPO Box 1123, Central, Hong Kong Special Administrative Region, People's Republic of China (office). *Telephone:* (852) 91373067 (office). *Fax:* (852) 28498099 (home).

YANG, Wei, MS, PhD; Chinese engineering scientist; *Director, National Natural Science Foundation of China;* b. 16 Feb. 1954, Beijing; ed Northwestern Polytechnical Univ., Tsinghua Univ., Brown Univ., USA; joined CCP 1976; Faculty mem. and Chair. Dept of Eng Mechanics, Tsinghua Univ., also Acting Dean, School of Aerospace 1978–2004, Dean 2004–05; Dir Ministry of Educ., Postgraduate Educ. Dept 2004–06; Pres. Zhejiang Univ. 2006–13; Dir Nat. Natural Science Foundation of China 2013–; Hon. DS (Brown Univ.) 2012. *Address:* National Natural Science Foundation of China, 83 Shuangqing Rd, Haidian, Beijing 310058, Zhejiang, People's Republic of China (office). *Telephone:* (10) 6231-1188. *E-mail:* Bic@nsfc.gov.cn (office). *Website:* www.nsfc.gov.cn (office).

YANG, Yong-eun; South Korean professional golfer; b. 15 Jan. 1972, Jeju-do; m. Ju Pak Young 1999; three c.; served with S Korean Army; professional golfer, Korean Professional Golfers' Asscn (PGA) Tour, Japan Golf Tour, European Tour 2006–, PGA Tour 2008–; mem. Asian team Royal Trophy 2007; won Korean Tour event, SBS Championship 2002, Japan Golf Tour events, Sun Chlorella Classic 2004, Asahi Ryokuken Yomiuri Asolizuka 2004, Coca-Cola Tokai Classic 2005, Suntory Open 2006, Asian Tour event, Kolon Hana Bank Korea Open 2006, European Tour event, HSBC Champions 2006, PGA Tour events, The Honda Classic 2009, PGA Championship 2009; Rookie of Year, Korean PGA Tour 1997. *Address:* c/o IMG Korea, 5th Floor, Namdo Building 823–24, Yeoksam-Dong, Kangnam-Gu, Seoul, 135-080, South Korea. *Telephone:* (2) 558-8544. *Fax:* (2) 558-8540.

YANG, Yu-liang, BSc, PhD; Chinese chemist, academic and university administrator; *President, Fudan University;* b. Zhejiang; ed Fudan Univ.; post-doctoral researcher, Max Planck Inst. for Polymer Research 1986–88; mem. Faculty, Fudan Univ., Vice-Pres. for Research 1999–2006, Pres. Fudan Univ. 2009–; Dir Gen. Dept of Degree and Postgraduate Educ., State Council of People's Repub. of China 2006–09; Sr Adviser, Shanghai Municipal Govt; serves on the boards of several academic journals including Chinese Journal of Chemistry and Science in China; leads Nat. 973 Project and Nat. 863 Project; mem. Chinese Acad. of Sciences 2003; Cheung Kong Scholar, Nat. Scientific and Technological Progress Award, First Prize, Science and Tech. Progress Awards, China Petroleum and Chemical Corpn 2003, Second Prize 2004, Science and Tech. Progress Award, Ho Leung Ho Lee Foundation 2007, Outstanding Scientist Award, Qiushi Foundation 2008, amongst others. *Publications:* about 260 papers in professional journals on condensed matter physics and polymer science; several domestic and int. patents. *Address:* Office of the President, Fudan University, 220 Handan Road, Shanghai 200433, People's Republic of China (office). *Telephone:* (21) 65642222 (office). *E-mail:* xjshi@fudan.edu.cn (office). *Website:* www.fudan.edu.cn (office).

YANG, Yuanqing, MSc; Chinese computer industry executive; *Chairman and CEO, Lenovo Group;* b. 12 Nov. 1964; ed Univ. of Science and Tech. of China; joined Lenovo Group 1989, CEO 2001, later Pres. and CEO Lenovo Group Ltd, Exec. Chair. 2004–09, CEO 2009–, Chair. 2011–; mem. New York Stock Exchange (now NYSE Euronext) Int. Advisory Cttee, Nat. Youth Asscn Cttee; mem. Bd of Dirs China's Entrepreneurs' Asscn; Guest Prof., Univ. of Science and Tech. of China; named by Forbes Asia as Asian Businessman of the Year by BusinessWeek magazine as one of the Stars of Asia, selected by Chinese media as one of China's Ten Star Entrepreneurs and Ten Most Valuable Managers, named by CCTV as a

Man of the Year 2004. *Address:* Lenovo Group, No. 6 Chuang Ye Road, Shangdi Information Industry Base, Haidian District, Beijing 100085, People's Republic of China (office). *Telephone:* (10) 58868888 (office). *E-mail:* info@lenovo.com (office). *Website:* www.lenovo.com (office).

YANG, Zhengwu; Chinese politician; b. Jan. 1941, Longshan Co., Hunan Prov.; joined CCP 1969; Deputy Sec. CCP Longshan Co. Cttee 1970, Sec. 1970–77; Sec. CCP Tujia-Miao Autonomous Prefectural Cttee, Hunan Prov., Xiangxi 1985–90, Deputy Magistrate, Intermediate People's Court 1985–90; mem. Standing Cttee CCP Hunan Prov. Cttee 1985–90, Deputy Sec. CCP Hunan Prov. Cttee 1990–98, Sec. 1998; Chair. Standing Cttee of People's Congress 1999–; Chair. Comm. for Comprehensive Man. of Social Security 1993–; Gov. of Hunan Prov. 1995–98; Alt. mem. 12th CCP Cen. Cttee 1982–87, mem. 13th CCP Cen. Cttee 1987–92, 14th CCP Cen. Cttee, 15th CCP Cen. Cttee 1997–2002, 16th CCP Cen. Cttee 2002–07. *Address:* Provincial People's Congress, Changsha, Hunan Province, People's Republic of China (office).

YANG, Zhenhuai; Chinese government official; b. Jan. 1928, Anhui; s. of Yang Licuo and Wu Dingshu; m. Yang Duanyi 1960; one s. one d.; joined CCP 1950; Vice-Minister for Water Resources and Electric Power 1983–88, Minister for Water Resources 1988–93; Sec.-Gen. State Flood Control HQ 1986–88, Deputy Head 1988; Deputy Head State Leading Group for Comprehensive Agric. Devt 1990; Vice-Chair. Environmental and Resources Protection Cttee; Hon. Vice-Chair. All-China Environment Fed. (ACEF); Alt. mem. 14th CCP Cen. Cttee 1992–97; mem. 9th Standing Cttee of NPC 1998–2003, Vice-Chair. Agric. and Rural Affairs Cttee 1998–2003. *Leisure interests:* reading history, geology, humane studies. *Address:* c/o All China Environment Federation, 6th Floor, HuaBiao Building, Hepingli Dongcheng, Beijing 100013, People's Republic of China (office).

YANG, Zhiguang; Chinese artist; b. 11 Oct. 1930, Shanghai; s. of Yang Miaocheng and Shi Qinxian; m. Ou Yang 1958; two d.; ed Cen. Acad. of Fine Art; Vice-Pres. and Prof., Guangzhou Acad. of Fine Arts; mem. Council, Chinese Artists' Asscn; mem. Acad. of Traditional Chinese Painting; does traditional Chinese figure painting, calligraphy and seal-making; Artist-in-Residence, Griffis Art Center, Conn., USA 1990; Gold Medal winner, 7th Vienna World Youth Festival, for picture Sending Food in Heavy Snow 1959, US China Outstanding Contribution Award 2012. *Publications:* Skill of Chinese Traditional Figure Painting, Selections of Portraits, Chinese Water Colours, Yang Zhiguang's Sketches in China's North-west, Portraits of Modern Chinese Artists, Painting Selections of Mr and Mrs Yang Zhiguang. *Leisure interests:* calligraphy, seal-making, poetry. *Address:* Guangzhou Institute of Fine Art, No. 257, Chang Gang Dong Lu Street, Haizhu District, Guangzhou, People's Republic of China (office). *Telephone:* (20) 84017598 (home). *Fax:* (20) 84017417 (home).

YANG, Zhuangsheng; Chinese business executive; *General Manager, Chairman and Chief Executive Officer, Science-Technology Group;* b. Dec. 1942; ed Univ. of Int. Business and Econs; Gen. Man., Chair. and CEO Science-Technology (SCITECH) Group 1991–. *Address:* Saite Dasha, 19 Jianguomenwai Da Jie, Beijing 100004, People's Republic of China (office).

YANGIBAEV, Baxadir; Uzbekistani politician; *Chairman of the Council of Ministers of the Sovereign Republic of Qoraqalpog'iston;* b. 1960, Beruni dist, Kara-Kalpak ASSR, Uzbek SSR, USSR; ed Tashkent Highways Inst., Tashkent State Econs Univ., specializing as Engineer-Constructor; economist responsible for highways repairs and construction in Beruni dist 1982, worked in various Komsomol and CP cttees 1982–93, Man. Insp., Head of Econ.-Analytical Dept of Qoraqalpog'iston br. of Tadbirkorbank 1993–95, Aide to the Chair. of Council of Ministers of Sovereign Repub. of Qoraqalpog'iston 1995–96; First Deputy Chair., Chief Dept of Cen. Bank of Uzbekistan for Qoraqalpog'iston 1996–99, Head of regional br. in Qoraqalpog'iston of Gallabanka; Minister of Finance, Sovereign Repub. of Qoraqalpog'iston 2002–06, Chair. Council of Ministers 2006–; mem. Council of Ministers of Uzbekistan; fmr Gov. To'rtku'l Dist. *Address:* Office of the Chairman, Council of Ministers of the Republic of Qoraqalpog'iston, 230102 Qoraqalpog'iston, Nukus, Dustlik Gazari 96, Uzbekistan (office). *Telephone:* (361) 222-05-01 (office); (361) 222-00-14 (office). *Fax:* (361) 222-26-46 (office). *E-mail:* info@sovminrk.gov.uz (office). *Website:* sovminrk.gov.uz (office).

YANGLING, Duoji; Chinese politician and academic; b. 24 April 1931, Batang Co., Sichuan Prov.; s. of Yang Yong-an and Basang-wengmo; m. Qumu-a Ying 1954; two s. one d.; Vice-Gov. Sichuan Prov. 1979–81; Perm. Sec. CCP Cttee, Tibet Autonomous Region 1981–86; Vice-Chair. People's Govt 1982–83; Alt. mem. 12th CCP Cen. Cttee 1982–87; Chair. Tibet Br., CPPCC 1983–86; Vice-Chair. and Vice-Sec. of Party, Sichuan CPPCC 1986; del. to 7th People's Congress of China 1988–92; Del. to 11th Congress of CCP 1980–82, 12th 1982–87, 13th 1987–92; Chair. Tibetan Studies Assn, Sichuan Prov.; Dean Acad. of Tibetan Studies, Sichuan Prov. 1990–; Ed. Tibetology Research, History of Kong Tibetan 1996–. *Leisure interest:* reading. *Address:* Office of the Vice-Chairman of the Chinese People's Consultative Council, No. 25 Hong Zhao Bi Street, Chengdu, Sichuan, People's Republic of China (office). *Telephone:* (28) 6753780 (home). *Fax:* (28) 663393.

YANIN, Valentin Lavrentyevich, DHist; Russian archaeologist; *Head Chair of Archaeology, Moscow University;* b. 6 Feb. 1929; m.; ed Moscow State Univ.; jr then sr researcher Moscow Univ. 1954–, Prof. 1963–, also Head Chair. of Archaeology, Moscow Univ.; researcher of history and archaeology of Middle Age Russia and of old manuscripts; Chair. of Bd Russian Humanitarian Scientific Fund (RGNF) 1996–; Corresp. mem. USSR (now Russian) Acad. of Sciences 1966, mem. 1990, mem. Presidium 1991–2002; Hon. Citizen of Novgorod; Lenin Prize, USSR State Prize. *Publications include:* Money and Weight Systems of Medieval Russia 1956, Novgorod Posadniki 1962, I Have Sent You a Birch Bark 1965, Act Stamps of Old Russia X–XV Centuries 1970, Novgorod Feudal Ancestral Lands 1982, Novgorod Acts XII–XV Centuries 1991. *Leisure interest:* collecting old vocal recordings. *Address:* RGNF, Yaroslavskaya str. 13, 129366 Moscow, Russia. *Telephone:* (495) 283-55-40 (office); (495) 335-54-28 (home).

YANKILEVSKY, Vladimir Borissovich; Russian/French artist; b. 15 Feb. 1938, Moscow, Russia; s. of Boris Yankilevsky and Rosa Yankilevskaya; m. Rimma Solod 1959; one d.; ed Moscow Secondary Art School and Moscow Polygraphic Inst.; took part in Manège exhbn of 1962; participated in first officially permitted Exhbn of

avant-garde artists 1975; first retrospective in Moscow 1978; first retrospectives in the West (New York and Bochum Museum, Germany) 1988; first participation in Sotheby's Auction in Moscow 1988; retrospectives in Moscow 1987, Paris 1991, Tretyakov Gallery, Moscow 1995–96, Neuhoff Gallery, New York 1996, Mané-Katz Museum, Haifa 2001, La femme à côté de la mer, Galerie Dina Vierny, Paris 2001, Artiste et son modèle, Group 2 Gallery, Brussels 2002, Collagen, Museum Bochum 2002, The Space of Experience, Sam Brook Gallery, Moscow 2003, Mutants, Krokin Gallery, Moscow 2003, Moment of Eternity, Ekaterina Cultural Foundation, Moscow and State Russian Museum, St Petersburg 2007, Métamorphoses, Galerie Le Minotaure, Paris 2009, Anatomy of Feelings, The Mall Galleries and Aktis Gallery, London 2010, Early Works, Aktis Gallery, London 2013; Art Critics' Prize 'Maître', Moscow 2007. *Animation work includes:* The World of Tales 1973, I Fly to You 1977, I Am with You Again 1977. *Television:* Good Evening, Moscow (Moscow, TV Gallery) 1996, Portraits of Artists-Nonconformists (Moscow, TV Gallery, Culture Channel) 2001. *Publications:* Retrospective 1958–1988 1988, Autoportraits 1992, Retrospective 1995–96 1995, Retrospective 1996, Radierungen: Anatomie der Gefühle; Stadt – Masken; Mutanten (Sodom und Gomorra) 1999, Maleri, Collage, Grafik 1999, Retrospective 2001, Variations on the Other – A Digital-Analog Monograph on the Work of Vladimir Yankilevsky (co-ed by David Riff) 2002, I dve figury … Tales for My Friend (in Russian) 2003, Moment of Eternity 2007, Métamorphoses 2009, Anatomy of Feelings 2010. *Leisure interest:* photography. *Address:* 230 rue St Charles, 75015 Paris, France (home). *Telephone:* 1-45-58-21-57 (home). *Fax:* 1-45-58-21-57. *E-mail:* yankilevsky@gmail.com. *Website:* www.vladimiryankilevsky.com.

YANNARAS, Christos, PhD, DrTheol; Greek philosopher and academic; *Professor Emeritus of Philosophy, Panteion University of Political and Social Studies;* b. 10 April 1935, Athens; ed Univ. of Athens, Univ. of Bonn, Germany, Univ. of Paris (Sorbonne), France, Faculty of Theology, Aristotle Univ. of Thessaloniki, Faculté des Lettres et Sciences Humaines, Sorbonne; Visiting Prof., Catholic Univ. of Paris 1971–73, Univ. of Geneva, Switzerland 1977–79, Univ. of Lausanne, Switzerland 1978–79, Univ. of Crete (Rethymnon) 1979–82; Prof. of Philosophy, Panteion Univ. of Political and Social Studies, Athens 1982–2005, Prof. Emer. 2005–; mem. Hellenic Authors' Soc., Acad. Int. des Sciences Humaines, Brussels, Belgium; Hon. DPhil (Belgrade), Hon. DD (St Vladimir's Orthodox Theological Seminary, New York), (Holy Cross Coll., Boston) 2011. *Publications include:* more than 60 books, including Critical Ontology (3rd edn) 1995, The Real and the Imaginary in the Political Economy (2nd edn) 1996, Heidegger and the Areopagite (4th edn) 1998, The Linguistic Boundaries of Realism in Metaphysics 1999, The Inhuman Character of Human Rights (3rd edn) 2000, The Freedom of Morality (3rd edn) 2002, Discontinuity in Philosophy (5th edn) 2002, Cultural Diplomacy (2nd edn) 2003, Postmodern Metaphysics (2nd edn) 2004, The Relational Ontology 2004, Variations on the Song of Songs (6th edn) 2005, Culture as the Central Problem in Politics (2nd edn) 2005, Orthodoxy and the West (5th edn) 2006, The Religionization of the Ecclesial Event (2nd edn) 2007, Person and Eros (6th edn) 2007; translated into many European languages. *Address:* 84 Plastira Street, 171 21 Nea Smyrni, Athens, Greece (home). *Telephone:* (210) 935-3697 (office). *Fax:* (210) 935-3697 (office). *E-mail:* anpa@uom.gr (office).

YANO, Akiko; Japanese musician; b. 1955, Tokyo; m. Sakamoto Ryuichi; ed classical training; child piano prodigy; familiar with jazz, pop and R&B at early age; working musician in Tokyo club scene during high school and began singing at this time; played on many albums as session musician in Japan; appeared in concert with Tin Pan Alley; recorded track album by Little Feat, Los Angeles; first solo album Japanese Girl 1976; participated in Yellow Magic Orchestra world tour 1979–80; double solo album co-produced by herself and her husband titled Gohan Ga Dekitayo (Dinner's Ready!) 1980. *Albums include:* Nagatsuki Kan Nazuki 1976, I Rohani Konpeitou 1977, To Ki Me Ki 1978, Gohan Ga Dekitayo 1980, Tadaima 1981, Ai Ga Nakuchane 1982, O.S.O.S. 1984, Brooch 1986, Granola 1987, Welcome Back Akiko Yano 1989, Super Folk Song 1992, Love Is Here 1993, Elephant Hotel 1994, Oui Oui 1997, Ego Girl 1999, Home Journey Girl 2000, Reverb 2002, Honto No Kimochi 2004, Hajimete No Yano Akiko 2006, Akiko 2008, Ongakudo 2010, Yano Akiko, Imawano Kiyoshirō o Utau 2013. *Address:* c/o Sony Music Entertainment Inc., 550 Madison Avenue, New York, NY 10022-3211, USA. *Website:* www.akikoyano.com.

YANO, Kaoru, MSc; Japanese electronics industry executive; *Chairman, NEC Corporation;* b. 23 Feb. 1944; ed Univ. of Tokyo, Stanford Univ., USA; joined NEC Corpn 1966, based in USA 1985–90, Gen. Man. Transmission Div. 1990–94, Exec. Gen. Man. Transmission Operations Unit 1994–95, Assoc. Sr Vice-Pres. 1995–99, Pres. NEC USA Inc. 1998–2000, Sr Vice-Pres. 1999–2002, mem. Bd of Dirs 2000–, Deputy Pres. NEC Networks Co. 2000–02, Pres. NEC Networks Co. 2002–03, Exec. Vice-Pres. NEC Corpn 2002–04, Sr Exec. Vice-Pres. and Rep. Dir 2004–06, Pres. and Rep. Dir 2006–10, Chair. and Rep. Dir 2010–12, Chair. 2012–. *Address:* NEC Corporation, 7-1, Shiba 5-chome, Minato-ku, Tokyo 108-8001, Japan (office). *Telephone:* (3) 3454-1111 (office). *Fax:* (3) 3798-1510 (office). *E-mail:* info@nec.com (office). *Website:* www.nec.com (office).

YANOFSKY, Charles, PhD; American biologist and academic; *Morris Herzstein Professor Emeritus of Biology, Stanford University;* b. 17 April 1925, New York, NY; s. of Frank Yanofsky and Jennie Kopatz Yanofsky; m. 1st Carol Cohen 1949 (died 1990); three s.; m. 2nd Edna Crawford 1992; ed City Coll. of New York and Yale Univ.; Research Asst in Microbiology, Yale Univ. 1951–53; Asst Prof. of Microbiology, Western Reserve Univ. 1954–58; Assoc. Prof., Dept of Biological Sciences, Stanford Univ., Prof., Dept of Biological Sciences 1961–, Morris Herzstein Prof. of Biology 1967, now Prof. Emer.; Pres. Genetics Soc. of America 1969, American Soc. of Biological Chemists 1984; Career Investigator American Heart Assscn 1969–95; mem. NAS, American Acad. of Arts and Sciences; Foreign mem. Royal Soc. 1985–; Fellow, European Acad. of Sciences 2004; Hon. mem. Japanese Biochemical Soc. 1985–; Hon. DSc (Univ. of Chicago) 1980, (Yale Univ.) 1981; Eli Lilly Award in Bacteriology 1959, US Steel Award in Molecular Biology 1964, Howard Taylor Ricketts Award 1966, Albert Lasker Award for Basic Medical Research 1971, Selman A. Waksman Award 1972, Louisa Gross Horwitz Prize 1976, Townsend Harris Medal, City Coll. of New York, Mattia Award, Roche Inst. 1982, Genetics Soc. of America Medal 1983, Gairdner Foundation Award 1985, Thomas Hunt Morgan Medal, Genetics Soc. of America 1990, Passano Award 1992, William C. Rose Award of the ASBMB 1997, Abbott-ASM Lifetime Achievement

Award 1998, Nat. Medal of Sciences 2003. *Publications:* more than 400 scientific articles in Proceedings of Nat. Acad. of Sciences, etc. *Leisure interests:* tennis, growing orchids. *Address:* Department of Biological Sciences, Stanford University, Stanford, CA 94305 (office); 725 Mayfield Avenue, Stanford, CA 94305, USA (home). *Telephone:* (650) 725-1836 (office); (650) 857-9057 (home). *Fax:* (650) 725-8221 (office). *E-mail:* yanofsky@stanford.edu (office). *Website:* med.stanford.edu/profiles/faculty/Charles_Yanofsky (office).

YANSANÉ, Kerfalla; Guinean economist and politician; *Minister of Mines and Geology;* fmr Gov. Banque Centrale de la République de Guinée; many roles as int. econ. consultant, including assignments with World Bank, African Devt Bank, UN Econ. Comm. for Africa, UNDP, Int. Lawyers and Economists against Poverty, Toronto, Canada; fmr Vice-Chair. African Econ. Research Consortium, Nairobi, Kenya; fmr Chair. Operations Cttee, African Capacity Building Foundation, Harare, Zimbabwe; fmr Lead Consultant, New Partnership for Africa's Devt African Peer Review Mechanism; Minister of the Economy and Finance 2010–14, of Mines and Geology 2014–. *Address:* Ministry of Mines and Geology, BP 295, Conakry, Guinea (office). *Telephone:* 300-41-38-33 (office). *Fax:* 300-41-49-13 (office).

YANUKOVYCH, Viktor Fedorovych, DEcon; Ukrainian politician and fmr head of state; b. 9 July 1950, Yenakiyevo, Donetsk Oblast; m. Lyudmyla Oleksandrivna Yanukovych; two s.; ed Donetsk Polytechnic Inst., Ukrainian Acad. of Foreign Trade; worked in a variety of early jobs including welder, Yenakiyevo metal works 1969–70, fitter and mechanic in automobile factory 1972–76, dir of transport depot 1976–84; mem. CP of Soviet Union 1980–91; moved to Donetsk 1984, held exec. positions at transport cos; fmr Dir-Gen. of major production firms including Donbastransremont, Ukrvuhlepromtrans, Donetsk Oblast Motor Transport Territorial Production Asscn 1994–96; Deputy Gov., then First Deputy Gov. of Donetsk Oblast State Admin 1996–97, Gov. 1997–2002; Chair. Donetsk Oblast Council 1999–2001 (resgnd); Prime Minister of Ukraine 2002–7 Dec. 2004, 28 Dec. 2004–5 Jan. 2005, 2006–07; unsuccessful presidential cand. 2004; Pres. of Ukraine 2010–14 (fled the capital for Kharkiv following popular protests, then travelled to Crimea, eventually to southern Russia, impeached by Parl. Feb. 2014, warrant for arrest issued, placed on US sanction list March 2014); Chair. Party of Regions 2003–10; Ind. 2010–; Prof., mem. Acad. of Econ. Sciences of Ukraine; Pres. Nat. Olympic Cttee of Ukraine 2002–05; mem. Presidium Nat. Acad. of Sciences of Ukraine; Merited Worker of Ukrainian Transport, Order of Merit, 3rd Class 1998, 2nd Class 2000, 1st Class 2002, Order 'Miner's Award' 3, 2, 1 Class, Order 'Miner's Glory' 3, 2, 1 Class, Certificate from the Cabinet of Ministers of Ukraine 2000, Order of Saint Nestor 1998, Order of St Prince Volodmyr, 3rd Class 1998, 2nd Class 2004, 1st Class 2010, Order of St Daniyel of Moscow 2004, Order of St Sergius, 1st Class 2004, Grand Croix, Légion d'honneur 2010, Order of the Precious Wand (Mongolia) 2011, Order of St Mashtots (Armenia) 2011, Order of José Martí (Cuba) 2011, Order Ismoili Samoni (Tajikistan) 2011. *Leisure interests:* sport (especially tennis), hunting, pigeon raising.

YAO, Ming; Chinese professional basketball player (retd); b. 12 Sept. 1980, Shanghai; s. of Yao Zhiyuan and Fang Fengdi; m. Ye Li; ed Shanghai Sports Coll.; center; played for Chinese Basketball Asscn Shanghai Sharks 1997–2002; drafted first overall by Nat. Basketball Asscn (NBA) Houston Rockets 2002; retd 2011; mem. Chinese Olympic team 2000 Sydney, 2004 Athens; carried Olympic Flame into Tiananmen Square during Olympic torch relay August 2008; led Chinese delegation during Olympic opening ceremony; mem. Chinese nat. team, Beijing Summer Olympics 2008; Chinese Basketball Asscn (CBA) Most Valuable Player 2001, 2002; CBA Sportsmanship Award 2002; selected for NBA All-Rookie team 2002; selected for NBA All-Star Game 2003, 2004, 2005, 2006, 2007; Laureus World Newcomer of the Year 2003, Laureus China Prominent Achievement of the Year 2011. *Publications:* Yao: A Life in Two Worlds (with Ric Bucher) 2004. *Address:* c/o Houston Rockets, Toyota Center, 1510 Polk Street, Houston, TX 77002, USA.

YAO, Yan; Chinese engineer and business executive; *General Manager and President, China National Building Materials Group;* b. Shanghai; successively held posts of Supt of Building Architecture Station, China Building Materials Acad., Pres. Asst, Supt of Cement and New Material Research Inst., Pres. and Deputy Gen. Man. China Nat. Building Materials Group, currently Dir, Gen. Man., Pres. and Vice-Sec. Party Cttee; Pres. China Building Materials Acad. *Address:* China National Building Materials Group, 2 South Zi Zhu Yuan Road, Beijing 100048, People's Republic of China (office). *Telephone:* (10) 88416688 (office); (10) 68720842 (office). *Fax:* (10) 68422743 (office). *E-mail:* cnbmadmin@cnbm.com.cn (office). *Website:* www.cnbm.com.cn (office).

YAO, Zhonghua; Chinese artist; b. 17 July 1939, Kunming, Yunnan; s. of the late Yao Penxien and Wang Huiyuan; m. Ma Huixian 1969; two s.; ed Cen. Acad. of Fine Arts; one-man show, Beijing 1980, Cité Int. Arts, Paris 1985 and exhbns in Paris and Eastern Europe; numerous group exhbns in China, also China Oil Paintings of Present Age Exhbn, New York, USA 1987, Melbourne, Sydney, Australia 1987, Wan Yu Tang Art Gallery, Hong Kong 1989; group exhbn Beijing Art Gallery 1992; one-man exhbn Taiwan 1992, Calif., USA 1995; mural for Parl. Hall, Yunnan People's Congress; mem. Council China Artists' Asscn; Vice-Pres. Yunnan Painting Inst. *Works include:* Oh, the Land!, Sani Minority's Festival, The Yellow River, Zhenghe's Voyage, The Jinsha River Flowing beside the Jade Dragon Mountain, Chinese Ink and Water. *Publications:* paper on painter Dong Xi Wen, in Chinese Oil Painting and Art Research 1990, Selected Works of Yao Zhonghua 1993. *Leisure interests:* music, literature. *Address:* c/o China Art Networks, 7/F, Xinzhong Mansion, Gongti Beilu, Beijing, People's Republic of China.

YAQUB, Muhammad, PhD; Pakistani banker and economist; b. 1937, Jalandar, India; s. of Haji Muhammad Shah and Bibi Karim; m. Nasreen Yaqub; two s. one d.; ed Punjab Univ., Yale Univ., Princeton Univ., USA; mem. Pakistan Taxation Comm. 1966–72; Asst Dir, Research Dept State Bank of Pakistan 1966–68, Deputy Dir 1968–69, Sr Deputy Dir 1969–72, Sr Prin. Officer, Dir Research Dept 1975, Gov. 1993–99; Sr Economist and Resident Rep., IMF, Saudi Arabia 1975, Fund Resident Adviser to Saudi Arabian Govt, IMF 1977, Div. Chief, Middle Eastern Dept IMF 1977–80, Asst Dir 1981–82, IMF Rep. to Paris Club, London Club, OECD

and co. aid consortia; Consultant IMF, Washington; Prin. Econ. Adviser, Special Section, Ministry of Finance 1992–93; Gov. State Bank of Pakistan 1993–99; has headed IMF missions to numerous Middle Eastern countries; mem. Bd of Dirs MCB Bank. *Publications include:* Major-Macro Economic Policy Issues in Pakistan. *Address:* c/o Board of Directors, MCB Bank, 16th Floor, MCB Tower, I.I Chundrigar Road, Karachi 74000, Pakistan (office).

YARK, Col Damehane; Togolese police officer and politician; *Minister of Security and Civil Protection;* b. 31 Dec. 1963, Worgou, Tône Dist; Dir-Gen. Gendarmerie nationale (police force) 2008–12; Minister of Security and Civil Protection 2012–. *Address:* Ministry of Security and Civil Protection, rue Albert Sarraut, Lomé, Togo (office). *Telephone:* 22-22-57-12 (office). *Fax:* 22-22-61-50 (office). *E-mail:* info@republicoftogo.com (office).

YARMOSHYN, Uladzimir Vasilyevich; Belarusian politician and engineer; b. 26 Oct. 1942, Pronsk, Ryazan Region, Russia; m.; two c.; ed Novocherkassk Polytech. Inst., Leningrad Civil Aviation Acad.; turner, Electric Locomotive plant, Novocherkassk; Sr Engineer, Chief Mechanical Engineer, Deputy Dir Minsk Civil Aviation plant 1965–90; Chair. Exec. Cttee Dist Soviet of People's Deputies, Minsk 1990; Deputy Chair. Minsk City Exec. Cttee, also Head Cttee on Housing and Power Eng 1990–92; First Deputy Chair. then Chair. Minsk City Exec. Cttee 1995–2000; mem. Council in Nat. Ass.; Chair. Council of Ministers 2000–01; Head of Belorussian Reps, Mobil Telesystems 2002–03; lived in Moscow for a short period; with Vnesheconombank from 2003; supervised building of Minsk-Arena sporting complex c. 2009; Hon. Citizen of Minsk.

YAROSHENKO, Fedir O.; Ukrainian politician; various positions within Ministry of Finance, including First Deputy Minister of Finance 2002–04, Chair. State Tax Admin of Ukraine 2004, Deputy Chair. –2010, Minister of Finance 2010–12. *Address:* c/o Ministry of Finance, 01008 Kyiv, vul. M. Hrushevskoho 12/2, Ukraine.

YAROV, Yuri Fedorovich; Russian politician; b. 2 April 1942, Mariinsk, Kemerovo Oblast; m.; one s. one d.; ed Leningrad Tech. Inst., Leningrad Eng Econ. Inst.; worked in factories in Latvia 1964–68, Leningrad oblast 1968–76; Dir factory Burevestnik 1978–85; First Sec. Gatchina City CPSU Cttee (Leningrad oblast) 1985–87; Deputy Chair. Exec. Cttee Leningrad oblast Soviet of Deputies 1987–89, Chair. 1989–90; Chair. Leningrad oblast Soviet of People's Deputies 1990–91; People's Deputy of Russian Fed. 1990–92; Deputy Chair. Supreme Soviet of Russia 1991–92; Deputy Prime Minister 1992–96; Presidential Rep. to Fed. Council; Deputy Head of Presidential Admin 1996–97, First Deputy 1997–98; Plenipotentiary Rep. of Pres. of the Russian Fed. in Federation Council 1998–99; Chair. Exec. Cttee of CIS 1999–2004. *Address:* c/o Executive Committee of Commonwealth of Independent States, 220000 Minsk, vul. Kirava 17, Belarus (office).

YARROW, Sir Eric Grant, 3rd Bt (cr. 1916), MBE, DL, FRSE; British business executive (retd); b. 23 April 1920, Glasgow; s. of the late Sir Harold Yarrow, 2nd Bt and Eleanor Etheldreda Yarrow; m. 1st Rosemary Ann Young 1951 (died 1957); one s. (deceased); m. 2nd Annette Elizabeth Françoise Steven 1959 (divorced 1975); three s.; m. 3rd Joan Botting 1982; ed Marlborough Coll., Glasgow Univ.; served apprenticeship with G. and J. Weir Ltd; army service in Burma 1939–45, Maj. Royal Engineers 1945; trained with English Electric Co. 1945–46; Asst Man., Yarrow and Co. Ltd 1946, Dir 1948, Man. Dir 1958–67, Chair. 1962–85, Pres. 1985–86; Chair. Yarrow (Shipbuilders) Ltd 1962–79; Dir Clydesdale Bank 1962–91, Deputy Chair. 1975–85, Chair. 1985–91; Dir Standard Life Assurance 1958–90, Nat. Australia Bank Ltd 1987–91; mem. Council, Royal Inst. Naval Architects 1957–, Vice-Pres. 1965, Hon. Vice-Pres. 1972; mem. Gen. Cttee Lloyd's Register of Shipping 1960–87; Prime Warden, Worshipful Co. of Shipwrights 1970–71; Deacon, Incorporation of Hammermen of Glasgow 1961–62; fmr mem. Council of Inst. Engineers and Shipbuilders in Scotland; Chair. Exec. Cttee Princess Louise Scottish Hosp., Erskine 1980–86, Hon. Pres. 1986–; Pres. Scottish Convalescent Home for Children 1958–70, Burma Star Asscn in Scotland 1989–2011; Officer, Most Venerable Order of the Hosp. of St John of Jerusalem. *Leisure interest:* family life. *Address:* Craigrowan, Porterfield Road, Kilmacolm, Renfrewshire, PA13 4PD, Scotland. *Telephone:* (1505) 872067.

YARUSH, Dmytro; Ukrainian politician; *Leader, Right Sector;* b. 30 Sept. 1971, Dniprodzerzhynsk, Ukrainian SSR, USSR; m. Olha Yarush; one s. two d.; ed High School No. 24, Dniprodzerzhynsk, State Univ. of Educ., Drohobych; drafted and served two years in Soviet army as a private 1989–91; as student, mem. Young Pioneers, later of Countrywide Leninist Communist Youth League (youth-based sub-orgs of CPSU); mem. People's Movt of Ukraine 1989–94, Tryzub 1994– (Leader 2005–); Leader, Right Sector (formed with Tryzub as its core) 2013–; arrest ordered by Basmanny Court, Moscow on charges of publicly inciting terrorism, placed on int. wanted list by Russian Fed. March 2014;*Website:* pravyysektor.info (office); www.facebook.com/d.yarosh.

YASHIMA, Toshiaki; Japanese energy industry executive; Man.-Dir Tohoku Electric Power Co. Inc. 1997, apptd Pres. 1998, Chair. –2010; fmr Chair. Tohoku Econ. Fed., now Hon. Chair.; Vice-Pres. Fed. of Electric Power Cos (FEPC) 1999, Co-Vice-Chair. –2001; Dir Japan Nuclear Fuel Ltd –2001; mem. Bd Energy Conservation Center (ECCJ) 1999–2001, Japan Productivity Center for Socio-Econ. Devt (JPC-SED); mem. Advisory Cttee UNU Global Seminars. *Address:* c/o Tohoku Electric Power Company Inc., 7-1 Honcho 1-chome, Aoba-ku, Sendai, Miyagi 980-8550, Japan. *Telephone:* (2) 2225-2111. *Website:* www.tohoku-epco.co.jp.

YASIN, Yevgeny Grigoryevich, DEconSc; Russian politician, economist and academic; *Professor, Higher School of Economics;* b. 7 May 1934, Odessa; s. of Grigory Yasin and Yevgenia Yasina; m. Lydia Yasina (née Fedoulova); one d.; ed Odessa Inst. of Construction Eng, Moscow State Univ.; worked USSR Cen. Dept of Statistics 1963–73, Researcher, Cen. Inst. of Econs and Math., USSR (now Russian) Acad. of Sciences 1973–89; Head of Div. State Comm. on Econ. Reform, USSR Council of Ministers (Abalkin Comm.) 1990–91; one of authors of econ. programme 500 Days; Dir-Gen. Direction on Econ. Policy of Russian Union of Industrialists and Entrepreneurs 1991; f. and Dir Expert Inst. of Russian Union of Industrialists and Entrepreneurs 1992–93; mem. Council of Enterprise of Pres. of Russia 1992; Plenipotentiary Rep. of Govt in Parl. 1992–93; Head of Analytical

Centre of Pres. 1994–; Minister of Econs of Russia 1994–97, Minister Without Portfolio 1997–98; Prof., Higher School of Econs 1992–, Scientific Head 1998–; Head of govt legislation drafting teams 1992–97. *Address:* Higher School of Economics, Malaya Yakimanka str. 2/1, Moscow, Russia. *Telephone:* (495) 921-79-83; (495) 928-92-90.

YASSUKOVICH, Stanislas Michael, CBE; British/American banker and business executive; *Chairman, S.M. Yassukovich & Co. Ltd;* b. 5 Feb. 1935, Paris, France; s. of Dimitri Yassukovich and Denise Yassukovich; m. Diana Townsend 1961; two s. one d.; ed Deerfield Acad., Mass. and Harvard Univ., USA; U.S. Marine Corps. 1957–61; joined White, Weld and Co. 1961, London Office 1962, Branch Man. 1967–69, Gen. Partner, New York 1969–73, Man. Dir, London 1969–73; Man. Dir European Banking Co. SA Brussels 1983–85, Chief Exec. European Banking Group 1983–85; Chair. Merrill Lynch Europe Ltd 1985–89, Hemingway Properties 1993–; Vice-Chair. Jt Deputy Chair. London Stock Exchange 1986–89, Bristol and West Bldg Soc. (now Bristol & West PLC) 1991–2000, ABC Int. Bank 1993–; currently Chair. S.M. Yassukovich & Co. Ltd; Chair. Securities Asscn 1988–91; Chair. Cragnotti & Partners Capital Investment (UK) 1991–96, Park Place Capital 1994–, Henderson EuroTrust PLC 1995–, Easdaq SA 1997–99, Manek Investment Man. Ltd 1997–; Deputy Chair. Flextech PLC 1989–97, South West Water (now Pennon Group PLC) 1993–2000; Dir Royal Nat. Theatre 1991–96, Chair. City Disputes Panel 1993–99; Dir (non-exec.) Henderson Group PLC 1990–98, Telewest PLC 1998–, Atlas Capital Ltd 1999–. *Leisure interests:* hunting, shooting and polo. *Address:* S.M. Yassukovich & Co. Ltd, 42 Berkeley Square, London, W1J 5AW, England (office). *Telephone:* (20) 7318-0825 (office). *E-mail:* smycoltd@aol.com (office).

YASTRZHEMBSKY, Sergey Vladimirovich, CandHistSc; Russian politician, journalist and diplomatist; b. 4 Dec. 1953, Moscow; m. Anastassia Yastrzhembskaya; three c.; ed Moscow State Inst. of Int. Relations, Inst. of Int. Workers' Movt; jr researcher, Acad. of Social Sciences Cen. Cttee CPSU 1979–81; on staff journal Problems of the World and Socialism (Prague) 1981–89; Sr staff-mem. Int. Div. Cen. Cttee CPSU 1989–90; Deputy Ed.-in-Chief Megapolis (journal) 1990–91, Ed.-in-Chief VIP journal 1991–92; Dir Dept of Information and Press, Russian Ministry of Foreign Affairs 1992–93; Amb. to Slovakia 1993–96; Press Sec. to Pres. Boris Yeltsin 1996; Deputy Head Pres. Yeltsin's Admin. 1997–98; Vice-Chair. Moscow Govt 1998–99; Asst to Pres. Vladimir Putin (q.v.) 2000–08; Special Envoy to the EU 2004; Rank II Order of the White Cross (Slovakia); Russian Orthodox Church Order of St Daniil; 850th Anniversary of Moscow Commemorative Medal. *Publications:* Social Democracy in the Contemporary World 1991; essays and articles on current events, contemporary devt of Portugal and European social democracy, and relations between Russia and EU. *Leisure interests:* tennis, stamp collecting, reading, hunting, downhill skiing, photography. *Address:* c/o Office of the President, 103132 Moscow, Staraya pl. 4, Russia (office).

YASUKAWA, Hideaki; Japanese business executive; trained as engineer and watch designer; joined Suwa Seikosha (renamed Seiko Epson Corpn) 1955, apptd Dir 1976, Man.-Dir 1981–85, Sr Man.-Dir 1985–87, Exec. Vice-Pres. 1987–91, Pres. 1991–2001, Chair. 2001–05, Dir and Advisor 2005–06; Chair. Nagano Employers' Asscn; mem. Nippon Keidanren, Japan Business Fed.; Order of the Sacred Treasure, Gold and Silver Star 2002 Medal of Honour with a Blue Ribbon 1996. *Address:* c/o Seiko Epson Corporation, 3-3-5 Owa, Suwa, Nagano 392-8502, Japan. *E-mail:* info@epson.com.

YASUOKA, Okiharu; Japanese politician; *Minister of Justice;* b. 11 May 1939; ed Hibiya High School, Tokyo, Legal Trainee of Supreme Court of Japan (grad. of 19th Class), Faculty of Law, Chuo Univ.; mem. House of Reps (Kagoshima Dist 1) 1972–; Judge, Kagoshima Dist Court 1972–78; Parl. Vice-Minister, Nat. Land Agency (Ohira Cabinet) 1978–80, Parl. Vice-Minister of Finance (Suzuki Cabinet) 1980–84; Chair. Standing Cttee on Construction, House of Reps (second Nakasone Cabinet) 1984–87, Deputy Sec.-Gen. LDP 1987, Chair. Cttee on Planning, HQ for Political Reform, LDP 1989, Special Cttee on Relocation of the Diet, House of Reps 1993, Finance Cttee, LDP 1996, Sr Dir Finance Cttee, House of Reps 1996, Sr Deputy Chair. Policy Research Council, LDP 1997, Acting Chair. HQ for Implementation of Educational Reform, LDP 1997, Chair. Research Comm. on Judiciary System, LDP 1998, Special Comm. on Promotion of Comprehensive Plan for Financial Revitalization, LDP 1998, Sr Dir Special Cttee on Financial Stabilization, House of Reps 1998, Chair. Research Comm. on Constitution, House of Reps 2000, Chief Sec. Nat. Vision Project HQ, LDP 2001, Acting Chair. HQ on Urgent Countermeasures to Stabilize the Financial System, LDP 2003, Chair. Research Comm. on Constitution, LDP 2003, Sr Dir Special Cttee for Research on Constitution of Japan, House of Reps 2005–07, Chair. Research Comm. on Antimonopoly Laws, LDP 2005–07, Deputy Chair. Jt Gen. Meeting of Both Houses 2007–08, Supreme Adviser, Research Comm. on Antimonopoly Laws 2007, Acting Chair. Council on Constitution 2007–08; Chief Judge, Judge Impeachment Court 2007–08; Minister of Justice 2000–01, 2008–. *Leisure interests:* jogging, swimming. *Address:* Ministry of Justice, 1-1-1, Kasumigaseki, Chiyoda-ku, Tokyo, 100-8977 Japan (office). *Telephone:* (3) 3580-4111 (office). *Fax:* (3) 3592-7011 (office). *E-mail:* webmaster@moj.go.jp (office). *Website:* www.moj.go.jp (office).

YATHOTOU, Pany; Laotian politician and fmr central banker; *President of the National Assembly;* Cabinet mem. 1987–98; Chair. Cen. Bank 1988–90, Gov. 1990–92, Gov. Bank of the Lao People's Democratic Repub. 1995–97; mem. Nat. Ass. 2001–, Chair. Cttee of Ethnic Affairs and Deputy Pres. Ass. 2001–10, Pres. Ass. 2010–; mem. Politbureau Cen. People's Democratic Repub. 1995–97; Chair. Cttee of the Lao People's Revolutionary Party. *Address:* Office of the President, National Assembly of the Lao People's Democratic Republic, Vientiane, Laos (office). *Website:* www.na.gov.la (office).

YATIM, Dato' Rais bin, MA, LLB, PhD; Malaysian politician; *Minister of Information, Communications and Culture;* b. 15 April 1942, Jelebu, Negeri Sembilan; m. Datin Masnah Mohamat; three s. one d.; ed Univs of Northern Illinois, Singapore and London; lecturer at ITM, School of Law and also managed own law firm in Kuala Lumpur 1973; mem. Bar Council 1973; mem. Parl. 1974; Parl. Sec. Ministry of Youth, Sport and Culture 1974; Deputy Minister of Law 1976, of Home Affairs 1978; elected to State Ass., Negeri Sembilan 1978; Menteri Besar, Negeri Sembilan 1978; Minister of Land and Regional Devt 1982, of Information 1984–86, of Foreign Affairs 1986–87; Advocate and Solicitor, High

Court of Malaysia 1988–; returned to law practice, Kuala Lumpur 1988–; mem. United Malays' Nat. Org. (UMNO) Supreme Council of Malaysia 1982–; Deputy Pres. Semangat 1989–; Minister in Prime Minister's Dept 1999; Minister of Foreign Affairs 2008–09, of Information, Communications and Culture 2009–; mem. Civil Liberty Cttee Bar Council, Kuala Lumpur 1996–98. *Publications:* Faces in the Corridors of Power 1987, Freedom under Executive Power in Malaysia 1995, Zaman Beredar Pesaka Bergilir 1999. *Leisure interests:* photography, writing, travel. *Address:* Ministry of Information, Communications and Culture, Tingkat 5, Wisma TV, Angkasapuri, Bukit Putra, 50610 Kuala Lumpur (office); 41 Road 12, Taman Grandview, Ampang Jaya, 68000 Ampang, Selangor, Malaysia (home). *Telephone:* (3) 22825333 (office); (3) 4569621 (home). *Fax:* (3) 22848115 (office). *E-mail:* azmi@kpkk.gov.my (office); drrais@pc.jaring.my (home). *Website:* www.kpkk.gov.my (office).

YATSENYUK, Arseniy Petrovych, PhD; Ukrainian lawyer and politician; *Interim Prime Minister;* b. 22 May 1974, Chernivtsi; m. Tereziya Victorivna Hur 1970; two d.; ed Chernivtsi State Univ. and Kyiv Univ. of Trade and Econs; Pres. Yurek Ltd (law firm), Chernivtsi 1992–97; consultant to credit dept, Aval Jt Stock Postal Pensions Bank, Kyiv 1998, Adviser to Chair. of Bd 1998–2001, Deputy Chair. of Bd Aug.–Sept. 2001; Minister of Economy, Autonomous Repub. of Crimea, Simferopol 2001–03; First Deputy Chair. Nat. Bank of Ukraine 2003–05; First Deputy Gov. Odesa Oblast March–Sept. 2005; Minister of Economy 2005–06, of Foreign Affairs 2007; Deputy Head, Presidential Secr. 2006–07; Chair. Verkhovna Rada 2007–08; mem. Nat. Security and Defence Council 2007; Founder Front of Changes political party 2007 (merged into Fatherland 2013), Open Ukraine Benevolent Foundation; Head of the Political Council, Fatherland United Opposition 2012–; Interim Prime Minister 2014–. *Address:* Office of the Cabinet of Ministers, 01008 Kyiv, vul. M. Hrushevskoho 12/2 (office); Fatherland United Opposition (Batkivshchyna Obyednana Opozytsiya), 01133 Kyiv, bulv. Lesï Ukraïnky 26/615; Open Ukraine International Charitable Organization, 04071 Kyiv, vul. Verkhniy Val 4A, Ukraine. *Telephone:* (44) 254-29-20 (office); (44) 255-21-15; (44) 220-18-40; (44) 286-42-36. *Fax:* (44) 254-33-70 (office); (44) 285-69-07. *E-mail:* web@kmu.gov.ua (office); sector@byti.org.ua. *Website:* www.kmu.gov.ua (office); byut.com.ua; www.openukraine.org.

YATSKEVICH, Boris Alexandrovich, CandGeol; Russian geologist; b. 7 Jan. 1948, Lignice, Poland; ed Voronezh State Univ.; Sr Technician, Sr Geologist, Chief Geologist Ukhta geological expedition, Komi Autonomous Repub. 1972–86; chief geologist Polar–Urals production geological co. Vorkuta 1986–90; Head of Div. State Cttee on Geology RSFSR 1990–92; Deputy Chair. State Cttee on Geology and use of Mineral Wealth 1992–96; First Deputy Minister of Natural Resources Russian Fed. 1996–99, Minister 1999–2001; mem. Observation Council ALROSA (Diamonds of Russia and Sakha). *Address:* c/o Ministry of Natural Resources of Russian Federation, Bolshaya Gruzinskaya str. 4/6, 123812 Moscow, Russia (office).

YAU, Carrie, BSocSc; Hong Kong civil servant; *Permanent Secretary for Home Affairs;* b. (Tsang Ka Lai), 4 June 1955; d. of Tsang Hin Yeung and Tsang Choon Kwa; m. Francis Yau; one s.; ed Maryknoll Sisters' School, Diocesan Girls' School, Univ. of Hong Kong; joined Hong Kong Govt as an Admin. Officer 1977, various posts in maj. policy areas, Govt Spokeswoman, Chief Sec.'s Office 1994–95, Dir of Admin. 1997–2000, Sec. for Information Tech. and Broadcasting 2000–02, Perm. Sec. for Health, Welfare and Food 2002–06, Perm. Sec. for Food and Environmental Hygiene of Health, Welfare and Food 2006–07, Perm. Sec. for Home Affairs 2007–; Chair. Bd of Review (Film Censorship), Steering Cttee on Cyberport; Vice-Chair. Broadcasting Authority; mem. Business Advisory Cttee, Services Promotion Strategy Group, Steering Cttee for Third Generation Mobile Service. *Leisure interests:* singing, hiking, family activities. *Address:* Office of the Permanent Secretary of Home Affairs, 31/F, Southern Centre, 130 Hennessy Road, Wanchai, Hong Kong Special Administrative Region, People's Republic of China (office). *Telephone:* 2835-2056 (office). *Fax:* 2591-6002 (office). *E-mail:* hab1@hab.gov.hk (office). *Website:* www.hab.gov.hk (office).

YAU, Shing-tung, PhD, FAAS; Chinese mathematician and academic; *William Casper Graustein Professor of Mathematics, Harvard University; Director, The Institute of Mathematical Sciences, The Chinese University of Hong Kong;* b. 4 April 1949, Shantou, Guangdong Prov.; s. of Chen ying Chiu and Yeuk Lam leung; Yu-yun Kuo, Isaac Chiu Yau and Michael Chiu; ed Univ. of California, Berkeley; Asst Prof. of Math., State Univ. of New York, Stony Brook 1972–73, Distinguished Visiting Prof. 1990; Prof. of Math., Stanford Univ. . 1974–79; Prof. of Math., Inst. for Advanced Study, Princeton NJ 1979–84; Chair and Prof. of Math., Univ. of California, San Diego 1984–87; Visiting Prof. and Sid Richardson Centennial Chair in Math., Univ. of Texas, Austin 1986; Prof. of Math., Harvard Univ. 1987–, Higgins Prof. (Chair Prof.) 1997–2000, William Casper Graustein Prof. 2000–, Chair. Math. Dept 2008–; Fairchild Distinguished Scholar, Calif. Inst. of Tech. 1990; Wilson T. S.Wang Distinguished Visiting Prof., The Chinese Univ. of Hong Kong 1991–92, Adjunct Prof. of Math. 1994–2003, Dir Inst. of Math. Sciences 1994–, Distinguished Prof.-at-Large 2003–; Special Chair, Nat. Tsinghua Univ., Hsinchu, Taiwan 1991–92; Eilenberg Visiting Prof., Columbia Univ., New York 1999; mem. Bd of Math. Sciences, National Acad. of Science –1989); Mem.-at-Large Council of the American Math. Soc. 1990–92; mem. Scientific Advisory Council Math. Sciences Research Inst. –1989; Ed.-in-Chief Journal of Differential Geometry 1980–, Methods and Application of Analysis 1994–, Asian Journal of Mathematics 1997–; Ed. Communications in Mathematical Physics 1982–99, Mathematical Research Letters, 1993–, Advances in Mathematics 1994–, Journal of Mathematical Physics 1997–; mem. Editorial Advisory Bd Methods and Applications of Analysis, 1993–, Communications in Analysis and Geometry 1993–; mem. American Acad. of Arts and Sciences 1982; Academic Sinica 1984, NAS 1993, New York Acad. of Science, American Physical Soc., Soc. for Industrial and Applied Math.; Foreign mem. Chinese Acad. of Sciences 1995, Russian Acad. of Sciences 2003, Accad. Nazionale dei Lincei; Fellow, American Math. Soc. 2012; Hon. Prof., Fudan Univ. 1983–, Chinese Acad. of Sciences 1983, Hangzhou Univ. 1987–, Tsinghua Univ. 1987–, Nankai Univ. 1993–, Beijing Univ. 1998–, Univ. of Science and Tech. of China 1999–, Zhejiang Univ. 2002–; Hon. mem. Academic Cttee Inst. of Math., Chinese Acad. of Sciences 1980–; Hon. Ed. Communications in Information and Systems 2001–; Hon. Fellow, Shaw Coll. of The Chinese Univ. of Hong Kong 2007; Hon. DSc (Chinese Univ. of Hong Kong) 1981, (Chao Tung Univ.)

1997, (Nat. Tsinghua Univ., Beijing) 2000, (Macao Univ.) 2002, (Zhejing Univ.) 2003, (Hong Kong Science and Tech. Univ.) 2004, (Cen. Univ. of Taiwan) 2005, (Polytechnic Univ., Brooklyn) 2005, (Nat. Taiwan Univ.) 2006, (Lehigh Univ.) 2009, (Nat. Cheng Kung Univ.) 2010; Hon. Dr of Math. (Univ. of Waterloo) 2011; Hon. MA (Harvard) 1987; Sloan Fellow 1975–76, California Scientist of the Year 1979, Veblen Prize 1981, Carty Prize, Nat. Acad. 1981, Guggenheim Fellowship 1982, Fields Medal, Int. Math. Union, Warsaw 1982 (presented 1983), America's 100 Brightest Scientists Under 40, Science Digest 1984, MacArthur Fellow 1985, American Math. Soc. Lecturer 1986, CraAoord Prize, Royal Swedish Acad. 1994, John Harvard Fellow, Univ. of Cambridge 1996, US Nat. Medal of Science 1997, Bowen Lecturer, Univ. of California, Berkeley 1997, Run Run Shaw Distinguished Lecturer, The Chinese Univ. of Hong Kong 1998, Bergman Lecturer, Stanford Univ. 1999, Radamacher Lecture, Univ. of Pennyslvania 1999, Int. Scientific and Technological Co-operation Award 2003, Wolf Prize in Math. (co-recipient) 2010. *Publications:* The Shape of Inner Space: String Theory and the Geometry of the Universe's Hidden Dimension (co-author) 2010; numerous articles in math. journals on partial differential equations, the Calabi conjecture in algebraic geometry, the positive mass conjecture of general relativity theory, and real and complex Monge-Ampère equations. *Address:* Department of Mathematics, Harvard University, One Oxford Street, Cambridge, MA 02138, USA (office); The Institute of Mathematical Sciences, Unit 601, 6/F, Academic Building No. 1, The Chinese University of Hong Kong, Shatin, Hong Kong Special Administrative Region, People's Republic of China. *Telephone:* (617) 495-0836 (Harvard) (office); 2609-8038 (Hong Kong) (office). *Fax:* 2603-7636 (Hong Kong (office). *E-mail:* yau@math.harvard.edu (office); yau@ims.cuhk.edu.hk (office). *Website:* math.harvard.edu (office); www.math.cuhk.edu.hk (office); www.doctoryau.com.

YAVLINSKII, Grigorii Alekseevich, PhD, CEconSc; Russian politician and economist; b. 10 April 1952, Lviv, Ukrainian SSR; m. Elena Yavlinskaya; two s.; ed Plekhanov Inst. of Econ., Moscow; electrician Lviv Co., Raduga 1968–69; Sr Researcher, Research Inst. of Man., Ministry of Coal Industry, Moscow 1976–80; Head of Div. Research Inst. of Labour 1980–84; Deputy Chief, Chief of Div., Chief of Dept of Man. USSR State Labour Cttee 1984–89; Chief of Div. State Cttee on Econ. Reform USSR Council of Ministers 1988–90; mem. Pres.'s Political Advisory Council 1990–; Deputy Chair. Council of Ministers of Russian Fed., Chair. State Cttee on Econ. Reform 1990, author of econ. programme 500 days July–Nov. 1990; Econ. Counsellor of Prime Minister of Russia 1991; Chair. of Council of Scientific Soc. EPI-CENTRE (Cen. for Political and Econ. Studies) 1991–; mem. Econ. Council of Pres. of Kazakhstan 1991–; Deputy Chair. USSR Cttee on Operational Man. of Nat. Econ. Aug.–Dec. 1991; mem. Political Advisory Council of Pres. Gorbachev Oct.–Dec. 1991; co-leader (with Y.U. Boldyrev and V. Lukin) of pre-election bloc (later political movt then political party) Yabloko Russian Democratic Party (Rossiisskaya demokraticheskaya partiya 'Yabloko') 1993, Leader 1995–2008, also party Chair. in Duma; mem. State Duma (Parl.) 1993; cand. in presidential elections 1996, 2000; Int. Prize for Freedom 2004. *Achievements:* Ukraine Jr Boxing Champion 1967, 1968. *Publications:* Russia–The Search for Landmarks 1993, Incentives and Institutions: The Transition to a Market Economy in Russia 2000; over 60 books on economy of USSR, numerous articles. *Address:* Yabloko Russian Democratic Party (Rossiisskaya demokraticheskaya partiya 'Yabloko'), 119034 Moscow, per. M. Levshinskii 7/3, Russia (office). *Telephone:* (495) 201-43-79 (office). *Fax:* (495) 292-34-50 (office). *E-mail:* info@yabloko.ru (office). *Website:* www.yabloko.ru (office).

YAWER, Ghazi Mashal Ajil al-; Iraqi engineer and business executive; b. 1958, Mosul; m.; three c.; ed Petroleum and Minerals Univ., Saudi Arabia, Georgetown Univ., USA; prominent mem. of Shammar tribe; left Iraq in mid-1980s; Vice-Pres. Hicap Tech. Co., Riyadh, –2003; apptd to Governing Council 2003, Interim Pres. 2004–05; Vice-Pres. of Iraq 2005–06. *Address:* c/o Office of the Vice-President, Baghdad, Iraq (office).

YAYI, Boni, PhD; Benin economist, banker and head of state; *President;* b. 1952, Tchaourou; m. Chantal Yayi; five c.; ed Nat. Univ. of Benin, Univ. of Dakar, Senegal, Univ. of Orleans and Paris Univ., France; worked for Cen. Bank of the States of West Africa (BCEAO) becoming Deputy Dir 1980–88; Deputy Dir for Professional Devt, West African Centre for Banking Studies, Dakar 1988; worked in office of Pres. of Benin in charge of monetary and banking policies 1992–94; Pres. West African Devt Bank 1994–2006; Pres. of Benin 2006–, also Minister of Defence 2012–13; Chair. African Union 2012–; Chevalier, Ordre Nat. de Mérite (France), Officier, Ordre Nat. de Burkina Faso, Grand Officier, Ordre Nat. de Benin, Commdr, Ordre Nat. de Mali, de Niger, de Senegal. *Address:* Office of the President, BP 1288, Cotonou, Benin (office). *Telephone:* 21-30-00-90 (office). *Fax:* 21-30-06-36 (office). *Website:* www.gouv.bj (office); www.boniyayi.bj.

YAZDI, Ibrahim, PhD; Iranian politician; b. c. 1933; m.; two s. four d.; studied and worked as physician in USA for sixteen years; close assoc. of Ayatollah Khomeini during exile in Neauphlé-le-Château, France Oct. 1978–Feb. 1979; mem. Revolutionary Council during Feb. 1979 revolution; Deputy Prime Minister with responsibility for Revolutionary Affairs Feb.–April 1979; Minister of Foreign Affairs April–Nov. 1979; Special Emissary of Ayatollah Khomeini on Prov. Problems 1979; Supervisor Keyhan Org. 1980–81; Deputy in Parl. for Tehran 1980–84; mem. Foreign Affairs, Health and Welfare Parl. Comms; WHO Adviser 1991; Sec.-Gen. Liberation Movt of Iran 1995–2011; arrested and imprisoned several times Dec. 2009, Oct. 2010–March 2011. *Publications:* Final Efforts in Terminal Days: Some Untold Stories of the Islamic Revolution of Iran 1984, Principles of Molecular Genetics 1985, Mutational Changes in Genetic Materials and Repair Systems 1989, The Ills of the Human Heart 1994; papers on herbal and traditional medicine, carcinogenics, the nucleic acid of cancer cells and Islamic and social topics. *Address:* 21 Touraj Lane, Valiasr Avenue, Tehran 19666, Iran. *Telephone:* (21) 2042558. *Fax:* (21) 2042558.

YAZGHI, Muhammad al-, LenD; Moroccan politician, lawyer and newspaper executive; b. 28 Sept. 1935, Fez; m. Balafrej Souada 1972; two s.; ed Moulay Youssef Coll., Lycée Gouraud, Univ. of Rabat and Ecole Nat. d'Admin., Paris; Dir of Budget, Ministry of Finance 1957–60; Dir Al-Moharir (daily paper) 1975–81, Liberation (daily paper) 1989–; First Sec. Moroccan Press Union 1977–93; Deputy in Parl. 1977–; mem. Political Bureau, Union Socialiste des Forces Populaires (USFP) 1975–91, Joint Vice-Sec. 1992, First Sec. –2007 (resgnd); Minister of Territorial Admin, the Environment, Urban Planning and Housing, then Minister of Territorial Administration, Water Resources and the Environment –2007; Minister of State 2007. *Publications:* articles in magazines and journals. *Leisure interests:* reading, travel. *Address:* c/o Parliament of Morocco, Chambre des Représentants, Avenue Mohamed V, Rabat (office).

YAZICI, Hayati, BS; Turkish politician and lawyer; *Minister of Customs and Trade;* b. 1952, Rize; m.; two c.; ed Istanbul Univ.; served as judge and freelance lawyer 1976–2002; elected mem. Grand Nat. Ass. representing Istanbul 2002; Deputy Prime Minister 2007–09, Minister of Customs and Trade 2011–; Co-founder, Bd Mem. and Deputy Chair. (Organizational Affairs), AKP (Adalet ve Kalkinma Partisi/Justice and Devt Party). *Address:* Ministry of Customs and Trade, Dumlupinar Boulevard 151, Eskisehir Yolu 9 Km.06530, Çankaya, Ankara, Turkey (office). *Telephone:* 449-10-00 (office). *E-mail:* bilgi@gtb.gov.tr (office). *Website:* www.gtb.gov.tr (office); www.hayatiyazici.com.tr.

YAZOV, Marshal Dmitri Timofeevich; Russian military official (retd); b. 1923; ed Frunze Mil. Acad. and Mil. Acad. of Gen. Staff; entered Soviet army 1941–; active service 1941–45; command posts 1945–76; Deputy Commdr of Far Eastern Mil. Dist 1976–79; Commdr of Cen. Group Forces in Czechoslovakia 1979–80; Deputy to USSR Supreme Soviet 1979–89; Commdr of Cen. Asian Mil. Dist 1980; Deputy Minister of Defence Feb.–June 1987, Minister of Defence and Head of Armed Forces 1987–91; mem. of Cen. Cttee of Kazakh CP 1987–87; mem. Presidential Council 1990–91; Cand. mem. of Cen. Cttee of CPSU 1981–91; fmr mem. Politburo; rank of Marshal 1990; arrested 1991, for participation in attempted coup d'état, charged with conspiracy 1992; on trial 1993; released 1994; Chief Mil. Adviser, Ministry of Defence 1998; Chair. Marshal G. Zhukov Memorial Cttee. *Leisure interests:* theatre, poetry. *Address:* Ministry of Defence, ul. Myasnitskaya 37 Moscow 105175, Russia (office). *Telephone:* (495) 296-39-66 (office). *Fax:* (495) 296-84-36 (office). *Website:* www.mil.ru (office).

YE, Gongqi; Chinese administrator; b. 1930; ed Shanghai High School; joined CCP 1948; Deputy Dir of Shanghai Light Industry Bureau 1976–; Vice-Mayor Shanghai 1985; Chair. Shanghai Municipal 9th and 10th People's Congress; Chair. Shanghai Consumers Asscn 2004–; Sr Consultant China Shipping (Group) Co.; Pres. Shanghai Asscn for Int. Friendly Contact. *Address:* Shanghai Consumers Association, 14th Floor, No. 301 Zhaojiabang Road Shanghai 200032, People's Republic of China (office).

YE, Liansong; Chinese politician and engineer; b. 1935, Shanghai; ed Jiaotong Univ., Shanghai; engineer, Shijiazhuang Municipal Diesel Plant 1960–80; Vice-Mayor Shijiazhuang 1982–85; mem. Standing Cttee Hebei Prov. CCP Cttee 1983–2000, Deputy Sec. 1998–2000; Vice-Gov. Hebei Prov. 1985–93, Gov. 1993–98; Alt. mem. 13th Cen. Cttee CCP 1987–92, mem. 14th Cen. Cttee 1992–97, 15th CCP Cen. Cttee 1997–2002; Deputy to 8th NPC 1993–98. *Address:* c/o Office of the Governor, Hebei Provincial Government, 1 Weiming Jie Street, Shijiazhuang City, People's Republic of China (office).

YE, Rutang; Chinese politician; b. 20 March 1940, Wenling Co., Zhejiang Prov.; s. of Ye Mei and Chen Jiaoru; m. Liu Wenbin 1968; one s. two d.; ed Tsinghua Univ.; Minister of Urban and Rural Construction and Environmental Protection 1985–88; Vice-Chair. Environmental Protection Cttee of State Council 1985–88; Vice-Minister of Construction 1988–98; Vice-Chair. Chinese Soc. of Science and Tech. for Social Devt 1991–2001; Dir Dongjiang Environmental Co. Ltd; Vice-Chair. Environment and Resources Protection Cttee, 10th NPC 2003–; Pres. Architectural Soc. of China 1992. *Leisure interests:* calligraphy, swimming. *Address:* Dongjiang Environmental Company, Shenzhen High-Tech Industrial Park North, Long Hill Road, Shenzhen 518057, People's Republic of China (office). *Telephone:* (86) 755-86676186 (office). *Fax:* (86) 755-86676006 (office). *Website:* www.szdongjiang.com (office).

YE, Shaolan, (Ye Qiang); Chinese singer, actor and playwright; b. Sept. 1943, Beijing; s. of Ye Shenglan; ed China Acad. of Traditional Operas, Cen. Acad. of Drama; started learning Peking Opera at age of 9; actor, dir, playwright; Art Dir Zhanyou Peking Opera Troupe, PLA Beijing Mil. Command; mem. Exec. Council of Chinese Dramatists Asscn; won 1st Nat. Theatre Plum Blossom Award 1984; Fulbright Int. Scholar; New York Lincoln Center Life Achievement Award. *Peking operas include:* Lu Bu and Diao Chan, Luo Cheng, Story of the Willow Tree, A Meeting of Heroes, Butterfly Lovers. *Recordings include:* Selected Arias of Ye Shaolan 1995. *Address:* c/o Zhanyou Peking Opera Troupe, People's Liberation Army, Beijing Command, Beijing, People's Republic of China (office).

YE, Weilin; Chinese writer; b. 1935, Huiyang Co., Guangdong Prov.; s. of Ye Wei; m. Chen Jieni; two c.; joined PLA 1950; Chair. Hainan Writers' Asscn 1990–; also writes film screenplays. *Publications:* The Blue Mulan Rivulet, On the River without Navigation Marks, The First Farewell, Passing the Night at Meiziguo. *Address:* Hunan Branch of the Writers' Association, Changsha City, Hunan Province, People's Republic of China (office).

YE, Xiaogang; Chinese composer; *Vice President, Central Conservatory of Music,;* b. 23 Sept. 1955, Shanghai; s. of Ye Chunzi and Ho Ying; m. Xu Jing 1987; ed Eastman School of Music, USA (postgraduate); Vice-Pres. Cen. Conservatory of Music, Beijing 2009–, Chair. Composition Division; piano concerto Starry Sky was premiered during opening ceremony of Beijing Olympic Games by pianist Lang Lang, August 2008; mem. China Fed. of Literature and Art; Vice Chair. Chinese Musicians Asscn; mem. Council, China Film Workers Asscn; Fellow Metropolitan Life Foundation, Pennsylvania Council of the Arts 1996; mem. judging penal, numerous nat. and int. competitions including Himalayas Cup Int. Piano Composition Competition, Luxembourg Int. Composition Competition; Alexander Tcherepnin Prize 1982, Japan Dance Star Ballet Prize 1986, Ministry of Culture Ou Yongxi Excellent Music Education Award. *Compositions:* Xi Jiang Yue Symphony 1984, Horizon Symphony 1985, Piano Ballade 1987, Dance Drama: The Love Story of Da Lai VI 1988, Last Paradise, Song of the Earth, Twilight in Tibet, My Far Away Nanjing, Nine Horses. *Address:* Central Conservatory of Music, 43 Baojiajie, Beijing 100031, People's Republic of China (office). *E-mail:* ao@ccom.edu.cn (office). *Website:* en.ccom.edu.cn (office).

YEANG, Dato' (Darjah Mulia Panguan Negeri) Ken, AADipl, PhD, RIBA; Malaysian architect and academic; *Principal, Llewelyn Davies Yeang and T. R. Hamzah & Yeang Sdn. Bhd.;* b. 6 Oct. 1948, Penang; ed Architectural Asscn, London, UK, Univ. of Pennsylvania, USA, Wolfson Coll., Cambridge, UK; Prin.

T. R. Hamzah & Yeang Sdn. Bhd. 1976–; External Examiner, Univ. of Moratuwa 1986–87, Universiti Sains Malaysia 1988–89, 2000–01; Adjunct Prof. Univ. of Malaya, Royal Melbourne Inst. of Tech. 1993–, Univ. of Hawaii at Manoa 1999–, Univ. of NSW 2000–; AIA Assoc. Prof. (Graham Willis Visiting Professorship), Univ. of Sheffield 1994–2004; Provost's Distinguished Visitor, Univ. of Southern California 1999; Hon. Fellow, Singapore Inst. of Architects 1998; Hon. FAIA 1999; Hon. Academician Int. Acad. of Architecture (Sofia) 2000; Norway Award 1992, Far Eastern Econ. Review Innovation Award 1998, Auguste Perret Prize 1999, Asia Pacific Distinguished Scholar Award 1999, Enterprise 50 Award 1999, Prinz Claus Fonds Award 1999, Sir Robert Mathew Award 2000. *Publications:* Bioclimatic Skyscrapers 1994, Designing with Nature 1995, The Skyscraper Bioclimatically Considered: A Design Primer 1997, The Green Skyscraper: The Basis for Designing Sustainable Intensive Buildings 1999. *Address:* Brook House, Torrington Place, London, WC1E 7HN, England (office). *Telephone:* (20) 7637-0181 (office). *Fax:* (20) 7637-8740 (office). *E-mail:* trhy@tm.net.my (office). *Website:* www .trhamzah-yeang.com/main.htm (office); www.ldavies.com (office).

YEDDYURAPPA, B(okanakere) S(iddalingappa), BA; Indian politician and government official; b. 27 Feb. 1943, Bookanakere village, Mandya Dist, Karnataka; s. of Siddalingappa Yediyurappa and Puttathayamma Yediyurappa; m. Smt. Maithra Devi Yediyurappa 1967 (died 2004); two s. three d.; mem. Bharatiya Janata Party (BJP); represents Shikaripura in Karnataka Legis. Ass.; first-div. clerk in social welfare dept 1965; clerk, Veerabhadra Shastri's Shankar rice mill, Shikaripur 1965–67; set up hardware shop in Shimoga; Sec. Rashtriya Swayamsevak Sangh's Shikaripur unit 1970–72; Pres. Taluk unit, Jan Sangh 1972–75; Pres. Town Municipality of Shikaripur 1975; imprisoned during Emergency in India 1975–77, lodged in Bellary and Shimoga jails; Pres. Shikaripur Taluk unit of BJP 1980–85, Pres. Shimoga Dist unit of BJP 1985–88, Pres. BJP unit, Karnataka 1988; first elected to Lower House of Karnataka Legislature 1983, has represented Shikaripur constituency five times, mem. Eighth, Ninth, Tenth and Eleventh Legis. Ass (Lower House) of Karnataka, Leader of Opposition, Tenth Ass., lost election 1999, nominated by BJP to become mem. Legis. Council (Upper House) of Karnataka; helped H. D. Kumaraswamy of Janata Dal (Secular) party bring down coalition govt of Dharam Singh, Kumaraswamy formed govt with help of BJP in Karnataka; Deputy Chief Minister and Minister of Finance in Kumaraswamy's Govt 2006–07, Chief Minister of Karnataka (prior to collapse of coalition govt) 12–19 Nov. 2007 (first BJP mem. to become Chief Minister of a South Indian state), 2008–11 (resgnd); arrested and charged with illegally selling govt land 2011. *Address:* c/o Office of the Chief Minister, Room No. 323, Vidhana Soudha, Bangalore 560 001, Karnataka, India.

YEFIMOV, Air Marshal Aleksandr Nikolayevich, MSc; Russian air force officer (retd); b. 6 Feb. 1923, Kantemirovka, Voronezh Oblast; ed Voroshilovograd Mil. Air Acad., Mil. Acad. of Gen. Staff; joined CPSU 1943; served in Soviet army 1941; fought on the Western and on 2nd Byelorussian Fronts at Vyazma, Smolensk, in Byelorussia, Poland and Germany 1942–45; by July 1944 had flown about 100 missions and was made Hero of the Soviet Union; completed his 222nd mission on 8 May 1945; awarded second Gold Star; held various command posts 1945–69; First Deputy C-in-C, Soviet Air Defence Forces 1969–91; Deputy to Supreme Soviet 1946–50, 1974–89; rank of Air Marshal 1975; Commdr of Soviet Air Force and Deputy Minister of Defence 1984–91, Mil. Insp.-Adviser, Ministry of Defence 1991; Chair. CIS Interstate Comm. on use of space and control of air services 1992–96, Council for co-operation with war veterans' unions 1995–; mem. CPSU Cen. Cttee 1986–90; USSR People's Deputy 1989; Hero of the Soviet Union 1944, 1945, Order of Lenin (twice), Order of the Red Banner (five times), Aleksandr Nevsky Order, Merited Mil. Pilot of USSR 1970 and other decorations. *Publication:* Over the Field of Battle 1976. *Address:* c/o Ministry of Defence, Myasnitskaya str. 37, 101000 Moscow, Russia. *Telephone:* (495) 293-31-76.

YEFUNI, Sergey Naumovich; Russian anaesthesiologist and physiologist; *Director-General, Institute of Hyperbaric Medicine;* b. 24 Jan. 1930; m.; two s.; ed Second Moscow Inst. of Medicine; head of surgery div., municipal hosp. 1954–56; researcher First Moscow Inst. of Medicine 1959–63; Sr Researcher, Head of Lab. All-Union Research Cen. of Surgery, USSR Acad. of Medical Sciences 1963–78, Head of Dept 1978–93; Dir-Gen. Inst. of Hyperbaric Medicine 1993–; Corresp. mem. USSR (now Russian) Acad. of Sciences 1979, mem. 1992; research in physiology of breathing, practical problems of anaesthesia, effect of anaesthesia on cardio-vascular system; mem. United Scientific Council on complex problem Physiology of Man and Animals; Chair. Comm. Acad. (now Inst.) of Sciences Problems of Hyperbaric Oxygenation; lives in USA; USSR State Prize. *Address:* Institute of Hyperbaric Medicine, 119435 Moscow, Russia (office). *Telephone:* (495) 246-49-87 (office); (495) 201-43-68 (home).

YEGOROV, Vladimir Konstantinovich; Russian politician, philosopher and journalist; *Rector, Russian Academy of State Service;* b. 30 Oct. 1947, Kanash, Chuvash ASSR; m.; one s.; ed Kazan State Univ.; Deputy Ed. Molodoi Komsomolets, also Head, Dept of Propaganda, Cen. Comsomol Cttee 1974–85; Rector, Gorky. Inst. of Literature in Moscow 1985–87; Deputy Head, Div. of Culture, Ideological Dept, CPSU Cen. Cttee 1987–90; Asst to Pres. Mikhail Gorbachev (q.v.) on Problems of Culture and Religion 1990–91; Chief Scientific Researcher, Analytical Centre at Ministry of Science 1992–96; Prof. Russian Acad. of State Service 1993–; mem. Co-ordination Council, My Motherland; Dir Russian State Library 1996–98; Minister of Culture Russian Fed. 1998–2000; Rector Russian Acad. of State Service 2000–. *Publications:* books including History in our Lives, Intelligentsia and Power, The Star Turns Pale: Reflections on Russian History, From Deadlock to Uncertainty, Many Faces of Russia, numerous articles. *Address:* Academy of State Service, Vernadskogo prosp. 84, 117606 Moscow, Russia. *Telephone:* (495) 436-90-12 (office).

YEH, Chu-Lan, LLB; Taiwanese politician; b. 13 Feb. 1949, Miaoli Co.; m. Cheng Nan-jung (died 1989); one d.; ed Fu Jen Catholic Univ.; Dir Business Dept, United Advertising Co. Ltd 1979–89; mem. Legislative Yuan 1990–2000, Convener Home and Nations Cttee, Foreign and Overseas Chinese Affairs Cttee, Judiciary Cttee, Deputy Convener Democratic Progressive Party Caucus 1992, Gen. Convener 1995; Minister of Transportation and Communications 2000–02; Chair. Council for Hakka Affairs 2002–04; Vice-Premier and Minister of Consumer Protection Comm. 2004–05; Acting Mayor of Kaohsiung 2005–06; mem. Cen. Standing Cttee, Democratic Progressive Party. *Address:* Deng Liberty Foundation, 3F, No. 11, Aly

3, Ln 106, Sec. 3, Minquan E. Road, Songshan District, Taipei 105, Taiwan. *Telephone:* (2) 25468766. *Fax:* (2) 27160758 (office). *E-mail:* nylon407@gmail.com. *Website:* www.nylon.org.tw.

YEHOSHUA, Abraham B., MA; Israeli writer and academic; *Professor of Comparative and Hebrew Literature, University of Haifa;* b. 9 Dec. 1936, Jerusalem; s. of Yakov Yehoshua and Malka Rosilio; m. Rivka Kirsninski 1960; two s. one d.; served in paratroopers unit 1954–57; Dir Israeli School in Paris 1964; Gen. Sec. World Union of Jewish Studies, Paris 1963–67; Dean of Students, Haifa Univ. 1967–72, Prof. of Comparative and Hebrew Literature 1972–; Visiting Prof., Harvard Univ., USA 1977, Univ. of Chicago 1988, 1997, 2000, Princeton Univ. 1992–; Co-Ed. Keshet 1965–72, Siman Kria 1973–, Tel Aviv Review 1987–; active mem. Israeli Peace Movt; Dr hc (Hebrew Union Coll.) 1990, (Tel-Aviv Univ.) 1998, (Univ. of Turin) 1999, (Bar Ilan Univ.) 2000, (Scuola Normale Superiore di Pisa) 2012; Brener Prize 1983, Alterman Prize 1986, Bialik Prize 1989, Booker Prize 1992, European B'nai B'rith Award 1993, Israel Prize 1995, Prix Médicis étranger (for a translated work for The Retrospective) 2012. *Film adaptations of novels and stories include:* The Lover, Facing the Forests, Continuing Silence, Mr Mani, Open Heart, A Voyage to the End of the Millennium, Early in the Summer of 1970. *Plays:* A Night in May 1969, Last Treatments 1973, Possessions 1992, The Night's Babies 1993. *Publications:* Death of the Old Man (short stories) 1963, Facing the Forest (short stories) 1968, Three Days and a Child (short stories) 1970, Early in the Summer of 1970 (novella) 1973, Two Plays 1975, The Lover (novel) 1977, Between Right and Right (essays) 1980, A Late Divorce (novel) (Flaiano Int. Poetry Prize, Italy 1996) 1982, Possessions 1986, Five Seasons (novel) (Nat. Jewish Book Award 1990, Cavour Prize, Italy 1994) 1988, The Wall and the Mountain (essays) 1988, Mister Mani (novel) (Israeli Booker Prize 1992, Nat. Jewish Book Award 1993, Wingate Prize, UK 1994) 1990, The Return from India 1994, Open Heart (novel) 1994, A Voyage to the End of the Millennium (novel) (Koret Prize) 1997, The Terrible Power of a Minor Guilt (essays) 1998, The Liberated Bride (novel) (Napoli Prize, Lampedusa Prize) 2001, The Mission of the Human Resource Man (novel) 2004, A Woman in Jerusalem (Los Angeles Times Book Prize for Fiction) 2006, Friendly Fire (novel) 2007. *Address:* 33 Shoshanat Ha-Carmel, Haifa, 34322, Israel. *Telephone:* 4-8370001. *Fax:* 4-8375569. *E-mail:* bulli@research.haifa.ac.il (home).

YEKHANUROV, Yuriy Ivanovych; Ukrainian politician and economist; b. 23 Aug. 1948, Belkachi, Yakut ASSR (now the Repub. of Sakha—Yakutiya), Russian Fed.; s. of Ivan Mikhailovich Yekhanurov and Galina Mikhailovna Yekhanurova; m. Olena Lvivna Yekhanurova; one s.; ed Kyiv Construction Tech. Coll.; Higher School of Econ. State Planning, Kyiv Inst. of Nat. Econs, Academic Research Econ. Inst. of State Planning; master, then head of workshop, Chief Engineer, Dir, Kyivmiskbur Co. 1967–77, Head of Kyivmiskbudkomplekt Co. 1977–88; Head, Buddetal Co. 1977–88; Deputy Chief, Golovkyivmiskbud Co. 1988–91; elected to Kyiv City Rada (Council) 1990; Head of State Econ. Council, Cabinet of Ministers 1991–92; Deputy Head of Bd of Verkhovna Rada (Parl.) 1992; Deputy Head of Kyiv City Admin. 1992–93; Deputy Minister of the Economy 1993–94; Head of State Property Fund 1994–97; Minister of Economy Feb.–July 1997; Head of State Cttee on Entrepreneurship Devt 1997–98; mem. Verkhovna Rada 1998–, Deputy Head, Cttee on Econ. Policy, Man. Economy, Property and Investment 1998–99; First Deputy Prime Minister 1999–2001; Deputy Head of Presidential Admin 2001, 2004, re-elected mem. Verkhovna Rada for Our Ukraine bloc 2002, Head of Parl. Cttee on Industrial Policy and Entrepreneurship 2002; Deputy Head of Viktor Yushchenko's presidential campaign team 2004; Head of Cen. Exec. Cttee, Our Ukraine People's Union party March 2005; Gov. Dnipropetrovsk Oblast April—Sept. 2005; apptd Acting Prime Minister Sept. 2005, Prime Minister Sept. 2005–06; Minister of Defence 2007–09; apptd first Deputy Head of the Presidential Secr. 2009. *Publications:* more than 60 publs on econs. *Address:* c/o Our Ukraine, 04070 Kyiv, vul. Borychiv Tik 22A, Ukraine. *E-mail:* info@yekhanurov.com; yekhanurov_u@ukr.net. *Website:* www.yekhanurov.info.

YELLAND, David, BA, AMP; British business executive and fmr journalist; *Partner, Brunswick Group LLP;* b. 14 May 1963, Harrogate, N Yorks., England; s. of John Michael Yelland and Patricia Ann McIntosh; m. 1st Tania Farrell 1996 (died 2006); one s.; m. 2nd Charlotte Marjorie Elston 2010; one d.; ed Brigg Grammar School, Lincs., Univ. of Coventry, Harvard Business School, USA; grad. trainee, Westminster Press 1985; trainee reporter, Buckinghamshire Advertiser 1985–87; industrial reporter, Northern Echo 1987–88; gen. news and business reporter, North West Times and Sunday Times 1988–89; city reporter, Thomson Regional Newspapers 1989–90; joined News Corpn 1990; city reporter, then City Ed. The Sun 1990–92, New York Corresp. 1992–93, Ed. 1998–2003; Deputy Business Ed. Business Ed., then Deputy Ed. New York Post 1993–98; Sr Vice-Pres. News Corpn, New York 2003–04; Vice-Pres. Weber Shandwick Worldwide (public relations consultancy) 2004–06; Partner, Brunswick Group LLP 2006–; Trustee, Action on Addiction 2012–; Campaign UK Media Achiever of the Year 2002. *Publication:* The Truth About Leo (novel) 2010. *Leisure interests:* writing, reading, recovering, swimming, Manchester City Football Club. *Address:* Brunswick Group LLP, 16 Lincoln's Inn Fields, London, WC2A 3ED, England (office). *Telephone:* (20) 7404-5959 (office). *Fax:* (20) 7936-7730 (office). *E-mail:* dyelland@brunswickgroup .com (office). *Website:* www.brunswickgroup.com (office).

YELLEN, Janet Louise, PhD; American economist, academic and central banker; *Chairwoman, Board of Governors, Federal Reserve System;* b. 13 Aug. 1946, Brooklyn, New York; d. of Julius Yellen and Anna Ruth Yellen (née Blumenthal); m. George Arthur Akerlof 1978; one s.; ed Brown Univ., Yale Univ.; Grad. Fellow, NSF 1967–71; Asst Prof. of Econs, Harvard Univ. 1971–76; consultant, Div. of Int. Finance, Bd of Govs of US Fed. Reserve System 1974–75, economist, Trade and Financial Studies section 1977–78; consultant, US Congressional Budget Office, Washington, DC 1975–76; Research Affiliate, Yale Univ. 1976; Lecturer, LSE 1978–80; Asst Prof. of Econs, School of Business Admin., Univ. of California, Berkeley 1980–82, Assoc. Prof. 1982–85, Prof., Haas School of Business 1985, Bernard T. Rocca Jr Prof. of Int. Business and Trade 1992, Eugene E. and Catherine M. Trefethen Prof. of Business Admin, now Prof. Emer., fmr mem. Haas Econ. Analysis and Policy Group; mem. Bd of Govs US Fed. Reserve System 1994–97; Chair. Council of Econ. Advisers 1997–99, also Chair. Econ. Policy Cttee of OECD; Pres. and CEO Fed. Reserve Bank of San Francisco 2004–10, Vice-Chair. Bd of Govs Fed. Reserve System 2010–14, Chair. 2014–;

Research Fellow, MIT 1974; mem. Panel of Econ. Advisers, US Congressional Budget Office 1993; mem. Advisory Panel on Econs NSF 1977–78, 1991–92; mem. Brookings Panel on Econ. Activity 1987–88, 1990–91, Sr Adviser 1989–; Lecturer on Macroeconomic Theory, Yrjö Jahnsson Foundation, Helsinki 1977–78; mem. Council on Foreign Relations 1976–81, American Econ. Asscn; Guggenheim Fellow 1986–87; Fellow, American Acad. of Arts and Sciences 2001–, Yale Corpn 2000–; Assoc., Journal of Econ. Perspectives 1987–91; Hon. Woodrow Wilson Fellow 1967; Maria and Sidney Rolfe Award for Nat. Econ. Service, Women's Econ. Roundtable 1997, Wilbur Lucius Cross Medal, Yale Univ. 1997, Adam Smith Award, Nat. Asscn for Business Economics 2010; ranked by Forbes magazine amongst The World's Most Powerful People (72nd) 2013. *Publications include:* The Limits of the Market in Resource Allocation (co-author) 1977, contrib. articles to professional journals. *Address:* Board of Governors of the Federal Reserve System, 20th Street and Constitution Avenue, NW, Washington, DC 20551, USA (office). *Telephone:* (202) 452-3000 (office). *Website:* www.federalreserve.gov (office).

YEMELYANOV, Aleksei Mikhailovich, DEcon; Russian politician and economist; b. 15 Feb. 1935; ed Moscow Univ.; mem. CPSU 1959–90; Lecturer, Prof., Head of Chair Moscow Univ.; mem. Russian Agric. Acad.; USSR People's Deputy 1989–91; Deputy Chair. Cttee on Agric. Problems, USSR Supreme Soviet 1989–91; mem. Pres. Council 1992–; Pres.-Rector Russian State Acad. of State Service 1994–2000, Prof. Dept of Econs 2000–; active participant of democratic movt; mem. of State Duma (Parl.) 1993–95. *Publications:* scientific works and articles on agricultural reforms in Russia. *Address:* Russian Agricultural Academy, Bolshoi Kharitonyevsky per. 21, 107814 Moscow; Academy of State Service, Vernadskogo prosp. 84, 117606 Moscow, Russia. *Telephone:* (495) 923-40-90 (Agricultural Acad.); (495) 436-94-24 (Acad. of State Service).

YEMELYANOV, Stanislav Vasilevich, DTechSc; Russian management specialist; b. 18 May 1929, Voronezh; s. of Vasilii Yemelyanov and Ludmila (née Chepkova) Yemelyanova; m. Olga Yemelyanova 1952; one s. one d.; ed Moscow Univ.; with Inst. of Control Problems, USSR (now Russian) Acad. of Sciences 1952–76, with Inst. for Systems Analysis 1976– (Dir 1991–), mem. Acad. 1984, mem. Presidium 1988, Acad.-Sec., Dept of Informatics, Computer Science and Automation 1990–; Gen. Dir Int. Inst. for Man. Science 1976–; Head of Chair of Nonlinear Dynamics and Control Processes, Moscow State Univ.; Chair of Engineering Cybernetics, Moscow Steel and Alloys Inst.; mem. editorial Bd Differential Equations, Automatic and Remote Control, Problems of Theory and Practice of Management, Dynamics and Control; research into variable structure control theory; holder of about 100 patents; Lenin Prize 1972, USSR State Prize 1980, Council of USSR Ministers Prize 1981, Russian Fed. State Prize 1994. *Publications:* 7 books; 250 journal articles. *Address:* International Institute for Management Science, Shchepkina Street 8, 129090 Moscow (office); Academic Zelinskii str. 38/8, Apt 69, Moscow, Russia (home). *Telephone:* (495) 208-91-06 (office); (495) 135-54-69 (home). *Fax:* (495) 938-16-74.

YEMENIDJIAN, Alex, MA; American business executive; *Chairman and CEO, Armenco Holdings LLC;* ed California State Univ., Northridge, Univ. of Southern California; Man. Partner, Parks, Palmer & Yemenidjian; joined Metro-Goldwyn-Mayer (MGM) Grand Inc., Las Vegas 1989, Chief Financial Officer 1994–98, Pres. and COO 1995–99, mem. Bd of Dirs 1999–2005, Dir MGM Grand Inc. (now MGM MIRAGE), Santa Monica 1989–, Chair. and CEO 1999–2005; Chair. and CEO Armenco Holdings LLC 2005–; Exec. Tracinda 1990–97, 1999; Chair., Pres. and CEO Tropicana Las Vegas Hotel & Casino, Inc. 2009–, Pres. and CEO Tropicana Las Vegas, Inc. 2013–; Chair. and CEO Hotel Ramada of Nevada; Chair. United Armenian Fund; Ind. Dir Kirk Kerkorian's Lincy Foundation 1989–, Guess Inc. 2005–; Trustee, Baron Investment Funds Trust 2006–, Baron Select Funds, Mutual Funds; Co-Chair. Imagine the Arts Campaign at California State Univ., Northridge 2005–. *Address:* Armenco Holdings LLC, 1925 Century Park East, Los Angeles, CA 90067-2701, USA (office). *Telephone:* (310) 788-3000 (office).

YEN, Ching-Chang, LLB, MA; Taiwanese politician; b. 7 April 1948, Tainan; m.; one s. one d.; ed Nat. Taiwan Univ., Univ. of Michigan, USA; joined Ministry of Finance 1972, Sr Customs Officer, Taipei Customs Bureau 1972–73, Specialist, Dept of Customs Admin. 1973–77, Sr Specialist in Secr. 1977–78, 1980–84, Exec. Sec. Legal Comm. 1984–85, Taxation and Tariff Comm. 1985–92, Deputy Minister of Finance 1996–2000, Minister of Finance 2000–02; Deputy Dir-Gen. First Bureau, Office of the Pres. 1992–93, Dir-Gen. 1993–96; Prof., Nat. Taiwan Univ., Nat. Chengchi Univ. and Soochow Univ. 1981–86; first Amb. of Taiwan WTO 2002–05; Chair. and CEO Yuanta Financial Holding Co., Ltd (fmrly Fuhwa Financial Holding Co.) 2005–; Eisenhower Fellowship, USA 1995; Chevalier, Ordre nat. du Mérite 1998, Order of Brilliant Star with Grand Cordon in 2005; Class One Merit Medal, Exec. Yuan 2000. *Publications:* Anti-dumping Act and Customs Policy 1981, Legal Problems of Sino-American Trade Negotiations 1987, Unveiling GATT: Order and Trend of Global Trade 1989, International Economic Law 1991, Laws and Regulations of International Economic Relations 1995, Taxation Law 1998, Understanding and Appreciating French Wines 1997; (in English) Taiwan Trade and Investment Law 1994. *Address:* Yuanta Financial Holding Co., Ltd, 9F, No. 4, Section 1, Chung-Hsiao W. Road, Taipei, Taiwan (office).

YEN, Gen. Ming; Taiwanese army officer and politician; *Minister of National Defense;* b. 14 Nov. 1949; ed Repub. of China Air Force Acad., Nat. Defense Univ.; spent long career in Repub. of China Air Force (ROCAF) including as Wing Chief, later Superintendent, ROCAFA, Chief of Staff of Combined Logistics Command, Commdr, ROCAF Logistics Command, Deputy Commdr, later Commdr, Deputy Chief of Staff and Chief of Staff ROCAF Command HQ, Commanding Gen. of ROCAF 2011–13, Chief of Gen. Staff Jan.–Aug. 2013; Minister of Nat. Defense 2013–; attained rank of Gen. 2008. *Address:* Ministry of National Defense, 2/F, 164 Bo Ai Road, Taipei 10048, Taiwan (office). *Telephone:* (2) 23116117 (office). *Fax:* (2) 23144221 (office). *Website:* www.mnd.gov.tw (office).

YENTOB, Alan, LLB; British television executive; *Creative Director, BBC;* b. 11 March 1947, London; s. of Isaac Yentob and Flora Yentob (née Khazam); one s. one d. by Philippa Walker; ed King's School, Ely, Univ. of Grenoble, France, Univ. of Leeds; BBC gen. trainee 1968, Producer/Dir 1970–, including Omnibus 1973–75, Ed. Arena 1978–85, Head of Music and Arts, BBC-TV 1985–88, Controller, BBC 2 1988–93, BBC 1 1993–97, BBC Dir of Programmes 1997–98, BBC Dir of TV

1998–2000, of Drama, Entertainment and Children's Programmes 2000–04, Creative Dir, BBC 2004–; presenter of arts series Imagine (BBC 1) 2003–; mem. British Film Inst. Production Bd 1985–93, British Screen Advisory Council, Advisory Cttee, Council Royal Court Theatre; Chair. Inst. of Contemporary Arts –2010; Gov. Nat. Film School 1998–; mem. S Bank Bd 1999–2008, Int. Acad. of Television Arts and Sciences; Trustee, Architecture Foundation 1992–2000, Timebank 2001–04, Kids Co.; Hon. Fellow RCA, RIBA, Royal TV Soc. *Leisure interests:* swimming, books. *Address:* BBC Television, Television Centre, Wood Lane, London, W12 7RJ, England (office). *Telephone:* (20) 8743-8000 (office). *Website:* www.bbc.co.uk (office).

YEO, Cheow Tong, BEng; Singaporean politician; b. 1947; m.; three d.; ed Anglo-Chinese School, Univ. of Western Australia; worked in Econ. Devt Bd 1972–75; joined LeBlond Makino Asia Pte. Ltd (LMA) as Staff Engineer 1975, subsequently promoted to Eng Man., then Operations Dir; Man. Dir LMA and subsidiary co., Pacific Precision Castings Pte. Ltd 1981–85; MP for Hong Kah 1984–; Minister of State for Health and for Foreign Affairs 1985–87; Acting Minister for Health, Sr Minister of State for Foreign Affairs 1987–90, of Health 1990–94, for Community Devt 1991–94, for Trade and Industry 1994–97, of Health and for the Environment 1997–99; Minister for Communications and Information Tech. 1999–2001; Minister of Transport 2001–06 (resgnd). *Address:* Yew Tee PAP Branch, Block 608, #01-103, Choa Chu Kang Street 62, Singapore 680608, Singapore (office). *Telephone:* 67606233 (office). *Fax:* 6760 2133 (office). *E-mail:* ctyeo@yewtee.org.sg (office). *Website:* www.parliament.gov.sg (office).

YEO, George Yong-Boon, BA, MBA; Singaporean politician; b. 13 Sept. 1954, Singapore; m. Jennifer Leong Lai Peng 1984; one d. three s.; ed Univ. of Cambridge, UK, Singapore Command and Staff Coll., Harvard Business School, USA; fmr Signals Officer, Singapore Air Force, later Head Air Plans Dept, Chief of Air Staff 1985; Dir Jt Operations and Planning, Ministry of Defence 1986–88, rank of Brig.-Gen. 1988; mem. Parl. 1988–; Minister of State for Finance and Minister of State for Foreign Affairs 1988–90; Acting Minister for Information and the Arts and Sr Minister of State for Foreign Affairs 1990–91; Minister for Information and the Arts 1991–99; Second Minister for Foreign Affairs 1991–94; Minister for Health 1994–97; Second Minister for Trade and Industry 1997–99, Minister for Trade and Industry 1999–2004; Minister of Foreign Affairs 2004–11; mem. Harvard Business School Visiting Cttee 1998–2004; Adviser Sun Yat Sen Nanyang Memorial Hall. *Leisure interests:* reading, swimming, jogging. *Address:* c/o Ministry of Foreign Affairs, Tanglin, 248163 Singapore (office).

YEOH, Michelle, BA; Malaysian actress; b. (Nee Yeoh Choo-Keng), 6 Aug. 1962, Ipoh, Perak; m. Dickson Poon 1988 (divorced 1992); ed Royal Acad. of Dance, London; fmr Bond girl in Tomorrow Never Dies 1997; deported and barred from entering Myanmar after playing role of freed democracy leader Aung San Suu Kyi in film, The Lady, about her life June 2011; Chevalier, Légion d'honneur 2007. *Films include:* Owls vs. Dumbo 1984, In the Line of Duty 2 1985, The Target 1985, Magnificent Warriors 1987, Easy Money 1987, The Heroic Trio 1993, Police Story 3 1992 (Part 2 1993), Butterfly Sword 1993, Heroic Trio 2: Executioners 1993, Seven Maidens 1993, Tai-Chi 1993, Wonder Seven 1994, The Stunt Woman 1996, The Soong Sisters 1997, Tomorrow Never Dies 1997, Moonlight Express 1999, Crouching Tiger, Hidden Dragon 2000, The Touch 2002, Fei ying 2004, Memoirs of a Geisha 2005, Fearless 2006, Sunshine 2007, Far North 2007, Purple Mountain 2008, The Children of Huang Shi 2008, The Mummy: Tomb of the Dragon Emperor 2008, Babylon A.D. 2008, True Legend 2010, Reign of Assassins 2010, Kung Fu Panda 2 (voice) 2011, The Lady 2011. *Television includes:* Jackie Chan Adventures (series) 2002. *Address:* c/o United Talent Agency, Inc., 9560 Wilshire Blvd, Suite 500, Beverly Hills, CA 90212, USA. *Telephone:* (310) 273-6700. *Fax:* (310) 247-1111.

YEOH, Tan Sri Dato' Seri Tiong Lay; Malaysian chartered builder and business executive; *Executive Chairman, YTL Corporation Berhad;* m.; seven c.; ed Chong Hwa Ind. High School, Kuala Lumpur; Founder and Exec. Chair. YTL Corpn Berhad (conglomerate with interests in construction, utilities, hotels, property Devt and technology); Fellow, Chartered Inst. of Building, Australian Inst. of Building, Faculty of Building (UK); PSM, SPMS, DPMS, KMN, PPN, PJK, Order of the Rising Sun, Gold Rays with Neck Ribbon 2008; Hon. DEng (Heriot-Watt), Hon. DBA (Universiti Malaysia Sabah). *Address:* YTL Corporation Berhad, 11th Floor, Yeoh Tiong Lay Plaza, 55 Jalan Bukit Bintang, 55100 Kuala Lumpur, Malaysia (office). *Telephone:* (3) 2142-6633 (office). *Fax:* (3) 2143-3192 (office). *E-mail:* info@ytl.com.my (office). *Website:* www.ytl.com.my (office).

YEOMANS, Donald Keith, BA, MS, PhD; American astronomer; *Supervisor, NASA Jet Propulsion Laboratory;* b. 3 May 1942, Rochester, NY; s. of George E. Yeomans and Jessie Yeomans; m. Laurie Robyn Ernst; one s. one d.; ed Middlebury Coll., Univ. of Maryland; Supervisor, Computer Sciences Corpn 1973–76; Sr Research Astronomer, NASA Jet Propulsion Lab. 1976–92, Supervisor 1992–; Discipline Specialist, Int. Halley Watch 1982–89; Chief Investigator, NASA Comet Mission 1987–91, Near-Earth Asteroid Rendezvous Mission 1994–2001, Multi-Comet Flyby Mission 1997–2002, Comet Impact Mission 1999–2006; Project Scientist for Asteroid Sample Return Mission 1998–; Man. NASA Near-Earth Object Program Office 1998–; mem. American Astronomical Soc.; American Inst. of Aeronautics and Astronautics Space Achievement Award 1985, NASA Exceptional Service Medal 1986, Distinguished Service Medal 2009, named NASA/JPL Senior Research Scientist 1993. *Publications include:* Comet Halley: Once in a Lifetime 1985, The Distant Planets 1989, Comets: A Chronological History of Observation, Science, Myth and Folklore 1991. *Address:* Jet Propulsion Lab #301-150, 4800 Oak Grove Drive, Pasadena, CA 91109-8001, USA (office). *Telephone:* (818) 354-4321 (office). *E-mail:* donald.k.yeomans@jpl.nasa.gov (office). *Website:* www.jpl.nasa.gov (office).

YÉPEZ NAJAS, Mauricio; Ecuadorean economist; ed Pontificia Universidad Católica de Quito, Univ. of Colorado, Williams Coll., USA; Gov. Cen. Bank of Ecuador –2004, Dir 2004–; Minister of the Economy and Finance 2004–05. *Address:* c/o Ministry of the Economy and Finance, Avda 10 de Agosto 1661 y Jorge Washington, Quito, Ecuador (office).

YEREMIN, Yuri Ivanovich; Russian theatre director and drama instructor; *Acting and Directing Instructor, Institute for Advanced Theatre Training;* b. 9 March 1944, Kolomna, Moscow Region; s. of Evdokiya Fillippovna Yeremina; m.

Nina Petrovna Yeremina 1974; one s. one d.; with Youth Theatre, Rostov-on-Don 1973–77; Gorky Drama Theatre, Rostov-on-Don 1978–80; Cen. Army Theatre, Moscow 1981–87; Dir Pushkin Theatre, Moscow 1987–2000; Acting and Directing Instructor, Inst. for Advanced Theatre Training, Harvard Univ., USA 1997–; mem. Faculty Moscow Art Theater School USA; US debut with production of The Paper Gramophone, Hartford Stage Co. 1989; Ward No. 6, dramatic adaptation of Chekhov story, performed at int. drama festivals in USA, France, Italy, Switzerland, Belgium, UK and Canada 1989–91; Vice-Pres. Int. Asscn of Theatre Producers 1991–; People's Artist of Russia 1986, Order for Literature and Art (France) 1989. *Recent productions include:* The Possessed (Dostoevsky adaptation) 1989, Black Monk (Chekhov adaptation) 1990, At Kingdom Gate (Hamsun) 1991, Erick XIV (Strindberg) 1992, The Ghosts (De Filippo) 1992, The History of one Staircase (Buero Valejo) 1993, To Moscow! To Moscow! (adaptation of Chekhov's Three Sisters) 1994, Madame Bovary (Flaubert adaptation) 1994, The Inspector (Gogol) 1994, King Oedipus (Sophocles) 1995. *Productions at American Repertory Theater (Cambridge, Mass.):* The Idiot (Dostoevsky) 1998, Ivanov (Chekhov) 1999, Three Farces and a Funeral (based on Chekhov's comedies) 2000, Othello (Shakespeare) 2001, Silver Age (Roshchin) 2001. *Leisure interests:* painting, writing. *Address:* A. R. T./MXAT Institute, Loeb Drama Center, 64 Brattle Street, Cambridge, MA 02138, USA (office); 7 Soviet Army Street, Apt. 213, 01827 Moscow, Russia. *Telephone:* (617) 496.2000 ext. 8890 (Cambridge) (office); (495) 281-83-20 (home); (495) 299-41-36. *E-mail:* institute@amrep.org (office); yuryer@mail.ru (home). *Website:* www.amrep.org/iatt (office).

YERGIN, Daniel, PhD; American writer and business executive; *Chairman, Cambridge Energy Research Associates;* ed Yale Univ., Univ. of Cambridge (Marshall Scholar), UK; taught at Harvard Business School and John F. Kennedy School of Govt, Harvard Univ.; Chair. Cambridge Energy Research Assocs; Dir US-Russian Business Council, Atlantic Partnership, New America Foundation; Global Energy Analyst, NBC, CNBC; mem. Bd US Energy Asscn, Advisory Bd US Sec. of Energy; mem. Nat. Petroleum Council, Russia Acad. of Oil and Gas; mem. Cttee on Studies, Council on Foreign Relations; Trustee Brookings Inst.; fmr Chair. US Dept of Energy Task Force on Strategic Energy Research and Devt; Pres.'s Medal, Repub. of Italy 2005; Dr hc (Univs of Houston and Missouri); US Energy Asscn Award. *Publications:* Shattered Peace: Origins of the Cold War and the National Security State 1978, Energy Future: Report of the Energy Project at the Harvard Business School (with Robert Stobaugh) 1981, Dependence Dilemma 1984, The Prize: The Epic Quest for Oil, Money and Power (Pulitzer Prize for Gen. Nonfiction 1992) 1993 (also PBS/BBC documentary series), Russia 2010 and What It Means for the World (with Thane Gustafson) 1995, Commanding Heights: Battle for the World Economy (with Joseph Stanislaw) (also PBS/BBC documentary series—CINE Golden Eagle Award, New York Festivals Gold World Medal). *Address:* Cambridge Energy Research Associates, 55 Cambridge Parkway, Cambridge, MA 02142, USA (office). *Telephone:* (617) 866-5000 (office). *Fax:* (617) 866-5900 (office). *E-mail:* akipp@cera.com (office). *Website:* www.cera.com (office).

YÉRIMA, Denis Ali; Benin politician; *Minister of National Defence;* Préfet, Borgou and Alibori Départements 2008–13; Minister of Nat. Defence 2013–. *Address:* Ministry of National Defence, BP 2493, Cotonou, Benin (office). *Telephone:* 21-30-08-90 (office). *Fax:* 21-30-18-21 (office).

YEROFEYEV, Victor Vladimirovich; Russian writer and critic; b. 19 Sept. 1947, Moscow; m. Veslava (née Skura) Yerofeyeva; one s.; ed Moscow Univ.; expelled from USSR Writers' Union for participation in almanac Metropol, membership restored in 1986; lecturer Maxim Gorky Literature Inst.; seminars on Modern Russian Literature at Univ. of South Calif.; contribs to Moscow News, Moscow Magazine, New York Review of Books; mem. Bd Russian PEN Centre; named Man of the Year by Moscow Magazine 1990. *Publications:* Anna's Body and End of the Russian Avant-garde (collection of short stories) 1980, Life with an Idiot (novel) 1980, Russian Beauty (novel) 1981, In the Maze of Cursed Questions (collection of essays) 1990, The Pocket Apocalypse 1993, Collected Works (3 vols) 1994–95, The Doomsday 1996, Men 1997, Five Rivers of Life 1998, Encyclopedia of the Russian Soul 2000. *Leisure interest:* travelling. *Address:* 1st Smolensky per. 9, Apt 1, Moscow, Russia. *Telephone:* (495) 241-02-08.

YERSHOV, Yuri Leonidovich, DMathSci; Russian scientist and mathematician; b. 1 May 1940, Novosibirsk; m.; three c.; ed Novosibirsk State Univ.; jr, sr researcher, then Head of Div. Inst. of Math., Siberian br., USSR (now Russian) Acad. of Sciences 1963–85, corresp. mem. Russian Acad. of Sciences 1970, mem. 1991; Rector Novosibirsk Univ. *Publications:* numerous scientific publs including monographs. *Address:* Novosibirsk State University, Pirogova str. 2, 630090 Novosibirsk, Russia (office). *Telephone:* (3832) 35-78-08 (office); (3832) 35-51-75 (home).

YESENBAYEV, Mazhit Tuleubekovich, CandEcon, Docent; Kazakhstani politician, engineer and economist; *Chairman, Agency for Competition Protection (Antimonopoly Agency);* b. 28 April 1949, Pavlodar; m.; three c.; ed Kazakh Polytechnic Inst., Almaty; fmr Gov. Cen. Karaganda Region; apptd Minister of Finance 1999–2001, of Economy and Trade 2002–03, of Industry and Trade 2003; Presidential Aide on Econ. Affairs 2003; Akim of Akmolinskaya Oblast 2004–08; Chair. Agency for Competition Protection (Antimonopoly Agency) 2008–; First Pres. Order 1997, Parasat Order 1999. *Publications:* more than 50 publs on issues of territorial production arrangements, education process optimization, current competition policy and its prospects. *Leisure interests:* judo, alpine skiing, tennis, reading. *Address:* #4 Entrance, House of Ministries Building, 010000 Astana, Kazakhstan (office). *Telephone:* (7172) 749068 (office). *Fax:* (7172) 749637 (office). *E-mail:* m.yessenbayev@azkrk.kz (office). *Website:* (office).

YESIMOV, Akhmetzhan S.; Kazakhstani politician; *Mayor of Almaty;* b. 1950; ed Kazakh Inst. of Agric., Acad. of Social Sciences, Moscow, Russia; mechanical engineer 1979–80; worked for econ. orgs in Almaty Region 1979–90; First Vice-Chair., State Agricultural and Industrial Cttee 1990–91; First Deputy Minister of Agric. of Kazakh SSR 1991–92; Head of Almaty Regional Admin 1992–94; Deputy Prime Minister of Kazakhstan 1994–96, State Sec. of Kazakhstan 1996, First Deputy Prime Minister and Chair. of State Cttee on Investments 1996–06; Minister of Agric. 2001–06; fmr Amb. and Head of Perm. Del. of Kazakhstan to

NATO, Brussels, Belgium; Mayor of Almaty 2008–. *Address:* Office of the Mayor, Almaty, Kazakhstan (office).

YESIN, Sergey Nikolayevich; Russian writer; *Rector, Maxim Gorky Literary Institute;* b. 18 Dec. 1935, Moscow; s. of Nikolai Yesin and Zinaida (née Afonina) Saprykina; m. Valentina Ivanova; ed Moscow State Univ.; debut as journalist, corresp. Moskovsky Komsomolets, Ed.-in-Chief Krugozor 1972–74; ed. Drama Broadcasting Div. State TV and Broadcasting Cttee 1974–81; Rector Maxim Gorky Literary Inst. 1992–, Prof. 1993; a Founder Club of Ind. Writers 1992; Founder and Vice-Pres. Acad. of Russian Literature 1996; Chair. Int. Union of Social Asscns of Bibliophiles 1997–; State Order of Friendship 1996, Sholokhov Literary Award 2000, Moscow Literary Award. *Publications include:* Recollections of August, Memoirs of a Forty-Year-Old, The Imitator, The Spy, Standing in the Doorway, Gladiator 1987, Characters 1990, Selected Stories 1994, In the Season of Salting Pickles 1994, The Current Day 1994, The Mars Eclipse 1994, Tutor 1996, The Power of Culture 1997, Selected Stories 1998, Literary Diaries 1999, 2000, 2001, 2002, Death of Titan 2002, Companion Thoughts 2002, Marburg. *Leisure interests:* building dachas, home maintenance. *Address:* Maxim Gorky Literary Institute, Tverskoy Boulevard 25, 103104 Moscow; Stroiteley str. 4, korp. 6, Apt. 43, 117311 Moscow, Russia (home). *Telephone:* (495) 202-84-22 (office); (495) 930-35-45 (home); (495) 203-01-01. *Fax:* (495) 202-76-88 (office); (495) 203-60-91. *E-mail:* liternity@litinstitut.ru (office); rectorat@litinstitut.ru (home). *Website:* www.litinstitut.ru (office).

YESSENIN-VOLPIN, Alexander Sergeyevich; Russian mathematician, philosopher and poet; b. 5 Dec. 1924, Leningrad (now St Petersburg); s. of poet Sergey Esenin and Nadiezhda Volpina; m. 2nd V. B. Volpina; m. 2nd I. G. Kristi; m. 3rd 1994; one c.; studied at Faculty of Math., Moscow Univ. 1941–46; arrested for his poetry and committed to mental asylum 1949; in exile Karaganda, Kazakh SSR 1950; amnestied 1953; wrote numerous articles on logic and math. and translated extensively; worked at USSR Acad. of Sciences Inst. of Scientific and Tech. Information 1961–72; dissident activity 1959–; emigrated 1972; Sakharov Prize. *Publications include:* A Free Philosophical Treatise 1959, A Leaf of Spring 1959, 1961, Open Letter to Solzhenitsyn 1970, Report on Committee on Rights of Man 1971, On the Logic of Moral Sciences (in English) 1988; numerous articles in Western and Russian scientific journals (after 1990s). *Leisure interests:* logic, philosophy. *Address:* 1513 North Shore Road, 2nd Floor, Revere, MA 02151, USA (home). *Telephone:* (781) 289-1072 (home).

YEUTTER, Clayton K., BS, JD, PhD; American lawyer, business executive and fmr government official; *Senior Advisor, Hogan Lovells LLP;* b. 10 Dec. 1930, Eustis, Neb.; m. 1st Lillian Jeanne Vierk (died); two s. two d.; m. 2nd Cristena Lynn Bach; three d.; ed Univ. of Nebraska, Lincoln; served in USAF 1952–57; ran family farm from 1957; Prof., Dir Agricultural Tech. Assistance Programme in Bogotá, Colombia 1968–70; Asst Sec. of Agric. for Marketing & Consumer Services, US Govt 1973–74, for Int. Affairs and Commodity Programs 1974–75; Deputy Special Trade Rep. 1975–77, US Trade Rep. 1985–88; Sec. of Agric. 1989–91; Chair. Republican Nat. Cttee 1991–92; Counsellor to the Pres. for Domestic Policy 1992; Sr Adviser, Hogan & Hartson LLP (law firm), Washington, DC 1993–; Pres. and CEO Chicago Mercantile Exchange 1978–85; mem. Bd Dirs Burlington Capital Group 2004–, Neogen Corpn; fmr mem. Bd of Dirs Weyerhaeuser Corpn, ConAgra Foods, Texas Instruments, B.A.T. Industries (London), Zurich Financial Services, Caterpillar Inc., FMC Corpn, OppenheimerFunds and others; eight hon. degrees; numerous nat. and int. awards. *Publications:* dozens of articles on trade policy and agricultural policy. *Address:* Hogan Lovells, Columbia Square, 555 13th Street, NW, Washington, DC 20004, USA (office). *Telephone:* (202) 637-5674 (office). *Fax:* (202) 637-5910 (office). *E-mail:* clayton.yeutter@hoganlovells.com (office). *Website:* www.hoganlovells.com/cyeutter (office).

YEVTUSHENKO, Yevgeniy Aleksandrovich; Russian poet, writer and academic; *Distinguished Professor, Department of English, University of Tulsa;* b. 18 July 1933, Zima, Irkutsk Region; m. 1st Bella Akhmadulina 1954 (divorced); m. 2nd Galina Sokol 1962; one s.; m. 3rd Jan Butler 1978; two s.; m. 4th Maria Novikova 1986; two s.; ed Moscow Literary Inst.; geological expeditions with father to Kazakhstan 1948, the Altai 1949–50; literary work 1949–; mem. Editorial Bd of Yunost magazine 1962–69; People's Deputy of the USSR 1989–91; Sec. USSR Writers' Union 1986–91; Vice-Pres. Soviet PEN Cttee; moved to Tulsa, Okla, USA in mid-1990s, currently Distinguished Professor in the Department of English, Univ. of Tulsa; sometime Prof. Pittsburgh Univ. USA, Univ. Autónoma de Santo Domingo, Dominican Rep.; USSR Cttee for Defence of Peace Award 1965, Order of Red Banner of Labour, Badge of Honour, USSR State Prize 1984. *Films directed include:* Kindergarten 1983, Stalin's Funeral 1987; acted in Ascent (film on Tsiolkovsky). *Publications include:* poetry: Scouts of the Future (collected verse) 1952, The Third Snow (lyric verse) 1955, The Highway of Enthusiasts 1956, Zima Junction 1956, The Promise (collected verse) 1960, Moscow Goods Station, The Nihilist, The Apple 1960–61, Do the Russians Want War?, Babi Yar 1961, The Heirs of Stalin, Fears 1962, A Sweep of the Arm 1962, Tenderness 1962, A Precocious Autobiography 1963, The City of Yes and the City of No, Bratskaya Hydro-Electric Power Station 1964, Letter to Yesenin 1965, Italian Tears, A Boat of Communication, Poems Chosen by the Author 1966, Collection of Verses: Yelabuga Nail, Cemetery of Whales 1967, That's What Is Happening to Me 1968, It's Snowing White 1969, Kazan University 1971, I am of Siberian Stock 1971, The Singing Domba 1972, Stolen Apples 1972, Under the Skin of the Statue of Liberty (play) 1972, Intimate Lyrics 1973, A Father's Hearing 1975, 1978, From Desire to Desire 1976, Love Poems 1977, People of the Morning 1978, Winter Station 1978, A Dove in Santiago: A Novella in Verse 1978, Heavy Soils 1979, The Face Behind the Face 1979, Ivan the Terrible and Ivan the Fool 1979, Berries (novel) 1981, Ardabiola (short story) 1981, Almost at the End (prose and verse) 1985, A Wind of Tomorrow (essays) 1987, Fatal Half Measures 1989, The Collected Poems 1952–90 1991, Farewell to Red Banner 1992, Twentieth Century Russian Poetry (compiler) 1994, Don't Die Before You're Dead (novel) 1996, My Very, Very... (poetry) 1996; photography: Divided Twins: Alaska and Siberia, Invisible Threads, Shadows and Faces. *Address:* Department of English, Zink Hall 346, 800 South Tucker Drive, Tulsa, OK 74104, USA. *Telephone:* (918) 631-2856. *E-mail:* yevgeny-yevtushenko@utulsa.edu.

YEVTUSHENKOV, Vladimir Petrovich, DEcon; Russian economist and business executive; *Chairman, AFK Sistema;* b. 25 Sept. 1948, Kamenshchina,

Smolensk region; m.; one s. one d.; ed D. Mendeleev Moscow Chemical Eng Inst., Moscow State Univ.; Deputy Dir and Chief Engineer Karacharovo Factory of Plastics, Moscow 1975–82; Chief Engineer, First Deputy CEO Polymerbyt Research and Manufacturing Asscn 1982–87; Head Tech. Dept, then Chief Dept of Science and Tech., Moscow City Exec. Cttee 1987–90, Head Cttee on Science and Tech. 1990–93; Founder and Pres. AFK Sistema (jt stock financial holding corpn) 1993–95, Chair. 1994–2005, Pres. 2005–06, Chair. 2006–; mem. Bureau of Bd of Dirs Russian Union of Industrialists and Entrepreneurs 2000–, Head of Cttee on Industrial Policy 2001–; mem. Presidium of Bd of Dirs, Russian Chamber of Commerce and Industry 2002–, Head of Russian-Arab Business Council 2003–; Chair. Bd of Trustees, Russian Museum Devt Fund 2004. *Leisure interests:* hunting, tennis. *Address:* AFK Sistema, 13 Mokhovaya Street, 125009 Moscow, Russia (office). *Telephone:* (495) 228-15-01 (office). *Fax:* (495) 629-12-52 (office). *E-mail:* chairman@sistema.ru (office). *Website:* www.sistema.com (office); www.sistema.com (office).

YEZHEL, Adm. (retd) Mykhailo Bronislavovych; Ukrainian politician and fmr naval officer; b. 19 Oct. 1952, Sloboda-Yaltushkivska, Barskyi Dist, Vinnytsia Oblast; m. Natalya Klimentivna; one s. one d.; fmrly served in Soviet Pacific Fleet 1975–93; joined Ukrainian Navy 1993, becoming Deputy C-in-C 1996–2000, C-in-C 2001–03; Adviser to Viktor Yanukovych June–Dec. 2007; Insp., Main Inspectorate of Ministry of Defence 2008; Minister of Defence 2010–12; adviser to Pres. Viktor Yanukovych 2012–. *Address:* c/o Office of the President, 01220 Kyiv, vul. Bankova 11, Ukraine (office). *Telephone:* (44) 255-73-33 (office). *Fax:* (44) 293-61-61 (office). *E-mail:* president@adm.gov.ua (office).

YHAP, Laetitia, DFA; British artist; b. 1 May 1941, St Albans, Herts., England; d. of Leslie Neville Yhap and Elizabeth Yhap (née Kogler); one s.; ed Camberwell School of Arts and Crafts, Slade School of Fine Art, Univ. Coll. London; Artist-in-Residence, Chatham House Grammar School, Ramsgate 1981; works in public collections in UK; mem. of London Group 1971–; exhibited in many nat. and museum-curated shows, British Council, Arts Council, Contemporary Art Soc. etc.; Leverhume Research Award 1962–63, John Moores Prize 1973. *Leisure interests:* music, attending concerts, playing badminton, choral singing.

YHOMBI-OPANGO, Brig.-Gen. Jacques-Joachim; Republic of the Congo army officer and fmr head of state; b. 1939; trained in French army; fmr military attaché at Congolese Embassy, Moscow; Chief of Staff, People's National Army 1968–73, Insp.-Gen. 1973–74; Sec.-Gen. of Council of State with rank of Minister 1974–75, Council of State Delegate responsible for Defence and Security 1974–75; Pres. of Republic, Pres. Council of Ministers, Pres. Mil. Council of Congolese Labour Party 1977–79; arrested 1979, detained 1979–84, released from detention Nov. 1984, rearrested Sept. 1987; Prime Minister of Congo 1993–96; fmr Leader Rassemblement pour la défense et le développement (RDP); fmr Leader Rassemblement pour la démocratie et le développement (RDD); Order of Nat. Flag (N Korea) 1978. *Address:* c/o Office of the Prime Minister, Brazzaville, Republic of the Congo.

YI, Huiman, MA; Chinese business executive; *Vice-Chairman, Executive Director and President, Industrial & Commercial Bank of China Limited;* ed Guanghua School of Man., Peking Univ.; joined Industrial & Commercial Bank of China Ltd (ICBC) 1985, apptd mem. of Sr Man. 2005, served in several positions at ICBC, including Deputy Head of Zhejiang Br., Deputy Head and Head of Jiangsu Br., and Head of Beijing Br., Sr Exec. Vice-Pres. Industrial & Commercial Bank of China Ltd 2008–13, Pres. May 2013–, Vice-Chair. and Exec. Dir July 2013–, concurrently Chair. Industrial and Commercial Bank of China (Malaysia) Berhad. *Address:* Industrial & Commercial Bank of China Ltd, 55 Fuxingmennan Dajie, Xicheng Qu, Beijing 100140, People's Republic of China (office). *Telephone:* (10) 66106070 (office). *Fax:* (10) 66106053 (office). *E-mail:* ir@icbc.com.cn (office). *Website:* www.icbc.com.cn (office).

YI, Jun, MSc; Chinese engineer and business executive; *Chairman, China State Construction Engineering Corporation;* ed studied Construction Project Man. at Cardiff Univ. and at Taylor Woodrow Ltd, UK, Chongqing Inst. of Construction and Eng; Dir and Gen. Man. China State Construction Contracting Co. 1993–2001, Vice-Pres. and mem. Party Cttee of China State Construction Engineering Corpn (CSCEC) 2001–02, Chair. and Pres. China State Construction International Co. Ltd 2002–, Chief Engineer, CSCEC 2005–, Pres. CSCEC and mem. Party Cttee of CSCEC 2005–11, Chair. and Sec. Party Leadership Group 2011–; Exec. Dir Fourth Council of China Int. Econ. Co-operation Soc.; Pres. Chartered Inst. of Building in China; Vice Chair. China Construction Industry Asscn, China Asscn of Construction Enterprise Man., China Civil Eng Soc., China Int. Contractors Asscn, China Asscn of Trade Services; Nat. Model Worker, Nat. Excellent Project Man., Excellent Party Mem. of Cen. and State Organs. *Address:* China State Construction Engineering Corporation, CSCEC Mansion, 15 Sanlihe Road, Haidian District, Beijing 100037, People's Republic of China (office). *Telephone:* (10) 88082888 (office). *Fax:* (10) 88082888 (office). *E-mail:* info@cscec.com (office); ir@cscec.com.cn (office). *Website:* www.cscec.com (office).

YIIN, Chii-ming, BS, MBA, PhD; Taiwanese economist and politician; *Minister of the Council for Economic Planning and Development;* b. 2 June 1952; m.; one s. one d.; ed Nat. Chiao Tung Univ., Nat. Chengchi Univ.; Sr Specialist, Council for Econ. Planning and Devt, Exec. Yuan 1978–1985; Dir Industrial Devt Bureau, Ministry of Econ. Affairs 1985–90, Deputy Dir-Gen. 1990–94, Dir-Gen. 1994–97, Deputy Minister of Econ. Affairs 1997–2005, Minister 2008–09, adviser to Exec. Yuan 2005–06, Minister without Portfolio 2009–11, Minister of the Council for Econ. Planning and Devt 2012–; Chair Prof., Chung Hua Univ. 2007–08. *Address:* Council for Economic Planning and Development, 3 Baoqing Rd, Zhongzheng District, Taipei 10020, Taiwan (office). *Telephone:* (2) 23165300 (office). *Fax:* (2) 23700415 (office). *Website:* www.cepd.gov.tw (office).

YILMAZ, A. Mesut; Turkish politician; b. 6 Nov. 1947, Istanbul; s. of Hasan Yilmaz and Güzide Yilmaz; m. Berna Müren; two s.; ed Istanbul High School for Boys, Faculty of Political Studies, Ankara and in London and Cologne; fmr company dir in pvt. business sector; Deputy for Rize 1983–; Minister of Culture and Tourism 1986–87, of Foreign Affairs 1987–90, Prime Minister of Turkey June–Nov. 1991, 1996, 1997–98; Deputy Prime Minister and Minister of State–2002; fmr Chair. Anavatan Partisi–ANAP (Motherland Party), Vice-Chair. EDU. *Address:* c/o Başbakanlık, Bakanlıklar, Ankara, Turkey.

YILMAZ, Durmus, MA; Turkish fmr central banker; b. 1947, Uşak; ed City Univ., London, Univ. Coll., London; joined Cen. Bank of Turkey 1980, worked in Foreign Debt Rescheduling, Exchange Rates and Foreign Exchange Reserve Man. 1993, Deputy Dir Foreign Exchange Transactions Div. 1995, Dir Interbank Money Market Div. 1996; Dir Balance of Payments Div. 1996, Deputy Exec. Dir Markets Dept to supervise Foreign Exchange Risk Man., Credits, Foreign Exchange and FX Banknotes Markets and Open Market Operations 2002, Exec. Dir Workers' Remittances (Non-Resident FX Deposits) Dept 2003, mem. Bd 2003–06, Gov. 2006–11. *Address:* c/o Central Bank of the Republic of Turkey, Head Office, Istiklal Cad. 10 Ulus, 06100 Ankara, Turkey (office).

YILMAZ, İsmet, MA, PhD; Turkish lawyer and politician; *Minister of National Defence;* b. 10 Dec. 1961, Sivas; m.; three c.; ed Faculty of Maritime Studies, Istanbul Tech. Univ., Faculty of Law, Istanbul Univ., World Maritime Univ., Malmö, Sweden, Inst. of Social Sciences, Marmara Univ., Inst. of Social Sciences, Ankara Univ.; worked for 20 years as engineer and accountant in the public and private sectors; Undersecretary of Maritime Affairs 2002; Minister of Transport and Communications May–Aug. 2007; Undersecretary, Ministry of Culture and Tourism 2007; mem. Büyük Millet Meclisi (Parl.) 2011–; Minister of Nat. Defence 2011–; fmr Vice-Chair. Turk Telekom; mem. Justice and Development Party (AKP). *Address:* Ministry of National Defence, 06100 Ankara, Turkey (office). *Telephone:* (312) 4186419 (office). *Fax:* (312) 4184737 (office). *Website:* www.msb.gov.tr (office).

YIN, Jiaxu, MA, MBA; Chinese engineer and business executive; *Chairman, China North Industries Group Corporation (NORINCO Group);* ed Univ. of Chongqing; fmr Gen. Man. CSG Automobile Co. Ltd; Pres. and Sec., Changan Automobile Group Co. (CAC) from 1998, Man. Yuzhou Gear Factory, Chair. and Pres. Changan Minsheng APLL Logistics Co. Ltd 2004–10; fmr Vice-Gen. Man. and Vice-Pres. China South Industries Group Corpn and China North Industries Group Corpn (NORINCO Group), Chair. 2013–; Dir Admin. Office and Deputy Gen. Dir Southwest Industries Bureau of China Industries Co.; Chair. Nanjing CMSC Logistics Co. Ltd; Exec. Dir Chongqing Changan Automobile Co. Ltd 1998–, South Automobile Corpn Ltd; Dir, Jiangling Motors Corpn Ltd. *Address:* China North Industries Group Corporation, No. 10 Chedaogou, Haidian Dist, Beijing 100089 (office); 46 Sanlihe Road, Beijing 100821, People's Republic of China (office). *Telephone:* (10) 68594210 (office); (10) 68787608 (office). *Fax:* (10) 68594232 (office); (10) 68594555 (office). *E-mail:* webmaster@cngc.com.cn (office). *Website:* www.norinco.com (office).

YIN, Jun; Chinese politician; *Chairman of Standing Committee, Yunnan Provincial People's Congress;* b. Sept. 1932, Eryuan, Yunnan Prov.; joined CCP 1949; Sec. CCP Xiaguan City Cttee, Yunnan Prov.; fmr Mayor of Xiaguan City; Sec. CCP Yunlong Co. Cttee, Yunnan Prov.; Chair. and Gov., Dali Bai Autonomous Pref., Yunnan Prov. 1982–84; Sec. Discipline Inspection Cttee, Yunnan CCP Prov. Cttee 1985; Deputy Sec. Yunnan Prov. Cttee 1990; Alt. mem. 12th CCP Cen. Cttee 1982–87, 13th CCP Cen. Cttee 1987–92; Chair. Standing Cttee Yunnan Prov. People's Congress 1993–; Deputy, 8th NPC 1993–98, 9th NPC 1998–2003; Del., 15th CCP Nat. Congress 1997–2002. *Address:* Dali Bai Autonomous Prefectural People's Government, Yunnan, People's Republic of China (office).

YIN, Weimin; Chinese government official; *Minister of Human Resources and Social Security;* b. 1953, Lingshou County, Hebei Prov.; ed Jilin Univ.; joined CCP 1973; Vice-Minister of Human Resources and Social Security 2000–07, Minister of Human Resources and Social Security 2007–; Deputy Dir CCP Cen. Cttee Org. Dept 2007–12; Dir State Admin of Civil Service 2008–; mem. 17th CCP Cen. Cttee 2007–12, 18th CCP Cen. Cttee 2012–. *Address:* Ministry of Human Resources and Social Security, 12 Hepinglizhong Jie, Dongcheng Qu, Beijing 100716, People's Republic of China (office). *Telephone:* (10) 84201114 (office). *Fax:* (10) 64218350 (office). *Website:* www.mohrss.gov.cn (office).

YIN, Wenying; Chinese entomologist and academic; *Professor, Institute of Plant Physiology and Ecology, Chinese Academy of Sciences;* b. Oct. 1923, Pingxiang Co., Hebei Prov.; ed Nat. Cen. Univ., Nanking, Cen. Univ. for Nationalities, Beijing and Zhongyang Univ.; worked at Inst. of Zoology, Shanghai, Inst. of Hydrobiology, Wuhan, Shanghai Inst. of Entomology, Chinese Acad. of Sciences; mem. Chinese Acad. of Sciences 1991; conducted research on fish parasites and fish disease prevention and treatment in the early stages of contamination; est. a new classification system according to her research; Two Nat. Natural Sciences Prizes, two Chinese Acad. of Sciences Prizes of Natural Sciences, four prizes both of the Nat. and Chinese Acad. of Sciences Prizes of Progress on Sciences and Tech., Ho Leung Ho Lee Life Sciences Award. *Publications:* China Animal Records: Original Tail Item 1999, Chinese Sub-tropical Soil Animals, Chinese Soil Animal Search Illustrated Handbook, Chinese Soil Animals; more than 130 research articles and four monographs. *Address:* Institute of Plant Physiology and Ecology, 300 Feng Lin Road, Shanghai 200032, People's Republic of China (office). *Telephone:* (21) 54924000 (office). *Fax:* (21) 54924015 (office). *E-mail:* wyyin@sibs.ac.cn (office). *Website:* www.sippe.ac.cn (office).

YIN, Zuoru; Chinese business executive; Pres. Kailuan (Group) Co. Ltd (coal mining co.) 2002–. *Address:* Kailuan (Group) Ltd Liability Corporation, 70 Xinhua Hua Dong Road, Tangshan 063018, People's Republic of China (office). *E-mail:* info@kailuan.com (office). *Website:* www.kailuan.com.cn (office).

YINGLUCK SHINAWATRA, BA, MA; Thai business executive and politician; b. 21 June 1967, San Kamphaeng; d. of Lert Shinawatra and Yindee Shinawatra; sister of fmr Prime Minister Thaksin Shinawatra; m. Anusorn Amornchat; one s.; ed Chiang Mai Univ., Kentucky State Univ., USA; worked at Shinawatra Directories Co. Ltd; mem. Cttee and Sec. Thaicom Foundation; fmr Pres. Advanced Info Service Public Co. Ltd (AIS) (mobile phone operator) before its sale to Singapore's Temasek Holdings; mem. Bd of Dirs SC Asset Corpn Public Co. Ltd (family business) 2004–, Chair. Exec. Cttee March 2006–, Acting Pres. Dec. 2006–09, Acting CEO 2009–11; also manages finances for opposition Pheu Thai Party; nominated by Pheu Thai Party as cand. for Prime Minister in 2011 elections (first woman to run for country's highest political office), Prime Minister 2011–14 (ordered to step down by Constitutional Court); Minister of Defence 2013–14; ranked by Forbes magazine amongst The World's 100 Most Powerful Women (59th) 2011, (30th) 2012, (31st) 2013. *Address:* SC Asset Corporation Plc, 1010 Shinawatra Tower, 3 Viphavadi Rangsit Road, Chatuchak, Bangkok 10900,

Thailand (office). *Telephone:* (2) 949-2333. *Fax:* (2) 949-2209. *E-mail:* info@scasset .com (office). *Website:* www.scasset.com.

YISHAI, Eliyahu; Israeli politician; b. 26 Dec. 1962, Jerusalem; m.; five c.; fmr Head of Interior Minister's bureau; acting Sec.-Gen., then Chair. Shas (Sephardic Torah Guardians) 1991; Dir-Gen. Shas-affiliated El ha-Ma'ayan Movt; elected to 14th Knesset (Parl.) 1996; Minister of Labour and Social Affairs 1996–2001, of Internal Affairs 2001–02, also Deputy Prime Minister 2001–02; Deputy Prime Minister 2002–13, Minister of Industry, Trade and Labour 2006–09, of the Interior 2009–13. *Address:* Shas, Beit Abodi, Rehov Hahida, Bene Beraq, Israel (office). *Telephone:* 2-6220661 (office). *Fax:* 2-6222412 (office).

YOAKAM, Dwight; American country singer, musician (guitar), songwriter and actor; b. 23 Oct. 1956, Pikeville, Ky; ed Ohio Univ.; solo artist 1978–; numerous tours; Acad. of Country Music Award for Best New Male Artist 1986, Music City News Country Award for Best Vocal Collaboration (for Streets of Bakersfield, with Buck Owens) 1988. *Films:* Red Rock West 1992, The Little Death 1995, Sling Blade 1996, Painted Hero 1996, The Newton Boys 1998, The Minus Man 1999, South of Heaven, West of Hell (also dir) 2000, Panic Room 2002, Hollywood Homicide 2003, 3-Way 2004, The Three Burials of Melquiades Estrada 2005, Wedding Crashers 2005, Bandidas 2006, Crank 2006, Four Christmases 2008, Crank: High Voltage 2009, The Last Rites of Ransom Pride 2009. *Television films:* Roswell 1994, Don't Look Back 1996, When Trumpets Fade 1998. *Recordings include:* albums: Guitars, Cadillacs, Etc., Etc. 1986, Hillbilly Deluxe 1987, Buenas Noches From A Lonely Room 1988, Just Looking For A Hit 1989, If There Was A Way 1990, La Croix D'Amour 1992, This Time 1993, Dwight Live 1995, Gone 1996, Under The Covers 1997, Come On Christmas 1997, A Long Way Home 1998, dwightyoakamacoustic.net 2000, Tomorrow's Sounds Today 2000, South Of Heaven, West Of Hell 2001, Population Me 2003, In Others' Words 2003, Blame The Vain 2005, Dwight Sings Buck 2007. *Address:* Gary Ebbins/Fitzgerald Hartley Company, c/o Etc. Etc. Communications, 7920 Sunset Blvd, Suite 460, Los Angeles, CA 90046, USA (office). *Website:* www.dwightyoakam.com.

YOCCOZ, Jean-Christophe, PhD; French mathematician and academic; *Professor, Collège de France;* b. 29 May 1957, Paris; ed Ecole Normale Supérieure, Paris and Ecole Polytechnique, Paris; mil. service in Brazil 1981–83; Attaché, then Head of Research, CNRS, l'Ecole Polytechnique 1979–88; Prof., University of Paris-Sud 1988–96; Prof., Collège de France 1996–; mem. Institut Universitaire de France 1990, Unité Recherche Associé 'Topology and Dynamics', CNRS, Acad. des sciences 1994, Brazilian Acad. of Sciences 1994; Assoc. mem. Third World Acad. of Sciences 2004–; Chevalier, Légion d'honneur 1995; Order of Scientific Merit (Brazil) 1998; Officier, l'Ordre nat. du Mérite 2000; Bronze Medal, CNRS 1984, IBM Math. Prize 1985, Cours de la Fondation Claude-Antoine PECCOT, Collège de France 1987, Salem Prize 1988, Invited Speaker, Kyoto Int. Congress 1990, Jaffe Prize, Acad. des sciences 1991, Fields Medal, Int. Congress of Mathematicians, Zürich 1994. *Publications:* numerous articles in math. journals on dynamical systems. *Address:* Collège de France, 3 rue d'Ulm, 75231 Paris Cedex 05, France (office). *Telephone:* 1-44-27-12-11 (office). *Website:* www.college-de -france.fr (office).

YODA, Alain Bédoum, LLB, DEcon; Burkinabè politician; *Minister of Foreign Affairs and Regional Co-operation;* b. 31 Dec. 1951, Komtoèga; m.; two c.; ed Univ. of Youndé, Cameroon, Univ. of Clermont Ferrand, France; with Ministry of Trade, Industry and Mines Jan.–March 1978, Ministry of Trade 1978–85, Tech. Adviser to Minister of Trade 1985; Econ. and Financial Adviser to Pres. of Burkina Faso 1985–87; Dir-Gen. Nagansgani Air Freight Co. 1986–92; assigned to Gen. Secr., Ministry of Transport and Communications 1992; Deputy, Nat. Ass. 1992–, Chair. Working Group on Mid-Term Review of Lomé IV Convention 1994, Finance and Nat. Ass. Integration Comm. 1996–97; Minister for Transport and Tourism 1997–2000, for Trade and the Promotion of Business and Crafts 2000–02, of Health 2002–08, of Foreign Affairs and Regional Co-operation 2008–. *Leisure interests:* swimming, board games, cinema, music, reading. *Address:* Ministry of Foreign Affairs and Regional Co-operation, rue 988, boulevard du Faso, 03 BP 7038, Ouagadougou, Burkina Faso (office). *Telephone:* 50-32-47-34 (office). *Fax:* 50-30-87-92 (office). *E-mail:* webmaster.mae@mae.gov.bf (office). *Website:* www.mae .gov.bf (office).

YOH-HAMURA, Shoei, BA (Econs); Japanese architect; *Design and Architectural Principal, Yoh and Architects;* b. 7 March 1940, Kumamoto City; ed Univ. of Keio, Tokyo, Wittenberg Univ., OH, USA; interior designer at Int. Design Associates, Tokyo 1964–67; project designer with Nic, Fukuoka 1967–70; Design and Architectural Prin. Yoh and Architects 1970–; Visiting Prof., Grad. School of Architecture, Urban Design and Preservation, Columbia Univ. 1992; Prof., Grad. School of Architecture and Urban Design, Keio Univ. 1996–2005; Mainichi Design Award 1983, Japan Inst. of Architects Award 1983, 1989, Architectural Inst. of Japan Award, IAKS Award 1993, City of Fukuoka Award 1994, Benedictus Award 1994, Fukuoka Pref. Award 1998, Wittenberg Fellow 2003. *Publications:* Ambient V Matrix 1970–1987 1987, Shoei Yoh – In Response to Natural Phenomena 1997, Calisthenics for Architecture 1997. *Leisure interest:* travel. *Address:* Shoei Yoh and Architects, 1-12-30 Heiwa, Minami-ku, Fukuoka-shi, 815-007, Japan (office). *Telephone:* (92) 521-4782 (office); (92) 521-4110 (home). *Fax:* (92) 521-6718 (office). *E-mail:* yohshoei@jade.dti.ne.jp (office).

YOKOMICHI, Takahiro, LLB; Japanese lawyer and politician; *Speaker, House of Representatives;* b. 3 Jan. 1941, Sapporo; ed Tokyo Univ.; worked as lawyer in pvt.; elected to House of Reps as mem. for Japan Socialist Party 1969, served five terms 1969–83; Gov. of Hokkaido 1983–95; joined Democratic Party of Japan 1995, fmr Vice-Pres.; mem. House of Reps for Hokkaido No. 1 constituency 1996–, Deputy Speaker 2005–09, Speaker 2009–. *Address:* Office of the Speaker, House of Representatives, 7-1, Nagata-cho, Chiyoda-ku, Tokyo 100-0014, Japan (office). *Telephone:* (3) 3581-5111 (office). *Website:* www.shugiin.go.jp (office); www .yokomichi.com (office).

YOKOYAMA, Shinichi; Japanese insurance industry executive; *Chairman and Representative Director, Sumitomo Life Insurance Company;* b. 1943; Vice-Pres. Sumitomo Life Insurance Co. –2001, Pres. 2001–03, Pres. and CEO 2003–07, Chair. and Rep. 2007–, Corp. Auditor of Sumitomo Chemical Co. Ltd; Standing Corp. Auditor of Shionogi & Co. Ltd 2008–; Chair. Life Insurance Asscn of Japan 2002–; mem. Bd Corp. Auditors, NEC Corpn 2003–. *Address:* Sumitomo Life

Insurance Co., 1-4-35 Shiromi, Chuo-ku, Osaka 540-8512, Japan (office). *Telephone:* (6) 6937-1435 (office). *E-mail:* info@sumitomolife.co.jp (office). *Website:* www.sumitomolife.co.jp (office).

YONATH, Ada E., BSc, MSc, PhD, FRSC; Israeli chemist and academic; *Martin S. and Helen Kimmel Professor of Structural Biology and Director, Helen and Milton A. Kimmelman Center for Biomolecular Structure and Assembly, Weizmann Institute of Science;* b. 22 June 1939, Jerusalem; ed Hebrew Univ. of Jerusalem, Weizmann, Inst. of Science; post-doctoral work at Carnegie Mellon Univ. 1969 and MIT 1970; returned to Weizmann Inst. of Science 1970, Assoc. Prof. 1984–88, Prof. 1988–, currently Martin S. and Helen Kimmel Prof. of Structural Biology, Dir Helen and Milton A. Kimmelman Center for Biomolecular Structure and Assembly 1989–, Chair. Dept of Structural Chem. 1989–92, of Dept of Structural Biology 1992–94; Head, Max Planck Research Units for Ribosomal Structure, Hamburg, Germany 1986–2004; Jt Ed. of numerous journals, including European Molecular Biology Organization (EMBO) Journal; mem. Israeli Acad. for Science and Humanities, NAS, European Acad. of Sciences, EMBO, Leopoldina – German Acad. for Sciences, American Acad. of Art and Sciences, Korean Acad. of Sciences and Tech., Int. Acad. of Astronautics, Int. Acad. for Microbiology; Hon. mem. Israeli Crystallographic Soc. 2001; Hon. Supreme Prof. of KEK, Photon Factory, Tsukuba, Japan 2010; Hon. Guest, Medical Univ., Baku, Azerbaijan 2012; Dr hc (Ben-Gurion Univ.) 2002, (Tel-Aviv Univ.) 2003, (Oxford) 2008, (Bar-Ilan Univ.) 2010, (Open Univ., Israel) 2011, (Fujou Univ., China) 2011, (Hebrew Univ.) 2011, (New York Univ.) 2011, (Oslo) 2011, (Toulouse) 2012, (Hamburg) 2012 (Mount Sinai Medical Univ., NYC) 2012, (Patras Univ., Greece) 2013, (Cambridge) 2013; Somach Sachs Award 1974, Kolthof Award 1990, European Crystallography Prize (first winner) 2000, Kilby Int. Award 2000, Israel Prize 2002, Harvey Prize 2002, Paul Ehrlich and Ludwig Darmstaedter Prize (with Harry Noller) 2007, Wolf Prize in Chem. (with George Feher) 2006–07, 2008, Albert Einstein World Award of Science, Princeton Univ. 2008, UNESCO-L'Oréal Award for European Woman in Life Science 2008, George E. Palade Gold Medal 2008, Linus Pauling Gold Medal, Stanford 2008, Nobel Prize in Chem. (with Venkatraman Ramakrishnan and Thomas A. Steitz) 2009, Eminent Scientists Award, Japan Soc. for the Promotion of Science 2010, Wilhelm Exner Medal, Austrian Asscn for SME (Oesterreichischer Gewerbeverein—OGV) (jtly) 2010, Erna Hamburger Prize, EFEL-WISH Foundation, Lausanne 2011, Gold Medal of Distinction, Prime Minister of India 2011, Maria Sklodowska-Curie Medal, Polish Chemical Soc. 2011, Pres. of Panama Award 2011, Cite of Florence Award 2011, Academia Sinica Award (Taiwan) 2012, Prakash S. Datta Medal, FEBS, Seville 2012. *Address:* Department of Structural Biology, Weizmann Institute of Science, Rehovot 76100, Israel (office). *Telephone:* (8) 9343028 (office). *Fax:* (8) 9344154 (office). *E-mail:* ada .yonath@weizmann.ac.il (office). *Website:* www.weizmann.ac.il/sb/faculty_pages/ Yonath/home.html (office).

YONEKURA, Hiromasa, MA, PhD; Japanese business executive; *Chairman, Sumitomo Chemical Company Ltd;* ed Faculty of Law, Univ. of Tokyo, Duke Univ., USA; joined Sumitomo Chemical Co. Ltd 1960, Rep., New York Office 1969–72, Gen. Man. Foreign Dept 1983–86, Gen. Man. Corp. Planning Office 1986–91, Dir and Gen. Man. Organic Chemicals Div. 1991–92, Gen. Man. Basic Chemicals Admin Office in charge of Organic Chemicals Div. 1992–93, Gen. Man. Basic Chemicals Admin Office in charge of Inorganic Chemicals and Organic Chemicals Divs 1993–94, Gen. Man. Planning and Coordination Office of Basic Chemicals Sector and Petrochemicals and Plastics Sector 1994–95, Man. Dir in charge of Planning and Coordination Office of Basic Chemicals Sector and Petrochemicals Div. of Petrochemicals and Plastics Sector 1995–97, Man. Dir with additional responsibility for Corp. Planning and Coordination Office 1997–98, Sr Man. Dir in charge of Corp. Planning and Coordination Office 1998–2000, Pres. Sumitomo Chemical Co. Ltd 2000–09, Chair. 2009–; Chair. Bd of Councillors Nippon Keidanren (Japan Business Fed.); fmr Chair. AOC Holdings Inc.; fmr Vice-Chair. Rabigh Refining & Petrochemical Co., currently Deputy Chair.; Vice-Chair. Japan-US Business Council. *Address:* Sumitomo Chemical Co. Ltd, 27-1, Shinkawa 2-chome, Chuo-ku, Tokyo 104-8260, Japan (office). *Telephone:* (3) 5543-5102 (office). *Fax:* (3) 5543-5901 (office). *E-mail:* info@sumitomo-chem.co.jp (office). *Website:* www.sumitomo-chem.co.jp (office).

YONGYUTH, Wichaidit; Thai politician and political scientist; *Deputy Prime Minister and Minister of Interior;* b. 15 July 1942, Surat Thani; ed Chulalongkorn Univ., Nat. Inst. of Devt Admin; fmr Deputy Minister of Interior; fmr Dir-Gen. Dept of Lands; fmr Chair. of Metropolitan Electricity Authority; fmr Chair. Audit Cttee of Govt Lottery Office; Deputy Minister to Sudarat Keyuraphan, Health Minister 2003–05; Advisor to Minister of Interior 2008; Leader Pheu Thai Party 2008–; Deputy Prime Minister and Minister of Interior 2011–. *Address:* Ministry of Interior, Thanon Ratchabophit, Wat Ratchabophit, Phra Nakhon, Bangkok 10200, Thailand (office). *Telephone:* (2) 222-1141 (office). *Website:* www.moi.go.th (office).

YONLI, Paramanga Ernest, PhD; Burkinabè politician, agricultural economist and diplomatist; b. 31 Dec. 1956, Tansarga, Tapoa Prov.; m.; ed Univ. of Benin, Univ. of Paris I (Panthéon-Sorbonne), France, Nat. Inst. of Agric., Paris-Grignon, Ouagadougou Univ., Univ. of Groningen, Netherlands; conducted research into food security and marketing; mem. Congress for Democracy and Progress (CDP) party; Dir of Prime Minister's Office Feb.–Sept. 1996; subsequently Minister of the Civil Service and Institutional Devt; Prime Minister of Burkina Faso 2000–07 (resgnd); elected to Nat. Ass. from Tapoa Prov. as CDP cand. May 2007 (resgnd); Amb. to USA 2008–11. *Publication:* Stratégies paysannes en matière de sécurité alimentaire et commercialisation céréalière – le rôle des banques de céréales dans le Nord du Plateau Central du Burkina Faso (Agricultural Strategies in the Field of Food Security and the Commercialisation of Cereal Production – The Role of Cereal Banks in the North of the Central Plateau of Burkina Faso) (thesis). *Address:* Ministry of Foreign Affairs and Regional Co-operation, Rue 988, Blvd du Faso, 03 BP 7038, Ouagadougou 03, Burkina Faso (office). *Telephone:* 50-32-47-34 (office). *Fax:* 50-30-87-92 (office). *E-mail:* webmaster.mae@mae.gov.bf (office). *Website:* www.mae.gov.bf (office).

YOO, Chong-ha; South Korean politician and diplomatist; *President, Korean Red Cross;* b. 28 July 1936; m.; three c.; ed Seoul Nat. Univ., Bonn Univ.; joined Ministry of Foreign Affairs 1959, Third Sec., Embassy in Bonn 1963–68, Consul, Chicago May–Oct. 1968, Islamabad 1968–71, Dir SE Asia Div. Ministry of Foreign Affairs 1971–74, Counsellor, Embassy in Washington, DC 1974–77, Deputy Dir-

Gen. American Affairs Bureau, Ministry of Foreign Affairs 1977–78, Dir-Gen. 1978–80, Minister, Embassy in London 1980–83, Amb. to Sudan 1983–85, Asst Minister for Econ. Affairs, Ministry of Foreign Affairs 1985–87, Amb. to Belgium 1987–89, to EC Feb.–Dec. 1989, Vice-Minister of Foreign Affairs 1989–92, Perm. Rep. to UN, New York 1992–94; Sr Adviser to Pres. for Foreign Policy and Nat. Security 1994–96; Minister of Foreign Affairs 1996–98; currently Pres. Korean Red Cross; Order of Service Merit (Red Stripes). *Address:* Korean Red Cross, Sopa-ro 145, Jung-gu, Seoul 100-043, South Korea (office). *E-mail:* international@ redcross.or.kr (office). *Website:* www.redcross.or.kr (office).

YOOBAMRUNG, Capt. Chalerm; Thai police officer and politician; *Minister of Labour;* b. 10 June 1947; m.; three s.; mem. Parl.; fmr police capt. and Minister of Justice; cand. in election for Gov. of Bangkok Metropolitan Admin 2004; Minister of the Interior 2008; Deputy Prime Minister 2012–13; Minister of Labour 2013–. *Address:* Ministry of Labour, Thanon Mitmaitri, Dindaeng, Bangkok 10400, Thailand (office). *Telephone:* (2) 232-1421 (office). *Fax:* (2) 246-1520 (office). *E-mail:* webmaster@mol.go.th (office). *Website:* www.mol.go.th (office).

YOON, Jeung-hyun, BA, MA; South Korean banking executive and politician; ed Seoul Nat. Univ., Univ. of Wisconsin, USA; Dir Int. Finance Div., Ministry of Finance 1983–86, Banking Div. 1986–87, Financial Policy Div. 1987–89, Dir-Gen. Tax and Customs Office 1992, Securities Bureau 1992–94, Finance Bureau 1994, Dir-Gen. Financial Policy Bureau, Ministry of Finance and Economy 1994–96, Deputy Minister, Tax and Customs Office 1996–97, Financial Policy Bureau 1997–98; Dean, Nat. Tax Coll. 1998–99; Exec. Dir Asian Devt Bank 1999–2004; Chair. Financial Supervisory Comm. 2004–07; Minister of Strategy and Finance 2009–11, also Acting Prime Minister Aug.–Oct. 2010; Sr Adviser to Kim & Chang (law firm) 2008; mem. Nat. Econ. Advisory Council 2008–; Service Merit Medal 1978, Asian Banker Achievement Award 2006, Daesan Insurance Prize 2008. *Address:* c/o Ministry of Strategy and Finance, Government Complex II, 88 Gwanmunro, Gwacheon City, Gyeonggi 427-725, Republic of Korea.

YOON, Adm. Kwang-ung; South Korean politician; b. 13 Oct. 1942, Busan; ed Busan Commercial High School, Repub. of Korea Naval Acad., US Naval Command and Staff Coll., Repub. of Korea Nat. Defence Univ.; CO, ROKS Chungnam, Repub. of Korea Navy 1985–86, Dir Org. Div., Repub. of Korea Navy HQ 1987–89, Commdr Flotilla Five 1991–92, Naval Forces Devt Command 1996–97, C-in-C ROKFLT 1997–98, Vice-Chief of Naval Operations 1998–99; Dir Acquisition and Devt Bureau, Ministry of Nat. Defence 1995–96; Adviser, Hyundai Heavy Industries Co. Ltd 2000–03; Chair. Emergency Planning Comm., Office of the Prime Minister 2003–04; Adviser to the Pres. on Nat. Defence Jan.–July 2004; Minister of Nat. Defence July 2004–06 (resgnd); US Legion of Merit, Korean Order of Nat. Security Merit. *Address:* c/o Minister of National Defence, 1 Yongsan-dong 3-ga, Yeongsan-gu, Seoul 140-701, Republic of Korea. *E-mail:* cyber@mnd.go.kr.

YORDANOV, Svetoslav, BEcons; Bulgarian business executive; *Executive Director, Petrol AD;* b. 28 May 1960, Bourgas; ed Varna Univ. of Econs; fmr Deputy Chief Accountant, Neftochim, later becoming Financial Dir and Commercial Dir; fmr Exec. Dir, Multigroup AD; Exec. Dir, Petrol AD 1999–. *Address:* Petrol AD, 43 Cherni Vrah, 1407 Sofia, Bulgaria (office). *Telephone:* (2) 9690333 (office). *E-mail:* office@petrol.bg (office). *Website:* www.petrol.bg (office).

YORK, HRH The Duke of; (Prince Andrew Albert Christian Edward), (Earl of Inverness, Baron Killyleagh), KG, GCVO, CD, ADC, FRS; British; b. 19 Feb. 1960, London, England; s. of HM Queen Elizabeth II (q.v.) and Prince Philip, Duke of Edinburgh (q.v.); m. Sarah Ferguson 1986 (divorced 1996); two d., Beatrice Elizabeth Mary, b. 8 Aug. 1988, Eugenie Victoria Helena, b. 23 March 1990; ed Heatherdown Preparatory School, Ascot, Gordonstoun School, Scotland, Lakefield Coll. School, Ont., Canada, Britannia Royal Naval Coll., Dartmouth; joined Royal Navy as Seaman Officer, specializing as a pilot 1979, before entering Royal Naval Coll.; flying training with RAF Leeming, Yorks. and helicopter training at Royal Naval Air Station (RNAS) Culdrose, Cornwall; received Wings 1981; joined front-line unit 820 Naval Air Squadron and embarked in Anti-Submarine Warfare Carrier HMS Invincible; participated in Falklands conflict; rank of Lt 1984; Personal ADC to HM The Queen 1984; served as Flight Pilot in NAS, Type 22 Frigate HMS Brazen 1984–86; returned to 702 NAS as Helicopter Warfare Instructor 1987; joined Type 42 Destroyer HMS Edinburgh as Officer of the Watch 1988–89; returned to RNAS Portland to form HMS Campbeltown Flight; served as Flight Commdr, 829 NAS 1989–91; Army Command and Staff Course, Staff Coll., Camberley 1992; rank of Lt Commdr 1992; commanded Hunt Class Minehunter HMS Cottesmore 1993–94; Sr Pilot, 815 NAS, RNAS Portland 1995–96; joined Ministry of Defence, London as a staff officer, Directorate of Naval Operations 1997–99; rank of Commdr, with Diplomacy Section of Naval Staff, London 1999–2001; Special Rep. for Int. Trade and Investment 2001–11; rank of Hon. Capt. 2005, Hon. Rear Adm. 2010; Adm. of the Sea Cadet Corps 1992–; Col-in-Chief Staffordshire Regt 1989–, Royal Irish Regt 1992–, Royal NZ Army Logistic Regt, Small Arms School Corps, Royal Highland Fusiliers (Princess Margaret's Own and Ayrshire Regt), 9th/12th Royal Lancers (Prince of Wales's), Queen's York Rangers (1st American Regt), Royal Highland Fusiliers of Canada, Princess Louise Fusiliers, Canadian Airborne Regt (disbanded), Yorkshire Regt (14th/15th, 19th and 33rd/76th Foot); Royal Col of the Royal Highland Fusiliers, 2nd Bn Royal Regt of Scotland; Hon. Air Cdre, RAF Lossiemouth, Morayshire; Cdre-in-Chief of the Fleet Air Arml Adm. of the Sea Cadet Corps; Patron of more than 90 orgs, including Greenwich Hosp., Fight for Sight, Defeating Deafness, Jubilee Sailing Trust, Royal Aero Club; Trustee Nat. Maritime Museum, Greenwich; Chair. Trustees Outward Bound Trust; Capt. Royal and Ancient Golf Club of St Andrews; mem. Advisory Bd of Govs, Lakefield Coll. School; Cdre, Royal Thames Yacht Club; Elder Brother, Trinity House; Queen Elizabeth II Silver Jubilee Medal 1977, South Atlantic Medal, with Rosette 1982, NZ 1990 Commemoration Medal 1990, Queen Elizabeth II Golden Jubilee Medal 2002, Commemorative Medal for the Centennial of Saskatchewan 2005, Queen Elizabeth II Diamond Jubilee Medal 2012; Grand Cross of the Royal Norwegian Order of St Olav 1988, Order of the Fed. (UAE) 2010. *Address:* Buckingham Palace, London, SW1A 1AA, England. *Website:* www.royal.gov.uk; www.thedukeofyork.org.

YORK, Michael, OBE, BA; British actor; b. (Michael York-Johnson), 27 March 1942, Fulmer; s. of Joseph Gwynne and Florence Edith (neé Chown) Johnson; m. Patricia McCallum 1968; ed Univ. Coll. Oxford; with Dundee Repertory Co. 1964,

Nat. Theatre Co. 1965, guest lecturer; Chair. Calif. Youth Theatre; Chevalier Ordre nat. des. Arts et Lettres 1995; star on the Hollywood Walk of Fame. *Stage appearances include:* Any Just Cause 1967, Hamlet 1970, Outcry (Broadway) 1973, Ring Round the Moon 1975, Bent, Cyrano de Bergerac, Whisper in the Mind 1990, The Crucible 1991, Someone to Watch Over Me 1993. *Radio:* Jane Eyre 2002, Alice in Wonderland 2002, The Trial of Walter Raleigh 2003. *TV appearances include:* The Forsyte Saga, Rebel in the Grave, True Patriot, Much Ado About Nothing, Jesus of Nazareth, A Man Called Intrepid, For Those I Loved, The Weather in the Streets, The Master of Ballantrae, Space, The Far Country, Are You My Mother 1986, Ponce de León 1987, Knot's Landing 1987, The Four Minute Mile 1988, The Lady and the Highwayman 1988, The Heat of the Day 1988, A Duel of Love 1990, The Road to Avonlea 1990, Teklab 1994, September 1995, A Young Connecticut Yankee in King Arthur's Court 1995, Not of This Earth 1995, The Ring 1996, True Women 1996, The Ripper 1997, A Knight in Camelot 1998, Perfect Little Angels 1998, The Haunting of Hell House 2000, The Lot 2001, Founding Fathers, Founding Brothers, La Femme Musketeer 2004. *Films include:* The Taming of the Shrew 1966, Accident 1966, Red and Blue 1967, Smashing Time 1967, Romeo and Juliet 1967, The Strange Affair 1967, The Guru 1968, Alfred the Great 1968, Justine 1969, Something for Everyone 1969, Zeppelin 1970, La Poudre d'Escampette 1971, Cabaret 1971, England Made Me 1971, Lost Horizon 1972, The Three Musketeers 1973, Murder on the Orient Express 1974, Great Expectations 1974, Conduct Unbecoming 1974, The Four Musketeers 1975, Logan's Run 1976, Seven Nights in Japan, The Last Remake of Beau Geste 1977, The Island of Dr Moreau 1977, Fedora 1977, The Riddle of the Sands 1978, Final Assignment 1979, Success is The Best Revenge 1984, Dawn 1985, Vengeance 1986, The Secret of the Sahara 1987, Imbalances 1987, Lethal Obsession 1987, The Return of the Musketeers 1988, Till We Meet Again 1989, The Heat of the Day 1989, The Night of the Fox 1990, Eline Vere 1990, Duel of Hearts 1990, The Wanderer 1991, The Long Shadow 1991, Wide Sargasso Sea 1991, Rochade 1991, Discretion Assured 1993, The Shadow of a Kiss 1994, Fall from Grace 1994, Gospa 1995, Goodbye America 1996, Austin Powers 1996, Dark Planet 1996, Wrongfully Accused 1998, One Hell of a Guy 1998, The Omega Code 1999, Borstal Boy 2000, Megiddo 2001, Austin Powers in Goldmember 2002, Moscow Heat 2004. *Music:* Christopher Columbus: A Musical Journey 2002, Enoch Arden (Tennyson/Strauss) 2003. *Publications:* The Courage of Conviction (contrib.) 1986, Voices of Survival (contrib.) 1987, Travelling Player (autobiog.) 1991, Accidentally on Purpose (autobiog.) 1992, A Shakespearean Actor Prepares 2000, Dispatches From Armageddon 2002. *Address:* c/o Andrew Manson, 288 Munster Road, London, SW6 6BQ, England. *Telephone:* (20) 7386-9158. *Fax:* (20) 7381-8874. *Website:* www .michaelyork.net (office).

YORKE, James A., PhD; American mathematician, physicist and academic; *Distinguished University Professor of Mathematics and Physics, Institute for Physical Sciences and Technology, University of Maryland;* b. 1941, Plainfield, NJ; ed Columbia Coll., Columbia Univ., Univ. of Md; Research Assoc., Inst. for Physical Sciences and Tech. (IPST), Univ. of Md 1966–67, Research Asst Prof. 1967–69, Research Assoc. Prof. 1969–73, Prof. 1973–, has held jt appointments with Math. 1976– and Physics 2000–, Acting Dir IPST 1985–88, Dir 1988–2001, Distinguished Univ. Prof. of Math. and Physics 1995–; Expert (part-time), Nat. Cancer Inst. 1978–79; mem. Editorial Bds International Journal of Bifurcation and Chaos, Journal of Complex Systems Chaos, Solitons and Fractals, SIAM Journal of Applied Dynamical Systems (SIADS), Journal of Difference Equations and Applications; best known to gen. public for jtly coining the math. term 'chaos' with T. Y. Li in a 1975 paper entitled Period Three Implies Chaos; mem. American Math Soc., Math Asscn of America, Soc. for Industrial and Applied Math. (SIAM); Fellow, AAAS 1998, American Physical Soc. 2003; Guggenheim Fellow 1980, 38th Annual Chaim Weizmann Memorial Lecturer, Weizmann Inst., Rehovot, Israel 1997, First recipient, Univ. of Md Regents Faculty Award for Excellence in Research/Scholarship 1998, American Physical Soc. Centennial Speaker 1998–99, Distinguished Alumnus Award, Univ. of Md Coll. of Computer, Math, and Physical Sciences 2002, Japan Prize (jtly with Benoit Mandelbrot) 2003. *Publications:* Gonorrhea Transmission: Dynamics and Control 1984, Dynamics: Numerical Explorations (co-author) 1994, Coping with Chaos (co-author) 1994, Chaos: An Introduction to Dynamical Systems (co-author) 1997; more than 300 articles in scientific journals. *Address:* Institute for Physical Sciences and Technology, University of Maryland, College Park, MD 20742-2431, USA (office). *Telephone:* (301) 405-4875 (office). *Fax:* (301) 314-9363 (office). *E-mail:* yorke2@ipst.umd.edu (office). *Website:* www.umd.edu (office); yorke.umd.edu (office); www.chaos.umd .edu (office).

YORKE, Thomas (Thom) Edward; British singer, songwriter and musician (guitar, keyboards); b. 7 Oct. 1968, Wellingborough, Northamptonshire, England; one s.; ed Univ. of Exeter; mem. and lead singer, On A Friday 1985, renamed Radiohead 1991–; also designer of record sleeves; numerous tours, festivals and television appearances; guest vocalist with Drugstore on White Magic for Lovers and El President 1998; guest vocalist with Velvet Goldmine 1998, MTV's 120 Minutes Live 1998; other collaborations include UNKLE, P. J. Harvey; founding mem. Atoms for Peace 2009–; Q Award for Best Act in the World Today 2001, 2002, 2003. *Recordings include:* albums: with Radiohead: Pablo Honey 1993, The Bends 1995, OK Computer (Grammy Award for Best Alternative Music Performance) 1997, Kid A (Grammy Award for Best Alternative Music Album) 2000, Amnesiac 2001, I Might Be Wrong (live recordings) 2001, Hail To The Thief 2003, In Rainbows (Ivor Novello Album Award 2008, Grammy Award for Best Alternative Music Album 2009) 2007, The King of Limbs 2011; solo: The Eraser 2006. *Address:* Courtyard Management, 21 The Nursery, Sutton Courtenay, Abingdon, Oxford-shire OX14 4UA, England (office). *Website:* www.radiohead.com.

YORONGAR, Ngarledjy; Chadian politician and editorial director; *Leader, Fédération Action pour le République-Parti fédération;* m.; five c.; ed schools and univs in Chad, Canada and France; civil servant and govt official; also worked for int. orgs including OECD, Science and Educ. Admin. and Financial Office in Zaire, Int. Insurance Inst. (IIA) in Cameroon; Cand. in Presidential Elections 1996, 2001; campaigner against human rights violations and corruption, arrested numerous occasions including 1996 and on winning 2001 elections, imprisoned 1998–99; currently Leader, Fédération Action pour le République–Parti fédération; Fed. Exec. Co-ordinator of Federalist Party; Pres. of Foundation for the Respect of Law and Liberties (FORELLI); Editorial Dir of newspapers La Roue and Le Phare

Républicain. *Publication:* Tchad: le Proces d'Idriss Deby. *Address:* Fédération Action pour la République–Parti fédération, BP 4197, N'Djamena, Chad (office). *Fax:* 22-51-78-60 (office). *E-mail:* yorongar@gmail.com (office). *Website:* www .yorongar.com.

YOSANO, Kaoru, LLB; Japanese politician; b. 22 Aug. 1938; ed Faculty of Law, Tokyo Univ.; joined Japan Atomic Power Co. 1963; mem. House of Reps (Tokyo 1st Dist) 1976–2009; Parl. Vice-Minister of Int. Trade and Industry 1985–89; Chair. Parl. Cttee on Commerce and Industry 1989–90, Cttee on Science and Tech. 1990–94; Minister of Educ. 1994; Deputy Chief Cabinet Sec. 1996–98; Minister of Int. Trade and Industry 1998–2005; Minister of State for Econ. and Fiscal Policy and Financial Services 2005–06; Deputy Chair., Policy Research Council, Liberal Democratic Party 1995–2004, Chair. 2004–06; Chief Cabinet Sec. Aug.–Sept. 2007; State Minister in charge of Econ. and Fiscal Policy and for Regulatory Reform 2008–09; Minister of Finance and Minister of State for Financial Affairs and for Econ. and Fiscal Policy 2009. *Address:* ; c/o Liberal-Democratic Party, 1-11-23, Nagata-cho, Chiyoda-ku, Tokyo 100-8910, Japan.

YOSELIANI, Otar Davidovich; Georgian film director; b. 2 Feb. 1934, Tbilisi; s. of David Yoseliani and Maria Yoseliani (née Mikaberidze); m. Rita Semenova 1956; one d.; ed Moscow Univ., Moscow Cinema Inst.; worked as sailor and miner; Tbilisi film studio 1959–76; teacher of cinema, Tbilisi Acad. of Fine Arts; working in France 1982–. *Films include:* Avril 1962, La Chute des Feuilles (Fipresci Prize, Cannes) 1966, Il était une fois un merle chanteur (Best Foreign Film of the Year, Italy) 1970, Pastorale (Fipresci Prize, Berlin) 1976, Sept pièces pour le cinéma noir et blanc 1982, Euskadi 1983, Les favoris de la lune (Grand Prix, Venice Festival) 1984, Le petit monastère en Toscane 1988, Et la lumière fut (Grand Prix, Venice Festival) 1989, Hunting Butterflies (Tarkovsky Prize 1993) 1992, Georgia Alone (TV documentary) 1994, Les Brigandeurs 1996, In Vino Veritas 1999, Lundi matin (Monday Morning) 2002, Jardins en automne 2006, Chantrapas 2010. *Leisure interest:* speleology. *Address:* Mitskewitch 1 korp., 1 Apt 38, 380060 Tbilisi, Georgia; 14 rue de Rivoli, 75004 Paris, France. *Telephone:* (32) 38-50-58 (Tbilisi); 1-40-26-07-18 (Paris).

YOSHIDA, Saori; Japanese wrestler; b. 5 Oct. 1982, Tsu Mie; d. of Eikatsu Yoshida; ed Chukyo Univ.; gold medal, World Championships Chalkida 2002, New York 2003, Budapest 2005, Guangzhou 2006, Baku 2007, Tokyo 2008, Herning 2009, Moscow 2010, Istanbul 2011; gold medal, World Univ. Championships 2002; gold medal, Women's 55kg Freestyle, Asian Games, Busan 2002, Doha 2006, Guangzhou 2010; gold medal, Women's 55kg Freestyle, Olympic Games, Athens 2004, Beijing 2008, London 2012; won 100th consecutive contest Sept. 2006, defeated after 119th consecutive victory by Marcie Van Dusen during Team World Cup series, Beijing 2008; coached by Kazuhito Sakae; Female Wrestler of the Year 2002, Athlete of the Year, Japan Sports Awards 2007. *Leisure interests:* singing karaoke songs. *Address:* Japanese Wrestling Association, Kishi Memorial Hall, 1-1-1 Jinnan, Shibuya-ku, Tokyo 150-8050, Japan. *Telephone:* (3) 3481-2354. *Fax:* (3) 3481-2356. *E-mail:* wrestling@japan-sports.or.jp. *Website:* www.japan-wrestling .jp.

YOSHIMOTO, Banana; Japanese writer; b. (Mahoko Yoshimoto), 24 July 1964, Tokyo; d. of Takaaki Yoshimoto; ed Nihon Univ.; mem. Japan Writers' Assocn; Minister of Educ. Award for New Artists 1988, Scanno Prize 1993, Fendissime Literary Prize 1996, Maschera d'argento Prize 1999. *Publications include:* Mūn raito shadou (Moonlight Shadow) 1986, Kicchen (Kitchen) (Izumi Kyoka Literary Prize 1986, Kaien Magazine New Writer Prize 1987) 1987, Tugumi (Goodbye Tsugumi) (Yamamoto Shugoro Literary Prize 1989) 1988, Pineapple Pudding, N.P. 1990, Fruit Basket, Tokage (Lizard) 1993, Amrita (Murasaki-shikibu Prize 1995) 1994, Furin to nanbei (Asleep) (Bunkamura Duet Magot Literary Prize 2000) 2000, Hardboiled/Hard Luck 2005, Mizuumi (The Lake 2011) 2005. *E-mail:* admin@ yoshimotobanana.com (office). *Website:* www.yoshimotobanana.com.

YOSHIMOTO, Takashi; Japanese medical research scientist and university administrator; ed Tohoku Univ.; began teaching career at School of Medicine, Tohoku Univ. 1981, Assoc. Prof. 1982–88, Prof., Dept of Neurosurgery 1988–, Dir Univ. Hosp. 1999, Dean Grad. School of Medicine 2001–02, Pres., Tohoku Univ. 2002–08; Chair. Japan Neurosurgical Soc. 2003–; mem. Liaison Cttee for Cerebral Neurology, Science Council of Japan 1994–, Cttee of Nat. Inst. for Academic Degrees 1996–; Devt and Promotion for Medical Care in the 21st Century Cttee, Ministry of Health, Labour and Welfare 2002–; Int. mem. American Assocn of Neurological Surgeons 1998–; Active mem. Academia Eurasiana Neurochirurgica 2000–; Award of the Japanese Stroke Soc. 1979, Gold Medical Award, School of Medicine, Tohoku Univ. 1984, Nikkei BP Tech. Award, Medical and Bio Section 2000. *Address:* c/o Tohoku University, 2-1-1 Katahira, Aoba-ku, Sendai 980-8577, Japan (office).

YOSHIMURA, Yukio, BA (Econs); Japanese business executive and fmr international organization official; *Executive Officer and Head of Government Affairs, Citigroup Japan Holdings Corporation;* b. 9 June 1947, Nishinomiya; s. of Kazuo Yoshimura and Itoko Iijima; m. Tomoko Shibazaki 1977; three s.; ed Tokyo Univ.; Dir Int. Orgs Div., Ministry of Finance 1991–92, Int. Banking Div. 1992–95; Counsellor, Minister's Secr., in charge of Int. Public Relations 1995–96, Deputy Dir-Gen. Int. Finance Bureau 1996–97; Exec. Dir for Japan, IMF 1997–2001; Sr Adviser to Pres. World Bank Group 2001–02, Vice-Pres. and Special Rep. for Japan 2002–07; Man. Dir, Govt Affairs, Citibank Japan Ltd 2007–08, mem. Bd of Dirs 2008–12; Head of Govt Affairs, Nikko Citi Holdings Inc. 2008–, renamed Citigroup Japan Holdings Corpn, also Exec. Officer; mem. Basle Cttee on Banking Supervision 1984–85; Alt. Exec. Dir World Bank 1988–91; Exec. Dir Inter-American Investment Corpn 1990–91; mem. Group of Ten Working Party on Electronic Money 1996–97. *Address:* Shin Marunouchi Building, 1-5-1 Marunou-chi, Chiyoda-ku, Tokyo 100-6524, Japan (office). *E-mail:* yuyoshi@mc.rosenet.ne.jp (home). *Website:* www.citigroup.jp (office).

YOSHINO, Yasuo; Japanese insurance industry executive; b. 5 Oct. 1939; Deputy Pres. Sumitomo Life Insurance Co. 1997, Chair. 2001–07, Adviser 2007–; Pres. Exec. Bd E Asian Insurance Congress (EAIC) 2002–04; mem. Council Int. Inst. for Advanced Studies Japan 2004–; Corp. Auditor, Matsushita Electric Industrial Co. Ltd (now Panasonic Corpn) 2003–. *Address:* Sumitomo Life Insurance Co., 1-4-35 Shiromi, Chuo-ku, Osaka 540-8512, Japan (office). *Telephone:* (6) 6937-1435

(office). *E-mail:* info@sumitomolife.co.jp (office). *Website:* www.sumitomolife.co.jp (office).

YOST, R. David, MBA; American business executive; ed US Air Force Acad., Univ. of California, Los Angeles; joined Kauffman-Lattimer, Columbus, Ohio 1974, served in a variety of operational, sales and exec. positions, including Pres., Exec. Vice-Pres. Operations 1995–97, Co-COO; CEO AmeriSource Health Corpn 1997–2001, Chair. 2000–01, CEO AmerisourceBergen Corpn (cr. through merger of Bergen Brunswick Corpn and AmeriSource Health Corpn) 2001–11, Pres. 2001–02, 2007–11; mem. Bd of Dirs Tyco International 2009–, ITT Exelis Inc., Marsh & McLennan Companies 2012–; Trustee, Penn Medicine, US Air Force Academy Endowment Bd. *Address:* c/o Board of Directors, Marsh & McLennan Companies, 1166 Avenue of the Americas, New York, NY 10036, USA.

YOU, Si-Kun, BA; Taiwanese politician; b. 25 April 1948, Yilan Co.; m. Yang Pao-yu 1978; two s.; ed Chih-Leei Coll. of Business, Tung-hai Univ. Dept of Political Science; mem. Seventh Taiwan Prov. Ass. 1981, Eighth 1985; co-f. Democratic Progressive Party (DPP) 1986, elected to First Cen. Standing Cttee 1986, Second 1987, Third 1988, Fourth 1989, Sec. Gen. DPP HQ 1999–2000, Chair. 2006–07 (resgnd); Yilan Co. Magistrate 1990–97; Exec. Campaign Man. and Chief Spokesperson for DPP cand. Chen Shui-bian's Presidential Campaign 2000; Vice-Premier of Taiwan 2000, also Sec. Gen. Office of the Pres. 2001–05; Premier of Taiwan 2002–05; Sec.-Gen. to the Pres. 2005–; Founder and Chair. Lan-yang Cultural and Educ. Foundation 1990–97, Chair. Taipei Rapid Transit Corpn 1998; Chair. Taiwan-India Co-operation Council 2006–. *Publications:* The Resignation of Tangwai Assemblymen 1985, The Road to Democracy: The Love for Native Land 1989. *Address:* Democratic Progressive Party (DPP), 10/F, 30 Beiping East Road, Taipei, Taiwan (office). *Telephone:* (20) 23929989 (office). *E-mail:* foreign@dpp.org .tw (office). *Website:* www.dpp.org.tw (office).

YOU, -Gen. Xigui; Chinese army officer; b. 1939, Dingzhou, Hebei Prov.; joined PLA 1958, CCP 1960; Deputy Dir Logistics Dept, Cen. Guard Div. 1980–82, Div 1982–98; rank of Maj.-Gen. 1990, Lt-Gen. 1997, Gen. 2004; personal bodyguard to Pres. Jiang Zemin 1994; fmr acting Dir Cen. Bodyguards Bureau PLA, Dir 1999–; Alt. mem. 15th CCP Cen. Cttee 1997–2002, 16th CCP Cen. Cttee 2002–07, Deputy Dir Cen. Health Cttee 1998–. *Address:* People's Liberation Army, c/o Ministry of National Defence, Jingshanqian Jie, Beijing, People's Republic of China (office).

YOUN, Kong-hi (Victorinus), STD, DD; North Korean ecclesiastic; b. 8 Nov. 1924, Jinnampo City; s. of (Peter) Sang Youn and (Victoria) Sang Sook Choi; ed St Willibrord's Maj. Seminary, Dok-Won, N. Korea, Urban Coll., Rome, Gregorian Univ., Rome; ordained priest 1950; Asst Priest, Cathedral of Seoul (Myong-Dong) 1950; Chaplain, Pusan UN POW Camp 1951, Vice-Pres. Catholic Library, Pusan 1953; teacher, Song-Shin (Holy Ghost) Middle and High School 1954; Sec. Catholic Conf. of Korea 1960; ordained Bishop 1963–; Ordinary of Su-Won Diocese 1963; Admin. Seoul Archdiocese 1967; Archbishop and Ordinary of Kwangju Archdiocese 1973, Archbishop Emer. 2000; Rep. Kwangju Catholic Coll. Foundation 1974; Chair. Episcopal Conf. of Korea 1975; Rep. of Episcopal Cttee of Bicentennial of Catholic Church in Korea 1980; Episcopal Moderator, Justice and Peace Cttee 1979. *Publication:* Radio Message 1963. *Leisure interest:* mountain climbing. *Address:* Kwangju Catholic University, Nampeong, PO Box 101, Naju-si, Jeonnam 520-710, Republic of Korea. *Telephone:* (61) 337-2181. *Fax:* (61) 337-2185. *E-mail:* vkyoun@mail.kjc.ac.kr (office).

YOUNES, Ahmad Hammoud; Syrian government official; b. 1950, Ras al-Maarra, Damascus; m.; four c.; ed Damascus Univ.; employed in the judiciary and occupied several posts including that of Chief of Econ. Security Court of Damascus; Chair. Cen. Comm. of Control and Inspection 1997–2009; Minister of Justice 2009–11 (resgnd with rest of cabinet at Pres.'s request following popular protests). *Address:* c/o Ministry of Justice, rue al-Nasr, Damascus, Syria.

YOUNG, Bob; Canadian software industry executive; *CEO, Lulu Enterprises;* b. 19 Jan. 1954; three c.; ed Univ. of Toronto; began career as sales and marketing exec. in computer industry 1976; co-f. Red Hat to develop and market Linux open-source operating software 1995, CEO 1995–1999; founder and CEO Lulu Enterprises; acquired Hamilton Tiger Cats of Canadian Football League 2003. *Publication:* Under the Radar 1999. *Leisure interests:* family holidays, fly-fishing. *Address:* Lulu Enterprises, 3131 RDU Center Drive, Suite 210, Morrisville, NC 27560, USA (office). *Website:* www.lulu.com (office).

YOUNG, Sir Colville Norbert, Kt, GCMG, MBE, JP, DPhil; Belizean government official and academic; *Governor-General;* b. 20 Nov. 1932, Belize City; s. of Henry Oswald Young and Adney Wilhelmina Young (née Waite); m. Norma Eleanor Trapp 1956; three s. one d.; ed Univ. of West Indies, Univ. of York; Prin. St Michael's Coll., Belize 1974–76; Lecturer in English and Gen. Studies Belize Tech. Coll. 1976–86; Pres. Univ. Coll. of Belize 1986–90, lecturer 1990–93; Gov.-Gen. of Belize 1993–; Hon. PhD (York) 2003; Arts Faculty Prize, Univ. Coll. of the West Indies 1959, Student of the Year, Univ. Coll. of the West Indies 1960, Outstanding Teacher's Award 1987. *Compositions include:* Misa Caribeña, Tiger Dead (folk opera), Ode to Independence (secular cantata for mixed voices and orchestra). *Publications:* Creole Proverbs of Belize 1980, Caribbean Corner Calling 1988, Language and Education in Belize 1989, Pataki Full 1990, From One Caribbean Corner (poetry) 1983, contrib. drama and poetry in various anthologies, articles in various publs. *Leisure interests:* creative writing, playing and arranging steel band music, musical composition. *Address:* Belize House, Belmopan, Belize. *Telephone:* (822) 2521 (office), (822) 3081 (office). *Fax:* (822) 2050 (office). *E-mail:* govgenbz@btl .net (office).

YOUNG, Rev. Frances Margaret, OBE, PhD, FBA; British academic; *Professor Emerita, Department of Theology, University of Birmingham;* b. (Frances Margaret Worrall), 25 Nov. 1939, Frome, Somerset; d. of A. Stanley Worrall and Mary Frances Worrall (née Marshall); m. Robert Charles Young 1964; three s.; ed Bedford Coll., Univ. of London, Girton Coll. Cambridge and Chicago Divinity School; Research Fellow, Clare Hall, Cambridge 1967–68; temporary lecturer, Univ. of Birmingham 1971–73, Lecturer 1973–84, Sr Lecturer 1984–86, Edward Cadbury Prof. 1986–2005, Prof. Emer. 2005–; Head, Dept of Theology 1986–95; Head of School of Philosophy and Theology 1989–93; Dean Faculty of Arts 1995–97; Pro-Vice-Chancellor 1997–2002; ordained Methodist Minister 1984; Hon. DD (Univ. of Aberdeen) 1994, Hon. DTheol (MF Norwegian School of Theology)

2008, Hon. DUniv (Oxford Brookes Univ.) 2010. *Publications:* Sacrifice and the Death of Christ 1975, Can These Dry Bones Live? 1982, From Nicaea to Chalcedon 1983 (second edn 2010), Face to Face: A Narrative Essay in the Theology of Suffering 1985, The Art of Performance 1990, The Theology of the Pastoral Letters 1994, Biblical Exegesis and the Formation of Christian Culture 1997, Cambridge History of Early Christian Literature (co-ed.) 2004, Cambridge History of Christianity: Origins to Constantine (co-ed.) 2006, Brokenness and Blessing 2007, Holiness and Mission (with Morna Hooker) 2010, Exegesis and Theology in Early Christianity 2012. *Leisure interests:* walking, cycling, camping, travel, music, poetry, literature. *Address:* 142 Selly Park Road, Birmingham, B29 7LH, England. *Telephone:* (121) 472-4841. *E-mail:* francesmyoung@gmail.com.

YOUNG, Rt Hon. Sir George (Samuel Knatchbull), 6th Bt, PC, CH, MA, MPhil; British politician; *Chief Whip in the House of Commons and Parliamentary Secretary to the Treasury;* b. 16 July 1941, Oxford, England; s. of Sir George Peregrine 'Gerry' Young, 5th Bt and Elisabeth Knatchbull-Hugessen; m. Aurelia Nemon-Stuart 1964; two s. two d.; ed Eton Coll., Christ Church, Oxford, Univ. of Surrey; Economist, Nat. Econ. Devt Office 1966–67; Kobler Research Fellow, Univ. of Surrey 1967–69; Econ. Adviser, Post Office Corpn 1969–74; Councillor, London Borough of Lambeth 1968–71; mem. Greater London Council for London Borough of Ealing 1970–73; MP for Acton 1974–83, for Ealing Acton 1983–97, for NW Hampshire 1997–, mem. House of Commons Comm. 2009–12, Speaker's Cttee for the Ind. Parl. Standards Authority 2009–12, contested Speaker election 2009, mem. Public Accounts Comm. 2010–12, Parl. and Political Service Honours Cttee 2012–; Opposition Whip 1976–79; Parl. Under-Sec. of State, Dept of Health and Social Security 1979–81, Dept of Environment 1981–86; Dir Lovell Partnerships 1987–90; Comptroller of HM Household 1990; Minister of State, Dept of Environment 1990–94; Financial Sec. to HM Treasury 1994–95; Sec. of State for Transport 1995–97; Opposition Front Bench Spokesman for Defence 1997–98; Shadow Leader of the House of Commons 1998–2000, 2009–10; Leader of the House of Commons and Lord Privy Seal 2010–12; Chief Whip in the House of Commons and Parl. Sec. to the Treasury 2012–; Patron, Tory Reform Group; Conservative. *Publications:* Accommodation Services in the UK 1970–80, Tourism, Blessing or Blight? 1973. *Leisure interests:* bicycling, Queens Park Rangers Footvall Club. *Address:* House of Commons, Westminster, London, SW1A 0AA (office); Constituency Office, 2 Church Close, Andover, SP10 1DP, England (office). *Telephone:* (20) 7219-6665 (London) (office); (1264) 401401 (Andover) (office). *E-mail:* sirgeorge@sirgeorgeyoung.org.uk (office); george.young.mp@parliament .uk (office). *Website:* www.parliament.uk/biographies/commons/george-young/ 25225 (office); sirgeorgeyoung.org.uk.

YOUNG, Ian, AO, BE (Hons), MEngSc, PhD, FTSE; Australian civil engineer, academic and university administrator; *Vice-Chancellor, Australian National University;* ed James Cook Univ., North Queensland; began academic career at Max Planck Institut für Meteorologie, Hamburg Germany; later Prof. of Civil Eng, Univ. of New South Wales; consultant to USN and offshore oil and gas industry in Australia, Asia and N America; Exec. Dean of Faculty of Eng, Computer and Math. Sciences, Univ. of Adelaide 1999–2003, also held position as Pro Vice-Chancellor (International) for part of this time; Vice-Chancellor Swinburne Univ. of Tech. 2003–11; Vice-Chancellor ANU 2011–; fmr Chair. Education Australia Ltd; fmr Dir IDP Education Pty Ltd; mem. Australian Qualifications Framework Council 2009–11; Fellow, Acad. of Technological Sciences and Eng; Hon. Fellow, Inst. of Engineers Australia; numerous awards, including C.N. Barton Medal, Lorenz G. Straub Medal, Centenary Medal for services to Australian Society 2003. *Publications:* three books and more than 100 papers in peer-reviewed journals on coastal and ocean engineering and physical oceanography. *Address:* Office of the Vice-Chancellor and President, University Executive Building 10, Chancelry, The Australian National University, Canberra, ACT 0200, Australia (office). *Telephone:* (2) 6125-2510 (office). *Fax:* (2) 6257-3292 (office). *E-mail:* vc@anu.edu.au (office). *Website:* www.anu.edu.au (office).

YOUNG, James R; American business executive; *Chairman, President and CEO, Union Pacific Corporation;* m. Shirley Young; three c.; ed Univ. of Neb.; joined Union Pacific Railroad Co. 1978, various roles in man., finance and operations, becoming Asst Vice-Pres. of Re-Eng 1994–95, Vice-Pres. of Re-Eng and Design 1995, Vice-Pres. Customer Service Planning & Quality 1997, Vice-Pres. Finance & Quality, Sr Vice-Pres., Corp. Treas. 1998–99, Sr Vice-Pres. Finance and Corp. Controller 1999, Exec. Vice-Pres. and Chief Financial Officer 1999–2004, Pres. and COO Union Pacific Railroad Co. 2004–05, mem. Bd of Dirs Union Pacific Corpn 2005–, Pres. and CEO 2005–, also Chair. 2007–; Dir Grupo Ferroviario Mexicano, Asscn of American Railroads, Creighton Univ., Joslyn Art Museum, Univ. of Neb. Medical Center. *Address:* Union Pacific Corpn, 1400 Douglas Street, Omaha, NE 68179-1001, USA (office). *Telephone:* (402) 544-5000 (office). *Fax:* (402) 501-2133 (office). *Website:* www.up.com (office).

YOUNG, Michael K., BA, JD; American lawyer, university administrator and fmr government official; *President and Professor of Law, University of Washington;* m. Suzan Young; three c.; ed Brigham Young Univ., Harvard Law School; Law Clerk, US Supreme Court, Washington, DC 1977–78; Assoc. Prof., then Prof., then Fuyo Prof. of Japanese Law, Columbia Univ. 1978–98, also Dir Center for Japanese Legal Studies, Center for Korean Legal Studies; Deputy Legal Adviser to US Dept of State 1989–91, Deputy Under-Sec. for Econ. and Agricultural Affairs 1991–93, Amb. for Trade and Environmental Affairs 1992–93; Dean and Lobingier Prof. of Comparative Law and Jurisprudence, George Washington Univ. Law School 1998–2004; Pres. and Distinguished Prof. of Law, Univ. of Utah 2004–11, Pres. Emer. and Distinguished Prof. of Law 2011–; Pres. and Prof. of Law, Univ. of Washington 2011–; Visiting Scholar, Faculty of Law, Univ. of Tokyo, Japan 1978–80, 1983; Visiting Prof., Nihon Univ., Tokyo 1985, Waseda Univ., Tokyo 1989; mem. US Comm. on Int. Religious Freedom 1998–2005, Brown v. Bd of Educ. 50th Anniversary Comm.; fmr mem. US Judicial Conf. Cttee on Int. Judicial Relations; fmr mem. Bd of Visitors, USAF Acad.; mem. Council on Foreign Relations, Worldwide Univs Network 2011, Asscn of American Univs 2011, Asscn of Pacific Rim Univs 2011, Asscn of Public and Land-grant Univs 2011, Asscn of Governing Bds of Colls and Univs 2011, Pac-12 Conf. of Chief Exec. Officers 2011; Fellow, POSCO Research Inst. 1996, American Bar Foundation; Order of St Michael of the Wing (Portugal) 2007; Honored Alumni of the Year, Coll. of Humanities, Brigham Young Univ. 1995, Award for Excellence in Ethics, Utah Valley State Univ. 2004, Award of Excellence in Educ., Utah Hispanic Chamber of Commerce 2005, Communicator of the Year Award, Utah Chapters of the Public Relations Soc. of America and Int. Asscn of Business Communicators 2005, Award for Distinguished Service in Promoting Religious Freedom, Int. Center for Law Religious Studies, Brigham Young Univ. 2005, Distinguished Service Award, J. Reuben Clark Soc., Los Angeles Chapter 2006, Award in Recognition of Excellence in the Promotion of Int. Religious Freedom, Church of Jesus Christ of Latter-Day Saints 2006, Helping Hands Award, Utah Youth Village 2006, US-China Educational Collaboration Leadership Award, Chinese Asscn for Science and Tech. (USA) 2008, Int. Leader of the Year, World Trade Asscn of Utah 2008, Distinguished Service Award, LDS Int. Asscn 2011. *Publications:* Foreign Acquisitions in Japan: Hurdling the Ultimate Barrier (co-author) 1985, American Lawyers in Japan: Opportunities and Obstacles for Clients and Practitioners 1989, Ho wa Nichibei wo Hedateru Ka? (Does Law Create a Separation Between Japan and the United States?) 1990, Trilateral Perspectives on International Legal Issues: Relevance of Domestic Law & Policy (ed.) 1996, Japanese Law in Context: Readings in Society, The Economy, and Politics (co-author) 2002, International Environmental Law: Cases, Materials, Problems (co-author) (second edn) 2011, The Fundamentals of U.S. Trade Law and Policy (second edn) 2011; numerous articles in both English and Japanese in professional journals and in newspapers and popular journals. *Address:* Office of the President, University of Washington, 301 Gerberding Hall, Box 351230, Seattle, WA 98195, USA (office). *Telephone:* (206) 543-5010 (office). *Fax:* (206) 616-1784 (office). *E-mail:* pres@uw.edu (office); pres@u.washington.edu (office). *Website:* www.washington.edu/president (office).

YOUNG, Michael W., BS, PhD; American geneticist, biologist and academic; *Richard and Jeanne Fisher Professor and Vice-President for Academic Affairs, The Rockefeller University;* b. 1949, Miami, Fla; m. Laurel Eckhardt; two d.; ed Univ. of Texas; Postdoctoral Researcher, Stanford Univ. School of Medicine 1975–78; Asst Prof., The Rockefeller Univ. 1978–84, Assoc. Prof. 1984–88, Prof. 1988–, Vice-Pres. for Academic Affairs and Richard and Jeanne Fisher Prof. 2004–; Investigator, Howard Hughes Medical Inst. 1987–96; Head of Rockefeller unit of NSF's Science and Tech. Center for Biological Timing 1991–2001; mem. NAS; Fellow, American Acad. of Microbiology; Neuroscience Prize, Peter and Patricia Gruber Foundation 2009, Louisa Gross Horwitz Prize, Columbia Univ. (co-recipient) 2011, Massry Prize 2012, Gairdner Int. Award 2012, Wiley Prize in Biomedical Science 2013, Shaw Prize in Life Science and Medicine (co-recipient) 2013. *Publications:* numerous papers in professional journals. *Address:* Young M Laboratory, The Rockefeller University, 1230 York Avenue, New York, NY 10065, USA (office). *E-mail:* michael.young@rockefeller.edu (office). *Website:* www.rockefeller.edu/ research/faculty/labheads/MichaelYoung (office).

YOUNG, Neil, (Bernard Shakey); Canadian singer, songwriter and musician (guitar); b. 12 Nov. 1945, Toronto, Ont.; m. Pegi Young; one s. one d.; fmr lead singer, The Squires; with Buffalo Springfield 1966–69; with Crosby, Stills, Nash and Young 1969–74; solo artist with own backing group, Crazy Horse 1969–; Grammy Award for Best New Artist 1970, Melody Maker Poll Winner for Best Int. Group 1971, MTV Video Award 1989, Rolling Stone Critics' Award for Best Album 1989, Bay Area Music Award for Outstanding Album 1993, Q Award for Best Live Act 1993, Juno Award for Best Producer 2006, Americana Award for Artist of the Year 2006, Grammy Award for Best Rock Song (for Angry World) 2011, inducted into Rock and Roll Hall of fame 1995 (as solo artist) and 1997 (as mem. of Buffalo Springfield). *Films:* Journey Through the Past (dir) 1974, Rust Never Sleeps (dir) 1979, Human Highway (writer and dir) 1982, Made in Heaven (actor) 1987, '68 (actor) 1988, Freedom (actor) 1989, Love at Large (actor) 1990, Weld (actor) 1990, Year of the Horse (exec. producer) 1997, Greendale (writer, dir, actor, producer) 2003, Neil Young: Heart of Gold 2006, CSNY/Déjà Vu (writer, dir, score) 2008. *Recordings include:* albums: with Buffalo Springfield: Buffalo Springfield 1967, Last Time Around 1968; with Crosby, Stills, Nash and Young: Déjà Vu 1970, Four Way Street 1971; solo: Neil Young 1969, Everybody Knows This Is Nowhere 1969, After The Goldrush 1970, Crazy Horse 1971, Harvest 1972, Journey Through The Past 1972, Time Fades Away 1973, On The Beach 1974, Tonight's The Night 1975, Zuma 1975, Long May You Run 1976, American Stars 'N' Bars 1977, Comes A Time 1978, Rust Never Sleeps 1979, Live Rust 1980, Where The Buffalo Roam (OST) 1980, Hawks & Doves 1980, Re-ac-tor 1981, Trans 1983, Everybody's Rockin' 1983, Old Ways 1985, Landing On Water 1986, Life 1987, This Note's For You 1988, Freedom 1989, Ragged Glory 1990, Arc 1991, Weld 1991, Harvest Moon 1992, Unplugged 1993, Sleeps With Angels 1994, Mirror Ball 1995, Dead Man (OST) 1996, Broken Arrow 1996, Year Of The Horse 1997, Silver & Gold 2000, Are You Passionate? 2002, Greendale (OST) 2003, Prairie Wind (Juno Award for Best Adult Alternative Album 2006) 2005, Living With War 2006, Chrome Dreams II 2007, Fork in the Road 2009, Le Noise 2010, Psychedelic Pill 2012. *Publication:* Waging Heavy Peace (memoir) 2012. *Address:* c/o Elliot Roberts, Lookout Management, 1460 Fourth Street, Suite 210, Santa Monica, CA 90404, USA (office). *Website:* www.neilyoung.com.

YOUNG, Richard Stuart; British photographer; b. 17 Sept. 1947, Welwyn Garden City, Herts., England; s. of the late David Young and Hilda Ellison; m. 1st Riita Sinikka Harju 1975 (died 1983); two s.; m. 2nd Susan Manije Walker 1985; one d.; photographer 1974–; opened Richard Young Gallery in West London with his wife, Susan Young 2008; lives and works in London and world-wide; Dr hc (Univ. of the Arts London) 2013; Ischia Art Award 2012. *Television:* subject of a four-part Sky Arts documentary, Celebrity Exposed: The Photography of Richard Young 2012. *Publications:* By Invitation Only 1981, Paparazzo 1989, Shooting Stars 2004. *Leisure interests:* films, travel, books, music, good food. *Telephone:* (20) 7937-8911. *E-mail:* info@richardyounggallery.co.uk (office); office@ richardyoungonline.com (office). *Website:* www.richardyounggallery.co.uk (office); www.richardyoungonline.com (office).

YOUNG, Rosie Margaret, CBE, MD, FRCP, FRCPE, FRCP (Glas), FRACP; British medical specialist and academic; *Honorary Professor of Medicine, University of Hong Kong;* b. 23 Oct. 1930, Hong Kong; d. of Yeung Shun Hang and Shiu Shui Ying; ed Univ. of Hong Kong; Prof. of Medicine, Univ. of Hong Kong, Hon. Prof. of Medicine 2000–; Dean, Faculty of Medicine, Univ. of Hong Kong 1983–85, Pro-Vice-Chancellor 1985–93; Chair. Medical Council of Hong Kong 1988–96; Chair. Hong Kong Educ. Comm. 1993–98; Overseas Adviser, Royal Coll. of Physicians of Edin. 1987–93; mem. Council Royal Australasian Coll. of Physicians

1993–96; JP in Hong Kong 1971; Hon. Fellow, Newnham Coll. Cambridge 1988; Gold Bauhinia Star (Hong Kong); Hon. DSc (Hong Kong Univ.) (Open Learning Inst. of Hong Kong) 1995, (City Univ. of Hong Kong) 2006. *Publications include:* more than 100 articles in int. medical journals, mostly on diabetes, CHO metabolism and endocrinology. *Address:* Room 413, Professorial Block, Queen Mary Hospital, Pokfulam, Hong Kong Special Administrative Region, People's Republic of China (office). *Telephone:* 2255-4253 (office). *Fax:* 2816-2863 (office). *E-mail:* rttyoung@hkucc.hku.hk (office). *Website:* www.hku.hk (office).

YOUNG, Simone Margaret, AM; Australian conductor; *Music Director and General Manager, Staatsoper Hamburg;* b. 2 March 1961; m. Greg Condon; two d.; ed Sydney Conservatorium of Music; Conductor, Vienna Staatsoper, Bastille (Paris), Berlin Staatsoper, Cologne Opera, Royal Opera House (London), Metropolitan Opera (New York), Houston Grand Opera, Los Angeles Opera, New York Philharmonic Orchestra, Oslo Philharmonic Orchestra, Munich Philharmonic Orchestra, Maggio Musicale (Florence), ORF Radio Orchestra Vienna, NDR Hanover, NHK Symphony Orchestra (Japan), Hamburg Philharmonic Orchestra Sydney, Melbourne and West Australian Symphony Orchestras; Chief Conductor, Bergen Philharmonic Orchestra 1999–2002; Music Dir, Opera Australia 2001–05; Music Dir and Gen. Man. Hamburg State Opera 2005–, Prin. Musical Dir Hamburg Philharmonic State Orchestra 2005–; Prof. of Music and Theatre, Hamburg Univ. 2006–; First Guest Conductor Gulbenkian Orchestra, Lisbon 2007–; Chevalier, Ordre des Arts et des Lettres; Hon. DMus (Monash Univ.) 1998, (Univ. of New South Wales) 2001; Young Australian of the Year 1987, Goethe Medal, Goethe Inst. 2005, Conductor of the Year, Opernwelt magazine 2006, Schleswig-Holstein Brahms Prize 2008. *Repertoire includes:* opera: Rigoletto, Tosca, La Traviata, Oberto, Der fliegende Holländer, Der Rosenkavalier, Macbeth, Elektra, La Bohème, Cavalleria rusticana, Pagliacci, Tales of Hoffmann, Il Trovatore, Lohengrin, Eugène Onegin, Salomé, Fidelio, Peter Grimes, Wozzeck, La Juive, Der Ring des Nibelungen, Die Meistersinger von Nürnberg, Die Fledermaus, Die Frau ohne Schatten, Faust, Ariadne auf Naxos, Simon Boccanegra, Tannhäuser, Falstaff, Don Carlos, Andrea Chenier, Tristan und Isolde, The Marriage of Figaro, Don Giovanni, Lulu, Otello; extensive symphonic repertoire, including works of Mahler, Strauss, Wagner, Brahms, Beethoven, Bruckner and Bartók. *Address:* Arts Management Pty Ltd, Level 1, 405 Elizabeth Street, Surry Hills, NSW 2010, Australia (office); c/o Hamburgische Staatsoper, Große Theaterstraße 34, 20354 Hamburg, Germany. *Telephone:* (2) 9211-9422 (office). *Fax:* (2) 9211-9466 (office). *E-mail:* enquiries@artsmanagement.com.au (office). *Website:* www.artsmanagement.com.au (office); www.hamburgische -staatsoper.de.

YOUNG, William L., BSc, MBA; Canadian business executive; *Chairman, Magna International Inc.;* ed Queen's Univ., Kingston, Ont., Harvard Univ.; Partner in European practice of Bain & Co 1981–88; Founding Partner, Westbourne Management Group 1988–; Co-founder and Man. Partner, Monitor Clipper Partners (pvt. equity firm) 1998–; mem. Bd of Dirs Magna International Inc. 2011–, Chair. 2012–; Chair. Bd of Trustees, Queen's Univ., Kingston 2006–12, Chair. Emer. 2012–; mem. Bd of Dirs Monitor Co, Barnyard Industries Inc. and several other pvt. cos. *Address:* Magna International Inc., 337 Magna Drive, Aurora, ON L4G 7K1, Canada (office). *Telephone:* (905) 726-2462 (office). *Fax:* (905) 726-7164 (office). *E-mail:* info@magnaint.com (office). *Website:* www .magnaint.com (office); www.magna.com (office).

YOUNG OF GRAFFHAM, Baron (Life Peer), cr. 1984, of Graffham in the County of West Sussex; **David Ivor Young,** PC, LLB, DL; British politician and business executive; *Chairman, Young Associates Ltd.;* b. 27 Feb. 1932, London; s. of the late Joseph Young and of Rebecca Young; m. Lita Marianne Shaw 1956; two d.; ed Christ Coll., Finchley and Univ. Coll. London; admitted solicitor 1955; solicitor, Malcolm Slowe, London 1955–56; Exec. Great Universal Stores 1956–61; Chair. Eldonwall Ltd 1961–74, Mfrs Hanover Property Services Ltd 1974–80; Chair. Greenwood Homes Ltd 1976–82; Dir Centre for Policy Studies 1979–82; Special Adviser Dept of Industry 1979–82, of Educ. and Science 1981–82; Chair. Manpower Services Comm. 1982–84; mem., Chair. NEDC 1982–89; Minister without Portfolio 1984–85, Sec. of State for Employment 1985–87, for Trade and Industry and Pres. of Bd of Trade 1987–89; Deputy Chair. Conservative Party 1989–90; Head of Research Project on Tax Simplification, Centre for Policy Studies 2001; Dir Salomon Inc. 1990–94; Head Supervisory Task Force Salomon Bros 1991; Chair. Cable and Wireless 1990–95; Chair. Young Associates Ltd 1996–; Chair. British Org. for Rehabilitation by Training 1975–80 (Pres. 1980–82), Int. Council of Jewish Social and Welfare Services 1981–84, EU–Japan Asscn 1991–97, UCL Council 1995–, London Philharmonic Trust 1995–98, Chichester Festival Theatre Co. Ltd 1997–, Business for Sterling; Pres. Jewish Care 1990–97, Inst. of Dirs 1993–, Nat. Fed. of Enterprise Agencies 1994–98, W Sussex Econ. Forum 1996–; Dir of numerous cos and orgs including Young Assocs Ltd, Acacia City Ltd, Autohit PLC, Elfin Systems Ltd, Pixology Ltd, Pere UK, London Active Man.; Digital Camera Co. Ltd; Industrial Adviser, English Industrial Estates Corpn 1979–80, Special Adviser, mem. 1980–82; DL (W Sussex) 1999; Hon. FRPS 1981; Hon. Fellow Univ. Coll., London 1988. *Publication:* The Enterprise Years: A Businessman in the Cabinet 1990. *Leisure interests:* music, book collecting, photography. *Address:* House of Lords, London, SW1A 0PW; Young Associates Ltd, Harcourt House, 19 Cavendish Square, London, W1G 0PL, England. *Telephone:* (20) 7219-5353 (House of Lords); (20) 7447-8800 (office). *Fax:* (20) 7447-8849 (office). *E-mail:* young@youngassoc.com (office).

YOUNG OF OLD SCONE, Baroness (Life Peer), cr. 1997, of Old Scone in the County of Perthshire; **Barbara Scott Young,** MA; British environmentalist and administrator; *Chairman, Care Quality Commission;* b. 8 April 1948, Scone; d. of George Young and Mary Young (née Scott); ed Perth Acad., Univ. of Edinburgh, Univ. of Strathclyde; Sector Admin. Greater Glasgow Health Bd 1973–78; Dir of Planning and Devt, St Thomas's Health Dist 1978–79; Dist Gen. Admin. NW Dist Kensington, Chelsea and Westminster Area Health Authority 1979–82; Dist Admin. Haringey Health Authority 1982–85; Dist Gen. Man. Paddington and N Kensington Health Authority 1985–88, Parkside Health Authority 1988–91; Chief Exec. Royal Soc. for the Protection of Birds 1991–98, Vice-Pres. 2000–; Chair. English Nature 1998–2000; Vice-Chair. of BBC 1998–2000; Chief Exec. Environment Agency 2000–08; Chair. Care Quality Comm. 2008–; Pres. Inst. of Health Services Man. 1987–88, British Trust for Ornithology 2005–; Vice-Pres. Flora and

Fauna International 1998–; mem. BBC Gen. Advisory Council 1985–88, UK Round Table on Sustainable Devt 1995–, World Council Birdlife International 1994–98 (Vice-Pres.) 1999–; Trustee, Inst. of Public Policy Research 1999–; Patron Inst. of Ecology and Environmental Man. 1993–; Hon. Fellow, Sydney Sussex Coll., Cambridge 2003, Geologists Asscn, Linnean Soc., Inst. of Agricultural Eng; Hon. mem. Royal Inst. of Chartered Surveyors, Chartered Inst. of Water and Environmental Man.; CIWEM Chartered Environmentalist 2004; Eminent Fellow, Inst. of Agricultural Eng 2004; Hon. DUniv (Stirling) 1995, (Herts.) 1997, (Open Univ., Aberdeen, St Andrews, York) 2000; Hon. DSc (Cranfield) 1998; Green Ribbon Award 2000. *Publications:* What Women Want (contrib.) 1990, Medical Negligence (contrib.) 1990. *Leisure interests:* cinema, gardening. *Address:* Care Quality Commission, 7th Floor, New Kings Beam House, 22 Upper Ground, London, SE1 9BW, England (office). *Telephone:* (300) 0616161 (office). *E-mail:* info@cqc.org.uk (office). *Website:* www.cqc.org.uk (office).

YOUSFI, Youcef, PhD; Algerian politician and diplomatist; *Minister of Energy and Mining;* b. 2 Oct. 1941, Batna; m.; three c.; ed Ecole Nationale Supérieure des Industries Chimiques, France, Université de Nancy, France; fmr Sr Lecturer, then Prof. of Chemical Eng Ecole Nationale Polytechnic d'Alger; fmr Prof. of Chemical Eng and Dir Chem. Inst., Houari Boumediene Univ. of Science and Tech., concurrently served as adviser on petroleum affairs to Ministry of Industry and Energy; fmr Vice-Pres. of Marketing, Sonatrach (nat. petroleum co.), CEO 1985; Chair. Bd, Mines, Petroleum and Hydraulics Participating Fund 1988; Chief of Staff to the Pres. Liamine Zéroual 1996–97; mem. Nat. Peoples's Ass. 1997; Minister of Energy and Mines 1997–99; Chair. OPEC 1998–99; Minister of Foreign Affairs 1999–2000, Minister-Del. to Chief of Govt 2000–01; Amb. to Canada 2001–06; Amb. and Perm. Rep. to UN, New York 2006–08; Amb. to Tunisia 2008–10; Minister of Energy and Mining 2010–; Acting Prime Minister March– April 2014. *Address:* Ministry of Energy and Mining, BP 677, Tower A, Val d'Hydra, Alger-Gare, Algiers, Algeria (office). *Telephone:* (21) 73-23-40 (office). *Fax:* (21) 48-85-57 (office). *E-mail:* info@memalgeria.org (office). *Website:* www .mem-algeria.org (office).

YOUSIFI, Haza al-; Yemeni judge; Chief of Supreme Judicial Council 2012–. *Address:* Supreme Judicial Council, San'a, Yemen (office).

YOUSSEF, Maj.-Gen. Nasser; Palestinian government official and military officer; fmr Dir Gen Palestinian Nat. Security Forces; Head of Security Forces in Gaza Strip and West Bank 1994; Minister of the Interior, Palestinian Authority (PA) 2005;. *Address:* c/o Ministry of the Interior, Gaza, Palestinian Autonomous Areas (office).

YOUSSOUF, Mahamoud Ali; Djibouti politician; *Minister of Foreign Affairs and International Cooperation;* Amb. to Egypt –2001; Minister-Del. of Int. Cooperation 2001; Minister of Foreign Affairs and Int. Cooperation 2005–. *Address:* Ministry of Foreign Affairs, International Cooperation and Parliamentary Relations, Bd Cheick Osman, BP 1863, Djibouti (office). *Telephone:* 352471 (office). *Fax:* 353049 (office). *Website:* www.djibdiplomatie.dj (office).

YOUSSOUFI, Abd ar-Rahman al-; Moroccan politician and lawyer; b. 8 March 1924, Tangiers; m. Hélène Youssoufi; ed Univs of Paris, Poitiers and Nice, Int. Inst. for Human Rights, Strasbourg; activist in union and independence movts; mem. Istiqlal –1959; left to help set up Union nat. des forces populaires (UNFP), later Union Socialiste des forces populaires (USFP); Asst to Medhi Ben Barka; imprisoned 1959 for anti-state activities; given 2-year prison sentence in political trial in 1963; went into exile in France after release in 1964; spokesman for African and Arab nationalist campaigns and human rights; returned to Morocco early 1980s; Sec. Gen. USFP 1992–93 (left party leadership and went into exile again in protest at outcome of 1993 gen. elections); returned to Morocco 1995 to resume Sec. Gen. post; Prime Minister of Morocco 1998–2002; Grand Collier Ordre de Boyacq, Grande Croix Extraordinaire avec Plaque d'Or Ordre du Congrès (Colombia). *Leisure interests:* reading, walking, theatre, music. *Address:* c/o Office of the Prime Minister, Palais Royal, Le Méchouar, Rabat, Morocco.

YOUSUF, Mohammad; Pakistani professional cricketer; b. (Yousuf Youhana), 27 Aug. 1974, Lahore, Punjab; m. Tania (now Fatima) Yousuf; middle order right-handed batsman; right-arm off-break bowler; plays for Bahawalpur 1996–97, Water and Power Devt Authority 1997–98, Pakistan 1998–2010, Pakistan Int. Airlines 1999–2002, Lahore Blues 2000–01, ZTBL 2002–03, Lahore 2003–04, Lahore Badshahs 2004–07, Lancs. 2008, Islamabad Leopards 2010, Lahore Lions 2010, Warwicks. 2011, Asia XI; Test debut 1996/97; Test debut: S Africa v Pakistan, Durban 26 Feb.–2 March 1998; One-Day Int. (ODI) debut: Zimbabwe v Pakistan, Harare 28 March 1998; T20I debut: England v Pakistan, Bristol 28 Aug. 2006; has played in 90 Tests and scored 7,530 runs (24 centuries, 33 half-centuries), highest score 223, average 52.29; ODIs: 288 matches, 9,720 runs (15 centuries, 64 half-centuries, average 41.71, strike rate 75.10), highest score 141 not out; Capt. of Test team for tour of NZ 2009; banned indefinitely from Test cricket by Pakistan Cricket Bd, along with Younus Khan, for "infighting" during tour of Australia March 2010, announced retirement from int. cricket 27 March 2010, ban later lifted, called back to squad for rest of Test series against England Aug. 2010; CNN-IBN Cricketer of the Year 2006, Wisden Cricketer of the Year 2007, ICC (Int. Cricket Council) Test Cricketer of the Year 2007, named in Test Team of the Year 2007. *Achievements include:* broke West Indian batsman Sir Vivian Richards' world record for the most Test runs (1,788) in a single calendar year 2006; holds record of scoring the most runs without being dismissed in ODIs, 405 against Zimbabwe in Zimbabwe 2002–03; third Pakistani batsmen to surpass 6,000 runs in Test cricket; has scored a 27-ball fifty in Test cricket, third fastest by any player. *Address:* c/o Pakistan Cricket Board, Gaddafi Stadium, Lahore 54600, Pakistan. *Telephone:* (42) 571-7231. *Fax:* (42) 571-1860. *E-mail:* info@pcboard.com .pk. *Website:* www.pcboard.com.pk/home.html.

YOVCHEV, Tsvetlin, MA (Econ), PhD; Bulgarian politician and academic; *Deputy Prime Minister and Minister of the Interior;* b. 7 May 1964, Pleven; ed Nikola Vaptsarov Naval Acad., Varna, Erasmus University, Rotterdam and St Clement of Ohrid Univ., Sofia (Jt Master Programme); Marine Engineer, Navigation Maritime Bulgare 1987–92; Chief Power Engineer, Gara Iztok Car Repair Factory 1992–93; consecutively occupied all managerial positions in Nat. Security Service (NSS) 1993–2007, successively Head of Dept, Head of the Field and Deputy Dir NSS; Dir Gen. Counterintelligence Gen. Directorate, SANS

2008–09; Chair. State Agency for Nat. Security 2009–11 (resgnd); Lecturer, Univ. of Library Studies and Information Technologies 2011–; Advisor to the Council of Ministers 2011–12; Chief of the Cabinet to the Pres. of 2012–13; Deputy Prime Minister and Minister of the Interior 2013–. *Address:* Ministry of the Interior, 1000 Sofia, ul. 6-ti Septemvri 29, Bulgaria (office). *Telephone:* (2) 982-25-74 (office). *Fax:* (2) 982-20-47 (office). *E-mail:* info@mvr.bg (office). *Website:* www.mvr.bg (office).

YSTAD, Vigdis, DPhil; Norwegian academic; *Professor of Scandinavian Literature, University of Oslo;* b. 13 Jan. 1942, Verdal; d. of Ottar Ystad and Guri Todal; m. 1st Asbjørn Liland 1962; m. 2nd Daniel Haakonsen 1971; one s. one d.; ed Univs of Trondheim and Oslo; Lecturer, Univ. of Oslo 1974, Prof. of Scandinavian Literature 1979–, mem. Univ. Bd 1990–92; Chair. Council for Research in the Humanities 1985; Chair. Bd Centre for Advanced Study, Norwegian Acad. of Science and Letters 1992–93; Vice-Chair. Nat. Acad. of Dramatic Art 1993–96; mem. Norwegian Research Council 1979–85, Norwegian Govt Research Cttee 1982–84; mem. Norwegian Acad. of Science and Letters, Norwegian Acad. for Language and Literature, Royal Swedish Acad. of Letters, History and Antiquities 2004, Kungliga Vetenskaps-Societeten 2004; mem. Bd Nat. Acad. of Art 2000–02, Oslo Acad. of Art 2000–02, Nansenskolen, Lillehammer 2001–; Gen. Ed. Henrik Ibsens skrifter 1998–; Kt of St Olav (1st Class) 2012. *Publications include:* Kristofer Uppdals Lyrikk 1978, Henrik Ibsens Dikt 1991, Sigrid Undset: Et kvinneliv-'livets endeløse gåde' 1993, Ibsens dikt og drama 1996, Contemporary Approaches to Ibsen, Ibsen studies (ed.). *Address:* Centre for Ibsen Studies, Box 1116, Blindern, 0316 Oslo (office); Thomas Heftyes gt. 56b, 0267 Oslo, Norway (home). *Telephone:* 22-85-91-65 (office); 22-55-94-66 (home). *Fax:* 22-85-91-69 (office). *E-mail:* a.v.ystad@ibsen.uio.no (office).

YU, Darvish; Japanese professional baseball player; b. 16 Aug. 1986, Habikino, Osaka; s. of Farzad Darvishsefad and Ikuyo Darvishsefad; m. Saeko Darvish 2007; one s.; professional debut 2005; Japanese nat. team debut at Asian Baseball Championship, Taiwan 2007, also appeared for nat. team at 2008 Beijing Olympics and World Baseball Classic, Los Angeles 2009; pitcher for Hokkaido Nippon Ham Fighters 2005–; f. Yu Darvish Water Fund (charity) 2007; awards include Asia Series Most Valuable Player 2006, Eiji Sawamura Award 2007. *Address:* Hokkaido Nippon Ham Fighters, 1-3 Hitsujigaoka, Toyohira-ku, Sapporo, Hokkaido, Japan (office). *Website:* darvish-yu.jp.

YU, Guangzhong, MA; Taiwanese academic, poet, critic, translator and essayist; b. 9 Sept. 1928, Nanjing City, Jiangsu Prov.; m. Wo Chun Fan 1956; four d.; ed Univ. of Iowa, USA; Chief Ed. of Blue Stars and Modern Literature; Prof., Taiwan Normal Univ., Chinese Univ. of Hong Kong; Kuang Hua Chair. Prof. of English, Nat. Sun Yat-sen Univ. 1998, now Prof. Emer.; Pres. Taipei Chinese Centre, PEN Int. 1990–99; Hon. Fellow, Hong Kong Trans. Soc. 1991; Australian Cultural Award 1972, Best Books of the Year 1994, 1996, 1998, 2000 (Taiwan), 1998 (Hong Kong), Nat. Poetry Prize, Wu San-Lian Prose Prize and others. *Publications include:* Elegy of Boatman, Stalactite, Blue Plume, Sirius, White Jade Bitter Gourd, A Tug of War with Eternity, Dream and Geography, Selected Poetry of Yu Guangzhong Vols I and II, The Child of Dogwood–A Life of Yu Guangzhong 1999, The Old Man and the Sea (trans.), The Importance of being Earnest (trans.), Lust for Life (trans.) Bartleby the Scrivener (trans.), Modern English and American Poetry (trans.), Ou Shen. *Leisure interests:* travel, hiking, music, museums, maps. *Address:* Foreign Literature Institute, Sun Yat-sen University, 135 Xingang Road, Guanzhou 510275, Guangdong Province, People's Republic of China. *Telephone:* (7) 5564908 (home); (20) 84112828. *Fax:* (20) 84039173. *E-mail:* adpo@zsu.edu.cn (office). *Website:* www.zsu.edu.cn (office).

YU, Han; Chinese business executive; *President and Chief Operating Officer, Maruhan Corporation;* joined Chisan Co. Ltd 1988–90; joined Maruhan Co. Ltd 1990, Dir and Shizuoka Sales Div. Chief 1992–2001, Dir and Business Exec. Chief 2001–05, Man. Dir and Sales Div. Chief 2005–06, Vice-Pres. Maruhan Corpn 2006–08, Pres. and COO 2008–. *Address:* Maruhan Corporation, 231 Seiryu-cho, Demachi, Imadegawa, Kamigyo-ku, Agaru, Kyoto 602-0822, Japan (office). *Telephone:* (75) 252-0011 (office). *Fax:* (75) 252-0018 (office). *E-mail:* info@maruhan.co.jp (office). *Website:* www.maruhan.co.jp (office).

YU, Hua, MA; Chinese writer; b. 3 April 1960, Gaotang, Shandong Prov.; m. Chen Hong; one s.; worked as a dentist for five years; writer 1983–; James Joyce Foundation Award 2002 (first Chinese to win award). *Publications include:* in trans: Leaving Home at Eighteen 1984, To Live (Grinzane Cavour Award, Italy) 1992, Chronicle of a Blood Merchant 1995, The Past and the Punishments 1996, Shouting in the Drizzle, Events of the World Are Like Smoke, One Kind of Reality, An Incident, Mistake at Riverside, Brothers 2005, China in Ten Words (essays) 2011.

YU, Junbo; Chinese politician; *Deputy Secretary, Beijing Municipal Committee;* b. Feb. 1941, Anshan, Liaoning Prov.; joined CCP 1977; mem. Standing Cttee CCP Haicheng Co. Cttee, Liaoning Prov., Deputy Sec. CCP Haicheng Co. Cttee; Vice-Magistrate of Haicheng Co. Liaoning Prov.; Deputy Sec., then Sec. Haicheng Cttee, Anshan Municipal Cttee; Vice-Mayor of Anshan City; Sec. Jinxi Municipal Cttee, Chair. Standing Cttee, Jinxi People's Congress; mem. Standing Cttee CCP Liaoning Prov. Cttee 1990, Dir Organizational Dept 1990; mem. Standing Cttee CCP Beijing Municipal Cttee 1996–, Deputy Sec. 1997–; Chair. Beijing Municipal People's Congress 2001–07; Del., 15th CCP Nat. Congress 1997–2002; Deputy, 9th NPC 1998–2003. *Address:* Beijing Municipal People's Congress, Beijing, People's Republic of China (office).

YU, Lu; Chinese theoretical physicist; *Professor, Institute of Physics, Chinese Academy of Sciences;* b. Zhenjiang, Jiangsu Prov.; ed Kharkov State Univ., USSR (now Ukraine); fmr researcher, Inst. of Theoretical Physics, Chinese Acad. of Sciences, currently Prof., Inst. of Physics; Head of Condensed Matter Physics Section, Int. Centre for Theoretical Physics, Trieste, Italy –2002; first Dir Interdisciplinary Centre of Theoretical Studies, Beijing 2002–06; Academician, Third World Acad. of Sciences 1990, Chinese Acad. of Sciences 1999; Fellow, American Physics Soc. 2005; Tate Medal for Leadership in Int. Physics 2007. *Publications:* three books and 200 papers in professional journals. *Address:* The Institute of Physics, Chinese Academy of Sciences, PO Box 603, Beijing 100190, People's Republic of China (office). *Telephone:* (10) 82649325 (office). *Fax:* (10) 82640073 (office). *E-mail:* lyu@iphy.ac.cn (office).

YU, Min; Chinese nuclear physicist; b. Aug. 1926, Ninghe Co., Hebei Prov.; ed Beijing Univ.; mem. Dept of Math. and Physics, Academia Sinica 1985–; known for work on theory of nuclear weapons; Hon. Special Nat. Prizes of Sciences and Tech. 1987, 1989, Two Bombs, One Satellite Achievement Medal. *Address:* c/o Chinese Academy of Sciences, 52 Sanlihe Rd, Beijing 100864, People's Republic of China.

YŪ, Miri; South Korean (b. Japanese) writer, playwright and essayist; b. 22 June 1968, Kanagawa, Japan; one s.; fmr actress and Asst Dir Tokyo Kid Brothers theatre group; Co-founder Seishun Gogetsu To (The May Youth Group) theatre group 1986–; Kishida Kunio Drama Prize, Izumi Kyoka Prize, Noma Bungei Newcomer Literature Prize. *Plays:* Sakana no matsur (play, trans. as Fish Festival) 1993, Himawari no hitsugi (play, trans. as The Sunflowers' Coffin) 1993, Green Bench (play) 1993,. *Publications:* Ishi ni oyogu sakana (novel, trans. as Fish Swimming in Stone) 1994, Kazoku no hyōhon (essays, trans. as Family Disunity) 1995, Yū Miri no jisatsu (essays, trans. as Yū Miri's 'Suicide') 1995, Mado no aru shoten kara (essays, trans. as From the Bookshop with a Window) 1996, Full House (novel) 1996, Kazoku Shinema (novel, trans. as Family Cinema) (Akutegawa Prize) 1997, Mizube no yurikago 1997, Kaisetsu 1997, Kamen no kuni 1998, Gold Rush (novel) 1998, Inochi (memoir) 2000, Tamashii 2001, Ikiru 2001. *Website:* yu-miri.jp.

YU, Myeong-hee, PhD; South Korean microbiologist and academic; *Principal Research Scientist and Director, 21C Frontier R&D Program, Functional Proteomics Center, Korean Institute of Science and Technology;* ed Univ. of California, Berkeley, USA; Post-doctoral research at MIT, Boston, USA; returned to South Korea in 1985; Investigator, Nat. Creative Research Initiatives, Korean Ministry of Science and Tech., Prin. Research Scientist, Korean Inst. of Science and Tech. 2000–, Head of 21C Frontier R&D Program, Functional Proteomics Center 2002–; Ed.-in-Chief Microbiological Soc. of Korea 2002; mem. Editorial Bd Molecules and Cells, 1993–, Journal of Biochemistry and Molecular Biology 1999–, On-line Journal; mem. Scientific Program, Korea UNESCO Cttee 1999–; Regional Sec. of Gender, Science and Tech., Asia and Pacific Rim, UNESCO 1999–2001; mem. Asia-Pacific Int. Molecular Biology Network 1998, Korean Acad. of Sciences 2002, Korean Soc. for Biochemistry and Molecular Biology, Korean Soc. of Molecular and Cellular Biology, American Soc. for Biochemistry and Molecular Biology 2002, Nat. Acad. of Science and Tech. 2002–; Distinguished Publication Award, Korean Fed. of Science and Eng Socs 1995, Mockam Award, First Korea Research Inst. of Bioscience and Biotechnology Award 1996, Korean Soc. of Molecular Biology 1996, L'Oréal-UNESCO Women in Science Award 1998, 50th Seoul City Cultural Award 2001, Order of Science and Tech., Ungbi Medal 2004. *Publications:* numerous articles in scientific journals on conformational transition process of proteins. *Address:* Korea Institute of Science and Technology, 39-1 Hawolgok-Dong, Seongbuk-gu, Seoul 136-791, South Korea (office). *Telephone:* (2) 958-5114 (office). *E-mail:* mhyu@kist.re.kr (office). *Website:* www.kist.re.kr (office).

YU, Nick Rongjun; Chinese playwright and director; *Deputy General Manager, Shanghai Dramatic Arts Centre;* b. July 1971, Anhui Prov.; ed Shanghai Theatre Acad.; Dir Shanghai Dramatic Arts Centre, Shanghai Univ. Theatre Festival 2004–, Shanghai Int. Contemporary Theatre Festival; currently Deputy Gen. Man. Shanghai Dramatic Arts Centre; versions of his plays have been performed in Singapore, Japan, Turkey, UK, Canada, South Korea, Germany, Italy, Greek, Israel, Egypt, Denmark, Sweden, Austria, Poland and USA; has also translated several plays and musicals from English into Mandarin. *Plays include:* The Insane Asylum is Next Door to Heaven, Last Winter 2000, www.com 2001, A Very Serious Matter 2002, The Salty Taste of Cappuccino 2002, Behind the Lie 2003, Perfume 2003, Midnight at Havana Club 2004, Dog's Face 2004, Activated Charcoal 2004, Love in a Fallen City 2005, A Winter Tale of Two Cities 2005, A Man Among Women 2005, Sighing 2006, Cry to Heaven 2007, The Angel in Wheelchair 2007, Drift 2007, The Dream of the Red Chamber 2007, Street Angel 2008, Dust to Dust 2008, Heartquake 2008, 1977 2009, Das Kapital 2009, Boatmen 2010, Massage 2011, A Piano in the Factory 2011, Ballet Jane Eyre 2012; trans. into Mandarin include The Vagina Monologues (by Eve Ensler) 2006, I Love You, You're Perfect, Now Change (by Joe DiPietro and Jimmy Roberts) 2007, The Apocalypse 2012, Glorious Day 2012, Johann Strauss in 1872 2012, The Captain 2013. *Television:* Together For Life. *Address:* Shanghai Dramatic Arts Centre, 288 Anfu Lu, Xuhui, Shanghai 200031, People's Republic of China (office). *Telephone:* (21) 64738667 (office).

YU, Qiuyu; Chinese writer and critic; b. 1946, Yuyao, Zhenjiang Prov.; ed Shanghai Acad. of Drama; fmrly Prof. and Pres. Shanghai Drama Acad.; Vice-Pres. Shanghai Dramatists Asscn; only Chinese scholar invited to attend UNESCO World Cultural Heritage Forum 2005; host Qiuyu Moment talk show, Hong Kong Phoenix TV Station 2006–; guest lecturer on Chinese culture and world civilization at many prestigious insts including Harvard Univ., Yale Univ., Univ. of Madrid, Washington Congress Library; numerous prizes, including Chinese Nat. Writers Lu Shun Prize, China Publisher Prize, Shanghai Outstanding Literary Work, Taiwan Reader Best Book (two consecutive years), Jin Shi Tong Most Influential Book Award, Taiwan Platinum Author Award, Most Popular Author Award in Malaysia. *Publications:* A Bitter Journey Through Culture 1992, Notes From the Hills 1995, Cold River 1999, Draft History of Dramatic Theories, Dramatic Aesthetic-Psychology, A Narration of the History of Dramatic Culture in China, A Sigh Of a Thousand Years 2000, Travel No End 2001, A Life Borrowed 2004. *Address:* Shanghai Academy of Drama, Shanghai, People's Republic of China (office).

YU, Shumin; Chinese business executive; *President, Hisense Group;* Pres. Hisense Group Co. Ltd (f. as Qingdao No. 2 Radio Factory in 1969, now has two listed cos, Hisense Electric Co. Ltd and Hisense Kelon Electrical Holdings Co. Ltd), Chair. Hisense Electric Appliance Co. Ltd; mem. CCP; Deputy to ninth and tenth People's Congress of Shandong Prov.; ranked by Fortune magazine amongst the 50 Most Powerful Women in Business outside the US (38th) 2010, (37th) 2011. *Address:* Hisense Group Co. Ltd, Hisense Tower, 17 Donghaixi Road, Qingdao 266071, Shandong Province, People's Republic of China (office). *Telephone:* (532) 83878888 (office). *Fax:* (532) 83872882 (office). *E-mail:* service@hisense.com (office); master@hisense.com (office). *Website:* www.hisense.com (office); www.hisense-transtech.com.cn (office).

YU, Xubo, EMBA; Chinese business executive; *President, China National Cereals, Oils and Foodstuffs Corporation (COFCO);* ed Univ. of Int. Business and Econs, China Europe Int. Business School; worked in USA for many years; joined China Nat. Cereals, Oils and Foodstuffs Corpn (COFCO) 1988, mem. Bd of Dirs and Pres. COFCO 2008–. *Address:* China National Cereals, Oils and Foodstuffs Corporation, 19F, COFCO Fortune Plaza No. 8, Chao Yang Men South Street, Chao Yang District, Beijing 100020, People's Republic of China (office). *Telephone:* (10) 85006637 (office). *Fax:* (10) 85006637 (office). *E-mail:* cofco-news@cofco.com (office). *Website:* www.cofco.com (office).

YU, Gen. Yongbo; Chinese army officer and party official; b. 1931, Wafangdian, Liaoning Prov.; joined PLA 1947, soldier, Liaoxi-Shenyang Campaign, Northeast China Winter Offensive 1947, Beijing-Tianjin Campaign 1947, Southwest China Campaign 1947; joined CCP 1948; Deputy Head, Div. Propaganda Team, Field Army, PLA Services and Arms 1949; Sec.-in-Charge, Propaganda Dept, PLA Regimental Office, Korea 1950; Chief, Propaganda Div. (unnamed PLA Unit) 1963, Regimental Political Commissar 1967, Deputy Div. Political Commissar 1969, Div. Political Commissar 1972; Political Commissar, PLA Guangzhou Mil. Region 1983; Dir Political Dept, PLA Nanjing Mil. Region 1985–89; rank of Lt.-Gen. PLA 1988, Gen. 1993; Deputy Dir PLA Gen. Political Dept 1989–92, Dir 1992–2004; mem. Cen. Mil. Comm. of People's Repub. of China 1993–; mem. 14th CCP Cen. Cttee 1992–97; Deputy Head Work Group for Placement of Demobilized Army Officers 1993; Deputy Head Leading Group for Suppressing Smuggling 1993; Vice-Chair. PLA Election Cttee 1997; mem. 13th CCP Cen. Cttee 1987–92, 14th CCP Cen. Cttee 1992–97 (mem. Cen. Mil. Comm. 1992–97), 15th CCP Cen. Cttee 1997–2002; mem. 8th NPC 1993–98, 9th NPC 1998–2003. *Address:* People's Liberation Army Headquarters, c/o Ministry of National Defence, Jingshanqian Jie, Beijing, People's Republic of China (office).

YU, Youxian; Chinese publisher; b. 1937, Penglai Co., Shandong; ed Nankai Univ.; joined CCP 1955; Teaching Asst, Chinese Language Dept, Nankai Univ. 1963, later becoming Head of Academic Research Section and Head of Teaching Reform Team; Ed. Henan People's Publishing House 1964, later Deputy Dir and Dir of Editorial Sub-Cttee, Asst Publr 1981, later Deputy Chief Ed., Publr, Chief Ed.; Deputy Head of Publicity, CCP Cttee, Henan Prov. 1984–86; Dir Educ. Comm., Henan Prov. 1986; Vice-Gov. Henan Prov. 1988–2000; Commr of State Admin of Press and Publs 1999; Commr, Nat. Copyright Admin of China 1999–; Pres. Publishers Asscn of China (now China Publication Asscn) –2011; mem. CCP Central Comm. for Discipline Inspection, 15th CCP Nat. Congress 1997; mem. Wisers China Advisory Bd 2008–. *Address:* c/o Press and Publications Administration, State Council, Beijing, People's Republic of China (office).

YU, Zhen; Chinese politician; b. 1936, Haiyang, Shandong Prov.; ed Jilin Technological Univ.; joined CCP 1956; Dir Machinery Industry Bureau, Ministry of Light Industry mid-1980s, Vice-Minister of Light Industry 1985–93; Pres. China Nat. Light Industrial Machinery Corpn 1983–85, China Nat. Council of Light Industry 1993–98; Vice-Minister, State Econ. and Trade Comm. 1998–2003; Hon. Pres. China Machinery Industry Fed.; Del., 13th CCP Nat. Congress 1987–92, 14th CCP Nat. Congress 1992–97; Alt. mem. 15th CCP Cen. Cttee 1997–2002; mem. 10th CPPCC Nat. Cttee 2003–. *Address:* c/o State Economics and Trade Commission, Beijing, People's Republic of China (office). *Telephone:* 8396250 (office).

YU, Zhengsheng; Chinese politician; *Chairman, National Committee, Chinese People's Political Consultative Conference (CPPCC);* b. April 1945, Shaoxin City, Zhejiang Prov.; ed Harbin Mil. Eng Inst.; joined CCP 1964; technician, No. 6 Radio Factory, Zhangjiakou City, Hebei Prov. 1967; Deputy Dir Electronics Application Research Inst., Ministry of Electronics Industry 1967, Deputy Dir-Gen. Planning and Construction Dept 1967; Vice-Chair. Exec. Council of Welfare Fund for the Handicapped 1984; Deputy Sec. CCP Yantai City Cttee and Vice-Mayor of Yantai City 1985, Mayor 1987; Sec. CCP Qingdao City Cttee and Mayor of Qingdao City 1993; Vice-Minister of Construction 1997–98, Minister 1998–2001; Sec. CCP Hubei Prov. Cttee 2001–02, Chair. Standing Cttee Hubei Provincial People's Congress 2002–07; Sec. CCP Shanghai Municipal Cttee 2007–12; Alt. mem. 14th CCP Cen. Cttee 1992; mem. 15th CCP Cen. Cttee 1997–2002, 16th CCP Cen. Cttee 2002–07, 17th CCP Cen. Cttee 2007–12, 17th CCP Politburo 2007–12; mem. 18th CCP Cen. Cttee 2012–, 18th CCP Politburo 2012–, 18th CCP Politburo Standing Cttee 2012–; Chair. Nat. Cttee Chinese People's Political Consultative Conf. (CPPCC) 2013–. *Address:* Standing Committee, Chinese Communist Party Politburo, Quanguo Renmin Diabiao Dahui, Zhongguo Gongchan Dang, 1 Zhongnanhai, Beijing, People's Republic of China. *Website:* cpc.people.com.cn (office).

YU, Gen. Zhenwu; Chinese air force officer; b. 1931, Kuangdian Co., Liaoning Prov.; ed PLA Air Force Aviation School; joined CCP 1947; Regt Chief Navigating Officer, PLA Air Force 1951; took part in Liaoxi-Shengyang and Peiping-Tientsin Campaigns and served with Chinese People's Volunteers in Korean War 1953; Group Commdr PLA Air Force 1954–55; Corps Chief Officer in charge of firing training 1957; Regt Commdr 1964; Deputy Div. Commdr 1969–73; Deputy Dir Mil. Training Dept PLA Air Force 1973–77, Dir 1977–79; Corps Commdr 1979–83; Commdr Air Force of Guangdong Mil. Dist 1983–85; Deputy Commdr PLA Air Force 1985–95, Commdr 1995–97, now Deputy Sec.; Alt. mem. 12th and 13th CCP Cen. Cttees 1982–92; mem. Standing Cttee, 9th NPC 1998–2003; rank of Lt.-Gen. 1988, Gen. 1996. *Address:* c/o Ministry of National Defence, Jingshanqian Jie, Beijing, People's Republic of China (office).

YUAN, Enfeng; Chinese folk singer; b. 22 Jan. 1940, Shaanxi Prov.; d. of Yuan Zaiming and Li Dexian; m. Sun Shao, composer; one s. two d.; ed Dong Yangshi Elementary School, Xian; joined Cultural Troupe of Provincial Broadcasting Station 1951; participated in over 3,000 performances, including numerous solo concerts and 1,000 radio and TV programmes; appearances abroad include Romania, Bulgaria, fmr Czechoslovakia, fmr USSR, Japan, Thailand, Philippines and USA; Hon. Dir and Chief. Folk Music Section, Shaanxi Broadcasting Station 1986–; Vice-Chair. Shaanxi TV Station; mem. Chinese Musicians' Asscn; mem. of Bd, Shaanxi Br., Chinese Cultural Exchange Centre; mem. of many other official orgs; State Actress Award 1987, May Day Labour Medal Award 1993. *TV film:* Silver Bell. *Compositions (with Sun Shao) include:* Millet is Delicious and Caves are Warm, Nowhere is Better than Our North Shaanxi; many recordings and song books; 300 songs on record, cassette and compact disc. *Leisure interests:* table tennis, fabric weaving. *Address:* Folk Music Section, Provincial Broadcasting and Television Station, Xian, Shaanxi, People's Republic of China (office). *Telephone:* (29) 7852689 (office).

YUAN, Guiren; Chinese academic and politician; *Minister of Education;* b. Nov. 1950, Guzhen, Anhui Prov.; ed Beijing Normal Univ.; fmrly Prof. of Philosophy, Vice-Pres., Sec. CCP Cttee, Beijing Normal Univ.; Asst Mayor of Beijing and Dir Beijing Educational Comm. 1998–99; Pres. Beijing Normal Univ. 1999–2001; Vice-Minister of Educ. 2002–09, Minister of Educ. 2009–; mem. CCP Central Comm. for Inspection 2007–12; mem. 17th CCP Cen. Cttee 2007–12, 18th CCP Cen. Cttee 2012–. *Publications:* Zhexue (Philosophy), Ren de Zhexue (The Philosophy of Man), Guanli Zhexue (The Philosophy of Management), Deng Xiaoping Lilun Gailun (Introduction to Deng Xiaoping's Theory). *Address:* Ministry of Education, 37 Damucang Hutong, Xidan, Beijing 100816, People's Republic of China (office). *Telephone:* (10) 66096114 (office). *Fax:* (10) 66011049 (office). *E-mail:* english@moe.edu.cn (office). *Website:* www.moe.edu.cn (office).

YUAN, Li; Chinese insurance industry executive; b. 1962; engaged in insurance sector from 1984; worked in China Insurance Regulatory Comm. 1998–2006, Chair. Asst and Spokesman 2006; Vice-Chair. China Life Insurance Co. Ltd –2011, Chair. 2011–12 (resgnd), Pres. China Life Insurance (Group) Co. 2011–12 (resgnd). *Address:* c/o China Life Insurance (Group) Co. Ltd, 16 Chaowai Avenue, 23rd Floor Chinalife Building, Chaoyang District, Beijing 100020, People's Republic of China. *E-mail:* info@chinalife.com.cn.

YUAN, Longping; Chinese agronomist; b. 7 Sept. 1930, De'an, Jiangxi Prov.; s. of Yuan Xin-Lie and Hua Jing; m. Deng Ze 1964; three s.; ed Southwest Agriculture Inst.; teacher, Hunan Prov. 1964–; Researcher, Hunan Acad. of Agricultural Sciences 1971; Technical Adviser, International Rice Institute 1980–81; Deputy, 5th NPC 1978–83; Sr Rice Breeder Agric. Acad. of Hunan Prov. 1981–; mem. Standing Cttee 6th CPPCC 1982–88; Deputy Leader Nat. Hybrid Rice Experts Advisory Group 1982; Dir Hybrid Rice Research Centre under the Hunan Acad. of Agricultural Sciences 1985–; Int. Chief Consultant, FAO 1991; Vice-Chair. CCP 7th Hunan Prov. Cttee; Fellow, Chinese Acad. of Eng; Gold Medal, UN World Property Org. 1985, Laureate of Science Prize, UNESCO 1987, Rank Prize for Food 1988, Magsaysay Prize 2001, Wolf Foundation Prize in Agriculture 2004, World Food Prize 2004, French Agriculture Achievement Medal 2010, Confucius Peace Prize 2012. *Leisure interests:* violin, swimming. *Address:* Hunan Academy of Agricultural Sciences, Mapoling, Furong District, Changsha 410125, Hunan Province, People's Republic of China (office). *Telephone:* (731) 4080755 (office). *Fax:* (731) 4691877 (office). *E-mail:* lpyuan@public.cs.hn.cn (office).

YUAN, Maozhen; Chinese energy industry executive; fmrly with State Power Corpn; Chair. China Southern Power Grid Co. Ltd 2003–10; mem. Bd of Dirs China Electricity Council; Hon. Vice-Chair. State Power Information Network. *Address:* c/o China Southern Power Grid Co. Ltd, 6 Huasui Road, Zhujiang Xincheng, Tianhe District, Guangzhou 510623, People's Republic of China (office).

YUAN, Gen. Shoufang; Chinese army officer; b. Jan. 1939, Jilin City, Jilin Prov.; ed PLA Political Acad.; joined PLA 1958, CCP 1962; Deputy Regimental Political Commissar, later Regimental Political Commissar, PLA 1975–80; Dir Political Dept, Army (or Ground Force), PLA Services and Arms 1991; Deputy Dir Political Dept of Jinan Mil. Area Command 1991–95, Dir 1995–96; Asst Dir PLA Gen. Political Dept 1996, Deputy Dir 1996–; mem. 14th CCP Cen. Comm. for Discipline Inspection 1992–97, Alt. mem. 15th CCP Cen. Cttee 1997–2002, 16th CCP Cen. Cttee 2002–07; rank of Maj.-Gen. 1988, Gen. 2000. *Address:* People's Liberation Army General Political Department, Beijing, People's Republic of China (office).

YUAN, Weimin; Chinese sports administrator and civil servant; b. July 1939, Suzhou, Jiangsu Prov.; ed Nanjing Inst. of Physical Culture; joined Jiangsu Prov. Men's Volleyball Team 1958; joined CCP 1962; joined Chinese Men's Volleyball Team 1962; Chief Coach, Chinese Women's Volleyball Team; Vice-Chair. All-China Sports Fed.; Vice-Chair. Chinese Olympic Cttee 1985–2000, Chair. 2000–05; Pres. Chinese Volleyball Asscn, Chinese Football Asscn 1992–2005, Asian Fed. for Wushu 1994–2000, Council of Physical Culture and Sports Science Soc. of China 1995; Exec. Vice-Chair. Asian Volleyball Fed. 1976–84, Chair. 1997–2001; Vice-Chair. State Comm. for Physical Culture and Sports 1984–98; Deputy Dir State Gen. Admin. for Sports 1998–2000, Dir 2000–04; Exec. Pres., Beijing Organizing Cttee for 2008 Summer Olympics; Alt. mem. CCP 12th Cen. Cttee 1982–87, mem. 13th CCP Cen. Cttee 1987–92, 14th CCP Cen. Cttee 1992–97, Alt. mem. CCP 15th Cen. Cttee 1997–2002, mem. 16th CCP Cen. Cttee 2002–07; introduced to Volleyball Hall of Fame 2007; Hon. Prof., Nanjing Inst. of Physical Culture 1992. *Publication:* My Way of Coaching. *Address:* Beijing Organizing Committee for the 2008 Summer Olympics, Beijing Olympic Tower, 267 Beisihuanzhonglu, Haidian, Beijing 102008, People's Republic of China (office).

YUAN, Zhongyi, MA; Chinese archaeologist (retd); b. 1932, Jiangsu Prov.; m. Liu Yu; one d.; ed East China Teachers' Univ.; led excavations of Terracotta Warriors, Xian; fmr Vice-Dir Shaanxi Prov. Archaeological Research Inst. and Curator Qin Shi Huang's Terracotta Army Museum; Del. 5th People's Congress, Council of China; Outstanding Prof. of Shaanxi Prov., First Class of Nat. Excellence for book on Qin Dynasty Pottery Inscriptions and other book awards. *Publications:* Studies of the Terracotta Army at Qin Shi Huang's Mausoleum, Pottery Inscriptions of the Qin Dynasty, The Pits of Terracotta Warriors and Horses of Qin Shihuang Mausoleum – An Excavation of No. 1 Pit, An Excavation Report on the Bronze Chariots and Horses of Qin Shihuang Mausoleum. *Leisure interest:* handwriting. *Address:* c/o Qin Shi Huang's Terracotta Army Museum, Lintong, Xian, People's Republic of China.

YUASA, Joji; Japanese composer and professor of music; *Professor Emeritus of Music, University of California, San Diego;* b. 12 Aug. 1929, Koriyama City; s. of Daitaro Yuasa and Otoe Yuasa; Rena Yuasa (MDr), Ryuhei Yuasa (painter); m. Reiko Suzuki 1958; one s. one d.; ed Asaka High School, Keio Univ.; orchestral works commissioned by Kousevitzky Music Foundation 1974, Inst. for Research and Co-ordination in Acoustics and Music 1988, Suntory Music Foundation and by orchestras in Japan, Germany and Finland; resident on Berlin Artist Program (DAAD) 1976–77; Prof. of Music, Univ. of California, San Diego 1981–94, Prof. Emer. 1994–; Visiting Prof. of Music, Nihon Univ. 1994–; Visiting Prof., Tokyo Coll. of Music; mem. Experimental Workshop, Tokyo 1952; featured composer,

Festival of the Arts of this Century, Hawaii 1970, Pacific Music Festival, Sapporo 1990, Music Today Festival, Tokyo 1992; mem. Int. Jury for World Music Days, Int. Soc. for Contemporary Music (ISCM) 1971, 1983, 1992, 2001; Composer-in-Residence, Centre for Music Experiment, Univ. of California at San Diego 1976, NSW Conservatorium of Music, Australia 1980, Univ. of Toronto, Canada 1981; resident at Institut Royal de la Culture Amazighe 1987, Civitella Ranieri Foundation 2002; a leader for Int. Composers' Workshops, Amsterdam 1984, 1992; Artistic Dir Int. Comm. Series for Orchestral Composition, Suntory Hall 1999–2011; Medal with Purple Ribbon 1997; nine awards from ISCM 1971–2005, Odaka Prizes for Orchestra 1972, 1988, 1997, 2003, Kyoto Music Prize Grand Prix 1995, Suntory Music Prize 1996, Japan Acad. Prize 1999, Imperial Prize 1999. *Film scores:* Ōsōshiki (The Funeral) (dir Yuzo Itami), Fukuro no Shiro (The Castle of Owls) (dir Mazathiro Shinoda). *Compositions include:* Projection for string quartet I & II 1971, 1985, Time of Orchestral Time 1976, Scenes from Basho (suite) 1980–89, Revealed Time for viola and orchestra 1986, Cosmos Haptic II for piano 1986, Nine Levels by Ze-Ami for chamber ensemble and quadraphonic tape 1988, Eye on Genesis II for orchestra 1992, Piano Concertino 1994, Symphonic Suite: The Narrow Road into the Deep North: Basho 1995, Libera me, in Requiem of Reconciliation 1995, Violin Concerto 1996, Cosmic Solitude 1997, Chronoplastic II for Orchestra 1999, Chronoplastic III for orchestra 2001, Projection for string trio 2002, Cosmos Haptic V for orchestra 2002, Eyes on Genesis III for orchestra 2005, Koto Uta (songs) from Buson's Five Haiku 2006, Projection for Chamber Orchestra 2008. *Radio:* Comet Ikeya (Prix Italia for stereophonic section) 1966, Ai to Shura (Prix Italia for stereophonic section) 1967 and others. *Television:* Yoshinobu Tokugawa (NHK) 1999 and others. *Publications:* To the Cosmology of Music 1981, A Half of the Life – Towards the Open Horizon of Music 1999, The World of Joji Yuasa 2004. *Leisure interests:* skiing, reading. *Address:* Tokyo Concerts, Belx Shinjuku Building, II Plaza 6F, Aisumi cho23, Shinkjuku Ku, Tokyo 160-0005 (office); 7-16-21-101 Ikegami, Ohta-ku, Tokyo 146-0082, Japan (home). *Telephone:* (3) 3226-9755 (office); (3) 3754-8710 (home). *Fax:* (3) 3226-9882 (office); (3) 3754-8710 (home). *E-mail:* info@tokyo-concerts.co.jp (office). *Website:* www.tokyo-concerts.co.jp (office).

YUDASHKIN, Valentin Abramovich; Russian fashion designer; b. 14 Oct. 1963, Bakovka, Moscow Region; m. Marina Vladimirovna Yudashkina; one d.; ed Moscow Industrial Pedagogical Inst.; Founder and Artistic Dir Vali-Moda 1987, Founder and Dir Velentin Yudashkin Presents Co. 1989; participated in maj. fashion shows, including Paris 1990–92, Los Angeles (Beverly Hills Hilton), Israel, Egypt, Italy, etc.; costume designer to several Moscow Theatre New Opera productions; est. Valentin Yudashkin House of Fashion 1993; mem. Paris Haute Couture Syndicate 1996; Honoured Art Worker of Russian Fed. 1999, Nat. Painter of Russia 2005, Chevalier, Ordre des Arts et des Lettres (France) 2007. *Address:* Valentin Yudashkin Fashion House, Kutuzovsky pr. 19, 121151 Moscow, Russia. *Telephone:* (495) 240-11-89 (office). *Fax:* (495) 240-43-01 (office). *E-mail:* nosova.i@ yudashkin.com (office). *Website:* www.yudashkin.com (office).

YUDHOYONO, Kristiani (Ani) Herrawati; Indonesian; *First Lady;* b. 6 July 1952, Jogjakarta; d. of Sarwo Edhie Wibowo and Sunarti Sri Hadiyah; m. Susilo Bambang Yudhoyono 1976; two s.; Nat. Amb. for HIV/AIDS, speaker at numerous events including UNESCO Regional Confs in Support of Global Literacy, Beijing, China 2007; Hon. Chair. Asscn for the Eradication of Tuberculosis Indonesia; Patron of numerous orgs including Indonesia Reading Foundation, White Ribbon Alliance for Safe Motherhood (Indonesia), Family Welfare Movt, Women's Int. Club, Jakarta, Nat. Crafts Agency; UN Environment Programme Global Leadership Award 2007, Golden Pin Award, Regional Microcredit Summit 2008. *Address:* Office of the President, Gedung Bina Graha Lt. 2, Jalan Veteran 16, Jakarta, Indonesia (office).

YUDOF, Mark George, AB, LLB; American lawyer, academic and university administrator; b. 30 Oct. 1944, Philadelphia, Pa; m. Judith Lynn Yudof (née Gomel) 1965; one s. one d.; ed Univ. of Pennsylvania, Univ. of Pennsylvania Law School; law clerk to Judge Robert A. Ainsworth, US Court of Appeals Fifth Circuit 1968–69; Assoc. Gen. Counsel of the Comm. of ABA to Study the Fed. Trade Comm. 1969; Research Assoc. Harvard Center for Law and Educ. 1969–70, Sr Staff Attorney 1970–71; Asst Prof. of Law, Univ. of Texas at Austin 1971–74, Prof. 1974–97, Assoc. Dean of the Law School 1979–84, Dean 1984–94, James A. Elkins Centennial Chair in Law 1983–97, John Jeffers Research Chair in Law 1991–94, Exec. Vice Pres. and Provost, Univ. of Texas at Austin 1994–97; Pres. and Prof. (Law School), Univ. of Minnesota 1997–2002, Pres. Emer. 2002–; Chancellor and Prof. (Law School), Univ. of Texas System 2002–08, Lee Hage and Joseph D. Jamail Regents Chair in Higher Educ. Leadership 2002–08, Charles Alan Wright Chair in Fed. Courts 2002–08; Pres. Univ. of California 2008–13; Chair. Council of Public Univ. Pres. and Chancellors 2007; mem. Bd of Dirs World Council on Information Tech. 2004–07, HealthTronics 2005–, Fellow, American Acad. of Arts and Sciences 2001–, American Bar Foundation, Texas Bar Foundation; Visiting Prof., Univ. of California, Berkeley Law School 1977, Univ. of Michigan Law School 1982; fmr Visiting Fellow, Univ. of Warwick, UK; mem. American Law Inst., Pres.' Council on Service and Civic Participation 2006–; Hon. Fellow, Queen Mary and Westfield Coll., Univ. of London 1990; Hon. Guest Prof., Fudan Univ. 2000, Peking Univ. Law School 2000; Jewish Nat. Fund Tree of Life Award (co-winner with wife) 1993, Univ. of Pennsylvania Law Alumni Award of Merit 1999, Odyssey Award, Big Brothers Big Sisters of Greater Minneapolis 2001, John R. Hogness Award, Asscn of Academic Health Center 2003, James Wilson Award, Univ. of Pennsylvania Law School 2004. *Publications include:* When Government Speaks 1983, Legal Deskbook for Administrators of Independent Colleges and Universities 1984, Gender Justice (jtly) 1987, Educational Policy and the Law (jtly) 2002; numerous book chapters and articles in professional journals. *Leisure interest:* collecting antique maps. *Address:* c/o Office of the President, University of California, Franklin Building, 1111 Franklin Street, Oakland, CA 94607-5200, USA.

YUE, Denise, (Denise Yue Chung-yee), JP, MPA; Hong Kong civil servant and politician; *Secretary for the Civil Service;* b. 1952, Hong Kong; ed Belilios Public School, Univ. of Hong Kong, Harvard Univ., USA; joined Admin. Service 1974, served in various bureaux and depts, including as Deputy Dir of Regional Services 1991–92, Deputy Sec. for Trade and Industry 1992–93, Dir-Gen. of Industry 1993–95, Sec. for Trade and Industry 1995–98, Sec. for the Treasury 1998–2002,

Perm. Sec. for Commerce, Industry and Tech. (Commerce and Industry) 2002–06, Sec. for the Civil Service 2006–; Gold Bauhinia Star 2001. *Address:* Civil Service Bureau, 10/F, West Wing, Central Government Offices, 11 Ice House Street, Central, Hong Kong Special Administrative Region, People's Repub. of China (office). *Telephone:* 2810-2741 (office). *Fax:* 2868-5069 (office). *E-mail:* csbts@csb .gov.hk (office). *Website:* www.csb.gov.hk (office).

YUEN, Woo-Ping; Chinese film director, actor and choreographer; b. (Yuan He-Ping), 1945, Guangzhou, Canton; s. of Yuen Hsiao-Tien; born into a family of Peking Opera artists, learned martial arts; worked with Jackie Chan (q.v.), Donnie Yen, Ng See Yuen. *Films directed include:* Snake in the Eagle's Shadow 1978, Magnificent Butcher 1979, Drunken Master 1979, Dreadnaught 1981, Drunken Tai-Chi 1984, Mismatched Couples 1985, Tiger Cage 1988, In the Line of Duty 4 1989, Tiger Cage 2 1990, Tiger Cage 3 1991, The Wicked City 1992, Last Hero in China 1993, The Tai Chi Master 1993, The Iron Monkey 1993, Heroes Among Heroes 1993, Wing Chun 1994, Fist of Legend 1994, Fiery Dragon Kid 1995, Tai Chi 2 1996, True Legend 2010. *Films acted in include:* Miracle Fighters 1982, Mismatched Couples 1985, Eastern Condors 1986, Wicked City 1992, Cinema of Vengeance 1994, The Grandmaster 2013. *Films choreographed include:* Fist of Legend 1994, Black Mask 1996, The Matrix 1999, Crouching Tiger, Hidden Dragon 2000, Kill Bill 2003, Kill Bill 2 2004, Kung Fu Hustle 2004, House of Fury 2005, Fearless 2006, The Forbidden Kingdom 2008, Ninja Assassin 2009, Man of Tai Chi 2013. *Television:* produced TV Series The Practice 1976.

YULDASHEV, Bekhzod, PhD; Uzbekistani nuclear physicist, politician and administrator; *Adviser-Consultant, International Atomic Energy Agency, Vienna;* b. 9 May 1945, Tashkent; m.; two s.; ed Tashkent Univ., Moscow Univ.; research in particle and nuclear physics, non-proliferation problems, Jt Inst. of Nuclear Research, Dubna, USSR 1968–71; Sr Researcher, Physical Tech. Inst., Tashkent 1972–83, Head of Lab. 1984–90; Dir-Gen. Inst. of Nuclear Physics 1990–2006; mem. Parl. 2000–05; Senator 2005–06; Adviser-Consultant, IAEA, Vienna 2006–; Visiting Prof., Univ. of Washington, Seattle 1977–78, 1980–81, 1989–90, Stanford Univ., Calif. 2006–07; Visiting Fellow, Indiana Univ. 1997, USA, Univ. of Cambridge, UK 2004; mem. Scientific Council Jt Inst. of Nuclear Research, Dubna; mem. Uzbekistan Acad. of Sciences (Pres. 2000–05), Kazakhstan Nat. Acad. of Sciences; mem. American Physical Soc., Islamic Acad. of Sciences; Hon. Fellow, Indiana Univ. 1997; Hon. Prof., Samarkand Univ. 2005; Order 'For Glorious Work'; Dr hc (Jt Inst. of Nuclear Research, Dubna) 2004; State Prize in Science and Tech. 1983, ECO Prize in Science and Tech. 2004. *Publications:* more than 300 papers in int. physics journals. *Address:* International Atomic Energy Agency, PO Box 200, Wagramer str. 5, Vienna 1400, Austria (office). *Telephone:* (1) 2600-24674 (office). *E-mail:* b.yuldashev@iaea.org (office); yuldbekh@gmail.com (office). *Website:* www.iaea.org (office).

YUMASHEV, Valentin Borisovich; Russian politician and journalist; b. 15 Dec. 1957, Perm; m. 1st; one d.; m. 2nd Tatiana Dyachenko (d. of fmr Pres. Yeltsin,); ed Moscow State Univ.; errand boy newspaper Komsomolskaya Pravda 1976; corresp., sr corresp. newspaper Komsomolskaya Pravda 1978–87; Moskovsky Komsomolets 1987–89; took part in election campaign of Boris Yeltsin to Supreme Soviet 1988, 1992, 1996; Head of Div., Ed., Deputy Ed.-in-Chief Ogonyok 1987–96; Adviser to Russian Press on mass media 1996–; Head of Admin Pres. Yeltsin 1997–98; apptd Adviser to Boris Yeltsin 1998; helped Pres. Yeltsin in writing memoirs. *Leisure interest:* tennis. *Address:* c/o Office of the President, Staraya pl. 4, Moscow 103132, Russia (office). *Telephone:* (495) 910-10-89 (office); (495) 206-60-88 (office).

YUMKELLA, Kandeh K., BSc, MSc, PhD; Sierra Leonean politician and UN official; *Director-General, United Nations Industrial Development Organization (UNIDO);* m.; several c.; ed Njala Univ. Coll., Univ. of Illinois, USA; held several academic and research positions in USA; Minister for Trade, Industry and State Enterprises, Sierra Leone 1994–95; Special Adviser to Dir-Gen. UNIDO 1996, Dir Africa and Least Developed Countries Regional Bureau 1996–2000, UNIDO Rep. and Dir Regional Industrial Devt Centre 2000–03, Sr Adviser to Dir-Gen. 2003–05, Dir-Gen. UNIDO 2005–; Special Rep. of the Sec.-Gen. for Sustainable Energy for All, UN 2012–; currently also Chair. UN-Energy. *Publications include:* co-author of numerous books, articles and staff papers on int. trade and devt issues. *Address:* United Nations Industrial Development Organization, Vienna International Centre, Wagramerstr. 5, PO Box 300, 1400 Vienna, Austria (office). *Telephone:* (1) 260260 (office). *Fax:* (1) 2633011 (office). *E-mail:* unido@unido.org (office). *Website:* www.unido.org (office).

YUN, Byung-se, MA; South Korean politician; *Minister of Foreign Affairs and Trade;* b. 3 Aug. 1953, Seoul; m.; one d.; ed Seoul Nat. Univ., School of Advanced Int. Studies, Johns Hopkins Univ., USA; joined Ministry of Foreign Affairs (MOFA) 1977, Consul, Consulate-Gen. in Sydney 1984, Counsellor, Perm. Mission to UN, New York 1990, Dir, N America Div. I, MOFA 1994, Minister-Counsellor, Embassy in Singapore 1995, Deputy Dir-Gen., Asian and Pacific Affairs Bureau, Ministry of Foreign Affairs and Trade (MOFAT) Feb.–July 1999, Deputy Dir-Gen., N American Affairs Bureau, MOFAT July 1999, Minister, Perm. Mission to UN Secr. and Int. Orgs in Geneva 2000, Minister, Embassy in Washington, DC 2002, Sr Coordinator, Nat. Security Council 2004–06, Deputy Minister of Foreign Affairs 2006, Sr Presidential Sec. for Foreign, Security and Unification Policy 2006, Minister of Foreign Affairs and Trade 2013–; Sr Adviser, Law Offices of Kim & Chang 2009; Visiting Prof., Grad. School of Int. Studies, Sogang Univ., Seoul 2009; mem. 18th Presidential Transition Cttee Sub-Cttee on Foreign Affairs, Nat. Defence and Unification 2013; Service Merit Medal 1992, Order of Service Merit (Yellow Stripes) 2005. *Address:* Ministry of Foreign Affairs and Trade, 37, Sejong-no, Seoul 110–787, South Korea (office). *Telephone:* (2) 2100-2114 (office). *Fax:* (2) 2100-7999 (office). *E-mail:* web@mofat.go.kr (office). *Website:* www.mofat.go.kr (office).

YUN, Gongmin; Chinese business executive; *President and CEO, China Huadian Corporation;* b. Sept. 1950, Inner Mongolia; ed Tsinghua Univ.; Chief of Yikezhao Banner of Inner Mongolia; Gen. Sec. Yikezhao Banner Cttee of CCP; Asst to the Pres. of Inner Mongolia Autonomous Region, Vice-Pres. Inner Mongolia Autonomous Region; Gen. Sec. Taiyuan Municipal Cttee of CCP; Vice-Gov. Shanxi Prov.; Vice-Gen. Sec. Shanxi Prov. Cttee of CCP; Deputy Chair. and Chair. Labour Union of Shenhua Group Corpn Ltd; Pres. and CEO China Huadian Corpn and Deputy

Sec. Party Leadership Group 2008–. *Address:* China Huadian Corporation, 2 Xuanwumennei Street, Xicheng District, Beijing 100031, People's Republic of China (office). *Telephone:* (10) 83566036 (office). *E-mail:* info@chd.com.cn (office). *Website:* www.chd.com.cn (office).

YUN, Jong-yong, BA; South Korean business executive; *Company Adviser, Samsung Electronics Company Limited;* b. 21 Jan. 1944, Youngchun, Kyoung-buk; m.; one s. one d.; ed Seoul Nat. Univ., MIT Sloan School, USA; joined Samsung Group 1966, with Samsung Electronics Co. Ltd 1969–, Head of Tokyo office 1977–80, Head of TV Business Div. 1980–81, Head of Video Business Div. 1981–85, Head of Research and Devt Div. 1985–88, Vice-Pres. Electronics Group 1988–90, Vice-Pres. and Rep. Dir Consumer Electronics Business Group 1990–92 (Pres. and Rep. Dir 1992–96), Pres. and CEO Samsung Electronics Co. Ltd 1996–99, Vice-Chair. and CEO 1999–2008, Co. Adviser 2008–; Pres. and CEO Samsung Electro-Mechanics Co. Ltd 1992, Samsung Display Devices Co. Ltd 1993, Samsung Japan HQ 1995; Chair. Nat. Acad. of Eng of Korea, Fed. of Korean Information Industries; Prize for Most Successful CEO in Korea (Korea Man. Asscn) 1999, Gold Medal for Contrib. to Industry 1992, Outstanding Achievement in Man. (Inst. of Inc. Engineers) 1998, Asia's Businessman of the Year (Fortune) 2000, CEO's Choice Award, Asia Business Leader Awards 2002. *Leisure interest:* golf. *Address:* Samsung Electronics Co. Ltd, 250 2-ga Taepyeong-no, jung-gu, Seoul 740-10 Hannam-dong, Yongsan-gu, Seoul 100-742, Republic of Korea (office). *Telephone:* (2) 727-7114 (office). *Fax:* (2) 727-7985 (office). *E-mail:* j-npr@samsung.co.kr (office). *Website:* www.samsung.com (office).

YUNIUPINGU, (James) Galarrwuy, AM; Australian community leader and business executive; *Chairman, Gumatj Association Inc.;* b. 30 June 1948, Melville Bay, nr Yirrkala, Gove; ed Mission School, Yirrkala, Methodist Bible Coll., Brisbane; active in Gumatj Clan's land struggle in 1960s; joined Interim Northern Land Council 1975, Chair. 1977–80, 1983–2002; Chair. Gumatj Asscn Inc. 1983–; Public Officer/Dir Yunupingu Industries 1983–; Chair. YBE Pty Ltd 1988–92; Co-Chair. Aboriginal Devt Consultative Forum 2000; Dir Garrangali Crocodile Farm 1991–, Gawpu Marine 1991–; mem. Australian Crocodile Farmers Asscn 1990–, Council for Aboriginal Reconciliation 1991–96; Exec. Dir Yothu Yindi 1992–; Yothu Yindu Foundation 1998–; Gumatj Clan Leader 1979–; also singer and songwriter; Australian of the Year 1978, honoured as one of Australia's Nat. Living Treasures 1998. *Publication:* Our Land Is Our Life. *Leisure interests:* fishing, hunting, songwriting, Australian Rules Football. *Address:* Gumatj Association Inc., PO Box 1220, Nhulunbuy, NT 0880, Australia (office).

YUNUS, Muhammad; Bangladeshi banker and academic; *Chairman, Yunus Centre;* b. 28 June 1940; m. Afrizi Yunus; one d.; ed Vanderbilt Univ., USA; Prof. of Econs, Chittagong Univ. 1976; f. Grameen Bank Project, pioneering microcredit loans to those in extreme poverty Dec. 1976, changed to ind. bank, Grameen Bank Sept. 1983, Man. Dir and CEO 1983–2011; currently Chair. Yunus Centre; f. Nagorik Shakti political party 2007; Dir UN Foundation; mem. Int. Advisory Group, Fourth World Conf. on Women, Beijing 1993–95, Advisory Council for Sustainable Econ. Devt 1993, UN Expert Group on Women and Finance, Prague Inst. for Global Urban Devt, UNESCO, Mahatma Gandhi Center for Global Nonviolence and numerous others; Founding Man. Dir Grameen Telecom 1995–, Grameen Capital Management Ltd 1998–, Grameen IT Park Ltd 2000–, Grameen Star Education Ltd 2002–, Grameen Information Highways Ltd 2002–; dir numerous Int. cos and foundations;; Hon. LLD (Warwick) 1996; Independence Day Award, Pres.'s Award and Cen. Bank Award (all Bangladesh), Ramon Magsaysay Award (Philippines), Aga Khan Award for Architecture, Mohamed Shabdeen Award for Science (Sri Lanka), World Food Prize (USA), Nobel Peace Prize (jtly with Grameen Bank) 2006, Presidential Medal of Freedom 2009, US Congressional Gold Medal 2010, St. Vincent de Paul Award 2011. *Publications include:* Creating a World Without Poverty: How Social Business Can Transform Our Lives 2008. *Address:* Yunus Centre, Grameen Bank Bhaban, Mirpur-2, Dhaka 1216, Bangladesh (office). *Telephone:* 2-801-1138 (office). *E-mail:* yunus@yunuscentre.org (office). *Website:* www.muhammadyunus.org.

YURKO, Allen; American business executive; *Partner, Compass Partners International Ltd;* b. 1951; ed Lehigh Univ., Baldwin-Wallace Coll.; early career in finance and accounting positions with Joy Manufacturing Co. and Eaton Corpn; Chief Financial Officer Mueller Holdings –1988; several management positions at Siebe including COO 1992–94, CEO 1994–98; CEO Invensys PLC (following merger of Siebe and BTR) 1998–2001; Pnr, Compass Pnrs Int. Ltd 2001–. *Address:* Compass Partners International Ltd, 4 Grosvenor Place, 3rd Floor, London, SW1X 7HJ, England (office). *Telephone:* (20) 7761-2000 (office). *Fax:* (20) 7761-2020 (office). *Website:* www.compasspartners.co.uk (office).

YURSKY, Sergei Yurievich; Russian actor, stage manager, film director and writer; b. 16 March 1935, Leningrad (now St Petersburg); s. of the late Yuriy Yursky and Eugenia Romanova; m. Natalia Tenyakova; one d. Daria Yurskaia 1973; ed Leningrad Univ., Leningrad Theatrical Inst.; worked for Gorky Theatre, Leningrad 1957–79, Mossoviet Theatre 1978– and other theatres in Moscow, Paris and Brussels; acted in films 1960–; one-man performances in 70 cities in USSR 1965–, in Czechoslovakia 1985, Japan 1986, France 1987, 1991, Italy 1987, Switzerland 1989, Israel 1992, Belgium 1993, USA 1994, Germany 1994; world tour with programme 'Pushkin and Others' 1999, including USA, Japan, Germany, France, England and Scotland; with programme 'From the First Person' to USA, Canada, Israel, Lithuania 2002 and Israel, Canada, Denmark, Belgium 2003; Order of Honour 1995; People's Artist of the RSFSR 1987, Gold Mask (Moscow) 1998, Pres. of Russia Prize 2003, Mikhel Chekhov Medal. *Stage roles:* over 60, including Chatsky (Woe from Wit) 1963, Tousenbach (Three Sisters) 1965, Victor Frank (Price) 1968, Henry IV (Henry IV) 1969, Molière (Molière; also dir) 1973, Groznov (Truth is Good, but Happiness is Better; also dir) 1980, Ornifle (Ornifle or Draught; also dir) 1986, King Beranger (The King is Dying, Ionesco) 1992, Azriel (Dibouk!) 1992, Glov (after Gamblers XXI, Gogol; also dir) 1992, Le Baron Cazou (Les Amants Puérils) 1993, Old Man (after Ionescu, also dir) 1994, Foma Opiskin (after Dostoevsky) 1995, Vogler (After The Rehearsal, Bergman) 1996, Malkovic (The Provocation, after Vatsetis; also dir), Libero Bocca (Ferrous Class) 1999, Jazda (The Nobody) 2002, The Dressing Room in the Bath House (also dir) 2006. *Radio appearances include roles in:* The Master Builder (also dir) 1996, The Chairs (also dir) 2000. *Television work includes:* Eugene Onegin (eight episodes) 1998, The Bald Singer (also dir) 2008. *Films:* A Man from Nowhere 1969,

The Golden Calf 1968, The Little Tragedies 1980, The Fall of Condor 1984, Love and Pigeons 1985, The Abyss 1987, The Picture 1989, Chernov/Chernov (also screenplay and dir) 1990 (Prizewinner, Karlovy Vary/Carlsbad Film Festival 1990), The Silencer 1993, Le Bonheur 1993, The Queen Margot 1997, Oligarkh 2003, Event with Doctor Leczin (screenplay and dir). *Publications:* Who Keeps the Pause 1977, enlarged edn 1989, During the Timeless Times (short stories) 1989, Recognizing (poetry), The Jest (poetry) 1997, The Contents of the Box (short stories) 1999, Play the Life 2002, Spotikatch (35 stories) 2001–03, The Heat All Time 2003, The Attempt to Reflect 2003, The Home Joys 2004. *Leisure interests:* cat Satik. *Address:* Theater Mossovet, B. Sadovaja 16, Moscow (office); Gagarinsky per. 35, Apt 4, 119002 Moscow, Russia. *Telephone:* (495) 699-44-37 (office); (499) 241-52-71.

YUSGIANTORO, Purnomo, BSc, MS, PhD; Indonesian politician and international organization official; *Minister of Defence;* b. 16 June 1951, Semarang, Cen. Java; m.; three c.; ed Bandung Inst. of Tech., Univ. of Colorado, USA; worked with several int. think tanks during 1980s; energy consultant with World Bank (IBRD) and Asian Devt Bank 1988–2000; fmr Deputy Gov. Nat. Resilience Inst. (Lemhannas); adviser, Minister of Energy 1993–98; Minister for Energy and Mineral Resources 2000–09, Minister of Defence 2009–; fmr Gov. OPEC, Vienna, Pres. OPEC Conf. and Acting Sec.-Gen. OPEC 2004; fmr Lecturer in Econs and Man., Atmajaya Univ., Jakarta and univs in USA; Co-founder Indonesian Inst. for Energy Econs. *Address:* Ministry of Defence, Jalan Medan Merdeka Barat 13–14, Jakarta Pusat 10200, Indonesia (office). *Telephone:* (21) 3456184 (office). *Fax:* (21) 3440023 (office). *E-mail:* postmaster@dephan.go.id (office). *Website:* (office).

YUSHCHENKO, Viktor Andriyovich, CandEconSc; Ukrainian economist, banker, politician and fmr head of state; *Chairman, Our Ukraine (Nasha Ukraina);* b. 23 Feb. 1954, Khoruzhivka, Sumy Oblast; s. of Andriy Andriyovych Yushchenko and Varvara Tymofiyovna Yushchenko; m. Kateryna Mykhailivna Yushchenko; two s. three d.; ed Ternopil Inst. of Finance and Econ., Ukrainian Inst. of Econs and Agricultural Man.; economist, Br. Dir USSR State Bank, Ulianivskyi Dist, Sumy Oblast 1976–85, Deputy Dir of Agric. Credits, Ukrainian Br. of USSR State Bank 1985–87; Dept Dir Ukrainian Bank (fmrly Ukrainian Agro-Industrial Bank) 1987–91, First Deputy Chair. 1991–93; Gov. Nat. Bank of Ukraine 1993–99; Prime Minister of Ukraine 1999–2001; Founder and Chair. Nasha Ukraina (Our Ukraine) coalition 2002–, mem. Parl. 2002–04; Pres. of Ukraine 2005–10; mem. Ukrainian Acad. of Econ. Sciences, Acad. of Econ. and Cybernetics; Kt, Order of the Three Stars (First Class), Grand Collar of the Order of Vytautas the Great, Kt Grand Cross, Grand Order of King Tomislav (Croatia) 2007, Grand Cross, Order of Polonia Restituta 2009, Order 'For Merits' of Class III 1996, Order of Heydar Aliyev (Azerbaijan) 2008, Order of the White Rose of Finland 2006, Order of the Golden Fleece (Georgia) 2009, Order of Victory St George (Georgia) 2009, Order of the White Eagle (Poland) 2005, Royal Order of the Seraphim (Sweden) 2008, Order of Merit (Hungary) 2008; Dr hc (Mohyla Acad.— Nat. Univ. of Kyiv, Ostroh Acad.), (Univ. of Maria Curie-Sklodowska) 2000, (Catholic Univ. of Lublin) 2009; Global Finance Award 1997, State Prize Laureate Science and Technology 1999, Man of the Year 'Wprost' 2004, Chatham House Prize, UK 2005. *Publications:* more than 250 articles and research papers in Ukrainian and int. journals. *Leisure interests:* painting, pottery, wood-carving, beekeeping. *Address:* Our Ukraine (Nasha Ukraina), 04070 Kyiv, vul. Borychiv Tik 22a, Ukraine (office). *Telephone:* (44) 206-60-97 (office). *Website:* www.razom.org.ua (office).

YUSHKIAVITSHUS, Henrikas Alguirdas; Russian/Lithuanian international civil servant; b. (Henrikes Alguirdas Yushkiavitshus), 30 March 1935, Siauliai, Lithuania; s. of Zigmas Yushkiavitshus and Stefa Biknevitchiutè; m. Elena Samuilytè 1961; one d.; ed Leningrad Electrotechnical Communication Inst.; Dir Technological Dept Lithuanian Radio and TV 1960–66; Dir Tech. Centre, Int. Radio and TV Org. 1966–71; Vice-Chair USSR State Cttee for TV and Radio 1971–90; Chair. Interministerial Cttee for Radio and TV Devt and mem. Interministerial Cttee for Satellite Communications 1971–90; Asst Dir-Gen. for Communication, Information and Informatics, UNESCO 1990–2001, Chargé de mission UNESCO 2001; Corresp. mem. Russian Eng Acad.; mem. Int. Acad. of Electrotechnical Sciences, Fed. Tenders Comm. 2004–; Fellow, Soc. of Motion Picture and TV Engineers, USA; Hon. Academician, Russian Acad. of Information; recipient of several Soviet and Russian decorations etc.; Order of Gediminas, Lithuania 1996; Dr hc (Int. Inst. for Advanced Studies in Systems Research and Cybernetics, Canada); Emmy Directorate Award, US Nat. Acad. of TV Arts and Sciences. *Publications include:* contribs to professional journals. *Leisure interests:* tennis, reading, music.

YUSON, Alfred, (Krip Yuson); Philippine writer; b. 1947; fmr Henry Lee Irwin Professorial Chair, Ateneo de Manila Univ., now teaches fiction and poetry; literary confs, festivals and reading tours world-wide; columnist, The Philippine Star and Philippine Graphic magazine; Philippines Ed., MANOA: A Pacific Journal of International Writing (Univ. of Hawaii); Founding mem., Philippine Literary Arts Council, Creative Writing Foundation, Inc., Manila Critics' Circle; Chair. UMPIL (Writers Union of the Philippines); bd mem. Movie and Television Ratings and Classification Bd; Rockefeller Foundation residency, Italy 2003, SEAWrite (SouthEast Asian Writers) Award for Lifetime Achievement 1992, Stalwart of Art & Culture Award 2003, Carlos Palanca Memorial Awards for Literature Hall of Fame, FAMAS Award, Catholic Mass Media Award. *Play:* Luto, Linis, Laba (Qbd Ink, The Writer's Center, Bethesda, USA) 2003. *Publications include:* 22 books, including three novels, short fiction, poetry and essay collections: Sea Serpent (poetry) 1980, Dream of Knives (poetry) 1986, The Great Philippine Jungle Energy Cafe (novel) (Palanca Grand Prize for the Novel) 1987, Confessions of a Q.C. house-husband and other privacies 1991, Trading in Mermaids (poetry) 1993, Voyeurs and Savages (novel) 1998, Mothers Like Elephants (poetry) 2000, Luto, Linis, Laba (play) (Carlos Palanca Memorial Awards for Literature 2000), The Word on Paradise (essays) 2001, The Philippines: Islands of Enchantment (non-fiction) 2002, Hairtrigger Loves: 50 Poems on Woman (poetry) 2002, Ang Walong Kuwento (short stories) 2002, The Music Child (novel) 2008. *Address:* c/o The Philippine Star, 13th Corner Railroad Street, Port Area, 1016 Manila, Philippines (office). *Telephone:* (2) 527-7901 (office). *E-mail:* tmendoza@philstar.com.ph (office).

YUSUF, Abdulqawi Ahmed, DrIur, DèsSc; Somali lawyer, academic and judge; *Judge, International Court of Justice;* ed Somali Nat. Univ., Centre for Studies and Research in Int. Law, Hague Academy of Int. Law, Netherlands, Grad. Inst. of Int. Studies, Univ. of Florence, Italy, Univ. of Geneva, Switzerland; barrister, Supreme Court of Somalia 1974–; Lecturer in Int. Law, Faculty of Law, Somali Nat. Univ. 1974–80, Chair. Public Law Dept 1976–78; adviser to Govt on int. legal matters; mem. various govt advisory bodies on legislation; Asst Prof., Faculty of Law, Univ. of Geneva 1981–83; Visiting Lecturer on public int. law and int. econ. law at univs and academic insts including Univ. of Siena, Italy 1984, Institut universitaire d'études du développement, Geneva 1984, Univ. of Florence 1985, Univ. of Milan-Bocconi, Italy 1990, Int. Devt Law Inst., Rome 1990, 1991, 1992, 1995, Univ. of Turin, Italy 1991, 1992, UNITAR Fellowship Programme in Int. Law, Hague Acad. of Int. Law, The Netherlands 1993, 1994, 1996, 1999, Thessaloniki Inst. of Public Int. Law and Int. Relations 2004; Rep. and Head, New York Office of UNCTAD 1992–94; Sr Liaison Officer, UN Programme of Action for Least Developed Countries, New York 1992–94, Head of Legal Policies Section, Tech. Programme, Geneva June–July 1992, Legal Officer, Tech. Div., Geneva 1981–88; Legal Adviser and Dir Legal Service, UNIDO 1994–98, Acting Man. Dir Country Programmes and Funds Mobilization Div. 1997–98, Asst Dir-Gen. and Special Adviser on African Affairs 1998–2001; Legal Adviser and Dir Office of Int. Standards and Legal Affairs, UNESCO, Paris 2001–; *ad hoc* Judge, Int. Court of Justice in case concerning Certain Questions of Mutual Assistance in Criminal Matters (Djibouti v. France), Judge 2009–; Rep. of Somalia to Third UN Conf. on the Law of the Sea 1975–81; mem. Somali del. to OAU Summit 1974, to Afro-Asian Legal Consultative Cttee 1975, 1976, to Arab-League Summit 1976; Expert Adviser, UNCTAD negotiations on a Draft Int. Code of Conduct on the Transfer of Tech. 1982–85, UN negotiations on a Convention on Biological Diversity 1990–91; Expert Adviser and UNCTAD Rep. at GATT Uruguay Round Trade Negotiations on TRIPS 1989–91; Legal Adviser to Industrial Devt Bd and Gen. Conf. of UNIDO 1994–98, to Int. Centre for Genetic Eng and Biotechnology, Trieste, Italy 1994–97, to Exec. Bd and Gen. Conf. of UNESCO 2001–, to UNESCO Intergovernmental Oceanographic Cttee and to World Heritage Cttee of Convention concerning the Protection of the World Cultural Natural Heritage 2001–, to UNESCO negotiations on the following conventions: Convention on the Protection of the Underwater Cultural Heritage, Convention for the Safeguarding of Intangible Cultural Heritage, Int. Convention against Doping in Sport, Convention on the Protection and Promotion of the Diversity of Cultural Expression 2001–06; mem. Comm. on Environmental Law, Int. Union for Conservation of Nature (IUCN); mem. Academic Council Doctoral School of Int. Law, Univ. of Paris 1 (Sorbonne), France, Int. Curatorium of Thessaloniki Inst. of Public Int. Law and Int. Relations, Greece; Founder and Gen. Ed. African Yearbook of International Law/Annuaire Africain de droit international; mem. Editorial Advisory Bd Asian Yearbook of International Law; mem. Inst. of Int. Law (Institut de droit int.), Geneva, Soc. française de droit int.; Founding mem. African Asscn of Int. Law, African Foundation for Int. Law (Chair. Exec. Cttee). *Publications:* author or co-author of several books and numerous articles dealing with various aspects of int. law. *Address:* International Court of Justice, Peace Palace, Carnegieplein 2, 2517 KJ, The Hague, The Netherlands (office). *Telephone:* (70) 302-2323 (office). *Fax:* (70) 364-9928 (office). *E-mail:* info@ icj-cij.org (office). *Website:* www.icj-cij.org (office).

YUSUF, Hamza; American theologian; *President, Zaytuna College;* b. (Mark Hanson), 1959, Walla Walla, Wash.; m.; five c.; ed Imperial Valley Coll., San Jose State Univ.; converted to Islam 1973 at age 17; moved to UAE to study Islam 1979–83; Co-founder and Exec. Dir Zaytuna Islamic Inst. (now Zaytuna Coll.), Calif. 1996, currently Pres. *Address:* Zaytuna College, 2515 Hillegass Ave, Berkeley, CA 94704, USA (office). *Telephone:* (510) 356-4760 (office). *Fax:* (510) 356-4768 (office). *E-mail:* info@zaytuna.org (office). *Website:* www.zaytunacollege .org (office).

YUSUF, Salim, OC, MD, MBBS, DPhil, FRSC, FRCPC; Canadian (b. Indian) physician and professor of medicine; *Director, Population Health Research Institute, McMaster University;* b. 26 Nov. 1952, Kottarakkara, Kerala, India; ed Bangalore Univ., St John's Medical Coll., Bangalore, Univ. of Oxford, UK; Registrar, Gen. Medicine and Cardiology, John Radcliffe Hosp., Oxford 1982; Registrar, Cardiology, Harefield Hosp. Regional Cardiac Centre, Middx 1982–84; Scientific Project Officer, NIH, Bethesda, Md, USA 1984, later Chair., working group for Women's Health clinical trial, Clinical Asst Prof., Uniformed Services Univ. Health Sciences 1987–88, Acting Chief of Clinical Trials Br., Nat. Heart, Lung and Blood Inst. 1991–92; Prof. of Medicine and Dir, Div. of Cardiology, McMaster Univ. 1992–, also Dir, Population Health Research Inst. 2000–, concurrently Heart and Stroke Foundation of Ontario/Marion W. Burke Chair in Cardiovascular Disease, McMaster Univ.; Vice-Pres. of Research and Chief Scientific Officer, Hamilton Health Sciences 1998–2000; Visiting Prof., Univ. of Sydney, Australia 1998, Cleveland Clinic Foundation 2000, St John's Medical Coll., Bangalore; Ed. Journal of Evidence-Based Cardiology, Textbook of Evidence-Based Cardiovascular Medicine; Fellow Int. Acad. of Cardiovascular Sciences; mem. American Coll. of Cardiology, Canadian Cardiovascular Soc., American Heart Asscn, Canadian Inst. of Academic Medicine, Int. Acad. of Cardiovascular Sciences, American Soc. of Clinical Investigation; mem. World Heart Fed. (Pres.-elect 2013–); Hon. Fellow, Polish Cardiac Soc. 1995, Venezuelan Cardiac Soc. 1999; Sr Scientist, Canadian Insts of Health Research; over 20 nat. and int. awards for research including Durrer Lecturer 1988, NIH Group Award 1992, Indo-Canadian Chamber of Commerce Professional of the Year 1996, Int. Soc. of Thrombosis and Hemostasis Sol Sherry Lecturer Award 1999, Canadian Cardiovascular Soc. Lifetime Research Achievement Award 1999, Prix Galien Canada Research Award 2001, Lucian Award for Cardiovascular Research 2002, British Cardiac Soc. Paul Wood Silver Medal 2003, IACS Medal of Merit 2011, J. Allyn Taylor Int. Prize in Medicine 2013, Canada Gairdner Wightman Award 2014; inducted into Canadian Medical Hall of Fame 2014. *Publications:* more than 300 papers. *Address:* McMaster University, Faculty of Health Sciences, Hamilton Health Sciences Corporation, 237 Barton Street East, Hamilton, ON L8L 2X2, Canada (office). *Telephone:* (905) 297-3781 (office). *Fax:* (905) 521-1166 (office). *E-mail:* yusufs@ mcmaster.ca (office). *Website:* fhs.mcmaster.ca (office).

YUTHASAK, Gen. Sasiprapha; Thai politician and fmr military officer; *Deputy Prime Minister;* b. 8 Jan. 1937, Bangkok; s. of Lt-Gen. Att Sasiprapha and Jumroon Sasiprapha; m. Khunying Orapan Sasiprapha; three c.; ed St Gabriel's Coll., Chulachomklao, Royal Military Acad., Nat. Defence Coll. of Thailand; served in Royal Thai Army, Maj.-Gen. for Army Reserve Force Students Chief of Staff 1985–90, Lt-Gen. 1990–96, Gen. 1996–; Dir-Gen. for Office of Policy and Planning, Ministry of Defence 1996, Perm. Sec. 1996–98; joined Thai Rak Thai Party, elected as party list MP; Deputy Defence Minister 2001–05, Minister of Defence 2011–12, Deputy Prime Minister 2012–; Pres. Nat. Olympic Cttee; Kt Grand Cross (First Class), Most Exalted Order of the White Elephant 1987, Kt Grand Cordon (Special Class), Most Noble Order of Crown of Thailand 1989, Kt Grand Cordon (Special Class) 1993, Grand Companion (Third Class, Higher Grade), Most Illustrious Order of Chula Chom Klao 1997. *Address:* c/o Office of the Prime Minister, Government House, Thanon Phitsanulok, Dusit, Bangkok 10300, Thailand (office). *Telephone:* (2) 281-4040 (PM office) (office). *Fax:* (2) 282-5131 (PM office) (office). *E-mail:* opm@opm.go.th (office). *Website:* www.opm.go.th (office).

YUZHANOV, Ilya Arturovich, CandEcon; Russian economist, politician and business executive; *Chairman, Polymetal Open Joint Stock Company;* b. 7 Feb. 1960, Leningrad (now St Petersburg); m.; three c.; ed Leningrad State Univ.; teacher, lecturer in Leningrad insts 1982–90; Chief Specialist, Leningrad Cttee on Econ. Reforms 1990–91; Head of Dept, First Deputy Chair. Cttee on Econ. Devt, St Petersburg 1991–94; Chair. Cttee on Land Resources of St Petersburg 1994–97; Chair. State Cttee on Land Resources of Russian Fed. 1997–98; Minister on Land Policy, Construction and Communal Econs May–Sept. 1998; Minister of Antimonopoly Policy and Support for Entrepreneurship 1999–2004; Chair. Supervisory Council NOMOS-Bank 2004–06, mem. Bd Dirs 2006–; Chair. Polymetal Open Jt Stock Co. 2008–; mem. Bd Dirs jt stock cos, including Unified Energy System of Russia 2000–08, NOVATEK 2006–09, Uralkalii 2006–, Kirovsky Zavod 2006–09, Alrosa 2009–; Medal in Commemoration of 850th Anniversary of Founding of Moscow 1997, Merited Economist of Russian Fed. 2000, Best Ind. Dir in Russia 2007. *Publications:* monographs and numerous articles in journals and newspapers on antimonopoly and other problems in econs. *Leisure interest:* sport. *Address:* NOMOS-Bank, Verkhnyaya Radishchevskaya str. 3, Moscow 109240, Russia (office). *Telephone:* (495) 725-32-30 (office). *Fax:* (495) 797-32-50 (office). *E-mail:* yuzhanov_ia@nomos.ru (office). *Website:* www.nomos.ru (office); www .polymetal.ru (office).

YZERMAN, Steve; Canadian sport organization executive and professional ice hockey player (retd); *Vice-President and General Manager, Tampa Bay Lightning Hockey Club;* b. 9 May 1965, Cranbrook, BC; m.; three d.; ed Bell High School, Nepean, Ont.; played Jr hockey with Peterborough Petes of Ont. Hockey League 1981–83; drafted fourth overall in 1983 Nat. Hockey League (NHL) Entry Draft by Detroit Red Wings; named team capt. 1986, longest serving capt. in NHL history; won three Stanley Cup Championships with Red Wings 1997, 1998, 2002; became 11th player to score 600 goals in NHL 1999 (692 career goals); has scored 1,755 career points, finished second in Red Wings history and sixth in NHL history; played for Canada in World Championships 1989, 1990, World Cup 1996, Winter Olympics 1998, 2002 (winner Gold Medal); retd 2006; Vice-Pres. Detroit Red Wings 2006–10; Vice-Pres. and Gen. Man. Tampa Bay Lightning 2010–; Gen. Man. for Hockey Canada at 2007 and 2008 IIHF World Championships, Exec. Dir for Hockey Canada for 2010, 2014 Winter Olympics; Lester B. Pearson Award 1989, Conn Smythe Trophy 1998, Frank J. Seike Trophy 2000, Bill Masterton Memorial Trophy 2003, Lester Patrick Award 2006; named to NHL All-Rookie Team 1984; named to 10 NHL All-Star Games, missing one due to injury 1999, elected to Hockey Hall of Fame 2009. *Address:* Office of the Vice-President and General Manager, Tampa Bay Lightning Hockey Club, St. Pete Times Forum, 401 Channelside Drive, Tampa, FL 33602, USA (home). *Telephone:* (813) 301-6500 (office). *Website:* lightning.nhl.com (office).

Z

ZABLUDOWICZ, Chaim 'Poju'; Finnish business executive and art collector; *Chairman and CEO, Tamares Investment Group;* b. 6 April 1953, Helsinki; s. of Shlomo Zabludowicz; m. Anita Zabludowicz; four c.; ed Svenska Samskolan i Tammerfors (Swedish-speaking school), Tel-Aviv Univ., Israel; raised in Tampere; trained with commercial bank in Frankfurt, Germany before joining Tamares Investment Group, Chair. and CEO 1990–; Chair. BICOM (Britain Israel Communications and Research Centre); mem. Jewish Leadership Council; holds Pocal Industries, Scranton, Pa, USA and br. in Gouldsboro, Pa; other business interests in the Middle East; exhibits pvt. art collection in Chalk Farm, N London 2007; has collected Young British Artists, including works by Tracy Emin; mem. European Advisory Bd of Citigroup, Bd of Dirs GEMS (Asia Pacific pvt. equity fund), Advisory Bd of Stratos Ventures (Finnish-based early stage venture capital fund); Trustee, The Zabludowicz Collection (a leading contemporary art collection); Co-founder (with his wife) Zoo Art Fair. *Address:* Tamares Investment Group, 41 Dover Street, London, W1S 4NS, England (office). *Telephone:* (20) 7629-6636 (office). *Fax:* (20) 7629-4244 (office). *E-mail:* poju@tamares.com (office). *Website:* www.tamares.com (office); www.zabludowiczcollection.com.

ZACHAU, Hans G., Dr rer. nat; German molecular biologist and academic; *Professor Emeritus of Physiological Chemistry, Adolf-Butenandt-Institut der Ludwig-Maximilians-Universität;* b. 16 May 1930, Berlin; s. of Erich Zachau and Gertrud Zachau; m. Elisabeth Vorster 1960; three s.; ed Univs of Frankfurt am Main and Tübingen; Postdoctoral Fellow, MIT and Rockefeller Univ. 1956–58; Max-Planck-Inst. für Biochemie, Munich 1958–61; Inst. für Genetik, Cologne 1961–66; Prof. of Physiological Chemistry and Head of Inst., Univ. of Munich 1967–98, Prof. Emer. 1998–; Chancellor Orden pour le mérite 1992–2006; mem. Deutsche Akad. der Naturforscher Leopoldina, Austrian, Russian and Bavarian Acads, Academia Europaea; Hon. mem. American Soc. of Biological Chemists 1978; Grosses Bundesverdienstkreuz mit Stern 1983, Orden pour le Mérite 1981, Bayerischer Verdienstorden 1989; Richard Kuhn Medaille 1968, Otto Warburg Medaille 1989, Maximiliansorden 1991. *Publications:* numerous publs in professional journals. *Address:* Adolf-Butenandt-Institut der Ludwig-Maximilians-Universität, Molekularbiologie, Schillerstrasse 44, 80336 Munich (office); Pfingstrosenstr. 5a, 81377 Munich, Germany (home). *Telephone:* (89) 218075429 (office); (89) 7147575 (home). *Fax:* (89) 218075425 (office); (89) 74141735 (home). *E-mail:* zachau@med.uni-muenchen.de. *Website:* www.med.uni-muenchen.de/biochemie/zachau (office).

ZACKHEOS, Sotirios, MA; Cypriot diplomatist and business executive; *Executive Director, RCB Bank Limited;* b. 24 Jan. 1950, Nicosia; m.; two c.; ed Univ. of Athens and Stanford Univ., USA; Counsellor Embassy, Moscow 1979–85; Amb. to China (also accred to Japan, Pakistan, The Philippines and Mongolia) 1989–93; Dir of Econ. Affairs, Foreign Ministry 1993, of Political Affairs 1995; Perm. Rep. to UN, Geneva 1996–97, Amb., Perm. Rep. to UN, New York 1997–2003, Perm. Sec. 2003–; Chair. Fourth Cttee (Special Political and Decolonization) 1999; High Commr (non-resident) to St Lucia, Grenada and Trinidad & Tobago 1997–2003; Amb. (non-resident) to Suriname 1997–2003; Perm. Sec., Ministry of Foreign Affairs 2003–07; Pres. European Arab Interactive Forum; Chair. S. Zackheos & Assocs Ltd (consultancy); currently Exec. Dir RCB Bank Ltd; ad hoc special envoy of Pres. of Cyprus to Russia; Vice-Pres. Cyprus GCC Countries Business Asscn; Head of Greek-Cypriot del. for negotiations with the Turkish-Cypriots on the issue of Security and Guarantees 2008–12; Grand Cross, Order of the Phoenix (Greece), Golden Order for Services in Diplomacy (Slovenia); Pancyprian Asscn of Florida Man of the Year Award 2003. *Publications:* Cyprus Diplomacy: A Personal Testimony (in Greek, English and Russian) 2010; contribs to Anthology of Young Cypriot Poets, Justice Pending: Indigenous Peoples and Other Good Causes; numerous articles in Cypriot newspapers. *Address:* Chapo Central, Michalakopoulou Tower, 25 Michalakopoulou Street, Office M203-204, 1075 Nicosia, Cyprus (office). *Telephone:* (22) 818385 (office). *Fax:* (22) 666744 (office). *E-mail:* s.zackheos@cytanet.com.cy (office).

ZACKIOS, Gerald M.; Marshall Islands politician and lawyer; ed Int. Maritime Law Inst.; Senator for Arno –2011; Attorney-Gen. 1995–2001; Minister of Foreign Affairs and Minister in Assistance to the Pres., then Minister of Foreign Affairs 2001–08, also of Trade 2001–07. *Address:* c/o Ministry of Foreign Affairs and Trade, PO Box 1349, Majuro, MH 96960, Marshall Islands.

ZADERNYUK, Andrei Fedorovich; Russian engineer; b. 26 July 1943, Orsk, Orenburg region; ed Krasnoyarsk Polytech. Inst., Gorky (Nizhnii-Novgorod) Lobachevsky State Univ.; metal worker, sr technician Krasnoyarsk-26 1962–66; Sr Technician, Master, Sr Engineer Krasnoyarsk Ore Chem. plant 1966–77; Chief Energy Specialist Production Union of Volga oil pipeline Nizhnii-Novgorod 1977–92; Dir Dept of Power Energy Complex Admin. of Nizhnii-Novgorod region; Vice-Gov. Nizhnii-Novgorod Region 1992–97; Chair. Fed. Energy Comm. of Russian Fed. 1997–2001; Sign of Hon., Order of the Friendship of Peoples; Labour Veteran Medal. *Address:* c/o Federal Energy Commission, Kitaigorodsky pr. 7, 103074 Moscow, Russia (office).

ZADORNOV, Mikhail Mikhailovich, Cand.Econ.; Russian politician and banker; *President and Chair, VTB 24 Bank;* b. 4 May 1963, Moscow; s. of Mikhail Zadornov and Raisa Zadornova; m. Natalya Zadornova 1982; one d.; ed G. Plekhanov Inst. of Nat. Econ.; one of authors Programme of Econ. Reforms 500 Days; mem. State Comm. on Econ. Reform, Russian Council of Ministers 1990–91; mem. State Duma (Parl.) (Yabloko faction) 1993–97, 1999–2003, re-elected as ind. 2003–; Chair., Cttee on Budget, Taxation, Banks and Finances 1994–97; Minister of Finance 1997–99; Special Rep. of Pres. Boris Yeltsin, rank of First Deputy Prime Minister, in negotiations with int. financial orgs 1998–99; Deputy Chair. Cttee on Budget and Taxes, Chair. Sub-Cttee on Monetary Policy, Exchange and Capital Control and the Activities of the Cen. Bank of the Russian Fed. 1999–2003; Pres. and Chairman VTB24 (jt stock bank) 2005–. *Publications:* more than 20 books; numerous articles on Russia's financial problems. *Leisure interest:* playing football. *Address:* VTB24, 101000 Moscow, 35, Ul. Myasnitskaya, Russia. *Telephone:* (495) 777-24-24 (office). *Fax:* (495) 980-46-66 (office). *E-mail:* info@vtb24.ru (office); www.vtb24.ru/en/ (office).

ZAERA-POLO, Alejandro; Spanish architect; *Co-founder and Director, Foreign Office Architects;* b. 17 Oct. 1963, Madrid; m. Farshid Moussavi; ed Escuela Técnica Superior de Arquitectura de Madrid, Harvard Univ. Grad. School of Design, USA; worked at Office for Metropolitan Architecture, Rotterdam 1991–93; moved to work in London, UK 1993; has worked for Rem Koolhaas, Rotterdam, Netherlands, Zaha Hadid, London, Renzo Piano, Genoa Italy; fmr Unit Master at Architectural Asscn School of Architecture; fmr Visiting Critic, UCLA, Columbia Univ., New York, Princeton Univ., School of Architecture, Madrid, Yokohama School of Architecture; co-f. Foreign Office Architects with Farshid Moussavi (q.v.) 1992, later Dir, rep. Britain, Architectura Biennale, Venice 2002, co. dissolved 2011; est. Alejandro Zaera-Polo Architecture (AZPA), London 2011 (renamed Alejandro Zaera-Polo & Maider Llaguno Architecture (AZPML) 2013); holder of Berlage Chair, Delft Univ. for six years; Dean, Berlage Inst. 2002–06, School of Architecture at Princeton Univ. 2012– (Visiting Prof. 2008); first Norman Foster Visiting Prof., Yale Univ. 2009; fmr adviser, Quality Comm. for Architecture, Barcelona, Urban Age Think Tank of the LSE; contrib. El Croquis, Quaderns, A. D.; Enric Miralles Prize for Architecture 2003, Kanagawa Prize for Architecture in Japan 2003, RIBA Int. Award 2004, 2005, 2006, Lion Award for Topography, 9th Venice Architecture Biennale 2004, Charles Jencks Award for Architecture 2005, RIBA European Award 2008, European Business Award for the Environment 2008, Urban Land Inst. Award for Excellence 2008, RIBA Award 2009, Civic Trust Award 2010, Int. Council of Shopping Centres Award 2010, Int. Architecture Award 2010. *Works include:* Foreign Office Architects: Osanbashi Yokohama Int. Passenger Terminal, Japan 1995–2002, Bluemoon Hotel, Groningen, The Netherlands 1999–2000, Police HQ, La Villajoyosa, Spain 2000–03, Coastal park with outdoor auditoriums, Barcelona, Spain 2000–04, HQ for Dulnyouk Publrs, Paju, South Korea 2000–05, Municipal Theatre, Torrevieja, Spain 2000–06, John Lewis dept store and Cineplex and pedestrian bridges, Leicester, UK 2000–08, mixed-use extension of West Quay II retail centre, Southampton 2002–, La Rioja Tech. Transfer Centre, Logrono 2003–07, Trinity EC3 office complex, City of London 2003–, Bamboo Bldg, social housing in Madrid 2004–07, villa in Pedralbes, Barcelona 2004–08, D-38 Office Complex, Barcelona 2004–09, Spanish Pavilion at 2005 Int. Expo, Aichi 2004–05, Meydan Retail Complex and Multiplex, Istanbul 2005–07, Ravensbourne Coll. on the Greenwich Peninsula, London 2005–, Hadspen Gardens, Somerset, UK 2005–, The Palace Residential Towers, Busan, South Korea 2006–11, Museum of Contemporary Art, Cleveland, Ohio 2006–, KL Central Plot D Residential Towers, Kuala Lumpur 2006–, Sevenstone Quarter mixed-use complex, Sheffield, UK 2007–, Euston Station, London 2008–, Birmingham New Street Station 2008–; AZPML: Birmingham New Street Redevelopment, Birmingham 2007–, Gapyong Community Centre, South Korea 2010–, 2014 ISAF Sailing World Championship Facilities, Santander, Spain 2011–, Hosp. Universitari Arnau de Vilanova, Lleida, Spain 2011–, BioPol Science Centre, Barcelona 2011–, Locarno Palazzo del Cinema, Switzerland 2013–. *Publications:* has published extensively as a critic in professional magazines world-wide; work featured in El Croquis, Quaderns, A+U, Arch+, Harvard Design Magazine; contribs to numerous publs. *Address:* AZPML, 55 Curtain Road, London EC2A 3PT, England (office). *Telephone:* (20) 7033-6480 (office). *Fax:* (20) 7033-6481 (office). *E-mail:* lon@azpml.com (office). *Website:* azpml.com (office).

ZAEV, Zoran; Macedonian politician; *Chairman, Social Democratic Alliance of Macedonia;* b. 8 Oct. 1974, Strumica; mem. Social Democratic Union of Macedonia (SDSM) 1996–; Pres. regional admin of the party in Strumica region for two mandates, Deputy Chair. SDSM 2008–13, Chair. 2013–; mem. Macedonian Ass. 2003–05; Mayor of Strumica 2005–; Leader of the Opposition; arrested along with five co-workers for alleged abuse of office and imprisoned July 2008, released by order of Pres. Branko Crvenkovski. *Address:* Social Democratic Alliance of Macedonia (Socijaldemokratski sojuz na Makedonija), 1000 Skopje, Bihakjka 8, Former Yugoslav Republic of Macedonia (office). *Telephone:* (2) 3293100 (office). *Fax:* (2) 3293109 (office). *E-mail:* president@sdsm.org.mk (office). *Website:* www.sdsm.org.mk (office).

ZAFAR, Muhammad Wasi, BA, LLB; Pakistani politician and lawyer; b. 12 Jan. 1949, Punjab; m.; two s. one d.; ed Univ. of Punjab, Lahore; practising lawyer 1972–; Advocate of Dist Court 1972, of High Court 1974, of Supreme Court 1983; Sec., Lahore High Court Bar Asscn 1982–83; mem. Punjab Bar Council 1983–88; elected to Punjab Prov. Ass. 1988, re-elected 1993, mem. of Cabinet and Special Asst to Punjab Chief Minister; elected to Nat. Ass. 2002; Minister of Law, Justice and Human Rights 2004. *Address:* c/o Ministry of Law, Justice and Human Rights, Block S&R, Pakistan Secretariat, Islamabad, Pakistan (office).

ZAGAJEWSKI, Adam, BA, MA; Polish writer, poet and academic; *Ferdinand Schevill Distinguished Service Professor, John U. Nef Committee on Social Thought, University of Chicago;* b. 21 June 1945, Lvov; s. of Tadeusz Zagajewski and Ludwika Zagajewska; m. Maria Zagajewska; ed Jagiellonian Univ., Kraków; first published poetry and essays in literary reviews in 1960s; became known as leading poet of 'Generation of 1968'; first collection of poems 1972; lived in France and joined staff of Zeszyty Literackie 1982–2002; Assoc. Prof. of English, Creative Writing Program, Univ. of Houston, USA 1988–2007; Prof. of Social Thought, Univ. of Chicago 2007, currently Ferdinand Schevill Distinguished Service Prof.; mem. Polish Writers' Asscn, PEN Club; co-ed. Zeszyty Literackie; Dr hc (Jagiellonian Univ.) 2012; Koscielscy Foundation Award 1975, Andrzej Kijowski Award 1987, Alfred Jurzykowski Foundation Award 1989, Guggenheim Fellowship 1992, Int. Vilenica Prize (Slovenia) 1996, Tomas Transtromer Prize (Sweden) 2000, Neustadt Int. Prize for Fiction 2004, Zhongkun Int. Poetry Prize (China) 2013. *Publications include:* collections of poetry: Komunikat (Communique) 1972, Sklepy miesne (Meat Shops) 1975, Letter: An Ode to Multiplicity 1983, Jechac do Lwowa (Travelling to Lvov) 1985, Plotno (The Canvas) 1990, Ziemia ognista (The Fiery Land) 1994, Pragnienie (Desire) 2000, Powrót (Without End) 2003, Anteny 2005, Unseen Hand 2009, Wiersze wybrane 2010; novels: Cieplo, zimno (Warm and Cold) 1975, Cienka kreska (The Thin Line) 1983, Absolute Pitch (in German) 1983; short stories: Two Cities 1991; essays: Swiat nie przedstawiony (The Unpresented World, with Julian Kornhauser) 1974, Drugi oddech (Second Wind) 1978, Solidarnosc i samotnosc (Solidarity and Solitude) 1986, W cudzym pieknie (In the Beauty of Others) 1998, Obrona żarliwości (In Defence of Fervour) 2002, Poeta rozmawia z filozofem 2007. *Leisure interests:* walking, reading. *Address:* John U. Nef Committee on Social Thought, Division of the Social Sciences, University of Chicago, 1130 East 59th Street, Chicago, IL 60637, USA (office). *Telephone:* (773) 702-8410 (office). *E-mail:* adamz@uchicago.edu (office). *Website:* socialthought .uchicago.edu (office).

ZAGALLO, Mário Jorge Lobo; Brazilian professional football manager and fmr professional footballer; b. 9 Aug. 1931, Maceió; inside forward; began footballer career with América FC 1948–49; player for Fluminese, Flamengo 1950–58, Botafogo 1958–65; played for Brazil 1958–64 (33 appearances, five goals), played in World Cup Final 1958, 1962; Man. clubs: Botafogo 1966–70, Fluminense 1971–72, Flamengo 1972–74, 1984–85, 2000–01, Botafogo 1975, 1978–79, 1986–87, Al Hilal 1978–79, Vasco da Gama 1980–81, 1990–91, Bangu 1988–89, Portuguesa 1999–2000; first footballer to attain World Championship as player and then man.; coached Brazilian football team for 1970, 1974 and 1998 World Cups, adviser to nat. coach Brazil 1994–99, 2006; nat. coach Kuwait 1976–78, Saudi Arabia 1981–84, UAE 1989–90; brief return to manage Brazil nat. team for Nov. 2002 friendly against S Korea in Seoul while successor to outgoing man. was sought; FIFA World Cup winning man. 1970, FIFA Confederations Cup winning man. 1997. *Address:* c/o Confederação Brasileira de Futebol, Rua de Alfandega 70 20, 070-001 Rio de Janeiro, Brazil. *E-mail:* comunicacao@cbf.com.br. *Website:* www.cbf .com.br.

ZAGHEN, Paolo, PhD; Brazilian economist and banker; b. Crema, Italy; ed Univ. of São Paulo, Univ. of Calif., Berkeley; Pnr-Dir Lucro DTVM Ltd 1988–91; Open Market Dir Banespa Securities and Exchange Brokers; Financial, Admin. and Public Relations Dir Paranapanema Mining, Industry and Construction 1994–96; Dir Cen. Bank 1996–2000; Pres. Bank of Brazil SA 2000–02 (resgnd). *Address:* c/o Banco do Brasil SA, Setor Bancário Sul, SBS, Quadro 4, Bloco C, Lote 32, 70089-900 Brasília DF, Brazil (office).

ZAGLADIN, Vadim Valentinovich; Russian politician; b. 23 June 1927, Moscow; m. Janetta Rogacheva; one s. three d.; ed Moscow Inst. of Int. Relations; taught at Moscow Inst. of Int. Relations 1949–54; editorial work on various journals 1954–64; editorial post in Prague 1960–64; mem. CPSU 1955–91; mem. Int. Dept, Cen. Cttee of CPSU 1964–67, Deputy Head 1967–82, First Deputy Head 1982–88; mem. Cen. Auditing Cttee 1971–76; cand. mem. Cen. Cttee of CPSU 1976–81, mem. 1981–90; Deputy, Supreme Soviet of USSR and Sec. Foreign Affairs Cttee 1981–89; Chair. Section of Global Problems of Scientific Council of Pres., USSR (now Russian) Acad. of Sciences 1981–; Deputy Chair. Parl. Group of USSR 1981–88; Adviser to fmr Pres. Gorbachev (q.v.) 1988–91; Adviser to Pres. of Int. Foundation for Socio-Econ. and Political Studies (Gorbachev Foundation) 1992–; mem. Russian Acad. of Natural Sciences 1992–; Vice-Pres. Asscn for Euro-Atlantic Co-operation 1991–. *Publications:* over 30 books and numerous articles on political problems. *Address:* Starokonuchenny 26, Apt. 43, 121002 Moscow, Russia. *Telephone:* (495) 241-87-33.

ZAGLER, Wolfgang L., PhD; Austrian scientist, electrical engineer and academic; *Professor, Vienna University of Technology;* b. 1951, Vienna; joined Institut für Industrielle Elektronik und Materialwissenschaften 1976, laid foundation for establishing a perm. ten-person Working Group on Rehabilitation Technology called 'fortec'; currently Prof., Vienna Univ. of Tech. and Head of fortec; Wilhelm Exner Medal, Austrian Asscn for SME (Oesterreichischer Gewerbeverein—OGV) (jtly) 2007. *Achievements include:* carried out research and devt of automatic seam following devices for precision welding equipment using optical pattern recognition; also developed a reading machine for assisting blind and visually impaired persons. *Publications:* Computers and Assistive Technology: ICCHP '98 Proceedings of the XV IFIP World Computer Congress (co-ed.) 1998, Computers Helping People with Special Needs: 10th International Conference, ICCHP 2006, Linz, Austria (Proceedings) 2006, Computers Helping People with Special Needs (with Joachim Klaus, Klaus Miesenberger and Dominique Burger); Strafvollzugsrecht. Österreichisches Recht; numerous papers in professional journals. *Address:* fortec – Rehabilitationstechnik, Favoritenstraße 11/029, 1040 Vienna, Austria (office). *Telephone:* (1) 58801-42900 (office); 664-60588-4290 (mobile). *Fax:* (1) 58801-42999 (office). *E-mail:* zagler@fortec.tuwien .ac.at (office); wolfgang.zagler@tuwien.ac.at (office); zw@fortec.tuwien.ac.at (office). *Website:* www.tuwien.ac.at (office).

ZAHAR, Mahmoud az-; Palestinian physician and government official; b. 1945; m.; four c.; ed Cairo Univ., Ain Shams Univ.; Co-founder, spokesperson, and official Islamic Resistance Movement (Hamas: Harakat al-Muqawama al-Islamiyya); Minister of Foreign Affairs 2006 (resgnd). *Address:* c/o Islamic Resistance Movement (Hamas—Harakat al-Muqawama al-Islamiyya), Gaza, Palestinian Autonomous Areas.

ZAHIR, Ahmed, BA; Maldivian politician and journalist; b. 26 Sept. 1945; m.; one s. two d.; teacher until 1978; journalist for Reuters and Asia Week –1978; fmr Project Officer (Marubeni), Dept of Tourism and Foreign Investment, Asst Dir Tourism Section, then Dir, Dir-Gen. Dept of Tourism; Deputy Minister Ministry of Tourism, Attorney-Gen.'s Office; fmr Minister of Transport and Shipping, of Transport and Communications, of Justice; mem. People's Majlis (Parl.), Deputy Speaker –2004, Speaker 2004–08, chaired numerous standing cttees; mem. Bd of Dirs Maldives Nat. Ship Man. Ltd; mem. Maldives Press Council, Judicial Service Comm. 2008–; fmr Publr and Ed. Hafta weekly newspaper; led three parl. dels including the first Maldivian parl. del. to an int. conf.; Presidential Award for Meritorious Work in Journalism 1980, Golden Pen Award on 50th Anniversary of Maldivian Journalism 1993. *Publication:* A Guide Book on Saudi Arabia. *Address:* c/o People's Majlis Secretariat, Medhuziyaaraiy Magu, Malé 20-080, Maldives.

ZAHIR, Maj.-Gen. Mohamed; Maldivian army officer; m. Fathimath Amira; four s. one d.; ed Hendon Police Coll., London, UK, Naval Postgraduate School, Monterey, Calif., USA, Sr Execs in Nat. and Int. Security Program, John F. Kennedy School of Govt, USA; joined civil service and worked in various Govt Depts before enlisting in Maldives Nat. Defence Force (MNDF—fmrly Nat. Security Service (NSS)) 1978, promoted to rank of Sergeant and commissioned as officer 1980, undertook various command positions within different units of MNDF, Deputy Chief of Staff, MNDF –1996, also commanded MNDF Defence Inst. for Training and Educ. (fmrly known as NSS Training Unit), promoted to rank of

Brig., Chief of Staff, MNDF 1996–2008, promoted to rank of Maj.-Gen. 2004, Chair. MNDF Advisory Council; Nat. Security Adviser to Pres. Mohamed Nasheed 2008–10; Medal for Exceptional Bravery 1988, Presidential Medal, Distinguished Service Medal, Dedicated Service Medal, Medal of Honour 2008. *Address:* c/o Office of the President, Boduthakurufaanu Magu, Malé 20-05, Maldives.

ZAHIR, Umar; Maldivian politician; Minister of Construction and Public Works –2004; Minister of Home Affairs and Environment 2004–05. *Address:* c/o Ministry of Home Affairs and Environment, Huravee Building, 3rd Floor, Ameer Ahmed Magu, Malé, Maldives.

ZAHRA, Trevor; Maltese writer and illustrator; b. 16 Dec. 1947, Zejtun; m. Stella Zahra (deceased); one s. one d.; ed Teachers' Coll. of Educ.; mem. Maltese Acad. of Writers; Council mem. Nat. Book Council; Medal for Services to the Repub. (Malta) in recognition for commitment to children's literature 2004; First Prize, Book Club, Malta 1974, co-winner Rothmas Award 1975, Nat. Literary Award (fourteen times). *Publications include:* Il-Pulena tad-Deheb (adventure story) 1971, Eden (poety) 1972, Il-Ghar tax-Xelter (adventure story) 1972, Dawra Durella (poetry for children) 1972, Dwal fil-Fortizza (adventure story) 1973, Is-Surmast (novel) 1973, Il-Praspar ta' Kuncett u Marinton (humorous short stories) 1974, Il-Kaxxa taz-Ziju (adventure story) 1974), Taht il-Weraq tal-Palm (novel) 1974, Praspar Ohra ta' Kuncett u Marinton (humorous short stories) 1975, Hdejn in-Nixxiegha (novel) 1975, Grajjiet in-Nannu Cens (humorous short stories) 1975), Qamar Ahdar (adventure story) 1976, Villa Siko-Sao 1977, Hmistax-il Numru 1977, Meta Jaqa' c-Cpar 1978, Il-Miraklu tal-Gizirana 1981, It-Tmien Kontinent 1981, Trid Kukkarda Hamra f'Gieh il-Biza'? 1982, Il-Praspar Kollha ta' Kuncett u Marinton 1983, Darba Kien Hemm Sultan 1984, LogHob Merill 1985, Qrempucu f'Belt il-Gobon 1985, Il-Ktieb tal-Fenek l-Ahmar 1986, Holm tal-Milied? 1987, Kliem ix-Xih 1988, Rigal tal-Milied 1989, Stella, Jien u HU 1990, Tlieta f'Wiehed 1994, Is-Surmast 1994, Fuklar Qadim u Bnadar Imcarrta 1995, Is-Seba' Trongiet Mewwija 1995, Hanut tal-Helu 1995, Lubien 1996, Taht Sema Kwiekeb 1997, Naqra Storja Zghra 1997, Sib it-Tezor 1999, Passiggata 1999, Mar id-Dawl 1999, Borma Minestra 1999, Koronata Traskurata 2000, Provenz 2000, Zvelajrin 2001, Mincott Hajt Iswed 2001, X'Tixtiequ Jaghmel il-Fenek? 2002, Din l-Art u Kull ma Fiha 2002, Il-Kotba ghat-Tfal 2002, Kieku Kieku 2005, Sfidi 2005, Kemm Naf Inpingi 2005, Ojnk Ojnk 2005, Krispella 2005, Il-Genn li jzommni f'Sikkti (autobiog.) 2008, Il-Hajja Sigrieta tan-Nanna Genoveffa (novel) 2008, Principessa 2009, Xi Jhobb jiekol id-Dragun 2009, 'Il Boghod mill-Habs 2009, Penumbra (short stories) 2010, Hadd Ma Jista' Jidhak (children's fiction) 2010; numerous translations and workbooks. *Address:* 23 Qrempuc Street, Marsaskala MSK- 2205, Malta. *Telephone:* (356) 21632944. *E-mail:* zahratrevor@gmail.com. *Website:* www.trevorzahra.com.

ZAHRADNÍK, Rudolf, DSc, DipEng; Czech physical chemist and academic; *Honorary President, Academy of Sciences of the Czech Republic;* b. 20 Oct. 1928, Bratislava; s. of Rudolf Zahradník and Jindřiška Zahradníková; m. Milena Zahradníková; one d.; ed Czech Tech. Univ., Prague; scientific worker Inst. of Hygiene and Occupational Diseases, Prague 1952–61, Inst. of Physical Chem. and Electrochem., Acad. of Sciences, Prague 1961–93; Prof., Charles Univ., Prague 1967–; Guest Prof. Univs of Würzburg 1965, Darmstadt 1966, Groningen 1967, Osaka 1977, Basel 1981, Vanderbilt Univ. 1990; Dir Jaroslav Heyrovský Inst. of Physical Chem. and Electrochem. Prague 1990–93; Pres. Czech Acad. of Sciences 1993–2001, Hon. Pres. 2001–; Pres. Czech Learned Soc. 1994–97; mem. many academic and scientific socs including Int. Acad. of Quantum Molecular Sciences 1982–, World Asscn of Theoretical Organic Chemists, European Acad. of Arts, Science and Literature, Ed. Council Special Journals; Hon. mem. Swiss and German Chemical Socs; Cross of Honour (First Class) for Science and Arts (Austria) 1999; Dr hc (Dresden, Fribourg, Pardubice, Georgetown, Prague, Bratislava, Clarkson, Waterloo, Montreal); Jaroslav Heyrovský Golden Plaque Czech Acad. of Sciences 1990, Medal for Merit, Prague 1998. *Publications:* Organic Quantum Chemistry Problems (with P. Cársky) 1973, Elements of Quantum Chemistry (with R. Polák) 1976, Intermolecular Complexes (with P. Hobza) 1988, Thinking as Passion (with Lenka Jaklová) 1998, Rule of Sense 2002, Laboratory Diary 2008. *Leisure interests:* serious music and literature. *Address:* J. Heyrovský Institute of Physical Chemistry of the ASCR, v.v.i., Dolejškova 3, 182 23 Prague 8 (office); Heřmanova 37, 170 00 Prague 7, Czech Republic (home). *Telephone:* (2) 86583029 (office). *Fax:* (2) 33382004 (home). *E-mail:* rudolf.zahradnik@jh-inst.cas .cz (office). *Website:* www.jh-inst.cas.cz (office).

ZAIDI, Syed Nasim Ahmed, PhD, MPA; Indian civil servant; b. 6 July 1952, Dehradun; s. of Aquil Ahmad and Hasnain Ahmad (née Fatima); m. Umm E. Rabab Zaidi; ed Indian Inst. of Finance, John F. Kennedy School of Govt, Harvard Univ., USA; joined Indian Admin. Service (IAS) from UP cadre 1976, first posting as Asst Collector of Unnao district, subsequent posts include Jt Sec. in Civil Aviation Ministry, Commr of Bareilly Devt Authority, Collector of Ghaziabad and Farukkhabad districts in UP, Dir Gen. of Civil Aviation (Perm. Rep. of India on Council of Int. Civil Aviation Org. 2005–08), retd from IAS as Sec. to Govt of India in Ministry of Civil Aviation 2012; Election Commr 2012–; Mason Fellow for Public Policy, Harvard Inst. for Int. Devt. *Publications:* several papers in scientific and admin. journals. *Address:* Election Commission of India, Nirvachan Sadan, Ashoka Road, New Delhi 110 001, India (office). *Telephone:* (11) 23720013 (office); (11) 23717035 (office); (11) 23074243 (home). *Fax:* (11) 23355631 (office). *E-mail:* nasimzaidi@eci.gov.in (office). *Website:* www.eci.nic.in (office).

ZAINUDDIN, Tun Daim, LLB; Malaysian business executive, lawyer and fmr politician; b. 29 April 1938, Alor Star, Kedah State; ed Sultan Abdul Hamid Coll., St Xavier's Inst., Penang, Lincoln's Inn, London, UK; called to the Bar, Lincoln's Inn, London 1959; worked in chambers of Pillai & Co., later in chambers of Shearn Delamore; private legal practice, Kota Bharu, Kelantan 1960–62; joined Malaysian Civil Service as a Magistrate in Johor Baru, Johor 1962–63, Sessions Court Judge, Muar, Johor 1963–64, Deputy Public Prosecutor in Ipoh, Perak 1964–65; returned to Kuala Lumpur and joined law firm of Allen & Gledhill 1965–68; est. own law practice of Daim & Gamany 1968–69; first business venture in salt production 1969, then plastics production, later land and property devt with founding of Syarikat Maluri Sdn Bhd 1971; Owner Indo-Suez (renamed Malaysian-French Bank) 1981, exchanged majority stake for a smaller stake in the larger United Malayan Banking Corpn; Founder-Chair. Int. Commercial Banking Group 2001–; fmr Chair. Peremba, Fleet Holdings, Syarikat Televisyen Malaysia (TV3), Rakyat First Merchant Bankers; Visiting Scholar, Univ. of

California, Berkeley, USA 1977–79, Harvard Inst. of Int. Devt 1991–92; Visiting Fellow, Univ. of Cambridge, UK 2002–03; mem. Dewan Negara (Senate) 1980–82; mem. Dewan Rakat (House of Reps) for Kuala Muda, Kedah 1982–86, for Merbok, Kedah 1986–2004; Minister of Finance 1984–91; Treas. of UMNO 1984, Barisan Nasional 1985; apptd Exec. Dir Nat. Econ. Action Council 1997; Econ. Adviser to Prime Minister Mahathir bin Mohammad; Minister of Finance Jan.–Nov. 1999, Minister of Finance and Minister of Special Functions Dec. 1999–2001; mem. Lembaga Pemegang Amanah Yayasan Pelaburan Bumiputra 1984–91; Chair. Northern Growth Triangle project (IMT-GT) between Thailand, Indonesia and Malaysia and Special Rep. for East Asean Growth (EAGA) between Philippines, Brunei, Indonesia and Malaysia 1992–2000, Labuan Devt Authority 1992–2000, Kumpulan Ladang-Ladang Perbadanan Kedah Sdn Bhd 1997–98, Internal Audit Cttee Asian Football, Kuala Lumpur; apptd Vice-Chair. Malaysian Business Council (Majlis Perdagangan Malaysia) 1991; Jt Chair. Langkawi Devt Authority; Founder-mem. Malaysian Wetlands Foundation 1997–99; mem. Bd of Govs, East-West Center, Hawaii, USA 2002–, mem. East-West Center Audit Cttee, Bd of Trustees, Multimedia Univ., Malaysia, Coca-Cola's Malaysia Advisory Group 2009–; Adjunct Prof., Univ. Utara Malaysia 1991–98; Pro-Chancellor Univ. Sains Malaysia 1994–98; spends most of his time in Africa, engaging African govts on economy and planning; hon. doctorates from local univs; several distinguished awards by local rulers, Highest Distinguished Award, Govt of Repub. of Benin 2006, Int. Business Leader Award, African Investor magazine 2006, Distinguished Assoc., Asia-Europe Inst., Univ. of Malaya 2011. *Publications:* Asian Economic Co-operation Agenda for the 1990's 1990, Managing Business: My Personal Experience 1995, Daim – The Man behind the Enigma 1995, Daim, Insan Di Sebalik Enigma 1996, Daim Speaks His Mind 1996, Daim Yang Diam, Sebuah Biografi 1997, War of Deception: The Facts and Fallacies about the War in Iraq 2004. *Leisure interests:* travelling, reading and writing on general global issue. *Address:* ICB Banking Group, Kuala Lumpur, Malaysia (office). *Telephone:* (3) 6201-6051 (office). *Fax:* (3) 6201-6053 (office). *E-mail:* kugan@icbglobal.com.my (office). *Website:* www.icbankingroup.com (office); daimzainuddin.com.

ZAITSEV, Vyacheslav Mikhailovich (Slava); Russian fashion designer and couturier; *President and Chief Designer, Slava Zaitsev Fashion House;* b. 2 March 1938, Ivanovo; s. of Mikhail Yakovlevich Zaitsev and Maria Ivanovna Zaitseva; one s.; ed Moscow Textile Inst.; chief designer, All-Union Fashion House 1965–78; chief designer, Moscow Fashion House 'Slava Zaitsev' 1982–, Pres. 1991–; participates in Paris fashion shows 1988–; shows collections world-wide; Prof., Moscow Textile Inst.; has exhibited paintings in USA, Belgium, UK and Germany; Pres. Nat. Acad. of Fashion Industry; Academician, Russian Acad. of Arts; Hon. Citizen of Paris 1988, Ivanovo 1996; Order of St Constantine the Great 1996; Order 'For Services to the Fatherland', IVth Degree 1998; Constantine Order of St George 2002; Medal 'For Labour Valour' 1974, 'Badge of Honour' 1980, Medal 'Veteran of Labour' 1987, First Prize, 'Golden Mannequin' for Fashion Week in Moscow 1995, Medal 'For Merits in Development of Design' 2002, Medal 'Professional of Russia' 2004, Nat. Award 'Best of the Best' 2004, Large Silver Medal numbered outstanding figure of world culture of Sergei Diaghilev 2006, Medal 'Professional of Russia' 2006, Best Designer Award (Japan) 1989, Laureate of State Prize of Russian Fed. *Publications:* The Changing Fashion 1980, This Many-Faced World of Fashion 1980. *Leisure interest:* painting. *Address:* Moscow Fashion House, Prospekt Mira 21, 129110 Moscow, Russia (office). *Telephone:* (495) 971-11-22 (office). *Fax:* (495) 281-55-75 (office). *E-mail:* slava@zaitsev.info (office). *Website:* www.zaitsev.info (office).

ZAITSEV, Yury Vladimirovich, DTechSc; Russian engineer and diplomatist; b. 2 Aug. 1933, Moscow; m.; two d.; ed Kuibyshev Moscow Inst. of Construction Eng, Diplomatic Acad. Ministry of Foreign Affairs; Sr researcher Centre for Inst. of Scientific Information on Construction and Architecture, USSR Acad. of Construction and Architecture 1958–59, Research Inst. of Concrete and Reinforced Concrete 1959–64; Prof., Head of Chair., Pro-Rector All-Union Polytechnic Inst. by correspondence 1964–90; Chair. Comm. on Problems of Citizenship at Supreme Soviet, then with Russian Presidency 1990–92; mem. Supreme Soviet of Russian Fed. 1990–93; Perm. Rep. of Russia at int. orgs in Vienna 1992–97; First Deputy Head, Internal Policy Dept of Pres. Yeltsin's Admin 1997–98; mem. Acad. of Tech. Sciences, Acad. of Natural Sciences, Acad. of Eng. *Publications include:* 18 monographs, textbooks, over 200 articles in scientific journals. *Address:* c/o Office of the President, Staraya pl. 4, Moscow 103132, Russia.

ZAKAREISHVILI, Paata; Georgian politician and government official; *State Minister, responsible for Reconciliation and Civic Equality;* b. 4 Aug. 1958, Tbilisi; m.; four c.; ed Kazan State Univ., Russian SFSR, Tbilisi Ecclesiastical Academy and Seminary; Head of Div. of Religious Rights Protection, State Cttee on Human Rights and People-to-People Relations 1992–95; Head of Comm. for Protection of Civilians in Conflict Zone, Missing Persons and Prisoners of War during Georgian–Abkhazian conflict 1992–97; Adviser to Council of Ministers of Autonomous Repub. of Abkhazia on issues of Internally Displaced Persons and Refugees 1995; Forced Migration Project Coordinator, Open Society Foundation, New York 1995–97; Head of Staff, Cttee for Nat. Minority Issues and Human Rights Protection, Parl. of Georgia 1995–2000; Deputy Chair. Penitentiary Dept of Georgia 2000–01; mem. Exec. Bd Open Society Inst.– Georgia 2000–04; mem. Tbilisi Sakrebulo (City Council) 2002–06; Georgian Co-ordinator, California Univ. (Irvine) Georgian–Abkhazian Civil Dialogue project 1995–2012; Georgian Co-ordinator of Conciliation Resources (London), Georgian–Abkhazian projects and Georgian Co-ordinator of the 'Shlaining Process' 1998–2012; Chair. Inst. for Study of Nationalism and Conflict 2009–12; State Minister, responsible for Reintegration 2012–14, for Reconciliation and Civic Equality 2014–. *Address:* Office of the State Minister, responsible for Reconciliation and Civic Equality, 0134 Tbilisi, Ingorokva str. 7, Georgia (office). *Telephone:* (32) 298-92-56 (office). *Fax:* (32) 292-16-50 (office). *E-mail:* press@smr.gov.ge (office). *Website:* www.smr.gov.ge (office).

ZAKARIA, Fareed, BA, PhD; American editor, academic, writer and television presenter; *Editor-at-Large, Time Magazine;* b. India; m. Paula Throckmorton Zakaria; two s. two d.; ed Yale and Harvard Univs; Lecturer on Int. Politics and Econs, Harvard Univ., also Head of Project on the Changing Security Environment; Adjunct Prof., Columbia Univ., New York, Case Western Reserve Univ., Cleveland, OH; Man. Ed. Foreign Affairs journal 1992–2000; Ed. Newsweek Int. 2000–10, columnist, Newsweek (USA); Host and Man. Ed. Foreign Exchange with Fareed Zakaria (PBS Series) 2006–07; political commentator, ABC News 2006–07;

host of Fareed Zakaria GPS, TV show on foreign affairs for CNN 2008–; Ed.-at-Large, Time Magazine 2010–; columnist, Washington Post 2001–; wine columnist for Slate (webzine); mem. Bd Trilateral Comm., IISS, Shakespeare and Co., The Century Asscn; Overseas Press Club Award, Deadline Club Award, Edwin Hood Award, India Abroad Person of the Year 2009, Padma Bhushan 2010. *Publications include:* From Wealth to Power: The Unusual Origins of America's World Role, The American Encounter: The United States and the Making of the Modern World (co-ed.), The Future of Freedom 2003, The Post-American World 2008; contrib. to publs including The New York Times, The New Yorker and The Wall Street Journal. *Address:* CNN, 1 Constitution Avenue, NE, Washington, DC 20002-5618, USA (office). *Website:* globalpublicsquare.blogs.cnn.com (office); www.fareedzakaria.com (office).

ZAKARIYA, Abdul Hameed; Maldivian business executive; Chair. Maldives Industrial Fisheries Co. 2004–06. *Address:* c/o Maldives Industrial Fisheries Co. Ltd, Hilaalee Magu, Maafannu, Malé, Maldives (office).

ZAKAYEV, Akhmed Khalidovich; Russian/Chechen rebel leader; b. 26 April 1956, Kirovskiy, Kazakh SSR, USSR; ed graduated from acting and choreography schools in Voronezh and Moscow; worked as actor at a Grozny theatre, specialized in Shakespearean roles; Chair. Chechen Union of Theatrical Actors 1991; field commdr, Chechen rebel movt 1994–96; 'Minister for Culture', Chechen Repub. of Ichkeriya' 1994; 'Deputy Prime Minister and Special Overseas Envoy' 1997–2002; 'Minister for Foreign Affairs' 1997–2007; 'Prime Minister of Chechen Repub. of Ichkeriya' Nov. 2007–; living with immediate family in exile in London, UK since Jan. 2002, arrested in Poland Sept. 2010, but returned to London.

ZAKHARCHENKO, Nikolai Petrovich; Russian energy industry executive; b. 1934; joined Surgutneftegas 1987, mem. Bd of Dirs 1996–2007, fmr First Deputy Dir-Gen., Chair. 2006–07; adviser to Sibneft. *Address:* c/o OJSC Surgutneftegas, 1 Kukuevitskogo Street, 628400 Surgut, Tyumen, Russia.

ZAKHARCHENKO, Maj. Gen. Vitaliy Yuriyovych; Ukrainian police officer and politician; b. 20 Jan. 1963, Kostyantynivka, Donetsk Oblast; m. Lyudmyla Zakharchenko; two c.; ed Riga br. of Minsk Higher School of Interior of USSR; began career in police of Donetsk Oblast 1981; held leading positions in State Tax Admin in Poltava Oblast 2008–10, Head of State Tax Admin of Ukraine 2010–11; Minister of Internal Affairs 2011–14 (suspended by parl.). *Address:* c/o Ministry of Internal Affairs, 10124 Kyiv, vul. Ak. Bohomoltsya 10, Ukraine. *E-mail:* mail@centrmia.gov.ua.

ZAKHAROV, Aleksander Vladimirovich; Russian business executive; b. 3 Oct. 1955, Moscow; m.; three c.; ed G. Plekhanov Moscow Inst. of Nat. Econs, All-Union Acad. of Foreign Trade; expert, sr consultant USSR Chamber of Industry and Commerce 1976–89; Deputy Rep. USSR Chamber of Industry and Commerce in Bulgaria 1989–91; Deputy Dir Centre on Interbank Currency Accounts USSR State Bank (Gosbank) Sept.–Dec. 1991; Dir Moscow Interbank Currency Exchange 1992–. *Leisure interests:* poetry, football. *Address:* Moscow Interbank Currency Exchange, B. Kislovskiy per. 13, 103009 Moscow, Russia. *Telephone:* (495) 234-48-11 (office). *Fax:* (495) 234-48-46. *Website:* www.micex.com.

ZAKHAROV, Mark Anatolievich; Russian theatre and film director and academic; *Artistic Director, Lenkom Theatre;* b. 13 Oct. 1933, Moscow; m. Nina Lapshinova; one d.; ed Lunacharsky Theatre Inst. (now Russian Acad. of Theatre Arts); actor since 1955; performed at Perm Regional Drama Theatre, Moscow Gogol Theatre; actor and Stage Dir, Moscow Theatre of Miniatures 1960–64, student theatre of Moscow State Univ. 1964–65; Stage Dir Moscow Satire Theatre 1965–73; Artistic Dir Lenkom Theatre (fmrly Moscow Theatre of Leninsky Komsomol) 1973–; teacher, Prof., Russian Acad. of Theatre Arts 1979–; mem. Pres.'s Council 1996–98; participated in making one of the most popular Russian films, The White Sun Over the Desert; People's Artist of the USSR 1988, State Prize of the USSR 1987, State Prizes of Russia 1992, 1997, 2003. *Plays directed include:* The Bankrupt by Alexander Ostrovsky 1967, Til by Grigory Gorin (after Charles de Koster) 1974), Juno and Avos by Andrey Voznesensky and Audrey Rybnikov 1981, Three Girls in Blue by Lyudmila Petrushevskaya 1985, Dictatorship of Conscience by Mikhail Shatrov 1986, The Commemorative Prayer by Grigory Gorin (after Sholom Aleihem) 1989, Wise Man by Alexander Ostrovsky 1989, The Marriage of Figaro by Beaumarchais 1993, The Seagull by Anton Chekhov 1994, Royal Games by Grigory Gorin 1995, Barbarian and Heretic (after Fyodor Dostoyevsky) 1997, The Mistification (after Dead Soles by Nickolay Gogol) 1998, The City of Millionaires by Eduardo de Philippo 2000, The Joker Balakirev by Grigory Gorin 2001, Va-Bank (after The Last Sacrifice by Alexander Ostrovsky) 2004. *Television films directed include:* Ordinary Wonder 1976, That Very Munchhausen 1979, The House That Swift Built 1983, The Formula of Love 1984, To Kill the Dragon 1989. *Film scripts:* author or co-author of scripts written for famous Russian films, includi The Star of Fascinating Happiness, Sannikov's Land. *Publications:* Contacts on Diverse Levels 1988, Super-Profession 2000; more than 100 articles on drama and on politics. *Address:* 6 Malaya Dmitrova str., Moscow, Russia (office). *Telephone:* (495) 699-12-61 (office). *Fax:* (495) 234-99-64 (office). *E-mail:* nimfa@lenkom.ru (office); lenkom1971@mail.ru (office). *Website:* lenkom.ru (office).

ZAKHAROVA, Svetlana; Ukrainian ballet dancer; *Principal Dancer, Bolshoi Ballet;* b. 10 June 1979, Lutsk; trained at Kiev Choreographic School for six years; obtained second prize for performance of Bluebird pas de deux, Int. Young Dancers Competition, St Petersburg 1995; admitted to Vaganova Ballet Acad. 1995–96; joined Mariinsky Ballet, St Petersburg 1996, promoted to soloist 1997, toured world-wide with Kirov in UK, USA, Germany, Austria, The Netherlands, Australia, Japan –2003; Prin. Dancer, Bolshoi Ballet, Moscow 2003–; Golden Mask Award (Best Female Role in Ballet) 1999, 2000, People of Our City Award of St Petersburg (for achievements in ballet) 2001, Honored Artist of Russia 2005, Benois de la Danse Int. Dance Asscn Prize 2005, People's Artist of Russia 2008. *Repertoire includes:* Princess Florentine in The Sleeping Beauty 1996, soloist in Tchaikovsky Pas de Deux 1996, The Dying Swan 1996, Maria in The Fountain of Bakhchisarai 1996, Masha in The Nutcracker 1996, Gulnara in Le Corsaire 1997, title role in Giselle 1997, the Bride in Les Noces 1997, Queen of the Dryads in Don Quixote 1997, Waltz and Mazurka Girl in Chopiniana 1997, friend of Juliet in Romeo and Juliet 1997, Aurora in The Sleeping Beauty 1998, Terpsichore in Apollo 1998, soloist in Serenade 1998, Odette-Odile in Swan Lake 1998, Poem of Ecstasy

1998, 1st Movt in Symphony in C 1999, Medora in Le Corsaire 1999, Nikiya in La Bayadère 1999, Diamonds in Jewels 2000, title role in Manon 2000, Kitri in Don Quixote 2000, soloist in Now and Then 2001, soloist in The Young Lady and The Hooligan 2001, Zobeide in Scheherazade 2001, Juliet in Romeo in Juliet 2002, soloist in Paquita Grand Pas 2003, soloist in Etudes 2003. *Address:* Bolshoi Theatre, 103009 Moscow, 1, Teatralnaya Square, Russia. *E-mail:* mail@svetlana -zakharova.com. *Website:* www.svetlana-zakharova.com; www.bolshoi.ru.

ZAKHILWAL, Muhammad Omar, BA, MA, PhD; Afghan economist, academic and government official; *Minister of Finance;* ed Univ. of Winnipeg, Queen's Univ., Kingston, Carleton Univ., Canada; fmr Prof. of Econs, Carleton Univ., Ottawa, Canada; fmr Sr Research Economist, Statistics Canada; fmr mem. Man. Bd Inst. for Afghan Studies, Ottawa; fmr Chief Policy Adviser, Afghan Ministry of Rural Rehabilitation and Devt; Acting Minister of Transport 2008; fmr Pres. and CEO Afghanistan Investment Support Agency; fmr mem. Supreme Council of da Afghanistan Bank (Afghanistan Cen. Bank); Acting Minister of Finance –2009, Minister of Finance 2010–; teacher of econs, Kabul Univ. *Publications include:* numerous articles and research papers on political, economic and social issues in newspapers and journals. *Address:* Ministry of Finance, Pashtunistan Wat, Kabul, Afghanistan (office). *Telephone:* (20) 2004199 (office). *Fax:* (20) 2103439 (office). *E-mail:* info@mof.gov.af (office). *Website:* www.mof.gov.af (office).

ZAKIS, Juris, DrSc; Latvian solid-state physicist; *Rector, Higher School of Social Technologies;* b. 4 Nov. 1936, Ogre; s. of Roderickh Zakis and Eugenia Zake; m. Anita Zake 1976; three s. two d.; ed Univ. of Latvia, Rīga; Prof., Univ. of Latvia 1978–2000, Prof. Emer. 2000–, Pro-Rector 1984–87, Rector 1987–2000; Pres. Rectors' Council of Latvia 1995–98; USSR People's Deputy 1989–91; mem. Parl. 1995–97; mem. Latvian Acad. of Sciences; Rector Higher School of Social Technologies (STA) 2004–; Latvian State Medal (Order) of Three Stars 2000, Lithuanian State Medal (Order) of Gedimino 2001; Merited Scientist of Latvia 1986, State Emer. Scientist 2002. *Publications:* numerous articles on physics of disordered solids and on higher educ. policy. *Leisure interests:* skiing, linguistics. *Address:* Sociālo Technoloģiju Augstskola, Bezdeligu iela 12, 1048 Riga, Latvia (office). *Telephone:* (2) 2929-9188 (home). *Fax:* (2) 6727-0228 (office). *E-mail:* juris .zakis@apollo.lv (office). *Website:* www.sta-edu.lv (office).

ZALAZNICK, Lauren, BA; American television executive and producer; *Executive Vice-President, NBCUniversal;* m.; three c.; ed Brown Univ.; Pres. Bravo Media, Oxygen Media 2004–08, has exec. responsibility for iVillage, also leads NBC Universal's environmental initiative, Green is Universal, oversaw launch of Bravo's suite of broadband services, including BravoTV.com, OUTzoneTV.com, BrilliantButCancelled.com and TelevisionWithoutPity.com, Pres. NBC Universal Women and Lifestyle Entertainment Networks 2008–10, Chair. Entertainment & Digital Networks and Integrated Media 2011–13, oversaw Bravo Media, Oxygen Media, Style Media, Telemundo Media, mun2, Sprout and TVOne, the digital properties DailyCandy, Fandango, Television Without Pity and iVillage, and the Integrated Strategic Marketing group, Exec. Vice-Pres., NBCUniversal 2013–, continues to oversee Fandango and DailyCandy; mem. NBCUniversal Foundation Bd, Chair. Women At NBCU Advisory Bd; mem. New York City Mayor Michael R. Bloomberg's MediaNYC2020, Brown Univ. Women's Leadership Council, Brown Univ. Creative; Trustee, Corpn of Brown Univ.; named by TIME magazine as one of the TIME 100, The World's Most Influential People 2009, named by Vanity Fair to their New Establishment list, ranked by Fortune magazine amongst the 50 Most Powerful Women in Business in the US (48th) 2009, (46th) 2010, (43rd) 2011, (48th) 2012, named by The Paley Center for Media one of the original 'She's Making Media' honorees 2011, inducted into Broadcasting & Cable Hall of Fame 2012. *Films include:* Sublet (producer) 1991, Poison (actress and assoc. producer) 1991, Swoon (actress, exec. producer and line producer) 1992, Jumpin' at the Boneyard (line producer) 1992, Getting In (aka Student Body) (line producer) 1994, Safe (producer) 1995, Kids (co-producer) 1995, Girls Town (producer) 1996, Zoolander (exec. producer) 2001, Final Cut: The Making and Unmaking of Heaven's Gate (exec. producer) 2004. *Television includes:* Dottie Gets Spanked (producer) 1993, The RuPaul Show (series, exec. producer) 1996, 1996 VH1 Fashion Awards (exec. producer) 1996, 1998 VH1 Fashion Awards (exec. producer) 1998, Random Play (exec. producer, episode 1.2) 1999, 100 Greatest Women of Rock & Roll (exec. producer) 1999, Pop Up Video (series, exec. producer and supervising producer) 2000, Rock of Ages (series, exec. producer) 2000, It's Only Rock 'n' Roll (exec. producer) 2000, Sound Affects (exec. producer) 2000, Animal Trax (series, exec. producer) 2001, Name That Video (series, exec. producer) 2001, Bands on the Run (series, exec. producer) 2001, 100 Greatest Teen Stars (mini-series, exec. producer) 2006. *Address:* NBC Universal, 30 Rockefeller Plaza, New York, NY 10112, USA (office). *Telephone:* (212) 664-4444 (office). *Fax:* (212) 664-4085 (office). *E-mail:* info@nbcuni.com (office). *Website:* www.nbcuni.com (office).

ZALM, Gerrit; Dutch economist, politician, international organization official and business executive; b. 6 May 1952, Enkhuizen; ed Amsterdam Free Univ.; mem. staff, Econs Affairs section, Budget Preparation Div., Ministry of Finance 1975, Head of Section 1977, Head of Div. 1978, Head of Cen. Review Secr. 1980, Deputy Dir for Budgetary Affairs and Head of Budget Preparation Div. 1981; Deputy Dir for Gen. Econs Policy, Ministry of Econ. Affairs 1983–85, Dir 1985–88 (also mem. Econ. Policy Cttee of EC); Deputy Dir Cen. Planning Bureau 1988–89, Dir 1989 (also mem. Council for Econ. Affairs, Socio-Econs Council, Bd Cen. Econs Comm., Cen. Statistics Comm., Budgetary Margins Study Group and Advisory mem. Advisory Council on Govt Policy); Prof. of Econs Policy, Amsterdam Free Univ. 1990; mem. Parl. and Chair. People's Party for Freedom and Democracy (VVD) Parl. Group 2002–03; Minister of Finance 1994–2003, Minister of Finance and Deputy Prime Minister 2003–07; Sr Advisor, Permira 2007–08; Chief Economist DSB Bank NV June 2007–08; Chief Financial Officer Dec. 2007–08; Chair. of Trustees, Int. Accounting Standards Cttee Foundation 2008; CEO of bank resulting from merger of Dutch state-owned ABN Amro and Fortis Netherlands 2009–. *Address:* c/o International Accounting Standards Committee Foundation, 30 Cannon Street, London, EC4M 6XH, England.

ZAMA, Francis; Solomon Islands politician; b. 3 July 1956, Hopongo Village, Rendova Island; fmrly with Solomon Islands Cen. Bank; fmr Prin. Tax Inspector, Ministry of Finance; MP for South New Georgia/Rendova/Tetepare, Western Province constituency 2001–; Minister of Finance and Treasury 2003–06, of Educ. March–July 2003, Nov.–Dec. 2007, of Justice and Legal Affairs Oct.–Nov. 2007;

Chair. Public Accounts Comm., Ministry of Finance, Nat. Reform and Planning 2007; mem. People's Alliance Party. *Address:* c/o National Parliament of Solomon Islands, PO Box G19, Vavaya Ridge, Honiara, Solomon Islands (office). *Telephone:* 23424 (office). *Fax:* 24272 (office). *E-mail:* www.parliament.gov.sb (office).

ZAMACHOWSKI, Zbigniew; Polish actor; b. 17 July 1961, Brzeziny; m. 1st Anna Komornicka (divorced); two s. two d.; m. 2nd Aleksandra Justa (divorced 2012); partner Monika Richardson; ed State Higher Film, TV and Theatre School, Łódź; performed at The Studio Theatre 1985–97; actor at National Theatre, Warsaw 1997–; best known as the voice of Shrek in the Polish version of Shrek (series); Aleksander Zelwerowicz Award 1993, Gdańsk Film Festival Prize for Best Actor, in Zawrócony 1994, Felix European Film Award, Wiktor Prize 1992, 1993, 1997. *Theatre includes:* Płatonow 1992, Amadeus 1993, Wujaszek Wania 1993, Don Juan 1996, Ildefonsjada 1996, Za i przeciw (Taking Sides) 1997, Ślub 1998, Kartoteka (The Card Index) 1999, Wesele (The Wedding) 2000, A Midsummer Night's Dream 2000. *Films:* Wielka majówka 1981, Pierscien i róza 1987, Matka Królów 1987, Ucieczka 1987, Prywatne sledztwo 1987, Les possédés 1988, Zabij mnie, glino 1988, Niezwykla podróz Baltazara Kobera 1988, Sztuka kochania 1989, Bal na dworcu w Koluszkach 1990, Korczak 1990, Ucieczka z kina 'Wolnosc' 1990, Seszele 1991, 30 Door Key 1991, Three Colours: Blue 1993, Tak tak 1993, Naprawde krotki film o milosci, zabijaniu i jeszcze jednym przykazaniu 1993, Straszny sen Dzidziusia Górkiewicza 1994, Three Colours: White 1994, Three Colours: Red 1994, Pestka 1995, Pulkownik Kwiatkowski 1995, Odwiedz mnie we snie 1996, Taranthriller 1997, Szczesliwego Nowego Jorku 1997, Pulapka 1997, Demony wojny wedlug Goi 1998, Love Me and Do Whatever You Want 1998, Darmozjad polski 1998, 23 1998, With Fire and Sword 1999, Pierwszy milion 2000, Prymas – trzy lata z tysiaca 2000, Cabin Fever 2000, Proof of Life 2000, Weiser 2001, Lightmaker 2001, Hi, Tereska 2001, Station 2001, The Hexer 2001, The Pianist 2002, Squint Your Eyes 2002, Distant Lights 2003, The Birch-Tree Meadow 2003, Cialo 2003, Zhoorek 2003, Zróbmy sobie wnuka 2003, Skazany na bluesa 2005, Czas surferów 2005, Diabel (short) 2005, The Call of the Toad 2005, Dublerzy 2006, Nadzieja 2007, The Ballad of Piotrowski 2007, Janek (short) 2008, The Offsiders 2008, Luxury (short) 2008, Popieluszko. Wolnosc jest w nas 2009, Operation Dunaj 2009, Within the Whirlwind 2009, Fundacja Kultura (The Foundation) (short) 2009, Esterhazy (short) (voice) 2009, Randka w ciemno 2010, Projekt dziecko, czyli ojciec potrzebny od zaraz 2010, Objects in Mirror are Closer Than They Appear (short) 2010, Father, Son & Holy Cow 2011, Aftermath 2012, Stacja Warszawa 2013, Walesa: Man of Hope 2013, Gabriel 2013, Lauf Junge lauf 2013, Jack Strong 2014. *Television:* Rycerze i rabusie (series) 1984, Zmiennicy (series) 1986, Ludozerca (short) 1987, Boczny tor (film) 1988, Zad wielkiego wieloryba (film) 1988, Dekalog: The Ten Commandments (mini-series) 1989, Sauna (film) 1992, Le clandestin (film) 1994, Reverted (film) 1994, Slawa i chwala (mini-series) 1998, 13 posterunek (series) 1998, Sto minut wakacji (film) 2001, Wiedzmin (mini-series) 2002, Inferno Below (film) 2003, Rodzinka (series) 2004, Niania (series) 2006, Przybyli ulani (film) 2006, Kryptonim Gracz (film) 2008, Naznaczony (series) 2009, Czarnobyl. Cztery Dni W Kwietniu (film) 2011, Do Dzwonka Cafe (series) 2012. *Address:* c/o Agata Domagata, ul. F. Schillera 6 m.12, 00-248 Warsaw, Poland. *Telephone:* (48) 501094390. *E-mail:* agat8@idea.net.pl.

ZAMAGNI, Stefano; Italian economist; *Professor of Economics, University of Bologna;* b. 4 Jan. 1943, Rimini; m. Vera Negri 1968; two d.; ed Univ. of Milan, Univ. of Oxford, UK; Assoc. Dir and Adjunct Prof., Bologna Center, Johns Hopkins Univ. 1977–; Prof. of Econs, Univ. of Bologna 1985–, Chair. Dept of Econs 1985–88, 1991–94, Dean Faculty of Econs 1994–96, Co-ordinator PhD Programme in Econs 1989–93; Pres. Int. Catholic Migration Comm., Geneva 1999–; Vice-Pres. Italian Econ. Asscn 1989–92, State Vic. Bank Visiting Prof., Deakin Univ., Geelong, Australia; McDonnell Visiting Scholar, Wider, Helsinki, Finland; Co-Ed. Economia Politica (quarterly) 1983–, Italian Economic Papers 1990–, Journal of International and Comparative Economics, Ricerche Economiche; mem. Exec. Cttee Int. Econ. Asscn 1989–, Pontifical Council on Justice and Peace 1992–, Scientific Cttee, J. Maritain Int. Inst. 1995–, Bd of Dirs UNIBANCA 1999–, Scientific Cttee, Rosselli Foundation, Turin, Bd of Dirs Hosp. Bambino Gesù, Rome 2000–; pres. not-for profit governmental agency 2007–12; mem. Acad. of Sciences; Paul Harris Fellow, Rotary International 1995; Hon. Citizen of Rosario and Mar del Plata, Argentina; Kt, Order of St Gregory the Great (Holy See); Hon. DEcon (Univ. F. de Vicoria, Madrid); Accad. Lincei Award, St Vincent Prize in Econs, Capri Prize in Econs 1995, Golden Sigismondo Prize 1997, Gold Medal, Pio Manzu Int. Centre 1998, Gold Medal, Cooperative Credit 2005. *Publications:* Microeconomic Theory 1987, The Economic Theories of Production 1989, History of Economic Thought 1991, Value and Capital—Fifty Years Later (with L. McKenzie) 1991, Firms and Markets 1991, Man – Environment and Development: Toward a Global Approach 1991, The Economics of Crime and Illegal Markets 1993, The Economics of Altruism 1995, An Evolutionary Dynamic Approach to Altruism 1996, Technological Change: Time-Use Policies and Employment 1996, Globalization as Specificity of Post-Industrial Economy 1997, Civil Economy and Paradoxes of Growth in Post-Fordist Societies 1997, Civil Economy, Cultural Evolution and Participatory Development 1999, The Economics of Corruption and Illegal Markets (co-author) 1999, Financial Globalization and the Emerging Economies (co-author) 2000, Time in Economic Theory (with E. Agliardi) 2004, Toward a New Economic Theory of Cooperative Firm 2005, Economic Theory and Interpersonal Relations (with P. Sacco) 2006, Civil Economy (with L. Bruni) 2007, Markets, Money and History (co-ed. with Scazzieri and Sen) 2008, Avarice – The Passion of Having 2009, The Cooperative Enterprise (with Vera Zamagni) 2010, The Economics of Common Good 2010, Family and Work 2012, Handbook on the Economics of Reciprocity and Social Enterprises 2013. *Leisure interests:* sports, theatre, classical music. *Address:* Department of Economics, University of Bologna, Piazza Scaravilli 2, 40126 Bologna, Italy (office). *Telephone:* (051) 2098665 (office). *Fax:* (051) 2098040 (office). *E-mail:* bruna.bordoni@unibo.it (office); stefano.zamagni@unibo.it (home).

ZAMBELLO, Francesca, BA; American opera and theatre director; *Artistic Director, Washington National Opera;* b. 24 Aug. 1956, New York; d. of Charles Carmine and Jean Sincere Zambello; ed American School of Paris, Moscow Univ., Colgate Univ.; Asst Dir, Lyric Opera of Chicago 1981–82, San Francisco Opera 1983–84, later Artistic Adviser; Artistic Dir, Skylight Music Theatre 1984–91; Gen. and Artistic Dir, Glimmerglass Opera, New York 2010–; fmr Artistic Adviser, Washington Nat. Opera, Artistic Dir 2013–; guest producer, Met, Chicago Lyric

Opera, La Scala, ROH, Paris Opera, San Francisco Opera, Teatro La Fenice, Savonlinna Festival, Houston Grand Opera, Nat. Opera of Iceland, Seattle Opera, San Diego Opera, Opera Theatre of St Louis, Rome Opera, Théâtre Municipal de Lausanne, Teatro Regio, Greater Miami Opera, Pesaro Festival, Parma and Wexford Festival; has worked on theatre productions in London's West End and New York's Broadway; fmr Visiting Prof., Harvard Univ., Univ. of Calif., Berkeley; Dr hc (Colgate Univ.); Chevalier des Arts et des Lettres; Medal for Service to Culture, Russian Fed.; three Olivier Awards from London Soc. of Theatres and two Evening Standard Awards for Best Musical and Best Opera. *Works directed include:* The Makropolous Case (Skylight Opera Theater) 1984, Albert Herring (Savonlinna Opera Festival, Finland) 1984, Fidelio (Houston Grand Opera) 1984, (Washington Opera) 2003, The Mikado (Nat. Opera of Iceland) 1985, Tosca (Nat. Opera of Puerto Rico) 1985, 1986, (Earl's Court Arena, London) 1991, Carmen (Texas Opera Theater) 1986, (Skylight Opera Theater) 1988, (ROH) 2006, 2010, The Barber of Seville (Nat. Opera of Iceland 1986, (Santa Fe Opera) 1994, Faust (Houston Grand Opera) 1986, (San Francisco Opera) 1987, (Seattle Opera and San Diego Opera) 1988, Beatrice di Tenda (Teatro La Fenice, Venice) 1987, L'Elisir d'Amore (Teatro Regio, Parma) 1988, 1992, The Devil and Kate (Wexford Festival) 1988, Salome (Houston Grand Opera) 1988, (Lyric Opera of Chicago) 2006, Don Giovanni (New Israeli Opera, Tel-Aviv) 1988, (ROH) 2002, 2003, La Bohème (San Francisco Opera) 1988, (Teatro Regio, Parma) 1991, (Royal Albert Hall) 2004, 2006, Idomeneo (Chicago Early Music Opera) 1989, Rigoletto (San Francisco Opera) 1989, War and Peace (Seattle Goodwill Festival) 1990, (Opéra Nat. de Paris) 2000, 2005, La Traviata (Skylight Opera Theater) 1990, (Roman Arena of the Orange Festival, France) 1993, (Bordeaux Opera) 1997, Les Troyens (Los Angeles Music Center Opera) 1991, (Met) 2003, Lucia di Lammermoor (Dublin Grand Opera) 1991, (Met) 1992, The Sorrows of Young Werther (Santa Fe Opera) 1992, Il Pirata (Zurich Opera) 1992, (Théâtre Municipal de Lausanne) 1993, Romulus Hunt (Met) 1993, Falstaff (Göteborg Opera, Sweden) 1993, The Midsummer Marriage (New York City Opera) 1993, Cherevichki (Wexford Festival) 1993, Orphée (American Repertory Theater, Harvard) 1993, Jenůfa (San Francisco Opera) 2001, (Dallas Opera) 1993, 2004, Khovanshchina (ENO) 1994, 2003, Blond Eckbert (Santa Fe Opera) 1994, Billy Budd (Grand Théâtre de Genève) 1994, (ROH) 1995, (Opéra Nat. de Paris) 1996, 2001, (Washington Opera and Teatro Regio, Parma) 2004, Street Scene (Houston Grand Opera) 1994, (Theater des Westens) 1995, Arianna (ROH) 1995, Tannhäuser (Royal Danish Opera, Copenhagen) 1995, Die Meistersinger von Nürnberg (Royal Danish Opera, Copenhagen) 1996, The Tales of Hoffmann (Staat Theater, Aalto) 1996, Emmeline (Santa Fe Opera) 1996, (New York City Opera) 1998, Paul Bunyan (Aldeburgh Festival) 1997, (ROH) 1999, Turandot (Opéra Nat. de Paris) 1997, 1999, Iphigénie en Tauride (Glimmerglass Opera) 1997, The Bartered Bride (ROH) 1998, 2001, Boris Godunov (ENO) 1998, (Canadian Opera Co.) 2002, (Paris Opera) 2005, Dialogues des Carmélites (Saito Kinen Festival, Japan) 1998, (Santa Fe Opera and Opéra Nat. de Paris) 1999, (Opéra Nat. de Paris) 2004, Tristan and Isolde (Seattle Opera) 1998, The Flying Dutchman (Bordeaux Opera) 1998, 2002, Madama Butterfly (Grand Théâtre de Genève) 1998, (Pittsburgh Opera) 2002, (San Diego Opera) 2003, (Houston Grand Opera) 2004, Aida (Grand Théâtre de Genève) 1999, Otello (Bayerisches Staatsoper) 1999, Peter Grimes (Netherlands Opera, Amsterdam) 2000, 2004, Luisa Miller (San Francisco Opera) 2000, (Dallas Opera) 2005, Thérèse Raquin (Dallas Opera) 2001, (L'Opéra de Montréal) 2002, (San Diego Opera) 2003, Of Mice and Men (Bregenz Festival and Washington Opera) 2001, (Houston Grand Opera) 2002, The Queen of Spades (ROH) 2001, Florencia en el Amazons (Houston Grand Opera) 2001, (Seattle Opera) 2005, Lady Macbeth of Mtsensk (Opera Australia) 2002, Die Walküre (Washington Opera) 2003, Alcina (New York City Opera) 2003, West Side Story (Bregenz Festival) 2003, 2004, The Little Prince (Houston Grand Opera) 2003, (Skylight Music Theater) 2004, (Boston Lyric Opera and New York City Opera) 2005, Queen of Spades (Grand Théâtre de Genève) 2003, (ROH) 2006, Guillaume Tell (Opéra Nat. de Paris) 2003, Fiery Angel (Bolshoi Theater) 2004, Der fliegende Holländer (Lithuanian Opera, Vilnius) 2004, Tibet Through the Red Box (Seattle Children's Theater) 2004, An American Tragedy (Met) 2005, Porgy and Bess (Washington Opera) 2005, Cyrano de Bergerac (Met) 2005, (ROH and Met) 2006, The Love for Three Oranges (Opera Australia) 2005, Das Rheingold (Washington Opera) 2006, Carmen (ROH) 2009, 2013, The Little Mermaid (Broadway), Little House on the Prairie (Guthrie), First Wives Club (Old Globe), Cyrano (La Scala), Die Walküre (San Francisco) 2011, Don Giovanni (ROH) 2012, Otello (Munich) 2012, Les Troyens (Met) 2012–13, Show Boat (Washington) 2013. *Leisure interests:* skiing, tennis, hiking. *Address:* c/o Caroline Woodfield, Opus Artists Ltd, 470 Park Avenue South, 9th Floor North, New York, NY 10016, USA (office); 257 West 52nd Street, 4th floor, New York, NY 10019, USA (office). *Telephone:* (212) 584-7580 (office); (646) 736-2900 (office). *Fax:* (646) 300-8280 (office). *E-mail:* cwoodfield@opus3artists.com (office); francesca@francescazambello.com (office); fzambello@mac.com (home); Jtantleff@paradigmagency.com (office). *Website:* www.opus3artists.com (office); www.francescazambello.com.

ZAMBRANO, Lorenzo H., BS, MBA; Mexican business executive; *Chairman and CEO, CEMEX SAB de CV;* ed Tecnológico de Monterrey, Stanford Univ., USA; joined CEMEX 1968, CEO 1985–, Chair. 1995–; Chair. Tecnológico de Monterrey 1997–2012; mem. Bd of Dirs IBM; mem. Int. Advisory Bd Citigroup; Stanford Grad. School Ernest Arbuckle Award 1998; Woodrow Wilson Award for Corporate Citizenship 2005, Americas Soc. Gold Medal for Distinguished Service 2005. *Address:* CEMEX SAB de CV, Avenida Ricardo Margáin Zozaya 325, Colonia Valle del Campestre, San Pedro Garza García 66265, Nuevo León, Mexico (office). *Telephone:* (81) 8888-8888 (office). *Fax:* (81) 8888-4417 (office). *E-mail:* info@cemex.com (office). *Website:* www.cemex.com (office).

ZAMFIR, Gheorghe; Romanian musician (pan-pipes); b. 6 April 1941, Găeşti, nr Bucharest; m. Marie-Noele Zamfir; ed self-taught and Bucharest Acad. of Music (studied under Fănică Luca); graduated in conducting at Ciprian Porumbescu Conservatory, Bucharest 1968; toured numerous countries in Europe as student and won first prize in many int. competitions; conductor of 'Ciocîrlia' Folk Ensemble in Bucharest 1969; Prof. of Pan-Pipes 1970; formed own orchestra 1970; numerous trips to Europe, Australia, S America, Canada and USA. *Recordings include:* Hora Romanilor & Tiganiada, Magic of the Panpipe, Legenda Romaneasca (muzica populara), Casa de discuri Media services, Romania, Gheorghe Zamfir en France (CD of popular music), Les Années 70, Mes Plus Belles Doina,

Pan d'Amour – Kiss From a Rose, Recording with Gheorghe Zamfir – Archive, Music by Candlelight 1983, Romance 1984, Harmony 1987, The Lonely Shepherd 1988, A Return To Romance 1988, Doina din Arges 1990, Christmas at Notre Dame Basilica 1992, Panflute & Organ 1995, Harmony – Zauber der Panflöte (Beliebte Melodien) 1997, Magic of the Panpipes 2001, Like a Breeze 2008, Spirit of the Andes 2008. *Address:* Postfach 202364, 20216 Hamburg, Germany (office). *Telephone:* (40) 4800808 (office). *Fax:* (40) 484443 (office). *E-mail:* info@gheorghe-zamfir.com (office). *Website:* www.gheorghe-zamfir.com.

ZAMMIT DIMECH, Hon. Francis, MA, LLD; Maltese politician and lawyer; b. 23 Oct. 1954, St Julian's; s. of George Zammit and Anne Dimech; ed St Aloysius Coll. and Univ. of Malta; called to the Bar 1980; Pres. Students' Rep. Council of Univ. 1978–79; Vice-Pres. Democratic Youth Community of Europe 1981–83; Nationalist Party MP 1987–, Chair. Legislation Cttee 2008–10, Foreign and European Affairs 2010–12; Minister of Foreign Affairs Nov. 2012–March 2013; mem. Maltese Parl. Del. to Parl. Ass. of Council of Europe 1987–92; Parl. Sec., later Minister for Transport and Communications 1990–92, 1992–94; Minister for the Environment 1994–96, 1998–2002; Shadow Minister and Opposition Spokesman on Public Works and Environment 1996–98; Pres. Exec. Council Nationalist Party 1997–99; Minister for Resources and Infrastructure 2002–03, for Tourism 2003–04, for Tourism and Culture 2004–08; Chair. Editorial Bd Zaghzugh 1986–87; Ed. Il-Poplu Magazine 1988–90. *Publications include:* Poll of '76 1980, The Untruth Game 1986, Eddie – The People's Choice 1987. *Leisure interests:* reading, broadcasting, theatre, swimming. *Address:* 7 St Julian's Hill, St Julian's, STJ 1342, Malta (home). *Telephone:* 21313501 (home). *E-mail:* francis@fzdadvocates.com (office). *Website:* www.fzdadvocates.com (office).

ZANATI, Zanati Muhammad az-; Libyan government official; Sec. of Gen. People's Congress (Mutamar Al Sha'ab Al Aam), Tripoli 1992–2008. *Address:* c/o General People's Congress (Qaat Ach. Chaab), PO Box 2554, Tripoli, Libya (office).

ZANDANSHATAR, Gombojav, MA; Mongolian politician; *Minister of External Relations;* b. 6 March 1970, Baatsagaan sum, Bayankhongor Prov.; m.; two c.; ed State People's Econs Inst., Russia, Maastricht Univ., Netherlands; mem. research staff, Coll. of Market Study 1992–93, Lecturer 1993–95; Expert Economist, Bank of Agric. 1995–96, Head of Foreign Relations and Co-operation Dept 1996–98, Man. 1998–99; Man., Training Center, Bank of Mongolia 1999, Bank of Mongolia Rep. to Bank of Agric. 1999–2000, Deputy Dir Bank of Agric. 2000–03; Vice Minister, Ministry of Agric. 2003–04; mem. Mongolian Great Khural (Parl.) 2004–; Minister of External Relations 2009–. *Address:* Ministry of External Relations, Enkh Taivny Örgön Chölöö 7a, Sükhbaatar District, Ulan Bator, Mongolia (office). *Telephone:* (11) 262788 (office). *Fax:* (11) 322127 (office). *E-mail:* mongmer@magicnet.mn (office). *Website:* www.mfat.gov.mn (office).

ZANDER, Edward J., BS, MBA; American engineer and telecommunications industry executive; b. 12 Jan. 1947, Brooklyn, New York; m. Mona Zander; two c.; ed Rensselaer Polytechnic Inst., Boston Univ.; engineer with Raytheon Co. 1968–73; Sr Man. Data Gen. 1973–82; fmr Sr Man. Apollo Computer Co.; joined Sun Microsystems 1987, later becoming Pres. and COO –2002; Man. Dir Silver Lake Pnrs (private equity firm) 2002–03; CEO Motorola Inc. 2004–07, Chair. 2004–08; mem. Bd of Dirs Eagleview Technologies 2008–, Seagate Tech. 2002–04, Time Warner 2007; mem. Science Advisory Bd, Rensselaer Polytechnic Inst., Advisory Bd, Boston Univ. School of Man.; mem. Econs Club Chicago, Exec. Club Chicago, Commercial Club Chicago. *Address:* c/o Board of Directors, EagleView Technologies, 2525 220th St SE, Suite 203, Bothell, WA 98021, USA.

ZANDER, Michael, QC, FBA; British legal scholar and academic; *Professor Emeritus of Law, London School of Economics;* b. 16 Nov. 1932, Berlin, Germany; s. of Walter Zander and Margaret Zander; m. Elizabeth Treeger 1965; one s. one d.; ed Royal Grammar School, High Wycombe, Jesus Coll. Cambridge and Harvard Law School; Sullivan & Cromwell, New York 1958–59; admitted solicitor of Supreme Court 1962; Asst Lecturer, LSE 1963, Lecturer 1965, Sr Lecturer 1970, Reader 1970, Prof. of Law 1977–98, Prof. Emer. 1998–, also mem. of Staff Manheim Centre for Criminology; Convenor (Head) 1984–88, 1997–98; Legal Corresp., The (Manchester) Guardian 1963–88; mem. Royal Comm. on Criminal Justice 1991–93, Home Office's PACE Strategy Bd 2007–; Hon. LLD (King's Coll. London) 2010. *Publications:* Lawyers and the Public Interest 1968, Cases and Materials on the English Legal System 1972, 2007, A Bill of Rights 1975, 1997, Legal Services for the Community 1978, The Law-Making Process 1980, 2004, The Police and Criminal Evidence Act 1984, 1995, 2005, A Matter of Justice 1989, The State of Justice 2000. *Leisure interests:* swimming (daily), the cello (not daily). *Address:* 12 Woodside Avenue, London, N6 4SS, England (home). *Telephone:* (20) 8883-6257 (home). *E-mail:* mandbzander@btinternet.com (home). *Website:* www.lse.ac.uk/collections/mannheim (office).

ZANE, Billy; American actor; b. 24 Feb. 1966, Chicago, Ill.; s. of William Zane Sr; m. Lisa Collins 1988 (divorced 1995); ed American School, Switzerland; moved to Hollywood 1984; stage appearances in American Music, New York, The Boys in the Backroom (Actors' Gang, Chicago). *Films:* Back to the Future 1985, Critters 1986, Dead Calm 1989, Back to the Future Part II 1989, Megaville 1990, Memphis Belle 1990, Blood and Concrete: A Love Story 1991, Millions, Femme Fatale 1991, Posse 1993, Orlando 1993, Sniper 1993, Flashfire, Tombstone 1993, The Silence of the Hams 1994, Cyborg Agent, Only You 1994, Tales from the Crypt Presents: Demon Knight 1995, Reflections in the Dark, Danger Zone 1995, The Phantom 1996, This World – Then the Fireworks 1996, Head Above Water 1996, Titanic 1998, Taxman 1999, Morgan's Ferry 1999, Cleopatra 1999, Hendrix 2000, Invincible 2001, The Diamond of Jeru 2001, The Believer 2001, Sea Devils 2002, Vlad 2003, Imaginary Grace 2003, Silver City 2004, Three 2004, Dead Fish 2004, Big Kiss 2004, The Pleasure Drivers 2005, The Last Drop 2005, BloodRayne 2005, Mem-o-re 2005, Kurtlar vadisi: Irak 2006, Three 2006. *Television:* (series) Twin Peaks, Cleopatra; (films) Brotherhood of Justice, The Case of the Hillside Stranglers 1989, Lake Consequence, Running Delilah, The Set Up. *Address:* Creative Artists Agency, 9830 Wilshire Boulevard, Beverly Hills, CA 90212, USA (office).

ZANGANEH, Bijam Namdar, MSc; Iranian civil engineer and politician; *Minister of Petroleum;* b. 1953, Kermanshah; ed Univ. of Tehran; fmr Lecturer, Dept of Eng, Khajeh Nasir Toosi Univ. of Tech.; Deputy Minister of Culture and Islamic Guidance 1980, Minister of Agric. 1983–88, of Energy 1988–97, of Petroleum 1997–2005, 2013–; fmr Chair. Heavy Equipment Production Co.; mem.

Expediency Council 1996. *Address:* Ministry of Petroleum, Hafez Crossing, Taleghani Avenue, Tehran 15936-57919, Iran (office). *Telephone:* (21) 66152606 (office). *Fax:* (21) 66154977 (office). *E-mail:* public-relations@nioc.ir (office). *Website:* www.mop.ir (office).

ZANGPO, Jigme; Bhutanese politician; *Speaker, National Assembly;* mem. Nat. Ass. from Monggar, Speaker 2013–. *Address:* Tshogdu Chenmo Secretariat, Gyelyong Tshokhang, PO Box 139, Thimphu, Bhutan (office). *Telephone:* (2) 322729 (office). *Fax:* (2) 324210 (office). *E-mail:* sdhendup@nab.gov.bt (office). *Website:* www.nab.gov.bt (office).

ZANINI, Marco; Italian fashion designer; *Creative Director, Halston;* began career as First Asst at Lawrence Steele; fmr First Asst to Domenico Dolce at Dolce & Gabbana; First Designer, Versace's Women's Wear, Ready to Wear and Haute Couture lines, where he worked with Donatella Versace –2007; Creative Dir, Halston 2007–. *Address:* Halston LLC, 1350 Avenue of the Americas, Suite 2025, New York, NY 10019, USA (office). *Telephone:* (212) 282-1200 (office). *Fax:* (212) 786-6775 (office). *E-mail:* info@halston.com (office). *Website:* www.halston.com (office).

ZANKER, Paul, DPhil; German archaeologist and academic; *Professor Emeritus of Classical Archeology, Scuola Normale Superiore di Pisa;* b. 7 Feb. 1937, Konstanz; ed Univ. of Munich, Univ. of Freiburg, Univ. of Rome, Italy; with Deutsches Archäologisches Inst. Rome 1963, Dir 1996–; Asst, Univ. of Bonn 1964; Lecturer, Univ. of Freiburg 1967; Prof., Univ. of Göttingen 1972; Prof. of Classical Archaeology, Univ. of Munich 1976; Prof. of Classical Archeology, Scuola Normale Superiore, Pisa, Italy, now Prof. Emer.; mem. Inst. of Advanced Study, Princeton, NJ, USA; mem. Bayerische Akad. der Wissenschaften, British Acad., Academia Europaea (London), Deutsches Archäologisches Inst. *Publications:* Wandel der Hermesgestalt 1965, Forum Augustum 1968, Forum Romanum 1972, Porträts 1973, Studien zu den Augustus-Porträts, Band 1: Der Actium-Typus 1973, Klassizistische Statuen. Studien zur Veränderung des Kunstgeschmacks in der römischen Kaiserzeit 1974, Provinzielle Kaiserporträts. Zur Rezeption der Selbstdarstellung des Princeps 1983, Augustus und die Macht der Bilder 1987, Die Trunkene Alte. Das Lachen der Verhöhnten 1988, The power of images in the age of Augustus (trans. by Alan Shapiro) 1988, Pompeji. Stadtbild und Wohngeschmack 1995, Stadtbild und Bürgerbild im Hellenismus (co-ed.) 1995, Die Maske des Sokrates. Das Bild des Intellektuellen in der Antiken Kunst 1995, Eine Kunst für die Sinne. Zur Bildwelt des Dionysos und der Aphrodite 1998, Mit Mythen leben. Die Bilderwelt der römischen Sarkophage (co-author) 2004, Die Apotheose der römischen Kaiser. Ritual und städtische Bühne 2004. *Address:* Meiserstrasse 10, 80333 Munich, Germany.

ZANNA, Mark P., BA, PhD, FRSC; Canadian social psychologist and academic; *University Professor, Department of Psychology, University of Waterloo;* ed Yale Univ.; Asst Prof., Princeton Univ. 1970–75; Assoc. Prof., Univ. of Waterloo 1975–79, Prof. 1979–2004, Inaugural Univ. Prof. 2004–, Prof. of Health Studies (Cross-Appointment) 1986–, Chair. Div. of Social Psychology 1978–79, 1989–91, 1992–93, 2002–03, Assoc. Chair./Undergraduate Affairs, Dept of Psychology 1983–86, Deputy Chair. Dept of Psychology 1986–88, 2008, Chair. 1997–2000, 2009–, mem. Senate 2000–03, mem. Bd of Dirs Center for Applied Health Research 1984–88; Visiting Assoc. Prof., Stanford Univ. 1979; Visiting Prof., Princeton Univ. 1981, McGill Univ. 1986, Univ. of Minnesota 1995, Univ. of California, Santa Cruz 1996, Univ. of Exeter, UK 1998; collaborative work on Int. Tobacco Control Policy Survey; Consulting Ed. Social Psychology Quarterly 1977–79, Journal of Personality 1977–79, 1982–97, Journal of Personality and Social Psychology 1978–86, 1990–, Canadian Journal of Behavioural Science 1978–79, 1982–90, Journal of Experimental Social Psychology 1978–79, 1982–91, Review of Personality and Social Psychology 1983–93, Journal of Consumer Psychology 1991–2000, Personality and Social Psychology Bulletin 1994–97, Basic and Applied Social Psychology 1994–2010, Group Processes and Intergroup Relations 1997–, Political Psychology 2002–10; Assoc. Ed. Journal of Experimental Social Psychology 1980–81; Co-Ed. Ontario Symposium on Personality and Social Psychology 1981–; Ed. Advances in Experimental Social Psychology 1990–; President-Elect, President, Past President, SPSP, 1996–1998; Pres. President, SESP, 1985, Soc. of Personality and Social Psychology (first Canadian), Int. Soc. of Experimental Social Psychology (first Canadian); mem. Canadian Psychological Asscn (mem. Bd of Dirs 1990–91), American Psychological Asscn (APA) Div. 8: Soc. of Personality and Social Psychology (mem. Exec. Cttee APA 1992–94), APA Div. 9: Soc. for the Psychological Study of Social Issues (SPSSI) (mem. Council SPSSI 1985–8), APA Div. 35: Soc. for the Psychology of Women, APA Div. 3: Div. of Experimental Psychology, Asscn for Psychological Science (fmrly American Psychological Soc.), American Asscn of Applied and Preventive Psychology, Eastern Psychological Asscn, Midwestern Psychological Asscn, Soc. of Experimental Social Psychology (mem. Exec. Cttee 1982–85); Fellow, Canadian Psychological Asscn 1978, American Psychological Asscn 1979 (Div. 8/SPSP 1980, Div. 9/SPSSI 1982, Div. 35/SPW 2002, Div. 3/DEP); Fellow-Elect, Center for Advanced Studies in the Behavioral Sciences 1982; Charter Fellow, Asscn for Psychological Science 1988, American Asscn of Applied and Preventive Psychology 1991; Departmental Honours with Exceptional Distinction, Yale Univ. 1966, NSF Grad. Fellow, Yale Univ. 1966–70, Otto Klineberg Intercultural and Int. Relations Prize, SPSSI 1992, Donald O. Hebb Award for Distinguished Contribs to Psychology as a Science, CPA 1993, Kurt Lewin Fellow, Univ. of Amsterdam 1994, Raymond D. Fowler Award for Professional Devt of Grad. Students, American Psychological Asscn of Grad. Students 1996, Donald T. Campbell Award for Distinguished Research in Social Psychology, Soc. of Personality and Social Psychology 1997, Inaugural Excellence in Research Award, Univ. of Waterloo 2000, Inaugural Outstanding Performance Award, Univ. of Waterloo 2004, 2008, 2011, Inaugural Award for Excellence in Grad. Supervision, Univ. of Waterloo 2005, Distinguished Scientist Award, Soc. of Experimental and Social Psychology 2007, Inaugural Fellow, Soc. of Experimental and Social Psychology 2009, Kurt Lewin Award for Distinguished Scientific Contributions, SPSSI 2010, Service Award for Contribs to the Field of Personality/Social Psychology, SPSP 2010, Killam Prize in the Social Sciences, Canada Council for the Arts 2011. *Publications:* numerous papers in professional journals on the psychology of attitudes. *Address:* PAS 3048, Department of Psychology, University of Waterloo, Waterloo, ON N2L 3G1, Canada (office). *Telephone:* (519) 888-4567

(ext. 35799) (office); (519) 747-9366 (home). *Fax:* (519) 746-8631 (office). *E-mail:* mzanna@uwaterloo.ca (office). *Website:* www.psychology.uwaterloo.ca (office).

ZANNIER, Lamberto, DIur; Italian lawyer, diplomatist and international organization official; *Secretary-General, Organization for Security and Co-operation in Europe;* b. 1954; m.; two s. two d.; ed Univ. of Trieste, Italian Diplomatic Inst.; served with FAO Legal Office, Rome 1976–78; joined Ministry of Foreign Affairs in 1978, worked on Multilateral Econ. Co-operation Desk, Second Sec., Embassy in Abu Dhabi 1979–82 First Sec. (for Multilateral Affairs), Embassy in Vienna 1982–87, with Political Affairs Div. then Office of Sec.-Gen., Ministry of Foreign Affairs 1987–91; seconded to NATO as Head of Disarmament, Arms Control and Cooperative Security Section 1991–97; Deputy Chief of Mission, Perm. Mission to OSCE, Vienna, Chair. for negotiations on Adaptation of the Treaty on Conventional Armed Forces in Europe 1997–2000; Rep. Exec. Council of Org. for Prohibition of Chemical Weapons 2000–02; Dir OSCE Conflict Prevention Centre 2002–06; worked on EU common foreign and security policy, Ministry of Foreign Affairs 2006–08; UN Sec.-Gen.'s Special Rep. for Kosovo and Head of Mission, UN Interim Admin. Mission in Kosovo (UNMIK) 2008–11; Sec.-Gen. OSCE 2011–. *Publications include:* numerous publs and articles on arms control, peace-keeping and security co-operation. *Address:* Organization for Security and Co-operation in Europe (OSCE), Wallnerstrasse 6, 1010 Vienna, Austria (office). *Telephone:* (1) 514-36-0 (office). *Fax:* (1) 514-36-96 (office). *E-mail:* info@osce.org (office). *Website:* www.osce.org (office).

ŽANTOVSKÝ, Michael; Czech diplomatist, politician, scientist, translator and author; *Ambassador to UK;* b. 3 Jan. 1949, Prague; s. of Jiří Žantovský and Hana Žantovská; m. 1st Kristina Žantovská (divorced 2000); one s. one d.; m. 2nd Jana Žantovská; one s. one d.; ed Charles Univ., Prague, McGill Univ., Montreal; scientific worker in a research inst., Prague 1973–80; freelance translator and interpreter 1980–88; Prague Corresp., Reuters 1988–89; activist for ind. creative org. Open Dialogue 1988; Founder mem. restored PEN 1989; Press Spokesman for Centre of Civic Forum 1989–90; mem. Advisory Bd to Pres. Václav Havel 1990–91; Press Spokesman to Pres. 1991–92; with Ministry of Foreign Affairs Aug. 1992; Amb. of Czech and Slovak Fed. Repub. to USA 1992, Amb. of Czech Repub. to USA 1993–97; mem. Senate 1996–2002, Chair. Senate Comm. for Foreign Affairs, Defence and Security 1996–2002; Amb. to Israel 2003–09, to UK 2009–; mem. Civic Democratic Alliance (ODA) 1997–, Chair. March–Nov. 1997, 2001, Vice-Chair. 1998–2001; mem. Bd of Supervisors OPS Prague – 'European City of Culture 2000' 1999–2001. *Publications include:* papers in scientific journals on psychological motivation and sexual behaviour, author of lyrics and translator of numerous works of fiction, drama and poetry. *Leisure interest:* tennis. *Address:* Embassy of the Czech Republic, 26–30 Kensington Palace Gardens, London, W8 4QY, England (office). *Telephone:* (20) 7243-1115 (office). *Fax:* (20) 7727-9654 (office). *E-mail:* london@embassy.mzv.cz (office). *Website:* www.mzv.cz/london (office).

ZANUSSI, Krzysztof; Polish film director and scriptwriter; b. 17 June 1939, Warsaw; s. of Jerzy Zanussi and Jadwiga Zanussi; m. Elżbieta Grocholska; ed Warsaw and Kraków Univs and Łódź Higher Film School; Dir TOR State Film Studio 1967–; Lecturer, Stage Dept of Higher State School of Film, TV and Drama, Łódź 1970–72; Prof. Univ. of Silesia; has directed numerous short feature films; Vice-Chair., Polish Film Asscn 1971–81; Pres. European Fed. of Film Dirs (FERA) 1990–; mem. Polish Acad. of Arts and Sciences, PEN Club, European Film Acad., Pontificia Accademia delle Arti e Lettere, The Int. Fed. of Film Critics (Fipresci) Moscow 2002; Kt's Cross of Order of Polonia Restituta, Gold Cross of Merit 1981, Chevalier de l'Ordre des Sciences et Lettres 1986; Dr hc (Moscow WGIC) 1998, (Minsk European Univ. Acad. of Arts, Bucharest); Best Director Cannes Film Festival 1980, Special Jury Prize, Venice Film Festival 1982, Grand Prix Venice 1984, State Prize 1st Class 1984, Grand Prix Moscow 2000. *Films include:* Death of Provincial (awards in Venice, Mannheim, Valladolid and Moscow) 1966, Structure of Crystals (award in Mar del Plata) 1969, Family Life (awards in Chicago, Valladolid and Colombo) 1971, Illumination (Grand Prize in Locarno 1973) 1973, The Catamount Killing (USA) (OCIC Prize, West Berlin Int. Film Festival) 1974, Quarterly Balance 1975, Camouflage (special prize, Tehran Int. Film Festival 1977, Grand Prix, Polish Film Festival 1977) 1977, Spiral (Prize of Journalists, V Polish Film Festival 1978, Cannes 1978, OCIC Prize) 1978, Wege in der Nacht (FRG) 1979, Constant Factor (Best Dir Cannes, OCIC Prize) 1980, Contract (Distribution Prize, Venice Film Festival) 1980, From a Far Country (Donatello Prize, Florence) 1980, Versuchung 1981, Imperative (Special Prize and Passinetti Award, Venice), The Unapproachable 1982, Year of the Quiet Sun (Grand Prix Golden Lion, Venice) 1984, The Power of Evil (OCIC Prize, Montreal) 1985, Wherever You Are (Oecumenical Prize, Moscow, Best Script and Act. European Award, Viareggio) 1989, Life for Life 1990, At Full Gallop (Special Jury Prize, Tokyo) 1995, Our God's Brother 1997, Life as a Fatal, Sexually Transmitted Disease (Grand Prix, Moscow Int. Film Festival) 2000, Supplement 2002, Julie Walking Home (exec. producer) 2002, Pregi (producer) 2004, Csoda Krakkóban (producer) 2004, Persona non Grata 2005, The Black Sun 2006, With an Open Heart 2008, Revisited 2009. *TV films:* Portrait of the Composer (prizes in Cracow, Leipzig), Face to Face 1967, Credit 1968, Pass Mark 1969, Mountains at Dark 1970, Role (FRG) 1971, Behind the Wall (Grand Prix, San Remo Int. Film Festival 1972) 1971, Hipotese (FRG) 1972, Nachtdienst (FRG) 1975, Penderecki Lutosławski Baird (documentary) 1976, Anatomiestunde (FRG) 1977, Haus der Frauen (FRG) 1978, Mein Krakau (documentary) 1979, Blaubart (FRG, Switzerland) (Prize, Venice Film Festival) 1984, Mia Varsavia 1987, Erloeschene Zeiten 1987, The Silent Touch 1993, Wrong Address (BBC) 1995, Don't Be Afraid (RAI) 1996, Weekend Stories 1995–2000. *Stage plays:* One Flew Over the Cuckoo's Nest 1977, Der König stirbt 1980, Mattatoiò 1982, Day and Night, Duo for One 1983, Hiòb, Les Jeux des Femmes (Paris) 1985, Alle Meine Sonne 1986, Giulio Cesare 1986, Alte Zeiten 1988, Koenig Roger 1988, Geburtstag der Infantin 1989, Regina dei Insort 1989, Death and the Maiden (Poznań and Berlin) 1994, Pl. Presidente (Rome, Florence) 1995, Re Pescatore (San Miniatò) 1996, L'uomo che vide (San Miniatò, Borgione) 1998, Herodias et Salomé (Rome) 1998, Amys Way (Essen) 1998, Parenti Terribili (Rome) 2002, Der Beweis (Cologne) 2002, Horrible Parents (Rome) 2002, Partners in Crime (Essen, Berlin) 2005 (Kiev) 2007, Duo (Novosibirsk) 2008, Medea (Syracuse) 2009, Rabbit Hole (Amberg) 2010. *Television:* Old Times (Harold Pinter) ARD 1988, L'Alouette (Jean Anouilh) TVP 2000, Casting Session 2003, Inner Voices 2008. *Publications:* Nowele Filmowe (short feature films) 1976, Scenariusze Filmowe (film scripts) 1978, Un rigorista nella fortezza assediata

1982, Scenariusze Filmowe (film scripts) II, III 1986, IV 1998, The Time to Die (autobiog.) 1997, Weekend Stories 1997, Between Kermess and Salon 1999, Six Scripts (USA) 2001. *Leisure interests:* travel, skiing, horse-riding. *Address:* Studio TOR, ul. Puławska 61, 02-595 Warsaw (office); ul. Kaniowska 114, 01-529 Warsaw, Poland (home). *Telephone:* (22) 8455303 (office); (22) 8392556 (home). *Fax:* (22) 8455303 (office). *E-mail:* tor@tor.com.pl (office). *Website:* www.tor.com.pl (office).

ZAORÁLEK, Lubomír; Czech politician; *Minister of Foreign Affairs;* b. 6 Sept. 1956; m. (divorced); three c.; ed Faculty of Philosophy, Jan Evangelista Purkyně Univ., Brno; script ed. Ostrava studio of Česká televize (Czech TV); worked for Československá socialistická strana (Czechoslovak Socialist Party) 1986–89; Founding mem. Občanské fórum (Civic Forum), Ostrava 1989, mem. Fed. Ass. as Forum's rep. 1990; elected to Ostrava Municipal Council 1990, mem. Town Council; Lecturer, Faculty of Philosophy, Univ. of Ostrava 1990–96; joined Česká strana sociálně demokratická (ČSSD—Czech Social Democratic Party) 1994, elected mem. Ostrava Town Council, also Chair. Culture Cttee; mem. Chamber of Deputies 1996–, Chair. 2002–06, served as Chair. Foreign Affairs Cttee; Minister of Foreign Affairs 2014–. *Address:* Ministry of Foreign Affairs, Loretánské nám. 101/5, 118 00 Prague 1, Czech Republic (office). *Telephone:* 224181111 (office). *Fax:* 224182048 (office). *E-mail:* podatelna@mzv.cz (office). *Website:* www.mzv.cz (office).

ZAOURAR, Hocine; Algerian photographer; b. 18 Dec. 1952, Birmandreiss; s. of Mohamed Zaourar and Khedidja Bourahla; teacher of photography, Ecole des Beaux-Arts, Algiers 1983–93; fmrly photojournalist Reuters; photojournalist Agence France-Presse, Algiers 1993–; World Press Photo People in the News, 1st Prize 1997, Prix Munn, Paris 1997, Prix Bayeux des correspondants de guerre 1998, Festival Int. du scoop et du journalisme, 1st Prize 1998. *Address:* c/o Agence France-Presse, 6 rue Abd al-Karim-el-Khettabi, Algiers; 5 Lotissement Tardithe, Birmandreiss, Algiers, Algeria (home). *Telephone:* 21-72-16-54 (office); 21-54-16-28 (home). *Fax:* 21-72-14-89 (office).

ZARB, Frank Gustav, MBA; American financial executive, insurance industry executive and fmr government official; *Senior Advisor and Managing Director, Hellman and Friedman LLC;* b. 17 Feb. 1935, New York; s. of Gustave Zarb and Rosemary Zarb (née Antinora); m. Patricia Koster 1957; one s. one d.; ed Hofstra Univ.; Graduate trainee, Cities Service Oil Co. 1957–62; Gen. Partner, Goodbody & Co. 1962–69; Exec. Vice-Pres., CBWL-Hayden Stone 1969–71, Exec. Vice-Pres. Hayden Stone 1972–73, 1977; Asst Sec., US Dept of Labor 1971–72; Assoc. Dir Exec. Office of the Pres., Office of Man. and Budget 1973–74; Admin., Fed. Energy Admin. 1974–77; Asst to the Pres. for Energy Affairs 1976; Gen. Pnr Lazard Frères 1977–88; Chair. and CEO Smith Barney, Harris Upham 1988–93, Smith Barney Shearson 1993; Chair., CEO Nat. Asscn of Securities Dealers 1997–2001; Sr Advisor and Man. Dir Hellman & Friedman LLC 2002–; also currently Chair. Promontory Financial Group, Nassau County Interim Finance Authority; Chair. NY State Comm. on Educ. Reform 2003–; Dir Securities Investor Protection Corpn 1988; Vice-Chair. Group Chief Exec. Travelers Inc. 1993–94; Chair., Pres., CEO Alexander & Alexander Services Inc., New York 1994–97; mem. Bd of Dirs Kraft Foods, Inc., fmr mem. Bd of Dirs American Int. Group (AIG) Inc. (Interim Chair. 2005), CS First Boston Inc., Council on Foreign Relations; Chair. Bd of Trustees, Hofstra Univ.; mem. US Presidential Advisory Cttee on Fed. Pay, US Investment Policy Advisory Cttee; Exec. in Residence, Columbia Univ.; Gerald R. Ford Foundation Distinguished Scholar Award, Hofstra Univ. *Publications:* The Stockmarket Handbook 1969, Handbook of Financial Markets 1981, The Municipal Bond Handbook. *Address:* Hellman and Friedman LLC, 375 Park Avenue, New York, NY 10152, USA (office). *Telephone:* (212) 871-6680 (office). *Fax:* (212) 871-6688 (office). *Website:* www.hf.com (office).

ZARDARI, Asif Ali; Pakistani business executive, politician and fmr head of state; *Co-Chairman, Pakistan People's Party;* b. 26 July 1955, Karachi, Sindh; s. of Hakim Ali Zardari; m. Benazir Bhutto 1987 (died 2007); one s. two d.; ed Cadet Coll. Petaro, Karachi, studied business in London, UK; mem. Nat. Ass. for Nawabshah 1990–93, 1993–96; imprisoned on blackmail charges 1990–93 (charges dropped); Fed. Minister of the Environment 1993; Fed. Minister for Investment 1995–96; imprisoned on corruption charges 1996–2004 (charges dropped); elected Senator 1997–99 (Parl. dissolved); Co-Chair. Pakistan People's Party (PPP) (following assassination of Benazir Bhutto) 2008–; Pres. of Pakistan 2008–13; Vice-Pres. Socialist International 2008–; Dir M/s Zardari Group (Pvt.) Ltd. *Leisure interests:* polo (fmr mem. Zardari Four polo team). *Address:* c/o Office of the President, Aiwan-e-Sadr, Islamabad, Pakistan; Pakistan Peoples Party, 8 Street 19, F-8/2, Islamabad, Pakistan (office). *Telephone:* (51) 2255264 (office). *Fax:* (51) 2282741 (office). *E-mail:* chairman@ppp.org.pk (office); ppp@comsats.net.pk (office). *Website:* www.ppp.org.pk (office).

ZARE, Richard Neil (Dick), BA, PhD, FRSC, FAAS, FMRS; American scientist and academic; *Marguerite Blake Wilbur Professor of Natural Science and Chairman, Department of Chemistry, Stanford University;* b. 19 Nov. 1939, Cleveland, Ohio; s. of Milton Zare and Dorothy Sylvia Zare (née Amdur); m. Susan Leigh Shively 1963; three d.; ed Harvard Univ., Univ. of California, Berkeley; Postdoctoral Research Assoc., Jt Inst. for Lab. Astrophysics, Univ. of Colorado 1964–65, Asst Prof., Dept of Physics and Astrophysics 1966–68, Assoc. Prof. 1968–69; Asst Prof., Dept of Chem., MIT 1965–66; Prof. of Chem., Columbia Univ. 1969–77, Higgins Prof. of Natural Science 1975–77; Prof. of Chem., Stanford Univ. 1977–, Marguerite Blake Wilbur Prof. in Natural Science 1987–, Shell Distinguished Prof. of Chem. 1980–85, Fellow 1984–86, Prof. of Physics 1992–, Chair. Dept of Chem. 2005–; Prof., Howard Hughes Medical Inst.; Christensen Fellow, St Catherine's Coll., Oxford 1982; Chair. Nat. Science Foundation Advisory Panel (Chem. Div.) 1980–82, Div. of Chemical Physics, American Physical Soc. 1985–86, NAS Panel on Science and Tech. Centers 1987; Chair. Nat. Research Council's Comm. on Physical Sciences, Math. and Applications 1992–95, Nat. Science Bd 1992–98; mem. Nat. Research Council's Cttee on Atomic and Molecular Science 1983–85, Directed Energy Weapons Study Panel of American Physical Soc. 1985–87, Govt-Univ.-Ind. Roundtable of NAS 1989–, Nat. Science Bd 1992–2000; Chair. Bd of Dirs Annual Reviews Inc. 1995–; Ed. Chemical Physics Letters 1982–85; mem. Editorial Advisory Bd Chemical Physics, Journal of Molecular Spectroscopy, Annual Reviews, Molecular Physics, Cambridge Univ. Press; mem. NAS 1976– (mem. Council 1995–), ACS, American Acad. of Arts and Sciences, American Philosophical Soc.; Fellow, American Physical Soc., Int. Advisory Bd,

Optical Soc. of America 1994–, Inst. of Physics 1999–; Foreign mem. Royal Soc. 1999, Royal Swedish Acad. of Eng Sciences 2005, Chinese Acad. of Sciences 2005, IVA, Indian Acad. of Sciences 2008, The Acad. of Sciences for the Developing World (TWAS) 2009; more than 100 distinguished lecturerships; Hon. Fellow, Chinese Chemical Soc. 2010, Hon. mem. Japan Soc. for Analytical Chem. 2011; Hon. DSc (Arizona) 1990, (Columbia) 2000, (State Univ. of W Georgia) 2001; Dr hc (Northwestern Univ.) 1993, (ETH, Zurich) 1993, (Uppsala) 2000, (Univ. of York) 2001, (Hunan Univ.) 2002, (Université Paul Sabatier) 2003, (Chalmers Inst. of Tech.) 2007, (Univ. of South Florida) 2013, Einstein Professorship, Chinese Acad. of Sciences 2011; numerous honours and awards, including Nat. Medal of Science 1983, Irving Langmuir Prize, American Physical Soc. 1985, Kirkwood Award Medal, Yale Univ. 1986, ACS Willard Gibbs Medal 1990, ACS Peter Debye Award 1991, NAS Award in Chemical Sciences 1991, Harvey Prize 1993, Dannie-Heineman Preis 1993, California Scientist of the Year 1997, Eastern Analytical Symposium Award 1997, NASA Exceptional Scientific Achievement Award 1997, ACS Award in Analytical Chem. 1998, Welch Award in Chem. 1999, ACS E. Bright Wilson Award in Spectroscopy 1999, ACS Nobel Laureate Signature Award for Grad. Educ. in Chem. 2000, Arthur L. Schawlow Prize in Laser Science, American Physical Soc. 2000, CaSSS Scientific Achievement Award 2000–01, ACS Charles Lathrop Parsons Award 2001, Madison Marshall Award 2001, Distinguished Chemist Award, ACS Sierra Nevada Section 2002, Wolf Prize in Chem. 2005, Chandler Medal, Columbia Univ. 2005, Pupin Medal "for service to the nation", Columbia Univ. School of Eng 2005, Oesper Award, Univ. of Cincinnati and Cincinnati Section of the ACS 2006, Dudley R. Herschbach Award for Excellence in Research in the field of Collision Dynamics, Dynamics of Molecular Collisions Meeting, Santa Fe 2007, James Flack Norris Award for Outstanding Achievement in the Teaching of Chem. 2004, ACS George C. Pimentel Award in Chemical Educ. 2008, F. Albert Cotton Award for Excellence in Chemical Research 2009, ACS Priestley Medal 2010, Pres.'s Award of Excellence in Science, Math., and Eng Mentoring 2010, R.B. Bernstein Award in Stereodynamics 2010, BBVA Foundation Frontiers of Knowledge Award in the Basic Sciences category 2010, ACS (Northeastern Section) Richards Medal 2010, King Faisal Int. Prize in Science (co-recipient) 2011, Torbern Bergman Medal 2012, Int. Science and Technology Cooperation Award, People's Republic of China 2012. *Publications include:* Angular Momentum 1988, Laser Experiments for Beginners 1995, Angular Momentum: Understanding Spatial Aspects in Chemistry and Physics and Companion to Angular Momentum (co-author) 1998, Annual Review of Analytical Chemistry, Vol. 1 (co-author) 2008, A Companion to Angular Momentum (co-author) 2009; more than 800 research articles. *Leisure interests:* chess, cooking, music, theatre. *Address:* Department of Chemistry, Stanford University, Room 133, Mudd Building, 333 Campus Drive, Stanford, CA 94305-5080 (office); 724 Santa Ynez Street, Stanford, CA 94305-8441, USA (home). *Telephone:* (650) 723-3062 (office). *Fax:* (650) 725-0259 (office). *E-mail:* zare@stanford.edu (office). *Website:* www.stanford.edu/group/Zarelab (office).

ZARIF, Farid; Afghan diplomatist and UN official; *Special Representative of the Secretary-General for Kosovo and Head, United Nations Interim Administration Mission in Kosovo (UNMIK);* b. 9 Jan. 1951; m. Alia Zarif; two s.; ed Faculty of Law and Political Science, Kabul Univ., Afghan Inst. of Diplomacy, Univ. of Oxford, UK (Postgraduate Diplomas in Int. Relations); joined Ministry of Foreign Affairs 1974, First Sec., later Charge d'Affaires, Embassy in Havana 1979–80, Amb. and Perm. Rep. to UN, New York 1981–87, Deputy Foreign Minister 1987–89; Prin. Foreign Policy Adviser to Pres. 1989–91; Sec.-Gen. Economic Advisory Council, Chambers of Commerce and Industry 1991–92; joined UN 1993, Referendum/Elections Coordinator UN missions in Eritrea and South Africa 1993 and 1995, Chief Elections Officer, UN Mission in Liberia (UNMIL) 1994–96, UN Deputy Humanitarian Coordinator in Iraq 1997–2000, fmr Chief, then Dir Office of Iraq Programme, New York, Chief of Staff, UN Assistance Mission for Iraq (UNAMI) 2004, then Chief of Staff and Acting Deputy Special Rep. of Sec.-Gen., UN Mission in Sudan (UNMIS), Dir Europe and Latin America Div., Dept of Peace-keeping Operations (DPKO) 2010, Special Rep. of Sec.-Gen. for Kosovo and Head, UN Interim Admin Mission in Kosovo (UNMIK) 2011–. *Address:* United Nations Interim Administration Mission in Kosovo (UNMIK) Headquaters, Industrial Zone, 10 000 Pristina, Kosovo (office); United Nations Interim Administration Mission in Kosovo (UNMIK), Department of Peace-keeping Operations, Room S-3727-B, United Nations, New York, NY 10017, USA (office). *Telephone:* (38) 5046045900 (Pristina) (office); (212) 967-3104 (New York) (office). *Fax:* (38) 5046045406 (Pristina) (office). *E-mail:* office-srsg@un.org (office). *Website:* www .unmikonline.org (office).

ZARZALEJOS NIETO, José Antonio; Spanish newspaper editor; *Director, ABC (newspaper);* fmrly Dir holding co. El Correo, owner of ABC as part of Vocento, Dir ABC 1998–. *Address:* ABC, Juan Ignacio Luca de Tena 7, 28027 Madrid, Spain (office). *Telephone:* (91) 3399000 (office). *Fax:* (91) 3203680 (office). *E-mail:* info@ abc.es (office). *Website:* www.abc.es (office).

ZATLERS, Valdis; Latvian surgeon and fmr head of state; *Chairman, Reform Party;* b. 22 March 1955, Rīga; m. Lilita Zatlere; three c.; ed Rīga Secondary School No. 50, Rīga Inst. of Medicine, Yale Univ. and Syracuse Univ., USA; served in Latvian Nat. Front 1988–89; practised medicine at Yale Univ., Syracuse Univ. and Keggi Orthopaedic Foundation, USA 1990–91; traumatologist and orthopaedist, Riga Hosp. No. 2 1979–85, Head of Traumatology Dept 1985–94; Dir Latvian Hosp. of Traumatology and Orthopaedics, Riga 1994–2007, Chair. of Bd 1998–2007; mem. Bd Latvian Popular Front 1988–89; Pres. of Latvia 2007–11; Founder and Chair. Zatlers' Reform Party (renamed Reform Party April 2012) 2011–; Chair. Latvian Asscn for Traumatology and Orthopaedics 2003–; f. Latvian Arthroscopy Asscn, Pres. 1990–93, Vice-Pres. 1994–98; mem. Int. Soc. of Arthroscopy, Knee Surgery and Orthopaedic Sports Medicine (ISACOS) 1993–; Patron European Acad. of Science and Art (Austria) 2009; Hon. mem. Georgian Asscn of Orthopaedics and Traumatology 1992, Univ. of Latvia 2009; Hon. Prof., Nat. Governance Acad. (Kazakhstan) 2008; Three-Star Order (Fourth Class) 2007, Stars, First Grade, with Chain (Latvia) 2007, Knightly Order Pro Merito Melitensi of the Sovereign Mil. Hosp. Order of St John of Jerusalem of Rhodes and of Malta 2008, Order of Special Service to the Fatherland (Uzbekistan) 2008, Order of Friendship, First Degree (Kazakhstan) 2008, Grand Order of King Tomislav, First Grade, with the Ribbon and Great Star (Croatia) 2008, Order of Yaroslav the Wise, First Grade (Ukraine) 2008, Order of the Three Stars, First Class 2008, Order of

Viesturs, First Grade (Latvia) 2008, Cross of Recognition, First Grade (Latvia) 2008, Victory Order of St George (Georgia) 2009, Heydar Aliyev Order with Chain (Azerbaijan) 2009, Ismoili Samoni Order with Chain (Tajikistan) 2009, Order and Chain of Isabel the Catholic (Spain) 2009, Order of the Cross of St Mary's Land (Estonia) 2009, Order of the White Rose 2010, Order of Vytautas the Great 2011, Order of Liberty (Ukraine) 2011; Dr hc (Yerevan State Univ., Armenia) 2009, (John Paul II Catholic Univ. of Lublin, Poland) 2010, (Univ. Stradiņša, Riga) 2010; Int. Arthroscopy Asscn Prize 1993, Medal of Honour, Local Govt of Miraflores, Lima, Peru 2008, Medal of Achievement, Baltic Defence Coll., Estonia 2009, Commemorative Medallion in honour of 90th anniversary of Latvian Border Guard 2009, Medal of Latvian Asscn of Reserve Officers 2010. *Address:* Reform Party (Reformu Partija), Vilandes iela 14-1/6, Riga 1050, Latvia (office). *Telephone:* 6728-3908 (office). *E-mail:* birojs@reformupartija.lv (office). *Website:* www .reformupartija.lv (office).

ZATULIN, Konstantin Fedorovich; Russian business executive and economist; *Director, Institute of CIS Countries;* b. 7 Sept. 1958, Batumi; m.; one d.; ed Moscow State Univ.; functionary, Cen. Komsomol Cttee 1988–89; Dir-Gen. Int. Asscn of Heads of Enterprises 1989–; Co-founder Moscow Stock Exchange; Chair. Bd Co.-Rostok; Pres. Moscow Exchange Union 1992–; mem. Bd Russian Party of Unity and Consent 1993–94; Chair. Businessman for New Russia Union 1993–, Cttee on CIS affairs and connections with compatriots 1994–; mem. State Duma (Parl.) 1993–95; mem. Govt Comm. on Compatriots Abroad 1994–; Dir Inst. for Problems of Diaspora and Integration (now Inst. of CIS Countries) 1996–; Chair. Fund for Devt of Econ. Reforms; Adviser to Mayor of Moscow 1997, Bd Moscow Fund of Presidential Programmes 2000–, Derzhava Movt 1998–, Sochi Friends Club 1998–; mem. Bd Otechestvo political org. 1998; Deputy of State Duma of Russian Fed. of IVth Convocation 2003–07, of Vth convocation 2007–; Awards of Russian Govt. *Address:* Institute of CIS Countries, B. Polyanka Street 7, 109180 Moscow (office); 1st Truzhenikov per. 17, Apt 79, Moscow, Russia (home). *Telephone:* (495) 959-34-51 (office); (495) 248-05-79 (home). *Fax:* (495) 959-34-49 (office). *E-mail:* institute@ zatulin.ru (office). *Website:* www.zatulin.ru (office).

ZATZ, Mayana, PhD; Israeli biologist and academic; *Professor of Genetics and Director, Centre for Studies of the Human Genome, University of São Paolo;* b. 1948; m.; two c.; ed Univ. of São Paolo and Univ. of California, Los Angeles, USA; moved with family to France where she lived until age seven, moved to Brazil 1955; post-doctoral work in Medical Genetics, UCLA; Prof. of Genetics, Dept of Biology, Inst. of Biosciences, Univ. of São Paulo and Dir Centre for Studies of the Human Genome 1969–, Rector of Research 2006–; Founder and Pres. Brazilian Muscular Dystrophy Asscn; mem. Int. Human Genome Project; mem. Conselho Nacional de Desenvolvimento Científico e Tecnológico, Science Acad. of the State of São Paulo, Brazilian Science Acad.; Research Award, Muscular Dystrophy Asscn (USA) 1986, Medal of Scientific and Technological Merit, Govt of State of São Paulo 2000, Nat. Order of Scientific and Technological Merit, Presidency of Repub. of Brazil 2000, L'Oréal-UNESCO For Women in Science Award 2001, Premio Claudia 2001, Prize in Basic Medical Sciences, Third World Acad. of Sciences 2004, Prêmio Hospitalar 2005, Prêmio Scopus 2007, Premio da Maçonaria 2007, Mulher Cidadã Bertha Lutz, Senado Federal 2008. *Publications:* more than 170 papers in scientific journals and approx. 150 articles in foreign magazines on genetics of neuromuscular diseases. *Address:* Department of Biology, Institute of Biosciences, University of São Paulo, Rua do Matão, 277 Sala 211, Travessa 14, 321-Butantã, 05508-900 São Paulo SP, Brazil (office). *Telephone:* (11) 3091-7563 (office). *Fax:* (11) 3091-7419 (office). *E-mail:* mayazatz@usp.br (office); ib@edu.usp.br (office). *Website:* www.ib.usp.br (office).

ZAVALA, Silvio, DenD; Mexican historian, diplomatist and academic; *Professor Emeritus, Colegio de México;* b. 7 Feb. 1909, Mérida, Yucatán; s. of Arturo Zavala and Mercedes Vallado; m. Huguette Joris 1951; one s. three d.; ed Univ. del Sureste, Univ. Nacional Autónoma de México and Univ. Central de Madrid, Spain; Centre of Historical Studies, Madrid 1933–36; Sec., Nat. Museum of Mexico 1937–38; Pres. Historical Comm. of Pan-American Inst. of Geography and History 1946–65; mem. Colegio de México 1940, Pres. 1963–66, Emer. Prof. 1981–; Dir Nat. Museum of History, Chapultepec 1946–54; Visiting Prof. Univ. de Puerto Rico 1945, Univ. de la Habana 1946; fmr Prof. of History of Social Insts of America, Univ. Nacional Autónoma de México; Visiting Prof., Mexico City Coll., Visiting Lecturer, Harvard Univ. 1953, Visiting Prof. Univ. of Washington (Seattle) and Ghent 1956; Chief, Section of Educ., Science and Culture of UN 1947; Founder and Dir Revista de Historia de América (review of Pan-American Inst. of Geography and History) 1938–65; Perm. del. to UNESCO 1956–62, mem. Exec. Council 1960–66, Vice-Pres. 1962–64; Vice-Pres. Int. Council of Human Sciences and Philosophy 1959–65, Pres. 1965–71; Amb. to France 1966–75; mem. Exec. Council, Int. Cttee for Historical Sciences; mem. Nat. Acad. of History and Geography, Mexican Acad. of History 1946, Mexican Acad. of Language 1976; Hon. Pres. Cttee for 450th Anniversary of Foundation of Mérida de Yucatán; Hon. Pres. 48th Int. Congress of Americanists 1994; Hon. mem. Historical Asscn England 1956, Royal Historical Soc., London 1957, American Historical Asscn, Washington, DC 1959, Academia Portuguesa da História 1987; Hon. Prof., Colegio de San Nicolás, Morelia, Inst. of Latin American Studies, Univ. of Texas; Grand Officier, Légion d'honneur 1973, Grand-Croix, Ordre nat. du Mérite 1975, Gran Cruz Orden Civil Alfonso X el Sabio 1983, Gran Cruz Orden Isabel la Católica 1997; Hon. DLitt (Columbia) 1954, (Ghent) 1956, (Toulouse) 1965, (Montpellier) 1967, (Seville) 1990, (Mexico) 1996, (Colima) 1996; Nat. Literary Prize, History Div., Mexico 1969, History Prize, Acad. du Monde Latin, Paris 1974, Arch. C. Gerlach Prize, Panamerican Inst. of Geography and History 1986, Aristotle Medal, UNESCO 1989, Citizen's Merit Medal, Mexico 1991, medals from Universidad Complutense and Panamerican Inst. of Geography and History, El Escorial, Spain 1992, Príncipe de Asturias Prize in Social Sciences 1993, Aguirre Beltrán Medal, Veracruz 1996, Benito Juárez Medal, Sociedad Mexicana de Geografía y Estadística 1997, Iberoamerican History Prize, VII Congress of Iberoamerican Asscn of History Academics, Rio de Janeiro 2000, Lifetime Career Award, Nat. Inst. of Anthropology and History 2008. *Publications:* Columbus' Discovery in Art, XIX and XX Centuries 1991, Bio-Bibliografía de S.Z. 1999 and many works on the Spanish colonization of America, Latin American history, New World history. *Address:* Montes Urales 310, Lomas de Chapultepec, Deleg. M. Hidalgo, México, DF, 11000 Mexico (home). *Telephone:* 5520-4418 (home); 5520-9317 (home). *Fax:* 5645-0464 (home). *E-mail:* mzavala@colmex.mx (office).

ZAVALA BAQUERIZO, Jorge Enrique; Ecuadorean lawyer and politician; b. 13 May 1922, Guayaquil; s. of Oswaldo Zavala Arbaiza and Ana C. Baquerizo Germán de Zavala; m. Carolina Egas Núñez de Zavala; four s.; ed Univ. de Guayaquil; Public Prosecutor, 2nd Criminal Tribunal of Guayas 1947; Prof. of Law, Univ. de Guayaquil; Provincial Counsellor Guayas 1956–58; Vice-Deputy of Guayas 1958–60; Pres. Guayaquil Coll. of Lawyers (twice); Constitutional Vice-Pres. of Republic of Ecuador 1968–72; Congressman Guayas Prov., First Nat. Congressman 1984–88; Pres. Congress 1987–88; Minister of Finance and Public Credit 1988–90; Pres. Acad. de Abogados de Guayaquil 1973–74, 1st Nat. Congress of Lawyers 1960, Nat. Comm. of Human Rights, XXV Curso Int. de Criminología; Vice-Pres. various legal confs; Prof. Univ. of Guayaquil and Catholic Univ. of Guayaquil; Del. of Sociedad Int. de Criminología; mem. Int. Lawyers' Comm., Int. Lawyers' Asscn, American Bar Asscn, American Judicature Soc., Int. Asscn of Penal Law, Exec. Cttee of World Habeas Corpus; Premio Código Civil 1940; Premio Código Penal 1944; Cotenta Prize for univ. work, Premio al Mérito Científico of Municipality of Guayaquil 1966, 1976; Orden al Mérito in the Grade of Gran Cruz. *Publications:* El Proceso Penal Ecuatoriano, Los Delitos contra la Propiedad, La Pena, Delitos contra la Fe Pública, La Victimiología, El Delito de Cheque sin Provisión de Fondos and other books on legal topics. *Address:* Zavala, Carmigniani & Illingworth Abogados, Edificio Amazonas, 8th Floor, General Cordova 401 y V.M. Rendon Guayaquil, Ecuador. *Telephone:* (4) 301007 (office). *Fax:* (9) 775527 (office). *E-mail:* zbzci@gye.satnet.net (office).

ZAVALA LOMBARDI, Fernando; Peruvian politician and economist; b. 16 Feb. 1971, Tacna; ed in Peru and UK; Deputy Minister of Economy and Finance 2004–05, Minister of Economy and Finance 2005–; Gov. for Peru, IDB 2005–06; Dir-Gen. Indecopi. *Address:* c/o Ministry of Economy and Finance, Jirón Junín 339, 4°, Circado de Lima, Lima 1, Peru (office).

ZAVARZIN, Col-Gen. Victor Mikhailovich; Russian army officer and politician; b. 28 Nov. 1948, Zaoleshenka, Kursk Region; m.; two d.; ed Ordzhonikidze Higher Gen. Army School, Frunze Mil. Acad., Acad. of Gen. Staff; Commdg posts in Middle Asia Command 1970–78; Head of Staff of Div. Far E Command 1981–85; Head of Staff, Deputy Commdr, Commdr of Div., Commdr Training Cen. Carpathian Command 1985–90; Commdr United Russian-Turkmen Armed Force in Turkmenistan 1993–94; Commdr United Peacekeeping Forces in Tajikistan 1996–97; Deputy, First Deputy Head of Staff Russian Army, responsible for co-operation with CIS countries April–Oct. 1997; Mil. Rep. of Russia to NATO HQ, Brussels Nov. 1997–99; led Russian mil. unit from Bosnia and Herzegovina to Kosovo, Yugoslavia 1999; elected to State Duma (Parl.) Yedinaya Rossiya faction 2003–. *Address:* State Duma, Okhotnyi ryad 1, 103265 Moscow, Russia (office). *Telephone:* (495) 292-83-10 (office). *Fax:* (495) 292-94-64 (office). *Website:* www .duma.ru (office).

ZAVGAYEV, Doku Gapurovich, CandEcon; Russian/Chechen politician and diplomatist; *Ambassador to Slovenia;* b. 22 Dec. 1940; mem. CPSU 1966–91; teacher at elementary school, mechanic, engineer of sovkhoz, man. Regional Union Selkhoztechnika, Dir sovkhoz Znamensky, Chair. Nadterechny Regional Exec. Cttee 1971–72; Chief Repub. Union of Sovkhozes 1972–75; Minister of Agric. of Checheno-Ingush SSR 1975–77; head of div., Second Sec. Checheno-Ingush Regional CP Cttee 1977–89; First Sec. Repub. CP Cttee 1989–91; Chair. Supreme Soviet of Checheno-Ingush Autonomous SSR 1990–91, mem. Cen. CPSU Cttee 1990–91; People's Deputy of RSFSR 1990–93; in Admin. of Pres. of Russia 1994–95; elected Pres. of Chechen Repub. 1995–96; Deputy, Council of Russian Fed. 1995–97; Amb. to Tanzania 1997–2004; Deputy Minister of Foreign Affairs 2004, Dir Gen. Ministry of Foreign Affairs 2004–09, Amb. to Slovenia 2009–; Order of Red Banner of Labour, Badge of Honour; awarded four medals. *Publication:* System of Agric. in Checheno-Ingush Republic. *Leisure interests:* walking, travelling. *Address:* Russian Embassy, 1000 Ljubljana, Tomšičeva 9, Slovenia (office). *Telephone:* (1) 4256875 (office). *Fax:* (1) 4256878 (office). *E-mail:* ambrus .slo@siol.net (office). *Website:* www.rus-slo.mid.ru (office).

ZAVOS, Panayiotis Michael, BA, MS, EdS, PhD; American reproductive specialist and andrologist; *President and CEO, ZDL, Inc.;* b. 23 Feb. 1944, Cyprus; m. Dr Panayota N. Zavos; three c.; ed Emporia State Univ., Kan. and Univ. of Minnesota, USA; long career as reproductive specialist; Founder, Dir and Chief Andrologist, Andrology Inst. of America; Co-Founder, Scientific Dir and Chief Embryologist, Kentucky Center for Reproductive Medicine; Pres. and CEO ZDL, Inc., Lexington, Ky; Prof., Univ. of Kentucky; mem. Editorial Bd American Soc. for Reproductive Medicine (ASRM), Infertility, and many others; thousands of scientific presentations world-wide; mem. ASRM, American Soc. of Andrology, European Soc. for Human Reproduction and Embryology, M.E. Fertility Soc., Japanese Fertility Soc. and numerous other professional socs; Hon. Prof., Chinese Acad. of Science; Distinguished Alumnus Award, Emporia State Univ., Distinquished Research Award, Univ. of Minnesota Outstanding Teacher Award, Emporia State Univ., Paul Harris Fellow, Rotary International, Distinguished Speaker, Middle East Fertility Soc. 2004. *Publications:* more than 500 specialist articles on reproduction and infertility. *Leisure interests:* golf, running, fishing. *Address:* ZDL Inc., 181 Southland Drive, Lexington, KY 40523, USA (office). *Telephone:* (859) 278-6806 (office). *Fax:* (859) 278-6906 (office). *E-mail:* zavos@ zavos.org (office). *Website:* www.zdlinc.biz (office); www.zavos.org (office); www .fertilityzone.net (office); www.aia-zavos.com (office).

ZAWADZKI, Włodzimierz, PhD; Polish scientist; b. 4 Jan. 1939, Warsaw; ed Warsaw Univ.; Prof. 1985; scientific worker and Prof., Inst. of Physics, Polish Acad. of Sciences (PAN) 1961–; with MIT, Cambridge, Mass, USA 1965–67, Ecole Normale Supérieure, Paris, France 1974; Visiting Prof., Linz Univ., Austria 1978, North Texas State Univ. 1980, Tech. Univ., Munich, FRG 1981, Innsbruck Univ., Austria 1983, Université des Sciences et Techniques du Languedoc Montpellier 1984; analyst for Polish weekly, Polityka; mem. Polish Physical Soc.; Annual Prize of Polish Science 1973, Maria Sklodowska-Curie Award 1977, State Prize (1st degree, collective) 1978, Mich. Univ. Award 1995, Marian Smoluchowski Medal 1997. *Publications:* more than 170 works on theory of semiconductors; also novels and collections of poetry, including Wanka-Wstanka 1990, Szekspir Socjalu 1991 and prose, including Wielki inkwizytor 1993. *Leisure interests:* literature, music, sports, skiing, tennis, basketball. *Address:* al. J. Ch. Szucha 11 m. 26, 00-580 Warsaw, Poland. *Telephone:* (22) 8410285. *E-mail:* zawad@ifpan.edu.pl.

ZAWAHIRI, Ayman Muhammad Rabi' az-, MS, DMed; Egyptian paediatrician, theologian and guerrilla leader; b. 19 June 1951, Maadi; grandson of Muhammad Rabi'a Zawahiri and Umayma Azzam; m. Azza Ahmed 1978 (died 2001); ed Cairo Univ.; mem. The Muslim Brotherhood (arrested for membership 1966); Founder Egyptian Islamic Jihad; imprisoned on firearms charge following Egyptian Pres. Sadat's assassination 1981–84; joined mujahidin troops fighting Soviet occupation forces in Afghanistan 1984; co-f. Int. Front for Fighting Jews and Crusaders (with Osama bin Laden) 1998; co-f. al Qa'ida; accused of planning bombings of US embassies in E Africa 1998; personal physician and political adviser to Osama bin Laden; fmr Leader Vanguards of Conquest Movt; assumed to be the figurehead of al Qa'ida following death of Osama bin Laden 2 May 2011, confirmed by press release from al Qa'ida's general command on 16 June; under worldwide sanctions by UN Security Council 1267 Cttee as a mem. or affiliate of al Qa'ida.

ZAYANI, Lt-Gen. (retd) Abdul Latif bin Rashid Al-, PhD; Bahraini international organization official and fmr army officer; *Secretary-General, Gulf Cooperation Council;* b. Muharraq; ed Royal Mil. Acad. Sandhurst and Aeronautical Eng Programme, Perth, UK, Air Force Inst. of Tech., Dayton, Ohio, Naval Postgraduate School, Monterey, Calif., Command and Gen. Staff Course, Fort Leavenworth, Kan. and Leaders in Devt Program, Harvard Univ., USA; commissioned as officer, Bahrain Defence Force 1973, numerous positions including Officer, 1st Royal Mechanized Bn, Royal Air Defence, Royal Bahraini Air Force, Dir of Planning and Org., Dir of Jt Operations, Asst Chief of Staff for Operations; Chief of Public Security, Ministry of the Interior 2004; Adviser with rank of Minister, Gen. Court of Ministry of Foreign Affairs 2010; Sec.-Gen., Gulf Cooperation Council 2011–; Chair. Jt Steering Cttee between Bahrain and UK; Chair. Devt and Regulation Cttee, Ministry of Foreign Affairs; fmr Prof. of Quantitative Methods, Univ. of Bahrain; fmr Prof. of Math. and Statistics, Univ. of Maryland, Bahrain; Efficiency Medal 2nd Class, Mil. Assessment Medal 1st Class, Bahrain Medal 3rd Grade, Shaikh Isa Medal 3rd Grade, Bahrain Medal 2nd Grade, Mil. Duty Medal, Hawar Medal 1st Grade, Liberation of Kuwait Medal 2nd Grade, Liberation of Kuwait Medal, Security Medal for Devotion to Duty 1st Class, Bahrain Medal 1st Grade, Sword of Honor along with title of Master Logistician from USA Army, Int. Police Leadership Award NPIA, UK 2010. *Leisure interests:* travel, fitness, sports. *Address:* Gulf Co-operation Council Building, King Khaled Road Diplomatic Area, PO Box 7153, Riyadh 11462 (office); Secretariat-General, Gulf Cooperation Council for the Arab States of the Gulf, PO Box 7153, Riyadh 11466, Saudi Arabia (office). *Telephone:* (1) 4827777 (office); (1) 4829015 (office). *Fax:* (1) 4829089 (office); (1) 4828008 (office). *E-mail:* dr.alzayani.off@gmail.com (office); info@gcc-sg.org (office). *Website:* www.gcc-sg.org (office).

ZAYCHANKA, Mikalay Petrovich; Belarusian economist and politician; b. 1948, Pogranichnyi, Maritime (Primorskii) Krai, Russia; ed Belarusian Polytechnic Inst.; Engineer then Sr Engineer, Inst. of Machine Planning, Acad. of Sciences of Belarusian SSR; Sr Economist and Jr Scientific Colleague, Inst. of Econs, Acad. of Sciences of Belarusian SSR; Sr Scientific Colleague, responsible for methodology, Scientific Research Inst. of Gosplan (State Planning Cttee); First Deputy Minister of the Economy 1997–03, Minister of the Economy 2003–09; Medal for Services to Labour. *Address:* c/o Ministry of the Economy, 220050 Minsk, vul. Bersona 14, Belarus (office).

ZBIDI, Abdelkarim, MD; Tunisian physician, academic and government official; b. 25 June 1950, Réjiche, Mahdia; ed Univ. Claude Bernard, Lyon, France; Foreign Asst Dr, Univ. of Medicine Grange Blanche, Lyon 1976–78; Teaching Asst, Univ. of Medicine of Sousse 1978–81, Assoc. Lecturer 1982–86, Teaching Prof. 1987–; Coordinator of High Health Technicians Training 1981–88, Head of Basic Sciences Dept 1982–89; Head of Functional Investigation Dept, Farhat Hached Hosp. of Sousse 1990–99, Dean, Faculty of Medicine 2005–08; Exec. of expert missions to IAEA 1992–; Chair. Physiology and Functional Investigation Coll., Ministry of Public Health 1994–97, Centre Univ. (Sousse, Monastir, Mahdia and Kairouan), Ministry of Higher Educ. 1995–99; Sec. of State to the Prime Minister for Scientific Research and Tech. 1999–2000; Minister of Public Health 2001, of Scientific Research and Tech. 2002, of Nat. Defence 2011–13; Chair. Public Health Hosp. 'RAZI' 2008–10, Scientific and Orientation Bd, Tech. Center of Sousse 2009–10; Founding mem. and Co-ordinator of Teaching, Medical School of Djibouti 2007–; mem. High-level Science and Technology Cttee to the Prime Minister 2009–10. *Publications:* 140 publs and 300 scientific papers. *Address:* c/o Ministry of National Defence, boulevard Bab Menara, 1008 Tunis, Tunisia (office).

ŽBOGAR, Samuel, BA; Slovenian diplomatist and politician; b. 5 March 1962, Postojna; m. Maja Žbogar; three c.; ed Faculty of Social Sciences, Univ. of Ljubljana; Sec. Foreign Students' Club, Inst. for Int. Scientific, Tech. and Cultural Cooperation 1986, adviser Dept of Neighbouring Countries 1987–90; Third Sec. Dept of Neighbouring Countries, Ministry of Foreign Affairs 1990, Counsellor and Sec. to Slovenian Del. at Int. Conf. on Fmr Yugoslavia 1991; Sec. Slovenian Rep. Office, EC Monitoring Mission in Zagreb 1991; Counsellor to the Minister and Sec. in the Office of the Sec.-Gen., Ministry of Foreign Affairs 1992; Chargé d'affaires a.i. and First Sec., Embassy in Beijing 1993–95; Counsellor to Govt and State Under-Sec. and Dir Dept for Africa, Asia, Latin America and the Pacific, Ministry of Foreign Affairs 1995–97; Deputy Perm. Rep. to UN, New York 1997–2001, Deputy Perm. Rep. to UN Security Council 1998–99; State Sec., Ministry of Foreign Affairs 2001–04; Amb. to USA 2004–08; Dir Inst. for Strategic Studies Oct.–Nov. 2008; Minister of Foreign Affairs 2008–12. *Leisure interest:* long distance running. *Address:* c/o Ministry of Foreign Affairs, 1001 Ljubljana, Prešernova 25, Slovenia.

ZBRUYEV, Alexander Victorovich; Russian actor; b. 31 March 1938, Moscow; m. Ludmila Savelyeva; one d.; ed Shchukin Higher School of Theatre Art; actor Moscow Theatre of Lininsky Comsomol 1961–; f. club and restaurant for actors 1998–; People's Artist of Russian Fed. 1989. *Films include:* My Junior Brother, Two Tickets for a Daytime Seance, Great Change, Romance for Those in Love, I Have You Alone, Circle, Wish for Love, Poor Sasha. *Plays include:* Optimistic Tragedy, Hamlet, Goodbye, Boys, The Day of the Wedding, My Poor Marat, 104 Pages About Love, Wizard, Gambler, The Last Night of the Last Tsar, The Barbarian and Heretic. *Leisure interests:* sports, cars. *Address:* Tverskaya str. 19, Apt. 76, 103050 Moscow, Russia (home). *Telephone:* (495) 299-99-34 (home).

ZECCHINI, Salvatore, MBA, PhD; Italian economist, government official and academic; b. 17 Nov. 1943, Palermo; m. Eliana de Leva 1971; one s. one d.; ed Columbia Univ., Univ. of Pennsylvania, Wharton School of Finance, Philadelphia, USA; economist, Research Dept Banca d'Italia, Dir Research Dept 1972–81, Dir 1981–84; Adviser to Govt of Italy 1978–84; Exec. Dir IMF 1984–89; Special Counsellor, OECD 1989–90, Asst Sec.-Gen. 1990–96, then Deputy Sec.-Gen.; Dir Centre for Co-operation of Economies in Transition 1990–96; Prof. of Int. Econ. Policy, Univ. of Rome 1997–; Econ. Adviser to Minister of Finance 1997–2000, to Minister of Industry and Trade 2001–09; Dir Public Investment Evaluation Centre 1997–98, Chair. Advisory Council of ICE (External Trade Agency) 2002–05; Chair. Gestore del Mercato Elettrico; Chair. Europex; Chair. IPI Inst. for Industrial Promotion. *Publications:* The Transition to a Market Economy (co-ed.) 1991, Lessons from The Economic Transition (ed.) 1996; articles in professional journals and books on econs and int. finance. *Leisure interests:* history, travel, hiking. *Address:* IPI Institute for Industrial Promotion, Via M. Pilsudski 124, 00197 Roma, Italy (office). *Telephone:* (06) 809721 (office). *Fax:* (06) 8072898 (office). *E-mail:* info@ipi.it (office). *Website:* www.ipi.it (office).

ZEDDA, Alberto; Italian conductor; *Artistic Director, Rossini Opera Festival;* b. 2 Jan. 1928, Milan; ed Univ. of Urbino; studied in Milan with Antonino Votto and Carlo Maria Giulini; debut as conductor, Milan 1956; teacher, Cincinnati Coll. of Music 1957–59; conductor with Deutsche Oper, Berlin 1961–63; with New York City Opera 1967–69; Covent Garden debut 1975; fmr Music Dir Festival della Valle d'Itria; Artistic Dir Teatro alla Scala, Milan 1992–93; currently Artistic Dir Rossini Opera Festival, Pesaro; guest conductor with numerous opera cos including La Scala, Milan, Vienna State Opera, La Fenice, Venice, San Francisco Opera, Royal Opera House, London, Mariinsky Theatre, St Petersburg; mem. Cttee Rossini Foundation, Pesaro; Hon. Pres. Deutsche Rossini Gesellschaft 2000. *Recordings include:* Bellini: Beatrice di Tenda 1986, Rossini: Tancredi 1994. *Address:* Rossini Opera Festival, Via Rossini, 24, 61121 Pesaro, Italy (office). *Telephone:* (0721) 3800213 (office). *E-mail:* rof@rossinioperafestival.it (office). *Website:* www.rossinioperafestival.it (office).

ZEDILLO PONCE de LEÓN, Ernesto, MA, MPhil, PhD, DEcon; Mexican economist, academic and fmr head of state; *Director, Center for the Study of Globalization, Yale University;* b. 27 Dec. 1951, Mexico City; s. of Rodolfo Zedillo Castillo and Martha Alicia Ponce de León; m. Nilda Patricia Velasco Núñez; five c.; ed Instituto Nacional Politécnico, Yale Univ., USA; joined Partido Revolucionario Institucional (PRI) 1971, with Instituto de Estudios Políticos, Económicos y Sociales (Iepes) (affil. to PRI); econ. researcher, Dirección Gen. de Programación Económica y Social; economist, Deputy Man. Econ. Research, Gen. Dir Trust Fund for the Renegotiation of Pvt. Firms' External Debt and Deputy Dir, Banco de Mexico (BANXICO) 1978–87; Prof. of Macroeconomics and Int. Econs, Instituto Nacional Politécnico and Colegio de México 1979–87; Under-Sec. of the Budget 1987–88, Sec. Budget and Econ. Planning 1988–92, Sec. of Educ. 1992–93; campaign man. for the late Luis Donaldo Colosio (fmr presidential cand.) 1993–94; Pres. of Mexico 1994–2000; Chair. UN High Level Panel on Financing for Devt 2000–01, Global Devt Network; Co-Chair. UN Comm. on Pvt. Sector and Devt 2004, Int. Task Force on Global Public Goods (sponsored by Govts of Sweden and France); Jt Coordinator UN Millennium Project's Task Force on Trade 2002–05; mem. Advisory Panel to Dir-Gen. WTO 2001–02, Trilateral Comm., Int. Advisory Bd of Council on Foreign Relations and Bd Dirs Inst. for Int. Econs, Int. Crisis Group Bd, High-Level Panel on Legal Empowerment of the Poor, Foundation Bd of World Econ. Forum, Club de Madrid, Group of Thirty Consultative Group on Int. Econ. and Monetary Affairs, Inc. (G-30), Washington, DC 2005–; UN Special Envoy for 2005 World Summit; Distinguished Visiting Fellow, Centre for Global Governance, LSE 2001; Distinguished Lecturer, Univ. of Miami 2001; Distinguished Collins Fellow, John F. Kennedy School of Govt, Harvard Univ. 2001; Prof. in the Field of Int. Econs and Politics and Dir Yale Center for the Study of Globalization, Yale Univ., USA 2002–; mem. Bd of Dirs Procter and Gamble, ALCOA, Union Pacific Corpn, Citigroup 2010–, Inst. for Int. Economics; mem. Int. Advisory Bd Coca Cola Co., MAGNA; mem. Editorial Bd Americas Quarterly; Trustee, Fundacion Carolina, Madrid; decorations from govts of 32 countries; Hon. LLD (Yale) 2001, (Harvard) 2003; Hon. DHumLitt (Miami) 2002; Dr hc (Massachusetts, Amherst) 2003; Wilbur Cross Medal, Democracy and Peace Award, Inst. of the Americas, Univ. of California, San Diego 2001, Franklin D. Roosevelt Freedom from Fear Award 2002, Tribuna Americana Award, Casa de America, Madrid, Spain 2002, Commencement Speaker, Harvard Univ. 2003, Gold Insigne, The Americas Soc. 2003, Berkeley Medal, Univ. of California, Berkeley 2004, Sustainable Devt Leadership Award, The Energy Resources Inst. (TERI), India 2006. *Address:* Yale Center for the Study of Globalization, Betts House, 393 Prospect Street, New Haven, CT 06511, USA (office). *Telephone:* (203) 432-1900 (office). *Fax:* (203) 432-1200 (office). *E-mail:* ernesto.zedillo@yale.edu (office); globalization@yale.edu (office). *Website:* www.ycsg.yale.edu (office).

ZEDKAIA, Iroij Jurelang; Marshall Islands politician and fmr head of state; s. of the late Leroij Atama Zedkaia (paramount chief of Majuro Atoll); began career as pharmacist; Iroij (traditional tribal chief), Majuro Atoll; Senator from Majuro, Nitijela (lower house of parl.), fmr Vice-Speaker, then Speaker 2008–09; Pres., Marshall Islands 2009–12; mem. Ailin Kein Ad (Our Islands). *Address:* c/o Office of the President, Government of the Republic of the Marshall Islands, POB 2, Majuro, MH 96960, Marshall Islands.

ZEFFIRELLI, Franco (Gian Franco Corsi); Italian theatre, opera and film director and set designer; b. 12 Feb. 1923, Florence; ed Liceo Artistico, Florence and Univ. of Florence School of Architecture; moved to Rome to debut as an actor in cinema and theatre 1946; met Luchino Visconti which proved crucial for his film and theatre training, hired as an asst and later as a set designer for production of William Shakespeare's Troilus and Cressida 1949, Tennessee Williams' A Streetcar Named Desire; worked as asst dir in various theatre productions and in films The Earth Trembles 1947, Bellissima 1951, Senso 1954; produced set designs for Romeo and Juliet, staged at the Old Vic Company, London 1960; staged, amongst others, productions of La Cenerentola by Gioachino Rossini 1953, La Traviata by Giuseppe Verdi with Maria Callas 1958; release of film The Taming of the Shrew 1967, Romeo and Juliet 1968; commissioned by leading opera houses world-wide, including Teatro alla Scala of Milan, The Met, New York, Covent Garden, London and Staatsoper, Vienna, to stage performances; numerous opera productions with artists including Maria Callas, Plácido Domingo, Luciano Pavarotti, Herbert Von Karajan, Leonard Bernstein, Carlos Kleiber; productions include Il Turco in Italia with Maria Callas, Aïda and La Bohéme at Teatro alla Scala, Milan, Carmen at the Staatsoper, Vienna, Tosca, Turandot, Falstaff and La Traviata at the Metropolitan, New York, Aïda, Il Trovatore, Carmen and Madama Butterfly in Verona, and two experiments in Busseto with small productions of Aïda and La Traviata; Aïda of Busseto brought to Moscow 2004, La Traviata of Busseto staged in Moscow and Tel-Aviv 2005 (also I Pagliacci); Teatro dell'Opera, Rome presented Don Giovanni 2006, followed by Aïda 2006; returned to Teatro dell'Opera, Rome for a new comeback of La Traviata 2007, Tosca 2008, I Pagliacci 2009, Falstaff 2010; production of Carmen at Arena of Verona 2009, Turandot 2010, also Aïda, Madama Butterfly, Carmen and Il Trovatore; new Turandot celebrated the opening of the Royal Opera House of Muscat, Sultanate of Oman 2011; presented Don Giovanni of Mozart at Arena of Verona 2012; made the film-opera of Cavalleria Rusticana by Pietro Mascagni and I Pagliacci by Ruggero Leoncavallo 1980; create film version of Verdi's La Traviata; also successful in the prose theatre, both in Italy and abroad, with works by Shakespeare: Hamlet with Giorgio Albertazzi, also performed in London, and Romeo and Juliet; other works include La Lupa by Verga, starring Anna Magnani, and pieces by contemporary authors: Who's Afraid of Virginia Woolf by Edward Albee, After the Fall by Arthur Miller, Due più due non fa più quattro by Lina Wertmüller, Sabato, Domenica e Lunedì by Eduardo, at the Old Vic, London and featuring Sir Laurence Olivier; Hon. KBE 2005; Prix des Nations 1976, Premio Colosseo, City of Rome 2009 and numerous others. Theatre: Romeo and Juliet (Old Vic, London) 1960, Othello (Stratford) 1961, Amleto (Nat. Theatre, London) 1964, After the Fall (Rome) 1964, Who's Afraid of Virginia Woolf (Paris) 1964, (Milan) 1965, La Lupa (Rome) 1965, Much Ado About Nothing (Nat. Theatre, London) 1966, Black Comedy (Rome) 1967, A Delicate Balance (Rome) 1967, Saturday, Sunday, Monday (Nat. Theatre, London) 1973, Filumena (Lyric, London) 1977, Six Characters in Search of an Author (London) 1992, Absolutely Perhaps! (London) 2003, Pagliacci (Teatro Carlo Felice, Genoa) 2011, Turandot (Royal Opera House, Sultanate of Oman) 2011, Pagliacci (Arena di Verona) 2012, Don Giovanni (Arena di Verona) 2012. Operas include: Lucia di Lammermoor, Cavalleria Rusticana, Pagliacci (Covent Garden) 1959, 1973, Falstaff (Covent Garden) 1961, L'Elisir d'amore (Glyndebourne) 1961, Don Giovanni, Alcina (Covent Garden) 1962, Tosca, Rigoletto (Covent Garden) 1964, 1966, 1973, (Metropolitan, New York) 1985, Don Giovanni (Staatsoper Wien) 1972, (Metropolitan, New York) 1990, Otello (Metropolitan, New York) 1972, Antony and Cleopatra (Metropolitan, New York) 1973, Otello (La Scala) 1976, La Bohème (Metropolitan, New York) 1981, Turandot (La Scala) 1983, 1985, (Metropolitan, New York) 1987, Don Carlos 1992, Carmen 1996, Aïda (New Theatre, Tokyo) 1997, (Busseto) 2000, La Traviata (Metropolitan, New York) 1998, Tosca (Rome) 2000, Il Trovatore (Arena di Verona) 2001, Aïda (Arena di Verona) 2002, La Bohème (La Scala) 2003, (Rome) 2003, Carmen (Arena di Verona) 2003, I Pagliacci (Covent Garden, London) 2003, (Tel-Aviv, Israel) 2005, Madama Butterfly (Arena Di Verona) 2004, Aïda (La Scala, Milan) 2006, La Traviata (Rome) 2007, I Pagliacci (Taormina) 2008, La Bohème (Tel-Aviv) 2008, Aïda (Tel-Aviv) 2009, I Pagliacci (Rome) 2009, Falstaff (Rome) 2010, Carmen (Arena di Verona) 2009, Turandot (Arena di Verona) 2010, Aïda (Arena di Verona) 2010, Madama Butterfl (Arena di Verona) 2010, Il Trovatore (Arena di Verona) 2010, Turandot (Royal Opera House of Muscat, Sultanate of Oman) 2011, Don Giovanni (Arena di Verona) 2012. Ballet: Swan Lake 1985; produced Beethoven's Missa Solemnis, San Pietro, Rome 1971. Films: The Taming of the Shrew 1966, Romeo and Juliet (five Nastri d'argento Awards, Italian cinematographic journalists) 1967, Brother Sun and Sister Moon 1973, The Champ 1979, Endless Love 1981, La Traviata 1983, Cavalleria Rusticana 1983, Otello 1986, The Young Toscanini 1987, Hamlet 1990, Storia di una capinera (Sparrow) 1993, Jane Eyre 1995, Tea with Mussolini 1998, Callas Forever 2002, Omaggio a Roma (short) 2009. Television includes: Florence, Days of Destruction (film) 1966, Jesus of Nazareth (mini-series) 1977, celebrative concert of the second century of the birth of Ludwig van Beethoven (RAI) held in St Peter's Basilica in the presence of Pope Paul VI. Publication: Zeffirelli by Zeffirelli (autobiog.) 1986 (second edn 2006). Address: Via Lucio Volumnio 45, 00178 Rome, Italy. Fax: (06) 7184213. E-mail: fzeffirelli@tin.it.

ZEGLIS, John D., LLB; American lawyer and telecommunications industry executive (retd); ed Univ. of Illinois, Harvard Law School; began legal career as Assoc., Sidley & Austin 1973, later becoming pnr –1984; joined AT&T Wireless Services, Inc. 1984, Corp. Vice-Pres. of Law 1984–86, Gen. Counsel 1984–96, Vice-Chair. and Pres. 1997–99, Chair. and CEO AT&T Wireless 1999-2004 (retd after AT&T Wireless acquired by Cingular Wireless LLC); mem. Bd of Dirs Helmerich and Payne Corpn, AMX Corpn, State Farm Insurance; fmr mem. Bd of Dirs Dynergy Corpn, Sara Lee Corpn, Georgia Pacific; fmr Sr Ed. Harvard Law Review; Chair. Bd of Trustees, George Washington Univ.; Trustee, Culver Educ. Foundation, Marshall County Community Fund, St. Joseph Medical Center of Plymouth, Ind.; mem. Bd Rural School and Community Trust, Washington; mem. Kellogg Advisory Bd, J.L. Kellogg Grad. School of Man.; mem. NW Univ., Univ. of Ill. Business Advisory Council. Address: c/o Board of Trustees, Culver Educational Foundation, 1300 Academy Road, Culver, IN 46511-1291, USA (office).

ZEIBOTS, Vice-Adm. Gaidis Andrejs; Latvian naval officer and radio and electronics engineer; Member of the Council, Rīga Shipyard; b. 26 June 1945, Valka Dist; m. Dzintra Zeibots; one d.; ed Naval Acad. of Radioelectronics, Leningrad (now St Petersburg), Russia, Coll. of Strategic Studies, George C. Marshall Centre, Germany, US Army War Coll., USA; Chief of Radio Eng Service of destroyer, Tallinn Naval Base, Estonia 1969–70, Liepaja Naval Base 1970–72; Exec. Officer of destroyer, Liepaja 1975–76, Commdr of frigate 1976–78; Deputy Chief of Staff, Missile Carrier Div., Baltic Naval Base 1980–86; Deputy Commdr Naval Base 1986–88; Commdr Naval Div., Gdynia, Poland 1988–91; C-in-C Latvian Naval Forces 1991–99; Exec. Sec. for NATO Integration, Ministry of Defence 1999–2002; Deputy Commdr and Operational Commdr Latvian Nat. Armed Forces 2002–03, Chief of Defence 2003–06; Advisor to Minister of Defence 2007–09; mem. Council, Rīga Shipyard 2009–; Norwegian Order of Royal Kts, Order of King Gedimins (Fourth Class), Orders from Estonia, Italy, Netherlands; Medal of Order of Three Stars, two Ministry of Defence Awards, NAF Commdr Medal, Naval Commdr Medal. Address: Rīga Shipyard, Gales Street 2, Rīga 1015, Latvia (office). Telephone: 67046317 (office). Fax: 67353452 (office). E-mail:

zeibots@riga-shipyard.com (office); office@eiroholdings.lv (office). Website: www.riga-shipyard.com (office).

ZEIDAN, Ali; Libyan politician and fmr diplomatist; b. 1950; served as Libyan diplomat during 1970s, including in India; defected 1980; est. Nat. Front for the Salvation of Libya, mem. –2011; served as Nat. Transitional Council's Europe envoy during uprising 2011; mem. Nat. Forces Alliance 2011–12; Ind. 2012–; elected for Jufra in Congressional election 2012; Prime Minister of Libya 2012–14. Address: c/o Office of the Prime Minister, Tripoli, Libya.

ZEIDANE, Zeine Ould, PhD; Mauritanian economist, banker and politician; b. 1966, Tamchekett; ed Univ of Nice, France; taught math. at Univ of Nice 1995–96 and Univ of Nouakchott 1996–97; Head of Treasury Dept, Gen. Bank of Mauritania 1997–98; Co-ordinator of Analysis and Econ. Synthesis, Ministry of the Economy and Devt 1998–2000; Economist, World Bank, Nouakchott 2000–02; Co-ordinator, Mauritanian Centre for Political Analysis 2002–04; Econ. Adviser to the Pres. 2003–04; Gov., Cen. Bank of Mauratania 2004–06; Prime Minister 2007–08 (resgnd); unsuccessful cand. in presidential elections 2007. Address: c/o Office of the Prime Minister, BP 237, Nouakchott, Mauritania (office).

ZEIDLER, Eberhard Heinrich, OC, OOnt, PA, DEng, DArch, FRAIC, RCA, OAA, MAIBC, OAQ; Canadian architect; b. 11 Jan. 1926, Braunsdorf, Germany; s. of Paul Zeidler and Dorothea Dabbert; m. Phyllis Jane Abbott 1957; one s. three d.; ed Bauhaus Weimar and Univ. Fridericiana, Karlsruhe Technische Hochschule; designer, Prof. Egon Eiermann, Karlsruhe 1949–50; Assoc. with Prof. Emanuel Lindner, Osnabrück 1950–51; emigrated to Canada 1951; Assoc.-in-Charge of Design, W. & W. R. L. Blackwell & Craig, Peterborough 1951–54; Partner, Blackwell, Craig & Zeidler Architects, Peterborough and Toronto 1954–57, Craig & Zeidler Architects, Peterborough and Toronto 1957–61, Craig, Zeidler & Strong, Peterborough and Toronto 1961–75, Zeidler Partnership/Architects, Toronto 1975–80, Zeidler Roberts Partnership/Architects, Toronto 1980–2001, Zeidler Grinnell Partnership 2001–03, Zeidler Partnership Architects 2003–, now Sr Partner Emer.; Hon. FAIA 1981; Gold Medal, Royal Architectural Inst. of Canada 1986; more than 100 nat. and int. awards. Projects include: Beth Israel Synagogue, Peterborough 1964, McMaster Univ. Health Science Centre, Hamilton, Ont. 1972, Ontario Place theme park (including Cinesphere), Toronto 1967–71, Walter C. Mackenzie Health Sciences Centre, Toronto 1975–86, Eaton Centre shopping mall and offices, with Bregman & Hamann Architects, Edmonton, Alberta 1977–81, Yerba Buena Gardens, San Francisco 1980–84, redevelopment of the Queen's Quay Terminal, Toronto 1979–83, Canada Place for Expo '86, Vancouver 1986, MediaPark Cologne 1990–2004, Raymond F. Kravis Center for the Performing Arts, West Palm Beach, Fla 1992, Toronto Centre for the Arts 1993, Living Arts Centre, Mississauga, Ont. 1997, Hosp. for Sick Children Atrium, Toronto 1993, Rogers Office Campus, Toronto 1992, York Univ. Accolade Project, Toronto 2005–06, Sherway Gardens Phase IV, Toronto 1989–90, Royal Victoria Hosp. Atrium, Barrie, Queen's Quay Terminal restoration, Toronto 1983, Markham Stouffville Hosp., Ont. 1990, Gladstone Hotel restoration 2002–03, Toronto Trump Int. Hotel and Tower, Toronto 2012. Publications: Healing the Hospital 1974, Multi-use Architecture in the Urban Context 1983, Zeidler Roberts Partnership – Ethics and Architecture 1999. Leisure interests: skiing, tennis. Address: Zeidler Partnership Architects, 315 Queen Street West, Toronto, ON M5V 2X2, Canada (office). Telephone: (416) 596-8300. Fax: (416) 596-1408. E-mail: ezeidler@zeidler.com (office); info@zeidler.com (office). Website: www.zeidler.com (office).

ZEILER, Gerhard; Austrian media executive; President, Turner Broadcasting System International; b. 20 July 1955; fmr freelance journalist; fmr press spokesman for Austrian Chancellors, Fred Sinowatz and Franz Vranitzky; Gen. Sec. ORF (broadcaster) 1986–1990; CEO Tele5 1990–92, RTL 2 1992–94, ORF 1994–98, RTL TV 1998–2005, RTL Group 2003–11; Pres. Turner Broadcasting System International 2011–; mem. Bd M6 TV station 2002–, Bertelsmann Foundation 2002–, Bertelsmann AG 2005–11. Address: Turner Broadcasting System International, c/o Time Warner Inc., One Time Warner Center, New York, NY 10019-8016, USA (office). Telephone: (212) 484-8000 (office). E-mail: info@turner.com (office). Website: www.turner.com (office).

ZEILINGER, Anton, PhD; Austrian physicist and academic; Scientific Director, IQOQI Institute of Quantum Optics and Quantum Information, Austrian Academy of Sciences; b. 20 May 1945, Ried/Innkreis; ed Bundesgymnasium Wien 13, Univ. of Vienna, Tech. Univ. of Vienna; Research Asst, Atominstitut Vienna with Prof. Helmut Rauch 1972–79, Asst Prof. 1979–83; Research Assoc. (Fulbright Fellow), Neutron Diffraction Lab., MIT, USA 1977–78, Assoc. Prof. of Physics (Visiting) 1981–83; Assoc. Prof., Tech. Univ. of Vienna 1983–90; Prof. of Physics (Lehrstuhlvertretung), Tech. Univ. of Munich 1988–89; Prof. of Experimental Physics, Univ. of Innsbruck 1990–99; Prof. of Experimental Physics, Univ. of Vienna 1999–, Dean of Faculty of Physics 2006–09, mem. Founding Convent, Univ. of Vienna 2002–03; Scientific Dir IQOQI Inst. of Quantum Optics and Quantum Information, Austrian Acad. of Sciences, Vienna 2004–; Guest Researcher (part-time), Institut Laue-Langevin, Grenoble, France 1974–89; regular summer research appointments at MIT 1983–90; Adjunct Full Prof. (part-time), Hampshire Coll., Amherst, USA 1986–89; Chaire Internationale, Collège de France, Paris 1995; Visiting Research Fellow, Merton Coll., Oxford, UK 1998, (part-time) 2010; Sr Humboldt Fellow, Humboldt Univ., Berlin, Germany 2001–04; est. a new postgraduate research inst. implemented as Inst. of Science and Tech. of Austria 2002, mem. Exec. Bd and Vice-Chair. Bd of Trustees, Inst. of Science and Tech. of Austria 2006–; mem. Editorial Bd Physical Review A 1994–2000, Foundations of Physics 1988–, New Journal of Physics 2006–08; Pres. Austrian Physical Soc. 1997–98, Int. Acad. Traunkirchen 2009–; Corresp. mem. Austrian Acad. of Sciences 1994, Full mem. 1998, mem. Planning and Strategy Cttee 2008–, Pres.-elect 2013; mem. Quantum Electronics and Optics Div., European Physical Soc. 1996–98, Academia Scientiarum et Artium Europaea 2000, Berlin-Brandenburg Acad. of Sciences 2002, German Acad. of Sciences Leopoldina 2005, Academia Europaea 2011; Foreign mem. Serbian Acad. of Sciences and Arts 2006, Acad. des Sciences, Institut de France 2009; Foreign Assoc. NAS 2013; Fellow, American Physical Soc. 1999, AAAS 2012; Hon. Prof., Univ. of Science and Tech. of China 1996; Hon. mem. Slovak Acad. of Sciences 2005; Decoration of Sciences and Arts (Austrian equivalent to the Order of Merit) 2001, Order pour le Mérite for Sciences and Arts (Germany) 2001, Great Cross of Merit with Star (Germany) 2009, Großer Tiroler Adler Orden 2013; Dr hc (Humboldt Univ., Berlin) 2005, (Gdansk Univ.,

Poland) 2006; numerous awards including Prize of the City of Vienna for the Encouragement of Young Scientists 1975, Prize for Jr Scientists, Kardinal Innitzer Foundation, Vienna 1979, Sir Thomas Lyle Lecturer, Univ. of Melbourne, Australia 1984, Prix Vinci d'Excellence, Fondation LVMH, Paris 1995, Colloquium Ehrenfestii, Univ. of Leiden, Netherlands 1996, 2004, Austrian Scientist of the Year 1996, European Lecturer, European Physical Soc. 1996, H.L. Welsh Lecture in Physics, Univ. of Toronto, Canada 1997, European Optics Prize, European Optical Soc. 1997, Schrödinger Lecturer, Trinity Coll., Dublin, Ireland 1999, Science Prize, City of Vienna 2000, Sr Humboldt Fellow Prize, Alexander von Humboldt Stiftung, Germany 2000, Johannes Kepler Prize, Science Prize of Upper Austria 2002, Niels Bohr Lecturer, Univ. of Copenhagen, Denmark 2003, Schrödinger Lecturer, Imperial Coll., London, UK 2003, Amos de-Shalit Memorial Lecturer, Weizmann Inst., Rehovot, Israel 2003, Sartorius Prize, Göttingen Acad. of Sciences, Germany 2003, Lorenz Oken Medal, Soc. of German Researchers and Physicians 2004, Descartes Prize, EC 2005, King Faisal Prize, Saudi Arabia 2005, Wilhelm Exner Medal, Austrian Asscn for SME (Oesterreichischer Gewerbeverein—OGV) (jtly) 2005, Rosenthal Lecturer, Yale Univ., USA 2006, Barut Memorial Lecturer, Bogazici Univ., Istanbul, Turkey 2006, Grand Gold Decoration, City of Vienna 2006, Quantum Electronics Prize, European Physical Soc. 2007, Asher Perez Memorial Lecturer, Technion, Haifa, Israel 2008, Newton Prize Lecture and Medal, Inst. of Physics, London 2008, Quantum Communication Award, Tamagawa Univ., Japan 2008; PITP Lecture on Quantum Phenomena, Pacific Inst. of Theoretical Physics, Vancouver, Canada 2009, Inaugural Kavli Colloquium, Kavli Inst. of Nanoscience, Delft Univ. of Tech., Netherlands 2009, Berlin Brandenburg Acad. of Sciences, Humboldt Univ., Berlin 2009, Celsius Lecturer, Uppsala Univ. 2010, Dvorak Memorial Lecturer, Univ. of Prague 2010, Ockham Lecturer, Merton Coll., Oxford 2010, Frontiers in Physics Lecturer, City Coll., CUNY 2010, Wolf Prize in Physics 2010, Van Fleck Lecturer, Univ. of Minnesota, USA 2011, Mark W. Zemansky Lecturer, City Coll. of New York 2011. *Publications include:* Matter Wave Interferometry. On the occasion of the 100th anniversary of E. Schrödinger's birth (co-ed.) 1988, Fundamental Problems in Quantum Theory. In Honor of Professor John A. Wheeler, Annals of the New York Academy of Sciences, Vol. 755 (co-ed.) 1995, The Physics of Quantum Information – Quantum Cryptography, Quantum Teleportation, Quantum Computation (co-ed.) 2000, Quantum Information – An Introduction to Basic Theoretical Concepts and Experiments, Springer Tracts in Modern Physics, Vol. 173 (co-ed.) 2001, Quantum Computation and Quantum Information Theory (co-ed.) 2001, Quantum [Un]speakables – From Bell to Quantum Information (co-ed.) 2002; more than 450 scientific publs, including more than 350 in peer-reviewed, ISI-ranked journals; popular science books: Einsteins Schleier 2003, Einsteins Spuk 2005, Dance of the Photons 2010. *Address:* Quantum Optics, Quantum Nanophysics, Quantum Information, University of Vienna, Boltzmanngasse 5, 1090 Vienna (office); Institute for Quantum Optics and Quantum Information, Austrian Academy of Sciences, Boltzmanngasse 3, 1090 Vienna, Austria (office). *Telephone:* (1) 4277-51201 (office). *Fax:* (1) 4277-29552 (office). *E-mail:* anton.zeilinger@univie.ac.at (office). *Website:* vcq.quantum.at/research/research-groups/zeilinger-group.html (office).

ZEINE, Ali Mahamane Lamine; Niger economist and politician; Dir of Cabinet of Pres. Mamadou Tandja –2003; Minister of the Economy and Finance 2003–10 (removed following coup d'état Feb. 2010, held under house arrest). *Address:* c/o Ministry of the Economy and Finance, BP 389, Niamey, Niger (office).

ZEITLIN, (Benjamin Harold) Benh; American filmmaker, composer and animator; b. 14 Oct. 1982, Queens, New York City, NY; s. of Steve Zeitlin and Amanda Dargan; ed Hastings-on-Hudson High School, Wesleyan Univ., Middletown, Conn.; began career as a filmmaker aged six when he and a friend made a Batman film; spent a summer in Prague working with a prominent animation artist; returned to USA to work in a pvt. Manhattan school helping elementary students create short films; co-f. Court 13 ind. collection of filmmakers 2004; moved to New Orleans while making his first short film, Glory at Sea 2008; Breakthrough Dir Award, Gotham Ind. Film Awards 2012, also received the inaugural Bingham Ray Award 2012, Smithsonian American Ingenuity Award for the Visual Arts 2012. *Films include:* Egg (short) 2005, The Origins of Electricity (short) 2006, Glory at Sea (short) 2008, Beasts of the Southern Wild (Caméra d'Or Award, Cannes Film Festival, Grand Jury Prize: Dramatic, Sundance Film Festival, Grand Jury Prize, Deauville American Film Festival, Los Angeles Film Festival Audience Award for Best Narrative Feature, Seattle Int. Film Festival Golden Space Needle Award for Best Dir) 2012; composer: Death to the Tinman (short) 2007. *E-mail:* josh@court13.com (office). *Website:* www.court13.com (office).

ZEKI, Semir, PhD, FRS, FMedSci; British neurobiologist and academic; *Professor and Head, Laboratory of Neurobiology, University College London;* m. Anne-Marie Claire; one s. one d.; ed Univ. Coll., London; joined teaching staff, Univ. Coll., London 1969, Prof., Dept of Anatomy and Embryology 1981, later Co-Head, Wellcome Lab. of Cognitive Neurology, currently Prof. of Neurobiology, Lab. of Neurobiology; Henry Head Research Fellow, Royal Soc., London 1975–80; fmr Visiting Prof. Univ. of Calif., Berkeley, USA; mem. Bd of Scientific Govs Scripps Scientific Research Inst., La Jolla, Calif., USA, Nat. Science Council of France; mem. Bd of Advisers Beit Memorial Trust; Ed. The Philosophical Transactions of the Royal Society; mem. Academia Europaea, European Acad. of Sciences and Arts; Foreign mem. American Philosophical Soc.; Fellow, Inst. for Neuroscience, New York; Trustee, Fight for Sight; Hon. DSc (Aston, Aberdeen); Hocart Prize, Royal Anthropological Inst. 1961, first Golden Brain Award, Minerva Foundation, Berkeley 1985, Science for Art Prize, LVMH 1991, Rank Prize in Optoelectronics 1992, Betty and David Koetser Foundation Prize 1997, King Faisal Int. Prize in Biology 2004, Erasmus Medal 2008. *Publications:* A Vision of the Brain 1993, La Quête de l'essentiel (co-author) 1995, Inner Vision – An Exploration of Art and the Brain 1999, Splendours and Miseries of the Brain 2008; numerous articles in scientific journals. *Address:* Department of Anatomy, University College London, Darwin Building, Gower Street, London, WC1E 6BT, England (office). *Telephone:* (20) 7679-7316 (office). *E-mail:* zeki.pa@ucl.ac.uk (office). *Website:* www.vislab.ucl.ac.uk (office); www.neuroesthetics.org (office).

ZELAYA ROSALES, José Manuel; Honduran politician and fmr head of state; b. 20 Sept. 1952, Catacamas, Olancho; s. of Jose Manuel Zelaya Ordoñez and Hortensia Esmeralda Rosales Sarmiento; m. Xiomara Castro Sarmiento; four c.; ed Nat. Honduran Univ.; trained as civil engineer; ranch owner; mem. Liberal Party of Honduras; Deputy in Nat. Congress 1985–, Chair. Natural Resources and Petroleum Cttee 1985–89; Minister for Investment, in charge of Honduran Investment Fund 1994–2002; Sec. Gen. Exec. Council for Advertising and Org. 1999–2004; Founder and Leader, Movimiento Esperanza Liberal (faction within Liberal Party) 2005–; Pres. of Honduras 2005–09; Chair. Bd of Dirs Asociación de Industriales de la Madera 1987–94; mem. Honduran Nat. Business Council (COEHP) 1987–94, Bd of Dirs Sogerin Bank. *Address:* c/o Office of the President, Palacio José Cecilio del Valle, Blvd Juan Pablo II, Tegucigalpa (office); Partido Liberal, Col. Miramonte, Tegucigalpa, Honduras (office).

ZELENSKAYA, Elena Emilyevna; Russian singer (soprano); b. 1 June 1961, Baku, Azerbaijan; ed Baku State Conservatory; soloist, Moscow Municipal Theatre New Opera 1991–96, Bolshoi Theatre 1996–; tours abroad 1992–; guest singer, Wiener Kammeroper 1992–; debut as Lady Macbeth in Lucerne, as Donna Elvira in Savonlinna Opera Festival (Finland), as Aida in Deutsche Oper Düsseldorf 1997, as Lisa in Queen of Spades in Berlin Oper, as Tosca in Norway. *Opera:* leading parts include Tatyana in Eugene Onegin, Yaroslavna in Prince Igor, Lady Macbeth in Macbeth, Amelia in Ballo in Maschera, Leonora in La Forza del Destino, Countess in Le Nozze di Figaro, Donna Elvira in Don Giovanni. *Address:* c/o APA Artist Management, 25E Frognal, London, NW3 6AR, England (office). *Telephone:* (20) 7794-7633 (office). *Fax:* (20) 7431-7320 (office).

ZELENSKY, Igor Anatolyevich; Russian ballet dancer; *Principal, Mariinsky Opera and Ballet Theatre;* b. 13 July 1969, Labinsk, Krasnodar Dist.; ed Tbilisi School of Choreography, Leningrad Vaganova School of Choreography; with Tbilisi Opera and Ballet Theatre 1988–89, Mariinsky Opera and Ballet Theatre 1988–, Prin. 1991–; dancer with New York City Ballet 1992–97; guest appearances with Royal Ballet, London 1996–; Prin. Guest Dancer Bayerische Staatsoper 2000; Grand Prix and Gold Medal Int. Competition of Ballet Artists, Paris 1990, Prix de Lumières of Italian Cinema, Honoured Artist of Russia 2000, Baltika prize 2001. *Ballets include:* Basil in Don Quixote, Siegfried in Swan Lake, Aki in Corsair, Solor in La Bayadère, Albert in Gisèle, leading roles in Romeo and Julliet, Apollo, Manon, Sleeping Beauty; numerous performances in Europe and the USA. *Address:* Mariinsky Theatre, Teatralnaya pl. 1, St Petersburg, Russia (office). *Telephone:* (812) 114-12-11 (office). *Website:* www.kirovballet.com (office).

ŽELEZNÝ, Jan; Czech fmr athlete; b. 16 June 1966, Mladá Boleslav; s. of Jaroslav Zelezny and Jana Zelezny; javelin thrower; fmr mechanic and army col; set five world javelin records; won 106 out of 135 competitions 1991–2001; current world record javelin throw (of 98.48m) at Jena 1996; World Champion 1992, 1995, 2001, bronze medal, Rome 1987, Seville 1999; silver medal, Olympic Games 1988, gold medal 1992, 1996, 2000; bronze medal, European Championships, Helsinki 1994, Gothenburg 2006; mem. IOC 2000–02, 2004–; Czech Athlete of the Year 1993, 1995, 2000, 2011, Men's European Athlete of the Year 1996, 2000, IAAF Athlete of the Year 2000, Medal of Merit, Czech Repub. 2001. *Leisure interests:* fishing, golf, tennis, fine wine. *Address:* c/o Czech Olympic Committee, Benešovská 6, 101 00 Prague 10, Czech Republic. *Telephone:* (2) 71730622. *Fax:* (2) 71731318. *E-mail:* info@olympic.cz. *Website:* www.olympic.cz/czech-republic; www.iaaf.org/athletes/czech-republic/jan-zelezny-3207.

ŽELEZNÝ, Vladimír, PhDr; Czech politician, publicist, manager and entrepreneur; *CEO, TV Barrandov;* b. 3 March 1945, Samara, Russia; s. of Theodor Zelezný and Alexandra Železný; m. 1st (divorced); two s.; m. 2nd; one s. one d.; ed Charles Univ., Prague; producer, Czechoslovak TV; student leader 1964–68; worked in radio, TV and newspapers 1970–89; spokesman of Civic Forum during Velvet Revolution 1989–91; Adviser to Prime Minister 1991–92; Founder and Dir-Gen. TV Nova 1993–2003; CEO TV Barrandov 2013–; has written and co-written over 100 popular science programmes for radio and TV; Senator 2002–04; mem. European Parl. (Independence/Democracy Group) 2004–09, mem. Cttee on Regional Devt, Substitute mem. Cttee on Agric. and Rural Devt, mem. Del. to EU-Russia Parl. Co-operation Cttee, Substitute mem. Del. for Relations with Israel; Vice-Pres. Intergroup Viticulture-Tradition-Quality; Founder and Vice-Pres. Franz Kafka Soc. and Franz Kafka Foundation, Prague; Head, Bd Trustees Galerie Foundation; Vice-Pres. B'nai B'rith Renaissance, Prague; mem. Bd KKL (Czech Repub.); Prize for the popularization of science, Czechoslovak Acad. of Science 1988. *Publications include:* screenplays, televised plays and books; several popular science studies, including Windows of the Universe Wide Open. *Leisure interests:* art collector, photographer, propagator of wineculture. *Address:* Dlouhá 12, 110 00 Prague 1, Czech Republic (office). *E-mail:* vladimir.zelezny@centrum.cz (office); v.zelezny@tanzberg.cz (office). *Website:* www.vladimirzelezny.cz (office).

ŻELICHOWSKI, Stanisław; Polish politician; b. 9 April 1944, Księżostany, Zamość Prov.; m.; one s. one d.; ed Dept of Forestry, Agric. Univ., Warsaw; began career in Presidium of Dist People's Council, Ostrołęka; Lecturer, Ciechanów Forest Inspectorate 1969; Forest Insp. Dwukoły Forest Inspectorate 1974; mem. Nat. Forestry Council; mem. United Peasants' Party (ZSL) 1970–89; mem. Tribunal of State 1989–91; mem. Main Exec. Cttee Polish Peasants' Party (PSL) and Pres. Prov. Bd of PSL, Ciechanów 1990–, mem. Comm. for Foreign Affairs; Deputy to Sejm (Parl.) 1985–89, 1991–; Minister of Environmental Protection, Natural Resources and Forestry 1993–97, of the Environment 2001–03; Vice-Chair. Parl. Cttee for Environmental Protection, Natural Resources and Forestry 1997–2001. *Leisure interests:* tourism, sports. *Address:* c/o Ministry of Environment, ul. Wawelska 52/54, 00-922 Warsaw, Poland (office).

ZELLICK, Graham John, CBE, QC (Hon.), MA, PhD, AcSS; British lawyer, academic, public servant and judge; *President, Valuation Tribunal for England;* b. 12 Aug. 1948, London, England; m. Jennifer Temkin 1975; one s. one d.; ed Christ's Coll., Finchley, London, Gonville & Caius Coll., Cambridge, Stanford Univ., USA; Lecturer in Laws, Queen Mary and Westfield Coll., Univ. of London 1971–78, Reader in Law 1978–82, Prof. of Public Law 1982–88, Dean Faculty of Laws 1984–88, Head, Dept of Law 1984–90, Drapers' Prof. of Law 1988–91, Sr Vice-Prin. and Acting Prin. 1990–91, Prin. 1991–98, Prof. of Law 1991–98, Prof. Emer. 1998–; Dean Faculty of Laws, Univ. of London 1986–88, Deputy Vice-Chancellor 1994–97, Vice-Chancellor and Pres. 1997–2003; Visiting Prof. of Law, Univ. of Toronto 1975, 1978–79; Visiting Scholar, St John's Coll. Oxford 1989; Visiting Prof., Queen Mary, Univ. of London 2007–12; barrister, Middle Temple 1992, Master of Bench 2001, Reader 2013; Chair. Criminal Cases Review Comm. 2003–08; mem. Competition

Comm. Appeal Tribunals 2000–03, Competition Appeal Tribunal 2003, Criminal Injuries Compensation Appeals Panel 2000–03, Investigatory Powers Tribunal 2013; Electoral Commr 2001–04; Ed. Public Law 1981–86; Founding Ed. European Human Rights Reports 1978–82; Gov. Tel-Aviv Univ.; Pres. W London (Reform) Synagogue 2000–06, Valuation Tribunal for England 2009–; Ford Foundation Fellow in Criminal Law and Policy, Stanford Law School 1970–71; Chair. Bd Govs Leo Baeck Coll. 2005–06, Bd Trustees, Richmond The American Int. Univ. in London 2005–06; Fellow, Inst. of Continuing Professional Devt 1998; mem. Court, Drapers' Co. 2000–, Master 2009–10; Academician, Acad. of Social Sciences 2000; Fellow, Heythrop Coll., Univ. of London 2005; Freeman, City of London 1992; Hon. Prof., School of Law, Univ. of Birmingham 2004–11; Hon. Fellow, Soc. of Advanced Legal Studies 1997–, Burgon Soc., Gonville and Caius Coll., Cambridge 2001, Leo Baeck Coll. 2007; Hon. FRAM 2003; Hon. LHD (New York) 2001; Hon. LLD (Richmond – The American Univ. in London) 2003, (Birmingham) 2006; Hon. DLit (Queen Mary, London) 2010. *Address:* Valuation Tribunal for England, Black Lion House, 45 Whitechapel Road, London, E1 1DU, England (office). *Telephone:* (20) 7426-3916 (office). *Fax:* (20) 7247-6598 (office). *E-mail:* president@vts.gsi.gov.uk (office). *Website:* www.valuationtribunal.gov.uk (office).

ZELLWEGER, Renée, BA; American actress; b. 25 April 1969, Katy, Tex.; d. of Emil Zellweger and Kjellfrid Zellweger; m. Kenny Chesney 2005 (annulled); ed Katy High School, Univ. of Texas. *Films include:* Dazed and Confused 1993, Reality Bites 1994, Love and a .45 1994, 8 Seconds 1994, The Low Life 1995, Empire Records 1995, The Whole Wide World 1996, Jerry Maguire 1996, Texas Chainsaw Massacre: The Next Generation 1997, Deceiver 1997, One True Thing 1998, A Price Above Rubies 1998, The Bachelor 1999, Me, Myself and Irene 2000, Nurse Betty (Golden Globe Award, Best Actress in a Comedy 2001) 2000, Bridget Jones' Diary 2001, Chicago (Golden Globe Award, Best Actress in a Musical 2003, Screen Actors' Guild Award, Best Actress 2003) 2002, Down With Love 2003, Cold Mountain (Golden Globe Award, Best Supporting Actress 2004, Critics' Choice Award, Best Supporting Actress 2004, BAFTA Award, Best Actress in a Supporting Role, Screen Actors Guild Best Supporting Actress Award 2004, Acad. Award, Best Supporting Actress 2004) 2003, Bridget Jones: The Edge of Reason 2004, Cinderella Man 2005, Miss Potter 2006, Bee Movie (voice) 2007, Leatherheads 2008, Appaloosa 2008, New in Town 2009, My One and Only 2009, My Own Love Song 2010. *Television includes:* Shake, Rattle and Rock Movie 1993, Murder in the Heartland 1994. *Address:* c/o John Carrabino, John Carrabino Management, 100 North Crescent Drive, Beverly Hills, CA 90210, USA (office).

ZELMANOV, Efim I., PhD; Russian mathematician and academic; *Professor of Mathematics, University of California, San Diego;* b. 7 Sept. 1955, Khabarovsk; ed Novosibirsk State Univ. and Leningrad State Univ.; apptd to staff, Novosibirsk State Univ.; Jr Researcher, Inst. of Math., USSR Acad. of Sciences, Novosibirsk 1980–85, Sr Researcher 1985–86, Leading Researcher 1986–87; left Soviet Union 1987; Prof., Univ. of Wisconsin-Madison, USA 1990–94; Prof., Univ. of Chicago 1994; Visiting Prof., Yale Univ. 1995; currently Prof. of Math., Univ. of California, San Diego; Medal of the Collège de France 1992, Fields Medal, Int. Congress of Mathematicians, Zürich 1994, Andre Aizenstadt Prize 1996. *Publications:* numerous articles in math. journals on combinatorial problems in non-associative algebra and group theory. *Address:* Department of Mathematics, University of California, San Diego, Applied Physics & Mathematics Building 7260, 9500 Gilman Drive, Department 0112, La Jolla, CA 92093-0112, USA (office). *Telephone:* (858) 534-2647 (office). *Fax:* (858) 534-5273 (office). *E-mail:* ezelmano@math.ucsd.edu (office). *Website:* math.ucsd.edu (office).

ZELNICK, Strauss, BA, JD, MBA; American business executive; *Chairman, ZelnickMedia LLC;* b. 26 June 1957, Boston; s. of Allan Zelnick and Elsa Lee Strauss; m. Wendy Belzberg 1990; two s.; ed Wesleyan and Harvard Univs; called to Bar NY 1984; Dir Int. TV Columbia Pictures Int. Corpn 1983–85, Vice-Pres. Int. TV 1985–86; Sr Vice-Pres. Corp. Devt Vestron Inc. 1986–87, Exec. Vice-Pres. 1987, Pres., COO 1988–89; Pres., COO Twentieth Century Fox 1989–93; Pres., CEO Crystal Dynamics 1993–95; Pres., CEO BMG Entertainment N America 1995–98, BMG Entertainment, New York 1998–2000 (resgnd); f. and Chair. ZelnickMedia LLC 2001–; Chair. (non-exec.) Take-Two Interactive Software 2007–; Trustee Wesleyan Univ. 1992–; mem. Bd of Dirs Covenant House 1995–2000, Insignia Financial Group, Inc., Carver Bancorp, Inc., UGO Networks, Inc. *Leisure interests:* squash, sailing, skiing. *Address:* ZelnickMedia LLC, 19 West 44th Street, 18th Floor, New York, NY 10036, USA (office). *Telephone:* (212) 223-1383 (office). *Fax:* (212) 223-1384 (office). *Website:* www.zelnickmedia.com (office).

ZELNIK, Patrick; French music industry executive; *President, Naïve;* b. 10 Nov. 1946, Paris; began his career at Polydor in 1972; met Richard Branson who offered to let him found Virgin France, Pres. and CEO Virgin France 1980–97, also launched Virgin Retail 1988; Founder and Pres. Champs Elysées Megastore 1988–2000; Founder and Pres. own label Naïve 1998– (produces multi-cultural goods in all styles of music: classical, jazz, pop, world, urban, and all formats: records, books, DVD), responsible for successes such as The Vivaldi Edition, and the breakthrough of Accentus, Anne Gastinel, Laurent Korcia and others, acquired labels Opus 111 and Ambroisie; Pres. UPFI 2000–04; Pres. Impala (ind. music cos' asscn) 2006–08, Co-Pres. (with Michel Lambot and Horst Weidenmüller) 2008–. *Address:* Naïve, 9 rue Victor Masse, 75009 Paris, France (office); Impala, Lamb House, Church Street, London, W4 2PD, England. *Telephone:* (7957) 227183 (mobile, UK). *E-mail:* contact@naive.fr (office); info@impalamusic.org (home). *Website:* www.impalamusic.org (office); www.naive.fr.

ZEMAN, Miloš; Czech politician and head of state; *President;* b. 29 Jan. 1944, Kolín; m. 2nd Ivana Bednarčíková; one s. (from previous marriage) one d.; ed School of Econs, Prague; teacher, School of Econs, Prague 1969–70; joined CP of Czechoslovakia 1968; expelled 1970; researcher Prognostic Inst., Prague 1971–89; Chair. Czech Social Democratic Party 1993–2001; Chair. of Parl. of Czech Repub. 1996–98; mem. Cttee of Socialist International 1997–2002; Chair. Cttee for Protection of Econ. Interests of Czech Repub., Cttee for Handicapped People 1998–; Prime Minister of Czech Repub. 1998–2002; presidential cand. 2003; f. Party of Civic Rights 2009–; Pres. of Czech Repub. 2013–. *Publications include:* Confession of a Former Prognosis Maker (with J. Bauer) 1995, Our Post-Totalitarian Crisis and Its Potential Cure 1992; many articles on econs in papers and magazines. *Leisure interests:* biking, cross-country skiing, science fiction, chess. *Address:* Office of the President, Pražský hrad, 119 08 Prague 1 (office);

Strana Práv Občanů, Opletalova 1418/23, Prague 1, 11000 Czech Republic (office). *Telephone:* 224371111 (office); 296515321 (office). *Fax:* 224373300 (office). *E-mail:* ladislav.jakl@hrad.cz (office). *Website:* www.hrad.cz (office).

ZEMECKIS, Robert L.; American film director, film producer and screenwriter; b. 14 May 1951, Chicago, Ill.; s. of Alphonse Zemeckis and Rose Zemeckis (née Nespeca); m. 1st Mary Ellen Trainor 1980 (divorced 2000); one s.; m. 2nd Leslie Harter 2001; two s.; ed Univ. of Southern California. *Films directed include:* The Lift 1972, Field of Honor 1973, I Wanna Hold Your Hand 1978, Used Cars 1980, Romancing the Stone 1984, Back to the Future 1985, Who Framed Roger Rabbit 1988, Back to the Future II 1989, Back to the Future III 1990, Death Becomes Her 1992, Forrest Gump 1994, Contact (also producer) 1997, What Lies Beneath (also producer) 2000, Cast Away (also producer) 2000, The Polar Express (also writer and producer) 2004, Beowulf (also producer) 2007, A Christmas Carol (also writer and producer) 2009, Flight (also producer) 2012. *Films produced include:* The Public Eye 1992, Trespass 1992, Demon Knight 1995, The Frighteners 1996, Bordello of Blood 1996, House on Haunted Hill 1999, Ritual 2001, Thir13en Ghosts 2001, Ghost Ship 2002, Matchstick Men 2003, Gothika 2003, Clink Inc. 2003, House of Wax 2005, The Prize Winner of Defiance, Ohio 2005, Last Holiday 2006, Monster House 2006, The Reaping 2007, Behind the Burly Q (exec. producer) 2010, Mars Needs Moms 2011, Real Steel 2011, Back for the Future (short) (exec. producer) 2011, Bound by Flesh (documentary) (exec. producer) 2012. *Television includes:* Tales from the Crypt (several episodes) 1989–96, Two-Fisted Tales 1991, Johnny Bago (series) 1993, W.E.I.R.D. World 1995, Perversions of Science (series) 1997, The 20th Century: The Pursuit of Happiness 1999. *Address:* c/o Gelfand, Rennert & Feldman, 1880 Century Park East, Suite 1600, Los Angeles CA 90067; South Side Amusement, Bldg 484, 100 Universal City Plaza, CA 91608, USA.

ZEMLIN, Jim; American computer industry executive; *Executive Director, Linux Foundation;* Brand Man., Western Wireless 1995–98; Co-founder and Dir of Marketing, Corio Inc. 1998–2000; Vice-Pres. of Marketing, Covalent Technologies 2000–04; Exec. Dir and Pres. Free Standards Group 2004–07 (group merged with Open Source Devt Labs (OSDL) to form the Linux Foundation), Exec. Dir Linux Foundation 2007–; adviser on open source strategy to various cos and governmental groups, including Hyperic, Zmanda, Chinese Open Source Promotion Union. *Address:* The Linux Foundation, 210 Fell Street, Suite 16, San Francisco, CA 94102, USA (office). *Telephone:* (415) 723-9709 (office). *Fax:* (415) 723-9709 (office). *E-mail:* info@linux-foundation.org (office). *Website:* www.linux-foundation .org (office).

ZEN ZE-KIUN, HE Cardinal Joseph, PhD, STL; Hong Kong ecclesiastic; *Bishop Emeritus of Hong Kong (Xianggang);* b. 13 Jan. 1932, Shanghai; ed Salesian Pontifical Univ.; ordained priest, Salesians of St John Bosco 1961; Coadjutor Bishop of Hong Kong (Xianggang) 1996; Bishop of Hong Kong (Xianggang) 2002–09, Bishop Emer. 2009–; cr. Cardinal 2006. *Address:* Catholic Diocese Centre 12F, 16 Caine Road, Hong Kong Special Administrative Region, People's Republic of China (office). *Telephone:* 2522-3677 (office). *Fax:* 2522-3749 (office). *E-mail:* hkcsco@catholic.org.hk (office). *Website:* www.catholic.org.hk (office).

ZENDER, J(ohannes) W(olfgang) Hans; German composer and conductor; b. 22 Nov. 1936, Wiesbaden; s. of Dr Franz Zender and Marianne Zender (née Fromm); m. Gertrud-Maria Achenbach 1962; ed Acad. of Music, Freiburg; studied composition and piano; Conductor, Freiburg im Breisgau 1959–63; Chief Conductor, Bonn City Theatre 1964–68; Gen. Dir of Music, Kiel 1969–72; Chief Conductor, Radio Symphony and Chamber Orchestras, Saarbrücken 1972–82; Gen. Dir of Music (Philharmonia and City Opera), Hamburg 1984–87; Chief Conductor Radio Chamber Orchestra, Netherlands Broadcasting Corpn; Prin. Guest Conductor, Opéra Nat., Brussels 1987–90; Prof. of Composition, Frankfurt Musikhochschule 1988–; Permanent Guest Conductor SWF Symphony Orchestra 1999–; Composer-in-Residence, Deutsches Symphonie-Orchester Berlin 2005–06; mem. Freie Akad. der Künste, Hamburg, Akad. der Künste, Berlin, Bayerische Akad. der Künste. *Major works include:* Canto I–VIII 1965–96, Zeitströme 1974, Mujinokyo 1975, Litanei 1976, Lo-Shu I–VI 1977–89, Hölderlin Lesen (string quartet) 1979–91, Dialog mit Haydn 1982, Stephen Climax (opera) 1979–84, Don Quixote (opera) 1989–91, Schubert's Winterreise (for soloists, choir, large orchestra and live electronics) 1993–97. *Publications:* Happy New Ears (essays) 1991, Wir steigen niemals in den selben Fluss (essays) 1996. *Leisure interests:* literature, art. *Address:* c/o Boosey and Hawkes, Aldwych House, 71–91 Aldwych, London, WC2B 4HN, England.

ZENG, Peiyan; Chinese politician and electronics engineer; *Chairman, China Center for International Economic Exchanges;* b. Dec. 1938, Shanghai; ed Tsinghua Univ., Beijing, CCP Cen. Cttee Cen. Party School; technician, later Chief of Research Project Group, Shanghai Electrical Appliances Inst., First Ministry of Machine-Building Industry 1962–64; technician, later Group Leader, Rectifier Research Office, Xi'an Switch and Rectifier Factory, First Ministry of Machine-Building Industry 1964–65, Group Leader, later Deputy Head and Deputy Chief Engineer, Xi'an Rectifier Inst. 1965–82; joined CCP 1978; Second then First Sec. Science and Tech. Counsellor's Office, Embassy, USA 1982–84; Head, Gen. Office then Dir-Gen. Planning Dept, Ministry of Electronics Industry 1984–88; Vice-Minister, Ministry of Electronics Industry 1987–88, Ministry of Machinery-Building and Electronics Industry 1988–92; Deputy Sec.-Gen. and Dir of Office (Minister) Cen. Finance and Econ. Leading Group 1992–; Vice-Minister, State Devt and Reform Comm. 1992–94, Minister 1994 (Sec. Leading Party Group 1998–2002); Deputy Dir Three Gorges Project Construction Cttee 1998–2000; Chair. China Center for Int. Econ. Exchanges 2008–; Dir Western Region Devt Office, State Council 2000–01, Head 2001–02; Deputy Leader, State Leading Group for Information 2001–02, Head, 2001–02; Vice-Premier, State Council 2003–08; Alt. mem. 14th CCP Cen. Cttee 1992–97, mem. 15th CCP Cen. Cttee 1997–2002, 16th CCP Cen. Cttee 2002–07, Political Bureau 2002–07. *Address:* China Center for International Economic Exchanges, 22 Xi'anmen Street, Xicheng District, Beijing 100017, People's Republic of China (office). *Fax:* (10) 83085207 (office). *Website:* www.cciee.org.cn (office).

ZENG, Qinghong; Chinese politician (retd); b. July 1939, Ji, Jiangxi Prov.; s. of Zeng Shan; ed Beijing Inst. of Tech.; joined CCP 1960; technician, No. 743 Army Unit, Group Army, PLA Services and Arms 1963–65; technician, No. 6 Office, No. 2 Dept, Second Acad., Seventh Ministry of Machine-Building Industry 1965–69, No.

2 Dept 1970–73; sent to do manual labour, Chikan Base, Army (or Ground Force), PLA Services and Arms 1969–70, Xihu Production Base, Hunan Prov. 1969–70; technician, Production Div., Comm. of Science, Tech. and Industry for Nat. Defence, Beijing 1973–79; Sec. Gen. Office, State Devt and Reform Comm. 1979–81; Deputy Div. Dir Gen. Office, State Energy Comm. 1981–82; worked in Liaison Dept, Foreign Affairs Bureau, Ministry of Petroleum Industry 1982–83; Deputy Man. Liaison Dept, China Nat. Offshore Oil Corpn 1983–84; Deputy Dir Foreign Affairs Bureau, Ministry of Petroleum Industry 1983–84; Sec. CCP Party Cttee, South and Yellow Seas Petroleum Corpn 1983–84; Deputy Head, later Head, Org. Dept, CCP Shanghai Municipal Cttee 1984–86, Sec.-Gen. Standing Cttee 1984–86, Deputy Sec. CCP Shanghai Municipal Cttee 1986–89; Deputy Dir, Gen. Office, 13th and 14th CCP Cen. Cttees 1989–93, Dir, Gen. Office, 14th CCP Cen. Cttee 1993–97, Sec. Work Cttee, Offices Under Cen. Cttee 1993–97, mem. 15th CCP Cen. Cttee 1992–97, Dir, Gen. Office, 15th CCP Cen. Cttee 1997–99, Dir Work Cttee, Offices Under Cen. Cttee 1997–99, Head, Org. Dept 1999–2002, Alt. mem. Politburo 1997–2002, mem. Politburo Secr. 1997, mem. 16th CCP Cen. Cttee 2002–07, Standing Cttee Politburo 2002–07, Sec.-Gen. 17th CCP Nat. Congress 2007–12; Chief Strategist to Pres. Jiang Zemin –2002; Vice-Pres. People's Repub. of China 2003–07 (retd). *Address:* c/o Central Committee of Chinese Communist Party, Beijing, People's Republic of China (office).

ZENG, Xianlin; Chinese government official; b. 1929, Anyue, Sichuan Prov.; ed Moscow Stalin Machine Tools and Tools Inst.; joined CCP 1947; spent over a decade as Dir and Deputy Engineer at Dalian Machine Tools Plant; Vice-Minister for Science and Tech. 1985–87, for State Planning Comm. 1986–87; Minister for Light Industry 1987–93; Alt. mem. 13th CCP Cen. Cttee 1987–92, 14th CCP Cen. Cttee 1992–97; Vice-Chair. Finance and Econ. Cttee of 9th NPC 1998–2003. *Address:* c/o Standing Committee of National People's Congress, Beijing, People's Republic of China.

ZENG, Yi; Chinese virologist and cancer research specialist; b. 8 March 1929, Jiexi, Guangdong Prov.; s. of Zeng Chin-yao and Chen Chai; m. Li Ze-lin 1953; one s. one d.; ed Shanghai No. 1 Medical Coll.; Vice-Pres. Chinese Acad. of Preventative Medical Science 1989; Deputy Dir AIDS Prevention Dept 1988–; Sr virologist, Inst. for Viral Disease Control and Prevention, Chinese Centre for Disease Control and Prevention; Fellow, Chinese Acad. of Sciences 1993–; Foreign mem. Russian Acad. of Medical Sciences 1993–; special interests: tumour viruses, relationship between EB virus and nasopharynx cancer, HIV and AIDS; several prizes including Ministry of Public Health Award 1990, Chen Jiageng Award 1991, Nat. Cttee of Sciences and Tech. Award 1996, 1998,. *Address:* Chinese Academy of Preventative Medicine, 10 Tiantan Xili, Beijing 100052 (office); Institute of Virology, 100 Ying Xin Jie, Beijing, People's Republic of China (office). *Telephone:* (10) 338621 (office). *E-mail:* zengy@public.bta.net.cn (office).

ZENNSTRÖM, Niklas, MSc; Swedish internet industry executive; *CEO, Atom-ico;* b. 1966; m.; ed Uppsala Univ., Univ. of Mich., USA; began career in business devt at Tele2 (telecom operator), launched (with Janus Friis) get2net (ISP) and everyday.com (also CEO); launched and served as CEO several cos including KaZaA (software co.), Joltid (software co.), Altnet (peer to peer network); Co-founder (with Janus Friis) and CEO Skype Technologies S.A (internet telephony co.) 2003–07, mem. of group that reacquired Skype from eBay, currently mem. Bd of Dirs; Co-founder (with Janus Friis) and Co-Chair. Joost N.V. 2007; Founding Pnr and CEO Atomico (venture capital group) 2006–; mem. Bd of Dirs Fon, Jolicloud, Rdio; Co-founder Zennström Philanthropies. *Leisure interests:* sailing, skiing, outdoor activities, travelling. *Address:* Atomico, 50 New Bond Street, London, W1S 1BJ, England (office). *E-mail:* contact@atomico.com (office). *Website:* www.atomico.com (office); www.skype.com; www.joost.com.

ZEPHANIAH, Benjamin Obadiah Iqbal; British poet, writer, dramatist, musician and singer and academic; *Professor of Poetry and Creative Writing, Brunel University;* b. 15 April 1958, Birmingham; ed Deykin Avenue Primary School, Birmingham Ward End Hall Comprehensive School, Birmingham Broad-way Comprehensive School, Birmingham Boreatton Park Approved School, Baschurch; Writer-in-Residence, Africa Arts Collective, Liverpool 1989, Hay-on-Wye Literature Festival 1991, Memphis State Univ., USA 1991–95, Keats House, Hampstead 2011–; currently Prof. of Poetry and Creative Writing, Brunel Univ.; numerous radio performances, acting roles, appearances; mem. Musicians' Union, Equity, Performing Rights Soc., Authors' Licensing and Collecting Soc.; Dr hc (Univ. of North London) 1998, (Univ. of West of England) 1999, (Staffordshire Univ.) 2001, (Oxford Brookes Univ.) 2002, (South Bank Univ., London) 2002, (Univ. of East London) 2003, (Univ. Coll. Northampton) 2003, (Open Univ.) 2004, (Univ. of Central England) 2005, Hon. DLitt (Westminster Univ.) 2006, (Univ. of Birmingham) 2008, (Univ. of Hull) 2010, (Univ. of Glamorgan) 2011; BBC Young Playwrights Festival Award 1988. *Recordings include:* albums: Rasta 1983, Us and Dem 1990, Back To Our Roots 1995, Belly Of The Beast 1996, Heading For The Door 2000, Naked 2006; singles: Dub Ranting (EP) 1982, Big Boys Don't Make Girls Cry 1984, Free South Africa 1986, Crisis 1992, Naked 2004. *Compositions include:* contrib. to Dancing Tribes (single, with Back To Base) 1999, Illegal (with Swayzak) 2000, What is In Between (with Mieko Shimizo) 2006, The Imagined Village 2007, The Police in Dub 2008, Skanny Skankny (Toddla T) 2009. *Plays:* Playing the Right Tune 1985, Job Rocking 1987, Delirium 1987, Streetwise 1990, The Trial of Mickey Tekka 1991; contrib. to periodicals, radio, TV and recordings, De Botty Business. *Radio plays:* Hurricane Dub 1988, Our Teacher's Gone Crazy 1990, Listen To Your Parents 2000, Face 2002. *Television play:* Dread Poets Society 1991, Peaky Blinders 2013. *Publications include:* fiction: Face 1999, Refugee Boy 2001, Teacher's Dead 2007; poetry: Pen Rhythm 1980, The Dread Affair 1985, Inna Liverpool 1988, Rasta Time in Palestine 1990, City Psalms 1992, Talking Turkeys 1994, Funky Chickens 1996, Propa Propaganda 1996, School's Out 1997, We Are Britain 2002, Too Black, Too Strong 2002, The Little Book of Vegan Poems 2002, Gangsta Rap 2004, My Story 2011, When I Grow Up 2011, Kung Fu Trip 2011, Liam 2012, Terror Kid 2014. *Leisure interests:* kung fu, tai chi, collecting bank notes. *Address:* c/o United Agents, 12–26 Lexington Street, London, W1F 0LE, England (office). *Telephone:* (20) 3214-0800 (office). *Fax:* (20) 3214-0801 (office). *E-mail:* info@unitedagents.co.uk (office). *Website:* unitedagents .co.uk (office); www.benjaminzephaniah.com.

ZEPPOS, Nicholas S., BA, JD; American lawyer and university administrator; *Chancellor, Vanderbilt University;* b. 1954, Milwaukee, Wis.; m. Lydia Howarth;

ed Univ. of Wisconsin, Madison; Practising Attorney, Wilmer, Cutler & Pickering, Washington, DC 1982–87; Prof., Vanderbilt Law School 1987, becoming Provost and Vice-Chancellor for Academic Affairs 2001, Chief Academic Officer 2002, Interim Chancellor 2007, Chancellor 2008–; fmr Chair. Scholars Cttee on Fed. Judiciary; fmr Chair. Rules Advisory Cttee US Court of Appeals for Sixth Circuit; Dir Nashville Area Chamber of Commerce, Nashville Alliance for Public Educ. *Address:* Office of the Chancellor, Vanderbilt University, 211 Kirkland Hall, Nashville, TN 37240, USA (office). *Telephone:* (615) 322-1813 (office). *Fax:* (615) 322-6060 (office). *E-mail:* chancellor@vanderbilt.edu (office). *Website:* www .vanderbilt.edu/chancellor (office).

ZERHOUNI, Elias Adam, MD; American (b. Algerian) physician, professor of radiology and fmr medical administrator; *Professor of Radiology and of Biomedical Engineering, School of Medicine, Johns Hopkins University;* b. Nedroma, Algeria; m. Nadia Azza; two s. one d.; ed Univ. of Algiers School of Medicine, Algeria; came to USA aged 24, naturalized US citizen 1990; Residency in Diagnostic Radiology, Johns Hopkins Univ. School of Medicine 1975–78, Chief Resident, Dept of Radiology 1977–78, Instructor 1978–79, Asst Prof. 1979–81, Assoc. Prof. 1985–92, Prof. of Radiology 1992– (Chair. of Dept 1996–2002), Prof. of Biomedical Eng (Secondary) 1995–2002, Exec. Vice-Dean, Vice-Dean for Clinical Affairs and Pres. Clinical Practice Asscn 1996–99, Vice-Dean for Research 1999–2000, Exec. Vice-Dean 2000–02, Martin Donner Prof. of Radiology and Prof. of Biomedical Eng (Secondary) 2000–02, 2009–, Chair. Russell H. Morgan Dept of Radiology and Radiological Science 2000–02; Asst Prof., Dept of Radiology, Eastern Va Medical School, Norfolk, Va 1981–83, Assoc. Prof. 1983–85; Dir Nat. Insts of Health (NIH) 2002–08; Asst Dir Body CT, The Johns Hopkins Hosp. 1978–81, Radiologist-in-Chief 1996–; Vice-Chair. and Dir Body Imaging Section, De Paul Hosp., Eastern Va Medical School 1982–85; Co-Dir, MRI and Body CT Coordinator of Clinical Research, The Johns Hopkins Medical Insts 1985–88, Dir Divs of Thoracic Imaging and MRI Dept of Radiology 1988–96; Dir Advanced Medical Imaging Inst., Norfolk 1991–92; Merrill Sosman Lecturer, Harvard Medical School, Boston, Mass 2001; est. Inst. for Cell Eng, Johns Hopkins Univ.; f. SurgiVision, Inc.; mem. NAS Inst. of Medicine, Bd of Scientific Advisors of the Nat. Cancer Inst. 1998–; Fellow, Int. Soc. of Magnetic Resonance Medicine 1998; American Roentgen Ray Soc. Gold Medal Award 1985, 1987, Paul Lauterbur Award for MRI Research 1989, 1993, Frank T. McClure Fellowship Award 1990–92, Royal Swedish Soc. of Radiology Centennial Speaker 1995, Fleischner Soc. Medal, London, UK 1997. *Publications:* author or co-author of more than 200 publs and 11 book chapters; eight patents. *Leisure interests:* playing the lute and piano, opera, tennis, scuba diving. *Address:* Whitaker Biomedical Engineering Institute, Johns Hopkins University School of Medicine, 720 Rutland Avenue, Baltimore, MD 21205, USA (office). *Telephone:* (410) 955-3131 (office). *Fax:* (410) 502-9814 (office). *Website:* www.bme.jhu.edu (office).

ZERROUGUI, Leila; Algerian lawyer, judge and UN official; *Special Represen-tative of the Secretary-General for Children and Armed Conflict, United Nations;* b. 1956, Souk-Ahras; ed Ecole Nationale d'Administration; Juvenile Judge and Judge of First Instance 1980–86, Appeal Court Judge 1986–97; legal adviser to Cabinet, Ministry of Justice 1998–2000; apptd to Supreme Court 2000; Deputy Special Rep. of Sec.-Gen. and Deputy Head, UN Org. Stabilization Mission in Democratic Republic of the Congo (MONUSCO) 2008–12, Special Rep. of UN Sec.-Gen. for Children and Armed Conflict 2012–; mem. Working Group on Arbitrary Detention under UN Human Rights Council 2001–, Chair.-Rapporteur Working Group 2003–08; Assoc. Prof., Ecole Supérieure de la Magistrature. *Address:* Office of the Special Representative of the Secretary-General for Children and Armed Conflict, United Nations, 405 East 42nd Street, New York, NY 10017, USA (office). *Telephone:* (212) 963-3178 (office). *Fax:* (212) 963-0807 (office). *Website:* childrenandarmedconflict.un.org (office).

ZETA-JONES, Catherine, CBE; British actress; b. 25 Sept. 1969, Swansea, Wales; d. of David James Jones; m. Michael Douglas (q.v.) 2000; one s. one d. *Stage appearances include:* The Pyjama Game, Annie, Bugsy Malone, 42nd Street, Street Scene, A Little Night Music, Broadway (Outer Critics Circle Award, Drama Desk Award, Tony Award for Best Leading Actress in a Musical 2010) 2009. *Television appearances include:* The Darling Buds of May (series) 1991, Out of the Blue 1991, The Cinder Path 1994, The Return of the Native 1995, Catherine the Great 1995, Titanic 1996. *Films:* Les 1001 nuits 1990, The Adventures of Young Indiana Jones: Daredevils of the Desert 1992, Christopher Columbus: The Discovery 1992, Splitting Heirs 1993, Blue Juice 1995, The Phantom 1996, The Mask of Zorro 1998, Entrapment 1999, The Haunting 1999, High Fidelity 2000, Traffic 2000, America's Sweethearts 2001, Chicago (BAFTA Award for Best Supporting Actress 2003, Screen Actors Guild Award for Best Supporting Actress 2003, Acad. Award for Best Supporting Actress 2003) 2002, Sinbad: Legend of the Seven Seas (voice) 2003, Intolerable Cruelty 2003, The Terminal 2004, Ocean's Twelve 2004, The Legend of Zorro 2005, No Reservations 2007, Death Defying Acts 2007, The Rebound 2009, Playing for Keeps 2012. *Address:* c/o Sam Fischer, Ziffren, Brittenham, Branca, Fischer, Gilbert-Lurie, Stiffelman & Cook LLP, 1801 Century Park West, Los Angeles, CA 90067-6406; c/o William Morris Agency, Inc., 1 William Morris Place, Beverly Hills, CA 90212, USA.

ZETI, Tan Sri Dato' Sri Akhtar Aziz, BSc, PhD; Malaysian economist and central banker; *Governor, Bank Negara Malaysia;* b. 1948; d. of Diraja Tun Ungku Aziz; m.; two c.; ed Univ. Malaya, Wharton School, Univ. of Pennsylvania, USA; served in the S-E Asian Research and Training Centre (SEACEN) 1979–1984; joined Bank Negara Malaysia (central bank) 1985, Rep. in London, UK 1989–94, Deputy Gov. 1995–1998, Acting Gov. 1998–2000, Gov. (first female in position) 2000–; Man. Dir Pengurusan Danaharta Nasional Bhd 1998–2000; mem. Bd of Dirs Khazanah Nasional Bhd 2000–08; apptd as panel mem. of UN task force to assess reform of global financial system 2008; Chair. Task Force for Islamic Finance and Global Financial Stability, Islamic Devt Bank 2009–; Chair. Inauguration Cttee, Islamic Financial Services Bd; headed launch of Malaysian global Islamic SUKUK; mem. Wharton Exec. Bd for Asia; Central Bank Gov. of the Year, Euromoney magazine 2003. *Address:* Bank Negara Malaysia, Jalan Dato' Onn, POB 10922, 50929 Kuala Lumpur, Malaysia (office). *Telephone:* (3) 26988044 (office). *Fax:* (3) 2912990 (office). *E-mail:* info@bnm.gov.my (office). *Website:* www .bnm.gov.my (office).

ZETSCHE, Dieter, DrIng; German automotive industry executive; *Chairman of the Board of Management, Daimler AG;* b. 5 May 1953, Istanbul, Turkey; ed Univs of Karlsruhe and Paderborn; joined Research Dept of Daimler-Benz AG 1976–81, Asst to Devt Man., Commercial Vehicles Business Unit 1981–84, Co-ordinator, Commercial Vehicle Devt Activities 1984–86, Sr Man. and Chief Engineer of Cross-Country Vehicle Unit 1986–87, Head of Devt Dept and Chief Engineer, Mercedes-Benz do Brasil 1987–89, mem. Man. Bd 1988–89, Pres. Mercedes-Benz Argentina 1989–91, Pres. Freightliner Corp., Portland, Ore., USA 1991–92, Deputy mem. Bd of Man., Mercedes-Benz AG and Chief Engineer, Devt Div., Passenger Cars Business Unit, 1992–95, mem. Bd of Man., Sales Div., Mercedes-Benz AG 1995–99, mem. Bd of Man., Sales Div., Daimler-Benz AG 1997–99, mem. Bd of Man., Sales Div., DaimlerChrysler AG 1998–99, mem. Bd of Man., Commercial Vehicle Div., DaimlerChrysler AG 1999, mem. Bd of Man., CEO and Pres. Chrysler Group 2000–05, Chair. Bd of Man. and Head, Mercedes Car Group, DaimlerChrysler AG (now Daimler AG after sale of Chrysler group to Cerberus Capital Management 2007), Stuttgart 2006–. *Address:* Daimler AG, 70546 Stuttgart, Germany (office). *Telephone:* (711) 170 (office). *Fax:* (711) 1722244 (office). *E-mail:* dialog@daimler.com (office). *Website:* www.daimler.com (office).

ZEWAIL, Ahmed H., BS, MS, PhD; American (b. Egyptian) chemist, physicist and academic; *Linus Pauling Chair Professor of Chemistry, Professor of Physics and Director, Physical Biology Center for Ultrafast Science and Technology and the National Science Foundation Laboratory for Molecular Sciences, California Institute of Technology;* b. 26 Feb. 1946, Damanhur, Egypt; m. Dema Zewail; four c.; ed Alexandria Univ., Univ. of Pennsylvania; IBM Postdoctoral Fellow, Univ. of California, Berkeley 1974–76; Asst Prof. of Chemical Physics, California Inst. of Tech. (Caltech) 1976–, Assoc. Prof. 1978–82; Prof. 1982–89, Linus Pauling Prof. of Chemical Physics 1990–94, Linus Pauling Prof. of Chem. and Prof. of Physics 1995–, Dir NSF Lab. for Molecular Sciences 1996–2007, Physical Biology Center for Ultrafast Science and Tech. 2005–; mem. Pres. Obama's Council of Advisers on Science and Tech. 2009–; US First Science Envoy to the Middle East 2009–; Founder Zewail City of Science and Tech., Cairo 2011; mem. NAS 1989, Third World Acad. of Sciences 1989, American Acad. of Arts and Sciences 1993, Acad. Européenne des Sciences, des Arts et des Lettres 1994, American Philosophical Soc. 1998, Pontifical Acad. of Sciences 1999, Indian Acad. of Sciences 2001, Chinese Acad. of Sciences 2009 and others; Foreign mem., Royal Soc. of London 2001, Russian Acad. of Sciences 2003, Royal Swedish Acad. of Sciences 2003, Royal Acad. of Belgium 2003, Acad. des sciences 2005, Royal Spanish Acad. of Sciences 2008, Azerbaijan Nat. Acad. of Sciences 2012; Fellow, American Physical Soc. 1982, AAAS 2000, ACS 2010; Foreign Fellow, Indian Nat. Science Acad. 2002; Hon. Fellow, Chemical Soc. of India 2000, Sydney Sussex Coll., Cambridge 2002; Hon. Foreign mem. Korean Acad. of Science and Tech. 2002; Hon. FRSC 2003, Islamic World Acad. of Sciences 2003, St Catherine's Coll., Oxford 2004; Hon. mem. European Acad. of Sciences 2004; Distinguished Chair of Science and Tech. Policy, United Nations Univ., Tokyo, Japan 2003–; Hon. Prof., Huazhong Univ., Wuhan, China 2004–; Fudan Univ., Shanghai 2004–; Hon. Chair, Univ. System of Taiwan, Taipei 2010–(20); Distinguished Prof., Alexandria Univ. 2010–; Hon. Prof., Eötvös Loránd Univ., ELTE, Budapest, Hungary 2010–; Grand Collar of the Nile (highest order of Egypt), Order of Merit (First Class), Sciences & Arts, Egypt, Order of Zayed, Highest Presidential Hon., State of UAE, Order of Cedar, Highest Rank of Comm., State of Lebanon, Order of Merit of Tunisia, Vatican Pontifical Acad. Insignia 2000, Order of the Two Niles, First Class (Sudan) 2004, Chevalier, Légion d'honneur 2012; hon. degrees from Univ. of Oxford, American Univ., Cairo, Egypt, Katholieke Univ., Leuven, Belgium, Univ. of Pennsylvania, USA, Univ. of Lausanne, Switzerland, Swinburne Univ., Australia, Arab Acad. for Science & Tech., Egypt, Alexandria Univ., Egypt, Univ. of New Brunswick, Canada, Univ. of Rome, Italy, Univ. of Liège, Belgium; Buck-Whitney Medal, King Faisal Int. Prize, Carl Zeiss Int. Award, Earl K. Plyler Prize, Wolf Prize in Chem., Bonner Chemiepreis, Herbert P. Broida Prize, Peter Debye Award, Robert A. Welch Award in Chem., Linus Pauling Medal, Benjamin Franklin Medal, E.O. Lawrence Award, Nobel Prize in Chem. 1999, ACS Priestly Medal 2011 and numerous other prizes and awards. *Publications:* Voyage Through Time: Walks of Life to the Nobel Prize (autobiog.) 2002, 50 ans du laser dans la ville lumière (Fifty Years of the Laser in the City of Light) 2010, seven books edited; approx. 400 scientific papers published. *Leisure interests:* reading, music, skiing. *Address:* California Institute of Technology, Arthur Amos Noyes Laboratory of Chemical Physics, Mail Code 127-72, 1200 East California Boulevard, Pasadena, CA 91125, USA (office). *Telephone:* (626) 395-6536 (office). *Fax:* (626) 792-8456 (office). *E-mail:* zewail@caltech.edu (office). *Website:* www.zewail.caltech.edu (office); www.zewailcity.edu.eg.

ZEWDE, Sahle-Work; Ethiopian diplomatist and UN official; *Director-General, United Nations, Nairobi;* b. 21 Feb. 1950; two s.; ed Univ. of Montpellier, France; Amb. to Senegal (also accred to Mali, Cape Verde, Guinea-Bissau, Gambia and Guinea) 1989–93, Amb. to Djibouti and Perm. Rep. to IGAD 1993–2002, Amb. to France and Perm. Rep. to UNESCO (also accred to Tunisia and Morocco) 2002–06, Perm. Rep. of Ethiopia to the African Union (AU) and UN ECA 2006–09, Dir-Gen. for African Affairs, Ministry of Foreign Affairs 2006–09, has represented Ethiopia in the Peace and Security Council of the AU 2006–; Special Rep. of the UN Sec.-Gen. and Head of UN Integrated Peacebuilding Office in the Cen. African Repub. (BINUCA) 2009–11, Dir-Gen. UN Office in Nairobi 2011–; Co-Chair. UN Security Council-AU Peace and Security Council jt meeting, New York April 2008; has attended most IGAD meetings, as well as OAU/AU summits and led the experts group in different partnership summits with Africa (China-India-EU-France-S America-Turkey), and has led OAU observer team in parl. and presidential elections in Mali 1991 and Niger 1993, 1996. *Address:* United Nations Office at Nairobi, PO Box 67578, Nairobi 00200, Kenya (office). *Telephone:* (20) 7621234 (office). *Website:* www.unon.org (office).

ZGONEA, Valeriu Ştefan, BA, MA; Romanian politician; *Chairman, Camera Deputaţilor (Chamber of Deputies);* b. 3 Sept. 1967, Craiova, Dolj Co.; ed 'Fraţii Buzeşti' Nat. Coll., Craiova, Univ. of Civil Eng, Bucharest, Nat. Inst. for Constructions, Univ. of Amsterdam, the Netherlands, American Council of Young Political Leaders, USA, Social Democrat Inst., Nat. Inst. of Admin, Nat. Defence Coll., Nat. Security Superior Coll.; employee at SC 'Construcţii Feroviare' SA, Craiova 1985, 1990–93; with Incertrans, Bucharest 1985–90; engineer with Compania Naţională 'CFR' SA 1994–2000; mem. Social Democrat Party of Romania (PDSR) 1996–, Pres. Youth Org. of PDSR, Dolj Co. 1999–2000, Vice-Pres. Exec. Cttee of Nat. Council of PDSR, mem. Exec. Bureau of PDSR, Dolj Co., Vice-Pres. Dolj Co. PSD Org. 2001, mem. Nat. Council of PDSR 2001–, Vice-Pres. PDSR 2010–; mem. Dolj Co. Council June–Nov. 2000; mem. Camera Deputaţilor (Chamber of Deputies) 2000–, mem. Cttee for Information, Tech. and Communications 2000–04, Exec. Cttee of Interparliamentary Union, Friendship Parl. Group with Armenia and Kuwait 2000–04, Vice-Leader of Parl. Group of PDSR 2004–08, mem. Cttee for European Integration 2004–08, Exec. Cttee of Interparliamentary Union of GB and NI 2004–08, Cttee for Public Admin, Territorial Devt and Environmental Balance 2004–08, EU Observer in European Parl. on behalf of Romania (Socialist and Social-Democrat Group) 2004–08, mem. Budget Cttee 2005, Questor, Chamber of Deputies Feb.–Sept. 2006, Sec., Camera Deputaţilor 2006–10, Vice-Chair. 2010–12, Chair. Parl. Group of PDSR May–July 2012, Chair. Camera Deputaţilor July 2012–. *Address:* Office of the Chairman, Camera Deputaţilor, Palatul Parlamentului, 050563 Bucharest, Palatul Parlamentului, str. Izvor 2–4, Sector 5, Romania (office). *Telephone:* (21) 4021444 (office). *Fax:* (21) 3126702 (office). *E-mail:* zgonea@gmail.com (office); secretar.general@cdep.ro (office). *Website:* www.cdep.ro (office).

ZHADOBIN, Lt-Gen. Yuri; Belarusian army officer and government official; *Minister of Defence;* b. 14 Nov. 1954, Dnipropetrovsk, Ukraine; ed Kazan Armour Command School, Malinovsky Acad. of Armoured Forces, Moscow; began mil. service 1972, moved through ranks from platoon leader to regt commdr 1976–90, various command posts in Belarusian civil defence and internal security troops within Ministry of Internal Affairs 1990–99, Deputy Minister of Internal Affairs and Commdr, Internal Troops 1999–2003, in charge of Belarusian Pres.'s Security Service 2003–07, Chair. State Security Cttee 2007–08, State Sec., Nat. Security Council 2008–09, Minister of Defence 2009–. *Address:* Ministry of Defence, 220034 Minsk, vul. Kamunistychnaya 1, Belarus (office). *Telephone:* (17) 297-12-12 (office). *Fax:* (17) 289-19-74 (office). *E-mail:* milcoop@mod.mil.by (office). *Website:* mod.mil.by (office).

ZHAI, Ruoyu; Chinese energy executive; b. 1947; ed Liaoning Univ.; joined Liaoning Power Plant 1966, becoming Deputy Dir, later Dir; Deputy Chief, Security and Environmental Protection Div., Ministry of Energy 1992, later Deputy Dir and Dir Supervisory Bureau, Ministry of Power Industry; fmr Head of Gen. Office, State Power Corpn; Gen. Man. Northeastern China br., Nat. Power Co. 1999, becoming Pres. North China Power Group 2000; Chair. and CEO Datang International Power Generation Co. Ltd –2010, also Gen. Man. China Datang Corpn 2002; Dir Buffalo Jayhawk China 2007–; Del. 10th NPC 2003; Del. CPPCC 2008; China CEO of the Year 2005, Asia Business Leader Awards. *Address:* c/o Datang International Power Generation Co. Ltd, 482 Guanganmennei Avenue, 8th Floor, Xuanwu District, Beijing 100053, China.

ZHAI, Taifeng; Chinese writer and party official; b. May 1933, Tangshan City, Hebei Prov.; ed Chinese People's Univ. 1955–57; joined CCP 1949; Vice-Chair. Beijing Fed. of Trade Unions 1981; Deputy Sec.-Gen. Propaganda Dept of CCP Cen. Cttee 1986, Sec.-Gen. and Vice-Dir 1991–; Vice-Pres. Chinese Writers' Asscn 1996; mem. 14th CCP Cen. Comm. for Discipline Inspection 1992–97; Del., 15th CCP Nat. Congress 1997–2002; mem. Standing Cttee 9th CPPCC Nat. Cttee 1998–2003. *Address:* c/o Propaganda Department, Chinese Communist Party Central Committee, Beijing, People's Republic of China (office).

ZHAN, Tao, PhD; Chinese mathematician and academic; *Director, Ministry of Education Management Information Centre;* b. April 1963, Shandong; Prof. of Pure Math., Shandong Univ. 1987, fmr Dean Dept of Math. and Vice-Pres. Shandong Univ., Pres. Shandong Univ. 2000–08; Pres. Jilin Univ. 2008–11; Dir, Ministry of Educ. Management Information Centre 2011–; has served as visiting prof. at univs in France, Netherlands and USA; fmr Vice-Pres. Shandong Youth Fed.; Deputy Dir Young Scientist Asscn of China; Standing mem. Chinese Asscn of Math., All China Youth Fed.; Chair. Shandong Asscn of Math.; numerous awards including Science and Tech. Prize for Young Scientists of China, Ministry of Educ., Science and Tech. Advancement Award, Univ. Science and Tech. Award of China, Nat. Award for Outstanding Teaching Achievement. *Address:* Management Information Centre, Ministry of Education, 37 Damucang Hutong, Xidan, Beijing 100816, People's Republic of China (office). *Telephone:* (10) 66096114 (office). *E-mail:* nglish@moe.edu.cn (office). *Website:* www.moe.edu.cn (office).

ZHANDOSOV, Oraz Aliyevich; Kazakhstani economist and politician; *Co-Chairman, Real Bright Road—Democratic Party of Kazakhstan (Naghyz Ak Zhol);* b. 26 Oct. 1961, Almaty; ; m.; one s. two d.; ed Econs Faculty, Moscow M. V. Lomonosov State Univ. University; Jr Academic Assoc., Inst. of Econs of Kazakh SSR 1987–91; worked at Higher Econ. Council, office of Pres. of Kazakhstan, first as consultant then as Deputy Head, Council of Econ. Consultants 1991–92; First Deputy Minister and Chair. Nat. Agency for Foreign Investment, Ministry of Economy 1993–94; First Deputy Chair. then Chair. Nat. Bank of Kazakhstan 1994–98; First Deputy Prime Minister of Kazakhstan and Chair. State Cttee for Investment 1998–99; Deputy Prime Minister and Minister of Finance Jan.–Oct. 1999; Pres. Kazakhstani Co. for Man. of Electric Networks (KEGOS) 1999–2000; Deputy Prime Minister 2000–01; Chair. Asscn of Financiers of Repub. of Kazakhstan 2001–02; Chair. Republican Agency for Regulation of Natural Monopolies and Protection of Competition 2003–04; Co-Chair. Real Bright Road—Democratic Party of Kazakhstan (Naghyz Ak Zhol) 2005–; mem. Presidium For a Just Kazakhstan Movt 2005–; mem. Political Council, Democratic Party of Kazakhstan Social Org. 2001–02. *Address:* Real Bright Road—Democratic Party of Kazakhstan (Naghyz Ak Zhol), 050010 Almaty, pr. Dostyk 123/7, Kazakhstan (office). *Telephone:* (727) 264-19-99 (office). *Fax:* (727) 260-73-34 (office). *E-mail:* info@akzhol-party.kz (office). *Website:* www.akzhol-party.kz (office).

ZHANG, Baifa; Chinese administrator; b. 1934, Xianghe Co., Hebei Prov.; joined CCP 1954; Vice-Minister of State Capital Construction Comm. 1976–82; Vice-Mayor of Beijing Municipality 1982–97; del. to 13th Cen. Cttee CCP 1987–91, 14th 1992; Standing Cttee mem. CCP 7th Beijing Municipal Cttee 1992–97; Exec. Vice-Pres. Beijing 2000 Olympics Bid Cttee 1991; Vice-Chair. Capital Planning and Construction Comm.; Adviser China Soong Ching Ling Foundation 2008–; took part in World Celebrity Golf Charity Tournament, Beijing 2005; IOC Olympic Order. *Address:* c/o Office of Vice-Mayor, Beijing Municipal Government, Beijing City, People's Republic of China (office).

ZHANG, Baoming; Chinese government official and mining engineer; *President, China Occupational Safety and Health Association;* b. Nov. 1940, Qiqihar, Heilongjiang Prov.; ed Fuxin Mining Inst.; technician, later Deputy Dir Haizhou Open-Cut Coal Mine, Fuxin Mining Admin 1960s–70s, Deputy Dir Fuxin Mining Admin 1982, later Dir; Section Chief, Designing Inst., Changchun Open-Cut Coal Mine 1978–82; joined CCP 1974; Vice-Minister of Coal Industry 1986–88, 1993–98; Deputy Gen. Man. China General Coal Corpn 1990–93; Dir State Admin of Coal Industry 1998–2000; Dir State Admin for Safe Production Supervision 2000–03; Pres. China Occupational Safety and Health Asscn 2002–; Alt. mem. 15th CCP Cen. Cttee 1997–2002. *Publications:* China Coal Industry Reform and Development. *Address:* China Occupational Safety and Health Association, No. 21 HePingLi North Street, Dong Cheng District, Beijing 100713, People's Republic of China (office). *E-mail:* cosha@cosha.org.cn (office). *Website:* (office).

ZHANG, Chaoyang, (Charles Zhang), PhD; Chinese business executive and inventor; *Chairman and CEO, Sohu.com;* b. 31 Oct. 1964, Xi'an, Shaanxi Prov.; ed Tsinghua Univ., Massachusetts Inst. of Tech., USA; Liaison Officer for MIT in Asia-Pacific Region 1993; Chief Rep. in China, Internet Securities 1995–; Founder of ITC and the inventor of the Chinese search engine Sohu; Chair. Bd and CEO Sohu.com 1998–; mem. All-China Fed. of Industry & Commerce 2003–; took part in Mount Everest expedition 2003 (reached height of 6,666 m); Tsung-Dao Lee Scholarship, selected by Asia Week as cover figure 1997, Time Digital Cyber Elite Top 50 1998, listed by China Youth Daily as one of Top Ten Information Tech. Men of the Year 1999–2001, named by Fortune Magazine as one of Top 25 New Corporate Stars 2001, Acad. of Man. Distinguished Exec. of the Year 2004, Ernst &Young Entrepreneur of the Year 2007. *Address:* Sohu.com, Internet Plaza, No.1 Park, Zhongguancun East Road, Haidian District, Beijing 100084, People's Republic of China (office). *Telephone:* (10) 62726666 (office). *Website:* corp.sohu .com (office).

ZHANG, Chunxian; Chinese government official; *Secretary, CCP Autonomous Regional Committee, Xinjiang Uygur Autonomous Region;* b. 1953, Yuzhou City, Henan Prov.; ed Dongbei Heavy Machinery School, Harbin Inst. of Tech.; joined PLA 1970, soldier, Wuhan Mil. Dist 1970–75; joined CCP 1972; Dir Industrial Machinery Dept Supervision Bureau, Ministry of Supervision 1991–92; Deputy Man., China Nat. Packaging Corpn 1992–93, Man. 1993–95, also Sec., CCP Party Cttee 1993–95; Asst Gov. Yunnan Prov. 1995–97; Vice-Minister of Transport 1998–2002, Minister of Transport 2002–05; Sec., CCP Provincial Cttee, Hunan Prov. 2005–10, also mem. CCP Provincial Cttee Standing Cttee 2005–10, Chair. 2006–10; Sec., CCP Autonomous Regional Cttee, Xinjiang Uygur Autonomous Region 2010–; mem. 16th CCP Cen. Cttee 2002–07, 17th CCP Cen. Cttee 2007–12, 18th CCP Cen. Cttee 2013–, also mem. 18th CCP Cen. Cttee Politburo 2012–. *Address:* Autonomous Regional Committee, Xinjiang Uygur Autonomous Region, Ürümqi 830000, People's Republic of China. *Website:* www.urumqi.gov.cn (office).

ZHANG, Cunhao, MSc; Chinese physical chemist; *Professor, Dalian Institute of Chemical Physics, Chinese Academy of Sciences;* b. (Chang Tsun-Hao), Feb. 1928, Wudi Co., Shandong Prov.; m. Chi Yunxia; two s.; ed Nanjing Cen. Univ., Nankai Univ., Univ. of Michigan, USA, Chinese Univ. of Hong Kong; joined China Democratic League 1952, CCP 1959; joined Dalian Inst. of Chemical Physics; Chinese Acad. of Sciences 1953, served in numerous positions including Assoc. Research Fellow, Research Fellow, Prof. 1962–, Vice-Dir 1979–83, Dir, 1986–90, Dir Chem. Div. 1994, mem. Praesidium of Gen. Ass. 1996; mem. Nat. Cttee China Asscn for Science and Tech. 1991–, Nat. Natural Science Fund Cttee; Del., 13th CCP Nat. Congress 1987–92, 14th CCP Nat. Congress 1992–97; Deputy Ed.-in-Chief of several scientific journals; Fellow, Chinese Acad. of Sciences 1980–, Third World Acad. of Sciences (now known as Acad. of Sciences for the Developing World) 1992–; Hon. Pres. Nat. Natural Science Foundation of China 1999–; Hon. DSc (Chinese Univ. of Hong Kong) 1998; Nat. Natural Sciences Award (2nd and 3rd Class) 1957, 1982, 1993, 1997, 1999; Chinese Acad. of Sciences Award 1980, 1985, 1989, 1991, 1996, 1997, Tan Kah-Kee Chem. Science Prize 2000; Ho Leung Ho Lee Prize for Science and Tech. Progress 2002. *Publications:* more than 90 research papers. *Leisure interests:* mountaineering, music, art. *Address:* Dalian Institute of Chemical Physics, Chinese Academy of Sciences, Dalian 116023, Liaoning Province (office); National Natural Science Foundation of China, 83 Shuangqing Road, Beijing 100085; Xinke Garden, Room 1-1306, Zhong Guan Cun, Beijing 100080, People's Republic of China. *Telephone:* (10) 62327134 (office); (10) 82522656 (home). *Fax:* (10) 82371297 (office). *E-mail:* zhangch@nsfc.gov.cn (office).

ZHANG, Dejiang; Chinese politician; *Chairman, NPC Standing Committee;* b. Nov. 1946, Tai'an Co., Liaoning Prov.; ed Yanbian Univ., Kim Il Sung Comprehensive Univ., Pyongyang, N Korea; sent to countryside, Taiping Brigade, Luozigou Commune, Wangqing Co., Jilin Prov. 1968–70; Sec. Propaganda Dept, CCP Communist Youth League of China Wangqing Co. Cttee 1970–72; mem. CCP 1971–; mem. Standing Cttee, CCP Party Cttee, Yanbian Univ. 1975–78, 1980–83, Vice-Chair CCP Revolutionary Cttee 1975–78, Vice-Pres. Yanbian Univ. 1980–83; Deputy Sec. CCP Yanji City Cttee 1983–85; Deputy Sec. CCP Yanbian Korean Autonomous Prefectural Cttee 1985–86, Sec. 1990–95; Vice-Minister of Civil Affairs 1986–90; Deputy Sec. CCP Jilin Prov. Cttee 1990–95, Sec. 1995–98; Chair. Jilin Prov. People's Congress 1998; Alt. mem. 14th CCP Cen. Cttee 1992–97, mem. 15th CCP Cen. Cttee 1997–2002, 16th CCP Cen. Cttee 2002–07, Politburo 2002–07; Sec., CCP Zhejiang Prov. Cttee 1998–2002, Guangdong Prov. 2002–07; mem. 17th CCP Cen. Cttee 2007–12, Politburo 2007–12; Vice-Premier State Council 2008–13; mem. 18th CCP Cen. Cttee 2012–, Politburo 2012–, Politburo Standing Cttee 2012–; Sec., Chongqing Municipal Cttee, CCP 2012–; Chair. Standing Cttee 12th NPC 2013–. *Address:* Great Hall of the People, West Edge, Tiananmen Square, Beijing, People's Republic of China (office). *Telephone:* (10) 88050813 (office). *Fax:* (10) 63070900 (office). *Website:* english.gov.cn/2008-03/16/content_921792.htm (office).

ZHANG, Delin; Chinese government and party official and engineer; b. Aug. 1939, Beijing; ed Tsinghua Univ.; joined CCP 1964; Vice-Pres. Gansu Polytechnical Univ. 1980–83, Sec. CCP Party Cttee 1983–85; Deputy Sec. CCP Harbin City Cttee, Heilongjiang Prov. 1985–90; Mayor of Harbin 1987–90; Deputy Sec., Ministry of Machine-Bldg and Electronics 1990–95; Deputy Sec. CCP Sichuan Provincial Cttee and Sec. CCP Chongqing City Cttee 1996; Sec. CCP Chongqing Mun. Cttee 1995–99; Mayor of Chongqing 1997–99; mem. 15th CCP Cen. Cttee

1997–2002, 16th CCP Cen. Cttee 2002–07; Deputy, 8th NPC 1993–98, 9th NPC 1998–2003; Vice-Chair. CPPCC Sub-cttee for Handling Proposals 2005–. *Address:* c/o Chinese Communist Party Chongqing Municipal Committee, Chongqing, Sichuan Province, People's Republic of China (office).

ZHANG, Dinghua; Chinese politician; b. June 1933, Shanxian Co., Henan Prov.; ed Northwest China Univ.; joined CCP 1956; worked for Qinghai Oil Prospecting Bureau; Deputy Head, Shengli Oilfield Prospecting Newspaper 1964; Dir Political Dept, CCP Cttee, Shengli Oilfield Command HQ 1970–79; Sec. CCP Dagang Petroleum Admin. Bureau Cttee; Dir Propaganda Dept CCP Tianjin Municipal Cttee, Sec. CCP Tianjin Mun. Comm. for Discipline Inspection; mem. 13th CCP Cen. Comm. for Discipline Inspection 1987; Vice-Sec. CCP Inner Mongolia Autonomous Regional Cttee 1988–91; apptd Vice-Pres. and First Sec. Secr. All-China Fed. of Trade Unions 1991–98; mem. Govt Del., Hong Kong Handover Ceremony 1997; Del., 13th CCP Nat. Congress 1987–92; mem. 14th CCP Cen. Cttee 1992–97, 15th CCP Cen. Cttee 1997–2002; Vice-Chair. Cttee for Internal and Judicial Affairs, NPC 1998–2003. *Address:* c/o National People's Congress, Great Hall of the People, Tian'anmen Square, Beijing, People's Republic of China (office).

ZHANG, Fangyou, MBA; Chinese engineer and automotive industry executive; *Chairman and General Manager, Guangzhou Automobile Industry Group;* b. Oct. 1956, Zengcheng, Guangdong Prov.; ed South China Normal Univ., Zhongshan Univ.; began career in 1974; joined CCP 1975; fmr Gen. Man. China Lounge Investments; Sec., Guangzhou Zengcheng Town (City) Govt 1991–95, Deputy Sec.-Gen. Guangzhou Municipal Govt and Office Dir of Automotive Industry Office 1996–97; joined Denway Motors Ltd 1997, Chair. 1998–99, Man. Dir 1999–2004; joined Guangzhou Automobile Group 1997, Chair. Guangzhou Automobile Industry Group 2000–, Exec. Dir Guangzhou Automobile Group Co. Ltd 2005–; Chair. Guangzhou Auto Group (Hong Kong) Ltd, China Lounge Investments Ltd; Ind. Dir, Guangzhou Dept Store Enterprises Group Co. Ltd; Dir, Guangzhou Honda Automobile Co. Ltd; mem. 6th and 9th Guangzhou Municipal Party Cttee; Del. to 8th and 10th Guangdong Party's Congress and to 11th Guangdong People's Congress; Figure of Chinese Economy 2007, Nat. Model Worker 2010. *Address:* Guangzhou Automobile Industry Group, 448–458 Dongfeng Middle Road, Guangzhou 510030, People's Republic of China (office). *Telephone:* (20) 83151380 (office). *Fax:* (20) 83150335 (office). *E-mail:* webmaster@gaig.com.cn (office). *Website:* www.gaig.com.cn (office).

ZHANG, Furong, BA, MA, PhD; Chinese banking executive; *Chairman of the Board of Supervisors, China Construction Bank;* ed Liaoning Finance and Econs Coll., Dongbei Univ. of Finance and Econs; joined People's Bank of China 1971; joined Industrial and Commercial Bank of China Ltd (ICBC) 1984, worked successively as Chief of Accounting Div. and Vice-Pres. ICBC Liaoning Br. 1986–94, concurrently served as Vice-Pres. ICBC Liaoning Br. and Pres. ICBC Dalian Br. 1994–97, Asst to the Pres. of ICBC and Gen. Man. of Human Resources Dept 1997–2000, Vice-Pres. ICBC 2000–05, Exec. Dir and Vice-Pres. ICBC 2005–10; Chair. Bd of Supervisors, China Construction Bank 2010–; Chair. and Dir (non-exec.) Industrial and Commercial Bank of China (Canada); Vice-Chair. Banking Accounting Soc. of China, Financial Planning Standards Council of China. *Address:* China Construction Bank, 25 Finance Street, Beijing 100032, People's Republic of China (office). *Telephone:* (10) 6759-7114 (office). *Fax:* (10) 6360-3194 (office). *E-mail:* info@ccb.cn (office). *Website:* www.ccb.cn (office).

ZHANG, Fusen; Chinese politician; b. March 1940, Shunyi Dist, Beijing Municipality; ed Tsinghua Univ., Beijing; joined CCP 1958; Chair. Tsinghua Students' Fed.; Head, Student Dept, CCP Communist Youth League of China, Beijing Municipal Committee, Deputy Sec. 1979; Exec. Deputy Sec. then Sec. CCP Haidian Dist Cttee of Beijing Municipality 1979–84; Sec. Commercial and Foreign Econ. Relations and Trade Work Cttee 1979; mem. Standing Cttee of CCP Beijing Mun. Cttee 1990; Deputy Sec., later Sec.-Gen. and Pres. Party School, CCP Xinjiang Uygur Autonomous Regional Cttee 1990; Vice-Minister of Justice 1995–97; Deputy Sec. CCP Beijing Municipal Cttee 1997–2001; Vice-Mayor of Beijing Municipality 1997–2000; Minister of Justice 2000–05; mem. 13th CCP Cen. Cttee 1987–92, 14th CCP Cen. Cttee 1992–97, 15th CCP Cen. Cttee 1997–2002, 16th CCP Cen. Cttee 2002–07; mem. 10th CPPCC Nat. Cttee Standing Cttee 2003–08, 11th CPPCC Nat. Cttee Standing Cttee 2008–13; Dir 11th CPPCC Cttee for Social and Legal Affairs 2008–13. *Address:* c/o Ministry of Justice, 10 Chaoyangmennan Dajie, Chao Yang Qu, Beijing 100020, People's Republic of China (office).

ZHANG, Gaoli; Chinese politician; *Vice-Premier;* b. Nov. 1946, Jinjiang, Fujian Prov.; ed Xiamen Univ.; joined CCP 1973; Deputy Sec. CCP Maoming City Cttee, Guangdong Prov.; Chair. Guangdong Econ. Comm. 1985–88; Vice-Gov. Guangdong Prov. 1988–93, Vice-Gov. and Acting Gov. 2001, Gov. 2002–03; First Sec. Shenzhen Garrison, CCP Party Cttee PLA Guangzhou Mil. Region 1998–2000; Chair. Standing Cttee Shenzhen Municipal People's Congress 2000; Deputy Sec. CCP Guangdong Prov. Cttee 1998–2001; Chair. Standing Cttee of Prov. People's Congress, Shandong Prov. 2003–07; Sec. CCP Tianjin Municipal Cttee 2007–12; Vice-Premier 2013–; Dir State Construction Comm. 2013–; Deputy Dir State Energy Comm. 2013–; Alt. mem. 15th CCP Cen. Cttee 1997–2002; mem. 16th CCP Cen. Cttee 2002–07, 17th CCP Cen. Cttee 2007–12, 17th CCP Politburo 2007–12, 18th CCP Cen. Cttee 2012–, Politburo 2012–, Politburo Standing Cttee 2012–. *Address:* Standing Committee, Chinese Communist Party Politburo, Quanguo Renmin Diabiao Dahui, Zhongguo Gongchan Dang, 1 Zhongnanhai, Beijing, People's Republic of China. *Website:* cpc.people.com.cn (office).

ZHANG, Gen. Gong; Chinese army officer and party official; b. 1935, Yuanping Co., Shanxi Prov.; joined PLA 1951, CCP 1961; Dir of Political Dept, Beijing Mil. Area Command 1985; rank of maj.-Gen. PLA 1988, Lt-Gen. 1990, Gen. 1998; Political Commissar, Beijing Mil. Area Command 1990, Chengdu Mil. Area Command 1992, PLA Acad. of Mil. Sciences 1993–2000; Del., 13th CCP Nat. Congress 1987–92, 7th PNC 1988–93; mem. 14th CCP Cen. Cttee 1992–97, 15th CCP Cen. Cttee 1997–2002; Deputy, 9th NPC 1998–2003; mem. Standing Cttee 10th CCP Cen. Cttee 2003–. *Address:* c/o Academy of Military Science of People's Liberation Army, Xianghongqi, Haidian District, Beijing, People's Republic of China (office).

ZHANG, Guoli; Chinese actor and director; b. 1955, Shaanxi; m. Deng Jie; with Sichuan People's Art Theatre 1983; with China Rail Arts Co. Drama Troupe,

Beijing 1993; Chair. Cttee for Chinese Young Film Workers 2006–; 4th Nat. Theatre Plum Blossom Award for Best Actor, MTV Grand Award for Best Dir 1995, Hundred-Flower Award for Best Actor 1996, 29th Golden Rooster Award for Best Actor 2013. *Films:* The Trouble-shooters 1988, The Strangers in Beijing 1996, A Long Sigh 2000, Cell Phone 2003, The 601st Phone Call 2006, Lady Cop & Papa Crook 2008, The Founding of a Republic 2009, The Monkey King: Uproar in Heaven 2012, Back to 1942 2012. *Television:* Hunchback Liu: The Prime Minister 1996, The Legend of Liulichang 1998, Emperor Kangxi Travelling Incognito 1999, Emperor Kangxi Travelling Incognito: A Sequel 2000, Golden Wedding (series) 2007 (14th Shanghai TV Festival Magnolia Best Actor Award 2008), Da Shenghuo 2008, Ganzou Nide Youyu 2008, The Bronze Teeth IV 2008, Better Dance 2010, 1942 2012, Tangshan Earthquake 2013, Spring Husband 2013. *Address:* China Rail Arts Company Drama Troupe, No.15, Erqijuchang Road, Fuxingmenwai, Beijing 100045, People's Republic of China (office).

ZHANG, Guoqing, PhD; Chinese engineer and business executive; b. 1964, Luoshan Co., Henan Prov.; ed Econs Man. Inst., Tsinghua Univ., Beijing, Harvard Business School, USA; joined CCP 1984; Vice-Pres. China North Industries Group Corpn (NORINCO Group) 1996–2004, Sec., CCP Party Cttee 1998–2004, Deputy Gen. Man. 1999–2008, mem. CCP Leading Party Group 1999–2013, Pres. NORINCO 2004–08, Gen. Man., Pres. and Deputy Sec. Leading Party, NORINCO Group 2008–13; Alt. mem. 17th CCP Cen. Cttee 2007–12, mem. 18th Cen. Cttee 2012–; Deputy Sec., Municipal Cttee, Chongqing Municipality, CCP 2013–. *Address:* c/o China North Industries Group Corporation, 46 Sanlihe Road, Beijing 100821, People's Republic of China. *E-mail:* webmaster@cngc.com.cn.

ZHANG, Huan, BA, MA; Chinese artist; b. 1965, An Yang City, He Nan Province; ed He Nan Univ., Kai Feng, Central Acad. of Fine Arts, Beijing; lives and works in Shanghai and New York; performance artist, sculptor and photographer; works held in numerous int. galleries including Museum of Modern Art, New York, Solomon R. Guggenheim Museum, New York, Museum of Fine Arts, Boston, Fukuoka Art Museum, Japan, Nat. Gallery of Australia, Centre Pompidou, Paris, Charles Saatchi Collection, London, Shanghai Art Museum, Museum of Contemporary Art, Barcelona, Israel Museum, Jerusalem. *E-mail:* zhanghuanstudio@gmail.com (office). *Website:* www.zhanghuan.com (office).

ZHANG, Jianguo, MEcons; Chinese banking executive; *Vice-Chairman, Executive Director and Executive President, China Construction Bank;* b. 1954; ed Tianjin Coll. of Finance and Econs; worked at Tianjin Br., People's Bank of China 1982–84; held several positions in Industrial and Commercial Bank of China 1984–2001, including Deputy Gen. Man. and Gen. Man. Int. Banking Dept, Deputy Gov. Tianjin Br., Deputy Gov. and Gov. Tianjin Econ. and Tech. Devt Area Br., and Deputy Man. Int. Banking Dept, Tianjin Br.; Vice-Pres. Bank of Communications Co. Ltd (BOCOM) 2001–04, Pres. and Vice-Chair. 2004–06; Vice-Chair. and Exec. Pres. China Construction Bank July 2006–, mem. Bd of Dirs Oct. 2006–. *Address:* China Construction Bank, 25 Finance Street, Xicheng Dist, Beijing 100032, People's Republic of China (office). *Telephone:* (10) 6759-7114 (office). *Fax:* (10) 6360-3194 (office). *E-mail:* info@ccb.com (office). *Website:* www .ccb.com (office).

ZHANG, Jie, PhD; Chinese physicist, university administrator and academic; *President, Shanghai Jiaotong University;* b. 1958; ed Inst. of Physics, Chinese Acad. of Sciences, Beijing; began career as research scientist at Inst. of Physics, Chinese Acad. of Sciences, Deputy Dir Inst. of Physics 1998–2003, Dir Chinese Spallation Neutron Source 2002–06, Dir-Gen. Bureau of Basic Sciences 2003–06; Pres. Shanghai Jiaotong Univ. 2006–; Alexander-von-Humboldt Research Fellow, Max-Planck-Institut für Quantenoptik, Germany 1989–90; Sr Research Scientist, Rutherford Appleton Lab., UK 1991–98; mem. Editorial Bd High Energy Density Physics, Chemical Physics Letters, Acta Physica Sinica; mem. Council and Co-Chair. Asscn of Asia Pacific Physical Socs, Asian Laser Network, Int. Workshop on Fast Ignition of Fusion Targets, OECD High Power Laser Cttee, and others; Academician Chinese Acad. of Sciences 2003; Alt. mem. 17th CCP Cen. Cttee 2007–12, 18th CCP Cen. Cttee 2012–. *Address:* Office of the President, Shanghai Jiaotong University, 1954 Hua Shan Road, Shanghai 200030, People's Republic of China (office). *Telephone:* (21) 62812444 (office). *Fax:* (21) 62821369 (office). *Website:* www.sjtu.edu.cn/english/index/index.htm (office).

ZHANG, Jike; Chinese table tennis player; b. 16 Feb. 1988, Qingdao, Shandong; debut in Int. Tournament, Hungary 2002; silver medal (singles, doubles and mixed doubles), gold medal (team), Asian Championship, Lucknow 2009; gold medal (team), World Team Cup, Linz 2009; silver medal (mixed doubles), bronze medal (doubles), World Championship, Yokohama 2009; gold medal (team), World Team Cup, Dubai 2010; silver medal (singles), Men's World Cup, Magdeburg 2010; gold medal (team), World Championship, Moscow 2010; gold medal (mixed doubles and team), Asian Games, Guangzhou 2010; gold medal (singles), Men's World Cup, Paris 2011; gold medal (singles), bronze medal (doubles), World Championship, Rotterdam 2011; gold medal (mixed doubles), Int. Table Tennis Fed. (ITTF) Pro Tour Grand Finals, London 2011; silver medal (singles), gold medal (team), Asian Championship, Macau 2012; gold medal (team), World Championship, Dortmund 2012; gold medal (singles and team), Olympic Games, London 2012; winner (singles): China Open 2010, German Open 2011, Slovenian Open and Korea Open 2012, winner (mixed doubles): Kuwait Open 2010, English Open, UAE Open, German Open, China Open, Slovenian Open 2011, Korea Open and Slovenian Open 2012. *Address:* c/o Chinese Table Tennis Association, C3 Longtan Road, Chongwen Qu, Beijing 100061, People's Republic of China. *Website:* tabletennis .sport.org.cn.

ZHANG, Jin; Chinese scientist and university professor; ed Tsinghua Univ., Beijing, Beijing Univ. of Aeronautics and Astronautics; specializes in computation of structural dynamics and mechanics of new complex materials for aviation industry; Guest Prof., MIT, USA; Prof., Beijing Univ. of Aeronautics and Astronautics (Beihang Univ.); Guest Research Fellow, Univ. of Calif., Berkeley, USA. *Publications include:* The Dynamic Mechanism and Application of New Complex Materials (co-author); scientific papers. *Address:* Beijing University of Aeronautics and Astronautics, 37 Xueyuan Road, Beijing 100083, People's Republic of China (office).

ZHANG, Junjiu; Chinese business executive; b. 1940, Funan, Anhui Prov.; Vice-Pres. China North Industries Group 1990–93; Deputy Gen. Man., later Gen. Man.

China Nat. Ordnance Industry Corpn 1994; Pres. China N Industries Group; mem. China Council for the Promotion of International Trade 1994; Vice-Chair. and First Sec. Secr. All-China Fed. of Trade Unions 1998–2002, Vice-Pres. Exec. Cttee 2002–05; Vice-Minister, State Comm. of Science, Tech. and Industry for Nat. Defence 1998–2003; Chair. Bd of Trustees, Beijing Univ. of Science and Eng 1995; Alt. mem. 14th CCP Cen. Cttee 1992–97; mem. 15th CCP Cen. Cttee 1997–2002, 16th CCP Cen. Cttee 2002–07. *Address:* c/o All-China Federation of Trade Unions, 10 Fuxingmenwai Street, Beijing 100865, People's Republic of China (office). *Website:* www.acftu.org.cn (office).

ZHANG, Kehui; Chinese politician; b. (Zhang Youyi), Feb. 1928, Zhanghua Co., Taiwan; m. Hong Xiaoling; ed Taiwan Teachers' Coll., Xiamen Univ., China; joined CCP 1948; cadre, Fujian-Guangdong-Jiangxi Border Column, PLA Co. Level 1949; Section Chief, United Front Work Dept, CCP Fujian Prov. Cttee 1950; Deputy Sec.-Gen. CPPCC Fujian Prov. Cttee 1950; Deputy Dir Overseas Chinese Affairs Office, Fujian Prov. 1950; joined Taiwan Democratic Self-Govt League 1979, Vice-Chair. Cen. Cttee 1992–96, Chair. 1997–; Head, Fed. of Taiwan Compatriots, Fujian Prov. 1980; Vice-Chair. CPPCC Fujian Prov. Cttee 1988; adviser, Asscn for Relations Across the Taiwan Straits 1990; Dir Taiwan Affairs Office of State Council 1990; Chair. 4th and 5th Councils, All-China Fed. of Taiwan Compatriots 1991–97, Hon. Chair. 6th Council 1997–; mem. Exec. Council, China Council for Promotion of Peaceful Reunification 1993, Pres. 1994–; adviser, Chinese Asscn of Int. Understanding 1999–; mem. Govt Del., Macao Hand-Over Ceremony, Macao Special Admin. Region Preparatory Cttee 1999; mem. Standing Cttee 8th NPC 1993–98; mem. 5th CPPCC Nat. Cttee 1978–83, 7th CPPCC Nat. Cttee 1988–93, Vice-Chair. 9th CPPCC Nat. Cttee 1998–2003, 10th CPPCC Nat. Cttee 2003–; mem. 13th CCP Cen. Cttee 1987–92, 14th CCP Cen. Cttee 1992–97. *Publications:* Taiwan Tales. *Address:* National Committee of Chinese People's Political Consultative Conference, 23 Taipingqiao Street, Beijing, People's Republic of China (office).

ZHANG, Li; Chinese real estate executive; *Co-Chairman and CEO, Guangzhou R&F Properties Group;* b. 1953, Guangdong; m.; one c.; Chief Man. Garden Village Hotel 1986; f. property co. with Hong Kong-born pnr Li Sze Lim in 1994, set up Guangzhou R&F Properties in 1996, listed on Hong Kong Stock Exchange 2005, currently Co-Chair. and CEO. *Address:* Guangzhou R&F Properties Group, 11-15/F, R&F Properties Building, 19 Jiaochangdong Road, Guangzhou 510055, Guangdong, People's Republic of China (office). *Telephone:* (20) 87302328 (office). *Fax:* (20) 87329029 (office). *E-mail:* myhome@rfchina.com (office). *Website:* www .rfchina.com (office).

ZHANG, Ligui; Chinese telecommunications executive; b. 1942; ed Beijing Univ. of Posts and Telecommunications; began career in telecommunications industry 1966; fmr Dir-Gen. Beijing Telecommunications Bureau; fmr Dir-Gen. Directorate-Gen. of Telecommunications, Ministry of Posts and Telecommunications; Dir-Gen. Gansu Posts and Telecommunications –2000; Pres. China Mobile Communications Corpn 2000–04 (retd). *Address:* c/o China Mobile Communications (Hong Kong) Ltd, 60/F The Centre, 99 Queen's Road Central, Hong Kong (office).

ZHANG, Ning; Chinese badminton player; b. 19 May 1975, Shenyang, Liaoning Prov.; ed Jingzhou Municipal Sports School, Liaoning and Liaoning Prov. Sports School; left home aged 12 to train full-time; joined prov. badminton team in 1989, nat. children's team in 1990 and nat. team in 1991; World Grand Prix results: winner, Women's Singles, Singapore Open 2001, Noonnoppi Korea Open 2002, 2004, Hong Kong Open 2003, Yonex German Open 2003, Proton Eon Malaysia Open 2004, Yonex Japan Open 2006, Aviva Open Singapore 2007; runner-up, Women's Singles, China Open 2002, Indonesia Open 2002, Singapore Open 2002, China Open 2006; World Championship results: semi-finalist, Women's Singles, Seville, Spain 2001, Gold Medal, Women's Singles, Birmingham, UK 2003; Gold Medals, Women's Singles, Olympic Games, Athens, Greece 2004, Beijing 2008; represented China as flag bearer, 2008 Summer Olympics closing ceremony; mem. Liaoning Badminton Club; ranked 4th in world 2008. *Leisure interests:* drawing, travelling, reading. *Address:* c/o Chinese Olympic Committee, 9 Tiyuguan Road, Beijing 100763, People's Republic of China. *Telephone:* (10) 67116669. *Fax:* (10) 67115858. *E-mail:* coc@olympic.cn. *Website:* en.olympic.cn.

ZHANG, Ping; Chinese politician; b. 1 Jan. 1946, Anhui Prov.; ed Anhui School of Banking; joined CCP 1979; accountant and Deputy Section Chief, People's Bank of China, Chaoxian Co., Anhui Prov. 1967–78; staff mem., Finance and Trade Office, Chaoxian Co. 1978–80; Sec., Research Office, Provincial People's Congress, Anhui Prov. 1981–85; Deputy Dir, later Dir, No. 2 Office, People's Govt, Anhui Prov. 1981–85; Deputy Dir, Provincial Planning Cttee, Anhui Prov. 1985–91; Dir, Provincial Econ. Information Centre, Anhui Prov. 1988–92; Acting Mayor, Wuhu City, Anhui Prov. 1992–93, Mayor 1993–95; Asst Gov., Anhui Prov. 1995–96, Vice-Gov. 1996–99; Sec.-Gen., People's Govt, Anhui Prov. 1996–97; mem. Standing Cttee, Anhui Prov. CCP Provincial Cttee 1999–2005, Deputy Sec. 1999–2005; Deputy, 9th NPC 1998–2003; Sec.-Gen., State Council 2005–08; Deputy Minister of Nat. Devt and Reform Comm. 2005, Minister 2008–13; alt. mem. 16th CCP Cen. Cttee 2002–07, mem. 17th CCP Cen. Cttee 2007–12. *Address:* c/o National Development and Reform Commission, 38 Yuetannan Jie, Xicheng Qu, Beijing 100824, People's Republic of China (office).

ZHANG, Ping; Chinese writer; b. Nov. 1954, Xi'an, Shanxi Prov.; ed Shanxi Teachers Univ.; teacher, Dongjie School, Xinjiang Co.; Shanxi Prov. 1976; Ed. then Head, Literature and Arts Div. Linfen Fed. of Literary and Art Circles; Assoc. Chief Ed. Spark Magazine; Vice-Chair. Shanxi Prov. Fed. of Literary and Art Circles; Vice-Chair. Chinese Writers' Asscn 2001–; 7th Nat. Award for Best Short Stories. *Publications:* The Law Rocks Fenxi County 1991, The Net of Heaven 1993, Choice 1997 (5th Mao Dun Prize 2000), Ambushed from all Sides 1999, The Murderer, Young Boys and Girls, Sister, Orphans' Tears, The Girl Opposite Me 2001, State Cadres 2004. *Address:* Shanxi Provincial Federation of Literary and Art Circles, Taiyuan, Shanxi Province, People's Republic of China (office).

ZHANG, Qingli; Chinese party official; *Director, Standing Committee, Provincial People's Congress, Hebei Province;* b. 1951, Dongping, Shandong Prov.; ed CCP Shandong Prov. Cttee Party School, Beijing Agricultural Univ.; began career as worker at fertilizer plant, Shandong Prov., Dongping Co. 1971–76; joined CCP 1973, mem. CCP Dongping Co. Cttee 1976–79, Standing Cttee Shandong Prov. 1976–79; Vice-Mayor, Dongyi City 1986–93, Mayor 1993–95; Chair., City People's Congress, Tai'an City 1997; sr positions in CCP regional cttees in Shandong Prov.

1997–98, Gansu Prov. 1998–99; Dir, City People's Congress, Lanzhou City 1999; mem. CCP Standing Cttee, Xinjiang Uygur Autonomous Region 1999–2004, Deputy Sec., CCP Regional Cttee 2004–06, Vice-Pres., People's Govt, Xinjiang Uygur 2005–; Sec. Man., Xinjian Group Co. of China 2002–05; Acting Sec., CCP Regional Cttee, Tibet Autonomous Region 2005–06, Sec. 2006–11; Dir, Standing Cttee, Provincial People's Congress, Hebei Prov. 2012–; mem. 16th CCP Central Cttee 2002–07, 17th CCP Central Cttee 2007–12, 18th CCP Cen. Cttee 2012–; Deputy, 10th NPC 2003–08. *Address:* Standing Committee, Provincial People's Congress, Shijiazhuang 05000, Hebei Province, People's Republic of China (office). *Website:* english.hebei.gov.cn/government.html (office).

ZHANG, Quanjing; Chinese politician; b. 1931, Pingyuan Co., Shandong Prov.; joined CCP 1949; Deputy Section Chief, CCP Dezhou Pref. Cttee; Deputy Sec. CCP Dezhou Municipal Cttee 1950–66; Div. Chief and Deputy Head, Org. Dept CCP Shandong Prov. Cttee 1971–86; mem. Standing Cttee and Head, Org. Dept CCP Shandong Prov. Cttee 1986–88; Sec. CCP Shandong Prov. Comm. for Inspecting Discipline 1988; Exec. Deputy Dir CCP Cen. Cttee Org. Dept 1991–94, Head 1994–99; Del., 13th, 14th and 15th CCP Nat. Congresses 1987–2002; mem. Standing Cttee 9th CPPCC Nat. Cttee 1998–2003; Deputy Head, CCP Cen. Cttee Party Building Directorate 1999–. *Address:* Party Building Directorate, Central Committee of Communist Party of China, Beijing, People's Republic of China (office).

ZHANG, Renzhi; Chinese landscape artist; b. 7 Dec. 1935, Hebei Prov.; s. of Zhang Pu and Zhang Chen; m. Lang Mei 1966; two s.; ed Cen. Art Inst.; joined Beijing Art Acad. as professional artist; jt exhbns, Xinxiang, Henan Prov., Macao, Beijing, Japan 1991, Exhbn of Buddhism 1991, Nat. Exhbn 1992, Beseto Arts Festival 1997, etc.; Wintertime Lotus and other works in collection of James Art Museum, Vermont State Univ., USA; Artist of the First Grade; Award of Excellence (for 'Quiet Valley'), Nat. Exhbn of Fine Arts 1991; prize for 'Lasting Forever' (burnt pine tree), Bronze Prize (for 'Mount Fanjing After Rain'), Nat. Exhbn of Fine Arts 1999. *Publications:* Zhang Renzhi's Album of Paintings, (Vol. 2) 1991, Collection of Landscape Paintings 2000. *Leisure interest:* travel. *Address:* Room 501, Building 2, Beijing Arts Institute, Chao Yang District, Beijing, People's Republic of China (office). *Telephone:* (10) 85973316 (office).

ZHANG, Ruimin, MBA; Chinese business executive and engineer; *Chairman and CEO, Haier Group;* b. Jan. 1949, Laizhou, Shandong Prov.; m.; one s.; ed China Science and Tech. Univ., Beijing; worker, Qingdao Construction Plant, Shandong Prov. 1968–75; Deputy Man., Qingdao Appliance Industry Co. 1982–88; Dir Qingdao Refrigerator Factory 1984–91 (renamed Qingdao Haier Group 1991), Chair. and CEO Haier Group 1991–; mem. 14th, 15th and 16th CCP Nat. Congresses 1992–; Alt. mem. 16th CCP Cen. Cttee 2002–07, 17th CCP Cen. Cttee 2007–12, 18th CCP Cen. Cttee 2012–; voted one of China's Top Ten Econ. Figures 2000, State Award for Excellent CCP Members 2001. *Address:* Haier Garden, Haier Industrial Park, Haier Lu, Haier Group, Qingdao 266101, Shandong Province, People's Republic of China. *Telephone:* (532) 8938888. *Fax:* (532) 8938666. *E-mail:* info@haier.com (office). *Website:* www.haier.com (office).

ZHANG, Shengman; Chinese banking executive; *Chairman, Asia Pacific Region, Citigroup Inc.;* b. 1957, Shanghai; ed Fudan Univ., McGill Univ., Montreal, Canada; Asst to Exec. Dir of World Bank (IBRD) 1983–87; section head and then Vice-Dir Dept of IBRD, Ministry of Finance 1987–92; Deputy Exec. Dir, then Exec. Dir IBRD 1992–95, Exec. Dir for China 1994–95, Sec. 1995–97, Man. Dir 1997–2005; Vice Chair. Global Banking, Citigroup Corp. and Investment Banking, New York 2006–09, also Chair. Citibank Public Sector Group, Chair. Asia Pacific Region 2009–. *Address:* Citigroup Inc., 399 Park Avenue, New York, NY 10022, USA (office). *Telephone:* (212) 559-1000 (office). *Fax:* (212) 793-3946 (office). *Website:* www.citibank.com (office).

ZHANG, Shiping; Chinese economist and business executive; *Chairman, Shandong Weiqiao Pioneering Group;* ed Anhui Coll. of Finance and Trading; Gen. Man. Chuangye Group (including its predecessor) 1996–98; Chair. Weiqiao Textile Co. Ltd (including its predecessor) 1998–2000; Dir Binzhou Weiqiao Technology Industrial Park Co. Ltd 2001–10; Chair. Aluminum Technology 2002–07, Chuangye Group, Hongqiao Holdings, Profit Long Investment, Weiqiao Pioneering (Hong Kong) Import & Export Co. Ltd; Chair. Shandong Weiqiao Chuangye Group Co. Ltd; currently Chair. Shandong Weiqiao Pioneering Group; Dir Shandong Hongqiao 1994–, Exec. Chair. China Hongqiao Group Ltd 2011–; Dir (non-exec.) Weiqiao Textile Co. Ltd, Zouping Supply and Marketing Investment Co. Ltd, Party Sec. Zouping County Supply and Marketing Co-operation Union; Deputy to 9th and 10th NPC; selected by the State Council as Nat. Model Worker 1995. *Address:* Shandong Weiqiao Pioneering Group, 1 Weifang Road, Zouping Economic Development Zone, Shandong 256200, People's Republic of China (office). *Telephone:* (543) 4161111 (office). *Fax:* (543) 4162000 (office). *E-mail:* wqcy@wqfz.com (office). *Website:* www.weiqiaocy.com (office).

ZHANG, Shuguang, BS, PhD; American (b. Chinese) biochemist, molecular biologist and academic; *Principal Investigator, Center for Bits and Atoms, Massachusetts Institute of Technology;* ed Sichuan Univ., Chengdu, Univ. of California, Santa Barbara (Regent Fellowship and a Grad. Mentor Fellowship); American Cancer Soc. Postdoctoral Fellow, Structural and Molecular Biology, MIT 1988–91, Research Scientist, Dept of Biology and Center for Biomedical Eng 1992–96, Prin. Research Scientist 1997–, Assoc. Dir Center for Biomedical Eng 1998–2012, Prin. Investigator, Center for Bits and Atoms 2012–; Visiting Prof., Tsinghua Univ., Beijing, Sichuan Univ., Chinese Acad. of Medical Science, Beijing, China Univ. of Petroleum, Qingdao; co-f. three startup cos, including 3DMatrix, Tokyo, Japan, Beaver Biosciences, Guanzhou, Beaver Nanotech, Suzhou, People's Repub. of China; mem. AAAS, American Soc. of Biochemistry and Molecular Biology, Human Genome Org. Americas, Protein Soc., New York Acad. of Sciences, Int. Soc. for the Study of Origin of Life; Foreign Corresp. mem. Austrian Acad. of Sciences; Fellow, Japan Soc. for Promotion of Science 2003, Japan Advancement for Medical Instrument 2005, American Inst. of Medical and Biological Eng; Hon. Prof. and Distinguished Changjiang Scholar, Sichuan Univ.; Hon. Prof., China Univ. of Petroleum; R&D100 Award 2004, his team's work on biosolar energy selected by Discover Magazine to be one of the Top 100 Science Stories in 2004, Guggenheim Fellow 2006, Wilhelm Exner Medal, Austrian Asscn for SME (Oesterreichischer Gewerbeverein—OGV) (jtly) 2006, numerous invited lectures.

Achievements include: discovered a self-assembling peptide system. *Publications:* Self-Assembling Peptide Systems in Biology, Engineering and Medicine (with A. Aggeli and N. Boden) 2001; 170 scientific articles, ten issued patents and 20 pending patent applications on self-assembling peptide systems. *Address:* Room E15-401, Center for Bits and Atoms, Massachusetts Institute of Technology, Cambridge, MA 02139-4307, USA (office). *Telephone:* (617) 258-7514 (office). *Fax:* (617) 253-7035 (office). *E-mail:* shuguang@mit.edu (office). *Website:* web.mit.edu/lms/www (office).

ZHANG, Siqing; Chinese judge; *Vice-Chairman, National Committee, Chinese People's Political Consultative Conference;* b. 1932, Luoyang City, Henan Prov.; m.; two d.; joined CCP 1952; Investigator, Cen.-South Section, Supreme People's Procuratorate 1952, Asst Judge, Northeast China Work Team; participant, Investigations and Trials of Japanese War Criminals; Investigator, Yangtze River Water Transport Procuratorate 1955; Procurator, Hubei Prov. People's Procuratorate; official, Public Security Dept, Hubei Prov. 1969–73, later Dir; Deputy Office Dir Higher People's Court (at prov. level), Hubei Prov. 1973–74, Vice-Pres. 1975, later Pres.; First Political Commissar, Armed Police Corps, Chinese People's Armed Police Force, Hubei Prov.; Sec. Political Science and Law Cttee, CCP Hubei Prov. Cttee; Deputy Procurator-Gen. Supreme People's Procuratorate of China 1985–93, Procurator-Gen. 1993–98; Alt. mem. 13th CCP Cen. Cttee 1987–92, mem. 14th CCP Cen. Cttee 1992–97, 15th CCP Cen. Cttee 1997–2002; Vice-Chair. 9th CPPCC Nat. Cttee 1998–2003, 10th CPPCC Nat. Cttee 2003–. *Leisure interests:* shadow boxing, swimming, calligraphy. *Address:* National Committee of Chinese People's Political Consultative Conference, 23 Taipingqiao Street, Beijing, People's Republic of China (office).

ZHANG, Tangmin; Chinese traditional medical practitioner and chemist; b. 19 March 1939, Kai Jai, Sichuan; s. of Zhang He Ming and Tao Kai Yun; m. Sun Ren Ping 1966; two s. one d.; ed Univ. of Science and Tech. of China; Asst Researcher, Inst. of Chem., Academia Sinica 1962–78, Asst Prof. 1978–87, Assoc. Prof. 1987; self-taught in traditional Chinese medicine 1964–; assigned to Beijing Xuanwu Hosp. 1981; opened own epilepsy clinic 1981. *Publications:* New Cure for Epilepsy, Can Epilepsy be Cured?, Fringe Science and Epilepsy, Discussions on the Cure for the Abdomen Type of Epilepsy; and other works on epilepsy. *Address:* Institute of Chemistry, Academia Sinica, Beijing 100080, People's Republic of China (office). *Telephone:* (10) 2553979 (office).

ZHANG, Wan Xin; Chinese petrochemicals industry executive and professor; *President, Creat Group Corporation;* b. 5 May 1930, Harbin; s. of Zhang Xinming and Sun Minying; m. Deng Yinin 1958; one s. one d.; ed Tsinghua Univ., Beijing, Dalin Univ.; Sr Vice-Pres. China Petrochemical Corpn (SINOPEC) 1983–88; Chair. and Pres. Int. Multi-Petrochemical Enterprise Ltd (IMPEL), Hong Kong 1989–94; Chair. and CEO Sino-American Corpn (SAAX) 1992; Pres. Creat Group Corpn 1995–; Vice-Chair. China Taiwan Study Asscn; Chair. MONTPEL 1992–97; Vice-Pres. Devt Research Centre, State Council; part-time Prof., Tsinghua Univ., Beijing; Alt. mem. 12th CCP Cen. Cttee 1982–87, 13th CCP Cen. Cttee 1987–92; Vice-Chair. China Chemical Eng and Industry Soc.; Prof., Shenzhen Univ. 1983–88, Tsinghua Univ. 1988–93; mem. CCP Cttee, Beijing Municipality 1981–83; Deputy Chief Exec. Econ., Tech. and Social Devt Research Center 1988, Vice-Pres. 1991; Vice-Chair. China Charity Foundation 1997–2002; Vice-Chair. China West Region Econ. Devt Asscn 1999–; Life Academician China Acad. of Sciences 2004–; Advanced Tech. Award from Beijing City Govt 1979, awarded Nat. Top Prize of State Cttee for Tech. Progress 1984. *Leisure interest:* listening to music, liberal arts. *Address:* 225 Chaoyangmen, Nei Dajie, Beijing 100010, People's Republic of China. *Telephone:* (10) 65270800; (10) 84721997. *Fax:* (10) 84721991. *E-mail:* zwx@creatgroup.com (office). *Website:* www.creatgroup.com (office).

ZHANG, Weiqing; Chinese politician; b. 1944, Lintong Co., Shaanxi Prov.; ed Peking Univ.; joined CCP 1972; Sec. CCP Communist Youth League of China Baode Co. Cttee, Shanxi Prov., Sec. CCP Baode Co. Cttee; Sec. CCP Huguan Co. Cttee, Shanxi Prov. 1975–83; Sec. Communist Youth League Shanxi Provincial Cttee 1982–83, Vice-Gov. Shanxi Prov. 1983–84; mem. Standing Cttee and Head Propaganda Dept, CCP Shanxi Prov. Cttee 1985–93; Vice-Minister, State Population and Family Planning Comm. 1994–98, Minister 1998–2008; Del., 14th CCP Nat. Congress 1992–97; mem. 15th CCP Cen. Cttee 1997–2002, 16th CCP Cen. Cttee 2002–07. *Address:* c/o State Population and Family Planning Commission, 14 Zhichun Lu, Haidan Qu, Beijing 100088, People's Republic of China (office). *Telephone:* (10) 62046622 (office). *Fax:* (10) 62051865 (office). *E-mail:* gjjsw@chinapop.gov.cn (office). *Website:* www.npfpc.gov.cn/en (office).

ZHANG, Wenkang; Chinese politician; b. April 1940, Nanhui Co., Shanghai; ed Shanghai No. 1 Medical Coll.; joined PLA 1962, CCP 1966; Lecturer, later Chief of Diving Physiology Office, later Dir Training Dept, later Assoc. Prof., later Vice-Pres., No. 2 Medical Univ. of the Chinese PLA 1962–90; Deputy Dir Health Dept, PLA Gen. Logistics Dept 1990–93; Vice-Minister of Public Health 1993–98, Minister 1998–2003 (resgnd); Dir State Admin of Traditional Chinese Medicine 1993–98, Drugs Licensing Cttee 1994; Deputy Head, Nat. Group for Narcotics Control 1997; mem. State Academic Degrees Cttee 1999; Pres. Chinese Medical Asscn 1999; mem. 15th CCP Cen. Cttee 1997–2002, 16th CCP Cen. Cttee 2002–07, Deputy Dir CCP Cen. Cttee Cen. Health Cttee 1998; Hon. Chair. Council of China Pharmaceutical Univ. 1995; Hon. Vice-Pres. Red Cross Soc. of China 1999. *Address:* c/o Ministry of Public Health, 1 Xizhinenwai Bei Lu, Xicheng Qu, Beijing, People's Republic of China (office).

ZHANG, Wenyue; Chinese politician; b. Oct. 1944, Pucheng Co., Fujian Prov.; ed Beijing Inst. of Geology; joined CCP 1965; Dir Geology and Mineral Resources Bureau of Sichuan Prov.; Dir-Gen. Office of Ministry of Geology and Mineral Resources 1986; Dir State Admin. on Mineral Resources 1989; Vice-Minister of Land and Resources (fmrly Geology and Mineral Resources) 1990–95; Deputy Sec. CCP Xinjiang Uygur Autonomous Regional Cttee 1996–2001; Vice-Chair. Xinjiang Uygur Autonomous Regional People's Govt 1999–2001; Deputy Sec. CCP Liaoning Prov. Cttee 2001–07, Sec. 2007–09; Chair. CPPCC Liaoning Prov. Cttee 2003–04; mem. CCP Cen. Comm. for Discipline Inspection 1992, 15th CCP Cen. Cttee 1997–2002, Alt. mem. 16th CCP Cen. Cttee 2002–07, mem. 17th CCP Cen. Cttee 2007–12; Acting Gov. Liaoning Prov. 2004, Gov. 2004–07; Deputy, 11th NPC 2008–13, Deputy Dir NPC Environmental and Resources Protection Cttee

2009–13. *Address:* c/o Liaoning CCP Provincial Committee, Shenyang, Liaoning Province, People's Republic of China (office).

ZHANG, Xianliang; Chinese writer and poet; b. 1936, Jiangsu; m. Yan Huili; one d.; fmr teacher in Beijing and Ningxia; in political disgrace 1957–79; mem. editorial staff Shuofang literary magazine in late 1970s; Cttee mem. CPPCC 1983; f. Ningxia Zhenbeipu West Studio; mem. Chinese Writers' Asscn (Vice-Pres. 1986); Best Novel of the Year Awards (China) 1981, 1983, 1984. *Publications:* Song of the Great Wind (poem) 1957, Soul and Flesh (aka A Herdsman's Story) 1981, Contemporary Chinese Short Stories (with Zhang Xian and others) 1984, Mimosa 1984, Prize-Winning Stories from China 1980–1981 (with others) 1985, Half of Man is Woman 1985, Yi Xiang Tian Kai (screenplay) 1986, Women Shi Shijie (screenplay) 1988, Getting Used to Dying 1989, Grass Soup 1992, My Bodhi Tree 1994. *Leisure interest:* Chinese calligraphy. *Address:* c/o Ningxia Writers' Association, Yinchuan City, People's Republic of China.

ZHANG, Xiaogang; Chinese steel industry executive; *President, Anshan Iron and Steel Group Corporation (Ansteel);* Pres. Anshan Iron and Steel Group Corpn (Ansteel), Chair. Angang Steel Co. Ltd; Vice-Chair. World Steel Asscn 2010–11, Chair. 2011–12. *Address:* Anshan Iron and Steel Group Corporation, 1 Huangang Road, Anshan 114021, Liaoning Province, People's Republic of China (office). *Telephone:* (412) 6723090 (office). *Fax:* (412) 6723080 (office). *E-mail:* office@ansteel.com.cn (office). *Website:* www.ansteelgroup.com (office).

ZHANG, Xiwu, DEng; Chinese engineer and mining executive; *Chairman, Shenhua Group;* worked as First Deputy Mine Head, later Mine Head, later Asst Bureau Chief, Dayan Coal Mining Bureau, Inner Mongolia; fmr mem. CCP Leadership Group and Deputy Chief of Bureau of Coal Industry, Jilin Prov. and Deputy Gen. Man. Northeast Inner Mongolia Coal Group Co.; served as mem. CCP Party Leadership Group, Pres. and Dir Shenhua Group, Vice-Pres. Shenhua Group, Chair., mem. CCP Cttee and Gen. Man. Shenhua Shendong Coal Co., Chair. and Standing mem. CCP Cttee of Shenhua Dongsheng Coal Co., Gen. Man. Fine Coal Business Dept, Shenhua Group, currently Sec. CCP Leadership Group and Chair. Shenhua Group Corpn Ltd, also Exec. Dir and Chair. China Shenhua; currently a Research Fellow. *Address:* Shenhua Group Corporation Ltd, Guohua Investment Plaza, 3 Dongzhimen South Street, Dongcheng District, Beijing 100007, People's Republic of China (office). *Telephone:* (10) 58133113 (office); (10) 58132001 (office); (10) 58132114 (office). *E-mail:* shjt@shenhuagroup.com.cn (office). *Website:* www.shenhuagroup.com.cn (office).

ZHANG, Xuanlong; Chinese business executive; *Chairman, Founder Group;* b. 1956, Quanzhou, Fujian Prov.; ed First Jr School of Quanzhou, Fujian; Gen. Man. Hong Kong Kingsoft Co. 1980; Gen. Man. and Vice-Chair. Tianjin Stone, a jt venture with Stone Group; as Vice-Chair. Founder Group, set up Super Chinese Card Dept and brought Founder Golden WPS software into the market 1990, currently Chair. Founder Group; Pres. Founder (Hong Kong) Co. Ltd and Deputy Pres. Founder Group 1992, Chair. Founder Holdings Ltd; f. PUC Founder (MSC) Berhad, Malaysia, Founder International Inc., Japan. *Address:* Peking University Founder Group, Founder Tower, Zhong Guan Cun, Haidian District, Beijing, People's Republic of China (office). *Website:* www.founder.com/en (office).

ZHANG, Xuezhong; Chinese politician; b. Feb. 1943, Lanzhou, Gansu Prov.; ed Lanzhou Univ.; joined CCP 1960; primary school teacher, Lanzhou Teachers' School; Sec. CCP Longnan Pref. Cttee 1961–89; People's Air Defence Office, Gansu Prov.; Office Sec., PLA Lanzhou Mil. Region (HQ) 1990; Sec. of Secr., Gen. Office of CCP Gansu Provincial Cttee 1990; Sec. CCP Fafang Commune Cttee, Wuwei Co., Sec. CCP Yuzhong Co. Cttee 1990; Deputy Sec. CCP Lanzhou Municipal Cttee 1990; Vice-Gov. Gansu Prov. 1990; Deputy Sec. CCP Tibet Autonomous Region Cttee 1990–94; Vice-Minister of Personnel 1994–2000, Minister 2000–02; Sec. CCP Sichuan Prov. Cttee 2002–06; Chair. Standing Cttee Sichuan Prov. People's Congress 2003–06; mem. 16th CCP Cen. Cttee 2002–07. *Address:* c/o Sichuan Provincial People's Congress, Chengdu, Sichuan Province, People's Republic of China (office).

ZHANG, Yan; Chinese diplomatist and government official; *Ambassador to India;* b. 3 Nov. 1950; m. Chen Wangxia; one d.; served with mission to Liberia 1978–83; with Ministry of Foreign Affairs 1983–96, Counsellor, Dept of Int. Orgs and Confs, Ministry of Foreign Affairs March–Aug. 1998; Dir-Gen. Foreign Affairs Office, Yunnan 1996–98; Sr Official, Asia Pacific Econ. Co-operation (APEC) 1998–99, Deputy Exec. Dir 2000, Exec. Dir 2001; Amb. to UN 2001–05; Dir-Gen. Dept of Arms Control and Disarmament, Ministry of Foreign Affairs 2005–07; Amb. to India 2007–. *Address:* Embassy of the People's Republic of China, Chanakyapuri, New Delhi 110 021, India (office). *Telephone:* (11) 26112345 (home). *Fax:* (11) 26885486 (office). *E-mail:* chinaemb_in@mfa.gov.cn (office). *Website:* www.chinaembassy.org.in (office).

ZHANG, Yimou; Chinese film actor and director; b. 1951, Xian, Shanxi Prov.; m. Xiao Hua 1982 (divorced 1990); ed Xian Middle School, Beijing Film Acad.; directed opening and closing ceremonies, Summer Olympics, Beijing 2008; Dr hc (City Univ. of Hong Kong) 2005. *Opera productions as director:* Turandot (Beijing) 1998, The First Emperor (Metropolitan Opera, New York) 2008. *Films include:* The Old Well (8th Golden Rooster Best Actor Award 1988), Red Sorghum (Hong Gaoliang), Raise the Red Lantern 1991, The Story of Qiu Ju 1992, Keep Cool 1997, Not One Less (Golden Lion, Venice) 1999, The Road Home 1999 (Grand Jury Prize, Berlin 1999), Happy Times 2001, Hero 2003, House of Flying Daggers (Best Foreign Language Film, Los Angeles Film Critics' Asscn) 2004, Riding Alone for Thousands of Miles 2005, Curse of the Golden Flower 2006, The Flowers of War 2011.

ZHANG, Yin, (Cheung Yan); Chinese business executive; *Chairwoman, Nine Dragons Paper Industries Company Limited;* b. Heilongjiang Prov.; d. of Cheung Deen; m. 2nd Ming Chung Liu; two c.; went to Hong Kong 1985, started career in waste paper trading with 30,000 yuan; moved to USA with husband 1990; f. America Chung Nam 1990; returned to Hong Kong 1995; Founder and Chair. Nine Dragons Paper Industries Co. Ltd, Dongguan, Guangdong Prov. 1996; mem. CPPCC 2007; Vice Chair. Women's Fed. of Commerce, All-China Fed. of Industry and Commerce; Hon. Citizen, City of Dongguan, Guangdong; Worldwide Chinese Amb. of Love 2006. *Address:* Nine Dragons Paper Industries Co. Ltd, Xinsha Port Industry Zone, Mayong Town, Dongguan 523147, Guangdong, People's Republic of

China (office). *Telephone:* (769) 88234888 (office). *Fax:* (769) 88824198 (office). *E-mail:* info@ndpaper.com (office). *Website:* www.ndpaper.com (office).

ZHANG, Youfu; Chinese ecologist; b. 21 May 1940, Jiangsu Prov.; s. of Zhang Changsheng and Zhong Yinlan; m. Xu Chunlan 1968; two s.; ed Nanking Univ., Chendu Inst. of Geography, Chinese Acad. of Sciences; has been engaged in research work on biological prevention of mudflow damage, soil and water conservation and forest ecology for over 20 years. *Publications:* numerous papers on mudflow, erosion, debris flow, landslides, disaster prevention, measures against debris flow, remote sensing information, etc. *Leisure interest:* photography. *Address:* Institute of Mountain Hazards and Environment, Chinese Academy of Science, PO Box 417, Chengdu 610041, Sichuan Province, People's Republic of China (office). *Telephone:* (28) 85228816 (office). *E-mail:* sdb@imde.ac.cn (office). *Website:* www.imde.ac.cn (office).

ZHANG, Youxi; Chinese engineer and mining industry executive; *Chairman, Datong Coal Mine Group Company Limited;* b. Dec. 1958; ed China Univ. of Mining and Tech., Central Party School; mine technician, tech. dir, production vice-mayor, gov., deputy chief engineer, Datong Mining Bureau, Baidong 1976–92, Deputy Dir, Jinwan Mine and mem. Party Cttee, Datong Mining Bureau 1992–97, Sec. of the Party Cttee and Deputy Dir, Yanya coal mine, Datong Mining Bureau 1997–98, Coal Mine Dir and Sec. of Party Cttee, Datong Mining Bureau 1998–2003, Deputy Gen. Man., Coal Mine Dir and Sec. of Party Cttee Datong Coal Ltd 2003–05, Vice-Chair. and Gen. Man. Datong Coal Industry Co. Ltd 2005–07, Deputy Gen. Man. Datong Coal Mine Group Co., Xuangang, Vice-Chair. and Gen. Man. coal company 2007–09, Chair. and Deputy Gen. Man. Datong Coal Mine Group gas and electric co. 2009–10, Deputy Gen. Man. Datong Coal Mine Group Co. Feb.–April 2010, Vice-Chair. and Gen. Man. Datong Coal Mine Group Co. Ltd 2010–11, Chair. and Party Sec. 2011–, Chair. Datong Coal Industry Ltd 2012–; Sec., Party Cttee, Zhangze Power Ltd 2013–; Vice-Pres. China Nat. Coal Asscn 2013–; sr expert, Shanxi Prov. Asscn; Deputy to NPC. *Address:* Datong Coal Mine Group Co. Ltd, 11 Dongmen Street, Datong 037003, People's Republic of China (office). *Telephone:* (352) 7868200 (office). *Fax:* (352) 7868201 (office). *E-mail:* dtmkjt@dtcoalmine.com (office). *Website:* www.dtcoalmine.com (office).

ZHANG, Yuan; Chinese film director; b. 1963; m. Ning Dai; ed Beijing Film Acad.; has directed music videos for leading Chinese rock singer Cui Jian; also producer and dir for MTV; has also made several documentaries. *Films:* Mama (Special Jury Prize, Nantes Film Festival 1991) 1990, Beijing Bastards 1992, The Square 1994, East Palace West Palace 1996, Seventeen Years (Best Dir, Venice Film Festival) 1999, Little Red Flowers 2006 (CICAE Award, Berlin Film Festival 2006) Dada's Dance 2008, Beijing Flickers 2013.

ZHANG, Yuliang; Chinese business executive; *Chairman and President, Greenland Holding Group;* fmrly with Shanghai Municipal Agricultural Comm. Residential Office; currently Chair. and Pres. Greenland Holding Group, Shanghai Greenland Construction (Group) Co. Ltd. *Address:* Greenland Holding Group, 700 Dapu Road, Shanghai 200023, People's Republic of China (office). *Telephone:* (21) 53188666 (office). *Fax:* (21) 53188660 (office). *E-mail:* info@greenlandsc.com (office). *Website:* www.greenlandsc.com (office).

ZHANG, Yun, PhD; Chinese economist and business executive; *Executive Vice-Chairman and President, Agricultural Bank of China;* ed Wuhan Univ.; served successively as Deputy Pres. Shenzhen br., Agricultural Bank of China, Deputy Pres. Guangdong br., and Pres. Guangxi Autonomous Region br., Exec. Asst Pres. and Gen. Man. Personnel Dept, Agricultural Bank of China 2001, Exec. Vice-Pres. Agricultural Bank of China 2001–09, Exec. Vice-Chair. and Pres. Agricultural Bank of China 2009–. *Address:* Agricultural Bank of China, 69 Jianguomen Nei Avenue, Dongcheng District, Beijing 100005, People's Republic of China (office). *Telephone:* (10) 85109619 (office). *Fax:* (10) 85108557 (office). *E-mail:* webmaster@intl.abocn.com (office); ir@abchina.com (office). *Website:* www.abchina.com (office).

ZHANG, Yunchuan; Chinese politician; b. 1946, Dongyang, Zhejiang Prov.; ed Harbin Inst. of Mil. Eng; joined CCP 1973; fmr technician, Factory No. 6214, Ministry of Machine Industry No. 6; mem. Standing Cttee, CCP Jiujiang City Cttee Jiangxi Prov. 1985–86, Vice-Mayor of Jiujiang City 1985–86; Commr Admin. Office and Deputy Sec. CCP Ganzhou Prefectural Cttee, Jiangxi Prov. 1986–91; mem. Standing Cttee CCP Jiangxi Prov. Cttee 1991–93; Asst to Gov. Jiangxi Prov. 1991–93, Vice-Gov. 1993–95; mem. Standing Cttee and Exec. Vice-Chair. Xinjiang Uygur Autonomous Region 1995–99, Deputy Sec. 1998–2001; Sec. Changsha Municipal Cttee 1999–2001; Vice-Gov. Hunan Prov. 2001, Acting Gov. 2001–02, Gov. 2002–03; Minister-in-Charge, Comm. of Science, Tech. and Industry for Nat. Defence (COSTIND) 2003–07; mem. 16th CCP Cen. Cttee 2002–07, 17th CCP Cen. Cttee 2007–12; Sec. CCP Hebei Prov. Cttee 2007–11; Chair. Standing Cttee, Hebei Provincial People's Congress 2008–11. *Address:* Hebei CCP Provincial Committee, Shijiazhuang, People's Republic of China (office). *Website:* www.hebei.gov.cn (office).

ZHANG, Yuzhuo, DEng; Chinese engineer and mining executive; *President and CEO, Shenhua Group;* worked as Deputy Dir Research Office, Beijing Mining Research Inst., China Coal Research Inst. (CCRI), later Asst Pres., Vice-Pres., Pres. and Deputy Party Sec. CCP Cttee of CCRI, later Deputy Dir Beijing Mining Research Inst.; conducted post-doctoral research in Dept of Mining and Environmental Eng, Southern Illinois Univ., Carbondale, USA and Univ. of Southampton, UK; served as Vice-Pres. Shenhua Group, currently Pres. and CEO, mem. CCP Leadership Group and Dir Shenhua Group Corpn Ltd, Exec. Dir and Vice-Chair. China Shenhua; currently a Research Fellow. *Address:* Shenhua Group Corporation Ltd, Guohua Investment Plaza, 3 Dongzhimen South Street, Dongcheng District, Beijing 100007, People's Republic of China (office). *Telephone:* (10) 58133113 (office); (10) 58132001 (office); (10) 58132114 (office). *E-mail:* shjt@shenhuagroup.com.cn (office). *Website:* www.shenhuagroup.com.cn (office).

ZHANG, Zhongwei; Chinese politician; b. Feb. 1942, Dujiangyan, Sichuan Prov.; ed CCP Cen. Cttee Cen. Party School; joined CCP 1960; Office Sec., CCP Zhongxing Dist Cttee, Sichuan Prov. 1958–64, Org. Dept, CCP Guanxian Co. Cttee, Sichuan Prov. 1959–64, CCP Wenjiang Prefectural Cttee, Sichuan Prov. 1962–74 (Deputy Sec., later Sec. CCP Communist Youth League of China Wenjiang Prefectural Cttee 1972–78); Sec. CCP Pengxian Co. Cttee, Sichuan Prov. 1978–82; Deputy Sec. CCP Wenjiang Prefectural Cttee 1982–83; mem.

Standing Cttee CCP Chengdu City Cttee, Sichuan Prov. 1983–87, Sec. Rural Work Cttee 1983–87; Deputy Head, Org. Dept, CCP Sichuan Prov. Cttee 1987–88; Dir Agriculture and Animal Husbandry Dept, Sichuan Prov. 1988–93; Vice-Gov. of Sichuan Prov. 1993–94, Acting Gov. 1997–99, Gov. 2000–07; mem. Standing Cttee CCP Sichuan Prov. Cttee 1994–97, Deputy Sec. Sichuan Prov. Cttee; mem. 16th CCP Cen. Cttee 2002–07. *Address:* c/o Office of the Governor, Sichuan Provincial People's Government, Chengdu, People's Republic of China (office).

ZHANG, Ziyi; Chinese actress; b. 9 Feb. 1979, Beijing; ed Beijing Dance Acad., Beijing Central Drama Coll. *Films:* Wo de fu qin mu qin (The Road Home) 1999 (Hundred Flowers Best Actress Award 2000), Wo hu cang long (Crouching Tiger, Hidden Dragon) 2000 (Golden Bauhinia Best Supporting Actress Award 2001, Golden Horse Film Festival Best Actress Award 2000, BAFTA Best Performance by an Actress in a Supporting Role 2001), Rush Hour II 2001, Shu shan zheng zhuan (The Legend of Zu) 2001, Musa 2001, Ying xiong (Hero) 2002 (Hong Kong Film Awards Best Supporting Actress Award 2003), Zi hudie (Purple Butterfly) 2003, Jopog manura II: Dolaon jeonseol (My Wife is a Gangster II) 2003, Shi mian mai fu (House of Flying Daggers) 2004 (BAFTA Best Performance by an Actress in a Leading Role 2005), 2046 (Best Actress, Hong Kong Film Critics' Soc. Awards 2005) 2004, Mo li hua kai (Jasmine) 2004 (Golden Rooster Best Actress Award 2004), Operetta tanuki goten 2005, Memoirs of a Geisha 2005 (BAFTA Best Performance by an Actress in a Leading Role 2006, Golden Globe Best Performance by an Actress 2006), The Banquet 2006, TMNT (voice) 2007, Mei Lanfang 2008, Horsemen 2009, Sophie's Revenge 2009, The Founding of a Republic 2009, Mo shu wai zhuan 2011, The Grandmasters 2012. *Address:* c/o Nine Muses and Apollo Inc., 525 Broadway, Suite 201, New York, NY 10012, USA (office). *Telephone:* (212) 431-2665 (office). *Fax:* (212) 431-2667 (office). *E-mail:* linglucas@aol.com (office).

ZHANG, Zongyan, MBA; Chinese engineer and business executive; *President, China Railway Construction Corporation;* ed Guanghua School of Man. of Peking Univ.; joined CRCC Group 1981, Deputy Gen. Man. China Railway 12th Bureau Group Co. Ltd 2002–05, Chair. and Sec. to CCP Cttee 2005–08, Chair. and Deputy Sec. 2008–09, Vice-Pres. China Railway Construction Corpn 2009–13, Pres. 2013–. *Address:* China Railway Construction Corporation, 40 Fuxing Road, Beijing 100855, People's Republic of China (office). *Telephone:* (10) 51888114 (office). *E-mail:* ir@crcc.cn (office). *Website:* www.crcc.cn (office).

ZHANG, Zuoji; Chinese politician; b. Jan. 1945, Bayan, Heilongjiang Prov.; ed Heilongjiang Univ.; joined CCP 1972; Vice-Pres. Party School, CCP State No. 123 Factory Cttee 1967–77; Sec. Political Dept, 5th Ministry of Machine-Building Industry 1977–87, Deputy Chief, Publicity Div. 1977–87; Deputy Sec. Org. Dept, Ministry of Ordnance Industry 1977–87; Deputy Dir Labour Bureau, Ministry of Labour and Personnel 1987–88, Dir Labour Force Admin. and Employment Dept 1988–91; Vice-Mayor of Xi'an City, Shaanxi Prov. 1991; Vice-Minister of Labour 1993–94; Deputy Sec.-Gen. State Council 1994–98; Minister of Labour and Social Security 1998–2003; Gov. Heilongjiang Prov. 2003–07; mem. Standing Cttee CCP Heilongjiang Prov. Cttee 2003–; mem. CCP Cen. Cttee Cen. Comm. for Discipline Inspection 1997, 16th CCP Cen. Cttee 2002–07, 17th CCP Cen. Cttee 2007–12; Dir 11th CPPCC Econ. Cttee 2008–. *Publications:* A Review of Labor Systems in Three East European Countries, The Reality, Difficulties and Countermeasures, Chinese Labor System in Reform. *Address:* CCP Provincial Committee, Harbin, Heilongjiang Province, People's Republic of China (office).

ZHANGKE, Jia; Chinese film director; b. 1970, Fenyang; m. Zhao Tao; a leading figure of the 'Sixth Generation' of Chinese film directors; jury mem. BigScreen Italia Film Festival, Kunming 2006. *Films include:* Xiaoshan huijia 1995, Xiao Wu (The Pickpocket) (Netpac Award, Berlin Int. Film Festival 1998, Golden Montgolfiere, Nantes Three Continents Festival 1998, New Currents Award, Pusan Int. Film Festival 1998, Dragons and Tigers Award, Vancouver Int. Film Festival 1998) 1997, Zhantai (Best Film, Buenos Aires Int. Festival of Independent Cinema 2001, Don Quixote Award and FIPRESCI Prize, Fribourg Int. Film Festival 2001, Golden Montgolfiere, Nantes Three Continents Festival, Young Cinema Award, Singapore Int. Film Festival 2001) 2000, Gong gong chang suo (In Public) (Grand Prix, Marseille Festival of Documentary Film 2002) 2001, Ren xiao yao (Unknown Pleasures) 2002, Shijie (The World) 2004. Sanxia haoren (Still Life) (Best Film, Durban Int. Film Festival 2007, Golden Lion, Venice Film Festival) 2006, Dong (Doc/It Award, Venice Film Festival) 2006, 24 City 2008, Cry Me a River 2008, Black Breakfast 2008, I Wish I Knew 2010, A Touch of Sin 2013.

ZHAO, Bandi; Chinese artist; b. 1963, Beijing; ed Cen. Acad. of Fine Arts, Beijing; painting, photography and installation work; has exhibited worldwide 1992–; best known for satirical photographs featuring toy pandas. *Address:* c/o ShanghART Main Gallery, 50 Moganshan Rd, Bldg 16, Shanghai 200060, People's Republic of China.

ZHAO, Gang; Chinese business executive; *President, China North Industries Group Corporation (NORINCO);* Pres. China North Industries Group Corpn (alternatively known as NORINCO) and China North Industries Corpn 2010–. *Address:* China North Industries Group Corporation (NORINCO), No. 10 Chedaogou, Haidian Dist, Beijing 100089 (office); China North Industries Group Corporation (NORINCO), 46 Sanlihe Road, Beijing 100821, People's Republic of China (office). *Telephone:* (10) 68594210 (office); (10) 68787608 (office). *Fax:* (10) 68594232 (office); (10) 68594555 (office). *E-mail:* webmaster@cngc.com.cn (office). *Website:* www.norincogroup.com.cn (office); www.norinco.com (office); www.cngc .com.cn (office).

ZHAO, Guangfa, MBA; Chinese engineer and business executive; *President and Executive Director, China Railway Construction Corporation Ltd;* b. Aug. 1952; ed Asia Int. Open Univ., Macao; joined China Railway Construction Corpn Ltd (CRCCG Group) 1970, served as Deputy Chief, then Chief and Deputy Sec. CCP Cttee of 18th Eng Bureau, Ministry of Railways (predecessor of China Railway 18th Bureau Group Co. Ltd) 1994–99, Dir and Deputy Sec. CCP Cttee of China Railway 18th Bureau Group 1999–2001, Chair. and Deputy Party Sec. China Railway 18th Bureau Group Co. Ltd 2001–04, Deputy Gen. Man. CRCCG 2004–07, Vice-Pres. 2007–09, Pres. and Exec. Dir 2009–. *Address:* China Railway Construction Corpn Ltd, 40 Fuxing Road, Haidian District, Beijing 100855, People's Republic of China (office). *Telephone:* (10) 51886971 (Directorate) (office); (10) 51889515 (Supervisory Bd) (office); (10) 52688600 (office); (10) 51888114 (office).

Fax: (10) 68217382 (office); (10) 52688302 (office). *E-mail:* ir@crcc.cn (office). *Website:* www.crccg.com (office); www.crcc.cn (office).

ZHAO, Guorong; Chinese chess player; b. 1961, Heilongjiang Prov.; Chinese Chess Master 1978; Chinese Chess Special Master 1987; winner, 2nd World Championships, Kunming 1991; Champion, First Chinese Chess Celebrity Championship 1997; AXF Int. Grandmaster;*Website:* chess.sport.org.cn.

ZHAO, Jianguo; Chinese business executive; *Chairman, China Southern Power Grid Company Ltd;* Vice-Pres. China Southern Power Grid Co. Ltd –2006, Pres. and CEO 2006–10, Chair. 2010–. *Address:* China Southern Power Grid Co. Ltd, 6 Huasui Road, Zhujiang Xincheng, Tianhe District, Guangzhou 510623, People's Republic of China (office). *Telephone:* (20) 3812-1958 (office); (20) 3812-1080 (office). *Fax:* (20) 3886-5670 (office); (20) 3812-0189 (office). *E-mail:* international@csg.cn (office). *Website:* www.csg.cn (office).

ZHAO, Leji; Chinese politician; *Head, CCP Central Committee Organization Department;* b. March 1957, Xi'ning, Qinghai Prov.; ed Peking Univ., Beijing; joined CCP 1975; teacher, later Deputy Dir Dean's Office, Qinghai Prov. Commerce School 1980–83; Deputy Dir Political Div., Commerce Dept, Qinghai Prov. 1983–84, Deputy Dir, later Dir Commerce Dept 1986–93 (also Sec. CCP Party Cttee), Dir Financial Dept 1993–94; Sec. CCP Qinghai Prov. Cttee 1984–86, 2003–07, Deputy Sec. 2000–03; Asst Gov. of Qinghai Prov. 1993–94, Vice-Gov. 1994–99, Acting Gov. 1999–2000, Gov. 2000–03; Sec. CCP Xining City Cttee, Qinghai Prov. 1997–98; Chair. Standing Cttee Qinghai Prov. People's Congress 2004–07; Sec. CCP Shaanxi Prov. Cttee 2007–12, also mem. Standing Cttee 2007–12; mem. 16th CCP Cen. Cttee 2000–07, 17th CCP Cen. Cttee 2007–12, 18th CCP Cen. Cttee 2012–, 18th CCP Cen. Cttee Politburo and Secr. 2012–; Head, CCP Cen. Cttee Organization Dept 2012–. *Address:* CCP Central Committee Organization Department, Zhongnanhai, Beijing, People's Republic of China (office). *Website:* cpc.people.com.cn (office).

ZHAO, Qizheng; Chinese politician; *Chairman,;* b. Jan. 1940, Beijing; s. of Zhao Jingyuan and Wan Shuxian; m. Zheng Shiting; one d.; ed China Univ. of Science and Tech.; joined CCP 1979; technician, later Sr Engineer 1963–74; Deputy Dir Shanghai Broadcasting Materials Factory 1982–84; Deputy Sec. Industrial Work Cttee, CCP Shanghai Municipal Cttee 1984, Deputy Head, later Head, Org. Dept 1984–86, mem. Standing Cttee 1986–91, Dir Dist Admin. Cttee 1993; Sec. Work Cttee CCP Pudong Dist Cttee, Shanghai 1992; Vice-Mayor of Shanghai 1993–98; Deputy Dir then Dir CCP Cen. Cttee Int. Communications Office 1998–; Deputy Dir, then Dir Information Office of State Council 1998–2005; mem. 16th CCP Cen. Cttee 2002–07; Vice-Chair. Foreign Affairs Cttee, CCP Cen. Cttee 2005–08, Chair. 2008–; Dean, School of Journalism and Communication, Renmin Univ. of China 2005–. *Publications:* America and American People in Chinese People's Eyes 2005, Introducing China to the Rest of the World 2006, A Friendly Dialogue between an Atheist and a Christian (with Luis Palau) 2008. *Address:* c/o State Council Information Office, 225 Chaoyangmen Neidajie, Beijing 100010, People's Republic of China. *Telephone:* (10) 6559-2339 (office). *Fax:* (10) 6559-2364 (office). *E-mail:* xuying@scio.gov.cn (office).

ZHAO, Ruichun; Chinese artist; b. Nov. 1935, Wenzhou, Zhejiang; s. of Zhao Loshu and Huang Shenghong; m. 1st 1956; one d.; m. 2nd Yun Xiuying; one d.; ed Chinese Cen. Fine Arts Inst.; Lecturer, Guangzhou Inst. of Fine Arts 1959–71; teacher, Chinese Cen. Fine Arts Inst. 1980–82; painter, Guangzhou Art Acad. 1984–, now Sr Painter; first one-man exhbn 1962; mem. Chinese Artists' Asscn, Chinese Engraving Asscn; Sec.-Gen. Chinese Asscn of Copper-Plate, Lithographic and Silkscreen Engraving; Ed.-in-Chief Modern Engraving; works exhibited in USA, Japan, UK, Australia, New Zealand, Ireland, Singapore, Denmark, Switzerland, Korea, Sweden, Thailand, Canada, USSR, Algeria, Italy and Taiwan. *Publications:* On Engraving Education 1981, Woodcut Techniques 1983, The Practice and Theory of Sketching 1986, Silk-screen Plate Techniques 1987. *Leisure interest:* Chinese cooking. *Address:* Guangzhou Academy of Painting, 130 Shuiyin Road, Guangzhou 510075, Guangdong Province (office); 609 Dongnan Mansion, Gongyuan Road, Wenzhou 325000, Zhejiang, People's Republic of China (home). *Telephone:* (20) 87724636 (office); (577) 88203025 (home). *Fax:* (577) 88203025 (home); (577) 88203026. *E-mail:* zrcit@sohu.com (office).

ZHAO, Shiping, BA; Chinese engineer and business executive; *Chairman, Yangquan Coal Industry (Group) Company Limited;* b. March 1955, Zuo Quan Co., Shanxi Prov.; mem. CCP 1985–; mem. Bd of Dirs and Gen. Man. Yangquan Coal Industry (Group) Co. Ltd 2006–12, Sec., Party Cttee and Chair. 2012–. *Address:* Yangquan Coal Industry (Group) Co. Ltd, 5 Beida Street, Yangquan 045000, Shanxi, People's Repub. of China (office). *Telephone:* (353) 7078728 (office). *Fax:* (353) 7078718 (office). *E-mail:* webmaster@ymjt.com.cn (office). *Website:* www .ymjt.com.cn (office).

ZHAO, Xizheng; Chinese power industry executive; *President, China Electricity Council;* b. 1942; ed Tsingua Univ.; Dir-Gen. Northeast Electric Power Admin Bureau and Pres. Northeast Electric Power Group Corpn 1989–93; Deputy Minister of Electric Power 1993–98; Exec. Vice-Pres. State Power Corpn of China (also known as State Grid Corpn of China) 1993–2003, CEO 2003; Pres. China Electricity Council 2004–; Chair. Presidium, China Fed. of Industrial Econs (CFIE); mem. CPPCC 2007. *Address:* China Electricity Council, No.1, Lane 2, Baiguang Road, Beijing 100761, People's Republic of China (office). *Website:* www .cec.org.cn (office).

ZHAO, Zhihao; Chinese government official; b. 1931, Longkou City, Huangxian Co., Shandong Prov.; joined CCP 1947; Sec. CCP Teng and Wenshang Co. Cttee 1958–82, CCP Qufu Normal Coll. Cttee 1982–83; Deputy Sec. CCP Shandong Prov. Cttee, Dir Gen. Office 1983–85; Sec. CCP Zibo Municipal Cttee 1985–88; Vice-Gov. Shandong Prov. 1988–89, Gov. 1989; mem. 14th CPP Cen. Cttee; NPC Deputy, Shandong Prov.; Deputy Sec. CCP Shandong Prov. Cttee 1988–94, Sec. 1994–2003, later Chair. Standing Cttee Prov. People's Congress, now Hon. Chair. *Address:* Shandong Provincial People's Congress, Jinan City, Shandong Province, People's Republic of China (office).

ZHAO, Zhongxian, DrSc; Chinese physicist; b. 30 Jan. 1941, Liaoning Prov.; s. of Zhao Desheng and Zhang Naibin; m. Zhou Yaqin 1967; two s.; ed Univ. of Science and Tech. of China; Researcher, Inst. of Physics, Acad. Sinica 1964–; Dir Nat. Lab. for Superconductivity 1991–2000; Chair. Scientific Council, Inst. of Physics 1999–;

mem. CPPCC Nat. Cttee 1993–98, 2003–07, 2008–13; Vice-Pres. China Asscn for Science and Tech. 2001–; Dir Working Cttee on Consultation and Evaluation of Chinese Academia Sinica 2000–08; mem. Presidium Chinese Acad. of Sciences 1998–2008; Vice-Pres. Chinese Physical Soc. 1994–2003, China Innovation Asscn 1996–; Fellow, Third World Acad. of Sciences 1987, Acad. of Ceramics (Int.) 1989, Chinese Acad. of Sciences 1991; mem. Council of Asscn of Asia Pacific Physical Soc. 1990–97; Special mem. China Center of Advanced Sciences and Tech. 1987; Hon. Fellow, India Materials Research Soc. 1991, China Materials Research Soc. 1996; Hon. DSc (Chinese Univ. of Hong Kong) 1988; Hon. Physics Award, Third World Acad. of Sciences 1986, Tan Kah-Kee Material Science Prize 1988, Natural Sciences Prize of China (1st Class) 1990, (2nd Class) 2002, Wang Dan-ping Science Prize 1992, Science and Tech. Progress Award, Ho Leung Ho Lee Foundation Physics Prize 1997, Award for Outstanding Achievement in Science and Tech., Chinese Acad. of Sciences 2005. *Leisure interests:* music, photography, calligraphy. *Address:* Institute of Physics, Chinese Academy of Sciences, Room D-420, Zhong Guan Cun, PO Box 603, Beijing 100080 (office); Building 17-105, Yan-Gui-Yuan, Zhong Guan Cun, Bei Er Tiao, Beijing 100080, People's Republic of China (home). *Telephone:* (10) 82649190 (office); (10) 82649361 (office); (10) 62564951 (home). *Fax:* (10) 82649486 (office); (10) 82649531 (office). *E-mail:* zhxzhao@aphy.iphy.ac.cn (office). *Website:* www.iphy.ac.cn (office).

ZHAPAROV, Akylbek Usenbekovich; Kyrgyzstani economist and politician; b. 14 Sept. 1964, Rybachye; ed Frunze (now Bishkek) Polytechnical Inst., Bishkek Financial-Econ. Acad.; worked in Automotive Highways and Roads Dept, Frunze Polytechnical Inst. 1986–91; Deputy Gen. Dir Tolkun org. 1991–92; Head, Youth Policy Dept, Office of the Pres. 1992–93; Head, Admin of Social Democratic Party of Kyrgyzstan 1993–95; Adviser to First Deputy Prime Minister 1995–96; Sec., Nat. Cttee for Securities, Office of the Pres. 1996–97; Chief Inspector, Ministry of Finance and Man. State Tax Inspectorate 1997–2000; Deputy, Zhogorku Kenesh (Parl.) 2000–05; Minister of Finance 2005–06 (resgnd), 2011–12, apptd Minister of Econ. Devt and Trade 2009, First Deputy Prime Minister 2009–10; Honoured Economist of the Kyrgyz Repub. 2002. *Address:* c/o Ministry of Finance, 720040 Bishkek, bul. Erkindik 58, Kyrgyzstan (office).

ZHARIKOV, Alexander Nikolayevich; Russian trade union official and engineer; b. 2 Jan. 1945, Arsenyevo; s. of Nicolai Philippovich Zharikov and Claudia Egorovna Gorodnicheva; m. 1st Olga Borisovna Suhova 1975 (deceased); one s.; m. 2nd Eva Shvachova; one s. one d.; ed Leningrad Shipbuilding Inst.; mil. service 1962–66; Sec. of Youth and Student Org. of Leningrad 1971–74; Chair. Student Council of USSR 1974–78; Vice-Pres. Int. Union of Students 1978–84; official, Int. Dept Cen. Cttee of CPSU 1984–88; Dir Int. Dept USSR All-Union Council 1988–90; Gen. Sec. World Fed. of Trade Unions (WFTU) 1990–2006; Hon. Prof. (Russian State Univ. of Humanitarian Science); Order of Honour (Russia) 1974. *Publications:* book on world student movt 1979; numerous articles on social issues, labour and trade union relations in newspapers and magazines. *Leisure interests:* swimming, collecting mushrooms, reading, skiing. *Address:* Branicka 112, 14701 Prague 4, Czech Republic (office). *Telephone:* (2) 44462140 (office). *Fax:* (2) 44461378 (office). *E-mail:* wftu@login.cz (office). *Website:* www.wftu.cz.

ZHARIKOV, Yevgeny Ilyich; Russian actor; b. 26 Feb. 1941, Moscow; s. of Ilya Melakhiyevich Zharikov and Anna Grigoryevna Zharikova; m. Natalia Gvozdikova; one s.; ed All-Union Inst. of Cinematography; mem. Union of Cinematographers 1968, Sec. 1999–; mem. Cinema Acad. Nica; Vice-Pres. Guild of Cinema Actors of Russia; f. Moscow Charity Foundation for Actors (Mercy); organized annual Int. Film Actors' Festival (Sozvezdiye) 1989–99; Pres. Yeugeny Zharikov Social Fund 1999–; Chair. Radio Kitt (Kino, Teatr, TV); mem. Exec. Bd Int. Fed. of Actors; mem. Int. Detective Club; Peoples' Artist of Russian Fed. 1979, USSR State Prize 1987, Order of Honour 1996, Order of Merit for Services to Country 2001. *Film roles include:* A esli eto lyubov? (What If This Is Love?) 1960, Ivanovo detstvo (Ivan's Childhood) 1962, Three Plus Two 1963, Russian for You 1966, Snegurochka (Snowgirl) 1969, Day of Angel, Born by Revolution, Trotsky 1993, Yuri the Long-Handed 1997, Salvation Army 2000, Blagoslovite zhenshchinu (Bless the Woman) 2003. *Leisure interests:* diving, hunting, fishing, sports, Russian and foreign classical literature, serious music. *Address:* Leninsky prospect 123, korp. 1, Apt. 589, 117513 Moscow, Russia (home). *Telephone:* (495) 438-12-97 (home). *Fax:* (495) 438-19-58 (home).

ZHELEV, Zhelyu Mitev, PhD; Bulgarian politician; b. 3 March 1935, Veselinovo/Shumen, Varna Region; s. of Mityu Zhelev and Yordanka Nedelcheva; m. Maria Ivanova Marinova 1966; two d.; ed Kliment Ohridski Univ. of Sofia; fmr librarian in Veselinovo; joined Bulgarian CP but expelled for criticism of Lenin 1964; unemployed 1966–72; initiator for establishment of Cttee for Ecological Protection of City of Ruse 1988; Co-Pres. Club for Protection of Glasnost and Restructuring (now Glasnost and Democracy Club) until Nov. 1989; Chair. UDF (opposition party) 1989–90; Pres. of Bulgaria 1990–97 (first Bulgarian pres. democratically elected in free elections 1992); Pres. Liberal Democratic Union 1998–; mem. Liberal International; Macedonian State Order 8 September 2010. *Publication:* Fascism 1981. *Leisure interests:* hiking, fishing. *Address:* c/o Office of the President, 2 Dondukov Boulevard, Sofia, Bulgaria. *Telephone:* 871767.

ZHENG, Silin; Chinese politician; *President, China Association of National Advertisers;* b. May 1940, Wu Co., Jiangsu Prov.; ed Taiyuan Science Univ.; joined CCP 1965; worked at Dandong Automobile Repair Plant, Liaoning Prov. 1965–81; Dir Dandong TV Parts Factory 1982–83; Vice-Mayor Dandong City 1983–85; Dir Comm. for Foreign Econ. Relations and Trade and Asst Gov., Liaoning Prov. 1985–89; Vice-Gov. Shaanxi Prov. People's Govt 1989–93; Vice-Minister of Foreign Trade and Econ. Co-operation 1993–94; Deputy Sec. 9th CCP Jiangsu Prov. Cttee 1994–98; Acting Gov. of Jiangsu Prov. 1994–95, Gov. 1995–98; Deputy Dir State Econ. and Trade Comm. 1998–2000; Minister of Labour and Social Security 2003–05; mem. ILO Social Protection Floor Advisory Group 2010–; Vice-Chair. NPC Foreign Affairs Cttee; Co-Chair. Canada-China Legislative Asscn; Executive Vice-Pres. China Enterprise Confed., China Enterprise Dirs Asscn; Founder and Pres. China Asscn of Nat. Advertisers 2005–; Alt. mem. 13th Cen. Cttee CCP 1987–92, mem. 14th Cen. Cttee 1992–97, 15th CCP Cen. Cttee 1997–2002 (Deputy Dir Cen. Work Cttee of Large Enterprises 2000–03), 16th CCP Cen. Cttee 2002–07. *Address:* China Association of National Advertisers, No.10 Xisanhuan Zhonglu, Haidian District, Beijing 100036, People's Republic of China (office). *Telephone:* (10) 88028766/ (office). *Website:* www.cananet.org.cn (office).

ZHENG, Wantong; Chinese politician; b. May 1941, Tianjin; ed Tianjin Teachers' Coll.; joined CCP 1960; high school teacher and cadre, Communist Youth League Hebei Dist Cttee, Tianjin 1961–68; cadre, CCP Hebei Dist Cttee, Tianjin 1974–78; cadre then Dir Gen. Office of CCP Tianjin Municipal Cttee 1978–83; Sec.-Gen. CCP Tianjin Municipal Cttee 1983–88; Guest Research Fellow, Tianjin Acad. of Social Sciences; Vice-Chair. and mem. Secr. All-China Fed. of Trade Unions 1988–93; Deputy Head, United Front Work Dept of CCP Cen. Cttee 1993–; mem. CCP Cen. Comm. for Discipline Inspection 1997–; Vice-Chair. 8th Exec. Cttee All-China Fed. of Industry and Commerce 1997–; Vice-Pres. China Overseas Friendship Asscn 1997–, First Council of Chinese Research Asscn for Economy and Society 2001–; Deputy Sec.-Gen. 8th CPPCC Nat. Cttee 1993–98, Sec.-Gen. 9th CPPCC Nat. Cttee 1998–2003, 10th CPPCC Nat. Cttee 2003–08, Vice-Chair. 11th CPPCC Nat. Cttee 2008–13; mem. 16th CCP Cen. Cttee 2002–07. *Address:* National Committee of Chinese People's Political Consultative Conference, 23 Taipingqiao Street, Beijing, People's Republic of China (office).

ZHENG, Wenxue; Chinese business executive; Chair. Kailuan (Group) Co. Ltd (coal mining co.) 2008–. *Address:* Kailuan (Group) Ltd Liability Corporation, 70 Xinhua Hua Dong Road, Tangshan 063018, People's Republic of China (office). *E-mail:* info@kailuan.com (office). *Website:* www.kailuan.com.cn (office).

ZHENG, Xiaoying; Chinese conductor and professor of music; *Artistic Director and Chief Conductor, Xiamen Philharmonic Orchestra;* b. 27 Sept. 1929, Shanghai; d. of Zheng Wei and Wen Siying; m. Liu Enyü 1947; one d.; ed China Central Conservatory of Music, Moscow P.I. Tchaikovsky State Conservatoire, USSR (now Russian Fed.); mem. song and dance troupe 1949; teacher and conductor, Cen. Conservatoire 1950–60, 1963–; conducted Cen. Conservatoire Chorus and Symphony Orchestra, Radio Orchestra of USSR 1961–63, Cen. Philharmonic, China Broadcasting Orchestra, Canberra Orchestra, Hong Kong Philharmonic; Chief Conductor Cen. Opera Theatre 1978–88; Founder, Musical Dir and Conductor Women's Chamber Orchestra, Capital Opera Inst. 1988; Artistic Dir and Chief Conductor Xiamen Philharmonic Orchestra 1998–; Artistic Dir 4th World Choir Games 2006, Xiamen; appeared at Hong Kong Performing Arts Festival, Savonlinna Opera Festival, Finland, Singapore Inaugural, Macao Int. Music Festival, Chinese Arts Festival; mem. Exec. Council Chinese Musicians' Asscn; numerous recordings; took part as torch bearer, Olympic Flame Relay, Xiamen, May 2008; Special Honour for Outstanding Women 1979, 1983, Nat. First Prize for Conductors 1981, La Donna nel Mondo (Italy) 1983, Médaille d'honneur des arts et des lettres (France) 1985, Olay Women's World Excellence Awards 2006. *Leisure interests:* travel, sports. *Address:* Central Conservatory, 43 Baojia Street, Beijing 100031 (office); Hai Tan Lu, Gulangyu, Xiamen 361002, People's Republic of China (home). *Telephone:* (592) 2061549 (Xiamen) (home); (610) 65520019 (Beijing) (home). *Fax:* (592) 2061549 (Xiamen) (home); (610) 65523164 (Beijing) (home). *Website:* www.xiaoying.com.cn.

ZHENOVACH, Sergey Vassilyevich; Russian theatre director; *Chief Artistic Director, Moscow Theatre on Malaya Bronnaya;* b. 15 May 1957, Potsdam, Germany; ed Krasnodar Inst. of Culture, Moscow Inst. of Theatre Arts; Dir Youth Theatre Studio Stroitel, Krasnodar 1979, 1982–83; army service 1979–82; teacher Moscow Inst. of Theatre Arts (now Russian Acad. of Theatre Arts) 1990–; Dir Moscow Theatre on Malaya Bronnaya 1992–96, Chief Artistic Dir 1996–; Mayor of Moscow Prize 1992, Golden Mask Prize 1996. *Stage productions include:* The Idiot, King Lear, The Abyss, Miller – Witch, Cheat and Matchmaker, Pannochka, Viy, Illusion, The Truth is Good but Happiness is Better, The Imaginary Invalid. *Address:* Moscow Theatre on Malaya Bronnaya, M. Bronnaya str. 4, 103104 Moscow, Russia (office). *Telephone:* (495) 290-67-31 (office).

ZHEVAGO, Konstantin; Ukrainian business executive; *Vice-Chairman, Supervisory Board, Ferrexpo Poltava Mining;* ed Kiev Inst. of Nat. Economy; Finance Dir Closed Jt Stock Co. Finance and Credit (bank) 1993, now Owner (now named CJSC Commercial Bank Finance and Credit); Man. Poltava Ore Mining and Enrichment Works 1994 (now Ferrexpo Poltava Mining), now Owner and Deputy Chair. Supervisory Bd, also Dir (non-exec.) Ferrexpo plc; also owns other cos including AvtoKraz and Rosava with interests in vehicles, tyres, pharmaceuticals, oil and gas; Deputy, Verkhovna Rada (Parl.) 1998–, mem. Yuliya Timoshenko Block political faction, mem. Parl. Cttee on Law Policy and Co-Chair. Parl. Group for Inter-Parl. Relations with Japan. *Address:* Supervisory Board, Ferrexpo Poltava Mining, Stroitelej Str., Komsomolsk 39802, Poltava region (office); c/o CJSC Commercial Bank Finance and Credit, 04050 Kiev, vul. Sichovykh Striltsiv 60, Ukraine. *Telephone:* (44) 490-68-70 (Bank). *Fax:* (44) 238-24-65 (Bank). *E-mail:* pgok@ferrexpo.com (office); common@fc.kiev.ua. *Website:* ferrexpo.poltava.ua (office); www.fc.kiev.ua.

ZHIGUNOV, Sergei V.; Russian actor and film producer; *Director-General, Shans Co. Mosfilm Cinema Corporation;* b. 2 Jan. 1963, Rostov-Don; ed Shchukin Theatre School; Dir.-Gen. Shans Co. Mosfilm Cinema Corpn; producer State Cttee on Radio and TV 1997–; Pres. Guild of Russian Film Actors 2000–; Russian Artist of Merit; Guild of Russian Film Actors prize 1997. *Films:* Chance 1984, The Right to Love 1986, Along the Main Street with Orchestra 1986, Gardemarines, Ahead! 1987, Trip to Wiesbaden 1989, Richard the Lionheart 1992, Knight Kennet 1993, Countess de Montsorot (producer) 1997, Nude (producer) 1998, What Did the Dead Say (producer) 1999, New Year in November (also producer) 2000. *Address:* 3d Gorogok 12, apt 106, Bolshevo 141090, Moscow region, Russia (home). *Telephone:* (495) 515-30-06 (home).

ZHILINSKY, Dmitry Dmitriyevich; Russian painter; b. 25 May 1927, Sochi; ed Moscow Inst. of Applied and Decorative Arts, Moscow State Surikov Inst. of Fine Arts; teacher Moscow State Surikov Inst. of Fine Arts 1951–74, Prof. 1968; Head of Chair Moscow State Inst. of Polygraphy 1974–81; mem. Exec. Bd USSR Artists' Union 1977; mem. USSR Acad. of Fine Arts 1988; Order, Friendship of Peoples 1994; Silver Medal, Acad. of Fine Arts 1966, Merited Worker of Arts of RSFSR 1983, RSFSR State Repin Prize 1985, Peoples' Artist of RSFSR 1987. *Address:* Russian Academy of Fine Arts, Prechistenka str. 21, 119034 Moscow, Russia (office). *Telephone:* (495) 210-36-65 (office).

ZHIRINOVSKII, Col Vladimir Volfovich, DPhil; Russian lawyer, politician and army officer; *Deputy Chairman, State Duma; Chairman, Liberal Democratic Party of Russia;* b. (Vladimir Eidelstein), 25 April 1946, Almatı, Kazakh SSR; m. Galina Alexandrovna Lebedeva; one s.; ed Inst. of Eastern languages (now Inst. of

Asian and African Countries) and Faculty of Law, Moscow M.V. Lomonosov State Univ. (MGU); officer, USSR Ministry of Defence, with Gen. Staff of Transcaucasian command 1970–72; with Int. Dept, Soviet Soc. of Friendship and Cultural Relations, Cttee for Peace 1973–75; with Office of Dean of Foreign Students, Higher School of Trade Union Movt 1975–77; legal consultant, Inyurcollegia 1977–83; Head of Legal Dept, Mir Publs 1983–90; f. Liberal-Democratic Party of Soviet Union (now of Russia—LDPR) 1989, Chair. 1990–, Chair. State Duma Parl. Group 1993–2000; mem. State Duma (Parl.) 1993–, Deputy Chair. 2000–; apptd Head of Russian del. to NATO Parl. Ass. 2002; unsuccessful cand. in Russian presidential elections 1991, 1996, 2000, 2008, 2012; attained rank of Col in Army Reserve 1995; Honorary Railwayman; Order of Merit for the Fatherland (4th Class), Order of Honour, Medal of Zhukov, 850th Anniversary of Moscow Medal, Medal of Merit in the Russian Population Census, 300th Anniversary of St Petersburg Medal, Medal Anatoliya Koni, Order 'For Personal Courage' (DMR), Order of Honour and Glory (Abkhazia); Distinguished Lawyer of the Russian Fed., Diploma of the Pres. of the Russian Fed. *Publications:* The Last Leap South 1993, Political Landscape of Russia 1995, Economic Ideas of a Politician 1996, Geopolitics and the Russian Question 1997, The Zhirinovsky Phenomenon in Russia 1998 and more than 100 other books and publs. *Leisure interests:* volleyball, swimming. *Address:* Gosudarstvennaya Duma (State Duma), 103265 Moscow, Okhotnyi ryad 1 (office); Liberal Democratic Party of Russia (Liberalno-demokraticheskaya partiya Rossii), 103045 Moscow, Lukov per. 9, Russia (office). *Telephone:* (495) 692-62-66 (Duma) (office); (495) 623-02-44 (LDPR) (office). *Fax:* (495) 697-42-58 (Duma) (office); (495) 692-92-42 (LDPR) (office). *E-mail:* stateduma@duma.gov.ru (office); info@ldpr.ru (office). *Website:* www.duma.gov.ru (office); www.ldpr.ru (office).

ZHISLIN, Grigory Yefimovich; Russian/British violinist and violist; *Professor, Hochschule für Musik, Würzburg;* b. 14 May 1945, Leningrad (now St Petersburg); s. of Yefim Zhislin and Sarra Zhislin; m. Valentina Murashova 1980; one s.; ed Moscow State Conservatory (pupil of Yuny Yankelevich); winner Int. Competitions of Paganini in Genoa 1967 and Queen Elizabeth in Brussels 1976; concerts in USSR and abroad 1966–; participated in major music festivals, including Maggio Musicale Fiorentina, Warsaw Autumn, Prague Spring, Kuhmi Chamber Music, Berliner Biennale, Pablo Casals in Puerto Rico, Paganini in Genoa and others; teacher, Kharkov Inst. of Arts 1971–73, Moscow Gnessin Pedagogical Inst. 1973–90, Prof. 1978–90; Royal Coll. of Music, London 1990–2004; Prof., Hochschule für Musik, Würzburg 1993–; Visiting Prof. Oslo Conservatory, Kraków Musik Akad., Warsaw Conservatory; masterclasses in USA, Italy, France, Finland, Sweden; Ordre du Mérite Culturel, Gloria Artist (Poland). *Recordings include:* Penderecki Viola Concerto/Cello Concerto No. 2 (Int. Classical Music Award for Best Contemporary Music Recording 2012) 2011. *Address:* Friedenstrasse 6A, 97072 Würzburg, Germany (home). *Telephone:* (931) 54772. *E-mail:* grig.zhislin@freenet.de (office).

ZHITINKIN, Andrei Albertovich; Russian theatre director; b. 18 Nov. 1960; ed Shchukin Theatre High School; Dir Mossoviet Theatre 1991–2001; apptd Chief Artistic Dir Drama Theatre, Malaya Bronnaya 2001; Merited Artist of Russia. *Plays include:* Dog's Waltz 1992, Yellow Angel 1993, All of a Sudden Last Summer 1994, My Poor Marat 1995, He Has Come 1996, Mon Ami 1997, Merchant of Venice 1999. *Address:* Malaya Bronnaya Theatre, Malaya Bronnaya str. 4, 103104 Moscow, Russia (office). *Telephone:* (495) 290-69-81 (office).

ZHONG, Jun; Chinese business executive; *President and CEO, China Southern Power Grid Company Ltd;* Pres. and CEO China Southern Power Grid Co. Ltd 2010–; mem. Nat. Cttee of the CPPCC. *Address:* China Southern Power Grid Co. Ltd, 6 Huasui Road, Zhujiang Xincheng, Tianhe District, Guangzhou 510623, People's Republic of China (office). *Telephone:* (20) 3812-1958 (office); (20) 3812-1080 (office). *Fax:* (20) 3886-5670 (office); (20) 3812-0189 (office). *E-mail:* international@csg.cn (office). *Website:* www.csg.cn (office).

ZHONG, Ming, FRSA; Chinese artist; b. 1949, Beijing; elected to Chinese Artists' Asscn 1980; founder mem. Beijing Oil Painting Research Asscn; achieved int. recognition with painting He is Himself—Sartre 1980; moved to UK 1984; exhibited at Open Exhbn of Royal Soc. of Painters in Watercolour, Bankside Gallery 1984; has also exhibited in Japan, Sweden, USA; speaker at int. symposium The Authentic Garden, Leiden, Netherlands 1990; returned to China 1998; worked as Dir, Shanghai Television and China Central Television. *Publications:* The Craft of Gardens (photographer) 1988; articles on art and cultural subjects in various periodicals. *Address:* 51 Sunningwell Road, Oxford, OX1 4SZ, England; Huanghua Road, Shanghai 201103, People's Republic of China.

ZHONG, Shengjian; Chinese real estate executive; *Chairman and CEO, Yanlord Land Group Limited;* b. 1958, Lufeng, Guangdong Prov.; moved to Singapore 1989; since 1980s has f. several trading, manufacturing, real estate and financial services cos spanning China, Singapore, Hong Kong, Indonesia, Malaysia and Australia; Founder, Chair. and CEO Yanlord Land Group Ltd early 1990s–; mem. Sichuan Singapore Trade and Investment Cttee, Network China; Hon. Citizen of Nanjing, Zhuhai and Shanwei; Hon. Business Adviser to Int. Enterprise Singapore (IE Singapore) for China 2004–07; White Magnolia Award for contribs to Municipal City of Shanghai 2005. *Address:* Yanlord Land Group Ltd, 9 Temasek Boulevard #36-02, Suntec City Tower Two, Singapore 038989 (office); Shanghai Yanlord Property Co. Ltd, 30F POS-Plaza No. 1600 Century Avenue, Pudong New Area, Shanghai 200122, People's Republic of China (office). *Telephone:* 63362922 (Singapore) (office); (21) 68768888 (Shanghai) (office). *Fax:* 62386256 (Singapore) (office); (21) 68765858 (Shanghai) (office). *Website:* www.yanlordland.com (office).

ZHOU, Deqiang; Chinese business executive; b. 1941; ed Nanjing Post and Telecommunications Coll.; joined CCP 1969; fmr Deputy Gen. Engineer, Beijing Trunk Exchange; fmr Deputy Chief, later Chief, Anhui Prov. Admin. Bureau of Post and Telecommunications 1984–94; Vice-Minister, Ministry of Information Industry 1994–2000; Gen. Man., China Telecommunications Group (China Telecom) 1998, also Dir, Chair. and CEO 2002–04 (retd); Ind. Dir Shenhua Group, TravelSky Technology Ltd 2010–; mem. CPPCC Econs Cttee 2003–08. *Address:* c/o TravelSky Technology Ltd, No.157, Dongsi West Street, Dongcheng District, Beijing 100010, People's Republic of China (office).

ZHOU, Ganzhi; Chinese architect; b. 1930, Suzhou, Jiangsu Prov.; ed Tsinghua Univ.; joined CCP 1952; Deputy Office Dir State Construction Comm.; Vice-Dir

City Planning Research Inst. of State Gen. Admin of City Construction; Acting Dir Tianjin City Planning Bureau; Sr Architect and Pres. China City Planning and Design Research Acad.; Vice-Minister of Urban and Rural Construction and Environment Protection; Vice-Minister of Construction 1952–98; worked on master plans for cities of Xi'an, Tianjin, Tangshan and Shenzhen; Prof. School of Architecture, Tsinghua Univ.; mem. Chinese Acad. of Sciences 1991–, Chinese Acad. of Eng 1994–; Hon. Pres. Urban Planning Soc. of China, Chinese Soc. of Landscape Architecture, Chinese Real Estate and Housing Research Asscn, Chinese Soc. of Urban Science. *Address:* c/o School of Architecture, Tsinghua University, Qinghua West Rd, Haidian, Beijing 100084, People's Republic of China (office). *Website:* www.arch.tsinghua.edu.cn/ (office).

ZHOU, Guangzhao, MS; Chinese nuclear physicist; b. 15 May 1929, Changsha City, Hunan Prov.; s. of Fengjiu Zhou and Zhen-zhao Tao; m. Zheng Aiqin 1955; one d.; ed Tsinghua Univ., Peking Univ.; joined CCP 1952; Lecturer, Physics Dept, Tsinghua Univ.; Researcher, Dubra Jt Nuclear Research Inst., Moscow, USSR 1957–60; Deputy Dir Theoretical Dept, later Dir and Chief Engineer, Nuclear Weapons Research Inst. 1961; Dir 9th Research Inst. of Second Ministry of Machine-Bldg Industry; Research Fellow and Dir Physics Research Inst. of Chinese Acad. of Sciences 1982, Vice-Pres. Chinese Acad. of Sciences 1984–87, Pres. 1987–97; Vice-Pres. China Physics Soc.; Vice-Chair. IUPAC 1993; mem. State Leading Group for Science and Tech. 1996; Chair. State Science and Tech. Comm. 1996; Alt. mem. 12th CCP Cen. Cttee 1982–85, mem. 1985–87, 13th CCP Cen. Cttee 1987–92, 14th CCP Cen. Cttee 1992–97, 15th CCP Cen. Cttee 1997–2002; Vice-Chair. Standing Cttee of 9th NPC 1998–2003; took part in making of China's first atomic bomb and hydrogen bomb; Hon. Pres. Chinese People's Asscn for Peace and Disarmament 1998; First Prize, State Award for Natural Sciences 1982, Meritorious Service Medal, CCP Cen. Cttee, State Council and Cen. Mil. Comm. 1999; Asteroid No. 3462, found in 1996 by Chinese astronomers, was named after Zhou Guangzhao 1996. *Publications:* Language Reform of China 1961, A Free Talk on Chinese Language 1992, Alphabets of the World 1993. *Leisure interests:* swimming, table tennis. *Address:* Chinese Academy of Sciences, 52 San Li He Road, 100864 Beijing, People's Republic of China (office). *Telephone:* (10) 8597203 (office).

ZHOU, Houjian; Chinese business executive; *Chairman, HiSense Group Corporation;* b. Aug. 1957, Qingdao, Shandong Prov.; ed Shandong Univ.; technician, Deputy Div. Head, Man.'s Asst, Vice-Man. then Man. Qingdao TV Plant 1982–94; Gen. Man. Qingdao HiSense Electric Co. 1994–95, Chair. 1995–, Chair. HiSense Group Corpn 1994–; Deputy 10th NPC 2003; awarded the Global Young Entrepreneurs Man. Talent Special Prize 1996, Nat. Wuyi Labour Medal 1998, named one of Top Ten Economic Figures in China 2000; Magnificent Ten Award 2005. *Leisure interests:* football, boxing. *Address:* HiSense Group Corporation, Qingdao, Shandong Province, People's Republic of China (office). *Telephone:* (532) 3861992 (office). *Fax:* (532) 3872882 (office). *E-mail:* master@hisense.com.cn (office). *Website:* www.hisense-transtech.com.cn (office).

ZHOU, Jichang, PhD; Chinese engineer and business executive; ed Tongji Univ., Beijing Jiaotong Univ.; joined China Communications Construction Co. Ltd 1977, Deputy Gen. Man. The First Highway Survey & Design Inst. of the fmr China Road and Bridge Corpn (a predecessor of the China Communications Construction Group Ltd) 1987–92 and Gen. Man. and Chair. China Road and Bridge Construction Co. (predecessor of China Road and Bridge Corpn) 1995–97, Gen. Man. China Road and Bridge Corpn 1997–2005, Chair. China Communications Construction Co. Ltd 2006–13, also Chair. ZPMC, CRBC International Co. Ltd (subsidiaries); Chair. Shanghai Zhenhua Heavy Industry (Group) Co. Ltd 2011–13. *Address:* c/o China Communications Construction Co. Ltd, B88 Andingmenwai Dajie, Beijing 100011; c/o China Communications Construction Co. Ltd, 85 Deshengmenwai Street, Xicheng District, Beijing 100088, People's Republic of China. *E-mail:* info@ccgrp.com.cn.

ZHOU, Jiping, MSc; Chinese oil industry executive; *Chairman, China National Petroleum Corporation (CNPC);* has worked in oil and gas industry since 1970s; Vice-Pres. China Nat. Oil & Gas Exploration and Devt Corpn (CNODC) 1996–97, Pres. Greater Nile Petroleum Operating Co. (Sudan) 1996–97, Pres. CNODC 1997–2001, Asst Pres. China Nat. Petroleum Corpn (CNPC) 2001, Pres. CNODC 2001–03, Vice-Pres. CNPC 2003–08, Vice-Chair. and Pres. PetroChina 2008–11, Pres. CNPC 2011–13, Acting Chair. March–April 2013, Chair. and Pres. April–July 2013, Chair. July 2013–. *Address:* China National Petroleum Corporation, 9 Dongzhimen North Street, Dongcheng District, Beijing 100007, People's Republic of China (office). *Telephone:* (10) 62094114 (office). *Fax:* (10) 62094205 (office). *E-mail:* admin_eng@cnpc.com.cn (office). *Website:* www.cnpc.com.cn (office).

ZHOU, Gen. Kunren; Chinese naval officer; b. Sept. 1937, Danyang Co., Jiangsu Prov.; ed PLA Political Acad. and PLA Univ. of Nat. Defence; joined PLA 1956; mem. CCP 1960–; Vice-Dir Political Dept of Navy; rank of Maj.-Gen. 1988; Political Commissar South Sea Fleet; Vice-Political Commissar, PLA Navy 1992, Political Commissar 1992; rank of Lt-Gen. 1993, Gen. 2000; Political Commissar, PLA Gen. Logistics Dept 1995–2002; Vice-Chair. 10th NPC Law Cttee 2003–; mem. 15th CCP Cen. Cttee 1997–2002. *Address:* National People's Congress Law Committee, Beijing, People's Republic of China (office).

ZHOU, Long, DMA; Chinese/American composer; b. 8 July 1953, Beijing; m. Chen Yi; ed Central Conservatory of Music, Beijing, Columbia Univ., USA; sent to rural state farm during Cultural Revolution; Composer-in-Residence, Nat. Broadcasting Symphony Orchestra of China 1983; moved to USA in 1985; Music Dir, Music from China, New York 1988–99; Music Alive! Composer-in-Residence, Seattle Symphony's Silk Road Project Festival with Yo-Yo Ma May 2002; commissions from Koussevitsky and Fromm Music Foundations, Chamber Music America and New York State Council on the Arts, and from ensembles including Bavarian Radio Symphony Orchestra, Tokyo and Brooklyn Philharmonics, New Music Consort, Pittsburgh New Music Ensemble, Peabody Trio and Kronos, Shanghai, Ciompi and Chester String Quartets and vocal ensemble Chanticleer; Visiting Prof. of Composition, Univ. of Missouri-Kansas City Conservatory of Music and Dance; fellowships from American Acad. of Arts and Letters, Nat. Endowment for the Arts and Guggenheim and Rockefeller Foundations, ASCAP Adventurous Programming Award 1999, Lifetime Achievement Award, American Acad. of Arts and Letters 2003, CalArts/Alpert Award in the Arts 2009, Barlow Int. Composition

Competition, Fifth Int. Composition Competition, d'Avray (France), Ensemblia Competition, Mönchengladbach (Germany). *Compositions include:* Poems from Tang, The Future of Fire, The Ineffable, Soul, Tian Ling, Spirit of Chimes, Dhyana, Ding, Madame White Snake (Pulitzer Prize for Music 2011). *Address:* c/o Music Department, Oxford University Press, Great Clarendon Street, Oxford, OX2 6DP, England.

ZHOU, Mingchen; Chinese business executive; ed Beijing Inst. of Foreign Trade (now Univ. of Int. Trade and Econs); fmr Vice-Pres. China Nat. Metals & Minerals Import & Export Corpn; fmr Pres. China Nat. Instrument Import & Export Corpn; apptd Dir China Nat. Cereals, Oils and Foodstuffs Import & Export Co. (COFCO) 1992, Chair. 1993–2006; Dir Xingda International Holdings Ltd 2005–11; Partner Uni-Quantum Private Equity Fund; ranked among Top 15 Influential Chinese Business Leaders by Asian Capital magazine 2004. *Address:* c/o Uni-Quantum Private Equity Fund, Room 906 Tower 3, China Central Place, No. 77 Jianguo Avenue, Chaoyang District, Beijing 100025, People's Republic of China (office).

ZHOU, Qiang, LLB, LLM; Chinese lawyer and government official; *President, Supreme People's Court; b.* 1960, Huangmei Co., Hubei Prov.; ed Southwest Univ. of Political Science and Law, Chongqing; began career with Ministry of Justice, several roles including Cadre, Policy Research Office 1985–89, Deputy Chief, Statute Bureau, Law and Statute Dept 1989–91, Chief, Statute Bureau 1991–93, Deputy Dir, Ministry of Justice Gen. Office 1993–95, Leader, Legal System Bureau 1995; mem. Communist Youth League of China Cen. Cttee Secr. 1995–97, co-Sec. 13th Cen. Cttee Secr. 1995, Exec. Sec. 1997–98, First Sec. 1998–2006; Deputy, 9th NPC 1998–2003, 10th NPC 2003–08, 11th NPC 2008–13, mem. NPC Internal and Judicial Affairs Cttee 1998–2003; Deputy Sec., Hunan CCP Prov. Cttee 2006–10, Sec. 2010–13; Acting Gov. Hunan Prov. 2006–07, Gov. 2007–10; Chair. Standing Cttee, Hunan Prov. People's Congress 2010–13; Pres. Supreme People's Court 2013–; mem. 16th CCP Cen. Cttee 2002–07, 17th CCP Cen. Cttee 2007–12, 18th CCP Cen. Cttee 2012–. *Address:* Supreme People's Court, Qianmen Dongdajie, Dongcheng District, Beijing, People's Republic of China (office). *Website:* en.chinacourt.org (office).

ZHOU, Qifeng; Chinese chemist, academic and university administrator; b. Oct. 1947; ed Peking Univ., Univ. of Massachusetts, USA; mem. of Faculty, Peking Univ. 1970–, Assoc. Prof. 1990, Prof. 1999, Pres. Peking Univ. 2008–13; Dir Grad. Student Affairs Office, Ministry of Educ. 2001–03; Dir State Academic Affairs Cttee 2001–03, Deputy Sec.-Gen. 2003–04; Pres. Jilin Univ. 2004–08; mem. Chinese Acad. of Sciences 1999–; mem. Nat. Natural Science Foundation of China 2004–. *Address:* c/o Peking University, College of Chemistry and Molecular Engineering, No. 5 Yiheyuan Road, Haidian District, Beijing 100871, People's Republic of China (office). *Website:* www.chem.pku.edu.cn (office).

ZHOU, Shengxian; Chinese politician; *Minister of Environmental Protection; b.* Dec. 1949, Wuzhong, Ningxia Hui Autonomous Region; ed Wuzhong Teachers' Coll. and CCP Cen. Cttee Cen. Party School; joined CCP 1972; teacher Weizhou Middle School, Tongxian Co. 1969–79; Deputy Magistrate Tongxian Co. 1981–83; Sec. CCP Tongxian Co. Cttee 1983–86; Sec. CCP Xiji Co. Cttee 1986–89; Vice-Chair. People's Govt of Ningxia Hui Autonomous Region 1993–2003; Deputy Dir State Admin. for Forestry 1999–2000, Dir 2000–05 (also Sec. CCP Leading Party Group 2000–05); Minister, Environmental Protection Admin. 2005–08, Minister of Environmental Protection 2008–; Alt. mem. 16th CCP Cen. Cttee 2002–07, mem. 17th CCP Cen. Cttee 2007–12, 18th CCP Cen. Cttee 2012–. *Address:* Ministry of Environmental Protection, No. 115 Xizhimennei Nanxiaojie, Xicheng District, Beijing 100035, People's Republic of China (office). *Telephone:* (10) 66556006 (office). *Fax:* (10) 66556010 (office). *E-mail:* info@mep.gov.cn (office). *Website:* english.mep.gov.cn (office).

ZHOU, Shouwei; Chinese engineer and petroleum industry executive; *Vice-President, China National Offshore Oil Corporation Ltd (CNOOC); b.* 1950; ed SW Petroleum Inst.; joined China National Offshore Oil Corpn (CNOOC) 1983, Deputy Gen. Man. China Offshore Oil Bohai Corpn (subsidiary co.), Gen. Man. Tianjin Br., CNOOC China Ltd, Exec Dir 1999–, Exec. Vice-Pres. 1999–2002, Pres. 2002–09, currently Vice-Pres. CNOOC Ltd, also Dir CNOOC International Ltd, Exec Dir CNOOC Engineering Co. Ltd (subsidiary co.) 1999–, Chair. 2003, Chair. CNOOC Southeast Asia Ltd (subsidiary co.) 2003–, Chair. Offshore Oil Engineering Co. Ltd 2003–10; mem. Chinese Acad. of Eng (Energy and Mining Div.) 2009–; Pres., 7th Council of China Petroleum & Petrochemical Equipment Industry Asscn 2010–. *Address:* CNOOC China Ltd, PO Box 4705, 25 Chao Yangmen North Street, Dongcheng District, Beijing 100010, People's Republic of China (office). *Telephone:* (10) 84521604 (office). *Fax:* (10) 64602503 (office). *Website:* www.cnoocltd.com (office).

ZHOU, Tienong; Chinese politician; b. Nov. 1938, Shenyang, Liaoning Prov.; ed Peking Univ.; teaching asst, Harbin Technological Univ. 1960–61; Assoc. Prof., Northeast Heavy Machinery Coll. 1961–83; Vice-Mayor of Qiqihar, Heilongjiang Prov. 1983–91; Asst to Gov. Heilongjiang Prov. 1991, Vice-Gov. 1991–98; Vice-Chair. Cen. Cttee of Kuomintang Revolutionary Cttee 1992–97, Chair. 2007–12; Pres. Sixth Council of China Council for Promotion of Peaceful Reunification 1999–; Adviser Chinese Asscn of Int. Understanding 1999–; mem. 7th CPPCC Nat. Cttee 1988–93, Standing Cttee 8th CPPCC Nat. Cttee 1993–98, Vice-Chair. 9th CPPCC Nat. Cttee 1998–2003, 10th CPPCC Nat. Cttee 2003–08; Vice-Chair. 11th NPC Standing Cttee 2008–13. *Address:* Standing Committee of the National People's Congress, 23 Taipingqiao Street, Beijing, People's Republic of China (office).

ZHOU, Weizhi, (Zhou Liangji, He Lishan); Chinese politician and musician; *Chairman, Chinese Culture Federation; b.* 1916, Dongtai Co., Jiangsu Prov.; m. Wang Kun; two s.; joined CCP 1938; Dir Central Songs and Dance Troupe; Pres. Cen. Experimental Drama Theatre; Dir Arts Dept of Ministry of Culture; Vice-Minister, then Acting Minister of Culture; Vice-Chair. Chinese Musicians Asscn; Chair. China Fed. of Literary and Art Circles 1996–2006, Hon. Chair. 2006–11; currently Chair. Chinese Culture Fed.; mem. Standing Cttee 7th CPPCC Nat. Cttee 1988–93; Del., 8th CCP Nat. Congress 1962–67, 12th CCP Nat. Congress 1982–87. *Compositions include:* songs: Put on the Bayonet, Frontline March. *Address:* c/o Ministry of Culture, Jia 83, Donganmen Bei Jie, Dongcheng Qu, Beijing 100701, People's Republic of China (office).

ZHOU, Wenzhong; Chinese diplomatist; b. Aug. 1945, Jiangsu Prov.; m.; one d.; ed Univ. of Bath and London School of Econs, UK; staff mem., Beijing Diplomatic Service Bureau 1970–73, univ. studies 1973–75, staff mem., Dept of Trans. and Interpretation, Ministry of Foreign Affairs 1975–78, Attaché, then Third Sec., Washington, DC 1978–83, Second Sec., Deputy Div. Dir, then Div. Dir Dept of Translation and Interpretation, Ministry of Foreign Affairs 1983–87, Deputy Consul Gen., San Francisco 1987–90, Amb. to Barbados and Antigua and Barbuda 1990–93, Deputy Dir-Gen. N American and Oceanic Affairs Dept, Ministry of Foreign Affairs 1993–94, Consul Gen., Los Angeles 1994–95, Deputy Chief of Mission, Embassy in Washington, DC 1995–98, Amb. to Australia 1998–2001; Asst Minister of Foreign Affairs 2001–03, Vice-Minister of Foreign Affairs 2003–05; Amb. to USA 2005–10. *Address:* c/o Ministry of Foreign Affairs, 2 Chaoyangmen, Nan Dajie, Chao Yang Qu, Beijing 100701, People's Republic of China (office). *Telephone:* (10) 65961114 (office). *Fax:* (10) 65962146 (office). *E-mail:* webmaster@ mfa.gov.cn (office). *Website:* www.fmprc.gov.cn (office).

ZHOU, Xiaochuan, PhD; Chinese economist and central banker; *Governor, People's Bank of China; b.* 29 Jan. 1948, Dongan, Heilongjiang Prov.; s. of the late Zhou Jiannan; ed Beijing Chemical Eng Inst., Tsinghua Univ.; worker, Beijing Inst. of Automation; Deputy Dir Inst. of Chinese Econ. Reform Research 1986–87; mem. State Council Econ. Policy Group 1986–87; Asst Minister of Foreign Trade and Econ. Co-operation 1986–89; mem. Nat. Cttee on Econ. Reform 1986–91; Deputy Gov. People's Bank of China (PBOC) 1991–95, 1996–98, Gov. 2002–, mem. Policy Comm. 2000– (also CCP Sec.); Dir State Admin of Foreign Exchange 1995–98; Pres. China Construction Bank 1998–2000; Chair. China Securities Regulatory Comm. 2000–02; Prof., Tsinghua Univ. School of Man., Grad. School PBOC, Univ. of Science and Tech. of China Business School; mem. Group of Thirty Consultative Group on Int. Econ. and Monetary Affairs, Inc. (G-30), Washington, DC; mem. 16th CCP Cen. Cttee 2002–07, 17th CCP Cen. Cttee 2007–12; Vice-Chair. 12th CPPCC Nat. Cttee 2013–; Hon. Pres. Univ. of Science and Tech. of China Business School; ranked by Forbes magazine amongst The World's Most Powerful People (48th) 2009, (11th) 2010, (15th) 2011. *Publications include:* more than 12 monographs and 100 journal articles on econ. reform including Rebuilding the Relationship Between the Enterprise and the Bank (Sun Zhifang Economics Thesis Prize 1994), Marching Toward an Open Economic System (An Zijie Int. Trade Publication Award 1994), Social Security: Reform and Policy Recommendations (Sun Zhifang Economics Thesis Prize 1997). *Leisure interest:* tennis. *Address:* People's Bank of China, 32 Chenfang Jie, Xicheng Qu, Beijing 100800, China (office). *Telephone:* (10) 66194114 (office). *Fax:* (10) 66015346 (office). *E-mail:* master@pbc.gov.cn (office). *Website:* www.pbc.gov.cn (office).

ZHOU, Xuhong; Chinese engineer, academic and university administrator; *President, Chongqing University; b.* 1956, Hunan Prov.; ed Hunan Univ.; Asst Engineer, China State Construction Eng Corpn 1982–84; Assoc. Prof., Civil Eng Dept, Hunan Univ. 1986–94, Prof. 1994–96, also Vice-Dean, Civil Eng Dept 1994–96, Head, Civil Eng Grad. School 1996–99, Vice-Pres. Hunan Univ. 1999–2002; Pres. Changan Univ. 2002–06; Pres. Lanzhou Univ. 2006–13; Pres. Chongqing Univ. 2013–; Vice-Pres. China Steel Structure Asscn; mem. Chinese Acad. of Eng; Nat. Science Progress Award, Hubei Prov. Science Progress Award, Chinese Univs Science Progress Award, Hunan Prov. Teaching Achievements Prize. *Publications:* over 60 research papers in nat. and int. journals. *Address:* Office of the President, Chongqing University, 174 Shazhengjie, Shapingba, Chongqing 400030, People's Republic of China (office). *Website:* international.cqu .edu.cn (office).

ZHOU, Xun; Chinese actress and singer; b. 18 Oct. 1976, Quzhou, Zhejiang; d. of Zhou Tianning and Chen Yiqin; ed Zhejiang Arts Inst. *Films include:* Old Grave 1991, Nü'er Hong 1994, Temptress Moon 1995, The Pampered Wife 1995, My Rice Noodle Shop 1998, The Emperor and the Assassin 1999, Suzhou River 2000, Beijing Bicycle 2001, Hollywood Hong Kong 2001, A Pinwheel Without Wind 2002, Where Have All the Flowers Gone 2002, Balzac and the Little Chinese Seamstress (Paris Film Festival Best Actress Award 2002) 2002, A West Lake Moment 2004, Beauty Remains 2004, Baobei in Love (Chinese Director's Association Award for Best Actress 2004) 2004, Stolen Life 2005, Perhaps Love (Hong Kong Film Critics Society Award for Best Actress 2005, Hong Kong Film Award for Best Actress 2006, Golden Bauhinia Award for Best Actress 2006, Golden Horse Award for Best Actress 2006) 2005, The Banquet (Hong Kong Film Award for Best Supporting Actress 2007, Golden Bauhinia Award for Best Supporting Actress 2007) 2006, Ming Ming 2006, The Equation of Love and Death (Asian Film Award for Best Actress 2009) 2008, Painted Skin 2008, All About Women 2008, The Message 2009, Confucius 2010, True Legend 2010, The Founding of a Party 2011, The Flying Swords of Dragon Gate 2011. *Television includes* Hongchufang 1997, Palace of Desire 1998, Taiping Tianguo 1998, Jingtan Fengyun 1998, Lüvi Hongniang 1999, April Rhapsody 1999, Kaixin Jiuhao 1999, Yuanlai Yijiaren 1999, Love Story in Shanghai 2000, Jinqian Bense 2000, Xin Wang 2000, Ripening Orange 2001, The Legend of the Condor Heroes 2002, Beach 2003, Fashion Family 2003. *Recordings:* albums: Summer 2003, Come Across 2005. *Address:* c/o Huayi Brothers Artist Agency, Huayi Brothers Media Corporation, Shunyi, Tianzhu, Wenyu River, Lou Tai Duan, Beijing, 101312, People's Republic of China (office). *Telephone:* (86) 10-6457-9338 (office). *E-mail:* stars@huayimedia.com (office). *Website:* www.hbstars .com (office).

ZHOU, Yaohe, DrSciTech; Chinese metallurgist; b. 30 May 1927, Beijing; ed Yaohua High School, Tsinghua Univ., Beijing, Moscow Institute of Steel and Iron, USSR; Pres. Casting Soc. of China Machinery Eng Soc. and Chair. Int. Soc. of Casting; Prof., Northwest Polytechnic Univ.; currently Prof. School of Materials Science and Eng, Shanghai Jiao Tong Univ.; Fellow, Chinese Acad. of Sciences 1991–; Nat. Science and Tech. Advancement Award, Nat. Invention Award and five ministerial awards. *Publications:* more than 200 publs in scientific journals. *Address:* Shanghai Jiao Tong University, Shanghai, People's Republic of China (office). *Website:* www2.sjtu.edu.cn (office).

ZHOU, Yongkang; Chinese politician; b. Dec. 1942, Wuxi City, Jiangsu Prov.; ed Beijing Petroleum Inst.; joined CCP 1964; intern and technician, Geological Survey Team, No. 673 Factory, Daqing, Heilongjiang Inst. 1967–70; Brigade Leader, Regional Office and technician, Geological Survey Regt, Liaohe Oil Exploration Campaign HQ 1970–73 (also Sec. CCP Party Br.), Dir Geophysical Survey Div., Liaohe Oil Exploration Bureau 1973–76, Deputy Dir Political Dept

1976–79, Deputy Dir-Gen. Liaohe Petroleum Exploration Bureau 1979–83 (also Party Sec. Drilling HQ and Geophysical Survey Div., CCP Party Cttee), Commdr Geophysical Survey Div. 1979–83, Dir-Gen. Liaohe Petroleum Exploration Bureau 1983–85 (also Deputy Sec. CCP Party Cttee); Mayor of Panjin City, Liaoning Prov. 1983–85, Vice-Sec. CCP Panjin City Cttee 1983–85; Vice-Minister of Petroleum Industry 1985–88; Deputy Gen. Man. China Nat. Petroleum Corpn 1988–96, Gen. Man. 1996–98 (also Sec. CCP Leading Party Group); Gen. Man. Head Office of China Petroleum and Natural Gas Company 1996–98; Commdr Tarim Oil Exploration Campaign HQ 1989–96 (also Sec. CCP Party Cttee 1989–90); Sec. CCP Dongying City Cttee, Shandong Prov. 1988–96; Dir-Gen. Petroleum Admin, Shengli, Shandong Prov. 1988–96 (Sec. CCP Party Cttee); Minister of Land and Resources 1998–99 (also Sec. CCP Leading Party Group); Sec. CCP Sichuan Prov. Cttee 1999–2002; State Councillor 2003–08; Minister of Public Security 2002–07; Alt. mem. 14th CCP Cen. Cttee 1992–97, mem. 15th CCP Cen. Cttee 1997–2002, 16th CCP Cen. Cttee 2002–07, 16th CCP Politburo 2003–07, CCP Politburo Secr. 2002–07, 17th CCP Cen. Cttee 2007–12, 17th CCP Politburo Standing Cttee 2007–12, Sec. Political and Legis. Affairs Cttee, CCP Cen. Cttee 2007–12 (retd); under investigation into corruption 2013–14; ranked by Forbes magazine amongst The World's Most Powerful People (29th) 2011. *Address:* Chinese Communist Party, Beijing, People's Republic of China (office). *Website:* english.cpc.people.com .cn (office).

ZHOU, Zhongshu, BA; Chinese business executive; *President, China National Metals and Minerals Corporation (Minmetals Corporation);* b. Nov. 1952, Xuzhou, Jiangsu Prov.; ed Shanghai Inst. of Foreign Languages; Deputy Dir 7th Dept, China Nat. Metals and Minerals Corpn (Minmetals Corpn) 1985, successively promoted to Exec. Pres. Minmetals Brazil 1988, Gen. Man. Minmetals 1990, Asst to the Pres. 1993–94, Sr Vice-Pres. Minmetals 1994, Pres. 2004–, Chair. Minmetals Devt Co.; Co-Chair. China Business Summit. *Address:* Minmetals Corporation, Building B, 5 Sanlihe Road, Haidian District, Beijing 100044, People's Republic of China (office). *Telephone:* (10) 68495888 (office). *Fax:* (10) 68335570 (office). *E-mail:* zc@minmetals.com.cn (office). *Website:* www.minmetals .com (office).

ZHOU, Zhuping, MEng; Chinese accountant and business executive; *Chairman of the Board of Supervisors, China Pacific Insurance (Group) Co. Ltd;* ed Tianjin Univ.; began career at Baosteel 1994, served as Dir of Finance Dept and Vice-Pres. Baosteel International Economic & Trading Co. Ltd, Deputy Chief Financial Officer Baosteel International Trade Corpn, Deputy Gen. Man. Baoshan Iron & Steel Trading Co. Ltd, Dir of Operations, Baosteel Group Corpn, Gen. Man. Baosteel Group Enterprise Development Corpn, Pres. Baosteel Development Co. Ltd, Deputy Dir of Planning and Finance Dept, Shanghai Baosteel Group Corpn, Sec. to Bd of Dirs, Baoshan Iron & Steel Co. Ltd, Vice-Financial Pres. Shanghai Baosteel International Economics & Trading Co. Ltd, Vice-Pres. Trading Br. of Baoshan Iron & Steel Co. Ltd, currently Chair. Baosteel Group Finance Co. Ltd, Baosteel Finance Co. Ltd and Fortune Investment Co. Ltd, Supervisor of Bd of Supervisors, Baoshan Iron & Steel Co. Ltd 2006–, Deputy Gen. Man., Shanghai Baosteel Group Corpn 2008–, Vice-Pres. 2009–; fmr Deputy Dir Finance Dept, Luzhong Metallurgical Mining Co.; Chair. Bd of Supervisors, China Pacific Insurance (Group) Co. Ltd 2010–; mem. CCP. *Address:* China Pacific Insurance (Group) Co. Ltd, 190 Yincheng Zhong Road, Shanghai 200120, Shanghai Province, People's Republic of China (office). *Telephone:* (21) 58776688 (office). *Fax:* (21) 68870922 (office). *E-mail:* info@cpic.com.cn (office). *Website:* www.cpic.com.cn (office).

ZHOU, Gen. Ziyu; Chinese army officer; b. 1935, Wucheng, Shandong Prov.; joined PLA 1951, CCP 1955; political instructor, Air Force Aviation School, rose to rank of Political Commissar, Maj.-Gen. of PLA Air Force 1988, Gen. 1996; Deputy Dir PLA Gen. Political Dept 1993–2000; Deputy Sec. CCP Cen. Comm. for Discipline Inspection 1997–2002; Deputy, 8th NPC 1993–98; mem. 15th CCP Cen. Cttee 1997–2002; mem. CPPCC Nat. Cttee, Standing Cttee 2003–. *Address:* c/o Central Committee of the Chinese Communist Party, Zhongnanhai, Beijing, People's Republic of China (office).

ZHU, Fushou, BEng, MBA; Chinese automotive industry executive; *General Manager and CEO, Dongfeng Motor Company Limited;* ed Anhui Inst. of Tech., Zhongnan Univ. of Econs and Law; joined Dongfeng Motor Co. Ltd 1984, Deputy Man. Dir Wheel Co., Dongfeng Motor Co. Ltd 1994–97, Deputy Gen. Man. Dongfeng Motor Wheel Co. Ltd 1997–99, Chair. and Gen. Man. Dongfeng Motor Wheel Co. Ltd 1999–2000, Gen. Man. and Sec. Party Cttee of Light Duty Vehicle Plant, Dongfeng Automobile Co. Ltd Feb.–Oct. 2000, Deputy Gen. Man. Dongfeng Motor Co. Ltd, Gen. Man., Sec. Party Cttee of Automobiles Subsidiary Co. of Dongfeng Automobile Co. Ltd 2000–02, mem. Standing Cttee of the Party Cttee of Dongfeng Motor Co. Ltd and Gen. Man. Dongfeng Automobile Co. Ltd 2001–03, Gen. Man. 2003–05, Vice-Pres. Dongfeng Motor Co. Ltd 2005–10, Dir (non-exec.) 2004–10, Pres. and Exec. Dir 2010–11, Gen. Man. and CEO 2011–; honoured as a sr engineer 1997. *Address:* Dongfeng Motor Co. Ltd, 29 Baiye Road, Wuhan, Hubei 430015, People's Republic of China (office). *Telephone:* (719) 8226-962 (office). *Fax:* (719) 8226-845 (office). *E-mail:* info@dfmc.com.cn (office). *Website:* www.dfmc.com .cn (office).

ZHU, Gaofeng; Chinese politician and telecommunications engineer; b. May 1935, Ningbo, Zhejiang Prov.; ed Tsinghua Univ., Leningrad Telecommunication Eng Inst., USSR; joined CCP 1964; technician, engineer, Sr Engineer and Chief Engineer, Ministry of Posts and Telecommunications 1958–82; Vice-Minister of Posts and Telecommunications 1982–95; Vice-Chair. and mem. Praesidium of Chinese Acad. of Eng 1994–; Chair. China Communications Standards Asscn 2002; Teacher, School of Econs and Man., Beijing Univ. of Posts and Telecommunications. *Address:* Beijing University of Posts and Telecommunications, 10 Xitucheng Road, Beijing 100038, People's Republic of China. *Website:* www.buptsem.cn (office).

ZHU, Jimin; Chinese business executive; *Chairman and Party Secretary, Shougang Corporation;* served as Deputy Gen. Man. and Gen. Man. Shougang Gen. Co., currently Chair. and Party Sec. Shougang Corpn, Vice-Chair. Shougang Gen. Co. –2002, Chair. 2002–, Chair. Beijing Shougang Co. Ltd, Shougang Jingtang Iron & Steel United Co. Ltd. *Address:* Shougang Corporation, Shijingshan Road, Beijing 100041, People's Republic of China (office). *Telephone:*

(10) 88291381 (office). *Fax:* (10) 88294300 (office). *E-mail:* info@shougang.com.cn (office). *Website:* www.shougang.com.cn (office).

ZHU, Mengyi; Chinese real estate executive; *Chairman, Hopson Development Holding Ltd;* b. 1959, Fengshun, Guangdong Prov.; Chair. Hopson Development Holding Ltd, Guangdong Zhujiang Investment, Tianjin Real Estate; mem. 11th CPPCC Nat. Cttee 2008–13. *Address:* Hopson Development Holding Ltd, 16/F Zhujiang Investment Building, 421 Zhujiang East Road, Zhujiang New City, Guangzhou 510623, Gaungdong, People's Republic of China (office). *E-mail:* info@ hopson.com.cn (office). *Website:* www.hopson.com.cn (office).

ZHU, Mingshan; Chinese jurist; b. May 1937, Jiutai Co., Jilin Prov.; two s.; ed People's Univ., Beijing; joined CCP 1961; exiled to countryside during Cultural Revolution 1966–76; judge, Criminal Court, Supreme People's Court 1978–82, Vice-Pres. 1982–83, Vice-Pres. Supreme People's Court 1983–2003 (title of Grand Justice); Vice-Chair. NPC Cttee for Internal and Judicial Affairs 2006–. *Address:* c/o Supreme People's Court, 27 Dongjiaomin Xiang, Beijing 100745, People's Republic of China (office).

ZHU, Qingshi, FRSC; Chinese physical chemist, university administrator and academic; *Founding President, South University of Science and Technology of China;* b. Feb. 1946, Chengdu, Sichuan Prov.; ed Univ. of Science and Tech. of China; workman, later planner, Xining Mountain-River Machine Tool Foundry, Qinghai Prov. 1968–74; trainee Research Fellow and Asst Research Fellow, Qinghai Salt Lake Inst., Chinese Acad. of Sciences (CAS) 1974–84, transferred to Dalian Inst. of Chemical Physics, CAS, working successively as leader of research group, dir of research lab., Assoc. Research Fellow and Research Fellow; teacher and researcher, Univ. of Science and Tech. of China (USTC) 1994–96, Vice-Pres. 1996–98, Pres. 1998–2008; Founding Pres. South Univ. of Science and Technology of China 2009–; Visiting Scholar, Univ. of Calif., Santa Barbara, MIT; Guest Scientist, Brookhaven Nat. Lab., USA, Nat. Research Council of Canada; Guest Prof., Univ. of Grenoble, Univ. of Dijon, Univ. of Paris-Sud, France, Univ. of Helsinki, Finland; Guest Research Fellow, Royal Soc., worked at Univs of Cambridge, Oxford and Nottingham, UK; Exec. mem. Bd of Dirs China Soc. of Chem.; mem. Bd of Dirs Br. of Physical Chem., IUPAC; Vice-Chair. China Soc. of Scientific History, Asscn of East Asia Research Univs, China Soc. of Dialectics of Nature; Deputy to 8th and 9th NPC; Vice-Pres. Anhui Prov. Asscn of Science and Tech.; Academician, CAS 1991; Fellow, Third World Acad. of Sciences 2001; SOCP Award for Achievements in Asia 1994, Thompson Memorial Award, Spectrochimica Acta 1994. *Publications:* Green Chemistry 1998, The Collected Works of Qinghsi Zhu 2000, Dynamics of Quantum Transitions in Laser Field (co-author) 2000; more than 140 articles and papers. *Address:* Office of the President, South University of Science and Technology of China, Xili Xueyuan Road, Nanshan District, Shenzhen 518055, People's Republic of China (office). *Telephone:* 755-8801 0000 (office). *Website:* www.sustc.edu.cn (office).

ZHU, Rongji; Chinese engineer and government official (retd); b. 20 Oct. 1928, Changsha City, Hunan Prov.; m. Lao An; one s. one d.; ed Tsinghua Univ., Beijing; fmr Deputy Head Production Planning Office, joined CCP 1949; NE China Dept of Industries; Group Head and Deputy Chief of Div., State Planning Comm. 1952–58, engineer 1958–69; sent for re-educ. during Cultural Revolution 1970–75; Deputy Chief Engineer, Pipeline Bureau, Ministry of Petroleum Industry 1975–79; Dir Industrial Econs Inst., Chinese Acad. of Social Sciences 1975–79; Div. Chief and Deputy Head of Bureau, State Econ. Comm. 1982, Vice-Minister in charge of State Econ. Comm. 1983–87; Vice-Mayor of Shanghai 1987–90; a Vice-Premier, State Council 1991–98, Premier 1998–2003, Dir State Council Production Office 1991; mem. Standing Cttee Political Bureau of CCP Cttee 1993–2003; Gov. People's Bank of China 1993–95; Head State Steering Group of Science, Tech. and Educ. 1998; Chair. Cttee for Construction of Three Gorges Project 1998; mem. Govt Del., Macao Hand-Over Ceremony, Macao Special Admin. Region Preparatory Cttee 1999. *Publication:* Zhu Rongji on the Record: The Road to Reform: 1991–1997 (memoir) 2013. *Leisure interest:* Peking Opera. *Address:* c/o State Council, Xi Changan Jie, Beijing, People's Republic of China (office).

ZHU, Senlin; Chinese politician; b. 1930, Chuansha Co., Shanghai; ed Qinghua Univ.; Deputy Sec.-Gen. and Dir-Gen. Gen. Office Guangzhou City Cttee of CCP 1981–; later Deputy Sec. Guangzhou City Cttee of CCP and Mayor of Guangzhou City; mem. Guangdong Provincial Cttee of CCP and Sec. Guangzhou City Party Cttee; Deputy Sec. Guangzhou Provincial Party Cttee, Acting Gov. 1991–93, Gov. of Guangdong Prov. 1992–96; Chair. Guangdong Provincial People's Congress 1996–2001; Alt. mem. 13th CCP Cen. Cttee 1987–92, 14th CCP Cen. Cttee 1992–97; Deputy to 7th, 8th and 9th NPC 1988–2003. *Address:* 305 Central Dongpeng Road, Guangzhou, People's Republic of China.

ZHU, Xiaohua; Chinese mathematician and academic; b. 1968; currently Prof., School of Math. Sciences, Peking Univ., Beijing; Chair. Organizing Cttee, Pacific Rim Complex Geometry Conf. 2006; expert in studies on complex differential geometry; Int. Centre for Theoretical Physics (ICTP) Prize 2005. *Publications:* numerous papers in professional journals. *Address:* School of Mathematical Sciences, Peking University, Beijing 100871, People's Republic of China (office). *Fax:* (10) 62751801 (office). *E-mail:* xhzhu@math.pku.edu.cn (office). *Website:* www .math.pku.edu.cn (office).

ZHU, Xiaohua; Chinese government official; b. 23 Jan. 1940, Xi'an, Shanxi Prov.; m. Li Yazhi 1962; three s.; ed Shanghai Univ. of Finance and Econs; with People's Bank of China 1979–90, positions include Deputy Dir, Financial Research Division, Deputy Pres. Shanghai Office, Deputy Gov. People's Bank of China 1993–96; Special Appointee IMF 1991–92; apptd Deputy Dir Science and Tech. Dept, State Family Planning Comm. 1992; Deputy Dir Econs Dept, Xinhua News Agency, Hong Kong 1992–93; Dir-Gen. State Admin of Foreign Exchange Control 1993–96; Chair. and CEO China Everbright Holdings Co. Ltd, Hong Kong 1996–99; charged with corruption; expelled from CCP Aug. 2002; convicted of bribery and sentenced to 15 years' imprisonment Oct. 2002.

ZHU, Xu; Chinese actor; b. Feb. 1930, Shenyang, Liaoning Prov.; actor, Beijing People's Arts Theatre 1952–. *Films include:* Drum Singers 1987, The Last Eunuch 1991, Xin Xiang 1993, The King of Masks (Best Actor, Tokyo Film Festival) 1996, Shower 1999, Beijing Herbs 2000, Gua Shua 2001, Osama no kampo 2004, Lan

2009, We See You in Heaven 2009. *Address:* Beijing People's Arts Theatre, Beijing, People's Republic of China (office).

ZHU, Xun; Chinese state official; b. 1930, Funing Co., Jiangsu Prov.; ed China People's Univ. and in USSR; joined CCP 1946; Vice-Minister of Geology and Minerals 1982–85, Minister 1985–94; Alt. mem. 12th CCP Cen. Cttee 1982, mem. 1985–87, mem. 13th CCP Cen. Cttee 1987–92, 14th CCP Cen. Cttee 1992–97; Sec.-Gen. 8th Nat. Cttee CPPCC 1994–98; Chair. Cttee for Liaison with Hong Kong, Macao, Taiwan and Overseas Chinese Affairs, 9th CPPCC Nat. Cttee 1998–2003; Hon. mem. Int. Hydrogeologists' Asscn 1989; Hon. Academician, Russian Acad. of Natural Sciences 1996, of Int. Euro-Asian Acad. of Sciences 1999; Boris Yeltsin Friendship Medal 1999. *Publications:* Introduction to Ore-Seeking Philosophy, Mineral Resources in China, Geo-science and Sustainable Development. *Leisure interests:* swimming, walking, music, film. *Address:* c/o National Committee of Chinese People's Political Consultative Conference, 23 Taipingqiao Street, Beijing, People's Republic of China (office). *Telephone:* (10) 66191803 (office); (10) 68321977 (home). *Fax:* (10) 66191616 (office).

ZHU, Yanfeng; Chinese automobile industry executive and government official; *Vice-Governor, Jilin Province;* b. 1961, Fenghua City, Zhejiang Prov.; ed Zhejiang Univ.; joined CCP 1982; joined China FAW Group Corpn as technician 1983, served as Deputy Dir Research Dept, Metering Div. 1986, Dir Foreign Econ. Div. 1994–97, Vice-Pres. China FAW Group Corpn 1997–98, Exec. Vice-Pres. 1998–99, Pres. 1999–2007, also Pres. FAW Sedan Co. 1997; Chair. Tianjin Automobile Group Corpn 2002–06; Vice-Gov. Jilin Prov. 2007–, also Deputy Sec. of Provincial CCP Cttee; Alt. Mem. 16th CCP Cen. Cttee 2002–07, 17th CCP Cen. Cttee 2007–12, 18th CCP Cen. Cttee 2012–; Chair. CIFE Presidium. *Address:* Office of the Vice Governor, Changchun 130011, Jilin Province, People's Republic of China (office). *Website:* www.jl.gov.cn (office).

ZHU, Yinghuang, MA; Chinese journalist, translator and academic; *Professor of Journalism and Communications, Tsinghua University;* b. 28 Dec. 1943, Shanghai; m. Yao Xiang 1972; one d.; ed Fudan Univ., Stanford Univ., USA; mem. teaching faculty, Shandong Normal Univ. 1977; Ed.-in-Chief China Daily 1993–2004, Ed.-in-Chief Emer. 2004–; took part in translation work of Basic Law of Hong Kong Special Admin. Region 1987–88; currently Prof. of Journalism and Communications, Tsinghua Univ.; also Prof., China Communication Univ.; Doctoral tutor, China Communications Univ.; mem. CPPCC 2003–08; Vice-Chair. China Translation Asscn, China Pacific Econ. Cooperation Cttee; Special Adviser to China-US Exchange Foundation; Outstanding Journalist of China 1984. *Publications:* Translations: Inside Stories of Macao and Singapore, The Memoirs of Dwight Whip, The Rich and Super Rich, Socialist Democratic Parties in Western Europe, Three Generations of a Newspaper Tycoon. *Address:* c/o China Daily, 15 Huixin Dongjie, Chao Yang Qu, Beijing 100029, People's Republic of China (office). *Telephone:* (10) 64995027 (office); (10) 64280990 (home). *Fax:* (10) 64918377 (office). *E-mail:* yhzhu@chinadaily.com.cn (office). *Website:* www.chinadaily.com.cn (office).

ZHU, Yongpeng, BEng; Chinese engineer and business executive; b. 1950, Shanghai; ed Electric Power Eng Dept, Northeast Dianli Univ.; began career in electric power industry 1968; joined CCP 1981; professor-level Sr Engineer with governmental special allowance issued by the State Council; served as Deputy Shift Supervisor, Heilongjiang Hulin Power Plant; successively, Technician, Asst Engineer, Engineer and Deputy Div. Chief in Tech. Div., Electric Power Production Dept, Ministry of Water Conservancy and Electric Power, as Div. Chief of Integrated Man. Div. of Electric Power Dept, Ministry of Energy, as Exec. Vice-Pres. and mem. Leading Party Group, later Pres. and Sec. Leading Party Group, China Longyuan Power Group Corpn, Ministry of Electric Power, as Vice-Chair., Pres. and Sec. Leading Party Group, GD Power Development Co. Ltd, as Exec. Vice-Pres. and mem. Party Group, as Vice-Gen. Man. China Guodian Group 2002–08, as Pres. and Assoc. Sec. Leading Party Group, China Guodian Corpn, Chair. and Gen. Man. 2007–13, Chief Legal Advisor 2008–13; Dir (non-exec.) China Longyuan Power Group Corpn Ltd 2009–13. *Address:* c/o China Guodian Corporation, 6–8 Fuchengmen Bei Street, Beijing 100034, People's Republic of China. *E-mail:* cgdcb@cgdc.com.cn.

ZHU, Yuli; Chinese government official; Dir State Bureau of Tech. Supervision 1990–93; Deputy Dir Econ. and Trade Office State Council 1991, Dir of Gen. Office of State Council's Leading Group for 'Year of Quality, Variety and Economic Results' 1992; Vice-Minister of Aerospace 1992–93; Pres. Aviation Industries of China 1993–99; mem. 15th CCP Cen. Cttee 1997–2002; mem. 9th Standing NPC Cttee 1998–2003; Deputy Dir 10th NPC Environment and Resources Protection Cttee 2003–. *Address:* Environment and Resources Protection Committee, National People's Congress, Beijing, People's Republic of China (office).

ZHUKOV, Aleksandr Dmitreyevich, MBA; Russian politician and economist; *First Deputy Chairman, State Duma (Parliament);* b. 1 June 1956, Moscow; s. of Dmitrii Anatolyevich Zhukov; m. Yekaterina Zhukova; one s.; ed Moscow State Univ., Harvard Univ., USA; mem. All-Union Research Inst. of Systems Studies and State Cttee on Science and Tech. –1980; mem. Chief Currency Econ. Dept, USSR Ministry of Finance 1980–91; Vice-Pres. Avtotractorexport Co., Ministry of Foreign Trade 1991–93; mem. State Duma (Parl.) 1993–2004, Chair. Cttee on Budget, Taxes, Banks and Finance 1997–2003, First Deputy Chair. 2012–; Deputy Chair. of Govt 2004–11; Pres. Russian Chess Fed. 2003–09, Russian Olympic Cttee 2010–; Order of Honour 2003, Order of Merit for the Fatherland (Fourth Class) 2006, (Third Class) 2011, Order of Friendship 2007; Diploma of the Pres. of Russia 2009. *Address:* Office of the State Duma (Parliament), 103265 Moscow, Okhotny Riad 1, Russia (office). *Telephone:* (495) 692-17-85 (office). *Fax:* (495) 692-86-00 (office). *Website:* www.duma.ru (office).

ZHUMALIYEV, Kubanychbek Myrzabekovich; Kyrgyzstani politician and scientist; b. 26 April 1956, Kichik-Ak-Zhol, Osh Oblast; ed Ryazan' Radio Tech. Inst.; worked as scientific researcher in Frunze Polytechnical Inst. 1978–86, Inst. of Physics Nat. Acad. of Sciences 1986–88; Exec. Dir Scientific Cen. Zhalyn Acad. of Sciences 1988–92; Chair. State Cttee of Science and New Tech. 1992–94; First Vice-Minister of Educ. and Science 1994–95; First Deputy to Sec. of State 1995–96; Head, Admin. of Pres. Akayev 1996–98; Prime Minister of Kyrgyzstan 2001; Gov., Jalal-Abad Oblast 1998–2001; Minister of Transport and Communications 2001–02; Deputy Prime Minister 2002; mem. Nat. Acad. of Sciences. *Address:* c/o

Ministry of Transport and Communications, 720017 Bishkek, Isanova 42, Kyrgyzstan.

ZHURKIN, Vitaliy Vladimirovich, DPhil, DHist; Russian political scientist; *Honorary Director, Institute of Europe, Russian Academy of Sciences;* b. 14 Jan. 1928, Moscow; m. Dina Zhurkina 1961 (died 1997); one s.; ed Moscow Inst. of Int. Relations; Ed. USA: Economics, Politics, Ideology (journal); Deputy Dir USA and Canada Inst. 1971–87; Founder and Dir Inst. of Europe, USSR (now Russian) Acad. of Sciences 1987–99, Hon. Dir 1999–, Sec., Dept of Int. Relations, Acad. of Sciences 1991–97, Corresp. mem. USSR (now Russian) Acad. of Sciences 1984, mem. 1990; mem. Academia Europaea 1990, World Acad. of Art and Science 1994; USSR State Prize 1980; ten govt decorations. *Publications include:* works on the political and mil. aspects of contemporary int. relations, International Conflicts 1972, UN Study on Deterrence 1985, Building Greater Europe 1990, EU: Foreign Policy, Security, Defence 1998, European Security and Defence 2005, European Army -Defeats and Victories: EU Common Security and Defence Policy 2012. *Leisure:* trekking, collecting books. *Address:* Institute of Europe, 125993 Moscow, 11-3, Mokhovaya Street, Russia (office). *Telephone:* (495) 203-73-43 (office). *Fax:* (495) 200-42-98 (office). *E-mail:* europe@ieras.ru (office).

ZHVANETSKY, Mikhail Mikhailovich; Russian writer; *Artistic Director, Moscow Miniature Theatre;* b. 6 March 1934, Odessa; s. of Emmanuil Moiseevich Zhvanetsky and Raisa Yakovlevna Zhvanetskaya; m.; two s. one d.; ed Odessa Inst. of Naval Eng; worked as technician and engineer, Prodmash factory, Odessa shipbuilding yard 1956–64; literary work 1964–; wrote short stories for Comedy Theatre of A. Raikin; f. Odessa Miniature Theatre (with R. Kartsev and V. Ilchenko) 1970; performed readings of short stories 1970–; stories banned because of criticism of state; Founder and Artistic Dir Moscow Miniature Theatre 1988–; Founder and Ed. Magazin journal 1991; Hon. Citizen of Odessa; Triumph Prize 1994. *Publications include:* Meetings in the Streets 1977, A Year For Two (short stories) 1989, My Life, Stay with Me (novel) 1989, Wir brauchen Helden! (short stories) 1992, My Odessa 1993 (short stories), Complete Works 2001; also stories in newspapers and periodicals. *Address:* Moscow Miniature Theatre, 125047 Moscow, 1st Tverskaya-Yamskaya 16 (office); 125047 Moscow, Lesnaya Str. 4, Apt 63, Russia (home). *Telephone:* (495) 250-37-21 (office).

ZI, Huayun; Chinese dancer and researcher; b. 10 March 1936, Tianjin City; d. of Zi Yaohua and Tong Yijun; m. Wang Shouyin 1960; one s. one d.; ed Tianjin Nankai High School, Beijing Normal Univ., Beijing Cen. Drama Coll.; dancer, China Cen. Dance Ensemble 1950–; Dir and Sr Fellow Dance Research Inst. of Chinese Arts Acad. 1987–; Chief Ed. The Art of Dance; Del. CPPCC 2002–; prizes include Gold Medal (for Tibetan Dance), 3rd World Youth Festival, Berlin 1950, Bronze Medal (for Flying Apsara), 5th World Youth Festival, Warsaw 1955, Prize for Excellent Performance, 1st Nat. Dancing Competition 1984. *Publications:* Dance and I 1987, Chinese and Foreign Artists 1989, Introduction to Choreology (co-author) 1991, Treatises on Choreology (co-author), The Rise and Development of Chinese Folk Dance during the Past 50 Years 1992, Collection of Essays of Hua Yun 1994, Fantasy of Dance 1995, Graceful Life 1997, The Art of Dance and Theory of Dance 1998, The Chinese Dance 1999, Studying Keeps You Young for Ever 2000. *Address:* Dance Research Institute, Chinese Academy of Arts, 17 Qianhai Xijie, Beijing 100009, People's Republic of China (office).

ZIA, Begum Khaleda; Bangladeshi politician; *Chairman, Bangladesh Jatiyatabadi Dal (Bangladesh Nationalist Party);* b. 15 Aug. 1945; d. of the late Iskander Majumder and of Begum Taiyaba Majumder; m. Capt. Ziaur Rahman (later Pres. of Bangladesh) 1960 (deceased); two s.; ed Surendranath Coll., Dinajpur; held captive during Bangladesh's war of independence; Vice-Chair. Bangladesh Jatiyatabadi Dal (Bangladesh Nationalist Party) (BNP) 1982–84, Chair. 1984–; helped to form seven-party alliance leading to ousting of Pres. Ershad from power 1990; Prime Minister of Bangladesh 1991–96, 2001–06, Minister in charge of Armed Forces Div., Cabinet Div., Chittagong Hill Tracts Affairs, Defences, Establishment, Power, Energy and Mineral Resources, Primary and Mass Educ. 2001–06; Chair. SAARC 1993–95, 2005–; ranked by Forbes magazine amongst 100 Most Powerful Women (14th) 2004, (29th) 2005, (33rd) 2006. *Publications:* Together for Better Tomorrow: Speeches of Begum Khaleda Zia 1992, Visions for the Future: Selected Speeches of Begum Khaleda Zia 2002. *Leisure interests:* reading, listening to music, gardening. *Address:* Bangladesh Nationalist Party, Banani Office, House 23, Road 13, Dhaka, Bangladesh (office). *Telephone:* (2) 8819525 (office). *Fax:* (2) 8813063 (office). *E-mail:* bnpbd@e-fsbd.net (office). *Website:* www.bnpbd.com (office).

ZIBARI, Hoshyar az-, BA, MA; Iraqi politician; *Minister of Foreign Affairs;* b. 1953, Aqra, Iraqi Kurdistan; four s. one d.; ed Univ. of Jordan, Univ. of Essex, UK; responsible for Kurdish Student Soc. in Europe, Chair. Overseas Student Cttee, UK 1978–80; participated in armed resistance campaign against regime of Saddam Hussein 1980–88; elected to Cen. Cttee, Kurdistan Democratic Party (KDP) 1979, Chief Foreign Rep. 1988–91 (acted as a spokesman during the 1991 Gulf War), mem. Political Bureau and Chief Rep. of Kurdistan Front in Europe 1989, liaised with coalitions' Operation Provide Comfort and Mil. Coordinating Centre, Zakho, Iraqi Kurdistan 1991–95, Head of KDP Int. Relations Bureau 1992–2003; mem. Kurdistani Nat. Ass. 1992–; elected to Exec. Council Iraqi Nat. Congress (INC) 1992, Head of Int. Relations of the Iraqi Opposition 1992, mem. INC Leadership Council 1999, mem. Iraqi Opposition Coordination and Follow-Up Cttee 2002; Prin. Negotiator in Kurdish peace talks that produced Washington Peace Agreement between KDP and Patriotic Union of Kurdistan 1998; Interim Minister of Foreign Affairs 2003–05, Minister of Foreign Affairs 2005–. *Address:* Ministry of Foreign Affairs, opposite State Organization for Roads and Bridges, Karradat Mariam, Baghdad, Iraq (office). *Telephone:* (1) 537-0091 (office). *E-mail:* press@iraqmofa.net (office). *Website:* www.mofa.gov.iq (office).

ZICO; Brazilian professional football coach, fmr professional football player and fmr politician; b. (Arthur Antunes Coimbra), 3 March 1953, Rio de Janeiro; s. of José Antunes Coimbra and Matilde da Silva Coimbra; m. Sandra de Sá Coimbra; three s.; playmaker/attacking midfielder; youth player for Flamengo 1967–71; sr player for Flamengo 1971–83, 1985–89 (212 appearances, 123 goals, won Rio State Championship 1972, 1974, 1978, 1979, 1979 (special), 1981, 1986, Brazilian Championship 1980, 1982, 1983, 1987, Libertadores Cup 1981, Intercontinental Cup 1981), Udinese 1983–85, Sumitomo Metals, Japan 1991–92, Kashima Antlers,

Japan 1992–94 (won J League 1st Stage Championship 1993); player, Brazilian nat. team 1976–88, played in World Cup 1978, 1982, 1986, 72 caps, 52 goals; won Beach Soccer World Championship 1995, 1996, American Cup Beach Soccer 1995, 1996; became a politician on retirement and apptd Minister of Sport; retd from politics and launched new J League, Japan; Asst Coach to Mário Zagallo (q.v.), World Cup 1998; Man. Kashima Antlers 1999, Japan nat. team 2002–06 (won Asian Cup 2004), Fenerbahçe, Turkey 2006–08 (won Turkcell Super League 2006/07, Turkish Super Cup 2007), FC Bunyodkor, Uzbekistan 2008–09 (won Uzbekistani Cup 2008, Uzbek League 2008), PFC CSKA Moscow, Russia 2009 (won Russian Super Cup 2009, Russian Cup 2008/09), Olympiacos FC, Greece 2009–10, Iraq Nat. Team 2011–12; 'Bola de Ouro' Brazilian Footballer of the Year, Placar Magazine (Brazil) 1974, 1982, Silver Ball, Placar Magazine (Brazil) 1974, 1975, 1977, 1982, 1987, set goal record in a single season as Flamengo player (49 goals) 1974 (56 goals) 1976, Rio State Championship Top Scorer (30 goals) 1975, (27 goals) 1977, (19 goals) 1978, (26 goals) 1979, (Special, 34 goals) 1979, (21 goals) 1982, South American Footballer of the Year, El Mundo (Venezuela) 1977, 1981, Brazilian Championship Top Scorer (21 goals) 1980, (21 goals) 1982, Libertadores Cup Best Player 1981, Libertadores Cup Top Scorer (11 goals) 1981, Intercontinental Cup Best Player 1981, World Footballer of the Year, Guerin Esportivo (Italy), El Mundo (Venezuela), El Balón (Spain), Placar Magazine (Brazil) 1981, Brazilian Top Scorer of the Year (59 goals) 1982, World Cup Bronze Shoe 1982, World Cup All-Star Team Player 1982, South American Footballer of the Year, El Mundo (Venezuela), El Gráfico (Argentina) 1982, Player of the Year, World Soccer 1983, Premier Player of the Year, Italian League 1983/84 1984, second highest scorer of Italian League (19 goals) 1984, Third Best Player of the Year, World Soccer Magazine 1984, Japan Soccer League record for goals scored in consecutive matches (11 goals in 10 straight matches) 1992, Top Scorer in Flamengo's history (568 goals), Top Scorer in Maracaná Stadium's history (333 goals), Beach Soccer World Championship Top Scorer (12 goals) 1995, Beach Soccer World Championship Best Player 1995, Third Best Brazilian Player of 20th Century 1999, IFFHS 7 Best Players in South America in 20th Century 1999, IFFHS Players of the 20th Century 1999, France Football Players of the 20th Century, World Soccer Players of the 20th Century, inducted into FIFA Hall of Fame 2000, named in FIFA 100 2004, Prize Golden Foot Award (Legend of Football) 2006. *Address:* Zico's Soccer Centre, Avenida Miguel Antônio Fernandes, nº 700 Recreio dos Bandeirantes, Rio de Janeiro RJ, Brazil (office). *Telephone:* (21) 24902431 (office). *E-mail:* centrodefutebolzico@hotmail.com (office). *Website:* www.ziconarede.com.br.

ŽIDAN, Dejan; Slovenian veterinary physician and politician; *Deputy Prime Minister and Minister of Agriculture and the Environment;* b. 16 Oct. 1967, Maribor; ed School for Animal Husbandry and Veterinary Technicians, Maribor, and later in Kamnik, Veterinary Faculty, Univ. of Ljubljana; completed traineeship at Reproduction Dept of Animal Husbandry and Veterinary Centre for Pomurje region, Murska Sobota; passed state examination at Ministry of Agric., Forestry and Food 1994; employed at Agromerkur, in the establishment's own veterinary clinic, and later at Nabergoj veterinary eng; began working at Reproduction Dept of regional unit, Animal Health Centre of Slovenia (AHCS), Murska Sobota 1995, Co-ordinator, later Head of AHCS regional unit, Murska Sobota 2000, in charge of regional unit of Nat. Veterinary Inst., Veterinary Faculty, Murska Sobota following reorganization of veterinary service; responsible for co-ordination of education of breeders and non-veterinary staff, Centre for Continuing Educ., Veterinary Faculty; Ed. Reja prašičev (Pig farming) magazine –2003; mem. Bd KG Rakičan d.d. 2003–13; Pres. Man. Bd, Panvita Group, KG Rakičan d.d. 2007–13; External Assoc., Veterinary Faculty, Ljubljana, elected as professional adviser for porcine health and reproduction 2003; reappointed mem. Animal Husbandry Council, Ministry of Agric., Forestry and Food 2007; Visiting Expert of Faculty of Agric., Univ. of Maribor 2007; Minister for Agric., Forestry and Food 2010–11; mem. Nat. Ass. 2011–, Chair. Cttee for Agric., Forestry, Food and the Environment; Deputy Prime Minister and Minister for Agric. and the Environment 2013–. *Address:* Ministry of Agriculture and the Environment, 1000 Ljubljana, Dunajska 22, Slovenia (office). *Telephone:* (1) 4789000 (office). *Fax:* (1) 4789021 (office). *E-mail:* gp.mkgp@gov.si (office). *Website:* www.mkgp.gov.si (office).

ZIDANE, Zinedine Yazid, (Zizou); French sports commentator and fmr professional footballer; *Adviser to the President, Real Madrid Football Club;* b. 23 June 1972, Marseille; s. of Ismail Zidane and Malika Zidane; m. Véronique Zidane; four s.; ed Centre de Formation de l'Asscn Sportive, Cannes; attacking midfielder; youth player, US Saint-Henri 1982–83, SO Septèmes-les-Vallons 1983–87, Cannes 1987–88; sr player, AS Cannes 1988–92 (61 games, six goals), Bordeaux 1992–96 (139 games, 28 goals, won UEFA Intertoto Cup 1995), Juventus, Turin 1996–2001 (151 games, 24 goals, won Serie A 1996/97, 1997/98, Italian Super Cup 1997, European Super Cup 1996, Intercontinental Cup 1996, UEFA Intertoto Cup 1999), Real Madrid (transferred for record £45 million fee) 2001–06 (155 games, 37 goals, won La Liga 2002/03, Spanish Super Cup 2001, 2003, UEFA Champions League 2001/02 (scored winning goal), European Super Cup 2002, Intercontinental Cup 2002); mem. French nat. team 1994–2004, 2005–06 (108 games, 31 goals), in winning team FIFA World Cup 1998, UEFA European Championship 2000, Capt. 2005–06; announced retirement from int. football Aug. 2004, announced return to int. football Aug. 2005, announced retirement from football 2006; Co-owner brasserie Nulle part ailleurs, Bordeaux; football commentator, Canal+ 2006–; Adviser to Pres. of Real Madrid 2009–, regularly plays for Real Madrid Veterans team; Chevalier, Légion d'honneur 1998, Officier 2009; Ordre Nat. du Mérite (Algeria) 2006; Ligue 1 Best Young Player 1994, Ligue 1 Best Player 1996, UEFA Champions League Best Midfielder 1998, Ballon d'Or 1998, UEFA Euro Player of the Tournament 2000, Serie A Foreign Footballer of the Year 1997, 2001, Serie A Footballer of the Year 2001, Onze d'Or 1998, 2000, 2001, French Player of the Year 1998, 2002, FIFA World Player of the Year 1998, 2000, 2003, UEFA Club Footballer of the Year 2002, Don Balón Award Foreign Player of the Year in La Liga 2002, UEFA Team of the Year 2001, 2002, 2003, FIFA World Player of the Year 1998, 2000, 2003, UEFA European Championship Team of the Tournament 2000, 2004, UEFA Golden Jubilee Poll 2004, named in FIFA 100 2004, FIFA World Cup Golden Ball 2006, FIFPro World XI All-Star Team 2005, 2006. *Film appearance:* Astérix at the Olympic Games 2008. *Leisure interests:* music, tennis, boating, cooking, Formula 1 racing. *Address:* c/o Alain Migliaccio, Calle 131, No 46, El Plantio

Canada, 46182 Valencia, Spain. *E-mail:* publicite@sporever.fr. *Website:* www .zidane.net; www.zidane.fr.

ZIEDAN, Youssef, PhD; Egyptian academic, writer and novelist; *Director, Centre and Museum of Manuscripts, Bibliotheca Alexandrina;* b. 30 June 1958; one s. two d.; ed Univ. of Alexandria; Lecturer in Islamic Philosophy and History of Science, Damanhur Alexandria Univ. 1992–97; currently Dir Centre and Museum of Manuscripts, Bibliotheca Alexandrina; consultant to UNESCO, UN Econ. and Social Comm. for Western Asia (ESCWA), Arab League; Kuwait Foundation for the Advancement of Science Prize 1994, 2005. *Publications:* Itiqa' al-Bahrin (essays in literary criticism), Zil al Af'a (novel), Azazel (novel) (Int. Prize for Arabic Fiction (Arabic Booker) 2009) 2008, Al-Nabati (The Nabataean) (novel) 2010, Arabic Theology 2010; more than 50 works of philosophy, history of medicine and information science. *Address:* Bibliotheca Alexandrina, PO Box 138, El Shatby, Alexandria 21526 (office); c/o Dar El Shorouk, 8 Sibaweh El Masry Street, Nasr City, Egypt. *Telephone:* (3) 4839999 (ext. 1300) (Alexandria) (office); (2) 24023399 (Dar El Shorouk). *Fax:* (3) 4820461 (Alexandria) (office); (2) 24037567 (Dar El Shorouk). *E-mail:* youssef.ziedan@bibalex.org (home); secretariat@bibalex.org (office); ziedan@ziedan.com (home); dar@shorouk.com. *Website:* www.shorouk.com (office); www.ziedan.com.

ZIEGLER, Jean, DenD, DenScPol; Swiss academic, writer and politician; *Vice-President, Advisory Committee, United Nations Human Rights Council;* b. 19 April 1934, Berne; s. of Hans Ziegler and Léa Ziegler; m.; one s.; ed Univs of Geneva, Berne, Paris-Sorbonne and Columbia Univ. New York; with Swiss American Corpn New York 1959; Jr lawyer in training with Theodor Haffner, New York; Asst to Sec.-Gen. of Int. Comm. of Jurists; UN expert, Léopoldville and Elisabethville, Congo 1961–62; Research Assoc., Faculté de Droit, Inst. Africain de Geneva 1963; Prof., Inst. d'Etudes Politiques, Univ. of Grenoble 1967; Faculty of Law and Social and Econ. Sciences, Univ. of Berne 1969; Prof., Faculty of Econ. and Social Sciences, Univ. of Geneva and Univ. Inst. of Devt Studies 1975; Prof., Univ. of Paris I—Sorbonne 1983; numerous research tours in Africa, Latin America and Asia since 1963; City Councillor, Geneva 1963; mem. Swiss Nat. Council 1967–83, 1987–99; mem. Fed. Parl. for Geneva; mem. Cen. Cttee Swiss Socialist Party; mem. Exec. Council, Socialist Int.; UN Special Rapporteur for the Right to Food, Vice-Pres. Advisory Cttee of UN Human Rights Council 2009–; Chevalier, Ordre des Arts et des Lettres 1994; Dr hc (Univ. Mons-Hainault, Univ. of Paris VIII, Univ. de Savoie); Adlai Stevenson Peace Award 1964, Bruno Kreisky Peace Prize 2000, Pres.'s Gold Medal (Italy). *Publications include:* La contre-révolution en Afrique 1963, Vive le pouvoir! ou les délices de la raison d'Etat 1985, Sankara. Un nouveau pouvoir africain (with J. P. Rapp) 1986, Dialogue Est-Ouest (with Y. Popov) 1987, La Suisse lave plus blanc 1990, La victoire des vaincus, oppression et résistance culturelle 1991, Le bonheur d'être Suisse 1993, Il s'agit de ne pas se rendre (with Régis Debray) 1994, L'or du Maniéma (novel) 1996, La Suisse, l'or et les morts 1997, Les seigneurs du crime, les nouvelles mafia contre la démocratie 1999, La faim dans le monde racontée à mon fils 2001, Les Nouveaux Maîtres du Monde 2003, L'Empire de la honte 2005, La Haine de l'Occident 2009, Der Aufstand des Gewissens: Die nicht-gehaltene Festspielrede 2011, Destruction massive: Géopolitique de la faim, 2011; numerous book chapters, articles in reviews, journals, newspapers etc. *Leisure interests:* skiing, tennis, mountaineering. *Address:* PO Box 136, 1211 Geneva 4, Switzerland (office). *Telephone:* (22) 908-44-33 (office). *Fax:* (22) 908-62-76 (office). *E-mail:* jeziegler@vtxnet.ch (home); jean .ziegler@unige.ch (home). *Website:* www.unhchr.ch (office); www.righttofood.org (office).

ZIEGLER, Peter Alfred, PhD; Swiss academic and fmr petroleum industry consultant; b. 2 Nov. 1928, Winterthur; s. of Eugen Ziegler and Adelheid Riggenbach; m. Yvonne M. Bohrer 1960; two s.; ed Univ. of Zürich; began work in petroleum industry 1955; field geologist in Israel, Madagascar, Algeria; joined Shell Canada 1958; transferred to Shell Int. Petroleum Maatschappij BV, The Hague 1970; tech. adviser, North Sea exploration 1970–77, exploration consultant Europe, South America, Deputy Head, new ventures and exploration advice with worldwide responsibility 1982, sr exploration consultant 1984–88, ind. petroleum exploration consultant 1988–2004; Hon. Lecturer Univ. of Basel 1990–96, Prof. of Global Geology 1996–2000; Co-ordinator EUCOR-URGENT Project 1999–2003; mem. Royal Netherlands Acad., Academia Europaea, Polish Acad. of Arts and Sciences, Polish Acad. of Sciences, Russian Acad. of Natural Sciences; Life mem. Bureau Int. Lithosphere Programme; Hon. mem. Geological Soc. London, Polish Geological Soc., European Union of Geosciences, American Asscn of Petroleum Geologists; Dr hc (Moscow State Univ.) 1998, (Tech. Univ. Delft) 2001; Fourmarier Medal (Geological Soc. Belgium), Van Waterschot van der Gracht Medal (Royal Geological and Mining Soc. of the Netherlands), William Smith Medal (Geological Soc. London), J. Neville George Medal (Geological Soc. Glasgow), Leopold von Buch Medal (Deutsche Geologische Gesellschaft), Robert H. Dott Sr Memorial Award (American Asscn of Petroleum Geologists), Special Commendation Award (American Asscn of Petroleum Geologists), Piotr Leonidovich Kapitsa Medal (Russian Acad. of Natural Sciences), S. Müller Medal (European Geophysical Soc.) 1998. *Publications include:* Geological Atlas of Western and Central Europe 1982, Evolution of Arctic-North Atlantic and Western Tethys 1988, Evolution of Laurussia, A Study in Late Palaeozoic Plate Tectonics 1989, Geodynamics of Rifting (ed. and contrib.) 1992, Structure and Prospects of Alpine Basins and Forelands (ed. and contrib.) 1996, Peritethyan Rift and Wrench Basins and Passive Margins (ed. and contrib.) 2001, The Transmed Atlas: The Mediterranean Region from Crust to Mantle (ed. and contrib.) 2004. *Leisure interests:* gardening, hiking. *Address:* Kirchweg 41, 4102 Binningen, Switzerland (home). *Telephone:* (61) 4215535 (home). *Fax:* (61) 4215535 (home). *E-mail:* paziegler@magnet.ch (home).

ZIEGLER, Philip Sandeman, CVO, MA, FRHistS, FRSL; British writer; b. 24 Dec. 1929, Ringwood, Hants.; s. of Colin Louis Ziegler and Dora Ziegler (née Barnwell); m. 1st Sarah Collins 1960 (deceased); one s. one d.; m. 2nd Mary Clare Charrington 1971; one s.; ed Eton Coll., New Coll. Oxford; joined Foreign Office 1952, served Vientiane, Paris, Pretoria, Bogotá; Editorial Dir Collins Publishers 1972, Ed.-in-Chief 1979–80, resgnd when apptd to write official biog. of the late Earl Mountbatten; Chair. London Library 1979–85, Soc. of Authors 1988–90, Public Lending Right Advisory Cttee 1993–96; Hon. DLitt (Westminster Coll., Mo., USA) 1987, (Univ. of Buckingham) 2000; Chancellor's Essay Prize 1950,

Heinemann Award 1976. *Publications include:* Duchess of Dino 1962, Addington 1965, The Black Death 1969, William IV 1971, Omdurman 1973, Melbourne 1976, Crown and People 1978, Diana Cooper 1981, Mountbatten 1985, Elizabeth's Britain 1926 to 1986 1986, The Sixth Great Power: Barings 1762–1929 1988, King Edward VIII, The Official Biography 1990, Wilson: The Authorized Life of Lord Wilson of Rievaulx 1993, London at War: 1939–45 1994, Osbert Sitwell 1998, Britain Then and Now 1999, Soldiers: Fighting Men's Lives 1901–2001 2001, Rupert Hart-Davis: Man of Letters 2004, Edward Heath: The Authorised Biography 2010; editor: The Diaries of Lord Louis Mountbatten 1920–1922 1987, Personal Diary of Admiral the Lord Louis Mountbatten 1943–1946 1988, From Shore to Shore: The Diaries of Earl Mountbatten of Burma 1953–1979 1989, Brooks's: A Social History (with Desmond Seward) 1991, Legacy: the Rhodes Trust and the Rhodes Scholarship 2008. *Address:* 22 Cottesmore Gardens, London, W8 5PR, England (home). *Telephone:* (20) 7937-1903 (home). *Fax:* (20) 7937-5458 (home).

ZIEJKA, Franciszek, PhD, DHabil; Polish philologist, writer, academic and fmr university rector; *UNESCO Chair in Translation Studies and Intercultural Communication, Jagiellonian University;* b. 10 March 1940, Radłów; m. Maria Gluszek (deceased); two c.; ed Jagiellonian Univ., Kraków; academic, Jagiellonian Univ. 1963–, Inst. of Polish Philology 1963–, Head of Chair of History of 19th century Polish Literature, Prof. 1998–, Vice-Dir 1988–89, Dean of Philological Faculty 1990–93, Vice-Rector 1993–99, Rector 1999–2005; currently holds UNESCO Chair in Translation Studies and Intercultural Communication; Lector, Provençal Univ., Aix-en-Provence 1970–73, Univ. of Lisbon 1979–80; Lecturer, Inst. des Langues et Civilisations Orientales, Paris 1984–88; Chair. Coll. of Kraków Univ. Rectors 1999–2005; Deputy Chair. Conf. of Academic Rectors of Polish Schools (KRASP) 1999–2002, Chair. 2002–05; mem. United Peasant Party (ZSL) 1962–89, Solidarity Trade Union 1989–93, Social Cttee for the Renovation of Kraków Monuments 1993–; mem. Editorial Bd Ruch Literacki, Regiony, Studia Academiae Scientiarum Hungaricae; mem. Polish Acad. of Arts and Sciences 2002–, PEN-Club 2002–, Nat. Council for European Integration 2002–05; Hon. Citizen of Tarnów and Sanok; Chevalier des Palmes académiques 1994, Officier 2002; Kt's Cross of Order of the Rebirth of Poland; Officer's Cross of the Rebirth of Poland; Order of Cross of the South (Brazil) 2002; Gold Rays with Neck Ribbon of the Order of the Rising Sun (Japan) 2002; Grand Golden Cross for Services Rendered to the Repub. of Austria 2002; Dr hc (Pedagogical Univ. of Kraków, Pontifical Faculty of Theology, Wrocław) 2003, (Swietorzyska Acad.) 2004; awards from Minister of Nat. Educ., Tomasz Nocznicki Award, Miesięcznik Literacki Award, Zycie Literackie Award, Fundusz Literatury Award, Kazimierz Wyka Literary Award of the City of Kraków, Zygmunt Gloger Award and Medal, Wlodzimierz Tetmajer Award, Jan Stanislawski Award, Cracovian of the Year 2000, Scena Illustrata Premio Internazionale I migliore dell Anno 2000, Super Express Golden Wings Award 2000, Pro Meritis Medal, Int. Mauthausen Committee 2003. *TV screenplays include:* Origin of the Legend: The Panorama of Racławice 1981, Polish November 1983, Traugutt 1991. *Radio plays include:* It Happened During Carnival 1996, A Book of Stone About the Past 1996, You Will Be a Pearl for Poland… 1997. *Publications:* Polish and Provençal Studies 1977, The Panorama of Racławice 1984, The Golden Legend of Polish Peasants 1985, Paris and Young Poland 1993, Our Family in Europe 1995, Wyspiański's 'Wedding' in Polish Myths 1997, Poets—Missionaries—Scientists 1998, Mythes polonais. Autour de "La Noce" de Stanisław Wyspiański 2001, The City of Poets 2005, Gaudium veritatis 2005. *Address:* Uniwersytet Jagielloński, ul. Gołębia 24, 31-007 Kraków (office); ul. Lipińskiego 9/9, 30-349 Kraków, Poland (home). *Telephone:* (12) 4221033 (office); (12) 4226689 (office); (12) 2662315 (home). *Fax:* (12) 4226665 (office). *E-mail:* ziejka@if.uj.edu.pl (office). *Website:* www.uj.edu.pl (office).

ZIELENKIEWICZ, Wojciech Władysław, MSc, PhD, DSc; Polish physical chemist and academic; *Professor, Institute of Physical Chemistry, Polish Academy of Sciences;* b. 6 June 1933, Warsaw; s. of Edward Zielenkiewicz and Barbara Zielenkiewicz (née Szot); m. Anna Kostrzyńska; one s.; ed Univ. of Warsaw; researcher, Inst. of Physical Chem., Polish Acad. of Sciences, Warsaw 1955–, Asst, Lecturer 1955–65, Head, Microcalorimetry Lab. 1965–68, Calorimetry Dept 1968–, Asst Prof. 1966–71, Extraordinary Prof. 1971–87, Ordinary Prof. 1987–, Dir of Inst. 1973–90; Gen. Dir, Polish Acad. of Sciences (PAN) 1968–69, Deputy Gen. Sec. PAN 1969–72, Deputy Sec. PAN Mathematical, Physical and Chemical Sciences Dept 1972–80, Sec. of Dept 1984–89, mem. Presidium 1984–89; Titular mem. Thermodynamics Comm. of IUPAC 1977–87; Chair. Comm. of Metrology and Scientific Apparatus of Polish Acad. of Sciences; Ed.-in-Chief Bulletin of the Polish Acad. of Sciences, Chemical Sciences Section 1985–94, Int. Journal Scientific Instrumentation 1972–85, Scientific Instrumentation (Warsaw) 1986–91; Pres. Polish Asscn on Calorimetry and Thermal Analysis 1985–91, Hon. mem. 1991–; mem. Polish Chemical Soc., Polish Physical Soc., ACS, Int. Soc. Nucleosides, Nucleotides and Nucleic Acids, Int. Soc. of Biological Calorimetry; Corresp. mem. Polish Acad. of Sciences 1977–; Foreign mem. Real Academia de Ciencias y Artes de Barcelona 1975–; Commdr's Cross Order of Polonia Restituta; Banner of Works; Gold Cross of Merit and other decorations; awards of Science and Tech. Cttee of PAN, Calvet Medal 1991, W. Świętosławski Medal 1994. *Publications:* six monographs and more than 200 original scientific works in Polish and foreign journals. *Leisure interests:* hiking, reading. *Address:* Instytut Chemii Fizycznej PAN, ul. Kasprzaka 44/52, 01-224 Warsaw (office); ul. L. Schillera 8 m. 30, 00-248 Warsaw, Poland (home). *Telephone:* (22) 6324389 (office). *Fax:* (22) 6325276 (office). *E-mail:* zivf@ichf.edu.pl (office). *Website:* www.ichf.edu.pl (office).

ŻIEMELIS, Vidmantas; Lithuanian lawyer and politician; b. 4 Dec. 1950, Gailiskiai, Moletai Region; one d.; ed Vilnius State Univ.; mem. CPSU –1989, voluntarily withdrew from CP; workman, later legal adviser Amalgamation of Chem. Consumer Products 1977–81; Asst to Prosecutor at Vilnius Prosecutor's Office 1981–84; Prosecutor-Gen. Supervision Dept Prosecutor's Office Repub. of Lithuania 1984–90; involved in Sajudis Movt from late 1980s; mem. Council of Sajudis, Vilnius City 1989–90; elected Deputy of Supreme Soviet Repub. of Lithuania Feb. 1990; signatory March 11th Act on Re-establishment of Independence; mem. Seimas (Parl.) Repub. of Lithuania (Homeland Union Group 2004–12) 1992–2012, Chair. Sub-cttee on the Evaluation of the Legal System and the Seimas Drafts 2005–12, mem. Cttee on State Issues and Legal Affairs 1989–96, Cttee on Legal Affairs 2004–12, Comm. on Drug Addiction Prevention 2004–12, Comm. for Parl. Scrutiny of Intelligence Operations 2005–12; Minister of Interior 1996–98.

Address: c/o Seimas, Gedimino pr. 53, 01109 Vilnius, Lithuania. *E-mail:* vidmantas.ziemelis@lrs.lt.

ZIGLAM, Hassan; Libyan business executive and politician; ed univ. in USA; fmr exec., Libyan Nat. Oil Co.; pvt. practice as accountant; Minister of Finance 2011–12. *Address:* c/o Ministry of Finance, Tripoli, Libya (office).

ZIGUÉLÉ, Martin; Central African Republic politician and insurance company executive; b. 12 Feb. 1957, Paoua; m.; six c.; ed State Coll. of Bangui Rapids, Univ. of Bangui, Int. Inst. of Insurance, Yaoundé, Cameroon; mem. staff Insurance Dept, Ministry of Finance 1978; Asst Gen. Man., then Head various depts. state-owned insurance co. SIRIRI 1988–95; Prin. Insp. of Taxes, seconded to regional insurance co. CICARE; Dir for the Central African Republic, Banque des Etats de l'Afrique Centrale (BEAC); Prime Minister of the Central African Republic 2001–03. *Address:* c/o Office of the Prime Minister, Palais de la Renaissance, Bangui, Central African Republic (office).

ŽIKEŠ, Ivan; Czech business executive; *Vice-President, Association of Czech, Moravian and Silesian Real Estate Agencies (ARKCR);* b. 27 April 1945, Šternov; s. of the late Josef Žikeš and of Vera Žikeš; m. Vera Žikeš; two s.; ed Tech. Univ., Prague; mem. staff, Vodní stavby, Prague 1969–90; Acting Sec. and Owner Recom Reality 1990–; Vice-Pres. ARKCR. *Leisure interest:* golf. *Address:* Recom Reality s.r.o., Varšavská 13, 360 01 Karlovy Vary (office); ARKCR, Strašnická 3165/1b, 102 00, Prague 10, Czech Republic (office). *Telephone:* (3) 53228545 (Karlovy Vary) (office); (2) 72762953 (Prague) (office). *Fax:* (3) 53228546 (Karlovy Vary) (office); (2) 72771412 (Prague) (office). *E-mail:* zikes@recomreality.cz (office); arkcr@arkcr.cz (office). *Website:* www.recomreality.cz (office); www.arkcr.cz (office).

ZIKMUND, Miroslav; Czech writer and film producer; b. 14 Feb. 1919, Plzeň; s. of the late Antonín Zikmund and Magdalena Zikmund; m. Eva Mašková (divorced 1972); one s.; ed Univ. of Econs; Hon. Citizen Zlín 1994, Plzeň 1999, Koprivnice 2000; Dr hc (Tomas Bata Univ., Zlín) 2014; Order of the Repub. 1953; Golden Plaque Czech Acad. of Sciences 1965, Medal of Merit of Czech Repub. 1999, Gold Medal Silesian Univ. 1999, Gold Medal, Palacký's Univ. Olomouc 2009. *Films:* From Morocco to Kilimanjaro 1953, From the Equator to Table Mountain 1953, From Argentina to Mexico 1954, If There be Paradise on Earth 1962, Criss-cross Life 2002, Africa I, II. *Television:* numerous documentaries. *Publications:* Africa, Dreams and Reality (with Jiří Hanzelka) 1952, With the Czech Flag to Kilimanjaro, Conquer the Desert 1954, Over There Behind the River is Argentina 1956, Over the Cordilleras 1957, Great Waters Iguazu 1957, Amazon Head Hunters 1958, Between Two Oceans 1959, Crescent Upside Down 1961, Kashmir 1962, Turkey 1962, 2010, Syria 1963, Kurdistan 1963, Thousand and Two Nights 1967, Continent under the Himalayas 1969, Political Analysis of the USSR 1989, Ceylon 1991, Life of Dreams and Reality 1997, Blue Mauritius 1999, Afrika um den Tatra 2002, Elephants Live up to Hundred Years (co-author) 2002, Tomtoms of Time: New Guinea (co-author) 2002, Das grosse Wasser Iguassu 2003, Die Wüste besiegt 2006, Trap on the Equator: Indonesia (co-author) 2008, Legend H+Z (Vol. 1) 2010, Legend Z+H (Vol. 2) 2011. *Leisure interests:* genealogy, travelling. *Address:* Pod Nivami 2894, 760 01 Zlín, Czech Republic.

ZILLE, Helen, BA; South African politician and fmr journalist; *Premier of the Western Cape;* b. 9 March 1951; m. Johann Maree; two s.; ed Univ. of Witwatersrand; Political Corresp., Rand Daily Mail 1974–82, oversaw investigation into death of Steve Biko; Sr Partner, Zille Shandler Assocs (public policy consultancy) 1989–93; Dir of Communications, Univ. of Cape Town 1993–99; joined Democratic Party (later Democratic Alliance) 1995, Caucus Chair., Western Cape Prov. 2002, Caucus Leader 2002–03, Nat. Spokesperson 2004–07, Educ. Spokesperson 2004–07, Leader 2007–; mem. Prov. Parl. 1999–2004; Minister of Educ. in Western Cape Prov. 1999–2001; mem. Nat. Parl. 2004–06; Mayor of Cape Town 2006–09; Premier of the Western Cape 2009–; fmr Bd mem. Open Soc. Foundation, Ind. Media Diversity Trust, Black Sash; Newsmaker of the Year, Nat. Press Club 2006, World Mayor of the Year 2008. *Address:* Office of the Premier, First Floor, 7 Wale Street, Cape Town 8001, South Africa (office). *E-mail:* Premier .Premier@westerncape.gov.za (office). *Website:* www.westerncape.gov.za (office); www.da.org.za; www.helenzille.co.za.

ZILLMAN, John W., AO, BSc, BA, DPhil; Australian meteorologist; *Chairman, Australian Partnership for Advanced Computing;* b. 28 July 1939, Brisbane; ed Univ. of Queensland, Univ. of Melbourne, Univ. of Wisconsin, USA; Dir Australian Bureau of Meteorology 1978–2003; Perm. Rep. of Australia to WMO 1978–2004, mem. WMO Exec. Council 1979–2004, First Vice-Pres. 1987–95, Pres. 1995–2003; Chair. Commonwealth Heads of Marine Agencies 1994–2003; Fellow, Australian Acad. of Technological Sciences and Eng 1980–, Hon. Sec. 1990–94, Vice-Pres. 1995–98, Pres. 2003–06; Pres. Nat. Acads Forum 2005–06; Pres. Int. Council of Acads of Eng and Technological Sciences 2005; Chair. Australian Partnership for Advanced Computing 2005–; fmr mem. Prime Minister's Science, Eng and Innovation Council; Int. Meteorological Org. Prize 2005. *Address:* Office of the Chairman, Australian Partnership for Advanced Computing, CSIT Building, North Road, Australian National University, Canberra, ACT 0200, Australia (office). *Telephone:* (3) 9669-4250 (office). *Fax:* (3) 9669-4169 (office). *Website:* www .apac.edu.au (office).

ZIMBA, Lyonpo Yeshey, MA (Econs); Bhutanese politician; b. 10 Oct. 1952, Omladama, Punakha Dist; m. Thuji Zangmo; one s. three d.; ed Univ. of Wisconsin, USA; joined civil service in the Royal Secr. 1974, planning officer, Ministry of Planning 1977, Jt Sec. 1991; apptd Chair. Royal Monetary Authority (Cen. Bank) 1986; Chair. Bank of Bhutan; Minister of Finance 1998–2003; Prime Minister and Chair. Council of Ministers 2000–01, 2004–05; Minister of Trade and Industry 2003–04, 2005–07 (resgnd), of Works and Human Settlements 2008–13; Silver Medal for Scholastic Achievement, Gold Medal for Best All-Round Coll. Student, Red Scarf 1991, Druk Thuksey and Coronation Medals 1999. *Leisure interests:* nature, walking. *Address:* c/o Ministry of Works and Human Settlements, PO Box 791, Thimphu, Bhutan. *E-mail:* mowhs@mowhs.gov.bt.

ZIMERMAN, Krystian; Polish pianist and conductor; *Lecturer, Academy of Music, Basel;* b. 5 Dec. 1956, Zabrze; m. Maria Drygajło; one s. one d.; ed State Higher Inst. of Music, Katowice, student of Prof. Andrzej Jasiński; Lecturer, Acad. of Music, Basel, Switzerland 1996–; Founder and Conductor Polish Festival Orchestra 1999–; collaborated with conductors Abbado, Bernstein, von Karajan,

Ozawa, Muti, Maazel, Previn, Boulez, Mehta, Haitink, Skrowaczewski, Rattle and others; has performed in numerous European countries and the USA; numerous prizes in prin. pianist competitions in Poland and abroad including First Prize, Beethoven Competition, Hradec Kralové 1973, Grand Prix IX Chopin Int. Pianist Competition, Warsaw 1975, Chigiana's Acad. Award for Best Young Pianist of the Year, Siena 1985, Orfeusz (Critics' Award), Polish Artists of Music Asscn 1988, Grand Prix de Disque, French Acad. 1989, Int. Critics' Award 1989, Edison Classical Music Award for Best Concert 2007. *Recordings:* CD recordings include: works for piano and chamber music by Schumann, Grieg (with H. von Karajan), Mozart (with K. Danczowska), Schubert, Brahms, Chopin (with Polish Festival Orchestra – Chopin Piano Concertos), Liszt, Debussy and others, Bartók Piano Concertos (with Andsnes and Grimaud) (Midem Classical Music Award for Concertos 2006). *Address:* Opus 3 Artists, 470 Park Avenue South, 9th Floor North, New York, NY 10016, USA (office); Kernmatterstrasse 8B, 4102 Binningen, Switzerland. *Telephone:* (212) 584-7500 (office). *Fax:* (646) 300-8200 (office). *E-mail:* info@opus3artists.com (office). *Website:* www.opus3artists.com (office).

ZIMMER, Hans Florian; German film score composer; b. 12 Sept. 1957, Frankfurt am Main, Germany; m. Vicki Carolyn (separated); one d.; ed in England; mem. The Buggles (produced hit song Video Killed the Radio Star); pioneered use of digital synthesizers with computer tech. and traditional orchestras; mem. BMI. *Film scores:* Moonlighting 1982, Histoire d'O: Chapitre 2 1984, Success is the Best Revenge 1984, Insignificance 1985, Separate Vacations 1986, The Wind 1987, Terminal Exposure 1987, Rain Man 1988, Twister 1988, Taffin 1988, Spies Inc 1988, The Fruit Machine 1988, Burning Secret 1988, A World Apart (with Stanley Myers) 1988, Wiezien Rio 1989, Paperhouse 1989, Dark Obsession 1989, Black Rain 1989, Driving Miss Daisy 1989, Green Card 1990, Pacific Heights 1990, Nightmare at Noon 1990, Fools of Fortune 1990, Chicago Joe and the Showgirl 1990, Bird on a Wire 1990, Days of Thunder 1990, K2 (European version) 1991, Backdraft 1991, Regarding Henry 1991, Thelma & Louise 1991, Where Sleeping Dogs Lie 1992, The Power of One 1992, A League of Their Own 1992, Radio Flyer 1992, Toys 1992, Cool Runnings 1993, Calendar Girl 1993, Point of No Return 1993, True Romance 1993, Younger and Younger 1993, The House of the Spirits 1993, The Lion King (Acad. Award, Golden Globe) 1994, Africa: The Serengeti 1994, I'll Do Anything 1994, Renaissance Man 1994, Drop Zone 1994, Two Deaths 1995, Crimson Tide (Grammy Award) 1995, Nine Months 1995, Something to Talk About 1995, Beyond Rangoon 1995, Muppet Treasure Island 1996, Broken Arrow 1996, The Preacher's Wife 1996, The Whole Wide World, 1996, The Fan 1996, The Peacemaker 1997, As Good As It Gets 1997, The Last Days 1998, The Thin Red Line 1998, The Prince of Egypt 1998, Chill Factor 1999, Gladiator (Golden Globe) 2000, The Road to El Dorado 2000, Mission: Impossible II 2000, An Everlasting Piece 2000, Hannibal 2001, Pearl Harbor 2001, Riding in Cars with Boys 2001, Invincible 2001, Black Hawk Down 2001, Spirit 2002, The Ring 2002, Tears of the Sun 2003, Matchstick Men 2003, The Last Samurai 2003, Something's Gotta Give 2003, King Arthur 2004, Thunderbirds 2004, Shark Tale 2004, Lauras Stern 2004, Spanglish 2004, The Ring Two 2005, Madagascar 2005, Batman Begins 2005, The Weather Man 2005, The Little Polar Bear: The Mysterious Island (with Nick Glennie-Smith) 2005, Pirates of the Caribbean: Dead Man's Chest 2006, The Holiday 2006, Pirates of the Caribbean: At World's End 2007, The Simpsons Movie 2007, Casi divas 2008, Kung Fu Panda 2008, The Dark Knight (Grammy Award for Best Score Soundtrack Album for Motion Picture 2009, Classical BRIT Award for Soundtrack of the Year 2009) 2008, The Burning Plain 2008, Frost/Nixon 2008, Madagascar: Escape 2 Africa 2008, The Dark Knight Rises 2012, Man of Steel 2013. *Television scores:* Wild Horses 1985, First Born 1989, Millennium 1992, Space Rangers 1993, The Critic (theme) 1994, High Incident (theme) 1996, Die Motorrad-Cops: Hart am Limit 1999, El Candidato 1999, Carnivàle (series) 2003, Threat Matrix (series title theme) 2003, The Contender (series) 2005. *Recordings:* Wings of Film 2001, numerous soundtrack recordings. *Address:* Gorfaine/Schwartz Agency Inc., 4111 West Alameda Avenue, Suite 509, Burbank, CA 91505, USA (office). *Telephone:* (818) 260-8500 (office). *Website:* www.gsamusic.com (office).

ZIMMER, Robert Jeffrey, AB, PhD; American mathematician, academic and university administrator; *President, University of Chicago;* b. 5 Nov. 1947, New York City, NY; ed Brandeis Univ., Harvard Univ.; Lecturer, US Naval Acad. 1975–77; L.E. Dickson Instructor of Math., Univ. of Chicago 1977–79, Assoc. Prof. 1979–80, Prof. 1980–, becoming Max Mason Distinguished Service Prof. of Math. –2002, Pres. Math. Dept 1991–95, Pres. Univ. of Chicago 2006–, Chair. Bd Govs, Argonne Nat. Lab., Chair. Fermi Research Alliance LLC; Prof. of Math., Univ. of California, Berkeley 1981–83; Ford Foundation Prof. of Math. and Provost, Brown Univ. 2002–06; mem. Bd of Math. Sciences, Nat. Research Council 1992–95 (mem. Exec. Cttee 1993–95); mem. Bd of Dirs Chicago Council on Global Affairs; mem. Exec. Cttee Council on Competitiveness, Washington DC, Nat. Science Bd (governing body of NSF), Pres.'s Cttee on the Nat. Medal of Science 2008–10; Fellow, American Acad. of Arts and Sciences, AAAS. *Publications:* Ergodic Theory and Semisimple Groups 1984, Essential Results of Functional Analysis 1990; more than 80 math. research articles. *Address:* Office of the President, The University of Chicago, 5801 South Ellis Avenue, Suite 501, Chicago, IL 60637, USA (office). *Telephone:* (773) 702-8800 (office). *E-mail:* president@uchicago.edu (office). *Website:* president.uchicago.edu (office).

ZIMMERMAN, Jean, BA (Hons); American fashion industry executive; *Executive, Oscar de la Renta;* m.; several c.; ed Univ. of Florida; began career in sales promotion at Charles of the Ritz for four years; joined Bristol-Myers in new product marketing; later worked for Estée Lauder as Dir of Fragrance Marketing; joined Chanel as Dir of Beauté Marketing 1978, responsible for launching Chanel cosmetics in the US market, Exec. Vice-Pres., Chanel, Inc. –2005, mem. Operating Cttee, Global Coordinating Cttee, Strategic Advertising Cttee; f. own consulting firm, JHZ Creative Management, LLC; Man. Consultant, Fragrance Div., Oscar de la Renta, Exec. 2012–; mem. Bd of Dirs Cosmetic Executive Women (Chair. and Pres. for eight years), Fragrance Foundation; mem. Advertising Women of New York, The Fashion Group, New York Cttee for United Cerebral Palsy; mem. Advisory Board for Grad. Program and Adjunct Prof., Cosmetics and Fragrance Marketing and Man., Fashion Inst. of Tech., New York; mem. Auxiliary Bd Lenox Hill Hosp.; mem. Bd of Advisors, Kate Somerville Skin Care; Chair. Sprayology; The Cartier Scholarship Recognition Award, Fashion Inst. of Tech., The Cosmetic Executive Women Achiever Award, Alumni of Distinction Award, Univ. of Florida,

Leah E. Harrison Humanitarian Award, Children Protection Center, Montefiore Hosp. 2003. *Address:* Oscar de la Renta Ltd, 11 West 42nd Street, 25th Floor, New York, NY 10036, USA (office). *Telephone:* (212) 288-5810. *E-mail:* info@oscardelarenta.com (office). *Website:* www.oscardelarenta.com (office).

ZIMMERMANN, Frank Peter; German violinist; b. 27 Feb. 1965, Duisburg; m. Young Joo Zimmermann; two s.; ed Folkwang Musikhochschule, Essen, Staatliche Hochschule der Künste, Berlin and with Herman Krebbers in Amsterdam; made debut aged 10 playing Mozart's violin concerto in G major, K216 in Duisburg; now performs with all major orchestras in world and has undertaken extensive tours in Europe, USA, Japan and Australia; also gives worldwide recitals, with pianists Alexander Lonquich –1994 and Enrico Pace 1998– and with Heinrich Schiff (q.v.), Christian Zacharias, Piotr Anderszewski and Emanuel Ax; Founder, Trio Zimmerman with Antoine Tamestit and Christian Poltera; appeared with English Chamber Orchestra conducted by Sir Colin Davis at Buckingham Palace by special invitation of HRH The Prince of Wales 1991; soloist at Europa Concert given by Berlin Philharmonic under Bernard Haitink at Royal Albert Hall, London and televised live all over world 1993; Bundesverdienstkreuz 1 Klasse der Bundesrepublik Deutschland; Premio Accad. Musicale Chigiana, Siena 1990, Rheinischer Kulturpreis 1994, Musikpreis, City of Duisburg 2002; numerous awards and prizes for recordings. *Recordings include:* concertos of Tchaikovsky, Brahms, Beethoven, Mozart, Prokofiev, Sibelius, Mendelssohn, Dvořák, Glazunov, Berg, Britten, Hindemith, Dean, Bruch, Busoni, Saint-Saëns, Szymanowski, Weill, Ligeti and Stravinsky; with pianist Alexander Lonquich recorded all Mozart and Prokofiev sonatas and works by Ravel, Debussy, Janáček etc.; with pianist Enrico Pace, 6 Sonatas by J.S. Bach; with Heinrich Schiff, duo works for violin and cello by Honegger, Martinů, J.S. Bach, Ravel and Pintscher; with Trio Zimmermann, string trios by Beethoven, Mozart and Schubert. *Leisure interests:* gastronomy, sports, wine, arts, literature. *Address:* c/o Nymus Artists, 34 Avenue du Beau Sejour, 1180 Brussels, Belgium (office). *Telephone:* (2) 372-30-05 (office). *Fax:* (2) 372-30-06 (office). *E-mail:* jt@nymusartists.com (office). *Website:* www .nymusartists.com (office).

ZIMMERMANN, Reinhard, Dr iur; German legal scholar and academic; *Director, Max Planck Institute for Comparative and International Private Law;* b. 10 Oct. 1952, Hamburg; s. of Fritz Zimmermann and Inge Hansen; ed Univ. of Hamburg, Regional Appeal Court, Hamburg; W.P. Schreiner Chair of Roman and Comparative Law and Head of Dept Univ. of Cape Town 1981–88, Deputy Dean and Dean, Faculty of Law 1983–88; Vice-Pres. and Pres. Soc. of South African Teachers of Law 1984–86; Prof. of Roman Law, German Private Law and Comparative Legal History, Univ. of Regensburg 1988–, Dean, Faculty of Law 1994–96; Visiting Prof., Univ. of Edinburgh, Tulane Univ., Univ. of Stellenbosch, Univ. of California, Berkeley, Cornell Univ., Yale Law School, Univ. of Auckland; Max Rheinstein Visiting Prof., Univ. of Chicago Law School 1993; A.L. Goodhart Prof. of Legal Science, Univ. of Cambridge, UK 1998–99; Visiting Fellow, All Souls Coll., Oxford, UK; Dir Max Planck Inst. for Comparative and Int. Private Law 2002–; Affiliate Prof., Bucerius Law School 2008–; Pres. Studienstiftung des Deutschen Volkes 2011–; Chair. Zivilrechtslehrervereinigung 2011–, Gesellschaft für Rechtsvergleichung 2014–; Co-Ed. Rabels Zeitschrift für ausländisches und internationales Privatrecht, Zeitschrift für Europäisches Privatrecht, Schriftenreihe zur Europäischen Rechtsgeschichte; mem. Acad. of Arts and Sciences Goettingen, Bavarian Acad. of Arts and Sciences; Foreign mem. Royal Netherlands Acad. of Arts and Science, Royal Soc. of Edin., Accad. delle Scienze Torino, British Acad., Austrian Acad. of Sciences; Hon. Dr iur (Chicago) 1997, (Aberdeen) 2002, (Maastricht) 2006, (Lund) 2006, (Cape Town) 2006, (Edinburgh) 2007, (Lleida) 2007, (Stellenbosch) 2009, (McGill Univ., Montreal) 2010; Leibniz Prize 1996. *Publications include:* Richterliches Moderationsrecht oder Totalnichtigkeit? 1979, Das römisch-holländische Recht in Südafrika 1983, The Law of Obligations: Roman Foundations of the Civilian Tradition 1993, Southern Cross (with D. Visser) 1996, Itinera Fiduciae (with R.H. Helmholz) 1998, Good Faith in European Contract Law (with S. Whittaker) 2000, A History of Private Law in Scotland (two vols) (with K. Reid) 2000, Roman Law, Contemporary Law, European Law: The Civilian Tradition Today 2001, Zivilrechtswissenschaft und Schuldrechtsreform (with W. Ernst) 2001, Comparative Foundations of a European Law of Set-Off and Prescription 2002, Jurists Uprooted (with J. Beatson) 2004, Mixed Systems in Comparative Perspective (with K. Reid and D. Visser) 2004, The New German Law of Obligations 2005, Die Europäisierung des Privatrechts und die Rechtsvergleichung 2006, Oxford Handbook of Comparative Law (with M. Reimann) 2006, Digest of European Tort Law (with H. Koziol *et al.*) 2007, Störungen der Willensbildung beim Vertragsschluss 2007, Historisch-kritischer Kommentar zum BGB Vol. II (Parts II/1 and II/2) (with M. Schmoeckel and J. Rückert) 2007, Exploring the Law of Succession: Studies National, Historical and Comparative (with K. Reid and M. de Waal) 2007, The Draft Civil Code for Israel in Comparative Perspective (with K. Siehr) 2008, Handwörterbuch des Europäischen Privatrechts (with J. Basedow and K. J. Hopt) 2009, Digest of European Tort Law Vol. II (with H. Koziol *et al.*) 2011, Revision des Verbraucheracquis (with H. Eidenmüller *et al.*) 2011, Comparative Succession Law: Testamentary Formalities (with K. Reid and M. de Waal) 2011, Max Planck Encyclopedia of European Private Law (with J. Basedow and K. J. Hopt) 2012, Freedom of Testation/Testierfreiheit 2012, Judge and Jurist (with A. Burrows and D. Johnston) 2013, Historisch-kritischer Kommentar zum BGB Vol. III (Parts III/1 and III/2) (with M. Schmoeckel and J. Rückert) 2013. *Leisure interests:* field hockey, tennis, running, classical music. *Address:* Max-Planck-Institut für ausländisches und internationales Privatrecht, Mittelweg 187, 20148 Hamburg, Germany (office). *Telephone:* (40) 41900401 (office). *Fax:* (40) 41900402 (office). *E-mail:* r.zimmermann@mpipriv.de (office). *Website:* www.mpipriv.de (office).

ZIMPHER, Nancy L., BS, MA, PhD; American university administrator; *Chancellor, State University of New York;* b. 29 Oct. 1946, Gallipolis, OH; d. of the late Aven Denzle Zimpher and of Elsie Gordon Zimpher (née Hammond); m. 1st William Fletcher Zimpher; one s.; m. 2nd Kenneth R. Howey 1987; ed Ohio State Univ.; fmr Exec. Dean Professional Colls and Dean Coll. of Educ., Ohio State Univ.; fmr Chancellor, Univ. of Wisconsin-Milwaukee, fmr mem. Faculty, School of Educ.; Pres. Univ. of Cincinnati (first woman) 2003–09; Chancellor, State Univ. of New York (first woman) 2009–; Pres. Holmes Partnership 1996–2001; fmr Co-Chair. Milwaukee Partnership Acad.; Co-Chair. Ohio Bd of Regents Articulation and Transfer Advisory Council; Chair. Urban Serving Univs 2005–; Chair. Nat.

Asscn of State Univs and Land-Grant Colls 2007– (fmr Chair. Comm. on Int. Programs); fmr Project Dir, Teacher Quality Grant, Dept of Educ.; fmr mem. American Council on Educ. Leadership Comm., Nat. Council for Accreditation of Teacher Educ.; fmr mem. Exec. Bd of American Asscn of Colls for Teacher Educ., Bd of Nat. Collegiate Athletic Asscn Div. One Exec. Cttee; mem. Cincinnati Business Cttee, A Greater Cincinnati Initiative Advisory Cttee; mem. Bd Greater Cincinnati Chamber of Commerce, Cincinnati Center City Devt Corpn, Greater Cincinnati Convention and Visitors Bureau, United Way of Greater Cincinnati, Uptown Consortium, Hebrew Union Coll.-Univ. of Cincinnati Ethics Center; YWCA Women of Achievement Award 1997, Ohio Women's Hall of Fame 1998, Outstanding Women of Achievement Educ. Award 2000, US Postal Service Women Putting Their Stamp on Metro Milwaukee Award 2003, Council for the Advancement and Support of Educ. Chief Exec. Leadership Award 2003, Asscn of Teacher Educators Distinguished Research Award, Edward C. Pomeroy Award for Outstanding Contribs to Teacher Educ., Virginia Commonwealth Univ. Distinguished Woman Scholar Award, US Postal Service Women's History Month Award 2004, YWCA Career Women of Achievement Award 2004, Ohio State Univ. Alumni Asscn Professional Achievement Award 2004. *Publications:* University Leadership in Urban School Renewal, A Time for Boldness: A Story of Institutional Change, Profiles of Preservice Teacher Education: Inquiry into the Nature of Programs, Creating a New Kind of University 2006, Recruiting, Preparing and Retaining Teachers for Urban Schools 2006, Boundary Spanners: A Key to Success in Urban P-16 University-School Partnerships; numerous chapters, articles and monographs. *Address:* Office of the Chancellor, State University of New York, State University Plaza, 353 Broadway, Albany, NY 12246, USA (office). *Telephone:* (518) 443-5355 (office). *Website:* www.suny.edu/chancellor (office).

ZINGRAFF, René; French business executive; *President, Fondation Institut Français de Mécanique Avancée;* b. 1936; ed Ecole Nationale Supérieure de Chimie et de Physique de Bordeaux; trained as chemical engineer; joined Michelin 1963, various man. positions including Dir of Quality, Mfg Plants in UK, Head of Sr Man. Personnel, Dir of Mfg Plants in N America 1983–86, Man. Pnr Compagnie Générale des Établissements Michelin (CGEM) 1986–2006; Chair. Bd of Dirs Siparex Associés 2006–; Pres. Fondation Institut Français de Mécanique Avancée 2006–. *Address:* Fondation Institut Français de Mécanique Avancée, Campus de Clermont-Ferrand les Cézeaux, BP 265, 63175 Aubière Cedex, France (office). *Telephone:* 4-73-28-80-63 (office). *Fax:* 4-73-28-80-88 (office). *E-mail:* fondation@ ifma.fr (office). *Website:* www.ifma.fr (office).

ZINKERNAGEL, Rolf Martin, PhD; Swiss professor of immunology; *Co-Head, Institute of Experimental Immunology, University Hospital, University of Zurich;* b. 6 Jan. 1944, Basel; m.; three c.; ed Mathematisch-Naturwissenschaftliches Gymnasium, Basel, Univ. of Basel, Univ. of Zurich, ANU, Canberra, Australia; intern, Surgical Dept, Clara-Spital Hosp., affiliated to Faculty of Medicine, Univ. of Basel 1969; Postdoctoral Fellow, Lab. for Electron Microscopy, Inst. of Anatomy, Univ. of Basel 1969–70; Postdoctoral Fellow, Inst. of Biochemistry, Univ. of Lausanne 1971–73; Visiting Fellow, Dept of Microbiology, John Curtin School of Medical Research, ANU, Canberra 1973–75; Assoc. mem. (Asst Prof.) Dept of Immunopathology, Research Inst. of Scripps Clinic, La Jolla, Calif., USA 1976–79, Adjunct Assoc. Prof., Dept of Pathology 1977–79, Full Prof., Dept of Immunopathology, Scripps Clinic and Research Foundation 1979; Assoc. Prof., Dept of Pathology, Univ. Hosp., Univ. of Zurich 1979–88, Full Prof. 1988–92, Co- Head, Inst. of Experimental Immunology 1992–; mem. numerous scientific advisory bodies including WHO Group of Experts in Vaccine Devt 1985–89, Advisory Council of Cancer Research Inst. 1988–; mem. editorial bds of immunology, pathology, microbiology and virology journals; mem. numerous professional orgs including Swiss Soc. of Allergy and Immunology 1971–76 (Pres. 1993–94, Hon. mem. 1996–), Academia Europea 1989–, European Network of Immunological Insts 1990–, Int. Soc. for Antiviral Research 1990–; Fellow, American Acad. of Microbiology 1996; Foreign Fellow, NAS 1996, Australian Acad. of Sciences 1996, American Acad. of Arts and Sciences 1998, Royal Soc. 1998, Acad. Royale de Médicine, Belgium 1998, Berlin-Brandenburgische Akad. der Wissenschaften 1998; Dr hc (Liège, ANU) 1996, (Oslo, Québec, Genoa) 1997, (Latvian Univ., Riga, Agricultural Univ. of Warsaw) 1998; Inst. for Cancer Research Award 1987; Nobel Prize for Medicine or Physiology 1996. *Publications:* numerous articles in learned journals. *Address:* Department of Pathology, University Hospital, Institute of Experimental Immunology, Schmelzbergstrasse 12, 8091 Zürich, Switzerland (office). *Telephone:* (44) 2552989 (office). *Fax:* (44) 2554420 (office). *E-mail:* rolf .zinkernagel@usz.ch (office). *Website:* www.unizh.ch/pathol/experimentelle -immunologie/pti_rzi_cv_e.html (office).

ZINKEVICIUS, Zigmas; Lithuanian philologist; b. 4 Jan. 1925, Juodausiai, Ukmerge Region; m. Regina Zinkeviciene; two c.; ed Vilnius State Univ.; lab. Asst Vilnius State Univ. 1946–50, Prof., Chair of Lithuanian Language 1950–56, Deputy Dean, Chair of Philology and History 1956–68, Prof., Head, Dept of Lithuanian Language 1967–88; Dir Inst. of Lithuanian Language 1995–96; Minister of Educ. and Science, Lithuanian Repub. 1996–98; Chair. Christian-Democratic Party (LKDP); consultant for educ. and science to Lithuanian Pres. 1998; main research in history of Lithuanian language, dialects and Baltic philology; mem. Swedish Royal Acad. of Letters, History and Antiques, Lithuanian Acad. of Sciences, Norwegian Acad. of Sciences, Lithuanian Catholic Acad. of Sciences 1991, Latvian Acad. of Science 1990; mem. Editorial Bd Baltistica Periodical; J. G. Herder Award. *Publications:* over 60 books, over 1000 articles in Lithuanian and foreign languages. *Address:* Justiniskiu 41-24, 2056 Vilnius, Lithuania (home). *Telephone:* (370) 52-41-08-77.

ZINMAN, David Joel; American conductor; *Music Director, Tonhalle Orchester Zürich;* b. 9 July 1936, New York; s. of Samuel Zinman and Rachel Ilo (née Samuels) Zinman; m. 1st Leslie Heyman (deceased); one s. one d.; m. 2nd Mary Ingham 1974; one s.; ed Oberlin Conservatory, Ohio and Univ. of Minnesota; studied conducting at Berkshire Music Center, Tanglewood and with Pierre Monteux; Asst to Monteux 1961–64; Music Dir, Nederlands Kamerorkest 1964–77; Music Dir, Rochester Philharmonic Orchestra, New York 1974–85, Baltimore Symphony Orchestra 1985–98; Prin. Guest Conductor, Rotterdam Philharmonic Orchestra 1977–79, Chief Conductor 1979–82; Music Dir, Tonhalle Orchester Zürich 1995–(2014); Music Dir, Aspen Music Festival and School 1997–2010; numerous recordings; Grand Prix du Disque, Edison Award, Gramophone Best

Selling Record (Górecki) 1993, Gramophone Award (Jungle Book) 1994, three Grammy Awards, Deutschen Schallplatten Prize, Peabody Medal 1996, MIDEM Classical Artist of the Year Award 2008. *Address:* Harrison Parrott, 5–6 Albion Court, London, W6 0QT, England (office); c/o Pippa Pawlik, PPPR Music PR, Ebnet 5, 8126 Zumikon, Switzerland (office). *Telephone:* (20) 7229-9166 (office); 43 288 0540 (office). *Fax:* (20) 7221-5042 (office). *E-mail:* info@harrisonparrott.co.uk (office); pippapawlik@musique-cordiale.com (office). *Website:* www .harrisonparrott.com (office); www.davidzinman.org.

ZINNI, Gen. Anthony, BA, MA; American diplomatist, academic, business executive and fmr military commander; *Executive Vice-President, DynCorp International LLC;* b. 1947, Philadelphia; ed Vilanova Univ.; joined US Marine Corps 1961, infantry officer 1965, rising to rank of Gen.; active service in Viet Nam (injured 1970), Philippines, Mediterranean, Caribbean, Korea, Turkey, Iraq, Soviet Union, Kenya; Head Unified Task Force Somalia in Operation Restored Hope 1992–93, supervised withdrawal of US forces 1995, also Asst to Special Envoy to Somalia; Deputy Commanding Gen. US Marine Corps. Combat Devt Command, Quantico, Va 1992–94, Commanding Gen. 1st Marine Expeditionary Force 1994–96; Commdr US Cen. Command 1997–2000, in charge of mil. forces in 25 countries in Middle East, Africa and fmr USSR; Head of Persian Gulf forces 1997–2000, Commdr in charge of Operation Desert Fox, Iraq 1998; retd from mil. Aug. 2000; fmr academic positions include Stanley Chair in Ethics, Va Mil. Inst., Nimitz Chair, Univ. of Calif., Berkeley, Hofheimer Chair, Jt Forces Staff Coll., Weissberg Chair in Int. Studies, Beloit Coll., Harriman Prof. of Govt, Coll. of William and Mary; mem. Bd Reves Center for Int. Studies, Coll. of William and Mary, Center for Responsible Leadership and Governance, Villanova Univ.; has worked with Inst. on Global Conflict and Cooperation, Univ. of Calif., US Inst. of Peace and Henri Dunant Centre for Humanitarian Dialogue, Geneva; Pres. Center for Middle East Devt, UCLA; Distinguished Advisor, Center for Strategic and Int. Studies, Washington 2000–; US Envoy to Middle East 2001–03; has participated in diplomatic missions to Somalia, Pakistan, Ethiopia and Eritrea; mem. mem. Council on Foreign Relations; mem. Bd of Dirs BAE Systems, Inc 2002–, Chair. 2009–12; Executive Vice-Pres. Dyncorp International 2007–; Defense Distinguished Service Medal, Defense Superior Service Medal (with two oak leaf clusters), Bronze Star Medal with Combat "V", Purple Heart; non-military awards include Papal Gold Cross of Honor, Union League's Abraham Lincoln Award, Italic Studies Institute's Global Peace Award, Distinguished Sea Service Award from Naval Order of US, Eisenhower Distinguished Service Award from Veterans of Foreign Wars, Chapman Award from Marine Corps Univ Foundation, Penn Club Award, St. Thomas of Villanova Alumni Medal. *Publications include:* Battle Ready (with Tom Clancy and Tony Koltz) 2004, The Battle for Peace (with Tony Koltz) 2006, Leading the Charge: Leadership Lessons from the Battlefield to the Boardroom (with Tony Koltz) 2009. *Address:* DynCorp International LLC, 3190 Fairview Park Drive, Suite 700, Falls Church, VA 22042, USA (office). *Telephone:* (571) 722-0210 (office). *Website:* www.dyn-intl.com (office).

ZINSOU, Emile Derlin; Benin physician and fmr head of state; b. 23 March 1918; ed Ecole Primaire Supérieure, Ecole Africaine de Médecine, Dakar and Faculté de Médecine, Paris; represented Dahomey in French Nat. Ass.; fmr Vice-Pres. Assemblée de l'Union française, Senator, Territorial Council; fmr Minister of Economy and of The Plan; fmr Amb. to France; Pres. Supreme Court of Dahomey; Minister of Foreign Affairs 1961–63, 1965–67; Pres. of Dahomey (now Benin) 1968–69; sentenced to death in absentia 1975; pardoned Aug. 1989; Leader Union Nationale pour la Démocratie et le Progrès; Grand Croix Ordre Nat., Dahomey; Grand Officier de la Légion d'honneur and numerous other decorations.

ZINZINDOHOUÉ, Armand; Benin politician; Cabinet Dir, Ministry of Transport and Public Works 2006–07, Del. Minister to the Pres. for Transport and Public Works 2007–08; Minister of the Interior and Public Security 2008–10; Pres. Friends of Radio Maranatha Asscn 2000–. *Address:* c/o Ministry of the Interior and Public Security, BP 925, Cotonou, Benin (office).

ZIOBRO, Zbigniew; Polish lawyer and politician; b. 18 Aug. 1970, Krakow; ed Jagiellonian Univ., Krakow; legal training at regional prosecutor's office in Katowice; worked for investigative bodies including Gen. Customs Inspectorate, Krakow; f. Katon Asscn and Help Centre for Victims of Crime and Social Pathology 1999; wrote communal draft of penal code 2000; fmr Adviser to Minister of Internal Affairs and Admin; elected to Sejm, Deputy Minister of Justice 2001, fmr Vice-Chair., Legislative Comm. and Special Comm. for Changes to Codifications; Minister of Justice 2005–07. *Address:* c/o Law and Justice Party, ul. Nowogrodzka 84/86, 02-018 Warsaw, Poland (office). *Telephone:* (22) 6215035 (office). *Fax:* (22) 6216767 (office). *E-mail:* biuro@pis.org.pl (office). *Website:* www.pis.org.pl (office).

ZIRNBAUER, Martin, MSc, DPhil; German theoretical physicist and academic; *Professor, University of Cologne;* b. 25 April 1958, Moosburg, Bavaria; ed Technical Univ. of Munich, Univ. of Oxford, UK; mem. Balliol Coll., Oxford 1979–82; Research Assoc., Max Planck Inst. for Nuclear Physics, Heidelberg 1982–84; Research Assoc., California Inst. of Tech., USA, Weingart Prize Fellowship 1984–87, Asst Prof. 1988; Assoc. Prof. (C3) for Theoretical Physics, Univ. of Cologne 1987–95, Full Prof. (C4) for Theoretical Physics 1996–, Dean of Physics (Vorsitzender der Fachgruppe) 2007–08, mem. Cttee Previewing Faculty Appointments (Beirat für Berufungsangelegenheiten) 2005–; Founding Dir (Gründungssprecher) Transregional Collaborative Research Centre 'Symmetries and Universality in Mesoscopic Systems' (SFB/TR 12, Cologne-Bochum-Essen-Warsaw) 2003–06; mem. Scientific Cttee, Max Planck Inst. for Math., Bonn 2004–, Scientific Cttee, Mathematisches Forschungsinstitut Oberwolfach 2010–; Deputy Chair. Bonn-Cologne Grad. School of Physics and Astronomy 2007–12, Chair. 2012–; mem. St John's Coll., Cambridge, UK 2008–; Assoc. Ed., Nuclear Physics B: Field Theory and Statistical Mechanics 2004–; mem. German Nat. Science Acad. 'Leopoldina' 2007; ranked among the top ten high school graduates of the Fed. State of Bavaria 1976, gifted student scholarship, Bavarian State Govt (Bayerische Begabtenförderung) 1976–79, Scholar of the German Nat. Scholarship Foundation 1976–82, Gottfried Wilhelm Leibniz Prize, German Science Foundation 2009, Max Planck Medal, Deutsche Physikalische Gesellschaft 2012. *Publications:* numerous papers in professional journals. *Address:* Room 206, Institute for Theoretical Physics, Department of Physics, University of Cologne, Zülpicher Str. 77, 50937 Cologne, Germany (office). *Telephone:* (221) 4704302 (office). *Fax:*

(221) 4702189 (office). *E-mail:* zirnbauer@uni-koeln.de (office). *Website:* www.thp .uni-koeln.de (office).

ZIVA, Vladimir P.; Russian conductor; *Artistic Director and Principal Conductor, Moscow Symphony Orchestra;* b. 7 March 1957, Arkhangelsk; m. Anna Ziva; two s.; ed Leningrad State Conservatory, Moscow State Conservatory; asst to principal conductor Symphony Orchestra of Moscow Philharmonics 1984–87; teacher Moscow State Conservatory 1988–89; Artistic Dir and Chief Conductor Nizhne-Novgorod Philharmonic Orchestra 1988–2000; principal conductor St Petersburg Mussorgsky Theatre of Opera and Ballet 1990–92; Artistic Dir and Principal Conductor Moscow Symphony Orchestra 2000–; co-founder Krasnodar Opera Co. 2003–; also currently Artistic Dir and Chief Conductor, South Jutland Symphony Orchestra; repertoire comprises classical and modern music; opera stage productions, in collaboration with B. Pokrovsky, include The Turn of the Screw, Albert Herring by B. Britten, Snow Maiden by P. Tchaikovsky; Hon. Artist of Russia, Conductor of the Year 1996, 1997; State Prize of Russian Federation 1995. *Address:* Moscow Symphony Orchestra, 191285 Moscow, Mosfilmovskaya 1, Russia (office). *Telephone:* (499) 143-97-13 (office). *E-mail:* msorchestra@gmail .com (office). *Website:* www.moscowsymphony.ru (office).

ŽIVKOVIĆ, Zoran; Serbian politician; b. 22 Dec. 1960, Nis; m.; one s. one d.; ed Bora Stankovic Grammar School, Nis and Belgrade Two-Year College of Econs; set up pvt. co. 1988; Pres. City Cttee of Democratic Party, Nis 1993–95; Rep. to Nat. Ass. of Repub. of Serbia 1993–97; Mayor of Nis 1996–2003; Founding mem., Deputy Chair., First Vice-Pres. and currently Deputy Pres. Democratic Party; Minister of the Interior, Fed. Govt of Yugoslavia –2003; Prime Minister of Serbia and Montenegro 2003–04. *Address:* c/o Office of the Prime Minister, 11000 Belgrade, Andrićev venac 1, Serbia (office).

ZIYAD, Abu Amr, BA, MA, PhD; Palestinian academic, politician and government official; b. 1950, Gaza City; m.; four c.; ed Damascus Univ., Syria, Georgetown Univ., USA; early career as teacher, Bahrain, Oman, Syria; elected mem. Palestinian Legis. Council (PLC) 1996 (ind.), re-elected 2006, Chair. PLC Political Cttee, mem. PLO-CC; Minister of Culture 2003, of Foreign Affairs March–June 2007; Prof. of Political Science, Birzeit Univ., Ramallah, West Bank 1985–; has done work for Centre for Policy Analysis on Palestine, Washington, DC and Centre for Palestine Research and Studies, Nablus; Pres. Palestinian Council on Foreign Relations; organised talks between the 12 major Palestinian factions within West Bank and Gaza to determine direction of intifada 2002; frequently serves as mediator between Hamas and Fatah. *Publications:* several books on books on Islamist movts and politics in Gaza 1948-67 including Islamic Fundamentalism in the West Bank and Gaza: Muslim Brotherhood and Islamic Jihad, Civil Society and Democratization in Palestine, The Significance of Jerusalem: A Muslim's Perspective and Emerging Trends in Palestinian Strategic Thinking and Practice. *Address:* c/o Ministry of Foreign Affairs POB 1336, Ramallah; POB 4017, Gaza, Palestinian Autonomous Areas (office).

ŽIŽEK, Slavoj, PhD; Slovenian sociologist, philosopher and critic; *Senior Researcher, Institute of Sociology, University of Ljubljana;* b. 21 March 1949, Ljubljana; m. 1st Renata Salecl; m. 2nd Analia Hounie 2004; ed Univ. of Ljubljana, Univ. Paris-VIII, France; moved to France early 1970s; prevented from gaining post at Univ. of Ljubljana after his degree thesis was deemed politically suspect 1975, spent next few years undertaking nat. service in Yugoslav army, eventually became involved with group of Slovenian scholars studying psychoanalytic theory of Jacques Lacan; researcher Inst. for sociology, Univ. of Ljubljana 1979–, now Sr Researcher; Prof. of Philosophy and Psychoanalysis European Graduate School, Saas-Fee, Switzerland; Int. Dir Birkbeck Inst. for the Humanities, Birkbeck, Univ. of London; Visiting Prof. Dept of Psychoanalysis, Univ. of Paris-VIII 1982–83, 1985–86, Centre for the Study of Psychoanalysis and Art, SUNY Buffalo 1991–92, Univ. of Minnesota 1992, Tulane Univ., New Orleans 1993, Cardozo Law School, New York 1994, Columbia Univ., New York 1995, Princeton Univ. 1996, New School for Social Research, New York 1997, Univ. of Michigan, Ann Arbor 1998, Georgetown Univ., Washington 1999; cand. for Liberal Democracy of Slovenia in 1990 presidential elections; participated in over 350 symposia worldwide; f. Pres. Soc. for Theoretical Psychoanalysis, Ljubljana. *Television:* The Pervert's Guide to Cinema (three-part documentary, More 4 channel, UK) 2006. *Publications include:* The Sublime Object of Ideology 1989, For They Know Not What They Do: Enjoyment as a Political Factor 1991, Looking Awry: An Introduction to Jacques Lacan through Popular Culture 1991, Everything You Always Wanted to Know About Lacan (But Were Afraid to Ask Hitchcock) (ed) 1992, Enjoy Your Symptom! Jacques Lacan in Hollywood and Out 1992, Tarrying With the Negative: Kant, Hegel and the Critique of Ideology 1993, Mapping Ideology (ed) 1994, The Metastases of Enjoyment: Six Essays on Woman and Causality (Wo Es War) 1994, The Indivisible Remainder: An Essay on Schelling and Related Matters 1996, Gaze and Voice as Love Objects (co-ed.) 1996, The Plague of Fantasies 1997, The Abyss of Freedom: Ages of the World (co-ed) 1997, The Ticklish Subject: The Absent Centre of Political Ontology 1999, Contingency, Hegemony, Universality: Contemporary Dialogues on the Left (co-ed) 2000, The Art of the Ridiculous Sublime, On David Lynch's Lost Highway 2000, The Fragile Absolute or Why the Christian Legacy is Worth Fighting For 2000, On Belief 2001, The Fright of Real Tears: Kieslowski and the Future 2001, Did Somebody Say Totalitarianism? Five Essays on the (Mis)Use of a Notion 2001, Opera's Second Death 2001, Welcome to the Desert of the Real 2002, Revolution at the Gates: Žižek on Lenin, the 1917 Writings 2002, The Puppet and the Dwarf 2003, Organs Without Bodies: On Deleuze and Consequences 2003, Iraq: The Borrowed Kettle 2004, Interrogating the Real 2005, The Universal Exception 2006, Neighbors and Other Monsters (in The Neighbor: Three Inquiries in Political Theology) 2006, The Parallax View 2006, Living in the End Times 2010; series ed.: Analecta, Wo es war, SIC; numerous essays; contrib. articles to newspapers, journals and websites, including London Review of Books, Guardian Unlimited. *Address:* Institute of Sociology, University of Ljubljana, Kardeljeva ploščad 5, 1000 Ljubljana, Slovenia (office). *Telephone:* (1) 5805100 (office). *Fax:* (1) 5805101 (office). *E-mail:* szizek@yahoo.com (home); slavoj.zizek@ fdv.uni-lj.si (office). *Website:* www.fdv.uni-lj.si (office); ics.leeds.ac.uk/zizek.

ŽIŽIĆ, Zoran; Montenegrin politician; mem. Socialist People's Party of Montenegro (Socijalistička Narodna Partija Crne Gore—SNP); Prime Minister of the Fed. Govt of Yugoslavia 2000–01 (resgnd in protest against extradition of Slobodan Milosevic by Serbian authorities); mem. Fed. Parl. of Serbia and Montenegro (fmr

Fed. Govt of Yugoslavia) 2003–06. *Address:* Assembly of Serbia and Montenegro, Trg Nikole, Pašića 13, Belgrade 11000; c/o Socijalistička Narodna Partija Crne Gore, Vaka Djurovica 5, 81000 Podgorica, Montenegro. *Telephone:* (81) 272421.

ZLATANOVA, Zinaida, LLM; Bulgarian politician; *Deputy Prime Minister and Minister of Justice;* b. 24 July 1973, Sofia; ed German Language School, Sofia, Sofia Univ. St Kliment Ohridski; work experience includes, amongst others, Dir of Directorate for Coordination of EU Affairs and Int. Financial Insts of Council of Ministers; fmr Head of EU Integration Unit, Ministry of Environment and Water, fmr Sr Expert, EU Integration and Int. Cooperation Dept; Head of EC Representation in Bulgaria 2008–13; Deputy Prime Minister and Minister of Justice (also in charge of EU Funds Absorption) 2013–. *Address:* Council of Ministers, 1594 Sofia, bul. Dondukov 1 (office); Ministry of Justice, 1040 Sofia, ul. Slavyanska 1, Bulgaria. *Telephone:* (2) 940-29-99 (Council) (office); (2) 923-75-55 (Ministry of Justice) (office). *Fax:* (2) 980-21-01 (Council) (office); (2) 981-91-57 (Ministry of Justice) (office). *E-mail:* gis@government.bg (office); pr@justice.government.bg (office). *Website:* www.government.bg (office); www.justice.government.bg (office).

ZLITNI, Abd al-Hafid Mahmud al-; Libyan banker and politician; fmr Minister of Econs and Trade; fmr Gov. Cen. Bank of Libya; Chair. Arab Bank for Investment and Foreign Trade 1988; Acting Chair. Nat. Oil Corpn 2001–02, Chair. 2002–07; Deputy Sec., Gen. People's Cttee (Deputy Prime Minister) 2007–09, Sec. for Finance and Planning 2009–11; Deputy Chair. Libyan Investment Corpn 2007–; Chair. Al Masraf (commercial bank in UAE). *Address:* Arab Bank for Investment and Foreign Trade, PO Box 46733, ARBIFT Building, Hamdan Street, Tourist Club Area, Abu Dhabi, United Arab Emirates (office).

ŻMIJEWSKI, Artur; Polish artist, filmmaker and photographer; b. 26 May 1966, Warsaw; ed Warsaw Acad. of Fine Arts, diploma at studio of Prof. Grzegorz Kowalski; Bursar, Gerrit Rietveld Academie, Amsterdam 1995; Guarene Arte exhibition (Prize of the Fondazione Sandretto Re Rebaudengo Per L'Arte for his work 'An Eye for an Eye') 2001; his 'Repetition' was shown in Polish Pavilion at the Venice Biennale 2005; Bursar, DAAD Artists in Residence, Berlin 2007–08, prepared latest project 'Democracies'; creates installations, photographs of objects, video realizations and films; fmr Ed. Czereja magazine; art critic and curator; Dir Seventh Berlin Biennale; Ordway Prize, New Museum, New York and Creative Link for the Arts 2010. *Address:* c/o Fundacja Galerii Foksal, Górskiego 1A, 00-033 Warsaw, Poland. *Telephone:* (22) 8265081. *E-mail:* mail@fgf.com.pl. *Website:* www .fgf.com.pl.

ZOBEL DE AYALA, Jaime; Philippine business executive; b. 18 July 1934; s. of Alfonson Zobel de Ayala and Carmen Pfitz y Henero; m. Beatriz Miranda 1985; two s. five d.; ed La Salle Univ., Madrid, Harvard Univ.; with House of Ayala 1958– (renamed Ayala Corpn 1967), Pres. and Chair. 1983–2005, Chair. Emer. 2006–; Amb. to UK 1970–75; fmr Adviser to Pres. Aquino; Chevalier des Arts et des Lettres; Hon. LLD (Univ of Philippines) 1991. *Leisure interests:* photography, scuba diving. *Address:* Ayala Corporation, 7/F Makati Stock Exchange Building, Ayala Avenue, 1254 Makati, Metro Manila 1200, Philippines (home).

ZOELLICK, Robert Bruce, BA, JD; American lawyer, business executive and fmr government official; *Chairman, International Advisory Board, Goldman Sachs;* b. 25 July 1953, Evergreen Park, Ill.; s. of William T. Zoellick and Gladys Zoellick; m. Sherry Lynn Ferguson 1980; ed Swarthmore Coll., Harvard Law School and Kennedy School of Govt, Harvard Univ.; Special Asst to Asst Attorney-Gen., Criminal Div., Dept of Justice 1978–79; fellowship to Hong Kong 1980; pvt. law practice 1981–82; Vice-Pres., Asst to Chair. and CEO Bd Fannie Mae 1983–85, Exec. Vice-Pres. Housing and Law 1993–97; Special Asst to Deputy Sec., Deputy Asst Sec. for Financial Insts Policy, Counsellor to Sec. and Exec. Sec. Treasury Dept 1985–88; Counsellor with rank of Under-Sec. Dept of State 1989–92, Under-Sec. for Econ. and Agricultural Affairs 1991–92; Deputy Chief of Staff, Asst to Pres. 1992–93; Olin Prof. of Nat. Security Affairs, US Naval Acad. 1997–98; Pres. and CEO Center for Strategic and Int. Studies 1998–99; US Trade Rep. 2001–05; Deputy Sec. of State and COO Dept of State 2005–06; Vice-Chair., Int., Goldman Sachs Group Inc., New York 2006–07, Chair. Int. Advisory Bd 2013–; Pres. World Bank Group, Washington, DC 2007–12; mem. Bd of Dirs Temasek Holdings (sovereign wealth fund of Singapore), Alliance Capital, Said Capital, German Marshall Fund US; Dir Aspen Inst. Strategy Group; mem. Int. Advisory Bd Rolls-Royce Group; Kt Commdr's Cross (Germany); Hon. DHumLitt (St Joseph's Coll., Rensselaer, Ind.); Distinguished Service Award, Treasury Dept, Alexander Hamilton Award, State Dept, Department of Defense Medal for Distinguished Public Service, ranked by Forbes magazine amongst The World's Most Powerful People (63rd) 2009, (45th) 2010, (49th) 2011. *Address:* Goldman Sachs, 200 West Street, #200, New York, NY 10282, USA (office). *Telephone:* (212) 902-1000 (office). *Website:* www.goldmansachs.com (office).

ZOGBY, James, BA, PhD; American political analyst and international organization executive; *President, Arab American Institute;* b. 19 Nov. 1945, New York, NY; m. Eileen Patricia McMahon; five c.; ed Le Moyne Coll., Temple Univ.; Pres. Arab American Inst. 1985–; Co-Pres. Builders for Peace 1993; Chair. Forum on Palestinian Economy, Casablanca Econ. Summit 1994; Co-Convenor Nat. Democratic Ethnic Coordinating Cttee; elected to Democratic Nat. Cttee's Exec. Cttee as Rep. of Nat. Democratic Ethnic Coordinating Cttee 1999, Chair. Resolutions Cttee; mem. Bd American Civil Liberties Union, Nat. Immigration Forum, Council on Foreign Relations; mem. Human Rights Watch Middle East Advisory Cttee; currently Sr Analyst, Zogby International; lectured on Middle East Issues, US-Arab relations, and history of Arab American community; Co-founder Palestinian Human Rights Campaign; Co-founder and Exec. Dir American-Arab Anti-Discrimination Cttee; Co-founder and Nat. Endowment for the Humanities Post-doctoral Fellow, Princeton Univ. 1976; Hon. LLD (Le Moyne); Distinguished Public Service Award. *Television:* host of Viewpoint with James Zogby on Abu Dhabi TV and Link TV, USA. *Publications:* books include What Ethnic Americans Really Think, and What Arabs Think: Values, Beliefs and Concerns, Arab Voices: What They Are Saying to Us, and Why it Matters 2010; author of 'Washington Watch' newspaper column 1992–. *Address:* Arab American Institute, 1600 K Street NW, Suite 601, Washington, DC 20006, USA (office). *Telephone:* (202) 429-9210 (office). *Fax:* (202) 429-9214 (office). *E-mail:* jzogby@ aaiusa.org (office). *Website:* www.aaiusa.org (office); www.zogby.com.

ZOHAR, Israel; Israeli artist; b. 7 Feb. 1945, Oktubinsk, USSR; m. 1st Ruth Bregman 1966 (divorced 1974); m. 2nd Arna Meyuhas 1974 (divorced 1982); m. 3rd Wendy Caron 1984; m. 4th Layil Barr; five s. one d.; ed Bezalel Acad. of Art, Jerusalem and with artists A. Yaskil and Ernst Fuchs; lectured at Hebrew Univ. Jerusalem 1979; maj. works include portraits of HRH The Princess of Wales 1990, Henry Catto (fmr US Amb. to UK) 1990, 24ft x 8ft painting of Jacob's Ladder for Music Festival, Exeter Cathedral, UK 1992, portrait of Anne Frank, Music Festival, Bad Kissingen 1992, portrait of Edith Sitwell for Hampstead Festival, London 1995; also writes, adapts and directs plays for theatre including Thomas Mann's Death in Venice (Duke of Cambridge, London), Brecht's The Jewish Wife (Cockpit, London), works by Strindberg, Chekhov, Sartre, Dostoevsky for Café Theatre, London, etc. *Address:* c/o Catto Gallery, 100 Heath Street, London, NW3 1DP, England.

ZOLL, Andrzej, PhD, DHabil; Polish professor of law; *Commissioner for Citizens' Rights;* b. 27 May 1942, Sieniawa; m.; one s.; ed Jagiellonian Univ., Kraków; Asst, Criminal Law Dept, Jagiellonian Univ., Kraków 1964–75, Asst Prof. of Criminal Law 1975–88, Extraordinary Prof. 1988–91, Ordinary Prof. 1991–; Judge, Constitutional Tribunal 1989–97, Pres. 1993–97; Vice-Chair. State Election Comm. 1989, Chair. 1990–93; Chair. Legislation Bd attached to the Prime Minister 1998–2000; Commr for Citizens' Rights 2000–; Commdr's Cross, Order of Polonia Restituta 1997, Great Cross of Merit with Star (Germany) 1997, Golden Star on Ribbon of Order of Merit (Austria) 1997, Great Duke Gedymin Order (Lithuania) 1997; Dr hc (Mainz Univ.) 1996, (Vilnius Univ.) 2003. *Publications:* more than 170 works on penal law, philosophy of law and constitutional law including Materialnoprawna problematyka warunkowego umorzenia postępowania karnego 1973, Okoliczności wyłączające bezprawność czynu 1982, O normie prawnej w prawie karnym 1990, Komentarz do kodeksu karnego (co-author) 1998. *Leisure interests:* mountaineering, classical music, books. *Address:* Commissioner for Citizens' Rights Office, al. Solidarności 77, 00-090 Warsaw, Poland (office). *Telephone:* (22) 5517700 (office). *E-mail:* brpoinf@brpo.gov.pl (office). *Website:* www.brpo.gov.pl (office).

ZOLLER, Peter, PhD; Austrian theoretical physicist and academic; *Professor of Physics, University of Innsbruck; Scientific Director, Institute for Quantum Optics and Quantum Information, Austrian Academy of Sciences;* b. 16 Sept. 1952; m. Johanna Zoller; two s. one d.; ed Gymnasium, Innsbruck, Univ. of Innsbruck; Max Kade Fellow, Univ. of Southern California, Los Angeles, USA 1978–79; Asst Prof., Univ. of Innsbruck 1977–90, Habilitation 1981, tenure 1981–, Prof. of Physics, Inst. for Theoretical Physics 1994–, Head of Inst. 1995–99, Vice-Dean of Studies 2001–04; Scientific Dir Inst. for Quantum Optics and Quantum Information, Austrian Acad. of Sciences, Innsbruck 2003–; Jt Inst. for Lab. Astrophysics (JILA) Visiting Fellow, Univ. of Colorado, USA 1981–82, 1988, Prof. of Physics and JILA Fellow, Jt Inst. for Lab. Astrophysics (JILA) 1991–94, JILA Adjoint Fellow 1994–; Guest Prof., Univ. Paris-Sud, Orsay, France 1986; Chair Prof., Tsinghua Univ., Beijing, People's Repub. of China; Yan Jici Chair Professorship, Univ. of Science and Tech. of China, Heifei 2004; Lorentz-Prof., Leiden Univ. March–June 2005; Guest Prof., Institut Henri Poincaré, Paris 2006; Distinguished Fellow, Max Planck Inst. of Quantum Optics, Garching, Germany 2012–13; Speaker, Sonderforschungsbereich Quantum Control and Measurement, Innsbruck 1999–; mem. Advisory Bds ITAMP, Harvard Univ. 1996–99, Max Planck Inst. for Quantum Optics, Garching 2001–, BEC Inst., Trento, Italy 2003–, Perimeter Inst., Canada 2005, Chinese Nat. Lab., Univ. of Science and Tech. of China 2005–, Arnold Sommerfeld Centre, LMU, Munich 2005–; mem. Int. Advisory Cttee for Inst. of Theoretical Physics, Beijing, Chinese Acad. of Sciences 2005–; Div. Assoc. Ed. Physical Review Letters 1994–98; Ed. Reviews of Modern Physics (Atomic Physics, Quantum Optics and Quantum Information) 1999–2003; Corresp. mem. Austrian Acad. of Sciences 1999–2001, mem. 2001–; mem. Austrian Physical Soc., Optical Soc. of America, NAS 2008, Royal Netherlands Acad. of Arts and Sciences 2008, Spanish Royal Acad. of Sciences 2009, German Acad. of Sciences Leopoldina 2010, European Acad. of Sciences 2012, Academia Europaea 2013; Fellow, American Physical Soc. 1993; Dr hc (Free Univ. of Amsterdam) 2012; Award of the City of Innsbruck 1981, Ludwig-Boltzmann Award, Austrian Physical Soc. 1983, Wittgenstein Award, Austrian Fed. Ministry of Science and Austrian Science Foundation 1998, Max Born Award, Optical Soc. of America 1998, Schrödinger Prize, Austrian Acad. of Sciences 1998, Sr Humboldt Award 2000, K. Innitzer Award 2001, Loeb Lecturer, Harvard Univ. 2004, Max Planck Medal, German Physical Soc. 2005, Niels Bohr/UNESCO Gold Medal 2005, Sixth Int. Quantum Communication Award 2006, Dirac Medal 2006, Dirac Medal, ICTP Trieste 2006, BBVA Foundation Frontiers of Knowledge Award in Basic Sciences (Spain) 2008, Wissenschaftspreis der Stiftung Südtiroler Sparkasse 2009, Benjamin Franklin Medal, Franklin Inst. 2010, Blaise Pascal Medal, European Acad. of Sciences 2011, Hamburg Prize for Theoretical Physics 2011, ERC Synergy Grant (shared with I. Bloch, E. Altman and J. Dalibard) 2012, David Ben Gurion Medal 2013, Wolf Prize in Physics (co-recipient) 2013. *Publications:* Quantum Noise, A Handbook of Markovian and Non-Markovian Quantum Stochastic Methods with Applications to Quantum Optics (co-author) 2004; numerous scientific papers in professional journals. *Address:* Institute for Theoretical Physics, University of Innsbruck, Technikerstraße 25, 6020 Innsbruck, Austria (office). *Telephone:* (512) 507-4780 (office). *Fax:* (512) 507-9815 (office). *E-mail:* peter.zoller@uibk.ac.at (office). *Website:* www.uibk.ac.at/th-physik/people/staffdb/354190.xml (office); bozon.uibk .ac.at/qo/zoller (office).

ZOLOTOV, Yuri Alexandrovich, DrChem; Russian chemist; *Principal Researcher, Kurnakov Institute of General and Inorganic Chemistry;* b. 4 Oct. 1932, Vysokovskoe, Moscow Region; m.; one s.; ed Moscow State Univ.; researcher, Deputy Dir, Head of Lab., Inst. of Geochemistry and Analytical Chem. 1958–89; Dir N Kurnakov Inst. of Gen. and Inorganic Chem. 1989–99, currently Prin. Researcher; Distinguished Prof., Moscow Univ.; Corresp. mem., USSR (now Russian) Acad. of Sciences 1970, mem. 1987–; main research in analytical chem., extraction of inorganic compounds, ion chromatography; Hon. Mem. Japan Soc. of Analytical Chem. 1991, Göteborg Royal Soc. of Art and Sciences, Sweden 1999; Dr hc (Kiev) 1994, (Krasnodar) 2002, (Ufa) 2012; Prize of USSR Council of Ministers 1985, USSR State Prize 1972, State Prize of Russia 1991, 2000, Prize of Russian Govt 2010, Hanus Medal, Prague 2012. *Publications:* 49 books, 870 scientific papers. *Leisure interests:* fishing, writing. *Address:* N. Kurnakov Institute of General and Inorganic Chemistry, 31 Leninsky prosp., 119991 Moscow, Russia

(office). *Telephone:* (495) 633-84-92 (office); (499) 132-20-10 (home). *Fax:* (495) 952-34-20 (office). *E-mail:* zolotov@igic.ras.ru (office).

ZONG, Qinghou; Chinese food industry executive; *Chairman and CEO, Hangzhou Wahaha Group;* b. 1945, Hangzhou, Zhejiang Prov.; m. Shi Youzhen; one d.; spent 17 years on Zhejiang state farms; returned to Hangzhou to take marketing position; hired to run sales dept of school-run business in Shangcheng Dist, Hangzhou 1987; launched Wahaha Nutritional Food Factory with two retd teachers to produce children's nutritional drinks 1989, merged with Hangzhou Canning Food Factory to form Hangzhou Wahaha Group Corpn 1991, merged with three cos in Fulin to support construction of Three Gorges area and form Wahaha Fulin Co., entered jt venture with Danone Group to form five new subsidiaries 1996, CEO Wahaha Group (largest beverage co. in China) –2007 (resgnd as Chair. of the jt venture); Del. to NPC 2002–; State Spark Second Prize, State Science Comm. 1992, recognized as a China Man. Master 1994, State Award for Excellent Operation Mans, Wu-Yi Medal, China Fed. of Trade Unions, Award for Nat. Model Worker, Fed. of Trade Unions 1995, Honoured Shuangduikou Excellent Personnel, Zhejiang Prov. 1998, honorary titles include: Nat. Excellent Entrepreneur, Nat. Excellent Manager, Model of Patriotism to Support the Armed Forces, Outstanding Model of Socialism with Chinese Characteristics, The First Chinese Entrepreneurs Entrepreneurship Prize, named by Forbes as China's richest man 2010. *Address:* Hangzhou Wahaha Group, 160 Qingtai Street, Hangzhou 310009, Zhejiang, People's Republic of China (office). *Telephone:* 86032866 (office). *Fax:* 86846000 (office). *E-mail:* whh@wahaha.com.cn (office). *Website:* en.wahaha .com.cn (office).

ZONGO, Tertius, MEconSc; Burkinabè diplomatist, civil servant and academic; b. 18 May 1957, Kougoudgou, Boulkiemdé Prov.; m.; three c.; ed Inst. of Enterprises Admin., Nantes, France; Head of Accounts, Nat. Office of Crops 1983–85, Dir-Gen. 1985–88; Sec.-Gen. Chamber of Commerce, Industry and Crafts 1986; Prof. of Accounting, Business Economy and Financial Analysis, Univ. of Ouagadougou; Chief of Dept Multilateral Co-operation 1988–92; Dir-Gen. of Co-operation, Ministry of Finances and Planning 1992; Gov. of Burkina Faso to World Bank (IBRD), Int. Monetary Fund (IMF), African Devt Bank, Islamic Devt Bank; Minister of Budget and Planning 1996–97, of Economy and Finance 1997–2000; Govt Spokesman 1996–2000; Amb. to USA 2002–07; Prime Minister of Burkina Faso 2007–11 (resgnd), reappointed 13 Jan.–18 April 2011; Kt and Officer of the Nat. Order. *Publications:* numerous contribs to papers on agric. and devt. *Leisure interests:* reading, sports. *Address:* c/o Office of the Prime Minister, 03 BP 7027, Ouagadougou 03, Burkina Faso. *Telephone:* 50-32-48-89. *Website:* www .gouvernement.gov.bf.

ZÖPEL, Christoph, PhD; German politician, economist, publisher and academic; b. 4 July 1943, Gleiwitz; s. of Kurt Zöpel and Martha Zöpel (née Grohla); m. Barbara Rössler 1969; one s. two d.; ed Minden, Westphalia, Free Univ. Berlin, Ruhr Univ., Bochum; mem. SDP 1964–, Deputy Chair. SDP in Landtag 1975–78, mem. Exec. Cttee 1986–95, mem. Presidium 1992–95; City Councillor, Bochum 1969–72; mem. Landtag of Land North Rhine/Westphalia 1972–1990, Minister for Fed. Affairs 1978–80, for Rural and Urban Devt 1980–85, for Urban Devt, Housing and Transport 1985–90; mem. Bundestag 1990–2005, mem. Cttee on Foreign Affairs 1990–99, 2002–05, Deputy Chair. Cttee on the Affairs of the EU 1991–92, Minister of State, Fed. Foreign Office 1999–2005; mem. Parl. Ass. OSCE 1994–99; Deputy Mem. N Atlantic Ass. 1998–99; Chair. Cttee on the Economy, Social Cohesion and the Environment, Socialist Int. 2000–; Prof., German-Jordanian Univ., Amman; Assoc. Prof., EBZ Business School, Univ. of Applied Sciences; Hon. Prof., Technische Universität Dortmund. *Publications include:* Weltstadt Ruhr, Essen 2005, Politik mit 9 Milliarden Menschen in einer Weltgesellschaft, Berlin 2008. *Address:* Kastanienweg 4, 44799 Bochum, Germany (home). *Telephone:* (30) 20654830 (office); (234) 30765798 (home). *Fax:* (30) 97005061 (office). *E-mail:* christoph.zoepel@t-online.de (office). *Website:* www.christoph-zoepel.de.

ZORAMTHANGA, Shri Pu, BA; Indian politician; *President, Mizo National Front;* b. 13 July 1944, Samthang village; s. of Darphunga Zoramthanga and Vanhnuaichhingi Zoramthanga; m. Roneihsangi Rohlira 1988; one s. one d.; ed Champhai Gandhi Memorial High School and Imphal D.M. Coll., Manipur; Sec. to Pres. Pu Laldenga, Leader of Mizo Nat. Front 1969–75, exiled with Pu Laldenga to Pakistan 1972–76, Foreign Rep. 1972–76; Minister of Finance and Educ., Mizoram State Govt 1987–90; Pres. Mizo Nat. Front 1990–; Chief Minister of Mizoram 1998–2008. *Address:* Mizo National Front, Aizawl 796 001, India (office).

ZORE, Edward J., BS, MS; American insurance industry executive; b. 5 July 1945, Milwaukee, Wis.; m. Diane Zore (neé Widemshek) 1967; two d.; ed Univ. of Wisconsin-Milwaukee; joined Investment Dept, Northwestern Mutual 1969, various positions 1969–90, Chief Investment Officer 1990–98, Chief Financial Officer 1995–98, elected Exec. Vice-Pres. 1995, apptd Head of Life and Disability Insurance Operations 1998, mem. Bd Trustees 2000–, Pres. 2000–01, Chair. and CEO 2001–10 (retd), Dir, Northwestern Mutual Wealth Man. Co., Northwestern Investment Man. Co., Northwestern Long Term Care Insurance Co., Northwestern International Holdings, Inc., Northwestern Mutual Series Fund, Northwestern Mutual Foundation, Chair. Russell Investment Group, Tacoma, Wash. (subsidiary of Northwestern Mutual); mem. Bd of Dirs Frank Russell Co., Manpower Inc., American Council of Life Insurers; mem. The Business Roundtable and Conf. Bd; mem. Bd Children's Hosp. of Wis. Inc., Competitive Wis., Froedtert Health System, Greater Milwaukee Cttee, Medical Coll. of Wis., Metropolitan Milwaukee Asscn of Commerce, Susan G. Komen Breast Cancer Foundation Inc., United Performing Arts Fund, United Way, Wisconsin Policy Research Inst.; mem. Advisory Bd Zilber Neighborhood Initiative; Trustee YMCA of Metropolitan Milwaukee; Hon. mem. Bd Million Dollar Round Table Foundation. *Address:* Northwestern Mutual, 720 East Wisconsin Avenue, Milwaukee, WI 53202-4797, USA (office). *Telephone:* (414) 271-1444 (office). *Fax:* (414) 299-7022 (office). *E-mail:* info@northwesternmutual.com (office). *Website:* www .northwesternmutual.com (office).

ZORIN, Leonid Genrikhovich; Russian playwright and writer; b. 3 Nov. 1924, Baku, Azerbaijan; s. of Genrikh Zorin and Polina Zorin; m. 1st 1951 (deceased); m. 2nd Tatjana Pospelova 1985; one s.; ed Azerbaijan State Univ., M. Gorky Inst. of Literature in Moscow; with Baku Russian Drama Theatre; later freelance, mem. USSR Union of Writers 1941–, Int. PEN Club, Russian PEN Centre, Russian Acad.

of Cinema, Science and the Arts; Grand Prix for the best film script Grandmaster (Festival in Kranje, Yugoslavia), Golden Medal for filmscript Peace to the Newcomer, Venice Film Festival 1961, Prize of All-Union Contest of Playwrights Revival of Russia (for Moscow Nest) 1995, (for Lusgan) 1997, Laureate of Apollon Igoziev-Price 2003, Prize of the Russian Authors Org. 2006. *Plays:* more than 49 produced in 16 countries, including Decembrists, Kind Men, The Coronation, The Deck, Warsaw Melody, The Copper Grandmother, The Quotation, The Perished Plot, The Infidelity, The Carnival, The Moscow Nest, Lusgan, The Warsaw Melody 1997, Tsar's Hunt, Roman Comedy, The Invisibles 1999, The Maniac 2000, The Misprint 2001, The Outcome 2002, The Detectives 2003. *Film scripts:* 15 including A Man from Nowhere, The Law, Peace to the Newcomer, Grandmaster, Transit, The Friends and the Years, Pokrovskye Gates, Tsar's Hunt, Hard Sand 2002. *Publications:* (novels and short stories) Old Manuscript 1983, Wanderer 1987, The Topic of the Day 1992, Proscenium 1997, The Plots 1998, The Teetotaller (Banner Prize, Apollon Grigorjev Prize) 2001, The Auction (collection of novels and stories) 2001, Whip (Banner Prize) 2002, Jupiter 2002, Oblivion 2004; numerous essays; Theatre Fantasy (collection of plays) 1974, Selected Plays (2 vols) 1986, The Green Notebooks (collection of essays etc.), The Curtain of the Millennium (collection of later plays) 2002, The Sansara (novel) 2004, The Will of Yzand (humorous book) 2005, The Prose (collection of novels and short stories) in two vols, The Parting March (humorous book) 2005, The National Idea 2006, The Letters from Petersburg 2006. *Leisure interests:* reading, chess. *Address:* Krasnoarmeyskaya str. 21, Apt. 73, 125319 Moscow, Russia. *Telephone:* (495) 151-43-33 (home).

ZORIN, Vladimir Yuryevich; Russian politician; b. 9 April 1948, Moscow; m.; three s. one d.; ed Tashkent Inst. of Nat. Econs, Acad. of Public Sciences at Cen. CP Cttee; fmr teacher; People's Deputy of Uzbekistan 1990, Deputy Perm. Rep., Cabinet of Ministers, Repub. of Uzbekistan to Govts of USSR and Russian Fed. 1991–93; fmr consultant on finance, regional policy and investments in various commercial cos; Deputy, then First Deputy Head Territorial Dept of Fed. Organs of Exec. Power, Chechen Repub.; Co-ordinator Exec. Cttee Int. Movt of Democratic Reforms on Relationship with CIS States 1991–93; mem. State Duma 1995–99; Deputy Head of Govt Del. on Peace Talks in Chechnya 1996; Chair. Perm. Cttee on Problems of Fed. and Regional Policy; Pres. Russian Asscn of Theory and Modelling of Int. Relations; mem. Political Council of Our Home is Russia Movt 1994–99; Deputy Rep. Plenipotentiary of Russian Pres. to Volga Fed. Dist 2000–01, Minister of Fed. Problems, Nat. and Migration Policy, then Minister without Portfolio, in charge of Nationalities Policy 2002–04. *Publications:* Chechen Conflict (1991–96): Estimate, Analysis and Ways of Solution, and numerous other publs on politics, history and sociology. *Leisure interests:* chess, painting, Russian folk and classical music, table tennis. *Address:* c/o Office of the Government, Krasnopresnenskaya nab. 2, 103274 Moscow, Russia (office).

ZORKIN, Valerii Dmitrievich, DJur; Russian lawyer, academic and judge; *Chairman, Constitutional Court;* b. 18 Feb. 1943, Maritime (Primorskii) Krai; widower; one d.; ed Faculty of Law, Moscow State Univ.; Sr Lecturer in Law, Moscow State Univ. 1964–67, Asst Prof. 1967–79; Prof. of Constitutional Law and Theory of State, Law Acad. of the USSR Ministry of Internal Affairs 1979–86, Prof. of Public Legal Disciplines 1986–; led group of experts on Constitutional Comm. 1990–91; Judge, Constitutional Court Oct. 1991, Chair. Nov. 1991–93 (resgnd), re-elected 2003, 2006–; Merited Lawyer of the Russian Fed. 2000, Order of Merit for the Fatherland (Third Class) 2008, (Second Class) 2011; Diploma of the Pres. of the Russian Fed. 2008. *Address:* Constitutional Court of the Russian Federation (Konstitutsionnyi Sud Rossiiskoi Federatsii), 190000 St Petersburg, pl. Dekabristov 1, Russia (office). *Telephone:* (812) 404-33-11 (office). *E-mail:* ksrf@ksrf.ru (office). *Website:* www.ksrf.ru (office).

ZORRILLA, Concepción (China); Uruguayan actress, director and producer; b. 14 March 1922, Montevideo; d. of José Luis Zorrilla de San Martin; ed Royal Acad. of Dramatic Art, London, UK; worked with Ars Pulchra group, Uruguayan Ind. Theatre; later worked as journalist and as actress and Dir Nat. Theatre of Uruguay; f. with Antonio Larreta and Enrique Guarnero, Theatre of City of Montevideo 1961; directed show Canciones para mirar, New York 1965 and later in Buenos Aires; staged Jacobo Langsner's El Tobogán and Neil Simon's Plaza Suite, Montevideo 1969; has made several films in Argentina; Dir, Como en casa (TV show); newscaster, Radio Belgrano; noted theatrical appearances including one-woman show Hola, hola, un, dos, tres (toured Argentina, Venezuela and USA) and as Emily in Spanish-language version of William Luce's The Belle of Amherst throughout Latin America and in USA 1981; Chevalier, Légion d'honneur 2008; Ciudadano Ilustre de la Ciudad de Buenos Aires 2004. *Films include:* Heroína (Heroine) 1972, Triángulo de cuatro (Triangle of Four) 1975, Darse cuenta (Best Actress, Havana Film Festival) 1984, Contar hasta diez (Count to Ten) 1985, Pobre mariposa (Poor Butterfly) 1986, El Verano del potro (Summer of the Colt) 1991, La Peste (The Plague) 1992, Fotos del alma (Pictures of the Soul) 1995, Conversaciones con mamá (Silver St George for Best Actress, Moscow Int. Film Festival) 2004, Elsa y Fred (Silver Condor for Best Actress, Argentinean Film Critics Asscn) 2005, Tres de corazones 2007, Tocar el cielo 2007, Sangre del pacífico 2008. *Television includes:* Leandro Leiva, un soñador 1995, Ricos y famosos 1997, El Arcángel 1997, Gasoleros 1998, Piel naranja años después 2004, Los Roldán 2004, Mujeres asesinas 2005, Vidas robadas 2008.

ZOU, Yu; Chinese lawyer and government official; b. 3 Oct. 1922, Guangdong Prov.; m. Xue Xialiang 1953; three s. two d.; ed Inst. of Shaanbei; Deputy Dir Public Security Dept Jilin City 1938–49; Deputy Garrison Commdr Shanton Dist 1949–53; Political Commissar Shanton Mil. Sub-Command 1957–75; First Deputy Dir Guangdong Prov. Public Security Dept, Commr Shanton Dist, Leader Guangdong Prov. Govt 1950–77; Dir State Seismological Bureau, State Council 1978–80; Head China Acad. of Sciences 1978–80; Vice-Minister of Justice 1982–83, Minister 1983–88; Pres. Nat. Lawyers Asscn 1986–91; Pres. China Univ. of Political Science and Law 1985–88; mem. Standing Cttee, NPC 1983–88; Deputy Dir Internal and Judicial Affairs Cttee NPC 1988–93; Pres. China Law Soc. 1991–97; mem. Exec. Cttee LAWASIA 1991, Vice-Pres. 1993; Adviser Internal and Judicial Affairs Cttee. *Publications:* The Strategic Meaning of Spreading Basic Legal Knowledge among the People 1986, The Social Position and Meaning of Civil Conciliation 1987, Dictionary of Jurisprudence 1991. *Leisure interests:* music, painting, calligraphy. *Address:* No. 6 Nam Dajie, Xizhimen, Beijing 100035, People's Republic of China. *Telephone:* (10) 6033363. *Fax:* (10) 6032251.

ZOU'BI, Moneef Rafe' Abdel-Hamid, BEng, MSc, PhD; Jordanian engineer and scientific researcher; *Director-General, Islamic World Academy of Sciences;* b. 30 Dec. 1963, Amman; s. of Rafe' Abdul Hamid Zou'bi and Wadha Sharif Zou'bi; m. Dr Basma A. S. Dajani; two s. one d.; ed Bishop's School, Amman, Beeston Coll., Nottingham, UK, Univs of Brighton and Loughborough, UK, Univ. of Malaya, Kuala Lumpur, Malaysia; Resident Engineer, Jordan Royal Corps of Engineers 1988–90; Tech. Affairs Officer, Islamic World Acad. of Sciences 1990–91, Tech. Affairs Dir 1991–95, Deputy Exec. Dir 1995–98, Dir-Gen. 1998–, Chief Ed. Newsletter of the Islamic Acad. of Sciences; Grad. mem. ICE (UK), Inst. of Structural Engineers (UK); mem. Asscn of Engineers (Jordan), Licensing Execs Soc., Jordan Computer Soc., Jordanian Friends of Archaeology Asscn, Arab Youth Forum, Royal Automobile Club of Jordan, US-Islamic World Forum, Rosenberg Int. Water Forum; Hon. Prof., East Kazakhstan State Univ. 2012, Tatarstan Acad. of Sciences Medal 2007, CICA Medal 2012. *Publications include:* Health, Nutrition and Development in the Islamic World (co-author) 1995, Water in the Islamic World (co-author) 1995, An Overview of the Islamic Academy of Sciences 1999, Science Education and Technology Management in the Islamic World (co-author) 2000, Personalities Noble (ed.) 2000, Information Technology for Development in the Islamic World (co-author) 2001, Biotechnology and Genetic Engineering for Development in the Islamic World (co-author) 2004, Materials Science and Technology and Culture of Science (co-author) 2004, Islamic World Academy of Sciences Outreach 2005, Energy for Sustainable Development (co-ed.), Science and Technology for Socioeconomic Developemnt (co-ed.) 2006, Higher Education Excellence (co-ed.) 2009; numerous specialist articles. *Leisure interests:* walking, photography, calligraphy, travel, cinema, reading. *Address:* Islamic World Academy of Sciences, PO Box 830036, Amman 11183 (office); 54 Oqba Bin Nafe' Street, Jabal Amman, Fourth Circle, Jordan (home). *Telephone:* (6) 5522104 (office); (6) 5932043 (home). *Fax:* (6) 5511803 (office). *E-mail:* ias@go.com.jo (office); mrzoubi@yahoo.com (home). *Website:* iasworld.org (office).

ZOUIOUECHE, Nazim Charif Eddine; Algerian engineer and oil company executive; *Chairman, Medex Petroleum;* b. 19 Feb. 1940, Algiers; m. Fariel Essid 1971; two s.; ed Ecole Nat Supérieure des Télécommunications, Ecole Nat. Supérieure du Pétrole, Paris; telecommunications engineer, Ministry of Telecommunications 1965–68; production engineer, Elf/Aquitaine 1968–71; Man. Hassi-Messaoud Dist 1971–76; Dir Production Div. Sonatrach 1976–79, Exec. Vice-Pres. and Man. Dir Sonatrach, in charge of Hydrocarbons Div. 1979–85, CEO Transmediterranean Pipeline Co. 1985–93, Chief of Staff Sonatrach 1994–95, Dir-Gen. 1995–98; Chair. Observatoire Méditerranéen pour l'Energie 1995–97; currently Chair. Medex Petroleum; mem. Bd Alfor Drilling Co. (SEDCO/Sonatrach Jt co.) 1977–82. *Leisure interests:* bridge, tennis, horse riding, jogging. *Address:* Medex Petroleum Ltd, Tour de l'Horloge, 4 place Louis Armand, 75603 Paris Cedex 12, France. *Telephone:* 1-73-02-03-55. *Fax:* 1-72-76-25-99. *E-mail:* contact@medexoil.com.

ZOUMARA, Côme; Central African Republic government official; ed École des hautes études internationales, Paris; fmr Adviser to Pres. on Global Defence and Coordinator of Nat. Comm. on Disarmament, Demobilization and Rehabilitation of Ex-Fighters of Central African Repub.; Minister of Foreign and Francophone Affairs and Regional Integration 2006. *Address:* c/o Ministry of Foreign and Francophone Affairs and Regional Integration, Bangui, Central African Republic (office).

ZOUMBOULAKIS, Petros I.; Greek artist, stage designer and professor of plastic arts; b. 19 April 1937, Athens; ed Polytechnic School of Athens; participant in numerous group exhbns in Greece, including Nat. Gallery; work also shown in group exhbns abroad including São Paulo Bienal 1969, Int. Exhbn of Visual Arts, Moscow 1988, 5th Int. Biennale, Cairo 1994, 1st Int. Biennale of Art (CIAC), Rome 1995, Plein Air, Varna 1999, 3ème Biennale Méditerranéene des Arts de la Ville de Tunis 2004; designer of scenery and costumes for both theatre and cinema; illustrator of textbooks used in Greek schools; teacher in applied arts, drawing, colour and stage design, Doxiadis School of Interior Design 1964–86; works in Nat. Gallery, Ministry of Educ. Collection and many public and pvt. collections at home and abroad; Acad. Award, Acad. of Arts-Letters-Sciences of Greece 2011. *Address:* Tsimiski 2, 11471 Athens (Studio); Evrou 18-20, 15234 Athens, Greece (home). *Telephone:* (1) 3630028 (Studio); (1) 6842088 (home). *Fax:* (1) 3630028 (office). *E-mail:* zoubmar@yahoo.gr (home).

ZSÁMBÉKI, Gábor; Hungarian theatrical manager and director; *Director, Katona József Theatre;* b. 30 Dec. 1943, Pécs; s. of János Zsámbéki and Judit Almásy; two d.; ed Faculty of Directing, Budapest Acad. of Dramatic Art and Film Art; Gen. Man. Csiky Gergely Theatre, Kaposvár 1974–78; Prof., Faculty of Acting and Directing, Budapest Acad. of Dramatic Art and Film Art 1978–; Head Dir, Budapest Nat. Theatre 1978–82; Art Dir Katona József Theatre, Budapest 1982–89, Gen. Man. and Stage Dir 1989; Stage Dir Theater Tribühne, Stuttgart 1988–2002, Katona József Theatre, Budapest 2003–; Pres. Union des Théâtres de l'Europe, Paris 1998–2002; mem. MITOS21; Chevalier, Ordre des Arts et des Lettres 2004; BITEF Prize (for The Government Inspector) 1989, French Critics' Prize for Best Foreign Production (for Ubu Roi, Théâtre de l'Odéon, Paris) 1990, Best Foreign Production (for The Government Inspector), Caracas Int. Festival 1990, Merited Artist of the Hungarian Repub., Kossuth Prize 1988, and other awards. *Productions:* about 150, including classics (Goldoni, Shakespeare, Gogol, Chekhov etc.), modern works (Jarry, Wesker, Gombrowicz) and world premières of contemporary Hungarian plays (Halleluyah by Kornis, The Imposter, Chicken-head, Bump by Spiró); productions in Cuba, Czechoslovakia, Finland, Germany, Israel, Norway. *Address:* Petőfi s. u. 6, 1052 Budapest, Hungary (office). *Telephone:* (1) 318-3269 (office). *Fax:* (1) 318-3952 (office). *E-mail:* katona@elender.hu (office). *Website:* www.katonajozsefszinhaz.hu (office).

ZU GUTTENBERG, Karl-Theodor; German politician; b. 5 Dec. 1971, Munich; m.; two d.; ed Univ. of Bayreuth; fmr freelance journalist for Die Welt; mem. Kulmbach Dist Council 2002; mem. Bundestag (Christian Social Union—CSU) 2002–; mem. CSU Gen. Secr. 2008–09; Fed. Minister of Econs and Tech. 2009, of Defence 2009–11 (resgnd); fmr Man. Pnr, Guttenberg GmbH, Munich. *Address:* Fritz-Hornschuch-Str. 13, 95326 Kulmbach, Germany (office). *E-mail:* kt@zuguttenberg.de. *Website:* www.zuguttenberg.de.

ZUAITER, Abbas Farouq, BSBA; American//Palestinian business executive; m. Samar Zuaiter; ed Georgetown Univ., USA; Chief Financial Officer and Head of Fixed Income, Currency and Commodity Trading, AFN Associates, Inc. 1991–94; Assurance and Business Advisory Partner, PricewaterhouseCoopers LLP 1992–2002; COO and Chief Financial Officer, Soros Fund Management 2002–12; Man. mem. Zuaiter Capital Holdings, LLC; currently adviser to the Soros family; mem. Arab Fund for Arts and Culture. *Address:* Zuaiter Capital Holdings, LLC, 888 7th Avenue, New York, NY 10106, USA (office). *Telephone:* (212) 586-3800 (office).

ZUBAK, Krešimir; Bosnia and Herzegovina politician; *Chairman, New Croatian Initiative;* b. 29 Nov. 1947, Doboj; m.; two c.; ed Sarajevo Univ.; worked in judicial bodies of Bosnia and Herzegovina; Pres. of Higher Court in Doboj; mem. del. of Croatian population to sign the Washington Agreement and Vienna Agreement; First Pres. of Fed. of Bosnia and Croatia 1994–97; fmr Croatian Co-Chair. of Bosnia and Herzegovina; Chair. New Croatian Initiative (Nova Hrvatska Inicijativa—NHI) following split from Croat Democratic Union of Bosnia and Herzegovina (HDZBiH) 1998–. *Address:* Nova Hrvatska Inicijativa, Sime Milutinovića 2/II, Sarajevo, Bosnia and Herzegovina (office). *Telephone:* (33) 214602 (office). *Fax:* (33) 214603 (office). *E-mail:* nhi@nhi.ba (office).

ZUBAKIN, Semen Ivanovich; Russian politician; b. 4 May 1952, Verkh-Uimon; m.; two s. one d.; ed All-Union Inst. of Finance and Econs; Asst forestry warden Altai Territory 1972–74; inspector, then Sr Economist, Deputy Head Dept of State Insurance, Gorno-Altai Autonomous Territory 1976–86; inspector, then head of div., Deputy Chair. Cttee on Finance Altai Repub. 1986–91; Deputy Supreme Soviet, Altai Repub.; Chair. Perm. Comm. on Problems of Econ. Reform and Property 1992, Deputy State Ass. 1993; Chief Controller Control Dept, Ministry of Finance of Russian Fed. for Altai Repub. 1994; Chair. of Govt Altai Repub. 1997–2001; mem. State Duma 1995–97; mem. Council of Fed., Russian Fed. 1997–2001; Chair. Russia's Democratic Choice Party, Altai Repub. Div. 1997–. *Address:* c/o Government of Altai Republic, E. Palkina str. 1, 659700 Gozno-Altaisk, Russia (office).

ZUBAKOV, Vice-Adm. Yurii Antonovich; Russian politician and diplomatist; *Deputy Secretary, National Security Council;* b. 27 Nov. 1943, Chita; s. of Anton Vasilievich Zubakov and Maria Fyoderovna Zubakov; m. Tatiana Michailovna; one s. one d.; ed KGB Higher School; on staff USSR KGB 1966–89; Deputy Head of sector Cen. CPSU Cttee 1989–90; on staff USSR Security Council 1990–91; Deputy Dir Foreign Intelligence Service USSR (later Russia) 1991–96; Deputy Minister of Foreign Affairs 1996–98; Minister 1998–99; Amb. to Lithuania 2000–03, to Moldova 2003–04; Deputy Sec. Nat. Security Council 2004–. *Leisure interests:* classical music, theatre. *Address:* National Security Council, 103132 Moscow, Ipat'yevski per. 4/10, Russia.

ZUBEIR WAKO, HE Cardinal Gabriel; Sudanese ecclesiastic; *Archbishop of Khartoum;* b. 27 Feb. 1941, Mboro; ed St Paul's Nat. Major Seminary, Tore River, Pontifical Urban Univ. and Pontifical Lateran Univ., Rome, Italy; ordained priest 1963; Bishop of Wau 1974–79; Coadjutor Archbishop of Khartoum 1979–81; Archbishop of Khartoum 1981–; cr. Cardinal (Cardinal Priest of Sant'Atanasio a Via Tiburtina) 2003; participated in Papal Conclave 2005, 2013. *Address:* PO Box 49, 11111 Khartoum, Sudan (office). *Telephone:* (11) 782174 (office); (11) 780939 (office). *Fax:* (11) 783518 (office).

ZUBERBÜHLER, Daniel; Swiss lawyer and banking regulator; b. 5 Oct. 1948, Bern; m. Lorna Austin; one d., three s.; ed Univ. of Berne; Legal Officer, Eidgenössische Bankenkommission (Swiss Fed. Banking Comm.) 1976–77, Head of Legal Service 1977–86, Vice-Dir 1986–88, Deputy Dir 1988–96, Dir 1996–2008; mem. Group of Experts for amendment of Swiss Penal Code on money laundering 1988–90, Financial Action Task Force on money laundering 1989–94, Tripartite Group of Banking, Securities and Insurance supervisors 1993–95, Working Party 3 of Int. Org. of Securities Comm. (IOSCO) 1990–96, Basel Cttee on Banking Supervision, BIS 1996–2010, Tech. Cttee of IOSCO 2009–11, Financial Stability Bd Standing Cttee on Supervisory and Regulatory Co-operation; Vice-Chair. Swiss Financial Market Supervisory Authority (FINMA) 2009–11; Sr Financial Consultant, KPMG Switzerland 2012–13; mem. Bd of Dirs, Banca Popolare di Sondrio (Suisse), EFG International. *Leisure interests:* jogging, cycling, skiing, listening to modern jazz, political cabaret. *Address:* Sonnenbergstrasse 3, 3013 Berne, Switzerland. *Telephone:* (78) 7104874. *E-mail:* d.zuberbuehler@hispeed.ch.

ZUBKOV, Viktor Alekseyevich, PhD; Russian government official and business executive; *Chairman, OAO Gazprom;* b. 15 Sept. 1941, Arbat village, Kushvinskii Dist, Sverdlovsk Oblast; m.; one d.; ed Leningrad (now St Petersburg) Agricultural Inst.; began career in state farm network, Leningrad Oblast including Gen. Dir Pervomaiskoye Sovkhoz Union 1967–85; various roles within CP including First Sec. Priozersk Cttee and First Deputy Chair. Leningrad regional Cttee 1985–91; Deputy Chair. External Relations Cttee, St Petersburg City Council 1992–93; Deputy Chair. Fed. Tax Service and Head, State Tax Inspectorate, St Petersburg 1993–99; Deputy Minister for Tax 1999–2001; Deputy Minister of Finance 2001–04; Chair. Financial Monitoring Service, Ministry of Finance 2004–07; Chair. of the Govt (Prime Minister) 2007–08, (Acting) 7–8 May 2012, First Deputy Chair. of the Govt (First Deputy Prime Minister) 2008–12; Russian Special Presidential Rep. for Co-operation with Gas Exporting Countries Forum 2012–; Chair. OAO Gazprom 2008–, Chair. Man. Cttee and Dir Gen. Gazprom Gazomotornoye Toplivo 2012–14; Honoured Economist of the Russian Fed. 2001, Hon. Citizen of the Leningrad Region 2009; Ceremonial dagger, Order of the Badge of Honour 1975, Order of the Red Banner of Labour 1981, Medal 'Veteran of Labour' 1986, Order of Merit for the Fatherland (Fourth Class) 2000, (Third Class) 2006, (Second Class) 2008, Order of Holy Prince Daniel of Moscow (First Class) (Russian Orthodox Church) 2011; Diploma of the Govt of the Russian Fed. 1998, ranked 84th in a survey of Russia's most influential politicians 2006. *Address:* OAO Gazprom, ul. Nametkina 16, V-420, GSP-7, 117997 Moscow, Russia (office). *Telephone:* (495) 719-30-01 (office). *Fax:* (495) 719-83-33 (office). *E-mail:* gazprom@gazprom.ru (office). *Website:* www.gazprom.com (office).

ZUCKER, Jeffrey (Jeff), BA; American television executive; *President, CNN Worldwide;* b. 9 April 1965, Homestead, Fla; s. of Arlene Zucker; m. Caryn Stephanie Zucker (née Nathanson) 1996; two s. one d.; ed North Miami Sr High School, Harvard Coll.; became ed. school paper and teenage freelance reporter for

The Miami Herald newpaper while a teenager attending N Miami Sr High School; participated in Northwestern Univ. Nat. High School Inst. Program for journalism; Pres. The Harvard Crimson 1985–86; hired by NBC to research material for coverage of Olympic Games in Seoul, S Korea 1988; field producer for The Today Show 1989, Exec. Producer 1992–93, 1994–2000; Pres. NBC Entertainment 2000–03, Pres. NBC Entertainment, News & Cable Group 2003–04, Pres. NBC Universal Television Group (following merger with Vivendi Universal) 2004–05, CEO NBC Universal Television Group 2005–07, CEO NBC Universal Inc. 2007–10; Pres. CNN Worldwide Jan. 2013–. *Address:* CNN Center, 190 Marietta Street NW, Atlanta, GA 30303, USA (office). *Website:* www.cnn.com (office).

ZUCKERBERG, Mark Elliot; American computer scientist and business executive; *Co-Founder and CEO, Facebook, Inc.;* b. 14 May 1984, White Plains, NY; s. of Edward Zuckerberg and Karen Zuckerberg; m. Priscilla Chan 2012; ed Ardsley High School, Phillips Exeter Acad., Harvard Univ.; began programming in middle school; took graduate course in programming at Mercy Coll. mid-1990s; co-f. Facebook (with Harvard classmates Dustin Moskovitz, Eduardo Saverin and Chris Hughes) 2004 and moved to Palo Alto, Calif.; f. Start-up: Education foundation 2010; ranked by Vanity Fair magazine on its list of the Top 100 "most influential people of the Information Age" (23rd) 2009, (first) 2010, chosen as No. 16 in New Statesman's annual survey of the world's 50 most influential figures 2010, ranked by Forbes magazine amongst The World's Most Powerful People (40th) 2010, (ninth) 2011, (25th) 2012, (24th) 2013, TIME magazine's Person of the Year 2010. *Achievements include:* became world's youngest billionaire. *Address:* Facebook, Inc., 1601 South California Avenue, Palo Alto, CA 94304, USA (office). *Telephone:* (650) 543-4800 (office). *Fax:* (650) 543-4801 (office). *Website:* www .facebook.com/markzuckerberg (office).

ZUCKERMAN, Mortimer (Mort) Benjamin, BA, LLM, MBA; American (b. Canadian) real estate developer, publisher and editor; *Chairman and Editor-in-Chief, US News and World Report, L.P.;* b. 4 June 1937, Montreal, Québec; s. of Abraham Zuckerman and Esther Zuckerman; ed McGill Univ., Pennsylvania Univ., Harvard Univ.; Sr Vice-Pres. Cabot, Cabot and Forbes 1965–69; Lecturer, then Assoc. Prof., Harvard Univ. Grad. School of Design 1966–74; Visiting Lecturer, Yale Univ. 1967–69; Chair. Boston Properties Co. 1970–; Dir RET Income Foundation 1976–79, Property Capital Trust Co. 1979–80; Pres., Chair. Atlantic Monthly Co., Boston 1980–; Chair. and Ed.-in-Chief US News and World Report 1984–; Propr, Chair. and Co-Publisher, New York Daily News. *Address:* US News and World Report L.P., 450 West 33rd Street, 11th Floor, New York, NY 10001 (office); Boston Properties, 800 Boylston Street at the Prudential Center, Boston, MA 02199-8103, USA (office). *Telephone:* (212) 716-6800 (office). *Website:* www.usnews.com (office); www.bostonproperties.com (office).

ZUGAZA MIRANDA, Miguel; Spanish museum director; *Director, Prado Museum;* b. 1964, Durango, Vizcaya; ed Universidad Complutense de Madrid; Deputy Dir Reina Sofia Museum of Contemporary Art, Madrid, then Dir 1994–96; Dir Museum of Fine Arts, Bilbao 1996–2002; Dir Prado Museum, Madrid 2002–. *Address:* Museo del Prado, Sede Administrativa, c/ Ruiz de Alarcón 23, 28014 Madrid, Spain (office). *Telephone:* (91) 3302800 (office). *Fax:* (91) 3302857 (office). *E-mail:* direccion.museo@museodelprado.es (office). *Website:* www.museodelprado .es (office).

ŽUGIĆ, Radoje, MEconSc, PhD; Montenegrin economist, politician and central banker; *Minister of Finance;* b. 3 April 1961, Novakovići, Žabljak; m.; three c.; ed Univ. of Podgorica, Univ. of Belgrade; Financial Dir Auto-Moto Asscn of Montenegro 1986; Sec., Directorate of Public Revenues 1992–96; Dir for payment system operations in Montenegro, Podgorica Br., ZOP (Clearing and Payments Agency) 1999–2001; Acting Dir Pension and Disability Insurance Fund 2004–2005, Dir 2005; fmr Deputy Dir-Gen. for Payment System Operations, Central Bank of Montenegro, Gov. 2010–12; Minister of Finance 2012–; Coordinator, Interbank Cttee for Payment System Reform; fmr mem. Parl. of Montenegro and Parl. of State Union of Serbia and Montenegro; fmr Dir Podgorička Banka, Prva Banka Crne Gore; fmr Chair. Servisimport, Central Depositary Agency, Lovćen Insurance. *Address:* Ministry of Finance, 81000 Podgorica, Stanka Dragojevića 2, Montenegro (office). *Telephone:* (20) 403105 (office). *Fax:* (20) 224450 (office). *E-mail:* mf@mif.gov.me (office). *Website:* wwww .mf.gov.me (office).

ZUHUROV, Shukurjon; Tajikistani engineer and politician; *President, Assembly of Representatives (Majlisi Namoyandagon);* b. 16 April 1954, Panj Dist, Khatlon Oblast; m.; five c.; ed Moscow Inst. of Land Use Planning Engineers, Russian Acad. of Public Admin; began career as engineer and geodesist, Khatlon Oblast; mem. Ass. of Reps (Majlisi Namoyandagon) for Qubodiyon Dist 2005–06, Pres. Ass. of Reps 2010–; Minister of Labour and Social Security 2006–10; mem. People's Democratic Party of Tajikistan (Xizbi Xalkii Demokratii Tojikston); Award of Supreme Council of Tajikistan 1985, Order of Friendship 1998, Order of Honour. *Address:* Office of the President, Majlisi Namoyandagon (Assembly of Representatives), 734051 Dushanbe, Xiyoboni Rudaki 42, Tajikistan (office). *Telephone:* (372) 21-23-66 (office). *Fax:* (372) 21-92-81 (office). *E-mail:* mejparl@parliament .tojikiston.com (office). *Website:* parlament.tj (office).

ZUKERMAN, Pinchas; Israeli violinist, violist and conductor; *Music Director, National Arts Centre Orchestra, Canada;* b. 16 July 1948, Tel-Aviv; s. of Yehuda Zukerman and Miriam Zukerman; m. 1st Eugenia Rich 1968 (divorced); two d.; m. 2nd Tuesday Weld 1985 (divorced); m. 3rd Amanda Forsyth 2004; ed Israel Conservatory, Acad. of Music, Tel-Aviv, Juilliard School of Music, New York with Ivan Galamian; debut in New York with New York Philharmonic 1969, in UK at Brighton Festival 1969; concert and recital performances throughout USA and Europe; debut as conductor, London 1970; appearances as conductor with orchestras world-wide; has performed at Spoleto, Pablo Casals and Edinburgh Festivals; Dir S Bank Summer Music 1978–80; Musical Dir St Paul Chamber Orchestra 1980–87; Prin. Conductor Dallas Symphony Orch. 1993–95 Prin. Guest Conductor Int. Summer Music Festival 1990–95; Music Dir Baltimore Symphony Orchestra Summer MusicFest 1997–99; Music Dir Nat. Arts Centre Orchestra, Canada 1998–; Principal Guest Conductor, Royal Philharmonic Orchestra, London 2009–; Hon. DMus (Brown Univ.) 1989; winner Leventritt Competition 1967, Isaac Stern Award for Artistic Excellence (Nat. Arts Awards) 2002, Grammy Award for Best Chamber Music Performance 1980, Grammy Award for Best Classical

Performance, Instrumental Soloist without Orchestra 1981. *Film soundtracks:* Prince of Tides, Critical Care. *Address:* Kirshbaum Demler & Associates, Inc., 711 West End Avenue, Suite 5KN, New York, NY 10025, USA (office); National Arts Centre Orchestra, 53 Elgin Street, Ottawa, ON K1P 5W1, Canada (office). *E-mail:* info@kirshdem.com (office). *Telephone:* (613) 232-5713 (office). *Website:* www.nac -cna.ca (office).

ZULEEG, Manfred (Friedrich), DJur; German academic and fmr international judge; b. 21 March 1935, Creglingen; s. of Ludwig Zuleeg and Thea Zuleeg (née Ohr); m. Sigrid Feuerhahn 1965; three s. one d.; ed Univs of Erlangen and Hamburg and Bologna Center, Johns Hopkins Univ.; Research Asst, Inst. for Law of the European Communities, Univ. of Cologne 1962–68, Sr Lecturer 1968–71; Prof. of Public Law and Law of the European Communities, Univ. of Bonn 1971–78; Prof. of Public Law, including European and Public Int. Law, Univ. of Frankfurt 1978–88, Jean Monnet Chair of European Law 1998–2003; Judge, Court of Justice, European Communities 1988–94; Research Fellow, Univ. of California, Berkeley 1969–70, Visiting Prof. 1996; Dr hc (Athens). *Publications:* Die Rechtsform der Subventionen 1965, Das Recht der Europäischen Gemeinschaften im innerstaatlichen Bereich 1969, Subventionskontrolle durch Konkurrentenklage 1974, Der rechliche Zusammenhalt der Europäischen Union 2004; contrib. to other works. *Leisure interests:* jogging, mountaineering, literature. *Address:* c/o J. W. Goethe-Universität, Senckenberganlage 31, 60054 Frankfurt am Main, Germany (office).

ZULFA, Mariyam, BA, MBA, PhD; Maldivian lawyer and government official; m.; one s. one d.; ed Univ. of Western Australia, Waikato Univ., Curtin Univ.; fmr Dir Selected Islands Devt, later Dir Non-Formal Educ. Centre; lectured in tourism law, Australia 2009; Man. Partner, Duckham and Co. Lawyers, Malé April–Nov. 2010, currently in pvt. law practise; Minister of Tourism, Arts and Culture 2010–12. *Address:* c/o Ministry of Tourism, Arts and Culture Ghazee Building, 1st Floor, Ameer Ahmed Magu, Malé 20-05, Maldives.

ZULUAGA ESCOBAR, Oscar Iván, BA, MA; Colombian business executive and politician; b. 3 Feb. 1957, Pensilvania, Caldas; ed Liceo de Cervantes, Universidad Javeriana, Univ. of Exeter, UK; elected Councillor in Pensilvania 1988–90, Mayor of Pensilvania 1990–92; Chair. ACESCO SA steel co. 1992–2001; launched campaign for Senate and won one of biggest votes in country 2001; supported candidacy of Alvaro Uribe Velez for Pres. of Colombia, Presidential Sr Advisor 2006–07; Minister of Finance and Public Credit 2007–10; fmr mem. several bds, including Nat. Fed. of Merchants (Federación Nacional de Comerciantes—FENALCO), Colombian Fed. of Metalworkers (Federación Colombiana de Industrias Metalúrgicas—Fedemetal), Colombo-Venezuelan Chamber of Commerce; fmr rep. of Colombian Iron and Steel Industry; fmr Nat. Pres. Asscn Internacionale des Étudiants en Sciences Economiques et Commerciales (AIE-SEC)-COLOMBIA; winner, Concurso Nacional de Tesis Universitarias under the heading 'Portfolio Investment Actions', Nat. Asscn of Financial Insts 1983, honoured as one of "10 Best Young Executives of Colombia", Jr Chamber of Colombia (Bogotá Chapter) 1997, chosen by Congress as Best Minister of the Cabinet 2007, selected as one of five Best Finance Ministers of Latin America. *Address:* c/o Ministry of Finance and Public Credit, Carrera 8A, No. 6-64, Of. 305, Bogotá, DC, Colombia (office).

ZUMA, Jacob; South African politician and head of state; *President;* b. 12 April 1942, Inkandla, KwaZulu-Natal; joined African Nat. Congress (ANC) 1959; mem. Umkhonto WeSizwe 1962 after ANC banned 1960, arrested 1963, sentenced to ten years' imprisonment; helped re-establish ANC underground structures, Natal Prov. 1973–75; left South Africa 1975; mem. ANC Nat. Exec. Cttee 1977, Deputy Chief Rep., Mozambique –1984, Chief Rep. 1984–87; Head of Underground Structures ANC Head Office, Lusaka, Zambia, 1987, Chief Intelligence Dept, mem. political and mil. council mid-1980s; returned to S Africa after legalization of ANC 1990, Chair. South Natal Region 1990, Deputy Sec.-Gen. ANC 1991, Nat. Chair. 1994–97, Deputy Pres. 1997–2007, Pres. 2007–; Deputy Pres. of South Africa 1999–2005; mem. Exec. Cttee Econ. Affairs and Tourism for KwaZulu Natal Gov. 1994–99, Chair. ANC in KwaZulu 1994–, est. and patron KwaZulu Reconstruction and Devt Project Bursary Fund; arrested and charged with rape Dec. 2005, found not guilty May 2006, charges of corruption dropped Sept. 2006, recharged by Nat. Prosecuting Authority, charges ruled invalid Sept. 2008, charges reinstated by court Jan. 2009, charges dropped April 2009; Pres. of South Africa 2009–; Hon. DLitt (Fort Hare Univ.) 2001, Hon. DBA (Univ. of Zululand) 2001, Hon. DPhil (Medical Univ. of Southern Africa) 2001; Nelson Mandela Award for Outstanding Leadership (USA) 1998. *Address:* The Presidency, Union Buildings, West Wing, Government Avenue, Pretoria 0001 (office); African National Congress of South Africa, PO Box 61884, Marshalltown 2107, South Africa (office). *Telephone:* (12) 3005200 (office); (11) 3761000 (office). *Fax:* (12) 3238246 (office); (11) 3761134 (office). *E-mail:* president@po.gov.za (office). *Website:* www.gov.za/president/index .html (office); www.anc.org.za (office).

ZUMTHOR, Peter; Swiss architect; b. 1943, Basel; ed Schule für Gestaltung, Basel, Pratt Inst., USA; apprenticeship in cabinet-making; architect, Dept for the Care and Presentation of Monument, Canton Graubünden 1968; tutor, Univ. of Zurich 1978; pvt. practice, Haldenstein, Graubünden 1979–; Visiting Prof., Southern Calif. Inst. of Architecture, USA 1988; workshop leader, Granz Summer School, Austria 1989; Davis Critic, Tulane Univ., USA 1992; Prof., Acad. of Architecture, Mendriso 1996; Fellow, Bayerische Akad. der Schönen Künste, Germany 2003; Hon. mem. Bund Deutscher Architekten, Germany; Hon. Fellow, American Inst. of Architects 2004; Foreign Hon. Fellow, American Acad. of Arts and Sciences 2009; Dr hc in Architettura (Univ. degli Studi di Ferrara, Italy) 2003; Auszeichnung guter Bauten im Kanton Graubünden 1987, 1994, Heinrich Tessenow Medal, Hanover Tech. Univ., Germany 1989; Gulam 1991, Int. Architecture Prize, Neues Bauen in den Alpen 1992, 1995, Best Building, 10 vor 10 1993, Int. Prize, Stone Architecture, Italy 1995, Erich-Schelling Architecture Prize, Germany 1996, Carlsberg Architecture Prize 1998, Pritzker Prize 2009. *Works include:* Churwalden Elementary School, Graubünden 1983, House Räth, Graubünden 1983, Atelier Zumthor, Graubünden 1986, St Benedict Chapel, Graubünden 1989, Chur Art Museum, Graubünden 1990, Gugalun House, Graubünden 1994, Thermal Baths Vals, Graubünden 1996, Bregenz Art Museum, Austria 1997, Topography of Terror, Int. Exhbn and Documentation Centre, Germany 1997, UK 1997, Swiss Pavilion, Expo 2000, Germany 1997–2000,

Kolumba, Erzbischöfliches Diözesanmuseum, Germany 1997–2006, Field Chapel to St Nikolaus von der Flüe, Mechernich, Germany 2007, Kolumba Art Museum, Cologne, Germany 2007, Benedict Chapel, Sumvitg, Graubünden. *Publications include:* Three Concepts 1997, Peter Zumthor Works: Buildings and Projects 1979–1997 (with Helene Binet) 1998, Thinking Architecture 1998, Swiss Sound Box, Kunsthaus Bregenz 1999. *Address:* Süesswingel 20, 7023 Haldenstein, Switzerland (office). *Telephone:* (81) 3549292 (office). *Fax:* (81) 3539293 (office). *E-mail:* arch@zumthor.ch (office).

ZUMWINKEL, Klaus, MS, Dr rer. pol; German logistics industry executive; b. 1943; ed Münster Univ., Wharton Business School, Univ. of Pa, USA; Man. Consultant McKinsey & Co., Düsseldorf and NY 1974–79, Pnr and mem. German Man. Group 1979–84, Sr Pnr and mem. Worldwide Man. Group 1984–85; Chair. Quelle Group, Fürth 1985–90; Chair. Deutsche Bundespost 1990–95; Chair., Bd of Man., Deutsche Post World Net 1990–2008 (resgnd); Chair. Supervisory Bd Deutsche Telekom 2003–08 (resgnd). *Address:* c/o Deutsche Post AG, Charles-de-Gaulle Strasse 20, 53113 Bonn, Germany (office).

ZÚÑIGA CHAVES, Guillermo, MSc; Costa Rican politician; early position with Fitch Cen. America (business ratings co.); served as Costa Rican Gov. at IBRD and Inter-American Devt Bank (IABD); mem. Bd of Dirs Banco Central de Costa Rica, Nat. Comm. on Prevention of Risks and Attention of Emergencies; Minister of Finance 2006–09. *Address:* c/o Ministry of Finance, Edif. Antigüo Banco Anglo, Avda 2a, Calle 3a, San José, Costa Rica (office).

ZUNZI, (pseudonym of Wong Kei-kwan); Chinese political cartoonist; b. 1955, Hong Kong; m. Chan Ya; ed Chinese Univ. of Hong Kong; worked briefly as print journalist before concentrating on political cartoons; works appear in mass-circulation Chinese-language publs in Hong Kong including Ming Pao (daily), People's Monthly, Apple Daily, Next (weekly magazine). *Works include:* Black Material, Grandpa Deng (about Deng Xiao-ping), 100 Caricatures of China, Hong Kong and Taiwan Politicians, A Biography of Mr Legislator, The New Leader. *Address:* Ming Pao Daily News, Block A, Ming Pao Industrial Centre, 15/F, 18 Ka Yip St, Chai Wan, Hong Kong Special Administrative Region, People's Republic of China (office).

ZUQUILANDA, Patricio; Ecuadorean politician; fmr Amb.; Minister of Foreign Affairs 2003–05; Chancellor 2005–07; Chair. Andean Council of Foreign Ministers 2003–04. *Address:* c/o Ministry of Foreign Affairs, Avenida 10 de Agosto y Carrión, Quito, Ecuador (office).

ZUR HAUSEN, Harald, DSc, MD; German virologist, medical scientist and academic; b. 11 March 1936, Gelsenkirchen, Westphalia; ed Gymnasium in Vechta, Univs of Bonn, Hamburg and Düsseldorf; Research Fellow, Univ. of Düsseldorf 1962–65, Children's Hosp. of Philadelphia, USA 1966–69; Sr Scientist, Inst. for Virology, Univ. of Wurzburg 1969–72; Chair. and Prof., Inst. of Clinical Virology, Univ. of Erlangen-Nurnberg 1972–77; Chair. and Prof., Inst. of Virology, Univ. of Freiburg 1977–83; Prof., Scientific Dir and Chair. Man. Bd, German Cancer Research Center 1983–2003, Prof. Emer. 2003–; Great Cross of Merit 2004; hon. degrees from Univs of Chicago, Umeå, Prague, Salford, Helsinki, Erlangen-Nuremberg and Salerno; Robert Koch Prize and Medal 1975, Charles Mott Prize 1986, Paul Ehrlich-Ludwig Darmstadter Prize 1994, Virchow Medal 2000, San Marino Prize for Medicine 2002, William B. Coley Award 2006, Gairdner Foundation Int. Award 2008, Nobel Prize in Medicine (jtly) 2008. *Achievements include:* discovered how human papilloma virus (HPV) induces cervical cancer which led to devt of a vaccine that helps prevent the disease. *Publication:* Infections Causing Human Cancer 2006. *Address:* German Cancer Research Center, Im Neuenheimer Feld 280, 69120 Heidelberg, Germany (office). *Telephone:* (6221) 420 (office). *Fax:* (6221) 422995 (office). *Website:* www.dkfz.de (office).

ZURABOV, Aleksander Yuryevich, C.ECON.SC.; Russian banker; b. 1956, Leningrad (now St Petersburg); m.; two c.; ed Moscow Inst. of Man., Acad. of Int. Trade; with Research Inst. of Marine Transport 1977–89; lecturer Acad. of Int. Trade 1989–91; Head of Div., Head of Dept, mem. Bd of Dirs Konversbank 1991–94; Chair. Bd of Dirs, Trust and Investments Bank, also Deputy Chair. Bd of Dirs, MENATEP Bank 1994–95, Pres. and Chair. Bd MENATEP 1996–; Chair. Bd of Dirs Russian Standard Bank 1999–2000; First Deputy Dir-Gen. Aeroflot 1999–. *Address:* MENATEP, Dubininskaya str. 17A, 113054 Moscow, Russia. *Telephone:* (495) 235-90-03 (office).

ZURABOV, Mikail Yuryevich; Russian engineer, government official and diplomatist; *Ambassador to Ukraine;* b. 3 Oct. 1953, Leningrad; m. Yuliya; one s. one d.; ed Moscow State Inst. of Man.; lecturer Moscow Inst. of Man. 1975–78; teacher Moscow Higher School of Montage 1981–82; engineer Moscow Research Inst. Orgtechstroi 1982–83; Sr Researcher and Head of Lab., All-Union Research Inst. of Montage Tech. 1983–88; Deputy Head Montage Co. Mospromtechmontage 1988–92; Dir-Gen. Jt Stock Insurance Co. Max 1992, also Dir-Gen. Medical Insurance Co. Max-M 1994–98; First Deputy Minister of Public Health May–Sept. 1998, Minister of Public Health and Social Devt 2004–07; adviser on social problems to Pres. 1998–99; Amb. to Ukraine 2010–; Chair. Bd of Dirs Konversbank; fmr Chair. Pension Fund of Russian Fed. *Address:* Russian Embassy, 03049 Kyiv, Povitroflotskyi pr. 27, Ukraine (office). *Telephone:* (44) 244-09-63 (office). *Fax:* (44) 246-34-69 (office). *E-mail:* embrus@public.icyb.kiev.ua (office). *Website:* www.embrus.org.ua (office).

ZUROVCIK, Danielle Renee, MSc, PhD; American mechanical engineer, academic and entrepreneur; *CEO, Worldwide Innovative Healthcare, Inc. (WiCare);* ed Massachusetts Inst. of Tech.; Founder and CEO Worldwide Innovative Healthcare, Inc. (WiCare); Judges' Choice Award, MC 2012 Innovation Expo, Student Poster First Place Prize Award, IEEE GHTC, First Place, Advamed MedTech Conf. Business Pitch Competition, MIT IDEAS Global Challenge Award Winner, Selected Program Participant, Founders' Skills Accelerator @ MIT Sloan, Member of the Month, Engineering 4 Change, Invited Talk, CMU-UAEM Global Health Conf., Second Place, IEEE Presidents' Change the World Competition, World Technology Network Award (Health and Medicine) 2010. *Publications:* numerous papers in professional journals. *Address:* Massachusetts Institute of Technology, 77 Massachusetts Avenue, Cambridge, MA 02139-4307, USA (office). *Telephone:* (617) 253-1000 (office). *E-mail:* drz@mit.edu (office); drz@

wicaresolutions.com. *Website:* web.mit.edu/drz/www/aboutme.html (office); www .wicaresolutions.com (office).

ŽUŽUL, Miomir, PhD; Croatian politician and diplomatist; b. 1955, Split; m.; four c.; fmr Amb. to USA; Minister of Foreign Affairs 2003–05 (resgnd); King Legacy Award for Outstanding Int. Service 2000. *Address:* c/o Ministry of Foreign Affairs, trg Nikole Šubića Zrinskog 7–8, 10000 Zagreb, Croatia.

ZVEREVA, Natalia (Natasha); Belarusian fmr professional tennis player; b. 16 April 1971, Minsk, Byelorussian SSR, USSR; d. of Marat Zverev and Nina Zvereva; winner, doubles French Open (with Larisa Neiland) 1989, (with Gigi Fernandez) 1992–95, 1997, Wimbledon (with Larisa Neiland) 1991, (with Gigi Fernandez) 1992–94, 1997, US Open (with Pam Shriver) 1991, (with Gigi Fernandez) 1992, 1995, 1996; winner mixed doubles Australian Open 1990, 1995, doubles (with Gigi Fernandez) 1993–94, 1997; four-time Olympian 1988–2000; bronze medallist in doubles (mem. Unified Team), Olympic Games, Barcelona, Spain 1992; winner doubles Pan Pacific (with Gigi Fernandez) 1996; 80 WTA Tour doubles titles; currently Capt. Belarus Fed Cup team; five-time winner of WTA Tour Doubles Team of the Year Award. *Leisure interests:* listening to music, watching water polo, table tennis, nightclubs, reading, cooking, farming. *Address:* c/o Belarus Tennis Association, 220030 Minsk, ul. Gertsena, 2A, Belarus. *Telephone:* (172) 26-93-74. *Fax:* (172) 26-98-23. *E-mail:* beltennis@yahoo.com. *Website:* www.tennis.by.

ZVONAREVA, Vera Igorevna; Russian professional tennis player; b. 7 Sept. 1984, Moscow; d. of Igor Zvonarev and Natalya Bykova; ed Russian State Univ. of Physical Educ., Diplomatic Acad. of Ministry of Foreign Affairs, Moscow; introduced by her mother to tennis at Chajka sports club aged six; played first career event on ITF (Int. Tennis Fed.) Circuit 1999; turned professional 2000; played first WTA (Women's Tennis Assn) main draw at Moscow 2000; won one singles title on ITF Circuit; winner ITF/Moscow 2000, ITF/Naples, Fla, USA 2002, Bol 2003, Memphis 2004, 2005, Cincinnati 2008, Birmingham 2008, Guangzhou 2008, Prague 2008, Indian Wells 2009, Pattaya City 2009, 2011, Doha 2011; reached finals of WTA Tour Championships 2008; Grand Slam results: quarter-finalist, French Open 2003, semi-finalist, Australian Open 2009, 2011, finalist, Wimbledon 2010, finalist, US Open 2010; bronze medallist, Olympic Games, Beijing 2008; winner Women's Doubles, Moscow (with Myskina) 2004, Berlin (with Likhovtseva) 2005, US Open (with Dechy) 2006, Indian Wells Auckland (with Likhovtseva) 2006, (with Azarenka) 2009; winner Mixed Doubles, US Open (with Bob Bryan) 2004, Wimbledon (with Ram) 2006; mem. Federation Cup Team for Russia 2003–04, 2008, 2011; participated in UNESCO Regional Conf. 'Political Involvement of Women in the Caucasus' 2008, named Promoter of Gender Equality under the partnership 2009; works with Int. Rett Syndrome Foundation. *Leisure interests:* travelling, volleyball, hockey, computers, reading, music. *Address:* c/o Women's Tennis Association, One Progress Plaza, Suite 1500, St Petersburg, FL 33701, USA. *Telephone:* (727) 895-5000. *Fax:* (727) 894-1982. *E-mail:* zvonareva .ru@mail.ru. *Website:* www.wtatennis.com; www.zvonareva.ru.

ZVYAGINTSEV, Andrei; Russian actor and film director; b. 6 Feb. 1964, Moscow; ed Moscow State Inst. of Theatre Arts; actor, Epigone Theatre at Central House of Actors; Int. Venice Film Festival Golden Lion 2003. *Play:* A Month in the Country (actor). *Films:* Reflection (actor), Genuine Threat (actor), Queen Margo (actor), The Return (dir) (Int. Venice Film Festival Best Debut Feature) 2003, The Banishment (dir) 2007, Elena (dir) 2011. *Television:* episode of Chyornaya komnata, 'Obscure' (dir and producer) 2000. *Leisure interest:* swimming.

ZWANZIG, Robert Walter, MS, PhD; American chemical physicist, scientist and academic; *Scientist Emeritus, Laboratory of Chemical Physics, National Institutes of Health;* b. 9 April 1928, Brooklyn, New York; s. of Walter Zwanzig and Bertha Weil Zwanzig; m. Francis Ryder Zwanzig 1953; one s. one d.; ed Polytechnic Inst. of Brooklyn, Univ. of Southern California and California Inst. of Tech.; Research Fellow, Yale Univ. 1951–54; Asst Prof. of Chem., Johns Hopkins Univ. 1954–58; Physical Chemist Nat. Bureau of Standards, Washington, DC 1958–66; Research Prof., Inst. for Physical Science and Tech., Univ. of Maryland 1966–80, Distinguished Prof. of Physical Science 1980–88, Prof. Emer. 1988–; Research Chemist, NIH Lab. of Chemical Physics from 1988, now Scientist Emer.; mem. NAS, ACS; Silver Medal, US Dept of Commerce, ACS Peter Debye Award in Physical Chem. 1976, Irving Langmuir Award in Chemical Physics 1984, ACS Joel Hildebrand Award 1994. *Publications:* Non-Equilibrium Statistical Mechanics 2001; more than 140 articles in scientific periodicals. *Address:* Laboratory of Chemical Physics, National Institutes of Health, Building 5, Room 120, Bethesda, MD 20892-0520 (office); 5314 Sangamore Road, Bethesda, MD 20816, USA (home). *Telephone:* (301) 496-8048 (office). *Fax:* (301) 496-0825 (office). *E-mail:* zwanzig@ sunder.niddk.nih.gov (office). *Website:* www.niddk.nih.gov (office).

ZWAVELING, Albert, MD, PhD; Dutch professor of surgery (retd); b. 21 July 1927, Schoonebeek; s. of Jan H. Zwaveling and Engeline F. (née Hinnen) Zwaveling; m. 1st Susanna M. van Soest 1952 (died 1966); one s.; m. 2nd Anna M. F. Bloem 1969; two s.; ed State Univ. of Utrecht, University Hosp., Leiden; mil. doctor (rank of maj.) 1954–57; Gen. Practitioner in Indonesia 1957–58; surgical trainee, Leiden 1958–63; Fellow in Oncology, Univ. of Wis., USA 1963–64; Jr Consultant 1964–68; Assoc. Prof. of Surgical Oncology, Leiden Univ. 1968–72, Prof. of Surgery 1972; Head, Dept of Surgery, Univ. Hosp., Leiden 1981–; Chair. Concilium Chirurgicum Utrecht 1985, Medical Staff Hosp., Leiden 1986; mem. Royal Netherlands Acad. of Sciences 1979, Medical Adviser 1972–; Hon. mem. Dutch Soc. of Oncology 1986, Dutch Asscn of Surgery 1987, Dutch Asscn of Surgical Oncology 1991; awarded Rotgans Medal of Nat. Cancer Inst. 1963, Zwanenberg Award 1969. *Publications:* Dutch Textbook of Oncology, Dutch Textbook of Surgery; 6 monographs on oncology, mainly cancer; more than 120 scientific papers. *Leisure interests:* collecting plastic art, gardening. *Address:* University Hospital, Leiden (office); Vlietpark 4, 2355 CT Hoogmade, Netherlands (home). *Telephone:* (71) 5018622 (home). *Fax:* (71) 5018622 (home). *E-mail:* a.zwaveling@inter.ne.net (home).

ZWERENZ, Gerhard; German writer; b. 3 June 1925, Gablenz; s. of Rudolf Zwerenz and Liesbeth Zwerenz; m. Ingrid Hoffman 1957; one d.; ed Univ. of Leipzig; worked as coppersmith 1939–42; army service 1942–44, deserted to join Red Army 1944; POW in Minsk, USSR 1944–48; obliged to serve with GDR police 1948–50; studied at Leipzig Univ. 1952–56; first published 1956; expelled from CP, fled to W Berlin 1957; mem. Bundestag 1994–; Ernst Reuter Prize 1975, Carl-von-

Ossietzky-preis 1986, Alternativer Büchnerpreis 1991. *Publications:* 65 books including Aufs Rad geflochten 1959, Die Liebe der toten Männer 1959, Heldengedenktag 1964, Rasputin 1970, Der Widerspruch 1974, Die West-deutschen 1977, Die Ehe der Maria Braun 1979, Der langsame Tod des Rainer-Werner Fassbinder 1982, Rechts und dumm? 1993, Links und lahm 1994, Krieg im Glashaus 2000, Sklavensprache und Revolte. Der Bloch-Kreis und seine Feinde in Ost und West (with Ingrid Zwerenz) 2004. *Address:* Brunhildenstieg 18, 61389 Schmitten, Germany. *Telephone:* (6082) 1078.

ZWICK, Charles John, BS, PhD; American banker and economist; b. 17 July 1926, Plantsville, Conn.; s. of Louis C. Zwick and Mabel Zwick (née Rich); m. Joan Cameron 1952; one s. one d.; ed Univ. of Connecticut and Harvard Univ.; Instructor, Univ. of Conn. 1951, Harvard Univ. 1954–56; Head, Logistics Dept RAND Corpn 1956–63, mem. Research Council 1963–65; Asst Dir US Bureau of the Budget, Washington, DC 1965–68, Dir 1968–69; Pres. Southeast Banking Corpn, Miami 1969, Chair. and CEO –1982; fmr Dir Manville Corpn and numerous other cos; fmr Chair. Pres.'s Comm. on Mil. Compensation; Trustee, Carnegie Endowment for Int. Peace, Chair.; mem. Reserve City Bankers Asscn, The Conference Bd, Council of the Int. Exec. Service Corps, Econ. Soc. of S. Fla, Council of 100; Founding Trustee, Collins Center for Public Policy, Miami, now Trustee Emer. *Address:* c/o Collins Center for Public Policy, New World Tower, 100 North Biscayne Blvd., Suite 1900, Miami, FL 33132, USA (office).

ZWICK, Edward, AB, MFA; American film director and producer; b. 8 Oct. 1952, Chicago; m. Liberty Godshall; ed Harvard Univ.; Exec. Producer The Bedford Falls Co. (film production co.). *Films include:* About Last Night 1986, Glory 1989, Leaving Normal 1992, Legends of the Fall 1994, Courage Under Fire 1996, The Siege 1998, The Last Samurai 2003, Blood Diamond 2006, Defiance 2008, Love and Other Drugs 2010. *Television includes:* thirtysomething (series) (exec. producer) 1987–91, Once and Again (writer and exec. producer) 1999–2002. *Address:* The Bedford Falls Company, 409 Santa Monica Blvd, Santa Monica, CA 90401, USA (office). *Telephone:* (310) 394-5022 (office).

ZWICKEL, Klaus; German trade union official; b. 31 May 1939, Heilbronn; apprentice toolmaker, Nordheim; regional admin. IG Metall-Gewerkschaft für Produktion und Dieustleistung im D6B; mem. Nat. Cttee 1986, Deputy Leader 1989–93, Leader 1993–2003; Pres. Int. Metalworkers' Fed.; Deputy Chair. Supervisory Bd Volkswagen AG 1996–; mem. Supervisory Bd (Deputy Chair. 1996–) Vodafone. *Address:* c/o IG Metall, Lyoner Str. 32, 60519 Frankfurt am Main, Germany.

ZWIRNER, David; American gallery owner and art dealer; *Director, David Zwirner Gallery;* b. 1974, Winnipeg, Canada; f. David Zwirner Gallery, Green Street, SoHo, New York City 1993 (relocated to Chelsea 2002); Co-founder and Partner (with Iwan Wirth), Zwirner & Wirth Gallery, New York City 2000–09; opened gallery in Mayfair, London 2012; mem. The Royal Art Lodge, Winnipeg. *Publications:* numerous catalogues and monographs. *Address:* David Zwirner Gallery, 525 West 19th Street, New York, NY 10011, USA (office). *Telephone:* (212) 727-2070 (office). *Fax:* (212) 727-2072 (office). *E-mail:* info@davidzwirner.com (office). *Website:* www.davidzwirner.com (office); www.zwirnerandwirth.com (office).

ZYAZIKOV, Murat Magometovich; Russian politician; b. 10 Sept. 1957, Osh, Kyrgyzstan; m.; three s.; ed Checheno-Ingush State Univ. (now Chechen State Univ.), KGB Acad.; worked in CP admin at local level 1980–81; served in army 1981–83; numerous positions in KGB 1984–92; Deputy Minister of Security for Ingushetiya 1992, Deputy Head of FSB Ingushetiya Office, then Head of Security Council 1992–96; Deputy Head of FSB Astrakhan Office, also mem. Comm. for Solution of Conflicts in Northern Caucasus 1996–2002; Deputy Presidential Envoy, South Russia Fed. Okrug Jan.–April 2002; elected Pres. Repub. of Ingushetiya 2002–05, appointed Pres. Repub. of Ingushetiya 2005–08 (resgnd); numerous civil and mil. awards and medals. *Address:* 366720 Ingushetiya, Magas, Dom Pravitelstva, Russia (office). *Telephone:* (8734) 55-11-55 (office). *Fax:* (8734) 55-11-55 (office). *E-mail:* murad@ingushetia.ru (office). *Website:* ingushetia.ru (office).

ŻYLIS-GARA, Teresa; Polish singer (soprano); *Professor of Lyric Art, State Higher School of Music, Łódź;* b. 23 Jan. 1930, Landwarow, nr Wilno (now Vilnius, Lithuania); m.; one c.; ed State Higher School of Music, Łódź with Prof. Olga Olgina; won inter-school competition in Warsaw; operatic debut in titles roles in Halka (Moniuszko), Madame Butterfly (Puccini) and as Giulietta in Les contes d'Hoffmann (Offenbach); soloist, Kraków Philharmonic 1954–58 and Kraków Opera 1958–59; foreign contracts in operas: Oberhausen 1961–63, Städtische Bühnen, Dortmund 1963–65, Deutsche Oper am Rhein, Düsseldorf 1965–70; debuts abroad at Glyndebourne Festival as Octavian in Rosenkavlier (Strauss) 1965, Paris Opera as Donna Elvira in Don Giovanni (Mozart) 1966, Salzburg Festival 1968, San Francisco Opera 1968, Metropolitan Opera, New York 1968, Royal Opera House, Covent Garden as Violetta in La Traviata (Verdi) 1968, Vienna Opera 1970, Aix-en-Provence Festival 1972, Nat. Theatre, Prague 1974, Orange Festival 1975, Nat. Theatre, Budapest 1976, Great Theatre, Warsaw 1976, La Scala, Milan 1977, Bolshoi Theatre, Moscow 1978, Teatro Colón, Buenos Aires 1981; regular performances at Metropolitan Opera, New York, Berlin, Hamburg, Munich, La Scala, Milan, Staatsoper, Vienna and several times at Mozart Salzburg Festival under Herbert von Karajan; repertoire includes prin. roles in operas by Mozart, Verdi, Puccini, R. Strauss, Chausson, Tchaikovsky and others; has sung with artists such as Franco Corelli, Placido Domingo, Luciano Pavarotti and José Cameras; has worked with directors including Franco Zeffirelli and conductors such as Herbert von Karajan, Karl Böhm, Carl-Maria Giulini and many others; song recitals have included Richard Strauss's Four Last Songs, Mercadante's Il Giuramento, Airs d'Opéras slaves, Rossini's Mose in Egitto; renowned for interpretation of works by Szymanowski; master-classes in inter-pretation and vocal technique in Poland, France, Monaco and USA; Prof. of Lyric Art, State Higher School of Music, Łódź 1999; Kt's Cross, Order of Polonia Restituta 1975, Commdr's Cross, Order of Polonia Restituta 2000; Dr hc (Karol Lipinski Music Acad., Wrocław) 2000; Gold Medal for roles of Mimi in Puccini's La Bohème and Fiordiligi in Mozart's Così fan tutte, Opera Bellas Artes, Mexico City 1967, Nat. Prize, Ministry of the Arts and Culture 1975, Winner, All-Polish Competition of Young Vocalists, Warsaw, Prime Minister's Prize (First Class)

1979, Prix de la Saison de l'Opera for "an extraordinary interpretation of Desdemona in Otello", Associación Verdiana Teatro Colon Buenos Aires 1981, Max Reinhardt Medal, Salzburg Opera Festival, Prix d'honneur de la Ville de Pont St Esprit (France) for musical educ. of the young, Medal of the Music Acad. of Łódź on its 50th anniversary 1999, Nat. Prize 'Gloria Artis', Ministry of the Arts and Culture 2006. *Recordings include:* Mozart's Don Giovanni, Chausson's Le Roi Arthus, Richard Strauss' Ariadne auf Naxos, Bach's St Matthew Passion, Dvořak's Requiem, Verdi's Messa da Requiem, Mahler's Das Klagende Lied, and songs by Canteloube, Chopin, Duparc, Fauré, Karlowicz, Lalo, Moniuszko, Paderewski and Szymanowski. *Leisure interests:* gardening, reading poetry and historical novels.

ŽYLIUS, Rimantas, MA; Lithuanian business executive and politician; b. 24 June 1973, Klaipėda; m.; ed Vilnius Univ.; Head of Travel Insurance Div., Preventa (insurance co.) 1994–96; Adviser to Prime Minister on Information Soc. Devt 1999–2000; Sr Adviser to Parl. Information Soc. Devt Cttee 2000–02; fmr Public and Research Sectors Man., Metasite (man. consultancy) 2002–03; Solution Architect, Hewlett-Packard 2003–09; Deputy Minister of the Economy 2009–11, Minister 2011–12; Founder mem. Knowledge Economy Forum. *Address:* c/o Ministry of the Economy, Gedimino pr. 38, Vasario 16-osios g. 2, Vilnius 01104, Lithuania.

ZYPRIES, Brigitte; German politician; b. 16 Nov. 1953, Kassel; in-service training, Giessen Land Court 1978–80; mem. academic staff, Univ. of Giessen 1980–1985; Deputy Head of Div., State Chancellery, Hessen 1985–88; mem. academic staff, Fed. Constitutional Court 1988–90; Head of Div., Lower Saxon State Chancellery 1991–95, Head of Dept 1995–97, State Sec. for Women, Labour and Social Affairs 1997–98; State Sec. Fed. Ministry of the Interior 1998–2002; Chair. of State Sec. Cttee for Man. of Modern State-Modern Admin. Fed. Govt Programme 1999–2002; Fed. Minister of Justice 2002–09; mem. of Parl. 2005–. *Address:* Deutscher Bundestag, Platz der Republik 1, 11011 Berlin, Germany (office). *Telephone:* (30) 22774099 (office). *Fax:* (30) 22776125 (office). *E-mail:* brigitte.zypries@bundestag.de (office). *Website:* www.brigitte-zypries.de (office).

ZYUGANOV, Gennadii Andreyevich, DPhil; Russian politician; *Chairman, Central Committee, Communist Party of the Russian Federation;* b. 26 June 1944, Mymrino Village, Orel Oblast; m. Nadezhda Zyuganova; ed Orel Pedagogical Inst., Acad. of Social Sciences of Cen. CPSU Cttee; worked as secondary school teacher 1961–65; CP and trade union functionary 1967; First Sec., Dist, City, Regional Komsomol Cttees of Orel 1971–74, Sec., Second Sec., Head of Propaganda Div. Orel Regional CPSU Cttee 1974–83; Instructor and Head of Propaganda Div. Cen. CPSU Cttee 1983–89; Deputy Head of Ideology Div., Cen. CPSU Cttee 1989–90; mem. Politburo, Sec., Cen. Cttee of CP of Russian Fed. 1990, Chair. Cen. Exec. Cttee CP of Russian Fed. 1993–; Chair. Co-ordination Cttee of Patriotic Forces of Russia 1992–, Co-Chair. Duma of Russian Nat. Sobor 1992–; Co-Chair. Political Council of the Front of Nat. Salvation 1992–; Chair. Union of Communist Parties-Communist Party of the Soviet Union (UCP-CPSU) 2001–; mem. State Duma (Parl.) of Russia 1993–; CP presidential cand. 1996, 2000, 2008, 2012; mem. Parl. Ass. of the Council of Europe 1996–. *Publications:* Russia and the Contemporary World 1995, Russia, My Homeland (The Ideology of State Patriotism) 1997. *Address:* Communist Party of the Russian Federation (Kommunistechiskaya Partiya Rossiiskoi Federatsii—KPRF), 103051 Moscow, per. M. Sukharevskii 3/1, Russia (office). *Telephone:* (495) 692-87-44 (office). *Fax:* (495) 692-68-54 (office). *E-mail:* ck@kprf.ru (office). *Website:* kprf.ru (office); www.zyuganov.kprf.ru.